BLOCKBUSTER VIDEO® GUIDE TO MOVIES AND VIDEOS 1996

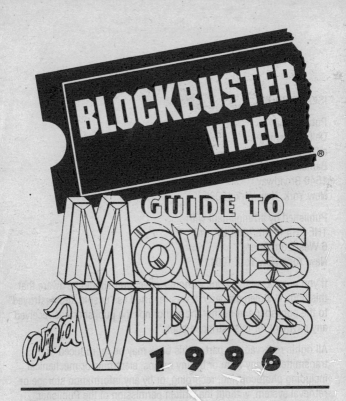

BLOCKBUSTER VIDEO®

GUIDE TO MOVIES and VIDEOS 1996

Edited by Ron Castell

Senior Vice President
Blockbuster Entertainment Group,
a Viacom Company

Produced by The Philip Lief Group, Inc.

ISLAND BOOKS

Published by
Dell Publishing
a Division of
Bantam Doubleday Dell Publishing Group, Inc.
1540 Broadway
New York, New York 10036

Published by arrangement with
THE PHILIP LIEF GROUP, INC.
6 West 20th Street
New York, New York 10011

ISBN: 0-440-22114-5

Printed in the United States of America

Published simultaneously in Canada

September 1995

10 9 8 7 6 5 4 3 2 1

CONTRIBUTORS

Peter Napolitano
George Robinson
Arnie Bernstein
Michael Gingold
Michael Podwill
Raymond Stehle
David Licata
Joel Weinberg
Jo Manning
Chris Koseluk
Paula Hunt
Chris Pangborn
Marshall Fine
Felicia Feaster
Brent Walker
Kevin Filipski
Paul Sammon
Mark Cerulli
Gary Marmorstein
Elizabeth Judd
Jim Kline
David Lugowski
Lee Mercer
Paul Fries
Susan Osborn
Gary Sunshine
Mary Kalamaras
Naomi Starr
Jennifer Hirshlag
Claudia HCQ Sorsby
Harold Rabinowitz
Ed Grant
Sterling Rome
Karen O'Hara
Clif Garboden
Charles Cassady
Kalle Matso
Christine Meola
Mark Smoyer
Dean Wei
Aaron Leventman
Peter Coyne
Chris Grunden
Jim Earp
Andrea Posner
Jack Sanchez
Sean Carr
Michael Zam
Jill Dearman
Gary Harner
David Yanover
Gerry Wild
Jim Ridley

SENIOR EDITORS

Claudia HCQ Sorsby
Susan Osborn

EDITORS

Sheila Gaffney
Sona Vogel
Barbara Sullivan
Peter Napolitano
George Robinson
Pam Loeser
Michelle Tempesta
Karen O'Hara

PRODUCTION EDITOR

Kelli Daley

COPY EDITOR

Brice Stephenson

EDITORIAL ASSISTANTS

Mary Kalamaras
Anne Pierce

Kelley Williams
Erwin Lerner
Jae Wolf
Beth Stevens
Alana Osborn-Lief

PROOFREADERS

Kristen Bowen
Kalea Chapman
Sharon Deokule
Helaine Feldman
Steven Kutz
Gayle Manero
Jennifer Manlowe

Andrew Freiser
Joyce Nolan
Sarah Picchi
Alda Trabucchi
Luise Trabucchi

DESIGN

Martin Lubin

DATABASE MANAGEMENT

Jim Bristol
Alex Mecs

TYPESETTING

N.K. Graphics

CONTENTS

INTRODUCTION

Welcome to the second, revised and updated edition of *The Blockbuster Video® Guide to Movies and Videos.*

We have made several changes in the new edition and many of these changes were suggested by readers who took the time to call or write to Blockbuster with their suggestions. Several readers contacted us regarding titles that we had not included in the 1995 edition. Everyone who wrote to us (and we received literally hundreds of cards and letters) received a personal response either from myself or a member of our editorial staff. Keep those cards and letters coming!

When movies first arrived at the dawn of the twentieth century, they were seen as an amusing oddity that provided a few moments of pleasure for the unsophisticated. Back then, even the most zealous advocates of motion pictures could not have predicted the cultural impact that this new medium would eventually make. Today, in America and throughout the world, movies are a fundamental part of life.

How significant a role do movies play in our lives?

Most of us can probably remember what movie we saw on our first date!

Many can recall the first movie they ever saw.

And when Clark Gable took off his shirt in *It Happened One Night* and revealed that he wore no undershirt, millions of Gable wannabes gave up on undershirts.

Movies are a haven, allowing us to escape to a new world for a few hours. For decades, the stars created by the Hollywood dream machine have been more familiar to us than many of the people we actually work and play with.

A badge of distinction at one time was to have a home with a private screening room. Up to the late 1970s, that badge was only worn by a privileged few, mainly in Hollywood. But the explosion of video technology has made it possible for virtually everyone to have a screening room at home. With your screening room in place, you have access (courtesy of your nearby video rental store) to thousands of the best (and worst) movies Hollywood ever produced. The *Blockbuster Video® Guide to Movies and Videos* is your individual road map to the best (and yes, even the worst) on-screen entertainment available.

Since the opening of our doors in 1985, Blockbuster has become the standard by which all other video stores are judged. Blockbuster buys, stocks, and rents more movies than any other chain worldwide. When it comes to knowing movies and what folks like to see at home, Blockbuster is the acknowledged leader in its field.

Who then is better suited to compile a guide to what's available on video than Blockbuster?

In compiling this book, our one guiding principle has been to put together a reference that we would like to use at our stores. A book that would be accurate, dependable, and conveniently organized. We've even included reviews of episodes from some of your favorite TV shows that are now on video. We believe you are holding the most comprehensive and meticulous guide to movies and videos yet published.

Ultimately, our goal has been to give pleasure to film lovers. Therefore, our writers and editors have approached this daunting task with equal parts of knowledge and wit. We have all worked hard and with good humor to try to create an entertaining and fun-to-read guide for browsing or reference. If you like movies, then the *Blockbuster Video® Guide to Movies and Videos* should be as indispensable to your VCR as your remote control. Keep in mind, though, that not every movie listed in this guide as available on video can be rented from your local Blockbuster Video® store.

Once again, special thanks to Blockbuster movie experts Mike Clarke, Steve Menke, and Gordon Smith, who brought so much of their love and knowledge of movies to this guide. And again—special thanks to all our readers who called and wrote with both praise and constructive criticism of the first edition.

We hope you find our guide as much fun to read as the movies you rent and buy. Now, hit the play button and let's go to the movies . . . at home.

Ron Castell
Editor-in-Chief
Blockbuster Video® Guide
to Movies and Videos

How to Use This Book

The *Blockbuster Video® Guide to Movies and Videos* is organized alphabetically by word to help you find the movies you are interested in as quickly and as easily as possible. Spaces between words are recognized, so *I Was a Teenage Werewolf* comes before *In the Heat of the Night.* Numbers are alphabetized by where they would appear if spelled out. Abbreviations, such as *Dr.* or *Mr.*, appear as they are written, so *Dr. Who and the Daleks* comes right before *Dracula.*

In English, articles at the beginning of words are ignored, so that *The Maltese Falcon* is listed as *Maltese Falcon, The* and appears under *M.* In foreign-language titles, however, we've kept the articles in front, so *La Balance* is under *L.*

Each review includes the following information:

- **Title**
- **Year:** Year of release.
- **Origin of production:** When other than American.
- **Star rating:** From five stars to one star.
- **Review:** Nearly every review contains a brief synopsis of the plot and an evaluation or appreciation of the movie's quality. We also have included warnings to parents on material that may be inappropriate for children.
- **Cast list**
- **Director**
- **Genre:** The categories are as follows:

  ACT = action and adventure
  COM = comedy, including stand-up concerts
  CRI = crime and mystery
  DOC = documentary
  DRA = drama
  FAM = appropriate for the whole family
  HOR = horror
  MUS = musicals and concerts
  SFI = science fiction and fantasy

WST = Western

Many movies listed under FAM also have an additional designation to indicate what category they are, such as comedy or drama.

■ **MPAA rating:** The Motion Picture Association of America has been rating movies for audience suitability since 1968. The ratings system has been changed occasionally, and we have endeavored to use the current codes. They are as follows:

G General Audiences: All ages admitted.

PG Parental Guidance suggested: Some material may not be suitable for children.

PG-13 Parents Strongly Cautioned: Some material may be inappropriate for children under 13.

R Restricted: Children under 17 require accompanying parent or adult guardian.

NC-17 No Children Under 17 Admitted (age may vary in certain areas).

In keeping with Blockbuster's emphasis on children and family viewing, movies rated NC-17 (and the older equivalent, X) are not included in this book.

■ **Running time:** Listed in minutes.

■ **Video availability:** Denoted by a V. Please keep in mind that movies both old and new are constantly being released to video; our listing is up to date as of press time, but you should check with your local Blockbuster store to see what has become available.

■ **Alternative titles:** Often a movie is known by more than one title. We list these at the end of the review, enabling you to track down a movie that has been retitled for video or re-released with a new title. They are marked a.k.a. ("also known as").

We also have included short essays on movie series, such as the *Tarzan* movies, describing the overall series and listing its titles.

In addition to the alphabetical listing of reviews, the Blockbuster Video® guide is indexed by actor, director, category and star rating. We have also included a separate index of family films. And, for your convenience, we have designed our indexes in our exclusive Video Tracker format. A box next to each title for you to check makes it easy for you to keep a running record of the films you've seen and the ones you want to see.

A

A Brivele der Mamen 1938 Polish ★★★ Cinematic time capsule of a world soon to disappear under the crush of Nazism. Soap opera story follows both a Polish Jew who immigrates to America, and the mother he leaves behind. A Yiddish-language film, most interesting for historical value. (a.k.a. *A Letter from Mama*) C: Lucy Gehrman, Misha Gehrman. D: Joseph Green. DRA 100m.

A-Haunting We Will Go 1942 ★★ Weak Laurel and Hardy outing, as the two become mixed up with gangsters who trick them into taking charge of a coffin which gets mixed up with one used by a magician. C: Stan Laurel, Oliver Hardy. D: Alfred Werker. COM 68m.

A Nos Amours 1983 French ★★★★ A teenager (Bonnaire) turns to promiscuity to escape the battleground of her constantly warring family. Excellent performances, but often difficult to watch. Director Pialat plays Bonnaire's emotionally wrecked father. C: Sandrine Bonnaire, Dominique Besnehard, Maurice Pialat. D: Maurice Pialat. DRA [R] 99m. v

A Nous La Liberté 1931 French ★★★★ Musical send-up of industrial society follows two prison escapees—one of whom becomes a phonograph manufacturing magnate. Charming and funny, though dated in parts. Considered by many as inspiration for Chaplin's *Modern Times*. C: Raymond Cordy, Henri Marchand. D: Rene Clair. MUS 87m. v

Aaron Loves Angela 1975 ★★★ *Romeo and Juliet/West Side Story* rehash tells the story of an innocent, star-crossed young couple, involving Aaron (Hooks), who is black, and Angela (Cara), who is Puerto Rican. Set against violent, drug-ridden streets of Harlem. Well acted, with music by José Feliciano. C: Kevin Hooks, Irene Cara, Moses Gunn, Robert Hooks, Ernest Jackson, José Feliciano. D: Gordon Parks. DRA [R] 98m. v

Aaron Slick from Punkin Crick 1952 ★★★ Big-city rat sets his sights on a small town widow in this early '50s musical. Placid, easygoing songs. (a.k.a. *Marshmallow Moon*) C: Alan Young, Dinah Shore, Adele Jergens, Robert Merrill. D: Claude Binyon. MUS 95m.

Abandon Ship! 1957 British ★★★★ On the lifeboat of a sunken luxury liner, officer (Power) faces an awful decision: Will the weak have to be sacrificed so that the strong may live? Intense, harrowing adventure drama. Later remade as *The Last Survivors*. (a.k.a. *Seven Waves Away*) C: Tyrone Power, Mal Zeterling, Lloyd Nolan, Stephen Boyd. D: Richard Sale. DRA 100m.

Abandoned 1949 ★★★ Uncovering an adoption scam while helping a young woman (Storm) find her sister's illegitimate baby jeopardizes a reporter's career and credibility. Bad guy Burr is the main attraction here. C: Gale Storm, Dennis O'Keefe, Raymond Burr, Marjorie Rambeau, Jeff Chandler. D: Joe Newman. CRI 79m.

Abar, the First Black Superman 1977 *See* **In Your Face**

Abbott and Costello Go To Mars 1953 ★★ Two buffoons trigger a rocket ship launch and wind up flying through space. Buffoonery carries through to the title—Bud and Lou actually land on Venus! C: Bud Abbott, Lou Costello, Robert Paige, Mari Blanchard, Martha Hyer. D: Charles Lamont. COM 77m. v

Abbott and Costello In Hollywood 1945 ★★★ Behind-the-scenes comedy features Abbott and Costello as barbershop proprietors in Tinseltown. Basically a promo piece for MGM, this is packed with cameo appearances by the studio stable. Younger kids may enjoy the clowning. C: Bud Abbott, Lou Costello, Frances Rafferty, Dean Stockwell. D: S. Simon. COM 83m. v

Abbott and Costello In The Foreign Legion 1950 ★★★ Basic Abbott and Costello adventure built around a tough drill sergeant and mirages in the Algerian desert. Equally enjoyable is Slezak as the sergeant. C: Bud Abbott, Lou Costello, Patricia Medina, Walter Slezak, Douglass Dumbrille. D: Charles Lamont. COM 80m.

Abbott and Costello Meet Captain Kidd 1952 ★★★ Swashbuckling nonsense as Abbott and Costello go in search of the title pirate's secret treasure. In between the songs and humor of the two stars, Laughton chews the scenery with wild abandon. Youngsters will get a few chuckles. C: Bud Abbott, Lou Costello, Charles Laughton, Hillary Brooke, Leif Erickson. D: Charles Lamont. COM 70m. v

Abbott and Costello Meet Dr Jekyll And Mr Hyde 1952 ★★★ Robert Louis Stevenson probably spun wildly in his grave over this production. In another of their horror film spoofs, Bud and Lou are 18th-century American detectives in London chasing down the literary legend, played by Karloff. Kids will enjoy. C: Bud Abbott, Lou Costello, Boris Karloff, Craig Stevens, Helen Westcott. D: Charles Lamont. COM 77m. v

Abbott and Costello Meet Frankenstein 1948 ★★★★½ Maybe the pair's best movie, plunking the boys down in the hair-raising world of Count Dracula (Lugosi), who wants to borrow Lou's brain to put in Frankenstein's monster. A guilty pleasure for adults, great for kids. C: Bud Abbott, Lou Costello, Bela Lugosi, Lon Chaney Jr., Glenn Strange. D: Charles Barton. COM 83m. v

Abbott and Costello Meet The Invisible Man 1951 ★★★★ Abbott and Costello play bumbling detectives who help to prove an innocent boxer (Franz) has been framed for murder in this fun sci-fi/mystery/comedy. Highlights include convincing special effects by John Fulton, the camera ace who also did trick photography for the original *Invisible Man*. C: Bud Abbott, Lou Costello, Nancy Guild, Arthur Franz, Adele Jergens, Sheldon Leonard. D: Charles Lamont. COM 82m. v

Abbott and Costello Meet The Keystone Kops 1955 ★★½ Two goofy innocents are tricked into buying a bottom-of-the-barrel movie studio. A nice homage to the silent era. Mack Sennett, father of the Keystone Kop comedies, makes a cameo appearance. C: Bud Abbott, Lou Costello, Fred Clark, Lynn Bari, Mack Sennett, Sam Flint. D: Charles Lamont. COM 79m.

Abbott and Costello Meet the Killer 1949 ★★★½ Lots of slamming doors and falling corpses are strewn through this horror spoof. This time Abbott and Costello follow Karloff's trail while he's trying to get his hands on Lou at the same time. Silly, not quite up to par, but the kids will enjoy the histrionic humor. C: Bud Abbott, Lou Costello, Boris Karloff, Lenore Aubert, Gar Moore. D: Charles Barton. COM 84m. v

Abbott and Costello Meet the Mummy 1955 ★★★ When Abbott and Costello go hunting for lost Egyptian treasures, they get involved with live crooks and a mummy returned from the dead. Typical for the Abbott and Costello horror films, with a few good yuks. C: Bud Abbott, Lou Costello, Marie Windsor, Michael Ansara, Richard Deacon. D: Charles Lamont. COM 79m. v

Abby 1974 ★★★ Possessed minister's wife causes him embarrassment in this African-American variation on *The Exorcist*. Worth watching for a few genuine thrills. C: Carol Speed, William Marshall, Terry Carter. D: William Girdler. HOR 92m.

Abdication, The 1974 British ★★ In the 17th century, Sweden's Queen Christina converts to Catholicism, abdicates, and falls in love with a cardinal. Turgid costumer. C: Liv Ullman, Peter Finch, Cyril Cusack, Paul Rogers, Michael Dunn. D: Anthony Harvey. DRA [PG] 103m.

Abducted 1985 ★★★½ Haggerty gives a sensitive performance as the father of a young man who kidnaps a woman and disappears into the Pacific Northwest forest. C: Dan Haggerty, Roberta Weiss, Lawrence King Phillips. D: Boon Collins. CRI 87m.

Abduction 1975 ★★ Wealthy West Coast heiress is taken hostage by social revolutionaries and eventually bonds with her captors. Sound familiar? Exploitation feature (based on a novel written *before* the famous kidnapping!) dramatizes the Patty Hearst scandal. C: Gregory Rozakis, Judith-Marie Bergan, David Pendleton, Leif Erickson, Dorothy Malone. D: Joseph Zito. DRA [R] 100m. v

Abduction from the Seraglio, The 1986 ★★★★ Elegant production of Mozart's comic opera, set in a Turkish harem, with a Spanish nobleman trying to rescue his lady love from the evil Pasha. Sung in German with English subtitles. C: Deon Van Der Walt, Oliver Tobias, Inge Neilsen. MUS 140m. v

Abductors, The 1957 ★★½ Fact-based story about a pair of wily bandits who decide to steal and then ransom Abraham Lincoln's remains. Trivia note: Bad guy McLaglen is director McLaglen's dad. C: Victor McLaglen, George Macready, Fay Spain. D: Andrew McLaglen. CRI 80m.

Abdulla the Great 1956 ★★★ Kendall plays a model who rebuffs the advances of a mideast monarch, and falls for a young revolutionary. Middling attempt at high adventure. (a.k.a. *Abdullah's Harem*) C: Kay Kendall, Sydney Chaplin, Gregory Ratoff. D: Gregory Ratoff. ACT 89m.

Abe Lincoln in Illinois 1939 ★★★★★ Fine, beautifully acted story of the Great Emancipator's early career and romantic relationships, from Robert E. Sherwood's Pulitzer Prize-winning play. Massey and Gordon excel as Lincoln and wife Mary Todd. C: Raymond Massey, Gene Lockhart, Ruth Gordon, Mary Howard, Howard da Silva. D: John Cromwell. DRA 110m. v

Abhijan 1962 *See* **Expedition, The**

Abie's Irish Rose 1946 ★★ A young Irishwoman marries into a Jewish family, creating predictable havoc. Old chestnut tackled by veteran comic director Sutherland. C: Joanne Dru, Richard Norris, Michael Chekhov, Eric Blore. D: A. Sutherland. DRA 96m.

Abilene Town 1946 ★★★½ Stalwart marshal in 1879 steps in to break up bitter range war. Quickly paced, entertaining Scott Western. C: Randolph Scott, Ann Dvorak, Edgar Buchanan, Rhonda Fleming, Lloyd Bridges. D: Edwin L. Marin. WST 90m. v

Abominable Dr. Phibes, The 1971 British ★★★★★ A horribly scarred man (Price) seeks vengeance against the doctors who failed to save his wife—by visiting lethal versions of the Biblical plagues upon them. Price has a field day in this engaging, off-the-wall chiller. C: Vincent Price, Joseph Cotten, Hugh Griffith, Terry-Thomas, Virginia North. D: Robert Fuest. HOR 94m.

About Face 1952 ★★½ Musical based on the hit film and play *Brother Rat*, about high jinks in military school. Score by Tobias and Rose. C: Gordon MacRae, Eddie Bracken, Dick Wesson, Phyllis Kirk, Joel Grey. D: Roy Del Ruth. MUS 94m.

About Last Night . . . 1986 ★★★ Yuppie comedy features Lowe and Moore as on-again, off-again Chicago couple trying to figure out the parameters of their relationship. Shallow adaptation of David Mamet's play *Sexual Perversity in Chicago*, with Belushi providing ribald comic relief. C: Rob Lowe,

Demi Moore, James Belushi, Elizabeth Perkins. D: Edward Zwick. COM [R] 113m. V

About Mrs. Leslie 1954 ★★★½ Ryan and Booth infuse warmth and sincerity into this unabashed soaper about a financier's relationship with a nightclub singer. Routine script, outstanding performances. C: Shirley Booth, Robert Ryan, Marjie Millar, Alex Nicol, Henry Morgan, Ellen Corby. D: Daniel Mann. DRA 104m.

Above and Beyond 1952 ★★★ This biographical film about the pilot who dropped the atomic bomb on Hiroshima chronicles his training and mission and its effect on his personal life. Overly long, but interesting character study. C: Robert Taylor, Eleanor Parker, James Whitmore, Jim Backus. D: Melvin Frank, Norman Panama. DRA 122m.

Above Suspicion 1943 ★★★ An Oxford professor (MacMurray) and his new bride (Crawford) are an unlikely pair of spies on their honeymoon in Paris. Lots of suspense as they work with British agents in a scheme against the Nazis. C: Joan Crawford, Fred MacMurray, Conrad Veidt, Basil Rathbone, Reginald Owen. D: Richard Thorpe. DRA 91m. V

Above The Law 1988 ★★★★ Action film debut for former L.A. bodyguard/martial arts master Seagal. He keeps the bodycount high as a Chicago cop fighting a CIA-sponsored drug gang. Stylish action sequences, but Seagal needed further acting experience. C: Steven Seagal, Pam Grier, Sharon Stone, Henry Silva. D: Andrew Davis. ACT [R] 99m. V

Above the Rim 1994 ★★★½ A high school basketball hero (Martin) is torn between a club owner (Shakur) and Shakur's mysterious older brother (Leon), a former b-ball star himself. Clichéd situation, but the characters are neatly played and the basketball sequences are terrific. C: Duane Martin, Leon, Tupac Shakur, David Bailey, Tonya Pinkins, Marlon Wayans. D: Jeff Pollack. DRA 93m.

Above Us The Waves 1956 British ★★★ Well-acted British adventure about a fleet of submarines trying to destroy a Nazi warship. The pseudodocumentary style enhances the story, although the film sometimes takes its own heroics too seriously. C: John Mills, John Gregson, Donald Sinden. D: Ralph Thomas. ACT 92m.

Abraham Lincoln—The New Birth of Freedom 1993 ★★★½ Adequate, politically correct children's documentary of the "Great Emancipator," narrated by Andrew Young. DOC 60m. V

Abraham Lincoln 1930 ★★½ Episodic, cradle-to-grave drama embalms rather than immortalizes Lincoln. Notable only as Griffith's first talkie and for Huston's standout performance. C: Walter Huston, Una Merkel, Edgar Dearing, Russell Simpson. D: D. W. Griffith. DRA 97m. V

Abraxas, Guardian of the Universe 1990 ★★½ Retired professional wrestler Jesse "The Body" Ventura takes a movie star turn as law officer patrolling two galaxies, battling both ecological troubles and the escapades of his crooked ex-partner. Low-level science fiction action with a few thrills. C: Jesse Ventura, Sven Ole-Thorsen, Marjorie Bransfield, James Belushi. D: Damian Lee. SFI [R] 90m. V

Abroad With Two Yanks 1944 ★★★½ Two Marines (O'Keefe and Bendix) run rampant through Australia in pursuit of the same woman (Walker). High-energy gags and playful spirit buoy this easygoing comic romp. C: William Bendix, Dennis O'Keefe, Helen Walker, John Loder. D: Allan Dwan. COM 81m. V

Absence of Malice 1981 ★★★★ A reporter (Field) maligns a reputed con (Newman) in print, then finds she may have brought about the downfall of an innocent man. Sharply structured intrigue and graceful star performances bring a refreshing dose of humanity to cynical surroundings. C: Paul Newman, Sally Field, Bob Balaban, Melinda Dillon, Luther Adler, Wilford Brimley. D: Sydney Pollack. DRA [PG] 116m. V

Absent Minded Professor, The 1961 ★★★★ Genial Disney fantasy casts MacMurray as a mild-mannered genius who discovers flying rubber (flubber), enabling cars to fly, etc. Nifty special effects. Followed by *Son of Flubber.* C: Fred MacMurray, Nancy Olson, Keenan Wynn, Tommy Kirk, Ed Wynn. D: Robert Stevenson. FAM/COM [G] 97m. V

Absinthe 1929 *See* **Madame X**

Absolute Beginners 1986 British ★★★½ Music-video director Temple delivers eye-popping visuals in this musical feature about teen life in '50s London. Terrific tunes include great Bowie title track. C: Eddie O'Connell, Patsy Kensit, David Bowie, James Fox, Ray Davies, Anita Morris. D: Julien Temple. MUS [PG-13] 107m. V

Absolute Strangers 1991 ★★★★ Winkler is very good in this gripping abortion drama about the husband of an incapacitated pregnant woman and his attempt to save her life even if it means terminating her pregnancy. Playwright Robert Anderson's script is well crafted and provocative. C: Henry Winkler, Karl Malden, Richard Kiley, Patty Duke. D: Gilbert Cates. DRA 100m. TVM

Absolutely Positive 1991 ★★★★½ Absorbing, trenchant documentary profiles a diverse group of people living with AIDS. Brave, generous individuals relate their true tales of coping; the universal humanity of each of them hits home with shattering impact. DOC

Absolutely the Best of the Soupy Sales Show ★★★★½ Choice clips from the brilliant 1960s kiddie show, which combined clever wit with utter lunacy. White Tooth, Black Fang, Pookie and all the rest are here, lovingly preserved. COM 50m. V

Absolution 1978 British ★★★ Twisted tale of a teacher/priest (Burton) at boys' boarding school forced into committing murder by a manipulative pupil (Guard). Slow-moving plot is somewhat forced, but the performances are interesting. Written (in typical game-playing fashion) by Anthony Shaffer. C: Richard Burton, Dominic Guard, Dai Bradley. D: Anthony Page. CRI [R] 95m. V

Abyss, The 1989 ★★★ Fine cast highlights this otherwise waterlogged adventure of a crew of oil-well riggers attempting to rescue a damaged submarine. Good underwater cinematography, but slow and overlong. Oscar winner for Visual Effects. C: Ed Harris, Mary Elizabeth Mastrantonio, Michael Biehn, Leo Burmester, Todd Graff, Chris Elliott. D: James Cameron. SFI [PG-13] 140m. V

Academy Awarded Winners—Animated Short Films 1983 ★★★★ Six Oscar-winning cartoons ranging in style from the satirical "Munro" to the lyrical "Moonbird." Very entertaining for all ages. COM 60m. V

Acapulco Gold 1978 ★★½ Gortner smuggles drugs in and out of Hawaii. Some magnificent location scenery. C: Marjoe Gortner, Robert Lansing, Ed Nelson. D: Burt Brinckerhoff. DRA [PG] 105m.

Accattone 1961 Italian ★★★★ Gritty tale of criminal underworld follows a small-time hood trying to come to terms with the directions his life has taken. First film from Italian director Pasolini (adapted from his own novel) makes effective use of real locations and documentary-style shooting. C: Franco Citti, Franca Pasut, Roberto Scaringella. D: Pier Paolo Pasolini. CRI 116m. V

Accent on Youth 1935 ★★★★ Twist on May-December affairs de coeur as older playwright (Marshall) is unlikely beneficiary of the affections of his younger secretary (Sidney). Humor has aged a little around the edges, but there still are some sweet laughs to savor in this breezy comedy adapted from a popular Broadway show. C: Sylvia Sidney, Herbert Marshall. D: Wesley Ruggles. COM 77m.

Acceptable Levels 1983 British ★★★½ Hard-hitting study of the conflict in Ireland from a Catholic perspective, detailing a conspiracy to suppress a damning act of violence caught on-camera by a British TV crew. A good political drama, if not a balanced one. C: Kay Adshead, Andy Rashleigh, Patrick Higgins. D: John Davies. DRA 103m.

Acceptable Risks 1986 ★★★★ Dennehy scores as a plant manager, ordered to cut costs and skimp on safety, who fights politicians to rescue his town. C: Brian Dennehy, Cicely Tyson, Kenneth McMillan. D: Rick Wallace. DRA 97m. TVM

Accident 1967 British ★★★ Psychological drama about married Oxford professor (Bogarde) who becomes infatuated with an attractive student. Adaptation of Harold Pinter's play keeps his trademarks—obscure motivations and confusing plot twists. C: Dirk Bogarde, Stanley Baker, Jacqueline Sassard, Delphine Seyrig, Michael York, Vivian Merchant, Harold Pinter. D: Joseph Losey. DRA 105m. V

Accidental Tourist, The 1988 ★★★★ Shattered by the violent death of his son, a travel writer (Hurt) withdraws from the world until an eccentric charmer (Oscar-winner Davis) brings him out of his shell. Adapted from the Anne Tyler best-seller, it's a witty, poignant, and tenderly romantic story. C: William Hurt, Kathleen Turner, Geena Davis, Amy Wright, David Ogden Stiers, Ed Begley Jr. D: Lawrence Kasdan. DRA [PG] 121m. V

Accidents 1988 Australian ★★★ Surgical invention is stolen from scientist (Albert) by corporate bigwig, who plans to market the device to terrorists. Mild suspense picture. C: Edward Albert, Leigh Taylor-Young, Jon Cypher. D: Gideon Amir. CRI [R] 90m. V

Accidents Will Happen 1939 ★★★ A claims adjustor (Reagan) investigates an insurance fraud. Quick pace and neat characterizations in a trim little package. C: Ronald Reagan, Gloria Blondell. D: William Clemens. DRA 62m.

Accomplices, The 1959 Italian ★★½ A woman can't choose between her two lovers until a murder makes the decision for her. A lot of heavy breathing. C: Sandro Luporini, Sandro Fizzotro. D: Gianni Vernuccio. DRA 93m.

Accursed, The 1958 British ★★½ Members of a military unit are dying off one by one, which motivates those remaining to find the murderer. Somewhat tame, given the premise. C: Donald Wolfit, Robert Bray, Jane Griffiths, Christopher Lee. D: Michael McCarthy. CRI 78m.

Accused 1958 *See* **Mark of the Hawk, The**

Accused of Murder 1956 ★★★ Honest cop (Brian) gets tangled up in a murderous affair when he falls for sultry Ralston. Seductive setup to a familiar melodrama. C: Vera Hruba Ralston, David Brian, Sidney Blackmer. D: Joseph Kane. DRA 74m.

Accused 1936 British ★★★½ Glamorous mystery set in a Parisian nightclub. Desmond and del Rio play two firebrands competing for Fairbanks; one gets knocked off. Slick entertainment has some sizzle. C: Douglas Fairbanks, Jr., Dolores Del Rio, Florence Desmond. D: Thorton Freeland. DRA 83m.

Accused, The 1948 ★★★★ A prim schoolteacher (Young) kills an amorous student, then covers her crime. Neat psychological thriller, well acted by intriguingly cast star. C: Loretta Young, Robert Cummings, Wendell Corey, Sam Jaffe. D: William Dieterle. DRA 101m.

Accused, The 1988 ★★★★ Intense, hard-hitting exploration of rape and its victims is a sharp indictment of the American legal system. When a tough young woman (Foster) is gang-raped, prosecutor (McGillis) treats the case as a routine plea-bargain, until Foster's outrage makes her reconsider. Extraordinarily moving, with an Oscar-winning performance by Foster. Sadly, based on a true story. C: Jodie Foster, Kelly McGillis, Bernie Coulson, Leo Rossi. D: Jonathan Kaplan. CRI [R] 110m. V

Ace Eli and Rodger of the Skies 1973 ★★½ A battle-scarred stunt pilot (Robertson) barnstorms through the early '20s, with his son (Shea) eager to follow in his footsteps. Highlight is the fabulous aerial photography; Peters' screen debut. Based on a story by Steven Spielberg. C: Cliff Robertson, Pamela Franklin, Eric Shea, Rosemary Murphy, Bernadette Peters, Alice Ghostley. D: Bill Sampson. ACT [PG] 92m.

Ace High 1969 Italian ★★★ Outlaw (Wallach) runs wild south of the border while doing anything he can to get his hands on some ill-gotten gains. Low-voltage, low-budget Italian spoof of Western-genre conventions. C: Eli Wallach, Terence Hill, Bud Spencer, Brock Peters, Kevin McCarthy. D: Giuseppe Colizzi. WST 120m. V

Ace in the Hole 1951 *See* **Big Carnival, The**

Ace of Aces 1933 ★★★½ Melodramatic but interesting antiwar film, in which a young sculptor (Dix) is shamed into enlisting during WWI as a pilot, and winds up a celebrated war hero. Chronicle of his reaction makes for a better than average aviation thriller. C: Richard Dix, Elizabeth Allan, Ralph Bellamy, Theodore Newton. D: J. Ruben. ACT 76m.

Ace Ventura: Pet Detective 1994 ★★½ When football's Miami Dolphins' beloved porpoise mascot is kidnapped, private eye Carrey tracks it down. The rubber-faced star spews scatological and lewd jokes. Preadolescents will love this one. C: Jim Carrey. COM V

Aces & Eights 1936 ★★★½ Authentic look at gamblers of the Old West, as McCoy plays a straight gambler foiling a cheat. C: Tim McCoy, Luana Walters, Wheeler Oakman. WST 54m.

Aces Go Places 2 1983 China ★★★ Chinese send-up of James Bond has a charming slapstick quality. C: Sam Hui, Sylvia Chang, Carl Mak. D: Eric Tsang. COM 100m.

Aces High 1977 British ★★★★ Excellent cast heads solid old-fashioned war drama recounting the adventures of a crack group of WWI airmen. Steeped in clichés of older war films, but making no apologies. C: Malcolm McDowell, Christopher Plummer, Simon Ward, Peter Firth. D: Jack Gold. ACT [PG] 104m.

Aces: Iron Eagle III 1992 ★★★½ An improvement over the first two installments in the *Iron Eagle* series, Chappy (Gossett, Jr.) this time shapes up a crew of WWII veterans to rescue a small village from parasitic drug dealers. Surprisingly suspenseful. C: Louis Gossett, Jr., Rachel McLish, Christopher Cazenove, Horst Buchholz. D: John Glen. ACT [R] 93m.

Acorn People, The 1981 ★★★½ A camp counselor establishes a unique and tender relationship with a group of disabled children. Tender and well played. C: Ted Bessell, LeVar Burton, Cloris Leachman. D: Joan Tewkesbury. DRA 100m. TVM

Acorraldo ★★★½ Violent but also touching tale of a vicious cross-country manhunt with a tender love story. C: Julieta Rosen, Sergio Jimenez, Claudio Abregon. CRI 90m. V

Across 110th Street 1972 ★★★½ What's the biggest mistake a Harlem street gang can make? Stealing $300,000 from the Mafia. Quinn is a racist police captain caught in the middle of the resulting bloodbath. Fast-moving and violent with a capital V. C: Anthony Quinn, Yaphet Kotto, Anthony Franciosa, Richard Ward. D: Barry Shear. ACT [R] 102m. V

Across the Bridge 1957 British ★★★★ A corrupt business magnate (Steiger) leads Scotland Yard authorities on an international chase after he illegally helps himself to a healthy bundle of money. Sharp-edged cast really delivers the goods—particularly Steiger, whose neurotic performance is a doozy. C: Rod Steiger, David Knight, Bernard Lee. D: Ken Annakin. ACT 103m.

Across the Great Divide 1977 ★★★½ Orphans (Rattray and Hall) trek to Oregon to claim their rightful inheritance. Logan's the con artist who hustles them. 1870s period piece boasts magnificent Rockies scenery, glimpses of wilderness and animal life. Appealing family film, but not much in the way of plot. C: Robert Logan, Heather Rattray, Mark Edward Hall. D: Stewart Raffill. FAM/ACT [G] 102m. V

Across the Pacific 1942 ★★★★ *Maltese Falcon* veterans reunite in a classic pre-WWII adventure. American ex-officer (Bogart) sails for China to enlist with the Nationalist forces, tangling with a pro-Japanese spy (Greenstreet) and falling in love (with Astor) en route. C: Humphrey Bogart, Mary Astor, Sydney Greenstreet, Victor Sen Yung, Keye Luke. D: John Huston. DRA 98m. V

Across the Tracks 1991 ★★★½ Back from reform school, a teenager (Schroder) becomes a star of the high school track team, but develops conflict with his older brother (Pitt). Intelligent, thought-provoking drama on the troubles of teen youth. Released to video in two versions, one rated R and the other PG-13. C: Rick Schroder, Brad Pitt, Carrie Snodgress. D: Sandy Tung. DRA [R,PG-13] 101m. V

Across the Wide Missouri 1951 ★★★ Gable and Montalban are 19th-century pioneers going West. The location shooting looks great, but the story makes for a bumpy and inconsistent ride. C: Clark Gable, Ricardo Montalban, John Hodiak, Adolphe Menjou. D: William Wellman. WST 78m. V

Act of Love 1953 ★★ Lonely G.I. (Douglas) and a destitute French woman (Robin) begin a doomed romance in 1944 Paris. Sentimental and slow; viewed today, ending looks trite rather than tragic. Based on Alfred Hayes' novel *The Girl on the Via Flaminia.* C: Kirk Douglas, Dany Robin, Barbara Laage, Robert Strauss, Brigitte Bardot. D: Anatole Litvak. DRA 108m.

Act of Murder, An 1948 ★★★★½ March gives a fine performance as a judge on trial for the mercy killing of his wife (Eldridge). Sincere, finely tuned drama. C: Fredric March, Florence Eldridge, Edmond O'Brien, Geraldine Brooks. D: Michael Gordon. DRA 91m.

Act of Piracy 1990 ★★½ Gang of modern-day pirates (led by Sharkey) plunders wealthy Busey's yacht. But the scalawags also kidnap Busey's children, so the heroic father heads out on a rescue mission. Action feature offers genre-formulated entertainment. C: Gary Busey, Belinda Bauer, Ray Sharkey. D: John Cardos. ACT [R] 101m. V

Act of the Heart 1970 Canadian ★★★½ A young farm woman's religious fanaticism manifests itself in forbidden love for Montreal priest, with tragic results for both of them. Fascinating character study, but flawed ending weakens film. C: Genevieve Bujold, Donald Sutherland. D: Paul Almond. DRA [PG] 103m.

Act of Vengeance 1974 *See* **Rape Squad**

Act of Vengeance 1986 ★★½ When he challenges the president of the United Mine Workers, a man and his family are killed. So-so dramatization of real-life event, despite strong cast. C: Charles Bronson, Ellen Burstyn, Wilford Brimley, Ellen Barkin, Keanu Reeves. D: John Mackenzie. DRA 95m. TVM V

Act of Violence 1949 ★★★★ A young soldier (Ryan), home from WWII, tries to track down an informer (Heflin) from prison camp. Slick and tense throughout. Nice go by the star cast. C: Van Heflin, Robert Ryan, Janet Leigh, Mary Astor, Phyllis Thaxter. D: Fred Zinnemann. DRA 82m.

Act of Violence 1979 ★★★★ Career-minded Montgomery experiences liberating feelings after divorce—until she's attacked by a vicious gang of muggers and forced to reconsider many formerly held beliefs. Tough-minded film with an uncompromising performance from Montgomery. (a.k.a. *Deadline Assault*). C: Elizabeth Montgomery, James Sloyan, Sean Frye, Roy Poole. D: Paul Wendkos. DRA 100m. TVM V

Act One 1963 ★★★½ Backstage look at playwright Moss Hart's early career, based on his autobiography. Lacks verve of the book, but it's still an interesting stroll down the Great White Way. Robards is fine as Hart's partner George S. Kaufman. C: George Hamilton, Jason Robards, George Segal, Eli Wallach, Sam Levene, Jack Klugman. D: Dore Schary. DRA 110m.

Acting on Impulse 1993 ★★★½ Tongue-in-cheek thriller about a schlock movie star (Fiorentino) mixed up in a real-life murder. Good performances, fast pacing. C: Linda Fiorentino, C. Thomas Howell, Nancy Allen, Paul Bartel, Isaac Hayes. D: Sam Irvin. CRI 93m. TVM V

Action for Slander 1938 British ★★★ British major sues two fellow officers who've accused him of cheating at cards. A bit talky, but solid cast helps. C: Clive Brook, Ann Todd, Margaretta Scott, Arthur Margetson, Ronald Squire. D: Tim Whelan. DRA 84m. V

Action in Arabia 1944 ★★★ WWII melodrama about U.S. journalist (Sanders) in Damascus who learns Arabs are collaborating with the Nazis. Low-budget adventure. C: George Sanders, Virginia Bruce, Gene Lockhart, Robert Armstrong. D: Leonide Moguy. DRA 72m. V

Action in the North Atlantic 1943 ★★★★ The heroics of the American Merchant Marine in WWII are lauded in this action drama about a ship running supplies through U-boat infested waters to Russia. Bogart and Massey are perfect as the first mate and captain of embattled vessel. C: Humphrey Bogart, Raymond Massey, Alan Hale, Julie Bishop, Ruth Gordon, Sam Levene. D: Lloyd Bacon. ACT 127m. V

Action Jackson 1988 ★★★ Weathers flexes his way through the mean streets of Detroit as a cop out to get even with an evil auto magnate (Nelson). Complicated plot doesn't always make sense, but memorable stunts almost make up for it. C: Carl Weathers, Craig T. Nelson, Vanity, Sharon Stone. D: Craig Baxley. ACT [R] 95m. V

Action of the Tiger 1957 British ★★★½ Occasionally exciting romp about an unlikely action hero (Johnson) liberating refugees from Albania. Lom is the best of an intriguing cast. C: Van Johnson, Martine Carol, Herbert Lom, Sean Connery. D: Terence Young. ACT 94m.

Actors and Sin 1952 ★★★½ Pair of short movies about show business. "Actors Blood" stars Robinson as a washed-up actor with a famous daughter. "Woman of Sin" features Albert as an agent peddling a nine-year-old girl's racy manuscript. Second half's sparkling satire makes it worthwhile. C: Edward G. Robinson, Eddie Albert, Marsha Hunt, Alan Reed, Dan O'Herlihy. D: Lee Garmes. DRA 86m. V

Actor's Revenge, An 1963 Japanese ★★★★ Kabuki female impersonator wreaks glorious vengeance on three men who ruined his parents. Shot in CinemaScope, the movie is a glittering visual feast featuring razor-sharp editing and dazzling Technicolor palette. A must for Japanese film fans. C: Kazuo Hasegawa, Ayako Wakao. D: Kon Ichikawa. DRA 110m. V

Actress, The 1953 ★★★★ Nostalgic, sweetly funny account of a young woman's (Simmons) struggle for an acting career against the wishes of her father (Tracy). Adapted from Ruth Gordon's autobiographical play *Years Ago.* Fine sparring by Simmons and Tracy. C: Spencer Tracy, Jean Simmons, Teresa Wright,

Anthony Perkins, Mary Wickes. D: George Cukor. DRA 91m.

Ada 1961 ★★★★ Entertaining melodrama about determined wife (Hayward) pushing husband (Martin) into governor's mansion. Zesty climb-to-the-top soaper, with fine Haywood, especially in climactic state senate showdown. C: Susan Hayward, Dean Martin, Wilfrid Hyde-White, Martin Balsam. D: Daniel Mann. DRA 109m.

Adam 1983 ★★★★ A little boy is kidnapped and murdered in this story, based on an actual incident in Florida. Travanti and Williams are excellent as the anguished parents who push for reform in child disappearance laws. Heartbreaking and timely; the boy's real-life father, John Walsh, went on to host TV's *America's Most Wanted.* C: Daniel J. Travanti, JoBeth Williams, Martha Scott, Richard Masur. D: Michael Tuchner. CRI 97m. TVM V

Adam and Evalyn 1949 British ★★★½ A gambling man (Granger) winds up caring for a young woman when her father dies—with the usual complications. Warmhearted, pleasant affair. (a.k.a. *Adam and Evelyne*) C: Jean Simmons, Stewart Granger, Wilfrid Hyde-White. D: Harold French. DRA 92m.

Adam and Evelyne 1949 *See* **Adam and Evalyn**

Adam at 6 A.M. 1970 ★★★★ A spirited young California college professor takes off for the summer to do manual labor in Missouri. Intelligent, well-rounded story, with excellent performances. C: Michael Douglas, Lee Purcell, Joe Don Baker, Grayson Hall, Meg Foster. D: Robert Scheerer. DRA [PG] 100m. V

Adam Had Four Sons 1941 ★★★½ Bland, overplotted soap about governess (Bergman) who raises Baxter's sons. She suffers nobly for the clan, largely because of seductress Hayward who muscles in. Worthy only for Bergman's warmth and Hayward's fire. C: Ingrid Bergman, Warner Baxter, Susan Hayward, Fay Wray. D: Gregory Ratoff. DRA 81m.

Adam: His Song Continues 1986 ★★½ True story about the parents of a lost child and their efforts to start up a nationwide network for missing children. Lesser sequel to 1983's *Adam.* C: Daniel J. Travanti, JoBeth Williams, Richard Masur, Martha Scott. D: Robert Markowitz. DRA 100m. TVM

Adam's Rib 1949 ★★★★★ Sparkling comedy classic stars Hepburn and Tracy in one of their best screen pairings, as married attorneys arguing different sides of the same murder case. A terrific supporting cast and the stylish, witty screenplay (by real-life husband-and-wife writing team of Gordon/Kanin) make for must-see viewing. C: Spencer Tracy, Katharine Hepburn, David Wayne, Judy Holliday, Tom Ewell, Jean Hagen. D: George Cukor. COM 101m. V

Adam's Rib 1994 Russia ★★★½ Four women learn to live in a small apartment that they must share during hard, but exhilarating times in post-communist Russia. D: Vyacheslav Krishtofovich. DRA 77m. V

Adam's Woman 1972 U.S. ★★★ Wrongly convicted Bridges tries to escape from a brutal 19th-century Australian penal colony. Mills, in a terrific performance as the reform-minded governor, quietly steals the show. (a.k.a. *Return of the Boomerang*) C: Beau Bridges, John Mills, Jane Merrow. D: Philip Leacock. DRA 116m.

Addams Family—Ghost Town 1991 ★★★½ Four entries from the animated series inspired by the New Yorker cartoons and the live-action TV series. Crudely drawn, but full of wicked humor. FAM/COM 90m. V

Addams Family—Left in the Lurch 1991 ★★★½ More animated adventures of the unusually gruesome, but good-natured clan. Often amusing, despite flat visuals. FAM/COM 90m. V

Addams Family, The 1991 ★★★½ A sinister lawyer schemes to pilfer the fortune of America's favorite macabre family by placing an imposter Uncle Fester in their midst. A bit overproduced, but good performances (especially Ricci as Wednesday) help convey some of the lunacy of the '60s sitcom as well as the demented humor of Charles Addams' original cartoons. Followed by a sequel. C: Anjelica Huston, Raul Julia, Christopher Lloyd, Dan Hedaya, Elizabeth Wilson, Judith Malina, Christina Ricci. D: Barry Sonnenfeld. COM [PG-13] 102m. V

Addams Family, The—Vol. 1 ★★★★ Episodes of the zany TV series that brought Charles Addams' creations to life. Classic comedy that's part of our culture (snap, snap). C: Carolyn Jones, Jackie Coogan, Blosom Rock, John Astin, Ken Weatherwax, Lisa Loring, Ted Cassidy, Felix Silla. FAM/COM 45m. V

Addams Family, The—Vol. 2 ★★★★ Two episodes from the TV series, with those "creepy, kooky" eccentrics in fine form. Features "Morticia Joins the Ladies League" and "Fester's Punctured Romance." C: Carolyn Jones, John Astin, Jackie Coogan, Blossom Rock, Ken Wetherwax, Lisa Loring, Ted Cassidy, Felix Silla. FAM/COM 45m. V

Addams Family, The—Vol. 3 ★★★★ More inspired lunacy from the oddball TV series. Features "The Addams Family Tree" and "Gomez the Politician." C: Carolyn Jones, John Astin, Ken Weatherwax, Lisa Loring, Jackie Coogan, Blossom Rock, Ted Cassidy, Felix Silla. FAM/COM 45m. V

Addams Family, The—Vol. 4 ★★★★ Morbid Morticia (Jones) is featured in this delightful pairing of two episodes from the TV series, including "New Neighbors Meet the Addams Family" and "Morticia the Matchmaker." C: Carolyn Jones, John Astin, Ken Weatherwax, Lisa Loring, Jackie Coogan, Blossom Rock, Ted Cassidy, Felix Silla. FAM/COM 45m. V

Addams Family, The—Vol. 5 ★★★★ Fans of the vintage TV series (or the recent movies) will want to catch Astin as "Green-Eyed Gomez," paired with "Wednesday Leaves Home." C: Carolyn Jones, John Astin, Ken Weatherwax, Lisa Loring, Jackie Coogan, Blossom Rock, Ted Cassidy, Felix Silla. FAM/COM 45m. V

Addams Family, The—Vol. 6 ★★★★ Two episodes from the 1960s TV series, featuring one of the best: "Lurch Learns to Dance." Also: "The Adams Family Meets the VIP's." C: Carolyn Jones, John Astin, Ken Weatherwax, Lisa Loring, Jackie Coogan, Blossom Rock, Ted Cassidy, Felix Silla. FAM/COM 45m. V

Addams Family Values 1993 ★★★½ A murderous gold digger (Cusack) sets her sights on Uncle Fester (Lloyd)'s fortune, while Wednesday (Ricci) and Pugsley (Workman) are sent to wreak havoc on a posh summer camp. The cast obviously has a ball sprinting from gag to gag in this second big-screen installment. Erratic but wickedly funny. C: Anjelica Huston, Raul Julia, Christopher Lloyd, Christina Ricci, Joan Cusack, Jimmy Workman. D: Barry Sonnenfeld. COM [PG-13] 94m. V

Addict 1971 ★★★★ Highly original comedy about drug addiction (yes, *comedy*), with George Segal giving a stand-out performance as a NYC hairdresser resorting to crime to support his heroin habit. Wonderfully irreverent treatment of a serious subject. (a.k.a. *Born to Win*) C: George Segal, Karen Black, Paula Prentiss, Hector Elizondo, Robert De Niro. D: Ivan Passer. COM [R] 100m. V

Adding Machine, The 1969 U.S. ★★★ Bookkeeper (O'Shea) turns to violence when he's replaced by a computer. Fantasy satire based on the Elmer Rice play is uneven but still interesting. Diller gets chance at serious role, and does fine. C: Milo O'Shea, Phyllis Diller, Billie Whitelaw. D: Jerome Epstein. COM [PG] 100m.

Address Unknown 1944 ★★½ Studio propaganda piece about a German-American revisiting the Fatherland during WWII and being brainwashed into becoming a Nazi. Nice sets and photography by master designer/director Menzies. C: Paul Lukas, Mady Christians, Morris Carnovsky. D: William Menzies. DRA 72m.

Adele Hasn't Had Her Dinner Yet 1978 *See* **Dinner for Adele**

Adios Amigo 1976 ★★½ Inane slapstick comedy follows escapades of two black con artists in the Old West. Occasionally amusing. C: Fred Williamson, Richard Pryor, James Brown, Mike Henry. D: Fred Williamson. COM 87m. V

Adios, Sabata 1971 Italian ★★ Opportunistic lone wolf (Brynner) uses the Mexican revolution to get his hands on gold. Spaghetti-Western sequel to *Sabata*; followed by *The Return of Sabata*. C: Yul Brynner, Dean Reed. D: Frank Kramer. WST [PG] 104m.

Adjuster, The 1991 Canadian ★★★★ Quirky tragicomedy about an intense, obsessed insurance adjuster who inevitably winds up having sex with his clients, and his voyeuristic wife, who makes a living censoring pornographic films. Provocative fantasy is not for everyone, but performances are strong. C: Elias Koteas, Arsinee Khanjian, Maury Chaykin, Gabrielle Rose. D: Atom Egoyan. DRA [R] 102m. V

Admirable Crichton, The 1957 British ★★★★ When a group of upper-crust British families are shipwrecked it's a resourceful butler who maintains an orderly life. His attentiveness brings romantic interest from both a wealthy young woman and another family servant. Funny and charming (a.k.a *Paradise Lagoon*). C: Kenneth More, Diane Cilento, Cecil Parker, Sally Ann Howes, Martita Hunt. D: Lewis Gilbert. COM 94m.

Admiral Was a Lady, The 1950 ★★★ Hendrix hands in her naval stripes and finds that the sharks on land are more dangerous than those at sea as she's pursued by a bunch of ne'er-do-wells. Breezy trifle provides some amusement. C: Edmond O'Brien, Wanda Hendrix, Rudy Vallee. D: Albert Rogell. COM 87m. V

Adolescent, The 1979 French ★★★ Another of Moreau's occasional outings as director is a well-meaning though monotonously executed tale of a French girl whose early teen years are shaped by events of WWII. (a.k.a. *L'Adolescente*). C: Laetitia Chauveau, Simone Signoret, Edith Clever, Jacques Weber, Francis Huster. D: Jeanne Moreau. DRA 90m.

Adorable Creatures 1956 French ★★★ The men and women of a small French town keep ending up in the wrong bed. Darrieux and Carol add to this mild little sex farce. C: Daniel Gelin, Martine Carol, Edwige Feuillere, Danielle Darrieux. D: Christian Jaque. COM 108m.

Adorable Julia 1962 French ★★★ Though married to a theatrical producer (Boyer), aging actress (Palmer) indulges in an affair with a much younger romantic interest (Sorel). Their liaison, however, does not end happily. Frothy adaptation of work by Somerset Maugham whips up a soap opera soufflé. C: Lilli Palmer, Charles Boyer, Jean Sorel. D: Alfred Weidenmann. DRA 94m.

Adrift 1993 ★★½ After being rescued from near drowning in a river, a young woman finds her benefactor falling in love with her. Simplistic tale that veers ineptly between comedy and drama. C: Kate Jackson, Kenneth Welsh, Bruce Greenwood. DRA 92m. V

Advance to the Rear 1964 ★★★★ During the Civil War, a Confederate spy dupes bumbling Union soldiers out of a shipment of gold bullion. Rollicking Western/comedy with slapstick fun. C: Glenn Ford, Stella Stevens, Melvyn Douglas, Joan Blondell, Jim Backus. D: George Marshall. WST 97m.

Adventure 1945 ★★½ A vagabond seaman (Gable) flirts with a staid librarian (Garson). The two stars were mismatched, with no script support. Gable's first post-WWII movie, famous for ad slogan: "Gable's back and Garson's got him!," but neither star shines in this disappointing comedy. C: Clark Gable, Greer Garson, Joan Blondell, Thomas Mitchell. D: Victor Fleming. COM 125m. V

Adventure in Baltimore 1949 ★★★ Turn-of-the-century comedy has a liberated young woman (Temple) ruffling the feathers of her pompous family with her outrageous ideas about love. Nothing new, particularly, but a pleasant cast. (a.k.a. *Bachelor Bait*) C: Shirley Temple, John Agar, Robert Young. D: Richard Wallace. COM 89m.

Adventure in Diamonds 1940 ★★★ Familiar faces lend believability to this adventure about an African jewel heist. Otherwise, standard studio fare. C: George Brent, Isa Miranda, Nigel Bruce. D: George Fitzmaurice. CRI 76m.

Adventure in Manhattan 1936 ★★★ Suave jewel thief (Owen) finds that his burglaries are being predicted by a criminologist (McCrea) hired by a newspaper. Interesting, early film noir. (a.k.a. *Manhattan Madness*) C: Jean Arthur, Joel McCrea, Reginald Owen, Thomas Mitchell. D: Edward Ludwig. CRI 73m.

Adventure in the Hopfields 1954 British ★★★½ After breaking a treasured piece of her mother's porcelain, a girl takes a job on a farm, where she learns a lesson about people's capacity for cruelty. Literate kids' film, with slightly dark British edge. C: Mandy Miller, Mona Washbourne, Hilda Fenemore. D: John Guillermin. FAM/DRA 60m.

Adventure in Washington 1941 ★★½ Senator (Marshall) gives a young thug a break and sets him to work as a pageboy. Sincere, if rather dated. C: Herbert Marshall, Virginia Bruce, Gene Reynolds. D: Alfred Green. DRA 84m.

Adventure Island 1947 ★★★ Marooned on a deserted island, a group of people are driven to violence by its crazed, self-proclaimed ruler. Kelly and cast provide some interesting moments. Remake of *Ebb Tide*. C: Rory Calhoun, Rhonda Fleming, Paul Kelly. D: Peter Stewart. ACT 66m.

Adventure of Sherlock Holmes' Smarter Brother, The 1978 ★★★½ Wilder (in his first attempt as writer/director) plays the younger sibling of London's famous sleuth. Hired by chanteuse (Kahn), he tries to overcome Sherlock's shadow by solving a mystery. Fair spoof, with good comic cast, energy and a sense of fun. Watch out for the hilarious fog-shrouded duel with oversize boots atop careening coaches. (a.k.a. *Sherlock Holmes' Smarter Brother*) C: Gene Wilder, Madeline Kahn, Marty Feldman, Dom DeLuise, Leo McKern. D: Gene Wilder. COM [PG] 91m. V

Adventurers, The 1952 *See* **Fortune in Diamonds**

Adventurers, The 1970 ★ Trashy, tedious adaptation of trashy, tedious Harold Robbins novel about a destructive playboy. Great cast totally wasted. C: Bekim Fehmiu, Candice Bergen, Ernest Borgnine, Olivia de Havilland, Leigh Taylor-Young, Rossano Brazzi. D: Lewis Gilbert. DRA [PG] 191m. V

Adventures in Babysitting 1987 ★★★½ A quiet evening of babysitting becomes anything but when sitter Shue drags her two young charges along to rescue a friend stranded on the mean streets of Chicago. Director's debut is lively, appealing teen comedy. C: Elisabeth Shue, Maia Brewton, Keith Coogan, Anthony Rapp, Vincent Phillip D'Onofrio, Penelope Ann Miller. D: Chris Columbus. COM [PG-13] 102m. V

Adventures of a Private Eye 1987 ★★★ A fun romp through the hard-boiled private eye film clichés of the past, with Neil as the detective looking for Dors' blackmailer. C: Christopher Neil, Suzy Kendall, Diana Dors. D: Stanley Long. COM 96m.

Adventures of a Taxi Driver 1976 British ★★ Dorky cabdriver is continually propositioned by his clients. This other 1976 *Taxi Driver* is part farce, part whodunit, and not totally competent. C: Barry Evans, Judy Geeson, Adrienne Posta, Diana Dors. D: Stanley Long. COM 89m.

Adventures of a Two-Minute Werewolf, The ★★★ A young horror movie buff is turned into a werewolf by one of his favorite movies. Mildly diverting fluff. C: Lainie Kazan, Melba Moore, Barrie Youngfellow. FAM/COM 60m. V

Adventures of a Young Man 1962 ★★½ Beymer stars as fictional creation Nick Adams in this episodic adaptation of several of writer Ernest Hemingway's autobiographical short stories. Complex, labyrinthine production. (a.k.a. *Hemingway's Adventures of a Young Man*). C: Richard Beymer, Diane Baker, Corinne Calvet, Dan Dailey, Arthur Kennedy, Ricardo Montalban, Susan Strasberg, Jessica Tandy, Eli Wallach, Paul Newman. D: Martin Ritt. DRA 145m.

Adventures of Arsene Lupin 1956 French ★★★ Colorful caper film, with Lamourex as the Robin Hood-like jewel thief targeting the German aristocracy before WWI. Stylish, lively. C: Robert Lamoureux, O.E. Hasse, Lisolotte Pulver. D: Jacques Becker. DRA 103m.

Adventures of Babar 1970 ★★★★ Animated features of the beloved elephant and his friends in their charming adventures. FAM/ACT 60m.

Adventures of Babar—Vol. 2 1970 ★★★½ That noble elephant and children's story favorite returns in this loveable assortment of animated tales. FAM/ACT 60m. V

Adventures of Babar—Vol. 3 1970 ★★★½ The animated elephant's adventures continue.

Will please all pint-sized fans of the first two, while evoking some smiles from their captive adults. FAM/ACT 60m. v

Adventures of Baron Munchausen, The 1989 ★★★½ Eighteenth-century adventure tale stars Neville in title role, traveling to moon, seas and beyond. Marvelous to look at, with dreamlike design, but lack of clear plotting undercuts stylish gloss; star-packed cast can't overcome script troubles. Story previously filmed in 1943 and 1961. C: John Neville, Eric Idle, Sarah Polley, Oliver Reed, Jonathan Pryce, Uma Thurman. D: Terry Gilliam. SFI [PG] 126m. v

Adventures of Barry Mckenzie, The 1972 Australian ★★★½ In this rambunctious adventure, a boorish, ill-mannered clan from Australia gets into all kinds of trouble when they travel to England. Aims for crude, lowbrow laughs and scores. Director's debut. Sequel: *Barry McKenzie Holds His Own.* C: Barry Crocker, Barry Humphries, Peter Cook, Spike Milligan. D: Bruce Beresford. COM 114m.

Adventures of Buckaroo Banzai Across the Eighth Dimension, The 1984 ★★★½ Jumbled story finds run-of-the-mill neurosurgeon-jetcar-driver-rock-star (Weller) saving Earth from the evil Dr. Lizardo (Lithgow). Superb cast portrays comic book characters in a film that should have been much better. A cult favorite nonetheless. (a.k.a. *Buckaroo Banzai*) C: Peter Weller, John Lithgow, Ellen Barkin, Jeff Goldblum, Christopher Lloyd. D: W. D. Richter. SFI [PG] 103m. v

Adventures of Bullwhip Griffin, The 1966 ★★★★ Proper English butler saves the day for his aristocratic masters in this Western spoof set during the California Gold Rush of 1849. McDowell has great fun as the butler. Good family viewing; stresses positive values. C: Roddy McDowall, Suzanne Pleshette, Karl Malden, Harry Guardino, Richard Haydn. D: James Neilson. FAM/COM 110m. v

Adventures of Captain Fabian 1951 ★★ Shallow adventure on the high seas, with a sea captain (Flynn) involved with an innocent woman imprisoned for murder. C: Errol Flynn, Micheline Presle, Agnes Moorehead, Vincent Price. D: William Marshall. ACT 100m. v

Adventures of Casanova 1948 ★★★ The people of Sicily call upon Casanova (de Cordova) to lead a revolution against evil rulers. Period piece with plenty of adventure. C: Arturo Cordova, Lucille Bremer, Turhan Bey. D: Roberto Gavaldon. ACT 83m.

Adventures of Charlie and Cubby, The ★★★½ Unusual example of Soviet Union children's fare. Technically adept puppet animation makes these slender tales of Charlie the Crocodile and his best chum, Cubby, worth trying. FAM/DRA 60m. v

Adventures of China Smith 1953 ★★★½ An American hero (Duryea) gets caught up in a series of adventures and intrigue in mysterious yet modern Singapore. C: Dan Duryea. ACT 60m. v

Adventures of Don Juan 1949 ★★★★ Flynn's last epic is a self-parodying swashbuckler chronicling Don Juan's adventures across Spain and England, plus a romantic subplot involving queens and commoners. Crackerjack action and a light touch make for a satisfying treat. Oscar for Best Costumes. C: Errol Flynn, Viveca Lindfors, Robert Douglas, Alan Hale, Ann Rutherford, Raymond Burr. D: Vincent Sherman. ACT 111m. v

Adventures of Droopy Featuring "Wags to Riches," The 1943 ★★★½ Seven short cartoons starring that loveable, if bumbling, hound. FAM/COM 53m. v

Adventures of Ford Fairlane, The 1990 ★★ Crass comic Clay stars as a detective investigating the suspicious death of a heavy metal singer. Few laughs amidst all the crudeness. C: Andrew Dice Clay, Wayne Newton, Priscilla Presley, Gilbert Gottfried, Ed O'Neill. D: Renny Harlin. COM [R] 100m. v

Adventures of Frontier Freemont, The 1976 ★★★½ A 19th-century city dweller (Haggerty) abandons the urban world and seeks harmony in nature. Familiar mountain-man adventure delivers wholesome quotient of friendly animals and lush scenery. C: Dan Haggerty, Denver Pyle. D: Richard Friedenberg. FAM/DRA 106m.

Adventures of Gallant Bess 1948 ★★★ A rodeo performer trains a wild horse and comes into conflict with his girlfriend. Pleasant, undemanding horse opera with all ending quite happily. C: Cameron Mitchell, Audrey Long. D: Lew Landers. WST 73m.

Adventures of Gerard, The 1970 British ★★ Bumbling officer takes the fall for Napoleon's wartime blunders in this surreal but flawed adaptation of Arthur Conan Doyle's story. Directed by the visually imaginative Skolimowski, with Wallach as Napoleon. C: Peter McEnery, Claudia Cardinale, Eli Wallach, Jack Hawkins, John Neville. D: Jerzy Skolimowski. COM 91m.

Adventures of Hajji Baba, The 1954 ★★★½ Young blade (Derek) gets an eyeful of sheik's enchanting—but promised—daughter (Stewart) and promptly sweeps her off her feet; the sheik vows revenge. Handsome, occasionally exciting production, with leads perfect for desert romance. C: John Derek, Elaine Stewart. D: Don Weis. ACT 94m.

Adventures of Huck Finn, The 1993 ★★★ Disney's turn to tackle Twain classic pairs a too sophisticated Huck (Wood) with a too young Jim (Vance) and omits some key incidents. So-so version, with a surprisingly heavy-handed emphasis on abuse and violence. C: Elijah Wood, Courtney Vance, Robbie Coltrane, Jason Robards. D: Stephen Sommers. FAM/DRA [PG] 107m. v

Adventures of Huckleberry Finn, The 1960

★★★★½ Terrific, energetic interpretation utilizes old-time Hollywood character actors to perfection. Young Hodges may not be ideally cast as Huck, but Moore is smashing as Jim. Randall shines as a villain. Excellent all around. C: Eddie Hodges, Archie Moore, Tony Randall, Patty McCormack, Neville Brand. D: Michael Curtiz. FAM/DRA 108m. V

Adventures of Huckleberry, Finn, The 1981 ★★ Uninspired 1981 version of Twain's classic story of Mississippi boyhood. Try another take on this popular story. C: Kurt Ida, Dan Monahan, Brock Peters, Forrest Tucker, Larry Storch. D: Jack Hively. FAM/DRA 97m. TVM V

Adventures of Huckleberry Finn 1984 ★★★★ American Playhouse version of Twain's classic is energized by bright performances of Day as bad boy Huck and Williams as Jim, the fugitive slave, as they raft down the Mississippi River. Intelligent, enjoyable fare for both adults and children. C: Patrick Day, Jim Dale, Frederic Forrest, Lillian Gish, Barnard Hughes, Samm-Art Williams, Butterfly McQueen. D: Peter Hunt. FAM/DRA 105m. V

Adventures of Ichabod and Mr. Toad, The 1949 ★★★★½ Outstanding pair of Disney animated movies. A witty, beautiful adaptation of Kenneth Grahame's children's classic *The Wind in the Willows* has irrepressible Toad on trial for motorcar theft. *Legend of Sleepy Hollow* is an exciting version of the Washington Irving tale, highlighted by Ichabod Crane's encounter with the Headless Horseman. Voices of: Bing Crosby, Basil Rathbone, Eric Blore. D: Jack Kinney, Clyde Geronimi, James Algar. FAM/ACT [G] 68m.

Adventures of Jack London, The 1943 *See* **Jack London**

Adventures of Marco Polo, The 1938 ★★★ Tongue-in-cheek treatment of the Venetian explorer's discoveries of spaghetti, fireworks, and the road to the East. The humor often falls flat, while all-American Cooper is miscast as Polo and Norwegian Gurie is miscast as a Chinese princess. C: Gary Cooper, Sigrid Gurie, Basil Rathbone, Binnie Barnes, Alan Hale. D: Archie Mayo. DRA 100m.

Adventures of Mark Twain, The 1944 ★★★ Versatile March plays Samuel Langhorne Clemens in this entertaining chronicle of the popular writer's life from youth to old age. Engaging, although it lacks Twain's biting wit and glosses over his often disagreeable temperament. C: Fredric March, Alexis Smith, Donald Crisp, Alan Hale, C. Aubrey Smith, John Carradine, Percy Kilbride. D: Irving Rapper. DRA 130m. V

Adventures of Mark Twain, The 1985 ★★★ Tom Sawyer, Huck Finn, and Becky Thatcher join originator Mark Twain on a ride to Halley's Comet. En route, Twain spins some of his more popular yarns. Mainly a showcase for Vinton's marvelous Claymation techniques, though the story does offer an unusual glimpse into a less "animated" side of Twain. Voices of: James Whitmore, Chris Ritchie, Gary Krug, Michele Mariana. D: Will Vinton. FAM/DRA [G] 90m.

Adventures of Martin Eden, The 1942 ★★★½ Jack London's novel comes alive as a sailor (Ford) struggles to become a writer. Very entertaining, especially Ford's performance. C: Glenn Ford, Claire Trevor, Evelyn Keyes, Dickie Moore. D: Sidney Salkow. DRA 87m.

Adventures of Milo and Otis, The 1989 Japanese ★★★½ Moore's comical narration enlivens this dog-and-cat-on-the-road story; diverting for both adults and children. C: Voice of Dudley Moore. D: Masanori Hata. FAM/COM [G] 76m. V

Adventures of Milo in the Phantom Tollbooth, The 1970 *See* **Phantom Tollbooth, The**

Adventures of Nick Carter 1972 ★★★ Nick investigates the death of a friend in this update of the classic detective series. Supporting cast of familiar faces delivers the goods. C: Robert Conrad, Shelley Winters, Broderick Crawford, Dean Stockwell. D: Paul Krasny. CRI 72m. TVM

Adventures of Ozzie and Harriet, The 1956 ★★★½ Classic episodes of the TV series that practically defined an era—with many supporting roles for future stars. C: Ozzie Nelson, Harriet Nelson. COM 60m. V

Adventures of Ozzie and Harriet, The 1964 ★★★ "Ricky's Horse" and "Ozzie The Babysitter," episodes from the beloved TV sitcom. C: Ozzie Nelson, Harriet Nelson. FAM/COM 55m. V

Adventures of Picasso, The 1978 Swedish ★★ Parody of art world and figures from '20s Paris never amounts to much. Picasso, Gertrude Stein, and Alice B. Toklas are three of many figures skewered in this mess. C: Gosta Ekman, Hans Alfredson, Margaretha Krook. D: Tage Danielsson. COM 88m. V

Adventures of Priscilla, Queen of the Desert, The 1994 Australian ★★★★ Three flamboyant entertainers (two transvestites and a transexual) leave the big city of Sydney for a job in the country, leading to classic fish-out-of-water situations. Funny, loony, gay-oriented comedy won't be everyone's cup of tea (but the Oscar-winning costumes are FABULOUS!). C: Terence Stamp, Hugo Weaving, Guy Pearce, Bill Hunter. D: Stephen Elliot COM [R]

Adventures of Robin Hood, The 1938 ★★★★★ Lavish adventure film shot in glorious Technicolor features charming, athletic Flynn at the top of his form, as he and his band of merry men rob from the rich and give to the poor. Thrilling swordfight (with Rathbone) climaxes one of the greatest Hollywood action films ever made. Oscars for Best Score, Art Direction, and Editing. C: Errol Flynn, Olivia de Havilland, Basil Rathbone, Claude Rains,

Eugene Pallette, Alan Hale, Una O'Connor. D: Michael Curtiz, William Keighley. ACT 102m. V

Adventures of Robinson Crusoe, The 1952 Mexican ★★★½ Surrealist director Buñuel's decidedly straightforward telling of the Daniel Defoe classic about a 17th-century castaway and his battles with cannibals, mutineers, and his own faith. O'Herlihy was nominated for an Oscar after U.S. release in 1954. (a.k.a. *Robinson Crusoe*) C: Dan O'Herlihy, Jaime Fernandez. D: Luis Buñuel. DRA 90m.

Adventures of Sadie, The 1955 British ★★★ The sexy exploits of a woman (Collins) who becomes the object of lust for three lonely men stranded on a tropical isle. Leering comedy with appealing young star. C: Joan Collins, George Cole, Kenneth More, Hermione Gingold. D: Noel Langley. COM 88m.

Adventures of Scaramouche 1964 French ★★★½ Cynical swordsman Scaramouche is out to avenge his brother's murder. Stewart Granger's *Scaramouche* is still the classic, but this costume epic manages to hold its own. C: Gerald Barray, Michele Giradon, Gianna Maria Canale, Alberto de Mendoza, Jose Bruguera. D: Antonio Isasi Isasmendi. ACT 98m.

Adventures of Sherlock Holmes, The 1939 ★★★★½ Classic mystery thriller as a dashing Holmes (Rathbone) saves England's crown jewels from Professor Moriarity (Zucco). Well done! C: Basil Rathbone, Nigel Bruce, George Zucco, Ida Lupino, Alan Marshal. D: Alfred Werker. CRI 86m. V

Adventures of Sinbad, The 1979 ★★★½ Short, animated version of the derring-do of Arabian superhero Sinbad to recover a lost magic lamp. Somewhat slow, which may cause younger children to lose interest, but gets credit for nice animation. FAM/ACT 47m. V

Adventures of Smilin' Jack 1943 ★★★★ Based on Zack Moseley's popular comic-strip character, adventurous tale of pilot Smilin' Jack Martin's dazzling raids over World War II China. C: Tom Brown, Sidney Toler. ACT 90m. V

Adventures of Superman 1942 ★★★ Six animated shorts featuring the famous superhero, produced by the noted cartoonist Max Fleischer. FAM/ACT 55m. V

Adventures of Tartu 1943 British ★★★½ WWII drama has a British spy (Donat) coming to the aid of Czechoslovakia in destroying a Nazi poison gas factory. Fair mix of adventure, thriller, and comedy; saving grace is Donat's inspired performance. (a.k.a. *Tartu*) C: Robert Donat, Valerie Hobson, Glynis Johns. D: Harold S. Bucquet. DRA 103m. V

Adventures of Teddy Ruxpin 1986 ★★★ Teddy Ruxpin and Grubby the Octopede embark upon a treasure hunt and become tangled in intrigue on the desert. Charming fun for toddlers. FAM/ACT 46m. V

Adventures of the Wilderness Family, The 1976 ★★★★ Urban pioneers find beauty—and problems—in their attempt to live a simple, more rewarding life in the Rocky Mountains. Well photographed and naturally acted. Lessons for the whole family make for a positive viewing experience. C: Robert Logan, Susan Damante Shaw. D: Stewart Raffill. FAM/DRA [G] 100m. V

Adventures of Tom Sawyer, The 1938 ★★★★★ The definitive film version of Twain's great book about growing up in a small town on the Mississippi in the mid-1800s. Wonderful acting from stars to bit players; Jory as Injun Joe is memorably creepy. Hollywood classic runs the gamut from humor to pathos. C: Tommy Kelly, Jackie Moran, Ann Gillis, May Robson, Walter Brennan, Victor Jory, Spring Byington, Margaret Hamilton. D: Norman Taurog. FAM/DRA 93m. V

Adventuress, The 1946 *See* **I See a Dark Stranger**

Adventurous Blonde 1937 ★★★½ On her honeymoon, to the dismay of her newlywed hubby cop (MacLane), reporter Torchy Blaine (Farrell) gets wind of a murder and is soon on the case. Snappy entry in series of *Torchy Blaine* movies gets fresh, wisecracking performances and direction. C: Glenda Farrell, Barton MacLane, Anne Nagel. D: Frank McDonald. COM 60m.

Adversary, The 1973 Indian ★★★★½ University student (Chatterjee) ends studies to support his family after his father dies. Forced to take menial labor in the swelter of Calcutta's inner city, he grows deeply embittered over his unexpected fate. Moving study of dreams denied packs an emotional wallop. (a.k.a. *Siddharta and the City*) C: Dhritiman Chatterjee, Krishnanbose, Jaysree Roy, Devraj Roy. D: Satyajit Ray. DRA 100m.

Advice to the Lovelorn 1933 ★★★½ A crass columnist takes over the Lonelyhearts column and twists it to his advantage. Tart-tongued Tracy leads a fine ensemble cast. Based on the Nathaniel West novella *Miss Lonelyhearts* and remade as *Lonelyhearts* in 1958 (with Montgomery Clift in Tracy's role). C: Lee Tracy, Sally Blane, Sterling Holloway. D: Alfred Werker. DRA 62m.

Advise and Consent 1962 ★★★★ A Presidential appointee must be confirmed by a very suspicious and cautious Senate. An utterly contemporary portrait that holds power to this day. Look for Laughton at his best. C: Henry Fonda, Don Murray, Charles Laughton, Walter Pidgeon, Peter Lawford, Gene Tierney, Franchot Tone, Lew Ayres, Burgess Meredith, Paul Ford. D: Otto Preminger. DRA 139m. V

Aerial Gunner 1943 ★★★ Typical WWII basic training yarn about two buddies (Morris and Arlen) and the woman (Lita) who comes between them. Lively action scenes are worth the wait. C: Richard Arlen, Chester Morris, Lita Ward. D: William Pine. ACT 78m.

Aerograd 1935 USSR ★★★★½ In the

midst of WWII, the Russian military faces off against Japanese forces bent on destroying a fledgling Siberian settlement. Despite Soviet propaganda typical for the era, a tense war story emerges, along with some genuinely thrilling moments. (a.k.a. *Frontier* and *Air City*) C: Semyon Shagaida, Stepan Shkurat. D: Alexander Dovzhenko. DRA 81m.

Aerosmith—The Making of "Pump" 1990 ★★★★ Behind-the-scenes look at the making of "Pump," Aerosmith's triumphant album. Look for insightful comments from band and production team, with some head-banging outtakes. C: Aerosmith. MUS 110m. V

Aerosmith—Things That Go Pump in the Night ★★★ Assortment of clips from the concert arena and recording studio, featuring the ever-enduring rock band. C: Aerosmith. MUS 45m. V

Affair in Havana 1957 ★★★ A gold-digging woman has to choose between the songwriter she loves and the handicapped man she is married to. Interesting for its early look at Cassavetes. C: John Cassavetes, Raymond Burr, Sara Shane. D: Laslo Benedek. CRI 77m.

Affair in Monte Carlo 1953 British ★★★ Standard romance features widowed Oberon in Monte Carlo trying to woo gambler Todd away from the gaming tables. Gets some pizzazz from glamorous locales. C: Merle Oberon, Richard Todd. D: Victor Saville. DRA 75m.

Affair in Reno 1957 ★★★ Private eye (Singleton) falls hard for publicity man (Lund). Film features an intriguing twist on role playing and an eyeful of atmospheric locales. C: John Lund, John Archer, Doris Singleton. D: R. G. Springsteen. DRA 75m.

Affair in Trinidad 1952 ★★★½ Chanteuse (Hayworth) teams up with brother-in-law (Ford) to solve husband's murder. Good star chemistry and colorful atmosphere make for entertaining intrigue. C: Rita Hayworth, Glenn Ford, Alexander Scourby. D: Vincent Sherman. DRA 98m. V

Affair, The 1973 ★★★½ Songwriter (Wood), stricken with polio, finds first love with lawyer (Wagner). Old-fashioned tearjerker with attractive stars, some insight. C: Natalie Wood, Robert Wagner, Bruce Davison. D: Gilbert Cates. DRA [PG] 74m. TVM V

Affair to Remember, An 1957 ★★★★½ Romantic tearjearker about a star-crossed couple (Grant and Kerr) who fall in love on an ocean voyage. Tip-top romance is the nearest thing to heaven among weepies. *Sleepless in Seattle* paid a witty, perceptive tribute to this classic portrait of a love affair. See them both. C: Cary Grant, Deborah Kerr, Richard Denning, Cathleen Nesbitt. D: Leo McCarey. DRA 115m. V

Affair with a Stranger 1953 ★★★½ An adopted child is caught in the middle between a divorcing couple. Average soap opera enlivened by good cast. C: Jean Simmons, Victor Mature, Jane Darwell. D: Roy Rowland. DRA 89m.

Affairs of Annabel, The 1938 ★★★½ A movie star (Ball) keeps falling for publicist's lamebrained schemes to keep her name in the papers. Cheerful Hollywood comedy, a good role for Lucy. Followed by *Annabel Takes a Tour*. C: Jack Oakie, Lucille Ball, Ruth Donnelly. D: Ben Stoloff. COM 68m. V

Affairs of Cellini 1934 ★★★½ 16th-century Florentine love quadrangle between artist Cellini who loves a peasant who is mistress to a duke whose wife, in turn, is having an affair with Cellini. Lots of musketeer-like dueling and chandelier swinging keep it fun. C: Constance Bennett, Fredric March, Frank Morgan, Fay Wray, Jessie Ralph. D: Gregory La Cava. DRA 80m.

Affairs of Dobie Gillis, The 1953 ★★★½ Diverting musical campus nonsense has a rare film appearance by top Broadway director/choreographer Fosse. Source for TV sitcom. C: Debbie Reynolds, Bobby Van, Bob Fosse, Hans Conreid. D: Don Weis. MUS 74m. V

Affairs of Susan, The 1945 ★★★½ Actress (Fontaine) is loved to distraction by four men (Abel, Brent, DeFore, O'Keefe) who all view her differently. Pleasing star vehicle for Fontaine. C: Joan Fontaine, George Brent, Dennis O'Keefe, Don DeFore, Walter Abel. D: William Seiter. COM 110m.

Affairs of the Heart 1994 ★★★ Even-keeled advisor to the lovelorn loses her cool when she falls head-over-heels in love. C: Amy Lynn Baxter, Michael Montana. D: Ernest G. Sauer. COM 90m. V

Affectionately Yours 1941 ★★½ Marital comedy about an overseas correspondent (Morgan) who comes rushing home when his wife (Oberon) files for divorce because she thinks he's having an affair. Lightweight fun. C: Merle Oberon, Dennis Morgan, Rita Hayworth, Ralph Bellamy. D: Lloyd Bacon. COM 90m.

Afraid of the Dark 1992 British ★★★½ A police officer's young son and blind wife become key figures during the hunt for a killer who stalks sightless victims. Unusual mystery offers many plot twists and some tense psychological moments. C: James Fox, Fanny Ardant, Paul McGann. D: Mark Peploe. CRI [R] 91m. V

Africa Addio 1966 Italian ★★½ Basically, this exposé of African tribes and their customs is heavy on senseless violence and short on actual fact. (a.k.a *Africa Blood and Guts*) C: Franco Prosperi. D: Gualtiero Jacopetti. DRA 122m.

Africa Screams 1949 ★★★ Funny, albeit dated, material finds Abbott and Costello in the heart of Africa on safari, searching for a cache of diamonds and finding a lot of standard gags along the way. Look for appearances by Stooges Besser and Shemp Howard. Good for younger audiences. C: Bud Abbott, Lou Costello, Hillary Brooke, Max Baer, Clyde Beatty. D: Charles Barton. COM 79m. V

Africa—Texas Style 1967 ★★★ A pair of American cow wranglers (O'Brian and Mills) try to round up and rescue wild animals in a Kenya game reserve. This rather plotless film is mainly an excuse for some excellent wildlife footage; it spawned a short-lived TV series, called *Cowboys in Africa.* C: Hugh O'Brian, John Mills, Nigel Green. D: Andrew Marton. ACT 109m. V

African Dream, An 1990 ★★★★ In 1906 Africa, an English-educated local man (Kani) and a recent colonial transplant (Aldridge) form a friendship that transcends social barriers. Fine drama, with standout performances. C: Kitty Aldridge, Dominic Jephcott, John Kani. D: John Smallcombe. DRA [R] 94m. V

African Elephant, The 1972 ★★★½ An intriguing look at one of nature's most enigmatic creatures, as documentary examines elephants' habits and odd behavior. (a.k.a. *King Elephant*) D: Simon Trevor. DOC 92m.

African Lion, The 1955 ★★★★ The title feline is shown in its natural habitat through the change of seasons. One of Disney's best documentaries, this film has drama, humor, suspense, and action. D: James Algar. DOC 75m.

African Queen, The 1951 ★★★★★ Bogart and Hepburn in two of their best roles (he won his only Oscar) as an earthy riverboat captain and a stiff missionary, thrown together in a life-and-death trip down a dangerous river in Africa during WWI. Great romance, wonderful humor thanks to James Agee and John Huston's perfect script (from C.S. Forester's novel), and stars with perfect chemistry. C: Katharine Hepburn, Humphrey Bogart, Robert Morley, Theodore Bikel. D: John Huston. DRA 105m. V

African Rage 1985 ★★ Quinn does an unexpected turn as a dying nurse who schemes to abduct an African president. C: Anthony Quinn, John Phillip Law, Simon Sabela. D: Peter Collinson. ACT 105m. V

African Treasure 1952 ★★½ Smugglers disguised as geologists flock into the diamond mines of Africa and raise the suspicions of Bomba the Jungle Boy. For the kiddies. (a.k.a. *Bomba and the African Treasure*) C: Johnny Sheffield, Laurette Luez, Lyle Talbot. D: Ford Beebe. FAM/ACT 70m.

After Dark, My Sweet 1990 ★★★½ Ex-pugilist (Patric) gets mixed up in a kidnapping plot after falling under the spell of a glamorous widow (Ward) and her cohort (Dern). Moody, well-acted adaptation of Jim Thompson's novel, with an absorbing lead-in. C: Jason Patric, Rachel Ward, Bruce Dern. D: James Foley. DRA [R] 114m. V

After Hours 1985 ★★★★ A late-night pickup in an uptown coffee shop turns into a date from hell for staid Manhattanite Dunne when he follows Arquette into Soho and confronts total lunacy. Edgy comedy from Scorsese is best suited for those who can handle bizarre humor; a cult classic. C: Griffin Dunne, Rosanna Arquette, Linda Fiorentino, Tommy Chong, Cheech Marin, Teri Garr, John Heard, Catherine O'Hara. D: Martin Scorsese. COM [R] 97m. V

After Midnight With Boston Blackie 1943 ★★★½ On a tip from a prisoner Blackie finds a cache of stolen diamonds, then is the likeliest murder suspect when his tipster mysteriously dies. Amiable whodunit, with cult star Savage good as the prisoner's daughter. C: Chester Morris, Ann Savage. D: Lew Landers. CRI 64m.

After Midnight 1989 ★★ Collection of three horror stories, framed by a psychology professor who believes that the best way to understand fear is to experience it. His theory seems to need a little work. C: Jillian McWhirter, Pamela Segall, Ramy Zada. D: Ken and Jim Wheat. DRA [R] 90m. V

After Office Hours 1935 ★★★ Newspaper editor (Gable) and reporter (Bennett) dig up the dirt on a hot crime story while taking digs at each other. Sub-par script by the usually brilliant Mankiewicz. C: Constance Bennett, Clark Gable, Billie Burke, William Demarest. D: Robert Z. Leonard. DRA 75m.

After the Fall of New York 1985 ★★★ In post-apocalyptic Gotham, desperate survivors search for a way to begin life anew. C: Valentine Monnier, Edmund Purdom, Anna Kanakis. D: Martin Dolman. SFI [R] 95m. V

After the Fox 1966 British ★★★ To conceal a daring gold robbery, a con artist (Sellers) poses as a pompous film director shooting a movie in a small Italian village. Inconsistent comedy, written by Neil Simon; Mature, spoofing his own star image, gets most of the laughs. C: Peter Sellers, Victor Mature, Britt Ekland, Martin Balsam. D: Vittorio De Sica. COM 103m. V

After the Promise 1987 ★★★½ During the Depression, a laborer (Harmon), ill-equipped to deal with bureaucracies and the legal system, fights for custody of his sons after his wife's death. Above-average weepie; based on a true story. C: Mark Harmon, Diana Scarwid. D: David Greene. DRA 93m. TVM V

After the Rehearsal 1984 Swedish ★★★★ Dense character study originally made for Swedish television. During a production of Strindberg's *Dream Play*, theater director (Josephson) becomes entangled with the actress daughter of a former lover. Not among Bergman's best, but still of interest. C: Ingmar

Bergman, Erland Josephson, Ingrid Thulin, Lena Olin. D: Ingmar Bergman. DRA [R] 72m. V

After the Shock 1990 ★★½ Quickie film, rushed out after the 1989 San Francisco earthquake. Film documents the sensations of living through an earthquake as a group of Northern California residents make the most of their fifteen minutes of fame. C: Yaphet Kotto, Rue McClanahan, Jack Scalia, Richard Crenna. D: Gary Sherman. ACT 92m. TVM V

After the Thin Man 1936 ★★★★½ Second installment in the popular *Thin Man* series chronicles a San Francisco murder investigated by husband and wife detectives Nick and Nora Charles. Sophisticated leads and an engaging, if incidental, storyline make for a top-drawer blend of comedy and mystery. C: William Powell, Myrna Loy, James Stewart, Elissa Landi, Jessie Ralph, Sam Levene. D: W. S. Van Dyke II. CRI 113m. V

Afterburn 1992 ★★★★ The wife of a deceased pilot sues the company that allegedly sent him up in a faulty jet. True-life story benefits from an intelligent script and Dern's powerhouse performance. C: Laura Dern, Robert Loggia, Victor Spano. D: Robert Markowitz. DRA [R] 105m. TVM V

Aftermath: A Test of Love 1991 ★★★ After his wife is murdered and son seriously hurt, a doctor (Chamberlain) works to heal his family from grief. Movie delivers its message in consistent, intimate fashion appropriate to the small screen. DRA TVM

Aftershock 1990 ★★★ In this futuristic tale, an alien travels to earth for serenity but instead finds herself battling a wildly despotic, techno-fascist government. C: Elizabeth Kaitan, Christopher Mitchum, Richard Lynch. D: Frank Harris. SFI [R] 90m. V

Afurika Monogatari 1983 *See* **Green Horizon, The**

Against a Crooked Sky 1975 ★★★ Pint-size version of John Wayne film *The Searchers* follows young man on quest for his sister who's been kidnapped by hostile Native Americans. Standard Western action, appropriate for child audiences, except for some questionable racial attitudes (talk to your kids first). C: Richard Boone, Stewart Peterson. D: Earl Bellamy. FAM/WST [G] 89m. V

Against All Flags 1952 ★★★½ Good but not great swashbuckler casts Flynn as an English soldier fighting his way into a pirate's fort in order to woo fiery O'Hara. Smooth direction and attractive leads partially offset predictable plotline. Remade as *The King's Pirate*. C: Errol Flynn, Maureen O'Hara, Anthony Quinn, Mildred Natwick. D: George Sherman. ACT 83m.

Against All Odds 1984 ★★★½ Broke ex-athlete (Bridges) takes job offered by former teammate (Karras, in chilling performance) and begins search for disappeared heiress (Ward). Bridges' investigation ultimately unravels tangled knot of deception and treachery. Style-ambitious remake of *Out of the Past*. C: Rachel Ward, Jeff Bridges, James Woods, Alex Karras, Richard Widmark, Dorian Harewood, Swoosie Kurtz. D: Taylor Hackford. DRA [R] 128m. V

Against Her Will: An Incident in Baltimore 1992 ★★★ When a young woman is institutionalized for questionable reasons, a lawyer takes on the local government on her behalf. Fine work by the tireless Matthau. C: Walter Matthau, Harry Morgan, Susan Blakely, Brian Kerwin. D: Delbert Mann. DRA 100m. TVM

Against the Drunken Cat Paws 1975 Taiwanese ★★ Vengeance tale of a young blind woman who studies to become a martial arts expert in order to punish men who had previously attacked her. C: Chia Ling, Ou-Yang Ksiek. D: Ting Skan-Si. ACT 94m. V

Against the Wind 1948 British ★★★★ An elite squad of English saboteurs in WWII are parachuted behind enemy German lines to lend support to the French Underground. Absorbing, well-made espionage thriller with semidocumentary feel. C: Robert Beatty, Simone Signoret, Jack Warner, Gordon Jackson. D: Charles Crichton. DRA 96m.

Agatha 1979 ★★★ Movie attempt to solve the mystery of the whodunit novelist's real-life 11-day disappearance. Redgrave delivers a sensitive, nuanced performance, but Hoffman is miscast as the brash reporter who tracks her down. Flat drama lacks suspense, despite a brilliantly evoked 1926 British spa town setting. C: Dustin Hoffman, Vanessa Redgrave, Timothy Dalton. D: Michael Apted. CRI [PG] 98m. V

Agatha Christie—Affair Of The Pink Pearl, The 1983 ★★★½ Married detective couple (Annis and Warwick) stumble onto mystery after attending a party in the London suburb of Wimbledon. Someone's lifted a guest's strand of pink pearls, and the pair is after "whodunit." Glossy British feast for Christie fans. C: Francesca Annis, James Warwick, Reece Dinsdale. D: Paul Annett. CRI 51m. V

Agatha Christie's The Man in the Brown Suit 1989 ★★★ American woman traveling in the Middle East gets involved in a jewel heist and murder. Capable cast and decent story. C: Rue McClanahan, Tony Randall, Edward Woodward, Stephanie Zimbalist, Ken Howard. D: Alan Grint. CRI 100m. TVM

Age Isn't Everything 1991 ★★★ A young man gives up his dream of being an astronaut to be a business exec. As a result, he begins to age at an accelerated rate. Some fun; but overemphasis on film's message weighs it down. (a.k.a. *Life in the Food Chain*) C: Jonathan Silverman, Robert Prosky, Rita Moreno, Paul Sorvino. D: Douglas Katz. COM [R] 91m. V

Age of Consent 1969 Australian ★★★½ A

middle-aged artist (Mason) finds inspiration in a young girl, to the dismay of the citizens of a small Australian village. Offbeat film by master British director Powell, with a vintage Mason performance and hauntingly lovely Australian landscape making up for a so-so script. C: James Mason, Helen Mirren. D: Michael Powell. DRA [R] 103m.

Age of Innocence, The 1993 ★★★★ Scorsese's lavish adaptation of Edith Wharton's novel set in 1870s New York, incisively measures (and condemns) the city's aristocracy. Prominent lawyer (Day-Lewis) becomes engaged to a proper young woman (Ryder) but desires her more worldly, sensuous older cousin (Pfeiffer). C: Daniel Day-Lewis, Michelle Pfeiffer, Winona Ryder. D: Martin Scorsese. DRA 138m.

Age-Old Friends 1989 ★★★★ Nursing home resident (Cronyn) lives through flirtations with nurses and delicate visits with his hostile daughter (played by Cronyn's real-life daughter Tandy). But his deepest concern is caring for his senile friend (Gardenia). Touching production with heartfelt performances. C: Hume Cronyn, Vincent Gardenia, Tandy Cronyn. D: Allan Kroeker. DRA 89m. TVM V

Agency 1981 Canadian ★★★ Latest political "gate" involves subliminal manipulation, as party candidate (Mitchum) devises a scheme to brainwash TV viewers into voting for him. Mitchum is dandy. (a.k.a. *Mind Games*) C: Robert Mitchum, Lee Majors, Valerie Perrine. D: George Kaczender. DRA [R] 93m. V

Agent 8 3/4 1965 British ★★★★ An out-of-work British writer finds that instead of being hired as a junior exec at a glass manufacturer, he's been employed as a secret agent. Delightful spy spoof. (a.k.a. *Hot Enough for June*) C: Dirk Bogarde, Sylva Koscina, Leo McKern, Robert Morley. D: Ralph Thomas. COM 98m.

Agent for H.A.R.M 1966 ★★★½ Low-key Bond spoof, as secret agents (Corey and Richman) try to protect a scientist (Esmond) looking for a cure for a disease that turns people into fungi. Good atmosphere thanks to Oswald, who directed many of the better *Outer Limits* episodes. C: Mark Richman, Wendell Corey, Carl Esmond, Barbara Bouchet. D: Gerd Oswald. COM 84m.

Agent on Ice 1985 ★★½ Both the Mob and the CIA stalk an ex-agent who has attempted to erase his past. Scenes which are supposedly set in Hungary were actually shot in New Jersey—*need we say more?* C: Tom Ormeny, Clifford David, Matt Craven. D: Clark Worswick. CRI [R] 96m.

Agnes of God 1985 ★★★★ Fonda, Bancroft, and Tilly act their hearts out in drama of naive young nun who gives birth and kills the baby. Did she know what was happening? Psychiatrist Fonda must determine Tilly's sanity to prove her innocence. Mysterious, tantalizing puzzle. C: Jane Fonda, Anne Bancroft, Meg Tilly. D: Norman Jewison. DRA [PG-13] 99m. V

Agony and the Ecstasy, The 1965 ★★★½ Lavish saga of the painting of the Sistine Chapel with Heston as Michelangelo, Harrison as Pope Julius II. Beautiful scenery and earnest detail, though it takes its time. First 20 minutes are an excellent documentary on the artist's work. Based on the Irving Stone novel. C: Charlton Heston, Rex Harrison, Diane Cilento, Harry Andrews. D: Carol Reed. DRA 140m. V

Agrippina 1985 ★★★★ The Cologne Opera and the London Baroque Players perform Handel's opera about the scheming empress Agrippina. In Italian, conducted by Arnold Ostman. C: Barbara Daniels, David Kuebler, Gunter Von Kannen. MUS 160m. V

Aguirre: The Wrath of God 1972 German ★★★★½ Compelling historical adventure with Kinski as a mad 16th-century Spanish conquistador leading explorers through the Amazon jungles in search of El Dorado. Rich in detail, with haunting mix of beauty and horror. C: Klaus Kinski, Ruy Guerra, Del Negro, Helena Rojo. D: Werner Herzog. DRA 94m. V

Ah, Wilderness 1935 ★★★★ One summer at the turn of the century, a boy comes to terms with adolescence and life in O'Neill's tender coming-of-age comedy. Based on the play drawn from the youth he wished he'd had. Still wonderful after all these years. C: Wallace Beery, Lionel Barrymore, Aline MacMahon, Mickey Rooney. D: Clarence Brown. DRA 98m. V

Aida 1953 Italian ★★★ Adaptation of Verdi's brilliant, famed opera provided early film break for Loren, who plays the Ethiopian princess. Renata Tebaldi sings gloriously for her. C: Sophia Loren, Lois Maxwell, Luciano Marra. D: Clemente Fracassi. MUS 96m.

Aida 1983 ★★★★ Classic Verdi opera about an Ethiopian slave in love with an Egyptian army officer. A compelling performance. C: Maria Chiara, Nicola Martinucci, Fiorenza Cossotto, Giuseppe Scandola. MUS 160m. V

Ain't Misbehavin' 1955 ★★★½ Wealthy playboy (Calhoun) falls for a chorus dancer (Laurie). Harmless fun; Twin Peaks fans will be amused to see Laurie as a scantily clad floozy. C: Rory Calhoun, Piper Laurie, Jack Carson, Mamie Van Doren. D: Edward Buzzell. MUS 82m.

Air America 1990 ★★★ Two pilots (Gibson, Downey) fly the unfriendly skies over Cambodia during the Vietnamese war. No reservations on this airline: It's run by the CIA, supplying secret missions. The Thai locations are beautiful, the stunts are energetic, but the story is as thin as a jungle mist. C: Mel Gibson, Robert Downey Jr., Nancy Travis. D: Roger Spottiswoode. ACT [R] 113m. V

Air Cadet 1951 ★★★ Boot camp saga of

raw Air Force recruits initiated by hard-bitten sergeant. Handsome cast in studio-engineered vehicle. C: Stephen McNally, Gail Russell, Rock Hudson. D: Joseph Pevney. DRA 94m.

Air City 1935 See **Aerograd**

Air Force 1943 ★★★★ A B-17 Flying Fortress crew fights its way from Manila to the Coral Sea. Hawks created one of the best aerial battle films of WWII with newsreel footage, Howe's Oscar-nominated cinematography, and a hard-driving story. C: John Garfield, John Ridgely, Gig Young, Arthur Kennedy. D: Howard Hawks. ACT 124m. V

Air Mail 1932 ★★★★ The early days of air mail delivery are chronicled in this splendid ensemble piece guided by the sure-handed Ford. Solid story and thrilling aerial footage; packs quite a wallop. C: Pat O'Brien, Ralph Bellamy, Slim Summerville. D: John Ford. ACT 83m.

Air Raid Wardens 1943 ★★½ Laurel and Hardy vs. the Nazis. Rejected by their draft board, the comedy duo become Civil Defense workers who frustrate—as only they can—an enemy scheme to take over a magnesium factory. C: Stan Laurel, Oliver Hardy, Edgar Kennedy. D: Edward Sedgwick. COM 68m. V

Air Supply—Live in Hawaii ★★½ Australian pop band perform their classics live in the desert. Not bad if you're a fan; helped by the laser light show. C: Air Supply. MUS 75m. V

Air Up There, The 1993 ★★★ To save a college basketball team, Bacon goes to Africa, where he hopes to discover a new hoop star. Innocuous comedy unfortunately treats indigenous Africans like smiling children. Bacon's amiable performance saves this one. C: Kevin Bacon, Charles Gitonga Mainah. D: Paul Michael Glaser. COM

Airborne 1993 ★★★ Forced to move to Cincinnati with his family, California kid McDermott finds Ohioians are unimpressed with his surfing prowess, so he becomes an in-line skater to win friends and influence people. Formula entertainment for the preteen market. C: Shane McDermott, Chris Conrad, Brittney Powell. D: Rob Bowman. DRA [PG] 91m. V

Airplane! 1980 ★★★★ A frenetically funny, gag-laden spoof of the airplane disaster movies as a pilotless plane heads for doom until a shaky ex-pilot (Hays) takes the controls. Deadpan delivery from Stack, Graves, Bridges, and Nielsen adds to the hysterics. C: Robert Hays, Julie Hagerty, Robert Stack, Lloyd Bridges, Peter Graves, Kareem Abdul-Jabbar, Leslie Nielsen. D: Jim Abrahams, Daivd Zucker, Jerry Zucker. COM [PG] 88m. V

Airplane II, The Sequel 1982 ★★★ A lunatic bomber books passage on the first space shuttle excursion and once again the skies are ripe for spoofing. Almost as frantic as the first, but doesn't feel as fresh. C: Robert Hays, Julie Hagerty, Lloyd Bridges, Peter Graves, William Shatner. D: Ken Finkleman. COM [PG] 84m. V

Airport 1970 ★★★★★ First-class aviation disaster flick as airport manager (Lancaster) and a big-name cast deal with a crippling snowstorm, a bomb-carrying depressive, and a little-old-lady stowaway (Supporting Actress Oscar-winner Hayes). What a night! Big and very entertaining, based on Arthur Hailey's best-seller. C: Burt Lancaster, Dean Martin, George Kennedy, Helen Hayes, Jean Seberg, Jacqueline Bisset, Van Heflin, Maureen Stapleton. D: George Seaton. DRA [G] 137m. V

Airport '75 1974 ★★★★ Sillier, but still entertaining sequel to *Airport*. A flight attendant (Black) flies jumbo jet when both pilots are killed in a freak accident. Big '70s cast runs gamut from Swanson to Reddy. Not surprisingly, it's hard to tell where the genuine suspense ends and the camp appeal begins—one shot of Karen Black piloting a 747 says it all. High-flying excitement. C: Charlton Heston, Karen Black, George Kennedy, Efrem Zimbalist Jr., Helen Reddy, Gloria Swanson, Linda Blair, Dana Andrews, Sid Caesar, Myrna Loy. D: Jack Smight. DRA [PG] 107m. V

Airport '77 1977 ★★ Grab your seat cushions! Lemmon is the pilot of a jumbo jet that plummets into the sea. This is the third film in the series of airplane disaster soap operas that, thankfully, gave way to spoofs. C: Jack Lemmon, Lee Grant, Brenda Vaccaro, George Kennedy, James Stewart, Joseph Cotten, Olivia de Havilland, Darren McGavin, Christopher Lee. D: Jerry Jameson. DRA [PG] 113m. V

Airport '79—The Concorde 1979 ★★★ The world's most luxurious airplane is in danger of mid-air destruction. The fourth, final, and most hilarious of the airplane disaster films is pure camp, yet seems to have been done in earnest. C: Alain Delon, Susan Blakely, Robert Wagner, Sylvia Kristel, George Kennedy. D: David Lowell. DRA 103m.

A.K. 1985 French/Japanese ★★★★ In this unusual "Making of..." documentary, master French filmmaker Chris Marker brings his own camera onto the set of Akira Kurosawa's *Ran*; the filming of the Kurosawa epic becomes an opportunity for a witty, insightful rumination on the very nature of the filmmaking process. D: Chris Marker. DOC 75m.

AKA Cassius Clay 1970 ★★★ Account of charismatic heavyweight champion benefits from Ali's presence, Richard Kiley's narration. D: Jim Jacobs. DOC 85m.

Akira 1989 Japanese ★★★★ Riveting, if violent, animated feature centers on futuristic motorcycle gang inadvertently becoming involved with secret government project. Amazing production designs, bone-crunching action and mind-boggling finale add up to exciting Asian cross between *Blade Runner* and *Mad Max*. Definitely for adults. D: Katsuhiro Otomo. SFI 124m. V

Akira Kurosawa's Dreams 1990 Japanese ★★★★ Kurosawa turned to his own dreams for the vignettes in this uneven, though visually beautiful episodic film. Not all parts work, but what does is often fascinating. One sequence features director's admirer Martin Scorsese as Vincent van Gogh. C: Akira Terao, Mitsuko Baisho, Mieko Harada, Martin Scorsese. D: Akira Kurosawa. DRA [PG] 120m. V

Aku Aku 1961 ★★★½ Writer/anthropologist Thor Heyerdahl meets with the native inhabitants of Easter Island and finds a number of surprises in store for him. Often fascinating documentary is good educational fare. DOC 86m.

Al Capone 1959 ★★★★ Uncompromising, often gritty documentary-style biography about the rise and fall of notorious Chicago gangster Al Capone during Prohibition. Steiger's title role performance is on target, all smoldering swagger and attitude. Nifty gangster movie. C: Rod Steiger, Fay Spain, James Gregory, Martin Balsam, Nehemiah Persoff. D: Richard Wilson. CRI 104m. V

Al Jennings of Oklahoma 1951 ★★★½ Sincere, unassuming Western about a bad guy trying to turn over a new leaf. Duryea shines in this departure from his usual gruff persona. C: Dan Duryea, Gale Storm. D: Ray Nazarro. WST 79m.

Aladdin 1992 ★★★★½ Disney does the Arabian Nights to a turn, largely thanks to Williams' dazzling verbal dexterity as the genie (great animation and a fun score help, too). A treat for the whole family. Oscars for Best Musical Score and Best Song ("A Whole New World"). C: Voices of Scott Weinger, Robin Williams, Gilbert Gottfried. D: John Musker, Ron Clements. FAM/MUS [PG] 90m. V

Aladdin and His Lamp 1952 ★★ When a boy cleans a tarnished lamp, up pops the grateful, long imprisoned genie. Familiar adaptation of the classic fable; pretty much just for the kids. C: Patricia Medina, Richard Erdman, John Sands. D: Lew Landers. FAM/MUS 67m.

Aladdin and His Magic Lamp 1985 ★★★½ Delightful animated version of classic Arabian Nights tale. Less lavish than more famous 1992 version. FAM/ACT 70m. V

Alakazam the Great 1961 Japanese ★★★ Fun animated tale of a magical monkey and his fantastic exploits. Good children's adventure. Voices of: Jonathan Winters, Frankie Avalon. D: Lee Kresel. FAM/ACT 84m. V

Alambrista! 1977 ★★★★ A young Mexican boy sneaks across the border into America. Seeking an income to help his family, he encounters exploitation. Sensitive and effective social drama. C: Domingo Ambriz, Trinidad Silva, Linda Gillin, Ned Beatty. D: Robert M. Young. DRA 110m.

Alamo Bay 1985 ★★★½ Influx of Vietnamese immigrants angers residents of a Texas coastal town, who try to stop it. Even-handed, if unenthralling look at contemporary intolerance. C: Amy Madigan, Ed Harris, Ho Nguyen, Donald Moffat. D: Louis Malle. DRA [R] 99m. V

Alamo, The 1960 ★★★½ Davy Crockett (Wayne), Jim Bowie (Widmark), William Travis (Harvey) and nearly 200 Texans struggling for independence at a San Antonio mission-garrison are wiped out after a lengthy siege by the Mexican Army in 1836. Long and windy historical saga with a memorable climax. Oscar for Best Sound; score by Dimitri Tiomkin. C: John Wayne, Richard Widmark, Laurence Harvey, Richard Boone, Frankie Avalon, Chill Wills. D: John Wayne. WST 161m. V

Alamo, The—Thirteen Days to Glory 1987 ★★½ Outnumbered Texas volunteers in 1836 lose their lives at the San Antonio mission in their fight for independence from Mexico. Vacant re-creation of historic Lone Star battle. C: James Arness, Brian Keith, Raul Julia, Alec Baldwin, Lorne Greene. D: Peter Werner, Burt Kennedy. WST 180m. TVM V

Alamut Ambush, The 1986 England ★★★½ A British spy with superhuman intelligence goes up against an international gang of cutthroats. Not bad, but not particularly memorable. C: Terence Stamp, Michael Culver. D: Ken Grieve. ACT [PG-13] 94m. V

Alan & Naomi 1992 ★★★½ Fourteen-year-old Brooklyn boy (Haas) helps his young neighbor (Zaoui), a Jewish war refugee, emerge from the shell she's built around herself as a reaction to Nazis' killing of her father in France. Lovely performances from these two talented young people salvage disappointing script. C: Lukas Haas, Vanessa Zaoui, Michael Gross. D: Sterling Van Wagenen. FAM/DRA [PG] 95m. V

Alaska Boy 1969 *See* **Joniko and the Kush Ta Ta**

Alaska Seas 1954 ★★★ Salmon packer hires old buddy and business partner just sprung from jail—but the men don't see eye to eye. Fine cast in melodramatic remake of *Spawn of the North*. C: Robert Ryan, Jan Sterling, Brian Keith. D: Jerry Hopper. DRA 78m.

Albino 1970 ★★★ A deranged albino leads a gang of African terrorists. Standard action, but Lee's performance will raise goose bumps. C: Christopher Lee, Trevor Howard, Sybil Danning. D: Jurgen Goslar. ACT 85m. V

Albuquerque 1948 ★★★ Tyrannical uncle drives young ranch hand to the brink. For Scott fans, with strong supporting cast a plus. C: Randolph Scott, Barbara Britton, Gabby Hayes, Lon Chaney Jr. D: Ray Enright. WST 89m.

Alcatraz 1975 ★★★★ Comprehensive documentary, narrated by William Conrad, looks at history of famous island prison and some of its most notorious residents. Uprising of 1946, 1962 prisoner escape, and Native-American takeover are some of the historical highlights. Voice of William Conrad. DOC 54m.

Alcatraz: The Whole Shocking Story 1980 ★★★½ The fact-based story of a man sent to Alcatraz at a very early age, and the long years which he spent planning one escape after another. Riveting insights into prison life. C: Michael Beck, Art Carney, Alex Karras, Telly Savalas, Ronny Cox. D: Paul Krasny. ACT 200m. TVM

Alchemist, The 1985 ★★ In the mid-19th century, a man is cursed into forever living the life of an animal—until he's restored a century later by a mysterious woman who strongly resembles his lost love. A pseudo-Gothic piece that sat on the shelf for four years before it was finally released. C: Robert Ginty, Lucinda Dooling. D: James Amante. HOR [R] 84m. V

Alex and the Gypsy 1976 ★★★ A loser bailbondsman (Lemmon) falls for a gypsy (Bujold) who is up against a murder charge. Quirky, offbeat but confused story, with a strong cast. C: Jack Lemmon, Genevieve Bujold, James Woods. D: John Korty. CRI [PG] 99m.

Alex in Wonderland 1970 ★★★½ Self-conscious comedy focuses on the dilemma of Hollywood director (Sutherland) searching for a follow-up to his successful first film. Mazursky's second directing effort, after hit *Bob & Carol & Ted & Alice*, scathingly pokes fun at late '60s Hollywood as he ponders his role in it. C: Donald Sutherland, Ellen Burstyn, Viola Spolin, Federico Fellini, Jeanne Moreau. D: Paul Mazursky. COM [R] 109m. V

Alex: The Life of a Child 1986 ★★★★ A young girl fights a losing battle with cystic fibrosis. Engrossing, sincere production adapted from Frank DeFord's book about his daughter's ordeal. C: Bonnie Bedelia, Craig T. Nelson, Gennie James, Danny Corkill. D: Robert Markowitz. DRA 104m. TVM

Alexa: A Prostitute's Own Story 1988 ★★ A hooker becomes romantically involved with a playwright, choosing theatrical career over tricks. Lacks credibility. C: Christine Moore, Kirk Baily, Tom Voth, Ruth Collins. D: Sean Delgado. ACT [R] 81m. V

Alexander 1968 French ★★★ Oddball little fable about a widowed farmer who falls asleep; entire town tries to wake him. Well-trained pooch nearly steals the show from its human co-stars in this cute, if forgettable story. C: Philippe Noiret, Francoise Brion, Marlene Jobert. D: Yves Robert. DRA [G] 89m.

Alexander Hamilton 1931 ★★★½ Biography of first U.S. Secretary of the Treasury. Film is done on a grand scale, with emphasis on Hamilton's patriotic fervor. Arliss hams it up throughout in his own inimitable style. C: George Arliss, Doris Kenyon, Montagu Love. D: John Adolfi. DRA 73m.

Alexander Nevsky 1938 Russian ★★★★★ Eisenstein's celebrated movie mythologizing the Russian Grand Duke Nevsky's defeat of the invading Teutonic knights in 1242, with parallels to the rise of 1930s Germany. Dynamic visuals, along with a rousing Prokofiev score, render the entire film—and especially the extended Battle on the Ice sequence—a classic. C: Nikolai Cherkassov, Nikolai Okhlopkov. D: Sergei Eisenstein. DRA 107m. V

Alexander the Great 1955 ★★★ Burton in a blond wig stars as the fourth-century B.C. Macedonian hero who alternately conquers foes and females in this endless sandy epic punctuated by scenes of battle and philosophy. Talented cast. C: Richard Burton, Fredric March, Claire Bloom, Danielle Darrieux. D: Robert Rossen. DRA 135m. V

Alexander: The Other Side of Dawn 1977 ★★½ Hustler turns tricks on the mean L.A. streets in order to survive and becomes involved with a teen prostitute. Sequel to *Dawn: Portrait of a Teenage Runaway*. Down and dirty, with so-so acting. C: Leigh McCloskey, Eve Plumb, Earl Holliman, Juliet Mills. D: John Erman. DRA 100m. TVM

Alexander's Ragtime Band 1938 ★★★★ Romance and musical merriment abound in this colorful ragtime-era backstage tale featuring great Irving Berlin songs. Highlights include "Now It Can Be Told" and title song. Good stars, wonderful tunes. C: Tyrone Power, Alice Faye, Don Ameche, Ethel Merman, Jack Haley. D: Henry King. MUS 109m. V

Alfie 1966 British ★★★★½ In the role that made him a star, Caine plays a lecherous Cockney Lothario in London's swinging '60s, casually breaking the hearts of all the pretty young "birds" he meets. Ribald comedy (with pathos at its core), based on Bill Naughton's play, is fast paced and energetic. Music by Bacharach/David is part of movie history. C: Michael Caine, Shelley Winters, Julia Foster, Millicent Martin, Vivien Merchant, Denholm Elliott. D: Lewis Gilbert. COM [PG] 113m. V

Alfie Darling 1975 *See* **Oh, Alfie**

Alfred the Great 1969 British ★★½ Purported film biography of Alfred of Wessex, leader of England during the 9th century, who tried to unite the British countryside. Extravagant costume drama, with some good battle sequences. C: David Hemmings, Michael York, Prunella Ransome, Colin Blakely, Ian McKellen. D: Clive Donner. ACT [PG] 122m.

Alfredo, Alfredo 1972 Italian ★★★ Forgettable Italian comedy, notable only for early Hoffman: He's a nebbishy banker who extracts himself from one bad marriage, then leaps right into another. Lackluster. C: Dustin Hoffman, Stefania Sandrelli, Carla Gravina. D: Pietro Germi. COM [R] 98m. V

Algiers 1938 ★★★★ A fugitive (Boyer)

finds safety in the Casbah of Algiers, until tempted out of hiding by Lamarr. Smoldering romantic drama. Boyer never said "Come with me to the Casbah," but his performance did inspire the cartoon character Pepe Le Pew. Remade as *Casbah*. A remake of the French *Pepe Le Moko*. C: Charles Boyer, Sigrid Gurie, Hedy Lamarr, Alan Hale. D: John Cromwell. DRA 96m. V

Ali Baba and the Forty Thieves 1944 ★★★½ A spirited classic about a prince (Hall) who disguises himself as a thief to regain his birthright and finds a secret cave. Lavish production has mostly camp value now. C: Maria Montez, Jon Hall, Scotty Beckett, Turhan Bey. D: Arthur Lubin. ACT 87m. V

Ali Baba Goes to Town 1937 ★★★★ Song and dance man (Cantor) is transported to time of Arabian Nights in funny musical frolic. Nice production values, good Cantor showcase. C: Eddie Cantor, Tony Martin, Roland Young, John Carradine, Louise Hovick. D: David Butler. MUS 81m.

Ali—Fear Eats the Soul 1974 German ★★★★ A quiet, ironic story of a love affair between a sixtyish German charwoman and a younger Arab mechanic. Works well as a commentary on social mores and racial prejudice. C: Brigitte Mira, El Hedi Salem, Barbara Valentin, Rainer Werner Fassbinder. D: Rainer Werner Fassbinder. DRA 94m. V

Alias a Gentleman 1948 ★★★ When oil is found on an ex-con's farm, his old pals try to cash in by bringing in a woman they claim is his long-lost daughter. Late, relatively weak Beery vehicle designed to tug at the heartstrings, as well as get laughs. C: Wallace Beery, Tom Drake, Gladys George. D: Harry Beaumont. COM 76m.

Alias Boston Blackie 1942 ★★★½ Third in the *Boston Blackie* series has Blackie entertaining inmates with a magic show, and caught up in a daring escape by an innocent convict desperate to clear his name. Enjoyable entry. C: Chester Morris, Adele Mara, Richard Lane. D: Lew Landers. CRI 67m.

Alias Jesse James 1959 ★★★★ A cowardly insurance sales rep (Hope) sells a life policy to Jesse James and then goes West to guard his client. An entertaining, lighthearted comedy-Western. C: Bob Hope, Rhonda Fleming, Wendell Corey. D: Norman McLeod. COM 92m.

Alias Nick Beal 1949 ★★★★ A modern retelling of the classic tale of *Faust*. Here, honest politician (Mitchell) is tempted to follow the advice of suave devil (Milland) who's assisted by the sultry (Totter). Effective twist on the famous allegory. C: Ray Milland, Audrey Totter, Thomas Mitchell. D: John Farrow. DRA 93m.

Alias Smith and Jones 1970 ★★★ At the turn of the century, two old-fashioned rogues struggle to stay ahead of the law. TV series pilot à la *Butch Cassidy and the Sundance Kid*. C: Peter Deuel, Ben Murphy, Earl Holliman. D: Gene Levitt. COM 90m. TVM

Alice 1984 ★★★★ Fun, oddball musical in which a young woman faints when she witnesses an assassination and awakens in a strange new world, à la Alice in Wonderland. C: Sophie Barjae, Jean-Pierre Cassel, Susannah York. D: Jacek Bromski. MUS 80m. V

Alice 1991 ★★★ A bored rich woman (Farrow), unfulfilled with a life of shopping and lunching, begins to disappear after visiting a Chinese doctor. Terrific cast alone is worth seeing. C: Mia Farrow, Alec Baldwin, Blythe Danner, Judy Davis, William Hurt, Keye Luke, Joe Mantegna, Bernadette Peters. D: Woody Allen. COM [PG-13] 106m. V

Alice Adams 1935 ★★★★½ A young, small-town woman, desperate to be accepted in society and ashamed of her humble family, finds herself courted by a wealthy beau. Poignant drama adapted from Booth Tarkington's Pulitzer Prize-winning novel. Hepburn gives a touching performance as the dream-spinning Alice and MacMurray is just right as her down-to-earth suitor. Famous dinner scene is hilarious and tragic. C: Katharine Hepburn, Fred MacMurray, Fred Stone, Evelyn Venable, Hattie McDaniel, Charlie Grapewin. D: George Stevens. DRA 99m. V

Alice Doesn't Live Here Anymore 1974 ★★★★ Burstyn shines in an Oscar-winning performance as a young widow who heads west with her wisecracking 11-year-old son (deadpan-funny Lutter) to rebuild her life. The source of TV's *Alice*. Look for Jodie Foster in an early appearance. C: Ellen Burstyn, Kris Kristofferson, Alfred Lutter, Diane Ladd, Jodie Foster, Harvey Keitel. D: Martin Scorsese. DRA [PG] 112m. V

Alice in the Cities 1974 German ★★★★ An American photojournalist goes on the road in Germany with a precocious abandoned child. Memorable tale of culture clash, enhanced by evocative cinematography. C: Rudiger Vogler, Yela Rottlander, Lisa Kreuzer, Chuck Berry. D: Wim Wenders. DRA 110m. V

Alice in Wonderland 1933 ★★★ All-star version of Lewis Carroll fantasy classic hides cast behind elaborate makeup, so look sharp. There's talent everywhere in this big production, but not much spark. C: Charlotte Henry, Richard Arlen, Gary Cooper, W. C. Fields, Cary Grant, Edward Everett Horton, Baby LeRoy, Edna May Oliver, Jack Oakie. D: Norman McLeod. FAM/DRA 77m.

Alice in Wonderland 1950 British ★★★½ Lewis Carroll's heroine goes down the rabbit hole and encounters a world of puppets in this charming, intelligent version of the classic tale. C: Carol Marsh, Pamela Brown, Bunin Puppets. D: Dallas Bower. FAM/DRA 80m. V

Alice in Wonderland 1951 ★★★★ Disney animated version of Lewis Carroll's classic story entertains thanks to some exquisite character depictions, notably that Cheshire Cat. Fine tunes, too. Voices of Kathryn Beaumont, Ed Wynn, Richard Haydn, Sterling Holloway, Jerry Colonna. D: Clyde Geronimi, Hamilton Luske, Wildred Jackson. FAM/DRA 75m. V

Alice in Wonderland 1985 ★★ Musical version of the Lewis Carroll classic, with cast of Broadway and television stars in overblown production with disappointing score. A much-heralded but unsuccessful extravaganza. C: Natalie Gregory, Red Buttons, Sammy Davis, Jr., Jonathan Winters, Roddy McDowall, Telly Savalas, Carol Channing. D: Harry Harris. FAM/DRA 94m. TVM V

Alice, or the Last Escapade 1977 French ★★★½ Subtle thriller with a woman finding herself stranded in a mysterious house after her car breaks down. Evocative and dreamlike, with an extra creepy finale. C: Sylvia Kristel, Charles Vanel, Jean Carmet. D: Claude Chabrol. DRA 93m.

Alice, Sweet Alice 1977 ★★★½ When young Shields (in her film debut) is brutally murdered, her family and community are plunged into a sea of suspicion, Catholic guilt, and further slayings. Dark, shocking religious-themed horror film. (a.k.a. *Holy Terror* and *Communion*). C: Brooke Shields, Tom Signorelli, Paula Sheppard, Mildred Clinton, Lillian Roth. D: Alfred Sole. HOR [R] 96m. V

Alice to Nowhere 1986 ★★★★ Taut adventure about a nurse pursued through the Australian countryside because she unknowingly carries the loot from a bungled heist. Unrelenting suspense and some truly exciting chase scenes through the Australian outback jazz up this satisfying action tale. C: John Waters, Rosie Jones, Ebsen Storm, Steve Jacobs, Ruth Cracknell. D: John Power. ACT 210m. V

Alice's Adventures in Wonderland 1972 ★★½ All-star British cast croons John Barry songs in this musical retelling of Lewis Carroll's beloved classic *Alice in Wonderland*. Faithful, inoffensive rendition of the oft-filmed tale. C: Fiona Fullerton, Michael Crawford, Ralph Richardson, Flora Robson, Peter Sellers, Dudley Moore, Michael Jayston. D: William Sterling. FAM/MUS [G] 100m. V

Alice's Restaurant 1969 ★★★★ Satirical look at trials and tribulations of being young and a member of the counterculture in the late '60s. Insightful comedy is based on the popular song by Guthrie, here in his only major film appearance. C: Arlo Guthrie, Pat Quinn, James Broderick. D: Arthur Penn. COM [PG] 111m. V

Alien 1979 ★★★★ Space explorer (Hurt) is attacked by an alien creature, which spawns through his body, and proceeds to terrorize remaining crew members. Simple plot but full-throttle scares, Oscar-winning special effects, and sleek art direction make for a terrific cinematic roller-coaster ride. Two sequels followed. C: Tom Skerritt, Sigourney Weaver, John Hurt, Ian Holm, Harry Dean Stanton. D: Ridley Scott. SFI [R] 116m. V

Aliens 1986 ★★★★ Cameron's stunning *Alien* sequel is pure action excitement. Ripley (Weaver) returns to the Alien's planet with a bunch of ultramacho Marines (and a kid!) to wipe out the beast once and for all, or at least until *Alien*^{3}. Won an Oscar for Visual Effects. C: Sigourney Weaver, Carrie Henn, Michael Biehn, Paul Reiser, Lance Henriksen. D: James Cameron. SFI [R] 138m. V

Alien^3 1992 ★★★½ Last of the *Alien* trilogy finds a crewcut Weaver on a grim prison planet, where she must once again battle those pesky creatures. Dark, pseudoreligious imagery doesn't quite work, but there is some effective, dizzying camerawork. C: Sigourney Weaver, Charles Dutton, Charles Dance, Paul McGann, Brian Glover. D: David Fincher. SFI [R] 115m. V

Alien Contamination 1981 ★★★½ Bacteria from outer space contaminate two astronauts returning from Mars. Tense and gripping, with good space and medi-tech effects. C: Ian McCulloch, Marino Mase, Louise Monroe. D: Lewis Coates. SFI [R] 90m. V

Alien Dead, The 1982 ★★★½ When a meteorite crashes into a houseboat, killing the inhabitants, the victims are transformed into flesh-eating zombies. C: Buster Crabbe, Ray Roberts, Linda Lewis, Dennis Underwood. D: Fred Olen Ray. HOR 89m. V

Alien Factor, The 1978 ★★★ So-so tale of a town terrorized by aliens emerging from a crashed spaceship, but with special effects worth seeing. C: Don Leifert, Tom Griffith, Dick Dyszel. D: Don Dohler. SFI 82m. V

Alien from L.A. 1988 ★★½ A Valley girl (Ireland) winds up in the lost city of Atlantis. California Valspeak humor; fans of Bill and Ted should enjoy it. C: Kathy Ireland, Thom Matthews. D: Albert Pyun. COM [PG] 88m. V

Alien Intruder 1992 ★★ Four prisoners in space are sent to find out why several exploratory missions haven't come back, and get back a now empty ship. Elements of virtual reality were added to make this story sexy, but all they do is make it explicit. Poorly (but violently and graphically) done. C: Billy Dee Williams, Tracy Scoggins, Maxwell Caulfield. D: Ricardo Jacques Gale. SFI [R] 90m. V

Alien Nation 1988 ★★★★ Xenophobic, seen-it-all cop (Caan) teams up with an extraterrestrial lawman (Patinkin) to find the alien who killed his partner. Fine performances by the leads and many clever touches carry the film. Made into a TV series. C: James Caan, Mandy Patinkin, Terence Stamp. D: Graham Baker. SFI [R] 89m. V

Alien Prey 1983 ★★½ An alien invades a girls' dormitory in search of protein; the human-flesh kind. Hair-raising. C: Barry Stokes, Sally Faulkner, Glory Annan. D: Norman J. Warren. SFI 85m. V

Alien Private Eye 1990 ★★★ Adventures of a extra-terrestrial private eye, searching for a black disk of enormous power. C: Nikki Hill, Cliff Abuddell, Brenda Winston. D: Vik Rubenfeld. SFI 90m. V

Alien Seed 1989 ★★★ A gripping tale of a woman seeking to avenge her sister's death at the hands of aliens. C: Erik Estrada, Heidi Paine, Steven Blade. D: Bob James. SFI 88m. V

Alien Space Avenger 1992 ★★★ Four escaped alien convicts come to Earth, pursued by a intergalactic bounty hunter. C: Robert Prichard, Gina Mastrogiacomo. D: Richard W. Haines. SFI 80m. V

Alien Terror 1968 ★★★ What happens when aliens take over the body of a vicious serial killer? Not many good things. C: Boris Karloff, Enrique Guzman, Crista Linder. D: Jack Hill. HOR 75m. V

Alien Thunder 1973 *See* **Dan Candy's Law**

Alien Women 1970 ★★ The exploits of James Ward, the spy who thrives on sexual adventure, pitted against an army of sexually potent women. C: Dawn Addams, James Robertson Justice. D: Michael Cort. ACT 86m. V

Alienator 1989 ★★★ Intergalactic prison escapee (Hagen) lands on Earth and is tracked by a space cop (Teagan), sent by an evil alien warden (Vincent, in a chilling performance). Fun cast lifts so-so sci-fi thriller. C: Jan-Michael Vincent, John Phillip Law, Ross Hagen, Teagan, P.J. Soles. D: Fred Olen Ray. SFI 93m. V

Aliens Are Coming, The 1980 ★★★ Alien creatures set out from their dying planet to find a new home. Good, campy fun. C: Tom Mason, Eric Braeden, Max Gail. D: Harvey Hart. SFI 100m. TVM V

Aliens, Dragons, Monsters & Me ★★★★ Fascinating profile of legendary movie animator Ray Harryhausen, the filmmaker responsible for genre classics like *The 7th Voyage of Sinbad*, *Jason and the Argonauts* and *Clash of the Titans*. A visual delight. DOC

Alison's Birthday 1979 ★★★ A young woman celebrates her 19th birthday with her family, but discovers that some of them are devil worshippers. C: Joanne Samuel, Lou Brown. D: Ian Coughlan. HOR 99m. V

Alive 1992 ★★★★ Gripping, gory and true—a rugby team's plane crashes high in the Andes, leaving the survivors with a brutal choice: feed on their dead, or die. Rugged scenery and tight performances make this an intense showcase of the will to live. C: Ethan Hawke, Vincent Spano, Josh Hamilton. D: Frank Marshall. ACT [R] 126m. V

All About Ah Long 1989 Chinese ★★★ Touching film that traces a former gangster's path from prison back to his reconciliation with an estranged wife and son. C: Sylvia Chang, Chow Yun Fat. D: To Kai-Fung. DRA 106m. V

All About Eve 1950 ★★★★★ Scintillating comedy/drama takes incisive look at Broadway life through story of aging star, Margo Channing (Davis) and her ambitious protegé Eve Harrington (Baxter). A brilliantly witty script and unsurpassed ensemble acting make this film one of the very best ever. Divine Bette runs gamut from superbly timed comedy to moving vulnerability. Winner of six Oscars including Best Picture, Direction, Screenplay (both Mankiewicz), and Supporting Actor (Sanders). C: Bette Davis, Anne Baxter, George Sanders, Celeste Holm, Gary Merrill, Thelma Ritter, Marilyn Monroe, Hugh Marlowe, Gregory Ratoff. D: Joseph L. Mankiewicz. COM 138m. V

All-American Boy, The 1973 ★★½ An unpolished boxer (Voight) will do whatever's necessary to make the U.S. Olympic team. Breathtaking scenery, lovingly photographed. C: Jon Voight, E.J. Peaker, Ned Glass, Anne Archer. D: Charles Eastman. DRA [R] 118m.

All-American Murder 1991 ★★★½ Odd black comedy/mystery, as a detective (Walken) tries to prove that a student with a pyromaniacal past (Schlatter) is innocent of a campus murder. Good potential hampered by too many arty camera shots and too much graphic violence. C: Christopher Walken, Charlie Schlatter. D: Anson Williams. CRI [R] 90m. V

All American, The 1953 ★★★ A prize athlete (Curtis) is torn between spending time with his girlfriend and his duty to the football team. Weighted more toward the romance than the pigskin. (a.k.a. *The Winning Way*) C: Tony Curtis, Lori Nelson, Richard Long, Mamie Van Doren. D: Jesse Hibbs. DRA 83m.

All Ashore 1953 ★★★ Shore leave deposits Navymen Mickey and Co. on the mainland and in search of women. Rooney is exuberant as usual, with Haymes in charge of most of the vocals. C: Mickey Rooney, Dick Haymes, Peggy Ryan. D: Richard Quine. MUS 80m.

All at Sea 1958 British ★★★★ Seasickness-prone heir of a seafaring family takes charge of a decrepit English amusement pier. Engaging British comedy is a low-key treat. (a.k.a. *Barnacle Bill*) C: Alec Guinness, Irene Browne, Percy Herbert. D: Charles Frend. COM 87m.

All Creatures Great and Small 1974 British ★★★★★ Hopkins is an eccentric veterinarian and Ward his apprentice in this memoir from the life of English vet James Herriot. Rich in incident and brimming with character; wonderful viewing for the entire family. C: Simon Ward, Anthony Hopkins, Lisa Harrow. D: Claude Whatham. FAM/DRA 92m. TVM

All Dogs Go to Heaven 1989 ★★★ Weak story of dog sent back to Earth from Heaven to do good deed is further hindered by feeble musical score. Bluth's animation is brilliant, though. Voices of Burt Reynolds, Loni Anderson, Judith Barsi, Dom DeLuise, Charles Nelson Reilly, Melba Moore. D: Don Bluth. FAM/MUS [G] 85m. V

All Fall Down 1962 ★★★★ A young boy (de Wilde) who idolizes his older, selfish brother (Beatty) watches as he exploits an emotionally fragile woman (Saint). Good performances highlight solid script by William Inge, adapted from James Leo Herlihy's novel. C: Warren Beatty, Eva Marie Saint, Karl Malden, Angela Lansbury, Brandon de Wilde. D: John Frankenheimer. DRA 110m. V

All God's Children 1980 ★★★★ A judge (Widmark) excites controversy when he must rule on a busing ordinance for area schoolchildren. Strong cast and tactful direction make the most of a timely issue. Provocative and compelling. C: Richard Widmark, Ned Beatty, Ossie Davis, Ruby Dee. D: Jerry Thorpe. DRA 97m. TVM V

All Hands On Deck 1961 ★★½ CinemaScope musical features bizarre pairing of sailors (Boone and Hackett) on a free-spirited romp. Pre-*Jeannie* Eden is the love interest here. C: Pat Boone, Buddy Hackett, Dennis O'Keefe, Barbara Eden. D: Norman Taurog. MUS 98m.

All I Desire 1953 ★★★½ Stanwyck thrives in this period soap opera of a prodigal mother returning to her family after years of neglect. Emotional and well crafted. C: Barbara Stanwyck, Richard Carlson, Lyle Bettger, Maureen O'Sullivan. D: Douglas Sirk. DRA 70m.

All I Want for Christmas 1991 ★★½ Brother and sister (Randall and Birch) want to get their divorced parents to reconcile in time for Christmas. Catch Bacall and Nielsen's turns as, respectively, kids' grandmother and department store Santa and ignore the rest of this sappy, unbelievable story. C: Harley Jane Kozak, Jamey Sheridan, Ethan Randall, Kevin Nealon, Thora Birch, Leslie Nielsen, Lauren Bacall. D: Robert Lieberman. FAM/DRA 92m. V

All in a Night's Work 1961 ★★★½ A publishing executive (Martin) sets his amorous sights on a beautiful employee (MacLaine), setting off a complicated comic chain. Lightweight romantic comedy—almost too light. C: Dean Martin, Shirley MacLaine, Charlie Ruggles, Cliff Robertson. D: Joseph Anthony. COM 94m.

All in the Family 20th Anniversary Special 1991 ★★★½ Nostalgic moments with cast and guest stars plus classic clips. Good for fans of Archie and the gang, unmemorable otherwise. C: Carroll O'Connor, Jean Stapleton, Rob Reiner, Sally Struthers. D: David S. Jackson. COM 74m. TVM V

All Mine to Give 1956 ★★★★ Orphaned children in turn-of-the-century Wisconsin must be doled out to neighbors by their eldest sibling in order to survive. Well-acted, terrific, heartbreakingly true story of endurance and courage spares no grim details. C: Cameron Mitchell, Glynis Johns, Patty McCormack. D: Allen Reisner. FAM/DRA 102m. V

All My Sons 1948 ★★★★ Family agonizes over a son's death in WWII and revelation of father's involvement in selling defective airplane parts during the war. Powerful adaptation of Arthur Miller's play heightens emotional impact of Robinson as father and Lancaster as war-scarred son. C: Edward G. Robinson, Burt Lancaster, Mady Christians. D: Irving Reis. DRA 94m.

All Night Long 1961 British ★★★½ Jazz version of *Othello.* He's a trumpeter/bandleader and Desdemona is the band's singer. Iago's the drummer. Interesting to watch, if not altogether successful. The music—Brubeck, Mingus, Hayes, Dankworth—is good. C: Patrick McGoohan, Marti Stevens, Betsy Blair, Keith Michell, Richard Attenborough. D: Basil Dearden. DRA 95m.

All Night Long 1981 ★★★ An executive (Hackman) is demoted to managing an all-night drugstore that's a magnet for every neighborhood wacko. Frustrations lead to affair with blonde next door (Streisand). Quirky romantic comedy runs out of steam early. Watchable for Hackman's subtle, offbeat performance. C: Gene Hackman, Barbra Streisand, Diane Ladd, Dennis Quaid. D: Jean-Claude Tramont. COM 100m. V

All of Me 1934 ★★★½ A teacher (March) gets mixed up with an unlucky criminal (Raft) and gets a lesson in the dark side of life. Implausible but entertaining melodrama. C: Fredric March, Miriam Hopkins, George Raft. D: James Flood. DRA 75m.

All of Me 1984 ★★★★½ Magical mix-up finds the spirit of a selfish, just-deceased woman (Tomlin) sharing the body of a stuffy attorney (Martin). The two battle for control of his body as they attempt to put her where she belongs. Winning comedy, highlighted by Martin's hilarious performance. C: Steve Martin, Lily Tomlin, Victoria Tennant. D: Carl Reiner. COM [PG] 93m. V

All Over Town 1937 ★★ Two vaudevillians (Olsen and Johnson) and their trained seal save a bankrupt theater in this dated low-budget comedy. C: Ole Olsen, Chic Johnson, Mary Howard, Franklin Pangborn, James Finlayson. D: James Horne. COM 52m. V

All Quiet on the Western Front 1930 ★★★★★ Powerful anti-war classic on the horrors of WWI caused great controversy on its release in 1930. Based on Eric Maria Remarque's novel, it portrays a group of German students facing disillusionment and death in the carnage of the trenches. Dark, moody visual poetry and emotionally potent story earned Best Picture and Director Oscars and a respected niche in film history. C: Lew

Ayres, Louis Wolheim, John Wray, Slim Summerville. D: Lewis Milestone. DRA 103m. v

All Quiet on the Western Front 1978 ★★★★ 1970s TV remake of the '30s classic on Germans facing the horrors of WWI. Good, but despite big budget and long running time, still fails to match its epic predecessor. C: Richard Thomas, Ernest Borgnine, Patricia Neal, Ian Holm, Donald Pleasence. D: Delbert Mann. DRA 131m. TVM v

All Screwed Up 1976 Italian ★★★½ This comedy, about naive Sicilians corrupted after moving to Milan, is one of Wertmuller's lesser-known efforts. Themes such as class divisions and the war between the sexes get a halfhearted airing. Best scene is a ballet in a slaughterhouse. C: Luigi Diberti, Nino Bignamini, Lina Polito. D: Lina Wertmuller. COM [PG] 105m. v

All-Star Reggae Session 1988 ★★★★ Rock/reggae all-stars gather in Jamaica, birthplace of reggae music. C: Jimmy Cliff, Ziggy Marley, Neville Brothers, Carlos Santana, The Wailers. MUS 60m. v

All-Star Salute to the Improv, An 1988 ★★★½ Comedy club The Improv turns 15. Stand-up greats are in top form. C: Robert Klein, Billy Crystal, Robin Williams. COM 60m. v

All That Heaven Allows 1955 ★★★★ A widow (Wyman) employs a young gardener (Hudson), then falls for him, causing small-town scandal. Slick soaper with fine cast tugs at heartstrings while scoring points against evils of gossip and small-mindedness. C: Jane Wyman, Rock Hudson, Agnes Moorehead, Conrad Nagel. D: Douglas Sirk. DRA 89m.

All That Jazz 1980 ★★★★ Famed Broadway choreographer/director Fosse's brilliant, Felliniesque take on his own life and career. An unusual, dark, and modern musical; the dancing is dazzling, especially the stunning opening sequence, danced to "On Broadway." C: Roy Scheider, Jessica Lange, Ann Reinking, Leland Palmer, Ben Vereen, Erzsebet Foldi, John Lithgow, Nicole Fosse. D: Bob Fosse. MUS [R] 123m. v

All That Money Can Buy 1941 *See* **Devil and Daniel Webster, The**

All the Brothers Were Valiant 1953 ★★★ Two brothers, both New England whalers, clash when one wants to go after treasure instead of whales. A typical adventure yarn. C: Robert Taylor, Stewart Granger, Ann Blyth, Keenan Wynn, James Whitmore, Lewis Stone. D: Richard Thorpe. DRA 101m.

All the Fine Young Cannibals 1960 ★★ Murky soap opera about two young lovers who marry others and despite their subsequent unhappiness, decide to lie in the beds they've made. Enjoy Bailey's role as blues singer. Loosely based on life of jazz trumpet player Chet Baker. Early pairing of real-life couple Wood and Wagner. C: Robert Wagner, Natalie Wood, Susan Kohner, George Hamilton, Pearl Bailey. D: Michael Anderson. DRA 112m.

All the Gold in the World 1961 French ★★★ Farm family refuses to sell potentially lucrative parcel of land to oily developers from the big city. Though a distinctly minor piece, its polished surface makes it agreeable. C: Bourvil, Philippe Noiret, Claude Rich, Colette Castel, Françoise Dorleac. D: Rene Clair. DRA 100m. v

All the Kind Strangers 1974 ★★½ Orphan children seek new parents to replace their dead ones; candidates who don't make the cut meet gruesome ends. Disturbing shocker. C: Stacy Keach, Samantha Eggar, John Savage, Robby Benson, Arlene Farber. D: Burt Kennedy. HOR 74m. v

All the King's Horses 1934 ★★ Silly musical about an actor posing as the king of a fictitious nation. Needs some tuning. C: Carl Brisson, Mary Ellis, Edward Everett Horton, Eugene Pallette. D: Frank Tuttle. MUS 87m.

All the King's Men 1949 ★★★★★ Life of backwoods politician who rises from local office to Southern governor's mansion and becomes increasingly ruthless and corrupt along the way, as seen through eyes of journalist (Ireland). Dynamic performances by Crawford as Huey Long-like figure and McCambridge as his mistress (both Oscar winners) stand out in this first-rate adaptation of Robert Penn Warren's Pulitzer Prize-winning novel. Oscar for Best Picture. C: Broderick Crawford, Joanne Dru, John Ireland, Mercedes McCambridge, John Derek. D: Robert Rossen. DRA 109m. v

All the Marbles 1981 ★★½ Two-bit promoter convinces two beautiful women wrestlers he can take them to the top of their profession. Offbeat character comedy's best moments are in the ring, especially the finale. C: Peter Falk, Vicki Frederick, Laurene Landon, Burt Young. D: Robert Aldrich. COM [R] 113m. v

All the Mornings of the World 1994 French ★★★★ Lavish period drama of the tempestuous relationship between the master cellist/composer Saint Colombe (Marielle) and his pupil Marin Marais (Depardieu). Depardieu's real-life son Guillaume plays Marin Marais as a young man. Handsome and thoughtful, with generous attention to the music itself. (a.k.a. *Tous Les Matins du Monde*) C: Jean-Pierre Marielle, Gerard Depardieu, Anne Brochet, Guillaume Depardieu. D: Alain Corneau. DRA 114m. v

All the President's Men 1976 ★★★★★ *Washington Post* reporters Woodward and Bernstein crack the Watergate case. Just about everything in this based-on-fact thriller comes off perfectly, including the chilling atmosphere of paranoia and the down-to-earth performances of Redford and Hoffman. C: Robert Redford, Dustin Hoffman, Jason Robards, Jack Warden, Martin Balsam, Hal Holbrook, Jane Alexander, Ned Beatty. D: Alan J. Pakula. DRA [PG] 139m. v

All the Right Moves 1983 ★★★ A high school football star (Cruise) hopes to get out of his depressed mill town by winning a college scholarship. Although not particularly imaginative or plausible, this drama is alternately charming and frustrating, and offers some fine game sequences. Craig Nelson (TV's Coach) is outstanding as Cruise's high school football coach. C: Tom Cruise, Craig T. Nelson, Lea Thompson. D: Michael Chapman. DRA [R] 90m. v

All the Vermeers in New York 1990 ★★★ Intriguing, avant-garde drama about a Wall Street broker infatuated by a young French woman who resembles a Vermeer painting. A fascinating and sometimes repellent examination of urban angst. C: Emmanuelle Chaulet, Stephen Lack, Grace Phillips. D: Jon Jost. DRA 90m. v

All the Way, Boys 1973 Italian ★★ Dumb follow-up to *They Call Me Trinity* and *Trinity is Still My Name* follows same cast members through inane comedy about airplanes in South American. Extremely sappy. C: Terence Hill, Bud Spencer, Cyril Cusack. D: Giuseppe Colizzi. COM [PG] 105m. v

All the Way Home 1963 ★★★★½ In early-20th-century America, a small-town family find their lives change in many ways following the passing of household patriarch. Adapted from James Agee's novel *A Death in the Family*, this moving story benefits from the many strengths of its talented ensemble. C: Jean Simmons, Robert Preston, Aline MacMahon, Pat Hingle. D: Alex Segal. DRA 103m.

All the Way 1957 *See* **Joker Is Wild, The**

All the Young Men 1960 ★★★ A squad of Marines is overrun by Chinese in this intelligent Korean war drama. Racism rears its head when a black GI (Poitier) takes command of his unit. "Hip" cast includes comedian Sahl, singer Darren, and heartthrob Ladd. C: Alan Ladd, Sidney Poitier, James Darren, Mort Sahl. D: Hall Bartlett. DRA 87m.

All These Women 1964 Swedish ★★ A sour comedy about a classical violinist with a satyr complex—he's compelled to bed every woman he sees. Even Bergman called this stiff exercise "a bloody nasty film." (a.k.a. *Now About All These Women*) C: Jarl Kulle, Harriet Andersson, Bibi Andersson. D: Ingmar Bergman. COM 80m.

All Things Bright and Beautiful 1979 British ★★★★ Lovely film for the whole family, based on the true experiences of Yorkshire veterinarian/writer James Herriot during his long career. Gentle beauty of country scenery is an added plus. C: John Alderton, Lisa Harrow, Colin Blakely. D: Eric Till. DRA [G] 94m.

All This and Heaven Too 1940 ★★★★ Classy costume drama from Rachel Field novel tells tale of a governess (Davis) falling for married nobleman (Boyer) in 1800s France. Stars work well together in effective tearjerker. C: Bette Davis, Charles Boyer, Barbara O'Neil, Jeffrey Lynn, Virginia Weidler, Helen Westley. D: Anatole Litvak. DRA 141m. v

All This and World War II 1976 ★★★ Strange pseudodocumentary combines WWII newsreel films with a sound track composed of songs made famous by the Beatles. Footage is interesting, as are the diverse artists covering the Lennon/McCartney songs. D: Susan Winslow. MUS [PG] 88m.

All Through the Night 1942 ★★★½ Bogie takes on another ring of Nazi spies, this time as a gambler in gangster-ridden New York. Light spy thriller features funnymen Silvers and Gleason for laughs and Lorre for menace. C: Humphrey Bogart, Conrad Veidt, Kaaren Verne, Jane Darwell, Frank McHugh, Peter Lorre, Judith Anderson, William Demarest, Jackie Gleason, Phil Silvers. D: Vincent Sherman. DRA 107m. v

All Tied Up 1994 ★★★ Three women kidnap a lecherous playboy (Galligan) to teach him a thing or two about feelings. Silly sex farce. C: Zach Galligan, Teri Hatcher, Lara Harris, Tracy Griffith. D: John Mark Robinson. COM [R] 90m. v

All Together Now 1975 ★★★★ Sincere drama about college student struggling to keep family intact after parents die. Well-crafted; based on true story. C: John Rubinstein, Glynnis O'Connor. D: Randal Kleiser. DRA 78m. TVM

Allan Quartermain And The Lost City Of Gold 1986 ★★ Go anywhere adventurer Quatermain (Chamberlain) heads into the bush to rescue his brother. Campy follow-up to *King Solomon's Mines,* hampered by a poor story and poorer production values. C: Richard Chamberlain, Sharon Stone, James Earl Jones, Henry Silva. D: Gary Nelson. ACT 100m. v

Allegheny Uprising 1939 ★★★½ Swiftly paced, absorbing item features Wayne as the man who organizes a band of American colonists against a crooked gun-runner (Donlevy) and a cruel British officer (Sanders). Really a pre-Revolutionary Western, set in Ohio. C: John Wayne, Claire Trevor, George Sanders, Brian Donlevy, Chill Wills. D: William Seiter. ACT 81m. v

Allegro Non Troppo 1977 Italian ★★★★ Italian takeoff on *Fantasia* offers a grab bag of cartoons illustrating various pieces of classical music, framed by live-action sequences featuring ragtag orchestra. Highlights include "Valse Triste" and "Bolero." Lively and imaginative animation. D: Bruno Bozzetto. COM [PG] 75m. v

Alligator 1980 ★★★★ Wickedly entertaining modern monster movie doesn't take itself too seriously but avoids camp. The old chestnut about 'gators in the sewers is taken to its horrific and hilarious extreme as a giant specimen runs amok in a Midwestern city. Witty screenplay by John Sayles. C: Robert Forster, Robin Riker, Michael V. Gazzo, Perry Lang, Jack Carter, Dean Jagger, Sue Lyon. D: Lewis Teague. HOR [R] 92m. v

Alligator II: The Mutation 1990 ★ Tedious sequel has none of the original's wit, despite presence of Bologna as an L.A. cop tracking a giant 'gator through the city's waterways. Chiller marked by poor scripting and weak special effects. C: Joseph Bologna, Dee Wallace Stone. D: Jon Hess. HOR [PG-13] 92m. v

Alligator Eyes 1990 ★★★ Moody road movie thriller about a blind mystery woman who hitches a ride with four strangers, ensnaring them in her private revenge scheme. The psychological mind games are fascinating, though the facile denouement doesn't ring true. C: Annabelle Larsen, Roger Kabler. D: John Feldman. DRA [R] 101m. v

Alligator Named Daisy, An 1957 British ★★★★ Breezy comedy about a salesman whose unexpected acquisition of a pet alligator leads to complications. Surprisingly funny. C: Diana Dors, Donald Sinden, Stanley Holloway, Margaret Rutherford, Stephen Boyd. D: J. Thompson. COM 88m.

Alligator People, The 1959 ★★★ Good cast and atmosphere help this chiller, clearly influenced by *The Fly*, about an accident victim given reptile genes to restore his health, only to become a half-human, half-alligator monstrosity. Not bad, but hampered by ridiculous conclusion. C: Beverly Garland, George Macready, Lon Chaney, Jr. D: Roy Ruth. HOR 74m.

Alligator Shoes 1981 Canadian ★★★ A family affair: writing, directing, producing, and acting all courtesy of the Borris clan. Focus is on a slippery con artist brother hustling his way through working-class Toronto. Cute idea could have used more polish. C: Garry Borris, Ronalda Jones, Clay Borris, Rose Maltais-Borris. D: Clay Borris. DRA 98m.

Allman Brothers Band, The—Live at Great Woods 1992 ★★★★ Southern rock at its best, as the Allman Brothers Band plays its full repertoire under the stars. C: Allman Brothers. MUS 90m. v

Allnighter, The 1987 ★½ Sexy coeds go for broke during senior week. Trashy. C: Susanna Hoffs, Dedee Pfeiffer, Joan Cusack, Michael Ontkean. D: Tamar Simon Hoffs. COM [PG-13] 95m. v

Allonsanfan 1974 Italian ★★★★ Entertaining effort from Italy's Taviani brothers features Mastroianni as an early 19th-century man involved with radicals he wants no part of. Fine performance from Mastroianni in well-told story. C: Marcello Mastroianni, Laura Betti, Lea Massari, Mimsy Farmer, Claudio Cassinelli, Renato de Carmine. D: Paolo Taviani, Vittorio Taviani. DRA 115m. v

Allotment Wives 1945 ★★½ Federal agent foils wartime scheme to bilk gullible servicemen out of their paychecks. Old-fashioned social commentary. C: Kay Francis, Paul Kelly, Otto Kruger. D: William Nigh. DRA 83m.

All's Fair 1989 ★ Lamebrained comedy about sexist business execs who get their comeuppance when their wives and lovers challenge them to a war game battle. C: George Segal, Sally Kellerman, Robert Carradine, Jane Kaczmarek, Lou Ferrigno. D: Rocky Lane. COM [PG-13] 90m. v

Almanac of Fall 1993 ★★★ Talky, extremely serious drama bout marital tensions is set completely in the couple's apartment. C: Sandor Kardos. D: Bela Tarr. DRA 119m. v

Almost an Angel 1990 ★★ Sentimental fantasy stars Hogan as a crafty thief who, when given a chance to be redeemed by The Almighty himself (Heston), begins doing good deeds. Hogan, who also scripted, has a hard time generating laughs in this sugary comedy. C: Paul Hogan, Elias Koteas, Linda Kozlowski, Charlton Heston, Joe Dallesandro. D: John Cornell. COM [PG] 98m. v

Almost Angels 1962 ★★★½ Gentle film about the friendship of two young boys who sing in the Vienna Boys Choir and face a crisis when the voice of one of them begins to crack. Pleasant, undemanding family viewing. C: Peter Weck, Hans Holt. D: Steve Previn. FAM/DRA 85m. v

Almost Perfect Affair, An 1979 ★★½ At the Cannes Film Festival, a young producer falls in love with the wife of an Italian movie magnate. Picturesque romantic adventure. C: Keith Carradine, Monica Vitti, Raf Vallone, Christian de Sica. D: Michael Ritchie. COM [PG] 92m. v

Almost Pregnant 1992 ★★½ A desperate married couple goes to any lengths, including swapping bed partners with the neighbors, to have a baby. Silly, sexy comedy delivers lots of low-brow, leering humor and nudity. C: Tanya Roberts, Jeff Conaway, Joan Severance, Dom DeLuise. D: Michael DeLuise. COM [R] 92m. v

Almost Summer 1978 ★★½ Teenybopper comedy combines high school hijinks and puppy love. Good young cast. C: Bruno Kirby, Lee Purcell, Didi Conn, Tim Matheson. D: Martin Davidson. COM [PG] 88m.

Almost You 1985 ★★½ While his wife recovers from a car accident, a fidgety urbanite begins to question his marriage and eye the beautiful young nurse caring for his bedridden spouse. Slow-moving character comedy. C: Brooke Adams, Griffin Dunne, Karen Young, Marty Watt, Spalding Gray. D: Adam Brooks. COM [R] 91m. v

Almost 1990 ★★★ Abandoned by her husband, a shy woman (Arquette) loses herself in romance books until the perfect suitor comes into her life, only he may just be a figment of her imagination. Low-keyed, but a few laughs.

C: Rosanna Arquette, Bruce Spence. D: Michael Pattinson. COM [PG] 87m. V

aloha, bobby and rose 1975 ★★★ When he's unwittingly involved in local crime, an L.A. mechanic and his girlfriend take off for Mexico. Tense, nicely done. C: Paul LeMat, Dianne Hull. D: Floyd Mutrux. DRA [PG] 88m.

Aloha Summer 1988 ★★ A group of boys come of age in the late '50s, this time in Hawaii. Great surfing. C: Chris Makepeace, Yuji Okumoto, Tia Carrere. D: Tommy Lee Wallace. DRA [PG] 98m. V

Aloma of the South Seas 1941 ★★★★ Spectacular MGM production set in Tahiti, with a couple (Lamour and Hall) shielding their love against evil chieftains and volcanos. Lavish use of music, color, and exotic locales in a bigger-than-life entertainment. C: Dorothy Lamour, Jon Hall. D: Alfred Santell. CRI 77m.

Alone in the Dark 1982 ★★★½ Sharply done shocker almost transcends maniac-on-the-loose standards with style, scares and effective satirical humor. The villains here are four escaped mental patients who terrorize their doctor at his home during a power blackout. C: Jack Palance, Donald Pleasence, Martin Landau. D: Jack Sholder. HOR [R] 92m. V

Alone in the T-Shirt Zone 1986 ★★½ The psychological results of abandonment are explored in this tale of a T-shirt artist running from his problems. Unmemorable. C: Michael Barrack, Taylor Gilbert, Bill Barron. D: Mikel B. Anderson. COM 81m.

Alone on the Pacific 1963 Japanese ★★★★ Compelling, true story of Kenichi Horie and his lone voyage across the Pacific Ocean from Osaka to San Francisco in a 19-foot yacht. Well-mounted Japanese production with vivid cinematic value and comedic turns told in flashbacks ashore. C: Yujiro Ishihara, Kinuyo Tanaka, Masayuki Mori. D: Kon Ichikawa. ACT 100m.

Along Came a Spider 1969 ★★★★ Taut suspense film about a scientist's widow's relationship with the colleague who may have been responsible for her husband's death. C: Suzanne Pleshette, Ed Nelson. D: Lee Katzin. DRA 92m. TVM

Along Came Jones 1945 ★★★★ Easygoing cowpoke (Cooper) is misidentified as wanted outlaw (Duryea), and is pursued by both the law and the real badman himself. Laid-back, enjoyable cowboy spoof gave Cooper a rare opportunity to poke fun at his own screen image. C: Gary Cooper, Loretta Young, William Demarest, Dan Duryea. D: Stuart Heisler. COM 93m. V

Along the Great Divide 1951 ★★★½ When a convict escapes from prison, sheriff (Douglas) braves a ferocious sandstorm to bring him to justice. Terrific scenery and sandstorm effects enliven this sprawling Western. C: Kirk Douglas, Virginia Mayo, John Agar, Walter Brennan. D: Raoul Walsh. WST 88m. V

Alpha Beta 1973 British ★★★★ Long-married couple (Finney and Roberts) play sadistic mind games with one another in the course of their union's rapid demise. Well-acted, high-strung dramatics along the lines of *Who's Afraid of Virginia Woolf?* C: Albert Finney, Rachel Roberts. D: Anthony Page. DRA 67m. V

Alpha Caper, The 1973 ★★★½ After being forced to retire, a discouraged parole officer (Fonda) decides to pull off a big gold heist. Good action, superior cast. C: Henry Fonda, Leonard Nimoy, Larry Hagman. D: Robert Lewis. CRI 73m. TVM

Alpha Incident, The 1977 ★★½ Alien organism spreads terror. Fun low-budget rubbish. C: Ralph Meeker, Stafford Morgan. D: Bill Rebane. HOR [PG] 86m. V

Alphabet City 1984 ★★★ A tough young man lives a life of crime on New York City's Lower East Side. Stylish slice-of-life drama loses on plot but wins big with intriguing Spano. C: Vincent Spano, Kate Vernon, Michael Winslow, Zohra Lampert. D: Amos Poe. CRI [R] 95m. V

Alphabet Murders, The 1966 British ★★★ Spoof of Agatha Christie's Hercule Poirot novel *The A.B.C. Murders*. Following a murderous trail, Poirot (Randall) uncovers a killer who is offing victims in alphabetical order. Attempt at mystery humor doesn't work as well as Christie's precision plotting. C: Tony Randall, Anita Ekberg, Robert Morley. D: Frank Tashlin. CRI 91m. V

Alphaville 1965 French ★★★ Futuristic detective story has Constantine searching for missing scientist while battling all-controlling computer. Blending of science fiction, comic book capers, and film noir seems a bit dated now, but was revolutionary in its day. C: Eddie Constantine, Anna Karina, Akim Tamiroff. D: Jean-Luc Godard. SFI 100m. V

Alpine Fire 1987 Romansh ★★★ Living in a remote farming region, a deaf teenager painfully deals with adolescence while a compassionate sister struggles with his needs. C: Thomas Nook, Johanna Lier, Dorothea Moritz, Rolf Illig. D: Fredi M. Murer. DRA [R] 115m.

Alsino and the Condor 1982 Nicaraguan ★★★★ A young Central American boy (Esquivel) dreams of flying free like a condor to escape poverty and civil war. Intense, enchanting allegorical tale touched with magical realism; lovely to look at. Oscar nominee, Best Foreign Film. C: Dean Stockwell, Alan Esquivel, Carmen Bunster. D: Miguel Littin. DRA [R] 90m. V

Altered States 1980 ★★★½ When a scientist (Hurt) explores his primal nature he finds he regresses farther back than planned. Paddy Chayefsky wrote the novel *and* script but had his name removed from the latter after conflicts with Russell. Hurt's fine performance and the psychedelic special effects carry it, despite a weak finish. A cult favorite. C: William Hurt, Blair Brown, Bob Balaban, Charles Haid. D: Ken Russell. SFI [R] 103m. v

Alvarez Kelly 1966 ★★★½ Neutral Civil War mercenary's loyalties are divided when a Confederate guerrilla kidnaps him to steal cattle for the South. Rugged performances from Widmark and Holden. C: William Holden, Richard Widmark, Janice Rule. D: Edward Dmytryk. WST 116m. v

Alvin Purple 1974 Australian ★★½ This amiable sex farce follows the exploits of a young Melbourne man (Blundell) who—for reasons unstated in the movie—women find completely irresistible. The talented cast of comedic actors tries hard to keep the thin material afloat. C: Graeme Blundell, George Whaley, Penne Hackforth-Jones. D: Tim Burstall. COM [R] 97m. v

Alvin Rides again 1974 Australian ★★ Feeble sequel to *Alvin Purple* has the irresistible young man (Blundell) switching places with a lookalike gangster. Silly farce. C: Robin Copping, Graeme Blundell, Alan Finney, Brionny Behets. D: David Bilcock. COM 89m. v

Always 1985 ★★★★ Intimate comedy explores the relationships of three different couples as they converge on a Los Angeles estate for a holiday weekend. Revealing character comedy, fascinating realism. C: Henry Jaglom, Patrice Townsend, Joanna Frank, Allan Rachins. D: Henry Jaglom. COM [R] 105m. v

Always 1989 ★★★½ Sentimental fantasy romance about a hot shot firefighting pilot (Dreyfuss) and the radio dispatcher (Hunter) who's in love with him. After he dies in a crash, he returns to act as guardian angel to young pilot (Johnson) on the same base. Sweet remake of WWII film *A Guy Named Joe*. Good leads. C: Richard Dreyfuss, Holly Hunter, John Goodman, Brad Johnson, Audrey Hepburn. D: Steven Spielberg. DRA [PG] 123m. v

Always a Bride 1954 British ★★★ Complications ensue when a federal officer gets involved with a crime ring and an alluring blonde. Harmless comedy. C: Peggy Cummins, Terence Morgan. D: Ralph Smart. COM 83m.

Always Goodbye 1938 ★★★ A woman (Stanwyck) secretly follows the destiny of the love child she gave up for adoption years earlier. Serviceable remake of *Gallant Lady*, boosted by sterling Stanwyck. C: Barbara Stanwyck, Herbert Marshall, Cesar Romero, Binnie Barnes. D: Sidney Lanfield. DRA 75m.

Always in My Heart 1942 ★★★ In this melodrama, Huston gives a fine performance as an unjustly convicted felon who returns to his hometown hoping to reconcile with his family. Film debut of teenage singer Warren; title song nominated for Oscar. C: Kay Francis, Walter Huston, Gloria Warren, Una O'Connor. D: Jo Graham. DRA 92m.

Always Leave Them Laughing 1949 ★★★ Typecast Berle plays a comedian whose career undergoes highs and lows in this backstage drama. Ex-burlesque star Lahr (better known as the Lion in *The Wizard of Oz*) recreates some memorable routines. Remade, sort of, by Billy Crystal as *Mr. Saturday Night*. C: Milton Berle, Virginia Mayo, Ruth Roman, Bert Lahr, Alan Hale. D: Roy Del Ruth. DRA 116m.

Always Together 1948 ★★★ A movie fanatic (Reynolds) inherits a fortune. Comedy noteworthy for cameo appearances by the likes of Humphrey Bogart and Errol Flynn, who figure in celluloid dream life. C: Robert Hutton, Joyce Reynolds, Jack Carson, Dennis Morgan, Janis Paige, Alexis Smith. D: Frederick de Cordova. COM 78m.

Amadeus 1984 ★★★★★ Speculative account of the fall of Mozart (Hulce) as orchestrated by his nemesis, the less talented Salieri (Abraham), who feels that God has scorned him and his devotion and instead rewarded the loutish boy. Lavish production, adapted by Peter Schaffer from his play, is a meditation on the nature of genius, and won Oscars for Best Picture, Director, Actor (Abraham), Screenplay, Costumes, Art Design, Make Up, Art Direction, and Sound. C: F. Murray Abraham, Tom Hulce, Elizabeth Berridge, Simon Callow, Jeffrey Jones. D: Milos Forman. DRA [PG] 158m. v

Amarcord 1974 Italian ★★★★★ Zesty satire re-creates the '30s Italy of Fellini's youth by following adventures and misadventures of town residents while foreshadowing the advent of fascism. Sparkling and lusty; one of director's best. Oscar winner for Best Foreign Film. C: Magali Noel, Bruno Zanin, Pupella Maggio. D: Federico Fellini. COM [R] 127m. v

Amateur Night at the Dixie Bar and Grill 1979 ★★★½ Locals put on a country-western talent show at a swinging joint in the South. Tapestry of interesting characters and good local color keep it compelling. C: Victor French, Candy Clark, Sheree North, Jamie Farr, Henry Gibson, Tanya Tucker, Don Johnson, Dennis Quaid. D: Joel Schumacher. COM 100m. TVM

Amateur, The 1982 Canadian ★★½ Espionage thriller places computer expert (Savage) behind the Iron Curtain as he seeks revenge against terrorists. Strong cast. C: John Savage, Christopher Plummer, Marthe Keller. D: Charles Jarrott. ACT [R] 112m. v

Amazing Adventure 1937 British ★★★½ A modest little do-good comedy about a wealthy young man (Grant) who bets that he can survive for a year without touching his inheritance. Based on E. Phillips Openheim's novel. (a.k.a. *Romance and Riches* and *The Amazing Quest of Ernest Bliss*) C: Cary Grant, Mary Brian. D: Alfred Zeisler. COM 63m. v

Amazing Colossal Man, The 1957 ★★★

Heroic army colonel finds himself at ground zero of a "plutonium bomb" test, which effects his growth hormones in a big way. Once enraged, he attacks Las Vegas! Cheap effects add to the fun. One of Gordon's best. Birthed *War of the Colossal Beast.* C: Glenn Langan, Cathy Downs. D: Bert I. Gordon. SFI 79m. V

Amazing Dobermans, The 1976 ★★★½ Amusing family fare concerns ex-con (Astaire) assisting undercover agent (Franciscus) by unleashing exceptionally smart dogs on petty crooks. Second-best film in series that includes *The Daring Dobermans* and *The Doberman Gang* (the pick of this particular litter). C: James Franciscus, Barbara Eden, Fred Astaire, Jack Carter. D: David and Byron Chudnow. FAM/ACT [PG] 99m. V

Amazing Doctor Clitterhouse, The 1938 ★★★½ Doctor (Robinson) infiltrates a crime gang for a psychological research project, then finds it hard to quit. Dated but jovial comedy, with nice work by the two stars. C: Edward G. Robinson, Humphrey Bogart, Claire Trevor, Donald Crisp. D: Anatole Litvak. COM 87m.

Amazing Grace and Chuck 1987 ★★½ Efforts of one young boy, a little league baseball player, to stop the nuclear arms race. Amazingly, athletes from around the world join him, and the President is moved to act. Well-intentioned film falters badly. C: Jamie Lee Curtis, Alex English, Gregory Peck. D: Mike Newell. FAM/DRA [PG] 116m. V

Amazing Grace 1974 ★★★ Stand-up comedienne Mabley stars as a sassy Baltimore mother so fed up with the way things are run in her neighborhood she runs as her own candidate for mayor. Curious but uneven comedy offers one of the few good looks at Mabley's talents. C: Moms Mabley, Slappy White, Moses Gunn, Rosalind Cash. D: Stan Lathan. COM [G] 99m.

Amazing Howard Hughes, The 1977 ★★★½ TV biography exploring the fantastic achievements and bizarre deterioration of the enigmatic millionaire. Jones and Feldshuh are slightly miscast as Hughes and Hepburn, but note intelligent performance by Flanders as long-suffering Hughes associate. C: Tommy Lee Jones, Ed Flanders, Tovah Feldshuh. D: William Graham. DRA 119m. TVM V

Amazing Mr. Blunden, The 1972 British ★★★★ Via the wonder of time travel, sympathetic ghost (Naismith) brings two children back to pre-Victorian era England and to the aid of two other children in dire distress. Wonderfully atmospheric ghost story with good period detail. C: Laurence Naismith, Lynne Frederick, Diana Dors. D: Lionel Jeffries. FAM/DRA [G] 100m. V

Amazing Mr. Williams 1939 ★★★½ Soon-to-be-married man wants to help a wronged woman clear her name, but his efforts don't sit well with his fiancée (Blondell). Well-played romantic comedy. C: Melvyn Douglas, Joan Blondell, Ruth Donnelly. D: Alexander Hall. COM 80m.

Amazing Mrs. Holliday, The 1943 ★★½ Sentimental WWII nonsense has missionary Durbin mixed up with Chinese orphans. Star sings pleasantly, as always. C: Deanna Durbin, Edmond O'Brien, Barry Fitzgerald. D: Bruce Manning. MUS 96m.

Amazing Quest of Ernest Bliss 1937 *See* **Amazing Adventure**

Amazing Spiderman, The 1977 ★★★ A young man develops weird powers after being bitten by a spider, and uses them to fight crime. Launched an irregular series; good for kids. C: Nicholas Hammond, Lisa Eilbacher, Michael Pataki. D: E.W. Swackhamer. SFI 94m. TVM

Amazing Stories: Book Four 1991 ★★★★ Several episodes of Spielberg's lavish TV series were edited into an entertaining home video package. C: Sam Waterston, Helen Shaver, Dick Cavett, Sid Caesar. D: Martin Scorsese, Donald Petrie, Paul Michael Glaser. SFI [PG] 75m. V

Amazing Transparent Man, The 1960 ★★ A demented scientist with the secret of invisibility uses it on an ex-con he hires to steal radioactive material. The ex-con, however, prefers banks. Ultracheap trash. C: Douglas Kennedy, Marguerite Chapman. D: Edgar Ulmer. SFI 58m. V

Amazon 1992 ★★★ Familiar, ecologically aware adventure flick involves an on-the-lam businessman joining forces with a Brazilian woman to help save the rain forest from greedy exploiters. Outstanding element is the fact that partial proceeds from the sale of this video go to support the Rainforest Action Network. C: Kari Vaananen, Robert Davi, Rae Dawn Chong. D: Mika Kaurismaki. DRA [R] 88m. V

Amazon Women on the Moon 1987 ★★ Collection of comedy sketches parodying commercials, sexual mores, television, and old movies misses more than it hits. Only Begley's son of the Invisible Man is truly funny, while the title sequence (a '50s science fiction spoof) falls completely flat. C: Rosanna Arquette, Ralph Bellamy, Carrie Fisher, Griffin Dunne, Steve Guttenberg, Michelle Pfeiffer, Paul Bartel, Henny Youngman. D: Joe Dante, Carl Gottlieb, Peter Horton, John Landis. COM [R] 85m. V

Amazon Women 1979 *See* **Gold of the Amazon Women**

Amazons 1986 ★ Evil sorcerers and tall naked women flounder through this hopelessly inept fantasy about superstrong femmes questing for a magic amulet. They should have searched for a script instead. C: Windsor Taylor Randolph, Penelope Reed, Joseph Whipp. D: Alex Sessa. SFI [R] 76m. V

Ambassador Bill 1931 ★★★ Hokey yarn

about an Oklahoma rancher (Rogers) assigned to an overseas ambassador's post, where he befriends the country's young king and charms everyone with his plain talkin' common sense. Ridiculous plot can't overshadow Rogers's signature style. C: Will Rogers, Greta Nissen, Ray Milland. D: Sam Taylor. COM 68m. V

Ambassador, The 1984 ★★★★ Intriguing story of international proportions follows American Mideast emissary (Mitchum) who is forced to deal with crises between Israelis and Palestinians, as well as domestic affairs of his cheating spouse. Sharp dramatics give this real impact. Last theatrical film for Rock Hudson. C: Robert Mitchum, Ellen Burstyn, Rock Hudson, Donald Pleasence. D: J. Lee Thompson. DRA [R] 97m. V

Ambassador's Daughter, The 1956 ★★★ While on R&R in Paris, American soldier (Forsythe) meets and woos the daughter of a powerful ambassador (de Havilland). Romantic comedy pushes all the right buttons, thanks to studio stable of filmmaking wizards. C: Olivia de Havilland, John Forsythe, Myrna Loy, Adolphe Menjou. D: Norman Krasna. COM 102m.

Amber Waves 1980 ★★★★ Stranded together in a small town in the Midwest, a farmer (Weaver) and a model (Russell) discover their world of differences. Marvelous clash of well-plumbed characters in a strong, thoughtful drama. Winningham won an Emmy. C: Dennis Weaver, Kurt Russell, Mare Winningham. D: Joseph Sargent. DRA 105m. TVM

Ambition 1991 ★★ A ruthless writer "befriends" a paroled psycho (Clancy, in a good scary-sad turn), plotting to push him over the edge and pen a tell-all best-seller about the bloody results. Star Phillips scripted this thriller—a neat idea inanely executed. C: Lou Diamond Phillips, Clancy Brown, Cecilia Peck, Haing S. Ngor. D: Scott Goldstein. CRI [R] 99m. V

Ambulance, The 1990 ★★½ New York-based mystery thriller centers on a series of unexplained disappearances. A sub-standard effort by cult director Cohen, despite the unlikely presence of Jones and Buttons in support roles. C: Eric Roberts, James Earl Jones, Megan Gallagher, Janine Turner, Red Buttons. D: Larry Cohen. CRI [R] 95m. V

Ambush 1949 ★★★½ A Native American tracker trails a missing woman. Somewhat dated, but entertaining, Western. C: Robert Taylor, John Hodiak, Arlene Dahl, Jean Hagen. D: Sam Wood. WST 89m.

Ambush at Cimarron Pass 1958 ★★½ After the Civil War, a cavalry officer and a bunch of rebels bury their differences in order to repel an Indian attack. Pretty soggy, but it's fun to watch the extremely green Eastwood. C: Scott Brady, Margia Dean, Clint Eastwood. D: Jodie Copelan. WST 73m.

Ambush at Tomahawk Gap 1953 ★★ Three misfits, fresh out of prison, are stymied by some unfriendly Apaches when they try to recover their hidden loot. B-Western. C: John Hodiak, David Brian. D: Fred Sears. WST 73m.

Ambush Bay 1966 ★★★ Marines race against the clock to complete a mission on a Japanese-occupied island. WWII film stays busy enough to hold attention. C: Hugh O'Brian, Mickey Rooney. D: Ron Winston. ACT 109m.

Ambush in Leopard Street 1962 British ★★ Old pro thief assembles a motley crew for one last job, but things go awry. C: James Kenney, Michael Brennan, Bruce Seton, Norman Rodway, Jean Harvey, Pauline Delany. D: J. Henry Piperno. CRI 60m.

Ambush Murders, The 1967 ★★ Third in the series of smutty Matt Helm spy spoofs finds ol' Dino wandering through the Mexican jungles in search of a hijacked flying saucer. Tired, lame, and not even a good bad movie. C: Dean Martin, Senta Berger, Janice Rule. D: Henry Levin. COM 102m. V

Ambush Murders, The 1981 ★★★ An attorney tries to win justice for an African-American activist framed for killing two police officers. Standard story, but competently told; based on a true story. C: James Brolin, Dorian Harewood, Alfre Woodward, Amy Madigan. D: Steven Hilliard Stern. CRI 98m. TVM V

Amelia Earhart 1976 ★★★★ Inspiring biography with strong work by Clark as the famed aviatrix. Takes heroine from her struggle to make her mark in a male-dominated profession through early triumphs. A valuable portrait. C: Susan Clark, John Forsythe, Catherine Burns. D: George Schaefer. DRA 150m. TVM

America 1924 ★★★★ Epic, silent D. W. Griffith re-creation of the Revolutionary War revolves around a patriot rider who romances the daughter of an English loyalist. Simple story frames familiar legends (including Paul Revere's ride). Large in scope, with marvelous battle sequences and attention to period detail. C: Neil Hamilton, Carol Dempster, Erville Alderson, Lionel Barrymore. D: D.W. Griffith. DRA 93m.

America 1986 ★★★ A cable station bounces its signal off the moon, with earth-shaking consequences. Tame satire. C: Zack Norman, Tammy Grimes, Michael J. Pollard. D: Robert Downey. COM [R] 90m. V

America, America 1963 ★★★★½ During the 1890s, a Greek boy comes to America and builds a new life for himself despite many hardships. Intelligent and emotionally charged re-creation of turn-of-the-century immigrants' struggles. Director Kazan based this on his uncle's true story. Won Oscar for Best Art Direction/Set Direction. C: Stathis Giallelis, Frank Wolff, Elena Karam, Lou Antonio. D: Elia Kazan. DRA 168m. V

America at the Movies 1976 ★★★ In celebration of the Bicentennial, the American Film

Institute put together a compilation of clips from Hollywood classics. A fun, if somewhat disorganized reminder of our love affair with movies. DOC [PG] 116m.

America 3000 1986 ★★★ Hundreds of years after a nuclear war, women are in charge of a primitive society. C: Chuck Wagner, Laurene Landon. D: David Engelbach. COM [PG-13] 94m.

American Anthem 1986 ★ A lemon of a vehicle for Olympic gold-medal gymnast Gaylord about, (surprise!) a gymnast stumbling over obstacles on the road to success. C: Mitch Gaylord, Janet Jones, Michelle Phillips. D: Albert Magnoli. DRA 100m. V

American Aristocracy, An 1916 ★★★★ Silent comedy features the versatile Fairbanks as an independent spirit who shakes up the carefully composed structure of a sophisticated New England family. Great fun, with delightful athletic feats from the star. C: Douglas Fairbanks, Sr., Jewel Carmen, Charles de Lima, Albert Parker. D: Lloyd Ingraham. COM 75m.

American Autobahn 1984 ★★★ A young writer becomes a fugitive from the Mob when he attempts to expose an undercover weapons operation. That's director Jim Jarmusch (*Stranger in Paradise*) in a supporting role. C: Jan Jalenak, Michael Von Der Goltz, Jim Jarmusch. D: Andre Degas. DRA 90m. V

American Blue Note 1991 ★★★ A good cast distinguishes this trite story of struggling jazz musicians from the New Jersey suburbs. C: Peter MacNicol, Trini Alvarado, Charlotte D'Amboise. D: Ralph Toporoff. DRA [PG-13] 90m. V

American Boyfriends 1989 Canadian ★★★ Modest sequel to *My American Cousin* about a Canadian college student (Langrick) maturing during a trip to Oregon for her cousin's wedding. Sweet and appealing, though it drags a bit. C: Margaret Langrick, John Wildman, Jason Blicker. D: Sandy Wilson. COM [PG-13] 90m. V

American Christmas Carol, An 1979 ★★★ Dickens' oft-filmed tale of miserly Scrooge encountering three ghosts on Christmas Eve, updated to Depression-era New England. Winkler labors hard under tons of latex makeup. C: Henry Winkler, David Wayne, Dorian Harewood. D: Eric Till. DRA 98m. TVM V

American Clock, The 1993 ★★★★ Playwright Arthur Miller's series of sketches about the Great Depression is uneven, but beautifully performed by a dream cast. Full of sharply observed details, but lacks a strong plot or characters to hold it together. (a.k.a. *Arthur Miller's The American Clock*) C: Roberts Blossom, Eddie Bracken, Mary McDonnell, Darren McGavin, Estelle Parsons, John Randolph, Tony Roberts, Jim Dale, Kelly Preston. D: Bob Clark. DRA 120m. TVM

American Cyborg—Steel Warrior 1994 ★★★ Pumped-up Lara does his best to save the world from a renegade robot in this standard actioner, with heavy violence. C: Joe Lara, Nicole Hansen, John Ryan. D: Boaz Davidson. ACT [R] 92m. V

American Dream 1981 ★★★½ Intelligent, well-done story of a family moving from the suburbs to integrated inner-city Chicago. C: Stephen Macht, Karen Carlson, Hans Conried. D: Mel Damski. DRA 90m. TVM V

American Dream 1990 ★★★★½ When Hormel meatpacking plant workers go on strike, the very legitimacy of unions is called into question. Director Kopple documents this heartbreaking strike, undermined by divisiveness within the union. Won the Academy Award for Best Documentary. D: Barbara Kopple. DOC [PG-13] 100m. V

American Dreamer 1984 ★★★ A conk on the head makes a mousey housewife (Williams), who dreams of being a mystery novelist, wake up in Paris believing she is her favorite fictional character. Lightweight adventure comedy, with charming performances by Williams and Conti. C: JoBeth Williams, Tom Conti, Giancarlo Giannini, Coral Browne. D: Rick Rosenthal. COM [PG] 105m. V

American Eagle 1990 ★★★ Deranged Vietnam vet stalks his former army buddies, who try to track him down. Low-budget suspense. C: Asher Brauner, Robert F. Lyons, Kai Baker, Vernon Wells. D: Robert J. Smawley. DRA [R] 92m. V

American Empire 1942 ★★★★ Handsome Western about three cattle ranchers whose friendships are tested when one becomes a rustler. Flavorful, with exciting action sequences. C: Richard Dix, Leo Carrillo, Preston Foster. D: William McGann. WST 82m. V

American Flyers 1985 ★★★★ Cycling drama focuses on the relationship between two brothers (Costner, Grant), one of whom is dying, training for a bicycle race. Good-natured, old-fashioned entertainment benefits from likable cast and excellent racing footage, particularly during the climactic marathon. Written by bike movie specialist Steve (*Breaking Away*) Tesich. C: Kevin Costner, David Marshall Grant, Rae Dawn Chong, Alexandra Paul. D: John Badham. DRA [PG-13] 113m. V

American Friend, The 1977 U.S. ★★★★★ A picture framer (Ganz) becomes involved with a murderous art smuggler (Hopper). Combination road picture/film noir often frighteningly funny, spiced with bleak philosophy of human nature. Look for cameos by various directors. C: Dennis Hopper, Bruno Ganz, Lisa Kreuzer, Gerard Blain. D: Wim Wenders. DRA 127m. V

American Friends 1993 ★★★ Cute, but trifling tale of a mild-mannered Englishman (Palin) pursued by two American vacationers in the Swiss Alps. C: Michael Palin, Connie Booth. D: Tristram Powell. DRA [PG] 95m. V

American Gangster, The 1992 ★★★★ Ruthlessly separating fact from fiction, this documentary about the roots of organized crime in America traces the careers of such legends as Bugsy Siegel, Lucky Luciano, and John Dillinger. DOC 45m. V

American Gigolo 1980 ★★★½ Cool, stylish portrait of a male prostitute was Gere's first big role. When an ex-client is murdered he can't get the alibi he needs from the woman with whom he has fallen in love (Hutton). Sleazy story with problematic hero, but good performances. C: Richard Gere, Lauren Hutton, Hector Elizondo, Nina Van Pallandt. D: Paul Schrader. DRA [R] 117m. V

American Gothic 1987 ★★ This formulaic hack-'em-up horror film about terrorized youths on an isolated island gets some juice from the eccentric cast (Steiger, De Carlo, Pollard) playing the demented family of villains. C: Rod Steiger, Yvonne De Carlo, Michael J. Pollard. D: John Hough. HOR [R] 90m. V

American Graffiti 1973 ★★★★½ Loving homage to small-town America is a funny and nostalgic look at teen coming-of-age rituals involved in cruising the strip on one last Friday night after high school graduation. Highlighted by a rocking soundtrack and winning performances from the amazing cast of young actors, who all went on to stardom. C: Richard Dreyfuss, Ron Howard, Paul Le Mat, Charles Martin Smith, Cindy Williams, Candy Clark, Mackenzie Phillips, Wolfman Jack, Harrison Ford, Suzanne Somers. D: George Lucas. COM [PG] 112m. V

American Guerilla in the Philippines 1950 ★★★★ Serious WWII film describes the American effort to aid Filipinos in their resistance to Japanese occupation. Notwithstanding occasional soapy melodramatics, director Lang manages to pack a visual wallop, bringing realism to the battle scenes through superb use of location photography. C: Tyrone Power, Micheline Prelle, Tom Ewell. D: Fritz Lang. ACT 105m.

American Heart 1993 ★★★★½ Moving, intelligent tale of aimless drifter (Bridges) and his troubled teenage son (Furlong). He reluctantly takes him in and the two try to put their lives back together with tragic results. Superbly acted and directed. C: Jeff Bridges, Edward Furlong. D: Martin Bell. DRA [R] 114m. V

American Hot Wax 1978 ★★★½ Nostalgic tribute to '50s rock 'n' roll tells true story of pioneering disc jockey Alan Freed with guest stints by many greats of the period. Entertaining. C: Tim McIntire, Fran Drescher, Jay Leno, Laraine Newman, Chuck Berry, Jerry Lee Lewis. D: Floyd Mutrux. MUS [PG] 91m.

American in Paris, An 1951 ★★★★½ Kelly's the title character, an artist torn between his wealthy patron and the woman he loves. Classic MGM musical. Caron is charming in her film debut, the Gershwin songs are timeless, and the landmark, 18-minute ballet finale is justly famous for its use of color and impressionistic decor. Film's six Oscars include Best Picture (the first musical to win in 15 years) and a special Oscar for Kelly. C: Gene Kelly, Leslie Caron, Oscar Levant, Georges Guetary, Nina Foch. D: Vincente Minnelli. MUS 115m. V

American Justice 1986 ★★★ The two stars of TV's *Simon and Simon* play different roles in this story of a slavery ring preying on illegal aliens near the Mexican border. Fair, if unoriginal drama. (a.k.a. *Jackals*) C: Jack Lucarelli, Gerald McRaney, Wilford Brimley, Jameson Parker, Jeannie Wilson. D: Gary Grillo. DRA [R] 92m.

American Madness 1932 ★★★★ Interesting fable of a bank president (Huston) contending with the Great Depression. Smartly written comedy/drama shows Capra defining his trademark style. Fine work by Huston. C: Walter Huston, Pat O' Brien, Kay Johnson. D: Frank Capra. DRA 81m.

American Me 1992 ★★★ Olmos tries, in his directorial debut, to show how low self-esteem and generations of poverty among Chicanos can lead to criminal behavior. Using raw brutality and graphic violence, he portrays the life of a sometime repentant gang member and crime kingpin. Based on a true story. C: Edward James Olmos, William Forsythe, Pepe Serna, Danny De La Paz. D: Edward James Olmos. CRI [R] 125m. V

American Nightmare 1983 ★★½ Violent, nasty tale of a youth looking for his sister in the New York underworld. C: Lawrence Day, Lora Stanley, Lenore Zann. D: Don McBrearty. DRA 85m. V

American Ninja 1985 ★★½ Military martial artist (Dudikoff) stationed in the Philippines uncovers plot on his own Army base to sell arms to corrupt South Americans. Okay karate sequences bogged down by witless plot and performances. C: Michael Dudikoff, Steve James, Judie Aranson. D: Sam Firstenberg. ACT [R] 96m. V

American Ninja 2: The Confrontation 1987 ★★★ First sequel in this series is a marked improvement over initial offering, as patriotic black-belt (Dudikoff) and sidekick (James) return to find themselves embroiled with a Caribbean drug lord (Conway) who's genetically altering U.S Marines into unstoppable ninja assassins. Dudikoff still can't act, but fans will enjoy the mayhem. C: Michael Dudikoff, Steve James, Larry Poindexter. D: Sam Firstenberg. ACT [R] 90m. V

American Ninja 3: Blood Hunt 1989 ★ Third installment in *American Ninja* series is so bad that even original star Dudikoff didn't show up. Instead, charisma-less Bradley takes on sinister criminal (Gortner). The pits. C: David Bradley, Steve James, Marjoe Gortner. D: Cedric Sundstrom. ACT [R] 90m. V

American Ninja 4: The Annihilation 1991 ★

Fourth (and final, we hope) entry in the series has Dudikoff returning as martial arts patriot, this time freeing captive Americans held prisoner by vicious Arabs. Witless bore doesn't even deliver the hand-to-hand goods. C: Michael Dudikoff, David Bradley. D: Cedric Sundstrom. ACT [R] 99m. v

American Pop 1981 ★★★ Bakshi's animation epic looks at four generations of an American family and their experiences with the music world. Beautiful at some points, routinely animated in others, this suffers from superficial plot development. Great soundtrack, though. C: Voices of Ron Thompson, Marya Small, Jerry Holland. D: Ralph Bakshi. DRA [R] 97m.

American Romance, An 1944 ★★★★ A mythic depiction of the American Dream, as an immigrant (Donlevy) rises from nothing to the top of industrial capitalism. Immense production is a fascinating example of the nation's optimistic mood toward the end of WWII. C: Brian Donlevy, Ann Richards. D: King Vidor. DRA 122m.

American Roulette 1988 British ★★ An exiled Latin American president (Garcia) goes on the run from assassins. Bewildering thriller runs on star power. C: Andy Garcia, Kitty Aldridge, Susannah York. D: Maurice Hatton. DRA [R] 102m. v

American Soldier, The 1970 German ★★★ In Fassbinder's homage to Philip Marlowe and Hollywood gangster films, a hired gun (Scheydt) carries out assassinations without a trace of emotion. Although somewhat cold and uninvolving, the climactic shoot-out is an impressive, balletically staged set piece. C: Karl Scheydt, Elga Sorbas, Jan George, Margarethe Von Trotta. D: Rainer Werner Fassbinder. CRI 80m. v

American Success Company, The 1979 ★★★½ Uneven but rewarding black comedy finds a disillusioned corporate drone (Bridges) giving the world a taste of its own medicine. Well-acted big business satire is caustically anti-establishment and may not be for all tastes. (a.k.a. *American Success*, and *Success*) C: Jeff Bridges, Belinda Bauer, Ned Beatty, Bianca Jagger. D: William Richert. COM [PG] 94m.

American Success 1979 *See* **American Success Company, The**

American Summer, An 1990 ★★★ Against his will, midwestern teen whose parents separate is sent to West Coast where he becomes immersed in beach culture. C: Michael Landes, Brian Austin Green, Joanna Kerns. DRA [PG-13] 100m. v

American Tail, An 1986 ★★★½ Fievel, the adorable Russian mouse, gets separated from his family while immigrating to the United States. Spielberg's first animated film, set at the end of the 19th century. Followed by a sequel and a TV series. Voices of Dom DeLuise, Christopher Plummer, Nehimiah Persoff, Madeline Kahn. D: Don Bluth. FAM/DRA [G] 80m. v

American Tail: Fievel Goes West, An 1991 ★★★★ Fans of the first Fievel the mouse feature, both young and old, will enjoy watching him and his family make their fortune in the Wild West. Stewart's marvelous as the addled sheriff. Voices of Philip Glasser, James Stewart, Dom DeLuise, Amy Irving, John Cleese, Jon Lovitz. D: Phil Nibbelink, Simon Wells. FAM/COM [G] 74m. v

American Tiger 1990 ★★★½ College student wrongfully accused of murder teams up with an exotic dancer to find the actual killer. C: Donald Pleasence, Mitch Gaylord, Victoria Prouty. D: Martin Doleman. ACT 93m. v

American Tragedy, An 1931 ★★★½ Sturdy filming of Theodore Dreiser's novel, made memorable by a brilliant Sidney as the forlorn, pregnant girlfriend of social climber (Holmes). See it for Sidney. Remade as *A Place in the Sun* in 1951. C: Sylvia Sidney, Frances Dee, Phillip Holmes. D: Josef von Sternberg. DRA 95m.

American Way, The 1988 *See* **Riders of the Storm**

American Werewolf in London, An 1981 ★★★★ In-your-face horror comedy, with Naughton as a young traveler bitten by a werewolf and fated to suffer its curse. Packed with scares and laughs—and Oscar-winning Rick Baker makeup—as Landis deftly coordinates horror and humor. C: David Naughton, Jenny Agutter, Griffin Dunne. D: John Landis. HOR [R] 97m. v

Americana 1981 ★★★★ Allegorical story of a Vietnam vet who undertakes to fix a dilapidated merry-go-round in a hostile Kansas town. Made independently by Carradine, and with great conviction. C: David Carradine, Barbara Hershey. D: David Carradine. DRA 90m. v

Americanization of Emily, The 1964 ★★★★ During WWII, a U.S. soldier (Garner) provides his superiors with liquor, food, and female companionship—little realizing he's being set up as the first casualty of the upcoming Normandy invasion. Intriguing black comedy tackles an unlikely subject; written by Paddy Chayefsky. Andrews has a nice turn as Garner's love interest. C: James Garner, Julie Andrews, Melvyn Douglas, James Coburn, Keenan Wynn. D: Arthur Hiller. COM 117m. v

Americano, The 1916 ★★★½ While working in South America, a young American engineer (Fairbanks) becomes embroiled in local uprising. Excellent silent adventure is a great showcase for the dashing Fairbanks. C: Douglas Fairbanks Sr. D: John Emerson. ACT

Americano, The 1955 ★★★ Standard western situated South-of-the-Border this time, where Ford fends off bad guys in Brazil. C: Glenn Ford, Cesar Romero. D: William Castle. ACT 85m. v

Americathon 1979 ★★ In 1998 America must hold a benefit to raise money to pay its bills. Satire of '70s America is narrated by George Carlin; best part of this comedy is the interesting cast. C: Harvey Korman, John Ritter, Nancy Morgan, Peter Riegert, Fred Willard. D: Neil Israel. COM [PG] 88m. V

Amerikaner Schadchen 1940 Yiddish ★★★★ Sprightly musical comedy about a millionaire playboy (Fuchs) who decides to take up matchmaking. C: Leo Fuchs, Judith Abarbanel, Judel Dubinsky. D: Edgar G. Ulmer. MUS 87m.

Amin—The Rise and Fall 1981 Kenya ★★ Voyeuristic chronicle of the acts of murder and torture perpetrated by the infamous dictator. He might as well be wearing a hockey mask. C: Joseph Olita, Geoffrey Keen. D: Sharad Patel. DRA [R] 101m. V

Amityville—A New Generation 1993 ★★½ Another evil artifact from the notorious manse—this time a haunted mirror—wreaks havoc among a group of artists when one installs it in their loft. Tries for psychological horror and only occasionally succeeds, though a few scenes deliver the chills. C: Ross Partridge, Lala Sloatman, David Naughton, Richard Roundtree, Terry O'Quinn. D: John Murlowski. HOR [R] 92m. V

Amityville Curse, The 1989 Canadian ★★ After moving into an old Long Island home, three couples learn the place has been haunted ever since a priest was murdered there years before. Another sequel to *The Amityville Horror* rehashes series formula. C: Kim Coates, Dawna Wightman. D: Tom Berry. HOR [R] 92m. V

Amityville 4: The Evil Escapes 1990 ★★ Rehash of haunted-house standards as Duke and family are plagued by evil forces until exorcists are called in to help. Professionally done. C: Patty Duke, Jane Wyatt, Frederic Lehne. D: Sandor Stern. HOR [R] 95m. TVM V

Amityville Horror, The 1979 ★★ Brolin and Kidder are dismayed to find supernatural pests infesting their new abode. Several uninspired shocks later, a priest (Steiger) arrives for some spiritual extermination. Based on "true" story, with requisite grotesqueries. Spawned a whole lot of sequels! C: James Brolin, Margot Kidder, Rod Steiger. D: Stuart Rosenberg. HOR [R] 114m. V

Amityville 1992: It's About Time 1992 ★★★ Better-than-average series entry in which a clock from the fateful house creates horrors in the home of its new owners. Benefits from a somewhat subtler approach than its predecessors—until expected, climactic special effects blowout. C: Stephen Macht, Shawn Weatherly, Megan Ward. D: Tony Randel. HOR [R] 95m. V

Amityville 3D 1983 ★★ A mild improvement over the previous installments, with skeptical Roberts moving into the creepy abode and slowly becoming convinced of the evil dwelling there. On video, this lacks the 3-D special effects that originally attracted moviegoers. C: Tony Roberts, Tess Harper, Robert Joy, Candy Clark, Meg Ryan. D: Richard Fleischer. HOR [PG] 98m. V

Amityville II: The Possession 1982 ★ Appalling prequel is based on a shocking mass murder that really occurred in the Amityville house (with Magner as the unbalanced son who ultimately turns on his family) but adds subplots about demonic takeover and incest that render it implausible and offensive. C: Burt Young, Rutanya Alda. D: Damiano Damiani. HOR [R] 104m. V

Among the Living 1941 ★★★½ Dekker is terrifically double cast as twin brothers: one insane who commits series of murders after being locked up for years, the other wrongly blamed and out to prove his own innocence. Frantic pacing gets carried away, but still an intriguing crime drama. C: Albert Dekker, Susan Hayward, Frances Farmer. D: Stuart Heisler. DRA 68m.

Amongst Friends 1993 ★★★½ Friends' loyal connections are put to the test when their gang turns to crime. Stylistic flourishes give a sleek look to an otherwise age-old tale. C: Steve Parlavecchio, Joseph Lindsay, Patrick McGaw. D: Rob Weiss. CRI [R] 88m. V

Amor Bandido 1981 Brazilian ★★★★ Fact-based drama about a police officer's daughter who turns to prostitution, then gets involved with a murderer. Gritty, realistic portrait of Rio underworld life, from the director of *Dona Flor and her Two Husbands.* C: Paulo Gracindo, Cristina Ache. D: Bruno Barreto. CRI 90m. V

Amore 1948 Italian ★★★½ Magnani takes on two roles here. In "The Miracle" she's convinced her unborn child is the Second Coming. In "The Human Voice," based on a play by Cocteau, she is deserted by her lover. At times a bit overemotional, but ultimately powerful and quite moving. C: Anna Magnani, Federico Fellini. D: Roberto Rossellini. DRA 90m. V

Amore 1977 ★★★ Major makeover turns wealthy curmudgeon into handsome Italian cinema idol. C: Joseph Bottoms, Greg Taylor, Judy Davis. D: Igor Auzins. COM [PG] 82m. V

Amorous Adventures of Moll Flanders, The 1965 British ★★★★ Vivacious orphan (Novak) longs for love and respect in 18th-century England, and ends up embroiled in one salacious liaison after another. Spirited comedy could use a little more spice, but still an entertaining romp. C: Kim Novak, Richard Johnson, Angela Lansbury, George Sanders, Vittorio De Sica, Lilli Palmer, Leo McKern. D: Terence Young. COM 126m. V

Amorous Mr. Prawn, The 1962 British ★★★ Good-natured farce in which military property is converted into a tourist hotel by general's wife while he's away on business.

Sprightly ensemble cast; Carmichael is especially good. C: Joan Greenwood, Cecil Parker, Ian Carmichael. D: Anthony Kimmins. COM 89m.

Amos 1985 ★★★½ A fiesty old man winds up in a nursing home, where he's determined to investigate mysterious goings-on. Well-written mystery drama, with a terrific Douglas. C: Kirk Douglas, Elizabeth Montgomery, Dorothy McGuire, Pat Morita. D: Michael Tuchner. DRA 95m. TVM V

Amos and Andrew 1993 ★★ A prize-winning black playwright, mistaken for a burglar, is imprisoned in his own home by police. Realizing their mistake, they coerce a two-bit crook into kidnapping the writer so they can save him and save face. Cage's kooky characterization is the brightest spot in an otherwise painful comedy. C: Nicolas Cage, Samuel L. Jackson, Dabney Coleman, Michael Lerner. D: E. Max Frye. COM [PG-13] 96m. V

Amsterdam Affair, The 1968 British ★★★½ When a writer is implicated in the murder of his mistress, a detective bucks the conventional wisdom by keeping the case alive. Good mystery, filmed on location. C: Wolfgang Kieling, William Marlowe, Catherine Schell. D: Gerry O'Hara. CRI 91m.

Amsterdam Kill, The 1978 ★★ Mitchum bounces from London to Amsterdam to Hong Kong as a drug agent trying to smash a heroin pipeline. Pacing is slow, Mitchum looks tired, and the dialogue is flat or unintentionally funny. C: Robert Mitchum, Bradford Dillman, Richard Egan, Leslie Nielsen, Keye Luke. D: Robert Clouse. ACT [R] 90m. V

Amsterdamned 1988 Dutch ★★★ Serial killer prowls streets of Amsterdam as police detective tries to stop the slaughter. Interesting use of location in otherwise routine splatter film. C: Huub Stapel, Monique Van de Ven. D: Dick Maas. HOR [R] 114m. V

Amy 1981 ★★★★ Dedicated teacher (Agutter, in a sharp, beautiful performance) leaves her husband to work with deaf and blind children. Turn-of-the-century period piece is intelligently written, appealing to children and parents alike. C: Jenny Agutter, Barry Newman, Kathleen Nolan, Margaret O'Brien, Nanette Fabray. D: Vincent McEveety. FAM/DRA [G] 100m. V

Amy Fisher: My Story 1992 ★★ Story of the "Long Island Lolita," who shot the wife of her alleged lover, Joey Buttafuoco. Steamy and soapy, in liberal doses. One of three TV-movies that came out almost simultaneously, this one is the version authorized by Amy. (a.k.a. *Lethal Lolita—Amy Fisher: My Story*) C: Noelle Parker, Ed Marinaro. D: Bradford May. DRA 100m. TVM

Amy Fisher Story, The 1993 ★★★½ If there can be a "best" of the infamous trio of network movies based on the "Long Island Lolita" case, this is it. Barrymore's tongue-in-cheek portrayal of the teenager who gets involved with a car mechanic, and then shoots his wife, makes this fun trash viewing for those still interested in the much publicized case. C: Drew Barrymore, Anthony John Denison, Harley Jane Kozak. D: Andy Tennant. DRA 96m. TVM V

Ana and the Wolves 1972 Spanish ★★★½ Symbol-laden drama of a naive governess terrorized by ravenous brothers in dilapidated mansion. For Saura, the brothers are Franco's Spain: the overt governmental criticism makes the allegory hard to swallow, though it has some biting moments. C: Geraldine Chaplin, Fernando Fernan-Gomez, Jose Maria Prada, Jose Vivo. D: Carlos Saura. DRA 100m. V

Anastasia 1956 ★★★★½ Bergman's Oscar-winning portrayal of a woman claiming to be the Czar's daughter Anastasia, survivor of the Bolshevik Revolution. Hayes lends great support as the exiled grand duchess who must decide if the claim is fake or not. Their long scene together is a tour de force. Brynner's good too; a classy historical mystery. C: Ingrid Bergman, Yul Brynner, Helen Hayes, Akim Tamiroff, Martita Hunt. D: Anatole Litvak. DRA 106m. V

Anastasia: The Mystery Of Anna 1986 ★★★★ Intelligent, well-produced historical drama of Anna Anderson (Irving), who insisted she was Anastasia, the lost daughter of Russia's last Czar (Sharif). De Havilland's grand duchess is her best work since the '40s. Compelling, fact-based drama about a real-life mystery woman. C: Amy Irving, Olivia de Havilland, Omar Sharif, Jan Niklas, Claire Bloom, Elke Sommer, Susan Lucci, Rex Harrison. D: Marvin J. Chomsky. DRA 210m. TVM V

Anatomist, The 1961 British ★★ Macabre black comedy about grave robbing. Boasts a supreme Grand Guignol role for Sim. C: Alastair Sim, George Cole, Jill Bennett. D: Leonard William. HOR 73m.

Anatomy of a Marriage 1964 French ★★★½ Experimental film shows the events preceding the breakup of a marriage from the separate and distinct points of view of two spouses. In effect, there are two films in one; first we see wife's point of view, then the husband's. Interesting, if not entirely successful. C: Jacques Charrier, Marie-Jose Nat, Georges Riviere, Macha Meril. D: Andre Cayatte. DRA 193m.

Anatomy of a Murder 1959 ★★★★½ A lawyer (Stewart) reluctantly takes on the case of a serviceman on trial for killing the alleged rapist of his wife (Remick). Crackerjack courtroom thriller with sexual content, bold for its time. Grand cast includes O'Connell and Arden lending a welcome comic touch as Jimmy's sidekicks. Even the score (by Duke Ellington, no less) is great. C: James Stewart, Lee Remick, Ben Gazzara, Arthur O'Connell, Eve Arden, George C. Scott. D: Otto Preminger. DRA 160m. V

Anatomy of a Seduction 1979 ★★★½ Forty-something divorced woman initiates romance with her college-aged son's favorite pal, who is also the child of her own best friend. C: Susan Flannery, Jameson Parker, Rita Moreno. D: Steven Hilliard Stern. DRA 96m. v

Anatomy of Terror 1974 ★★★ Years after the Korean War, former P.O.W. nearly drowns in long-buried memories of a dark wartime deed. C: Paul Burke, Polly Bergen. DRA 74m. v

Anchors Aweigh 1945 ★★★½ Two sailors (Kelly and Sinatra) on leave help a woman (Grayson) get an audition with a famous conductor (Iturbi). Harmless grab bag of popular songs and operetta schmaltz, notable for Kelly's magical dance with cartoon Jerry (the mouse of Tom and Jerry fame). C: Frank Sinatra, Kathryn Grayson, Gene Kelly, Jose Iturbi, Dean Stockwell. D: George Sidney. MUS 141m. v

And a Nightingale Sang 1990 ★★★★½ At the end of the Blitz, a London couple tries to prevent the war from separating them. Tender tale, starkly countered by brutal bombing sequences. C: Joan Plowright. DRA 90m. v

And Baby Makes Six 1979 ★★★½ A woman with grown-up children discovers that she is pregnant again, and clashes with her husband who wants to put child-rearing behind him. Probing, good-natured drama. Wonderful Dewhurst. C: Colleen Dewhurst, Warren Oates, Mildred Dunnock, Timothy Hutton. D: Waris Hussein. DRA 97m. TVM v

And Baby Makes Three 1949 ★★★ Complications abound when a divorced woman (Hale) discovers she's pregnant by her ex-husband. Rather dated comedy tries hard. C: Robert Young, Barbara Hale, Robert Hutton, Billie Burke. D: Henry Levin. COM 84m.

. . . And God Created Woman 1956 ★★★★ In the film that launched Bardot as an international sex symbol, she plays an 18-year-old newlywed with wandering eyes. Shot on location in steamy St. Tropez. C: Brigitte Bardot, Curt Jurgens, Jean-Louis Trintignant, Christian Marquando. D: Roger Vadim. DRA 92m. v

And God Created Woman 1988 ★★ Although it has the same title and was directed by Vadim, not a remake of Bardot's sensational 1956 film. An aspiring rock star (De Mornay) strikes a deal with her politician lover so she can be released from prison. Contrived, with a trite ending. C: Rebecca De Mornay, Vincent Spano, Frank Langella, Donovan Leitch. D: Roger Vadim. DRA [R] 100m. v

. . . And God Spoke 1994 ★★★ Sophomoric, but occasionally hilarious, spoof of biblical epics, set in Hollywood during production of unusual take on the Old and New Testaments. Highlight is veteran TV kiddie host Sales as Moses! C: Michael Riley, Stephen Rappaport, Soupy Sales, Lou Ferrigno, Eve Plumb. D: Arthur Borman. COM [R] 83m. v

And Hope to Die 1972 French ★★★★ A Frenchman (Trintignant) flees France and joins a Canadian gang, which uses him in a big heist. Existential gangster film with a decidedly European flavor. Nice turn by Ryan as the boss. Don't expect speed, but the payoff is substantial. C: Robert Ryan, Tisa Farrow, Jean-Louis Trintignant. D: Rene Clement. CRI [PG] 95m. v

And I Alone Survived 1978 ★★★ Woman fights to survive plane crash that leaves her stranded in the Sierra Nevadas. C: Blair Brown, David Ackroyd, Vera Miles. D: William Graham. DRA 90m. v

And Justice for All 1979 ★★★ Manic attack on the American legal system, with its deal-making, dishonest practices, and outright corruption. Pacino, in an inflated performance, plays an honest lawyer trying to buck the system. A flawed, troublesome drama. Lahti's feature film debut. C: Al Pacino, Jack Warden, John Forsythe, Lee Strasberg, Christine Lahti, Craig T. Nelson. D: Norman Jewison. DRA [R] 117m. v

And Millions Will Die 1973 ★★ Bsehurt must race to find a nerve gas bomb that's about to go off somewhere in Hong Kong. Weak thriller. C: Richard Basehart, Susan Strasberg, Leslie Nielsen. D: Leslie Martinson. ACT 96m.

And No One Could Save Her 1973 ★★★ Good cast elevates routine thriller about heiress (Remick) whose husband disappears on his way to Ireland. DRA

And Nothing But the Truth 1982 British ★★★ When a Welsh farmer takes on the government, a documentary filmmaker (Jackson) and a reporter (Finch) come to his aid. Stiff, but earnest indictment of media manipulation, with good performances from both leads. (a.k.a. *Giro City*) C: Glenda Jackson, Jon Finch, Kenneth Colley. D: Karl Francis. DRA 90m. v

And Now for Something Completely Different 1972 British ★★★★ Off-the-wall British comedy troupe Monty Python redo most popular routines from their legendary BBC television series. Includes all the classic Python sketches from "The Dead Parrot" to "The Lumberjack Song." A full dose of the group's irreverent humor. C: Graham Chapman, John Cleese, Eric Idle, Terry Gilliam, Terry Jones, Michael Palin. D: Ian McNaughton. COM [PG] 89m. v

And Now Miguel 1966 ★★★★ Ten-year-old Mexican boy proves to his father that he can be a good, trustworthy sheepherder. Slow-moving, but excellent film for family viewing; based on an award-winning children's story. C: Pat Cardi, Michael Ansara, Guy Stockwell. D: James Clark. FAM/DRA 95m.

And Now My Love 1975 French ★★★½ Man and woman from different political/social/cultural backgrounds meet and fall in love despite all odds. Pure soap opera plot, but Lelouch and cast make the most of predictable material. C: Marthe Keller, Andre Dussollier, Charles Denner, Gilbert Becaud. D: Claude Lelouch. DRA [PG] 121m. V

And Now the Screaming Starts 1973 British ★★★½ Stylish horror film about a newlywed couple's move into a seriously haunted house. Chilling. C: Peter Cushing, Stephanie Beacham, Herbert Lom, Patrick Magee. D: Roy Ward Baker. HOR [R] 87m. V

And Now Tomorrow 1944 ★★½ Ladd achieved star status in this clichéd tale of a rich society woman (Young) who falls in love with the doctor who's trying to cure her deafness. From the best-seller by Rachel Field. Interesting trivia: Raymond Chandler has a writing credit. C: Alan Ladd, Loretta Young, Susan Hayward, Barry Sullivan, Beulah Bondi. D: Irving Pichel. DRA 85m.

And Quiet Flows the Don 1957 Russian ★★★★ Involving study of Russian life as WWI and the 1917 Revolution sweep through the life of one rural family. A moving adaptation of Mikhail-Sholokov's novel. C: Ellina Bystritskaya, Pyotr Glebov. D: Sergei Gerasimov. DRA 107m.

And So They Were Married 1936 ★★★½ Pleasant fluff about a widow (Astor) and widower (Douglas) marrying despite their children's objections. Harmless and diverting. C: Melvyn Douglas, Mary Astor. D: Elliott Nugent. COM 74m.

And So They Were Married 1944 *See* **Johnny Doesn't Live Here Any More**

And Soon the Darkness 1970 British ★★★ A pair of nurses on a bicycling holiday in France are stalked by a killer. Atmospheric psychosexual thriller. C: Pamela Franklin, Michele Dotrice, Sandor Eles. D: Robert Fuest. DRA [PG] 94m. V

And the Angels Sing 1944 ★★★ Two members of a female singing group (Lamour, Hutton) get involved with their sax player (MacMurray, who started out as a big-band sax player in real life). Innocuous musical comedy, highlighted by Hutton's raucous delivery of "Bluebirds in My Belfry!" C: Dorothy Lamour, Fred MacMurray, Betty Hutton, Diana Lynn. D: George Marshall. MUS 96m.

And the Band Played On 1993 ★★★★½ Far-ranging exposé of governmental mishandling of AIDS, from the earliest cases to the late '80s. Expert rendering of scientific issues surrounding crisis with no winners, but some genuine heroes. Strong, persuasive drama, from the acclaimed non-fiction book by Randy Shilts. C: Matthew Modine, Alan Alda, Phil Collins, Richard Gere, Glenne Headly, Anjelica Huston, Swoosie Kurtz, Steve Martin, Ian McKellan, Lily Tomlin. D: Roger Spottiswoode. DRA [PG-13] 140m. TVM V

And the Sea Will Tell 1991 ★★★ True story of two couples and murder in the South Seas is given rather heavy-handed treatment. C: Richard Crenna, Rachel Ward, Hart Bochner, James Brolin. D: Tommy Wallace. DRA 200m. TVM

And the Ship Sails On 1984 Italian ★★★★ In 1914, an oceanliner sets sail carrying the ashes of an opera diva which are to be scattered by her entourage once they're at sea. The usual oddball Fellini types are on display, as is the director's magic touch. C: Freddie Jones, Barbara Jefford, Victor Poletti, Janet Suzman. D: Federico Fellini. DRA [PG] 130m. V

And the Wild, Wild Women 1958 Italian ★★★½ Badly dubbed women's prison drama, worth seeing for Italian film divas Magnani and Massina in their only screen teaming. C: Anna Magnani, Giulietta Massina, Myriam Bru, Renato Salvatori. D: Renato Castellani. DRA 110m. V

And Then There Were None 1945 ★★★★★ The first and best screen version of Agatha Christie's novel, with ten guests on an isolated island being killed off one by one. Plenty of suspense and a dream cast, helped by the light touch of director Clair. Remade several times as *Ten Little Indians*. C: Barry Fitzgerald, Walter Huston, Louis Hayward, Roland Young, June Duprez, C. Aubrey Smith, Judith Anderson, Mischa Auer, Richard Haydn. D: Rene Clair. CRI 97m. V

And Then You Die 1987 ★★★★ The leader of a Canadian coke-dealing empire (Welsh) must contend with rival dealers and police interference when a Mafia chief is murdered. An unusually suspenseful thriller is made more absorbing by its exploration of the complex web of relationships in the gangster hierarchy. Inspired by *The Long Good Friday*. C: Kenneth Welsh, R.H. Thomson, Wayne Robson, Tom Harvey, Graeme Campbell. D: Francis Mankiewicz. ACT [R] 115m. V

And You Thought Your Parents Were Weird! 1991 ★★★½ Kids bring their dead dad's spirit back and place it in the robot he was working on at the time of his demise. Mildly amusing entry in the *Honey, I...* sweepstakes may be a little dark for the younger tykes. C: Joshua Miller, Edan Gross, Marcia Strassman, Alan Thicke. D: Tony Cookson. FAM/COM [PG] 92m. V

Anderson Platoon, The 1967 French ★★★★ A look at the day-to-day lives of G.I.s in a U.S. Army platoon fighting and dying in the early years of the Vietnam War. This Oscar-winning French documentary vividly captures the sights, sounds, and feelings of jungle combat. D: Pierre Schoendorffer. DOC 58m. V

Anderson Tapes, The 1971 ★★★★ Connery shines as a tough ex-convict planning to loot an entire luxury building in New York's snooty Upper East Side. Walken makes his screen debut under Lumet's lightning-fast direction. C: Sean Connery, Dyan Cannon, Martin Balsam, Alan King, Margaret Hamilton,

Christopher Walken. D: Sidney Lumet. ACT [PG] 98m. v

Anderson's Angels 1976 *See* **Chesty Anderson, USN**

Andersonville Trial 1970 ★★★★ Shocking and intelligent adaptation of MacKinlay Kantor's book, exposing the atrocities of the American Civil War's most notorious prison camp. C: Martin Sheen, William Shatner, Buddy Ebsen. D: George C. Scott. DRA 150m. v

Andrei Rublev 1965 Russian ★★★★★ On the surface, this is the history of the famous 15th-century Russian icon painter told in exquisite images. But Tarkovsky's subtext is a bold message about individual freedom, which caused Soviet authorities to ban the film for several years. Considered a modern Russian classic. C: Anatoli Solonitzin, Ivan Lapikov, Nikolai Grinko. D: Andrei Tarkovsky. DRA [R] 185m. v

Andrei Tarkovsky, the Genius, the Man, the Legend 1988 Russian ★★★★ Imaginative portrait of the brilliant and complex Russian genius, sparking more questions than it can possibly answer. D: Michal Leszczylowski. DOC 101m. v

Andrew Dice Clay— "No Apologies" 1993 ★★ Vulgar comedian performs headline-grabbing material at Long Island's Westbury Music Fair. C: Andrew Dice Clay. COM 65m. v

Andrews' Raiders 1956 *See* **Great Locomotive Chase, The**

Androcles and the Lion 1952 ★★★★ Though burdened by some slow spots, Bernard Shaw's adaptation of this famed Aesop's fable is enjoyable family fare. Young is the title character, an early Christian who makes friends with a lion after removing a thorn from the beast's paw. Younger viewers will enjoy the slapstick, while adults will appreciate Shaw's wit. C: Jean Simmons, Alan Young, Victor Mature, Maurice Evans, Elsa Lanchester, Robert Newton. D: Chester Erskine. FAM/COM 105m. v

Android 1982 ★★★★ Entertaining science fiction satire set aboard a spaceship, where a mad doctor (Kinski) teaches the near-human robot (Opper) about Earth. When intergalactic fugitives arrive, the robot decides to take matters into his mechanical hands. Clever script and snappy acting distinguish this nifty work. C: Klaus Kinski, Don Opper, Brie Howard. D: Aaron Lipstadt. SFI [PG] 80m. v

Andromeda Strain, The 1971 ★★★ Scientists work against the clock to contain and destroy a lethal virus from outer space. Fine premise and performances undermined by overlong treatment. Based on the Michael Crichton novel. C: Arthur Hill, David Wayne, James Olson, Kate Reid, Paula Kelly. D: Robert Wise. SFI [G] 130m. v

Andrzej Wajda—A Portrait 1989 Polish ★★★★ The camera turns inward in this intense look at the renowned Polish director. Well-done. DOC 76m. v

Andy 1965 ★★★★ Insightful study of the daily hardships of a mentally retarded man, with a marvelous performance by Alden. Sensitive handling avoids mushy pitfalls. C: Norman Alden, Tamara Daykarhonova. D: Richard Sarafian. DRA 86m.

Andy Griffith Show, The—Special Holiday Release ★★★½ Come home to this warm and sentimental collection of three episodes focusing on the holidays. C: Andy Griffith. COM 71m. TVM

Andy Griffith Show, The ★★★★ Three holiday episodes from the classic TV show, featuring Andy, Opie, Barney, and Aunt Bea. Includes "Christmas Story," "Sermon for Today" and "Family Visit." C: Andy Griffith. D: Andy Griffith. FAM/COM 71m. TVM v

---

Andy Hardy In its heyday, MGM liked to aim its films at Main Street, USA. As Andy Hardy, Mickey Rooney was the teen next door, perpetually fascinated by girls and cars. Although he first essayed the role in *A Family Affair* (1937), with crusty Lionel Barrymore as his gruff but understanding father, the immensely likable, if somewhat predictable series actually begins with 1938's *You're Only Young Once*. The films also showcase numerous MGM starlets, including Judy Garland, Lana Turner, and Esther Williams.

A Family Affair (1937)
You're Only Young Once (1938)
Judge Hardy's Children (1938)
Love Finds Andy Hardy (1938)
Out West With the Hardys (1938)
The Hardys Ride High (1939)
Andy Hardy Gets Spring Fever (1939)
Judge Hardy and Son (1939)
Andy Hardy Meets Debutante (1940)
Andy Hardy's Private Secretary (1940)
Life Begins for Andy Hardy (1941)
The Courtship of Andy Hardy (1942)
Andy Hardy's Double Life (1942)
Andy Hardy's Blonde Trouble (1944)
Love Laughs at Andy Hardy (1946)
Andy Hardy Comes Home (1958)

Andy Hardy Comes Home 1958 ★★½ In this late entry Andy Hardy, now a corporate lawyer, returns home to battle a greedy landowner. Tries to capture the old magic. C: Mickey Rooney, Patricia Breslin, Fay Holden, Cecilia Parker, Sara Haden. D: Howard Koch. FAM/COM 80m.

Andy Hardy Gets Spring Fever 1939 ★★★ Seventh in the Hardy series. Enthusiastic Andy (Rooney) gets a crush on his drama teacher and writes a starring part for himself in the school play. Warm and funny, as usual, but no glitter. C: Lewis Stone, Mickey Rooney, Cecilia Parker, Fay Holden, Ann Rutherford, Sara Haden. D: W. S. Van Dyke II. FAM/COM 85m. v

Andy Hardy Meets Debutante 1940 ★★★★

The Andy Hardy film everyone remembers, costarring Judy Garland as a sophisticated New Yorker who steals his heart. Garland sings two songs, including "I'm Nobody's Baby." Ninth in the series, and one of the best. C: Mickey Rooney, Lewis Stone, Fay Holden, Cecilia Parker, Judy Garland, Sara Haden, Ann Rutherford. D: George B. Seitz. FAM/COM 86m. V

Andy Hardy's Blonde Trouble 1944 ★★★★ Andy Hardy (Rooney) can't keep his mind on his college texts for all the fresh-faced young women passing his way. Dad comes to the rescue. Excellent series entry, the squeaky-clean charm in full gear. C: Mickey Rooney, Lewis Stone, Fay Holden, Sara Haden, Bonita Granville, Keye Luke, Herbert Marshall. D: George B. Seitz. FAM/COM 107m.

Andy Hardy's Double Life 1942 ★★★ Number thirteen in the long-running Andy Hardy series. Swimming champion Esther Williams makes her first film appearance in this story of Andy's college freshman year. Warm and amusing addition to the Hardy family saga. C: Mickey Rooney, Lewis Stone, Cecilia Parker, Ann Rutherford, Sara Haden, Esther Williams. D: George B. Seitz. FAM/COM 92m. V

Andy Hardy's Private Secretary 1941 ★★★ Tenth in Hardy family series and film debut of actress/singer Grayson. She gets to trill "Voices of Spring" while working as his much put-upon social secretary. The usual stuff, but fun. C: Mickey Rooney, Lewis Stone, Fay Holden, Sara Haden, Kathryn Grayson. D: George B. Seitz. FAM/COM 101m.

Andy Kaufman—Sound Stage 1985 ★★★ Future household name, Elayne Boosler, makes an appearance in this "best of" stand-up performance by Kaufman. C: Andy Kaufman. COM 60m.

Andy Kaufman Special, The 1979 ★★★½ Impersonations of Ed Sullivan and Elvis Presley highlight this talented comedian's original and irreverent stand-up. C: Andy Kaufman, Cindy Williams. D: Tom Trbovich. COM 59m.

Andy Warhol's Bad 1971 ★★★½ Demented black comedy stars Baker as a Queens housewife who makes ends meet by hiring out women as assassins. Warhol's most mainstream effort has a cult following, but many will find it distasteful. C: Carroll Baker, Perry King, Susan Tyrrell. D: Jed Johnson. COM 107m. V

Andy Warhol's Dracula 1974 Italian ★★★ Revisionist (to say the least) retelling of the legend of the Count, who seeks the blood of "ware-gins" but has a hard time finding any with studly Dallesandro around. Occasionally funny, more often gross, though the climax is undeniably memorable. C: Udo Kier, Joe Dallesandro, Vittorio De Sica. D: Paul Morrissey. HOR [R] 106m. V

Andy Warhol's Frankenstein 1974 Italian ★★ Gross-out update of Mary Shelley's horror classic stars Kier as the maddest mad doctor yet, stitching together body parts in his quest to make a man. Sex, violence, and black humor galore. C: Joe Dallesandro, Monique Van Vooren. D: Paul Morrissey. HOR [R] 95m. V

Angel 1937 ★★★ No sparkling "Lubitsch touch" or Dietrich magic in this thin story of a lady who leaves her English lord husband for another man while on vacation. Did nothing to prevent Dietrich from being named "Box Office Poison" in 1937. C: Marlene Dietrich, Herbert Marshall, Melvyn Douglas, Edward Everett Horton, Laura Hope Crews. D: Ernst Lubitsch. DRA 91m.

Angel 1984 *See* **Danny Boy**

Angel 1984 ★★★ Honor student Wilkes goes to high school by day, works as Hollywood Boulevard hooker by night—until a serial killer sets his sights on her. Good action and not too exploitative. C: Donna Wilkes, Cliff Gorman, Susan Tyrrell, Rory Calhoun, Dick Shawn. D: Robert Vincent O'Neil. ACT [R] 92m. V

Angel and the Badman 1947 ★★★★ Character-driven Western about a gunslinger (Wayne) who is nursed back to health by a Mormon family, and offered redemption in the process. Focusing on love story rather than gunplay, the Duke gets a real chance to act. Very satisfying. Compare with 1985's *Witness.* C: John Wayne, Gail Russell, Harry Carey. D: James Edward Grant. WST 100m. V

Angel at My Table, An 1991 New Zealand ★★★★★ Fox gives an expansive but finely tuned performance as a New Zealand woman who survives a tortuous youth, including many years in a mental hospital, to become an acclaimed author. Based on Janet Frame's autobiographies, Campion's challenging masterwork was originally released as a three-part television series. C: Kerry Fox, Alexia Keogh, Karen Fergusson. D: Jane Campion. DRA [R] 160m. V

Angel Baby 1961 ★★★½ Good melodrama about faith healers has occasional punch, with a spicy Southern milieu and a gothic feel. Reynold's debut. C: Hubert Cornfield, George Hamilton, Salome Jens, Mercedes McCambridge, Joan Blondell, Burt Reynolds. D: Paul Wendkos. DRA 97m.

Angel City 1980 ★★★ Family of migrant workers, trapped working in a seamy Florida labor camp, are terrorized by its overseer in this present-day *Grapes of Wrath.* C: Ralph Waite, Paul Winfield, Jennifer Warren, Jennifer Jason Leigh. D: Philip Leacock. DRA 90m. TVM V

Angel Dusted 1981 ★★★★ Solid drama describes the toll a teenager's drug use takes on his entire family. Stapleton does extraordinary work, playing off her real-life son (Putch). C:

Jean Stapleton, Arthur Hill, John Putch, Helen Hunt. D: Dick Lowry. DRA 98m. TVM

Angel Face 1953 ★★★½ A demented, rich young woman (Simmons) causes the violent deaths of her family members in this suspenseful psychological study. Solid performances by Simmons and by Mitchum, as a working-class ambulance driver lured into the mystery. C: Robert Mitchum, Jean Simmons, Herbert Marshall, Jim Backus, Barbara O'Neil, Leon Ames. D: Otto Preminger. CRI 91m.

Angel From Texas, An 1940 ★★★ A rube (Albert) gets swindled while trying to buy his girlfriend's way into an acting career. Innocuous comedy should appeal to Reagan aficionados: He plays an unscrupulous theater producer. C: Eddie Albert, Wayne Morris, Rosemary Lane, Jane Wyman, Ronald Reagan. D: Ray Enright. COM 69m.

Angel Heart 1987 ★★★½ Hired to locate a missing man, a private detective (Rourke) gets involved with a bizarre New Orleans religious cult. Unsettling, disturbing psychological study contains an infamous sex scene (slightly cut in theaters, restored on video) involving much nudity, blood, and chickens. C: Mickey Rourke, Robert De Niro, Lisa Bonet. D: Alan Parker. CRI [R] 112m. V

Angel in a Taxi 1959 Italian ★★★½ Painless comedy of little orphan (Marietto) who decides to adopt a ballerina as his mother after seeing her picture in the papers. De Sica is charming in a triple role. C: Vera Cecova, Vittorio De Sica, Marietto. D: Antonio Leonviola. DRA 89m. V

Angel in Exile 1948 ★★★ Unusual Western about an ex-con believed to have miraculous powers. Interesting. C: Philip Ford, John Carroll, Adele Mara. D: Allan Dwan. WST 90m.

Angel in Green 1987 ★★½ During WWII, a missionary nun (Dey) has an affair with military official (Boxleitner) on a South Pacific island. Modern soap opera, masquerading as a classic '40s WWII movie. C: Bruce Boxleitner, Susan Dey, Milo O'Shea. D: Marvin J. Chomsky. DRA 100m. V

Angel in my Pocket 1969 ★★★½ A small-town preacher interferes in local politics, with comic results. Not much of a stretch from his TV work for Griffith, but pleasant just the same. C: Andy Griffith, Lee Meriwether, Jerry Van Dyke, Kay Medford. D: Alan Rafkin. COM [G] 105m.

Angel Levine, The 1970 ★★★★ A Jewish tailor (Mostel) is surprised by a black angel (Belafonte) who has arrived to redeem his wretched life. Well-done adaptation of Bernard Malamud's short story is directed with poignant humor and insight. C: Zero Mostel, Harry Belafonte, Ida Kaminska, Milo O'Shea, Eli Wallach, Anne Jackson. D: Jan Kadar. DRA [PG] 104m.

Angel of Vengeance 1981 *See* **Ms. 45**

Angel of Vengeance 1988 *See* **War Cat**

Angel on My Shoulder 1946 ★★★★ In order to become human again, a murdered gangster (Muni) makes a deal with the devil (Rains) to trade places with an honest judge. Fun change of pace for Muni really works. Later remade for TV. C: Paul Muni, Anne Baxter, Claude Rains. D: Archie Mayo. DRA 100m. V

Angel on My Shoulder 1980 ★★½ A deceased criminal comes back to earth in the body of a district attorney. Remake of classic comic fantasy. C: Peter Strauss, Richard Kiley, Barbara Hershey, Janis Paige. D: John Berry. COM 100m. TVM

Angel on the Amazon 1948 ★★ Silly jungle picture about a woman (Ralston) who suffers a tragedy, seeks solace in nature, and stops aging. When a plane crash survivor falls in love with her, her biological clock starts ticking again. Unintentionally funny. C: George Brent, Vera Ralston, Constance Bennett, Brian Aherne. D: John Auer. DRA 86m.

Angel Passed over Brooklyn, An 1957 *See* **Man Who Wagged His Tail, The**

Angel River 1986 ★ Repulsive action film about a bandit (Sanchez) who kidnaps and rapes a homesteader (Johnson), who then falls in love with him. C: Lynn-Holly Johnson, Salvador Sanchez. D: Sergio Greene. ACT 91m.

Angel Street 1940 *See* **Gaslight**

Angel III—Final Chapter, The 1988 ★★ This time the reformed streetwalker learns that her younger sister is caught up in prostitution. Time to whip out that gun and exact more revenge! Fun exploitation fare and the latest, but not last, of the *Angel* films. C: Mitzi Kapture, Maud Adams, Richard Roundtree, Kin Shriner. D: Tom De Simone. ACT [R] 100m. V

Angel Town 1990 ★★ Kickboxing champion interrupts his university studies to combat a series of depraved street thugs. Action material cannot transcend its racist caricature villains. C: Olivier Gruner, Theresa Saldana, Peter Kwong. D: Eric Karson. ACT [R] 90m. V

Angel Unchained 1970 ★★ A biker gang protects a hippie commune against small town roughnecks. Good cast in biker movie following in the wake of *Easy Rider*. C: Don Stroud, Luke Askew, Larry Bishop, Tyne Daly. D: Lee Madden. ACT [PG] 92m.

Angel Who Pawned Her Harp, The 1954 British ★★★ Bittersweet comedy about an angel (Cilento) who enters the life of a pawnshop owner (Aylmer). Better than the title. C: Felix Aylmer, Diane Cilento. D: Alan Bromly. COM 76m.

Angel Wore Red, The 1960 ★★★½ Beautifully photographed tale set during the Spanish Civil War. A priest (Bogarde) has left the church after his affair with a prostitute (Gardner), and now they're joined in political struggle. Fine cast. C: Ava Gardner, Dirk Bogarde, Joseph Cotten, Vittorio De Sica. D: Nunnally Johnson. DRA 99m.

Angela 1977 Canadian ★★ Years after he is kidnapped, son falls in love with his ex-hooker mother; neither knows the other's identity. Soap opera, despite the cast. C: Sophia Loren, Steve Railsback, John Huston. D: Boris Sagal. DRA 91m. v

Angele 1934 French ★★★★ Bored with life in the French countryside where she lives with her overbearing father, a young woman goes to Paris and is beguiled by a streetwise hustler. Solid character-driven drama that thrives on excellent performances from the ensemble. Based on a novel by Jean Giono. C: Orane Demazis, Fernandel, Henri Poupon, Edouard Delmont. D: Marcel Pagnol. DRA 130m. v

Angelo, My Love 1983 ★★★★ Charming docudrama about the contemporary gypsy community in New York City, focusing on Angelo Evans, a 12-year-old living by his wits. Intriguing and steady delivery. Good work by authentic amateur cast. C: Angelo Evans, Mike Evans, Steve Tsigonoff, Millie Tsigonoff. D: Robert Duvall. DRA [R] 115m. v

Angels' Alley 1948 ★★½ The Bowery Boys vs. a gang of car thieves. Middle series entry. DRA

Angels' Brigade 1979 ★★ Female vigilantes convert a van into a war bus and go after drug pushers. Plenty of violent action. C: Jack Palance, Neville Brand, Jim Backus, Peter Lawford, Jacqueline Cole, Susan Kiger, Sylvia Anderson. D: Greydon Clark. ACT [PG] 97m. v

Angels Die Hard 1970 ★★★ When a mining disaster overwhelms small town, a gang of motorcycle riders defies stereotypes and lends a helping hand. Unusual approach to biker pictures carries a message with the revving engines. Different from others in the genre. C: Tom Baker, William Smith, Connie Nelson. D: Richard Compton. ACT [R] 86m. v

Angels From Hell 1968 ★★ An embittered Vietnam veteran assembles a biker army and invades a small town. Countercultural fantasy. C: Tom Stern, Arlene Martel, Ted Markland. D: Bruce Kessler. ACT [R] 86m. v

Angels Hard as They Come 1972 ★★★½ Episodic plotless tale of bikers on the open road both satirizes and succumbs to the conventions of the motorcycle genre. Demme's production has some seemingly authentic dialogue and situations performed by a superior cast. C: James Iglehart, Gilda Texter, Gary Busey. D: Joe Viola. ACT [R] 86m. v

Angels in Disguise 1949 ★★★ Bowery Boys vs. local gangsters. Typical fun. C: Leo Gorcey, Huntz Hall, Gabriel Dell. D: Jean Yarbrough. COM 63m.

Angels in the Outfield 1951 ★★★★ The Pittsburgh Pirates can't seem to win a game, until Heaven lends a hand. Classic baseball comedy, with Douglas terrific as the curmudgeonly manager. Remade in 1994. C: Paul Douglas, Janet Leigh, Keenan Wynn, Spring Byington, Lewis Stone, Ellen Corby, Donna Corcoran. D: Clarence Brown. COM 102m. v

Angels of Darkness 1956 Italian ★★½ The sentimental story of three prostitutes after their bordello is torn down. C: Linda Darnell, Anthony Quinn, Valentina Cortese. D: Giuseppe Amato. DRA 84m.

Angels of the City 1989 ★★★½ The memory of a sorority prank quickly fades away when two college students witness a brutal shooting and place themselves in danger by becoming a street lord's next target. C: Lawrence Hilton-Jacobs, Kelly Galindo, Cynthia Cheston. D: Lawrence Hilton-Jacobs. ACT 90m.

Angels One Five 1954 British ★★½ Realistic but plodding WWII story, told from the point of view of the experts in the control room who guide and monitor RAF flyers in the air. C: Jack Hawkins, Michael Denison, John Gregson. D: George O'Ferrall. ACT 98m.

Angels over Broadway 1940 ★★★★ An embezzler on the verge of suicide (Qualen) is befriended by an alcoholic writer (Mitchell), a gambling shill (Fairbanks Jr.) and his sharp girlfriend (Hayworth) in this tale of four losers joining forces to outhustle some cardsharps. Nonconforming mixture of humor, drama, and caustic dialogue make for a small gem. C: Douglas Fairbanks Jr., Rita Hayworth, John Qualen,Thomas Mitchell. D: Ben Hecht, Lee Garmes. DRA 75m. v

Angels Wash Their Faces, The 1939 ★★★½ Sequel to *Angels with Dirty Faces*, this time with a D.A.'s son trying to clear a gang member of false arson charges. Sheridan and the Dead End Kids provide continuity, but Reagan is no Cagney or O'Brien. C: Ann Sheridan, Dead End Kids, Frankie Thomas, Bonita Granville, Ronald Reagan, Margaret Hamilton, Marjorie Main. D: Ray Enright. DRA 84m.

Angels with Dirty Faces 1938 ★★★★½ Cagney and O'Brien play buddies from a tough New York neighborhood who grow up on opposite sides of the law. One becomes a murdering gangster, the other a priest trying to keep the local kids from emulating the life of crime. The archetypal gangster film. C: James Cagney, Pat O'Brien, Humphrey Bogart, Dead End Kids, Ann Sheridan. D: Michael Curtiz. DRA 97m. v

Angi Vera 1978 Hungarian ★★★★½ In 1948, a bright but apolitical young woman enrolls in a Communist Party school. Initially suspicious of the Party, she has an affair with her group leader that triggers a shocking about-face. This haunting, chillingly brilliant depiction of political indoctrination is one of a kind. C: Veronika Papp, Erzsi Paszior, Eva Szabo, Laszlo Horvath. D: Pal Gabor. DRA 96m. v

Angie 1993 ★★★★ Warm and witty tale of a working-class woman from Queens (Davis) who gets pregnant and decides to keep the baby, even though she doesn't have a husband. As her loyal best friend, Turturro steals the picture. C: Geena Davis, Stephen Rea, James Gandolfini, Aida Turturro, Philip Bosco. D: Martha Coolidge. DRA [R] 107m.

Angry Breed, The 1969 ★★ This breed includes a Vietnam veteran who wants to be a screenwriter, an outlaw biker who wants to be an actor, a square movie producer, and his daughter. Unmemorable, at best. C: Jan Sterling, James MacArthur, William Windom. D: David Commons. DRA 89m.

Angry Harvest 1986 West German ★★★★★ Highly charged WWII story about a wealthy Jewish escapee from a concentration camp-bound train (Trissenaar) who takes refuge with a Polish farmer (Stahl). First her protector, he imprisons her when she rejects his love. Deeply felt, complex drama. C: Armin Mueller-Stahl, Elisabeth Trissenaar. D: Agnieszka Holland. DRA 102m. v

Angry Hills, The 1959 ★★★½ War film has journalist (Mitchum) in the Balkans fighting the Nazis. Mitchum's solid performance anchors this adaptation of the novel by Leon Uris. C: Robert Mitchum, Elisabeth Mueller, Stanley Baker, Gia Scala, Theodore Bikel. D: Robert Aldrich. ACT 105m.

Angry Joe Bass 1976 ★★★½ Tension erupts into violence in a twist and turn story of a Native American who stands firm and defends his fishing rights. C: Henry Bal, Molly Mershon. D: Thomas G. Reeves. DRA 82m.

Angry Red Planet, The 1960 ★★★ Spaceship returning from Mars runs into trouble when attacked by a gaggle of monsters. Inventive special effects and some really bizarre alien creatures will please fans of low-budget science fiction movies. C: Gerald Mohr, Nora Heyden, Les Tremayne. D: Ib Melchior. SFI 84m. v

Angry Silence, The 1960 British ★★★★ Politically uncertain story about a factory worker (Attenborough) who is used as a pawn in a union strike. Some good performances, though film seems a bit afraid of its material. C: Richard Attenborough, Pier Angeli, Michael Craig. D: Guy Green. DRA 95m.

Anguish 1988 Spanish ★★★½ A twisted mother-son team (he cuts out eyes for her) turns out to be inspiration for a *real* psycho. Novel twist on slasher genre is often scary (and gory) until some silly implausibilities in final third. C: Zelda Rubinstein, Michael Lerner. D: Bigas Luna. HOR [R] 89m. v

Animal Behavior 1989 ★ Love blooms in academia when a music professor (Assante) and an animal researcher specializing in chimpanzees (Allen) fall for each other. Badly edited from a poor script. The stars (including the chimp!) probably wish they'd burned the film negative. C: Karen Allen, Armand Assante, Holly Hunter, Josh Mostel. D: H. Anne Riley. FAM/COM [PG] 97m. v

Animal Called Man, An 1987 ★★★ Things get out of hand for two greedy crooks who find that the bloodthirsty outlaw gang they've joined has put them in more danger than they bargained for. C: Vassilli Karis, Craig Hill, Gillian Bray. D: Robert Mauri. WST 83m.

Animal Crackers 1930 ★★★★½ One of the Marx Brothers' finest. Story revolves around thieves and a stolen oil painting, but is really just an excuse to let the four crazies indulge in their usual manic hijinks. This is the one featuring Groucho singing "Hooray for Captain Spaulding." C: Groucho Marx, Harpo Marx, Chico Marx, Zeppo Marx, Margaret Dumont, Lillian Roth. D: Victor Herman. COM 98m. v

Animal Farm 1955 British ★★★½ Animated version of George Orwell's allegory examines the political fallout after barnyard animals try to run things on their own. Straight-forward adaptation has its moments, though it suffers by altering the original ending. Good for junior high school kids and up. D: Joy Batchelor, John Halas. DRA 73m. v

Animal House 1978 ★★★★ The party animals of Delta fraternity are on the loose and no woman (or can of beer) at Faber College is safe. Quintessential college comedy delivers big laughs despite vulgar, sophomoric humor. Belushi steals the show as Bluto, the biggest slob of them all. (a.k.a. *National Lampoon's Animal House*) C: John Belushi, Tim Matheson, John Vernon, Verna Bloom, Donald Sutherland. D: John Landis. COM [R] 109m. v

Animal Instincts 1992 ★★½ Under the influence of an aphrodisiac, the wife of a voyeuristic policeman entertains many lovers—one of whom is a politician running a campaign against smut. Little substance in a film unsuccessfully striving for erotic titillation. C: Maxwell Caulfield, Mitch Gaylord, Shannon Whirry, John Saxon, David Carradine, Jan-Michael Vincent. D: Alexander Gregory Hippolyte. DRA [R] 94m. v

Animal Kingdom, The 1932 ★★★★ Intelligent adaptation of the Philip Barry play about a tradition-bound man (Howard) who is enlightened by an affair with a free spirit (Harding), but marries his social equal (Loy) with tragic results. Still a keen observation of society and morals. C: Ann Harding, Leslie Howard, Myrna Loy, Ilka Chase. D: Edward H. Griffith. DRA 95m. v

Animals, The 1970 ★★½ Barbaric Western about a woman who gets revenge against the men who raped her. C: Henry Silva, Keenan Wynn, Michele Carey. D: Ron Joy. WST [R] 86m.

Animalympics 1979 ★★★ Animated spoof of the Olympics, featuring voices of several Hollywood stars in animal guise. Funny but overlong, becoming a tad wearisome and repetitious; but when it's funny it's really very funny. Voices of Billy Crystal, Gilda Radner, Harry Shearer. D: Steven Lisberger. FAM/COM 78m. v

Anita—Dances of Vice 1987 German ★★★½ Iconoclast von Praunheim revives (literally) the legendary and outrageous Anita Berber, a dancer during Germany's Weimar era. Witty but fragmented. C: Lotti Huber, Ina Blum, Mikhael Honesseau. D: Rosa von Praunheim. DRA 85m. V

Ann Jillian Story, The 1988 ★★★ TV personality Jillian stars in her own biography, chronicling her comeback in show business after a devastating bout with breast cancer. Sincere production has more going for it than usual disease movie clichés. C: Ann Jillian, Tony Lo Bianco, Viveca Lindfors. D: Corey Allen. DRA 95m. TVM V

Ann Vickers 1933 ★★★ Long-suffering prison social worker (Dunne) rises to a position of influence, only to see her lover incarcerated. Dunne lends dignity to this soggy drama; from the Sinclair Lewis novel. C: Irene Dunne, Walter Huston, Bruce Cabot, Edna May Oliver. D: John Cromwell. DRA 72m.

Anna 1951 Italian ★★★½ Lusty Italian spectacle in flashback form explores a woman's stormy relationships prior to becoming a nun. Involving and worthwhile. C: Silvana Mangano, Raf Vallone, Vittorio Gassman. D: Alberto Lattuada. DRA 95m.

Anna 1987 ★★★★ Exiled from her native Czechoslovakia, screen actress (Kirkland) takes novice talent (Porizkova) under her wing, then watches angrily as the protégé eclipses the star. Clever twist on *All About Eve* and countless other backstage stories. Kirkland was nominated for Best Actress Oscar. C: Sally Kirkland, Paulina Porizkova, Robert Fields. D: Yurek Bogayevicz. DRA [PG-13] 101m. V

Anna Akhmatova File, The 1990 Russian ★★★½ A close and personal look into the impact and influence of banned Soviet poet Anna Akhmatova, whose poem "Requiem" inspired many people suffering oppression under Stalin. D: Semeon Aranovitch. DRA 65m.

Anna and the King of Siam 1946 ★★★★ Original, nonmusical adaptation of Anna Leonowens' autobiography of her experiences as a British governess at the court of King Mongkut in the 19th century. A different perspective from the familiar Rodgers and Hammerstein version, but uniformly excellent. C: Irene Dunne, Rex Harrison, Linda Darnell, Lee J. Cobb, Gale Sondergaard. D: John Cromwell. DRA 129m. V

Anna Christie 1923 ★★★½ Silent version of Eugene O'Neill's play about a woman with a shady past who tries to find solace, redemption, and love in her relationship with a seaman. This film precedes Garbo's talkie. C: Blanche Sweet, George Marion. D: John Griffith Wray. DRA 95m.

Anna Christie 1930 ★★★★ On the waterfront, a former prostitute tries to turn her life around without being defeated by her alcoholic father and an Irish sailor. Famous as Garbo's first talkie, Eugene O'Neill's play was cleaned up considerably for the screen. Stagy, but absorbing. C: Greta Garbo, Charles Bickford, Marie Dressler. D: Clarence Brown. DRA 92m. V

Anna Karenina 1935 ★★★★★ Garbo is Tolstoy's tragic heroine in this touching romance about the wife of a cold Russian nobleman (Rathbone) who falls in love with a handsome cavalry officer (March) and gives up her son (Bartholomew) to run away with him. Garbo previously filmed a silent version, *Love*. C: Greta Garbo, Fredric March, Freddie Bartholomew, Maureen O'Sullivan, May Robson, Basil Rathbone. D: Clarence Brown. DRA 96m. V

Anna Karenina 1948 British ★★★ Leigh plays Tolstoy's doomed romantic who destroys her life out of love for a Russian count (Moore). Lush, often visually stunning production and talented cast don't quite bring it to the Garbo level, but they try. C: Vivien Leigh, Ralph Richardson, Kieron Moore. D: Julien Duvivier. DRA 90m.

Anna Karenina 1985 ★★★ Lavish version of Tolstoy's classic stars Bisset as the tragic heroine; highlighted by Scofield's portrayal of riveting Karenin. C: Jacqueline Bisset, Christopher Reeve, Paul Scofield. D: Simon Langton. DRA [PG] 96m. TVM V

Anna Lucasta 1949 ★★★½ Goddard's tough portrayal of a Brooklyn streetwalker mixed up in her brother-in-law's scam sparks this cleaned-up version of Philip Yordan's play. Remade in 1958 with an all-black cast, as originally intended. C: Paulette Goddard, Oscar Homolka, John Ireland, Broderick Crawford, William Bishop. D: Irving Rapper. DRA 86m.

Anna Lucasta 1958 ★★★½ Solid remake of the 1949 movie, about a young hooker (Kitt) forced to marry for money by her family. Playwright Philip Yordan adapted his own play again; this time it's an all-black cast, as originally intended. Ingram and Davis are the standouts this time. C: Eartha Kitt, Sammy Davis, Jr., Frederick O'Neal, Rex Ingram. D: Arnold Laven. DRA 97m.

Anna of Brooklyn 1960 *See* **Fast and Sexy**

Anna to the Infinite Power 1984 ★★★ A telepathic youngster finds that she is one of a set of clones with unusual powers. Good for younger viewers. C: Dina Merrill, Martha Byrne, Jack Gilford. D: Robert Wiemer. SFI 101m. V

Annabel Takes A Tour 1938 ★★★ A wacky actress (Ball) reluctantly embarks upon a publicity junket cooked up by her frenzied press agent (Oakie) to pump up her sagging career. Sequel to *The Affairs of Annabel*. C: Lucille Ball, Jack Oakie, Ruth Donnelly. D: Lew Landers. COM 67m.

Annapolis Story, An 1955 ★★ Two brothers are on their way to the Korean War and in love with the same woman. Soapy drama. C: John Derek, Diana Lynn, Kevin McCarthy. D: Don Siegel. DRA 81m. v

Anne of Avonlea 1988 Canadian ★★★★★ Wonderfully evocative sequel to *Anne of Green Gables* continues the adventures of young teacher Anne Shirley. Here, she meets the man of her dreams and loses her heart. Rewarding fare for entire family. Based on the books by L.M. Montgomery. C: Megan Follows, Colleen Dewhurst, Frank Converse. D: Kevin Sullivan. FAM/DRA 224m. TVM v

Anne of Green Gables 1934 ★★★★ Anne Shirley loved this role so much, she kept the name for her own, and why not? It made her a star, playing the heroine of this children's classic of a spunky orphan and the kindly old folks who take her in. Charming. Followed by *Anne of Windy Poplars*; remade for Canadian TV in 1985. C: Anne Shirley, Tom Brown, O. P. Heggie, Helen Westley. D: George Nicholls Jr. FAM/DRA 79m.

Anne of Green Gables 1985 Canadian ★★★★ Fine adaptation of oft-filmed story details Follows' journey from childhood and adoption by farming siblings, through first pangs of young adult romance. Great family viewing. Originally broadcast in two episodes, "A New Home" and "A Bend in the Road." Sequel: *Anne of Avonlea.* C: Megan Follows, Colleen Dewhurst, Patricia Hamilton. D: Kevin Sullivan. FAM/DRA 202m. TVM v

Anne of the Indies 1951 ★★★½ Colorful swashbuckler with a twist: The pirate leader is a woman (Peters). More costumes than story, but it delivers the goods. C: Jean Peters, Louis Jourdan, Debra Paget, Herbert Marshall. D: Jacques Tourneur. ACT 81m.

Anne of the Thousand Days 1969 ★★★★ England's Henry VIII (Burton) splits with the Catholic Church so that he can divorce his wife and marry Anne Boleyn (Bujold), but tires of her and has her framed for adultery. Strong performances supplemented by handsome Renaissance flavor and court intrigue. Oscar for Costumes. C: Richard Burton, Genevieve Bujold, Irene Papas, Anthony Quayle. D: Charles Jarrott. DRA [PG] 145m. v

Anne of Windy Poplars 1940 ★★½ Character familiar from *Anne of Green Gables* returns, becoming a school vice president and running into local interference. Not as strong as the earlier story, but still interesting. C: Anne Shirley, James Ellison, Henry Travers. D: Jack Hively. DRA 88m.

Annie 1982 ★★★½ Movie version of the Broadway musical megahit, based on the comic strip *Little Orphan Annie.* Our heroine (Quinn) starts out in AN orphanage run by heavy-drinking Miss Hannigan (Burnett), then moves on to stay with millionaire Warbucks (Finney) who helps search for her parents. Big, belligerently cheerful musical, with good work by Finney, Quinn, and Reinking. C: Albert Finney, Carol Burnett, Aileen Quinn, Bernadette Peters, Tim Curry, Ann Reinking. D: John Huston. MUS [PG] 128m. v

Annie Get Your Gun 1950 ★★★★ Big, brassy, energetic adaptation of Irving Berlin's musical chronicles the life and times of the famed performing sharpshooter, Annie Oakley (Hutton) and her romance with marksman Frank Butler (Keel). Rousing tunes, including "No Business Like Show Business," pack a colorful production (the score won an Oscar). Quintessential family viewing. C: Betty Hutton, Howard Keel, Louis Calhern, Edward Arnold, Keenan Wynn. D: George Sidney. MUS 107m.

Annie Hall 1977 ★★★★★ Woody Allen's intelligent and wryly funny examination of love recounts his affair with the irresistible Annie (Keaton), a flighty would-be nightclub singer who almost becomes the love of his life. Winner of four Oscars, for Best Picture, Director, Actress, and Screenplay; a modern classic. Don't miss Jeff Goldblum's one line during an LA party. C: Woody Allen, Diane Keaton, Tony Roberts, Paul Simon, Shelley Duvall, Carol Kane, Colleen Dewhurst, Christopher Walken. D: Woody Allen. COM [PG] 93m. v

Annie Oakley 1935 ★★★★ Vigorous biography of the sharpshooting star of Buffalo Bill's Wild West Show and her sporadic romance with Frank Butler. Firmly directed, with snappy dialogue. C: Barbara Stanwyck, Preston Foster, Melvyn Douglas. D: George Stevens. WST 100m. v

Annihilators, The 1985 ★ Vietnam vets use their training to clean up a crime-ridden city. Extremely violent. C: Christopher Stone, Andy Wood, Lawrence Hilton-Jacobs. D: Charles E. Sellier Jr. ACT [R] 87m. v

Anniversary, The 1968 British ★★½ A tyrannical widow insists her three sons commemorate her wedding anniversary, and uses the celebration to belittle and blackmail them. Weird black comedy's funniest moments unintentionally come from Davis' scenery-chewing performance. C: Bette Davis, Sheila Hancock, Jack Hedley. D: Roy Baker. COM 95m.

Another Chance 1989 ★★½ Womanizer finds himself in danger when he gets simultaneously involved with two very different women. C: Bruce Greenwood, Vanessa Angel, Frank Annese, Jeff East, Anne Ramsey. D: Jerry Vint. COM [R] 99m. v

Another Country 1984 British ★★★★ Everett is outstanding as a young upper-class homosexual whose insensitive treatment at British public school sows seeds for his eventual defection to the USSR; Firth isn't far behind as his only real friend. Loosely based on life of spy Guy Burgess. A lush, beautiful film; compelling and thoughtful. C: Rupert Everett, Colin Firth, Michael Jenn, Robert Addie, Cary Elwes. D: Marek Kanievska. DRA [PG] 90m. v

Another Dawn 1937 ★★★½ An officer (Flynn), still grieving for his lover killed in WWI, meets a woman who reminds him of her. Set in Africa, with plenty of trimmings thrown in, including a really great score. C: Kay Francis, Errol Flynn. D: William Dieterle. DRA 73m.

Another 48 HRS 1990 ★★ Disappointing sequel to the 1982 comedy again finds detective (Nolte) reluctantly teamed with convict (Murphy)—this time to nab an elusive kingpin. No story to speak of, just a mishmash of loud and destructive action scenes. C: Eddie Murphy, Nick Nolte, Brion James, Kevin Tighe. D: Walter Hill. COM [R] 95m.

Another Language 1933 ★★★★½ Biting romantic drama in which a wife (Hayes) struggles to be accepted by her husband's family, a bunch of society snobs led by their matriarch (Hale). Acted to perfection. C: Helen Hayes, Robert Montgomery, Louise Hale, Margaret Hamilton, Henry Travers. D: Edward Griffith. DRA 77m.

Another Man, Another Chance 1977 French ★★★ Love story set in the 1870s American West between two bruised souls: a veterinarian and a young Frenchwoman whose spouses were murdered. Trifle soft around the edges, but sincere and well-meaning. C: James Caan, Genevieve Bujold. D: Claude Lelouch. DRA [PG] 132m. V

Another Man's Poison 1951 British ★★★ An English mystery writer living in the creepy Yorkshire moors poisons her husband and lover. Little indication that Davis and Rapper were the pair that worked together on the classic *Now, Voyager*, but Davis keeps this one watchable. C: Bette Davis, Gary Merrill, Emlyn Williams. D: Irving Rapper. DRA 89m.

Another Pair of Aces: Three of a Kind 1991 ★★★ Sequel to *Pair of Aces* spotlights a Texas Ranger (Kristofferson) and a safecracker (Nelson) as they defend a friend against a murder rap. Charismatic leads are the whole show. Slightly raunchier, unedited version is available on video. C: Willie Nelson, Kris Kristofferson, Rip Torn. D: Bill Bixby. CRI 93m. TVM V

Another Part of the Forest 1948 ★★★½ Scheming Hubbard clan plots against each other mercilessly in well-acted but dark Southern period drama. Based on Lillian Hellman's prequel to *The Little Foxes*. C: Fredric March, Dan Duryea, Edmond O'Brien, Ann Blyth, Florence Eldridge, John Dall. D: Michael Gordon. DRA 107m.

Another Stakeout 1993 ★★★½ Down-to-earth detectives (Dreyfus and Estevez) have trouble blending in when they are assigned to stake out a ritzy neighborhood. Second time out for the detective pairing lacks the spark of *Stakeout*, their first. O'Donnell, as a sassy D.A., is a welcome addition to this comedy/thriller outing. C: Richard Dreyfuss, Emilio Estevez, Rosie O'Donnell. D: John Badham. DRA 108m.

Another Thin Man 1939 ★★★★ Even though they've just had a baby, Nick and Nora Charles can't resist solving a murder at a Long Island mansion. Third lark in this classic series keeps the laughs and thrills coming, aided by a strong supporting cast, as usual. C: William Powell, Myrna Loy, C. Aubrey Smith, Virginia Grey, Otto Kruger, Marjorie Main, Ruth Hussey. D: W.S. Van Dyke II. CRI 105m. V

Another Time, Another Place 1958 ★★½ Dreary soap opera notable only as an early vehicle for Connery. He's a married British journalist in WWII involved with an American newspaper writer (Turner). When he's killed, she goes to Cornwall in an attempt to comfort his widow. Corny and unbelievable. C: Lana Turner, Barry Sullivan, Glynis Johns, Sean Connery. D: Lewis Allen. DRA 98m. V

Another Woman 1988 ★★★★ Philosophy professor (Rowlands) seems to have it all but is devoid of emotional attachments. When she discovers she can listen in on the therapist working upstairs, her eavesdropping leads to startling revelations about her own life. Fascinating, thought-provoking adult drama from Allen. C: Gena Rowlands, Mia Farrow, Ian Holm, Blythe Danner, Gene Hackman, Sandy Dennis. D: Woody Allen. DRA [PG] 81m. V

Another You 1991 ★★½ Forced to perform community service, con man (Pryor) finds himself in charge of a pathological liar (Wilder). Dollar signs form in his eyes when Wilder is mistaken for a millionaire heir. Dull comedy lacks energy and laughs. C: Richard Pryor, Gene Wilder, Mercedes Ruehl, Stephen Lang, Vanessa Williams. D: Maurice Phillips. COM [R] 98m. V

Antarctica 1984 Japanese ★★★½ Breathtaking photography is the highlight of this thoughtful adventure about a marooned expedition and the fate of a team of sled dogs. One of the all-time Japanese box-office champs. C: Ken Takakura, Masako Natsume, Keiko Oginome. D: Koreyoshi Kurahara. DRA 112m.

Anthony Adverse ★★★★½ Continent-spanning historical romance about an illegitimate youth (March) and his many adventures in the early 1800s, including marrying an aspiring opera singer (de Havilland). An entertaining spectacle, with misunderstandings, murder, and Napoleon. Sondergaard makes a stunning debut as a double-crossing housekeeper, and won an Oscar for Best Supporting Actress. Film also won Oscars for Score and Cinematography. From Hervey Allen's novel. C: Fredric March, Olivia de Havilland, Donald Woods, Gale Sondergaard, Anita Louise, Edmund Gwenn, Claude Rains, Louis Hayward, Akim Tamiroff. D: Mervyn Le Roy. DRA 141m. V

Antigone 1962 Greek ★★★★ Sophocles'

tragedy is opened up for the big screen, using gorgeous Greek scenery to achieve a sense of spectacle. More important, the script is faithful, and the acting, especially by Papas, is excellent. C: Irene Papas, Manos Katrakis, Maro Kontou, Nikas Kazis, Ilia Livikou. D: George Tzavellas. DRA 93m.

Antonia: A Portrait of a Woman 1974 ★★★★ Documentary look at conductor Antonia Brico, who carved out a career in male-dominated orchestral community. Personalizes Brico's overcoming prejudice and sexism to triumph at the podium. D: Judy Collins, Jill Godmilow. DOC 58m.

Antonia & Jane 1991 British ★★★★ Jealousy rears its head when best of friends, whose destinies have taken very different paths, envy each other's lifestyles. Quirky comedy with refreshingly different characters. C: Saskia Reeves, Imelda Staunton, Brenda Bruce. D: Beeban Kidron. COM [R] 75m. V

Antonio 1973 ★★★ An eccentric American tycoon gives an impoverished South American potmaker a new car that brings him nothing but trouble. Parable has a few amusing moments to its credit. C: Trini Lopez, Larry Hagman, Noemi Guerrero. D: Claudio Guzman. DRA 81m.

Antonio das Mortes 1969 Brazilian ★★★ This Brazilian "Cinema Novo" spaghetti-Western is the true story of a hired killer employed by the rich who turns the tables and fights for the poor against social wrongs. A bloody, metaphysical, and politically radical movie full of stylized action which many find tough going. C: Mauricio do Valle, Odete Lara, Othon Bastos, Hugo Carvana. D: Glauber Rocha. WST 100m. V

Antony and Cleopatra 1973 ★★½ Shakespeare's drama—about Marc Antony's life after Caesar and his dalliance and disgrace with the Egyptian queen—gets a competent but ho-hum treatment. Primarily for diehard history buffs. C: Charlton Heston, Hildegard Neil, Eric Porter, Fernando Rey. D: Charlton Heston. DRA 160m. V

Ants and Panic at Lakewood Manor 1977 *See* **It Happened at Lakewood Manor**

Any Man's Death 1990 ★★½ Reporter discovers that a former Nazi war criminal has been living in anonymity in Africa. Quasi-morality play performed by interesting cast. C: John Savage, William Hickey, Mia Sara, Ernest Borgnine. D: Tom Clegg. DRA [R] 105m. V

Any Number Can Play 1949 ★★★½ The bad news of one day's events all but destroys a local gambling joint boss. Gable and Smith (as his wife) sparkle in this jaunty melodrama. Yes, that is Dwayne Hickman (Dobie Gillis) as their son. C: Clark Gable, Alexis Smith, Wendell Corey, Audrey Totter, Mary Astor, Lewis Stone. D: Mervyn Le Roy. DRA 112m. V

Any Number Can Win 1963 French ★★★½ Bandits scheme to rob the local bank. Gabin and Delon are just fine, and the Riviera is spectacular in this slick caper. Good fun had by all. C: Jean Gabin, Alain Delon. D: Henri Verneuil. COM 108m.

Any Second Now 1969 ★★★½ Husband is ready to bump off his wife, but a twist of fate provokes a change of mind. Good chemistry between the embattled couple rings true most of the way. Nice dark turn by Granger. C: Stewart Granger, Lois Nettleton. D: Gene Levitt. DRA 97m.

Any Wednesday 1966 ★★★½ Lively comedy of a Wall Street whiz (Robards) and his mistress (Fonda), who encounter romantic scheduling problems when their love nest is discovered. Old-fashioned Broadway sex farce is well played and appropriately silly. C: Jane Fonda, Jason Robards, Dean Jones, Rosemary Murphy. D: Robert Ellis Miller. COM 109m. V

Any Which Way You Can 1980 ★★★ Eastwood is back as a bar brawler, now matched up against a supertough opponent (Smith). Fists fly and orangutan antics abound. Popular sequel to *Every Which Way But Loose*, but the lunacy wears a bit thin. C: Clint Eastwood, Sondra Locke, Geoffrey Lewis, Harry Guardino, Ruth Gordon. D: Buddy Van Horn. COM [PG] 116m. V

Anyone Can Play 1968 Italian ★★½ Four women get together and try to solve their problems in love. Stunning leads struggle with self-conscious sex farce. C: Ursula Andress, Virna Lisi, Jean-Pierre Cassel. D: Luigi Zampa. COM 88m.

Anything Can Happen 1952 ★★½ Transplanted Russian tries to make a go of it in America. Comedy/drama tailored for Ferrer, who really goes to town. C: Jose Ferrer, Kim Hunter, Kurt Kasznar, Eugenie Leontovich. D: George Seaton. DRA 107m.

Anything for Love 1974 *See* **11 Harrowhouse**

Anything for Love 1993 ★★★ When a teen musician (Haim) successfully escapes into the female gender to avoid a bully's fist, his curiosity is piqued and he decided to stay—for a while. C: Corey Haim. COM 90m.

Anything Goes 1936 ★★★½ First of two versions of Cole Porter's Broadway smash, with fine songs ("You're the Top," "I Get a Kick Out of You," etc.). Rather leaky shipboard plot, but with Merman from the original cast, who cares? (a.k.a. *Tops Is The Limit*) C: Bing Crosby, Ethel Merman, Charlie Ruggles, Ida Lupino. D: Lewis Milestone. MUS 92m.

Anything Goes 1956 ★★★ Crosby tries this Cole Porter musical one more time. Score is full of interpolations from other Porter shows as well as from other composers. C: Bing Crosby, Jeanmaire, Donald O'Connor, Mitzi Gaynor. D: Robert Lewis. MUS 106m.

Anything to Survive 1990 ★★★½ A family is shipwrecked off the Alaskan coast and left to fend for themselves in this surprisingly good tale of survival. Spectacular locale shooting. C: Robert Conrad, Matthew LeBlanc. D: Zala Dalen. DRA 100m. TVM

Anzacs: The War Down Under 1985 Australian ★★★½ Group character study looks at an Australian-New Zealand Army Corps platoon during WWI. Interesting historic detail and splendid acting ensemble, with future *Crocodile Dundee* star Hogan providing effective comic relief. C: Paul Hogan, Andrew Clarke, Megan Williams, Jon Blake. D: George Miller. ACT 165m. V

Anzio 1968 French ★★★ Mitchum plays a war correspondent covering the Allied assault on the beaches of Italy in WWII. A strong cast and big, noisy battles partly offset the film's frustratingly slow pace. C: Robert Mitchum, Peter Falk, Robert Ryan, Earl Holliman. D: Edward Dmytryk. DRA [PG] 117m. V

Apache 1954 ★★★ Lancaster portrays an Apache warrior in a one-man fight against expansionist U.S. government. Melodramatic script makes what was a true story a little hard to swallow. C: Burt Lancaster, Jean Peters, John McIntire. D: Robert Aldrich. WST 86m. V

Apache Ambush 1955 ★★★ Immediately after the Civil War, a group of soldiers driving cattle get involved with the fate of a cache of guns; everything ends with a giant shoot-out. Unusual premise makes an offbeat Western. C: Bill Williams, Richard Jaeckel, Alex Montoya, Movita, Adele August, Tex Ritter, Ray "Crash" Corrigan. D: Fred F. Sears. WST 68m.

Apache Drums 1951 ★★½ Town besieged by Indians looks to shady gambler (McNally) for help. Standard Western with good performances from the leads. C: Stephen McNally, Coleen Gray, Willard Parker. D: Hugo Fregonese. WST 75m.

Apache Gold 1965 German ★★★½ The Apaches and opportunistic bandits vie for gold. Nice locale shooting and intriguing little story goes quite a ways in this offbeat Western. C: Lex Barker, Mario Adorf, Pierre Brice. D: Harald Reinl. WST 91m.

Apache Rifles 1964 ★★★ The Apaches are threatening the settlers and it's the cavalry to the rescue. Audie is the captain in charge of rounding up the tribe. Not bad. C: Audie Murphy, Michael Dante, Linda Lawson. D: William Witney. WST 92m.

Apache Territory 1958 ★★½ A heroic cowpoke (Calhoun) manages to drive away Apache marauders and lead surviving settlers to safety. Formulaic Western. C: Rory Calhoun, Barbara Bates. D: Ray Nazarro. WST 75m.

Apache Uprising 1965 ★★★ Rory matches wits with Apaches and bandits. Local color provided by a unique cast of veteran Western actors. C: Rory Calhoun, Corinne Calvet, John Russell, Lon Chaney Jr. D: R. G. Springsteen. WST 90m.

Apache War Smoke 1952 ★★½ A stagecoach attack by marauding Apaches leads to all-out war with the settlers. B-movie Western with A-movie cast. C: Gilbert Roland, Robert Horton, Glenda Farrell. D: Harold Kress. WST 67m.

Apache Warrior 1957 ★★½ Apache vows revenge when his brother is killed by the white man. Low-voltage Western. C: Keith Larsen, Jim Davis. D: Elmo Williams. WST 74m.

Apache Woman 1955 ★ A diplomat (Bridges) steps in to mediate Indian settler troubles and soon falls for a woman of mixed blood. Quickie Corman production, mainly good for a few (unintentional) laughs. C: Lloyd Bridges, Joan Taylor, Lance Fuller. D: Roger Corman. WST 83m. V

Aparajito 1957 Indian ★★★★★ This understated and moving coming-of-age film involves an impoverished Indian family and their son's preparation for higher education in Calcutta. Ray's second film in *Apu* trilogy after *Pather Panchali.* Followed by *The World of Apu.* (a.k.a. *The Unvanquished*) C: Pinaki San Gupta, Smaran Ghosal. D: Satyajit Ray. DRA 108m. V

Apartment for Peggy 1948 ★★★★ Cute campus comedy with attractive leads and great comic support from Gwenn and Lockhart as older guardian angels of postwar newlyweds (Holden and Crain). C: Jeanne Crain, William Holden, Edmund Gwenn, Gene Lockhart. D: George Seaton. COM 99m.

Apartment, The 1960 ★★★★★ Biting, if dated satire on interoffice politics concerns a lowly corporate employee (Lemmon) trying to get ahead by loaning his apartment to boss (MacMurray) for illicit affairs. Multiple Oscar winner (Oscars for Best Picture, Best Director, Best Story, and Screenplay) is alternately tender and ironic, romantic and grim. Another bittersweet gem from acclaimed writer/director Wilder. C: Jack Lemmon, Shirley MacLaine, Fred MacMurray, Ray Walston, Jack Kruschen. D: Billy Wilder. COM 125m. V

Apartment Zero 1989 British ★★★½ A hypnotically creepy and slyly witty psychosexual thriller. A repressed English film buff (Firth), living in Buenos Aires, becomes obsessed with the possibly psychopathic American (Bochner) he takes in as a boarder. C: Colin Firth, Hart Bochner, Dora Bryan. D: Martin Donovan. DRA 124m. V

Ape Man, The 1943 ★ Lugosi, in one of his hammiest turns, plays a scientist who transforms himself into a half-man, half-ape killer, then goes out with a real gorilla to kill people for an antidote. Shlocky. C: Bela Lugosi, Louise Currie, Wallace Ford, Henry Hall. D: William Beaudine. HOR 63m. V

Ape, The 1940 ★★ Karloff gives a decent performance as an insane small-town doctor who dons an ape skin and murders locals, draining their spinal fluid to help cure a polio victim. Low budget, familiar plotting are major drawbacks. C: Boris Karloff, Gertrude Hoffman, Henry Hall, Maris Wrixon. D: William Nigh. HOR 62m. v

Apocalypse Now 1979 ★★★★★ Coppola's stunning, mystical, Vietnam War epic about a burned-out soldier (Sheen) and his secret mission to kill a C.O. gone mad (Brando). Lush location photography and awesome sets give this film a surreal look from start to finish, though it is confusing at times. Based on Joseph Conrad's *Heart of Darkness*. C: Marlon Brando, Robert Duvall, Martin Sheen, Frederic Forrest. D: Francis Ford Coppola. DRA [R] 153m. v

Apology 1986 ★★★ An avant-garde artist (Warren) starts up a confessional phone message line, and a demented caller begins committing murders to give himself confessional material. Film tries to rise above standard stalker fare, but seems dependent upon its sex and violence. Written by playwright Mark (*Children of a Lesser God*) Medoff. C: Lesley Ann Warren, Peter Weller, John Glover. D: Robert Bierman. CRI 98m. TVM v

Appaloosa, The 1966 ★★★ Brando is painfully self-conscious as a cow wrangler who pursues a sadistic Mexican bandit after his horse is stolen. Solid supporting performances offset Brando's overdone anguish. Visually rich; based on the novel by Robert MacLeod. C: Marlon Brando, Anjanette Comer, John Saxon. D: Sidney Furie. WST 99m. v

Appearances 1990 ★★★ Midwestern family grapples but never really comes to terms with the death of a son. Pilot for a TV show that got scuttled in development. C: Scott Paulin, Wendy Phillips, Ernest Borgnine. D: Win Phelps. DRA 100m. TVM

Applause 1929 ★★★★ Important early sound drama about a washed-up burlesque queen (Morgan) and her daughter (Peers). Classic tearjerker seems crude now, but it was a groundbreaking production in its day, thanks to innovative direction and sound effects. Tragic stage star Morgan gives a heartbreaking performance. C: Helen Morgan, Joan Peers. D: Rouben Mamoulian. DRA 78m.

Apple Dumpling Gang, The 1975 ★★★ Kids may enjoy this silly Disney comedy, set in the Wild West, with Knotts and Conway as slapstick crooks teamed with a gambler's gold-prospecting children. Was a surprise hit, spawning a sequel, *The Apple Dumpling Gang Rides Again*. C: Bill Bixby, Don Knotts, Tim Conway, Susan Clark. D: Norman Tokar. FAM/COM [G] 100m. v

Apple Dumpling Gang Rides Again, The 1979 ★★★ Knotts and Conway return as inept bandits in this loose sequel to Disney's *Apple Dumpling Gang*. Like the first film, packed with slapstick routines, double-takes, pratfalls, and other tried-and-true kiddie pleasers. C: Tim Conway, Don Knotts, Tim Matheson, Kenneth Mars. D: Vincent McEveety. FAM/COM [G] 88m.

Appleseed 1988 Japanese ★★★½ Animated Japanese sci-fi takes place in a futuristic, post-WW III city of Olympus, where two members of an elite SWAT team battle ruthless terrorists equipped with heavily armored "powersuits." A good introduction to the "female crimefighter" genre of Japanese animation. D: Kazuyashi Katayama. SFI 70m. v

Appointment for Love 1941 ★★★★ Deft romantic comedy has newlyweds (Boyer and Sullavan) occupying separate apartments while they juggle their busy schedules. Scintillating dialogue is smartly delivered by charismatic leads. C: Charles Boyer, Margaret Sullavan, Rita Johnson. D: William Seiter. COM 89m.

Appointment in Honduras 1953 ★★ Well-meaning but contrived story of an American (Ford) who enlists bad guys to help him to save a Central American country. Harmless, but hardly entertainment. C: Ann Sheridan, Glenn Ford, Zachary Scott. D: Jacques Tourneur. DRA 79m. v

Appointment, The 1969 ★★★ Sharif plays a great legal mind who isn't bright enough to see that he's fallen for a woman who's going to bring him down. Ultrasudsy melodrama. C: Omar Sharif, Anouk Aimee, Lotte Lenya. D: Sidney Lumet. DRA [R] 100m.

Appointment, The 1982 ★★★ Evil forces exploit the psycho-kinetic talents of a father and his gifted musician daughter. Great cast. C: Edward Woodward, Jane Merrow. D: Lindsey C. Vickers. HOR 90m.

Appointment with Danger 1951 ★★★★ A postal inspector (Ladd) cracks a mail fraud conspiracy. Don't let the wimpy-sounding mail angle fool you; the stakes are high in this good, hard-boiled film noir. Also, Webb and Morgan make this a must-see for *Dragnet* fans. C: Alan Ladd, Phyllis Calvert, Paul Stewart, Jan Sterling, Jack Webb, Harry Morgan. D: Lewis Allen. DRA 89m.

Appointment with Death 1988 ★★½ Ustinov reprises the role of Agatha Christie's Belgian detective Hercule Poirot, investigating the murder of a disliked widow (Laurie) at a Holy Land archaeological site. Uninspired direction in what is probably the worst of the Ustinov Poirot films. C: Peter Ustinov, Lauren Bacall, Carrie Fisher, John Gielgud, Piper Laurie, Hayley Mills. D: Michael Winner. CRI [PG] 103m. v

Appointment with Fear 1985 ★★ Slasher schlocker about a menaced babysitter, this time being stalked by the possessed father of her young charge. Adds little to the genre except unintentional humor. C: Michelle Little, Michael Wyle, Kerry Remsen, Douglas Rowe, Garrick Dowhen. D: Alan Smithee (Ramzi Thomas). HOR [R] 98m.

Appointment with Venus 1951 *See* **Island Rescue**

Apprenticeship Of Buddy Kravitz, The 1974 Canadian ★★★★½ Schemer without a conscience, raised in Montreal's Jewish ghetto during the '40s, pulls out all the stops to rise to the top. Funny, winsome drama/comedy provides a ruthless performance by Dreyfuss as the fascinating, not completely repugnant title character. Based on Mordecai Richler's novel. C: Richard Dreyfuss, Micheline Lanctot, Jack Warden, Randy Quaid, Denholm Elliott. D: Ted Kotcheff. COM 121m. V

April Fool's Day 1986 ★★ The producer of the *Friday the 13th* sequels and the director of *When a Stranger Calls* made this nice-try attempt at kidding the slasher genre. A group of vacationing college kids falls victim to murders that may or may not be practical jokes. C: Deborah Foreman, Griffin O'Neal, Clayton Rohner. D: Fred Walton. HOR [R] 90m. V

April Fools, The 1969 ★★½ A middle-aged stockbroker (Lemmon) falls for Deneuve and decides he must be with her, despite the fact that she's married to his boss. Heavy-handed attempt to revive the romantic screwball comedy falls short of its goal. C: Jack Lemmon, Catherine Deneuve, Myrna Loy, Charles Boyer, Peter Lawford, Harvey Korman, Sally Kellerman. D: Stuart Rosenberg. COM [PG] 95m.

April in Paris 1952 ★★★ A chorus girl (Day), mistakenly sent to Europe as "cultural ambassador," finds love with a bureaucrat (Bolger) en route. Not the sunniest Day, though title tune is a bright spot. C: Doris Day, Ray Bolger, Claude Dauphin. D: David Butler. MUS 100m. V

April Love 1957 ★★ A juvenile delinquent (Boone) is sent to a farm in Kentucky and is reformed by Jones. Wholesome musical, '50s style. C: Pat Boone, Shirley Jones. D: Henry Levin. MUS 97m.

April Morning 1988 ★★★★ A young man awakens to adulthood just as the American colonies are preparing to fight for their independence. A compelling and thoughtful portrait of life in Revolutionary times. Based on Howard Fast's novel. C: Tommy Lee Jones, Robert Urich, Chad Lowe, Susan Blakely. D: Delbert Mann. DRA 100m. TVM

April Showers 1948 ★★ The story of a family in vaudeville, their act, and papa's propensity toward drink. Well-acted but predictable backstage drama. C: Jack Carson, Ann Sothern, Robert Alda, S. Z. Sakall. D: James Kern. DRA 94m.

Aquaman 1985 ★★★ A fun, eight-cartoon collection of Aquaman's battles with undersea evil. FAM/SFI 60m.

Arabella 1969 Italian ★★ A con artist cranks up her fleecing operations because of a special need: Her grandmother owes a fortune in taxes. Silly, limp comedy, improved somewhat by a solid international cast. C: Virna Lisi, James Fox, Margaret Rutherford, Terry-Thomas. D: Adriano Barocco. COM [PG] 91m.

Arabella 1984 ★★★★ A wonderful interpretation of Strauss' opera conducted by Bernard Haitink and performed by the Glyndebourne Festival Opera Company. C: Ashley Putnam, Gianna Rolandi, Regina Sarfaty. MUS 160m.

Arabesque 1966 ★★★★ A university language expert (Peck) travels to London, where he inadvertently gets caught up with spies, intrigue and Loren. A fun, stylish thriller, fast-paced and intricately plotted. C: Sophia Loren, Gregory Peck. D: Stanley Donen. ACT 105m. V

Arabian Adventure 1979 British ★★½ The stern ruler of an emirate offers his daughter's hand to a young prince, if the lad finds a rare and magical rose. Fair action, but a knockoff of many predecessors. C: Christopher Lee, Milo O'Shea, Puneet Sira, Emma Samms, Peter Cushing, Mickey Rooney, Capucine. D: Kevin Connor. ACT [G] 98m.

Arabian Nights 1942 ★★★ When Montez is kidnapped by an evil caliph, Sabu rides through the desert to rescue her. Heavy on the corn by today's standards, but still a lot of fun with its campy sets, costumes, and histrionics. C: Jon Hall, Maria Montez, Sabu, Leif Erickson, Turhan Bey. D: John Rawlins. ACT 86m. V

Arachnophobia 1990 ★★★★ Steven Spielberg's longtime producer Marshall shows some of his mentor's touch in this tale of deadly tropical spiders invading a peaceful American town. Slick and not too deep but full of solid jumps and well-timed humor. C: Jeff Daniels, Harley Kozak, John Goodman, Julian Sands. D: Frank Marshall. HOR [PG-13] 110m. V

Arcade 1993 ★★½ A new virtual reality game is sucking up youthful souls, and only a brave teenage couple can stop it. Attractive computer graphics spice up the routine plotting and characters. C: Megan Ward, Peter Billingsley, John De Lancie, Sharon Farrell, Seth Green. D: Albert Pyun. SFI 85m.

Arch of Triumph 1948 ★★★ In Paris after WWII, a survivor searches for the Nazi who abused him. Meanwhile, he falls in love. A slow but interesting story, based on Erich Maria Remarque's novel. Remade for TV. C: Ingrid Bergman, Charles Boyer, Charles Laughton, Louis Calhern. D: Lewis Milestone. DRA 132m. V

Arch of Triumph 1985 ★★½ Remake of the story of the liberation of Paris from the Nazis and the lives of two young people in love. Still slow, but done by another good cast. C: Anthony Hopkins, Lesley-Anne Down, Donald Pleasence, Frank Finlay. D: Waris Hussein. DRA 95m. TVM

Archer's Adventure 1985 ★★★★ Exciting tale of a brave Australian lad and his horse as they cross the land down under on their way to a big race. Good for both adults and children; especially pleasurable for animal lovers. C: Brett Como, Robert Coleby, Nicole Kidman. D: Denny Lawrence. FAM/ACT 120m. v

Archie: To Riverdale and Back Again 1990 ★★ Adventures of Archie, Veronica, Jughead, and the gang from the timeless comic strip in live action. C: Christopher Rich, Karen Kopins. D: Dick Lowry. COM 100m. TVM

Architecture of Frank Lloyd Wright, The ★★★½ Anne Baxter narrates this inspiring study of the renowned and gifted American architect, Frank Lloyd Wright. DOC 75m.

Are Husbands Necessary? 1942 ★★★ A married couple who are constantly at each other's throats decide to adopt a baby as a means of making peace. Silly little comedy that has bright moments. C: Ray Milland, Betty Field. D: Norman Taurog. COM 79m.

Are Parents People? 1925 ★★★★ Charming, light silent comedy about the effects of a couple's impending divorce on their daughter (Bronson). Skillful direction and believable characters make for a remarkably fresh and sensitive story. C: Betty Bronson, Adolphe Menjou, Florence Vidor. D: Malcolm St. Clair. COM 60m.

Are You in the House Alone? 1978 ★★½ Teenage student (Beller), alone in an empty house, vulnerable to any wacko out running loose, is terrorized in usual horror movie fashion. Fine performance from Beller. C: Kathleen Beller, Blythe Danner, Tony Bill, Dennis Quaid, Scott Colomby. D: Walter Grauman. HOR 96m. v

Are You with It? 1948 ★★★½ Corny but good-natured musical about a math genius (O'Connor) who uses his powers to save his pal's carnival. C: Donald O'Connor, Olga San Juan. D: Jack Hively. MUS 90m.

Aretha Franklin—The Queen of Soul ★★★½ Interviews, rare footage, and the performance of several hit songs showcase the inspiring talent of Aretha Franklin. C: Aretha Franklin. MUS 60m.

Argentine Nights 1940 ★★½ With creditors on their heels, the Ritz Brothers and the Andrews Sisters take off for Argentina. Some zany fun and snappy music. C: Ritz Brothers, Andrews Sisters, Constance Moore. D: Albert Rogell. MUS 74m.

Aria 1988 British ★★ Frustrating compilation of operatic "music videos," with roster of top-flight directors showing uneven affinity for giving dramatic life to favorite arias. C: John Hurt, Theresa Russell, Nicola Swain, Jack Kaylee, Bridget Fonda. D: Bill Bryden, Nicolas Roeg, Charles Sturridge, Jean-Luc Godard, Robert Altman. MUS 90m. v

Ariel 1989 Finnish ★★★★ Laid-off blue collar mine worker takes to the highway to find the meaning of life. Completely offbeat directorial style makes this a bizarre but immensely watchable comedy. C: Turo Pajala, Susanna Haavisto. D: Aki Kaurismaki. DRA 74m. v

Arise, My Love 1940 ★★★★ A reporter (Colbert) and aviator (Milland) make an unlikely couple who keep meeting at various points during the early days of WWII. Charming comedy/drama was a subtle wake-up call to America about events in Europe. Oscar for Best Story. C: Claudette Colbert, Ray Milland. D: Mitchell Leisen. DRA 113m.

Aristocats, The 1970 ★★★★ Animated children's film, from Disney, features Gabor as the voice of a mother feline who is catnapped by a cruel servant, and transported to the country along with her three kittens. Charming and visually inventive. Voices of Eva Gabor, Maurice Chevalier, Scatman Crothers, Sterling Holloway, Phil Harris. D: Wolfgang Reitherman. FAM/DRA [G] 78m.

Arizona Heat 1988 ★★ A cop, respectful of the law, is called to rein in the vigilante-style violence of a fellow officer investigating a series of weird murders. C: Michael Parks, Denise Crosby, Hugh Farrington. D: John G. Thomas. ACT [R] 91m. v

Arizona Kid, The 1939 ★★★ During the Civil War, a Union captain (Rogers) in Missouri must deal with groups of Confederate bandits, one of whom may be a friend of his. An unusually dark story for the singing cowboy, and Rogers does well with it. C: Roy Rogers, George "Gabby" Hayes, Jack Ingram, David Kerwin. D: Joseph Kane. WST 61m. v

Arizona Mission 1956 *See* **Gun the Man Down**

Arizona Raiders, The 1936 ★★½ Crabbe (of *Flash Gordon* fame) plays a clueless outlaw who squirms his way out of a hanging in this forgettable comic Western. Based on a novel by Zane Grey. C: Buster Crabbe, Raymond Hatton, Johnny Downs, Marsha Hunt. D: James Hogan. WST 59m. v

Arizona Raiders 1965 ★★½ In this remake of *The Texas Rangers*, Murphy plays a Confederate officer who goes after Quantrill's Raiders in Arizona. Plenty of action, but not much of it is fresh. C: Audie Murphy, Michael Dante, Ben Cooper, Buster Crabbe, Gloria Talbott. D: William Witney. WST 88m. v

Arizona Ripper 1985 *See* **Bridge Across Time**

Arizona to Broadway 1933 ★★ New to the big city, a young woman from the sticks meets up with a smooth con artist. Some fun. C: James Dunn, Joan Bennett. D: James Tinling. DRA 66m.

Arizona 1940 ★★★ A tough-as-nails frontier woman teams up with a traveler from back East, and together they clean out villains from Arizona territory. Ambling story but nice chemistry between Arthur and Holden. C: Jean Arthur, William Holden. D: Wesley Ruggles. WST 121m. v

Ark of the Sun God . . . Temple of Hell, The

1982 ★ Cynical hero battles evil Mideastern caricatures in this unabashed plundering of *Indiana Jones* formulas, plots, and characters. Racist inanity. C: David Warbeck, John Steiner, Susie Sudlow, Alan Collins. D: Anthony M. Dawson. ACT 95m. V

Arkansas Traveler, The 1938 ★★½ When her newspaper publisher husband dies, a widow meets a stranger who helps her to keep the paper going. Well done and pleasant, if forgettable. C: Bob Burns, Fay Bainter, Jean Parker. D: Alfred Santell. DRA 85m.

Armed and Dangerous 1986 ★★ Bumbling security guards (Candy and Levy) manage to uncover a smuggling ring run by a mobster (Loggia). Two talented comedians work hard to make this material funny, but they're saddled with a lame script. C: John Candy, Eugene Levy, Robert Loggia, Meg Ryan. D: Mark Lester. COM [PG-13] 88m. V

Armed Response 1986 ★★★ A Japanese mob boss enlists the talents of a private eye to find his stolen antique jade. Good action and a stylish throwback to old-time mysteries. C: David Carradine, Lee Van Cleef, Mako, Lois Hamilton. D: Fred Olen Ray. CRI [R] 86m. V

Armored Attack 1943 *See* **North Star, The**

Armored Car Robbery 1950 ★★★★ After McGraw's partner is killed by Talman and his gang, the angered cop begins picking off crooks one by one when they pull off another armored car heist. Full of suspense and terrific action, this is a real nail-biter. C: Charles McGraw, Adele Jergens, William Talman. D: Richard Fleischer. CRI 61m. V

Armored Command 1961 ★★ Hard to swallow war film about a sexy Nazi spy (Louise, before her *Gilligan's Island* years) involved with a group of G.I.s. C: Howard Keel, Tina Louise, Burt Reynolds. D: Byron Haskin. DRA 105m. V

Army Brats 1984 ★★ War-like battles between children and parents of a military family. C: Akkemay, Frank Schaafsma, Geert De Jong. D: Ruud Van Hemert. COM 103m. V

Army of Darkness 1993 ★★★★½ Second, bigger-budgeted sequel to *The Evil Dead* continues the quest for the magic book that can lay to rest the undead. A wild mix of camp humor and special effects, with typically kinetic direction by Raimi. C: Bruce Campbell, Embeth Davidtz, Marcus Gilbert, Ian Abercrombie, Richard Grove. D: Sam Raimi. HOR [R] 80m. V

Arnelo Affair, The 1947 ★★ With her marriage on the rocks, a lawyer's wife is drawn to her husband's nightclub-owner client. A dark and seedy little murder mystery. C: John Hodiak, George Murphy, Frances Gifford, Dean Stockwell, Eve Arden. D: Arch Oboler. CRI 86m.

Arnold 1973 ★★ The tape-recorded voice of a dead man plays havoc with a number of his heirs. Murder mystery combined with black comedy; probably not to everyone's taste. C: Stella Stevens, Roddy McDowall, Elsa Lanchester, Farley Granger, Victor Buono. D: Georg Fenady. COM [PG] 96m. V

Around the World in 80 Days 1956 ★★★★½ Phileas Fogg bets his gentlemen's club members that he can circumnavigate the globe in 80 days, so he sets out accompanied by his hapless valet (Cantinflas) and unknowingly pursued by a detective (Newton) who thinks he's robbed the Bank of England. Fun, star-studded adventure with just enough tongue-in-cheek humor to keep it all buoyant. Based on the Jules Verne tale; Won Oscars for Best Picture, Score, Screenplay, Cinematography, and Editing. C: David Niven, Cantinflas, Shirley MacLaine, Robert Newton. D: Michael Anderson. ACT 179m. V

Around the World in 80 Ways 1988 ★★★★ Two scheming brothers take their father on a worldwide excursion entirely created in their back yard. Crazy Australian comedy, pleasing at every turn, thanks to wildly imaginative scripting and inventive direction. C: Philip Quast, Allan Penney, Diana Davidson, Kelly Dingwall, Gosia Dobrowolska. D: Stephen MacLean. COM [R] 90m. V

Around the World Under the Sea 1966 ★★½ Scientists go underwater to conduct earthquake experiments. Docudrama is ho-hum viewing for adults, just barely passable for children. C: Lloyd Bridges, Shirley Eaton, David McCallum, Brian Kelly, Keenan Wynn. D: Andrew Marton. FAM/DRA [G] 117m. V

Around the World 1943 ★★★ Kay Kyser and his fabulous "Kollege of Musical Knowledge" go on a worldwide wartime tour to entertain the troups. Lots of good music and a period glimpse of America at war. C: Kay Kyser, Mischa Auer, Joan Davis. D: Allan Dwan. MUS 80m. V

Arousers, The 1970 ★★½ Hunter works out impotency troubles by indulging himself in a killing spree. Hunter's performance belongs in another film—he's several notches above the routine sex and violence script. (a.k.a. *Sweet Kill* and *A Kiss from Eddie*) C: Tab Hunter, Nadyne Turney. D: Curtis Hanson. DRA 85m. V

Arrangement, The 1969 ★★ Melodrama about a wealthy advertising executive (Douglas) whose deep unhappiness leads him to try to commit suicide. Failing that, he falls into an affair with a coworker (Dunaway). Kazan adapted his own novel. C: Kirk Douglas, Faye Dunaway, Deborah Kerr, Hume Cronyn. D: Elia Kazan. DRA [R] 126m. V

Arrest Bulldog Drummond 1939 ★★★ The dashing crime-fighting adventurer gets into hot water with the police. Good entry from the terrific mystery series. C: John Howard, Heather Angel, H.B. Warner. D: James Hogan. CRI 115m. V

Arrival, The 1990 ★★ An alien power restores an elderly man's health, while simultaneously creating new problems for him. C:

John Saxon, Joseph Culp, Robin Frates. D: David Schmoeller. HOR [R] 107m. V

Arrivederci, Baby 1966 ★★ A ruthless schemer who's amassed a fortune by murdering a string of wealthy female benefactors meets his match in a woman who's planning the same fate for him. Lethargic black farce done in by a lethally unfunny script. C: Tony Curtis, Rosanna Schiaffino, Lionel Jeffries, Zsa Zsa Gabor, Nancy Kwan. D: Ken Hughes. COM 105m. V

Arrogant, The 1987 ★★ Fugitive criminal takes hitchhiker for a ride. C: Sylvia Kristel, Gary Graham. D: Philippe Blot. ACT [R] 86m. V

Arrow in the Dust 1954 ★★★ An army deserter takes on the identity of a dead commander and leads a wagon train during an Indian attack. Good Western action. C: Sterling Hayden, Coleen Gray, Keith Larsen. D: Lesley Selander. WST 80m.

Arrowhead 1953 ★★★ After a peace treaty is broken, a frontier scout and an Apache chief fight to the death. Well-mounted standard Western; controlled performances by Stone and Keith offset Heston's overacting. C: Charlton Heston, Jack Palance, Katy Jurado, Brian Keith, Milburn Stone. D: Charles Marquis Warren. WST 105m. V

Arrowsmith 1931 ★★★★ A medical researcher (Coleman) devotes himself to finding a cure for the plague, but when an epidemic breaks out, he must choose between rresearch and actual treatment. Well-acted drama, based on the Sinclair Lewis novel (Lewis actually saw it, and thought it was a good interpretation). C: Ronald Colman, Helen Hayes, Richard Bennett, Myrna Loy, Beulah Bondi. D: John Ford. DRA 95m. V

Arruza 1972 ★★★½ Compelling documentary about the life of the famous bullfighter. Anthony Quinn narrates. D: Budd Boetticher. DOC 90m. V

Arsenal Stadium Mystery, The 1939 British ★★★★ During a soccer match, a star player is poisoned. Not only whodunit, but how? A witty, sharp, and taut murder mystery. C: Leslie Banks, Greta Gynt. D: Thorold Dickinson. CRI 85m.

Arsene Lupin 1932 ★★★★ Detective story pairs Barrymore brothers in their first screen appearance together, as a French Duke (John) and Parisian police chief (Lionel), one of whom may be the masterful jewel thief of the title. High-class crook picture with a sense of humor. C: John Barrymore, Lionel Barrymore, Karen Morley. D: Jack Conway. CRI 84m.

Arsenic and Old Lace 1944 ★★★★½ Screwball horror-comedy stars Grant as a harried young man who discovers his sweet old aunts are actually poisoning lonely old men with their homemade elderberry wine. Fast-paced, often hilarious black comedy boasts a first-class cast that's clearly enjoying the material. Colorized version available. Based on Kesselring's popular Broadway play. C: Cary Grant, Priscilla Lane, Raymond Massey, Peter Lorre, Jack Carson, Josephine Hull, Jean Adair. D: Frank Capra. COM 118m. V

Art of Love, The 1965 ★★½ A fledgling artist, so poor he can't afford to eat, fakes his own suicide to spark interest in his work. Dismal black comedy. C: James Garner, Dick Van Dyke, Elke Sommer, Angie Dickinson, Ethel Merman. D: Norman Jewison. COM 99m.

Art of Tom and Jerry III: The Chuck Jones Years 1994 ★★★ Thirty-five shorts about famous cartoon characters created by renowned animator. COM 300m. TVM V

Arthur 1981 ★★★★½ A spoiled, drunken millionaire (Moore) risks forfeiting his fortune when he falls for a working-class woman (Minnelli). Spirited comedy with Moore endearing as title character. Gielgud took home a Best Supporting Oscar for his hilarious turn as Arthur's acerbic valet. Followed by a sequel. C: Dudley Moore, Liza Minnelli, John Gielgud, Geraldine Fitzgerald, Jill Eikenberry. D: Steve Gordon. COM [PG] 97m. V

Arthur 2—On the Rocks 1988 ★★★ Pale sequel finds lovable Arthur (Moore) still rich and still a lush but now married to Minnelli and preparing to start a family. That is, until his former fiancée's father conspires to leave him penniless. C: Dudley Moore, Liza Minnelli, John Gielgud, Geraldine Fitzgerald, Kathy Bates. D: Bud Yorkin. COM [PG] 113m. V

Arthur and the Square Knights of the Round Table 1984 ★★ Animated feature about Camelot, from Australia, features funny knights, silly dragons, and conventionally insipid damsels. DRA 80m. V

Arthur Miller's The American Clock *See* **The American Clock**

Arthur the King 1985 *See* **Merlin and the Sword**

Arthur's Hallowed Ground 1984 ★★ A cricket field is saved from destruction by an elderly man. C: Michael Elphick, Jimmy Jewel, Jean Boht. D: Freddie Young. DRA 75m. V

Article 99 1992 ★★½ Well-meaning but obvious story about idealistic doctors in Reagan-era veterans' hospitals trying to buck a heartless system to give good care. Efforts at satire fall flat; preachy and hard to swallow. C: Ray Liotta, Kiefer Sutherland, Forest Whitaker, Lea Thompson, John C. McGinley, Kathy Baker, Eli Wallach. D: Howard Deutch. DRA [R] 99m. V

Artists and Models Abroad 1938 ★★★½ A female musical revue and their manager (Benny) are stranded in Paris, and a Texas oilman comes to their rescue. Nice musical comedy, smartly paced and aided by a top cast. C: Jack Benny, Joan Bennett, Mary Boland. D: Mitchell Leisen. MUS 90m.

Artists and Models 1937 ★★★½ Modest musical with unusual pairing of dramatic actress Lupino with comic Benny. Ida plays a phony society dame, hoodwinking advertising exec Benny. Catch the "Public Enemy" dance number, staged by then-unknown Vincente Minnelli. No relation to the Martin-Lewis vehicle. C: Jack Benny, Ida Lupino, Richard Arlen, Gail Patrick, Judy Canova, Martha Raye, Connee Boswell, Ben Blue. D: Raoul Walsh. MUS 97m.

Artists and Models 1955 ★★★★ Above-par comedy has Lewis suffering from wacky dreams which cartoonist (Martin) turns into his own comic strips. Loud and frenetic—enjoyment level will depend on viewer's tolerance for Lewis's manic antics. C: Dean Martin, Jerry Lewis, Shirley MacLaine, Dorothy Malone. D: Frank Tashlin. COM 109m. V

Artur Rubinstein—Love of Life 1975 ★★★★★ Oscar winner for Best Documentary offers an affectionate look at the life of pianist Artur Rubinstein, focusing on his impending retirement and the resplendent memories of his distinguished career. Sheer delight for music lovers. D: François Reichenbach, S.G. Patris. DOC 91m. V

As If It Were Raining 1963 French ★★ A traveler in Spain gets mixed up in a plot to embezzle funds. Routine. C: Eddie Constantine, Henri Cogan, Elisa Montes. D: Jose Monter. DRA 85m. V

As Is 1986 ★★★ A young writer (Carradine), stricken by AIDS, is cared for by his stalwart photographer lover (Hadary). Unfortunately, this looks too much like a filmed play, on which it was based, rather than a movie. Mature theme and language. C: Jonathan Hadary, Robert Carradine, Alan Scarfe, Colleen Dewhurst, Joanna Miles. D: Michael Lindsay-Hogg. DRA 86m. V

As Long As They're Happy 1957 British ★★★ All heck breaks loose when a wealthy London stockbroker opens his plush home to an American singer. Fun satire that moves along. C: Janette Scott, Jean Carson, Diana Dors. D: J. Thompson. MUS 76m.

As Summers Die 1986 ★★★ Slow-moving tale of an underdog lawyer in 1959 Louisiana small town, taking on local heavyweights by representing a poor black woman in a land struggle. Davis rises to the occasion with her usual grit. C: Scott Glenn, Jamie Lee Curtis, Bette Davis. D: Jean-Claude Tramont. DRA 87m. TVM

As the Sea Rages 1960 ★★½ An American (Robertson) arrives on the Greek coast, where villagers conspire to sabotage his diving business. German production contains some marvelous scenery, but script founders on the rocks. (a.k.a. *Raubfischer in Hellas*) C: Maria Schell, Cliff Robertson, Cameron Mitchell. D: Horst Haechler. DRA 74m.

As You Desire Me 1932 ★★★½ Oddly fascinating drama of an amnesiac (Garbo), falling in love again with her former husband (Douglas). Interesting cast, enjoyable drama. C: Greta Garbo, Melvyn Douglas, Erich von Stroheim, Hedda Hopper. D: George Fitzmaurice. DRA 71m. V

As You Like It 1936 British ★★★★½ In his first Shakespearean film, Olivier takes on the part of Orlando, chasing the love of his life, Rosalind (Bergner), in Vienna. Deftly played comedy that fans of the Bard will enjoy. Set design is just wonderful. C: Elizabeth Bergner, Laurence Olivier, Sophie Stewart, Henry Ainley. D: Paul Czinner. COM 96m. V

As Young As You Feel 1951 ★★★½ The incomparable and crotchety Woolley plays a 65-year-old, forcibly retired employee who gets his revenge by impersonating the company's president and saving the business from bankruptcy. Social satire is agreeable without being preachy. C: Monty Woolley, Thelma Ritter, David Wayne, Jean Peters, Constance Bennett, Marilyn Monroe. D: Harmon Jones. COM 77m.

Ascent to Heaven 1951 Mexican ★★★★ Would-be groom takes a bus ride to his home village so his mother's will can be settled. Temptation, of course, travels with him. Good satire with the usual surreal fun from director Buñuel. (a.k.a. *Mexican Bus Ride*) C: Lilia Prado, Carmelita Gonzalez, Esteban Marquez. D: Luis Buñuel. COM 85m. V

Ash Wednesday 1973 ★★ Off-beat saga of a middle-aged woman (Taylor) who undergoes massive plastic surgery to regain her former appearance and her husband's interest. Beware of the stomach-turning operating room scenes. C: Elizabeth Taylor, Henry Fonda, Helmut Berger. D: Larry Peerce. DRA [R] 99m. V

Ashanti: Land of No Mercy 1979 ★★½ After his wife (Johnson) is kidnapped by a slave trader (Ustinov), missionary (Caine) sets out on a multination trek to rescue her. Exotic locales and talented cast, but not much else. (a.k.a. *Ashanti*) C: Michael Caine, Peter Ustinov, Beverly Johnson, Omar Sharif, Rex Harrison, William Holden. D: Richard Fleischer. DRA [R] 102m. V

Ashes and Diamonds 1958 Polish ★★★★★ Depiction of post-WWII destruction in Poland focuses on antihero Cybulski, who is chosen to assassinate a Communist party official. Known as the Polish James Dean, Cybulski gives a flamboyant performance. This gutsy, inspiring film is considered a Polish cinema classic. C: Zbigniew Cybulski, Ewa Krzyzanowska. D: Andrzej Wajda. DRA 105m. V

Ashes and Embers 1983 ★★ After the war, grandmother and friends help African-American Vietnam soldier understand his past and his present as a vet of color in America. D: Haile Gerima. DRA 120m. V

Ashik Kerib 1988 Russian ★ A wandering troubadour travels for 1,000 days and nights in hope of earning enough money to marry.

Based on Mikhail Lermontov's story. C: Yuri Goyan, Veronika Metonidze, Levan Natroshvill. D: Sergei Paradjanov. DRA 75m. V

Ask Any Girl 1959 ★★★★ To tame his playboy brother (Young), a staid businessman (Niven) conspires with their assistant (MacLaine) to make his sibling fall in love and marry her. Spirited comedy, with bubbly performances from all three leads. C: David Niven, Shirley MacLaine, Gig Young, Rod Taylor. D: Charles Walters. COM 101m. V

Aspen Extreme 1992 ★★ Tale of life on the cutting edge of a Colorado ski resort offers some exciting mountainside action, but nothing worth watching off the slopes. C: Paul Gross, Peter Berg, Finola Hughes. D: Patrick Hasburgh. DRA [PG-13] 118m. V

Asphalt Jungle, The 1950 ★★★★★ A gang of jewel thieves plans a carefully detailed heist that ultimately goes very, very wrong. Taut nailbiter of a crime story with uniformly excellent performances. Huston's razor-sharp direction is right on the money. Also offered an early career break for Monroe. Remade three times: *The Badlanders*, *Cairo*, and *Cool Breeze*. C: Sterling Hayden, Louis Calhern, Jean Hagen, James Whitmore, Sam Jaffe, Marilyn Monroe. D: John Huston. CRI 112m. V

Asphyx 1972 British ★★★★ Effective period chiller with convincing acting, artful but unpretentious storytelling and a unique story line: Inventor (Stephens) finds that he can photograph the spirit of death and attempts to capture it to achieve eternal life. (a.k.a. *Spirit of the Dead*) C: Robert Stephens, Robert Powell, Jane Lapotaire. D: Peter Newbrook. HOR [PG] 96m. V

Assam Garden, The 1985 British ★★★★ A shy, bereaved woman (Kerr) forms a friendship with an Indian neighbor (Jaffrey) while tending her dead husband's garden. Kerr's lovely performance, in a rare post-1970 appearance, makes this must-see fare for fans of *Masterpiece Theatre*. C:Deborah Kerr, Madhur Jaffrey, Alec McCowen. D: Mary McMurray. DRA 92m.

Assassin 1973 British ★★★ Government agents plan the execution of a spy in the Air Ministry. Routine British suspense. C: Ian Hendry, Edward Judd. D: Peter Crane. ACT 83m.

Assassin 1989 ★★ A rebel cyborg is programmed to murder American politicians. C: Robert Conrad, Karen Austin, Richard Young. D: Sandor Stern. SFI [PG-13] 94m. V

Assassin of Youth 1937 ★★ A young reporter infiltrates a circle of dopers to write an article. Extremely low-budget, unintentionally laughable midnight movie. (a.k.a. *"Marijuana"*) C: Luana Walters, Arthur Gardner, Dorothy Short. D: Elmer Clifton. DRA 80m.

Assassin, The 1953 British ★★½ Police get involved in a high-level manhunt in Venice after WWII. Routine action and a little romance on the side. C: Richard Todd, Eva Bartok. D: Ralph Thomas. CRI 90m.

Assassin, The 1961 Italian ★★★ A dealer of antiques is arrested and charged with murder, and he gets to like the celebrity. Nifty blend of comedy and drama. C: Marcello Mastroianni, Salvo Randone. D: Elio Petri. CRI 105m.

Assassination 1987 ★★ Secret Service agent (Bronson) is assigned to protect First Lady (Ireland—Code Name: One Mama) and ultimately shields her from a would-be assassin. Plenty of explosions, low-level sexual tension and violence. C: Charles Bronson, Jill Ireland, Stephen Elliott. D: Peter Hunt. ACT [PG-13] 88m. V

Assassination Bureau, The 1968 British ★★★½ An international gang of killers wreaks havoc by assassinating whomever they consider deserving. A journalist (Riggs) dares their leader (Reed) to have his own group try and kill him, and he accepts the challenge. Good fun in a turn-of-the-century comedy; based on a story by Jack London. C: Oliver Reed, Diana Rigg, Telly Savalas, Curt Jurgens, Philippe Noiret. D: Basil Dearden. COM [PG] 106m. V

Assassination Game, The 1992 ★★ This wildly improbable tale pairs a CIA and a KGB agent in the foiling of an assassination attempt. Long on espionage clichés but short on new ideas. C: Robert Rusler, Theodore Bikel, Denise Bixler, Doug Wert. D: Jonathan Winfrey. ACT [R] 83m. V

Assassination of Trotsky, The 1972 French ★★★ In Mexico City, Russian Revolutionary leader Leon Trotsky is hiding out from Stalinist agents. At last, one gets through. A strangely impassive film that seems to have its own particular agenda. C: Richard Burton, Alain Delon, Romy Schneider. D: Joseph Losey. DRA [R] 90m. V

Assassination Run, The 1980 ★★ German terrorists' plan to blackmail former British intelligence agent involves kidnapping his wife. C: Malcolm Stoddard, Mary Tamm, Sandor Eles. D: Ken Hannam. ACT 111m. V

Assassins de l'Orde, Les Law Breakers 1971 French ★★ Brutal police kill an innocent man. C: Jacques Brel, Catherine Rouvel. D: Marcel Came. CRI 100m. V

Assault and Matrimony 1987 ★★★ In this deadly funny, slapstick comedy, battling spouses go to outrageous extremes to eliminate each other. C: Jill Eikenberry, Michael Tucker. D: James Frawley. COM [PG] 95m. TVM V

Assault Force 1980 *See* **ffolkes**

Assault of the Killer Bimbos 1988 ★ Vigilantes engage in lewd law enforcement. The title's the best part. C: Karen Nielsen, Debi Thibeault, Lisa Schmidt. D: Gorman Bechard. COM [R] 90m. V

Assault of the Party Nerds 1989 ★★ Wimpy fraternity brothers throw the party of a lifetime. Not exactly a black-tie affair. C: Linnea Quigley, Troy Donahue, Richard Gabai. D: Richard Gabai. COM [R] 82m. V

Assault of the Rebel Girls 1959 ★ Cuban women smuggle weapons to rebels (led by

Flynn) during Castro's revolution. Dull attempt at adventure was, sadly, Flynn's last film. C: Errol Flynn, Beverly Aadland, John MacKay. D: Barry Mahon. ACT 66m. V

Assault on a Queen 1966 ★★ Gang uses a submarine to apprehend and rob a luxury oceanliner. Despite script from the usually reliable Rod Serling, this third-rate Sinatra caper is neither funny nor charming. Neat Ellington jazz score, though. C: Frank Sinatra, Virna Lisi, Tony Franciosa. D: Jack Donohue. CRI 106m. V

Assault on Agathon 1975 British ★★ An Interpol agent (Minardos), investigating an international drug deal, stumbles across a conspiracy to begin new global revolution. Tiresome, familiar plot, barely jazzed up by stunning Greek island locales. C: Nico Minardos, Nina Van Pallandt, Marianne Faithfull. D: Laslo Benedek. ACT 95m. V

Assault on Precinct 13 1976 ★★★★★ A truly creepy thriller about a nearly abandoned precinct in Los Angeles that is besieged by a violent gang of youths. Superb acting and some on-target black humor make this a modern-day classic. Carpenter seems to have been inspired by Hawks' *Rio Bravo.* C: Austin Stoker, Darwin Joston, Laurie Zimmer. D: John Carpenter. ACT [R] 91m. V

Assault on the Wayne 1970 ★★½ Commander of U.S. submarine *Anthony Wayne* must deal with double agents among officers and crew. Able cast but no surprises. C: Leonard Nimoy, Lloyd Haynes, William Windom. D: Marvin Chomsky. ACT 74m.

Assault, The 1986 Dutch ★★★★★ Only surviving member of a family destroyed by the Nazis looks back on his childhood in hope of exorcising his psychological demons. Tough and emotionally wrenching. Oscar for Best Foreign Film. C: Derek DeLint, Marc Van Uchelen, Monique Van DeVen. D: Fons Rademakers. DRA [PG] 126m. V

Assault with a Deadly Weapon 1982 ★★½ Thugs terrorize city when mayor cuts down number of police on the streets. C: Richard Holliday, Sandra Foley, Lamont Jackson. D: Arthur Kennedy. ACT 86m. V

Assault 1971 *See* **In the Devil's Garden**

Assignment in Brittany 1943 ★★½ Free French soldier (Aumont) bears a resemblance to a Nazi commander, which he uses to help the underground. Familiar story, adapted from Helen MacInnes's WWII thriller, made watchable by Aumont's sturdy performance. C: Pierre Aumont, Susan Peters. D: Jack Conway. ACT 96m.

Assignment K 1968 British ★★ An espionage agent (Boyd) becomes disenchanted by double agents all around him, including his mistress (Sparv). Downbeat spy thriller. C: Stephen Boyd, Camilla Sparv, Michael Redgrave, Leo McKern. D: Val Guest. ACT 97m.

Assignment—Paris 1952 ★★ Reporter (Andrews), working at the Paris bureau of the *Herald-Tribune*, is mistaken for a spy. Cold War espionage thriller never gels, despite a fine supporting cast and a good score by George Duning. C: Dana Andrews, Marta Toren, George Sanders. D: Robert Parrish. ACT 85m.

Assignment Terror 1970 Spanish ★ An alien invader (Rennie) exploits the powers of movie/mythic monsters (Dracula, et al), only to be stopped by a werewolf, the monster with a conscience. Truly dumb attempt at international horror. (a.k.a. *Dracula vs. Frankenstein*) C: Michael Rennie, Karin Dor. D: Tulio Demicheli. HOR 86m.

Assignment, The 1978 Swedish ★★½ Swedish attaché (Plummer) gets in over his head when he tries to straighten out a crisis in South America. Melodrama briefly enlivened by the suave, smooth Rey. C: Christopher Plummer, Thomas Hellberg, Carolyn Seymour, Fernando Rey. D: Mats Arehn. DRA 92m. V

Assignment to Kill 1968 ★★★ O'Neal, doing a Coburnesque turn, is an insurance investigator sent to Switzerland to check out a crooked financier. Stylish international thriller with a solid supporting cast. C: Patrick O'Neal, Joan Hackett, John Gielgud, Herbert Lom. D: Sheldon Reynolds. ACT 102m.

Assisi Underground, The 1984 ★★½ Escaping from Nazi persecution, Jewish refugees are hidden away in the Catholic monasteries of Assisi, Italy. Exciting story gets by-the-numbers treatment, despite excellent cast. C: Ben Cross, James Mason, Irene Papas, Maximilian Schell. D: Alexander Ramati. DRA [PG] 115m. V

Associate, The 1982 French, German ★★★★ Sparkling comedy about a Milquetoast businessman (Serrault) who creates a fictitious partner to give his company some much-needed panache. The scheme works a little too well, resulting in wonderfully inventive complications. C: Michel Serrault, Claudine Auger, Catherine Alric. D: Rene Gainville. COM 94m.

Asterix and Cleopatra 1985 ★★ Asterix vs. the queen of the Nile. SFI 72m. V

Asterix in Britain ★★ Asterix deflects Caesar's army from invading Britain. Some violence. SFI 85m. V

Asterix the Gaul 1985 ★★ Asterix vs. Roman warriors. Some violence. Not for all tastes. SFI 67m. V

Asterix vs. Caesar ★★ In order to rescue Falbala and her prince, Asterix once again takes on the Roman army. Some violence. SFI 85m. V

Astonished Heart, The 1950 British ★★★ Noel Coward adapted his own play about a psychiatrist cheating on his wife with a former school chum of hers. Takes itself much too seriously. C: Noel Coward, Celia Johnson, Margaret Leighton. D: Terence Fisher, Anthony Darnborough. DRA 92m.

Astro-Zombies 1967 ★ Scientist (Carradine) creates deadly zombies out of his freshly killed victims. Familiar, ultracheap horror. (a.k.a. *Space Zombies* and *Space Vampires*)

C: Wendell Corey, John Carradine. D: Ted V. Mikels. HOR [PG] 83m. v

Astronaut, The 1971 ★★½ To maintain government funding, NASA-like officials persuade an ex-flyer (Markham) to impersonate an astronaut who died during space voyage. Solid idea given overly solemn, melodramatic treatment. C: Monte Markham, Susan Clark. D: Robert Michael Lewis. DRA 72m.

Asylum of Satan 1976 ★ Cheapie set in a hospital run by a Satanist, who wants to use a female patient as a sacrifice. In between, there's a series of gory axe murders. Lurid and gruesome, but rarely frightening. C: Charles Kissinger, Carla Borelli, Nick Jolley. D: William Girdler. HOR [PG] 82m. v

Asylum 1972 British ★★★★ *Psycho* author Robert Bloch scripted this well-mounted anthology of horror tales told by mental patients. Best segment: living dolls that kill. Good cast and direction. (a.k.a. *House of Crazies*) C: Barbara Parkins, Richard Todd, Peter Cushing, Britt Ekland, Herbert Lom. D: Roy Ward Baker. HOR [PG] 100m. v

At Close Range 1986 ★★★★ Dark, hard-edged tale, based on a true story, of a seductively murderous gang kingpin (Walken) whose sons want to emulate him—and who ultimately become his victims. Tough material, with characters who are fascinating but off-putting. C: Sean Penn, Christopher Walken, Mary Stuart Masterson, Christopher Penn, Kiefer Sutherland, Crispin Glover. D: James Foley. CRI [R] 115m. v

At Dawn We Die 1936 *See* **Tomorrow We Live**

At First Sight 1978 *See* **Love at First Sight**

At Good Old Siwash 1940 *See* **Those Were the Days**

At Gunpoint 1955 ★★★½ A nonviolent shopkeeper (MacMurray) accidentally kills a would-be robber, then, as sheriff, has to defend his village against the robber's avenging brothers. Better than average *High Noon*-type Western, with MacMurray surprisingly good as a Western hero. C: Fred MacMurray, Dorothy Malone, Walter Brennan. D: Alfred Werker. WST 81m. v

At Gunpoint 1990 ★★ Serial murderer tracked by FBI agent. C: Frank Kanig, Tain Bodkin, Scott Claflin. D: Steven L. Harris. ACT 88m. v

At Long Last Love 1975 ★★ Director's tribute to '30s art deco musicals stumbles and falls flat as a pancake with leather-lung stars murdering great Cole Porter songs as silly plot of mismatched society couples rambles on. Then—at long last—it's over. A notably famous flop. C: Burt Reynolds, Cybill Shepherd, Madeline Kahn, Duilio Del Prete, Eileen Brennan. D: Peter Bogdanovich. MUS 118m.

At Mother's Request 1987 ★★★ Sturdy true-crime drama about a millionaire's murder, orchestrated by his socialite daughter (Powers). No-frills treatment has impact. C: Stefanie Powers, Doug McKeon, John Woods, E.G. Marshall, Frances Sternhagen. D: Michael Tuchner. CRI 208m. v

At Play in the Fields of the Lord 1991 ★★★½ Modern-day missionaries from the U.S. face reluctant converts and a crisis of faith in the Amazon jungle, while Berenger, a part-Cherokee pilot, joins the tribal society. Ambitious on-location epic is too long, but gets better as it goes. C: Tom Berenger, Aidan Quinn, Kathy Bates, John Lithgow, Daryl Hannah, Tom Waits. D: Hector Babenco. DRA [R] 190m. v

At Sword's Point 1952 ★★★½ A spirited tale that reworks *The Three Musketeers* by recounting the swashbuckling adventures of their offspring. Lavish sets and stunning Technicolor. C: Cornel Wilde, Maureen O'Hara, Dan O'Herlihy, Alan Hale Jr. D: Lewis Allen. ACT 81m. v

At the Circus 1939 ★★★½ Crazy Marx Brothers try to save a circus from bankruptcy in this uneven attempt to recapture the zany glory of their earlier films. Long-suffering Margaret Dumont does get shot from a cannon, though, and Groucho sings his famous song, "Lydia the Tattooed Lady." Some of Harpo's gags were devised by Buster Keaton. C: Groucho Marx, Chico Marx, Harpo Marx, Margaret Dumont, Eve Arden, Nat Pendleton. D: Edward Buzzell. COM 87m. v

At the Earth's Core 1976 British ★★★ Victorian scientists burrow their way to the center of the Earth to find it inhabited by giant reptilian beasties and protohumans. Game cast and fun effects highlight this adaptation of the Edgar Rice Burroughs book. C: Doug McClure, Peter Cushing, Caroline Munro. D: Kevin Connor. SFI 90m. v

At the Jazz Band Ball 1993 ★★★★ Great moments from the height of the Jazz Age, including performances by Duke Ellington, Louis Armstrong, and Bo Jangles. MUS 60m. v

At War with the Army 1950 ★★★½ Following supporting roles in the *My Friend Irma* pictures, Martin and Lewis became main players in this film. Dean's a military man who hooks up with a new recruit (Lewis) to solve romantic troubles. Zany antics abound, as one might expect. Silly, but younger audiences might enjoy. C: Dean Martin, Jerry Lewis, Polly Bergen. D: Hal Walker. COM 93m. v

Atalia 1985 Hebrew ★★★ Love between older war widow and young man, set on a kibbutz. C: Michal Bat-Adam, Yftach Katzur, Dan Toren. D: Akiva Tevet. DRA 90m. v

Athena 1954 ★★★½ Unusual MGM bodybuilding musical about a family of health and exercise fanatics, including cheerful Powell and perky Reynolds. Offbeat tuner features fun number, "I Never Felt Better." C: Jane Powell, Debbie Reynolds, Edmund Purdom, Vic Damone, Louis Calhern. D: Richard Thorpe. MUS 96m. v

Atlanta Child Murders, The 1985 ★★★★ Lengthy chronicle of the investigation and subsequent 1982 conviction of Wayne Williams for the notorious series of murders (mostly of black children) in Atlanta in the late '70s. Some powerful issues are raised by Abby Mann's script, and there are knockout performances by Torn and Robards. C: Jason Robards, James Earl Jones, Martin Sheen, Rip Torn, Morgan Freeman. D: John Erman. DRA 245m. TVM

Atlantic City 1944 ★★★ At the turn of the century, a nervy impresario (Taylor) sets out to make "Atlantic City" synonymous with "entertainment." Spirited little musical, hopping with interludes by Louis Armstrong, Paul Whiteman, many others. C: Brad Taylor, Constance Moore, Charley Grapewin, Jerry Colonna. D: Ray McCarey. MUS 87m.

Atlantic City 1980 Canadian ★★★★★ An aging, washed-up numbers runner (Lancaster) on the back streets of Atlantic City returns to the action to help a young woman (Sarandon) mixed up with the underworld. Poignant character study, spiced with offbeat romance, features a great performance by Lancaster and Sarandon's grown-up sensuality. C: Burt Lancaster, Susan Sarandon, Michel Piccoli. D: Louis Malle. DRA 104m. V

Atlantis, the Lost Continent 1961 ★ A young fisherman faces danger and intrigue in the final days of the fabled city before it slips into the deep. Even the special effects are below sea level on this one. C: Anthony Hall, Joyce Taylor, John Dall. D: George Pal. ACT 91m. V

Atlas 1961 ★★★½ Greek hero Atlas (Forest) must choose between fighting for the rich or the poor. Cult horror director Corman switches to the sword-and-sandal genre, with unintentionally comic results. Forest looks like he needs more time in the gym. C: Michael Forest, Frank Wolff, Barboura Morris. D: Roger Corman. ACT 80m.

Atoll K, Robinson Crusoeland 1950 *See* **Utopia**

Atom Age Vampire 1961 Italian ★ Another loony Italian horror film about a mad scientist who restores the beauty of an accident victim, then kills other young women for healthy replacement cells. Unbelievably bad, with hilarious English-language dubbing. C: Alberto Lupo, Susanne Loret. D: Anton Majano. HOR 87m.

Atom Man vs. Superman—Complete ★★ Fifteen-tale series about criminal genius Lex Luthor's malign adventures in Metropolis. C: Kirk Alyn, Tommy Bond, Noel Neill. D: Spencer Gordon Bennet. SFI 252m. V

Atomic Cafe, The 1982 ★★★★½ Amazing assemblage of government and educational films from the '50s shows how the U.S. tried to ease its citizens into the atomic era and the idea of possible nuclear annihilation. Thorough documentary of government propaganda effort elicits howls of both laughter and terror. C: Jayne Loader, Pierce Rafferty. D: Kevin Rafferty. DOC 92m. V

Atomic City, The 1952 ★★★ A Los Alamos scientist teams up with the feds to recover his kidnapped son. Interesting post-atomic bomb footage and lack of pretension compensate for tame script. C: Gene Barry, Nancy Gates. D: Jerry Hopper. ACT 85m. V

Atomic Kid, The 1954 ★★ Hilariously dated comedy features Rooney as a bomb blast survivor who becomes radioactive. There's more than one bomb on screen here. Notable mostly as an early story credit for future director Blake Edwards. C: Mickey Rooney, Robert Strauss. D: Leslie Martinson. COM 86m. V

Atomic Man, The 1956 British ★★★ A nuclear accident makes a man's brain radioactive, enabling him to be seven seconds ahead of his friends and enemies. Goofy English espionage, adapted from Charles Eric Maine's novel *The Isotope Man*, rises above its B-picture budget. C: Gene Nelson, Faith Domergue. D: Ken Hughes. SFI 78m.

Atomic Submarine, The 1959 ★★★ U.S. atomic sub in Arctic waters encounters an alien spaceship that can move underwater. Cult thriller with sturdy, familiar low-budget cast and solid script. C: Arthur Franz, Dick Foran, Tom Conway, Brett Halsey. D: Spencer Gordon Bennet. SFI 80m. V

Ator, the Fighting Eagle 1983 ★ Italian sword-and-sorcery entry displays musclebound O'Keefe sleepwalking and flexing against Evil. Martial arts in a mythic Middle Ages, with heaving bosoms and a lot of hair. C: Miles O'Keefe, Sabrina Siani. D: David Hills. ACT [PG] 98m. V

Atraccion Peculiar 1988 Argentine ★★ Comedic adventures of two men transformed into transvestites. C: Alberto Olmedo, Jorge Porcel. COM 90m. V

Attack and Retreat 1965 *See* **Italiano Brava Gente**

Attack Force Z 1981 Australian ★★★ An Australian military unit in WWII is sent to rescue a Japanese defector downed in a plane crash in the South Pacific. Not-bad action adventure, notable mostly as an early vehicle for Gibson and Neill. C: John Phillip Law, Sam Neill, Mel Gibson. D: Tim Burstall. ACT 84m. V

Attack of the Beast Creatures 1985 ★ Carnivorous beasts attack the passengers of a luxury liner stranded on a deserted island. C: Robert Nolfi, Robert Lengyel, Julia Rust. D: Michael Stanley. HOR 82m. V

Attack of the Crab Monsters 1957 ★★½ Giant crustaceans take on the psyches of their victims and terrorize a group of scientists stranded on an island. Not bad, though the big crabs aren't especially convincing. C: Richard Garland, Pamela Duncan. D: Roger Corman. HOR 68m.

Attack of the 50 Ft. Woman 1958 ★★ After encountering a gigantic alien, a scorned wife takes on enormous proportions, exacting her revenge on her cheating husband and his trampy mistress. The worst special effects imaginable and some pretty bad acting have made this a camp classic. Awful fun. Remade for TV. C: Allison Hayes, William Hudson. D: Nathan Juran. SFI 60m. V

Attack of the 50 Ft. Woman 1993 ★★★½ A downtrodden woman (Hannah) grows to gargantuan size after exposure to a UFO, and takes revenge on her male chauvinist husband. Mild remake of the 1958 camp classic would have been better off with someone like Bette Midler in the lead. C: Daryl Hannah, Daniel Baldwin, William Windom, Christi Conaway. D: Christopher Guest. SFI [R] 90m. TVM V

Attack of the Giant Leeches 1959 ★★ Title tells all, except that the fake-looking, slimy monsters are actually intelligent and the main characters are involved in a love triangle. Low-budget silliness. C: Ken Clark, Yvette Vickers, Jan Shepard. D: Bernard Kowalski. HOR 62m.

Attack of the Killer Tomatoes 1979 ★★½ Thousands of tomatoes grow giant size and terrorize the good citizens of San Diego to avenge the way they've been mistreated. Low-budget, campy sci-fi parody has a cult following; it's spawned two sequels and an animated cartoon show. C: David Miller, Sharon Taylor, George Wilson. D: John De Bello. COM [PG] 87m. V

Attack of the Mayan Mummy 1963 ★ Post-life regression goes haywire when a subject takes a scientist back to ancient Mexican ruins—and their proprietorial residents. Patched and botched horror job, good for a laugh. C: Richard Webb, Nina Knight. D: Jerry Warren. HOR 77m.

Attack of the Puppet People 1958 ★★ Low-budget horror about a dollmaker who can make humans doll-sized. Substandard fare from schlockmeister Gordon. C: John Agar, John Hoyt, June Kenney, Scott Peters. D: Bert Gordon. HOR 78m.

Attack of the Swamp Creature 1975 ★★ The citizens of a small town are attacked by a scientist who has changed himself into a bog monster. C: Frank Crowell, Patricia Allison. D: Arnold Stevens. HOR 96m. V

Attack on Terror: The FBI vs. the Ku Klux Klan 1975 ★★★ Investigation into the murder of three civil rights workers in 1964 leads to the discovery of a conspiracy by the Klan. Loosely adapted from Don Whitehead's account (with FBI files as source). Uneven script has a foregone conclusion, but still rings true. C: Ned Beatty, John Beck, Billy Green Bush, Dabney Coleman, Andrew Duggan, Wayne Rogers, George Grizzard, Rip Torn. D: Marvin J. Chomsky. DRA 215m. TVM

Attack on the Iron Coast 1968 ★★★ During WWII, Bridges leads a Canadian commando team against a German naval installation on the French coast. Watchable British action film. C: Lloyd Bridges, Andrew Keir, Sue Lloyd. D: Paul Wendkos. ACT [G] 89m.

Attack! 1956 ★★★★ Gritty antiwar film still packs a wallop, as soldiers under an incompetent commander (Albert) face certain death during the Battle of the Bulge. One of director Aldrich's toughest films—which is saying plenty—and a favorite of the French New Wave directors. C: Jack Palance, Eddie Albert, Lee Marvin. D: Robert Aldrich. DRA 107m.

Attic, The 1979 ★★★ A spinster (Snodgress) is both nursemaid and virtual slave to her crippled, mad dad (Milland); can she break away without murdering him? Psychological horror reaches for depth but not far enough. Points for ambition, if not execution. C: Carrie Snodgress, Ray Milland, Rosemary Murphy. D: George Edwards. DRA [PG] 97m. V

Attic, The: The Hiding of Anne Frank 1988 ★★★★½ Marvelous drama features a quietly magnetic performance by Steenburgen as unsung Dutch heroine Miep Gies, who risked her life hiding the family of Anne Frank from the Nazis in Amsterdam. Tense drama never falters. C: Mary Steenburgen, Paul Scofield, Huub Stapel. D: John Erman. DRA 95m. TVM V

Attica 1980 ★★★★ A reenactment of one of American history's most notorious prison uprisings, in upstate New York in 1971. A riveting, multifaceted drama that confronts viewers' sympathies and ethical standards. Based on Tom Wicker's book *A Time to Die*. C: Charles Durning, George Grizzard, Glynn Turman, Morgan Freeman. D: Marvin J. Chomsky. DRA 97m. TVM V

Attila 1958 Italian ★ Quinn is Attila preparing to defeat Valentinian's army and sack Rome. Howlingly bad epic, left on shelf for four years before American release, with too brief appearance by Loren. Listen for Quinn's puzzling Bronx accent. Camp fun. (a.k.a. *Attila the Hun*) C: Anthony Quinn, Sophia Loren, Irene Papas. D: Pietro Francisci. ACT 83m.

Attila the Hun 1958 *See* **Attila**

Au Hasard, Balthazar 1966 France ★★★★★ One of the director's best is a magical parable of love, told from an unlikely point of view, that of a donkey who witnesses and suffers from the stupidity of humans. Lyrical and often tragic. C: Anne Wiazemsky, François Lafarge, Philippe Asselin, Nathalie Joyaut. D: Robert Bresson. DRA 95m. V

Au Revoir, Les Enfants 1987 French ★★★★★ Powerful story, based on Malle's childhood in Nazi-occupied France. When a new student enters a rural Catholic school, he receives special care from the priests. Gradually it's learned that the boy is a Jew in hiding. Develops slowly toward tragic conclusion. One of Malle's best. C: Gaspard Manesse, Raphael Fejto, Francine Racette. D: Louis Malle. DRA [PG] 103m.

Audrey Rose 1977 ★★½ Intriguing premise is played entirely too low-key, as Hopkins tries to convince Beck and Mason that their child is the reincarnation of (as he repeatedly refers to her) "my daughter, Audrey Rose." The cast helps, but not enough. C: Marsha Mason, John Beck, Anthony Hopkins. D: Robert Wise. HOR [PG] 113m. V

Aunt Mary 1979 ★★★ True-life story of Mary Dobkin (Stapleton), a Baltimore activist who became locally prominent coaching sandlot baseball. Potential tearjerker grounded by tough, earthy performances, especially by Balsam. C: Jean Stapleton, Martin Balsam, Harold Gould. D: Peter Werner. DRA 100m. TVM

Auntie Lee's Meat Pies 1992 ★★ A meat-pie maker sends her five nieces in search of her special ingredient—young men. C: Karen Black, Pat Morita, Pat Paulsen, Huntz Hall. D: Joseph F. Robertson. COM [R] 100m. V

Auntie Mame 1958 ★★★★½ Bright, uproarious antics of a madcap aunt (Russell) and her young nephew. Liberal vs. conservative theme gives unity to hilarious episodes, as Auntie Mame shows her naive ward how to "live, live, live!" Great star performance by Russell. Based on the hit novel and play by Patrick Dennis; later became the basis for the musical *Mame.* C: Rosalind Russell, Forrest Tucker, Coral Browne, Fred Clark, Peggy Cass. D: Morton Da Costa. COM 144m. V

Aurora 1984 ★★★ Desperate to get money for her seeing-impaired son's operation, Loren hits up old flames for cash, ultimately zeroing in on Travanti. Soap opera goes extra-thick on the treacle. Loren's real son plays her boy, her stepson is the producer, and her niece has a cameo. C: Sophia Loren, Daniel Travanti, Edoardo Ponti, Philippe Noiret. D: Maurizio Ponzi. DRA 100m. TVM

Aurora Encounter 1985 ★★ Kind alien visits western town at turn of the century. C: Jack Elam, Peter Brown, Carol Bagdasarian, Dottie West. D: Jim McCullough, Sr. SFI [PG] 90m. V

Austeria (The Inn) 1984 Polish ★★ Polish Jews seek shelter in an inn when pursued by Russian Cossacks. D: Jerzy Kawalerowicz. DRA 110m. V

Austerlitz 1960 *See* **Battle of Austerlitz, The**

Author! Author! 1982 ★★★★ Playwright Pacino finds himself in charge of five kids when his flighty wife takes off with another man. He struggles to keep the family together amid the turmoil of mounting a new play. It's Pacino's show all the way in this sweet, low-key character comedy. C: Al Pacino, Dyan Cannon, Tuesday Weld, Alan King, Bob Elliott, Ray Goulding. D: Arthur Hiller. COM [PG] 100m. V

Autobiography of a Princess 1975 British ★★★★ Early Merchant-Ivory effort focuses on England-India relations as an Indian princess (Jaffrey) and British gentleman (Mason) meet for tea. Articulate and evocative, but a mite dull. Script by Ruth Prawer Jhabvala (*Howards End*). C: James Mason, Madhur Jaffrey. D: James Ivory. DRA 60m.

Autobiography of Miss Jane Pittman 1974 ★★★★½ Sweeping adaptation of Ernest J. Gaines' novel about American life from the Civil War through the '50s, as remembered by an 110-year-old former slave. A superb epic, memorable for its almost unbearable brutality and Tyson's monumental performance in the title role. Winner of nine Emmy Awards. C: Cicely Tyson, Barbara Chaney, Richard Dysart, Katherine Helmond. D: John Korty. DRA 106m. TVM V

Autopsy 1976 Italian ★★ When a student begins researching suicides and murders, people start disappearing. C: Mimsy Farmer, Ray Lovelock. D: Armando Crispino. HOR [R] 90m. V

Autumn Afternoon, An 1962 Japanese ★★★★½ Set against a backdrop of modernized, Westernized Japan, a father's sadness and loss as he reluctantly surrenders his only daughter to marriage reaches epic proportions. Prime example of the stylistic purity that made Ozu a master. C: Chishu Ryu, Shima Iwashita. D: Yasujiro Ozu. DRA 115m. V

Autumn Born 1979 ★★ Soft-core feature stars murdered Playboy Playmate Stratten (subject of Bob Fosse's film biography *Star '80*) as the helpless captive of a cruel guardian who keeps her under his sadistic thumb. Cinematic curio. C: Dorothy R. Stratten. DRA 76m. V

Autumn Leaves 1956 ★★★½ A middle-aged woman (Crawford) marries a younger man (Robertson) who becomes unhinged when his father and wife come for a surprise visit. Tense melodrama benefits from psychological twist. Nat King Cole sings title tune. C: Joan Crawford, Cliff Robertson, Vera Miles, Lorne Greene. D: Robert Aldrich. DRA 108m. V

Autumn Marathon 1979 Russian ★★ An English professor in Leningrad becomes confused by the demands of his wife, his mistress, his students, and his colleagues. C: Oleg Basilashvili, Natalia Gundareva. D: Georgy Danelia. DRA 100m. V

Autumn Sonata 1978 Swedish ★★★★ Bergman and Bergman collaborated late in their careers on this heated drama about parental psychological tyranny. Bergman is a successful concert pianist whose self-absorption has permanently scarred Ullmann, her devoted ugly-duckling daughter. Their harrowing confrontation is masterfully played by the two actresses. C: Ingrid Bergman, Liv Ullmann. D: Ingmar Bergman. DRA [PG] 97m. V

Autumn's Tale, An 1987 Chinese ★★ A young woman seeks help from her tough cousin to regain the affections of her boyfriend from Hong Kong. C: Cherie Chung, Chow Yun Fat. D: Mabel Cheung. DRA 98m. V

Avalanche 1978 ★★★ An entrepreneur (Hudson) opens a lavish ski lodge just in time for an avalanche. Outstanding special effects clash with poor acting in this unsuccessful attempt to ride the coattails of the '70s box-office fascination with disasters. C: Rock Hudson, Mia Farrow. D: Corey Allen. ACT [PG] 91m. V

Avalanche Express 1979 ★★ CIA agent (Marvin) has to get a KGB defector (Shaw) to safety—by train. Shaw's last role, Robson's last film, derailed by a poor story and production. C: Lee Marvin, Robert Shaw, Linda Evans, Maximilian Schell, Joe Namath. D: Mark Robson. ACT [PG] 87m. V

Avalon 1990 ★★★ Highly touted Russian Jewish immigrant family saga goes downhill from spectacular opening sequence. Wonderful performance by Mueller-Stahl as clan patriarch can't salvage what is in truth a very dull script and a film that is too talky, too long, and not well cast. C: Aidan Quinn, Elizabeth Perkins, Armin Mueller-Stahl, Joan Plowright, Lou Jacobi, Elijah Wood. D: Barry Levinson. DRA [PG] 126m. v

Avant Garde and Experimental Films ★★★★ Great collection of several famous avant garde films, including Buñuel's and Dali's "Un Chien Andulou", Ivens' and Franken's "Regen", and Welles' "The Hearts of Age." DRA 74m. v

Avanti! 1972 ★★★★½ An uptight American businessman (Lemmon) travels to Italy to claim his late father's body and ends up letting his hair down with the daughter (Mills) of his father's mistress. Lively, bittersweet black comedy, spiritedly played by Lemmon and Mills. C: Jack Lemmon, Juliet Mills, Clive Revill, Edward Andrews. D: Billy Wilder. COM [R] 144m. v

Avengers, The *See* **The Day Will Dawn**

Avenging Angel 1985 ★★ Inevitable sequel to *Angel* features Russell as ex-teen prostitute turned law student. When cop hero from first film is murdered, Russell and buddy Calhoun go bad guy hunting! Exploitation all the way. Sequel: *Angel III—The Final Chapter*. C: Betsy Russell, Rory Calhoun, Susan Tyrrell, Ossie Davis. D: Robert Vincent O'Neil. ACT [R] 94m. v

Avenging Disco Godfather, The *See* **Disco Godfather**

Avenging Force 1986 ★★★½ After the son of a prominent African-American politician (James) is killed during an assassination attempt, dad's old comrade-in-arms (Dudikoff) comes out of retirement to battle secret reactionary organization. Solid action feature with a strong antiracist message and some thrilling sequences. C: Michael Dudikoff, Steve James. D: Sam Firstenberg. ACT [R] 104m.

Avenging Spirit 1978 *See* **Dominique**

Avenging, The 1992 ★★ Man, indicted for crime he didn't commit, escapes prison and tracks down fellow who framed him. C: Michael Horse, Efrem Zimbalist, Jr., Sherry Hursey. D: Lyman Dayton. WST 90m. v

Aviator, The 1985 ★★ Moody 1920s-era mail pilot (Reeve) crash-lands faulty plane, then crash-romances his dreamgirl (Arquette). Pair quickly move on with their adventure and end up lost in woods, battling bears. No kidding! C: Christopher Reeve, Rosanna Arquette, Jack Warden, Sam Wanamaker, Tyne Daly. D: George Miller. DRA [PG] 98m.

Aviator's Wife, The 1981 French ★★★★½ One of Rohmer's best efforts (and the first installment of his "Comedies and Proverbs" series), in which a jealous lover is driven to track his girlfriend's every move. Full of engaging conversation, lighter-than-air humor, and intellectual fireworks. Not to be missed. C: Philippe Marlaud, Marie Riviere. D: Eric Rohmer. COM [PG] 104m.

Awakening of Candra, The 1983 ★★ Horrifying, real-life story of newlyweds whose honeymoon is disrupted by a murderer. C: Richard Jaeckel, Cliff DeYoung, Blanche Baker. D: Paul Wendkos. DRA 96m. v

Awakening of Cassie, The 1986 ★★ A young artist meets an art gallery owner and experiences five extraordinary days with him. C: P. J. Soles, David Hedison, Richard Deacon. DRA 97m. v

Awakening, The 1980 ★ Bram Stoker's novel *The Jewel of the Seven Stars* becomes an unintentionally laughable chiller about a young woman possessed by the spirit of an Egyptian queen unearthed by her archaeologist father (Heston). Played way too straight; the old mummy movies were more fun. C: Charlton Heston, Susannah York. D: Mike Newell. HOR [R] 101m. v

Awakenings 1990 ★★★★½ A shy but determined neurologist (Williams) manages to bring several catatonic patients out of their decades-long deep freeze, and suddenly they have lives, minus many years. High-powered cast, headed by the ever-versatile De Niro, energizes miraculous true story. Be warned, though; they do not live happily ever after. Based on Oliver Sacks's book. C: Robert De Niro, Robin Williams, Julie Kavner, Penelope Ann Miller, Max Von Sydow. D: Penny Marshall. DRA [PG-13] 120m. v

Away All Boats 1956 ★★½ Chandler commands an attack transport unit in the South Pacific, preparing his men to go into battle. Stiff and superpatriotic WWII action at sea. Good supporting cast. C: Jeff Chandler, George Nader, Julie Adams, Lex Barker. D: Joseph Pevney. ACT 114m. v

Awful Dr. Orloff, The 1961 Spanish ★★ A doctor performs suspicious operations on young women to provide body parts for his mangled daughter. Stylish horror flick has a cult following. C: Howard Vernon, Conrado Sanmartin. D: Jess Franco. HOR 95m.

Awful Truth, The 1937 ★★★★★ Delightful screwball comedy has unhappy couple (Grant, Dunne) divorcing so that they can both marry someone else, then doing everything they can to interfere with the other's upcoming nuptial plans. The sort of hilarious Hollywood farce they just don't make anymore, with comic timing raised to an art form. Oscar for Best Director. C: Irene Dunne, Cary Grant, Ralph Bellamy. D: Leo McCarey. COM 92m. v

Ay, Carmela! 1991 Spanish ★★★★½ Saura's Spanish Civil War tragedy is a neglected triumph. A theatrical troupe of husband, wife, and dim-witted sidekick perform for the Republican cause but get trapped behind fascist lines. This moving meditation on political responsibility features a force-of-nature performance by Maura that lights up the screen. C: Carmen Maura, Andres Pajares, Gabino Diego. D: Carlos Saura. DRA [PG-13] 105m. v

B

Babar: The Movie 1989 Canadian-French ★★★½ Jean and Laurent de Brunhoff's captivating creation, Babar the Elephant, appears in his first feature-length cartoon. Toddlers won't mind the crude animation; adults should keep a magazine handy. Voices of Gordon Pinsent, Gavin Magrath, Sarah Polley. D: Alan Bunce. FAM/DRA [G] 70m. V

Babbitt 1934 ★★½ Second film version (the first was a silent, done in 1924) of the celebrated Sinclair Lewis novel about small-town, small-minded America bears little likeness to the original story; retooled as a vehicle for the saucer-eyed Kibbee. C: Guy Kibbee, Aline MacMahon. D: William Keighley. DRA 74m.

Babe 1975 ★★★★ Sensitive, well-acted tear-jearker tells the true story of the legendary athlete Babe Didrickson Zaharias (Clark). Features an Emmy-winning performance by Clark and a solid job by ex-football player Karras as Babe's husband. C: Susan Clark, Alex Karras, Slim Pickens. D: Buzz Kulik. DRA 100m. TVM

Babe, The 1992 ★★★ In the best tradition of the Hollywood film biography, Babe Ruth's life is sanitized somewhat for family viewing. Goodman triumphs, however, as the complex "Bambino," capturing the baseball hero's essence both as man and enduring legend. Entertaining. C: John Goodman, Kelly McGillis, Trini Alvarado, Bruce Boxleitner. D: Arthur Hiller. DRA [PG] 115m. V

Babe Ruth Story, The 1948 ★★★ Long before John Goodman, Bendix did a commendable job portraying the life, and loves, of baseball's greatest superstar. A bit sappy, but a good feel for what the man was like. C: William Bendix, Claire Trevor, Charles Bickford, Sam Levene, William Frawley. D: Roy Del Ruth. DRA 107m. V

Babes in Arms 1939 ★★★★ The original Rooney/Garland "Hey kids, let's put on a show!" musical features the duo as perky protégés of retired vaudevillians, now ready to hit the boards themselves. Most of Rodgers and Hart's original Broadway music is gone, but this is still a shiny songfest. Fun family viewing. C: Mickey Rooney, Judy Garland, Charles Winninger, Guy Kibbee. D: Busby Berkeley. FAM/MUS 91m. V

Babes in Toyland 1934 ★★★★½ Victor Herbert's Mother Goose operetta has Bo Peep forced to marry the wicked Barnaby unless Laurel and Hardy can save her. Ideal fantasy for kids; fun for grown-ups, too, as stars' humor keeps the whimsy from becoming too cloying. (a.k.a. *The March of the Wooden Soldiers*) C: Stan Laurel, Oliver Hardy, Charlotte Henry, Henry Kleinbach, Felix Knight. D: Gus Meins, Charles Rogers. MUS 73m.

Babes in Toyland 1961 ★★½ Lush Disney interpretation of Victor Herbert's popular fantasy operetta. Wynn steals the show from young lovers Kirk and Funicello. Also see the 1934 Laurel and Hardy version. C: Ray Bolger, Tommy Sands, Annette Funicello, Ed Wynn. D: Jack Donohue. FAM/MUS 105m. V

Babes in Toyland 1986 ★★ Cloying, mediocre Leslie Bricusse score makes this slick retread of Victor Herbert's charming operetta a major disappointment. What was wrong with the original songs, only two of which remain? Skip it! C: Drew Barrymore, Richard Mulligan, Eileen Brennan, Keanu Reeves, Pat Morita. D: Clive Donner. FAM/MUS 150m. TVM V

Babes on Broadway 1941 ★★★½ Rousing "let's put on a show" nonsense makes a zippy vehicle for Mickey and Judy. Good musical numbers include "How About You" and "Hoe Down," and Mickey does an uncanny Carmen Miranda impersonation. Film ends poorly, though. C: Mickey Rooney, Judy Garland, Fay Bainter, Virginia Weidler, Donna Reed. D: Busby Berkeley. MUS 121m. V

Babette Goes to War 1959 French ★★½ Bardot, working for the British in 1940, is sent back to Paris to romantically a bait Nazi general and forestall London blitz. Picture tries to be light, but ends up heavy-footed. C: Brigitte Bardot, Jacques Charrier. D: Christian Jaque. COM 106m.

Babette's Feast 1987 Danish ★★★★★ Oscar-winning adaptation of an Isak Dinesen short story is sheer delight. In 18th-century Denmark, two elderly, devout sisters allow their expatriate French chef to prepare a sumptuous meal. The feast ultimately reveals family secrets in series of wonderful twists. Not to be missed. C: Stephane Audran, Jean-Philippe Lafont, Bibi Andersson, Birgitte Federspiel. D: Gabriel Axel. DRA [G] 102m. V

Baby and the Battleship, The 1956 British ★★★ Forerunner of the *Three Men and a Cradle* films, with Attenborough and Mills as two sailors hiding and caring for an Italian infant aboard ship. Mild service comedy is helped by good ensemble acting. C: John Mills, Richard Attenborough, Andre Morell, Michael Hordern. D: Jay Lewis. COM 96m.

Baby Blood *See* **The Evil Within**

Baby Blue Marine 1976 ★★★ Examination of small-town values begins after Vincent, as a Marine kicked out of boot camp, returns home impersonating a hero. Vincent wears his usual craggy opacity, and the photography is splendid. C: Jan-Michael Vincent, Glynnis O'Connor, Katherine Helmond, Richard Gere. D: John Hancock. DRA [PG] 90m.

Baby Boom 1987 ★★★★ A high-powered ad exec (Keaton) finds her life turned upside down when a long-lost relative's infant is put in her care. Formula comedy delivers laughs thanks to a snappy script and Keaton's comic ability. C: Diane Keaton, Harold Ramis, Sam Shepard, Sam Wanamaker, James Spader. D: Charles Shyer. COM [PG] 110m. V

Baby Comes Home 1980 ★★½ Dewhurst and Oates play middle-aged parents now raising their fourth child in this sequel to *And Baby Makes Six*. Wears thin quickly, but is helped by solid performances. C: Colleen Dewhurst, Warren Oates, Mildred Dunnock. D: Waris Hussein. DRA 100m. TVM

Baby Doll Murders, The 1992 ★★½ A sadistic killer always leaves a child's doll at the scene of his crimes. One investigator uncovers links among the murder victims and realizes his partner's spouse is probably next on the deadly list. Straightforward crime thriller. C: Jeff Kober, Melanie Smith, John Saxon, Tom Hodges. D: Paul Leder. CRI [R] 90m. V

Baby Doll 1956 ★★★★ Considered brash and vulgar at the time for its portrayal of a backwards Mississippi family, and the con artist who tries to exploit them, this is still steamy drama. Based on a Tennessee Williams story. C: Karl Malden, Carroll Baker, Eli Wallach, Mildred Dunnock, Rip Torn. D: Elia Kazan. DRA [R] 115m. V

Baby Face Harrington 1935 ★★★ A timid straight-arrow (Butterworth) is mistaken for a mobster, which gets him in hot water with both the real Mob and the cops. Mild comedy is helped immeasurably by marvelous supporting cast. C: Charles Butterworth, Una Merkel, Eugene Pallette, Harvey Stephens. D: Raoul Walsh. COM 61m.

Baby Face Nelson 1957 ★★★ Gangland activities in the 1930s, with Rooney chewing scenery as Nelson, and Jones playing a sultry moll. Rooney is too cherubic but still energetic, matching Siegel's high-voltage direction on a shoestring budget. C: Mickey Rooney, Carolyn Jones, Cedric Hardwicke. D: Don Siegel. CRI 85m.

Baby Face 1933 ★★★ Stanwyck plays a saloon gal who literally sleeps her way to top of society in this once scandalous but now rather moralistic look at how a woman can succeed in business. Watch for a young John Wayne in a supporting role. C: Barbara Stanwyck, George Brent, Donald Cook, Margaret Lindsay, John Wayne. D: Alfred E. Green. DRA 72m. V

Baby Girl Scott 1992 ★★ When a young couple's first child is dangerously premature, they discover the emotions that really hold them together. C: John Lithgow, Mary Beth Hurt, Linda Kelsey. D: John Korty. DRA 97m. V

Baby, It's You 1983 ★★★★ Amusing, sensitive romantic comedy about a middle-class Jewish teenager (Arquette) attracted to a blue-collar Roman Catholic young man (Spano) in '60s New Jersey suburbia. Lots of charm here, sharp observation of the period. C: Rosanna Arquette, Vincent Spano, Matthew Modine, Robert Downey Jr., Fisher Stevens. D: John Sayles. COM [R] 105m. V

Baby Love 1969 British ★★ A flirtatious young woman uses her sexual wiles to put an entire household under her spell. Meager drama. C: Ann Lynn, Linda Hayden, Keith Barron, Derek Lamden, Diana Dors. D: Alastair Reid. DRA [R] 98m. V

Baby M 1988 ★★★★ Well-done docudrama follows the explosive Mary Beth Whitehead case. Williams is riveting as the surrogate mother who reneges on her contract to bear a child for an affluent couple (Shea, Strasser) after the baby is born. C: JoBeth Williams, John Shea, Dabney Coleman, Bruce Weitz, Robin Strasser, Anne Jackson. D: James Sadwith. DRA 200m. TVM

Baby Maker, The 1970 ★★★ A straitlaced, childless couple (Groom and Wilcox-Horne) hire a Malibu hippie (Hershey) to be a surrogate mother. Sensitive treatment, but the characters lack depth, and the dialogue is weighed down by tinny "lifestyle" speeches. Scott Glenn's debut. C: Barbara Hershey, Colin Wilcox-Horne, Sam Groom, Scott Glenn, Jeannie Berlin. D: James Bridges. DRA [R] 109m. V

Baby of the Bride 1991 ★★ Older newlyweds contend with an unexpected discovery: at 53, she is pregnant with their first (her fifth) child. C: Rue McClanahan, Ted Shackelford, Kristy McNichol. D: Bill Bixby. COM 93m. TVM V

Baby on Board 1991 ★★½ An unassuming New York cabbie finds his life turned upside-down when a Mafia princess on the run accidentally leaves her young daughter in his cab. Action chase comedy revs high on sentiment but low on laughs. C: Judge Reinhold, Carol Kane, Geza Kovacs, Alex Stapley, Holly Stapley, Errol Slue. D: Francis A. Schaeffer. COM [PG] 90m. V

Baby . . . Secret of the Lost Legend 1985 ★★★ The baby dinosaur—a brontosaurus—discovered by Katt and Young is adorable, but taking it from its very protective mother is a big mistake! McGoohan is the villain in this uneven film, which veers from cute to violent too easily. May scare younger children. C: William Katt, Sean Young, Patrick McGoohan. D: B.W.L. Norton. FAM/ACT [PG] 95m.

Baby Snakes 1983 ★★ Zappa's home movie, featuring 15 Zappa compositions. Though many other musicians and colleagues are present, they rarely come between the filmmaker and the camera. With neat Claymation. C: Frank Zappa, Ron Delsener, Joey Psychotic. D: Frank Zappa. MUS 183m. V

Baby Take a Bow 1934 ★★★½ When her formerly felonious father is wrongly accused of stealing, little Shirley Temple pouts, smiles, sings and dances her innocent daddy out of the pokey. Temple's first starring feature is sweet and entertaining. Young children adore it. C: Shirley Temple, James Dunn, Claire Trevor. D: Harry Lachman. FAM/MUS 76m. V

Baby the Rain Must Fall 1964 ★★★½ A country singer on parole for stabbing a man returns home to his wife and daughter, but can't seem to shake his reckless habits. Emotionally hard-hitting, with strong performances. C: Lee Remick, Steve McQueen, Don Murray. D: Robert Mulligan. DRA 100m. V

Baby, The 1973 ★★½ Weird mix of horror and psychodrama, with a social worker (Comer) discovering that Roman's been rearing her now-teenaged son as an infant. Offbeat, but never quite as engrossing or scary as it wants to be. C: Anjanette Comer, Ruth Roman. D: Ted Post. HOR [PG] 80m. V

Babycakes 1989 ★★½ A tubby mortuary worker (Lake) is surprised to find love with the handsome Sheffer in this remake of Percy Adlon's *Sugarbaby*. Lake is undeniably charming, but the movie lacks the openness and sensuality of the German original. C: Ricki Lake, Craig Sheffer. D: Paul Schneider. DRA 100m. TVM V

Babyfever 1994 ★★★★ When a group of liberated women meet for a baby shower, the talk is frank and funny. No plot to speak of, but articulate dialogue and interesting characters make this an off-beat treat. C: Victoria Foyt, Dinah Lenney, Frances Fisher, Matt Salinger, Eric Roberts. D: Henry Jaglom. COM 110m.

Baby's Day Out 1994 ★★★ Mildly amusing Hughes offering, about a baby who eludes kidnappers through a series a mishaps. Sort of a *Home Alone* for toddlers. C: Joe Montegna, Joe Pantoliano, Brian Haley. D: Patrick Read Johnson. COM [PG] 98m.

Babysitter, The 1969 ★★ As the title character, Wymer seduces her employer, the prominent local D.A. Tries to be titillating, but tame by contemporary standards. C: Patricia Wymer, George Carey, Ann Bellamy. D: Don Henderson. COM [R] 70m.

Babysitter, The 1975 Italian ★★ A babysitter (Schneider) finds herself tricked into the kidnapping of her ward. Plodding European-made feature; insipid acting and worse direction. (a.k.a. *The Raw Edge*). C: Maria Schneider, Sydne Rome, Vic Morrow, Robert Vaughn. D: Rene Clement. CRI 111m.

Bacall on Bogart ★★ Profile of Humphrey Bogart, narrated by Lauren Bacall, includes outtakes, film clips, and recollections of friends. C: Lauren Bacall, Humphrey Bogart. DOC 90m. V

Bach and Broccoli 1986 ★★ When a man's orphaned niece is returned to foster care, he discovers how important she was to him. C: Mahee Paiement, Raymond Legault. D: Andre Melancon. FAM/DRA 96m. V

Bachelor and the Bobby-Soxer, The 1947 ★★★★ Hoping to cure her starry-eyed baby sister (Temple) of a teenaged crush, a judge (Loy) sentences a playboy (Grant) to escort the adolescent. Great fun, with clever repartee between Grant and Loy and one of Temple's best post-child star roles. Oscar for Best Screenplay—to Sidney Sheldon! C: Cary Grant, Myrna Loy, Shirley Temple, Rudy Vallee. D: Irving Reis. COM 95m. V

Bachelor Apartment 1931 ★★★½ Neat little comedy about a debonair bachelor (Sherman) who is both pursuer and pursued. Silent star Murray plays one of his admirers. C: Lowell Sherman, Irene Dunne, Mae Murray. D: Lowell Sherman. COM 77m. V

Bachelor Bait 1934 ★★ Organizer of lonely-hearts club finds romance with assistance of his secretary. C: Stuart Erwin, Rochelle Hudson. D: George Stevens. COM 75m. V

Bachelor Bait 1949 *See* **Adventure in Baltimore**

Bachelor Father, The 1931 ★★★ Smith repeated his stage role as an elderly, much-married English gentleman who seeks out his three illegitimate adult children (Davies, Milland, and Quartaro) in this solid adaptation of Edward Childs Carpenter's play. C: Marion Davies, Ralph Forbes, C. Aubrey Smith, Ray Milland. D: Robert Z. Leonard. DRA 90m.

Bachelor Flat 1961 ★★ Terry-Thomas is a British professor on leave in America, trying to fend off the inappropriate attentions of his hostess's daughter (Weld). Some good sight gags. C: Tuesday Weld, Richard Beymer, Celeste Holm, Terry-Thomas. D: Frank Tashlin. COM 91m.

Bachelor in Paradise 1961 ★★★ Lesser Hope comedy finds Old Ski Nose as an author who's the only single man in a neighborhood full of married couples. His attempts to document the community lead to some humorous situations. C: Bob Hope, Lana Turner, Janis Paige, Jim Hutton, Paula Prentiss, Agnes Moorehead. D: Jack Arnold. COM 109m. V

Bachelor Mother 1939 ★★★★½ Madcap romp of a virtuous woman (Rogers) who finds an abandoned baby on her doorstep and must cope with everyone thinking she's the infant's mother. Excellent example of '30's Hollywood humor; directed by noted comedy screenwriter Kanin. Fun for the entire family. Later remade as *Bundle of Joy*. C: Ginger Rogers, David Niven, Charles Coburn. D: Garson Kanin. COM 82m. V

Bachelor Party, The 1957 ★★★★ Deft slice-of-life drama about louts giving bachelor party for a bookkeeper. Bleak, well scripted by Paddy Chayefsky. Jones steals it with her portrait of a party girl. C: Don Murray, E. G. Marshall, Jack Warden, Patricia Smith, Carolyn Jones, Larry Blyden. D: Delbert Mann. DRA 93m.

Bachelor Party 1984 ★★★½ Before Hanks

says "I do," his buddies plan the bachelor party to end all bachelor parties. Sophomoric gross-out comedy works on its own level, especially the flippant, throwaway performance by young Hanks. C: Tom Hanks, Tawny Kitaen, Adrian Zmed, George Grizzard. D: Neal Israel. COM [R] 105m. v

Back Door to Heaven 1939 ★★★ A poor young man must choose between a life of crime with easy money and one of hard work with poverty. Mixture of familiar '30s themes of drama and social commentary, effectively realized. C: Wallace Ford, Aline MacMahon, Van Heflin. D: William Howard. CRI 85m.

Back Door to Hell 1964 ★★½ This film about G.I.s under MacArthur's command in the Philippines is adequate, though familiar, and the first of several collaborations between director Hellman and actor (and occasional screenwriter) Nicholson. C: Jimmie Rodgers, Jack Nicholson, John Hackett. D: Monte Hellman. ACT 68m.

Back From Eternity 1956 ★★½ An airliner crashes in the South American jungle, and the survivors must learn to cooperate and work their way back to civilization. Cheesy melodrama is a variation on several older movies, including *Five Came Back*. Ryan is excellent as the alcoholic pilot, though. C: Robert Ryan, Anita Ekberg, Rod Steiger. D: John Farrow. ACT 97m. v

Back From the Dead 1957 ★★ On her honeymoon, Castle becomes possessed by the evil spirit of her husband's dead first wife. Bafflingly and weird horror tale, part *Rebecca*, part *Blithe Spirit*. C: Peggie Castle, Arthur Franz. D: Charles Warren. HOR 79m.

Back Home 1990 British ★★★ When World War II ends, an adolescent girl who had been staying in America for safety returns to her family in England. Fair family drama. C: Hayley Mills, Hayley Carr, Rupert Frazer, Jean Anderson, Brenda Bruce. D: Piers Haggard. DRA 103m. TVM v

Back in the USSR 1991 ★★★ An American (Whaley) vacationing in Moscow is caught up in a search for a stolen rare book. Despite its authentic locations and status as the first American film shot entirely in Russia, glasnost cannot save this weakly scripted mystery. C: Frank Whaley, Natalya Negoda, Roman Polanski. D: Deran Serafian. CRI [R] 88m. v

Back Roads 1980 ★★½ A prostitute and inept pugilist butt heads, then steal each other's hearts as they travel across America together. Pleasant enough, but easily forgettable. C: Sally Field, Tommy Lee Jones, David Keith. D: Martin Ritt. COM 94m. v

Back Street 1932 ★★★★ First of three versions of the Fannie Hurst weepie, with Dunne suffering nobly as the longtime mistress of married industrialist (Boles). Well-acted, landmark melodrama. C: Irene Dunne, John Boles, ZaSu Pitts, Jane Darwell. D: John Stahl. DRA 89m.

Back Street 1941 ★★★½ Second version of Fannie Hurst's romance about an executive (Boyer) who marries another woman while his mistress (Sullavan) refuses to let their relationship end. Good chemistry between the leads animates this soap opera. C: Margaret Sullavan, Charles Boyer, Richard Carlson, Frank McHugh, Tim Holt. D: Robert Stevenson. DRA 89m.

Back Street 1961 ★★★ Fannie Hurst's three-hankie story of heroine's lengthy affair with wealthy married man is given glossy, fashion-plate treatment that almost overwhelms the simple story. Hayward's trapped beneath the glitter. C: Susan Hayward, John Gavin, Vera Miles. D: David Miller. DRA 107m. v

Back to Bataan 1945 ★★★★ While waiting for American reinforcements during WWII, stalwart officer (Wayne) organizes a Filipino guerrilla platoon and leads raids on Japanese troops. Solid war picture with some exciting action scenes. Wayne is at his rugged best. C: John Wayne, Anthony Quinn, Beulah Bondi. D: Edward Dmytryk. ACT 95m. v

Back to God's Country 1953 ★★★ A boat captain (Hudson) must fight the brutal Canadian tundra and defend his wife (Henderson) and cargo from slimy Cochran. Okay action-adventure, inferior to similar pictures but oddly enjoyable. C: Rock Hudson, Marcia Henderson, Steve Cochran, Hugh O'Brian. D: Joseph Pevney. ACT 78m.

Back to Hannibal: The Return of Tom Sawyer and Huckleberry Finn 1990 ★★ Grown-up Tom and Huck, as attorney and journalist, attempt to exonerate ex-slave Jim in the murder of Becky Thatcher's husband. The actors comport themselves with as much dignity as possible. C: Raphael Sbarge, Megan Follows, William Windom, Paul Winfield, Ned Beatty. D: Paul Krasny. DRA 92m. TVM

Back to School 1986 ★★★★ Seeking respect from his college-bound son, a self-made millionaire (Dangerfield) decides to follow him and get a degree himself. Lots of good Dangerfield one-liners make this spoof of higher education a laugh-filled treat. C: Rodney Dangerfield, Sally Kellerman, Burt Young, Robert Downey Jr., Ned Beatty. D: Alan Metter. COM [PG-13] 91m. v

Back to the Beach 1987 ★★★ Frankie and Annette are 20 years older but their comeback vehicle is as harmlessly silly as any of their "beach party" films. Multitude of cameos by sitcom and '60s music stars make this a must for nostalgia buffs. C: Frankie Avalon, Annette Funicello, Connie Stevens, Don Adams, Bob Denver, Alan Hale, Jerry Mathers, Tony Dow, Barbara Billingsley, Edd Byrnes. D: Lyndall Hobbs. MUS [PG] 92m. v

Back to the Forest 1989 Japanese ★★★ When a devouring business conglomerate sets its sights on a peaceful forest, one brave sprite leads his animal friends in a fight to save their home. Amiable message film for kids through animation. D: Yoshio Koruda. FAM/DRA 75m. v

Back to the Future 1985 ★★★★ A 1980s high school student (Fox) treks to the 1950s via a time machine built by a scientist (Lloyd). Once there, he must fix up his future parents to guarantee his own existence! Charming, silly, and occasionally wicked humor marks a nifty blend of science fiction and comedy, and Fox shines throughout. Two sequels followed. C: Michael J. Fox, Christopher Lloyd, Crispin Glover, Lea Thompson, Thomas F. Wilson. D: Robert Zemeckis. COM [PG] 116m. v

Back to the Future Part II 1989 ★★★ Rehash of *Back to the Future* has Fox and Lloyd taking time traveling Delorean through past, present, and future. Concepts originated in *Part I* get worked over without much freshness and film quickly grows tired. Shot simultaneously with *Part III*. C: Michael J. Fox, Christopher Lloyd, Lea Thompson, Thomas F. Wilson, Elisabeth Shue. D: Robert Zemeckis. COM [PG] 108m. v

Back to the Future Part III 1990 ★★★★ Another trip to the past—this time to the Old West, where Fox must save Lloyd from gunslingers. Terrific chase sequence combines anachronisms, stunts, and special effects for an exciting climax that nicely caps the *Back to the Future* series. C: Michael J. Fox, Christopher Lloyd, Mary Steenburgen, Thomas F. Wilson, Lea Thompson, Elisabeth Shue, Richard Dysart. D: Robert Zemeckis. COM [PG] 118m. v

Back to the Wall 1959 French ★★★ Moreau is an unfaithful wife, flaunting her infidelity and her lavish clothes, until a murder scheme threatens to catch up with her. Classy thriller gives Moreau an early role that later became her trademark. Worth a look. C: Gerard Oury, Jeanne Moreau. D: Edouard Molinaro. CRI 94m.

Backbeat 1994 ★★★½ Intriguing chronicle of the early days of the Beatles (1960), particularly concentrating on John Lennon and Stu Sutcliffe, the group's original bassist. Honest, episodic portrait. C: Sheryl Lee, Steven Dorff, Ian Hart, Gary Bakewell, Chris O'Neill, Scot Williams, Kai Weisinger, Carlton Williams, Sharif Rashed, Spike Lee. D: Iain Softley. MUS 100m.

Backdraft 1991 ★★★½ Two brothers (Russell and Baldwin) on the same fire department bicker melodramatically while pyrotechnics and De Niro, as an arson investigator, steal the show. Spectacular special effects highlight this ode to fire and firemen (but mostly fire). C: Kurt Russell, William Baldwin, Robert De Niro, Donald Sutherland, Jennifer Jason Leigh, Scott Glenn, Rebecca De Mornay. D: Ron Howard. DRA [R] 135m. v

Backfield in Motion 1991 ★★★½ A single mom (Arnold) tries to start a high school mother-son football league. Pleasant comedy, with likable Roseanne. C: Roseanne Arnold, Tom Arnold, Colleen Camp, Conchata Ferrell. D: Richard Michaels. COM 95m. TVM v

Backfire 1950 ★★★ MacRae and a nurse (Mayo) search for their pal (O'Brien), who's been kidnapped by a high-rolling mobster. Tight, well-paced thriller, though one expects MacRae to burst into song. C: Virginia Mayo, Gordon MacRae, Edmond O'Brien, Viveca Lindfors, Ed Begley. D: Vincent Sherman. CRI 91m.

Backfire 1988 U. S. ★★★★ A wealthy, unbalanced Vietnam veteran (Fahey) is slowly being driven mad, but by whom? Slick and entertaining psychological thriller develops a neat set of thrills. C: Karen Allen, Keith Carradine, Dean Martin, Dinah Manoff. D: Gilbert Cates. CRI [R] 90m. v

Background to Danger 1943 ★★★★ Trying to stop Turkish forces from allying with the Nazis during WWII, an American spy (Raft) heads overseas to deal with a German agent (Greenstreet) and a Turkish official (Lorre). Energetically paced, well-done wartime intrigue. C: George Raft, Brenda Marshall, Sydney Greenstreet, Peter Lorre. D: Raoul Walsh. ACT 81m. v

Backlash 1947 ★★ Travis tries to frame spouse Rogers for murder he committed. Overly familiar but watchable, this quickie took a full 17 days to film. C: Jean Rogers, Richard Travis. D: Eugene Forde. CRI 66m.

Backlash 1956 ★★★ Surviving a massacre by Apaches, Widmark searches for his father, who sold out his family and partners. Ambitious psychological western, written by genre craftsman Borden Chase (*Red River*, etc.). C: Richard Widmark, Donna Reed. D: John Sturges. WST 84m.

Backlash 1987 Australian ★★½ Australian cops (Argue and Miller) have difficulty escorting an insolent aborigine (Carides), accused of castrating and murdering her rapist boss, across the Outback. Obscure drama takes a stab at racial and sexual themes; interesting but unsatisfying. C: David Argue, Gia Carides, Lydia Miller. D: Bill Bennett. DRA [R] 89m. v

Backstab 1990 ★★½ After his wife passes away, an architect (Brolin) becomes involved with a married woman who draws him into a web of murder. Weak rehash of *Fatal Attraction*'s plot gets routine and unsurprising treatment. C: James Brolin, Dorothee Berryman, Meg Foster, Isabelle Truchon, June Chadwick, Brett Halsey. D: James Kaufman. DRA [R] 91m. v

Backstage at the Kirov 1984 ★★★½ The famed Russian dance troupe is shown rehearsing and performing *Swan Lake*. Interesting more for its rare glimpse at the large international artists' group than for its beautiful dancing. C: Galina Mezentxseva, Konstantin Zaklinsky. D: Derek Hart. DOC 80m. V

Backtrack 1989 ★★★½ An assassin (Hopper) is assigned to kill Foster (who witnessed a previous murder) but falls in love with her and can't follow through. Uneven mob thriller features a tremendous cast, including several unbilled appearances (like Joe Pesci's). C: Dennis Hopper, Jodie Foster, Dean Stockwell, Vincent Price, John Turturro, Charlie Sheen, Bob Dylan. D: Dennis Hopper. CRI [R] 105m. V

Bad and the Beautiful, The 1952 ★★★★½ A ruthless Hollywood producer (Douglas) is remembered by an actress (Turner), a director (Sullivan), and a writer (Powell) who were made and then discarded by him. Biting, brilliant drama takes a jaundiced inside look at the film industry (Douglas' character was reputedly based on David O. Selznick). Oscars for Best Supporting Actress (Grahame), Screenplay, Costumes, Art Direction, and Cinematography. C: Kirk Douglas, Lana Turner, Dick Powell, Gloria Grahame, Barry Sullivan, Walter Pidgeon, Gilbert Roland. D: Vincente Minnelli. DRA 123m. V

Bad Attitude 1993 ★★ Cop in search of partner's murderer falls in love with woman who turns out to be implicated in the killing. C: Leon, Gina Lim. D: Bill Cummings. ACT 87m. V

Bad Bascomb 1946 ★★ A blustery but soft-hearted bank robber (Beery) leads Mormons through the mountains. Decent direction and photography fail to compensate for cloying script. C: Wallace Beery, Margaret O'Brien, Marjorie Main. D: S. Simon. WST 110m.

Bad Behavior 1993 ★★★ Suburban intrigue in a lower-class English neighborhood includes references to a shifty con artist, a housewife's midlife crisis, and a disputable bathroom remodeling. Sorely lacks a screenplay. C: Stephen Rea, Sinead Cusack. D: Les Blair. COM [R] 103m. V

Bad Blood 1981 New Zealand ★★★★ Exciting man-hunt drama about a New Zealand farmer/murderer (Thompson) used by the Nazis for propaganda purposes during WWII. An early gem from director Newell (*Four Weddings and a Funeral*). C: Jack Thompson, Carol Burns, Donna Akersten, Denis Lill. D: Mike Newell. CRI 104m. V

Bad Blood 1987 French ★★★ Allegorical attempt at AIDS drama involves an attempt to steal medicine that cures a rare blood disorder. Interesting in parts; mostly notable for appearance of the talented Binoche. C: Michel Piccoli, Denis Lavant, Juliette Binoche. D: Leos Carax. DRA [R] 128m.

Bad Blood 1989 ★★½ A psycho mother (Raymond) can't let go of her grown son (Patrick), much to the chagrin of her daughter-in-law (Blair). Potentially interesting erotic thriller with all the trimmings (including considerable nudity). (a.k.a. *A Woman Obsessed*) C: Gregory Patrick, Linda Blair, Ruth Raymond, Troy Donahue. D: Chuck Vincent. DRA [R] 104m.

Bad Boy 1949 ★★½ Chip-on-his-shoulder teenager (Murphy) is sent to a ranch for delinquent boys, where the director learns the boy thinks he killed his own mother. A contrived, film noir *Boys Town* that still manages to produce some tension. (a.k.a. *The Story of Danny Lester*) C: Lloyd Nolan, Jane Wyatt, Audie Murphy, James Gleason, Dickie Moore. D: Kurt Neumann. DRA 86m.

Bad Boys 1982 ★★★★ Very violent, street-wise tale of two rival gang leaders who begin a vicious cycle of revenge leading to a prison confrontation. Diverse, convincing characters and powerful work by Penn and Morales make this a superior look at disenfranchised urban youth. Sheedy's film debut. C: Sean Penn, Reni Santoni, Esai Morales, Ally Sheedy. D: Rick Rosenthal. CRI 123m. V

Bad Channels 1992 ★★ A big-headed alien takes over a radio station and uses music-video hallucinations (don't ask) to entrap women, whom it then shrinks to a foot high. Chintzy, nonsensical horror comedy, though a couple of the musical numbers are fun. C: Paul Hipp, Martha Quinn, Aaron Lustig, Ian Patrick Williams. D: Ted Nicolaou. HOR [R] 90m. V

Bad Company 1931 ★★½ A mobster (Cortez) infiltrates a rival gangster's operation by having his attorney marry the rival's sister (Twelvetrees), but the plan backfires. Creaky crime film, still watchable for Cortez's theatrical villainy. C: Ricardo Cortez, Helen Twelvetrees, John Garrick. D: Tay Garnett. CRI 75m.

Bad Company 1972 ★★★★ Personality opposites Bridges and Brown team up in 1863 for a series of robberies that divert them from Civil War conflicts. Alternately funny and thrilling, this action-packed historical film flourishes under marvelously energetic direction and an offbeat lead duo. C: Jeff Bridges, Barry Brown, Jim Davis. D: Robert Benton. ACT [PG] 94m. V

Bad Company 1995 ★★★½ Company guilty of toxic waste poisoning hires an ex-CIA agent (Fishburne) to bribe the judge on the pending lawsuit. Overly complex but stylish thriller, with strong performances. C: Laurence Fishburne, Ellen Barkin, Frank Langella, Spalding Gray, David Ogden Stiers. D: Damian Harris. CRI [R] 108m. V

Bad Day at Black Rock 1954 ★★★★½ A crippled war veteran (Tracy) steps off a train at a sleepy western town and discovers a deadly secret when he tries to find the father of the soldier who saved his life during battle. Tense drama keeps a quick, suspenseful pace, leading to a dynamic finale; a striking adaptation of "Bad Time at Hondo," by Howard Breslin. C: Spencer Tracy, Robert Ryan, Anne Francis, Dean Jagger, Walter

Brennan, Ernest Borgnine, Lee Marvin. D: John Sturges. WST 82m. V

Bad Dreams 1988 ★ The young survivor of a Jonestown-type massacre hallucinates that the dead cult leader is coming back to get her. Or *are* they hallucinations? Owes a large debt to the *Nightmare on Elm Street* films, with a slick look that is at odds with its cheapjack storytelling. C: Jennifer Rubin, Bruce Abbott, Richard Lynch, Harris Yulin, Susan Ruttan. D: Andrew Fleming. HOR [R] 84m. V

Bad For Each Other 1953 ★★ Matured by Army service, a physician (Heston) learns there's more to his Pennsylvania hometown than the society people he derides. Updated, Americanized variation of A. J. Cronin's *The Citadel* drowns in suds, though Heston is surprisingly believable. C: Charlton Heston, Lizabeth Scott, Dianne Foster, Mildred Dunnock, Marjorie Rambeau. D: Irving Rapper. DRA 83m.

Bad Georgia Road 1977 ★★ Law officers and competing criminals try to track down rum runners for control of their loot. C: Royal Dano. D: John C. Broderick. ACT [R] 85m. V

Bad Girl 1931 ★★★½ Boy and girl meet at Coney Island, get married, have baby, become estranged, are reunited. Though quite melodramatic, this early talkie was quite popular and was nominated for several Academy Awards, including Best Picture and Best Director. C: Sally Eilers, James Dunn, Minna Gombell. D: Frank Borzage. DRA 90m.

Bad Girls 1994 ★★ Four prostitutes form a gun-toting gang in this feminist western. Draws a blank, due to modern tone at odds with period setting. Talented cast is wasted. C: Madeleine Stowe, Mary Stuart Masterson, Andie MacDowell, Drew Barrymore, Dermot Mulroney, Robert Loggia. D: Jonathan Kaplan. WST [R] 99m. V

Bad Girls Dormitory 1984 ★★ Exploitation picture details brutal goings-on in another female prison. Sleazy. C: Carey Zuris, Teresa Farley. D: Tim Kincaid. ACT 95m. V

Bad Girls from Mars 1990 ★ Panting bedroom frolics of an actress from Europe purportedly in Hollywood to star in a sci-fi movie. Dud. C: Edy Williams, Brinke Stevens, Jay Richardson. D: Fred Olen Ray. SFI [R] 86m. V

Bad Girls in the Movies 1986 ★★ Film clips about notorious women in films including convicts and prostitutes. What you see is what you get. C: David Carradine, Yvonne De Carlo, Gene Autry. DRA 56m. V

Bad Guys 1986 ★ Suspended from the force, two young cops (Baldwin and Jolly) become professional wrestlers. Steroids and bum jokes, for hard-core pro wrestling fans only. C: Adam Baldwin, Mike Jolly, Ruth Buzzi. D: Joel Silberg. COM [PG] 87m. V

Bad Influence 1990 ★★★½ Creepy Lowe aids financial analyst (Spader) in a barroom altercation, then slowly takes over his life. Faustian script tightens the suspense and Spader's sense of helplessness; excellent performances from both leads. C: Rob Lowe, James Spader, Lisa Zane. D: Curtis Hanson. CRI [R] 99m. V

Bad Lieutenant 1992 ★★★½ A deeply corrupt cop (Keitel) gets one last chance at redemption when he investigates the brutal rape of a nun. Extremely violent depiction of one man's hell is notable for Keitel's brave performance. C: Harvey Keitel, Frankie Thorn, Paul Hipp. D: Abel Ferrara. CRI [R] 91m. V

Bad Lord Byron 1951 British ★★ On his deathbed, the great poet recalls his adventures and loves. Price is miscast in this stilted, episodic costume piece. Greenwood, as a stunning Lady Caroline Lamb, almost makes up for the rest of the picture. C: Dennis Price, Joan Greenwood, Mai Zetterling. D: David Macdonald. DRA 85m.

Bad Man of Brimstone 1938 ★★★ Crusty old Beery renounces his criminal ways after reunion with son. Sentimental Western tailor-made for Beery; look for Wallace's half brother Noah in supporting role. Script is by Richard Maibaum, who wrote early James Bond movies. C: Wallace Beery, Virginia Bruce, Dennis O'Keefe, Lewis Stone, Guy Kibbee, Bruce Cabot. D: J. Ruben. WST 90m.

Bad Man, The 1941 ★★★ A south-of-the-border bandit (Beery) aids a longtime pal (Barrymore) and two young lovers (Day and Reagan). Western comedy makes a fair vehicle for Beery, lighter and more likable here than usual. C: Wallace Beery, Lionel Barrymore, Laraine Day, Ronald Reagan, Henry Travers. D: Richard Thorpe. WST 70m.

Bad Manners 1984 ★★ When one of five children in orphanage is adopted, the four left attempt to return their "brother" to the orphanage. C: Martin Mull, Karen Black, Anne DeSalvo. D: Bobby Houston. COM [R] 85m. V

Bad Man's River 1972 Italian ★★ Van Cleef and cronies are offered $1 million to blow up a Mexican arsenal, but Lollobrigida is always there to stop them. Spanish-produced Western comedy can't decide what it wants to be. C: Lee Van Cleef, James Mason, Gina Lollobrigida. D: Eugenio Martin. WST [PG] 92m. V

Bad Medicine 1985 ★★ Med school reject (Guttenberg) heads south of the border to attend a fifth-rate med school, but suffers a crisis of conscience when he sees the locals in dire need. Slapstick. C: Steve Guttenberg, Alan Arkin, Julie Hagerty, Bill Macy, Julie Kavner, Gilbert Gottfried. D: Harvey Miller. COM [PG-13] 97m. V

Bad Men of Missouri 1941 ★★ The Younger Brothers are forced into criminal activity to confront slimy carpetbaggers. Appealing cast in a thoroughly fictionalized attempt to recast Western villains as heroes. C: Dennis Morgan, Jane Wyman, Wayne Morris, Arthur Kennedy, Victor Jory. D: Ray Enright. WST 74m.

Bad Men of Tombstone 1949 ★★★½ Bleak, unsentimental Western about a pair of irredeemable gunslingers. Surprisingly violent for its time, though filmmakers clearly condemn the behavior they chronicle. Interesting shoot-'em-up. C: Barry Sullivan, Marjorie Reynolds, Broderick Crawford, Fortunio Bonanova, Guinn "Big Boy" Williams, John Kellogg. D: Kurt Neumann. WST 74m. v

Bad News Bears Go To Japan, The 1978 ★★ Band of misfits goes international as an unscrupulous promoter attempts to turn their appeal into big bucks for himself. Lackluster third film in the series strikes out by adding nothing new to the lineup. C: Tony Curtis, Jackie Earle Haley, Tomisaburo Wakayama. D: John Berry. COM [PG] 102m. v

Bad News Bears in Breaking Training, The 1977 ★★★½ The foul-mouthed little leaguers return a little sappier and a lot cleaner as their ace hitter takes the team on the road to the Astrodome, where he convinces his estranged father to helm the team. Not as memorable as the original, but still a solid outing. C: William Devane, Jackie Earle Haley, Jimmy Baio. D: Michael Pressman. COM [PG] 97m. v

Bad News Bears, The 1976 ★★★★½ Beer-guzzling pool man turns a bunch of misfits into a contending little league team thanks to a female fastballer. Walter and Tatum are a winning combo as this good-natured satire scores big with a hilarious, insightful story. C: Walter Matthau, Tatum O'Neal, Vic Morrow, Joyce Van Patten, Jackie Earle Haley. D: Michael Ritchie. COM [PG] 102m. v

Bad Ronald 1974 ★★★ A family moves into their new home, unaware that a demented teenage killer has taken refuge and secretly observes them from his hidden room. Seems a bit long, but very suspenseful. C: Scott Jacoby, Pippa Scott, Dabney Coleman, Kim Hunter. D: Buzz Kulik. HOR 78m. TVM v

Bad Seed, The 1956 ★★★★ If six-year-old (McCormack) is as sweet as mother thinks she is, why does everyone around her die? Gripping suspense from Maxwell Anderson play, with good cast sinking their teeth into the taut script. C: Nancy Kelly, Patty McCormack, Eileen Heckart. D: Mervyn Le Roy. DRA 129m. v

Bad Seed, The 1985 ★★★ Okay remake of 1956 thriller about a malevolent child and hysterical mother lacks the impact of the original, but gets by just the same. C: Blair Brown, Lynn Redgrave, David Carradine, Richard Kiley, David Ogden Stiers. D: Paul Wendkos. DRA 100m.

Bad Sleep Well, The 1960 Japanese ★★★★ A rising corporate star (Mifune) marries the company president's daughter, looking for revenge for his father's murder. Complex, scathing indictment of corporate corruption. C: Toshiro Mifune, Takeshi Kato, Masayuki Mori. D: Akira Kurosawa. DRA 152m. v

Bad Taste 1988 New Zealand ★★★ Aliens wipe out a small seaside New Zealand town, collecting humans for a fast-food chain back home. A low-budget spoof, as crazy as it sounds. C: Peter Jackson, Pete O'Herne. D: Peter Jackson. SFI 90m. v

Bad Timing: A Sensual Obsession 1980 British ★★★★ A psychiatrist becomes obsessed with a loose woman. Fascinating and provocative. C: Art Garfunkel, Theresa Russell, Harvey Keitel, Denholm Elliott, Daniel Massey. D: Nicolas Roeg. DRA [R] 129m.

Badge of Marshal Brennan, The 1957 ★★½ On-the-lam outlaw (Davis) stops running to impersonate a lawman who's near death, and seeks redemption when he goes up against gunslinging rustlers. Watchable Western, with craggy Davis in solid form. C: Jim Davis, Arleen Whelan, Lee Van Cleef. D: Albert C. Grannaway. WST 74m.

Badge of the Assassin 1985 ★★★★½ When radicals knock off a pair of cops patrolling Harlem, a detective (Kotto) and a district attorney (Woods) enter an absorbing investigation to find the murderers. Tense, exciting drama, bolstered by strong performances. Based on a true case. C: James Woods, Yaphet Kotto, Alex Rocco, Pam Grier, Rae Dawn Chong. D: Mel Damski. CRI 96m. TVM v

Badge or the Cross, The 1973 ★★½ Police Sgt. Sam Cavanaugh (Kennedy) figures he can better serve the community by trading his gun for a clerical collar and becoming Father Cavanaugh. This sudsy movie begat the early-'70s TV series *Sarge*, also starring Kennedy. C: George Kennedy, Ricardo Montalban. D: Richard Colla. DRA

Badge 373 1973 ★★½ Quasi-sequel to *The French Connection* stars Duvall in Gene Hackman's role, battling Mob forces and Puerto Rican gunrunners. Plenty of hard-nosed action; catch former cop Egan (whose exploits inspired *The French Connection*) in supporting role. C: Robert Duvall, Verna Bloom, Henry Darrow. D: Howard Koch. ACT [R] 116m. v

Badlanders, The 1958 ★★★½ A pair of Arizona outlaws nearly outwit each other in their plot to steal a massive goldmine shipment. Remake of *The Asphalt Jungle* in a Western setting, filled with exciting action sequences. C: Alan Ladd, Ernest Borgnine, Katy Jurado. D: Delmer Daves. WST 83m. v

Badlands

Badlands 1973 ★★★★ Dreamy teen (Spacek) narrates, romance-novel style, her life on the run with a garbage collector/psychopath (Sheen), who leads her on a trail of violence to Montana's Badlands. Very effective. Loosely based on the Starkweather and Fugate killings of the 1950s. C: Martin Sheen, Sissy Spacek, Warren Oates. D: Terence Malick. CRI [PG] 97m. v

Badlands of Dakota 1941 ★★½ Young

Stack wins out against older brother Crawford for Rutherford's affections, but has a tougher time as sheriff taming the territory. Decent B-Western, though Stack and Crawford are never quite believable as the Holliday Brothers. C: Robert Stack, Ann Rutherford, Richard Dix, Frances Farmer, Broderick Crawford. D: Alfred Green. WST 74m.

Badman's Country 1958 ★★ Loopy Western pits good guys Pat Garrett, Wyatt Earp, and Buffalo Bill against bad guy Butch Cassidy (played by Brand). C: George Montgomery, Buster Crabbe, Neville Brand. D: Fred Sears. WST 68m.

Badman's Territory 1946 ★★★ A Texas sheriff (Scott) encounters a famed outlaw gang while searching for his younger brother. Routine western might please oater fans. Available in original black-and-white and colorized editions. C: Randolph Scott, Ann Richards, George "Gabby" Hayes, Ray Collins. D: Tim Whelan. WST 79m. V

Baffled 1972 ★★½ Nimoy plays a race car driver with a sixth sense concerning danger to people in his field of vision. Excellent cast raises silly material a notch or two. C: Leonard Nimoy, Susan Hampshire, Vera Miles, Rachel Roberts. D: Phillip Leacock. ACT 101m. V

Bagdad Cafe 1988 West German ★★★★ A staid German traveler (Sagebrecht) walks out on her husband in the middle of the Mojave desert and ends up at a dreary little roadside rest stop run by sassy Pounder. Offbeat character comedy features winning performances, especially by Palance as an esoteric artist. C: Marianne Sagebrecht, CCH Pounder, Jack Palance, Christine Kaufmann. D: Percy Adlon. COM [PG] 91m. V

Bagdad 1949 ★★ A British-educated princess (O'Hara) returns home to the title city upon her father's assassination, then helps a tribal leader, accused of the murder, prove his innocence. Silly swashbuckler with stunning O'Hara and Technicolor. C: Maureen O'Hara, Paul Christian, Vincent Price. D: Charles Lamont. ACT 82m.

Bahama Passage 1941 ★★★ Cosmopolitan Madeleine Carroll wants to stay on lovely West Indies isle, but complications ensue when Hayden steps onto the sand. Slight romance is easy to look at, with lovely settings and a sterling supporting cast, including teenaged Dorothy Dandridge. C: Madeleine Carroll, Sterling Hayden, Flora Robson, Leo G. Carroll. D: Edward Griffith. DRA 83m.

Bail Jumper 1990 ★★ Comedic adventures of an ex-con and gangster who falls in love and moves to New York. C: Eszter Balint, Joie Lee. D: Christian Faber. COM 96m. V

Bail Out 1990 ★★ Bounty hunters try to find a kidnapped heiress. C: Linda Blair, David Hasselhoff, John Vernon. D: Max Kleven. ACT [R] 88m. V

Bailiff, The 1954 *See* **Sansho the Bailiff**

Bailout at 43,000 1957 ★★ A test pilot (Payne) suffers a crisis of conscience after refusing to try a new ejection seat. Service drama means to be stirring but just hangs there. C: John Payne, Karen Steele, Constance Ford. D: Francis Lyon. DRA 78m. V

Bait 1954 ★★ Romantic triangle creates trouble for panting goldminers, and the woman who comes between them. Classically sleazy B-picture. Interesting pretitle Lucifer sequence. C: Cleo Moore, Hugo Haas, John Agar. D: Hugo Haas. DRA 79m.

Baja Oklahoma 1988 ★★★½ When she's not involved in an ill-fated love affair, a Texas barmaid writes songs and dreams of country-western stardom. Energetic, appealing period piece. Excellent music. C: Lesley Ann Warren, Peter Coyote, Swoosie Kurtz, Billy Vera, Julia Roberts, Willie Nelson, Emmylou Harris. D: Bobby Roth. DRA 100m. TVM V

Baker's Hawk 1976 ★★★★ An elderly, reclusive man (Ives) is victimized by vigilantes, then has to swallow his pride and accept help, in turn helping a young man (Montgomery) to mature. Sweet, easy-to-take Western drama for the whole family. Majestic scenery. C: Clint Walker, Burl Ives, Lee H. Montgomery, Diane Baker. D: Lyman Dayton. WST [G] 98m. V

Baker's Wife, The 1938 French ★★★★½ After moving to rural France, a gifted baker refuses to whip up another loaf until his unfaithful wife is returned to him. The townsfolk, desperate for bread, take it upon themselves to reconcile the couple. Charming, classic comedy. C: Raimu, Ginette Leclerc, Charles Moulin. D: Marcel Pagnol. COM 124m. V

Balalaika 1939 ★★★ After the Revolution, Russian exiles celebrate life in Paris. Elegantly produced operetta with a dozen songs tailor-made for Eddy and company. Music by Herbert Stothart. C: Nelson Eddy, Ilona Massey, Charles Ruggles, Frank Morgan. D: Reinhold Schunzel. MUS 91m. V

Balboa 1982 ★★ A ruthless tycoon (Curtis) manipulates everyone around him while trying to win back his former flame (Lynley); meanwhile, the paradise-like title resort is turning into Sodom-on-the-Sea. Racy melodrama was released theatrically in 1986 after failing as a TV miniseries. C: Tony Curtis, Carol Lynley, Jennifer Chase, Chuck Connors, Sonny Bono. D: James Polakof. DRA 92m. V

Balcony, The 1963 ★★★★ When revolution breaks out in the streets, patrons and law officials led by Falk create a mutiny of their own by taking over a brothel, run by Winters. Good cast enlivens this adaptation of Jean Genet's play. C: Shelley Winters, Peter Falk, Lee Grant, Ruby Dee, Leonard Nimoy. D: Joseph Strick. DRA 87m. V

Ball of Fire 1941 ★★★★★ Delicious screwball comedy about gangster's moll Sugarpuss O'Shea (Stanwyck) hiding out in a house filled with seven moth-eaten professors and a linguistics expert (Cooper). Marvelously witty and appealing, with Stanwyck living large. C: Gary Cooper, Barbara Stanwyck, Oscar Homolka, Dana Andrews, Dan Duryea, S. Z. Sakall, Richard Haydn, Henry Travers, Gene Krupa. D: Howard Hawks. COM 111m. V

Ballad in Blue 1966 British ★★½ Ray Charles, playing himself, befriends a blind boy and helps him get his life together. About a third of the movie is concert footage, with the singer/pianist at his best; remainder is a bad B-movie. (a.k.a. *Blues for Lovers*) C: Ray Charles, Tom Bell, Mary Peach. D: Paul Henreid. DRA 67m. V

Ballad of a Bounty Hunter 1970 ★★ When the brother of the woman a bounty hunter loves turns to crime, the hunter's compelled to track him down, despite his personal feelings. C: James Philbrook, Maria Silva. D: Joaquin L. Romero Marchent. ACT 83m. V

Ballad of a Gunfighter 1964 ★★ The head of a robbery gang and a gunslinger have it out over women and money. C: Marty Robbins, Bob Barron, Joyce Reed. D: Bill Ward. WST 84m. V

Ballad of A Soldier 1959 Russian ★★★★ In the midst of WWII, a Russian soldier falls in love with a rural woman. Simple, well-told, unpretentious love story also works as condemnation of war. C: Vladimir Ivashov, Shanna Prokhorenko. D: Grigori Chukrai. DRA 89m.

Ballad of Andy Crocker, The 1969 ★★★ A Vietnam soldier (Majors) comes home from the war to find life has gone on without him. Long before such features as *Coming Home* and *Welcome Home*, this movie deftly handled delicate material about Vietnam vets. C: Lee Majors, Joey Heatherton, Jimmy Dean, Agnes Moorehead, Marvin Gaye. D: George McCowan. DRA 73m.

Ballad of Cable Hogue, The 1970 ★★★★ Abstract, playful tale about a loner (Robards) who builds a town in the remote desert. Martin and Oates are classic Western villains, and other characters are eccentric and enigmatic. C: Jason Robards, Stella Stevens, David Warner. D: Sam Peckinpah. WST [R] 121m.

Ballad of Death Valley ★★ Illegal Mexican aliens seeking sanctuary hold a farmer and his daughter captive; violence ensues. C: Montgomery Wood, Giuliano Gemma, Fernando Sancho. D: Duccio Tessari. ACT 91m. V

Ballad of Gregorio Cortez, The 1982 ★★★½ Fact-based tale set in 1901, with a massive force of Texas Rangers pursuing a Mexican cowboy for killing a sheriff. Story of bigotry and language barriers is realistically told from multiple perspectives. C: Edward James Olmos, James Gammon. D: Robert Young. WST [PG] 99m.

Ballad of Josie, The 1967 ★★½ Strained Western comedy about a ranch widow (Day) trying to raise sheep. Try another Day. C: Doris Day, Peter Graves, George Kennedy, Andy Devine. D: Andrew McLaglen. WST 102m.

Ballad of Little Jo, The 1993 ★★★½ Earnest tale of a woman who goes west disguised as a man. Amis is interestingly androgynous, but Greenwald backs away from some of the more intriguing implications of the material. C: Suzy Amis, Bo Hopkins, Ian McKellan, Rene Aberjonois, Carrie Snodgress. D: Maggie Greenwald. DRA [R] 124m. V

Ballad of Narayama, The 1958 Japanese ★★★★ Stylized arthouse film focuses on an old Japanese tradition of taking the old and frail out to Mount Narayama and leaving them to die of exposure, for the good of the community. Tanaka, a fixture of Japanese cinema for many years, stands out in a good cast. C: Kinuyo Tanaka, Teiji Takahashi, Yuko Mochizuki. D: Keisuke Kinoshita. DRA 98m.

Ballad of Narayama, The 1983 Japanese ★★★ A retelling of the '58 version, this time done more naturalistically. Emphasis is on a son who battles wintry weather, but leaves his mother to die in the wilderness. C: Ken Ogata, Sumiko Sakamota, Tonpei Hidari, Shoichi Ozawa. D: Shohei Imamura. DRA 129m. V

Ballad of the Sad Cafe, The 1991 ★★★½ Strange film about an even stranger Georgia community of eccentrics and misfits that is certainly for specialized viewing tastes only. Ends with a male vs. female, no-holds-barred, bloody bar fight. The acting is superb; from material by Carson McCullers and Edward Albee. C: Vanessa Redgrave, Keith Carradine, Rod Steiger. D: Simon Callow. DRA [PG-13] 100m. V

Ballbuster ★★ On investigating a murder, a detective finds that the supposed victim is still very much alive and her loan-sharking spouse is behind some brutal business. Violence-laden crime film. C: Ivan Rogers, Bonnie Paine, W. Randolph Galvin, Bill Shirk, Brenda Banet. D: Eddie Beverly, Jr. CRI 100m. V

Baltimore Bullet, The 1980 ★★ Coburn and protégé Boxleitner are stylish pool sharks shooting and loving their way toward a match against pool king Sharif. Smarmy comedic variation on *The Hustler*. C: James Coburn, Omar Sharif, Bruce Boxleitner, Ronee Blakley. D: Robert Ellis Miller. COM [PG] 103m. V

Bambi 1942 ★★★★★ One of the great Disney animated features, recounting the adventures of Bambi and other woodland creatures as they deal with threats from fire and humans. Superb animation, great voice work, and an unforgettable story line. D: David Hand. FAM/DRA [G] 69m. V

Bamboo Prison, The 1954 ★★ An American POW agrees to become an informer for his North Korean captors, only to secretly gather anti-Communist information. Tired propaganda material, given a bit of verve by veteran director Seiler. C: Robert Francis, Dianne Foster, Brian Keith, E. G. Marshall. D: Lewis Seiler. ACT 80m.

Bamboo Saucer, The 1967 ★★★ American and Soviet officials want to check out and hush up a possible UFO crash in the People's Republic of China, with everybody tiptoeing around everyone else. Decent script compensates for the shoestring budget. Duryea's last film. (a.k.a. *Collision Course*) C: Dan Duryea, John Ericson, Lois Nettleton. D: Frank Telford. SFI [G] 103m. V

Banacek 1972 ★★½ An insurance investigator (Peppard) is hired to check out the mysterious disappearance of an armored Brinks truck in the Southwest. Served as pilot for TV series of same name. (a.k.a. *Detour to Nowhere*) C: George Peppard, Christine Belford. D: Jack Smight. CRI 100m. TVM

Banana Monster 1973 *See* **Schlock**

Banana Peel 1965 French ★★★ Moreau and Belmondo make a fine comedic-romantic pair, vaguely reminiscent of Myrna Loy and William Powell, who pull a con on obscenely wealthy Frobe. Enjoyable, but violent. C: Jeanne Moreau, Jean-Paul Belmondo, Gert Frobe. D: Marcel Ophuls. COM 97m.

Bananas 1971 ★★★★½ A nebbish (Allen) becomes a political activist to impress a woman and winds up dictator of a South American banana republic. Freewheeling, gag-filled Allen at his craziest satirizes everything from politics to religion to television sports, with hysterical results. C: Woody Allen, Louise Lasser, Carlos Montalban, Howard Cosell. D: Woody Allen. COM [PG] 82m. V

Band of Angels 1957 ★★★ Civil War epic from the Robert Penn Warren novel about a mysterious Southern gentleman (Gable) in love with a woman of mixed ancestry (De Carlo). Poitier stands out as a strong-willed slave in this otherwise murky costume piece. C: Clark Gable, Yvonne De Carlo, Sidney Poitier, Efrem Zimbalist Jr. D: Raoul Walsh. DRA 127m. V

Band of Outsiders 1964 French ★★★★ A woman (Karina) enlists two thugs to commit a robbery, but mistakenly gets her aunt killed instead. Entertaining send-up with great deadpan humor, including a Bob Fosse dance routine, bad miming, and a slam-bang tour of the Louvre. Great fun. C: Anna Karina, Sami Frey, Claude Brasseur. D: Jean-Luc Godard. CRI 95m. V

Band of the Hand 1986 ★★½ A pack of teenage thugs becomes a crack team of vigilantes fighting to rid Miami of drug dealers in this first directing effort from former *Starsky and Hutch* star Glaser. Glossy *Miami Vice* look courtesy of producer Michael Mann. C: Stephen Lang, Michael Carmine, Lauren Holly, John Cameron Mitchell. D: Paul Michael Glaser. ACT [R] 109m. V

Band Wagon, The 1953 ★★★★★ Sparkling musical, one of the pinnacles of the MGM era. Fading film star (Astaire) tries for a Broadway comeback. Fabray and Levant as squabbling screenwriters, Buchanan as an egotistical director, and Charisse as a temperamental dancer create a marvelous atmosphere of spontaneous gaiety, enhanced by a great Schwartz and Dietz score. C: Fred Astaire, Cyd Charisse, Oscar Levant, Nanette Fabray, Jack Buchanan. D: Vincente Minnelli. MUS 112m. V

Bandido 1956 ★★★ During the 1916 Mexican rebellion, a mercenary (Mitchum) helps a rebel leader (Roland) defeat a gunrunner (Scott) and his gang. Tense action-Western, with good script by Earl Felton. C: Robert Mitchum, Zachary Scott, Gilbert Roland, Ursula Thiess. D: Richard Fleischer. WST 92m.

Bandit of Sherwood Forest, The 1946 ★★★ Wilde is Robin Hood's son, determined to stop the evil Regent from usurping the throne from England's rightful king. Eye-pleasing photography and handsome, athletic star in top form. Adapted from Paul Castleton novel *Son of Robin Hood*. C: Cornel Wilde, Anita Louise, Edgar Buchanan. D: George Sherman, Henry Levin. ACT 86m.

Bandit of Zhobe, The 1959 British ★★ A 19th-century East Indian chieftain (Mature) avenges his wife's death by fighting British colonial rulers. CinemaScope is the only attraction here. C: Victor Mature, Anthony Newley. D: John Gilling. ACT 80m.

Bandits 1986 French ★★★ An ex-con (Yanne) sets out to avenge his wife's murder while looking after his daughter (Marie-Sophie L.), who's in love with a jewel thief. Atmospheric fantasy, with more drama than thrills. C: Jean Yanne, Marie-Sophie L.(Lelouch). D: Claude Lelouch. DRA 98m. V

Bandits of Corsica, The 1953 ★★★½ Sequel to 1942 *The Corsican Brothers* revisits saga of the swashbuckling twin brothers (Greene) fighting to bring democratic rule to 19th-century Corsica. Greene makes a nice old-fashioned hero in the Douglas Fairbanks style. C: Richard Greene, Paula Raymond, Raymond Burr, Lee Van Cleef. D: Ray Nazarro. ACT 81m.

Bandits of Orgosolo 1964 Italian ★★★½ A shepherd, wrongly accused of murder, flees to the mountains, where he becomes a bandit. Solid sociopolitical drama reminiscent of the Italian neorealist films of the '40s. C: Michele Cossu, Peppeddu Cuucu, Vittorina Pisano. D: Vittorio De Seta. DRA 98m. V

Bandolero 1968 ★★★ A Texas outlaw saves his brother from hanging and the pair escape with a female hostage into Mexican bandit territory. Gloomy, but agreeable entertainment with interesting casting of Stewart and Martin. C: James Stewart, Dean Martin, Raquel Welch, George Kennedy. D: Andrew V. McLaglen. WST [PG] 106m. V

Bang-Bang Kid, The 1968 Spanish ★★★★

Fun send-up of the Western has a bumbling inventor (Bosley) and his robot, the Bang-Bang Kid, battling a corrupt sheriff (Madison) who lives like a feudal lord at the turn of the century. Witty comedy makes for ideal family entertainment. (a.k.a. *Bang Bang*) C: Guy Madison, Tom Bosley. D: Stanley Prager. FAM/COM 78m. v

Bang Bang! Marrakesh 1966 *See* **Bang, Bang, You're Dead!**

Bang, Bang, You're Dead! 1966 British ★★½ A tourist (Randall) gets mixed up with criminals (Lom and Kinski) while vacationing in Marrakesh. Spy spoof strives for wackiness but ends up falling flat. Good supporting cast, though. (a.k.a. *Bang Bang! Marrakesh* and *Our Man in Marrakesh*) C: Tony Randall, Senta Berger, Terry-Thomas, Herbert Lom, Wilfrid Hyde-White. D: Don Sharp. COM 92m.

Bang Bang 1968 *See* **Bang-Bang Kid, The**

Bang the Drum Slowly 1973 ★★★★★ Superlative buddy film, with De Niro as a dying catcher trying to make it through one more season, and the team's star pitcher (Moriarty) as his best friend. Roster of superb supporting players headed by Gardenia as hard-boiled manager. Funny, tragic, classic baseball drama—one of the best sports films made. Danny Aiello's film debut. C: Michael Moriarty, Robert De Niro, Vincent Gardenia, Phil Foster, Danny Aiello. D: John Hancock. DRA [PG] 98m. v

Bang! You're Dead 1954 *See* **Game of Danger**

Banjo on My Knee 1936 ★★★★ Stanwyck makes a rare foray into song and dance in this life-on-the-Mississippi riverboat musical, packed full of multiple plotlines and some exuberant songs. Plain old-fashioned fun. C: Barbara Stanwyck, Joel McCrea. D: John Cromwell. MUS 96m. v

Bank Dick, The 1940 ★★★★★ Best of Fields' films, penned by the comedian under pseudonym, Mahatma Kane Jeeves. He's a bystander who becomes a bank guard after inadvertently foiling a robbery. From there, Fields takes an insane ride through a world of embezzlement, shrewish relatives, a movie studio, and even a beefsteak mine! Fields' nasty edges are at their sharpest in this classic film. C: W. C. Fields, Cora Witherspoon, Una Merkel, Jessie Ralph, Franklin Pangborn. D: Eddie Cline. COM 73m. v

Bank Robber 1993 ★★ Contemporary version of Robin Hood with a twist: this Robin Hood steals from the rich but is also rooked by the poor. C: Judge Reinhold, Lisa Bonet, Patrick Dempsey. COM [R] 90m. v

Bank Shot 1974 ★★ Criminal genius (Scott) devises a foolproof plan for the perfect bank robbery: steal the entire building. Slow-moving caper comedy can't steal any laughs. Based on Donald E. Westlake's novel. C: George C. Scott, Joanna Cassidy. D: Gower Champion. COM [PG] 83m.

Banker, The 1989 ★★½ Mild-mannered banker by day, crossbow-toting killer by night, maverick vigilante (Regehr) hunts down prostitutes, while hard-nosed cop (Forster) tries to stop the brutal string of murders. Violent, formulaic thriller. C: Robert Forster, Duncan Regehr, Richard Roundtree. D: William Webb. CRI [R] 95m. v

Bannerline 1951 ★★★½ A wet-behind-the-ears reporter (Brasselle) goes up against political corruption in his town in this message drama, which blends comedy and romance. The plot isn't exactly original, but it's buoyed by some fine, natural performances. C: Keefe Brasselle, Sally Forrest, Lionel Barrymore, Lewis Stone. D: Don Weis. DRA 88m.

Banning 1967 ★★★½ A ritzy country club is the site of adultery, dirty dealings, gambling, and sex, sex, sex in this vice-packed soap opera. Slick production and cast make up for a rather messy script. C: Robert Wagner, Anjanette Comer, Jill St. John, Guy Stockwell, James Farentino, Susan Clark, Gene Hackman. D: Ron Winston. DRA 102m.

Banyon 1971 ★★★½ A not-so hard-boiled private detective (Forster), who drinks tea instead of liquor, is suspected of murder. Well done, with a tight script and good Depression-era setting (inspired by Warner Brothers' '30s gangster films). Pilot for a TV series. C: Robert Forster, Darren McGavin, Jose Ferrer. D: Robert Day. CRI 97m. TVM

Banzai Runner 1986 ★★ When a cop's brother is killed by a group of wealthy men who consider themselves above the law, the cop seeks revenge. C: Dean Stockwell, John Shepherd, Charles Dierkop. D: John G. Thomas. CRI 88m. v

Barabbas 1961 ★★★½ Murderer/thief Barabbas (Quinn), whose place on the cross was preempted by Christ, comes to terms with his conscience and converts to Christianity. Cluttered epic contains spectacle elements and violence, especially gladiator scenes. C: Anthony Quinn, Silvana Mangano, Arthur Kennedy, Jack Palance, Ernest Borgnine, Katy Jurado. D: Richard Fleischer. DRA 134m. v

Baraka 1993 ★★★ Visual collage shows Earth evolving and humankind's interdependence with our environment. Stunning images throughout, reminiscent of *Koyaanisqatsi* and *Powaqqatsi*. D: Ron Fricke. DOC 96m.

Barbarella 1968 French ★★★ A space-traveling heroine (Fonda)'s adventures in the 41st century, as seen through the eyes of 1960s corporate psychedelia. A visual eyeful, but little else. Cult favorite based on the popular French comic book. Don't miss the opening credits. C: Jane Fonda, John Phillip Law, Milo O'Shea, David Hemmings, Marcel Marceau, Claude Dauphin. D: Roger Vadim. SFI [PG] 98m. v

Barbarian and the Geisha, The 1958 ★★ Adventure and romance await the first American diplomat to 1850s Japan. Not without its moments, but ultimately ineffective. C: John

Wayne, Eiko Ando, Sam Jaffe. D: John Huston. DRA 104m. V

Barbarian Queen 1985 Italian ★ Enraged female warriors seek revenge against those who've captured their men. Nudity, blood, tedium. C: Lana Clarkson, Frank Zagarino, Katt Shea Ruben, Dawn Dunlap, Susana Traverso. D: Hector Olivera. SFI 71m. V

Barbarian Queen II—The Empress Strikes Back 1989 Italian ★★ Sword 'n' sorcery hokum concerns a princess wrongly imprisoned by her evil brother, joining up with female rebels to regain her kingdom. C: Lana Clarkson, Greg Wrangler, Rebecca Wood. D: Joe Finley. SFI 87m. V

Barbarian, The 1933 ★★★★ A tourist (Loy) is wooed by an Egyptian tour guide (Novarro) in this hot-house romance. Noted for its sultry exoticism and charming leads. Look for the nude bathing scene, considered quite daring in its day. (a.k.a. *A Night in Cairo*) C: Ramon Novarro, Myrna Loy, Reginald Denny, Louise Hale, C. Aubrey Smith, Edward Arnold, Hedda Hopper. D: Sam Wood. DRA 82m.

Barbarians at the Gate 1992 ★★★★½ Dirty dealing unfolds as several high-stakes financiers vie for the multimillion-dollar buyout of conglomerate R.J Reynolds. Delicious big-business satire, based on a true story, frantically proving that truth is stranger and much funnier than fiction when the subject is corporate America. From the best-seller by Bryan Burroughs and John Helyar. C: James Garner, Jonathan Pryce, Peter Riegert, Joanna Cassidy. D: Glenn Jordan. COM [R] 105m. TVM V

Barbarians, The 1987 ★★ Bad movie traditions pass their plebeian torch in this sword-and-sorcery anti-epic. Body-building twins the Paul brothers follow in the tradition of their muscular predecessors, starring as siblings battling their evil captor. C: David Paul, Peter Paul. D: Ruggero Deodato. ACT [R] 88m. V

Barbarosa 1982 ★★★★ An elusive outlaw takes a naive boy under his wing in this lighthearted Western, featuring a surprisingly good performance from Nelson. C: Willie Nelson, Gary Busey, Isela Vega, Gilbert Roland. D: Fred Schepisi. WST [PG] 90m. V

Barbary Coast Gent 1944 ★★★½ A charming gentleman crook (Beery) leaves 1880s San Francisco's gold-crazed Barbary Coast and winds up trying to go straight in Nevada's gold rush. Vintage Beery, in a typically smooth-talking role. C: Wallace Beery, Binnie Barnes, John Carradine, Chill Wills. D: Roy Del Ruth. WST 87m.

Barbary Coast, The 1974 ★★★½ A turn-of-the-century detective (Shatner) works with a casino owner (Cole) to uncover a blackmailer in San Francisco's Barbary Coast. Lightweight, entertaining period piece; pilot for a short-lived TV series. C: William Shatner, Dennis Cole, Lynda Day George, Bill Bixby. D: Bill Bixby. WST 100m.

Barbary Coast 1935 ★★★★ Colorful turn-of-the-century San Francisco tale about a saloon belle (Hopkins) grappling with a wealthy scoundrel (Robinson). Brennan stands out in excellent supporting cast, and McCrea looks good, as usual. Rousing, full-blooded yarn. C: Miriam Hopkins, Edward G. Robinson, Joel McCrea, Walter Brennan. D: Howard Hawks. ACT 90m. V

Barber of Seville 1973 German ★★★★ The definitive film adaptation of the Italian opera, both faithful to the source and cinematically inspired. C: Teresa Berganza, Hermann Prey, Luigi Alva, Enzo Dara, Paolo Montarsolo. D: Ernst Wild. MUS 141m. V

Barcelona 1994 ★★★★ An American living in Spain must deal with his visiting cousin, cheating girlfriend, and other distractions. Another witty, quirky comedy from the director/screenwriter of *Metropolitan*. C: Taylor Nichols, Christopher Eigeman, Tushka Bergen, Mira Sorvino. D: Whit Stillman. COM [PG-13] 101m. V

Bare Essence 1982 ★★★ Melodrama mixes up a heady brew of perfume industry and romance in this sudsy adaptation of Meredith Rich's novel. Unspectacular glimpse into the world of the "beautiful people" led to a short-lived TV series. C: Bruce Boxleitner, Linda Evans, Genie Francis, Lee Grant, Donna Mills, John Larroquette. D: Walter Grauman. DRA 200m. TVM

Bare Essentials 1991 ★★½ Minimal script combines with minimal costumes as an uptight, urban couple, hoping to get away from it all on a tropical vacation, gets stranded on a remote island inhabited by two very sexy castaways. Predictable comedy teases rather than pleases. C: Gregory Harrison, Lisa Hartman, Mark Linn-Baker. D: Martha Coolidge. COM [PG] 94m. TVM V

Barefoot Contessa, The 1954 ★★★★ A director (Bogart) manipulates the career of a barefoot Spanish cabaret dancer (Gardner) and turns her into a Hollywood movie star. A bitter Cinderella story—her prince can't give her everything—is a juicy, classic mid-'50s melodrama with a wonderful Bogart turn. C: Humphrey Bogart, Ava Gardner, Edmond O'Brien, Marius Goring, Rossano Brazzi, Valentina Cortesa. D: Joseph L. Mankiewicz. DRA 128m. V

Barefoot Executive, The 1971 ★★★½ Mailroom employee (Russell) finds a chimpanzee with the ability to pick TV shows that will be popular. The chimp, naturally, is promoted to his own windowed executive office in this amiable Disney spoof of TV ratings. C: Kurt Russell, Joe Flynn, Harry Morgan, Wally Cox, John Ritter. D: Robert Butler. FAM/COM [G] 92m. V

Barefoot in the Park 1967 ★★★★ Frothy Neil Simon comedy about newlyweds (Fonda and Redford) and their adjustments to married life in Greenwich Village. Irresistible easy-going fun with charismatic stars and charming support from Natwick and Boyer. C: Robert Redford, Jane Fonda, Charles Boyer, Mildred Natwick. D: Gene Saks. COM [G] 106m. V

Barefoot Mailman, The 1951 ★★★½ Saga of an early pioneer mailman (Courtland) blazing a trail through Florida with a con artist and a lady along for the journey. Some thrills and pretty scenery, shot on location in Silver Springs, Florida. C: Robert Cummings, Terry Moore, Will Geer. D: Earl McEvoy. ACT 83m.

Barefoot Savage 1952 *See* **Sensualita**

Barfly 1987 ★★★★ Unsavory, violent, profane, semiautobiographical film (based on the life of Charles Bukowski) set in down-at-heels L.A., about hard-bitten boozers. Rourke, as the slovenly drunk who's also a poet, and Dunaway, an alcoholic lady down on her luck, turn in powerful performances. Raw, gritty drama. C: Mickey Rourke, Faye Dunaway, Alice Krige. D: Barbet Schroeder. DRA [R] 100m. V

Baritone 1985 Polish ★★ A celebrated baritone inexplicably loses his voice when he returns to his hometown for a birthday celebration. C: Zbigniew Zapasiewicz. D: Janusz Zaorski. DRA 100m. V

Barjo 1994 French ★★ Marriage on the rocks, as viewed by wife's brother. C: Anne Brochet. D: Jerome Boivin. DRA 85m. V

Barkleys of Broadway, The 1949 ★★★½ Astaire and Rogers reunited (after a 10-year separation) in this slight Comden/Green script loosely based on their own careers. High point: Climactic dance to Gershwin's "They Can't Take That Away From Me," originally introduced by the pair in 1937's *Shall We Dance.* C: Fred Astaire, Ginger Rogers, Oscar Levant, Billie Burke. D: Charles Walters. MUS 110m. V

Barnaby and Me 1977 Australian ★★★½ Family fare about a con artist who falls in love with an Australian woman and her daughter's pet koala, while being chased by gangsters. Typical romantic adventure story with an unusual setting. C: Sid Caesar, Juliet Mills. D: Norman Panama. FAM/COM [G] 90m. TVM V

Barnacle Bill 1941 ★★★★ A grizzled sailor (Beery) tries to stay out of the clutches of a woman (Main) bent on marrying him. Main and Beery are a lot of fun in their feisty, combative roles. C: Wallace Beery, Marjorie Main, Leo Carrillo, Virginia Weidler, Donald Meek. D: Richard Thorpe. DRA 98m. V

Barnacle Bill 1958 *See* **All at Sea**

Barnum 1986 ★★ Story of rise to fame and power of co-founder of Barnum and Bailey Circus, Phineas T. Barnum. C: Michael Crawford. D: Terry Hughes. DRA 113m. V

Baron and the Kid, The 1984 ★★ When an expert pool player meets his son for first time, they combine their energies to open their own pool hall. C: Johnny Cash, June Carter Cash, Greg Webb. D: Gary Nelson. DRA 101m. V

Baron Blood 1972 Italian ★★★ A dark castle is purchased by a wheelchair-bound entrepreneur (Cotten) who plans to restore it—until an evil ancestor comes back to life and gets in the way. Bava sets the mood, but few surprises. C: Joseph Cotten, Elke Sommer. D: Mario Bava. HOR [PG] 90m. V

Baron Münchausen 1943 German ★★★★½ Commissioned by Hitler's right-hand man Goebbels to celebrate the German film studio UFA's 25th anniversary, this is a nationalistic look at Germany's legendary liar, shown here as a ladies' man who is always loyal to the Fatherland. Brilliant performances and imaginative visual effects highlight this Nazi curio. Story done in 1961 as *The Fabulous Baron Münchausen* and in 1989 as the *Adventures of Baron Münchausen.* C: Hans Albers, Brigitte Horney. D: Josef Von Baky. ACT 110m. V

Baron of Arizona, The 1950 ★★★½ Typically weird Fuller drama about a shrewd, rapacious 19th-century businessman (Price) who has an elaborate plan to gain ownership of Arizona. Low-budget picture features a fun, over-the-top performance from Price; based on a true story. C: Vincent Price, Ellen Drew, Beulah Bondi. D: Samuel Fuller. WST 90m.

Baroness and the Butler, The 1938 ★★★★ Rich woman (Annabella), the prime minister's daughter, has a debonair butler (Powell) who moonlights as an opposition party member of the Hungarian parliament; the expected romantic and comic entanglements ensue. The Budapest locations and clever political content make this solid entertainment. Powell as usual shines. C: William Powell, Annabella, Helen Westley, Henry Stephenson, Joseph Schildkraut. D: Walter Lang. COM 75m.

Baron's African War, The 1943 ★★★½ An American (Cameron) battles a host of villains, including Nazis and corrupt Arabs in the wilds of Africa. Exciting adventure is a reedited version of a Republic Studios serial, released as *Secret Service in Darkest Africa.* C: Rod Cameron, Joan Marsh. D: Spencer Bennet. ACT 100m.

Barquero 1970 ★★★½ A vicious, murderous outlaw (Oates) gets more than he bargained for from a ferry operator (Van Cleef) in this modernized, bloody Western. Intense, with excessive violence, in the Peckinpah and Leone tradition. C: Lee Van Cleef, Warren Oates, Forrest Tucker, Kerwin Mathews, Mariette Hartley. D: Gordon Douglas. WST [PG] 115m.

Barretts of Wimpole Street, The 1934 ★★★★½ Charming, lavishly produced biography of love-matched poets Elizabeth Barrett (Shearer) and Robert Browning (March) in 19th-century England. Handsome costume romance with trademark MGM sheen. Remade in 1957. C: Norma Shearer, Fredric March, Charles Laughton, Maureen O'Sullivan, Una O'Connor. D: Sidney Franklin. DRA 110m. V

Barretts of Wimpole Street, The 1957 U.S. ★★★½ Love affair of 19th-century British poets Elizabeth Barrett (Jones) and Robert Browning (Gielgud) gets another well-textured production. This one's fine, but the 1934 version still reigns. C: Jennifer Jones, John Gielgud, Bill Travers, Virginia McKenna. D: Sidney Franklin. DRA 105m.

Barricade 1939 ★★★ The American consulate in North China is under siege by Mongolian rebels, while within a newsman and a woman with a past find romance. A story covered in countless Westerns is transposed to an exotic setting. Troubled production resulted in numerous editing problems; great fun for blooper hunters. C: Alice Faye, Warner Baxter, Charles Winninger, Arthur Treacher, Keye Luke. D: Gregory Ratoff. ACT 71m.

Barricade 1950 ★★★ A corrupt miner (Massey) tangles with two fugitives and a lawyer who, often being forced to accept his hospitality, try to end his corrupt operation. Loose remake of the 1941 sea picture *The Sea Wolf*; features good performances. C: Dane Clark, Ruth Roman, Raymond Massey. D: Peter Godfrey. WST 75m.

Barrier 1966 Polish ★★★ So-so drama follows a group of young adults in Poland as they react to the changing world around them. Some cinematic flourishes fascinate; others fall flat. C: Joanna Szczerbic, Jan Nowicki. D: Jerzy Skolimowski. DRA 84m.

Barry Lyndon 1975 British ★★★★½ William Thackeray's tale of a ne'er-do-well Irish soldier of fortune (O'Neal) whose marriage to a wealthy young widow (Berenson) assures his social position but ultimately dooms him. A leisurely, sumptuous costume drama sparked by great direction and performances. Oscars for Best Cinematography, Score, Art Direction/Set Direction, and Costume Design. C: Ryan O'Neal, Marisa Berenson, Patrick Magee, Hardy Kruger. D: Stanley Kubrick. DRA [PG] 185m. V

Barry Mackenzie Holds His Own 1974 Australian ★★★ Campy yarn, a sequel to *The Adventures of Barry Mackenzie*, concerns Transylvanian Count Barry and his twin brother (Crocker in a dual role) as they rescue a damsel in distress (Humphries, in a drag role) who has been kidnapped to the count's country. C: Barry Humphries, Barry Crocker, Donald Pleasence. D: Bruce Beresford. ACT 93m. V

Bartleby 1972 British ★★★★ A stubborn, odd clerk (McEnery) refuses to give up his job when he's fired. The small drama becomes an epic story of the modern alienated man who ultimately is ground down and loses his spirit. Fine performances in a story with many subtle charms. A brooding, intelligent adaptation and updating of Herman Melville's novella. C: Paul Scofield, John McEnery. D: Anthony Friedmann. DRA 79m. V

Barton Fink 1991 ★★★½ During the '40s, a playwright (Turturro), whose first play chronicled the struggles of ordinary people, tries his hand at Hollywood and winds up with a colossal case of writer's block. An odd exercise in dark humor, full of the Coen brothers' trademark visual style. Doesn't completely work, but Turturro and Goodman are wonderful. C: John Turturro, John Goodman, Judy Davis, Michael Lerner. D: Joel Coen. COM [R] 116m.

Based on an Untrue Story 1993 ★★★ Humorous parody of TV movies based on true stories. C: Morgan Fairchild, Harvey Korman, Dyan Cannon. D: Jim Drake. COM 90m. TVM V

Bashful Elephant, The 1962 German ★★½ A Hungarian orphan searches for a new home in Austria with a dog and an elephant along for the quest. Sweet story dampened only by a romantic subplot that doesn't really belong in a children's fairy tale. C: Stuart McGowan, Molly Mack. D: Dorrell McGowan. FAM/DRA 82m.

Basic Instinct 1992 ★★★★ A San Francisco cop (Douglas) becomes attracted to a murder suspect (Stone), a sexy, outrageous novelist whose fiction closely parallels real crimes. Steamy, suspenseful pulp; controversial for its portrayal of bisexuality and Stone's interrogation scene. C: Michael Douglas, Sharon Stone, George Dzundza, Jeanne Tripplehorn, Dorothy Malone. D: Paul Verhoeven. CRI [R] 123m. V

Basic Training 1971 ★★★★ Fascinating cinema-verite look at the Army training process, with drill sergeants breaking down misfit recruits and turning them into soldiers. You'll never look at *Sands of Iwo Jima* the same way again! D: Frederick Wiseman. DOC 89m.

Basic Training 1986 ★ The battle between the sexes and the B-movie sinks to new lows as a cadre of buxom ladies, led by Dusenberry, overcome lascivious Pentagon officials. C: Ann Dusenberry, Rhonda Shear, Angela Aames. D: Andrew Sugerman. COM [R] 85m. V

Basileus Quartet 1982 French/Italian ★★★★ When one member of a string quartet dies, a young violinist is hired as a replacement. The remaining veterans find their lives altered as the newcomer challenges their stagnant ways. Story unfolds quietly; deeply moving at times. C: Pierre Malet, Hector Alterio, Omero Antonutti. D: Fabio Carpi. DRA 120m. V

Basket Case 1982 ★★★ A young man and his deformed Siamese twin (whom he keeps in a basket) seek revenge on the doctors who separated them. Very low-budget but one-of-a-kind (until the subsequent sequels) horror film mixes extreme gore with the blackest of humor. C: Kevin Van Hentenryck, Terri Susan Smith, Beverly Bonner. D: Frank Henenlotter. HOR [R] 89m. v

Basket Case 2 1990 ★★★ Though it lacks the dark streak of the original, this follow-up is almost as much fun, with Van Hentenryck and his twisted twin brother finding a haven at a home for freaks and taking on antagonistic outsiders. C: Kevin Van Hentenryck, Annie Ross, Jason Evers. D: Frank Henenlotter. HOR [R] 90m. v

Basket Case 3 1991 ★★★ This time, the gang of freaks takes a road trip and runs afoul of the law while Belial sires 12 mutant children from one mother. Obviously, not for all tastes, but Henenlotter's perverse sense of horror and humor still works. C: Kevin Van Hentenryck, Annie Ross, Gil Roper. D: Frank Henenlotter. HOR [R] 90m. v

Basketball Fix, The 1951 ★★★½ Obvious but well-done morality tale of a debt-ridden jump-shooter doing a favor for a bookie. Will he find the courage to do the right thing? C: John Ireland, Marshall Thompson, Vanessa Brown, William Bishop. D: Felix Feist. DRA 65m. v

Bastard, The 1978 ★★★ First part of a trilogy, based on John Jake's novels, concerns an illegitimate Englishman who, unacknowledged by his noble father, journeys to America and joins the Revolution—on the American side. Average romantic/historic miniseries. C: Andrew Stevens, Noah Beery, Peter Bonerz, Tom Bosley, Kim Cattrall, Buddy Ebsen, Lorne Greene. D: Lee H. Katzin. DRA 189m. TVM v

Bat People 1974 ★★★ A biologist (Moss) on his honeymoon gets bitten by a bat and turns into a bloodthirsty night flyer. Occasionally stomach-turning horror, with good special effects. (a.k.a. *It Lives By Night*) C: Stewart Moss, Marianne McAndrew, Michael Pataki. D: Jerry Jameson. HOR 95m. v

Bat, The 1959 ★★★ A mystery writer, summering in a spooky mansion, watches as the town is terrorized by a murderous hooded figure. A faithful adaption of Rinehart's novel (also a 1926 play). C: Vincent Price, Agnes Moorehead. D: Crane Wilbur. HOR 80m. v

Bat 21 1988 ★★★★ An American pilot (Hackman), used to seeing the war from far above, is downed in Vietnam. His only hopes of escape are his wits and the efforts of an intrepid air controller (Glover) with whom he has radio contact. Good acting sparks tense action; based on a true story. C: Gene Hackman, Danny Glover, Jerry Reed, David Marshall Grant. D: Peter Markle. DRA [R] 106m. v

Bat Whispers, The 1930 ★★½ Relic thriller about a mysterious killer "the Bat" preying upon an unsuspecting populace. Striking set design and atmospheric visuals. Remake of silent film *The Bat.* C: Chester Morris, Una Merkel, Chance Ward. D: Roland West. HOR 84m. v

Bataan 1943 ★★★ An American patrol in the Philippines holds out against all odds in a mission to destroy a key Japanese bridge. A rough, realistic feel and the desperate plight of the G.I.s make this one of the more engaging WWII Pacific theater films. C: Robert Taylor, George Murphy, Thomas Mitchell, Lloyd Nolan, Desi Arnaz. D: Tay Garnett. DRA 105m. v

Bates Motel 1987 ★★ A weak continuation of the *Psycho* story, with the infamous motel now playing host to a just-released mental patient (Cort). An especially dumb chiller. C: Bud Cort, Jason Bateman, Moses Gunn. D: Richard Rothstein. HOR 100m. TVM

Bathing Beauty 1944 ★★★½ Songwriter (Skelton) is suspicious of his swimming teacher fiancée (Williams). Splashy musical, a cheerful mix of Red's slapstick and Esther's backstrokes. Exciting water ballet finale. C: Red Skelton, Esther Williams, Basil Rathbone, Ethel Smith, Xavier Cugat, Harry James and his orchestra. D: George Sidney. MUS 101m. v

Batman 1989 ★★★★ Burton's darkly entertaining retelling of the comic classic. Keaton gives a brooding performance as the Caped Crusader and Nicholson's Joker is a show stealer. Imaginative special effects and a terrifically turbo Batmobile. C: Jack Nicholson, Michael Keaton, Kim Basinger, Robert Wuhl, Pat Hingle. D: Tim Burton. ACT [PG] 126m. v

Batman: Mask of the Phantom 1994 ★★★ The legendary crime fighter is mistaken for a superhuman killer who has eliminated several policemen. Sophisticated animated thriller, but too shrill and violent for kids. Voices of Kevin Conroy, Dana Delany, Hart Bochner, Mark Hamill, Stacy Keach, Jr., Efrem Zimbalist, Jr., Abe Vigoda. D: Eric Randomski, Bruce W. Timm. ACT 76m.

Batman Returns 1992 ★★★★ Sequel to 1989 smash *Batman* introduces Penguin (DeVito) and Catwoman (Pfeiffer) as nemeses of Caped Crusader (Keaton). Muddled plot follows billionaire's evil plan to elect Penguin mayor of Gotham City. Picture's redeemed by terrific Pfeiffer and Burton's visual genius. Too grisly for children. C: Michael Keaton, Danny DeVito, Michelle Pfeiffer, Christopher Walken. D: Tim Burton. ACT [PG-13] 126m. v

Batman—The Movie 1966 ★★★½ Film version of popular '60s TV series stars West and Ward as the Dynamic Duo, defending Gotham City when villains Joker, Penguin, Catwoman, and Riddler unite. Marked by the TV show's deliberately campy humor, production plays on dual level to kids and grownups. C: Adam West, Burt Ward, Burgess Meredith, Cesar Romero, Frank Gorshin, Lee Meriwether. D: Leslie Martinson. FAM/ACT 104m.

Batmania from Comics to Screen 1990 ★★½ This history of the cowled one, from doodle on paper to campy television show, culminating with the "60s celluloid effort. More than the average person wants to know about the Caped Crusader, but some interesting bits should satisfy his big fans. C: Charles Boyer, John Loder, Merle Oberon. DOC 45m. V

Batmen of Africa 1936 ★★★½ Republic Studios' first cliffhanger is a classic serial reedited to feature length, with Beatty and his companion (King) searching the Dark Continent to save King's sister from winged batmen. (a.k.a. *Darkest Africa*) C: Clyde Beatty, Manuel King, Elaine Shepard. D: B. Eason, Joseph Kane. ACT 100m.

Battered 1979 ★★ Three marriages are destroyed by domestic violence. C: Mike Farrell, Karen Grassle, Le Var Burton. D: Peter Werner. DRA 95m. V

batteries not included 1987 ★★ Sentimental tale of oldsters (Cronyn and Tandy, brilliant as always) helped in their dealings with an unscrupulous landlord by pint-sized aliens. C: Hume Cronyn, Jessica Tandy, Elizabeth Pena, Dennis Boutsikaris. D: Matthew Robbins. FAM/SFI [PG] 107m. V

Battle Angel 1992 Japanese ★★★ Animated science fiction involves a cyborg bounty hunter who must choose between love for her human savior and loyalty to a cause. Extremely violent cartoon (*not* for children) that genre fans will enjoy. SFI 65m. V

Battle at Apache Pass, The 1952 ★★★½ Peaceable Indian chief Cochise (Chandler) fights dishonest American soldiers and his Apache enemy Geronimo (Silverheels). Chandler, reprising his role in *Broken Arrow*, is a nicely fleshed-out Indian hero in this decent Western with some zesty fight scenes. C: Jeff Chandler, John Lund, Beverly Tyler, Richard Egan, Hugh O'Brian. D: George Sherman. WST 85m.

Battle at Bloody Beach 1961 ★★★ A civilian (Murphy) is caught up in a guerrilla fight against the Japanese during WWII, offering supplies and aid to the insurgent Filipinos while tracking down his missing wife. A worthwhile picture for war film buffs. (a.k.a. *Battle on the Beach*) C: Audie Murphy, Gary Crosby, Dolores Michaels. D: Herbert Coleman. ACT 83m.

Battle Beneath the Earth 1967 British ★★★½ Matinee sci-fi classic that plays upon the old legend of digging to China. This time it's Chinese communists who are engineering the invasion of America via underground tunnels. A lot of campy fun. C: Kerwin Mathews, Viviane Ventura. D: Montgomery Tully. SFI 112m. V

Battle Beyond the Stars 1980 ★★★ *Magnificent Seven/Seven Samurai* superimposed onto low-budget space sets, via master recycler Roger Corman. Relatively decent effects, a good cast of B-movie regulars, and a John Sayles script make this quickie homage enjoyable viewing. C: Richard Thomas, John Saxon, Robert Vaughn, George Peppard, Sybil Danning, Sam Jaffe. D: Jimmy T. Murakami. SFI [PG] 104m. V

Battle Beyond the Sun 1963 ★★★ Russian sci-fi opus of war between dueling superpowers was bought and recut into an American film by Roger Corman and Francis Ford Coppola (credited as T. Colchart). Dumb, but offers a rare glimpse of Soviet special effects. (a.k.a. *Nebo Zowet*) C: Edd Perry, Arla Powell. D: Thomas Colchart. SFI 75m.

Battle Circus 1953 ★★ An inept drama set in a mobile surgical unit in the Korean War. An Army nurse (Allyson) falls for a world-weary major (Bogart), in this dull and unfunny precursor to the comedy M*A*S*H. Bogie's good, though. C: Humphrey Bogart, June Allyson, Keenan Wynn. D: Richard Brooks. DRA 90m. V

Battle Cry 1955 ★★★★ Well-done, episodic story about a WWII Marine unit in the Pacific. Full of box-office stars (Van Heflin, Hunter, Whitmore), romance, and lots of action. Based on Leon Uris's novel. C: Van Heflin, Aldo Ray, Tab Hunter, Dorothy Malone, Anne Francis, Raymond Massey, James Whitmore. D: Raoul Walsh. ACT 150m. V

Battle Flame 1959 ★★★ During the Korean War, an Army nurse (Edwards) and a Marine (Brady) find love interrupted when she and several other American nurses are captured by the North Koreans. Not an exceptional battlefront romance, but the two leads make a good team. C: Scott Brady, Elaine Edwards, Robert Blake. D: R. G. Springsteen. DRA 78m.

Battle for the Falklands 1984 ★★★ TV film retraces the 1982 British invasion of the Falkland Islands. Solidly informative. DRA 110m. V

Battle for the Planet of the Apes 1973 ★★ The fifth and last in the *Apes* cycle finds human mutants trying to overthrow the simian ruling class. Totally exhausted, with lazy acting. For *Apes* lovers only. Evolved into a short-lived TV series. C: Roddy McDowall, Natalie Trundy, Severn Darden, Paul Williams, Claude Akins, John Huston. D: J. Lee Thompson. SFI [G] 96m. V

Battle Hell (Yangtse Incident) 1957 ★★ Chinese communists attack a British war vessel on the Yangtze in 1949. Based on a true incident. C: Richard Todd, Akim Tamiroff, Keye Luke. D: Michael Anderson. ACT 113m. V

Battle Hymn 1957 ★★★ Factual tale of a former WWII pilot (Hudson) who becomes a minister and establishes an orphanage in war-torn Korea. Overblown and rambling, but Hudson is appealing. C: Rock Hudson, Martha Hyer, Anna Kashfi, Dan Duryea. D: Douglas Sirk. ACT 108m.

Battle in Outer Space 1960 Japanese ★★ Earth is ready to take on all comers in this low-budget sci-fi movie. Poor special effects and stiff performances—save this for "Backseat Drive-In" night. C: Ryo Ikebe, Kyoko Anzai. D: Inoshiro Honda. SFI 74m.

Battle of Algiers 1966 Italian ★★★★ Engrossing but biased docudrama about the Algerian battle for independence from France. Covers the period 1954-1962 in great detail. Documentary style, Morricone's music, and compelling action make this controversial film undeniably effective. C: Yacef Saadi, Jean Martin, Brahim Haggiag. D: Gillo Pontecorvo. DRA 125m. V

Battle of Austerlitz, The 1960 French ★★½ Director Gance returns to his favorite subject, Napoleon, in this screen epic of the emperor's great battle. Awesome cast suffers from amateurish dubbing. (a.k.a. *Austerlitz*) C: Claudia Cardinale, Martine Carol, Leslie Caron, Vittorio De Sica, Jean Marais, Jack Palance, Orson Welles. D: Abel Gance. ACT 180m. V

Battle of Britain, The 1969 British ★★★ A who's who of British cinema in the '70s headlines this homage to the RAF and their heroic duels with the Luftwaffe in WWII. Despite stellar cast and big budget, the dogfights steal the show. C: Harry Andrews, Michael Caine, Trevor Howard, Curt Jurgens, Kenneth More, Laurence Olivier, Christopher Plummer, Michael Redgrave, Ralph Richardson, Robert Shaw, Susannah York. D: Guy Hamilton. DRA [G] 132m.

Battle of El Alamein 1968 Italian ★★★½ Unusual twist has sympathetic Germans and Italians fighting the British in the Sahara during WWII. Tensions between the two Axis armies make this interesting to watch, as does the good guys vs. bad guys reversal. C: Frederick Stafford, Ettore Manni, Robert Hossein, Michael Rennie. D: Calvin Padget. ACT [PG] 105m.

Battle of Midway, The 1942 ★★★★ The first WWII documentary actually shot during combat, this Oscar-winner features thrilling war footage filmed under fire by director Ford himself. The flag-waving narration dates it, but it's a very stirring film nevertheless. Voices of Henry Fonda, Donald Crisp, Jane Darwell. D: John Ford. DOC 20m.

Battle of Neretva, The 1971 Yugoslavian ★★★ All-star cast re-creates the 1943 invasion of Yugoslavia by Nazi forces. The European version was well received (it was nominated for Best Foreign Film by the Academy); however, the American release was unnecessarily trimmed, making for a confusing story line. C: Yul Brynner, Sergei Bondarchuk, Curt Jurgens, Sylva Koscina, Franco Nero, Orson Welles. D: Veljko Bulajic. DRA [G] 106m.

Battle of Rogue River 1954 ★★★ Oregon settlers try to strike a pact with the local Indians, with the usual misunderstandings. Tame Western offers colorful scenery. C: George Montgomery, Richard Denning, Martha Hyer. D: William Castle. WST 71m.

Battle of San Pietro, The 1944 ★★★★★ Powerful WWII documentary presents an unvarnished look at the ravages of war, through battle footage shot in Italy. Huston's camerawork is particularly fine here. D: John Huston. DOC 43m. V

Battle of the Bulge 1965 ★★★ The historic setback when German Panzers broke through Allied lines in WWII is portrayed in this brash and noisy battle epic. Exciting action and strong performances by Fonda, Shaw, and Ryan. C: Henry Fonda, Robert Shaw, Robert Ryan, Telly Savalas, Dana Andrews, George Montgomery, Pier Angeli, Charles Bronson. D: Ken Annakin. ACT 141m. V

Battle of the Coral Sea 1959 ★★★½ Trapped on a Japanese island in WWII, a Navy captain (Robertson) leaks strategic information through enemy lines. Taut action picture is worth a look. C: Cliff Robertson, Gia Scala, Teru Shimada. D: Paul Wendkos. ACT 80m.

Battle of the March Line 1978 *See* **Great Battle, The**

Battle of the Rails 1949 French ★★★½ French railway workers aid the Resistance during WWII. Inspiring story uses nonactors and actual locations to achieve a flawless sense of authenticity. Realistic drama, made even more newsreel-like by the use of a narrator (Boyer). C: Clarieux, Daurand, Deagneaux, Tony Laurent, Charles Boyer. D: Rene Clement. DRA 87m. V

Battle of the Sexes, The 1960 British ★★★★ A staid chief accountant (Sellers)'s thoughts turn to murder when an overly officious efficiency expert begins meddling in his business at a British textile plant. Sellers shines in this slight, but sly, macabre comedy, buttressed by an ace supporting cast. Adapted from James Thurber's short story "The Catbird Seat." C: Peter Sellers, Robert Morley, Constance Cummings. D: Charles Crichton. COM 90m. V

Battle of the Villa Fiorita, The 1965 British ★★★½ Two middle-aged lovers run off to Italy and brave the disapproval of their stick-in-the-mud kids. Not for the cynical, this overly romantic melodrama is good fun. Lavish production and beautiful Italian locations make for a sweeping affair. C: Maureen O'Hara, Rossano Brazzi, Richard Todd, Phyllis Calvert. D: Delmer Daves. DRA 111m.

Battle of the Worlds 1961 Italian ★★½ A runaway planet's orbit is in a direct line to deliver a death blow to Earth. Rains and several other brilliant scientists are called to get Earth out of the mess. Hint: We survive. C: Claude Rains, Maya Brent, Bill Carter. D: Anthony Dawson. SFI 84m.

Battle Stations 1956 ★★★ Cast of old reliables prepare to take on the Japanese in a standard war story that fails to excite. Battle scenes aren't too hot, either. C: John Lund, William Bendix, Keefe Brasselle, Richard Boone. D: Lewis Seiler. ACT 81m.

Battle Stripe 1950 *See* **Men, The**

Battle Taxi 1955 ★★½ The always watchable Hayden heads a helicopter rescue squadron during the Korean War. Fairly predictable tale. C: Sterling Hayden, Arthur Franz, Marshall Thompson. D: Herbert Strock. ACT 82m.

Battle, The 1934 French ★★ Unpleasant and inappropriate casting typical of the time finds Boyer and Oberon as a Japanese couple; he's a naval officer who wants her to do some spying on the British. Curious antique, a quality effort in its day. C: Charles Boyer, John Loder, Merle Oberon. D: Nicolas Farkas. DRA 85m. V

Battle Zone 1952 ★★★ Heavy-handed rhetoric infuses this war film about two photographers who pursue the same woman when they're not at the front. Attractive leads do their best to brighten this Korean War saga. C: John Hodiak, Linda Christian, Stephen McNally. D: Lesley Selander. ACT 82m.

Battleaxe, The 1962 British ★★½ Unsubtle farce about the attempts of a man (Matthews) to take his fiancée (Ireland) to court for breach of promise, on account of his future mother-in-law's meddling in his romantic life. C: Jill Ireland, Francis Matthews. D: Godfrey Grayson. COM 66m.

Battleforce 1978 *See* **Great Battle, The**

Battleground 1949 ★★★½ American G.I.s fight WWII's Battle of the Bulge in this lean studio drama, shot just after the war. Fresh memories brought a realistic look and feel to the production, which garnered Oscars for Best Screenplay and Cinematography. C: Van Johnson, John Hodiak, Ricardo Montalban, George Murphy, Denise Darcel, James Whitmore. D: William Wellman. DRA 118m. V

Battleground 1967 ★★ Disturbance between U.S. marshall and his old friend, now leader of a gang of tramps. C: Telly Savalas, Warren Oates, Stuart Whitman. D: Don Medford. COM 72m. V

Battleship Potemkin 1925 Russian ★★★★★ Perhaps the most influential film of all time. Silent masterpiece deals with the Revolution of 1905, climaxing with the massacre on the Odessa Steps (still being duplicated in movies to this very day). Thrilling, edge-of-your-seat entertainment. (a.k.a. *Potemkin*) C: Alexander Antonov, Vladimir Barsky. D: Sergei Eisenstein. DRA 65m. V

Battlestar: Galactica 1978 ★★★ They took the TV series about interplanetary hot rodders (commanded by Lorne Greene) and blew up several episodes into 35-mm hoping to cash in on the *Star Wars* craze. C: Richard Hatch, Dirk Benedict, Lorne Greene, Ray Milland, Patrick MacNee, Lew Ayres, Jane Seymour. D: Richard Colla. SFI [PG] 125m. V

Battling for Baby 1993 ★★★ A newborn granddaughter arouses competitive maternal feelings in her grandmothers (Pleshette and Reynolds). Not wildly original, but well-played by the two veterans. Cox isn't bad, either, as the mother of the child. C: Suzanne Pleshette, Debbie Reynolds, Courteney Cox. D: Art Wolff. DRA 93m. TVM V

Battling Bellhop, The *See* **Kid Galahad**

Battling Hoofer *See* **Something to Sing About**

Bawdy Adventures of Tom Jones, The 1976 British ★★★ Stage musical of the Fielding book is not a worthy successor to the Albert Finney classic *Tom Jones*. Still, the lusty material offers a few laughs. C: Nicky Henson, Trevor Howard, Joan Collins, Terry-Thomas, Georgia Brown. D: Cliff Owen. MUS [R] 89m. V

Baxter 1989 French ★★★★ Bizarre story of a fascist canine, told through the dog's point of view. After murdering one owner and attempting to kill the infant of another, Baxter is adopted by a preadolescent Hitler admirer. Black comedy with a twisted but funny outlook. C: Lise Delamare, Jean Mercure. D: Jerome Boivin. DRA 82m. V

Bay Boy, The 1984 Canadian-French ★★★ A mother (Ullman) is concerned about her restless son (Sutherland), who is beginning to outgrow their small Canadian town during the 1930s. Well-intentioned, if unoriginal drama. C: Liv Ullmann, Kiefer Sutherland, Peter Donat. D: Daniel Petrie. DRA [R] 107m. V

Bay of Blood 1971 Italian ★★★★ Four vacationers are menaced by a violent maniac. A true triumph of style over substance; many later horrormeisters were strongly influenced by Bava and his techniques. Unusual, to say the least. Quite violent. (a.k.a. *Twitch of the Death Nerve*) C: Claudine Auger, Luigi Pistilli, Claudio Volonte. D: Mario Bava. HOR [R] 85m. V

Bay of Saint Michel, The 1963 British ★★★ Deceit and betrayal mark this action-adventure fare about three military mercenaries on the trail of lost Nazi riches. Okay, but played too safe. (a.k.a. *Operation Mermaid*) C: Keenan Wynn, Mai Zetterling. D: John Ainsworth. ACT 73m.

Bayou Romance 1986 ★★ When an artist (Potts) becomes heir to an old Louisiana property, she finds herself being wooed by two suitors—a doctor and a mysterious Gypsy. Cinematic soap opera, straight from the pages of popular romance novels. C: Annie Potts, Paul Rossilli, Michael Ansara, Barbara Horan. D: Alan Myerson. DRA 105m. V

Baywatch: Panic at Malibu Pier 1989 ★★★ Male and female lifeguards patrol the beaches of Malibu. Pilot for popular syndicated TV show features a well-built cast in various stages of undress. C: David Hasselhoff, Parker Stevenson, Shawn Weatherly, Billy Warlock. D: Richard Compton. ACT 96m. TVM V

Be Beautiful but Shut Up 1957 French ★★★ Young smugglers get their hands on hot money and live the easy life. French takeoff of American-style juvenile delinquent movies. C: Mylene Demongeot, Henri Vidal, Isabelle Miranda. D: Henri Verneuil. DRA 94m.

Be My Guest 1965 British ★★★ Quirky musical about a vacationing young man (Hemmings) who is targeted as a sucker by the producers of a fake music contest. Wide array of talented musical guests (including Jerry Lee Lewis) sustains interest. C: David Hemmings, Stephen Marriot, Andrea Monet. D: Lance Comfort. MUS 82m.

Be Yourself 1930 ★★★ A quick-witted nightclub singer falls for a softhearted prizefighting palooka. An odd little antique created primarily to showcase the talents of Brice. C: Fanny Brice, Robert Armstrong. D: Thornton Freeland. DRA 77m.

Beach Babes from Beyond 1993 ★ Three aliens enter a bikini contest on Earth. The title says it all. C: Joe Estevez, Don Swayze, Joey Travolta. D: Ellen Cabot. SFI [R] 78m. V

Beach Ball 1965 ★★★ Silly beach movie lacks Frankie and Annette, but the formula's still there. Great cameos by major mid-'60s pop bands: The Four Seasons, The Supremes, and The Righteous Brothers. C: Edd Byrnes, Chris Noel, Robert Logan. D: Lennie Weinrib. MUS 83m.

Beach Blanket Bingo 1965 ★★★½ Fifth and best go-around of the "beach party" series is a hodgepodge of low comedy, '60s camp, and silly plot twists involving a mermaid. But any film which pits Lynde and Rickles in insult-to-insult combat should not be ignored. C: Frankie Avalon, Annette Funicello, Paul Lynde, Harvey Lembeck, Don Rickles, Linda Evans, Buster Keaton. D: William Asher. MUS 96m. V

Beach Boys: An American Band, The 1985 ★★★½ Documentary of the classic rock 'n' roll band aims not to offend and succeeds. Old TV clips are fascinating. D: Malcolm Leo. DOC [PG-13] 103m. V

Beach House 1982 ★★ There's barely a plot to be found in this routine teens-hit-the-sand outing. New Jersey kids meet up with a group from Philadelphia, and proceed to live the high life for one romantic summer. C: Ileana Seidel, Kathy McNeil, Richard Duggan, John Cosola. D: John A. Gallager. COM 76m. V

Beach Party 1963 ★★★½ Fun and sun nonsense, with Cummings studying teenagers' behavior, was a surprise smash hit and spawned numerous follow-ups. Frankie and Annette were the most popular musical team since Astaire and Rogers. C: Frankie Avalon, Annette Funicello, Bob Cummings, Dorothy Malone, Harvey Lembeck, Morey Amsterdam. D: William Asher. MUS 98m. V

Beach Red 1967 ★★★★ Marines in WWII attempt to establish a beachhead on a South Pacific island held by the Japanese. Honest account of the brutalities of war and military realities. C: Cornel Wilde, Rip Torn, Burr De Benning, Patrick Wolfe. D: Cornel Wilde. ACT 105m. V

Beachcomber, The 1938 British ★★★★ Real-life husband and wife Laughton and Lanchester star in Somerset Maugham's story of a missionary who reforms a drunk in the Dutch East Indies. Excellent performances all around. Remade in 1955. C: Charles Laughton, Elsa Lanchester, Tyrone Guthrie, Robert Newton. D: Erich Pommer. DRA 87m. V

Beachcomber, The 1955 British ★★★½ A prudish woman (Johns) falls for a good-for-nothing bum (Newton). Somerset Maugham story benefits from tropical locale and excellent performances from the leads. First version appeared in 1938. C: Glynis Johns, Robert Newton, Donald Sinden, Michael Hordern, Donald Pleasence. D: Muriel Box. DRA 82m.

Beaches 1988 ★★★★ Midler and Hershey play two unlikely longtime friends who stick together through good times and bad. Unabashedly sentimental film that will affect even the most jaded viewer. Bialik is a hoot as the young Midler. C: Bette Midler, Barbara Hershey, John Heard, Lainie Kazan, Mayim Bialik. D: Garry Marshall. DRA [PG-13] 123m. V

Beachhead 1954 ★★★½ During WWII, four Marines in the Pacific take on a perilous assignment in the jungles of Bougainville. Above-average heroics. C: Tony Curtis, Frank Lovejoy, Mary Murphy. D: Stuart Heisler. ACT 89m.

Beaks—The Movie 1987 ★★ Violent birds, attacking people around the world, also descend upon a journalist and her camera operator boyfriend investigating the situation. C: Christopher Atkins, Michelle Johnson. D: Rene Cardona, Jr. HOR 86m. V

Beans of Egypt, Maine, The *See* **Forbidden Choices**

Bear Island 1980 British ★★½ While stationed at a frozen North Pole meteorological station, Sutherland and company catch gold fever and murder reigns supreme. So-so adaptation of Alistair MacLean's novel does boast a truly talented cast. C: Donald Sutherland, Vanessa Redgrave, Richard Widmark, Christopher Lee, Barbara Parkins, Lloyd Bridges. D: Don Sharp. ACT [PG] 102m. V

Bear, The 1984 ★★½ Fictionalized biography of legendary Alabama football coach Bear Bryant. Busey's interpretation of the Bear is earnest but the script is unconvincingly saccharine. C: Gary Busey, Cynthia Leake, Harry Dean Stanton, Jon-Erik Hexum. D: Richard Sarafian. DRA [PG] 112m.

Bear, The 1989 French ★★★★ Rousing adventure of two bears (one an orphan, the other an adult) in the wild, and their adversaries: men with guns. Superbly photographed, with excellent "acting" by the animals; timely (but offhand) messages on environmental preservation. D: Jean-Jacques Annaud. FAM/DRA [PG] 92m. V

Bear Who Slept through Christmas, The 1983 ★★ In order to see what Christmas is like, a bear stays awake through winter in this animated feature, followed by a series of Ted E. Bear storybook adventures. Voices of Tom Smothers, Arte Johnson, Barbara Feldon. FAM/DRA 60m. V

Bears and I, The 1974 ★★½ Lovely nature photography distinguishes this Disney film about a Vietnam veteran who raises three feisty little bear cubs while aiding Native Americans fighting for land rights. Pleasant entertainment, but not very deep. C: Patrick Wayne, Chief Dan George, Andrew Duggan, Michael Ansara. D: Bernard McEveety. FAM/DRA 89m. V

Beast from Haunted Cave 1960 ★★½ A cobweb-covered, many-legged beast interrupts thieves attempting to escape with their loot. Low-budget and generally unexciting, but has some good moments. C: Michael Forest, Sheila Carol. D: Monte Hellman. HOR 64m.

Beast from 20,000 Fathoms, The 1953 ★★★★ Rudely awakened by a nuclear blast, Ray Harryhausen's "rhedosaurus" leaves the Arctic for his old stomping ground—Manhattan! All heck ensues until the climactic scene in Coney Island. Very entertaining, with landmark effects. The model for giant-reptiles-run-amok movies. Based on a Ray Bradbury story. C: Paul Christian, Paula Raymond, Cecil Kellaway, Lee Van Cleef. D: Eugene Lourie. SFI 80m. V

Beast in the Cellar, The 1971 British ★★★ Two spinsters lock their demented brother in the basement. Old-fashioned horror flick is not eerie enough to be totally effective, but the performances are worthwhile. The American version is 15 minutes shorter. C: Beryl Reid, Flora Robson, John Hamill. D: James Kelly. HOR [R] 101m. V

Beast Must Die, The 1974 British ★★★★ A millionaire (Lockhart) tries to trap a werewolf by inviting him—and other guests—to a party at his remote castle. Good, tense suspense, loosely based on the story "There Shall Be No Darkness" by James Blish. (a.k.a. *Black Werewolf*) C: Calvin Lockhart, Peter Cushing, Charles Gray. D: Paul Annett. HOR [PG] 93m. V

Beast of Blood 1970 *See* **Beast of the Dead, The**

Beast of Budapest, The 1958 ★★½ After his father's death, a son opens his eyes to the evil of the Communist regime in Hungary. Odd little film with emphasis on the propaganda. C: Gerald Milton, John Hoyt, Greta Thyssen, Robert Blake. D: Harmon Jones. DRA 72m.

Beast of Hollow Mountain, The 1956 Mexican ★★★ A sleepy Western town is threatened by an evil monster. One of the first horror Westerns, and not bad. C: Ismael Rodriguez, Guy Madison, Patricia Medina. D: Edward Nassour. HOR 80m.

Beast of Morocco, The 1968 *See* **Hand of Night, The**

Beast of The City, The 1932 ★★★★ A gritty policeman (Huston) takes on the Mob and a gangster's moll (Harlow). An effective and absorbing tale that sets out to glorify police officers, rather than criminals, according to the opening statement by then-President Hoover. C: Walter Huston, Jean Hersholt, Wallace Ford, Mickey Rooney. D: Charles Brabin. CRI 87m.

Beast of the Dead, The 1970 ★★ A headless monster is on the loose as a mad doctor searches for a new head for his creation. Sequel to *Mad Doctor of Blood Island.* (a.k.a. *Beast of Blood*) C: John Ashley, Eddie Garcia, Beverly Miller. D: Eddie Romero. HOR 90m.

Beast of Yucca Flats, The 1961 ★★ Horror cult fave Johnson is exposed to nuclear testing and goes bonkers, wreaking havoc on the good folks in Yucca Flats. There are no words to describe Tor's performance. C: Douglas Mellor, Tor Johnson, Barbara Francis. D: Coleman Francis. HOR 60m.

Beast, The 1988 ★★★★ During the Soviet-Afghan war, an extremist Soviet tank commander leads his squadron to suicidal lengths. One soldier decides to leave and switches loyalties to the Afghan rebels. Well told, if predictable war drama that gives a unique perspective to the much-debated conflict. C: Jason Patric, Steven Bauer, George Dzundza, Stephen Baldwin. D: Kevin Reynolds. ACT [R] 109m. V

Beast with Five Fingers, The 1946 ★★★½ A dead man's mysteriously severed hand leaves his coffin to prey on those he left behind. Lorre is in fine form as a raving psychotic. Strikingly eerie at times. C: Robert Alda, Peter Lorre, Andrea King. D: Robert Florey. HOR 89m. V

Beast Within, The 1982 ★★ Extensive, often gruesome makeup effects and a dependable supporting cast give a bit of a lift to this silly shocker, with teenaged Clemens, the product of a monstrous rape, becoming a murderous creature himself. C: Ronny Cox, Bibi Besch, Paul Clemens. D: Philippe Mora. HOR [R] 98m. V

Beastmaster, The 1982 ★★★ All warriors can fight; this one (Singer) can telepathically communicate with animals, and use them to battle an evil magician (Torn). Lots of special effects and some amazing animal stunts spice up the silly story, which attracted an incredibly huge audience through TV showings. Followed by a sequel. C: Marc Singer, Tanya Roberts, Rip Torn, John Amos. D: Don Coscarelli. ACT [PG] 120m. V

Beastmaster 2: Through the Portal of Time 1991 ★★★ The Beastmaster (Singer) is back, this time in present day L.A. on a mission of revenge. Yes, the animals are still listening! More of the same. C: Marc Singer,

Kari Wuhrer, Sarah Douglas, Wings Hauser. D: Sylvio Tabet. ACT [PG-13] 107m. V

Beasts 1972 U.S.-Filipino ★★★ Typical mad-scientist shenanigans with a heavy borrowing from H.G. Wells's *Island of Lost Souls*, as castaway (Ashley) encounters human-animal mutations being created and hunted on a remote island. Cheap and tacky, but not without its entertaining elements. (a.k.a. *Twilight People*) C: John Ashley, Pat Woodell, Charles Macaulay, Pam Grier, Jan Merlin. D: Eddie Romero. HOR [PG] 84m.

Beasts 1983 ★★ Yet another variation on the humans-are-the-real-animals theme, with a camping couple set upon by savage attackers of both kinds in the Rockies. Low-budget, low-interest thriller. C: Tom Babson, Kathy Christopher, Vern Potter. HOR 92m. V

Beasts Are in the Streets, The 1978 ★★ Wild beasts escape from an animal park and terrorize the locals. Interesting idea, given campy treatment. C: Carol Lynley, Dale Robinette. D: Peter Hunt. HOR 104m. V

Beat, The 1988 ★★ A sensitive young boy attends a tough NYC high school. Through his poetry he spreads joy and wonder, forever changing the lives of the other students. Hopeful but somewhat unreal*to say the least*. C: John Savage, David Jacobson, Kara Glover. D: Paul Mones. DRA [R] 102m. V

Beat Street 1984 ★★½ Inner-city teens find creative release in wholesome activities such as graffiti and breakdancing. Naive script with some energetic musical interludes. C: Rae Dawn Chong, Guy Davis, Jon Chardiet. D: Stan Lathan. MUS [PG] 106m. V

Beat the Devil 1954 ★★★★ Spy thriller satire about group of schemers out to strike it rich. Cult comedy has a devoted following, though it never hit big at the time it was made. Sly screenplay by Huston and Truman Capote, able cast, and lovely Venice locations. C: Humphrey Bogart, Jennifer Jones, Gina Lollobrigida, Robert Morley, Peter Lorre. D: John Huston. COM 89m. V

Beatlemania the Movie 1981 *See* **Beatlemania**

Beatlemania 1981 ★ Popular stage show filmed live has four unknowns impersonating John, Paul, George, and Ringo. (a.k.a. *Beatlemania The Movie*) C: Mitch Weissman, Ralph Castelli, David Leon, Tom Teeley. D: Joseph Manduke. MUS [PG] 90m. V

Beatrice *See* **Passion of Beatrice, The**

Beau Brummel 1924 ★★★½ Barrymore is a a delight as a dandy whose love was forced to marry another, leaving him with a grudge against high society. Silent with organ accompaniment. C: John Barrymore, Mary Ator, Irene Rich, Willard Louis, Carmel Myers, Alec B. Francis, William Humphries. D: Harry Beaumont. DRA 117m.

Beau Brummel 1954 U.S. ★★★½ Rise and fall of a 19th-century court dandy (Granger) who becomes an indispensable friend to the Prince of Wales (Ustinov)—soon to be George IV—but undermines his success with pride and vanity. Entertaining costume drama. C: Stewart Granger, Elizabeth Taylor, Peter Ustinov, Robert Morley. D: Curtis Bernhardt. DRA 113m. V

Beau Geste 1939 ★★★★ Terrific French Foreign Legion tale, taken from P.C. Wren's classic adventure, about three brothers who run away together to avoid a family scandal. Shot in Yuma, Arizona, with tense and exciting action sequences, plus the unforgettable Cooper charm. Remade in 1966. C: Gary Cooper, Ray Milland, Robert Preston, Brian Donlevy, Susan Hayward, J. Carroll Naish, Broderick Crawford. D: William Wellman. ACT 114m. V

Beau Geste 1966 ★★★ Adventure-seeking brothers join the French Foreign legion. Remake of the classic tale suffers from miscasting and bland direction, although Telly has a few good moments as a dirty, rotten commander. C: Telly Savalas, Guy Stockwell, Doug McClure, Leslie Nielsen. D: Douglas Heyes. ACT 103m.

Beau James 1957 ★★★★ Hope gives a stylish performance as flamboyant Mayor Jimmy Walker in this colorful evocation of Prohibition-era New York. Surprisingly touching and memorable. C: Bob Hope, Vera Miles, Paul Douglas, Alexis Smith, Darren McGavin. D: Melville Shavelson. DRA 105m.

Beau Pere 1981 French ★★★★ After taking in his dead lover's seductive 14-year-old daughter, a piano player finds himself falling in love with her. Potentially tasteless material is handled with humor and sensitivity. C: Patrick Dewaere, Ariel Besse, Maurice Ronet, Nathalie Baye. D: Bertrand Blier. DRA 124m. V

Beauties of the Night 1954 French ★★★★ Charming fantasy involves a composer whose dream-life takes him through romance in a variety of eras. Lyrical and entertaining. (a.k.a *Les Belles-de-Nuit*) C: Gerard Philipe, Martine Carol, Gina Lollobrigida. D: Rene Clair. DRA 84m.

Beautiful Blonde from Bashful Bend, The 1949 ★★★ After pulling the trigger on a law officer, a saloon singer (Grable) holes up in a Western town where she's mistaken for the new school teacher. Last Hollywood feature for director Sturges and well below his finest efforts. Has its share of charm and fun, but overall too forced. C: Betty Grable, Cesar Romero, Rudy Vallee, Olga San Juan, Sterling Holloway. D: Preston Sturges. COM 76m. V

Beautiful but Dangerous 1952 *See* **She Couldn't Say No**

Beauty and the Beast 1946 French ★★★★★ Classic rendition of beloved, oft-filmed fairy tale romance features Day and Marais in title roles. Cocteau's visuals are masterly, with his use of light and surreal images achieving painterly effects. Highly recommended masterpiece. C: Jean Marais, Josette Day, Marcel Andre. D: Jean Cocteau. DRA 90m. V

Beauty and the Beast 1963 ★★ Little-known version of the classic story has a medieval princess (Taylor) looking out for the interests of an unfortunate prince who turns into a werewolf by night. Excellent makeup (by Jack Pierce, inventor of the original Frankenstein look) is the strongest point of this rendition. C: Joyce Taylor, Mark Damon, Eduard Franz. D: Edward Cahn. FAM/DRA 77m.

Beauty and the Beast 1991 ★★★★★ The old tale of a charming girl betrothed against her will to a "beast" who turns out to be more human than anyone suspects gets the Disney treatment, with inventive animation, great voice work, and a perky Ashman/Menken score. Stunning return to form for the Disney animators, this was the first animated feature ever nominated for the Best Picture Oscar, and rightly so. Won Oscars for Title Song and Best Score. Delightful. Later the basis for a Broadway musical. Voices of Paige O'Hara, Robby Benson, Jerry Orbach, Angela Lansbury, David Ogden Stiers. D: Gary Trousdale, Kirk Wise. FAM/MUS [G] 90m. V

Beauty and the Devil 1952 French ★★★★ Worthy updating of Goethe's *Faust*, with Simon capably playing both Faust and Mephisto (no easy task). The black and white photography is quite striking; a visual and literary treat. C: Michel Simon, Gerard Philippe, Nicole Besnard. D: Rene Clair. DRA 81m.

Beauty and the Robot, The 1960 *See* **Sex Kittens Go to College**

Beauty for Sale 1933 ★★★★ A naive young woman (Evans) falls for a wealthy married man (Kruger). Very good Kruger, striking cinematography, and tasteful direction. C: Madge Evans, Alice Brady, Otto Kruger, Una Merkel, May Robson, Hedda Hopper. D: Richard Boleslawsky. DRA 87m.

Beauty for the Asking 1939 ★★★ A beautician (Ball), jilted by a social climber (Knowles), gets her revenge by starting a lucrative cosmetics company funded by her ex's new rich wife (Inescort). Flimsy cold cream love-triangle, with a pleasing performance by Ball. C: Lucille Ball, Patric Knowles, Frieda Inescort. D: Glenn Tryon. DRA 68m. V

Beauty School 1993 ★ Exotic dance routines and other excuses for stripping make up most of the running time of this weak comedy about a businessman's search for the perfect women to model his specially made brassiere. C: Sylvia Kristel, Kevin Bernhardt, Kimberly Taylor, Jane Hamilton. D: Ernest G. Sauer. COM 95m. V

Bebe's Kids 1992 ★★★★ A man's romantic plans go up in smoke when his date brings along her brood of obnoxious and unruly children. Animated feature, built around characters created by the late African-American comedian Robin Harris, is a fun-filled, offbeat treat. Voices of Faizon Love, Nell Carter, Tone Loc, Myra J., Vanessa Bell Calloway, Wayne Collins. D: Bruce Smith. COM [PG-13] 74m. V

Bebo's Girl 1964 Italian ★★★½ Girl dumps boy for another boy—this one in jail. Cardinale is just fine as the young woman who falls for a troubled ex-war hero. Nicely done. C: Claudia Cardinale, George Chakiris. D: Luigi Comencini. DRA 106m.

Because He's My Friend 1978 Australian ★★★★ Parents find life with their retarded child to be both heartbreaking and rewarding. Poulsen is excellent as the young boy. Warmhearted drama is insightful and entertaining. C: Karen Black, Keir Dullea, Jack Thompson, Warwick Poulsen. D: Ralph Nelson. DRA 93m. TVM

Because of Him 1946 ★★★½ An ambitious young woman (Durbin) hopes to engineer her success through the patronage of one of Broadway's greatest actors (Laughton). Pleasant light comedy lets Durbin sing and Laughton act, and both do it well. C: Deanna Durbin, Franchot Tone, Charles Laughton, Helen Broderick. D: Richard Wallace. COM 88m.

Because of You 1952 ★★½ Man does not suspect that his new wife is an ex-convict. Once the secret is out, she returns to her old ways. Good performance by Young. C: Loretta Young, Jeff Chandler, Alex Nicol, Frances Dee. D: Joseph Pevney. DRA 95m.

Because They're Young 1960 ★★★½ Earnest, idealistic young teacher tries to get to know his "difficult" students and fails miserably. Clark, in his film debut, is well cast as the teacher, but Weld steals the show. C: Dick Clark, Michael Callan, Tuesday Weld, Victoria Shaw, Doug McClure, James Darren. D: Paul Wendkos. DRA 102m.

Because You're Mine 1952 ★★★ A tenor (Lanza) gets drafted into the Army, and falls for his sergeant's sister (Morrow). Service comedy with opera trimmings. Good Lanza showcase. C: Mario Lanza, James Whitmore, Doretta Morrow, Spring Byington. D: Alexander Hall. MUS 101m. V

Becket 1964 ★★★★★ Becket (Burton), friend to libidinous Henry II (O'Toole), is appointed archbishop of Canterbury as a puppet bureaucrat but becomes an adversary when he insists on taking his job seriously. Opulent costume drama, powered by dynamic performances by two leads (O'Toole played Henry again, in *The Lion in Winter*). Edward Anhalt won an Oscar for his screenplay adaptation of Jean Anouilh's play. C: Richard Burton, Peter O'Toole, John Gielgud, Donald Wolfit, Martita Hunt, Pamela Brown, Felix Aylmer. D: Peter Glenville. DRA 148m. V

Becky Sharp 1935 ★★★½ Hopkins shines as the title character, an enterprising minx striving for romance and fortune in 18th-century

England. First full-length Technicolor film is an appealing condensation of Thackeray's brilliant novel *Vanity Fair.* C: Miriam Hopkins, Frances Dee, Cedric Hardwicke, Billie Burke. D: Rouben Mamoulian. DRA 83m. v

Becoming Colette 1992 U.S. ★★ The supposedly true story of the 19th-century French author who came to renown after wresting her identity and her erotic writings from her tyrannical husband. A dainty, flimsy attempt at literate soft porn. C: Klaus Maria Brandauer, Mathilda May, Virginia Madsen, Paul Rhys, Jean-Pierre Aumont. D: Danny Huston. DRA [R] 97m. v

Bed and Board 1970 French ★★★½ The fourth chapter in Truffaut's autobiographical "Antoine Doinel" cycle finds Leaud married to the beautiful Jade and domesticated to within an inch of his life. Not much happens, but Leaud's humorous encounters with adulthood and responsibility radiate Truffaut's typically Gallic charm. C: Jean-Pierre Leaud, Claude Jade, Hirolo Berghauer. D: Francois Truffaut. DRA [PG] 97m.

Bed of Roses 1933 ★★★★ Randy romp about two young women, just released from reform school, on the make for guys with an unlimited cash flow. Bennett is charming as the girl with a heart of gold. Sharp, devious comedy from master La Cava. C: Constance Bennett, Joel McCrea, Pert Kelton, Franklin Pangborn. D: Gregory La Cava. COM 67m.

Bed-Sitting Room, The 1969 British ★★★½ Surreal supposition of what England would be like after nuclear war as the few remaining survivors attempt to reestablish some semblance of society. Bizarre, non sequitur British comedy more appealing for its outrageous images than its humor. C: Rita Tushingham, Ralph Richardson, Peter Cook, Dudley Moore, Harry Secombe, Spike Milligan, Michael Hordern, Mona Washbourne. D: Richard Lester. COM 90m.

Bedazzled 1967 British ★★★½ The devil (Cook) barters for the soul of a frumpy cook (Moore) by offering him seven wishes. Vignette comedy doesn't always work, but comics Cook and Moore generate lots of laughs. Raquel Welch as Lust also stands out. C: Peter Cook, Dudley Moore, Eleanor Bron, Raquel Welch. D: Stanley Donen. COM 107m. v

Bedelia 1946 British ★★★½ Atmospheric piece surrounding an unsuspecting man who marries a lovely woman with a dark past. Old black widow story is given fresh life with a probing, psychological approach. C: Margaret Lockwood, Ian Hunter. D: Lance Comfort. DRA 92m.

Bedevilled 1955 ★★★½ A young man studying for the clergy shields a shady nightclub singer from the law. Colorful Parisian locales animate this brooding melodrama. C: Anne Baxter, Steve Forrest, Simone Renant. D: Mitchell Leisen. DRA 85m.

Bedford Incident, The 1965 ★★★★ Conflict erupts on a surveillance submarine off the shore of Greenland, with the gruff captain (Widmark) challenged by reporter (Poitier) and doctor (Balsam). Good example of a Cold War thriller, expertly acted. C: Richard Widmark, Sidney Poitier, Martin Balsam, Wally Cox, James MacArthur, Donald Sutherland. D: James B. Harris. ACT 102m. v

Bedknobs and Broomsticks 1971 ★★★½ Clever mix of live action and animation, with Lansbury adorable as a good witch who enlists her powers to help the Allied effort in WWII. Minor Disney, enlivened by Lansbury. Don't miss the animated soccer match! C: Angela Lansbury, David Tomlinson, Roddy McDowell, Sam Jaffe. D: Robert Stevenson. FAM/COM [G] 112m. v

Bedlam 1946 ★★★★ An actress (Lee) antagonizes the wrong people in 18th-century England and is made a Bedlam inmate, encountering odd and frightening characters. Karloff is head of the asylum. Moody drama, produced by the talented Val Lewton. C: Boris Karloff, Anna Lee, Ian Wolfe, Richard Fraser. D: Mark Robson. HOR 79m. v

Bedroom Eyes 2 1989 ★★½ A stockbroker (Hauser) takes up with a woman (Blair) to spite his cheating wife, but ends up in hot water when the lover is killed. Change of lead actors doesn't bring any improvement over dull original. C: Wings Hauser, Kathy Shower, Linda Blair. D: Chuck Vincent. CRI [R] 85m. v

Bedroom Eyes 1986 ★★★ A businessman (Gilman) becomes a suspect when the woman he has been peeping at through a bedroom window is murdered. Uninvolving thriller bogs down in ridiculous attempts to be erotic. C: Dayle Haddon, Kenneth Gilman, Barbara Law, Christine Cattall. D: William Fruet. CRI 90m. v

Bedroom Window, The 1987 ★★★★ An architect (Guttenberg) tries to cover for his boss's wife (with whom he has had an affair) when she witnesses a murder, but he finds himself the prime target of the investigation. Edge-of-the-seat suspense in this Hitchcock-influenced thriller. C: Steve Guttenberg, Elizabeth McGovern, Isabelle Huppert, Wallace Shawn. D: Curtis Hanson. CRI [R] 113m. v

Bedtime for Bonzo 1951 ★★★ In an effort to prove that character is developed by one's surroundings, a chimpanzee is raised by a professor as if it were his own child. A mild romp with some genuine laughs, the film achieved cult status when its leading man became President of the U.S. C: Ronald Reagan, Diana Lynn, Walter Slezak, Jesse White. D: Frederick De Cordova. COM 83m. v

Bedtime Story, A 1933 ★★★½ A playboy's love life is threatened when he has to take care of an abandoned baby. Stylish, vintage musical comedy, with irrepressible Chevalier and jaunty musical numbers. C:

Maurice Chevalier, Helen Twelvetrees, Baby LeRoy, Edward Everett Horton. D: Norman Taurog. MUS 87m.

Bedtime Story 1941 ★★★★ Playwright (March) has two problems: completing his next work and trying to keep his acting spouse (Young) from retiring so she can star in the new production. Sparkling backstage comedy, brimming with good humor. March and Young are a terrific duo. C: Fredric March, Loretta Young, Robert Benchley, Eve Arden. D: Alexander Hall. COM 85m.

Bedtime Story 1963 ★★★★ Two con artists each feel the other is encroaching on his territory; they decide to settle their dispute by betting which one can bilk a rich widow first. Clever caper comedy enhanced by the unusual comic teaming of Brando and Niven. See the 1988 remake, *Dirty Rotten Scoundrels*, for a fun comparison. C: Marlon Brando, David Niven, Shirley Jones, Dody Goodman. D: Ralph Levy. COM 99m. V

Been Down So Long It Looks Like Up to Me 1971 ★★½ A beatnik gets hazed by students on a '50s college campus. Staid treatment of an interesting topic; based on Richard Fariña's novel. C: Barry Primus, Linda DeCoff, Susan Tyrrell, Bruce Davison, Raul Julia. D: Jeffrey Young. DRA [R] 90m.

Beer Drinker's Guide to Fitness and Filmmaking, The 1988 ★★★½ Fun autobiographical closeup on irreverent filmmaker's eccentric world. C: Fred G. Sullivan, Polly Sullivan, Tate Sullivan. D: Fred G. Sullivan. DOC [PG] 84m. V

Beer 1985 ★★½ An ad executive designs a foolproof method to market beer. Pedestrian screenplay and performances dilute this stale spoof of the business world. C: Loretta Swit, Rip Torn, Kenneth Mars, David Alan Grier, Dick Shawn. D: Patrick Kelly. COM [R] 83m. V

Bees, The 1978 ★★ A swarm of South American killer bees infests the U.S. A-swarm with overwrought performances. C: John Saxon, Angel Tompkins, John Carradine. D: Alfredo Zacharias. HOR [PG] 86m. V

Beethoven 1936 French ★★★★ Visually impressive study of the brilliant composer's troubled life and struggle with deafness. Director of *Napoleon* utilizes his mastery of camerawork to bring this difficult story to life. (a.k.a. *Beethoven's Great Love*) C: Harry Baur, Jean-Louis Barrault, Marcel Dalio. D: Abel Gance. DRA 116m. V

Beethoven 1992 ★★★½ Grodin's kids talk him into keeping a puppy who grows into a St. Bernard, the title character. Fun film for kids and dog lovers (and surprisingly fun for other adults, too). Followed by a sequel. C: Charles Grodin, Bonnie Hunt, Dean Jones, Oliver Platt. D: Brian Levant. FAM/COM [PG] 87m. V

Beethoven's Great Love *See* **Beethoven**

Beethoven Lives Upstairs 1992 ★★★ Beethoven seen through the eyes of his landlady's young son, who develops a tender relationship with the talented composer. Glorious music. C: Neil Munro, Illya Woloshyn, Fiona Reid, Sheila McCarthy, Paul Soles. D: David Devine. FAM/DRA 52m. V

Beethoven's Nephew 1988 ★★★ The legendary musician (Reichmann) struggles to tame his rather wild nephew (Prinz). Lacks coherent purpose despite lovely music, settings, and costumes. C: Wolfgang Reichmann, Ditmar Prinz, Jane Birkin, Nathalie Baye. D: Paul Morrissey. DRA 103m. V

Beethoven's 2nd 1994 ★★★½ The charming Beethoven finds true love with another St. Bernard, Missy, and they add four puppies to their unsuspecting human family. Many doggie gags in this squeaky clean sequel to *Beethoven*. The puppies are adorable. C: Charles Grodin, Bonnie Hunt. COM

Beetlejuice 1988 ★★★★ When the efforts of two recently deceased yuppies fail to get rid of the new owners of their house, they turn to deranged spirit Beetlejuice (Keaton) to get the job done. Visually inventive and imaginative comedy features a manic performance by Keaton. C: Michael Keaton, Alec Baldwin, Geena Davis, Jeffrey Jones, Catherine O'Hara, Winona Ryder, Sylvia Sidney. D: Tim Burton. COM [PG] 92m. V

Beezbo 1985 ★★★½ A sweet creature from space suddenly becomes human and learns about human courtesy. C: Josh Williams, Melissa Clayton, Karen Renee. D: Robert C. Bailey. FAM/DRA 70m. V

Before Dawn 1933 ★★★★ Early mystery with all the quintessential elements: the creaky house, cookie-cutter suspects, multiple murders, and plot twists galore. A delight for whodunit fans. C: Stuart Erwin, Dorothy Wilson, Warner Oland, Dudley Digges, Jane Darwell. D: Irving Pichel. CRI 60m. V

Before I Hang 1940 ★★½ Karloff manages to rejuvenate himself with a blood transfusion, little knowing that the donor was a murderer whose traits he begins to assume. Familiar story starts strongly and is well acted, but slow-moving second half derails it. C: Boris Karloff, Evelyn Keyes, Bruce Bennett. D: Nick Grinde. HOR 70m. V

Before I Wake 1956 *See* **Shadow of Fear**

Before Stonewall 1984 ★★★★ Forceful chronicle of America's gay rights movement, prior to the famous late-'60s Greenwich Village demonstration. Illuminating and absorbing; allows both sides to air views. D: J. Scagliotti. DOC 87m. V

Before Sunrise 1995 ★★★★½ Exhilirating romantic comedy about two free spirits who meet on a train to Vienna and spend one eventful night together. As they talk, make love, and talk some more, the audience falls as much in love with them as they do with each other. A winner. C: Ethan Hawke, Julie Delpy. D: Richard Linklater. COM [R] 100m. V

Before the Revolution 1962 Italian ★★★★ A young man (Barilli), in his mid-20s, searching for answers to social and philosophical problems, embraces Marxist rhetoric and has a brief flirtation with revolutionary fervor. Energetic story of youthful explorations, solidly rooted in '60s political turmoil. C: Adriana Asti, Francisco Barilli. D: Bernardo Bertolucci. DRA 110m. V

Before Winter Comes 1969 British ★★★½ An unlikely romantic triangle emerges in a WWII refugee camp, when a British captain (Niven) and his Russian interpreter (Topol) both become involved with an Austrian widow. Unusual blend of comedy and drama succeeds thanks to strong performances. C: David Niven, Topol, Anna Karina, John Hurt, Anthony Quayle. D: J. Thompson. DRA [PG] 102m.

Beggarman, Thief 1979 ★★★½ Sequel to TV's first popular miniseries *Rich Man, Poor Man* continues the adventures and liaisons of novelist Irwin Shaw's fictional Jordache clan. The main action takes place during the glitz of the Cannes Film Festival, in a high-pitched soap opera that will please genre fans. C: Jean Simmons, Glenn Ford, Lynn Redgrave, Tovah Feldshuh, Andrew Stevens, Jean-Pierre Aumont, Anne Francis. D: Lawrence Doheny. DRA 200m. TVM

Beggars of Life 1928 ★★★★ Brooks is magnificent in this silent drama, as a young woman hiding from the police after shooting her adoptive father in self-defense. C: Wallace Beery, Louise Brooks, Richard Arlen, Roscoe Karns. D: William Wellman. DRA 80m. V

Beggar's Opera, The 1953 British ★★★★ Olivier swaggers magnificently as Macheath, the infamous highway robber and hero of this film version of John Gay's 18th-century comic opera. Superior cast distinguishes a somewhat uneven production. C: Laurence Olivier, Stanley Holloway, Dorothy Tutin, Hugh Griffith. D: Peter Brook. MUS 94m.

Beginner's Luck 1984 ★★★½ A shy law student is introduced to the ways of the world and women by his less-than-bashful buddies. Better-than-average "first-time" comedy garners bright performances from the leads. C: Sam Rush, Riley Steiner, Charles Homet. D: Frank Mouris. COM [R] 85m. V

Beginning of the End 1957 ★ Take a bunch of locusts, zap 'em with radiation, and you've got giant grasshoppers winging toward Chicago. Transparent plot and special effects. Good for laughs. C: Peggie Castle, Peter Graves. D: Bert I. Gordon. SFI 80m. V

Beguiled, The 1970 ★★★★ Seven females at a Confederate finishing school become predatory when they help a Union soldier recover from his wounds. Gothic Western melodrama, marked by a fine Eastwood performance. C: Clint Eastwood, Geraldine Page, Elizabeth Hartman. D: Don Siegel. DRA [R] 105m. V

Behave Yourself 1951 ★★★½ Pandemonium hits an unassuming couple's lives when they take in a stray dog, not knowing that a gangster wants the pooch for his own nefarious purposes. Enjoyable blend of thrills and laughs, deftly played by Granger and Winters. C: Farley Granger, Shelley Winters, William Demarest, Margalo Gilmore, Lon Chaney Jr., Elisha Cook Jr., Hans Conried. D: George Beck. COM 81m. V

Behind Enemy Lines 1986 ★★ As the Vietnam War enters its final days, a POW (Carradine) leads a group of captured soldiers past the Commies to freedom. Nonstop-action film follows *Rambo*'s tried-and-true formula. (a.k.a. *P.O.W. The Escape*) C: David Carradine, Charles R. Floyd, Mako, Steve James. D: Gideon Amir. ACT 91m. V

Behind Locked Doors 1948 ★★★½ A newspaperman finds a missing judge in an insane asylum—and has he got a story to tell. Tense, well-directed thriller gets the most out of potentially lurid material. C: Lucille Bremer, Richard Carlson, Douglas Fowley. D: Oscar (Budd) Boetticher. DRA 62m.

Behind That Curtain 1929 ★★★ A troubled wife dumps her spiteful husband for her boyfriend. Early talkie features one of the first incarnations of Charlie Chan. C: Warner Baxter, Lois Moran, Gilbert Emery, Boris Karloff. D: Irving Cummings. DRA 90m.

Behind the Door 1940 *See* **Man with Nine Lives, The**

Behind the Eight Ball 1942 ★★½ Behind the scenes at a summer theater lurks a psychotic killer, watching . . . and waiting. Slim plot serves a vehicle for Ritz Brothers and other entertainers. C: Ritz Brothers, Carol Bruce, Dick Foran, William Demarest. D: Edward Cline. MUS 60m.

Behind the Front 1926 ★★★½ Two WWI servicemen on leave chase after wine, women, and song. Good fun; worthy addition to the many popular Army buddy silent films of the '20s. Rowdy Beery's the show here, while the strong supporting cast adds to the hijinks. C: Wallace Beery, Mary Brian, Raymond Hatton, Richard Arlen. D: A. Sutherland. COM 60m.

Behind the High Wall 1956 ★★★ A weary prison warden is about to crack beneath the strain of his sick wife's complaining and the convicts' repeated escape attempts. Remake of *The Big Guy*—conflict, crisis, and all. C: Tom Tully, Sylvia Sidney, Betty Lynn, John Gavin. D: Abner Biberman. CRI 85m.

Behind the Mask 1932 ★★★ Offbeat, campy thriller has a government agent infiltrating a gang of narcotics pushers to expose a gangland boss. Good cast struggles in an uninspired production. C: Jack Holt, Constance Cummings, Boris Karloff. D: John Dillon. CRI 70m.

Behind the Rising Sun 1943 ★★ Anti-Japanese tract depicts a father trying to force his son to join the Japanese Army. Propaganda from the height of WWII, of interest only as an artifact of the times. C: Margo, Tom Neal, J. Carroll Naish, Robert Ryan. D: Edward Dmytryk. ACT 89m.

Behold a Pale Horse 1964 ★★★ After the Spanish Civil War concludes, a Loyalist continues a solo struggle until an official decides to put a stop to it. Potentially intriguing political allegory collapses under the weight of dialogue-heavy drama. C: Gregory Peck, Anthony Quinn, Omar Sharif, Mildred Dunnock. D: Fred Zinnemann. DRA 118m. v

Behold My Wife 1935 ★★★ Racism through a soft-focus lens: a Native American (Sidney) falls in love with a WASP (Raymond), whose family can't see beyond her color. Earnest Hollywood drama, passing for grit. C: Sylvia Sidney, Gene Raymond, Laura Hope Crews, Ann Sheridan. D: Mitchell Leisen. DRA 78m.

Being, The 1983 ★★ The state of Idaho is terrorized by a beast created out of nuclear waste. Broadly played horror/comedy sat on the shelves for years; main attraction here is the cast. C: Martin Landau, Jose Ferrer, Dorothy Malone, Ruth Buzzi. D: Jackie Kong. HOR [R] 82m. v

Being There 1979 ★★★★½ Insulated all his life, a childlike simpleton's (Sellers) only exposure to the real world has been TV. When he's finally forced out of his solitude he becomes Washington's new political messiah. Brilliant satire on media's role in modern society, adapted by Jerzy Kosinski from his novel. Douglas won an Academy Award for Best Supporting Actor. Don't miss the outtakes in the final credits. C: Peter Sellers, Shirley MacLaine, Melvyn Douglas, Jack Warden, Richard Dysart, Richard Basehart. D: Hal Ashby. COM [PG] 124m. v

Bela Lugosi Meets a Brooklyn Gorilla 1952 ★★ Marooned on a tropical island, a comedy team runs into a mad scientist (Lugosi), who turns one of them into a gorilla. The absolute pits—and fascinating for it. C: Bela Lugosi, Duke Mitchell, Sammy Petrillo. D: William Beaudine. COM 60m. v

Belarus File, The 1985 ★★★½ The ever-popular dectective Kojak (Savalas) is back, and now he must apprehend a murderer of Nazi concentration camp survivors. C: Telly Savalas, Suzanne Pleshette, Max von Sydow. D: Robert Markowitz. DRA 95m. v

Believe in Me 1971 ★★½ A straitlaced professional woman visits Greenwich Village and gets hooked on amphetamines. Typical Hollywood attempt at sophistication looks embarrassing today. C: Michael Sarrazin, Jacqueline Bisset, Jon Cypher. D: Stuart Hagmann. DRA [R] 90m.

Believers, The 1987 ★★★ Investigating a Santeria cult, a psychologist (Sheen) and his young son become embroiled in supernatural murder and sacrifice. Professionally made on every level, but handled in too straightforward a manner to really cut loose as a horror film. Still too much for children, though. C: Martin Sheen, Helen Shaver, Harley Cross, Robert Loggia, Elizabeth Wilson, Jimmy Smits. D: John Schlesinger. HOR [R] 114m. v

Belizaire the Cajun 1986 ★★★½ A feisty medicine man (Assante) defends himself against murder charges in the midst of a territorial conflict in 1880s Louisiana. Involving backwoods whodunit, combined with an affecting love story, boasts interesting characters and an unusual look at a unique American subculture. C: Armand Assante, Gail Youngs, Michael Schoeffling. D: Glen Pitre. DRA [PG] 101m. v

Bell' Antonio 1960 Italian ★★★ Minor comedy features Mastroianni as a man whose impotence is no longer a public joke after a young woman declares him her paramour. Unmemorable if slightly amusing Italian sex farce. C: Marcello Mastroianni, Claudia Cardinale. D: Mauro Bolognini. COM 101m. v

Bell, Book and Candle 1958 ★★★½ A modern-day witch (Novak) tries to snare a publisher (Stewart) in this film version of John van Druten's stage comedy. Lemmon shines as a whimsical warlock playing havoc with the street lights. C: James Stewart, Kim Novak, Jack Lemmon, Ernie Kovacs, Elsa Lanchester, Hermione Gingold. D: Richard Quine. COM 103m. v

Bell for Adano, A 1945 ★★★★ Faithful adaptation of John Hersey's enormously popular novel about the American WWII occupation of a small Sicilian village, and the commander's efforts to revitalize it by the return of the city-hall bell. Quiet, touching story. C: Gene Tierney, John Hodiak, William Bendix, Glenn Langan, Richard Conte. D: Henry King. DRA 103m.

Bell Jar, The 1979 ★★½ When her father dies, a teenager becomes mentally unhinged. Based on Sylvia Plath's novel. Unconvincing, but fans of the book will want to see it. C: Marilyn Hassett, Julie Harris, Anne Jackson, Barbara Barrie, Robert Klein. D: Larry Peerce. DRA [R] 113m. v

Bellboy, The 1960 ★★★½ Lewis shoots for Chaplin-like status in his first directorial effort, playing a bellboy for Miami's Fountainbleau Hotel in a series of silent gags. More like a string of short films revolving around Lewis' ineptness, this works in parts but never gels into anything substantial. Kids may enjoy it, though. C: Jerry Lewis, Alex Gerry, Bob Clayton, Sonny Sands. D: Jerry Lewis. COM 72m. v

Belle de Jour 1967 French ★★★★★ A wealthy woman (Deneuve) goes to work in a high-class Parisian brothel. Her clients and their requests grow continuously more bizarre, as do her sexual fantasies. A wickedly surreal concoction from Buñuel at his peak. C: Catherine Deneuve, Jean Sorel, Michel Piccoli, Genevieve Page. D: Luis Buñuel. DRA [R] 100m.

Belle Epoque 1992 Spanish ★★★★½ In 1931 Spain, an army deserter is taken in by an eccentric old man with four daughters, each of whom has a turn with the young visitor. Charming, sexy comedy, winner of the 1993 Academy Award for Best Foreign Film. C: Jorge Sanz, Fernando Fernan Gomez, Maribel Verdu, Ariadna Gil, Miriam Diaz-Aroca, Penelope Cruz. D: Fernando Trueba. COM [R] 108m. V

Belle Le Grand 1951 ★★★½ A gambling woman (Ralston) is willing to roll the dice to get her man. Tight, entertaining little Western features some refreshing role reversals. James Arness has a bit part in the fire scene. C: Vera Hruba Ralston, John Carroll, William Ching. D: Allan Dwan. WST 90m.

Belle of New York, The 1952 ★★★½ So-so musical with some pretty numbers, as a playboy (Astaire) courts a missionary (Vera-Ellen) in Gay '90s New York. C: Fred Astaire, Vera-Ellen, Marjorie Main, Keenan Wynn. D: Charles Walters. MUS 82m. V

Belle of the Nineties 1934 ★★★★ Irrepressible West does her take on the Gay '90s, making mincemeat of would-be suitors and a scheming villain in this period comedy. Notable for West's double entendres, rendition of "My Old Flame," and an early screen appearance of Duke Ellington's orchestra. Originally called *It's No Sin*, the title was changed at the behest of censors. C: Mae West, Johnny Brown, Warren Hymer. D: Leo McCarey. COM 73m. V

Belle of the Yukon 1944 ★★★½ Colorful musical features a rough-and-tumble saloon owner (Scott) reformed by his warmhearted, virtuous girlfriend (Lee). Bouncy cast keeps this humming. C: Randolph Scott, Gypsy Rose Lee, Bob Burns, Dinah Shore, Charles Winninger. D: William Seiter. MUS 84m.

Belle Starr 1941 ★★½ Sanitized version of the West's most infamous female criminal, who rode with Jesse James and Cole Younger and whose Oklahoma home became a refuge for outlaws. Hollywood fluff. C: Gene Tierney, Randolph Scott, Dana Andrews. D: Irving Cummings. WST 87m.

Belle Starr 1980 ★★★½ Montgomery is the latest to take on the legend of the notorious bandit—and she does a fine job. Creditable Western has Belle rubbing elbows with the James and Younger gangs. C: Elizabeth Montgomery, Cliff Potts, Michael Cavanaugh, Fred Ward. D: John Alonzo. WST 97m. TVM

Belle Starr's Daughter 1948 ★★★ After Belle is murdered, her daughter wants to settle the score with the killers. Nice character twist elevates standard tale of revenge. C: George Montgomery, Rod Cameron, Ruth Roman. D: Lesley Selander. WST 86m.

Belles of St. Trinians, The 1953 British ★★★★ Sim plays a dual role as the nutty headmistress of a "seminary for young ladies" (whose students are anything but) and her scheming bookie twin brother. Hysterical comedy, based on the cartoons of Ronald Searle, led to several *St. Trinians'* sequels. C: Alastair Sim, Joyce Grenfell, George Cole, Hermione Baddeley. D: Frank Launder. COM 86m. V

Belles on Their Toes 1952 ★★½ The continuing saga of the twelve Gilbreth children. Middling sequel to the more colorful *Cheaper by the Dozen*. C: Myrna Loy, Jeanne Crain, Debra Paget, Jeffrey Hunter, Edward Arnold, Hoagy Carmichael. D: Henry Levin. COM 89m.

Bellissima 1951 Italian ★★★½ An obsessive stage mother (Magnani) pushes her awkward daughter into a screen test. Anna's terrific in this interesting but spotty comic drama. C: Anna Magnani, Walter Chiari, Tina Apicella. D: Luchino Visconti. DRA 112m.

Bellman and True 1987 British ★★★★ A British computer expert becomes involved with bank robbers who want to use his skills to lift funds. The catch is, they're holding his son to ensure cooperation. Absorbing performances and some really intriguing moments sustain interest. C: Bernard Hill, Kieran O'Brien, Richard Hope. D: Richard Loncraine. CRI [R] 114m. V

Bellman, The 1947 French ★★★★ Creepy thriller about a man whose job it is to ring a bell and alert travelers to their whereabouts; instead of providing direction, he lures them to their deaths. Deliciously macabre film deserves more recognition. C: Lucien Coedel, Fernand Ledoux, Renee Faure, Madelaine Robinson. D: Christian Jaques. HOR 95m. V

Bells Are Ringing 1960 ★★★★ An answering-service operator gets involved with her clients' lives and loves. Broadway hit vehicle for Holliday, scripted by Comden and Green, comes to the screen with its star, and with most of its score intact. Outstanding songs: "Just in Time" and "The Party's Over." Holliday's last film. C: Judy Holliday, Dean Martin, Fred Clark, Eddie Foy Jr., Jean Stapleton, Frank Gorshin, Gerry Mulligan. D: Vincente Minnelli. MUS 126m. V

Bells of Rosarita 1945 ★★★½ All the Roy Rogers regulars are here, this time trying to save a young woman from being swindled by an unscrupulous circus impresario. Tuneful Western works like a charm. C: Roy Rogers, Dale Evans, George "Gabby" Hayes. D: Frank McDonald. WST 68m. V

Bells of San Angelo 1947 ★★★½ Evans takes center stage in this Rogers musical Western. She plays a novelist who gets herself and Rogers out of a jam, proving that the pen is mightier than the sword—or six-shooter, in this case. One of their better efforts. C: Roy Rogers, Dale Evans, Andy Devine. D: William Witney. WST 71m. V

Bells of San Fernando 1947 ★★★ During the time when California was a territory of Spain, a wicked ranch overseer, Juan, rules the San Fernando Valley. When he announces his engagement to Maria, she is outraged because she wants to marry Michael. But will Michael be able to rescue her in time? C: Donald Woods, Gloria Warren, Monte Blue. WST 75m. V

Bells of St. Mary's, The 1945 ★★★★ Father O'Malley (Crosby) is sent to a new parish school in this sequel to *Going My Way*. Strict Sister Benedict (Bergman) has her own way of running things. Sentimental and utterly charming. C: Bing Crosby, Ingrid Bergman, Henry Travers, William Gargan, Ruth Donnelly. D: Leo McCarey. DRA 126m.

Belly of an Architect, The 1987 British ★★★ An American architect (Dennehy) runs into trouble with his wife (Webb), his stomach, and his grasp on reality while visiting Rome. Typically blasé, refined, and academic Greenaway excursion delivers ornate visuals and fleeting existential truths. C: Brian Dennehy, Chloe Webb, Lambert Wilson. D: Peter Greenaway. DRA [R] 119m. V

Beloved Enemy 1936 ★★★★ An Englishwoman and an Irish rebel are in love but their warring countries are tearing them apart. Slick, well-done melodrama. C: Merle Oberon, Brian Aherne, Karen Morley, David Niven, Donald Crisp. D: H. Potter. DRA 86m.

Beloved Infidel 1959 ★★½ The '30s love story of Hollywood columnist Sheilah Graham and author F. Scott Fitzgerald, based on her book. Interesting romance, good period color. C: Gregory Peck, Deborah Kerr, Eddie Albert. D: Henry King. DRA 123m.

Beloved Rogue, The 1927 ★★★★½ Lavish, silent period piece about the 15th-century balladeer and adventurer, François Villon (Barrymore) focuses on his romance with a damsel in distress; Veidt as Louis XI makes a formidable adversary. Likable film is pure entertainment having little to do with history; Barrymore himself, however, thought he overacted. Judge for yourself. C: John Barrymore, Conrad Veidt, Marceline Day. D: Alan Crosland. DRA 99m.

Below the Belt 1980 ★★★★½ Low-budget comedy/drama follows the rise of waitress-turned-wrestler as she learns the rough-and-tumble ways of the sport and gets a chance at a championship bout. Realistic and genuinely touching portrayal of this colorful, if less-than-glamorous, profession. C: Regina Baff, Mildred Burke, John C. Becher. D: Robert Fowler. DRA [R] 92m. V

Below the Sea 1933 ★★★★ One of the first big-budget underwater spectaculars follows the hunt for gold aboard a sunken submarine. Tremendously watchable adventure, with crackerjack special effects; catch Bellamy's famous fight with an octopus. C: Ralph Bellamy, Fay Wray. D: Albert Rogell. ACT 78m.

Belstone Fox, The 1973 British ★★★★ Beautifully detailed children's film uses live animals as protagonists to wonderful effect. A friendship between a fox and a dog is threatened when cruel humans use them for sport. Not all sugar and spice, but thoughtful family fare. C: Eric Porter, Rachel Roberts, Jeremy Kemp, Bill Travers. D: James Hill. FAM/DRA 103m. V

Ben 1972 ★★★ A sickly young boy takes care of a rat. Pretty gory sequel to *Willard* is not for the kids. Michael Jackson sings the theme song. C: Lee Montgomery, Joseph Campanella, Arthur O'Connell, Rosemary Murphy, Meredith Baxter-Birney. D: Phil Karlson. HOR [PG] 95m. V

Ben-Hur 1926 ★★★★½ One of the great silent epics; during the time of Christ, two boyhood friends fall out over Roman politics. Climactic chariot race is a thrilling achievement. Remade with great success in 1959. Includes a primitive color sequence. C: Ramon Novarro, Francis X. Bushman, May McAvoy, Betty Bronson. D: Fred Niblo. DRA 148m. V

Ben-Hur 1959 ★★★★★ Jewish galley slave Ben-Hur (Heston) rescues a Roman (Hawkins) after a shipwreck and pledges revenge on his boyhood friend Messala (Boyd) who's become his mortal enemy. The definitive historical epic, featuring a spectacular sea battle and thrilling chariot race finale. Won 11 Oscars (a record), including Best Picture, Director, Actor (Heston), and Supporting Actor (Griffith). A true classic. C: Charlton Heston, Jack Hawkins, Stephen Boyd, Haya Harareet, Hugh Griffith, Martha Scott, Sam Jaffe. D: William Wyler. DRA 211m. V

Bend of the River 1952 ★★★★ Well-directed story about a reformed outlaw guiding settlers along the Oregon Trail and the conflict that arises when he runs into an old criminal cohort. Stewart is excellent, but Kennedy doesn't seem comfortable in cowboy boots. C: James Stewart, Julie Adams, Arthur Kennedy, Rock Hudson. D: Anthony Mann. WST 91m. V

Beneath the Planet of the Apes 1970 ★★★★ An astronaut (Franciscus) is sent to Earth to find the previous team of astronauts and discovers not only apes aboveground, but hideous mutants below, who pray to a stainless-steel god—an atom bomb. Imaginative sequel to *Planet of the Apes;* followed by *Escape from the Planet of the Apes*. Trivia note: This is the only *Apes* movie without Roddy McDowall. C: James Franciscus, Kim Hunter, Maurice Evans, Linda Harrison, Charlton Heston, Victor Buono. D: Ted Post. SFI [G] 95m.

Beneath the 12 Mile Reef 1953 ★★★ Off the Florida coast, bland lovebirds (Wagner and Moore) romance against the backdrop of two sponge-diving families battling the sea and each other. The underwater CinemaScope photography is unfortunately more interesting than the story. Ends with the requisite man vs. octopus battle. C: Robert Wagner, Terry Moore, Gilbert Ronald. D: Robert Webb. DRA 102m.

Benefit of the Doubt, The 1967 British ★★★ British documentary looks at the Vietnam War. Odd pastiche of documentary footage interspersed with a theatrical production; not forbidding as it sounds. An interesting '60s relic. C: Eric Allan, Mary Allen. D: Peter Whitehead. DOC 70m.

Bengal Brigade 1954 ★★½ A British officer (Hudson) is assigned to quell an uprising in India. Plodding, underwhelming spectacle. C: Rock Hudson, Arlene Dahl, Ursula Thiess, Dan O'Herlihy, Michael Ansara. D: Laslo Benedek. ACT 87m.

Bengazi 1955 ★★ A police inspector and three assistants searching for stolen war supplies are attacked by natives and banished to a holy tomb. Action and adventure remain buried with them. C: Richard Conte, Victor McLaglen, Richard Carlson. D: John Brahm. ACT 78m.

Beniker Gang, The 1984 ★★★½ A teenager (McCarthy) leads an orphanage breakout with four younger cohorts and later supports them all by writing a newspaper advice column. Unusual, well-acted film is surprisingly effective; excellent for family viewing. C: Andrew McCarthy, Jennie Dundas. D: Ken Kwapis. FAM/DRA [G] 88m. V

Benjamin 1968 French ★★★ A young man sets out on his own and makes conquests of the beautiful Deneuve and Morgan. Costume drama, set in the 18th century, suffers from ambivalence—part sex romp, part identity search. C: Catherine Deneuve, Michele Morgan, Pierre Clementi, Michel Piccoli. D: Michel Deville. DRA [R] 100m.

Benjamin 1973 German ★★★½ Good--natured romp about a klutzy accountant who is mistaken for a ski champion. Breathtaking mountain footage, with a cast chock-full of real-life ski greats. C: Philip Sonntag, Helmut Trunz, Billy Kidd, Suzy Chaffee. D: Willy Bogner. COM 95m. V

Benji the Hunted 1987 ★★★ Heroic Benji has to survive by his considerable wits in the wild and look after orphaned cougar cubs in this later sequel to the very popular *Benji*. Not as much fun as the first couple, but he's still adorable. C: Red Steagall, Frank Inn. D: Joe Camp. FAM/DRA [G] 89m. V

Benji 1973 ★★★★ A remarkable and extremely lovable little mutt thwarts children's kidnapping and becomes a hero. This hard-to-resist modern dog story became an instant box-office hit, and spawned several sequels. Next was *For the Love of Benji*. C: Peter Breck, Deborah Walley, Edgar Buchanan. D: Joe Camp. FAM/DRA [G] 87m. V

Benny & Joon 1993 ★★★½ Simple grease monkey (Quinn) is worn out caring for his disturbed sister (Masterson). However, he feels new suitor (Depp), who courts her using silent movie routines, may be too crazy even for his sister. Sentimental, romantic comedy charms thanks to Depp's endearing performance. C: Johnny Depp, Mary Stuart Masterson, Aidan Quinn, Julianne Moore, Oliver Platt. D: Jeremiah Chechik. COM [PG] 98m. V

Benny Goodman Story, The 1955 ★★★ Allen made his feature film debut in this biography of the swing musician, which is long on music but short on facts. Lots of cameos, with Goodman himself playing on the soundtrack. C: Steve Allen, Donna Reed, Herbert Anderson, Gene Krupa, Lionel Hampton. D: Valentine Davies. DRA [G] 116m. V

Benny's Place 1982 ★★★★ Gossett shines as a middle-aged man feeling his years and losing his grip, both in the workplace and in his private life. Able supporting cast strengthens this well-done character study. C: Louis Gossett Jr., Cicely Tyson. D: Michael Schultz. DRA 100m. TVM

Benson Murder Case 1930 ★★★½ Palatable series entry has Philo Vance looking into the sordid lives of Long Island's rich and famous, searching for clues to the murder of a stockbroker. The ever-charming Powell and strong supporting cast give this a boost. C: William Powell, Natalie Moorhead, Eugene Pallette, Paul Lukas, Mischa Auer. D: Frank Tuttle. CRI 69m.

Berkeley in the Sixties 1991 ★★★ UCB campus was center of students' Free Speech Movement, and this documentary takes a straightforward approach, using newsreel and archival footage to show us those involved. D: Mark Kitchell. DOC 117m. V

Berkeley Square 1933 ★★★ An American goes to a previous life in London 200 years ago and falls in love. Tepid adaptation of Henry James' *The Sense of the Past*; its romance has not aged well. C: Leslie Howard, Heather Angel, Irene Browne. D: Frank Lloyd. DRA 84m.

Berlin Affair, The 1985 Italian ★★ Tawdry drama set in WWII Germany about a labored, none too believable lesbian love affair. Based on Junichiro Tanizuki's *The Buddhist Cross*, this embarrassing fizzle uses the tired Nazi angle to add a little kinkiness—but fails. C: Gudrun Landgrebe, Kevin McNally, Mio Takaki. D: Liliana Cavani. DRA [R] 97m. V

Berlin Alexanderplatz 1980 German ★★★★★ Fifteen-and-a-half hour epic about decadent pre-WWII Berlin has the fascination of a soap opera populated by whores, pimps, and murderers. Saga focuses on an ex-con (Lamprecht) who tries, but cannot go straight, and features stellar performances from Sukova and Schygulla.

Sprawling and hypnotic. C: Gunter Lamprecht, Hanna Schygulla, Barbara Sukowa. D: Rainer Werner Fassbinder. DRA 930m. TVM V

Berlin Blues 1989 ★★★★ Gripping story of a German chanteuse struggling to choose between two amorous men. C: Julia Migenes, Keith Baxter. D: Ricardo Franco. DRA [PG] 90m. V

Berlin Conspiracy, The 1991 ★★★ When a group of European terrorists try to transport a shipment of biological weapons, the CIA sends a team out after them. Jolting action. C: Marc Singer, Mary Crosby. D: Terence H. Winkless. ACT 83m. V

Berlin Correspondent 1942 ★★★ A beat reporter helps his girlfriend and her closely watched father to escape from the Nazis. Good Andrews, despite the usual propagandizing. C: Dana Andrews, Virginia Gilmore, Mona Maris, Sig Ruman. D: Eugene Forde. DRA 70m.

Berlin Express 1948 ★★★★ Suspenseful tale about representatives from four nations who plot to rescue a German statesman who's fallen into the hands of underground Nazis after WWII. This gripping movie uses a semidocumentary style and the landscape of war-torn Europe to heighten the drama. C: Merle Oberon, Robert Ryan, Paul Lukas, Robert Coote. D: Jacques Tourneur. DRA 86m. V

Berlin Tunnel 21 1981 ★★★★ An East German, desperate to get to freedom in the West, formulates a plan to dig a tunnel beneath the Berlin Wall. Slow at first, but once the plot kicks in this becomes a tense, neatly plotted thriller. C: Richard Thomas, Horst Buchholz, Jose Ferrer. D: Richard Michaels. DRA 150m. TVM

Bermuda Mystery 1944 ★★★ The family of a murdered man looks into the mystery surrounding his death. Surreal atmosphere and spunky cast lift this little whodunit. C: Preston Foster, Ann Rutherford, Charles Butterworth. D: Benjamin Stoloff. CRI 65m.

Bermuda Triangle, The 1978 ★★★ Docudrama looks at the mysterious ocean zone where dozens of ships, planes, and crews have vanished through alien intervention or electromagnetic phenomena. Thought-provoking, though low budget. DOC 94m. V

Bernadette of Lourdes 1961 French ★★★½ Young girl has a vision and is soon on the road to sainthood. Pleasant French production holds its own with the Jennifer Jones classic, *Song of Bernadette.* Rather moving. C: Daniele Ajoret, Nadine Alari. D: Robert Darene. DRA 90m.

Bernard and the Genie 1992 ★★★★ A down-on-his-luck art dealer believes his life can't get any stranger until he discovers one of his last remaining possessions contains a magical genie. Delightful British comedy rises above its premise, conjures up consistent laughs. C: Lenny Henry, Rowan Atkinson, Bob Geldof, Alan Cumming. D: Paul Welland. COM 75m. TVM V

Bernardine 1957 ★★★ A young man (Boone) and his mates try to impress Bernardine (Moore), the most perfect young woman they have ever seen. Coy, cloying film marked Boone's debut, as well as the long-awaited return (though last appearance) of Gaynor. C: Pat Boone, Terry Moore, Jane Gaynor, Dean Jagger. D: Henry Levin. COM 95m.

Bernhard, Sandra: Without You I'm Nothing 1990 ★★★ Strictly for Bernhard fans, this filmization of her popular off-Broadway one-person show mixes observations of relationships and the state of the world with musical numbers. Her talent is obvious, but her taste is questionable. C: Sandra Bernhard, Steve Antin, Lu Leonard. D: John Boskovich. COM [R] 90m. V

Berry Gordy's the Last Dragon 1985 ★★★ A young man strives to become the best kung-fu fighter in Harlem, but two neighborhood toughs stand in his way. Some fine action. C: Taimak, Thomas Ikeda, Julius Carry, Christopher Murney. D: Michael Schultz. DRA [PG-13] 108m. V

Bersork 1967 British ★★★ British cheapie features Joan as the head of a circus plagued by a series of grisly murders. Lurid little horror flick has a couple of neat twists but is memorable mostly for the still shapely Miss Crawford in a leotard. C: Joan Crawford, Ty Hardin, Diana Dors, Judy Geeson. D: Jim O'Connolly. HOR 96m. V

Berserker 1987 ★★★ On vacation, six college kids happen upon an ancient Scandinavian monster—a fierce Viking warrior that eats only human flesh. Grisly smorgasbord. C: Joseph Alan Johnson, Valerie Sheldon, Greg Dawson. D: Jef Richard. HOR [R] 85m. V

Bert Rigby, You're a Fool 1989 ★★★ Old-fashioned musical of a coal miner struggling to make it as a song-and-dance man. Agreeable showcase for West End London and Broadway star Lindsay. C: Robert Lindsay, Robbie Coltrane, Anne Bancroft, Corbin Bernsen. D: Carl Reiner. MUS [R] 94m. V

Beryl Markham: A Shadow on the Sun 1988 ★★★ Miniseries portrays '30s aviator/adventurer Beryl Markham (Powers). Markham's autobiography is fascinating and provides a rare look at a true Renaissance woman. (a.k.a. *Shadow on the Sun*) C: Stephanie Powers, Claire Bloom, Frederic Forrest. D: Tony Richardson. ACT 192m. TVM V

Best Boy 1979 ★★★★½ Documentarist Wohl's 52-year-old retarded cousin Philly is subject of this often moving, almost too personal study. Heartbreaking but inspiring in its depiction of his family's difficulties and its demonstration of Philly's laborious education. Oscar for Best Documentary. D: Ira Wohl. DOC 105m. V

Best Defense 1984 ★★ Weak satire of the

defense industry switches back and forth from an engineer's (Moore) misadventures in developing a new war weapon to the Army lieutenant (Murphy) stuck inside the resulting lemon in the Middle East. C: Dudley Moore, Eddie Murphy, Kate Capshaw, George Dzundza. D: Willard Huyck. COM [R] 94m. V

Best Enemies 1986 ★★★ The story of an impassioned young man, his lover and his best friend during the storm days of the late '60s. Good drama. C: Sigrid Thornton, Paul Williams, Judy Morris, Brandon Burke. D: David Baker. DRA 96m. V

Best Foot Forward 1943 ★★★½ Loosely based on the Broadway show, new plot has Ball playing herself, tricked into being a cadet's date at the school dance. Worth seeing just for the film debuts of Walker and Allyson. Energetic dance numbers staged by Charles Walters. C: Lucille Ball, William Gaxton, Virginia Weidler, Nancy Walker, Gloria DeHaven, June Allyson. D: Edward Buzzell. MUS 95m. V

Best Friends 1982 ★★★½ Live-in lovers/-screenwriters (Hawn and Reynolds) finally tie the knot, then come to regret it on the trip to meet each others's parents. Charming interplay of two stars makes it work. C: Burt Reynolds, Goldie Hawn, Jessica Tandy, Barnard Hughes, Audra Lindley, Keenan Wynn, Ron Silver. D: Norman Jewison. COM [PG] 108m. V

Best Intentions, The 1992 Swedish ★★★★ Autobiographical script by Ingmar Bergman, originally developed for Swedish television, focuses on the turbulent marriage of his parents, a seminarian (Froler) who weds a wealthy woman (August). Uncompromising look at familial interactions, with keen performances by the leads. In real life, Pernilla August is the spouse of director August. C: Samuel Froler, Pernilla August, Max von Sydow, Ghita Norby. D: Bille August. DRA 182m. V

Best Kept Secrets 1984 ★★★★ After her cop husband is denied a much deserved promotion, Duke discovers the police department has blacklisted him because of her work helping Central American refugees. Political drama benefits from tight scripting and a fine performance by Duke. C: Patty Duke Astin, Peter Coyote, Frederic Forrest, Meg Foster. D: Jerrold Freedman. DRA 94m. V

Best Legs in the 8th Grade 1984 ★★★ As a little boy he was a nerd. Now he's a hotshot attorney, and when he meets up with his 8th-grade crush, he falls for her all over again. A cute little comedy with fresh performances. C: Tim Matheson, James Belushi, Annette O'Toole, Kathryn Harrold. D: Tom Patchett. COM 60m. V

Best Little Girl in The World, The 1981 ★★★★ A beloved high schooler suffers in secret from a serious case of anorexia. Compelling disease exposé, wrenching drama. Superior all the way, including fabulous early work by Leigh. C: Charles Durning, Eva Marie Saint, Jennifer Jason Leigh, Melanie Mayron, Viveca Lindfors. D: Sam O'Steen. DRA 90m. TVM V

Best Little Whorehouse in Texas, The 1982 ★★½ The madam of a down-home brothel and her sheriff lover come to blows with a TV evangelist trying to close the place down. Pallid adaptation of the Broadway hit, despite likable stars. Durning's "Side Step" steals the show. C: Burt Reynolds, Dolly Parton, Dom DeLuise, Charles Durning, Jim Nabors. D: Colin Higgins. MUS [R] 114m. V

Best Man, The 1964 ★★★★½ Political skullduggery in spades, as presidential candidates (Fonda and Robertson) sling the mud during their party convention. Sharply observed Gore Vidal screenplay, from his Broadway play, with Tracy outstanding as the lame duck President. C: Henry Fonda, Cliff Robertson, Edie Adams, Margaret Leighton, Shelley Berman, Lee Tracy, Ann Sothern. D: Franklin J. Schaffner. DRA 103m.

Best of Enemies, The 1961 British ★★½ A British commander (Niven) constantly bumps into his Italian opposite number (Sordi) as they battle and blunder their way through a WWII campaign in Italy. Two strong performances, but not enough laughs for a victory. C: David Niven, Michael Wilding, Harry Andrews, Alberto Sordi. D: Guy Hamilton. COM 104m.

Best of Everything, The 1959 ★★★½ Three career women try to make it in New York City. Slick, glitzy soap opera taken from the pages of Rona Jaffe's '50s best-seller has it all. Entertaining, but rather dated now. C: Hope Lange, Stephen Boyd, Suzy Parker, Diane Baker, Martha Hyer, Joan Crawford, Brian Aherne, Louis Jourdan. D: Jean Negulesco. DRA 121m.

Best of Sledge Hammered, The 1988 ★★★ A quartet of episodes featuring the adventures of the dimwitted detective Sledge Hammer. Lots of laughs in "All Shook Up," "Witless," "Wild About Hammer" and "Under the Gun." C: David Rasche, Anne-Marie Martin, Harrison Page. D: Martha Coolidge. COM 100m. V

Best of Soupy Sales ★★★½ The madcap, slapstick kiddy host of all time, strutting his stuff for kids and adults who have fond memories of him. C: Soupy Sales, White Fang, Pookie. COM 53m. TVM

Best of the Badmen 1951 ★★★½ Fallen good-guy colonel (Ryan) goes up against bad-guy detective (Preston). Enter the James and Younger gangs, who go to bat for the colonel. The two Roberts make worthy adversaries in this offbeat Western. C: Robert Ryan, Claire Trevor, Robert Preston, Walter Brennan. D: William D. Russell. WST 84m. V

Best of the Best 1989 ★★★ U.S. karate team travels to Korea to take on their dreaded national team. The brutal contest becomes a personal grudge match for one American, whose brother died at his opponent's hands. Strictly by the numbers, but popular enough to warrant a sequel. C: Eric Roberts, James Jones, Sally Kirkland, Christopher Penn, Louise Fletcher. D: Bob Radler. ACT [PG-13] 95m. v

Best of Times, The 1986 ★★ Convinced that his life is a shambles because he blew the big high school football game, a mousy car salesman (Williams) convinces all involved to restage the game 20 years after the fact. Funny at times, but quirky character comedy never really connects. C: Robin Williams, Kurt Russell, Pamela Reed, Holly Palance, Donald Moffat. D: Roger Spottiswoode. COM [PG-13] 105m. v

Best Place to Be, The 1979 ★★★ Sprawling soap opera has Reed making her TV comeback in grand style as a widow who tries to turn her life around. Cast is in fighting shape, although the overlapping stories could be trimmed. Best taken in multiple doses. C: Donna Reed, Efrem Zimbalist, Jr., Betty White, Timothy Hutton. D: David Miller. DRA 202m. TVM v

Best Revenge 1983 ★★★ Tough drug smugglers make a daring escape from a Moroccan prison and plot revenge against their informers. Tough lurid action. C: Levon Helm, Moses Znaimer, Alberta Watson, John Rhys-Davies. D: John Trent. ACT [R] 92m. v

Best Seller 1987 ★★★ Former cop, now author (Dennehy) receives a unique proposal from a retired killer-for-hire (Woods), who's got the goods on a prominent business magnate. Dennehy follows Woods's story into a dark underworld in this straightforward thriller, which is distinguished by the intense strength of its two co-stars. C: James Woods, Brian Dennehy, Victoria Tennant. D: John Flynn. CRI [R] 95m. v

Best Things in Life Are Free, The 1956 ★★★½ Minor musical chronicles the songwriting legacy of Tin Pan Alley tunesmiths DeSylva, Brown, and Henderson. Enjoyable on its own level, with many memorable ditties (including "Sonny Boy" and "Birth of the Blues"). C: Gordon MacRae, Dan Dailey, Ernest Borgnine, Sheree North. D: Michael Curtiz. MUS 104m.

Best Years of Our Lives, The 1946 ★★★★★ Three returning GIs (March, Andrews, and Russell) have difficulty adjusting in post-WWII America. This sensitive commentary on the pressures of civilian life for vets earned eight Oscars, including: Best Picture, Director, Screenplay, Actor (March), Editing, and Score. Russell, a veteran, won two Oscars, one for his supporting role and a special one for inspiring other handicapped veterans. C: Fredric March, Myrna Loy, Teresa Wright, Dana Andrews, Virginia Mayo, Harold Russell, Hoagy Carmichael, Gladys George. D: William Wyler. DRA 170m. v

Bethune 1977 Canadian ★★★★ Above-average biography of the Canadian surgeon, Dr. Norman Bethune, who combined medical prowess with political actions, including helping the Chinese army during Mao Tse-tung's march to power. Made for Canadian television. C: Donald Sutherland, Kate Nelligan. D: Eric Till. DRA 88m. TVM

Betrayal from the East 1945 ★★★ Wisecrackng Tracy leads the U.S. war effort against the Japanese. The usual cinematic propaganda. C: Lee Tracy, Nancy Kelly. D: William Berke. ACT 82m.

Betrayal of the Dove 1992 ★★★ A divorced woman (Slater) believes that her best friend (LeBrock) has introduced her to the ideal date (Zane); but is she right or not? Fair drama; script written by Robby Benson. C: Helen Slater, Billy Zane, Kelly LeBrock, Harvey Korman. D: Strathford Hamilton. DRA [R] 93m. v

Betrayal 1983 British ★★★★ Riveting, painful story of an adulterous love affair. Told backwards, it begins two years after the affair has ended, and ends with the affair just beginning. Fine acting by Irons and Kingsley, working from Harold Pinter's screenplay (adapted from his own play). C: Jeremy Irons, Ben Kingsley, Patricia Hodge. D: David Jones. DRA [R] 95m. v

Betrayed 1944 *See* **When Strangers Marry**

Betrayed 1954 ★★ Turner sizzles as a nightclub singing Mata Hari, denounced as a Nazi informer, working for the Dutch underground. Otherwise a sickly spy film which neither an aging Gable nor location filming could revive. C: Clark Gable, Lana Turner, Victor Mature, Louis Calhern, Wilfred Hyde-White, Ian Carmichael. D: Gottfried Reinhardt. DRA 108m. v

Betrayed 1988 ★★★ A ditsy FBI agent (Winger) falls in love with the right-wing fanatic (Berenger) she is supposed to investigate; his racist/terrorist organization has been linked to the murder of a radio talk show host. Disturbing and violent suspense thriller needed a more coherent script. C: Debra Winger, Tom Berenger, John Heard, Betsy Blair, John Mahoney. D: Costa-Gavras. CRI [R] 127m.

Betrayed Women 1955 ★★½ Prisoners learn they aren't going to get any breaks from the sadistic warden in this lurid women's prison film. Nothing new. C: Carole Mathews, Beverly Michaels, Peggy Knudsen. D: Edward Cahn. DRA 70m.

Betsy, The 1978 ★★ Even as he nears retirement, a successful auto manufacturer continues to fuel controversy, in the boardroom and at home. Great cast and lots of glitz; from the novel by Harold Robbins. C: Laurence Olivier, Robert Duvall, Katharine Ross, Tommy Lee Jones, Jane Alexander, Lesley-Anne Down. D: Daniel Petrie. DRA [R] 125m. v

Betsy's Wedding 1990 ★★★★ Good-natured, funny comedy about the father of the bride (Alda) getting mixed up with organized crime to finance wedding of his daughter (Ringwald). Strong subplot, with a policewoman (Sheedy) romanced by a Mob underling (LaPaglia) almost upstages the rest of the film. C: Alan Alda, Madeline Kahn, Anthony Lapaglia, Joe Pesci, Molly Ringwald, Ally Sheedy. D: Alan Alda. COM [R] 94m. V

Better Late Than Never 1982 ★★★ Two down-and-out oldsters learn that one of them will be named guardian of an obnoxious, but very rich, ten-year-old heiress. Even the talented stars can't coax many laughs from this slow-moving formula comedy. C: David Niven, Art Carney, Maggie Smith. D: Bryan Forbes. COM [PG] 95m. V

Better Off Dead 1985 ★★★ Lovelorn Cusack makes a complete fool of himself over a high school crush and decides to end it all. Wacky, black teen comedy loaded with off-the-wall gags. C: John Cusack, David Ogden Stiers, Kim Darby. D: Steve Holland. COM [PG] 87m. V

Better Tomorrow, A 1986 Hong Kong ★★★★ Two brothers are on opposite sides of the law. The plot means little in this terrifically charged action piece from Woo, a master of choreographed violence. At the time, Hong Kong's biggest financial success, and still a prime example of Woo's work. C: Chow Yun-fatt, Leslie Cheung, Ti Lung. D: John Woo. ACT 95m. V

Betty 1992 French ★★★½ When a drunken woman is taken in by a female stranger, an unusual, potentially dangerous relationship develops. Enigmatic psychological thriller holds the attention, but may be too murky for some. C: Marie Trintignant, Stephane Audran. D: Claude Chabrol. DRA 100m. V

Betty Blue 1986 French ★★★½ Schizophrenic Dalle takes aspiring novelist Anglade to Paris in a violent search for fame and adventure. Confused, flashy melodrama with a heavy quotient of sex and violence. C: Jean-Hugues Anglade, Beatrice Dalle. D: Jean-Jacques Beineix. DRA 121m. V

Betty Ford Story, The 1987 ★★★½ Story of the former First Lady's battle with alcohol/prescription drug dependency makes earnest drama, helped by Rowlands' Emmy-winning performance. Inspiring. C: Gena Rowlands, Josef Sommer, Nan Woods. D: David Greene. DRA 100m.

Between Friends 1983 ★★★★ Two divorcés, both middle-aged but otherwise different in every way, become friends and help each other through their mid-life crises. Great star chemistry, solid drama. Good watching. C: Elizabeth Taylor, Carol Burnett, Barbara Rush. D: Lou Antonio. DRA 105m. TVM V

Between God, the Devil and a Winchester 1972 ★★ Angry cowboys go at each other with ferocity on the great plains. Gruesome and pointless western. C: Gilbert Roland, Richard Harrison. D: Dario Silvester. WST 98m. V

Between Heaven and Earth 1993 French ★★★ A rising journalist has a casual affair and when she becomes pregnant her unborn baby communicates with her, telling her he'd rather not be born into such an unhappy world. Intriguing and thought provoking. C: Carmen Maura, Jean-Pierre Cassel, Didier Bezace, Samuel Mussen, Andre Delvaux. D: Marion Hansel. DRA 80m. V

Between Heaven and Hell 1956 ★★½ A bigoted Southerner, stationed in the Pacific, learns that his survival in boot camp and combat during WWII depends on a revised view of his fellow men. Heavenly intentions, but formula scripting paves the road to hell. C: Robert Wagner, Terry Moore, Broderick Crawford, Buddy Ebsen, Harvey Lembeck. D: Richard Fleischer. DRA 95m. V

Between Midnight and Dawn 1950 ★★★½ Gritty nail biter about tough cops in pursuit of escaped cons. Lots of action and great exterior shooting. O'Brien is marvelous, as usual. C: Mark Stevens, Edmond O'Brien, Gale Storm. D: Gordon Douglas. ACT 89m.

Between the Lines 1977 ★★★★ The staff of an underground newspaper ponder their fate when a publishing empire buys their counterculture tabloid. Strong performances from a talented young acting ensemble keep this comedy/drama intriguing. C: John Heard, Lindsay Crouse, Jeff Goldblum, Jill Eikenberry, Marilu Henner. D: Joan Micklin Silver. COM [R] 101m. V

Between Time And Eternity 1960 German ★★★ When a woman (Palmer) discovers she is dying, she sets out to make up for lost time and learns about herself in the process. Old warhorse back in action. C: Lilli Palmer, Willy Birgel. D: Arthur Rabenalt. DRA 98m.

Between Two Women 1944 ★★★½ Boy next door Dr. Red Adams (Johnson) sweet-talks two women through medical crises. Gentle tale features DeHaven singing "I'm in the Mood for Love." C: Van Johnson, Lionel Barrymore, Gloria DeHaven, Keenan Wynn, Marilyn Maxwell, Keye Luke. D: Willis Goldbeck. DRA 83m.

Between Two Women 1986 ★★★★½ Outstanding picture has mother (Dewhurst) and daughter-in-law (Fawcett) coming to blows, then weathering adversity together. Both actresses do a fine job of etching real characters in this uncommonly fine exploration of a common situation. C: Farrah Fawcett, Colleen Dewhurst, Michael Nouri. D: Jon Avnet. DRA 95m. TVM

Between Two Worlds 1944 ★★★★ A group of men and women find themselves on a mysterious ship, then realize they're dead. Interesting remake of the play *Outward Bound*, with an outstanding cast of veteran character actors. C: John Garfield, Eleanor Parker, Sydney Greenstreet, Faye Emerson, Paul Henreid, Sara Allgood, Edmund Gwenn. D: Edward Blatt. DRA 112m.

Between Us Girls 1942 ★★★½ Mom (Francis) and daughter (Barrymore) share secrets about the men they're seeing. Amiable romantic comedy. C: Kay Francis, Diana Barrymore, Robert Cummings, Andy Devine, John Boles. D: Henry Koster. COM 89m.

Between Wars 1985 ★★★ The story of a young doctor serving with the Australian Army during WWI action and after. Intriguing and intelligent. C: Corin Redgrave, Judy Morris, Gunter Meisner, Arthur Dignam. D: Michael Thornhill. DRA 97m. V

Beulah Land 1980 ★★½ During the Civil War, a Southern belle (Warren) clings to her plantation against all odds. Overheated epic with a familiar story line and threadbare production values. C: Lesley Ann Warren, Michael Sarrazin, Don Johnson, Eddie Albert, Hope Lange, Meredith Baxter Birney. D: Harry Falk, Virgil W. Vogel. DRA 267m. TVM V

Beverly Hillbillies, The 1993 ★★ Lame remake of the popular TV series retells the story of poor mountaineer Jed Clampett's relocation to Beverly Hills after striking it rich with oil. Leachman is wasted as Granny and only Tomlin's overofficious Hathaway drums up any laughs. C: Diedreich Bader, Dabney Coleman, Erika Eleniak, Cloris Leachman, Lily Tomlin, Rob Schneider. D: Penelope Spheeris. COM [PG] 93m. V

Beverly Hills Bodysnatchers 1989 ★★★ A mad scientist teams up with a mortician and they concoct a serum that's supposed to bring the dead back to life. Ghoulish fun results when they bring back a mafia chieftain who goes after them. Gorshin and Tayback are hilarious. C: Vic Tayback, Frank Gorshin, Rodney Eastman, Warren Selko, Brooke Bundy. D: Jon Mostow. COM [R] 85m. V

Beverly Hills Brats 1989 ★★ Neglected rich kid engineers his own kidnapping so his parents will give him some attention. His ruse ends up turning real when both he and the kidnapper are abducted by two crooks. Slight comedy doesn't live up to its premise. C: Peter Billingsley, Martin Sheen, Terry Moore, Burt Young. D: Dimitri Sotirakis. COM [PG-13] 90m. V

Beverly Hills Cop III 1994 ★★★ The franchise is getting a little tired as Murphy goes back to California to solve a murder in an amusement park. Less than amusing. C: Eddie Murphy, Judge Reinhold, Hector Elizondo, Theresa Randle. D: John Landis. COM [R] 103m.

Beverly Hills Cop II 1987 ★★★½ Detroit's craziest cop (Murphy) returns to Beverly Hills when the precinct's police lieutenant gets shot at while jogging. His investigation leads to drug smugglers. Sporadically funny sequel gets by mostly on the talents of its star. C: Eddie Murphy, Judge Reinhold, Jurgen Prochnow, Ronny Cox, Brigitte Nielsen, Dean Stockwell. D: Tony Scott. ACT [R] 103m. V

Beverly Hills Cop 1984 ★★★★½ A streetwise Detroit cop (Murphy) finds things somewhat different when he hits the clean streets of Beverly Hills looking for his friend's murderers. Terrific blend of action and comedy uses Murphy's comic talents perfectly. Followed by two sequels. C: Eddie Murphy, Judge Reinhold, John Ashton, Lisa Eilbacher, Ronny Cox, Bronson Pinchot. D: Martin Brest. COM [R] 105m. V

Beverly Hills, 90210—The Graduation 1993 ★★ Overaged actors playing high school students finally get their diplomas and head for another series. Phony baloney plot twists can't salvage this overwrought soap opera. C: Jason Priestley, Shannen Doherty, Luke Perry, Brian Austin Green, Tori Spelling. DRA 118m. TVM V

Beverly Hills, 90210 1990 ★★★½ Members of a Minnesota family move to La-La Land and find their values challenged by the glitz and money of their new environment. Better than expected. Basis for the popular TV series. C: Luke Perry, Jason Priestley, Brian Austin Green, Shannen Doherty, Tori Spelling. DRA 90m. TVM V

Beverly Hills Vamp 1988 ★★★½ Ekland is a madam by day and a vampire by night. Amusing spoof is better than many more serious films in the genre; aims to please and succeeds. C: Eddie Deezen, Britt Ekland. D: Fred Olen Ray. COM [R] 90m. V

Beverly Sills in Verdi's La Traviata 1976 ★★★★ The opera superstar plays Violetta in this Verdi opera masterpiece. Excellent and stirring. In Italian with English subtitles. C: Beverly Sills. MUS 144m. V

Beware, My Lovely 1952 ★★★½ A psycho handyman terrorizes his employer. Well-done thriller with good performances. C: Ida Lupino, Robert Ryan, Taylor Holmes. D: Harry Horner. DRA 77m. V

Beware of a Holy Whore 1971 German ★★★½ The holy whore is cinema itself, and Fassbinder's autobiographical movie on moviemaking is bluntly honest about the creative process. Set at a seaside hotel, where cast and crew practice psychological and sexual terrorism on each other when the camera isn't rolling. Movie's intensity makes this a harsh yet fascinating viewing experience. C: Eddie Constantine, Hanna Schygulla, Margarethe von Trotta. D: Rainer Werner Fassbinder. DRA 110m.

Beware of Blondie 1950 ★★½ When Dagwood's boss, Mr. Dithers, goes on vacation, he puts the irrepressible Bumstead in charge. Fun and games as usual in this, the last *Blondie* film. C: Penny Singleton, Arthur Lake. D: Edward Bernds. COM 66m.

Beware of Children 1961 British ★★ A young couple inherits a small fortune and opens a summer camp for kids. Contrived. C: Leslie Phillips, Geraldine McEwan. D: Gerald Thomas. COM 80m.

Beware of Pity 1946 British ★★★★ Motivated by pity, a soldier proposes marriage to an ailing young baroness, who learns the bitter truth in the midst of her joy. Quite poignant and moving throughout. C: Lilli Palmer, Albert Lieven, Cedric Hardwicke, Gladys Cooper. D: Maurice Elvey. DRA 102m.

Beware, Spooks! 1939 ★★★ An ambitious young amusement park policeman takes on a bunch of outrageous con artists. A consistently good and high-powered comedy, with Brown excellent as the buffoon who shapes up. C: Joe E. Brown, Mary Carlisle, Clarence Kolb, Marc Lawrence. D: Edward Sedgwick. COM 68m.

Bewitched 1945 ★★★½ The harrowing story of a schizophrenic (Thaxter) who commits a murder and later has absolutely no recollection of it. Taut, intense drama. C: Phyllis Thaxter, Edmund Gwenn, Horace McNally, Henry Daniels Jr. D: Arch Oboler. CRI 65m.

Beyond a Reasonable Doubt 1956 ★★★ A novelist (Andrews) pretends to be a murderer to get a behind-the-scenes look at the court system, but then can't prove his own innocence. Despite the startling twist ending, implausible development makes this one of Lang's lesser works. C: Dana Andrews, Joan Fontaine, Sidney Blackmer. D: Fritz Lang. CRI 80m.

Beyond Atlantis 1973 U.S. ★★ Imaginative but silly look at the fabled lost underwater society—including a plot to kidnap women! When all is said and done, it's all wet. C: Patrick Wayne, John Ashley, Leigh Christian, George Nader. D: Eddie Romero. ACT [PG] 90m. V

Beyond Evil 1980 ★★ A young married couple moves into an old mansion rumored to be haunted. Some good, frightful nonsense wrapped up in a story that's been told thousands of times. C: John Saxon, Lynda Day George, Michael Dante. D: Herb Freed. HOR [R] 98m. V

Beyond Fear 1978 ★★ A real estate salesman stumbles upon a murder plot, and when the killer finds out, he breaks into the realtor's home and holds his family hostage. Beyond pointless. C: Michel Bouquet, Michael Constantine, Marilu Tolo. D: Yannick Andrei. ACT 92m. V

Beyond Glory 1948 ★★★ A WWII vet (Ladd), now a West Point instructor, is wrongly charged with misconduct. The cast does a good job with mediocre material. C: Alan Ladd, Donna Reed. D: John Farrow. DRA 82m.

Beyond Justice 1992 ★★ After a wealthy emir (Sharif) kidnaps his grandson and spirits him to the Mideast, the boy's worried CEO mom (Alt) hires a mercenary (Hauer) to get him back. From there on out, guns blaze away in one violent action sequence after another. C: Rutger Hauer, Carol Alt, Omar Sharif, Elliott Gould. D: Duccio Tessari. ACT [R] 113m. V

Beyond Mombasa 1957 U.S. ★★ During the Mau Mau uprising in Kenya, an American is killed and his brother seeks vengeance. Ordinary adventure set in an exotic locale. C: Cornel Wilde, Donna Reed, Leo Genn, Christopher Lee. D: George Marshall. ACT 90m.

Beyond Obsession 1985 ★★½ Strange love triangle develops between an ex-diplomat, a beautiful and enigmatic young woman and an American engineer. Fascinating cast can't save the overdone script. C: Marcello Mastroianni, Tom Berenger, Eleanora Giorgi, Michel Piccoli. D: Liliana Cavani. DRA 110m. V

Beyond Reason 1977 ★★½ A psychologist dedicates himself to the treatment of the criminally insane. Savalas's first writing-directing effort, not released theatrically. C: Telly Savalas, Laura Johnson, Diana Muldaur. D: Telly Savalas. DRA [PG] 88m. V

Beyond Reasonable Doubt 1980 New Zealand ★★★★ A remorseless police officer (Hemmings) convicts a farmer (Hargreaves) for a pair of murders on circumstantial evidence. Hemmings stands out in this New Zealand production, based on a true story; book by David Yallop. C: David Hemmings, John Hargreaves. D: John Laing. CRI 117m. V

Beyond the Blue Horizon 1942 ★★ Marooned on a tropical island, a young girl matures with only a chimpanzee and a tiger for company. Rescued years later, she inherits a fortune. Typical Lamour-in-sarong treatment that touches, at times, on absurdity. C: Dorothy Lamour, Richard Denning, Jack Haley. D: Alfred Santell. COM 76m.

Beyond the Door II 1979 Italian ★★★ Unrelated to the original (aside from its Italian background) and certainly superior to it, this chiller about a possessed young boy terrorizing his mother is enlivened by the stylish direction of veteran scaremeister Bava. C: Daria Nicolodi, John Steiner. D: Mario Bava. HOR [R] 90m. V

Beyond the Door 1975 U.S. ★ Wretched *Exorcist* ripoff from Italy has all the "shocking" trappings (pea-soup vomiting, screeching profanity, etc.) but none of the style or terror. This time, the victim of demonic possession is Mills, a long way from *Nanny and the Professor*. C: Juliet Mills, Richard Johnson. D: Oliver Hellman. HOR [R] 97m. V

Beyond the Forest 1949 ★★ "What a dump." This is the movie that classic line comes from. It also describes the film in general, as Davis gets involved in a murky murder story. Only for diehard fans. C: Bette Davis, Joseph Cotten, David Brian, Ruth Roman. D: King Vidor. DRA 94m. V

Beyond the Law 1968 Italian ★★★ An outlaw makes a miraculous reformation and becomes a sheriff. But as soon as a big shipment of silver comes in he takes it and takes off. Solidly entertaining Western and Van Cleef is lots of fun. C: Lee Van Cleef, Antonio Sabato, Lionel Stander. D: Giorgio Stegani. WST 94m. V

Beyond the Limit 1983 ★★ Adaptation of

Graham Greene's *The Honorary Consul* obsesses over a brooding and somewhat threatening love triangle in the midst of a sweltering South American city. Not without moments of intensity, but generally a tedious affair. C: Michael Caine, Richard Gere, Bob Hoskins, Elpidia Carrillo. D: John Mackenzie. DRA [R] 103m. V

Beyond the Poseidon Adventure 1979 ★★ The S.S. *Poseidon* is still capsized and there are still passengers trapped inside. Now two salvage teams fight for the ship's precious cargo—gold and plutonium. Mediocre special effects and zigzag script make this a watery sequel. C: Michael Caine, Sally Field, Telly Savalas, Peter Boyle, Jack Warden, Shirley Knight, Shirley Jones, Karl Malden, Mark Harmon, Veronica Hamel. D: Irwin Allen. ACT [PG] 115m. V

Beyond the Stars 1989 ★★★ An unhappy youth (Slater) teams up with a down-and-out ex-astronaut (Sheen) who shows him a bizarre lunar secret he's kept under wraps. Fair sci-fi effort, with good performances by all, weakened by a poor script. (a.k.a. *Personal Choice*) C: Christian Slater, Martin Sheen, F. Murray Abraham, Sharon Stone. D: David Saperstein. SFI 94m. V

Beyond the Time Barrier 1960 ★★ During a test flight, a pilot breaches the fifth dimension and lands in the 21st century, where civilization has moved entirely underground. Science fiction at its most primitive. C: Robert Clarke, Darlene Tompkins. D: Edgar Ulmer. SFI 75m.

Beyond the Walls 1984 Israeli ★★★ Routine prison drama involving Arab and Israeli criminals, forced by their crimes to spend time in confinement. Strictly routine stuff that leaves heavy-duty issues dormant. C: Arnon Zadok, Muhamad Bakri. D: Uri Barbash. DRA [R] 104m. V

Beyond, The *See* **7 Doors of Death**

Beyond Therapy 1987 ★★ Exploration of the New York City psyche, seen through the relationship between bisexual Goldblum and neurotic Haggarty, as told to their respective therapists. Christopher Durang, with Altman's help, adapts his stage play into an unfocused mishmash of vignettes. C: Julie Hagerty, Jeff Goldblum, Glenda Jackson, Tom Conti, Christopher Guest, Genevieve Page. D: Robert Altman. COM [R] 93m.

Beyond This Place 1959 *See* **Web of Evidence**

Beyond Tomorrow 1939 ★★★ Three hoary angels (Carey, Smith, and Winninger) intervene when a singer (Carlson) hits it big on the radio and leaves his love (Parker) for a big-city sophisticate (Vinson). Heavenly lightness. C: Richard Carlson, Jean Parker, Harry Carey, C. Aubrey Smith, Charles Winninger, Maria Ouspenskaya. D: Edward A. Sutherland. COM 84m. V

B.F.'s Daughter 1948 ★★ Amazingly wooden, characterless adaptation of satirical Marquand novel, brought to life somewhat by Stanwyck's performance as a rich woman who marries a poor economics professor (Heflin) and finances his success in New Deal Washington. C: Barbara Stanwyck, Van Heflin, Charles Coburn, Keenan Wynn. D: Robert Z. Leonard. DRA 108m.

Bhowani Junction 1956 U.S. ★★★★ Interesting drama about the divided loyalties of a half-English/half-Indian woman (Gardner) who loves an English military man but also has deep feelings for her country. Marvelous use of locations in India; well acted and directed. C: Ava Gardner, Stewart Granger, Bill Travers. D: George Cukor. DRA 110m. V

Bible, The 1966 Italian ★★★ Actually, it goes only as far as Abraham and Isaac, but why quibble? Huston's stark, spare treatment moves at a stately pace, and it doesn't really work; but there are scattered joys throughout—primarily the director's acting turn as Noah, and Scott as Abraham, bellowing his consternation at the Almighty. C: George C. Scott, John Huston, Richard Harris, Michael Parks, Ulla Bergryd, Ava Gardner, Stephen Boyd, Peter O'Toole, Franco Nero. D: John Huston. DRA 174m. V

Bicycle Thief, The 1948 Italian ★★★★★ Classic Italian neorealist film of a father and son in search of a stolen bicycle in war-torn Rome. Simply told drama is a moving study of the human condition under extreme circumstances. A cinema landmark, which won a special Oscar. C: Lamberto Maggiorani, Lianella Carell, Enzo Staiola. D: Vittorio De Sica. DRA 89m. V

Big Bad John 1990 ★★ Sheriff (Dean), in pursuit of his wayward daughter, is chased across the country by vicious rednecks. Oddball cast and good soundtrack (with Dean reprising the smash title hit, Charlie Daniels, and Willie Nelson, etc.) can't save this clinker. C: Ned Beatty, Jack Elam, Bo Hopkins, Jimmy Dean. D: Burt Kennedy. ACT [PG-13] 90m.

Big Bad Mama II 1987 ★★ The continuing adventures of a gangster mother (Dickinson) during the Great Depression. Here she and her grown daughters tackle corrupt politicians. An unintended spoof of the classic Mob genre. C: Angie Dickinson, Robert Culp, Danielle Brisebois. D: Jim Wynorski. ACT [R] 85m. V

Big Bad Mama 1974 ★★★½ Entertaining exploitation film follows a sexy outlaw mother (Dickinson) with two daughters who share her penchant for robbing banks. Some nudity, lots of violence, game cast. C: Angie Dickinson, Tom Skerritt, William Shatner. D: Steve Carver. ACT [R] 84m. V

Big Bang, The 1990 ★★★ People from all walks of life are asked questions about subjects ranging from sex to universe's origin, hence the title. Toback gets some interesting answers from his carefully handpicked cross-section. D: James Toback. DOC [R] 81m. v

Big Beat, The 1958 ★★½ Fantabulous music by Fats Domino, The Four Aces, The Mills Brothers, and others upstages a weak story of a recording executive racing around to sign up the artists. C: William Reynolds, Andra Martin, Gogi Grant, Rose Marie, Hans Conried. D: Will Cowan. MUS 81m.

Big Bet, The 1985 ★★ A teen with an overactive imagination (Sloane) wagers that he can seduce a minister's daughter in one week. Weak teen-sex farce, but Kristel provides some bright spots as a lascivious older neighbor. C: Sylvia Kristel, Kim Evenson, Lance Stone, Ron Thomas. D: Bert I. Gordon. COM 90m. v

Big Bird Cage, The 1972 ★★ The leader of a revolutionary group (Grier) recruits new members by getting herself thrown into prison. Semisatirical jab at the women-in-prison genre, with the usual sadism and nudity. Inferior sequel to *The Big Doll House*. C: Pam Grier, Anitra Ford, Sid Haig. D: Jack Hill. ACT [R] 93m. v

Big Blockade, The 1942 British ★★★ Interesting bit of propaganda detailing the importance of blockading Germany in order to win WWII. British stars shine in a series of documentary-style sketches. C: Michael Redgrave, Leslie Banks, Will Hay, John Mills, Robert Morley, Marius Goring, Michael Rennie, Michael Wilding. D: Charles Frend. DRA 77m.

Big Blue, The 1988 U.S. ★★½ Long, stunning underwater sequences dominate this story of two rival deep-sea divers who are crazy for dolphins; Arquette's role is almost an afterthought. Pretentious and muddled, but the photography is pretty. C: Jean-Marc Barr, Jean Reno, Paul Shenar, Griffin Dunne. Rosanna Arquette. D: Luc Besson. DRA [PG] 118m. v

Big Bluff, The 1955 ★★½ An opportunist turns to murder when the heiress he's married recovers from a "terminal" illness. Good, low-budget suspense. C: John Bromfield, Martha Vickers, Robert Hutton. D: W. Wilder. DRA 70m.

Big Boodle, The 1957 ★★½ A Havana casino employee (Flynn) discovers plates belonging to counterfeiters, which sends him on a chase through the city's dark underworld. Interesting pictures of pre-Castro Cuba, but over-the-hill Flynn can't do much with the meager plot. (a.k.a. *Night in Havana*) C: Errol Flynn, Pedro Armendariz, Rossana Rory. D: Richard Wilson. CRI 83m.

Big Bounce, The 1969 ★ A real bad news veteran hires on at a small California motel and lives (barely) to regret it. Muddled and gloomy. C: Ryan O'Neal, Leigh Taylor-Young, James Daly, Robert Webber, Lee Grant, Van Heflin. D: Alex March. DRA [PG] 102m. v

Big Boy 1930 ★★½ An African-American jockey (Jolson in blackface) wins big at the track. Wildly dated but lighthearted adaptation of Jolson's hit Broadway show. C: Al Jolson, Claudia Dell, Louise Closser Hale, Lloyd Hughes. D: Alan Crosland. MUS 69m.

Big Brawl, The 1980 ★★½ A Chinese cafe owner's son (Chan) goes after gangsters in Chicago. Kung fu silliness, with some entertaining comedy. C: Jackie Chan, Jose Ferrer, Kristine De Bell. D: Robert Clouse. ACT [R] 95m. v

Big Broadcast of 1938, The 1938 ★★★ Radio revue offers mixed bag of skits and songs, including two funny Fields's routines and Hope singing his signature tune, "Thanks for the Memories," in his feature debut. C: W. C. Fields, Martha Raye, Dorothy Lamour, Shirley Ross, Bob Hope, Ben Blue. D: Mitchell Leisen. MUS 90m.

Big Broadcast of 1937, The 1936 ★★★½ Thin plot (Ross as radio announcer squabbling with tenor Forrest) is just an excuse for another radio revue as one great performer after another does their thing; Burns and Allen steal the show. Fun for nostalgia buffs. Third of series. C: Jack Benny, George Burns, Gracie Allen, Bob Burns, Martha Raye, Shirley Ross, Ray Milland. D: Mitchell Leisen. MUS 102m.

Big Broadcast of 1936, The 1935 ★★★★ Series of novelty numbers strung together by Oakie as a radio singer chased by Roberti. Great lineup of talent: Burns and Allen, Merman blasting "It's the Animal in Me," tap dancer Bill Robinson and, of all things, the Vienna Boys' Choir! Second in series. C: Jack Oakie, George Burns, Gracie Allen, Lyda Roberti, Wendy Barrie, Ethel Merman, Charlie Ruggles, Mary Boland, Bill Robinson. D: Norman Taurog. MUS 97m.

Big Broadcast, The 1932 ★★★★ First of a popular series that allowed Hollywood to exploit radio talent while proving its superiority. Forget the plot, about a singer (Crosby) and millionaire (Erwin) in love with same woman (Hyams), and enjoy great stars doing signature numbers: Smith ("When the Moon Comes Over the Mountain"), Calloway ("Minnie the Moocher"), and The Boswell Sisters ("Shout, Sister Shout"). C: Bing Crosby, Kate Smith, George Burns, Gracie Allen, Cab Calloway, The Mills Brothers, The Boswell Sisters. D: Frank Tuttle. MUS 87m.

Big Brown Eyes 1936 ★★★ A smooth private detective (Grant) and his wisecracking girlfriend (Bennett) conspire to catch a gang of jewel thieves in this pleasant mystery. C: Joan Bennett, Cary Grant, Walter Pidgeon, Isabel Jewell, Lloyd Nolan. D: Raoul Walsh. CRI 77m.

Big Bus, The 1976 ★★½ On its initial voyage the world's most luxurious and first nuclear-powered tour bus encounters every mishap imaginable. Overblown spoof of disaster films predates *Airplane!* C: Joseph Bologna, Stockard Channing, John Beck, Lynn Redgrave, Jose Ferrer, Ruth Gordon, Richard Shull, Sally Kellerman, Ned Beatty, Bob Dishy, Richard Mulligan, Larry Hagman. D: James Frawley. COM [PG] 88m. V

Big Business Girl 1931 ★★½ Can a young woman build her own career and support her singing fiancé? Some fun and excellent work by Young. C: Loretta Young, Ricardo Cortez, Jack Albertson, Joan Blondell. D: William A. Seiter. COM 75m.

Big Business 1988 ★★★½ It's double trouble when Midler and Tomlin play dual roles as two sets of identical twins, mismatched and switched at birth. Now the country twins are converging on the city to protest a business action by the rich urban twins. High-energy comic performances keep this farce moving. C: Bette Midler, Lily Tomlin, Fred Ward, Edward Herrmann. D: Jim Abrahams. COM [PG] 98m. V

Big Bust-Out, The 1973 ★ Four women, held captive in a Mideast prison, escape while disguised as domestic help at an abbey, then take time to battle a prostitution ring. Exploitation feature is heavy on violence. C: Vonetta McGee, Monica Taylor, Gordon Mitchell. D: Richard Jackson. ACT 75m.

Big Cage, The 1933 ★★ Old-time circus adventure, this one starring real-life circus impresario Clyde Beatty. Best for its animal sequences and solid cast of supporting stars. C: Clyde Beatty, Anita Page, Mickey Rooney, Andy Devine. D: Kurt Neumann. ACT 82m.

Big Caper, The 1957 ★★½ A couple of con artists move into a town and pretend they're married to set up a big rip-off. Small-time suspense, but handled well. C: Rory Calhoun, Mary Costa, James Gregory. D: Robert Stevens. DRA 84m.

Big Carnival, The 1951 ★★★★★ Brilliant, cynical story of a coal miner caught in a mountain cave-in and slowly dying as a reporter (Douglas) milks the story for his own gain. Terrific performances, including Sterling as the miner's wife. Downbeat, but unforgettable. (a.k.a. *Ace in the Hole*) C: Kirk Douglas, Jan Sterling, Bob Arthur, Porter Hall, Frank Cady. D: Billy Wilder. DRA [R] 112m.

Big Cat, The 1949 ★★★ Deep in a mountainous paradise, ranchers find themselves constantly at odds with each other. Beautiful locations and credible cast. C: Lon McCallister, Preston Foster, Forrest Tucker. D: Phil Karlson. WST 75m. V

Big Chief, The 1960 French ★★★½ French version of O. Henry's famous short story, "The Ransom of Red Chief," about the kidnapping of a bratty child who drives his kidnappers bonkers. Fernandel's clowning is always fun, whatever the excuse. C: Fernandel, Gino Cervi, Papouf, Jean-Jacques Delbo, Noelle Norman. D: Henri Verneuil. FAM/COM 105m.

Big Chill, The 1983 ★★★★½ Seven friends, who went to college together in the late '60s, gather after the funeral of a mutual friend for a poignant reunion that reveals how they've changed. An entertaining and superbly coordinated ensemble piece, by turns wistful, witty, and uplifting. Justly renowned for its terrific soundtrack of '60s classics. C: William Hurt, Glenn Close, Jeff Goldblum, Tom Berenger, Kevin Kline, Mary Kay Place, Meg Tilly, JoBeth Williams. D: Lawrence Kasdan. DRA 103m.

Big Circus, The 1959 ★★★½ Action and intrigue at a nearly bankrupt circus is made interesting by the exceptionally talented cast (Lorre is the standout). Spectacle triumphs over plot in this likable extravaganza. C: Victor Mature, Red Buttons, Rhonda Fleming, Kathryn Grant, Vincent Price, Peter Lorre, David Nelson, Gilbert Roland, Steve Allen. D: Joseph Newman. DRA 108m.

Big City Blues 1932 ★★★ When a small-town yokel takes on Manhattan, he's in for a range of experiences—including his first love affair. Nicely done, and the cast is great (including an early Bogie appearance). C: Joan Blondell, Eric Linden, Inez Courtney, Guy Kibbee, Humphrey Bogart, Ned Sparks. D: Mervyn LeRoy. DRA 65m.

Big City, The 1937 ★★★ Gritty drama about a Russian immigrant (Tracy) involved in a taxi cab war. Makes up for holes in plot with sheer speed and energy. C: Spencer Tracy, Luise Rainer, Eddie Quillan, William Demarest, Regis Toomey. D: Frank Borzage. DRA 80m.

Big City, The 1948 ★★ Three New York bachelors act as "mentor" to a young woman, then fall in love with their creation. Syrupy sweet, but at least there's no aftertaste. C: Margaret O'Brien, Robert Preston, Danny Thomas, George Murphy, Betty Garrett. D: Norman Taurog. COM 103m.

Big City, The 1963 Indian ★★★★ Strict class and caste rules are broken when a Calcutta man is forced to let his wife take a job to support their family. Ray, India's master film director, does a fine job with this sensitive material. C: Madhabi Mukherjee, Anil Chatterjee. D: Satyajit Ray. DRA 122m.

Big Clock, The 1948 ★★★★ A reporter (Milland) working for a true-crime magazine finds himself the prime suspect in a murder he must solve for his editor (Laughton). Suspenseful and satisfying film noir, with an edgy blend of dark humor and tension. Remade in 1987 with espionage setting as *No Way Out.* C: Ray Milland, Charles Laughton, Maureen O'Sullivan, George Macready, Rita Johnson. D: John Farrow. CRI 95m.

Big Combo, The 1955 ★★ Police squad cracks down on a local crime syndicate. Heavy on the violence and light on entertainment. C: Cornel Wilde, Jean Wallace, Brian Donlevy, Richard Conte. D: Joseph H. Lewis. ACT 89m. v

Big Country, The 1958 ★★★★ Energetic, all-star Wild West show about an ex-sea captain (Peck) who goes West to marry Baker but gets distracted by a range war between feuding cattle ranchers. Ives won an Academy Award for Best Supporting Actor. C: Gregory Peck, Charlton Heston, Jean Simmons, Carroll Baker, Burl Ives, Chuck Connors, Charles Bickford. D: William Wyler. WST 168m. v

Big Crimewave, The 1986 ★★★ A disgruntled young man moves out of his tiny flat and ventures to Kansas where he hopes to become a famous writer of crime movies. Funny moments along the way. C: John Paizs, Darrel Baran, Eva Covacs. D: John Paizs. COM 80m. v

Big Cube, The 1969 ★★ A young girl devises an excellent plan for murdering her stepmother: feed her large doses of LSD. As lurid as it sounds. C: Lana Turner, George Chakiris, Richard Egan, Dan O'Herlihy. D: Tito Davison. DRA [PG] 98m.

Big Day, The 1957 *See* **No Time to Be Young**

Big Deal on Madonna Street 1956 Italian ★★★★½ Hilarious caper comedy involves a gang of novice crooks and criminal has-beens who plot the perfect crime. Naturally everything that can go wrong does, in great comic twists. Superb pacing. Remade as *Crackers*. C: Vittorio Gassman, Marcello Mastroianni, Renato Salvatori, Rossana Rory. D: Mario Monicelli. COM 91m. v

Big Doll House, The 1971 ★★★ Exploitation "women-in-prison" feature from producer Corman proved to be something of a groundbreaker. Bottom line: Female inmates revolt against sadistic guards in an orgy of sex and violence. Self-parodying movie makes for some entertaining viewing. (a.k.a. *Women's Penitentiary I*) C: Judy Brown, Roberta Collins, Pam Grier. D: Jack Hill. CRI [R] 93m. v

Big Easy, The 1987 ★★★★ A Mafia murder brings together homicide detective (Quaid) and assistant D.A. (Barkin), who launch a romance marked by ethical debate. Sexy, original thriller, with spicy New Orleans atmosphere. C: Dennis Quaid, Ellen Barkin, Ned Beatty, John Goodman, Charles Ludlam. D: Jim McBride. CRI [R] 101m. v

Big Fisherman, The 1959 ★★½ The life and times of St. Peter, with special emphasis on his dealings with an Arab princess. Major studio epic, with spectacle outweighing substance. C: Howard Keel, John Saxon, Susan Kohner, Herbert Lom, Martha Hyer. D: Frank Borzage. DRA [G] 180m.

Big Fix, The 1978 ★★★★ A former hippie turned private detective (Dreyfuss) tries to solve a murder among a group of former Berkeley revolutionaries. Fairly suspenseful film gets originality points for placing '40s film noir structure in a post-'60s campus setting. C: Richard Dreyfuss, Susan Anspach, Bonnie Bedelia, John Lithgow, F. Murray Abraham. D: Jeremy Paul Kagan. CRI [PG] 108m. v

Big Gag, The 1987 ★★ Comedians travel the world over to play silly tricks on people. When they knock on your door, pretend to be out. C: Danuta, Caroline Langford, Cyril Green. D: Yuda Barkan. COM [R] 84m. v

Big Gamble, The 1961 ★★½ While trekking across Africa in a rather undependable truck, a couple of gadabouts start a carting business for fun and profit. An interesting premise that works at times, as both comedy and adventure. C: Stephen Boyd, Juliette Greco, David Wayne, Sybil Thorndike. D: Richard Fleischer. COM 100m.

Big Girls Don't Cry . . . They Get Even 1992 ★★★ A teenager takes to the road when her dysfunctional family begins to drive her crazy. Teenagers will enjoy this angst-filled comedy about the revolt of one of their own. C: Hillary Wolf, David Strathairn, Margaret Whitton, Griffin Dunne. D: Joan Micklin Silver. COM [PG] 98m. v

Big Gusher, The 1951 ★★ A group of oil workers are under a tight deadline to strike it big. Well intended, but flat. C: Wayne Morris, Preston Foster, Dorothy Patrick. D: Lew Landers. DRA 68m.

Big Guy, The 1939 ★★½ Through an unexpected course of events, a young prisoner gets involved in a jail break that leads to murder. Good old-style convict story. C: Jackie Cooper, Victor McLaglen, Ona Munson. D: Arthur Lubin. DRA 78m.

Big Hand for the Little Lady, A 1966 ★★★★ Unpretentious comic Western about married homesteaders (Fonda and Woodward) suddenly thrown into a high-stakes poker game. Very entertaining, with a neat ending. C: Henry Fonda, Joanne Woodward, Jason Robards, Charles Bickford, Burgess Meredith, Paul Ford, Kevin McCarthy. D: Fielder Cook. WST 95m.

Big Hangover, The 1950 ★★ An up-and-coming lawyer tries to make it with the cocktail party set—but he's allergic to liquor. Muddled and not as funny as it should be. C: Van Johnson, Elizabeth Taylor, Leon Ames, Edgar Buchanan, Rosemary De Camp. D: Norman Krasna. COM 82m.

Big Heat, The 1953 ★★★★ An honest homicide detective sets out to find who's behind the car bomb that killed his wife and winds up investigating Mob infiltration within the police ranks. Taut, suspenseful film noir, with a surprising amount of violence. C: Glenn Ford, Gloria Grahame, Jocelyn Brando, Lee Marvin, Carolyn Jones, Jeanette Nolan. D: Fritz Lang. CRI 90m. v

Big House, The 1930 ★★★★ Inspired by an actual prison riot, this grim, hard-hitting story examines inmate society and how it fosters fatalism and criminal behavior. One of the first and most popular prison movies. Oscars for Best Screenplay and Sound. C: Wallace Beery, Chester Morris, Robert Montgomery, Lewis Stone. D: George Hill. CRI 86m.

Big House, U.S.A. 1955 ★★ To recover a stolen cache of money, a couple of tough cons bust out of the pen. Interesting casting, but otherwise typical prison melodrama. C: Broderick Crawford, Ralph Meeker, Charles Bronson, Lon Chaney Jr. D: Howard Koch. ACT 82m.

Big Jack 1949 ★★ A couple of aging ne'er-do-wells and their adventures in pre-Revolutionary America. Curious film, significant as Beery's final screen performance. C: Wallace Beery, Marjorie Main, Edward Arnold, Richard Conte. D: Richard Thorpe. COM 85m.

Big Jake 1971 ★★★ An aging cattle baron heads up a prairie trek to deliver a ransom to the outlaw who carried off his grandson. Agreeable but violent Western, with Wayne still awesome in his twilight. Solid performance by Boone. C: John Wayne, Richard Boone, Maureen O'Hara, Patrick Wayne, Bobby Vinton. D: George Sherman. WST [PG] 110m. V

Big Jim McLain 1952 ★★½ Wayne is out of his element as a hard-nosed government agent who will stop at nothing to catch Communist spies on the loose in the Hawaiian Islands. Lots of pretty scenery to complement the action, though. C: John Wayne, James Arness, Nancy Olson, Veda Ann Borg, Hans Conried. D: Edward Ludwig. ACT 90m. V

Big Job, The 1965 British ★★★★ Good British comic crime caper with a nifty plot twist: When the crooks get out of jail, they discover a police station has been built where they buried the loot. C: Sidney James, Sylvia Syms, Dick Emery, Joan Sims, Jim Dale. D: Gerald Thomas. COM 88m.

Big Knife, The 1955 ★★★ The ruthless edge of Hollywood is explored in this cynical story of a star (Palance) who wants better scripts and the parasitic show-biz types who surround him. Heavy-handed drama, loosely based on the play by Clifford Odets. C: Jack Palance, Ida Lupino, Shelley Winters, Rod Steiger, Ilka Chase, Wendell Corey. D: Robert Aldrich. DRA 111m.

Big Land, The 1957 ★★ Reluctant cooperation between Texas cattlemen and grain farmers hungry to profit from a statewide railroad. Some big stars in a small film. C: Alan Ladd, Virginia Mayo, Edmond O'Brien. D: Gordon Douglas. ACT 92m.

Big Leaguer, The 1953 ★★ A slugging rookie third baseman tries out at the New York Giants' training camp. A film made specially—if not solely—for baseball lovers. C: Edward G. Robinson, Vera-Ellen, Jeff Richards, Richard Jaeckel. D: Robert Aldrich. DRA 70m.

Big Lift, The 1950 ★★★★ Fact-based account of an American pilot (Clift) during the postwar Berlin airlift. Successful as entertainment, and fascinating as a pictorial record, film was shot almost entirely on location in West Berlin. C: Montgomery Clift, Paul Douglas, Cornell Borchers. D: George Seaton. DRA 120m.

Big Meat Eater, The 1983 Canadian ★★★ Interplanetary splatter musical about radioactive body parts. As bizarre as it sounds. C: George Dawson, Andrew Gillies. D: Chris Windsor. MUS 82m.

Big Mouth, The 1967 ★★★½ An unassuming bungler inadvertently gets mixed up in a hunt for a missing cache of diamonds. Ample laughs in this typical outing for the meister of mania. C: Jerry Lewis, Harold J. Stone, Susan Bay. D: Jerry Lewis. COM 107m. V

Big Night, The 1951 ★★ When his father is beaten by gangsters, a teenager goes out for revenge. Peculiar but interesting account of one rambunctious young man against the world. C: John Barrymore Jr., Preston Foster, Howland Chamberlain, Joan Lorring, Dorothy Comingore. D: Joseph Losey. DRA 75m.

Big Noise, The 1944 ★★ Laurel and Hardy play special detectives assigned to deliver a new weapon to Washington. Repeats some priceless routines, but a clinker on the whole. C: Stan Laurel, Oliver Hardy, Arthur Space, Veda Ann Borg. D: Malcolm St. Clair. COM 74m.

Big One: The Great Los Angeles Earthquake, The 1990 ★★ Los Angeles is battered mercilessly by a series of incredible earthquakes. Standard disaster film, replete with the usual personal profiles in tragedy. C: Joanna Kerns, Ed Begley Jr., Dan Lauria, Richard Masur, Joe Spano. D: Larry Elikann. DRA 200m. TVM

Big Operator, The 1959 ★★ A labor union leader with ties to the syndicate fights back when Uncle Sam cracks down. Low-level Mob picture with few redeeming qualities. C: Mickey Rooney, Steve Cochran, Mamie Van Doren, Mel Torme, Jim Backus, Jackie Coogan. D: Charles Haas. DRA 91m.

Big Parade, The 1925 ★★★★½ A young man's life is changed when he goes off to fight in WWI. Powerful battle scenes make it unforgettable, and the wartime romance works almost as well. A classic silent masterpiece. C: John Gilbert, Renee Adoree, Hobart Bosworth. D: King Vidor. ACT 142m. V

Big Parade, The 1986 Chinese ★★★★ Preparing for China's National Day parade, four young men and two of their superiors build a sometimes volatile, sometimes close camaraderie. Excellent character study, marked by wonderful photography. C: Wang Xuegi, Sun Chun, Lu Lei, Wu Ruofu. D: Chen Kaige. DRA 103m.

Big Picture, The 1989 ★★★★ Cocky film

student (Bacon) thinks his award-winning short will be his ticket to Hollywood success, but discovers it isn't that easy. Funny, dead-on exposé of show business won't please everyone, but those familiar with the film industry will laugh long and hard. C: Kevin Bacon, Emily Longstreth, J. T. Walsh, Jennifer Jason Leigh, Michael McKean. D: Christopher Guest. COM [PG-13] 100m. V

Big Pond, The 1930 ★★★ The black sheep of an aristocratic French family (Chevalier), posing as a Venetian gondolier, falls in love with an American heiress (Colbert) whose suspicious father gets him a job in his chewing gum factory. Likable musical pokes fun at Americans abroad and at home. C: Maurice Chevalier, Claudette Colbert, George Barbier. D: Hobart Henley. MUS 75m.

Big Punch, The 1948 ★★ When a boxer refuses to throw a fight, the syndicate frames him for murder. Insipid and predictable. C: Wayne Morris, Gordon MacRae, Lois Maxwell. D: Sherry Shourds. DRA 80m.

Big Red One, The 1980 ★★★★½ Tough, semiautobiographical account of the legendary First Infantry Division in WWII; a grizzled sergeant (Marvin) leads four young riflemen as everyone dies around them. Intensely personal film succeeds on many levels; Fuller both wrote and directed. C: Lee Marvin, Mark Hamill, Robert Carradine. D: Samuel Fuller. ACT [PG] 113m. V

Big Red 1962 ★★★★ A young boy (Payant) goes to work for a dog breeder (Pidgeon) and finds true friendship and loyalty with Big Red, a purebred Irish setter. Beautifully filmed in Quebec's countryside and wilderness areas. Based on the popular boys' novel by Jim Kjelgaard. C: Walter Pidgeon, Gilles Payant, Emile Genest. D: Norman Tokar. FAM/DRA 89m. V

Big Risk, The 1960 French ★★ To spare his family further grief, a mobster gives himself up to the police. Slow moving, and somewhat ineffective usage of the steamy Belmondo. C: Jean-Paul Belmondo, Lino Ventura, Marcel Dalio. D: Claude Sautet. DRA 111m.

Big Score, The 1983 ★★★ After a large pile of cash disappears from a drug bust, a Chicago cop (Williams) has to clear his name with his fellow officers—and do battle with the crooks who think he's got their loot. Solid low-budget actioner. C: Fred Williamson, John Saxon, Richard Roundtree, Nancy Wilson. D: Fred Williamson. ACT [R] 88m. V

Big Shakedown, The 1934 ★★★ After her husband becomes involved with organized crime, Davis decides the marriage is over. Minor Warner Brothers production is a good example of studio output at that period. C: Bette Davis, Ricardo Cortez, Glenda Farrell, Charles Farrell. D: John Dillon. DRA 64m.

Big Shot, The 1942 ★★½ Fair story of a third-rate criminal (Bogart) who is double-crossed by a one-time accomplice. Excellent cast distinguishes this otherwise routine gangster film. C: Humphrey Bogart, Irene Manning, Susan Peters. D: Lewis Seiler. CRI 82m.

Big Shots 1987 ★★ Trouble abounds when a pint-sized innocent from the suburbs befriends a savvy street kid and their adventures involve them with a hired killer. Weak blend of action and comedy. C: Ricky Busker, Darius McCrary, Robert Joy, Robert Prosky, Jerzy Skolimowski, Paul Winfield. D: Robert Mandel. COM [PG-13] 93m. V

Big Show, The 1961 ★★½ A circus owner dies, and his sons fight each other to take over the business. Compelling at times and generally well done. C: Esther Williams, Cliff Robertson, Nehemiah Persoff, Robert Vaughn. D: James Clark. DRA 113m.

Big Sky, The 1952 ★★★★ A well-done screen adaptation of A.B. Guthrie, Jr.'s novel about Kentucky mountain trappers and a perilous 1830 expeditionary keelboat trade journey up the Missouri River. Exciting and amiable wilderness drama. C: Kirk Douglas, Dewey Martin, Elizabeth Threatt, Arthur Hunnicutt. D: Howard Hawks. WST 121m. V

Big Sleep, The 1946 ★★★★★ One of the great crime films, despite its labyrinthine plot. Bogart is Raymond Chandler's detective antihero Philip Marlowe, investigating a murder while sexually sparring with the seductive Bacall. Moody film noir ambiance radiates throughout, marked by a fine cast, atmospheric direction, and a thoroughly dark sense of humor. William Faulkner has a scriptwriting credit. Remade in 1978. C: Humphrey Bogart, Lauren Bacall, John Ridgely, Martha Vickers, Dorothy Malone, Elisha Cook Jr. D: Howard Hawks. CRI 114m. V

Big Sleep, The 1978 British ★★★ Mitchum plays Raymond Chandler's Philip Marlowe, trying to cut through a complex web to solve a murder while looking after a rich man's unbalanced daughters. Though faithful to Chandler's story, relocating the setting to London dilutes some of the original flavor. C: Robert Mitchum, Sarah Miles, Candy Clark, Oliver Reed, Richard Boone, James Stewart, Joan Collins, Edward Fox, John Mills. D: Michael Winner. CRI [R] 101m. V

Big Steal, The 1949 ★★★★★ Cracker-jack film noir about a tough guy (Mitchum) trying to clear himself of robbery charges, while chasing the real thief across Mexico. Tough, tense, and full of surprises. C: Robert Mitchum, Jane Greer, William Bendix, Ramon Novarro. D: Don Siegel. CRI 71m. V

Big Store, The 1941 ★★★½ Zany detective Groucho is called in to save a department store. Film has a few high points, as in Groucho's singing "Sing While You Sell." C: Groucho Marx, Chico Marx, Harpo Marx,

Tony Martin, Virginia Grey, Margaret Dumont. D: Charles Riesner. COM 83m. V

Big Street, The 1942 ★★★ Damon Runyon fare in which a shy busboy (Fonda) falls for a selfish nightclub singer (Ball), who hardly knows he exists. She comes to her senses only after suffering a crippling accident. Strong against-type performances by Fonda and Ball, but the story wallows in sentimentality. C: Henry Fonda, Lucille Ball, Barton MacLane, Eugene Pallette, Agnes Moorehead, Sam Levene, Ray Collins, Hans Conried. D: Irving Reis. DRA 88m. V

Big Time 1988 ★★★ Singer Tom Waits appears in a special performance in Los Angeles. Waits plays all kinds of weird and funny characters and belts out numerous songs in his wheezy, raspy voice. Excellent for Waits fans. C: Tom Waits. D: Chris Blum. MUS [PG] 87m. V

Big Tip Off, The 1955 ★★ Shady dealings between a newspaper columnist and a powerful Mob boss. Some colorful characterizations in an otherwise murky film. C: Richard Conte, Constance Smith, Bruce Bennett. D: Frank McDonald. DRA 79m.

Big T.N.T. Show, The 1966 ★★★ An all-star tunefest, featuring performances by Joan Baez, Ray Charles, Bo Diddley, and more. Excellent music. C: David McCallum, Roger Miller, Joan Baez, Ike Turner, Tina Turner, Bo Diddley, The Ronettes, Ray Charles. D: Larry Peerce. MUS 93m.

Big Top Pee-Wee 1988 ★★★ TV's strangest kids' show host plays a farmer who becomes entangled with circus folk. Golino is attractive as the trapeze artist who is his love interest. Mainly for kids and fans of Herman. C: Pee-Wee Herman, Penelope Ann Miller, Kris Kristofferson, Valeria Golino. D: Randal Kleiser. FAM/COM [PG] 120m. V

Big Town Girl 1937 ★★★½ Fleeing from her violent husband, a singer (Trevor) poses as a countess. Very good B-feature, with a mighty fine performance from Claire. C: Claire Trevor, Donald Woods, Alan Dinehart. D: Frank R. Strayer. DRA 68m.

Big Town, The 1987 ★★★ A crapshooter (Dillon) comes to Chicago in the late '50s, looking for big-time dice games, and gets involved with a married stripper (Lane). Powerful cast looks great, but unfortunately has little to do. C: Matt Dillon, Diane Lane, Tommy Lee Jones, Tom Skerritt, Lee Grant, Bruce Dern. D: Ben Bolt. DRA [R] 109m. V

Big Town 1947 ★★ The old one about a major newspaper editor in all-out fight to chase the Mob out of town. Good guy-bad guy scenario receives sturdy but uninspiring treatment. C: Philip Reed, Hillary Brooke. D: William Thomas. DRA 60m.

Big Trail, The 1930 ★★★★ The movie that launched Wayne's career is a wagon train epic that pits him against murderers, Native American warriors, and unforgiving terrain in a sequel to *The Oregon Trail*. Wayne's potential is apparent. C: John Wayne, Marguerite Churchill. D: Raoul Walsh. WST 110m. V

Big Trees, The 1952 ★★★½ Set in turn-of-the-century California, greedy lumbermen (led by Douglas) battle homesteaders for possession of the redwood forests. Remake of *Valley of the Giants* is slight and predictable, but it has a lighthearted appeal. C: Kirk Douglas, Eve Miller, Patrice Wymore, Edgar Buchanan. D: Felix Feist. WST 89m. V

Big Trouble in Little China 1986 ★★★½ A tough trucker (Russell) gets mixed up in the mystical wedding plans of Chinatown's 2000-year-old Godfather—who needs a green-eyed bride to acquire immortality. Slam-bang special effects and stunts (as well as an outrageous sense of humor) keep this moving. A cult classic. C: Kurt Russell, Kim Cattrall, Dennis Dun, James Hong. D: John Carpenter. ACT [PG-13] 100m. V

Big Trouble 1986 ★★★ Desperate for cash to fund his three sons's tuition to Yale, an insurance rep (Arkin) agrees to help sultry D'Angelo murder her husband (Falk) and collect the life insurance. Comic remake of *Double Indemnity* is sporadically funny at best. Pairing of Arkin and Falk worked much better in he In-Laws. C: Peter Falk, Alan Arkin, Beverly D'Angelo, Charles Durning, Robert Stack. D: John Cassavetes. COM [R] 93m. V

Big Wave, The 1960 Japanese ★★★ Two young men, friends since childhood, come into conflict because they both like the same girl. Leisurely paced and quite interesting, really. C: Sessue Hayakawa, Ichizo Itami, Mickey Curtis. D: Tad Danielewski. DRA 60m.

Big Wednesday 1978 Japanese ★★★★ Carefree pals on the California seaside encounter the pitfalls of growing up at the advent of the Vietnam War. Full of energy, surfing, and natural, charismatic performances (particularly from Busey and Katt), but the "surfing as a metaphor for life" angle doesn't quite work. C: Jan-Michael Vincent, William Katt, Gary Busey, Lee Purcell. D: John Milius. DRA [PG] 120m. V

Big Wheel, The 1949 ★★½ After his father dies in a racing car accident, a young man decides to race cars, too. Predictable in many ways, but the cast is fine and the action keeps things on track. C: Mickey Rooney, Thomas Mitchell, Spring Byington. D: Edward Ludwig. ACT 92m.

Big Zapper 1973 British ★★½ A private eye and her hapless assistant share countless adventures. Cheerful, lighthearted rendition of a popular British comic strip. C: Linda Marlowe, Gary Hope. D: Lindsay Shonteff. COM [R] 94m.

Big 1988 ★★★★ A frustrated youngster's wish to be older comes true thanks to a magical carnival fortune-telling machine. Charming fantasy comedy; Hanks is perfect as the child in a man's body. C: Tom Hanks, Elizabeth Perkins, John Heard, Jared Rushton, Robert Loggia, Mercedes Ruehl. D: Penny Marshall. COM [PG] 104m.

Bigamist, The 1953 ★★★★ One of the few women to sit in the Hollywood director's chair, Lupino's fine film noir crime drama is the only time she also directed herself. Sympathetic story of a man who falls in love with and marries two women. C: Edmond O'Brien, Joan Fontaine, Ida Lupino, Edmund Gwenn, Jane Darwell. D: Ida Lupino. DRA 80m.

Bigfoot 1987 ★★ It's Sasquatch from Disney! All kinds of silly things happen when a pair of Bigfoots (Bigfeet?) meet up with an anthropologist and a couple of kids. Pleasant enough for families. C: Colleen Dewhurst, James Sloyan, Gracie Harrison. D: Danny Huston. FAM/COM 100m. TVM

Bigger than Life 1956 ★★★½ When a teacher (Mason) becomes addicted to drugs, both he and his family suffer. Well done and gripping. Mason is excellent. C: James Mason, Barbara Rush, Walter Matthau. D: Nicholas Ray. DRA 95m.

Biggest Bundle Of Them All 1968 ★★½ A big gangster, now retired, is kidnapped by other crooks so he can mastermind a large platinum heist. Solid cast tries hard to hold together a flimsy script. C: Robert Wagner, Raquel Welch, Vittorio De Sica, Edward G. Robinson, Godfrey Cambridge. D: Ken Annakin. COM 110m.

Biggles: Adventures in Time 1985 British ★★★★ Mild-mannered, modern-day New Yorker (Hyde-White) leaps back in time to help his soulmate, a British WWI ace pilot named Biggles (Dickson). Novel use of the time travel device holds up, often providing humor with its action. Anglophiles may enjoy it most. Based on characters of Capt. W.E. Johns. C: Neil Dickson, Alex Hyde-White, Fiona Hutchinson, Peter Cushing. D: John Hough. ACT 88m. V

Bikini Beach 1964 ★★★ Third entry in the *Beach Party* series has Frankie competing for Annette's affections with British singing star, The Potato Bug. Mild, '60s-style comedy typical of the series. Mostly notable for an appearance by very young Stevie Wonder. C: Frankie Avalon, Annette Funicello, Keenan Wynn, Martha Hyer, Harvey Lembeck, Don Rickles, Little Stevie Wonder. D: William Asher. COM 100m. V

Bikini Carwash Company, The 1992 ★ A hick car wash owner shares his profits with his main attraction: bikini-clad car cleaners. Lots of slow motion and pointless strutting. C: Joe Dusic, Neriah Napaul, Suzanne Browne. D: Ed Hansen. COM [R] 90m. V

Bikini Carwash Company II, The 1993 ★ When an evil mogul works to eradicate their car-cleaning business, a group of beach bunnies start their own lingerie home-shopping network. More of a plotline, but even dumber than the original. C: Suzanne Browne, Neriah Napaul, Rikki Brando, Greg Raye. D: Gary Orona. COM [R] 94m. V

Bilitis 1977 French ★★ A young lady, a student at an elite girls' school, gets her first lessons in sex and love. Just an excuse for the standard soft-core applesauce. C: Patti D'Arbanville, Mona Kristensen, Bernard Giraudeau. D: David Hamilton. DRA [R] 95m.

Bill and Coo 1947 ★★½ Very odd and quite interesting indeed: a love story with a cast made up entirely of birds. Enormously unusual, to say the least! D: Dean Riesner. DRA 61m. V

Bill & Ted's Bogus Journey 1991 ★★★½ Sequel to *Bill & Ted's Excellent Adventure* finds Reeves and Winter making postmortem pals with Death after being killed by evil look-alike robots sent from the future. Totally goofball humor and most excellent special effects in an entertainingly idiotic comedy. C: Keanu Reeves, Alex Winter, William Sadler, Joss Ackland, George Carlin, Pam Grier. D: Peter Hewitt. COM [PG] 98m. V

Bill & Ted's Excellent Adventure 1989 ★★★½ Fun-loving teenage buddies travel through time to study for a history exam. For good-natured silliness, it's hard to beat. Followed by a sequel. C: Keanu Reeves, Alex Winter, George Carlin. D: Stephen Herek. COM [PG] 90m. V

Bill Cosby— "Himself" 1983 ★★★★ Cosby onstage in top form, getting ample mileage out of the kind of cozy, nonconfrontational routine his fans expect, most of it satirizing the cute foibles of family life. Clean, no surprises. D: Bill Cosby. COM [PG] 104m. V

Bill of Divorcement, A 1932 ★★★★ Barrymore is affecting as a man who returns home after confinement in a mental institution on the day his wife (Burke) divorces him. His despondency is eased by the renewal of his relationship with his daughter (Hepburn, in her first film). Wonderful cast, in a fine melodrama. Remade in 1940. C: John Barrymore, Katharine Hepburn, Billie Burke. D: George Cukor. DRA 74m. V

Bill of Divorcement, A 1940 ★★★ After a long absence, a man gets to know his now grown daughter. Solid remake of the 1932 classic, with O'Hara and Menjou playing the Hepburn and Barrymore roles. No slouches, these two, but the production can't escape the shadow of the original. C: Maureen O'Hara, Adolphe Menjou, Fay Bainter, Herbert Marshall, Dame May Whitty, C. Aubrey Smith. D: John Farrow. DRA 74m.

Bill: On His Own 1983 ★★★★ Follow-up to movie *Bill* continues the story of a retarded adult (Rooney) as he forays into the world. A college student (Hunt) serves as Rooney's teacher, while filmmaker (Quaid) continues looking out for his friend. Sensitive and thoughtful family viewing. C: Mickey Rooney, Helen Hunt, Teresa Wright, Dennis Quaid. D: Anthony Page. FAM/DRA 97m. TVM V

Bill 1981 ★★★★ After almost half a century in an asylum, a mentally retarded adult (Rooney) has to learn how to live in the world outside. Effective drama garnered Rooney a well deserved Emmy. C: Mickey Rooney, Dennis Quaid, Largo Woodruff. D: Anthony Page. DRA 97m. TVM V

Billie 1965 ★★½ A gifted high school athlete (Duke) is surrounded by parents, teachers, and a boyfriend who all wish she'd act more ladylike. Energetic but dated comedy. C: Patty Duke, Warren Berlinger, Jim Backus, Jane Greer, Billy De Wolfe. D: Don Weis. COM 86m. V

Billion Dollar Brain 1967 British ★★ A former CIA agent journeys to Finland and gets involved in a psychopathic attempt at world conquest. Beautiful location shooting wasted on utter nonsense. Third in series, after *The Ipcress File* and *Funeral in Berlin.* C: Michael Caine, Karl Malden, Ed Begley, Oscar Homolka, Francoise Dorleac. D: Ken Russell. DRA 111m.

Billion Dollar Hobo, The 1977 ★★ In order to collect his multimillion-dollar inheritance, a dimwit must live his life as a hobo. Conway makes some fun out of a silly script. C: Tim Conway, Will Geer. D: Stuart McGowan. COM [G] 96m.

Billionaire Boys Club 1992 ★★★ A bunch of rich, spoiled college kids get mixed up in fraud, embezzlement, and murder. True story makes for interesting courtroom drama. C: Judd Nelson, Fredric Lehne, Raphael Sbarge. D: Marvin J. Chomsky. DRA 94m. TVM V

Billy Bathgate 1991 ★★★★ In the '30s, a streetwise kid (Dean) works his way into the organization of Dutch Schultz (Hoffman). But the vicious Mob life isn't the escape from poverty he expects. Highly polished, handsome, yet somehow less-than-compelling drama, dominated by Hoffman's strong performance. Screenplay by Tom Stoppard, based on the novel by E.L. Doctorow. C: Dustin Hoffman, Nicole Kidman, Loren Dean, Bruce Willis. D: Robert Benton. DRA [R] 107m. V

Billy Budd 1962 U.S. ★★★★ Herman Melville's allegorical tale of moral right vs. lawful justice, about a conscientious sailor (Stamp) aboard a 1797 British warship who kills its sadistic master-at-arms (Ryan), is turned into a straightforward drama of good vs. evil. Well done, with powerful performances. C: Robert Ryan, Peter Ustinov, Melvyn Douglas, Terence Stamp, David McCallum. D: Peter Ustinov. DRA 123m. V

Billy Crystal—Don't Get Me Started 1986 ★★★½ Comedian Billy Crystal portrays his most engaging characters in a blend of absurd documentary and classic stand-up. Adding to the many laughs is a stream of guest stars. C: Billy Crystal, Rob Reiner, Christopher Guest. D: Billy Crystal. COM 60m. V

Billy Crystal—Midnight Train to Moscow 1989 ★★★½ Comedian Billy Crystal's famous 1989 comedy concert at Moscow's Pushkin Theater. Lots of laughs and some poignant moments as well. Good going. C: Billy Crystal. D: Paul Flaherty. COM 72m. V

Billy Galvin 1986 ★★★ Billy wants to be a construction worker like his father, who wants him to be anything but. Involving drama, good performances. C: Karl Malden, Lenny Von Dohlen, Joyce Van Patten. D: John Gray. DRA [PG] 99m. V

Billy in the Lowlands 1979 ★★ Tormented by the need to "find" himself, a young loser breaks out of prison to search for his estranged father. Well-meaning but quite confused. C: Henry Tomaszewski, Paul Benedict, David Morton. D: Jan Egleson. DRA 88m.

Billy Jack Goes to Washington 1977 ★★½ The famous, idealistic karate expert journeys to Washington to fight corruption in national politics. Good to a point, then starts to ramble. C: Tom Laughlin, Delores Taylor, Sam Wanamaker, Lucie Arnaz, E. G. Marshall. D: Tom Laughlin. ACT 155m.

Billy Jack 1971 ★★½ He may be half Indian, but he's all Green Beret when he's forced to defend his reservation's school against local bigots. A cult hit that picked up on a character from *Born Losers.* Two sequels followed, *The Trial of Billy Jack* and *Billy Jack Goes to Washington.* C: Tom Laughlin, Delores Taylor. D: T. C. Frank. ACT [PG] 115m. V

Billy Joel—Live at Yankee Stadium 1990 ★★★½ Billy Joel's fabulous 1990 rock concert at New York's glorious Yankee Stadium. Includes the tunes from his "Storm Front" album plus special footage detailing Joel's fondness for Yankee Stadium. Well done. C: Billy Joel. MUS 80m. V

Billy Liar 1963 British ★★★★ In a small British town, an undertaker's clerk dreams constantly of other lives he'd like to be living. Intriguing character study soars with a high-quality cast. C: Tom Courtenay, Julie Christie, Wilfred Pickles, Mona Washbourne, Ethel Griffies, Finlay Currie. D: John Schlesinger. DRA 96m.

Billy Madison 1995 ★★½ Moronic son (Sandler) of a millionaire (McGavin) is forced to repeat grammar school in order to inherit fortune. One of several "dumb is good" comedies; one of the more obnoxious ones, with Sandler terrorizing his sweet, six-year-old classmates. C: Adam Sandler, Darren McGavin, Bradley Whitford, Josh Mostel. D: Tamra Davis. COM [PG-13] 88m. V

Billy Rose's Jumbo 1962 ★★★★ Enjoyable musical, with Durante delightful as the owner of a near-bankrupt circus, flanked by his loving daughter (Day) and perennial fiancée (Raye). Sentimental period charmer, with grand Rodgers and Hart score. Nice spice from Raye. (a.k.a. *Jumbo*) C: Doris Day, Stephen Boyd, Jimmy Durante, Martha Raye. D: Charles Walter. MUS 127m.

Billy the Kid vs. Dracula 1966 ★★ When Dracula arrives out West, he takes up with a pretty ranch owner—who happens to be the fiancée of Billy the Kid. A real hoot, and vintage Carradine. C: Chuck Courtney, John Carradine, Melinda Plowman. D: William Beaudine. HOR 95m.

Billy the Kid 1989 ★★★½ Romanticized retelling of the legend of the notorious Southwest cattle thief and murderer, William H. Bonney. Watchable Western, with good outdoor photography. C: Val Kilmer, Julie Carmen, Duncan Regehr, Wilford Brimley. D: William Graham. WST 96m. V

Billy Two Hats 1974 ★★½ Uneven Western about a grizzled bandit (Peck) recruiting a younger man (Arnaz) for one last job. Peck is very good. C: Gregory Peck, Desi Arnaz Jr., Jack Warden. D: Ted Kotcheff. WST [PG] 99m.

Biloxi Blues 1988 ★★★★ Boot camp in Mississippi is quite a jolt for Brooklyn-born Broderick, especially as he must contend with a slightly psychotic drill sergeant. Neil Simon continues the comic coming-of-age saga he started in *Brighton Beach Memoirs* with a funny yet poignant look at basic training. Walken is terrific as the crazed sergeant. C: Matthew Broderick, Christopher Walken, Matt Mulhern, Corey Parker, Penelope Ann Miller. D: Mike Nichols. COM [PG-13] 105m.

Bimbo the Great 1961 German ★★ When his wife is found murdered, a high-wire circus star conducts his own investigation. Standard Big Top bonanza, including the obligatory fiery conflagration. C: Claus Holm, Germaine Damar, Elma Karlowa, Marina Orschel. D: Harold Philipp. CRI 96m.

Bingo Long Traveling All-Stars & Motor Kings, The 1976 ★★★★ Absorbing comedy about an all-black baseball team that defects from the Negro League and sets out on its own, traveling the countryside and challenging local white teams. Powerhouse cast deftly handles the comedy and drama of this offbeat, thought-provoking film. C: Billy Dee Williams, James Earl Jones, Richard Pryor, Ted Ross. D: John Badham. COM [PG] 111m. V

Bingo 1991 ★★½ Family film about a runaway circus pooch who is befriended by a lonely boy. Though separated by a family move, the mutt and his master are ultimately reunited. Harmless pull at the heartstrings for your children and Fido. C: Cindy Williams, David Rasche. D: Matthew Robbins. FAM/DRA [PG] 90m. V

Biography of a Bachelor Girl 1935 ★★★ A beautiful and demure portrait painter publishes her surprisingly amorous autobiography. Interesting adaptation of a hit Broadway play. C: Ann Harding, Robert Montgomery, Edward Everett Horton, Edward Arnold, Una Merkel. D: Edward Griffith. DRA 82m.

Bionic Showdown: The Six Million Dollar Man and the Bionic Woman 1989 ★★★ The famous restructured superhumans take on bad guys everywhere. Loads of fun, thanks to plenty of action and outstanding production values. C: Lindsay Wagner, Lee Majors, Richard Anderson, Josef Lee. D: Alan Levi. ACT 100m. TVM

Biquefarre 1983 French ★★★½ Semi-documentary about French farmers struggling to keep their land. Earnest, if sometimes plodding. Sequel to 1948's *Farrebique.* C: Henri Rouquier, Maria Rouquier, Roger Malet. D: George Rouquier. DRA 90m.

Birch Interval 1978 ★★★★ A young Amish girl faces the trials and traumas of growing up and falling in love. Excellent family drama, well played. C: Eddie Albert, Rip Torn, Ann Wedgeworth. D: Delbert Mann. FAM/DRA [PG] 104m. V

Bird 1988 ★★★★½ Inspired acting by Whitaker dominates this marvelous film biography of saxophone legend Charlie Parker, who made beautiful music but whose personal life was a drug-filled shambles. Evocative settings, terrific jazz, and spot-on, realistic performances give an authentic feel to the story. C: Forest Whitaker, Diane Venora, Michael Zelniker. D: Clint Eastwood. DRA [R] 161m. V

Bird of Paradise 1932 ★★★ Unambitious South Seas romance pairs McCrea with a native princess (Del Rio). Harmless, if not exactly memorable. Remade in 1951. C: Joel McCrea, Dolores Del Rio, John Halliday, Lon Chaney Jr. D: King Vidor. DRA 82m. V

Bird of Paradise 1951 ★★★ High-budget remake of the 1932 adventure adds little to the original. This time around, the restless natives steal the show from the romantic plot. C: Louis Jourdan, Debra Paget, Jeff Chandler, Everett Sloane. D: Delmer Daves. DRA 100m.

Bird on a Wire 1990 ★★★½ Somewhat mechanical chase/comedy finds Gibson and Hawn on the run from a group of dangerous drug dealers who'll stop at nothing to eliminate them. Main claim to fame is shot of Gibson's naked backside. C: Mel Gibson, Goldie Hawn, David Carradine. D: John Badham. COM [PG-13] 110m. V

Bird With the Crystal Plumage, The 1970 Italian ★★½ Expatriate living in Rome witnesses a hideous crime and becomes a target himself. Stylized horror, only for die-hard Argento fans. (a.k.a. *The Phantom of Terror*) C: Tony Musante, Suzy Kendall, Eva Renzi. D: Dario Argento. ACT [PG] 98m. V

Birdman of Alcatraz 1962 ★★★★ Based on the true story of Robert Stroud (Lancaster), a double murderer who was incarcerated in solitary confinement for 53 years, studied ornithology, and eventually became an expert in bird diseases. Subplot of the inhumanity of penal system isn't as strong as the character study of Stroud, which Lancaster turns into something almost profound. C: Burt Lancaster, Karl Malden, Thelma Ritter, Betty Field, Neville Brand, Edmond O'Brien, Telly Savalas. D: John Frankenheimer. DRA 143m. V

Birds and the Bees, The 1956 ★★½ A naive millionaire falls under the spell of a seductive cardsharp (Gaynor). Remake of the classic comedy *The Lady Eve* turns a silk purse into a sow's ear. C: Mitzi Gaynor, David Niven, George Gobel, Reginald Gardiner. D: Norman Taurog. COM 94m.

Birds Do It 1966 ★★½ After a maintenance man at a nuclear plant gets ionized by accident, he discovers that he can fly. Silly comedy based on a silly premise. For the kids. C: Soupy Sales, Tab Hunter, Arthur O'Connell. D: Andrew Marton. FAM/COM 95m.

Birds of Prey 1973 ★★★ An Army pilot, a veteran of WWII, wages a private war against a band of vicious kidnappers. Good action, including some nifty helicopter chase scenes. C: David Janssen, Elayne Heilveil, Ralph Meeker. D: William Graham. ACT 81m. V

Birds, the Bees and the Italians, The 1966 Italian ★★★½ A group of friends share experiences, partners, and beds in a little Italian town. Dated but amusing sex comedy. C: Virna Lisi, Gastone Moschin, Nora Ricci. D: Pietro Germi. COM 100m.

Birds, The 1963 ★★★★½ Hitchcock's widely imitated shocker (based on the Daphne du Maurier tale), zeros in on a small town where millions of birds seem to have declared war on people, launching a terrifying series of attacks. This would be even more intense if only the script (written by Evan Hunter, better known as Ed McBain) were as good as the special effects. C: Rod Taylor, Tippi Hedren, Suzanne Pleshette, Jessica Tandy. D: Alfred Hitchcock. HOR [PG-13] 119m. V

Birdy 1984 ★★★★½ After the Vietnam War, an unlikely friendship between two young, blue-collar Philadelphians takes dramatic turns as the mentally unstable Modine drifts out of reality and Cage seeks to bring him back. A harrowing, uncompromising film with an unforgettable ending. Based on the novel by William Wharton. C: Matthew Modine, Nicolas Cage. D: Alan Parker. DRA [R] 120m. V

Birgit Haas Must Be Killed 1981 French ★★ A German terrorist is the target of an especially ruthless secret agent. Some good tension. C: Philippe Noiret, Jean Rochefort, Lisa Kreuzer. D: Laurent Heynemann. ACT 105m.

Birth of a Nation, The 1915 ★★★★★ D.W. Griffith's Civil War masterpiece, based on Thomas Dixson's *The Clansman,* spans the beginning of the conflict to Reconstruction focusing on two families, the Southern Camerons and Northern Stonemans. The battle scenes are justifiably famous, as are some detailed family scenes, but "heroic" Ku Klux Klan members rescuing the white damsel from black kidnappers is an embarrassing reminder of Griffith's politics. C: Lillian Gish, Mae Marsh, Henry Walthall, Miriam Cooper, Wallace Reid. D: D. W. Griffith. DRA 159m. V

Birth of the Beatles 1979 ★★ Unknowns were cast as the four boys from Liverpool in this dramatization of their early days as a rock group. Interesting primarily because of the impact of the real Beatles. C: Stephen MacKenna, Rod Culbertson, John Altman, Ray Ashcroft. D: Richard Marquand. MUS 100m. TVM

Birth of the Blues 1941 ★★★½ Entertaining but false look at the roots of jazz in New Orleans, seen from a purely white (Crosby's) point of view. But the songs are invigorating ("St. Louis Blues," "Tiger Rag," title tune) and Martin gets a rare screen chance to shine. C: Bing Crosby, Mary Martin, Brian Donlevy, Eddie "Rochester" Anderson. D: Victor Schertzinger. MUS 85m.

Birthday Party, The 1968 British ★★★½ A roomer at a boarding house is set upon by a couple of strangers. Intriguing though sometimes difficult screen version of Harold Pinter's play. C: Robert Shaw, Patrick Magee, Dandy Nichols. D: William Friedkin. DRA [G] 127m.

Biscuit Eater, The 1940 ★★★★ The friendship between a white boy and a black boy is cemented when they choose the runt of a litter and dedicate themselves to training it to become a champion bird dog. Excellent family entertainment has aged very well. Remade in 1972. C: Billy Lee, Cordell Hickman, Helene Millard. D: Stuart Heisler. FAM/DRA 83m.

Biscuit Eater, The 1972 ★★★ The adventures of two boys, one white and one black, and their hunting dog. Routine execution (by Disney) of an intriguing original story. C: Earl Holliman, Johnny Whitaker, George Spell, Lew Ayres, Godfrey Cambridge, Patricia Crowley. D: Vincent McEveety. FAM/DRA [G] 90m.

Bishop Murder Case 1930 ★★½ Detective Philo Vance (Rathbone) goes after a killer who leaves nursery rhymes near his victims. A sturdy early entry in the detective genre. C: Basil Rathbone, Leila Hyams, Roland Young, George Marion. D: Nick Grinde. CRI 91m.

Bishop's Wife, The 1947 ★★★★ A minister (Niven) and his wife (Young) are struggling to found a new parish. Enter an angel (Grant), whose heavenly intervention profoundly affects the couple's life. Charming fantasy with wonderful performances. Wooley is great in support. C: Cary Grant, Loretta Young, David Niven, Monty Woolley, James Gleason, Gladys Cooper, Elsa Lanchester. D: Henry Koster. COM 109m. V

Bitch, The 1979 British ★ A proprietor of a London nightclub (Collins) tries everything to keep her place going. The only question is:

What's worse, Joan's acting or sister Jackie's writing? It's a toss-up. Sequel to *The Stud.* C: Joan Collins, Kenneth Haigh, Michael Coby, Ian Hendry. D: Gerry O'Hara. DRA [R] 93m. v

Bite the Bullet 1975 ★★★★½ At the turn of the century, a motley group of cowpokes engage in a contest involving a grueling 600-mile marathon horserace. Offbeat, epic Western. Hackman and Coburn excel. Fine location photography. C: Gene Hackman, Candice Bergen, James Coburn, Ben Johnson, Ian Bannen, Jan-Michael Vincent. D: Richard Brooks. WST [PG] 131m. v

Bitter Creek 1954 ★★ When his brother is murdered out West, a man takes off to seek revenge. Purely routine Western with the usual share of action. C: Bill Elliott, Carleton Young, Beverly Garland, Claude Akins. D: Thomas Carr. WST 74m.

Bitter Harvest 1981 ★★★★ When his cattle start dying from a mysterious disease, a young dairy farmer has to fight hard for his farm's survival. Tense, affecting drama; fact-based story received Emmy nominations for directing and writing. C: Ron Howard, Art Carney, Tarah Nutter, Richard Dysart. D: Roger Young. DRA 98m. TVM v

Bitter Moon 1994 ★★★½ Black comedy has a wheelchair-bound hack writer (Coyote) and his wife (Seigner) trying to seduce a more reserved couple (Grant and Scott-Thomas). Good performances from Hugh and Kristen boost this wildly uneven contribution from director Polanski. C: Peter Coyote, Emmanuelle Seigner, Hugh Grant, Kristin Scott-Thomas. D: Roman Polanski. DRA [R] 139m.

Bitter Rice 1948 Italian ★★★★ Female rice pickers work hard by day and make *amore* by night. This movie catapulted the young Mangano to stardom and is a lesser-known neorealist classic. C: Silvana Mangano, Vittorio Gassman, Raf Vallone. D: Giuseppe De Santis. DRA 107m. v

Bitter Sweet 1933 British ★★½ In 19th-century Vienna, a violinist and a dancer fall in love and marry—and then Tragedy (no doubt jealous of their happiness) strikes. Noel Coward's first major work as a composer may creak now, but many considered it excellent at the time. C: Anna Neagle, Fernand Graavey, Miles Mander. D: Herbert Wilcox. MUS 93m.

Bitter Sweet 1940 ★★★½ Lavish version of the Noel Coward operetta about a young English woman (MacDonald) falling for her Viennese vocal coach (Eddy). Over-the-top MGM production retains several songs from the original production, including "I'll See You Again." C: Jeanette MacDonald, Nelson Eddy, George Sanders, Felix Bressart, Sig Ruman. D: W.S. Van Dyke II. MUS 94m. v

Bitter Tea of General Yen, The 1932 ★★★★ A missionary (Stanwyck) falls for the fascinating Chinese warlord (Asther) who holds her captive. Somewhat bizarre; still hypnotic and compelling. C: Barbara Stanwyck, Nils Asther, Gavin Gordon, Toshia Mori. D: Frank Capra. DRA 89m. v

Bitter Tears of Petra Von Kant, The 1972 German ★★★½ Unsettling drama of the problems of a lesbian (Carstensen) with her new romantic interest, Hermann, and her unfaithful lover. Stark, claustrophobic, and difficult; one of Fassbinder's more sadistic features. C: Margit Carstensen, Hanna Schygulla, Irm Hermann, Eva Mattes. D: Rainer Werner Fassbinder. DRA 124m. v

Bitter Victory 1957 French ★★ Two soldiers, one of whom suspects the other of having an affair with his wife, are sent on a secret mission in war-torn Libya. Tame melodrama. C: Richard Burton, Curt Jurgens, Ruth Roman, Christopher Lee. D: Nicholas Ray. DRA 82m.

Bittersweet Love 1976 ★★ The world collapses for a pair of young newlyweds when they discover they had the same father. Excellent production values are undone by a weak script. C: Lana Turner, Robert Lansing, Celeste Holm, Robert Alda, Meredith Baxter Birney. D: David Miller. DRA [PG] 92m. v

Bix: An Interpretation of a Legend 1990 Italian ★★★½ Film biography of the legendary jazz trumpeter Bix Beiderbecke. Good jazz account, by a masterful director. C: Bryant Weeks, Emile Levisetti, Sally Groth, Mark Collver. D: Pupi Avati. MUS 100m. v

Black Abbot, The 1963 German ★★½ Weird tale of a bizarre monk who kills anyone within range of his mysterious buried treasure. Gory nonsense. C: Joachim Fuchsberger, Dieter Borsche. D: Franz Gottlieb. HOR 95m.

Black and White in Color 1976 French ★★★★ French traders living in a remote African village at start of WWI enlist local tribesmen to attack a nearby German fort. Droll satire on nationalism won an Academy Award as Best Foreign Film. C: Jean Carmet, Catherine Rouvel, Jacques Spiesser. D: Jean-Jacques Annaud. DRA [PG] 90m. v

Black Angel 1946 ★★½ Shock and horror greet an alcoholic when he sets out to find his wife's killer. Guess who? Fine performances. C: Dan Duryea, June Vincent, Peter Lorre, Broderick Crawford. D: Roy Neill. CRI 80m.

Black Bart 1948 ★★½ A glamorous señorita gets involved with a few outlaws and winds up sabotaging their plans to hold up a bank. A solid Western that doesn't take itself too seriously. C: Yvonne De Carlo, Dan Duryea, Jeffrey Lynn, Percy Kilbride. D: George Sherman. WST 80m.

Black Beauty 1946 ★★★ Extremely loose adaptation of Anna Sewell's classic set in Victorian England. Story of a girl's love for her horse is pleasant but unremarkable. Good children's viewing. C: Mona Freeman, Richard Denning, Evelyn Ankers. D: Max Nosseck. FAM/DRA 74m.

Black Beauty 1971 British ★★★½ A spirited horse is sold to increasingly brutal masters in this classic children's story, which sticks faithfully to the original Sewell novel. When it seems things just can't get any worse, the poor animal's luck finally changes. Whew! Good children's viewing. C: Mark Lester, Walter Slezak. D: James Hill. FAM/DRA [G] 109m. V

Black Belly of the Tarantula 1972 Italian ★ The police are called in to investigate a number of mysterious murders at an exclusive health and beauty club. Thoroughly uninspiring. C: Giancarlo Giannini, Stefania Sandrelli, Barbara Bouchet. D: Paolo Cavara. DRA [R] 88m.

Black Belt Jones 1974 ★★★ When mobsters attempt to muscle in on a Los Angeles martial arts dojo, the owner retaliates. Bloodless but occasionally funny, with plenty of action. C: Jim Kelly, Gloria Hendry, Scatman Crothers. D: Robert Clouse. ACT [R] 87m. V

Black Bird, The 1975 ★★★ Loving, but weak comic follow-up to *The Maltese Falcon* begins 30 years after the original with Sam Spade, Jr., on the trail of the elusive bird. Presence of a few cast members from the original adds to the fun. C: George Segal, Stephane Audran, Lionel Stander, Lee Patrick, Elisha Cook Jr. D: David Giler. COM [PG] 98m. V

Black Bounty Killer, The 1975 *See* **Boss Nigger**

Black Buccaneer, The 1962 *See* **Rage of the Buccaneers, The**

Black Caesar 1973 ★★½ Williamson updates Edward G. Robinson for the '70s, playing an African-American gangster who rises from the ghetto to become the head of a Harlem crime syndicate. C: Fred Williamson, Art Lund, Julius W. Harris, Gloria Hendry. D: Larry Cohen. CRI [R] 92m. V

Black Camel, The 1931 ★★½ When a starlet is murdered in Honolulu, Charlie Chan arrives on the scene and catches the culprit. Early entry in the *Chan* series, and quite efficient. C: Warner Oland, Sally Eilers, Bela Lugosi, Dorothy Revier, Robert Young. D: Hamilton MacFadden. CRI 71m.

Black Castle, The 1952 ★★½ When his friends are tormented and murdered by a lunatic count, a mysterious knight seeks revenge. Pointless action adventure. C: Richard Greene, Boris Karloff, Stephen McNally, Paula Corday, Lon Chaney Jr. D: Nathan Juran. ACT 81m.

Black Cat, The *See* **Kuroneko**

Black Cat, The 1934 ★★★★½ A doctor and his wife are held against their will in a house of satanic worship. Though this first teaming of Karloff and Lugosi bears no resemblance to Edgar Allan Poe's tale, it's still marvelous. Stylish and tense, with some terrific performances. C: Boris Karloff, Bela Lugosi, David Manners, Jacqueline Wells. D: Edgar G. Ulmer. HOR 66m. V

Black Cat, The 1941 ★★★ A dying cat lover calls upon her entire family to visit her in her creaking mansion. All the elements are here: the haunted house, the pelting rainstorm, the ensemble cast. Lots of fun. C: Basil Rathbone, Hugh Herbert, Broderick Crawford, Bela Lugosi, Gale Sondergaard, Gladys Cooper. D: Albert Rogell. HOR 70m.

Black Cauldron, The 1985 ★★★★ Entertaining and beautifully animated Disney tale involves a young man's search for the mystical Black Cauldron and his attempts to protect this magic pot from the evil Horned King. Not Disney's finest, but more than adequate storytelling. Younger audiences and fantasy fans should enjoy. Voices of Grant Bardsley, Susan Sheridan, John Hurt. D: Ted Berman, Richard Rich. FAM/SFI [PG] 80m.

Black Christmas 1975 Canadian ★★★ A forerunner to the slasher-film trend of the '80s, this one makes effective use of many of its devices as a maniac preys on a sorority during holiday break. Clever direction and a surprise ending elevate the standard material. C: Olivia Hussey, Keir Dullea, Margot Kidder, John Saxon, Andrea Martin. D: Bob Clark. HOR [R] 100m. V

Black Cross 1960 Polish ★★ During the Middle Ages, a vicious band of knights pillage their way across Poland. Far from gripping, but a fine portrayal of Polish life at the time. C: Urszula Modrzynska, Grazyna Staniszewska. D: Aleksander Ford. ACT 175m.

Black Dakotas, The 1954 ★★ A group of shiftless cow wrangler con artists try to outwit some Indians and wind up under attack. Standard Western punctuated by occasional action. C: Gary Merrill, Wanda Hendrix. D: Ray Nazarro. WST 65m.

Black Dragon of Manzanar 1943 ★★ During WWII, federal agents mix it up with agents from Japan. Serial-style action keeps it moving. Edited from a real serial, *G-Men Vs. the Black Dragon.* C: Rod Cameron, Roland Got, Constance Worth. D: William Witney. ACT 100m.

Black Dragons 1942 ★ Thanks to help from a Nazi surgeon (Lugosi), Japanese saboteurs pose as Americans; then Lugosi takes his revenge. Incoherent; colorization only makes matters worse. C: Bela Lugosi, Joan Barclay, Clayton Moore. D: William Nigh. HOR 61m. V

Black Eagle 1988 ★★½ Low-rent espionage adventure may disappoint martial arts fans—while there's plenty of mayhem, most of it comes from bombs and bullets rather than karate chops. Still, the climactic duel between the evil KGB agent (Van Damme) and the noble CIA agent (Kosugi) ranks with the best. C: Sho Kosugi, Jean Claude Van Damme. D: Eric Karson. ACT [R] 93m. V

Black Fist, Black Streetfighter 1989 *See* **Homeboy**

Black Force ★★ Vigilante nonsense involving two brothers, with the emphasis on martial arts action. Familiar plot concerns civic-minded citizens banding together to slaughter criminals. C: Un Watson, Warhawk Tanzania, Malachi Lee. D: Michael Fink. ACT 82m. V

Black Fox: Adolph Hitler 1962 ★★★★ Documentary detailing Hitler's rise to power. Filled with newsreels of the time as well as comparisons of the Nazi dictator to a medieval folk character called Reynard the Fox. Quite well done: Oscar for Best Documentary. D: Louis Stoumen. DOC 89m. V

Black Friday 1940 ★★★ Fast-paced, energetic blend of horror and gangster movies, as a doctor (Karloff) transplants part of a dying criminal's brain into the head of a professor, who takes on the thug's identity. C: Boris Karloff, Bela Lugosi, Anne Nagel. D: Arthur Lubin. HOR 70m.

Black Fury 1935 ★★★ An immigrant coal miner finds himself in the middle of a labor dispute instigated by a corrupt union. Familiar social commentary scenario for Muni, although not his finest. C: Paul Muni, Karen Morley, William Gargan. D: Michael Curtiz. DRA 95m. V

Black Gestapo, The 1975 ★ Violent, racist black exploitation film about a quasimilitary organization bent on rooting out the "White Devil" from American society. Mixes karate, sex, and guns for sleazy, sadistic results. C: Rod Perry, Charles P. Robinson, Phil Hoover. D: Lee Frost. ACT [R] 89m. V

Black Girl 1972 ★★★½ A young dancer and her two half-sisters make life miserable for Uggams, in this perceptive look at life in an African-American family which emphasizes the difficult integration of foster children. C: Brock Peters, Leslie Uggams, Claudia McNeil, Ruby Dee. D: Ossie Davis. DRA [PG] 97m.

Black Gold 1947 ★★½ A young Indian couple, living on a reservation, discover oil and adopt a Chinese baby who grows up to become a champion jockey. Lots of heartfelt emotion; comes off pretty well. C: Anthony Quinn, Katherine DeMille, Elyse Knox, Hall. D: Phil Karlson. DRA 92m.

Black Gold 1963 ★★ A rookie oil prospector strikes it rich in the Oklahoma fields. Thoroughly typical little adventure yarn. C: Philip Carey, Diane McBain, Claude Akins. D: Leslie Martinson. ACT 98m.

Black Gunn 1972 ★★★ Routine black exploitation film has a nightclub owner (Brown) gunning for the men who killed his brother. Landau's villainous turn adds some class. C: Jim Brown, Martin Landau, Brenda Sykes, Luciana Paluzzi. D: Robert Hartford-Davis. ACT [R] 98m.

Black Hand 1950 ★★★ Dancer Kelly plays it straight as a young man in turn-of-the-century New York who must avenge the murder of his parents by the Black Hand, later to become famous as the Mafia. Middle-of-the-road crime drama. C: Gene Kelly, J. Carroll Naish, Teresa Celli. D: Richard Thorpe. CRI 93m.

Black Hole, The 1979 ★★★ Disney's attempt to cash in on *Star Wars* mania features Schell as an unhinged scientist in search of the title entity. Notable only for its fine effects. Good cast wasted on one-dimensional characters in a tiresome story line. C: Maximilian Schell, Anthony Perkins, Robert Forster, Joseph Bottoms, Yvette Mimieux, Ernest Borgnine. D: Gary Nelson. SFI [PG] 97m. V

Black Horse Canyon 1954 ★★½ A rancher (Blanchard) hires a couple of cowpokes to help train a wild stallion. Pleasant enough Western. C: Joel McCrea, Mari Blanchard, Race Gentry. D: Jesse Hibbs. WST 81m.

Black Jack 1973 ★★ Three radicals steal a bunch of nuclear weapons, planning to blow up Fort Knox—as a political statement, of course. Weak comedy, at best. De Wilde's last film. (a.k.a. *Wild in the Sky*) C: Georg Standford Brown, Brandon de Wilde, Keenan Wynn, Tim O'Connor, James Daly, Dick Gautier, Robert Lansing. D: William Naud. CRI [PG] 87m.

Black Klansman, the 1966 ★ Wretched low-budget film concerning a light-skinned African-American who infiltrates the KKK after they murder his daughter. Far from a serious examination of its subject, treatment here is consistently cheap and inflammatory. (a.k.a. *I Crossed the Line*) C: Richard Gilden, Rima Kutner. D: Ted V. Mikels. DRA 88m. V

Black Knight, The 1954 U.S. ★★ Virtue is its own reward in this medieval rouser about a swordmaker exposing corruption within King Arthur's court. Ladd seems a bit self-conscious. C: Alan Ladd, Patricia Medina, Andre Morell, Harry Andrews, Peter Cushing. D: Tay Garnett. ACT 85m.

Black Legion 1936 ★★★★ After Bogart loses an expected promotion to someone from an ethnic minority, a Ku Klux Klan-like organization takes advantage of his frayed emotions and convinces him to join their ranks. Compelling drama, taken directly from a then-notorious, real-life incident in Detroit. Bogie turns in a strong performance as the confused lead. C: Humphrey Bogart, Erin O'Brien-Moore, Dick Foran, Ann Sheridan. D: Archie Mayo. DRA 83m.

Black Like Me 1964 ★★★★ A white journalist dyes his skin to discover what it's like to be a black man in '60s America. Punch of the original, provocative premise seems a bit diluted after 30 years, but it's still relevant. Based on John Griffin's book. C: James Whitmore, Roscoe Lee Browne, Lenka Petersen, Sorrell Booke, Will Geer, Al Freeman Jr. D: Carl Lerner. DRA 110m. V

Black Lizard 1968 Japanese ★★★½ Bizarre, highly stylized film defies synopsis, but it involves homosexuality, cross-dressing, and perverse violence. Typical Yukio Mishima and definitely not to all tastes, unless his writing is your cup of tea. C: Akihiro Maruyama, Isao Kimura, Yukio Mishima. D: Kinji Fukasaku. DRA 90m. V

Black Magic 1944 ★★½ The solicitous Chinese detective Charlie Chan (Toland) investigates murder at a séance held by fortune-tellers. Serial entry, showing signs of wear and tear. (a.k.a. *Meeting at Midnight*). C: Sidney Toler, Mantan Moreland, Frances Chan. D: Phil Rosen. CRI 67m.

Black Magic 1949 ★★★ A nefarious necromancer conspires to seize power in 18th-century Italy. Welles (as the magician Cagliostro) provides an apt focal point for this gaudy, colorful, and complex period piece. C: Orson Welles, Akim Tamiroff, Nancy Guild, Raymond Burr. D: Gregory Ratoff. DRA 105m. V

Black Magic 1991 ★★★½ Unable to escape nightmares involving his dead cousin, a young man becomes involved with the cousin's ex-girlfriend and begins to suspect that she is a witch. Lightweight fare lifted by the talents of Reinhold and Ward. C: Rachel Ward, Judge Reinhold, Anthony La Paglia, Brion James. D: Daniel Taplitz. CRI [PG-13] 94m. V

Black Magic M-66 1987 Japanese ★★★½ Despite its supernatural title, this is actually an animated science fiction/action film. The story centers on a crusading photojournalist who learns that "M-66 robots" (sophisticated marionettes with terrible strength and amazing agility) are on the rampage in a futuristic Japan. Lively entertainment builds to a nail-biting climax. D: Takayuki Sawaura. SFI 48m.

Black Magic Woman 1991 ★★ An art gallery owner (Hamill) has a one-night stand with a gorgeous woman (Apollonia); when he then spurns her, she puts a curse on him. Neither sexy nor scary enough. C: Mark Hamill, Apollonia, Amanda Wyss. D: Deryln Warren. HOR [R] 91m. V

Black Mama, White Mama 1972 U.S. ★★ Chained to each other, two female prisoners, one black and one white, bust out of a Philippines jail. *The Defiant Ones* does more justice to the same theme. C: Pam Grier, Margaret Markov, Sid Haig. D: Eddie Romero. ACT [R] 87m.

Black Marble, The 1980 ★★★★ A tough cop (Prentiss) and a washed-up detective (Foxworth) work together and fall in love. Well acted drama. Script by Joseph Wambaugh, from his novel. C: Robert Foxworth, Paula Prentiss, Harry Dean Stanton, James Woods, Michael Dudikoff, Christopher Lloyd. D: Harold Becker. DRA [PG] 110m. V

Black Moon 1975 French ★★★ Intriguing if somewhat baffling fantasy about a young woman who drives her car into another dimension. Lots of striking imagery, with frequent allusions to Lewis Carroll. Anyway, it's different. C: Cathryn Harrison, Therese Giehse, Alexandra Stewart, Joe Dallesandro. D: Louis Malle. SFI [R] 100m.

Black Moon Rising 1986 ★★★½ Enjoyable adventure about a master thief who sets his sights on a high-tech car, which happens to be stored at the top of a skyscraper. From horror specialist John Carpenter's screenplay, with top-notch special effects. C: Tommy Lee Jones, Linda Hamilton, Robert Vaughn, Richard Jaeckel. D: Harley Cokliss. CRI [R] 100m. V

Black Narcissus 1947 British ★★★★★ A nun (Kerr) and five sisters turn a remote Himalayan palace, perched on the edge of a cliff, into a school and hospital. Eventually, the harmony of the nuns' work is threatened by spiritual unrest. Brilliant color photography and outstanding performances heighten the tension between physical repression and spiritual freedom. Oscars for Cinematography and Art Direction. Based on the novel by Rumer Godden. C: Deborah Kerr, David Farrar, Sabu, Jean Simmons, Kathleen Byron, Flora Robson. D: Michael Powell, Emeric Pressburger. DRA 100m. V

Black Oak Conspiracy 1977 ★★ A worker innocently stumbles onto a mining company conspiracy that involves, among others, the local sheriff. Fact-based tale delivers standard suspense. C: Jesse Vint, Karen Carlson, Albert Salmi, Seymour Cassel. D: Bob Kelljan. DRA [R] 92m. V

Black Orchid, The 1959 ★★★½ The title flower is a gangster's widow (Loren), who encouraged her late husband in a life of crime and who now sees a chance to redeem herself when a friendly widower (Quinn) proposes. Italian family melodrama. C: Sophia Loren, Anthony Quinn, Ina Balin. D: Martin Ritt. DRA 96m. V

Black Orpheus 1959 Brazilian-French ★★★★★ Reworking of the Orpheus and Eurydice legend, set during Rio de Janeiro's famed carnival. Amid frenzied atmosphere, music, and costumes, a streetcar conductor meets a woman from rural Brazil and begins an ill-fated romance. Stunning drama, with a memorable score. Oscar winner for Best Foreign Film. C: Breno Mello, Marpessa Dawn, Lea Garcia. D: Marcel Camus. DRA 103m. V

Black Patch 1957 ★★ Familiar premise of innocence maligned, as a marshal sets out to clear himself of a murder charge. Somber Western plods along without distinction. C: George Montgomery, Diane Brewster, Sebastian Cabot. D: Allen Miner. WST 83m.

Black Pirate, The 1926 ★★★★½ Silent film shot in primitive Technicolor almost singlehandedly defined the swashbuckler genre; it has all the ingredients we now expect from pirate movies, served up at a delirious pace. Fairbanks is athletic and charming in the title role. Terrific fun. C: Douglas Fairbanks, Sr., Bille Dove, Anders Randolf, Donald Crisp. D: Albert Parker. ACT 85m. V

Black Pirates, The 1954 Mexican ★★ A

motley crew of pirates get involved in a hunt for gold. Unextraordinary story delivered by a competent cast. C: Anthony Dexter, Martha Roth, Lon Chaney, Jr. D: Allen Miner. ACT 72m. V

Black Rain 1988 Japanese ★★★★ Radioactive fallout in postwar Japan slowly but steadily destroys a family that survived Hiroshima; a deeply moving and haunting character study. C: Yoshiko Tanaka, Kazuo Kitamura, Etsuko Ichihara. D: Shohei Imamura. DRA 123m. V

Black Rain 1989 ★★★½ A New York detective (Douglas) and his partner (Garcia) travel to Osaka to track down a dangerous Yakuza enforcer who escaped from their custody. Fast moving and visually stunning. C: Michael Douglas, Andy Garcia, Ken Takakura, Kate Capshaw, John Spencer. D: Ridley Scott. ACT [R] 125m. V

Black Rainbow 1991 British ★★★★ A clairvoyant (Arquette) claims to know the identity of a murderer, and is pursued by a reporter (Hulce). Effective, unusual blend of drama and murder mystery, with Robards a standout as Arquette's tippling father. C: Rosanna Arquette, Jason Robards, Tom Hulce. D: Mike Hodges. CRI [R] 103m. V

Black Raven, The 1943 ★★½ While stranded at the Black Raven Inn, a number of travelers witness a murder. So-so mystery. C: George Zucco, Wanda McKay, Noel Madison, Glenn Strange. D: Sam Newfield. CRI 64m. V

Black Robe, The 1991 Canadian ★★★½ Brutally honest look at the culture clash between Indians and Europeans in 17th-century Canada, as a young priest endures an excruciating wintertime canoe trip to bring salvation to a tribe of Hurons. Stark, violent scenes are juxtaposed against beautiful natural settings. C: Lothaire Bluteau, August Schellenberg. D: Bruce Beresford. DRA [R] 101m. V

Black Rodeo 1972 ★★★½ Unique documentary about a rodeo that takes place in—of all places—Harlem. A truly fascinating achievement, with music by Ray Charles, B.B. King, and others. C: Archie Wycoff, Clarence Gonzalez. D: Jeff Kanew. DOC [G] 87m.

Black Room, The 1935 ★★★★ Condemned by villagers for sinister activities, evil Karloff assumes the identity of his noble twin brother after secretly murdering him. Excellently acted dual role for Karloff. C: Boris Karloff, Marian Marsh, Robert Allen. D: Roy William Neill. HOR 67m. V

Black Rose, The 1950 ★★½ A Saxon scholar and warrior (Power) embarks upon a muddled series of adventures in Asia in the 1200s. Some good action scenes can't redeem the lackluster plot. C: Tyrone Power, Cecile Aubry, Orson Welles, Jack Hawkins, Michael Rennie, Herbert Lom. D: Henry Hathaway. ACT 120m.

Black Roses 1988 ★★ A horrible heavy metal band plays a small town and turns the teens into killers, making parents an endangered species. Ex-Vanilla Fudge drummer Appice plays the lead singer. Interesting makeup effects. C: John Martin, Ken Swofford, Julie Adams, Sal Viviano. D: John Fasano. HOR [R] 90m. V

Black Sabbath 1964 Italian ★★★½ Boris hosts three creepy vignettes of horror, and even steps in during the bloodsucking finale. Still some chills after all these years. C: Boris Karloff, Mark Damon, Suzy Anderson. D: Mario Bava. HOR 99m. V

Black Scorpion, The 1957 ★★★½ Giant venomous insects crawl out of their nice warm volcano and go out hunting humans in this sci-fi shocker with superb special effects. C: Richard Denning, Carlos Rivas, Mara Corday. D: Edward Ludwig. HOR 88m. V

Black Shampoo 1975 ★ Takeoff on Warren Beatty's *Shampoo*, set in an African-American hair salon on Sunset Strip. Basically a mindless excuse for disturbingly cruel violence and raunchy sex. C: John Daniels, Tanya Boyd. D: Greydon Clark. DRA [R] 90m. V

Black Shield of Falworth, The 1954 ★★★★ Curtis is a medieval knight fighting for love and honor in this well-made, colorful version of Howard Pyle's *Men of Iron*. Famous for Curtis's utterance, "Yonda lies the castle of my fodda," in perfect Brooklynese. C: Tony Curtis, Janet Leigh, David Farrar, Barbara Rush, Herbert Marshall. D: Rudolph Mate. ACT 99m.

Black Six, The ★ Dumb biker film about six black Vietnam vets avenging one of their brothers killed by a white gang; holds the dubious distinction of casting former football players as bikers. Strictly amateur film-making. C: Joe Greene, Gene Washington, Mercury Morris, Willie Lanier. D: Matt Cimber. ACT 84m. V

Black Sleep, The 1956 ★★ A mad surgeon (Rathbone) experiments on human subjects while seeking to cure his catatonic wife. Great cast of horror veterans lifts this horror opus. C: Basil Rathbone, Akim Tamiroff, Lon Chaney, John Carradine, Bela Lugosi. D: Reginald LeBorg. HOR 81m. V

Black Spurs 1965 ★★ Familiar, old-fashioned western about a bounty hunter brought in to help a scheming railroad baron. Standard action, served up by an interesting cast of familiar faces from decades of shoot-'em-ups. Darnell's swan song. C: Rory Calhoun, Terry Moore, Linda Darnell, Scott Brady, Lon Chaney, Jr., Bruce Cabot, Richard Arlen, DeForest Kelley. D: R.G. Springsteen. WST 81m.

Black Stallion Returns, The 1983 ★★★ Reno's beloved horse is stolen by an Arab chieftain and he's determined to get him back. Sequel to *The Black Stallion* is not its equal, but the further adventures of this duo are still worth watching. C: Kelly Reno, Vincent

Spano, Terri Garr, Woody Strode. D: Robert Dalva. FAM/ACT [PG] 103m. v

Black Stallion, The 1979 ★★★★½ Lyrical, superbly photographed story of a shipwrecked boy (Reno) and the magical wild Arabian stallion he tames and later rides to victory. Rooney shines (and was Oscar-nominated) as the horse's trainer. A gem of a movie, from Walter Farley's popular children's novel. Perfect for the whole family. C: Kelly Reno, Mickey Rooney, Teri Garr, Clarence Muse, Hoyt Axton. D: Carroll Ballard. FAM/ACT [G] 118m. v

Black Starlet ★★ In this boring, exploitative story, an impressionable young woman makes an easy transition from Chicago's South Side to the sex-and-drugs circuit in Hollywood. C: Juanita Brown, Eric Mason, Rockne Tarkington. DRA [R] 90m. v

Black Sunday 1961 Italian ★★★ A witch (Steele) returns from the dead to seek vengeance on those who burned her at the stake. Atmospheric horror, marred somewhat by contrived script and performances. Horror fans, take note: this was Bava's debut as a director. C: Barbara Steele, John Richardson, Ivo Garrani. D: Mario Bava. HOR 83m. v

Black Sunday 1977 ★★★★ The leader of the Black September terrorist cell (Keller) teams up with a deranged pilot (Dern) to explode the Goodyear blimp at the Super Bowl. Can a super tough Mossad agent (Shaw) stop them in time? Well made and downright scary. C: Robert Shaw, Bruce Dern, Marthe Keller, Fritz Weaver. D: John Frankenheimer. ACT [R] 143m. v

Black Swan, The 1942 ★★★★ A swashbuckling pirate (Power) sets out to rescue a damsel (O'Hara) in this beautifully made sea yarn. Lots of action and Oscar-winning cinematography by Leon Shamroy. C: Tyrone Power, Maureen O'Hara, Laird Cregar, Thomas Mitchell, George Sanders, Anthony Quinn. D: Henry King. ACT 85m.

Black Tent, The 1957 British ★★ A wounded WWII British soldier recuperates from the fighting in Libya by spending time with a group of nomadic Arabs—and making time with the sheik's daughter. A romantic drama that's somewhat implausible. Shot well, though. C: Anthony Steel, Donald Sinden, Anna Sandri, Donald Pleasence. D: Brian Hurst. DRA 93m.

Black Tights 1960 French ★★★★ Chevalier provides narration as the best screen and stage dancers of the time hoof it through four choreographed stories. Colorful treat for ballet fans. C: Cyd Charisse, Moira Shearer, Zizi Jeanmaire, Roland Petit. D: Terence Young. MUS 115m. v

Black Tuesday 1954 ★★★★ Two Death Row convicts on the run (Robinson and Graves) evade police and take hostages. Robinson updates his tough-as-nails gangster persona to good effect. Tense melodrama boasts crackling dialogue and gripping suspense. C: Edward G. Robinson, Peter Graves, Jean Parker. D: Hugo Fregonese. CRI 80m.

Black Vampire 1973 ★★★ Moody, original chiller about a vampirized professor (Jones) who takes up with his assailant's wife (Clark). Intelligent and atmospheric, though heavily cut from the original version, titled *Ganja and Hess.* (a.k.a. *Double Possession* and *Blood Couple*) C: Duane Jones, Marlene Clark, Bill Gunn, Sam Wayman, Leonard Jackson. D: Bill Gunn. HOR [R] 83m. v

Black Venus 1983 ★ Loose adaptation of stories by Balzac follows Jones as she sleeps her way through late 19th-century Paris. Great costumes and sets; lousy script and bad acting. C: Josephine Jacqueline Jones, Jose Antonio Ceinos. D: Claude Mulot. DRA [R] 110m. v

Black Watch, The 1929 ★★★★ Early action-adventure spectacle from director Ford places McLaglen in India during WWI, serving as a spy in the court of an exotic princess (Loy). Fast-paced fun in the *Gunga Din* tradition. Remade in 1953 as *King of the Khyber Rifles.* C: Victor McLaglen, Myrna Loy. D: John Ford. ACT 91m.

Black Water Gold 1969 ★★½ The promise of a fortune in gold prompts a rather unsavory group of rivals to undertake a joint recovery expedition. Underwater excitement that at times rises above board in entertainment. C: Ricardo Montalban, Keir Dullea, Lana Wood, Bradford Dillman, France Nuyen. D: Alan Landsburg. ACT 75m.

Black Werewolf 1974 *See* **Beast Must Die, The**

Black Whip, The 1956 ★★ A cow wrangler distinguishes himself by saving the lives of a number of women. Uneventful Western. C: Hugh Marlowe, Coleen Gray, Angie Dickinson. D: Charles Warren. WST 77m.

Black Widow 1954 ★★ Rogers plays against type as a villainous actress who murders the protégé of a Broadway producer (Cotton) and stands by while police suspect him of being the killer. This dull mystery is the most convincing argument that Ginger was better off dancing. C: Ginger Rogers, Van Heflin, Gene Tierney, George Raft, Peggy Ann Garner, Reginald Gardiner, Cathleen Nesbitt. D: Nunnally Johnson. CRI 95m.

Black Widow 1987 ★★★ An investigator for the Justice Department (Winger) believes she's onto a woman (Russell) who kills the rich men she marries. A stylish thriller. C: Debra Winger, Theresa Russell, Sami Frey, Dennis Hopper, Nicol Williamson. D: Bob Rafelson. DRA [R] 98m. v

Black Windmill, The 1974 British ★★★ Spy thriller presents Caine in a familiar role as a British agent, this time struggling to rescue his son from kidnappers. Good action sequences and intelligent use of European locations. C: Michael Caine, Donald Pleasence, Janet Suzman, Delphine Seyrig. D: Don Siegel. CRI [PG] 102m. V

Black Zoo 1963 ★ A psychopath, the owner of his own private zoo, trains his animals to kill people. A truly wretched horror film. C: Michael Gough, Virginia Grey. D: Robert Gordon. HOR 88m.

Blackbeard, the Pirate 1952 ★★★★ Colorful version of the classic high-seas yarn. Newton is larger-than-life as the notorious pirate. Lots of fun. C: Robert Newton, Linda Darnell, William Bendix, Richard Egan, Irene Ryan. D: Raoul Walsh. ACT 99m. V

Blackbeard's Ghost 1968 ★★★½ Ustinov, as the ghost of the notorious pirate, chews on the scenery with great gusto as he helps his descendants foil developers and keep their ancestral home. Unpretentious, pleasant family entertainment enlivened by slapstick turns. C: Peter Ustinov, Dean Jones, Suzanne Pleshette, Elsa Lanchester. D: Robert Stevenson. FAM/COM [G] 106m. V

Blackboard Jungle 1955 ★★★★½ A teacher (Ford) at a tough New York City school works to gain the respect of his juvenile delinquent pupils and their hoodlum leader (Morrow) in this gritty, intense adaptation of Evan Hunter's book. Bill Haley and the Comets provide "Rock Around the Clock" over the opening credits. C: Glenn Ford, Anne Francis, Vic Morrow, Louis Calhern, Sidney Poitier, Richard Kiley. D: Richard Brooks. DRA 101m. V

Blackenstein 1974 ★ A paraplegic Vietnam veteran thinks he's found salvation when a modern Dr. Frankenstein gives him a new arm and leg. But the inevitable tragedy ensues, which is nothing compared to the violence done to the classic story by this cheap ripoff. C: John Hart, Ivory Stone, Andrea King, Liz Renay. D: William A. Levy. HOR 87m. V

Blackjack Ketchum, Desperado 1956 ★★½ The quiet life eludes a one-time gunman when he's forced to shoot it out one more time. Routine Western distinguished by an excellent cast. C: Howard Duff, Victor Jory, Maggie Mahoney. D: Earl Bellamy. WST 76m.

Blackmail 1929 British ★★★★½ Hitchcock's first sound film involves a woman (Ondra) who murders her would-be attacker, and then must contend with her own guilt and the demands of a seedy extortionist. Full display of Hitchcock's style, compares favorably with his later work. Ondra's lines were dubbed by Joan Barry. C: Anny Ondra, Sara Allgood, John Longden, Cyril Ritchard. D: Alfred Hitchcock. CRI 86m. V

Blackmail 1939 ★★★ An innocent man (Robinson) is blackmailed and sent to prison. Robinson does a Swell job; gripping suspense. C: Edward G. Robinson, Gene Lockhart, Guinn Williams, Ruth Hussey. D: H. Potter. CRI 81m.

Blackout 1940 *See* **Contraband**

Blackout 1978 Canadian ★★ New York City's 1977 electrical blackout enables several criminals (some of them violent) to indulge themselves. Confused mishmash punctuated by violence and weird humor. C: Jim Mitchum, Robert Carradine, Belinda Montgomery, June Allyson, Jean-Pierre Aumont, Ray Milland. D: Eddy Matalon. ACT [R] 86m. V

Blackout 1985 ★★★½ Cop (Widmark) thinks he's spotted a suspected murderer (Carradine) 10 years after the grisly slaughter of the man's family. Solid performances from dependable leads carry this suspenseful outing. C: Richard Widmark, Keith Carradine, Michael Beck, Kathleen Quinlan. D: Douglas Hickox. DRA 99m. TVM V

Blackwell's Island 1939 ★★★½ To get the inside scoop on a clever racketeer, a reporter (Garfield) arranges to have himself put in jail. A solid, quick little crime story, with good work from Garfield. C: John Garfield, Rosemary Lane, Dick Purcell, Victor Jory. D: William McGann. CRI 71m.

Blacula 1972 ★★★ Marshall gives a terrific performance as an African prince who was bitten by the original Dracula and rises again in 1972 L.A. One of the best of the black exploitation films, eschewing cheap thrills for honest terror and hip humor. C: William Marshall, Denise Nicholas, Vonetta McGee. D: William Crain. HOR [PG] 92m. V

Blade 1973 ★★ When a psychopathic woman hater goes into his dance, a tough New York detective cuts in. Some gritty action. C: John Marley, Jon Cypher, Kathryn Walker, Rue McClanahan. D: Ernest Pintoff. ACT [R] 79m. V

Blade in Hong Kong 1985 ★★★ When his father is targeted for assassination in Hong Kong, a young detective sets out to find the gangsters responsible. Nice location color, fine action. C: Terry Lester, Leslie Nielsen, Nancy Kwan, Anthony Newley. D: Reza Badiyi. CRI 96m. V

Blade in the Dark, A 1983 ★★½ Seeking peace and quiet, a talented young composer moves into a remote villa only to find himself involved in murder. So-so shocker. C: Andrea Occhipinti, Anny Papa. D: Lamberto Bava. HOR 96m. V

Blade Master, The 1984 Italian ★★½ An ancient superwarrior is charged with protecting planet Earth from a rather strange atomic weapon. Silly rather than serious. C: Miles O'Keeffe, Lisa Raines Foster. D: David Hills. SFI [PG] 92m. V

Blade of Satan's Boy *See* **Satan's Book**

Blade Runner 1982 ★★★★½ In 21st-century L.A., a former lawman (Ford) tracks down superhuman androids who escaped enslavement. Stunningly beautiful, intelligent, and action-packed. From Philip K. Dick's novel *Do Androids Dream of Electric Sheep?* Often imitated, never replicated. Director's cut eliminates Ford's voice-over and features additional footage. C: Harrison Ford, Rutger Hauer, Sean Young, Edward James Olmos, Daryl Hannah. D: Ridley Scott. SFI [R] 122m. V

Blades of Courage 1987 ★★★ A young girl, going nowhere in her small town, turns to figure skating as a means of escape. Well handled. C: Christianne Hirt, Colm Feore, Stuart Hughes. D: Randy Bradshaw. DRA 98m. V

Blades 1989 ★★½ At a luxurious suburban country club, a lethal lawn mower slices and hooks the unsuspecting golfers—until three duffers try to stop it. Silly. C: Robert North, Jeremy Whelan, Victoria Scott. D: Thomas R. Rondinella. HOR [R] 99m. V

Blame It on Rio 1984 ★★ Caine can't keep his hands off his best friend's daughter when they travel south during Carnival time. Labored remake of French comedy *One Wild Moment* is too sexy for children and only passingly funny for adults. C: Michael Caine, Joseph Bologna, Valerie Harper, Michelle Johnson, Demi Moore. D: Stanley Donen. COM [R] 90m. V

Blame It on the Bellboy 1992 British ★★ Confusion abounds when an addlebrained bellboy at a posh Venice hotel mixes up messages to three guests (one a hitman) with similar sounding names. Innocuous comedy features great scenery. C: Dudley Moore, Bronson Pinchot, Bryan Brown, Patsy Kensit. D: Mark Herman. COM [PG-13] 79m. V

Blame It on the Night 1984 ★★ Story of a rock star trying to win over his straitlaced son. Rolling Stones fans alert: Mick Jagger co-wrote the story, with the director. C: Nick Mancuso, Byron Thames, Leslie Ackerman. D: Gene Taft. MUS [PG-13] 85m. V

Blanche Fury 1948 British ★★★½ Seduction, marriage, and murder, as a scheming governess plots to do away with the wealthy (and unsuspecting) British country squire she has wed. Well-crafted, Gothic melodrama. C: Stewart Granger, Michael Gough, Maurice Denham. D: Marc Allegret. DRA 95m.

Blank Check 1994 ★★½ A young boy cashes a $1 million blank check, and finds himself running from G-men and mobsters alike. *Home Alone*-inspired romp has the violence but not the heart of its predecessor. Too many zeroes. C: Brian Bonsall, Karen Duffy, Miguel Ferrer, James Rebhorn, tone Loc. D: Rupert Wainwright. COM 93m. V

Blaze of Noon 1947 ★★★ High-flying pilot (Holden) has two loves—his work and Baxter. Somewhat talky, but the flying sequences are fun. C: Anne Baxter, William Holden, Sonny Tufts, William Bendix, Sterling Hayden. D: John Farrow. DRA 91m.

Blaze O'Glory 1930 ★★★½ Uneasy mixture of music and courtroom drama in which former song-and-dance men, now soldiers, stand trial for murder; flashbacks recall their good old days, with emphasis on big production numbers. Contrast of tones is well-done, if a bit odd. C: Eddie Dowling, Betty Compson, Ferdinand Schumann-Heink, Frank Darro. D: Renaud Hoffman, George J. Crone. MUS 78m.

Blaze 1989 ★★★½ All about the affair between New Orleans stripper Blaze Starr and feisty, maverick Louisiana governor Earl Long. Doesn't quite succeed as an insightful look into the dangerous and volatile mix of love and politics, but Newman has some fun moments. Davidovich's memorable starring debut. C: Paul Newman, Lolita Davidovich. D: Ron Shelton. DRA [R] 117m. V

Blazing Forest, The 1952 ★★½ Trouble starts when a well-heeled landowner (Moorehead) mixes it up with a bunch of rough timbermen. Some nifty romance and a swell fire keep things sizzling. C: John Payne, Agnes Moorehead, Richard Arlen, William Demarest. D: Edward Ludwig. DRA 90m.

Blazing Saddles 1974 ★★★★★ Madcap Western spoof is a no-holds-barred gagfest. Little is appointed the first black sheriff of all-white Rock Ridge, in a plot to chase the townspeople from their homes. Kahn stops the show as a sexy, Dietrich-like salon singer. Then up-and-coming comedy writers Richard Pryor and Andrew Bergman had their hands in the script. C: Cleavon Little, Gene Wilder, Harvey Korman, Madeline Kahn, Slim Pickens, Alex Karras. D: Mel Brooks. COM [R] 93m. V

Bleak House 1985 ★★★★ Dickens's classic tale of intrigue and affairs in the London Court of Chancery. This BBC production is atmospheric and fine all around, with special credit due to the outstanding cast. C: Denholm Elliott, Lucy Hornak, Philip Franks, Diana Rigg. D: Ross Devenish. DRA 391m. V

Bless the Beasts and Children 1972 ★★★½ Ecological drama of troubled teens on a journey to save doomed buffalo. Well acted, but too earnest. C: Billy Mumy, Barry Robins, Miles Chapin. D: Stanley Kramer. DRA [PG] 109m. V

Blessed Event 1932 ★★★★ A wiseguy gossip columnist can't keep himself out of trouble. Charming, fast moving, and utterly delightful from start to finish. C: Lee Tracy, Mary Brian, Dick Powell, Frank McHugh, Ruth Donnelly. D: Roy Del Ruth. COM 78m. V

Bleu 1993 *See* **Blue**

Blind Alley 1939 ★★★★ A psychologist (Bellamy), held hostage by escaped convicts, subjects one of his captors to hypnosis. Excellent, psychological film noir begins in high gear and just gets better and better, as it delves into the memories of a violent man. Remade as *The Dark Past*. C: Chester Morris, Ralph Bellamy, Ann Dvorak. D: Charles Vidor. CRI 71m.

Blind Alley 1985 *See* **Perfect Strangers**

Blind Date 1959 *See* **Chance Meeting**

Blind Date 1987 ★★½ Willis (in his film debut) thinks he's in for a night of heaven when he's matched on a blind date with Basinger. However his night becomes a living hell when he ignores the warning not to let her drink. Slapstick comedy of destruction unravels long before it's over. C: Bruce Willis, Kim Basinger, John Larroquette, William Daniels. D: Blake Edwards. COM [PG-13] 95m. v

Blind Faith 1990 ★★★ Best-selling Joe McGinniss true-crime book becomes a standard potboiler, with Urich as a loving family man who kills his wife. Doesn't sustain its length; originally shown in two parts. C: Robert Urich, Joanna Kerns, Robin Strasser, Dennis Farina, Joe Spano. D: Paul Wendkos. CRI 200m. TVM

Blind Fear 1988 ★★½ Killers play a cat-and-mouse game while stalking a blind woman (Hack) at an abandoned country inn. Abundant clichés and Hack's limitations sink this thriller. C: Shelly Hack, Jack Langedyk, Kim Coates, Heidi Von Palleske. D: Tom Berry. CRI [R] 87m. v

Blind Fury 1990 ★★★½ Sightless Vietnam vet (Hauer) rescues his buddy's son from an evil gambling kingpin (Willingham) and fights his way cross-country to reunite father and son. Highly entertaining and Hauer's samurai stunts are faster than the eye. C: Rutger Hauer, Brandon Call, Lisa Blount. D: Phillip Noyce. ACT [R] 86m. v

Blind Husbands 1919 ★★★½ A doctor and his wife vacationing in the Alps meet an infamous Lothario who seduces the wife while charming the husband. Von Stroheim's first silent hit shows the irony, bitterness, and extravagance for which he became famous. C: Erich von Stroheim, Gibson Gowland, Sam De Grasse. D: Erich von Stroheim. DRA 8 reels.

Blind Justice 1986 ★★★ A man's life is destroyed when he's falsely accused of rape. Powerful and sobering modern-day nightmare. C: Tim Matheson, Lisa Eichhorn, Mimi Kuzyk, Tom Atkins. D: Rod Holcomb. DRA 94m. TVM

Blind Man's Bluff 1991 ★★★½ When a blind professor is accused of murdering his neighbor, he prepares his own hands-on defense. Neat suspense. C: Robert Urich, Lisa Eilbacher, Patricia Clarkson, Ken Pogue, Ron Perlman. D: James Quinn. HOR [PG-13] 86m. TVM v

Blind Rage 1983 Philippine ★★★ Five kung fu masters—each one blind—decide to rob a Filipino bank. A fascinating premise that's brought off with humor and panache. C: D'urville Martin, Leo Fong, Fred Williamson. D: Efren C. Pinon. ACT [R] 81m. v

Blind Side 1993 ★★★½ Hauer is well-cast as a mysterious blackmailer, who stalks De Mornay and Silver after their involvement in a hit-and-run accident. Intriguing thriller runs out of steam midway. C: Rutger Hauer, Rebecca De Mornay, Ron Silver. D: Geoff Murphy. CRI [R] 100m. v

Blind Spot 1947 ★★★ A mystery writer gets implicated in the murder of his publisher. Exciting plot and fine B-movie cast—worth a look. C: Chester Morris, Constance Dowling, Steven Geray, Sid Tomack. D: Robert Gordon. CRI 73m.

Blind Spot 1993 ★★★★ Another in a long line of strong Woodward TV-film performances, this time as a congresswoman who doesn't know about her daughter's drug problem. Woodward was Emmy-nominated for this incisive drama. C: Joanne Woodward, Laura Linney, Reed Diamond, Fritz Weaver. D: Michael Toshiyuki Uno. DRA 100m. TVM v

Blind Terror 1971 *See* **See No Evil**

Blind Trust 1987 French ★★★★ Intriguing thriller involving a career criminal and an undercover cop who steal an armored car, not realizing a guard is locked in back. Hard-hitting crime story, well told and acted. C: Marie Tifo, Pierre Curzi, Yvan Ponton, Jacques Robert Gravel. D: Yves Simoneau. DRA [PG-13] 86m. v

Blind Vengeance 1990 ★★½ When a man is murdered by a group of white supremacists, his friend sets out to avenge him. Solid action and workmanlike performances. C: Gerald McRaney, Marg Helgenberger, Lane Smith. D: Lee Philips. ACT [R] 100m. TVM

Blind Vision 1991 ★★½ Timid Von Dohlen spies on his beautiful neighbor through a camera lens, which leads him into trouble when one of her lovers turns up dead. A lukewarm study of secret sexual obsessions. C: Louise Fletcher, Ned Beatty, Lenny Von Dohlen, Deborah Shelton. D: Shuki Levy. CRI 92m. v

Blindfold: Acts Of Obsession 1994 ★★½ Young woman cannot control her participation in erotic intrigue. C: Shannen Doherty, Judd Nelson. DRA [R] 91m. v

Blindfold 1966 ★★★ Hodgepodge of comedy and suspense, as a prominent psychiatrist is enlisted by the CIA to treat a disturbed scientist threatening national security. Campy espionage thriller. C: Rock Hudson, Claudia Cardinale, Jack Warden. D: Philip Dunne. CRI 102m.

Blindman 1972 Italian ★★ A large number of Italian mail-order brides have been kidnapped, and "Big Daddy" Blindman seeks revenge. Nonsensical little oddity: would you believe Ringo Starr in a cameo as a Mexican peasant? . . . C: Tony Anthony, Ringo Starr, Agneta Eckemyr. D: Ferdinando Baldi. WST [R] 105m.

Blindsided 1992 ★★½ Blinded during an errant drug sting, A crooked cop (Fahey) meets an adventuress (Sara) at a resort and finds himself up to his neck in a different kind of danger. The setup has potential, but the script never delivers in this cable-released thriller. C: Jeff Fahey, Mia Sara, Ben Gazzara. D: Tom Donnelly. CRI 93m. TVM v

Blink 1994 ★★★ A violin player (Stowe) has her sight restored just in time to witness a murder, and she is then stalked and tormented by the killer. Predictable thriller, despite a talented cast. C: Madeleine Stowe, Aidan Quinn, Laurie Metcalf, James Remar, Peter Friedman. D: Michael Apted. CRI [R] 106m. v

Bliss of Mrs. Blossom, The 1968 U.S.-British ★★★★½ The neglected wife (MacLaine) of an English brassiere manufacturer keeps a lover in her attic—for years. MacLaine shines in this wonderfully absurd comedy; sheer joy from beginning to end. C: Shirley MacLaine, Richard Attenborough, James Booth, John Cleese. D: Joseph McGrath. COM [PG] 93m. v

Bliss 1985 Australian ★★★½ A family man sees his life very differently after a near-death experience, and his new perspective leads him on a strange journey in search of bliss. Original, offbeat comedy from Australia. C: Barry Otto, Lynette Curran, Helen Jones. D: Ray Lawrence. COM [R] 112m. v

Blithe Spirit 1945 British ★★★★½ Noel Coward's stage bauble gets a fine adaptation, with a sterling cast, as a hilarious medium (Rutherford) calls forth the ghost of a gentleman's dead wife (Hammond). Sophisticated dialogue, clever special effects. C: Rex Harrison, Constance Cummings, Kay Hammond, Margaret Rutherford. D: David Lean. COM 96m. v

Blob, The 1958 ★★★ A ravenous creature from outer space threatens small town and it's up to a teen (McQueen) and his squeaky clean friends to stop it. Not very exciting or scary, but good campy fun all the same. McQueen's starring debut. Beware the sequel, *Beware! The Blob*, directed by Larry Hagman. Remade in 1988. C: Steven McQueen, Aneta Corseaut. D: Irvin Yeaworth Jr. SFI 80m. v

Blob, The 1988 ★★★ Updated retelling of the campy original, with some significant changes: the gooey stuff is man-made, the teenagers are not angels, and this blob is scary. Ounce for ounce, more horror than its predecessor. Fine effects and gore galore. C: Shawnee Smith, Donovan Leitch, Ricky Goldin, Kevin Dillon. D: Chuck Russell. SFI [R] 92m. v

Block Busters 1944 ★★½ Muggs, Gimpy, and the rest of the fabled East Side Kids take on assorted city hoodlums and Nazi spies. Good fun and part of an entertainment series classic. C: Leo Gorcey, Huntz Hall, Gabriel Dell. D: Wallace Fox. COM 60m.

Block-Heads 1938 ★★★★ Blissfully unaware that WWI has been over for 20 years, Laurel is still defending the trenches until Hardy comes to take him home, resulting in the usual pandemonium. Among the best of their vehicles. C: Stan Laurel, Oliver Hardy, Billy Gilbert, James Finlayson. D: John G. Blystone. COM 75m. v

Blockade 1938 ★★★★ The Spanish Civil War comes alive in this action romance. Good performances and a tight script. C: Madeleine Carroll, Henry Fonda, Leo Carrillo. D: William Dieterle. DRA 85m.

Blockhouse, The 1973 British ★★★ Seven men trapped in a German bunker during WWII struggle to survive over the course of six years. Unusual dramatic role for Sellers, but the claustrophobic setting leads to a rather pretentious viewing experience. C: Peter Sellers, Charles Aznavour, Per Oscarsson, Peter Vaughan. D: Clive Rees. DRA 88m. v

Blonde Bait 1956 British ★★½ A blowsy blonde breaks out of a women's prison and becomes a show girl. Glum and predictable. C: Beverly Michaels, Jim Davis, Joan Rice. D: Elmo Williams. DRA 70m.

Blonde Blackmailer 1958 British ★★½ Once he's out of prison, an ex-con determines to find the gang that framed him. Stilted, stiff, and stuffy. C: Richard Arlen, Susan Shaw. D: Charles Deane. CRI 58m.

Blonde Crazy 1931 ★★★★ Cagney and Blondell are a couple of less-than-expert con artists in this perfectly tuned, feather-light crime comedy. Fast, witty dialogue, agreeable tunes, and a top-drawer supporting cast keep this one floating on air. (a.k.a. *Larceny Lane*) C: James Cagney, Joan Blondell, Louis Calhern, Ray Milland. D: Roy Del Ruth. COM 81m. v

Blonde Dynamite 1950 ★★½ The Bowery Boys, led by the indomitable Slip Mahoney (Gorcey), tangle with a gang of sleek con artists. Plenty of laughs and silliness. C: Leo Gorcey, Huntz Hall, Gabriel Dell, Adele Jergens. D: William Beaudine. COM 66m.

Blonde Fever 1944 ★★½ After years of a tedious marriage, a middle-aged gentleman falls in love with a brassy greasy-spoon waitress. Even with a decent cast, adds up to a pleasant but predictable comedy. C: Philip Dorn, Mary Astor, Felix Bressart, Gloria Grahame. D: Richard Whorf. COM 69m.

Blonde for a Day 1946 ★★ A crime reporter stumbles onto big doings by the Mob. Small-time suspense, with a credible cast. C: Hugh Beaumont, Kathryn Adams. D: Sam Newfield. COM 67m.

Blonde in a White Car 1960 *See* **Nude in a White Car**

Blonde Venus 1932 ★★★★ A former singer (Dietrich), married to a dull Englishman (Marshall), returns to the stage and takes up with a rich Englishman (Grant). With its glossy photography and Dietrich in a gorilla suit singing "Hot Voodoo" you can forgive the weak story. C: Marlene Dietrich, Herbert Marshall, Cary Grant, Dickie Moore. D: Josef von Sternberg. DRA 89m. v

Blondes at Work 1938 ★★★ No one knows why Torchy Blane, reporter, is always scooping the competition. Could it be her big cop boyfriend? Good fun and a nice, crusty cast led by Farrell. C: Glenda Farrell, Barton MacLane, Tom Kennedy, Carole Landis. D: Frank McDonald. COM 63m.

Blondie Chic Young's comic strip was a natural for a film series, with its bumbling husband, clever wife, and hard-headed boss with his overbearing wife. Columbia kicked it off with 1938's *Blondie,* featuring Penny Singleton in the title role, Arthur Lake memorably giddy as Dagwood, and Jonathan Hale as Mr. Dithers. Low-budget but brisk, the films suffer a bit from repetition and cast changes in the early '40s, but overall the entries are cheerful and amusing.

Blondie (1938)
Blondie Meets the Boss (1939)
Blondie Takes a Vacation (1939)
Blondie Brings Up Baby (1939)
Blondie On a Budget (1940)
Blondie Has Servant Trouble (1940)
Blondie Plays Cupid (1940)
Blondie Goes Latin (1941)
Blondie in Society (1941)
Blondie Goes to College (1942)
Blondie's Blessed Event (1942)
Blondie for Victory (1942)
It's a Great Life (1943)
Footlight Glamour (1943)
Leave It to Blondie (1945)
Life With Blondie (1946)
Blondie's Lucky Day (1946)
Blondie Knows Best (1946)
Blondie's Big Moment (1947)
Blondie's Holiday (1947)
Blondie in the Dough (1947)
Blondie's Anniversary (1947)
Blondie's Reward (1948)
Blondie's Secret (1948)
Blondie's Big Deal (1949)
Blondie Hits the Jackpot (1949)
Blondie's Hero (1950)
Beware of Blondie (1950)

Blondie 1938 ★★★½ Amusing low-budget comedy adapted from the popular comic strip about the misadventures of a typical suburban couple, Blondie (Singleton) and Dagwood (Lake) Bumstead. First of 28 films in sturdy, likable series. C: Penny Singleton, Arthur Lake, Gene Lockhart, Jonathan Hale. D: Frank Strayer. COM 68m. V

Blondie and Dagwood—It's a Great Life *See* **It's a Great Life**

Blondie Brings Up Baby 1939 ★★★ Dagwood and Blondie have a son! How will the bumbling Bumsteads ever recover from the arrival of Baby Dumpling? Frenetic and uproarious. C: Penny Singleton, Arthur Lake, Larry Simms, Jonathan Hale. D: Frank Strayer. COM 67m.

Blondie for Victory 1942 ★★½ The Bumsteads do their part for the war effort. Typical lighthearted hilarity in this ongoing series. COM

Blondie Goes Latin 1941 ★★½ Blondie adds a little south-of-the-border spice to Bumstead life in small-town America. Mambo, anyone? COM

Blondie Goes to College 1942 ★★½ Blondie gets it into her head to get a little more into her head. Schooltime fun with the Bumsteads. Watch for young Lloyd Bridges. COM

Blondie Has Servant Trouble 1940 ★★½ The Bumsteads are coming up in the world. As always, complications ensue. Good fun throughout. COM

Blondie Hits the Jackpot 1949 ★★ Suddenly things are really going Blondie's way—and all the Bumsteads are beneficiaries. Typical series laughs. COM

Blondie in Society 1941 ★★½ More adventures of the Bumstead family as they meet the elite. Veterans Frawley and Kennedy add to the fun. COM

Blondie in the Dough 1947 ★★ Big bucks and Bumsteads don't always mix. More laughs but at this point the series is showing its age. COM

Blondie Johnson 1939 ★★★ A tough young woman gets involved with the mob and the rackets. But after a good run, she pays for her life of crime. An entertaining early comedy/drama that showcases Blondell's considerable talent. C: Joan Blondell, Chester Morris, Allen Jenkins, Sterling Holloway, Mae Busch. D: Ray Enright. COM 67m.

Blondie Knows Best 1946 ★★½ Even more adventures of Blondie, Dagwood, and their lovable offspring, Alexander and Cookie. The usual good times with this batty bunch of Bumsteads. COM

Blondie Meets the Boss 1939 ★★★ Blondie puts her best foot forward on behalf of Dagwood. Mr. Dithers of the office may not be amused, but we are. COM

Blondie of the Follies 1932 ★★★½ Two Follies stars fall for the same fella (Montgomery). Superbly talented cast (led by Durante and Davies) make this a special little film. C: Marion Davies, Robert Montgomery, Billie Dove, Jimmy Durante, ZaSu Pitts. D: Edmund Goulding. COM 90m.

Blondie on a Budget 1940 ★★★ The Bumstead household feels the pinch when Blondie tightens her belt. Early fun in the series. COM

Blondie Plays Cupid 1940 ★★½ Love is in the air—and Blondie is quick to take note. Young Glenn Ford adds to the fun. COM

Blondie Takes a Vacation 1939 ★★½ Even the harried Bumsteads need a break now and then. Freed from their usual routine, Blondie and her brood wreak havoc upon a sleepy resort town. Lotsa laughs. COM

Blondie's Anniversary 1947 ★★½ The Bumsteads' road may get bumpy at times, but Dagwood and Blondie will always travel together. Mark the event with a "joy" ride of your own. COM

Blondie's Big Deal 1949 ★★½ Blondie is never one to keep something small. Series is getting a little long in the tooth, and it shows. COM

Blondie's Big Moment 1947 ★★½ The irrepressible Mrs. Bumstead keeps everyone hopping. Cute addition to this lengthy series. COM

Blondie's Blessed Event 1942 ★★½ Is there another Bumstead on the way? If you're expecting a smile from Blondie, you won't be disappointed. COM

Blondie's Hero 1950 ★★½ Everyone looks for inspiration wherever it can be found. With Blondie Bumstead, the search is a guaranteed giggle getter! Still, it's clear this is a late entry in the series. COM

Blondie's Holiday 1947 ★★ A blessed respite from the usual absurdity. Of course Blondie seizes the opportunity to generate more glee. COM

Blondie's Lucky Day 1946 ★★★ Good fortune (?) knocks on Blondie's door when Dagwood loses his job! Chuckle along with America's favorite suburbanites. COM

Blondie's Reward 1948 ★★½ No one is more deserving of the best things in life than the charming and good-hearted Blondie Bumstead. Still fun, although late in the life of this series. COM

Blondie's Secret 1948 ★★★ Blondie tries her best to keep news under wraps. Torment for Mrs. B—but a tickler to watch! COM

Blood Alley 1955 ★★★ Wayne and Bacall smuggle Chinese refugees past the Communists in this hackneyed action film. Wellman and the two stars have done a lot better elsewhere. C: John Wayne, Lauren Bacall, Paul Fix, Mike Mazurki, Anita Ekberg. D: William Wellman. ACT 115m. V

Blood and Black Lace 1965 Italian ★★½ Mystery surrounds the ghastly murders of a half-dozen fashion models. Unduly gruesome, derivative suspense/horror entry. C: Cameron Mitchell, Eva Bartok. D: Mario Bava. HOR 90m. V

Blood & Guts 1978 Canadian ★★½ Young man tries to prove himself after joining the pro wrestling circuit. No surprises in this rehash of well-worn material. C: William Smith, Micheline Lanctot. D: Paul Lynch. DRA [PG] 92m. V

Blood and Lace 1971 ★★½ Caretakers of a sinister orphanage are the suspects in a rash of murders. Thin, low-budget creepfest. C: Gloria Grahame, Melody Patterson, Vic Tayback. D: Philip Gilbert. HOR [PG] 87m.

Blood & Orchids 1986 ★★★★ When a hasty conviction is sought against four Hawaiians charged with rape, a tenacious police officer suspects a frame-up. Frenzied courtroom drama right out of the tabloids. C: Kris Kristofferson, Jane Alexander, Sean Young, Jose Ferrer, Susan Blakely, Richard Dysart. D: Jerry Thorpe. DRA 200m. TVM

Blood and Roses 1961 Italian ★★½ When a vampire takes over the body of her covetous female descendant mayhem ensues. Vague horror tale based on Sheridan Le Fanu's *Carmilla*. C: Mel Ferrer, Elsa Martinelli. D: Roger Vadim. HOR 74m. V

Blood and Sand 1922 ★★★★ A dashing matador (Valentino) faces death in the ring, and is loved by two beautiful women (Lee and Naldi). A silent-era classic that made him a star. Made again in 1941 and 1989. C: Rudolph Valentino, Lila Lee, Nita Naldi. D: Fred Niblo. DRA 92m. V

Blood and Sand 1941 ★★★★ A gorgeous color remake of the 1922 silent classic. Power takes over the Valentino role with gusto. Remade in 1989. C: Tyrone Power, Linda Darnell, Rita Hayworth, Nazimova, Anthony Quinn, J. Carrol Naish, John Carradine, George Reeves. D: Rouben Mamoulian. DRA 125m. V

Blood and Sand 1989 Spanish ★★½ Remake of the frequently told tale about a hot-blooded toreador whose head is turned by success and a woman who tempts him away from his wife. Overt sex and flashy bullfighting can't compensate for lack of originality. C: Chris Rydell, Sharon Stone, Ana Torrent. D: Javier Elorrieta. DRA [R] 96m. V

Blood and Steel 1959 ★★½ U.S. sailors support partisans in freeing prisoners from a Japanese-occupied island. Standard heroics in mediocre WWII entry. C: John Lupton, James Edwards, Brett Halsey. D: Bernard Kowalski. DRA 63m.

Blood Arrow 1958 ★★★ A scout, a trapper, and a gambler band together to help a young Mormon woman transport a supply of smallpox serum past a warring Indian tribe. Average Western driven more by character than by action. C: Scott Brady, Paul Richards, Phyllis Coates. D: Charles Warren. WST 75m.

Blood Barrier 1979 British ★★★ Mexicans are illegally transported into California, to the dismay of a U.S. Border Patrol officer. Promising idea marred by undernourished plot and an unsatisfying climax. C: Telly Savalas, Danny Paz, Eddie Albert. D: Christopher Leitch. ACT [R] 86m.

Blood Bath 1966 ★★½ A vampire posing as an artist selects his models as victims. Grisly patchwork chiller; in general a hodgepodge. C: Jack Hill, William Campbell, Jonathan Haze. D: Stephanie Rothman. HOR 80m. V

Blood Beach 1981 ★★ A monstrous menace sucks beachgoers down into the sand—or, as the ads put it, "Just when you thought it was safe to go back into the water, you can't get to it." Rather bloodless, in both senses of the word, but enlivened by an offbeat approach. C: John Saxon, David Huffman, Mariana Hill. D: Jeffrey Bloom. HOR [R] 92m. V

Blood Beast from Outer Space 1965 British ★★★½ To save their dying planet, space aliens kidnap an Earth woman to breed with. Orderly British science fiction story deals maturely with theme. (a.k.a. *Night Caller from Outer Space*) C: John Saxon, Maurice Denham, Patricia Haines, Jack Carson. D: John Gilling. SFI 84m.

Blood Couple 1973 *See* **Black Vampire**

Blood Evil, Nightmare of Terror *See* **Demons of the Mind**

Blood Evil *See* **Demons of the Mind**

Blood Feud 1979 Italian ★★★ A widow (Loren) is torn between a good lawyer (Mastroianni) and a bad gangster (Giannini). The stars and director should have been an ideal mix, but all are undone by the weak script. (a.k.a. *Revenge*) C: Sophia Loren, Marcello Mastroianni, Giancarlo Giannini. D: Lina Wertmuller. DRA [R] 112m. V

Blood Feud 1983 ★★★★½ Attorney General Robert Kennedy leads an investigation into Teamster president Jimmy Hoffa's ties to the criminal underworld. Superior TV movie succeeds as history and drama. Outstanding performance by Blake. C: Robert Blake, Cotter Smith, Danny Aiello, Edward Albert, Brian Dennehy, Ernest Borgnine, Jose Ferrer, Forest Tucker. D: Mike Newell. DRA 200m. TVM

Blood Fiend *See* **Theatre of Death**

Blood from the Mummy's Tomb 1972 British ★★½ Explorers who broke into an ancient Egyptian royal tomb are murdered piecemeal. Unduly complex thriller sans mummy. C: Michael Carreras, Andrew Keir, Valerie Leon. D: Seth Holt. HOR [PG] 94m.

Blood In, Blood Out *See* **Bound by Honor**

Blood in the Face 1991 ★★★★ Blood-curdling documentary about extreme right-wing groups, like the Ku Klux Klan, Aryan Nation, and Nazi party. Most effective when detailing their hate campaigns. D: Anne Bohlen, Kevin Rafferty, James Ridgeway. DOC 75m. V

Blood in the Streets 1975 Italian ★★½ A warden (Reed) is forced to release a prisoner in exchange for his kidnapped wife. Standard Euro-thriller does have a few effective chase scenes. C: Oliver Reed, Agostina Belli, Fabio Testi. D: Sergio Sollima. ACT [R] 111m.

Blood Mania 1970 ★★ A would-be heiress murders her tycoon father only to learn she's not in his will. Sub-standard chiller fable. C: Peter Carpenter, Maria De Aragon, Vicki Peters. D: Robert Vincent O'Neil. DRA [R] 88m. V

Blood Money 1933 ★★★★ A giddy debutante (Dee) comes between a corrupt social-climbing bail bondsman (Bancroft) and his associate (Anderson). Snappy, stylish '30s underworld drama. C: George Bancroft, Frances Dee, Judith Anderson. D: Rowland Brown. DRA 65m.

Blood Money 1988 *See* **Clinton and Nadine**

Blood of a Poet, The 1930 ★★★★ Cocteau presents a series of surrealist episodes that describe the Poet's role as hero, his relationship to his Muse, and his suicide for the sake of artistic immortality. A seminal surrealist movie. C: Lee Miller, Pauline Carton, Odette Talazac. D: Jean Cocteau. DRA 55m. V

Blood of Dracula 1957 ★★ An unwitting pupil at a girls' school is converted to vampirism by an evil teacher. Minor second bill fodder lacks bite. C: Sandra Harrison, Gail Ganley, Jerry Blaine. D: Herbert L. Strock. HOR 71m. V

Blood of Dracula's Castle 1969 ★ A vampire and his wife keep a group of strangely compliant girls shackled in their basement. Cheapie shocker, laughably bad. C: John Carradine, Paula Raymond. D: Al Adamson. HOR 84m. V

Blood of Heroes, The 1990 ★★★ Rugged, bloody action film combining elements of *Rollerball* and *Mad Max*. In a postapocalyptic future a group of nomadic athletes, led by Hauer, struggle for survival as they compete in a savage game. (a.k.a. *The Salute of the Juggler*) C: Rutger Hauer, Joan Chen. D: David Peoples. ACT [R] 91m. V

Blood of Others, The 1984 ★★½ At the start of WWII, a young French woman experiences conflicting passions for her absent Resistance boyfriend and a kindhearted German. Soapy, less than successful adaptation of Simone de Beauvoir's novel. C: Jodie Foster, Michael Ontkean, Sam Neill, Lambert Wilson. D: Claude Chabrol. DRA 130m. TVM V

Blood of the Condor 1969 Bolivian ★★★ Angry drama posits the notion that the U.S. Peace Corps sanctions sterilization programs of indigenous women in Third World countries. Film is full of anti-American sentiment and revolutionary zeal; it's considered a landmark of leftist cinema. A compelling if transparently biased work. C: Marcelino Yanahuaya, Benedicta Mendoza Huenca, Vincente Salinas. D: Jorges Sanjines. DRA 74m.

Blood of the Vampire 1958 British ★★★ An imprisoned physician and a vampiric convict team up in a quest for blood. Gore and blood abound in sluggish horror fare. C: Donald Wolfit, Barbara Shelley. D: Henry Cass. HOR 84m. V

Blood on Satan's Claw, The 1971 British ★★★★ Evocative period horror film about a cult of devil-worshipping children that springs up around the discovery of the title artifact. Creepy and explicit (though often cut), with Hayden memorable as the group's voluptuous young leader. C: Patrick Wymark, Linda Hayden. D: Piers Haggard. HOR [R] 101m. V

Blood on the Arrow 1964 ★★½ Western parents set out to save their son who was carried off by Apaches. Tedious sagebrush action film. C: Dale Robertson, Martha Hyer, Wendell Corey. D: Sidney Salkow. WST 91m.

Blood on the Moon 1948 ★★★★ Excellent cast highlights this dark Western that finds a noble drifter (Mitchum) torn between love and friendship, and caught in the middle of a war between ranchers and homesteaders. Absorbing drama captures film noir atmosphere in the Old West. C: Robert Mitchum, Barbara Bel Geddes, Robert Preston, Walter Brennan, Phyllis Thaxter. D: Robert Wise. WST 88m. V

Blood on the Streets 1974 *See* **Borsalino and Company**

Blood on the Sun 1945 ★★★ In pre-WWII Japan, a reporter (Cagney) uncovers Japanese plans for world domination. He's pursued by their government and military, who want to prevent him from escaping to America with the information. Propaganda disguised as drama, but very watchable. C: James Cagney, Sylvia Sidney, Wallace Ford, Rosemary De Camp, Robert Armstrong. D: Frank Lloyd. DRA 98m. V

Blood Red 1989 ★★ A railroad tycoon (Hopper) tries to strong-arm his railroad through the land of immigrant families in California. Good direction can't make up for the weak script and low production values, but the cast, including Julia Roberts in her first screen role, is interesting to watch. C: Eric Roberts, Giancarlo Giannini, Dennis Hopper, Burt Young. D: Peter Masterson. WST [R] 91m. V

Blood Relations 1989 ★★ A young woman (Danier), visiting her fiancé's family, discovers that they are involved in murder plots and worse. Undistinguished thriller only intermittently builds tension. C: Jan Rubes, Lydie Denier, Kevin Hicks, Lynne Adams, Ray Walston. D: Graeme Campbell. HOR [R] 88m. V

Blood Relatives 1978 French ★★★★ A clandestine incestuous relationship has fatal results. Cold but well-handled thriller, tastefully rendered. C: Donald Sutherland, Aude Landry, Lisa Langlois, Stephane Audran, Donald Pleasence. D: Claude Chabrol. CRI [R] 100m. V

Blood River 1991 ★★★★ On the run from a murder charge, a young desperado forms an unlikely bond with a crotchety loner. Intriguing character Western, scripted by John Carpenter. C: Rick Schroder, Wilford Brimley, Adrienne Barbeau. D: Mel Damski. WST 100m. TVM

Blood Rose 1969 French ★★½ After a fire deforms her face, a woman's artist husband contrives to rebuild it. Inferior French entry. C: Philippe Lemaire, Anny Duperey. D: Claude Multo. HOR [R] 87m.

Blood Salvage 1990 ★★½ Twisted shocker about a demented garbage collector who starts accumulating people, with the intention of selling their body parts. Sufficiently gruesome to recommend to those with a stomach for these things and to warn those without. C: Danny Nelson, Lori Bridsong, John Saxon, Ray Walston, Evander Holyfield. D: Tucker Johnston. HOR [R] 90m. V

Blood Simple 1985 ★★★★½ A husband's simple attempt to have his wife and her lover killed turns into a complex demonstration of Murphy's Law. Modern film noir, via the Coen brothers, offers very bloody black humor, along with some striking visual scenes. C: John Getz, Frances McDormand, Dan Hedya, Samm-Art Williams. D: Joel Coen. CRI [R] 96m. V

Blood Sisters 1986 ★ Sorority women think it would be a lark to spend the night in a haunted house—they're dead wrong. Slasher-film offers nothing new, nothing scary. C: Amy Brentano, Marla MacHart, Brigete Cossu, Randy Mooers. D: Roberta Findlay. HOR [R] 85m. V

Blood Sweat and Fear 1975 Italian ★★ Majestic Italian scenery highlights this otherwise routine crime drama in which a driven young narcotics officer determinedly hunts a major drug lord. Uninvolving. C: Lee J. Cobb, Franco Gasparri. D: Stevio Massi. CRI [R] 90m.

Blood Tide 1982 ★★ A good cast flounders (and occasionally overacts) in this soggy opus about a mythological sea monster that terrorizes a Greek island. Nice photography can't save this ludicrous film. C: James Earl Jones, Jose Ferrer, Lila Kedrova, Mary Louise Weller, Martin Kove. D: Richard Jeffries. HOR [R] 82m. V

Blood Ties 1986 Italian ★★★½ an American architect in Italy (Davis) is drawn into an assassination plot by the Mafia in order to save his father. Twisty, absorbing story builds a paranoid atmosphere well. C: Brad Davis, Tony Lo Bianco, Vincent Spano, Barbara De Rossi, Maria Conchita Alonso. D: Giacomo Battiato. CRI 98m. V

Blood Vows—The Story of a Mafia Wife 1988 ★★ She says, "I do," then finds out what his "family" does. She should have known better. You do now. C: Melissa Gilbert, Joe Penny, Eileen Brennan, Anthony Franciosa. D: Paul Wendkos. CRI 95m. TVM

Blood Wedding 1981 Spanish ★★★★ Harndsome adaptation of Federico Garcia Lorca's play is a fine combination of ballet and cinema. Revenge story takes place during rehearsals interspersed with interviews. For flamenco aficionados especially. C: Antonio Gades, Cristina Hoyos, Juan Antonio Jimenez. D: Calos Saura. DRA [R] 71m. V

Bloodbrothers 1978 ★★★½ Examination of life in an Italian-American family, focusing on the ethos of machismo among its men. Gere's role is one of his best, as his character's sensitive aspirations conflict with the family's working-class values. Powerful writing by Richard Price from his own novel. (a.k.a. *A Father's Love*) C: Richard Gere, Paul Sorvino, Tony Lo Bianco, Lelia Goldoni, Marilu Henner, Danny Aiello. D: Robert Mulligan. DRA [R] 120m. V

Bloodeaters 1980 ★★ A toxic chemical agent is dispersed on a cannabis harvest and turns farmers into rampaging killer zombies. Bloodcurdling cheapie. C: Charles Austin,

Beverly Shapiro. D: Chuck McCrann. HOR [R] 84m.

Bloodfist 1989 ★★½ When his brother is killed, a kickboxer swears vengeance. Florid martial arts fare with abundant violent action for fans. C: Don Wilson, Michael Shaner. D: Terence H. Winkless. ACT [R] 86m. V

Bloodfist 2 1991 ★★½ A master kickboxer tries to penetrate an impregnable fortress on a distant island. Low-budget flying feet thrills. Violence and profanity. C: Don Wilson, Maurice Smith, Timothy Baker, James Warring. D: Andy Blumenthal. ACT [R] 85m. V

Bloodfist III—Forced to Fight 1991 ★★½ An unjustly incarcerated kickboxer steps in when ruthless inmates assault his chum. Fast-paced martial arts fare with feral battles. Some profanity. C: Don Wilson, Richard Roundtree, Richard Paul. D: Paul Ziller. ACT [R] 90m. V

Bloodhounds of Broadway 1952 ★★★ Stagey '20s gangster comedy/musical follows the adventures of a roguish ne'er-do-well trying to get out of hot water on a cold New Year's night. Funny, Runyonesque characters are everywhere; Gaynor's in top form. C: Mitzi Gaynor, Scott Brady, Mitzi Green. D: Harmon Jones. COM 90m.

Bloodhounds of Broadway 1989 ★★★½ A leggy rube goes to New York in the '20s and, aided by mobdom, becomes a burlesque headliner. Fair comedy/musical, based on stories by Damon Runyon; slick production. C: Matt Dillon, Madonna, Jennifer Grey, Rutger Hauer, Randy Quaid, Julie Hagerty, Anita Morris. D: Howard Brookner. COM [PG] 90m. V

Bloodline 1979 ★ Hepburn's inheritance of a highly valuable Swiss pharmaceutical company puts her life in jeopardy in this awful adaptation of a Sidney Sheldon novel. Fine cast is wasted in this unredeeming, trashy melodrama. C: Audrey Hepburn, Ben Gazzara, James Mason, Michelle Phillips, Omar Sharif, Romy Schneider, Irene Papas, Beatrice Straight. D: Terence Young. DRA [R] 116m. V

Bloodmatch 1991 ★★ Martial arts opus in which would-be action star Matthews plays a karate expert in search of his brother's killer. C: Benny Vrquidez, Thom Matthews. D: Albert Pyon. ACT 87m. V

Bloodsport 1987 ★★½ True story of an American ninja (Van Damme) who tries to win a brutal martial arts competition. Bloody, mindless actioner had the dubious distinction of introducing its star to U.S. audiences. For fans of the "Muscles from Brussels." C: Jean Claude Van Damme, Donald Gibb, Forest Whitaker. D: Newt Arnold. ACT [R] 92m. V

Bloodstone—Subspecies II 1993 ★★ The heroine of the first *Subspecies* fights the vampire curse (and the villain who gave it to her) while her sister travels to Romania to find her. Director Nicolaou tries to cover the thin plot with gobs of atmosphere, but succeeds only sporadically. C: Anders Hove, Denice Duff. D: Ted Nicolaou. HOR [R] 107m. V

Bloodsuckers 1971 ★★½ An English gentleman falls under the spell of vampires on a Greek island. Jumbled plot patched together as a psychotic horror tale. C: Patrick MacNee, Peter Cushing. D: Robert Hartford Davis. HOR [R] 90m. V

Bloody Birthday 1981 ★★ Typical '80s horror film, with lots of blood and not too much thought. Three prepubescents embark on a murderous rampage because they were born during a lunar eclipse. More silly than scary; the main interest is an early (and unclothed) appearance by Julie Brown. (a.k.a. *Creeps*) C: Susan Strasberg, Jose Ferrer, Lori Lethin, Joe Penny, Michael Dudikoff. D: Ed Hunt. HOR [R] 85m. V

Bloody Mama 1970 ★★ During the '30s, Ma Barker (Winters) leads her violent brood through a series of crimes before their inevitable shoot-'em-up demise. Fine cast of rising stars gives great support to Winters' lead, but the ensemble can't rise above the often mindless exploitation script. C: Shelley Winters, Don Stroud, Pat Hingle, Robert DeNiro, Bruce Dern. D: Roger Corman. DRA [R] 90m. V

Bloomfield 1972 *See* **Hero, The**

Blossoms in the Dust 1941 ★★★½ Noble drama of a woman who starts an orphanage after the death of her own child. Determined Garson tearjerker with a good cast and glossy production. C: Greer Garson, Walter Pidgeon, Felix Bressart, Marsha Hunt. D: Mervyn Le Roy. DRA 114m. V

Blow Out 1981 ★★★★ A movie sound effects man (Travolta) inadvertently records a car accident, and after playing back the tape discovers the possibility of a murder and a political cover-up. An engrossing web of suspense and intrigue, with well-developed characters. Based loosely on Michelangelo Antonioni's *Blowup*. C: John Travolta, Nancy Allen, John Lithgow, Dennis Franz. D: Brian De Palma. CRI [R] 108m. V

Blowing Wild 1953 ★★★½ Oily romantic triangle, between a crude tycoon (Quinn), his scheming wife (Stanwyck), and his best friend (Cooper), who rekindles his romance with the wife. Melodramatic star vehicle, watchable mainly for Stanwyck's performance. C: Gary Cooper, Barbara Stanwyck, Ruth Roman, Anthony Quinn. D: Hugo Fregonese. DRA 92m. V

Blown Away 1994 ★★★★ Taut suspense film about a duel between Boston bomb squad cops, led by Bridges, and an imaginative psycho (Jones). Jones is a little over the top, but the whole thing is great fun. C: Jeff Bridges, Tommy Lee Jones, Lloyd Bridges, Forest Whitaker. D: Stephen Hopkins. ACT [R] 120m.

Blowup 1966 British ★★★★ A London fashion photographer's aimless, decadent lifestyle is disturbed when he suspects images on a negative he has shot may be evidence of murder. Antonioni's alienated, existential drama isn't as trendy as it once was (back when the sex and nudity were shocking), but it can still trigger a healthy debate: What did happen? Based on a short story by Julio Cortazar. Awarded Best Film at Cannes '67. C: Vanessa Redgrave, David Hemmings, Sarah Miles. D: Michelangelo Antonioni. DRA 102m. V

Blue 1968 ★★½ A hard-hearted young Mexican-raised American has no use for anybody until circumstances force him to trust someone, or else. Standard Western. C: Terence Stamp, Joanna Pettet, Karl Malden, Ricardo Montalban, Joe De Santis, Sally Kirkland. D: Silvio Narizzano. WST 113m. V

Blue 1993 French ★★★★ When her husband and daughter are killed in a car crash, Binoche tries to use this bleak opportunity to free herself from her past, beginning a new life in Paris and struggling against memories and revelations that won't go away. Intense psychological probing coupled with dark, sensuous cinematography make this an intriguing item. Binoche's work is stellar. First in the director's "Three Color" trilogy; followed by *White* and *Red*. (a.k.a. *Bleu*) C: Juliette Binoche, Benoit Regnant, Florence Pernel, Charlotte Very, Helene Vincent. D: Krzysztof Kieslowski. DRA [R] 98m. V

Blue Angel, The 1930 German ★★★★★ Aging, punctilious bourgeois (Jannings) comes under the spell of a cheap cabaret singer (Dietrich) and allows himself to be increasingly and utterly degraded by his attraction to her. A harrowing drama, tawdry and stylized. This is the role that rocketed Dietrich to Hollywood and the picture in which she sings "Falling in Love Again." Her first collaboration with Sternberg is a must-see, though it's no pleasure cruise. Remade in 1959. C: Marlene Dietrich, Emil Jannings. D: Josef von Sternberg. DRA 103m. V

Blue Angel, The 1959 ★ An amoral chanteuse (Britt) seduces and ruins a professor (Jurgens). An unnecessary, atrocious remake of the Dietrich classic. C: May Britt, Curt Jurgens, Theodore Bikel. D: Edward Dmytryk. DRA 107m.

Blue Bird, The 1940 ★★★ Children's fantasy follows a young girl (Temple) in search of the Blue Bird of Happiness. Somewhat stiff and overproduced adaptation of a popular play. C: Shirley Temple, Spring Byington, Nigel Bruce, Gale Sondergaard. D: Walter Lang. FAM/MUS 83m. V

Blue Bird, The 1976 Russian ★★ Much ballyhooed U.S.-Soviet co-production of a musical fantasy about children's search for the elusive Blue Bird of Happiness. Big-name stars look uncomfortable in dumb costumes. A detente disappointment. C: Todd Lookinland, Patsy Kensit, Elizabeth Taylor, Jane Fonda, Ava Gardner, Cicely Tyson, George Cole, Will Geer, Robert Morley. D: George Cukor. FAM/MUS [G] 99m.

Blue Blood 1951 ★★½ An aged racehorse trainer wants to revive his flagging career. Uninspired tale doesn't make it through the stretch. C: Bill Williams, Jane Nigh. D: Lew Landers. DRA 72m.

Blue Chips 1994 ★★★★ A college basketball coach (Nolte) uses questionable recruiting tactics to field a winning team. Typical sports story is given gung-ho treatment by director Friedkin. Nolte is excellent emulating the over-the-top Bobby Knight coaching style. Very entertaining; the superstar cameos make it an extra treat. C: Nick Nolte, Mary McDonnel, J.T. Walsh, Ed O'Neill, Alfre Woodard, Shaquille O'Neal, Bob Cousy. D: William Friedkin. DRA [PG-13] 108m. V

Blue City 1986 ★ Brat-packer Nelson is obnoxious and unsympathetic as a young hood who heads home to Blue City, Florida to avenge the mysterious death of his father. Revenge tale tries for a stylish look. Based on a Ross MacDonald thriller. C: Judd Nelson, Ally Sheedy, David Caruso, Paul Winfield, Anita Morris. D: Michelle Manning. CRI [R] 83m. V

Blue Collar 1978 ★★★★ Three frustrated workers on a Detroit auto assembly line cross over into crime. Rough-and-ready film about men on the edge, cleanly and unsentimentally acted by Pryor, Keitel, and Kotto. Schrader's directorial debut. C: Richard Pryor, Harvey Keitel, Yaphet Kotto, Ed Begley, Jr. D: Paul Schrader. CRI [R] 114m. V

Blue Dahlia, The 1946 ★★★★ A war veteran who returns to an unfaithful wife is suspected of murder when she winds up dead. Screenplay by hard-boiled novelist Raymond Chandler gives this satisfying, stylish thriller a really mean bite. C: Alan Ladd, Veronica Lake, William Bendix, Howard da Silva. D: George Marshall. CRI 99m.

Blue de Ville 1986 ★ A feisty girl and her shy pal strike out on the road. Thin, disagreeable pilot for a television series aimed at the youth market. C: Jennifer Runyon, Kimberley Pistone, Mark Thomas Miller. D: Jim Johnston. DRA 95m. TVM V

Blue Denim 1959 ★★ Generation gap drama about a teenage couple (Lynley and de Wilde) who must come to terms with the young woman's pregnancy and their parents' interference. Competent performances can't save the dated attitudes of this film. C: Carol Lynley, Brandon de Wilde, Macdonald Carey, Marsha Hunt. D: Philip Dunne. DRA 89m.

Blue Fin 1979 Australian ★★★ An at-odds father and son set sail on a sea hunt for an evasive tuna catch. Tepid Australian family fare. C: Hardy Kruger, Greg Rowe, Elspeth Ballantyne. D: Carl Schultz. FAM/ACT [PG] 93m.

Blue Fyre Lady 1983 ★★★ A vigorous young woman leaves her family and takes a job at a stable, where she's put in charge of a promising race horse called Blue Fyre Lady. Some nice moments. C: Cathryn Harrison, Mark Holden, Peter Cummins. D: Ross Dimsey. DRA 96m. v

Blue Gardenia 1953 ★★★ An innocent woman (Baxter) is accused of murder. She must clear her name with the help of an ace reporter (Conte) looking for a scoop. Beyond the then-innovative casting of a female lead, not exactly a groundbreaking mystery. C: Anne Baxter, Richard Conte, Ann Sothern, Raymond Burr, Nat King Cole. D: Fritz Lang. CRI 90m.

Blue Grass of Kentucky 1950 ★★★ Love between the offspring of two rival horse-breeding families settles old feuds. Standard generational dramatics. C: Bill Williams, Jane Nigh. D: William Beaudine. DRA 71m.

Blue Hawaii 1961 ★★★½ Elvis is a tour guide to giggling schoolgirls in hopping Honolulu. The plot's nonsensical, but pretty scenery, Lansbury, and 15 decent songs make it palatable, even to non-Presley fans. C: Elvis Presley, Joan Blackman, Angela Lansbury. D: Norman Taurog. MUS 101m. v

Blue Hotel, The 1977 ★★★ In a small hotel far out on the Nebraska frontier, a young Swedish immigrant is the inadvertent cause of senseless violence. Effective adaptation of the Stephen Crane story. Hosted by Henry Fonda. C: David Warner, James Keach, John Bottoms, Rex Everhart. D: Jan Kadar. DRA 55m. v

Blue Hour, The 1991 German ★★★½ When her boyfriend takes off, a sweet young woman becomes romantically involved with a male prostitute. Interesting, offbeat character study. C: Andreas Herder, Dina Leipzig. D: Marcel Gisler. DRA 87m. v

Blue Ice 1993 ★★★★ A former spy (Caine) runs a hopping London jazz club until he meets an ambassador's wife, who forces him back into his deadly profession. A well-done, '60s-style thriller. Look for the Rolling Stone's drummer Charlie Watts in the house band. C: Michael Caine, Sean Young, Ian Holm, Bobby Short. D: Russell Mulcahy. CRI [R] 96m. v

Blue Iguana, The 1988 ★★ Two wayward IRS agents dispatch a bounty hunter to heist laundered money from a South American bank. Lame "kitchen sink" spoof. C: Dylan McDermott, Jessica Harper, James Russo, Tovah Feldshuh, Dean Stockwell. D: John Lafia. COM [R] 88m. v

Blue Knight, The 1973 ★★★★½ With four days left to retirement, an L.A. cop (Holden) becomes obsessed with hunting down the murderer of a prostitute. Adapted from the popular Joseph Wambaugh novel, this film is charged by realism and psychological undertones. Holden copped an Emmy. C: William Holden, Lee Remick, Joe Santos, Sam Elliott. D: Robert Butler. CRI 103m. TVM

Blue Lagoon, The 1949 British ★★★½ The first adaptation of H. deVere Stacpoole's novel. Marooned for several years on a tropical island, two youngsters (Simmons and Houston) fend off smugglers, become lovers, and have a child. Tender idyll is limpid but pretty, with vivid Fijian locales. Remade in 1980. C: Jean Simmons, Donald Houston, Cyril Cusack. D: Frank Launder. DRA 101m.

Blue Lagoon 1980 ★★ Shipwrecked as children, Shields and Atkins unravel the mysteries of a desert island, the sea, and their bodies as they grow into their teens. Inane to be sure, but a crowd-pleaser. C: Brooke Shields, Christopher Atkins, Leo McKern. D: Randal Kleiser. DRA [R] 104m. v

Blue Lamp, The 1950 British ★★★★ Scotland Yard detectives search for a cop killer in this well-respected British police film. Gripping suspense, with fantastic chase sequences and well-sketched good and bad guys. Led to long-running British TV series *Dixon of Dock Green.* C: Jack Warner, Jimmy Hanley, Dirk Bogarde. D: Basil Dearden. CRI 84m.

Blue Light, The 1932 German ★★★ Riefenstahl starred and directed in this fable of an Alpine mountain woman who engages in a doomed affair with Weimann. Routine tale with sumptuous background; however, the film so impressed Hitler that he asked her to make Nazi propaganda films, including her notorious *Triumph of the Will.* C: Leni Riefenstahl, Mathias Weimann, Beni Fuhrer. D: Leni Riefenstahl. DRA 77m.

Blue Manhattan 1970 *See* **Hi, Mom!**

Blue Max, The 1966 ★★★½ Ruthless WWI German ace (Peppard) competes for the "Blue Max" flying award and with his commander (Mason) for his wife's (Andress) affections. Great flying and music soar above an inane storyline. C: George Peppard, James Mason, Ursula Andress, Jeremy Kemp. D: John Guillermin. DRA 155m. v

Blue Monkey 1987 ★★★ A monstrous giant insect menaces a hospital. Old-fashioned shocker manages to close well. Neither this, nor the former title *Green Monkey* have any relevance. C: Steve Railsback, Gwynyth Walsh, Susan Anspach, Joe Flaherty. D: William Fruet. HOR [R] 97m. v

Blue Movies 1987 ★ Juvenile farce about two losers who decide to become producers of a porn film; in the process they tangle with a famous adult star and the Mafia. C: Larry Linville, Steve Levitt, Lucinda Crosby, Darien Mathias. D: Ed Fitzgerald. COM [R] 92m. v

Blue Murder at St. Trinian's 1958 British ★★★½ A jewel thief eludes capture by hiding out at a private school inhabited by wacky female pupils— much to his regret. Skillful, zany comedy with a pleasant cast; part of the popular *St. Trinian's* series. C: Alastair Sim, Joyce Grenfell, Terry-Thomas, George Cole. D: Frank Launder. COM 86m. v

Blue Sierra 1946 *See* **Courage of Lassie**

Blue Skies Again 1983 ★★★ A plucky female attempts to break into major league baseball. Earnest and topical. C: Harry Hamlin, Robyn Barto, Mimi Rogers, Andy Garcia. D: Richard Michaels. DRA [PG] 91m. v

Blue Skies 1946 ★★★★ Romantic rivalry plot provides a chance for Crosby and Astaire to perform a bunch of grand Irving Berlin songs, including "Heat Wave" and "Puttin on the Ritz." A sunny delight. C: Bing Crosby, Fred Astaire, Joan Caulfield, Billy de Wolfe, Olga San Juan. D: Stuart Heisler. MUS 104m. v

Blue Sky 1994 ★★★★ Jones and Lange are a mismatched married couple; He's a repressed army scientist, and she's a nymphomaniac. Together, their explosive relationship makes for intense, satisfying viewing, against and early 1960s backdrop. Richardson's last film, made in 1991. Lange won an Oscar (in 1994) as Best Actress for her tremendous performance. C: Jessica Lange, Tommy Lee Jones, Amy Locane, Chris O'Donnell. D: Tony Richardson. DRA [PG-13] 101m. v

Blue Steel 1990 ★★½ A rookie cop (Curtis) finds out that the upscale beau of her dreams (Silver) is really the serial killer terrorizing New York. Stylish but shallow. C: Jamie Lee Curtis, Ron Silver, Clancy Brown, Louise Fletcher. D: Kathryn Bigelow. ACT [R] 103m. v

Blue Sunshine 1977 ★★★ Bad acid (LSD, if you need ask) is killing trippers ten years after the fact. The police zero in on the man they think is responsible. Occasionally compelling thriller is nowhere near as dumb as it sounds. C: Zalman King, Deborah Winters. D: Jeff Lieberman. DRA [R] 94m. v

Blue Thunder 1983 ★★★ Lively techno-thriller about an L.A. police pilot (Scheider) who brings down the empire of a crime lord (McDowell) with a high-tech helicopter. Terrific aerial photography. Later the basis for a TV series. C: Roy Scheider, Malcolm McDowell, Candy Clark, Daniel Stern, Warren Oates. D: John Badham. ACT [R] 110m. v

Blue Veil, The 1951 ★★★★ When a WWI widow (Wyman) loses her only child, she becomes a children's caretaker in order to devote her entire life to the young. She takes a succession of posts, setting up an episodic film which manages to be warm and engaging, largely due to the fine cast. C: Jane Wyman, Charles Laughton, Joan Blondell, Richard Carlson, Agnes Moorehead, Audrey Totter, Cyril Cusack, Natalie Wood, Vivian Vance. D: Curtis Bernhardt. DRA 113m.

Blue Velvet 1986 ★★★★ An innocent young man (MacLachlan) helps a nightclub singer (Rossellini), and is caught up in a bizarre subculture under the floorboards of a conservative logging town. Lynch often tries too hard with his mix of kitsch and depravity, but Hopper's kinky sadist is a tour de force. C: Kyle MacLachlan, Isabella Rossellini, Dennis Hopper, Laura Dern, Hope Lange, Dean Stockwell. D: David Lynch. CRI [R] 120m. v

Blue Water, White Death 1971 ★★★ Documentary on that most notable of all feared sea creatures: the great white shark. Good underwater footage. D: Peter Gimbel, James Lipscomb. DOC [G] 99m.

Blue, White and Perfect 1941 ★★★½ Private shamus Michael Shayne tangles with secret espionage saboteurs smuggling industrial diamonds. Gripping formula film set in early WWII. C: Lloyd Nolan, Mary Hughes, Helene Reynolds. D: Herbert Leeds. ACT 73m.

Blue Yonder, The 1986 ★★★½ A youth travels fifty years back in time, where he and his air ace grandfather are tempted to alter history. Nostalgic Disney fare. (a.k.a. *Time Flyer*) C: Peter Coyote, Art Carney. D: Mark Rosman. FAM/ACT 90m. v

Bluebeard 1944 ★★★★ A deranged Parisian painter kills models after painting their likenesses, while developing an affection for a clever young woman. Atmospheric, effective thriller boosted by a suitably creepy performance by Carradine. C: John Carradine, Jean Parker, Nils Asther, Iris Adrian. D: Edgar G. Ulmer. HOR 73m. v

Bluebeard 1962 French ★★★★ Chabrol's antihero is a perfect bourgeois gentleman, with a wife and mistress who, nevertheless, is driven to destroy beauty in the shape of women. Bluebeard's crimes are kept at a distance, making his motives rather obscure. Minor Chabrol. (a.k.a. *Landru*) C: Charles Denner, Michele Morgan, Danielle Darrieux, Hildegarde Neff, Stephane Audran. D: Claude Chabrol. DRA 108m. v

Bluebeard 1972 ★★ Burton is the rogue who just can't get enough. Campy attempt to cash in on the leading ladies' drawing power. C: Richard Burton, Raquel Welch, Virna Lisi, Joey Heatherton, Nathalie Delon. D: Edward Dmytryk. DRA [R] 128m. v

Bluebeard's Eighth Wife 1938 ★★★ Oft-married millionaire playboy (Cooper) meets his match in a gold digger (Colbert). Comedy is less than the sum of the considerable talents involved. C: Claudette Colbert, Gary Cooper, David Niven, Edward Everett Horton. D: Ernst Lubitsch. COM 80m.

Blueberry Hill 1988 ★★★ After her father dies, a young woman learns about him from a local blues singer. Sensitive and thoughtful, but best for jazzy soundtrack. C: Jennifer Rubin, Carrie Snodgress, Matt Lattanzi, Margaret Avery. D: Strathford Hamilton. DRA [R] 93m. v

Bluegrass 1988 ★★½ A feisty horse-breeder (Ladd) is determined against tough odds to win the Kentucky Derby. Watchable, if a bit sappy. C: Cheryl Ladd, Brian Kerwin, Anthony Andrews, Mickey Rooney, Wayne Rogers, Diane Ladd. D: Simon Wincer. DRA 200m. TVM

Blueprint for Murder 1953 ★★★½ A man (Cotton) suspects his sister-in-law (Peters) may be responsible for the poisonings of two of his relatives. Serviceable "perfect crime" whodunit with efficient plot twists and a suspenseful ending. C: Joseph Cotten, Jean Peters, Gary Merrill, Mae Marsh. D: Andrew Stone. CRI 76m.

Blueprint for Robbery, A 1961 ★★★ A veteran thief accomplishes a robbery caper, but his associates ill-advisedly want to split the loot right away. Tame heist tale, effective in spots. C: J. O'Malley, Robert Wilke. D: Jerry Hopper. CRI 87m.

Blues Brothers, The 1980 ★★★★ Jake and Elwood Blues (Belushi and Aykroyd) embark on a quest to reform their band and raise enough money to save their childhood orphanage. Wild, fun mix of crass humor, destruction, and soulful music numbers by James Brown, Aretha Franklin, and Cab Calloway. C: John Belushi, Dan Aykroyd, Cab Calloway, John Candy, Carrie Fisher, Ray Charles, Aretha Franklin, James Brown. D: John Landis. COM 133m. V

Blues Busters 1950 ★★★½ Top Bowery Boys entry features cheerful delinquent Jones (Hall) transformed into a swinging crooner. Above-average fare for the popular, long-running series. C: Leo Gorcey, Huntz Hall, Gabriel Dell. D: William Beaudine. COM 68m. V

Blues for Lovers *See* **Ballad in Blue**

Blues in the Night 1941 ★★★★ Downbeat, effective study of jazz musicians and their transient life. Features two stunning songs by Johnny Mercer and Harold Arlen: the title number and "This Time the Dream's On Me." Watch for director Elia Kazan as clarinetist. C: Priscilla Lane, Richard Whorf, Betty Field, Lloyd Nolan, Jack Carson, Elia Kazan. D: Anatole Litvak. MUS 88m.

Blume In Love 1973 ★★★★ A philandering divorce lawyer realizes the error of his ways when his wife splits and he attempts to regain her love. Angst comedy of relationships, deftly handled with bite and intelligence. C: George Segal, Susan Anspach, Kris Kristofferson, Marsha Mason, Shelley Winters, Paul Mazursky. D: Paul Mazursky. COM [R] 115m. V

BMX Bandits 1983 ★★★ Bike-riding youngsters use their skills to foil some silly crooks. Good stuff for small fry, with plenty of great BMX bicycle stunts. Look for featured role by future star Nicole Kidman in this Australian kiddy caper. C: Nicole Kidman, David Argue, John Ley. D: Brian Trenchard-Smith. FAM/ACT 92m. V

Boarding School 1983 German ★ Silly comedy about students at a private school who pose as brothel employees, hoping to win the hearts of the boys at the school next door. Grade-Z European sex farce. C: Nastassja Kinski, Gerry Sundquist. D: Andre Farwagi. COM [R] 100m. V

Boardwalk 1979 ★★★½ The 50th anniversary celebration of an aged couple on Coney Island is marred by street gang violence. Occasionally moving study of how urban unease affects the elderly, with an unexpected climax. C: Ruth Gordon, Lee Strasberg, Janet Leigh. D: Stephen Verona. DRA 98m.

Boat is Full, The 1961 German ★★★½ Well-intentioned WWII story involves Jewish refugees from Nazi Germany who face new prejudices when they arrive in Switzerland. Not as thought provoking as it could be, but interesting nonetheless. C: Tina Engel, Curt Bois, Renate Steiger. D: Markus Imhoof. DRA 104m. V

Boat People 1983 Hong Kong ★★★★ A Japanese photojournalist in postwar Vietnam is devastated by the wretched plight of the boat people. Agonizing study of glaring realities compared to officialdom's hype. C: Lam Chicheung, Cora Miao. D: Ann Hui. DRA [R] 106m. V

Boatniks, The 1970 ★★★½ A Coast Guardsman (Morse) can't cope with the demands of his new job controlling traffic in Newport Harbor. All's well that ends well though when, despite his blundering, he captures a passel of jewel thieves. Family fun that doesn't make great demands on the intellect. C: Robert Morse, Stefanie Powers, Phil Silvers. D: Norman Tokar. FAM/ACT [G] 99m. V

Bob & Carol & Ted & Alice 1969 ★★★★ The new sexual freedom of the '60s faces off against America's traditional mores as two couples decide to take their friendship a step further and into the bedroom. Mazursky, in his directorial debut, captures the mood and pop culture of the time. C: Natalie Wood, Robert Culp, Elliott Gould, Dyan Cannon. D: Paul Mazursky. COM [R] 104m. V

Bob Le Flambeur 1955 French ★★★★½ Gangster drama is an unheralded classic. Duchesne plays an aging thief who plans one last heist—hitting the Deauville casino. Ingenious plotting weaves Duchesne's personal life with his criminal masterminding, building to a surprise ending. Slyly witty thriller. C: Roger Duchesne, Isbel Corey. D: Jean-Pierre Melville. CRI 97m. V

Bob Mathias Story, The 1954 ★★★½ Biography of the two-time Olympic decathlon champion. Inoffensive, low-budget account with the noted athlete playing himself. C: Bob Mathias, Ward Bond, Melba Mathias. D: Francis Dlyon. DRA 80m.

Bob Roberts 1992 ★★★★ A folksinger (Robbins) running for Senate captivates America and manipulates the media via song and crowd-pleasing right-wing rhetoric. Robbins, making his debut as writer/director, is right on target with this sly political satire. C: Tim Robbins, Giancarlo Esposito, Ray Wise. D: Tim Robbins. COM 102m. V

Bobbie Jo and the Outlaw 1976 ★★½ A drive-in waitress takes off with a crook who launches a crime wave. Unduly violent, derivative cheapie. C: Marjoe Gortner, Lynda Carter, Jesse Vint. D: Mark L. Lester. ACT [R] 89m. V

Bobbikins 1960 British ★★★ A baby talks like a grown-up and provides stock market tips, to the astonishment of his parents. Mildly amusing fantasy with an original contrivance. C: Max Bygraves, Shirley Jones, Steven Stocker, Billie Whitelaw. D: Robert Day. COM 89m.

Bobby Deerfield 1977 ★★ A world-class auto racer (Pacino) falls in love with a young woman, then learns that she's fatally ill. Even Pacino can't save this soap opera. C: Al Pacino, Marthe Keller, Anny Duperey. D: Sydney Pollack. DRA [PG] 123m. V

Bobby Ware Is Missing 1955 ★★★ A law officer and the parents of a vanished teenager go in search of his kidnappers. Routine melodrama. C: Neville Brand, Arthur Franz, Jean Willes. D: Thomas Carr. CRI 67m.

Bobo, The 1967 British ★★★ Down on his luck, Sellers is so desperate to find work as a singing matador he accepts a challenge to seduce Barcelona's famed courtesan in exchange for a gig. Slow-paced comedy, with Sellers giving a real oddball performance. C: Peter Sellers, Britt Ekland, Rossano Brazzi. D: Robert Parrish. COM 103m. V

Boccaccio '70 1962 Italian ★★★★ Anthology of three tales. Fellini's satire on virtue "The Temptation of Dr. Antonio" features Ekberg as a billboard figure who becomes mortal; Visconti's "The Job" stars Schneider as a wife rebelling against her oppressive husband; De Sica's "The Raffle" involves a milquetoast who wins love in a lottery. The first two shine; the final one is just all right. C: Anita Ekberg, Sophia Loren, Romy Schneider. D: Vittorio De Sica, Luchino Visconti, Federico Fellini. COM 165m.

Bodies, Rest & Motion 1993 ★★★½ A group of young people contemplate their aimless lives and chances for connections in a dreary Arizona town. Lively performances from Cates and Fonda keep the goings-on from getting too maudlin. Stoltz co-produced. C: Phoebe Cates, Bridget Fonda, Tim Roth, Eric Stoltz. D: Michael Steinberg. DRA [R] 94m. V

Bodily Harm 1991 ★★ Surgeon and patient cook up dangerous negligence scam that goes awry. C: Joe Penny, Lisa Hartman, Kathleen Quinlan. D: Tom Wright. HOR 100m. V

Body and Soul 1926 ★★★★ A minor classic, featuring the outstanding Paul Robeson in dual roles: as a preacher with evil in his heart and as his pious brother. Fascinating silent curio. C: Paul Robeson. D: Oscar Micheaux. DRA 60m. V

Body and Soul 1947 ★★★★★ A Jewish boxer (Garfield) fights his way to the top, only to find he must sell himself to a gambler to get a chance at the title. Powerful drama, with Garfield giving a knockout performance and James Wong Howe's Oscar-winning camerawork providing striking boxing scenes. An Oscar also went to Francis Lyon and Robert Parrish for Editing. C: John Garfield, Lilli Palmer, Hazel Brooks, Anne Revere, William Conrad. D: Robert Rossen. DRA 104m. V

Body and Soul 1981 ★ An insult to the 1947 film of which this is a remake. Classic boxing story is transferred to an African-American milieu, with large doses of sex and hyperbolic violence. Muhammed Ali is definitely the main attraction. C: Muhammed Ali, Leon Isaac Kennedy, Jayne Kennedy, Peter Lawford. D: George Bowers. DRA [R] 109m. V

Body Beat 1988 ★★★ When a proper dance academy sinks under its debt, its owners turn to a jazz instructor to shake things up. Fun music and dance. C: Tony Fields, Galyn Gorg, Eliska Krupa, Steve La Chance, Paula Nichols. D: Ted Mather. COM [PG] 90m. V

Body Beneath, The 1983 ★★ A jaded preacher organizes an army of ghouls who prey on the life blood of God-fearing people. More garish than ghoulish. C: Gavin Reed, Jackie Skarvellis, Susan Heard. D: Andy Milligan. HOR 85m. V

Body Chemistry 1990 ★ Married sex researcher (Singer) has a fling with his coworker (Pescia), then tries to break it off but can't shake her threats. Terrible rip-off of *Fatal Attraction* is neither original nor arousing. C: Marc Singer, Lisa Pescia, Mary Crosby. D: Kristine Peterson. CRI [R] 84m. V

Body Chemistry 2 (Voice of a Stranger) 1991 ★★ Pescia's sex psychologist returns to host a talk show, and her alluring advice leads an ex-policeman into a game of deadly sex with her. This unremarkable study in eroticism is barely better than its predecessor. C: Lisa Pescia, Gregory Harrison, Morton Downey Jr. D: Adam Simon. CRI [R] 84m. V

Body Disappears, The 1941 ★★½ A professor's chemical experiment can turn humans invisible. Forgettable silliness tries hard for laughs. C: Jeffrey Lynn, Jane Wyman, Edward Everett Horton. D: Ross Lederman. COM 72m.

Body Double 1984 ★★★½ A young man (Wasson) watches a woman (Griffith) disrobing in a Hollywood hillside home, which leads to his witnessing a murder and seeking clues within the porno industry. De Palma combines Hitchcock fixations and violent sexual obsessions with a complex plot that's simultaneously repulsive and engrossing. C: Craig Wasson, Gregg Henry, Melanie Griffith, Deborah Shelton. D: Brian De Palma. CRI [R] 114m. V

Body Heat 1981 ★★★★ Femme fatale (Turner) lures lawyer (Hurt) into murdering her rich husband (Crenna). Modern film noir borrows from earlier films, but concocts a surprise ending all its own. Highlight: torrid sex scenes between Hurt and Turner that match the steamy Florida locale. C: William Hurt, Kathleen Turner, Richard Crenna, Ted Danson, Mickey Rourke. D: Lawrence Kasdan. CRI [R] 113m. V

Body Language 1992 ★★★ A deranged secretary (Locklear) plots her boss's murder between coffee breaks. Fans of *Melrose Place* will enjoy Heather's over-the-top performance in this lurid thriller. C: Heather Locklear, Linda Purl, Edward Albert. D: Arthur Allan Seidelman. CRI [R] 100m. TVM V

Body Melt 1994 Australian ★★★★ Gross-out horror film from Down Under is energetic and colorful, with some memorably quirky characters; all it needed was a coherent script. Story centers on a health farm, where vitamin treatments have disgusting side effects. C: Gerard Kennedy, Andrew Daddo, Ian Smith, Vince Gil, Regina Gaigalas. D: Philip Brophy. HOR 82m.

Body of Evidence 1988 ★★★★ A police pathologist's wife suspects he may be a serial murderer. Solid suspense; Campanella co-wrote the script, too. C: Margot Kidder, Barry Bostwick, Tony Lo Bianco. D: Roy Campanella II. CRI 100m. TVM

Body of Evidence 1993 ★ Courtroom murder trial of Madonna is an excuse for witless s&m sex scenes involving broken glass, hot wax, and other accoutrements. C: Madonna, Willem Dafoe, Joe Mantegna, Anne Archer, Frank Langella. D: Uli Edel. CRI [R] 139m. V

Body of Influence 1992 ★★ A Beverly Hills psychiatrist becomes dangerously involved with an unbalanced female client. Blah low-budget sexual thriller. C: Nick Cassavetes, Shannon Whirry, Sandahl Bergman, Don Swayze. D: Gregory Hippolyte. CRI [R] 96m. V

Body Parts 1991 ★★ Fahey gets a new arm after losing one in a car accident, only to find it has a violent personality all its own. Slick production and earnest acting can't hide the silliness and ultimate predictability of this story. C: Jeff Fahey, Lindsay Duncan, Kim Delaney, Brad Dourif. D: Eric Red. HOR [R] 88m. V

Body Rock 1984 ★★½ A ghetto cad drops his girl and his friends for success as an emcee at a trendy break-dance nightclub. Low-grade music-video thrills, badly in need of ear plugs. And Lamas can't dance! C: Lorenzo Lamas, Vicki Frederick. D: Marcelo Epstein. DRA [PG-13] 93m. V

Body Slam 1987 ★★½ A down-and-out promoter mistakenly originates a new twist on professional wrestling. Laid-back, predictable sports comedy. C: Dirk Benedict, Tanya Roberts, Roddy Piper, Capt. Lou Albano, Charles Nelson Reilly. D: Hal Needham. COM [PG] 90m. V

Body Snatcher, The 1945 ★★★★½ A doctor engages the services of unscrupulous Karloff to steal bodies from a cemetery for medical school studies. Karloff's exceptionally sinister performance places this among the horror classics. Based on a short story by Robert Louis Stevenson. C: Boris Karloff, Bela Lugosi, Henry Daniell, Edith Atwater. D: Robert Wise. HOR 77m. V

Body Snatchers 1993 ★★★½ Third version of story updates it to a U.S. military base in the '90s, with aliens infiltrating Earth by duplicating people. Stylish and nasty paranoia from Ferrara, but still not up to the 1956 original (titled *Invasion of the Body Snatchers*). C: Gabrielle Anwar, Meg Tilly, Forest Whitaker, Lee Ermey, Terry Kinney, Billy Wirth. D: Abel Ferrara. SFI 87m. V

Bodyguard 1948 ★★½ A man wrongfully charged with a killing sets out to clear his name. Standard crime melodrama. C: Lawrence Tierney, Priscilla Lane, Philip Reed. D: Richard Fleischer. CRI 62m.

Bodyguard, The 1992 ★★½ Houston's film debut, as she plays a megastar menaced by death threats; she hires a bodyguard (Costner) to protect her and they fall in love. Limp script, without suspense, and confusing plot didn't seem to bother Houston's hordes of fans, who ate it up. Good songs. C: Kevin Costner, Whitney Houston, Gary Kemp, Bill Cobbs, Ralph Waite. D: Mick Jackson. DRA [R] 130m. V

Bodyhold 1949 ★★½ A wrestler and his female companion try to rid his sport of racketeering. Formula B-movie fare. C: Willard Parker, Lola Albright, Hillary Brooke. D: Seymour Friedman. CRI 63m.

Boeing Boeing 1965 ★★★ A womanizing journalist (Curtis) leads three different flight attendants to believe they're engaged to him, which keeps his Parisian apartment quite lively. Chaos ensues when their flight schedules start to change. Silly comedy, more hectic than funny. C: Jerry Lewis, Tony Curtis, Dany Saval, Christiane Schmidtmer, Thelma Ritter. D: John Rich. COM 102m. V

Bofors Gun, The 1968 ★★★★½ A hard-drinking Irishman (Williamson) resorts to extreme measures to destroy a young British corporal. Scalding look at the effects of the conflict in Ireland, and a plum role for Williamson. Tough, spiky script, brilliantly acted all around by a first-rate cast. C: Nicol Williamson, Ian Holm, David Warner. D: Jack Gold. DRA 106m.

Bog 1984 ★ Murky thriller evokes more than its share of unintentional laughs as a thawed Arctic swamp monster terrorizes a group of tourists foolish enough to travel through his marsh lands. Production's shoestring budget really shows. C: Gloria De Haven, Aldo Ray, Marshall Thompson. D: Don Keeslar. HOR 90m. V

Boggy Creek II 1989 ★★ Picturesque but low-energy sequel to the semidocumentary

Legend of Boggy Creek. Here, Pierce leads an expedition into the bayou to find the lurking ape-man, but the action doesn't perk up until the final reels. C: Cindy Butler, Charles B. Pierce. D: Charles B. Pierce. HOR [PG] 93m. v

Bogie 1980 ★★★ Biography of distinguished, Oscar-winning film actor Humphrey Bogart, who died of throat cancer in 1957. This is a somewhat superficial tribute to the versatile star who appeared in numerous and memorable screen classics. C: Kevin J. O'Connor, Kathryn Harrold, Ann Wedgeworth. D: Vincent Sherman. DRA 100m. TVM v

Bohemian Girl, The 1936 ★★★ Comic operetta starring Laurel and Hardy as bumbling Gypsies, raising a foundling girl who's really a princess. Cheerful Stan and Ollie fun. C: Stan Laurel, Oliver Hardy, Thelma Todd. D: James W. Horne, Charles Rogers. COM 90m. v

Boiling Point 1993 ★★★ No-nonsense U.S. Treasury agent (Snipes) tracks down a killer con artist who gunned down his friend on the force. Solid performances make the weak plot easy to overlook. C: Wesley Snipes, Dennis Hopper, Lolita Davidovich, Tony Lo Bianco, Valerie Perrine. D: James B. Harris. ACT [R] 93m. v

Bold and the Brave, The 1956 ★★½ Dime-a-dozen war film concerning three G.I.s on the Italian front. Outside of an energetic Rooney performance, there's little to recommend. C: Wendell Corey, Mickey Rooney, Don Taylor. D: Lewis Foster. ACT 87m.

Bold Caballero, The 1936 ★★★ After being framed for murder, Zorro (Livingston) clears his name and fights a corrupt official in 19th-century southern California. Average action film is the first sound feature for the dashing avenger. C: Robert Livingston, Heather Angel, Sig Rumann. D: Wells Root. ACT 69m. v

Bolero: An Adventure in Ecstasy 1984 *See* **Bolero**

Bolero 1934 ★★★ Egotistical owner of a swank Parisian nightclub (Raft) falls in love with his gold-digging dancing partner (Lombard). Separated during WWI, they're reunited afterward and dance the Bolero one last time together. Mildly fun and better than their reteaming in *Rumba*. C: George Raft, Carole Lombard, Sally Rand, William Frawley, Ray Milland. D: Wesley Ruggles. DRA 83m.

Bolero 1982 French ★★½ Confusing and often unintentionally campy look at a family of European musicians from the '20s through '70s, further hampered by lackluster plotting. C: James Caan, Geraldine Chaplin, Nicole Garcia. D: Claude Lelouch. DRA 173m. v

Bolero 1984 ★ Bo loses her virginity in Spain. More erotic ramblings from husband John, mastermind of their *Tarzan* collaboration. (a.k.a. *Bolero: An Adventure in Ecstasy*) C: Bo Derek, George Kennedy. D: John Derek. DRA [R] 106m. v

Bomb at 10:10 1966 Yugoslavian ★★½ A man breaks out of a German prison camp and aids resistance fighters in killing POW commanders. Forgettable prefab WWII patchwork. C: George Montgomery, Rada Popovic. D: Charles Damic. DRA 86m.

Bomb in the High Street 1964 British ★★★½ Thieves create a diversion from the scene of their heist by staging a bogus bomb scare. Straightforward British crime drama. C: Ronald Howard, Terry Palmer. D: Terence Bishop. CRI 60m.

Bomba the Jungle Boy Johnny Sheffield made his film debut playing Boy in the *Tarzan* films, so when Walter Mirisch wanted someone to play the hero of Roy Rockwood's kids books, he was a natural choice. Unfortunately, the 11 films that result are pretty formulaic, though leavened by the presence of Peggy Ann Garner as Bomba's friend. Kids will probably enjoy these jungle adventures, but adults may find them a bit tedious.

Bomba the Jungle Boy (1949)
Bomba on Panther Island (1949)
The Lost Volcano (1950)
The Hidden City (1950), a.k.a. Bomba and the Hidden City
Bomba and the Elephant Stampede (1951)
African Treasure (1952)
Bomba and the Jungle Girl (1952)
Safari Drums (1953)
The Golden Idol (1954)
Killer Leopard (1954)
Lord of the Jungle (1959)

Bomba and the African Treasure 1952 *See* **African Treasure**

Bomba and the Elephant Stampede 1951 ★★★½ The jungle boy (Sheffield) makes war against ivory poachers. Competent low-budget action, mainly for kids. C: Johnny Sheffield, Donna Martell, Edith Evanson. D: Ford Beebe. FAM/ACT 71m.

Bomba and the Hidden City 1950 *See* **Hidden City, The**

Bomba and the Jungle Girl 1952 ★★★ A teenager orphaned in the jungle seeks to gain knowledge of his parents' whereabouts. Routine juvenile adventure yarn; about par for the series. C: Johnny Sheffield, Karen Sharpe, Walter Sande. D: Ford Beebe. FAM/ACT 70m.

Bomba on Panther Island 1949 ★★★ Bomba the jungle boy has to slay a panther that primitive islanders worship as a deity. Average entry for the series. For the kiddies. C: Johnny Sheffield, Allene Roberts, Lita Baron. D: Ford Beebe. FAM/ACT 76m.

Bomba the Jungle Boy 1949 ★★★ First of the twelve-film series, starring Sheffield as a younger version of Tarzan (the character was taken from Roy Rockwood's comic strip). Here, he befriends photographers on safari in dangerous terrain and rescues a young woman (Garner). Fun for the kids. C: Johnny Sheffield, Peggy Ann Garner, Smoki Whitfield, Charles Irwin. D: Ford Beebe. FAM/ACT 70m.

Bombardier 1943 ★★★½ A Flying Fortress bombing crew trainee gets toughened up by missions over Japan. Standard WWII heroics; quickly paced action. C: Pat O'Brien, Randolph Scott, Anne Shirley, Eddie Albert, Robert Ryan. D: Richard Wallace. ACT 99m. V

Bombay Talkie 1970 Indian ★★★ Inside look at the Indian film industry is notable chiefly as an early collaboration for the team of Ivory, Merchant, and Prawer-Jhabvala. A western writer (Kendal) searches for romance in Bombay but ends up in a complicated love triangle. C: Shashi Kapoor, Jennifer Kendal, Zia Mohyeddin. D: James Ivory. DRA [PG] 110m. V

Bombers B-52 1957 ★★★ An Air Force sergeant takes umbrage when a playboy pilot woos his daughter. Superficial service melodrama with watchable aerial footage. C: Natalie Wood, Karl Malden, Marsha Hunt, Efrem Zimbalist, Jr., Dean Jagger. D: Gordon Douglas. DRA 106m.

Bombs Away 1986 ★★★ Everything's fine at the little Mom 'n Pop war surplus store—until the government sends them a working atomic bomb! Some explosive comedy, along with typical yuks from McCormick. C: Michael Huddleston, Pat McCormick. D: Bruce Wilson. COM 90m. V

Bombs Over Burma 1942 ★★½ A dedicated Chinese patriot works as a spy for her country during WWII. Forgettable spy flick. C: Anna May Wong, Noel Madison, Dan Seymour. D: Joseph Lewis. DRA 62m.

Bombshell 1933 ★★★★½ Harlow is the star looking for a new image, Tracy her conniving publicist who will stop at nothing to keep her name in the news. One of Harlow's best performances, in a hilarious satire of the mechanics of the '30s Hollywood studio system. C: Jean Harlow, Lee Tracy, Frank Morgan, Franchot Tone, Una Merkel, Pat O'Brien, C. Aubrey Smith. D: Victor Fleming. COM 95m. V

Bombsight Stolen *See* **Cottage to Let**

Bon Voyage Charlie Brown (and Don't Come Back!) 1980 ★★★★ Charming, animated adventure features Charlie Brown and the "Peanuts" gang as exchange students who find romance and intrigue in Paris. C: Voices of Daniel Anderson, Casey Carlson, Patricia Patts. D: Bill Melendez. FAM/COM [G] 76m. V

Bon Voyage! 1962 ★★½ An American family vacationing abroad gets into scrapes but somehow muddles through. Competently acted but simplistic Disney movie, with its full complement of laughs. C: Fred MacMurray, Jane Wyman, Michael Callan, Deborah Walley, Tommy Kirk. D: James Neilson. FAM/COM 131m. V

Bonanza: The Next Generation 1988 ★★½ Hoss and Little Joe Cartwright's offspring head out to the Ponderosa with their great uncle (Ireland). TV movie mediocrity on the hoof. C: John Ireland, Robert Fuller, Barbara Anderson, Michael Landon, Jr. D: William Claxton. WST 100m. TVM

Bond Street 1948 British ★★★ Anthology film tells four stories revolving around pieces of a bride's trousseau. Good cast with somewhat overdone material. C: Jean Kent, Roland Young, Kathleen Harrison, Derek Farr, Hazel Court. D: Gordon Parry. DRA 109m.

Bonfire of the Vanities, The 1990 ★ A hit-and-run accident in the south Bronx turns the life of a wealthy white businessman upside down. Embarrassingly bad adaptation of Tom Wolfe's best-selling satirical novel. C: Tom Hanks, Bruce Willis, Melanie Griffith, Morgan Freeman, Kim Cattrall. D: Brian De Palma. DRA [R] 126m. V

Bonjour Tristesse 1958 ★★★ Preminger's second attempt to make Seberg a star failed in this reworking of Françoise Sagan's novel about a girl who attempts to sabotage the relationship between her playboy father and his mistress. Impaired by shaky adaptation and some ludicrous dialogue. C: Deborah Kerr, David Niven, Jean Seberg. D: Otto Preminger. DRA 94m. V

Bonnie and Clyde 1967 ★★★★★ A treatise on the mythologizing of criminals, and one of the first popular movies to feature graphic violence. Brilliantly mixes sympathy with cynicism as it charts the career of the ruthless Barrows Gang, the exploits of which both appalled and fascinated Depression-era America. Acting, editing, and direction now look classical, but it was all quite radical for Hollywood at the time. C: Warren Beatty, Faye Dunaway, Michael J. Pollard, Gene Hackman, Estelle Parsons. D: Arthur Penn. CRI 111m. V

Bonnie Parker Story, The 1958 ★★★½ A bored waitress (Provine) takes up with a hoodlum on a crime spree. B-movie account of a doomed criminal. C: Dorothy Provine, Jack Hogan. D: William Witney. ACT 81m.

Bonnie Prince Charlie 1948 British ★★★ In 1745, Prince Charles (Niven), member of the Stuart family that had ruled Great Britain for centuries, returns from exile to try and reclaim the throne. Handsomely mounted but bungled historical pageant is slow-moving and unduly long. C: David Niven, Margaret Leighton, Jack Hawkins. D: Anthony Kimmins. DRA 118m.

Bonnie Scotland 1935 ★★★½ Laurel and Hardy join the Scottish army and somehow wind up in India. Sounds preposterous and it is—brilliantly so, the Stan and Ollie way. C: Stan Laurel, Oliver Hardy, June Lang, James Finlayson. D: James W. Horne. COM 81m. V

Bonnie's Kids 1972 ★★½ Some tough kids in a tough neighborhood get involved in sex, larceny, and murder. Low level thrills. C: Tiffany Bollings, Scott Brady, Robin Mattson, Steve Sandor. D: Arthur Marks. CRI [R] 107m. V

Bonzo Goes to College 1952 ★★★ A prodigious chimpanzee helps to win a football game. Madcap monkey business with okay cast. That's David Janssen in a bit role. C: Maureen O'Sullivan, Charles Drake, Edmund Gwenn, Gigi Perreau, Irene Ryan. D: Frederick de Cordova. COM 80m.

Boob Tube, The 1974 ★ Thinly scripted spoof of soap operas in which a TV station spices up its programming with the accent on sex. C: John Alderman, Sharon Kelly. COM [R] 90m. V

Boogens, The 1981 ★★★★ An abandoned mine is reopened, freeing deadly little creatures called "boogens." Well made, with enough built-in chills to satisfy. C: Rebecca Balding, Fred McCarren, Anne-Marie Martin. D: James Conway. HOR [R] 95m. V

Boogeyman, The 1980 ★★½ A young woman who witnessed a murder in a mirror finds that the looking glass now contains a malevolent spirit. Former Fassbinder collaborator Lommel tries for artsiness and comes up instead with a laughable, splattery bore. Followed by a sequel. C: Suzanna Love, Ron James, John Carradine. D: Ulli Lommel. HOR [R] 86m. V

Boogeyman II 1983 ★★ A Hollywood producer wants to make a movie about the experiences of the survivor of the murders in the previous *Boogeyman* movie. Feeble slasher flick. C: Suzanna Love, Shana Hall. D: Bruce Starr. HOR 80m. V

Boogie Man Will Get You, The 1942 ★★★½ Eccentric scientists set out to develop a race of supermen in an attempt to aid the Allies in WWII. Lively horror film spoof with several familiar faces in the cast. C: Boris Karlof, Peter Lorre, Jeff Donnell, Larry Parks. D: Lew Landers. HOR 66m.

Book of Love 1991 ★★ Typical coming-of-age comedy set in the '50s about a group of teenaged boys preoccupied with girls, cars, and emulating James Dean. When the new kid in town moves in on the school's blonde bombshell, she uses him to make her boyfriend jealous. Not very memorable. C: Chris Young, Keith Coogan, Josie Bissett, Tricia Leigh Fisher. D: Robert Shaye. COM [PG-13] 86m. V

Book of Numbers 1973 ★★★½ Underworld African-Americans operate a numbers scam in the '30s. Occasionally entertaining but erratic crime tale set in the country. C: Raymond St. Jacques, Phillip Thomas, Freda Payne. D: Raymond St. Jacques. CRI [R] 80m.

Boom in the Moon 1945 Mexican ★★ A bumbler is hoodwinked into flying to the moon. Mexican-made comedy, of interest to Keaton loyalists. C: Buster Keaton, Angel Garasa. D: Jaime Salvador. COM 83m. V

Boom Town 1940 ★★★½ Two wildcatters (Gable and Tracy) strike it rich on the oilfields but their friendship is threatened by two women (Colbert and Lamarr). Low-budget story gets big-budget star treatment. C: Clark Gable, Spencer Tracy, Claudette Colbert, Hedy Lamarr, Frank Morgan, Lionel Atwill, Chill Wills. D: Jack Conway. DRA 120m. V

Boom! 1968 U.S. ★★ Ponderous drama from Tennessee Williams play about a wealthy, terminally ill woman (Taylor) ministered to by "guardian angel" poet (Burton). The symbolism is as heavy as Liz's makeup. C: Elizabeth Taylor, Richard Burton, Noel Coward, Joanna Shimkus, Michael Dunn. D: Joseph Losey. DRA [PG] 113m.

Boomerang 1934 British ★★★ Mediocre mystery, about a blind author trying to save his wife from a blackmail scheme. C: Lester Matthews, Nora Swinburne. D: Arthur Maude. CRI 82m.

Boomerang! 1947 ★★★★½ Terrific drama based on an actual event, in which the wrong man is fingered for murder of small-town minister. Andrews gives an intelligent performance as the D.A. committed to learning the truth. Sharp script and documentary style add to the realism. C: Dana Andrews, Jane Wyatt, Lee J. Cobb, Arthur Kennedy, Sam Levene, Ed Begley, Karl Malden. D: Elia Kazan. CRI 88m.

Boomerang 1960 West German ★★★½ Flawed-but-provocative crime heist drama, with safecrackers turning on one another when their scheme goes awry. Weidenmann directs with flair. C: Hardy Kruger, Mario Adorf, Horst Frank. D: Alfred Weidenmann. CRI 92m.

Boomerang 1992 ★★★ Change-of-pace comedy for Murphy, who plays a selfish, womanizing marketing executive upon whom the tables are turned with the arrival of a sexy, aggressive female boss (Givens). C: Eddie Murphy, Halle Berry, Robin Givens, David Alan Grier, Grace Jones, Geoffrey Holder, Eartha Kitt, Melvin Van Peebles. D: Reginald Hudlin. COM [R] 118m. V

Boost, The 1988 ★★★ The boost is that snort of cocaine that gets you happily through the day. Woods plays a sales rep who needs to get happier and happier; Young's the wife who follows him into the downward spiral of addiction. Predictable story energized by Woods' intense performance. C: James Woods, Sean Young, John Kapelos, Steven Hill. D: Harold Becker. DRA [R] 95m. V

Boot Hill 1969 Italian ★★½ Saddle pals team up against frontier badmen. It's tomato sauce and spicy meatballs in meandering spaghetti-Western, alternately funny and violent. C: Terence Hill, Bud Spencer, Woody Strode, Victor Buono, Lionel Stander. D: Giuseppe Colizzi. WST [PG] 87m.

Bootleg 1989 ★★½ On an unusual assignment, a tough private eye finds himself involved with corrupt politicians. Mildly entertaining. C: Ray Meagher. D: John Prescott. CRI 82m. V

Bootleggers 1974 ★★★ Rural moonshiners compete with each other as they run their goods to Tennessee. Boisterous action comedy set during the Depression. C: Paul Koslo, Dennis Fimple, Slim Pickens, Jaclyn Smith. D: Charles Pierce. COM [PG] 101m.

Boots And Saddles 1937 ★★★ When a young English aristocrat wants to sell the ranch he has inherited, Autry transforms him into a true-blue westerner. C: Gene Autry, Smiley Burnette, Judith Allen. D: Joseph Kane. WST 54m. V

Boots Malone 1952 ★★★★ A seedy drifter (Holden) turns his life around when he begins training an aspiring jockey (Stewart). Holden gives a moving performance. C: William Holden, Johnny Stewart, Ed Begley, Harry Morgan. D: William Dieterle. DRA 103m.

Bop Girl 1957 ★★ A pop psychologist believes that calypso music will replace rock 'n' roll. And Picasso was a plastic surgeon. Tuneful nonsense. C: Judy Tyler, Bobby Troup, Margo Woode. D: Howard Koch. MUS 79m.

Bopha! 1993 ★★★½ Drama about a black policeman battling apartheid in South Africa was dated immediately by events, which is unfortunate because the film is earnest and intelligent. C: Danny Glover, Malcolm McDowell, Alfre Woodard, Marius Weyers. D: Morgan Freeman. DRA [PG-13] 120m. V

Border Heat 1988 ★★ A vagrant (Moore) helps organize illegal workers in struggle against sadistic rancher (Vernon) and corrupt union official (White). Superficial handling of material kills off any dramatic potential. (a.k.a. *Deadly Stranger*) C: Darlanne Fluegel, Michael J. Moore, John Vernon. D: Max Kleven. DRA 93m. V

Border Incident 1949 ★★★½ Immigration agents create a diversion to contain the smuggling of illegal aliens into Texas from Mexico. Effectively done, tense crime drama. Good performance by Montalban. C: Ricardo Montalban, George Murphy, Howard da Silva. D: Anthony Mann. CRI 92m.

Border Phantom 1937 ★★½ Cowpoke Steele solves Western mystery involving ghosts. Unmemorable Western from the popular B-movie star. C: Bob Steele, Harley Wood, Don Barclay. D: S. Roy Luby. WST 59m.

Border Radio 1988 ★★★½ A rock star steals a lot of money from some thugs and winds up running for his life. Offbeat rock and roll drama, appealing cast. C: John Doe, Dave Alvin, Chris Shearer, Luana Anders. D: Allison Anders. DRA 88m. V

Border River 1954 ★★★ In the waning days of the Civil War, a rebel officer is dispatched to purchase guns from Mexico. Offbeat B-Western, with okay action and characterizations. C: Joel McCrea, Yvonne De Carlo, Pedro Armendariz. D: George Sherman. WST 80m.

Border Shootout 1990 ★★★½ A veteran sheriff bumps heads with a naive young rancher who's just been deputized when the town decides to hang a couple of cowpokes believed to be rustlers. Solid Western action. C: Cody Glenn, Jeff Kaake, Glenn Ford, Michael Ansara. D: C. J. McIntyre. WST 110m. V

Border Street 1948 Polish ★★★★ Strong, sincere though occasionally overplayed drama about conditions Polish Jews endured after being forced into ghettos during WWII. C: Maria Broniewsha, Mieczyslewa Cwiklinsha, Jerzy Lesczynshi. D: Alexander Ford. DRA 110m. V

Border, The 1981 ★★★½ Corrupt patrol guards on the border at El Paso victimize poor, illegal Mexican wetbacks. Nicholson is the good cop, Keitel one of the many bad cops. Well-meaning but simplistic drama. C: Jack Nicholson, Harvey Keitel, Valerie Perrine, Warren Oates. D: Tony Richardson. DRA [R] 107m. V

Borderline 1950 ★★★½ Two undercover agents on the same case, each believing the other is a criminal, fall in love. Thriller is uneven in tone, but the deft playing of the leads carries it off. C: Fred MacMurray, Claire Trevor, Raymond Burr. D: William Seiter. CRI 88m.

Borderline 1980 ★★★ A U.S. border patrolman (Bronson) pursues an elusive killer trafficking in illegal aliens. Standard Bronson action yarn. C: Charles Bronson, Bruce Kirby, Burt Remsen, Ed Harris. D: Jerrold Freeman. ACT 97m.

Bordertown 1935 ★★★★ Davis plays a lower-class woman who kills her husband (Pallette) when she falls for lawyer Muni and then goes to pieces. Her scene on the witness stand is pure Davis: nervous, mannered, and fascinating. C: Paul Muni, Bette Davis, Eugene Pallette, Margaret Lindsay. D: Archie Mayo. DRA 90m.

Borgia Stick, The 1966 ★★★½ A couple tries to free themselves from ties to a pervasive crime syndicate. Improbable suspense/thriller holds interest. Excellent cast. C: Don Murray, Inger Stevens, Barry Nelson, Fritz Weaver. D: David Lowell Rich. CRI 100m.

Boris and Natasha 1992 ★★ Those Russian spies from the "Rocky and Bullwinkle" cartoons are now embodied by Kellerman and Thomas, sans moose and squirrel. Also missing, however, is the wit and fun of the TV series. Made for theaters, but wound up on cable instead. (June Foray, the voice of Rocky and Natasha, makes a quick appearance.) C: Sally Kellerman, David Thomas, Andrea Martin, Alex Rocco. D: Charles Martin Smith. COM [PG] 88m. V

Boris Godunov 1954 ★★★★ Faithful rendition of Mussorgsky's opera about 16th-century Russian tsar benefits from colorful costumes, strong settings, and fine performances. A real treat for opera fans. C: Alexander Pirogov. MUS 108m. V

Born Again 1978 ★★ Jones portrays Charles Colson, special counsel to President Nixon and Watergate co-conspirator, who, after a prison term, turns to Christianity. Bland biography neither inspires nor informs. C: Dean Jones, Anne Francis, Jay Robinson, Dana Andrews, Raymond St. Jacques, George Brent. D: Irving Rapper. DRA [PG] 110m. V

Born American 1986 U.S. ★★ A trio of robust Americans accidentally cross into Russia for sport, then find themselves held there against their will. Inept hokum about Cold War is as inane as the premise. C: Mike Norris, Steve Durham, David Coburn. D: Renny Harlin. ACT [R] 93m. V

Born Free 1966 British ★★★★ Popular, sentimental tale of Adamson family raising the lioness Elsa in Africa. Oscar to John Barry for Best Score and Title Song. Followed by *Living Free*. C: Virginia McKenna, Bill Travers. D: James Hill. FAM/DRA 95m. V

Born in East L.A. 1987 ★★★ Bumbling Los Angeles Chicano (Marin) gets caught without identification in an INS raid, and before you can say deported, he finds himself stranded in Mexico. Laugh-filled comedy makes strong points about U.S. immigration policy and its treatment of Latinos. C: Cheech Marin, Daniel Stern, Paul Rodriguez, Jan-Michael Vincent. D: Cheech Marin. COM [R] 85m. V

Born Innocent 1974 ★★½ A young girl is sent to juvenile hall where she's forced to adjust to an often terrifying environment. Graphic at times and goes for shock value. C: Linda Blair, Joanna Miles, Kim Hunter, Richard Jaeckel. D: Donald Wrye. DRA 92m. TVM V

Born Losers 1967 ★★½ A half-breed attempts to save a young girl from a gang of marauding bikers. Violent, tasteless chopper flick introduced Billy Jack character to the screen. C: Tom Laughlin, Elizabeth James. D: T. C. Frank. ACT 112m. V

Born on the Fourth of July 1989 ★★★★★ The second film in Stone's Vietnam trilogy (between *Platoon* and *Heaven and Earth*) tells the true story of Ron Kovic, from his picket-fence youth to his tour of duty, then to his postwar years of hospitalization, family strife, and political activism. A heartbreaking, emotionally brutal American nightmare, charged by Cruise's forceful performance in the lead. Won Oscars for Best Director and Editing. C: Tom Cruise, Willem Dafoe, Raymond J. Barry, Kyra Sedgwick. D: Oliver Stone. DRA [R] 145m. V

Born Reckless 1959 ★★½ A broncobuster appoints himself protector of a platinum-blond siren. Tuneful, predictable bad-girl B-movie. Put the blame on Mamie. C: Mamie Van Doren, Jeff Richards. D: Howard Koch. DRA 79m.

Born To Be Bad 1950 ★★★½ An iniquitous woman (Fontaine) feigns innocence to trick a millionaire (Scott) into marriage, and then takes up with a novelist (Ryan) before the two men discover her sinister nature. Well handled, but Ray was forced to tack on a contrived ending to please censors. C: Joan Fontaine, Robert Ryan, Joan Leslie, Mel Ferrer, Zachary Scott. D: Nicholas Ray. DRA 94m. V

Born To Be Loved 1959 ★★★ An aged music professor plays cupid to an oddly matched couple. Restrained, light romantic fare. C: Carol Morris, Vera Vague, Hugo Haas. D: Hugo Haas. DRA 82m.

Born to Dance 1936 ★★★★ Nifty Cole Porter musical about an ambitious chorus dancer (Powell) helped along by a sailor (Stewart). Jimmy croons "Easy to Love" and Eleanor tap-dances up a storm in this endearing lark. C: Eleanor Powell, James Stewart, Virginia Bruce, Una Merkel, Frances Langford, Buddy Ebsen. D: Roy Del Ruth. MUS 102m. V

Born to Kill 1947 ★★★★ Unflinchingly brutal film noir, about a psychotic husband who's after his bride's money, while also eyeing her sister. Grim but worthwhile. Tierney is brilliantly evil. C: Claire Trevor, Lawrence Tierney, Walter Slezak, Audrey Long, Elisha Cook, Jr. D: Robert Wise. CRI 92m. V

Born to Race 1988 ★ Hoodlums kidnap an engineer (Heasley) who has invented an extraordinary new engine. Boneheaded movie uses the stock car circuit for an excuse to show lots of hot cars and nude women. C: Joseph Bottoms, Marc Singer, George Kennedy, Marla Heasley, McGrady. D: James Fargo. ACT [R] 95m. V

Born to the West 1937 ★★★½ A naive cowpoke (Wayne) falls under the influence of rustlers. It takes his law officer cousin (Brown), to pull the Duke back from their nefarious hands. Entertaining B-Western, based on a Zane Grey story. Wayne's fans will enjoy this prestar vehicle. (a.k.a. *Hell Town*) C: John Wayne, Marsha Hunt, Johnny Mack Brown, Monte Blue, Syd Saylor, Alan Ladd. D: Charles Barton. WST 50m. V

Born to Win *See* **Addict**

Born Yesterday 1950 ★★★★★ A D.C. bigshot (Crawford) hires a cynical reporter (Holden) to tutor his delightfully dim mistress (Holliday). Great fun, based on Garson Kanin's play. Holliday, recreating her Broadway role, steals the show and earned a Best Actress Oscar. Not to be missed. Remade in 1993. C: Judy Holliday, William Holden, Broderick Crawford, Howard St. John. D: George Cukor. COM 103m. V

Born Yesterday 1993 ★★★½ Remake of the quintessential not-so-dumb-blonde comedy classic. A vulgar tycoon's mistress (Griffith) gets a quick education from a brainy reporter (Johnson), and vice versa. Certainly the 1950 Judy Holliday Cadillac will always lead, but the story holds up pleasantly here. C: Melanie Griffith, John Goodman, Don Johnson, Edward Herrmann. D: Luis Mandoki. COM [PG] 100m. v

B.O.R.N. 1989 ★★ The diabolical Body Organ Replacement Network appropriates human body parts by devious means. Tedious, minor scarefare. C: Ross Hagen, P. J. Soles, William Smith, Russ Tamblyn. D: Ross Hagen. HOR [R] 90m. v

Borrower, The 1991 ★★★½ A murderer from another planet receives a tough punishment—life on earth, where he causes some folks to lose their heads. Slam-bang plot and special effects. C: Rae Dawn Chong, Don Gordon, Antonio Fargas. D: John McNaughton. HOR [R] 97m. v

Borrowers, The 1973 ★★★★ Heartwarming fantasy from the classic children's tale about a boy's discovery of a tiny family living beneath the floorboards of Victorian house. Veteran Broadway cast in charming adaptation. C: Eddie Albert, Judith Anderson, Tammy Grimes, Barnard Hughes, Beatrice Straight. D: Walter Miller. FAM/DRA 78m.

Borsalino 1970 French ★★★★ Belmondo and Delon do charming star turns as a pair of small-time hoods who become gangster bigwigs in '30s. Low-key humor and great fashion sense make it work. Followed by a sequel. C: Jean-Paul Belmondo, Alain Delon, Michel Bouquet, Catherine Rouvel. D: Jacques Deray. CRI [R] 125m. v

Borsalino and Company 1974 French ★★½ Weak sequel to *Borsalino* features Delon as a gangster struggling with heroin and control for power in the criminal underground of '30s Marseilles. Stale rehash of familiar gangster movie clichés. (a.k.a. *Blood on the Streets*) C: Alain Delon, Catherine Rouvel, Ricardo Cusiolla, Rene Kolldehoff, Daniel Ivernel. D: Jacques Deray. CRI 110m.

Bosambo 1935 *See* **Sanders of the River**

Bosna! 1994 French ★★★½ One-sided documentary on the war in Bosnia advocates U.S. intervention to stop the nation's suffering. Strident, graphic, sometimes powerful. D: Bernard-Henri Levy, Alain Ferrari. DOC 117m.

Boss Nigger 1975 ★★★ Typical Williamson vehicle has Fred as a bounty hunter in the Old West. Campy exploitation film is not as offensive as the title would suggest. (a.k.a. *Boss* and *The Black Bounty Killer*) C: Fred Williamson, D'Urville Martin, R.G. Armstrong. D: Jack Arnold. WST [PG] 92m. v

Boss, The 1956 ★★★★ A WWI veteran fights corruption in his home town. Solid work from all concerned, especially Payne. C: John Payne, William Bishop, Gloria McGhee. D: Byron Haskin. CRI 89m.

Boss' Wife, The 1986 ★★★ A young stockbroker (Stern) wants to impress his boss (Plummer), but the boss' wife (Dombasle) just wants him. Not too bad, but talented cast doesn't really rise above the threadbare plot and silly situations. C: Daniel Stern, Arielle Dombasle, Fisher Stevens, Melanie Mayron, Martin Mull, Christopher Plummer. D: Ziggy Steinberg. DRA [R] 83m. v

Boss 1975 *See* **Boss Nigger**

Boss's Son, The 1978 ★★★★ Son goes to work in his father's factory, and is upset when he finds he has to start from the bottom. Quiet, solid work from writer/director Roth; this sleeper pays dividends. C: Asher Brauner, Rudy Solari, Rita Moreno, Piper Laurie. D: Bobby Roth. DRA 97m. v

---

Boston Blackie Blackie is another one of those reformed thieves who is constantly outsmarting the police and solving crimes for them. As incarnated by Chester Morris in 14 films for Columbia, he is a charming rogue, and the films are snappy B-movie whodunits.

Meet Boston Blackie (1941)
Confessions of Boston Blackie (1941)
Alias Boston Blackie (1942)
Boston Blackie Goes Hollywood (1942)
After Midnight With Boston Blackie (1943)
The Chance of a Lifetime (1943)
One Mysterious Night (1944)
Boston Blackie Booked on Suspicion(1945)
Boston Blackie's Rendezvous (1945)
A Close Call for Boston Blackie (1946)
The Phantom Thief (1946)
Boston Blackie and the Law (1946)
Trapped by Boston Blackie (1948)
Boston Blackie's Chinese Venture (1949)

Boston Blackie and the Law 1946 ★★★ Killer escapes from a women's prison and it's Blackie to the rescue. Morris is amusing even though things get a little stale by film's end. Fair to middling offering in this series. C: Chester Morris, Trudy Marshall. D: D. Lederman. CRI 70m.

Boston Blackie Booked on Suspicion 1945 ★★★½ Blackie discovers a body and soon finds he is a suspect for murder. Numerous neat plot twists and quick pace keep this afloat. C: Chester Morris, Lynn Merrick. D: Arthur Dreifuss. CRI 66m.

Boston Blackie Goes Hollywood 1942 ★★★★ The cops think Blackie is transporting a missing diamond as he visits Tinseltown. One of the best *Blackie*'s is helped along by nice ensemble playing and terrific atmosphere. C: Chester Morris, George Stone, Forrest Tucker. D: Michael Gordon. CRI 68m.

Boston Blackie's Chinese Venture 1949 ★★★ Blackie is under investigation for a series of Chinatown murders, so he goes underground to solve the crimes. Last *Blackie* film is one of the weakest. C: Chester Morris, Joan Woodbury. D: Seymour Friedman. CRI 59m.

Boston Blackie's Rendevous 1945 ★★★½ A killer (Cochran) escapes from prison and goes on a murderous rampage. Blackie must use all his wiles to catch him. Exciting, darker than usual Blackie fare. C: Chester Morris, Nina Foch, Steve Cochran. D: Arthur Dreifuss. CRI 64m.

Boston Strangler, The 1968 ★★★★ Intelligent police procedural describes in documentary style the search for the real-life mass murderer of the early '60s. Curtis is chillingly believable as the mild-mannered psychopath. C: Tony Curtis, Henry Fonda, George Kennedy, Mike Kellin, Hurd Hatfield, Sally Kellerman. D: Richard Fleischer. CRI [R] 116m. V

Bostonians, The 1984 ★★½ 19th-century period piece. Young suffragette orator (Potter) is pursued by a conservative Southern lawyer (Reeve) and a lesbian older woman (Redgrave). A Merchant-Ivory-Jhabvala adaptation of Henry James's novel. C: Christopher Reeve, Vanessa Redgrave, Madeleine Potter, Jessica Tandy, Nancy Marchand, Linda Hunt. D: James Ivory. DRA 120m. V

Botany Bay 1953 ★★★½ On a prison ship heading for Australia, a wrongly convicted doctor (Ladd) clashes with the evil captain (Mason). Lavish costume drama, set in the late 18th century, creaks at times but Mason's performance saves the day. C: Alan Ladd, James Mason, Patricia Medina, Cedric Hardwicke. D: John Farrow. DRA 94m.

Both Sides of the Law 1954 British ★★★½ Dry, tasteful account of life in the precinct for London policewomen. Movie's realism has look and feel of a documentary. Engaging all the way. C: Peggy Cummins, Terence Morgan. D: Muriel Box. DRA 94m.

Bottom of the Bottle, The 1956 ★★★½ Strange melodrama, set in border town. Attorney tries to help his alcoholic, on-the-lam brother flee authorities. Good beginning fizzles but Johnson is compelling as the bad brother. C: Van Johnson, Joseph Cotten, Ruth Roman, Jack Carson. D: Henry Hathaway. DRA 88m.

Bottoms Up 1977 ★★★½ Amusing songfest about Hollywood promoter who finds work for friends by passing them off as British aristocrats. C: Adam Janas, Sparky Abrams, Adrain Ayres, Kathleen Johnson. D: Karl Rawicz. MUS [R] 90m. V

Boudu Saved From Drowning 1932 French ★★★★ Pulled from the Seine by a middle-class bookseller after a suicide attempt, Simon is invited to live with his savior and proceeds to upend his household. Simon's portrayal of an inveterate bohemian is peerless. This much-loved early Renoir classic was remade as *Down and Out in Beverly Hills*. C: Michel Simon, Charles Granval, Marcelle Hania. D: Jean Renoir. DRA 87m. V

Boulevard Nights 1979 ★★ Chicano youths try to stay out of trouble in gang-infested East L.A. Yniguez and De La Paz, playing brothers, are sympathetic but basically uninteresting. Limp direction. C: Richard Yniguez, Marta Du Bois, Danny De La Paz. D: Michael Pressman. CRI [R] 102m. V

Bound and Gagged: A Love Story 1993 ★★½ When a lesbian thinks her bisexual girlfriend is about to dump her, she kidnaps her and takes her for a wild, crime-filled spree. Quirky, trashy rip-off of *Thelma and Louise* ends with the memorable quote: "It is better to have loved and lost than to shove a screwdriver up your nose"! C: Elizabeth Saltarelli, Ginger Lynn Allen, Steve Mulkey, Karen Black. D: Daniel Appleby. DRA [R] 101m. V

Bound by Honor 1993 ★★★½ Sometimes gripping prison film, based on the real-life experiences of poet Jimmy Santiago Baca. However, this portrait of a Chicago drug addict whose half-brother is a narcotics detective is marred by overlength and gratuitous violence. (a.k.a. *Blood In, Blood Out*) C: Damian Chapa, Jesse Borrego, Benjamin Bratt, Enrique Castillo. D: Taylor Hackford. CRI [R] 180m. V

Bound for Glory 1976 ★★★★½ Carradine scores high marks in Hal Ashby's visually stunning biography of singer/activist Woody Guthrie, who took to the rails in Depression-era America and chronicled in words and music the lives of the poor and downtrodden. Lyrical, powerful film. Oscars for Best Cinematography and Score. C: David Carradine, Ronny Cox, Melinda Dillon, Gail Strickland, Randy Quaid. D: Hal Ashby. DRA [PG] 147m. V

Bounty Hunter, The 1954 ★★★ Scott goes after criminals in order to make his fortune. C: Randolph Scott, Dolores Dorn, Marie Windsor. D: Andre de Toth. ACT 90m.

Bounty Hunter, The 1989 ★★½ Vietnam vet (Ginty) looks into the murder of a Native-American buddy. His investigation leads to an angry sheriff who isn't too pleased with the bounty hunter's snooping. Violent, predictable fare was also directed by the star. C: Robert Ginty, Bo Hopkins, Loeta Waterdown, Melvin Holt. D: Robert Ginty. ACT [R] 90m.

Bounty Killer, The 1965 ★★★½ Duryea sets a town on end as a ruthless bounty killer. His smarmy performance keeps this oater interesting. Watch for the many Western old-timers in the cast. C: Dan Duryea, Rod Cameron, Audrey Dalton, Richard Arlen, Buster Crabbe. D: Spencer Bennet. WST [R] 92m.

Bounty Man, The 1972 ★★★½ The bounty man (Walker) chases a killer, while losing his girlfriend and his freedom. Bleak script and good cast make for good, off-the-beaten-path viewing. C: Clint Walker, Richard Basehart, Margot Kidder. D: John Llewellyn Moxey. ACT 73m. TVM V

Bounty, The 1984 ★★★½ Third *Mutiny on the Bounty* go-round is handsome and literate and the physical detail is often breathtaking. Hopkins makes a wonderfully venal Captain Bligh, and his scenes with Gibson really crackle. C: Mel Gibson, Anthony Hopkins, Laurence Olivier, Edward Fox, Daniel Day-Lewis, Liam Neeson. D: Roger Donaldson. DRA [PG] 130m. V

Bounty Tracker 1993 ★★½ Always the essence of cool professionalism, a tough bounty hunter gets hot under the collar when he runs into the outlaw who shot his brother. Middling adventure. C: Lorenzo Lamas, Matthias Hues, Cyndi Pass, Paul Regina, Whip Hubley. D: Kurt Anderson. ACT [R] 90m. V

Bouquet of Barbed Wire ★★★ When his daughter gets married—and gets pregnant—a big time publishing executive finds himself in a jealous rage that threatens his whole family. Heartfelt family emotions. C: Frank Finlay, James Aubrey, Sheila Allen, Susan Penhaligon. D: Tom Wharmby. DRA 343m. V

Bourne Identity, The 1988 ★★★★ A secret agent suffering from amnesia (Chamberlain) flees with a woman he's kidnapped (Smith) to escape assassins while trying to reestablish his identity. TV adaptation of Robert Ludlum's novel effectively captures author's taut espionage thrills. C: Richard Chamberlain, Jaclyn Smith, Anthony Quayle, Donald Moffat, Denholm Elliott. D: Roger Young. CRI 188m. TVM V

Bowery at Midnight 1942 ★★★ Lugosi is ideally cast as a psychiatrist who by night is an evil criminal in the streets of New York. Cheap but atmospheric yarn will make eerie viewing for some but will trigger a few guffaws from everybody else. C: Bela Lugosi, John Archer, Wanda McKay. D: Wallace Fox. HOR 63m.

Bowery Blitzkrieg 1941 ★★½ Gorcey tries to push Jordan off the streets and into the boxing ring. The usual yuks prevail in this East Side Kids entry. COM

Bowery Bombshell 1946 ★★★½ Sach becomes a suspect in a bank robbery, so the Boys go underground and track down the real culprits. One of the better entries in this series, directed by film noir veteran Karlson. COM

Bowery Boys, The/Dead End Kids/East Side Kids After starting out as the juvenile delinquent supporting cast in Broadway hit *Dead End* and moving to Hollywood for Sam Goldwyn's 1937 adaptation of the Sidney Kingsley play, the guys stuck around the movie business for another 21 years and some 86 films. As the Dead End Kids, they appeared in six films at Warner Brothers after their debut for Goldwyn, including classy Cagney and Garfield vehicles like *Angels with Dirty Faces* and *They Made Me a Criminal*. A seeminngly endless series of lowbrow comedies for Universal and Monogram followed, under a variety of appellations and with varying casts of characters.

The Dead End Kids Dead End (1937)
Crime School (1938)
Angels With Dirty Faces (1938)
They Made Me A Criminal (1939)
Hell's Kitchen (1939)
Angels Wash Their Faces (1939)
On Dress Parade (1939)
The Dead End Kids and Little Tough Guys
Little Tough Guy (1938)
Call a Messenger (1939)
You're Not So Tough (1940)
Give Us Wings (1940)
Hit the Road (1941)
Mob Town (1941)
Tough as They Come (1942)
Mud Town (1943)
Keep 'Em Slugging (1943)
East Side Kids East Side Kids (1940)
Boys of the City (1940)
That Gang of Mine (1940)
Pride of the Bowery (1941)
Flying Wild (1941)
Bowery Blitzkrieg (1941)
Spooks Run Wild (1941)
Mr. Wise Guy (1942)
Let's Get Tough (1942)
Smart Alecks (1942)
'Neath Brooklyn Bridge (1942)
Kid Dynamite (1943)
Clancy Street Boys (1943)
Ghosts on the Loose (1943)
Mr. Muggs Steps Out (1943)
Million Dollar Kid (1944)
Follow the Leader (1944)
Block Busters (1944)
Bowery Champs (1944)
Docks of New York (1945)
Mr. Muggs Rides Again (1945)
Come Out Fighting (1945)
Bowery Boys Live Wires (1946)
In Fast Company (1946)
Bowery Bombshell (1946)
Spook Busters (1946)
Mr. Hex (1946)
Hard Boiled Mahoney (1947)
News Hounds (1947)
Bowery Buckaroos (1947)
Angel's Alley (1948)
Jinx Money (1948)
Smuggler's Cove (1948)
Trouble Makers (1948)
Fighting Fools (1949)
Hold That Baby! (1949)
Angels in Disguise (1949)

Master Minds (1949)
Blonde Dynamite (1950)
Lucky Losers (1950)
Triple Trouble (1950)
Blues Busters (1950)
Bowery Battalion (1951)
Ghost Chasers (1951)
Let's Go Navy (1951)
Crazy Over Horse (1951)
Hold That Line (1952)
Here Come the Marines (1952)
Feudin' Fools (1952)
No Hold Barred (1952)
Jalopy (1953)
Loose in London (1953)
Clipped Wings (1953)
Private Eyes (1953)
Paris Playboys (1954)
The Bowery Boys Meet the Monsters (1954)
Jungle Gents (1954)
Bowery to Baghdad (1955)
High Society (1955)
Spy Chasers (1955)
Jail Busters (1955)
Dig That Uranium (1956)
Crashing Las Vegas (1956)
Fighting Trouble (1956)
Hot Shots (1956)
Hold That Hypnotist (1957)
Spook Chasers (1957)
Looking For Danger (1957)
Up In Smoke (1957)
In the Money (1958)

Bowery Boys Meet the Monsters, The 1954 ★★★ Later entry tries and, sort of, succeeds as the Boys run afoul of evil scientists. Look for TV's Grandma Walton (Corby) in a small role. C: Leo Gorcey, Huntz Hall. D: Edward Bernds. COM 65m.

Bowery Buckaroos 1947 ★★½ The Boys go West and run into trouble. Endearingly silly as usual, but weak. C: Leo Gorcey, Huntz Hall, Bobby Jordan, Gabriel Dell. D: William Beaudine. COM 66m. V

Bowery Champs 1944 ★★★ Gorcey is a reporter who is hot onto a murder investigation. Of course, the Boys help make things go haywire. Jordan pops up in a cameo. C: Leo Gorcey, Huntz Hall, Billy Benedict, Gabriel Dell. D: William Beaudine. COM 62m.

Bowery, The 1933 ★★★ Coarse Beery and courtly Raft play saloon owners in Gay '90s New York competing for business and the same woman (Wray). Walsh captures colorful Lower East Side beer halls and personalities in this action-packed film. C: Wallace Beery, George Raft, Jackie Cooper, Fay Wray, Pert Kelton. D: Raoul Walsh. DRA 90m.

Bowery to Bagdad 1954 ★★★ One of the most imaginative and ludicrous films in the series has Genie (Blore) whisking away the gang to Baghdad. Funny premise doesn't really pan out. C: Leo Gorcey, Huntz Hall, Joan Shawlee, Eric Blore. D: Edward Bernds. COM 64m.

Bowery to Broadway 1944 ★★★ Thin plot about rival theatrical producers serves as a means to show a cavalcade of stars. Typical revue show of the WWII period. C: Jack Oakie, Donald Cook, Maria Montez, Louise Allbritton, Turhan Bey, Andy Devine, Rosemary DeCamp, Frank McHugh, Ann Blyth. D: Charles Lamont. MUS 94m.

Boxcar Bertha 1972 ★★★ In Arkansas during the Depression, a young drifter (Hershey) gets involved with a group of train robbers. Early, interesting Scorsese effort. C: Barbara Hershey, David Carradine, Barry Primus, John Carradine. D: Martin Scorsese. DRA [R] 90m. V

Boxing Helena 1993 ★ A young woman is abducted by a psychotic who begins a slow process of dismembering her. Gruesome allegorical fantasy, intended first for Madonna and later, Kim Basinger. Lynch is the daughter of director David Lynch, and tries to emulate his surrealist, dreamlike style. Repeat: tries. C: Julian Sands, Sherilyn Fenn, Bill Paxton, Art Garfunkel, Betsy Clark. D: Jennifer Chambers Lynch. DRA [R] 105m. V

Boy 1969 Japanese ★★★★ Chillingly told tale, based on fact, about a young Japanese boy whose parents train him to fall against moving cars and fake injury in order to collect damages from the drivers. Psychological study of child abuse is one of Oshima's major works. C: Tetsuo Abe, Fumio Watanabe, Akiko Koyama. D: Nagisa Oshima. DRA 97m.

Boy and His Dog, A 1976 ★★★★ Black comedy follows a post-nuclear-holocaust boy (Johnson) and his intelligent, telepathic dog as they search for food and girls until they stumble upon a subterranean, totalitarian society. Offbeat sci-fi fun and a cult favorite. From the Harlan Ellison novella. C: Don Johnson, Susanne Benton, Jason Robards. D: L.Q. Jones. SFI [R] 90m. V

Boy and the Pirates 1960 ★★★½ A young boy is transported to a pirate ship where he finds things aren't as enchanting as he thought. Nice fantasy yarn, good for the kids. C: Charles Herbert, Susan Gordon, Murvyn Vye. D: Bert Gordon. FAM/ACT 82m.

Boy Cried Murder, The 1966 British ★★★½ Boy-cries-wolf story set in an Italian resort, as a boy claims he witnessed murder but nobody believes him—except the murderer. Pale remake of 1949 classic *The Window*. C: Veronica Hurst, Phil Brown, Beba Loncar, Frazer MacIntosh, Tim Barrett. D: George Breakston. CRI 86m.

Boy, Did I Get a Wrong Number! 1966 ★★½ And how! Unpleasant farce casts Hope as real estate agent ogling a visiting sex symbol (Sommer). C: Bob Hope, Elke Sommer, Phyllis Diller. D: George Marshall. COM 100m. V

Boy Friend, The 1971 British ★★★★ On

Broadway, this was a zippy send-up of '20s musicals. Russell's fun, flamboyant adaptation has a film producer watch an amateur stage production, then dream how he'd film it. Lots of inventive Busby Berkeley-style numbers and ebullient performances; Glenda Jackson makes a hilarious, unbilled appearance as a spiteful, arrogant star. C: Twiggy, Christopher Gable, Tommy Tune. D: Ken Russell. MUS [G] 137m. V

Boy from Indiana 1950 ★★★ A boy, a girl, and a horse. Typical horse racing story given a tasteful, if not overly exciting treatment. Good family fare. C: Lon McCallister, Lois Butler, Billie Burke. D: John Rawlins. FAM/ACT 66m.

Boy from Oklahoma, The 1954 ★★★½ A peace-loving sheriff (Rogers) manages to enforce the law and still have time for his lady (the winsome Olson). Low-key Western has a certain charm. One of Will, Jr.'s better vehicles. C: Will Rogers, Jr., Nancy Olson, Lon Chaney, Jr., Merv Griffin. D: Michael Curtiz. WST 88m.

Boy in Blue, The 1986 Canadian ★★½ Rags-to-riches story about a 19th-century Canadian rower (Cage) who revolutionized the sport. Tepid tale gets in way of interesting characterizations. C: Nicolas Cage, Cynthia Dale, Christopher Plummer. D: Charles Jarrott. DRA [R] 97m. V

Boy in the Plastic Bubble, The 1977 ★★★★ A young man, born with all kinds of immunity deficiencies, is compelled to live in a highly controlled plastic "bubble." Interesting and sincere. Travolta does wonderfully. C: John Travolta, Glynnis O'Connor, Robert Reed, Diana Hyland, Ralph Bellamy. D: Randal Kleiser. DRA 96m. TVM V

Boy Meets Girl 1938 ★★★½ Frantic spoof of movie business follows screenwriters (Cagney and O'Brien) looking for a hot new idea. Funny, though it creaks a bit. C: James Cagney, Pat O'Brien, Marie Wilson, Ralph Bellamy, Frank McHugh, Ronald Reagan. D: Lloyd Bacon. COM 86m. V

Boy Meets Girl 1984 French ★★★★ A loner who wanders Paris streets meets and romances a young woman who has been cast off by her boyfriend. Odd but intriguing drama with moments of strange humor, played largely without dialogue. C: Denis Lavant, Mireille Périer, Carroll Brooks, Elie Poicard. D: Leos Carax. DRA 100m. V

Boy Named Charlie Brown, A 1969 ★★★★ First "Peanuts" animated feature chronicles angst-ridden Charlie Brown's attempt to find success when he enters a national spelling bee. Sweet tale of personal growth tempered by wry comedy. Voices of Peter Robbins, Pamelyn Ferdin, Glenn Gilger. D: Bill Melendez. FAM/COM [G] 85m. V

Boy of the Streets 1937 ★★★ Young punk (Cooper) takes after his sleazy politico dad in this often corny coming-of-age story. Film manages to redeem itself with some true grit. C: Jackie Cooper, Maureen O'Connor, Kathleen Burke, Marjorie Main. D: William Nigh. FAM/DRA 75m.

Boy on a Dolphin 1957 ★★★½ Aquatic treasure hunt tale gets boost from gorgeous Greek scenery and the equally gorgeous Loren, in U.S. film debut. C: Alan Ladd, Sophia Loren, Clifton Webb, Laurence Naismith. D: Jean Negulesco. DRA 111m.

Boy Ten Feet Tall, A 1963 British ★★★★ After his parents are killed in an air strike, a youngster must trek alone across Africa to get to his aunt's home in Durban. Entertaining film for children, with gorgeous scenery. Robinson is good in a supporting role. (a.k.a. *Sammy Going South*) C: Edward G. Robinson, Fergus McClelland, Constance Cummings. D: Alexander Mackendrick. FAM/DRA [G] 118m.

Boy! What a Girl 1946 ★★★★ Young man in drag becomes the most popular woman in town. This behind-the-scenes musical features an all African-American cast and lively direction. Moore has star quality as the "girl," and the jitterbugging is pretty racy for 1946. A little-seen gem. C: Tim Moore, Duke Williams, Elwood Smith. D: Arthur Leonard. MUS 70m.

Boy Who Caught a Crook 1961 ★★½ A newsboy is pursued by a thief who thinks the kid has his missing loot. The title explains the rest. C: Wanda Hendrix, Roger Mobley, Don Beddoe. D: Edward Cahn. CRI 72m.

Boy Who Could Fly, The 1986 ★★ Sentimental nonsense about an autistic boy (Underwood) who thinks he can fly, helped by a young newcomer to the neighborhood (Deakins). Tries to be oh-so-sensitive. C: Lucy Deakins, Jay Underwood, Bonnie Bedelia, Fred Savage, Colleen Dewhurst. D: Nick Castle. DRA [PG] 114m. V

Boy Who Cried Bitch, The 1991 ★★★★½ Grim story of a psychotic 12-year-old (Cross) whose mental illness overwhelms his mother and who gets only the most half-hearted psychiatric care. An uncompromising look at deeply disturbing human issues, played with compassion by an excellent cast. C: Harley Cross, Karen Young, Dennis Boutsikaris, Moira Kelly. D: Juan Campanella. DRA 101m.

Boy Who Cried Werewolf, The 1973 ★★½ A teenager realizes his father is a werewolf. A thriller for those who don't wish to be *too* scared. C: Kerwin Mathews, Elaine Devry, Scott Sealey. D: Nathan Juran. HOR [PG] 93m.

Boy Who Had Everything, The 1984 Australian ★★★ A college student (Connery) seems to have life in the palm of his hand, until his girlfriend and growing pains make him see differently. Too precious to be effective. Connery's mom is Cilento (both on-and off-screen) and his real-life dad is 007 himself. C: Jason Connery, Diane Cilento. D: Stephen Wallace. DRA [R] 94m.

Boy Who Stole a Million, The 1960 British ★★★½ Young boy decides to help out his debt-burdened dad by turning to crime. Mildly amusing family fare. C: Maurice Reyna, Virgilio Texera. D: Charles Crichton. FAM/COM 64m.

Boy with Green Hair, The 1948 ★★★★ Fable about orphaned boy who becomes an outcast when his hair turns green is almost a classic. Surprisingly tough and tender film transcends its quirky premise in a big way. Director Losey's first feature. C: Dean Stockwell, Pat O'Brien, Robert Ryan, Barbara Hale. D: Joseph Losey. DRA 82m. V

Boyfriends and Girlfriends 1987 French ★★★★ Sixth film in Rohmer's "Comedies and Proverbs" series involves two women who become friends, then begin entangling themselves in shared romances. Charming and delightfully witty tale that relies more on whim than conventional plotting to carry the story. C: Emmanuelle Chaulet, Sophie Renoir. D: Eric Rohmer. COM [PG] 102m. V

Boys From Brazil, The 1978 ★★★½ An at-large former Nazi officer (Peck) attempts DNA cloning of Hitler to rejuvenate the Third Reich; Olivier is wonderful as the Nazi-hunter on his trail. Attempt to make a serious thriller can only go so far with silly mad scientist premise. Based on Ira Levin's novel. C: Gregory Peck, Laurence Olivier, James Mason, Lilli Palmer, Uta Hagen, Rosemary Harris, Anne Meara, Denholm Elliott, Steve Guttenberg. D: Franklin J. Schaffner. DRA [R] 127m. V

Boys from Syracuse, The 1940 ★★★ Rodgers and Hart musical from Shakespeare's *Comedy of Errors* is a broad mistaken-identity farce focusing on two pairs of twins in ancient Greece. Raye is funny. C: Allan Jones, Joe Penner, Martha Raye, Rosemary Lane, Irene Hervey, Eric Blore. D: A. Sutherland. MUS 73m.

Boys in Company C, The 1978 ★★★★ Low-budget look at five Marine draftees doing their tour of duty in Vietnam. Realistic film on "grunts" in combat has fewer pyrotechnics and more detail than most big-budget films on the same war. C: Stan Shaw, Andrew Stevens, James Canning, Michael Lembeck. D: Sidney J. Furie. DRA [R] 127m. V

Boys in the Band, The 1970 ★★★★ Eight friends throw a birthday party; the honoree's "gift" is an attractive young man. One of the first American films to deal with homosexuality in a straightforward manner. Retains the punch, humor, and pathos of Mort Crowley's successful Broadway play. C: Kenneth Nelson, Cliff Gorman, Leonard Frey, Laurence Luckinbill, Frederick Combs. D: William Friedkin. DRA [R] 119m. V

Boys Next Door, The 1985 ★★ Bleak, extremely violent film about two sociopathic, alienated young men—Sheen and Caulfield—going bad in a big way on a weekend spree in Los Angeles. Graphic and ugly. C: Maxwell Caulfield, Charlie Sheen, Christopher McDonald, Patti D'Arbanville, Moon Zappa. D: Penelope Spheeris. CRI [R] 88m. V

Boys' Night Out 1962 ★★★★ To satisfy their amorous whims, four Manhattan business execs decide to share a penthouse apartment and staff it with Novak who, unbeknownst to them, is a sociology student researching their habits. Clever sex comedy with invigorating performances. C: Kim Novak, James Garner, Tony Randall, Howard Duff, Janet Blair, Patti Page, Zsa Zsa Gabor. D: Michael Gordon. COM 115m.

Boys of Paul Street 1969 Hungarian ★★★★ Lyrical antiwar film, as children try to take over a vacant lot in Budapest. Inspired performances make the message more poignant. Director Fabri was a major figure in the Hungarian New Wave Cinema of the '60s. C: Anthony Kemp, Robert Efford. D: Zoltan Fabri. DRA [G] 108m.

Boys of St. Vincent, The 1994 ★★★★ Engrossing documentary about a difficult and controversial topic: the sexual molestation of young boys by Catholic priests. Both sides are fairly presented as the viewer is allowed to make up his own mind. DOC V

Boys of the City, The 1940 ★★★ The East Side Kids are led to a gothic mansion as they try to solve the mystery of a judge's mysterious death. Worth a look for fans of film noir director Lewis. C: Leo Gorcey, Bobby Jordan, Sunshine Morrison. D: Joseph Lewis. COM 65m.

Boys on the Side 1995 ★★★★ Three fugitives from justice travel cross-country to Arizona, bonding en route. Surprisingly effective comedy/drama, with three crackerjack performances from the stars. C: Whoopi Goldberg, Mary-Louise Parker, Drew Barrymore, James Remar. D: Herbert Ross. COM [R] 115m. V

Boys, The 1961 British ★★★½ Well-meaning attorney tries to determine the motives of four young men who commit heinous crimes. British angry-young-man film is slightly bloated by its social conscience, but still engaging. C: Richard Todd, Robert Morley, Felix Aylmer, Wilfred Brambell. D: Sidney Furie. DRA 123m.

Boys, The 1991 ★★★½ Two writer/partners face tragedy when they find that one of them is dying from breathing the other's secondhand smoke. True story, written by William Link (of Link & Levinson), benefits from strong performances by Woods and Lithgow. C: James Woods, John Lithgow, Joanna Gleason, Alan Rosenberg. D: Glenn Jordan. DRA 100m. TVM

Boys Town 1938 ★★★★ Father Flanagan (Tracy) labors to build a community for wayward boys and reform a cocky teenage hoodlum (Rooney) in this effective tearjerker. Oscar to Tracy (Best Actor) and Script. Sequel: *Men of Boys Town*. C: Spencer Tracy,

Mickey Rooney, Henry Hull, Gene Reynolds. D: Norman Taurog. DRA 96m. v

Boyz N the Hood 1991 ★★★★ Singleton's taut, gut-wrenching debut about a young man's tumultuous coming of age in the mean streets of Los Angeles, where he contends with a strong father and a core of friends that threatens to disintegrate. A simple, violent story told with care. C: Larry Fishburne, Ice Cube, Cuba Gooding, Jr., Nia Long, Angela Bassett. D: John Singleton. DRA [R] 112m. v

Braddock: Missing in Action III 1988 ★★ A Vietnam vet (Norris) goes back to Southeast Asia to look for his Vietnamese wife. What could have been an intriguing thriller/love story becomes just another martial arts flick, as Chuck battles hordes of soldiers. C: Chuck Norris, Aki Aleong, Roland Harrah III. D: Aaron Norris. ACT [R] 101m. v

Brady Bunch Movie, The 1995 ★★★½ Surprisingly sprightly feature film version of the cult 70's TV sitcom, about a "perfect" family comprised of two parents, six kids, and a maid named Alice. The fashions, fads, and mores of the period are intact, even though the film is set in the 90's. No plot to speak of (mainly fragments borrowed from best-known episodes), just silly, harmless fun. C: Shelley Long, Gary Cole, Christopher Daniel Barnes, Henriette Mantel, RuPaul. D: Betty Thomas. COM [PG-13] 95m. v

Brady Girls Get Married, The 1981 ★★½ This pilot to the quickly canceled *The Brady Brides* series will be a disappointment to Brady fans (it's hard to believe Marcia would end up with such a loser) and detractors alike. But for the diehards, it's one of the few times the entire cast was included in a reunion. C: Robert Reed, Florence Henderson, Ann B. Davis, Maureen McCormick, Barry Williams, Christopher Knight, Mike Lookinland, Susan Olsen, Jerry Houser, Eve Plumb. D: Peter Baldwin. FAM/COM 100m. TVM

Brady's Escape 1984 U.S. ★★½ An Air Force pilot (Savage) is shot down over Hungary in WWII. Hungarian cowboys rescue him and try to smuggle him past Nazis. Interesting premise goes nowhere. (a.k.a. *The Long Ride*) C: John Savage, Kelly Reno, Ildiko Bansagi. D: Pal Gabor. ACT 92m. v

Brain Damage 1988 ★★★ Bizarrely compelling comic horror film, from the maker of *Basket Case*, about a young man's addiction to a brain-eating parasite that injects him with hallucinogens. Works as both a metaphor for drug dependency and a witty, gory shocker. C: Rick Herbst, Gordon MacDonald, Jennifer Lowry. D: Frank Henenlotter. HOR [R] 89m. v

Brain Dead 1990 ★★★½ Entrusted to unlock the mind of catatonic Cort, a doctor (Pullman) finds himself trapped in a nightmare of madness and multiple realities. Unusually ambitious low-budget chiller, with an above-average cast, keeps one guessing and gasping throughout. C: Bill Pullman, Bill Paxton, George Kennedy, Bud Cort. D: Adam Simon. HOR [R] 85m. v

Brain Donors 1992 ★★½ Farce about a shyster lawyer and two zany cohorts taking over a ballet company. Homage to the Marx Brothers doesn't make it despite high energy and outrageous gags. C: John Turturro, Bob Nelson, Mel Smith. D: Dennis Dugan. COM [PG] 79m. v

Brain Eaters, The 1958 ★★ Fuzzy, spongy, parasite things from the middle of the Earth bore to the surface and attach themselves to human necks, turning their hosts into zombielike slaves. Loosely based on Robert Heinlein's *The Puppet Masters*. The bearded alien is Leonard Nimoy! C: Joanna Lee, Jody Fair. D: Bruno Sota. SFI 60m. v

Brain from Planet Arous, The 1957 ★★★½ An evil brain takes over the body of an Earthling (Agar) in an effort to take over the planet. Luckily a good alien brain takes over the body of something close by—his dog! Interesting twist on an old plot; oddly appealing. A camp classic. C: John Agar, Joyce Meadows. D: Nathan Juran. HOR 71m. v

Brain Machine, The 1956 British ★★½ A scientist embroiled in a drug-smuggling scheme is harassed by an obnoxious machine which reads people's thoughts. Low-tech terror, of some curio value. C: Patrick Barr, Elizabeth Allan. D: Ken Hughes. HOR 72m.

Brain Smasher: A Love Story 1993 ★ Lame-brained comedy featuring Clay as a bouncer unwittingly entrusted with the protection of a fashion model from a band of ninjas. C: Andrew Dice Clay, Teri Hatcher. D: Albert Pyun. COM [PG-13] 88m. v

Brain That Wouldn't Die, The 1960 ★★½ Doctor keeps the nagging, severed head of his lover alive while he searches for the right body. A truly sick film. Has its followers; may have been before its time. C: Herb Evers, Virginia Leith. D: Joseph Green. HOR 70m. v

Brain, The 1965 German ★★★½ Kept alive in a scientist's laboratory, an evil brain outsmarts his keeper. Decent remake of *Donovan's Brain*. (a.k.a. *Vengeance*) C: Peter Van Eyck, Anne Heywood. D: Freddie Francis. HOR 83m. v

Brain, The 1969 French ★★★ Niven masterminds a train robbery, only to find several other crooks have the same idea. Zany late '60s heist comedy works best if you don't look through the holes in the plot. Dynamite cast. C: David Niven, Jean-Paul Belmondo, Bourvil, Eli Wallach. D: Gerard Oury. COM [G] 100m. v

Brainscan 1994 Canadian-U.S. ★★★ Computer-nerd (Furlong) finds himself turning into a murderer while playing an addictive new game called Brainscan. Intriguing premise falls short of the mark, due to inferior f/x and hammy Rider-Smith as the villainous

Trickster. C: Edward Furlong, Frank Langella, T Rider-Smith, Amy Hargreaves. D: John Flynn. SFI [R] 95m. V

Brainstorm 1983 ★★★½ An extraordinary invention, which reads into the human soul, may fall into the hands of a ruthless colleague in this implausible but better than average sci-fi thriller. The special effects, courtesy of Trumbull, are the real stars. Wood's last film (she died during filming). C: Christopher Walken, Natalie Wood, Louise Fletcher, Cliff Robertson. D: Douglas Trumbull. SFI [PG] 106m. V

Brainwashed 1961 German ★★★½ Nazis interogate Austrian doctor (Jurgens) who fights to maintain his sanity. Slow-paced but interesting psychological drama. C: Curt Jurgens, Claire Bloom. D: Gerd Oswald. DRA 102m.

Brainwaves 1982 ★★★★ Intriguing low-budgeter about a young woman (Love) whose frightening flashbacks after a brain operation link her to a murder victim. Nicely played thriller. C: Keir Dullea, Suzanna Love, Tony Curtis, Vera Miles. D: Ulli Lommel. HOR [PG] 83m. V

Bram Stoker's Dracula 1992 ★★★★ Coppola retells the classic vampire story in grand style, with breathtaking visuals, a strong cast, and a palpable sense of erotic menace. Oldman is excellent as the alternately vulnerable and vicious Count. Only problem: too much of everything. Deservedly won Oscars for costumes, makeup, and sound editing. C: Gary Oldman, Winona Ryder, Anthony Hopkins, Keanu Reeves, Cary Elwes, Tom Waits. D: Francis Ford Coppola. HOR [R] 128m. V

Bramble Bush, The 1960 ★★★ Trashy melodrama about a doctor with a past (Burton) returning to Cape Cod to heal the wounds of his past. Somehow Dickinson and Carson manage to breathe life into this hot air. C: Richard Burton, Barbara Rush, Jack Carson, Angie Dickinson. D: Daniel Petrie. DRA 104m. V

Brand New Life, A 1973 ★★★★½ Terrific drama, with impressive performances by Leachman and Balsam as a middle-aged, childless couple faced with wife's unexpected pregnancy. Surprisingly touching and credible. C: Cloris Leachman, Martin Balsam, Marge Redmond, Gene Nelson, Mildred Dunnock. D: Sam O'Steen. DRA 74m. TVM

Branded 1950 ★★★½ Pressured by outlaws, Ladd tells old man (Bickford) that he is his missing son, but his change of heart has a surprise outcome. Good strong drama, well played. C: Alan Ladd, Mona Freeman, Charles Bickford. D: Rudolph Mate. WST 94m. V

Brannigan 1975 British ★★★★ The Duke decks half of London hunting an escaped criminal. His bare-knuckles brawling contrasts nicely with his staid Scotland Yard partner (Attenborough). A rollicking adventure. C: John Wayne, Richard Attenborough, Judy Geeson, Mel Ferrer, Lesley-Anne Down. D: Douglas Hickox. ACT [PG] 111m. V

Brasher Doubloon, The 1947 ★★★★ Philip Marlowe (Montgomery) tries to uncover the mystery of a rare coin which has caused several killings. Compact Chandler story makes for an eerie atmospheric production. Worth watching. Previously filmed as *Time to Kill*. C: George Montgomery, Nancy Guild, Conrad Janis. D: John Brahm. CRI 72m.

Brass Bottle, The 1964 ★★½ Genie (Ives)) is ready to serve a reluctant Randall in this lamebrained comedy. Ironically, Eden became TV's *Jeannie* the same year. C: Tony Randall, Burl Ives, Barbara Eden. D: Harry Keller. COM 89m.

Brass Legend, The 1956 ★★★★ Underrated Western about cowardice and small-town prejudice from cult director Oswald. O'Brian and Burr are excellent as the hero and villain; more here than meets the eye. C: Hugh O'Brian, Nancy Gates, Raymond Burr. D: Gerd Oswald. WST 79m.

Brass Target, The 1978 ★★½ Complex thriller stretches a theory that Patton was assassinated by his staff to create a farfetched plot about a great gold caper. Occasionally plodding, but von Sydow is a great villain. C: John Cassavetes, Sophia Loren, George Kennedy, Max von Sydow, Robert Vaughn, Bruce Davison, Patrick McGoohan. D: John Hough. ACT [PG] 111m.

Bravados, The 1958 ★★★★ Grave, heroic epic stars Peck as a rancher in pursuit of his wife's murderers. King's direction is uncompromising in this grim parable about the folly of revenge and brutality. C: Gregory Peck, Joan Collins, Stephen Boyd. D: Henry King. WST 99m.

Brave Bulls, The 1951 ★★★★ Entertaining look at life behind the scenes and in the ring with a bullfighter is heightened by uniformly excellent performances. Unusual slice-of-life film, punctuated by exciting bullfighting sequence. C: Mel Ferrer, Miroslava, Anthony Quinn. D: Robert Rossen. DRA 108m.

Brave Little Toaster, The 1987 ★★★½ When a young boy is missing, his beloved household appliances come to the rescue. If kids can accept the premise, they'll enjoy this attractively drawn cartoon, with cute songs by Van Dyke Parks. Voices of Jon Lovitz, Timothy E. Day, Deanna Oliver. D: Jerry Rees. FAM/ACT 90m. V

Brave New World 1980 ★★★ Tepid and overlong TV treatment of the Aldous Huxley classic about life in the 25th century. Cast is a Who's Who of '70s cult-movie stars. C: Keir Dullea, Bud Cort, Julie Cobb, Victoria Racimo. D: Burt Brinckerhoff. SFI 150m. TVM

Brave One, The 1956 ★★★★ When a boy's pet bull is dragged off to the bull ring, the boy goes to the animal's rescue. Heartwarming, well-written story, with solid family appeal. Won an Oscar for Best Original Screenplay; since it had been written by blacklisted Dalton Trumbo, under the pen name "Robert Rich," he was only able to receive the award years later. C: Michel Ray, Rodolfo Hoyos, Fermin Rivera. D: Irving Rapper. FAM/DRA 100m.

Brave Warrior 1952 ★★★ Struggling settler (Hall) faces off against surrounding Indian tribes. Jay (Tonto) Silverheels is the standout in this otherwise forgettable tale. C: Jon Hall, Jay Silverheels, Michael Ansara. D: Spencer Bennet. WST 73m.

Brazil 1985 ★★★★ Monty Python meets Orwell: A visually stunning picture of a repressively bureaucratic society and one man's attempt to escape from it. Imaginative, surreal black comedy. C: Jonathan Pryce, Kim Greist, Robert De Niro, Katherine Helmond, Ian Holm, Bob Hoskins, Michael Palin, Ian Richardson. D: Terry Gilliam. COM [R] 131m. V

Bread and Chocolate 1978 Italian ★★★★ Charming episodic comedy about the adventures of Manfredi, an Italian immigrant trying to find fortune and acceptance in Switzerland. Manfredi carries the film with a happy goofball style. C: Nino Manfredi, Anna Karina, Johnny Dorelli. D: Franco Brusati. COM 107m.

Bread, Love and Dreams 1954 Italian ★★★★ Vittorio is pursued by Gina in this charming sex comedy; it's easy to see why legendary filmmaker De Sica was a matinee idol in '30s Italy. C: Vittorio De Sica, Gina Lollobrigida. D: Luigi Comencini. COM 90m.

Break in the Circle 1957 British ★★★ Cold War yarn has a scientist (Goring) casting his lot with a reluctant boatsman (Tucker) in trying to escape from East Germany. Pedestrian acting and direction never let this take flight. C: Forrest Tucker, Eva Bartok, Marius Goring. D: Val Guest. DRA 72m.

Break In 1980 *See* **Loophole**

Break of Hearts 1934 ★★★½ A young composer weds a world famous conductor, but their marriage leads to heartache. Moving story, fine cast. C: Katharine Hepburn, Charles Boyer, John Beal, Jean Hersholt. D: Philip Moeller. DRA 78m. V

Break the News 1938 British ★★★★ Underrated musical has Chevalier and Buchanan as rival chorus dancers, vying for the attentions of the shallow star (Knight). Funny, inventive plot twists—the boys literally start a revolution! Remake of Clair's French *La Morte en Fuite*. C: Maurice Chevalier, Jack Buchanan, June Knight, Marta Labarr, Gertrude Musgrove. D: Rene Clair. MUS 72m.

Break to Freedom 1955 British ★★★½ Another POW camp escape movie that is tasteful and at times, moving. Able direction from action veteran Gilbert. C: Anthony Steel, Jack Warner, Robert Beatty. D: Lewis Gilbert. DRA 88m.

Breaker! Breaker! 1977 ★ Norris is searching for his little brother (Augenstein) in a backwater town run by a crooked judge (Murdock). Another in the endless *Trucker vs. Smokey* movies from the late '70s. C: Chuck Norris, George Murdock, Terry O'Connor. D: Don Hulette. ACT [PG] 86m. V

Breaker Morant 1980 Australian ★★★★½ Riveting, flawlessly made film about a controversial real-life British court-martial during the Boer War. Sterling performances and high drama. Won Australian Oscar for Best Film; Thompson won for Best Actor. C: Edward Woodward, Jack Thompson, John Waters, Bryan Brown. D: Bruce Beresford. DRA [PG] 107m. V

Breakfast at Tiffany's 1961 ★★★★½ Hepburn is delightful as flighty Holly Golighty searching for romance in New York. Charming realization of Truman Capote's story. Only sour note is Mickey Rooney's distasteful portrayal of Japanese upstairs neighbor. C: Audrey Hepburn, George Peppard, Patricia Neal, Buddy Ebsen, Mickey Rooney, Martin Balsam. D: Blake Edwards. COM 114m. V

Breakfast Club, The 1985 ★★★★ The quintessential John Hughes teen flick about disgruntled students from various cliques who bond during detention in the school library. A shrewd, funny film that knows how to push the right buttons. C: Emilio Estevez, Judd Nelson, Molly Ringwald, Anthony Michael Hall, Ally Sheedy, Paul Gleason. D: John Hughes. DRA [R] 92m. V

Breakfast for Two 1937 ★★★½ Fizzy screwball comedy about a Texas heiress taming an irresponsible playboy. Marshall and Stanwyck are great fun. C: Barbara Stanwyck, Herbert Marshall, Glenda Farrell, Eric Blore. D: Alfred Santell. COM 67m.

Breakfast in Hollywood 1946 ★★★ Based on a popular radio show, this dull story rates points for zippy cameos (the Nat King Cole Trio, Spike Jones, etc.). Otherwise, dated and none too interesting. C: Tom Breneman, Bonita Granville, Beulah Bondi. D: Harold Schuster. MUS 91m. V

Breakfast in Paris 1981 Australian ★★ Two love-wary singles meet in Paris and, as luck would have it, end up in each other's arms. Pointless piffle makes the best of the locale but has all the feeling of a picture postcard. C: Barbara Parkins, Rod Mullinar. D: John Lamond. DRA 85m. V

Breakfast with Les and Bess 1984 ★★½ A married couple—he's an ex-sports writer and she's an ex-reporter—broadcast a daily society radio show from their plush apartment. Some laughs. C: Dick Van Dyke, Cloris Leachman. COM 89m. TVM V

Breakheart Pass 1976 ★★★½ A railroad agent investigates a string of mysterious murders aboard a westbound troop train. Good Bronson Western set in 1873. From a book by Alistair MacLean. C: Charles Bronson, Ben Johnson, Richard Crenna, Jill Ireland, Charles Durning. D: Tom Gries. WST [PG] 95m. V

Breakin' II: Electric Boogaloo 1984 ★★★ Dickey is in a fight to save the arts center from being demolished. So . . . she puts on a show. Amusing bits of stereotypical humor and spectacular dancing save the day . . . and the show. C: Adolfo Quinones, Lucinda Dickey. D: Sam Firstenberg. MUS [PG] 94m. V

Breakin' 1984 ★★★ Young woman (Dickey) wants to break free from dreary waitress job and dance, dance, dance. Monster hit cashed in on the *Flashdance* formula and dance craze. Inspired a popular sequel *Breakin' II*. C: Adolfo Quinones, Lucinda Dickey. D: Joel Silberg. MUS [PG] 87m. V

Breaking All the Rules 1985 Canadian ★★★ Teenage escapades at an amusement park start out with hopes of romance but turn into a clash with low-life jewel thieves. Slow-moving comedy. C: Carl Marotte, Carolyn Dunn. D: James Orr. COM [R] 91m. V

Breaking Away 1979 ★★★★★ A frequently hilarious, always endearing portrait of four recent high school graduates in Indiana trying to maintain their friendship as each begins to find his place in the real world. It's fun to see future stars Stern and Quaid in early roles, but Dooley and Barrie, as parents, may be the film's most delightful assets. Steve Tesich won a richly deserved Oscar for Best Original Screenplay. C: Dennis Christopher, Dennis Quaid, Daniel Stern, Jackie Earle Haley, Barbara Barrie, Paul Dooley. D: Peter Yates. DRA [PG] 100m. V

Breaking Glass 1980 English ★★★½ Good cast lifts rags-to-riches musical about the New Wave punk craze of the late '70s. Highlighted by amusing digs at the music biz and a howling performance by Pryce as a sax player. C: Phil Daniels, Hazel O'Connor, Jonathan Pryce. D: Brian Gibson. MUS [PG] 94m. V

Breaking Home Ties 1987 *See* **Norman Rockwell's Breaking Home Rules**

Breaking In 1989 ★★★★ Involving buddy comedy has veteran safecracking pro Reynolds revealing the tricks of his trade to eager young upstart, Siemaszko. John Sayles' script and Forsyth's direction emphasize character over comedy with pleasing results. C: Burt Reynolds, Casey Siemaszko, Sheila Kelley, Albert Salmi. D: Bill Forsyth. COM [R] 95m. V

Breaking Loose 1989 ★★ When his girlfriend is kidnapped by a vicious motorcycle gang, a young surfer has no choice but to fight back. Dreadfully violent. C: Peter Phelps, Vince Martin, Abigail, David Ngoobujjarra. D: Rod Hay. ACT 88m. V

Breaking Point 1950 ★★★ Cash-poor skipper (Garfield) in Key West rents his boat to arms smugglers. Remake of Hemingway's *To Have and Have Not* (and remade again as *The Gun Runners*). Not as good as original, but better than subsequent film. C: John Garfield, Patricia Neal, Phyllis Thaxter. D: Michael Curtiz. DRA 97m.

Breaking Point 1976 Canadian ★★½ Svenson runs from the mob after he snitches on them in court. Typical action flick. C: Bo Svenson, Robert Culp, John Colicos. D: Bob Clark. ACT [R] 92m. V

Breaking Point 1989 ★★★ Nazis tell American officer (Bernsen) the war is over and he's in a friendly hospital. Remake of *36 Hours*. C: Corbin Bernsen, Joanna Pacula, John Glover. D: Peter Markle. ACT 90m. TVM V

Breaking the Rules 1992 ★ Terminally ill young man takes buddies on road trip. C: Jason Bateman, C. Thomas Howell, Jonathan Silverman, Annie Potts. D: Neal Israel. CRI [PG-13] 100m. V

Breaking the Sound Barrier 1952 British ★★★½ Documentary-style drama about first jets, the men who flew them, and the obsessed aircraft manufacturer who set out to prove that sound barrier could be broken. Technically impressive although dramatically stiff. C: Ralph Richardson, Ann Todd, Nigel Patrick, Dinah Sheridan, Denholm Elliott. D: David Lean. DRA 109m.

Breaking Up Is Hard to Do 1979 ★★★½ Six malcontented men share a summer house and discuss divorce, marriage, and longing. Occasionally absorbing and unconventional, told from a male point of view. C: Robert Conrad, Ted Bessell, Jeff Conaway, Billy Crystal. D: Lou Antonio. DRA 150m. TVM V

Breaking with Old Ideas 1975 ★★★½ In rural China, villagers struggle with new ideas about education. A controversial and captivating study from the People's Republic of China. D: Li Wen-Hua. DRA 126m. V

Breakout 1975 ★★★½ To save a prisoner (Duvall) from a Mexican penitentiary, a chopper pilot (Bronson) swoops down for a rescue. Zesty action thriller that overcomes difficulties in plot logic by blasting away everything in sight. Fun in its own way. C: Charles Bronson, Robert Duvall, Jill Ireland, John Huston, Sheree North, Randy Quaid. D: Tom Gries. ACT [PG] 96m. V

Breakthrough 1950 ★★★½ Standard boot camp story has new recruits loving and fighting all the way to the front. Exciting action and well-developed performances give the old story a boost. C: David Brian, John Agar, Frank Lovejoy. D: Lewis Seiler. DRA 91m.

Breakthrough 1978 West German ★ German sergeant (Burton) saves the life of an American colonel (Mitchum) after a failed plot to kill Hitler. A sequel to *Cross of Iron*, this wastes the talents of its fine cast. C: Richard Burton, Robert Mitchum, Rod Steiger, Curt Jurgens. D: Andrew V. McLaglen. DRA [PG] 115m. V

Breath of Scandal, A 1960 ★★ A strong-willed Romanian princess (Loren) refuses to marry the royal mate chosen by her parents after she falls in love with an American diplomat. Period costume comedy, highlighted by Lansbury and Chevalier. Based on Molnar's play *Olympia*. C: Sophia Loren, John Gavin, Maurice Chevalier, Isabel Jeans, Angela Lansbury. D: Michael Curtiz. COM 98m. V

Breathing Fire 1991 ★★★ With an innocent girl's life on the line, a heroic young kickboxer tries his best to save her. Effective martial arts actioner. C: Bolo Yeung, Jerry Trimble, Jonathan Ke Quan. D: Lou Kennedy. ACT [R] 86m. V

Breathing Lessons 1994 ★★★★ Anne Tyler's Pulitzer Prize-winning novel gets a gentle and respectful treatment in this skillful movie. On a day of travel to a funeral, the 28-year marriage of Garner and Woodward is examined through the lens of the people they meet on the road. Nice chemistry between leads, capable supporting cast. C: James Garner, Joanne Woodward. D: John Erman. DRA 120m. TVM V

Breathless 1959 French ★★★★★ Landmark film, based on a François Truffaut story. Belmondo is terrific as a cop-killer hiding out in Paris with his American girlfriend (Seberg). This film noir parody reinvented cinematic grammar with innovative editing. Great realistic shots of Paris life. Remade in 1983. C: Jean Seberg, Jean-Paul Belmondo, Daniel Boulanger, Liliane David. D: Jean-Luc Godard. CRI 90m. V

Breathless 1983 ★★ Energetic but misguided remake of Godard's New Wave classic. This time Gere plays the charismatic bad boy on the run from the law with French girlfriend Kaprisky. Fun, but ultimately pointless. C: Richard Gere, Valerie Kaprisky, Art Metrano, John P. Ryan. D: Jim McBride. CRI [R] 105m. V

Breed Apart, A 1984 ★★ Boothe is mountaineer hired to rob bald eagle's nest of rare breed specimens, clashing with conservationist Hauer. Muddled ecological drama spiced up with a little action and romance. Notable for magnificent scenery. C: Rutger Hauer, Powers Boothe, Kathleen Turner, Donald Pleasence. D: Philippe Mora. DRA [R] 95m. V

Breezy 1973 ★★★½ May-December romance has a weary older man (Holden) falling for a kooky hippie girl (Lenz). Underrated Eastwood film delivers unexpected delights. C: William Holden, Kay Lenz. D: Clint Eastwood. DRA [R] 108m.

Brenda Starr 1976 ★★½ Dime-store script and direction doom this adaptation of Dale Messick's comic strip heroine. St. John seems out of her league in the jungles of Brazil. Hammy cast does make for some amusing moments. C: Jill St. John, Jed Allan, Sorrell Booke, Victor Buono. D: Mel Stuart. ACT 78m. TVM

Brenda Starr 1992 ★ This good-looking botch of Dale Messick's comic strip took years to be released . . . and disappeared without a whimper. Story has artist (Peck) going into his cartoon and getting involved with his heroine's life. C: Brooke Shields, Timothy Dalton, Tony Peck, Diana Scarwid. D: Robert Ellis Miller. ACT [PG] 94m. V

Brewster McCloud 1970 ★★★★ Absurdist comedy centers around a boy's ambition to build wings and sail through the Houston Astrodome. Left-field humor and disenfranchised hero may be off-putting; others find it hilarious. C: Bud Cort, Sally Kellerman, Michael Murphy, William Windom, Shelley Duvall, Rene Auberjonois, Stacy Keach, Margaret Hamilton. D: Robert Altman. COM [R] 101m. V

Brewster's Millions 1935 British ★★★★ Man inherits a fortune with one stipulation—he must first spend $500,000 in just 30 days. Witty version of a much-filmed comic story, with some elaborate musical numbers and fiesta scenes thrown in for the sheer fun of it. C: Jack Buchanan, Lili Damita, Nancy O'Neil. D: Thornton Freeland. COM 80m.

Brewster's Millions 1945 ★★★★ Delightful comedy about a returning G.I. who stands to receive a major inheritance with one catch: He must first spend $1 million within two months in order to qualify! Remade in 1985 as a vehicle for Richard Pryor. C: Dennis O'Keefe, Helen Walker, Eddie Anderson, June Havoc, Gail Patrick, Mischa Auer. D: Allan Dwan. COM 79m. V

Brewster's Millions 1985 ★★★ A minor league pitcher (Pryor) learns he'll inherit a huge fortune if he can spend one million dollars in one month. The laughs are sporadic at best in Pryor's remake of this familiar story. C: Richard Pryor, John Candy, Lonette McKee, Stephen Collins, Jerry Orbach, Pat Hingle, Tovah Feldshuh, Hume Cronyn. D: Walter Hill. COM [PG] 97m. V

Brian's Song 1970 ★★★★★ True story of the friendship between Chicago Bears football players Gale Sayers (Williams) and Brian Piccolo (Caan), a teammate dying of cancer. A deeply emotional and heartfelt drama, brought to life by an excellent script and moving performances. C: James Caan, Billy Dee Williams, Jack Warden, Judy Pace, Shelley Fabares. D: Buzz Kulik. DRA [G] 73m. TVM V

Bribe, The 1949 ★★★½ Government man (Taylor) is driven into a tizzy by beautiful singer (Gardner) in this film noir tale. Excellent cast nearly transcends trite material and aimless direction. C: Robert Taylor, Ava Gardner, Charles Laughton, Vincent Price, John Hodiak. D: Robert Z. Leonard. DRA 98m.

Bridal Path, The 1959 Scottish ★★★½ Young Scot islander searches the mainland for a lassie to marry. Utterly charming. C: Bill Travers, Bernadette O'Farrell, Alex MacKenzie, Eric Woodburn. D: Frank Launder. DRA 95m.

Bride Came C.O.D., The 1941 ★★★★ Cagney is delivery pilot who finds unlikely cargo in the form of Davis, a bride on the run from holy wedlock. Chemistry between Cagney and Davis is impeccable and the results are hilarious. C: James Cagney, Bette Davis, Stuart Erwin, Eugene Pallette, Jack Carson. D: William Keighley. COM 93m. V

Bride Comes Home, The 1935 ★★★★ Short-of-cash socialite (Colbert) uses her connections to help a sophisticate (Young) and an average guy (MacMurray), but gets caught in romantic triangle instead. Amiable comedy glides along with bright performances. C: Claudette Colbert, Fred MacMurray, Robert Young. D: Wesley Ruggles. COM 82m.

Bride for Sale 1949 ★★★ So-so comedy about tax expert (Colbert) wooed by a fake millionaire (Young). The stars are willing, the script is weak. C: Claudette Colbert, Robert Young, George Brent. D: William Russell. COM 87m.

Bride Goes Wild, The 1948 ★★★ Fast-and-loose children's author (Johnson) pretends to be widowed father (of Jenkins) so he can court straitlaced schoolteacher (Allyson). Good mix of slapstick and humor. C: Van Johnson, June Allyson, Butch Jenkins, Hume Cronyn, Una Merkel, Arlene Dahl. D: Norman Taurog. COM 98m.

Bride in Black, The 1990 ★★★ Silly melodrama about lonely woman (Lucci) who meets the man of her dreams and is devastated when he is killed on her wedding day. She vows to find the killer. Another "born to suffer" role for Lucci. C: Susan Lucci, David Soul, Finola Hughes. D: James Goldstone. DRA 100m. TVM

Bride Is Much Too Beautiful, The 1956 French ★★ Simple country woman Bardot becomes a renowned fashion model. Designed to exploit Bardot's sexy image, the film effectively achieves its superficial purpose. C: Brigitte Bardot, Micheline Presle, Louis Jourdan. D: Fred Surin. DRA 90m.

Bride of Boogedy, The 1987 ★★★ Lonely ghost haunts the home of an obnoxious family in this sequel to a TV pilot. Masur and Levy are very good in this overwrought comedy. C: Richard Masur, Mimi Kennedy. D: Oz Scott. COM 100m. TVM

Bride of Frankenstein, The 1935 ★★★★½ Dr. Frankenstein is at it again, this time creating a mate for his monster. Classic sequel to *Frankenstein* humanizes the creature while still providing plenty of scares. Highlighted by Lanchester's eerie performance as the "bride." C: Boris Karloff, Colin Clive, Valerie Hobson, Ernest Thesiger, Elsa Lanchester, Una O'Connor, John Carradine. D: James Whale. HOR 75m. V

Bride of Re-Animator 1990 ★★★ Follow-up to the cult hit *Re-Animator* finds Dr. West (Combs, terrific again) venturing into Frankenstein territory, attempting to create a living woman from body parts. Not as fresh or witty as the first, but swift (and extremely gruesome) fun. C: Jeffrey Combs, Bruce Abbott, Claude Jones. D: Brian Yuzna. HOR [R] 99m. V

Bride of the Gorilla 1951 ★★ Overseer of a tropical plantation (Burr) kills his employer but falls under native curse, leading him to think he's a gorilla. Good performances, average horror flick. C: Raymond Burr, Barbara Payton, Lon Chaney, Jr. D: Curt Siodmak. HOR 76m. V

Bride of the Monster 1955 ★ Mad scientist (Lugosi) attempts to create a race of superhumans and menaces reporter (King) in a swamp-bound mansion. Ultracheap and generally inept. C: Bela Lugosi, Tor Johnson, Tony McCoy, Loretta King. D: Edward D. Wood, Jr. HOR 78m. V

Bride of Vengeance 1949 ★★★ Ponderous historical drama about the Borgia family in medieval Italy. Generally unsuccessful but intriguing costume drama. C: Paulette Goddard, John Lund, Macdonald Carey, Raymond Burr. D: Mitchell Leisen. DRA 91m.

Bride, The 1974 *See* **House that Cried Murder, The**

Bride, The 1985 ★★½ Revisionist remake of *Bride of Frankenstein* suffers from pallid performances by Sting as the good doctor and Beals as his creation; Brown as male creature and Rappaport as circus performer he befriends come off better. Scares eclipsed by ineffective moralizing. C: Sting, Jennifer Beals, Clancy Brown, David Rappaport, Geraldine Page, Quentin Crisp. D: Franc Roddam. HOR [PG-13] 118m. V

Bride Walks Out, The 1936 ★★½ Former model and newlywed (Stanwyck) with tastes beyond the modest salary brought home by her devoted husband (Raymond) veers toward a millionaire (Young), then realizes her mistake and returns to domestic life. Marital comedy. C: Barbara Stanwyck, Gene Raymond, Robert Young, Ned Sparks, Helen Broderick, Hattie McDaniel. D: Leigh Jason. COM 81m.

Bride Wore Black, The 1968 French ★★★★ Truffaut's Hitchcock salute, complete with Bernard Hermann score. A woman (Moreau) tracks down and kills the men who killed her husband (accidentally) on their wedding day. Doesn't entirely work as a suspense thriller, but still entertaining and interesting. C: Jeanne Moreau, Claude Rich, Jean-Claude Brialy, Michel Bouquet. D: Francois Truffaut. CRI 108m. V

Bride Wore Boots, The 1946 ★★½ Marital farce about horse-crazy Stanwyck's attempts to break in her greenhorn spouse Cummings. Leads try hard in one-joke story. C: Barbara Stanwyck, Robert Cummings, Diana Lynn, Peggy Wood, Robert Benchley, Natalie Wood. D: Irving Pichel. COM 86m. V

Bride Wore Red, The 1937 ★★ Familiar Crawford "working her way up the ladder" story. This time she's a cabaret singer posing as a society girl to snag a rich husband. C: Joan Crawford, Franchot Tone, Robert Young, Billie Burke, Reginald Owen. D: Dorothy Arzner. DRA 103m. v

Brides of Dracula 1960 British ★★★ Baroness keeps vampire son chained in castle until he is unwittingly released by visitor to prey on local women. Above-average production values keep this from being just another in a long line of sequels. C: Peter Cushing, Martita Hunt, Yvonne Monlaur, Freda Jackson. D: Terence Fisher. HOR 86m. v

Brides of Fu Manchu, The 1966 British ★★★½ Lee reprises one of his best roles as the maniacal Fu. This time he and his scientists have the world on the brink of the apocalypse. Lee flourishes in this otherwise second-rate sequel. C: Christopher Lee, Douglas Wilmer, Marie Versini. D: Don Sharp. ACT 94m.

Brideshead Revisited ★★★★★ The series that launched Irons and Andrews in America. A marvelously restrained, yet emotionally compelling story of a young Englishman who becomes involved with a rapidly deteriorating British family and finds he can do nothing to save them. Beautifully shot and sumptuously designed, with a wonderful cast. Based on the novel by Evelyn Waugh. C: Jeremy Irons, Anthony Andrews, Laurence Olivier, Claire Bloom. DRA 588m. TVM v

Bridge Across Time 1985 ★★★ After London Bridge is moved to Arizona, law officials are puzzled by a series of murders, until they realize the killer is the ghost of Jack the Ripper! Television movie plays silly premise in laughably earnest fashion. (a.k.a. *Arizona Ripper* and *Terror at London Bridge*) C: David Hasselhoff, Stepfanie Kramer, Adrienne Barbeau, Rose Marie. D: E.W. Swackhamer. CRI 100m. TVM

Bridge at Remagen, The 1969 ★★★ War movie and history buffs will appreciate this well-acted and red-blooded action film based on the Allied fight to capture a key bridge from the Nazis in WWII. Otherwise pretty predictable fare. C: George Segal, Robert Vaughn, Ben Gazzara, Bradford Dillman, E. G. Marshall. D: John Guillermin. ACT [PG] 115m. v

Bridge of San Luis Rey, The 1944 ★★½ Ponderous adaptation of Wilder's novel tracing lives of five people killed when a rope bridge breaks in 18th-century Peru. C: Lynn Bari, Nazimova, Louis Calhern, Akim Tamiroff, Francis Lederer, Blanche Yurka. D: Rowland Lee. DRA 89m.

Bridge on the River Kwai, The 1957 British ★★★★★ Led by their by-the-book C.O. (Guinness), British POWs in a Japanese labor camp build a bridge that will carry enemy troops and arms through the Burmese jungle. As much a character study of Guinness and Hayakawa—playing the equally stubborn Japanese commander—as a commentary on the futility of war. Based on Pierre Boulle's novel. Won Oscars for Best Picture, Director, Actor (Guinness), Cinematography, Editing, Scoring, and Screenplay. C: William Holden, Alec Guinness, Jack Hawkins, Sessue Hayakawa. D: David Lean. DRA [PG] 162m. v

Bridge, The 1960 German ★★★ Underaged boys are drafted into Hitler's army to stave off the advancing Allies. An uncompromising look at Nazi horrors has earnest performances and a gritty subject that make this tough viewing. C: Folker Bohnet, Fritz Wepper, Michael Hinz. D: Bernhard Wicki. DRA 100m.

Bridge to Silence 1989 ★★★½ After surviving a car crash in which her husband died, a hearing-impaired widow (Matlin) tries to fend off her mother's attempt to gain custody of her daughter. Slick soap opera works due to strong performances from Matlin and Remick. C: Lee Remick, Marlee Matlin, Michael O'Keefe, Josef Sommer, Phyllis Frelich. D: Karen Arthur. DRA 100m. TVM v

Bridge to the Sun 1961 U.S. ★★★ An American woman (Baker) contends with prejudice and illness in Japan during WWII when she elects to stay with her Asian husband. Provocative subject matter given generally melodramatic treatment. C: Carroll Baker, James Shigeta, James Yagi. D: Etienne Perier. DRA 113m.

Bridge Too Far, A 1977 British ★★★ Attenborough's bland re-creation of Operation Market Garden, the ill-fated WWII Allied campaign to capture strategic bridges. Star-studded cast can't do much with plodding story line. C: Dirk Bogarde, James Caan, Michael Caine, Sean Connery, Edward Fox, Elliott Gould, Gene Hackman, Anthony Hopkins, Liv Ullmann, Laurence Olivier, Ryan O'Neal, Robert Redford, Maximilian Schell. D: Richard Attenborough. DRA [PG] 175m. v

Bridges at Toko-Ri, The 1954 ★★★★ Oscar-winning special effects highlight Robson's compelling adaptation of James Michener's novel, with pilot Holden torn between duty and conscience during the Korean War. Riveting flying sequences—the climactic bombing sequence helped inspire the Death Star raid in *Star Wars*. C: William Holden, Grace Kelly, Fredric March, Mickey Rooney. D: Mark Robson. ACT 103m. v

Brief Encounter 1945 British ★★★★★ One of the most romantic films ever made, adapted by Noel Coward from his play. Howard and Johnson, both in solid but dull marriages, both middle class and middle aged, are helplessly drawn together. Brilliantly acted and directed; one of the truly memorable screen love stories. C: Celia

Johnson, Trevor Howard, Stanley Holloway, Joyce Carey. D: David Lean. DRA 86m. V

Brief Encounter 1974 ★ Painfully misguided remake of David Lean's inspired romantic drama, as bad as its predecessor is good. A low point in Burton's checkered screen career. C: Richard Burton, Sophia Loren. D: Alan Bridges. DRA 103m. TVM

Brief History of Time, A 1992 U.S. ★★★★ Fascinating chronicle of British scientist Stephen Hawking, who has not allowed debilitating Lou Gehrig's Disease to prevent him from continuing his work in quantum physics. Director Morris allows viewers to enter the world of this genius and make sense of it as well. D: Errol Morris. DOC [G] 84m. V

Brief Vacation, A 1973 Italian ★★★★ A poor Calabrian woman is so overworked by her husband that she collapses from TB and is sent to a sanitarium, where she discovers a more refined world via a handsome lover. Bolkan's bravura performance brings this simple, affecting story to life. C: Florinda Bolkan, Renato Salvatori. D: Vittorio De Sica. DRA [PG] 106m.

Brigadoon 1954 ★★★★ Film version of Lerner and Loewe's haunting stage musical, about an American finding love in an enchanated Scottish town which only awakens for a day every 100 years. The story still weaves its magic, the music is charming, and Kelly and Charisse dancing to "Heather on the Hill" are delightful. C: Gene Kelly, Van Johnson, Cyd Charisse. D: Vincente Minnelli. FAM/MUS 108m. V

Brigand of Kandahar, The 1965 British ★★★ A soldier (Reed) faces native uprisings in a Victorian Indian outpost. Quirky direction tries to cover the total lack of a story line. C: Ronald Lewis, Oliver Reed, Yvonne Romain. D: John Gilling. DRA 81m.

Brigand, The 1952 ★★ Dexter plays both Spanish king and his commoner look-alike who becomes involved with royal affairs. Lots of costumes but stiff dialogue and listless plot development. C: Anthony Dexter, Anthony Quinn, Gale Robbins. D: Phil Karlson. DRA 94m.

Brigham Young 1940 ★★★ The great Mormon leader and his followers on their epic journey to Utah. An admirable effort that isn't quite all it should be. Power and Darnell provide a romantic spark. C: Tyrone Power, Linda Darnell, Dean Jagger, Brian Donlevy, John Carradine, Jane Darwell, Mary Astor, Vincent Price. D: Henry Hathaway. DRA 114m.

Bright Angel 1991 ★★★★ A disconnected boy (Mulroney) assists a drifting girl (Taylor) in her plan to get her brother out of jail. Isolated Big Sky Country locations add credibility to the desperation of the lead characters. C: Dermot Mulroney, Lili Taylor, Sam Shepard, Burt Young, Valerie Perrine. D: Michael Fields. DRA [R] 94m. V

Bright Eyes 1934 ★★★★½ Irresistible child star Temple shines in one of her first films, the story of an orphan caught in a custody battle. And if that's not enough, we have "On the Good Ship Lollipop," too! Dunn and Withers are exceptional. C: Shirley Temple, James Dunn, Judith Allen, Jane Withers. D: David Butler. FAM/DRA [PG] 90m. V

Bright Leaf 1950 ★★★½ Cooper stars as a tobacco farmer who battles rivals, woos Bacall, and ends up as cigarette baron. Nicely acted drama. C: Gary Cooper, Lauren Bacall, Patricia Neal, Jack Carson, Donald Crisp. D: Michael Curtiz. DRA 110m.

Bright Lights, Big City 1988 ★★★ Midwesterner Fox is undone by high living when he gets swept into the cocaine-fueled life of New York's yuppie fast lane. An earnest but somewhat shallow adaptation of Jay McInerney's best-seller, features a first-rate performance by Sutherland as Fox's substance-abusing friend. C: Michael J. Fox, Kiefer Sutherland, Phoebe Cates, Swoosie Kurtz, Frances Sternhagen, John Houseman, Jason Robards, Dianne Wiest. D: James Bridges. DRA [R] 108m. V

Bright Lights 1935 ★★★½ Eccentric couple (Brown and Dvorak), on their way to the big time, split up. Typical breathless Warner Brothers pace fights clichés. C: Joe E. Brown, Ann Dvorak, Patricia Ellis. D: Busby Berkeley. DRA 83m.

Bright Road 1953 ★★★ Dandridge takes an interest in several students and their problems in a small-town school. Belafonte's first film. C: Dorothy Dandridge, Harry Belafonte, Robert Horton. D: Gerald Mayer. DRA 69m.

Bright Victory 1951 ★★★★ When Kennedy is blinded during WWII combat, he believes his life is over. Sent to rehab unit, he grows bitter until Dow arrives and gives him courage to go on. Well-handled drama of human spirit that doesn't overplay sentimental aspects. Look for very young Rock Hudson in bit part. C: Arthur Kennedy, Peggy Dow, Julie Adams, James Edwards, Will Geer. D: Mark Robson. DRA 97m.

Brighton Beach Memoirs 1986 ★★★½ Coming of age in 1937 Brooklyn isn't easy when your family and your aunt's live under the same roof—but it can be funny. Neil Simon's first entry in his autobiographical series charms, even though Danner and Ivey are miscast as Jewish matrons. Followed by *Biloxi Blues* and *Broadway Bound*. C: Blythe Danner, Bob Dishy, Jonathan Silverman, Judith Ivey, Jason Alexander. D: Gene Saks. COM [PG-13] 110m. V

Brighton Rock 1947 British ★★★★ The ruthless teenage leader of a racetrack gang (Attenborough) commits murder, using an innocent waitress as his alibi. Afraid she'll expose him, he marries her, hoping to drive her to suicide. Brutal and effective; based on the novel by Graham Greene. C: Richard Attenborough, Carol Marsh, Hermione Baddeley. D: John Boulting. CRI 86m.

Brighton Strangler, The 1945 ★★★ Actor (Loder) becomes a demented strangler—thrown over the top by a Nazi air raid. Decent thriller, but strains for credibility. C: John Loder, June Duprez, Michael Angel. D: Max Nosseck. CRI 67m.

Brighty of the Grand Canyon 1967 ★★★ A grizzled old prospector (Foran) and his spunky little mule discover gold in the Grand Canyon. Taken from a popular children's book, story is slow-going but pleasant enough, with great Southwestern scenery. C: Joseph Cotten, Pat Conway, Karl Swensen. D: Norman Foster. FAM/WST 90m. V

Brimstone and Treacle 1982 British ★★★ Uneven thriller with dark religious underpinnings and a demonic performance by Sting as a cunning stranger who sweet-talks his way into the household of an atheist hymn composer with a devout wife and comatose daughter. The rocker sings the closing theme. C: Sting, Denholm Elliott, Joan Plowright, Suzanna Hamilton. D: Richard Loncraine. DRA [R] 85m. V

Brimstone 1949 ★★★ When a cattle rustler and his brood cause trouble, a marshal goes undercover to put a stop to the gang. Typical B-Western action. C: Rod Cameron, Walter Brennan, Forrest Tucker. D: Joseph Kane. WST 90m.

Bring 'Em Back Alive 1932 ★★★½ Real-life Great White Hunter Buck dramatizes his jungle exploits. Huge hit upon its release, now remembered for its corny style and cleverly edited sleight-of-hand. Much later, it became a TV series. C: Frank Buck. D: Clyde Elliott. DOC

Bring Me the Head of Alfredo Garcia 1974 ★★★★ Corrupt millionaire hires down-and-out bar owner Oates to kill the man who slept with his daughter. The guy's already dead, so Oates brings back the next best thing—his head, but other would-be killers want it too. Bloody and filled with trademark Peckinpah violence. C: Warren Oates, Isela Vega, Gig Young, Robert Webber, Helmut Dantine, Kris Kristofferson. D: Sam Peckinpah. ACT [R] 113m. V

Bring Me the Head of Dobie Gillis 1988 ★★★ Reprise of cult TV show *The Many Lives of Dobie Gillis* suffers from the usual reunion malaise as a middle-aged Dobie is tempted by the beautiful Thalia (Stevens). Amiable enough, but the old show's far more fun. C: Dwayne Hickman, Bob Denver, Connie Stevens. D: Stanley Cherry. COM 100m. TVM

Bring on the Girls 1945 ★★★ Musical tells tale of millionaire (Bracken) impersonating a sailor to test Lake's love for him. Yvonne De Carlo is a hatcheck attendant; comedy band Spike Jones & City Slickers is a plus. C: Veronica Lake, Sonny Tufts, Eddie Bracken, Marjorie Reynolds. D: Sidney Lanfield. MUS 92m.

Bring on the Night 1984 British ★★★★ Straightforward documentary about ex-Police member Sting's new band benefits from great music making; high point is finale, the group's first live show in Paris. Entertaining sidebar to Sting's "Dream of the Blue Turtles" album. C: Sting. D: Michael Apted. DOC [PG-13] 97m. V

Bring Your Smile Along 1955 ★★★ Tin Pan Alley romance has Towers and Brasselle teaming up to write songs for Laine, who shines in a rare star turn. Pretty standard musical fare; Edwards' directing debut. C: Frankie Laine, Keefe Brasselle, Constance Towers, Jack Albertson. D: Blake Edwards. MUS 83m.

Bringing Up Baby 1938 ★★★★★ An eccentric heiress (Hepburn) chases a forgetful zoologist (Grant) who is chasing an important dinosaur bone stolen by her dog. They also chase a leopard—named Baby. Terrific star chemistry (and rotten singing) are only part of perhaps the greatest screwball comedy ever. C: Cary Grant, Katharine Hepburn, Charlie Ruggles, May Robson, Barry Fitzgerald. D: Howard Hawks. COM 102m. V

Brink of Life 1958 Swedish ★★★ Despite the heavy-hitting cast, this is minor Bergman, a look at a group of women and their interactions in a maternity ward. Too much brooding hampers routine story. C: Eva Dahlbeck, Ingrid Thulin, Bibi Andersson, Erland Josephson, Max von Sydow. D: Ingmar Bergman. DRA 84m.

Brink's Job, The 1978 ★★★★ Fact-based fable about a gang of ragtag losers who somehow manage to pull off the heist of a lifetime. Endearing performances make this enchanting and comic. C: Peter Falk, Peter Boyle, Warren Oates, Gena Rowlands, Paul Sorvino. D: William Friedkin. COM [PG] 103m. V

Britannia Hospital 1982 British ★★★★ British satire presents a hospital beset by countless woes as it attempts to prepare for a visit by the Queen. Frantic comedy scores often and hard with its irreverent humor. C: Leonard Rossiter, Graham Crowden, Malcolm McDowell, Joan Plowright, Jill Bennett. D: Lindsay Anderson. COM [R] 111m. V

Britannia Mews 1949 *See* **Forbidden Street, The**

British Agent 1934 ★★★½ A British agent (Howard) is mesmerized by a Soviet (Francis) in this witty rendering of the days leading up to the Russian Revolution. Kay is worth the price of admission alone. C: Kay Francis, Leslie Howard, William Gargan, J. Carroll Naish, Cesar Romero. D: Michael Curtiz. DRA 81m.

British Intelligence 1940 ★★★½ Karloff is a butler by day and spy by night in a British war official's residence, where a German woman (Lindsay) is staying as a guest. Lindsay makes a savvy adversary to Karloff's villain in this entertaining espionage caper. Remake of *Three Faces East.* C: Boris Karloff, Margaret Lindsay. Maris Wrixon, Holmes Herbert. D: Terry Morse. DRA 62m.

Broadcast News 1987 ★★★★½ A look behind the scenes at a network news bureau where the anchor's a dumb pretty boy, the producer an obsessive perfectionist, and the best reporter has no on-camera charisma. Lively mix of comedy, drama, and romantic triangle, with knockout performances by Hunter, Hurt, and Brooks. C: William Hurt, Albert Brooks, Holly Hunter, Robert Prosky, Joan Cusack, Jack Nicholson. D: James L. Brooks. COM [R] 132m. V

Broadminded 1931 ★★★½ This comedy was a vehicle for the trademark "gosh shucks" style of Brown. Lugosi has a great cameo as a man whose hotdog is stolen. Generally pleasant and amusing. C: Joe E. Brown, William Collier, Jr., Margaret Livingston, Thelma Todd, Bela Lugosi. D: Mervyn LeRoy. COM 72m.

Broadway 1929 ★★★½ A gangster reminisces about his younger days of thrills and spills. Memorable mainly for its technically innovative camerawork and photography. Remade in 1942. C: Glenn Tryon, Evelyn Brent, Merna Kennedy, Robert Ellis. D: Paul Fejos. DRA 105m.

Broadway 1942 ★★★★ Famous dancer (Raft) returns to his old haunts and remembers his days as a young hoofer during Prohibition. Loose remake of 1929 film, parallels Raft's own life in many ways; many terrific numbers. C: George Raft, Pat O'Brien, Janet Blair, Broderick Crawford, Marjorie Rambeau, S. Z. Sakall. D: William Seiter. MUS 91m.

Broadway Bad 1933 ★★★½ A dancer (Blondell) is slandered by her slimy husband (Cortez), so she turns the tables and uses the publicity for star coverage. Punchy Warner Brothers melodrama. Rogers stands out in a supporting role. C: Joan Blondell, Ricardo Cortez, Ginger Rogers. D: Sidney Lanfield. DRA 61m.

Broadway Bill 1934 ★★★★ Cheery comedy about a reformed gambler (Baxter) who risks everything on a racehorse named Broadway Bill. Lovely support by Loy as Baxter's loyal sister-in-law. Remade by Capra as *Riding High.* C: Warner Baxter, Myrna Loy, Walter Connolly, Helen Vinson, Margaret Hamilton. D: Frank Capra. COM 100m. V

Broadway Bound 1992 ★★★★ Third in Neil Simon's autobiographical trilogy focuses on a weary Brooklyn matriarch (Bancroft), based on his mother, and her broken dreams. Not as effective as *Brighton Beach Memoirs* or *Biloxi Blues*, but still well worth seeing. (a.k.a. *Neil Simon's Broadway Bound*) C: Anne Bancroft, Hume Cronyn, Jonathan Silverman, Jerry Orbach, Michele Lee, Corey Parker. D: Paul Bogart. COM 100m. TVM V

Broadway Danny Rose 1984 ★★★★ Warm, funny showbiz comedy about a loser talent agent (Allen) with a big heart. His adventures with a tough cookie (Farrow) and her boozy singer boyfriend (Forte) have an oddball sweetness that's charming. C: Woody Allen, Mia Farrow, Nick Apollo Forte. D: Woody Allen. COM [PG] 85m. V

Broadway Gondolier 1935 ★★★½ Highly charged musical has pretty boy singer (Powell) hounding a Belascoesque producer (Menjou) for his big break. Director Bacon squeezes everything he can out of rehashed Warners' formula. C: Dick Powell, Joan Blondell, Adolphe Menjou. D: Lloyd Bacon. MUS 98m.

Broadway Limited 1941 ★★ Young actress (Woodworth) suffers embarrassment as the result of a publicity stunt gone haywire. Weak backstage fluff. Despite McLaglen and Pitts, this film is lifeless. C: Dennis O'Keefe, Victor McLaglen, Marjorie Woodworth, ZaSu Pitts, Patsy Kelly. D: Gordon Douglas. DRA 74m.

Broadway Melody of 1940 1940 ★★★★ Plot about partners (Astaire and Murphy) fighting over love interest (Powell) doesn't get in the way of marvelous Cole Porter songs performed to a fare-thee-well by Fred and Eleanor. Highlight: "Begin the Beguine." C: Fred Astaire, Eleanor Powell, George Murphy, Frank Morgan. D: Norman Taurog. MUS 103m. V

Broadway Melody of 1938 1937 ★★★½ Boardinghouse full of Broadway hopefuls provides backdrop for pleasant musical numbers by all-star cast. Powell's energetic, as usual, and this *Melody* includes Judy's classic rendition of "Dear Mr. Gable/You Made Me Love You." C: Robert Taylor, Eleanor Powell, Judy Garland, Sophie Tucker, Binnie Barnes, Buddy Ebsen. D: Roy Del Ruth. MUS 113m. V

Broadway Melody of 1936 1935 ★★★★ Snappy tap-fest for Powell hung on slim plot of a Broadway columnist (Benny) blackmailing a producer (Taylor). Great dance numbers include "Broadway Rhythm" and "You Are My Lucky Star." Delightful musical. C: Jack Benny, Eleanor Powell, Robert Taylor, Una Merkel, Buddy Ebsen. D: Roy Del Ruth. MUS 105m. V

Broadway Melody, The 1929 ★★★ Antique sound musical, winner of Best Picture Oscar. Sibling chorus girls (Love and Page) vie for song and dance man (King). Stagy and dated, but the songs, including "You Were Meant For Me," are as good as new. C: Bessie Love, Anita Page, Charles King. D: Harry Beaumont. MUS 111m. V

Broadway Musketeers 1938 ★★★½ Three childhood friends look for a break on the Great White Way. The plot creaks and groans but still has its moments; Sheridan walks away with acting honors. Remake of *Three on*

a Match. C: Margaret Lindsay, Ann Sheridan, Marie Wilson. D: John Farrow. DRA 62m.

Broadway Rhythm 1944 ★★½ MGM revue doesn't have the big stars one expects from such films, but does have the old Broadway producer (Murphy) having troubles putting on a show. One gorgeous song: Kern and Hammerstein's "All the Things You Are." C: George Murphy, Ginny Simms, Charles Winninger, Gloria De Haven, Nancy Walker, Tommy Dorsey Orchestra. D: Roy Del Ruth. MUS 111m. V

Broadway Serenade 1939 ★★★ Songwriter Ayres and singer MacDonald must struggle to keep their two-career marriage together. Dated musical, notable for Busby Berkeley finale. C: Jeanette MacDonald, Lew Ayres, Ian Hunter, Frank Morgan, Rita Johnson. D: Robert Z. Leonard. MUS 114m. V

Broadway Through a Keyhole 1933 ★★★½ Brisk direction bolsters this tale of a gangster's love for a cabaret singer. Dated but entertaining. C: Constance Cummings, Russ Columbo, Paul Kelly, Blossom Seeley, Gregory Ratoff, Texas Guinan. D: Lowell Sherman. DRA 90m.

Broadway to Hollywood 1933 ★★★ Spanning 50 years and three generations, this showbiz saga has marvelous atmosphere. Rooney, 10 at the time, steals every scene he's in. Nelson Eddy's film debut. C: Alice Brady, Frank Morgan, Jackie Cooper, Russell Hardie, Madge Evans, Mickey Rooney. D: Willard Mack. MUS 85m.

Broken Arrow 1950 ★★★★ Widowed Indian agent Tom Jeffords attempts to make a lasting peace with war chief Cochise and the Chiricahua Apaches in the 1870s. Fine Stewart western, told from the Native Americans' perspective, helped change the way Native Americans are portrayed in westerns. C: James Stewart, Jeff Chandler, Debra Paget, Will Geer. D: Delmer Daves. WST 93m. V

Broken Blossoms 1919 ★★★★ Tragic, sentimental story of a Chinese boy's (Barthelmess) "pure" love and concern for a white girl (Gish) abused by her evil father (Crisp). Excellent acting and direction keep the film from becoming morbid or overly melodramatic. C: Lillian Gish, Richard Barthelmess, Donald Crisp. D: D. W. Griffith. DRA 88m. V

Broken Chain, The 1993 ★★★★ Two Native American braves find their friendship threatened by the French and Indian Wars, during the 1700's. Handsome, engrossing history lesson, courtesy of Turner Entertainment's "Native American Series" of telefilms. C: Eric Schweig, Wes Studi, Pierce Brosnan, Graham Greene, Buffy Sainte-Marie. D: Lamont Johnson. DRA 100m. TVM V

Broken Journey 1948 ★★★ Good cast in familiar story of plane crash victims' struggle to survive. C: Phyllis Calvert, Margot Grahame, James Donald, Francis L. Sullivan, Derek Bond, David Tomlinson. D: Ken Annakin. DRA 89m.

Broken Lance 1954 ★★★★ Iron-fisted cattle baron (Tracy) finds the control he once wielded over his family and business slipping through his fingers. An excellent Tracy is the highlight in this sometimes melodramatic sagebrush remake of *House of Strangers*. C: Spencer Tracy, Robert Wagner, Jean Peters, Richard Widmark, Katy Jurado, Hugh O'Brian, E.G. Marshall. D: Edward Dmytryk. WST 96m. V

Broken Land, The 1962 ★★★ Sheriff (Taylor) gets pleasure out of making everybody miserable in this cheaply made Western. Look for Nicholson in an uncharacteristic role as Taylor's whipping boy. C: Kent Taylor, Dianna Darrin, Jody McCrea, Jack Nicholson. D: John Bushelman. WST 60m.

Broken Lullaby 1932 ★★★★ After taking a life in midst of WWI battle, French soldier is filled with remorse and tries to make it up to dead enemy's sweetheart, whom he grows to love himself. Intriguing drama gracefully handles difficult emotions.(a.k.a. *The Man I Killed*) C: Lionel Barrymore, Nancy Carroll, ZaSu Pitts. D: Ernst Lubitsch. DRA 77m.

Broken Rainbow 1985 ★★★★½ Forced relocation of Navajo Indians from Arizona makes for unusually strong documentary that makes no bones about its pro-Navajo stance. Narrated by Martin Sheen; Oscar for Best Documentary. Voice of Burgess Meredith. D: Maria Florio, Victoria Mudd. DOC 70m.

Broken Sky 1982 Swedish ★★★ Teenage girl has to make hard decisions during her coming of age. Story never quite jells. Director Thulin (*Wild Strawberries*) authored the screenplay. C: Susanna Kall, Thommy Berggren. D: Ingrid Thulin. DRA 96m.

Bronco Billy 1980 ★★★★ An heiress flees from her ill-advised wedding and joins a ragtag Wild West show run by a self-made matinee cowboy hero. Whimsical satire refreshes as it delights. Eastwood's broad performance is a hoot. C: Clint Eastwood, Sondra Locke, Geoffrey Lewis, Scatman Crothers. D: Clint Eastwood. COM [PG] 117m. V

Bronco Buster 1952 ★★★½ Capable rodeo story concerns a young buckaroo (Brady) in love with the girlfriend (Holden) of his tutor (Lund). Brisk direction from Western master Boetticher makes for a good show. C: John Lund, Scott Brady, Joyce Holden, Chill Wills. D: Budd Boetticher. WST 81m.

Bronk 1975 ★★★ Pilot for TV series has cop (Palance) battling his superiors and the Mob after his partner dies mysteriously. Palance is always interesting, but this is nothing special. C: Jack Palance, Henry Beckman, Tony King. D: Richard Donner. ACT 74m. TVM

Brontë 1983 Irish ★★★★ Harris flies solo as Charlotte Brontë in this noble, if stagy attempt at re-creating the great writer's life. An unusual, one-woman film shot on location in

Ireland. C: Julie Harris. D: Delbert Mann. DRA 88m.

Brontë Sisters, The 1979 French ★★★ Big, lush, and boring biography of famed literary sisters that goes nowhere despite megatalented ensemble. Great costumes and sets can't cover slow plot development. C: Isabelle Adjani, Marie-France Pisier, Isabelle Huppert. D: Andre Techine. DRA 115m.

Bronx Executioner, The 1986 ★★★ Far into the future, gangs of roving Androids fight it out with their human rivals until the humans call upon robot replicants to help them. Interesting effects and some chills. C: Gabriel Gori, Chuck Valenti, Margie Newton, Rob Robinson. D: Bob Collins. SFI 88m. V

Bronx Tale, A 1993 ★★★★ Young boy growing up in '60s NYC is torn between loyalty to his busdriver father (De Niro) and local gangster (Palmintieri, who wrote script and source material). De Niro's directorial debut owes a lot—in fact, too much—to Scorsese. C: Robert De Niro, Chazz Palminteri, Francis Capra, Lillo Brancato. D: Robert De Niro. DRA [R] 122m. V

Bronx War, The 1991 ★★ Violent, unlikely tale of a drug dealer with a heart of gold. Urban drama uneasily vacillates between mayhem and social consciousness-raising. C: Joseph, Fabio Urena, Charmaine Cruz, Andre Brown. D: Joseph B. Vasquez. DRA [R] 91m. V

Brood, The 1979 Canadian ★★★½ Cronenberg's finest hour in the low-budget arena, exploring the psychology of rage as disturbed Eggar, under the tutelage of unorthodox doctor Reed, literally gives birth to the murderous children of her anger. Graphic, intelligent, and terrifying. C: Oliver Reed, Samantha Eggar, Art Hindle. D: David Cronenberg. HOR [R] 92m. V

Broth of a Boy 1959 Irish ★★★★ Quiet, insightful tale of a TV exec trying to do a story on the birthday of the world's oldest man, with the sly senior citizen wanting his share of the spoils. Intelligent story, with quaint Irish locale. C: Barry Fitzgerald, Harry Brogan. D: George Pollock. COM 77m.

Brother, Can You Spare a Dime? 1975 ★★★ Depression-era documentary juxtaposes newsreels with Hollywood fiction. D: Philippe Mora. DOC [PG] 106m. V

Brother from Another Planet, The 1984 ★★★★ This imaginative film stars an excellent Morton as a mute alien whose silence is variously misinterpreted by Earthlings. More a social commentary with humor than a sci-fi film. Brilliantly written by Sayles. A fine example of quality on a low, low budget. C: Joe Morton, Darryl Edwards, Steve James. D: John Sayles. SFI 109m. V

Brother John 1970 ★★★★ Enigmatic Poitier stirs up a small Southern town where he's hailed as the Messiah by some and feared by others. A fascinating fantasy. C: Sidney Poitier, Will Geer, Bradford Dillman, Beverly Todd, Paul Winfield. D: James Goldstone. DRA [PG] 94m. V

Brother Minister: The Assassination of Malcolm X 1995 ★★★½ Hard-hitting, somewhat exploitative documentary attempts to prove that Louis Farrakhan orchestrated Malcolm X's death in 1965. Browne narrates assortment of clips and interviews which hold interest. C: Roscoe Lee Browne. D: Jack Baxter, Jefri Aalmuhammed. DOC 120m.

Brother Orchid 1940 ★★★★ When gangster Robinson's former territory is usurped by Bogart, the ex-bad guy takes refuge in an order of monks. Great tongue-in-cheek genre parody, expertly played by two leads. Montages were created by future director Don Siegel. Some violence. C: Edward G. Robinson, Ann Sothern, Humphrey Bogart, Ralph Bellamy, Donald Crisp. D: Lloyd Bacon. COM 87m. V

Brother Rat 1938 ★★★ Capers and conundrums of three cadets (Reagan, Morris, and Albert) at Virginia Military Institute and Albert's efforts to conceal existence of his expectant wife. Albert stands out in role he created on Broadway. Remade as *About Face.* C: Priscilla Lane, Wayne Morris, Jane Bryan, Eddie Albert, Ronald Reagan, Jane Wyman. D: William Keighley. COM 90m.

Brother Rat and a Baby ★★★ Sequel to *Brother Rat* continues the story of three buddies at the Virginia Military Institute who are now graduating, with Albert possibly returning as a football coach. Comic spark isn't as bright, but still entertaining. C: Priscilla Lane, Wayne Morris, Eddie Albert, Jane Bryan, Ronald Reagan, Jane Wyman. D: Ray Enright. COM 87m.

Brother Sun, Sister Moon 1973 Italian ★★★ Account of the life of St. Francis of Assisi (Faulkner), who rejects his wealthy family after a spiritual epiphany and clashes with the Pope (Guinness). Flower child flavor enhanced by Donovan's music. C: Graham Faulkner, Judi Bowker, Leigh Lawson, Alec Guinness, Valentina Cortese. D: Franco Zeffirelli. DRA 120m. V

Brotherhood of Satan 1971 ★★★ Small town is besieged by witches and other things that go bump in the night. Pretty silly . . . but not without some hair-raising moments. C: Strother Martin, L.Q. Jones. D: Bernard McEveety. HOR [PG] 92m. V

Brotherhood of the Rose 1988 ★★★ Two men (Strauss and Morse) find their friendship is threatened by duty to the CIA. Rambling, though Mitchum steals every scene he's in. C: Robert Mitchum, Perter Strauss, Connie Sellecca, David Morse, M. Emmet Walsh. D: Marvin J. Chomsky. ACT [PG] 103m. TVM V

Brotherhood, The 1968 ★★★½ Tale of generational conflict within the Mafia can't avoid comparisons with *The Godfather*, released four years later. Large and generally able cast is headed by Douglas, who seems miscast as a veteran mafioso. Still, an entertaining drama with plenty of intrigue. C: Kirk Douglas, Alex Cord, Irene Papas, Luther Adler. D: Martin Ritt. DRA [PG] 96m. V

Brotherly Love 1969 British ★★★★ Little-known English film is hilarious send-up of the snooty upper-class behavior on display in one *veddy* British household. Amusing ensemble cast features standout performances from York and O'Toole. (a.k.a. *Country Dance*) C: Peter O'Toole, Susannah York, Michael Craig, Harry Andrews, Cyril Cusack. D: J. Thompson. COM [R] 112m.

Brothers in Arms 1988 ★★ This poor rip-off of *Deliverance* pits two feuding brothers who join together to defend themselves against lethal religious fanatics high in the Rockies. Decently made, in spite of unsavory story. C: Todd Allen, Dedee Pfeiffer. D: George Jay Bloom III. ACT [R] 95m. V

Brothers in Law 1957 British ★★★★ A newly graduated lawyer (Carmichael), hired by a distinguished but doddering barrister (Malleson), learns more about law from a "professional" defendant (Terry-Thomas) than his employer. Lighthearted English comedy makes enjoyable fun of the legal profession. C: Richard Attenborough, Ian Carmichael, Terry-Thomas. D: Roy Boulting. COM 94m.

Brothers Karamazov, The 1931 *See* **Karamazov**

Brothers Karamazov, The 1958 ★★★★ Four brothers (Brynner, Basehart, Shatner, and Salmi) in 19th-century Russia are tormented by their cruel, loutish father until he's killed by one of them. Brooks' adaptation and direction of Fyodor Dostoyevsky's family saga is faithful but rather slow moving. Shatner's film debut. C: Yul Brynner, Maria Schell, Claire Bloom, Lee J. Cobb, Richard Basehart, William Shatner. D: Richard Brooks. DRA 147m. V

Brother's Keeper 1992 ★★★★★ Riveting documentary about the notorious case of the Ward brothers, illiterate farmers in upstate New York, one of whom stood trial for performing a mercy killing on the other. Film takes anthropological approach in describing the profoundly isolated lives of simple men who seem to come from a previous century. Poignant, suspenseful, and fascinating. D: Joe Berlinger, Bruce Sinofsky. DOC 80m. V

Brothers Lionheart, The 1977 ★★★ Medieval brothers fight for love and glory in this obscure Scandinavian adventure/fantasy. A different viewing experience that's not easy to get into, but develops a nice rhythm of its own. For older children. C: Staffan Gotestam, Lars Soderdahl, Allan Edwall. D: Olle Hellbron. FAM/ACT [G] 108m.

Brothers O'Toole, The 1973 ★★½ Clunky Western comedy, with Three Stooges-like humor, has something to do with gold hunting and rescuing women from bad men. The idiosyncratic Carroll, and the always weird Conreid, add to the overall strangeness; may appeal to children. C: John Astin, Steve Carlson, Pat Carroll, Hans Conried. D: Richard Erdman. WST [G] 94m. V

Brothers Rico, The 1957 ★★★★ Businessman (Conte) learns that gangsters are after his two brothers. He tries to find and warn them, but discovers that the Mob has been using him to track them down. Worthwhile, unusual story, tense but with little actual violence. Based on a George Simenon novel. C: Richard Conte, Dianne Foster, Kathryn Grant, James Darren. D: Phil Karlson. CRI 92m.

Brothers 1977 ★★★ An honorable attempt at portraying '60s militant Angela Davis' relationship with convict George Jackson goes awry due to slapdash filming and a clinker of a script. Film's few good passages can't redeem its overall shoddiness. C: Bernie Casey, Vonetta McGee, Ron O'Neal. D: Arthur Barron. DRA [R] 104m.

Browning Version, The 1951 British ★★★★ Repressed, unpopular boarding school teacher (Redgrave) is saddled with an unfaithful wife (Kent). Faithful adaptation of Terence Rattigan's potent but cramped play energized by Redgrave's brilliant performance. C: Michael Redgrave, Jean Kent, Nigel Patrick, Brian Smith, Wilfrid Hyde-White. D: Anthony Asquith. DRA 90m. V

Browning Version, The 1994 British ★★★½ Updated remake of the 1951 film with Finney in fine form as an unpopular schoolmaster reevaluating his life. Story (from a 1939 Terence Rattigan play) seems contrived now, but the ending is still quite moving. C: Albert Finney, Greta Scacchi, Matthew Modine. D: Mike Figgis. DRA [R] 97m.

Brubaker 1980 ★★★ Redford is miscast as tough warden who disguises himself as a prisoner to investigate crime and corruption in the system. Based on a true story, this tries for gritty reality but remains largely predictable. C: Robert Redford, Yaphet Kotto, Jane Alexander, Murray Hamilton, Morgan Freeman. D: Stuart Rosenberg. DRA [R] 127m. V

Bruce Lee Fights Back From The Grave 1979 ★★ Martial arts and sci-fi hybrid in which Bruce Lee, the un-dead, returns to battle Black Angel of Death. C: Bruce Lee. D: Umberto Lenzi. ACT 97m. V

Bruce, Lenny: The Performance Film ★★★★ Black-and-white footage of Bruce's next-to-last performance before his suicide in 1966 shows flashes of the comedian's brilliance, but much of his routine is taken up by his obsession with his ongoing legal battles. Includes the cartoon *Thank You Mask Man.* C: Lenny Bruce. COM V

Brutal Glory 1990 ★★½ Kid McCoy, a tough street kid, stops at nothing to attain his goal of becoming a championship boxer. Inspiring and tough. C: Robert Vaughn, Leah Pinsent. D: Koos Roets. DRA 96m. V

Brute Force 1947 ★★★★½ When a sadistic prison guard's (Cronyn) tactics become unbearable, a group of inmates stage a riot where no one—even fellow convicts—is spared. Realistic and gritty: Tremendous ensemble handles difficult assignments well in an often disturbing drama. C: Burt Lancaster, Hume Cronyn, Charles Bickford, Yvonne De Carlo, Ann Blyth. D: Jules Dassin. CRI 98m.

Brute Man 1946 ★★★★ All-American actor (Hatton) who acquired a rare, disfiguring glandular disease—acromegaly—stars in this tale of a deformed murderer going after the classmates who caused his disfigurement. Very loosely based on Hatton's own experiences. An unusual but worthwhile film. C: Tom Neal, Rondo Hatton, Jane Adams. D: Jean Yarbrough. DRA 60m. V

B.S. I Love You 1971 ★★ A young TV executive (Kastner) seduces a mother and her daughter, his boss, and his fiancée in a brash display of sexual prowess. Unoriginal premise. C: Peter Kastner, Joanna Cameron. D: Steven Stern. COM [R] 99m.

Buccaneer, The 1938 ★★★ Adventure with March as a pirate dedicated to the American cause during the War of 1812. Plenty of the usual DeMille pageantry and dazzle, along with some unusual patriotic polemics. C: Fredric March, Franciska Gaal, Margot Grahame, Akim Tamiroff, Walter Brennan, Anthony Quinn. D: Cecil B. DeMille. ACT 124m.

Buccaneer, The 1958 ★★½ Pirate Jean Lafitte (Brynner) is forced into an antagonistic alliance with Andrew Jackson (Heston) to help win the War of 1812. Stiff remake of DeMille's 1938 swashbuckler, directed by his (then) son-in-law Quinn. C: Yul Brynner, Charlton Heston, Claire Bloom, Charles Boyer, Inger Stevens, Henry Hull, E.G. Marshall, Lorne Greene. D: Anthony Quinn. ACT 121m. V

Buccaneer's Girl 1950 ★★★½ High seas tale boasting plenty of swashbuckling to please pirate lovers stars De Carlo as a singer who falls in love with a pirate in New Orleans. Rousing adventure with loads of charm. C: Yvonne De Carlo, Philip Friend, Elsa Lanchester. D: Frederick de Cordova. ACT 77m.

Buchanan Rides Alone 1958 ★★★★ Gripping Western has outsider (Scott) fighting corrupt border-town locals as he makes his way from Texas to Mexico. Well-constructed drama compensates for lack of big-budget thrills with constant plot twists: Let's hear it for brains over bucks. C: Randolph Scott, Craig Stevens. D: Budd Boetticher. WST 78m.

Buck and the Preacher 1972 ★★ Poitier's directorial debut is adequate in this story of ex-slaves moving West, but while his characters are definitely intriguing, they're not altogether likable. C: Sidney Poitier, Harry Belafonte, Ruby Dee, Cameron Mitchell. D: Sidney Poitier. WST [PG] 102m. V

Buck Benny Rides Again 1940 ★★★★ Benny and cast from his radio show head West, where the anything but roughneck Benny tries to prove to Drew that he was born with boots on. Still fresh and funny, and a good chance to see what all those voices looked like. C: Jack Benny, Ellen Drew, Andy Devine, Phil Harris, Virginia Dale, Dennis Day, Eddie "Rochester" Anderson. D: Mark Sandrich. COM 82m.

Buck Privates Come Home 1947 ★★★½ WWII is over and Bud and Lou are civilians now, smuggling a European war orphan stateside. Sentimental comedy builds to a funny car chase. C: Bud Abbott, Lou Costello, Tom Brown, Joan Fulton. D: Charles Barton. COM 78m. V

Buck Privates 1941 ★★★★ Bud and Lou enlist in the Army by accident, then provide comic defense from ordinary romance subplot. Great Abbot and Costello routines plus Andrews Sisters performing "Boogie Woogie Bugle Boy." The boys' first starring feature and one of their best. C: Bud Abbott, Lou Costello, Lee Bowman, Alan Curtis, The Andrews Sisters. D: Arthur Lubin. COM 85m. V

Buck Rogers in the 25th Century 1979 ★★★ The comic book hero (Gerard) returns in this genial science fiction tale released theatrically and spun out into a TV series. Hokey, but kids will enjoy. C: Gil Gerard, Pamela Hensley, Erin Gray. D: Daniel Haller. FAM/SFI [PG] 90m. V

Buck Rogers: Space Vampire 1980 ★★★ Rogers (Gerard) dukes it out with an intergalactic bloodsucker. Fair special effects, but somewhat tedious to stay with. C: Gil Gerard, Erin Gray, Tim O'Connor, Christopher Stone. D: Larry Stewart. FAM/SFI 47m.

Buckaroo Banzai 1984 *See* **Adventures of Buckaroo Banzai Across the Eighth Dimension, The**

Bucket of Blood, A 1959 ★★★½ B-movie perennial Miller is a scream in this horror/comedy about would-be beatnik artist who uses human bodies in his sculptures. Very much a film of its time, but witty writing and acting make it perennially enjoyable. C: Dick Miller, Barboura Morris. D: Roger Corman. HOR 66m. V

Buckeye and Blue 1988 ★★½ A Civil War hero becomes a real rascal, living a brawling outlaw life. Rock 'em sock 'em western. C: Robyn Lively, Jeffrey Osterhage, Rick Gibbs, Michael Horse. D: J. C. Compton. WST [PG] 94m. V

Buckskin 1968 ★★★ A frontier sheriff (Sullivan) comes to the aid of homesteaders battling a corrupt, imperious cattle baron (Corey). Ordinary Western features an extraordinary cast. C: Barry Sullivan, Joan Caulfield, Wendell Corey, Lon Chaney, Jr. D: Michael Moore. WST (G) 97m. V

Buckskin Frontier 1943 ★★★½ Two men, one a railroad pioneer, the other a freight company owner terrified of losing his business, clash over development of the 19th-century Western frontier. Strong drama with good cast. C: Richard Dix, Jane Wyatt, Albert Dekker, Lee J. Cobb, Victor Jory. D: Lesley Selander. WST 74m. V

Bucktown 1972 ★★★½ Good example of a 1970's blaxploitation thriller, with Williamson as the vigilante leader of African-Americans fed up with racial violence in a small Southern town. Dreadful as drama, intriguing as social document. C: Fred Williamson, Pam Grier. D: Arthur Marks. ACT (R) 94m. V

Bud and Lou 1978 ★★ Somber biography, with Korman and Hackett as comedy team Abbott and Costello, showing no flair for the team's famous humor. Not so hot. C: Harvey Korman, Buddy Hackett, Michele Lee, Arte Johnson, Robert Reed. D: Robert C. Thompson. COM 98m. TVM V

Buddies 1983 Australian ★★★½ One of the first AIDS-themed dramas, this story revolves around a volunteer "buddy" to a lonely hospitalized man who is slowly succumbing to the virus. A touching feature that occasionally suffers from low-budget production woes. C: Colin Friels, Kris McQuade, Harold Hopkins, Dennis Miller. D: Arch Nicholson. DRA 99m.

Buddy Buddy 1981 ★★★ When a paid assassin and a forsaken husband, out to commit suicide, share adjoining hotel rooms, neither seems to be able to finish his intended task. Comedy saved by its talented stars. C: Jack Lemmon, Walter Matthau, Paula Prentiss, Klaus Kinski. D: Billy Wilder. COM (R) 98m. V

Buddy Holly Story, The 1978 ★★★★½ Solid musical biography of the bespectacled rock 'n' roll legend, and Busey is uncanny in the lead. All music was performed by the actors; the score adaptation by Joe Penzetti won an Oscar. Some glaring liberties are taken with the facts, though. C: Gary Busey, Charles Martin Smith, Don Stroud. D: Steve Rash. MUS (PG) 113m. V

Buddy System, The 1983 ★★★ Single mom Sarandon, seeking to find a life after divorce, strikes up a friendship with quirky, but likable Dreyfuss. Her young son then tries to push them toward a romance. Slow-moving but pleasant; saved by strong performances. C: Richard Dreyfuss, Susan Sarandon, Nancy Allen, Jean Stapleton. D: Glenn Jordan. COM (PG) 110m. V

Buffalo Bill 1944 ★★★½ Amiable epic Western about the famed Indian scout, buffalo hunter, and Wild West showman. Generally entertaining, with a good cast. C: Joel McCrea, Maureen O'Hara, Linda Darnell, Thomas Mitchell, Anthony Quinn. D: William Wellman. WST 90m. V

Buffalo Bill and the Indians 1976 ★★★½ Film shows us Buffalo Bill as the merchant of his own myth. Not Altman's most cogent work, but full of terrific performances. Adapted from Arthur Kopit's excellent play, *Indians*; full title, *Buffalo Bill and the Indians, or Sitting Bull's History Lesson* C: Paul Newman, Joel Grey, Kevin McCarthy, Burt Lancaster, Geraldine Chaplin, Harvey Keitel. D: Robert Altman. WST (PG) 135m. V

Buffet Froid 1980 French ★★★★ Mix of black comedy and film noir starts with Depardieu's penknife embedded in a subway train passenger. From there it's a surreal, dizzying ride of murder and odd coincidences. Great film of a somewhat confusing story. C: Gerard Depardieu, Bernard Blier, Jean Carmet, Genevieve Page. D: Bertrand Blier. CRI 95m.

Buffy the Vampire Slayer 1992 ★★ A vacuous high school cheerleader discovers her heritage destines her to be a modern vampire killer. And worst of all, it's going to interfere with the prom. Disappointing comedy gets a few laughs from its goofy premise. C: Kristy Swanson, Donald Sutherland, Paul Reubens, Rutger Hauer, Luke Perry. D: Fran Rubel Kuzui. COM (PG-13) 86m. V

Bug 1975 ★★½ Not a film for the squeamish; sci-fi horror has huge, grotesque bugs that spit fire unleashed on planet after an earthquake. Undeniably stupid, but holds some laughs for devotees of the invasion genre. Best watched very late at night. Final film of producer William Castle. C: Bradford Dillman, Joanna Miles. D: Jeannot Szwarc. HOR (PG) 100m. V

Bugle Sounds, The 1941 ★★★½ An old-time cavalry sergeant and traditionalist (Beery) fights against mechanical innovations in the new-fangled Army and saves the day at the end. Patriotic premise celebrates history of American forces. Solid entertainment. C: Wallace Beery, Marjorie Main, Lewis Stone, Donna Reed. D: S. Simon. DRA 101m. V

Bugles in the Afternoon 1952 ★★★½ A cavalry officer, demoted as a coward, redeems himself at Custer's Last Stand. Well-paced Western with attractive landscapes. C: Ray Milland, Forrest Tucker, George Reeves. D: Roy Rowland. WST 85m. V

Bugs Bunny Superstar 1975 ★★★★½ Orson Welles narrates this documentary recollection of the golden era of the Warner Brothers cartoon unit. Interviews with famed denizens of Termite Terrace like Chuck Jones and Friz Freleng are interspersed with classic Bugs Bunny cartoons. A must for adults and kids alike. Voice of Mel Blanc. D: Larry Jackson. FAM/COM 91m. V

Bugs Bunny/Road Runner Movie, The 1979 ★★★★ Classic cartoons from Warner Brothers' stable. Includes "Duck Amuck" and "What's Opera, Doc?" and features Wile E. Coyote, Pepe Le Pew, Elmer Fudd, and the rest of the gang. Great fun for all. (a.k.a. *Great American Bugs Bunny—Road Runner Chase.*) Voice of Mel Blanc. D: Chuck Jones, Phil Monroe. FAM/COM [G] 98m. V

Bugs Bunny's 3rd Movie—1001 Rabbit Tales 1982 ★★★½ Compilation featuring Chuck Jones' classic "One Froggy Evening," as well as Yosemite Sam, Tweety Bird, Speedy Gonzalez, and other favorite Warner Brothers cartoon characters. Fun viewing, as always. C: Voice of Mel Blanc. D: David Detiege, Art Davis, Bill Perez. FAM/COM [G] 74m. V

Bugsy, Dutch, and Al—The Gangsters 1991 ★★★ Documentary on federal government's pursuit of Prohibition crime syndicates. Superficial treatment. DOC 60m. V

Bugsy 1991 ★★★★½ Marvelously elegant portrait of starstruck gangster Bugsy Siegel and his passionate affair with actress Virginia Hill, as well as his vision for creating Las Vegas. Startling mix of humor and violence. Oscars for Costumes and Art Direction-Set Design. C: Warren Beatty, Annette Bening, Harvey Keitel, Ben Kingsley, Elliott Gould, Joe Mantegna. D: Barry Levinson. CRI [R] 135m. V

Bugsy Malone 1976 British ★★★ A truly original movie: A spoof of '30s gangster movies, done as an all-kiddy musical. Watch as machine guns fire whipped cream and young Foster croons a torch song; it's bizarre, silly fun. Music by Paul Williams. C: Scott Baio, Florrie Dugger, Jodie Foster. D: Alan Parker. FAM/MUS [G] 94m. V

Build and Marry 1932 *See* **Trunks of Mr. O.F., The**

Bull Durham 1988 ★★★★ Veteran minor league catcher (Costner) tries to help rookie pitcher (Robbins) with his game; Sarandon also wants to contribute to the young player's experience. Sexy, intelligent baseball comedy. C: Kevin Costner, Susan Sarandon, Tim Robbins. D: Ron Shelton. COM [R] 108m. V

Bulldog Drummond At the beginning of the sound era, Ronald Colman portrayed the eponymous hero with a polish and wit unknown to the original stories. When Paramount revived the series in the mid-'30s, John Howard played a slightly stiffer but still dapper Drummond, with John Barrymore as Scotland Yard's Inspector Neilsen. Howard was followed by Ron Randell, Tom Conway, and lastly Walter Pidgeon. Though a short-lived attempt was made to bring Drummond back as a proto-James Bond in the 1960s, these were always fun crime thrillers with snap and crackle.

Bulldog Drummond (1929)
The Return of Bulldog Drummond (1934)
Bulldog Jack (1934)
Bulldog Drummond Escapes (1937)
Bulldog Drummond at Bay (1937)
Bulldog Drummond Comes Back (1937)
Bulldog Drummond's Revenge (1937)
Bulldog Drummond's Peril (1938)
Bulldog Drummond in Africa (1938)
Bulldog Drummond's Secret Police (1939)
Bulldog Drummond's Bride (1939)
Arrest Bulldog Drummond (1939)
Bulldog Drummond at Bay (1947)
Bulldog Drummond Strikes Back (1947)
The Challenge (1948)
13 Lead Soldiers (1948)
Calling Bulldog Drummond (1951)
Deadlier Than the Male (1967)
Some Girls Do (1969)

Bulldog Drummond at Bay 1937 British ★★★ H.C. McNeile's fictional British detective Bulldog goes up against foreign saboteurs trying to swipe the plans for a British airplane. Doesn't pack the wallop of other Drummond fare, but passable. C: John Lodge, Dorothy Mackaill, Victor Jory. D: Norman Lee. CRI 62m.

Bulldog Drummond at Bay 1947 ★★★ Later entry in the classic *Bulldog Drummond* detective series, with Randell as the dapper British sleuth, tracking a murderer this time around. C: Ron Randell, Anita Louise, Pat O'Moore. D: Sidney Salkow. CRI 70m.

Bulldog Drummond Comes Back 1937 ★★★½ Sophisticated detective Drummond (Howard) and his Scotland Yard sidekick Nielson (Barrymore) try to find Bulldog's kidnapped fiancée. Barrymore's multiple disguises alone are worth the price of admission. C: John Barrymore, John Howard, Louise Campbell, Reginald Denny. D: Louis King. CRI 119m. V

Bulldog Drummond Escapes 1937 ★★★ Drummond gets entangled in a romantic web, falling in love with the aristocratic Angel under his protection. Milland makes a terrific Drummond. C: Ray Milland, Guy Standing, Heather Angel. D: James Hogan. CRI 65m. V

Bulldog Drummond in Africa 1938 ★★★½ Drummond's Scotland Yard pal Nielson (Warner) is kidnapped and only suave ex-military man Bulldog (Howard) and his smart fiancée (Angel) can save Nielson from the wilds of Africa. Well-done sleuth picture. C: John Howard, Heather Angel, H. B. Warner, J. Carroll Naish, Reginald Denny, Anthony Quinn. D: Louis King. ACT 115m. V

Bulldog Drummond Strikes Back 1947 ★★★ Fourteenth chapter in the saga of larger-than-life amateur British sleuth Drummond, who this time unmasks phony heiress. Teems with good times and snappy action. C: Ron Randell, Gloria Henry, Pat O'Moore. D: Frank McDonald. CRI 65m.

Bulldog Drummond 1929 ★★★★½ British WWI hero and gentleman adventurer Drummond (Colman) helps an American woman (Bennett) rescue her uncle from the clutches of an evil insane-asylum doctor. Colman's first talkie was also the first of a series of films based on Herman Cyril McNeile's character. Highly entertaining, stylish adventure. C: Ronald Colman, Joan Bennett, Montagu Love, Claud Allister. D: F. Jones. DRA 89m.

Bulldog Drummond's Bride 1939 ★★★½ British adventurer and sleuth Drummond (Howard) must delay his nuptials to nab bank robbers fleeing across Europe. Final fast-paced entry in original *Drummond* series. CRI v

Bulldog Drummond's Peril 1938 ★★★★ A murderer interrupts Drummond's impending marriage in fast-paced mystery involving a criminal scheme to manufacture fake diamonds. Barrymore returns as Scotland Yard detective, Col. Nielson; as fun to watch as ever. A top-notch effort. CRI v

Bulldog Drummond's Revenge 1937 ★★★★ The dapper British detective (Howard) battles some agents trying to steal British bomb formula. Ever-lively teaming of Barrymore and Howard makes this one of better picks in the *Bulldog Drummond* series. CRI

Bulldog Drummond's Secret Police 1939 ★★★½ Slightly gothic-style entry in the series with a mad professor and a weird castle; Carroll has fun playing three parts. CRI v

Bulldog Jack 1934 British ★★★★ Amusing Pennington (Hulbert) must help ailing Drummond (Fleming) in foiling international jewel thieves while rescuing his sidekick Angel (Wray). Very funny hijinks in this clever installment. C: Jack Hulbert, Ralph Richardson, Fay Wray, Athole Fleming. D: Walter Forde. CRI 73m.

Bullet for a Badman 1964 ★★★½ Ex-lawman (Murphy) framed for murder, escapes prison and goes after ex-friend and crook (McGavin) who wants revenge for Murphy's having married his ex-wife. Film boasts pretty scenery and some unusual plot twists. It could be said "ex" marks the plot. C: Audie Murphy, Darren McGavin, Ruta Lee. D: R.G. Springsteen. WST 80m.

Bullet for Joey, A 1955 ★★★½ Cold War thriller about a gangster (Van Eyck) stalking an American physicist (who holds the secret to the atom bomb) and the efforts of a Canadian policeman (Robinson) to stop him. Incredible plot is redeemed by very credible acting. C: Edward Robinson, George Raft, Audrey Totter, Peter Van Eyck. D: Lewis Allen. CRI 85m.

Bullet for Pretty Boy, A 1970 ★★½ Gory revisionist gangster biography of Charles "Pretty Boy" Floyd (teen idol Fabian). Violent film follows basically good Floyd's descent into crime. C: Fabian Forte, Jocelyn Lane, Astrid Warner. D: Larry Buchanan. CRI [PG] 91m.

Bullet for Sandoval, A 1970 Italian ★★★ An angry father (Hilton) goes after the man (Borgnine) he holds responsible for his child's death in Mexico. Spaghetti-Western is hopelessly corny with dubbed English dialogue but boasts good production values and supercharged action. C: Ernest Borgnine, George Hilton, Alberto De Mendoza. D: Julio Buchs. WST [PG] 96m. v

Bullet for Stefano 1950 Italian ★★★½ An Italian Robin Hood (Brazzi) saves his lady love (Cortese) from marriage and fights for justice until criminal life spoils him. Well-done 19th-century romantic adventure. C: Rossano Brazzi, Valentina Cortese. D: Duilio Coletti. ACT 96m.

Bullet for the General, A 1968 Italian ★★½ Spaghetti-Western about an American soldier of fortune (Castel) who participates in Mexican Revolution when he's hired by Volonte and Kinski. Fair action picture. C: Gian Maria Volonte, Lou Castel, Klaus Kinski. D: Damiano Damiani. WST 95m. v

Bullet is Waiting, A 1954 ★★★½ Sheriff and prisoner are stranded in desert with young woman and her father. Uncommon psychological study. C: Jean Simmons, Rory Calhoun, Brian Aherne. D: John Farrow. WST 82m.

Bulletproof 1987 ★★ A tough, retired L.A. cop Frank "Bulletproof" McBain (Busey)—he keeps the bullets removed from his body in a mason jar—goes south of the border to fight Communist terrorists. Silly action film, with plenty of smash-ups and gunplay. C: Gary Busey, Darlanne Fluegel, Henry Silva. D: Steve Carver. ACT [R] 93m. v

Bullets or Ballots 1936 ★★★★ Feigning his own dismissal, undercover cop Robinson infiltrates MacLane's gang. Sturdy, well-done gangster drama. C: Edward G. Robinson, Joan Blondell, Barton MacLane, Humphrey Bogart, Frank McHugh. D: William Keighley. CRI 82m. v

Bullets Over Broadway 1994 ★★★★ Funny, perceptive look at the theatre world of the 1920's stars Cusack as a young playwright dealing with a bootlegger backer, a meddling bodyguard, and a difficult diva (Weist, who walks away with the movie—and her second Oscar for Best Supporting Actress). Allen's most entertaining film since *Hannah and Her Sisters*. C: John Cusack, Dianne Weist, Chazz Palminteri, Mary Louise Parker, Jennifer Tilly, Tracey Ullman, Jim Broadbent. D: Woody Allen. COM [R] 85m. v

Bullfighter and the Lady, The 1950 ★★★★ Arrogant American (Stack) visiting Mexico decides to become a bullfighter and asks country's premiere matador (Roland) to teach him. Compelling drama heightened by exciting bullfighting scenes. C: Robert Stack, Joy Page, Gilbert Roland, Katy Jurado. D: Budd Boetticher. DRA 87m. v

Bullfighters, The 1945 ★★½ Chaos erupts south of the border when private detectives Laurel and Hardy arrive in Mexico and Laurel just happens to resemble a famous matador. Duo's last American feature. C: Stan Laurel, Oliver Hardy, Margo Woode, Richard Lane. D: Mal St. Clair. COM 61m. V

Bullies 1986 Canadian ★ *Deliverance*-type revenge tale of killer hillbillies and a man seeking vengeance for their torture of his family. Violent. C: Jonathan Crombie, Janet-Laine Green, Stephen Hunter. D: Paul Lynch. ACT [R] 96m. V

Bullitt 1968 ★★★★½ THE police chase film! Hard-boiled San Francisco detective (McQueen) hunts down the killer of a government witness. Precedent-setting action scenes and the mother of all high-speed car chases. C: Steve McQueen, Robert Vaughn, Jacqueline Bisset, Don Gordon, Robert Duvall. D: Peter Yates. ACT [PG] 113m. V

Bullseye! 1989 ★★ Two con-men (Caine, Moore) impersonate look-alike research scientists to profit from their discoveries. Silly farce wastes its charismatic stars. John Cleese has an unbilled bit part near the finale. C: Michael Caine, Roger Moore, Sally Kirkland. D: Michael Winner. COM [PG-13] 89m. V

Bullshot 1983 British ★★★½ Parody of the long-running British *Bulldog Drummond* series, with a "Bullshot" Crummond (Shearman) immersed in almost as many romances and adventures as the original British sleuth. Appealing comedy; based on the play by Shearman, White, and House. C: Alan Shearman, Diz White, Ron House. D: Dick Clement. COM [PG] 84m. V

Bullwhip 1958 ★★★½ A man falsely accused of murder (Madison) must choose between marriage to feisty Fleming or execution. Some good laughs and romance result when he makes the obvious choice. Handsome production delivers the escapist goods. Remade as *Goin' South* (1978). C: Guy Madison, Rhonda Fleming. D: Harmon Jones. WST 80m.

Bump in the Night 1991 ★★★½ The son of an alcoholic writer (Baxter-Birney) is kidnapped by Reeve for use in child pornography. Somewhat sensationalized, but not without tension. C: Meredith Baxter-Birney, Christopher Reeve, Geraldine Fitzgerald, Shirley Knight, Wings Hauser. D: Karen Arthur. CRI 100m. TVM

Bunco 1976 ★★★ Two boisterous members of the LAPD bunco squad get involved in all kinds of misadventures—with all kinds of ridiculous people. Some fun thanks to the appealing cast. C: Tom Selleck, Robert Urich, Donna Mills. D: Alexander Singer. COM 60m. TVM V

Bundle of Joy 1956 ★★★ Tongues start to wag when unmarried salesclerk Reynolds shows up with a baby, and the pressure is on for her and boyfriend Fisher to tie the knot. Mildly amusing update of *Bachelor Mother* gets most of its energy from Reynolds. C: Debbie Reynolds, Eddie Fisher, Adolphe Menjou, Tommy Noonan. D: Norman Taurog. COM 98m. V

Bunker, The 1981 ★★★★ Historical drama goes underground to Hitler's bunker during the final days of Nazi Germany. Hopkins is superb as Hitler, in an Emmy-winning performance. Captivating drama. C: Anthony Hopkins, Piper Laurie, Richard Jordan, Susan Blakely, Cliff Gorman. D: George Schaefer. DRA 150m. TVM

Bunny Lake Is Missing 1965 ★★★★ Imaginative psychological mystery has a young mother reporting her daughter's disappearance, and a skeptical police inspector unable to prove the child ever existed. Downbeat, but strong cast buoys implausible storyline. C: Laurence Olivier, Carol Lynley, Keir Dullea, Noel Coward, Martita Hunt. D: Otto Preminger. CRI 107m.

Bunny O'Hare 1972 ★★ Davis and Borgnine disguise themselves as hippies to pull a string of bank robberies. Little real wit or humor; must be seen to be believed. C: Bette Davis, Ernest Borgnine, Jack Cassidy, John Astin. D: Gerd Oswald. COM [PG] 91m.

Bunny's Tale, A 1985 ★★★ In 1963, journalist Gloria Steinem (Alley) goes undercover as a Playboy Bunny to research an article. Interesting look at one of the roots of Steinem's feminism. C: Kirstie Alley, Cotter Smith, Joanna Kerns, Delta Burke. D: Karen Arthur. DRA 97m. TVM V

Buona Sera, Mrs. Campbell 1968 ★★★ Three American WWII vets (Lawford, Silvers, Savalas) have been separately supporting their wartime lover (Lollobrigida) and her daughter for years; each believes he's the father. Their 20-year reunion in Italy is the catalyst for this goofy, fun farce. C: Gina Lollobrigida, Peter Lawford, Shelley Winters, Phil Silvers, Telly Savalas, Lee Grant. D: Melvin Frank. COM [PG] 113m. V

'Burbs, The 1989 ★★ Complacent suburbanites suspect a new neighbor may be up to something sinister and begin to take drastic measures to discover what it might be. Silly, oddball comedy. C: Tom Hanks, Bruce Dern, Carrie Fisher, Rick Ducommun, Corey Feldman. D: Joe Dante. COM [PG] 101m. V

Burden of Dreams 1982 ★★★★ Documentary about making of Werner Herzog's *Fitzcarraldo* is in many ways better than the film itself; director Herzog's megalomania eclipses that of fictional character he's recreating. Blank raises thorny questions about risking one's life—and other's lives—for art. C: Klaus Kinski, Mick Jagger, Jason Robards Jr., Werner Herzog. D: Les Blank. DOC 94m. V

Burden of Proof, The 1992 ★★★ Disappointing, overlong version of Scott Turow's best-seller. Elizondo seems miscast as a lawyer who has to cope with his wife's suicide and the barrage of problems it sets into motion; Dennehy steals the show. C: Hector Elizondo, Brian Dennehy, Mel Harris, Stefanie

Powers, Victoria Principal. D: Mike Robe. DRA 200m. TVM v

Bureau of Missing Persons 1933 ★★★★ A woman goes to the Bureau of Missing Persons to find her missing husband; newly assigned cop (O'Brien) is so taken with her that he doesn't notice she's wanted for murder. He then stages her funeral, hoping she'll attend. Somehow, it all works; genuinely amusing. C: Bette Davis, Lewis Stone, Pat O'Brien, Allen Jenkins, Ruth Donnelly, Glenda Farrell. D: Roy Del Ruth. COM 73m. v

Burglar 1987 ★★★ Offbeat ex-con Goldberg is conned into committing one last crime—but she's innocent when it comes to murder. Whoopi does her thing, providing plenty of laughs in an otherwise flat story. C: Whoopi Goldberg, Bob Goldthwait, G. W. Bailey, Lesley Ann Warren. D: Hugh Wilson. ACT [R] 103m. v

Burglars, The 1972 French ★★★½ An international cast and beautiful Greek setting boost this caper film of a burglary, masterminded by Belmondo, which gradually unravels. Fast-paced production. French remake of 1956 *The Burglar.* C: Jean-Paul Belmondo, Omar Sharif, Dyan Cannon. D: Henri Verneuil. CRI [PG] 117m.

Buried Alive 1984 ★★ Sick twist on *Psycho* has taxidermist Modesto committing unspeakable acts with the tools of his craft. A gross-out. C: Sam Modesto, Ann Cardin. D: Joe D'Amato. HOR 90m.

Buried Alive 1990 ★★★ Sadistic doctor Vaughn lures young women to his house of horrors. Horror film stalwarts Pleasence and Carradine deliver creepy performances in this weird chiller. C: Robert Vaughn, Donald Pleasence, Karen Witter, John Carradine. D: Gerard Kikoine. HOR 97m. v

Burke and Wills 1986 Australian ★★★½ In 1860, two explorers (Thompson and Havers) set out on a doomed expedition to cross the Australian continent and back. Flashbacks of men's lives in England and Ireland intercut with their desert transverse make compelling drama. C: Jack Thompson, Nigel Havers, Greta Scacchi. D: Graeme Clifford. DRA [PG-13] 140m.

Burma Convoy 1941 ★★★½ A trucker (Bickford) running supplies to soldiers over the Burma Road has his retirement delayed as he contends with hijackers and murderers on the treacherous route. Workman-like action-drama. C: Charles Bickford, Evelyn Ankers, Cecil Kellaway, Keye Luke, Turhan Bey. D: Noel Smith. ACT 72m.

Burmese Harp, The 1956 Japanese ★★★★½ At the end of WWII, a Japanese man becomes obsessed with burying war dead and ultimately turns to Buddhism. Fascinating antiwar drama, memorable and compelling. (a.k.a. *Harp of Burma*) C: Rentaro Mikuni, Shoji Yasui. D: Kon Ichikawa. DRA 116m. v

Burn! 1970 Italian ★★★★ A 19th-century slave revolt on a Portuguese-held island in the Caribbean is whipped up by British ambassador (Brando) for political reasons. Extraordinary exposé, although the story gets tangled. C: Marlon Brando, Evaristo Marquez, Renato Salvatori, Tom Lyons. D: Gillo Pontecorvo. ACT [PG] 113m. v

Burn, Witch, Burn! 1962 British ★★★★ Solid British thriller, with credible story line and real scares. Professor (Wyngarde) finds wife (Blair) is dabbling in dark arts; his disbelief in the occult leads to all hell breaking loose. Based on Fritz Leiber's story "Conjure Wife." (a.k.a. *Weird Woman* and *Night of the Eagle*) C: Janet Blair, Peter Wyngarde, Margaret Johnston. D: Sidney Hayers. HOR 90m.

Burndown 1990 ★★★½ A Southern sheriff (Firth) and a reporter (Moriarty) trail a rapist and serial killer who's leaving radioactive corpses in his wake. Admittedly bizarre B-movie premise nevertheless makes a suspenseful thriller with an environmental message. C: Peter Firth, Cathy Moriarty, Michael McCabe. D: James Allen. CRI [R] 87m. v

Burning an Illusion 1982 British ★★★★ Black Englishwoman finds herself drawn to radical movements after institutional sexism and racism take their toll on her psyche. Interesting social film with good performances, though telling isn't as strong as thematic convictions. C: Cassie MacFarlane, Victor Romero, Beverley Martin. D: Menelik Shabbazz. DRA 101m.

Burning Bed, The 1984 ★★★★ Fawcett proves she can really act in this meaty, real-life drama about a battered wife driven to murder her abusive husband by setting him on fire while he sleeps. An intelligent script and affecting performances all around. C: Farrah Fawcett, Paul Le Mat, Richard Masur. D: Robert Greenwald. DRA 95m. TVM v

Burning Bridges 1990 ★★½ Weepy melodrama of an adulterous woman (Baxter-Birney) destroying head and home as she pursues scorching passion with her doctor. C: Meredith Baxter-Birney, Nick Mancuso. D: Sheldon Larry. DRA 96m.

Burning Cross, The 1974 *See* **Klansman, The**

Burning Hills, The 1956 ★★½ Western features Hunter as a cowhand who takes refuge from rustlers and a cattle baron's son in a homestead with miscast Wood. Based on a Louis L'Amour novel. C: Tab Hunter, Natalie Wood, Skip Homeier, Earl Holliman, Claude Akins. D: Stuart Heisler. WST 94m.

Burning Man, The 1981 *See* **Dangerous Summer, A**

Burning Question, The 1936 *See* **Reefer Madness**

Burning Rage 1984 ★★★ A poverty-stricken town of coal miners and their families fall victim to a series of fires that burn in the empty coal shafts under their homes. Moving story, interesting cast. C: Barbara Mandrell, Eddie Albert, Tom Wopat, Bert Remsen. D: Gilbert Cates. DRA 100m. V

Burning Secret 1988 ★★★½ Aristocratic soldier recuperating from a WWI injury uses a woman's ill son to gain her affections, only to emotionally abandon the needy child once romance is sparked. Beautifully photographed and literary, Brandauer is excellent, but Dunaway is miscast. C: Faye Dunaway, Klaus Maria Brandauer, Ian Richardson. D: Andrew Birkin. DRA [PG] 107m. V

Burning, The 1981 ★★ A camp custodian disfigured by a teenage prankster turns killer and seeks revenge on a summer camp. Has all the corniness and gore (compliments of makeup wizard Tom Savini) that make for classic teenage exploitation horror; Holly Hunter's film debut. C: Brian Matthews, Leah Ayres, Brian Backer, Jason Alexander. D: Tony Maylam. HOR [R] 90m. V

Burnt Offerings 1976 ★★ Familiar haunted house tale as family rents creepy old mansion for the summer, only to find themselves under attack from the spirit world. Spooky atmosphere and ho-hum plot. C: Karen Black, Oliver Reed, Bette Davis, Burgess Meredith, Eileen Heckart. D: Dan Curtis. HOR [PG] 116m. V

Burroughs 1986 ★★★ Worshipful documentary on the Beat writer William S. Burroughs. Personality, rather than literary, oriented. DOC 60m.

Bury Me an Angel 1971 ★★★½ A motorcycle vigilante (Peabody) sets out—with a shotgun—to find her brother's murderer. Original vision and good direction are the key elements of this woman's biker film. C: Dixie Peabody, Terry Mace, Clyde Ventura, Dan Haggerty. D: Barbara Peeters. ACT [R] 90m. V

Bus Is Coming, The 1971 ★★½ A black ex-G.I. returns home and investigates his brother's murder. Unsubtle, with mediocre acting. C: Mike Sims, Stephanie Faulkner, Burl Bullock, Sandra Reed. D: Wendell J. Franklin. DRA [PG] 102m. V

Bus Riley's Back in Town 1965 ★★★ Town bad boy (Parks) returns from Navy stint determined to succeed and to win back his rich girlfriend (Ann-Margaret). Heavy-handed, disjointed drama, but with some good cameos. C: Ann-Margaret, Michael Parks, Janet Margolin, Kim Darby, Jocelyn Brando, Larry Storch, David Carradine. D: Harvey Hart. DRA 93m.

Bus Stop 1956 ★★★★½ Naive cowboy (Murray) is so smitten by charms of street-smart saloon singer (Monroe) that he wants to marry her on the spot—whether she agrees or not. Excellent script and performances (particularly by Monroe) place this comedy/drama near the top of her output. High point: her torchy rendition of "That Old Black Magic." (a.k.a. *The Wrong Kind of Girl*) Adapted from William Inge play. C: Marilyn Monroe, Don Murray, Arthur O'Connell, Betty Field, Eileen Heckart, Hope Lange. D: Joshua Logan. COM 94m. V

Bush Christmas 1947 Australian ★★★½ Well-done family drama of Australian children tracking horse thieves through the Outback. The children deliver refreshingly natural performances in this pleasant adventure. C: Chips Rafferty, John Fernside. D: Ralph Smart. FAM/ACT 76m.

Bushbaby, The 1970 ★★★ A young girl (Brooks) visiting Africa is mistakenly believed to have been kidnapped by a former family servant (Gossett). Her pet bushbaby, a small and mischievous marsupial animal, contributes to the general mayhem. Children's film with little adult appeal. C: Margaret Brooks, Louis Gossett, Jr., Laurence Naismith. D: John Trent. FAM/COM 101m. V

Bushfire Moon 1987 *See* **Christmas Visitor, The**

Bushido Blade, The 1979 Japanese ★★★½ Samurai steals a prized sword that a Yokohama shogun meant as a gift for U.S. Navy Commander Perry to cement U.S.-Japan treaty relations in 1854. Period swordplay and martial arts combine with sporadic decapitation. Boone's last feature. C: Richard Boone, Frank Converse, James Jones, Toshiro Mifune, Mako. D: Tom Kotani. ACT [R] 104m. V

Bushwackers, The 1952 ★★½ A Civil War vet returned from battle vows to give up guns, but is forced to fight for his love (Malone) and champion the cause of settlers terrorized by bad guys led by greedy land magnate (Chaney). Conventional story wastes Malone's talents. C: Dorothy Malone, John Ireland, Wayne Morris, Lon Chaney, Jr. D: Rod Amateau. WST 70m.

Business as Usual 1988 British ★★★½ Moving drama of a British woman who fights harassment at her workplace and is fired. She then draws national attention to the treatment of women. May be too heavy-handed for some; others will appreciate director/writer Barrett's intelligent examination of personal politics in this heavily slanted script. C: Glenda Jackson, John Thaw, Cathy Tyson. D: Lezli-An Barrett. DRA [PG] 89m. V

Busman's Honeymoon *See* **Haunted Honeymoon**

Buster 1988 British ★★★½ Pop star Collins makes film debut as notorious bank robber Buster Edwards, who only wants a happy home life with wife (Walters). Somewhat precious but good work by stars, good songs (including "Two Hearts, One Mind" and "Groovy Kind of Love"). C: Phil Collins, Julie Walters, Larry Lamb, Stephanie Lawrence, Anthony Quayle. D: David Green. MUS [R] 95m. V

Buster and Billie 1974 ★★★½ Love conquers all as a "fast" country high school girl in 1948 Georgia falls in love with a sensitive boy in her class. Campus romance narrative, effectively acted. C: Jan-Michael Vincent, Joan Goodfellow, Pamela Sue Martin. D: Daniel Petrie. DRA [R] 100m. v

Buster Keaton Story, The 1957 ★★ Lightweight, unfunny biography of the amazing silent-film comedian. Outrageous fictionalization of the facts of Keaton's life. C: Donald O'Connor, Ann Blyth, Rhonda Fleming, Peter Lorre. D: Sidney Sheldon. DRA 91m.

Bustin' Loose 1981 ★★★★ Ex-convict Pryor reluctantly agrees to drive teacher Tyson and her school bus full of difficult children cross-country. In the process he gains new insight into his own life. Pryor (who also wrote the story) gives a touching, funny performance in this tenderhearted comedy. C: Richard Pryor, Cicely Tyson, Robert Christian. D: Oz Scott. COM 94m. v

Busting 1974 ★★★½ Two L.A. vice cops (Gould, Blake) take on a Mob boss (Garfield) by themselves when they're thwarted by the system. Standard vigilante drama with dynamic action sequences. C: Elliott Gould, Robert Blake, Allen Garfield, Antonio Fargas. D: Peter Hyams. CRI [R] 92m. v

Busy Body, The 1967 ★★★½ A gangster's patsy finds himself in hot water when he can't locate a corpse on which a million dollars has been concealed. Frantic farce keeps the laughs coming fast and furiously—thanks to Caesar's incessant mugging. Pryor's film debut. C: Sid Caesar, Robert Ryan, Anne Baxter, Kay Medford, Jan Murray, Richard Pryor, Dom DeLuise, Godfrey Cambridge, Marty Ingels, Bill Dana, George Jessel. D: William Castle. COM 90m.

But Not For Me 1959 ★★★★ Sophisticated urban romance casts Gable as a theatrical producer, torn between young Baker and older Palmer. One of the King's final films. Remake of *Accent on Youth*. C: Clark Gable, Carroll Baker, Lilli Palmer, Barry Coe, Lee J. Cobb. D: Walter Lang. DRA 105m. v

Butch and Sundance: The Early Days 1979 ★★★½ Meandering prequel fictionalizes the famed outlaws' early careers as robbers. Ambitious and not without humor, but doesn't measure up to attractive personality of movie on which it's based. C: William Katt, Tom Berenger, Brian Dennehy, Jill Eikenberry. D: Richard Lester. WST [PG] 111m. v

Butch Cassidy and the Sundance Kid 1969 ★★★★★ William Goldman's humorous account of two wisecracking Hole-in-the-Wall Gang bank and train robbers who flee with a schoolteacher to Bolivia to resume their careers. Landmark "buddy" Western, much imitated and laced with priceless moments. Oscars for Best Song, Best Screenplay. C: Paul Newman, Robert Redford, Katharine Ross, Strother Martin, Henry Jones, Cloris Leachman, Kenneth Mars. D: George Roy Hill. WST [PG] 112m. v

Butcher's Wife, The 1991 ★★½ Clairvoyant Southern beauty Moore marries a dour butcher from Greenwich Village. When she moves back to New York with him she changes the lives of everyone in the neighborhood. Comedy fantasy tries too hard to be magical and comes off insincere. C: Demi Moore, Jeff Daniels, George Dzundza, Mary Steenburgen, Frances McDormand. D: Terry Hughes. COM [PG-13] 107m. v

Butley 1974 British ★★★★ A tour de force, with Bates reprising his Broadway role as an amoral college professor whose private life is a shambles. A serious drama with some very funny turns. Pinter's directorial debut, of Simon Gray's Broadway hit. C: Alan Bates, Jessica Tandy, Richard O'Callaghan. D: Harold Pinter. DRA [R] 127m.

Buttercup Chain, The 1971 British ★ Privileged young lovers tempt fate with their licentiousness. Appealing European photography. C: Hywel Bennett, Leigh Taylor Young, Jane Asher. D: Robert Miller. DRA [R] 95m.

Butterfield 8 1960 ★★★★ John O'Hara's tough novel about a NYC prostitute is turned into MGM gloss about a call girl/model crazy to be suburban. Best scenes: the opening "morning after," complete with lipstick message in the mirror; and Liz grinding her Oscar-winning heel into Harvey's foot. C: Elizabeth Taylor, Laurence Harvey, Eddie Fisher, Dina Merrill, Mildred Dunnock, Betty Field, Kay Medford. D: Daniel Mann. DRA 110m. v

Butterflies Are Free 1972 ★★★★ Much to the horror of his mother, a soft-spoken blind man falls in love with offbeat neighbor. Winning adaptation of Leonard Gershe's Broadway hit features strong performances all around—especially Heckart, who won Best Supporting Oscar. C: Goldie Hawn, Edward Albert, Eileen Heckart, Mike Warren. D: Milton Katselas. COM [PG] 109m. v

Butterfly 1982 U.S. ★★ James M. Cain's tough crime tale involving incest, murder, and atonement ends up as garbage in this awful and unintentionally campy rendition. Its high spot is Orson Welles's cameo. C: Stacy Keach, Pia Zadora, Orson Welles, Lois Nettleton, Edward Albert. D: Matt Cimber. CRI [R] 105m. v

Buy & Cell 1988 ★★½ Unscrupulous stockbroker's greedy ways send him to prison, where he establishes a multimillion-dollar business from behind bars. Weak comedy relies on broad stereotypes. C: Robert Carradine, Michael Winslow, Malcolm McDowell, Roddy Piper, Ben Vereen. D: Robert Boris. COM [R] 95m. v

Buy Me That Town 1941 ★★★½ Nolan is a criminal who saves pals on the lam by buying a bankrupt town to serve as a gangster haven. Silly fun, though satire never hits the bull's-eye. C: Lloyd Nolan, Constance Moore, Albert Dekker. D: Eugene Forde. COM 70m.

Buying Time 1989 ★★★ Teenage gamblers become involved in murder and are forced to go undercover in order to catch the killers. Engaging. C: Dean Stockwell, Jeff Schultz, Leslie Toth, Michael Rudder. D: Mitchell Gabourie. CRI [R] 97m. v

Bwana Devil 1952 ★★ Fin de siécle Africa provides logical setting for a pair of ravenous lions out to dine on terrorized railroad workers. Silly jungle yarn, remarkable mainly as the first 3-D feature. C: Robert Stack, Barbara Britton, Nigel Bruce. D: Arch Oboler. DRA 79m.

By Candlelight 1934 ★★★ A valet impersonates his employer to win the affections of a lady he thinks is a countess. Passable urbane fluff. C: Paul Lukas, Elissa Landi, Nils Asther. D: James Whale. COM 70m.

By Dawn's Early Light 1990 ★★★½ Tense Cold War thriller about America and USSR on the brink of nuclear war after an accidental missile attack on Russia. Packs some punch. Based on William Prochnau's *Trinity Child.* C: Powers Boothe, Rebecca De Mornay, James Earl Jones, Martin Landau, Darren McGavin, Rip Torn. D: Jack Sholder. DRA 100m. TVM

By Design 1982 Canadian ★★½ Lesbian couple decide to have a baby and set out to find the perfect man to be the father. Clumsy attempt at a hip black comedy doesn't quite deliver. C: Patty Duke Astin, Sara Botsford. D: Claude Jutra. COM 90m. v

By Love Possessed 1961 ★★★ Sudsy saga, based on James Gould Cozzens's novel centers on a bored housewife (Turner), her failing marriage to impotent Robards, and her affair with Zimbalist, Jr., Robards' partner. Talky, episodic melodrama, but Robards shines. C: Lana Turner, Efrem Zimbalist, Jr., Jason Robards, George Hamilton, Thomas Mitchell, Barbara Bel Geddes, Carroll O'Connor. D: John Sturges. DRA 115m. v

By the Light of the Silvery Moon 1953 ★★★★ Nostalgic family musical about returning doughboy (MacRae) and girl-next-door fiancée (Day). Cheerful Americana, nicely served by adorable leads and excellent supporting cast. C: Doris Day, Gordon MacRae, Leon Ames, Rosemary DeCamp, Mary Wickes. D: David Butler. MUS 100m. v

By Whose Hand? 1932 ★★★½ Snappy little B-movie murder mystery set on L.A.-S.F. express train. Minor but fun. C: Ben Lyon, Barbara Weeks, William V. Mong, Ethel Kenyon. D: Ben Stoloff. CRI 63m.

By Your Leave 1935 ★★★½ Aspiring Don Juan keeps finding himself back home. Morgan is amusing as husband with roving eye but honest feet. C: Frank Morgan, Genevieve Tobin, Gene Lockhart, Margaret Hamilton, Betty Grable. D: Lloyd Corrigan. COM 81m.

Bye, Bye, Birdie 1963 ★★★★ Exuberant, inventive transfer of Broadway musical, using real-life Army drafting of Elvis Presley as its plot premise. Knockout presence of Ann-Margret helped by strong stage holdovers Van Dyke and Lynde. Songs include "Put on a Happy Face," "Got a Lot of Living to Do," and "Kids." C: Dick Van Dyke, Janet Leigh, Ann-Margret, Maureen Stapleton, Paul Lynde, Jesse Pearson, Bobby Rydell, Ed Sullivan. D: George Sidney. MUS 112m. v

Bye Bye Blues 1990 Canadian ★★★★ Warm homefront tearjerker of expectant mother (Jenkins) stationed in India with physician husband. Nicely directed by Wheeler with insightful, appealingly feminist edge. Soft in spots but not too sappy; good acting, too. C: Rebecca Jenkins, Luke Reilly, Stuart Margolin, Kate Reid, Michael Ontkean. D: Anne Wheeler. DRA [PG] 110m. v

Bye Bye Braverman 1968 ★★★ Four New York writers encounter one misadventure after another as they attempt to attend a colleague's funeral. Offbeat comic mishmash. C: George Segal, Jack Warden, Joseph Wiseman, Sorrell Booke, Jessica Walter, Phyllis Newman, Zohra Lampert, Godfrey Cambridge, Alan King. D: Sidney Lumet. COM 109m.

Bye Bye Brazil 1980 Brazilian ★★★★ Freewheeling road movie is a picaresque saga of a two-bit traveling sideshow that plays to Brazil's backwater towns. Laced with mild political commentary about the incursion of TV into people's lives, movie is humorous and engagingly upbeat. C: Jose Wilker, Betty Faria. D: Carlos Diegues. COM [R] 105m. v

Bye Bye, Love 1995 ★★★½ Uneven, often funny, look at three divorced fathers who meet weekly at McDonald's to pick up their children and discuss their efforts to restructure their lives. Highlight is Quaid's blind date with an obnoxious woman (Garofalo) who asks him, "Do you know how long veal stays in your colon?" C: Matthew Modine, Randy Quaid, Paul Reiser, Janeane Garofalo, Amy Brenneman, Rob Reiner, Eliza Dushku. D: Sam Weisman. COM [PG-13] 107m. v

C

C-Man 1949 ★★★ Treasury Department customs agent (Jagger) gets involved with sinister thief and murderer (Carradine). Lively B-movie. C: Dean Jagger, John Carradine. D: Joseph Lerner. CRI 75m.

Cabaret 1972 ★★★★★ Smash Kander and Ebb musical has a young, American woman in pre-WWII Berlin caught in a web of decadence and deception while singing her heart out. A Broadway adaptation that improves on the original with Fosse's kinetic camera work and Minnelli's bravura performance (Oscar for Best Actress). Not a happy musical, but a brilliant one. Film's eight Oscars include Director and Supporting Actor (Grey). Based on Christopher Isherwood's *Berlin Stories*. C: Liza Minnelli, Michael York, Helmut Griem, Joel Grey, Marisa Berenson. D: Bob Fosse. MUS [PG] 124m. V

Cabbage Patch Kids First Christmas ★★½ Animated feature cashing in on doll craze follows the stuffed moppets as they leave their enchanted land to search for the true meaning of Christmas. Cloying seasonal entertainment. FAM/COM 30m. V

Cabeza de Vaca 1993 Spanish ★★★½ Sixteenth-century Spanish explorer is shipwrecked off Florida coast and suffers both deprivation and torture. Documentary filmmaker Echevarria takes Native Americans' side in this overlong but compelling historical drama. (a.k.a. *Cow's Head*) C: Juan Diego, Daniel Gimenez Cacho, Roberto Soscba, Carlos Castanon, Gerardo Villarreal. D: Nicolas Echeverria. DRA [R] 108m. V

Cabin Boy 1994 ★★ An effete snob (Elliot) mistakes fishing vessel for yacht and a group of crusty fisherfolk force him to work, making his life miserable. Several *Late Night with David Letterman* alumni worked on this shallow farce. C: Chris Elliot, Ritch Brinkley, James Gammon, Brian Doyle-Murray, Brion James. D: Adam Resnick. COM 80m.

Cabin in the Cotton, The 1932 ★★★½ Seductive daughter (Davis) of plantation owner chases after sharecropper (Barthelmess). Bette in first bad-girl role makes this melodrama watchable. Contains her famous (and favorite) line: "Ah'd love t' kiss ya, but ah jes' washed mah hair!" C: Richard Barthelmess, Dorothy Jordan, Bette Davis, Hardie Albright. D: Michael Curtiz. DRA 77m.

Cabin in the Sky 1943 ★★★★ All-black folk musical has gambler (Anderson) succumbing to temptress (Horne) while wife (Waters) gallantly suffers and gets the best songs ("Happiness is Just A Thing Called Joe," "Taking a Chance on Love"). Hopelessly stereotyped, but gives legendary talent rare chance to perform. First film for Minnelli. C: Eddie Anderson, Lena Horne, Ethel Waters, Louis Armstrong, Duke Ellington. D: Vincente Minnelli. MUS 99m. V

Cabinet of Caligari, The 1962 ★★★ Young woman finds herself at the mercy of a sadistic, bearded stranger when she takes refuge at a desolate mansion. Remake of 1919 classic silent relies on violence and perversion for its thrills. C: Dan O'Herlihy, Glynis Johns, Richard Davalos, Estelle Winwood. D: Roger Kay. HOR 104m.

Cabinet of Dr. Caligari, The 1919 German ★★★★★ Justifiably famous silent chiller helped define Germany's Expressionist trend in filmmaking, with the title villain using hypnotism to drive an innocent man to kill. An unremarkable story is made unforgettable through striking visuals. C: Werner Krauss, Conrad Veidt. D: Robert Wiene. HOR 52m.

Cabiria 1914 Italian ★★★★ During the second Punic War, a young slave (Quaranta) experiences tribulations and love in Rome. Classic, innovative silent spectacle has influenced directors from D.W. Griffith to Fellini. C: Italia Manzini, Lidia Quaranta, Bartolomeo Pagano. D: Piero Fosco. DRA 123m. V

Cabiria 1957 *See* **Nights of Cabiria**

Caboblanco 1980 ★★½ Tight-lipped barkeep in Peru (Bronson), watches parade of humanity wander in and out of his saloon in search of missing gold, among other things. Bald-faced imitation of *Casablanca* runs its course without originality or dramatic effect. C: Charles Bronson, Jason Robards, Dominique Sanda, Fernando Rey, Simon MacCorkindale, Gilbert Roland. D: J. Thompson. DRA [R] 87m.

Cactus 1986 Australian ★★★ A young woman (Huppert) visiting Australia faces blindness as a result of a car accident. She meets a blind cactus grower (Menzies) who helps her through the crisis and they fall in love. Some wonderful moments, but slow pace works against the story. C: Isabelle Huppert, Robert Menzies. D: Paul Cox. DRA 96m. V

Cactus Flower 1969 ★★★ Philandering dentist Matthau gets involved with sweet young thing Hawn while finding himself falling for his assistant Bergman. Adapted from Broadway play, this comedy has some funny moments though humor is extremely dated. Hawn won Oscar for Best Supporting Actress. C: Ingrid Bergman, Walter Matthau, Goldie Hawn, Jack Weston. D: Gene Saks. COM [M/PG] 103m. V

Caddie 1976 Australian ★★★½ Period piece set in Depression-era Australia. A woman (Morse) abandoned by her husband must work in a bar to support her children. A few too many clichés, but fine acting and an upbeat ending. C:

Helen Morse, Takis Emmanuel, Jack Thompson. D: Donald Crombie. DRA 107m. V

Caddy, The 1953 ★★★ Looney caddy Lewis teaches the game to reluctant protégé Martin. Lame vehicle for duo, highlight is their duet, "That's Amore." C: Dean Martin, Jerry Lewis, Donna Reed, Fred Clark. D: Norman Taurog. COM 95m. V

Caddyshack 1980 ★★★★ Golf course swarming with snobs and uncouth caddies is chewed up by rich put-down artist (Dangerfield) and a cute gopher. Low-brow comedy at its best, with perfectly outrageous performances from Chase, Knight, and Murray. Followed by a sequel. C: Chevy Chase, Rodney Dangerfield, Ted Knight, Michael O'Keefe, Bill Murray. D: Harold Ramis. COM [R] 98m. V

Caddyshack II 1988 ★★★ Uncouth slobs vie for acceptance at exclusive country club. Sequel to 1980 goofball classic tries ethnicity slant but doesn't make par. C: Jackie Mason, Dyan Cannon, Robert Stack, Dina Merrill, Chevy Chase, Dan Aykroyd, Randy Quaid, Jonathan Silverman. D: Allan Arkush. COM [PG] 98m. V

Cadence 1991 ★★ Sheen directs son Charlie as a young troublemaker who finds himself the only white soldier among blacks in an Army brig and in conflict with volatile warden Martin. Over-emotional drama tries for genuine intensity, but misses. C: Charlie Sheen, Martin Sheen, Larry Fishburne, Michael Beach, Ramon Estevez. D: Martin Sheen. DRA [PG-13] 97m. V

Cadillac Man 1990 ★★★ Ideal Williams vehicle casts comic as hustling car salesman taken hostage by his lover's deranged husband (Robbins). Alternately funny and tense at first, but then it goes out with a whimper. C: Robin Williams, Tim Robbins, Pamela Reed, Fran Drescher, Zack Norman, Annabella Sciorra, Lori Petty. D: Roger Donaldson. COM [R] 97m. V

Caesar and Cleopatra 1945 British ★★★★ Julius Caesar tries to civilize the wilful princess Cleopatra in a faithful and sparkling (if a mite stagebound) adaptation of Bernard Shaw's play. Cast is top-notch; a rare opportunity to see Claude Rains in a full-size role worthy of him. C: Claude Rains, Vivien Leigh, Stewart Granger, Flora Robson. D: Gabriel Pascal. DRA 123m. V

Cafe Au Lait 1994 French ★★★½ A young mulatto Parisian woman is torn between a rich, black African and a poor, white Jewish man (director Kassovitz) in this feisty comedy with an amused tone. Diverting. C: Mathieu Kassovitz. D: Mathieu Kassovitz. COM

Cafe Express 1981 Italian ★★★ An espresso bootlegger on the Milan-Naples express train must constantly outmaneuver conductors and police. Manfredi is terrific in this uneven comedy, in a role almost identical to that he played in *Bread and Chocolate*. C: Nino Manfredi, Adolfo Celi, Vittorio Mezzogiorno. D: Nanni Loy. COM 90m. V

Cafe Metropole 1937 ★★★★ American playboy down on his luck in Paris passes himself off as a Russian prince to woo an heiress and clear a gambling debt. Breezy, sophisticated comic romance; entertaining script. C: Loretta Young, Tyrone Power, Adolphe Menjou, Gregory Ratoff, Charles Winninger, Helen Westley. D: Edward Griffith. COM 84m.

Cafe Romeo 1992 ★★★ Six young friends congregate at a NYC coffeehouse to share their troubles and dreams in this old-fashioned romantic comedy. Nicely played, though somewhat awkward and unfocused. C: Catherine Mary Stewart, Jonathan Crombie, Michael Ironside, John Cassini. D: Rex Bromfield. DRA [R] 93m. V

Cafe Society 1939 ★★★★ On a bet a spoiled socialite (Carroll) marries a reporter (MacMurray) to humiliate him, then falls for him. Vivacious, stylish '30s comedy performed with sophistication and wit. C: Madeleine Carroll, Fred MacMurray, Shirley Ross, Jessie Ralph. D: Edward Griffith. COM 83m.

Cage of Gold 1950 British ★★★ An unscrupulous man allows his wife to believe him dead, waits until she marries again, then reappears intent on blackmail. Slow starter—wait for the payoff. C: Jean Simmons, David Farrar, James Donald, Herbert Lom. D: Basil Dearden. DRA 83m.

Cage of Nightingales 1947 French ★★★ Inspirational teacher at reform school. Noel also wrote the script for this good minor drama. C: Noel-Noel, Micheline Francey, George Biscot. D: Jean Dreville. DRA 78m.

Cage, The *See* **Mafu Cage, The**

Cage 1989 ★★½ Ferrigno gives an unexpectedly good performance as a brain-damaged Vietnam vet drawn into the underworld as a cage fighter, but this sleazy affair is flat out brain-dead. Extremely violent. C: Lou Ferrigno, Reb Brown, Michael Dante, James Shigeta. D: Lang Elliott. ACT [R] 101m. V

Caged Fury 1948 ★★½ Circus setting offers myriad opportunities for a lunatic murderer to run rampant. Not bad for low-budget fare. C: Richard Denning, Sheila Ryan, Buster Crabbe. D: William Berke. CRI 60m.

Caged Heat 1974 ★★★½ Abuses suffered by female inmates at hands of wheelchair-bound warden. Tongue-in-cheek tone, feminist slant, and young director Demme all add up to one of the better entries in the genre. (a.k.a. *Renegade Girls*) C: Juanita Brown, Erica Gavin, Roberta Collins, Rainbeaux Smith, Barbara Steele. D: Jonathan Demme. ACT [R] 84m.

Caged in Paradiso 1989 ★★ Convict and his wife are sentenced to remote deserted island. When hubby disappears, woman must carry on by herself. Dismal survival pic. C: Irene Cara, Peter Kowanko, Joseph Culp, Paula Bond. D: Michael Snyder. ACT [R] 90m. v

Caged Terror 1972 ★ Vacationing urban couple are set upon by backwoods barbarians. When wife is raped, husband seeks revenge. C: Percy Harkness, Elizabeth Suzuki, Leon Morenzie. D: Barrie Angus McLean. ACT 76m. v

Caged 1950 ★★★★ Naive widow (Parker) is sent to women's prison on minor violation, where she encounters nightmarish conditions. Best of the lady convict pictures, with a fine cast, including Moorehead as sympathetic warden and Emerson as brutal matron. Tough and chilling. C: Eleanor Parker, Agnes Moorehead, Hope Emerson, Jan Sterling, Betty Garde, Ellen Corby, Jane Darwell, Lee Patrick. D: John Cromwell. DRA 96m.

Cagney & Lacey 1981 ★★★½ A pair of undercover detectives investigate the murder of a Hasidic diamond broker. Smart pilot for the hit series focuses on the relationship between the two partners. C: Loretta Swit, Tyne Daly, Joan Copeland. D: Ted Post. CRI 100m. TVM

Cahill—United States Marshal 1973 ★★ When his son takes to a life of crime, the town's marshal (Wayne) is on the spot. A late Wayne. C: John Wayne, George Kennedy, Gary Grimes, Neville Brand. D: Andrew McLaglen. WST [PG] 103m.

Cain and Mabel 1936 ★★ Overproduced vanity production financed by Davies' lover William Randolph Hearst. Gable's a boxer, Davies a musical star pretending to love him. Fascinating testament to Hearst's folly. C: Marion Davies, Clark Gable, David Carlyle, Ruth Donnelly, Pert Kelton. D: Lloyd Bacon. MUS 90m.

Caine Mutiny Court-Martial, The 1988 ★★★★ Outstanding courtroom drama, based on Wouk's Pulitzer Prize winning novel and Broadway play about a compulsive naval commander whose crew mutinies during a storm at sea. Davis and Bogosian shine in pivotal roles; superior drama. C: Eric Bogosian, Jeff Daniels, Brad Davis, Peter Gallagher. D: Robert Altman. DRA [PG] 100m. TVM

Caine Mutiny, The 1954 ★★★★★ Early in WWII, a naval lieutenant (Johnson) seizes command of a minesweeper from unstable Captain Queeg (Bogart), and is later court-martialed. Powerful stuff, both at sea and in the courtroom. Adapted from Herman Wouk's play, which was based on his Pulitzer Prize-winning novel. C: Humphrey Bogart, Jose Ferrer, Van Johnson, Robert Francis, Fred MacMurray, E.G. Marshall, Lee Marvin. D: Edward Dmytryk. DRA 125m. v

Cairo 1942 ★★★ Movie-star (MacDonald) is mistaken for an enemy spy during WWII, in a muddled mixture of musical comedy and espionage intrigue. Jeanette's last major MGM vehicle (she would make a comeback several years later at the studio). C: Jeanette MacDonald, Robert Young, Mona Barrie, Reginald Owen, Ethel Waters. D: W.S. Van Dyke II. MUS 101m. v

Cairo 1963 British ★★★ Robbers set out to heist King Tutankhamen's jewels from Cairo's museum. Sturdy remake of *The Asphalt Jungle*. C: George Sanders, Richard Johnson. D: Wolf Rilla. CRI 91m.

Cal 1984 British ★★★½ O'Connor's debut feature is an uneven, but ultimately moving story of young IRA assassin (Lynch) who falls in love with widow of one of his victims (Mirren), with tragic results. Mirren's intelligent performance is a marvel of sensuality. C: Helen Mirren, John Lynch, Donal McCann. D: Pat O'Connor. DRA [R] 104m. v

Calamity Jane 1953 ★★★★½ Buoyant musical, with a sunny performance by Day as the buckskin belle who pledges to bring a famous actress to remote Deadwood City. Day and Keel are great together. Opening sequence, completely sung, is a wonder. Terrific score includes Oscar-winning ballad, "Secret Love." C: Doris Day, Howard Keel, Allyn Ann McLerie, Philip Carey. D: David Butler. MUS 101m. v

Calamity Jane 1984 ★★★½ Gritty, realistic account of Wild West markswoman Calamity Jane. Alexander's credible and poignant interpretation of the legend makes for memorable and touching historical drama. C: Jane Alexander, Frederic Forrest, Ken Kercheval, Talia Balsam, Sara Gilbert. D: James Goldstone. DRA 96m. TVM v

Calamity Jane and Sam Bass 1949 ★★½ An outlaw on the run for murder crosses trails with a plucky frontierswoman. Mainly notable for some unusual casting choices in a B-Western. C: Yvonne De Carlo, Howard Duff, Lloyd Bridges. D: George Sherman. WST 85m.

Calcutta 1947 ★★★½ Pilot combs the markets and hotels of Calcutta in search of his buddy's killers. Watchable intrigue, with solid acting by Ladd. C: Alan Ladd, Gail Russell, William Bendix, June Duprez. D: John Farrow. DRA 83m.

Calendar Girl 1993 ★★½ Three young men with overactive hormones travel from Nevada to Hollywood hoping to meet Marilyn Monroe. Lightweight comedy heavy on nostalgia but thin on laughs. C: Jason Priestley, Jerry O'Connell, Gabriel Olds. D: John Whitesell. COM [PG-13] 95m. v

California 1946 ★★★ During early California gold rush, a man and woman cross paths with people opposing statehood for selfish ends. Conventional Hollywood sagebrush glamour piece. C: Barbara Stanwyck, Ray Milland, Barry Fitzgerald, Anthony Quinn. D: John Farrow. WST 97m.

California Conquest 1952 ★★★½ When the Russians contrive to annex Mexican-ruled

California territory, Spanish Californians unite to abort the takeover. Acceptable B-Western highlights sidebar of early U.S. history. C: Cornel Wilde, Teresa Wright. D: Lew Landers. WST 79m.

California Dreaming 1979 ★★½ Pale reprise of '60s beach-blanket movies, with Christopher as the Eastern outsider trying desperately to fit in with the cool California surfing crowd. Means well, but it's pretty slow. C: Dennis Christopher, Glynnis O'Connor. D: John Hancock. DRA 93m. V

California Kid, The 1974 ★★★½ Tidy thriller about a sadistic vigilante sheriff who runs highway speeders off mountain hairpin turns. Compact, well-executed drama with tense performances by Sheen and Morrow. C: Martin Sheen, Vic Morrow, Michelle Phillips, Nick Nolte. D: Richard Heffron. CRI 78m.

California Split 1974 ★★★★ Robert Altman's compelling film involves a pair of on-the-edge compulsive gamblers caught up in their respective lifestyles. Improvisational element lends air of authenticity to rambling character studies skillfully realized by Segal and Gould. C: George Segal, Elliott Gould. D: Robert Altman. DRA [R] 108m.

California Straight Ahead 1937 ★★★½ An enterprising truck driver proposes a cross-country race to demonstrate that trucks can beat trains. Solid, high-spirited action. C: John Wayne, Louise Latimer. D: Arthur Lubin. ACT 67m.

California Suite 1978 ★★★★ All-star show based on Neil Simon's stage comedy tracks progress of four couples during their stays in Beverly Hills hotel. Dozens of great lines, succinct excellence from Matthau and Caine, and Oscar-winning turn from Smith (Supporting Actress) overcome vain attempts at slapstick and soapy emotion. C: Jane Fonda, Alan Alda, Maggie Smith, Michael Caine, Walter Matthau, Elaine May, Richard Pryor, Bill Cosby. D: Herbert Ross. COM [PG] 103m. V

Caligula 1980 ★★ Roman emperor Caligula's bestial reign graphically depicted, replete with blood, violence, nudity, and stomach-turning situations; an expensive production, and talented cast wasted (writer Vidal refused credit). R-version loses a lot of coherence, with substantial cuts from unrated original. C: Malcolm McDowell, Peter O'Toole, Helen Mirren, John Gielgud. D: Tinto Brass. DRA [R] 105m. V

Call a Messenger 1939 ★★★ The rowdy Dead End Kids take straight jobs as telegraph messengers and thwart a stickup attempt. Tightly paced entry in the series. C: Billy Halop, Huntz Hall, William Benedict, David Gorey, Buster Crabbe. D: Arthur Lubin. COM 65m.

Call Her Savage 1932 ★★★½ Bow lights up the screen in this ill-conceived melodrama about a half-Indian, half-white woman, abandoned by a lout, and forced to work the streets. A camp classic. C: Clara Bow, Gilbert Roland, Thelma Todd. D: John Dillon. DRA 88m.

Call Him Mr. Shatter 1976 British ★ Over-the-hill hit man (Whitman) proves his mettle against martial arts fiends in Hong Kong. Sets a new low for kung-fu flicks! Troubled production went through three directors and three cinematographers to make this mess. (a.k.a. *Shatter*) C: Stuart Whitman, Ti Lung, Lily Li, Peter Cushing. D: Michael Carreras. ACT [R] 90m. V

Call It a Day 1937 ★★★½ Spring fever interrupts a day in the life of a wacky British family. Good cast shines in sprightly comedy. C: Olivia de Havilland, Ian Hunter, Alice Brady, Anita Louise. D: Archie Mayo. COM 89m.

Call Me a Cab 1963 *See* **Carry on Cabbie**

Call Me Anna 1990 ★★★½ Dramatization of Patty Duke's autobiography is a courageous self-portrait, from years as child star on. Duke plays herself as an adult suffering from manic depression. Interesting and sincere. C: Patty Duke, Howard Hesseman, Millie Perkins, Karl Malden. D: Gilbert Cates. DRA 100m. TVM

Call Me Bwana 1963 ★★★ Hope in Africa, tussling with natives, wild animals, and Anita Ekberg. Lots of pretty scenery, sophomoric humor. C: Bob Hope, Anita Ekberg, Edie Adams. D: Gordon Douglas. COM 103m. V

Call Me Madam 1953 ★★★★ Broadway belter Merman is at full tilt in this faithful adaptation of Irving Berlin's hit stage musical. Plot involves a lively Washingtonian hostess who is appointed ambassador to a tiny European country, à la real-life Washingtonian Perle Mesta. What counts are great songs superbly sung, including "You're Just in Love," and "It's a Lovely Day Today." C: Ethel Merman, Donald O'Connor, George Sanders, Vera Ellen. D: Walter Lang. MUS 117m.

Call Me Mister 1951 ★★★ Agreeable WWII Broadway musical updated to Korean conflict and twisted into vehicle for Grable as she and GI husband (Dailey) squabble while entertaining troops. Unbilled Bobby Short performs "Going Home Train." C: Betty Grable, Dan Dailey, Danny Thomas, Dale Robertson, Jeffrey Hunter. D: Lloyd Bacon. MUS 95m.

Call Me 1988 ★★½ A bored female reporter welcomes an obscene phone caller and is plunged into a nightmare world of drugs, sex, and corruption. Charbonneau turns in a credible performance, but the muddled story line loses tension. C: Patricia Charbonneau, Patti D'Arbanville, Sam Freed, Boyd Gaines. D: Sollace Mitchell. DRA [R] 98m. V

Call Northside 777 1948 ★★★★ Investigating a routine assignment, a reporter (Stewart) stumbles on evidence of police cover-up in a cop's murder and attempts to clear an innocent man convicted of the crime. Gripping drama, shot in documentary style. (a.k.a. *Calling Northside 777)*. C: James Stewart, Richard Conte, Lee J. Cobb, E.G. Marshall. D: Henry Hathaway. CRI 111m.

Call of the Wild 1935 ★★★★ High adventure in the frozen North as Hollywood adapts Jack London's timeless classic. Worthwhile and entertaining; somewhat ahead of its time. Remade in 1972 and 1976. C: Clark Gable, Loretta Young, Jack Oakie. D: William Wellman. FAM/DRA 81m.

Call of the Wild 1972 ★★★ Jack London's classic Yukon adventure gets pictorially pleasing treatment, but it drags compared to the 1935 Clark Gable version. Best performance: the dog's! C: Charlton Heston, Michele Mercier, Rik Battaglia. D: Ken Annakin. ACT [PG] 100m. V

Call of the Wild, The 1976 ★★★½ Solid version of Jack London's story about a young tenderfoot and his heroic sled dog, caught up in the hurly-burly of the 1903 Yukon gold rush. A good example of the old adage about dogs stealing scenes. C: John Beck, Bernard Fresson, Donald Moffat. D: Jerry Jameson. FAM/DRA 100m. TVM V

Call Out the Marines 1942 ★★★½ A couple of Marine roughnecks take on foreign agents and a dockside vamp. Rollicking comedy action; lots of coarse fun. C: Edmund Lowe, Victor McLaglen, Binnie Barnes, Franklin Pangborn. D: Frank Ryan, William Hamilton. COM 67m.

Call the Cops 1976 *See* **Find the Lady**

Callan 1974 British ★★½ Woodward is an undercover spy fighting the system while trying to fulfill his murderous assignment in this movie adaptation of the popular British TV series. Development seems to take forever. (a.k.a. *The Neutralizer*) C: Edward Woodward, Eric Porter. D: Don Sharp. ACT 106m.

Callaway Went Thataway 1951 ★★★½ Two promoters (MacMurray and McGuire), unable to locate a former cowpoke movie star whose serials have made it big on TV, hire his former stand-in (Keel plays both parts) instead. Fine performances, including some fun star cameos. (a.k.a. *The Star Said No*) C: Fred MacMurray, Dorothy McGuire, Howard Keel, Jesse White, Natalie Schafer. D: Norman Panama, Melvin Frank. COM 81m.

Caller, The 1987 ★★★½ McDowell and Smith are locked together in a lonely cabin, far from anyone else. They begin playing psychological games with each other, leading to a strange outcome. Starts off well but doesn't know when to end. C: Malcolm McDowell, Madolyn Smith. D: Arthur Allan Seidelman. DRA [R] 90m. V

Calling Bulldog Drummond 1951 ★★★½ Retired British adventurer Hugh Drummond gets back into action to foil a gang of archcriminals. Light mystery par for the durable series. C: Walter Pidgeon, Margaret Leighton, Robert Beatty, David Tomlinson, Peggy Evans. D: Victor Saville. CRI 80m.

Calling Dr. Death 1943 ★★★ When the unfaithful wife of a prominent physician (Chaney, Jr.) is murdered, he is among the many suspects—and he's not sure he didn't do it. Low-budget mystery's tight direction and cast make up for an uneven script. First in the *Inner Sanctum* series. C: Lon Chaney Jr., Ramsay Ames. D: Reginald LeBorg. CRI 63m.

Calling Dr. Gillespie 1942 ★★★ The curmudgeonly head of medicine (Barrymore) at an urban hospital trains a protegeé, and an insane ex-patient prowls the wards. Solid entry for the *Dr. Kildare* series (minus Ayres as Kildare). C: Lionel Barrymore, Philip Dorn, Donna Reed. D: Harold Bucquet. DRA 84m.

Calling Dr. Kildare 1939 ★★★ Kildare signs up for outpatient care at Blair General and calls on crusty old Gillespie when he's involved in murder. Second in the popular doctor series. C: Lew Ayres, Lionel Barrymore, Laraine Day, Lana Turner. D: Harold Bucquet. DRA 86m.

Calling Homicide 1956 ★★★ A cop killing leads a detective (Elliott) to a modeling school and extortion. Tidy, effective mystery successfully produced on a low budget. C: Bill Elliott, Kathleen Case. D: Edward Bernds. CRI 61m.

Calling Northside 777 1948 *See* **Call Northside 777**

Calling Philo Vance 1940 ★★★ Remake of *The Kennel Murder Case*, with the suave private eye investigating the murder of a manufacturing magnate and discovering Axis spies among the dead man's domestic help. Workmanlike effort, with wartime espionage thrown in. C: James Stephenson, Margot Stevenson. D: William Clemens. CRI 62m.

Caltiki, the Immortal Monster 1959 Italian ★★½ A fiendish creature terrorizes archaeologists on an expedition in Mexico. Juvenile thrills with an amorphous gelatin monster on tap. C: John Merivale, Didi Sullivan. D: Robert Hampton. HOR 76m.

Calypso Heat Wave 1957 ★★★ Musical dance numbers by '50s artists dominate Hollywood plot of a parasitic crook who muscles in on a young man's record production enterprise. Watch for Alan Arkin as one of the Tarriers. C: Johnny Desmond, Merry Anders, Joel Grey, The Treniers, The Tarriers, The Hi Lo's, Maya Angelou. D: Fred Sears. MUS 86m.

Calypso Joe 1957 ★★½ A television actor and his airline hostess wife bicker, then patch things up. Crowd-pleasing songfest set in South America. C: Herb Jeffries, Angie Dickinson, Edward Kemmer. D: Edward Dein. MUS 76m.

Came a Hot Friday 1985 ★★★½ In 1949 two con artists work their way across New Zealand fleecing race track bettors and wooing women. This film has an abundance of charm and easy style. C: Peter Bland, Philip Gordon. D: Ian Mune. COM [PG] 101m. V

Camel Boy, The 1984 ★★★ Animated adventure of boy and pet camel traveling across a desert in the early 1900s. Unexceptional children's feature. FAM/ACT 78m. V

Camelot 1967 ★★ Romantic Lerner/Loewe musical treatment of King Arthur/Guinevere/Lancelot triangle is sabotaged by elephantine production, though Redgrave is charming. Won Oscars for sets, costumes, and scoring. C: Richard Harris, Vanessa Redgrave, Franco Nero, David Hemmings. D: Joshua Logan. MUS [G] 180m. V

Camera Buff 1983 Polish ★★★★ Amateur filmmaker graduates from home movies to political documentaries, which ultimately gets him in trouble with government authorities. Though not terribly original, this well-told Polish satire film conveys genuine love for art and power of cinema. C: Jerzy Stuhr, Malgorzata Zabkowska, Ewa Pokas. D: Krzstof Kieslowski. COM 112m.

Cameraman, The 1928 ★★★★½ A bumbling documentary cameraman (Keaton) can't seem to get his love life in focus. Keaton's genius makes this vintage silent comedy a laugh riot. C: Buster Keaton, Marceline Day. D: Edward Sedgwick. COM 69m. V

Cameron's Closet 1987 ★★ Supernatural horror film (based on Gary Brandner novel) squanders good idea with muddled plotting and lousy effects. Youngster's fears of monster-in-the-closet turn out to be very real; his mom (Harris) and a detective (Smith) try to stop it. C: Cotter Smith, Mel Harris, Chuck McCann, Tab Hunter. D: Armand Mastroianni. HOR 90m. V

Camila 1984 Argentine ★★★ Fact-based story of doomed love involves a wealthy Argentine young woman entangled with a Jesuit priest. Defying social conventions, they flee, with the authorities in pursuit. Not bad, but not as deep as it thinks it is. C: Susu Pecoraro, Imanol Arias. D: Maria Bemberg. DRA 105m. V

Camilla 1994 ★★★ Tandy is the sole reason to watch this sentimental drama, as a sheltered woman forms a bond with a young musician (Fonda). Jessica's next-to-last performance is beautifully judged, making material look better than it is. C: Jessica Tandy, Bridget Fonda, Elias Koteas, Hume Cronyn, Graham Greene. D: Deepa Mehta. COM [PG-13] 90m.

Camille 1936 ★★★★½ One of the great romantic films. Luminous Garbo is Dumas' doomed courtesan, loved by well-to-do Taylor, who sacrifices her happiness for his well-being. Bad guys—Daniell, and Barrymore—have the most fun, but Cukor gets brilliant performances from everyone but Taylor, who is handsome as a tailor's dummy. C: Greta Garbo, Robert Taylor, Lionel Barrymore, Laura Hope Crews, Henry Daniell, Jesse Ralph. D: George Cukor. DRA 110m.

Camille 1984 British ★★★½ Alexandre Dumas' tale of the tragic courtesan who sacrifices all for her guileless lover. Remake of Garbo's 1936 classic is better than most remakes, with a great cast. C: Greta Scacchi, Colin Firth, John Gielgud, Billie Whitelaw, Ben Kingsley, Denholm Elliott. D: Desmond Davis. DRA 100m. TVM

Camille Claudel 1989 French ★★★ Historical fact-based story of French sculptor (Adjani) and her passionate romance with great sculptor and artist Pierre Rodin (Depardieu). Sumptuous production values and good acting, but direction only skims surface of complicated story. C: Isabelle Adjani, Gerard Depardieu. D: Bruno Nuytten. DRA [R] 159m. V

Camille 2000 1969 ★ Heroine enchants a Roman nobleman, but her heart belongs to a commoner. Soft-core rip-off of the classic Dumas tale, most notable for terrible dubbing. C: Daniele Gaubert, Eleanora Rossi-Drago, Nino Castelnuovo, Philippe Forquet. D: Radley Metzger. DRA [R] 115m. V

Camorra 1985 Italian ★★½ A group of Naples mothers takes the law into their own hands when they become fed up with local mob and drug dealers. Unusual combination of preaching and action. C: Angela Molina, Harvey Keitel. D: Lina Wertmuller. CRI [R] 94m. V

Camouflage 1977 Polish ★★★★ A cynical scholar and idealistic younger colleague at summer language school clash over politics. Comedic parable of Poland under communism; Zanussi finds insights as plentiful as laughs. C: Piotr Garlicki, Zbignieu Zapasiewicz. D: Krzysztof Zanussi. COM 106m. V

Camp Cucamonga 1990 ★★ Dopey movie about summer at a coed wilderness camp. Almost everyone's a familiar face from a popular TV comedy series, but they can't do enough with the stale jokes and the stereotypical characterizations. C: John Ratzenberger, Sherman Hemsley, G. Liddy. D: Roger Duchonwny. COM 100m. TVM

Camp on Blood Island, The 1958 British ★★½ Unaware Japan has surrendered, a barbaric POW commandant vows to kill every Allied prisoner. Horrific, sadistic WWII drama of questionable intent. C: Andre Morell, Carl Mohner. D: Val Guest. DRA 81m.

Campbell's Kingdom 1958 British ★★★ Amid the vast splendor of the Canadian Rockies, a landowner clashes with a corrupt contractor out to construct a big dam near his oil-rich property. Updated Western with requisite action and romance. C: Dirk Bogarde, Stanley Baker. D: Ralph Thomas. WST 102m.

Campus Man 1987 ★★ Inoffensive trifle about college student (Dye) who struggles against all odds to publish a calendar of campus hunks. Fairchild and the other authority figures do their best to squash the fun, but—

as always—beefcake triumphs. C: John Dye, Steve Lyon, Morgan Fairchild. D: Ron Casden. COM [PG] 94m. V

Can-Can 1960 ★★★ Cole Porter's Broadway bonbon dealing with origins of the racy French dance and attempts to suppress it. Some good songs: "C'est Magnifique," "I Love Paris," "It's All Right With Me." Good dancing best appreciated in the letterboxed edition. C: Frank Sinatra, Shirley MacLaine, Maurice Chevalier, Louis Jourdan, Juliet Prowse. D: Walter Lang. MUS 131m. V

Can Hieronymus Merkin Ever Forget Mercy Humppe and Find True Happiness? 1969 British ★★½ A variety performer's midlife crisis prompts him to recall his bygone sexual past. Self-indulgent surrealism. C: Anthony Newley, Joan Collins, Milton Berle, George Jessel, Stubby Kaye. D: Anthony Newley. DRA [R] 106m.

Can I Do It . . . 'Til I Need Glasses? 1977 ★ Threadbare assemblage of sketches about sex. The humor, especially the swinging and swapping jokes, dates badly. C: Moose Carlson, Walter Olkewicz, Robin Williams. D: I. Robert Levy, Victor Dunlap. COM [R] 72m. V

Can It Be Love 1992 ★ Love has little to do with this sophomoric sex comedy about two teens looking for action. C: Richard Beaumont, Maryann Mixon, Jennifer Langdon, Blake Pickett. D: Peter Maris. COM [R] 90m. V

Can She Bake a Cherry Pie? 1983 ★★½ When her husband dumps her, Black takes up with Emil. Free-flowing relationship comedy whips up a few laughs, despite unfocused story. C: Karen Black, Michael Emil. D: Henry Jaglom. COM 90m. V

Can Tropical Rainforests Be Saved? 1992 ★★★½ Documentary addresses the serious problem of disappearing tropical rainforests, and seeks solutions. Well-done, in-depth investigation, with some startling footage. DOC 40m. V

Can You Feel Me Dancing? 1986 ★★★½ A blind teenager (Bateman) tries to lead her own life and free herself from her overprotective parents. Predictable drama, but better than most of its kind. C: Justine Bateman, Jason Bateman, Max Gail. D: Michael Miller. DRA 90m. TVM V

Can You Hear the Laughter? The Story of Freddie Prinze 1979 ★★★ True story of Puerto Rican comic Freddie Prinze, who rose to overnight TV stardom but tragically committed suicide. Loving account of sad story. C: Ira Angustain, Kevin Hooks. D: Burt Brinckerhoff. DRA 96m. TVM V

Canadian Pacific 1949 ★★★½ A railroad surveyor torn between two loves and beset by Indians constructs a train link through a wilderness pass in the Rockies. Decent outdoor action film. C: Randolph Scott, Jane Wyatt. D: Edwin Marin. ACT 95m.

Canadians, The 1961 ★★★½ Mounties thwart efforts of several corrupt Canadians to attack a band of Sioux fleeing the bloody aftermath of Custer's last stand. Entertainment-focused revisionist history, shot in Canada. C: Robert Ryan, John Dehner, Torin Thatcher, Teresa Stratas. D: Burt Kennedy. ACT 85m.

Canaris 1954 German ★★★ The head of German intelligence attempts to remove Adolf Hitler from power in the '30s. Fact-based, multi-leveled production. (a.k.a. *Canaris, Master Spy*) C: O. E. Hasse, Barbara Rutting. D: Alfred Weidenmann. ACT 92m.

Canaris, Master Spy 1954 *See* **Canaris**

Canary Murder Case 1929 ★★★ One of the first talkies, which started out as a silent, debuts suave detective Philo Vance as he investigates the death of a singer. Powell heads up fine cast. C: William Powell, Louise Brooks, Jean Arthur. D: Malcolm Clair. CRI 81m.

Cancel My Reservation 1972 ★★ Hope quips his way through this tedious mystery comedy in which he plays a talk show host who gets mixed up in the murder of a millionaire rancher. Very little to laugh about. Based on a Louis L'Amour novel. C: Bob Hope, Eva Marie Saint, Ralph Bellamy, Keenan Wynn. D: Paul Bogart. COM [G] 99m. V

Candid Candid Camera 1985 ★★★★ Without the restraints of TV censors, the master of the hidden camera, Alan Funt, puts a host of naked beauties in unlikely situations in hopes of getting a rise out of his unsuspecting victims. Entertaining for uninhibited fans of the series. COM 55m. V

Candidate for Murder 1962 British ★★★½ Edgar Wallace story concerns an insane man attempting to murder his actress wife. Well-rendered narrative provides decent suspense. C: Michael Gough, Erika Remberg. D: David Villiers. CRI 60m.

Candidate, The 1972 ★★★★★ Idealistic attorney (Redford) runs for the Senate only to find he must make compromises and play political games if he wants to win. Intelligent, ironic look at American politics, highlighted by excellent performances all around. Oscar for Best Original Screenplay by Jeremy Larner. C: Robert Redford, Peter Boyle, Don Porter, Karen Carlson, Melvyn Douglas. D: Michael Ritchie. DRA [PG] 109m.

Candleshoe 1978 ★★★ Street waif (Foster) poses as heiress to an English estate in order to get inside and look for a hidden treasure. Hayes, in her final film, is the elderly hoodwinked grandmother. C: David Niven, Jodie Foster, Helen Hayes, Leo McKern. D: Norman Tokar. FAM/DRA [G] 101m. V

Candy 1968 U.S. ★★ Forced spoof about lovely young woman pursued by most of the cast members. Worth seeing for all-star cast. C: Ewa Aulin, Richard Burton, Marlon Brando, Charles Aznavour, James Coburn, John Huston, Walter Matthau, Ringo Starr, John Astin. D: Christian Marquand. COM [R] 115m.

Candy Man, The 1969 ★★★ A jaded British narcotics dealer in Mexico City contrives to abduct an American film actress's child. Thriller offers Sanders in his twilight. C: George Sanders, Leslie Parrish. D: Herbert Leder. CRI [G] 98m.

Candy Mountain 1987 Canadian ★★★ Downbeat road film about a young, ambitious musician seeking a master guitar maker. Appearances by notable singers, although production lacks star power. C: Kevin O'Connor, Harris Yulin, Tom Waits. D: Robert Frank, Rudy Wurlitzer. DRA [R] 90m. V

Candy Stripe Nurses 1974 ★★ Roger Corman's series of nursing sex romps winds up with this lesser entry. Title tells the idea and familiar Corman cast does the rest. Do not resuscitate. C: Candice Rialson, Robin Mattson. D: Allan Holleb. COM [R] 80m.

Candy Tangerine Man, The 1975 ★★ A weemingly respectable businessman is actually a pimp. Ridiculous yet entertaining low-grade actioner. An unsung guilty pleasure. C: John Daniels, Tom Hankerson. D: Matt Cimber. ACT [R] 93m. V

Candyman 1992 ★★★★ Clive Barker's story "The Forbidden" inspired this gripping, frightening film in which grad student Madsen, researching urban legends, uncovers a mythical killer who proves to be very real. Intelligent and refreshingly free of gimmicks; Madsen is terrific. C: Virginia Madsen, Tony Todd, Vanessa Williams. D: Bernard Rose. HOR [R] 98m. V

Candyman: Farewell to the Flesh 1995 ★ Grotesque, bee-filled corpse of one-time slave terrorizes modern-day New Orleans. Gruesome, cheaply made sequel to 1992 film. C: Tony Todd, Kelly Rowan, Timothy Carhart, Veronica Cartwright. D: Bill Condon. HOR [R] 99m. V

Cannery Row 1982 ★★★ Adaptation of John Steinbeck's stories *Cannery Row* and *Sweet Thursday* features Nolte as marine biologist who romances devil-may-care Winger. Despite engaging leads and character actor ensemble, film suffers from meandering and occasionally confusing plot development. C: Nick Nolte, Debra Winger, Audra Lindley. D: David S. Ward. COM [PG] 120m. V

Cannibal Attack 1954 ★★★ Jungle Jim (Weissmuller) battles unscrupulous foreigners out to swindle cobalt from a tribe of cannibals. Tangled but entertaining *Jungle Jim* yarn. C: Johnny Weissmuller, Judy Walsh. D: Lee Sholem. ACT 69m.

Cannibal Girls 1973 Canadian ★★★ Horror spoof includes a vignette about a couple stuck in a weird town whose poshest restaurant serves patrons—on the menu. Facetious Canadian low-budget parody, with many twists and turns. C: Eugene Levy, Andrea Martin. D: Ivan Reitman. COM [R] 84m.

Cannibal Women in the Avocado Jungle of Death 1988 ★★★½ A feminist anthropologist (former *Playboy* model Tweed), is sent by the CIA on an expedition to find a legendary tribe of man-eating cannibal women. Comic adventure revolves around a series of offbeat gags: For example, should men be consumed with guacamole or clam dip? C: Adrienne Barbeau, Bill Maher, Shannon Tweed, Karen Mistal. D: J.D. Athens. COM [PG-13] 90m. V

Cannon for Cordoba 1970 ★★★½ A U.S. Army captain (Peppard) on the Texas border in 1912 leads his troops against a wily Mexican bandido harboring a stolen cannon. Familiar Western sparked with action. C: George Peppard, Giovanna Ralli, Raf Vallone. D: Paul Wendkos. WST [PG] 104m.

Cannon 1971 ★★★½ Is a friend's murder related to corruption in a small New Mexico town? The portly private detective (Conrad) investigates in this well-received pilot for the hit series. Above-average mystery yarn laden with subplots. C: William Conrad, Vera Miles, Keenan Wynn. D: George McCowan. CRI 99m. TVM

Cannonball 1976 ★★★ Freewheeling race-car drivers compete for a $100,000 prize in the Trans-American Grand Prix from Los Angeles to New York. Thrill-packed car crashes and stunts dominate formula action-adventure. C: David Carradine, Veronica Hamel, Judy Canova. D: Paul Bartel. ACT [PG] 94m. V

Cannonball Run, The 1981 ★★ Reynolds in yet another coast-to-coast car race, accompanied by every actor he ever worked with. Pointless crash-up comedy. Followed by a sequel. C: Burt Reynolds, Roger Moore, Farrah Fawcett, Dom DeLuise, Dean Martin, Sammy Davis Jr., Jamie Farr, Peter Fonda, Bianca Jagger, Molly Picon. D: Hal Needham. COM [PG] 96m. V

Cannonball Run II 1983 ★★ More cross-country antics from Burt and fellow celebrities. Silly and rambling. C: Burt Reynolds, Dom DeLuise, Shirley MacLaine, Marilu Henner, Dean Martin, Sammy Davis Jr., Ricardo Montalban, Jim Nabors, Charles Nelson Reilly, Telly Savalas, Jamie Farr. D: Hal Needham. COM [PG] 109m. V

Canon City 1948 ★★★★ Documentary-style account of convicts who break out of Colorado State Penitentiary. Compact, aggressive melodrama is well presented. Photographed on actual locations. C: Scott Brady, Jeff Corey. D: Crane Wilbur. CRI 82m.

Can't Buy Me Love 1987 ★★★ A high school nerd (Dempsey) is so desperate to be accepted by the in-crowd he hires the school beauty (Peterson) to be his girlfriend. Mechanical and moralistic, but there's enough high-spirited comedy to hold one's interest. C: Patrick Dempsey, Amanda Peterson. D: Steve Rash. COM [PG-13] 94m.

Can't Help Singing 1944 ★★★½ Determined young woman (Durbin) travels west in search of lost love (Paige). Period musical with good Jerome Kern score. Fans of the star won't want to miss her in color. C: Deanna Durbin, Robert Paige, Akim Tamiroff. D: Frank Ryan. MUS 89m.

Can't Stop the Music 1980 ★★ Nostalgic for late '70s? Here's the cure: a mega disco musical loosely based on the Village People's rise to pop music fame. Peerless flop has undeniable camp appeal. C: Valerie Perrine, Bruce Jenner, Steve Guttenberg, Tammy Grimes. D: Nancy Walker. MUS [PG] 118m. v

Canterbury Tale, A 1944 British ★★★★ A British soldier, an American soldier, and a local woman converge on an English town and try to uncover the identity of a mysterious nighttime marauder, the "Glue Man." Charming Powell-Pressburger collaboration marked by excellent camerawork. C: Eric Portman, Sheila Sim. D: Michael Powell, Emeric Pressburger. DRA 123m.

Canterville Ghost, The 1944 ★★★★ Jovial British fantasy of a cowardly ghost (Laughton) doomed to haunt his castle until a descendant (Young) performs a deed of bravery. Laughton is a splendid ham; fun family viewing. Remade in 1986. C: Charles Laughton, Robert Young, Margaret O'Brien, Una O'Connor, Peter Lawford. D: Jules Dassin. FAM/COM 96m.

Canterville Ghost, The 1986 ★★½ Charmless retread of the charming 1944 film. Gielgud shines as the bombastic, cowardly ghost, but the rest of the cast (especially Wass as the father) is inadequate. Be careful: dangerous ghostly tricks may give youngsters foolish ideas. C: John Gielgud, Ted Wass, Alyssa Milano, Andrea Marcovicci, Harold Innocent. D: Paul Bogart. FAM/COM 96m. v

Canvas 1992 ★★★ Uneven suspense drama about a struggling artist drawn into the Mob via his brother's failed business deal. C: Gary Busey, John Rhys-Davies, Vittorio Rossi, Nick Cavaiola. D: Alain Zoloum. CRI [R] 94m. v

Canyon Crossroads 1955 ★★★½ Bandits target a uranium prospector when he makes a strike. Basehart offers a convincing performance in this true-to-form Western. C: Richard Basehart, Phyllis Kirk. D: Alfred Werker. WST 83m.

Canyon Passage 1946 ★★★★ Andrews and Donlevy compete for Hayward's charms in the pioneering Old West. Enjoyable oater features good action, scenery, and Hoagy Carmichael's own rendition of his song "Ole Buttermilk Sky." C: Dana Andrews, Brian Donlevy, Susan Hayward, Lloyd Bridges. D: Jacques Tourneur. WST 92m.

Canyon River 1956 ★★½ Montgomery is a cattle drover besieged by outlaws and Indians. Cut 'n' paste horse opera is not exactly a stampede of originality. C: George Montgomery, Marcia Henderson, Peter Graves. D: Harmon Jones. WST 80m.

Cape Canaveral Monsters 1960 ★★ A couple killed in an auto accident become possessed by evil aliens bent on destroying the U.S. space program. Director Tucker also unleashed *Robot Monster* on an unsuspecting world. C: Scott Peters, Linda Connell. D: Phil Tucker. HOR 69m.

Cape Fear 1961 ★★★★ Gripping thriller involving a lawyer (Peck), his wife, and daughter, who are terrorized by Mitchum, an ex-con who blames Peck for his jail term. Good shocks and Mitchum's sadistic turn make this an exemplary adaptation of the John D. MacDonald novel. Remade in 1991. C: Gregory Peck, Robert Mitchum, Polly Bergen, Martin Balsam, Telly Savalas. D: J. Lee Thompson. CRI 106m. v

Cape Fear 1991 ★★★★ Remake of the 1962 feature stars heavily tattooed De Niro as a psychopathic prison parolee come to exact revenge on an attorney (Nolte), his wife (Lange) and daughter (Lewis). Tense, very frightening and very violent. Includes terrific performances and cameos from Mitchum, Peck, and Balsam, who all appeared in the original. C: Robert De Niro, Nick Nolte, Jessica Lange, Juliette Lewis, Joe Don Baker, Robert Mitchum, Gregory Peck, Martin Balsam. D: Martin Scorsese. CRI [R] 128m. v

Cape Town Affair, The 1967 ★★★ Pickpocket mistakenly steals purse containing purloined microfilm, then must deal with spies who want it back. Mediocre remake of Sam Fuller's film noir classic *Pickup on South Street* was shot in South Africa. C: Claire Trevor, James Brolin, Jacqueline Bisset. D: Robert Webb. ACT 103m.

Caper of the Golden Bulls, The 1967 ★★ Ex-crook Boyd forced to assist gang planning bank robbery during famed "running of the bulls" in Pamplona, Spain. Suspenseful climax saves this average heist film. C: Stephen Boyd, Yvette Mimieux. D: Russell Rouse. CRI 104m. v

Capone 1975 ★★★ Slick exploitation biography follows rise and fall of legendary Chicago mobster Al Capone (Gazzara, with stuffed cheeks). Emphasis is on action and atmosphere. C: Ben Gazzara, Susan Blakely, Harry Guardino, John Cassavetes, Sylvester Stallone. D: Steve Carver. CRI [R] 101m.

Capone 1989 ★ Dismal recap of famed gangster's life. Sharkey works hard but writer and director don't. C: Keith Carradine, Ray Sharkey, Debrah Farentino, Jayne Atkinson, Charles Haid. D: Michael Pressman. CRI [R] 96m. v

Caprice 1967 ★★★ Stylishly mod espionage comedy about a cosmetics exec (Day) who uncovers an international spy ring. Not Doris's most seamless romp, but it sure is fun, '60s style. C: Doris Day, Richard Harris, Ray Walston. D: Frank Tashlin. COM 98m.

Capricious Summer 1968 Czech ★★★★ Low-key period comedy of two itinerant carnival performers who shake up a small town. Charming example of Czech New Wave before the Soviet Union moved in. C: Rudolph Hrusinsky, Vlastimil Brodsky, Mila Myslikova. D: Jiri Menzel. COM 75m.

Capricorn One 1978 ★★★★ Astronauts (Brolin, Waterston, and Simpson) have a secret the government does not want them to share, ever. Combination of science fiction, action/chase, and conspiracy genres may not always be credible, but it's effective and fun. C: Elliott Gould, James Brolin, Hal Holbrook, Sam Waterston, Karen Black, O.J. Simpson, Telly Savalas. D: Peter Hyams. ACT [PG] 118m. V

Captain America 1979 ★★ Comic book superhero Captain America must stop a crazed extortionist, who, if not given the oodles of cash he demands, will blow up Phoenix. Mindless, simple entertainment. Followed by a sequel. C: Reb Brown, Heather Menzies. D: Rod Holcomb. ACT 98m. TVM V

Captain America II 1979 ★★ The Marvel hero (Brown) returns, this time to stop evil terrorists wielding a deadly drug. Lifeless story fails to capture the excitement of the comic book series. C: Reb Brown, Connie Sellecca, Christopher Lee. D: Ivan Nagy. ACT 88m. TVM V

Captain Apache 1971 British-Spanish ★★★ A Union Army officer uncovers plot to steal land from Indians. Welcome humor and good supporting cast. C: Lee Van Cleef, Carroll Baker, Stuart Whitman. D: Alexander Singer. WST [PG] 94m.

Captain Blackjack 1951 U. S. ★★★ Superior locations and actors fail to elevate pedestrian yarn of drug smugglers plying their trade on the Spanish Riviera. Standard action film. C: George Sanders, Herbert Marshall, Agnes Moorehead. D: Julien Dunvivier. ACT 90m.

Captain Blood 1935 ★★★★½ Surgeon Peter Blood (Flynn), falsely accused of treason, first becomes a slave, and then a pirate. Quintessential swashbuckler is a marvelously exciting adventure yarn that made the dashing Flynn and lovely de Havilland instant stars in their first of eight films together. Based on the novel by Rafael Sabatini. C: Errol Flynn, Olivia de Havilland, Basil Rathbone, Lionel Atwill, Guy Kibbee. D: Michael Curtiz. ACT 120m. V

Captain Blood 1960 French ★★½ Poor variation on the revered Errol Flynn swashbuckler has Marais foiling an evil plot aimed at King Louis XIII. Adequate costumes and cinematography almost overcome the simplistic script. C: Jean Marais, Elsa Martinelli. D: Andre Hunebelle. ACT 95m.

Captain Boycott 1947 British ★★★½ Nineteenth-century tale of poverty-stricken Irish farmers banding together to defeat brutal landowners. Terrific British cast enlivens otherwise erratic, jumbled historical drama. C: Stewart Granger, Kathleen Ryan, Alastair Sim. D: Frank Launder. DRA 92m.

Captain Carey, U.S.A. 1950 ★★★★ Former American military officer returns to Italy to locate the spy whose informing destroyed the lives of villagers. Above-average WWII vet movie. Notable for theme song "Mona Lisa," which won Oscar. C: Alan Ladd, Wanda Hendrix. D: Mitchell Leisen. DRA 83m.

Captain Caution 1940 ★★★ During the War of 1812, a young girl allows patriotic Mature to use her dead father's ship to fight the British. No-nonsense naval adventure features bit performance by soon-to-be famous Alan Ladd. C: Victor Mature, Louise Platt. D: Richard Wallace. ACT 85m.

Captain China 1949 ★★★ Ex-sea captain scours the ocean for the treacherous first mate who cost him command of his ship. Interesting melodrama. C: John Payne, Gail Russell, Lon Chaney Jr., Edgar Bergen. D: Lewis Foster. DRA 97m.

Captain Eddie 1945 ★★★ Famed flyer Eddie Rickenbacker (MacMurray) examines his life in flashback following a plane crash in the Pacific. Rather dull, slapdash biography, particularly considering the exciting source material. C: Fred MacMurray, Lynn Bari, Charles Bickford, Thomas Mitchell, Lloyd Nolan. D: Lloyd Bacon. DRA 107m.

Captain Falcon 1958 Italian ★★½ Swashbuckling Barker embarks on a mission to save a woman's homeland from bloodthirsty marauders. The most entertaining element is the lousy dubbing. C: Lex Barker, Rossana Rory. D: Carlo Campogalliani. ACT 97m.

Captain from Castile 1947 ★★★ In the 15th century, a dashing Spaniard seeks adventure with Cortez during the conquest of Mexico. Fine location shooting makes for genuine excitement at times. C: Tyrone Power, Jean Peters, Cesar Romero, Lee J. Cobb. D: Henry King. ACT 140m.

Captain from Koepenick 1933 ★★★★ Classic film version of satirical play about young man impersonating Prussian officer. Very funny and still timely. C: Max Adalbert, Willi Schur, Hermann Vallentin. D: Franz Schroeder. COM 96m.

Captain Fury 1939 ★★★ Brave Australian adventurer clashes with warden of brutal Aussie penal colony. Down-under backgrounds help camouflage routine story line in this brawling action movie. C: Brian Aherne, Victor McLaglen, Paul Lukas, John Carradine. D: Hal Roach. ACT 91m.

Captain Hates the Sea, The 1934 ★★½ Sea captain (Connolly), weary of steering the lives of his passengers more than his ship, is eager to reach land and never sail again. Episodic comedy was one-time matinee idol Gilbert's last film. C: Victor McLaglen, John Gilbert, Walter Connolly, Akim Tamiroff. D: Lewis Milestone. COM 93m.

Captain Horatio Hornblower 1951 British ★★★½ British naval officer (Peck) battles the Spanish and French during the Napoleonic Wars and eventually marries admiral's widow (Mayo). Well-done sea saga, from C.S. Forester's novels. C: Gregory Peck, Virginia Mayo. D: Raoul Walsh. ACT 117m. V

Captain Is a Lady, The 1940 ★★★ Financially-strapped seafarer dresses in drag to keep watch over his wife, who's been forced into a retirement home. Capable cast and crazy situation enhance this farce. C: Charles Coburn, Beulah Bondi, Helen Broderick, Billie Burke, Dan Dailey. D: Robert Sinclair. COM 63m.

Captain January 1936 ★★★½ Temple survives shipwreck, is rescued by crusty-but-kindhearted lighthouse keeper. Enjoyable song 'n' dance numbers might have been better served if film concentrated on story instead of sentiment. Shirley is quite good. C: Shirley Temple, Guy Kibbee, Slim Summerville, Buddy Ebsen. D: David Butler. MUS 76m. V

Captain John Smith and Pocahontas 1953 ★★½ Tensions and romances between English settlers and native Americans in Colonial America. Dull low-budget melodrama takes too long to recount the famed love affair between titled characters. C: Anthony Dexter, Jody Lawrance. D: Lew Landers. DRA 75m.

Captain Kidd and the Slave Girl 1954 ★★★ Title tells all, with search for lost treasure spicing up Gabor/Dexter love scenes. Resolutely routine swashbuckler. C: Anthony Dexter, Eva Gabor. D: Lew Landers. ACT 83m.

Captain Kidd 1945 ★★½ Slow-moving pirate yarn. Laughton is the main attraction as the late-18th-century pirate, raiding and double-crossing on the high seas. C: Charles Laughton, Randolph Scott, Barbara Britton, John Carradine. D: Rowland V. Lee. ACT 83m. V

Captain Kronos: Vampire Hunter 1974 British ★★★★ An English noble (Janson) dedicates himself to wiping out the plague of vampirism—with his deadly swords. Another handcrafted Hammer horror, with lots of action. A cult favorite. C: Horst Janson, John David Carson. D: Brian Clemens. HOR [R] 91m. V

Captain Lightfoot 1955 ★★½ The 19th-century Irish rebellion, as seen through the eyes of one of its heroes. Masterful cinematography and exquisite scenery perk up a less than enthralling tale. C: Rock Hudson, Barbara Rush. D: Douglas Sirk. ACT 91m.

Captain Midnight 1979 *See* **On the Air Live with Captain Midnight**

Captain Nemo and the Underwater City 1970 ★★★½ Shipwrecked passengers are held captive by famed Jules Verne character in fabulous underwater city, where they undergo various adventures. Poor miniature effects mar otherwise okay fantasy. C: Robert Ryan, Chuck Connors, Nanette Newman. D: James Hill. ACT [G] 105m.

Captain Newman, M.D. 1963 ★★★★ Dedicated Army shrink Peck clashes with military bureaucracy as he tries to help troubled soldiers at a U.S. base during WWII. Irreverent, offbeat comedy drama with Darin affecting as a disturbed war hero. Based on Leo Rosten's best-seller. C: Gregory Peck, Angie Dickinson, Tony Curtis, Eddie Albert, Bobby Darin, Larry Storch, Robert Duvall. D: David Miller. DRA 126m. V

Captain of the Clouds 1942 ★★★★ In WWII, cocky Canadian bush pilot (Cagney) proves too independent for the Royal Canadian Air Force, but still demonstrates heroism on a civilian mission. Entertaining war story with good training sections and flight photography. C: James Cagney, Dennis Morgan, Alan Hale. D: Michael Curtiz. ACT 113m.

Captain Pirate 1952 ★★★½ Reformed buccaneer returns to piracy to uncover the imposter who's framing him for crimes. Energetic swashbuckler was based on Rafael Sabatini's novel *Captain Blood Returns*. C: Louis Hayward, Patricia Medina. D: Ralph Murphy. ACT 85m.

Captain Ron 1992 ★★ A suburbanite hopes to find adventure on the high seas when he inherits an old sailing craft, but he inadvertently hires a drunken wastrel to pilot the craft. Situation comedy that should have stowed away more laughs before setting sail. C: Kurt Russell, Martin Short, Mary Kay Place. D: Thom Eberhardt. COM [PG-13] 99m. V

Captain Scarlett 1953 ★★½ Greene is an avenging force out to right wrongs perpetrated by evil noblemen after the Napoleonic Wars in southern France. Robin Hood-type costume drama. C: Richard Greene, Leonora Amar. D: Thomas Carr. ACT 75m.

Captain Sinbad 1963 ★★★½ Arabian Nights fantasy adventure with good special effects. Energetic and enterprising. C: Guy Williams, Heidi Bruhl. D: Byron Haskin. FAM/ACT [G] 86m. V

Captain Sirocco 1949 *See* **Pirates of Capri, The**

Captain Tugboat Annie 1945 ★★★ Low-budget reworking of *Tugboat Annie* has female skipper (Darwell) attempting to adopt young boy, getting full-grown man (because of paperwork error) instead. Starpower manages to bail out this leaky tub. C: Jane Darwell, Edgar Kennedy. D: Phil Rosen. COM 60m.

Captains Courageous 1937 ★★★★★ Spectacular adventures of a spoiled rich kid (Bartholomew), who learns about life when he falls off a cruise liner and is picked up by a Portuguese trawler. Rapport between the boy and a weathered fisherman (Tracy, who won an Oscar) is wonderful. Engrossing, lively drama, based on Rudyard Kipling's book; especially suitable for children. Remade in 1977. C: Spencer Tracy, Freddie Bartholomew, Melvyn Douglas, Lionel

Barrymore, Mickey Rooney, John Carradine. D: Victor Fleming. FAM/DRA 116m.

Captains Courageous 1977 ★★★ Spoiled rich kid (Kahn) is rescued at sea by a fishing ship, slowly matures into manhood through hard work in this remake of the classic 1937 film based on the Kipling story. Malden is good as the crusty skipper. C: Karl Malden, Jonathan Kahn, Ricardo Montalban, Fritz Weaver, Fred Gwynne. D: Harvey Hart. DRA 110m. TVM

Captain's Paradise, The 1954 British ★★★★ Amiable sea captain shuttles between Tangier and Gibraltar, where he has a different wife in each port. Nice performance by Guinness; exotic locales enhance one-note story line in this wry British comedy. C: Alec Guinness, Yvonne De Carlo, Celia Johnson. D: Anthony Kimmins. COM 89m. V

Captain's Table, The 1958 British ★★★ Uncouth cargo skipper (Gregson) is promoted to captain of luxury liner and creates mayhem as he tries to adapt to his sophisticated new surroundings. Energetic British comedy of manners. (a.k.a. *Shenanigans*) C: John Gregson, Peggy Cummins, Donald Sinden. D: Jack Lee. COM 89m. V

Captive City, The 1952 ★★★½ Forsythe is crusading newspaperman uncovering small-town Mafia corruption. Solid little documentary-like crime film. C: John Forsythe, Joan Camden. D: Robert Wise. CRI 90m.

Captive Girl 1950 ★★★ Rugged explorer (and ex-Tarzan) Weissmuller battles evil hunter Crabbe (another ex-Tarzan) over sunken African treasure. Low-budget thrills distinguish this juvenile adventure film, the best entry in the *Jungle Jim* series. C: Johnny Weissmuller, Buster Crabbe. D: William Berke. ACT 73m.

Captive Heart, The 1946 British ★★★★½ A Czech captain (Redgrave) with false British papers is thrown into a WWII POW camp. Intelligent writing and a terrific cast help make this one of the best British war films. C: Michael Redgrave, Mervyn Johns, Basil Radford, Jack Warner, Gordon Jackson. D: Basil Dearden. DRA 108m. V

Captive Hearts 1987 ★★½ Two American flyers are held prisoner in a remote Japanese village during WWII, one falling in love with a local maiden. Trite interracial romance story. C: Noriyuki "Pat" Morita, Chris Makepeace. D: Paul Almond. DRA [PG] 97m. V

Captive Wild Woman 1943 ★★★ Carradine's at his sinister best as a scientist who transforms a jungle ape into a beautiful woman whose animal instincts get the better of her. Entertaining, but hampered by plot digressions and overuse of stock footage. C: John Carradine, Evelyn Ankers, Acquanetta. D: Edward Dmytryk. HOR 61m.

Capture of Big Foot 1979 ★★ A sleazy businessman attempts to apprehend the mysterious monster to exploit it in this low-budget, generally uninteresting attempt to cash in on the '70s Bigfoot craze. C: Stafford Morgan, Katherine Hopkins, Richard Kennedy, Otis Young, George Rowe. D: Bill Rebane. HOR 92m.

Capture, The 1950 ★★★½ Innocent man is chased into Mexico for robbery he didn't commit, while pursuing detective slowly realizes he may be after the wrong man. Absorbing if lower-key film noir. C: Lew Ayres, Teresa Wright. D: John Sturges. DRA 91m.

Captured 1933 ★★★½ Howard suffers through WWI combat and a German POW camp only to discover, on his return home, that his best friend and his wife were lovers. Reliable cast salvages creaky romance and obvious story line. C: Leslie Howard, Douglas Fairbanks Jr., Paul Lukas, Margaret Lindsay. D: Roy Del Ruth. DRA 72m.

Car 54, Where Are You? 1994 ★★ Toody and Muldoon protect a key witness so he can testify against Mob boss. Feature reprise of the classic TV show brings back several cast regulars but gives an obvious, campy handling. Not the brightest shtick. C: David Johansen, John C. McGinley, Fran Drescher, Nipsey Russell, Rosie O'Donnell. D: Bill Fishman. COM 89m.

Car 99 1935 ★★★½ When a gangster wreaks havoc with police radios, the law has a difficult time tracking him down. Routine B-movie crime drama has its moments and boasts a good early performance by MacMurray. C: Fred MacMurray, Guy Standing, Ann Sheridan, Frank Craven, William Frawley. D: Charles Barton. CRI 60m.

Car, The 1977 ★★½ A small Southwestern town is bedeviled by a satanic automobile. Slick but tediously absurd thriller is composed primarily of hit-and-run sequences. C: James Brolin, Kathleen Lloyd. D: Elliot Silverstein. HOR 95m.

Car Trouble 1986 British ★★★½ A philandering wife becomes the center of a media frenzy when—during the throes of passion—she and her lover get stuck in her husband's precious sports car. Most of the laughs in this one-joke premise come from Walters's "daffy performance." C: Julie Walters, Ian Charleson, Vincenzo Ricotta, Stratford Johns. D: David Green. COM [R] 93m. V

Car Wash 1976 ★★★½ Episodic comedy follows the exploits of the funky workers at a Los Angeles car wash. Hit-and-miss series of comedic interludes benefits from game cast and a memorable sound track. C: Richard Pryor, George Carlin, Irwin Corey, Melanie Mayron, Garrett Morris. D: Michael Schultz. COM [PG] 97m. V

Caravaggio 1986 ★★★ Low-budget but lush fantasy biography of the Italian Baroque painter emphasizes his homosexuality and scandalous life. Great looking, but enigmatic filmmaker Jarman avoids straightforward storytelling. C: Nigel Terry, Sean Bean, Tilda Swinton. D: Derek Jarman. DRA 97m. V

Caravan 1934 ★★★ Operetta with Young as Countess Wilma who must marry to receive her inheritance. Full of spectacle. C: Loretta Young, Charles Boyer. D: Erik Charrell. MUS 101m.

Caravans 1978 U.S. ★★★ In 1948, junior American diplomat (Sarrazin) searches in and around Iran for senator's daughter (O'Neill). Lavishly produced romantic drama based on the James Michener novel. C: Anthony Quinn, Jennifer O'Neill, Michael Sarrazin, Christopher Lee, Joseph Cotten. D: James Fargo. DRA [PG] 123m.

Carbine Williams 1952 ★★★★ Effective biography of man (Stewart) who invented the lightweight rifle, his troubles with the law, and the love of his supportive family. Strong performances by Stewart and Corey. C: James Stewart, Jean Hagen, Wendell Corey, James Arness. D: Richard Thorpe. DRA 91m.

Carbon Copy 1981 ★★ A business executive, hiding the fact that he's Jewish, fears the appearance of his illegitimate African-American son will destroy his fast-track corporate career. Washington's first film. C: George Segal, Denzel Washington, Susan St. James, Jack Warden, Paul Winfield. D: Michael Schultz. COM [PG] 90m. V

Card, The 1952 *See* **Promoter, The**

Cardiac Arrest 1980 ★★★ San Francisco police are hot on the trail of a mad killer whose modus operandi is removal of his victims' hearts. Routine thriller is no heart-stopper. C: Garry Goodrow, Mike Chan. D: Murray Mintz. CRI [PG] 90m.

Cardinal Richelieu 1935 ★★★★ Profile of the nefarious cardinal who maintained control over Louis XIII. Arliss in yet another of his classic historical epics. A truly superb production. C: George Arliss, Maureen O'Sullivan, Edward Arnold, Cesar Romero. D: Rowland Lee. DRA 83m.

Cardinal, The 1963 ★★★ Preminger's film chronicles the rise of humble Irish-Catholic American priest to a high position in College of Cardinals. All-star cast fails to lift this shallow drama above soap opera level. C: Tom Tryon, John Huston, Romy Schneider, Carol Lynley, Raf Vallone, Burgess Meredith, Ossie Davis, John Saxon. D: Otto Preminger. DRA 175m. V

Care Bears Adventure in Wonderland!, The 1987 Canadian ★★½ The animated bear family travels to Wonderland with Alice in this sequel to *The Care Bears Movie.* Pablum for the kiddies. C: Bob Dermer, Eva Alamos, Dan Hennessy. D: Raymond Jafelice. FAM/DRA [G] 76m. V

Care Bears Movie, The 1985 Canadian ★★★ Voices of Mickey Rooney and Georgia Engel and songs by Carole King make this the best of the three Care Bears movies, but it's still a long advertisement for the stuffed toys and only for very young children. C: Mickey Rooney, Georgia Engel. D: Arna Selznick. FAM/DRA [G] 75m. V

Care Bears Movie II: A New Generation 1986 ★★ Blatant commercialism: an overt ad for the toys that spawned this series of movies is the only point in this installment of the *Care Bears* trilogy. C: Maxine Miller, Pam Hyatt, Hadley Kay. D: Dale Schott. FAM/DRA [G] 77m. V

Career Girl 1959 ★★½ Busty young starlet tries to make it in Hollywood. Sordid low-budget melodrama features legendary *Playboy* Playmate pioneer Wilkinson. C: June Wilkinson, Charles Keane. D: Harold David. DRA 61m.

Career Opportunities 1991 ★★ John Hughes' teen comedy concerns loser (Whaley) who gets job as department store's night watchman and discovers richest girl in town (Connelly) hiding out there; on the same night there is a break-in. Single joke pushed far too long. C: Frank Whaley, Jennifer Connelly, Dermot Mulroney. D: Bryan Gordon. COM [PG-13] 85m. V

Career 1959 ★★★ Show business story of a likable, ambitious actor (Franciosa) determined to make it as a star on Broadway. A not entirely successful adaptation of the play of the same name, with some awkward and incongruous storylines. C: Dean Martin, Anthony Franciosa, Shirley MacLaine, Carolyn Jones. D: Joseph Anthony. DRA 105m.

Carefree 1938 ★★★★½ Astaire is a psychiatrist, Rogers his screwball patient. Romance develops. Interesting attempt to extend stars' range (and mollify Rogers' desire for a serious acting career). Great Irving Berlin songs, and swell comedy stuff. Best number: "Change Partners." C: Fred Astaire, Ginger Rogers, Ralph Bellamy, Jack Carson, Franklin Pangborn. D: Mark Sandrich. MUS 83m. V

Careful, He Might Hear You 1984 Australian ★★★★ Depression-era story told from the viewpoint of a young boy who is a pawn in a custody battle between two aunts. Moving, with surprising dénouement. Based on the novel by Sumner Locke Elliot. C: Wendy Hughes, Robyn Nevin, John Hargreaves. D: Carl Schultz. DRA [PG] 113m. V

Caretaker, The 1964 *See* **Guest, The**

Caretakers, The 1963 ★★★★ Lurid yet entertaining melodrama charts schizophrenic Bergen's recovery through "enlightened" mental hospital. Tense direction, tart performances, shabby script; one of Crawford's final legitimate films before her career spiraled into low-budget horror pictures. C: Robert Stack, Joan Crawford, Polly Bergen, Janis Paige, Constance Ford, Herbert Marshall. D: Hall Bartlett. DRA 97m.

Carey Treatment, The 1972 ★★★★ Boston doctor tries to save the good name of a fellow healer accused of killing a patient while performing an abortion. Complex, well-done mystery. C: James Coburn, Jennifer O'Neill, Pat Hingle. D: Blake Edwards. CRI [PG] 101m.

Cargo to Capetown 1950 ★★½ Shanghaied onto an African-bound tramp steamer, a young man falls in love. Standard adventure sleaze sparked by a decent cast. C: Broderick Crawford, John Ireland, Ellen Drew. D: Earl McEvoy. ACT 80m.

Caribbean 1952 ★★½ Eighteenth-century romance on the high seas as a pirate tangles with rivals in the Caribbean and excites the love of an exotic woman. Passable swashbuckler. Watch for Hardwicke as a pirate! C: John Payne, Arlene Dahl, Cedric Hardwicke. D: Edward Ludwig. ACT 97m.

Caribbean Mystery, A 1983 ★★★★ When a British army officer is murdered at an elegant Bahamian resort, Agatha Christie's redoubtable Miss Marple (Hayes) is brought in to find the guilty party. Good work by all in high-level suspense; the script was co-written by Sue Grafton. C: Helen Hayes, Jameson Parker, Barnard Hughes, Maurice Evans, Beth Howland, Swoosie Kurtz. D: Robert Lewis. CRI 100m. TVM

Cariboo Trail 1950 ★★★ Two prospectors dig for riches in British Columbia during the 1890s Gold Rush. Beautifully filmed (in Colorado) and well acted by a cast of hardy notables. C: Randolph Scott, Karin Hayes, Victor Jory. D: Edwin Marin. DRA 81m. V

Carl Sandburg—Echoes and Silences 1982 ★★★★ Life and times of the great Midwest American poet. A thoughtful, compelling, and altogether outstanding portrayal by Cullum. Worth a look. C: John Cullum, Michael Higgins, Frances Conroy. D: Perry Adato. DRA 119m. TVM

Carlito's Way 1993 ★★★★ De Palma and Pacino resume their *Scarface* ways, this time spinning a yarn of an ex-con, ex-drug dealer trying to straighten out his life and seize the love of a good woman (Miller). Above-average gangster flick, with kudos to Pacino and Penn. C: Al Pacino, Sean Penn, Penelope Ann Miller. D: Brian De Palma. CRI [R] 145m. V

Carlton-Browne of the F.O. 1959 *See* **Man in a Cocked Hat**

Carmen 1983 Spanish ★★★★★ Superb reworking of Bizet's opera sets the story against the background of a dance troupe preparing a new theatrical production. The ensuing love and war between cast members and director mirrors the opera's plot. Excellent dance sequences. C: Antonio Gades, Laura Del Sol. D: Carlos Saura. MUS [R] 99m. V

Carmen 1984 French ★★★★ Opera buffs will enjoy this colorful version of Bizet's opera involving unfaithful Gypsy and the adoring Spanish soldier who pursues her. Great costumes and sets, with fine performances by Migenes-Johnson and Domingo. C: Julia Migenes-Johnson, Placido Domingo, Ruggero Raimondi, Faith Esham. D: Francesco Rosi. MUS [PG] 152m. V

Carmen Jones 1954 ★★★★ Unusual updating of Bizet's *Carmen* set in black Army unit during WWII with Oscar Hammerstein lyrics set to original music. Melodramatic and a bit artificial, but Dandridge (dubbed by Marilyn Horne), is sizzling and Bailey's big number is a knockout. Dandridge's Oscar nomination was the first for an African American in a leading role. C: Dorothy Dandridge, Harry Belafonte, Pearl Bailey, Diahann Carroll. Voice of Marilyn Horne. D: Otto Preminger. MUS 105m.

Carmilla 1989 ★★★½ One of many screen adaptations of J. Sheridan Le Fanu's novel about a lesbian vampire is less bloody and erotic than most, but benefits from decent production and a good cast. Made for Shelley Duvall's *Nightmare Classics* cable series. C: Meg Tilly, Ione Skye, Roddy McDowell, Roy Dotrice. D: Gabrielle Beaumont. HOR 60m. TVM V

Carnal Knowledge 1971 ★★★★ Nichols' lacerating look at the sex lives of buddies Nicholson and Garfunkel from college to middle age was a groundbreaking film and is still a penetrating character drama. Ann-Margret's poignant performance as a good-hearted bimbo won her an Oscar nomination. C: Jack Nicholson, Candice Bergen, Art Garfunkel, Ann-Margret, Rita Moreno. D: Mike Nichols. DRA [R] 98m. V

Carnegie Hall 1947 ★★★★ Forget the plot of an immigrant mother (Hunt) pushing her son to be a classical pianist and instead relish wonderful performances by stellar group of concert artists including Artur Rubinstein, Lily Pons, Jascha Heifetz, and Rise Stevens. C: Marsha Hunt, William Prince, Frank McHugh, Martha O'Driscoll. D: Edgar Ulmer. MUS 134m.

Carnival 1953 French ★★★ Offbeat melodrama of a widowed puppeteer and daughter, hiding out in circus because his father-in-law wants to take the child. C: Fernandel, Jacqueline Pagnol, Pauline Carton. D: Marcel Pagnol. DRA 100m.

Carnival in Costa Rica 1947 ★★½ A young Costa Rican gentleman runs into trouble with his parents when he returns home with his American fiancée. Premise is rather thin, but the music makes up for it. C: Dick Haymes, Vera-Ellen, Cesar Romero, Celeste Holm, Anne Revere. D: Gregory Ratoff. MUS 95m.

Carnival in Flanders 1936 French ★★★★ When word comes that foreign troops are approaching, "brave" men hide, leaving their women to greet the invaders. One of the most popular foreign films of the '30s is also one of the most charming. C: Françoise Rosay, Jean Murat, Louis Jouvet. D: Jacques Feyder. DRA 90m. V

Carnival of Sinners 1947 French ★★★★ An artist sells his soul to the devil. Clever fantasy could also be allegory about collaborationists in occupied France. (a.k.a. *La Main du Diable*) C: Pierre Fresnay, Josseline Gael, Palau, Noel Roquevert. D: Maurice Tourneur. DRA 83m.

Carnival of Souls 1962 ★★★★ A young woman appears to survive a car accident, but finds herself in a strange limbo, haunted by spectral ghouls. Creepy cult classic, with evocative imagery, is perfect for late-night video viewing. C: Candace Hilligoss, Sidney Berger, Frances Feist. D: Herk Harvey. HOR 84m. V

Carnival Rock 1957 ★★ Typical love triangle involves a jealous nightclub owner, a sexy singer, and a dissipated gambler. Nice music, particularly by The Platters. C: Susan Cabot, Dick Miller, The Platters. D: Roger Corman. MUS 80m. V

Carnival Story 1954 ★★ In Germany, a young woman joins the circus as a trapeze artist and in short time is wooed by two smitten fellow workers. Slow, despite the high-wire antics. Baxter is cast standout. C: Anne Baxter, Steve Cochran, George Nader. D: Kurt Neumann. DRA 94m. V

Carnosaur 1993 ★★ Roger Corman's answer to *Jurassic Park* ladles on the gore while telling a similar story of a scientist (Ladd) creating genetically cloned dinosaurs. The dino special effects look cheesy, but Ladd is fun as she chews even more scenery than the monsters do. C: Diane Ladd, Clint Howard, Harrison Page, Ned Bellamy. D: Adam Simon. HOR [R] 83m.

Carny 1980 ★★★★ A dark love triangle in a carnival setting; a runaway (Foster) comes between friends (Busey and Robertson). Steamy and atmospheric, with good acting and musical score. C: Gary Busey, Jodie Foster, Robbie Robertson, Meg Foster. D: Robert Kaylor. DRA [R] 104m. V

Caro Diario 1994 Italian ★★★★½ Funny, perceptive collection of random thoughts/vignettes from the life of actor/director Moretti, Italy's answer to Woody Allen. Begins with a motorcycle tour of Rome, then progresses into an autobiographical account of Moretti's recent struggle with cancer. Mood magically remains lighthearted throughout — a remarkable achievement. C: Nani Moretti, Renato Carpentieri, Jennifer Beals. D: Nani Moretti. COM 100m. V

Carolina Cannonball 1955 ★★½ Zany hillbilly (Canova) gets involved with a hit squad of foreign operatives. Canova's antics are good for a few laughs in this pleasant little comedy yuck-fest. C: Judy Canova, Andy Clyde. D: Charles Lamont. COM 74m.

Carolina Skeletons 1991 ★★★★ A Vietnam veteran Marine officer (Gossett) returns to his rural Southern birthplace to clear the name of his brother, executed for the murder of two white girls three decades earlier. Suspenseful adaptation of an award-winning novel contains taut mystery elements. C: Louis Gossett Jr., Bruce Dern. D: John Erman. CRI [R] 100m. TVM

Caroline? 1989 ★★★★½ Classy, Emmy-winning mystery about a woman (Zimbalist) who has been presumed dead; when she reappears and claims an inheritance, her identity is challenged. Excellent cast, suspenseful story. Based on the novel *Father's Arcane Daughter*, by E.L. Konigsberg. C: Stephanie Zimbalist, Pamela Reed, George Grizzard, Patricia Neal, Dorothy McGuire. D: Joseph Sargent. DRA 100m. TVM V

Carousel 1956 ★★★★½ Classic Rodgers and Hammerstein musical comes to the screen with most of its heartbreaking drama and music intact. Amusement park barker MacRae tries to change his life when he marries Jones, with tragic results. Maine locations add much to those glorious songs: "If I Loved You," "Soliloquy," "You'll Never Walk Alone." The musical itself is based on Ferenc Molnar's play *Liliom*, which was filmed in 1930 and 1934. C: Gordon MacRae, Shirley Jones, Cameron Mitchell, Barbara Ruick. D: Henry King. MUS 105m. V

Carpenter, The 1989 ★★★ Unusual chiller about a woman recovering from a breakdown and the deranged handyman who murderously intercedes in her life. But is he real? Not entirely successful, but has its share of creepy (and gory) moments. C: Wings Hauser, Pierce Lenior, Barbara Ann Jones, Lynne Adams. D: David Wellington. HOR [R] 85m. V

Carpetbaggers, The 1964 ★★★½ Trashy tale, from Harold Robbins' novel, about an ambitious Hollywood entrepreneur loosely based on Howard Hughes. Ladd appears (in his last film) as cowboy star Tom Mix. Overdone but entertaining. C: George Peppard, Carroll Baker, Alan Ladd, Bob Cummings, Martha Hyer, Elizabeth Ashley, Lew Ayres, Martin Balsam. D: Edward Dmytryk. DRA 150m.

Carrie 1952 ★★★ Mundane adaptation of Theodore Dreiser novel *Sister Carrie* features Jones as late-19th-century Chicago woman who rises through social ranks with help of Olivier. Great sets and costumes but otherwise an unmemorable effort. C: Jennifer Jones, Laurence Olivier, Miriam Hopkins, Eddie Albert. D: William Wyler. DRA 118m. V

Carrie 1976 ★★★★ De Palma put his and Stephen King's names on the map with his stylish adaptation of King's novel about a put-upon high school student who telekinetically lashes out at her tormentors. Spacek is both sympathetic and frightening in the title role. C: Sissy Spacek, Piper Laurie, Amy Irving, Nancy Allen, Betty Buckley, William Katt, John Travolta. D: Brian De Palma. HOR [R] 98m. V

Carrier, The 1987 ★★★½ A strange plague

that dissolves people on contact strikes a small Michigan town, and locals relentlessly pursue possible disease-carriers. Weird, violent, but well-made independent film may achieve cult status. C: Gregory Fortescue, Stevie Lee. D: Nathan J. White. DRA [R] 90m. V

Carrington V.C. 1955 *See* **Court Martial**

Carry On *See* **Carry on Admiral**

Carry on Admiral 1957 British ★★★ After imbibing too much, a British naval officer and a government official end up switching jobs. Silly, witless farce only goes so far on premise. Not part of the *Carry On* series. (a.k.a. *The Ship Was Loaded*). C: David Tomlinson, Peggy Cummins, Alfie Bass, Ronald Shiner. D: Val Guest. COM 89m.

Carry On Cabbie 1963 British ★★★ Feeling ignored, a woman starts up her own taxi-cab firm to compete with her husband's. Innocuous entry in the *Carry On* series. (a.k.a. *Call Me a Cab*) C: Sidney James, Hattie Jacques, Kenneth Conner, Charles Hawtrey, Esma Cannon, Liz Fraser, Milo O'Shea. D: Gerald Thomas. COM 91m.

Carry on Camping 1972 British ★★½ An entry in Britain's popular *Carry On* series involving the great outdoors and the great unwashed—hippies on the trail. Some lightweight fun. C: Sidney James, Kenneth Williams, Joan Sims, Barbara Windsor. D: Gerald Thomas. COM [R] 89m.

Carry on Cleo 1965 British ★★½ A spoof on the Cleopatra story as performed by Britain's notable *Carry On* cut-ups. Fun and games by an adequate—if not stellar—troupe. C: Amanda Barrie, Sidney James, Kenneth Williams, Joan Sims. D: Gerald Thomas. COM 91m. V

Carry on Constable 1960 British ★★★ In a British precursor to America's *Police Academy* series, the *Carry On* comics wreak havoc as they join the ranks of law enforcement. Typical *Carry On* humor, with a few tepid laughs. C: Sidney James, Eric Barker, Kenneth Connor, Hattie Jacques, Joan Sims, Shirley Eaton. D: Gerald Thomas. COM 86m.

Carry on Doctor 1968 British ★★★ A bumbling practitioner continually finds himself in trouble at the country hospital where he's in residency. The diagnosis is nonstop, lowbrow shenanigans in another gag-filled entry in the popular British comedy series. C: Frankie Howard, Kenneth Williams, Jim Dale, Barbara Windsor. D: Gerald Thomas. COM [PG] 95m. V

Carry on Henry VIII 1972 British ★★ This time the *Carry On* crew lampoons the famous randy king. A few chuckles, but not among their finest offerings. C: Sidney James, Kenneth Williams, Joan Sims, Barbara Windsor. D: Gerald Thomas. COM [PG] 90m.

Carry on Nurse 1959 British ★★★★ Uproarious *Carry On* adventures in a large hospital. One of the best in the series and a big hit in America. C: Kenneth Connor, Shirley Eaton, Joan Sims, Kenneth Williams, Wilfrid Hyde-White, Joan Hickson, Jill Ireland. D: Gerald Thomas. COM 84m. V

Carry On Sergeant 1959 British ★★★½ The *Carry on* contingent joins the Royal army—score a point for the enemy! Very funny at times. C: William Hartnell, Bob Monkhouse, Shirley Eaton, Dora Bryan. D: Gerald Thomas. COM 88m.

Carry on Spying 1965 British ★★★ Enemy agents steal a crucial formula, and the *Carry On* spoof spies go after them. Lively takeoff of espionage adventures. C: Kenneth Williams, Barbara Windsor, Bernard Cribbins. D: Gerald Thomas. COM 88m.

Carry On, Up the Khyber 1968 British ★★★½ One of the better *Carry On* films takes place in Victorian-era Egypt as residents try to discover what Scottish troops are wearing beneath those kilts. Silly and ribald, though fun at its own level. C: Sidney James, Kenneth Williams, Charles Hawtrey, Roy Castle, Joan Sims. D: Gerald Thomas. COM 87m.

Cars That Ate Paris, The 1974 Australian ★★★ Director's first effort focuses on inhabitants of town in Australia who increase commerce by deliberately causing motor accidents and then reselling anything and anyone salvageable. Absurd black comedy appeals to those with macabre taste. C: Terry Camilleri, John Meillon. D: Peter Weir. COM 91m. V

Carson City 1952 ★★★½ Fed up with traveling by stagecoach, on which bandits have apparently declared open season, a financier organizes construction of a railroad. Typically agreeable Western enhanced by crackerjack performances. C: Randolph Scott, Raymond Massey. D: Andre de Toth. WST 87m.

Cartel 1990 ★★ A pilot (O'Keefe), framed for murder, takes the law into his own hands in breaking up the syndicate. Nasty, brutal film abounds with violence and nudity. C: Miles O'Keefe, Don Stroud, Crystal Carson, Suzanne Slater. D: John Stewart. ACT [R] 100m. V

Carthage in Flames 1959 Italian ★★½ Details of the war between Rome and Carthage. A fair action epic that slips in a little romance for good measure. C: Jose Suarez, Pierre Brasseur. D: Carmine Gallone. ACT 96m. V

Cartouche 1964 French ★★★★ Fun, action-filled send-up of swashbuckling movies puts Belmondo in the role of an 18th-century French Robin Hood. Cardinale shines in support. De Broca knows his cliches. C: Jean-Paul Belmondo, Claudia Cardinale. D: Philippe De Broca. COM 115m.

Carve Her Name With Pride 1958 British ★★★★ Film biography of Violette Szabo, who continually risked her life while working for the French Resistance during WWII. Absorbing drama, with an excellent lead performance by McKenna. C: Virginia McKenna,

Paul Scofield, Jack Warner, Denise Grey. D: Lewis Gilbert. DRA 119m.

Casablanca 1942 ★★★★★ During WWII, the American owner of a Casablanca watering hole (Bogart) finds love and patriotism rekindled when his former inamorata (Bergman) and her Resistance hero husband (Henreid) seek his help. Romantic drama par excellence with outstanding performances all around, a wonderful score (including the memorable "As Time Goes By") and one of the best movie endings ever. Oscars for Best Picture, Director, and Screenplay. C: Humphrey Bogart, Ingrid Bergman, Paul Henreid, Claude Rains, Conrad Veidt, Peter Lorre, Sydney Greenstreet, Dooley Wilson, S.Z. Sakall. D: Michael Curtiz. DRA [PG] 102m. V

Casanova 1987 ★★★ Chamberlain is the 18th-century ladies' man looking back on his life of romantic adventure. Tongue-in-cheek flavor adds some spice to otherwise standard sex romp. C: Richard Chamberlain, Faye Dunaway, Ornella Muti, Hanna Schygulla. D: Simon Langton. DRA 122m. TVM V

Casanova & Co. 1978 *See* **Some Like It Cool**

Casanova Brown 1944 ★★★½ Freshly divorced Cooper, about to remarry, learns that first wife (Wright) is pregnant so he steals the child from hospital and raises it himself. Cooper looks uncomfortable playing light comedy, but he's amusing. Previously filmed twice before, in 1930 and 1939, as *Little Accident*, based on Floyd Dell and Thomas Mitchell's play. C: Gary Cooper, Teresa Wright, Frank Morgan, Anita Louise. D: Sam Wood. COM 94m. V

Casanova in Burlesque 1944 ★★★½ Dignified Shakespearean professor takes off for the summer and, unbeknownst to all, performs with a burlesque troupe. Typical Brown: lots of raucous fun and high energy. C: Joe E. Brown, June Havoc, Dale Evans. D: Leslie Goodwins. COM 74m.

Casanova '70 1965 French ★★★ Mastroianni is typecast as Italian lover who needs risks to find sex exciting; so finding the right woman isn't such good news. Funny, but somewhat dated sex comedy. C: Marcello Mastroianni, Virna Lisi, Michele Mercier, Marisa Mell. D: Mario Monicelli. COM 113m.

Casanova's Big Night 1954 ★★★★ A Romeo with credit problems (Price) switches places with a tailor's apprentice (Hope) who takes his new role to Venice. C: Bob Hope, Joan Fontaine, Basil Rathbone, Raymond Burr, Vincent Price. D: Norman McLeod. COM 86m. V

Casbah 1948 ★★★½ The life, loves, and adventures of a classic casbah thief. Interesting musical remake of the heralded *Algiers*. Martin and Lorre are especially good. C: Yvonne De Carlo, Tony Martin, Peter Lorre. D: John Berry. MUS 94m.

Cascarrabias 1930 *See* **Grumpy**

Case Against Brooklyn, The 1958 ★★ A rookie cop takes on a notorious Brooklyn gambling ring. Well-done, if predictable, little B-movie story. C: Darren McGavin, Maggie Hayes. D: Paul Wendkos. CRI 82m.

Case Against Mrs. Ames, The 1936 ★★½ Justice on trial, as district attorney falls in love with a beautiful woman accused of murdering her husband. The elegant Ms. Carroll brightens this ofttold tale. C: Madeleine Carroll, George Brent, Arthur Treacher, Beulah Bondi. D: William Seiter. CRI 85m.

Case of Deadly Force, A 1986 ★★★★ When police kill a man in custody after he was wrongly arrested, it's up to a lone attorney to get past the cover-up and find the truth. Based on a true story; told with spareness and excellent use of detail. C: Richard Crenna, John Shea, Lorraine Toussaint, Frank McCarthy. D: Michael Miller. CRI 95m. V

Case of Dr. Laurent, The 1958 French ★★½ The story of a doctor in rural France and his crusade for natural childbirth. Heralded for its rather stark birthing scenes. C: Jean Gabin, Nicole Courcel. D: Jean-Paul LeChanois. DRA 91m.

Case of Libel, A 1983 ★★★ The McCarthy era is dramatized in this true story about an accused Communist's lawsuit against an influential newspaper columnist. Mundane but competent. C: Daniel J. Travanti, Edward Asner, Gordon Pinsent, Lawrence Dane. D: Eric Till. DRA 90m. V

Case of Mrs. Loring, The 1959 *See* **Question of Adultery, A**

Case of Rape, A 1974 ★★★★ Suburban housewife (Montgomery) finds brutal rape the first of many violations as she's victimized by court system, untrusting husband, etc. Strong social drama makes some striking points along the way. C: Elizabeth Montgomery, William Daniels. D: Boris Sagal. DRA 100m.

Case of the Black Cat, The 1936 ★★★½ Perry Mason investigates the murder of an old man who had just made major changes in his will. Strong entry in the series, aided by solid cast. C: Ricardo Cortez, June Travis, Jane Bryan. D: William McGann. CRI 65m.

Case of the Curious Bride, The 1935 ★★★½ A woman claims that she's being blackmailed by her husband—but he's been dead for years. A rather bemused Perry Mason gets to the bottom of things. Watch for young Errol Flynn as a murder victim. C: Warren William, Margaret Lindsay. D: Michael Curtiz. CRI 80m.

Case of the Hillside Stranglers, The 1989 ★★★ Slow-moving tale never quite captures the terror of real-life L.A. killings. Crenna is excellent, though. C: Richard Crenna, Dennis Farina. D: Steven Gethers. CRI 91m. V

Case of the Howling Dog, The 1934 ★★★½ Trouble brews when two men insist they are married—to the same woman! Early Perry Mason thriller with sedate William as the sleuth and a fine cast of character pros. C: Warren William, Mary Astor. D: Alan Crosland. CRI 75m.

Case of the Lucky Legs, The 1935 ★★★½ When an unscrupulous beauty contest promoter makes off with ill-gotten gains, it's up to ace attorney Perry Mason to save the day. Minor but entertaining courtroom drama with some good moments. C: Warren William, Genevieve Tobin. D: Archie Mayo. CRI 76m.

Case of the Red Monkey 1955 British ★★½ Police are called in to solve a series of murders in which the victims are all atomic scientists. Solid sleuthing, British style. C: Richard Conte, Rona Anderson. D: Ken Hughes. CRI 73m.

Case of the Stuttering Bishop, The 1937 ★★★ There's some question as to whether or not an heiress is real or an impostor. When in doubt, call on Perry Mason! One of the series' weaker efforts. C: Donald Woods, Ann Dvorak. D: William Clemens. CRI 70m.

Case of the Velvet Claws, The 1936 ★★★½ Perry Mason goes off on his honeymoon . . . and is promptly charged with murder! Satisfying blend of mystery and humor. C: Warren William, Claire Dodd. D: William Clemens. CRI 60m.

Casey's Shadow 1977 ★★★½ Matthau brings his usual professional polish to this tale of a horse trainer raising three kids after his wife dies. Sentimental material is saved by the star's grittiness. C: Walter Matthau, Alexis Smith, Robert Webber. D: Martin Ritt. FAM/DRA [PG] 117m. v

Cash McCall 1959 ★★★ Garner is a successful business executive who romances Wood, daughter of his failing rival Jagger. Minor soap opera, buoyed by the ever-appealing Garner. C: James Garner, Natalie Wood, Nina Foch, Dean Jagger, E.G. Marshall. D: Joseph Pevney. DRA 116m. v

Cash on Delivery 1956 British ★★½ Winters stands to inherit a fortune, but only if she can keep her ex-husband's new wife from bearing a child. Mundane melodrama. (a.k.a. *To Dorothy a Son*) C: Shelley Winters, John Gregson. D: Muriel Box. DRA 82m.

Casino Murder Case 1935 ★★★ Another Philo Vance mystery has the intrepid detective (Lucas) investigating murders at Skipworth's mansion. The plot itself is something of a mystery at times. C: Paul Lukas, Alison Skipworth, Rosalind Russell, Eric Blore, Leo G. Carroll, William Demarest. D: Edwin Marin. CRI 85m.

Casino Royale 1967 British ★★★½ Aging James Bond (Niven) chooses a successor from a host of Bond wannabes in this sprawling, big-budget spy spoof. Boasts a promising cast, but incoherent and only intermittently funny. Niven was novelist Fleming's original choice for the movie Bond. C: Peter Sellers, Ursula Andress, David Niven, Orson Welles, Joanna Pettet, Woody Allen, Deborah Kerr, William Holden, Charles Boyer, John Huston, George Raft, Jean-Paul Belmondo, Jacqueline Bisset. D: John Huston, Robert Parrish, Joe McGrath, Val Guest. COM 130m.

Casque D'or 1956 ★★★★ Woodworker Reggiani defies potential dangers from underworld leader Dauphin after engaging in romance with Signoret. Lushly photographed and intelligently told story with good performances from ensemble. (a.k.a. *Golden Marie*) C: Simone Signoret, Serge Reggiani, Claude Dauphin. D: Jacques Becker. DRA 96m.

Cass Timberlane 1947 ★★★★ A lower-class young woman is transformed when she marries an older, small-town judge. Strong drama in the best Hollywood tradition, combining high production values and able stars. From the novel by Sinclair Lewis. C: Spencer Tracy, Lana Turner, Zachary Scott, Mary Astor. D: George Sidney. DRA 119m. v

Cassandra Crossing, The 1976 British ★★★ Scenic Italy and France and a solid cast are the highlights of this disaster movie centering on a lethal virus carried aboard a train as it approaches a rickety bridge. Diverting enough, and with a few tense moments, but nothing new for the genre. C: Richard Harris, Sophia Loren, Burt Lancaster, Ava Gardner, Martin Sheen, O.J. Simpson. D: George P. Cosmatos. ACT [R] 129m.

Cast a Dark Shadow 1955 British ★★★★ Bogarde murders his wife, only to discover there is no inheritance. Consequently, he turns attentions to wealthy former barkeep Lockwood. Some good suspense in this thrilling twist on the Bluebeard story. C: Dirk Bogarde, Margaret Lockwood, Mona Washbourne, Kathleen Harrison. D: Lewis Gilbert. CRI 84m.

Cast a Deadly Spell 1991 ★★★½ Witty and effective marriage of horror and private eye stories, with detective (Ward) in '40s L.A. encountering monsters and magic in his search for a stolen mystic book. Heavily influenced by author H.P. Lovecraft. C: Fred Ward, David Warner, Julianne Moore, Alexandra Powers. D: Martin Campbell. HOR [R] 92m. v

Cast a Giant Shadow 1966 ★★★ American military lawyer (Douglas) aids Israel in its 1947 war against the Arabs. Romantic view of the early years of the Jewish state lacks focus but works well as a fictional biography. C: Kirk Douglas, John Wayne, Frank Sinatra, Yul Brynner, Senta Berger, Angie Dickinson, Luther Adler, Topol. D: Melville Shavelson. DRA 142m.

Cast a Long Shadow 1959 ★★ An alcoholic wanders into a Western town and claims to be the long-lost son of a deceased cattleman. Footweary tale that ambles off to nowhere. C:

Audie Murphy, Terry Moore. D: Thomas Carr. WST 82m.

Castaway 1986 ★★★ Executive Reed advertises for woman to share tropical paradise and wedded bliss, dreaming of sexual abandon. Unfortunately, partner Donohoe doesn't share his dreams. Director Roeg does well with tired material. C: Oliver Reed, Amanda Donohoe. D: Nicolas Roeg. DRA [R] 118m. V

Castaway Cowboy, The 1974 ★★★½ Texan (Garner) stranded on Hawaiian island in 1850s helps farmer Miles keep her land out of clutches of evil Culp. Mild Disney fare brightened by appealing Garner. C: James Garner, Vera Miles, Robert Culp. D: Vincent McEveety. FAM/DRA [G] 91m.

Castaways on Gilligan's Island, The 1979 ★★ At long last rescued, Gilligan, the skipper, the Howells, and all the others return to Gilligan's Island with plans to turn it into a tourist haven. For those who really loved the show. C: Bob Denver, Alan Hale Jr., Jim Backus, Natalie Schafer, Russell Johnson, Dawn Wells, Tom Bosley. D: Earl Bellamy. COM 74m.

Castilian, The 1963 Spanish ★★ Idealistic young nobleman rouses his people and leads them in battle against foreign invaders. A swashbuckler that buckles far too fast. C: Cesar Romero, Alida Valli, Frankie Avalon, Broderick Crawford. D: Javier Seto. ACT 129m.

Castle in the Desert 1942 ★★★½ Chan (Toler) and several other guests visit a remote Mojave Desert castle, where several murders occur. Dungeons, secret passages, and plenty of red herrings make this final Twentieth Century-Fox *Chan* entry an entertaining whodunit. C: Sidney Toler, Arleen Whelan. D: Harry Lachman. CRI 62m. V

Castle Keep 1969 ★★★ A medieval castle filled with rare art is the pawn in a deadly game of possession between American and German soldiers. Good action throughout in this solid WWII adventure. C: Burt Lancaster, Peter Falk, Patrick O'Neal, Jean-Pierre Aumont, Al Freeman Jr., Bruce Dern. D: Sydney Pollack. ACT 105m.

Castle of Blood 1964 French ★★★ To win a wager, a poet spends a night in a castle from which no one has ever returned alive. Alternately suspenseful and silly, this tries too hard to frighten. (a.k.a. *The Castle of Terror*) C: Barbara Steele, George Riviere, Margaret Robsahm. D: Antonio Margheriti. HOR 85m.

Castle of Cagliostro 1980 ★★★★ Kids and adults alike will enjoy this amusing Japanese animated adventure, which follows the exploits of master thief Wolf, who's out to reestablish a rightful heir to the throne of a small European country called Cagliostro. Action and comedy are the prime ingredients here. FAM/ACT 100m. V

Castle of Evil 1966 ★★ Assembled on a remote island for the reading of a will, a group of heirs is slain—one victim at a time. Odd little horror story that chooses its moments. C: Scott Brady, Virginia Mayo. D: Francis D. Lyon. HOR 81m. V

Castle of Fu Manchu, The 1968 ★ The notorious Fu Manchu is working on a diabolical scheme to place the entire planet Earth in a deep freeze. This is one chiller guaranteed to leave you cold. C: Christopher Lee, Richard Greene. D: Jess Franco. HOR [PG] 92m.

Castle of Purity 1974 ★★★½ Crazy father locks up daughters to protect them from evils of sex. Ripstein's first feature borrows heavily from Buñuel, to good purpose. C: Claudio Brook, Rita Macedo. D: Arturo Ripstein. COM 116m.

Castle of Terror, The 1964 *See* **Castle of Blood**

Castle of the Living Dead 1964 Italian ★★ The nefarious Count Drago mummifies all who dare to visit his castle. Low-level thriller noteworthy as Donald Sutherland's film debut. C: Christopher Lee, Gala Germani, Donald Sutherland. D: Herbert Wise. HOR 90m.

Castle on the Hudson 1940 ★★★★ Remake of *20,000 Years in Sing Sing* features Garfield as prison inmate who challenges reforms of new warden O'Brien. Fine cast of character actors fills out this well-acted telling of prison film conventions. C: John Garfield, Pat O'Brien, Ann Sheridan, Burgess Meredith. D: Anatole Litvak. CRI 77m.

Castle, The 1968 German ★★★★ Kafka's tale of a surveyor who cannot reach the leaders of a strange town. Schell is well cast, directing is showy. C: Maximilian Schell, Cordula Trantow. D: Rudolf Noelte. DRA 90m. V

Casual Sex? 1988 ★★★½ A pair of young women, Thompson and Jackson, go to a California health resort to escape the danger-fraught singles scene. Their aerobic and amorous adventures aren't particularly memorable, but there's some fun to be had in this unpretentious comedy. C: Lea Thompson, Victoria Jackson, Andrew Dice Clay, Mary Gross. D: Genevieve Robert. COM [R] 87m. V

Casualties of Love: The "Long Island Lolita" Story 1993 ★★ Yet another Amy Fisher saga, this one told from Joey Buttofucco's point of view. Former TV hunk Scalia has gone far away from his past persona. For serious Amyphiles only. C: Jack Scalia, Alyssa Milano, Phyllis Lyons. D: John Herzfeld. DRA 100m. TVM V

Casualties of War 1989 ★★★½ Private in Vietnam refuses to allow a cover-up of the rape and murder of an innocent woman by members of his unit. De Palma uses his flair for graphic violence to deliver a strong moral lesson. C: Michael J. Fox, Sean Penn, Thuy Thy Le, Don Harvey, John Leguizamo. D: Brian De Palma. DRA [R] 120m. V

Cat and Mouse 1975 French ★★★★ Comedic thriller follows Parisian police detective's attempt to solve a murder case that has too many suspects. Well-made mystery features strong performances and great scenery. C: Michele Morgan, Serge Reggiani, Jean-Pierre Aumont, Philippe Leotard. D: Claude Lelouch. CRI [PG] 107m. V

Cat and the Canary, The 1927 ★★★★ The original, silent example of the "old dark house" genre involves strange goings-on in a shadowy manor during the reading of deceased master's will. Originally a stage play, the movie is greatly enhanced by the director's prowess; remade often. C: Laura LaPlante, Tully Marshall. D: Paul Leni. HOR 70m.

Cat and the Canary, The 1939 ★★★★ A remake of the 1927 film that began the whole haunted house movie genre where frightened folks spend a night in a spooky mansion. This one stars Bob Hope in the role that established his film career. A superb mixture of comedy and chills. C: Bob Hope, Paulette Goddard, Gale Sondergaard. D: Elliott Nugent. COM 74m.

Cat and the Canary, The 1978 British ★★★½ Respectable, serious version of the classic haunted house story, with Lynley as an heiress to a fortune coveted by murderous relatives. Good cast. C: Carol Lynley, Honor Blackman, Michael Callan, Wendy Hiller, Wilfrid Hyde-White, Olivia Hussey, Edward Fox. D: Radley Metzger. CRI [PG] 90m. V

Cat and the Fiddle, The 1934 ★★★★ Jerome Kern/Otto Harbach operetta is lovingly transferred to the screen for MacDonald's first MGM musical. Navarro's a composer who vies with Morgan for her attentions. Finale in color. Includes "The Night Was Made For Love" and "She Didn't Say Yes." C: Jeanette MacDonald, Ramon Novarro, Frank Morgan, Charles Butterworth, Jean Hersholt. D: William K. Howard. MUS 88m. V

Cat Ballou 1965 ★★★★ Freewheeling Western spoof takes title schoolmarm (Fonda) from young innocent to desperado gang leader. Marvin bagged the Oscar for Best Actor playing dual roles as a drunken gunslinger and the notorious outlaw he finally brings to justice. Rousing, fun-filled comedy. C: Jane Fonda, Lee Marvin, Michael Callan, Dwayne Hickman. D: Elliot Silverstein. WST 95m. V

Cat Chaser 1989 ★★½ McGillis, married to head of Latin American secret police force, finds unwanted trouble when a former lover reenters her life. Choppy, confusing story helped by a good cast. Based on Elmore Leonard book. C: Kelly McGillis, Peter Weller, Charles Durning. D: Abel Ferrara. DRA [R] 93m. V

Cat Creature, The 1973 ★★★½ A bizarre cat god turns all kinds of people into victims during its search for a powerful gold relic. High-quality horror story offers eerie atmosphere in a tight little package. C: Meredith Baxter, David Hedison, Gale Sondergaard, Stuart Whitman, Keye Luke, John Carradine. D: Curtis Harrington. HOR 72m.

Cat Creeps, The 1946 ★★ Minor horror thriller about a feline that lives on inside the body of a dead woman. More frivolous than frightening. C: Noah Beery Jr., Lois Collier. D: Erle Kenton. HOR 58m.

Cat From Outer Space, The 1978 ★★★ An alien cat with super powers needs help to replace its damaged spaceship. Harmless children's fantasy/comedy may remind viewers of the superhit *E.T.* (which came out four years later). C: Ken Berry, Sandy Duncan, McLean Stevenson, Harry Morgan, Roddy McDowall. D: Norman Tokar. FAM/SFI [G] 103m. V

Cat Girl 1957 British ★★ Psychic link between a young woman and a murderous leopard form the basis for a prolonged reign of terror. Decent horror premise goes unrealized. C: Barbara Shelley, Robert Ayres. D: Alfred Shaughnessy. HOR 69m. V

Cat o' Nine Tails 1971 Italian ★★ One-time detective, now blind, teams up with a cub reporter to hunt down a serial killer. A whole lot of blood and gore and violence. C: Karl Malden, James Franciscus, Catherine Spaak. D: Dario Argento. CRI [PG] 112m. V

Cat on a Hot Tin Roof 1958 ★★★★ Ives plays the dying patriarch of a lust-ridden and greedy family eager to get their hands on his money. Newman plays his alcoholic son, married to sexually repressed Taylor. Some of the overt sexuality of the original Tennessee Williams play has been tempered, but the level of electricity is still quite high. Remade in 1984. C: Elizabeth Taylor, Paul Newman, Burl Ives, Jack Carson, Judith Anderson, Madeleine Sherwood. D: Richard Brooks. DRA 108m. V

Cat on a Hot Tin Roof 1984 ★★★½ Adaptation of the Tennessee Williams play with Lange as Maggie the Cat, married to an alcoholic ex-football player (Jones). More faithful than the 1958 version but not as steamy. C: Jessica Lange, Tommy Lee Jones, Rip Torn, David Dukes. D: Jack Hofsiss. DRA 122m. V

Cat People 1942 ★★★ Young man marries Serbian woman who turns into ferocious cat at night, attacking those who cross her by day. Haunting atmosphere gives film its overall creepy effect. Basis for 1982 remake. C: Simone Simon, Kent Smith. D: Jacques Tourneur. HOR 73m. V

Cat People 1982 ★★★ Remake of the 1942 classic, with Kinski one of the last survivors of a race of beings who transform into felines in the heat of passion. Kinski and McDowell are fine, and the movie is stylish, sexy, and gruesome, if sometimes emotionally cold. C: Nastassia Kinski, Malcolm McDowell, John Heard, Annette O'Toole, Ruby Dee, Ed Begley Jr., John Larroquette. D: Paul Schrader. HOR [R] 118m. V

C.A.T. Squad 1986 *See* **Stalking Danger**

Cat, The 1966 ★★ When he's separated from his parents on a camping trip, a young boy is attacked by a trespasser, then saved by a tame mountain lion. Woefully tedious. C: Peggy Ann Garner, Barry Coe. D: Ellis Kadison. DRA 87m.

Cat Women of the Moon 1954 ★★ Lunar expedition discovers an advanced subterranean civilization of women in black leotards and heavy eyeliner. Maybe the best so-bad-it's-good film ever. C: Sonny Tufts, Victor Jory, Marie Windsor. D: Arthur Hilton. SFI 64m. V

Catamount Killing 1974 German ★★½ A small-town bank manager and his girlfriend rob the bank, then they find it difficult to escape. Some good suspense amid the Green Mountains of Vermont. C: Horst Buchholz, Ann Wedgeworth, Polly Holliday. D: Krzysztof Zanussi. CRI 93m.

Catastrophe ★★ William Conrad narrates this superficial documentary about eight natural and technological disasters, from the Hindenburg to the Dust Bowl. DOC

Catch Me a Spy 1971 British ★★★ After her husband is arrested for espionage, Jobert finds herself sucked into the world of Cold War spying. Despite some good laughs, this would-be spy thriller never amounts to much. (a.k.a. *To Catch a Spy*). C: Kirk Douglas, Marlene Jobert, Trevor Howard, Tom Courtenay. D: Dick Clement. ACT 81m. V

Catch-22 1970 ★★★½ In the Mediterranean during WWII, Air Force Captain Yossarian (Arkin) and others try to hold on to their lives and their sanity amid wartime madness. Uneven but moving blackly comic adaptation of Joseph Heller's modern-classic anti-war novel, with terrific cast. C: Alan Arkin, Martin Balsam, Richard Benjamin, Arthur Garfunkel, Jack Gilford, Bob Newhart, Anthony Perkins, Paula Prentiss, Martin Sheen, Jon Voight, Orson Welles. D: Mike Nichols. DRA [R] 121m. V

Catch Us If You Can 1965 *See* **Having a Wild Weekend**

Catered Affair, The 1956 ★★★½ A cab driver (Borgnine) is tormented by his wife (Davis) into giving their daughter (Reynolds) a lavish wedding he can't afford. Serious, well-written comedy/drama (Gore Vidal did the script), from Paddy Chayevsky's TV play. C: Ernest Borgnine, Bette Davis, Debbie Reynolds, Rod Taylor, Barry Fitzgerald. D: Richard Brooks. DRA 94m. V

Catherine & Co. 1975 French ★★½ An ambitious young prostitute incorporates herself. Some fun, mostly fluff. C: Jane Birkin, Patrick Dewaere, Jean-Pierre Aumont. D: Michel Boisrond. COM 99m.

Catherine the Great 1934 British ★★★½ Antique retelling of the Russian czarina's rise to power, despite a miserable royal marriage. Rather stilted; those interested in the subject should check out Marlene Dietrich's *The Scarlet Empress*. C: Elisabeth Bergner, Douglas Fairbanks, Jr., Flora Robson. D: Paul Czinner. DRA 92m. V

Catholics 1973 ★★★★ An isolated Irish monastery clings to old ways. Sheen plays the Vatican emissary sent to modernize them; Howard their recalcitrant abbott. Strong if talky drama, adapted by Brian Moore from his novel. (a.k.a. *The Conflict*) C: Trevor Howard, Martin Sheen, Raf Vallone, Cyril Cusack. D: Jack Gold. DRA 86m. TVM V

Cathy's Child 1979 Australian ★★½ Alcoholic journalist rediscovers his sense of justice and sobriety after becoming involved in a baby custody fight. Congested Australian melodrama. C: Michelle Fawdon, Alan Cassell, Bryan Brown, Harry Michael. D: Donald Crombie. DRA 89m.

Cathy's Curse 1976 French-Canadian ★★ *Exorcist* rip-off about a little girl and her family terrorized by the spirit of her dead aunt, who possesses her doll and then the child herself. Script and effects are equally unconvincing. C: Alan Scarfe, Beverley Murray, Randi Allen, Roy Witham. D: Eddy Matalon. HOR 90m. V

Catlow 1971 ★★★★ In the Old West, a robber (Brynner) is determined to pull off a million-dollar gold theft. Funny, rip-roaring yarn, based on a Louis L'Amour novel. C: Yul Brynner, Leonard Nimoy, Richard Crenna, Daliah Lavi, Jo Ann Pflug. D: Sam Wanamaker. WST [PG] 103m. V

Catman of Paris 1946 ★★ Silly horror B-movie: Esmond turns into a cat at night, sucks blood, and generally makes a pest of himself. C: Carl Esmond, Lenore Aubert, Adele Mara. D: Lesley Selander. HOR 65m.

Cat's Eye 1985 ★★★ Trilogy of Stephen King stories works more often than not, thanks in large part to strong casting, especially Woods as the subject of an unorthodox quit-smoking program and McMillan as a gambler who makes a deadly bet with Hays. C: Drew Barrymore, James Woods, Alan King, Kenneth McMillan, Robert Hays. D: Lewis Teague. HOR 94m. V

Cat's Paw, The 1934 ★★★ Missionary's son returns from China and gets involved with corrupt politicians. Some silly situations and laughter courtesy of Lloyd, but otherwise a misfire. C: Harold Lloyd, Una Merkel. D: Sam Taylor. COM 90m.

Catskill Honeymoon 1949 Yiddish ★★★ Semi-documentary set at a Borscht Belt hotel, featuring a lengthy variety show of the old kind, a veritable Yiddish vaudeville. Mainly of historical interest. C: Michal Michalesko, Jan Bart, Bas Sheva, Max Boyzk, Rose Boyzk, Bobby Colt. D: Josef Berne. COM 93m.

Cattle Annie and Little Britches 1980 ★★★½ In 1893, two young Eastern women charm surviving members of Dalton and Doolin gangs into committing more bank robberies. A bit lean in places but saved by excellent cast, with Plummer outstanding in her first film. Based on Robert Ward's novel. C: Burt Lancaster, Rod Steiger, Amanda Plummer, Diane Lane. D: Lamont Johnson. WST [PG] 95m.

Cattle Drive 1951 ★★★★ A teenager, the spoiled son of a wealthy land baron, learns a lot about life and friendship when he's sent along on a cattle drive. A solid story and a fine cast, particularly McCrea. C: Joel McCrea, Dean Stockwell, Leon Ames, Chill Wills. D: Kurt Neumann. WST 77m.

Cattle Empire 1958 ★★★½ Recognizing an opportunity to take revenge against those who sent him to jail, a trail boss agrees to lead a new cattle drive. Good Western action and fine work from McCrea. C: Joel McCrea, Gloria Talbott. D: Charles Warren. WST 83m.

Cattle King 1963 ★★★½ Questions over grazing rights pit two powerful ranchers against each other. Familiar story benefits from a fine cast, led by major star Taylor. C: Robert Taylor, Joan Caulfield, Robert Loggia. D: Tay Garnett. WST 88m.

Cattle Queen of Montana 1954 ★★★½ Title character (Stanwyck) fights off marauding Indians and evil land baron. Average Western benefits from Barbara's spitfire performance and gorgeous location photography. C: Barbara Stanwyck, Ronald Reagan. D: Allan Dwan. WST 88m. V

Cattle Town 1952 ★★ Ranchers returning from the Civil War find their land occupied by hordes of squatters. Sedentary, low-budget Western. C: Dennis Morgan, Philip Carey, Amanda Blake, Rita Moreno, Merv Griffin. D: Noel Smith. WST 71m.

Caught 1949 ★★★ A model (Bel Geddes) marries a powerful but unstable millionaire (Ryan). She flees her oppressive life by falling in love with a sympathetic doctor (Mason), but is forced to return to her husband when she finds she's pregnant. Polished, moody melodrama. Mason's Hollywood debut. C: James Mason, Barbara Bel Geddes, Robert Ryan. D: Max Ophuls. DRA 90m. V

Caught in the Draft 1941 ★★★★½ Movie star (Hope), trying to dodge the WWII draft, enlists by accident. Very funny Army farce never lets up with tailor-made sight gags, wisecracks. One of Bob's best. C: Bob Hope, Dorothy Lamour, Eddie Bracken. D: David Butler. COM 82m. V

Cauldron of Blood 1967 Spanish ★ Yet another variation on the story of a sculptor (Karloff) whose human figures include the genuine article, thanks to his psychopathic wife (Lindfors). Tedious waste of Karloff, who died prior to its release. C: Boris Karloff, Viveca Lindfors, Jean-Pierre Aumont. D: Edward Mann. HOR [PG] 95m. V

Cause for Alarm 1951 ★★★½ Housewife tries to save herself from potential murder charge when her jealous husband sends an incriminating letter to the D.A., then dies. Little real suspense, but film moves at a good clip and boasts clever surprise ending. C: Loretta Young, Barry Sullivan, Margalo Gillmore. D: Tay Garnett. CRI 73m. V

Cavalcade 1933 ★★★★½ Chronicle of the lives of a British family and their servants from the turn of the century to the Depression; based on Noel Coward's play. Sweeping yet detailed saga won Oscars for Best Picture and Director. C: Diana Wynyard, Clive Brook, Margaret Lindsay, Una O'Connor. D: Frank Lloyd. DRA 110m. V

Cavalier, The 1928 ★★½ A mysterious masked man (Talmadge) rescues Bedford on her way to New Spain. Stilted early talkie, with Talmadge (Douglas Fairbanks, Sr.'s former stand-in) a game but unheroic hero. C: Richard Talmadge, Barbara Bedford, Nora Cecil, David Torrence. D: Irvin Willat. WST 69m.

Cavalry Scout 1951 ★★ The adventures of a scout who recovers stolen property and romances frontier women. Typical trail story with little to surprise. C: Rod Cameron, Audrey Long, Jim Davis, James Arness. D: Lesley Selander. WST 78m.

Cave of Outlaws 1951 ★★½ Released at last from prison, an outlaw returns to the caves where he'd stashed his loot. Minor Western includes some highly interesting photography on location at the Carlsbad Caverns. C: Macdonald Carey, Alexis Smith, Edgar Buchanan, Victor Jory. D: William Castle. WST 75m.

Caveman 1981 ★★★½ Prehistoric man (Starr) leads his own tribe of fellow misfits. Dinosaur gags abound in this loopy and visually entertaining spoof. C: Ringo Starr, Barbara Bach, John Matuszak, Shelley Long, Dennis Quaid, Jack Gilford. D: Carl Gottlieb. COM [PG] 92m. V

Cavern, The 1966 ★★½ Six soldiers and a young girl, seeking safety during a bombing attack, find themselves trapped inside an Italian cave. Claustrophobic WWII tale. C: Rosanna Schiaffino, John Saxon, Brian Aherne, Peter Marshall, Larry Hagman. D: Edgar Ulmer. DRA 83m.

CB4—The Movie 1993 ★★★ Hip parody of rap culture as a middle-class kid assumes the identity of a tough-talking convict to bolster the success of his musical group. Comedy's satirical edge not always sharp, but it keeps rocking. C: Chris Rock, Allen Payne, Phil Hartman. D: Tamra Davis. COM [R] 88m. V

C.C. and Company 1970 ★★½ In Namath's first major role, he plays a mild-mannered motorcyclist who tries to fend off a biker gang and the come-ons of fashion expert (Ann-Margret). Except for a few well-done comic turns (and some unintentional ones) this action/comedy rarely rises above its premise. Some nudity. (a.k.a. *Chrome Hearts*) C: Joe Namath, Ann-Margret. D: Seymour Robbie. COM [PG] 91m. V

Cease Fire 1985 ★★½ Years after the Vietnam War, a couple of vets remain tormented by their experiences. Has its moments. C: Don Johnson, Lisa Blount. D: David Nutter. DRA [R] 97m. V

Ceiling Zero 1935 ★★★★ Devil-may-care pilot (Cagney) flirts with Travis and danger until his freewheeling ways catch up with him, disastrously. O'Brien is his order-barking commander in this exciting star vehicle. Filmed again as *International Squadron*. C: James Cagney, Pat O'Brien, June Travis. D: Howard Hawks. DRA 95m. V

Celebration at Big Sur 1971 ★★★ Documentary filming of a folk-rock festival at the famous California seaside locale. Some big names, including Joan Baez and Crosby, Stills, Nash & Young, and some fine music. C: Joan Baez, Crosby, Stills, Nash & Young, Joni Mitchell, John Sebastian, Mimi Farina. D: Baird Bryant, Johanna Demetrakas. DOC [PG] 82m.

Celeste 1981 German ★★★★ Handsome attempt to film the memoirs of Marcel Proust's devoted housekeeper Celeste Alberet (Mattes). Jurgens is the novelist. Adlon adds some interesting directorial flourishes to an unusual story. C: Eva Mattes, Jurgen Arndt. D: Percy Adlon. DRA 107m. V

Celia—Child of Terror 1989 ★★★ Despite the title, this Australian production is less concerned with horrific effects than psychological chills. Set in the '50s, it centers on a young girl whose inability to deal with reality leads to trauma and terror. C: Rebecca Smart, Nicholas Eadie, Victoria Longley, Mary-Anne Fahey. D: Ann Turner. DRA 110m. V

Céline and Julie Go Boating 1974 French ★★★★½ A magician and a librarian visit a strange house and get caught up in the residents' lives. An unusual and lyrical tale, adapted from Henry James' stories. The film develops on its own terms, with an often dreamlike quality. Quite marvelous. C: Dominique Labourier, Juliet Berto, Bulle Ogier, Marie-France Pisier, Barbet Schroeder. D: Jacques Rivette. DRA 192m.

Cell 2455, Death Row 1955 ★★ Through skillful use of the judicial appeals system, a convicted murderer continually postpones his execution. Slow-moving knockoff of real-life events of murderer Caryl Chessman. C: William Campbell, Kathryn Grant, Vince Edwards. D: Fred Sears. CRI 77m.

Cellar Dweller 1988 ★★ Slack, unscary creature feature suffers from low-budget production and unimaginative scripting, though the monster (the creation of a long-dead cartoonist that comes to life and terrorizes current residents of the artist's old mansion) isn't bad. C: Deborah Mullowney, Vince Edwards, Yvonne De Carlo. D: John Carl Buechler. HOR 78m. V

Cemetery Club, The 1992 ★★★★ Trio of middle-aged widows band together for strength and comfort as they hope for one more chance at love. Offbeat character comedy features engaging performances by wonderful cast. C: Ellen Burstyn, Olympia Dukakis, Diane Ladd, Danny Aiello, Lainie Kazan, Christina Ricci. D: Bill Duke. COM [PG-13] 107m. V

Cemetery Girls 1971 *See* **Vampire Hookers**

Centennial Summer 1946 ★★★ Knock-off of *Meet Me in St. Louis* with Crain and Darnell as sisters in 1876 Philadelphia during the Centennial Exposition. Includes lovely Jerome Kern songs "All Through the Day," "In Love In Vain," and "Up With the Lark." C: Jeanne Crain, Cornel Wilde, Linda Darnell, Walter Brennan, Constance Bennett, Dorothy Gish. D: Otto Preminger. MUS 102m.

Center of the Web 1992 ★★★ A victim of mistaken identity helps the CIA by keeping up the facade to catch a dangerous assassin. When the tables turn he is soon running from the Mob *and* the government, in this moderately exciting thriller. The villainous Davi steals the show. C: Robert Davi, Charlene Tilton, Tony Curtis. D: David Prior. ACT [R] 88m. V

Centerfold Girls, The 1974 ★★★½ A young psychotic decides to kill all the women who ever posed for a nude centerfold. Riveting at times, with an excellent cast. C: Andrew Prine, Tiffany Bolling, Aldo Ray. D: John Peyser. CRI [R] 93m. V

Central Airport 1933 ★★½ Post-WWI home-front account of a love triangle at an aerial circus. A real relic, but check out those aerial acrobatics! C: Richard Barthelmess, Sally Eilers, Tom Brown, Glenda Farrell. D: William Wellman. ACT 75m.

Central Park 1932 ★★★ A series of spirited, highly entertaining stories about people in New York City's famous park. Quite well done and still interesting to watch. C: Joan Blondell, Guy Kibbee, Wallace Ford. D: John Adolfi. DRA 61m.

Central Park 1989 ★★★★½ Charming documentary takes a look at New York City's Central Park over the course of one spring day, from sunrise to sunset, from joggers and dog walkers to a political fight over building new tennis courts. One of Wiseman's gentlest films. D: Frederick Wiseman. DOC 180m.

C'era Una Volta *See* **More Than a Miracle**

Ceremony, The 1963 ★★½ Rather than die at the hands of a Tangier executioner, a bank robber breaks out of jail with the help of his brother. A little less moralizing and more action would have helped. C: Laurence Harvey, Sarah Miles. D: Laurence Harvey. CRI 105m.

Certain Fury 1985 ★★ When two women

are mistaken for a couple of violent prostitutes, they decide to flee for their lives. Confusing. C: Tatum O'Neal, Irene Cara, Peter Fonda. D: Stephen Gyllenhaal. DRA [R] 88m. V

Certain Sacrifice, A 1980 ★★ A rape victim seeks out her assailant and murders him according to a rather bizarre ritual. Noteworthy mainly as Madonna's film debut. C: Madonna Ciccone, Jeremy Pattnosh. D: Stephen Lewicki. CRI 60m. V

Certain Smile, A 1958 ★★★ Love among the rich and adulterous on the French Riviera, from the Françoise Sagan best-seller, as a nubile teenager (Carere) falls for her suave married uncle (Brazzi). The goings-on are upstaged by beautifully filmed vistas of France; popular Johnny Mathis theme song won an Oscar nomination. C: Rossano Brazzi, Joan Fontaine, Christine Carere, Bradford Dillman. D: Jean Negulesco. DRA 106m.

Cesar and Rosalie 1972 French ★★★★ Tired of her live-in lover, middle-aged French woman has affair with sexy younger man who then befriends the lover. Pleasant love triangle told with liberal sense of humor. Montand is particularly good as Schneider's liberal mature mate. C: Yves Montand, Romy Schneider, Sami Frey, Isabelle Huppert. D: Claude Sautet. DRA [R] 110m. V

Cesar 1936 French ★★★★★ Concluding episode of Marcel Pagnol's classic trilogy (the others being *Marius* and *Fanny*) in which Marius returns from the sea, discovers he has a grown son and is eventually reunited with his love, Fanny. Moving finale to refreshingly realistic, yet still romantic triumvirate of tales. C: Raimu, Pierre Fresnay, Orane Demazis, Charpin. D: Marcel Pagnol. DRA 117m. V

C'est la Vie 1990 French ★★★ Handsome, quasi-sequel to the popular *Entre Nous* continues the semi-autobiographical story of the director's mother. At the end of the '50s, a woman decides to divorce her husband, so she and her daughters go away for the summer. Eventually, the mother begins a new romantic relationship. Again, Kurys manages to convey a child's-eye view of the world surprisingly well. C: Nathalie Baye, Richard Berry, Zabou, Julie Bataille. D: Diane Kurys. DRA 110m.

Cet Obscur Objet du Désir 1977 *See* **That Obscure Object of Desire**

Chad Hanna 1940 ★★½ An inside look at a circus troupe in 19th-century New York State. Beautiful to look at, but little more. C: Henry Fonda, Dorothy Lamour, Linda Darnell, Guy Kibbee, Jane Darwell, John Carradine. D: Henry King. DRA 86m.

Chain Gang Killings, The 1985 ★★½ Two shackled prisoners are on the lam after escaping from a brutal chain gang—one prisoner is black, the other white. Plodding and lamebrained; not to be confused with *The Defiant Ones*. C: Ian Yule, Ken Gampu. D: Clive Harding. ACT 99m. V

Chain Lightning 1950 ★★★ A jet manufacturer (Massey) hires an ex-WWII pilot (Bogart) to test the prototype he hopes to sell to the Air Force. Run-of-the mill flight drama does feature some good special effects. C: Humphrey Bogart, Eleanor Parker, Raymond Massey. D: Stuart Heisler. DRA 94m.

Chain of Evidence 1957 ★★★½ Murdered: one businessman. In relentless pursuit of killer: one dedicated policeman. Murder mystery sustains suspense. C: Bill Elliott, Don Haggerty. D: Paul Landres. CRI 64m.

Chain Reaction 1980 Australian ★★½ When a worker at an atomic plant is seriously harmed in an accident, some of his colleagues start talking up the danger of nuclear power. A relevant topic handled with intelligence. C: Steve Bisley, Arna-Maria Winchester. D: Ian Barry. DRA 87m. V

Chained 1934 ★★ Lavishly produced but improbable romantic triangle. Crawford, wife to wealthy Kruger, yearns for Gable, with whom she'd had a passionate shipboard fling before her marriage. Fun for Crawford and Gable fans; others can pass. C: Joan Crawford, Clark Gable, Otto Kruger, Una O'Connor, Akim Tamiroff. D: Clarence Brown. DRA 73m. V

Chained Heat 1983 U.S. ★★★½ First-rate camp classic, as chubby convict (Blair) is thrown into prison overseen by sleazy warden (Vernon) who frolics with prisoners in his jailhouse jacuzzi. Priceless dialogue, brisk pace make this Sequel to *Concrete Jungle* one of the best women-in-chains flicks ever. C: Linda Blair, John Vernon, Sybil Danning, Tamara Dobson, Stella Stevens, Edy Williams. D: Paul Nicolas. ACT [R] 97m. V

Chained Heat 2 1993 ★★ Run-of-the-mill female prisoner flick is disappointing story of Amazonian warden (Nielsen) running secret coke factory out of Prague prison. Sequel can't compete with original's sleazy energy. C: Brigitte Nielsen, Paul Koslo, Kimberley Kates, Kari Whitman. D: Lloyd Simandl. ACT [R] 98m. V

Chains of Gold 1992 ★★★½ Social worker (Travolta) rescues a young boy from a drug-running street gang. Colorful performances and direction make for tangy entertainment. C: John Travolta, Marilu Henner, Bernie Casey, Hector Elizondo. D: Rod Holcomb. DRA [R] 95m. V

Chairman, The 1969 ★★ An American scientist is sent to China on a highly confidential mission. Plodding, but star-studded cast helps. C: Gregory Peck, Anne Heywood, Arthur Hill. D: J Thompson. DRA [PG] 102m.

Chalk Garden, The 1964 British ★★★★ Mysterious governess Kerr brings love into the lives of Evans and her troubled teenage granddaughter Mills. Based on Enid Bagnold's play, sensitively brought to the screen. C: Deborah Kerr, Hayley Mills, Edith Evans, John Mills. D: Ronald Neame. DRA 104m. V

Challenge for Robin Hood, A 1968 British ★★ Another retelling of the Robin Hood legend. Harmless, breezy and somewhat entertaining. Best perhaps for children. C: Barrie Ingham, James Hayter. D: C. Richards. FAM/ACT [G] 85m.

Challenge of the Masters 1989 ★★½ As reward for winning a kung fu contest, son of martial arts master is given new teacher who trains him to defend friends and honor. Average martial arts yarn. C: Liu Chia-Hui, Chen Kuan-Tai, Chiang Yang, Liu Chia-Yung. D: Liu Chia-Liang. ACT 97m. v

Challenge, The 1982 ★★★½ An American boxer (Glenn) becomes involved with a Japanese family, descendants of renowned samurai warriors. Entertaining action piece; co-scripted by John Sayles. C: Scott Glenn, Toshiro Mifune, Donna Kei Benz. D: John Frankenheimer. ACT 108m. v

Challenge to Be Free 1978 ★★ In the Arctic, a fur trapper stays one step ahead of the law. A singular idea, weakly produced. C: Mike Mazurki, Vic Christy. D: Tay Garnett. DRA [G] 90m. v

Challenge to Lassie 1949 ★★★½ In 19th-century Edinburgh, a faithful pet keeps returning to the grave of his dead master, over the objections of a mean-spirited town official. Based on a true story; later remade as *Greyfriars Bobby*. Simple tale is hard to resist. C: Edmund Gwenn, Donald Crisp, Geraldine Brooks, Reginald Owen. D: Richard Thorpe. FAM/DRA [G] 77m. v

Challenge to White Fang 1987 ★★ Dog steals the show in this good vs. evil story pitting a gold prospector against a white-collar crook, but it's still lightweight and skippable. C: Franco Nero, Virna Lisi, Harry Carey Jr. D: Lucio Fulci. FAM/ACT [PG] 89m. v

Challenge 1976 ★ Murder a man's entire family, and he's apt to seek revenge. Brutal and ghastly. C: Earl Owensby, William T. Hicks. D: Martin Beck. ACT [PG] 90m. v

Challenger 1990 ★★★ The planning, liftoff, and ultimate tragedy of the *Challenger* space shuttle voyage of 1986. Quite well done and truly heartrending. C: Karen Allen, Barry Bostwick, Brian Kerwin, Peter Boyle. D: Glenn Jordan. DOC 144m.

Chamber of Horrors 1940 British ★★½ A psychopathic murderer is hunted down and ultimately discovered in a wax museum. A little shock, a little schlock, and a cast that's filled with surprises. C: Leslie Banks, Lilli Palmer, Cathleen Nesbitt. D: Norman Lee. HOR 80m.

Chameleon Street 1992 ★★★★ A resourceful young black man confronts racism and other societal prejudices by contriving new identities for himself. Low-budget satire that is always provocative, if not always funny. C: Wendell B. Harris Jr., Angela Leslie. D: Wendell B. Harris Jr. COM [R] 95m. v

Champ for a Day 1953 ★★½ Aging boxer tracks down the murderer of his best friend. Interesting little film with solid cast. C: Alex Nicol, Audrey Totter, Charles Winninger, Hope Emerson. D: William Seiter. CRI 90m.

Champ, The 1931 ★★★★ Sentimental weepie about a washed-up fighter (Beery) who returns to the ring to save face for his devoted son (Cooper) was a huge hit when first released. Beery won an Oscar as Best Actor, and the movie won for Best Original Story. Remade in 1979. C: Wallace Beery, Jackie Cooper, Irene Rich. D: King Vidor. DRA 87m.

Champ, The 1979 ★★★ Voight is a washed-up boxer who risks his life making a comeback in order to win custody of his son in this sentimental remake of the 1931 classic. A calculated tearjerker. C: Jon Voight, Faye Dunaway, Ricky Schroder, Jack Warden, Joan Blondell. D: Franco Zeffirelli. DRA [PG] 121m. v

Champagne 1928 British ★★ Silly story about a rich girl whose father pretends to be poor to teach her a lesson. Even Hitchcock disliked this film. Flat champagne indeed. C: Betty Balfour, Jean Bradin, Gordon Harker. D: Alfred Hitchcock. DRA 93m.

Champagne Charlie 1944 ★★★ Chronicle of the major personalities of the 19th-century British music hall. Long-winded but tuneful and ultimately entertaining. C: Tommy Trinder, Betty Warren, Stanley Holloway. D: Cavalcanti. MUS 107m.

Champagne Charlie 1989 Canadian ★★ The real-life story of the special gent who, in the 1860s, introduced that delightful bubbly stuff to America. C: Hugh Grant, Megan Gallagher, Megan Follows, Stephane Audran. D: Allen Eastman. DRA 200m. TVM

Champagne for Caesar 1950 ★★★★ Professor (Colman) makes a mint on the TV quiz show circuit. Amusing spoof; Price is priceless as a stuffy, malevolent soap sponsor. C: Ronald Colman, Celeste Holm, Vincent Price, Art Linkletter. D: Richard Whorf. COM 115m. v

Champagne Murders, The 1967 French ★★★½ Fuzzy characters and their doings are the backbone of a suspense plot about a wealthy eccentric who may be a killer. Plenty of red herrings. C: Anthony Perkins, Maurice Ronet, Stephane Audran. D: Claude Chabrol. CRI 98m.

Champagne Waltz 1937 ★★ It's jazz vs. serious music as opera star (Swarthout) spars with band leader (MacMurray). C: Gladys Swarthout, Fred MacMurray, Jack Oakie. D: A. Sutherland. MUS 87m.

Champion 1949 ★★★★★ Douglas gives a championship performance as a brutal boxer fighting his way up through the ranks, and sparing no one, in or out of the ring. His on-screen breakdown is a show stopper. Editing by Harry Gerstad won an Oscar. C: Kirk Douglas, Marilyn Maxwell, Arthur Kennedy, Ruth Roman. D: Mark Robson. DRA 99m. v

Champions 1983 British ★★★ A jockey and his horse both face serious illnesses, but together they rally and win a big race. A straightforward account of a true story. Inspiring. C: John Hurt, Edward Woodward, Ben Johnson, Kirstie Alley. D: John Irvin. DRA [PG] 115m.

Champions: A Love Story 1979 ★★½ A couple of teenagers meet and fall in love during competition for the American figure-skating title. Good skating, but no surprises. C: Shirley Knight, Tony Lo Bianco. D: John Alonzo. DRA 100m. TVM

Champions Forever 1989 ★★★ Heavyweight boxers Ali, Frazier, Holmes, Norton, and Foreman are deified thanks to interviews and highlights of their bouts. Magnetism of quintet (especially Ali) offsets too-serious slant; boxing fans should add a star. D: Dimitri Logothetis. DOC 87m. V

Chan is Missing 1982 ★★★★ Intriguing, low-budget comedy/mystery follows the exploits of a pair of Chinese cab drivers as they search through San Fransisco's Chinatown for mysterious man who has stolen their money. Taut directing highlights this unique cinematic sojourn. C: Wood Moy, Marc Hayashi, Laureen Chew, Judy Mihei. D: Wayne Wang. COM 80m. V

Chance at Heaven 1933 ★★★ A young man breaks off his engagement to a sweet young woman in order to marry a society brat. Curious and somewhat somber, but young McCrea and Rogers are fine. C: Ginger Rogers, Joel McCrea, Andy Devine, Betty Furness. D: William Seiter. DRA 70m.

Chance Meeting 1959 British ★★★★ Thoughtful murder mystery incorporates a look at the class system in England, as an artist finds the world closing in on him when he is wrongly accused of murder. Baker and Kruger are brilliant as detective and suspect, respectively. (a.k.a. *Blind Date*) C: Hardy Kruger, Stanley Baker, Micheline Presle. D: Joseph Losey. CRI 96m.

Chance of a Lifetime, The 1943 ★★★½ Boston Blackie (Morris) has his hands full when convicts are released into his care. Solid entry in the popular crime series. C: Chester Morris, Eric Rolf. D: William Castle. CRI 65m.

Chance of a Lifetime 1950 British ★★★★ Harassed boss (Radford) lets complaining workers run his factory to give them a taste of his problems. Realistically etched comedy/drama carries a flinty conviction. Superbly acted, seamlessly executed. C: Alan Osbiston, Basil Radford, Kenneth More. D: Bernard Miles. DRA 89m.

Chance 1989 ★★ Two detectives (Haggerty, Hilton-Jacobs) set a trap for murderous jewel thieves, only to become caught themselves. Routine. C: Dan Haggerty, Lawrence Hilton-Jacobs, Addison Randall, Roger Rodd, Charles Ganis, Pamela Dixon. D: Addison Randall, Charles Kanganis. ACT 90m. V

Chances Are 1989 ★★★ Labored fantasy concerns young man (Downey, Jr.) who suddenly realizes his girlfriend's mother (Shepherd) used to be his wife in his previous life, which means he's dating his daughter! Comic misfire tries too hard to be funny and poignant. C: Cybill Shepherd, Robert Downey Jr., Ryan O'Neal, Mary Stuart Masterson, Josef Sommer, Susan Ruttan. D: Emile Ardolino. COM [PG] 108m. V

Chances 1931 ★★★★ Two WWII English officers (Fairbanks, Jr. and Bushell), who are also brothers, romance the same woman (Hobart) while on leave in Florida. Tidy entertainment handled with skill and sensitivity; Fairbanks is terrific. C: Douglas Fairbanks Jr., Rose Hobart, Anthony Bushell. D: Allan Dwan. DRA 72m.

Chandler 1972 ★★½ Alcoholic shamus turned security guard (Oates) is hired to watch a ganglord's mistress (Caron) and falls for her. Below-average detective yarn. C: Warren Oates, Leslie Caron, Gloria Grahame. D: Paul Magwood. CRI [PG] 88m.

Chandu the Magician 1932 ★★½ When a diabolical maniac threatens the world with a death ray, Chandu (Lugosi) uses his mystical powers to stop him. Substandard B-serial silliness. C: Marcel Varnel, Edmund Lowe, Bela Lugosi. D: William Menzies. SFI 70m.

Chanel Solitaire 1981 U.S. ★★ Soapy biography of renowned fashion designer Coco Chanel (Pisier) concentrates on her romances and rise to riches. Glossy and stylish, but empty. C: Marie-France Pisier, Timothy Dalton, Rutger Hauer, Karen Black. D: George Kaczender. DRA [R] 124m. V

Chang 1927 ★★★★ Silent nature documentary, set in the wilds of Thailand (then known as Siam), focuses on a family's battle to co-exist with brutal elephants ("chang"). From the future creators of *King Kong*. D: Merian C. Cooper, Ernest B. Schoedsack. DOC 67m. V

Change of Habit 1969 ★★½ Elvis' last film, and a serious one at that. He's a ghetto doctor working with three novice nuns, one of whom (Moore) may not take her final vows. Not bad. C: Elvis Presley, Mary Tyler Moore, Barbara McNair, Edward Asner. D: William Graham. DRA [G] 97m. V

Change of Heart 1943 ★★★ A songwriter (Hayward) is ripped off by an unscrupulous music publisher (Carroll); then they fall in love. Tuneful fluff improved by 25-year-old Hayward. (a.k.a. *Hit Parade of 1943*) C: John Carroll, Susan Hayward, Gail Patrick, Eve Arden, Dorothy Dandridge. D: Albert Rogell. MUS 90m.

Change of Mind 1969 ★★★ A dying white district attorney's brain is implanted into a black man's body. Good cast prevails over incredible premise. And, there's a bonus; Duke Ellington did the soundtrack. C: Raymond St. Jacques, Susan Oliver, Leslie Nielsen. D: Robert Stevens. DRA [R] 103m.

Change of Seasons, A 1980 ★★★½ Suffering middle-aged blues, college professor Hopkins has affair with much younger Derek. In return, Hopkins' wife MacLaine takes on lover of her own. Well acted, though uneventful mid-life crises comedy/drama. C: Shirley MacLaine, Anthony Hopkins, Bo Derek, Michael Brandon. D: Richard Lang. COM [R] 102m. V

Changeling, The 1979 Canadian ★★★★ After the death of his wife and child, Scott moves into an old house that proves to be inhabited by a restless ghost. Supernatural drama is directed and acted with compelling conviction; the "automatic writing" scene is a highlight. C: George C. Scott, Trish Van Devere, Melvyn Douglas, Jean Marsh. D: Peter Medak. HOR [R] 113m. V

Changes 1993 ★★★ Ladd is a glamorous, divorced TV anchorperson living in New York. Nouri is a glamorous widower surgeon living in Los Angeles. Can they make their romance work in a glamorous fashion? Soaper, based on Danielle Steele's popular romance novel, will please its intended audience. C: Cheryl Ladd, Michael Nouri. D: Charles Jarrott. DRA 96m. V

Chant of Jimmy Blacksmith, The 1978 Australian ★★★★ Powerful, disturbing exploration of racism based on a true incident in Australia circa 1900. A mixed-blood aborigine (Lewis) goes on a murderous rampage when he realizes he'll never be accepted into white society. Quite violent, but effective and well acted. From Thomas *Schindler's List* Keneally's novel. C: Tommy Lewis, Freddy Reynolds, Jack Thompson. D: Fred Schepisi. DRA 124m.

Chantilly Lace 1993 ★★★½ Three reunions of seven women over one year provide ample opportunities for the talented cast to emote, back-bite, and trade quips. Static, but entertaining. Largely improvised. C: Lindsay Crouse, Martha Plimpton, Ally Sheedy, Talia Shire, Helen Slater, Jill Eikenberry, JoBeth Williams. D: Linda Yellen. DRA [R] 102m. TVM V

Chapayev 1934 Russian ★★★½ Uneducated peasant becomes hero during Russian Revolution. Obvious propaganda piece, but often stirring, with some painstakingly detailed battle scenes. C: Boris Bobochkin, Leonid Kmit. D: Sergei Vasiliev, Georgi Vasiliev. DRA 95m.

Chaplin 1992 British ★★★ Robert Downey Jr. transforms himself into the Little Tramp in a stunning performance that's the highlight of this overlong, episodic biography of the silent screen star. Little dramatic momentum, but Downey is a delight to watch. C: Robert Downey Jr., Dan Aykroyd, Geraldine Chaplin, Anthony Hopkins, Milla Jovovich, Kevin Kline, Diane Lane, Penelope Ann Miller, Marisa Tomei. D: Richard Attenborough. DRA [PG-13] 135m. V

Chaplin Revue, The 1958 ★★★★½ Solid introduction pieces together three classic shorts: *A Dog's Life* (1918), *Shoulder Arms* (1918), and *The Pilgrim* (1923) with Chaplin providing new music score, sound effects and narration. Last is best with Charlie a criminal pretending to be a minister. COM 119m. V

Chapman Report, The 1962 ★★★ Adaptation of best-seller based on Kinsey Report findings concerns sex researchers who survey the erotic practices of suburban women. Glitzy soap opera is often outright salacious, but Cukor's pro direction and highly skilled cast make it watchable. C: Efrem Zimbalist Jr., Shelley Winters, Jane Fonda, Claire Bloom, Glynis Johns, Andrew Duggan, Cloris Leachman, Chad Everett. D: George Cukor. DRA 125m.

Chappaqua 1966 ★★★ A heroin addict hallucinates as he goes through withdrawal. Visually impressive but superficial handling of actual experience of the director/star Rooks. C: Jean-Louis Barrault, Conrad Rooks, William Burroughs, Allen Ginsburg, Ravi Shankar, Ornette Coleman. D: Conrad Rooks. DRA 92m.

Chapter Two 1979 ★★ Talky adaptation of quasiautobiographical Neil Simon play. Story concerns a widowed writer whose love for his deceased wife interferes with his courtship of an appealing divorcé. C: James Caan, Marsha Mason, Valerie Harper, Joseph Bologna. D: Robert Moore. COM [PG] 124m. V

Charade 1963 ★★★★ Nifty suspense comedy features debonair Grant enlisted by widow Hepburn to help find a cache of riches hidden by her murdered husband. Cat-and-mouse timing is expertly played by ensemble. C: Cary Grant, Audrey Hepburn, Walter Matthau, James Coburn, George Kennedy. D: Stanley Donen. COM 113m. V

Charge at Feather River, The 1953 ★★★ Army prisoners rescue two women abducted by Indians. Routine Western packed with action scenes to take advantage of original 3-D format. C: Guy Madison, Vera Miles, Frank Lovejoy. D: Gordon Douglas. WST 96m.

Charge of the Black Lancers 1961 Italian ★★★½ Patriot fights for his country and against his traitorous brother. Invigorating costume drama with fine production values. C: Mel Ferrer, Yvonne Furneaux. D: Giacomo Gentilomo. ACT 97m.

Charge of the Light Brigade, The 1936 ★★★★½ Hollywood fudged on the location of the 27th Lancers' famous Crimean cavalry charge, and took some liberties with Alfred Lord Tennyson's romantic poem to create a thrilling adventure classic. Flynn is the commander bent on revenge who begins the ill-fated charge, and de Havilland his love. C:

Errol Flynn, Olivia de Havilland, Patric Knowles, Donald Crisp, David Niven, Spring Byington. D: Michael Curtiz. ACT 115m. V

Charge of the Light Brigade, The 1968 British ★★★★ The legendary, doomed British charge at Balakava, Turkey in the Crimean War in 1854. Scathing attack on military thinking and the absurdity of war. Well acted, with excellent animated sequences. C: David Hemmings, Vanessa Redgrave, John Gielgud, Harry Andrews, Trevor Howard. D: Tony Richardson. ACT [PG-13] 130m. V

Charge of the Model Ts, The 1976 ★★½ A WWI German agent tries to sneak into the U.S. with a weapon-rigged motorcar. Silly family comedy. C: John David Carson, Louis Nye, Arte Johnson. D: Jim McCullough. FAM/COM [G] 94m.

Charing Cross Road 1935 British ★★★ Somewhat creaky musical has youths trying to crash society. C: John Mills, June Clyde, Derek Oldham. D: Albert De Courville. MUS 72m.

Chariots of Fire 1981 British ★★★★★ Critics and public alike went crazy over this sophisticated, turn-of-the-century sports drama based on the true story of two British runners (a Scottish missionary and a Jewish Cambridge student) who compete in the 1924 Olympics. Oscars for Best Picture, Original Screenplay, Costumes, and the very popular score by Vangelis. C: Ben Cross, Ian Charleson, Nigel Havers, Cheryl Campbell, Ian Holm, John Gielgud, Brad Davis. D: Hugh Hudson. DRA [PG] 124m. V

Chariots of the Gods? 1974 ★★★ Based on Erich Von Daniken's book, this pseudo-documentary theorizes benevolent aliens visited and upgraded ancient civilizations. Not terribly convincing, but does include some nice cinematography of exotic locales. For the *In Search Of* set. D: Harold Reinl. SFI [G] 98m. V

Charles & Diana: A Palace Divided 1992 ★★★ Typical "behind the palace doors" soap opera recycles every tabloid story about the Prince of Wales's ill-fated marriage. Oxenberg portrayed Diana in 1982's idyllic *The Royal Romance of Charles and Diana*, forming a sort of video "before and after." (a.k.a. *Charles & Diana: Unhappily Ever After*) C: Roger Rees, Catherine Oxenberg, Benedict Taylor. D: John Power. DRA 100m. TVM V

Charles & Diana: A Royal Love Story 1982 ★★★½ The courtship and marriage of the Prince of Wales and Lady Diana Spencer. Fine film biography captures attendant hoopla. C: David Robb, Caroline Bliss, Christopher Lee, Rod Taylor, Margaret Tyzack, Mona Washbourne. D: James Goldstone. DRA 100m. TVM

Charles & Diana: Unhappily Ever After *See* **Charles & Diana: A Palace Divided**

Charles and Lucie 1982 French ★★★★ Two elderly people—a junk dealer and a cleaner—lose their money in a scam and find themselves falling in love as they run from authorities. Offbeat romance is sweet and touching at times, with an eccentric sense of reality. C: Daniel Ceccaldi, Ginette Garcin, Jean-Marie Proslier. D: Nelly Kaplan. DRA 97m.

Charles, Dead or Alive 1972 Swiss ★★★★ Wealthy Swiss industrialist gives up his opulent life and goes to live with a band of nonconformists in the countryside. Candid slice-of-life tale with an intriguing point of view about roles in society at large. Well acted by fine ensemble. C: François Simon, Marcel Robert, Marie-Claire Dufour, Andre Schmidt. D: Alain Tanner. DRA 93m.

Charleston 1978 Italian ★ Odd little comedy about an imprisoned art thief (Spencer) who wants out. The story line is convoluted, to say the least. C: Bud Spencer, James Coco, Herbert Lom. D: Marcello Fondato. COM 77m.

Charley and the Angel 1973 ★★★½ A cold shopkeeper (MacMurray) in the Depression undergoes a change of heart when he discovers his days on Earth are numbered. Whimsical, sentimental, and entertaining. C: Fred MacMurray, Cloris Leachman, Harry Morgan, Kurt Russell. D: Vincent McEveety. FAM/DRA [G] 94m. V

Charley One-Eye 1973 ★★★ An Indian outcast (Thinnes) and a black Union Army deserter (Roundtree) come together in the desert. Long two-person drama has tragic elements. C: Richard Roundtree, Roy Thinnes. D: Don Chaffey. WST [R] 107m.

Charley Varrick 1973 ★★★★½ A professional thief (Matthau) robs a small-town bank only to learn the loot is Mob money. Superior caper thriller with nifty ending; wonderful Matthau. C: Walter Matthau, Joe Don Baker, Felicia Farr. D: Don Siegel. CRI 111m. V

Charley's Aunt 1941 ★★★★ Slyly amusing Benny is an Oxford goofball who poses as his own maiden aunt in order to chaperon his buddies and their girls. This version of Brandon Thomas' often-filmed play is the funniest, moving at a breakneck, farcical pace. Entire cast exudes comic energy, with Benny a standout. C: Jack Benny, Kay Francis, Anne Baxter, Edmund Gwenn. D: Archie Mayo. COM 81m.

Charlie and the Great Balloon Chase 1978 ★★★½ A boy and his grandpa sail cross-country in a hot-air balloon, realizing the old man's life-long dream. Cheerful family yarn. C: Jack Albertson, Adrienne Barbeau, Slim Pickens. D: Larry Elikann. FAM/DRA 98m. TVM V

Charlie Bubbles 1968 ★★★½ A working-class writer's successful novel catapults him to fame, fortune, and ultimate boredom. Interesting, off-beat character study is Finney's directorial and Minelli's screen debut. C: Albert Finney, Colin Blakely, Billie Whitelaw, Liza Minnelli. D: Albert Finney. DRA 91m.

Charlie Chan The 20th Century-Fox *Charlie Chan* films may be the definitive Hollywood film series, faithfully intelligent, clever, and brisk mysteries that are solidly entertaining, if unambitious. Chan, created by Earl Derr Biggers, and first played by Warner Oland, is the top homicide detective on the Honolulu Police, dogged by his large brood of children, particularly would-be detective Number One Son, Lee (Keye Luke). When Oland died in 1937, he was replaced by Sidney Toler, whose Chan is more avuncular, and Victor Sen Yung came on board as Number Two Son, Jimmy. Unfortunately, after 1942's *Castle in the Desert*, one of the best films in the series, Fox dropped the films. They landed at Monogram, where the series continued for seven years. When Toler died, he was replaced by Roland Winters and the series wound down in 1949.

Behind That Curtain (1929)
Black Camel (1931)
Charlie Chan In London (1934)
Charlie Chan in Paris (1935)
Charlie Chan in Egypt (1935)
Charlie Chan in Shanghai (1935)
Charlie Chan's Secret (1936)
Charlie Chan at the Circus (1936)
Charlie Chan at the Race Track (1936)
Charlie Chan at the Opera (1936)
Charlie Chan at the Olympics (1937)
Charlie Chan on Broadway (1937)
Charlie Chan at Monte Carlo (1938)
Charlie Chan in Honolulu (1938)
Charlie Chan in Reno (1939)
Charlie Chan at Treasure Island (1939)
Charlie Chan in City in Darkness (1939)
Charlie Chan in Panama (1940)
Charlie Chan's Murder Cruise (1940)
Charlie Chan at the Wax Museum (1940)
Murder Over New York (1940)
Dead Men Don't Tell (1941)
Charlie Chan in Rio (1941)
Castle in the Desert (1942)
Charlie Chan in the Secret Service (1944)
The Chinese Cat (1944)
Black Magic (1944),
a.k.a. Meeting at Midnight
The Jade Mask (1945)
The Scarlet Clue (1945)
The Shanghai Cobra (1945)
The Red Dragon (1945)
Dark Alibi (1946)
Shadows Over Chinatown (1946)
Dangerous Money (1946)
The Trap (1947)
The Chinese Ring (1947)
Docks of New Orleans (1948)
The Shanghai Chest (1948)
The Golden Eye (1948)
The Feathered Serpent (1948)
Sky Dragon (1949)

Charlie Chan and the Curse of the Dragon Queen 1981 ★★½ The wicked Dragon Queen puts a curse on the sage Chinese detective and his number-one grandson. Talented cast at work in comedy spoof. C: Peter Ustinov, Lee Grant, Angie Dickinson, Richard Hatch, Brian Keith, Michelle Pfeiffer, Roddy McDowall, Rachel Roberts. D: Clive Donner. COM [PG] 97m. V

Charlie Chan and the Golden Eye 1948 *See* **Golden Eye, The**

Charlie Chan at Monte Carlo 1938 ★★½ Chan investigates a difficult case at the famed Riviera casino. Superjudicious use of logical clues leaves the audience guessing in this entry for the mystery series. C: Warner Oland, Keye Luke, Virginia Field. D: Eugene Forde. CRI 71m.

Charlie Chan at the Circus 1936 ★★★ The Chan family's revelry at the Big Top is disrupted by a killer ape. Show-time three-ring mystery featuring the aphoristic Asian sleuth. C: Warner Oland, Keye Luke, George and Olive Brasno, Francis Ford. D: Harry Lachman. CRI 72m.

Charlie Chan at the Olympics 1937 ★★★★ Chan pursues a vital aircraft guidance system from Honolulu to the Berlin Olympics via various modes of transportation—including the Nazi dirigible *Hindenburg*. First-rate Chan undertaking, with plenty of excitement. C: Warner Oland, Keye Luke. D: H. Bruce Humberstone. CRI 71m.

Charlie Chan at the Opera 1936 ★★★★ Prime Chan mystery, with Chan (Oland) trying to solve a series of murders committed during opera performances. Opera singer and mental asylum escapee (Karloff) heads the list of suspects, with police sergeant (Demarest) counterpointing Chan's deliberate thoughtfulness. Fake opera written by Oscar Levant. C: Warner Oland, Boris Karloff, Keye Luke, Charlotte Henry, Nedda Harrigan, William Demarest. D: H.Bruce Humberstone. CRI 66m.

Charlie Chan at the Race Track 1936 ★★★½ Chan foils crooks who are doping racehorses from a prominent stable. Above-average, fast-moving Chan entry. C: Warner Oland, Keye Luke, Helen Wood. D: H.Bruce Humberstone. CRI 70m.

Charlie Chan at the Wax Museum 1940 ★★★★ Chan (Toler) must dodge poison darts to solve a murder at a wax museum, with vengeful gangster (Lawrence) and a mad scientist among the suspects. One of the better Toler entries in the series, with the museum providing an effectively eerie setting. C: Sidney Toler, Sen Yung, Joan Valelrie. D: Lynn Shores. CRI 64m. V

Charlie Chan at Treasure Island 1939 ★★★★ After an author friend commits suicide on a plane, Chan tangles with a lunatic astrologer at the San Francisco Fair. Polished cat-and-mouse Chan sleuther, with good atmospherics. C: Sidney Toler, Cesar Romero, Pauline Moore, Sen Yung. D: Norman Foster. CRI 75m.

Charlie Chan Carries On 1931 ★★★½ When a rich American tourist is killed aboard an oceangoing cruise ship, fellow passenger Charlie Chan investigates the murder. One of the first *Charlie Chan* films, this is an entertaining little mystery. C: Warner Oland, John Garrick, Marguerite Churchill. D: Hamilton MacFadden. CRI 76m

Charlie Chan in City in Darkness 1939 ★★★½ While reuniting with old military chums in Paris, Charlie tangles with a fifth columnist. Propaganda cum mystery in representative Chan outing. C: Sidney Toler, Lynn Bari, Richard Clarke. D: Herbert Leeds. CRI 75m.

Charlie Chan in Egypt 1935 ★★★★ Chan's on the trail of crooks after Pharaoh Tutankhamen's treasure. Above-average mystery in the series features young Hayworth. C: Warner Orland, "Pat" Paterson, Thomas Beck, Rita Casino (Hayworth), Jameson Thomas. D: Louis King. CRI 65m.

Charlie Chan in Honolulu 1938 ★★★ The Chinese detective goes after a waterfront killer in Hawaii. Toler replaces the deceased Oland in this entry for the mystery series. C: Sidney Toler, Phyllis Brooks, Sen Yung, Eddie Collins, John King. D: Bruce Humberstone. CRI 68m.

Charlie Chan in London 1934 ★★★½ The Asian crime-buster (Oland) investigates a homicide at a stately country manor. Earl Derr Biggers' man of many sayings is in top form here. Watch for a young Ray Milland. C: Warner Oland, Drue Leyton, Alan Mowbray, Raymond Milland. D: Eugene Forde. CRI 79m.

Charlie Chan in Panama 1940 ★★★½ Chan goes undercover in a race against time to stop saboteurs from dynamiting the Panama Canal. Superior, entertaining entry with Charlie in disguise. C: Sidney Toler, Jean Rogers, Kane Richmond, Lionel Atwill, Sen Yung. D: Norman Foster. CRI 67m.

Charlie Chan in Paris 1935 ★★★★ Chan (Oland) and Number One Son (Luke) chase a murderous counterfeiter. Solid entry, boosted by Oland's performance in the series, and an exciting finale in the Paris sewers. C: Warner Oland, Mary Brian, Erik Rhodes, Keye Luke. D: Lewis Seiler. CRI 72m. V

Charlie Chan in Reno 1939 ★★★½ The ace Chinese sleuth unravels a puzzle involving the murder of an estranged spouse suing for divorce. Charlie gets the culprit in the end; the fun is in the watching. Above average. C: Sidney Toler, Ricardo Cortez, Phyllis Brooks, Sen Yung. D: Norman Foster. CRI 70m.

Charlie Chan in Rio 1941 ★★★½ Chan (Toler) arrives in the Sugar Loaf town to arrest a nightclub singer, but when she turns up dead he investigates. Average entry is a remake of the earlier *The Black Camel*. C: Sidney Toler, Mary Beth Hughes, Victor Jory, Sen Yung. D: Harry Lachman. CRI 62m. V

Charlie Chan in Shanghai 1935 ★★★ Chan investigates drug smuggling in his hometown. The ninth talkie entry for this popular mystery series. C: Warner Oland, Irene Hervey, Keye Luke. D: James Tinling. CRI 70m.

Charlie Chan in the Secret Service 1944 ★★★ The brilliant Chinese investigator is called in when an inventor is murdered for a secret formula. Two-bowl popcorn entry for the long-running mystery series. C: Sidney Toler, Mantan Moreland, Benson Fong. D: Phil Rosen. CRI 64m. V

Charlie Chan on Broadway 1937 ★★★★ Charlie hobnobs with underworld denizens, gossip columnists, and nightclub habitués while tracking a murderer. First-rate Chan film with plenty of puzzles and clues. C: Warner Oland, Keye Luke, Joan Marsh, J. Edward Bromberg, Leon Ames. D: Eugene Forde. CRI 68m.

Charlie Chan's Murder Cruise 1940 ★★★ Chan boards a cruise ship in search of clues to the Honolulu homicide of a Scotland Yard detective. Seaworthy puzzler for the popular sleuth. C: Sidney Toler, Sen Yung, Marjorie Weaver, Lionel Atwill, Robert Lowery. D: Eugene Forde. CRI 75m.

Charlie Chan's Secret 1936 ★★★½ When a wealthy business tycoon's son is murdered, Charlie Chan rounds up the usual suspects to find the killer. Good entry in the *Charlie Chan* series with some fun moments. C: Warner Oland, Rosina Lawrence, Charles Quigley, Henrietta Crosman, Edward Trevor. D: Gordon Wiles. CRI 71m. V

Charlie Chaplin Carnival 1938 ★★★★½ Early genius of Chaplin on display in four shorts, circa 1916-17: *Behind the Screen*, *The Count*, *The Fireman*, and *The Vagabond*. Only drawbacks are some distracting sound effects and music. C: Charlie Chaplin, Edna Purviance, Eric Campbell. D: Charles Chaplin. COM 100m. V

Charlie Chaplin Cavalcade 1938 ★★★★★ Three great Chaplin silent comedy shorts, 1916-17: *One A.M.*, *The Floorwalker*, and *The Rink*. Superb early-period Little Tramp. COM 75m.

Charlie Chaplin Festival 1938 ★★★★★ Top collection of four Chaplin silent comedies: *The Adventurer*, *The Cure*, *Easy Street*, and *The Immigrant*. Extraordinary exhibition by an extraordinary genius. COM 96m.

Charlie McCarthy, Detective 1956 ★★★ Entertainer/ventriloquist Edgar Bergen and his famous wisecracking dummy help a police inspector (Kennedy) solve a publisher's mysterious murder. Improbable blend of comedy and whodunit succeeds as entertainment. C: Edgar Bergen, Charlie McCarthy,

Constance Moore, Louis Calhern. D: Frank Tuttle. COM 60m. v

Charlie Muffin 1979 British ★★★★ A wily, individualistic British secret agent (Hemmings) annoys his stodgy bosses and gets involved with a would-be Russian defector. Intelligently done espionage thriller with an astounding climax. C: David Hemmings, Sam Wanamaker, Ian Richardson, Ralph Richardson. D: Jack Gold. ACT 109m. TVM

Charlie, the Lonesome Cougar 1967 ★★★½ True-life adventure about a magnificent wild animal, superbly filmed in its natural habitat. For the whole family. FAM/ACT 75m. v

Charlie's Angels 1976 ★★½ A trio of comely detectives capitalize on their allure to trap the murderer of a wine tycoon. Breezy, lightweight pilot, basis for smash TV series. C: Kate Jackson, Farrah Fawcett-Majors, Jaclyn Smith. D: John Llewellyn Moxey. CRI 78m. TVM

Charlotte Forten's Mission 1984 *See* **Half Slave, Half Free 2**

Charlotte's Web 1973 ★★★★ E.B. White's children's classic of prize pig Wilbur saved by Charlotte the spider. Tender animated fable of friendship that will appeal to all ages. Voices of Debbie Reynolds, Henry Gibson, Paul Lynde, Agnes Moorehead, Charles Nelson Reilly. D: Charles Nichols, Iwao Takamoto. FAM/DRA [G] 94m. v

Charly 1968 ★★★★½ A retarded man is briefly cured (and raised to the level of genius) by a scientific experiment in this improbable but wonderful fantasy. Oscar-winner Robertson's moving performance as the title character (and Bloom's support) makes it touching drama. Based on Daniel Keyes' novel *Flowers for Algernon*. C: Cliff Robertson, Claire Bloom, Lilia Skala, Dick Van Patten. D: Ralph Nelson. DRA [PG] 106m. v

Charming Sinners 1929 ★★★ Emotional drama adapted from W. Somerset Maugham's *The Constant Wife*, in which a socialite (Chatterton) contrives to get even with her philandering husband (Brook). C: Ruth Chatterton, Clive Brook, William Powell, Laura Hope Crews, Florence Eldridge. D: Robert Milton. DRA 85m.

Charro! 1969 ★★ An ex-badman is held responsible for stealing a cannon. The Pelvis sans wiggle in a dramatic role which turns out to be a drab Western. C: Elvis Presley, Ina Balin, Victor French. D: Charles Marquis Warren. WST [G] 98m. v

Chartroose Caboose, The 1960 ★★★ A droll, retired railroad conductor harbors a runaway couple in his unusual home—a modified green caboose. Sentimental, featherweight comedy with songs by Bee. C: Molly Bee, Ben Cooper. D: William Reynolds. COM 75m.

Chase 1985 ★★½ A lawyer (O'Neill) finds herself opposing her former boyfriend in a murder case she is assigned to defend. The plot complications are predictable, and the performances uninspired. C: Jennifer O'Neill, Michael Parks, Richard Farnsworth, Robert S. Woods. D: Rod Holcomb. CRI 90m. v

Chase a Crooked Shadow 1958 British ★★★★ In a fiendish scheme to trick an heiress (Baxter) out of her inheritance, a man (Todd) impersonates her dead brother. Well-acted, Hitchcockian suspense melodrama competently handled; surprise ending is worth the wait. C: Richard Todd, Anne Baxter, Herbert Lom. D: Michael Anderson. CRI 87m.

Chase for the Golden Needles, The *See* **Golden Needles**

Chase Me Charlie 1932 ★★½ A compilation of Charlie Chaplin's early silent efforts that attempts to build a story around his antics which doesn't do the comic clown justice—with much better showcases of his work available elsewhere. C: Charlie Chaplin, Edna Purvidince, Ben Turpin. COM 61m.

Chase, The 1946 ★★★ A battle-fatigued ex-GI runs afoul of a gangster in Cuba and falls for his wife. Atmospheric film noir with a surprise twist. C: Robert Cummings, Michele Morgan, Steve Cochran, Peter Lorre. D: Arthur Ripley. CRI 86m.

Chase, The 1966 ★★★ Muddled, overwrought drama about bigoted Texas town's reactions to home-town boy Redford's escape from jail. Great cast flounders in clichéd script by Lillian Hellman. C: Marlon Brando, Jane Fonda, Robert Redford, Angie Dickinson, James Fox, Robert Duvall, E.G. Marshall, Miriam Hopkins, Martha Hyer. D: Arthur Penn. DRA 135m. v

Chase, The 1991 ★★★★ Fact-based movie emphasizes action as a Colorado news team follows the trail of an escaped convict. Good performances and solid direction make this a riveting thriller. C: Casey Siemaszko, Ben Johnson. D: Paul Wendkos. CRI [PG-13] 100m.

Chase, The 1994 ★★ Related only by title to the 1966 Marlon Brando-Robert Redford thriller, with Sheen as an escaped convict kidnapping a wealthy man's daughter, and embarking on a desperate journey to freedom. C: Charlie Sheen, Kristy Swanson, Henry Rollins. D: Adam Rifkin. ACT [PG-13] 94m. v

Chaser, The 1938 ★★★½ Brisk B-comedy about ambulance-chasing shyster falling for woman who can't stand him. Pleasant. C: Dennis O'Keefe, Ann Morriss, Lewis Stone, Nat Pendleton. D: Edwin L. Marin. COM 73m.

Chasing Dreams 1982 ★★ Farmboy copes with the pressures of college by going out for the baseball team, where he blossoms. Maudlin romance. C: Therese Conte, David Brown. D: Sean Roche. DRA 105m.

Chastity Belt, The 1968 *See* **On My Way to the Crusades, I Met a Girl Who...**

Chastity 1969 ★★★ A pitiable young woman goes on the road to find herself—and love. Cher, in her solo acting debut, rises well above material Sonny Bono wrote for her. C: Cher, Barbara London, Tom Nolan. D: Alessio DePaola. DRA [PG] 98m.

Chato's Land 1972 Spanish ★★½ A renegade half-breed Apache in 1870s New Mexico wreaks havoc on a vengeful posse after him for a questionable killing. Unrelenting blood and gore in over-long, infernal Western. C: Charles Bronson, Jack Palance, Richard Basehart, Jill Ireland. D: Michael Winner. WST [PG] 97m. V

Chattahoochee 1990 ★★★ Korean War veteran Oldman has a breakdown and finds himself in a nightmarish mental institution. Grim drama about violence and neglect in '50s psychiatric hospitals. C: Gary Oldman, Dennis Hopper, Frances McDormand, Pamela Reed, Ned Beatty. D: Mick Jackson. DRA [R] 96m. V

Chattanooga Choo Choo 1984 ★★★ A bumbler has to earn his inheritance by restoring the famed train and taking it on a last overnight run. Sophomoric gloss with a lively cast. C: Barbara Eden, George Kennedy, Melissa Sue Anderson, Joe Namath. D: Bruce Bilson. COM [PG] 102m. V

Chatterbox 1936 ★★★ Mild star vehicle has a naive country girl (Shirley) seeking a stage career. Painless comedy. C: Anne Shirley, Phillips Holmes, Erik Rhodes, Margaret Hamilton, Lucille Ball. D: George Nicholls, Jr. COM 68m.

Chatterbox 1943 ★★★½ A mild-mannered radio cowboy star (Brown) with a fear of horses visits a dude ranch for the publicity and becomes a hero with the help of a wacky hick (Canova). Hilarious comedy, skillfully played by two pros. C: Joe E. Brown, Judy Canova, Rosemary Lane. D: Joseph Santley. COM 76m.

Che! 1969 ★★ Argentinian Communist revolutionary and guerrilla leader Che Guevara helps organize Fidel Castro's Cuban coup. Undeniably revisionist history; slow moving and high blown. Famous for Palance's turn as Fidel. C: Omar Sharif, Jack Palance, Cesare Danova, Robert Loggia. D: Richard Fleischer. DRA [PG] 96m.

Cheap Detective, The 1978 ★★★ Falk does Bogart in Neil Simon's homage to *The Maltese Falcon*, et al. A parade of star turns keeps things interesting, though ultimately not altogether hilarious. C: Peter Falk, Ann-Margret, Eileen Brennan, Sid Caesar, Stockard Channing, James Coco, Dom DeLuise, Louise Fletcher, John Houseman, Madeline Kahn, Fernando Lamas, Marsha Mason, Phil Silvers. D: Robert Moore. COM [PG] 92m. V

Cheaper by the Dozen 1950 ★★★★ Gently funny, true story of the turn-of-the-century Gilbreth family, including efficiency expert papa (Webb), his patient wife (Loy), and their 12 children. Episodic, but charming. Sequel: *Belles on Their Toes*. C: Clifton Webb, Myrna Loy, Jeanne Crain, Mildred Natwick. D: Walter Lang. COM 85m.

Cheaper to Keep Her 1980 ★★ An attorney retains a private eye to keep tabs on ex-husbands slow in alimony payments. Substandard. C: MacDavis, Tovah Feldshuh, Ian McShane, Priscilla Lopez, Rose Marie, Jack Gilford. D: Ken Annakin. DRA [R] 92m. V

Cheaters, The 1945 ★★★★ When a hoity-toity family invites an underfed thespian to their home for Christmas dinner, the clan learns a few lessons in humility. Charming comedy with sweet moral center, nicely played by a good cast. C: Joseph Schildraut, Billie Burke, Eugene Pallette, Ona Munson. D: Joseph Kane. COM 87m.

Cheatin' Hearts 1993 ★★★½ Modest slice-of-life story about a Southwestern housewife questioning her own troubled marriage while arranging her daughter's wedding. Kirkland gives a restrained, underrated performance. (a.k.a. *Paper Hearts*) C: Sally Kirkland, James Brolin, Kris Kristofferson, Pamela Gidley. D: Rod McCall. DRA [R] 90m. V

Cheats, Youthful Sinners, The 1984 *See* **Les Tricheurs**

Check and Double Check 1930 ★ The various misadventures of handymen Amos 'n' Andy. Weak, dated film based on popular, long-running radio show featuring two bumbling African-Americans played by white actors. C: Freeman Gosden, Charles Correll, Sue Carol, Duke Ellington. D: Melville Brown. COM 77m. V

Check Is in the Mail, The 1986 ★★ A suburban family gets fed up with the trappings of society and completely seal themselves off from the rest of the world. Talented cast is the main attraction of this dim-witted comedy. C: Brian Dennehy, Anne Archer, Hallie Todd, Dick Shawn. D: Joan Darling. COM 91m.

Checkered Flag or Crash 1977 ★★ Race car drivers compete in a 1,000-mile marathon in the Philippines. Vehicular thrills are the main attraction. C: Joe Don Baker, Susan Sarandon, Larry Hagman. D: Alan Gibson. ACT [PG] 95m.

Checkers 1937 ★★★ Withers gets mixed up with the racetrack crowd, thanks to her feckless uncle. Good for kids. C: Jane Withers, Stuart Erwin, Una Merkel. D: H. Bruce Humberstone. FAM/COM 79m.

Checking Out 1989 ★★½ An ounce of prevention becomes a life's obsession for family man Daniels, when the death of his best buddy convinces him to go on a megahealth binge. Weird black comedy never gels. C: Jeff Daniels, Melanie Mayron, Michael Tucker. D: David Leland. COM [R] 95m. V

Checkpoint 1957 British ★★★ Suspenser

set in world of auto racing mixes sports with industrial espionage. Competent if unmemorable. C: Anthony Steel, Odile Versois, Stanley Baker, James Robertson Justice, Maurice Denham. D: Ralph Thomas. DRA 84m.

Cheech and Chong—Get Out of My Room 1985 ★★★½ Wacked-out compilation of videos features the stoner comedy duo performing four different comedy/musical routines including: "Get Out of My Room," "I'm Not Home Right Now," "Love Is Strange," and "Born in East L.A." Perfect way to enjoy this team in small doses. C: Cheech Marin, Tommy Chong. D: Cheech Marin. COM 53m. V

Cheech & Chong—Still Smokin' 1983 ★★½ Doper duo heads to Amsterdam to save an endangered film festival by taking to the stage and performing their nightclub routines. Slipshod attempt with not a spark to be found. C: Cheech Marin, Tommy Chong, Shirleen Stroker. D: Tommy Chong. COM [R] 94m. V

Cheech & Chong—Up in Smoke 1978 ★★★★ Feature debut for the comedy team, a freewheeling, hilarious trip. No mind-boggling plotline, just the boys embarking on a journey to find the best smoke available as they elude a maniacal, sadistic cop. Refreshingly funny and irreverent. C: Cheech Marin, Tommy Chong, Edie Adams, Stacy Keach, Strother Martin. D: Lou Alder. COM [R] 87m. V

Cheech & Chong's Next Movie 1980 ★★½ Second film effort by the spaced-out comedy team follows them as they search for new highs while evading the police. They do what they do and draw some laughs. C: Cheech Marin, Tommy Chong, Evelyn Guerrero, Betty Kennedy. D: Tommy Chong. COM [R] 95m. V

Cheech & Chong's Nice Dreams 1981 ★★★ The comedy team plays potheads using an ice cream truck to peddle a special brand of home-grown herb around Los Angeles. One of their funnier film efforts, but still a mixed treat at best. C: Cheech Marin, Tommy Chong, Evelyn Guerrero, Paul Reubens, Stacy Keach. D: Tommy Chong. COM [R] 88m.

Cheech & Chong's The Corsican Brothers 1984 ★★½ Far-out comedy team puts on the puffy shirts in this costume comedy remake of Dumas tale about brothers, separated at birth, who feel everything the other feels. The duo go up in smoke out of their drug-humor milieu. C: Cheech Marin, Tommy Chong, Roy Dotrice, Rikki Marin, Edie McClurg, Rae Dawn Chong. D: Tommy Chong. COM [PG] 91m. V

Cheerleaders, The 1972 ★★ A naive teenager (Fondue) joins a busy group of seductive cheerleaders. Asinine sex comedy that seems to know it's asinine; an interesting approach. C: Stephanie Fondue, Denise Dillaway, Jovila Bush, Debbie Lowe. D: Paul Glickler. COM [R] 84m. V

Cheers for Miss Bishop 1941 ★★★★ Scott gives a subtle, moving performance as a Midwest teacher sacrificing personal happiness for her students. It provides heartwarming and inspirational viewing. C: Martha Scott, William Gargan, Edmund Gwenn, Sterling Holloway. D: Tay Garnett. DRA 94m. V

Cheetah 1989 ★★★ American teenagers living with their scientist parents in Africa adopt an orphaned cheetah and make friends with a Masai youngster, but still have trouble adjusting to a new country and an alien culture. Simple but educational film for children and adults, from Disney. C: Keith Coogan, Lucy Deakins. D: Jeff Blyth. FAM/DRA [G] 80m. V

Chernobyl: The Final Warning 1991 U.S. ★★★ Drama about a surgeon (Voight) who goes to the Ukraine to aid the victims of the Chernobyl nuclear disaster. Sincere effort, but heavy going at times. (a.k.a. *Final Warning*) C: Jon Voight, Jason Robards, Sammi Davis. D: Anthony Page. DRA 100m. TVM

Cherokee Strip 1940 ★★★ An appointed marshal to a small frontier town sets out to trap a notorious outlaw and his gang. Compact, if predictable Dix feature. C: Richard Dix, Florence Rice, Victor Jory. D: Lesley Selander. WST 86m.

Cherry Hill High 1977 ★ Five high school seniors compete to see who can lose their virginity in the most interesting manner. Slightly more original than the usual teen sex outing, due to the locales chosen. C: Linda McInerney, Nina Carson. D: Alex E. Goiten. COM [R] 92m. V

Cherry 2000 1988 ★★ When Andrews loses his automaton companion, he recruits toughie tracker Griffith to lead him through the *Road Warrior*-like frontier to find a worthy surrogate. Uninspired, unoriginal tale with some passable action sequences. C: Melanie Griffith, Ben Johnson, Harry Carey, Jr., David Andrews. D: Steve DeJarnatt. SFI [PG-13] 99m. V

Chess Players, The 1978 Indian ★★★★ In 1856 India, two Indian men passionately play chess while around them the British Raj takes over. Overlong, but well-observed film which uses chess rivalry as metaphor for political drama of the time. Directed by Ray with his usual attention to human detail. C: Richard Attenborough, Sanjeev Kumar, Saeed Jaffrey. D: Satyajit Ray. DRA 135m.

Chesty Anderson, USN 1976 ★★★ Bosom jokes run rampant in this lighthearted (and light-headed) naval farce; the plot finds Anderson (Eubank) intent on retrieving her sister, kidnapped by a kinky senator. Good supporting actors (Crothers, Willard, Carey). (a.k.a. *Anderson's Angels*) C: Shari Eubank, Rosanne Katon, Scatman Crothers, Fred Willard, Timothy Carey. D: Ed Forsyth. COM [R] 88m.

Cheyenne Autumn 1964 ★★★★ Uprooted by the U.S. government to an Oklahoma reservation, Cheyenne Indians embark on a perilous 1500-mile trek back to their Wyoming home ground. Ford's last Western, from a true 1860s incident, is imposing, eventful frontier entertainment. Based on the Mari Sandoz novel. C: Richard Widmark, Carroll Baker, Karl Malden, Dolores Del Rio, Sal Mineo, Edward G. Robinson, James Stewart, Ricardo Montalban, Gilbert Roland, Arthur Kennedy, John Carradine. D: John Ford. WST 155m. V

Cheyenne Social Club, The 1970 ★★★ Valiant efforts all around—including Kelly's only Western directorial credit, and amiable performances by Fonda and Stewart —boost this comedy about a cowhand who inherits a bordello. Later a Broadway musical. C: Henry Fonda, James Stewart, Shirley Jones, Sue Ane Langdon. D: Gene Kelly. WST [PG] 103m.

Cheyenne 1947 ★★★ A frontier gambler is deputized to catch a stagecoach bandit and falls for his wife. True-to-form Western. (a.k.a. *The Wyoming Kid*) C: Dennis Morgan, Jane Wyman, Janis Paige, Alan Hale, Arthur Kennedy. D: Raoul Walsh. WST 100m.

Chicago Calling 1951 ★★★ An alcoholic stands by for a crucial telephone contact regarding news of his daughter and estranged wife, injured in an automobile accident. Interesting premise, with a tremendous performance from Duryea. C: Dan Duryea, Mary Anderson. D: John Reinhardt. DRA 74m.

Chicago Confidential 1957 ★★★ Efforts to expose labor union corruption in the Windy City unite an unlikely team of crusading reporters (Keith and Garland). Genre big-city potboiler, fun for late-night munching. C: Brian Keith, Beverly Garland. D: Sidney Salkow. DRA 73m.

Chicago Deadline 1949 ★★★ An idealistic metropolitan journalist launches a newspaper crusade against murderous racketeers. Clichés abound, and the actors tend to mug a bit. Enjoyable. C: Alan Ladd, Donna Reed, June Havoc, Arthur Kennedy. D: Lewis Allen. DRA 87m.

Chicago Joe and the Showgirl 1990 British ★★★ True story of American soldier-crook (Sutherland) gone AWOL during WWII and his crime spree with a British vamp (Lloyd) ending in murder. Lloyd carries this uneven low-budget drama/fantasy. C: Kiefer Sutherland, Emily Lloyd, Patsy Kensit. D: Bernard Rose. CRI [R] 105m. V

Chicago Story 1981 ★★★½ A lawyer defends a man wrongfully accused of wounding a little girl in a sniper-related shooting. Thoughtful story. C: Vincent Baggetta, Dennis Franz, Craig T. Nelson. D: Jerry London. DRA 100m. TVM

Chicago Syndicate 1955 ★★★ A principled accountant tries to expose a multibillion-dollar criminal syndicate operating behind a respectable front. Prototype racket-busting melodrama fun; to watch. C: Dennis O'Keefe, Abbe Lane, Xavier Cugat. D: Fred Sears. DRA 83m.

Chicken Chronicles, The 1977 ★★½ A high school senior (Guttenberg) is obsessed with losing his virginity. Title comes from fast food restaurant in which he and his friends work. Mild comedy, Guttenberg's debut. C: Steven Guttenberg, Ed Lauter, Lisa Reeves, Phil Silvers. D: Francis Simon. COM [PG] 94m. V

Chicken Every Sunday 1948 ★★★½ Period comedy about a family-run boarding house in Tucson. The hard-working mother (Holm) keeps things running while the father (Dailey) tries one unsuccessful get-rich-quick scheme after another. Engaging family fare. C: Dan Dailey, Celeste Holm, Alan Young, Natalie Wood. D: George Seaton. FAM/COM 91m.

Chief Crazy Horse 1955 ★★★ Sympathetic portrait of the great Dakota Sioux chief who defeated Custer at Little Bighorn. Mature is athletic and suitably commanding as Crazy Horse, but the script holds him back. C: Victor Mature, Suzan Ball, John Lund. D: George Sherman. WST 86m.

Chiefs 1983 ★★★½ In 1962, the new police chief (Williams) in a sleepy Southern town reopens a 40-year-old murder case, unsettling certain citizens, Heston among them. Taut, well-handled drama. C: Charlton Heston, Paul Sorvino, Billy Dee Williams, Keith Carradine, Wayne Rogers, Brad Davis. D: Jerry London. CRI 200m. TVM V

Chikamatsu Monogatari 1954 Japanese ★★★★★ Based on a popular 17th-century Japanese puppet play, memorable film follows the tragic romance of a lowly worker and his employer's pious wife. Ravishing cinematography and straight-from-the-heart acting propel one of Mizoguchi's best-loved films. (a.k.a. *Crucified Lovers*). C: Kazuo Hasegawa, Kyoko Kagawa, Yoko Minamida. D: Kenji Mizoguchi. DRA 91m.

Child Bride of Short Creek 1981 ★★★½ An older man in a polygamous Arizona Mormon community decides to take a 15-year-old bride, only to be challenged by his son, a recently returned Korean War vet. Unusual, well-made drama based on a true incident. C: Christopher Atkins, Diane Lane, Conrad Bain, Helen Hunt. D: Robert Lewis. DRA 95m. TVM V

Child in the House 1956 British ★★★½ Girl of divorced parents goes to live with her aunt and uncle, bringing a fresh perspective on the world to their lives. Good acting raises this above its soap opera plotting. C: Phyllis Calvert, Eric Portman, Stanley Baker, Dora Bryan, Joan Hickson. D: C. Raker Endfield. DRA 90m.

Child in the Night 1990 ★★★ A scared eight-year-old boy who witnessed a murder (within his family) must testify at the trial and a psychologist (Williams) works with the child to get his cooperation. Good performances. C: JoBeth Williams, Tom Skerritt, Elijah Wood, Darren McGavin. D: Mike Robe. CRI 93m. TVM

Child Is Born, A 1940 ★★★½ A convicted murderess (Fitzgerald) is about to give birth in a maternity hospital. Tearjerker boasts a splendid performance by Fitzgerald in this remake of 1932's *Life Begins*, which starred Loretta Young. C: Geraldine Fitzgerald, Jeffrey Lynn, Gladys George, Spring Byington, Eve Arden. D: Lloyd Bacon. DRA 79m.

Child Is Waiting, A 1963 ★★★★ Interesting casting helps somber drama of a psychologist (Lancaster) and music teacher (Garland) at a school for retarded children. Judy's dramatic performance is impressive. C: Burt Lancaster, Judy Garland, Gena Rowlands. D: John Cassavetes. DRA 102m.

Child of Darkness, Child of Light 1991 ★★½ Two teenagers become subject to immaculate conception—but one's baby may have been spawned by Satan. Chiller can't conceal too many borrowings from *The Omen*; Penny and Datillo as the young mothers come off best. Based on James Patterson's novel *Virgin*. C: Anthony Dennison, Brad Davis, Sydney Penny, Kristin Datillo. D: Marina Sargenti. HOR [PG-13] 85m. TVM V

Child of Satan 1976 *See* **To the Devil—A Daughter**

Child Stealer, The 1979 ★★★½ A frank examination of an emotionally-charged issue—parents who abduct their children from the homes of their former spouses. C: Beau Bridges, Blair Brown. D: Mel Damski. DRA 104m. TVM

Child Under a Leaf 1974 Canadian ★★½ An unhappily married woman (Cannon) is too indecisive to leave her violent husband (Campanella) for her devoted lover (Pilon), the father of her newborn child. Disaster is foreshadowed early, so there are few surprises. C: Dyan Cannon, Joseph Campanella, Donald Pilon. D: George Bloomfield. DRA [R] 88m. TVM

Children Nobody Wanted, The 1981 ★★★½ Inspirational story of college student becoming foster parent. Pfeiffer shows star quality in early role. C: Fred Lehne, Michelle Pfeiffer, Matt Clark. D: Richard Michaels. DRA 104m.

Children of a Lesser God 1986 ★★★★½ A teacher of hearing-impaired children (Hurt), becomes intrigued by an intelligent, isolated and deaf janitor (Matlin), and they fall in love. Never sentimental drama thrives thanks to strong cast and excellent direction. Matlin won an Oscar for Best Actress. Based on Mark Medoff's Tony Award-winning play. C: William Hurt, Marlee Matlin, Piper Laurie, Philip Bosco. D: Randa Haines. DRA [R] 110m. V

Children of An Lac, The 1980 ★★★★ Compelling, well-acted drama based on the actual experiences of actress Balin, who was instrumental in airlifting hundreds of children from a Vietnamese orphanage before the fall of Saigon in 1975. C: Shirley Jones, Ina Balin, Beulah Quo. D: John Llewellyn Moxey. DRA 100m.

Children of Divorce 1980 ★★★ Divorce from the viewpoint of the children of three broken homes. Ordinary drama, despite some good acting. C: Barbara Feldon, Lance Kerwin, Stacey Nelkin, Bily Dee Williams. D: Joanna Lee. DRA 96m. V

Children of Hiroshima 1952 Japanese ★★★★ Shindo mixes documentary and fiction in grim tale of a teacher who returns to Hiroshima seven years after the A-bomb was dropped. Powerful and painful. C: Nobuko Otowa, Chikako Hoshawa, Niwa Saito, Jukichi Uno. D: Kaneto Shindo. DRA 97m.

Children of Paradise 1943 French ★★★★★ Mime Barrault falls in unrequited love with heartless Arletty in one of cinema's genuine masterpieces. Sumptuous production provides breathtaking view of 19th-century Paris. Remarkably, shot during the Nazi occupation. Written by noted poet Jacques Prevert. C: Jean-Louis Barrault, Arletty, Pierre Brasseur, Albert Remy. D: Marcel Carne. DRA 189m. V

Children of Sanchez, The 1978 Mexican-U.S. ★★ Philandering Mexican widower (Quinn) neglects his children, with tragic results. Heavy-handed domestic drama, with one asset: Chuck Mangione's catchy score. C: Anthony Quinn, Dolores Del Rio, Katy Jurado. D: Hall Bartlett. DRA [R] 117m. V

Children of the Corn 1984 ★ Stephen King's short story is padded to feature length and further burdened with ludicrous dialogue and clichéd situations. Horton and Hamilton are a none-too-bright couple terrorized by a cult of killer kids. Followed by a sequel. C: Peter Horton, Linda Hamilton. D: Fritz Kiersch. HOR [R] 94m. V

Children of the Corn II 1992 ★★ Belated sequel is, if nothing else, slightly better than the original. The evil youngsters are still up to their murderous supernatural tricks and, while the story is muddled and explanations vague, there are a few good isolated scares. C: Terence Knox, Paul Scherrer. D: David F. Price. HOR [R] 93m. V

Children of the Damned 1964 British ★★ Some of the original alien children have survived the ending of *Village of the Damned* and now they pool their power for protection—and revenge. Weak sequel to the outstanding original. C: Ian Hendry, Alan Badel, Barbara Ferris. D: Anton Leader. HOR 90m. V

Children of the Night 1992 ★★★★½ A young schoolteacher and a teenaged girl team up to stop an invasion of vampires taking over their town. Moody, eerie horror film, with some unusual special effects and well-placed dashes of humor. C: Karen Black, Pe-

ter DeLuise, Ami Dolenz, Garrett Morris, Maya McLaughlin. D: Tony Randel. HOR [R] 90m.
Children of Theatre Street, The 1977 ★★★★★ Documentary about renowned Kirov Ballet School in Leningrad, whose graduates include Baryshnikov and Nureyev. Narration by Princess Grace of Monaco. Must-see film for ballet lovers and aspiring dancers. Outstanding. D: Robert Dornhelm, Earle Mack. DOC 92m. V
Children Shouldn't Play with Dead Things 1972 ★★★½ Young filmmaking troupe looking to conjure up real horrors for their latest production get more than they bargain for when they raise the hungry dead. Offbeat comic chiller. C: Alan Ormsby, Anya Ormsby. D: Benjamin Clark. HOR [PG] 91m. V
Children, The 1980 ★★ While traveling on their school bus, a group of kids pass through a radioactive cloud, transforming them from lovable tykes to terrifying monsters who burn victims alive with hugs. Silly and poorly done science fiction/horror thriller. C: Martin Shakar, Gil Rogers. D: Max Kalmanowicz. HOR [R] 89m.
Children, The 1990 British ★★★ Kingsley and Novak work surprising well together, but they can't compensate for this tedious story about his clandestine affair, conducted on the eve of his wedding, with a friend's teen-age daughter. From an Edith Wharton novel. C: Ben Kingsley, Kim Novak, Siri Neal, Geraldine Chaplin, Joe Don Baker, Karen Black. D: Tony Palmer. DRA 90m.
Children's Hour, The 1962 ★★★ Drama adapted from Lillian Hellman's play about schoolteachers (Hepburn, MacLaine) accused of lesbianism by vicious student. More explicit remake of *These Three* is, ironically, less effective. MacLaine's good, though. C: Audrey Hepburn, Shirley MacLaine, James Garner, Miriam Hopkins, Fay Bainter. D: William Wyler. DRA 108m. V
Child's Play 1972 ★★★ A teacher (Bridges) in a Catholic boys boarding school watches strange happenings among the students and suspects another instructor of inciting trouble. Psychological drama with some bite. Based on the play by Robert Marasco. C: James Mason, Robert Preston, Beau Bridges. D: Sidney Lumet. DRA [PG] 100m.
Child's Play 1988 ★★★ Chucky the deadly doll is introduced in this hit shocker, possessed by a dead serial killer (Dourif, who also does the doll's voice) and terrorizing young Vincent. The material is silly, but it's done with such panache you can't help but go along for the ride. Led to several sequels. C: Catherine Hicks, Chris Sarandon, Alex Vincent, Brad Dourif, Dinah Manoff. D: Tom Holland. HOR [R] 88m. V
Child's Play 2 1991 ★★ Vincent thought he'd killed the evil Chucky, but you can't keep a good villain down, and he returns to stalk the boy and his foster family. This sequel contains little you can't predict (or can believe), though it's swiftly and stylishly directed. C: Alex Vincent, Jenny Agutter, Gerrit Graham, Christine Elise. D: John Lafia. HOR [R] 84m. V
Child's Play 3 1991 ★★ It's many years later, and the young protagonist of this series is now at military school—and guess who's coming to visit? There are a few effective moments here (mostly toward the end), but the formula's wearing awfully thin. C: Justin Whalin, Perrey Reeves, Jeremy Sylvers. D: Jack Bender. HOR [R] 90m. V
Chilling, The 1991 ★ Flesh-eating zombies, cryogenically preserved, come to life and terrorize Kansas City. No-budget no-brainer. Run! C: Linda Blair, Dan Haggerty, Troy Donahue. D: Deland Nuse, Jack Sunseri. HOR [R] 95m. V
Chilly Scenes of Winter 1979 *See* **Head Over Heels**
Chimes at Midnight 1966 ★★★★★ Young Prince Henry V explores the seamy side of life in 15th-century England as part of his preparation to inherit the crown. Welles' last masterpiece might be the finest Shakespeare on film. Battle of Shrewsbury is without peer as medieval battle sequence; Welles as Falstaff is both bawdy and affecting. C: Orson Welles, Jeanne Moreau, Margaret Rutherford, John Gielgud. D: Orson Welles. DRA 115m.
China 1943 ★★½ A callous American oil representative (Ladd) takes a courageous stand against murder by Japanese soldiers in China. Anti-Japanese propaganda thinly disguised as drama. C: Loretta Young, Alan Ladd, William Bendix. D: John Farrow. DRA 79m.
China Clipper 1936 ★★★½ O'Brien is good as a pilot obsessed with his vision of commercial airlines circling the globe. Based on the actual 1935 heroic flight of Pan American plane, this movie has a gritty, honest feel to it. C: Pat O'Brien, Beverly Roberts, Humphrey Bogart, Marie Wilson. D: Ray Enright. ACT 85m.
China Corsair 1951 ★★½ American ship's engineer (Hall) finds himself marooned on an island off the coast of China. High-seas adventure flick; Borgnine's debut. C: Jon Hall, Lisa Ferraday, Ernest Borgnine. D: Ray Nazzaro. ACT 67m.
China Cry 1990 ★★★★ Daughter (Nickson-Soul) of wealthy Shanghai physician (Shigeta) experiences Japanese invasion of China in 1941, and Communist terror 10 years later. Compelling drama based on Nora Lamm's autobiography. C: Julia Nickson-Soul, Russell Wong, James Shigeta. D: James F. Collier. DRA [PG-13] 103m. V
China Doll 1958 ★★½ Romance blossoms between American Air Force captain (Mature) and young woman servant (Hua) he buys and

later marries. Sincere, well-intentioned film enlivened by climactic flying action sequence. C: Victor Mature, Li Hua, Bob Mathias, Stuart Whitman. D: Frank Borzage. DRA 88m.

China Gate 1957 ★★★½ Mixed bag of soldiers attack Communist munitions dump deep in Indochina. Fast-moving action, interesting political slant, good Dickinson. Cole sings the title song. C: Gene Barry, Angie Dickinson, Nat King Cole. D: Samuel Fuller. ACT 97m. V

China Girl 1942 ★★★½ Wartime action drama set in Burma stars Montgomery as an adventurer who falls in love with Eurasian schoolteacher (Tierney) and battles nefarious spies for the encroaching Japanese. Action never flags. C: Gene Tierney, George Montgomery, Lynn Bari, Victor McLaglen. D: Henry Hathaway. ACT 95m.

China Girl 1987 ★★★½ Modern Shakespeare: Juliet is from Chinatown, Romeo from Little Italy, and their clans are warring street gangs. Violent, moody New York City background adds tension, and innovative direction avoids clichés. C: James Russo, Richard Panebianco, Sari Chang. D: Abel Ferrara. DRA [R] 90m. V

China Is Near 1968 Italian ★★★★ Working-class couple try to seduce members of aristocratic family to improve their own social and economic status. Early work by director is occasionally flat, but more often, film works as hilarious sex farce with political overtones. C: Glauco Mauri, Elda Tattoli, Paolo Graziosi. D: Marco Bellocchio. COM 108m.

China Lake Murders, The 1989 ★★★★ An exciting and well-paced action piece that pits a visiting cop (Parks) against a local sheriff (Skerritt) in the investigation of a series of mysterious killings. Great desert scenery. C: Tom Skerritt, Michael Parks. D: Alan Metzger. ACT [PG-13] 89m. TVM V

China Moon 1994 ★★★ Unassuming man falls under the spell of a beautiful woman and kills her husband. Tepid thriller benefits from Harris and Stowe as the star-crossed lovers. Good, steamy performances. C: Ed Harris, Madeleine Stowe, Benecio Del Toro, Charles Dance. D: John Bailey. CRI [R] 99m.

China 9, Liberty 37 1978 ★★★½ Western about man saved from hanging by evil railroad barons so he can carry out murder of a former gunfighter opposed to railroad. Different and pretty well done. (a.k.a. *Gunfire*) C: Warren Oates, Fabio Testi, Jenny Agutter, Sam Peckinpah. D: Monte Hellman. WST [R] 102m.

China Seas 1935 ★★★★ Action and adventure aboard Chinese riverboat captained by Gable who has his hands full with buccaneer Beery, heart-of-gold Harlow, and aristocratic Russell. Lots of fun even though plot is farfetched. C: Clark Gable, Jean Harlow, Wallace Berry, Rosalind Russell, Lewis Stone, Robert Benchley, C. Aubrey Smith, Hattie McDaniel. D: Tay Garnett. DRA 88m. V

China Sky 1945 ★★½ Heroic physicians (Scott and Warrick) treat Chinese peasants in remote hill village under attack by Japanese. So-so adaptation of Pearl Buck story. C: Randolph Scott, Ruth Warrick, Anthony Quinn, Ellen Drew. D: Ray Enright. DRA 78m.

China Syndrome, The 1979 ★★★★ Gripping, timely thriller about a threatened nuclear plant meltdown. Suspenseful drama builds to almost unbearable tension as TV reporter Fonda and engineer Lemmon (both Oscar-nominated) try to expose a cover-up at the plant. C: Jane Fonda, Jack Lemmon, Michael Douglas, Scott Brady. D: James Bridges. DRA [PG] 123m. V

China Venture 1953 ★★★½ Commando Marines are sent into Chinese jungle on a rescue mission at the end of WWII. Surprisingly exciting adventure yarn. C: Edmond O'Brien, Barry Sullivan, Jocelyn Brando. D: Don Siegel. ACT 83m.

China's Little Devils 1945 ★★★ Chinese urchins aid downed American flyers in this sentimental WWII drama. Appealing and heart-tugging tale. C: Harry Carey, Paul Kelly. D: Monta Bell. DRA 74m.

Chinatown 1974 ★★★★★ A private eye (Nicholson) in '30s L.A. is hired by a mysterious woman to spy on her husband, and is drawn into a complicated case of murder and intrigue. Superb revival of film noir, with an Oscar-winning script by Robert Towne. Sequel: *The 2 Jakes*. C: Jack Nicholson, Faye Dunaway, John Huston, John Hillerman, Diane Ladd, Burt Young. D: Roman Polanski. CRI [R] 131m. V

Chinese Boxes 1984 ★★★ After American drug dealer Patton's fellow heroin smugglers turn up dead in Berlin, he becomes involved with gunrunners. Deliberately nihilistic low-budget feature is too self-aware for its own good. C: Will Patton, Adelheid Arndt, Gottfried John, Robbie Coltrane. D: Christopher Petit. ACT 87m. V

Chinese Cat, The 1944 ★★★ Chan (Toler) must find a murderer among a greedy group trying to get their hands on a diamond-studded statue. This low-budget *Chan* entry made for Monogram suffers from a lesser script and direction, though Toler is still effective in the title role. C: Sidney Toler, Benson Fong, Joan Woodbury. D: Phil Rosen. CRI 65m. V

Chinese Connection 1972 Hong Kong ★★★ In turn-of-the-century Shanghai, a master martial artist hunts his teacher's killers. Although the dubbing is weak, it's a fine Lee powerhouse karate vehicle. C: Bruce Lee, Miao Ker Hsiu. D: Lo Wei. ACT [R] 90m.

Chinese Ghost Story, A 1987 Cantonese ★★★½ Ancient China is the setting for a love story between a male student and a female ghost. Uneven blend of laughs, romance, and thrills was entertaining enough to spawn two sequels. C: Leslie Cheung, Wong Tsu Hsien, Wu Ma. D: Ching Siu Tung. DRA 93m. V

Chinese Ring, The 1947 ★★½ Charlie Chan is out to solve the murder of a wealthy Chinese aristocrat, Average formula mystery; Winters's debut as the Asian detective. C: Roland Winters, Warren Douglas, Victor Sen Yung, Louise Currie. D: William Beaudine. CRI 65m.

Chinese Roulette 1976 German ★★★★ Vicious satire about a young paraplegic (Schober), who lures her parents—and their lovers—to a country home for a weekend of psychological games. Alternately funny and horrifying. C: Margit Carstensen, Ulli Lommel, Anna Karina, Andrea Schober. D: Rainer Werner Fassbinder. COM 96m. V

Chinese Web, The 1978 ★★½ Spiderman ventures to China to help clear a government official who is wrongly accused of selling military secrets during WWII. Some tense moments. C: Nicholas Hammond, Robert F. Simon. D: Don McDougall. SFI 95m. TVM V

Chino 1973 Italian ★★½ Spaghetti-western filmed in Spain stars Bronson as a half-breed rancher who would like to mind his own business and care for his horses, but is distracted by bad guys. Based on a novel by Lee Hoffman. (a.k.a. *The Valdez Horses*) C: Charles Bronson, Jill Ireland. D: John Sturges. WST [PG] 98m. V

Chip Off the Old Block 1944 ★★★ Comedy-star vehicle for O'Connor, playing a teenager who comes to the big city to break into musical theater. Blyth makes a charming debut as his girlfriend, in this happy-go-lucky tale. C: Donald O'Connor, Peggy Ryan, Ann Blyth, Helen Broderick. D: Charles Lamont. COM 82m.

Chips, the War Dog 1993 ★★★ WWII raw recruit with a fear of dogs is assigned to handle a large German shepherd. Likable Disney fare, pleasantly suitable for family viewing. C: Brandon Douglas, Ned Vaughn, William Devane. D: Ed Kaplan. FAM/COM 91m. TVM V

Chisum 1970 ★★★ Vibrant Western about a rancher (Wayne) defending his territory. Wayne is a pleasure to watch, though his is only one of several story lines, including one that follows a vengeful Billy the Kid. C: John Wayne, Forrest Tucker, Christopher George, Ben Johnson, Lynda Day. D: Andrew V. McLaglen. WST [G] 111m. V

Chitty Chitty Bang Bang 1968 ★★★½ Children's fantasy musical about flying car is probably best enjoyed by those who saw it when both it and they were young. It's hard to get off the ground now. Based on the novel by (no kidding) Ian *James Bond* Fleming. C: Dick Van Dyke, Sally Ann Howes, Lionel Jeffries, Benny Hill. D: Ken Hughes. MUS [G] 142m. V

Chloe in the Afternoon 1972 French ★★★★½ Last of Rohmer's "Six Moral Tales" involves happily married man who is tempted by beguiling charms of unconventional girl. Wispy plot delivered with suitably light touch. C: Bernard Verley, Zouzou, Françoise Verley. D: Eric Rohmer. COM [R] 97m. V

Chocolat 1989 French ★★★★ A woman reminisces about her childhood as the daughter of French colonists in Africa; the resulting story is a perceptive look at race relations through the eyes of an eight-year-old. Strong acting and direction. C: Isaach DeBankole, Giulia Boschi, Francois Cluzet, Cecile Ducasse. D: Claire Denis. DRA [PG-13] 105m. V

Chocolate Soldier, The 1941 ★★★ Married opera stars (Eddy and Stevens) test each other's fidelity with elaborate disguises. Musical adaptation of Molnar's play, *The Guardsman*, could have used more songs. C: Nelson Eddy, Rise Stevens, Nigel Bruce, Florence Bates. D: Roy Del Ruth. MUS 102m. V

Chocolate War, The 1988 ★★★★ Low-budget but well-done, tense adaptation of Robert Cormier's novel about an idealistic Catholic high school student who refuses to take part in an annual fundraising event, and is caught in a schoolwide power struggle. C: John Glover, Mitchell Ilan Smith, Bud Cort, Adam Baldwin. D: Keith Gordon. DRA [R] 103m. V

Choice of Arms 1983 French ★★★★ Retired gangster Montand's comfortable life with his wife Deneuve is threatened by escaped convict Depardieu. Good character study marked by fine performances. C: Yves Montand, Catherine Deneuve, Gerard Depardieu. D: Alain Corneau. DRA 114m. V

Choice of Weapons 1976 *See* **Dirty Knight's Work**

Choice, The 1981 ★★ A mother (Clark) sees her own history repeating itself as her unmarried daughter (Warren) must choose between aborting or keeping her baby. Credible acting, but an insipid story. C: Susan Clark, Jennifer Warren, Mitchell Ryan, Largo Woodruff. D: David Greene. DRA 96m. V

Choices 1981 ★★★ A hearing-impaired youngster (Carafotes) becomes depressed when his handicap keeps him off the football team. Well-meaning and nicely played. Moore's film debut. C: Paul Carafotes, Victor French, Lelia Goldoni, Demi Moore, Billy Moses. D: Silvio Narizzano. DRA 90m.

Choirboys, The 1977 ★ Cruel and crude antics of L.A. cops are the raison d'être of this tasteless black comedy. Loosely based on Joseph Wambaugh's novel (he disowned this production). C: Charles Durning, Louis Gossett Jr., Perry King, Randy Quaid, James Woods, Burt Young. D: Robert Aldrich. DRA [R] 120m. V

C.H.O.M.P.S. 1979 ★★½ A computer-controlled watchdog, a.k.a. Canine HOMe

Protection System, the brainchild of a young inventor (Eure), saves a small firm from going under, but it then becomes the target of a hostile takeover. Weak comedy. C: Wesley Eure, Valerie Bertinelli, Conrad Bain, Chuck McCann, Red Buttons, Jim Backus. D: Don Chaffey. FAM/CRI [G] 90m. v

Choose Me 1984 ★★★★ Film-noirish story of romantic entanglements, set in a Los Angeles where anything goes. Bujold is terrific as a radio call-in psychologist who has more love problems than anyone she counsels. Director Rudolph's quirky style, however, is an acquired taste. C: Genevieve Bujold, Keith Carradine, Lesley Ann Warren, Rae Dawn Chong, John Larroquette, John Considine. D: Alan Rudolph. DRA [R] 106m. v

Chopper Wars ★★ Gung-ho Vietnam War documentary about helicopters with special emphasis on "recon by fire." DOC 60m. v

Chopping Mall 1986 ★★ Security robots go on a rampage after hours at a galleria and terrorize—you guessed it—partying teenagers who've sneaked in. Despite a couple of laughs and some good effects, this horror cheapie quickly becomes as mechanical as its villains. (a.k.a. *Killbots*) C: Kelli Maroney, John Terlesky, Paul Bartel, Mary Woronov. D: Jim Wynorski. HOR [R] 77m. v

Chorus Line, A 1985 ★★★½ Screen adaptation of famed Broadway musical about dancers auditioning for chorus of show, exposing their innermost secrets and dreams of success. Much of the genius got lost in uneasy transition from stage to screen, but the movie's still very enjoyable. C: Michael Douglas, Alyson Reed, Terrence Mann, Vicki Frederick, Audrey Landers, Gregg Burge, Nicole Fosse, Janet Jones. D: Richard Attenborough. MUS [PG-13] 118m. v

Chorus of Disapproval, A 1989 British ★★★½ After his wife passes away, Irons moves to a small British coast town where he becomes involved with local theatrical troupe. Small scale, meandering film revolves around romances and misunderstandings within thespian crowd. Well done, with good humor. C: Jeremy Irons, Anthony Hopkins, Prunella Scales, Sylvia Syms, Patsy Kensit. D: Michael Winner. COM [PG] 99m. v

Chosen Survivors 1974 ★★★ Vampire bats threaten the lives of ten people chosen to test the effects of thermonuclear war. Fine cast in acceptable formula horror film. C: Jackie Cooper, Alex Cord, Richard Jaeckel. D: Sutton Roley. HOR [PG] 99m.

Chosen, The 1982 ★★★★ Religious differences threaten the friendship between two Jewish boys (Hasidic Benson and liberal Miller) in '40s Brooklyn. A well-made, warm-hearted family drama based on Chaim Potok's novel. C: Maximilian Schell, Rod Steiger, Robby Benson, Barry Miller. D: Jeremy Paul Kagan. FAM/DRA [PG] 107m. v

Chosen, The 1983 *See* **Holocaust: 2000**

Christ Stopped at Eboli 1979 *See* **Eboli**

Christian Licorice Store, The 1971 ★★½ A depressed Hollywood tennis player (Bridges) searches for the answer to life's mysteries in this offbeat comedy. Cameos pop up all over the place to keep it going. C: Beau Bridges, Maud Adams, Gilbert Roland, McLean Stevenson. D: James Frawley. COM 90m.

Christian the Lion 1976 ★★★½ A lion born in captivity is returned to the wild through the efforts of wildlife experts (Travers and McKenna). Real-life animal expert George Adamson joins in. Charming family docudrama. C: Bill Travers, Virginia McKenna, George Adamson, Anthony Bourke. D: James Hill, Bill Travers. FAM/DRA 87m. v

Christiane F. 1982 German ★★★ A 13-year-old heroin junkie turns to prostitution to support her habit. Realistic portrait nearly collapses under its own good intentions. David Bowie appears in brief concert sequence. C: Nadja Brunkhorst, Thomas Haustein. D: Ulrich Edel. DRA [R] 130m. v

Christina 1974 ★★★ Suspense film about a beautiful woman (Parkins) who offers a strange man (Haskell) money to marry her, then disappears just as he falls in love. Somewhat baffling mystery doesn't completely satisfy. C: Barbara Parkins, Peter Haskell, James McEachin. D: Paul Krasny. DRA [PG] 95m.

Christine Jorgensen Story, The 1970 ★½ Biographical drama about Christine Jorgensen (Hansen) who was the first man to undergo a successful gender-changing operation. Flawed script holds it back. C: John Hansen, Joan Tompkins. D: Irving Rapper. DRA [R] 89m.

Christine 1983 ★★★½ Stylish, streamlined adaptation of Stephen King's novel about a '58 Plymouth Fury with an evil soul that takes over the life of high school outcast Gordon. Fast paced, with good acting and terrific special effects, even if it's never truly terrifying. C: Keith Gordon, John Stockwell, Alexandra Paul, Robert Prosky, Harry Dean Stanton. D: John Carpenter. HOR [R] 110m. v

Christmas Carol, A 1938 ★★★★ Top-drawer production of Dickens' classic tale of the miser (Owen) who gets his comeuppance on an unforgettable Christmas Eve. Excellent emoting by the talented cast, especially Lockhart as Cratchit. C: Reginald Owen, Gene Lockhart, Kathleen Lockhart, Leo G. Carroll, Ann Rutherford. D: Edwin L. Marin. FAM/DRA 70m. v

Christmas Carol, A 1951 British ★★★★★ Sim is *the* memorable Scrooge, almost as if he were born to play the part of the miserable old tightwad. Well-mounted production is probably the most popular and well-known film version of the Dickens classic. (a.k.a. *Scrooge*) C: Alastair Sim, Jack Warner, Kathleen Harrison, Mervyn Johns, Hermione Baddeley, Michael Hordern. D: Brian Desmond Hurst. FAM/DRA 86m. v

Christmas Carol, A 1984 ★★★★ Yes, Virginia, another version of Dickens' holiday perennial—but this one's a sugarplum, lovingly produced. Scott makes an effective Scrooge, learning the true meaning of Christmas in one restless evening. Second only to the Alastair Sim version. C: George C. Scott, Frank Finlay, Edward Woodward, Roger Rees, Angela Pleasence, Susannah York. D: Clive Donner. FAM/DRA 100m. TVM

Christmas Coal Mine Miracle, The 1977 ★★½ Coal mine cave-in, thanks to owner wilfully ignoring safety regulations, traps several miners on Christmas Eve. Predictable, sentimental survival story is nothing special. (a.k.a. *Christmas Miracle in Caulfield, U.S.A.*) C: Kurt Russell, Melissa Gilbert, Barbara Babcock, Mitchell Ryan. D: Jud Taylor. FAM/DRA 97m. TVM V

Christmas Comes to Willow Creek 1989 ★★½ Reteaming of *Dukes of Hazzard* stars Schneider and Wopatas as two feuding brothers trucking Christmas trees to a remote Alaskan village. Gets stuck pretty early on. C: John Schneider, Tom Wopat, Kim Delaney. D: Richard Lang. ACT 95m. TVM V

Christmas Eve 1947 ★★★ An elderly woman (Harding) about to be judged incompetent calls her ne'er-do-well heirs home for Christmas. Sentimental story juggles comedy and drama with some success. C: George Brent, George Raft, Randolph Scott, Joan Blondell, Ann Harding. D: Edwin Marin. DRA 90m.

Christmas Eve 1986 ★★★★ A terminally ill, wealthy grandmother (Young) invites her squabbling clan home for the holidays. Sentimental tearjerker with old pro Loretta making the visit well worthwhile. C: Loretta Young, Ron Leibman, Trevor Howard, Arthur Hill. D: Stuart Cooper. DRA 100m. TVM

Christmas Holiday 1944 ★★★★ Durbin stars in an atypical role of New Orleans nightclub singer whose love for convict (Kelly) leads to life of crime. Surprisingly effective change of pace for winsome star with grand Frank Loesser song, "Spring Will Be a Little Late This Year." C: Deanna Durbin, Gene Kelly, Gale Sondergaard, Gladys George. D: Robert Siodmak. DRA 92m.

Christmas in Connecticut 1945 ★★★★ Phony homemaker magazine columnist (Stanwyck) has to come up with an instant husband, baby, and country home when she's roped into entertaining WWII vet (Morgan) over the holidays. Pleasant seasonal comedy with fine work by star. C: Barbara Stanwyck, Dennis Morgan, Sydney Greenstreet, Reginald Gardiner, S.Z. Sakall, Una O'Connor. D: Peter Godfrey. COM 102m. V

Christmas in Connecticut 1992 ★★★ Updated remake of the 1945 Stanwyck comedy, with Cannon as a phony TV talk show host talked into doing a "good deed" for holiday publicity. Stick with Barbara. Arnold's inauspicious feature-length directing debut. C: Dyan Cannon, Kris Kristofferson, Tony Curtis. D: Arnold Schwarzenegger. COM 100m. TVM V

Christmas in July 1940 ★★★★½ Clerk (Powell) and his girlfriend (Drew) think he's won a contest and buy presents for the entire neighborhood, then learn his friends have tricked him. Lively Sturges comedy, with a colorful collection of supporting players. C: Dick Powell, Ellen Drew, Raymond Walburn, William Demarest, Franklin Pangborn. D: Preston Sturges. COM 67m. V

Christmas Kid, The 1968 Spanish ★★★ A gunfighter (Hunter), who was born on Christmas day, tries to find out his real identity. Offbeat character study set in the Southwest is an out-of-the-ordinary ride. C: Jeffrey Hunter, Louis Hayward. D: Sidney Pink. WST 89m.

Christmas Lilies of the Field 1979 ★★★½ A soldier (Williams) returns to visit the nuns for whom he helped build a church and finds himself constructing an orphanage. Sequel to *Lilies of the Field*. Inspirational, with a sense of humor. C: Billy Dee Williams, Maria Schell. D: Ralph Nelson. DRA 98m. TVM V

Christmas Miracle in Caulfield, U.S.A. 1977 *See* **Christmas Coal Mine Miracle, The**

Christmas Mountain 1980 ★★★ Blizzard of '88 is the setting for this inspirational Christmas story about an old cowboy geezer who learns the true meaning of the season from a widow and her large brood of children. Earnest seasonal offering. C: Slim Pickens, Mark Miller, Barbara Stanger. D: Pierre Moro. FAM/WST 90m.

Christmas Story, A 1983 ★★★★½ Warm, funny comedy of a 1940's boy (Billingsley) setting his heart on a Red Ryder BB gun as a Yuletide gift. Has developed into a baby boomer Christmas classic. From columnist Jean Shepherd's memoirs. Followed by *A Summer Story*. C: Peter Billingsley, Darren McGavin, Melinda Dillon. D: Bob Clark. COM [PG] 98m. V

Christmas That Almost Wasn't, The 1966 Italian ★★★ A despicable misanthrope (Brazzi) decides to kidnap Santa Claus and ruin Christmas. Somewhat clumsy film benefits from appealingly tuneful songs (and fond memories of those who saw this at 60s-70s kiddie matinees). C: Rossano Brazzi, Paul Tripp, Sonny Fox, Mischa Auer. D: Rossano Brazzi. MUS [G] 88m. V

Christmas to Remember, A 1978 ★★★★½ A country couple (Robards and Saint) take in their city-dwelling grandson during the holidays. Heartwarming seasonal gem with a touching script, strong performances, and nice Depression-era flavor. C: Jason Robards, Eva Marie Saint, Joanne Woodward. D: George Englund. FAM/DRA 96m. TVM V

Christmas Tree, The 1969 ★★★ A rich

man (Holden) must deal with his young son's impending death. This tearjerking holiday pudding is a trifle soggy. (a.k.a. *When Wolves Cry*) C: William Holden, Virna Lisi, Brook Fuller, Bourvil. D: Terence Young. DRA [G] 110m. V

Christmas Visitor, The 1987 Australian ★★★½ Inspiring Christmas story set in the 1890s Australian Outback. Drought is everywhere, and a badly needed miracle is sought. Worthwhile holiday charmer. (a.k.a. *Bushfire Moon*) C: Dee Wallace Stone, John Waters. D: George Miller. FAM/DRA 98m.

Christmas Wife, The 1988 ★★★★ Two great actors in a tightly focused character study of a widower hiring a woman to be his companion during the Yuletide vacation. Modestly winning. C: Jason Robards, Julie Harris. D: David Jones. DRA 73m. V

Christmas Without Snow, A 1980 ★★★½ Curmudgeonly choir master (Houseman) befriends a bereaved widow (Learned) and makes her part of the church community. Pleasant movie with good performances. C: Michael Learned, John Houseman. D: John Korty. DRA 96m. TVM V

Christopher Columbus 1949 British ★★★★ Classic Columbus saga, loaded with big studio pageantry. March makes a sympathetic hero, obsessed with his vision of a round world. No ocean greyhound, but memorable. C: Fredric March, Florence Eldridge. D: David MacDonald. DRA 104m. V

Christopher Columbus 1985 ★★★ Lavish, lengthy try at dramatizing the voyage to the New World with authentic reproductions of Columbus' ships highlighting a static script and an all-star cast with too little to do. Byrne is adequate as Christopher; Dunaway overwrought as Isabella. Edited from a six-hour TV miniseries. C: Gabriel Byrne, Faye Dunaway, Oliver Reed, Max von Sydow, Nicol Williamson, Eli Wallach, Jose Ferrer, Raf Vallone. D: Alberto Lattuada. DRA 135m. V

Christopher Columbus—The Discovery 1992 U.S. ★★★ Fifteenth-century Genoese explorer sails across the Atlantic to pioneer a shorter route to the spice-rich East Indies. Elaborate spectacle of historical voyage flawed by uneven performances. C: Marlon Brando, Tom Selleck, George Corraface, Rachel Ward. D: John Glen. DRA [PG-13] 121m. V

Christopher Strong 1933 ★★★ Independent, high-flying aviatrix Hepburn falls in love with a married man (Clive) and becomes pregnant. Hepburn's second film is notable only for her performance. Watch for her in a glimmering lamé gown with antennae. C: Katharine Hepburn, Colin Clive, Billie Burke, Helen Chandler. D: Dorothy Arzner. DRA 77m. V

Chrome and Hot Leather 1971 ★★ Green Beret seeks revenge when his fiancée is killed by a motorcycle gang. Dreadful film goes down like stale beer. C: William Smith, Tony Young, Peter Brown, Marvin Gaye. D: Lee Frost. ACT [PG] 91m. V

Chrome Hearts 1970 *See* **C.C. and Company**

Chrome Soldiers 1992 ★★★½ Hero (Busey) returns from the Gulf War to find his brother dead and his hometown gutted by drug dealers. He recruits four buddies, also Vietnam vets, to clean up the town. More than meets the eye here, Busey and company rise to the occasion. C: Gary Busey, Ray Sharkey, William Atherton. D: Thomas J. Wright. ACT [R] 92m. TVM V

Chronicles of Narnia—Prince Caspian and the Voyage of the Dawn Treader 1989 British ★★★½ Second of a BBC trilogy based on C.S. Lewis' children's fables (about a young prince who enlists four kids to help overthrow his dad, the crooked king) here given passable treatment; fun for older children. C: Barbara Kellerman, Jeffrey Perry, Richard Dempsey, Sophie Cook, Jonathan Scott, Sophie Wilcox. D: Alex Kirby. FAM/SFI 174m. TVM V

Chronicles of Narnia—Silver Chair, The 1989 British ★★★½ Third film in the BBC trilogy based on C.S. Lewis' book of children's stories; well-done (if lengthy) production will engage older kids and parents alike. C: Barbara Kellerman, Jeffrey Perry, Richard Dempsey, Sophie Cook, Jonathan Scott, Sophie Wilcox. D: Alex Kirby. FAM/SFI 174m. TVM

Chronicles of Narnia—The Lion, the Witch and the Wardrobe, 1989 British ★★★★ C.S. Lewis' masterful fantasy brought to life; first of three BBC films dramatizes one of Lewis' best-known tales, about a witch who turns all who oppose her into stone and the children who overcome her. Beautifully produced. C: Barbara Kellerman, Jeffrey Perry, Richard Dempsey, Sophie Cook, Jonathan Scott. D: Alex Kirby. FAM/SFI 174m. TVM

Chronique d'un Ete 1960 French ★★★★★ Anthropologist/filmmaker Rouch turns his attention from "primitive" peoples to Parisians, asking the question: "Are you happy?" A landmark documentary, both funny and poignant; it offers a unique snapshot of the French people. D: Jean Rouch, Edgar Morin. DOC 90m.

Chronopolis 1982 ★★★★ Animated sci-fi fantasy about immortal inhabitants of future outerspace city trying to manipulate time. Strange and fascinating. D: Piotr Kamler. SFI 70m. V

Chronos 1985 ★★½ New Age video wallpaper with Stonehenge, the pyramids, and music by Michael Stern. DOC 40m. V

Chu Chu and the Philly Flash 1981 ★★ Comedy about two hustlers (Arkin and Burnett), who inadvertently get involved with the Mob. Too bad the film's not as good as its stars. C: Alan Arkin, Carol Burnett, Jack Warden, Danny Aiello, Danny Glover, Ruth Buzzi. D: David Lowell Rich. COM [PG] 102m. V

Chubasco 1968 ★★★½ A fishing boat captain (Egan) becomes incensed when one of his crew (Jones), a former beach bum, gets involved with his daughter (Strasberg). Ably played, with turbulent man-against-nature action scenes at sea. C: Richard Egan, Christopher Jones, Susan Strasberg, Ann Sothern. D: Allen Miner. DRA 100m.

Chuck Berry Hail! Hail! Rock 'n' Roll 1987 ★★★★★ Lively profile of great rock 'n' roll star at age 60, with legends Roy Orbison, Bruce Springsteen, and Keith Richards stopping by. Berry energetically performs his old standards in this excellent, involving documentary. C: Chuck Berry, Keith Richards, Eric Clapton, Robert Cray, Etta James, Julian Lennon, Linda Ronstadt. D: Taylor Hackford. DOC 121m. V

C.H.U.D. 1984 ★★★ A photographer (Heard) and a soup kitchen owner (Stern) discover that missing homeless people are mutating into cannibalistic monsters beneath the streets. Sharp writing and acting make this scarier and wittier than the premise suggests. Followed by a sequel. C: John Heard, Daniel Stern, Kim Greist, Christopher Curry, John Goodman. D: Douglas Cheek. HOR [R] 88m. V

C.H.U.D. II 1989 ★ Graham's body is infected with "C.H.U.D. enzymes" that make him ambulatory, cannibalistic—and contagious. Idiotic, sitcom-level horror comedy has nothing to do with the first *C.H.U.D.*, and intelligent viewers shouldn't have anything to do with this sequel. C: Brian Robbins, Bill Calvert, Gerrit Graham, Robert Vaughn, Bianca Jagger. D: David Irving. HOR [R] 84m. V

Chuka 1967 ★★½ Revisionist Western about a world-weary gunfighter (Taylor) who intervenes in a battle between soldiers and Arapaho Indians. Disappointing Western gets caught in crossfire. C: Rod Taylor, John Mills, Ernest Borgnine, Luciana Paluzzi, James Whitmore, Louis Hayward. D: Gordon Douglas. WST 105m. V

Chump at Oxford, A 1940 ★★★ A couple of street cleaners save the day in an attempted bank robbery and are rewarded with a college education at Oxford. Slow in getting started, the film picks up steam as it goes along, resulting in some fine comic moments. C: Stan Laurel, Oliver Hardy, James Finlayson. D: Alfred Goulding. COM 83m. V

Church, The 1990 Italian ★★★½ Evil spirits possess a European cathedral, trapping and killing innocent victims inside. Schematic story is too reminiscent of the *Demons* films (produced, like this one, by Dario Argento), but Soavi manages some striking images and shocking gore. C: Tomas Arana, Hugh Quarshie, Barbara Cupisti, Antonella Vitale. D: Michele Soavi. HOR [R] 110m. V

Chushingura 1962 Japanese ★★★★★ The forced suicide of a young lord goads his samurai retainers into exacting revenge against the feudal lords responsible. Classic of the Japanese cinema, lavishly produced and beautifully filmed. Originally shown in two parts. C: Koshiro Matsumoto, Yuzo Kayama, Toshiro Mifune. D: Hiroshi Inagaki. DRA 108m.

C.I.A.: Code Name Alexa 1992 ★★ A terrorist is reprogrammed by the feds to turn against her mentor, a diabolical crime boss, who is threatening to destroy America. As dumb as it sounds. C: Lorenzo Lamas, O.J. Simpson, Kathleen Kinmont, Michael Bailey Smith, Jeff Griggs. D: Joseph Merhi. ACT [R] 93m. V

Ciao! Manhattan *See* **Edie in Ciao! Manhattan**

Ciao Professore! 1994 Italian ★★★★ A grade-school teacher in an impoverished suburb of Naples, Italy has a beneficial effect on his students. Sort of a Mediterranean *To Sir, With Love*: funny and charming. Some profanity. C: Paolo Villaggio. D: Lina Wertmuller. COM [R] 91m. V

Cigarette Girl from Mosselprom, The 1924 Russian ★★★½ A young working-class woman becomes an overnight movie star in this silent satire of '20s Russian life and film movements. C: Yulia Solntseva. D: Yuri Zhelyabuzhsky. COM 78m.

Cimarron 1931 ★★★½ Western saga from Edna Ferber novel (Dix and Dunne) of settlers in Oklahoma territory. Impressive scope, but dated acting style hobbles it now. First Western to win Best Picture Oscar; also won for Best Screenplay. C: Richard Dix, Irene Dunne. D: Wesley Ruggles. WST 125m. V

Cimarron 1960 ★★★½ Epic Western about an Oklahoma homesteader family, the Cravats, settling in the prairie from 1890 to 1915. Based on an Edna Ferber story. C: Glenn Ford, Maria Schell, Anne Baxter, Arthur O'Connell, Russ Tamblyn, Mercedes McCambridge, Vic Morrow, Aline MacMahon. D: Anthony Mann. WST 147m. V

Cimarron Kid, The 1951 ★★½ Gunfighter (Murphy) is persuaded to hang up his six-guns by the love of a good woman. So what else is new? Pretty stale trail mix. C: Audie Murphy, Beverly Tyler, Hugh O'Brian. D: Budd Boetticher. WST 84m.

Cincinnati Kid, The 1965 ★★★ New Orleans cardsharp McQueen challenges rival Robinson to high-stakes poker game. There's a little romance on the side but it's the game that provides tension and drama here, with a knowing performance by Blondell as the dealer. C: Steve McQueen, Ann-Margret, Edward G. Robinson, Karl Malden, Tuesday Weld, Joan Blondell, Rip Torn, Jack Weston, Cab Calloway. D: Norman Jewison. DRA 105m. V

Cinderella 1950 ★★★★★ Disney version of fairy tale about girl with a slipper and a dream. Imaginative additions include mice as allies against the wicked stepmother; their creation of dress for heroine is film's highlight. Lovely animation, cute songs including

"Bibbidi-Bobbidi-Boo." A must for youngsters of all ages. Voices of Ilene Woods, Eleanor Audley, Mike Douglas, Verna Felton. D: Wilfred Jackson, Hamilton Luske, Clyde Geronimi. FAM/MUS [G] 76m. v

Cinderella 1964 ★★★★ Rodgers and Hammerstein's version of fairy tale boasts lovely, memorable songs, including "Ten Minutes Ago," "Impossible," and "In My Own Little Corner." Musical's stagy style is so dated that now it's part of the charm. Sweetly marvelous, romantic tunefest. C: Lesley Ann Warren, Ginger Rogers, Walter Pidgeon, Celeste Holm, Jo Van Fleet. D: Charles S. Dubin. MUS 83m. TVM v

Cinderella, Italian Style *See* **More Than a Miracle**

Cinderella Jones 1946 ★★½ A not-so-bright woman (Leslie) must find a brainy husband or lose a huge inheritance. She enrolls in the local college and finds just the guy. Minor comedy with pleasant songs. C: Joan Leslie, Robert Alda, S.Z. Sakall, Edward Everett Horton, Ruth Donnelly. D: Busby Berkeley. COM 88m.

Cinderella Liberty 1973 ★★★★ A kindly sailor (Caan) on shore leave falls in love with a hooker (Mason) who's having a tough time raising her illegitimate son. Sentimental but satisfying, with superior performances. C: James Caan, Marsha Mason, Eli Wallach, Kirk Calloway, Burt Young, Dabney Coleman, Sally Kirkland. D: Mark Rydell. DRA [R] 117m. v

Cinderfella 1960 ★★½ Sex-switched fairy tale with Lewis as Anderson's stepson helped by fairy godfather Wynn in his pursuit of princess Alberghetti. Boring, over-produced fantasy. C: Jerry Lewis, Ed Wynn, Judith Anderson, Anna Maria Alberghetti, Count Basie. D: Frank Tashlin. COM 88m. v

Cindy 1978 ★★★★ Unusual musical updating of the Cinderella story is set in WWII Harlem with a dynamic black cast, catchy tunes, and effective choreography. Woodard's a real charmer as the poorly dressed heroine aching for a better life. C: Clifton Davis, Charlaine Woodard, Scoey Mitchell, Nell Carter, Alaina Reed. D: William Graham. MUS 100m. TVM

Cinema Paradiso 1989 Italian ★★★★½ In the years following WWII, a Sicilian boy attaches himself to a small-town movie projectionist. A simple, beautiful homage to the art of cinema, which deservedly won the Oscar for Best Foreign Film. Wonderful family viewing (even with subtitles). A longer director's cut is also available. C: Philippe Noiret, Jacques Perrin, Salvatore Cascio. D: Giuseppe Tornatore. FAM/DRA [PG] 123m. v

Circle of Children, A 1977 ★★★★ Alexander's restrained, intelligent performance as affluent volunteer in school for emotionally disturbed youngsters makes this inspiring entertainment. Roberts lends fine support as veteran teacher resentful of Jane's presence. C: Jane Alexander, Rachel Roberts, David Ogden Stiers. D: Don Taylor. DRA 100m. TVM

Circle of Danger 1951 British ★★★ Melodramatic chase adventure follows an American in England, investigating the mysterious death of his brother in WWII. Not too suspenseful, but involving nevertheless. C: Ray Milland, Patricia Roc. D: Jacques Tourneur. DRA 86m.

Circle of Deceit 1981 French ★★★★★ While covering war in Lebanon, journalist Ganz agonizes over whether to remain a witness to events or try and help victims. Gripping tale of ethics under extreme duress. Shot on location during Lebanese Civil War. (a.k.a. *False Witness*) C: Bruno Ganz, Hanna Schygulla, Jerzy Skolimowski. D: Volker Schlondorff. DRA [R] 108m.

Circle of Deception, A 1961 British ★★★ Allied officer (Dillman) parachutes into France with classified information for the Resistance, but his superiors have set him up to be captured. Tingly espionage thriller. C: Bradford Dillman, Suzy Parker, Harry Andrews. D: Jack Lee. DRA 100m.

Circle of Friends 1995 ★★★★ Charming tale of an unusual romance between a strong-willed wallflower (Driver) and a handsome youth (O'Donnell) in 1950's Ireland. Driver's performance is a winner. From Maeve Binchy's novel. C: Chris O'Donnell, Minnie Driver, Geraldine O'Rawe, Colin Firth. D: Pat O'Connor. COM [PG-13] 112m. v

Circle of Iron 1978 ★★★½ A young man must endure numerous tests to possess a sacred book. Above-par martial arts Zen fantasy. Scripted by Sterling Silliphant and based on an idea by Bruce Lee, just before he died. C: David Carradine, Jeff Cooper, Roddy McDowall, Eli Wallach, Christopher Lee. D: Richard Moore. ACT [R] 102m. v

Circle of Love 1964 ★★ Uninspired version of the love classic *La Ronde*, scripted by Jean Anouilh, describing a circle of seduction and love. Goes around, gets nowhere. C: Jane Fonda, Jean-Claude Brialy, Catherine Spaak. D: Roger Vadim. DRA 110m. v

Circle of Two 1981 Canadian ★★ Parents of teenager are horrified when she takes up with aging artist even though the relationship is platonic. Comedy/drama attempts to give some insight into both youth and experience. C: Richard Burton, Tatum O'Neal. D: Jules Dassin. COM [PG] 90m. v

Circle of Violence: A Family Drama, A 1986 ★★★ Depressing problem drama, with a housewife (Weld) separated from her husband and taking her frustrations out on her elderly mother (Fitzgerald). The intentions are good, but it sinks into soap opera tedium. C: Tuesday Weld, Geraldine Fitzgerald, River Phoenix. D: David Greene. DRA 104m.

Circuitry Man 1990 ★★★½ When L.A.'s smog gets out of control, the inhabitants move underground, but a bodyguard (Wheeler-Nicholson) has to deliver a shipment of electronic chips, the drug of the future, to New York. Will she make it alive? Inventive plot with many twists. C: Dana Wheeler-Nicholson, Jim Metzler, Lu Leonard, Vernon Wells. D: Steven Lovy. SFI [R] 85m. V

Circumstantial Evidence 1945 ★★★½ An innocent man is about to be executed in the electric chair in this trim and tense crime melodrama. C: Michael O'Shea, Lloyd Nolan. D: John Larkin. CRI 68m.

Circus Clown, The 1934 ★★★ Star vehicle for wide-mouthed comic Brown as the son of an ex-circus clown who decides to join his father's old cronies. Pleasant entertainment, enlivened by Brown's talent for acrobatics. Good family viewing. C: Joe E. Brown, Dorothy Burgess, William Demarest. D: Ray Enright. FAM/COM 63m.

Circus of Horrors 1960 British ★★★★ A twisted plastic surgeon (Diffring) and his nurse use a bizarre traveling circus as a front for their criminal enterprises. Well made and atmospheric. C: Anton Diffring, Erika Remberg, Donald Pleasence. D: Sidney Hayers. HOR 88m. V

Circus Queen Murder, The 1933 ★★★½ Menjou is eminently acceptable as sleuth investigating killings in a traveling show. Snappy. C: Adolphe Menjou, Greta Nissen. D: R. W. Neill. CRI 63m.

Circus, The/A Day's Pleasure 1928 ★★★★½ Almost feature-length *The Circus* is paired with an earlier short: in first, Chaplain's a clown smitten with unrequited love for a bareback rider; in second, he's a family man out for a disaster-prone Sunday. Hilarious, if occasionally uneven. Note: During the first Oscar presentation, Chaplin was given a special Oscar for "versatility and genius in writing, acting, directing, and producing" *The Circus*. C: Charlie Chaplin, Allen Garcia, Merna Kennedy. D: Charles Chaplin. COM 105m. V

Circus World 1964 ★★★½ Big Top story offers nothing new but still entertains. A circus owner (Wayne) pines for lost love (Hayworth) as he tries to save his troubled show. Includes exciting circus fire sequence. C: John Wayne, Rita Hayworth, Claudia Cardinale, Lloyd Nolan, Richard Conte. D: Henry Hathaway. DRA 132m. V

Cisco Pike 1972 ★★★ A has-been rock star (Kristofferson) gets blackmailed by a corrupt narcotics cop (Hackman). Slow but not half bad. C: Kris Kristofferson, Karen Black, Gene Hackman, Harry Dean Stanton. D: B. Norton. CRI [R] 94m. V

Citadel, The 1938 U.S. ★★★★½ Beautifully written tale of doctor trading moral values for monetary gain, from A.J. Cronin novel. Donat portrays inner struggle well, as wife Russell and best friend Harrison register their distaste for his changed personality. Terrific supporting cast. C: Robert Donat, Rosalind Russell, Ralph Richardson, Rex Harrison, Emlyn Williams. D: King Vidor. DRA 112m. V

Citizen Cohn 1992 ★★★★ Woods has a field day with the meaty role of Roy Cohn in this biography of the shark-like lawyer who was Senator McCarthy's aide in the '50s, a media celebrity in the '70s, and who died of AIDS in the '80s. Adapted from the best-seller by Nicholas von Hoffman and energized by a top-notch supporting cast. C: James Woods, Joe Don Baker, Joseph Bologna, Ed Flanders, Frederic Forrest, Lee Grant, Pat Hingle, Tovah Feldshuh. D: Frank Pierson. DRA [R] 115m. TVM V

Citizen Kane 1941 ★★★★★ Groundbreaking cinematic masterpiece remains as fresh and exciting today as upon initial release. Chronicling rise and fall of Hearst-like newspaper magnate, film makes innovative use of flashback, deep-focus photography, newsreel footage, and editing. Then-unknown Mercury Theater cast is uniformly excellent. Welles' directing debut won Oscar for Screenplay, but surprisingly not Best Picture! C: Orson Welles, Joseph Cotten, Everett Sloane, Dorothy Comingore, Ray Collins, George Coulouris, Ruth Warrick, Agnes Moorehead, William Alland, Erskine Sanford, Paul Stewart. D: Orson Welles. DRA [PG] 119m. V

Citizens Band 1977 ★★★★ Group of CB radio enthusiasts from a small Midwestern town use their gadgets to eavesdrop on one another, leading to comical adventures. Excellent script, fine low-key performances and imaginative situations brighten this early effort from Oscar-winning director Demme. (a.k.a. *Handle with Care*) C: Paul LeMat, Candy Clark, Ann Wedgeworth, Marcia Rodd, Ed Begley, Jr. D: Jonathan Demme. COM [PG] 98m.

City Across the River 1949 ★★★ Brooklyn juvenile gang story, adapted from hardhitting bestseller *The Amboy Dukes*. Tony Curtis debuted as a gang member. C: Stephen McNally, Thelma Ritter, Richard Jaeckel. D: Maxwell Shane. DRA 90m.

City Beneath the Sea 1953 ★★★ Romantic adventure about treasure-seeking deep-sea divers (Ryan and Quinn) who come upon the submerged Caribbean city of Port Royal. Vivid Technicolor photography of lush tropical island locale. C: Robert Ryan, Mala Powers, Anthony Quinn. D: Budd Boetticher. ACT 87m.

City Beneath the Sea 1970 ★★★½ Futuristic tale of a fledgling undersea city trying to survive while threatened by various dangers, including an approaching asteroid. Good special effects and production values. Scripted by John Meredyth Lucas. C: Robert Wagner, Stuart Whitman, Joseph Cotten. D: Irwin Allen. SFI [G] 98m. TVM V

City for Conquest 1940 ★★★★ Boxer Cagney sacrifices career and health for younger brother Kennedy. Sentimental hokum is distinguished by one of Cagney's finest performances. Good support by Sheridan as jaded dancer. C: James Cagney, Ann Sheridan, Frank Craven, Arthur Kennedy, Donald Crisp, Frank McHugh, Elia Kazan, Anthony Quinn. D: Anatole Litvak. DRA 101m.

City Girl 1984 ★★★★ A young woman (Harrington) builds a career as a photographer while having her ups and downs with a series of men. Realistic, uncompromising, and witty. A sleeper gem with a strong performance by Harrington. C: Laura Harrington, Joe Mastroianni, Carole McGill, Peter Riegert, Colleen Camp. D: Martha Coolidge. DRA 85m.

City Heat 1984 ★★★ Macho superstars Reynolds and Eastwood ham it up as they spoof their own screen images. A tough cop and a private investigator trade barbs while they battle gangsters during Prohibition. C: Clint Eastwood, Burt Reynolds, Jane Alexander, Madeline Kahn, Rip Torn, Irene Cara, Richard Roundtree, Tony Lo Bianco. D: Richard Benjamin. CRI [PG] 97m.

City in Fear 1980 ★★★★ A psychotic killer on a rampage (Rourke in his film debut) confides in a jaded newspaper columnist (Janssen in his last film role) as he goes about his grisly deeds. Thriller features an excellent cast and a well-written, realistic script. C: David Janssen, Robert Vaughn, Perry King, Mickey Rourke. D: Allan Smithee (Jud Taylor). CRI 150m. TVM

City Lights 1931 ★★★★★ Silent masterpiece mixes humor with sentiment as the Little Tramp falls in love with blind flower girl (Cherrill) and vows to restore her sight. Simple story packs an emotional punch; culminates in classic fade-out. Perfect for the whole family. C: Charlie Chaplin, Virginia Cherrill, Hank Mann, Harry Myers. D: Charles Chaplin. FAM/COM [G] 86m. V

City Limits 1985 ★★ Futuristic action, set in a world devastated by plague and overrun by hoods on motorbikes. Messy, less than interesting sci-fi. Good cast. C: Darrell Larson, John Stockwell, Kim Cattrall, Rae Dawn Chong, Robby Benson. D: Aaron Lipstadt. SFI [PG-13] 85m. V

City News 1983 ★★ Cartoonist on an alternative newspaper draws his fantasy relationship with a young woman, the closest he gets to realizing it. Tries too hard to be funny. C: Elliot Crown, Nancy Cohen, Thomas Trivier. D: David Fishelson, Zoe Zinman. COM 65m.

City of Bad Men 1953 ★★★½ Set in 1890s Nevada during the Corbett-Fitzsimmons boxing match, as a trio of bad guys plan to steal the fight receipts. Interesting twist on traditional Western formula. C: Jeanne Crain, Dale Robertson, Richard Boone, Lloyd Bridges. D: Harmon Jones. WST 82m.

City of Blood 1988 South African ★★★½ Unusual murder mystery/horror film has a doctor chasing a serial killer; this solid sleeper deals with South Africa's racial issues directly and intelligently. C: Joe Stewardson, Ian Yule, Susan Coetzer. D: Darrell Roodt. HOR [R] 96m. V

City of Fear 1959 ★★½ B-movie thriller follows a demented escaped convict who's carrying around a canister filled with deadly radioactive material. Some suspense. C: Vince Edwards, Lyle Talbot, Patricia Blair. D: Irving Lerner. DRA 81m.

City of Fear 1966 British ★★½ A journalist travels to Hungary to smuggle out anti-Communists with the help of former refugees. None-too-thrilling caper picture. C: Paul Maxwell, Terry Moore, Marisa Mell. D: Peter Bezencenet. DRA 90m.

City of Hope 1991 ★★★★ Sayles' sprawling drama of inner-city crime and corruption explores their effect on lives of locals, from politicians to laborers. Loosely plotted and overlong, but full of rich characterizations and wonderful performances. C: Vincent Spano, Tony Lo Bianco, Joe Morton, John Sayles, Angela Bassett, David Strathairn, Jace Alexander, Todd Graff. D: John Sayles. DRA [R] 129m. V

City of Joy 1992 British ★★★ Swayze gives it his all but is miscast as a troubled physician who goes to India for spiritual guidance and finds inner peace by helping others. Ponderous, preachy story is enlivened by excellent supporting performances. C: Patrick Swayze, Pauline Collins, Om Puri, Art Malik. D: Roland Joffe. DRA [PG-13] 134m. V

City of Sadness, A 1989 Taiwanese ★★★★★ Family carves out a struggling existence in '40s Taiwan, which has gone from Japanese to Chinese occupation. Hou's brilliantly layered epic is the first part of a proposed "history of Taiwan" trilogy; second film, the equally good *The Puppetmaster* (1993), is actually a prequel. C: Tony Leung, Hsin Shu-fen, Kao Jai. D: Hou Hsiao-hsien. DRA 155m.

City of Shadows 1955 ★★½ Rackets boss (McLaglen) gets one-upped by clever newsboys in this undistinguished saga of the big city. C: Victor McLaglen, Kathleen Crowley. D: William Witney. DRA 70m.

City of Song 1931 *See* **Farewell to Love**

City of Women 1981 Italian ★★★★ Womanizer Mastroianni dreams up a city of women, where he finds both pleasure and comeuppance for his libertine ways. Over-the-top social satire that audiences either love or hate. C: Marcello Mastroianni, Anna Prucnal, Donatella Damiani. D: Federico Fellini. COM [R] 139m. V

City on a Hunt 1953 *See* **No Escape**

City on Fire 1979 Canadian ★★ After a summerlong drought, what's the last thing a town needs? An oil refinery fire, of course. Weak disaster movie with the requisite starry cast. C: Barry Newman, Henry Fonda, Ava Gardner, Shelley Winters, Susan Clark, Leslie Nielsen, James Franciscus. D: Alvin Rakoff. ACT [R] 101m.

City Slickers 2: Legend of Curly's Gold 1994 ★★★½ Crystal and friends go back out West and run into Palance playing his own evil twin brother, looking for buried treasure in this sequel to the surprise hit. C: Billy Crystal, Jack Palance, Jon Lovitz, Daniel Stern, Patricia Wettig. D: Paul Weiland. COM [PG-13] 116m.

City Slickers 1991 ★★★★ Three New Yorkers escape mid-life crises by going on a cattle drive led by Palance, who won a Best Supporting Oscar for his endearing performance. Countless comic moments blend riotously with engaging story. Followed by a sequel. C: Billy Crystal, Daniel Stern, Bruno Kirby, Jack Palance, Josh Mostel, David Paymer, Patricia Wettig. D: Ron Underwood. COM [PG-13] 112m. V

City Streets 1931 ★★★★ Original screenplay by Dashiell Hammett about a carnival worker (Cooper) who falls in love with a mobster's daughter (Sidney) and their efforts to escape syndicate influence. Solid gangster melodrama, with stylish camerawork. Sidney's first film. C: Gary Cooper, Sylvia Sidney, Paul Lukas, Guy Kibbee. D: Rouben Mamoulian. CRI 82m.

City Streets 1938 ★★★ A caring grocer (Carillo) impoverishes himself by selling his store so that a wheelchair-bound orphan (Fellows) can have a needed operation. Handkerchief drencher, with endearing performances. C: Edith Fellows, Leo Carrillo, Tommy Bond, Mary Gordon. D: Albert Rogell. DRA 68m.

City That Never Sleeps 1953 ★★★ A married Chicago policeman (Young) can't decide whether or not to leave his wife after he falls in love with another woman (Powers). Dated melodrama benefits from fine use of city-at-night atmosphere. C: Gig Young, Mala Powers, Edward Arnold, Chill Wills. D: John Auer. DRA 90m.

City, The 1971 ★★ The hardworking, grizzled mayor of a Southwestern city overcomes problems in this pilot for a failed TV series. Below-average Quinn. C: Anthony Quinn, Skye Aubrey, E.G. Marshall. D: Daniel Petrie. DRA 100m. TVM

City, The 1977 ★★★ Police hunt for a psychotic killer determined to murder a popular country-western singer. Suspenseful story. C: Robert Forster, Don Johnson. D: Harvey Hart. CRI 78m. TVM

City Without Men 1943 ★★½ Women waiting and hoping that their men will get parole huddle together in a boardinghouse near a prison. Formula potboiler, appealing Darnell. C: Linda Darnell, Michael Duane, Sara Allgood, Edgar Buchanan, Glenda Farrell, Margaret Hamilton, Rosemary DeCamp. D: Sidney Salkow. DRA 75m.

Civil War, The 1990 ★★★★★ Ken Burns' profoundly moving, nine-part archival re-creation of the sights and sounds of the American Civil War weaves photos, music and the words of its participants into one of the most important historical journals ever filmed. Not to be missed. D: Ken Burns. DOC 540m. V

Civilization 1916 ★★★★ In this silent anti-war parable, a vision of Christ on the battlefield of an unnamed country stops a war. Stands the test of time; well worth seeing. C: Howard Hickman, Enid Markey, J. Barney Sherry, Lola May. D: Thomas Ince. DRA 102m. V

Clair de Femme 1979 French ★★½ Montand and Schneider give it their all as melancholy, middle-aged lovers. Based on a novel by Romain Gargol. C: Yves Montand, Romy Schneider, Lila Kedrova. D: Costa-Gavras. DRA 103m.

Claire of the Moon 1993 ★★½ Writer at a women's literary retreat finds herself attracted to another writer. Lesbian love story tries to be matter-of-fact, but winds up being tedious and talky instead. C: Trisha Todd, Karen Trumbo, Faith McDevitt, Sheila Dickinson, Damon Craig. D: Nicole Conn. DRA 108m. V

Claire's Knee 1971 French ★★★★½ Brialy agonizes over whether or not to touch the object of his affection—the right knee of a friend's daughter. Charming study of comic longing is fifth in Rohmer's "Six Moral Tales." C: Jean-Claude Brialy, Aurora Cornu, Beatrice Romand. D: Eric Rohmer. COM 106m. V

Clairvoyant, The 1934 British ★★★★ A music-hall mindreader (Rains) begins to experience genuine precognition. Eerie character drama with top-drawer Rains. (a.k.a. *The Evil Mind*) C: Claude Rains, Fay Wray. D: Maurice Elvey. DRA 80m.

Clambake 1967 ★★½ Rich kid (Presley) wants to get out from under father's all-controlling thumb, so he switches places with water-skiing instructor. Not exactly the most intellectually demanding film of its era, but Elvis fans shouldn't care. One of three Presley musicals that year. C: Elvis Presley, Shelley Fabares, Will Hutchins, Bill Bixby, Gary Merrill. D: Arthur Nadel. MUS 100m. V

Clan of the Cave Bear, The 1986 ★★ Silly Neanderthal drama, based on Jean Auel's popular novel, casts Hannah as a beautiful blonde outcast shunned by her tribe of swarthy cavemen. Determined to prove her worth, she becomes a warrior and shaman. Preposterous but good for a giggle. C: Daryl Hannah, Pamela Reed. D: Michael Chapman. DRA [R] 98m. V

Clara's Heart 1988 ★★★ Sentimental family fare about wise, good-hearted Jamaican housekeeper who helps a troubled boy through his parents' separation. Whoopi's charm and skill hold this together. C: Whoopi

Goldberg, Michael Ontkean, Kathleen Quinlan, Neil Patrick Harris, Spalding Gray. D: Robert Mulligan. FAM/DRA [PG-13] 108m. v

Clarence 1991 ★★★ An inept guardian angel gets one more chance to prove his mettle by traveling to Earth to save a suicidal woman. Familiar formula makes for slow-moving, overly sentimental comedy. C: Robert Carradine, Kate Trotter. D: Eric Till. COM [G] 92m. v

Clarence and Angel 1980 ★★★½ Unlikely duo of friends, kung fu aficionado (Cardova) and shy, illiterate Southern classmate (Brown), team up to help each other through school. Obscure, low-budget film worth watching for fine acting and touching story. C: Darren Brown, Mark Cardova, Cynthia McPherson. D: Robert Gardner. FAM/DRA 75m. v

Clarence, the Cross-Eyed Lion 1965 ★★★½ A lion unable to hunt because of bad eyesight is taken in by an animal refuge center and becomes a family pet. Entertaining family film set in Africa spawned popular TV show *Daktari*. C: Marshall Thompson, Betsy Drake, Richard Haydn. D: Andrew Marton. FAM/DRA [G] 120m. v

Clash by Night 1952 ★★★★ Woman with a past (Stanwyck) returns to home town and settles down to marry a mild fisherman (Douglas), but is wooed by tough-guy Ryan who senses she needs a real man. Clifford Odets' story bolstered by Stanwyck's standout performance. C: Barbara Stanwyck, Paul Douglas, Robert Ryan, Marilyn Monroe. D: Fritz Lang. DRA 105m. v

Clash of Steel 1962 French ★★★½ French king Henry of Navarre loses his throne in this energetic period-piece production featuring beautifully choreographed, fancy swordplay and energetic acting. C: Gerard Barray, Gianna Canale. D: Bernard Borderie. ACT 79m.

Clash of the Titans 1981 British ★★½ Perseus (Hamlin), the mortal of son of Zeus (Olivier), must overcome various mythological beasties to fulfill his destiny. Boring yarn (even Olivier seems to be sleepwalking) made endurable only by Ray Harryhausen's special effects. C: Harry Hamlin, Laurence Olivier, Maggie Smith, Claire Bloom, Burgess Meredith, Sian Phillips, Ursula Andress. D: Desmond Davis. DRA [PG] 118m. v

Class 1983 ★★ McCarthy unwittingly begins an affair with the beautiful mother (Bisset) of his prep school roommate (Lowe). It's all quite improbable, but that's the fun of this unpretentious wisp of hormonal overload. C: Andrew McCarthy, Rob Lowe, Jacqueline Bisset, Stuart Margolin, Cliff Robertson, John Cusack, Joan Cusack. D: Lewis John Carlino. COM [R] 98m. v

Class Act 1992 ★★★½ Trouble in the classroom as tough street hood and straight-A nerd switch places. Winning personalities of rap stars Kid n' Play make this slight comedy fun. C: Christopher Reid, Christopher Martin, Meshach Taylor, Karyn Parsons, Rhea Perlman. D: Randall Miller. COM [PG-13] 100m. v

Class Action 1990 ★★★½ Veteran lawyer Hackman files class-action suit against an auto company only to find himself facing daughter Mastrantonio (who's representing the defendant) in court. Fairly obvious drama, but Hackman and Mastrantonio make it very watchable. C: Gene Hackman, Mary Elizabeth Mastrantonio, Larry Fishburne, Donald Moffat, Jonathan Silverman. D: Michael Apted. DRA [R] 110m. v

Class of '44 1973 ★★★ The young men from *Summer of '42* are back again, this time in college, facing the usual romantic entanglements. Entertaining, but nowhere near the original. C: Gary Grimes, Jerry Houser, Oliver Conant. D: Paul Bogart. DRA [PG] 95m. v

Class of Miss MacMichael, The 1978 British ★★ Stoic teacher at school for troubled students attempts to make a difference. Uneven comedy/drama irritates more than entertains. C: Glenda Jackson, Oliver Reed, Michael Murphy. D: Silvio Narizzano. DRA [R] 99m. v

Class of 1984 1982 ★★½ Psychotic student (Van Patten) and cronies make life miserable for well-meaning teacher (King) in this dreary, over-the-top updating of *Blackboard Jungle*. Followed by equally trashy sequel *Class of 1999*. C: Perry King, Merrie Ross, Roddy McDowall, Timothy Van Patten, Michael J. Fox. D: Mark L. Lester. DRA [R] 93m. v

Class of 1999 1990 ★★★ When the students get out of hand, school authorities send in an android faculty—who have their own brutal ideas on classroom discipline. Inventive sequel to *Class of 1984*. C: Bradley Gregg, Traci Lin, Malcolm McDowell, Stacy Keach, Pam Grier. D: Mark L. Lester. ACT [R] 99m. v

Class of Nuke 'Em High 1986 ★ New Jersey school begins to mass produce mutants thanks to residual nuclear waste from a nearby toxic dump. C: Samuel Weil, Janelle Brady. D: Richard Haines. SFI [R] 81m. v

Class of Nuke 'Em High Part II: Subhumanoid Meltdown 1991 ★ Sinister, evil Nukamama Corporation is manufacturing subhumanoids for slave labor. Lumpy horror stew throws in a mad scientist, a boyish hero, scantily clad women and inept special effects. C: Brick Bronsky, Lisa Gaye. D: Eric Louzil. HOR [R] 95m. v

Class of '63 1973 ★★★★ Couple at college reunion realize their marriage is in trouble when wife meets old flame. Hackett's performance is terrific in well-written drama. C: Cliff Gorman, Joan Hackett, James Brolin. D: John Korty. DRA 74m. TVM v

Claudelle Inglish 1961 ★★★½ Bored young farm woman tantalizes the men in her life and lives to regret it. Lurid melodrama, based on Erskine Caldwell story. C: Diane McBain, Arthur Kennedy. D: Gordon Douglas. DRA 99m.

Claudia 1943 ★★★★ Charming domestic comedy has newlywed McGuire, ill-prepared for married life, growing up quickly while husband Young tries to cope. Two leads play off each other beautifully. Dorothy's film debut. C: Dorothy McGuire, Robert Young, Ina Claire, Reginald Gardiner. D: Edmund Goulding. COM 91m.

Claudia and David 1946 ★★★½ McGuire reprises her debut role as Claudia, a young wife who's not quite grown up. Young plays her long-suffering but loving spouse. Sequel concerns their married life in Connecticut suburbs as they cope with having a child. Appealing and well acted. C: Dorothy McGuire, Robert Young, Mary Astor, Gail Patrick. D: Walter Lang. DRA 78m.

Claudine 1974 ★★★★ Uplifting, gentle comedy has single, inner-city mom Carroll falling in love with refuse collector Jones as he ponders what kind of role model he can be to her six kids. Well-made family film dealing with complicated issues. C: Diahann Carroll, James Earl Jones. D: John Berry. COM [PG] 92m.

Claw Monsters, The 1955 ★★ A mad scientist defends his diamond mines via native superstitions and a gang of Neanderthal-like mercenaries. Reedit of serial called *Panther Girl of the Kongo*. Pretty silly by any name. C: Phyllis Coates, Myron Healey. D: Franklin Adreon. ACT 100m.

Claws 1985 ★ Young farmer is repeatedly attacked by mutant cats. It would be camp if it weren't so stupid. Scratch this from your list. C: Jason Roberts, Brian O'Shaugnessy. HOR 84m. V

Clay Pigeon, The 1949 ★★★½ A sailor (Williams) wakes up with amnesia, discovers he's about to be court-martialled for treason and that he was responsible for the death of a friend. Superior B-movie suspense thriller is neatly done and satisfying. C: Bill Williams, Barbara Hale, Martha Hyer. D: Richard Fleischer. DRA 63m.

Clay Pigeon 1971 ★★½ A Vietnam vet is used as a decoy by a ruthless federal agent trying to nab a notorious drug dealer. Flawed script made watchable by nice ensemble acting in the supporting cast. C: Lane Slate, Tom Stern, Telly Savalas, Robert Vaughn, Burgess Meredith. D: Tom Stern. DRA [R] 97m.

Clean and Sober 1988 ★★★★ Needing a place to lie low, a yuppie cocaine addict (Keaton) hides out in a rehab clinic where a counselor (Freeman) and fellow patient (Baker) force him to confront the truth about his addiction. Keaton is superb in his first dramatic role; tough, well-done drama. C: Michael Keaton, Kathy Baker, Morgan Freeman. D: Glenn Gordon Caron. DRA [R] 124m. V

Clean Slate 1981 *See* **Coup de Torchon**

Clean Slate 1994 ★★★ Carvey plays it relatively straight as a detective with a rare form of amnesia that causes him to forget his previous life every morning. Mildly amusing comedy, but the dog steals the film. C: Dana Carvey, Victoria Golino, James Earl Jones, Kevin Pollak, Michael Gambon, Michael Murphy, Olivia D'Abo. D: Mick Jackson. COM 107m.

Clear All Wires 1933 ★★★★ A manipulative, hustling newsman (Tracy), who prefers making news to reporting it, gets sent to Russia by his exasperated editor. Fast-talking Tracy is terrific in this sharp comedy. Gleason is good too as Tracy's enterprising sidekick. C: Lee Tracy, Benita Hume, Una Merkel, James Gleason. D: George Hill. COM 78m.

Clear and Present Danger 1994 ★★★½ CIA superhero Jack Ryan (Ford) becomes aware of an illegal goverment plot against Columbian drug dealers. Second Tom Clancy thriller to star Ford (after *Patriot Games*) is again well done. C: Harrison Ford, Anne Archer, Willem Dafoe, James Earl Jones. D: Phillip Noyce ACT [PG-13] 114m. V

Clearcut 1991 Canadian ★★★★ Angered by a paper mill's destruction of a forest, Native American (Greene) kidnaps the mill's manager, after liberal lawyer (Lea) loses attempt to block matters in court. Some surprising violence, but Greene excels in fine drama. C: Ron Lea, Graham Greene, Red Crow. D: Richard Bugajski. DRA [R] 98m. V

Cleo From 5 to 7 1962 French ★★★½ Singer wanders streets of Paris as she awaits the results of biopsy. An intriguing character study, notable for being set in "real" time. Would be better if director had chosen more compelling heroine. C: Corinne Marchand, Antoine Bourseiller, Michel Legrand, Anna Karina, Eddie Constantine, Jean-Luc Godard. D: Agnes Varda. DRA 90m.

Cleopatra 1934 ★★★★½ Colbert makes a fetching queen of the Nile in this grandiose DeMille production with a welcome sense of humor. Sexy shipboard seduction scene with Marc Antony (Wilcoxon) is a highlight. Intelligent script, good performances. C: Claudette Colbert, Warren William, Henry Wilcoxon, Joseph Schildkraut, C. Aubrey Smith. D: Cecil B. DeMille. DRA 100m. V

Cleopatra 1963 ★★ Mammoth, overlong epic, with Taylor's Egyptian queen embroiled in a power struggle with Roman emperor Caesar (Harrison) and lover Marc Antony (Burton). More notable for the offscreen Taylor/Burton love affair than anything on film. Even the spectacle scenes are a letdown. C: Elizabeth Taylor, Richard Burton, Rex Harrison, Roddy McDowall, Hume Cronyn, Pamela Brown. D: Joseph L. Mankiewicz. DRA [G] 251m. V

Cleopatra Jones 1973 ★★½ Black exploitation flick stars towering Dobson as a karate-chopping agent hot on the trail of crime godmother (Shelley Winters). Average comic-book actioner. C: Tamara Dobson, Bernie Casey, Shelley Winters, Esther Rolle. D: Jack Starrett. ACT [PG] 89m. v

Cleopatra Jones and the Casino of Gold 1975 ★★★½ A statuesque Interpol agent travels to Hong Kong to foil a drug empress (Stevens). Glossy, sexy actioner features karate, great sets, and attitude, plus Dobson's outrageous, retina-searing wardrobe. Better than the first. C: Tamara Dobson, Stella Stevens. D: Chuck Bail. ACT [R] 96m. v

Cleopatra's Daughter 1960 Italian ★★★ The empress' daughter and her machinations in the Egyptian court. Bloated, overproduced epic is extremely violent. C: Debra Paget, Ettore Manni, Robert Alda. D: Richard McNamara. DRA 102m.

Clerks 1994 ★★★★ Low-budget, but prize-winning comedy set in New Jersey convenience store where two young men discuss sex, videos, sex, food, sex, prices, and sex. Cumulative effect is funny and charming, but the easily offended should be forewarned. Filmed in black-and-white. C: Brian O'Halloran, Jeff Anderson, Lisa Spoonauer. D: Kevin Smith. COM [R] 89m. v

Client, The 1994 ★★★½ A young boy witnesses a suicide and hears a confession that puts his life in danger. Terrific cast brings Grisham novel to life, despite flaccid direction. C: Susan Sarandon, Tommy Lee Jones, Mary-Louise Parker, Anthony LaPaglia. D: Joel Schumacher. CRI [PG-13] 120m.

Cliff Cemetery 1951 French ★★★½ Interesting short film about funeral practices among the Dogon tribe of Mali, focusing on sacrifices to the water god and unusual burial procedures. D: Jean Rouch. DOC 20m.

Cliffhanger 1993 U.S. ★★★★ Spectacular mountain vistas star as mountain climber (Stallone) matches wits with ultrabad guy (Lithgow). Enjoyable, though dizzying for the acrophobic. A perfect rental for the dog days of summer. C: Sylvester Stallone, John Lithgow, Michael Rooker, Janine Turner, Paul Winfield. D: Renny Harlin. ACT [R] 113m. v

Cliffhangers—Adventures from the Thrill Factory ★★★½ Critic Leonard Maltin discusses popular action serials from the golden age of Hollywood with clips of famous stunts and performances. Fun stuff. DOC 46m. v

Clifford 1994 ★ Disastrously unfunny farce in which Grodin is stuck with care of his manic, mischievous 10-year-old nephew (played by the adult Short). Filmed several years earlier. C: Martin Short, Charles Grodin, Mary Steenburgen, Dabney Coleman, G. D. Spradlin, Anne Jeffreys. D: Paul Flaherty. COM [PG] 89m.

Climax, The 1944 ★★★ A crazy opera house doctor (Karloff) is driven over the edge by a soprano (Foster) whose voice reminds him of a woman he killed. Gothic melodrama entertains if not taken too seriously. C: Boris Karloff, Gale Sondergaard, Susanna Foster, Turhan Bey. D: George Waggner. DRA 86m.

Climb an Angry Mountain 1972 ★★★ Lawman (Parker), a widower raising his children on a ranch in the Rockies, is given orders to arrest a Native American who's wanted for murder. Solid outdoor adventure features lots of pretty mountain scenery. C: Barry Nelson, Fess Parker. D: Leonard Horn. WST 97m. TVM

Clinging Vine, The 1926 ★★★½ Lighthearted comedy stars Joy as a smart career woman who hides her talents to make her boss look good, then gives up all for love. Well-made, stylish production. C: Leatrice Joy, Tom Moore, Tody Claude. D: Paul Sloane. COM 71m.

Clinic, The 1985 Australian ★★★ Sly and naughty look at events in an Australian clinic for venereal diseases. Ramshackle mixture of comedy and drama won't please everyone, but the vulgar humor is often very funny. For more broadminded audiences. C: Chris Haywood, Simon Burke. D: David Stevens. COM 92m. v

Clinton and Nadine 1988 ★★★½ Amiable drug smuggler (Garcia) enlists aid of heart-of-gold prostitute (Barkin) in avenging the murder of his brother, which gets them both involved in Central American arms scheme. Well-done thriller. (a.k.a. *Blood Money*) C: Andy Garcia, Ellen Barkin, Morgan Freeman. D: Jerry Schatzberg. CRI 110m. TVM v

Clipped Wings 1953 ★★★½ The Bowery Boys join the Air Force by mistake while visiting a friend stationed at a base. One of the best in the series, fast-moving and enjoyable. C: Leo Gorcey, Huntz Hall, David Condon. D: Edward Bernds. COM 65m. v

Clive of India 1935 ★★★★ Star-filled biography of the legendary empire-builder Robert Clive, played to an exquisite turn by the suave Colman. Semihistorical adventure concentrates on his romance and marriage, omitting some key historical facts. Lavish production, exotic settings, good trooping. C: Ronald Colman, Loretta Young, Colin Clive, C. Aubrey Smith, Cesar Romero, Leo G. Carroll. D: Richard Boleslawski. DRA 90m.

Cloak and Dagger 1946 ★★★ Muted spy thriller has American physics professor Cooper going undercover in Nazi Germany to find abducted atomic scientist. Lesser Lang's still watchable. C: Gary Cooper, Lilli Palmer, Robert Alda. D: Fritz Lang. DRA 106m. v

Cloak & Dagger 1984 ★★★★ Young boy (Thomas) calls on his spy buddy/imaginary friend (Coleman) to help him save the country from evil spies. Both appropriate for children and entertaining for adults. Dabney's dandy in the dual role of average dad and adventurous spook. Remake of *The Window*. C: Henry Thomas, Dabney Coleman, Michael Murphy. D: Richard Franklin. FAM/ACT [PG] 101m. v

Cloak Without Dagger 1957 *See* **Operation Conspiracy**

Clock, The 1945 ★★★★½ Touching WWII romance with Garland and Walker meeting, falling in love, then marrying in 24-hour period. Judy is heartbreaking in dramatic debut. Scene in restaurant after rushed wedding a high point. C: Judy Garland, Robert Walker, James Gleason, Keenan Wynn. D: Vincente Minnelli. DRA 91m. V

Clockmaker, The 1973 French ★★★★ Aging clockmaker investigates murder of his son with same precision he brings to his craft. Debut feature from director is solid character study with impressive performance from Noiret in title role. C: Philippe Noiret, Jean Rochefort, Jacques Denis. D: Bertrand Tavernier. CRI 105m.

Clockwise 1986 British ★★★½ An uptight headmaster (Cleese), consumed with rules and punctuality, loses his composure when a trip to deliver a speech about his educational methods collapses into chaos. Cleese's talent for physical comedy and quick pacing compensate for the thin story. C: John Cleese, Penelope Wilton, Alison Steadman. D: Christopher Morahan. COM [PG] 96m. V

Clockwork Orange, A 1971 ★★★★½ Sadistic youth Alex (McDowell) and his droogs (friends) terrorize innocents until Alex is caught and "reformed." Kubrick's satiric vision of juvenile delinquency in the near future, via the Anthony Burgess novel, is extremely disturbing and often difficult to watch. McDowell is frighteningly good. C: Malcolm McDowell, Patrick Magee, Adrienne Corri. D: Stanley Kubrick. SFI [R] 137m. V

Clonus Horror, The 1978 *See* **Parts: The Clonus Horror**

Close Call for Boston Blackie, A 1946 ★★ A questionable lady gets the popular series detective Boston Blackie framed for murder in this rather lame comic mystery. CRI

Close Call for Ellery Queen 1942 ★★½ Detective Ellery Queen (Gargan) gets involved in the investigation of a crime ring after a millionaire is murdered. So-so series installment. C: William Gargan, Margaret Lindsay, Charley Grapewin. D: James Hogan. CRI 65m.

Close Encounters of the Third Kind 1977 ★★★★★ A Spielberg knockout, this adult sci-fi yarn features a superb Dreyfuss as the ordinary guy mysteriously summoned to be the first human to meet aliens. Dazzling special effects and Oscar-winning cinematography contribute to the film's grand scale. C: Richard Dreyfuss, Melinda Dillon, Teri Garr, Francois Truffaut. D: Steven Spielberg. SFI [PG] 135m. V

Close My Eyes 1991 British ★★★★ Striking, uneven, but well-rendered drama about incest. Brother and sister Owen and Reeves, prone to surprisingly intense flirting, eventually begin a no-holds-barred affair. Engrossing, intelligent, well-acted, with Rickman (as Reeves' husband) a standout. C: Alan Rickman, Clive Owen, Saskia Reeves. D: Stephen Poliakoff. DRA [R] 105m. V

Close to Eden 1992 Russian ★★★★ Wonderful clash-of-cultures story about a Mongolian herdsman who brings home a stranded Russian truck driver. Thoughtful and beautifully filmed. (a.k.a. *Urga*) C: Badema Byaertu, Vladimir Gostukhin. D: Nikita Mikhalkov. DRA [PG] 109m. V

Close to My Heart 1951 ★★★½ Nature loses to nurture in this sentimental story of a couple (Milland and Tierney) who adopt a baby with less than noble parentage. Well-acted soaper. C: Ray Milland, Gene Tierney, Fay Bainter. D: William Keighley. DRA 90m.

Closely Watched Trains 1966 Czech ★★★★½ Unusual coming-of-age comedy set against specter of WWII German occupation about a young railway dispatcher's sexual initiation while involved in the Czech resistance movement. Oscar for Best Foreign Film. One of the finest of the Czech New Wave. C: Vaclav Neckar, Jitka Bendova. D: Jiri Menzel. COM 89m. V

Closer, The 1991 ★★ On eve of his retirement, a powerhouse sales rep puts his would-be successors through hell before picking one to replace him. Aiello recreates his stage performance from Louis La Russo II's play *Wheelbarrow Closers* in familiar and predictable drama. C: Danny Aiello, Michael Pare, Justine Bateman. D: Dimitri Logothetis. DRA [R] 87m. V

Closet Land 1991 ★★ Enigmatic drama about a supposedly subversive children's author (Stowe) being grilled by government interrogator Rickman. Though the stars give their all to this two-character adaptation, it remains opaque. C: Madeleine Stowe, Alan Rickman. D: Radha Bharadwaj. DRA [R] 95m. V

Cloud Dancer 1980 ★★★ Acrobatic flying pilot (Carradine) worries his friends and family with his life-threatening exploits. Wonderful aerial footage, but goes on far too long for its slim storyline. C: David Carradine, Jennifer O'Neill, Joseph Bottoms, Colleen Camp. D: Barry Brown. DRA [PG] 108m. V

Cloudburst 1951 British ★★★½ Cipher genius and WWII vet (Preston) goes after the criminals who accidentally killed his wife during the commission of a crime. Suspenseful thriller, with powerful Preston. C: Robert Preston, Elizabeth Sellars, Harold Lang. D: Francis Searle. CRI 83m.

Clouded Yellow, The 1951 British ★★★★ Thriller set in England's Lake District stars Howard as a former secret service agent relegated to working for an eccentric butterfly collector. When the collector is murdered, trouble starts. Superior, gripping chase drama. C: Jean Simmons, Trevor Howard,

Barry Jones, Kenneth More. D: Ralph Thomas. CRI 85m.

Clouds over Europe 1939 British ★★★★½ As war mounts, Britain's closely guarded fighter plan secrets are snatched by enemies. A fighter jock and Scotland Yard detective team up to crack espionage ring. Crackling WWII suspense drama, with great performance by Richardson. (a.k.a *Q Planes*). C: Laurence Olivier, Ralph Richardson, Valerie Hobson. D: Tim Whelan. ACT 100m. ᴠ

Clown Murders, The 1975 Canadian ★★½ Halloween party is the setting for a fake kidnapping. Thriller provided early dramatic role for Candy, and he stands out in an otherwise mediocre cast. C: Stephen Young, Susan Keller, Lawrence Dane, John Candy. D: Martyn Burke. CRI 96m. ᴠ

Clown, The 1952 ★★★½ Skelton in rare dramatic role as washed-up comic alienating loyal son (Considine in fine performance). Very sentimental, but some affecting moments. Remake of *The Champ*. C: Red Skelton, Tim Considine, Jane Greer. D: Robert Z. Leonard. DRA 91m. ᴠ

Clowns, The 1971 Italian ★★★★ Film essay on circus clowns is part interview, part documentary and part recreation. Fellini's collage style is both affectionate and satirical. Originally shot for Italian television. C: Mayo Morin, Lima Alberti. D: Frederico Fellini. DRA [G] 91m. TVM ᴠ

Club Extinction 1990 German-Italian-French ★★★½ Nasty but entertaining update of the classic *Dr. Mabuse*, about a Berlin suicide spate linked to a mad scientist (Bates) and his vacation resort. Beals sleepwalks through her role of an enticing billboard model. (a.k.a. *Dr. M.*) C: Alan Bates, Jennifer Beals, Jan Niklas, Hans Zischler. D: Claude Chabrol. CRI [R] 112m. ᴠ

Club Havana 1945 ★★½ Ensemble drama with music ("Besame Mucho," "Tico Tico," etc.) set in fashionable nightclub. Surprisingly bland low-budgeter. C: Tom Neal, Margaret Lindsay, Don Douglas. D: Edgar Ulmer. DRA 62m.

Club Med 1983 ★★½ Beautiful people hang around beautifully at a Club Med resort in Mexico. Aimless, but pretty to look at. C: Alan Thicke, Jim Carrey, Bill Maher, Rita Coolidge, Ronnie Hawkins. D: David Mitchell. DRA 60m. ᴠ

Club Paradise 1986 ★★½ A high-strung Chicago fireman hopes to retire and run a beach-front tropical resort, but instead inherits an island full of trouble. Sporadic laughs from usually more reliable talent. C: Robin Williams, Peter O'Toole, Rick Moranis, Twiggy, Adolph Caesar, Eugene Levy, Andrea Martin, Mary Gross. D: Harold Ramis. COM [PG-13] 96m. ᴠ

Club, The 1994 Canadian ★★★½ At a high school dance, a clutch of teenagers are pitted against their deepest fears by a demonic young man. Well-intentioned but only sporadically effective psychological horror. C: Joel Wyner, Andrea Roth, Rino Romano, Zack Ward, Kim Coates. D: Breton Spencer. HOR [R] 88m.

Clue 1985 ★★½ Mystery comedy based on the popular board game finds Colonel Mustard, Professor Plum and company faced with murder when they gather at an ominous Victorian mansion. Scatterbrained attempt to capture the game's spirit gives movie different possible endings, all of which are included on video. C: Lesley Ann Warren, Eileen Brennan, Tim Curry, Christopher Lloyd, Madeline Kahn, Michael McKean, Martin Mull, Colleen Camp, Howard Hesseman. D: Jonathan Lynn. COM [PG] 96m. ᴠ

Clue of the New Pin 1960 British ★★½ Heavy-handed mystery drama unravels a supposedly perfect crime. Not too sharp. C: Paul Daneman, Bernard Archard. D: Allan Davis. CRI 58m.

Clue of the Silver Key 1961 British ★★★ A Scotland Yard inspector (Lee) is baffled by a series of murders, but not for long. Nicely made mystery drama; from an Edgar Wallace story. C: Bernard Lee, Finlay Currie. D: Gerald Glaister. CRI 59m.

Cluny Brown 1946 ★★★★½ A plumber's niece and a Czech immigrant find love and turmoil in wartime England. Superbly written and performed comedy sneaks up on you. Nothing much happens, except caring for these characters immensely. May be Jones's best performance. C: Jennifer Jones, Charles Boyer, Peter Lawford, C. Aubrey Smith, Reginald Owen, Richard Haydn. D: Ernst Lubitsch. COM 100m.

C'mon, Let's Live a Little 1967 ★★★ Campus musical hijinks galore. A singer (Vee) goes back to college and falls in love with the dean's daughter (De Shannon). Lively romp with '60s music. C: Bobby Vee, Jackie De Shannon, Eddie Hodges, John Ireland Jr., Patsy Kelly, Kim Carnes. D: David Butler. MUS 85m.

Coach 1978 ★★½ A sexy young woman (Crosby) hired by mistake to coach a boys' high school basketball team, turns them into winners. C: Cathy Lee Crosby, Michael Biehn, Keenan Wynn. D: Bud Townsend. COM [PG] 100m. ᴠ

Coach of the Year 1980 ★★★½ A wounded Vietnam vet coaches a team of delinquent boys from his wheelchair. Conrad's very good. C: Robert Conrad, Erin Gray. D: Don Medford. DRA 100m. TVM

Coal Miner's Daughter 1980 ★★★★★ Oscar-winner Spacek (who did her own singing) is a virtual reincarnation of country star Loretta Lynn, as she brings this biographical film brilliantly to life. She's helped by an insightful script, perceptive direction, and pithy supporting performances. C: Sissy Spacek, Tommy Lee Jones, Beverly D'Angelo. D: Michael Apted. DRA [PG] 124m. v

Coast Guard 1939 ★★★ Two rugged coastguardsmen fight over the same woman, then a plane crash maroons one of them in the snow. Stock action-packed hokum. C: Randolph Scott, Frances Dee, Ralph Bellamy. D: Edward Ludwig. ACT 72m.

Coast of Skeletons 1964 British ★★★ American diamond magnate's African enterprise is aborted, and a former police inspector (Todd) is called in to investigate. Okay mystery action story. From a character created by Edgar Wallace in *Saunders of the River.* C: Richard Todd, Dale Robertson, Marianne Koch. D: Robert Lynn. ACT 91m.

Coast to Coast 1980 ★★★½ Brawny trucker (Blake) contends with creditors after his rig, and a runaway ostensible mental patient (Cannon) as a traveling companion. Watchable but forced road story with a few chuckles. C: Dyan Cannon, Robert Blake, Michael Lerner. D: Joseph Sargent. COM [PG] 95m. v

Cobb *See* **Ty Cobb Story, The**

Cobb 1994 ★★★½ Jones roars through this bio of baseball great Ty Cobb, giving a magnificent performance. Wuhl is the sportswriter chosen to sweeten up Ty's story. Film tells unvarnished truth, but, since Cobb remains an unsympathetic monster throughout, its appeal is limited. C: Tommy Lee Jones, Robert Wuhl, Lolita Davidovich. D: Ron Shelton. DRA [R] 130m. v

Cobra 1986 ★★ Rogue cop Stallone is called in when incompetent police don't have what it takes to foil a vicious cult on a murdering spree. It's *Rambo*with a badge and a haircut. Plenty of action. C: Sylvester Stallone, Brigitte Nielsen, Reni Santoni. D: George P. Cosmatos. ACT 87m. v

Cobra Strikes, The 1948 ★★½ Trouble follows when a robber interferes with an inventor. Cheapie of the B-movie variety. C: Sheila Ryan, Richard Fraser. D: Charles Reisner. CRI 62m.

Cobra, The 1968 Spanish ★ Secret service operative (Andrews) tangles with Middle Eastern opium traffickers. C: Dana Andrews, Anita Ekberg. D: Mario Sequi. ACT [R] 93m.

Cobra Woman 1944 ★★★★ Camp classic has Montez playing twin sisters (one good, one bad) in Arabian Nights-type tale. Evil twin is high priestess famed for "King Cobra" mating dance that must be seen to be believed. C: Maria Montez, Jon Hall, Sabu, Edgar Barrier, Lon Chaney Jr. D: Robert Siodmak. DRA 70m.

Cobweb, The 1955 ★★★ Intricately plotted tale of behind-the-scenes goings-on in mental institution. Overheated with some embarrassing acting by Bacall, Widmark. C: Richard Widmark, Lauren Bacall, Gloria Grahame, Charles Boyer, Lillian Gish, John Kerr, Susan Strasberg, Oscar Levant. D: Vincente Minnelli. DRA 125m. v

Coca-Cola Kid, The 1985 Australian ★★★ American go-getter arrives in Australia to bring a small soda company up to corporate speed. The laid-back manner of the company soon has him climbing the walls. Funny scenario highlighted by Scacchi's scene-stealing performance. C: Eric Roberts, Greta Scacchi. D: Dusan Makavejev. COM [R] 98m. v

Cocaine Cowboys 1979 ★★ Rockers deal in drugs between gigs. And the beat goes on. Filmed at Warhol's Long Island digs. C: Jack Palance, Tom Sullivan, Andy Warhol. D: Ulli Lommel. DRA [R] 90m. v

Cocaine Fiends, The 1936 ★★ Underworld dealer attempts to get a brother and sister addicted to cocaine. Decidedly unintentionally camp cautionary tale is downright silly. C: Noel Madison, Sheila Manners. D: William O'Connor. DRA 68m. v

Cocaine: One Man's Seduction 1983 ★★★½ Drug addiction drama, with a fine performance by Weaver as a successful realtor who gets hooked on cocaine. Slightly melodramatic, but effective. C: Dennis Weaver, Karen Grassle, Pamela Bellwood, David Ackroyd. D: Paul Wendkos. DRA 97m. TVM v

Cocaine Wars 1986 ★★★ Lone DEA agent (Schneider) strikes out after the South American coke titan who abducted his girlfriend. Typical. C: John Schneider, Kathryn Witt. D: Hector Olivera. ACT [R] 82m. v

Cockeyed Cavaliers 1934 ★★★ Burlesque team Wheeler and Woolsey romp through 16th century as a pair of bumpkins mistaken for court doctors, who then exploit their good fortune. Snappy pace and music help the slapstick. C: Bert Wheeler, Robert Woolsey, Thelma Todd, Franklin Pangborn. D: Mark Sandrich. COM 70m. v

Cockeyed Cowboys of Calico County 1970 ★★★ Turn-of-the-century blacksmith (Blocker) eagerly awaits a mail-order bride. Good cast looking lost under the spreading chestnut tree in this feeble comedy/Western. C: Dan Blocker, Nanette Fabray, Jim Backus, Wally Cox, Mickey Rooney, Marge Champion, Jack Cassidy. D: Ranald MacDougall. COM [G] 99m.

Cockeyed Miracle, The 1946 ★★★ Ghost (Morgan) returns from heaven to resolve family problems. Affable cast transcends fantasy story reminiscent of *It's a Wonderful Life.* C: Frank Morgan, Keenan Wynn, Audrey Totter. D: S. Simon. COM 81m.

Cockfighter 1974 ★★★½ Story of a man who trains roosters to fight for sport, in which the central character's thoughts serve as voice-over guide to the story, though he never speaks. Intriguing experiment; may be too violent for some tastes. C: Warren Oates, Harry Dean Stanton, Troy Donahue. D: Monte Hellman. DRA [R] 84m. v

Cockleshell Heroes, The 1956 British ★★★½ Elite squad of U.S. Marines invade the port of Bordeaux by canoe in a dangerous mission to blow up Nazi battleships. Heroic, fact-based WWII story is suspenseful and tense. C: Jose Ferrer, Trevor Howard, Anthony Newley. D: Jose Ferrer. ACT 97m.

Cocktail Molotov 1980 French ★★★★ Rite of passage of a teenage French girl in 1968 Venice who gets involved with political radicals. Sequel to *Peppermint Soda*; engaging, humorous nostalgia with an appealing cast. C: Elise Caron, Philippe Lebas. D: Diane Kurys. DRA [R] 100m.

Cocktail 1988 ★★ Cruise, trained by cocktail guru/life practitioner Brown is a novice bartender who needs a rich woman to bankroll his own bar, but falls for penniless waitress. Silly unrealistic movie that scores high with teenage Cruise fans. C: Tom Cruise, Bryan Brown, Elisabeth Shue, Lisa Banes. D: Roger Donaldson. DRA [R] 103m. V

Cocoanut Grove 1938 ★★★ Chicago saxophonist (MacMurray) auditions his band at the storied Hollywood night spot. Fluff musical with forgettable plot and songs. C: Fred MacMurray, Harriet Hilliard, The Yacht Boys, Ben Blue, Eve Arden. D: Alfred Santell. MUS 85m.

Cocoanuts, The 1929 ★★★★ The Marx Brothers' first film is a reworking of their Broadway stage hit about a greedy hotel manager trying to cash in on the rising value of Florida real estate. Not all the material transfers smoothly from stage to screen, but the film still has hilarious moments. C: Groucho Marx, Harpo Marx, Chico Marx, Zeppo Marx, Kay Francis, Margaret Dumont. D: Robert Florey. COM 96m. V

Cocoon 1985 ★★★★ Florida retirees discover a fountain-of-youth miracle water created by aliens! This low on sci-fi, high on humanity fable boasts probably the most experienced acting cast ever assembled, with a stellar Ameche in his Oscar-winning role. Warm and endearing, but a bit too saccharine at times. C: Steve Guttenberg, Brian Dennehy, Don Ameche, Wilford Brimley, Hume Cronyn, Maureen Stapleton, Jessica Tandy, Gwen Verdon, Jack Gilford. D: Ron Howard. SFI [PG-13] 117m. V

Cocoon: The Return 1988 ★★★ Uninspired sequel follows elderly friends led by Ameche as they return to earth from brief space sojourn, and must decide whether to remain here. Cast is still great. C: Steve Guttenberg, Don Ameche, Hume Cronyn, Wilford Brimley, Jessica Tandy, Maureen Stapleton, Gwen Verdon, Elaine Stritch, Jack Gilford. D: Daniel Petrie. SFI [PG] 116m. V

Code Name—Emerald 1985 ★★★ The Germans capture an American officer in Paris. He knows Allied D-Day plans, and a bold agent (Harris) must stop him from talking. Old-fashioned WWII stuff. C: Max von Sydow, Horst Buchholz, Helmut Berger, Eric Stoltz. D: Jonathan Sanger. ACT [PG] 95m. V

Code Name: Minus One 1976 *See* **Gemini Man**

Code Name: Operation Crossbow 1965 *See* **Operation Crossbow**

Code Name, Red Roses 1969 Italian ★★★½ American agent in WWII infiltrates German lines on sabotage mission. Cliched plot executed by an adequate cast. Made in Italy. (a.k.a. *Red Roses for the Führer*) C: James Daly, Pier Angeli. D: Fernando DiLeo. ACT 97m.

Code of Honor 1990 ★★★½ McGillis takes on the military establishment when she investigates the officers who derailed her cadet brother's career. Good suspense drama. C: Alec Baldwin, Wings Hauser, Kelly McGillis, Alfre Woodward, Kevin Dobson. D: David Greene. DRA 105m. TVM V

Code of Scotland Yard 1946 British ★★★★ After escaping from Devil's Island, Homolka becomes a London shopowner. But his new life in the antiques business depends on whether his past will catch up to him. Entertaining little drama. (a.k.a. *The Shop at Sly Corner*) C: Oscar Homolka, Muriel Pavlov, Kathleen Harrison, Diana Dors. D: George King. DRA 90m.

Code of Silence 1985 ★★½ Tough ("When I want your opinion, I'll beat it out of you") cop (Norris) takes on Chicago's mobsters. Standard right-wing action film. C: Chuck Norris, Henry Silva, Molly Hagan, Dennis Farina. D: Andrew Davis. ACT [R] 100m. V

Code of the Secret Service 1939 ★★½ Treasury agents trail counterfeiters to Mexico in this sequel to *Secret Service of the Air*. Jerky serial action with Reagan as Lt. "Brass" Bancroft. C: Ronald Reagan, Eddie Foy Jr. D: Noel Smith. ACT 58m.

Code 7 Victim 5 1964 British ★★★ Operative looks into a murder committed in South Africa. Passable, fast-paced action-filled adventure. C: Lex Barker, Ronald Fraser. D: Robert Lynn. ACT 88m.

Code 645 1948 ★★★ G-men tangle with a fiendish archcriminal on the loose. Modest reedited Republic serial with pre-Lone Ranger Moore sans mask. C: Yakima Canutt, Clayton Moore. D: Fred Brannon. ACT 100m.

Code Two 1953 ★★★ Three Los Angeles Police Academy trainees track the culprits who killed a fellow student. Routine plot telegraphs the action. C: Ralph Meeker, Sally Forrest, Keenan Wynn. D: Fred Wilcox. CRI 69m.

Codename: Kyril 1988 British ★★★★ Russian KGB operative (Charleson) learns his intelligence hierarchy plans to use him as a scapegoat. Fine spy drama unfolds slowly as it becomes more intriguing. Excellent performance by Woodward as the bad guy. Adaptation of John Trenhaile's *A Man Called*

Kyril. C: Edward Woodward, Ian Charleson, Denholm Elliott. D: Ian Sharp. ACT 115m. TVM V

Codename—Wildgeese 1984 German ★★ Mercenaries undertake a mission to demolish fortified opium warehouses in Thailand. Well-paced, with comic-book violence. C: Lewis Collins, Lee Van Cleef, Ernest Borgnine, Klaus Kinski. D: Anthony M. Dawson. ACT 101m. V

Coffee, Tea or Me? 1973 ★★★½ Perky flight attendant commuting between Los Angeles and London juggles two husbands. Above-par comedy about a double life. Only drawback is the faint finale. C: Karen Valentine, John Davidson. D: Norman Panama. COM 73m. TVM

Coffy 1973 ★★★½ A nurse (Grier) feigns addiction in order to infiltrate the drug gang responsible for her sister's death. Nudity and ruthless violence abound in one of Grier's better black exploitation pics. C: Pam Grier, Booker Bradshaw. D: Jack Hill. ACT [R] 91m. V

Cohen and Tate 1989 ★★ Ultraviolent tale of two at-odds paid assassins sent to snatch small boy who witnessed his parents' murder by the mob. Drags from action scene to action scene. C: Roy Scheider, Adam Baldwin. D: Eric Red. CRI [R] 86m. V

Coins in the Fountain 1990 ★★½ Glossy remake of the 1954 *Three Coins in the Fountain*, about a trio of gorgeous women who seek—and find—love and romance in Rome. Fun fluff. C: Loni Anderson, Stepfanie Kramer, Shanna Reed, Anthony Newley. D: Tony Wharmby. DRA 100m. TVM

Cold Comfort 1990 ★★★★ A father plans to give his daughter an 18th-birthday present she'll never forget: an escaped convict he's holding hostage. Askew comedy provides both laughs and chills with its dark premise. C: Maury Chaykin, Margaret Langrick, Paul Gross. D: Vic Sarin. COM [R] 88m. V

Cold Feet 1984 ★★½ Two wary casualties of past romantic failures ignore their attraction to each other as they continue to enter into ill-fated relationships. Low-key comedy. C: Griffin Dunne, Marcia Chibas, Blanche Baker. D: Bruce Van Dusen. COM [PG] 91m. V

Cold Feet 1989 ★★★ Wacky modern comedy/western revolves around a scheme to bring a cache of jewels into the United States in a horse's stomach. Odd assortment of characters tend to be as grating as they are funny in this hit-and-miss venture. C: Keith Carradine, Sally Kirkland, Tom Waits, Rip Torn. D: Robert Dornhelm. COM [R] 94m. V

Cold Front 1990 ★★★ Sheen is a determined American cop dispatched to Vancouver and partnered with Ontkean to solve a murder involving a paid assassin turned serial killer. Thriller delivers fair amount of suspense. C: Martin Sheen, Michael Ontkean, Beverly D'Angelo, Kim Coates. D: Paul Bnarbic. CRI [R] 94m. V

Cold Heaven 1992 ★★★ A wayward wife's husband dies in an accident—but the body vanishes. Is it because she resisted a miraculous vision the year before? Brooding, supernatural marital drama seems palpably uncomfortable with itself. Based on a Brian Moore novel. C: Theresa Russell, Mark Harmon, Talia Shire. D: Nicolas Roeg. DRA [R] 104m. V

Cold Night's Death, A 1973 ★★★★ Eerie phenomena interrupt scientific monkey research at remote mountain laboratory. Well-done terror yarn with a worthwhile surprise twist. C: Robert Culp, Eli Wallach. D: Jerrold Freedman. HOR 73m. TVM

Cold River 1981 ★★½ Two young people find danger and adventure in the wild Adirondacks. Locales dominate the cast in a weak outdoor tale. C: Suzanne Weber, Pat Petersen, Richard Jaeckel. D: Fred G. Sullivan. FAM/ACT [PG] 94m. V

Cold Room, The 1984 ★★½ Low-budget movie about a college student who finds danger behind the Iron Curtain. Diluted from Jeffrey Caine's novel. C: George Segal, Amanda Pays. D: James Dearden. DRA 95m. V

Cold Sassy Tree 1989 ★★★★½ Period Southern romance with widower Widmark deciding to marry Northerner Dunaway three weeks after wife's death, to family's dismay. Sensitive adaptation of Olive Ann Burns' novel with two stars in fine form. C: Faye Dunaway, Richard Widmark, Neil Patrick Harris, Frances Fisher. D: Joan Tewkesbury. DRA 97m. TVM V

Cold Steel 1987 ★★ Psychopath plagues a young police officer (Davis) seeking to avenge his father's grisly murder. No surprises in this crime story. C: Brad Davis, Sharon Stone, Jonathan Banks, Adam Ant. D: Dorothy Ann Puzo. CRI [R] 91m. V

Cold Sweat 1971 French ★★½ Peace-loving American (Bronson), enjoying life in idyllic France, is forced into dope smuggling by smoothie mobster (Mason). Familiar yarn, with Bronson delivering his usual laid-back tough guy performance. The Riviera looks dreamy, though. Based on Richard Matheson's *Ride the Nightmare.* C: Charles Bronson, Liv Ullmann, James Mason, Jill Ireland. D: Terence Young. ACT [PG] 94m. V

Cold Turkey 1971 ★★★★ Crackling, cruel satire about a small Midwestern town that will win a giant cash prize if everybody in it quits smoking. No-holds-barred exposure of human foibles is wickedly funny and expertly played. C: Dick Van Dyke, Pippa Scott, Bob Newhart, Vincent Gardenia, Barnard Hughes, Jean Stapleton. D: Norman Lear. COM [PG] 99m. V

Cold Wind in August, A 1961 ★★★★ Poignant drama of tender love between a dejected 30ish stripper (Albright) and a slum teenager (Marlowe). Smartly directed, sexually frank, and featuring a sensitive, multilayered performance by Albright. C: Lola

Albright, Scott Marlowe, Herschel Bernardi. D: Alexander Singer. DRA 80m.

Colditz Story 1957 British ★★★★ Suspenseful account of the Nazis' supposedly impregnable prison, Colditz castle, and the efforts of various Allied prisoners to escape. Replete with fascinating detail, and based on the personal experiences of author P.D. Reid. C: John Mills, Eric Portman, Lionel Jeffries, Ian Carmichael, Theodore Bikel. D: Guy Hamilton. ACT 93m. V

Cole Younger, Gunfighter 1958 ★★★ The famed gunslinger finds his reputation repeatedly challenged in 1870s Texas. Moderate, rugged Western gunplay fiction. C: Frank Lovejoy, James Best, Abby Dalton. D: R.G. Springsteen. WST 78m.

Collector, The 1965 ★★★★ A psychopathic butterfly collector (Stamp) adds a beautiful art student (Eggar) to his collection in this disturbing but well-made story of obsession and possession. Both compelling and chilling. From John Fowles' novel. C: Terence Stamp, Samantha Eggar, Mona Washbourne. D: William Wyler. DRA 119m. V

Collector's Item 1989 ★★★½ Musante runs into Antonelli, a woman he had seduced many years before. This chance encounter leads to unexpected circumstances and occasional terror in this offbeat suspense drama. C: Tony Musante, Laura Antonelli, Florinda Bolkan. D: Giuseppe Patroni Griffi. DRA 99m. V

Colleen 1936 ★★★½ Typical Keeler/Powell musical romance without genius of Busby Berkeley to help them out. Veteran character actor Herbert steals film as drunken millionaire. C: Dick Powell, Ruby Keeler, Jack Oakie, Joan Blondell. D: Alfred Green. MUS 89m.

College 1927 ★★★½ Keaton plays a smart college student who decides to become a football hero to win the love of his sweetheart. Not prime Keaton, but loaded with sightgags. C: Buster Keaton, Ann Cornwall. D: James W. Horne. COM 60m. V

College Coach 1933 ★★★½ Mild-mannered chemistry student (Powell) becomes the prize player of a rough football coach (O'Brien). Brisk tale of corruption in collegiate sports. That's USC's John Wayne in a walk-on. C: Dick Powell, Ann Dvorak, Pat O'Brien. D: William Wellman. DRA 75m.

College Confidential 1960 ★★ Chaos ensues in a small town after a sociology professor (Allen) conducts a Kinsey-like sex survey on campus. Spicey stuff for its time masquerading as an "exposé." Impressive guest appearances. C: Steve Allen, Jayne Meadows, Mamie Van Doren, Walter Winchell, Herbert Marshall, Mickey Shaughnessy. D: Albert Zugsmith. DRA 91m.

College Holiday 1936 ★★★ Boland hires Benny to recruit guinea pigs for love experiment she's conducting, but he hires a bunch of college entertainers instead who make enough money to buy an old hotel and everyone's happy. Foolish fluff. C: Jack Benny, George Burns, Gracie Allen, Mary Boland, Martha Raye. D: Frank Tuttle. COM 88m.

College Humor 1933 ★★★½ Professor at small Midwestern college (Crosby) and football Lothario (Arlen) fall for the same young woman (Carlisle) in this modest campus musical, complete with the requisite football game finale. Light and harmless. C: Bing Crosby, Jack Oakie, George Burns, Gracie Allen, Mary Carlisle, Richard Arlen. D: Wesley Ruggles. MUS 80m.

College Swing 1938 ★★ Gracie inherits a college and turns it into venue for vaudevillians. Great cast and premise. C: George Burns, Gracie Allen, Martha Raye, Bob Hope, Edward Everett Horton, Ben Blue, Betty Grable, John Payne. D: Raoul Walsh. MUS 86m. V

Collision Course 1967 *See* **Bamboo Saucer, The**

Collision Course 1975 ★★★ Those in search of a quick lesson on the Korean War conflict between Douglas MacArthur (Fonda) and Harry Truman (Marshall) will find this worthwhile. Those in search of gripping drama should look elsewhere, despite the earnestness of the two stars. C: Henry Fonda, E.G. Marshall, Andrew Duggan, Lucille Benson. D: Anthony Page. DRA 100m. TVM

Collision Course 1987 ★★½ Cop buddy movie about two opposites (Leno and Morita) who band together to break a car smuggling ring. Some action and sporadic laughs in this easily dismissed comedy. C: Jay Leno, Pat Morita. D: Lewis Teague. COM 100m. TVM

Colonel Blimp 1943 *See* **Life and Death of Colonel Blimp**

Colonel Chabert 1994 French ★★★★ Title character (Depardieu) returns from war, after 10 years presumed missing, to find his wife in second, unhappy marriage. Her divorce proceedings are the core of this literate, fascinating drama, beautifully acted. From a novel by French literary giant, Honore de Balzac. Depardieu's experienced with the "missing man's return" theme, from his previous film *The Return of Martin Guerre*. C: Gerard Depardieu, Fanny Ardant, Fabrice Luchini, Andre Dussollier. D: Yves Angelo. DRA 110m. V

Colonel Effingham's Raid 1946 ★★★½ Retired Georgia Confederate colonel (Coburn) deploys soldierly expertise to preserve corrupt town's historical landmark. Capable second feature largely carried by Coburn. Many funny moments. C: Charles Coburn, Joan Bennett. D: Irving Pichel. COM 70m. V

Colonel Redl 1985 German ★★★★ In early 1900s, a military official rises to the top ranks of the Austro-Hungarian empire despite his Jewish background and homosexuality. Engrossing, partly true story is second in a trilogy including *Mephisto* and *Hanussen.* C: Klaus Maria Brandauer, Armin Mueller-Stahl. D: Istvan Szabo. DRA [R] 143m. V

Color Me Dead 1969 U.S. ★★★ Dying man (Tryon) races against time to catch the killer who fatally poisoned him. Inferior remake of *D.O.A.*, but still a good premise with plenty of tension throughout. C: Tom Tryon, Carolyn Jones. D: Eddie Davis. CRI [R] 91m. V

Color of Money, The 1986 ★★★★ Twenty-five years after *The Hustler,* Scorsese brings Newman back for a sequel in a colorful story of the now over-the-hill pool shark who takes a talented kid (Cruise) under his wing and shows him how to play the game. Oscar for Best Actor to Newman. C: Paul Newman, Tom Cruise, Mary Elizabeth Mastrantonio, Helen Shaver, John Turturro. D: Martin Scorsese. DRA [R] 119m. V

Color of Night 1994 ★★ Willis is a New York psychiatrist who moves to Los Angeles after a patient commits suicide. There he throws himself into a sexually charged, dangerous relationship with a mysterious woman (March). Ludicrous, overheated melodrama serves mainly as an excuse for Willis to take his clothes off. The video version includes six minutes of nudity cut for theatrical release. C: Bruce Willis, Jane March, Ruben Blades, Lesley Ann Warren. D: Richard Rush. CRI [R] 123m. V

Color of Pomegranates, The 1969 ★★★★ Armenian poet-martyr Sayat Nova's life is given avant-garde treatment; Paradjanov jettisons narrative for selection of beautifully textured images. More like a visual poem than a conventional film. C: Sophico Chiaourelli, V. Galstian. D: Sergei Paradjanov. DRA 80m. V

Color Purple, The 1985 ★★★★ Spielberg's earnest screen adaptation of Alice Walker's powerful novel about a poor black woman abused by her brutal husband was praised as moving drama by some, judged as superficial and glib by others. Affecting performances (particularly Winfrey, in her screen debut) and lush cinematography are the highlights here. C: Danny Glover, Whoopi Goldberg, Margaret Avery, Oprah Winfrey, Adolph Caesar, Larry Fishburne. D: Steven Spielberg. DRA [PG-13] 154m. V

Colorado Territory 1949 ★★★★ Fugitive convict (McCrea) plans a final robbery before reforming. Solid fast-paced outdoor action story. Walsh's Western remake of *High Sierra.* C: Joel McCrea, Virginia Mayo, Dorothy Malone, Henry Hull. D: Raoul Walsh. WST 94m.

Colors 1988 ★★★★ In first film to accurately portray the brutal realities of the Los Angeles gangs, aging cop Duvall must temper and teach young rookie Penn the realities of life on the street. Performances are stark, Hopper's direction is solid. C: Sean Penn, Robert Duvall, Maria Conchita Alonso. D: Dennis Hopper. CRI [R] 127m. V

Colors of War, The 1971 ★★★ Clips from WWII combat films directed by John Huston and William Wyler, and narrated by James Stewart. Two volume set. D: John Huston. DOC 60m. V

Colossus of New York, The 1958 ★★½ Man transplants his dead scientist son's brain into a huge robot which runs amok in Gotham. No surprises in this comic-book bosh with laughable plot holes. C: John Baragrey, Mala Powers, Otto Kruger. D: Eugene Lourie. SFI 70m.

Colossus of Rhodes, The 1960 Italian ★★★½ Leone's directorial flair is on view in this well-produced epic about slaves against noblemen in ancient Greece. C: Rory Calhoun, Lea Massari, Georges Marchal. D: Sergio Leone. ACT 128m.

Colossus: The Forbin Project 1970 ★★★★ Superintelligent and independent-minded computer overrides its masters in effort to achieve global control. A high-brow and thought-provoking cautionary fable. Nicely acted by little-known ensemble. (a.k.a. *The Forbin Project*) C: Eric Braeden, Susan Clark. D: Joseph Sargent. SFI 100m. V

Colt .45 1950 ★★★ When gun vendor Scott's supply of Colt 45s is stolen by a band of outlaws, he must save the day by retrieving the weapons. Plenty of action follows! (a.k.a. *Thundercloud*) C: Randolph Scott, Zachary Scott, Ruth Roman, Lloyd Bridges. D: Edwin Marin. WST 74m.

Columbo: Murder By the Book 1971 ★★★½ Trench-coated detective (Falk) investigates the murder of a mystery writer. Engaging TV-movie version of the successful television series. Writer Steven Bochco later created *Hill Street Blues, L.A. Law* and *NYPD Blue.* C: Peter Falk, Jack Cassidy, Martin Milner, Rosemary Forsyth. D: Steven Spielberg. CRI 79m. V

Columbo: Prescription Murder 1967 ★★★★ Unkempt, unrelenting but unfailingly polite detective (Falk) attempts to uncover the killer of the wife of a cocky psychiatrist (Barry). Multiple subplots and red herrings make this a treat. Columbo's debut; adapted by authors Levinson and Link from their Broadway play. C: Peter Falk, Gene Barry, Nina Foch, Katherine Justice, William Windom. D: Richard Irving. CRI 99m. V

Column South 1953 ★★★ Union cavalry officer during the Civil War sides with hostile Navajos in an effort to end bloodshed. Durable but slow-moving Murphy second feature. C: Audie Murphy, Joan Evans. D: Frederick De Cordova. WST 85m.

Coma 1978 ★★★★ New surgeon (Bujold) at a large city hospital becomes suspicious when too many patients start lapsing into comas. Edge-of-your-seat medical thriller ably handled by Crichton from Robin Cook's novel. C: Genevieve Bujold, Michael Douglas, Elizabeth Ashley, Rip Torn, Richard Widmark. D: Michael Crichton. DRA [PG] 113m. V

Comanche 1956 ★★★ Warring Comanches carry off a prominent Spaniard's daughter in 1875 New Mexico, and a cavalry scout (Andrews) intervenes to bring peace. Competent Western action film. C: Dana Andrews, Kent Smith, Linda Cristal. D: George Sherman. WST 87m.

Comanche Station 1960 ★★★★ Western marshal (Scott) heads up a perilous rescue mission to find his wife, who was abducted by Comanches. Typically above-par Scott adventure. Taut and gripping. C: Randolph Scott, Nancy Gates, Claude Akins. D: Budd Boetticher. WST 74m.

Comanche Territory 1950 ★★★ Knife-wielding frontiersman Jim Bowie comes to the aid of Comanches at the mercy of land-grabbing white men. Nothing special in intent or delivery. Big Jim must've stopped by on his way to the Alamo. C: Maureen O'Hara, Macdonald Carey, Will Geer. D: George Sherman. WST 76m.

Comancheros, The 1961 ★★★★ Gambling, guns, and booze are the enemy, and a Texas ranger (Wayne) is determined to clean house in Indian territory. Absorbing and well-made. Wayne in his element. C: John Wayne, Stuart Whitman, Lee Marvin, Ina Balin. D: Michael Curtiz. WST 107m. V

Combat Academy 1986 ★★½ Rambunctious delinquents sent to military academy where they continue their rampage of practical joking. Lame, juvenile comedy and silly, over-the-top performances. C: Keith Gordon, Jamie Farr, Sherman Hemsley, John Ratzenberger. D: Neal Israel. COM 96m. V

Combat Squad 1953 ★★½ A frightened young recruit proves himself under fire during the Korean War. Thin wartime rite of passage. C: John Ireland, Lon McCallister. D: Cy Roth. ACT 72m.

Combination Platter 1993 ★★★★ An illegal Hong Kong immigrant, working at a Chinese eatery in Queens, tries to become a U.S. citizen by marrying an American woman. Modest comedy-drama tackles some tough questions with disarming charm. C: Jeff Lau, Colleen O'Brian. D: Tony Chan. COM 84m. V

Come and Get It 1936 ★★★★ Brooding Edna Ferber period piece dealing with the greed and family conflicts of a Midwestern lumber town. It's all here—money, power, and romance. Oscar for Best Supporting Actor went to Brennan. C: Edward Arnold, Joel McCrea, Frances Framer, Walter Brennan, Andrea Leeds. D: Howard Hawks, William Wyler. DRA 99m. V

Come and See 1985 Russian ★★★★ Soviet youth witnesses firsthand horrors of Nazi onslaught during WWII. Grim, relentless account of wartime brutality and anarchy. C: Alexei Kravchenko, Olga Mironova. D: Elem Klimov. DRA 142m.

Come Back, Charleston Blue 1972 ★★★ In this unworthy sequel to *Cotton Comes to Harlem*, detectives Coffin Johnson and Gravedigger Jones investigate white and black gangs vying for Harlem's heroin traffic. Violent. C: Raymond St. Jacques, Godfrey Cambridge, Jonelle Allen. D: Mark Warren. CRI [PG] 100m.

Come Back, Little Sheba 1952 ★★★★½ Booth won a well-deserved Oscar in this drama of an unhappy marriage unmasked by college boarder Moore's probings. Lancaster is excellent as Booth's drunken husband. Adapted from William Inge's play. C: Shirley Booth, Burt Lancaster, Terry Moore, Richard Jaeckel. D: Daniel Mann. DRA 99m. V

Come Back to the Five and Dime, Jimmy Dean, Jimmy Dean 1982 ★★★★ Six old friends and a mysterious stranger (Black) gather in a run-down Texas convenience store, where one of them (Dennis) claims to have given birth to film star James Dean's child. Weak Broadway play is given strong performances, by an excellent cast under Altman's incisive direction. The final credit sequence is a knockout. C: Sandy Dennis, Cher, Karen Black, Sudie Bond, Kathy Bates. D: Robert Altman. DRA [PG] 109m. V

Come Blow Your Horn 1963 ★★★★ Man-about-town Sinatra takes in younger brother Bill and shows him the ropes in this film version of Neil Simon's first play. Diverting, with a confident Frank at the helm. C: Frank Sinatra, Tony Bill, Lee J. Cobb, Molly Picon, Barbara Rush, Jill St. John. D: Bud Yorkin. COM 115m. V

Come Dance with Me! 1960 French ★★★½ When her dentist husband is charged with killing a woman he picked up in a bar, a sexy Frenchwoman (Bardot) tracks down the actual murderer. Deft merging of comedy and mystery. C: Brigitte Bardot, Henri Vidal. D: Michel Boisrond. COM 91m.

Come Fill the Cup 1951 ★★★★ A newspaperman Cagney tries to overcome alcoholism, with the help of a friend (Gleason) who's been there. Powerful performances more than make up for the implausible script. C: James Cagney, Phyllis Thaxter, Gig Young, Raymond Massey. D: Gordon Douglas. DRA 113m.

Come Fly with Me 1963 ★★ Three attractive flight attendants are determined to marry well. Vacant hijinks aloft; easy viewing. C: Hugh O'Brian, Pamela Tiffin, Dolores Hart, Lois Nettleton, Karl Malden. D: Henry Levin. COM 109m.

Come Live With Me 1941 ★★★½ Struggling American writer (Stewart) marries a beautiful Austrian woman (Lamarr) to prevent her deportation. Engaging romantic comedy. Predictable but well done by all. C: James

Stewart, Hedy Lamarr. D: Clarence Brown. COM 86m.

Come 'n Get It 1980 *See* **Lunch Wagon**

Come Next Spring 1956 ★★★★ After eight years of drifting, an Arkansas farmer returns to home and hearth. Warm countrified drama is smartly done. C: Ann Sheridan, Steve Cochran, Walter Brennan. D: R.G. Springsteen. DRA 92m.

Come-On, The 1956 ★★★ Hardened confidence artist (Baxter) gets embroiled in a homicide case. Baxter's spirited performance overcomes banal crime yarn. C: Anne Baxter, Sterling Hayden, John Hoyt, Jesse White. D: Russell Birdwell. CRI 83m.

Come Out Fighting 1945 ★★★ The East Side Kids add a young lady and a judge's son to their ranks. Okay entry for the cheerful juvenile series, and the final installment before being remade as *The Bowery Boys*. C: Leo Gorcey, Huntz Hall, Billy Benedict, Gabriel Dell. D: William Beaudine. COM 62m.

Come See the Paradise 1990 ★★★ Appealing love story set during one of U.S.'s darkest moments, the shameful internment of Japanese-Americans during WWII. Though flawed by lack of continuity, merits watching both for history lesson and Tomita's enchanting performance. C: Dennis Quaid, Tamlyn Tomita, Sab Shimono. D: Alan Parker. DRA 135m. V

Come September 1961 ★★★★ A millionaire (Hudson) is outraged that Lollobrigida is using his villa as a hotel when he's not around. Surprisingly amusing sex comedy, thanks to attractive stars and a droll script. C: Rock Hudson, Gina Lollobrigida, Sandra Dee, Bobby Darin, Walter Slezak, Joel Grey. D: Robert Mulligan. COM 112m.

Come Spy With Me 1967 ★★½ Intelligence agent tangles with killers in Jamaica. Empty would-be spy spoof. Good Caribbean locales. C: Troy Donahue, Andrea Dromm, Albert Dekker. D: Marshall Stone. ACT 85m.

Come to the Stable 1949 ★★★★ Young and Holm are WWII refugee nuns in New England, trying to raise money to build a children's hospital. Sentimental fable with a charming cast; good Christmas fare. C: Loretta Young, Celeste Holm, Hugh Marlowe, Elsa Lanchester. D: Henry Koster. FAM/DRA 94m.

Comeback, The 1979 British ★ An American singer reviving his flagging career gets caught up in a string of grisly murders. Bloody and unduly long crime tale. C: Jack Jones, Pamela Stephenson. D: Pete Walker. CRI 100m. V

Comeback Trail, The 1974 ★★½ Two B-movie producers (McCann and Staats) star a washed-up cowboy hero (Crabbe) in a box office flop they intend to turn into an insurance windfall. Economical farce with numerous film buff jokes and guest appearances. Originally filmed in the '70s, but not released until 1982. C: Chuck McCann, Buster Crabbe, Robert Staats, Ina Balin. D: Harry Hurwitz. COM 80m.

Comedians, The 1967 ★★ Stars are unable to energize this muddled adaptation of Graham Greene's novel about political plotting in Haiti under the Papa Doc Duvalier dictatorship. C: Elizabeth Taylor, Richard Burton, Alec Guinness, Peter Ustinov, Paul Ford, Lillian Gish, Raymond St. Jacques, James Earl Jones, Cicely Tyson. D: Peter Glenville. DRA 148m. V

Comedy of Terrors, The 1964 ★★★½ Minor but very amusing horror comedy boasts solid lineup of genre veterans. Funeral parlor owner (Price) and unwilling henchman (Lorre) bump off various victims to boost business, including one (Rathbone) who won't stay down. C: Vincent Price, Peter Lorre, Boris Karloff, Basil Rathbone, Joe E. Brown. D: Jacques Tourneur. HOR 84m. V

Comes a Horseman 1978 ★★★ In post-WWII Montana a greedy cattle baron (Robards) wants another rancher's (Fonda's) land. A big oil company wants everybody's land. Fonda and Caan just want to fall in love. Contemporary but cliched Western does feature a gem of a performance by Farnsworth (who received an Oscar nomination for his work). C: Jane Fonda, James Caan, Richard Farnsworth, Jason Robards, George Grizzard, Mark Harmon. D: Alan J. Pakula. WST [PG] 118m. V

Comet Over Broadway 1938 ★★½ Murder forces a stage actress (Francis) to choose between her career and her family. Fatuous backstage soap opera with unintentional laughs. C: Kay Francis, Ian Hunter, Donald Crisp. D: Busby Berkeley. DRA 69m.

Comfort and Joy 1984 British ★★★★ Abandoned by his girlfriend, a Glasgow DJ goes out in search of something that will give life meaning, and stumbles into the middle of an inter-family ice cream war. Typical Forsyth comedy—charming, with quirky, memorable characters, and more than a little to say about the world at large. C: Bill Paterson, Eleanor David. D: Bill Forsyth. COM [PG] 93m. V

Comfort of Strangers, The 1991 Italian ★★★★ While on a second honeymoon in Venice, trying to invigorate a stale marriage, Richardson and Everett encounter a mysterious couple (Walker and Mirren). Dark, unnerving story builds, through repetition and oddity, to a shocking finale. Written by Harold Pinter. C: Christopher Walken, Natasha Richardson, Rupert Everett, Helen Mirren. D: Paul Schrader. DRA [R] 102m. V

Comic Book Confidential 1990 U.S. ★★★ Engaging view of underground comic book creators, including Robert Crumb and Harvey Pekar. Makes point about illustrators as social commentators. D: Ron Mann. DOC 85m. V

Comic Strip Hero 1967 *See* **Killing Game, The**

Comic, The 1969 ★★★★ Underrated look at the world of silent film comedy from the point of view of a self-destructive genius, well played by Van Dyke. Funny re-creations of slapstick alternate with searing dramatic scenes. C: Dick Van Dyke, Michele Lee, Mickey Rooney, Cornel Wilde. D: Carl Reiner. DRA [PG] 96m. v

Comin' at Ya! 1981 Italian ★★ Reformed outlaw goes after the three desperados who abducted his betrothed. Inferior spaghetti-Western spoof with 3-D tricks. C: Tony Anthony, Gene Quintano. D: Ferdinando Baldi. WST [R] 91m. v

Comin' Round the Mountain 1951 ★★½ Two goofs (Abbott and Costello) get involved with feuding hillbillies. Corny entry for the legendary duo. C: Bud Abbott, Lou Costello, Dorothy Shay. D: Charles Lamont. COM 77m.

Coming Apart 1969 ★★½ Unstable New York psychoanalyst secretly films troubled female visitors and his own breakdown, in his apartment. So pathetic, it's mesmerizing. C: Rip Torn, Viveca Lindfors, Sally Kirkland. D: Milton Ginsberg. DRA 110m.

Coming Home 1978 ★★★★★ Compelling Vietnam War-era drama chronicles the awakening of one woman (army wife Fonda) when she falls in love with a paraplegic veteran (and anti-war activist) Voight while her husband (Dern) goes to war. An important film about the effects of the war at home. Oscars for Best Actor (Voight), Actress, and Original Screenplay. C: Jane Fonda, Jon Voight, Bruce Dern, Robert Carradine. D: Hal Ashby. DRA [R] 127m. v

Coming-Out Party 1934 ★★½ Her parents object when a debutante (Dee) is romanced by a jazz musician (Raymond). Weary tale of uptowners and ham 'n' eggers. C: Frances Dee, Gene Raymond, Alison Skipworth, Nigel Bruce. D: John Blystone. DRA 79m.

Coming Soon 1983 ★★★ Entertaining compilation of coming-attractions trailers from Universal horror films, hosted by Jamie Lee Curtis. Quality of the material varies, but stick with it for the final entry, Hitchcock's wonderfully witty *Psycho* trailer. C: Jamie Lee Curtis. D: John Landis. HOR 55m. v

Coming Through 1985 British ★★½ D.H. Lawrence's courtship of wife-to-be Frieda von Richthofer is interwoven with a modern story about a man who struggles to understand Lawrence's writings. Branagh and Mirren are splendid as the combative literary couple, but slow-moving film captures nothing of Lawrence's passion. See the Australian film *Kangaroo* for a different view of Lawrence and Frieda. C: Kenneth Branagh, Helen Mirren. D: Peter Fleming. DRA 80m.

Coming to America 1988 ★★★★ African royalty meets African-American womanhood in this light but engaging Murphy vehicle. When the prince (Murphy) arrives in Queens to find a bride he gets his regal head turned around. Fun comedy, most famous for humor columnist Art Buchwald's successful plagiarism suit. C: Eddie Murphy, Arsenio Hall, James Earl Jones, John Amos, Madge Sinclair. D: John Landis. COM [R] 116m. v

Coming Up Roses 1986 British ★★★ Small-town satire as people band together to save the local movie theater by growing mushrooms inside! Not bad; dialogue spoken in Welsh. C: Dafydd Hywel, Iola Gregory. D: Stephen Bayly. COM [PG] 90m. v

Command Decision 1948 ★★★★ Gable leads an A-list cast as a rugged brigadier general in charge of an Air Force mission against a secret Nazi target. Taut direction and rousing score enhance the impact of this powerful film about the moral dilemmas forced upon men in war. C: Clark Gable, Walter Pidgeon, Van Johnson, Brian Donlevy, Charles Bickford, John Hodiak, Cameron Mitchell. D: Sam Wood. ACT 112m. v

Command, The 1954 ★★★ Cavalry medic leads a wagon train through hostile Indian territory in Wyoming. Durable second-string Western, the first in CinemaScope. C: Guy Madison, Joan Weldon, James Whitmore. D: David Butler. WST 88m.

Commando 1985 ★★★ High-body-count tale has ex-commando Schwarzenegger back in action when his daughter (Milano) is kidnapped by a bloodthirsty South American general (Hedaya) seeking power and revenge. C: Arnold Schwarzenegger, Rae Dawn Chong, Dan Hedaya, Alyssa Milano. D: Mark L. Lester. ACT [R] 90m. v

Commandos Strike at Dawn, The 1942 ★★★½ When German troops attack his homeland, a Norwegian (Muni) works with British forces to save his compatriots. Star power helps this minor war drama do more than its now bygone purpose as a morale booster for the WWII home front. C: Paul Muni, Anna Lee, Lillian Gish, Cedric Hardwicke, Ray Collins, Rosemary DeCamp. D: John Farrow. ACT 100m. v

Commissar 1967 Soviet ★★★★ An anti-Semitic commissar is forced to hide out with Jewish peasants to keep her pregnancy secret from her comrades. More accomplished than most Russian films of the Communist era, this moving drama was banned by its government and not seen in this country until 1988. C: Nouna Mordyuhova, Rolan Byhov. D: Alexander Askoldov. DRA 105m. v

Commitments, The 1991 British ★★★★ Rambunctious tale of ambitious Irish youths who form a soul band is high-spirited fun. Features great music, a witty script, energetic direction and exuberant performances. C: Robert Arkins, Michael Aherne, Angeline Ball, Maria Doyle, Dave Finnegan. D: Alan Parker. DRA [R] 116m. v

Common Bonds 1991 ★★★ Social science is the bad guy in this predictable tale of two subjects of an experimental project who decide to buck the system. C: Brad Dourif, Rae Dawn Chong, Michael Ironside. D: Allan A. Goldstein. DRA 109m. V

Common Ground 1990 ★★★½ Story of the desegregation of Boston's public schools centers on two opposing mothers—well-played by Curtin and Pounder. Fair treatment of a highly volatile issue, but hurt by casting mistakes. Based on J. Anthony Lukas' Pulitzer-Prize-winning book. C: Jane Curtin, CCH Pounder, Richard Thomas, James Farentino. D: Mike Newell. DRA 200m. TVM

Common Threads: Stories From the Quilt ★★★★★ Tales behind the many panels that made up the AIDS quilt, which was laid out on the Mall in Washington, D.C. Almost unbearably emotional in its personalizing of the AIDS epidemic; narrated by Dustin Hoffman. Oscar for Best Documentary. D: Robert Epstein, Jeffrey Friedman. DOC 80m. V

Communion 1977 *See* **Alice, Sweet Alice**

Communion 1989 ★★★ True story of author Whitley Strieber who claims he was abducted and tormented by aliens. Slow and uneven, but Walken is compelling as a man unsure of his sanity. Adapted by Strieber from his best-seller. C: Christopher Walken, Lindsay Crouse, Frances Sternhagen. D: Philippe Mora. SFI [R] 103m. V

Company Business 1991 ★★★ Adventure/comedy featuring a CIA agent (Hackman) who must escort KGB agent (Baryshnikov) to a spy swap. When things don't go as planned, they must become allies to stay alive. Set in post-Cold War Eastern Europe, the film settles for standard action instead of exploring its interesting premise. C: Gene Hackman, Mikhail Baryshnikov, Terry O'Quinn. D: Nicholas Meyer. ACT [PG-13] 99m. V

Company of Wolves, The 1984 British ★★★★ Fascinating early work from director Jordan, adapting the Red Riding Hood story into a parable of lost innocence and the temptation of animal urges. Atmospheric and scary; a thinking person's werewolf film. C: Angela Lansbury, David Warner, Stephen Rea. D: Neil Jordan. HOR [R] 95m. V

Company She Keeps, The 1950 ★★★½ A parole officer and ex-con vie for the same man. Moody melodrama benefits from gritty script and good performances by Scott and Greer as the adversaries. C: Lizabeth Scott, Jane Greer, Dennis O'Keefe. D: John Cromwell. DRA 83m.

Competition, The 1980 ★★★ Irving and Dreyfuss compete for a classical piano scholarship in a predictable romantic drama. Musical sequences are obviously faked. C: Richard Dreyfuss, Amy Irving, Lee Remick, Sam Wanamaker. D: Joel Oliansky. DRA [PG] 123m. V

Compleat Beatles, The 1982 ★★★★ Chronological summing up of the Fab Four's extraordinary run at the top of the rock music world. Generous supply of little-seen clips and snippets of many great songs make for a breezy, intelligent overview of John's, Paul's, George's and Ringo's influence on popular culture. Narrated by Malcolm McDowell. D: Patrick Montgomery. DOC 190m. V

Compliments of Mr. Flow 1941 French ★★★½ Wily safecracker lives life of luxury in jail, compliments of his outside criminal connections. Clever farce goes off the rails occasionally, but is good fun. C: Fernand Gravet, Edwige Feuillere, Louis Jouvet. D: Robert Slodmak. COM 80m.

Compromising Positions 1985 ★★★★ Sarandon stars as a journalist turned homemaker investigating the murder of a promiscuous Long Island dentist. Charming cast makes this suburban comedy quirkily appealing. C: Susan Sarandon, Raul Julia, Edward Herrmann, Judith Ivey, Mary Beth Hurt, Joe Mantegna, Joan Allen. D: Frank Perry. COM [R] 99m. V

Compulsion 1959 ★★★★ Fictionalized account of the notorious '20s Leopold-Loeb case. College students (Stockwell, Dillman), convinced of their intellectual superiority, kidnap and murder a boy for fun. Courtroom drama highlighted by excellent acting and direction. *Rope* and *Swoon* also tell the story. C: Orson Welles, Dean Stockwell, Bradford Dillman, Diane Varsi, E.G. Marshall. D: Richard Fleischer. CRI 103m.

Computer Dreams 1988 ★★ Amanda Pays shows viewer the world of computer animation from graphics to consumer product design. Interesting but dated. C: Amanda Pays. DOC 58m. V

Computer Killers 1973 *See* **Horror Hospital**

Computer Visions 1991 ★★ Applications of "the latest" in computer-aided animation are shown in daily-life situations. Some helpful material, but technology has passed it by. DOC 30m. V

Computer Wore Tennis Shoes, The 1970 ★★★ A college student (Russell) is accidentally implanted with a computer-capacity brain, then chased by a mob led by Romero. Goofy Disney comedy; harmless time-waster for the very young. Remade for TV in 1995. Sequel: *Now You See Him, Now You Don't.* C: Kurt Russell, Cesar Romero, Joe Flynn. D: Robert Butler. COM [G] 91m. V

Comrade X 1940 ★★★½ American newspaperman (Gable) tries to defrost icy reserve of a Russian street car conductor (Lamarr). Charming tale of opposites attracting benefits from romantic sparks between Gable and Lamarr. C: Clark Gable, Hedy Lamarr, Felix Bressart, Oscar Homolka, Eve Arden. D: King Vidor. COM 90m. V

Comrades of Summer, The 1992 ★★★★ A self-absorbed baseball manager's last chance to remain in the game is to relocate to Russia and prepare a miserably inept gang of athletes for Olympic competition. Strong script and spirited cast make this comedy a winner. C: Joe Mantegna, Natalya Negoda, Michael Lerner. D: Tommy Lee Wallace. COM [R] 90m. V

Conagher 1991 ★★★½ Elliott plays a cowhand who comes to the aid of abandoned frontier wife Ross. Good-looking and well-played adaptation of novel by Louis L'Amour. C: Sam Elliott, Katharine Ross. D: Reynaldo Villalobos. WST 117m. TVM V

Conan the Barbarian 1982 ★★ Adventures of a muscle-bound hero (Schwarzenegger) seeking vengeance for the murder of his parents. Barbarism, misogyny, and stilted dialogue abound; unintentionally hilarious. C: Arnold Schwarzenegger, Sandahl Bergman, James Earl Jones, Mako, Max von Sydow. D: John Milius. ACT [R] 129m. V

Conan the Destroyer 1984 ★★½ Another ponderous vehicle for the sword-wielding hero. This time Conan and three sidekicks (Walter, Mako, Chamberlain) search for a magic crystal. C: Arnold Schwarzenegger, Grace Jones, Wilt Chamberlain, Mako, Sarah Douglas. D: Richard Fleischer. ACT [PG] 101m. V

Concentration Camp 1939 U.S.S.R. ★★★½ An underground labor group escapes from the clutches of Nazi Germany. Although basically Communist propaganda, this gritty, realistic film offers an interesting, well-done look at Hitler's war machine. C: O. Jakov, S. Shirokova, S. Mezhinsky, I. Kudriatsev. D: A. Macharet. DRA 60m.

Concerning Mr. Martin 1937 ★★★★ Innocent young woman is conned by a sleazy club owner, and she enlists the aid of a thief to recover her money. Well-made thriller provides plenty of fun and excitement. C: Wilson Barrett, William Devlin, Marjorie Peacock. D: Roy Kellino. CRI 59m.

Concert for Bangladesh, The 1971 ★★★★ Simple presentation of famous all-star rock concert to benefit flood-ravaged country. Many top-notch performances include those of Bob Dylan and Eric Clapton. C: George Harrison, Ringo Starr, Eric Clapton, Bob Dylan, Ravi Shankar. MUS [G] 90m. V

Concerto 1946 *See* **I've Always Loved You**

Concrete Cowboys 1979 *See* **Ramblin' Man**

Concrete Jungle, The 1960 British ★★★★ Hard-hitting study of criminal life, about a perennial con (Baker) pulling off a racetrack heist, then trying to hold on to the loot while in prison. Great performance from Baker, fine direction. (a.k.a. *The Criminal*) C: Stanley Baker, Sam Wanamaker, Margit Saad. D: Joseph Losey. CRI 86m.

Condemned 1929 ★★★ Man condemned to Devil's Island falls in love with the warden's wife. Early prison movie hasn't aged too well thanks to old-fashioned performance styles. Good in its day, though. C: Ronald Colman, Ann Harding. D: Wesley Ruggles. DRA 86m.

Condemned of Altona, The 1963 ★★★½ A wealthy German (March), facing death attempts to sort out his affairs and settle his problems with his sons. Tough order: one's an insane Nazi (Schell), the other a callous playboy (Wagner). Melodrama based on a play by Jean-Paul Sartre. C: Sophia Loren, Fredric March, Robert Wagner, Maximilian Schell. D: Vittorio DeSica. DRA 114m.

Condorman 1981 British ★★ Cartoonist (Crawford) adopts the persona of Condorman, his comic book character, to rescue beautiful, defecting Russian spy (Carrera). Reed is the villain out to thwart them both. Silly, tedious effort hampered by poor premise and so-so acting. C: Michael Crawford, Oliver Reed, Barbara Carrera. D: Charles Jarrott. FAM/ACT [PG] 90m. V

Conduct Unbecoming 1975 British ★★★½ Old-fashioned courtroom drama, concerning an alleged assault of a British officer's widow in India's northwest frontier in the late 19th century. Dated but engrossing, with outstanding performances. C: Michael York, Richard Attenborough, Stacey Keach, Trevor Howard, Christopher Plummer, Susannah York. D: Michael Anderson. DRA 107m.

Conductor, The ★★★½ Distinguished classical music conductor (Gielgud) returns to homeland in Poland to conduct local orchestra. Tempers clash and the music soars in this intriguing entry by the great Polish director Wadja. Good performance by Gielgud despite inept dubbing. DRA V

Coneheads, The 1993 ★★★½ Aykroyd, Curtin, and Burke are back as the "French" family next door, late of the planet Remulak. Familiar schtick will satisfy die-hard fans of this popular *Saturday Night Live* segment; others may find its one-note joke lacking. C: Dan Aykroyd, Jane Curtin, Chris Farley, Garrett Morris, Phil Hartman. D: Steve Barron. COM [PG] 87m. V

Coney Island 1943 ★★★★ Bright, colorful period musical with Grable showing off her legs as night club singer promoted into Broadway star by con artist Montgomery. Remade with Grable in 1950 as *Wabash Avenue*. C: Betty Grable, George Montgomery, Cesar Romero, Charles Winninger, Phil Silvers. D: Walter Lang. MUS 96m.

Confess, Dr. Corda 1958 German ★★ Innocent doctor tries to clear himself of his mistress' murder. Stiff performances, especially the miscast Kruger. C: Hardy Kruger, Elisabeth Mueller. D: Josef Baky. CRI 81m.

Confession 1937 ★★★★ Soapy thriller served up with striking continental flair by director May. Singer Francis kills rat (Rathbone), who once separated her from family, when he starts making advances to daughter Bryan years later. Good acting and striking cinematography. C: Kay Francis, Basil Rathbone, Ian Hunter, Donald Crisp, Laura Hope Crews. D: Joe May. CRI 86m.

Confession, The 1970 ★★★★ Costa-Gavras' follow-up to his international hit *Z* concerns devoted Communist party member tortured by party leaders into false confession. Harrowing study of interrogation is difficult to sit through due to stark brutality. Those who remain with it will find the experience rewarding. C: Yves Montand, Simone Signoret, Gabriele Ferzetti. D: Costa Gavras. DRA [PG] 138m.

Confessions of a Nazi Spy 1939 ★★★½ Well-paced but somewhat bland thriller, shot in interesting semidocumentary style by Litvak, has G-man routing American Nazi ring. Robinson, Lederer, and Lukas (doing a Hitler imitation) are all fine. C: Edward Robinson, Francis Lederer, George Sanders, Paul Lukas, James Stephenson, Sig Rumann. D: Anatole Litvak. DRA 102m.

Confessions of a Newlywed 1941 French ★★★★ An entomologist's assistant is engaged to his boss' daughter, but doesn't quite know what to do next. Amusing, witty, well-handled comedy, features a good cast and fun story. C: Raimu, Sylvia Bataille, Pierre Brasseur. D: Leo Joannon. COM 80m.

Confessions of a Peeping John 1970 *See* **Hi, Mom!**

Confessions of a Police Captain 1972 Italian ★★★½ An honest cop (Balsam) fights corruption while trying to capture vicious mobsters. Balsam is fine in this standard cop story. C: Martin Balsam, Franco Nero. D: Damiano Damiani. CRI [PG] 104m. V

Confessions of a Rogue 1948 French ★★★★ Jouvet plays the rogue, in six different guises, who tries to sell museums to gullible investors. Sharp, witty farce has a terrific cast. Jouvet is marvelous. C: Louis Jouvet, Suzy Delair, Annette Poivre, Jane Marken. D: Constantin Geftman. COM 84m.

Confessions of a Serial Killer 1987 ★★★ Surprisingly effective low-budget horror entry, with captured murderer Burns recounting his violent exploits. Based on the same true case that inspired the superior *Henry: Portrait of a Serial Killer*, this film alternates between the gratuitous and the gripping. C: Robert A. Burns, Dennis Hill. D: Mark Blair. HOR 85m. V

Confessions of Amans, The 1977 ★★★★ Tutor falls for his student's attractive mother. This warm and intelligent rite-of-passage saga was made for only $20,000! Producers used several costumes from *El Cid*. C: William Bryan, Michael St. John, Susannah MacMillan. D: Gregory Nava. DRA 90m.

Confessions of Boston Blackie 1941 ★★★½ Blackie busts up a ring of murderers disguised as an art forgery racket. Exciting early series entry is full of twists and turns, as Blackie stays barely ahead of the killers and the law. C: Chester Morris, George E. Stone, Harriet Hilliard (Nelson), Richard Lane. D: Edward Dmytryk. CRI

Confessions of Felix Krull, The 1958 German ★★★½ A lowly Parisian hotel employee has a wonderful time rising to the top of society. Entertaining adaptation of Thomas Mann novel. C: Horst Buchholz, Lilo Pulver. D: Kurt Hoffman. COM 107m.

Confessor 1973 ★★★½ Symbolistic story of the lost American Dream features an all-knowing confessor trying to help a woman come to terms with the sterility of her mate. Often funny parable (made in the darkest days of the Vietnam War) doesn't date well but is worth a look. C: Robert Waterhouse, Helen Dream. D: Edward Bergman. COM 83m.

Confidence 1979 Hungarian ★★★★ Married (though not to each other) pair have to pose as husband and wife to slip through Nazi lines, and they fall in love. Another intriguing, humanistic look at WWII by Hungarian director Szabo (*Mephisto*). C: Ildiko Bansagi, Peter Andorai, Karoly Csaki. D: Istvan Szabo. DRA 117m.

Confidential 1935 ★★★½ Nifty little B-picture about a G-man (Cook) going to the ends of the earth after a dangerous criminal (Naish). C: Donald Cook, Evalyn Knapp, J. Carrol Naish, Warren Hymer. D: Edward L. Cahn. CRI 67m.

Confidential Agent 1945 ★★★★ Espionage during the Spanish Civil War. Graham Greene's moving story is brought to life by solid performances. C: Charles Boyer, Lauren Bacall, Peter Lorre, Katina Paxinou. D: Herman Shumlin. DRA 118m.

Confidential Report 1955 *See* **Mr. Arkadin**

Confidentially Connie 1953 ★★★½ Pregnant wife tries to steer her passive husband out of his unrewarding teaching job. Amusing fluff features likable performances by Leigh and Calhern. C: Van Johnson, Janet Leigh, Louis Calhern, Walter Slezak, Gene Lockhart. D: Edward Buzzell. COM 74m.

Confidentially Yours 1983 French ★★★★ Falsely charged with murder, realtor Trintignant hides out while his secretary Ardant plays sleuth to clear him. Truffaut's final feature, while not his sharpest, is still entertaining fare. C: Jean-Louis Trintignant, Fanny Ardant, Philippe Laudenbach. D: Francois Truffaut. CRI [PG] 110m. V

Conflagration 1958 Japanese ★★★★ Troubled man reacts to hypocrisy and corruption by torching a beautiful temple. Ichikawa's adaptation of Yukio Mishima's novel *The Temple of the Golden Pavilion* is compelling and exquisitely photographed. (a.k.a. *Enjo* and *The Flame of Torment*.) C: Raizo Ichikawa, Tatsuya Nakadai, Ganjiro Nakamura, Yoko Uraji, Tanie Kitabayashi. D: Kon Ichikawa. DRA 96m. V

Conflict 1939 French ★★★½ A Married woman adopts her sister's illegitimate child. When sister meets another man and falls in love the real father of the child shows up and demands to be paid off. Sensitive melodrama is given tasteful treatment. C: Corinne Luchaire, Annie Ducaux, Claude Dauphin. D: Leonide Moguy. DRA 94m.

Conflict 1945 ★★★½ Man plots to kill his wife so he can marry her sister. Convoluted melodrama with a terrific cast. C: Humphrey Bogart, Alexis Smith, Sydney Greenstreet. D: Curtis Bernhardt. DRA 86m.

Conflict of Wings 1954 *See* **Fuss Over Feathers**

Conflict, The 1973 *See* **Catholics**

Conformist, The 1970 Italian ★★★★★ Trintignant as a repressed homosexual trying to survive within fascist regime of WWII-era Italy. His conscience is put to the test when he is ordered to assassinate a former teacher. Compelling character and social study, tensely directed by Bertolucci. C: Jean-Louis Trintignant, Stefania Sandrelli, Dominique Sanda. D: Bernardo Bertolucci. DRA [R] 108m. V

Congress Dances 1931 ★★★½ A prince tries to keep his king away from vital cabinet meetings by distracting him with beautiful women. German musical set in 19th-century Austria and as tasty as a Viennese pastry. In both English and German versions. C: Lilian Harvey, Conrad Veidt, Willy Fritsch. D: Erik Charell. MUS 92m. V

Congress of Penguins, The 1994 ★★★½ Ecology is focus of unusual documentary set in Antarctica. Hundreds of penguins march across the screen, with narration voicing their "thoughts", criticizing mankind's abuse of nature. Interesting, but after an hour, enough already. D: Hans-Ulrich Schlumpf. DOC 91m.

Conjugal Bed, The 1963 French ★★★★ After his wife bears a child, husband finds himself no longer needed in their marriage. More accurate Italian title is *Queen Bee*; either way, it's subversively funny. C: Ugo Tognazzi, Marina Vlady, Walter Giller. D: Marco Ferreri. COM 90m.

Connecticut Yankee, A 1931 ★★★★ Contemporary New Englander goes back in time to King Arthur's court. Mark Twain's classic story gets the Will Rogers treatment with caustic wit and dated drolleries. Still very funny. Remade twice. C: Will Rogers, Maureen O'Sullivan, Myrna Loy, Frank Albertson. D: David Butler. COM 95m. V

Connecticut Yankee in King Arthur's Court 1949 ★★★½ Singer gets knocked out, wakes up in Camelot, mistaken for wizard. Mark Twain's social satire turned into easygoing Crosby musical with lackluster songs. C: Bing Crosby, Rhonda Fleming, Cedric Hardwicke, William Bendix, Henry Wilcoxon. D: Tay Garnett. COM 108m. V

Connecting Rooms 1971 British ★★½ Three self-deluding losers come together in a seedy suburban London boardinghouse. Slow, dismal, and creaky melodrama. C: Bette Davis, Michael Redgrave, Kay Walsh. D: Franklin Gollings. DRA 103m.

Connection, The 1961 ★★★★ A documentary filmmaker hangs around a bunch of junkies waiting for a fix from their "connection," and is tempted to try drugs himself. Acclaimed '60s independently produced film. C: William Redfield, Warren Finnerty, Jerome Raphael. D: Shirley Clarke. DRA 115m. V

Conquered City, The 1962 Italian ★★★½ In an Athens Hotel near the end of WWII, a British major (Niven) holds the fort, amidst people of various different nationalities. Solid wartime drama. C: David Niven, Ben Gazzara, Michael Craig, Martin Balsam, Lea Massari. D: Joseph Anthony. DRA 87m.

Conquering Horde, The 1931 ★★★ When Texas resists U.S. government directives after the Civil War, the President hires an amiable Texan to calm the ruffled feathers. Dated Western popular when first released. C: Richard Arlen, Fay Wray, Ian MacLaren, Frank Rice. D: Edward Sloman. WST 73m.

Conqueror, The 1953 ★★★ Wayne improbably cast as Genghis Khan in epic tale of Mongols vs. Tartars with Hayward as kidnapped princess. Full of dreadful dialogue that's so out of place, it's funny. C: John Wayne, Susan Hayward, Pedro Armendariz, Agnes Moorehead, William Conrad. D: Dick Powell. DRA [G] 111m. V

Conqueror Worm, The 1968 British ★★★★ Groundbreakingly graphic and intense shocker set in the 1600s, with Ogilvy seeking vengeance against the corrupt Witchfinder General, Matthew Hopkins (a real-life character). Price, in an uncharacteristically low-key performance, is terrific as the villain. (a.k.a. *The Witchfinder General.*) C: Vincent Price, Ian Ogilvy, Hilary Dwyer. D: Michael Reeves. HOR 87m. V

Conquerors, The 1932 ★★★ Sixty years in the life of a struggling family, who make it rich in the banking business. Transparent carbon of Edna Ferber's *Cimarron*, with a good cast trapped in a mundane script. (a.k.a. *Pioneer Builders*) C: Richard Dix, Ann Harding, Edna May Oliver, Guy Kibbee. D: William Wellman. DRA 86m.

Conquest 1937 ★★★ The emperor Napoleon (Boyer) takes up with the Polish countess Walewska (Garbo). Superb performances by a top-tiered cast struggling to overcome a lifeless script. C: Greta Garbo, Charles Boyer, Reginald Owen, Henry Stephenson, Alan Marshal, Dame May Whitty, Leif Erickson, Maria Ouspenskaya. D: Clarence Brown. DRA 113m. V

Conquest 1983 ★★ Warriors Ilias and Maxz battle evil sorceress Ocron, who has plunged their land into darkness by covering the sun. Cheesy foreign sci-fi. C: Jorge Rivero, Andrea Occhipinti. D: Lucio Fulci. SFI [R] 92m. V

Conquest of Everest, The 1953 British

★★★★ Pulse-pounding account of Edmund Hillary's successful expedition to reach Mount Everest's summit; made even more exciting fact that it's real life. Stunningly photographed. DOC 78m. V

Conquest of Space 1954 ★★★ The U.S. Army seeks to conquer a new territory—Mars. Solid George Pal special effects enhances an interesting plot. C: Eric Fleming, William Hopper, Ross Martin, Joan Shawlee. D: Byron Haskin. SFI 80m. V

Conquest of the Earth 1980 ★★ Spaceship commander Greene helps scientist Reed battle Cyclons who've attacked earth. Cobbled-together episodes of TV series *Battlestar Galactica.* C: Lorne Greene, Kent McCord, Barry Van Dyke. D: Sidney Hayers. SFI 99m. V

Conquest of the Planet of the Apes 1972 ★★★ Enslaved ape McDowall rallies his simian comrades to revolution. Answers the nagging question: How did apes come to rule Earth? Fourth in the *Apes* cycle and devolving fast. Followed by *Battle for the Planet of the Apes.* C: Roddy McDowall, Don Murray, Ricardo Montalban. D: J. Lee Thompson. SFI [PG] 87m. V

Conrack 1974 ★★★★ Simple but moving story of young white schoolteacher devoted to helping disadvantaged black students on an island off the South Carolina coast. Based on writer Pat Conroy's own experiences and his book, *The Water Is Wide.* C: Jon Voight, Paul Winfield, Hume Cronyn, Madge Sinclair. D: Martin Ritt. DRA [PG] 111m. V

Consenting Adult 1985 ★★★★½ College student Tubb alienates parents when he discloses his homosexuality. By TV standards, this is courageous drama—intelligently acted with restraint and taste. Thomas very impressive as woman torn between husband and son. Based on best-selling Laura Z. Hobson novel. C: Marlo Thomas, Martin Sheen, Barry Tubb, Talia Balsam. D: Gilbert Cates. DRA 94m. TVM V

Consenting Adults 1992 ★★½ Spacey and Miller move next door to Kline and Mastrantonio. Mutual flirtations lead to spouse swapping and Kline being framed for murder. Simplistic plot and gaping holes pockmark this uninvolving thriller; has real "so bad it's funny" potential. C: Kevin Kline, Mary Elizabeth Mastrantonio, Kevin Spacey, Rebecca Miller, Forest Whitaker, E. G. Marshall. D: Alan J. Pakula. CRI [R] 99m. V

Consequence, The 1977 German ★★★★ Popular actor (Prochnow in memorable performance) sent to prison because of affair with underage youth is pursued by warden's handsome teenage son. Touching gay love story may surprise only those familiar with director's later action-oriented pictures. C: Jurgen Prochnow, Ernst Hannawald, Walo Luond. D: Wolfgang Peterson. DRA 100m.

Consolation Marriage 1931 ★★★ Left by their lovers, Dunne and O'Brien take consolation in each other. Years later their marriage is threatened when the original sweethearts return. Predictable soap opera given some depth by better than average cast. C: Irene Dunne, Pat O'Brien, Myrna Loy. D: Paul Sloane. DRA 82m. V

Conspiracy of Hearts 1960 British ★★★★ Nuns hide Jewish children from the Nazis in an Italian convent. Nice direction and believable performances give tried and true story fresh life. Good nail-biter. C: Lilli Palmer, Sylvia Syms, Yvonne Mitchell. D: Ralph Thomas. DRA 116m.

Conspiracy, The 1973 *See* **Le Complot**

Conspiracy—The Trial of the Chicago 8 1987 ★★★★ Intriguing, solidly acted docudrama of the trial of the radicals charged with disrupting the 1968 Democratic National Convention in Chicago. Interviews with actual members of the Chicago Eight are mixed with dramatized footage. C: Peter Boyle, Elliott Gould, Robert Carradine, Martin Sheen. D: Jeremy Paul Kagan. DRA 118m. V

Conspirator 1949 British ★★★ Cold War-era drama features the two Taylors as an English Army officer and his American wife. Liz is thrown off guard when she learns Robert is a Communist spy. Strains credibility. C: Robert Taylor, Elizabeth Taylor, Honor Blackman, Wilfrid Hyde-White. D: Victor Saville. DRA 85m. V

Conspirators, The 1944 ★★★★ A cloak-and-dagger potboiler in WWII Lisbon. Though the story elements are all familiar, Lamarr and the rest of the great cast admirably manage to energize the proceedings. C: Hedy Lamarr, Paul Henreid, Sydney Greenstreet, Peter Lorre. D: Jean Negulesco. DRA 101m.

Constance 1984 New Zealand ★★½ Attractive schoolteacher lets love of classic Hollywood movies swamp her life, leading to a tragic outcome. Disappointing handling of premise. C: Donogh Rees, Shane Briant, Judie Douglass. D: Bruce Morrison. DRA 104m.

Constant Factor, The 1980 Polish ★★★ Intellectual, nonconformist mountain climber winds up being a window washer in Communist Poland. Thoughtful story and characterizations. C: Tadeusz Bradecki, Zofia Mrozowska. D: Krzysztof Zanussi. DRA 96m.

Constant Husband, The 1955 British ★★★½ Harrison is an amnesic bigamist who would rather go to jail than face his seven angry wives; sparkling comedy. C: Rex Harrison, Kay Kendall, Margaret Leighton, Cecil Parker, Michael Hordern, Robert Coote. D: Sidney Gilliat. COM 88m.

Constant Nymph, The 1943 ★★★★ Literate love triangle: Fontaine deeply in love with self-centered composer Boyer, who marries socialite Smith instead. Outstanding performances by all three players. C: Charles Boyer, Joan Fontaine, Alexis Smith, Charles Coburn,

Dame May Whitty, Peter Lorre. D: Edmund Goulding. DRA 112m.

Constantine and the Cross 1962 Italian ★★★½ Christians vs. Romans, 4th century A.D. Well-made epic offers exciting battle scenes and intelligent performances. C: Cornel Wilde, Christine Kaufmann. D: Lionello Felice. DRA 120m.

Consuming Passions 1988 U.S. ★★★ Success eludes chocolate factory trainee until he stumbles on a formula that makes the confections irresistible. Unfortunately, the secret ingredient is human beings. Slow-moving, black comedy not without laughs. C: Vanessa Redgrave, Jonathan Pryce, Sammi Davis. D: Giles Foster. COM [R] 98m. V

Contagion 1987 ★★ Man enters a haunted mansion where careerist phantoms advocate murder for getting ahead in business. Silly chiller sermonizes about the "contagion" of greed and lust, the latter illustrated explicitly by seductive girl ghosts. C: John Doyle, Nicola Bartlett, Nathy Gaffney, Ray Barrett. D: Karl Zwicky. HOR 90m. V

Contempt 1964 French ★★★★ Bizarre comedy about movie business with Palance as a crude producer, Lang (in self-parody) as director, and Bardot as star of the film-within-the-film. Unreal at times, but worth the ride. Look for Godard's cameo as Lang's assistant. C: Brigitte Bardot, Jack Palance, Michel Piccoli, Fritz Lang. D: Jean-Luc Godard. COM 102m. V

Continental Divide 1981 ★★★ Belushi plays a curmudgeonly Chicago newspaper columnist (based on Mike Royko) who travels to Rocky Mountains and falls for naturalist Brown. Scenic romantic comedy. C: John Belushi, Blair Brown. D: Michael Apted. COM [PG] 103m. V

Contraband 1940 British ★★★★ Veidt and Hobson, stars of *The Spy in Black*, are reunited as a Danish sea captain and agent who unveil secret operations of WWII spies. Well-crafted story with a lot of spunk. (a.k.a. *Blackout*) C: Conrad Veidt, Valerie Hobson, Hay Petrie. D: Michael Powell. DRA 92m.

Contract on Cherry Street 1977 ★★★★ Sinatra makes his TV-film debut in this made-to-order crime drama, about a New York cop out to avenge his partner's murder. Grabs attention throughout, and Frank's fine. C: Frank Sinatra, Harry Guardino, Martin Balsam, Michael Nouri. D: William A. Graham. CRI 150m. TVM

Contract 1980 Polish ★★★★ Rabid black comedy uses a disastrous wedding reception as metaphor for confused morality in Poland. As parents drink themselves into oblivion, their children present themselves as carbon copies. Zanussi keeps highly charged politics in check. C: Leslie Caron, Maja Komorowska. D: Krzysztof Zanussi. COM 114m. V

Control 1987 ★★★ Psychological survival experiment in a fallout shelter goes awry when a real nuclear emergency occurs. Tedious drama. C: Burt Lancaster, Kate Nelligan, Ben Gazzara, Andrea Ferreol, Jean Benguigui. D: Guiliano Montaldo. DRA 83m. TVM V

Conversation Piece 1974 Italian ★★ Aging American academic Lancaster is caught up in sexual intrigue when a middle-aged siren (with young lover) and her sexy daughter move in upstairs. Dry and talky despite the sensational subject matter. C: Burt Lancaster, Silvana Mangano, Helmut Berger, Claudia Cardinale. D: Luchino Visconti. DRA [R] 112m. V

Conversation, The 1974 ★★★★★ Absorbing drama about a surveillance expert (Hackman) whose investigation of an unusual client apparently turns up a murder plot. Tense development underscored by effective use of background sound leaves viewer on edge throughout, with shattering plot twist at climax. Hackman is terrific in one of Coppola's best. Look for a small appearance by Harrison Ford, and a scene with Garr cut from most TV prints. C: Gene Hackman, Frederic Forrest, John Cazale, Allen Garfield, Cindy Williams, Teri Garr, Harrison Ford. D: Francis Coppola. DRA [PG] 113m. V

Convict 99 1938 British ★★★ Rascally schoolteacher is mistakenly chosen to become warden of a prison. Soon he turns the jail into a business with the prisoners in charge. Strange comedy/drama has good premise. C: Will Hay, Moore Marriott, Googie Withers. D: Marcel Varnel. COM 91m.

Convicted 1986 ★★★ Wrong man drama about innocent Larroquette mistakenly imprisoned for rape, and wife Wagner seeking the true criminal. Standard drama; good Larroquette. C: John Larroquette, Lindsay Wagner. D: David Lowell Rich. DRA 104m. TVM V

Convicts Four 1962 ★★★ Prisoner becomes an artist. Gazzara is good in the lead, surrounded by offbeat supporting cast. C: Ben Gazzara, Stuart Whitman, Ray Walston, Vincent Price, Rod Steiger, Broderick Crawford, Sammy Davis, Jr. D: Millard Kaufman. DRA 105m.

Convicts 1991 ★★★★ A young boy (Haas) learns about injustice in the Louisiana cornfields of 1902, as he watches a senile plantation owner (Duvall) survive by exploiting convict labor. Duvall's brilliant performance gets strong support from Haas, Jones, and Horton Foote's script (from his play). Harsh, gripping drama. C: Robert Duvall, Lukas Haas, James Earl Jones. D: Peter Masterson. DRA 95m. V

Convoy 1978 ★★★★ High-speed feud between good ol' boy trucker (Kristofferson) and a tough backwater cop (Borgnine), based on the country hit by C.W. McCall. Director Peckinpah makes 16-wheelers do things never thought possible. C: Kris Kristofferson, Ali MacGraw, Ernest Borgnine, Burt Young. D: Sam Peckinpah. ACT [PG] 106m. V

Coogan's Bluff 1968 ★★★★ Vintage Eastwood as a lanky Arizona deputy taking on the wilds of New York City to run down a murderer. Great culture clash between the straight-shooting, simple cowboy and the sophisticated denizens of the Big Apple. Basis of TV series, *McCloud*. C: Clint Eastwood, Lee J. Cobb, Susan Clark, Betty Field. D: Don Siegel. CRI [R] 100m. V

Cook, the Thief, His Wife & Her Lover, The 1990 French ★★★½ Perverse, extremely stylized film; Mirren is the adulterous wife, Gambon her vicious thug-husband, and Howard her lover in this graphic, sometimes sickening revenge tale. Greenaway is an acquired taste; not for everyone. Definitely not for children. C: Helen Mirren, Michael Gambon. D: Peter Greenaway. DRA [R] 100m. V

Cookie 1989 ★★★½ Finally out of prison, mobster (Falk) must contend with his sassy, teenage daughter (Lloyd) who's anxious to follow in his footsteps. Lackluster comedy gains some muscle from scene-stealing lead performances. C: Peter Falk, Dianne Wiest, Emily Lloyd, Brenda Vaccaro, Lionel Stander, Jerry Lewis, Bob Gunton, Ricki Lake. D: Susan Seidelman. COM 93m. V

Cool as Ice 1991 ★★ Rapper Vanilla Ice made his embarrassing debut as big-screen star in this silly story about a man who loves both his motorcycle and a pretty girl. For fans only. C: Vanilla Ice, Kristin Minter, Michael Gross. D: David Kellogg. DRA [PG] 95m. V

Cool Hand Luke 1967 ★★★★ A defiant convict (the very cool Newman) rebels against harsh injustices of the chain gang in this gritty and blackly comic prison drama. Oscar for Best Supporting Actor to Kennedy, but slyly funny Martin is just as good. C: Paul Newman, George Kennedy, J.D. Cannon, Strother Martin, Jo Van Fleet, Wayne Rogers, Harry Dean Stanton, Dennis Hopper. D: Stuart Rosenberg. DRA [PG] 129m. V

Cool Runnings 1993 ★★★½ Good-natured, often very funny film about the unlikely bobsled team from Jamaica and their efforts to compete in the 1992 Winter Olympics at Albertville. Candy's their coach. C: John Candy, Doug E. Doug, Leon, Malik Yoba, Rawle Lewis. FAM/COM [PG] 98m. V

Cool World 1992 ★★½ Distinctly adult cartoon, with cartoonist (Byrne) lured into a world inhabited by his creation (Basinger) so she can escape and become human. Mix of live action and typically wild Bakshi animation. C: Gabriel Byrne, Kim Basinger, Brad Pitt. D: Ralph Bakshi. DRA [PG-13] 101m. V

Cooley High 1975 ★★★ High school hijinks à la *American Grafitti*. Well-handled mix of comedy and drama, with a soundtrack of Motown gold. C: Glynn Turman, Lawrence Hilton-Jacobs, Garrett Morris. D: Michael Schultz. DRA [PG] 107m. V

Coonskin 1975 ★★★½ Video title is *Streetfight*. Wild, shocking collection of animated and real life vignettes, from legendary animator Bakshi, on the subject of being African-American. Zany, lampooning spirit, often intentionally offensive. C: Barry White, Charles Gordone, Scatman Crothers. D: Ralph Bakshi. COM [R] 83m. V

Cop 1988 ★★★ Detective Woods' personal and professional relationships suffer from his obsession with a serial murderer. Strong performance by Woods competes with overdose of blood and profanity. C: James Woods, Lesley Ann Warren, Charles Durning. D: James Harris. CRI [R] 110m. V

Cop and a Half 1993 ★★ Odd, rather weak vehicle for Reynolds has him chaperoning a tyke who is deputized by local cops after he becomes a key witness in a drug case. C: Burt Reynolds, Norman D. Golden II, Ruby Dee, Holland Taylor, Ray Sharkey. D: Henry Winkler. COM [PG] 93m. V

Cop au Vin 1984 French ★★★★ Crippled mom and her mail carrier son plot revenge against evictors. Typically caustic Chabrol film: unhinged characters, suspenseful plotting, and wry social commentary. Sequel: *Inspecteur Lavadin*. C: Jean Poiret, Stephane Audran, Michael Bouquet. D: Claude Chabrol. CRI 110m.

Copacabana 1947 ★★★ An unscrupulous agent (Marx) tries to turn his one client (Miranda) into a star. Lackluster musical, with two unique leads mixing like oil and water. Groucho's first solo acting effort. Choose from original black-and-white or colorized. C: Groucho Marx, Carmen Miranda, Steve Cochran, Gloria Jean. D: Alfred E. Green. MUS 92m. V

Copper Canyon 1950 ★★★½ Gunslinger leads group of Civil War vets in settling Western territory. Solid cast and beautiful photography elevate average story. C: Ray Milland, Hedy Lamarr, Macdonald Carey. D: John Farrow. WST 84m. V

Cops and Robbers 1973 ★★★ Two frustrated cops decide that bending the law is no longer enough, and cross over into a life of crime. Bologna is decent. C: Cliff Gorman, Joseph Bologna, Shepperd Strudwick. D: Aram Avakian. ACT 89m. V

Cops and Robbersons 1994 ★★★ It's the mismatched partners gambit: Chase is cast as a charmless bumbler yet again, a suburbanite with a dysfunctional family whose home is taken over for a stakeout by a hard-as-nails cop (Palance). Good direction buoys familiar material. C: Chevy Chase, Jack Palance, Dianne Wiest, Robert Davi, David Barry Gray, Jason James Richter. D: Michael Ritchie. COM [PG] 93m.

Coquette 1929 ★★★ Young Southern flapper falls for the wrong man. Stiff, old-fashioned melodrama was Pickford's first talking movie and showcased a then-newfangled style for her. Her performance won her the

Best Actress Oscar. C: Mary Pickford, John Mack Brown. D: Sam Taylor. DRA 75m. V

Cordelia 1980 French ★★★ A flirtatious Quebec woman is accused of killing her husband. Earnest dramatization of a true story. C: Louise Portal, Gaston Lepage, Pierre Gobeil. D: Jean Beaudin. DRA 118m.

Corinna, Corinna 1994 ★★★½ A widower (Liotta) hires a housekeeper (Goldberg) to look after his daughter. Unsurprisingly, she brings new life into a house in mourning. Goes a long way on the charm of the leads. C: Whoopi Goldberg, Ray Liotta, Tina Majorino, Don Ameche, Joan Cusack, Larry Miller, Jenifer Lewis. D: Jessie Nelson. DRA 115m.

Corn Is Green, The 1945 ★★★★ Bright youth in Welsh mining town is rescued from poverty by idealistic schoolteacher played with skill by Davis. Entertaining, but shows its literary roots. C: Bette Davis, John Dall, Nigel Bruce, Joan Lorring, Mildred Dunnock. D: Irving Rapper. DRA 115m. V

Corn Is Green, The 1978 ★★★★½ Terrific remake of 1945 paean to education as Hepburn teaches Welsh coal miner Saynor how to surmount his upbringing. Kate's great in this part. Location photography a plus. C: Katharine Hepburn, Ian Saynor, Bill Fraser, Patricia Hayes. D: George Cukor. DRA 93m. V

Cornbread, Earl and Me 1975 ★★★ When a black high school basketball star is mistakenly shot by police, his family fights a cover-up to clear his name. Fine cast is unable to enliven this earnest but uninspired drama. C: Moses Gunn, Bernie Casey, Rosalind Cash, Larry Fishburne. D: Joe Manduke. DRA [PG] 95m. V

Cornered 1945 ★★★★ French-Canadian pilot Powell travels the globe to track down the Nazi responsible for his French wife's death in this crafty, taut revenge tale in the film noir tradition. Satisfying action. C: Dick Powell, Walter Slezak, Micheline Cheirel. D: Edward Dmytryk. CRI 102m. V

Coroner Creek 1948 ★★★½ Man sets out to avenge the death of his fiancée and recover loot stolen in Indian attack. His anger is abated by the appearance of a new love on the horizon. Solid Western all the way, with a splendid cast. C: Randolph Scott, Marguerite Chapman. D: Ray Enright. WST 93m.

Corpse Came C.O.D., The 1947 ★★½ When a dead body shows up in an actress' home, two warring reporters (Brent and Blondell) quickly jump on the case. Stars add punch to minor whodunit. C: George Brent, Joan Blondell, Adele Jergens, Una O'Connor. D: Henry Levin. DRA 87m.

Corpse Vanishes, The 1942 ★★★ Once again, a mad scientist (Lugosi) attempts to save a loved one; here he abducts young brides in quest to provide eternal youth for his own aged wife. Typical of Lugosi's Poverty Row output, though slightly better than usual. C: Bela Lugosi, Luana Walters. D: Wallace Fox. HOR 64m. V

Corregidor 1943 ★★★ Two doctors vie for the affections of a third (Landi) during famous WWII siege in the Pacific. Weak drama, little action. C: Otto Kruger, Elissa Landi, Donald Woods. D: William Nigh. DRA 73m.

Corridor of Mirrors 1948 British ★★★½ Strange artist, obsessed with the past, marries a beautiful young woman, but their idyllic life is shattered by a murder. Atmospheric, lyrical story pays dividends to those with patience. C: Eric Portman, Edana Romney. D: Terence Young. DRA 105m.

Corridors of Blood 1958 British ★★★ Karloff adds juice to tale of a doctor who becomes addicted to anesthetics, falling in with graverobbers (including Lee) to support his habit. Good period atmosphere also helps bolster stolid storytelling. C: Boris Karloff, Betta St. John, Christopher Lee. D: Robert Day. HOR 89m. V

Corrupt 1983 Italian ★★★★ Bizarre crime thriller about the psychological relationship between a corrupt NYC narc (Keitel) and a murderer (Lydon, a.k.a. Johnny Rotten of The Sex Pistols). Slow-paced but effective mind-game caper. C: Harvey Keitel, Nicole Garcia, Sylvia Sidney. D: Roberto Faenza. CRI [R] 99m. V

Corsair 1931 ★★★½ When a college man is rejected by the woman he loves because he is too dull, he goes to work as a bootlegger for her rascal of a father. Early, oddball gangster film has enough twists and turns to keep things lively. C: Chester Morris, Thelma Todd, Frank McHugh, Emmett Corrigan. D: Roland West. DRA 75m.

Corsican Brothers, The 1941 ★★★★ Alexander Dumas' classic tale of swashbuckling twins psychically linked no matter how far apart they are. An energetic Fairbanks excels in the dual role. C: Douglas Fairbanks Jr., Ruth Warrick, Akim Tamiroff. D: Gregory Ratoff. ACT 112m.

Corvette K-225 1943 ★★★★½ Title names a kind of Canadian warship depicted in this action-packed story of a naval convoy's dangerous journey to Russia. Much of the astounding photography was taken in the midst of actual battles by a team of intrepid filmmakers. C: Randolph Scott, James Brown, Ella Raines, Barry Fitzgerald. D: Richard Rossen. ACT 99m.

Corvette Summer 1978 ★★★½ A high school student (Hamill) tracks car thief to Las Vegas but gets sidetracked when he falls in love with a call girl (Potts). Overlooked coming-of-age story, hurt by inappropriate title, has real comedy and real warmth. C: Mark Hamill, Annie Potts, Eugene Roche. D: Matthew Robbins. COM [PG] 105m. V

Cosmic Eye, The 1985 ★★★★ Charming animated film about three extraterrestial musicians who visit Earth in an effort to spread peace throughout the world. Ambitious message piece is sincere and its execution is impressive. Food for thought for both children and adults. C: Dizzy Gillespie, Maureen Stapleton. D: Faith Hubley. SFI 72m. V

Cosmic Man Appears in Tokyo, The 1956 *See* **Mysterious Satellite, The**

Cosmic Man, The 1959 ★★★½ A man from another planet lands on Earth to save the human race and he finds it hard to convince us. Medium sci-fi; flawed, but worth seeing. C: Bruce Bennett, John Carradine, Angela Greene. D: Herbert Greene. SFI 72m. V

Cottage to Let 1941 British ★★★ Plodding WWII espionage tale involving a Nazi plot to steal an inventor's plans for a hidden bombsight. (a.k.a. *Bombsight Stolen*) C: Alastair Sim, Leslie Banks, John Mills, Michael Wilding. D: Anthony Asquith. CRI 90m.

Cotton Club, The 1984 ★★★ Overlong and only intermittently successful musical epic tells parallel stories about a white musician (Gere) and a black dancer (Hines) who get involved with the mob. Stunning visuals, great music, and terrific dance numbers, but the story is a bust. C: Richard Gere, Gregory Hines, Diane Lane, Lonette McKee, Bob Hoskins, Nicolas Cage, Fred Gwynne, Gwen Verdon. D: Francis Ford Coppola. DRA [R] 127m. V

Cotton Comes to Harlem 1970 ★★★½ Two undercover detectives (Cambridge, St. Jacques) investigate a corrupt Harlem preacher (Lockhart) and search for a stash of money in this entertaining crime-comedy based on Chester Himes' book. Sequel: *Come Back, Charleston Blue*. Davis' directorial debut. C: Godfrey Cambridge, Raymond St. Jacques, Redd Foxx. D: Ossie Davis. COM [R] 97m. V

Couch Trip, The 1988 ★★★½ Lunatic Aykroyd goes on the lam from the funny farm, travels west and convinces the denizens of Beverly Hills he's a renowned radio psychologist. Fast-paced direction and sly performances provide plenty of laughs. C: Dan Aykroyd, Walter Matthau, Charles Grodin, Donna Dixon. D: Michael Ritchie. COM [R] 97m. V

Counsellor-at-Law 1933 ★★★★★ Early Wyler triumph, with Barrymore in one of his greatest performances as Jewish lawyer facing personal and professional crises. Set in a few rooms but never stage-stuck. Supple, adult Hollywood cinema based on Elmer Rice's play. C: John Barrymore, Bebe Daniels, Doris Kenyon, Isabel Jewell, Melvyn Douglas, Thelma Todd. D: William Wyler. DRA 82m.

Count Dracula 1971 Italian ★★★ European production is more faithful to Bram Stoker's novel about a vampire (Lee) than most previous movies but suffers from cheapjack production and uncertain direction. Good cast. C: Christopher Lee, Herbert Lom, Klaus Kinski. D: Jess Franco. HOR [PG] 98m. V

Count Five and Die 1958 British ★★★½ American agent and his British superiors mislead the Nazis into believing the Allies will land in Holland. Intelligent spy caper generates some thrills. C: Jeffrey Hunter, Nigel Patrick, Ann-Marie Duringer. D: Victor Vicas. ACT 92m.

Count of Monte Cristo, The 1934 ★★★★½ Edmond Dantes escapes prison and seeks revenge on those who set him up. Dumas' classic gets A-one early Hollywood swashbuckler treatment. Nicely handled on all accounts, and still mighty entertaining. C: Robert Donat, Elissa Landi, Louis Calhern, Sidney Blackmer. D: Rowland V. Lee. ACT 119m. V

Count of Monte Cristo, The 1974 ★★★★ Faithful filming of Dumas novel with Chamberlain perfectly cast as Edmond Dantes, the French soldier unjustly imprisoned for many years. Upon escaping, he assumes a new identity to exact his revenge. Handsome production with one jarring note: Curtis. C: Richard Chamberlain, Tony Curtis, Trevor Howard, Louis Jourdan, Donald Pleasence, Kate Nelligan. D: David Greene. DRA 104m. V

Count Three and Pray 1955 ★★★½ Yankee soldier returns to his Southern hometown and tries to make a go of it as the local minister. Tasteful, interesting drama was Woodward's fine film debut. C: Van Heflin, Joanne Woodward, Raymond Burr. D: George Sherman. DRA 102m.

Count Yorga, Vampire 1970 ★★★½ Energetic, scary and funny opus about a modern bloodsucker (Quarry) in California luring women to become his undead brides. Quarry is fine as the domineering villain. C: Robert Quarry, Roger Perry, Donna Anders. D: Bob Kelljan. HOR [R] 90m. V

Count Your Blessings 1959 ★★½ Adaptation of Nancy Mitford's novel *The Blessing* has a nine-year-old boy (Stephens) plot to reunite his estranged parents (Kerr and Brazzi) with the assistance of family friend (Chevalier). Shot in Paris. C: Deborah Kerr, Rossano Brazzi, Maurice Chevalier. D: Jean Negulesco. COM 102m.

Count Your Bullets 1972 ★★★½ Gunslinger rescues young Native-American woman from a U.S. Army attack and leads her to safety. Violent, but also smart and different. (a.k.a. *Cry For Me, Billy*) C: Cliff Potts, Oaxchitl, Harry Dean Stanton. D: William A. Graham. WST [R] 92m.

Countdown at Kusini 1976 Nigerian ★★★ Sincere story about the liberation of a small, fictional African country. Some exciting moments and well intentioned, with moving performances. C: Ruby Dee, Ossie Davis, Greg Morris. D: Ossie Davis. DRA 101m.

Countdown 1968 ★★★★ Fictionalized account of the first moon landing, with emphasis on the people affected most: the astronauts, their families, and colleagues. Effective ensemble acting and good, realistic script. C: Robert

Duvall, James Caan, Charles Aidman, Ted Knight. D: Robert Altman. DRA 102m. v

Counter-Attack 1945 ★★★½ The Allies sneak behind Nazi lines, sabotaging their fortifications. Sure-handed performances and direction elevate this wartime tale. C: Paul Muni, Marguerite Chapman, Larry Parks. D: Zoltan Korda. ACT 90m.

Counterfeit Traitor, The 1962 ★★★★ Holden plays an oil importer coerced into serving as an Allied agent against the Gestapo in WWII. Based on the exploits of masterspy Eric Erickson, the film is solid, if unexciting, espionage fare. C: William Holden, Lilli Palmer, Hugh Griffith, Eva Dahlbeck. D: George Seaton. DRA 140m. v

Counterfeiters of Paris, The 1962 French ★★★½ Trying to get out of the prostitution business, two men begin careers as counterfeiters. They bring on an old hand (Gabin) to oversee operations. Breezy caper movie is helped considerably by the marvelous cast. (a.k.a. *Money, Money, Money*) C: Jean Gabin, Bernard Blier, Martine Carol, Francoise Rosay. D: Gilles Grangier. CRI 99m.

Counterpoint 1968 ★★ Nazis capture a world-famous conductor (Heston) so he will lead a VIP concert. Maestro Heston? Sounds dangerous. C: Charlton Heston, Maximilian Schell, Kathryn Hays, Leslie Nielsen. D: Ralph Nelson. DRA 107m.

Countess Dracula 1972 British ★★★ A countess assumes the identity of her daughter and finds she needs fresh blood to maintain her youthful appearance. Not bad, actually. Chilling beauty treatment. C: Ingrid Pitt, Nigel Green, Peter Jeffrey, Lesley-Anne Down. D: Peter Sasdy. HOR [PG] 94m.

Countess from Hong Kong, A 1967 British ★★½ Loren, a stowaway on oceanliner, encounters diplomat Brando, then pretends to be the noblewoman of title. Romantic misfire with old-fashioned script, leaden direction. Sad, since this is Chaplin's last film. C: Marlon Brando, Sophia Loren, Sydney Chaplin, Tippi Hedren, Margaret Rutherford. D: Charles Chaplin. DRA [G] 108m.

Country 1984 ★★★★ Realistic, probing drama of the problems of modern-day farmers: unsympathetic bureaucrats, bank loan officers, and the weather. Sterling performances, especially by Lange as a strong farmwife who holds it all together. C: Jessica Lange, Sam Shepard, Wilford Brimley. D: Richard Pearce. DRA [PG] 109m. v

Country Dance 1969 *See* **Brotherly Love**

Country Doctor, The 1936 ★★★½ Backwoods doctor (Hersholt) fights small-town prejudice to build a much needed hospital. And he gets to deliver quintuplets, too. Sentimental but nicely told. Don't try to resist it, you can't. C: Jean Hersholt, June Lang, Slim Summerville. D: Henry King. DRA 93m.

Country Girl, The 1954 ★★★★½ Crosby, in a riveting performance, is alcoholic singer on comeback trail with help of wife Kelly and director Holden. Excellent adaptation of Clifford Odets play won Oscars for star Kelly and Seaton's script adaptation. C: Bing Crosby, Grace Kelly, William Holden. D: George Seaton. DRA 104m. v

County Chairman, The 1935 ★★★ Rogers plays an attorney involved in an election for County Prosecutor, against corrupt incumbent who has no plans to give up his job. Rambling comedy/drama is not Rogers' best, but still charms. C: Will Rogers, Evelyn Venable, Kent Taylor, Louise Dresser, Mickey Rooney. D: John Blystone. COM 85m.

County Fair 1933 British ★★ To win big stakes, gamblers sedate a racehorse, raising the ire of the locals. Minor, predictable fare. C: John Arledge, Mary Lou Lender, J. Farrell MacDonald. D: Howard Bretherton. DRA 71m.

Coup de Grace 1976 French ★★★ Bored and stifled Countess (von Trotta) falls for a common soldier who doesn't return her affection. Interesting period talkfest about social and sexual conflicts arising out of WWI. C: Margarethe Trotta, Matthias Habich. D: Volker Schlondorff. DRA 96m.

Coup de Tete *See* **Hot Head**

Coup de Torchon 1981 French ★★★★½ Black comedy resets Jim Thompson's pulp thriller *Pop. 1280* in '30s colonial Africa. Police Chief (Noiret) hopes to bring serenity to his town, but learns that murder helps him meet his goals. (a.k.a. *Clean Slate.*) C: Philippe Noiret, Isabelle Huppert, Stephane Audran. D: Bertrand Tavernier. CRI 128m. v

Coup de Ville 1990 ★★½ Transporting a car from their father in Michigan to their mother in Florida forces three estranged brothers to spend time together and to face their long-seated animosities. Mixture of character comedy, '60s nostalgia and road humor eventually runs out of gas quickly. C: Patrick Dempsey, Arye Gross, Daniel Stern, Alan Arkin. D: Joe Roth. COM [PG-13] 99m. v

Courage 1986 ★★★★ A Queens housewife (Loren), the guilt-ridden mother of a drug addict, willingly goes undercover for the Drug Enforcement Agency. Laudable drama, based on a true story, with a tough, gritty performance by Loren. C: Sophia Loren, Billy Dee Williams, Hector Elizondo. D: Jeremy Paul Kagan. DRA 141m. TVM v

Courage Mountain 1990 U.S./French ★★★ Heidi (Caton), sent to pre-WWII Italy for schooling, winds up in an orphanage from hell when war breaks out. She and her schoolmates, abetted by her loyal soldier friend Peter (Sheen), escape over the Alps. Overdone, sometimes preposterous film is nevertheless suspenseful and appealing. C: Juliette Caton, Charlie Sheen, Leslie Caron. D: Christopher Leitch. FAM/DRA [PG] 92m. v

Courage of Black Beauty 1957 ★★★ Heart

warming story of a boy (Crawford) and the horse he raises from a colt. Nothing special, but good for family viewing. C: John Crawford, Diane Brewster. D: Harold Schuster. FAM/DRA 80m. V

Courage of Lassie 1946 ★★★½ After hero Lassie helps in war effort, fourteen-year-old friend (Taylor) helps canine hero readjust to life back home. One of Lassie's best, and Elizabeth's great, too. (a.k.a. *Blue Sierra*) C: Elizabeth Taylor, Frank Morgan, Tom Drake. D: Fred Wilcox. DRA [G] 93m. V

Courage of the West 1937 ★★★½ Texas Ranger learns his father is the head of the outlaw gang he is pursuing. Musical Western star Baker beat out Roy Rogers for this role! C: Bob Baker, Lois January, J. Farrell MacDonald. D: Joseph H. Lewis. WST 56m.

Court Concert, The 1936 German ★★★★ In 19th-century Vienna, a young chanteuse learns her father is the king of Austria. Charming, elegant German musical was an early effort from legendary Hollywood director Sirk. C: Martha Eggerth, Johannes Heesters, Kurt Meisel. D: Douglas Sirk. MUS 85m.

Court Jester, The 1956 ★★★★★ Delicious Kaye romp set in Merrie Olde England, with star as an imposter caught in court intrigue. Sterling support from Lansbury as a daffy princess, Rathbone spoofing his own bad-guy image, Johns, Natwick. Great for the youngsters, who will get a kick out of terrific "pellet with the poison" routine. Easily Kaye's best film. C: Danny Kaye, Glynis Johns, Basil Rathbone, Angela Lansbury, Mildred Natwick, John Carradine. D: Norman Panama, Melvin Frank. COM 101m. V

Court Martial 1955 British ★★★½ Did officer pilfer military funds? And what role did nasty wife play? Tense, watchable courtroom drama kept simmering by Asquith, with Niven in fine form. (a.k.a. *Carrington V.C.*) C: David Niven, Margaret Leighton, Maurice Denham. D: Anthony Asquith. CRI 105m. V

Court-Martial of Billy Mitchell, The 1955 ★★★★ Compelling courtroom drama based on 1925 case of Army general who accurately predicted air war with Japan. Cooper, excellent in lead, is well matched by Steiger as prosecuting attorney. C: Gary Cooper, Charles Bickford, Ralph Bellamy, Rod Steiger, Elizabeth Montgomery. D: Otto Preminger. DRA 100m. V

Court-Martial of Jackie Robinson, The 1990 ★★★ Braugher is impressive in this story of the future baseball hero who runs into racism in the Army when he's court-martialed for challenging segregationist policies. C: Andre Braugher, Daniel Stern, Ruby Dee, Bruce Dern. D: Larry Peerce. DRA 93m. TVM V

Court Martial of Major Keller, The 1961 British ★★★½ Courtroom drama has soldier (Payne) on trial for killing his cowardly commanding officer. Intriguing material. C: Laurence Payne, Susan Stephen, Ralph Michael. D: Ernest Morris. DRA 69m.

Courtney Affair, The 1947 British ★★★½ Young aristocrat falls for the housemaid and causes family furor when he marries her. Sentimental soap opera covers 45 years in their lives. Well-made romance through the years. (a.k.a. *The Courtneys of Curzon Street*) C: Anna Neagle, Michael Wilding, Coral Browne. D: Herbert Wilcox. DRA 112m.

Courtneys of Curzon Street, The 1947 *See* **Courtney Affair, The**

Courtship 1986 ★★★★ Wonderful story of pre-WWI courtship in small Texas town as traveling sales representative (Converse-Roberts) woos upperclass Foote. Foote's affecting performance gives this period drama real strength. From her father Horton Foote's trilogy of plays. *On Valentine's Day* and *1918* follow. C: Hallie Foote, Amanda Plummer, William Converse-Roberts. D: Howard Cummings. DRA 85m. V

Courtship of Andy Hardy, The 1942 ★★★ Andy has eyes for the lovely daughter (Reed) of a divorcing couple. Complications arise when his father the judge (Stone) handles the divorce. Earnest series entry. C: Mickey Rooney, Lewis Stone, Fay Holden, Ann Rutherford, Donna Reed. D: George Seitz. COM 93m.

Courtship of Eddie's Father, The 1963 ★★★★ Charming comedy with tyke (Howard) helping widower father (Ford) find new bride. Glenn gets the girl, but the kid steals the movie. Spawned TV series. C: Glenn Ford, Ron Howard, Shirley Jones, Stella Stevens, Dina Merrill. D: Vincente Minnelli. COM 117m. V

Cousin Angelica 1974 Spanish ★★★★ Loyalist family is split apart by Spanish Civil War. Vazquez is remarkable as a middle-aged man and (in flashbacks) the boy he was in the '30s. Photography strikingly evokes Spanish painting. C: Jose Luis Lapez Vazquez, Lina Canalejas. D: Carlos Saura. DRA 105m.

Cousin Bobby 1991 ★★★★ Intriguing portrait of director Demme's (*Silence of the Lambs*) cousin, Robert Castle, an Episcopal priest in Harlem who prides himself on his radical activism. Some heavy-handed use of race riot montages, but when it focuses on its subject, it's riveting. Castle went on to play Tom Hank's dad in *Philadelphia*. D: Jonathan Demme. DOC 70m. V

Cousin, Cousine 1976 French ★★★★ A man and a woman, cousins by marriage, at an on-going series of family functions decide they were made for each other and begin an affair much to the consternation of their spouses. Breezy comedy became an international hit and spawned an American remake (*Cousins*). C: Marie-Christine Barrault, Victor

Lanoux, Marie-France Pisier. D: Jean-Charles Tacchella. COM [R] 95m. V

Cousins, The 1959 French ★★★★ Two cousins (one from the city and one from the country) go to the Sorbonne together. In time, the country boy falls under influence of his self-absorbed city relative. Despite creaky, overly schematic premise, this is a compelling drama with sinister undertones. C: Jean-Claude Brialy, Gerard Blain, Juliette Mayniel. D: Claude Chabrol. DRA 112m.

Cousins 1989 ★★★ In between family weddings and funerals, Danson and Rosselini begin an affair to get even with their unfaithful spouses (Young and Peterson), only to discover that they might actually be in love with one another. A pleasant if cloying multigenerational comedy. Based on *Cousin, Cousine.* C: Ted Danson, Isabella Rossellini, Sean Young. D: Joel Schumacher. COM [PG-13] 110m. V

Cover Girl 1944 ★★★★½ Hayworth as chorus girl turned model must decide between Broadway stardom and the hoofer she loves (Kelly). What counts here is wonderful dancing, lovely Jerome Kern songs ("Long Ago and Far Away") and smashing cast. Rita's big dance number to title song is one of her finest moments on screen. C: Rita Hayworth, Gene Kelly, Lee Bowman, Phil Silvers, Eve Arden. D: Charles Vidor. MUS 107m. V

Covered Wagon, The 1923 ★★★★ Wagon train pioneers brave hostile Indians and other perils on the way to Western territory. Silent epic was a pioneer in its own right. Gorgeous photography offsets the leisurely pace. C: J. Warren Kerrigan, Lois Wilson, Alan Hale. D: James Cruze. WST 98m. V

Cow and I 1961 French ★★★½ Country bumpkin enlists the help of a cow to escape from a prison camp. Light, amusing romp is Fernandel's show all the way. C: Fernandel. D: Henri Verneuil. COM 98m.

Cowboy and the Lady, The 1938 ★★★ Rodeo rider (Cooper) and adventurous politician's daughter (Oberon) who's switched places with her maid elope to Texas. Dusty social satire, saved by charm of leads. C: Gary Cooper, Merle Oberon, Patsy Kelly, Walter Brennan. D: H.C. Potter. COM 91m. V

Cowboy Canteen 1944 ★★★½ Ranch owner opens entertainment complex on his spread to entertain the GIs. Episodic Western spin on Hollywood Canteen is boosted by the appearances of several legendary Western stars. C: Charles Starrett, Jane Frazee, Vera Vague. D: Lew Landers. WST 72m.

Cowboy from Brooklyn, The 1938 ★★★½ Streetwise crooner (Powell) needs to pose as genuine cowpoke in order to get plum radio gig. Light, rather silly musical somehow manages to be entertaining. C: Dick Powell, Pat O'Brien, Priscilla Lane, Ann Sheridan, Ronald Reagan. D: Lloyd Bacon. DRA 80m.

Cowboy Way 1994 ★★★½ When their friend disappears in big bad Manhattan, two rodeo cowpokes (Sutherland and Harrelson) ride their horses into town and . . . you can guess the rest. Sutherland displays real comic talent in this light entertainment. C: Kiefer Sutherland, Woody Harrelson, Dylan McDermott, Ernie Hudson. D: Gregg Champion. COM [PG-13] 98m.

Cowboy 1958 ★★★★ Evocative Western based on Frank Harris' book, involving the author as a dude who learns about life on the range from a tough trail boss during a big roundup. Impressive, atmospheric Western thoughtfully entertains. C: Glenn Ford, Jack Lemmon, Anna Kashfi. D: Delmer Daves. WST 92m.

Cowboys, The 1972 ★★★½ An aging rancher (Wayne) must break in a bunch of schoolkids as wranglers after his cowhands leave for California gold hunt. Dern and Wayne an exciting pairing in this stylized and action-packed Western. C: John Wayne, Roscoe Lee Browne, Bruce Dern, Colleen Dewhurst, Slim Pickens, A. Martinez. D: Mark Rydell. WST [PG] 128m. V

Crack House 1989 ★★½ Gangs, drugs, and tough cops vie for control of the streets of L.A. Unimaginative shoot-'em-up with unfulfilled dramatic pretensions. C: Jim Brown, Anthony Geary, Richard Roundtree, Angel Tompkins. D: Michael Fischa. DRA [R] 91m. V

Crack in the Mirror 1960 ★★★ Lawyers representing accused murderers find their own lives resemble those of their clients. Pretentious trick of using three lead actors in double roles damages credibility of otherwise interesting tale of deceit and murder. C: Orson Welles, Juliette Greco, Bradford Dillman. D: Richard Fleischer. DRA 97m.

Crack in the World 1965 ★★★★ Underground nuclear testing causes a section of the Earth to blast off into outer space. Lushly photographed with some imaginatively realized optical effects. C: Dana Andrews, Janette Scott, Kieron Moore. D: Andrew Marton. SFI 96m.

Crack-Up 1937 ★★★½ Airline worker (Lorre) bribes a test pilot (Donlevy) for plans of an experimental airplane. Uneven drama features terrific special effects and a wonderfully offbeat performance from Lorre. C: Peter Lorre, Brian Donlevy, Helen Wood. D: Malcolm St. Clair. DRA 71m.

Crack-Up 1946 ★★★★ Underrated film noir story of an art expert (O'Brien) trying to investigate possible forgeries while recovering from memory black-out. Involved plot and tight direction keep the suspense. C: Pat O'Brien, Claire Trevor, Herbert Marshall. D: Irving Reis. CRI 93m. V

Cracker Factory, The 1979 ★★★★ Wood is marvelous as a neurotic, alcoholic housewife unable to handle daily life, in and out of a psychiatric hospital she calls "the cracker factory." Based on Joyce Rebeta-Burditt's novel. C: Natalie Wood, Perry King, Vivian Blaine, Shelley Long. D: Burt Brinckeroff. DRA 100m. TVM V

Cracking Up 1983 ★ A plethora of characterizations from Lewis, but not many laughs as he pieces together a story about a clumsy depressive seeking help from a psychiatrist. Repetition of gags defeats director's comedic intentions. (a.k.a. *Smorgasbord*). C: Jerry Lewis, Herb Edelman, Milton Berle, Sammy Davis Jr. D: Jerry Lewis. COM [PG] 91m. V

Cradle Will Fall, The 1983 ★★★ Effective TV thriller about a D.A. (Hutton) in danger after witnessing a murder. C: Lauren Hutton, Ben Murphy, James Farentino. D: John Llewellyn Moxey. CRI 103m. V

Craig's Wife 1936 ★★★★½ Russell is outstanding as middle-class spouse whose devotion to home and material possessions overwhelm her love for husband Boles. Fascinating character study that refuses to demonize its unsympathetic subject. Fine cast brings out deeper implications of situation. Remade as *Harriet Craig*. C: Rosalind Russell, John Boles, Billie Burke, Jane Darwell, Thomas Mitchell. D: Dorothy Arzner. DRA 75m. V

Cranes Are Flying, The 1957 Russian ★★★★ After her sweetheart goes off to WWII, woman marries his cousin, enduring an unhappy relationship with him until she can rebuild her life. Simple, tender story of tragic love. Beautifully photographed, well acted and directed. C: Tatiana Samoilova, Alexei Batalov. D: Mikhail Kalatozov. DRA 94m. V

Crash and Burn 1990 ★★★ In the future, the world is run by a giant corporation, staffed by humanoids—except for a lone holdout TV station. Interesting plot, done with flair. C: Paul Ganus, Ralph Waite, Megan Ward. D: Charles Band. SFI 85m. V

Crash Dive 1943 ★★★ Lightweight romantic drama about triangle involving two submarine officers (Power and Andrews) and Baxter. Most watchable for exciting underwater battle finale; the film won an Oscar for Special Effects. C: Tyrone Power, Anne Baxter, Dana Andrews, Dame May Whitty. D: Archie Mayo. ACT 105m. V

Crash of Silence 1953 British ★★★★½ The mother of a deaf girl (Miller) must make some tough decisions about her upbringing. Groundbreaking social drama may seem a bit dated today, but it's still effective due to fine performances, especially from Miller, who plays herself in this true story. (a.k.a. *Mandy*) C: Phyllis Calvert, Mandy Miller, Jack Hawkins. D: Alexander Mackendrick. DRA 93m.

Crashing Hollywood 1937 ★★★★ Needing help with a gangster script, neophyte screenwriter Tracy hires dim-witted ex-con Guilfoyle, who proceeds to base his story on an actual robbery he committed. Fast-paced, above-par comedy. C: Lee Tracy, Joan Woodbury, Paul Guilfoyle. D: Lew Landers. COM 60m.

Crater Lake Monster, The 1977 ★★ David Allen's nifty monster effects (an aquatic dinosaur hatched by a meteor) are the only highlight of this painfully slow, pedestrian chiller. Unfortunately, they're at the end. C: Richard Cardella, Glenn Roberts. D: William R. Stromberg. HOR [PG] 85m. V

Craving, The 1986 ★ The last of Naschy/-Molina's many Spanish werewolf films to see U.S. release is a tedious affair in which the hairy antihero battles a female vampire. Atmospheric. C: Paul Naschy, Julie Saly. D: Jack Molina. HOR [R] 93m. V

Crawling Eye, The 1958 British ★★★ Hiding out in a cloud over a Swiss mountain are enormous alien eyeballs who, for unexplained reasons, behead humans. Uneven effects and many plot holes hamper this otherwise entertaining film. Spawned from the British TV series *The Trollenberg Terror*. C: Forrest Tucker, Laurence Payne, Janet Munro. D: Quentin Lawrence. SFI 85m. V

Crawlspace 1986 ★★ Former Nazi Kinski creeps around behind the walls of the apartment house he owns, spying on and murdering his female tenants. Tacky cheapie nonetheless manages to scare up a few claustrophobic chills. C: Klaus Kinski, Talia Balsam. D: David Schmoeller. HOR [R] 86m. V

Crazies, The 1973 ★★★ Pennsylvania townspeople infected by a biological plague battle National Guard troops sent in to help them. Derivative but peppy chiller with requisite violence. (a.k.a. *Code Name: Trixie*) C: Lane Carroll, W.G. McMillan. D: George Romero. HOR 103m. V

Crazy Desire 1964 Italian ★★★½ Middling Italian romantic comedy has middle-aged Tognazzi falling for much younger Spaak. Airy entertainment. C: Ugo Tognazzi, Catherine Spaak. D: Luciano Salce. COM 108m.

Crazy From the Heart 1991 ★★★★ Charming, offbeat romance with school principal Lahti attracted to Mexican janitor Blades, while her narrow-minded town gossips. Simple, but affectingly performed. C: Christine Lahti, Ruben Blades. D: Thomas Schlamme. DRA 120m. TVM V

Crazy House 1985 *See* **Goodbye, New York**

Crazy in Love 1992 ★★★½ Rambling comedy looks at romantic entanglements of three generations of women living in Pacific Northwest. Sweet, if unexceptional feature benefits from good casting. C: Holly Hunter, Gena Rowlands. D: Martha Coolidge. COM 93m. TVM V

Crazy Jack and the Boy 1973 *See* **Silence**

Crazy Love 1987 *See* **Love Is a Dog from Hell**

Crazy Mama 1975 ★★★★ An off-kilter comedy about three generations of women (Sothern, Leachman, Purl) who take a joy ride from the West Coast to Arkansas in the rockin' and rollin' '50s, committing crimes and picking up men along the way. Leachman turns in a particularly fine performance in this rollicking, thoroughly enjoyable escapist fantasy. C: Cloris Leachman, Stuart Whitman, Ann Sothern, Jim Backus. D: Jonathan Demme. COM [PG] 81m. v

Crazy People 1990 ★★½ Ad exec Moore goes berserk and winds up in a sanitarium where he devises a series of hilariously truthful ads. Unfortunately, slow-moving comedy's only real laughs come from the totally honest and outrageous ads. C: Dudley Moore, Daryl Hannah, Paul Reiser, Mercedes Ruehl. D: Tony Bill. COM [R] 91m. v

Crazy Ray, The 1923 ★★★★ Scientist sets off ray in Paris that temporarily freezes most of the population. Delightful early silent film is both gentle social satire and infectious romance. C: Henri Rollan, Albert Prejean, Marcel Vallee. D: Rene Clair. COM 62m. v

Crazy Wheels 1986 *See* **Dirt Bike Kid, The**

Crazylegs 1953 ★★½ Mild sports comedy with Elroy "Crazylegs" Hirsch playing himself on and off the field. (a.k.a. *Crazylegs.*) C: Elroy Hirsch, Lloyd Nolan, Joan Vohs. D: Francis Lyon. COM 87m.

Creation of the Humanoids 1962 ★★½ In the future, man creates "humanoids" to do the dirty work; but a tough cop (Megowan) watches as the droids slowly take over, and then—insult added to injury!—his sister falls for one. Low-budget production values. C: Don Megowan, Frances McCann. D: Wesley E. Barry. SFI 75m. v

Creator 1985 ★★★ Disjointed but likable comedy, thanks to good cast that steams past oversentimental patches. O'Toole is college professor attempting to clone his dead wife, while his assistant (Spano), falls for student (Madsen). Based on Jeremy Leven's novel. C: Peter O'Toole, Mariel Hemingway, Vincent Spano, Virginia Madsen. D: Ivan Passer. COM [R] 108m. v

Creature 1985 ★★ A vicious extraterrestrial stowaway gorily eliminates members of a deep-space rescue team one at a time. Sound familiar? Blatant *Alien* clone, right down to its female lead. Saved from the abyss by Kinski's demented performance. C: Stan Ivar, Wendy Schaal, Klaus Kinski. D: William Malone. SFI [R] 97m. v

Creature From Galaxy 27 1958 *See* **Night of the Blood Beast**

Creature From the Black Lagoon 1954 ★★★★ Scientists searching the Amazon for fossil remains discover Gill-Man, and live to regret it. One of the best-known '50s monster movies is exciting and colorful; scenes of the creature swimming beneath an oblivious Adams are highlights. Originally presented in 3-D; followed by *Revenge of the Creature* and *The Creature Walks Among Us*. C: Richard Carlson, Julia Adams, Richard Denning. D: Jack Arnold. HOR [G] 80m. v

Creature From the Haunted Sea 1960 ★★ To cover his tracks, a gangster circulates stories about a sea monster, which turn out to be true. A low-budget comedy, vintage Corman all the way. C: Antony Carbone, Betsy Jones Moreland. D: Roger Corman. SFI 76m. v

Creature Walks Among Us, The 1956 ★★½ Poor second sequel to *Creature From the Black Lagoon* has Gill-Man captured and caged, then subjected to reconstructive surgery to try to make him more human. Diminishing returns. C: Jeff Morrow, Leigh Snowden. D: John Sherwood. HOR 79m. v

Creature Wasn't Nice, The 1981 ★★★ A spacecraft with only one woman aboard (Williams) is invaded by an alien monster. Loony satire of *Alien* genre, with a wacky send-up by Nielson as the deadpan commander. (a.k.a. *The Spaceship, Naked Space*) C: Cindy Williams, Bruce Kimmel, Leslie Nielson. D: Bruce Kimmel. COM [PG] 88m. v

Creatures 1973 *See* **From Beyond the Grave**

Creepers 1985 Italian ★★★ Argento returns to girls'-school-slayings territory: A lovely young student (Connelly) uses her empathy with insects to track a killer. Hampered by heavy cutting for U.S. release and some laughable moments, this gory shocker still delivers the goods for horror fans. C: Jennifer Connelly, Donald Pleasence. D: Dario Argento. HOR [R] 82m. v

Creepers, The 1971 *See* **In the Devil's Garden**

Creeping Flesh, The 1972 British ★★★★ A distinguished doctor (Cushing) brings the remains of the "missing link" back to England, where it's stolen by his rival brother (Lee) and brought back to life, killing all within reach. Innovative and effective, worth seeing for horror masters Cushing and Lee. C: Peter Cushing, Christopher Lee. D: Freddie Francis. HOR [PG] 94m. v

Creeping Unknown, The 1956 British ★★★★ Upon returning to Earth, astronaut succumbs to a radical type of space sickness that turns him into a grotesque monster. A solid and intelligent sci-fi film in every respect. The first of the "Quatermass" films, followed by *Enemy from Space, Five Million Years to Earth,* and *Quatermass Conclusion.* C: Brian Donlevy, Margia Dean. D: Val Guest. SFI 78m.

Creepozoids 1987 ★★ Military escapees stumble onto an old research lab and all hell breaks loose. Tries to come off as a sci-fi thriller and misses by a mile. C: Linnea Quigley, Ken Abraham, Michael Aranda, Richard Hawkins. D: David De Coteau. HOR [R] 72m. v

Creeps 1981 *See* **Bloody Birthday**

Creepshow 2 1987 ★★ Another round of King-inspired tales, but the style is flatter and the stories are predictable. A wooden Indian avenges his owners' murder; a hit-and-run victim refuses to die; and (the best piece)

teens are menaced by a monster in a lake. C: Lois Chiles, George Kennedy, Dorothy Lamour. D: Michael Gornick. HOR [R] 89m. v

Creepshow 1982 ★★★★ Stephen King-scripted anthology features tales of a vicious monster in a crate, lethal roaches, and vengeance from beyond the grave. Frightening and funny, with Romero perfectly capturing the visual style of the EC horror comics that inspired this film. C: Hal Holbrook, Adrienne Barbeau, Fritz Weaver, Leslie Nielsen, E. G. Marshall, Ed Harris, Ted Danson. D: George A. Romero. HOR [R] 120m. v

Cria! 1977 Spanish ★★★★ Torrent is brilliant as a nine-year-old grappling with adults less mature than she is. Another moving and thoughtful tale of middle-class Spanish life by Carlos Saura. C: Geraldine Chaplin, Ana Torrent. D: Carlos Saura. DRA 105m. v

Cricket, The 1983 Italian ★★ Portrait of life on the edge as older woman marries a young cafe owner. Pulpy complications abound when the woman's adult daughter from previous marriage enters the scene. Standard at best; fun sleaze at worst. C: Anthony Franciosa, Virna Lisi, Renato Salvatori, Clio Goldsmith. D: Alberto Lattuada. DRA 90m. v

Cries and Whispers 1972 Swedish ★★★★ In 1900, two sisters aid a dying third sibling and her maid. Intense drama of human suffering, beautifully acted and directed. Won Oscar for Sven Nykvist's cinematography. C: Liv Ullmann, Ingrid Thulin, Harriet Andersson, Erland Josephson, Henning Moritzen. D: Ingmar Bergman. DRA 94m. v

Crime Against Joe 1956 ★★★ A young artist (Bromfield) pushed to the edge by failure, goes on a bender and wakes up to learn he's accused of murdering a woman he just met. Routine mystery lacks polish. C: John Bromfield, Julie London. D: Lee Sholem. CRI 69m.

Crime & Punishment, USA 1959 ★★★ A poor student (Hamilton, in his screen debut) kills a miserly pawnbroker and is driven made by guilt. Condensed version of Dostoyevsky classic lacks psychological edge. C: George Hamilton, Mary Murphy, Frank Silvera, Marian Seldes. D: Denis Sanders. DRA 78m.

Crime and Punishment 1935 ★★★★ Little-seen Sternberg is good example of how directorial inventiveness could overcome Hollywoodization of Dostoyevsky's classic novel. While original story is truncated to cat-and-mouse chase between murderer Lorre and inspector Arnold (both excellent), Sternberg's flourishes and Ballard's cinematography give this some weight. C: Edward Arnold, Peter Lorre, Marian Marsh. D: Josef von Sternberg. DRA 88m. v

Crime and Punishment 1970 ★★★½ Poor student robs and murders a pawnbroker, and is driven mad by guilt. Interesting Russian adaptation of the oft filmed Dostoyevsky novel. Tasteful and heavy as borscht. C: Georgi Taratorkin, Viktoria Fyodorova, Irina Gosheva. D: Lev Kulidzhanov. DRA 200m.

Crime Doctor What if the nation's leading expert on criminal behavior were himself a gangster? Max Marcin's radio series posed this question, with Dr. Ordway a brilliant forensic psychologist recovering from a case of amnesia to find out that he once had been a criminal himself. Columbia picked up the film rights to the radio show and introduced Warner Baxter as Ordway in 1943 in *Crime Doctor*. The series continued for another nine crisp mysteries.

Crime Doctor (1943)
Crime Doctor's Strangest Case (1943)
Shadows in the Night (1944)
Crime Doctor's Courage (1945)
Crime Doctor's Warning (1945)
Crime Doctor's Man Hunt (1946)
Just Before Dawn (1946)
The Millerson Case (1947)
Crime Doctor's Gamble (1947)
Crime Doctor's Diary (1949)

Crime Doctor 1943 ★★★½ Inspired by a popular radio show. An amnesiac-turned-psychiatrist (Baxter) learns he has led a previous life as a gangster and must stand trial. Cleverly handled. C: Warner Baxter, Margaret Lindsay. D: Michael Gordon. CRI 66m.

Crime Gives Orders 1938 *See* **Hunted Men**

Crime in the Streets 1956 ★★★½ Frustrated teen plots murder and gets involved with compassionate social worker. Cassavetes, repeating TV role, is so riveting you almost forget he's too old for the part. Well directed, earnest, but unimaginative. Based on Reginal Rose's teleplay. C: James Whitmore, John Cassavetes, Sal Mineo. D: Donald Siegel. CRI 91m. v

Crime of Monsieur Lange, The 1935 French ★★★★★ Anarchic masterpiece follows a lowly printing house worker's decision to murder his boss for the company's good. Jacques Prevert's subtle script, Renoir's limpid direction, sublime acting, and rigorous intelligence permeate every frame of this classic, which has not dated in nearly 60 years. C: Rene Lefevre, Jules Berry, Florelle. D: Jean Renoir. DRA 90m. v

Crime of Passion 1957 ★★★½ An ambitious wife (Stanwyck) will stop at nothing to promote her husband. Barbara excels as a modern-day Lady Macbeth, but the script lets her down. C: Barbara Stanwyck, Sterling Hayden, Raymond Burr, Fay Wray. D: Gerd Oswald. DRA 84m. v

Crime Story 1985 ★★★★ Series pilot pits a former cop (Farina) against the Mafia during the 1960s. Well-paced, exciting movie derives much of its drama from fine character acting by a talented cast. C: Dennis Farina, Anthony Dennison, Stephen Lang, Darlanne Fluegel. D: Abel Ferrara. CRI 96m. V

Crime Wave 1954 ★★★½ Ex-con Nelson wants to stay clean but is pressured by former associates who want him back, while policeman Hayden doesn't believe he's sincere. Routine crime drama; colorful performances. C: Sterling Hayden, Gene Nelson, Phyllis Kirk, Charles Bronson. D: Andre Toth. CRI 74m.

Crime Without Passion 1934 ★★★★ Brilliant but jealous lawyer (Rains, who is superb) tries to outsmart system after shooting mistress. Features justly famous opening montage by Slavko Vorkapich. C: Claude Rains, Margo Whitney. D: Ben Hecht, Charles MacArthur. CRI 72m.

Crimes and Misdemeanors 1989 ★★★★★ Profoundly disturbing, yet entertaining Allen opus has two plotlines: Happily married doctor Landau plots to murder mistress Huston, while documentary filmmaker Allen vies with famous louse Alda for Farrow's affections. Potent drama successfully mixed with uproarious comedy in one of Woody's best films. C: Woody Allen, Martin Landau, Mia Farrow, Alan Alda, Anjelica Huston, Jerry Orbach, Sam Waterston, Claire Bloom, Joanna Gleason. D: Woody Allen. COM 104m. V

Crimes at the Dark House 1940 British ★★★½ A Victorian landowner kills his wife and installs a crazed look-alike in her place. Overwrought melodrama is based on Wilkie Collins' novel *The Woman in White*. Slaughter gives a typically way out performance as the murderous husband. C: Tod Slaughter, Sylvia Marriott, Hilary Eaves. D: George King. DRA 65m. V

Crimes of Dr. Mabuse, The 1933 *See* **Testament of Dr. Mabuse, The**

Crimes of Passion 1984 ★★★ A successful fashion designer (Turner) enjoys a kinky double-life as streetwalker, loved by unhappily married Laughlin and hunted by manic street preacher Perkins. Typically over-the-top satire on sex by Russell is wildly uneven, often funny, and sometimes merely laughable. C: Kathleen Turner, Anthony Perkins, Annie Potts, Bruce Davison. D: Ken Russell. DRA 101m. V

Crimes of the Heart 1986 ★★★★ Three sisters gather to celebrate one of their birthdays as another's arrested for attempted murder, while their father lies dying. Meanwhile, there's Mom's suicide to deal with, and . . . Kooky Southern comedy from Pulitizer Prize-winning Beth Henley play has its moments, mostly due to Spacek's inspired performance. C: Diane Keaton, Jessica Lange, Sissy Spacek, Sam Shepard, Tess Harper. D: Bruce Beresford. COM 105m. V

Criminal Code, The 1931 ★★★ Caught in the web of an obsessed district attorney an innocent man goes to jail. Huston is powerful as prison warden in Hawks' tense predecessor to *Scarface*. C: Walter Huston, Phillips Holmes, Constance Cummings, Boris Karloff. D: Howard Hawks. CRI 98m. V

Criminal Court 1946 ★★★½ Lawyer (Conway) accidentally kills blackmailing nightclub owner (Armstrong) and then defends blackmailer's victim (O'Driscoll) when she is accused of murder. Hard-hitting, fast-paced little courtroom drama. C: Tom Conway, Martha O'Driscoll, Robert Armstrong. D: Robert Wise. CRI 63m. V

Criminal Justice 1990 ★★★½ Career criminal (Whitaker) is identified—incorrectly—as the purse snatcher who disfigured a prostitute, and the prosecutor (Grey) must figure out the contradictions. Excellent performances boost this indictment of the justice system. C: Forest Whitaker, Jennifer Grey, Rosie Perez, Anthony La Paglia. D: Andy Wolk. CRI [R] 92m. TVM V

Criminal Law 1989 ★★½ Oldman (in good performance) is a defense attorney who wins acquittal for wealthy Bacon, accused of serial murders. Oldman comes to realize a serious miscarriage of justice has occurred, but is caught between legal ethics and his own morals. C: Gary Oldman, Kevin Bacon, Joe Don Baker, Tess Harper. D: Martin Campbell. CRI [R] 113m. V

Criminal Lawyer 1951 ★★★ A crooked lawyer (O'Brien) turns to the bottle after failing the Bar exam, but straightens up to defend a friend accused of murder. Modest courtroom melodrama. C: Pat O'Brien, Jane Wyatt. D: Seymour Friedman. DRA 74m.

Criminal Life of Archibaldo de la Cruz, The 1955 Mexican ★★★ Disturbed man believes he has the power to decide who shall live and who shall die. Psychological drama is not the best Buñuel, but benefits greatly from his dark and strange touches. C: Ernesto Alonso, Miroslava Stern. D: Luis Buñuel. DRA 91m. V

Criminal, The *See* **The Concrete Jungle**

Crimson Cult, The 1968 British ★★ Karloff is wasted as a witchcraft expert involved in satanic rituals in a small English town. Saved by Karloff's talented presence. C: Christopher Lee, Boris Karloff, Mark Eden, Virginia Wetherell, Barbara Steele. D: Vernon Sewell. HOR [PG] 87m.

Crimson Kimono, The 1959 ★★★ L.A. homicide detectives (Corbett and Shigeta) tracking stripper's murderer become rivals when they both fall for witness (Shaw). Murder mystery gets tension from racial theme. C: Victoria Shaw, Glenn Corbett, James Shigeta. D: Samuel Fuller. CRI 82m.

Crimson Pirate, The 1952 ★★★★ Good pirate (Lancaster) wields swords, swings on ropes, and breaks hearts of the lovely maidens in this fabulous swashbuckler. Good fun for the entire family, with plenty of color and slapstick to please the kids. C: Burt Lancaster, Eva Bartok, Nick Cravat, Christopher Lee. D: Robert Siodmak. ACT 104m. V

Crimson Romance 1934 ★★★½ American pilot (Lyon) joins the German air force with his native-born friend (Bush) and feels conflicting loyalties when WWI breaks out. Odd action drama with von Stroheim strutting about in a monocle. C: Ben Lyon, Sari Maritza, Erich von Stroheim. D: David Howard. DRA 72m.

Cripple Creek 1952 ★★★ B-Western has Montgomery and sidekick Courtland as undercover federal agents infiltrating a gang planning to smuggle gold out of a mine. Standard. C: George Montgomery, Karin Booth, Richard Egan. D: Ray Nazarro. WST 78m.

Crisis at Central High 1981 ★★★½ Historic 1957 integration case in Little Rock, Arkansas, told from white teacher Woodward's point of view. As such, it's one-dimensional with black students little more than window dressing in what should have been their story. C: Joanne Woodward, Charles Durning, Henderson Forsythe. D: Lamont Johnson. DRA 120m. TVM V

Crisis 1950 ★★½ Stodgy tale of U.S. doctor Grant, admirably sober but misused, forced to treat Latin American dictator. Ferrer relies on flashy technique. Brooks's first directorial effort just plain dull. C: Cary Grant, Jose Ferrer, Paula Raymond, Signe Hasso, Ramon Novarro, Gilbert Roland. D: Richard Brooks. DRA [PG-13] 95m.

Criss Cross 1949 ★★★★½ Down-and-out security guard (Lancaster) is lured into crime by his sultry ex-wife (De Carlo). Sizzling film noir, loaded with style. C: Burt Lancaster, Yvonne De Carlo, Dan Duryea. D: Robert Siodmak. CRI 87m.

CrissCross 1992 ★★★ Abandoned by her Vietnam War-veteran husband, working-class mother Hawn copes with raising her 12-year-old son alone in 1969 Florida. Well-intentioned but inert drama. C: Goldie Hawn, Arliss Howard, Keith Carradine. D: Chris Menges. DRA [R] 101m. V

Critical Condition 1986 ★★ A crisis at a medical institution leads con artist Pryor to be mistaken for a doctor; everyone then counts on him to take charge of the situation. Pryor manages some laughs, but even he has trouble keeping this feeble comedy alive. C: Richard Pryor, Rachel Ticotin, Ruben Blades, Joe Mantegna, Sylvia Miles. D: Michael Apted. COM [R] 99m. V

Critic's Choice 1962 ★★★ So-so comedy from Ira Levin play about drama critic and his playwright wife. Two stars are hard put to make characters likable, but they manage. Note: Inspired by real-life *Herald Tribune* drama critic Walter Kerr and his wife, Jean Kerr. C: Bob Hope, Lucille Ball, Marilyn Maxwell, Rip Torn, Jessie Royce Landis. D: Don Weis. COM 100m. V

Critters 1986 ★★★ Alien killer hedgehogs terrorize a Kansas family until a couple of deadpan humanoid aliens arrive to hunt them down. Borrows heavily from *Gremlins*, *Brother from Another Planet*, and many others, but combines the elements creatively and with humor. Spawned three sequels. C: Dee Wallace Stone, M. Emmet Walsh, Scott Grimes. D: Stephen Herek. SFI [PG-13] 86m. V

Critters 2 1988 ★★ This time the pesky alien hedgehogs terrorize a whole town. Weak sequel to the okay original. (To be fair, there's not much to work with here.) Two sequels followed. C: Scott Grimes, Liane Curtis. D: Mick Garris. SFI [PG-13] 87m. V

Critters 3 1991 ★★★ Evil furry little creatures invade an apartment house, hungry for the residents. Third *Critters* film, with okay special effects, hampered by a predictable story. C: Aimee Brooks, Leonard DiCaprio. D: Kristine Peterson. HOR [PG-13] 86m. V

Critters 4 1992 ★★★ The befanged little hairballs are back, infesting a space salvage ship. Suspenseful and satisfyingly scary. C: Don Keith Opper, Brad Dourif, Angela Bassett. D: Rupert Harvey. HOR [PG-13] 94m. V

Crocodile 1979 ★ A mammoth reptile flattens everything in its path while, in true *Jaws* tradition, a heroic trio set out to stop it. The cheap special effects are good for a few laughs, but mostly this Malaysian import is numbingly inept. C: Nat Puvanai, Tany Tim. D: Sompote Sands. HOR [R] 95m. V

Crocodile Dundee 1986 Australian ★★★★ After escorting American reporter Kozlowski around Australian outback, wiry guide Hogan heads to New York City where wildlife has distinctively different look. Enormous box office hit, this fish-out-of-water story thrives on Hogan's droll comic skills. C: Paul Hogan, Linda Kozlowski, John Meillon. D: Peter Faiman. COM [PG-13] 98m. V

Crocodile Dundee II 1988 U.S. ★★★ Lesser follow-up to previous hit switches formula: This time reporter Kozlowski follows adventurer Hogan from Manhattan to his home turf in Australia and they get involved with international drug dealers. Jokey showcase for Hogan's comic talents. C: Paul Hogan, Linda Kozlowski, John Meillon, Charles Dutton. D: John Cornell. COM [PG] 110m. V

Cromwell 1970 British ★★ Chronicle of 17th-century Puritan revolutionary who deposed English King Charles I. Huge battles, Oscar-winning costumes, and sweeping cinematography can't rouse this behemoth. C: Richard Harris, Alec Guinness, Robert Morley, Dorothy Tutin, Frank Finlay, Timothy Dalton. D: Kenneth Hughes. DRA [G] 139m. V

Cronos 1992 Mexican ★★★★ Mexico City antiques dealer finds an ancient device that confers immortality on whoever possesses it, with one small drawback: it turns you into a vampire. A dying millionaire wants it badly enough to send his nephew (Perlman) to kill for it. Imaginative blend of many genres (comedy, horror, thriller) makes for unique viewing experience. Available in Spanish or English-dubbed. C: Federico Luppi, Ron Perlman, Margarita isabel, Claudio Brook. D: Guillermo Del Toro. HOR [G] 92m. v

Crook, The 1971 French ★★★★ A shady lawyer masterminds a bank robbery, but the plan goes awry. A surprisingly cold, cynical tale by the usually sentimental Lelouch; Trintignant is superb, plot construction ingenious. C: Jean-Louis Trintignant, Daniele Delorme, Christine Lelouch. D: Claude Lelouch. CRI [G] 120m.

Crooked Hearts 1991 ★★★½ A family is torn at the seams by rival brothers (Berg, D'Onofrio), both prone to failure. Incisive and beautifully acted, but, since all the characters are losers, ultimately depressing. From Robert Boswell's novel. C: Vincent D'Onofrio, Jennifer Jason Leigh, Peter Berg, Peter Coyote, Juliette Lewis, Cindy Pickett. D: Michael Bortman. DRA [R] 112m. v

Crooklyn 1994 ★★★½ An African-American family struggles in the '70s to recover from turmoil of the '60s. Apparently autobiographical film from Lee features his trademarks: in-your-face controversy about racial attitudes and choppy narrative style. C: Alfre Woodard, Delroy Lindo, David Patrick Kelly, Zelda Harris. D: Spike Lee. DRA [PG-13] 112m.

Crooks and Coronets 1969 British ★★★½ A gangster schemes to rob heirloom-filled mansion, but has second thoughts when he befriends the inhabitants. Entertaining caper comedy. (a.k.a. *Sophie's Place*) C: Telly Savalas, Edith Evans, Warren Oates, Cesar Romero. D: Jim O'Connolly. COM [PG] 106m. v

Crooks Anonymous 1962 British ★★★ Reform-minded thief (Phillips) joins 12-step program for criminals, but they just can't stand all that talent going to waste. Ridiculous comedy is Christie's screen debut. C: Leslie Phillips, Stanley Baxter, Wilfrid Hyde-White, Julie Christie. D: Ken Annakin. COM 87m.

Cross Country 1983 ★★ After a high-priced prostitute turns up dead, detective Ironside follows the trail across Canada left behind by suspect Beymer. Uninvolving murder mystery, with seamy settings. C: Richard Beymer, Nina Axelrod, Michael Ironside. D: Paul Lynch. CRI [R] 95m. v

Cross Creek 1983 ★★★★ Fleeing broken marriage, author Marjorie Kinnan Rawlings settles in the bayou country where she gets to know the locals, falls in love, and writes *The Yearling*. Excellent, leisurely paced story with an exceptional cast. C: Mary Steenburgen, Rip Torn, Alfre Woodard, Peter Coyote, Joanna Miles, Ike Eisenmann. D: Martin Ritt. DRA [PG] 115m. v

Cross My Heart 1987 ★★★ O'Toole and Short embark on their third date armed only with the bad advice of friends and family. A minor pleasure but film's gentle humor often has the sting of truth. C: Martin Short, Annette O'Toole, Paul Reiser, Joanna Kerns. D: Armyan Bernstein. COM [R] 91m. v

Cross of Fire 1989 ★★★★ Heard makes his mark in this 1920s period piece, a memorable biography of the appallingly charismatic Ku Klux Klan Grand Dragon D.C. Stephenson. C: John Heard, Mel Harris, Lloyd Bridges, Kim Hunter. D: Paul Wendkos. DRA 200m. TVM v

Cross of Iron 1977 British ★★★½ A German battalion on the Eastern front in 1943 retreats before Russians. led by battle-shy commander (Schell) who lies to secure medal. War's morally and physically destructive nature is explored with an emphasis on violence. Sequel: *Breakthrough*. C: James Coburn, Maximilian Schell, James Mason, David Warner, Senta Berger. D: Sam Peckinpah. DRA [R] 132m. v

Cross of Lorraine, The 1943 ★★★★ Two French soldiers (Aumont and Kelly) are duped into surrendering after the fall of France in a remarkably brutal portrait (for its day) of concentration camp life. Film is made particularly chilling by Peter Lorre's portrayal of a Nazi sergeant who revels in torture. C: Jean-Pierre Aumont, Gene Kelly, Cedric Hardwicke, Peter Lorre, Hume Cronyn. D: Tay Garnett. ACT 90m.

Crossed Swords 1978 ★★★ Mediocre adaptation of classic Mark Twain switched-identity story, *The Prince and the Pauper*. Lester too old for dual leading role, and miscast on top of that. Splendid sets, photography, and many star cameo appearances can't elevate this one. (a.k.a. *The Prince and the Pauper.*) C: Mark Lester, Oliver Reed, Raquel Welch, Ernest Borgnine, George C. Scott, Rex Harrison, Charlton Heston. D: Richard Fleischer. FAM/DRA [PG] 113m. v

Crossfire 1933 ★★★ Weird hybrid of gangster tale and western features Keene as a lawman fighting mob forces intent on framing his best friend for murder. David O. Selznick produced this modest programmer. C: Tom Keene, Betty Furness, Edgar Kennedy. D: Otto Brower. WST 55m.

Crossfire 1947 ★★★★½ War veteran goes berserk and begins randomly shooting Jewish victims, then leads law enforcement through citywide hunt. Gritty, determined crime drama that handles emotionally charged subject with dexterity. Cast is outstanding. C: Robert Young, Robert Mitchum, Robert Ryan, Gloria Grahame, Sam Levene. D: Edward Dmytryk. DRA 86m. v

Crossing Delancey 1988 ★★★★ New York career woman (Irving) can't get her lovable Jewish grandmother (Bozyk) to stop matchmaking. Her latest choice is a pickle maker (Riegert). Their nonromance is charmingly played; Bozyk is particularly endearing performance. C: Amy Irving, Reizl Bozyk, Peter Riegert, Jeroen Krabbe, Sylvia Miles. D: Joan Micklin Silver. COM 97m. V

Crossing the Bridge 1992 ★★★ Three friends make a drug deal involving a trip to Canada, without realizing how it will change their lives. Earnest but slow-moving and predictable. C: Josh Charles, Jason Gedrick, Stephen Baldwin. D: Mike Binder. DRA 103m. V

Crossing the Line 1991 U.S. ★★★½ An out-of-work coal miner (Neeson) unhappily fights bare-knuckled for ready cash in depressed Scotland. Brawler of a film has some surprising twists and turns. C: Liam Neeson, Joanne Kilmer, Ian Bannen, Hugh Grant. D: David Leland. DRA 93m. V

Crossing, The 1992 ★★★ Young woman must choose between staying in a small town or moving to the big city with artist boyfriend. Compelling characters, interesting coming-of-age story. C: Russell Crowe, Robert Mammone, Danielle Spencer. D: George Ogilvie. DRA 92m. V

Crossing to Freedom 1990 ★★½ A man (O'Toole) who hates children finds himself smuggling them out of occupied France during WWII. O'Toole steals the show—in fact, he IS the show! Remake of better 1942 Monty Woolley film, *The Pied Piper*. C: Peter O'Toole, Mare Winningham. D: Norman Stone. DRA 100m. TVM

Crossover Dreams 1985 ★★★½ Story of an ambitious salsa singer (Blades) from NYC's Spanish Harlem who wants to make it "downtown" is predictable and formulaic, but the music, and Blades' natural performance are terrific. C: Ruben Blades, Shawn Elliot, Tom Signorelli. D: Leon Ichaso. MUS 85m. V

Crossroads 1938 French ★★★½ Rich industrialist (Vanel), shell-shocked after WWI, is blackmailed; but he can't remember what happened. Twisty plot, intriguing but inconclusive. Remade in U.S. in 1942. C: Charles Vanel, Jules Berry, Suzy Prim. D: Kurt Bernhardt. DRA 73m.

Crossroads 1942 ★★★★ American remake of 1938 French film. Amnesiac American diplomat in prewar Paris (Powell) is blackmailed by Trevor and Rathbone who convince him that he was a criminal. Effective melodrama with a mystery twist. C: William Powell, Hedy Lamarr, Claire Trevor, Basil Rathbone. D: Jack Conway. DRA 84m.

Crossroads 1986 ★★★½ Julliard guitarist who prefers the blues (Macchio) heads South with old-time blues musician (Seneca) who's sold his soul to the devil—on a quest for "forgotten" manuscripts of legendary bluesman Robert Johnson. Excellent score highlights average road musical. C: Ralph Macchio, Joe Seneca, Jami Gertz, Joe Morton. D: Walter Hill. MUS [R] 100m. V

Crosswinds 1951 ★★★ Adventurer (Payne) seeks shipment of gold that went down in a plane near New Guinea and encounters exotic dangers. Modest treasure-hunting tale. C: John Payne, Rhonda Fleming, Forrest Tucker. D: Lewis Foster. DRA 93m.

Crow, The 1994 ★★★★ Adaptation of underground comic classic about superhero from beyond the grave; he's come back to avenge his murder and be reunited with his fiancée. Will probably be remembered as the film on which Brandon Lee was killed. C: Brandon Lee, Ernie Hudson, Michael Wincott, David Patrick Kelly. D: Alex Proyas. ACT [R] 100m. V

Crowd Roars, The 1932 ★★★ Family drama of an unscrupulous father forcing his son into boxing—and into the arms of the Mob. Okay story and stars. C: James Cagney, Joan Blondell, Ann Dvorak, Guy Kibbee, Frank McHugh. D: Howard Hawks. DRA 85m.

Crowd Roars, The 1938 ★★★½ Boxer (Taylor) and manager-father (Morgan) get involved with murder and crime czar (Arnold). Punchy genre fare. Remake: *Killer McCoy*. C: Robert Taylor, Edward Arnold, Frank Morgan, Maureen O'Sullivan, Lionel Stander, Jane Wyman. D: Richard Thorpe. CRI 92m.

Crowd, The 1928 ★★★★★ Silent film classic about just another unimportant little man doomed to be mediocre, lost in the city's great crush of humanity. Considered highly innovative in its day, and still extremely impressive. C: Eleanor Boardman, James Murray, Bert Roach. D: King Vidor. DRA 104m. V

Crowded Sky, The 1960 ★★★ Those aboard a military plane and a jet liner are unaware that they are headed for a mid-air collision. Superficial thriller concerns itself with "interior drama." C: Dana Andrews, Rhonda Fleming, Efrem Zimbalist, Jr., John Kerr, Troy Donahue, Patsy Kelly. D: Joseph Pevney. ACT 105m.

Crucible of Horror 1971 British ★★ Sadist (Gough) makes life hell for his wife and daughter to the point where they kill him—but he returns nonetheless to torment them anew. Unimaginative direction. C: Michael Gough, Sharon Gurney. D: Viktors Ritelis. HOR [PG] 91m. V

Crucible, The 1957 French ★★★★ Strikingly cinematic foreign-made version of Arthur Miller's Salem witch-hunt drama with Montand and Signoret effective as victims of savage prejudice. Intended as indictment of McCarthyism. C: Simone Signoret, Yves Montand, Mylene Demongeot. D: Raymond Rouleau. DRA 140m.

Crucifer of Blood, The 1991 British ★★★½ Heston plays Sherlock Holmes in this mystery of two ex-soldiers with something to hide, and their comrade, bent on vengeance. Adapted from a play by Paul Giovanni based in turn on

Conan Doyle's "The Sign of Four"; solid Sherlock suspenser. C: Charlton Heston, Richard Johnson, Susanna Harker, Simon Callow, James Fox. D: Fraser C. Heston. CRI 105m. TVM V

Crucified Lovers *See* **Chikamatsu Monogatari**

Cruel Sea, The 1953 British ★★★★ A dramatic feature with a documentary feel on the courageous men serving aboard a Royal Navy corvette on convoy duty in WWII. Well crafted and acted, with noteworthy performance by Hawkins and a very early look at Elliot. C: Jack Hawkins, Donald Sinden, Denholm Elliott, Virginia McKenna, Alec McCowen. D: Charles Frend. DRA 121m. V

Cruel Story of Youth 1960 ★★★★ Teenagers meet their fate after blackmailing several men and playing sexual games together. Oshima's disturbing second feature was clearly influenced by Godard: long takes, hand-held camera, alienated youth. Stands on its own, however. (a.k.a. *Naked Youth.*) C: Miyuki Kuwano, Yoshiko Kuga, Yusuke Kawazu. D: Nagisa Oshima. DRA 96m. V

Cruel Tower, The 1956 ★★★½ High-steel workers fight and love. Standard but muscular. C: John Ericson, Mari Blanchard, Charles McGraw. D: Lew Landers. DRA 79m.

Cruising 1980 ★ Dishonest, offensive thriller with Pacino as homophobic undercover cop decked out in chains and leather to attract killer of homosexuals. Fails on all levels, regardless of viewers' politics. C: Al Pacino, Paul Sorvino, Karen Allen, Don Scardino. D: William Friedkin. DRA [R] 102m. V

Crusades, The 1935 ★★★½ Cecil B. DeMille medieval extravaganza follows Richard the Lionheart (Wilcoxon), battling infidels, and avoiding marriage to French princess (Young). Much pomp and pomposity. C: Loretta Young, Henry Wilcoxon, Ian Keith, Katherine DeMille, C. Aubrey Smith. D: Cecil B. DeMille. DRA 123m.

Crush, The 1993 ★★ A magazine writer (Elwes) is stalked by a disturbed teenager (Silverstone), who is obsessively in love with him. Generic *Fatal Attraction* clone substitutes hornets for dead bunnies. C: Cary Elwes, Alicia Silverstone, Jennifer Rubin. D: Alan Shapiro. CRI [R] 89m. V

Crusoe 1988 ★★★★ Slave trader Crusoe (Quinn), is shipwrecked on a secluded island, where he struggles daily to survive and comes to terms with his relationship with a cannibal (Sapara). Overlooked, intriguing version of the Defoe novel with fine performances. C: Aidan Quinn, Ade Sapara. D: Caleb Deschanel. DRA [PG-13] 95m. V

Cry Baby Killer, The 1958 ★★★ Crazed killer takes three hostages and waits it out in a storeroom as crowd gathers to watch ordeal. Moderately successful look at American voyeurism. Brief cameo by Corman as a news camera operator; Nicholson's film debut. C: Harry Lauter, Jack Nicholson, Carolyn Mitchell. D: Jus Addiss. CRI 62m.

Cry-Baby 1990 ★★★½ Goody-goody Locane is tempted by sin in the form of black-jacketed Depp in this parody of '50s rock 'n' roll movies. Good cast plays it to the hilt, though story lacks any real bite. Great cameo appearances add to the energetically goofy aura. C: Johnny Depp, Amy Locane, Polly Bergen, Iggy Pop, Ricki Lake, Traci Lords, Troy Donahue, Joey Heatherton, David Nelson. D: John Waters. MUS [PG-13] 86m. V

Cry Blood, Apache 1970 ★ Dreadful gold-lust tale about tattered prospectors who kill a bunch of Indians. Told in flashback by elder McCrea. C: Jody McCrea, Dan Kemp, Joel McCrea. D: Jack Starrett. WST [R] 82m. V

Cry Danger 1951 ★★★★ A convict (Powell) is set up and sent up the river; when he gets released, he's out for revenge. Taut actioner. C: Dick Powell, Rhonda Fleming, William Conrad. D: Robert Parrish. ACT 80m. V

Cry for Happy 1961 ★★★ Four Navy photographers (Ford, O'Connor, Shigeta, and Douglas) meet four geishas and help them found an orphanage. Saccharine comedy. C: Glenn Ford, Donald O'Connor, Myoshi Umeki. D: George Marshall. COM 110m.

Cry for Help: The Tracey Thurman Story, A 1989 ★★★★½ Sitcom star McKeon proves herself formidable actress in searing study of battered wife vainly seeking police protection. Interesting flashback/trial structure culminating in devastating climax. One of the better true-crime TV movies. C: Nancy McKeon, Dale Midkiff. D: Robert Markowitz. DRA 100m.

Cry For Me, Billy 1972 *See* **Count Your Bullets**

Cry Freedom 1987 British ★★★★ True story about white South African journalist Donald Woods (Kline), who supports black activist Steven Biko (Oscar-nominated Washington, in a fiery performance) and flees the country to tell Biko's story after he dies in prison. Ambitious epic focuses too much on Woods but tells an important story. C: Kevin Kline, Penelope Wilton, Denzel Washington, Alec McCowen, Zakes Mokae, Ian Richardson. D: Richard Attenborough. DRA [PG] 157m. V

Cry from the Mountain 1985 ★★½ Religious propaganda from the Billy Graham Ministry cloaked in the guise of an adventure story about a father and son who take a kayak trip to Alaska. Scenery's great; preaching may be a turn-off. C: James Cavan, Wes Parker, Chris Kidd, Billy Graham, Rita Walter. D: James F. Collier. FAM/DRA [PG] 78m. V

Cry from the Streets, A 1959 British ★★★½ Documentary-style drama about London social workers and the homeless children they try to help. Well meaning. C: Max Bygraves, Barbara

Murray, Kathleen Harrison. D: Lewis Gilbert. DRA 99m.

Cry Havoc 1943 ★★★½ Occasionally effective women-at-war flick with top-flight cast as American nurses stationed on island of Bataan during WWII. Wispy Sullavan seems out of place here, but hard-edged Southern is terrific. C: Margaret Sullavan, Joan Blondell, Ann Sothern, Fay Bainter, Marsha Hunt, Ella Raines, Connie Gilchrist. D: Richard Thorpe. ACT 97m.

Cry in the Dark, A 1988 U.S. ★★★★ True story of Australian woman damned by press and public (and ultimately accused of murder) after her baby was carried off by a wild dog. Stern and unsentimental, but Streep gives a bravely flinty performance as the unlikable victim whose stoic religious beliefs made her an unsympathetic public figure. C: Meryl Streep, Sam Neill. D: Fred Schepisi. DRA [PG-13] 121m. V

Cry in the Night, A 1956 ★★½ Mentally unhinged Burr, obsessed with Wood and her boyfriend, turns from voyeurism to kidnapping. Potboiler suspense doesn't offer much insight or many surprises. C: Edmond O'Brien, Brian Donlevy, Natalie Wood, Raymond Burr. D: Frank Tuttle. DRA 75m.

Cry in the Wild, A 1990 ★★★★ Teenage boy (Rushton, in an excellent performance) survives a plane crash in northern California and must make do by his wits and wilderness skills. Weakened by unnecessary subplot, but still a gripping tale. C: Jared Rushton, Pamela Sue Martin, Ned Beatty. D: Mark Griffiths. FAM/ACT [PG] 82m. V

Cry of the Banshee 1970 British ★★★ A brutal witchhunter (Price) picks the wrong woman to hunt—she hexes him and his family. Stylish and gripping. C: Vincent Price, Elisabeth Bergner, Hugh Griffith. D: Gordon Hessler. HOR [PG] 87m. V

Cry of the City 1948 ★★★★½ Superb film noir by one of best directors of the genre. Boyhood friends grow up into cop and criminal. Splendid acting includes scary support from Emerson. A familiar story given first-class treatment. C: Victor Mature, Richard Conte, Fred Clark, Shelley Winters, Betty Garde, Debra Paget, Hope Emerson. D: Robert Siodmak. CRI 95m.

Cry of the Hunted 1953 ★★½ Policeman (Sullivan) chases escaped convict (Gassman) through Louisiana swamps in this low-budget chase picture with Cajun spice. C: Vittorio Gassman, Barry Sullivan, Polly Bergen, William Conrad. D: Joseph Lewis. CRI 80m.

Cry Terror 1958 ★★★½ Tense thriller about psycho Steiger who forces family man Mason to help him plant a bomb on a plane for extortion purposes. Mason's daughter Portland makes a brief appearance. C: James Mason, Rod Steiger, Inger Stevens, Neville Brand, Angie Dickinson, Jack Klugman. D: Andrew Stone. CRI 96m.

Cry the Beloved Country 1951 British ★★★★ Hard-hitting apartheid drama features a stellar Poitier as clergyman faced with a moral crisis in his own country. C: Canada Lee, Charles Carson, Sidney Poitier, Joyce Carey. D: Zoltan Korda. DRA 120m. V

Cry Uncle! 1971 ★★★★ Outrageous detective spoof with investigator Garfield getting into all sorts of sordid trouble as he pursues the clues to a blackmailing case. Salacious, wickedly funny sex comedy. C: Allen Garfield, Madeleine De La Roux, Davin Goldenberg. D: John G. Avildsen. COM [R] 87m. V

Cry Vengeance 1954 ★★★½ Innocent ex-cop and ex-con (Stevens) goes after the criminals who framed him and killed his family. Mediocre suspense drama. C: Mark Stevens, Martha Hyer. D: Mark Stevens. CRI 83m. V

Cry Wolf 1947 ★★★½ Fair mystery with Stanwyck literally climbing the walls as widow trying to claim inheritance in spooky family mansion. C: Barbara Stanwyck, Errol Flynn, Geraldine Brooks, Richard Basehart. D: Peter Godfrey. DRA 83m.

Crying Game, The 1992 British ★★★★½ After a kidnapping attempt goes sour, an IRA terrorist (Rea) hides in London where he becomes involved with the hostage's lover (Davidson). Unusual, adult, and very distinct drama, highlighted by complicated character relationships and outstanding performances. Notorious for its "secret" but good enough to survive even if you know the twist. Oscar winner for Best Original Screenplay. C: Stephen Rea, Jaye Davidson, Miranda Richardson, Forest Whitaker. D: Neil Jordan. DRA [R] 112m. V

Crystal Ball, The 1943 ★★★ After losing a beauty contest, Goddard tries her luck at telling fortunes and gets entangled in a real estate racket. Thin comedy with pie-throwing finale. C: Paulette Goddard, Ray Milland, Virginia Field, Gladys George, William Bendix. D: Elliott Nugent. COM 81m.

Crystal Force 1990 ★★ Grieving daughter buys magical crystal that promises good things, but delivers just the opposite. Low-budget horror manages a few scares. C: Katherine McCall, John Serrdakue, Tony C. Burton. D: Laura Keats. HOR 82m. V

Crystal Heart 1985 ★★ Young man who must live in regulated environment without germs falls for rock singer. Bland romance, punctuated with silly, if energetic, music videos from Kitaen. C: Tawny Kitaen, Lee Curreri, Lloyd Bochner. D: Gil Bettman. DRA [R] 103m. V

Cthulhu Mansion 1990 ★ Young punks on the run kidnap a magician and his daughter and hole up at his mansion, where they're terrorized by supernatural forces. Jumbled, silly shocker with uneven effects and only a slight resemblance to the H.P. Lovecraft stories it's supposedly based on. C: Frank Finlay, Melanie Shatner, Marcia Layton, Brad Fisher. D: J.P. Simon. HOR [R] 95m. V

Cuba 1979 ★★ Old-fashioned epic romance has British mercenary Connery rekindling affair with Adams during the Cuban revolution. Well-done, and beautiful to look at. C: Sean Connery, Brooke Adams, Jack Weston, Hector Elizondo, Denholm Elliott, Lonette McKee. D: Richard Lester. DRA [R] 121m. V

Cuban Love Song, The 1931 ★★★½ Twist on *Madame Butterfly* has Marine Tibbett falling for Havana peanut-vendor Velez, then ditching her to return to girlfriend Morley back home. Nice mix of music and melodrama was radio/opera star Tibbett's last film. C: Lawrence Tibbett, Lupe Velez, Ernest Torrence, Jimmy Durante. D: W.S. Van Dyke. MUS 80m.

Cuban Pete 1946 ★★★ Second-tier musical about Cuban orchestra leader trying to make it big in the Big Apple; most notable as Arnaz's screen debut. C: Desi Arnaz, Beverly Simmons, Don Porter. D: Jean Yarbrough. MUS 61m.

Cujo 1983 ★★★ One of the better Stephen King films, with Wallace and her young son terrorized in their broken-down car by a rabid Saint Bernard. Played straight and free of gimmicks, building to some genuinely pulse-pounding moments. C: Dee Wallace, Danny Pintauro, Daniel Hugh Kelly. D: Lewis Teague. HOR [R] 93m. V

Cul-De-Sac 1966 British ★★★★ Bizarre group of characters inhabit this weird Polanski comedy/drama. A duo of fleeing gangsters take refuge with and end up tormenting timid business exec and his wife. Stylish and effective. C: Donald Pleasence, Francoise Dorleac, Lionel Stander, Jacqueline Bisset. D: Roman Polanski. DRA 111m.

Culpepper Cattle Co., The 1972 ★★½ Self-conscious rite of passage for 16-year-old boy who finds his manhood on a trail-drive. Director Richards forces a lot of empty style and violence on viewers. C: Gary Grimes, Billy Green Bush, Luke Askew, Bo Hopkins. D: Dick Richards. WST [PG] 92m. V

Cup Final 1992 Israeli ★★★★ Captured Israeli soldier and Palestinian leader find their love for soccer has meaning in world deadened by war. The war/sport metaphor is laid on with a trowel but the film is still a surprisingly engaging view of a horrific contemporary crisis. C: Moshe Ivgi. D: Eran Riklis. DRA 107m.

Curée 1966 *See* **Game is Over, The**

Curiosity Kills 1990 ★★★ Convoluted but often tense story about young artist neighbors who team up to snare the paid assassin living in their building, but quickly find that they're in over their heads. C: C. Thomas Howell, Rae Dawn Chong. D: Colin Bucksey. CRI [R] 86m. TVM V

Curly Sue 1991 ★★★ Ragtag, pint-size hustler tries to light a romantic fire between her scruffy guardian and a successful, sophisticated lawyer they've been conning. Sometimes funny, sometimes misdirected blend of slapstick and sentimentality. C: James Belushi, Kelly Lynch, Alisan Porter. D: John Hughes. COM [PG] 102m. V

Curly Top 1935 ★★★★ Orphan Temple plays matchmaker for older sister Hudson and millionaire Boles. Classic Temple vehicle introduced song *Animal Crackers*, and is one of several films based on Jean Webster's *Daddy Long Legs*. C: Shirley Temple, John Boles, Rochelle Hudson, Jane Darwell, Arthur Treacher. D: Irving Cummings. MUS 74m. V

Curse 4 1992 ★★ Young monk Van Patten and his monastic brothers tangle with an unleashed evil spirit in their midst. Originally filmed as *Catacombs*, this sequel-that-isn't is stronger as a religious drama than as a horror movie. C: Jeremy West, Ian Abercrombie, Timothy Van Patten, Laura Schaefer. D: David Schmoeller. HOR [R] 84m. V

Curse of Dark Shadows 1971 *See* **Night of Dark Shadows**

Curse of Frankenstein, The 1957 British ★★★★ Vivid British retelling of Shelley's classic story—Young Baron Frankenstein (Cushing) creates a hideous monster (Lee) from dead body parts. This is Hammer's first color horror film, and still one of the best. C: Christopher Lee, Peter Cushing, Hazel Court. D: Terence Fisher. HOR 83m. V

Curse of King Tut's Tomb, The 1980 ★★ Some say the discovery of Tutankhamen's tomb caused inexplicable catastrophes. Does this movie make its case? Sensationalist rendering of the 1922 excavation in Egypt, with Burr prominently miscast as a Cairo villain. C: Robert Ellis, Harry Andrews, Eva Marie Saint, Raymond Burr. D: Philip Leacock. HOR 98m. TVM V

Curse of the Black Widow 1976 ★★ By-the-numbers thriller about giant killer spider in L.A. (a.k.a. *Love Trap*) C: Anthony Franciosa, Donna Mills, June Allyson, Patty Duke. D: Dan Curtis. HOR 97m. TVM V

Curse of the Cat People, The 1944 ★★★★ Wise's directorial debut, sequel to Val Lewton's *Cat People*. Little girl creates make-believe world to make up for her father's lack of interest in her. Wonderfully evocative glimpse of a child's imagination, ends up somewhere between fantasy and horror. C: Robert Wise, Simone Simon, Kent Smith. D: Gunther Fritsch. HOR 70m. V

Curse of the Demon 1957 British ★★★★½ Ancient curse is killing people off, but criminal psychologist refuses to believe it. Startling thriller that still packs a punch. (a.k.a. *Night of the Demon*.) C: Dana Andrews, Peggy Cummins. D: Jacques Tourneur. HOR 83m. V

Curse of the Golem 1967 *See* **It**

Curse of the Pink Panther 1983 ★ Embarrassing entry into *Pink Panther* series attempts to replace Sellers with inept American detective Wass. C: Ted Wass, David Niven, Robert Wagner, Herbert Lom, Capucine, Robert Loggia. D: Blake Edwards. COM [PG] 110m. V

Curse of the Queerwolf 1987 ★★★½ A full moon means queer horror for a macho guy after he's bitten on the behind by a transvestite werewolf. Campy comedy; those who can accept the premise will find themselves howling. C: Michael Palazzolo, Kent Butler, Taylor Whitney. D: Mark Pirro. COM 90m. V

Curse of the Werewolf, The 1961 British ★★★ Boy is possessed by spirit of the werewolf. Strong performances by all and above-average production values keep this from being routine. C: Clifford Evans, Oliver Reed. D: Terence Fisher. HOR 91m. V

Curse, The 1987 ★ H.P. Lovecraft's story "The Colour Out of Space" becomes an ineffective exercise in gross-out shocks, with Akins' family falling victim to mutations after a meteor crashes on their farm. (a.k.a. *The Farm*) C: Wil Wheaton, Claude Akins, John Schneider. D: David Keith. HOR [R] 90m. V

Curse II: The Bite 1989 U.S. Italian ★★ A young man is bitten by a radioactive snake and grows lethal serpentine heads on his hands. Ludicrous, faux sequel wastes Schoelen in a mess of gross-out effects. C: Jill Schoelen, J. Eddie Peck, Bo Svenson, Jamie Farr, Al Fann. D: Fred Goodwin (Federico Prosperi). HOR 97m.

Curtain Rises, The 1939 French ★★★ Paris Conservatory teacher (Jouvet) tries to get to bottom of murder. Exceptionally vivid atmosphere of bohemian Parisian society and Jouvet's presence are the pluses. C: Louis Jouvet, Claude Dauphin, Janine Darcey. D: Marc Allegret. CRI 90m.

Curtain Up 1952 British ★★★★ Clever, funny look at a minor theater group coping with a dithering, neophyte playwright (Rutherford). Lovely interplay between caustic director Morley and Rutherford makes this a treat. C: Robert Morley, Margaret Rutherford, Kay Kendall, Joan Rice. D: Ralph Smart. COM 85m.

Custer of the West 1968 Spanish-U.S. ★★★ The famed general's life, from early adulthood to his "last stand." Some stunning visuals, but lumbers like a buffalo until the climactic battle scene. Originally in Cinerama. (a.k.a. *Good Day for Fighting*) C: Robert Shaw, Mary Ure, Jeffrey Hunter, Robert Ryan, Ty Hardin. D: Robert Siodmak. WST [G] 140m.

Cutter's Way 1981 ★★★★ A Vietnam veteran (Heard) talks his buddy (Bridges) into helping him track a murderer. Good performances but somewhat easygoing attitude undercuts interesting mystery. Based on Newton Thornburg's novel *Cutter and Bone*. C: Jeff Bridges, John Heard, Lisa Eichhorn. D: Ivan Passer. DRA [R] 105m. V

Cutting Class 1989 ★★ A string of brutal murders has perpetual horror heroine Schoelen worried: Is the killer her boyfriend (Pitt) or an unbalanced admirer (Leitch)? Ungainly mix of horror and satire with a few good moments. C: Donovan Leitch, Jill Schoelen, Roddy McDowall, Brad Pitt. D: Rospo Pallenberg. HOR [R] 91m. V

Cutting Edge, The 1991 ★★★ Hockey star whose career is cut short by an injury teams up with prima donna ice skater who needs a partner. Stars play well together and their skating is a treat to watch. C: D. B. Sweeney, Moira Kelly, Roy Dotrice, Terry O'Quinn. D: Paul Michael Glaser. DRA [PG] 101m. V

Cyborg 1989 ★ Van Damme vehicle set in a *Blade Runner/Road Warrior*-esque future has the Muscles from Brussels taking on sadistic street gangs. Cheesy sets and effects, with gratuitous violence in place of action. C: Jean-Claude VanDamme, Deborah Richter, Vincent Klyn. D: Albert Pyun. SFI [R] 86m. V

Cynara 1932 ★★★ Barrister (Colman) has affair with shopkeeper (Barry) who despairs when he returns to his wife (Francis). Once considered high-toned, but hasn't aged well. C: Ronald Colman, Kay Francis. D: King Vidor. DRA 78m.

Cynthia 1947 ★★½ Unlikely starring vehicle for Taylor as an overprotected, sickly young woman who turns to music for solace and learns how to live her own life. Treacly and overlong. C: Elizabeth Taylor, George Murphy, S. Z. Sakall, Mary Astor, Spring Byington. D: Robert Z. Leonard. FAM/DRA 98m.

Cyrano de Bergerac 1950 ★★★★ Ferrer won an Oscar in the title role of Rostand's classic play of a romantic cavalier who yearns for the love of Roxanne. Careful production marred only by weak supporting cast. Remade with Gerard Depardieu in 1990; Rostand's play also basis for 1987 Steve Martin film *Roxanne*. C: Jose Ferrer, Mala Powers, William Prince, Morris Carnovsky. D: Michael Gordon. DRA 112m. V

Cyrano de Bergerac 1990 French ★★★★½ Wonderful adaptation of Rostand's play in which Depardieu plays the lover who pines for unattainable Roxanne (Brochet). Thoughtful production is respectful and at times inspired. Anthony Burgess supervised translation of English subtitles. Rostand's original play was written as protest against the outcome of the Dreyfus court-martial. C: Gerard Depardieu, Anne Brochet. D: Jean-Paul Rappeneau. DRA [PG] 138m. V

D

D-Day the Sixth of June 1956 ★★★★ Allied landing at Normandy during WWII is the backdrop for a love triangle involving a young woman (Wynter) and two officers—one American (Taylor), one British (Todd). Imposing invasion photography highlights above-par war tale. C: Robert Taylor, Richard Todd, Dana Wynter. D: Henry Koster. DRA 106m. v

D2: The Mighty Ducks 1994 ★★½ Labored sequel in which Estevez's head is swelled by success of team in first film—he has been selected to coach U.S. Peewee Olympics team—leading all of them to brink of on-ice disaster which is only prevented when they realize what made them win in the first place—teamwork. C: Emilio Estevez Kathryn Erbe, Michael Tucker, Jan Rubes, Carsten Norgaard, Maria Ellingsen. D: Sam Weisman. COM [PG] 106m. v

Da 1988 ★★★ Returning to Ireland for his father's funeral, Sheen talks with the old man's ghost as they reminisce about good times and bad. Adapted from Hugh Leonard's play; stagy but well acted. C: Barnard Hughes, Martin Sheen. D: Matt Clark. DRA [PG] 102m. v

Dad 1989 ★★★ Yuppie exec Danson bonds with his dying father (Lemmon) in this formulaic tearjerker. Glibly sentimental. C: Jack Lemmon, Ted Danson, Olympia Dukakis, Kathy Baker, Kevin Spacey, Ethan Hawke. D: Gary David Goldberg. DRA [PG] 117m. v

Dadah Is Death 1988 ★★★½ A parent's nightmare comes true for a mother (Christie) battling to save the life of her son, condemned to death for drug smuggling in Malaysia. Grim and realistic, but a bit too long. Based on the true story of an Australian family. C: Julie Christie, Victor Banerjee. D: Jerry London. DRA 200m. TVM

Daddy Long Legs 1955 ★★★½ Jean Webster's children's story converted into December-May romance as waif Caron's education is financially assisted by anonymous guardian Astaire. Two stars' dancing styles don't match, but there's a nifty song, "Something's Gotta Give." C: Fred Astaire, Leslie Caron, Thelma Ritter, Terry Moore. D: Jean Negulesco. MUS 125m. v

Daddy Nostalgia 1990 French ★★★★ Writer (Birkin) travels home to be with her ailing father (Bogarde), and she begins to appreciate him as a person and a father. Touchingly realistic family drama, with stellar performances and a good script. C: Dirk Bogarde, Jane Birkin. D: Bertrand Tavernier. DRA 105m. v

Daddy's Dyin'. . . Who's Got the Will? 1990 ★★★★ Refreshingly eccentric black comedy unites a misfit Texan family as its patriarch nears death. Thrives on over-the-top performances all around, particularly those of Bridges and D'Angelo. C: Beau Bridges, Keith Carradine, Beverly D'Angelo, Tess Harper, Judge Reinhold. D: Jack Fisk. COM [PG-13] 97m. v

Daddy's Gone A-Hunting 1969 ★★★ In this semisleazy thriller a happily married mother and child are terrorized by the woman's crazed ex-boyfriend. Well-plotted tension. C: Carol White, Paul Burke, Scott Hylands. D: Mark Robson. CRI [PG] 108m. v

Daffy Duck's Movie: Fantastic Island 1983 ★★★★ Amusing compilation of old Warner Brothers cartoons brings a whole range of familiar animated characters into play. All the favorites are here! Voice of Mel Blanc. D: Fritz Freleng. FAM/COM [G] 78m. v

Daffy Duck's Quackbusters 1989 ★★★★ Delightful animated spoof on popular *Ghostbusters* film, with energetic Daffy joining forces with friends Porky Pig and Bugs Bunny to rid clients of annoying supernatural forces. Voice of Mel Blanc. D: Greg Ford. FAM/COM [G] 79m. v

Daisy Kenyon 1947 ★★★½ Who will shopgirl Crawford pick: rich man Fonda or poor man Andrews? Standard romantic contrivance with some heat generated by Joan's emoting. C: Joan Crawford, Ruth Warrick, Peggy Ann Garner. D: Otto Preminger. DRA 99m.

Daisy Miller 1974 ★★ Cybill Shepherd plays a naive young American heiress on European Grand Tour who comes to a tragic end in Rome. Production values high, but basically an overreaching, attempt at filming Henry James' subtle novella. C: Cybill Shepherd, Barry Brown, Cloris Leachman, Mildred Natwick, Eileen Brennan. D: Peter Bogdanovich. DRA [G] 93m. v

Dakota 1945 ★★★ Rugged cowboy (Wayne) weds railroad magnate's daughter (Ralston), and intervenes when land war erupts between homesteaders and railroad. Middle-of-the-road Republic star Western. C: John Wayne, Vera Hruba Ralston, Walter Brennan, Ward Bond, Ona Munson. D: Joseph Kane. WST 82m.

Dakota 1988 ★★★½ Runaway (Phillips) becomes a ranch hand in Texas and learns to face his problems. Wholesome drama, with solid work by young Phillips and spectacular cinematography. C: Lou Diamond Phillips, Eli Cummins, Dee Dee Norton. D: Fred Holmes. DRA [PG] 96m. v

Dakota Incident 1956 ★★★½ Stagecoach passengers try to survive repeated attacks by marauding Plains Indians. Formulaic Western saved by good acting. C: Linda Darnell, Dale Robertson, John Lund. D: Lewis R. Foster. WST 88m. v

Daleks—Invasion Earth 2150 A.D. 1966 British ★★★★ Dr. Who (Cushing) travels to the future with his family and battles evil Dalek aliens, who've turned all earthlings into zombies.

Good fun. Fans of the cult TV series will be in warp drive! Sequel to *Dr. Who and the Daleks*. (a.k.a. *Invasion Earth 2150 A.D.*) C: Peter Cushing, Bernard Cribbins, Andrew Keir, Ray Brooks, Jill Curzon. D: Gordon Flemyng. SFI 84m. V

Dallas 1950 ★★★½ In post-Civil War Southwest, former Confederate officer seeking vengeance rids town of gunslingers. Capable Cooper vehicle with Roman as love interest. C: Gary Cooper, Ruth Roman, Raymond Massey. D: Stuart Heisler. WST 94m.

Dam Busters, The 1954 British ★★★★½ During WWII, British intelligence originates a scheme to destroy the Ruhr Valley dams in Northwest Germany. Fascinating war drama with plenty of thrills. C: Richard Todd, Michael Redgrave, Ursula Jeans. D: Michael Anderson. DRA 119m. V

Damage 1992 British ★★★½ Gripping study of the power of sexual obsession, ably directed by Malle from Josephine Hart best-seller. Irons falls for son's fiancée (Binoche), setting in motion a monstrous tragedy. Oscar nominee Richardson excellent as the betrayed wife. C: Jeremy Irons, Juliette Binoche, Miranda Richardson, Rupert Graves, Leslie Caron. D: Louis Malle. DRA [R] 111m. V

Dames 1935 ★★★★ The old "let's put on a show" plot gets the fabled Berkeley treatment. Brilliant production numbers including "Dames" and "I Only Have Eyes For You" (featuring hundreds of Ruby Keelers). Songwriter Sammy Fain appears as—a songwriter. C: Joan Blondell, Dick Powell, Ruby Keeler, ZaSu Pitts, Guy Kibbee. D: Ray Enright. MUS 95m. V

Damien—Omen II 1978 ★★★ Our young Antichrist is now 13 and living with relatives, none of whom know his powers until he shows them. Production and effects are solid, if not original. Followed by *The Final Conflict*. C: William Holden, Lee Grant, Lew Ayres, Sylvia Sidney, Jonathan Scott-Taylor. D: Don Taylor. HOR [R] 107m. V

Damn the Defiant! 1962 British ★★★½ British naval officer and first mate come to blows while fighting Napoleon's fleet. Exciting seafaring actioner with excellent sparring by Guinness and Bogarde. C: Alec Guinness, Dirk Bogarde, Maurice Denham, Anthony Quayle. D: Lewis Gilbert. ACT 93m. V

Damn Yankees 1958 ★★★★ Joe Hardy (Hunter) sells his soul to devil Walston for chance to help Washington Senators beat that New York team. Exuberant Broadway musical comes to screen with most of its score and cast intact, including sizzling Verdon as temptress Lola. Her striptease to "Whatever Lola Wants" is film's highlight. C: Tab Hunter, Gwen Verdon, Ray Walston, Russ Brown, Jean Stapleton. D: George Abbott, Stanley Donen. MUS 110m. V

Damnation Alley 1977 ★★ After a nuclear war, a small band of survivors roam the devastation, seeking out other humans battling mutants along the way. Could be more exciting. C: Jan-Michael Vincent, George Peppard, Dominique Sanda, Paul Winfield. D: Jack Smight. SFI [PG] 87m. V

Damned Don't Cry, The 1950 ★★★½ Tailor-made Crawford vehicle about tough gal from the wrong side of the tracks using her looks to make good till bad-guy Brian crosses her. Entertaining soap opera suffers from lack of strong leading man for Joan to play off of. C: Joan Crawford, Steve Cochran, Kent Smith, Richard Egan. D: Vincent Sherman. DRA 103m.

Damned, The 1962 *See* **These Are the Damned**

Damned, The 1969 Italian ★★★★★ Unforgettable, difficult, often disturbing drama of a German industrialist family under the rise of Nazism. Decadent at some points, near operatic at others with uncompromising performances by a strong cast. Not an easy film to watch, but compelling. C: Dirk Bogarde, Ingrid Thulin, Helmut Griem, Helmut Berger. D: Luchino Visconti. DRA [R] 150m. V

Damsel in Distress, A 1937 ★★★★ American dancer (Astaire) woos British aristocrat. Benefits from Gershwin gems "A Foggy Day," "Nice Work If You Can Get It," "Things Are Looking Up," and surprisingly good support and dancing from Burns and Allen, who prove to be marvelous dancers. Scripted by P.G. Wodehouse. C: Fred Astaire, George Burns, Gracie Allen, Joan Fontaine, Constance Collier. D: George Stevens. MUS 101m. V

Dan Candy's Law 1973 Canadian ★★★ Accused of murdering a Mountie, a Cree Indian flees the authorities—pursued by investigator Sutherland. Enjoy this one for the spectacular Canadian countryside. (a.k.a. *Alien Thunder*) C: Donald Sutherland, Kevin McCarthy, Chief Dan George, Jean Duceppe, Jack Creely, Francine Racette. D: Claude Fournier. ACT [PG] 90m.

Dance, Fools, Dance 1931 ★★★ Gable and Crawford sizzle as two people on opposite sides of the law—she's a reporter willing to do almost anything to make it; he's the target of her hunt. C: Joan Crawford, Cliff Edwards, Clark Gable. D: Harry Beaumont. DRA 81m. V

Dance, Girl, Dance 1940 ★★★½ Love and career problems beset young nightclub dancers: O'Hara wants to be a ballerina and Ball hopes to hit it big in burlesque. Okay musical with protofeminist twist. Ball's performance is highlight. C: Maureen O'Hara, Louis Hayward, Lucille Ball, Ralph Bellamy, Maria Ouspenskaya. D: Dorothy Arzner. MUS 89m. V

Dance Hall 1941 ★★★ Romero is a dance-hall manager who falls for employee Landis. Cute, minor musical romance. C: Carole Landis, Cesar Romero. D: Irving Pichel. MUS 73m. V

Dance Hall 1950 British ★★★ Four working-class women find fun and romance at the local dance palace. Trivial, harmless, with a very young Petula. C: Natasha Parry, Diana Dors, Petula Clark, Jane Hylton. D: Charles Crichton. COM 78m. V

Dance Hall Racket 1953 ★★ Lenny Bruce's grade-Z home crime movie features him as gangster operating on fringe edges of seedy dance hall. Bruce's wife Harlowe and mother Marr also star. Bruce's hammy death scene is great fun. Director Tucker also helmed camp classic *Robot Monster*. C: Lenny Bruce, Honey Harlowe, Sally Marr. D: Phil Tucker. DRA 60m.

Dance of Death 1968 British ★★★½ Olivier's farewell stage performance, in a Strindberg play of an aging, cantankerous sea captain and his wife, whose marriage is a battlefield. Olivier gives a memorable and passionate performance. C: Laurence Olivier, Geraldine McEwan, Robert Lang, Carolyn Jones. D: David Giles. DRA [G] 138m.

Dance of the Damned 1988 ★★★ A vampire yearning to know about living in the daylight forges a tentative relationship with a stripper who wants to end her own life. Subdued, thoughtful horror drama with more characterization than usual for the genre. Remade as *To Sleep with a Vampire*. C: Cyril O'Reilly, Starr Andreef. D: Katt Shea Ruben. HOR [R] 83m. V

Dance of the Vampires 1967 *See* **Fearless Vampire Killers or: Pardon Me, But Your Teeth Are in My Neck, The**

Dance With a Stranger 1984 British ★★★★ Miranda Richardson gives a searing performance in this true story of a bar hostess who seduces a debauched young aristocrat and then kills him when he dumps her. Lean, unsentimental drama of romantic obsession. C: Miranda Richardson, Rupert Everett, Ian Holm. D: Mike Newell. DRA [R] 101m. V

Dance with Me Henry 1956 ★★½ Abbott and Costello run an entertainment park for kids, where some crooks have coincidentally hidden their loot. Their last film together. C: Bud Abbott, Lou Costello, Gigi Perreau. D: Charles Barton. COM 80m. V

Dancers 1987 ★★½ A caddish ballet dancer (Baryshnikov) sets his gaze on a naive ballerina (Browne) during preparation of a production of *Giselle*. Balletomanes will forgive the simplistic romance and cardboard characterizations, and thrill to the American Ballet's dancing. C: Mikhail Baryshnikov, Alessandra Ferri, Leslie Browne. D: Herbert Ross. MUS [PG] 99m. V

Dances with Wolves 1990 ★★★★★ Battle-weary Civil War veteran Costner decides to see the frontier before it is gone. Alone on the prairie, he befriends a roaming band of Sioux and learns the true meaning of "civilization." A modern epic, Costner's heartfelt directorial debut swept the Oscars—Best Picture, Director, Screenplay Adaptation, Score, Cinematography, and Editing. C: Kevin Costner, Mary McDonnell, Graham Greene. D: Kevin Costner. DRA [PG-13] 180m. V

Dancing in the Dark 1986 Canadian ★★★½ Henry is a model homemaker who slowly disintegrates beneath her shiny veneer, with ultimately fatal consequences. Slow-moving, occasionally black-humored character study works thanks to Henry's strong performance. C: Martha Henry, Neil Munro. D: Leon Marr. DRA [PG-13] 93m. V

Dancing Lady 1933 ★★★½ Star-studded backstage musical romance ostensibly stars Crawford, Gable, and Tone in tired triangle, but it's Astaire in film debut who dances off with the picture. Crawford's flat-footed attempt to partner him is unintentionally amusing. C: Joan Crawford, Clark Gable, Franchot Tone, May Robson, Nelson Eddy, Fred Astaire, Robert Benchley. D: Robert Z. Leonard. MUS 93m. V

Dancing Masters, The 1943 ★★½ Laurel and Hardy help young inventor (Bailey) win over his sweetheart's father by foiling some hoods in an insurance scam. Familiar comedy. C: Stan Laurel, Oliver Hardy, Margaret Dumont. D: Mal St. Clair. COM 63m.

Dancing Mothers 1926 ★★★ Silent tale featuring the "It" girl, Clara Bow, fast-living as a flapper who flies in the face of convention. Pleasant Jazz-age curio. C: Clara Bow, Alice Joyce, Norman Trevor. D: Herbert Brenon. COM 60m. V

Dandy in Aspic, A 1968 British ★★★ Spy thriller about British double agent (Harvey) ordered to murder another agent. Good premise marred by dull delivery. Director Mann died while filming and was replaced by Harvey. C: Laurence Harvey, Tom Courtenay, Mia Farrow, Lionel Stander. D: Anthony Mann. CRI [R] 107m. V

Danger: Diabolik 1967 Italian ★★★★ Thief is too clever for the cops, whom he outsmarts at every move. Stylish, witty mystery. (a.k.a. *Diabolik*.) C: John Phillip Law, Marisa Mell, Michel Piccoli, Terry Thomas. D: Mario Bava. CRI [PG-13] 99m. V

Danger Island *See* **Mr. Moto in Danger Island**

Danger Lights 1930 ★★★ Sweet-natured railroad engineer Wolheim loves Arthur but has his heart broken when she falls for roguish newcomer Armstrong. Guess who Arthur ends up with in the end? C: Jean Arthur, Robert Armstrong, Hugh Herbert. D: George B. Seitz, Louis Wolheim. DRA 73m. V

Danger—Love at Work 1937 ★★½ Young lawyer (Haley) needs the signature of wealthy eccentric (Boland) to close a deal, but she pushes him into marriage with her daughter (Sothern) instead. Low-budget screwball comedy. C: Ann Sothern, Jack Haley, Mary Boland, John Carradine, Edward Everett Horton. D: Otto Preminger. COM 81m.

Danger Patrol 1937 ★★★ Trucker who delivers nitroglycerine to oil fields forbids his daughter (Eilers) to marry a man (Beal) in the same risky occupation. Potentially dynamite story fails to ignite. C: Sally Eilers, John Beal, Harry Carey, Frank M. Thomas. D: Lew Landers. DRA 59m.

Danger Signal 1945 ★★★ Smooth scoundrel Scott charms his way into fiancée Emerson's family and then implicates them in murder in this routine drama. C: Zachary Scott, Faye Emerson, Rosemary DeCamp. D: Robert Florey. DRA 78m.

Dangerous 1935 ★★★★ Davis won first Oscar for showy role of drunken actress redeemed by architect Tone's love. Pure soap, with a script that defies credulity, but Bette does have her moments. C: Bette Davis, Franchot Tone, Margaret Lindsay. D: Alfred E. Green. DRA 72m. V

Dangerous Company 1982 ★★½ Prison drama about two men caught up in the system and what it does to them. Bridges plays the convict who finally smartens up and reforms. Based on a true story. C: Beau Bridges, Ralph Macchio, Karen Carlson, Carlos Brown. D: Lamont Johnson. CRI 98m.

Dangerous Corner 1934 ★★★½ In this stagy drama, a group of friends gather together to recount the long-past apparent suicide of a common friend. Worthwhile adaptation of J.B. Priestley play. C: Virginia Bruce, Conrad Nagel, Melvyn Douglas, Betty Furness. D: Phil Rosen. CRI 66m.

Dangerous Crossing 1953 ★★★½ When a woman's husband vanishes during a honeymoon ocean voyage, no one on the ship believes that he ever existed. Suspense picture fails to live up to its intriguing premise. Based on a John Dickinson Carr story; remade as *Treacherous Crossing*. C: Jeanne Crain, Michael Rennie. D: Joseph Newman. DRA 75m.

Dangerous Curves 1988 ★★½ Trouble ensues when two UCLA students agree to drive a sports car from Los Angeles to Lake Tahoe. Tame teen comedy. C: Robert Stack, Lesie Nielsen, Robert Romanus, Martha Quinn. D: David Lewis. COM [PG] 93m.

Dangerous Exile 1958 British ★★★ During the dark days of the French Revolution, an idealistic young monarchist (Jourdan) rescues royalty from the guillotine. Lots of color and action. C: Louis Jourdan, Belinda Lee, Keith Michell. D: Brian Hurst. ACT 90m.

Dangerous Female 1931 *See* **Maltese Falcon, The**

Dangerous Friend, A 1971 *See* **Todd Killings, The**

Dangerous Game 1993 ★★★½ Off-the-wall look at filmmaking by maverick Ferrara, with Madonna as actress whose real-life relationship with director (Keitel) and on-screen liaison with Russo begin to blur. As funky and sleazy as Ferrara's masterful *Bad Lieutenant*; not as compelling, but still well worth seeing. C: Madonna, Harvey Keitel, James Russo, Nancy Ferrara. D: Abel Ferrara. DRA [R] 109m. V

Dangerous Liaisons 1960 1959 French ★★★★ Choderlos de Laclos's oft-filmed tale of 18th-century sexual intrigue is updated to 1960 Paris, where jet-set marrieds (Moreau, Philipe) exchange partners, seduce innocents, etc. in perilous bedroom games. Offbeat and engrossing, with an outstanding jazz score (by this formidable trio: Thelonious Monk, Art Blakey, and Duke Jordan). Remade in 1988 as *Dangerous Liaisons*, with Glenn Close, and in 1989 as *Valmont*, with Annette Bening. C: Jeanne Moreau, Gerard Philipe, Jeanne Valerie, Annette Vadim, Jean-Louis Trintignant. D: Roger Vadim. DRA 106m. V

Dangerous Liaisons 1988 ★★★★½ Devious 18th-century aristocrats (Close and Malkovich) amuse themselves by trapping innocents in their web of sexual deceit and betrayal. Gorgeous and engrossing drama with magnificent cast. Close makes a memorable villain. Oscar-winning screenplay by Hampton from his play. Also filmed in 1989, as *Valmont*. C: Glenn Close, John Malkovich, Michelle Pfeiffer, Keanu Reeves, Uma Thurman, Mildred Natwick, Swoosie Kurtz. D: Stephen Frears. DRA [R] 120m. V

Dangerous Love 1988 ★ A psychopath videotapes then murders female clients of a dating service, and a geeky computer executive (Monoson) is suspected of the crimes. A *Peeping Tom* for the '80s that falls flat on its face. C: Lawrence Monoson, Brenda Bakke, Teri Austin, Anthony Geary, Elliott Gould. D: Marty Ollstein. CRI [R] 96m. V

Dangerous Mission 1954 ★★½ Originally shot in 3-D to capitalize on the exquisite Montana Glacier National Park scenery, a cop protects a witness from a band of gangsters. Undistinguished cat-and-mouse suspense fare. C: Victor Mature, Piper Laurie, William Bendix, Vincent Price. D: Louis King. CRI 75m.

Dangerous Moonlight 1941 British ★★★★ During Battle of Britain, a displaced Polish pianist goes on an apparent RAF suicide mission. Fine WWII romance/drama, well acted with first-rate score. (a.k.a. *Suicide Squadron*) C: Anton Walbrook, Sally Gray. D: Brian Hurst. DRA 83m.

Dangerous Moves 1984 Swiss ★★★★ Personal conflicts surround international chess tournament, pitting decrepit master against his youthful protege. Just what you'd expect from a film about chess—slow and deliberate but at times surprisingly riveting. Oscar for Best Foreign Film. C: Michel Piccoli, Alexandre Arbatt, Leslie Caron, Liv Ullmann. D: Richard Dembo. DRA 96m. V

Dangerous Obsession 1990 *See* **Mortal Sins**

Dangerous Summer, A 1981 Australian ★★½ Arsonists plot to sabotage a multimillion-dollar resort under construction in Australia's Blue Mountains by an American businessman (Skerritt). Good cast saves this disjointed drama. (a.k.a. *The Burning Man*) C: Tom Skerritt, Ian Gilmour, James Mason, Wendy Hughes. D: Quentin Masters. ACT 100m. V

Dangerous to Know 1938 ★★★★½ Typically terrific B-film from Florey. Ganglord ignores devoted mistress in favor of society woman. Excellent performances all around, and a memorably grim finale. C: Akim Tamiroff, Anna May Wong, Gail Patrick, Lloyd Nolan, Anthony Quinn. D: Robert Florey. CRI 70m.

Dangerous When Wet 1953 ★★★ While preparing to swim the English Channel, Williams is wooed by Lamas, her real-life spouse. Mildly amusing romantic comedy; highlight is the aquatic dance with cartoons Tom and Jerry. C: Esther Williams, Fernando Lamas, Jack Carson, Charlotte Greenwood, Denise Darcel. D: Charles Walters. MUS 95m. V

Dangerous Woman, A 1993 ★★★ Disappointing drama of plain-Jane Winger slowly going off her rocker. Strathairn is memorable, playing against type as a sleazy guy who takes advantage of her loneliness, but the film is mannered and slow. C: Debra Winger, Barbara Hershey, Gabriel Byrne, David Strathairn. D: Steven Gyllenhaal. DRA [R] 93m. V

Dangerously Close 1986 ★★ Teenage fascists terrorize their schoolmates in this ill-made morality tale. Arty effects can't disguise the fact that there's less going on here than meets the eye. C: John Stockwell, J. Eddie Peck, Carey Lowell. D: Albert Pynn. DRA [R] 96m. V

Dangerously They Live 1942 ★★★ Propaganda piece with home-front Nazis trying to track down an injured British agent carrying important documents. Entertaining film appropriate for its time. C: John Garfield, Nancy Coleman, Raymond Massey, Lee Patrick. D: Robert Florey. DRA 77m.

Dangers of the Canadian Mounted 1948 *See* **R.C.M.P. & the Treasure of Genghis Khan**

Daniel and the Devil 1941 *See* **Devil and Daniel Webster, The**

Daniel Boone, Trail Blazer 1956 ★★★½ Low-budget, low-key, but well-acted life of famed Indian fighter and wilderness settler Boone. C: Bruce Bennett, Lon Chaney, Jr. D: Albert Gannaway, Ismael Rodriquez. WST 76m.

Daniel Boone 1936 ★★★ The legendary woodsman guides a group of pioneers through the wilderness to Kentucky in this average actioner. C: George O'Brien, Heather Angel, John Carradine. D: David Howard. ACT 75m. V

Daniel 1983 ★★★★ Mixed-up children (Hutton and Plummer) of couple executed for treason in the '50s try to cope with the tragic consequences of those deaths and find meaning in their lives. Stellar performance by Hutton; an earnest, imperfect but fascinating film. Adapted from E.L. Doctorow's *The Book of Daniel*. C: Timothy Hutton, Mandy Patinkin, Lindsay Crouse, Edward Asner, Ellen Barkin, Tovah Feldshuh, Amanda Plummer. D: Sidney Lumet. DRA [R] 130m. V

Danielle Steel's Fine Things 1992 ★★½ Family saga based on the best-seller about a young woman who becomes a pawn in the conflict between her father and stepfather. Average miniseries with plenty of romantic suds. C: D.W. Moffett, Tracy Pollan, Cloris Leachman. DRA 145m. V

Danny 1979 ★★★½ Young girl (Page) cherishes an injured horse callously discarded by the spoiled daughter of a rich family. Charming film is predictable but still wonderful family viewing. C: Rebecca Page, Janet Zarish. D: Gene Feldman. FAM/DRA [G] 90m.

Danny Boy 1941 ★★ Todd is a Broadway star who returns to England to find abandoned husband and son. Musical melodrama. C: Ann Todd, Wilfred Lawson, Grant Tyler, David Farrar. D: Oswald Mitchell. MUS 67m.

Danny Boy 1984 Irish ★★★★ A saxophonist (Rea) witnesses a double slaying and becomes obsessed with avenging it. Packing a gun, he goes on a manhunt through the hills and dales of county Armagh. Jordan's stunning directorial debut packs a wallop. (a.k.a. *Angel*) C: Stephen Rea, Veronica Quilligan, Donal McCann. D: Neil Jordan. DRA [R] 92m. V

Dante's Inferno 1935 ★★½ Tracy is a fast-talking carnival barker whose devilish midway attraction ultimately leads to disaster. Minor allegory that overplays its message; notable mostly for early appearance of Rita Hayworth (then billed as Rita Cansino) in a dance sequence. C: Spencer Tracy, Claire Trevor, Henry Walthall, Scotty Beckett, Rita Cansino Hayworth. D: Harry Lachman. DRA 88m.

Danton 1983 Polish ★★★★ Poland's foremost director explores the Reign of Terror following the French Revolution and the ideological battle between Robespierre and Danton as an allegory for Poland's own political turmoil. Worthwhile, intelligent drama. C: Gerard Depardieu, Wojciech Pszoniak, Patrice Chereau. D: Andrzej Wajda. DRA [PG] 136m. V

Danzon 1992 Mexican ★★★ A telephone operator (Rojo) who's won awards for her dancing at the local ballroom journeys from Mexico City to Veracruz to find her vanished dance partner. Lively, good-natured picture with an infectious soundtrack. C: Maria Rojo, Carmen Salinas. D: Maria Novaro. DRA [PG-13] 103m. V

Darby O'Gill and the Little People 1959 ★★★★½ Leprechauns capture a boastful caretaker who falls down a well into their kingdom and are tricked into giving him three wishes. When he tells this tale, no one believes him! Cute, fun-filled fantasy with some scary special effects. C: Sean Connery, Albert Sharpe, Janet Munro, Estelle Winwood. D: Robert Stevenson. FAM/DRA [G] 90m. V

Darby's Rangers 1957 ★★★ U.S. commando unit trains in England and sees action in North

Africa and Sicily in WWII. Adequate battle scenes mixed with romantic interludes in the standard formula. One of Garner's first roles. C: James Garner, Jack Warden, Edward Byrnes, Stuart Whitman, David Janssen. D: William Wellman. DRA 122m. v

Dare to Be Truthful 1992 ★★½ A spoof on women in the news, starring MTV's Julie Brown. Lots of laughs. (a.k.a. *Medusa—Dare to Be Truthful*) C: Julie Brown, Bobcat Goldthwait, Carol Leifer. D: John Fortenberry. COM 51m.

Daring Dobermans, The 1973 ★★★½ Hoodlums train talented canines to pull off an inventive heist. Entertaining sequel to *The Doberman Gang* is fine family fun. C: Charles Knox Robinson, Tim Considine, David Moses. D: Bryon Ross Chudnow. FAM/ACT [G] 88m. v

Dario Argento's World of Horror 1985 ★★★½ Better-than-average filmmaker documentary centering on Italy's best-known, and most stylish, director of modern horror movies. A good introduction to Argento's work, it also features some gory sequences that were cut from U.S. releases of his films. C: James Franciscus, Karl Malden, Jessica Harper, Donald Pleasence, David Hemmings. D: Dario Argento. DOC 76m.

Dark Angel, The 1935 ★★★★ Thirties weepie, remake of blockbuster 1925 silent film about lovers whose lives are shattered by blindness. Excellent performances, with Oberon nominated for Best Actress Oscar. Film received Oscar for Art Direction. C: Fredric March, Merle Oberon, Herbert Marshall. D: Sidney Franklin. DRA 110m.

Dark Angel: The Ascent 1994 ★★★★ Offbeat account of a young demon (Featherstone) escaping from Hades to explore our world. Silly, but full of knowing humor and fun shocks; the only real problem is the obvious use of European locations as stand-ins for an American city. C: Angela Featherstone, Daniel Markel, Charlotte Stewart, Michael Genovese, Nicholas Worth. D: Linda Hassani. HOR [R] 83m.

Dark at the Top of the Stairs, The 1960 ★★★★ Preston heads flawless cast in William Inge drama of sexual tensions in small Oklahoma town during the '20s. Arden shines in unusual dramatic role as bossy sister of docile McGuire. C: Robert Preston, Dorothy McGuire, Eve Arden, Angela Lansbury, Shirley Knight. D: Delbert Mann. DRA 123m.

Dark Avenger, The 1955 *See* **Warriors, The**

Dark Backward, The 1991 ★★½ Perverse black comedy in which stand-up comedian Nelson only finds fame after he grows a third arm out of his back. Weird, with definite cult appeal. C: Judd Nelson, Lara Flynn Boyle, Bill Paxton, Wayne Newton, James Caan, Rob Lowe. D: Adam Rifkin. COM [R] 100m. v

Dark City 1950 ★★★ Heston's good in first Hollywood film as gambler who takes sap (DeFore) for small fortune, driving him to suicide. Colorful supporting cast, but Scott's torch songs fail to ignite and soft script mars film noir mood. C: Charlton Heston, Lizabeth Scott, Viveca Lindfors, Dean Jagger, Jack Webb, Ed Begley. D: William Dieterle. DRA 88m.

Dark Command 1940 ★★★★ Elaborate historical Western with marshal (Wayne) battling a band of guerrillas terrorizing post-Civil War Southwest. Sprawling, with an excellent cast. C: John Wayne, Claire Trevor, Walter Pidgeon, Roy Rogers, George Gabby Hayes, Marjorie Main. D: Raoul Walsh. WST 100m. v

Dark Corner, The 1946 ★★★★ Framed for murder, private eye Stevens and his secretary Ball must find the real killer before the cops close in. Fast-paced, satisfying thriller with bitter undercurrent. C: Lucille Ball, Clifton Webb, William Bendix, Constance Collier. D: Henry Hathaway. CRI 99m. v

Dark Crystal, The 1983 British ★★★½ Somber fantasy, with an all-puppet cast created by Henson's Muppet Factory, tells the mythic tale of a missing crystal shard which must be replaced before grotesque creatures destroy the world. Casts a spell, but more appropriate for adults than children, due to some frightening elements. Voices of Jim Henson, Frank Oz, Kathryn Mullen, Dave Goelz. D: Jim Henson, Frank Oz. SFI [PG] 94m. v

Dark End of the Street, The 1981 ★★★★ Low-budget independent film about an interracial group of teenage friends and their working-class Boston neighborhood. Realistic, often grim, with fine, natural acting. C: Laura Harrington, Henry Tomaszewski, Michelle Green. D: Jan Egleson. DRA 90m.

Dark Eyes of London 1939 *See* **Human Monster, The**

Dark Eyes 1987 Italian ★★★★ Sentimental love story has rich, bored Italian (Mastroianni) recounting in flashback his one great love: a Russian woman he met while vacationing away from his heiress wife. Inspired by Chekhov's short stories, film deftly combines farce and tragedy, with Mastroianni charming as middle-aged romantic who's traded love for material comfort. C: Marcello Mastroianni, Silvana Mangano, Marthe Keller. D: Nikita Mikhalkov. DRA [R] 118m. v

Dark Habits 1984 Spanish ★★★ Almodóvar sends up the sacred in this wickedly twisted tale of a junkie chanteuse who hides out at a convent populated by not-too-upstanding nuns with a taste for drugs, porn, and secular couture. Good for a laugh. C: Cristina Pascual, Carmen Maura, Julieta Serrano. D: Pedro Almodovar. COM 116m. v

Dark Half, The 1991 ★★★½ Intelligent, very scary adaptation of Stephen King's novel about a writer whose dark side manifests itself as a brutal killer. Hutton is excellent in the dual role, and Romero makes the premise both plausible and frightening. C: Timothy Hutton, Amy Madigan, Julie Harris, Robert Joy. D: George Romero. HOR [R] 121m. v

Dark Hazard 1934 ★★★½ Fine Robinson performance in decent drama about compulsive gambler. The reliable Tobin (as wife) and Farrell (as old girlfriend) lend good support. C: Edward G. Robinson, Genevieve Tobin, Glenda Farrell. D: Alfred Green. DRA 72m.

Dark Horse 1992 ★★★★ Teenager Meyers gets into trouble and is sentenced to weekends at horse farm for community service. Caring for horses gives her new slant on life and she begins to work out her problems. Well-done, nonpreachy, family entertainment. C: Mimi Rogers, Ed Begley, Jr., Ari Meyers, Samantha Eggar, Tab Hunter. D: Alfred Green. FAM/DRA 75m.

Dark Intruder 1965 ★★★★ TV pilot given theatrical release is a well-crafted, off-beat mystery thriller. A turn-of-the-century San Francisco criminologist (Nielsen) battles demonic forces trying to occupy the body of a socialite. Bizarre but satisfying. C: Leslie Nielsen, Judi Meredith, Werner Klemperer. D: Harvey Hart. CRI 59m.

Dark Journey 1937 British ★★★★ During WWI, English spy (Leigh) falls for her German contact (Veidt) when they meet in Stockholm. Sophisticated espionage romance with polished performances. C: Conrad Veidt, Vivien Leigh. D: Victor Saville. DRA 80m. v

Dark Mirror, The 1946 ★★★★ Clever whodunit with de Havilland as twin sisters, one shy, one brazen, mixed up in murder. Trick photography fairly advanced for its time. Star makes most of showy double role. Remade as TV movie. C: Olivia de Havilland, Lew Ayres, Thomas Mitchell, Richard Long. D: Robert Siodmak. DRA 85m. v

Dark Mirror 1984 ★★★ Twin sisters, one bad, one good, join forces to foil police investigation of murder that one of them committed. Seymour tries hard, but can't hold a candle to Olivia de Havilland in original 1946 version. C: Jane Seymour, Stephen Collins, Vincent Gardenia. D: Richard Lang. DRA 100m.

Dark Obsession 1989 British ★ Dull, heavy-handed morality tale of drunken aristocrats who accidentally kill young house maid. Muddled and preachy—even the extensive nudity can't liven this up. C: Gabriel Byrne, Amanda Donohoe, Michael Hordern. D: Nicholas Broomfield. DRA [R] 87m. v

Dark of the Night 1985 New Zealand ★★★ Woman gets a bargain used car that's haunted by its murdered former owner. Traditional ghost story with a feminist slant, and offbeat New Zealand locales. Based on "Mr. Wrong," an Elizabeth Jane Howard story Hitchcock once intended to film. C: Heather Bolton, David Letch. D: Gaylene Preston. HOR 88m. v

Dark of the Sun 1968 British ★★★★ Effective re-teaming of Taylor and Mimieux (*The Time Machine*), in a nail-biting yarn about an adventurer hired to retrieve a trainload of uncut diamonds in the Congo. C: Rod Taylor, Yvette Mimieux, Jim Brown, Kenneth More. D: Jack Cardiff. ACT [PG] 101m. v

Dark Page, The 1954 *See* **Scotch on the Rocks**

Dark Passage 1947 ★★★½ An innocent man convicted for murder, escapes from prison, undergoes plastic surgery, and sets out to find the killer. Fascinating Bogart behind the surgical tape. Nice star work. C: Humphrey Bogart, Lauren Bacall, Agnes Moorehead, Bruce Bennett. D: Delmer Daves. DRA 107m. v

Dark Past, The 1949 ★★★★ Tense, imaginative psychological drama, a remake of *Blind Alley*, with psychiatrist outwitting the killer holding him prisoner. A thrill at every turn and a fun '40s peek at the supposed workings of the criminal mind. C: William Holden, Nina Foch, Lee J. Cobb. D: Rudolph Mate. CRI 75m. v

Dark Places 1973 British ★★½ Good cast in tepid shocker, as heir to an estate, including spooky mansion, becomes possessed by psychopathic former owner and starts bumping off rivals for the fortune. None too scary or surprising. C: Christopher Lee, Joan Collins, Herbert Lom, Jane Birkin, Jean Marsh. D: Don Sharp. HOR [PG] 91m. v

Dark Sands 1937 British ★★½ A U.S. deserter (Robeson) hides out with an African tribe in this mediocre drama. C: Paul Robeson, Henry Wilcoxon, Wallace Ford. D: Thornton Freeland. DRA 75m. v

Dark Secret of Harvest Home 1978 ★★★★ New Yorker (Ackroyd) moves his family to New England town where mysterious fertility rituals threaten his life. Thomas Tryon's thriller novel, *Harvest Home*, makes a suspenseful film; Davis is hopelessly hammy as evil crone. C: David Ackroyd, Rosanna Arquette, Bette Davis, Rene Auberjonois, Michael O'Keefe. D: Leo Penn. HOR 200m. TVM v

Dark Shadows ★★½ Cross cuts are used effectively as vampire Barnabas Collins is revived in the present to terrorize and seduce various characters in this movie-length pilot for a revival of the '60s TV show. The look is slicker, but the material is just as pulpy. HOR v

Dark Side of the Moon, The 1990 ★★ The moon's effect on the Bermuda Triangle is explored in a space mission in this lame sci-fi effort. C: Will Bledsoe, Alan Blumenfeld, John Diehl, Robert Sampson, Joseph Turkel. D: D.J. Webster. SFI [R] 96m.

Dark Star 1971 ★★★★ Sci-fi satire answers the question: What is the most dangerous aspect of space life? The crew's agonizing boredom! That and a truly smart bomb with ideas of its own. Carpenter's first feature. A visual wonder considering its $60,000 budget. C: Dan O'Bannon, Dre Pahich. D: John Carpenter. SFI [G] 91m. v

Dark, The 1979 ★★ As if L.A. didn't have enough problems, now there's a psycho zombie killing at will. Low-budget outing. C: William Devane, Cathy Lee Crosby, Keenan Wynn, Vivian Blaine. D: John Cardos. HOR [R] 92m. v

Dark, The 1994 Canadian ★★★ Slick but often laughable monster movie, with a scientist (McHattie) and a vengeful fed (James) tracking a prehistoric beast lurking under a graveyard. The production is better than the contrived script deserves. C: Stephen McHattie, Brion James, Cynthia Belliveau, Jaimz Woolvett, Neve Campbell. D: Craig Pryce. HOR [R] 90m.

Dark Tower 1987 ★ An office building under construction is haunted by the murderous ghost of the husband of the structure's designer (Agutter). Hokey, unconvincing shocker wastes a good cast; directed pseudonymously by acclaimed cinematographer Freddie Francis. C: Michael Moriarty, Jenny Agutter, Carol Lynley, Theodore Bikel. D: Ken Barnett. HOR [R] 91m. v

Dark Victory 1939 ★★★★½ Classic woman's picture with Davis at top of her form as spoiled playgirl Judith Traherne, suffering from terminal brain tumor. Flawless support from Fitzgerald as loyal best friend and Brent as doctor who falls in love with his patient. Final fade-out with Max Steiner music throbbing in background is unforgettable. Remade twice. C: Bette Davis, George Brent, Geraldine Fitzgerald, Humphrey Bogart, Ronald Reagan. D: Edmund Goulding. DRA 106m. v

Dark Victory 1976 ★★★ Updated remake of Davis classic with Montgomery now TV producer suffering from brain tumor and falling for doctor Hopkins. Despite its lineage, this is run-of-the-mill weepie with little to recommend it. C: Elizabeth Montgomery, Anthony Hopkins, Michele Lee, Michael Lerner, Vic Tayback. D: Robert Butler. DRA 150m. TVM

Dark Waters 1944 ★★★★ Oberon, unstable after her parents' deaths, is victim of insidious plot in Louisiana bayous. Soggy mystery with few surprises. C: Merle Oberon, Franchot Tone, Thomas Mitchell, Fay Bainter. D: Andre de Toth. CRI 93m. v

Dark Wind, The ★★★ With no help from the FBI, Native-American cop (Phillips) tracks down murderous drug peddlers. Standard thriller with good ethnic sensibility. From the Tony Hillerman novel. C: Lou Diamond Phillips, Fred Ward, Gary Farmer. D: Errol Morris. CRI [R] 111m.

Darker than Amber 1970 ★★½ Travis McGee (Taylor), the private eye created by novelist John D. MacDonald, sets out to avenge murdered Kendall, who had a murky role in an elaborate con. Competent detective work. C: Rod Taylor, Suzy Kendall, Theodore Bikel, Jane Russell. D: Robert Clouse. CRI [PG] 97m.

Darkest Africa 1936 *See* **Batmen of Africa**

Darkman 1990 ★★★★ Who is Darkman? A mild-mannered scientist (Neeson) who is transformed into an avenging superhero after being exposed to his own experimental drug by really, really bad guys. Raimi's pastiche style always entertains and exhilarates. A B-movie at its best. C: Liam Neeson, Frances McDormand, Larry Drake. D: Sam Raimi. ACT 95m. v

Darktown Strutters 1974 ★★ An African-American, all-girl motorcycle gang searches for the kidnapped mother of one of their members. C: Trina Parks, Edna Richardson, Bettye Sweet. D: William Witney. DRA 85m. v

Darling, How Could You 1951 ★★ Parents who've been abroad try to get to know their kids, while the children worry about their parents' romance. Dusty adaptation of James Barrie's play. C: Joan Fontaine, John Lund. D: Mitchell Leisen. COM 96m.

Darling Lili 1970 ★★★★ Elaborate, entertaining musical with Julie in unusual role of WWI German spy posing as British music hall entertainer. Hudson is military officer she falls for in sexy romp that suffers from overlength. Outstanding Henry Mancini song: "Whistling in the Dark." C: Julie Andrews, Rock Hudson, Jeremy Kemp. D: Blake Edwards. MUS [G] 136m.

Darling 1965 British ★★★★½ Restless '60s model Christie cavorts in swinging London in search of thrills and success. Provocative and stylish indictment of those mod times; trendsetting visually and thematically. Christie's Oscar. C: Julie Christie, Dirk Bogarde, Laurence Harvey. D: John Schlesinger. DRA 122m. v

D.A.R.Y.L. 1985 ★★★ Young couple adopts a wunderkind—who happens to be a pint-sized robot. Entertaining romp, perfect for the younger set. C: Mary Beth Hurt, Michael McKean, Kathryn Walker, Colleen Camp. D: Simon Wincer. FAM/SFI [PG] 100m. v

Das Boat 1982 German ★★★★★ Tense, claustrophobic study of life aboard German U-boat during WWII that realistically portrays perils of life below the depths and conveys subtle antiwar message. Outstanding camerawork. Prochnow is stellar as submarine commander. (a.k.a. *The Boat.*) C: Jurgen Prochnow, Herbert Gronemeyer. D: Wolfgang Petersen. DRA [R] 145m. v

Date with an Angel 1987 ★★ During bachelor party for reluctant groom Knight, a broken-winged angel falls into swimming pool. After rescuing heavenly visitor, she rescues him. Cute premise, weak development. C: Michael E. Knight, Phoebe Cates, Emmanuelle Beart, David Dukes. D: Tom McLoughlin. COM [PG] 105m. v

Date With Judy, A 1948 ★★★★ Taylor and Powell compete for Stack in this sprightly family musical, stolen by Miranda teaching Beery the rumba while singing "Cuanto La Gusta." Taylor fans will enjoy her "It's a Most

Unusual Day." C: Wallace Beery, Jane Powell, Elizabeth Taylor, Carmen Miranda, Xavier Cugat, Robert Stack. D: Richard Thorpe. MUS 114m. v

Date With the Falcon, A 1941 ★★★½ Amateur sleuth (Sanders) keeps standing up his fiancee (Barrie) so he can rescue the kidnapped inventor of a synthetic diamond formula. Entertaining mystery yarn, with a large dollop of comedy. Second in the Falcon series. C: George Sanders, Wendy Barrie, James Gleason. D: Irving Reis. CRI 63m.

Daughter of Darkness 1990 ★★★½ A woman (Sara) travels to Budapest in search of the father she never knew and tangles with vampires, led by Perkins. Some good atmosphere and chills, but its made-for-TV status blunts Gordon's usual visceral approach. C: Mia Sara, Anthony Perkins, Robert Reynolds, Jack Coleman, Dezso Garas. D: Stuart Gordon. HOR [R] 93m. TVM

Daughter of Dr. Jekyll 1958 ★★ Lackluster, contrived follow-up to the classic story. When mysterious murders occur, title character (Talbott) thinks her father's evil side has been passed on to her. C: John Agar, Gloria Talbott. D: Edgar G. Ulmer. HOR 73m. v

Daughter of Luxury 1931 *See* **Five and Ten**

Daughter of Rosie O'Grady, The 1950 ★★★ At the turn of the century, young singer (Haver) wants to be a musical comedy star like her late mother, but father disapproves. Standard nostalgic period musical; look for young Debbie Reynolds as Haver's sister. C: June Haver, Gordon MacRae, Debbie Reynolds, Gene Nelson, S.Z. Sakall, Jane Darwell. D: David Butler. MUS 104m.

Daughter of Shanghai 1937 ★★★½ Wealthy merchant's daughter (Wong) seeks vengeance for her father's death and discovers a smuggling racket. Tidy mystery/melodrama with strong Wong. C: Anna May Wong, Charles Bickford, Buster Crabbe, Anthony Quinn. D: Robert Florey. DRA 63m.

Daughter of the Dragon 1931 ★★★ Complicated story of the infamous Fu Manchu's (Oland's) attempt to seek revenge on his arch enemy (Fletcher) for his wife's death during Chinese Boxer Rebellion. Well-staged thriller. C: Warner Oland, Anna May Wong, Sessue Hayakawa. D: Lloyd Corrigan. CRI 72m.

Daughter of the Streets 1990 ★★★½ A harried single mother (Alexander) realizes almost too late she's neglected her teenaged daughter (Zal), leaving her to find what companionship she can on the streets. Short on story but has two solid lead performances. C: Jane Alexander, Roxana Zal, Martha Scott, John Stamos, Harris Yulin, Peter White, Bryan Horrocks. D: Ed Sherin. DRA 96m.

Daughters Courageous 1939 ★★★★ Prodigal father Rains returns to family he abandoned and gets mixed welcome. Moving sequel to *Four Daughters* features Garfield in dashing performance as Lane's confident boyfriend. C: John Garfield, Claude Rains, Fay Bainter, Priscilla Lane, Rosemary Lane, Lola Lane, May Robson, Donald Crisp, Frank McHugh. D: Michael Curtiz. DRA 107m.

Daughters of Darkness 1971 Belgian ★★★½ Cult chiller reimagines real-life figure of bloodthirsty Countess Bathory (Seyrig) as a lesbian vampire who seduces an abusive husband and his wife at a seaside resort. Artier and more intelligent than one might expect. C: Delphine Seyrig, Daniele Ouimet. D: Harry Kumel. HOR [R] 87m. v

Daughters of Destiny 1954 French ★★½ Three great women (Lysistrata, Elizabeth I, and Joan of Arc) and their roles in history, served up in a series of short tales. An interesting effort, but no more. C: Claudette Colbert, Michele Morgan, Andre Clement. D: Marcel Pagliero. DRA 94m.

Daughters of Satan 1972 ★★½ Witches search for a new member to join their club. Pretty tame horror flick. C: Tom Selleck, Barra Grant. D: Hollingsworth Morse. HOR [R] 96m.

Daughters of the Dust 1991 ★★★★ A look at life among the Gullah people, descendants of slaves who preserve their African heritage on offshore islands of South Carolina and Georgia. Leisurely paced but lyrical and fascinating. C: Cora Day, Alva Rodgers. D: Julie Dash. DRA 113m. v

Dave 1993 ★★★★ Kline is a marvel as good-hearted, ordinary guy and dead ringer for the President who suddenly finds himself in the Oval Office. Hilarious throughout as he outwits his Machiavellian chief-of-staff (Langella) and woos the First Lady (Weaver). Terrific, feel-good fun. C: Kevin Kline, Sigourney Weaver, Frank Langella, Ben Kingsley, Kevin Dunn, Charles Grodin, Faith Prince. D: Ivan Reitman. COM 110m. v

David 1976 German ★★★★ Unflinching look at Nazi horrors through eyes of a Jewish teenager who lives to tell his tale. Atrocities are detailed; overall an enlightening and important glimpse of Nazi resistance from German viewpoint. C: Mario Fischel, Irene Vrkijan. D: Peter Lilienthal. DRA 106m. v

David 1988 ★★★★ Peters is excellent as the mother of a child almost burned to death, deliberately, by his father. Harrowing drama is based on a real-life story. C: Bernadette Peters, John Glover, George Grizzard. D: John Erman. DRA 100m. TVM

David and Bathsheba 1951 ★★★ Judaean king seizes Jerusalem and is pursued by the wife of one of his officers. Uninspired Old Testament spectacle. Lush production; stilted performances. C: Gregory Peck, Susan Hayward, Raymond Massey, Jayne Meadows. D: Henry King. DRA 116m. v

David and Lisa 1962 ★★★★ Independent, low-budget film tells an upbeat love story of two disturbed adolescents at a mental institution. Dullea and Margolin turn in touching performances as the teens; Da Silva plays a sympathetic psychiatrist. Slightly dated but still moving. C: Keir Dullea, Janet Margolin, Howard Da Silva, Clifton James. D: Frank Perry. DRA 94m. V

David Copperfield 1935 ★★★★★ Definitive version of Dickens' classic novel tells epic story of mistreated English lad growing up into man of the world. Superb cast captures vivid characters brilliantly, especially Fields as Mr. Micawber and Rathbone as dour Mr. Murdstone. Excellent way to introduce youngsters to English literature. C: Freddie Bartholomew, W.C. Fields, Basil Rathbone, Lionel Barrymore, Edna May Oliver, Maureen O'Sullivan, Lewis Stone, Jessie Ralph, Elsa Lanchester, Una O'Connor. D: George Cukor. DRA 131m. V

David Copperfield 1970 ★★★½ Story of young man's journey to independence and self-awareness. Adequate version of Dickens novel with Who's Who in the English Theatre cast. Pedestrian script loses much of original's charm. C: Robin Phillips, Susan Hampshire, Edith Evans, Michael Redgrave, Ralph Richardson, Laurence Olivier, Wendy Hiller, Emlyn Williams, Richard Attenborough. D: Delbert Mann. DRA 110m. TVM

David Harum 1934 ★★★½ Rogers delivers his classic homespun wit and wisdom playing a rancher who brings together lovebirds Venable and Taylor. Pleasant, folksy comedy. C: Will Rogers, Louise Dresser, Evelyn Venable, Stepin Fetchit. D: James Cruze. COM 83m.

David Holzman's Diary 1968 ★★★★ Extremely personal chronicle of a naive moviemaker who decides to document his life on film. Made on a shoestring; more a triumph of imagination than truly substantial autobiography by writer/director McBride. Still perceptive and funny. C: L.M. Carson, Eileen Dietz. D: Jim McBride. DOC 74m. V

Davy Crockett and the River Pirates 1956 ★★★½ Two episodes from the popular '50s TV series were spliced together for this story of Davy's rousing encounter with keelboater Mike Fink. Plenty of action; entertaining family fare. C: Fess Parker, Buddy Ebsen. D: Norman Foster. FAM/WST [G] 81m. V

Davy Crockett, Indian Scout 1950 ★★★ Frontiersman Montgomery, descendant of Davy, and his Indian sidekick Red Hawk (Reed) escort a wagon train through hostile territory in this fanciful, stereotypical Western yarn. C: George Montgomery, Ellen Drew. D: Lew Landers. WST 71m.

Davy Crockett, King of the Wild Frontier 1955 ★★★★ The exciting story of Davy Crockett (Parker) comes to life in this combination of several episodes of the popular '50s TV series. The action-filled, well-acted story is excellent for family viewing. C: Fess Parker, Buddy Ebsen, Hans Conried. D: Norman Foster. FAM/WST [G] 96m. V

Dawn at Socorro 1954 ★★★ Gunslinger (Calhoun) who's sworn off violence must battle his conscience when he's hunted by two outlaws in this poor man's *High Noon*. C: Rory Calhoun, Piper Laurie. D: George Sherman. WST 80m.

Dawn of the Dead 1979 ★★★★ Romero's sequel to his *Night of the Living Dead* is a masterpiece, combining shocking (and extremely gory) horror with dark satire. Four survivors of a zombie plague hole up in an abandoned shopping mall and must defend the temple of consumerism from the flesh eaters outside. C: David Emge, Ken Foree. D: George A. Romero. HOR [R] 130m. V

Dawn Patrol, The 1930 ★★★½ First version of the classic WWI tale of fighter pilots struggling against long odds, long hours, and rigid officers. Director Hawks, a former pilot himself, brings truthfulness to the material, though the 1938 remake plays better today. C: Richard Barthelmess, Douglas Fairbanks, Jr., Neil Hamilton, William Janney. D: Howard Hawks. ACT 95m.

Dawn Patrol, The 1938 ★★★★ Solid remake of 1930 film about the trials faced by a star-crossed aerial squadron in France during WWI. Outstanding performances, especially by Rathbone. C: Errol Flynn, Basil Rathbone, David Niven, Donald Crisp, Barry Fitzgerald. D: Edmund Goulding. DRA 108m. V

Dawning, The 1992 British ★★★½ In '20s Ireland, a naive young woman (Pidgeon) becomes involved with an IRA man (Hopkins) on the run. Slow-paced drama is beautifully and hauntingly shot. Top-notch cast, with Howard's last film appearance. C: Anthony Hopkins, Jean Simmons, Trevor Howard, Rebecca Pidgeon, Hugh Grant. D: Robert Knights. DRA [PG] 97m. V

Day After, The 1983 ★★★ Controversial TV movie detailing horrifying aftereffects of nuclear war on a quiet, Midwestern town. Sometimes heavy-handed and graphic but always grimly terrifying. C: Jason Robards, JoBeth Williams, Steve Guttenberg, John Cullum, John Lithgow, Amy Madigan. D: Nicholas Meyer. DRA 126m. V

Day and the Hour, The 1963 French ★★★½ A bourgeois woman becomes a Resistance fighter, falls for American flyer she's to smuggle to safety. Unexceptional plot enlivened by Signoret, superb reconstruction of WWII France and Henri Decae's eye-opening camera work. C: Simone Signoret, Stuart Whitman, Genevieve Page, Michel Piccoli. D: Rene Clement. DRA 110m. V

Day at the Races, A 1937 ★★★★★ The Marx Brothers come to the aid of a young woman at a sanitorium. She also happens to own a racehorse. Contains several of the Marxes' most inspired comic routines, as well as favorite foil Dumont. One of the Marx Brothers', and therefore comedy's, crowning achievements. C: Groucho Marx, Harpo Marx, Chico Marx, Allan Jones, Maureen O'Sullivan, Margaret Dumont, Sig Ruman. D: Sam Wood. COM 109m. V

Day for Night 1973 French ★★★★★ The off-camera activities of a motion picture cast and crew are dramatized in this lively Oscar winner for Best Foreign Film. Top-notch performances (including Truffaut as the director) highlight this homage to the many pitfalls and dramas of making art. C: Jacqueline Bisset, Jean-Pierre Aumont, Valentina Cortese, Francois Truffaut, Jean-Pierre Leaud. D: Francois Truffaut. DRA [PG] 116m. V

Day for Thanks on Waltons' Mountain, A 1982 ★★★½ Fans of the long-running TV series will enjoy this reunion story, centered on the family's efforts to gather for Thanksgiving. Michael Learned's character is absent and Wightman, not Richard Thomas, plays John-Boy. Wholesome, as always. C: Ralph Waite, Ellen Corby, Judy Norton-Taylor, Robert Wightman. D: Harry Harris. FAM/DRA 100m. TVM V

Day in October, A 1992 Danish ★★★ A WWII Danish resistance fighter falls in love with a Jewish woman prior to large-scale rescue of Jews from Denmark. Routine romantic melodrama enhanced mainly by novelty of seldom-seen historical events. C: D.B. Sweeney, Kelly Wolf, Tovah Feldshuh. D: Kenneth Madsen. DRA [PG-13] 96m. V

Day in the Country, A 1936 French ★★★★★ Leisurely paced film details family's excursion to French countryside, culminating in separate seductions of wife and daughter. Based on story by Guy de Maupassant, an insightful and visually stunning work. C: Jean Renoir, Sylvia Bataille, Georges Saint-Saens, Jacques Borel. D: Jean Renoir. DRA 40m. V

Day in the Death of Joe Egg, A 1971 British ★★★★ Black comedy of a teacher (Bates) and his wife (Suzman) trying to cope with their severely physically and brain-damaged son, whom they call Joe Egg, and whom they consider euthanizing. Peter Nichols' successful stage play translates well onto film, but the subject is not easy to laugh at even though the writing is humorous. C: Alan Bates, Janet Suzman, Elizabeth Robillard, Peter Bowles, Joan Hickson. D: Peter Medak. COM [R] 106m. V

Day of Fury, A 1956 ★★★★½ Western law officer is reluctant to arrest criminal who once saved his life. Tight drama with neat psychological twist. C: Dale Robertson, Mara Corday. D: Harmon Jones. WST 78m.

Day of the Animals 1977 ★★★ After the ozone layer has been destroyed, radiation drives the world's animals crazy and they menace a group of backpackers in the California mountains. Gory and violent but the animals give their all. (a.k.a. *Something Is Out There*) C: Christopher George, Lynda Day George, Leslie Nielsen, Michael Ansara. D: William Girdler. HOR [PG] 97m. V

Day of the Bad Man 1958 ★★½ Judge MacMurray stands his ground when the brothers of a man he's sentenced to hang besiege the jail. Limp Western drama. C: Fred MacMurray, Joan Weldon. D: Harry Keller. WST 81m.

Day of the Dead 1985 ★★½ Third film in Romero's series concerning zombies devouring people, this time underground. Unlike the legendary *Night of the Living Dead* and the entertaining *Dawn of the Dead*, this one has neither creative characters nor scares. C: Lori Cardille, Terry Alexander, Richard Libert. D: George A. Romero. HOR 100m. V

Day of the Dolphin, The 1973 ★★★½ Researcher (Scott) teaches the smiling aquatic mammals to talk, then faces a crisis when he learns they are also being trained as assassins. Diverting, but undermined by some unintentional silliness. C: George C. Scott, Trish VanDevere, Paul Sorvino, Fritz Weaver. D: Mike Nichols. ACT [PG] 104m. V

Day of the Jackal, The 1973 British ★★★★½ Excellent adaptation of Frederick Forsyth's novel about a professional assassin trailing French president Charles De Gaulle, focusing on the killer's preparations. A tense and engrossing nail-biter to the end. C: Edward Fox, Alan Badel, Terrence Alexander, Cyril Cusack, Eric Porter, Delphine Seyrig, Derek Jacobi. D: Fred Zinnemann. CRI [PG] 142m. V

Day of the Locust, The 1975 ★★★ Bleak drama about the nasty underbelly of '30s Hollywood as seen through the eyes of young artist Atherton. A grim indictment of greed and blind ambition, based on the novel by Nathanael West. C: Donald Sutherland, Karen Black, Burgess Meredith, William Atherton, Geraldine Page, Richard Dysart. D: John Schlesinger. DRA [R] 140m. V

Day of the Outlaw 1959 ★★★½ Big-time rancher (Ryan) and his small-time rival (Marshal) join forces when an outlaw (Ives) and his gang come to town. Tension-packed Western set in stark Wyoming winter. C: Robert Ryan, Burl Ives, Tina Louise. D: Andre DeToth. WST 91m.

Day of the Triffids, The 1963 British ★★★★ Meteor shower awes Earthlings until they realize not only has it caused global blindness but also has transformed select plants into mobile man-eaters. Don't be fooled by imitations, this is *the* killer-plants-from-outer-space movie. Based on John Wyndham's novel. C: Howard Keel, Nicole Maurey, Kieron Moore. D: Steve Sekely. SFI 95m. V

Day of Wrath 1943 Danish ★★★★½ Elderly woman, burned for being a witch, puts spell on a pastor. Later, pastor's wife becomes obsessed with her own handsome stepson and is eventually accused of witchcraft herself. Somber, brilliantly imagined study of superstition and repression. C: Thorkild Roose, Lisbeth Movin. D: Carl Dreyer. DRA [PG] 110m.

Day One 1989 ★★★★ Fascinating depiction of the Manhattan Project, the creation of the first atomic bomb. Tight script makes for a crisp telling of this important story, but unfortunately necessitates deletion or glossing over of some events. Strong cast. C: Brian Dennehy, David Strathairn, Michael Tucker, Hume Cronyn, Richard Dysart, Hal Holbrook, Barnard Hughes. D: Joseph Sargent. DRA 141m. TVM V

Day the Earth Caught Fire, The 1962 British ★★★★ Thoughtful early disaster film finds the Earth hurtling toward the sun. Why? Atomic testing, of course. The stress here is on the Earthlings' response to impending doom (there's time for wooing, thank goodness), not special effects. A welcome change. C: Edward Judd, Janet Munro, Leo McKern. D: Val Guest. SFI 95m. V

Day the Earth Stood Still, The 1951 ★★★★★ Extraterrestrial (Rennie) lands on Earth to impart an urgent message—live in peace or be annihilated—but politicians won't lend him their ears. Witty and humorous, while preaching the liberal side of McCarthy-era politics. C: Michael Rennie, Patricia Neal, Hugh Marlowe, Sam Jaffe. D: Robert Wise. SFI [G] 92m. V

Day the Fish Came Out, The 1967 Greek ★ Failed absurdist comedy/drama centers around an Aegean island that becomes a hotbed of American concern when two pilots and their cargo of atomic bombs turn up missing in the area. Camp surrealism. C: Tom Courtenay, Candice Bergen, Colin Blakely, Sam Wanamaker. D: Michael Cacoyannis. DRA 109m.

Day the Hot Line Got Hot, The 1969 French ★★★ An international crisis is precipitated when spies fool around with the red telephone/hot line that connects Washington D.C. to Moscow. Tepid comedy was Taylor's last film. (a.k.a. *Hot Line*) C: Robert Taylor, Charles Boyer, George Chakiris. D: Etienne Perier. COM [M/PG] 92m.

Day the World Ended, The 1956 ★★★ Survivors of a nuclear blast scrap amongst themselves while fighting off a three-eyed monster. Corman's directorial debut is suitably cheesy and fun, in that low-budget kind of way. C: Richard Denning, Lori Nelson, Adele Jergens. D: Roger Corman. SFI [PG] 82m.

Day They Robbed the Bank of England, The 1960 British ★★★★ Irish loyalists plan to rob the largest bank in England in 1901. Entertaining crime drama. C: Aldo Ray, Elizabeth Sellers, Peter O'Toole, Hugh Griffith. D: John Guillermin. CRI 85m.

Day-Time Wife 1939 ★★★ Light marital comedy has Darnell thinking husband Power is dating his secretary; she gets a job so she can date one of his colleagues. C: Tyrone Power, Linda Darnell, Warren William, Binnie Barnes, Wendy Barrie, Joan Davis. D: Gregory Ratoff. COM 71m.

Day Will Dawn, The 1942 British ★★★★ A British journalist mobilizes a Norwegian village to rout Nazi U-boat. Top-notch WWII adventure yarn. (a.k.a. *The Avengers*) C: Hugh Williams, Deborah Kerr, Griffiths Jones, Ralph Richardson. D: Harold French. ACT 99m.

Daybreak 1939 *See* **Le Jour Se Leve**

Daybreak 1946 British ★★★ An unemployed hangman (Portman) marries a vamp (Todd) who continues to have affairs while her husband is away. Manufactured story lacks film noir atmosphere it aims to create. C: Eric Portman, Ann Todd, Maxwell Reed. D: Compton Bennett. DRA 75m.

Daydreamer, The 1966 ★★★½ Mixture of live action and animation has young Hans Christian Anderson meeting the characters he would later write about. Capable family entertainment, but not of the polished variety. C: Ray Bolger, Paul O'Keefe, Jack Gilford, Margaret Hamilton. D: Jules Bass. FAM/DRA 98m. V

Days and Nights in the Forest 1969 India ★★★★½ Quartet of gentlemen vacationing in country are changed by contact with less sophisticated locals. Though designed to parody urban elitism, Ray's great humanity still pervades this romantic light satire. C: Soumitra Chatterjee, Sharmilia Tagore, Shubhendu Chatterjee. D: Satyajit Ray. DRA 115m.

Days of Glory 1944 ★★½ Russian peasants battle the Nazi war machine in this slow-moving, but well-acted, WWII Allied propaganda film. Peck plays his first starring role as the commander of the blitzkrieg-busting guerrillas. C: Gregory Peck, Alan Reed, Maria Palmer. D: Jacques Tourneur. DRA 86m.

Days of Heaven 1978 ★★★★ Landowner Shepard and laborer Gere romance Adams in this moody, turn-of-the century love triangle. Spectacularly beautiful cinematography by Nestor Almendros, who won an Oscar. C: Richard Gere, Brooke Adams, Sam Shepard, Linda Manz. D: Terrence Malick. DRA [PG] 94m. V

Days of Hope 1939 *See* **Man's Hope**

Days of Thrills and Laughter 1961 ★★★★½ Excellent compilation of silent movie clips, alternating between comic gems featuring the likes of Keystone Kops, Laurel and Hardy, and cliffhangers starring Pearl White, Douglas Fairbanks, etc. C: Stan Laurel, Oliver Hardy, Charlie Chaplin, The Keystone Kops. Compiled by Robert Youngson. COM 93m. V

Days of Thunder 1990 ★★★ Cruise reprises his patented underdog role in this stock car racing yarn. *Top Gun* on wheels, from the makers of the same geared toward fans of the same. Ludicrous fantasy buoyed only slightly by Duvall's good performance. C: Tom Cruise, Robert Duvall, Randy Quaid, Nicole Kidman. D: Tony Scott. DRA [PG-13] 107m. V

Days of Wine and Roses 1962 ★★★★★

Heartrending drama gives an unflinching look at the downward spiral of alcoholic husband and the wife he drags along with him. Lemmon and Remick are outstanding in uncompromising performances. Oscar to Henry Mancini and Johnny Mercer for title song. C: Jack Lemmon, Lee Remick, Charles Bickford, Jack Klugman. D: Blake Edwards. DRA 138m. v

Dazed and Confused 1993 ★★★★ Seventies Texas high school students party hearty to celebrate the end of another school year. Drug-laced humor accents this nostalgic, freewheeling and well-acted teen comedy. D: Richard Linklater. COM v

D.C. Cab 1984 ★★★½ While cruising Washington streets, gonzo band of cab drivers form unusual camaraderie as they struggle to keep their fledgling company together. Wild comedy keeps rolling along thanks to freewheeling script and funny ensemble cast. C: Adam Baldwin, Charlie Barnett, Irene Cara, Mr. T, Marsha Warfield. D: Joel Schumacher. COM [R] 100m. v

Dead Again 1991 ★★★★½ A detective (Branagh) trying to help a woman (Thompson) regain her memory gets involved with a famous murder from the '40s. Very unusual, modern film-noir handles double story line well. C: Kenneth Branagh, Emma Thompson, Andy Garcia, Derek Jacobi, Hanna Schygulla, Robin Williams. D: Kenneth Branagh. CRI [R] 107m. v

Dead Ahead: The Exxon Valdez Disaster 1993 U.S. ★★★½ Docudrama on the Exxon *Valdez* oilspill disaster plots the conflicts among Exxon, environmentalists, and Alaska residents. Thoughtful, provocative, and well-crafted story of environmental havoc. (a.k.a. *Disaster at Valdez*) C: John Heard, Christopher Lloyd, Rip Torn. D: Paul Seed. DRA [PG-13] 90m. TVM v

Dead-Alive 1993 ★★★½ New Zealand bachelor does battle with his mother's corpse. Amidst all the blood lies a campy film that pokes as much fun at horror pictures as it does at domineering mothers and the '50s. C: Timothy Balme, Diana Penalver, Ian Watkin. D: Peter Jackson. HOR [R] 85m. v

Dead and Buried 1981 ★ A mad doctor (Albertson) spends his days bringing corpses back to life—an activity made easier by the idiotic actions of the other characters, including the sheriff (Farentino). Dumb, gory horror film. C: James Farentino, Melody Anderson, Jack Albertson. D: Gary A. Sherman. HOR [R] 95m. v

Dead-Bang 1989 ★★★ L.A. cop (Johnson) investigates the murder of a fellow officer and suspects a clan of white supremacists might be involved. Durable shoot-'em-up with game Johnson, skillful direction. C: Don Johnson, Penelope Ann Miller, William Forsythe. D: John Frankenheimer. DRA [R] 102m. v

Dead Calm 1989 Australian ★★★★ A married couple (Neill and Kidman) recovering on their yacht from a recent tragedy, rescue a young man (Zane) who claims to be the sole survivor of a disaster; he proceeds to kidnap the wife. Frightening drama moves so rapidly that the plot holes are barely noticeable. C: Sam Neill, Nicole Kidman, Billy Zane. D: Phillip Noyce. CRI [R] 96m. v

Dead Connection 1993 ★★½ Negligible thriller about a rogue cop (Madsen) and a tough reporter (Bonet) tracking a serial killer. C: Michael Madsen, Lisa Bonet, Gary Stretch. D: Nigel Dick. CRI [R] 93m. v

Dead Don't Die, The 1975 ★ And neither do clichés. Voodoo sect plots to raise the dead and take over the world. Silly stuff from a director, writer (*Psycho*'s Robert Bloch), and cast who usually do better. C: George Hamilton, Ray Milland, Linda Cristal, Ralph Meeker. D: Curtis Harrington. HOR 74m.

Dead End Drive-In 1986 Australian ★★½ In a totalitarian vision of the future after global economic collapse in 1990(!), criminals and other less-than-productive citizens are consigned to a former drive-in that's now a kind of boot camp. Entertaining premise, but otherwise listless. Violence and nudity. C: Ned Manning, Natalie McCurry. D: Brian Trenchard Smith. SFI [R] 92m. v

Dead End Kids on Dress Parade, The 1939 *See* **On Dress Parade**

Dead End Kids 1986 ★★★★ Oddball avant-garde history of nuclear power, using comic skits and musical numbers to comment on man's self-destructive tendencies. Some scenes, like Brisbin's monologue with a dead chicken, are in bad taste; others hit their target with dead-on precision. C: David Brisbin, Ellen McElduff, Ruth Maleczech, George Bartenieff. D: JoAnne Akalaitis. COM 90m.

Dead End 1937 ★★★★½ On the lam for murder, a big-time gangster revisits the slums he grew up in—and those he grew up with. Graphic depiction of New York City's Lower East Side enhances this poignant, searing cinematic treatment of Sidney Kingsley's excellent play. The colorful cast is uniformly outstanding. First look at the fabulous Dead End Kids. C: Joel McCrea, Humphrey Bogart, Sylvia Sidney, Wendy Barrie, Claire Trevor, Marjorie Main, Huntz Hall, Leo Gorcey, Gabriel Dell. D: William Wyler. DRA 92m. v

Dead Heat on a Merry-Go-Round 1966 ★★★★ A crook (Coburn) seduces a psychologist and attempts to rob the Los Angeles Airport bank. Good blend of comedy and drama, with a dynamic performance from Coburn. Harrison Ford's film debut (he's a bellhop). C: James Coburn, Camilla Sparv, Aldo Ray, Rose Marie. D: Bernard Girard. CRI 107m. v

Dead Heat 1988 ★★★ A once-dead cop and his mortal partner do battle with evildoers. Mildly interesting blend of horror film and wisecracking thriller. C: Treat Williams, Joe

Piscopo, Lindsay Frost, Darren McGavin, Vincent Price. D: Mark Goldblatt. CRI [R] 86m. V

Dead Kids *See* **Strange Behavior**

Dead Man Out 1989 ★★★★ A psychiatrist (Glover) is hired to treat a psychotic Death Row prisoner (Blades) so he can be declared sane and executed. Volatile drama ignited by intense performances from the two stars. C: Danny Glover, Ruben Blades. D: Richard Pearce. DRA 87m. TVM V

Dead Man's Folly 1986 ★★★ Agatha Christie's sleuth Hercule Poirot infiltrates an American novelist's role-playing game of murder. A tepid whodunit. C: Peter Ustinov, Jean Stapleton, Constance Cummings. D: Clive Donner. CRI 100m.

Dead Men Don't Wear Plaid 1982 ★★★★ Fun homage to film noir, with a sexy woman (Ward) hiring a private eye (Martin) to uncover a scheme to steal a famous cheese recipe. The story line is done with a montage of old b&w films with new footage—see if you can guess who and what movie. C: Steve Martin, Rachel Ward, Reni Santoni, Carl Reiner. D: Carl Reiner. COM [PG] 91m. V

Dead of Night 1945 British ★★★★½ Each member of a group of people staying at a country inn has a frighteningly real nightmare; best involves a ventriloquist whose dummy comes to life. Classic scary treat that became the prototype of British horror anthologies. C: Basil Dearden, Sally Ann Howes, Googie Withers, Michael Redgrave, Basil Radford, Naunton Wayne. D: Alberto Cavalcanti, Basil Dearden, Robert Hamer, Charles Crichton. HOR 104m. V

Dead of Night 1972 *See* **Deathdream**

Dead of Winter 1987 ★★★½ Reasonably suspenseful thriller, with an actress (Steenburgen) hired to impersonate a dead woman, then held in a snowbound house against her will. The plot keeps twisting and turning to good effect, but eventually becomes predictable. C: Mary Steenburgen, Roddy McDowall, Jan Rubes. D: Arthur Penn. DRA [R] 100m. V

Dead People 1974 ★★ Horror story about the Messiah of Evil, who promises to have the living dead prowl the streets. Ghastly goings-on. (a.k.a. *Messiah of Evil*) C: Michael Greer, Marianna Hill, Royal Dano, Anitra Ford. D: Willard Huyck. HOR [R] 90m.

Dead Pit 1989 ★★½ The zombie results of a mad doctor's experiments were imprisoned in a hospital's basement decades ago, but a psychic patient believes they're about to rise again. Low-budget horror entry with some shocking, gruesome moments. C: Jeremy Slate, Steffen Gregory Foster, Danny Gochnauer, Cheryl Lawson. D: Brett Leonard. HOR [R] 95m.

Dead Poets Society 1989 ★★★★ Robin Williams' dynamic performance as a boys' prep school English teacher who inspires his students to pursue their dreams is the spark that brings this sometimes maudlin teen drama to life. Tom Schulman won an Oscar for his screenplay. C: Robin Williams, Robert Sean Leonard, Ethan Hawke. D: Peter Weir. DRA [PG] 128m. V

Dead Pool, The 1988 ★★★★ A sports pool bets on which luminaries on a list will die next, but someone starts cheating by killing them. When Dirty Harry's name is added, he jumps in with guns blazing. A solid fifth entry in the *Dirty Harry* series, with a macabre but hilarious car chase. C: Clint Eastwood, Patricia Clarkson, Liam Neeson. D: Buddy Van-Horn. CRI [R] 91m. V

Dead Reckoning 1947 ★★★★ When a war hero disappears, his army buddy (Bogart) sets out to find him. Solid, thrilling postwar tale with Bogart in his element. Fine supporting cast. C: Humphrey Bogart, Lizabeth Scott, Morris Carnovsky. D: John Cromwell. ACT 100m. V

Dead Ringer 1964 ★★★½ A down-and-out woman (Davis) kills her wealthy twin sister, then takes her place. Star has a field day in dual role, but movie is lurid and poorly produced. Remade for TV as *The Killer in the Mirror*. C: Bette Davis, Karl Malden, Peter Lawford, Estelle Winwood. D: Paul Henreid. DRA 116m. V

Dead Ringers 1988 Canadian ★★★★★ Irons, in a magnificent accomplishment, plays identical twin gynecologists whose mutual dependence on one another leads to deadly psychological games. Frightening, disturbing, and ultimately difficult to watch, but Iron's multi-layered performance has to be seen to be believed. C: Jeremy Irons, Genevieve Bujold, Heidi Von Palleske. D: David Cronenberg. DRA [R] 117m. V

Dead Solid Perfect 1988 ★★½ Duffer (Quaid) struggles to keep his career and love life in check as he pursues a perfect day on the links. Sports comedy/drama tees up a few good laughs but rarely gets into the swing of things. Based on Dan Jenkins' novel. C: Randy Quaid, Kathryn Harrold, Jack Warden. D: Bobby Roth. COM 97m. TVM V

Dead, The 1988 ★★★★ Director Huston's last film is a melancholy meditation on life and loveless marriage, vividly realized by a talented Irish cast. Slow going at times but richly detailed and poignant. Based on the story by James Joyce. C: Anjelica Huston, Donal McCann, Helena Carroll, Dan O'Herlihy, Donal Donnelly. D: John Huston. DRA [PG] 82m. V

Dead Zone, The 1983 ★★★★ A teacher (Walken) wakes up after an accident to find he has acquired the ability to foresee the future. As his value to society increases, his life crumbles. Surprisingly thoughtful and moving. Based on the Stephen King novel. C: Christopher Walken, Brooke Adams, Tom Skerritt, Herbert Lom, Colleen Dewhurst, Martin Sheen. D: David Cronenberg. HOR [R] 104m. V

Deadfall 1993 ★★ When a con man (Biehn) kills his father/partner by accident, he hooks up with his uncle's gang. Over-heated, muddled crime drama, directed by Francis Ford Coppola's nephew. C: Michael Biehn, Sarah Trigger, Nicolas Cage, James Coburn, Peter Fonda, Charlie Sheen, Talia Shire. D: Christopher Coppola. CRI [R] 98m. V

Deadhead Miles 1972 ★★★½ Independent filmmaker Zimmerman teamed with Terrence Malick (*Days of Heaven*) writing this offbeat road movie about a long-distance trucker and the people he encounters. Pleasant if meandering. Originally filmed in 1972, but not released for 10 years. C: Alan Arkin, Paul Benedict, Hector Elizondo, Charles Durning, Barnard Hughes, Loretta Swit, John Milius, Ida Lupino, George Raft. D: Vernon Zimmerman. DRA [R] 93m.

Deadlier than the Male 1957 French ★★★ World-weary Gabin plays the chump to ex-stepdaughter Delorme who plans to marry him and then kill him for his money. Slack pacing and no real suspense. C: Jean Gabin, Daniele Delorme. D: Julien Duvivier. DRA 104m.

Deadlier than the Male 1967 British ★★★ Bulldog Drummond (Johnson) investigates a suave criminal (Green) and two assassins (Sommer and Koscina) plotting to murder the competition in a big oil company deal. Tasteless black comedy attempts to update the famous detective. Sequel: *Some Girls Do.* C: Richard Johnson, Elke Sommer, Sylva Koscina. D: Ralph Thomas. CRI 101m.

Deadliest Art, The: The Best of the Martial Arts Films, The 1992 ★★★ Compilation of the genre's most memorable sequences of kicks, chops, and death blows, without all that unnecessary plot. Lives up to its title. C: Bruce Lee, Jackie Chan, Lee Van Cleef, Cynthia Rothrock, Sho Kosugi, Chuck Norris, Kareem Abdul-Jabbar, Jean-Claude Van Damme. DRA 90m. V

Deadliest Season, The 1977 ★★★★ A popular but violent ice hockey player (Moriarty) is brought up on charges of manslaughter after he severely injures another player during a game. A hard-hitting examination of a newsworthy subject. Streep's film debut. C: Michael Moriarty, Kevin Conway, Meryl Streep, Jill Eikenberry. D: Robert Markowitz. DRA 98m. TVM

Deadliest Sin, The 1956 British ★★½ When thief Chaplin abandons his partner and skips with the loot, the betrayed man tracks him down. Slipshod crime caper with trite moral ending. C: Sydney Chaplin, Audrey Dalton. D: Ken Hughes. CRI 77m.

Deadline Assault 1979 *See* **Act of Violence**

Deadline at Dawn 1946 ★★★½ A somewhat confusing murder mystery, as a young actress (Hayward) tries to help clear a sailor on leave (Williams) of murder. Lukas plays a wise old taxi driver. Some good moments, but too few of them. C: Susan Hayward, Paul Lukas, Jerome Cowan. D: Harold Clurman. CRI 82m. V

Deadline U.S.A 1952 ★★★★ A courageous editor (Bogart) fights the underworld and struggles to keep his paper from buckling under to pressure. Great performances; tight script is right on target. C: Humphrey Bogart, Kim Hunter, Ethel Barrymore, Ed Begley. D: Richard Brooks. DRA 87m.

Deadline 1987 German ★★ While on assignment in Lebanon, a journalist (Walken) finds himself embroiled in a mysterious nest of machinations. Complicated and confusing. C: Christopher Walken, Hywel Bennett. D: Nathaniel Gutman. ACT [R] 100m. V

Deadlock 1991 ★★½ In the future prisons have no fences—but prisoners must wear exploding necklaces that go off if they stray away from each other. Good premise, mundane execution. C: Rutger Hauer, Mimi Rogers, Joan Chen. D: Lewis Teague. ACT [R] 103m. TVM V

Deadly Affair, The 1967 ★★★★ Masterfully directed espionage film based on John Le Carre's *Call for the Dead* features a wonderful performance from Mason as a British agent investigating a coworker's suicide. Top-of-the-line spy thriller. C: James Mason, Simone Signoret, Maximilian Schell, Harriet Andersson, Lynn Redgrave. D: Sidney Lumet. CRI 107m.

Deadly Blessing 1981 ★★★ Bizarre murders in a rural town may be caused by supernatural force or by member of local cult. Despite some good performances and scares, the film itself seems unable to make sense of all the madness. C: Karen Jensen, Sharon Stone, Lois Nettleton, Ernest Borgnine. D: Wes Craven. HOR [R] 104m. V

Deadly Breed ★★½ A small-town police department is taken over by white supremacists. Soon, the whole countryside is in an uproar. Interesting idea collapses in this dull affair. DRA

Deadly Business, A 1986 ★★★★ By day, Arkin's the right-hand man to a polluting mob boss; by night, he's informing to the government about illegal toxic dumping. Harrowing true story convincingly told. C: Alan Arkin, Armand Assante, Michael Learned. D: John Korty. CRI 100m. TVM

Deadly Companions, The 1961 ★★★★ Shady gunslinger guides funeral procession of dance-hall entertainer's son on a dangerous passage through Apache country. Above-average fare is an early effort by Peckinpah. C: Maureen O'Hara, Brian Keith, Steve Cochran, Chill Wills. D: Sam Peckinpah. WST 90m. V

Deadly Dust, The *See* **Spiderman: The Deadly Dust**

Deadly Eyes 1982 ★★★ Over-grown rats menace a busy metropolis as romance develops between a health inspector (Botsford) and a science teacher (Groom). Okay horror flick reaches its peak when the critters attack a movie theater. (a.k.a. *The Rats*) C: Sam Groom, Sara Botsford, Scatman Crothers. D: Robert Clouse. HOR [R] 93m. V

Deadly Friend 1986 ★★ Mindless meld of two story lines. Begins harmlessly as a "boy genius and his cute robot" yarn and abruptly becomes a dark Frankenstein tale when Laborteaux revives his brain-dead girlfriend. Awful, despite a game Swanson. C: Matthew Laborteaux, Kristy Swanson, Anne Twomey, Anne Ramsey. D: Wes Craven. SFI [R] 91m. V

Deadly Hero 1975 ★★★½ Dedicated police officer (Murray) near the end of his career may lose it all when a woman whose life he saved comes forward with a bizarre accusation. Intriguing crime drama strained by unnecessary violence. C: Don Murray, Diahn Williams, James Earl Jones, Treat Williams. D: Ivan Nagy. CRI [R] 102m. V

Deadly Impact 1984 Italian ★★★ Two men from different worlds team up in ambitious plot to pilfer cash from Las Vegas casinos. Williamson plays the smooth operator, with Svenson cast as his antithesis. Footage of Vegas is well used. C: Bo Svenson, Fred Williamson. D: Larry Ludman. CRI 90m. V

Deadly Mantis, The 1957 ★ Enormous mantis, awakened from a polar deep freeze, wreaks havoc from the Arctic to New York City, where it meets its doom in the "Manhattan Tunnel"! The nadir of giant insect films, with dreadful effects and wooden acting. C: Craig Stevens, William Hopper. D: Nathan Juran. SFI 79m. V

Deadly Sanctuary 1970 ★★ Hard to believe the likes of Palance got involved in this sleazy sex/horror film about two orphaned young women who become involved in torture, murder, and other Marquis de Sade-inspired doings. C: Jack Palance, Romina Power, Akim Tamiroff, Klaus Kinski, Sylva Koscina. D: Jess Franco. HOR 93m.

Deadly Spawn, The 1983 ★★★½ A meteor crash releases toothy, sluglike creatures that terrorize a suburban household. Micro-budget monster movie isn't all that scary, but it has the good sense not to take itself very seriously. (a.k.a. *Return of the Alien's Deadly Spawn*) C: Charles George Hildebrandt, Tom DeFranco, Richard Lee Porter, Jean Tafler, Karen Tighe. D: Douglas McKeown. HOR [R] 78m.

Deadly Stranger 1988 *See* **Border Heat**

Deadly Strangers 1974 British ★★★½ A young woman (Mills) picks up a hitchhiker (Ward) after a mad strangler has escaped from a mental hospital. Are they one and the same? Well-acted psychological thriller. C: Hayley Mills, Simon Ward, Sterling Hayden. D: Sidney Hayers. CRI 93m. V

Deadly Surveillance ★★½ Police investigating drug world murders suspect cop's girlfriend may be involved. Some suspense, but Canadian-made actioner can't shake that seen-it-before feeling. DRA

Deadly Trackers, The 1973 ★★ A Texas sheriff hunts down the bandit killers of his family. Violent potboiler from Samuel Fuller short story goes awry on the trail. C: Richard Harris, Rod Taylor, Neville Brand. D: Barry Shear. WST [PG] 110m.

Deadman's Curve 1978 ★★★½ Biography of rock 'n' roll surfer boys Jan and Dean, who were plagued by personal tragedy. Well acted, modestly effective, with strong work by Davison and Hatch. C: Bruce Davison, Richard Hatch. D: Richard Compton. MUS 104m.

Deaf and Blind 1987 ★★★★★ Compilation of four poignant and thoughtful films (*Blind, Deaf, Multi-Handicapped,* and *Adjustment and Work*), showing the work of the Alabama Institute for the Deaf and Blind, a school for handicapped children ages five and up. These sensitive documentaries are among Wiseman's finest achievements. D: Frederick Wiseman. DOC 542m.

Deaf Smith and Johnny Ears 1973 Italian ★★★ Deaf-mute Quinn is befriended by Nero as both witness political turmoil in 1830s Texas. Good teaming of Quinn and Nero, though story tends to lose itself. (a.k.a. *Los Amigos*) C: Anthony Quinn, Franco Nero, Pamela Tiffin. D: Paolo Cavara. WST [PG] 91m.

Deal of the Century 1983 ★★★½ Slapdash screwball comedy about small-time con artist (Chase) trying to sell weapons to a Central American dictator. Satire never reaches comic potential, but fun cast gains some momentum. C: Chevy Chase, Sigourney Weaver, Gregory Hines, Vince Edwards. D: William Friedkin. COM [PG] 99m. V

Dealers 1989 British ★★ McGann and De Mornay are currency traders for London bank in this lightweight and forgettable story of business rivalry and romance. C: Paul McGann, Rebecca DeMornay, Derrick O'Connor. D: Colin Bucksey. DRA [R] 92m. V

Dealing: or The Berkeley-to-Boston Forty-Brick Lost-Bag Blues 1972 ★★★½ A Harvard student pays his tuition by selling grass (the potent kind). Uneven comedy makes a nostalgic time capsule, with Lithgow a hoot as a stoned hippie. From the novel by Robert and Michael Crichton. C: Robert F. Lyons, Barbara Hershey, John Lithgow, Charles Durning. D: Paul Williams. COM [R] 99m.

Dear America: Letters Home from Vietnam 1988 ★★★★ Actors movingly read from soldiers' actual correspondence. Perhaps too heavy on period pop songs, but a compelling and beautifully-realized account of soldiers' daily traumas. Made for HBO; later theatrical release. D: Bill Couturie. DRA [PG-13] 84m. V

Dear Brigitte 1965 ★★★ Family comedy as kid (Mumy) with penchant for picking winning horses blackmails father (Stewart) so he can meet his dream woman (Bardot). Good cast, weak premise. C: James Stewart,

Fabian, Glynis Johns, Billy Mumy, Ed Wynn. D: Henry Koster. COM 100m. V

Dear Dead Delilah 1972 ★★ Last screen role for Moorehead as a bedridden Southern matriarch with a fortune hidden on her estate. Gory ax murders ensue among greedy, treasure-hunting relatives. Uncut version concludes with nutty recap of killings to "Battle Hymn of the Republic." C: Agnes Moorehead, Will Geer, Michael Ansara. D: John Farris. HOR 97m. V

Dear Detective 1977 French ★★★★ Middle-aged female inspector gets help with murder investigation from her lover, a college professor. Fairly generic plotting, but obvious chemistry between French stars, Girardot and Noiret, turned this into an American hit. C: Annie Girardot, Philippe Noiret, Catherine Alric. D: Philippe DeBroca. CRI 105m.

Dear Detective 1979 ★★★ Vaccaro is a homicide police unit head who juggles the search for a killer who's targeting politicians with the demands of a budding love affair with a college professor. Remake of French film of same name. C: Brenda Vaccaro, Arlen Dean Snyder, Michael MacRae. D: Dean Hargrove. CRI 92m. TVM V

Dear Heart 1964 ★★★★ Two middle-aged delegates to a post office convention in New York City meet and fall in love. A charming, understated film, elegantly performed by Ford and Page. C: Glenn Ford, Geraldine Page, Angela Lansbury, Barbara Nichols, Mary Wickes. D: Delbert Mann. DRA 114m.

Dear Michael 1976 Italian ★★★★½ Outcast son of privileged family strikes back by having a child with loose-moraled girl. Terrific satire of the middle class is propelled entirely by letters. C: Mariangela Melato, Aurore Clement, Fabio Carpi. D: Mario Monicelli. COM 108m.

Dear Mr. Wonderful 1982 German ★★★★ A Jersey City man runs a bowling alley but aspires to be a singer. Incredibly, this very American-seeming, charming drama was made in Germany. (a.k.a. *Ruby's Dream*) C: Joe Pesci, Karen Ludwig, Evan Handler. D: Peter Lilienthal. DRA 115m.

Dear Ruth 1947 ★★★½ Amusing slice of Americana about young student (Freeman) who pretends to be her older sister (Caulfield) so she can write love letters and impress her heartthrob—an unsuspecting soldier (Holden). Adapted from hit Broadway play. *Dear Wife* and *Dear Brat* were sequels. C: Joan Caulfield, William Holden, Mona Freeman, Edward Arnold, Billy DeWolfe. D: William Russell. COM 95m.

Dear Wife 1949 ★★★ Sequel to *Dear Ruth* has Freeman once again conspiring, this time to get Holden to run for same Senate seat as her father (Arnold). C: Joan Caulfield, William Holden, Edward Arnold, Mona Freeman, Billy DeWolfe. D: Richard Haydn. COM 88m.

Death and the Maiden 1973 *See* **Hawkins on Murder**

Death and the Maiden 1994 ★★★★½ Tingling political thriller casts Weaver as a Chilean woman once raped and tortured during a now-fallen dictatorship. When a stranger stops at her home, she's convinced that he's the man who tormented her. Weaver's terrific, and so's Kingsley as her nemesis. From the play by Ariel Dorfman. C: Sigourney Weaver, Ben Kingsley, Stuart Wilson. D: Roman Polanski. DRA [R] 103m.

Death at Love House 1975 ★★★½ A lonely writer (Wagner) fixates on a dead movie star—until her spirit tries to kill him! Mediocre script, but delivers some genuine chills. Filmed at Harold Lloyd's estate. C: Robert Wagner, Kate Jackson, Sylvia Sidney, Joan Blondell, Dorothy Lamour, John Carradine. D: E.W. Swackhamer. HOR 74m. TVM V

Death Be Not Proud 1975 ★★★★ Wrenching tearjerker from John Gunther memoir of son's bout with terminal brain tumor. Benson does a fine job as the doomed 17-year-old, while Hill and Alexander show admirable restraint as stricken parents. C: Arthur Hill, Jane Alexander, Robby Benson. D: Donald Wrye. DRA 120m. TVM V

Death Becomes Her 1992 ★★★★ Eye-popping special effects highlight this wacky black comedy about two women who quest for eternal youth as they both try to win the love of a plastic surgeon. Solid laughs make this an attractive jaunt into the macabre. Oscar for Visual Effects. C: Meryl Streep, Goldie Hawn, Bruce Willis, Isabella Rossellini, Sydney Pollack. D: Robert Zemeckis. COM [PG-13] 103m. V

Death Before Dishonor 1987 ★★ Marine Sergeant (Dryer) is on a mission to take revenge on terrorists who killed his men and kidnapped his superior (Keith). Typical macho posturing in surface *Rambo* variation. C: Fred Dryer, Brian Keith, Paul Winfield. D: Terry J. Leonard. ACT [R] 95m. V

Death Drug 1986 ★★ PCP—otherwise known as angel dust—is the drug of choice in dead-end story of musician who sacrifices his talent for his drug. Inept and dull. C: Philip Michael Thomas, Rosalind Cash. D: Oscar Williams. DRA [PG-13] 73m. V

Death Game 1976 ★ Mean-spirited story about two crazed lesbians who take a man hostage for fun and psycho-games. Trash. (a.k.a. *The Seducers*) C: Sondra Locke, Colleen Camp, Seymour Cassel. D: Peter S. Traynor. CRI [R] 91m. V

Death Hunt 1981 ★★★½ Macho action thriller, as a trapper (Bronson) wrongly accused of murder runs from Mountie (Marvin). Some decent action sequences and good cinematography make it watchable, but beware of the disturbingly violent dog fight scene. C: Charles Bronson, Lee Marvin, Andrew Stevens, Angie Dickinson, Carl Weathers. D: Peter H. Hunt. ACT [R] 96m. V

Death in California, A 1985 ★★★★ A psychotic killer (Elliott) alternately terrorizes and seduces a wealthy woman (Ladd) in this bizarre but true story. Well-made, gripping drama, despite off-putting theme. C: Cheryl Ladd, Sam Elliott, Alexis Smith. D: Delbert Mann. CRI 200m. TVM

Death in Canaan, A 1978 ★★★★ Arthur Miller was just one of many Connecticut residents who rallied to the aid of a young man (Clemens) coerced by the police into admitting he'd murdered his mother. Taut, disturbing drama, based on an unfortunately true story. C: Stefanie Powers, Brian Dennehy, Paul Clemens, Tom Atkins, Jacqueline Brookes. D: Tony Richardson. CRI 120m. TVM

Death in Venice 1971 Italian ★★★★ Vivid, detailed adaptation of Thomas Mann's novella follows an artist (based on composer Gustav Mahler) in his obsessive quest for beauty in the form of a young boy he discovers during a summer in Venice. Memorable Mahler score adds to haunting atmosphere. C: Dirk Bogarde, Mark Burns, Marisa Berenson, Bjorn Andresen, Silvana Mangano. D: Luchino Visconti. DRA [PG] 131m. V

Death Kiss, The 1933 ★★★½ Confused, low-budget mystery of actor murdered while shooting a scene. Thin plot, but interesting insights into filmmaking. Marin's directorial debut is entertaining at times. C: Bela Lugosi, David Manners, Adrienne Ames. D: Edwin L. Marin. CRI 72m. V

Death of a Bureaucrat 1966 Cuban ★★★★ Lunatic satire of Castro's Cuba finds a young man unable to bury his uncle and hamstrung by the red tape after exhuming the body to get dead man's union card, which aunt needs to collect pension. On-target dissection of bureaucracy's impossible demands on individuals. COM V

Death of a Centerfold: The Dorothy Stratten Story 1981 ★★★ Curtis stars as the *Playboy* model who was murdered by her jealous husband (Weitz) just as she was beginning an acting career. Covers same ground as *Star 80*, a better film; interesting to compare the two. C: Jamie Lee Curtis, Bruce Weitz, Robert Reed. D: Gabrielle Beaumont. DRA 100m. TVM V

Death of a Cyclist 1955 ★★★★ Well-off professor leaves a bicyclist to die after his car hits him. Affecting parable of the chasm between rich and poor in Franco's Spain works as story with real characters, not just symbols. DRA

Death of a Gunfighter 1969 ★★★½ Gunplay ensues after marshal outgrows his usefulness to townfolk. Slowly paced, unconventional Western. C: Richard Widmark, Lena Horne, John Saxon, Carroll O'Connor. D: Allen Smithee. WST [M/PG] 100m. V

Death of a Prophet 1981 ★★★½ Drama about the last day in the life of an unnamed African-American leader. Low-budget documentary-style drama evokes life of Malcolm X, and effectively incorporates actual civil rights footage. Freeman is excellent. C: Morgan Freeman, Yolanda King. D: Woodie King Jr. DRA 60m. V

Death of a Salesman 1951 ★★★★★ Classic film version of Arthur Miller's Pulitzer Prize-winning play, with March as the tragic traveling salesman who realizes too late that he's sacrificed his wife and family for the road. Superb acting, across the board. C: Fredric March, Mildred Dunnock, Kevin McCarthy, Cameron Mitchell. D: Laslo Benedek. DRA 115m.

Death of a Salesman 1985 ★★★★ Hoffman captures the embattled little man Arthur Miller envisioned, in this touching, imaginatively realized production. Malkovich embodies the wistful loser son in this drama about the tragic distance between one man's illusions and the reality of his life. Solid (if stagey) rendition of a classic. C: Dustin Hoffman, Kate Reid, John Malkovich, Stephen Lang, Charles Durning. D: Volker Schlondorff. DRA 135m. TVM V

Death of a Scoundrel 1956 ★★★½ Down-and-out European cad (Sanders) comes to American to strike it rich by conning wealthy women. Messy combination of comedy, murder, and bad taste. (a.k.a. *The Loves and Death of a Scoundrel* and *The Loves of a Scoundrel*) C: George Sanders, Yvonne De Carlo, Zsa Zsa Gabor. D: Charles Martin. CRI 119m. V

Death of a Soldier 1985 Australian ★★★ In this WWII drama, an Army counsel (Coburn) tries to cop an insanity plea for an American soldier who brutally murdered three Melbourne women. The American military brass, meanwhile, want him hanged to curry favor with Australian allies. Wordy but intriguing film, based on a true incident. C: James Coburn, Bill Hunter, Maurie Fields. D: Philippe Mora. DRA [R] 90m. V

Death of an Angel 1986 ★★★ A female priest (Bedelia) goes to Mexico to save her daughter (Ludwig) from the clutches of a Mexican religious cult and its charismatic leader (Mancuso). Timely and well acted, but overdone fantasy makes plot hard to swallow. C: Bonnie Bedelia, Nick Mancuso, Pamela Ludwig. D: Petru Popescu. DRA [PG] 95m. V

Death of Her Innocence 1974 *See* **Our Time**

Death of Richie, The 1977 ★★★½ Teenager Benson's drug addiction leads to family tragedy. Overwrought drama worth seeing for Gazzara's bravura performance as father on trial for murdering his son. C: Ben Gazzara, Robby Benson, Eileen Brennan, Lance Kerwin. D: Paul Wendkos. DRA 100m. V

Death of Tarzan, The 1968 Czech ★★★★ A "wild man" is introduced to Czech society under Nazi rule and struggles to become more "civilized." Czechoslovakian production, which has nothing to do with the legendary jungle swinger, playfully and skillfully satirizes modern man's estrangement from his primative impulses. C: Rudolf Hrusinsky, Jana Stepankova, Martin Rusek. D: Jaroslav Balik. DRA

Death of the Empedocles, The 1988 West German ★★★★ A Greek philosopher falls from the grace of God. Austere, scholarly, historically accurate adaptation of the Holderlin play. D: Jean-Marie Straub, Daniele Huillete. DRA 132m.

Death of the Incredible Hulk, The 1990 ★★★ Is the green monster dead? Not by a long shot. Hulk fans and the younger set will love the pumped-up action. C: Bill Bixby, Lou Ferrigno. D: Bill Bixby. ACT 96m. V

Death on the Nile 1978 British ★★★½ Ustinov as Belgian detective Poirot travels to Egypt and faces shipful of suspects in Agatha Christie whodunit. Holds attention till satisfying conclusion, but numerous reenactments of crime border on the ludicrous. C: Peter Ustinov, Mia Farrow, David Niven, Bette Davis, Angela Lansbury, Maggie Smith, George Kennedy, Jack Warden, Lois Chiles, Olivia Hussey, Simon MacCorkindale, Jane Birkin. D: John Guillermin. DRA [PG] 135m. V

Death Race 2000 1975 ★★★ Forget drag racing—this sport gives drivers points for hitting people. Sci-fi actioner with a touch of tongue-in-cheek humor. C: David Carradine, Mary Woronov, Sylvester Stallone. D: Paul Bartel. ACT [R] 85m. V

Death Scream 1975 ★★★ Detective Julia investigates murder of young woman in which numerous witnesses stood by and did nothing as victim was stabbed to death. Lurid, poorly acted docudrama based on infamous NYC Kitty Genovese case. C: Raul Julia, Tina Louise, Art Carney. D: Richard Heffron. DRA 100m.

Death Sentence 1974 ★★★½ Juror Leachman, serving on murder case, suspects her husband of committing the crime. Moderately suspenseful, due to Leachman's convincing performance. C: Cloris Leachman, Laurence Luckinbill. D: E. W. Swackhamer. DRA 73m.

Death Ship 1980 Canadian ★ Survivors of an oceanliner disaster board the vessel that sank them, only to find it's an old Nazi torture ship with a bloodthirsty mind of its own. Ridiculous premise yields sluggish laughable chiller. C: George Kennedy, Richard Crenna, Nick Mancuso, Sally Ann Howes. D: Alvin Rakoff. HOR [R] 91m. V

Death Takes a Holiday 1934 ★★★★½ Poetically sad romance as Death comes to Earth to see why people fear him and falls for a morbid young woman. March and Venable work beautifully in delicate territory. Stylish direction by Leisen. Based on a play by Alberto Casella. C: Fredric March, Evelyn Venable, Guy Standing, Gail Patrick, Helen Westley, Henry Travers. D: Mitchell Leisen. DRA 78m.

Death Trap 1976 *See* **Eaten Alive**

Death Warrant 1990 Canadian ★★★ Van Damme is an undercover Mountie who infiltrates a prison to investigate the deaths of several inmates. An old adversary is transferred to the cell block and the sparks fly. Not bad as Van Damme's movies go . . . and certainly not as violent. C: Jean-Claude Van Damme, Robert Guillaume, Cynthia Gibb. D: Deran Serafian. ACT [R] 111m. V

Death Wish 1974 ★★★★ Mild-mannered architect (Bronson) becomes ruthless vigilante after his wife is murdered and daughter raped by N.Y.C. hoodlums. Remains the best of the countless blood-lusting vigilante films it spawned. Followed by too many sequels. C: Charles Bronson, Hope Lange, Vincent Gardenia, Steven Keats, William Redfield, Olympia Dukakis, Christopher Guest. D: Michael Winner. ACT [R] 93m. V

Death Wish II 1982 ★★ Vigilante (Bronson) does for L.A. exactly what he did for N.Y.C. in the original; shoot no-good hoodlum scum. Lifeless sequel with no purpose other than to show the effects of bullets on people and pad the principals' wallets. Followed by 3, 4 and 5. C: Charles Bronson, Jill Ireland, Vincent Gardenia, Anthony Franciosa, Larry Fishburne. D: Michael Winner. ACT [R] 93m. V

Death Wish 3 1985 ★ Bronson the vigilante remains in L.A. and, when the police prove to be unhelpful, again, resumes his gun-toting/hand-grenade-launching ways. Awful. Followed by *Death Wish 4* and *5*. C: Charles Bronson, Deborah Raffin, Ed Lauter, Martin Balsam. D: Michael Winner. ACT [R] 90m. V

Death Wish 4: The Crackdown 1987 ★ This time, Bronson takes aim at crack dealers and the body count soars. May try even fans of the previous three *Death Wishes*. There aren't enough bad things to say about this movie. C: Charles Bronson, Kay Lenz. D: J. Lee Thompson. ACT [R] 100m. V

Death Wish 5 1994 ★ Bronson's fiancée is killed, so he straps on his gun for vengeance again. For Bronson fans only. C: Charles Bronson, Lesley-Anne Down, Michael Parks, Saul Rubinek. D: Allan Goldstein. ACT [R] 90m. V

Deathdream 1972 Canadian ★★★½ A bereaved woman wills her Vietnam soldier son back from the dead. Unfortunately, he's become a blood-thirsty cannibal. Taut, low-budget thriller that delivers. (a.k.a. *Dead of Night*) C: John Marley, Richard Backus, Lynn Carlin. D: Bob Clark. HOR 90m. V

Deathmoon 1978 ★ Dumb chiller is far too tame to sustain any suspense, as witchcraft turns vacationer (Foxworth) into a werewolf. Hawaiian setting is a novelty. C: Robert Foxworth, Charles Haid, Joe Penny, France Nuyen. D: Bruce Kessler. HOR 90m.

Deathsport 1978 ★★★ Sequel to *Death Race 2000* once again features ruthless professional race car driver (Carradine) competing in a deadly futuristic road game in which contestants score points by flattening pedestrians and destroying their fellow contestants. Gorier and less fun than the original. C: David Carradine, Claudia Jennings, Richard Lynch. D: Allan Arkush. ACT [R] 90m. v

Deathstalker 1983 ★★ Beefcake warrior is out to save a princess (Benton) from an evil wizard. Somehow spawned three (and counting) sequels. C: Richard Hill, Barbi Benton. D: John Watson. SFI [R] 80m. v

Deathstalker II—Duel of the Titans 1987 ★★★ Princess enlists soldier in an effort to regain her throne. Amusing, campy quality helps *Stalker 2* eclipse the original. Much nudity and endearingly cheap production values. C: John Terlesky, Monique Gabrielle. D: Jim Wynorski. SFI [R] 85m. v

Deathstalker III 1989 ★★ Wizards and sorcery are the hallmarks of the *Deathstalker* series. This installment about a quest for three magic stones satirizes itself, but despite a few funny gags, the story is confused. (a.k.a. *Deathstalker III: The Warriors from Hell*) C: John Allen Nelson, Carla Hert, Thom Christopher. D: Alfonso Corona. SFI [R] 85m. v

Deathstalker III: The Warriors from Hell 1989 *See* **Deathstalker III**

Deathstalker IV 1991 ★★ An evil queen invites several of the universe's great warriors to her tournament in an attempt to create an invincible army. Lacks the charm of the previous films in this series. C: Rick Hill, Maria Ford, Michelle Moffett, Brent Baxter Clark. D: Howard R. Cohen. SFI [R] 85m.

Deathtrap 1982 ★★★½ A faded playwright (Caine), tired of being supported by his wife (Cannon), plots to steal a brilliant thriller written by ex-student (Reeve)—and even kill him, if necessary. Comic mystery has twists and surprises, but some real slow spots. Based on Ira Levin's Broadway play. C: Michael Caine, Christopher Reeve, Dyan Cannon, Irene Worth. D: Sidney Lumet. CRI [PG] 116m. v

Deathwatch 1982 French ★★★★ Futuristic thriller of man (Keitel) with a camera in his brain who befriends a dying woman (Schneider) and records her steady decline for TV. Intelligent sci-fi provides thought-provoking glimpse at media manipulation. C: Romy Schneider, Harvey Keitel, Harry Dean Stanton, Max von Sydow. D: Bertrand Tavernier. SFI [R] 128m. v

Debajo del Mundo (Under Earth) 1986 ★★★★½ Powerful chronicle, based on true story, of a Jewish clan in WWII Poland who survived in makeshift underground shelters. Vivid portrait of endurance against Nazis, anti-Semitism and fighting among themselves. Well worth seeking out. C: Sergio Renan, Barbara Mugica, Victor La Place. D: Beda Docampofeijoo. DRA 100m.

Decameron Nights 1953 British ★★★ Toothless version of Boccaccio's bawdy medieval *Decameron* stories features Jourdan on an episodic quest for romance with Fontaine. C: Joan Fontaine, Louis Jourdan, Binnie Barnes, Joan Collins. D: Hugo Fregonese. DRA 87m. v

Deceived 1991 ★★ After her husband is killed, a widow (Hawn) uncovers web of falsehoods proving that everything is not as it seems. Hawn is suprisingly believable in a serious role. C: Goldie Hawn, John Heard, Robin Bartlett, Beatrice Straight, Kate Reid. D: Damian Harris. CRI [PG-13] 108m. v

Deceivers, The 1988 British ★★ British officer (Brosnan) goes undercover to join a vicious religious sect in 1830s India. Based on a true story, but lacks credibility; slow pace and Brosnan, who seems like a fish in a tree here, don't help. C: Pierce Brosnan, Saeed Jeffrey, Shashi Kapoor, Keith Michell, David Robb. D: Nicholas Meyer. ACT [PG-13] 103m. v

December 7th—The Movie ★★★ WWII drama takes a hard look at the bungling that led to Pearl Harbor. Banned by the U.S. government for realistic scenes of race relations in the military and sympathetic views of Japanese-Americans. C: Walter Huston. D: John Ford. DRA 85m. v

December 1991 ★★★ The day after Pearl Harbor, five prep school friends try to decide whether going to war is more important than education. Endless debate fizzles to a meager end. C: Balthazar Getty, Jason London, Wil Wheaton. D: Gabe Torres. DRA [PG] 92m. v

Deception 1946 ★★★★ A concert pianist (Davis) can't shake the influence of her malevolent Svengali-like sponsor (Rains). Claude wipes the floor with Bette in this schmaltzy melodrama; his performance is truly memorable. C: Bette Davis, Claude Rains, Paul Henreid. D: Irving Rapper. DRA 112m. v

Deception 1993 ★★★½ Widow (MacDowell) treks the globe to locate her husband's missing money via clues left on baseball cards. Homage to thriller/romances like *Charade* boasts attractive stars, fun scenery. C: Andie MacDowell, Liam Neeson, Viggo Mortenson, Jack Thompson. D: Graeme Clifford. CRI [PG-13] 90m. v

Deceptions 1990 ★★★½ A homicide detective (Hamlin) investigates death of rich man whose widow grieves with a smile while she seduces Hamlin. Not bad, but not great. C: Harry Hamlin, Nicollette Sheridan, Robert Davi. D: Ruben Preuss. CRI [R] 105m. TVM v

Decision Against Time 1957 British ★★★½ British test pilot brazenly risks his life again and again for God, country, and the hell of it. Good Brit action drama with fine lead performance by Hawkins. C: Jack Hawkins, Elizabeth Sellars, Eddie Byrne, Donald Pleasence. D: Charles Crichton. ACT 87m.

Decision at Sundown 1957 ★★★½ Solid Western about rancher (Scott) out for revenge against the man responsible for his wife's suicide. Predictable at times, but still satisfying, with charismatic Scott heading a fine cast of character actors. C: Randolph Scott, Karen Steele. D: Budd Boetticher. WST 77m.

Decision Before Dawn 1951 ★★★½ In 1944, a German POW reenters his homeland on a spy mission for the Allies. Werner's excellent acting highlights thoughtful thriller. C: Gary Merrill, Oskar Werner, Richard Basehart, Hildegarde Neff. D: Anatole Litvak. DRA 119m.

Decks Ran Red, The 1958 ★★★½ A crew of cutthroat sailors attempts to take over a freighter but meets strong resistance from the ship's brutal captain. Offbeat high seas adventure with an excellent cast and intriguing plot twists. C: James Mason, Dorothy Dandridge, Broderick Crawford, Stuart Whitman. D: Andrew Stone. ACT 84m.

Decline and Fall of a Bird Watcher 1969 British ★★★ A tutor (Phillips) is seduced by his student's wealthy mom (Page). Mannered, hit-and-miss satire of British class consciousness, from a novel by Evelyn Waugh. C: Robin Phillips, Genevieve Page, Colin Blakely, Leo McKern. D: John Krish. COM [PG] 86m.

Decline of the American Empire, The 1986 Canadian ★★★★ Talky drama focuses on dinner gathering of university academics engaged in lively, confessional conversation about sex which disintegrates into personal attack and cruelty. Incisive look at the manners and mores of the intelligentsia. C: Dominique Michel, Dorothee Berryman, Louise Portal, Genevieve Rioux. D: Denys Arcand. DRA [R] 101m. v

Decline of Western Civilization, The 1981 ★★★★½ Probing documentary of the early-'80s L.A. punk rock scene. As social and musical document it's witty, scary, and, yes, touching. Highly recommended alternative viewing. Followed by *The Decline of Western Civilization II: The Metal Years.* C: Alice BagBand, Black Flag, Catholic Discipline, Circle Jerks. D: Penelope Spheeris. DRA [R] 100m. v

Decline of Western Civilization, The Part II: The Metal Years 1988 ★★★★ Spheeris' second rockumentary goes behind the scenes with heavy-metal bands, showcasing stage-weary veterans, adrenaline-charged newcomers, and loyal fans. Insightful. C: Joe Perry, Steven Tyler, Gene Simmons, Paul Stanley. D: Penelope Spheeris. DOC [R] 90m. v

Decoration Day 1992 ★★★★★ Outstanding drama of courage and honor marked by fine performances. Garner's a retired Southern judge who helps his old friend Cobbs regain the honor he lost in WWII and Ivey's the psychically wounded woman he encourages to keep on living. C: James Garner, Judith Ivey, Ruby Dee, Larry Fishburne. D: Robert Markowitz. FAM/DRA [PG] 99m. TVM v

Decoy for Terror 1966 *See* **Playgirl Killer**

Decoy, The 1953 British ★★½ Trite spy drama about a Scotland Yard agent (Broone) searching for an enemy agent carrying deadly explosives. C: Anthony Broone, Charlotte Rose, Miles Brook. D: David Collins. CRI 97m.

Deep Blue Sea, The 1955 British ★★★½ Wealthy matron Leigh can't resist having affair with working-class More in literate soap opera that tends to drag. Based on Terence Rattigan's play. C: Vivien Leigh, Kenneth More, Eric Portman, Emlyn Williams. D: Anatole Litvak. DRA 99m.

Deep Cover 1992 ★★★★ Experienced inner-city cop Fishburne goes undercover to expose a drug connection (Goldblum). But a taste of the high life has him wondering which side to choose. Fishburne is authentic, and Goldblum is eerily exact in this gritty thriller. C: Larry Fishburne, Jeff Goldblum, Charles Martin Smith, Clarence Williams III. D: Bill Duke. ACT [R] 107m. v

Deep End 1970 U.S. ★★★★½ A teenage boy working as an attendant in a London bath house becomes obsessed with an attractive female co-worker, resulting in many highly charged confrontations. Excellent, hauntingly disturbing erotic thriller from legendary Polish director Skolimowski; starts out slowly but builds to an intensely unsettling climax. C: Jane Asher, John Brown, Diana Dors. D: Jerzy Skolimowski. DRA [R] 88m.

Deep in My Heart 1954 ★★★½ Soggy musical biography of operetta composer Sigmund Romberg (Ferrer) saved by stellar cast in striking musical numbers. Highlights include Charisse's sinuous dance with James Mitchell, Gene Kelly dancing with brother Fred, and Ferrer playing all the parts in backers' audition of new show. C: Jose Ferrer, Merle Oberon, Helen Traubel, Howard Keel, Ann Miller, Cyd Charisse, Jane Powell, Fred Kelly, Vic Damone, Walter Pidgeon, Rosemary Clooney, Gene Kelly. D: Stanley Donen. MUS 133m. v

Deep in the Heart 1983 British ★★★½ Young British teacher is raped by a manipulative but charismatic Texan, then gradually slides into dementia while seeking vengeance. Well-handled, somewhat predictable British drama with many effective moments and strong lead performances by Young and Day. C: Karen Young, Clayton Day. D: Tony Garnett. DRA [R] 99m. v

Deep Red 1975 Italian ★★★½ One of Argento's best-known films is a very violent shocker (cut for U.S.) in which pianist Hemmings attempts to solve gruesome hatchet murders. Dazzling style makes up for story lapses; (a.k.a. *The Hatchet Murders.*) C: David Hemmings, Daria Nicolodi. D: Dario Argento. HOR [R] 100m. v

Deep Six, The 1958 ★★★ A Quaker draftee (Ladd) must prove to his outfit that his religious beliefs don't make him a coward. Interesting characters in an otherwise standard WWII drama. C: Alan Ladd, William Bendix, Keenan Wynn, James Whitmore, Joey Bishop, Efrem

Zimbalist, Jr., Dianne Foster. D: Rudolph Mate. ACT 105m. v

Deep Space 1987 ★★★ Low budget sci-fi action flick follows tough cop (Napier) hot on the trail of the alien that killed a fellow officer. Packs a few chills and close calls. C: Charles Napier, Ann Turkel, Julie Newmar. D: Fred Holen Ray. SFI [R] 95m. v

Deep, The 1977 ★★★ Soggy sea saga of rival divers (Nolte, Shaw, and Gossett) after a sunken load of morphine. Okay underwater photography, a mean moray eel, and Jacqueline Bisset are not enough to keep it afloat; violence and silly script sink it. Based on Peter Benchley's novel. C: Nick Nolte, Jacqueline Bisset, Robert Shaw, Louis Gossett Jr., Eli Wallach. D: Peter Yates. ACT [PG] 123m. v

Deep Valley 1947 ★★★★ Atmospheric melodrama of farm girl Lupino romanced by escaped convict. Starts slowly, then builds up steam to shattering climax. C: Ida Lupino, Wayne Morris, Dane Clark, Fay Bainter. D: Jean Negulesco. DRA 104m.

Deep Waters 1948 ★★★ Cutesy tale of a gruff fisherman befriending a young orphan boy who tries to fix him up with an attractive woman from the local town. Good cast drowns in a sea of contrived romantic complications. C: Dana Andrews, Jean Peters, Cesar Romero, Dean Stockwell, Anne Revere, Ed Begley. D: Henry King. DRA 85m.

DeepStar Six 1989 ★★½ Crew installing nuclear missiles underwater discovers a voracious sea creature doesn't take kindly to their efforts. Low-budget sci-fi horror is pretty soggy, but cast keeps bailing until the end. C: Greg Evigan, Nancy Everhard, Cindy Pickett. D: Sean S. Cunningham. SFI 103m. v

Deer Hunter, The 1978 ★★★★★ Controversial Vietnam War drama about young steelworkers who go to war and the women they leave behind. A stellar ensemble cast, stunning cinematography and scenes of undeniable power earned five Oscars, including Best Picture, Director, and Supporting Actor (Walken). C: Robert De Niro, John Cazale, John Savage, Meryl Streep, Christopher Walken. D: Michael Cimino. DRA [R] 183m. v

Deerslayer, The 1957 ★★ Leatherstocking (Barker) and Chingachgook (Rivas) rescue a trapper and his two beautiful daughters from the dangerous Hurons in this slapdash, poorly made version of Cooper's tale. C: Lex Barker, Forrest Tucker, Rita Moreno. D: Kurt Neumann. FAM/ACT 78m.

Deerslayer, The 1978 ★★½ Average version of Fenimore Cooper story featuring Forrest and Romero as Leatherstocking and Chingachgook. Stowe went on to play Cora Munro in the 1992 *Last of the Mohicans*. Otherwise, nothing special. C: Steve Forrest, Ned Romero, John Anderson, Madeleine Stowe. D: Richard Friedenberg. FAM/ACT 98m. v

Def By Temptation 1990 ★★★ Hip horror item with a black cast and crew eschews black exploitation clichés in favor of a fresh, stylish approach. Director/writer Bond plays a religious young man who visits Manhattan and encounters a deadly supernatural temptress. C: Cynthia Bond, Kadeem Hardison, James Bond III, Melba Moore, Samuel L. Jackson. D: James Bond III. HOR [R] 95m. v

Def-Con 4 1985 ★ Astronauts return to Earth from deep space to find their post-nuclear-holocaust planet in the hands of mutants, punks, and survivalists. A shameless—and worse, boring—rip-off of practically every postapocalypse film ever made. C: Lenore Zann, Maury Chaykin. D: Paul Donovan. SFI [R] 85m. v

Defection of Simas Kudirka, The 1978 ★★★★½ True story of a Lithuanian sailor who defected in 1970 in Portsmouth, New Hampshire, and was handed back to the Soviets. Arkin shines in his portrayal of Kudirka; director Rich won an Emmy. Powerful drama, superlative script. C: Alan Arkin, Richard Jordan, Donald Pleasence, Shirley Knight. D: David Rich. DRA 100m. TVM

Defector, The 1966 ★★★ A U.S. spy pretends to defect in this Cold War thriller. Clift does a fine job in his last movie, making it worth watching. C: Montgomery Clift, Hardy Kruger, Roddy McDowall. D: Raoul Levy. CRI 106m.

Defence of the Realm 1985 British ★★★★½ British journalists (Elliot and Byrne) uncover a major scandal leading to political disgrace for a member of Parliament. Tense adult drama explores moral implications of public's right to sensitive information. Excellent cast, with fine starring performance by Byrne. C: Gabriel Byrne, Greta Scacchi, Denholm Elliott. D: David Drury. DRA [PG] 96m. v

Defending Your Life 1991 ★★★½ Finding himself in a kitschy, homogenized limbo with charming Streep, newly deceased yuppie Brooks has to convince authorities he deserves his final reward instead of being sent back to Earth to do it all over again. Deftly played but without much bite. C: Albert Brooks, Meryl Streep, Rip Torn, Lee Grant, Buck Henry. D: Albert Brooks. COM [PG] 112m. v

Defenseless 1991 ★★★½ Defense lawyer (Hershey) is suspected of murder of her lover, who was also a client, while a shadowy figure trails every move she makes. Good ensemble enlivens a routine thriller. C: Sam Shepard, Barbara Hershey, Mary Beth Hurt, J.T. Walsh. D: Martin Campbell. CRI [R] 106m. v

Defiance 1980 ★★★½ A vicious Lower East Side gang contends with a loner seaman (Vincent) determined to wipe them out. Old-fashioned man-against-the-world story gets a kick from the strong supporting cast. C: Jan-Michael Vincent, Art Carney, Theresa Saldana, Danny Aiello, Rudy Ramos, Fernando Lopez. D: John Flynn. ACT [PG] 102m. v

Defiant Ones, The 1958 ★★★★★ Superior

drama about two handcuffed convicts (Poitier and Curtis) on the run from the law. Racial themes and Southern setting handled with insight. Oscars for Screenplay and Cinematography; later remade for television. C: Tony Curtis, Sidney Poitier, Theodore Bikel, Cara Williams, Lon Chaney, Jr. D: Stanley Kramer. CRI 97m. V

Deja Vu 1985 ★★½ The ghost of a dead ballerina (Smith) plagues a screenwriter (Terry) and his girlfriend (Smith, again). The title must refer to the seen-it-before thriller storyline, gamely hoisted by Smith. C: Jaclyn Smith, Nigel Terry, Shelley Winters, Claire Bloom. D: Anthony Richmond. DRA [R] 95m. V

Deliberate Stranger, The 1986 ★★★★ Harmon gives a chilling portrait of seductive serial killer Ted Bundy, one of the most notorious multiple murderers in American crime annals. A disturbing and well-acted drama. C: Mark Harmon, Frederic Forrest, George Grizzard. D: Marvin J. Chomsky. CRI 188m. V

Delicate Balance, A 1973 ★★★★ An elderly New England couple's peaceful home is invaded by one too many of their neurotic family and friends. Film of Albee's play remains somewhat stagebound, but that's a minor complaint; great cast. C: Katharine Hepburn, Paul Scofield, Lee Remick, Kate Reid, Joseph Cotten, Betsy Blair. D: Tony Richardson. DRA [PG] 132m.

Delicate Delinquent, The 1957 ★★★★ Sentimental, enjoyable comedy with Lewis trying to be a policeman. Jerry's mugging is controlled here. (Lewis' first film without Martin, with McGavin stepping into Dean's role after the pair's breakup.) C: Jerry Lewis, Darren McGavin, Martha Hyer. D: Don McGuire. COM 101m. V

Delicatessen 1991 French ★★★½ Unholy appetites are unleashed in a strange, post-apocalyptic apartment building featuring an even stranger house menu. Dark comedy has original look, thanks to sepia-toned image and imaginative set design; not for all tastes. C: Marie-Laure Dougnac, Dominique Pinon, Karin Viard. D: Marc Caro, Jean-Pierre Jeunet. COM 95m. V

Delightfully Dangerous 1945 ★★★½ Standard musical fluff with Powell as perky youngster trying to marry off burlesque queen sister Moore to befuddled Bellamy. Fifteen-year-old Jane shows off impressive pipes in Johann Strauss medley. C: Jane Powell, Ralph Bellamy, Constance Moore. D: Arthur Lubin. MUS 93m. V

Delinquents, The 1957 ★★½ Low-budget cautionary tale about a clean-cut teenager (Laughlin), drawn into a wild gang of toughs, then framed for robbery. Altman's first feature film. C: Tom Laughlin, Peter Miller, Rosemary Howard. D: Robert Altman. DRA 75m.

Delirious 1991 ★★ A soap opera scripter (Candy), knocked unconscious, wakes to find himself in his fictional TV town, where his own storylines begin to backfire. Neat premise and game cast are sabotaged by a weak script and dreadful direction. C: John Candy, Emma Samms, Mariel Hemingway, David Rasche, Raymond Burr. D: Tom Mankiewicz. COM [PG] 96m. V

Deliverance 1972 ★★★★½ Reynolds and friends start out on a leisurely canoeing trip that turns into a violent, backwater nightmare. May seem slow at the start but masterfully paced for the chilling final reel. Stellar performances from the excellent cast (Beatty and Cox's debuts). From the James Dickey novel. C: Jon Voight, Burt Reynolds, Ned Beatty, Ronny Cox. D: John Boorman. DRA [R] 109m. V

Delta Force, The 1986 ★★★ When Arab terrorists hijack an American passenger plane, it's up to antiterrorists (Marvin, Norris) to free the hostages. Military action film begins credibly, but then slips into unbelievable shoot-'em-up jingoism. Interesting passengers. C: Chuck Norris, Lee Marvin, Martin Balsam, Joey Bishop, Lainie Kazan, George Kennedy, Hanna Schygulla, Susan Strasberg, Shelley Winters. D: Menahem Golan. ACT [R] 129m.

Delta Force 2—Operation Stranglehold 1990 ★★½ Chuck Norris and his special unit are out to oust an evil Colombian drug lord. Sequel to the barely superior original can't compensate for the loss of Lee Marvin, no matter how many rounds of ammo are fired. C: Chuck Norris, John P. Ryan, Paul Perri. D: Aaron Norris. ACT [R] 110m. V

Delta Pi *See* **Mugsy's Girls**

Deluge, The ★★★★ The Swedish invasion of Poland in the 1600s and the partisans' valiant response is the subject of this mammoth five-hour, two-part adaptation of Nobel Prize-winner Henryk Sienkiewicz's novel *Quo Vadis*. Grandly scaled epic balances well-crafted battle scenes with the difficult affair between a soldier and a gentlewoman. DRA

Deluge 1933 ★★★★ A gigantic tidal wave obliterates N.Y., but a group of survivors stick together. Lost for many years, this film offers some nice surprises, including great special effects. C: Sidney Blackmer, Peggy Shannon. D: Felix Feist. ACT 70m.

Delusion 1980 ★ Senior citizen (Cotten) is cared for in old house by nurse, who reveals secrets behind mysterious series of murders. Mystery without a clue suffers from poorly packaged bundle of old movie clichés. C: Patricia Pearcy, David Hayward, John Dukakis, Joseph Cotten. D: Alan Beattie. DRA [R] 83m.

Delusion 1991 ★★★★ While on the run from people he's stolen money from, an embezzler (Metzler) picks up Rubin and her hired-killer boyfriend (Secor). Intriguing story of alienation is truly offbeat; benefits greatly from bleak Death Valley locations. C: Jim Metzler, Jennifer Rubin, Jerry Orbach. D: Carl Colpaert. CRI [R] 100m. V

Delusions of Grandeur 1971 French ★★★½

When a 17th-century nobleman orders one of his servants to infiltrate the royal palace, the servant ends up working for the king and queen as one of their most trusted advisors. Amusing French farce, with Montand leading a fine cast on a slapstick-laden romp. C: Yves Montand, Louis De Funes, Alice Sapritch. D: Gerard Oury. COM 105m.

Dementia 13 1963 ★★ Ax murderer is on the loose in mansion. Talky script is offset by occasional gory scene. Coppola's directorial debut. C: William Campbell, Luana Anders, Patrick Magee. D: Francis Ford Coppola. HOR 81m. V

Demetrius and the Gladiators 1954 ★★★ Sequel to *The Robe* follows former slave Demetrius (Mature) as he tries to keep a holy relic out of the hands of Caligula. A guilty pleasure—dumb but fun. C: Victor Mature, Susan Hayward, Michael Rennie, Debra Paget, Anne Bancroft, Ernest Borgnine. D: Delmer Daves. DRA 101m. V

Demolition Man 1993 ★★★½ Moderately amusing action film, with cop Stallone and crook Snipes as 20th-century antagonists who are frozen and then thawed out in the distant future. Noisy, violent, and a bit sophomoric, but fast and occasionally clever. C: Sylvester Stallone, Wesley Snipes. ACT V

Demon 1977 ★★★½ Shocking murders are being committed by people who claim "God told me to" and cop (Lo Bianco) tries to get to the bottom of it. Compellingly bizarre horror film gets *really* strange at the climax, with good jolts throughout. (a.k.a. *God Told Me To*) C: Tony Lo Bianco, Sandy Dennis, Sylvia Sidney, Deborah Raffin, Sam Levene. D: Larry Cohen. HOR [R] 95m.

Demon Keeper 1994 ★★ Once again, an attempt at a seance works all too well, raising a hellish monster that kills off the attendees. Rock-bottom, ridiculous horror film. C: Dirk Benedict, Edward Albert, Andre Jacobs, Adrienne Pearce, David Sherwood. D: Joe Tornatore. HOR [R] 71m.

Demon of Paradise 1987 ★ A creature from the low-budget lagoon is unleashed by fishermen using dynamite and terrorizes a Hawaiian resort. Chintzy monster movie lacks thrills and originality. C: Kathryn Witt, William Steis, Laura Banks, Leslie Huntly. D: Cirio H. Santiago. HOR [R] 84m.

Demon Planet, The 1965 *See* **Planet of the Vampires**

Demon Pond 1980 Japanese ★★★★ Eerie, elaborate Japanese fantasy has two parallel stories: One focuses on bewitched pond dwellers, and the other on mortals. Fascinating use of color and special effects ultimately defines the film. Bando, a Kabuki star, provides effective character nuances. Mandatory viewing for Japanese film devotees. C: Tomasaburo Bando, Hisashi Igawa, Tsutomu Yamasaki. D: Masahiro Shinoda. SFI 88m.

Demon Seed 1977 ★★★ A megacomputer designed to help humankind wants to run a few tests of its own—on the wife of a scientist (Christie)! Well done and scary—especially for married scientists. C: Julie Christie, Fritz Weaver. D: Donald Cammell. SFI [R] 97m. V

Demon Within, The 1972 ★★★ Powerful drama about a doctor using controversial shock therapy treatment on military personnel to curb aggressive behavior. (a.k.a. *The Happiness Cage* and *The Mind Snatchers.*) C: Christopher Walken, Ronny Cox. D: Bernard Girard. DRA 94m.

Demonic Toys 1991 ★ Producer Charles Band's rip-off of his own *Puppetmaster*. Possessed playthings terrorize a cop, a chicken delivery boy, and others in a deserted warehouse. C: Tracy Scoggins, Bentley Mitchum. D: Peter Manoogian. HOR [R] 86m. V

Demonios En El Jardin *See* **Demons in the Garden**

Demons 1985 Italian ★★★ Patrons at horror movie preview are terrorized by evil that spreads off the screen and traps them in the theater. Tense, gory, claustrophobic Italian shocker with an unfortunately implausible windup; directorial debut of genre master Mario Bava's son. C: Urbano Barberini, Natasha Hovey. D: Lamberto Bava. HOR 89m. V

Demons 2 1987 Italian ★★ This time, the flesh-eating fiends emerge from TV sets and terrorize an apartment complex. Too fragmented and implausible to match the original's power, though a few moments are gruesomely effective. C: David Knight, Nancy Brilli. D: Lamberto Bava. HOR [R] 88m. V

Demons in the Garden 1984 Spanish ★★★★ Sweeping drama follows three generations of a rural family after Spanish Civil War, mainly through ten-year-old Juanito, the delightful center of an extended family. Intelligent, lightly comic drama praised by European critics. C: Angela Molina, Ana Belen, Encarna Paso, Imanol Arias. D: Manuel Gutierrez Aragon. (a.k.a. *Demonios En El Jardin*) DRA 100m.

Demons of the Mind 1971 British ★★★★ Disturbing tale of a man (Hardy) keeping his grown son and daughter locked in a basement, fearing they'll inherit their deceased mother's madness. Nonetheless, violence ensues in this well-mounted period chiller. (a.k.a. *Blood Evil, Nightmare of Terror*) C: Paul Jones, Gillian Hills, Robert Hardy, Shane Briant, Patrick Magee. D: Peter Sykes. HOR [R] 89m.

Dempsey 1983 ★★★ By-the-numbers bio of the heavy-weight champ (Williams), from his autobiography. Good cast. C: Treat Williams, Sam Waterston, Sally Kellerman. D: Gus Trikonis. DRA 110m. TVM V

Denial 1991 ★ Confusing story about a woman mourning her late lover. Frustrating and bewildering mix of flashbacks and present tense narration. C: Robin Wright, Jason Patric, Rae Dawn Chong. D: Erin Dignam. DRA [PG] 103m. V

Dennis the Menace 1993 ★★½ Strangely violent and unimaginative rendering of the towheaded rascal's war with grumpy neighbor Mr. Wilson (Matthau). Based on the comic strip by Hank Ketcham. Despite the film's shortcomings, Matthau is a delight. C: Walter Matthau, Mason Gamble, Joan Plowright, Christopher Lloyd, Lea Thompson, Paul Winfield. D: Nick Castle. COM [PG] 96m. TVM V

Dentist on the Job 1961 *See* **Get on with It**

Deported 1950 ★★★½ An American expatriate gangster becomes involved with the European black market. Tough, taut B-movie suspense softened somewhat by romantic subplot. C: Jeff Chandler, Marta Toren, Claude Dauphin. D: Robert Siodmak. DRA 80m.

Deputy and the Congressman, The 1978 *See* **Deputy, The**

Deputy, The 1978 Spanish ★★★★ Socialist politician on the rise begins affair with young, handsome ex-convict. His wife soon joins them in the bedroom. One of the first Spanish films with explicit homosexual content is also interesting study of life in post-Franco Spain. Strong sexual content. (a.k.a. *El Diputado* and *The Deputy and the Congressman*). C: Jose Sacristan, Maria Luisa San Jose, Angel Pardo. D: Eloy de l'Iglesia. DRA 111m.

Der Purimshpiler 1937 Polish ★★★★ Engaging fable of a poor actor, his love for a woman, and her father's disapproval of their relationship. Simple, funny fare interspersed with delightful musical numbers. In Yiddish. (a.k.a. *The Jester* and *The Jewish Jester*) C: Zygmund Turkow, Miriam Kressyn, Hymie Jacobson, Max Bozyk, Berta Litwina. D: Joseph Green, Jan-Nowina Przybylski. MUS 90m.

Deranged 1974 ★★★★ Okay thriller based on true case of killer Ed Gein (as were *Psycho* and *The Texas Chainsaw Massacre*). Farmer (Blossom) can't handle mom's death, so he keeps body—and gets a few more. Helped by weird sensibility and humor, and Blossom's performance. C: Alan Ormsby, Roberts Blossom, Cosette Lee. D: Jeff Gillen. HOR [R] 82m. V

Derby 1971 ★★★½ Documentary explores a uniquely American pastime: roller derby. Nicely shaded, with goofiness and seriousness in equal measure. C: Charlie O'Connell, Mike Snell, Eddie Krebs. D: Robert Kaylor. DOC [PG] 91m. V

Derby Day 1952 *See* **Four Against Fate**

Dersu Uzala 1975 Japanese ★★★★★ An aged hunter, hired as guide for an expedition of Russian soldiers in Siberia, uses his skills and spiritual understanding of nature to save the men from death. An epic tale told in small, human details. Incredibly beautiful wilderness photography. Unforgettable. Oscar for Best Foreign Film. C: Maxim Munzuk. D: Akira Kurosawa. DRA 124m. V

Descending Angel 1990 ★★★★ Roberts is first-rate as a man forced to investigate whether or not his fiancée's Romanian immigrant father served in a WWII Nazi death camp. Works very well, despite overused theme. Lane and Scott are also very good. C: George C. Scott, Diane Lane, Eric Roberts. D: Jeremy Paul Kagan. CRI 98m. TVM V

Desert Attack 1960 British ★★★★ A German agent menaces an English ambulance officer and two nurses in a dangerous trek across the Libyan desert during WWII. Suspenseful psychological adventure. C: John Mills, Sylvia Syms, Anthony Quayle. D: J. Thompson. ACT 79m.

Desert Bloom 1986 ★★★★½ A sensitive teen (Gish) treads carefully in a dysfunctional household consisting of an ineffectual mother (Williams), a bitter, alcoholic stepfather (Voight), and an oversexed aunt (Barkin). Beautifully told coming-of-age film set against the stark background of Nevada desert atomic testing grounds in the '50s. C: Jon Voight, JoBeth Williams, Ellen Barkin, Annabeth Gish. D: EO Corr. DRA [PG] 103m. V

Desert Fox, The 1951 ★★★★ Mason shines as Field Marshall Rommel, German commander in North Africa in WWII, who, after his desert defeat, returns disillusioned to his homeland and joins the conspiracy to assassinate the Führer. Above average historical film biography. C: James Mason, Jessica Tandy, Cedric Hardwicke, Luther Adler, Leo G. Carroll, Richard Boone. D: Henry Hathaway. DRA 88m. V

Desert Fury 1947 ★★★½ Fine cast spruces up this routine western about a gambling house madam (Astor) trying to stop her daughter (Scott) from following in her footsteps. C: John Hodiak, Lizabeth Scott, Burt Lancaster, Mary Astor, Wendell Corey. D: Lewis Allen. WST 95m.

Desert Hawk, The 1950 ★★★ Okay Arabian Nights tale about a princess (De Carlo) who's tricked into marrying a blacksmith (Greene). Yes, that's Gleason as Aladdin, and future Three Stooger Besser as Sinbad! C: Yvonne De Carlo, Richard Greene, George Macready, Jackie Gleason, Joe Besser, Rock Hudson. D: Frederick de Cordova. ACT 77m.

Desert Hearts 1986 ★★★ Sensitive (but explicit) lesbian romance set on Reno dude ranch in the 1950s; Charbonneau is young woman who seduces older divorcée Shaver. C: Helen Shaver, Patricia Charbonneau, Audra Lindley. D: Donna Deitch. DRA [R] 96m. V

Desert Rats, The 1953 ★★★★ A British disciplinarian (Burton) commands a devil-may-care Aussie unit fighting Rommel in North Africa in WWII. (Mason recreates his *Desert Fox* role.) The boys from "down under" teach him a few things about courage. Fine acting all around. C: Richard Burton, James Mason, Robert Newton, Chips Rafferty. D: Robert Wise. DRA 88m. V

Desert Song, The 1953 ★★★ Lumbering

Sigmund Romberg operetta, with a mysterious hero (MacRae) in Africa, coming to warbling Grayson's rescue. Outstanding song: "One Alone." C: Gordon MacRae, Kathryn Grayson, Raymond Massey. D: H. Bruce Humberstone. MUS 110m. V

Design for Living 1933 ★★★★ A worldly woman (Hopkins) is loved by three men: an artist (Cooper), a playwright (March), and her benefactor (Horton), and doesn't want to hurt any feelings. Hecht's down-to-earth adaptation of Noel Coward's play charms. C: Gary Cooper, Frederic March, Miriam Hopkins, Edward Everett Horton, Franklin Pangborn, Jane Darwell. D: Ernst Lubitsch. COM 90m.

Design for Scandal 1941 ★★★½ Newsman Pidgeon whips up scandal involving lady judge Russell in dated, sexist comedy sparked by talented stars. C: Rosalind Russell, Walter Pidgeon, Edward Arnold, Guy Kibbee. D: Norman Taurog. COM 85m.

Designing Woman 1957 ★★★★ When sports writer Peck marries clothing designer Bacall, the couple suddenly must mix and match highly incompatible social sets. Charming comedy, smartly played by Peck and Bacall with style that recalls best of Tracy and Hepburn teamings. Writer George Wells won Oscar. C: Gregory Peck, Lauren Bacall, Dolores Gray, Sam Levene, Mickey Shaughnessy. D: Vincente Minnelli. COM 108m. V

Desire 1936 ★★★★ An exotic jewel thief (Dietrich) is wooed by a gullible American (Cooper) in sunny Spain. Charismatic stars add zest to the bubbly script. Highlight: Marlene chasing Gary. C: Marlene Dietrich, Gary Cooper, William Frawley, John Halliday, Akim Tamiroff. D: Frank Borzage. COM 96m. V

Desire and Hell at Sunset Motel 1992 ★★½ Nightmare comedy about a '50s couple who become involved in a murder plot en route to a Disneyland vacation. Works too hard to be offbeat; rarely hits satirical intent. C: Sherilyn Fenn, Whip Hubley, Paul Bartel. D: Alien Castle. COM 87m. V

Desire Me 1947 ★★★ Rare Hollywood film without director credit: studio tampering made George Cukor remove name; Jack Conway and Mervyn LeRoy directed the rest. Not awful, but Mitchum and Garson mix like beer and mouthwash as supposedly dead man reclaims wife from bounder (Hart) who left him behind during POW escape attempt. C: Robert Mitchum, Richard Hart, George Zucco Greer Garson. DRA 91m.

Desire Under the Elms 1958 ★★★½ Loren falls in love with her new elderly husband Ives' son by previous marriage (Perkins) in 19th-century New England. A slow-moving adaptation of the Eugene O'Neill play; Loren is miscast, but interestingly so. Worth seeing. C: Sophia Loren, Anthony Perkins, Burl Ives. D: Delbert Mann. DRA 111m. V

Desiree 1954 ★★ Brando is woefully miscast as Napoleon in this costume saturated epic that mixes history and fiction with wild abandon. Too talky for its own good and cast is largely wasted on a soap opera script. C: Marlon Brando, Jean Simmons, Merle Oberon, Michael Rennie, Cameron Mitchell, Cathleen Nesbitt, Carolyn Jones. D: Henry Koster. DRA 110m. V

Desk Set 1957 ★★★★ Hepburn's job as researcher for TV network is threatened by computer designed by Tracy in this amusing battle of the sexes. Two stars a delight to watch, ably supported by Blondell and Young. C: Spencer Tracy, Katharine Hepburn, Gig Young, Joan Blondell, Dina Merrill. D: Walter Lang. COM 103m. V

Despair 1979 West German ★★★★ Berlin chocolate factory owner schemes to swindle some insurance money by faking his death. Sharp dialogue and an ironic sensibility. Scripted by Tom Stoppard from Vladimir Nabokov's slyly comic novel. C: Dirk Bogarde, Andrea Ferreol. D: Rainer Werner Fassbinder. DRA 120m. V

Desperadoes, The 1943 ★★★★ Hoping to redeem his crooked past, a seasoned gunslinger (Ford) joins forces with a lawman (Scott) to wage war on the local bad guys. Familiar story line is handled surprisingly well by director and enhanced by superlative cast. C: Randolph Scott, Glenn Ford, Claire Trevor, Evelyn Keyes, Edgar Buchanan. D: Charles Vidor. WST 85m.

Desperados, The 1969 ★★½ Post-Civil War deserters turn outlaw and plunder the range. Crude, bloodthirsty Western made in Spain. C: Vince Edwards, Jack Palance, George Maharis, Sylvia Syms. D: Henry Levin. WST 90m. V

Desperate 1947 ★★★½ A truck driver and his wife are pursued by both cops and crooks after he witnesses a gangland murder. Taut, no-nonsense B-movie chase film enlivened by suspenseful pacing and a competent, appealing cast. C: Steve Brodie, Audrey Long, Raymond Burr. D: Anthony Mann. ACT 73m. V

Desperate Characters 1971 ★★★★ Overdone story of paranoid New Yorkers who no longer feel safe in their gentrified Brooklyn neighborhood. MacLaine's performance is probably one of her best, but the film is still depressing. C: Shirley MacLaine, Kenneth Mars, Sada Thompson. D: Frank D. Gilroy. DRA [R] 88m. V

Desperate Hours, The 1955 ★★★★ One family's terrifying ordeal at the hands of a trio of escaped convicts hiding out in surburbia. Interesting match-up pits March against Bogart. Good, taut stuff. C: Humphrey Bogart, Fredric March, Arthur Kennedy, Martha Scott, Gig Young. D: William Wyler. DRA 112m. V

Desperate Hours 1990 ★★½ Inferior remake of 1955 crime drama has a prison escapee (Rourke) leading a gang of cutthroats in ruthless attack on Hopkins and family. C:

Mickey Rourke, Anthony Hopkins, Mimi Rogers, Lindsay Crouse, Elias Koteas. D: Michael Cimino. CRI [R] 106m. V

Desperate Journey 1942 ★★★ Unlikely but entertaining exploits of five Allied airmen (including Flynn and Reagan) downed in WWII Poland. Feats such as stealing Goering's staff car in Berlin, as they fight their way to freedom, make for entertaining fluff! C: Errol Flynn, Raymond Massey, Ronald Reagan, Alan Hale, Arthur Kennedy. D: Raoul Walsh. DRA 108m. V

Desperate Moment 1953 British ★★★½ Adrift in Berlin when falsely accused of murder, a man (Bogarde) must prove his innocence before he is captured. Gritty, post-WWII drama transcends familiarity thanks to star's convincing performance. C: Dirk Bogarde, Mai Zetterling. D: Compton Bennett. DRA 88m.

Desperate Search 1952 ★★★½ Rescue team frantically combs the Canadian wilderness in search of two young survivors of a plane crash. Fast-paced adventure with effective romantic subplot, well handled by cult director Lewis and sparked by fine cast of B-movie veterans. C: Howard Keel, Patricia Medina, Jane Greer, Keenan Wynn. D: Joseph Lewis. DRA 73m.

Desperate Siege 1951 *See* **Rawhide**

Desperately Seeking Susan 1985 ★★★½ Conk on the head during a jaunt to Manhattan frees amnesiac housewife Arquette to assume free-spirited new identity. Steeped in downtown hip and storefront kitsch, this meandering caper's somewhat affected style might be off-putting for some viewers, but it's all in good fun. C: Rosanna Arquette, Madonna, Aidan Quinn, Robert Joy, Laurie Metcalf. D: Susan Seidelman. COM [PG-13] 104m. V

Destination Gobi 1953 ★★★★ World War II Navy troops join forces with local desert inhabitants to repel Japanese invaders. Intriguing war drama with many unusual twists, competently directed by Wise and featuring an excellent young cast headed by veteran Widmark in one of his most effective performances. C: Richard Widmark, Don Taylor, Darryl Hickman. D: Robert Wise. ACT 89m.

Destination Moon 1950 ★★★★ Simple, speculative story about the trials encountered by the first lunar expedition. Significant for its emphasis on the "sci" side of sci-fi and its absence of aliens, lost civilizations, etc. Co-scripted by Robert Heinlein. C: John Archer, Warner Anderson, Tom Powers. D: Irving Pichel. SFI 91m. V

Destination Tokyo 1943 ★★★★ Tense war drama involving WWII submarine crew patrolling waters outside Japan, preparing for attack on enemy forces. Grant holds his own in the lead, with excellent support from entire cast. C: Cary Grant, John Garfield, Alan Hale. D: Delmer Daves. DRA 136m. V

Destiny 1944 ★★★ After escaping from prison, convicted murderer Curtis hides out in country and meets blind farmer's daughter Jean. Originally developed as a sequence in *Flesh and Fantasy*, film has some interesting moments. C: Gloria Jean, Alan Curtis, Frank Craven. D: Reginald LeBorg. DRA 65m.

Destiny of a Man 1959 ★★★★½ After escaping from a Nazi prison camp, Russian man comes home to find his family have also been victimized by the horrors of war. Unflinchingly realistic view of the terrible impact of WWII. Very well done. C: Sergei Bondarchuk, Zinaids Kivienikova, Pavil Pakilk Boriskin. D: Sergei Bondarchuk. DRA 98m.

Destroy All Monsters! 1968 Japanese ★★★ Evil aliens enrage mutant Earth creatures, who then wreak worldwide destruction. The ultimate low-budget Japanese monster mash, featuring all your favorites: Godzilla, Rodan, Mothra, Ghidrah, plus giant snakes and spiders thrown in for good measure. Hilarious, trashy nonsense. C: Akira Kubo, Jun Tazaki. D: Ishiro Honda. HOR [G] 88m.

Destroyer 1943 ★★★½ Naval drama about an older sailor (Robinson) and his conflict with a young upstart (Ford). Well done, if unsurprising. C: Edward G. Robinson, Glenn Ford, Marguerite Chapman. D: William Seiter. DRA 99m. V

Destroyer 1988 ★★ Film crew goes to prison and is stalked by the ghost of an executed killer (Alzado). Even casting coup of Perkins and Alzado in the leads can't salvage this. C: Anthony Perkins, Lyle Alzado, Deborah Foreman. D: Robert Kirk. HOR 91m. V

Destructors, The 1974 British ★★★½ A U.S. drug enforcer (Quinn) is determined to dig up dirt on a drug dealer (Mason) in Paris. Better-than-average international intrigue. C: Anthony Quinn, Michael Caine, James Mason. D: Robert Parrish. ACT [PG] 89m. V

Destry Rides Again 1939 ★★★★★ Screen adaptation of Max Brand's story about a quiet sheriff who tries to keep the peace without gunplay in untamed, crooked Bottleneck while being wooed by a sultry dancehall singer. Expert comic Western wonderfully hits all the marks. A classic. C: James Stewart, Marlene Dietrich, Charles Winninger, Brian Donlevy, Una Merkel, Mischa Auer, Jack Carson, Billy Gilbert. D: George Marshall. WST 94m. V

Destry 1954 ★★★ A mild-mannered sheriff cleans up a Wild West town with his wits, not his guns. Fair remake of the 1939 classic *Destry Rides Again*. C: Audie Murphy, Mari Blanchard, Lyle Bettger, Thomas Mitchell. D: George Marshall. WST 95m.

Detective 1985 French ★★ Godard's homage to crime dramas is talk, talk, and more talk. There are more in-jokes and arcane movie references than can be digested in one viewing. Complicated comings and goings in a hotel setting result in one long riddle. C:

Claude Brasseur, Nathalie Baye, Jean-Pierre Leaud. D: Jean-Luc Godard. DRA 95m.

Detective Story 1951 ★★★★ Slice-of-life melodrama explores a day in the life of urban police station with Douglas outstanding as overworked cop. Dated, but packed with top-flight performances from Bendix, Parker, and especially Grant as a pathetic shoplifter. C: Kirk Douglas, Eleanor Parker, William Bendix, Lee Grant, Joseph Wiseman, Gladys George. D: William Wyler. DRA 103m.

Detective, The 1954 ★★★★½ Resourceful priest and amateur detective Father Brown (Guinness) attempts to retrieve a valuable church cross. A poignant and zany comedy/mystery, with Guinness reveling in the part of the legendary priest-detective. Based on the books by G.K. Chesterton. (a.k.a. *Father Brown*) C: Alec Guiness, Joan Greenwood, Peter Finch, Bernard Lee, Cecil Parker. D: Robert Hamer. COM 91m.

Detective, The 1968 ★★★★ Hard-edged portrayal by Sinatra as a tough, driven NYC cop overwhelmed with marital problems as he tries to solve the grisly murder of a homosexual. Gritty script unsparingly bares sleazy underside of police investigations, but seems rather dated now. C: Frank Sinatra, Lee Remick, Ralph Meeker, Jacqueline Bisset, William Windom, Jack Klugman, Robert Duvall. D: Gordon Douglas. CRI 114m.

Detour 1945 ★★★★½ Cult favorite follows a New York pianist who thumbs his way cross-country, joined by an underhanded lady hitchhiker intent on blackmailing him. Bleak film noir, aided greatly by low budget which inspired (and required) remarkable cinematic improvisation. C: Tom Neal, Ann Savage, Claudia Drake. D: Edgar G. Ulmer. CRI [PG] 67m. V

Detour to Nowhere 1972 *See* **Banacek**

Devi 1960 ★★★★ Religious Indian farmer convinces everyone that his daughter-in-law is a Hindu deity come to life. Intelligent, darkly humorous satire from one of India's master filmmakers. A welcome change of pace. Subtitled. (a.k.a. *The Goddess*) C: Chhabi Biswas, Sharmila Targore, Soumitra Chatterjee. D: Satyajit Ray. DRA

Devil and Daniel Webster, The 1941 ★★★★★ Entertaining rendition of Benet's classic short story features Arnold as attorney defending misguided farmer from delightfully satanic Huston. Fine production values and acting throughout; Oscars for cinematography, Herrmann's great score, and special effects. (a.k.a. *All That Money Can Buy* and *Daniel and the Devil.*) C: Edward Arnold, Walter Huston, James Craig, Anne Shirley, Jane Darwell, Simone Simon. D: William Dieterle. DRA 109m. V

Devil and Max Devlin, The 1980 ★★ Gould is dispatched by the devil to secure three more souls. Embarrassingly bad, poorly written so-called comedy from Disney. C: Elliott Gould, Bill Cosby, Susan Anspach. D: Steven Hilliard Stern. FAM/COM [PG] 95m. V

Devil and Miss Jones, The 1941 ★★★★½ A millionaire (Coburn) pretends to be a clerk in his own department store to investigate employee complaints. Sparkling comedy, scripted by Norman Krasna, explores class distinctions with intelligence and good humor. C: Jean Arthur, Charles Coburn, Robert Cummings, Spring Byington, Edmund Gwenn, S.Z. Sakall, William Demarest. D: Sam Wood. COM 92m. V

Devil and the Deep 1932 ★★★½ Submarine captain Laughton's wanton wife (Bankhead) has two lovers: Cooper and Grant. Overripe trash with powerhouse cast. Tallulah and Laughton chew the scenery shamelessly while Gary and Cary look amused. Worth catching. C: Tallulah Bankhead, Gary Cooper, Charles Laughton, Cary Grant. D: Marion Gering. DRA 78m.

Devil and the Ten Commandments, The 1962 French ★★★ The Lord's Top-10 list of do's and don'ts is dramatized one by one. Earnest episodical French production would have benefited from a dose of entertainment with its moralizing. C: Michel Simon, Lucien Baroux, Charles Aznavour. D: Julien Duvivier. DRA 143m.

Devil at 4 O'Clock, The 1961 ★★★½ An alcoholic, self-doubting missionary (Tracy), helped by three criminals, attempts to save leper children from an erupting volcano on a South Pacific island. The best is saved for last in this drawn-out adventure. C: Spencer Tracy, Frank Sinatra, Jean-Pierre Aumont, Kerwin Mathews. D: Mervyn LeRoy. DRA 126m. V

Devil Bat, The 1942 ★★ Lugosi is a mad doctor creating electrically englarged bats, trained to kill victims wearing a special after-shave! Only for mad Lugosi fans. C: Bela Lugosi, Suzanne Kaaren. D: Jean Yarbrough. HOR 68m. V

Devil by the Tail, The 1969 French Italian ★★★★ Concierge and mechanic at failing hotel disable cars of passing drivers to force them to stay. Flippant, highly amusing comedy. C: Yves Montand, Maria Schell, Jean Rochefort, Jean-Pierre Marielle, Claude Pieplu. D: Philippe de Broca. COM 93m.

Devil Commands, The 1941 ★★★½ Karloff is an obsessed scientist willing to do *anything* to communicate with his dead wife. A superb Karloff in a scary vehicle. C: Boris Karloff, Amanda Duff, Richard Fiske, Anne Revere. D: Edward Dmytryk. HOR 65m.

Devil Dogs of the Air 1935 ★★½ Two Marine Air Corps hot dogs are natural rivals in heroics and romance. Typical Warners' offering of the period. Best for its star chemistry. C: James Cagney, Pat O'Brien, Margaret Lindsay, Frank McHugh. D: Lloyd Bacon. ACT 85m. V

Devil Doll 1964 British ★★★★ A hypnotist/ventriloquist (Halliday) likes to put real souls into his dummies. Nifty little thriller, comparable to the better-known *Dead of Night*. C: Bryant Halliday, William Sylvester, Yvonne Romain. D: Lindsay Shonteff. HOR 80m. V

Devil-Doll, The 1936 ★★★★ An escaped convict (Barrymore) uses tiny devil dolls to seek out and kill people who have done him wrong. Imaginative thriller from the director of *Dracula*. C: Lionel Barrymore, Maureen O'Sullivan. D: Tod Browning. HOR 80m. V

Devil in Love, The 1968 Italian ★★ Splotchy farce about a pair of emissaries from Hell (Gassman and Rooney) during the Renaissance. Director Scola (*Le Bal, A Special Day*) went on to better things. C: Vittorio Gassman, Mickey Rooney, Claudine Auger. D: Ettore Scola. COM 97m.

Devil in the Flesh 1946 French ★★★★½ Lonely wife has an affair with a young man while her soldier husband is at war. Touching, intelligent, and provocative love story, set during WWI. Beautifully photographed. C: Gerard Philipe, Micheline Presle, Jacques Tati. D: Claude Lara. DRA 110m.

Devil in the Flesh 1986 Italian ★★★ Remake of 1946 film notorious for its groundbreaking sensuality, Bellocchio's version treats a beautiful, mentally troubled woman's torn passion for her terrorist lover and an inexperienced young boy. Explicitly erotic, though leads lack essential chemistry. C: Maruschka Detmers, Federico Pitzalis. D: Marco Bellocchio. DRA [R] 110m. V

Devil Is a Sissy, The 1936 ★★★½ English kid Bartholomew moves to America and tries to fit in with streetwise Cooper and Rooney. Simple, entertaining film showcasing three young stars. C: Freddie Bartholomew, Mickey Rooney, Jackie Cooper. D: W.S. Van Dyke II. DRA 92m.

Devil Is a Woman, The 1935 ★★★★½ Sternberg's last with Dietrich, as a coldhearted woman who destroys two men (Atwill and Romero). Stunning visuals, rueful humor, splendid acting: Atwill is very moving, and watch that close-up of Dietrich at the hospital. C: Marlene Dietrich, Lionel Atwill, Cesar Romero, Edward Everett Horton, Alison Skipworth. D: Josef Sternberg. DRA 83m.

Devil Is a Woman, The 1975 Italian ★★ Crazed mother superior (Jackson) wreaks havoc at a religious retreat. Murky exercise in the macabre gives Glenda a prime opportunity for scenery-chewing. C: Glenda Jackson, Adolfo Celi, Lisa Harrow. D: Dâmiano Damiani. HOR [R] 105m.

Devil Makes Three, The 1952 ★★★ American WWII veteran returns to Germany and becomes involved with the family that helped save his life. Interesting premise jeopardized somewhat by predictable situations and syrupy romantic angle. C: Gene Kelly, Pier Angeli, Richard Egan. D: Andrew Marton. DRA 96m.

Devil Never Sleeps, The *See* **Satan Never Sleeps**

Devil on Horseback, The 1954 British ★★★ Apprentice horseracing jockey (Spenser) shows great promise, but his ego gets in the way. Documentarist Frankel and good cast deliver professional but unexciting drama. C: Googie Withers, John McCallum. D: Cyril Frankel. DRA 88m. V

Devil Pays Off 1941 ★★½ World War II drama about a serviceman's attempts to track down spies who have infiltrated the Navy. B-movie quickie best saved for third-feature marathon-night viewing. C: J. Bromberg, Osa Massen. D: John Auer. DRA 56m.

Devil Probably, The 1977 French ★★★½ A disillusioned, world-weary Parisian bent on suicide seeks out the devil for assistance. Despairing examination of the dehumanizing effects of modern life. C: Antoine Monnier, Tina Irissari, Henri De Maublanc, Laelita Carcano. D: Stephane Tcholdieff. DRA 95m.

Devil-Ship Pirates, The 1964 British ★★★½ High-seas adventure set in 16th-century Europe, involving Spanish pirates looting English coastal towns. Colorful, lively British-produced yarn benefits from good cast and spirited, swashbuckling action. C: Christopher Lee, Andrew Keir. D: Don Sharp. ACT 89m.

Devil Strikes at Night, The 1959 German ★★★★½ True story of Bruno Ludke, a Gestapo official who murdered more than 70 women during WWII. Exciting thriller also provides a seldom-seen glimpse of the inner workings of Nazi officialdom, which deflected blame for the deaths on a lowly clerk. C: Claus Holm, Mario Adorf, Hannes Messemer. D: Robert Siodmak. CRI 97m.

Devil Thumbs a Ride, The 1947 ★★★½ Innocent motorist North picks up hitchhiker Tierney, only to find he's an amoral murderer. Tough performance by Tierney overcomes talky script in low-budget thriller. C: Lawrence Tierney, Ted North, Nan Leslie. D: Felix Feist. CRI 62m.

Devil Walks at Midnight, The 1972 *See* **Devil's Nightmare, The**

Devil's Bride, The 1968 British ★★★★½ Solid supernatural thriller pits nobleman (Lee) against satanist (Gray) in battle for a man's soul. Finale, subjecting heroes to all manner of demonic torment, is especially scary. Well-acted adaptation of Dennis Wheatley novel *The Devil Rides Out*. C: Christopher Lee, Charles Gray, Nike Arrighi. D: Terence Fisher. HOR [G] 95m.

Devil's Brigade, The 1968 ★★★ Unsuccessful knockoff of *The Dirty Dozen* provides neither the humor nor the excitement of the original. A group of thugs led by Holden trains to fight Nazis in WWII Norway, but ends up scaling the Italian Alps. C: William Holden, Cliff Robertson, Vince Edwards, Michael Rennie, Dana Andrews, Carroll O'Connor. D: Andrew V. McLaglen. ACT 130m. V

Devil's Brother, The 1933 ★★★★ Handsome production of operetta with L&H as bumbling assistants to notorious king of thieves. Good mix of potent comedy with charming musical sequences. One of the team's best. (a.k.a. *Fra Diavolo*) C: Stan Laurel, Oliver Hardy, Dennis King, Thelma Todd, James Finlayson. D: Hal Roach, Charles Rogers. MUS 88m.

Devil's Daughter, The 1992 Italian ★★★ Stylish horror film, produced and written by Dario Argento, has more mood and less gore than most, as Curtis (Jamie Lee's sister) finds herself pursued by evil cult. Somewhat overlong, but worth sticking with. (a.k.a. *The Sect.*) C: Kelly Leigh Curtis, Herbert Lom, Tomas Arana. D: Michele Soavi. HOR 112m.

Devil's Disciple, The 1959 British ★★★★ Snappy satire has colonists Lancaster (a minister) and Douglas (a cad) teaming up to dupe the English during the Revolutionary War. Adaptation of a G.B. Shaw play survives its transition to the big screen due to outstanding performances by the three principals. C: Burt Lancaster, Kirk Douglas, Laurence Olivier, Janette Scott, Eva LeGallienne, George Rose. D: Guy Hamilton. COM 83m. V

Devil's Envoys, The 1942 French ★★★★ Charming period fairy tale about a love affair that inflames the devil himself. A prelude to the masterful *Children of Paradise* with the same director, writer, and star. (a.k.a. *Les Visiteurs du Soir.*) C: Arletty, Jules Berry. D: Marcel Carne. DRA 120m.

Devil's Express 1940 *See* **Gang Wars**

Devil's Eye, The 1960 Swedish ★★★★ Satan recruits Don Juan from hell to corrupt a virtuous woman. Period comedy by Bergman contains excellent acting. C: Jarl Kulle, Bibi Andersson. D: Ingmar Bergman. COM 90m. V

Devil's General, The 1956 German ★★★½ Allegedly true story about German aviation ace who loses faith in both Hitler and Nazism. Keeps propaganda to minimum; engrossing. C: Curt Jurgens, Marianne Cook. D: Helmut Kautner. DRA 120m.

Devil's Hairpin, The 1957 ★★★ Car-racing adventure has director/star Wilde hamming it up as daredevil driver who learns some hard lessons while speeding for glory. Breathless action sequences, but predictable pit stops knock this one out of the winner's circle. C: Cornel Wilde, Jean Wallace, Mary Astor. D: Cornel Wilde. ACT 82m.

Devil's Imposter, The *See* **Pope Joan**

Devil's in Love, The 1933 ★★★½ A doctor falsely accused of murder joins the French Foreign Legion, but must still struggle to clear his name. Vintage courtroom drama benefits from unusual cast choices (Lugosi plays the prosecutor) and effective handling of standard story. Young is especially radiant. C: Loretta Young, Victor Jory, Vivienne Osborne, Bela Lugosi. D: William Dieterle. DRA 71m.

Devil's Island 1940 ★★★★ French doctor (Karloff) is banished to Devil's Island for helping treasonous soldier. He must survive barbaric conditions and preserve his humanity. Grim, well-acted prison drama with shining lead by stoic Karloff. C: Boris Karloff, Nedda Harrigan, James Stephenson. D: William Clemens. DRA 62m.

Devil's Mask, The 1946 ★★½ Relatively bland entry in the '40s *I Love a Mystery* series, based on popular radio show, this one involving occult-like shenanigans perpetrated by a mystery figure. C: Jim Bannon, Anita Louise. D: Henry Levin. CRI 66m.

Devil's Nightmare, The 1972 ★★½ A creepy mansion is site of bloody horror when seven travelers (representing the deadly sins) fall victim to an evil succubus there. Good-looking but predictable European production; villainess Blanc the only highlight among the cast. (a.k.a. *The Devil Walks at Midnight*) C: Erica Blanc, Jean Servais, Daniel Emilfork, Lucien Raimbourg. D: Jean Brismee. HOR 88m.

Devil's Own, The 1966 British ★★★ Traumatized by an encounter with witchcraft in Africa, a woman returns to England only to run into more wicked doings at private school where she works. Well-crafted though familiar tale of sacrifice and the supernatural. C: Joan Fontaine, Kay Walsh, Alec McCowen. D: Cyril Frankel. HOR 90m.

Devil's Playground 1937 ★★★½ High-seas romance adventure in which a diver battles to win back the woman in his life after he realizes she's fallen in love with another man. Potent combination of love and action with appealing cast and exciting underwater encounters. C: Richard Dix, Dolores Del Rio, Chester Morris. D: Erle Kenton. ACT 74m.

Devil's Playground, The 1976 Australian ★★★½ Young boys attending a Catholic boarding school, struggling to control their sexual impulses, are further traumatized by their priest mentors. Controversial Australian-produced drama is handled with intelligence and restraint by director/writer Schepisi. C: Arthur Dignam, Nick Tate. D: Fred Schepisi. DRA 107m. V

Devil's Rain, The 1975 ★★½ Borgnine leads a coven of satanists searching for a hidden book listing the names of souls promised to the devil. Schlocky but occasionally amusing horror flick, notable mostly for a climax in which all the cultists dissolve. C: William Shatner, Ernest Borgnine, Tom Skerritt, Ida Lupino, Eddie Albert, Keenan Wynn. D: Robert Feust. HOR [PG] 85m. V

Devils, The 1971 British ★★★½ Over-the-top story of nuns and witchcraft in 17th-century

France, via director Ken Russell. Frequent burnings at the stake, among other ghastly and vulgar goings-on. Based on Aldous Huxley novel, it has a point, somewhere. C: Vanessa Redgrave, Oliver Reed, Max Adrian, Gemma Jones. D: Ken Russell. DRA [R] 103m. v

Devil's Wanton, The 1949 Swedish ★★★ A desperate woman finds solace with man whose wife destroyed their marriage. One of many minor films Bergman made before hitting his stride in mid-'50s; interesting for glimpses of later themes and style. C: Doris Svedlund, Birger Malmsten, Eva Henning. D: Ingmar Bergman. DRA 72m. v

Devil's Widow, The 1972 ★★★ Aging jet-setter Gardner surrounds herself with younger lovers. Overly arty directing debut by McDowall. (a.k.a. *Tamlin*) C: Ava Gardner, Ian McShane, Stephanie Beacham, Cyril Cusack. D: Roddy McDowall. DRA [PG] 107m.

Devonsville Terror, The 1983 ★★½ The town of Devonsville begins to report creepy, satanic goings-on after an attractive new schoolteacher moves in. Solid performances across the board, but "witch's curse" story line is weakened by cloned climax from *Raiders of the Lost Ark*. C: Suzanna Love, Robert Walker, Donald Pleasence. D: Ulli Lommel. HOR 97m. v

Devotion 1946 ★★★½ Britain's fabulous Brontë family gets the Hollywood biography treatment, which stresses the sentimental aspects rather than the trio's literary genius. Powerhouse cast is main appeal. C: Olivia de Havilland, Ida Lupino, Paul Henreid, Sydney Greenstreet, Arthur Kennedy, Dame May Whitty. D: Curtis Bernhardt. DRA 107m.

D.I., The 1957 ★★★ Webb directed and starred creditably in the title role in this so-so character drama of a tough Marine drill sergeant determined to break a rebellious recruit. Many parts played by real "leathernecks." C: Jack Webb, Don Dubbins, Jackie Loughery. D: Jack Webb. DRA 106m. v

Diabolically Yours 1967 ★★★½ Wife and best friend believe rich man's amnesia is fake—who's playing with whom? Intriguing puzzle-mystery. C: Alain Delon, Senta Berger. D: Julien Duvivier. CRI [G] 94m.

Diabolik 1967 *See* **Danger: Diabolik**

Diabolique 1954 French ★★★★½ A disgruntled mistress and neglected wife plot to murder the sadistic schoolteacher who's caused them so much grief. With its legendary twist ending, this is the inspiration for many lesser suspense thrillers. (a.k.a. *Les Diaboliques*; Remade in the U.S. as *Reflections of Murder*). C: Simone Signoret, Vera Clouzot, Paul Meurisse, Charles Vanel. D: Henri-Georges Clouzot. CRI 100m. v

Diagnosis: Murder 1976 British ★★★★ The strange disappearance of his wife subjects a psychiatrist to intense scrutiny—both professional and criminal—as he struggles to solve the mystery. Adroit handling of subject, with many intensely chilling moments. Lee is in top form. C: Chrisopher Lee, Judy Geeson, Jon Finch. D: Sidney Hayers. CRI 95m.

Dial M for Murder 1954 ★★★★ Husband (Milland) plots to bump off young wife (Kelly) in order to inherit her fortune. Stars make a chilling couple in this minor but fine Hitchcock thriller. Originally filmed in 3-D. C: Ray Milland, Grace Kelly, Robert Cummings, John Williams. D: Alfred Hitchcock. CRI [PG] 105m. v

Dial 1119 1950 ★★½ A psychopath takes over a bar, threatening to kill the patrons. Slight B-movie has a few good moments, but bland cast can't compensate for overly melodramatic situations. C: Marshall Thompson, Virginia Field, Sam Levene. D: Gerald Mayer. DRA 75m.

Diamond Head 1962 ★★★½ Heston plays a domineering patriarch in this soap opera, set on a Hawaiian pineapple plantation. Mimieux, as the sister who dares marry a native, is the only family member who stands up to him. An unexceptional story, but scenic. C: Charlton Heston, Yvette Mimieux, George Chakiris, France Nuyen, James Darren, Aline MacMahon. D: Guy Green. DRA 107m. v

Diamond Horseshoe 1945 ★★★½ Actual nightclub of same name, owned by Billy Rose, is backdrop for backstage yarn of dancer (Grable) involved with doctor (Haymes). Colorful numbers, attractive stars. Hit song: "The More I See You." C: Betty Grable, Dick Haymes, Phil Silvers, William Gaxton, Carmen Cavallaro, Margaret Dumont. D: George Seaton. MUS 104m.

Diamond Hunters 1956 French ★★★★½ Socially diverse refugees escape from an authoritarian state and journey through the South American rainforests. Interesting, accessible adventure from the great Buñuel. (a.k.a. *Gina* and *Evil Eden*) C: Simone Signoret, Georges Marchal. D: Luis Buñuel. DRA 92m.

Diamond Jim 1935 ★★★★ Colorful period piece on the 1890s tycoon who lived for pleasure—and could afford it. Lots of fun and energy throughout. C: Edward Arnold, Jean Arthur, Binnie Barnes, Cesar Romero, Eric Blore. D: A. Sutherland. ACT 93m.

Diamonds 1972 Israeli ★★★★ English businessman Shaw hires ex-con Roundtree to assist him in plot to steal millions of dollars worth of precious jewels. A strong script, an interesting setting, and solid performances make this formula film work. C: Robert Shaw, Richard Roundtree, Shelley Winters, Barbara Hershey Seagull. D: Menahem Golan. CRI [PG] 108m. v

Diamonds and Crime 1943 *See* **Hi Diddle Diddle**

Diamonds Are Forever 1971 British ★★★★ Agent 007 (Connery) must stop a diamond smuggling ring headed by archenemy Blofeld

(Gray) who is using the gems to power a deadly space laser. Last classic Connery Bond features a clever script, a great score, and a way-out Vegas car chase. C: Sean Connery, Jill St. John, Lana Wood, Jimmy Dean. D: Guy Hamilton. ACT [PG] 119m. V

Diamonds for Breakfast 1968 British ★★ Wandering caper comedy with Mastroianni as penniless Russian aristocrat who gathers seven women to help him steal jewels lost by his ancestors. Slow moving. C: Marcello Mastroianni, Rita Tushingham. D: Christopher Morahan. COM [PG] 102m.

Diamonds of the Night 1964 Czech ★★★★ During WWII, two Jewish boys escape from a train on its way to the gas chambers, and spend a terrifying few days hoping to survive. Vivid atmosphere, eloquent direction, realistic acting, from the short-lived Czech New Wave. C: Antonin Kumbera. D: Jan Nemec, Ladislav Jansky. DRA 71m.

Diana: Her True Story 1993 British ★★★½ British TV-movie purporting to scrutinize the stormy royal romance and marriage of princelings Charles and Diana. One of the best of many "tell-all" dramas about royal couple, and also one of the harshest. Based on Andrew Morton's best-seller. C: Serena Scott Thomas, David Threlfall, Jemma Redgrave, Anne Stallybrass. D: Kevin Connor. DRA 180m. TVM V

Diane 1956 ★★ Trivial costume drama about the influence of courtesan Diane de Poitiers (Turner) on the King of France, and her affairs at his licentious court, including one with his son. C: Lana Turner, Pedro Armendariz, Roger Moore, Marisa Pavan, Sir Cedric Hardwicke. D: David Miller. DRA 110m. V

Diary for My Children 1982 Hungarian ★★★★½ A winner of many awards, this Hungarian drama brilliantly examines that country's recent history by chronicling three generations of the main character's family. Unsentimental and highly engrossing. C: Zsuzsa Czinkoczi, Anna Polony, Jan Nowicki. D: Marta Meszaros. DRA 107m.

Diary of a Bride 1948 *See* **I, Jane Doe**

Diary of a Chambermaid 1946 ★★ A rare misfire by the French master. A young maid must come to terms with her own struggles in the midst of turmoil in her own country. See this before you see Buñuel's superior version. C: Paulette Goddard, Hurd Hatfield, Burgess Meredith, Judith Anderson, Irene Ryan. D: Jean Renoir. DRA 87m. V

Diary of a Chambermaid 1964 French ★★★★½ Father of surrealism Buñuel reworks 1946 Renoir classic, casting Moreau as a jaded maid working for a sexually and politically perverse upper-class family. Scathing indictment of French bourgeoisie during rise of fascism in 1930s. C: Jeanne Moreau, Michel Piccoli, Georges Geret. D: Luis Buñuel. DRA 97m. V

Diary of a Country Priest 1950 French ★★★★½ Young priest tries unsuccessfully to inspire a parish in a remote country village. One of director Bresson's most harrowing, yet accessible works, a richly detailed study of loneliness, spiritual struggle, and commitment. C: Claude Laydu. D: Robert Bresson. DRA 115m. V

Diary of a Hitman 1992 ★★★½ Retiring hitman (Whitaker) is talked out of his last job by victim-to-be (Fenn). Interesting and well-directed character study disappeared from theaters quickly and undeservedly. The leads are excellent. C: Forest Whitaker, James Belushi, Lois Chiles, Sharon Stone, Sherilyn Fenn. D: Roy London. DRA [R] 90m. V

Diary of a Lost Girl 1929 German ★★★★½ G.W. Pabst's last silent feature reunites him with *Pandora's Box* star Brooks in a gripping account of a woman who is seduced and then abandoned, leading her to life of degradation. Uncompromising yet highly sympathetic, Pabst's original version was thought lost for decades until restored in 1984. C: Louise Brooks, Fritz Rasp. D: G.W. Pabst. DRA 100m. V

Diary of a Mad Housewife 1970 ★★★½ Snodgress dominates as the put-upon wife who must cope with her arrogant lover (Langella) and social-climbing, insensitive husband (Benjamin). Biting, satirical writing, but very much a film of its time; doesn't sit well in the postfeminist '90s. C: Carrie Snodgress, Richard Benjamin, Frank Langella. D: Frank Perry. DRA [R] 100m. V

Diary of a Madman 1963 ★★½ Magistrate (Price) kills one of his prisoners in self-defense, only to be possessed by the evil spirit that had inhabited the convict. Some scares, but mostly routine chiller set in 19th-century France, based on Guy de Maupassant story "Le Horla." C: Vincent Price, Nancy Kovack, Chris Warfield. D: Reginald LeBorg. HOR 96m. V

Diary of a Teenage Hitchhiker 1979 ★★ The moral of the story is: Don't accept rides from strangers. Sleazy film tries to tell an important message, but doesn't do it very well. C: Charlene Tilton, Dick Van Patten, Katherine Helmond. D: Ted Post. DRA 100m. TVM V

Diary of a Young Comic 1979 ★★★½ Fact-based story about struggling, stand-up Lewis as he moves from New York to Los Angeles. Insightful and funny. C: Richard Lewis, Stacy Keach, Dom DeLuise. D: Gary Weis. COM 67m. V

Diary of Anne Frank, The 1959 ★★★★½ True story of Jewish family hiding from Nazis in WWII Amsterdam, from play based on young Anne's diary during seclusion. Fine, inspirational drama with extraordinary performances by Schildkraut and Winters (Oscar for Best Supporting Actress). Only flaw is miscasting of inexperienced model Perkins as Anne. C: Millie Perkins, Joseph Schildkraut, Shelley Winters, Richard Beymer, Lou Jacobi, Ed Wynn. D: George Stevens. DRA 150m. V

Diary of Anne Frank, The 1980 ★★★★½ Strong remake of 1959 film with Gilbert touchingly real in title role of Jewish girl hiding from Nazis in Amsterdam attic with family. Fine supporting performances from Schell and Plowright. C: Melissa Gilbert, Maximilian Schell, Joan Plowright, Doris Roberts, James Coco, Clive Revill. D: Boris Sagal. DRA 100m. TVM

Diary of Oharu 1952 *See* **Life of Oharu, The**

Dick Tracy 1945 ★★½ The celebrated comic strip police detective hunts for the nefarious Splitface in this first nonserialized adventure featuring the characters created by Chester Gould. Made primarily for kiddie matinee audiences of the '40s. (a.k.a. *Splitface* and *Dick Tracy:Detective*) C: Morgan Conway, Anne Jeffreys. FAM/CRI V

Dick Tracy 1990 ★★★½ Beatty directs himself as the admirable detective out to rid the streets of crime. Pacino is wonderful, of course, and Madonna finally has the perfect role—a cartoon vamp. Great cameos, and an eye-popping comic-book look make this interesting. Oscars for Makeup, Art Direction, and Song, "Sooner or Later" by Stephen Sondheim. C: Warren Beatty, Madonna, Al Pacino, Glenne Headly, Charlie Korsmo, Mandy Patinkin, Charles Durning, Paul Sorvino, Dustin Hoffman. D: Warren Beatty. CRI [PG] 105m. V

Dick Tracy: Detective 1945 *See* **Dick Tracy**

Dick Tracy Meets Gruesome 1947 ★★★ The best in the series of early exploits featuring the comic strip police detective. Main appeal is Karloff as the sinister Gruesome, who uses a secret paralyzing formula to help him rob banks. Simplistic and cornball, but fun. (a.k.a. *Dick Tracy's Amazing Adventure* and *Dick Tracy Meets Karloff*) C: Boris Karloff, Ralph Byrd, Anne Gwynne. D: John Rawlins. FAM/CRI 65m. V

Dick Tracy Meets Karloff 1947 *See* **Dick Tracy Meets Gruesome**

Dick Tracy's Amazing Aventure 1947 *See* **Dick Tracy Meets Gruesome**

Dick Turpin 1925 ★★★★ Cowboy star Mix gets a change of scene as the notorious British robber in this entertaining early example of action filmmaking. C: Tom Mix, Kathleen Myers, Alan Hale. D: John Blystone. ACT 73m.

Die Die My Darling 1965 British ★★★½ Bizarre thriller boasts an unusual cast, led by Bankhead as an insane woman who traps her dead son's fiancée in her house, where the girl is tormented by various eccentrics. Unsubtle but entertaining. Bankhead's last film. (a.k.a. *Fanatic.*) C: Tallulah Bankhead, Stefanie Powers, Donald Sutherland. D: Silvio Narizzano. HOR 97m. V

Die Ewige Maske 1937 *See* **Eternal Mask, The**

Die Hard 1988 ★★★★ When elegant terrorists (Rickman, Godunov, and associates) hold an L.A. office building hostage, it's up to a wise-cracking cop (Willis) to foil their scheme. Loud, fast, and explosive. Hollywood action fun at its expensive best. C: Bruce Willis, Alan Rickman, Bonnie Bedelia, Alexander Godunov, Robert Davi. D: John McTiernan. ACT [R] 132m. V

Die Hard 2 1990 ★★★★ Beleaguered cop (Willis) finds himself matching wits with terrorists who have their sights on creating airport mayhem. Nonstop action, excellent effects, and a little twist keep things interesting. Not for those who have a fear of flying. Based on Walter Wager's novel *58 Minutes.* C: Bruce Willis, Bonnie Bedelia, William Atherton, Reginald VelJohnson, Franco Nero, Dennis Franz. D: Renny Harlin. ACT [R] 124m. V

Die Laughing 1980 ★ Taxi driver, accidentally involved in murder of nuclear scientist, becomes target of assassins. C: Robby Benson, Linda Grovenor, Charles Durning, Elsa Lanchester, Peter Coyote. D: Jeff Werner. COM [PG] 108m. V

Die, Monster, Die! 1965 ★★½ Young man visits British home of future father-in-law (Karloff) and finds that a recently landed meteorite is causing mutations among local animals and people. Atmospheric adaptation of H.P. Lovecraft story "The Colour Out of Space." C: Boris Karloff, Nick Adams, Freda Jackson, Patrick Magee. D: Daniel Haller. HOR 80m. V

Die Niebelungen 1923 German ★★★★★ Fritz Lang's classic silent film re-creates German mythology. In "Siegfried," the brave warrior slaughters dragon; in "Kriemheld's Revenge," Siegfried's widow takes arms against his killers. Epic telling achieves commanding level of Wagnerian opera. An unforgettable visual experience, with breathtaking set design based on 19th-century romantic paintings. C: Paul Richter, Margarete Schon. D: Fritz Lang. DRA 280m. V

Different Story, A 1979 ★★★½ A homosexual (King) marries a lesbian (Foster) to prevent his deportation, then they fall in love and have a baby. A rather strange story which probably has to be seen to be believed. Fine acting by Foster. C: Perry King, Meg Foster, Valerie Curtin, Peter Donat. D: Paul Aaron. DRA [PG] 107m. V

Digby—The Biggest Dog in the World 1974 British ★★½ An English sheepdog ingests, by accident, a formula created to increase the size of vegetables and grows thirty feet high. Charming fantasy spoiled by pedestrian special effects, but still okay viewing for children. C: Jim Dale, Spike Milligan, Milo O'Shea. D: Joseph McGrath. FAM/COM [G] 88m. V

Diggstown 1992 ★★★½ Hustler (Woods) bets nasty gambler (Dern) that his boxer (Gossett) can defeat 10 fighters within 24 hours. Mostly enjoyable (though boxing haters will tire of the fight sequences quickly), with Woods and Dern gleefully vying for sleaze honors. C: James Woods, Louis Gossett Jr., Bruce Dern, Oliver Platt. D: Michael Ritchie. DRA [R] 98m. V

Dillinger 1945 ★★★★ Excellent crime drama follows the exploits of the legendary triggerman, with the accent on legendary, not accuracy. Still, great fun. C: Edmund Lowe, Anne Jeffreys, Lawrence Tierney, Eduardo Ciannelli, Elisha Cook Jr. D: Max Nosseck. CRI 70m. V

Dillinger 1973 ★★★½ Milius' first feature is flamboyant funny biographical picture of notorious Depression-era bank robber, with Oates winningly laconic in title role. Runs out of gas in second half, but wonderful character bits by Johnson, Kanaly, Stanton, and a hilarious Dreyfuss keep it afloat. C: Warren Oates, Ben Johnson, Cloris Leachman, Michelle Phillips, Richard Dreyfuss, Harry Dean Stanton. D: John Milius. CRI [R] 106m. V

Dim Sum—A Little Bit of Heart 1985 ★★★★½ A traditional Chinese mother disapproves of her Americanized daughter's lifestyle and continually pressures her to find a husband. Refreshing comedy delivers gentle, warmhearted humor. C: Laureen Chew, Kim Chew, Victor Wong. D: Wayne Wang. COM [PG] 87m. V

Dimboola 1979 Australian ★★★★ Reporter retreats to small Australian town to write a story, but finds little peace as he is swept up in a large wedding party. Subtle, joyous film boasts excellent performances, especially Spence as the writer. C: Bruce Spence, Natalie Bate, Max Gillies, Bill Garner. D: John Duigan. COM 89m.

Dime with a Halo 1963 ★★★½ Impoverished street kids steal a dime from the church offering and use it to bet on the horses. Adroit mixture of sentiment and social commentary highlights this simple but effective Damon Runyonesque story. C: Roger Mobley, Barbara Luna. D: Boris Sagal. DRA 97m.

Dimples 1936 ★★★★ Who else but Shirley Temple? Period piece set in pre-Civil War New York City is an admirable showcase for the talented moppet. She's an orphan looking after her beloved, good-for-nothing grandfather, played to a turn by Morgan. C: Shirley Temple, Frank Morgan, Helen Westley, Stepin Fetchit. D: William A. Seiter. FAM/MUS [PG] 78m. V

Diner 1982 ★★★★ It's Baltimore, 1959, and a bunch of college kids, friends since childhood, try to face the confusing process of growing up. Good characters and interplay in a warm and funny story. Cast is a treasure trove of future stars—all unknown at the time. C: Steve Guttenberg, Daniel Stern, Mickey Rourke, Kevin Bacon, Timothy Daly, Ellen Barkin. D: Barry Levinson. DRA [R] 110m. V

Dingaka 1965 South Africa ★★★ Controversial story of tribal strife in the interior and black/white conflict in the cities of Africa. Slow moving, serious drama, quite a change from the writer/director of *The Gods Must Be Crazy*. C: Stanley Baker, Juliet Prowse. D: Jamie Uys. DRA 96m. V

Dingo 1994 Australian ★★★½ Frustrated musician who traps wild dogs on the Australian outback dreams of traveling to Paris to meet his idol (Davis). Offbeat, charming film, notable for Davis's only dramatic performance, filmed in 1991. C: Colin Friels, Miles Davis, Helen Buday, Bernadette Lafont. D: Rolf de Heer. DRA 108m.

Dining Room, The 1984 ★★★★ A parade of characters (all played by six actors) reveal their triumphs, foibles, and follies in a series of moving and funny vignettes. Intriguing and effective. Based on A.R. Gurney, Jr.'s play. C: John Shea, Francis Sternhagen. D: Allan Goldstein. COM 86m. TVM V

Dinner at Eight 1933 ★★★★★ Marvelous all-star comedy/drama, based on Kaufman/Ferber play, focuses on the private intrigues behind a society dinner. Tremendous direction and performances weave together several story lines. Remade for TV, but hold out for the original. C: John Barrymore, Wallace Beery, Marie Dressler, Jean Harlow, Lionel Barrymore, Lee Tracy, Billie Burke, Edmund Lowe, Jean Hersholt, Madge Evans. D: George Cukor. COM 111m. V

Dinner at Eight 1990 ★★★ Television remake of classic '30s comedy about social climbing and mores tries to match the wit and slyness of original, but can't capture the magic. C: Lauren Bacall, Charles Durning, Ellen Greene, Harry Hamlin, John Mahoney, Marsha Mason. D: Ron Lagomarsino. COM 95m. TVM V

Dinner at the Ritz 1937 British ★★★ This muddled drama features an international cast led by Annabella as a woman who tracks swindlers responsible for her financier father's bankruptcy and death. A polite little mystery. C: Annabella, Paul LuKas, David Niven. D: Harold Schuster. CRI 77m. V

Dinner for Adele 1978 Czech ★★★★ Wild detective spoof, with pulp detective Nick Carter in 1900 Prague: title character is a man-eating plant. Too many film buff in-jokes, but cheerful enough so others will stay with it. (a.k.a. *Nick Carter in Prague, Adele Hasn't Had Her Supper Yet.*) C: Michal Docolomansky, Rudolf Hrusinsky. D: Oldrich Lipsky. COM 100m.

Dino 1957 ★★★★ Delinquent (Mineo) has a serious attitude problem until girlfriend (Kohner) and social worker (Keith) help soften his edges. Good adolescent soaper with signature brooding by Mineo. Feature version of TV play which also starred Mineo. C: Sal Mineo, Brian Keith, Susan Kohner. D: Thomas Carr. DRA 96m. V

Dinosaur! ★★★½ Walter Cronkite leads an entertaining and educational excursion into the prehistoric world of dinosaurs. Both interesting and fun. DOC v

Dinosaurus! 1960 ★★★ Trials and tribulations of a caveman and two dinosaurs who inhabit a modern tropical island after being awakened from a deep sleep. Good, wholesome fun requiring little brain power from the viewer. Just don't expect *Jurassic Park.* C: Ward Ramsey, Kristina Hanson. D: Irvin Yeaworth Jr. SFI 85m. v

Dio Mio, Come Sono Caduto in Basso 1974 *See* **Till Marriage Do Us Part**

Diplomaniacs 1933 ★★★ Wheeler and Woolsey represent a Native American reservation at Geneva convention. Topical farce was big hit for popular comedy team. C: Bert Wheeler, Robert Woolsey, Marjorie White, Louis Calhern. D: William A. Seiter. MUS 62m. v

Diplomatic Courier 1952 ★★★★ Cold War espionage, with American and Russian agents duking it out on a European train ride from Salzburg to Trieste. Well-done political yarn features Lee Marvin, Charles Bronson, and Michael Ansara in unbilled bit parts. C: Tyrone Power, Patricia Neal, Hildegarde Neff, Karl Malden. D: Henry Hathaway. DRA 97m.

Dirigible 1931 ★★★ The U.S. Navy experiments with airships under harsh Antarctic conditions in this rather plodding adventure with some good action scenes. C: Jack Holt, Fay Wray, Ralph Graves. D: Frank Capra. DRA 93m.

Dirt Bike Kid, The 1986 ★★ Boy (Billingsley) has to learn how to control his unusual Yamaha motorbike (which behaves as if it had a mind of its own), and does battle with evil corporate types. (a.k.a. *Crazy Wheels.*) C: Peter Billingsley, Stuart Pankin, Anne Bloom. D: Hoite C. Caston. FAM/CRI [PG] 91m. v

Dirty Dancing 1987 ★★★★ Sheltered teen Grey finds romance with sexy dancer Swayze at Catskills resort in the '60s in popular fairy tale. Good dance numbers and attractive performers. Oscar for Best Song: "(I've Had) The Time of My Life." Great date movie. C: Jennifer Grey, Patrick Swayze, Jerry Orbach, Cynthia Rhodes, Jack Weston. D: Emile Ardolino. MUS [PG-13] 105m. v

Dirty Dingus Magee 1970 ★★★½ Cowpoke parody with Sinatra as a wisecracking fugitive outlaw running afoul of old adversary (Kennedy). Unsophisticated burlesque is fast paced and fun. C: Frank Sinatra, George Kennedy, Anne Jackson, Lois Nettleton, Jack Elam. D: Burt Kennedy. WST [PG] 90m.

Dirty Dishes 1982 French ★★★★ Droll comedy explores Parisian homemaker's rebellion from the drudgery of domesticity, the hilarious perils of supermarket shopping, and her eventual collapse into madness. Great comic touch by Laure. C: Carole Laure, Pierre Santini. D: Joyce Buñuel. COM [R] 96m. v

Dirty Dozen, The 1967 ★★★★½ Often imitated but never equaled, this rollicking buddy film recruits a band of criminals for a suicide mission in WWII Europe. Features classic performances by bad guys Marvin, Borgnine, Savalas, and Sutherland. C: Lee Marvin, Ernest Borgnine, Jim Brown, John Cassavetes, Robert Ryan, Charles Bronson, Donald Sutherland, George Kennedy, Telly Savalas. D: Robert Aldrich. ACT 151m. v

Dirty Dozen, The: The Next Mission 1985 ★★ Sequel has Marvin reprising an earlier role as he leads condemned GIs on a suicide raid to assassinate Hitler. Thinly plotted comic book heroics. C: Lee Marvin, Ernest Borgnine, Ken Wahl. D: Andrew V. McLaglen. ACT 97m. TVM v

Dirty Game, The 1966 Italian ★★★ World War II drama, basically a collection of separate incidents involving various characters in life-and-death situations. Episodic structure detracts from overall impact; genuinely appealing cast. C: Christian Jaque, Henry Fonda, Vittorio Gassman, Annie Girardot, Robert Ryan. D: Terence Young. DRA 91m.

Dirty Hands 1976 French ★★★½ The bodies pile up, then start walking around, as two lovers conspire to kill the woman's husband. Director Chabrol is a master at handling the subject, although this time unintentional humor creeps in to wreck the sinister mood. C: Rod Steiger, Romy Schneider. D: Claude Chabrol. CRI [R] 102m. v

Dirty Harry 1971 ★★★★ Eastwood's one-man assault on the Constitution begins in this first of the *Dirty Harry* series, when a tough cop, his hands tied by legal bureaucracy, becomes judge, jury, and executioner for a psychotic killer. Almost a classic. C: Clint Eastwood, Harry Guardino, Reni Santoni. D: Don Siegel. CRI [R] 102m. v

Dirty Knight's Work 1976 British ★★½ Modern-day society of knights may be responsible for series of mysterious murders in England. Erratic and not very funny. (a.k.a. *Choice of Weapons*) C: John Mills, Donald Pleasence, Barbara Hershey, David Birney, Margaret Leighton, Peter Cushing. D: Kevin Connor. COM [PG] 88m. v

Dirty Laundry 1987 ★★ An unassuming buffoon ends up with a ton of stolen money and some angry crooks after him thanks to a laundry bag mix-up. Silly and low-budget. C: Leigh McCloskey, Jeanne O'Brien, Frankie Valli, Sonny Bono. D: William Webb. COM [PG-13] 81m. v

Dirty Mary 1969 *See* **Very Curious Girl, A**

Dirty Mary, Crazy Larry 1974 ★★★½ A relentlessly paced thriller about auto racing, in which a star driver (Fonda) picks up young woman (George) and a mechanic (Roarke), and then holds up a supermarket. The remainder of film is an exuberant demolition derby. C: Peter Fonda, Susan George, Adam Roarke, Vic Morrow, Roddy McDowall. D: John Hough. ACT [PG] 91m. v

Dirty Money 1972 French ★★★ Melodrama

about bank robbers and drug traffickers. Melville's last film features some excellent actors. C: Alain Delon, Catherine Deneuve, Richard Crenna. D: Jean-Pierre Melville. CRI 98m.

Dirty Rotten Scoundrels 1988 ★★★★ Sophisticated Riviera con artist (Caine) and his rube competition (Martin) compete to fleece an American heiress. Much funnier than its 1964 predecessor, *Bedtime Story*, which had David Niven and Marlon Brando in the Caine and Martin roles. C: Steve Martin, Michael Caine, Glenne Headly. D: Frank Oz. COM [PG] 110m. V

Dirty Work 1992 ★★ A thoroughly unpleasant guy stalks and kills a drug dealer for his money, and then is chased himself. Okay for dedicated action fans. C: Kevin Dobson, John Ashton, Roxann Biggs. D: John McPherson. ACT 88m.

Disappearance of Aimee, The 1976 ★★★★½ Fascinating drama of '20s evangelist Aimee Semple McPherson's disappearance, allegedly by kidnapping, leading to court trial for fraud. Dunaway gives electric performance, matched by Davis as her domineering mother. C: Faye Dunaway, Bette Davis, James Sloyan, James Woods. D: Anthony Harvey. DRA 96m. TVM V

Disappearance, The 1977 Canadian ★★★★ Sutherland as a professional killer whose wife disappears, pursues the man he thinks is responsible. Stylized thriller is plagued by self-conscious psychologizing which slows it down—plodding! C: Donald Sutherland, Francine Racette, David Hemmings, David Warner, Christopher Plummer, John Hurt. D: Stuart Cooper. CRI [R] 80m. V

Disaster at Silo 7 1993 ★★★ Someone presses the wrong button at a missile silo and the race is on to prevent global nuclear tragedy. Not as tense as it sounds, but based on true incident. C: Perry King, Peter Boyle, Patricia Charbonneau. D: Larry Elikann. DRA 92m. TVM V

Disaster at Valdez 1993 *See* **Dead Ahead: The Exxon Valdez Disaster**

Disaster in Time 1992 ★★★½ Inconspicuous time travelers create confusion when they make a rest stop in a backwater town. Clever and entertaining sci-fi manages to avoid many of the clichés of the genre. (a.k.a. *Grand Tour*) C: Jeff Daniels, Ariana Richards. D: David Twohy. SFI 99m. V

Disciple, The 1915 ★★★★ William S. Hart stars and directs this silent involving a gun-toting preacher who tames a wild, crooked town and saves his wife from a vile gambler. Durable early Western. C: William S. Hart, Dorothy Dalton, Robert McKim. D: William S. Hart. WST 80m.

Disclosure 1994 ★★★★ Douglas is accused of sexually harrassing his new boss (Moore), but he's the true victim. High-tech, glossy thriller is exciting entertainment, but sends disturbing messages about men's view of women in power. Based on Michael Crichton's novel. C: Michael Douglas, Demi Moore, Donald Sutherland, Caroline Goodall, Roma Mafia, Dennis Miller. D: Barry Levinson. DRA [R] 128m. V

Disco Godfather ★★ Moore's final installment of his Dolemite trilogy mulches the excesses of the '70s Kung-fu, mobster and black exploitation melodramas. (a.k.a. *Avenging Disco Godfather, The*.) ACT

Discreet Charm of the Bourgeoisie, The 1972 French ★★★★★ Six guests for dinner are continually prevented from actually eating anything, because the director has something else in mind. Beautiful, surreal, and scathing social satire, the inimitable Buñuel way. Oscar for Best Foreign Film. Subtitled. C: Fernando Rey, Delphine Seyrig, Stephane Audran, Jean-Pierre Cassel, Michel Piccoli. D: Luis Buñuel. COM [PG] 100m. V

Dishonored 1931 ★★★ Lesser Dietrich/von Sternberg collaboration features the great Marlene as a Mata Hari-like spy during WWI. Not much to the thin plot, but fun to watch Dietrich work her way through costumes and co-stars. C: Marlene Dietrich, Victor McLaglen, Warner Oland. D: Josef von Sternberg. DRA 91m. V

Dishonored Lady 1947 ★★★ A psychologically disturbed magazine editor (Lamarr) is accused of murdering a former flame (Loder). Okay mystery vehicle for the glamourous star. C: Hedy Lamarr, Dennis O'Keefe, John Loder, William Lundigan. D: Robert Stevenson. CRI 85m. V

Disorder and Early Torment 1977 German ★★★★ A history professor is author Thomas Mann's alter ego during the darkest days of post-WWII Germany. Fascinating look at the great writer. C: Martin Held, Ruth Leuwerik, Sabine von Maydell, Frederic Meissner. D: Franz Seitz. DRA 85m.

Disorderlies 1987 ★★★ Mayhem abounds as rap group (The Fatboys) plays nursemaid to cantankerous millionaire Belamy, and saves him from the clutches of his devious, money-grubbing nephew. Lots of low-brow, slapstick humor. C: The Fat Boys, Ralph Bellamy, Anthony Geary. D: Michael Schultz. COM [PG] 87m. V

Disorderly Orderly, The 1964 ★★★½ Uneven romp for Lewis as a stumbling employee in nursing home/hospital. Best moments involve Jerry's physical reactions to other people's pain. C: Jerry Lewis, Glenda Farrell, Susan Oliver, Everett Sloane. D: Frank Tashlin. COM 90m. V

Disorganized Crime 1989 ★★½ Group of ex-cons come together to organize a small-town bank robbery, but soon one of them is arrested, and the others can't think on their feet. Talented ensemble cast. C: Hoyt Axton, Corbin Bernsen, Ruben Blades, Fred Gwynne,

Ed O'Neill, Lou Diamond Phillips. D: Jim Kouf. COM [R] 101m. v

Dispatch from Reuters, A 1940 ★★★½ Overly earnest biography of news agency founder who began with pigeon carriers. Good finale shows coverage of Lincoln's assassination. C: Edward G. Robinson, Edna Best, Eddie Albert. D: William Dieterle. DRA 89m.

Disraeli 1929 ★★★½ Stagy, verbose early talkie, but Oscar-winner Arliss is a pleasure to listen to. Life of British Prime Minister is interesting as he tries to buy Suez Canal; less so when he plays matchmaker for young lovers. C: George Arliss, Joan Bennett. D: Alfred E. Green. DRA 89m. v

Distance 1975 ★★★★ Benjamin and Woods struggle to keep their marriages intact while carving out military careers during the harsh times of the Cold War. Well-acted drama insightfully examines the stress of career soldiers. C: Paul Benjamin, Eija Pokkinen, James Woods, Polly Holliday. D: Anthony Lover. DRA [R] 94m.

Distant Drums 1951 ★★★½ An army officer fights a fierce guerrilla war against Seminole Indians in 1840s Florida. Lengthy, conventional Western entertainment with lackluster interludes offset by action. C: Gary Cooper, Mari Aldon, Richard Webb, Robert Barratt. D: Raoul Walsh. WST 101m. v

Distant Harmony—Pavarotti in China 1988 ★★★½ Great Italian tenor's first trip to China, where he performed in famed Great Hall, is documented in no-frills style that underscores meeting of Western and Eastern cultures. Exquisite music, attractive scenery. C: Luciano Pavarotti, Kallen Esperian. MUS [G] 85m. v

Distant Thunder 1973 Indian ★★★★½ Small town struggles through devastating famine. Powerful, unsentimental study of rural life in India is one of Ray's best. C: Soumitra Chatterji, Babita, Sandhya Roy. D: Satyajit Ray. DRA 100m. v

Distant Thunder 1988 U.S. ★★½ A traumatized Vietnam vet (Lithgow) who's become a hermit in the forests of the Pacific Northwest reunites with son (Macchio) he abandoned years ago. Talented cast tries hard. C: John Lithgow, Ralph Macchio, Reb Brown. D: Rick Rosenthal. DRA [R] 114m. v

Distant Trumpet, A 1964 ★★★½ Newly arrived cavalry officer at frontier outpost sternly prepares his troops for what they might confront in the new West. Solid, standard Western. C: Troy Donahue, Suzanne Pleshette, Kent Smith, Claude Akins. D: Raoul Walsh. WST 117m.

Distant Voices, Still Lives 1988 British ★★★★ Unusual, autobiographical memoir of director's youth in '40s England with abusive father and long-suffering mother. Notable for vivid soundtrack using popular songs of the period, juxtaposed with haunting cinematography. Not very effective as a narrative but impressive cinematic experiment. C: Freda Dowie, Peter Postlethwaite, Angela Walsh. D: Terence Davies. DRA [PG-13] 87m. v

Distinguished Gentleman, The 1992 ★★★½ Murphy delivers dozens of pointed barbs at D.C. politics with this salvo of somewhat obvious political humor. A penny-ante hustler cons his way into Congress when he finds out how much legislators can steal. C: Eddie Murphy, Lane Smith, Sheryl Lee Ralph, Joe Don Baker, Victoria Rowell, Charles Dutton. D: Jonathan Lynn. COM [R] 112m. v

Disturbance, The 1990 ★★ A young man is tormented not only by his domineering mother, but by a demon that seems to dwell within him and slaughters his girlfriends. Thoroughly routine low-budgeter with uninspired script, direction, and acting. C: Timothy Greeson, Lisa Geffreion. D: Cliff Guest. HOR 81m. v

Disturbed 1990 ★★ Asylum keeper (McDowell) has nasty habit of assaulting attractive female inmates, but one of his dead victims now appears to be haunting him. McDowell is fun, if predictably cast, but film becomes overwrought and obvious. C: Malcolm McDowell, Geoffrey Lewis, Pamela Gidley. D: Charles Winkler. HOR [R] 96m. v

Diva 1981 French ★★★★½ Stylish thriller has a Parisian bike postman and opera buff accidentally becoming embroiled in criminal underworld. A little bit arty at times, but a lot of fun anyway. Big cult splash for first-time director Beineix. C: Frederic Andrei, Wilhelmenia Wiggins Fernandez, Richard Bohringer. D: Jean-Jacques Beineix. CRI [R] 119m. v

Dive Bomber 1941 ★★★ Pre-Pearl Harbor flying film features Flynn as a medical researcher studying pilot blackouts during aerial maneuvers. Good flight scenes and dramatic moments enliven a somewhat talky picture. C: Errol Flynn, Fred MacMurray, Alexis Smith, Ralph Bellamy, Robert Armstrong. D: Michael Curtiz. DRA 129m. v

Divided Heart, The 1954 British ★★★★ Loving British couple finds their life in torment when their adopted son's mother, believed killed during WWII, reappears, demanding custody of her child. Top-notch British tearjerker realistically handles touchy dramatic subject. C: Cornell Borchers, Yvonne Mitchell, Alexander Knox. D: Charles Crichton. DRA 89m.

Divine 1935 ★★★½ Naive young woman from the country goes to Paris to become a dancer. Based on charming Colette story, Ophuls' uneven treatment is brightened by marvelous music-hall atmosphere. C: Simone Berriau, George Riguad, Catherine Fonteney. D: Max Ophuls. DRA 80m.

Divine Madness 1980 ★★★★ Bette Midler's concert film parodies show business conventions and the singer herself through series of outrageous sketches and songs. Mermaid outfits are unforgettable and film thrives on Miss M.'s infectious and boisterous energy. C: Bette Midler. D: Michael Ritchie. COM [R] 86m. V

Divine Nymph, The 1979 Italian ★★ Italian siren Antonelli is a sophisticated '20s mistress to two wealthy men in this largely undistinguished work. Film relies greatly on titillation to disguise lack of cinematic merit. C: Marcello Mastroianni, Laura Antonelli, Terence Stamp. D: Giuseppe Patroni Griffi. DRA 100m. V

Divine Waters 1985 ★★ Documentary on irreverent independent filmmaker John Waters has its moments, but it's definitely a matter of taste—as is much of his work. A fan must-see. C: Divine. D: John Waters. DOC 110m.

Divorce American Style 1967 ★★★★½ American marriage gets raked over the coals in this comic exposé as Van Dyke and Reynolds discover life after divorce may be just as miserable as life in an unhappy union. Searingly honest and hilarious. C: Dick Van Dyke, Debbie Reynolds, Jason Robards, Jean Simmons, Van Johnson, Lee Grant, Tom Bosley, Eileen Brennan. D: Bud Yorkin. COM 109m.

Divorce His, Divorce Hers 1973 ★★★½ Husband (Burton) tells his side of their divorce, wife (Taylor) hers. Not terribly exciting; has a good script but the thrust of the film is to serve as a showcase for two big stars. C: Elizabeth Taylor, Richard Burton, Carrie Nye, Barry Foster. D: Waris Hussein. DRA 148m. TVM V

Divorce—Italian Style 1962 Italian ★★★★½ Wonderful sex comedy involving a wealthy Sicilian husband (Mastroianni) who fantasizes about murdering his wife to run off with a nubile 16-year-old. Mastroianni is masterful as the disgruntled husband, backed by plenty of great comic action. Oscar for Best Screenplay. C: Marcello Mastroianni, Daniela Rocca, Stefania Sandrelli. D: Pietro Germi. COM 104m. V

Divorce of Lady X, The 1938 British ★★★½ Glossy mistaken identity caper has Oberon innocently spending the night in lawyer Olivier's hotel suite, only to be mistaken for wife of his best friend. Leads make flimsy story breezy. C: Merle Oberon, Laurence Olivier, Binnie Barnes, Ralph Richardson. D: Tim Whelan. COM 90m. V

Divorce Wars: A Love Story 1982 ★★★★ Selleck and Curtin show considerable dramatic flair as a couple whose marriage is on the rocks. Well-written drama. C: Tom Selleck, Jane Curtin, Joan Bennett, Viveca Lindfors, Candy Azzara. D: Donald Wrye. DRA 100m. TVM

Divorcee, The 1930 ★★★½ Fed-up wife (Shearer) of philanderer (Morris) decides to indulge in love affairs of her own. Gushy, though still entertaining soap opera that won Best Actress Oscar for intermittently wooden Shearer. C: Norma Shearer, Chester Morris, Robert Montgomery. D: Robert Z. Leonard. DRA 95m. V

Dixiana 1930 ★★★½ Antique, flamboyant operetta typical of early talkie extravangazas with Daniels as circus star involved with society beau (opera star Marshall). Worth seeing for color finale featuring legendary tap dancer Robinson. (Beware of TV prints that leave it out!) C: Bebe Daniels, Everett Marshall, Bert Wheeler, Robert Woolsey, Bill "Bojangles" Robinson. D: Luther Reed. MUS 98m. V

Dixie: Changing Habits 1983 ★★★★ Pleshette plays a New Orleans bordello owner who's caught plying her trade and sentenced to serve time at nun Leachman's convent. Surprisingly, the women end up teaching and helping each other. C: Suzanne Pleshette, Cloris Leachman, Geraldine Fitzgerald, Judith Ivey. D: George Englund. COM 100m. TVM V

Dixie Dynamite 1976 ★★ To avenge their father's death, two sisters enlist the help of a drunken biker (Oates) and run riot in a small Southern town. The kind of action movie Burt Reynolds used to do. C: Warren Oates, Christopher George, Jane Anne Johnstone. D: Lee Frost. ACT [PG] 88m. V

Dixie 1943 ★★½ Dan Emmett, writer of title tune, is subject of this unnecessary film biography. Mainly for Crosby fans. C: Bing Crosby, Dorothy Lamour, Billy DeWolfe, Marjorie Reynolds. D: A. Sutherland. MUS 89m.

Do Not Disturb 1965 ★★★ Middling comedy with Park Avenue matron Day transplanted to suburban England by hubby Taylor. There she meets dashing Fantoni with ensuing complications. Script is paint-by-numbers affair with few laughs. C: Doris Day, Rod Taylor, Hermione Baddeley. D: Ralph Levy. COM 102m.

Do Not Fold, Spindle or Mutilate 1971 ★★★½ Four old ladies create a fantasy woman, then sign her up with a computer dating service; but the joke turns sour when a psychotic single man isn't amused. Mild thriller's a must-see for fans of the veteran stars, all of whom are in top form. C: Helen Hayes, Myrna Loy, Sylvia Sydney, Mildred Natwick, Vince Edwards. D: Ted Post. CRI 71m. TVM

Do or Die ★★★ Two bodacious federal agents (former *Playboy* models Speir and Vasquez) battle a nasty crime boss (Morita) in this typical Sidaris thriller. C: Dona Speir, Roberta Vasquez, Pat Morita. D: Andy Sidaris. ACT [R] 90m. V

Do the Right Thing 1989 ★★★★★ Lee's most provocative film tells the story of the racial tensions between an Italian pizza shop owner and the local African-American kids that flare during the hottest day of summer in interracial Brooklyn neighborhood. Trenchant and tough; the ending is especially disturbing. C: Danny Aiello, Spike Lee, Ossie Davis, Ruby Dee, Giancarlo Esposito, John Turturro, Rosie Perez. D: Spike Lee. DRA [R] 120m. V

Do You Love Me? 1946 ★★★★ Reserved dean of a music college gets a makeover when a swinging dance band leader intimates the dean is frumpy. Diverting, easy-going musical-comedy brightened by O'Hara's charm and Haymes' vocals. C: Maureen O'Hara, Dick Haymes, Harry James. D: Gregory Ratoff. MUS 91m.

Do You Remember Love? 1985 ★★★★½ Emmy-winning Woodward's performance as college professor with Alzheimer's disease and surprisingly unsentimental script make for outstanding drama. Transcends disease-of-the-week genre with taste and style. C: Joanne Woodward, Richard Kiley, Geraldine Fitzgerald. D: Jeff Bleckner. DRA 100m. TVM

D.O.A. 1949 ★★★★½ Heart-racing drama follows unassuming businessman O'Brien as he frantically attempts to discover who poisoned him before the deadly toxin in his body takes effect. Stylishly directed film noir crackles from beginning to end. C: Edmond O'Brien, Pamela Britton, Luther Adler. D: Rudolph Mate. DRA 83m. V

D.O.A. 1988 ★★★ College professor (Quaid) has been poisoned; he tries to find who did it—and why—before he dies. Unsatisfying remake (and update) of 1949 film noir classic adds contrived ending. C: Dennis Quaid, Meg Ryan, Daniel Stern, Charlotte Rampling. D: Rocky Morton, Annabel Jankel. CRI [R] 104m. V

D.O.A.—A Right of Passage 1981 ★★★½ Documentary on punk rock in Britain and America, with delirious footage of untalented musicians giving it their all. Highlight is interviews with drug-stupefied Sid Vicious and Nancy Spungen. Good companion to *Sid and Nancy*. D: Lech Kowalski. DOC 90m. V

Doberman Gang, The 1972 ★★½ Clever guard dogs are further trained to rob banks. Action filled, but a somewhat unforgivable premise. C: Byron Mabe, Julie Parrish, Hal Reed. D: Byron Ross Chudnow. FAM/ACT [G] 85m. V

Doc Hollywood 1991 ★★★ En route to a lucrative cosmetic surgery practice in L.A., Fox is waylaid in small Southern town and finds himself ministering to the unusual ailments of eccentric locals. Romance rears its head in the person of acerbic Warner. No surprises, but clean fun. C: Michael J. Fox, Julie Warner, Bridget Fonda, Woody Harrelson, Barnard Hughes, Frances Sternhagen. D: Michael Clayton-Jones. COM [PG-13] 104m. V

Doc Savage: The Man of Bronze 1975 ★★★ Comic strip superhero Doc Savage (Ely) and his backup, The Fabulous Five, sojourn to South America to investigate the suspicious passing of Doc's dad. Campy adventure yarn that could have used a bigger budget (who couldn't?). More fun for kids than adults. C: Ron Ely, Pamela Hensley. D: Michael Anderson. ACT [G] 101m. V

Doc 1971 ★★★ Wyatt Earp and Doc Holliday get their Tombstone tale told again, this time in defiantly unglamourous fashion. Interesting, but glum. C: Stacy Keach, Harris Yulin, Faye Dunaway. D: Frank Perry. WST [PG] 96m. V

Docks of New York 1928 ★★★★★ The great silent director is in top form in this tale of a woman who attempts suicide, only to be saved by her admirer. A visual masterpiece. C: George Bancroft, Betty Compson, Olga Baclanova. D: Josef Von Sternberg. DRA 76m. V

Docteur Popaul 1972 *See* **High Heels**

Doctor and the Devils, The 1985 ★★★ An 18th-century doctor and a pack of grave robbers resort to nefarious methods to procure bodies for experiments. A macabre tale, from a vintage screenplay by Dylan Thomas. C: Timothy Dalton, Jonathan Pryce, Twiggy, Julian Sands, Stephen Rea, Patrick Stewart. D: Freddie Francis. HOR [R] 93m. V

Doctor at Large 1957 British ★★★½ Third installment in British *Doctor* series has Dr. Sparrow (Bogarde) job hunting after he antagonizes head surgeon Spratt (Justice) at posh hospital where he wants to practice. Bawdy medical comedy. C: Dirk Bogarde, Muriel Pavlow, Donald Sinden, James Robertson Justice, Shirley Eaton. D: Ralph Thomas. COM 95m. V

Doctor At Sea 1955 British ★★★ Dr. Sparrow (Bogarde) serves on passenger freighter carrying two young French women (Bardot and De Banzie) and tries to avoid the domineering captain (Justice). Sequel to *Doctor in the House* has its moments. C: Dirk Bogarde, Brigitte Bardot, Brenda deBanzie. D: Ralph Thomas. COM 93m. V

Doctor Blood's Coffin 1961 British ★★★★ Citizens of a lonely Welsh town are turned into human guinea pigs for twisted research experiments. The scenery is beautiful and the horror is chilling. C: Kieron Moore, Hazel Court. D: Sidney Furie. HOR 92m. V

Doctor Detroit 1983 ★★★½ Aykroyd blitzes the screen as a meek academic transformed into a bizarre crime lord. Strange tale won a cult following with its manic energy and odd sense of humor. C: Dan Aykroyd, Howard Hesseman, T.K. Carter, Donna Dixon, Lynn Whitfield, Fran Drescher. D: Michael Pressman. COM [R] 91m. V

Doctor Dolittle 1967 ★★ Weak adaptation of Hugh Lofting books, about a doctor (Harrison) who has a way with animals, nearly bankrupted Twentieth Century-Fox. Still, the film did win an Oscar for Best Special Effects, and Leslie Bricusse won an Oscar for Best Song for "Talk to the Animals." C: Rex Harrison, Samantha Eggar, Anthony Newley, Richard Attenborough. D: Richard Fleischer. FAM/MUS 145m. V

Doctor in Distress 1963 British ★★★ In Bogarde's last performance as amorous Dr. Sparrow, he pursues a reluctant model (Eggar) and helps out flinty Dr. Spratt (Justice), who amazes everyone by falling in love. Some nice sentimental touches. C: Dirk Bogarde, Samantha Eggar, James Robertson Justice. D: Ralph Thomas. COM 98m. V

Doctor in Love 1960 British ★★★★ Continuation of the British comedy series follows the misadventures of Dr. Richard Hare as his eye for the ladies gets him into all sorts of hot water. Likable formula comedy delivers a healthy dose of laughs. C: Michael Craig, James Robertson Justice, Virginia Maskell. D: Ralph Thomas. COM 93m.

Doctor in the House 1954 British ★★★½ Film spans five years at a London hospital, where new recruit Dr. Simon Sparrow (Bogarde) and other young physicians study their female patients' bodies for other than medical reasons. Fast-paced, good-natured humor. C: Dirk Bogarde, Muriel Pavlow, Kenneth More, Donald Sinden, Kay Kendall. D: Ralph Thomas. COM 92m. V

Doctor in Trouble 1970 British ★★★½ British comedy series goes to sea as it continues making fun of the medical profession, this time following the misadventures of Phillips, (continuing his role from *Doctor in Love* and *Doctor in Distress*) as he hides out during an ocean cruise. Justice and Morley provide most of the laughs. C: Leslie Phillips, Harry Secombe, James Robertson Justice, Robert Morley. D: Ralph Thomas. COM [R] 90m. V

Doctor Mordrid—Master of the Unknown 1992 ★★★★ Strange gatekeeper (Combs) keeps watch over a cosmic doorway in Manhattan. Fiery special effects add to this far-out tale. C: Jeffrey Combs, Yvette Nipar, Brian Thompson. D: Albert Band, Charles Band. SFI [R] 102m. V

Doctor of Doom 1962 ★ Wrestling women take on a mad scientist specializing in brain transplants and his creation, a murderous ape man. Too bad no one transplanted any brains into this one, but it does offer some so-bad-it's-good entertainment. Remade (if you can believe it) as *Night of the Bloody Apes*. HOR V

Doctor Rhythm 1938 ★★½ A doctor (Crosby) does a favor for a police friend (Devine) by playing bodyguard for a night, and naturally falls in love with the woman he guards (Carlisle). Light musical. C: Bing Crosby, Beatrice Lillie, Mary Carlisle, Sterling Holloway, Laura Hope Crews. D: Frank Tuttle. MUS 80m.

Doctor Socrates ★★★½ Small-town physician forced to treat fleeing gangsters ultimately outsmarts them by shooting them up with morphine. Punchy, well-directed if routine Warners' melodrama, with Muni, Dvorak and MacLane in fine form. C: Paul Muni, Ann Dvorak, Batton MacLane. D: William Dieter. DRA 70m.

Doctor Takes a Wife, The 1940 ★★★★ Charming mistaken identity comedy has Milland posing as Young's husband when people mistake them for man and wife. Likable stars play script with deft touch. C: Ray Milland, Loretta Young, Reginald Gardiner, Gail Patrick, Edmund Gwenn. D: Alexander Hall. COM 89m. V

Doctor, The 1991 ★★★★ When a top surgeon finds out he has throat cancer, he discovers the pain of being on the other end of the stethoscope. Fascinating and illuminating drama that's often touching. The cast is excellent. C: William Hurt, Christine Lahti, Elizabeth Perkins, Mandy Patinkin. D: Randa Haines. DRA [PG-13] 125m. V

Doctor X 1932 ★★★ Reporter and police track series of murders in which victims are cannibalized—could mad scientist (Atwill) be responsible? Great visuals, but story and comic relief in this early horror tale don't hold up as well. C: Lionel Atwill, Fay Wray, Lee Tracy, Preston Foster. D: Michael Curtiz. HOR 77m. V

Doctor Zhivago 1965 ★★★★½ Powerful, romantic epic based on Pasternak's classic novel of a doctor (Sharif) caught in the upheaval of the Russian Revolution and his tragic love for the beautiful, always-elusive Lara. The sweeping cinematography won an Oscar, as did the haunting score. The film won three others, and was nominated for both Best Picture and Best Director. C: Omar Sharif, Julie Christie, Geraldine Chaplin, Tom Courtenay, Alec Guinness, Siobhan McKenna, Ralph Richardson, Rod Steiger, Rita Tushingham. D: David Lean. DRA [PG] 200m. V

Doctor's Dilemma 1958 British ★★★★ In turn-of-the-century London, a devoted wife (Caron) must persuade physicians that her stricken roguish husband is worthy of treatment. Delightful comedy, adapted from the G.B. Shaw play. C: Dirk Bogarde, Leslie Caron, Alastair Sim, Robert Morley. D: Anthony Asquith. COM 99m.

Doctor's Wives 1970 ★ Attempt by a cheating wife (Cannon) to bed every doctor within arm's reach is cut short by her husband's gun. Overdramatized trials and tribulations of the medical professional proves to be a campy excursion into melodrama. C: Dyan Cannon, Richard Crenna, Gene Hackman, Rachel Roberts, Carroll O'Connor, Janice Rule, Diana Sands, Cara Williams, Ralph Bellamy. D: George Schaefer. DRA [R] 102m. V

Dodes'ka-den 1970 Japanese ★★★ A pastiche of life in Tokyo slums. Kurosawa, known for his superb historical epics, seems less comfortable with this piece of modern realism. Powerful images often overwhelm more intimate human stories. C: Yoshitaka Zushi, Tomoko Yamazaki. D: Akira Kurosawa. DRA 140m. V

Dodge City 1939 ★★★★ An Irish trail boss (Flynn) pins on a star to help tame a wild Kansas railroad town. Entertaining, action-packed big studio Western with a dandy climax. C: Errol Flynn, Olivia de Havilland, Ann Sheridan, Bruce Cabot, Frank McHugh, Alan Hale. D: Michael Curtiz. WST 105m. V

Dodsworth 1936 ★★★★½ Wyler's classic about a rich American entrepreneur trying to deal with success and his wife's material desires. Poignant adult drama highlighted by sensitive performances and intelligent script based on novel by Sinclair Lewis. C: Walter Huston, Ruth Chatterton, Mary Astor, Paul LuKas, David Niven, Maria Ouspenskaya, Spring Byington. D: William Wyler. DRA 90m. v

Dog Day 1983 French ★★★ American mobster (Marvin) holes up in a French farm house owned by a very peculiar family. Violent, offbeat thriller satirizes gangster mythology. C: Miou Miou, Lee Marvin, Victor Lanoux, Bernadette Lafont, Tina Louise. D: Yves Boisset. CRI 101m. v

Dog Day Afternoon 1975 ★★★★½ Offbeat drama, based on fact. Thwarted bank robber (Pacino), in need of money for his boyfriend's sex change operation, holes up in beseiged bank and becomes a media sensation. Funny, frightening, and unforgettable. Pacino is sensational and Lumet's direction deftly captures the city's manic energy. Oscar-winning screenplay. C: Al Pacino, John Cazale, Charles Durning, James Broderick, Chris Sarandon. D: Sidney Lumet. CRI [R] 125m. v

Dog Eat Dog 1964 U.S. ★★ Potboiler in which a stolen $1 million brings out the worst in all involved as they each try to make off with the loot. Mansfield is unintentionally hilarious, and the script is downright silly; improves when seen very late at night. C: Cameron Mitchell, Jayne Mansfield. D: Gustav Gavrin. ACT 86m. v

Dog of Flanders, A 1959 ★★★½ Dutch boy and his grandfather rescue brutalized dog and nurse it back to health. Later, when boy runs away, faithful dog tracks him down. Based on silent film previously made from 1872 novel by Ouida. Effective children's tearjerker is well produced. C: David Ladd, Donald Crisp, Theodore Bikel. D: James B. Clark. FAM/DRA 96m. v

Dog Soldier: Shadows of the Past 1991 ★★½ Adult animated sci-fi pits a deranged bad guy who stole a lethal virus against an ex-Green Beret hired by the government to get it back. Violent; best for fans of Japanese animation. D: Hiroyuki Ebata. SFI 45m. v

Dog Soldiers 1978 *See* **Who'll Stop the Rain**

Dogfight 1991 ★★★ Bet between Marines on leave to see who can find most unattractive date leads to unlikely love match between ugly duckling Taylor and young corporal Phoenix. Director Savoca scores again with quirky, slice-of-life story set during Vietnam era. C: River Phoenix, Lili Taylor, Holly Near, Brendan Fraser. D: Nancy Savoca. DRA 94m. v

Dogpound Shuffle 1975 Canadian ★★★½ A hobo lives off earnings of his dog—until dog is sent to the pound and he must scrape together money to get him back. Precious but watchable, especially for families. (a.k.a. *Spot*) C: Ron Moody, David Soul, Pamela McMyler. D: Jeffrey Bloom. FAM/DRA 98m. v

Dogs in Space 1987 Australian ★★½ Australian cult film that's choppy and loud but also engaging, funny, and sweet, featuring an assortment of lost souls sharing a Melbourne squat in the hippie '70s. The title refers to the name of their punk rock group. C: Michael Hutchence, Saskia Post. D: Richard Lowenstein. MUS [R] 109m. v

Dogs of Hell 1983 ★ Amateurish low-budgeter about a pack of murderous rottweilers terrorizing a small town; producer Owensby plays the sheriff trying to stop them. Originally in 3-D. C: Earl Owensby, Bill Gribble. D: Worth Keeter. HOR [R] 90m. v

Dogs of War, The 1981 British ★★★ Tough mercenaries, hired to overthrow a West African dictator, run amuck in this adaption of the Frederick Forsyth best-seller. Confused, violent film features another great psychopath role for Walken. C: Christopher Walken, Tom Berenger, Colin Blakely. D: John Irvin. ACT [R] 109m. v

Doin' Time on Planet Earth 1988 ★★★ Teenager becomes convinced he's really an alien with a mission: to lead his "people" back to their home planet. Warm, eccentric comedy. C: Nicholas Strouse, Andrea Thompson, Adam West, Hugh O'Brian, Roddy McDowall, Maureen Stapleton. D: Charles Matthau. COM [PG] 83m. v

Doing Time 1979 British ★★★★ Two career criminals find the outside prison so horrendous, they scheme to break back into the slammer. Funny, gag-laden British comedy is a delight throughout. (a.k.a. *Porridge*) C: Ronnie Barker, Richard Beckinsale. D: Dick Clement. COM 95m.

Dolemite 1975 ★★½ Ex-con gets even with his old cellmates. Bizarre mishmash of black exploitation and kung fu vixen cinema gives this a certain cheap and cheesy fun quality. C: Rudy Ray Moore, Jerry Jones, Lady Reed. D: D'Urville Martin. ACT [R] 91m. v

Dolemite II: The Human Tornado ★★½ Rudy is back (!) as a lady's man who teams up with a madame and a chorus of kung fu kicking women to chase the mob out of town. Mindless exploitation. (a.k.a. *The Human Tornado.*) ACT [R] 98m. v

Doll Face 1946 ★★★½ Burlesque stripper Blaine becomes big Broadway star. Okay musical with good cast. Hit song: Como's "Hubba Hubba Hubba." C: Vivian Blaine, Dennis O'Keefe, Perry Como, Carmen Miranda. D: Lewis Seiler. MUS 80m. v

$ (Dollars) 1972 ★★★★ Security expert (Beatty) sets up a safeguard system for a bank, then conspires with assistant (Hawn) to rob it. All style and no substance, but so what? Fast and furious entertainment with plenty of twists. C: Warren Beatty, Goldie Hawn. D: Richard Brooks. COM [R] 119m. v

Dollmaker, The 1984 ★★★★ During WWII, a poor Kentucky family must leave the hills and move to Detroit where the father (Helm) can get work. When the workers strike and the family is destitute, his long-suffering wife begins to realize her productive talents as an artist. Excellent production in a fine, affecting drama. Change-of-pace role for Fonda, and she's terrific. C: Jane Fonda, Levon Helm, Amanda Plummer, Geraldine Page. D: Daniel Petrie. DRA 140m. v

Dollman 1991 ★★★½ This future cop (Thomerson) is tough as nails, armed to the teeth—but since landing on Earth, he's a foot tall! Interesting premise and highly entertaining. C: Tim Thomerson, Jackie Earle Haley, Kamala Lopez. D: Albert Pyun. ACT [R] 86m. v

Dollman vs. Demonic Toys 1993 ★ Pint-size alien hero teams with one of the miniaturized babes from *Bad Channels* against the tiny toy terrors. Film is padded (even at just over an hour this follow-up somehow manages to be worse than all of its predecessors). HOR [R] 65m. v

Doll's House, A 1973 British ★★★★ Ibsen's masterpiece about a woman trying to break free from her husband's crushing hold is powerfully played by Bloom and Hopkins. Slightly stagy, but still provocative. C: Claire Bloom, Anthony Hopkins, Ralph Richardson, Edith Evans, Denholm Elliott. D: Patrick Garland. DRA [G] 105m. v

Doll's House, A 1973 British ★★★★ Fonda's take on the classic Ibsen play, giving her view of the 19th-century heroine's problems with a difficult husband. Unusual, to say the least. C: Jane Fonda, David Warner, Trevor Howard, Delphine Seyrig, Edward Fox. D: Joseph Losey. DRA 99m. v

Dolls 1987 ★★★ In this gimmicky story, various characters seek shelter from a storm in mansion with Rolfe and his malevolent dolls. Film is given evocative treatment by director Gordon. Nice special effects, too. C: Ian Patrick Williams, Carolyn Purdy-Gordon, Carrie Lorraine. D: Stuart Gordon. HOR [R] 77m. v

Dolly Sisters, The 1945 ★★★★ Grable and Haver shine as vaudeville sister act in pretty Technicolor bonbon with many song standards and good new tune, "I Can't Begin to Tell You." C: Betty Grable, John Payne, June Haver, S.Z. Sakall, Reginald Gardiner. D: Irving Cummings. MUS 114m.

Dolores Claiborne 1995 ★★★★½ Bates gives a bravura performance in this adaptation of Stephen King's novel about a Maine housekeeper who may or may not have killed her employer. Not as graphic or violent as most King stories, but just as terrifying. C: Kathy Bates, Jennifer Jason Leigh, Judy Parfitt, Christopher Plummer, David Strathairn, Eric Bogosian. D: Taylor Hackford. HOR [R] 131m. v

Dom Za Vesanje 1990 *See* **Time of the Gypsies**

Dominick and Eugene 1988 ★★★★ One brother is a medical student, the other is a mildly retarded garbage collector. Touching exploration of family loyalty and human relationships. Every bit as good as the more successful *Rain Man*. C: Tom Hulce, Ray Liotta, Jamie Lee Curtis, Todd Graff. D: Robert M. Young. DRA [PG-13] 111m. v

Dominique 1978 British ★★★ Woman turns up dead—maybe—and her greedy husband could be to blame. Dry thriller helped by great cast. (a.k.a. *Dominique Is Dead* and *Avenging Spirit*) C: Cliff Robertson, Jean Simmons, Jenny Agutter, Simon Ward, Ron Moody, Flora Robson. D: Michael Anderson. CRI [PG] 100m. v

Dominique Is Dead 1978 *See* **Dominique**

Domino Kid, The 1957 ★★★★½ Embittered Calhoun ruthlessly tracks the five men who murdered his father and destroyed the family's cattle ranch. Solid Western tale of revenge remains riveting throughout, thanks to above-average production and insightful realistic performances. C: Rory Calhoun, Kristine Miller. D: Ray Nazarro. WST 73m.

Domino Principle, The 1977 ★★½ A murderer (Hackman) is enlisted by a mysterious organization dedicated to assassinating politicians. The talented cast does their best with improbable material. C: Gene Hackman, Candice Bergen, Richard Widmark, Mickey Rooney, Eli Wallach. D: Stanley Kramer. CRI [R] 104m. v

Domino 1989 ★ Documentarian (Neilsen) obsesses about sex in this boring misfire. Talentless cast, pretentious directing, clichéd writing. C: Brigitte Nielsen, Daniela Alzone, Tomas Arana. D: Ivana Massetti. DRA [R] 95m. v

Don Giovanni 1979 ★★★★★ One of the best-ever opera films. Lavish, faithful, with magnificent singing and clear, legible subtitles. Mozart's masterpiece retells the famous Don Juan story and Losey's film makes a marvelous introduction to its glories. D: Joseph Losey. MUS 185m. v

Don Is Dead, The 1973 ★★ Quickie attempt to cash in on success of *The Godfather* with another tale of internecine Mafia wars is tedious, pointlessly violent. Waste of a good cast. C: Anthony Quinn, Frederic Forrest, Robert Forster. D: Richard Fleischer. CRI 96m. v

Don Juan 1926 ★★★★ Barrymore plays the famous lover, swashbuckler, and bon vivant in the court of Lucretia Borgia. One of the great silent films, played with gusto and verve by all. Film's reputation now largely due to first release which was released with synchronized score and sound effects. C: John Barrymore, Mary Astor, Estelle Taylor, Warner Oland, Myrna Loy, Hedda Hopper. D: Alan Crosland. DRA 171m. v

Don Juan, Mi Querido Fantasma 1990 *See* **Don Juan, My Love**

Don Juan, My Love 1990 ★★★½ Ghost of Don Juan arises from his grave for a 24-hour spree, changing places with a sleazy actor playing Don Juan in a local theatrical production. Mistaken identity creates a wealth of confusion in slapstick comedy that's a lot of fun. (a.k.a. *Don Juan, Mi Querido Fantasma*) COM 96m. V

Don Q, Son of Zorro 1925 ★★★★½ Swashbuckler Fairbanks rides high as the next-generation hero in this silent classic sequel to the 1920 film. A wonderful turn by Fairbanks in the dual role, featuring both his action and comic abilities. C: Douglas Fairbanks, Mary Astor, Donald Crisp, Warner Oland, Jean Hersholt. D: Donald Crisp. ACT 111m. V

Don Quixote 1973 ★★★½ Nureyev was slightly past his prime when he starred in and choreographed this historically valuable document. Ballet fans will be pleased, star's earlier *Swan Lake* is even better. C: Rudolf Nureyev, Robert Helpmann, Lucette Aldous. D: Rudolf Nureyev. MUS [G] 110m. V

Dona Flor and Her Two Husbands 1978 Brazilian ★★★★ Newly married to a kind but passionless husband, Flor (Braga) is visited by the naked ghost of her rotten but sexy louse of an ex. Erotic comedy most famous for Braga's sex scenes. C: Sonia Braga, Jose Wilker, Mauro Mendonca. D: Bruno Barreto. COM [R] 105m. V

Dona Herlinda and Her Son 1986 Mexican ★★★★ A seemingly sweet Mexican mama keeps her gay son at home by inviting his lover to move in, and further encouraging his other sexual dalliances. Bizarre treatment of the mothering instinct amusingly handled. C: Arturo Meza, Marco Antonio Trevino, Leticia Lupersio. D: Jaime Humberto Hermosillo. COM 90m. V

Dondi 1961 ★★½ Terribly sentimental tale about an Italian orphan boy who stows away in order to follow his G.I. friends back home. Adapted from a then-popular comic strip, this is hard to swallow and harder to watch. C: David Janssen, Patti Page, David Kory, Walter Winchell, Gale Gordon. D: Albert Zugsmith. FAM/DRA 100m.

Donkey Skin 1971 French ★★ From Charles Perrault's fairy tale about a newly widowed king who will only remarry a woman as lovely as his queen. Deneuve certainly fills the bill, but Demy's leaden touch sinks the wispy material. C: Catherine Deneuve, Jacques Perrin, Jean Marais, Delphine Seyrig. D: Jacques Demy. DRA 90m. V

Donner Pass—The Road to Survival 1978 ★★★½ Eighty-seven settlers from Illinois are trapped by snow in the Sierra Nevada in 1846. When food runs out, the survivors resort to cannibalism. TV movie about actual ill-fated wagon train pioneers emphasizes action over starvation. C: Robert Fuller, Andrew Prine, Diane McBain. D: James L. Conway. WST 98m. TVM V

Donovan Affair, The 1929 ★★★★ Early talkie combines mystery and comedy as a bullheaded inspector and his addlebrained assistant attempt to determine the killer of a debt-dodging gambler. Amusing early effort from Capra. C: Jack Holt, Dorothy Revier, William Collier, Jr., John Roche. D: Frank Capra. COM 83m.

Donovan's Brain 1953 ★★★★ Suspenseful adaptation of Curt Siodmak's novel, centering on a scientist (Ayres) who keeps the disembodied brain of a crooked millionaire alive and is taken over by its evil influence. Pulp premise made plausible by writer/director Feist and good cast. C: Lew Ayres, Gene Evans, Nancy Davis. D: Felix Feist. HOR 85m. V

Donovan's Reef 1963 ★★★½ A group of retired sailors find their island paradise in trouble when the very proper daughter of one of the buddies comes for a visit. A likable comedy. C: John Wayne, Lee Marvin, Elizabeth Allen, Jack Warden, Cesar Romero, Dorothy Lamour. D: John Ford. COM 109m. V

Don's Party 1976 Australian ★★★★½ Wickedly funny Australian satire involves a randy gathering of highly outspoken middle classers as they gather on election evening to watch the results. Sly humor and pointed direction fill this intellectual comedy with insight and humor. Based on David Williamson's play. C: John Hargreaves, Pat Bishop, Graham Kennedy, Veronica Lang. D: Bruce Beresford. COM 91m. V

Don't Answer the Phone 1980 ★★ Worth's bizarre performance is the only noteworthy aspect of this otherwise cheap, trashy shocker; he plays a psycho who constantly calls a radio psychiatrist when he's not out butchering female victims. C: James Westmoreland, Nicholas Worth, Flo Gerrish. D: Robert Hammer. HOR [R] 94m. V

Don't Be Afraid of the Dark 1973 ★★★½ A young couple (Darby and Hutton) inherit a house that's already occupied—by dangerous small creatures. A genuine fright. C: Kim Darby, Jim Hutton, William Demarest. D: John Newland. HOR 74m. TVM V

Don't Bother to Knock 1952 ★★★ Monroe is best part of this lesser drama, starring as hotel baby sitter whose mind becomes unhinged. Widmark saves her from suicide when Monroe thinks he's her dead boyfriend. Some good performances. Bancroft's first film. C: Richard Widmark, Marilyn Monroe, Anne Bancroft. D: Roy Baker. DRA 76m. V

Don't Cry, It's Only Thunder 1981 ★★★★ Fact-based drama about the efforts of an American soldier (Christopher) and a physician (St. James) to help Vietnam war orphans. Compelling wartime tale told with a minimum of sentiment. Based on a true story. C: Dennis Christopher, Susan St. James. D: Peter Werner. DRA [PG] 108m. V

Don't Drink the Water 1969 ★★½ Suspected of spying, American caterer (Gleason), wife, and daughter take asylum at U.S. embassy in Eastern Bloc nation of Vulgaria. Adaptation of Woody Allen's Broadway hit comedy fizzles on film. C: Jackie Gleason,

Estelle Parsons, Ted Bessell. D: Howard Morris. COM [G] 100m. V

Don't Give Up the Ship 1959 ★★★½ Lame-brained sailor (Lewis) loses a battleship and can't explain why or how it disappeared. Madcap mayhem, and a genuinely hilarious Lewis vehicle. C: Jerry Lewis, Dina Merrill, Diana Spencer, Gale Gordon. D: Norman Taurog. COM 89m.

Don't Go Near the Water 1957 ★★★½ Diverting WWII service comedy concerning the U.S. Navy press corps, trying to keep things lively on a remote Pacific island far away from the arena of action. Shaughnessy's foul-mouthed sailor and Clark's bombastic CPO bring in most of the laughs. C: Glenn Ford, Gia Scala, Anne Francis, Fred Clark, Eva Gabor, Keenan Wynn, Mickey Shaughnessy. D: Charles Walters. COM 102m. V

Don't Go to Sleep 1982 ★★★½ Selfish—and dead!—daughter wants her family to join her. Effective chiller. Good cast. C: Dennis Weaver, Valerie Harper, Ruth Gordon. D: Richard Lang. HOR 93m. TVM V

Don't Just Stand There 1968 ★★★ Debonair smuggler (Wagner) and companion (Moore) get in up to their ears in kidnapping and unfinished sex novels. Farce tries hard, gets points for stylishness. C: Robert Wagner, Mary Tyler Moore, Harvey Korman, Glynis Johns. D: Ron Winston. COM 100m.

Don't Knock the Rock 1956 ★★★ Rockers attempt to make community elders accept their music by reminding them how things were when they were young. Forget the plot and watch Bill Haley, Little Richard, The Treniers, and Dave Appell and His Applejacks bring the house down in this low-budget rock 'n' roll musical. C: Bill Haley, Alan Freed, Little Richard, Alan Dale, The Treniers. D: Fred Sears. MUS 84m.

Don't Let the Angels Fall 1969 Canadian ★★★★ A middle-class businessman questions his supposedly happy family life after succumbing to the charms of a young woman during a business trip. Insightful drama effectively addresses alienation and hopelessness in today's impersonal society. C: Arthur Hill, Sharon Acker, Charmion King, Jonathan Michaelson. D: George Kaczender. DRA 97m.

Don't Look Back 1967 ★★★★★ Pennebaker's brilliant documentary of Bob Dylan's 1965 English tour captures the singer/songwriter at his peak. Entertaining and worthwhile, even for non-Dylan fans. C: Bob Dylan, Joan Baez, Donovan, Alan Price. D: D.A. Pennebaker. MUS 96m.

Don't Look in the Basement 1973 ★ Deranged inmates take over mental institution. Flimsy characters, cheap effects, and inane plot development. C: William McGee, Annie MacAdam. D: S.F. Brownrigg. HOR [R] 94m. V

Don't Look Now 1973 British ★★★★ Bereaved father visiting Venice is haunted by the image of his drowned little daughter darting throughout the ancient, crumbling city. Tricky, adult horror drama, with intensely erotic relationship between Sutherland and Christie. Based on a Daphne du Maurier story. C: Julie Christie, Donald Sutherland. D: Nicolas Roeg. HOR [R] 110m. V

Don't Make Waves 1967 ★★★½ A salesman (Curtis) plots revenge on the woman who destroyed his car. Both Curtis and Tate are genuinely amusing in this madcap farce about the California lifestyle during the swingin' '60s. C: Tony Curtis, Claudia Cardinale, Sharon Tate, Robert Webber, Mort Sahl, Jim Backus, Edgar Bergen, Dave Draper. D: Alexander Mackendrick. COM 97m.

Don't Raise the Bridge, Lower the River 1968 ★★ Lewis plays an American schemer in England whose marriage goes on rocks when he turns home into a disco. Rather sour Lewis farce boasts delightful Terry-Thomas. C: Jerry Lewis, Terry-Thomas. D: Jerry Paris. COM [G] 99m. V

Don't Take It to Heart 1945 British ★★★★ Accidental explosion releases a spirit trapped in an ancient English manor, who then begins meddling in the affairs of all those around the castle. Whimsical British comedy/fantasy scares up lots of laughs with its offbeat humor. C: Richard Greene, Patricia Medina. D: Jeffrey Dell. COM 89m.

Don't Tell Her It's Me 1990 ★★ Shy, sickly artist Guttenberg yearns to meet attractive young writer Gertz. When his meddling sister Long contrives to transform him into a desirable hunk on a motorcycle, lame comedy/romance quickly runs out of gas. C: Steve Guttenberg, Jami Gertz, Shelley Long, Kyle MacLachlan. D: Malcolm Mowbray. COM [PG-13] 102m. V

Don't Tell Mom the Babysitter's Dead 1991 ★★★½ Kids must fend for themselves when Mom and Dad take off for Europe and the sitter suddenly passes away. Soon they realize freedom isn't all it's cracked up to be. Clunky and bland, it nonetheless provides some good laughs. C: Christina Applegate, Joanna Cassidy, John Getz. D: Stephen Herek. COM [PG-13] 103m. V

Don't Trust Your Husband 1948 *See* **Innocent Affair, An**

Don't Turn the Other Cheek 1974 Italian ★★★½ An unkempt Mexican bandido, a bogus Russian nobleman, and an idealistic Irish reporter team up during the revolution in Mexico. Entertaining, spaghetti-Western farce. C: Franco Nero, Lynn Redgrave, Eli Wallach. D: Duccio Tessari. WST [PG] 117m. V

Doolins of Oklahoma, The 1949 ★★★ Scott ably plays outlaw who tries to go straight, but just can't avoid the bad influences of the gang he leads. Plenty of action but run-of-the-mill story. C: Randolph Scott, George Macready, Louise Allbritton. D: Gordon Douglas. WST 90m.

Doom Asylum 1988 ★ Demented squatter in

an abandoned madhouse attacks youngsters who have invaded his turf. Substandard slasher. C: Patty Mullen, Ruth Collins. D: Richard Friedman. HOR [R] 77m. V

Doomwatch 1972 British ★★★ Ecologists inspect a Cornish fishing community where toxic waste has caused mutations in the inhabitants. Despite eerie atmosphere, it's more formulaic detective drama than horror, with grotesque villagers (properly) shown as victims, not monsters. Based on a British TV series. C: Ian Bannen, Judy Geeson, George Sanders. D: Peter Sasdy. DRA 90m. V

Door to Door 1984 ★★★ Two traveling sales reps scheme more than they sell as their misadventures land them in hot water with both authorities and customers. Slight comedy is mildly diverting. C: Ron Leibman, Arliss Howard, Jane Kaczmarek, Alan Austin. D: Patrick Bailey. COM [PG] 93m. V

Door with Seven Locks, The 1962 German ★★★ Creepy remake of *Chamber of Horrors* tells of man whose last will inspires desperate competition among his successors when he bequeaths to each a separate key to his treasure vault. C: Eddie Arent, Heinz Drache, Klaus Kinski. D: Alfred Vohrer. HOR 96m.

Doors, The 1991 ★★★½ The story of the famous rock group with special emphasis on the rise and fall of their charismatic leader, Jim Morrison (Kilmer). Lots of rock and drugs to go with it. Entertaining, but most effective on surface level as a re-creation of a period in time. C: Val Kilmer, Meg Ryan, Frank Whaley, Kevin Dillon, Kyle MacLachlan, Billy Idol. D: Oliver Stone. MUS [R] 135m. V

Doorway to Hell 1930 ★★★★½ Beer bootlegger Ayres hangs up his tommy gun and goes straight until rival rumrunners kill his kid brother. Rousing gangster film features lots of action peppered with ironic humor. Second film appearance by Cagney, who ignites the screen as Ayres' gangster lieutenant. C: Lew Ayres, Charles Judels, Dorothy Matthews, James Cagney. D: Archie Mayo. CRI 78m.

Doppelganger 1969 *See* **Journey to the Far Side of the Sun**

Dorian Gray 1971 Italian ★★ Updated remake of Oscar Wilde's famed novel features Berger as the playboy whose portrait ages, reflecting all his sins, while he remains young and handsome. Slow paced and dull. (a.k.a. *The Secret of Dorian Gray*) C: Helmut Berger, Richard Todd, Herbert Lom. D: Massimo Dallamano. DRA [R] 86m. V

Dorothy and Alan at Norma Place 1987 ★★★★½ Dorothy Parker was a talented writer and noted wit who held court at the famed Algonquin Roundtable in NYC in the '30s and '40s. This biography is a fresh and lively look at the spirit of Parker and of her life, full of her witticisms and phrases. C: Strawn Bovee, George LaFleur, Jared Rutter. DRA 120m. V

Dorothy in the Land of Oz ★½ Uninteresting further adventures of characters from *The Wizard of Oz*, in animated format. Pass on this one. FAM/DRA V

Dossier 51 1978 French ★★★★ A diplomat is the unwitting target of surveillance by his own side. Compelling spy tale of paranoia and betrayal. C: Francois Marthouret, Claude Mercault, Philippe Rouleau, Nathalie Juvet. D: Michel Deville. CRI 108m.

Dot and the Bunny 1983 Australian ★★★★ Australian animated feature follows little red-haired Dot as she searches for a missing baby kangaroo but meets up with a mixed-up rabbit that longs to be anything but a hare. Real-life backgrounds create a unique look for this endearing children's adventure tale. Voices of Drew Forsythe, Barbara Frawley, Ron Haddrick, Ann Haddy. D: Yoram Gross. FAM/DRA 80m.

Double Dragon 1994 ★★★½ Action-packed story based on popular video game is set in Los Angeles, circa 2007, where two teenagers (Dacascos, Wolf) are in a fight to the finish with the deadly Koga Shuko (Patrick). Pumped-up pacing and special effects deliver the goods. C: Robert Patrick, Mark Dacascos, Scott Wolf. D: James Yukich. ACT [PG-13] 99m. V

Double Dynamite 1951 ★★ In this labored comedy, a bank clerk is mistaken for a robber. Laughs rarely materialize. C: Frank Sinatra, Jane Russell, Groucho Marx. D: Irving Cummings. COM 80m. V

Double Edge 1991 U.S. ★★½ An aggressive reporter (Dunaway) is assigned to Jerusalem and becomes involved with both an Israeli officer and a family of Palestine Arabs. An even-handed treatment of the Israeli-Arab conflict, but the script lacks tension. Interviews with real political figures are an interesting touch. C: Faye Dunaway, Amos Kollek. D: Amos Kollek. DRA [PG-13] 85m. V

Double Exposure 1982 ★★★½ Photographer Callan has murderous nightmares that appear to be coming true in this complex, satisfying psychological thriller. C: Michael Callan, Joanna Pettet. D: William B. Hillman. CRI [R] 95m. V

Double Hit *See* **The Next Man**

Double Identity 1940 *See* **River's End**

Double Identity 1990 ★★★★ A college professor with a hidden criminal past (Mancuso) tries to restart his life in a new town with a new identity. The past, alas, all too soon catches up with him. Interesting drama, though a real downer. C: Nick Mancuso, Leah Pinsent, Patrick Bauchau, Anne Letourneau. D: Yves Boisset. DRA [PG-13] 92m. V

Double Impact 1991 ★★★ Two brothers (Van Damme x 2) join forces to avenge the murder of their parents. An entertaining rarity: a karate film with a sense of humor! C: Jean-Claude Van Damme, Geoffrey Lewis. D: Sheldon Lettich. ACT [R] 107m. V

Double Indemnity 1944 ★★★★★ Film noir

classic features MacMurray, brilliantly cast against type, as an insurance salesman duped into killing Stanwyck's husband. Robinson is MacMurray's loyal boss who gradually realizes something is amiss. Excellent adaptation of James M. Cain's novel by director Wilder and fellow crime writer Raymond Chandler. Remade (sort of) in 1981 as *Body Heat.* C: Barbara Stanwyck, Fred MacMurray, Edward G. Robinson, Porter Hall. D: Billy Wilder. CRI 107m. V

Double Jeopardy 1992 ★★★½ Sela Ward takes on defense of husband Boxleitner's old girlfriend Rachel Ward, accused of murder, and gradually realizes the past affair isn't over. Wildly improbable courtroom drama goes heavy on the passion, with some good performances. C: Rachel Ward, Sela Ward, Bruce Boxleitner, Sally Kirkland. D: Lawrence Schiller. DRA [R] 100m. TVM V

Double Life, A 1947 ★★★★ Backstage story, knowingly scripted by Garson Kanin and Ruth Gordon, features Colman as actor who finds his role as Shakespeare's "Othello" consuming his entire life. Oscars for Colman and Score by Miklos Rozsa. C: Ronald Colman, Signe Hasso, Shelley Winters, Edmond O'Brien. D: George Cukor. DRA 103m. V

Double Life of Veronique, The 1991 Polish ★★★½ The destinies of two identical women, one French and one Polish, who share the same name and looks merge in this uncanny mystery. Complex, textured work delivers a strong beginning, but lags in the finale. C: Irene Jacob, Wladyslaw Kowalski, Philippe Volter. D: Krzysztof Kieslowski. DRA 96m. V

Double Man, The 1967 British ★★½ A British spy extravaganza casts Brynner as both an American CIA agent seeking information about his son's skiing death and as his East German look-alike. The European footage is magnificent, especially the scenes in the Alps, but the ending is disappointing. C: Yul Brynner, Britt Ekland, Clive Revill. D: Franklin Schaffner. CRI 105m.

Double McGuffin, The 1979 ★★½ Lackluster mystery with group of small-town youths trying to foil the assassination of a foreign leader visiting the U.S. From producer of *Benji* movies and featuring voice-over narration by Orson Welles. Mainly for kids. C: Ernest Borgnine, George Kennedy, Elke Sommer, Vincent Spano. D: Joe Camp. FAM/CRI [PG] 100m. V

Double or Nothing 1937 ★★★½ Crosby, Raye, Devine, and Frawley all compete for $1 million in amusing musical. Highlight: Raye's comic striptease, "It's On, It's Off." C: Bing Crosby, Martha Raye, Andy Devine, William Frawley. D: Theodore Reed. MUS 95m.

Double Possession 1973 *See* **Black Vampire**

Double Suicide 1969 ★★★★ News dealer falls in love with courtesan, leaving neglected wife to run business. Shinoda's illuminating parable on the irrationality of desire works on many levels; visually impressive, with stylized sets and constantly moving camera. Director's wife Iwashita is superb playing both women. C: Kichiemon Nakamura, Shima Iwashita. D: Masahiro Shinoda. DRA 105m. V

Double Trouble 1966 ★★½ Is it ever! Elvis goes to Europe and gets mixed up with a band of jewel thieves. Typical Elvis vehicle. C: Elvis Presley, Annette Day. D: Norman Taurog. MUS 91m. V

Double Vision ★★½ A studious med student (Cattrall) assumes the identity of her wilder twin sister—who has disappeared in London—and soon finds herself involved in a lifestyle of depravity and murder. Rarely suspenseful adaptation of a Mary Higgins Clark short story. C: Kim Cattrall, Christopher Lee. CRI V

Double Wedding 1937 ★★★★ Loy and Powell took a break from the *Thin Man* series in this goofy romantic comedy. She designs clothing and he's an artist, and when they combine forces to fix up Loy's little sister they fall in love. Great slapstick, with an appealing conclusion that will disappoint only the most jaded viewer. C: William Powell, Myrna Loy, Florence Rice, Edgar Kennedy. D: Richard Thorpe. COM 87m. V

Doubting Thomas 1935 ★★★ Rogers wrangles with his wife (Burke) who wants to produce a variety show with her society friends. George Kelly's play *The Torch Bearers* was expanded to showcase Rogers' many talents. C: Will Rogers, Billie Burke, Alison Skipworth, Sterling Holloway, Gail Patrick. D: David Butler. COM 78m. V

Doughboys 1930 ★★★ Often overlooked comedy has Keaton accidentally enlisting in the Army and creating as much chaos behind the lines as on the front. Some funny moments in drag highlight his first talkie. (a.k.a. *Forward March*) C: Buster Keaton, Sally Eilers, Cliff Edwards. D: Edward Sedgwick. COM 80m. V

Doughgirls, The 1944 ★★★½ Sheridan, Smith, and Arden make good comic trio as sympathetic Army officers helping Carson and Wyman during WWII Washington honeymoon. Very slight, but amusing. C: Ann Sheridan, Alexis Smith, Jane Wyman, Eve Arden, Jack Carson. D: James Kern. COM 102m.

Dove, The 1974 ★★★★ Teenager embarks on global sailing trip. Mostly wholesome adventure based on true story, features fine cinematography in exotic ports of call. Ready to stir a young person's imagination. C: Joseph Bottoms, Deborah Raffin, Dabney Coleman. D: Charles Jarrott. DRA [PG] 105m. V

Down Among the Sheltering Palms 1953 ★★★ Army officer Lundigan gets romantically entangled with missionary's daughter Greer and native woman Gaynor, on a tropical South Sea island. Pleasant musical-comedy, highlighted by Harold Arlen and Ralph Blane's breezy score. C: William Lundigan, Jane Greer,

Mitzi Gaynor, David Wayne, Gloria DeHaven, Jack Paar. D: Edmund Goulding. MUS 87m.

Down and Dirty 1976 ★★★ Depressing drama concerns large family living in poverty outside Rome and the despicable patriarch (Manfredi) who exemplifies the clan's moral squalor. C: Nino Manfredi, Maria Bosco, Francesco Anniballi. D: Ettore Scola. DRA 115m.

Down and Out in Beverly Hills 1986 ★★★★ Dysfunctional wealthy family thrown into tumult by arrival of suicidal drifter (Nolte). Perfect casting infuses simple satire with wicked humor. C: Nick Nolte, Richard Dreyfuss, Bette Midler, Little Richard, Tracy Nelson. D: Paul Mazursky. COM [R] 103m. V

Down Argentine Way 1940 ★★★★ American heiress in hot pursuit of Ameche. First of several immensely entertaining Fox musical vehicles for Grable, with Miranda sensational in "South American Way." Unlikely Grable/Miranda team sparkles. C: Don Ameche, Betty Grable, Carmen Miranda, Charlotte Greenwood. D: Irving Cummings. MUS 94m. V

Down by Law 1986 ★★★★½ Lurie and Waits, framed in New Orleans, share a cell with the English mangling, irrepressible Benigni in this rambling jailbreak adventure. Consistently amusing, and beautifully photographed in black-and-white, it's an offbeat delight. C: Tom Waits, John Lurie, Roberto Benigni, Ellen Barkin. D: Jim Jarmusch. COM [R] 107m. V

Down Dakota Way 1949 ★★★★ Rogers and Evans ride to the rescue when a veterinarian, investigating a mysterious disease destroying the cattle herds, turns up dead. Above-average Western packs a load of action and thrills. C: Roy Rogers, Dale Evans, Pat Brady, Montie Montana, Elisabeth Risdon. D: William Whitney. WST 67m. V

Down Memory Lane 1949 ★★★★½ Humorist Allen hosts compilation of classic clips from the king of comedy, Mack Sennett, featuring a variety of silent bits as well as sound shorts from W.C. Fields and Bing Crosby. A laugh-filled treat, especially for film buffs. C: Steve Allen, Franklin Pangborn, Frank Nelson, Mack Sennett, W.C. Fields, Bing Crosby. D: Phil Karlson. COM 72m.

Down the Drain 1989 ★★★ Lawyer (Stevens) enlists some of his unsavory clientele to help him rob a bank. Diverting caper comedy only occasionally gets clogged. C: Andrew Stevens, John Matuszak, Teri Copley, Stella Stevens, Jerry Mathers. D: Robert C. Hughes. COM [R] 106m. V

Down to Earth 1932 ★★★★ A rich man (Rogers) pretends to go bankrupt to stop his family's spending spree. Warm, modest Rogers vehicle is a folksy treat. Sequel to *They Had To See Paris*. C: Will Rogers, Irene Rich, Dorothy Jordan. D: David Butler. COM 73m.

Down to Earth 1947 ★★★½ Hayworth cast as Greek mythology goddess of dance, Terpsichore, visiting Earth to help Parks put on a show. Earthbound musical helped by good dance numbers and Rita at her most ravishing, in glorious Technicolor. C: Rita Hayworth, Larry Parks, Marc Platt, Edward Everett Horton. D: Alexander Hall. MUS 101m. V

Down to the Sea in Ships 1922 ★★★ Family conflicts and romance engulf a New England whaling household. Fine use of location shooting and exciting whaling footage can't hoist uneventful story. Silent film is best remembered as feature debut of *It* girl Clara Bow. Remade in 1949. C: William Walcott, Marguerite Courtot, Clara Bow. D: Elmer Clifton. DRA 83m. V

Down to the Sea in Ships 1949 ★★★★ Lusty seafaring saga about generational conflict involving old salt Barrymore, scientifically educated newcomer Widmark, and captain's young grandson Stockwell. Fine direction and acting, with standout location footage and iceberg finale. C: Richard Widmark, Lionel Barrymore, Dean Stockwell, Cecil Kellaway, Gene Lockhart. D: Henry Hathaway. DRA 120m.

Down Twisted 1987 ★★½ A young American woman unwittingly becomes involved in a Central American caper when she's pursued by villains who think she has valuable artifact. Convoluted plot twists dominate overblown and cartoonish effort. C: Carey Lowell, Charles Rocket, Trudi Dochtermann. D: Albert Pyun. ACT [R] 89m. V

Down Under 1984 ★★ Two California boys enter the outback for predictable encounter with various things Australian. Narrated by Patrick MacNamee. C: Don Atkinson, Donn Dunlop, Patrick MacNee. DOC 90m. V

Downhill 1927 British ★★½ Silent melodrama about a worthy man's social decline. Creaky early Hitchcock effort. C: Ivor Novello, Ben Webster, Robin Irvine. D: Alfred Hitchcock. DRA 95m.

Downhill Racer 1969 ★★★★ Terrific film on skiers competing for World Cup/Olympics medals on the European circuit; chronicles the ups and downs of one ambitious, morally bankrupt young athlete from a lower-class background who is trying to make good. Brilliantly photographed; superbly underplayed by Redford. C: Robert Redford, Gene Hackman, Camilla Sparv, Dabney Coleman. D: Michael Ritchie. DRA [PG] 102m. V

Downstairs 1932 ★★★ Romantic intrigues in a baron's house revolve around the roguish butler (Gilbert). Good talkie effort by the charming star of silents. C: John Gilbert, Paul Lukas, Virginia Bruce, Hedda Hopper, Reginald Owen. D: Monta Bell. DRA 77m.

Downtown 1990 ★★½ Young cop Edwards from an affluent neighborhood is reassigned to the worst part of town, where he's partnered with inner-city detective Whitaker. C: Anthony Edwards, Forest Whitaker, Joe Pantoliano, David Clennon, Penelope Ann Miller. D: Richard Benjamin. CRI [R] 96m. V

Dr. Alien 1988 ★★ Dippy teen fantasy has a nerdlike freshman (Jacoby) becoming a ladies' man in an experiment conducted by his otherworldly biology teacher (Landers). A likable cast struggles with a predictable script. C: Judy Landers, Billy Jacoby, Olivia Barash, Linnea Quigley, Troy Donahue, Edy Williams. D: David De Coteau. HOR [R] 90m. v

Dr. Black and Mr. Hyde 1976 ★★★½ Kindly African-American physician Casey develops a potion to cure his kidney problem that instead turns him into a vicious white-skinned killer. Laughable take on the classic tale by Robert Louis Stevenson is low-budget camp at its best. (a.k.a. *The Watts Monster* and *Dr. Black and Mr. White*) C: Bernie Casey, Rosalind Cash. D: William Crain. HOR 88m. v

Dr. Black and Mr. White 1976 *See* **Dr. Black and Mr. Hyde**

Dr. Bull 1933 ★★★★ Rogers is delightful in title role as small-town physician who heals small minds and petty prejudices in addition to small and large sicknesses. Ford's folksy atmospherics suit bucolic humor well. C: Will Rogers, Marian Nixon, Ralph Morgan, Rochelle Hudson, Andy Devine. D: John Ford. DRA 75m.

Dr. Christian Jean Hersholt is probably best known for the Motion Picture Academy humanitarian award that bears his name, but for MGM and RKO, he was a dependable character actor, fatherly and warm. He brought those qualities to a radio series, *Dr. Christian*, in the mid-'30s, and two half-dozen B-movies RKO based on that series about small-town life, released between 1939 and 1941.

Meet Dr. Christian (1939)
The Courageous Dr. Christian (1940)
Dr. Christian Meets the Women (1940)
Remedy for Riches (1940)
Melody for Three (1941)
They Meet Again (1941)

Dr. Cyclops 1940 ★★★½ Well-mounted sci-fi thriller (the first in color) set in South America, where crazed scientist (Dekker) shrinks five visitors to a foot high. Resulting terrors (the doctor and now-giant animals) are convincingly realized with vivid effects. C: Albert Dekker, Thomas Coley, Janice Logan. D: Ernest B. Schoedsack. SFI 76m. v

Dr. Demento: 20th Anniversary Collection 1991 ★★★ Compilation video of cult disc jockey's favorite bizarre musical moments. Some strange laughs, but strictly for fans. MUS 60m. v

Dr. Ehrlich's Magic Bullet 1940 ★★★★ One of Hollywood's finest bios. Beautifully directed, with Robinson wonderful in gentle title role, and Kruger providing ace support. Best (but strangest) scene: discussing syphilis over dinner. C: Edward G. Robinson, Ruth Gordon, Otto Kruger, Donald Crisp, Maria Ouspenskaya. D: William Dieterle. DRA 103m.

Dr. Faustus 1968 British ★★ Marlowe's classic about medieval scholar Faustus exchanging his soul to Mephistopheles for the promise of a more passionate life. Thoroughly unmoving throughout. C: Richard Burton, Elizabeth Taylor, Andreas Teuber. D: Richard Burton, Nevill Coghill. DRA 93m. v

Dr. Giggles 1992 ★★ Every slasher cliché you thought had died in the mid-'80s is recycled in slick but empty-headed shocker about lunatic Drake (who thinks he's a doctor) carving his way through small-town teens. Alternately laughable and dull. C: Larry Drake, Cliff DeYoung. D: Manny Cotto. HOR [R] 99m. v

Dr. Gillespie's Criminal Case 1943 ★★★½ Dr. Kildare's crusty mentor (Barrymore) tries to aid a psychologically troubled murderer (Craven). Typically good medical series entry boasts a young supporting cast of future stars. C: Lionel Barrymore, Van Johnson, John Craven, Donna Reed, Keye Luke, Margaret O'Brien. D: Willis Goldbeck. CRI 89m.

Dr. Gillespie's New Assistant 1942 ★★★½ Three interns vie for the plum job of replacing Dr. Kildare. Well-produced medical drama, as you'd expect from the long-running series. C: Lionel Barrymore, Van Johnson, Susan Peters, Richard Quine, Keye Luke. D: Willis Goldbeck. DRA 87m.

Dr. Goldfoot and the Bikini Machine 1966 ★★½ Goofball comedy has wacky, greedy scientist Price manufacturing lovely, gold-digging robot-women. Hybrid of beach and sci-fi genres results in campy '60s fun. Sequel? Of course! *Dr. Goldfoot and the Girl Bombs.* C: Vincent Price, Frankie Avalon, Dwayne Hickman, Susan Hart. D: Norman Taurog. COM [G] 90m.

Dr. Goldfoot and the Girl Bombs 1966 Italian ★ A mad scientist (Price) tries to kill NATO generals by creating seductive woman robots, programmed to explode when their belly buttons are touched. Sophomoric comedy sequel to *Dr. Goldfoot and the Bikini Machine.* C: Vincent Price, Fabian, Franco Franchi, Laura Antonelli. D: Mario Bava. SFI 85m.

Dr. Heckyl and Mr. Hype 1980 ★★★★ Outrageous parody reverses the Robert Louis Stevenson classic by having repugnant foot doctor Reed turn into a suave charmer when he drinks a forbidden potion. This unlikely brew of horror and comedy is frequently hilarious. C: Oliver Reed, Sunny Johnson, Maia Danziger, Jackie Coogan. D: Charles B. Griffith. COM [R] 100m. v

Dr. Jekyll and Mr. Hyde 1920 ★★★★ Barrymore gives an outstanding performance as the mild-mannered doctor who turns into his vicious alter-ego Hyde. Silent version is highly effective. C: John Barrymore, Martha Mansfield, Brandon Hurst, Nita Naldi. D: John S. Robertson. HOR 63m. v

Dr. Jekyll and Mr. Hyde 1932 ★★★★½

March won an Oscar as the doctor who experiments with humanity's darker side, eventually becoming the murderous Hyde. Stylishly told adaptation of Robert Louis Stevenson's novel; 15 minutes of footage originally cut for rerelease have been restored. C: Fredric March, Miriam Hopkins, Rose Hobart. D: Rouben Mamoulian. HOR 96m. v

Dr. Jekyll and Mr. Hyde 1941 ★★★★ Retelling of Stevenson's oft-filmed classic of Victorian doctor transformed into a murderous beast by magic potion. Notable for atypical casting of Bergman—at her request—as the bad woman to Turner's good. Richly entertaining. C: Spencer Tracy, Ingrid Bergman, Lana Turner, Donald Crisp. D: Victor Fleming. HOR [G] 113m. v

Dr. Jekyll and Sister Hyde 1971 British ★★★★ Hammer adds an innovative twist to the old Robert Louis Stevenson tale with the good doctor turning into a woman for his/her deadly late-night jaunts. Great period production values and the Bates/Beswick casting is inspired—their resemblance is striking. C: Martine Beswick, Ralph Bates, Gerald Sim. D: Roy Ward Baker. HOR [PG] 94m. v

---

Dr. Kildare Max Brand is most remembered for his Westerns, but he worked in every genre imaginable, and his longest-running character is undoubtedly Dr. Kildare, an impulsive but goodhearted intern at Blair General Hospital. Introduced in the 1937 Paramount film, *Interns Can't Take Money*, with Joel McCrea as Kildare, the hospital setting offered inherent drama, which MGM was quick to pick up on. Beginning in 1938, Lew Ayres sparred with Lionel Barrymore, whose Dr. Gillespie held the hospital and the series together. In fact, after Ayres left the series in 1942 following *Dr. Kildare's Victory*, Barrymore continued for another six films.

Young Dr. Kildare (1938)
Calling Dr. Kildare (1939)
The Secret of Dr. Kildare (1939)
Dr. Kildare's Strange Case (1940)
Dr. Kildare Goes Home (1940)
Dr. Kildare's Crisis (1940)
The People vs. Dr. Kildare (1941)
Dr. Kildare's Wedding Day (1941)
Dr. Kildare's Victory (1942)
Calling Dr. Gillespie (1942)
Dr. Gillespie's New Assistant (1942)
Dr. Gillespie's Criminal Case (1943)
Three Men in White (1944)
Between Two Women (1944)
Dark Delusion (1947)

Dr. Kildare Goes Home 1940 ★★★½ Dr. Kildare (Ayres) tries to prove his medical abilities in his own hometown. Brisk addition to the popular Kildare caseload. C: Lew Ayres, Lionel Barrymore, Laraine Day. D: Harold S. Bucquet. DRA 78m.

Dr. Kildare's Crisis 1940 ★★★½ Kildare (Ayres) diagnoses his soon-to-be brother-in-law's illness as epilepsy. Is he right? Fine, typically well-mounted Kildare outing. C: Lew Ayres, Lionel Barrymore, Laraine Day, Robert Young. D: Harold S. Bucquet. DRA 75m.

Dr. Kildare's Strange Case 1940 ★★★½ Kildare (Ayres) must try experimental brain surgery to cure a patient. Solid entry in the fine medical series. C: Lew Ayres, Lionel Barrymore, Laraine Day, Shepperd Strudwick. D: Harold S. Bucquet. DRA 76m. v

Dr. Kildare's Victory 1942 ★★★½ A sick woman (Ayars) falls for the good doctor, but there's heart trouble ahead that Cupid can't fix. Good medical series entry; Ayres's last stint as Kildare. C: Lew Ayres, Lionel Barrymore, Ann Ayars, Robert Sterling. D: W.S. Van Dyke II. DRA 92m.

Dr. Kildare's Wedding Day 1941 ★★★½ Kildare (Ayres) plans to marry his longtime fiancee (Day), but fate intervenes. One of the best in the sturdy *Kildare* series. C: Lew Ayres, Lionel Barrymore, Laraine Day, Red Skelton, Fay Holden. D: Harold S. Bucquet. DRA 82m.

Dr. M. *See* **Club Extinction**

Dr. Mabuse, King of Crime 1922 German ★★★★½ Follow-up to *Dr. Mabuse, The Gambler* is actually the second half of the story begun in first film. Arch criminal Mabuse is now going mad in this silent classic of German expressionism. C: Rudolf KleinRogge, Gertrude Weicker. D: Fritz Lang. DRA 93m. v

Dr. Mabuse, the Gambler 1922 German ★★★★★ Silent espionage thriller enters the elaborate crime network of psychotic genius Mabuse. First installment of a two-part saga with *Dr. Mabuse, King of Crime*. Imaginative handling of decadent, high-tech mastermind clearly foreshadows the James Bond villains. C: Rudolf Klein-Rogge, Aud Nissen, Gertrude Welcker. D: Fritz Lang. CRI 120m. v

Dr. Minx 1975 ★★ Sordid erotic thriller centers on escapades of kinky academic (Williams) and her greedy lover. Lots of unintentional laughs here. Williams is the ex-Mrs. Russ Meyer. C: Edy Williams, Randy Boone. D: Howard Hikmet Avedis. ACT [R] 97m. v

Dr. No 1963 British ★★★★★ British agent 007 (Connery) with a "license to kill" travels to Jamaica to investigate the murder of another spy—and comes face-to-face with an evil genius (Wiseman) who is diverting American missiles from their flight paths. The movie that started the '60s spy craze is high-spirited fun and action all the way. C: Sean Connery, Ursula Andress, Joseph Wiseman, Jack Lord. D: Terence Young. ACT [PG] 111m. v

Dr. Otto and the Riddle of the Gloom Beam 1986 ★★★½ A mad doctor (Varney) changes his appearance several times to fulfill his plan to rule the world. Wacky, amusing comedy gave the star of the *Ernest* films his movie debut. C: Jim Varney, Glenn Petech, Myke Mueller, Jackie Welch. D: John R. Cherry III. COM [PG] 97m. V

Dr. Phibes Rises Again 1972 British ★★★½ Sequel to *The Abominable Dr. Phibes* is almost as good, with Price returning as the vengeful villain using ingenious methods to dispatch competitors for a potion with which he can revive his dead wife. Still pretty campy. C: Vincent Price, Robert Quarry, Peter Cushing, Terry-Thomas, Hugh Griffith. D: Robert Fuest. HOR [PG] 89m. V

Dr. Rhythm 1938 ★★★½ Crosby pretends to be a policeman to be close to his lady love (Carlisle). Congenial semi-musical, with a notable appearance by the great comic Lillie. C: Bing Crosby, Mary Carlisle, Beatrice Lillie, Andy Devine, Sterling Holloway. D: Frank Tuttle. MUS 80m.

Dr. Socrates 1935 ★★★★ A noble doctor (Muni) is forced to minister to the underworld. Fast-paced melodrama, with an excellent cast, offers a rare instance of Muni appearing without elaborate makeup. Remade in 1939 as *King of the Underworld.* C: Paul Muni, Ann Dvorak, Barton MacLane. D: William Dieterle. CRI 70m.

Dr. Strange 1978 ★★★ Marvel Comics' superhero must stop a wicked witch from snatching men's souls. Assisting him (and stealing the show) is a seen-it-all wizard. Not terrible, but cut-rate production values don't help. C: Peter Hooten, Clyde Kusatsu, Jessica Walter. D: Philip DeGuere. SFI 100m. V

Dr. Strangelove or: How I Learned To Stop Worrying and Love the Bomb 1964 British ★★★★★ Cold-war black comedy classic about an insane general launching nuclear attack on USSR. Sellers is brilliant in triple role of U.S. President, British officer, and eccentric title character, inventor of the Bomb. Highlights include phone call between President and Soviet leader and Pickens' final ride. C: Peter Sellers, George C. Scott, Sterling Hayden, Slim Pickens, Keenan Wynn. D: Stanley Kubrick. COM [PG] 93m. V

Dr. Syn 1937 British ★★★½ Arliss is a prim clergyman by day, pirate by night. Exciting tale, even if the star's a bit long in the tooth for swashbuckling. Remade as a Disney movie (*Dr. Syn, Alias the Scarecrow*) in 1964. C: George Arliss, Margaret Lockwood, John Loder. D: Roy William Neil. ACT 80m. V

Dr. Syn, Alias the Scarecrow 1964 ★★★½ McGoohan stars as a vicar by day and an avenger by night, righting wrongs in the time of England's George III. From three-part Disney TV series. Somewhat predictable family fare, but greatly enlivened by lead performance. C: Patrick McGoohan, George Cole, Tony Britton. D: James Neilson. FAM/ACT [G] 129m. V

Dr. Tarr's Torture Dungeon 1972 ★★½ Mexican production, based on Poe's story "The System of Dr. Tarr and Professor Feather," about a journalist discovering that the inmates of an asylum have literally taken it over. Weirdly stylish if minor effort, with copious erotic elements. C: Claudio Brook, Ellen Sherman. D: Jaun Lopez Moctezuma. HOR 88m. V

Dr. Terror's House of Horrors 1965 British ★★★½ Highly effective British trilogy centers around a fortune teller (Cushing) and his clients' very bloody (and short) futures. C: Peter Cushing, Christopher Lee, Max Adrian, Donald Sutherland. D: Freddie Francis. HOR 98m. V

Dr. Who and the Daleks 1965 British ★★★★ Dr. Who (Cushing) treats his friends to an excursion they won't forget—through outer space and distant time. Entertaining sci-fi, based on the long-running British TV series. C: Peter Cushing, Roy Castle, Jennie Linden. D: Gordon Flemyng. SFI 85m. V

Dracula 1931 ★★★★ First sound version of Bram Stoker's classic is still most famous, and made Lugosi's performance an enduring icon. Atmospheric. C: Bela Lugosi, David Manners, Helen Chandler, Dwight Frye. D: Tod Browning. HOR 75m. V

Dracula 1957 *See* **Horror of Dracula**

Dracula 1973 ★★★½ Palance is in fine form as the Count, terrorizing London and falling for Lewis. Opulent settings forsake some of the traditional creepiness, but a respectful adaptation of Stoker's story nonetheless. C: Jack Palance, Simon Ward, Nigel Davenport, Pamela Brown, Fiona Lewis. D: Dan Curtis. HOR 105m. TVM V

Dracula 1979 ★★ Misguided remake has a big budget and Langella reprising his Broadway performance as the vampire Count, but he's overwhelmed by flashy visuals and a dramatically empty—and pointlessly altered—interpretation of Stoker's story. C: Frank Langella, Laurence Olivier, Donald Pleasence, Kate Nelligan. D: John Badham. HOR [R] 109m. TVM V

Dracula A.D. 1972 British ★★★ As the title suggests, this Hammer entry finds the Count alive (?) and well in 1970s London, still pursued by Cushing as a modern-day Van Helsing. "Trendy" settings render this one silly—and dated, too. C: Peter Cushing, Christopher Lee, Stephanie Beacham, Michael Coles, Caroline Munro. D: Alan Gibson. HOR [PG] 98m.

Dracula and Son 1979 French ★★ The caped one, much to his horror, fathers a lad who shows no interest in following his dad's bloodsucking ways. Despite funny premise, tepid horror spoof has trouble scaring up laughs. C: Christopher Lee, Bernard Menez, Marie-Helene Breillat. D: Eduard Molinaro. COM [PG] 78m. V

Dracula Has Risen From the Grave 1968 British ★★★ After performing exorcism rites in front of Dracula's castle, priest becomes target of the Count's revenge. Somewhat predictable fare. C: Christopher Lee, Rupert Davies. D: Freddie Francis. HOR [G] 92m. V

Dracula—Prince of Darkness 1966 British ★★★½ Second entry in the British horror series (following *Horror of Dracula*) finds Lee, everyone's favorite bloodsucking count, terrorizing a quartet of wayward travelers who dare to venture into his castle. Sincere treatment of subject matter conjures up a few scares. C: Christopher Lee, Barbara Shelley, Andrew Keir. D: Terence Fisher. HOR 90m.

Dracula vs. Frankenstein 1970 *See* **Assignment Terror**

Dracula's Daughter 1936 ★★★ Sophisticated Baroness (Holden) has a thirst for blood of the living, enlists aid of psychiatrist to release her from this curse. Provocative sequel to Lugosi classic. C: Gloria Holden, Otto Kruger, Irving Pichel, Nan Grey, Hedda Hopper. D: Lambert Hillyer. HOR 70m. V

Dracula's Dog 1978 ★★½ An ancient follower of Dracula accompanies title pooch to America in search of the count's modern descendant. Not quite as bad as it sounds, but early inventiveness runs out. C: Jose Ferrer, Michael Pataki. D: Albert Band. HOR [R] 90m. V

Dracula's Widow 1988 ★★ Former softcore queen Kristel plays the Countess, who arrives in modern Los Angeles seeking a new mate and stakes out Von Dohlen. Occasionally gruesome, mediocre attempt to update the legend. C: Josef Sommer, Sylvia Kristel, Lenny Von Dohlen. D: Christopher Coppola. HOR [R] 85m. V

Dragnet 1954 ★★★ Sgt. Joe Friday and officer Frank Smith investigate the murder of an ex-convict. Webb's straightforward directing and acting style make his first attempt to bring his popular TV show to the big screen more a comedy than a crime drama. C: Jack Webb, Ben Alexander, Richard Boone. D: Jack Webb. CRI 88m. V

Dragnet 1987 ★★★ Spoofy updating of sober TV series finds Joe Friday's nephew, an LAPD detective, on the trail of a bizarre religious cult. Aykroyd's dead-on portrayal of Joe Friday is hilarious; the rest of the movie should have been arrested. C: Dan Aykroyd, Tom Hanks, Christopher Plummer, Harry Morgan, Alexandra Paul, Elizabeth Ashley, Dabney Coleman. D: Tom Mankiewicz. COM [PG-13] 106m. V

Dragon Chow 1987 ★★★ Newly arrived immigrants hope to succeed in their new home in Germany. Well-observed study of newcomers struggling to overcome seemingly insurmountable culture and language barriers. Director Schutte's feature debut. C: Bhasker, Ric Young, Buddy Uzzaman. D: Jan Schutte. DRA 75m. V

Dragon Fist ★★½ Kung fu expert seeks revenge for the killing of his master. Plenty of bone-crunching action for martial arts fans. ACT

Dragon Flies, The 1975 *See* **Man from Hong Kong, The**

Dragon Seed 1944 ★★★ Small Japanese village undergoes turmoil and change after invasion by Chinese forces. Overlong adaptation of Pearl S. Buck's novel, though good cast tries to make best of talky script. C: Katharine Hepburn, Walter Huston, Aline MacMahon, Turhan Bey, Hurd Hatfield, Agnes Moorehead, Akim Tamiroff. D: Jack Conway, Harold S. Bucquet. DRA 149m. V

Dragon: The Bruce Lee Story 1993 ★★★★ Well-done biography of the martial arts hero who died mysteriously at 33 examines his brief but spectacular career and his personal and professional struggles. Exciting action scenes and strong performances in a truly inspiring story. C: Jason Scott Lee, Lauren Holly, Robert Wagner, Michael Learned, Nancy Kwan. D: Rob Cohen. ACT [PG-13] 120m. V

Dragon vs. Needles of Death ★★½ Kung fu masters find themselves up against the deadliest foes: wristbands containing the needles of death. Genre martial arts film with a twist. ACT V

Dragon Wells Massacre 1957 ★★ Cynical gunslinger leads a wagon train on a perilous journey through bloodthirsty Apache territory. Clichéd Western offers no surprises. (a.k.a. *Dragoon Wells Massacre*) C: Barry Sullivan, Dennis O'Keefe, Katy Jurado, Sebastian Cabot. D: Harold Schuster. WST 88m.

Dragonfly 1976 *See* **One Summer Love**

Dragons Forever 1988 ★★★ In this martial-arts comedy, lawyer with a conscience helps fishers in fight against area takeover by chemical plant. Legendary kung fu star Chan and zesty action make this one watchable. C: Jackie Chan. D: Samo Hung. COM 88m.

Dragon's Showdown, The 1983 ★★½ A son is out to avenge the honor of his parents after he witnesses their murders. Plenty of action within ritualized format. C: Dragon Lee. D: Godfrey Ho. ACT [R] 90m. V

Dragonslayer 1981 ★★★½ Medieval fantasy yarn of a fledgling wizard (MacNicol) whose destiny it is to rub out the large mythic lizard. Excellent effects and an all too brief appearance by Richardson are the highlights, but overall heavy and dreary. Too violent for young children. C: Peter MacNicol, Caitlin Clarke, Ralph Richardson. D: Matthew Robbins. SFI [PG] 110m. V

Dragonwyck 1946 ★★★★ Tierney plays innocent country dweller who marries a rich cousin with a dark secret. Gothic suspense yarn with psychotic flourishes from Price. Adapted from Anya Seton's best-seller. C: Gene Tierney, Walter Huston, Vincent Price, Anne Revere, Spring Byington, Jessica Tandy. D: Joseph Mankiewicz. HOR 103m.

Dragoon Wells Massacre 1957 *See* **Dragon Wells Massacre**

Drama of Jealousy, A 1970 *See* **Pizza Triangle, The**

Dramatic School 1938 ★★★ Rainer gives awkward portrayal as stagestruck acting novice struggling to make good in marriage and career. Rest of cast tries hard, but sentimental story seems contrived. C: Luise Rainer, Paulette Goddard, Alan Marshal, Lana Turner, Genevieve Tobin. D: Robert Sinclair. DRA 80m.

Drango 1957 ★★½ Civil War veteran Chandler hangs up his Union blues and travels south to restore order to a Georgian town he destroyed during the war. Shadowy Western fails to wring deeper meaning from its story. C: Jeff Chandler, Joanne London, Donald Crisp. D: Hall Bartlett, Jules Bricken. WST 92m.

Draughtsman's Contract, The 1982 British ★★★½ When a rich woman hires a virile artist to draw her estate, she compensates him with sexual favors. Cryptic film of sex, murder, and art in period England. Difficult and cold, though Greenaway fans claim it's brilliant. C: Anthony Higgins, Janet Suzman, Hugh Fraser. D: Peter Greenaway. DRA [R] 103m. V

Draw! 1984 ★★★½ Drunken sheriff tries to bring has-been gunfighter to justice. Amusing showdown Western with a light touch. C: Kirk Douglas, James Coburn. D: Steven Hilliard Stern. WST 90m. TVM V

Dream a Little Dream 1989 ★ Young and old trade places in this forgettable body-switch comedy. Feldman is getting nowhere with dream girl Salenger until Robards steps in to help. Will bore both the young and the young at heart. C: Corey Feldman, Meredith Salenger, Jason Robards, Piper Laurie, Harry Dean Stanton. D: Marc Rocco. COM [PG-13] 114m. V

Dream Date 1989 ★★★ A teenager prepares for her first date, and her overprotective father fears her escort will be as rambunctious as he was at that age. Light comedy, lively cast. C: Clifton Davis, Tempest Bedsoe. D: Anson Williams. COM 96m. TVM V

Dream for Christmas, A 1979 ★★★½ Heartwarming story of black country pastor and his family who move from Arkansas to Los Angeles to take over a poor congregation housed in physically deteriorating church about to be razed. Inspiring '50s period piece stresses positive family values. C: Hari Rhodes, Beah Richards, Lynn Hamilton, Juanita Moore. D: Ralph Senensky. FAM/DRA 96m. TVM V

Dream Girl 1948 ★★½ An unhappy woman (Hutton) enjoys her Walter Mitty-like dreams until one threatens to become real. Tepid comedy based on play by Elmer Rice. C: Betty Hutton, Macdonald Carey. D: Mitchell Leisen. COM 85m.

Dream Lover 1986 ★★★ Undistinguished, fluffy scientific thriller about a dream researcher aiding the murder investigation of a New York woman who has killed an intruder. C: Kristy McNichol, Ben Masters, Justin Deas. D: Alan J. Pakula. CRI [R] 105m. V

Dream Machine, The 1991 ★★ Wish fulfillment teen comedy shows Haim purchasing a Porsche for next to nothing. It turns out there's a murdered man in the trunk and the killer is still at large, but story maintains a party's-on attitude regardless. C: Corey Haim, Evan Richards. D: Lyman Dayton. COM [PG] 86m. V

Dream of Kings, A 1969 ★★★★ A poetic Greek immigrant (Quinn) living in Chicago tries to raise money to take his sick son back to Greece. Stevens plays a widow who's attracted to Quinn. Emotional and exuberant, but also more than a tad sentimental. C: Anthony Quinn, Irene Papas, Inger Stevens, Sam Levene. D: Daniel Mann. DRA [R] 107m. V

Dream of Passion, A 1978 Greek ★★½ Prententious modern-day version of Greek tragedy *Medea* with actress Mercouri becoming obsessed by American Burstyn, imprisoned in Athens for murdering three children. Two women's intense emoting has little impact, due to stagy script. C: Melina Mercouri, Ellen Burstyn. D: Jules Dassin. DRA [R] 106m. V

Dream Team, The 1989 ★★★★ Four lunatics are let loose on the streets of New York City when their doctor gets mugged during a field trip to a baseball game. Delightful wacky comedy never at a loss for laughs, thanks to clever scripting and looney performances. C: Michael Keaton, Christopher Lloyd, Peter Boyle, Dennis Boutsikaris, Lorraine Bracco. D: Howard Zieff. COM [PG-13] 113m. V

Dream to Believe 1985 ★★½ Modern, MTV-type musical is a Cinderella story of gymnast D'Abo surmounting all odds to win championship and Prince Charming (Reeves). Good concept. (a.k.a. *Flying.*) C: Rita Tushingham, Keanu Reeves, Olivia D'Abo. D: Paul Lynch. MUS 96m. V

Dream Wife 1953 ★★½ Executive (Grant) strays from independent wife (Kerr) and pretends to marry an Eastern princess (St. John) primarily interested in pleasing men. What was once sophisticated comedy now seems a bit dated. C: Cary Grant, Deborah Kerr, Walter Pidgeon, Betta St. John. D: Sidney Sheldon. COM 101m.

Dreamboat 1952 ★★★½ Former screen team (Rogers and Webb) have different reactions when their movies air on TV. One of the better Hollywood comedies satirizing its small-screen nemesis. C: Ginger Rogers, Clifton Webb, Jeffrey Hunter, Anne Francis, Elsa Lanchester. D: Claude Binyon. COM 83m.

DreamChild 1985 British ★★★★ Browne plays Alice Liddell, inspiration for Lewis Carroll's *Alice in Wonderland.* At age 80, Alice visits New York for centennial of Carroll's birth, only to be haunted by his creations. Masterful star performance and original conception with fascinating dream sequences. C:

Coral Browne, Ian Holm, Peter Gallagher, Caris Corfman. D: Gavin Millar. DRA [PG] 90m. V

Dreamer of Oz, The: The Frank L. Baum Story 1990 ★★★★ More or less true story of creator of *The Wizard of Oz*, well played by Ritter. Standard rags-to-riches story given boost by imaginative use of Baum's characters. Wholesome family fare. C: John Ritter, Annette O'Toole, Rue McClanahan. D: Jack Bender. FAM/DRA 100m. TVM

Dreamer 1979 ★★½ An underdog risks all to win the championship in his chosen sport—bowling! Not bad *Rocky*-in-bowling-shoes tale. C: Tim Matheson, Susan Blakely, Jack Warden. D: Noel Nosseck. DRA [PG] 86m.

Dreaming Lips 1937 British ★★★½ Rich but bored wife of well-known orchestra conductor throws caution to the wind by having an affair with troubled violinist. High-strung performances fill out the soap opera plot, with good lead by Bergner. C: Elisabeth Bergner, Raymond Massey, Felix Aylmer. D: Paul Czinner. DRA 69m. V

Dreams Lost, Dreams Found 1987 ★★★ After her husband dies, an American woman goes to her ancestral Scottish homeland where romance awaits. Handsome trifle, produced by Harlequin Romances. C: Kathleen Quinlan, David Robb. D: Willi Patterson. DRA 97m. TVM V

Dreams 1955 Swedish ★★★½ A model agency owner (Dahlbeck) and her protegee (Andersson) travel throughout Sweden looking for love and fullfillment with a variety of men. Middling Bergman. (a.k.a. *Journey Into Autumn*) C: Eva Dahlbeck, Harriet Andersson, Gunnar Bjornstrand. D: Ingmar Bergman. DRA 86m. V

Dreamscape 1983 ★★★★ Having nightmares? Don't worry, these doctors will send someone (Quaid) *into* your bad dreams and make them stop! Nifty plot and special effects. C: Dennis Quaid, Max Von Sydow, Christopher Plummer, Eddie Albert, Kate Capshaw. D: Joseph Ruben. SFI [PG-13] 99m. V

Dress Gray 1986 ★★★ Gay cadet is murdered at military academy, with the expected clash between guilt and honor. Suspenseful but stiff mystery. Adaptation by Gore Vidal. C: Alec Baldwin, Hal Holbrook, Lloyd Bridges. D: Glenn Jordan. DRA 192m. TVM V

Dressed to Kill 1946 ★★★½ When plates stolen from the Bank of England begin to show up in London, Holmes is hot on the trail. Final teaming of Rathbone and Bruce; they make it work splendidly, as usual. C: Basil Rathbone, Nigel Bruce, Patricia Morison. D: Roy Neill. CRI 72m. V

Dressed to Kill 1980 ★★★★ A cheating housewife (Dickinson) and a prostitute (Allen) who finds a body are stalked by a cross-dressing killer in New York. Liberal borrowings from Hitchcock add to a suspenseful, memorable thriller. C: Michael Caine, Angie Dickinson, Nancy Allen. D: Brian De Palma. CRI [R] 105m. V

Dresser, The 1983 British ★★★★ A jaded, brilliant Shakespearean actor (Finney) grows more and more reliant upon the faithful qualities of his devoted dresser (Courtney). Memorable backstage drama, outstanding leads. C: Albert Finney, Tom Courtenay, Edward Fox, Eileen Atkins. D: Peter Yates. DRA [PG] 119m. V

Dressmaker, The 1988 British ★★★★ Plain, timid Horrocks falls for an American G.I. in wartime Liverpool and sets off a terrible tragedy. Plowright and Whitelaw were in their acting prime as her two unmarried aunts, one a swinger, the other repressed. Good, unsentimental evocation of the period. C: Joan Plowright, Billie Whitelaw, Peter Postlethwaite, Jane Horrocks. D: Jim O'Brien. DRA 89m. V

Drifter, The 1988 ★★★½ An interior designer picks up a hitchhiker for a night of passion, only to find he won't get out of her life afterwards. Low-budget thriller from a woman's perspective. C: Kim Delaney, Timothy Bottoms, Miles O'Keeffe. D: Larry Brand. CRI [R] 89m. V

Drifting 1983 ★★★½ Young film director battles homophobia and internal pressures. First Israeli film to deal with openly gay themes. Resists sensationalism and is generally successful. C: Jonathan Sagalle, Ami Traub, Ben Levine. D: Amos Guttman. DRA 83m. V

Drifting Weeds 1959 *See* **Floating Weeds**

Drive a Crooked Road 1954 ★★½ A grease monkey (Rooney) finds himself in hot water with a gangster (Kelly) when he falls for moll (Foster). Slow-moving melodrama never gets out of first gear. C: Mickey Rooney, Dianne Foster, Kevin McCarthy. D: Richard Quine. DRA 82m.

Drive, He Said 1972 ★★★½ Jack Nicholson's directorial debut, the trials and travails of a college basketball team on the road. Strong performances from Dern and Black. C: William Tepper, Karen Black, Michael Margotta, Bruce Dern, Robert Towne. D: Jack Nicholson. DRA [R] 90m.

Drive-In 1976 ★★★½ Low-budget effort about lowlife antics of patrons of Texas drive-in theater including lovers, robbers, rednecks, and rock 'n' rollers. Spoofy disaster flick provides a continual stream of laughs. C: Lisa Lemole, Glen Morshower. D: Rod Amateau. COM [PG] 96m. V

Driver, The 1978 ★★★★½ In this idiosyncratic chase film, a professional driver of getaway cars (O'Neal) is pursued by a strange detective (Dern). The relentless action, spectacular chase sequences and clever double-crosses make an ebullient film. C: Ryan O'Neal, Bruce Dern, Isabelle Adjani. D: Walter Hill. ACT [PG] 131m. V

Driver's Seat, The 1975 Italian ★★ Misguided story for true Taylor fans only: a woman is determined to do herself harm, travels to Rome and is harassed by dangerous men along the way. Deeply botched arty fluff. (a.k.a. *Psychotic*) C: Elizabeth Taylor, Ian Bannen, Mona Washbourne, Andy Warhol. D: Giuseppe Patroni Griffi. DRA [R] 102m. v

Driving Force 1989 ★ Big ol' trucker wreaks havoc on postnuclear road hogs. This is road kill meant to be *Road Warrior*. Mucho violence. C: Sam Jones, Catherine Bach, Don Swayze. D: A.J. Prowse. ACT [R] 90m. v

Driving Miss Daisy 1989 ★★★★½ A calm, quiet and sturdy black man is hired to be chauffeur to an argumentative, aging Southern lady. Over many years they develop an unspoken devotion to each other. Fascinating characters, good historical evocation. A truly wonderful experience and worthy of its Oscars for Best Picture, Actress (Tandy), Screenplay, and Makeup. C: Jessica Tandy, Morgan Freeman, Dan Aykroyd, Patti LuPone, Esther Rolle. D: Bruce Beresford. DRA [PG] 99m. v

Drop Dead Fred 1991 ★★ An imaginary childhood friend wreaks havoc in young woman's life when he returns to her after the breakup of her marriage. Maniacal performance by Mayall only plus in this otherwise childish comedy. C: Phoebe Cates, Rik Mayall, Marsha Mason, Tim Matheson, Carrie Fisher. D: Ate DeJong. COM [PG-13] 103m. v

Drop-Out Mother 1988 ★★★ Successful public relations exec hangs up her suit to devote all her time to being housewife and mom. Entertaining diversion. C: Valerie Harper, Wayne Rogers, Carol Kane, Kim Hunter. D: Charles S. Dubin. COM 95m. TVM v

D.R.O.P. Squad 1994 ★★★½ Stands for Deprogramming and Restoration of Pride in this Spike Lee-produced piece about black activists fighting for better depiction in the media, beginning with upscale African-American ad execs. Well-intentioned but preachy. C: Eriq LaSalle, Vondie Curtis-Hall, Vanessa Williams. D: David Johnson. DRA

Drop Zone 1994 ★★★★ Snipes is U.S. marshall pursuing gang of sky divers trying to steal information on undercover drug agents. Full of stunning aerial stunts and fast-paced action. C: Wesley Snipes, Gary Busey, Yancy Butler, Michael Jeter, Corin Nemec, Kyle Secor. D: John Badham. ACT [R] 102m. v

Drowning by Numbers 1991 British ★★★½ Three women drown their husbands and escape detection thanks to a friendly coroner. More entertaining than usual Greenaway puzzle, with lively cast. C: Joan Plowright, Bernard Hill, Juliet Stephenson, Joely Richardson. D: Peter Greenaway. DRA [R] 121m. v

Drowning Pool, The 1975 ★★★½ Slow sequel to *Harper* features Newman again playing the Ross MacDonald detective, coming to the aid of an ex-lover (Woodward). Whodunit homage lacks its precursor's sparkle; saving grace is Newman's charm. C: Paul Newman, Joanne Woodward, Anthony Franciosa, Melanie Griffith. D: Stuart Rosenberg. CRI [PG] 109m. v

Drugstore Cowboy 1989 ★★★★ A group of young junkies rob drugstores to support their habits. Humorous, gritty film doesn't take sides, offering a fresh look at society's problem children. Lynch and Dillon are excellent as a pair of stoned lovers. Based on inmate James Fogle's unpublished autobiography. C: Matt Dillon, Kelly Lynch. D: Gus Van Sant Jr. DRA [R] 104m. v

Drum 1976 ★ This sequel to *Mandingo* set in pre-Civil War bordello in New Orleans is yet another wallow in bad taste and lurid cinematic excess. C: Warren Oates, Ken Norton, Pam Grier. D: Steve Carver. DRA [R] 89m. v

Drum Beat 1954 ★★★★ Former Indian fighter tries to make peace with an Oregon tribal chief. Bronson fine as the Modoc chieftain in this colorful action-packed Western. C: Alan Ladd, Audrey Dalton, Marisa Pavan, Charles Bronson. D: Delmer Daves. WST 111m. v

Drum, The 1938 *See* **Drums**

Drums Along the Mohawk 1939 ★★★★½ The peaceful life of settlers is threatened by the Revolutionary War. Rousing Colonial saga is one of the best films depicting the birth of the United States. Glorious Technicolor epic masterfully directed by John Ford. C: Claudette Colbert, Henry Fonda, Edna May Oliver, John Carradine, Jessie Ralph. D: John Ford. ACT 104m. v

Drums in the Deep South 1951 ★★½ Two West Point cadets find their rivalry extending to the Civil War battlefield as they fight on opposite sides. Standard war melodrama. C: James Craig, Barbara Payton, Guy Madison. D: William Menzies. DRA 90m. v

Drums 1938 British ★★★★ Young Sabu uses his jungle skills to help British soldiers in 19th-century India. Colorful action. (a.k.a. *The Drum*) C: Sabu, Raymond Massey, Valerie Hobson. D: Zoltan Korda. DRA 96m. v

Drunken Angel 1949 ★★★ Alcoholic physician comes under spell of gangster he treats for gunshot wound. Early (and lesser) Kurosawa meanders for much of its length—only Mifune's intensity holds it together. Video print has difficult-to-read subtitles. C: Toshiro Mifune, Takashi Shimura. D: Akira Kurosawa. DRA 102m.

Dry White Season, A 1989 ★★★½ In the '70s, a white South African schoolteacher (Sutherland) comes to an understanding of the true horrors of apartheid. Well-intentioned drama stays strangely distant but tries very hard. Best is Brando in a small role as a bombastic barrister. C: Donald Sutherland, Janet Suzman, Zakes Mokae, Susan Sarandon, Marlon Brando. D: Euzhan Palcy. DRA [R] 105m. v

Du Barry, Woman of Passion 1930 ★★½ Courtesan Madame Du Barry wielded true power as mistress of France's King Louis XV.

Dated studio attempt to re-create atmosphere of the 18th century still holds interest. C: Norma Talmadge, William Farnum, Conrad Nagel. D: Sam Taylor. DRA 90m.

Du-beat-e-o 1984 ★★ A director (Sharkey) is ordered by mob backers to complete rock 'n' roll film by next day. Pumped-up rock mélange is a curiosity piece. C: Ray Sharkey, Joan Jett. D: Alan Sacks. COM 84m. V

Du Rififi Chez des Hommes 1954 *See* **Rififi**

DuBarry Was a Lady 1943 ★★★★ Waiter Skelton passes out, wakes up as King Louis XV of France in 18th century, dueling with mistress DuBarry (Ball). Enjoyable comedy from Cole Porter Broadway musical with only two songs remaining: "Friendship" and "Do I Love You?" C: Red Skelton, Lucille Ball, Gene Kelly, Virginia O'Brien, Zero Mostel, Tommy Dorsey. D: Roy Del Ruth. MUS 112m. V

Duchess and the Dirtwater Fox, The 1976 ★★ Grating blend of comedy and music features Hawn as music hall floozie and Segal as bumbling card shark who, against their better judgment, find themselves teaming up. Skimpy, labored Western spoof. C: George Segal, Goldie Hawn. D: Melvin Frank. WST [PG] 104m. V

Duchess of Idaho 1950 ★★★ Williams finds herself swimming in both water and romance in Sun Valley. Whisper of a plot has her help a roommate with romantic troubles, and soon Williams has her own. Amiable performances help. Look for Powell in her last film appearance. C: Esther Williams, Van Johnson, John Lund, Eleanor Powell, Lena Horne. D: Robert Z. Leonard. MUS 98m. V

Duck Soup 1933 ★★★★★ Groucho plays nincompoop Rufus T. Firefly, leader of the tiny country of Freedonia, who declares war on a neighboring state for no discernible reason. A classic farce lampooning political leaders, war, and unquestioned nationalism. Contains many of the Marx Brothers' best gags—including the famous Groucho/Harpo mirror sequence. Arguably the greatest of the Marx Brothers films. C: Groucho, Harpo, Chico, and Zeppo Marx, Margaret Dumont, Louis Calhern, Edgar Kennedy. D: Leo McCarey. COM 72m. V

Duck Tales: The Movie—Treasure of the Lost Lamp 1990 ★★★★ Uncle Scrooge McDuck, with his three nephews, goes on an expedition looking for a magical lamp. Surprisingly good feature version of the Disney cartoon TV series. Effective animation, imaginative story, and funny characters. Voices of Alan Young, Christopher Lloyd, Rip Taylor, Chuck McCann. D: Bob Hathcock. FAM/COM [G] 73m. V

Duck, You Sucker 1972 Italian ★★★★½ This sprawling adventure takes place during the Mexican revolution. Steiger is superb as a peasant thief who's talked into the war by an Irish munitions specialist (Coburn). Leone's action sequences are in rare form. Well worth seeing. (a.k.a. *A Fistful of Dynamite*) C: Rod Steiger, James Coburn. D: Sergio Leone. ACT [PG] 138m. V

Dude Goes West, The 1948 ★★★★ Brooklynite Albert travels to Nevada during the lawless days of 1876 and ends up becoming a ruthless gunslinger while vying for the love of man-hating Storm. Effective blend of comedy and Western action highlighted by Albert's lively, winning performance. C: Eddie Albert, Gale Storm, James Gleason, Binnie Barnes. D: Kurt Neumann. COM 87m.

Dude Ranger, The 1934 ★★★★ A city slicker must prove his mettle out West when he comes to the rescue of a ranch foreman's daughter besieged by a bandit. Fast-moving Western based on a Zane Grey story. C: George O'Brien, Irene Hervey, Smiley Burnett. D: Edward F. Cline. WST 68m.

Dudes 1988 ★★★½ When an urban punker falls victim to a pack of vile rednecks, his buddies decide to avenge his murder. Offbeat mixture of modern-day punks and traditional Western values rustles up enough laughs for those simpatico to these subcultures. C: Jon Cryer, Daniel Roebuck, Catherine Mary Stewart. D: Penelope Spheeris. COM [R] 90m. V

Duel 1971 ★★★★½ Motorist (Weaver) is terrorized by a big rig for no apparent reason. Spielberg's directorial debut is gripping and suspenseful, and almost without dialogue. Will be of special interest to any Spielberg fan. C: Dennis Weaver, Tim Herbert. D: Steven Spielberg. ACT [PG] 90m. TVM V

Duel at Apache Wells 1957 ★★ After roaming the frontier for four years, cow wrangler Cooper returns home to Arizona only to discover he must fight for ownership of his father's cattle ranch. Low-budget Western. C: Anna Maria Alberghetti, Ben Cooper, Jim Davis. D: Joe Kane. WST 70m.

Duel at Diablo 1966 ★★★½ In seeking revenge for the death of his wife, a Native American triggers an all-out war between the cavalry and the Indians. Offbeat Western features solid performances from Garner and Poitier. C: James Garner, Sidney Poitier, Bibi Andersson, Dennis Weaver. D: Ralph Nelson. WST 130m. V

Duel at Silver Creek, The 1952 ★★★★ Ruthless claim jumpers resort to murder, and it's up to the Silver Kid to "right the wrong." Above-average oater thanks to quick-draw direction by Siegel. One of Marvin's earliest appearances. C: Audie Murphy, Stephen McNally, Faith Domergue, Lee Marvin. D: Don Siegel. WST 77m.

Duel in the Jungle 1954 British ★★★ An insurance adjuster follows a dead man, who is very much alive somewhere in Africa. Good performances; has its moments. C: Dana Andrews, Jeanne Crain, David Farrar. D: George Marshall. DRA 102m.

Duel in the Sun 1946 ★★★★ Selznick

wanted to top *Gone with the Wind* with this one, but in falling short, he still created one hell of a show. Jones plays a seductress who gnaws at the already tenuous threads barely holding a range family together. Stellar cast is outstanding. C: Jennifer Jones, Gregory Peck, Joseph Cotten, Lionel Barrymore, Lillian Gish, Herbert Marshall, Walter Huston, Butterfly McQueen, Charles Bickford. D: King Vidor. WST 138m. V

Duel of Hearts 1992 British ★★★ Nineteenth-century romantic suspense from prolific pen of Barbara Cartland shows what a strong-minded young woman can do when she sets her mind to do it—in this case, save her lover from the evil machinations of his cousin. Charming and enjoyable romp. C: Alison Doody, Michael York, Geraldine Chaplin, Billie Whitelaw, Richard Johnson. D: John Hough. DRA 95m. TVM V

Duel of the Seven Tigers 1980 ★★★ Nine of the world's great kung fu masters get ready for a showdown in this martial arts spectacular. A genre pleaser for fans of all ages. C: Cliff Lok, Ka Sa Fa. D: Yeung Kuen. ACT 93m. V

Duel of the Titans 1961 Italian ★★★ Ancient Rome, according to legend, was founded by Romulus (Reeves) and Remus (Scott), two men raised by wolves. A competent-if-uninspired telling of their story, and how virtue overcomes corruption and tyranny. C: Steve Reeves, Gordon Scott, Virna Lisi. D: Sergio Corbucci. ACT 88m. V

Duel, The 1964 ★★½ Soviet adaptation of a Chekhov drama focuses on the mundane life of a Yalta administrator who, feeling trapped in his relationship with his mistress, desperately searches for escape. Will appeal to foreign film fanatics. C: Lyudmila Shagalova, Oleg Strizhenov, Vladimir Druzhnikov, Aleksandr Khvylya. D: Tatyana Berezantseva, Lev Rudnik. DRA 93m.

Duellists, The 1978 British ★★★★ In Napoleonic Europe, a trivial slight sends two French officers on an endless quest to kill one another; along the way each becomes the other's chief reason for living. Carradine and Keitel are surprisingly effective and exquisite from beginning to end. C: Keith Carradine, Harvey Keitel, Edward Fox, Cristina Raines, Tom Conti, Albert Finney. D: Ridley Scott. DRA [PG] 101m. V

Duet for One 1986 ★★★½ Violin virtuoso Andrews is diagnosed with multiple sclerosis. Her life falls apart till she seeks help from psychiatrist von Sydow. Maudlin soap opera worth watching for bravura performance by Julie in dramatic role. C: Julie Andrews, Alan Bates, Max von Sydow, Rupert Everett, Liam Neeson. D: Andrei Konchalovsky. DRA [R] 108m. V

Duffy 1968 U.S. ★★ Con artist (Coburn) conspires with half-brothers to rob their millionaire father. Eye-popping Tangier scenery can't compensate for absurd, smirky plot. C: James Coburn, James Mason, James Fox, Susannah York. D: Robert Parrish. COM [PG] 101m.

Duffy's Tavern 1945 ★★ Popular '40s radio show comes to the big screen with little fanfare and the thinnest of plots as a parade of screen stars visit the popular watering hole to save it from extinction. C: Barry Sullivan, Marjorie Reynolds, Bing Crosby, Dorothy Lamour, Alan Ladd, Betty Hutton, Eddie Bracken, Veronica Lake, Robert Benchley, Paulette Goddard, Brian Donlevy. D: Hal Walker. COM 97m.

Duke of West Point, The 1938 ★★★½ A rambunctious cadet discovers it takes more than fast talk to succeed at the Army's most prestigious academy. Drama enjoyably mixes romance and morality as it explores the rigors of the legendary military institute. C: Louis Hayward, Joan Fontaine, Richard Carlson. D: Alfred Green. DRA 109m.

Dulcimer Street 1948 British ★★★★ London slum dwellers rally around neighbor accused of murder. Reliable and interesting Attenborough and Sim lead fine cast; features moody direction and Dickensian flavor from comedy master Gilliat. C: Richard Attenborough, Alastair Sim, Fay Compton. D: Sidney Gilliat. DRA 112m.

Dulcinea 1962 Spanish ★★ When the dying Don Quixote mistakes barmaid as the love of his life, she takes up his cause and travels the countryside to help the poor and sick. Low-budget costume drama relies more on words than action. C: Millie Perkins, Cameron Mitchell, Folco Lulli. D: Vicanie Escriva. DRA 102m.

Dulcy 1940 ★★★½ Featherweight comedy about a flighty woman and her disastrous attempts to help further her financé's career. Sothern sparkles in title role and gets good support from the rest of the seasoned comic cast. C: Ann Sothern, Ian Hunter, Roland Young, Reginald Gardiner, Billie Burke. D: S. Simon. COM 64m.

Dumb and Dumber 1994 ★★★★ Hit comedy is virtually nothing but a string of gags exploiting the limited intelligence of characters played by Carrey and Daniels. However, most of it is howlingly funny, with the most effective toilet humor in comedy history. Snobs will not be amused, but others will love it. C: Jim Carrey, Jeff Daniels, Lauren Holley, Teri Garr. D: Peter Farrelly. COM [PG-13] 106m. V

Dumbo 1940 ★★★★½ Animated film is at its best in this Disney classic of a little elephant who discovers he can fly. Charming film, marred only by the casual racism of the period in the crows' musical number. Otherwise, a pure delight. D: Ben Sharpsteen. FAM/MUS [G] 63m. V

Dune 1984 ★★ Visionary adaptation of the dense Frank Herbert novel about the struggle to control the titular desert planet. Additional footage and narration added for the TV presentation (with Lynch credited under the pseudonym Allen Smithee). Both versions are bloated misfires. C: Kyle MacLachlan, Francesca Annis, Brad Dourif, Jose Ferrer, Linda Hunt, Virginia Madsen, Silvana Mangano, Max von Sydow, Sting, Sian Phillips. D: David Lynch. SFI [PG-13] 137m. V

Dunera Boys, The 1988 Australian ★★★½ A group of Jewish refugees are arrested in London as suspected Nazi spies and exiled to an Australian prison camp. Mind-boggling tale is worth a look, even though some of it's slow going. Filmed in Australia. C: Joseph Spano, Bob Hoskins, Joseph Furst. D: Ben Lewin. DRA 150m. V

Dungeonmaster, The 1983 ★ Weak fantasy tale of a girl held hostage and the attempts to rescue her. Notable mainly for the presence of seven different directors. C: Paul Bradford, Jeffrey Byron, Leslie Wing, Richard Moll. D: Charles Band. SFI [PG-13] 80m. V

Dunkirk 1958 British ★★★½ Realistic account of the evacuation of 337,000 trapped British and Allied troops from a Northern France seaport in 1940. Well-staged re-creation of actual rescue operation with good acting. C: John Mills, Robert Urquhart, Ray Jackson. D: Leslie Norman. DRA 113m.

Dunwich Horror, The 1970 ★★★½ One of the better film versions of H.P. Lovecraft's work; student (Dee) falls under the spell of black magician (Stockwell). Creepy, well-paced supernatural horror story with an intense climax. C: Sandra Dee, Dean Stockwell, Ed Begley, Sam Jaffe. D: Daniel Haller. HOR [PG] 87m. V

Duplicates 1992 ★★★ A young couple's missing son turns up with a new family and no memory of his past. Parents' search for the reason leads to a frightening climax. Provocative, absorbing setup. C: Gregory Harrison, Kim Greist, Cicely Tyson, Lane Smith, William Lucking, Scott Hoxby, Kevin McCarthy. D: Sandor Stern. SFI [PG-13] 92m. TVM V

Dust 1985 French ★★★★ Repressed woman murders her father after he beds his black foreman's wife. South Africa is setting for unusual, bleak study of isolation that moves from reality to fantasy in blink of an eye. Taut direction, strong acting by Birkin. C: Jane Birkin, Trevor Howard. D: Marion Hansel. DRA 87m. V

Dust Be My Destiny 1939 ★★★★ Social outcast Garfield finds love after he's been arrested for vagrancy. Familiar melodramatic plotline aided by appealing leads and a strong supporting cast. C: John Garfield, Priscilla Lane, Alan Hale, Frank McHugh. D: Lewis Seiler. DRA 88m.

Dust Devil 1992 ★★★ Director Stanley's follow-up to *Hardware* is a visually striking tale in which a woman, fleeing a bad marriage, encounters a bloodthirsty desert wanderer who's actually supernatural being. Well acted, with intriguing mythological undertones. D: Richard Stanley. HOR [R] V

Dusty 1987 Australian ★★★½ Touching film set in the Australian Outback concerns an old man and the wild dog he tries to tame. Surprisingly effective. C: Bill Kerr, Noel Trevarthen, Carol Burns. D: John Richardson. DRA 89m. V

Dutch 1991 ★★½ Blue-collar bozo O'Neill makes the mistake of agreeing to drive his girlfriend's incorrigible, spoiled son from Atlanta to Chicago for a holiday visit. As expected, disaster strikes every step of the way. Familiar formulaic comedy. C: Ed O'Neill, Ethan Randall, JoBeth Williams. D: Peter Faiman. COM [PG-13] 108m. V

Dutchman 1966 British ★★★★½ Tawdry white woman terrorizes a reserved African-American man during a New York subway ride. Effective exploration of racial tension heightens provocative premise in this searing British drama based on LeRoi Jones' play. C: Shirley Knight, Al Freeman Jr. D: Anthony Harvey. DRA 55m.

Dybbuk, The 1937 Polish ★★★★ Deceased young man's spirit enters his beloved's body in this recently restored film based on classic Yiddish play. Stagy, claustrophobic, but haunting. C: Leon Liebgold, Lili Liliana. D: Michal Waszynsky. DRA 120m. V

Dying Room Only 1973 ★★★★ Surprisingly engaging mystery revolves around a couple traveling through desert to L.A. They stop at a roadside cafe, where the husband mysteriously disappears from the washroom. C: Cloris Leachman, Ross Martin, Ned Beatty. D: Phillip Leacock. CRI 74m. TVM V

Dying Young 1991 ★★★½ Roberts finds meaning in life after taking a job as a nurse/companion to leukemia patient (Scott). Soap opera material, designed for Roberts; bring a hankie and enjoy. C: Julia Roberts, Campbell Scott, Vincent Phillip D'Onofrio, Colleen Dewhurst, Ellen Burstyn. D: Joel Schumacher. DRA [R] 115m. V

Dynamite Chicken 1971 ★★ Jumbled panache of dated comedy sketches. Only Pryor, doling out one-liners as he fools with a basketball, scores any laughs. C: Richard Pryor, John Lennon, Yoko Ono, Sha Na Na, Joan Baez, Ron Carey, Andy Warhol, Paul Krassner, Leonard Cohen, Malcolm. D: Ernie Pintoff. COM 76m.

Dynamite Women 1975 *See* **Great Texas Dynamite Chase, The**

Dynamo 1980 ★★½ Advertising exec decides to destroy her rival by promoting kung fu master Li. Don't let the offbeat packaging fool you: Li and Co. deliver the usual chops. C: Bruce Li, Mary Han, James Griffiths. D: Hwa I Hung. ACT [R] 81m. V

E

Each Dawn I Die 1939 ★★★½ An up-and-coming newshound is tagged with a phony manslaughter charge and hardened beyond recognition by a vicious penal system. Classic Cagney in convict mold, supported by a fast-moving script. C: James Cagney, George Raft, George Bancroft, Jane Bryan. D: William Keighley. DRA 92m. V

Eagle and the Hawk, The 1933 ★★★★ Heartfelt, beautifully acted anti-war film casts March and Grant as members of a WWI British flying squad. One is appalled at the atrocities of war; the other can't wait to get into battle. Fine aerial footage complements the on-ground drama. C: Fredric March, Cary Grant, Carole Lombard, Jack Oakie. D: Stuart Walker. ACT 68m.

Eagle and the Hawk, The 1950 ★★★★ Two U.S. government agents are sent south of the border to stop France from invading Texas during the Mexican revolution. Excellent action sequences and effective photography enhance solid B-movie adventure. (a.k.a. *Spread Eagle*) C: John Payne, Rhonda Fleming, Dennis O'Keefe, Thomas Gomez, Fred Clark. D: Lewis Foster. ACT 104m.

Eagle Has Landed, The 1977 ★★★½ Playing on an Irishman's (Sutherland's) anti-British sentiments, Nazis Caine and Duvall recruit him in a plot to assassinate Churchill. Good cast carries off taut WWII espionage drama. C: Michael Caine, Donald Sutherland, Robert Duvall, Jenny Agutter, Donald Pleasence, Jean Marsh. D: John Sturges. DRA [PG] 134m. V

Eagle in a Cage 1971 British ★★★★ Story of Napoleon's exile on St. Helena, with Haigh giving an impressive performance in the title role and Gielgud equally fine as his jailer. Serious if talky historical fare. C: John Gielgud, Ralph Richardson, Billie Whitelaw, Kenneth Haigh, Moses Gunn, Ferdy Mayne. D: Fielder Cook. DRA [PG] 98m.

Eagle Squadron 1942 ★★★½ Six American pilots join the RAF, helping Britain fend off the Nazis. Rousing war adventure features effective aerial sequences, some of it documentary footage. C: Robert Stack, Eddie Albert, Diana Barrymore, Nigel Bruce, Jon Hall, Evelyn Ankers, Gladys Cooper, Mary Carr. D: Arthur Lubin. ACT 109m.

Eagle, The 1925 ★★★★ When his family's lands are taken away, a Russian Cossack turns into a latter-day Robin Hood. Valentino is at his peak in this silent costume drama as he exudes sensuality while fighting on the side of righteousness. C: Rudolph Valentino, Vilma Banky, Louise Dresser, Albert Conti. D: Clarence Brown. DRA 81m. V

Eagle's Brood, The 1936 ★★★½ Hopalong Cassidy (Boyd) decides to help an aged outlaw find his long-lost grandson, over the protest of high-minded townsfolk. Solid entry in the B-Western series. C: William Boyd, Jimmy Ellison, William Farnum. D: Howard Bretherton. WST 61m.

Eagle's Wing 1979 British ★★½ A renegade Comanche and a fur trapper are at odds as they grapple for ownership of a valuable white mustang. British-made Western artifice is as offbeat as it is pretentious. C: Martin Sheen, Sam Waterston, Caroline Langrishe, Harvey Keitel, Stephane Audran, John Castle, Jorge Luke. D: Anthony Harvey. WST [PG] 111m. V

Earl Carroll Vanities 1945 ★★★½ Low-budget, mundane musical with Moore as princess slumming in musical comedy. Arden brightens dull proceedings with trademark wisecracks. C: Dennis O'Keefe, Constance Moore, Eve Arden, Otto Kruger. D: Joseph Santley. MUS 91m.

Earl of Chicago, The 1940 ★★★ Montgomery was cast against type as Chicago gangster who inherits a British earldom and tries to change his life, but kills a man and hangs for it. Complex story put over by solid performances. C: Robert Montgomery, Edward Arnold, Reginald Owen, Edmund Gwenn. D: Richard Thorpe. COM 85m.

Early Autumn *See* **St. Petersburg, The**

Early Frost, An 1985 ★★★★ TV breakthrough for its frank, powerful depiction of AIDS victim and parents' wrenching struggle to cope with their son's homosexuality and illness. Honest and emotional drama highlighted by sensitive performances. C: Aidan Quinn, Gena Rowlands, Ben Gazzara, Sylvia Sidney. D: John Erman. DRA 97m. TVM V

Early Spring 1956 Japanese ★★★½ Bored with work and his wife, a young man has an affair that paradoxically saves his marriage. Ozu's straightforward style pushes simple story to great dramatic heights. Not the director's best, but well worthwhile. C: Ryo Ikebe, Chikage Awashima, Keiko Kishi. D: Yasujiro Ozu. DRA 108m.

Early Summer 1951 Japanese ★★★★ Anecdotal tale of close-knit family's gradual disintegration when daughter decides to marry. Absolutely charming, beautifully directed film shows Ozu at peak of his powers. As always, plot is subordinate to character, which shouldn't deter viewer from this deliberate film's richness. C: Setsuko Hara, Ichiro Sugai, Chishu Ryu, Kuniko Miyake. D: Yasujiro Ozu. DRA 135m. V

Early to Bed 1936 ★★★½ Caspar Milquetoast (Ruggles) is a fearless crusader while sleepwalking, single-handedly tangling with a ruthless gang. Cute light comedy with fun performances from the leads. C: Mary Boland, Charlie Ruggles, George Barbier, Gail Patrick, Robert McWade, Lucien Littlefield. D: Norman McLeod. COM 75m.

Earrings of Madame de . . . , The 1953 French/Italian ★★★★★ A woman pawns earrings her husband (Boyer) gave her, setting in motion a chain of events that leads to tragedy. A truly great film, dazzling and moving in its examination of the empty lives of the idle rich. Brilliantly acted and directed. C: Danielle Darrieux, Charles Boyer, Vittorio de Sica, Jean Debucourt. D: Max Ophuls. DRA 105m.

Earth 1930 Russian ★★★★ Soviet farmers' collective protects its fields from uncooperative owners. Visually striking silent, made as obvious propaganda by Dovzhenko but filled with artistry and genuine warmth toward its long-suffering characters. C: Semyon Svashenko, Stephan Shkurat, Mikola Nademsky. D: Alexander Dovzhenko. DRA 69m. V

Earth Entranced 1970 ★★★½ Brazilian writer (Filho) gets involved in his country's politics, which proves to be his downfall. Pretentious and polemical but obviously heartfelt and often gripping. C: Jardel Filho, Jose Lewgoy, Glauce Rocha. D: Glauber Rocha. DRA 110m.

Earth Girls Are Easy 1989 ★★★½ Three aliens who land in hairdresser Davis' pool get amazing makeovers and a lesson in San Fernando Valley living. Sporting a couple of musical numbers, including Brown's wickedly satirical "Cause I'm A Blonde," this is lightweight, frothy fun. C: Geena Davis, Jeff Goldblum, Julie Brown, Charles Rocket, Jim Carrey, Damon Wayans, Michael McKean. D: Julien Temple. COM [PG] 100m. V

Earth vs. the Flying Saucers 1956 ★★★★ Aliens from a dying planet need a new world to colonize. Naturally, they choose Earth. Ray Harryhausen effects, an intelligent script, and a very satisfying climax help make this one of the best Earth vs. invaders from space movies. C: Hugh Marlowe, Joan Taylor, Donald Curtis, Morris Ankrum. D: Fred F. Sears. SFI 83m. V

Earth vs. the Spider 1958 ★★ Gigantic arachnid, believed dead by its P.T. Barnum-like displayers, comes back to life at the high school sock hop. Awful filmmaking at its best, from the man (Gordon) who never tired of the oversized thing theme. (a.k.a. *The Spider.*) C: Ed Kemmer, June Kenny, Geene Persson. D: Bert I. Gordon. SFI 72m. V

Earthbound 1981 ★★★★ A dead man's ghost returns to help his widow (Leeds) catch his murderer. Remake of 1920 silent film is an entertaining, modest mystery which uses its gimmick to good effect. C: Burl Ives, Christopher Connelly, Meredith MacRae, Joseph Campanella, Todd Porter, Marc Gilpin, Elissa Leeds, John Schuck, Stuart Pankin. D: James Conway. DRA [PG] 94m.

Earthling, The 1980 Australian ★★★ Schroder plays an orphan lost in the Australian bush and befriended by reclusive cancer victim Holden who teaches him Outback survival skills. Breathtaking Aussie landscapes leave the most lasting impression. C: William Holden, Ricky Schroder, Jack Thompson, Olivia Hamnett. D: Peter Collinson. DRA [PG] 102m. V

Earthquake 1974 ★★★½ Box office smash about Los Angeles disaster and impact on the lives of several individuals. Oscar-winning special effects and all-star cast. C: Charlton Heston, Ava Gardner, George Kennedy, Genevieve Bujold, Lorne Greene, Marjoe Gortner. D: Mark Robson. ACT [PG] 129m. V

Earth's Final Fury 1980 *See* **When Time Ran Out . . .**

Earthworm Tractors 1936 ★★★½ A tractor salesman (Brown) plies his trade on his trusting neighbor (Kibbee), with disastrous results. Zany star vehicle has its moments, particularly when Brown moves Kibbee's house with tractor—while the family eats dinner. C: Joe E. Brown, June Travis, Guy Kibbee, Dick Foran, Carol Hughes, Gene Lockhart, Olin Howland. D: Ray Enright. COM 69m.

Easiest Way, The 1931 ★★★½ Poor shop employee (Bennett) becomes a model, then mistress to several men (Menjou, Montgomery) in pre-Code drama that straddles the fence between condemning and condoning her behavior. Dated, but fascinating. C: Constance Bennett, Adolphe Menjou, Robert Montgomery, Anita Page. D: Jack Conway. DRA 86m.

East and West 1924 Austrian ★★★★ Charming silent comedy about Jewish-American flapper (Picon) who finds herself in an Eastern European *shtetl*, filled with Orthodox Jewish men. Picon teaches boxing, lifts weights and dances the shimmy. C: Molly Picon, Jacob Kalish, Sidney M. Goldin, Saul Nathan, Laura Glucksman, Eugen Neufeld, Johannes Roth. D: Sidney M. Goldin, Ivan Abramson. COM 85m.

East End Chant 1934 *See* **Limehouse Blues**

East L.A. Warriors 1989 ★★ As L.A. suffers through another gang war, a mobster (Hilton-Jacobs) plots to turn the situation to his advantage. Director and cast do nothing with potentially explosive material. C: Lawrence Hilton-Jacobs, Tony Bravo, Kamar Reyes, William Smith. D: Addison Randall. ACT 90m. V

East of Eden 1955 ★★★★★ Towering adaptation of Steinbeck's epic novel, focusing on good son/bad son rivalry with Biblical overtones. Dean, as misunderstood rebel Cal epitomizes the troubled youth syndrome with a charismatic performance, while Van Fleet makes the most of her brief, Oscar-winning role as a bordello madam. Beautiful cinematography should be seen in letterbox version. Remade as a TV miniseries. C: James Dean, Julie Harris, Raymond Massey, Jo Van Fleet, Burl Ives, Richard Davalos. D: Elia Kazan. DRA 114m. V

East of Eden 1981 ★★★★½ Multipart remake of the classic 1955 filming of Steinbeck novel is more complete than its predecessor, dramatizing the early life of patriarch Adam Trask (Bottoms) and his wayward wife (Seymour), as well as the later rivalry of their two sons. Stands on its own as powerful storytelling, with a riveting, Emmy-winning performance by Seymour. C: Jane Seymour, Timothy Bottoms, Bruce Boxleitner, Anne Baxter, Lloyd Bridges. D: Harvey Hart. DRA 240m. TVM V

East of Sumatra 1953 ★★★½ Chandler is a mining engineer caught between greedy employers and restless natives. Two-fisted adventure, set on tropical island. C: Jeff Chandler, Marilyn Maxwell, Anthony Quinn, Suzan Ball, Peter Graves. D: Budd Boetticher. ACT 82m.

East of the Bowery *See* **Follow the Leader**

East of the River 1940 ★★★ Two brothers, one good (Lundigan), one bad (Garfield), vie for the same woman (Marshall). Routine Gotham soaper. C: John Garfield, Brenda Marshall, Marjorie Rambeau, William Lundigan. D: Alfred E. Green. DRA 73m.

East Side Kids 1940 ★★½ Street-kid-turned-detective (Ames) helps a gang of well-meaning youths to straighten up. Sentimental potboiler misses the popular spark of its *Dead End* cousins. C: Harris Berger, Hally Chester, Frankie Burke, Leon Ames. D: Robert F. Hill. DRA 62m. V

East Side of Heaven 1939 ★★★★ A crooning cab driver (Crosby) finds an abandoned infant in his backseat, causing confusion for him and his fianceé (Blondell). Diverting, sunny musical with Bing at his most charming. C: Bing Crosby, Joan Blondell, Mischa Auer, Irene Hervey, C. Aubrey Smith, Baby Sandy. D: David Butler. MUS 90m.

East Side, West Side 1949 ★★★ Glossy melodrama of troubles in marriage of upper-class Manhattan couple Mason and Stanwyck. Gardner registers strongly as Mason's object of affection. C: Barbara Stanwyck, James Mason, Ava Gardner, Van Heflin, Cyd Charisse, Gale Sondergaard, William Frawley, Nancy Davis. D: Mervyn LeRoy. DRA 110m. V

Easter Parade 1948 ★★★★★ Marvelous MGM musical has little to do with Easter, but it doesn't matter. Dancer (Astaire) has trouble with new dance partner (Garland) after old one (Miller) jilts him. Film's 17 Irving Berlin standards give both stars ample opportunity to shine. Highlights: "Stepping Out With My Baby," "A Couple of Swells," "Drum Crazy." C: Judy Garland, Fred Astaire, Peter Lawford, Ann Miller. D: Charles Walters. MUS 103m. V

Easy Come, Easy Go 1947 ★★ So she can keep funding his habit, Irish gambler (Fitzgerald) doesn't want daughter (Lynn) to marry. Harmless drama. C: Barry Fitzgerald, Diana Lynn, Sonny Tufts, Dick Foran, Frank McHugh, Allen Jenkins. D: John Farrow. DRA 77m.

Easy Come, Easy Go 1967 ★★ Elvis plays a Navy diver after sunken treasure. Best for Presley fans. C: Elvis Presley, Dodie Marshall, Pat Priest, Elsa Lanchester, Frank McHugh. D: John Rich. MUS 95m. V

Easy Go 1930 *See* **Free and Easy**

Easy Life, The 1963 Italian ★★★★ Eccentric playboy shows his eager protégé how to live it up, with tragic results. Gassman and Trintignant are magnificent in this moving drama that paints a disturbing picture of permissive modern society. C: Vittorio Gassman, Catherine Spaak, Jean-Louis Trintignant, Luciana Angiolillo. D: Dino Risi. DRA 105m.

Easy Living 1937 ★★★★★ Classic screwball farce starts with working girl Arthur getting hit in the head with cast-off sable coat, then plot spins wildly till all of New York is involved in madcap adventures of modern-day Cinderella. Famous food fight in automat is just one highlight of comic gem with wickedly funny Preston Sturges script. C: Jean Arthur, Edward Arnold, Ray Milland, Franklin Pangborn, William Demarest, Mary Nash, Luis Alberni. D: Mitchell Leisen. COM 86m.

Easy Living 1949 ★★★★ Football player (Mature) nearing the end of his career puts his health on the line for his self-centered wife (Scott). Surprisingly moody, atmospheric melodrama takes a shot at the often ruthless world of professional sports. Ball gives a fine performance as loyal team secretary. C: Victor Mature, Lizabeth Scott, Lucille Ball, Sonny Tufts, Lloyd Nolan. D: Jacques Tourneur. DRA 77m. V

Easy Money 1983 ★★★½ Fine vehicle for Dangerfield as obnoxious nobody who must clean up his act in order to inherit a fortune. Lots of laughs for fans of the no-respect comedy. C: Rodney Dangerfield, Joe Pesci, Geraldine Fitzgerald, Taylor Negron, Jennifer Jason Leigh, Tom Ewell. D: James Signorelli. COM 95m. V

Easy Rider 1969 ★★★★½ Two guys on motorcycles (Hopper and Fonda) hit the road to find out what America's all about. A prototypical film of youth in turmoil and a vivid evocation of an era. After his turn as a drunken lawyer, Nicholson was on his way to stardom. C: Peter Fonda, Dennis Hopper, Jack Nicholson, Karen Black. D: Dennis Hopper. DRA [R] 94m. V

Easy to Love 1953 ★★★½ Esther works as typist by day, aquacade star by night in slight MGM swimfest with Johnson, Martin, and Bromfield all vying for star's affections. Brilliant Busby Berkeley water ballets culminate with fireworks finale that must be seen to be believed. C: Esther Williams, Van Johnson, Tony Martin, John Bromfield, Carroll Baker. D: Charles Walters. MUS 96m. V

Easy to Take 1936 ★★★½ Children's talent show host (Howard) gets appointed guardian of spoiled rich kid with attractive older sister (Hunt). Unassuming comedy with a light touch. C: Marsha Hunt, John Howard, Eugene Pallette. D: Glenn Tryon. COM 66m.

Easy to Wed 1946 ★★★ Lightweight Technicolor musical remake of *Libeled Lady*. An heiress sues a newspaper for libel; Ball steals the show as the ready-to-wed fiancée of newspaper editor Wynn. C: Van Johnson, Esther Williams, Lucille Ball, Keenan Wynn, Cecil Kellaway, June Lockhart. D: Edward Buzzell. MUS 110m.

Easy Virtue 1927 British ★★ Married woman's boyfriend commits suicide, and she must deal with the aftermath. A yawn, but of interest to Hitchcock buffs. C: Isabel Jeans, Franklin Dyall, Eric Bransby Williams, Ian Hunter, Robin Irvine. D: Alfred Hitchcock. DRA 79m. V

Easy Way, The 1952 *See* **Room for One More**

Eat a Bowl of Tea 1989 ★★★½ When the U.S. lifts its WWII ban on Chinese female immigrants, a family of males looks forward to marriage. Low-key and perceptive, but the story meanders through several slow spots. C: Cora Miao, Russell Wong, Victor Wong, Lau Siu Ming. D: Wayne Wang. COM [PG-13] 104m. V

Eat Drink Man Woman 1994 Taiwanese ★★★★ Deft Chinese generation gap comedy about a retired Taiwanese cook whose three daughters try his patience and understanding. Another gem from the director of *The Wedding Banquet*. C: Chen-Lien Wu, Sihung Lung, Kuei-Mei Yang, Yu-Wen Wang. D: Ang Lee. COM 123m.

Eat My Dust 1976 ★★½ Car saga about a pair of grease monkeys and their wheels. Don't bother to fasten your seat belts for this cheap retread. C: Ron Howard, Christopher Norris, Warren Kemmerling, Rance Howard, Clint Howard, Corbin Bernsen. D: Charles B. Griffith. COM [PG] 89m. V

Eat the Peach 1986 Irish ★★★ Out-of-work Irish buddies concoct scheme to build "Wall of Death" for motorcycles. Ingratiating little comedy rides Elvis idolatry theme rather heavily, but entertains all the way through. C: Stephen Brennan, Eamon Morrissey, Catherine Byrne, Niall Toibin. D: Peter Ormrod. COM 95m. V

Eat the Rich 1987 British ★★ A revolutionary serves bourgeois restaurant diners what they deserve: human flesh. Dark comedy not to everyone's (or anyone's) taste. C: Nosher Powell, Lanah Pellay, Fiona Richmond, Ronald Allen, Sandra Dorne. D: Peter Richardson. COM 92m. V

Eaten Alive 1976 ★★★½ Hooper's follow-up to *Texas Chainsaw Massacre* has some of the same nightmare intensity, as maniac (Brand) murders guests at his isolated hotel and feeds them to his pet alligator. Gruesome, with black-humor touches. (a.k.a. *Death Trap*, *Horror Hotel*, *Legend of the Bayou* and *Starlight Slaughter*) C: Neville Brand, Mel Ferrer, Carolyn Jones, Robert Englund, Stuart Whitman. D: Tobe Hooper. HOR [R] 96m. V

Eating 1990 ★★★★ Engaging examination of group of diverse women gathered for birthday party, who discuss life and food. Joyous and often funny celebration serves up good portions of insightful humor. C: Frances Bergen, Lisa Richards, Nelly Alard, Mary Crosby. D: Henry Jaglom. COM [R] 110m. V

Eating Raoul 1982 ★★★★ Mundane couple finance dream restaurant by inviting moneyed swingers home and then killing them for their cash. Played with sadistic glee, the comic absurdity is always in sharp focus. C: Paul Bartel, Mary Woronov, Robert Beltran, Buck Henry, Ed Begley Jr., Hamilton Camp. D: Paul Bartel. COM [R] 83m. V

Ebb Tide 1937 ★★★ Shipwreck victims land on a remote island ruled by a psycho (Nolan). Somewhat stilted, but still rousing. Made again as *Adventure Island*. C: Frances Farmer, Ray Milland, Oscar Homolka, Lloyd Nolan, Barry Fitzgerald, David Torrence. D: James Hogan. DRA 94m.

Eboli 1979 Italian ★★★★½ Based on Carlo Levi's autobiographical account of an antifascist writer growing to accept the people he lives among during exile in '30s southern Italy. Rosi's understated direction and Volonte's multishaded performances help cover rough transitions from editing of three and a half-hour Italian TV series. (a.k.a. *Christ Stopped at Eboli*; this second edited version is nearly twice as long.) C: Gian Maria Volonte, Irene Papas, Paolo Bonicelli, Alain Cuny, Lea Massari. D: Francesco Rosi. DRA 120m.

Ebony, Ivory and Jade 1979 ★★ A cadre of Las Vegas performers and showgirls are assigned by the government to protect a scientist pursued by terrorists. This pilot for a series that was never made requires a major suspension of disbelief. ACT TVM

Ebony Tower, The 1987 ★★★★½ Young wanderer (Rees) disturbs idyll of aged painter (Olivier) who's hidden himself from world in French château, comforted by two young, very lovely art students. Superb adaptation of John Fowles' novel; with some nudity. C: Laurence Olivier, Roger Rees, Greta Scacchi. D: Robert Knight. DRA 90m. V

Echo of Barbara 1961 ★★★½ Burlesque dancer (Connell) impersonates ex-con's abandoned daughter to gain hidden robbery money. Suspenseful low-budget drama with good cast. C: Mervyn Johns, Maureen Connell, Paul Stassino. D: Sidney Hayers. DRA 58m.

Echo Park 1985 ★★½ Young, would-be Hollywood stars and artists living in seedy building near downtown L.A. share fortunes and heartaches. Lots of talk, much of it tiresome, but actors, particularly fetching Dey and musclebound Bowen, keep it diverting. C: Susan Dey, Thomas Hulce, Michael Bowen, Christopher Walker. D: Robert Dornhelm. COM [R] 92m. V

Echoes in the Darkness 1987 ★★★★ Based on true story about Svengali-like private school teacher who has affair with, then murders, a colleague and takes off with her children. Effectively creepy. C: Peter Coyote, Stockard Channing, Robert Loggia, Peter Boyle. D: Glenn Jordan. DRA 234m. V

Echoes of a Summer 1976 ★★★½ A stricken 12-year-old helps her parents cope with her impending death. Multi-hankie tearjerker makes the most of a very effective Foster performance. (a.k.a. *The Last Castle*) C: Richard Harris, Lois Nettleton, Jodie Foster, Geraldine Fitzgerald. D: Don Taylor. DRA [G] 99m.

Echoes of Paradise 1986 Australian ★★ Cheated-on wife, taking dull vacation to Thailand has fling of her own. Poor direction and acting, though Lone makes an awfully fetching Bali dancer. C: Wendy Hughes, John Lone, Steven Jacobs, Peta Toppano. D: Philip Noyce. DRA [R] 90m. V

Eclipse, The 1962 French ★★★ Early Antonioni love story about a couple with little in common is an intriguing, often difficult analysis of relationships between men and women. Vitti's marvelous presence holds it together despite ambiguous imagery. Last in trilogy, after *L'Avventura* and *La Notte*. (a.k.a. *L'Eclisse*) C: Alain Delon, Monica Vitti, Francesco Rabal. D: Michelangelo Antonioni. DRA 123m. V

Ecstasy 1933 Czech ★★★ Tale of a woman's affair (notorious for scenes of a skinny-dipping pre-Hollywood Lamarr) was a milestone in the battle against screen censorship. More famous for its scandal than for its story. C: Hedy Lamarr, Jaromir Rogoz. D: Gustav Machaty. DRA 88m. V

Ecstasy of Young Love 1936 ★★★½ A impoverished teenager sets out to obtain a pair of shoes for his ladylove. Slight but charming romance with an otherworldly feel. C: Vasa Jalovec, Jarmila Berankova, Jar Vojta, Vojtova Mayerova. D: J. Rovensky. DRA 75m.

Ed Wood 1994 ★★★★½ The true story of Ed Wood, Jr., arguably the worst director in Hollywood history, makes a fine, funny film. Depp hits his stride in the title role as a movie buff with a yen for wearing nylons and angora sweaters, and Landau won an Oscar for Best Supporting Actor for his sublimely touching performance as Wood's favorite actor, Bela Lugosi. Filmed in glorious black-and-white, and also won an Oscar for Best Makeup. Makes a great double feature with Wood's classic, all-time-worst film, *Plan 9 From Outer Space*. C: Johnny Depp, Martin Landau, Patricia Arquette, Sarah Jessica Parker, Bill Murray, Jeffrey Jones. D: Tim Burton. COM [R] 120m. V

Eddie and the Cruisers 1983 ★★★ Cult rock musical has Pare as a rising '60s star whose untimely end starts investigation years later. Some good songs by John Cafferty. Sequel followed. C: Tom Berenger, Michael Pare, Joe Pantoliano, Matthew Laurance, Ellen Barkin. D: Martin Davidson. MUS [PG] 92m. V

Eddie and the Cruisers II—Eddie Lives! 1989 ★★ Long-presumed-dead rock star comes back to collect royalties; some more good songs. C: Michael Pare, Marina Orsini, Bernie Coulson, Matthew Laurance. D: Jean-Claude Lord. MUS [PG-13] 106m. V

Eddie Cantor Story, The 1953 ★★½ Multimedia star Cantor was manic, funny, talented, and yes, an acquired taste. Watching cute but intensely annoying Brasselle, whose mimic job somehow failed to make him a star, is like listening to nails on a blackboard. Nice vaudeville atmosphere, though. C: Keefe Brasselle, Marilyn Erskine, Aline MacMahon, Marie Windsor. D: Alfred Green. DRA 116m.

Eddie Macon's Run 1983 ★★½ An escaped convict (Schneider) struggles to make it to Mexico by hard-nosed police officer (Douglas). Lightweight, familiar fare. C: Kirk Douglas, John Schneider, Lee Purcell, Leah Ayres. D: Jeff Kanew. ACT [PG] 95m. V

Eddie Murphy Raw 1987 ★★½ Stand-up comedy concert film was actually edited for theatrical release to avoid NC-17 rating. The monologue remains an endless stream of profanities, and it all becomes somewhat numbing. Murphy's hard-core fans won't mind. C: Eddie Murphy. D: Robert Townsend. COM [R] 93m. V

Eddy Duchin Story, The 1956 ★★★½ Musical weepie with Power as real-life pianist Duchin caught in tragic romance with stunningly beautiful Novak. Theme music from Chopin is memorable, as is manipulative tugging of heartstrings. C: Tyrone Power, Kim Novak, Victoria Shaw, James Whitmore. D: George Sidney. MUS 123m. V

Edge of Darkness 1943 ★★★★ Above average WWII studio picture on the Norwegian resistance fighting the Nazis, led by trawler Flynn and his loving fiancée Sheridan. Gripping story with strong romantic leads and a stage-trained supporting cast. C: Errol Flynn, Ann Sheridan, Walter Huston, Nancy Coleman, Helmut Dantine, Judith Anderson, Ruth

Gordon, John Beal, Roman Bohnen. D: Lewis Milestone. DRA 120m. v

Edge of Darkness 1986 ★★★½ Detective hunting his daughter's killer happens upon conspiracy involving nuclear power plant and the government. British miniseries, with very good performances by all. C: Joe Don Baker, Bob Peck, Joanne Whalley-Kilmer. D: Martin Campbell. CRI 307m. v

Edge of Doom 1950 ★★★½ Priest's violent murder is catalyst for compelling portrait of the disturbed youth (Granger) who committed the crime. Depressing, but gripping. (a.k.a. *Stronger Than Fear*) C: Dana Andrews, Farley Granger, Joan Evans, Mala Powers, Adele Jergens. D: Mark Robson. DRA 99m.

Edge of Eternity 1959 ★★★½ Sheriff's deputy (Wilde) goes on a manhunt for a murderer (Shaughnessy) holding a lovely hostage (Shaw). Contemporary Western has routine script, but exciting chase scenes with stunning canyon climax. C: Cornel Wilde, Victoria Shaw, Mickey Shaughnessy, Edgar Buchanan, Rian Garrick, Jack Elam. D: Don Siegel. WST 80m.

Edge of Sanity 1989 British ★★★ Another adaptation of the Jekyll and Hyde story, this time with Perkins performing both roles. Though film drags a bit, its star shows off his ability to appear completely insane while self-consciously maintaining an edge of subtle wit. C: Anthony Perkins, Glynis Barber, Sarah Maur-Thorp, David Lodge, Ben Cole, Lisa Davis. D: Gerard Kikoine. HOR [R] 85m. v

Edge of the City 1957 ★★★ Friendship of black and white dock workers leads to tragedy. Strong performances compensate for average script. C: John Cassavetes, Sidney Poitier, Jack Warden, Ruby Dee, Kathleen Maguire, Ruth White. D: Martin Ritt. DRA 85m.

Edge of the World, The 1937 British ★★★★½ Haunting, almost mythical melodrama about family tragedy during evacuation of isolated Shetland isle. MacGinnis, Laurie, Currie lead excellent cast. Stunning location shooting, all masterfully guided by Powell. C: Niall MacGinnis, Belle Chrystall, John Laurie, Finlay Currie, Eric Berry. D: Michael Powell. DRA 74m.

Edge, The 1968 ★★★½ Disillusioned radical activists gather at a farm to do drugs, make love, argue, and complain about changing times. Frustrating but compelling portrait of the '60s era. Weiss is a standout. C: Jack Rader, Tom Griffin, Jeff Weiss, Anne Waldman Warsch, Paul Hultberg. D: Robert Kramer. DRA 100m.

Edie in Ciao! Manhattan 1972 ★★ Semi-documentary look at the brief life of Andy Warhol star Edie Sedgwick, who appears topless in footage from two unfinished movies. Crude and tasteless, of interest only to 60's pop culture fans. (a.k.a. *Ciao! Manhattan*) C: Edie Sedgwick, Baby Jane Holzer, Viva, Roger Vadim. D: John Palmer, David Weisman. DOC [R] 84m. v

Edison, the Man 1940 ★★★★ Far superior sequel to *Young Tom Edison* follows the Wizard of Menlo Park through poverty and marriage until his invention of the light bulb. Tracy, as the very human, determined inventor, is particularly solid in this pleasurable film biography. Educational and entertaining. C: Spencer Tracy, Rita Johnson, Lynne Overman, Charles Coburn, Gene Lockhart, Henry Travers, Felix Bressart. D: Clarence Brown. DRA 108m. v

Edith and Marcel 1983 French ★★★ Brief but intense romance between singer Edith Piaf (Bouix) and boxer Marcel Cerdan (played by his son, Jr.), recounted with flair but decided sentimentality by Lelouch. We never care about this couple; in fact, the subplot's romance is much more watchable. C: Evelyne Bouix, Marcel Cerdan, Jr., Jacques Villeret, Jean-Claude Brialy, Charles Aznavour. D: Claude Lelouch. DRA 140m. v

Educating Rita 1983 British ★★★★ Walters enchants as Cockney hairdresser who cajoles professor Caine into teaching her about the literary world. In the process, she lifts him out of his professional doldrums. Tight, charming comedy. C: Michael Caine, Julie Walters, Michael Williams, Maureen Lipman. D: Lewis Gilbert. COM [PG] 110m. v

Education of Sonny Carson, The 1974 ★★★½ The story of Sonny Carson, a black man from the harsh streets of Brooklyn. Blunt depiction of ghetto life in '50s and '60s remains interesting and provocative. C: Rony Clanton, Don Gordon, Joyce Walker, Paul Benjamin. D: Michael Campus. DRA [R] 104m. v

Edvard Munch 1976 ★★★★ Impressive biography of Norwegian painter whose most famous work, "The Scream," was indicative of his constant struggle with depression and madness during his tragic life. Overlong, but beautifully acted. C: Geir Westby, Gro Fraas, Johan Halsborg, Lotte Teig. D: Peter Watkins. DRA 215m. v

Edward and Caroline 1952 French ★★★★ Up-and-coming pianist and wife pick the worst time to fight: right before a recital where he will introduce himself to high society. Very funny, consistently engaging comedy handled with the perfect light touch by Becker. C: Daniel Gelin, Anne Vernon, Betty Stockfield. D: Jacques Becker. DRA 90m.

Edward, My Son 1949 British ★★★½ Father (Tracy) recalls the events that led to his son's suicide. Experiment in melodrama features Tracy relating his pain directly to the audience. Reliable cast and director in departure from studio norm; a curiosity. C: Spencer Tracy, Deborah Kerr, Ian Hunter, James Donald, Mervyn Johns, Felix Aylmer, Leueen McGrath. D: George Cukor. DRA 112m.

Edward Scissorhands 1990 ★★★★½ A Scissor-appendaged boy (Depp) is whisked to suburbia by gracious Avon lady (Wiest). Irresistible parable of adolescent ostracism, with great effects and startlingly sensitive performances throughout. C: Johnny Depp, Winona Ryder, Dianne Wiest, Vincent Price, Alan Arkin, Anthony Michael Hall, Kathy Baker, Brian Larkin. D: Tim Burton. DRA [PG-13] 100m. V

Edward II 1992 British ★★★★ Visionary interpretation of Christopher Marlowe's 16th-century drama about a homosexual king, with characters in modern dress and with contemporary gay sensibilities. May be too violent for some. C: Steven Waddington, Andrew Tiernan, Tilda Swinton, Nigel Terry. D: Derek Jarman. DRA [R] 91m. V

Eegah! 1963 ★ A giant prehistoric creature (Kiel) kidnaps a young woman. Awful mess stars on many "all-time-worst" movie lists, so at least it's famous. Good title, too. C: Arch Hall, Jr., Marilyn Manning, Richard Kiel. D: Nicholas Merriwether (Arch Hall, Sr.). SFI 92m. V

Effect of Gamma Rays on Man-in-the-Moon Marigolds, The 1972 ★★★★ A high school girl ignores the demands of her alcoholic mother (Woodward) to work on her city-wide science fair entry, the first step in her ticket to a better life. Appealing, well-directed drama with a stunning performance by Woodward. C: Joanne Woodward, Nell Potts, Roberta Wallach, Judith Lowry. D: Paul Newman. DRA [PG] 100m.

Effi Briest 1974 German ★★★★½ A daughter's arranged marriage leads to an affair; the jealous husband then kills her lover in a duel. Fassbinder at peak of his powers: handsome b&w photography enhances richly textured period piece. C: Hanna Schygulla, Wolfgang Schenck, Karl-Heinz Bohm, Ulli Lommel, Lilo Pempeit. D: Rainer Werner Fassbinder. DRA 135m. V

Efficiency Expert, The 1992 Australian ★★★½ Hopkins is staid but sympathetic business consultant in '60s Australia hired to improve operations at a family shoe factory run on old-fashioned values. Folksy, low-key farce enlivened by Hopkins' witty performance. (a.k.a. *Spotswood.*) C: Anthony Hopkins, Alwyn Kurts, Russell Crowe, Angela Punch McGregor, Ben Mendelsohn, Bruno Lawrence. D: Mark Joffe. COM [PG] 97m. V

Egg 1988 ★★★ Simpleminded young man leads well-ordered life in small Dutch village. Picturesque landscapes add ambience to story so laid back it might fall over. Pleasant enough, but minor. C: Johan Leysen, Marijke Vengelers. D: Danniel Danniel. DRA 58m.

Egg and I, The 1947 ★★★★ Genial, folksy comedy, based on Betty MacDonald's best-seller, with Park Avenue matron (Colbert) talked into running chicken farm with country-loving husband (MacMurray). Excellent performances all around; debut of characters Ma and Pa Kettle (Main, Kilbride), later spun off into film series of their own. C: Claudette Colbert, Fred MacMurray, Marjorie Main, Percy Kilbride. D: Chester Erskine. COM 108m. V

Eglantine 1972 ★★★★ An 11-year-old boy stays with his female relatives during the summer of 1895 and learns about love and life from his 80-year-old grandmother (Tessier, in a marvelous performance). Fetching, nostalgic coming-of-age charmer. C: Valentine Tessier, Claude Dauphine, Odile Versois, Micheline Luccioni. D: Jean-Claude Brialy. DRA 90m.

Egon Schiele—Excess and Punishment 1981 ★★★½ Depressing but vivid biography of painter Schiele (Carriere) whose work was condemned as pornography in his native Austria. Stunning cinematography and effective performances. C: Mattieu Carriere, Jane Birkin, Nina Fallenstein. D: Herbert Vesely. DRA 93m.

Egyptian, The 1954 ★★ Sensitive physician (Purdom) in ancient Egypt receives enlightenment. A laughable soap opera but looks great and has a score cowritten by Alex North and Bernhard Herrmann. C: Edmund Purdom, Jean Simmons, Victor Mature, Gene Tierney, Michael Wilding, Peter Ustinov, John Carradine. D: Michael Curtiz. DRA 140m. V

Eiger Sanction, The 1975 ★★★ Espionage combines with mountain climbing in this tale of a former operative (Eastwood) now an art teacher, recruited by a CIA-like agency to terminate the killers of one of their agents. Swiss Alpine action can't fill holes in this cheesy script based on the Trevanian novel. C: Clint Eastwood, George Kennedy, Vonetta McGee, Jack Cassidy, Thayer David. D: Clint Eastwood. ACT [R] 125m. V

8 1/2 1963 Italian ★★★★★ Fellini's autobiographical masterwork probes the world of a confused film director (Mastroianni), struggling with questions of life and art while working on his next project. Whirlwind of ideas and subplots coalesce perfectly under Fellini's magnificent cinematic hand. Oscars for Best Foreign Film and Best Costumes. C: Marcello Mastroianni, Claudia Cardinale, Anouk Aimee, Barbara Steele. D: Federico Fellini. DRA 135m. V

Eight Bells 1935 ★★★½ Nautical romance, with Sothern as a stowaway on her fiancé's ship, finding herself attracted to another man (Bellamy). Ann's charm makes it palatable. C: Ann Sothern, Ralph Bellamy, Catharine Doucet, Franklin Pangborn. D: Roy William Neill. DRA 69m.

Eight Iron Men 1952 ★★★½ Eight GIs pinned down by Germans in a destroyed Italian hamlet hold out for reinforcements. Emphasis is on character with occasional ghastly war humor. C: Bonar Colleano, Lee Marvin,

Richard Kiley, Nick Dennis, Arthur Franz, Mary Castle. D: Edward Dmytryk. DRA 80m.

Eight Men Out 1988 ★★★★ The 1919 Chicago White Sox were the best team in baseball and a "sure bet" to win the World Series. But they blew the series instead, taking a Mob payoff in exchange for victory. Evocative period drama and a tragic look at loss of innocence. Labor of love for Sayles and a fine job all around. C: John Cusack, Clifton James, Michael Lerner, Christopher Lloyd, John Mahoney, Charlie Sheen, David Strathairn, D.B. Sweeney, Michael Rooker. D: John Sayles. DRA [PG] 119m. V

8 Million Ways to Die 1986 ★ Disappointing thriller about an embittered ex-cop (Bridges) hauled into an unwanted murder investigation by a prostitute (Arquette). Unsympathetic characterizations and self-conscious dialogue detract from the work of these usually admirable talents. C: Jeff Bridges, Rosanna Arquette, Alexandra Paul, Andy Garcia. D: Hal Ashby. CRI [R] 115m. V

Eight O'Clock Walk 1952 British ★★★★ An innocent cab driver (Attenborough) is accused of murdering a little girl. Tense, well-acted mystery builds to a terrific courtroom finale. C: Richard Attenborough, Cathy O'Donnell, Derek Farr, Ian Hunter. D: Lance Comford. DRA 87m.

Eight on the Lam 1967 ★★ Widower bank teller (Hope) suspected of embezzling $10,000. Gags aim low—and miss. Normally reliable comics Diller and Winters go down with sinking ship. C: Bob Hope, Phyllis Diller, Jonathan Winters, Jill St. John, Shirley Eaton. D: George Marshall. COM 106m.

8 Seconds 1994 ★★★½ Perry is the late rodeo rider Lane Frost, struggling atop bulls in the spotlight while trying to win his father's love outside the ring. A routine sports tale, but Perry has some good moments, and kids will undoubtedly enjoy. C: Luke Perry, Stephen Baldwin, James Rebhorn, Carrie Snodgresss, Red Mitchell. D: John G. Avildsen. DRA 104m.

18 Again! 1988 ★★★ A birthday wish and car accident allow an octogenarian to inhabit the body of his teenaged grandson. Burns charms during his short screen appearance and Schlatter does a great impression of the aging comedian in this body-switching comedy. C: George Burns, Charlie Schlatter, Tony Roberts, Red Buttons, Jennifer Runyon. D: Paul Flaherty. COM [PG] 100m. V

Eighteen Jade Arhats, The ★★½ When the sacred Arhat power is transmitted to the wrong man, all hell breaks loose. For martial arts fans everywhere. ACT V

Eighth Day of the Week 1959 Polish ★★★★½ Classic, supressed anti-Communist film with Cybulski and Ziemann as a married couple victimized by Socialist bureaucracy in Warsaw. Beautifully acted, with flashes of wry humor through the wrenching drama. Most prints are in German because of government restrictions, an ironic comment on the film's veracity. C: Sonja Ziemann, Zbigniew Cybulski, Ilse Steppat, Burn Krueger. D: Alexander Ford. DRA 84m.

Eighties, The 1986 *See* **Golden Eighties**

Eighties, The 1989 ★★★ Offbeat musical set in Brussels shopping mall. Audacious idea by Akerman is unfortunately given perfunctory treatment. Most of the musical numbers are silly and disjointed, with only the elaborate set making any comedic points. C: Aurore Clement, Lio, Magali Noel, Pascale Salkin. D: Chantal Akerman. MUS 86m. V

80 Blocks from Tiffany's ★★½ Filmmaker Gary Weiss ventures from Manhattan glitz to the subterranean world of Bronx street gangs in this would-be social documentary. Unfortunately, he lacks insight into the world of its subjects. DOC 72m. V

84 Charing Cross Road 1987 ★★★★★ An outgoing New Yorker (Bancroft) maintains a 20-year correspondence with a reserved London bookseller (Hopkins). United by their love of literature, they develop a unique cross-cultural friendship. This intelligent and entertaining movie boasts two excellent performances. Based on Helene Hanff's memoirs and play. C: Anne Bancroft, Anthony Hopkins, Judi Dench, Jean DeBaer, Mercedes Ruehl. D: David Jones. DRA [PG] 100m. V

84 Charlie Mopic 1989 ★★★★½ A Vietnam movie with a difference: The story is told by a two-man motion picture (mopic) camera crew recording a routine reconnaissance mission that turns dangerous. The realistic perspective, complete with sometimes jolting handheld camera, makes it compelling. C: Jonathan Emerson, Nicholas Cascone, Jason Tomlins, Christopher Burgard, Glenn Morshower, Richard Brooks, Byron Thames. D: Patrick Duncan. ACT [R] 95m. V

Eijanaika 1981 Japanese ★★★★ The mass hysteria surrounding the fall of the Tokugawa Shogunate is seen through the eyes of two peasants. Showcase for Imamura's trademark blend of violence and eroticism in a dark, biting treatment of the causes and human toll of revolution. C: Shigeru Izumiya, Ken Ogata, Shigeru Tsuyuguchi. D: Shohei Imamura. DRA 151m. V

El Amor Brujo 1986 ★★★ Third in a trilogy of Spanish dance films—following *Blood Wedding* and *Carmen*—translates its tempestuous love story into passionate dance numbers complemented by spectacular musical accompaniment. Mainly for diehard dance fans. C: Antonio Gades, Christina Hoyos, Laura Del Sol. D: Carlos Saura. MUS [PG] 100m. V

El Bruto 1952 Mexican ★★★★ An evil landlord's stooge falls in love with the daughter of a man he murdered. Hard-hitting drama, with a ferocious performance from Jurado. A good early look at some of the future themes of filmmaking giant Bunuel. C: Pedro Armendariz, Katy Jurado, Andres Soler. D: Luis Bunuel. DRA 83m. V

El Cid 1961 ★★★½ Legendary 11th-century warrior Cid rids Spain of Moors. One of the better epics and certainly one of the biggest. Heston is stalwart in the title role. C: Charlton Heston, Sophia Loren, Raf Vallone, Genevieve Page. D: Anthony Mann. DRA 184m. V

El Condor 1970 ★★★ Two conmen look for hidden gold in Mexico. Atmospheric western, but it needs a stronger leading man than ex-quarterback Brown. C: Jim Brown, Lee Van Cleef, Patrick O'Neal, Mariana Hill. D: John Guillermin. WST [R] 102m. V

El Diablo 1990 ★★★½ Aging gunfighter and a teacher set out to save a young girl from a dangerous outlaw. Comic twists and pleasing performances enliven slow-moving comedy Western. C: Anthony Edwards, Louis Gossett, Jr., John Glover, M.C. Gainey, Miguel Sandoval, Sarah Trigger, Robert Beltran, Joe Pantoliano. D: Peter Markle. WST [PG-13] 115m. TVM V

El Diputado 1978 *See* **Deputy, The**

El Dorado 1967 ★★★★ An aging gunfighter (Wayne) and a drunken sheriff (Mitchum) are allies in a turf war. A top-notch cowboy movie, and comic touches perfectly accent the action. C: John Wayne, Robert Mitchum, James Caan, Edward Asner, Michele Carey, Christopher George. D: Howard Hawks. WST 126m. V

El Greco 1966 Italian-French ★★★½ Gorgeous photography enriches this dramatically feeble bio of the legendary Spanish painter (Ferrer). C: Mel Ferrer, Rosanna Schiaffino. D: Luciano Salce. DRA 95m.

El Manosanta Esta Cargado★★★ The wild and wacky Manosanta on a non-stop romp through all kinds of jobs and all kinds of wild affairs with an assortment of women. Some raucous fun. C: Alberto Omedo, Adriana Brodsky, Silvia Perez, Susana Romero. D: Hugo Sofovich. COM 116m. V

El Mariachi 1993 ★★★★ First effort from Rodriguez, as famous for its minuscule budget as for its rich, inventive story, has a mariachi mistaken for a gangster. An exuberant, stylish tale. C: Carlos Gallardo, Consuelo Gomez, Peter Marquardt. D: Robert Rodriguez. ACT [R] 83m. V

El Mundo Del Talisman 1987 Spanish ★★★½ A lovely animated exploration of the galaxies of space. In Spanish. FAM/SFI 80m.

El Nino Y El Papa 1987 Spanish ★★★ A Mexican boy separated from his mother during an earthquake seeks help from the Pope and finds adventure along the way. DRA 90m.

El Norte 1983 Mexican ★★★★★ Brother and sister flee Guatemala and political persecution for the imagined paradise of Los Angeles. Story sympathetically traces their adaptation to The North with a hypnotic visual style and remarkable compassion. Highly recommended. C: Zaide Silvia Gutierrez, David Villalpando, Ernesto Gomez Cruz, Alicia del Lago, Heraclio Zepeda, Stella Quan, Lupe Ontiveros. D: Gregory Nava. DRA [R] 139m. V

El Professor Hippie 1969 Argentinian ★★★ Middle-aged professor stays in tune with students' thinking, much to his superiors' consternation. Huge Argentinian box-office hit is lightweight concoction that steers clear of any depth. Veteran comic Sandrini is entire show. C: Luis Sandrini, Soledad Silveyra. D: Fernando Ayala. COM 95m.

El Super 1979 ★★★★½ A sensitive portrait of a Cuban exile (Hidalgo-Gato) working as a superintendent in a Manhattan apartment building, trying to make it in a cold new world, tormented by homesickness and his outsider status. A simple, melancholy film with fine, nuanced performances. C: Raymundo Hidalgo-Gato, Zully Montero, Elizabeth Pena. D: Leon Ichaso, Orlando Jimenez-Leal. DRA 90m. V

El: This Strange Passion 1955 ★★★★ Pious, celibate Catholic in his 40s marries beautiful young woman only to be consumed by jealousy. Quintessential—and essential—Buñuel has all the trademarks: scathing humor, satiric swipes at the Church, and continual subversion of cinematic conventions. C: Arturo De Cordova, Delia Garces, Luis Baristain. D: Luis Buñuel. COM 100m.

Eleanor and Franklin 1976 ★★★★★ Marvelous dramatization of early lives of Franklin Delano Roosevelt and wife Eleanor, culminating in former's presidency, with definitive performances by Herrmann and Alexander. Remarkably accurate for TV, based on Pulitizer Prize-winning biography by Joseph P. Lash that humanizes these larger-than-life legends of American politics. Followed by sequel. C: Jane Alexander, Edward Herrmann, Rosemary Murphy, Pamela Franklin, David Huffman, MacKenzie Phillips, Lilia Skala, Ed Flanders, Anna Lee, Linda Purl, Linda Kelsey, Lindsay Crouse. D: Daniel Petrie. DRA 208m. TVM

Eleanor and Franklin: The White House Years 1977 ★★★★★ Sequel to *Eleanor and Franklin* continues the Roosevelts' story into the White House for four elected terms, 1932-1945, covering the Depression and WWII. Consistently enlightening entertainment represents TV filmmaking at its finest. Handsome production elements, literate script, and impeccable performances. C: Jane Alexander, Edward Herrmann, Rosemary Murphy, Walter McGinn, Blair Brown, David Healy, Anna Lee, Mark Harmon, Linda Kelsey, Peggy McKay, Donald Moffat. D: Daniel Petrie. DRA 152m. TVM

Eleanor, First Lady of the World 1982 ★★★★ Sitcom star Stapleton displays dramatic talents in well-written account of Mrs.

Roosevelt's life after FDR's death in 1945. Effectively captures Eleanor's refusal to retire into obscurity and her subsequent impact on social issues. C: Jean Stapleton, E.G. Marshall, Coral Browne, Joyce Van Patten, Gail Strickland, Kenneth Kimmins, Richard McKenzie, Kabir Bedi. D: John Erman. DRA [G] 96m. TVM v

Eleanor Roosevelt Story, The 1965 ★★★★ Informative, absorbing documentary about one of the most vital and important women of our century. This Oscar winner is narrated by Archibald MacLeish, Eric Sevareid, and Francis Cole. D: Richard Kaplan. DOC 91m. v

Electra Glide in Blue 1973 ★★★★ Arizona highway motorcycle cop tries to make sense of the random violence of his job and the height discrimination he faces. Thoughtful, quirky but violent. C: Robert Blake, Billy "Green" Bush, Elisha Cook, Jr. D: James William Guercio. DRA [PG] 113m. v

Electric Dreams 1984 ★★★ Computer is jealous of owner's love affair. Cute post-*2001: A Space Odyssey* idea, generates enough sweetness to keep going. C: Lenny Von Dohlen, Maxwell Caulfield. D: Steve Barron. COM [PG] 95m. v

Electric Horseman, The 1979 ★★★½ Fallen rodeo star (Redford), now reduced to hawking breakfast food, rescues beloved horse from Vegas promoters and heads out to desert. A reporter (Fonda) follows the story and falls for Redford. Slight and sometimes obvious drama gets a boost from strong leads. C: Robert Redford, Jane Fonda, Valerie Perrine, Willie Nelson. D: Sydney Pollack. DRA [PG] 120m. v

Electronic Monster, The 1957 British ★★★ An actress's death unlocks the door to bizarre experiments using high voltage. Quirky sci-fi delivers some thrills. (a.k.a. *Escapement.*) C: Rod Cameron, Mary Murphy, Meredith Edwards, Peter Illing. D: Montgomery Tully. SFI 72m. v

Elegant Criminal, The 1992 ★★★★ Fictional treatment of real-life French gadabout of the 19th century, a charming cad who died on the guillotine. Flashbacks reveal his sordid, adventurous past of professional romance, murder, and petty thievery. C: Daniel Auteuil, Jean Poiret, Jacques Weber. D: Francis Girod. CRI 120m. v

Element of Crime, The 1985 ★★★★ Futuristic thriller has a police officer (Elphick) hypnotized to return to murder scene, becoming one with the killer to catch him. Imaginative blend of sci-fi and film noir in which all the characters are morally implicated in the crimes. Wonderfully eerie. C: Michael Elphick, Esmond Knight, Meme Lei. D: Lars Von Trier. CRI 104m. v

Elena and Her Men 1956 French ★★ Exiled Polish princess must choose between three very different suitors. Very minor Renoir has attractive case and a few chuckles but little else. (a.k.a. *Paris Does Strange Things* and *Elena et les Hommes.*) C: Ingrid Bergman, Jean Marais. D: Jean Renoir. COM 98m.

Elena et les Hommes 1956 *See* **Elena and Her Men**

Eleni 1985 ★★★½ A Greek-American journalist returns to the old country to learn more about the post-WWII execution of his mother at the hands of Communists. A true and intriguing story, with powerful work by Nelligan at the emotional center. C: Kate Nelligan, John Malkovich, Linda Hunt, Oliver Cotton. D: Peter Yates. DRA [PG] 117m. v

Elephant 1972 *See* **African Elephant, The**

Elephant Boy 1937 British ★★★★½ Classic Flaherty docudrama that made a star out of young mahout Sabu as a boy in harmony with nature and with his elephant. Shows signs of age, but still effective and disarming. A must-see. C: Sabu, Allan Jeayes, D. Williams. D: Zoltan Korda, Robert Flaherty. DRA 80m. v

Elephant Man, The 1980 ★★★★ Dreamlike retelling of story of hideously disfigured 19th century Englishman John Merrick, brilliantly acted and directed. Based on actual accounts, not the Broadway play. C: Anthony Hopkins, John Hurt, Anne Bancroft, John Gielgud, Freddie Jones. D: David Lynch. DRA [PG] 125m. v

Elephant Walk 1954 ★★★ Taylor wasted as Finch's wife in mundane drama of her difficulties adjusting to life on his Ceylon plantation. Climactic elephant stampede is well done. C: Elizabeth Taylor, Dana Andrews, Peter Finch, Abraham Sofaer. D: William Dieterle. DRA 103m. v

Elephant's Child 1985 ★★★★½ Nicholson does a marvelous job narrating this tale of a curious little elephant from Kipling's classic *Just So Stories.* Voice of Jack Nicholson. D: Mark Sottnick. FAM/DRA 30m.

Elevator to the Gallows 1958 *See* **Frantic**

11 Harrowhouse 1974 British ★★½ American diamond merchant (Grodin) is robbed, so he in turn robs an international diamond syndicate. Reasonably pleasant caper spoof. (a.k.a. *Anything for Love*) C: Charles Grodin, Candice Bergen, James Mason, Trevor Howard, John Gielgud. D: Aram Avakian. COM 95m. v

Eliza Frazer 1976 ★★★½ York is a shipwrecked Englishwoman captured by Australian aborigines. Comic adventure tale, with some delightful sequences. Based on a true story. C: Noel Ferrier, Susannah York, Trevor Howard. D: Tim Burstall. COM 130m.

Elizabeth of Ladymead 1948 British ★★★★ Thoughtful and captivating historical set pieces tell the story of four English women (all played by Neagle) over the course of four different wars (1854, 1903, 1919, 1946) and their returning husbands. Fine performances, with touches of humor. C: Anna Neagle, Hugh Williams, Michael Laurence, Bernard Lee, Nicholas Phipps, Isabel Jeans. D: Herbert Wilcox. DRA 97m.

Elizabeth the Queen *See* **Private Lives of Elizabeth and Essex, The**

Ella Cinders 1926 ★★★★ Funny silent updating of the Cinderella story with Moore as victim of tyrannical stepmother and stepsisters. When she wins talent contest and goes to Hollywood, the tables are turned. Or are they? Adds some neat twists to old story and star is charming. C: Colleen Moore, Lloyd Hughes, Vera Lewis, Doris Baker, Emily Gerdes, Jed Prouty. D: Alfred Green. COM 60m.

Ellery Queen 1975 ★★★½ Manfred B. Lee and Frederic Dannay's crafty shamus returns to help his police officer father solve the murder of a fashion designer. Moderately successful attempt to borrow look and feel of a '40s hard-boiled drama. C: Jim Hutton, David Wayne, Ray Milland, Kim Hunter, Monte Markham, John Hillerman, John Larch, Tim O'Connor. D: David Greene. CRI 78m. TVM

Ellery Queen and the Murder Ring 1941 ★★ Queen (Bellamy) helps his police officer father (Grapewin) solve a murder in the local hospital. Scattered sleuth series entry. C: Ralph Bellamy, Margaret Lindsay, Charley Grapewin, Blanche Yurka. D: James Hogan. CRI 65m.

Ellery Queen and the Perfect Crime 1941 ★★½ Queen (Bellamy) solves the murder of a businessman who sold phony stocks. About average for this detective series. C: Ralph Bellamy, Margaret Lindsay, Charley Grapewin, Spring Byington. D: James Hogan. CRI 68m.

Ellery Queen, Master Detective 1940 ★★★ First appearance of Bellamy as detective Queen, tracking down killer at a health spa. Flimsy entry in flat series of gumshoe films. C: Ralph Bellamy, Margaret Lindsay, Charley Grapewin, James Burke, Michael Whalen, Marsha Hunt, Fred Niblo, Charles Lane, Douglas Fowley, Katherine DeMille. D: Kurt Neumann. CRI 66m.

Ellery Queen's Penthouse Mystery 1941 ★★½ Queen (Bellamy) helps his father (Grapewin) solve the slaying of a Chinese vaudevillian. So-so series entry. C: Ralph Bellamy, Margaret Lindsay, Charley Grapewin, Anna May Wong, James Burke. D: James Hogan. CRI 69m.

Ellis Island 1984 ★★★ TV miniseries chronicles persons and events affected by historic New York Bay immigration station in the 1900s. Retread but affecting nonetheless. Filmed on location. C: Richard Burton, Faye Dunaway, Peter Riegert, Ben Vereen, Melba Moore, Ann Jillian, Claire Bloom. D: Jerry London. DRA 327m. TVM V

Elmer Gantry 1960 ★★★★★ Oscar-winning turn by Lancaster as evangelist who hooks up with Simmons, sends girlfriend Jones into life of prostitution, and finds himself being investigated by journalist Kennedy. Jones also nabbed Oscar, as did Brooks' adaptation of the Sinclair Lewis novel. C: Burt Lancaster, Jean Simmons, Dean Jagger, Arthur Kennedy, Shirley Jones. D: Richard Brooks. DRA 146m. V

Elmer the Great 1933 ★★★★ Cute comedy features baseball player (Brown) whose penchant for stretching the truth gets him in trouble with mobsters who want him to help throw the World Series. Adapted from Ring Lardner-George M. Cohan play. Fine for younger viewers. C: Joe E. Brown, Patricia Ellis, Frank McHugh, Claire Dodd, Preston Foster, Russell Hopton, Sterling Holloway, Emma Dunn, J. Carroll Naish. D: Mervyn LeRoy. COM 74m.

Elopement 1951 ★★★ When his daughter elopes, a fussy father goes on the prowl to break them up. Trim comedy showcase for Webb's dapper wit. C: Clifton Webb, Anne Francis, Charles Bickford, William Lundigan, Evelyn Varden, Margalo Gillmore. D: Henry Koster. COM 82m.

Elusive Corporal, The 1962 French ★★★ French soldiers captured by Nazis dream of escape. Almost a remake of *Grand Illusion*, but without that film's profound subtlety. C: Jean-Pierre Cassel, Claude Brasseur, Claude Rich, Jean Carmet. D: Jean Renoir. DRA 105m. V

Elusive Pimpernel, The 1950 *See* **Fighting Pimpernel, The**

Elvira—Alabama's Ghost ★★ TV's scream queen unearthed this early-'70s rarity about a dead magician returning to life when a musician steals his secrets. Odd little low-budgeter may be the first to feature an undead, motorcycle rock band. HOR V

Elvira Madigan 1967 Swedish ★★★★½ Sumptuously rendered romance, based on a true story, concerns married army officer who runs off with tightrope walker. With a soundtrack by Mozart and dreamy photography. A lyrical, upbeat film. C: Pia Degermark, Thommy Berggren. D: Bo Widerberg. DRA 89m. V

Elvira, Mistress of the Dark 1988 ★★ The TV horror character travels to her Massachusetts hometown to collect inheritance. Ultracampy star can't conjure laughs out of this comedy's musty double-entendres and threadbare plot. C: Elvira, Susan Kellermann, Jeff Conaway, Edie McClurg. D: James Signorelli. COM [PG-13] 96m. V

Elvis 1979 ★★★½ The story of the King, from his early days to the big, big time. Russell really pulls it off, and the story, in general, comes across in style. C: Kurt Russell, Shelley Winters, Pat Hingle, Season Hubley. D: John Carpenter. DRA [G] 117m. TVM V

Elvis and Me 1988 ★★★ Priscilla Presley's tell-all tale of life with "The King." Midkiff gives reasonable interpretation. Soundtrack performed by country singer Ronnie McDowell. C: Dale Midkiff, Susan Walters, Jon Cypher, Linda Miller. D: Larry Peerce. MUS 187m. TVM V

Elvis and the Beauty Queen 1981 ★★★½ The King has a fling with a pageant contestant. Undistinguished "true confession" soap opera; worth a look for Johnson and/or Elvis fans. C: Don Johnson, Stephanie Zimbalist. D: Gus Trikonis. DRA 100m. TVM

Elvis on Tour 1972 ★★★½ Fair concert film, with Elvis just at the beginning of his decline. Not his best, but a must-see for hardcore fans. C: Elvis Presley. D: Pierre Adidge, Robert Abel. MUS [G] 93m. V

Elvis: That's the Way It Is 1970 ★★★★½ Presley's historic comeback concert in Las Vegas gets definitive documentary preservation, with a fine mix of backstage and performance footage. Great intro for Elvis neophytes. C: Elvis Presley. D: Denis Sanders. MUS [G] 97m. V

Embarassing Moments 1930 ★★★ Kennedy pretends to be married to avoid her father's choice of suitor. Dizzy comedy has an improbable premise but an amusing cast, with Harlan the standout as Merna's snobbish dad. C: Reginald Denny, Merna Kennedy, Otis Harlan. D: William James Craft. COM 60m.

Embassy 1972 British ★★★ Spy thriller about the efforts of an American agent (Roundtree) to elude a KGB assassin (Connors) and smuggle a would-be defector (von Sydow) out of the Mideast. Some fine acting, especially by Connors. Too much talk. (a.k.a. *Target: Embassy*) C: Richard Roundtree, Chuck Connors, Max von Sydow, Ray Milland, Broderick Crawford, Marie-Jose Nat. D: Gordon Hessler. ACT [PG] 90m.

Embraceable You 1948 ★★★½ Getaway car driver (Clark) maims Brooks leaving scene of a murder, then falls in love with her. Contrived, but emotionally compelling tearjerker. C: Dane Clark, Geraldine Brooks, S.Z. Sakall, Wallace Ford. D: Felix Jacoves. DRA 80m.

Embryo 1976 ★★★ A scientist (Hudson) "grows" an artificial woman from an egg—but she's nobody's dream date! Imaginative thriller. (a.k.a. *Created To Kill.*) C: Rock Hudson, Diane Ladd, Barbara Carrera, Roddy McDowall. D: Ralph Nelson. SFI [PG] 108m. V

Emerald Forest, The 1985 ★★★★ When engineer (Boothe) and family are on assignment in the Amazon, his young son (Boorman, the real-life son of the director) is abducted by natives. Boothe searches for years, while Boorman assimilates. Well-told tale highlighted by a fine Boothe and stunning locale. C: Powers Boothe, Meg Foster, Charley Boorman, Dira Pass. D: John Boorman. DRA [R] 113m. V

Emergency Call 1953 *See* **Hundred Hour Hunt**

Emergency Hospital 1956 ★★★ One night in a L.A. hospital's emergency room is the frame for this episodic film, focusing on a doctor (Lindsay) fending off the advances of a devil-may-care playboy (Palmer). Thin stuff, but well played. C: Walter Reed, Margaret Lindsay, John Archer, Byron Palmer, Rita Johnson, Jim Stapleton. D: Lee Sholem. DRA 62m.

Emigrants, The 1971 Swedish ★★★★★ Swedish family endures the rugged harshness of the New World after leaving their homeland in the 1850s. Leisurely, loving look at settler couple and their fierce will. Von Sydow and Ullmann are brilliant, as are Troell's directing and photography. Sequel, *The New Land*, is equally good. Presented together on television, dubbed, as *The Emigrant Saga.* C: Max von Sydow, Liv Ullmann, Eddie Axberg, Allan Edwall. D: Jan Troell. DRA [PG] 148m. V

Emil 1938 ★★★½ Young boy organizes other children to find and stop a thief who preys on juvenile victims. First of many versions of famous German children's classic isn't the best, but Williams is charming as title character. (a.k.a. *Emil and the Detectives*) C: George Hayes, Mary Glynne, John Williams, Clare Greet. D: Milton Rosmer. FAM/CRI 63m.

Emil and the Detectives 1938 *See* **Emil**

Emil and the Detectives 1964 ★★★★ En route to Berlin, a young lad is drugged and robbed. He pursues the thief, eventually enlisting hundreds of children to help him. Second and best version of children's detective story. Has a sweet, goofy charm that is irresistible for both children and adults. C: Walter Slezak, Bryan Russell, Roger Mobley, Heinz Schubert. D: Peter Tewksbury. FAM/CRI 99m. V

Emily 1976 ★★ After learning that her mother is really a prostitute, distraught student (Stark) turns to an artist, and the artist's boyfriend and husband to console herself. Erotica debut in softcore is the main attraction. C: Koo Stark, Sarah Brackett, Victor Spinetti. D: Henry Herbert. DRA 84m. V

Eminent Domain 1991 ★★★½ Polish politician (Sutherland) is inexplicably dismissed from his post. Investigation is not only futile, but deadly. Kafkaesque bureaucratic nightmare, effectively suspenseful. C: Donald Sutherland, Anne Archer, Jodhi May, Paul Freeman, Francoise Michaud. D: John Irvin. DRA [PG-13] 102m. V

Emma 1932 ★★★★½ Simple, beautifully acted story of elderly nanny Dressler and her developing relationship with employer Hersholt. Star's uncanny ability to merge comedy with pathos makes this very special, heartwarming entertainment. C: Marie Dressler, Richard Cromwell, Jean Hersholt, Myrna Loy,

John Miljan, Leila Bennett. D: Clarence Brown. DRA 73m.

Emma's Shadow 1988 Danish ★★★ Rich girl runs away, given refuge by poor sewer worker in '30s Copenhagen. Modest story finds all its charms in youngster Kruse; otherwise generic and predictable. C: Borje Ahlstedt, Line Kruse, Henrik Larsen. D: Soeren Kragh-Jacobsen. DRA 93m.

Emperor and A General, The 1968 ★★★½ During the final hours of WWII, Japan's War Minister (Mifune) takes drastic measures to prevent Emperor Hirohito from surrendering. Factual drama has thrilling moments, but a predictable ending. C: Toshiro Mifune, So Yamamura, Chishu Ryu, Takashi Shimura. D: Kihachi Okamoto. DRA 158m.

Emperor Caligula 1983 ★ Cavalcade of debauchery and gory excess charts the lifestyle of history's most infamous pervert. A thinly disguised splatter film, will test the stomachs of the most dedicated sleazehound. C: David Cain Haughton, Joan McCoy, Laura Gemser. D: David Hills. ACT [R] 100m. V

Emperor Jones, The 1933 ★★★ Robeson stars as train porter elevated to ruler of Caribbean isle in adaptation of Eugene O'Neill play. Stiff, clunky production suffers from low budget and rewriting to showcase Robeson's singing. C: Paul Robeson, Dudley Digges, Frank Wilson, Fredi Washington. D: Dudley Murphy. DRA 72m. V

Emperor of Peru, The 1982 *See* **Odyssey of the Pacific**

Emperor of the North Pole 1973 *See* **Emperor of the North, The**

Emperor of the North, The 1973 ★★★★½ A compelling adventure about the Depression pits a sadistic train conductor (Borgnine), who vows to kill all tramps who stow away on his train, against a hobo (Marvin) determined to flout him. This deadly serious contest makes for a tense symbolic tale about freedom and repression, with some superbly realized moments of black humor. (a.k.a. *Emperor of the North Pole*) C: Lee Marvin, Ernest Borgnine, Keith Carradine, Charles Tyner, Harry Caesar, Malcolm Atterbury, Simon Oakland, Matt Clark, Elisha Cook Jr. D: Robert Aldrich. ACT 118m.

Emperor Waltz, The 1948 ★★★★ Underrated, charming operetta has Crosby trying to sell a phonograph to Emperor Franz Joseph of Austria. Delightful departure from Wilder's usual hard-boiled style. Perhaps Crosby's best performance. C: Bing Crosby, Joan Fontaine, Roland Culver, Lucile Watson, Richard Haydn, Sig Ruman. D: Billy Wilder. MUS 106m. V

Emperor's Candlesticks, The 1937 ★★½ In this adaptation of Baroness Orczy's novel, two pre-WWI spies (Rainer and Powell) on opposing sides scamper across Europe and fall in love. Expensive, handsome production. C: William Powell, Luise Rainer, Robert Young, Maureen O'Sullivan, Frank Morgan, Emma Dunn, Douglass Dumbrille. D: George Fitzmaurice. DRA 89m.

Empire of the Ants 1977 ★★ Ants bigger than Buicks (they ate radioactive waste) threaten Collins and others on a remote vacation island. Total schlock from master schlockateer Gordon. From an H.G. Wells story. *Them* remains the definitive big-insect movie. C: Joan Collins, Robert Lansing, Albert Salmi, John David Carson. D: Bert I. Gordon. SFI [PG] 89m. V

Empire of the Night, The 1963 ★★★½ Constantine is a saloon singer trying to stop hoodlums from taking over his nightclub. Suspenseful crime drama with interesting atmosphere. C: Eddie Constantine, Elga Andersen, Genevieve Grad. D: Pierre Grimblat. CRI 90m.

Empire of the Sun 1987 ★★★★ Pampered British boy (Bale) is left on his own after being separated from his parents in early WWII China, as Japan invades. Often touching dramatic epic highlighted by solid acting, especially by Bale and Malkovich. Scripted by Tom Stoppard from J.G. Ballard's autobiographical novel. C: Christian Bale, John Malkovich, Miranda Richardson, Nigel Havers. D: Steven Spielberg. DRA [PG] 152m. V

Empire State 1988 ★★★ Desperate characters converge on a club called the Empire State. One thing leads to another, culminating (naturally) in lots of action, heavy on the violence. C: Ray McAnally, Cathryn Harrison, Martin Landau. D: Ron Peck. ACT [R] 104m. V

Empire Strikes Back, The 1980 ★★★★★ Leia, Luke, Han, and those droll droids continue their intergalactic struggle against the Evil Empire. Masterful storytelling manages to weave several plotlines, further develop the main characters, *and* introduce the slippery Calrissian and Zen master Yoda. Mesmerizing effects, even on TV. The darkest and best of the trilogy. Sequel to *Star Wars* and followed by *Return of the Jedi*. C: Mark Hamill, Harrison Ford, Carrie Fisher, Billy Dee Wiliams. D: Irvin Kershner. SFI [PG] 124m. V

Employees' Entrance 1933 ★★★½ Fast-paced look at day-to-day life in a big city department store and employee struggles with a merciless floorwalker. Dated but snappy. C: Warren William, Loretta Young, Wallace Ford, Alice White, Allen Jenkins. D: Roy Del Ruth. DRA 75m. V

Empress and I, The 1933 ★★★½ German Empress' beautician (Harvey) is mistaken for Her Highness (Christians) in sophisticated musical with expressionistic sets. Perhaps a bit esoteric for contemporary taste, but fascinating. C: Mady Christians, Charles Boyer, Lilian Harvey, Maurice Evans. D: Friedrich Hollander. MUS

Empress Yang Kwei Fei, The 1955 *See* **Princess Yang Kwei Fei, The**

Empress Yank Kwei Fei 1955 *See* **Princess Yang Kwei Fei**

Empty Canvas, The 1964 French ★★½ Laughable melodrama from Alberto Moravia novel has Bette doing her utmost to save artist son Buchholz from obsessive love for Spaak. C: Bette Davis, Horst Buchholz, Catherine Spaak, Isa Miranda. D: Damiano Damiani. DRA 118m. v

Enchanted April 1935 ★★★ Four women renting an Italian villa for a month to escape men and London are set upon by various nutty visitors. Adaptation of play by Kane Campbell, from Elizabeth von Arnim's novel is a mixture of syrup and soap. Sophisticated remake appeared in 1991. C: Ann Harding, Frank Morgan, Katharine Alexander, Reginald Owen, Jane Baxter, Ralph Forbes, Jessie Ralph, Charles Judels, Rafaela Ottiano. D: Harry Beaumont. DRA 66m.

Enchanted April 1991 British ★★★★ Two starchy Englishwomen leave their husbands at home and go off for a quiet month in the Italian countryside that turns out to be not so quiet. Pleasant comedy drama nicely delivered and, yes, enchanting. Remake of 1935 movie by same title. C: Josie Lawrence, Miranda Richardson, Joan Plowright, Polly Walker, Alfred Molina, Jim Broadbent, Michael Kitchen. D: Mike Newell. COM [PG] 101m. v

Enchanted Cottage, The 1945 ★★★★ Sentimental fairy tale story of a man horribly disfigured by war and a very plain young woman who share love and happiness together. The Pinero play was also a 1924 silent film. Oscar nomination for music. C: Dorothy McGuire, Robert Young, Herbert Marshall, Mildred Natwick. D: John Cromwell. DRA 91m. v

Enchanted Forest 1945 ★★★★ Lost young boy is tutored by a wise old hermit in the ways of nature in an untouched forest glade. Charming, low-key, and innocent. Best-known example of Cinecolor process. C: Edmund Lowe, Brenda Joyce, Billy Severn, Harry Davenport. D: Lew Landers. DRA 78m. v

Enchanted Island 1958 ★★ Two British sailors living among cannibals on a South Seas island. One of them is in love with a native princess. Unenchanting adaptation of Melville's *Typee*. C: Dana Andrews, Jane Powell, Don Dubbins, Arthur Shields. D: Allan Dwan. DRA 94m. v

Enchantment 1948 ★★★★ Niven misses chance at love with father's ward (Wright), years later encourages WWII ambulance driver Keyes not to make same mistake with soldier Granger. Handsomely produced, well-acted, classy tearjerker. C: David Niven, Teresa Wright, Evelyn Keyes, Farley Granger, Jayne Meadows, Leo Carroll. D: Irving Reis. DRA 102m. v

Encino Man 1992 ★★½ Caveman (Fraser) is unearthed by two teens (Shore and Astin), thawed out, and taken to school as an exchange student. Enjoyable foolishness is damaged by occasional moralizing. C: Sean Astin, Brendan Fraser, Pauly Shore, Megan Ward, Mariette Hartley, Michael DeLuise. D: Les Mayfield. COM [PG] 89m. v

Encore 1952 British ★★★ Three directors team up for three different Somerset Maugham tales in a sequel to *Trio*. A mixed bag but *Winter Cruise* is the most memorable and funniest. C: Nigel Patrick, Roland Culver, Kay Walsh, Glynis Johns, Peter Graves, Margaret Vyner. D: Pat Jackson, Anthony Pelissier, Harold French. DRA 85m. v

Encounter at Raven's Gate 1988 ★★★★ Small Australian town is upended by all manner of calamities. Good performances in this gripping study of people under fire. C: Steven Vidler, Celine Griffin. D: Rolf De Heer. SFI [R] 85m. v

Encounter with the Unknown 1973 ★★ Supposedly fact-based film about various bizarre phenomena (ghosts, ancient curses, etc.) is cheap looking and padded with flashbacks, but gets a little cachet from Rod Serling narration. C: Rosie Holotick, Gary Brockette, Gene Ross. D: Harry Thomason. DOC [PG] 87m. v

End of a Day, The 1939 ★★★★ Retirement home for actors becomes elderly thespians' final stage. Lyrical study of twilight years, with Jouvet at top of his form. C: Victor Francen, Louis Jouvet, Michel Simon. D: Julien Duvivier. DRA 94m.

End of August, The 1982 ★★ Shallow adaptation of Kate Chopin's once-sensational novel, *The Awakening*. Bored society wife takes bohemian lover in turn-of-the-century New Orleans in order to experience sexual fulfillment she cannot find with her husband. Prettily photographed but disappointing. C: Sally Sharp, Lilia Skala, David Marshall Grant, Kathleen Widdoes. D: Bob Graham. DRA [PG] 104m. v

End of Desire 1958 French-Italian ★★★ Period soaper stars Schell as a woman whose husband is carrying on with the maid under her very nose. Good performances. Based on a story by Guy de Maupassant. (a.k.a. *One Life*) C: Maria Schell, Christian Marquand, Pascale Petit, Ivan Desny. D: Alexandre Astruc. DRA 86m.

End of Innocence, The 1990 ★★★ Cannon's tour de force as writer/director/actress wavers uncertainly between drama and comedy. She gives strong, emotional performance as woman driven over the edge by family demands who finally straightens herself out at drug rehab clinic. C: Dyan Cannon, John Heard, Bridget Fonda, Rebecca Schaeffer. D: Dyan Cannon. DRA [R] 102m. v

End of St. Petersburg, The 1927 ★★★★½ Youngster moves from rural Russia to the city, where he is caught up in 1917 Revolution. Silent film masterpiece, brilliantly directed, using actual settings and real armed forces for gigantic action sequences. Superlative use of cinema as propaganda. C: Ivan Chalelov. D: Vanvlov Pudovkin. DRA

End of Summer, The 1961 ★★★★½ Aging merchant shocks his three adult daughters by rekindling his relationship with a former mistress. Ozu's penultimate film is also one of his greatest, teeming with grace, humor, subtlety, depth. A loving view of humanity's shortcomings. (a.k.a. *Early Autumn.*) C: Ganjiro Nakamura, Setsuko Hara, Yoko Tsukasa. D: Yasujiro Ozu. DRA 103m.

End of the Affair, The 1955 British ★★★ Kerr and Johnson are adulterous lovers in WWII romance set during London blitz. Desperate to keep her lover safe, devout Kerr makes a pact with God and breaks off the affair, without telling Johnson why. Well acted but overlong. Based on popular Graham Greene novel. C: Deborah Kerr, Van Johnson, John Mills, Peter Cushing, Michael Goodliffe. D: Edward Dmytryk. DRA 106m.

End of the Game 1976 German-Italian ★★★½ Stylized, intriguingly indecipherable mystery about rival sleuths (Voight, Bisset) investigating a 30-year-old murder. Sutherland has a cameo—as a corpse! The script was co-written by Swiss playwright Friedrich (*The Visit*) Duerrenmatt. (a.k.a. *Getting Away With Murder*) C: Jon Voight, Jacqueline Bisset, Martin Ritt, Robert Shaw, Donald Sutherland. D: Maximilian Schell. CRI [PG] 103m.

End of the Line 1988 ★★½ When an old freight depot is closed, disappointed railroad workers (Brimley and Helm) steal a train engine and head for corporate headquarters in Chicago to protest. Lovingly displays down-home qualities of its stars, but stays predictable. C: Wilford Brimley, Levon Helm, Mary Steenburgen, Barbara Barrie, Kevin Bacon, Holly Hunter, Bob Balaban. D: Jay Russell. DRA [PG] 103m. V

End of the River, The 1947 British ★★½ A young South American Indian (Sabu) stands trial for murder. Produced by the famed directing team of Eric Powell and Emeric Pressburger, but only some of their adventurousness shows. C: Sabu, Esmond Knight, Bibi Ferreira. D: Derek Twist. DRA 80m.

End of the Road, The 1936 ★★★½ A song-and-dance man (Lauder) won't give up show business despite personal tragedy and financial ruin. Film is an entertaining showcase for British music hall star Lauder, who's wonderful. C: Harry Lauder, Ruth Haven, Bruce Seton. D: Alex Bryce. MUS 72m.

End of the Road, The 1954 ★★★★ Retired factory worker (Currie) is made to feel useless and unwanted by his son and daughter-in-law. Attempt to deal with the problems of aging is marred by sentimentality. Good performance by Currie. C: Finlay Currie. D: Wolf Rilla. DRA 76m.

End of the Trail 1932 ★★★★ A 19th-century Army officer (McCoy) is unjustly court-martialed, then dedicates his life to clearing himself and helping the maligned Indian nation. Outstanding Western is unique in its humanized depiction of Native Americans. C: Tim McCoy, Luana Walter, Wheeler Oakman. D: Ross Lederman. WST 61m.

End of the Trail 1936 ★★★★ A cattle rustler (Holt) risks his life to avenge the murder of his ladylove's brother. Downbeat Western with attractive antihero was ahead of its time and makes for interesting viewing. C: Jack Holt, Louise Henry, Douglass Dumbrille, Guinn "Big Boy" Williams. D: Erle C. Kenton. WST 72m.

End of the World in Our Usual Bed in a Night Full of Rain, The 1978 *See* **Night Full of Rain, A**

End of the World 1962 *See* **Panic in Year Zero!**

End Play 1975 ★★★½ Two brothers, a seaman and a terminally ill paraplegic, both suspect each other of being a serial killer. Satisfying mystery with an effective surprise ending. C: George Mallaby, John Waters, Ken Goodiet, Delvene Delaney. D: Tim Burstall. DRA 80m.

End, The 1978 ★★★½ Terminally ill man (Reynolds) hospitalized after suicide attempt gets some help from fellow patient (DeLuise). Leads create powerful synergy in surprisingly despairing black comedy. C: Burt Reynolds, Sally Field, Dom DeLuise, Joanne Woodward, Kristy McNichol, Robby Benson, David Steinberg, Norman Fell, Carl Reiner, Pat O'Brien, Myrna Loy. D: Burt Reynolds. COM [R] 100m. V

Endangered Species 1982 ★★★ New York cop bites off more than he can chew when he investigates a series of cattle mutilations out West. Thriller is based on a real-life incident. C: Robert Urich, JoBeth Williams, Paul Dooley, Hoyt Axton, Peter Coyote. D: Alan Rudolph. DRA [R] 97m. V

Endless Game, The 1989 British ★★★½ Cold War thriller in which a British secret agent (Finney) searches for his agent/lover's killer and stumbles upon an international conspiracy. Complex spy offering highlighted by musical score from Ennio Morricone. C: Albert Finney, George Segal, Derek DeLint, Ian Holm, Kristin Scott Thomas. D: Bryan Forbes. CRI [PG-13] 123m. V

Endless Love 1981 ★ Grotesque, morbid film about obsessive teenage love of Hewitt for Shields. She is more inert than usual, and he is a good match. Adult cast looks suitably embarrassed. Cruise's film debut. C: Brooke Shields, Martin Hewitt, Shirley Knight, Don Murray, Richard Kiley, Beatrice Straight, James Spader, Tom Cruise, Jami Gertz. D: Franco Zeffirelli. DRA [R] 115m. V

Endless Night 1971 British ★★★ Newly married British chauffeur (Bennett) and his rich American wife (Mills) move into the house of their dreams, but are nearly frightened to death. Weak adaptation of Agatha Christie novel hurt by miscast Mills. C: Hayley Mills, Hywel Bennett, Britt Ekland, George Sanders. D: Sidney Gilliat. CRI 95m. V

Endless Summer, The 1966 ★★★★ Dazzlingly golden photography highlights documentary on surfing all over the world. As a worshiper of the sport, Brown shot, directed, and edited—and it shows. Intelligent and droll, this isn't just for surfing fans. D: Bruce Brown, Mike Hynson, Robert August. DOC 90m. V

Endless Summer II—The Journey Continues 1994 ★★★½ It's been 27 years, but the search for the perfect wave goes on, this time with a new generation of tanned, toned beachboys. Stunning photography, but rather irritating narration. Surf fans will love it. Brief nudity. D: Bruce Brown, Patrick O'Connell, Robert Weaver. DOC [PG] 107m. V

Endurance ★★ Clips from oddball Japanese game show, where contestants submit themselves to unthinkable physical torture and mental anguish in pursuit of nominal prizes. For those who find humor in watching others experience degrading pain and humiliation. COM 90m. V

Enemies, A Love Story 1989 ★★★★ A somber Jewish intellectual (Silver), a refugee who spent the war years hiding from the Nazis, comes to postwar Coney Island and gets himself involved with three different women (two of whom are his wives!). Adaptation of an I.B. Singer story of loss, libido and loyalty. Beautifully done. C: Anjelica Huston, Ron Silver, Lena Olin, Margaret Sophie Stein, Alan King. D: Paul Mazursky. DRA [R] 119m. V

Enemies of Progress 1934 ★★★½ Communist propaganda drama, with Livanov as a Czarist army officer refusing to accept the Bolshevik Revolution, then trying to incite local peasants to revolt. Pedantic, but interesting as an historical document. C: Livanov, Gardin, Taskin. D: Nicolai Beresnyev. DRA 80m.

Enemy Agent 1940 ★★★½ Nazi agents and G-men vie for top-secret plans in the possession of an innocent architect (Cromwell). Modestly entertaining espionage. C: Richard Cromwell, Helen Vinson, Robert Armstrong, Marjorie Reynolds. D: Lew Landers. ACT 61m.

Enemy Below, The 1957 ★★★★ They broke the mold with this classic U-boat vs. destroyer duel set in the South Atlantic in WWII. Mitchum and Jurgens are perfect as the ships' commanders locked in a tense naval chess game to the death. Good pacing and suspense to spare. C: Robert Mitchum, Curt Jurgens, Theodore Bikel, Doug McClure. D: Dick Powell. DRA 98m. V

Enemy Mine 1985 ★★★ Mortal enemies (one human, one alien) stranded on the same harsh planet must overcome their mutual hatred to survive. At times slow and cheap-looking (except for Gossett's reptilian makeup), but generally a competent action adventure. C: Dennis Quaid, Louis Gossett, Jr., Brion James, Richard Marcus. D: Wolfgang Petersen. SFI [PG-13] 108m. V

Enemy of the People, An 1977 ★★★★ McQueen surprisingly good in very different role for him as a doctor who exposes deadly water pollution in his small town. Script by Arthur Miller adapted from Ibsen's play is top-notch. Durning, as McQueen's adversary and brother, is excellent. C: Steve McQueen, Charles Durning, Bibi Andersson, Richard Bradford, Robin Pearson Rose, Richard Dysart. D: George Schaefer. DRA 103m.

Enemy of the People, An 1989 Indian ★★★ Ibsen's classic play about a doctor who defies townspeople by taking a stand against pollution has been updated and reset in Bengal. Interesting ideas, but inadequately developed. (a.k.a. *Garashatru.*) C: Soumitra Chatterjee, Dhritiman Chatterjee, Ruma Guhathakurta, Mamata Shankar, Dipankar Dey. D: Satyajit Ray. DRA [G] 100m.

Enforcer, The 1951 ★★★★ When tough D.A. (Bogart) decides to bust up a crime gang, boss (Sloane) does his ruthless best to stop him. Robust cops-and-robbers story, with Bogey at his best. C: Humphrey Bogart, Everett Sloane, Zero Mostel. D: Bretaigne Windust. CRI 87m. V

Enforcer, The 1976 ★★★½ Tough plainclothes cop Dirty Harry (Eastwood) battles terrorists in San Francisco. Daly, as his new partner, proves a good foil to Eastwood's standard macho persona. Third of five Harry features. C: Clint Eastwood, Tyne Daly, Bradford Dillman, Harry Guardino. D: James Fargo. CRI [R] 96m. V

England Made Me 1973 British ★★★★½ Twin brother and sister (York and Neil) ingratiate themselves with a wealthy, corrupt industrialist (Finch) in '30s Nazi Germany. Intelligent, underrated film is both subtle and powerful, with smashing performances. From the Graham Greene novel. C: Peter Finch, Michael York, Hildegard Neil, Michael Hordern, Joss Ackland. D: Peter Duffell. DRA [PG] 100m.

English Without Tears 1948 *See* **Her Man Gilbey**

Enid Is Sleeping *See* **Over My Dead Body**

Enigma 1983 British ★★★½ A team of five KGB assassins sets out to eliminate five Russian dissidents. CIA agent (Sheen) uses the seductive charms of his ex-paramoor (Fossey) to gain info from top KGB chief (Neill). Terrific acting from a great cast helps an implausible plot. C: Martin Sheen, Brigitte Fossey, Sam Neill, Derek Jacobi. D: Jeannot Szwarc. ACT [PG] 101m. V

Enjo 1958 *See* **Conflagration**

Enola Gay 1980 ★★★ Ambitious but only

adequate television docudrama on the first atomic bomb drop. Familiar TV faces (Duffy, Crystal, Frank) play the key characters in the training for and flying of the fateful mission. C: Billy Crystal, Kim Darby, Patrick Duffy, Gary Frank. D: David Lowell Rich. DRA 150m. TVM V

Enormous Changes at the Last Minute 1983 ★★★½ Tangled relationships of three women living in New York City are explored in three separate but unequal dramas. Barkin's acting segment is the best of the lot; the others falter. John Sayles wrote screenplay from Grace Paley's story collection. C: Maria Tucci, Lynn Milgrim, David Strathairn, Ellen Barkin, Zvee Scooler, Kevin Bacon. D: Mirra Bank, Ellen Hovde. DRA 110m. V

Enrapture 1990 ★★★ An out-of-work actor becomes a chauffeur to a wealthy couple, and gets caught up in sex and murder. Trashy but twisty mystery. C: Kevin Thomsen, Ona Simms, Harvey Siegel. D: Chuck Vincent. CRI [R] 87m. V

Ensign Pulver 1964 ★★½ Quirky young officer (Walker) on WWII cargo ship in Pacific islands. Uneasy blend of comedy and drama misses high mark set by predecessor *Mister Roberts*. Several supporting players later became stars, including an already smirking Jack Nicholson. C: Robert Walker, Jr., Burl Ives, Walter Matthau, Tommy Sands, Millie Perkins, Kay Medford, Larry Hagman, Jack Nicholson, James Coco, James Farentino. D: Joshua Logan. COM 104m. V

Entangled 1993 ★★★ A struggling writer falls in love, but the affair may cost him dearly when he finds himself framed for murder. Formulaic melodrama. C: Pierce Brosnan, Judd Nelson. D: Max Fischer. ACT [R] 98m. V

Entebbe: Operation Thunderbolt 1976 *See* **Raid on Entebbe**

Enter Laughing 1967 ★★½ Carl Reiner adapted his Broadway comedy about becoming an actor in New York in the 1930s. Strains for laughs, but some memorable supporting performances. C: Reni Santoni, Jose Ferrer, Shelley Winters, Elaine May, Jack Gilford, Janet Margolin, David Opatoshu. D: Carl Reiner. COM 112m. V

Enter Madame 1935 ★★★ When a young man (Grant) marries an opera singer (Landi), he finds himself overshadowed by her fame. Romantic comedy gains a lot from Grant's deft touch. C: Elissa Landi, Cary Grant, Lynne Overman, Sharon Lynne. D: Elliott Nugent. COM 83m.

Enter the Dragon 1973 ★★★★ A Chinese martial arts expert goes undercover for the British to expose a drug lord. Hollywood-budgeted kung fu entry with espionage and plenty of foot and fist violence. Lee's last completed film made him an international star. C: Bruce Lee, John Saxon, Jim Kelly, Ahna Capri, Angela Mao. D: Robert Clouse. ACT [R] 98m. V

Enter the Game of Death 1980 ★★★ Bruce Lee encounters an army of kung fu masters on his way to an ancient treasure. Better-than-average martial arts film. C: Bruce Li. ACT 90m. V

Enter the Ninja 1981 ★★★ A Ninjitsu fighter battles an avaricious cabal seeking to monopolize global oil distribution. Well-staged martial arts fare with lots of bloody violence. C: Franco Nero, Susan George, Sho Kosugi, Christopher George. D: Menahem Golan. ACT [R] 99m. V

Entertainer, The 1960 British ★★★★ Olivier's tour-de-force portrayal of song-and-dance man Archie Leach at the end of his rope distinguishes this filming of John Osborne play. Also notable for film debuts of Bates, Finney, and future Mrs. Olivier, Plowright. C: Laurence Olivier, Brenda de Banzie, Roger Livesey, Joan Plowright, Alan Bates, Albert Finney. D: Tony Richardson. DRA 97m. V

Entertainer, The 1975 ★★★½ John Osborne's play gets another go-round in this downbeat tale of a mediocre song-and-dance man haunted by his father's superior talent. Lemmon's performance seems haunted by Olivier's in the 1960 version. Otherwise, not bad, with a nice turn by Bolger. Incidental songs by Marvin Hamlisch. C: Jack Lemmon, Ray Bolger, Sada Thompson, Tyne Daly. D: Donald Wrye. DRA 100m. TVM

Entertaining Mr. Sloane 1970 British ★★½ Joe Orton's black comedy about attractive, amoral young tenant who seduces middle-aged woman and her gay brother in their own home. Strong acting, but satire seemed fresher on stage. C: Beryl Reid, Harry Andrews, Peter McEnery, Alan Webb. D: Douglas Hickox. COM 94m. V

Enthusiasm 1931 ★★★★½ Documentary about Russian coal miners is justly celebrated not only for its accurate rendering of their lives but for its detailed and inventive soundtrack. D: Dziga Vertov. DOC 96m.

Entity, The 1982 ★★★★ Tormented woman repeatedly raped by evil spirit believes she's going crazy until parapsychologists prove the entity is real and destroy it. Sounds sleazy but is actually a suspenseful and complex thriller. C: Barbara Hershey, Ron Silver, Jacqueline Brooks. D: Sidney J. Furie. HOR [R] 125m. V

Entre Nous 1983 French ★★★★★ Kurys' personal, insightful examination of the long-time friendship that develops between two women in '50s France is a moving, articulate, and fully realized treatment of the complexities of two lives. Outstanding performances. C: Miou-Miou, Isabelle Huppert, Guy Marchand. D: Diane Kurys. DRA [PG] 110m. V

Epic that Never Was, The 1965 ★★★★ Fascinating documentary about aborted filming of Robert Graves' novel *I Claudius* with tantalizing clips of finished footage. Laughton's scenes, in particular, are revelatory. C: Charles Laughton, Flora Robson, Emlyn Williams, Merle Oberon, Robert Newton. DOC 74m.

Equinox 1971 ★★★½ A group of archaeology students, searching for their missing professor, runs into a posse of gruesome monsters and the devil. Ultracheap science fiction film has a game cast and some neat special effects. (a.k.a. *The Beast*) C: Edward Connell, Barbara Hewitt, Frank Boers Jr., Robin Christopher. D: Jack Woods. SFI 82m. V

Equinox 1993 ★★★★ A writer investigates two identical men living in the same city—one a hoodlum, the other a timid auto mechanic. Typically off-the-wall Rudolph comedy-drama. C: Matthew Modine, Lara Flynn Boyle, Fred Ward, Tyra Ferrell, Marisa Tomei, Lori Singer. D: Alan Rudolph. DRA [R] 110m. V

Equinox Flower 1958 ★★★★ When his daughter accepts a marriage proposal without his consent, old-fashioned dad feels slighted. One of Ozu's lightest, most frivolous pieces nonetheless contains many insights into human behavior. (a.k.a. *Higan-Gana*). C: Shin Saburi, Kinuyo Tanaka, Ineko Arima. D: Yasujiro Ozu. DRA 118m. V

Equus 1977 ★★★ A disturbed teenager has a strange obsession with horses, and his psychiatrist (Burton) tries to treat him. Peter Shaffer's stage success gets an interesting screen adaptation. C: Richard Burton, Peter Firth, Colin Blakely. D: Sidney Lumet. DRA [R] 138m. V

Eraserhead 1977 ★★★½ Director Lynch's debut film is a tale of a physically and psychologically bizarre family. Mesmerizing characters, fascinating shot composition, and a decent film if you can tolerate the long stretches without dialogue. C: John Nance, Charlotte Stewart, Jeanne Bates. D: David Lynch. HOR 90m. V

Erendira 1983 Mexican ★★★★ Novelist Gabriel Garcia Marquez wrote the screenplay to this dreamy fantasy about an innocent girl forced into prostitution by her grandmother. Hovers between fairy tale and magical reality. C: Irene Papas, Claudia Ohana, Michel Lonsdale, Oliver Wehe, Rufus. D: Ruy Guerra. DRA 103m. V

Eric 1975 ★★★★ Superior inspirational story of teenage athlete Savage refusing to succumb to terminal illness, with Neal giving fine performance as his courageous mother. Based on true story. C: Patricia Neal, John Savage, Claude Akins, Mark Hamill. D: James Goldstone. DRA 100m. TVM V

Erik the Viking 1989 ★★ A softhearted Viking (Robbins) decides to lay down his sword and embark on a mission to bring peace to the world. Weak script, but a hilarious supporting cast. C: Tim Robbins, Mickey Rooney, Eartha Kitt, John Cleese. D: Terry Jones. COM [PG-13] 104m. V

Ernest Goes to Camp 1987 ★★ Dumb-humor field day as Ernest P.Worrell is a camp counselor who, with help of some kids, fights off a construction company that threatens their camp. For kids only. First of a series. C: Jim Varney, Victoria Racimo, John Vernon, Iron Eyes Cody, Lyle Alzado. D: John R. Cherry 3rd. FAM/COM [PG] 92m. V

Ernest Goes to Jail 1990 ★★★ Always-annoying character Ernest Worrell (Varney) is mistaken for an organized crime boss and winds up in the slammer. Popular series has its following, and it's harmless fun. C: Jim Varney, Gailard Sartain, Bill Byrge, Barbara Bush, Randall "Tex" Cobb. D: John R. Cherry. FAM/COM [PG] 81m. V

Ernest Green Story, The 1990 ★★★½ Heartfelt tale about an African-American man's struggle against racism in Arkansas in the '50s. Insightful film well worth an expanded version. C: Morris Chestnut, CCH Pounder, Gary Grubbs, Tina Lifford. D: Eric Laneuville. DRA 101m.

Ernest Rides Again 1993 ★★ Fifth film in this interminable series involves subcretinous Ernest (Varney) with thieves who are after the British crown jewels. Ernest fans won't be disappointed. C: Jim Varney, Ron K. James, Duke Ernsberger, Jeffrey Pillars. D: John Cherry. FAM/COM [PG] 100m. V

Ernest Saves Christmas 1988 ★★ Second film in series has Ernest trying to find a successor for Santa when the man in the red suit decides to retire. Even worse than its predecessor. C: Jim Varney, Douglas Seale, Oliver Clark, Noelle Parker. D: John R. Cherry. FAM/COM [PG] 91m. V

Ernest Scared Stupid 1991 ★★ Fourth movie in series features more silliness as Ernest battles with evil demon that threatens his hometown. Title has it right. C: Jim Varney, Eartha Kitt. D: John R. Cherry. FAM/COM [PG] 93m. V

Ernie Kovacs: Between the Laughter 1984 ★★★ Little-known episode in famed TV comedian's life involving ex-wife's kidnapping of his two daughters during custody battle. Could just as well be about anybody. Standard TV soap fare. C: Jeff Goldblum, Melody Anderson, Cloris Leachman, Madolyn Smith, Edie Adams. D: Lamont Johnson. DRA [PG] 95m. TVM V

Eroica 1957 ★★★★★ Stories about war's stupidity debunk prevailing myths of heroism. Subtitled a "heroic symphony in two movements," it is one of most profound indictments of modern warfare ever filmed. Munk's penultimate film; tragically, he was killed in 1961 car crash. (a.k.a. *Heroism.*) C: Barbara Polomska, Leon Neiemzyk. D: Andrzej Munk. DRA 83m.

Errand Boy, The 1961 ★★★★ Better than

average Lewis vehicle with lovable klutz running amok in a movie studio. Collection of comic bits vary in quality but best ones are a scream. C: Jerry Lewis, Brian Donlevy, Howard McNear, Sig Ruman, Fritz Feld, Iris Adrian. D: Jerry Lewis. COM 92m. V

Escapade 1950 *See* **Utopia**

Escapade 1955 British ★★★★ The three sons of a world-renowned pacifist (Mills) steal a plane, in a daring scheme to bring their splitting parents back together. Intriguingly original plot and excellent acting. C: John Mills, Yvonne Mitchell, Alastair Sim, Andrew Ray, Jeremy Spenser. D: Philip Leacock. DRA 87m.

Escapade in Japan 1957 ★★★½ A young American trying to locate his parents in postwar Tokyo is helped by a Japanese youth. Beautiful location photography and an ultrayoung Eastwood make this highly watchable. C: Cameron Mitchell, Teresa Wright, Jon Provost, Roger Nakagawa, Clint Eastwood. D: Arthur Lubin. DRA 93m. V

Escape 1940 ★★★★ Glossy, entertaining melodrama has Shearer as countess in Nazi Germany helping Taylor's mother (Nazimova) escape from concentration camp. Norma's progression from spoiled aristocrat to fervent political activist is well done. C: Norma Shearer, Robert Taylor, Nazimova, Conrad Veidt, Felix Bressart, Bonita Granville, Blanche Yurka. D: Mervyn LeRoy. DRA 104m.

Escape 1948 British ★★★★ Atmospheric English locations and fine British supporting cast enhance story of an innocent man's imprisonment and subsequent dash from Dartmoor. Harrison is first-rate as the wronged hero. Remake of 1930 film. C: Rex Harrison, Peggy Cummins, William Hartnell, Norman Wooland, Jill Esmond, Frederick Piper, Marjorie Rhodes, Betty Ann Davies, Cyril Cusack. D: Joseph Mankiewicz. DRA 78m.

Escape Artist, The 1980 ★★★ Teenaged magician (O'Neal) takes on politicians who may have killed his father. Ambitious movie made by talented people with murky results. Gripping young O'Neal. C: Griffin O'Neal, Raul Julia, Teri Garr, Joan Hackett. D: Caleb Deschanel. COM [PG] 93m. V

Escape from Alcatraz 1979 ★★★★ Director Siegel and box-office big guy Eastwood effectively tackled this true story of the 1962 escape by three convicts from Alcatraz. Engrossing tale with taut action and a good cast; also Danny Glover's fine film debut. C: Clint Eastwood, Patrick McGoohan, Roberts Blossom, Fred Ward, Paul Benjamin. D: Don Siegel. ACT [PG] 112m. V

Escape from Fort Bravo 1953 ★★★★ A Union Arizona garrison commander protects a fugitive Rebel soldier and his female companion when Indians attack. Top Western feature filmed in Death Valley. Rip-roaring finale. C: William Holden, Eleanor Parker, John Forsythe, Polly Bergen, William Demarest. D: John Sturges. WST 98m. V

Escape from Iran: The Canadian Caper 1981 ★★★½ Absorbing tale of the Canadian Embassy officials who, in a daring move, saved six Americans from being taken hostage when the U.S. Embassy in Teheran was overrun. C: Gordon Pinsent, Chris Wiggins, Diana Barrington, Robert Joy, James B. Douglas. D: Lamont Johnson. DRA 100m. TVM

Escape from New York 1981 ★★★★ In the near future, Manhattan has been turned into a maximum security prison. When the President's plane crashes there, it's up to Snake Plissken (Russell impersonating Eastwood) to rescue the Commander-in-Chief. Exciting and humorous action; a cult classic. Director's cut also available. C: Kurt Russell, Lee Van Cleef, Ernest Borgnine, Donald Pleasence, Isaac Hayes, Adrienne Barbeau. D: John Carpenter. ACT [R] 99m. V

Escape from Sobibor 1987 ★★★★ Against immeasurable odds, a group of WWII death camp prisoners plot and execute a massive escape from their Nazi jailers. Sobering and graphic. Based on Richard Rashke's book. C: Alan Arkin, Joanna Pacula, Rutger Hauer, Hartmut Becker, Jack Shepherd. D: Jack Gold. ACT 120m. TVM V

Escape from the Bronx 1985 Italian ★★ A murderous real estate developer tries to clear out New York borough residents for his own evil ends, but the Bronxites don't take it sitting down. Slam-bang futuristic actioner. C: Henry Silva, Valerie d'Obici, Mark Gregory, Timothy Brent. D: Enzo G. Castellari. ACT [R] 89m. V

Escape from the Planet of the Apes 1971 ★★★★½ Apes (McDowall and Hunter) escape the nuclear destruction of their world by arriving in present-day L.A.—then face annihilation a second time when their human hosts' hospitality turns lethal. Exciting, thought provoking, and the best installment since the original entry. Followed by *Conquest of the Planet of the Apes.* C: Roddy McDowall, Kim Hunter, Bradford Dillman, Sal Mineo, Ricardo Montalban. D: Don Taylor. SFI [G] 97m. V

Escape from Yesterday 1939 ★★★½ Foreign Legion twist on Hugo's *Les Miserables*, with a murderer/fugitive (Gabin) fighting in North Africa while being pursued by a determined policeman (Le Vigan). Strong performances and direction breathe life into an old story. C: Jean Gabin, Annabella, Robert Le Vigan. D: Julien Duvivier. ACT 88m.

Escape from Zahrain 1962 ★★★ A band of revolutionaries tries to cross the Arabian desert, with the police in very hot pursuit. Good-looking, sandy actioner. C: Yul Brynner, Sal Mineo, Madlyn Rhue, James Mason, Jack Warden. D: Ronald Neame. ACT 93m.

Escape If You Can 1949 *See* **St. Benny the Dip**

Escape in the Desert 1945 ★★★ WWII-updated remake of Robert E. Sherwood's *The Petrified Forest*, with Dorn and Sullivan taken prisoner by renegade Nazis in a deserted desert diner. Can't compare with Leslie Howard/Humphrey Bogart version, but some interesting suspense. C: Philip Dorn, Helmut Dantine, Jean Sullivan, Alan Hale. D: Edward A. Blatt. ACT 81m.

Escape in the Sun 1956 ★★★ An eccentric millionaire hunts down his wife and her lover as if they were big game. Fair remake of *The Most Dangerous Game* with some attractive African locations. C: John Bentley, Martin Boddey, Vera Fusek. D: George Breakston. DRA 86m.

Escape Me Never 1947 ★★★½ Romantic tearjerker about a poor young woman (Lupino) who marries a poor composer (Flynn), who then betrays her with a rich woman. Remake of 1935 movie. Based on a stage play. C: Errol Flynn, Ida Lupino, Eleanor Parker, Gig Young, Reginald Denny, Isobel Elsom. D: Peter Godfrey. DRA 101m. V

Escape to Athena 1979 British ★★½ Wacky WWII comic adventure has Allied POWs joining forces with cultured Nazi Moore and Greek resistance leader Savalas. Competent action sequences, but otherwise just plain strange. C: Roger Moore, Telly Savalas, David Niven, Claudia Cardinale. D: George Pan Cosmatos. ACT [PG] 120m. V

Escape to Burma 1955 ★★★ Tough plantation owner (Stanwyck) must keep both wild animals, especially elephants and tigers, and a fugitive (Ryan) at bay. The setting—a tea plantation in Burma—is the most interesting part of this melodrama. C: Barbara Stanwyck, Robert Ryan, David Farrar, Murvyn Vye. D: Allan Dwan. DRA 86m. V

Escape to Freedom 1988 *See* **Judgment in Berlin**

Escape to Glory 1940 ★★★★ A U.S.-bound British freighter is in danger of being torpedoed by the Nazis, with a potpourri of passengers on board. Shipshape early WWII drama. (a.k.a. *Submarine Zone*) C: Constance Bennett, Pat O'Brien, John Halliday, Alan Baxter. D: John Brahm. DRA 74m.

Escape to Love 1986 ★★★½ Intrigue and romance aboard train bound for Paris, as young U.S. student and her lover are pitted against Polish KGB. Decent adventure drama with some passionate moments. C: Clara Perryman, Aharon Idale, Patricia Davis. D: Herb Stein. DRA 105m. V

Escape to the Sun 1972 British ★★½ Two Soviet Jews try to escape the Soviet Union; film deals with the after-effects of their failed attempt to hijack a plane. Strong premise and cast undermined by a weak script. C: Laurence Harvey, Josephine Chaplin, John Ireland, Lila Kedrova. D: Menahem Golan. ACT [PG] 94m. V

Escape to Witch Mountain 1975 ★★★★ Engaging Disney mystery/fantasy about two orphans with supernatural powers (Richards and Eisenmann) pursued by a powerful millionaire who wants to use them for his own evil ends. Suspenseful and entertaining. C: Kim Richards, Ike Eisenmann, Eddie Albert, Ray Milland, Donald Pleasence. D: John Hough. FAM/SFI [G] 97m. V

Escapes 1986 British ★ Five short *Twilight Zone*-type tales (each stupendously bad), with wraparound introductions and conclusions featuring the inimitable Price. Proves to be a major disappointment. C: Vincent Price, John Mitchum, Jerry Grisham, Todd Fulton, Lee Canfield, Roelle Mitchell. D: David Steensland. SFI 72m. V

Especially on Sunday 1993 Italian ★★★★ Gentle, satisfying trilogy of stories written by veteran Italian screenwriter Tonino Guerra, each dealing with love and loss. Most effective is title story, in which an aging roué tries to seduce a young woman, but is thwarted by her attentive boyfriend. C: Bruno Ganz, Ornella Muti, Philippe Noiret. D: Giuseppe Tornatore, Marco Tullio Giordana, Giuseppe Bertolucci, Francisco Barilli. DRA

Espionage Agent 1939 ★★★½ McCrea is a government agent on the trail of Nazi spies while traveling by rail in Europe. Stars excel in this topical WWII espionage adventure. C: Joel McCrea, Brenda Marshall, George Bancroft, Jeffrey Lynn, James Stephenson, Martin Kosleck. D: Lloyd Bacon. ACT 83m.

Espoir 1939 *See* **Man's Hope**

Esther and the King 1960 ★★½ When his queen dies, Persian emperor falls for Jewish woman and makes her new queen. She uses her influence to ultimately save her own people. Biblical epic creaks with wooden dialogue falling from mouths of badly costumed cast. C: Joan Collins, Richard Egan, Denis O'Dea, Sergio Fantoni. D: Raoul Walsh. DRA 109m.

Esther Waters 1948 British ★★ A 19th-century British scoundrel and his racy escapades with a bevy of women. Starts well, then turns to soft soap. C: Kathleen Ryan, Dirk Bogarde, Cyril Cusack, Ivor Barnard, Fay Compton, Mary Clare. D: Ian Dalrymple. ACT 108m.

E.T. The Extra-Terrestrial 1982 ★★★★★ Spielberg finds the magic formula for kids of all ages in this classic tale of a cute alien who lands in suburbia and the boy who befriends him. Oscars for Best Score, Sound, and Visual Effects don't begin to tell the half of it. Charming, sweet, and effective. C: Dee Wallace Stone, Henry Thomas, Peter Coyote, Drew Barrymore. D: Steven Spielberg. FAM/SFI [PG] 115m. V

Eternal Evil 1987 ★★★½ An experimental filmmaker is out of his league when he confronts a bevy of angry transient souls! Imaginative horror thriller. C: Karen Black, Winston Rekert, Lois Maxwell. D: George Mihalka. HOR [R] 85m. V

Eternal Husband, The 1946 French ★★★★ A widowed peasant (Raimu) discovers his child really belongs to another man, then becomes obsessed with exacting his revenge. Effective adaptation of Dostoyevsky's short novel was star's last film, and he's magnificent. (a.k.a. *L'Homme au Chapeau Rond*) C: Raimu, Aime Clariond, Lucy Valnor. D: Pierre Billon. DRA 90m.

Eternal Mask, The 1937 Austrian, Swiss ★★★★★ Expressionistic classic about a mentally unbalanced doctor who may or may not have developed a cure for meningitis. Film brilliantly visualizes protagonist's surrealistic inner turmoil, using startling sets and camera devices. (a.k.a. *Die Ewige Maske*) C: Peter Petersen, Mathias Wieman, Olga Tschechowa. D: Werner Hochbaum. DRA 74m.

Eternal Return, The 1943 French ★★★★ Update of Tristan and Isolde legend as an alternately playful and serious romantic fable has Cocteau written all over it: blatant stylization, plot driven by deus ex machina (the dwarf), and presence of the great Marais all stem from Cocteau's unique imagination. (a.k.a. *Love Eternal*) C: Jean Marais, Madeleine Sologne, Jean Murat. D: Jean Delannoy. DRA 100m. V

Eternal Sea, The 1955 ★★★½ When Admiral John Hoskins is injured at sea, he overcomes obstacles to become a war hero. Solid biography/war epic features a fine lead performance from Hayden. C: Sterling Hayden, Alexis Smith, Dean Jagger, Virginia Grey. D: John Auer. ACT 103m.

Eternally Yours 1939 ★★ Frustrated woman (Young) wed to professional magician (Niven) wants more romance and is continually frustrated by Niven's devotion to his unusual career. Minor fluff at best. C: Loretta Young, David Niven, Hugh Herbert, C. Aubrey Smith. D: Tay Garnett. COM 95m. V

Eternity 1989 ★★½ The eternal struggle between Good and Evil is embodied by crusading documentary filmmaker (Voight) and right-wing industrialist (Assante). The catch is that they were warring brothers in previous life. Confusing script, co-written by Voight. C: Jon Voight, Armand Assante, Wilford Brimley, Lainie Kazan. D: Steven Paul. DRA [R] 122m. V

Eternity of Love 1961 Japanese ★★★★ Trusting student (Tsukasa) marries her dominating teacher, with tragic results. Depressing but powerful drama of self-destructive love, with a strong performance from Tsukasa. C: Yoko Tsukasa, Tadao Takashima, Kiyoshi Kodama. D: Hiromichi Horikawa. DRA 100m.

Ethan Frome 1993 ★★★★ Farmer (Neeson) marries a dominating woman (Allen), but things change as Neeson gradually comes to love her cousin (Arquette). Well-told adaptation of Edith Wharton's story, with an intelligent, muted performance by Neeson. Fine use of New England scenery. C: Liam Neeson, Patricia Arquette, Joan Allen. D: John Madden. DRA [PG] 99m. V

Eubie! 1981 ★★★★ Brothers Gregory and Maurice Hines star in this Broadway tribute to ragtime composer Eubie Blake. Straightforward filming of the original stage show is packed with great dancing and timeless songs. C: Gregory Hines, Maurice Hines, Alaina Reed. D: Julianne Boyd. MUS 85m. V

Eureka 1983 ★★★ After striking it rich as a Yukon gold prospector, a reclusive man hordes his millions and successfully holds out from the world until it comes crashing in. Offbeat, stylish drama. C: Gene Hackman, Theresa Russell, Rutger Hauer, Ed Lauter, Mickey Rourke. D: Nicolas Roeg. DRA [R] 130m. V

Europa, Europa 1991 French ★★★★½ True story of Jewish boy (Hofschneider) who is mistaken for an Aryan and enrolled in a training school for Hitler Youth. Harrowing look at the Nazi war machine is also a blackly comic coming-of-age tale. C: Marco Hofschneider, Rene Hofschneider, Julie Delpy, Hanns Zischler, Klaus Abramowsky, Marta Sandrowicz. D: Agnieszka Holland. DRA [R] 115m. V

Europa's 1951 *See* **Greatest Love, The**

Europeans, The 1979 ★★★½ Rich period drama about a 19th-century New England family and its troubles with visiting European relatives. Fabulous to look at and a detailed rendering of the Henry James novel. C: Lee Remick, Robin Ellis, Wesley Addy, Lisa Eichhorn. D: James Ivory. DRA 90m. V

Eva 1965 British ★★★½ A well-to-do writer falls for an amoral woman (Moreau) who destroys his wife, his career, his health, and anything else she can get her hands on. Tired retread of *The Blue Angel*, with star's charisma a saving virtue. (a.k.a. *Eva, the Devil's Woman*) C: Jeanne Moreau, Stanley Baker, Virna Lisi, Nona Medici, Francesco Rissone, James Villiers. D: Joseph Losey. DRA 115m.

Eva, the Devil's Woman 1965 *See* **Eva**

Eve Knew Her Apples 1945 ★★★ Weak musical remake of *It Happened One Night* with Miller as runaway heiress on bus trip with journalist. C: Ann Miller, William Wright, Robert Williams, Ray Walker. D: Will Jason. MUS 64m.

Eve of Destruction 1991 ★★★ Scientist Soutendijk creates a robot bomb in her own image, and the result is mayhem. Poor Gregory Hines has to stop it. Solid special effects enhance a nifty plot. C: Gregory Hines, Renee Soutendijk, Kevin McCarthy. D: Duncan Gibbins. ACT [R] 101m. V

Eve of St. Mark, The 1944 ★★★½ A pair of lovers affected by the looming war in Europe. Lyrical annotation of tragedy of war. Based on Maxwell Anderson play. C: Anne Baxter, William Eythe, Michael O'Shea, Vincent Price, Dickie Moore. D: John M. Stahl. DRA 96m.

Eve Wants to Sleep 1961 ★★★★ Title character is a country-bred innocent sent to trade school in town where thieves and policemen are interchangeable and anarchy reigns. Entertaining, surreal comedy creates its own madcap world with its own disarming logic. C: Barbara Lass, Stanislaw Mikulski, Ludwik Benoit, Zygmunt Zintel. D: Tadeusz Chmielewski. COM 98m.

Evel Knievel 1972 ★★★ Biography of Knievel (Hamilton), the motorcyclist famed for jumping over cars and other large objects, captures only some of the stuntman's appeal. An unexceptional movie about an exceptional man. C: George Hamilton, Sue Lyon, Bert Freed, Rod Cameron. D: Marvin J. Chomsky. DRA [PG] 90m. V

Evelyn Prentice 1934 ★★★★ Powell and Loy as high-powered attorney and loving wife who accidentally become involved in murder case he's trying. Classy, engrossing melodrama, nicely acted. Great scene: reconciliation during morning exercises. C: William Powell, Myrna Loy, Una Merkel, Rosalind Russell, Isabel Jewell, Harvey Stephens, Cora Sue Collins. D: William K. Howard. DRA 80m. V

Even Cowgirls Get the Blues 1994 ★★★ A big-thumbed cowgirl/model (Thurman) hitchhikes her way on a psychedelic journey through the New West. The goofy absurdism of Tom Robbins' cult novel doesn't translate well to screen despite earnest efforts of cast and director. C: Uma Thurman, Rain Phoenix, Keanu Reeves, Pat Morita, Angie Dickinson. D: Gus Van Sant. COM [R]

Even Dwarfs Started Small 1968 German ★★★ Dwarfs in an asylum run amuck in this amorphous indictment of society's ills. Herzog often substitutes symbolic action for subtlety in this relentlessly single-minded film. Compare to Tod Browning's *Freaks*. C: Helmut Doring, Gerd Gickel, Paul Glauer, Erna Gschwnedtner, Gisela Hartwig. D: Werner Herzog. DRA 96m.

Evening in Byzantium, An 1978 ★★★½ Terrorist attack at Cannes Film Festival threatens lives of movie mogul Ford and his entourage. Slick pap from Irwin Shaw best-seller with better than average cast. C: Glenn Ford, Eddie Albert, Vince Edwards, Shirley Jones, Erin Gray, Harry Guardino, Patrick Macnee, Gregory Sierra, Michael Cole, Gloria DeHaven, George Lazenby, Christian Marquand, James Booth. D: Jerry London. DRA 200m. TVM

Event, An 1970 Yugoslavian ★★★½ Allegorical fable from Anton Chekhov short story about a Russian farmer and his small grandson traveling through a murky forest en route to selling their horse at the local fair. Slight, but haunting, with memorable atmosphere. C: Pavle Vujisic, Serdjo Mimica, Boris Dvornik. D: Vatroslav Mimica. DRA 93m.

Events 1970 ★★★ Low-budget cinema verité about the making of a porno film. A plotless excuse for women to sit around partially disrobed, discussing their "inner feelings." C: Ryan Listman, Joy Wener, Frank Cavestani, Marsha Rossa. D: Fred Baker. DRA [R] 84m.

Ever in My Heart 1933 ★★ Thirties romantic tearjerker. Kruger leaves wife Stanwyck during anti-German hysteria in WWI U.S. She goes to France to aid war effort and finds he's now a German spy. Dated and overly sentimental. Stars deserve better than this. C: Barbara Stanwyck, Otto Kruger, Ralph Bellamy, Ruth Donnelly, Frank Albertson. D: Archie Mayo. DRA 68m.

Ever Since Eve 1937 ★★★ Painfully dated comedy features Davies as an office worker who dresses down to avoid unwanted flirtations. After hours she's pursued by her boss, who doesn't realize the object of his attention is really his secretary. Davies' last feature. C: Marion Davies, Robert Montgomery, Frank McHugh, Patsy Kelly, Allen Jenkins, Louise Fazenda, Barton MacLane. D: Lloyd Bacon. COM 79m.

Ever Since Venus 1944 ★★★ Inventor of a no-stain, non-smear lipstick risks life and limb and $1,000 to get his product featured at a beauty fair. Ho-hum B-musical, worth seeing for rare appearance by famed band leader Hutton. C: Ina Ray Hutton, Hugh Herbert, Glenda Farrell, Ross Hunter, Alan Mowbray. D: Arthur Dreifuss. MUS 74m.

Evergreen 1934 British ★★★★ Matthews is delightful as musical comedy hopeful impersonating her once-famous, dead mother. Some dandy Rodgers and Hart songs help considerably, particularly "Dancing on the Ceiling." C: Jessie Matthews, Sonnie Hale. D: Victor Saville. MUS 90m. V

Eversmile, New Jersey 1989 ★★ Day-Lewis is itinerant dentist traveling through Patagonia with a mission: to raise the populace's level of dental hygiene. An entranced young woman (Jokovic), heeding her calling to dental profession, runs after him. Different, yes, indeed, but by no means interesting. C: Daniel Day-Lewis, Mirjana Jokovic, Gabriela Archer. D: Carlos Sorin. DRA [PG] 88m. V

Every Bastard a King 1970 Israeli ★★★½ Immediately prior to the Israeli-Arab Six-Day War, a pilot (Kotler) flies to Cairo to achieve peace with Abdel Nasser. Offbeat war drama is distinguished by gripping, impressive 20-minute tank battle scene. (a.k.a. *Every Man a King*) C: Pier Angeli, William Berger, Oded Kotler, Yehoram Gaon, Ori Levy. D: Uri Zohar. ACT [PG] 93m.

Every Day's a Holiday 1937 ★★★★ Mild Gay '90s comedy with West as con artist Peaches O'Day trying to expose police corruption in NYC. Script is tame by Mae's standards, but star can make anything suggestively funny. C: Mae West, Edmund Lowe, Charles Butterworth, Charles Winninger, Walter Catlett, Lloyd Nolan, Louis Armstrong,

Herman Bing, Chester Conklin. D: A. Edward Sutherland. COM 79m. V

Every Girl Should Be Married 1948 ★★★★ Soon-to-be real-life marrieds Drake and Grant star in this minor comedy about a woman whose eyes are set on a most reluctant bachelor. Though a routine comedy, players give it a nice comic touch. C: Cary Grant, Franchot Tone, Diana Lynn, Betsy Drake. D: Don Hartman. COM 84m. V

Every Man a King 1970 *See* **Every Bastard a King**

Every Man for Himself 1980 French ★★★½ Three characters try to exist in a mechanized, uncaring big city. Celebrated as Godard's return to past glory, but really begins a new, reflective direction. Mostly for fans willing to make an artistic leap with the director. (a.k.a. *Slow Motion*) C: Isabelle Huppert, Jacques Dutronc, Nathalie Baye, Roland Amstutz, Anna Baldaccini. D: Jean-Luc Godard. DRA 87m.

Every Man for Himself and God Against All 1975 German ★★★★ Mystical drama based on the true story of Kaspar Hauser, a boy who grew up in the wild, and was then confined for most of the rest of his life after he suddenly showed up in 1820s Nuremberg. (a.k.a. *The Mystery of Kaspar Hauser*) C: Bruno S., Walter Ladengast, Brigitte Mira, Willy Semmelrogge. D: Werner Herzog. DRA 110m. V

Every Night at Eight 1935 ★★★½ Three female singers join forces with orchestra leader Raft in climb to stardom. Good cast, two classic songs: "I Feel A Song Coming On" and "I'm in the Mood for Love." C: George Raft, Alice Faye, Frances Langford, Patsy Kelly, Herman Bing, Walter Catlett. D: Raoul Walsh. MUS 81m.

Every Time We Say Goodbye 1986 Israeli ★★ Early Hanks as an American pilot in 1942 Jerusalem who falls for a young Sephardic Jew. Despite getting pummeled by her brothers and insulted by her family in Ladino, love triumphs. Notable solely for Hanks' dramatic debut. C: Tom Hanks, Cristina Marsillach, Benedict Taylor, Anat Atzmon. D: Moshe Mizrahi. DRA [PG-13] 97m. V

Every Which Way but Loose 1978 ★★ Popular but dopey country-western comedy features Eastwood as a hard-drinking trucker with a pet orangutan chasing the love of his life to Colorado. Inexplicable success, followed by *Any Which Way You Can*. C: Clint Eastwood, Sondra Locke, Geoffrey Lewis, Beverly D'Angelo, Ruth Gordon. D: James Fargo. COM [PG] 119m. V

Every Woman's Man 1933 *See* **Prizefighter and the Lady, The**

Everybody Does It 1949 ★★★★ Would-be vocalist Holm wants a singing career, but much to everyone's surprise, her seemingly nonmusical husband (Douglas) proves to be the one with the stellar voice. Remake of *Wife, Husband and Friend* is a witty comedy with engaging cast. C: Paul Douglas, Linda Darnell, Celeste Holm, Charles Coburn, Millard Mitchell, Lucile Watson, John Hoyt, George Tobias. D: Edmund Goulding. COM 98m.

Everybody Sing 1938 ★★★ Musical misfire with great cast as residents of theatrical boarding house put on a show to advance their careers. Everyone tries too hard to enliven hackneyed script and the songs are mediocre. But Judy's energetic and Brice does Baby Snooks routine. C: Allan Jones, Judy Garland, Fanny Brice, Reginald Owen, Billie Burke. D: Edwin L. Marin. MUS 80m. V

Everybody Wins 1990 ★★★ Off-kilter prostitute (Winger) cajoles gumshoe (Nolte) into helping clear a man of a murder charge. Awkward, muddled detective mystery was Arthur Miller's first screenplay in almost 30 years. C: Debra Winger, Nick Nolte, Jack Warden, Judith Ivey. D: Karel Reisz. CRI [R] 97m. V

Everybody's All-American 1988 ★★★ Here's what really happened to the football hero and the college beauty queen when the band stopped playing and the crowds stopped cheering. Good performances, but somewhat longwinded. C: Jessica Lange, Dennis Quaid, Timothy Hutton, John Goodman, Carl Lumbly. D: Taylor Hackford. DRA [R] 127m. V

Everybody's Baby: The Rescue of Jessica McClure 1989 ★★★★½ Terrific re-creation of events surrounding rescue of 18-month-old baby trapped in well for close to 60 hours. Resists any heart-tugging or sentimentality as it pays tribute to tireless emergency workers while criticizing overzealous press. C: Beau Bridges, Pat Hingle, Roxana Zal, Patty Duke, Will Oldham, Whip Hubley. D: Mel Damski. DRA 100m. TVM

Everybody's Fine 1990 Italian ★★★ Retired Sicilian father journeys across Italy to visit his five grown-up children; expecting the best, getting the worst. Mastroianni is wonderful, though the storytelling is clumsy. C: Marcello Mastroianni, Marino Cenna, Roberto Nobile, Valeria Cavali, Norma Martelli, Salvatore Cascio. D: Giuseppe Tornatore. DRA [PG-13] 115m. V

Everything for Sale 1968 Polish ★★★★ Life on movie set becomes increasingly difficult after a film star's accidental death. Wajda's extremely personal tribute to actor Zbigniew Cybulski, who died in similar fashion. Probing commentary on filmmaking, friendship, and loyalty. C: Beata Tyszkiewicz, Elzbieta Czyzewska, Daniel Olbrychski, Andrzej Lapicki. D: Andrzej Wajda. DRA 105m.

Everything Happens at Night 1939 ★★★ Two reporters (Milland and Cummings) team up to track down missing Nobel Prize winner. Their partnership is really tested when both fall for skating star Henie. Though Henie's vehicle, Milland and Cummings give this some comic spark. C: Sonja Henie, Ray Milland, Robert Cummings, Alan Dinehart, Fritz Feld,

Jody Gilbert, Victor Varconi. D: Irving Cummings. COM 77m. V

Everything I Have Is Yours 1952 ★★½ Husband and wife (the Champions) suffer turmoil when he dances professionally and she wants to join him. Only starring vehicle for this team. C: Marge and Gower Champion, Dennis O'Keefe, Eduard Franz. D: Robert Leonard. MUS 92m.

Everything Is Thunder 1936 ★★★★ During WWI, a lady of the evening (Bennett) aids an escaped Canadian POW (Montgomery) in his attempt to cross the German border. Atmospheric, well-acted action-romance. C: Constance Bennett, Douglass Montgomery, Oscar Homolka. D: Milton Rosmer. ACT 76m.

Everything You Always Wanted to Know About Sex (But Were Afraid to Ask) 1972 ★★★★ Allen wrote, directed and starred in this episodic takeoff of Dr. David Reuben's book answering basic questions about you know what. Wilder's loopy love affair with a sheep is a classic. Each of seven sketches is over before it gets boring. C: Woody Allen, John Carradine, Lou Jacobi, Louise Lasser, Lynn Redgrave, Gene Wilder. D: Woody Allen. COM [R] 88m. V

Evil Altar 1988 ★ Unexciting low-budget horror film set in a town controlled by a satanist (Smith) who gains his power from human sacrifices. C: William Smith, Robert Z'Dar, Pepper Martin. D: Jim Winburn. HOR [R] 90m. V

Evil Dead, The 1983 ★★★★ An evil force is out to destroy four friends on vacation in the woods. Beautifully balances jokes with some of the scariest and grossest moments in horror history—particularly involving is the possessed woman in the basement. C: Bruce Campbell, Ellen Sandweiss, Betsy Baker, Hal Delrich, Sarah York. D: Sam Raimi. HOR 85m. V

Evil Dead 2, The 1987 ★★★ The demons are back to torment Campbell. A little disappointing and not as creepy as the first *Evil Dead*, but manic camera work, extreme gore, and delightful sense of humor make up for it. Followed by *Army of Darkness* C: Bruce Campbell, Sarah Berry, Dan Hicks, Kassie Wesley. D: Sam Raimi. HOR [R] 84m. V

Evil Eden 1956 *See* **Diamond Hunters**

Evil Mind, The 1934 *See* **Clairvoyant, The**

Evil of Frankenstein, The 1964 British ★★½ Lesser entry in the Hammer Frankenstein series finds the bad doctor bringing the monster back and enlisting a hypnotist to give it life, only for the mesmerist to use the creature to kill. Few surprises, poor makeup; beware extended U.S. TV version, which deletes some scenes. C: Peter Cushing, Duncan Lamont, Peter Woodthorpe, Sandor Eles. D: Freddie Francis. HOR 84m. V

Evil That Men Do 1985 ★★ Retired hit man (Bronson) returns to his killing ways when his friend is murdered. Standard Bronson actioner has that seen-it-before feeling. C: Charles Bronson, Theresa Saldana, Joseph Maher, Jose Ferrer, John Glover. D: J. Lee Thompson. ACT [R] 90m. V

Evil, The 1978 ★★★ A group of doctors, patients and students doing research at an old mansion fall victim to a demonic force determined to kill them all. Nothing new, but not bad, with decent cast; special effects vary in persuasiveness. C: Richard Crenna, Joanna Pettet, Andrew Prine, Victor Buono. D: Gus Trikonis. HOR [R] 90m. V

Evil Under the Sun 1982 British ★★★★ Agatha Christie's popular detective Hercule Poirot (Ustinov) descends on an exclusive seaside spa, where a colorful collection of upper crusts become murder suspects. Excellent cast and suspense. C: Peter Ustinov, Jane Birkin, Colin Blakely, Roddy McDowall, James Mason, Denis Quilley, Diana Rigg, Maggie Smith. D: Guy Hamilton. CRI [PG] 102m. V

Evil Within, The 1994 French ★★★★ A carnival performer becomes impregnated with a creature that talks to her psychically and forces her to kill for blood to feed it. Gory, compelling shocker is also surprisingly well-dubbed (including an uncredited Gary Oldman as the "baby's" voice!). (a.k.a. *Baby Blood*) C: Emmanuelle Escourrou, Jean-Francois Gallotte, Christian Sinniger, Francois Frapier, Theirry LePortier. D: Alain Robak. HOR [R] 82m.

Evilspeak 1982 ★★★½ A military school nerd (Howard) gets revenge on his classmates when he discovers an ancient book of magic. Tongue-in-cheek horror flick works its own peculiar spell. Recommended for fans of the genre. C: Clint Howard, R.G. Armstrong, Joseph Cortese. D: Eric Weston. HOR [R] 89m. V

Evita Peron 1981 ★★★½ First-class production values can't camouflage dramatically threadbare biography of Argentina's dictatorial First Lady, accused of hoarding great wealth at the expense of her people. Dunaway's over-the-top performance will impress some, amuse others. C: Faye Dunaway, James Farentino, Rita Moreno, Jose Ferrer, Pedro Armendariz Jr., Michael Constantine, Signe Hasso, Katy Jurado, Robert Viharo, Jeremy Kemp, John Dreelen, Marvin Miller, Virginia Gregg. D: Marvin Chomsky. DRA 200m. TVM

Ewok Adventure, The 1984 ★★★★ Two youngsters lost in space are aided by the lovable creatures created by George Lucas in *Return of the Jedi.* Terrific production values highlight this charming adventure; small fry will lap it up. Sequel: *Ewoks: The Battle For Endor.* C: Eric Walker, Warwick Davis, Fionnula Flanagan, Voice of Burl Ives. D: John Korty. FAM/SFI 100m. TVM V

Ewoks: The Battle for Endor 1985 ★★★½ Those funny, furry little creatures from *Return of the Jedi* are menaced by a nasty queen who wants to destroy them and their friends.

Geared for kids, although some scenes may be a bit intense for younger viewers. C: Warwick Davis, Aubree Miller, Sian Phillips. D: Jim and Ken Wheat, Wilford Brimley. FAM/ACT 98m. TVM V

Ex-Champ 1939 ★★★ Former boxer trains son and tries to keep him out of trouble. Okay melodrama. C: Victor McLaglen, Tom Brown, Nan Grey, Constance Moore. D: Phil Rosen. DRA 64m.

Ex-Lady 1933 ★★★½ Snappy script, well handled by Florey, with up-and-coming Davis in first leading lady showcase. Very pre-Code, as feminist wants love and sex but not marriage from boyfriend. C: Bette Davis, Gene Raymond, Frank McHugh, Claire Dodd, Ferdinand Gottschalk. D: Robert Florey. DRA 65m. V

Ex-Mrs. Bradford, The 1936 ★★★★ Divorced doctor (Powell) and mystery writer (Arthur) attempt to reclaim their marriage in the midst of a series of race track murders. Witty attempt to create another *Thin Man* pairing, with wisecracking Arthur very appealing. C: William Powell, Jean Arthur, James Gleason, Eric Blore. D: Stephen Roberts. CRI 80m. V

Excalibur 1981 British ★★★★ In their quest for the Holy Grail, King Arthur and his knights encounter the benevolent wizard Merlin and his witchy, alluring counterpart, Morgana. Sexy, slick epic never quite reaches its aspirations, but should entertain sword and sorcery fans. C: Nicol Williamson, Nigel Terry, Helen Mirren, Patrick Stewart, Cherie Lunghi, Liam Neeson. D: John Boorman. SFI [PG] 140m. V

Excessive Force 1993 ★★★ An undercover cop looking into the disappearance of $3 million worth of drugs soon runs up against an angry Mob boss who is also wondering what happened to the money. Violent action picture, with a great cast. C: Thomas Ian Griffith, Lance Henriksen, James Earl Jones, Burt Young. D: Jon Hess. ACT [R] 90m. V

Exclusive 1937 ★★★ Farmer is an aspiring reporter hired by same daily where her father (Ruggles) and boyfriend (MacMurray) are also journalists. A lively competition ensues when she tries to out-scoop the two men. Amusing, though below Farmer's talents. C: Fred MacMurray, Frances Farmer, Charlie Ruggles, Lloyd Nolan, Fay Holden, Ralph Morgan, Horace McMahon. D: Alexander Hall. COM 85m.

Exclusive Story 1936 ★★★½ Well-paced crime story capably done by Seitz, with Tone as likable newspaper lawyer out to nab Calleia (doing another memorably nasty gangster). C: Franchot Tone, Madge Evans, Stuart Erwin, Joseph Calleia, Robert Barrat, J. Farrell MacDonald, Louise Henry. D: George Seitz. DRA 75m.

Excuse My Dust 1951 ★★★★ Sprightly turn-of-the-century musical with Skelton mugging up a storm as a slow-witted inventor who claims to have perfected a horseless carriage. Lively production numbers grace a charming score by Arthur Schwartz and Dorothy Fields. C: Red Skelton, Sally Forrest, Macdonald Carey, Monica Lewis, William Demarest. D: Roy Rowland. MUS [G] 82m.

Execution of Private Slovik, The 1974 ★★★★½ Outstanding drama of WWII soldier executed for desertion in 1945. Sheen's glorious performance and a subtle, sensitive approach dignify this exceptional film. C: Martin Sheen, Mariclare Costello, Ned Beatty, Gary Busey, Matt Clark, Ben Hammer, Warren Kemmerling. D: Lamont Johnson. DRA 122m. TVM V

Execution of Raymond Graham, The 1985 ★★★½ When a young man is convicted of murder, his lawyers and his family stage a major effort to keep him alive. Riveting, intelligent drama. C: Jeff Fahey, Morgan Freeman, Laurie Metcalf. D: Daniel Petrie. DRA 96m. V

Executioner, The 1970 British ★★½ Thriller about an agent (Peppard) who begins to think that his colleague (Michell) is doublecrossing him and may be a double agent. C: Joan Collins, George Peppard, Judy Geeson, Oscar Homolka, Keith Michell. D: Sam Wanamaker. CRI [R] 107m.

Executioner, Part II, The 1984 ★ Police officer pursues self-styled vigilante. A mess; unrelated to any other *Executioner*. C: Christopher Mitchum, Aldo Ray. D: James Bryant. ACT [R] 115m. V

Executioner's Song, The 1982 ★★★★ The true story of Gary Gilmore. After his murder conviction, Gilmore fought to make sure the state would execute him. An absolutely fabulous performance by Jones. Mailer wrote the screenplay, adapting it from his book. C: Tommy Lee Jones, Rosanna Arquette, Christine Lahti, Eli Wallach, Walter Olkewicz. D: Lawrence Schiller. DRA 157m. TVM V

Executive Action 1973 ★★ Who killed J.F.K.? More ideas, interesting as a precursor to *JFK*. Thriller scripted by Dalton Trumbo. C: Burt Lancaster, Robert Ryan, Will Geer, John Anderson. D: David Miller. CRI [PG] 91m. V

Executive Suite 1954 ★★★★ Star-heavy cast makes most of multi-storied film of power struggles on board of furniture manufacturer. Farfetched but entertaining slice of company life. C: William Holden, June Allyson, Barbara Stanwyck, Fredric March, Walter Pidgeon. D: Robert Wise. DRA 104m. V

Exile Express 1939 ★★★½ A scientist is killed aboard a train in Europe, and his assistant (Sten) is now in grave danger. "Secret formula" espionage drama, nicely played. C: Anna Sten, Alan Marshal, Jerome Cowan. D: Otis Garrett. DRA 70m.

Exile, The 1947 ★★★½ King Charles II (Fairbanks, Jr.), exiled in Holland, romances a commoner (Montez). Fun swashbuckler with good production values and acting. C: Douglas Fairbanks Jr., Maria Montez, Paule Croset, Henry Daniell, Nigel Bruce, Robert Coote. D: Max Ophuls. DRA 95m.

Exiled to Shanghai 1937 ★★★½ Ford and Jagger are newsreel filmmakers, one of whom thinks he's discovered television. Inappropriately titled B-movie drama is swift and painless. C: Wallace Ford, June Travis, Dean Jagger. D: Nick Grinde. DRA 65m.

Exit Dragon, Enter Tiger 1976 ★★★ Film looks at the mysterious death of kung fu legend Bruce Lee. Exploitative venture trades on Lee's exploits to sustain audience interest. C: Bruce Li. ACT [R] 84m.

Exit to Eden 1994 ★★½ First (and hopefully last) sado-masochistic situation comedy stars Delany as "mistress" of S&M holiday spa. O'Donnell and Aykroyd are undercover cops in dominatrix garb, providing the film's only laughs. Poorly adapted from Anne Rice's novel. C: Dana Delany, Paul Mercurio, Rosie O'Donnell, Dan Aykroyd. D: Garry Marshall. COM [R] 113m. v

Exodus 1960 ★★★★ Otto Preminger's fine adaptation of Leon Uris' novel about the establishment of the state of Israel. Historical sweep and good performances with exciting episodes. Oscar-winning score. C: Paul Newman, Eva Marie Saint, Ralph Richardson, Peter Lawford, Lee Cobb, Sal Mineo. D: Otto Preminger. DRA 213m. v

Exorcist, The 1973 ★★★★½ A disturbed young priest tortured by self-doubt must face his fears when he undertakes the exorcism of a 12-year-old girl possessed by the devil. Terrifying adaptation of William Peter Blatty's best-seller features excellent cast and direction. Blatty won Oscar for Best Screenplay. Quite simply, the best of its kind. C: Ellen Burstyn, Max von Sydow, Linda Blair, Jason Miller, Lee J. Cobb, Kitty Winn, Jack MacGowran. D: William Friedkin. HOR [R] 120m. v

Exorcist II: The Heretic 1977 ★ Sequel finds Blair, still undergoing therapy four years later, being investigated by priest Burton, with the expected demonic shenanigans resulting. C: Richard Burton, Linda Blair, Louise Fletcher, Kitty Winn, James Earl Jones, Max von Sydow. D: John Boorman. HOR [R] 118m. v

Exorcist III, The 1990 ★★★ Gemini Killer leaves signs he may be a servant of the devil. Based on the novel by William Peter Blatty, picture unfolds nicely and Scott gives fine performance as tormented investigator. But we've been scared like this before. C: George C. Scott, Ed Flanders, Brad Dourif, Jason Miller, Nicol Williamson, Scott Wilson. D: William Peter Blatty. HOR [R] 105m. v

Expedition, The 1962 Indian ★ Drunken cabbie finds himself embroiled in intrigue with drug smugglers, prostitutes, and slave traders. One of Ray's weakest films: Chatterjee fatally miscast as the hero, and Ray seems entirely out of his usual humanist element. (a.k.a. *Abhijan*) C: Sourmitra Chatterjee, Waheeda Rehman. D: Satyajit Ray. DRA 150m.

Expensive Husbands 1937 ★★★★ Roberts is a movie starlet marrying a down-on-his-luck European prince for the publicity. Charming, clever fluff with a better-than-average script. C: Patric Knowles, Beverly Roberts, Allyn Joslyn. D: Bobby Connolly. DRA 62m.

Experience Preferred . . . but Not Essential 1983 British ★★★½ College student (Edmonds) takes summer job at Welsh hotel in 1962 and comes of age. Sweet English comedy surrounds heroine with funny eccentrics. C: Elizabeth Edmonds, Sue Wallace, Geraldine Griffith, Karen Meagher, Ron Bain, Alun Lewis, Robert Blythe. D: Peter Duffell. COM [PG] 80m. v

Experiment in Fear, An 1988 *See* **Monkey Shines**

Experiment in Terror 1962 ★★★★ Disturbed asthmatic kidnapper menaces the sister (Remick) of his hostage (Powers). Superb thriller. San Francisco never looked so frightening. C: Glenn Ford, Lee Remick, Stefanie Powers, Ross Martin. D: Blake Edwards. CRI 123m. v

Experiment Perilous 1944 ★★★★ A woman married to a wealthy psychopath falls in love with his psychiatrist, with violent consequences. Crisp, superbly directed melodrama. Lukas is exceptional as the dangerous husband. C: Hedy Lamarr, George Brent, Paul Lukas, Albert Dekker. D: Jacques Tourneur. CRI 92m. v

Experts, The 1989 ★★ Two hip disco operators (Travolta and Gross) are picked to train Soviet spies in American mores. Flat treatment of solid script idea. C: John Travolta, Arye Gross, Charles Martin Smith, Kelly Preston, Deborah Foreman. D: Dave Thomas. COM [PG-13] 94m. v

Explorers 1985 ★★★★ Three kids (Hawke, Phoenix, Presson) build a homemade spaceship and take off to . . . explore. Great fun for kiddies, from the director of *Gremlins*. C: Ethan Hawke, River Phoenix, Jason Presson, Amanda Peterson, Dick Miller. D: Joe Dante. FAM/SFI [PG] 109m. v

Explosion 1969 Canadian ★★½ After his brother is killed in Vietnam a teen flees to Canada to avoid draft, and turns to crime. Stolid melodrama. C: Don Stroud, Richard Conte, Gordon Thomson, Michele Chicoine, Cecil Linder, Robin Ward. D: Jules Bricken. DRA [PG] 96m.

Explosive Generation, The 1961 ★★ High school teacher Shatner gets himself in hot water for bringing sex education into his classroom. Relevant in it's time but now very dated. C: William Shatner, Patty McCormack, Billy Gray, Steve Dunne, Lee Kinsolving, Virginia Field, Phillip Terry, Edward Platt, Beau Bridges. D: Buzz Kulik. DRA 89m.

Exposed 1983 ★★★ A high-fashion model (Kinski) falls for concert violinist (Nureyev), but it turns out that he's involved with terrorists. A glitzy, ritzy ball of cotton candy, enhanced by the alluring leads. C: Nastassia

Kinski, Rudolf Nureyev, Harvey Keitel, Ian McShane. D: James Toback. DRA [R] 100m. v

Exposure 1991 Brazilian ★★ Photographer (Coyote) sinks deeper and deeper into the seedy side of Rio when he searches for the murderer of a prostitute. Slick treatment of sleaze. C: Peter Coyote, Tcheky Karyo, Amanda Pays, Raul Cortez. D: Walter Salles, Jr. CRI [R] 105m. v

Expresso Bongo 1960 British ★★★★ Talent agent Harvey—in kind of role he does so well—plays fast and loose with his clients and comes to well-deserved bad end. Richard is teenaged bongo player who becomes a star. Energetic performances and witty script. C: Laurence Harvey, Sylvia Syms, Yolande Donlan, Cliff Richard. D: Val Guest. DRA 108m.

Exquisite Corpses 1989 ★★★ Naive young musician moves to NYC and promptly falls for a homicidal woman. Brooding, offbeat comedy has some inspired moments. C: Zoe Tamerlaine Lund, Gary Knox, Daniel Chapman. D: Temistocles Lopez. COM 95m. v

Exterminating Angel, The 1962 Mexico ★★★★½ Guests at dinner party can't bear to leave. Only Buñuel could make such a movie: scintillating blend of surrealism, savage satire, and dry wit that remains one of Buñnuel's most satisfying films. C: Silvia Pinal, Enrique Rambal, Jacqueline Andere, Jose Baviera, Augusto Benedico. D: Luis Buñuel. COM 95m. v

Exterminator, The 1980 ★ Ginty plays an unhinged Vietnam vet who goes ballistic and kills members of a street gang who paralyzed his best friend. Extremely bloody film, similar to Charles Bronson's revenge epics. C: Christopher George, Samantha Eggar, Robert Ginty, Steve James. D: James Glickenhaus. ACT [R] 101m. v

Exterminator II 1984 ★½ A Vietnam veteran goes after street hoods with a flamethrower. Repugnant Bronson vigilante clone. C: Robert Ginty, Mario Van Peebles, Deborah Geffner, Frankie Faison. D: Mark Buntzman. ACT [R] 88m. v

Extra Girl, The 1923 ★★★★ Silent "small-town girl goes to Hollywood in search of fame" story is given some nice twists by star Normand. Made in midst of personal scandal, Normand's performance is touched with irony. Scene with lion roaming movie set is a classic. C: Mabel Normand, Ralph Graves, George Nichols. D: F. Richard Jones. COM 87m. v

Extraordinary Seaman, The 1969 ★★ In late '60s, four sailors encounter Royal Navy captain (Niven) still piloting his WWII ship. Comedy/fantasy needs water wings, concept flounders. C: David Niven, Faye Dunaway, Alan Alda, Mickey Rooney, Juano Hernandez, Jack Carter, Manu Tupou, Barry Kelley. D: John Frankenheimer. COM 80m.

Extreme Close-Up 1973 *See* **Sex Through a Window**

Extreme Close-Up 1990 ★★★★ Mourning his mother's death, a disconsolate boy reviews his family's home videos. Compelling drama, with a nifty ending. C: Blair Brown, Craig T. Nelson, Morgan Weisser, Samantha Mathis, Kimber Shoop, Kerrie Keane, Richard Libertini. D: Peter Horton. DRA 100m.

Extreme Justice 1993 ★★½ When a detective is suspended from the department for excessive violence, he is offered a job with an elite corps of the police—who believe in taking the law into their own hands. Brutal, violent film will please action fans. C: Lou Diamond Phillips, Scott Glenn, Chelsea Field, Yaphet Kotto. D: Mark L. Lester. ACT [R] 95m. v

Extreme Prejudice 1987 ★★★★ Texas sheriff Nolte must confront a childhood friend (Boothe) who has become a drug lord south of the border, and has been targeted by a fanatical group of federal agents. A solid story, quality performances, and raucous action sequences. C: Nick Nolte, Powers Boothe, Michael Ironside, Maria Conchita Alonso, Rip Torn, Clancy Brown. D: Walter Hill. ACT [R] 104m. v

Extremities 1986 ★★½ After she's raped, a woman avenges herself. Good adaptation of controversial play. Shocking drama. C: Farrah Fawcett, James Russo, Diana Scarwid, Alfre Woodard. D: Robert M. Young. DRA [R] 89m. v

Eye Creatures, The 1965 ★ Poor imitation of *Invasion of the Saucer Men*, adding explicit gore and nothing else to the story of aliens taking on heroic teenagers (including 30ish Ashley). C: John Ashley, Cynthia Hull, Warren Hammack, Chet Davis, Bill Peck. D: Larry Buchanan. HOR 80m.

Eye for an Eye, An 1966 ★★★ Two men, one blind, the other handicapped, act as one when they pair up to gain revenge against the person who murdered the latter man's family. Gimmicky but passable Western. (a.k.a. *Talion*) C: Robert Lansing, Patrick Wayne, Slim Pickens, Gloria Talbott, Strother Martin. D: Michael Moore. WST 106m. v

Eye for an Eye, An 1981 ★★★ Ex-cop Norris joins with a tenacious reporter to uncover a well-concealed drug smuggling operation. Plenty of choreographed violence, but a decent cast helps. C: Chuck Norris, Christopher Lee, Richard Roundtree, Maggie Cooper. D: Steve Carver. ACT [R] 106m. v

Eye of the Cat 1969 ★★★★ Feline horror, with cat hater (Sarrazin) visiting his crippled, pet-loving aunt, hoping to bilk her out of her fortune. Intensely watchable. Screenwriter Joseph Stefano also penned the screenplay to *Psycho*. C: Michael Sarrazin, Gayle Hunnicutt, Eleanor Parker, Tim Henry, Laurence Naismith. D: David Lowell Rich. HOR [PG] 102m.

Eye of the Devil 1967 British ★★★ A French nobleman uses ancient family black magic to ensure his vineyard's continued prosperity. Kerr lends some dignity to an otherwise ineffectual occult thriller. C: Deborah Kerr, David Niven, Donald Pleasence, Edward Mulhare,

Flora Robson, Emlyn Williams, Sharon Tate, David Hemmings, John Mesurier. D: J. Lee Thompson. HOR 92m.

Eye of the Needle 1981 ★★★★ Nazi spy (Sutherland) shipwrecked on remote shore, meets lonely British wife (Nelligan). Will his mission be accomplished? Suspenseful thriller, fine actors, exciting ride. From the Ken Follett novel. C: Donald Sutherland, Kate Nelligan, Ian Bannen, Christopher Cazenove, Philip Martin Brown. D: Richard Marquand. DRA [R] 112m. V

Eye of the Storm 1991 German ★★ Brothers traumatized by the unsolved slaughter of their parents run a creepy desert inn. When a suspicious good ol' boy and his young mistress check in, stage is set for murder. Fine actors can't make this contrived American Gothic work for an instant. C: Craig Sheffer, Bradley Gregg, Lara Flynn Boyle, Dennis Hopper. D: Yuri Zeltser. CRI [R] 98m. V

Eye of the Tiger 1986 ★★½ A Vietnam veteran seeks vengeance against sadistic bikers in yet another vigilante slay-fest. C: Gary Busey, Yaphet Kotto, Seymour Cassel, Bert Remsen. D: Richard Sarafian. ACT [R] 90m. V

Eye on the Sparrow 1987 ★★★½ A blind couple buck the system in order to adopt a child. Fact-based drama with good performances. C: Mare Winningham, Keith Carradine, Conchata Ferrell. D: John Korty. DRA [PG] 94m. TVM V

Eye Witness 1950 British ★★★ Montgomery directs and stars in this solid tale of an American lawyer in Britain who must track down the witness who can prove his friend innocent of murder. The clue: a book of poems. (a.k.a. *Your Witness*) C: Robert Montgomery, Felix Aylmer, Leslie Banks, Michael Ripper, Patricia Wayne. D: Robert Montgomery. CRI 104m.

Eyes in the Night 1942 ★★★★ First-rate, innovative whodunit featuring a blind detective and his seeing-eye dog. Zimmerman's first feature. C: Ann Harding, Edward Arnold, Donna Reed, Stephen McNally, Reginald Denny, Rosemary DeCamp, Mantan Moreland, Barry Nelson. D: Fred Zinnemann. CRI 80m.

Eyes of a Stranger 1981 ★★ *The Love Boat's* Tewes took her first feature as a TV news anchor tracking a psychopathic rapist/murderer. Offensive, low-budget junk nonetheless boasts a reasonably sympathetic performance by Leigh (in her film debut) as Tewes' sister. C: Lauren Tewes, Jennifer Jason Leigh, John DiSanti, Peter DuPre, Gwen Lewis. D: Ken Wiederhorn. HOR [R] 85m. V

Eyes of a Witness 1991 ★★ A self-centered industrialist journeys to Africa to coerce his philanthropic doctor daughter to come back to the U.S. Once on African soil, he's framed for murder. Fair drama, brightened by stunning African locations. C: Daniel Travanti, Jennifer Grey, Carl Lumbly, Daniel Gerroll, Eriq LaSalle. D: Peter Hunt. DRA 100m. TVM

Eyes of Hell 1961 Canadian ★★½ Hokey horror about an ancient mask with hypnotic powers that causes anyone who wears it to kill. The hallucination sequels were originally shot in 3-D, but even with this gimmick, the film is deadly dull. (a.k.a. *The Mask*) C: Paul Stevens, Claudette Nevins, Bill Walker, Anne Collings, Martin Lavut, Jim Moran. D: Julian Roffman. HOR [PG] 83m. V

Eyes of Laura Mars 1978 ★★★½ Violent photographs by commercial photographer (Dunaway) seem to be foreshadowing a series of gruesome murders. Some genuine suspense, but decadent characters are off-putting. C: Faye Dunaway, Tommy Lee Jones, Brad Dourif, Rene Auberjonois, Raul Julia, Rose Gregorio. D: Irvin Kershner. CRI [R] 103m. V

Eyes of Texas 1948 ★★★½ Unusually gripping Rogers Western with Roy as marshal up against a deadly real estate developer with a vicious pack of dogs as her henchmen. C: Roy Rogers, Andy Devine, Lynne Roberts. D: William Witney. WST 70m.

Eyes of the Amaryllis, The 1982 ★★½ Young girl (Byrne) goes to Nantucket Island to help care for her mentally ill grandmother and becomes involved in strange happenings. Detached, hard-to-get-into film from a Natalie Babbitt story. C: Ruth Ford, Martha Byrne, Guy Boyd. D: Frederick King Keller. FAM/COM 94m. V

Eyes of the Underworld 1943 ★★★½ Blackmailing mobsters threaten to expose police chief's (Dix) early prison record. Neatly executed crime yarn. C: Richard Dix, Wendy Barrie, Lon Chaney, Lloyd Corrigan, Don Porter, Billy Lee, Marc Lawrence. D: Roy William Neill. CRI 61m.

Eyes, the Mouth, The 1983 Italian ★★★ Unconventional Italian family becomes even more unhinged following son's suicide. Another in Bellocchio's chronicles of emotional messes lurches perfunctorily through gallery of obviously metaphorical stand-ins for state of Italy. C: Lou Castel, Angela Molina, Emmanuele Riva, Michel Piccoli. D: Marco Bellocchio. DRA [R] 100m. V

Eyes, the Sea and a Ball, The 1968 Japanese ★★★★ Schoolteacher (Natsuki) uses volleyball as means to reach his disinterested students. Inspirational "feel good" drama. C: Yosuke Natsuki, Mayumi Ozora, Kumeko Urabe. D: Keisuke Kinoshita. DRA 115m.

Eyes Without a Face 1959 *See* **Horror Chamber of Dr. Faustus, The**

Eyewitness 1970 *See* **Sudden Terror**

Eyewitness 1981 ★★★½ To get closer to television reporter (Weaver), janitor (Hurt) pretends to know the identity of the perpetrator of a murder that she has been covering. Unnecessary characters and subplot weaken thriller; script by Steve Tesich. C: William Hurt, Sigourney Weaver, Christopher Plummer, James Woods, Irene Worth, Morgan Freeman. D: Peter Yates. CRI [R] 102m. V

F

F for Fake 1973 ★★★★ What begins as a look at the work of master art forger Elmyr de Hory soon encompasses other famous fakes throughout this century, including Welles' own "War of the Worlds" radio broadcast. Playful pseudodocumentary is itself a fake, but if anyone can be pompous, overbearing, and still riveting, it's Welles. D: Orson Welles. DOC 85m.

F. Scott Fitzgerald and "The Last of the Belles" 1974 ★★★★ Imaginative pairing of two stories: that of author Fitzgerald and neurotic wife Zelda (Chamberlain, Danner) in post-WWI era juxtaposed with dramatization of his story "The Last of the Belles" (featuring Sarandon and Huffman). Well-acted, intriguing experiment. C: Richard Chamberlain, Blythe Danner, Susan Sarandon, David Huffman, Ernest Thompson, Richard Hatch, James Naughton, Brooke Adams. D: George Schaefer. DRA 100m. TVM

F. Scott Fitzgerald in Hollywood 1976 ★★★ Well-meaning attempt to dramatize *The Great Gatsby* author's perilous film writing career is sabotaged by miscasting of dour Miller in title role. Weld is smashing as wife Zelda, but film is uninvolving. C: Jason Miller, Tuesday Weld, Julia Foster, Dolores Sutton, Susanne Benton, Michael Lerner, Tom Ligon, John Randolph, James Woods. D: Anthony Page. DRA 100m. TVM

F/X 1986 ★★★★ Special effects wizard (Brown) is used by the feds to stage a mobster's murder. Entertaining and twisty, with clever effects proving things are never what they seem to be in the movies. Followed by *F/X2*. C: Bryan Brown, Brian Dennehy, Diane Venora, Cliff De Young, Mason Adams. D: Robert Mandel. ACT [R] 109m. V

F/X2 1991 ★★★ Movie effects maestro (Brown) uses his tricks to aid police again, and friend (Dennehy) lends a hand. Shoddy-looking duplicate of its predecessor, and previous one's cleverness is in short supply. C: Bryan Brown, Brian Dennehy, Rachel Ticotin, Joanna Gleason, Philip Bosco. D: Richard Franklin. ACT [PG-13] 107m. V

Fabiola 1951 Italian ★★★★½ Excellent historical spectacle, concerning a plot by the Roman aristocracy to massacre the Christians before the arrival of Constantine. Splendidly produced. Well worth seeing. C: Michele Morgan, Henri Vidal, Michel Simon, Gino Cervi. D: Alessandro Blasetti. ACT 96m.

Fable, A 1971 ★★★★ A violent civil rights activist (Freeman) takes his white ex-wife and her family hostage. Brutal, gripping drama from a LeRoi Jones play. Somewhat dated, but well acted. (a.k.a. *The Slave*) C: Al Freeman, Jr., Hildy Brooks, James Patterson. D: Al Freeman, Jr. DRA 80m.

Fabulous Baker Boys, The 1989 ★★★★½ Piano-playing brothers jazz up stale lounge act by adding sultry female singer who changes their lives as well as their act. Highlight is Oscar-nominated Pfeiffer's steamy rendition of "Making Whoopee" atop Jeff Bridges' Steinway, evoking Rita Hayworth's "Gilda." Taut, realistic love story. C: Jeff Bridges, Michelle Pfeiffer, Beau Bridges, Elie Raab. D: Steve Kloves. DRA [R] 116m. V

Fabulous Baron Munchausen, The 1961 Czech ★★★½ Animated film uses Gustave Doré drawings to bring to life the fabulous lies and tall tales of the fictitious baron. Visually stunning, but stories are uneven. C: Milos Kopecky, Jana Brejchova, Rudolph Jelinek, Jan Werich. D: Karel Zeman. FAM/ACT 84m. V

Fabulous Dorseys, The 1947 ★★★½ Big-band fans will enjoy this highly fictionalized biography of famous brothers playing themselves. Guest appearances by Bob Eberly, Art Tatum, and Helen O'Connell. Songs include "Green Eyes" and "Runnin Wild." C: Dorsey Brothers, Janet Blair, Paul Whiteman. D: Alfred E. Green. MUS 91m. V

Fabulous Joe, The 1947 ★★★ A henpecked hubby (Abel) is the laughingstock of his home. Lucky for him there's a talking dog to build him up! Fun and giggles aplenty. C: Marie Wilson, Walter Abel, Margot Grahame, Donald Meek. D: Bernard Carr, Harve Foster. COM 60m. V

Fabulous Suzanne, The 1946 ★★ Unlucky in love, a disillusioned young woman decides to back a more predictable animal—and makes a fortune picking the right racehorses. Nice idea that peters out halfway around the track. C: Barbara Britton, Rudy Vallee, Otto Kruger, Richard Denning, Veda Ann Borg. D: Steve Sekely. COM 71m.

Fabulous World of Jules Verne, The 1958 Czech ★★★★ Several Verne short stories are interwoven in fanciful, beautifully designed mix of live action and animation that will appeal to grown-ups as well as older children. C: Lubor Tolos, Arnost Navratil, Miroslav Holub, Zatloukalova. D: Karel Zeman. SFI 83m.

Face at the Window, The 1939 British ★★★ Overwrought but entertaining period chiller about mysterious killer terrorizing Paris. The bodies pile up and a scientist tries to revive one, and Slaughter gleefully overacts in this fun B-movie. C: Tod Slaughter, Marjorie Taylor, John Warwick. D: George King. HOR 65m. V

Face Behind the Mask, The 1941 ★★★★ Lorre is hideously burned in a tenement fire and forced to resort to crime, but falls in love with sightless woman, leading to further tragedy. Intriguing and well-acted with strong direction. C: Peter Lorre, Evelyn Keyes, Don Beddoe, George E. Stone, John Tyrell. D: Robert Florey. HOR 69m.

Face in the Crowd, A 1957 ★★★★½ Griffith is a backwoods man spotted by television exec Neal, who turns him into a star. Strong critique of television industry with persuasive script. Screen debut for Griffith and costar Remick. Filled with cameos of real TV celebrities. C: Andy Griffith, Patricia Neal, Anthony Franciosa, Walter Matthau, Lee Remick. D: Elia Kazan. DRA 126m. V

Face in the Rain, A 1963 ★★½ Things get tight for an American spy in WWII Italy when his mission collapses. Fast-paced suspense yarn. C: Rory Calhoun, Marina Berti, Niall MacGinnis, Massimo Giuliani. D: Irvin Kershner. ACT 91m.

Face of a Fugitive 1959 ★★★ Accused of a murder he did not commit, a man runs off to start a new life. Taut, efficient horse opera, and nice work by MacMurray. C: Fred MacMurray, Lin McCarthy, Dorothy Green, James Coburn, Alan Baxter, Myrna Fahey. D: Paul Wendkos. WST 81m.

Face of a Stranger 1991 ★★★★½ Class-conscious woman's picture with suddenly impoverished socialite Rowlands drawn into relationship with bag lady Daly. Compelling performances and intelligent script by playwright Marsha Norman make this superior drama. C: Tyne Daly, Gena Rowlands, Harris Yulin, Cynthia Nixon, Kevin Tighe, Seymour Cassel. D: Claudia Weill. DRA 100m.

Face of Another, The 1966 Japanese ★★★½ An accident victim receives a new face, so handsome that he seduces his own wife without her knowing the truth. Flawed, but worthwhile. C: Tatsuya Nakadai, Mikijiro Hira. D: Hiroshi Teshigahara. DRA 124m.

Face of Fear 1971 ★★★ When an Idaho schoolteacher learns she's dying from leukemia, she heads to San Francisco—but hard decisions await her. Excellent suspense and even a little intelligent laughter. C: Ricardo Montalban, Jack Warden, Elizabeth Ashley. D: George McCowan. DRA 72m.

Face of Fire 1959 ★★★½ Interesting story of man disfigured in fire while saving young child, and his subsequent problems. Quietly handled; Whitmore has some fine moments, but supporting cast is dull. C: Cameron Mitchell, James Whitmore, Bettye Ackerman, Royal Dano, Robert Simon, Richard Erdman. D: Albert Band. DRA 83m.

Face of Fu Manchu, The 1965 British ★★★★ The first in the imaginative British series about evil Emperor Fu (Lee), who's determined to expand his conquests. Lavish, lovely sets enhance the wild thrills of the chase in this entertaining '20s period piece. Sequel: *The Brides of Fu Manchu.* C: Christopher Lee, Nigel Green, James Robertson Justice, Howard Marion-Crawford, Tsai Chin, Walter Rilla. D: Don Sharp. HOR 96m.

Face of Marble 1946 ★★½ An eccentric scientist uses voodoo to bring the dead back to life. Perfect vehicle for Carradine, "master of the macabre." C: John Carradine, Claudia Drake, Robert Shayne, Maris Wrixon. D: William Beaudine. HOR 70m.

Face of Rage, The 1983 ★★★ Therapists decide to bring rape victims into direct contact with their assailants. Handled with engaging sensitivity and integrity. C: Dianne Wiest, George Dzundza, Jeffrey DeMunn, Danny Glover, Tom Waites. D: Donald Wrye. DRA 104m.

Face of the Frog 1959 German ★★★ A German police inspector goes in relentless pursuit of a notorious criminal known as "the Frog." Satisfying and hard-boiled, like an old-time serial. C: Joachim Fuchsberger, Fritz Rasp, Siegfied Lowitz, Joachen Brochmann. D: Harold Reinl. ACT 92m.

Face of the Screaming Werewolf 1959 Mexican ★★ Incoherent mishmash resulting from reediting of Mexican horror comedy that eliminates the (intentional) humor. Chaney plays an unearthed mummy that turns out to be a werewolf. C: Lon Chaney, Jr., Landa Varle. D: Gilberto Martinez Solares, Jerry Warren. HOR 60m.

Face of War, A 1967 ★★★½ This documentary uses location footage to portray a day in the life of the American forces in Vietnam. Interesting and informative. DOC 77m. V

Face the Music 1993 ★★★ Husband-and-wife musical team (Ringwald and Dempsey) falls apart as their marriage goes flat. When they are offered one big chance at fame, however, they cast aside their differences for the sake of posterity. C: Molly Ringwald, Patrick Dempsey, Lysette Anthony. D: Carol Wiseman. COM [PG-13] 93m. V

Face to Face 1952 ★★★½ Anthology of two well-done adaptations: Joseph Conrad's "The Secret Sharer," with Mason as neophyte captain who must deal with fugitive on board; and Stephen Crane's "Bride Comes to Yellow Sky," about sheriff Preston's attempt to civilize town. Engaging and well done. C: James Mason, Michael Pate, Robert Preston, Marjorie Steele. D: John Brahm, Bretaigne Windust. DRA 92m.

Face to Face 1967 Italian ★★★½ Volonte is an ailing professor who becomes intrigued, then transformed by an evil outlaw in this allegory of Italy's seduction and destruction at the hands of Adolf Hitler, transplanted to the American West. Those who make the connection might find it fascinating. For others, this is a standard spaghetti-Western. C: Gian-Maria Volonte, Tomas Milian, William Berger. D: Sergio Sollima. WST 110m.

Face to Face 1976 Swedish ★★★★ Psychiatrist Ullmann hides her neuroses under a cloak of professionalism in Bergman's harrowing treatment of mental breakdown. Beautifully multifaceted, hopeful film suggests that individual spirit and love, not psychiatry, have power to heal. Originally a four-part miniseries. C: Liv Ullmann, Erland Josephson, Gunnar Bjornstrand, Aino Taube-Henrikson, Kari Sylwan, Sif Ruud. D: Ingmar Bergman. DRA [R] 136m.

Faces in the Dark 1960 British ★★★★ Gregson, blinded in a light bulb accident, believes his wife and her lover are plotting to do away with him. Clever, chilling thriller with a dandy finish. C: John Gregson, Mai Zetterling, Michael Denison, John Ireland, Nanette Newman. D: David Eady. DRA 85m.

Faces 1968 ★★★★★ Cassavetes' well-made, highbrow soap opera dissects failing marriage with convincing insight and sympathy. Cassel and Carlin received Oscar nominations, as did Cassavetes' script. A critic's darling that did considerable box office despite its unfamiliar and sometimes discomforting art-house pacing. C: John Marley, Gena Rowlands, Lynn Carlin, Seymour Cassel, Fred Draper, Val Avery. D: John Cassavetes. DRA [R] 130m.

Facts of Life Down Under, The 1987 ★★ The cast of TV's *The Facts of Life* on an Australian holiday. Made for those who really love the show. C: Cloris Leachman, Lisa Whelchel, Nancy McKeon, Kim Fields, Mindy Cohn, Mackenzie Astin, Mario VanPeebles. D: Stuart Margolin. COM 100m.

Facts of Life Goes to Paris, The 1982 ★★ Those irrepressible young ladies from *The Facts of Life* TV show on a visit to the City of Light. Best for fans of the series. C: Charlotte Rae, Lisa Whelchel, Nancy McKeon, Kim Fields, Mindy Cohn, Frank Bonner, Roger Til. D: Asaad Kelada. COM 100m.

Facts of Life, The 1960 ★★★½ Middle-aged suburbanites (Hope and Ball) have an extramarital fling. Two old pros get a chance at grown-up material and do okay. C: Bob Hope, Lucille Ball, Ruth Hussey, Don DeFore. D: Melvin Frank. COM 103m.

Facts of Murder, The 1959 Italian ★★★★ Director Germi gives memorable performance as Roman police detective investigating sordid crime. Fast-paced study stocked with colorful characters. C: Claudia Cardinale, Pietro Germi, Franco Fabrizi. D: Pietro Germi. DRA 110m.

Fade-In 1968 ★★ Uninspired, self-serving melodrama shot on the location set of the trivial Silvio Narizzano Western *Blue*. The plot centers on production-crew member Loden's romantic fling. Interesting for its "movie about making a real movie" gimmick. (a.k.a. *Iran Cowboy*) C: Burt Reynolds, Barbara Loden, Noam Pitlik, Patricia Casey, James Hampton, Joseph Perry. D: Allen Smithee. DRA 93m.

Fade to Black 1980 ★★ Good horror premise goes awry thanks to exploitative approach and slack performance by Christopher, playing an introverted, obsessive movie buff who impersonates classic film characters in order to murder those who've done him wrong. C: Dennis Christopher, Linda Kerridge, Tim Thomerson. D: Vernon Zimmerman. HOR [R] 100m. V

Fahrenheit 451 1966 ★★★★½ Books are off limits in the Earth of the future. A fireman (Werner) assigned to burn them has a change of heart in this strong adaptation of Bradbury's enduring novel. (The title alludes to the exact temperature at which paper bursts into flame.) Mesmerizing; one of Truffaut's best. C: Julie Christie, Oskar Werner, Cyril Cusack, Anton Diffring. D: Francois Truffaut. SFI 111m. V

Fail-Safe 1964 ★★★★½ Gripping doomsday story of mistakenly launched American nuclear attack on Moscow and combined American-Soviet attempt to stop the unthinkable. Fonda is terrific as President facing ultimate decision. Same idea also done satirically in *Dr. Strangelove*. C: Henry Fonda, Walter Matthau, Fritz Weaver, Dan O'Herlihy. D: Sidney Lumet. DRA 111m. V

Falling of Raymond, The 1971 ★★ After he flunks high school English, a confused young man stalks his teacher. Tepid suspense and a lackluster script. C: Jane Wyman, Dean Stockwell, Dana Andrews. D: Boris Sagal. DRA 73m.

Fair Exchange 1936 British ★★★½ Cutesy detective comedy, with father/son sleuths out to one-up each other while investigating art theft. C: Patric Knowles, Roscoe Ates, Isla Bevan. D: Ralph Ince. COM 63m.

Fair Game 1987 ★★★ Australian exploitation picture concerns three kangaroo hunters who, while on a rampage in the Outback, decide to make a spunky wildlife sanctuary warden (Delaney) their next trophy. Escalating series of outrages handled with some flair, in otherwise standard melodrama. C: Cassandra Delaney, Peter Ford. D: Mario Andreacchio. ACT [R] 86m. V

Fair Wind to Java 1953 ★★★½ Change of pace for the usually genial MacMurray finds him playing a salty sea captain battling assorted hazards while searching for South Seas treasure. Not bad adventure yarn features exciting volcanic explosion climax. C: Fred MacMurray, Vera Ralston, Victor McLaglen, Robert Douglas, Philip Ahn. D: Joseph Kane. ACT 92m.

Faithful City 1952 Israeli ★★★★ An American (Smith) in post-WWII Israel befriends a bunch of Jewish orphans, winning their love and admiration. The children are adorable in this refreshing, inspirational story. C: Jamie

Smith, Ben Josef, John Slater. D: Joseph Leytes. DRA 86m.

Faithful in My Fashion 1946 ★★★ A soldier on furlough comes home for a visit, only to learn that his sweetheart is stuck on someone new. Pleasant comedy with an excellent cast. C: Donna Reed, Tom Drake, Edward Everett Horton, Spring Byington, Sig Ruman. D: Sidney Salkow. COM 81m.

Faithkeeper, The 1991 ★★★½ TV's Bill Moyers talks with Oren Lyons, who is the official historian or "faithkeeper" of his tribe, about Native Americans and their belief. Well-done. DOC 58m. V

Faithless 1932 ★★ Clunky melodrama about romantic ups and downs of spoiled society woman and her earnest, hardworking beau. C: Tallulah Bankhead, Robert Montgomery, Hugh Herbert, Louise Closser Hale, Henry Kolker. D: Harry Beaumont. DRA 76m.

Fake-Out 1982 ★★½ This movie tries to be all genres to all moviegoers with little success. Zadora is equally unconvincing as a Vegas singer who is raped and falls in love with a gangster, against whom she eventually is forced to testify. An obvious "vehicle" for Zadora's talents, with some well-done chase scenes. For fans only. C: Pia Zadora, Telly Savalas, Desi Arnaz Jr. D: Matt Cimber. ACT 89m. V

Fake, The 1953 British ★★½ An art investigator informs a noted portrait gallery that one of its da Vincis is an imitation. Predictable mystery manages a few nice touches here and there. C: Dennis O'Keefe, Coleen Gray, Guy Middleton, John Laurie. D: Godfrey Grayson. DRA 80m.

Fakes, The 1970 *See* **Hell's Bloody Devils**

Falcon, The After George Sanders played Michael Arlen's amateur detective and troubleshooter in the first three efforts (one of them a loose adaptation of Raymond Chandler's *Farewell My Lovely*), he turned the role over to his brother Tom Conway in a bizarre offering in which they played twin brothers, *The Falcon's Brother*. After that, Conway starred in nine more. Like so many of the series detective films, the *Falcon* movies are a splendid showcase for character actors as much as for their putative stars.

The Gay Falcon (1941)
A Date With the Falcon (1941)
The Falcon takes Over (1942)
The Falcon Strikes Back (1943)
The Falcon and the Co-eds (1943)
The Falcon in Danger (1943)
The Falcon in Hollywood (1944)
The Falcon in Mexico (1944)
The Falcon Out West (1944)
The Falcon in San Francisco (1945)
The Falcon's Alibi (1946)
The Falcon's Adventure (1946)
The Devil's Cargo (1948)
Appointment With Murder (1948)
Search for Danger (194)

Falcon and the Co-eds, The 1943 ★★★½ The Falcon saves the day after murder at a posh girls' school. Solid entry. C: Tom Conway, Jean Brooks, Rita Corday, Amelita Ward, Isabel Jewell, George Givot, Cliff Clark, Ed Gargan. D: William Clemens. CRI 68m.

Falcon and the Snowman, The 1985 ★★★½ Two old friends, one a drug dealer and the other a college washout, decide to make money by accepting a deal to spy for the Russians. A fascinating; provocative true story. Best is Penn's portrait of the enigmatic druggie. C: Timothy Hutton, Sean Penn, David Suchet, Lori Singer, Pat Hingle, Jennifer Runyon. D: John Schlesinger. DRA [R] 131m. V

Falcon in Danger, The 1943 ★★½ A plane crashes, people disappear—along with a small fortune in cash. A fairly disappointing entry in the *Falcon* series. C: Tom Conway, Jean Brooks, Elaine Shepard, Amelita Ward, Cliff Clark, Ed Gargan, Clarence Kolb, Richard Martin. D: William Clemens. CRI 70m.

Falcon in Hollywood, The 1944 ★★★★ The Falcon goes behind the scenes on the RKO studio lot to solve the mystery of an actor's murder. One of the campier episodes in the series, with some interesting scenes of moviemaking in the '40s. C: Tom Conway, Barbara Hale, Veda Ann Borg, Sheldon Leonard. D: Gordon Douglas. CRI 67m. V

Falcon in Mexico, The ★★★★ The Falcon goes south of the border to solve the murder of a prominent art-gallery owner. Solid thrills. C: Tom Conway, Mona Maris, Martha MacVicar, Nestor Paiva, Mary Currier, Emory Parnell, Pedro de Cordoba. D: William Berke. CRI 70m.

Falcon in San Francisco, The 1945 ★★★½ The Falcon hits the City by the Bay to bring down a ring of smugglers. Well-made and entertaining. C: Tom Conway, Rita Corday, Edward Brophy, Sharyn Moffett, Fay Helm, Robert Armstrong, Myrna Dell. D: Joseph H. Lewis. CRI 66m.

Falcon Out West, The 1944 ★★★½ A rancher's murder in NYC takes the Falcon to Texas to solve it. Solid entry. C: Tom Conway, Barbara Hale, Don Douglas, Carole Gallagher, Joan Barclay, Cliff Clark, Ed Gargan, Minor Watson, Lyle Talbot. D: William Clemens. CRI 64m.

Falcon Strikes Back, The 1943 ★★★★ The Falcon is framed for murder and must keep one step ahead of the law as he looks for the real killer. One of the better entries in the *Falcon* series. Trivia note: Conway's female co-star is Harriet Hilliard Nelson—Ozzie's wife. C: Tom Conway, Harriet Hilliard, Jane Randolph, Edgar Kennedy, Cliff Edwards, Rita

Corday, Wynne Gibson, Cliff Clark, Ed Gargan. D: Edward Dmytryk. CRI 66m.
Falcon Takes Over, The 1942 ★★★★ Rousing adventure has the Falcon (Sanders) involved with the ex-girlfriend of an economy-size ex-con. Remade as *Murder My Sweet* (1944) and *Farewell My Lovely* (1975). Based on Raymond Chandler's novel. C: George Sanders, Lynn Bari, James Gleason, Allen Jenkins, Helen Gilbert, Ward Bond, Edward Gargan, Anne Revere, George Cleveland, Hans Conried, Turhan Bey. D: Irving Reis. CRI 62m.
Falcon's Adventure, The 1946 ★★½ Conway's final Falcon entry has the detective protecting an inventor with a lucrative project. One of the series' lows. C: Tom Conway, Madge Meredith, Edward S. Brophy, Robert Warwick. D: William Berke. CRI 61m. V
Falcon's Alibi, The 1946 ★★½ A grande dame loses priceless jewels, and the Falcon is on the case. Plodding and fairly uninspired. C: Tom Conway, Rita Corday, Vince Barnett, Jane Greer, Elisha Cook, Jr., Emory Parnell, Al Bridge, Jason Robards, Sr., Jean Brooks, Myrna Dell. D: Ray McCarey. CRI 62m.
Falcon's Brother, The 1942 ★★★★ The Falcon and his brother team up to stop a South American assassination. Sanders' real-life brother Conway plays the Falcon's brother; Conway played the Falcon himself subsequently. C: George Sanders, Tom Conway, Jane Randolph, Don Barclay. D: Stanley Logan. CRI 63m. V
Falcon's Gold 1982 Canadian ★★★ Deep in the jungle, soldiers of fortune seek an ancient golden artifact with mystical powers. Colorful adventure. C: Simon MacCorkindale, John Marley, Louise Vallance, George Touliatos, Blanca Guerra, Jorge Reynaldo, Roger Cudney. D: Bob Schulz. ACT 90m. TVM
Falklands Task Force South 1990 ★★★½ Documentary follows British defense of the Falkland Islands against Argentinian attack. Exciting action footage was shot aboard the British flagship. DOC 114m. V
Fall From Grace 1990 ★★★ Gutsy performances by Peters and Spacey can't save this slick, surface story of televangelists Jim and Tammy Faye Bakker and the various scandals that destroyed their careers. C: Bernadette Peters, Kevin Spacey, Richard Herd, Beth Grant, John McLiam, Richard Paul, Travis Swords. D: Karen Arthur. DRA 100m. TVM
Fall Guy 1947 ★★★½ Young man (Penn) is framed for a murder that occurred during a night he can't remember. Oft-told tale, this time with good support from Armstrong as sympathetic cop. C: Clifford Penn, Teala Loring, Robert Armstrong, Elisha Cook, Jr. D: Reginald LeBorg. CRI 64m.
Fall of the Berlin Wall, The 1990 ★★½ This documentary traces the history of the Berlin Wall, its symbolism of the Cold War, and the joy of its collapse. An educational and inspiring look at a great moment. DOC 49m. V
Fall of the House of Usher 1960 ★★★★★ Top-notch horror film, suggested by Edgar Allan Poe's story. Damon plays a young man unlucky enough to enter Price's title abode. Stylish, spooky, ultimately thrilling in more ways than one. First of eight Corman/Price/Poe adaptations. (a.k.a. *House of Usher*) C: Vincent Price, Mark Damon, Myrna Fahey. D: Roger Corman. HOR 85m. V
Fall of the House of Usher, The 1982 ★★ An insane man (Landau) buries his sister alive—and is haunted by her. A stale rehashing of Poe's classic tale. C: Martin Landau, Robert Hays, Charlene Tilton, Ray Walston. D: James L. Conway. HOR [PG] 101m. V
Fall of the Roman Empire 1964 ★★★★ Marcus Aurelius dies trying to save Rome from itself. Power struggle ensues between his good adopted and evil natural sons (Boyd and Plummer, respectively). Unusually intelligent for the genre, with a standout performance by Mason. C: Sophia Loren, Stephen Boyd, Alec Guinness, James Mason, Christopher Plummer, John Ireland, Omar Sharif, Mel Ferrer. D: Anthony Mann. DRA 187m. V
Fallen Angel 1945 ★★★ Bad guy (Andrews) plans to move up in life by getting rid of his wife, but a brutal murder complicates things. Some modest thrills. C: Alice Faye, Dana Andrews, Linda Darnell, Charles Bickford, Anne Revere, Bruce Cabot, John Carradine. D: Otto Preminger. CRI 97m.
Fallen Angel 1981 ★★½ Distasteful, exploitative drama of child pornographer Masur and the innocents seduced into posing for him. C: Dana Hill, Melinda Dillon, Richard Masur, Ronny Cox. D: Robert Lewis. DRA 100m. TVM V
Fallen Angels—Volume 1 1993 ★★★½ Showtime produced this two-part series of film noir films. Tom Cruise debuts as director in *The Fighting Frammis*. *Murder Obliquely* features Dern and the always interesting Rickman. Busey steals the show in *Since I Don't Have You*. C: Isabella Rossellini, Laura Dern, Alan Rickman, Diane Lane, James Woods, Tim Matheson, Peter Gallagher, Gary Busey. D: Tom Cruise. DRA 90m. V
Fallen Angels—Volume 2 1993 ★★★½ Second part of the Showtime-produced tribute to film noir. *Dead End for Delia* features Gary Oldman. Tom Hanks gets his directing debut in *I'll Be Waiting*. Joe Mantegna is the man in *The Quiet Room*. C: Gary Oldman, Gabrielle Anwar, Meg Tilly, Tom Hanks, Bruno Kirby, Bonnie Bedelia, Joe Mantegna, Peter Gallagher. D: Tom Hanks. DRA 90m. V
Fallen Champ: The Untold Story of Mike Tyson 1993 ★★★½ Documentary covers the rise and fall of the great heavyweight champion from his tough childhood in Brooklyn

through the glory years as champ to his conviction for rape. Several revealing interviews only scratch the surface of this complex man. D: Barbara Kopple. DOC 93m. V

Fallen Idol, The 1948 British ★★★★★ The idol is a servant to a young boy in whose eyes the servant can do no wrong, despite being suspected of murder. A first-rate thriller from writer Graham Greene. C: Ralph Richardson, Michele Morgan, Bobby Henrey, Jack Hawkins. D: Carol Reed. DRA 92m. V

Fallen Sparrow 1943 ★★★½ Spanish Civil War veteran returns to New York City only to discover he's being pursued by ruthless Nazis who've murdered his best friend. Gripping but confused thriller features excellent, typically intense performance by Garfield as the half-crazy vet. C: John Garfield, Maureen O'Hara, Walter Slezak, Patricia Morison. D: Richard Wallace. DRA 94m. V

Falling Down 1993 ★★★ A tightly wound engineer goes on a violent spree, walking across Los Angeles with guns drawn. Meant as a metaphor for stress of modern life, but comes across as exploitative and shallow. C: Michael Douglas, Robert Duvall, Barbara Hershey, Frederic Forrest, Tuesday Weld, Dedee Pfeiffer. D: Joel Schumacher. DRA [R] 113m. V

Falling for the Stars 1984 ★★★ Farnsworth, a former stuntman himself, hosts this look at the most thrilling—and dangerous part of the movies. D: Richard Farnsworth. DOC 58m. V

Falling from Grace 1992 ★ Country music star comes home to Indiana and the troubled family he left behind. Rock star Mellencamp proves that his acting skills are no better than his abilities as director. C: John Mellencamp, Mariel Hemingway, Kay Lenz, Claude Akins. D: John Mellencamp. DRA [PG-13] 100m. V

Falling in Love 1984 ★★ Adulterous commuter love affair between Streep and De Niro is ho-hum all the way to Grand Central Station and back. Ambitious remake of *Brief Encounter* with happy ending. C: Robert De Niro, Meryl Streep, Harvey Keitel, Dianne Wiest. D: Ulu Grosbard. DRA [PG-13] 106m. V

Falling in Love Again 1980 ★★ Sullen Bronx everyman meets blonde preppie in tedious culture-clash romance. Michelle Pfeiffer's debut. C: Elliott Gould, Susannah York, Stuart Paul, Michelle Pfeiffer, Kaye Ballard, Robert Hackman. D: Steven Paul. DRA [PG] 103m. V

False Arrest 1992 ★★½ An innocent woman is wrongly convicted of involvement in Mafia murders. Frightening drama, based on a true story. C: Donna Mills, Robert Wagner, Dennis Christopher. D: Bill L. Norton. CRI 102m. V

False Colors 1939 ★★★ Hopalong Cassidy rides to the rescue of a woman threatened by a swindler—who may also be a murderer. Typical series entry. C: William Boyd, Jimmy Rogers, Robert Mitchum. D: George Archainbaud. WST 65m. V

False Face 1978 *See* **Scalpel**

False Identity 1990 ★★½ Scandal comes to a small town when an attempt to find the owner of a Purple Heart uncovers many secrets. C: Stacy Keach, Genevieve Bujold. D: James Keach. DRA [PG-13] 97m. V

False Paradise 1948 ★★★ Hopalong Cassidy defends the land of an elderly teacher from the bad guys in this series western. C: William Boyd, Rand Brooks. D: George Archainbaud. WST 59m. V

False Witness 1981 *See* **Circle of Deceit**

Falstaff 1976 ★★★½ John Pritchard conducts the London Philharmonic in a production of Nardi's classic opera, at the Glyndebourne Festival. Performed in Italian. C: Donald Gramm, Benjamin Luxon. MUS 123m. V

Falstaff 1983 ★★★★ Maestro Carlo Maria Giulani conducts Verdi's masterpiece with stirring vitality. C: Renato Bruson, Katia Ricciarelli. MUS 141m. V

Fame 1980 ★★★½ Talented cast of bright newcomers spark this mixed-bag story about students at N.Y. High School of Performing Arts. Cara's recording of the Oscar-winning title song was a huge hit. Later a widely praised TV series. C: Irene Cara, Lee Curreri, Eddie Barth, Laura Dean, Paul McCrane, Billy Hufsey, Gene Anthony Ray, Maureen Teefy. D: Alan Parker. MUS [R] 134m. V

Fame Is the Name of the Game 1966 ★★★ Freelance writer investigates murder of call girl in convoluted, drab mystery which led to weekly TV series. C: Tony Franciosa, Jill St. John, Jack Klugman, George Macready, Lee Bowman, Susan Saint James, Jack Weston, Robert Duvall, Nanette Fabray. D: Stuart Rosenberg. DRA 100m.

Fame Is the Spur 1946 British ★★ Overcoming an impoverished childhood, a young man fashions a career for himself in national politics. Redgrave's a treat, but the story is hardly compelling. C: Michael Redgrave, Rosamund John, Anthony Wager, Brian Weske, Hugh Burden. D: John Boulting, Roy Boulting. DRA 116m.

Family Affair, A 1937 ★★★★ Film that began the long, popular Andy Hardy series. Judge Hardy tries to solve family problems and works to get himself reelected. Fond, nostalgic look at small-town America. Barrymore and Byington's roles later taken over by Lewis Stone and Fay Holden. C: Lionel Barrymore, Mickey Rooney, Spring Byington, Cecilia Parker, Eric Linden, Julie Haydon, Charley Grapewin, Sara Haden. D: George Seitz. FAM/COM 69m.

Family Business 1986 French ★★★½ A thief who specializes in wall safes finds his family taking a hands-on approach to his career. Unusual comic effort from political thriller director Costa-Gavras falls flat, but has its amusing moments. C: Johnny Hallyday,

Fanny Ardant, Guy Marchand. D: Costa-Gavras. COM 98m.

Family Business 1989 ★★½ A seasoned veteran criminal (Connery) whose son (Hoffman) has left the business of crime, entices his grandson (Broderick) into continuing the family tradition. Considerable charm and talents of three leads compete with weak story. C: Sean Connery, Dustin Hoffman, Matthew Broderick, Rosana DeSoto. D: Sidney Lumet. CRI [R] 115m. V

Family Circus Christmas, A 1979 ★ Christmas brings wonder and delight when Dolly, PJ, Jeffy and Billy prepare for holiday festivities. Based on the popular comic. FAM/COM 60m. V

Family Circus Easter, A 1982 ★★★½ Billy, Dolly, and Jeff try to trap the elusive Easter bunny. Animated, includes a few short rabbit cartoons. FAM/COM 60m. V

Family Dog—Enemy Dog/Show Dog 1992 ★★★★ Tim Burton and Steven Spielburg worked together to present this charming, original fable, a dog look's at contemporary life. C: Danny Mann, Martin Mull, Molly Cheek. D: Chris Buck. FAM/COM 47m. V

Family for Joe, A 1990 ★★★½ When a judge threatens to split them up, four orphans get a homeless old codger to pretend he's their grandfather. The ploy works, and they all move in together. Interesting look at a kinder, gentler Mitchum. Good stuff. C: Robert Mitchum, Maia Brewton, Jarrad Paul, Jessica Player, Barbara Babcock, David Nelson, John Mitchum. D: Jeffrey Melman. COM 100m. TVM

Family Game, The 1983 Japanese ★★★★ The pressures of career, education, and family are examined in this biting satire of contemporary Japanese values as middle-class parents hire a tutor (Matsuda) for their backward son. Matsuda is a joy to watch as he takes over the household. C: Yusaku Matsuda, Juzo Itami, Saori Yuki, Ichirota Miyagawa. D: Yoshimitsu Morita. COM 107m. V

Family Honeymoon 1948 ★★ Widow with three kids remarries and takes her children along on the honeymoon. Though they try hard, neither Colbert nor MacMurray can lift this one-joke comedy above the initial premise. C: Claudette Colbert, Fred MacMurray, Rita Johnson, Gigi Perreau. D: Claude Binyon. COM 80m.

Family Hour Special—Animal Talk ★★★½ Well-acted package of three wild-life stories, geered towards older children. Includes Jack London's Call of the Wild, Sterling North's Rascal, and Mel Ellis' Flight of the White Wolf. C: Anthony Newley, Lance Kerwin, John Quade, Spencer Mulligan. D: Paul Asselin. FAM/DRA 45m. V

Family Hour Special—Out of Time ★★★½ Locane and Baldwin are two time-travelling youngsters finding out family secrets in 1851. Cute idea, well-done. C: Adam Baldwin, Amy Locane, R.D. Robb. D: Michael Schweitzer. FAM/DRA 45m. V

Family Jewels, The 1965 ★★★½ Child heiress Butterworth must pick her guardian from one of seven relatives, all played by Lewis. Enjoyment of this innocuous comedy will depend on fondness for star, who mugs up a storm no matter which character he's playing. C: Jerry Lewis, Donna Butterworth, Sebastian Cabot, Robert Strauss, Milton Frome. D: Jerry Lewis. COM 100m. V

Family Life 1972 ★★★½ Outstanding performances distinguish this story of a rebellious teenager (Ratcliff) victimized by her uncaring, unimaginative parents. (a.k.a. *Wednesday's Child*) C: Sandy Ratcliff, Bill Dean, Grace Cave. D: Ken Loach. DRA 105m. V

Family Matter, A 1991 ★★½ Alt gets married, then discovers her new husband killed her crime boss father. Film is as slow witted as the character she plays. C: Eric Roberts, Carol Alt, Eli Wallach. D: Stuart Margolin. CRI [R] 110m.

Family Nobody Wanted, The 1975 ★★ An impoverished minister and his wife adopt a large family of racially mixed children. Uplifting story that loses its spark. C: Shirley Jones, James Olson, Katherine Helmond. D: Ralph Senensky. DRA 72m.

Family of Spies 1990 ★★½ Navy officer John Walker, Jr. spied—over two decades—for the Soviet Union. Interesting look at a fascinating story. C: Powers Boothe, Lesley Ann Warren, Graham Beckel, Gordon Clapp, John M. Jackson, Jeroen Krabbe. D: Stephen Gyllenhaal. ACT 200m. TVM

Family Pictures 1993 ★★★½ Intense drama of suburban family torn apart by autistic child. Huston is shattering as mother unwilling to place her son in home. However, pat script fails to explain why this family can't survive its ordeal, while others do. C: Anjelica Huston, Sam Neill, Kyra Sedgwick, Dermot Mulroney,, Janet-Laine Green, Jamie Harrold. D: Philip Saville. DRA 200m. TVM

Family Plot ★★★★ A wacky psychic (Harris) and her sleuthing boyfriend (Dern) try to track down a missing heiress. Harris is wonderful and Devane is perfect as the oily foil. Hitchcock's last film is lighthearted fun. C: Karen Black, Bruce Dern, Barbara Harris, William Devane, Ed Lauter, Cathleen Nesbitt. D: Alfred Hitchcock. CRI [PG] 120m. V

Family Prayers 1993 ★★★½ Modest coming-of-age film, set in L.A. in 1969, about a boy approaching his bar mitzvah while his family falls apart because his father (Mantegna) is a compulsive gambler. Absorbing story and sensitive acting, marred slightly by some unseemly nostalgia. C: Joe Mantegna, Anne Archer, Tzyi Ratner-Strauber, Paul Reiser, Patti LuPone. D: Scott Rosenfelt. DRA [PG] 108m. V

Family Reunion 1981 ★★★★ Sentimental

Davis vehicle casts her as retired schoolmarm seeking to reunite family with help of precocious boy (Hyman, Bette's own grandson). One of Davis' better grande-dame performances. C: Bette Davis, J. Ashley Hyman, David Huddleston, John Shea, Roy Dotrice, David Rounds, Kathryn Walker, Roberts Blossom, Roberta Wallach, Jeff McCracken, Ann Lange, Paul Rudd. D: Fielder Cook. DRA 200m. TVM V

Family Rico, The 1972 ★★★ A Mob boss tries to come to terms with the various conflicting elements of his crime family. Powerful delivery courtesy of a potent cast. C: Ben Gazzara, Sal Mineo, Jo Van Fleet, James Farentino, Sian Allen, Dane Clark, Leif Erickson, Jack Carter. D: Paul Wendkos. ACT 73m.

Family Secret, The 1951 ★★★½ Golden boy Derek accidentally causes the death of his best friend. When he confesses to his family, they disagree over going to the police. Well-meaning social drama with a good cast. C: John Derek, Lee J. Cobb, Erin O'Brien-Moore, Jody Lawrance. D: Henry Levin. DRA 85m. V

Family Sins 1987 ★★★½ A family is torn apart by the escalating and ultimately tragic competitiveness a father creates between his sons. Very well acted. C: James Farentino, Jill Eikenberry, Andrew Bednarski. D: Jerrold Freedman. DRA 93m. V

Family, The 1970 Italian ★★½ A hardened ex-con (Bronson) sets off in relentless pursuit of the man who framed him. Nonstop action. (a.k.a. *Violent City*) C: Charles Bronson, Jill Ireland, Telly Savalas, Michel Constantin. D: Sergio Sollima. ACT 94m. V

Family, The 1987 Italian ★★★★ The ups and downs of life in a large middle-class Italian family unfold in the decades between the birth of baby Carlo (Gassman), and his 80th birthday. Slow but intriguing, warm-hearted drama. C: Vittorio Gassman, Fanny Ardant, Stefania Sandrelli, Philippe Noiret. D: Ettore Scola. DRA [PG] 128m. V

Family Ties Vacation 1985 ★★ Inimitable clan from the *Family Ties* TV series takes off for a visit to London. Nothing extraordinary, but some familiar faces. C: Meredith Baxter Birney, Michael Gross, Michael J. Fox, Justine Bateman, Tina Yothers, Derek Nimmo, John Moulder Brown. D: Will Mackenzie. COM 100m. TVM

Family Upside Down, A 1978 ★★★★ Retired couple is separated by husband's heart attack. Astaire shows long-neglected dramatic talent in effective tearjerker with terrific cast. C: Helen Hayes, Fred Astaire, Efrem Zimbalist Jr. D: David Lowell Rich. DRA 100m. V

Family Viewing 1989 ★★ A woman's affair with her stepson destroys the family. Sensitive treatment of a delicate issue. C: Michael McManus, Arsinee Khanjian. D: Atom Egoyan. DRA 86m. V

Family Way, The 1966 British ★★★★ Living with their family puts too much of a strain on young English married couple (Mills and Bennett). Sweet comedy scores with excellent cast and witty dialogue. Music by Paul McCartney. C: Hayley Mills, Hywel Bennett, John Mills, Marjorie Rhodes, Avril Angers, Murray Head. D: Roy Boulting. DRA 115m.

Famly Enforcer 1977 ★★★ A young man climbs the ladder of the underworld to the top, only to become the target of other ambitious hoodlums. C: Joseph Cortese, Joe Pesci, Lou Criscuolo. D: Ralph DeVito. CRI [R] 89m. V

Famous Five Get Into Trouble, The 1987 ★★★½ Based on the books by Enid Blyton, the story of a bicycle trip that becomes a kidnapping. Exciting and engrossing for all ages. C: Ove Sprogoe, Manfred Reddeman, Lily Broberg. D: Trine Hedman. FAM/ACT 90m. V

Fan, The 1949 ★★★ An adaptation of Oscar Wilde play *Lady Windemere's Fan* follows the misadventures of a Victorian woman whose reputation precedes her. She's using her daughter as a way up the social ladder. Great production values and costumes, but still a lackluster comedy from director Preminger. C: Jeanne Crain, Madeleine Carroll, George Sanders, Richard Greene. D: Otto Preminger. COM 89m.

Fan, The 1981 ★★★ Fan's admiration for screen and stage star (Bacall) turns deadly when his advances, via creepy letters, are rejected. Impressive cast, especially Bacall, adds glitter. C: Lauren Bacall, Michael Biehn, Maureen Stapleton, James Garner, Hector Elizondo. D: Edward Bianchi. CRI [R] 95m. V

Fanatics, The 1957 French ★★★ Choreographing the assassination of a Latin American dictator. Suspenseful political thriller enhanced by a first-rate cast. C: Pierre Fresnay, Michel Auclair, Gregoire Aslan, Betty Schneider. D: Alex Joffe. DRA 85m.

Fancy Pants 1950 ★★★★ Enjoyable retread of classic *Ruggles of Red Gap* casts Hope as British butler to Ball on trip to the Wild West. Two stars work well together in colorful comedy. C: Bob Hope, Lucille Ball, Bruce Cabot, Jack Kirkwood, Lea Penman, Eric Blore. D: George Marshall. COM 92m. V

Fandango 1985 ★★★★ In one final soul-searching journey, a group of college-age friends must face their uncertain future during the years of the Vietnam draft. Costner and Nelson are interesting. C: Kevin Costner, Judd Nelson, Sam Robards, Chuck Bush, Brian Cesak. D: Kevin Reynolds. DRA [PG] 91m. V

Fanfan the Tulip 1951 French ★★★½ French soldier (Philipe) in Louis XV's army swashbuckles through series of adventures. Stylish comedy; Lollobrigida and especially Philipe are wonderful. C: Gerard Philipe, Gina Lollobrigida, Noel Roquevert, Olivier Hussenot, Marcel Herrand, Sylvie Pelayo. D: Christian-Jaque. COM 104m.

Fangface ★★★ Two episodes of lukewarm TV animated series about a teenage werewolf. FAM/DRA 44m. v

Fangface II Spooky Spoofs 1978 ★★½ More adentures of the teenage nerd-turned-werewolf, from the feeble TV animated series. COM 45m. v

Fangs of Fate 1984 ★★★ Cattle rustlers take over a town by appointing an inexperienced sheriff. Only average silent Western, worth watching as a curiosity piece. C: Tom Kenna, Victoria Racimo. D: Joel M. Reed. WST [R] 86m. v

Fanny and Alexander 1983 Swedish ★★★★★ When ten-year-old Alexander's father dies, his mother remarries a taciturn minister, disrupting the boy's idyllic existence. Bergman's rich, multi-layered tribute to his own childhood is one of his most emotionally fulfilling films. Winner of four Oscars, including Best Foreign Film. C: Pernilla Allwin, Bertil Guve, Gunn Wallgren, Allan Edwall, Ewa Froling. D: Ingmar Bergman. DRA [R] 197m. v

Fanny by Gaslight 1944 *See* **Man of Evil**

Fanny Hill 1983 ★★★ Fair adaptation of the John Cleland novel concerning the erotic escapades of a wide-eyed young woman (Raines). A good cast and stunning period detail distinguish this telling of the tale. C: Lisa Raines, Oliver Reed, Wilfrid Hyde-White, Shelley Winters. D: Gerry O'Hara. DRA [R] 80m. v

Fanny 1932 French ★★★★½ Classic soap opera, the middle film of Pagnol's trilogy, in which the deserted, pregnant Fanny marries the elderly sailmaker Panisse, under the watchful eye of her lover's father (Raimu). Beautifully acted, although the sound and photography are a mite primitive. The other two films are *Marius* and *Cesar*. All three were combined and remade in 1961 as *Fanny*. C: Raimu, Pierre Fresnay, Charpin, Orane Demazis. D: Marc Allegret. DRA 128m. v

Fanny 1961 ★★★★½ Romance between a French sailor and the pregnant woman he leaves behind is the framework for this heartbreaking, beautifully photographed and acted adaptation of Marcel Pagnol's film trilogy (*Marius, Cesar,* and *Fanny*). Logan uses the score of the 1957 Broadway musical (based on the same material) as stunning background music for Marseilles locations. C: Leslie Caron, Maurice Chevalier, Charles Boyer, Horst Buchholz. D: Joshua Logan. DRA 133m. v

Fan's Notes, A 1972 Canadian ★★ The misadventures and psychological demise of a sensitive young man who rebels against prevailing definitions of American success and conformity. Confusing, and nowhere near as powerful as Exley's fine novel. C: Jerry Ohrbach, Burgess Meredith, Patricia Collins, Julia Ann Robinson, Rosemary Murphy. D: Eric Till. DRA [R] 100m. v

Fantasia 1940 ★★★★½ A milestone in the history of animation, this Disney feature offers eight episodes set to classical music. Mickey Mouse as the bedeviled Sorcerer's Apprentice is the high point. D: Ben Sharpsteen. FAM/MUS [G] 120m. v

Fantasies 1981 ★ Should have been called "Nightmares." Derek and Hooten try to make tourist haven out of tiny Greek isle. Filmed eight years before released, and proof that Derek (billed as Kathleen Collins) couldn't act when she was 16, either. C: Bo Derek, Peter Hooten, Anna Alexiadis. D: John Derek. COM [R] 81m. v

Fantasist, The 1986 Irish ★★½ Psychotic murderer lures his victims via obscene phone calls. A country woman in big city Dublin is his latest target. Graphic thriller helped out by Irish setting; some viewers may find the premise offensive. C: Christopher Cazenove, Timothy Bottoms, Moira Harris. D: Robin Hardy. CRI [R] 98m. v

Fantastic Animation Festival ★★★★ Good grab-bag of cutting edge animation, highlighted by Oscar-winning short, *Closed Monday*. COM 91m. v

Fantastic Comedy 1975 Romanian ★★★★ Pairing of two science fiction stories. The first is a comedy about a bumbling alien robot stranded on Earth. The second takes a darker look at an Earthling child used as a guinea pig by aliens out to create the perfect human. Expensive-looking, diverting, and imaginative. C: Dem Radulescu, Cornel Coman, Vasilia Tastaman. D: Ion Popescu-Gopo. COM 90m.

Fantastic Invasion of Planet Earth 1966 ★★ Somehow a young couple find themselves stranded in an eerie, empty town that's enclosed in a mysterious bubble. Odd little film that worked better in 3-D. C: Michael Cole, Deborah Walley, Johnny Desmond. D: Arch Oboler. SFI [PG] 91m.

Fantastic Planet 1973 French ★★★½ Animated feature set on the planet YGAM, where supersmart giant automatons keep humans as pets, until one rebels. Imaginative and fun, but may be a little too slow for younger viewers. D: Rene Laloux. SFI 72m. v

Fantastic Voyage 1966 ★★★★ Scientists perform precedent-setting microsurgery by reducing themselves in size and entering the patient in a minicapsule. Engaging take on the shrunken person theme peaks when the antibodies attack Welch. Oscars for Special Visual Effects, Art Direction, and Set Direction. C: Stephen Boyd, Raquel Welch, Edmond O'Brien, Donald Pleasence. D: Richard Fleischer. SFI 100m. v

Fantastic World of D.C. Collins, The 1983 ★★ Coleman plays an imaginative teenager who fantasizes that villainous strangers are pursuing him to recover a lost videotape. Seriously uninspired. C: Gary Coleman, Bernie Casey, Fred Dryer, Marilyn McCoo. D: Leslie Martinson. FAM/COM 96m. v

Fantastica 1980 Canadian ★★½ A beautiful young woman, the star of a musical revue, has a number of consuming love affairs. Somewhat dreamlike treatment of boundless youthful romance. C: Carole Laure, Lewis Furey, Serge Reggiani, Claudine Auger, John Vernon. D: Gilles Carle. DRA 104m.

Fantasy Double Bill, A ★★★★½ Marvelous double-bill of children's operas, both from Maurice Sendak picture-books: *Where the Wild Things Are and Higglety-Pigglety Pop.* Great introduction to an often off-putting art form. FAM/MUS 100m. V

Fantasy Island 1977 ★★★ An odd millionaire (Montalban) invites guests to his lush tropical island; there, amid gently swaying palm trees, all their fantasies come true. Entertaining source of the hit TV series. C: Ricardo Montalban, Bill Bixby, Sandra Dee, Peter Lawford, Carol Lynley, Hugh O'Brian, Eleanor Parker. D: Richard Lang. DRA 100m. TVM V

Fantasy Mission Force 1985 ★★★ Martial arts star Chan tries to recover stolen loot during WWII. Okay for this genre. C: Jackie Chan. DRA 90m. V

Far and Away 1992 ★★★½ Exquisitely photographed historical romance. Unlikely lovers-to-be escape troubles in Ireland to seek land and freedom in the New World. Enthusiastically acted by huge cast, who do their best with an old-fashioned story. C: Tom Cruise, Nicole Kidman, Thomas Gibson, Robert Prosky, Barbara Babcock, Colm Meaney. D: Ron Howard. DRA [PG-13] 140m. V

Far Country, The 1955 ★★★★ Rustlers and swindlers harass a quiet trail boss on a cattle drive to Alaska. Excellent outdoor Western adventure with vivid locales. C: James Stewart, Ruth Roman, Corinne Calvet, Walter Brennan, Jay C. Flippen, John McIntire, Harry Morgan. D: Anthony Mann. WST 97m. V

Far Country, The 1966 ★★★½ An old hatred does its best to destroy a flourishing new romance. At times compelling. C: Michael York, Sigrid Thornton. D: George Miller. DRA 115m.

Far East 1985 ★★ An expatriate Australian (Brown) runs bar in tumultuous Asian city, and is visited by old flame. Dim-witted stab at remaking *Casablanca*, with humdrum results. C: Bryan Brown, Helen Morse. D: John Duigan. DRA 105m.

Far From Home: The Adventures of Yellow Dog 1995 ★★★★ Boy and his dog are stranded in Canadian wilds during a boat trip. Exciting tale of survival makes fine family fare, particularly for canine afficionados; Borsos' final movie. C: Jesse Bradford, Mimi Rogers, Bruce Davison, Tom Bower. D: Phillip Borsos. FAM/ACT [PG] 81m. V

Far from Home 1989 ★★½ Vacation plans go awry when adolescent (Barrymore) finds herself terrorized by camp site killer. Typical thriller. C: Matt Frewer, Drew Barrymore, Richard Masur, Karen Austin, Susan Tyrrell, Anthony Rapp, Jennifer Tilly. D: Meiert Avis. CRI 86m. V

Far from the Madding Crowd 1967 British ★★★★ Ambitious farmgirl (Christie) in Victorian England and her destructive unrequited loves. Handsomely mounted version of Thomas Hardy novel with excellent performances by Bates and Finch. C: Julie Christie, Peter Finch, Terence Stamp, Alan Bates, Prunella Ransome. D: John Schlesinger. DRA 169m. V

Far Frontier, The ★★★ Rogers (with the aid of Trigger, his horse) foils a gang that brings deported outlaws back into the USA. Standard oater. C: Roy Rogers, Andy Devine, Clayton Moore, Gail Davis. WST 53m. V

Far Horizons, The 1955 ★★½ Typically fictionalized Hollywood history lesson explains famed Lewis and Clark expedition. Heavy on the scenery, weak on accuracy and action. Romantic subplot doesn't help. C: Fred MacMurray, Charlton Heston, Donna Reed, Barbara Hale, William Demarest. D: Rudolph Mate. DRA 108m.

Far North 1988 ★★★½ A family of Minnesotans deal with troubles on their farm. Low key, symbolic drama via Sam Shepard carries some insight. C: Jessica Lange, Charles Durning, Tess Harper, Donald Moffat, Ann Wedgeworth, Patricia Arquette. D: Sam Shepard. DRA [PG-13] 90m. V

Far Off Place, A 1993 ★★★½ American teenager living in Africa flees across Kalahari desert when her parents are slaughtered by elephant poachers. Accompanying her are a young Bushman and a teenage tourist whose father was also slain. Stunning cinematography, but extremely graphic violence for a children's film. C: Reese Witherspoon, Ethan Randall, Maximilian Schell, Jack Thompson, Sarel Bok, Robert Burke, Patricia Kalember, Daniel Gerroll, Miles Anderson. D: Mikael Salomon. FAM/ACT [PG] 105m.

Far Out Man 1990 ★★ Middle-aged hippie (Chong) in search of his '60s flame and their love child. Family enterprise features several Chongs and sorely needs gags. C: Tommy Chong, Shelby Chong, Paris Chong, C. Thomas Howell, Martin Mull, Rae Dawn Chong. D: Tommy Chong. COM [R] 84m. V

Far Out Space Nuts ★★½ Two episodes of obscure TV series with the two stars as bumbling astronauts. Only for diehard fans of Denver's *Gilligan's Island*. C: Bob Denver, Chuck McCann. COM 48m. V

Far Pavilions, The 1984 ★★★ A royal daughter betrothed to a Hindu prince and a patriotic British officer in 19th-century India fall in love. Stale story with lush settings and splendid costumes. C: Ben Cross, Amy Irving, John Gielgud, Omar Sharif. D: Peter Duffell. DRA 108m. V

Faraway, So Close 1993 German ★★★½ The angelic protagonists of *Wings of Desire* return: Ganz, the fallen angel now owns a pizza parlor; his erstwhile partner Sander becomes a mortal after saving a little girl. Overlong and a bit loopy, but sweet-natured and visually beautiful. Notable also as Mikhail Gorbachev's film debut. C: Otto Sander, Willem DaFoe, Bruno Ganz, Peter Falk, Lou Reed, Heinz Ruhmann, Horst Buchholz, Mikhail Gorbachev. D: Wim Wenders. DRA [PG-13] 140m. V

Farewell Again 1937 British ★★★ Human-interest heart tugger of British soldiers on short leave from horrors of the front. Moving and surprisingly effective. C: Leslie Banks, Flora Robson, Sebastian Shaw, Patricia Hilliard. D: Tim Whelan. ACT 81m.

Farewell Friend 1968 French ★★ Several French mercenaries just back from Algeria team up for robbery. Wooden adventure that drags for two hours wastes interesting cast. (a.k.a. *Honor Among Thieves*) C: Alain Delon, Charles Bronson, Olga Georges-Picot, Brigitte Fossey, Bernard Fresson. D: Jean Herman. DRA [PG] 115m.

Farewell My Concubine 1993 ★★★★ Two Peking Opera stars maintain lifelong friendship during turbulent times in China. Glossy, sumptuous production often sacrifices depth for epic sweep, but holds interest throughout. Opening sequences in children's opera school are extraordinarily compelling. C: Leslie Cheung, Zhang Fengyi, Gong Li, Lu Qi, Ying Da, Ge You, Li Chun. D: Chen Kaige. DRA 156m. V

Farewell, My Lovely 1975 British ★★★★½ A hulking gangster (O'Halloran) hires Philip Marlowe (Mitchum) to find his long-lost love, leading him into a complex plot littered with dead bodies. Raymond Chandler once said Mitchum was the perfect choice for his hard-boiled private eye. Remake of *Murder My Sweet* and *The Falcon Takes Over*. C: Robert Mitchum, Charlotte Rampling, John Ireland, Sylvia Miles, Jack O'Halloran. D: Dick Richards. CRI [R] 97m. V

Farewell to Arms, A 1932 ★★★★½ Glowing, tragic adaptation of Hemingway masterpiece, with Cooper and Hayes moving as ill-fated lovers caught in WWI maelstrom. Borzage's lush romanticism and Charles Lang's Oscar-winning cinematography make this a genuinely affecting tearjerker. Remade in 1957. C: Helen Hayes, Gary Cooper, Adolphe Menjou, Mary Philips. D: Frank Borzage. DRA 78m. V

Farewell to Arms, A 1957 ★★★½ Hemingway's novel of romance and sacrifice in WWI Italy is given elaborate but stilted filming in David O. Selznick production. Hudson and Jones miscast as wounded ambulance driver and the nurse he falls in love with. Remake of superior 1932 version. C: Rock Hudson, Jennifer Jones, Vittorio DeSica, Alberto Sordi, Mercedes McCambridge, Elaine Stritch, Oscar Homolka. D: Charles Vidor. DRA 152m.

Farewell to Love 1931 British ★★★ Minor musical romance with wealthy British woman (Stockfield) sponsoring a tempermental Neapolitan tenor (Kiepura) on his debut tour of England. (a.k.a. *City of Song*) C: Jan Kiepura, Betty Stockfield, Hugh Wakefield. D: Carmine Gallone. MUS 96m.

Farewell to Manzanar 1976 ★★★★½ Gripping true story of Japanese Americans in WWII internment camp has shattering impact. Large cast of Japanese actors shine in rare opportunity to carry a film. Standouts include Mako and Morita. C: Yuki Shimoda, Nobu McCarthy, Clyde Kusatsu, Mako, Akemi Kikiumura, Pat Morita, James Saito. D: John Korty. DRA 105m. TVM

Farewell to the King 1989 ★★★ WWII American deserter (Nolte) becomes king of a tribe of Borneo headhunters. Good concept is thwarted by poor direction by Milius but salvaged with colorful jungle visuals and plenty of action. C: Nick Nolte, Nigel Havers, James Fox, Marilyn Tokuda. D: John Milius. DRA 114m. V

Farinelli 1995 French-Italian ★★★½ Exotic tale of the 18th-century castrato singer, Carlo Broschi (Dionisi), who was a favorite with the ladies—despite his "shortcomings." Sumptuous production, but bizarre subject matter, not to all tastes. C: Stefanio Dionisi, Enrico Lo Verson, Jeroen Krabbe. D: Gerard Corbiau. DRA [R] 110m.

Farm, The 1987 ★★★ A young boy struggles to save his family from being possessed by evil aliens. Okay thriller. C: Wil Wheaton, John Schneider, Claude Akins. D: David Keith. HOR [R] 92m.

Farmer Takes a Wife, The 1935 ★★★★ Gaynor and Fonda (in film debut, repeating his stage role) make pleasing team in story of Erie Canal worker who romances cook and takes up farming. Stars are charming in well-made slice of Americana. Remade as musical in 1953. C: Janet Gaynor, Henry Fonda, Charles Bickford, Slim Summerville, Jane Withers. D: Victor Fleming. DRA 91m.

Farmer Takes a Wife, The 1953 ★★★½ A farmer woos his beloved in this musical remake of the 1935 romance set in Erie Canal country. Game cast re-creates feel of more leisurely paced bygone era. C: Betty Grable, Dale Robertson, Thelma Ritter, John Carroll. D: Henry Levin. MUS 80m. V

Farmer, The 1977 ★★ In postwar Georgia, callow ex-soldier tries to work his farm but gets mixed up with a local group of mobsters. A real misfire that never catches on. C: Gary Conway, Angel Tompkins, Michael Dante, George Memmoli, Ken Renard. D: David Berlatsky. ACT [R] 98m.

Farmer's Daughter, The 1940 ★★★ Raye is title character, a bumbling show business wanna-be who gets her big chance when the star gets sick. Predictable excuse for Martha's clowning. C: Martha Raye, Charlie Ruggles, Richard Denning, Gertrude Michael, William Frawley. D: James Hogan. COM 60m.

Farmer's Daughter, The 1947 ★★★★ Fresh off the farm, a Swedish woman becomes a congressman's housekeeper, and her outspoken, commonsense ideas soon have her running for Congress herself. Excellent comedy, done with Hollywood know-how and flair. Young won an Oscar for her charming performance. C: Loretta Young, Joseph Cotten, Ethel Barrymore, Charles Bickford. D: H.C. Potter. COM 97m. V

Farmer's Other Daughter, The 1973 ★★★ Predictable but diverting tale of farmer forced to "sell" his daughter in order to keep his land. C: Bill Michael, Harry Lovejoy, Judy Pennebaker. D: John Patrick Hayes. COM [PG] 84m. V

Farmer's Wife, The 1928 British ★★★ Despite all his efforts, a lonesome farmer can't find a wife—until he falls in love with his housekeeper. Interesting early (and silent) Hitchcock best known for its beautiful photography. C: Jameson Thomas, Lillian Hall-Davies, Gordon Harker. D: Alfred Hitchcock. COM 93m. V

Farrebique 1947 French ★★★★½ Year in the life of peasant family on farm in central France. Meticulous attention to everyday detail and stunningly beautiful photography are among the many accomplishments of Rouquier's unique documentary. A must-see masterpiece. D: Georges Rouquier. DOC 85m.

Farrell for the People 1982 ★★ An ambitious attorney (Harper) prosecutes a well-connected ex-convict who's accused of murder. Occasionally interesting, but inconsistent. C: Valerie Harper, Ed O'Neill, Gregory Sierra. D: Paul Wendkos. DRA 104m.

Fascist, The 1961 ★★★ Captured by militant fascist, professor gains upper hand on way back to Rome. Okay comedy/drama provides some laughs but strains for significance beneath the surface. C: Ugo Tognazzi, Georges Wilson, Stefania Sandrelli. D: Luciano Salce. DRA 102m.

Fashions 1934 ★★★★ Tasty bit of fluff with Powell and Davis as fast-talking Americans trying to make their mark as Parisian dressmakers. Highlight is Busby Berkeley production number "Spin a Little Web of Dreams." C: William Powell, Bette Davis, Verree Teasdale, Reginald Owen, Frank McHugh, Phillip Reed, Hugh Herbert. D: William Dieterle. MUS 78m. V

Fass Black ★★ Disco owner puts his life on the line to keep disco safe from the mob. Talk about courage in the face of adversity! Lame concept poorly executed. C: John Poole, Johnnie Taylor, Jeanne Bell. D: Martin D'urville. CRI 105m. V

Fast and Furious 1939 ★★★½ Fronting as rare book dealers, husband-and-wife detective investigate a murder at a beauty pageant. Last entry in this three-film series delivers the goods; intriguing fun. C: Franchot Tone, Ann Sothern, Ruth Hussey, John Miljan, Allyn Joslyn, Bernard Nedell, Mary Beth Hughes. D: Busby Berkeley. CRI 73m.

Fast and Loose 1930 ★★★ Star-crossed romance between pampered society woman (Hopkins in her screen debut) and auto mechanic features some fine dialogue by Preston Sturges. Adapted from Avery Hopwood's play *The Best People.* Watch for a brief appearance by then-unknown Carole Lombard. C: Miriam Hopkins, Frank Morgan, Ilka Chase, Charles Starrett. D: Fred Newmeyer. COM 75m.

Fast and Loose 1939 ★★★★ Rare book dealer detectives are hired by an eccentric tycoon to look for missing first editions. Best is the chemistry between Montgomery and Russell as husband-and-wife team, with a terrific supporting cast to add zip. C: Robert Montgomery, Rosalind Russell, Reginald Owen, Ralph Morgan, Etienne Girardot, Alan Dinehart, Jo Ann Sayers, Joan Marsh, Sidney Blackmer. D: Edwin L. Marin. CRI 80m.

Fast and Sexy 1960 Italian ★★★ A perky widow (Lollobrigida) returns to her hometown to find a new husband. Lollobrigida is delightful but Robertson, as an Italian, kills the comedic pace; there is a nice bit from director De Sica. (a.k.a. *Anna of Brooklyn*) C: Gina Lollobrigida, Dale Robertson, Vittorio De Sica, Carla Macelloni. D: Vittorio De Sica. COM 98m.

Fast and the Furious, The 1954 ★★½ A man (Ireland), framed for murder, flees and tries to stay a step ahead of the law. Ireland tries hard, but can't overcome unoriginal script. C: John Ireland, Dorothy Malone, Iris Adrian, Bruce Carlisle, Jean Howell, Larry Thor. D: Edwards Sampson, John Ireland. ACT 73m.

Fast Break 1979 ★★★ New York deli counterman (Kaplan) accepts job coaching basketball at Nevada college, bringing hometown street players with him. Predictable but enjoyable comedy. C: Gabriel Kaplan, Harold Sylvester, Mike Warren, Bernard King, Reb Brown. D: Jack Smight. COM [PG] 107m. V

Fast Charlie, The Moonbeam Rider 1979 ★★★ A disenchanted doughboy deserts his unit for a cross-country motorcycle race. Enduring comedy/drama nestled within credible re-creation of a bygone age. C: David Carradine, Brenda Vaccaro, L.Q. Jones, R.G. Armstrong, Jesse Vint. D: Steve Carver. ACT [PG] 99m.

Fast Company 1938 ★★★ A rare-book enthusiast (Douglas) teams up with his wife (Rice) to investigate a murder. An entertaining if slight plot that is sometimes witty. Spawned two more in series. C: Melvyn

Douglas, Florence Rice, Claire Dodd, Louis Calhern, George Zucco, Shepperd Strudwick, Dwight Frye, Nat Pendleton. D: Edward Buzzell. CRI 73m.

Fast Company 1953 ★★★ Bergen owns a horse that dances. Light, harmless musical comedy. C: Polly Bergen, Howard Keel, Marjorie Main, Nina Foch, Iron Eyes Cody. D: John Sturges. MUS 67m.

Fast Food 1989 ★★½ Two collegiate party animals open their own hamburger stand, challenging burger magnate Wrangler Bob (Varney) by adding their "secret sauce," an aphrodisiac. Run-of-the-mill sex comedy made palatable by good hamming. C: Clark Brandon, Randal Patrick, Tracy Griffith, Jim Varney, Michael J. Pollard, Traci Lords. D: Michael A. Simpson. COM [PG-13] 92m. V

Fast Forward 1984 ★★½ Old-fashioned saga of Midwest teenagers in the Big Apple, yearning to make good in show business. Difference is they breakdance instead of jitterbug. C: John Scott Clough, Don Franklin, Tamara Mark, Tracy Silver. D: Sidney Poitier. MUS [PG] 110m. V

Fast Friends 1979 ★★½ After her marriage falls apart, a young woman tries to establish herself in broadcasting. Nice try by a good cast, but far from captivating. C: Edie Adams, Dick Shawn, Carrie Snodgress, Mackenzie Phillips. D: Steven H. Stern. DRA 104m.

Fast Getaway 1991 ★★ Father and son have a grand time robbing banks until the law intervenes. C: Marcia Strassman, Corey Haim, Lisa Hansen, Leo Rossi. D: Spiros Razatos. COM [PG] 91m. V

Fast Gun 1993 ★★ Former CIA agent confronts a heavily armed town. C: Rick Hill, Kaz Garas, Robert Dryer, Brenda Bakke, Morgan Strickland. D: Cirio H. Santiago. CRI [R] 90m. V

Fast Lady, The 1962 British ★★½ A shy, gentle young man becomes a dashing Casanova when he buys himself a sleek old Bentley sedan. Predictable yet broadly funny (even silly) comedy. C: James Robertson Justice, Leslie Phillips, Stanley Baxter, Kathleen Harrison, Julie Christie, Eric Barker. D: Ken Annakin. COM 95m.

Fast Lane Fever 1982 ★★ Worker and well-known drag racer compete for a young woman. C: Terry Serio, Deborah Conway, Max cullen, Graham Bond. D: John Clark. ACT [R] 94m. V

Fast Money 1983 ★★ Three pilots attempt to make lots of money transporting drugs. C: Sammy Allred, Sonny Carl Davis, Lou Perry, Doris Hargrave. D: Doug Holloway. ACT 92m. V

Fast Talking 1986 ★★★★½ Prize-winning story of unhappy youth who whiles away his hours developing crazy schemes. Sensitive, uncommonly charming. C: Rod Zuanic, Tony Allylis, Chris Truswell. D: Ken Cameron. FAM/COM 93m. V

Fast Times at Ridgemont High 1982 ★★★★ One year in the lives of several students in a Southern California high school. Film was a surprise hit when released and continues to grow in stature with each passing year. Highlights in the standout cast include Leigh as the shy young girl who yearns to learn about sex and love and Penn as the stoned surfer who has pizza delivered to class. Funny, poignant adaptation by Cameron Crowe from his own book. C: Sean Penn, Jennifer Jason Leigh, Judge Reinhold, Robert Romanus, Brian Backer, Phoebe Cates, Ray Walston, Forest Whitaker, Pamela Springsteen, Martin Brest. D: Amy Heckerling. COM [R] 91m. V

Fast-Walking 1982 ★★★ A Prison guard (Woods) belongs behind bars as much as any criminal. Violent melding of black comedy and drama gives Woods a chance to trot out his patented sicko performance. C: James Woods, Tim McIntire, Kay Lenz, M. Emmett Walsh. D: James B. Harris. CRI [R] 116m. V

Fast Workers 1933 ★★ Construction worker rivals are fast on the job and when it comes to love. Weak vehicle for Gilbert and for Browning. Amusing erotic humor veers into poor melodrama. C: John Gilbert, Robert Armstrong, Mae Clarke, Muriel Kirkland, Vince Barnett, Virginia Cherrill, Sterling Holloway. D: Tod Browning. DRA 68m.

Faster Pussycat . . . Kill! Kill! 1966 ★★★½ Fast-paced cult favorite about three go-go dancers who go wild in California. Not for everybody, but it succeeds because of its gonzo humor and insight into the stranger, seamier side of life in the '60s. C: Tura Satana, Haji, Lori Williams. D: Russ Meyer. ACT 84m.

Fastest Guitar Alive, The 1968 ★★ Confederate soldiers rob the San Francisco mint, then must return gold to the government when they learn war is over. Originally intended as follow-up for Elvis to *Love Me Tender*, interesting now as one of Orbison's few film appearances. C: Roy Orbison, Sammy Jackson, Maggie Pierce, Joan Freeman. D: Michael Moore. COM 88m. V

Fastest Gun Alive, The 1956 ★★★½ Tense Western about a quiet shopkeeper (Ford), still well known as a once deadly gunslinger, who's drawn into a showdown with a notorious outlaw (Crawford) who's fast with a gun. Interesting psychological Western morality play, with excellent acting. C: Glenn Ford, Jeanne Crain, Broderick Crawford, Russ Tamblyn. D: Russell Rouse. WST 92m. V

Fat Chance 1975 *See* **Peeper**

Fat City 1972 ★★★★½ Alcoholic ex-boxer Keach, encouraged by young friend and protégé Bridges, attempts comeback, but it's too late. Excellent performances, with Tyrrell as boxer's girlfriend earning Oscar nomination for Best Supporting Actress. Solid, sharply etched character study. C: Stacy Keach, Jeff

Bridges, Susan Tyrrell, Candy Clark, Nicholas Colasanto. D: John Huston. DRA [PG] 100m. v

Fat Man and Little Boy 1989 ★★★½ The story of the building of the first atomic bomb, with emphasis on the organizing general (Newman) and the scientific genius (Schultz, as Robert Oppenheimer). An informative, well-acted film. C: Paul Newman, Dwight Schultz, John Cusack, Laura Dern. D: Roland Joffe. DRA 127m. v

Fat Man, The 1951 ★★★ A murder mystery under the Big Top featuring corpulent detective/hero from radio series. C: J. Scott Smart, Rock Hudson, Julie London, Clinton Sundberg, Jayne Meadows, Emmett Kelly. D: William Castle. CRI 77m.

Fata Morgana 1971 West German ★★★★ Ambitious documentary detailing man's continuing battle against nature. Shot primarily in the Sahara, Herzog's disturbing images are paradoxically beautiful to see; music by Leonard Cohen and Couperin adds to hallucinatory effect. D: Werner Herzog. DOC 78m.

Fatal Attraction 1980 Canadian ★★★½ Psychologist (Kellerman) and teacher (Lack) indulge in erotic fantasy games which escalate beyond their control. Suspenseful but uneven, with lapses in continuity. Nudity. C: Sally Kellerman, Stephen Lack, John Huston. D: Michael Grant. DRA 98m.

Fatal Attraction 1987 ★★★★½ Married attorney (Douglas) gets more than he bargained for after a dalliance with a book editor (Close) who *won't be ignored.* High-gloss '80s cautionary suspenser with good, tense result. A change of pace for Close, and she's terrifying. C: Michael Douglas, Glenn Close, Anne Archer, Ellen Latzen, Ellen Foley, Fred Gwynne. D: Adrian Lyne. CRI [R] 120m. v

Fatal Beauty 1987 ★★★ Undercover cop (Goldberg) is after the masterminds of a drug syndicate. Comedy/drama mostly for Whoopi's fans. C: Whoopi Goldberg, Sam Elliott, Ruben Blades, Harris Yulin, Brad Dourif. D: Tom Holland. COM [R] 104m. v

Fatal Charm 1992 ★★★ Romantic young woman hopes the mysterious boy she dreams about isn't a serial killer on the loose. C: Christopher Atkins, Amanda Peterson, Mary Frann. D: Alan Smithee. HOR [R] 90m. v

Fatal Charms ★★★½ Exotic dancer (Collins) smooths the way for an Italian detective trying to unravel a complicated kidnapping case. C: Joan Collins, Maurizio Merli. D: Stelvio Massi. DRA 85m. v

Fatal Chase 1987 *See* **Nowhere to Hide**

Fatal Confession: A Father Dowling Mystery 1987 ★★★ The crime-busting adventures of a parish priest/private eye and a brash young nun. Good treatment that became the good TV show. C: Tom Bosley, Tracy Nelson, Sada Thompson, Leslie Nielsen. D: Chris Hibler. ACT 104m.

Fatal Confinement 1964 ★★★★ After living alone with her daughter for over a decade, hermit-like woman must sell her property to big business. Wrenching Crawford. C: Joan Crawford, Paul Berg, Charles Bickford. D: Robert Guest. DRA 70m. v

Fatal Desire 1953 Italian ★★½ Sicilian village is a hotbed of adultery and vengeance in forgettable, non-musical version of Mascagni's opera *Cavalleria Rusticana.* C: Anthony Quinn, Kerima, May Britt, Ettore Manni, Umberto Spadaro. D: Carmine Gallone. DRA 80m.

Fatal Error 1987 ★★ Hauer plays a police detective investigating the killing of a fellow cop. Flat-footed flop. C: Rutger Hauer, Rijk de Googer. D: Rob Houwer. DRA 90m.

Fatal Exposure 1991 ★★★ In a mix-up at the photo lab, snapshots taken by a single mom (Winningham) are mistakenly turned over to a professional assassin. Decent thriller. C: Mare Winningham, Nick Mancuso, Christopher McDonald, Geoffrey Blake. D: Alan Metzger. CRI [PG-13] 100m. TVM v

Fatal Games 1984 ★★★ Grim murder mystery in which mad killer stalks elite female athletes at training academy. C: Sally Kirkland, Sean Masterson. D: Michael Elliot. CRI 88m. v

Fatal Hour, The 1940 ★★½ Fourth in a series of thrillers featuring detective Mr. Wong (Karloff), this time investigating the murder of a police officer. Karloff a pleasure. C: Boris Karloff, Marjorie Reynolds, Grant Withers, Charles Trowbridge, John Hamilton, Frank Puglia, Jason Robards Sr. D: William Nigh. CRI 67m.

Fatal Image, The 1990 ★★½ While vacationing in Paris, mother (Lee) and daughter (Bateman) are hunted by a killer who knows they accidentally caught his latest hit on videotape. Paris looks great. C: Michele Lee, Justine Bateman, Francois Dunoyer, Jean-Pierre Cassel, Sonia Petrovna. D: Thomas J. Wright. CRI 96m. v

Fatal Images 1989 ★★★ Fashion photographer tries to learn why her models all die after photo sessions using her new camera. C: Lane Coyle, Kay Schaver, David Williams. D: Dennis Devine. CRI 90m. v

Fatal Instinct 1993 ★★½ Gag-filled spoof of crime movies follows private eye Assante as he investigates Young and Nelligan. Silly laughs, but little substance. C: Sean Young, Armand Assante, Sherilyn Fenn, Kate Nelligan. D: Carl Reiner. COM [PG-13] 95m. v

Fatal Justice 1992 ★★★ Assassin hired by the CIA to kill an aging agent changes gears when her target turns out to be the father she hasn't seen for years. C: Joe Estevez, Suzanne Ager. D: Gerald Cain. ACT 90m. v

Fatal Mission 1989 ★★★ GI captures Chinese guerilla in Vietnam, then teams up with her to escape the enemy jungle. C: Tia Carrere, Peter Fonda, Mako. D: George Rowe. ACT [R] 84m. V

Fatal Pulse 1988 ★★½ A vicious killer stalks members of an exclusive sorority. C: Michelle McCormack, Ken Roberts, Joe Phelan. D: Anthony Christopher. HOR 90m. V

Fatal Skies 1990 ★★★ Eco-conscious students fight a man's efforts to unload toxic waste into the town's main water supply. C: Timothy Leary. D: Thomas Dugan. DRA 88m. V

Fatal Vision 1984 ★★★★ Green Beret (Cole), is accused of slaying his wife and family. He claims he's innocent, and grieving father-in-law (Malden) believes him—at first. Superior, fact-based drama, from Joe McGinnis' best-seller. C: Karl Malden, Eva Marie Saint, Gary Cole, Barry Newman, Andy Griffith, Wendy Schaal. D: David Greene. CRI 192m. TVM V

Fatal Witness, The 1945 ★★ When a well-heeled society woman is murdered, authorities scramble to nail her killer. Solid, minor suspense tale. C: Evelyn Ankers, Richard Fraser, George Leigh, Barbara Everest, Frederick Worlock. D: Lesley Selander. CRI 59m.

Fate 1990 ★★★ Young man imagines precisely how wonderful love will be, if only he can get the woman of his dreams to return his affections. C: Stuart Paul, Cheryl M. Lynn, Kaye Ballard. D: Stuart Paul. COM [PG-13] 115m. V

Fate Is the Hunter 1964 ★★½ Ford plays investigator ferreting out cause of airline tragedy in this run-of-the-mill drama. C: Glenn Ford, Nancy Kwan, Rod Taylor, Suzanne Pleshette, Jane Russell, Wally Cox. D: Ralph Nelson. DRA 106m.

Fate of Lee Khan, The ★★★ Action packed, gory depiction of rebellion against the Mongols during Yuan Dynasty. C: Angela Mao, Roy Chaid. D: Kinghu. ACT 107m. V

Fate Takes a Hand 1961 British ★★★ A sack of stolen mail resurfaces after 15 years in limbo—and has quite an effect on the various recipients. Interesting idea that plays quite well. C: Ronald Howard, Christina Gregg, Basil Dignam, Sheila Whittingham. D: Max Varnel. DRA 72m.

Father 1966 Hungarian ★★★½ Young man who has worshipped his late father visits people who knew him to shape a more realistic portrait. Often funny and affecting chronicle played out against backdrop of 1956 Communist uprising. Witty direction and use of music. C: Miklos Gabor, Daniel Erdelyi, Andras Balint. D: Istvan Szabo. DRA [PG-13] 96m. V

Father Brown *See* **The Detective**

Father Clements Story, The 1987 ★★★½ Gossett shines as a concerned priest who takes on the Catholic hierarchy in his attempt to adopt a troubled teenager. Routine yet heartfelt. C: Louis Gossett, Jr., Malcolm-Jamal Warner, Carroll O'Connor, Rosetta LeNorie, Leon Robinson, Ron McClarty. D: Ed Sherin. DRA 100m. V

Father Figure 1980 ★★★ Widower Linden struggles to reconcile with his estranged sons. Poignant family drama based on a novel by Richard Peck. C: Hal Linden, Timothy Hutton, Jeremy Licht, Martha Scott, Cassie Yates. D: Jerry London. DRA 95m. TVM V

Father Goose 1964 ★★★★ Grant's peaceful WWII lookout post on Pacific island becomes a living hell when a disabled plane crashes, leaving him in charge of teacher Caron and her young schoolgirls. Grant's lively performance keeps this spirited comedy funny throughout. C: Cary Grant, Leslie Caron, Trevor Howard, Jack Good. D: Ralph Nelson. COM 116m. V

Father Guido Sarducci Goes to College 1985 ★★★½ Beloved "Saturday Night Live" character takes his "Vatican Gossip Column" to University of California stage in this irreverent comedy concert. D: Steve Binder. COM 59m. V

Father Hood 1993 ★★ A small-time thief (Swayze) gets saddled with custody of his kids. Swayze's no comedian, but his charm helps. C: Patrick Swayze, Halle Berry, Diane Ladd. D: Darrell James Roodt. COM [PG-13] 90m. V

Father Is a Bachelor 1950 ★★★ Carefree bachelor becomes the unlikely father to five orphaned children and his parenting skills catch the romantic eye of a local judge's daughter. A serviceable, if limited comedy. C: Abby Berlin, William Holden, Coleen Gray, Mary Saunders, Stuart Erwin, Sig Ruman. D: Norman Foster. COM 84m.

Father Makes Good 1950 ★★★ Father protests the new milk tax by purchasing a family cow. Lots of laughs throughout this consistently agreeable entry in Walburn's series. C: Raymond Walburn, Walter Catlett, Barbara Brown, Gertrude Astor. D: Jean Yarbrough. COM 61m.

Father of a Soldier 1966 USSR ★★★★ Strong WWII drama about a Soviet farmer desperately searching for his wounded son. A daring antiwar tract that depicts fighting as a crime against nature. Powerful performances. (a.k.a. *Otets Soldata*) C: Sergei Zakariadze, Vladimir Privaltsev, Keto Bochorishvili. D: Revas Chkheidze. DRA 83m.

Father of the Bride 1950 ★★★★½ Immensely entertaining look, through charming, daffy dad's (Tracy's) eyes, at the frenzy and fanfare surrounding daughter Taylor's forthcoming marriage. Most of the cast plays straight man to Tracy's nagging in this delightful comedy of American manners. C: Spencer Tracy, Elizabeth Taylor, Joan Bennett, Billie Burke, Leo Carroll, Don Taylor. D: Vincente Minnelli. COM 93m. V

Father of the Bride 1991 ★★★★ A father faces his worst nightmare—planning the marriage of his daughter. This remake of the Spencer Tracy classic stays warm and funny throughout, thanks mostly to Martin. Short, as fastidious wedding planner, steals all of his scenes. C: Steve Martin, Diane Keaton, Martin Short, Kimberly Williams, Kieran Culkin, George Newbern, B.D. Wong, Peter Goetz, Kate MacGregor Stewart, Martha Gehman. D: Charles Shyer. COM [PG] 105m. V

Father Takes a Wife 1941 ★★★ Glamorous theater personality Swanson retires from the theater to marry rock-steady Menjou. She can't get show business out of her system though, and takes aspiring opera singer Arnaz under her tutelage. Fairly amusing premise, pumped up by talented cast. C: Adolphe Menjou, Gloria Swanson, John Howard, Desi Arnaz, Helen Broderick, Florence Rice, Neil Hamilton. D: Jack Hivley. COM 79m.

Father Takes the Air 1951 ★★½ Father (Walburn) joins a local flying school and inadvertently nabs a crook. Nice series fun and perfect for the hammy Walburn. C: Raymond Walburn, Walter Catlett, Florence Bates, Gary Gray. D: Frank McDonald. COM 61m.

Father Was a Fullback 1949 ★★★½ A college football coach has plenty of problems to tackle—on and off the field. Charming, sparkling clean comedy with a first-rate cast. C: Fred MacMurray, Maureen O'Hara, Betty Lynn, Rudy Vallee, Thelma Ritter, Natalie Wood. D: John M. Stahl. COM 84m.

Fathers and Sons 1992 ★★★ Father and son make an untimely move to a quiet Jersey suburb in the grips of a serial killer, where psychic Arquette warns dad of the son's rendezvous with the murderer. Decent though implausible thriller. Good Goldblum. C: Jeff Goldblum, Rosanna Arquette, Rory Cochrane. D: Paul Mones. CRI [R] 109m. V

Father's Dilemma 1952 Italian ★★★★ Winning combination of slapstick and heart-tugging comedy as Fabrizi scours Rome for his daughter's lost communion dress. C: Aldo Fabrizi, Gaby Morlay, Adrianna Mazzotti. D: Alessandro Blasetti. COM 88m.

Father's Little Dividend 1951 ★★★★ Sequel to *Father of the Bride* has Taylor expecting a bundle of joy to the uncertain delight of father Tracy, who hasn't yet recovered from the wedding. Light and charming. C: Spencer Tracy, Joan Bennett, Elizabeth Taylor, Don Taylor, Billie Burke. D: Vincente Minnelli. DRA 82m. V

Father's Love, A 1978 *See* **Bloodbrothers**

Father's Revenge, A 1987 ★★★★ When stewardess is held hostage by terrorists, her dad (Dennehy) is determined to see justice done, with or without the authorities. Superior TV drama, helped enormously by sterling Silver and Dennehy. C: Brian Dennehy, Ron Silver, Joanna Cassidy. D: John Herzfeld. DRA [R] 92m. V

Father's Wild Game 1950 ★★½ After railing at higher meat prices, Father (Walburn) decides it's better to hunt for the family dinner. Decidedly funny addition to the Walburn series. C: Raymond Walburn, Walter Catlett, Jane Darwell, Roscoe Ates, Ann Tyrrell. D: Herbert Leeds. COM 61m.

Fathom 1967 ★★★★ A satiric spy thriller with a cast of oddball characters. Welch is winning as a glamorous, sky-diving send-up of James Bond. The plot is superfluous—just enjoy this fun, campy romp. C: Tony Franciosa, Raquel Welch, Clive Revill, Greta Chi, Richard Briers, Ronald Fraser, Tony Adams. D: Leslie Martinson. COM 99m.

Fats Domino and Friends—Immortal Keyboards of Rock & Roll 1988 ★★★★ All-star cast performs such hits as "Blueberry Hill" and "Great Balls of Fire" in New Orleans concert. C: Fats Domino, Jerry Lee Lewis, Ray Charles. MUS 60m. V

Fatso 1980 ★★★ Obese DeLuise decides to lose weight when his cousin dies as result of his obsessive eating habits. Overly sentimental directorial debut for Bancroft doesn't cook up enough laughs to satisfy completely. C: Dom DeLuise, Anne Bancroft, Candice Azzara, Ron Carey. D: Anne Bancroft. COM [PG] 93m. V

Faust 1926 German ★★★★★ Classic silent version of the good, elderly doctor who sells his soul to the devil (Jannings, in a brilliant performance) for the gift of youth is still one of the very best. Stylish direction unsurpassed. C: Emil Jannings, Gosta Ekman, Camilla Horn, Wilhelm Dieterle. D: F.W. Murnau. DRA 117m.

Faust 1994 Czech ★★½ Famed animator Svankmajer stumbles with this dark, depressing variation of the Faust legend, as a Prague businessman falls victim to the Devil. Highlight: puppet animation sequence with baby turning into Satan. C: Petr Cepek. D: Jan Svankmajer. DRA 97m.

Favor, The 1994 ★★★ Kozak, bored in her marriage, asks her best friend (McGovern) a big favor: sleep with her high school flame to find out what she missed. Light romantic comedy, from the director of *Mystic Pizza*. C: Harley Jane Kozak, Elizabeth McGovern, Bill Pullman, Brad Pitt, Ken Wahl. D: Donald Petrie. COM 97m.

Favor, the Watch, and the Very Big Fish, The 1992 French ★★½ A photographer (Hoskins) looks for someone to pose as Jesus, and he finds a zany guy (Goldblum) who starts to get carried away with the role. Failed farce, despite game cast. C: Bob Hoskins, Jeff Goldblum, Natasha Richardson, Michel Blanc. D: Ben Lewin. COM [R] 89m. V

Fawlty Towers—The Complete Set 1992 ★★★★½ All twelve episodes of this hilarious British TV series are preserved in this four-volume set. Cleese is brilliant as the bumbling manger of a small hotel with Scales as his prim, super-efficient wife. C: John

Cleese, Prunella Scales, Connie Booth, Andrew Sachs. D: J.H. Davies. COM 360m. V

Fazil 1928 ★★★½ Silent, enjoyable desert sheik nonsense, attractively if impersonally shot by then-new director Hawks. Farrell barely pulls off sheik role. C: Charles Farrell, Greta Nissen, Mae Busch, Vadim Uraneff, Tyler Brooke, John Boles. D: Howard Hawks. DRA 88m.

FBI Girl 1951 ★★½ Federal agents nail a gang of extortionists. Routine action played by a competent cast. C: Cesar Romero, George Brent, Audrey Totter, Tom Drake, Raymond Burr. D: William Berke. ACT 74m.

FBI Murders, The 1992 ★★★★ Two mild-mannered homebodies turn inexplicably to a life of violent crime, and the FBI must be called in to catch them. Tense thriller delivers with a good cast and excellent script. C: Ronny Cox, Doug Sheehan, David Soul. D: Dick Lowry. CRI 95m. TVM V

F.B.I. Story, The—The FBI Versus Alvin Karpis, Public Enemy Number One 1974 ★★ The heat is on when FBI head J. Edgar Hoover (Yulin) dogs a notorious criminal. Exciting throwback to the good guy-bad guy films of Hollywood's golden age. C: Robert Foxworth, Kay Lenz, Gary Lockwood, Anne Francis, Harris Yulin, Chris Robinson, Eileen Heckart, Gerald McRaney, Whit Bissell, James B. Sikking. D: Marvin Chomsky. ACT 100m.

FBI Story, The 1959 ★★★★ Entertaining tribute to the FBI during J. Edgar Hoover's reign. Episodic film features Stewart as a lifer agent and covers the bureau's confrontations with the KKK, Baby Face Nelson, Dillinger, and the Nazis. Stewart is his usual fascinating self. C: James Stewart, Vera Miles, Murray Hamilton, Nick Adams, Diane Jergens. D: Mervyn LeRoy. ACT 149m. V

F.D.R., The Last Year 1980 ★★★★½ Robards captures the fighting spirit of the ailing president in this superb TV movie. Gripping, intensely moving drama of one of the most important periods in U.S. history. C: Jason Robards, Jr., Eileen Heckart, Kim Hunter. D: Anthony Page. DRA 153m.

Fe-Fi-Fo-Fun ★★★½ A charming take-off on the Rip Van Winkle story starring our favorite caveman, Fred Flintstone. FAM/COM 90m. V

Fear, Anxiety and Depression 1989 ★★ First director's outing for young Woody Allen wanna-be. He pines for a girl. Viewer pines for some action. C: Todd Solondz, Max Cantor, Alexandra Gersten. D: Todd Solondz. COM [R] 84m. V

Fear 1946 ★★½ After killing his professor, a student drives himself crazy with guilt. Echoes of *Crime and Punishment*, sans grandeur. Still, gripping at times. C: Peter Cookson, Warren William, Anne Gwynne, James Cardwell, Nestor Paiva. D: Alfred Zeisler. DRA 68m.

Fear 1979 *See* **Night Creature**

Fear 1990 ★★★ Psychic crime fighter (Sheedy) runs into unforeseen trouble when her latest murder case is perpetrated by another psychic. Interesting if goofy premise handled well. C: Ally Sheedy, Lauren Hutton, Michael O'Keefe. D: Rockne S. O'Bannon. CRI [R] 98m. TVM V

Fear Chamber, The 1971 Mexican ★★ Wacky story about volcanologist experiments inside an active volcano cave that holds strange powers. Quickie Mexican production was completed just before Karloff's death in 1968. C: Boris Karloff, Julissa, Carlos East, Isela Vega, Yerye Beirute. D: Juan Ibanez, Jack Hill. HOR 80m.

Fear City 1984 ★★ A very violent and creepy tale about a serial killer who targets hookers in New York City. The cast is good, but the story is sleazy and unpleasant. C: Tom Berenger, Billy Dee Williams, Jack Scalia, Melanie Griffith, Rae Dawn Chong. D: Abel Ferrara. ACT [R] 93m. V

Fear in the City 1987 ★★½ Competing New York crime factions clash violently in lurid action tale. C: Michael Constantine, Fred Williamson, Gianni Manera. D: Gianni Manera. CRI 90m. V

Fear in the Dark 1992 ★★★½ Documentary probes the minds of several masters of horror to uncover the sources of their inspiration. Nice assortment of directorial talent, but horror fans may prefer the films themselves. DOC 60m.

Fear in the Night 1947 ★★★★ Memorable psychological portrait of a man who dreams he has committed murder, only to wake to evidence that he has done just that. Mesmerizing thriller, adapted from Cornell Woolrich story. C: Paul Kelly, Ann Doran, Kay Scott, DeForest Kelley, Robert Emmett Keane. D: Maxwell Shane. CRI 72m.

Fear in the Night 1972 British ★★★ School for boys is the chilling setting for this British thriller about a skittish bride (Geeson) driven to plot a murder. The psychological motivation is far-fetched, but the story is well paced and absorbing. C: Judy Geeson, Joan Collins, Ralph Bates, Peter Cushing. D: Jimmy Sangster. CRI [PG] 94m. V

Fear Inside, The 1992 ★★★ Agoraphobic artist (Lahti) is terrorized in her own home (where else?) by psycho roomies. Strained suspense, saved by an excellent Lahti. C: Christine Lahti, Dylan McDermot, Jennifer Rubin. D: Leon Ichaso. CRI [R] 100m. V

Fear Is the Key 1972 British ★★★ When his family is killed in a mysterious plane crash, a man goes after those responsible. Reasonably taut thriller. C: Barry Newman, Suzy Kendall, John Vernon, Dolph Sweet, Ben Kingsley. D: Michael Tuchner. DRA [PG] 103m.

Fear No Evil 1969 ★★★ A strange antique mirror brings a scientist back to life when wielded by his fiancée. Engaging, sometimes compelling view of the supernatural. C: Louis

Jourdan, Bradford Dillman, Lynda Day, Marsha Hunt, Wilfried Hyde-White, Carroll O'Connor. D: Paul Wendkos. HOR 98m.

Fear No Evil 1981 ★★★ Straight-A high school student who is reincarnation of Lucifer uses his powers in struggle against good, including getting even with taunting fellow students and parents. Film stalls at times with seemingly aimless subplots. C: Stefan Arngrim, Elizabeth Hoffman, Kathleen Rowe McAllen, Frank Birney, Daniel Eden. D: Frank Laloggia. HOR [R] 96m. v

Fear of a Black Hat 1994 ★★★★ Goofy parody of rockumentaries, featuring fictional hard-core rappers, N.W.H. led by Cundieff as Ice Cold. Lower-budget than similar *CB4*, but much funnier. Has a well-deserved cult reputation. C: Rusty Cundieff, Larry B. Scott, Kasi Lemmons, Mark Christopher Lawrence. D: Rusty Cundieff. COM 86m.

Fear on Trial 1975 ★★★★ Devane plays blacklisted '50s radio personality John Henry Faulk in this fact-based political drama about personal tragedies of the McCarthy era. Strong script, unglamorized presentation, and a masterful performance by Scott as Faulk's lawyer Louis Nizer. C: George C. Scott, William Devane, Dorothy Tristan, John Houseman, Judd Hirsch, Lois Nettleton, Milt Kogan, Ben Piazza. D: Lamont Johnson. DRA 100m. TVM

Fear Stalk 1989 ★★ Just when a TV producer is getting her life together, she learns that she's being stalked by a lunatic. Sometimes chilling. D: Larry Shaw. ACT

Fear Strikes Out 1957 ★★★★ Biography of baseball player Jimmy Piersall, whose career comes to a halt because of a nervous breakdown. Perkins is at his neurotic best as Piersall; Malden is perfect as his overbearing father. C: Anthony Perkins, Karl Malden, Norma Moore, Adam Williams. D: Robert Mulligan. DRA 100m. v

Fearless 1993 ★★★½ A survivor of a terrible plane crash reexamines his life and the lives of all those he loves. Great performance by Perez. C: Jeff Bridges, Isabella Rossellini, Rosie Perez, Tom Hulce. D: Peter Weir. DRA [R] 122m. v

Fearless Fagan 1952 ★★ When a circus employee is drafted into the Army, he brings his lion with him. Minor comedy. C: Carleton Carpenter, Janet Leigh, Keenan Wynn, Richard Anderson, Ellen Corby, Barbara Ruick. D: Stanley Donen. COM 79m.

Fearless Fighters 1977 ★★½ When the bad guys offend the good guys, trouble follows. The usual acrobatics and face rearranging. Good location shooting in China. C: Lei Peng, Mu Lah. ACT [R] 83m.

Fearless Frank 1967 ★★ Voight, a bumbling innocent, is murdered, then reincarnated to avenge himself as a superhero. Low-budget satire helped by presence of various Second City TV comedians; Voight's film debut. (a.k.a. *Frank's Greatest Adventure*) C: Jon Voight, Monique Van Vooren, Joan Darling, Severn Darden, Anthony Holland, Lou Gilbert, David Steinberg, Nelson Algren. D: Philip Kaufman. COM [G] 83m.

Fearless Hyena, The 1979 ★★★ After witnessing the killing of his grandfather, young Chan becomes a martial arts expert and stalks the murderers. Better-than-average kung fu film has developed cult status. C: Jackie Chan. ACT 97m. v

Fearless Hyena, The—Part 2 1985 ★★★ Kung fu expert Chan is now with the Ying/Yang clan, who for several years have been pursued by a mysterious gang known as Heaven and Earth. Continuation of the saga of original *The Fearless Hyena*. C: Jackie Chan. ACT 90m. v

Fearless Vampire Killers or: Pardon Me, But Your Teeth Are in My Neck 1967 British ★★★★ Hilarious horror comedy pits hapless vampire slayer/professor (MacGowran) and assistant (Polanski) against evil count (Mayne) and his bloodsucking brood. Full of surprises, great scenery and enthusiastic performers, but beware of edited versions. One of the beautiful Sharon Tate's few film roles. Her scene in the bathtub with the old Hassidic vampire is a scream. (a.k.a. *Dance of the Vampires*) C: Jack MacGowran, Roman Polanski, Sharon Tate, Alfie Bass, Ferdy Mayne, Terry Downes. D: Roman Polanski. HOR 107m. v

Fearless Young Boxer 1973 ★★★ A young man becomes proficient in kung fu to gain revenge against his father's paid murderer. Martial arts entry features group gymnastics, a comic turn, and a slam-bang climax. ACT 94m. v

Fearmakers, The 1958 ★★ Dreadfully dated, paranoid effort about Korean War POW (Andrews) who returns to Washington public relations firm and discovers Commies! Well-directed, of historical interest, but marred by endless speechifying. Capturing crooks at Lincoln Memorial is laughable. C: Dana Andrews, Dick Foran, Mel Torme, Marilee Earle. D: Jacques Tourneur. DRA 83m.

Feast of the Devil 1987 ★★½ Woman searches for her sister and stumbles upon a deranged doctor who has mysteriously entranced the hordes of women who live in his castle. C: Krista Nell, Thomas Moore, Teresa Gimpera. D: John Lacy. HOR 90m. v

Feathered Serpent, The 1948 ★ One of the last of the Charlie Chan movies, about a stolen Mexican artifact. Series out of steam. C: Roland Winters, Keye Luke, Victor Sen Yung, Mantan Moreland, Carol Forman, Robert Livingston, Martin Garralaga, Nils Asther, Jay Silverheels. D: William Beaudine. CRI 68m.

Federal Agents vs. Underworld, Inc. 1949 ★★½ A federal agent battles a desperate archvillain and her cohorts who will stop at nothing to get their hands on a legendary archeological treasure. C: Carol Forman, Kirk Alyn, Rosemary La Planche. D: Fred C. Brannon. ACT 167m. V

Federal Hill 1994 ★★★½ Five young Italian-Americans hang out and find out about life in Providence, R.I. Okay character study, stolen by Turturro as thief with explosive temper. Shot in black-and-white; plans to colorize the film for theatrical release were abandoned after industry protests. C: Anthony De Sando, Nicholas Turturro, Libby Langdon, Robert Turano, Jason Andrews, Michael Raynor. D: Michael Corrente. DRA [R] 97m.

Federal Manhunt 1939 ★★★½ Imaginative criminals escape from Alcatraz by staging a mock wedding. Exciting B-movie chase film, modestly winning. C: Robert Livingston, June Travis, John Gallaudet. D: Nick Grinde. ACT 64m.

Fedora 1978 German ★★★★ Fascinating mystery of Garbo-like actress pestered by film producer Holden to make a comeback. Nothing is what it seems in this dreamlike movie with a stunning finish. From first part of Thomas Tryon's book *Crowned Heads*. C: William Holden, Marthe Keller, Hildegarde Knef, Jose Ferrer, Frances Sternhagen, Henry Fonda, Michael York, Mario Adorf. D: Billy Wilder. DRA [PG] 110m. V

Feds 1988 ★★★ DeMornay and *Saturday Night Live* refugee Gross play klutzy FBI recruits eager to prove their worth. Intentions are good, but results should be funnier. C: Rebecca De Mornay, Mary Gross, Fred Dalton Thompson, Ken Marshall, Larry Cedar. D: Dan Goldberg. COM [PG-13] 82m. V

Feel My Pulse 1928 ★★★★ Young woman inherits a fortune from her grandfather, with the stipulation she lead a germ-free life. Zany, rip-roaring silent comedy, expertly played and directed. C: Bebe Daniels, Richard Arlen, William Powell. D: Gregory La Cava. COM 86m.

Feet First 1930 ★★★ In his second sound feature, Lloyd reworks premise of his silent classic *Safety Last*, with uneven results. As a shoe salesman trying to impress a secretary, Lloyd ends up climbing the side of a building, but it's nothing like the famous sequence of the earlier (and better) feature. C: Harold Lloyd, Barbara Kent, Robert McWade, Lillian Leighton, Henry Hall. D: Clyde Bruckman. COM 83m.

Feet Foremost 1983 ★★★½ A well-to-do couple finds it hard to settle into their new house, which is haunted by a young girl. Twisty British shocker. C: Jeremy Kemp. D: Gordon Flemyng. HOR 60m. V

Felix in Outer Space ★★★½ Animated collection features Felix the Cat and his magic bag of tricks in "out-of-this-world" adventures. FAM/COM 55m. V

Felix the Cat—Movie, The 1991 ★★ Disappointing animated film filled with what seem to be leftovers from a number of cartoon adventure movies. Silly and skippable. FAM/COM 82m.

Felix's Magic Bag of Tricks ★★★½ When will the Professor ever learn that Felix will never part with his magic bag of tricks? Still, it's fun to watch him try. FAM/COM 60m. V

Fellini Satyricon 1969 Italian ★★★½ Director's usual originality cannot save stagy, excessive treatment of ancient Rome. Enormous sets and widescreen photography are impressive but fragmented story line demands perseverance. C: Martin Potter, Hiram Keller, Max Born, Capucine, Gordon Mitchell. D: Federico Fellini. DRA 129m. V

Fellini's Casanova 1976 Italian ★★★ Life of the infamous 18th-century seducer, as only Fellini could show it. Intentionally tedious and lifeless—the director found Casanova a cipher—but visually ravishing, with several eye-popping sets and costumes. May be heavy going for non-Fellini fans. C: Donald Sutherland, Tina Aumont, Cicely Browne, John Karlsen, Daniel Emilfork Berenstein. D: Federico Fellini. DRA [R] 158m.

Fellini's Roma 1972 Italian ★★★★ Fellini's exuberant, loving homage to the carnivalesque city of Rome. From his first knowledge of the Eternal City in boyhood to the present, Fellini sketches a delightful, fantastic portrait of the power of a place to inspire and move. (a.k.a. *Roma*) C: Peter Gonzales, Britta Barnes, Pia deDoses, Fiona Florence, Marne Maitland, Renato Giovannoli, Federico Fellini. D: Federico Fellini. DRA [R] 128m. V

Fellow Traveler 1989 British ★★★★ An evocative dramatization of show business in the McCarthy era, with screenwriter Silver and movie star Bochner as victims of blacklist. A gripping political and personal drama. C: Ron Silver, Hart Bochner, Imogen Stubbs, Daniel J. Travanti. D: Philip Saville. DRA 97m. V

Female 1933 ★★★★ Entertaining vehicle for Chatterton as autocratic auto exec; free-spirited Brent shows her that work isn't everything. Gender play adds spice to well-mounted production. C: Ruth Chatterton, George Brent, Ferdinand Gottschalk, Philip Faversham, Ruth Donnelly, Johnny Mack Brown, Lois Wilson, Gavin Gordon. D: Michael Curtiz. DRA [R] 60m. V

Female and the Flesh 1956 *See* **Light Across the Street, The**

Female Animal, The 1958 ★★★ Film star (languid Lamarr) shows gratitude to extra (numb Nader) who saved her life by hiring him as caretaker, but has regrets when both she and daughter (perky Powell) fall for him. Tiresome melodrama. C: Hedy Lamarr, Jane Powell, Jan Sterling, George Nader. D: Harry Keller. DRA 84m.

Female Fiends 1958 British ★★★½ A malevolent woman (Swinburne) uses amnesiac Barker in an elaborate scheme to claim her dead husband's inheritance. Involving mystery with a capable cast. (a.k.a. *The Strange Awakening*) C: Lex Barker, Carole Mathews, Nora Swinburne, Richard Molinas. D: Montgomery Tully. DRA 69m.

Female Jungle, The 1956 ★★★ Tough cop (Tierney) goes after killer of actress. Mansfield, billed as "Sex on the rocks!" and playing a nymphomaniac, provides only interest. C: Jayne Mansfield, Lawrence Tierney, John Carradine, Kathleen Crowley, Rex Thorsen, Burt Carlisle. D: Bruno VeSota. CRI 56m. V

Female on the Beach 1955 ★★★½ Trash classic with Crawford as wealthy widow meeting well-proportioned gigolo on beach, marrying him, then fearing for her life. Awful dialogue full of sexual innuendo that reaches new heights of unintentional humor. C: Joan Crawford, Jeff Chandler, Jan Sterling, Cecil Kellaway, Judith Evelyn, Natalie Schafer, Charles Drake. D: Joseph Pevney. DRA 97m.

Female Trouble 1975 ★★ Underground chronicle of rise and fall of a crime goddess (Divine), in Waters' early (i.e. raw), inimitable style. Violence, sex, and one-liners. Special trash. C: Divine, David Lochary, Edith Massey, Mink Stole. D: John Waters. COM 95m. V

Feminine Touch, The 1941 ★★★★ University professor noted for a book on jealousy finds himself a victim of his own theories. His wife suspects he's carrying on with another woman and the green-eyed monster raises its ugly head. A clever comedy of manners. C: Rosalind Russell, Don Ameche, Kay Francis, Van Heflin, Donald Meek, Gordon Jones, Robert Ryan. D: W.S. VanDyke II. COM 97m. V

Feminine Touch, The 1956 British ★★ The adventures of a group of student nurses at their first hospital assignment. Standard ups and downs. C: George Baker, Belinda Lee, Delphi Lawrence, Adrienne Corri, Diana Wynyard. D: Pat Jackson. DRA 91m.

Feminist and the Fuzz, The 1970 ★★ Sparks fly when a women's libber and a male chauvanist policeman become roommates. Some nice comic touches in an otherwise predictable setup. C: Barbara Eden, David Hartman, Jo Anne Worley, Herb Edeman, Julie Newmar, John McGiver, Farrah Fawcett, Harry Morgan. D: Jerry Paris. COM 90m.

Femme Fatale 1990 ★★ Tired of women, gynecologist and gigolo run away to remote village where they are put to work in brothel by horde of armed feminists. Too much of this outlandish, unsavory, and not very funny misogynistic fantasy expends its energy on the obvious. C: Colin Firth, Lisa Blount, Lisa Zane, Billy Zane. D: Andre Guttfreund. COM [R] 96m. V

Femmes de Personne 1986 French ★★ Success in the boudoir and in their professional lives gives four women little solace. Imperceptive "feminist" account with talented quartet of leading ladies. C: Marthe Keller, Jean-Louis Trintignant, Caroline Cellier. D: Christopher Frank. DRA 106m.

Fer-de-Lance 1974 ★★ A submarine is trapped fathoms beneath the ocean. Worse still, deadly snakes are let loose! Creepy. C: David Janssen, Hope Lange, Ivan Dixon, Jason Evers. D: Russ Mayberry. ACT 100m. TVM V

Fernandel the Dressmaker 1957 French ★★★ Being an everyday tailor is not enough for our hero (Fernandel), who wants to make it as a high-fashion designer. Popular comic actor has definite charm, but everything around him is formulaic. C: Fernandel, Suzy Delair, Francoise Fabian, Georges Chamarat. D: Jean Boyer. COM 95m. V

FernGully . . . The Last Rainforest 1992 ★★★★ When bulldozers threaten a magical rainforest, an enchanted human is coaxed into helping little creatures preserve their world. Ecological cartoon with lovely animation (and Williams as a manic bat) will please both adults and tykes. Voices of Tim Curry, Samantha Mathis, Christian Slater, Robin Williams, Cheech Marin, Tommy Chong. D: Bill Kroyer. FAM/DRA [G] 76m. V

Ferocious Female Freedom Fighters 1982 ★★★½ Like Woody Allen's *What's Up, Tiger Lily?*, a group of comedians and writers dubbed a low-budget martial arts film with sometimes hilarious results. A caveat: many of the jokes are crude or silly. C: Eva Arnaz, Barry Prima. D: Jopi Burnama. COM 74m. V

Ferris Bueller's Day Off 1986 ★★★★ Maddeningly irreverent teen (Broderick) cuts class for a day and plays cat and mouse with the dean (Jones), fleeing suburbia for an adventure-filled day in Chicago. Broderick winningly carries the film with excellent support, especially from the bubbly McClurg. Amusingly sharp teen comedy suffers only from caricatured depictions of adults. C: Matthew Broderick, Alan Ruck, Mia Sara, Jeffrey Jones, Edie McClurg. D: John Hughes. COM [PG-13] 103m. V

Ferry Cross the Mersey 1965 British ★★★ A Liverpool rock 'n' roll band enters a local music contest. This showcase for Gerry and the Pacemakers features eight of their hit songs, including the title cut. A genuine look at a bit of music history. C: Gerry and the Pacemakers, Cilla Black, The Fourmost, Jimmy Saville. D: Jeremy Summers. MUS 88m.

Ferry to Hong Kong 1959 British ★★★½ A captain cannot land his boat at any of Hong Kong's ports of call but proves his mettle during a typhoon. As usual, Welles and Jurgens are great, but the script is just average. C: Orson Welles, Curt Jurgens, Sylvia Syms, Jeremy Spenser. D: Lewis Gilbert. ACT 113m. V

Feud of the West 1937 ★★★ Chuckle-filled early western comedy. C: Hoot Gibson. COM 62m. V

Feud, The 1989 ★★★½ A family feud disrupts a tiny village. Bizarre black comedy is based on Thomas Berger novel of the same name. First film by director D'Elia. C: Rene Auberjonois, Ron McLarty, Joe Grifasi, Scott Allegrucci, Gale Mayron, David Strathairn, Lynne Killmeyer. D: Bill D'Elia. COM [R] 87m. v

Feudin' Fools 1952 ★★½ Slip, Satch, and the rest of the Bowery Boys tangle with a couple of tough con artists. Mostly silly stuff with moments of pure hysteria. C: Leo Gorcey, Huntz Hall, Bennie Bartlett, David Gorcey, Bernard Gorcey, Dorothy Ford, Lyle Talbot, Benny Baker, Russell Simpson, Bob Easton. D: William Beaudine. COM 63m.

Feudin', Fussin' and A-Fightin' 1948 ★★½ O'Connor's tap dancing is the main asset of this hillbilly musical. Plot has Donald as a traveling sales rep helping town win annual footrace. C: Donald O'Connor, Marjorie Main, Percy Kilbride, Penny Edwards. D: George Sherman. MUS 78m.

Fever 1989 Australian ★★★ A cop, his duplicitous wife, and her lover vie for a cache of cash. Taut modern film noir touches all the right, lurid bases. Fine no-name cast. C: Bill Hunter, Mary Regan, Gary Sweet. D: Craig Lahiff. CRI [R] 83m. v

Fever in the Blood, A 1961 ★★★ A murder trial serves as grandstanding vehicle for three ambitious gubernatorial candidates. Good cast, but flaccid melodrama weighs them down. C: Efrem Zimbalist, Jr., Angie Dickinson, Herbert Marshall, Don Ameche, Jack Kelly, Carroll O'Connor. D: Vincent Sherman. DRA 117m.

Fever Pitch 1985 ★★½ Reporter (O'Neal) can't shake his destructive gambling habit. Writer/director Brooks struggles to transcend bad dialogue and uninspired casting. C: Ryan O'Neal, Catherine Hicks, Giancarlo Giannini, Chad Everett. D: Richard Brooks. DRA [R] 95m. v

Few Days in the Life of I.I. Oblomov, A 1980 *See* **Oblomov**

Few Days with Me, A 1988 French ★★★ Unbalanced heir (Auteil) falls in love with ordinary waitress (Bonnaire). Even accomplished acting by the two leads cannot save Sautet's flimsy comedy/drama. C: Daniel Auteuil, Sandrine Bonnaire, Jean-Pierre Marielle, Dominique Lavanant, Danielle Darrieux, Tanya Lopert. D: Claude Sautet. COM [PG-13] 131m.

Few Good Men, A 1992 ★★★★ A young Navy lawyer (Cruise) investigates the suspicious death of a Marine at Guantanamo Bay. Great performances by stellar cast, particularly Nicholson as tough-as-nails marine colonel squaring off against young hot-shot Cruise. C: Tom Cruise, Jack Nicholson, Demi Moore, Kevin Bacon, Kiefer Sutherland, Kevin Pollak, James Marshall, J.T. Walsh, Wolfgang Bodison, Cuba Gooding Jr. D: Rob Reiner. DRA [R] 138m. v

ffolkes 1980 ★★★½ When terrorists seize two oil rigs in North Atlantic, the British government turns to oddball professional spy Moore to save the day. Moore is entertaining parodying his James Bond image. (a.k.a. *Assault Force* and *North Sea Hijack*) C: Roger Moore, James Mason, Anthony Perkins, Michael Parks. D: Andrew McLaglen. ACT [PG] 99m. v

Fickle Finger of Fate, The 1967 U.S. ★★★ A Spanish comedy/adventure about an innocent American engineer who becomes the fallguy in a European art smuggling racket in Madrid. The low budget shows, but the story is entertaining. C: Tab Hunter, Luis Prendes, Patty Shepard, Gustavo Rojo, Fernando Hilbeck. D: Richard Rush. COM 91m.

Fiction Makers, The 1967 ★★★½ In his usual suave and inimitable fashion, Simon Templer takes on the mob and puts his own life in danger to protect a famous author. C: Roger Moore, Sylvia Sims. ACT 102m. v

Fiddler on the Roof 1971 ★★★★ Faithful, reasonably successful filming of Broadway megahit musical. Tells touching story of Jewish dairyman in Czarist Russia trying to cling to tradition in a changing world. Location footage reduces some of the stage magic, but able cast performs marvelous score including "Sunrise, Sunset," "If I Were a Rich Man," "Matchmaker, Matchmaker." C: Topol, Norma Crane, Leonard Frey, Molly Picon, Paul Mann, Rosalind Harris, Michele Marsh, Neva Small, Candice Bonstein. D: Norman Jewison. MUS [G] 181m. v

Field of Dreams 1989 ★★★★½ Iowa farmer Costner hears a "voice" telling him if he builds a baseball field, it will bring the immortal Shoeless Joe Jackson and other baseball legends back from the dead. Like *Miracle on 34th Street*, this film is a wondrous, yet unsappy tribute to faith, and to holding fast to the beliefs of one's heart. Warmhearted glimpse of Americana for children of all ages. Adapted from W.P. Kinsella's book *Shoeless Joe*. C: Kevin Costner, Amy Madigan, Ray Liotta, James Earl Jones, Burt Lancaster. D: Phil Alden Robinson. FAM/DRA [PG] 106m. v

Field of Fire 1992 ★★★ The dense and foreboding Cambodian jungle is only one of the dangers that must be overcome in an attempt to rescue a high-ranking military expert trapped behind enemy lines. C: David Carradine. D: Christopher Santigo. ACT [R] 90m. v

Field, The 1990 British ★★★★ Stubborn Irish farmer stands to lose the land his family has worked for generations—and makes tragic, lunatic choices in trying to hold on to it. Sometimes overwrought, but carried by Harris' startlingly intense performance. C: Richard Harris, John Hurt, Tom Berenger, Sean Bean, Brenda Fricker. D: Jim Sheridan. DRA [PG-13] 110m. v

Fiend 1980 ★★ A murderer's corpse is brought back to life by an insectoid phantom. Amateurish acting, directing, and make-up sink this would-be shocker. C: Don Leifert, Richard Nelson, Elaine White, George Stover. D: Don Dohler. HOR 93m. V

Fiend, The 1972 ★★½ A religious cult made up of psychotics wreaks mental havoc on a confused and impressionable man who murders for "redemption." Unsettling. C: Ann Todd, Patrick Magee, Tony Beckley. D: Robert Hartford-Davis. HOR [R] 87m. V

Fiend Who Walked the West, The 1958 ★★ Fresh out of prison, a sadistic killer stalks and terrorizes some pals of his cellmate. It's *Kiss of Death* in a Western format. C: Hugh O'Brian, Robert Evans, Dolores Michaels, Linda Cristal, Stephen McNally. D: Gordon Douglas. WST 101m.

Fiendish Ghouls 1959 *See* **Flesh and the Fiends, The**

Fiendish Plot of Dr. Fu Manchu, The 1980 British ★★ Relentless Scotland Yard constable tracks diabolically evil Chinese lunatic before he can execute his plan to control the world. Sellers, in his last film, plays both lead roles, but can't muster any laughs in this insipid, dreary comedy. C: Peter Sellers, Helen Mirren, Sid Caesar, David Tomlinson. D: Piers Haggard. COM [PG] 100m. V

Fiercest Heart, The 1961 ★★★ In South Africa, Boers on trek to the Transvaal are aided by British deserters in violent encounters with Zulus. Minor feature with colorful battle sequences. C: Stuart Whitman, Juliet Prowse, Ken Scott, Raymond Massey, Geraldine Fitzgerald. D: George Sherman. ACT 91m.

Fiesta 1947 ★★★½ Montalban made debut in colorful musical nonsense, starring as a bullfighter who wants to be composer, and has him and Williams as unlikely twins. Worth seeing for Mexican locations and marvelous dance number "Fantasia Mexicana" staged by Eugene Loring. C: Esther Williams, Akim Tamiroff, Ricardo Montalban, John Carroll, Mary Astor, Cyd Charisse. D: Richard Thorpe. MUS 104m.

Fievel's American Tails Vol. 1—The Gift & A Case of the Hiccups 1993 ★★★ Two episodes of charming animated series inspired by *An American Tail*. Fans of Fievel will enjoy it. FAM/COM 47m. V

5th Avenue Girl 1939 ★★★ A millionaire (Connolly) makes a young homeless woman (Rogers) his choice for a daughter-in-law. Screwball misfire proves that even a great star and director can't save a weak script. C: Ginger Rogers, Walter Connolly, Tim Holt, Franklin Pangborn, James Ellison. D: Gregory LaCava. COM 83m. V

Fifth Chair, The 1945 *See* **It's in the Bag**

Fifth Day of Peace, The 1972 Italian ★★★ After WWI, armistice is declared, an apathetic group of pardoned German POWs roam war-torn roads of rural Italy. Transparent WWI story. C: Richard Johnson, Franco Nero, Bud Spencer, Michael Goodliffe. D: Guiliano Montaldo. DRA [PG] 95m. V

Fifth Floor, The 1980 ★★½ A party girl overdoses on drugs and winds up in a psycho ward, where an unbalanced attendant (Hopkins) takes a liking to her. Lurid thriller. C: Bo Hopkins, Dianne Hull, Patti D'Arbanville, Mel Ferrer. D: Howard Avedis. HOR [R] 90m. V

Fifth Horseman Is Fear, The 1965 Czech ★★★★ In Nazi-overrun Prague, Jewish doctor allows fugitive to hide in his home. Relentlessly downbeat but expertly filmed and acted. One of first Czech films to gain acceptance abroad. C: Jiri Sternwald, Miroslav Machacek, Olga Scheinpflugova, Josef Vinklar. D: Zbynek Brynych. DRA 100m.

Fifth Monkey, The 1990 ★★★★ Touching adventure of a poor hunter (Kingsley, marvelous as usual) determined to raise enough money to marry the woman he loves by selling snakeskins and monkeys. A slight, uplifting tale. C: Ben Kingsley, Mika Lins. D: Eric Rochat. DRA [PG-13] 93m. V

Fifth Musketeer, The 1979 Austrian ★★½ Twin brothers compromise the Crown in this swashbuckler of 17th-century France. Remake of *The Man in the Iron Mask*, distinguished by an excellent cast. C: Beau Bridges, Sylvia Kristel, Ursula Andress, Lloyd Bridges, Jose Ferrer, Rex Harrison, Olivia de Havilland. D: Ken Annakin. ACT [PG] 103m. V

Fifth Seal, The 1976 ★★★ Sympathetic WWII film about five Hungarian friends given freedom from a Communist dictatorship provided they beat a man about to die. C: Sandor Horvath. D: Zoltan Fabri. DRA 116m. V

55 Days at Peking 1963 ★★★½ Even with the chaos of the Boxer Rebellion raging all about them in 1900s China, Heston and Gardner find time for (but of course!) romance. Ambitious historical romantic epic juggles affairs of state and heart, with some marvelous camerawork throughout. C: Charlton Heston, Ava Gardner, David Niven, Flora Robson, John Ireland, Paul Lukas, Jacques Sernas. D: Nicholas Ray. DRA 150m.

Fifty Roads to Town 1937 ★★★ Ameche and Sothern fall in love while marooned at a snowbound cabin where mistaken identities and mixed motives abound. Easygoing romp. C: Don Ameche, Ann Sothern, Slim Summerville, Jane Darwell, John Qualen, Stepin Fetchit, Oscar Apfel. D: Norman Taurog. COM 81m.

52 Pick-Up 1986 ★★★½ An ordinary, married businessman (Scheider) becomes the target of a blackmail scheme after his tryst with a woman with a shady reputation. Sleazy, often implausible cat-and-mouser kept afloat by colorful villains. From the Elmore Leonard novel. C: Roy Scheider, Ann-Margret, Vanity, John Glover. D: John Frankenheimer. CRI [R] 111m. V

Fifty/Fifty 1992 ★★ Rival mercenaries (Hays

and Weller) shoot up a war-torn Latin American country while trying to woo a lovely local. Unfunny one-liners pose as humor, while lots of bullets try to pass for action. C: Peter Weller, Robert Hays, Charles Martin Smith, Ramona Rahman, Kay Tong Lim. D: Charles Martin Smith. COM [R] 90m. v

Fight for Jenny, A 1986 ★★★ Heartwrenching account of the real-life battle a young girl suffers when her mother marries a black man in a prejudiced southern town. C: Philip Michael Thomas, Lesley Ann Warren, Jean Smart. D: Gilbert Moses. DRA 95m. v

Fight for Life 1987 ★★★ A concerned father (Lewis) struggles to learn the truth about his daughter's illness. Effective TV movie, but might've fared better as a *Marcus Welby* episode. C: Jerry Lewis, Patty Duke, Morgan Freeman. D: Elliot Silverstein. DRA 104m.

Fight for Rome 1969 German ★★★½ The Emperor Justinian (Welles) struggles to maintain a crumbling Roman Empire. Mammoth, disjointed epic with an eclectic cast. (a.k.a. *Kampf um Rom*) C: Laurence Harvey, Orson Welles, Sylva Koscina, Honor Blackman, Harriet Andersson. D: Robert Siodmak. DRA 99m.

Fight for Us 1989 ★★½ Freed anti-Marcos activist and priest go up against political vigilantes who seek control of the Philippine government. Spirited struggle gives way to exciting danger and intrigue. C: Phillip Salvador, Dina Bonnevie, Bembol Roco. D: Lino Brocka. ACT [R] 92m. v

Fight for Your Lady 1937 ★★★½ Singer (Boles), jilted by society woman (Grahame), gets help from wrestling trainer (Oakie). Funny, low-budget musical. Excellent support from veteran character comics Rhodes and Gilbert. C: John Boles, Jack Oakie, Ida Lupino, Margot Grahame, Gordon Jones, Erik Rhodes, Billy Gilbert. D: Ben Stoloff. MUS 67m.

Fight for Your Life 1979 ★★½ Three prison escapees take a hostage and hightail it to the Canadian border. Go for the requisite action and you won't be disappointed. C: William Sanderson, Robert Judd, Lela Small. ACT [R] 89m. v

Fight to the Death 1983 Japan ★★★ An army of Kung Fu fighters pave the way for a Japanese invasion and World War II. Outstanding martial arts display by Van Clief. C: Bruce Tse, Chang Li, Ron Van Clief. D: Wang Lee. ACT 100m. v

Fight to Win ★★½ The psychological and physical trials of two karate masters vying for renowned statue. C: Richard Norton, Cynthia Rothrock, George Chung. D: George Chung. ACT 88m. v

Fighter Attack 1953 ★★★ An American Air Corps major (Hayden) is sent on a final mission over Italy. Summarily produced, WWII action, told in flashbacks. C: Sterling Hayden, J. Carroll Naish, Joy Page, Paul Fierro. D: Lesley Selander. ACT 80m. v

Fighter Squadron 1948 ★★★ A pilot's devotion to duty endangers his mens' lives. Clichéd, standard aerial adventure. Rock Hudson's screen debut. C: Edmond O'Brien, Robert Stack, John Rodney, Tom D'Andrea, Henry Hull. D: Raoul Walsh. ACT 96m.

Fighter, The 1952 ★★★ In Mexico, a fisherman (Conte) becomes a boxer to fund his revenge for his family's murder. Familiar story, but well done. C: Richard Conte, Vanessa Brown, Lee J. Cobb, Roberta Haynes. D: Herbert Kline. DRA 78m.

Fighters, The 1992 ★★★½ Compilation of historical and modern footage that puts the viewer in the cockpit of the F-4 Phantom, F-15 Eagle, and F-16 Falcon. Virtual reality effects are impressive; especially fun for those who are into video games. Monte Markham narrates. C: Monte Markham. DOC 50m. v

Fighting Back 1982 ★★★½ Vigilanteism runs rampant, as a Philadephia resident organizes the ultimate Neighborhood Watch program. Violent action, saved by the fine cast. C: Tom Skerritt, Patti LuPone, Michael Sarrazin, Yaphet Kotto. D: Lewis Teague. ACT [R] 98m. v

Fighting Black Kings 1976 ★★★½ Martial arts, kung fu, and karate experts are invited to the First International Karate Tournament. Showcase is a must for all martial arts fans. C: William Oliver, Charles Martin. ACT [PG] 90m.

Fighting Caravans 1931 ★★★½ Rousing tale of pioneers and wagon trains against the Indians. Based on Zane Grey story. C: Gary Cooper, Lili Damita, Ernest Torrence. D: Otto Brewer. WST 80m. v

Fighting Chance, The 1955 ★★★ A jockey and a horse trainer are rivals for the love of the same woman. Routine love triangle against a backdrop of horseracing. C: Rod Cameron, Julie London, Ben Cooper, Taylor Holmes, Bob Steele. D: William Witney. DRA 70m.

Fighting Choice 1986 ★★★ Epileptic teenager files a lawsuit against his parents for the right to have dangerous experimental surgery. Average treatment of a topical subject. C: Beau Bridges, Karen Valentine. D: Ferdinand Fairfax. DRA 104m.

Fighting Coast Guard 1951 ★★★½ Coast Guard team trains for military action during WWII. Above average wartime drama. C: Brian Donlevy, Forrest Tucker, Ella Raines, John Russell, Richard Jaeckel, William Murphy, Martin Milner, Steve Brodie, Hugh O'Brian. D: Joseph Kane. DRA 86m.

Fighting Devil Dogs, The 1938 ★★★½ The serialized adventures of two soldiers battling an evil scientist equipped with a high-tech airplane. Good, rollicking fun. C: Lee Powell, Herman Brix, Hugh Southern. D: John English. ACT 195m. V

Fighting Father Dunne 1948 ★★½ Catholic priest takes charge of slum boys in this '40s melodrama. Talented O'Brien good as Dunne, but screenplay needs a lot of work. C: Pat O'Brien, Darryl Hickman, Charles Kemper, Una O'Connor. D: Ted Tetzlaff. DRA 93m. V

Fighting Fools 1949 ★★★½ The Bowery Boys persuade a friend (Darro) to give up drinking and develop his boxing talents. Above-par entry for the series. C: Leo Gorcey, Huntz Hall, Gabriel Dell, Frankie Darro, Billy Benedict, David Gorcey, Benny Bartlett, Lyle Talbot, Evelynne Eaton, Bernard Gorcey. D: Reginald LeBorg. COM 69m.

Fighting Frontier 1943 ★★★½ Likable B-Western with good-guy Holt pretending to be a villain so he can bust up a gang of outlaws. Some good shoot-'em-up sequences. C: Tim Holt, Cliff Edwards, Ann Summers, Eddie Dew. D: Lambert Hillyer. WST 57m.

Fighting Gringo, The 1939 ★★★½ A self-appointed lawman (O'Brien) tries to clear a Mexican landowner of a false murder charge, while romancing his daughter. Well-produced Western with fine chase scenes. C: George O'Brien, Lupita Tovar, Lucio Villegas. D: David Howard. WST 59m.

Fighting Guardsman 1945 ★★★½ French Robin Hood-like rogue Parker robs the rich and gives to the poor. Parker's good deeds come into question when he falls for wealthy Louise. Based on Dumas' novel, this is full of colorful though routine action. C: Willard Parker, Anita Louise, Janis Carter, John Loder, Edgar Buchanan, George Macready. D: Henry Levin. ACT 84m.

Fighting Kentuckian, The 1949 ★★★½ Frontier hero (Wayne) comes to the aid of French settlers who are being deceived out of land. Nothing new, but well-made and engaging nevertheless. C: John Wayne, Vera Ralston, Philip Dorn, Oliver Hardy, Marie Windsor. D: George Waggner. WST 100m. V

Fighting Lawman, The 1953 ★★ In the Wild West, a rambunctious woman steals from a band of robbers. Bland script and paltry action. C: Wayne Morris, Virginia Grey, Harry Lauter, John Kellogg, Myron Healey, Dick Rich. D: Thomas Carr. WST 71m.

Fighting Mad 1976 ★★★★ Quiet farmer (Fonda) must ward off scheming landowner who wants his land. Interesting early Demme film pays off by focusing on character more than violence. Includes a steady performance by Fonda. C: Peter Fonda, Lynn Lowry, John Doucette, Philip Carey, Scott Glenn, Kathleen Miller. D: Jonathan Demme. ACT [R] 90m. V

Fighting Man of the Plains 1949 ★★★½ An ex-desperado sets out for revenge against his brother's killers. Adequate, formulaic Western. C: Randolph Scott, Bill Williams, Jane Nigh, Victor Jory. D: Edwin L. Marin. WST 94m.

Fighting O'Flynn, The 1949 ★★★ Fairbanks, Jr., cuts dashing figure as poor young adventurer foiling Napoleon's plans to invade 19th-century Ireland. Minor but entertaining swashbuckler. C: Douglas Fairbanks, Jr., Richard Greene, Helena Carter, Patricia Medina. D: Arthur Pierson. ACT 94m.

Fighting Pimpernel, The 1950 British ★★★★ Niven is the swashbuckling British nobleman who singlehandedly saves Parisian aristocrats from death during the French Revolution. Colorful, witty tale from Baroness Orczy's novel, *The Scarlet Pimpernel*, one of several filmings. (a.k.a. *The Elusive Pimpernel*) C: David Niven, Margaret Leighton, Jack Hawkins, Cyril Cusack, Robert Coote. D: Michael Powell, Emeric Pressburger. ACT 109m. V

Fighting Prince of Donegal, The 1966 ★★★★ British Disney swashbuckler about teenaged Irish prince (McEnery) who rescues his family from the encroaching, evil British in time of Elizabeth I. A fast-moving, colorful romp based on action novel *Red Hugh, Prince of Donegal*. C: Peter McEnery, Susan Hampshire, Tom Adams, Gordon Jackson. D: Michael O'Herlihy. FAM/ACT 110m. V

Fighting Ranger, The 1948 ★★★½ Plenty of shoot-'em-up action scenes highlight standard tale of a mild-mannered ranger (Brown) jolted into bravery when a gang of vicious criminals hits a small Western town. C: Johnny Mack Brown, Raymond Hatton. D: Lambert Hillyer. WST 57m.

Fighting Rookie, The 1934 ★★★ A young cop is asked to risk his life and his reputation by pretending to join the Mob. C: Jack La Rue. D: Spencer Gordon Bennet. CRI 65m. V

Fighting Seabees, The 1944 ★★★½ WWII adventure set in the South Pacific as Navy construction workers (Wayne and O'Keefe) hold up their end of the war while sparring over the same love interest (Hayward). Fairly typical, but engaging just the same. C: John Wayne, Susan Hayward, Dennis O'Keefe, William Frawley, Paul Fix. D: Edward Ludwig. ACT 100m. V

Fighting 69th, The 1940 ★★★★ A member of famed Irish WWI regiment (Cagney) progresses from cringing cowardice to heroic bravery under the watchful eyes of famed chaplain Father Duffy (O'Brien). Stirring, powerful battle scenes and moving screenplay make this an outstanding tribute to patriotism. C: James Cagney, Pat O'Brien, George Brent, Jeffrey Lynn, Alan Hale, Frank McHugh, Dennis Morgan. D: William Keighley. ACT 90m. V

Fighting Stallion, The 1926 ★★★½ A spirited, renegade horse is the object of four cowboys' desires in this gripping silent western with excellent photography. C: Yakima Canutt, Neva Gerber, Bud Osborne. WST 76m. V

Fighting Trouble 1956 ★★★ The Bowery Boys as newspaper stringers out to snap a photo of an elusive mobster. First entry without Gorcey spelled decline of the series. Only fair juvenile hijinx. C: Huntz Hall, Stanley Clements, Adele Jergens, Joseph Downing, Queenie Smith, David Gorcey. D: George Blair. COM 61m.

Fighting Trouper 1934 ★★★ A young mountie, disguised as a trapper strives to catch the killer of his buddy. Effective thriller. C: Kermit Maynard, Barbara Worth. D: Ray Taylor. CRI 50m.

Fighting Westerner, The 1935 *See* **Rocky Mountain Mystery**

Fighting Wildcats, The 1957 British ★★½ London gangsters get involved in Middle East intrigue. Dull nonsense in exotic setting. C: Keefe Brasselle, Kay Callard, Karel Stepanek, Ursula Howells. D: Arthur Crabtree. ACT 74m.

Fighting Youth 1935 ★★★ Radical politics competes with the gridiron in an unlikely story. Sheridan is a rebellious student who takes on the more conservative football quarterback Farrell and campus comedy abounds. Dated, but funny in a campy sort of way. C: Charles Farrell, June Martel, Andy Devine, J. Farrell MacDonald, Ann Sheridan, Edward Nugent. D: Hamilton MacFadden. COM 85m.

Figures in a Landscape 1970 British ★★ Lost in a landscape would be more accurate. Shaw and McDowell are on the lam for reasons unexplained. Shaw took over the script during filming and there's alleged to be some symbolism at work. But, like the film itself, deeper meaning eludes most viewers. C: Robert Shaw, Malcolm McDowell, Henry Woolf, Christopher Malcolm, Pamela Brown. D: Joseph Losey. DRA [PG] 95m.

File of the Golden Goose, The 1969 British ★★ An American agent and a Scotland Yard detective infiltrate a group of counterfeiters in London. C: Yul Brynner, Charles Gray, Edward Woodward, John Barrie, Adrienne Corri. D: Sam Wanamaker. CRI [PG] 105m.

File on Jill Hatch, The 1983 U.S. ★★★½ An African-American soldier stationed in England during WWII meets and marries a white Englishwoman. Enduring love in the face of racial trials and tribulations, portrayed with great sensitivity and intelligence. C: Joe Morton, Frances Tomelty, Gloria Foster, Penny Johnson, Tim Woodward, John Atkinson. D: Alastair Reed. DRA 180m.

File on Thelma Jordon, The 1949 ★★★½ Stanwyck in one of her best bad girl roles as murder suspect in love with D.A. Corey. Atmospheric film noir would have been better with stronger support for star. C: Barbara Stanwyck, Wendell Corey, Joan Tetzel, Stanley Ridges, Richard Rober, Paul Kelly. D: Robert Siodmak. DRA 100m.

Fillmore 1972 ★★★★ Grateful Dead, Jefferson Airplane, and Santana headline final concerts at San Francisco's famed rock venue. Genuine slice of early '70s life has great music and magnetic superpromoter Bill Graham. C: Bill Graham, The Grateful Dead, Santana, Jefferson Airplane. D: Richard T. Heffron. MUS [R] 105m.

Film House Fever 1986 ★★★½ Compilation that's just the ticket for cult film fans, including "She Devil on Wheels" and "The Warrior and the Sorceress." C: Jamie Lee Curtis, James Keach, David Carradine. HOR 58m. V

Filmgore 1983 ★★★ Collection of scary clips from truly horrifying films. Definitely not for the squeamish or faint of heart. D: Ken Dixon. HOR 85m. V

Final Alliance 1990 ★★ Drifter with pet puma seeks revenge against the vicious bike gang that killed his family. Violent. C: David Hasselhoff, John Saxon, Bo Hopkins. D: Mario Di Leo. ACT [R] 94m. V

Final Analysis 1992 ★★★ To understand a patient (Thurman)'s psychosis, a psychiatrist (Gere) questions her sister (Basinger), and is swept up in a web of intrigue. Film attempts Hitchcock-like suspense, but overdoes it with too many twists and turns. C: Richard Gere, Kim Basinger, Uma Thurman, Eric Roberts, Paul Guilfoyle. D: Phil Joanou. CRI [R] 125m. V

Final Approach 1991 ★★★ Fighter pilot (Sikking) ejects out of a top secret aircraft and winds up spilling his guts to a psychiatrist. Cast tries hard in this offbeat action film. C: James B. Sikking, Hector Elizondo, Madolyn Smith, Kevin McCarthy. D: Eric Steven Stahl. ACT [R] 100m. V

Final Assignment 1980 Canadian ★★ A Canadian TV news reporter (Bujold) must get past KGB interference to report about scientific experiments being performed on children in Russia. Far-fetched story was shot in Montreal as a stand-in for Moscow. C: Genevieve Bujold, Michael York, Burgess Meredith, Colleen Dewhurst. D: Paul Almond. DRA [PG] 92m. V

Final Chapter—Walking Tall 1977 ★★ Continuation of the story of controversial Tennessee lawman Buford Pusser (Svenson), a fighting, feisty country sheriff whose wife was gunned down by gangsters. Not anywhere near as effective as first two films about Pusser. C: Bo Svenson, Margaret Blye, Forrest Tucker, Lurene Tuttle, Morgan Woodward, Libby Boone. D: Jack Starrett. DRA [R] 112m.

Final Combat, The 1984 ★★★★ Survivor of nuclear war tries to build an airplane so he can search for a mate. Award-winning silent film. C: Pierre Jolivet, Fritz Wepper, Jean Reno. D: Luc Besson. SFI 93m. V

Final Comedown, The 1972 ★★½ A black radical's efforts to recruit white support falls apart, resulting in a bloody race war. Grim, sobering urban drama. C: Billy Dee Williams,

Martin D'urville, Celia Kay. D: Oscar Williams. ACT [R] 84m.

Final Conflict, The 1981 ★★★ Finale to *The Omen* saga has some good shock scenes, but follows a predictable pattern and loses steam toward the end. The now-grown Antichrist, Damien (Neill), attempts to obtain governmental position to solidify his evil power. C: Sam Neill, Rossano Brazzi, Don Gordon, Lisa Harrow, Mason Adams. D: Graham Baker. HOR [R] 108m. v

Final Countdown, The 1980 ★★★½ Modern-day aircraft carrier is time-warped to Pearl Harbor right before the Japanese attack. Will Douglas and crew become involved in the event and alter the course of history? Familiar *Star Trek/Twilight Zone* plot buoyed by game cast. C: Kirk Douglas, Martin Sheen, Katharine Ross, James Farentino, Charles Durning. D: Don Taylor. SFI [PG] 104m. v

Final Crash, The *See* **Steelyard Blues**

Final Cut 1988 ★★ When a movie crew goes on location in a treacherous swamp, not all of them make it out alive. C: Joe Rainer, Jordan Williams, Brett Rice. D: Larry Brown. ACT [R] 92m. v

Final Days, The 1989 ★★★★½ A Distinguished behind-the-scenes look at last stages of Richard Nixon's presidency from Bob Woodward/Carl Bernstein best-seller. Smith is an uncanny Nixon in an uncompromising, yet sympathetic portrait of a flawed politician caught in a scandal of his own making. C: Lane Smith, Richard Kiley, David Ogden Stiers, Ed Flanders, Theodore Bikel, Graham Beckel, James B. Sikking, Gregg Henry. D: Richard Pearce. DRA 150m.

Final Embrace 1992 ★★ When a rock singer is murdered, her distraught sister appeals to sensitive cops to help find killer. C: Robert Rusler, Nancy Valen, Dick Van Patten. D: Oley Sassone. CRI [R] 83m. v

Final Executioner, The 1983 ★★½ Post-nuclear world challenges the physical and emotional instincts of those remaining in a new and brutal society. C: William Mang, Marina Costa, Harrison Muller. D: Romolo Guerrieri. SFI 95m. v

Final Extra, The 1927 ★★★ A reporter is intent on exposing a ring of gunrunners while investigating the murder of a rival. A dramatic score keeps the action moving quickly in this silent film. C: Marguerite De La Motte, Grant Withers. D: James P. Hogan. CRI 76m.

Final Impact 1991 ★★½ An Ex-kickboxing champ trains young fighter to compete against his old nemesis. C: Lorenzo Lamas, Kathleen Kinmont, Jeff Langton. D: Joseph Merhi. ACT [R] 99m. v

Final Judgment 1992 ★★★ Priest fleeing erroneous murder rap encounters L.A.'s sex industry in search of actual murderer. C: Brad Dourif, Isaac Hayes, Karen Black. D: Louis Morneau. CRI [R] 90m. v

Final Justice 1984 ★★ An American lawman (Baker) decides to take justice into his own hands by heading to Italy to stop the Mafia in this silly action picture. Violence and profanity. C: Joe Don Baker, Rossano Brazzi, Patrizia Pellegrino. D: Greydon Clark. ACT [R] 90m.

Final Mission 1978 ★★ Cable production about a cop who tracks down his family. C: Richard Young, John Dresden, Christine Tudor. D: Cirio H. Santiago. CRI 97m. v

Final Notice 1989 ★★ A likable detective enlists the help of an attractive librarian to catch the maniac who's destroying both books and pretty women. Lukewarm thriller. C: Gil Gerard, Melody Anderson, Jackie Burroughs, Louise Fletcher, David Ogden Stiers, Steve Landesburg. D: Steven Hilliard Stern. CRI 88m. TVM v

Final Option, The 1982 British ★★½ A British Special Air Services officer (Collins) goes undercover to foil a terrorist plot to take over American Embassy. Quite violent, with a weak script, but Davis is wonderful as the passionate head of a no-nukes organization that's advancing its message by taking hostages. Widmark has a cameo as U.S. secretary of state. (a.k.a. *Who Dares Wins*) C: Lewis Collins, Judy Davis, Richard Widmark, Robert Webber. D: Ian Sharp. ACT [R] 125m. v

Final Programme, The 1973 ★★★ Odd futuristic action film about a man saving the world from his diabolical brothers, and himself from a flaky computer programmer. C: Jon Finch, Jenny Runacre, Sterling Hayden, Patrick Magee. D: Robert Fuest. COM [R] 85m. v

Final Romance, The 1988 ★★★½ Classical music/opera buffs will want to catch this bio of 19th-century tenor Julian Gayarre, well-played and sung by Carreras. C: Jose Carreras, Sydne Rome, Antonio Ferrandis, Mario Pardo. MUS 120m. v

Final Terror, The 1981 ★★★ Standard but well-shot horror film about young hikers in the woods falling victim to a maniacal killer. Most notable for a relatively low body count and presence of many up-and-comers (including debuting director Davis). C: John Friedrich, Adrian Zmed, Daryl Hannah, Rachel Ward. D: Andrew Davis. HOR [R] 90m. v

Final Test, The 1953 British ★★★½ Modest comedy of father and son who compete for woman's hand. Asquith shows grace with actors, though: Warner and Relph are likable, Morley gets in a few wicked bits, Allen is very charming. C: Jack Warner, Robert Morley, George Relph, Adrianne Allen. D: Anthony Asquith. COM 84m.

Final Verdict 1991 ★★★½ Young Burnette idolizes her lawyer father Williams, despite tensions in family caused by his defense of murderer. Period piece, set in 1919 Los Angeles, talky but well produced and well acted. Based on Adela Rogers St. John's remembrances of her father. C: Treat Williams, Glenn Ford, Olivia Burnette. D: Jack Fisk. DRA 93m. V

Final War, The 1960 Japanese ★★★★ Horrific speculation about the outbreak of widespread nuclear war, beginning with accidental bombing of South Korea by the U.S. Powerful antinuclear film, from a Japanese point of view. C: Tatsuo Umemiya, Yoshiko Mita, Yayoi Furusato. D: Shigeaki Hidaka. DRA 77m.

Find the Lady 1976 Canadian ★★ Inept cops search for kidnapped heiress. Silly shenanigans poorly done. (a.k.a. *Call the Cops* and *Kopek and Broom*) C: Lawrence Dane, John Candy, Mickey Rooney, Peter Cook. D: John Trent. COM 79m. V

Finders Keepers 1951 ★★★ When Ewell finishes his time in prison he's ready to straighten out his life, but these plans take an unexpected twist when his son finds a pile of money that nearly sends Ewell back to the pokey. Ewell is better then the material deserves. C: Tom Ewell, Julia Adams, Evelyn Varden, Dusty Henley. D: Frederick de Cordova. COM 74m.

Finders Keepers 1984 ★★ Everybody is after stolen loot hidden somewhere on a coast-to-coast train. Frantic slapstick generates some laughs, but often more obnoxious than funny. C: Michael O'Keefe, Beverly D'Angelo, Louis Gossett, Jr., Ed Lauter, David Wayne, Pamela Stephenson, Brian Dennehy. D: Richard Lester. COM [R] 96m. V

Finding the Way Home 1991 ★★★★½ Scott gives a bravura performance as a man suffering from temporary amnesia who is taken in by a camp of migrant workers and finds a home and meaning to his life. Elizondo is excellent, too. C: George C. Scott, Hector Elizondo, Julie Carmen, Beverly Garland, Julio Cedillo, Jose Alcala, David Hussey. D: Rod Holcomb. DRA 100m. TVM

Fine Gold 1988 ★★★½ Intense drama about a man (Stevens), falsely accused of embezzlement, trying to rebuild his life and clear his name. C: Andrew Stevens, Ray Walston, Ted Wass, Stewart Granger, Lloyd Bochner. D: J. Anthony Loma. DRA 91m. V

Fine Madness, A 1966 ★★★★ A fiercely nonconformist New York poet (Connery) runs afoul of an anal-retentive psychiatrist, who wants to lobotomize him. Zesty, often hilarious comedy/drama was jumbled by reediting but remains energetic and satisfying. An overlooked '60s gem. C: Sean Connery, Joanne Woodward, Jean Seberg, Patrick O'Neal, Colleen Dewhurst. D: Irvin Kershner. COM 104m. V

Fine Mess, A 1986 ★★ When they learn of a fixed horse race, doltish piano movers hope to make a fast buck, but instead incur the wrath of addlebrained mobsters. Messy, flat-footed slapstick. C: Ted Danson, Howie Mandel, Richard Mulligan, Stuart Margolin, Maria Conchita Alonso, Jennifer Edwards, Paul Sorvino. D: Blake Edwards. COM [PG] 104m. V

Fine Pair, A 1969 ★★ Hopeless tale of cop (Hudson) and jewel heist. One of Rock's weaker efforts. C: Rock Hudson, Claudia Cardinale, Thomas Milian, Leon Askin, Ellen Corby, Walter Giller. D: Francesco Maselli. COM [PG] 89m.

Fine Romance, A 1992 U.S. ★★★ Intriguing pairing of Andrews and Mastroianni as recently divorced strangers finding solace in new friendship comes off as oil meets water. Neither star is well served by fluffy script and slow-paced direction. Based on play *Tchin-Tchin*. C: Julie Andrews, Marcello Mastroianni, Ian Fitzgibbon, Jean-Pierre Castaldi, Jean-Jacques Dulon, Maria Machado, Catherine Jarret. D: Gene Saks. COM [PG-13] 83m. V

Finest Hour 1992 ★★★ Two gung-ho Navy SEALs vie for glory and the same woman in this low-budget action potboiler. Some rousing battle action sequences, but incoherent plot. C: Rob Lowe, Gale Hansen, Tracy Griffith. D: Shimon Dotan. ACT [R] 105m. V

Finest Hours, The 1964 ★★★★ Fascinating documentary about British prime minister Winston Churchill delves deeply into the great politician's unsettled childhood, career as soldier, and triumphs and tragedies as world leader in WWII. C: Orson Welles. DOC 116m. V

Finger of Guilt 1956 British ★★★½ When a film director (Basehart) receives increasingly menacing letters from a mysterious stranger claiming to be his lover, his career and marriage are jeopardized. Gripping thriller directed (pseudononymously) by blacklisted Losey. (a.k.a. *The Intimate Stranger*) C: Richard Basehart, Mary Murphy, Constance Cummings, Roger Livesey, Mervyn Johns, Faith Brook. D: Joseph Losey. CRI 85m.

Finger on the Trigger 1965 ★★½ After the Civil War, soldiers from the North and the South battle Indians for buried treasure. Well-played action. C: Rory Calhoun, James Philbrook, Todd Martin, Silvia Solar, Brad Talbot. D: Sidney Pink. ACT 89m. V

Finger Points, The 1931 ★★★½ Impoverished reporter Barthelmess accepts hush money from sharp gangland czar. Lumpy scripting but potently presented. Gable shows early star quality. C: Richard Barthelmess, Fay Wray, Regis Toomey, Robert Elliott, Clark Gable, Oscar Apfel. D: John Francis Dillon. CRI 88m.

Fingerman 1955 ★★★ Ex-con (Lovejoy) helps federal agents capture powerful crime boss (Tucker) in standard underworld thriller, which sports good performances. Cult star Carey a standout as nutso hitman. C: Frank Lovejoy, Forrest Tucker, Peggie Castle, Timothy Carey, Glenn Gordon, Evelynne Eaton. D: Harold Schuster. DRA 82m. V

Fingers at the Window 1942 ★★ Actor and girlfriend (Ayres and Day) on the trail of a string of ax murders. Dated mystery, creepy title. C: Lew Ayres, Laraine Day, Basil Rathbone, Walter Kingsford, Miles Mander, James Flavin. D: Charles Lederer. CRI 80m.

Fingers 1978 ★★★★ Keitel is compelling as concert pianist drawn into underworld by gangster father. He and Brown make the most out of unsympathetic characters. Strong direction by scriptwriter James Toback with unsettling sex-and-violence subtext. C: Harvey Keitel, Jim Brown, Tisa Farrow, Michael Gazzo, Tanya Roberts, Danny Aiello. D: James Toback. CRI [R] 91m. V

Finian's Rainbow 1968 ★★★½ Forties musical fantasy with dated script, but lovely score makes lumbering movie as leprechaun Steele turns bigot Wynn into a black man while Astaire searches for a pot of gold. Clark fetchingly sings "Look to the Rainbow," "That Ole Devil Moon," and "How Are Things in Glocca Morra," in her film debut. C: Fred Astaire, Petula Clark, Tommy Steele, Al Freeman, Jr., Don Francks, Keenan Wynn. D: Francis Coppola. MUS [G] 145m. V

Finish Line 1989 ★★ Brolin boys as father and son confronting the steroid craze in high school athletics. Makes its point but not especially interesting. C: James Brolin, Josh Brolin, Mariska Hargitay. D: John Nicolella. DRA 100m. TVM V

Finishing School 1933 ★★★★ Upper-class young woman runs into opposition from her mother when she brings her fiancé (a struggling intern) home. Intriguing family drama. C: George Nicholls, Jr., Frances Dee, Bruce Cabot, Ginger Rogers, Beulah Bondi, Billie Burke, John Halliday. D: Wanda Tuchock. DRA 73m. V

Finnegan Begin Again 1985 ★★★★ Two losers caught in luckless relationships meet on bus, then forge unusual friendship. Charming, if slight, comedy/drama benefits immensely from two stars at top of their form. C: Mary Tyler Moore, Robert Preston, Sylvia Sidney, Sam Waterston, David Huddleston, Bob Gunton. D: Joan Micklin Silver. COM 105m. V

Finnegan's Wake 1965 ★★★★ Dublin man visualizes his own death and his boozy friends who attend the wake. This ambitious attempt at filming one of the most unfilmable novels uses stock footage, animation, and live-action footage—and succeeds. Non-Joyce fans should proceed with caution, however. C: Page Johnson, Martin J. Kelly, Jane Reilly, Peter Haskell. D: Mary Ellen Bute. DRA 97m.

Fiorile 1994 Italian ★★★★ Multigenerational saga of a family whose past includes romance, the Napoleonic Wars, and a chest of gold. Beautifully mounted by the Taviani Brothers (*Night of the Shooting Stars*), with a real fairy-tale feeling. (a.k.a. *Wild Flowers*) DRA V

Fire! 1977 ★★★ An escaping convict starts a diversionary forest fire, putting residents in danger; where there's smoke, there's a very excited member of the star-studded cast. Effective disaster extravaganza. C: Ernest Borgnine, Vera Miles, Patty Duke Astin, Lloyd Nolan, Donna Mills, Alex Cord. D: Earl Bellamy. ACT 100m. TVM V

Fire Alarm 1932 ★★ A fireman discovers that the pretty typist he is wooing is no pushover. C: Johnny Mack Brown, Noel Frances. D: Karl Brown. DRA 68m. V

Fire and Ice 1983 ★★½ The beautiful warriors take on a ghastly collection of ghouls in prehistoric times. Shot in "Rotoscope" (which uses live models as armatures for the animation), this Bakshi production features graphic design by industry legend Frank Frazetta and a script by two popular comic book writers, Roy Thomas and Gerry Conway. D: Ralph Bakshi. SFI [PG] 81m. V

Fire & Ice 1987 German ★★★ Boy meets girl on the ski slopes. Damp storyline gets lift from action-packed ski footage. C: Suzy Chaffee, John Eaves. D: Willy Bogner. DRA [PG] 83m. V

Fire and Rain 1989 ★★★½ A Delta Airlines flight goes down at the Dallas/Fort Worth Airport. Better-than-average disaster film features the usual familiar faces in cameos. C: Charles Haid, John Beck, Tom Bosley, Penny Fuller, Robert Guillaume, David Hasselhoff, Susan Ruttan, Angie Dickinson. D: Jerry Jameson. DRA 89m. TVM V

Fire and Sword 1985 ★★★ Costumer about an English knight torn between love for an Irish princess and love of country. Swashbuckling adventure. C: Peter Firth, Leigh Lawson. D: Veith Von Furstenberg. ACT 84m. V

Fire Down Below 1957 British ★★★½ Familiar melodrama of tramp steamer crew (Mitchum and Lemmon) vying for affections of devious charmer (Hayworth). Powerhouse cast and beautiful Caribbean locations can't hoist only slightly above-average plot. C: Rita Hayworth, Robert Mitchum, Jack Lemmon, Herbert Lom. D: Robert Parrish. DRA 116m. V

Fire Festival 1985 *See* **Himatsuri**

Fire, Ice and Dynamite 1990 German ★ Wealthy man fakes his own death to save his fortune, then leaves instructions for a daredevil race to determine his heir. This film is long on stunts and explosives, but short on real excitement. C: Roger Moore, Shari Belafonte. D: Willy Bogner. ACT [PG] 107m. V

Fire in the Dark 1991 ★★★½ Dukakis does well with grim drama of elderly woman reluctantly giving up home to live with smothering daughter Wagner. Doesn't go much beyond parameters of TV drama, but has its touching moments. C: Olympia Dukakis, Lindsay Wagner, Jean Stapleton, Joan Leslie. D: David Jones. DRA 96m.

Fire in the Night 1985 ★★★ Beautiful, beguiling woman has trouble with an old-money Southern family when she pries into their sordid past. Small-town atmosphere does little to save this trite melodrama. C: John Martin, Graciela Casillas. D: John Soet. DRA 89m. v

Fire in the Sky 1993 ★★ Travis Wilson's account of his attempts to convince skeptics that his temporary disappearance was the result of alien abduction. Decent premise gone awry, due mostly to the supposed veracity of the tale. From Wilson's book *The Walton Experience.* C: D.B. Sweeney, Robert Patrick, Craig Sheffer, Peter Berg, James Garner. D: Robert Lieberman. SFI [PG-13] 107m. v

Fire in the Stone, The 1985 ★★★½ Three Australian boys band together and try to tolerate each other's company during search for stolen jewels in this disarming juvenile adventure tale. C: Paul Smith, Linda Hartley. D: Gary Conway. FAM/ACT 97m.

Fire in the Straw 1943 French ★★★½ Backstage story of a struggling actor who's envious of his son's sudden fame in the movies. Well-acted melodrama. C: Lucien Baroux, Orane Demazis, Jean Fuller. D: Jean Benoit-Levy. DRA 89m.

Fire Maidens of Outer Space 1955 British ★★ Low-budget schlock pits astronauts against spacewomen. C: Anthony Dexter, Susan Shaw, Paul Carpenter, Harry Fowler, Sydney Tafler. D: Cy Roth. SFI 80m.

Fire Next Time, The 1993 ★★★½ A Louisiana family (Nelson, Bedelia, and children) in the near future face trials as they travel to Canada seeking to escape from pollution and global warming. Harrowing, realistic, believably acted. C: Craig T. Nelson, Bonnie Bedelia, Richard Farnsworth. D: Tom McLoughlin. DRA 180m.

Fire Over England 1937 British ★★★½ The mighty Spanish Armada attempts to defeat Queen Elizabeth's royal navy in 1588. Lavish pageantry and appealing leads. C: Laurence Olivier, Flora Robson, Leslie Banks, Raymond Massey, Vivien Leigh. D: William K. Howard. DRA 89m. v

Fire Sale 1977 ★★ Frenzied, black comedy about department store owner and sons. C: Alan Arkin, Rob Reiner, Vincent Gardenia, Anjanette Comer, Kay Medford, Sid Caesar, Barbara Dana, Alex Rocco, Byron Stewart, Richard Libertini, Augusta Dabney. D: Alan Arkin. COM [PG] 88m.

Fire! Trapped on the 37th Floor 1991 ★★½ A number of people are trapped when The First Interstate Bank Building, one of L.A.'s tallest, becomes a blazing inferno. Flickering action. ACT

Fire with Fire 1986 ★★★ Sheffer is locked up in reform school; Madsen is emotionally imprisoned at a Catholic girls school across the way. Logistics aside, their love is inevitable. Low-key and pleasant, if predictable. Based on a true story. C: Craig Sheffer, Virginia Madsen, Jon Polito, Kate Reid. D: Duncan Gibbins. DRA 103m. v

Fire Within, The 1958 *See* **Time to Love and a Time to Die, A**

Fire Within, The 1963 French ★★★★½ An alcoholic writer (Ronet) contemplates suicide. Gripping, downbeat character study; one of Malle's best films. C: Maurice Ronet, Lena Skerla, Yvonne Clech, Jeanne Moreau. D: Louis Malle. DRA 108m. v

Fireback 1978 ★★★ When his wife is abducted by organized crime, a Vietnam vet goes haywire. Formula actioner with good work by Harrison. C: Richard Harrison, Bruce Baron. ACT 90m. v

Fireball 500 1966 ★★ Hot-rodder (Avalon) unknowingly transports moonshine during cross-country road race. For Avalon fans. C: Frankie Avalon, Annette Funicello, Fabian, Chill Wills, Harvey Lembeck, Julie Parrish. D: William Asher. ACT 92m.

Fireball Forward 1972 ★★★ A tough-as-nails general turns a company of WWII misfits into a crack unit. C: Ben Gazzara, Eddie Albert, Ricardo Montalban, Dana Elcar. D: Marvin Chomsky. ACT 100m. v

Fireball, The 1950 ★★★½ Little orphan (Rooney) runs away from school headed by priest (O'Brien), becomes roller derby champ until polio interrupts and teaches him lesson. Obvious, contrived, but saved by professional direction and energetic acting and action sequences. C: Mickey Rooney, Pat O'Brien, Beverly Tyler, Marilyn Monroe, Milburn Stone, Glenn Corbett. D: Tay Garnett. DRA 84m.

Fireballs 1990 ★★½ Love ignites in the firehouse when the new firefighters are women. C: Goren Kalezik, Mike Strapko. D: Mike Strapko. COM 89m. v

Firebird, The 1934 ★★★ Handsome love 'em and leave 'em actor is found murdered. Well acted, not so well written. C: Verree Teasdale, Ricardo Cortez, Lionel Atwill, Anita Louise, C. Aubrey Smith. D: Gilbert Miller. DRA 75m.

Firebird 2015 A.D. 1981 ★★ The gas shortage in the 21st century is so severe that cars are rounded up and demolished by the government in this futurist fantasy. A *Mad Max* rip off; if you like this, see the real thing. C: Darren McGavin, Doug McClure, Mary Beth Rubens. D: David Robertson. SFI [PG] 97m. v

Firebirds 1990 ★★½ Military hardware saga features helicopters destroying everything within a 50-mile radius of the target, just to be safe. *Top Gun* clone, stressing choppers over beleaguered actors who should have mutinied. C: Nicolas Cage, Tommy Lee Jones, Sean Young, Mary Ellen Trainor. D: David Green. ACT 86m. v

Firecracker 1971 ★★ Karate flick pits female martial artist against gang that killed her sister. Tedious. C: Jillian Kesner, Darby Hilton. ACT [R] 83m. v

Firecreek 1968 ★★★½ When farmer Stewart is elected sheriff of a small town, his inexperience is put to the test by a gang of outlaws led by Fonda. The performances are fine, as one would expect, but story runs out of gas. C: James Stewart, Henry Fonda, Inger Stevens, Gary Lockwood, Dean Jagger, Ed Begley, Jay C. Flippen, Jack Elam, Barbara Luna. D: Vincent McEveety. WST 104m. V

Firefight 1987 ★★★½ A maniac and his gang of cutthroats try to take over what is left of America after a Soviet nuclear attack. Only his ex-wife can muster the forces to stop him. C: James Pfeiffer, Janice Carraher. D: Scott Pfeiffer. ACT 89m. V

Firefly, The 1937 ★★★★ Lovely, gorgeously produced operetta about French spies during the Napoleonic war. Outstanding Rudolf Friml score includes "Donkey Serenade," well sung by Jones to MacDonald at her most charming. C: Jeanette MacDonald, Allan Jones, Warren William, Billy Gilbert, Henry Daniell, Douglass Dumbrille, George Zucco. D: Robert Z. Leonard. MUS 131m. V

Firefox 1982 ★★½ Eastwood thriller of a retired pilot assigned to liberate a high-tech aircraft from the Soviets and fly it to the West. Slow pacing at first offset later by good aerial action and battle sequences. C: Clint Eastwood, Freddie Jones, David Huffman, Warren Clarke. D: Clint Eastwood. ACT [PG] 136m. V

Firehawk 1992 ★★ Surviving a helicopter crash in Vietnam, the crew suspects that a traitor, not the Viet Cong, may have sabotaged their chopper. Run-of-the-mill action adventure. C: Martin Kove, Matt Salinger. D: Cirio H. Santiago. DRA 92m. V

Firehead 1991 ★★★½ Russian with the power to start fires at will attacks U.S. high-tech weapons factories, and becomes unwitting pawn in plot to start WWIII. C: Martin Landau, Christopher Plummer, Chris Lemmon. D: Peter Yuval. ACT 88m. V

Firehouse 1972 ★★★½ Brave rookie fireman (Roundtree) battles flames in buildings and racism in the firehouse in this pilot for TV series. Dramatically potent script overcomes cheap look. C: Richard Roundtree, Vince Edwards, Andrew Duggan, Richard Jaeckel, Val Avery, Paul Le Mat. D: Alex March. ACT [R] 73m. TVM V

Fireman, Save My Child 1932 ★★★ Brown is a firefighter whose fantasies of playing baseball get in the way of his day job. Not his funniest picture, but Brown has a few good turns. Fine for younger viewers. C: Joe E. Brown, Evalyn Knapp, Lillian Bond, Guy Kibbee, Virginia Sale. D: Lloyd Bacon. COM 67m.

Fireman Save My Child 1954 ★★★ Fire station run by loony Jones and assistant Hackett gets a new engine in turn-of-the-century San Francisco. Some fun songs and appropriate mayhem in this musical farce. C: Spike Jones, Buddy Hackett, Hugh O'Brian, Adele Jergens. D: Leslie Goodwins. COM 80m.

Firemen's Ball, The 1968 Czech ★★★ Party for retiring fire chief turns into succession of black comic vignettes. Obvious political allegory, often heavy-handed and cruel, but making pertinent observations on human behavior. Forman's last Czech film before coming to the U.S. C: Jan Vostrcil, Josef Svet, Vaclav Stockel, Maria Jezkova. D: Milos Forman. COM 73m. V

Firepower 1979 British ★★★½ Caribbean beachfront settings enhance this above-average thriller about a beautiful woman (Loren) seeking revenge for the murder of her husband. The plot seems needlessly complex, but the star-studded cast, glamorous locales, and constant explosions hold attention. C: Sophia Loren, James Coburn, O.J. Simpson, Eli Wallach. D: Michael Winner. ACT [R] 104m. V

Fires on the Plain 1959 Japanese ★★★★ WWII Japanese regiment struggles to make it through the Pacific campaign's final days. Ichikawa came to international prominence with this uncompromisingly clear-eyed look at war's horrors; acting, photography, music first-rate. C: Eiji Funakoshi, Osamu Takizawa, Mickey Curtis. D: Kon Ichikawa. DRA 105m. V

Fires Were Started 1943 British ★★★★½ Thrilling story of firemen battling blazes during the Blitz. Poet and documentarian Jennings brings a painter's eye to this material, using a non-professional cast (including many firefighters) and realistic re-enactments in his only feature-length film. C: George Gravett, Philip Dickson, Fred Griffiths, Loris Rey. D: Humphrey Jennings. DRA 80m.

Fires Within 1991 ★★★½ Political prisoner, released from Cuba, reunites with his family in Miami and finds their lives have changed during his absence. Intriguing idea, attractive cast, but unfulfilled screenplay. C: Jimmy Smits, Greta Scacchi, Vincent D'Onofrio. D: Gillian Armstrong. DRA [R] 90m. V

Firestarter 1984 ★★★ A young girl (Barrymore) can start fires with her mind, and the government wants her. The pyrotechnics are effective, and the story (by Stephen King) has a nice message about the importance of family. Unfortunately, rather predictable. C: David Keith, Drew Barrymore, George C. Scott, Martin Sheen, Heather Locklear, Art Carney, Louise Fletcher, Freddie Jones. D: Mark L. Lester. HOR [R] 113m. V

Firewalker 1986 ★★ Mercenaries (Norris and Gossett) embark on a quest to uncover Aztec loot. Norris takes aim at the comedy/adventure realm and winds up shooting nothing but blanks. Norris fans will be disappointed. C: Chuck Norris, Lou Gossett, Jr., Melody Anderson, Will Sampson. D: J. Lee Thompson. ACT [PG] 106m. V

Firing Line, The 1991 ★★★ Mercenary is hired to fight Sandinista-type rebels, but the tables turn when he decides to join their cause and help bring down the corrupt government. Decent action film. C: Reb Brown, Shannon Tweed. D: John Gale. ACT 93m. V

Firm, The 1993 ★★★★ Up-from-nothing lawyer (Cruise) lands dream job with small prestigious firm that has some skeletons in its wood-paneled closets. Full-blown Hollywood treatment of popular Grisham novel. Enjoyable suspense. C: Tom Cruise, Gene Hackman, Jeanne Tripplehorn, Holly Hunter, Ed Harris, Hal Holbrook, Wilford Brimley, David Strathairn, Gary Busey. D: Sydney Pollack. CRI [R] 154m. V

First Blood 1982 ★★★½ Stallone's first appearance as Rambo, a former Green Beret who was tortured in Vietnam and must now defend himself against a small-town cop (Dennehy) in the Pacific Northwest forests—his new 'Nam. The movie is jingoistic and improbable, but a must-see for fans of slick action adventures. C: Sylvester Stallone, Richard Crenna, Brian Dennehy, David Caruso. D: Ted Kotcheff. ACT [R] 96m. V

First Comes Courage 1943 ★★★½ WWII propaganda film concerns a Norwegian agent (Oberon) who poses as a collaborator to obtain intelligence from unsuspecting Nazis. Okay war espionage drama, if a bit somber in spots. C: Merle Oberon, Brian Aherne, Carl Esmond, Fritz Leiber, Erik Rolf. D: Dorothy Arzner. DRA 88m.

First Date 1989 Taiwanese ★★★½ Young man experiences growing pains in late-'50s Taiwan. Quiet, occasionally bullseye comedy also amusingly touches on Americanization of Far East. C: Chang Shi, Li Xing Wen. D: Peter Wang. COM 90m.

First Deadly Sin, The 1980 ★★★★ Sinatra's wife is dying (Dunaway in a hospital bed throughout), but first he has to track down a psychotic killer who is roaming New York. Takes its time, but worth it. Adapted from Lawrence Sanders' best-selling novel. C: Frank Sinatra, Faye Dunaway, David Dukes, Brenda Vaccaro, James Whitmore. D: Brian G. Hutton. DRA [R] 112m. V

First Family 1980 ★★★ Washington satire with Newhart as the West's most inept leader saddled with extremely neurotic clan. Redeemed by plethora of seasoned comedians and some on-target political gags. C: Bob Newhart, Gilda Radner, Madeline Kahn, Richard Benjamin, Bob Dishy. D: Buck Henry. COM 100m. V

First Great Train Robbery, The 1979 *See* **Great Train Robbery, The**

First Lady 1937 ★★★★ At the urging of his determined spouse, an upright Secretary of State enters the race for the presidency against an underhanded judge. Witty dialog is adapted from the political satire by George S. Kaufman and Katherine Dayton. C: Kay Francis, Anita Louise, Verree Teasdale, Preston Foster, Walter Connolly, Victor Jory, Louise Fazenda. D: Stanley Logan. COM 82m.

First Legion, The 1951 ★★★½ Odd, surprisingly dignified soap about a paralyzed priest who suddenly walks, and skeptical priest (Boyer) who must determine whether miracle has happened. Mushy ending, but very stylishly told; excellent acting, especially from Boyer. C: Charles Boyer, William Demarest, Lyle Bettger, Barbara Rush, Leo G. Carroll. D: Douglas Sirk. DRA 86m. V

First Love 1939 ★★★★ Durbin is enchanting in this Cinderella story about an orphaned waif living miserably in rich uncle's house till Prince Charming Stack notices her. Highlight is star's first screen kiss, which made headlines in its day. C: Deanna Durbin, Robert Stack, Helen Parrish, Eugene Pallette, Leatrice Joy, Marcia Jones, Frank Jenks. D: Henry Koster. DRA 84m.

First Love 1970 British ★★★½ Graceful and touching, if minor, tale of young lovers. Schell's direction shows sympathy for his talented cast. Slow, but affecting. C: Maximilian Schell, John Moulder Brown, Dominique Sanda, John Osborne. D: Maximilian Schell. DRA [R] 90m. V

First Love 1977 ★★ Director Darling's tale of college lovers Katt and Dey whose relationship is threatened by the girl's affair with an older gentleman. Unsatisfying despite its stars' innocent appeal and the story's scandalous undercurrent. C: William Katt, Susan Dey, John Heard, Beverly D'Angelo, Robert Loggia. D: Joan Darling. DRA [R] 92m. V

First Man into Space 1959 British ★★★ The first man into space returns to Earth and transforms into an evil, bloodthirsty monster. Manages to entertain despite its low budget and uneven acting. Owes much to the classic *The Creeping Unknown*. C: Marshall Thompson, Marla Landi, Bill Edwards. D: Robert Day. SFI 78m. V

First Men in the Moon 1964 British ★★★½ Outstanding Ray Harryhausen effects enliven this tale of a Victorian era expedition to the moon. From the H.G. Wells story. C: Edward Judd, Martha Hyer, Lionel Jeffries, Erik Chitty. D: Nathan Juran. SFI 103m. V

First Monday in October 1981 ★★★½ Prophetic comedy/drama from Lawrence and Lee Broadway play imagines first woman on the Supreme Court (Clayburgh) as a conservative in conflict with liberal justice Matthau. Bogs itself down in verbiage, but enjoyable for interplay of stars. C: Walter Matthau, Jill Clayburgh, Barnard Hughes, James Stephens. D: Ronald Neame. COM [R] 99m. V

First Name: Carmen 1983 French ★★★½ Clever, risqué, very loose adaptation of Bizet's *Carmen* shows title femme fatale as a lovely crook who incites passion in the heart of a cop. Godard appears as her film director uncle, a patient in a mental hospital. Best appreciated by Godard devotees. C: Maruschka Detmers, Jacques Bonnaffe, Myriem Roussel,

Christophe Odent, Jean-Luc Godard. D: Jean-Luc Godard. DRA 85m. V

First Nudie Musical, The 1976 ★★★ Contrived, silly nonsense about movie studio owner driven to producing pornographic musical with such attractions as "dancing dildoes." Goes limp after first 20 minutes. C: Bruce Kimmel, Stephen Nathan, Cindy Williams, Bruce Kimmel, Diana Canova, Alexandra Morgan, Leslie Ackerman. D: Mark Haggard. COM [R] 100m.

First of the Few, The 1942 *See* **Spitfire**

First Olympics: Athens 1896, The 1984 ★★★★ Reminiscent of *Chariots of Fire*, the stirring story of the organizers and promoters of the first modern Olympics. Engrossing and informative. C: Louis Jourdan, David Ogden Stiers, Honor Blackman, Angela Lansbury. D: Alvin Rakoff. DRA 280m.

First Power, The 1990 ★★★ Cop Phillips tries to stop a killer powered by evil forces. Excellent chases and fights, but that's all. C: Lou Diamond Phillips, Tracy Griffith, Jeff Kober. D: Robert Resnikoff. HOR [R] 98m. V

First Spaceship on Venus 1960 German ★★ Farcical German sci-fi effort about an exploratory trip to Venus. Dated and unintentionally funny. C: Yoko Tani, Oldrich Lukes, Ignacy Machowski, Julius Ongewe. D: Kurt Maetzig. SFI 78m. V

First Steps 1985 ★★½ A woman paralyzed in a car wreck is left to the care of a skillful specialist, who dedicates himself to her recovery. Emotionally uplifting at times. C: Judd Hirsch, Amy Steel, Kim Darby. D: Sheldon Larry. DRA 104m.

First Teacher, The 1965 Soviet ★★★★ Ex-soldier opens school in small town; after he falls for local girl, disaster strikes. Konchalovsky's first feature is a taut study of clashing mores. C: Bolot Beishenaliev, Natalia Arinbasarova. D: Andrei Mikhalkov-Konczlovsky. DRA 98m.

First Texan, The 1956 ★★½ Hero Sam Houston spurs Texas to victory in the war against Mexico. Nice job by veteran McCrea. C: Joel McCrea, Felicia Farr, Jeff Morrow, Wallace Ford. D: Byron Haskin. WST 82m.

First 36 Hours of Dr. Durant, The 1975 ★★½ Surgical resident's first day and a half on call at the hospital. What it takes to be a doc—in a dose that's effective and provocative. C: Scott Hylands, Katherine Helmond, Dana Andrews. D: Alexander Singer. DRA 72m.

First Time, The 1952 ★★★ Newlyweds Cummings and Hale face joys and financial woes, along with a few predictable moments of humor caring for their newborn child. Director Tashlin's fast-paced style moves the thin plot along. Good family viewing. C: Robert Cummings, Barbara Hale, Jeff Donnell, Mona Barrie, Cora Witherspoon. D: Frank Tashlin. COM 89m.

First Time, The 1969 ★★ Teenager tries (and tries) to lose his virginity. Clumsy mix of comedy and drama manages to vulgarize what should be touching story of boy's coming-of-age. C: Jacqueline Bisset, Wes Stern, Rick Kelman. D: James Neilson. DRA 90m. V

First Time, The 1983 ★★★ Virginal student's romantic escapades, as assisted by his roommate and a campus psychology professor. A little known sleeper, and a surprisingly amusing college comedy. C: Tim Choate, Krista Errickson, Marshall Efron, Wendy Fulton. D: Charlie Loventhal. COM [R] 96m. V

First to Fight 1967 ★★★ After being treated like a hero while on leave, a soldier cracks when he returns to his unit. Intriguing psychological slant on WWII with an impressive cast. C: Chad Everett, Marilyn Devin, Dean Jagger, Bobby Troup, Claude Akins, Gene Hackman. D: Christian Nyby. ACT 97m.

First Traveling Saleslady, The 1956 ★★ Rogers is an enterprising capitalist who heads out West with a bundle full of corsets to peddle. Plodding comedy notable mostly for an appearance by budding actor and future Oscar-winning director Eastwood. C: Ginger Rogers, Barry Nelson, Carol Channing, David Brian, James Arness, Clint Eastwood. D: Arthur Lubin. COM 92m.

First Turn-On, The 1983 ★★½ Four young people get trapped in a cave and, being two boys and two girls, decide to use the opportunity to discover their sexuality. C: Sheila Kennedy, Michael Sanville. D: Michael Herz. COM [R] 84m. V

First Yank into Tokyo 1945 ★★★ Plastic surgery enables an Army Air Corps flier to pass as a Japanese soldier and rescue an interned American. Dated, low-budget WWII fare. C: Tom Neal, Barbara Hale, Marc Cramer, Richard Loo, Keye Luke, Leonard Strong, Benson Fong. D: Gordon Douglas. DRA 82m. V

First Year, The 1932 ★★★½ The struggles of incompatible newlyweds make up most of this charming film's episodic plot, with Gaynor dissatisfied at Farrell's small-town preferences. The two stars have a potent chemistry. C: Janet Gaynor, Charles Farrell, Minna Gombell, Dudley Digges. D: William K. Howard. DRA 80m.

First, You Cry 1978 ★★★★ Moore gives a powerful dramatic performance in well-made biography of journalist Betty Rollin's mastectomy and her struggle to go on with her life. Star does admirable job of capturing the emotional phases of cancer: denial, anger, grief, acceptance. C: Mary Tyler Moore, Anthony Perkins, Richard Crenna, Jennifer Warren, Florence Eldridge, Don Johnson. D: George Schaefer. DRA 100m. TVM

Firstborn 1984 ★★★ Violent family affair from director Apted with Garr as an uncertain divorced mom who unwisely admits an evil beau into her home. A fine cast betrayed by a misguided script. C: Teri Garr, Peter Weller, Christopher Collet, Corey Haim, Robert Downey Jr. D: Michael Apted. DRA [PG-13] 103m. v

Fish Called Wanda, A 1988 ★★★★½ Spirited farce involves Kline and Curtis as lovers attempting to pull off heist by manipulating attorney Cleese and double-crossing partner Palin. Hilarious black comedy that constantly surprises; Kline won Oscar for Best Supporting Actor but the whole cast is razor sharp. C: John Cleese, Jamie Lee Curtis, Kevin Kline, Michael Palin. D: Charles Crichton. COM [R] 108m. v

Fish Hawk 1979 Canadian ★★½ Mawkish story of a down-and-out alcoholic Native American who befriends a lonely farmhand. So-so and not much more. C: Will Sampson, Charlie Fields, Geoffrey Bowes, Mary Pirle. D: Donald Shebib. FAM/DRA [G] 95m. v

Fish that Saved Pittsburgh, The 1979 ★★½ Quintessential bad '70s comedy involves a basketball team that uses astrology, woefully dated costumes, and music to win story-climaxing Big Game. Cast of big comedy and basketball names. C: Julius ("Dr.J") Erving, Stockard Channing, Jonathan Winters, Flip Wilson. D: Gilbert Moses. COM [PG] 104m. v

Fisher King, The 1991 ★★★★½ A former shock-radio host (Bridges), fallen on hard times, takes up with a street eccentric (Williams) who has his own sorrowful past. Colorful and fascinating, and as funny as it is sensitive. An elaborate, quirky charmer. Ruehl won Oscar as Best Supporting Actress. C: Robin Williams, Jeff Bridges, Amanda Plummer, Mercedes Ruehl, Michael Jeter. D: Terry Gilliam. DRA [R] 138m. v

F.I.S.T. 1978 ★★★ Director Jewison tries to get the most out of this tale of ruthless power politics in the teamster's union. Unfortunately, co-writer Stallone took the Hoffa-figure role for himself and managed to flatten honest efforts by the rest of the cast. C: Sylvester Stallone, Rod Steiger, Peter Boyle, Melinda Dillon, David Huffman. D: Norman Jewison. DRA [PG] 145m. v

Fist Fighter 1989 ★★½ The Fist Fighter goes to Central America to avenge the murder of his friend. Recycled junk. C: George Rivero, Edward Albert, Brenda Bakke. D: Frank Zuniga. ACT [R] 99m.

Fist in His Pocket 1966 Italian ★★★★★ A classic study of madness. The protagonist, superbly portrayed by Castel, murders his mother, drowns his younger brother, and has an unconsummated affair with his sister. Bellocchio's authoritative debut never stints in its disturbing presentation of a deranged family. C: Lou Castel, Paola Pitagora, Marino Mase, Liliana Gerace, Pier Luigi Troglio. D: Marco Bellochio. DRA 105m.

Fist of Honor 1992 ★★ A boxer seeks to avenge the death of his fiancée, a bad cop does a lady wrong, and the mob tries to take control of a city afire in this bone-crunching exercise in stupidity. C: Joey House, Sam Jones, Bubba Smith, Harry Guardino. D: Richard Pepin. ACT [R] 100m. v

Fist of Steel 1993 ★★★½ Tension mounts as a champion gladiator must risk his life to escape from a syndicate killer. C: Cynthia Khan, Dale Cook. D: Irvin Johnson. ACT 97m. v

Fist of Vengeance ★★★ A loyal Chinese officer faces off with an evil society and its hired samurai. C: Shoji Karada, Lu Pi Chen. ACT 90m.

Fistful of Dollars, A 1964 Italian ★★★★ First of Leone's three great spaghetti-Westerns (including *The Good, the Bad and the Ugly* and *For a Few Dollars More*). Eastwood as the "man with no name" made his name in movies with his portrayal of the unshaven cigar-smoking gunfighter. C: Clint Eastwood, Gian Maria Volonte, Marianne Koch, Mario Brega. D: Sergio Leone. WST [R] 101m. v

Fistful of Dynamite, A 1972 *See* **Duck, You Sucker**

Fists of Blood 1987 ★★½ With friend dead and girlfriend kidnapped, Jason Blade wields his marital arts justice. C: Eddie Stazak. D: Brian Trenchard-Smith. ACT 90m.

Fists of Bruce Lee ★★★½ Two master martial artists, one assassin, one cop, fight to the death in this action-packed battle against the mob. C: Bruce Li, Lo Lieh. ACT 90m.

Fists of Dragons 1969 Chinese ★★ Blood and mayhem, unhampered by any plot. For fans. D: Yeh Yung. ACT 92m.

Fists of Fury 1971 ★★★ Lee's first Hong Kong movie is about a young rural kung fu fighter who becomes a symbol of honor. Violent, formless martial arts production made palatable by Lee's flying acrobatics. C: Bruce Lee, Maria Yi, James Tien, Han Ying Chieh, Miao Ker Hsiu, Robert Baker. D: Lo Wei. ACT [R] 102m. v

Fists of Fury 2 1980 ★★½ Bruce Li vs. the Evil Organization; they try to kill him in a number of nasty ways, then go after his mother. Typically violent kung fu flick. C: Bruce Li. D: To Lo Po. ACT [R] 90m.

Fit to Kill 1993 ★★★ It's a tough job to protect an irreplaceable piece of ice, but it's up to two talented special agents to do it. C: Dona Speir, Julie Strain, Roberta Vasquez. D: Andy Sidaris. ACT [R] 94m. v

Fitzcarraldo 1982 ★★★★ Visually stunning tale of one man's obsessive efforts to drag a steamship over Amazonian mountains with the help of the natives. The herculean task of making the film is documented in the equally fascinating *Burden of Dreams.* Unusual but very satisfying film. C: Klaus Kinski, Claudia Cardinale, Jose Lewgoy, Miguel Angel Fuentes. D: Werner Herzog. DRA [PG] 150m. v

Fitzwilly 1967 ★★★½ Ingenious butler (Van Dyke) decides to organize a burglary ring to keep his grande dame employer

(Evans) afloat. Notable for an excellent supporting cast (including Feldon and Waterston), but could have been a lot funnier. C: Dick Van Dyke, Barbara Feldon, Edith Evans, John McGiver, Harry Townes, John Fiedler, Norman Fell, Cecil Kellaway, Sam Waterston. D: Delbert Mann. COM 102m.

Five 1951 ★★ The five survivors of a nuclear holocaust talk it out and do each other in. Outdated, pretentiously talky '50s atomic hysteria film with only relief from the melodrama the camera shots panning to the outdoors. C: William Phipps, Susan Douglas, James Anderson, Charles Lampkin, Earl Lee. D: Arch Oboler. DRA 93m.

Five Against the House 1955 ★★★★ Crooks band together to execute complicated robbery of Reno casino. Crackerjack caper film boasts good ensemble performances, nice location photography, and a tense climactic heist. Entertaining winner. C: Guy Madison, Kim Novak, Kerwin Mathews, William Conrad, Alvy Moore. D: Phil Karlson. DRA 84m.

Five and Ten 1931 ★★★½ A dime-store heiress (Davies) rejects her ardent suitor (Howard)—until he marries. Glossy melodrama, with a flashy performance by Davies. (a.k.a. *Daughter of Luxury*) C: Marion Davies, Leslie Howard, Richard Bennett. D: Robert Z. Leonard. DRA 88m.

Five Angles on Murder 1950 *See* **Woman in Question, The**

Five Branded Women 1960 ★★½ Quintet of Yugoslavian women, disgraced for mixing with Nazis, redeem themselves by becoming underground fighters. Dreadful misuse of extraordinary cast, sloppy storytelling. C: Van Heflin, Silvana Mangano, Jeanne Moreau, Vera Miles, Barbara Geddes, Richard Basehart, Harry Guardino, Carla Gravina, Alex Nicol, Steve Forrest. D: Martin Ritt. DRA 106m.

Five Came Back 1939 ★★★★ Engrossing jungle survival tale concerns band of passengers who must fight off headhunters, and each other, when their small plane crashes in the Amazon. Vivid characterizations, including rare dramatic role for Ball, add up to solid entertainment in still sturdy '30s actioner. C: Chester Morris, Lucille Ball, Wendy Barrie, John Carradine, Allen Jenkins, Joseph Calleia, C. Aubrey Smith, Patric Knowles. D: John Farrow. ACT 75m. V

5 Card Stud 1968 ★★½ One by one, the members of a lynching party meet their maker. Star-studded cast distinguishes this otherwise mediocre western. C: Dean Martin, Robert Mitchum, Inger Stevens, Roddy McDowall. D: Henry Hathaway. WST [PG] 103m. V

Five Corners 1988 ★★★½ Neighborhood anger and quirkiness in the Bronx, mid-'60s. Erratic comedy/drama has some sparkling sequences. John Patrick Shanley wrote the half bleak, half zany script. C: Jodie Foster, Tim Robbins, Todd Graff, John Turturro, Elizabeth Berridge, Rose Gregorio, Gregory Rozakis, John Seitz. D: Tony Bill. DRA [R] 92m. V

Five Day Lover 1961 French ★★★ Kept man who sleeps with his mistress's best friend has a field day hiding his secrets. Frantic, well-acted farce, still the weakest of DeBroca's trio of sex comedies. (*The Love Game* and *The Joker* are funnier.) (a.k.a. *Infidelity*) C: Jean Seberg, Micheline Presle, Jean-Pierre Cassel, Francois Perier. D: Philippe De Broca. COM 86m.

Five Days 1954 *See* **Paid to Kill**

Five Days from Home 1978 ★★½ Ex-con breaks out of prison, jeopardizing his upcoming official release date, in a desperate flight to be at the bedside of his ailing young son. Nothing special, but well intentioned. C: George Peppard, Neville Brand, Savannah Smith, Sherry Boucher, Victor Campos, Robert Donner. D: George Peppard. DRA [PG] 109m.

Five Days One Summer 1982 ★★★ An obsessive love affair between a Scottish doctor and a young woman who is not his wife. Sensitive portrait of a relationship, scenic Swiss Alps backdrop. C: Sean Connery, Betsy Brantley, Lambert Wilson, Jennifer Hilary. D: Fred Zinnemann. DRA 108m. V

Five Easy Pieces 1970 ★★★★½ A promising musician gives up on his talents and goes to work on an oil rig, but after many years the past is still with him. Fascinating, funny, sorrowful and compelling. Super Nicholson leads a fine cast. C: Jack Nicholson, Karen Black, Susan Anspach, Sally Struthers, Lois Smith. D: Bob Rafelson. DRA [R] 98m. V

Five Fighters from Shaolin ★★ Kickboxing extravaganza concerns efforts of five heroes to take back their temple from vicious nobleman. Typical. C: Chang Shen, Lung Kwan Wu. D: Ko Shu-How. ACT 88m. V

Five Finger Exercise 1962 ★★★ Weak, garbled adaptation of decent Peter Shaffer play with Russell overacting as smothering mother in love with daughter's piano teacher. C: Rosalind Russell, Jack Hawkins, Maximilian Schell, Richard Beymer, Lana Wood, Annette Gorman. D: Daniel Mann. DRA 109m.

5 Fingers 1952 ★★★★½ Fascinating spy melodrama about a valet at the British Embassy in Ankara who sells secrets to the Germans in WWII and eventually falls prey to his own double crosses. Like all Mankiewicz, a lot of intelligent talk, with an excellent Mason leading the fine cast. Based on a supposedly factual novel. C: James Mason, Danielle Darrieux, Michael Rennie, Walter Hampden, John Wengraf, Michael Pate. D: Joseph L. Mankiewicz. DRA 108m. V

Five Fingers of Death 1973 Chinese ★★½ Slimly plotted, poorly dubbed kung fu fest, as young martial artist must kick his way to becoming Chinese champion. Attractively packaged and fairly well performed. C: Lo Lieh, Wang Ping, Wang Ching-Feng. D: Cheng Chang Ho. ACT [R] 102m.

Five for Hell 1967 Italian ★★ The Dirty Dozen minus seven. Five misfits, each with a specialty unrelated to warfare, head behind enemy lines to thwart a Nazi offensive. Undistinguished, Italian-made WWII shoot-'em-up. C: Klaus Kinski, John Garko. D: Frank Kramer. ACT 88m. V

Five Gates to Hell 1959 ★★ Communist soldier (Brand) abducts two doctors and seven nurses from French Vietnam hospital, then gets more than he bargained for when they slaughter everything in sight. Clavell gives women grit and is sympathetic to Asian ways, but his direction is wanting. C: Neville Brand, Benson Fong, Shirley Knight, Ken Scott, John Morley, Dolores Michaels, Nancy Kulp, Irish McCalla. D: James Clavell. DRA 98m.

Five Golden Dragons 1967 British ★★★ An American ne'er-do-well (Cummings) in Hong Kong becomes embroiled in an international crime scheme. Too many clichés, but a great supporting cast. C: Robert Cummings, Margaret Lee, Brian Donlevy, Christopher Lee, George Raft, Dan Duryea. D: Jeremy Summers. ACT 93m. V

Five Golden Hours 1961 British ★★½ A con artist (Kovacs) worms his way into the lives of wealthy widows for fun and profit. Only occasionally amusing black comedy, but entertaining Ernie and seductive Charisse make an interesting pair. C: Ernie Kovacs, Cyd Charisse, George Sanders, Kay Hammond, Dennis Price, Finlay Currie, Ron Moody. D: Mario Zampi. COM 90m.

Five Graves to Cairo 1943 ★★★★ Crackling WWII thriller with Rommel (von Stroheim, of course) matching wits with spies in a hotbed of espionage in the Sahara. A change of pace for director Wilder who co-wrote the taut, literate script with Charles Brackett. C: Franchot Tone, Anne Baxter, Akim Tamiroff, Erich von Stroheim, Peter Van Eyck, Fortunio Bonanova. D: Billy Wilder. ACT 96m.

Five Guns West 1955 ★★★ The Confederate army dispatches five prisoners to trap a spy and waylay a stagecoach bearing Union gold. Low-budget Western; Corman's directorial debut. C: John Lund, Dorothy Malone, Touch (Mike) Connors, Jack Ingram. D: Roger Corman. WST 78m.

Five Heartbeats, The 1991 ★★★½ A '60s rhythm & blues group hits the top only to fall victim to drugs and infighting. Talented Townsend and cast. C: Robert Townsend, Michael Wright, Leon, Harry J. Lennix, Tico Wells, Diahann Carroll. D: Robert Townsend. MUS [R] 120m. V

Five Man Army, The 1970 ★★★ Quintet of ne'er-do-wells must slaughter several hundred to get their hands on half a million in gold headed for Mexican dictator. Routine spaghetti-Western lacks flair and social depth, but it's lively entertainment. C: Peter Graves, James Daly, Bud Spencer, Tetsuro Tamba, Nino Castelnuovo. D: Don Taylor. WST [PG] 107m.

Five Miles to Midnight 1962 ★★★ A man plans to fake his death so his wife can cash in a life insurance policy. Good Perkins, flimsy mystery. C: Tony Perkins, Sophia Loren, Gig Young, Jean-Pierre Aumont, Pascale Roberts. D: Anatole Litvak. CRI 110m.

Five Million Years to Earth 1968 British ★★★★ Deadly creatures from outer space are discovered buried beneath the London Underground subway system in this effective space thriller. C: James Donald, Barbara Shelley, Andrew Keir, Julian Glover, Maurice Good. D: Roy Ward Baker. SFI 98m.

Five of Me, The 1981 ★★★ Birney plays a Korean War vet and his five alter egos in this saga of a multiple-personality sufferer and the shrink who uncovers the awful source of the disorder. C: David Birney, Dee Wallace, Mitchell Ryan, John McLiam. D: Paul Wendkos. DRA 100m. TVM V

Five on the Black Hand Side 1973 ★★★½ Mother eventually follows the lead of her daughter and two sons in resisting the tyrannical ways of her husband and father, a middle-class barber. Well-intentioned African-American comedy has moments of wit and insight. C: Clarice Taylor, Leonard Jackson, Virginia Capers, D'Urville Martin, Glynn Turman, Godfrey Cambridge. D: Oscar Williams. COM [PG] 96m.

Five Pennies, The 1959 ★★★½ Soggy biography of '20s cornet player Red Nichols, enlivened by numerous standards of the period. Highlight: Armstrong and Kaye belting out "When the Saints Go Marching In." C: Danny Kaye, Barbara Bel Geddes, Tuesday Weld, Louis Armstrong, Bob Crosby, Ray Anthony, Shelley Manne, Bobby Troup. D: Melville Shavelson. MUS 117m. V

Five Star Final 1931 ★★★★½ Blistering indictment of yellow journalism, potently dished up by LeRoy. Editor is asked by paper owner to revive unsolved murder case without concern for effects on family involved. Marsh's acting is painfully stiff, but everyone else is topnotch. Remake: *Two Against the World.* C: Edward G. Robinson, H.B. Warner, Marian Marsh, George E. Stone, Ona Munson, Boris Karloff, Aline MacMahon. D: Mervyn LeRoy. DRA 89m.

Five Steps to Danger 1957 ★★★ Cold War spy yarn; a courier (Roman), carrying a coded message picks up a vacationer (Hayden), involving him in Soviet missile plot. The leads do well and the support is good, but tangled scripting and lackluster direction weigh it down. C: Ruth Roman, Sterling Hayden,

Werner Klemperer, Richard Gaines. D: Henry S. Kesler. ACT 80m.

5,000 Fingers of Dr. T, The 1953 ★★★½ Imaginative, quirky musical fantasy via Dr. Seuss which tells of a boy's nightmare about his dreaded piano teacher (Conried) who gets transformed into evil Dr. T, who forces boys to practice till they drop. Concert finale is great fun. C: Peter Lind Hayes, Mary Healy, Tommy Retting, Hans Conried. D: Roy Rowland. FAM/COM 88m.

Five Weeks in a Balloon 1962 ★★★½ Entertaining, mildly pleasant adventure film from a Jules Verne story set in 1862 about a balloon safari across Africa. Fine cast rates better than rather formulaic script. C: Red Buttons, Barbara Eden, Fabian, Cedric Hardwicke, Peter Lorre. D: Irwin Allen. FAM/ACT 101m. V

Fix, The 1984 ★★★ Trouble starts when the Feds go after some big time drug smugglers. Lots of action and suspense in this taut film. The good "B" cast does a fine job. C: Vince Edwards, Richard Jaeckel, Tony Dale, Julie Hill. D: Will Zens. ACT 95m. V

Fixed Bayonets 1951 ★★★★ A sensitive corporal must command a small infantry group protecting rear as U.S. Army withdraws through snowy pass in Korea. Admirably gritty saga, finely shot and directed; refuses to glamorize either soldiers or war. C: Richard Basehart, Gene Evans, Michael O'Shea, Richard Hylton, Craig Hill, James Dean. D: Samuel Fuller. ACT 92m.

Fixer, The 1968 ★★★★ In Tsarist Russia, a Jewish handyman (Bates) is imprisoned for the murder of a Christian child. Film is weighed down by grim and dreary prison sequences, but Bates' dignified performance does justice to acclaimed Bernard Malamud novel. C: Alan Bates, Dirk Bogarde, Georgia Brown, Hugh Griffith, Ian Holm, Jack Gilford. D: John Frankenheimer. DRA [PG-13] 132m. V

F.J. Holden, The 1977 Australian ★★★½ Title refers to Couzens' treasured race car, which becomes his obsession. Modest Australian drama with fine racing sequences. C: Paul Couzens, Eva Dickinson, Carl Stever. D: Michael Thornhill. DRA 105m.

Flame and the Arrow, The 1950 ★★★★ Entertaining Robin Hood-type saga set in medieval Italy with Lancaster as Dardo the Arrow, up against a malevolent warlord. Terrifically athletic and fun film. C: Burt Lancaster, Virginia Mayo, Robert Douglas, Aline MacMahon, Nick Cravat. D: Jacques Tourneur. ACT 88m. V

Flame and the Flesh, The 1954 ★★ Slick but shallow star vehicle for Turner who lures a handsome singer from his young fiancée but then undergoes a change of heart. Remake of the 1937 French movie. C: Lana Turner, Pier Angeli, Carlos Thompson, Bonar Colleano, Charles Goldner, Peter Illing. D: Richard Brooks. DRA 104m.

Flame Barrier, The 1958 ★★ Mysterious entity clings like a barnacle to U.S. satellite. What's a conscientious scientist to do? Sci-fi silliness, lent some gravity by the presence of Franz. C: Arthur Franz, Kathleen Crowley, Robert Brown, Vincent Padula. D: Paul Landres. SFI 70m.

Flame in the Streets 1961 British ★★★★ Union honcho (Mills) is the lone voice of reason when fellow workers threaten to strike after the hiring of a black foreman. Earnest attempt to deal with racism, dignified by a noble performance from Mills. C: John Mills, Sylvia Syms, Brenda de Banzie. D: Roy Baker. DRA 93m.

Flame Is Love, The 1979 ★★ Typical Barbara Cartland romance turned into overdone period melodrama about heiress en route to England who stays in Paris for a little romance and mystery. Dull performances drain the life out of this. C: Linda Purl, Shane Briant, Timothy Dalton, Richard Johnson. D: Michael O'Herlihy. DRA 98m. V

Flame of Araby 1951 ★★★ Arabian princess (O'Hara) determined to evade an arranged marriage makes herself the prize in a horse race, hoping she'll be won by heartthrob Chandler. O'Hara is luminous. C: Maureen O'Hara, Jeff Chandler, Maxwell Reed, Susan Cabot. D: Charles Lamont. ACT 77m.

Flame of Barbary Coast 1945 ★★★ Period melodrama with a Montana cattle rancher pursuing a San Francisco cafe singer and his fortune as a casino owner. Typical Republic Pictures feature includes 1906 earthquake. C: John Wayne, Ann Dvorak, Joseph Schildkraut, William Frawley, Virginia Grey. D: Joseph Kane. WST 91m. V

Flame of Calcutta 1953 ★★★ In 18th-century India, Darcel leads a revolt against the local despot. Typical Far East spectacle from producer Sam Katzman (the *Jungle Jim* TV series). C: Denise Darcel, Patric Knowles, Paul Cavanagh. D: Seymour Friedman. ACT 70m.

Flame of New Orleans, The 1941 ★★★½ Minor Dietrich film has the glamorous star forced to choose between affluent Young or hard-working Cabot, the man she really loves. Sumptuous production, but featherweight romance. This was the first American film for French director Clair. C: Marlene Dietrich, Bruce Cabot, Roland Young, Laura Hope Crews, Mischa Auer, Andy Devine. D: Rene Clair. COM 78m.

Flame of Stamboul 1951 ★★ Spies in old Istanbul, frenzy and bobbing burnooses. C: Richard Denning, Lisa Ferraday, Norman Lloyd, Nestor Paiva. D: Ray Nazarro. ACT 68m.

Flame of the Islands 1955 ★★★ A profitable Bahamas-based casino gains the unwanted attention of some greedy gangsters in sultry but predictable romantic thriller. De Carlo is great as the resident lounge singer, though. C: Yvonne De Carlo, Howard Duff, Zachary Scott, James Arness, Kurt Kasznar. D: Edward Ludwig. DRA 92m. V

Flame of the West 1945 ★★★★ Outstanding B-Western, with Brown as a peace-loving doctor forced to unpack the six-shooter after outlaws gun down the town sheriff. Rip-roaring action sequences. (a.k.a. *Flaming Frontier*) C: Johnny Mack Brown, Raymond Hatton, Joan Woodbury. D: Lambert Hilyer. WST 71m.

Flame of Torment, The 1958 *See* **Conflagration**

Flame over India 1959 British ★★★½ Trainload of British soldiers traveling through 19th-century India to protect Indian Prince from repeated rebel attacks. Diverting, well-paced adventure. (a.k.a. *Northwest Frontier*) C: Lauren Bacall, Kenneth More, Herbert Lom, Wilfrid Hyde-White. D: J. Lee Thompson. ACT 130m. V

Flame over Vietnam 1967 Spanish ★★★½ Interesting drama set in Vietnam during the French colonial period, with Barrios a determined nun leading orphaned children to safety with the help of a wounded pilot. C: Elena Barrios, Jose Nieto, Manodo Moran. D: Joe Lacy. DRA

Flame, The 1947 ★★ A woman agrees to set a man up for blackmail, but can't go through with it when she falls for him. Even the clichéd situations here overtax Ralston's perpetual air of befuddlement. C: Vera Ralston, John Carroll, Robert Paige, Broderick Crawford, Henry Travers, Constance Dowling. D: John Auer. CRI 97m.

Flame Within, The 1935 ★★½ Psychiatrist, against her better judgment, begins affair with patient's husband and suffers the consequences. Absorbing sudser, ably directed. C: Ann Harding, Herbert Marshall, Maureen O'Sullivan, Louis Hayward. D: Edmund Goulding. DRA 71m.

Flaming Feather 1951 ★★½ White villain leads band of Native Americans through rampage in the Southwest. Excellent cast (particularly angelic Rush), but politically backward. C: Sterling Hayden, Forrest Tucker, Barbara Rush, Arleen Whelan. D: Ray Enright. ACT 77m.

Flaming Frontier 1945 *See* **Flame of the West**

Flaming Frontier 1958 ★★ Cavalryman tries to end the fighting between his mother's and father's people. Laudable theme. C: Bruce Bennett, Jim Davis, Paisley Maxwell, Cecil Linder, Peter Humphreys. D: Sam Newfeld. ACT [G] 70m.

Flaming Star 1960 ★★★★ Presley is surprisingly effective in this tightly directed, well-scripted film about a half-white/half-Kiowa torn between his mother's tribe and white settlers. Excellent performances all around. Based on Huffaker's novel *Flaming Lance*. C: Elvis Presley, Barbara Eden, Steve Forrest, Dolores Del Rio, John McIntire. D: Don Siegel. WST 92m. V

Flamingo Kid 1984 ★★★★ In the early '60s, Dillon, a working-class kid from Brooklyn yearns for the posh life he sees at private club where he works as cabana boy, and is torn between an engineering scholarship and the quick buck Crenna holds out for him. Smart, funny coming-of-age story deftly handled. C: Matt Dillon, Richard Crenna, Hector Elizondo, Jessica Walter, Fisher Stevens, Janet Jones. D: Garry Marshall. COM [PG-13] 100m. V

Flamingo Road 1949 ★★★★ High camp melodrama of dancer Crawford's scheming love affairs in a small Florida town. Greenstreet proves her undoing. Stars tear through juicy script. Later remade as a TV movie and series. C: Joan Crawford, Zachary Scott, Sydney Greenstreet, David Brian, Gertrude Michael, Gladys George. D: Michael Curtiz. DRA 94m. V

Flamingo Road 1980 ★★★ Remake of 1949 Crawford melodrama, with carnival dancer Raines stranded in Florida town that sizzles with passion and gossip. Served as pilot for long-running TV series. C: John Beck, Cristina Raines, Howard Duff, Morgan Fairchild, Kevin McCarthy, Barbara Rush, Mark Harmon, Stella Stevens, Woody Brown, Melba Moore, Dianne Kay, Mason Adams. D: Gus Trikonis. DRA 100m. TVM V

Flap 1970 ★★ Quinn portrays an alcoholic, down-and-out Native American who decides to fight a one-man war against the U.S. government. Unintelligent and ineffective, with uneven acting and a marginal script. C: Anthony Quinn, Claude Akins, Tony Bill, Victor Jory, Shelley Winters. D: Carol Reed. DRA [PG] 106m.

Flareup 1969 ★★★ A dancer (Welch) is stalked from Las Vegas to L.A. by a deranged acquaintance who blames her for the collapse of his marriage. Tense, violent, and fast-paced. Good location filming. C: Raquel Welch, James Stacy, Luke Askew, Don Chastain, Ron Rifkin, Jean Byron. D: James Neilson. CRI [PG] 100m.

Flash and the Firecat 1975 ★★ Davis and Sembera joyride up and down the West Coast in search of the big heist. Cheapo *Bonnie and Clyde* ripoff in which the leads seem to be having a lot of fun. C: Roger Davis, Tricia Sembera, Dub Taylor, Richard Kiel, Joan Shawlee, Philip Bruns. D: Ferd Sebastian, Beverly Sebastian. ACT [PG] 84m.

Flash Gordon 1980 ★★★½ The evil Emperor Ming and his hordes of do-no-gooders wage interstellar war on the legendary comic strip/movie serial hero. Score by Queen and a fine performance by Muti are the high points in this film, half camp and half sci-fi adventure. C: Sam Jones, Melody Anderson, Topol, Max von Sydow, Ornella Muti, Brian Blessed,

Timothy Dalton. D: Mike Hodges. SFI [PG] 111m. v

Flash of Green 1985 ★★★ Journalist Harris becomes mired in investigation of a Florida land-development scam. Wonderful cast ends up plodding through a swampy script to a belated conclusion. Adapted from a book by John D. MacDonald. C: Ed Harris, Blair Brown, Richard Jordan, John Glover. D: Victor Nunez. DRA 122m. v

Flash, The 1990 ★★★ D.C. Comics' speedy superhero tries to save Capitol City from marauding motorcycle toughs in this fun TV pilot. Tongue-in-cheek humor, lavish sets and effects, and Shipp and Pays' chemistry add to the overall quality. C: John Wesley Shipp, Amanda Pays. SFI 94m. v

Flashback 1990 ★★ Young, yuppie FBI agent (Sutherland) is asked to bring in a '60s subversive (Hopper) who's been on the lam for decades. But the hippie pulls a fast one and sends the agent to jail in his stead. Silly and inconsequential, though Hopper seems to be having fun. C: Dennis Hopper, Kiefer Sutherland, Carol Kane, Cliff De Young, Paul Dooley. D: Franco Amurri. ACT [R] 108m. v

Flashdance 1983 ★★★½ Beals is welder by day, erotic dancer by night. Her dream? To dance with the Pittsburgh Ballet. Premise and script wooed audiences with kinetic MTV style and fairy-tale ambiance. Oscar for title song. Beals was doubled by Marine Jahan in dance scenes. C: Jennifer Beals, Michael Nouri, Lilia Skala, Sunny Johnson. D: Adrian Lyne. MUS [R] 96m. v

Flashpoint 1984 ★★★½ Two border patrol officers in Texas (Kristofferson and Williams) stumble upon a skeleton and a horde of cash that embroils them in an unsolved mystery. A suspenseful and action-filled adventure. C: Kris Kristofferson, Treat Williams, Rip Torn, Kevin Conway, Miguel Ferrer, Jean Smart. D: William Tannen. ACT [R] 95m. v

Flat Top 1952 ★★★ Navy carrier pilots respect their strict commander after surviving WWII combat thanks to his training. Newsreel aerial photography and well-paced action are combined to good effect. C: Sterling Hayden, Richard Carlson, Bill Phipps, Keith Larsen. D: Lesley Selander. DRA 85m. v

Flatbed Annie 1979 *See* **Flatbed Annie & Sweetiepie: Lady Truckers**

Flatbed Annie & Sweetiepie: Lady Truckers 1979 ★★★ Two truckers with gumption (Potts and Darby) struggle valiantly to keep their expensive rig from falling into the hands of repo men. A silly but likable precursor to female road buddy movies like *Thelma and Louise*. (a.k.a. *Flatbed Annie*) C: Annie Potts, Kim Darby, Harry Dean Stanton, Billy Carter. D: Robert Greenwald. DRA 100m. TVM v

Flatfoot 1978 ★★★ On the hunt for drug smugglers, a police inspector won't let anyone or anything—including the mafia—get in his way. C: Bud Spencer, Joe Stewardson, Werner Pochath, Dagmar Lassander. D: Steno. ACT [PG] 95m. v

Flatliners 1990 ★★★½ Cocky young med students experiment on each other to explore the big unknown—Death. Elaborate set design and music video style; near-death sequences keep it churning. C: Kiefer Sutherland, Julia Roberts, Kevin Bacon, William Baldwin, Oliver Platt. D: Joel Schumacher. DRA [R] 111m. v

Flavor of Green Tea over Rice, The 1953 Japanese ★★★★ Middle-aged couple without children are continually at odds until wife realizes her husband's importance when he's to leave town on business. Even with such slight material, Ozu fashions touching and true glimpses at real human behavior. C: Shin Saburi, Michiyo Kogure. D: Yasujiro Ozu. DRA 115m.

Flaxfield, The 1983 Belgian ★★★ Hard-headed elderly farmer disagrees with his son over how to run their farm. Set at turn of the century, offers visually pleasing vistas but very little drama or characterization. C: Vic Moeremans, Dora van der Groen, Rene van Sambeek. D: Jan Gruyaert. DRA 90m.

Flaxy Martin 1949 ★★½ Reformed attorney (Scott) ditches the mob, then falls for an ex-client's moll and gets framed for murder. Slick melodrama. C: Virginia Mayo, Zachary Scott, Dorothy Malone, Tom D'Andrea, Helen Westcott, Elisha Cook Jr. D: Richard Bare. ACT 86m.

Flea in Her Ear, A 1968 U.S. ★★ Lecherous lawyer (Harrison) has effect on various husbands and wives at luxury hotel. Generally unfunny slapstick. C: Rex Harrison, Rosemary Harris, Louis Jourdan, Rachel Roberts. D: Jacques Charon. COM [PG] 94m.

Fleet's In, The 1942 ★★★★ Frisky WWII musical with Holden as reputed Navy Romeo trying to seduce virginal Lamour while Hutton steals film in debut role as a mancrazy WAVE. Great songs include "Tangerine," "I Remember You," and "Arthur Murray Taught Me Dancing in a Hurry." C: Dorothy Lamour, William Holden, Eddie Bracken, Betty Hutton, Betty Rhodes, Leif Erickson, Cass Daley, Gil Lamb, Barbara Britton, Rod Cameron, Lorraine Rognan, Jimmy Dorsey Orchestra. D: Victor Schertzinger. MUS 93m.

Flesh 1932 ★★★★ Unpolished German wrestler (Beery) falls for woman whose own affair with a gangster leads to trouble for all. Better than average drama with good performances by leads and tight direction. C: Wallace Beery, Karen Morley, Ricardo Cortez, Jean Hersholt, Herman Bing, John Miljan. D: John Ford. DRA 95m.

Flesh + Blood 1985 ★★½ Adventure yarn set in Dark Ages has damsel (Leigh) kidnapped from princely fiancée by semisadistic rogue (Hauer), who she comes to love. Extremely graphic and not for the squeamish, this is Verhoeven's English language debut. (a.k.a. *The Rose and the Sword*) C: Rutger Hauer, Jennifer Jason Leigh, Tom Burlinson, Jack Thompson, Susan Tyrrell. D: Paul Verhoeven. ACT [R] 126m. V

Flesh & Blood 1951 British ★★★½ Three generations of an embattled Scottish family, with Todd in dual role. Admirable attempt at sweeping domestic melodrama contains some dramatic episodes. C: Richard Todd, Glynis Johns, Joan Greenwood, Andre Morell, Freda Jackson, James Hayter, George Cole, Michael Hordern. D: Anthony Kimmins. DRA 102m.

Flesh & Blood 1979 ★★★★ Adaptation of Pete Hamill novel about a young street-smart boxer (Berenger) with eyes on the heavyweight title. Well-done, with strong supporting performances, authentic boxing locales. C: Tom Berenger, Mitchell Ryan, Kristin Griffith, Denzel Washington, Suzanne Pleshette, John Cassavetes, Bert Remsen, Dolph Sweet. D: Jud Taylor. ACT 200m. TVM

Flesh and Bone 1993 ★★★★ A psychotic cowhand (Caan) discovers his son (Quaid) is in love with the sole survivor (Ryan) of a family he murdered when she was a child. Will she remember him? Suspenseful modern film noir buoyed by fine performances, especially Caan's. C: Dennis Quaid, James Caan, Meg Ryan. D: Steve Kloves. CRI [R] 127m. V

Flesh and Fantasy 1943 ★★★★ Unusual three-part movie linked by supernatural themes and presence of Benchley in each one. Field stars in first as ugly girl transformed by mask into beauty. Second features Robinson as victim of fortune teller's predictions. Third has Boyer as circus psychic haunted by Stanwyck. Robinson's tale is the best, but all are intriguing. C: Charles Boyer, Edward G. Robinson, Barbara Stanwyck, Robert Benchley, Betty Field, Robert Cummings, Thomas Mitchell, Charles Winninger. D: Julien Duvivier. DRA 93m.

Flesh and Flame 1959 *See* **Night of the Quarter Moon**

Flesh and Fury 1952 ★★★½ Curtis plays a hearing-and speech-impaired boxer torn between sexy exploiter (Sterling) and kindly newspaperwoman (Freeman). Nothing spectacular or insightful, but well presented; features good, restrained Curtis performance. C: Tony Curtis, Jan Sterling, Mona Freeman, Wallace Ford, Harry Guardino. D: Joseph Pevney. DRA 82m.

Flesh and the Devil 1927 ★★★★ Romantic triangle finds irresistible Garbo caught between a soldier and his friend. Garbo and Gilbert's impassioned love scenes are something to see in this absorbing and often exotic silent romance. C: John Gilbert, Greta Garbo, Lars Hanson, Barbara Kent. D: Clarence Brown. DRA 103m. V

Flesh and the Fiends, The 1959 British ★★★½ Effective, gruesome account of a scientist (Cushing) relying on graverobbers (Pleasance, Rose) to provide him with cadavers. (a.k.a. *Mania, Psycho Killers,* and *The Fiendish Ghouls.*) C: Peter Cushing, Donald Pleasance. D: John Gilling. HOR 74m.

Flesh and the Woman 1953 French ★★★ To escape his horrid wife a Parisian joins the Foreign Legion where he meets her exact double. Of course, Lollobrigida plays dual roles in tepid comedy that's a remake of 1934 French film, *Le Grand Jeu.* C: Gina Lollobrigida, Jean-Claude Pascal, Arletty, Raymond Pellegrin, Peter Van Eyck. D: Robert Siodmak. COM 102m.

Flesh Eaters, The 1964 ★★½ Low-budget sci-fi thriller features mad scientist on isolated island experimenting with flesh-eating sea fauna; a plane crash provides him with fresh victims. Violent. C: Rita Morley, Martin Kosleck. D: Jack Curtis. SFI 87m. V

Flesh Eating Mothers 1989 ★★½ In a beautiful suburban town, the peace is disturbed by a strange and horrific virus that affects, strangely enough, only adulterous women. About as silly as it sounds. C: Robert Lee Oliver, Donatella Hecht, Valorie Hubbard, Neal Rosen. D: James Aviles Martin. HOR 90m. V

Flesh Feast 1970 ★ Sad finale to Lake's career casts her as a mad scientist using maggots in experiments to restore youth. Unappetizing, to say the least, but climactic scene of her turning the maggots on Hitler must be seen to be believed. C: Veronica Lake, Phil Philbin, Heather Hughes, Chris Martell. D: Brad F. Grinter. HOR [R] 72m. V

Fleshburn 1983 ★ A Vietnam veteran, suffering terribly from nightmares of his battle experiences, escapes from an asylum and stalks his psychiatrists. Absolutely brutal and virtually without redemption. C: Steve Kanaly, Karen Carlson, Sonny Landham. D: George Cage. ACT [R] 91m. V

Fletch 1985 ★★★★ Smarmy reporter is hired to murder millionaire, which leads to cracking big time L.A. drug ring. Some fun sequences that wallow in silliness and provide plenty of comic opportunities for Chase in role tailored to his talents. Followed by *Fletch Lives.* C: Chevy Chase, Dana Wheeler-Nicholson, Tim Matheson, Geena Davis, Kenneth Mars. D: Michael Ritchie. COM [PG] 96m. V

Fletch Lives 1989 ★★★ Chase reprises Fletch character and this time heads to Louisiana where he inherits a mansion. This leads to murder investigation and a variety of disguises based on Southern stereotypes. Not as much fun as original. C: Chevy Chase, Hal Holbrook, Julianne Phillips, Cleavon Little. D: Michael Ritchie. COM [PG] 95m. V

Flicks 1985 ★★ Satirical Saturday afternoon at the movies compiles complete bill of cartoons, coming attractions, feature, B-movie, etc. For film buffs. C: Pamela Sue Martin, Joan Hackett, Martin Mull, Betty Kennedy. D: Peter Winograd. COM [R] 79m. V

Flight 1929 ★★★½ Two pilots competing in the air and in romance fly to Nicaragua to rescue U.S. Marines. Capra's early sound film may now seem dated but still shows undeniable command of medium. Script credited to director and to co-star Graves. C: Jack Holt, Ralph Graves, Lila Lee, Alan Roscoe, Harold Goodwin, Jimmy Cruze. D: Frank Capra. ACT 116m.

Flight Command 1940 ★★★½ Conceited trainee pilot (Taylor) wants to excel in a Navy flight unit. Flagwaving hokum enlivened by good cast. C: Robert Taylor, Ruth Hussey, Walter Pidgeon, Paul Kelly, Nat Pendleton, Shepperd Strudwick, Red Skelton, Dick Purcell. D: Frank Borzage. DRA 116m.

Flight for Freedom 1943 ★★½ Quasi-Amelia Earhart story, with imperious aviatrix romanced by cocky fellow flier and dull designer. Acting far overblown, and characterizations shallow. C: Rosalind Russell, Fred MacMurray, Herbert Marshall, Eduardo Ciannelli, Walter Kingsford. D: Lothar Mendes. DRA 99m.

Flight from Ashiya 1964 ★★★ Three pilots try to rescue the crew of a ship sunk in the Pacific. The minimal plotline is fleshed out with flashbacks to earlier rescue sequences in the three men's lives. Good acting. C: Yul Brynner, Richard Widmark, George Chakiris, Suzy Parker, Shirley Knight. D: Michael Anderson. DRA 100m.

Flight from Destiny 1941 ★★★★ Elderly professor (Mitchell) with six months to live decides to help young couple by murdering woman interfering with their attempt to reunite. Lynn's the weak link, but better than one might expect. Good direction; Mitchell and Fitzgerald are tops. C: Geraldine Fitzgerald, Thomas Mitchell, Jeffrey Lynn, James Stephenson, Mona Maris, Jonathan Hale. D: Vincent Sherman. DRA 73m.

Flight from Glory 1937 ★★★ Perils faced by company pilots whose job is to fly over Andes Mountains on daily runs between isolated mines and their home base. Intriguing B-movie suspenser plays like a low-budget inspiration for the later (and better known) *Only Angels Have Wings*. C: Chester Morris, Van Heflin, Whitney Bourne, Onslow Stevens. D: Lew Landers. DRA 67m. V

Flight From Terror *See* **Satan Never Sleeps**

Flight into Nowhere 1938 ★★★½ A daring pilot (Purcell) is grounded by his employer, yet refuses to stop flying, winding up on an African adventure. Rugged action-adventure with fine aerial footage. C: Jack Holt, Jacqueline Wells, Dick Purcell. D: Lewis D. Collins. ACT 65m.

Flight Lieutenant 1942 ★★★ Service melodrama about a reckless flyer (Ford) whose superior compares him to equally reckless dad (O'Brien). C: Pat O'Brien, Glenn Ford, Evelyn Keyes, Minor Watson, Larry Parks, Lloyd Bridges, Hugh Beaumont. D: Sidney Salkow. ACT 80m.

Flight 90: Disaster on the Potomac 1983 ★★½ Story of 1982 disaster off runway at Washington, D.C., with dramatic rescues in the freezing Potomac River. Handled with more sensitivity than most such disaster flicks. C: Richard Masur, Dinah Manoff, Donnelly Rhodes. D: Robert Lewis. ACT 104m.

Flight Nurse 1954 ★★ Leslie ministers to soldiers and falls in love in Korea. Korean War romance. C: Joan Leslie, Forrest Tucker, Jeff Donnell, Arthur Franz, Ben Cooper. D: Allan Dwan. ACT 90m.

Flight of Black Angel 1991 ★★★½ A deranged pilot steals a nuclear weapon and threatens to destroy Las Vegas. Tight, suspenseful script is kept aloft by superior performances. C: Peter Strauss, William O'Leary, James O'Sullivan, Michele Pawk, Michael Keys Hall. D: Jonathan Mostow. ACT [R] 102m. TVM V

Flight of Dragons 1982 ★★★ Acceptable, if undistinguished animation feature about intelligent lizards who bring a man back to their era. Visuals by Rankin/Bass productions. D: Arthur Rankin, Jr., Jules Bass. FAM/DRA 98m.

Flight of Rainbirds, A 1981 Dutch ★★★★ Thirtyish virgin dreams that God gives him ultimatum: have sex within a week or die. Funny tale of simple man in complex world enhanced by Krabbe's acting and de Jong's direction. C: Jeroen Krabbe, Marijke Merckens. D: Ate de Jong. COM 94m. V

Flight of the Doves 1971 British ★★★ Two children from Liverpool run away from their unkind stepfather to visit their Irish grandmother (McGuire), pursued by an uncle (Moody) with evil intentions and a trunk full of bizarre disguises. Has its funny moments, but not enough of them. C: Ron Moody, Jack Wild, Dorothy McGuire, Stanley Holloway, Helen Raye, William Rushton. D: Ralph Nelson. DRA [G] 105m.

Flight of the Eagle, The 1982 Swedish ★★★★½ True story of three Swedes, circa 1900, who make ill-fated attempt to reach North Pole by balloon. Troell's epic features evocative period settings, stunning photography, sublime acting. Even unfortunate dubbing can't harm it. Oscar nominee for Best Foreign Film. C: Max von Sydow, Goran Stangertz, S.A. Ousdal, Eva Von Hanno. D: Jan Troell. DRA 115m. V

Flight of the Grey Wolf 1976 ★★½ A tame wolf is mistakenly hunted as a killer, but is helped by a young friend. Appealing children's story. C: Jeff East, Bill Williams, Barbara Hale. FAM/DRA 83m. V

Flight of the Innocent, The 1994 Italian

★★★½ Mafia feud in Sicily causes young boy to flee with his pursuers hot on his trail. Calao tremendous as the boy; Carlei's first film is manipulative but effective transposition of our own formula chase pictures. C: Manuel Colao, Francesca Neri, Jacques Perrin. D: Carlo Carlei. CRI [R] 105m. V

Flight of the Intruder 1991 ★★ Vietnam War film sends U.S. carrier pilots on an unauthorized mission to bomb an air base in Hanoi. Except for hot aerial action and rugged acting by Dafoe, Glover, and Johnson the picture bombs instead. C: Danny Glover, Willem Dafoe, Brad Johnson, Rosanna Arquette, Tom Sizemore. D: John Milius. DRA 115m. V

Flight of the Lost Balloon 1961 ★★½ African bush adventure of hotdogger Thompson balloon-tracking missing explorer. C: Marshall Thompson, Mala Powers, James Lanphier, Douglas Kennedy. D: Nathan Juran. ACT 91m.

Flight of the Navigator 1986 ★★★½ *Explorers* meets *Hangar 18* as NASA investigates case of 12-year-old boy who takes an eight-year-long ride on alien spaceship. Cute, if a bit cloying. C: Joey Cramer, Veronica Cartwright, Cliff De Young, Sarah Jessica Parker, Howard Hesseman. D: Randal Kleiser. FAM/SFI 90m. V

Flight of the Phoenix 1966 ★★★★ When a plane crashes in the desert, survivors must overcome the elements and each other to rebuild the vehicle. A fine, thoughtful script and a stellar cast highlight this adventure drama of men pushed to the extreme. C: James Stewart, Richard Attenborough, Peter Finch, Hardy Kruger, Ernest Borgnine, Ian Bannen, Dan Duryea. D: Robert Aldrich. DRA 147m. V

Flight That Disappeared, The 1961 ★★★½ As three nuclear scientists prepare to deliver their report to the President, they are kidnapped by mysterious beings who may or may not be from the future. Odd but enjoyable little sci-fi film with a social conscience. C: Craig Hill, Paula Raymond, Dayton Lummis. D: Reginald LeBorg. SFI 71m.

Flight, The 1989 ★★★½ After making a departure from Athens, an American commercial airliner, with 153 passengers aboard, is taken over by terrorists. Some nifty action. C: Lindsay Wagner, Eli Danker, Sandy McPeak. D: Paul Wendkos. ACT 96m. TVM V

Flight to Berlin 1983 West German ★★★½ A man, who may or may not be guilty of murder, travels to title city to explore his past involvement with two sisters, one of whom is now dead. Enigmatic and stylish drama uses a cryptic story line to move from the offbeat to the surreal. Not for traditional tastes. C: Tusse Silberg, Paul Freeman, Lisa Kreuzer, Eddie Constantine. D: Christopher Petit. DRA 90m.

Flight to Fury 1966 ★★★½ On its way to the Philippines, a plane carrying a group of crafty diamond smugglers crashes. Nicholson wrote the script for this absorbing low-budget thriller, and stars as one of the thieves. C: Dewey Martin, Fay Spain, Jack Nicholson, Vic Diaz. D: Monte Hellman. ACT 73m. V

Flight to Hong Kong 1956 ★★½ Crime boss Calhoun takes one look at perfect woman Rush and realizes he has to betray his cronies to survive. Calhoun is appealing. C: Rory Calhoun, Barbara Rush, Dolores Donlon, Soo Yong. D: Joseph Newman. CRI 88m.

Flight to Mars 1951 ★★½ A joint news/-science expedition crash-lands on Mars and discovers a strange race living beneath the surface. Tame sci-fi thriller. C: Marguerite Chapman, Cameron Mitchell, Arthur Franz. D: Lesley Selander. SFI 72m. V

Flight to Nowhere 1946 ★★ Hoods and feds on the hunt for uranium. Screen Guild quickie (shot in 13 days) attempted to cash in on new awareness of nuclear destruction. C: Evelyn Ankers, Alan Curtis, Jack Holt, Jerome Cowan, Micheline Cheirel, John Craven, Inez Cooper, Hoot Gibson. D: William Rowland. ACT 75m.

Flight to Tangier 1953 ★★★½ When a plane carrying stolen money crashes, the various passengers scramble to get a share of the loot. An entertaining—if predictable—adventure drama. C: Joan Fontaine, Jack Palance, Corinne Calvet, Robert Douglas. D: Charles Marquis Warren. DRA 90m.

Flim Flam Man, The 1967 ★★★½ Aging Southern con artist (Scott) teaches the larcenous ropes to young pupil (Sarrazin). Episodic, charming and perceptive, with a jaunty score and great Scott. C: George C. Scott, Sue Lyon, Michael Sarrazin, Harry Morgan, Jack Albertson, Alice Ghostley, Albert Salmi, Slim Pickens. D: Irvin Kershner. COM 115m. V

Flintstone Christmas, A 1977 ★★★ When Santa comes up lame on Christmas Eve, Fred and Barney heroically take his place. Pleasant Yuletide fun from the cartoon family. FAM/COM 49m. V

Flintstone Files, The 1991 ★★★½ Three episodes from the famous television cartoon series. Fred, Barney, Wilma, Betty and the rest are here in fine form. Wonderful fun for kids of all ages. FAM/COM 75m. V

Flintstones, The 1994 ★★ It took 35 screenwriters to come up with a live-action version of the Hanna-Barbera cartoon. In spite of an enormously likable performance by Goodman as Fred Flintstone, this is pretty silly. Kids will like it, though. C: John Goodman, Elizabeth Perkins, Rick Moranis, Rosie O'Donnell, Kyle MacLachlan, Halle Berry, Elizabeth Taylor. D: Brian Levant. FAM/COM 92m.

Flipper 1963 ★★★★ Endearing film about a lovable dolphin and the fisherman's son (Halpin) who saves him and becomes his friend. Delightful family film teaches children importance of kindness to animals. Followed by two sequels and a TV series. C: Chuck Connors, Luke Halpin, Kathleen Maguire, Connie Scott. D: James Clark. FAM/DRA [G] 87m. v

Flipper's New Adventure 1964 ★★★★ Resourceful dolphin and his young friend Sandy (Halpin) head out to a deserted island when threatened by separation, immediately becoming involved with kidnappers and pirates. No sweat, they save the day! Well-done, nicely acted adventure drama for family viewing. C: Luke Halpin, Pamela Franklin, Helen Cherry, Tom Helmore, Brian Kelly. D: Leon Benson. FAM/DRA [G] 103m. v

Flipper's Odyssey 1966 ★★★½ Flipper is the whole show in this children's adventure film. In this one, the heroic dolphin is separated from his young friend (Halpin) and must find his way home. Terrific underwater photography captures Flipper's daring rescues. Good family viewing. C: Brian Kelly, Luke Halpin, Tommy Norden. D: Paul Landres. FAM/DRA 77m. v

Flirtation Walk 1934 ★★★ West Point cadet (Powell) woos an officer's daughter (Keeler). Ordinary plot can't be lifted by mediocre numbers; a Busby Berkeley-style musical without Busby Berkeley. C: Dick Powell, Ruby Keeler, Pat O'Brien, Ross Alexander, Guinn Williams, Henry O'Neill. D: Frank Borzage. MUS 98m. v

Flirting 1990 Australian ★★★★ Shy Australian boy and beautiful, headstrong Ugandan exchange student fall in love in touching comedy set in the mid '60s. Small-scale but charming sequel to *The Year My Voice Broke*. C: Noah Taylor, Thandie Newton, Nicole Kidman, Bartholomew Rose, Felix Nobis. D: John Duigan. COM [R] 100m. v

Flirting with Fate 1938 ★★ Touring vaudeville company winds up in South America without a way to get back home. Added to their woes are a gang of comic villains, led by Carrillo. A minor musical with predictable gags. C: Joe E. Brown, Leo Carrillo, Beverly Roberts, Wynne Gibson, Steffi Duna, Stanley Fields, Charles Judels. D: Frank McDonald. MUS 69m.

Floating Weeds 1959 Japanese ★★★★★ Ozu's remake of his own 1934 silent film. Story of actor reunited with his lover and their son after 12 years boasts director's characteristic painterly compositions and leisurely exposition. A hallmark of traditional Japanese filmmaking and one of Ozu's best (a.k.a. *Drifting Weeds*) C: Ganjiro Nakamura, Machiko Kyo, Haruko Sugimura, Ayako Wakao. D: Yasujiro Ozu. DRA 119m. v

Flood! 1976 ★★★½ A private helicopter pilot reluctantly goes to the aid of a small town flooded after a faulty dam gives way. Irwin Allen's calamity adventure is more interested in special effects than character development, but the film is compelling nonetheless. C: Robert Culp, Martin Milner, Barbara Hershey, Richard Basehart. D: Earl Bellamy. ACT 98m. TVM v

Flood Tide 1958 ★★½ Nader is framed for murder by the jealous son of a female admirer. Potentially interesting suspense film (part *Children's Hour*, part *Wrong Man*). C: George Nader, Cornell Borchers, Michel Ray, Judson Pratt. D: Abner Biberman. CRI 82m.

Floods of Fear 1959 British ★★ An escaped convict redeems himself when he acts decisively in a flood. Sentimental British drama. C: Howard Keel, Anne Heywood, Cyril Cusack, Harry H. Corbett, John Crawford. D: Charles Crichton. DRA 82m.

Flor Silvestre 1945 Spanish ★★★ Two families that have been friends for years suddenly find themselves enemies during Mexican Revolution. Del Rio is a particular delight in this melodramatic spectacle. C: Dolores Del Rio, Pedro Armendariz, Emilio Fernandez. D: Emilio Fernandez. DRA 94m.

Florence Nightingale 1985 ★★★ Biography spotlights the Victorian-era nurse, with Smith in title role. Lovely costumes and plausible dialogue; Bloom is magnificent, as usual. C: Jaclyn Smith, Timothy Dalton, Claire Bloom. D: Daryl Duke. DRA 104m.

Florentine Dagger, The 1935 ★★★½ A playwright (Woods), a descendant of the Borgias, believes he has inherited their murderous tendencies. When a murder does occur, both he and his leading lady (Lindsay) are suspects. Finely turned mystery features an excellent script and fast-paced direction. Based on Ben Hecht's novel. C: Donald Woods, Margaret Lindsay, C. Aubrey Smith. D: Robert Florey. CRI 70m.

Florian 1940 ★★ Brought together by their love for horses, working-class Young romances upper-crust Gilbert. Typical B-movie romance for its time. C: Robert Young, Helen Gilbert, Charles Coburn, Lee Bowman, Reginald Owen, Lucile Watson. D: Edwin L. Marin. COM 91m.

Florida Straits 1986 ★★½ A Cuban refugee (Julia) leads a modern-day treasure hunt for gold buried during the Bay of Pigs invasion. Uneven, occasionally thrilling adventure. C: Raul Julia, Fred Ward, Daniel Jenkins, Jamie Sanchez, Antonio Fargas. D: Mike Hodges. ACT [PG-13] 98m. TVM v

Floradora Girl, The 1930 British ★★★★ Operetta was huge stage hit both here and abroad. Film version has Gay '90s charm and early talkie crudeness, but works as comic vehicle for Davies. She's man-shy virgin who's taught the ropes by her friends till she snares a millionaire. (a.k.a. *The Gay Nineties*) C: Marion Davies, Lawrence Gray, Walter Catlett, Louis Bartels, Ilka Chase, Vivien Oakland, Jed Prouty, Sam Hardy. D: Harry Beaumont. MUS 80m.

Floundering 1994 ★★★ A down-out denizen of Venice Beach, California tries to keep his grip on reality as his life falls apart. Uneasy mix of drama and satire with confusing fantasy sequences. C: James Le Gros, Chief Fence, Steve Buscemi, John Cusack, Ethan Hawke. D: Peter McCarthy. DRA [R] 97m. v

Flower Drum Song 1961 ★★★½ Chinese generation-gap musical with middling Rodgers and Hammerstein score. Umeki is charming as mail-order bride competing with brassy Kwan for Shigeta's affections. Colorful San Francisco locations help lackluster production. C: Nancy Kwan, Jack Soo, James Shigeta, Miyoshi Umeki, Juanita Hall. D: Henry Koster. MUS 133m. v

Flowers in the Attic 1987 ★★ Four children are locked in the attic of a creepy estate by their evil mom (Tennant) and *her* evil mom (Fletcher). Why? Money, of course. Prunes the thrills From the V.C. Andrews best-seller. C: Louise Fletcher, Victoria Tennant, Kristy Swanson, Jeb Adams. D: Jeffrey Bloom. DRA [PG-13] 93m. v

Flowers of St. Francis 1950 Italian ★★★★★ Austere and thoughtful, light-years away from Hollywood religious epics, this is one of the great films of all time. Rossellini's earnest and touching examination of the faith of St. Francis and his followers is a must-see. D: Roberto Rossellini. DRA 75m.

Flowing Gold 1940 ★★★ Lackluster story of man hiding out in western oilfield and competing for love of local woman. Then-controversial actress Farmer provides sole interest now. C: John Garfield, Frances Farmer, Pat O'Brien, Raymond Walburn, Cliff Edwards, Tom Kennedy. D: Alfred Green. DRA 82m.

Fluffy 1965 ★★★ A scientist (Randall) goes in for a bit of lion taming; Jones is his love interest. Silly, but good-spirited and harmless. C: Tony Randall, Shirley Jones, Edward Andrews, Ernest Truex, Howard Morris, Dick Sargent. D: Earl Bellamy. FAM/COM 92m.

Flustered Comedy of Leon Errol, The 1939 ★★★★ A compilation of comedian Leon Errol's greatest film roles. If you don't know his work, here's an excellent introduction. C: Leon Errol, Vivian Tobin, Frank Faylen. COM 56m. v

Fly, The 1958 ★★★★ The original shocker about a doomed scientist (Hedison) whose big mistake is exchanging molecules with a fly during a teleportation experiment. The film holds up remarkably all the way to the stunning ending. Sequels are *Return of the Fly* and *Curse of the Fly*. C: Al (David) Hedison, Patricia Owens, Vincent Price, Herbert Marshall, Kathleen Freeman. D: Kurt Neumann. HOR 94m. v

Fly, The 1986 ★★★★ An experiment gone awry transforms mild-mannered scientist into a grotesque insect. This remake of the 1958 chiller often turns the stomach, but is worth it for the scares it delivers. Goldblum's performance is exceptional. Won Oscar for Makeup. Followed by sequel. Be very afraid. C: Jeff Goldblum, Geena Davis, John Getz. D: David Cronenberg. SFI [R] 96m. v

Fly II, The 1989 ★½ Gone is the horrifying yet touching romance of *The Fly* remake; now all we're left with are gooey special effects. Only for those with a cast-iron stomach. C: Eric Stoltz, Daphne Zuniga, Lee Richardson, John Getz. D: Chris Walas. HOR [R] 105m. v

Fly with the Hawk ★★★½ A young, emotionally impaired young boy is lost for a year in the woods. When he's found, he returns to civilization and, to everyone's joy, he's much stronger after his travail. Quite tender and well done. C: Peter Ferri, Peter Snook, Shelley Lynne Speigel. D: Robert Tanos. DRA 90m. v

Flying 1985 *See* **Dream to Believe**

Flying Aces, The 1939 *See* **Flying Deuces, The**

Flying Blind 1941 ★★ Arlen vs. foreign agents out to steal air defense secrets. C: Richard Arlen, Jean Parker, Marie Wilson. ACT 69m. v

Flying Deuces, The 1939 ★★★★ Laurel and Hardy join the French Foreign Legion, hoping to mend Ollie's broken heart. An enjoyable feature for the comic duo, highlighted by their rendition of "Shine on Harvest Moon." This is perfect for younger viewers. (a.k.a *The Flying Aces*) C: Stan Laurel, Oliver Hardy, Jean Parker, Reginald Gardiner, James Finlayson. D: A. Edward Sutherland. COM 67m. v

Flying Down to Rio 1933 ★★★★ Astaire and Rogers made film debut as second leads in this old-fashioned but elaborate musical, with Del Rio caught between two suitors in Brazil. Highlights are Astaire and Rogers dancing "The Carioca" and a bevy of dancing girls on wings of planes for the eye-popping finale. C: Dolores Del Rio, Gene Raymond, Ginger Rogers, Fred Astaire, Eric Blore, Franklin Pangborn. D: Thornton Freeland. MUS 89m. v

Flying Fontaines, The 1959 ★★★ High-wire walker romantically involved with showgirl in undistinguished, under-the-big-top drama. Some romance, a few thrills thanks to circus milieu. C: Michael Callan, Evy Norlund, Joan Evans, Joe deSantis, Roger Perry, Rian Garrick. D: George Sherman. DRA 84m.

Flying Fool, The 1929 ★★★★ Rousing action film captures the excitement of the adventure serial with its story of a daredevil pilot recruited to capture a murderer for the Secret Service. Full of atmosphere and old-time movie thrills. C: William Boyd, Marie Prevost, Russell Gleason. D: Taylor Garnett. ACT 73m.

Flying High 1931 ★★★½ Lahr's screen debut is main attraction in antique musical with Bert as aviator who accidentally breaks world record. Early example of Busby Berkeley's dance direction. C: Bert Lahr, Charlotte Greenwood, Pat O'Brien, Kathryn Crawford, Charles Winninger, Hedda Hopper, Guy Kibbee. D: Charles Riesner. MUS 80m.

Flying Irishman, The 1939 ★★ Larger-than-life biography about and starring "Wrong Way" Corrigan, whose aeronautical misadventures became part of contemporary folklore. C: Douglas Corrigan, Paul Kelly, Robert Armstrong, Gene Reynolds. D: Leigh Jason. DRA 72m.

Flying Leathernecks 1951 ★★★½ A squadron is whipped into shape by its commander (Wayne) and a softhearted officer (Ryan) takes exception to his disciplinarian ways. Good WWII action picture. C: John Wayne, Robert Ryan, Jay C. Flippen, Janis Carter, Don Taylor. D: Nicholas Ray. ACT 102m. V

Flying Missile, The 1950 ★★½ Sub commander (Ford) tries to implement use of guided missiles, but brings tragedy (to his best friend and to himself) after an unsanctioned test launch. Earnest postwar propaganda. C: Glenn Ford, Viveca Lindfors, Henry O'Neill, Jerry Paris, Richard Quine. D: Henry Levin. ACT 93m.

Flying Saucer, The 1950 ★★★ Red scare science fiction: UFO sightings are connected to Soviet aircraft. Notable as the first film to focus on UFOs, and to use the term "flying saucer." Highlighted by great cinematography. C: Mikel Conrad, Pat Garrison, Russell Hicks, Denver Pyle. D: Mikel Conrad. SFI 70m. V

Flying Saucers over Hollywood: The Plan 9 Companion 1993 ★★★ Documentary about 1959 cult sci-fi classic *Plan 9 from Outer Space*, perhaps the worst film ever made. Interviews with those who made it, and avid fans. Amusing. DOC 111m. V

Flying Serpent, The 1946 ★★ Archaeologist keeps treasure hunters at bay with deadly airborne creature. Goofy remake of Bela Lugosi's *Devil Bat*. C: George Zucco, Ralph Lewis, Hope Kramer, Eddie Acuff, Milton Kibbee. D: Sherman Scott. HOR 59m.

FM 1978 ★★★ Semieffective "hip" comedy about crazy group of disc jockeys rebelling against new station policy forbidding rock 'n' roll. Scattershot farce features good '70's soundtrack and appearances by then-hot rock stars. C: Michael Brandon, Martin Mull, Eileen Brennan, Cleavon Little, Cassie Yates. D: John A. Alonzo. COM 104m. V

Fog Island 1945 ★★ Creaky plot of various suspicious, greedy characters involved in murder, revenge and other treachery at fog-bound island mansion gets some juice from good cast of B-movie stalwarts. C: George Zucco, Lionel Atwill, Veda Ann Borg, Jerome Cowan, Sharon Douglas. D: Terry Morse. HOR 72m. V

Fog Over Frisco 1934 ★★★★ Ace craftsman Dieterle pulls out all technical stops on this amazing tale of thrill-crazy heiress who perpetrates securities fraud. So fast that last half may have you laughing from sheer excitement and not the fun but foolish plot. C: Bette Davis, Lyle Talbot, Margaret Lindsay, Donald Woods, Henry O'Neill, Arthur Byron, Hugh Herbert, Alan Hale, William Demarest. D: William Dieterle. DRA 68m.

Fog, The 1980 ★★★ A shipload of zombies comes in with the fog to wreak havoc on what used to be a peaceful town. Ambitious endeavor with eerie shots of the fog rolling in, but not one of Carpenter's most effective efforts. C: Adrienne Barbeau, Jamie Lee Curtis, Hal Holbrook, Janet Leigh, John Houseman. D: John Carpenter. HOR [R] 89m. V

Folies Bergere 1935 ★★★★ Song-and-dance man Chevalier poses as society dandy romancing Oberon while girlfriend Sothern fumes. Stylish musical has expert cast and buoyant script. Highlight is elaborate "Straw Hat" finale. C: Maurice Chevalier, Ann Sothern, Merle Oberon, Eric Blore, Ferdinand Munier. D: Roy Del Ruth. MUS 84m.

Folies Bergere 1958 French ★★½ French singer (Jeanmaire) and American husband (Constantine) compete professionally. Colorful, authentic atmosphere can't make up for dreadful script. C: Jeanmaire, Eddie Constantine, Nadia Gray, Yves Robert. D: Henri Decoin. MUS 90m.

Folies Bourgeoises *See* **The Twist**

Folks! 1992 ★★ Tasteless story about impoverished stockbroker (Selleck) whose senile parents agree to commit suicide so he can collect insurance. Ameche excellent, Ebersole very good in dopey movie. C: Tom Selleck, Don Ameche, Anne Jackson, Christine Ebersole. D: Ted Kotcheff. COM [PG-13] 107m. V

Follow a Star 1959 British ★★ Wisdom (who co-wrote script) is a starstruck amateur who allows fading music hall star Desmonde to coast on his talent. Slapstick, long on pathos and song. C: Norman Wisdom, June Laverick, Jerry Desmonde, Hattie Jacques, John Le Mesurier, Richard Wattis, Ron Moody. D: Robert Asher. COM 93m.

Follow Me, Boys! 1966 ★★★½ Sticky sweet Disney tale of young-at-heart MacMurray starting Boy Scout troop, then dedicating his life to helping young boys become "fine, upstanding men." Those nostalgic for days when such activity was as innocent as it appeared might like this. C: Fred MacMurray, Vera Miles, Lillian Gish, Charlie Ruggles. D: Norman Tokar. FAM/DRA [G] 120m. V

Follow Me Quietly 1949 ★★★★ A detective foils maniac strangler. Atmospheric and quick-paced thriller. C: William Lundigan, Dorothy Patrick, Jeff Corey, Nestor Paiva. D: Richard Fleischer. CRI 59m. V

Follow that Bird 1985 *See* **Sesame Street Presents: Follow That Bird**

Follow That Camel 1967 British ★★★ British farce against Foreign Legion backdrop. Nicely produced installment of *Carry On* series, with fun Silvers. C: Phil Silvers, Jim Dale,

Charles Hawtrey, Kenneth Williams. D: Gerald Thomas. COM 95m. v

Follow That Car 1980 ★★★ Three young people become unwilling FBI agents and wind up in an exciting car chase worth naming the movie after. C: Dirk Benedict, Tanya Tucker, Terri Nunn. D: Daniel Haller. ACT [PG] 96m. v

Follow That Dream 1962 ★★½ Presley and clan claim government property in Florida coveted by gangsters. Typical star vehicle. C: Elvis Presley, Arthur O'Connell, Anne Helm, Joanna Moore. D: Gordon Douglas. MUS 111m. v

Follow That Horse! 1960 British ★★★½ Unassuming diplomat goes on the adventure of his life when the scientist he's escorting turns out to be a spy and the secret plans in their possession end up being eaten by a horse. Madcap comedy delivers the laughs, thanks to spirited performances. C: David Tomlinson, Cecil Parker, Richard Wattis, Mary Peach, Dora Bryan. D: Alan Bromly. COM 80m.

Follow the Boys 1944 ★★★★ During WWII, each studio made an all-star revue pegged to a "let's entertain the boys" plot. This is Universal's and it's better than most, due to authentic footage of stars performing for actual troops. Acts range from Sophie Tucker to Orson Welles sawing Marlene Dietrich in half. C: Marlene Dietrich, George Raft, Orson Welles, Vera Zorina, Dinah Shore, W.C. Fields, Jeanette MacDonald, Maria Montez, Andrews Sisters, Sophie Tucker, Nigel Bruce, Gale Sondergaard. D: A. Edward Sutherland. MUS 122m.

Follow the Boys 1963 ★★★ Young wives and single women wait for sailors on the French Riviera. Amiable musical with luscious scenery and painless romance gags. C: Connie Francis, Paula Prentiss, Ron Randell, Janis Paige, Russ Tamblyn. D: Richard Thorpe. MUS 95m.

Follow the Fleet 1936 ★★★★½ Astaire eschews top hat and tails for sailor suit. Rogers gets her first (and only) solo tap dance. And together they make this tale of sailors trying to raise money to restore a ship a diverting delight. C: Fred Astaire, Ginger Rogers. D: Mark Sandrich. MUS 110m. v

Follow the Leader 1944 ★★½ The East Side Kids try to clear one of their own of bogus theft charges. Okay series entry. (a.k.a. *East of the Bowery*) C: Leo Gorcey, Huntz Hall, Gabriel Dell, Bobby Stone. D: William Beaudine. COM 64m.

Follow the Sun 1951 ★★½ Sentimentalized film biography of golfing great Ben Hogan doesn't have much punch. Only the most dedicated golf fans will find it interesting. C: Glenn Ford, Anne Baxter, Dennis O'Keefe, June Havoc. D: Sidney Lanfield. DRA 93m.

Follow Thru 1930 ★★½ Two women vie for the affections of a professional golfer. Fans of vintage Broadway musicals will enjoy this screen rendition. C: Charles Rogers, Nancy Carroll, Jack Haley, Eugene Pallette, Thelma Todd. D: Laurence Schwab. MUS 93m.

Follow Your Dreams 1983 *See* **Independence Day**

Follow Your Heart 1990 ★★½ Discharged Marine (Cassidy), whose own family died while he was at war, wanders into small town and discovers new family of quirky locals, one of whom (Stewart) provides romance. Star vehicle, a bit heavy on treacle. C: Patrick Cassidy, Catherine Mary Stewart. D: Noel Nosseck. DRA 96m. TVM

Following the Fuhrer 1986 German ★★½ Unusual mix of documentary and fictional footage frames this tale about a group of Third Reich members struggling to survive in Germany near the end of WWII. Heavy-handed dramatics hurt the credibility of this West German historical film. C: Renan Demirkan, Udo Lindenberg, Inga Humpe, Tana Schanzara, Gunter Lamprecht. D: Adolf Winkelmann. DRA 90m. TVM

Folly to Be Wise 1952 British ★★★★ Army chaplain Sim finds camp life a bit too dull for his tastes. Hoping to liven up the starchy surroundings, he concocts an unusual array of diversions for the troops. Sim sparkles in this witty military comedy. C: Alastair Sim, Elizabeth Allan, Roland Culver, Maritita Hunt. D: Frank Launder. COM 91m.

Food of the Gods, The 1976 ★★ Veteran schlockmeister Gordon trashes H.G. Wells' story, with painfully bad special effects to boot. A hunter (Gartner) discovers that a mysterious substance is causing woodland creatures to grow to gigantic size and attack humans. C: Marjoe Gortner, Pamela Franklin, Ida Lupino, Ralph Meeker. D: Bert I. Gordon. HOR [PG] 88m. v

Food of the Gods, The (Part 2) 1989 Canadian ★ In-name-only sequel about a university doctor whose experiments result in giant rats that terrorize the campus. Dialogue and special effects defy belief, though they are good for some unintended laughs. (a.k.a. *Gnaw.*) C: Paul Coufos, Lisa Schrage, Jackie Burroughs, Colin Fox. D: Damian Lee. HOR 90m. v

Fool for Love 1985 ★★★ Basinger and Shepard spar verbally and violently in a motel room on the fringes of the Mojave desert trying to work out their incestuous attraction. Basinger and Stanton acquit themselves well, but claustrophobic one-room setting works against drama. Based on Shepard's play. C: Sam Shepard, Kim Basinger, Harry Dean Stanton, Randy Quaid. D: Robert Altman. DRA [R] 108m. v

Fool Killer, The 1965 ★★★½ Runaway orphan (Albert) is befriended by a strange young man (Perkins) whom he comes to suspect is an ax murderer. Extremely well-acted period piece set in post-Civil War South. C: Anthony Perkins, Edward Albert, Dana Elcar, Henry Hull. D: Servando Gonzalez. DRA 100m. V

Foolin' Around 1980 ★★★ Misadventures of poor Oklahoma farmboy who goes to college, falls in love with a rich girl, and stops at nothing to win her heart. Cookie-cutter comedy is redeemed by talents of eager Busey and winsome O'Toole. C: Gary Busey, Annette O'Toole, Cloris Leachman, Eddie Albert, Tony Randall. D: Richard T. Heffron. COM [PG] 101m. V

Foolish Wives 1922 ★★★★½ Lavishly produced, well-scripted melodrama with a Monte Carlo setting. Von Stroheim is at his most seductive and sinister as a phony count who blackmails susceptible, indiscreet women. Fine acting by Busch. C: Erich von Stroheim, Maud George, Mae Busch, Cesare Gravina. D: Erich von Stroheim. DRA 107m. V

Fools 1970 ★ Witless tale of aging former movie star (Robards) falling for woman on the run from her ruthless husband. Corny soundtrack contributes to laughably dated, embarrassing love story. C: Jason Robards, Katharine Ross, Scott Hylands, Roy C. Jenson. D: Tom Gries. DRA [PG] 93m. V

Fools for Scandal 1938 ★★★ The usually effervescent Lombard is best part of this minor Parisian-based comedy. She's a movie star in the French capital who gets involved in an unlikely romance with Gravet, an aristocrat who's seen better days. Fun, but forgettable the moment it's over. C: Carole Lombard, Fernand Gravet, Ralph Bellamy, Allen Jenkins, Isabel Jeans, Marie Wilson. D: Mervyn LeRoy. COM 81m.

Fools of Fortune 1990 British ★★★½ Soap opera set in Ireland before and after WWII, chronicles horrible experiences of an Irish family at British hands. Good cast—Christie is outstanding—and sympathetically written, but uneven and rambling. C: Mary Elizabeth Mastrantonio, Iain Glen, Julie Christie. D: Pat O'Connor. DRA [PG-13] 104m. V

Fools' Parade 1971 ★★½ Misfire of a movie, yet boasts a sterling performance by Stewart as an ex-con menaced by his former prison guard. Sloppy script. C: James Stewart, George Kennedy, Anne Baxter, Strother Martin, Kurt Russell, William Windom, Kathy Cannon. D: Andrew McLaglen. DRA [PG] 98m.

Footlight Glamour 1943 ★★★ Blondie casts the daughter of Dagwood's boss in a play, jeopardizing her hubby's career. Predictable, light-hearted comedy, typical of the series. C: Penny Singleton, Arthur Lake. D: Frank Strayer. COM 75m.

Footlight Parade 1933 ★★★★★ Crackerjack Busby Berkeley musical with Cagney dynamic as stage-show producer racing against the clock to foil competitors from bankrupting his company. Triple threat finale numbers are knockouts: "Honeymoon Hotel," "By a Waterfall," and "Shanghai Lil" with Keeler cast improbably as Chinese femme fatale. Maybe the best of the Berkeley-Warner Bros. musical extravaganzas. C: James Cagney, Joan Blondell, Ruby Keeler, Dick Powell, Guy Kibbee. D: Lloyd Bacon. MUS [G] 104m. V

Footlight Serenade 1942 ★★★ Grable plays a dancer torn between beefcake suitors (Mature, Payne) in this breezy but minor musical. C: Betty Grable, Victor Mature, John Payne, Phil Silvers. D: Gregory Ratoff. MUS 80m. V

Footloose 1984 ★★★½ Rock musical has appealing cast, score, and style, as free-spirited teenager Bacon fights small-minded minister in town that hates dancing. C: Kevin Bacon, Lori Singer, John Lithgow, Dianne Wiest, Christopher Penn. D: Herbert Ross. MUS [PG] 107m. V

Footsteps 1972 ★★★ Irish-American football coach (Crenna) uses Vince Lombardi-like tactics on the field and even more aggressive tactics off, intimidating and infuriating colleagues at small college. Fairly adult drama—obvious, but worth a look. C: Richard Crenna, Joanna Pettet. D: Paul Wendkos. DRA 73m. TVM

Footsteps in the Dark 1941 ★★½ An aspiring crime novelist begins to solve a mystery in his spare time. Okay comedy/mystery, fun cast. C: Errol Flynn, Brenda Marshall, Ralph Bellamy, Alan Hale, Lee Patrick, Allen Jenkins. D: Lloyd Bacon. CRI 96m.

Footsteps in the Fog 1955 British ★★★½ Servant girl and employer match wits when she suspects him of murder. Taut psychological drama, convincing performances. C: Stewart Granger, Jean Simmons, Finlay Currie, Bill Travers, Ronald Squire. D: Arthur Lubin. CRI 90m.

For a Few Dollars More 1965 Italian ★★★★ The sequel to spaghetti-Western *A Fistful of Dollars* keeps up the pace by teaming a lanky, laconic gunslinger (Eastwood) with a dark rival to face off against a nasty bandit (Volonté) and his gang. The match-striking scene will make you cringe. C: Clint Eastwood, Lee Van Cleef, Gian Maria Volonte, Jose Egger, Mara Krup, Rosemarie Dexter, Klaus Kinski, Mario Brega. D: Sergio Leone. WST [R] 130m. V

For All Mankind 1989 ★★★★½ Superb footage from various NASA Apollo moon missions has been sharply edited into a single typical journey. Spectacular, awe-inspiring sights. Available on laser disc only. D: Al Reinert. DOC 90m.

For Better, For Worse 1954 British ★★★½ English newlyweds try to make a go of it. Familiar domestic comedy (adapted from Arthur Watkyn play) with sterling cast and some real laughs. C: Dirk Bogarde, Susan Stephen, Cecil Parker, Dennis Price, Eileen Herlie, Athene Seyler, Thora Hird, Sidney James. D: J. Thompson. COM 83m.

For Freedom 1940 British ★★★ Account of the sinking of the German battleship the *Graf Spee*, woven into the story of a father-son film company. Low-budget wartime drama draws heavily on actual newsreel footage. C: Will Fyffe, Anthony Hulme. D: Maurice Elvey Knight. DRA 87m.

For Heaven's Sake 1926 ★★★½ Lloyd reprised his bored young millionaire persona in this lesser silent comedy. This time he undergoes a change of heart after meeting a mission worker helping derelicts on Skid Row. Lloyd's first film for Paramount has a great chase scene, but overall this isn't his funniest. C: Harold Lloyd, Jobyna Ralston, Noah Young, James Mason, Paul Weigel. D: Sam Taylor. COM 86m.

For Heaven's Sake 1950 ★★★ A pair of angels debark from Heaven to save a young couple's marriage and see them through the birth of their first child. A cute fantasy with enjoyable turns by Webb and Gwenn as the ethereal visitors. C: Clifton Webb, Joan Bennett, Robert Cummings, Edmund Gwenn, Joan Blondell. D: George Seaton. COM 92m.

For Keeps 1988 ★ Teenage couple (Ringwald and Batinkoff) deals with unexpected pregnancy. Dull and wholly devoid of humor or romance. C: Molly Ringwald, Randall Batinkoff, Kenneth Mars, Miriam Flynn, Conchata Ferrell. D: John G. Avildsen. COM [PG-13] 98m. V

For Ladies Only 1981 ★ Harrison has neither the physique nor the dancing ability to pull off role of actor turned exotic dancer in Chippendales-like dance club. Movie is predictable beefcake trash. C: Gregory Harrison, Patricia Davis, Dinah Manoff, Louise Lasser, Lee Grant. D: Mel Damski. DRA 100m. TVM V

For Love Alone 1986 ★★★½ In Australia, circa 1930's, a rebellious student falls madly in love with her maverick instructor. C: Helen Buday, Sam Neill, Hugo Weaving. D: Stephen Wallace. DRA 102m. V

For Love of Ivy 1968 ★★½ When a lonely housekeeper decides to quit her job and move on, her employer's children scheme to find her a boyfriend so she'll stay. Interesting Hollywood attempt at African-American romance never really flies. C: Sidney Poitier, Abbey Lincoln, Beau Bridges, Carroll O'Connor. D: Daniel Mann. COM [G] 102m. V

For Love or Money 1963 ★★★ Superrich mom (Ritter) hires lawyer (Douglas) to find suitable husbands for her three daughters, and strenuously objects when he becomes romantically involved with one himself. Formulaic '60s farce boasts sturdy cast. C: Kirk Douglas, Mitzi Gaynor, Gig Young, Thelma Ritter, William Bendix, Julie Newmar. D: Michael Gordon. COM 108m. V

For Love or Money 1993 ★★★ Smarmy New York hotel concierge's dream of building his own hotel forces him to choose between the woman he's falling for and the man who could deliver the money he needs. Uneven comedy recommended only for Fox fans. C: Michael J. Fox, Gabrielle Anwar, Michael Tucker. D: Barry Sonnenfeld. COM [PG] 97m.

For Me and My Gal 1942 ★★★½ Minor Garland vehicle set in WWI has her, Murphy and Kelly (his debut) as vaudeville trio struggling to play the Palace. Full of patriotic schmaltz. Highlight: Garland and Kelly doing the title tune. C: Judy Garland, George Murphy, Gene Kelly, Ben Blue, Keenan Wynn. D: Busby Berkeley. MUS 104m. V

For Men Only 1952 ★★½ College professor (Henreid) contends with scandal caused by hazing death of a fraternity pledge. Well-meaning, star-directed melodrama. C: Paul Henreid, Kathleen Hughes, Russell Johnson, James Dobson, Margaret Field, Vera Miles, Douglas Kennedy, O.Z. Whitehead. D: Paul Henreid. DRA 93m.

For Pete's Sake 1974 ★★★½ Streisand is whole show in trite fluff about cab driver's wife getting in all sorts of trouble raising money to finance hubby's dreams. Star is great, but deserves better script. C: Barbra Streisand, Michael Sarrazin, Estelle Parsons, William Redfield, Molly Picon. D: Peter Yates. COM [PG] 90m. V

For Queen and Country 1988 British ★★★½ A soldier (Washington) returns home to engage a domestic enemy—racism, both personal and institutional. Stinging indictment at times a bit overwhelming. C: Denzel Washington, Dorian Healey, Amanda Redman, Sea Chapman, Bruce Payne. D: Martin Stellman. DRA [R] 105m.

For Richer, For Poorer 1992 ★★★½ Marvelous cast brings a lot to this breezy comedy about a wealthy eccentric (Lemmon) who gets rid of his money in order to revitalize his life. Jack's terrific. C: Jack Lemmon, Talia Shire, Joanna Gleason, Madeline Kahn, Jonathan Silverman. D: Jay Sandrich. COM 90m. TVM V

For Singles Only 1968 ★ Swingin' '60s nonsense about singles-only apartment complex. Silly. C: John Saxon, Mary Ann Mobley, Milton Berle, Lana Wood, Mark Richman, Chris Noel. D: Arthur Dreifuss. COM 91m.

For the Boys 1991 ★★★½ A bigshot USO singer (Midler) puts on all kinds of shows for the soldiers during WWII. Along the way she takes up with a brash, brassy egotistical comedian (Caan). Terrific Midler is all high energy and hot sauce, although the story is only okay. C: Bette Midler, James Caan, George Segal, Patrick O'Neal, Christopher Rydell, Norman Fell. D: Mark Rydell. MUS [R] 145m. V

For the Defense 1930 ★★★★ Chronicle of the noteworthy feats of a well-known New York criminal lawyer, William Fullom (Powell) in the first decades of the 20th century. It's Powell's show all the way, and he makes the most of it. Location shots of the N.Y. courts add to the credibility. C: William Powell, Kay

Francis, Scott Kolk. D: John Cromwell. DRA 62m.

For the First Time 1959 ★★★½ Lanza is temperamental opera singer falling in love with hearing-impaired young woman in breathtakingly photographed Capri. Manipulative tearjerker with good musical interludes. C: Mario Lanza, Johanna Von Koszian, Kurt Kasznar, Zsa Zsa Gabor, Hans Sohnker. D: Rudy Mate. DRA 97m. V

For the Love of Angela 1986 ★★★ Working-class woman must win over her wealthy future mother-in-law before she can marry the man of her dreams. C: Joyce Brothers, Sarah Rush, Barbara Mallory, David Winn. D: Rudy Vejar. DRA 105m. V

For the Love of Benji 1977 ★★★★ Terrific chase film, with the adorable mutt pursued through the crowded, boisterous streets of Athens by bad guys who want the secret formula tatooed on his paws. Great fun and good family fare. C: Benji, Patsy Garrett, Cynthia Smith, Allen Fiuzat, Ed Nelson. D: Joe Camp. FAM/DRA [G] 85m. V

For the Love of It 1980 ★★★ Fast-paced pursuit by assortment of villains who assume couple (Raffin and Conaway) hold secret to potentially deadly video game called "Doom's Day." Energetic screwball comedy. C: Deborah Raffin, Jeff Conaway, Barbi Benton, Don Rickles. D: Hal Kanter. COM 100m. TVM V

For the Love of Mary 1948 ★★★ In her last film, Durbin plays the switchboard operator at the White House. When phone lines get crossed, her love life gets inadvertently tangled up in Washington politics. Minor B-movie comedy. C: Deanna Durbin, Edmond O'Brien, Don Taylor, Jeffrey Lynn. D: Frederick de Cordova. COM 90m.

For the Love of Mike 1960 ★★★ Native American boy in New Mexico cares for animals, especially a horse, and hopes to contribute to his local parish. Sweet, sincere family film, maybe too sentimental for grown-ups. C: Richard Basehart, Stuart Erwin, Arthur Shields, Armando Silvestre. D: George Sherman. FAM/DRA 84m.

For Thee and Me 1975 *See* **Friendly Persuasion**

For Those in Peril 1944 British ★★★ A young man (Michael) joins the British air/sea rescue service in WWII, but is unhappy because he can't be in a more glamorous service. However, through various adventures he realizes the importance of his work. Rousing wartime flag waver. C: David Farrar, Ralph Michael, Robert Wyndham. D: Charles Crichton. DRA 67m.

For Those Who Think Young 1964 ★★ College comedy has students hanging out at local nightclub filled with aging celebrities. Dull goings-on, even with Ellen Burstyn (here going under the name Ellen McRae). C: James Darren, Pamela Tiffin, Tina Louise, Paul Lynde, Woody Woodbury, Ellen McRae. D: Leslie Martinson. COM 96m.

For Us, the Living 1983 ★★★★ Powerful film biography about civil rights martyr Medgar Evers (Rollins) is touching and penetrating. Cara is wife, Myrtle, who wrote biography on which film is based. An American Playhouse production. C: Howard Rollins Jr., Irene Cara, Margaret Avery, Roscoe Lee Browne, Paul Winfield. D: Michael Schultz. DRA 90m. TVM V

For Valor 1937 British ★★★½ War comedy follows two military families over the course of two campaigns as first fathers, then sons struggle to survive. Character-driven humor boasts some clever inventions—including having the same actors portray both the fathers and the sons. C: Tom Walls, Ralph Lynn, Veronica Rose. D: Tom Walls. COM 94m.

For Whom the Bell Tolls 1943 ★★★★ Hemingway's American adventurer (Cooper) fights alongside Spanish Civil War partisans. Solemn, slow-moving big-budget drama has great stars and color, but doesn't attain classic heights. Worth viewing, though. Oscar for Best Supporting Actress (Paxinou). C: Gary Cooper, Ingrid Bergman, Akim Tamiroff, Arturo de Cordova, Joseph Calleia, Katina Paxinou, Vladimir Sokoloff, Mikhail Rasumny, Fortunio Bonanova. D: Sam Wood. DRA 130m.

For Your Eyes Only 1981 British ★★★★ Bond (Moore) is dispatched to Greece to recover a top secret missile targeting unit from a sunken spy ship—but the Soviets want the device too. A tighter story and less reliance on gags makes this one of Moore's better Bonds. C: Roger Moore, Carole Bouquet, Topol, Lynn-Holly Johnson, Jill Bennett. D: John Glen. ACT [PG] 127m. V

For Your Love Only 1976 German ★★★ College student (Kinski) is blackmailed because of her affair with her professor. Routine melodrama. C: Nastassia Kinski, Christian Quadflieg, Judy Winter. D: Wolfgang Petersen. DRA 97m. V

Forbidden 1932 ★★★½ Early, atypical effort from director Capra is a strictly weepy affair, with mother (Stanwyck) relinquishing her illegitimate child to the father and his invalid wife. Forget Capra, see it for Stanwyck. C: Barbara Stanwyck, Adolphe Menjou, Ralph Bellamy, Dorothy Peterson, Henry Armetta. D: Frank Capra. DRA 81m.

Forbidden 1953 ★★★ A hired hood (Curtis) searches for a crime boss's wife, who turns out to be his old flame. Appealing leads Curtis and Dru in story set in Macao. C: Tony Curtis, Joanne Dru, Lyle Bettger, Marvin Miller, Victor Sen Yung. D: Rudolph Mate. DRA 85m.

Forbidden 1985 ★★★ Love story between Bisset, a German aristocrat who's with the anti-Nazi resistance, and Prochnow, a Jew she shelters in her Berlin apartment. Tense climax when Prochnow unexpectedly falls prey to the invading Russian army. Well done and moving. Based on true story. C: Jacqueline Bisset, Jurgen Prochnow, Irene Worth, Peter Vaughan. D: Anthony Page. DRA 116m. TVM V

Forbidden Cargo 1954 British ★★★ A customs officer (Patrick) is determined to keep drug smugglers from importing narcotics into England in this solid drama. Good performances. C: Nigel Patrick, Elizabeth Sellars, Terence Morgan, Jack Warner, Greta Gynt, Joyce Grenfell, Theodore Bikel. D: Harold French. CRI 83m.

Forbidden Choices 1994 ★★★½ A Woman married to a roughneck in the backwoods of Maine must struggle with many deprivations. An uneven adaptation of Carolyn Chute's novel; the original's rough edges have been smoothed out to the point of blandness. (a.k.a *Beans of Egypt, Maine, The*) C: Martha Plimpton, Rutger Hauer, Patrick McGaw, Kelly Lynch. D: Jennifer Warren. DRA [R] 99m. V

Forbidden Dance, The 1990 ★ Quickie Lambada musical about a Brazilian trying to save the rain forests tried to capitalize on brief dance craze. C: Laura Herring, Jeff James, Sid Haig, Richard Lynch. D: Greydon Clark. MUS [PG-13] 97m. V

Forbidden Fruit 1959 French ★★ Middle-aged loner falls in love with innocent young girl. Nothing new; sincere and maudlin, occasional bright spots. C: Fernandel, Francoise Arnoul, Sylvie. D: Henri Verneuil. DRA 97m. V

Forbidden Games 1951 French ★★★★½ In midst of WWII, a family of peasants shelters an orphaned Parisian child, who develops a touching friendship with their young son. Heartbreakingly realistic performances from two children touched by adult cruelty. Not to be missed: Academy Award for Best Foreign Film. C: Brigitte Fossey, Georges Poujouly, Louis Herbert. D: Rene Clement. DRA 90m. V

Forbidden Love 1982 ★★½ Against her better judgment, woman begins an affair with considerably younger man. Obvious attempt to exploit beauty of stars manages insight. (Watch for scene when Stevens brings his friends over for a swim at Yvette's.) C: Yvette Mimieux, Andrew Stevens, Lisa Lucas, Dana Elcar. D: Steven Hilliard Stern. DRA 96m. TVM V

Forbidden Music 1936 British ★★★ A singer (Tauber) persuades a Ruritanian duchess to lift the ban on music in her country. Excellent cast in old-style operetta. (a.k.a. *Land Without Music*) C: Richard Tauber, Jimmy Durante, Diana Napier, June Clyde. D: Walter Forde. MUS 80m.

Forbidden Nights 1990 ★★★½ American teacher (Gilbert) flouts local mores in China by falling in love with a local man. Admirable movie tackles anti-Asian racism. C: Melissa Gilbert, Robin Shou, Victor K. Wong. D: Waris Hussein. DRA 96m. TVM

Forbidden Paradise 1979 *See* **Hurricane**

Forbidden Planet 1956 ★★★★★ Futurized version of Shakespeare's *Tempest* finds Nielsen amid the only survivors of a spaceship wreck: Dr. Morbius (Pidgeon) and his daughter (Francis), along with their automaton assistant, Robby the Robot. No other sci-fi film would rival its intelligence and production values until *2001* in 1968. C: Walter Pidgeon, Anne Francis, Leslie Nielsen, Warren Stevens, Earl Holliman. D: Fred McLeod Wilcox. SFI [G] 98m. V

Forbidden Relations 1983 Hungarian ★ Grieving widow has affair with divorced man whom she discovers is her half brother. Dismal, unintentionally humorous attempt to make serious film about taboo subject. C: Lili Monori, Miklos B. Szekely, Mari Torocsik. D: Zsolt Kezdi-Kovacs. DRA 92m.

Forbidden Street, The 1949 British ★★★ Victorian melodrama with O'Hara as wealthy widow marrying beneath her. Andrews has dual role as both an artist and a lawyer. Film falters owing to poorly cast stars; supporting cast, however, is excellent. (a.k.a. *Britannia Mews*) C: Dana Andrews, Maureen O'Hara, Sybil Thorndike, Wilfrid Hyde-White, Fay Compton. D: Jean Negulesco. DRA 91m.

Forbidden Sun 1989 ★★ Coach (Hutton) and her gymnast trainees romp around Crete. When one youngster is raped, her friends exact their revenge. Crete looks great. C: Lauren Hutton, Cliff De Young, Renee Estevez. D: Zelda Barron. CRI [R] 88m. V

Forbidden Trails 1941 ★★★ Miner is lucky to have the Rough Riders behind him to straighten out some prairie price-gouging. C: Buck Jones, Tim McCoy, Raymond Hatton. D: Robert Bradbury. WST 54m. V

Forbidden World 1982 ★★ Limp follow-up to *Galaxy of Terror* featuring space explorers investigating alien skullduggery. (a.k.a. *Mutant*) Remake: *Dead Space*. C: Jesse Vint, June Chadwick, Dawn Dunlap, Linden Chiles. D: Allan Holzman. SFI [R] 82m. V

Forbidden Zone 1980 ★★ Strange doings on an alien planet where the inhabitants sing and dance and are ruled by a pint-sized leader (Villechaize). Fans of campy cult films will enjoy this one; filmed in b&w. C: Herve Villechaize, Susan Tyrrell, Viva. D: Richard Elfman. SFI [R] 75m. V

Forbin Project, The 1970 *See* **Colossus: The Forbin Project**

Force: Five 1981 ★★½ Martial arts squad to the rescue as dojo buddies team up to save young woman from the grip of evil cult leader. Lots of action, with a touch more nudity than most. C: Joe Lewis, Pam Huntington, Master Bong Soo Han, Richard Norton. D: Robert Clouse. ACT [R] 95m. V

Force of Arms 1951 ★★★ In the Italian theater during WWII a WAC nurse falls for her Army officer patient. Update of Hemingway's

A Farewell To Arms. (a.k.a. *A Girl for Joe*) C: William Holden, Nancy Olson, Frank Lovejoy, Gene Evans, Dick Wesson. D: Michael Curtiz. DRA 100m.

Force of Evil 1948 ★★★★½ Idealistic lawyer (Garfield) works for racketeer, only to find his own values corrupted as he descends into dark criminal underworld. Tough-minded film about moral issues marked by film noir style and a troubling performance from Garfield. C: John Garfield, Beatrice Pearson, Thomas Gomez, Roy Roberts, Marie Windsor. D: Abraham Polonsky. CRI 78m. V

Force of One, A 1979 ★★½ Martial arts expert (Norris) single-handedly rids a drug-infested town of its bad element. Norris keeps kicking, but there are few surprises. Sequel to *Good Guys Wear Black*. C: Chuck Norris, Jennifer O'Neill, Clu Gulager, Ron O'Neal. D: Paul Aaron. ACT [PG] 91m. V

Force on Thunder Mountain 1977 ★★★ A father and son on a camping trip find adventure with ancient indian myths and UFOs—and a new relationship with each other. C: Christopher Cain, Todd Dutson. FAM/ACT 93m. V

Force 10 from Navarone 1978 British ★★★ Commandos plan to sabotage bridge in Yugoslavia to thwart Nazis. Routine sequel to *The Guns of Navarone*. Ford's first starring role. C: Robert Shaw, Harrison Ford, Edward Fox, Franco Nero, Barbara Bach. D: Guy Hamilton. ACT 118m. V

Forced March 1990 U.S. ★★½ Film about the making of a film. Sarandon is an actor portraying a Hungarian hero killed in the Nazi death camps who tries to make sense of what happened in the Holocaust. Ambitious, well-intentioned film that goes nowhere. C: Chris Sarandon, Renee Soutendijk, Josef Sommer, John Seitz. D: Rick King. DRA 104m. V

Forced Vengeance 1982 ★★ Ex-Vietnam vet (Norris) takes on the mob in Hong Kong, where he's head security honcho at a casino. Scenic locale is highlight, but Norris's acting makes this for fans only. C: Chuck Norris, Mary Louise Weller, Camilla Griggs, David Opatoshu. D: James Fargo. ACT 103m. V

Ford: The Man and the Machine 1987 ★★½ Film biography of the automobile pioneer Henry Ford, based on Robert Lacey's best-seller. Robertson is somber in oddly depressing film. C: Cliff Robertson, Hope Lange, Heather Thomas, Michael Ironside, R.H. Thompson. D: Allan Eastman. DRA 200m. V

Foreign Affair, A 1948 ★★★★ Topical post-WWII comedy puts farmbred congresswoman Arthur in Berlin as U.S. government envoy, vying with ex-Nazi Marlene for Lund's attentions. Bright, witty script and good chemistry between dueling female stars makes up for dated satire. C: Jean Arthur, Marlene Dietrich, John Lund, Millard Mitchell, Peter Von Zerneck, Stanley Prager. D: Billy Wilder. COM 116m.

Foreign Affairs 1935 British ★★★½ An auto salesman (Lynn) and an aristocratic gambler (Walls) find themselves involved in the activities of a con artist in Nice. Walls and Lynn were a popular British comedy team in the '30s, and this was a good showcase for them. C: Tom Walls, Ralph Lynn. D: Tom Walls. COM 71m.

Foreign Affairs 1993 ★★★½ Alison Lurie's story of seemingly mismatched middle-aged lovers (a female academician and a sewage-plant engineer from Oklahoma) who meet on a plane to London is deliciously acted by Woodward and Dennehy. Appealing and mature. C: Joanne Woodward, Brian Dennehy, Eric Stoltz, Stephanie Beacham. D: Jim O'Brien. DRA 100m. TVM V

Foreign Body 1986 British ★★★½ An East Indian tourist visiting London pretends be a doctor and soon finds himself surrounded by scores of willing women. Old-fashioned sex comedy works well within its limitations. Enjoyable sleeper. C: Victor Banerjee, Warren Mitchell, Trevor Howard, Geraldine McEwan, Amanda Donohoe. D: Ronald Neame. COM [PG-13] 108m. V

Foreign Correspondent 1940 ★★★★½ An American journalist (McCrea) tracks down a spy ring run by the father (Marshall) of the woman he loves (Day). Another shamelessly entertaining tale of intrigue; watch for the famed windmill scene. Benchley, who co-wrote the script, and Sanders are splendid as Joel's sidekicks. C: Joel McCrea, Laraine Day, Herbert Marshall, George Sanders, Albert Basserman, Robert Benchley, Edmund Gwenn. D: Alfred Hitchcock. CRI 120m. V

Foreign Intrigue 1956 ★★★½ Steely-nerved press agent (Mitchum) investigates suspicious death of his shady boss, who was blackmailing foreign traitors. Effective Cold War melodrama benefits from offbeat storyline, inventive use of European locales. Based on a TV series. C: Robert Mitchum, Genevieve Page, Ingrid Thulin, Frederick O'Brady. D: Sheldon Reynolds. DRA 100m.

Foreign Student 1994 French ★★★★ An African-American student (Givens) at an elite Southern school in the segregated 1950s falls for a French exchange student, presenting obvious problems. Givens is charming in this intelligent, romantic comedy with a serious undertone. C: Marco Hofschneider, Robin Givens, Rick Johnson, Charlotte Ross, Edward Herrmann, Jack Coleman, Charles Dutton. D: Eva Sereny. COM 93m.

Foreigner 1978 ★★★ Secret agent, intending to meet his contact, discovers intrigue in New York night life. C: Eric Mitchell, Patti Astor. D: Amos Poe. DRA 90m. V

Foreman Went to France, The 1941 British ★★★½ Fact-based WWII tale, adapted from J.B. Priestly story, about a Welsh factory engineer caught up in German occupation of

Dunkirk while attempting to appropriate endangered top-secret French machinery. Exciting, documentary-style chase drama with comic touches. C: Tommy Trinder, Clifford Evans, Constance Cummings, Robert Morley, Mervyn Johns, Gordon Jackson, Ernest Milton. D: Charles Frend. DRA 88m.

Foreplay 1974 ★★½ Three extended comedy sketches focusing on sex and politics. C: Pat Paulsen, Jerry Orbach, Estelle Parsons, Zero Mostel. COM [R] 100m. V

Forest Rangers, The 1942 ★★★½ Goddard and Hayward are again rivals for a man (MacMurray). Decent if busy plotting, with Technicolor shown to advantage in forest blaze. Delightful hit song "I've Got Spurs That Jingle, Jangle, Jingle" added treat. C: Fred MacMurray, Paulette Goddard, Susan Hayward, Albert Dekker, Rod Cameron, Lynne Overman, Eugene Pallette. D: George Marshall. DRA 87m.

Forest, The 1983 ★★★½ Two couples camping in woods run afoul of a psychopathic killer and the ghosts of his murdered family. Interesting twists raise this above the crowd of low-budget slasher flicks. (a.k.a. *Terror in the Forest*) C: Dean Russell, Michael Brody, Elaine Warner, John Batis. D: Don Jones. HOR [R] 85m. V

Forever 1978 ★★★ Teenage girl has first experience with love. All moony and swoony, but it could have been worse, and its very modesty is engaging. Based on novel by Judy Blume. C: Stephanie Zimbalist, Dean Butler, John Friedrich, Diana Scarwid. D: John Korty. DRA 100m. TVM V

Forever Amber 1947 ★★★★ A beautiful young lady trades sex for security and power among the glitterati of Charles II's court. Action sequences breathe life into this sumptuous costumer. Sanders as Charles II is particularly enjoyable. C: Linda Darnell, Cornel Wilde, Richard Greene, George Sanders, Jessica Tandy, Anne Revere, Leo Carroll. D: Otto Preminger. DRA 140m. V

Forever and a Day 1943 ★★★★★ Wonderful saga of British house and its occupants over many years, elegantly served by brilliant all-star cast. Each vignette is self-contained, segueing seamlessly into the next with nary a dud among them. C: Edmund Goulding, Cedric Hardwicke, Frank Lloyd, Victor Saville, Robert Stevenson, Herbert Wilcox, Kent Smith, Ray Milland, Merle Oberon, Ida Lupino, Charles Laughton, Herbert Marshall, Claude Rains. D: Rene Clair. DRA 105m. V

Forever Darling 1956 ★★★½ Lukewarm big-screen expansion of stars' sitcom antics, with Lucy driving Desi to divorce till guardian angel (Mason) intercedes. Nothing much, but pleasant. C: Lucille Ball, Desi Arnaz, James Mason, Louis Calhern. D: Alexander Hall. COM 91m. V

Forever Evil 1986 ★★ Terrorized vacationers do battle with a murderous supernatural force. C: Red Mitchell, Tracey Huffman, Charles Trotter. D: Roger Evans. HOR 120m. V

Forever Fairytales—Brothers Grimm ★★★ Lushly animated adaptations of three Grimm classics: "The Fisherman and the Fish," "The Ice Witch," and "The Frog Princess." FAM/DRA 89m. V

Forever Fairytales—Charles Perrault ★★★ Vibrantly animated versions of Perrault's "The Dragon" and "Beauty and the Beast." FAM/DRA 59m. V

Forever Fairytales—Hans Christian Andersen ★★★ Animated versions of two Hans Christian Andersen rustic tales, "The Woodcutter's Wish" and "The Wild Swans." FAM/DRA 79m. V

Forever Fairytales—Rudyard Kipling ★★★★ Animation captures excitement of Kipling's "The Jungle Book," "The Tiny Oxen" and "The Magic Antelope." FAM/ACT 75m. V

Forever Female 1953 ★★★★ Rogers shines in witty backstage comedy about summer stock star who insists on playing parts too young for her. Very funny, with perceptive insight into self-deception. C: Ginger Rogers, William Holden, Paul Douglas, Pat Crowley, James Gleason. D: Irving Rapper. COM 93m. V

Forever, Lulu 1987 ★ Schygulla stars as an innocent who tumbles into unintelligible web of New York street intrigue. Introducing Baldwin in his debut and featuring Blondie front-woman Harry in a nonessential role. Meant to be hip. It's not. (a.k.a. *Crazy Street.*) C: Hanna Schygulla, Deborah Harry, Alec Baldwin, Paul Gleason. D: Amos Kollek. DRA [R] 86m. V

Forever Mary 1989 Italian ★★★½ Unorthodox teacher at a tough boys' reform school teaches his charges to accept a recently-arrived transvestite prostitute. Italian soap opera kept watchable by buoyant acting. C: Michele Placido, Francesco Benigno. D: Marco Risi. DRA 90m. V

Forever My Love 1962 German ★★½ The relationship between Emperor Franz Joseph and his empress Elizabeth in 19th-century Austria. Pleasant period piece, but nothing new. C: Romy Schneider, Karl Boehm, Magda Schneider, Vilma Degischer. D: Ernest Marischka. DRA 147m.

Forever Young 1983 ★★★ Coming-of-age story about a youngster who idolizes a priest, while sexual issues threaten his family life. Earnest drama. C: James Aubrey, Nicholas Gecks, Alec McCowen. D: David Drury. DRA 85m. V

Forever Young 1992 ★★★★ In 1939, his injured fiancée in a coma, test pilot Gibson agrees to be frozen for one year in an experiment. Thawed out over fifty years later, he embarks on an amazing adventure, and discovers love never dies. Tender, charming, heartfelt film. C: Mel Gibson, Jamie Lee Curtis, Elijah Wood, Isabel Glasser, George Wendt. D: Steve Miner. DRA [PG] 102m. V

Forget Mozart 1985 ★★★★ When the great

composer dies, inspector launches investigation into whether there was foul play. Great idea for a movie boasts lively execution and fascinating interplay of fact and conjecture. Sort of an anti-*Amadeus*. C: Armin Mueller-Stahl, Catarina Raacks. D: Salvo Luther. DRA 93m. V

Forgiven Sinner, The 1961 French ★★★½ Priest helps a shady woman deal with her anger toward life. Subtle, quirky performance by '60s heartthrob Belmondo. Insightful character study. (a.k.a. *Leon Marin, Priest*) C: Jean-Paul Belmondo, Emmanuele Riva, Patricia Gozzi, Irene Tunc. D: Jean-Pierre Melville. DRA 101m.

Forgotten One, The 1990 ★★½ An author moves into an old house and suffers ghostly phenomena, eventually uncovering the spirit of a pretty murder victim with whom he falls in love. Familiar tale gets a boost from O'Quinn's performance. C: Kristy McNichol, Terry O'Quinn. D: Phillip Badger. HOR [R] 98m. V

Forgotten Prisoners: The Amnesty Files 1990 ★★★ Silver is agent of Amnesty International digging into human-rights abuses in Turkey. Worthy stab at relevance lacks conviction beyond dutiful lip service to a serious subject. C: Ron Silver, Hector Elizondo, Roger Daltrey. D: Robert Greenwald. DRA 92m. TVM V

Forgotten, The 1989 ★★★ Returning band of Vietnam POWs is stalked through Europe by spies. A chance to enjoy the affable Keach brothers and their pals Carradine and Railsback, but implausible narrative defies viewer involvement. C: Keith Carradine, Steve Railsback, Stacy Keach, William Lucking, Pepe Serna. D: James Keach. ACT 96m. TVM V

Forgotten Tune for the Flute, A 1988 Russian ★★★½ A Russian functionary's boring existence is transformed when he falls in love with his nurse after heart surgery. Charming comedy/romance. C: Tatyana Dogileva, Leonid Filatov. D: Eldar Ryazanov. COM [PG-13] 131m.

Forgotten Warrior 1986 ★★★½ Veteran searches for traitorous soldier who shot him and killed his commanding officer back in Vietnam. C: Ron Marchini, Quincy Frazer, Sam T. Lapuzz, Joe Meyer. D: Nick Cacas. ACT [R] 76m. V

Forgotten Woman 1939 ★★★ Woman (Gurie) is wrongfully convicted and jailed. After four years, the D.A. who convicted her finds new evidence, and fights gangsters to clear her name. Serious sudser. C: Sigrid Gurie, William Lundigan, Eve Arden, Elizabeth Risdon, Virginia Brissac. D: Harold Young. CRI 63m.

Formula, The 1980 ★★★ A cop (Scott), looking into his friend's murder, discovers a plot to suppress production of a new synthetic oil. Dull mystery depends solely upon the colossal pairing of Brando and Scott, but even they can't overcome obvious script. C: George C. Scott, Marlon Brando, Marthe Keller, John Gielgud. D: John G. Avildsen. CRI 117m. V

Forrest Gump 1994 ★★★★ Charming, offbeat fable about a mildly retarded man who overcomes his handicap by dint of sheer concentration. As the "feel-good" movie of the year, it picked up six Oscars, including Best Picture, Director, Actor, and Adapted Screenplay. Hanks (the first man to win consecutive Best Actor awards since Spencer Tracy) gets to age 30 years, and is seen with U.S. presidents and other celebs through the magic of film. Sort of like *Zelig* with a heart. C: Tom Hanks, Robin Wright, Sally Field, Gary Sinise, Mykelti Williamson. D: Robert Zemeckis. DRA [PG-13]

Forsaking All Others 1934 ★★★ MGM pulled out the big guns for this star-filled soap opera. Gable silently loves Crawford for years, standing by her though she comes close to nuptials with Montgomery. The onscreen talent is huge; unfortunately the script is just routine. C: Clark Gable, Joan Crawford, Robert Montgomery, Charles Butterworth, Billie Burke, Rosalind Russell. D: W.S. Van Dyke II. DRA 84m. V

Fort Apache 1948 ★★★★★ A self-important and abrasive commander of a dangerous frontier outpost (Fonda) does what he thinks is right with violent results. Fonda gives an inspired and unforgettable performance in this elegant John Ford cavalry saga. Well paced and altogether absorbing post-Civil War Western that deserves its status as a classic. C: John Wayne, Henry Fonda, Shirley Temple, John Agar, Ward Bond, George O'Brien, Victor McLaglen. D: John Ford. WST 120m. V

Fort Apache, The Bronx 1981 ★★★★ Veteran cop (Newman) set in his ways, must face the changing realities of a tough job in an even tougher neighborhood. A talented cast and intelligent story line add to an already smart performance by Newman. C: Paul Newman, Edward Asner, Ken Wahl, Danny Aiello, Rachel Ticotin. D: Daniel Petrie. CRI [R] 120m. V

Fort Bowie 1958 ★★★ Marauding Apaches and internal romantic scheming jeopardize the survival of a U.S. cavalry fort. Pretty decent Western. C: Ben Johnson, Jan Harrison, Kent Taylor. D: Howard W. Koch. WST 80m.

Fort Defiance 1951 ★★½ Weary soldier returns from the Civil War, only to skirmish with Indians. Minor Western, boosted by competent performances. C: Dane Clark, Ben Johnson, Peter Graves, Tracey Roberts. D: John Rawlins. WST 81m.

Fort Massacre 1958 ★★★½ Wild West *Exodus*, as aging cavalry soldier (McCrea) leads white survivors of Indian attacks out of territory. Interesting Western with some odd, film noir overtones. C: Joel McCrea, Forrest Tucker, Susan Cabot, John Russell. D: Joseph M. Newman. WST 80m.

Fort Osage 1952 ★★ Professional swindlers

inadvertently start an Indian uprising. Watchable Western. C: Rod Cameron, Jane Nigh, Douglas Kennedy, Iron Eyes Cody. D: Lesley Selander. WST 72m.

Fort Ti 1953 ★★ Mid 1700s North American border wars: French-Canadians vs. local Indians. Another Sam Katzman quickie, memorable primarily for 3-D cinematography—duck that tomahawk! C: George Montgomery, Joan Vohs, Irving Bacon, James Seay. D: William Castle. ACT 73m.

Fort Utah 1968 ★★½ Ireland tries to subdue nemesis Brady, whose gang has taken over cavalry fort. Late-period oater from genre veteran Selander, aided by presence of grizzled performers. C: John Ireland, Virginia Mayo, Scott Brady, John Russell, Robert Strauss, James Craig, Richard Arlen, Jim Davis, Don "Red" Barry. D: Lesley Selander. WST 83m.

Fort Vengeance 1953 ★★½ Canadian Mounties track fur thieves, discovering too late that one among their own is a cold-blooded Indian killer. Western with some lush color photography. C: James Craig, Rita Moreno, Keith Larsen, Reginald Denny, Emory Parnell. D: Lesley Selander. WST 75m.

Fort Worth 1951 ★★★½ Gunslinger retires to edit local newspaper, then reinstates himself to take on an outlaw who shows no respect for journalism. Decent Western, with Scott at his craggiest, Thaxter at her most vibrant. C: Randolph Scott, David Brian, Phyllis Thaxter, Helena Carter. D: Edwin L. Martin. WST 80m.

Fortress 1985 Australian ★★★★ When teacher (Ward) and her young pupils are besieged by Aussie thugs in the Outback, they show their mettle by fighting back. Riveting survival drama with outstanding Ward. Suspenseful and too violent for younger viewers. C: Rachel Ward, Sean Garlick, Rebecca Rigg, Robin Mason. D: Arch Nicholson. ACT 90m. TVM V

Fortress 1993 ★★★★ An entertaining sci-fi thriller, with Lambert unjustly placed in a privatized maximum-security prison of the future, where high-tech torture and corruption are the order of the day. Violent, inventive, and a lot of fun. Followed by a sequel. C: Christopher Lambert, Loryn Locklin. D: Stuart Gordon. SFI [R] 95m. V

Fortunate Pilgrim 1988 ★★★★ Loren is mater familias who brings her family to New World to embrace the American dream. Italian immigrant saga based on Mario Puzo novel bursts with life and has added attraction of stunning score sung by Luciano Pavarotti. C: Sophia Loren, Edward James Olmos, John Turturro, Anna Strasberg. D: Stuart Cooper. DRA 192m. TVM

Fortune and Men's Eyes 1971 Canadian ★★★ A young man in a Canadian prison faces homosexual rape. Heavy-handed and lurid. C: Wendell Burton, Michael Greer, Zooey (David) Hall, Danny Freedman. D: Harvey Hart. DRA [R] 102m. V

Fortune Cookie, The 1966 ★★★★½ Matthau's over-the-top turn (Oscar for Best Supporting Actor) as an ambulance-chasing lawyer dominates entertaining, bristling comedy. Lemmon plays football cameraman talked into faking injury for insurance claim. First of five Lemmon/Matthau pairings to date. C: Jack Lemmon, Walter Matthau, Ron Rich, Cliff Osmond, Judi West. D: Billy Wilder. COM 125m. V

Fortune Dane 1986 ★★½ Police detective Dane (Weathers) must prove his innocence when falsely accused of murder. Nothing special. C: Carl Weathers, Adolph Caesar, Sonny Landham. D: Nicholas Sgarro. CRI [PG] 83m. TVM V

Fortune in Diamonds 1952 British ★★½ Stolen gems lure greedy, cutthroat trio to Africa at the turn of the century. Good comic cast. (a.k.a. *The Adventurers* or *The Great Adventure*) C: Dennis Price, Jack Hawkins, Siobhan McKenna. D: David MacDonald. ACT 74m.

Fortune, The 1975 ★★★½ Two less than brilliant con artists (Nicholson, Beatty) latch onto heiress Channing with intent to murder her and fleece her fortune. Great comic performance by Jack, but rest of slapstick black comedy falls flat, particularly in second half. C: Jack Nicholson, Warren Beatty, Stockard Channing, Scatman Crothers, Florence Stanley, Richard B. Shull. D: Mike Nichols. COM [PG] 88m.

Fortunes of Captain Blood, The 1950 ★★½ Tepid swashbuckler concerns famed pirate thwarting enemies by commandeering their own ship. Strictly by-the-numbers adventure fare with second-tier cast, few surprises. C: Louis Hayward, Patricia Medina, George Macready, Terry Kilburn. D: Gordon Douglas. ACT 91m.

Fortunes of War 1992 ★★★★ Idealistic young British professor (Branagh) and bride (Thompson) move to the Balkans in 1939, where he becomes involved in antifascist politics. Masterpiece Theatre series, based on Olivia Manning's autobiographical novels. Rather slow story with excellent performances. C: Kenneth Branagh, Emma Thompson, Rupert Graves. D: James Cellan Jones. DRA 350m.

40 Carats 1973 ★★★ Lackluster comedy from the Broadway hit about a 40-ish widow involved with a man half her age. Ingmar Bergman veteran Ullmann seems woefully out of place in this trifle. C: Liv Ullmann, Gene Kelly, Edward Albert, Binnie Barnes, Deborah Raffin. D: Milton Katselas. COM [PG] 110m. V

Forty Deuce 1982 ★★★ A young hustler (Bacon) tries to get drug money by selling a boy to a middle-aged man (Bean); his plans are disrupted when the kid dies. Bacon is excellent in a deliberately seedy story. Alan Browne adapted his own play. C: Orson Bean, Kevin Bacon, Mark Keyloun, Harris Laskaway, Tommy Citera. D: Paul Morrissey. DRA 89m.

48 Hrs. 1982 ★★★★ Slam-bang adventure has gruff-'n'-tough cop (Nolte) springing fast-talking con man (Murphy) from prison to help track down Murphy's escaped partner (Remar). Funny, energetic, and the film that made Murphy a movie star. Loaded with violence and profanity, though. Sequel: *Another 48 Hrs.* C: Nick Nolte, Eddie Murphy, Annette O'Toole, James Remar, Frank McRae. D: Walter Hill. COM [R] 97m.

Forty Guns 1957 ★★★½ New territorial marshal (Sullivan) of untamed Tombstone, Arizona faces lawlessness and a willful cattle queen (Stanwyck) who shields her wild brother from justice. Tolerable but peculiar tale given grandiose treatment. C: Barbara Stanwyck, Barry Sullivan, Dean Jagger, John Ericson, Gene Barry. D: Samuel Fuller. WST 80m.

Forty Little Mothers 1940 ★★★½ Effective change of pace for musical star Cantor casts him as an unemployed professor raising an abandoned baby at an all-girls school. Sentimental, but winning. C: Eddie Cantor, Judith Anderson, Rita Johnson, Ralph Morgan. D: Busby Berkeley. DRA 90m.

Forty Naughty Girls 1937 ★★ Hildegarde Withers mystery, the last in the series, puts the crime solver (Pitts) in a backstage setting to solve an actor's murder. Not the best in the Withers case files. C: ZaSu Pitts, James Gleason, Marjorie Lord. D: Edward Cline. CRI 63m.

49th Parallel 1941 British ★★★★ Nazi soldiers whose U-boat sinks off the coast of Canada try to find safety before they're captured. A gripping chase story that still thrills. The film won an Oscar for Best Story, but outstanding cast deserves equal mention. C: Anton Walbrook, Eric Portman, Leslie Howard, Raymond Massey, Laurence Olivier, Glynis Johns. D: Michael Powell. ACT 123m. V

Forty Pounds of Trouble 1963 ★★★½ Manager of gambling club copes with cute little girl thrust into his life. Family-style romp offers host of humorous character actors and extensive location filming at Disneyland. Innocuous remake of *Little Miss Marker.* C: Tony Curtis, Phil Silvers, Suzanne Pleshette, Larry Storch, Howard Morris, Stubby Kaye, Claire Wilcox, Jack Rue. D: Norman Jewison. COM 106m.

42nd Street 1933 ★★★★★ The classic backstage musical. Producers putting on a splashy new extravaganza have everything going for them until star (Daniels) sprains her ankle. Can chorus dancer (Keeler) save the play? Every show business cliché is played to perfection here. Busby Berkeley's choreography set a new standard, and the score is a toe-tapper. Years later the movie became a real Broadway musical. C: Warner Baxter, Ruby Keeler, George Brent, Bebe Daniels, Dick Powell, Ginger Rogers. D: Lloyd Bacon. MUS 90m. V

47 Ronin, The 1941 Japanese ★★★★½ One of many adaptations of a famous Japanese Kabuki story has 47 samurai vowing revenge on the men who tricked their leader into committing suicide; an engrossing tale of honor, filmed during WWII. Thoroughly entertaining, flawlessly directed. Sometimes shown in two parts. (a.k.a. *The Genroku Chusingara* and *Loyal 47 Ronin*). C: Chojuro Kawarazaki, Knemon Nakamura, Utaemon Ichikawa. D: Kenji Mizoguchi. DRA 225m. V

Forty Thousand Horsemen 1941 ★★★ WWI exploits of the Australian Light Horse brigade in Palestine. Well-organized, sincere war yarn. C: Chips Rafferty, Grant Taylor, Betty Bryant. D: Charles Chauvel. ACT 86m.

Forward March 1930 *See* **Doughboys**

Foul Play 1978 ★★★★ Amusing comedy/-romance entwines Hawn in assassination plot, with Chase—ever the charming oaf—assigned to protect her. Moore's scenes as hot-to-trot Britisher are legendary. C: Goldie Hawn, Chevy Chase, Burgess Meredith, Dudley Moore, Rachel Roberts, Eugene Roche, Marilyn Sokol, Billy Barty, Marc Lawrence, Brian Dennehy. D: Colin Higgins. COM [PG] 116m. V

Fountain, The 1934 ★★★ Moving performance by Harding rises above soap opera plot of wife torn between her duty to fragile, battle-scarred German husband (Lukas), and her love for English officer Aherne (her childhood sweetheart), held as prisoner of war in their home. C: Ann Harding, Brian Aherne, Paul Lukas, Jean Hersholt, Ian Wolfe. D: John Cromwell. DRA 83m.

Fountainhead, The 1949 ★★★½ Ayn Rand's controversial novel about individualism vs. conformity makes for fascinating, but frustrating drama. Cooper plays architect who'd rather blow up the building he designed than see his work corrupted by corporate meddling. Weird, stylized sets make no sense in supposedly conservative world that Gary's rebelling against. C: Gary Cooper, Patricia Neal, Raymond Massey, Kent Smith, Robert Douglas, Henry Hull. D: King Vidor. DRA 114m. V

Four Adventures of Reinette and Mirabelle 1986 French ★★★★ Two young women, one from the country, the other city-bred, share a Parisian flat and form a deep friendship based on zest for life and learning. Light, satisfying drama in four mini-episodes has depth in its sweet simplicity. C: Joelle Miquel, Jessica Forde, Philippe Laudenbach, Yasmine Haury, Marie Riviere, Beatrice Romand. D: Eric Rohmer. DRA 95m. V

Four Against Fate 1952 British ★★★ Four individuals engage in the sport of kings at Epsom Downs racetrack. Comedy and drama at play in account of human nature. (a.k.a.

Derby Day) C: Anna Neagle, Michael Wilding, Googie Withers, John McCallum. D: Herbert Wilcox. COM 84m.

Four Bags Full 1956 French ★★★★ Comedy about a pair of smugglers who try to outsmart the Nazis and sneak a butchered hog onto the black market in WWII France. Strong performances by French stars Bourvil and Gabin. C: Jean Gabin, Bourvil, Louis deFunes. D: Claude Autant-Lara. COM 82m. V

Four Clowns 1970 ★★★★★ Some of silent comedy's greatest moments, compiled with affection. Absolute must for fans of Keaton, Laurel and Hardy, and underpraised Chase. Classic and seldom-seen sequences alternate with equal hilarity. C: Stan Laurel, Oliver Hardy, Buster Keaton, Charley Chase. D: Robert Youngson. COM 97m.

4 D Man 1959 ★★★★ A scientist's experiments in matter transferral give him superhuman power and deadly impulses. Riveting, vintage science-fiction thriller. C: Robert Lansing, Lee Meriwether, James Congdon, Patty Duke. D: Irvin S. Yeaworth Jr. SFI 84m. V

Four Dark Hours 1937 *See* **Green Cockatoo, The**

Four Daughters 1938 ★★★★ Good tearjerker of title women (Lane sisters, Page), their doting father (Rains, delightful as always) and their suitors. Garfield is memorable in film debut as hard-luck composer. Followed by two sequels, remade as *Young at Heart.* C: Claude Rains, Rosemary Lane, Lola Lane, Priscilla Lane, Gale Page, John Garfield, Jeffrey Lynn. D: Michael Curtiz. DRA 90m. V

Four Days in July 1984 ★★★★ Two couples (one Protestant, the other Catholic) meet in a Belfast maternity ward with surprisingly funny results. As usual, Leigh provides low-key charm and understated wit. C: Brid Brennan, Desmond McAleer. D: Mike Leigh. COM 99m. V

Four Days Leave 1950 ★★★ On leave in Switzerland, a sailor's life takes an unexpected turn when he falls for a young woman he meets in a watch shop. Being in Switzerland, he enters a ski competition and this being a romance movie, he wins both the race and the object of his affections. Fun and forgettable. C: Cornel Wilde, Josette Day, Simone Signoret, Alan Hale Jr. D: Leopold Lindtberg. COM 98m.

Four Desperate Men 1960 Australian ★★★★ Doomsday drama about four on-the-lam crooks holding the fuse to a bomb that could blow up Sydney. Tense psychological interplay among the bad guys sets this apart from routine scare stories. (a.k.a. *The Siege of Punchgut*) C: Aldo Ray, Heather Sears. D: Harry Watt. CRI 104m.

Four Deuces, The 1975 ★★½ Palance is superb as the proprietor of the Four Deuces, a casino during Prohibition. The story of bootlegging activities however, never quite gets off the ground; it balances awkwardly between ironic humor and violence. Lynley provides the love interest as a broadly played gun moll. C: Jack Palance, Carol Lynley, Warren Berlinger, Adam Roarke. D: William Bushnell Jr. ACT [R] 87m. V

Four Eyes and Six-Guns 1992 ★★★½ Tenderfoot optometrist (Reinhold) from NYC fits Wyatt Earp (Ward) with specs so he can clean up Tombstone, Arizona. Cheerful Western comedy, charmingly acted. C: Judge Reinhold, Patricia Clarkson, Dan Hedaya, M. Emmet Walsh, Fred Ward. D: Piers Haggard. WST 92m. TVM V

Four Faces West 1948 ★★★½ Resolute sheriff tracks a young man who turned robber to prevent the loss of his family's ranch. Smart and well made, with excellent acting. (a.k.a. *They Passed This Way*) C: Joel McCrea, Frances Dee, Charles Bickford, Joseph Calleia. D: Alfred E. Green. WST 90m. V

Four Feathers, The 1939 British ★★★★★ Fabulous action epic of 1889 desert warfare; Richardson must prove himself under fire. Brilliantly acted; a classic of the genre. Based on best-selling A.E.W. Mason novel, filmed before in 1921 and 1929. Remade as *Storm Over the Nile* in 1956, and as a TV movie in 1977. C: John Clements, Ralph Richardson, Aubrey Smith, June Duprez, Donald Gray. D: Zoltan Korda. DRA 99m. V

Four Feathers, The 1977 ★★★★ Dishonored British officer (Bridges) redeems himself and saves his friends during war in the Sudan. Remake of the 1939 adventure yarn, succeeds via plenty of thrills, exotic locales, and fine acting. C: Beau Bridges, Robert Powell, Simon Ward, Jane Seymour. D: Don Sharp. ACT 95m. TVM V

Four for Texas 1963 ★★★ Bantering enemies Sinatra and Martin operate competing watering holes, then join forces against villainous banker Buono. Comic Western, worth a look as museum piece—for the way the men cavalierly treat Ekberg and Andress and for their constant winking at each other. And the Three Stooges to boot! C: Frank Sinatra, Dean Martin, Anita Ekberg, Ursula Andress, Charles Bronson, Victor Buono, Richard Jaeckel, Mike Mazurki, Jack Elam. D: Robert Aldrich. WST 124m. V

Four Friends 1981 ★★★★ Bittersweet, moving coming-of-age film centering on four Midwestern teenagers in 1961, who dream great dreams about their futures. Wasson excellent as one of three young men, a Yugoslavian immigrant; Thelen miscast as free-spirited young woman they all love. C: Craig Wasson, Jodi Thelen, Jim Metzler, Michael Huddleston, Reed Birney. D: Arthur Penn. DRA [R] 115m. V

Four Frightened People 1934 ★★½ Bubonic plague breaks out on ship, forcing survivors to flee in lifeboats. Then they face perilous trek through savage jungle. DeMille misfire is no epic, but rather routine, studio-bound curiosity. C: Claudette Colbert, Herbert Marshall, Mary Boland, Leo Carrillo, William Gargan. D: Cecil B. DeMille. DRA 78m.

Four Girls in Town 1956 ★★★ Hollywood hopefuls vie to fill part vacated by star. Unexciting cast, unoriginal screenplay, and busy score (including cloying theme), but with colorful ambiance and narrative drive. C: George Nader, Julie Adams, Gia Scala, Marianne Cook, Elsa Martinelli, Sydney Chaplin, Grant Williams, John Gavin. D: Jack Sher. DRA 85m.

Four Guns to the Border 1954 ★★ Western about bank robbers who pay (and pay) for their crime. Actor Richard Carlson's second outing as director incorporates familiar elements and cast (including Brennan, of course). C: Rory Calhoun, Colleen Miller, George Nader, Walter Brennan, Nina Foch. D: Richard Carlson. WST 82m.

Four Horsemen of the Apocalypse, The 1921 ★★★★½ Sprawling silent epic has Argentinean painter moving to France, defending that country during WWI, then discovering that his brother's joined the other side. Antiwar classic is exotically shot and succeeds with very downbeat tone. The movie that made Valentino a star. Remade in 1962. C: Rudolph Valentino, Alice Terry, Alan Hale, Jean Hersholt, Nigel deBrulier, Wallace Beery. D: Rex Ingram. DRA 114m.

Four Horsemen of the Apocalypse 1962 ★★½ Awkward remake of classic Valentino film. This time the hero finds himself by fighting in the WWII French Resistance. Overdone. C: Glenn Ford, Ingrid Thulin, Charles Boyer, Lee J. Cobb, Paul Henreid, Yvette Mimieux. D: Vincente Minnelli. DRA 153m. V

Four Hours to Kill 1935 ★★★½ A murderer bent on getting the man who squealed on him slips away from his guard and is loose in a vaudeville house. The action is confined to a single building, in this witty, exciting thriller. C: Richard Barthelmess, Joe Morrison, Helen Mack, Gertrude Michael, Dorothy Tree, Ray Milland, Roscoe Karns, John Howard, Noel Madison, Charles Wilson. D: Mitchell Leisen. CRI 71m.

Four Hundred Blows, The 1959 French ★★★★★ Truffaut's first feature and first installment in his partly autobiographical five-film series about French boy Antoine Doinel (Leaud). Here the protagonist is a 12-year-old delinquent reacting to and trying to escape from indifferent parents. Sensitive but not precious, with marvelous handheld photography of Paris and a strong musical score by Jean Constantin. C: Jean-Pierre Leaud, Claire Maurier, Albert Remy, Jeanne Moreau, Jean-Claude Brialy, Guy Decomble. D: Francois Truffaut. DRA 97m. V

Four in a Jeep 1951 Swiss ★★★½ A refugee (Lindfors) in post-WWII Vienna enlists the aid of four at-odds military police officers in the international zone. Fine performance by Lindfors marks solid entertainment. C: Viveca Lindfors, Ralph Meeker, Joseph Yadin, Michael Medwin. D: Leopold Lindtberg. DRA 97m.

Four Infernos to Cross 1975 ★★ Dramatic account of the sufferings of the Korean people under Japanese overlords in the early 20th century. Lots of martial arts action; otherwise slow going. C: Musung Kwak, Kyehee Kim. DRA 90m. V

Four Jacks and a Jill 1942 ★★★½ Strong cast has field day in otherwise weak musical about waif Shirley posing as famed European nightclub singer to get job. Highlight is Bolger's prizefight tap dance. C: Ray Bolger, Desi Arnaz, Anne Shirley, June Havoc, Eddie Foy Jr. D: Jack Hively. MUS 68m. V

Four Jills in a Jeep 1944 ★★★ Based on four female stars' true adventures on USO tour during WWII, this musical has diverting moments and the usual round of guest star spots. Trouble is, they all do numbers they've done better in other movies. C: Kay Francis, Carole Landis, Martha Raye, Mitzi Mayfair, Phil Silvers, Dick Haymes, Jimmy Dorsey, and His Orchestra, Betty Grable, Alice Faye, Carmen Miranda, George Jessel. D: William A. Seiter. MUS 89m.

Four Men and a Prayer 1938 ★★★½ Four brothers suspect that their military man father was murdered. In a freewheeling and often hilarious series of adventures, the brothers fan out over several continents, working together to find the killer. C: Loretta Young, Richard Greene, George Sanders, David Niven, C. Aubrey Smith, William Henry, J. Edward Bromberg, Alan Hale, Reginald Denny, John Carradine. D: John Ford. CRI 85m.

Four Mothers 1941 ★★½ Last of *Four Daughters* trilogy about closely knit Lemp family, with Rains as clan patriarch and real-life Lane sisters. Family averts serious financial crisis in this soap opera and last daughter gets happily "in the family way." C: Priscilla Lane, Rosemary Lane, Lola Lane, Gale Page, Claude Rains, Jeffrey Lynn, May Robson, Eddie Albert, Frank McHugh, Dick Foran. D: William Keighley. DRA 86m.

Four Musketeers, The 1975 ★★★★ Excellent, if somewhat darker sequel to *The Three Musketeers* (they were filmed at the same time) has all the elements of a first-rate swashbuckler: sword fights, fine costumes, humor, hammy acting, plus an evil Dunaway. Followed by *The Return of the Three Musketeers*. C: Oliver Reed, Raquel Welch, Richard Chamberlain, Frank Finlay, Michael York, Simon Ward, Faye Dunaway, Charlton Heston. D: Richard Lester. ACT [PG] 108m. V

Four Nights of a Dreamer 1972 French ★★★ Bresson transfers Dostoyevsky's *White Nights* to a modern Parisian setting as a painter falls in love with a young woman who's just lost her lover. Some find this film about being in love exquisitely beautiful; others think Bresson's rigorously austere style is a royal pain. C: Isabelle Weingarten, Guillaume Des Forets, Maurice Monnoyer. D: Robert Bresson. DRA 87m.

Four Poster, The 1952 ★★★★ Harrison and Palmer (then real-life spouses) are married couple who, from their wedding night in 1890, spend 35 years in the same rooms, with old four-poster in corner of bedroom. Warmth of De Hartog stage comedy (which starred Hume Cronyn and Jessica Tandy on Broadway) shines through, as does performers' chemistry. C: Rex Harrison, Lilli Palmer. D: Irving Reis. DRA 103m.

Four Rode Out 1969 ★★ Roberts is lawman tracking bank robber Mateos across the Southwest. Offbeat Western with a few nods at the hip '60s—the *19*60s, that is. C: Pernell Roberts, Sue Lyon, Leslie Nielsen, Julian Mateos. D: John Peyser. WST [R] 99m. V

Four Seasons, The 1981 ★★★ Alda wrote, directed, and starred in this cloying production in which four middle-aged suburban couples vacation together. Potential insights about love and marriage only skin the surface. C: Alan Alda, Carol Burnett, Len Cariou, Sandy Dennis, Rita Moreno, Jack Weston. D: Alan Alda. COM [PG] 108m. V

Four Sided Triangle 1953 British ★★ Scientist loses girlfriend to his best friend, so replicates her in the laboratory—only to discover replicant has the same elusiveness. Of interest largely for participation of notorious B-movie actress Payton, in dual role. C: James Hayter, Barbara Payton, Stephen Murray, John Eyssen, Percy Marmont. D: Terence Fisher. SFI 81m. V

Four Skulls of Jonathan Drake, The 1959 ★ Scientist tries to lift ancient curse on fiancée's family. Low-budget horror fare with some of the worst acting ever put on screen. Worth a look for bad-film aficionados. C: Eduard Franz, Valerie French, Henry Daniell, Grant Richards, Paul Cavanagh, Howard Wendell. D: Edward L. Cahn. HOR 70m.

Four Sons 1928 ★★★★½ Silent antiwar classic concerns Bavarian mother who loses three sons to combat and settles in United States with her last. One of director Ford's earliest films, featuring stunning location work in Germany. Based on I.A.R. Wylie novel. C: James Hall, Margaret Mann, Earle Foxe, Charles Morton, Francis X. Bushman Jr., George Meeker. D: John Ford. DRA 100m.

Four Sons 1940 ★★★ Remake of 1928 antiwar silent classic in which Leontovitch plays mother who loses three of her four sons in WWII; Ameche and Curtis play sons on opposing sides. Deflecting sympathy for Nazi Germany, 1940 film changed locale to Sudetenland in Czechoslovakia. C: Don Ameche, Eugenie Leontovich, Mary Hughes, Alan Curtis, George Ernest, Robert Lowery. D: Archie Mayo. DRA 89m.

Four Ways Out 1951 Italian ★★★½ Early Lollobrigida in one of her better films, a dark study of four participants in a robbery and its aftermath. (a.k.a. *La Citta Si Defende*) C: Gina Lollobrigida, Renato Baldini, Cosetta Greco, Paul Muller, Enzo Maggio. D: Pietro Germi. DRA 77m.

Four Weddings and a Funeral 1994 ★★★★ Sprightly comedy about Grant, an attractive but diffident perennial best man, and his pursuit of MacDowell, whom he encounters at the title occasions. Callow is a scream. C: Hugh Grant, Audie MacDowell, Kristin Scott Thomas, Simon Callow, James Fleet, John Hannah. D: Mike Newell. COM [R] 116m. V

Four Wives 1939 ★★★ Sequel to popular, acclaimed *Four Daughters* comes up short, with sister act having babies this time around. Wallows in sentimentality, only partly redeemed by Curtiz's strong direction and excellent performances from Rains and Albert. C: Claude Rains, Eddie Albert, Priscilla Lane, Rosemary Lane, Lola Lane, Gale Page, John Garfield, May Robson, Frank McHugh, Jeffrey Lynn. D: Michael Curtiz. DRA 110m.

Four's a Crowd 1938 ★★★★ A romantic comedy of errors finds Flynn, de Havilland, and Russell in a complicated love triangle. Flynn is surprisingly good in a rare comic role that keeps his swashbuckle in check. C: Errol Flynn, Olivia de Havilland, Rosalind Russell, Patrick Knowles, Hugh Herbert. D: Michael Curtiz. COM 91m.

Fourteen Hours 1951 ★★★★ More suspense than one expects in semidocumentary rendering of man on building ledge threatening to jump. Bel Geddes is dull but Basehart is in his element, and Hathaway's direction is slick. Grace Kelly's debut. C: Paul Douglas, Richard Basehart, Barbara Bel Geddes, Debra Paget, Agnes Moorehead, Robert Keith, Howard da Silva, Jeffrey Hunter, Martin Gabel, Grace Kelly, Jeff Corey. D: Henry Hathaway. DRA 92m.

1492: Conquest of Paradise 1992 ★★★ Italian Columbus (played by French Depardieu) persuades Spanish monarchs to fund his journey to find trade route to the East. Lavish, at least. C: Gerard Depardieu, Sigourney Weaver, Armand Assante, Frank Langella, Loren Dean, Angela Molina. D: Ridley Scott. DRA [PG-13] 142m. V

Fourth Man, The 1984 Dutch ★★★★ Alcoholic gay writer attends lecture by mysterious blond woman and finds himself strangely drawn to her—though she may have killed three other men and possibly intends him as her next victim. Glossy and original film with strong sense of erotic style. C: Jeroen Krabbe, Renee Soutendijk, Thom Hoffman, Dolf DeVries. D: Paul Verhoeven. ACT 104m. V

Fourth Protocol, The 1987 British ★★★½

Hypersuave Soviet agent (Brosnan) will nuke a U.S. military base in the U.K. unless British spy (Caine) can stop him. Solid espionage thriller, good cat and mouse. Scripted by Frederick Forsyth from his novel. C: Michael Caine, Pierce Brosnan, Joanna Cassidy, Ned Beatty. D: John Mackenzie. DRA [R] 119m. v

Fourth Story, The 1990 ★★★★ A woman (Rogers) hires earnest, klutzy detective (Harmon) to find her missing husband (DeYoung). Deftly directed thriller, full of delicious twists and surprises. Good psychological suspense. C: Mark Harmon, Mimi Rogers, Cliff DeYoung. D: Ivan Passer. DRA [PG-13] 91m. TVM v

Fourth War, The 1990 ★★★½ Tensions escalate between an American and a Russian colonel posted on opposite sides of the Czechoslovakian/East German border. Middling thriller directed with authority. C: Roy Scheider, Jurgen Prochnow, Tim Reid, Harry Dean Stanton, Lara Harris. D: John Frankenheimer. DRA [R] 91m. v

Fourth Wise Man, The 1985 ★★★½ Easter legend of wealthy physician who undertakes a journey to seek Christ. Good seasonal fare. C: Martin Sheen, Alan Arkin, Eileen Brennan, Ralph Bellamy. D: Michael Ray Rhodes. DRA 72m. v

Fowl Play ★★½ Odd trio seek gold at the first-ever cockfighting olympics. C: Ross Hagen, Nancy Kwan. D: Gus Trikonis. COM 80m. v

Fox and His Friends 1975 German ★★★★★ Fassbinder stars in this semiautobiographical melodrama as a naive homosexual circus performer exploited by his lover and friends when he wins a lottery. Poignant, powerful treatment of human cruelty, with documentary feel. C: Rainer Werner Fassbinder, Peter Chatel, Karlheinz Bohm, Adrian Hoven, Harry Baer. D: Rainer Werner Fassbinder. DRA 123m. v

Fox and the Hound, The 1981 ★★★½ Minor Disney animated feature about an improbable but lasting friendship between a fox and a foxhound. Not on a par with the great Disney classics, but fine for kids. Voices of Pearl Bailey, Mickey Rooney, Kurt Russell, Jack Albertson, Sandy Duncan. D: Art Stevens. FAM/COM [G] 83m. v

Fox, The 1968 ★★★★ Study of lesbian couple invaded by heterosexual Dullea raised eyebrows in 1968. Prettily filmed in Canada and featuring a sincere performance by Dennis, but ultimately diluted by circumspection that left much of the audience wondering what was so important. Based on novella by D.H. Lawrence. C: Sandy Dennis, Keir Dullea, Anne Heywood, Glyn Morris. D: Mark Rydell. DRA 110m.

Foxes 1980 ★★★½ Growing pains of four Valley girls who share an apartment in Los Angeles. Men come and go, but friendship (especially between Foster and Currie) prevails. Lighthearted film turns unexpectedly dark at end, almost as if it's another movie. C: Jodie Foster, Cherie Currie, Scott Baio, Sally Kellerman, Randy Quaid. D: Adrian Lyne. DRA [R] 106m. v

Foxes of Harrow, The 1947 ★★★ In 1820, a New Orleans misfit abandons his family in search of fame and fortune. Colorful but turgid interpretation of Yerby's best-seller. C: Rex Harrison, Maureen O'Hara, Richard Haydn, Victor McLaglen, Vanessa Brown, Patricia Medina, Gene Lockhart. D: John M. Stahl. DRA 117m.

Foxfire 1955 ★★★ New bride (Russell) of a struggling engineer (Chandler) has trouble settling down in an Arizona mining town. Fine, full-bodied love story. C: Jane Russell, Jeff Chandler, Dan Duryea. D: Joseph Pevney. DRA 92m.

Foxfire 1987 ★★★★ Poetic, skillful tribute to Appalachian folk, inspired by the Foxfire books, with Tandy radiant as mountain woman dealing with death of husband Cronyn while son Denver wants to sell family land. Based on the Broadway play. C: Jessica Tandy, Hume Cronyn, John Denver. D: Jud Taylor. DRA [PG] 118m. TVM v

Foxfire Light 1983 ★★★ Status-conscious woman threatens her daughter's relationship with a good-looking cowboy. C: Tippi Hedren, Leslie Nielsen, Lara Parker, Barry Van Dyke. D: Allen Baron. DRA [PG] 102m. v

Foxhole in Cairo 1961 British ★★★ Espionage in WWII Libya, with the Brits trying to outsmart "Desert Fox" Rommel and the Nazis. Not bad; the 18-year-old Michael Caine is billed 16th on cast list. C: James Robertson Justice, Adrian Hoven, Peter Van Eyck, Neil McCallum, Michael Caine. D: John Moxey. ACT 79m.

Foxstyle 1986 ★★★ An affluent nightclub owner leaves the city to rescue his ailing rural hometown. C: Chuck Daniel, Juanita Moore, Richard Lawson. D: Clyde Houston. DRA 84m. v

Foxtrap 1985 ★★½ Rugged adventurer sent to Italy to find missing person learns he's a pawn in a deadly game. Shallow, predictable action drama. C: Fred Williamson, Chris Connelly, Arlene Golonka, Donna Owen. D: Fred Williamson. ACT 89m. v

Foxtrot 1976 Mexican ★★ Strange saga of wealthy Romanian couple (O'Toole and Rampling) who flee impending European war for tropical island bliss. All's blissful indeed, until their servants revolt! C: Peter O'Toole, Charlotte Rampling, Max von Sydow, Jorge Luke, Claudio Brook. D: Arturo Ripstein. DRA [R] 91m. v

Foxy Brown 1974 ★★½ After a narcotics gang kills her drug-dealing brother and her cop boyfriend, vengeful woman poses as prostitute to destroy the mob. Ultraviolent *Coffy* sequel not one of black exploitation queen Grier's better efforts. C: Pam Grier, Peter Brown, Antonio Fargas, Terry Carter, Kathryn Loder. D: Jack Hill. ACT [R] 92m. V

F.P. 1 Doesn't Answer 1933 German ★★½ Aviation drama concerning the efforts of an enterprising French consortium to launch an airport floating platform at sea. Unique set design doesn't make up for thin plotting and lack of characterization. C: Hans Alberg, Sybille Schmitz, Paul Hartmann, Peter Lorre, Hermann Speelmans, Paul Westermeier, Arthur Peiser, Gustav Puttjer, Georg August Koch, Hans Schneider, Werner Schott, Erik Ode, Philip Manning. D: Karl Hartl. DRA 109m.

F.P. 1 1933 British ★★½ British remake of earlier German drama essentially uses the same plot of rivalries over control of a floating airstrip. Filmmakers rely on unusual locale for most of its appeal and ignore plot in this slow-moving drama. C: Leslie Fenton, Conrad Veidt, Jill Esmond. D: Karl Hartl. DRA 74m.

Fra Diavolo 1933 *See* **Devil's Brother, The**

Fragment of Fear 1971 British ★★½ A young writer's amateur investigation of his aunt's murder leads him to doubt his own sanity. Promising premise, and some energy. C: David Hemmings, Gayle Hunnicutt, Flora Robson, Wilfred Hyde-White, Daniel Massey, Roland Culver, Adolfo Celi, Mona Washbourne. D: Richard C. Sarafian. CRI [PG] 96m.

Fragrance of Wild Flowers, The 1979 Yugoslavian ★★★½ A prominent actor hopes to escape the pressures of stardom by becoming a recluse—but receives only more attention. Yugoslavian drama satirizes both the media and socialism. C: Ljuba Tadic, Sonja Divak, Nemanja Zivic. D: Srdjan Karanovic. DRA 92m.

Framed 1947 ★★½ Psychological drama with Ford as unemployed engineer set up by two thieves and forced to establish his innocence. Tight, talky script. C: Glenn Ford, Janis Carter, Barry Sullivan, Edgar Buchanan, Karen Morley. D: Richard Wallace. DRA 82m. V

Framed 1975 ★★★ Nashville gambler falsely imprisoned is paroled and bent on vengeance against crooked cops who set him up. Routine melodrama with gratuitous violence. C: Joe Don Baker, Conny Van Dyke, Gabriel Dell, John Marley, Brock Peters. D: Phil Karlson. CRI 106m. TVM V

Framed 1990 ★★★½ International intrigue catches up with an art forger (Goldblum) who may or may not have been deceived by his conniving girlfriend. Goldblum is marvelous in this comic adventure. Some adult situations. C: Jeff Goldblum, Kristin Scott Thomas, Todd Graff. D: Dean Parisot. COM [PG-13] 87m. TVM V

Fran 1985 ★★★ Gritty portrait of the unstable life of a welfare mom whose love affairs take her away from her needy kids. C: Noni Hazelhurst, Annie Byron. D: Glenda Hambly. DRA 92m. V

Frances 1982 ★★★½ The tragic, horrifying life and times of actress Frances Farmer (Lange), a beautiful young woman ascending to stardom—until she lost it all in a mental asylum. Realistic rendering sometimes painful to watch. Gripping performances by Lange and Stanley. C: Jessica Lange, Kim Stanley, Sam Shepard, Bart Burns. D: Graeme Clifford. DRA [R] 134m. V

Francis the Talking Mule Long before there was Mister Ed there was Francis. With the voice of Chill Wills, this smarter-than-average jackass led his not-as-bright friend Donald O'Connor through a variety of predictable hijinks in six films. Mickey Rooney replaced O'Connor in the final film in the series, *Francis in the Haunted House*.

Francis (1949)
Francis Goes to the Races (1951)
Francis Goes to West Point (1952)
Francis Covers the Big Town (1953)
Francis Joins the Wacs (1954)
Francis in the Navy (1955)
Francis in the Haunted House (1956)

Francis 1949 ★★★½ Naive army private (O'Connor) is befriended by a shrewd, talking mule (voice courtesy of Wills) whose unique talents go unrecognized by officers but whose assistance makes his human friend a decorated hero. The first of seven good-natured and simple comedies. C: Donald O'Connor, Patricia Medina, ZaSu Pitts, Chill Wills. D: Arthur Lubin. COM 91m. V

Francis Covers the Big Town 1953 ★★★ In this Man-Mule adventure, O'Connor and Francis become reporters for a big-city newspaper. They get the score on mob activities, but things look mighty grim when the bad guys try to get even. Typical *Francis* fare, and it doesn't get more complicated than that. Fine for youngsters. C: Donald O'Connor, Nancy Guild, Yvette Dugay, Gene Lockhart, William Harrigan, Gale Gordon, Chill Wills. D: Arthur Lubin. COM 86m.

Francis Gary Powers: The True Story of the U-2 Spy Incident 1976 ★★★½ Dramatized replay of the 1960 downing of U.S. spy plane over Soviet Union, purporting to take viewers behind the scenes as pilot Powers (Majors) is grilled by his Communist captors. Unexceptional despite excellent performances by Majors and Persoff. C: Lee Majors, Nehemiah Persoff, Noah Berry Jr., William Daniels, Lew Ayres, Brooke Bundy, Jim McMullen, Briff McGuire, James Gregory. D: Delbert Mann. ACT 100m. TVM

Francis Goes to the Races 1951 ★★★ This time Francis is a bookmaker (with predictions obtained from hooved relatives at the track.) Their insider information on horse racing causes some unwanted problems for his human pal, O'Connor—but was anything more to be expected? C: Donald O'Connor, Piper Laurie, Chill Wills. D: Arthur Lubin. COM 87m. V

Francis Goes to West Point 1952 ★★★ O'Conner, in trouble as usual thanks to Francis the Talking Mule, becomes an inadvertent military hero and ultimately goes to the famed academy—where there's even more trouble in store for him. Amiable but predictable. Leonard Nimoy appears briefly as a cadet. C: Donald O'Connor, Lori Nelson, Alice Kelley, William Reynolds, Palmer Lee, James Best, Les Tremayne, David Janssen, Chill Wills. D: Arthur Lubin. COM 81m.

Francis in the Haunted House 1956 ★★ In the last, and weakest of the *Francis* films, O'Connor hoofed it out of the series, as fellow MGM player Rooney took on the role of the fool for the mule. The duo wind up in a spooky old house, but there's not many laughs or scares to be found here. C: Mickey Rooney, Virginia Welles, James Flavin, Paul Cavanagh, Mary Kaye, David Janssen, Richard Deacon, Timothy Carey, Chill Wills. D: Charles Lamont. COM 80m.

Francis in the Navy 1955 ★★★ Sixth entry in Talking Mule series has O'Connor enlisting in Navy, accompanied by his four-legged friend. For Francis fans only. (O'Connor jumped ship from series after this, replaced by Mickey Rooney.) C: Donald O'Connor, Martha Hyer, Jim Backus, David Janssen, Clint Eastwood, Chill Wills. D: Arthur Lubin. COM 80m. V

Francis Joins the Wacs 1954 ★★★ Out of the military at last, O'Connor falls victim to an incredible military bungle when he's redrafted as a member of the Women's Army Corps. It could only happen in a *Francis* movie, but that's half the fun of the series. C: Donald O'Connor, Julia Adams, Mamie VanDoren, Chill Wills, ZaSu Pitts. D: Arthur Lubin. COM 95m. V

Francis of Assisi 1961 ★★★ Beloved 13th-century cleric founds his own order of peaceful monks and achieves sainthood. Dillman's performance highlights overall good cast, but film is overly ponderous. C: Bradford Dillman, Dolores Hart, Stuart Whitman, Cecil Kellaway, Finlay Currie, Pedro Armendariz. D: Michael Curtiz. DRA 111m.

Frankenhooker 1990 ★★★ After a lawnmower accident dismembers his fiancée, a young scientist aims to bring her back to life using body parts of prostitutes. Compellingly bizarre comedy/shocker revels in bad taste and warped sense of humor. C: James Lorinz, Patty Mullen, Charlotte Helmkamp, Shirley Stoler, Louise Lasser. D: Frank Henenlotter. HOR 90m. V

Frankenstein 1972 ★★★½ Faithful if undistinguished adaptation of the Shelley classic, with Foxworth as the doctor and Svenson as a sympathetic monster. Good acting makes up for the low-budget production; produced by *Dark Shadows'* Dan Curtis. C: Robert Foxworth, Bo Svenson, Susan Strasberg, Robert Gentry, Heidi Vaughn. D: Glenn Jordan. HOR 128m. TVM

Frankenstein 1993 ★★★½ Commendable attempt at more faithful adaptation of Shelley's novel is played too straightforwardly to be truly scary or affecting, though Quaid is good as the sometimes sympathetic creature. C: Randy Quaid, Patrick Bergin, John Mills, Lambert Wilson. D: David Wickes. HOR 117m. TVM V

Frankenstein (Restored) 1931 ★★★★½ Obsessed with unlocking the secrets of life and death, Dr. Frankenstein assembles a creature from dead body parts and brings it to life, only to have it turn on him. Horror classic made Karloff a star and spawned dozens of sequels. Restored version contains footage cut from the original because it was judged too frightening. C: Colin Clive, Mae Clarke, Boris Karloff, John Boles, Dwight Frye. D: James Whale. HOR 71m. V

Frankenstein and the Monster From Hell 1974 British ★★★ The Baron (Cushing) holes up in a sanitorium, stitching together a new monster (Prowse). The final, frightful entry in Hammer's *Frankenstein* series. C: Peter Cushing, Shane Briant, Madeline Smith, Dave Prowse, John Stratton. D: Terence Fisher. HOR [R] 93m. V

Frankenstein Conquers the World 1966 Japanese ★★★ A Tokyo scientist (Adams) combats the Frankenstein monster—except he's 60 feet tall and tosses helicopters around like pebbles. A must for '60s Japanese horror fans. C: Nick Adams, Tadao Takashima, Kumi Mizuno. D: Inoshiro Honda. HOR 87m.

Frankenstein Created Woman 1967 British ★★★ Baron Frankenstein (Cushing) is restored to life and returns the favor by reviving a drowned woman (Denberg). Unfortunately, he gives her the soul of a man wrongly executed—and he wants revenge. An effective and atmospheric Hammer installment. C: Peter Cushing, Susan Denberg, Robert Morris, Barry Warren, Thorley Walters, Duncan Lamont. D: Terence Fisher. HOR 92m.

Frankenstein Island 1981 ★ When hot-air balloonists crash-land on a mysterious island and meet a descendant of you-know-who, monstrous intrigue follows. Amateurish mess with no scares or suspense; a waste of the veteran cast. C: John Carradine, Andrew Duggan, Cameron Mitchell, Steve Brodie, Robert Clarke, Katherine Victor. D: Jerry Warren. HOR 97m. V

Frankenstein Meets the Space Monster 1965 ★★ Ridiculous dreck combines aliens kidnapping women in Puerto Rico with a robot astronaut gone haywire; he's eventually reprogrammed to battle the invaders. Truly awful, but entertains on a camp-classic level. C: James Karen, David Kerman, Nancy Marshall. D: Robert Gaffney. HOR 80m. V

Frankenstein Meets the Wolf Man 1943 ★★★½ Entertaining sequel to both *The Ghost of Frankenstein* and *The Wolf Man* has Chaney hunting down Frankenstein's diary which will free him from the curse of the werewolf. Ouspenskaya adds her usual flair for the supernatural. C: Lon Chaney Jr., Patric Knowles, Ilona Massey, Bela Lugosi, Maria Ouspenskaya, Lionel Atwill, Dwight Frye. D: Roy William Neill. HOR 72m. V

Frankenstein Must Be Destroyed! 1970 British ★★★½ The Baron (Cushing) has taken over an asylum and is furthering his research into transplanting brains—with horrific results. Gorily entertaining in the Hammer tradition. C: Peter Cushing, Simon Ward, Veronica Carlson, Freddie Jones. D: Terence Fisher. HOR [PG] 101m.

Frankenstein—1970 1958 ★★ Karloff stars as the great grandson of the infamous doctor, now trying to create a monster of his own with atomic energy. The muddled story makes this for die-hard fans only. C: Boris Karloff, Tom Duggan, Jana Lund, Donald Barry. D: Howard W. Koch. HOR 83m.

Frankenstein: The True Story 1973 ★★★★ A ghoulish retelling of Mary Shelley's tale with a handsome monster (Sarrazin) who starts to degenerate—and takes revenge for his condition. Innovative, beautifully photographed film that still packs some punch. C: James Mason, Leonard Whiting, Michael Sarrazin, David McCallum, Jane Seymour, Michael Wilding, Margaret Leighton, Ralph Richardson, Agnes Moorehead, John Gielgud, Tom Baker. D: Jack Smight. HOR 200m. TVM

Frankenstein Unbound 1990 ★★ Time-traveling scientist Hurt goes back to 1800s, where he encounters Mary Shelley, Dr. Frankenstein, and infamous creature. Corman's return to directing after 20 years is disappointing and story only occasionally involving. C: John Hurt, Raul Julia, Bridget Fonda, Nick Brimble, Jason Patric. D: Roger Corman. HOR 86m. V

Frankenstein's Daughter 1958 ★ Awful rip-off of the classic story. The doctor's descendant is actually male, though he does create a misshapen female monster (played by a man). Obvious low-budgeter bogged down by superfluous scenes involving teen cast. C: John Ashley, Sandra Knight, Donald Murphy, Sally Todd, Harold Lloyd Jr. D: Richard Cunha. HOR 85m. V

Frankie and Johnny 1936 ★★½ Famous song about romantic triangle inspires weak musical plagued by censorship problems. Broadway legend Morgan gives tepid performance, not helped by bland songs. C: Helen Morgan, Chester Morris, Lilyan Tashman, Florence Reed, Walter Kingsford. D: Chester Erskine. MUS 66m.

Frankie and Johnny 1965 ★★★½ Riverboat gambler Presley is torn between Douglas and Kovack. Features attractive river sets and good songs. C: Elvis Presley, Donna Douglas, Harry Morgan, Nancy Kovak, Sue Ane Langdon. D: Frederick deCordova. MUS 88m. V

Frankie and Johnny 1991 ★★★★ Terence McNally's play well served by excellent cast. Pfeiffer is a cynical waitress who expects nothing from life courted by Pacino, a lusty short-order cook just released from prison. Gritty and believable. C: Al Pacino, Michelle Pfeiffer, Hector Elizondo, Nathan Lane, Kate Nelligan. D: Garry Marshall. DRA 118m.

Frank's Greatest Adventure 1967 *See* **Fearless Frank**

Frantic 1958 French ★★★★ An adulterous affair leads to murder in this tidy, suspenseful thriller. Malle's debut as a feature director isn't perfect, but it's helped greatly by Moreau's star-making performance and Miles Davis' improvised score. (a.k.a. *Elevator to the Gallows*; *Lift to the Scaffold*; and *Ascenseur pour L'echafaud*) C: Jeanne Moreau, Maurice Ronet, Georges Poujouly. D: Louis Malle. DRA 92m. V

Frantic 1988 ★★★½ An innocent mistake by American surgeon Ford leads to the kidnapping of his wife (Buckley) in Paris. When local police find his story hard to swallow, he enlists aid of young French woman (Seigner). Tight suspense; Ford and Seigner are admirable. C: Harrison Ford, Emmanuelle Seigner, Betty Buckley, John Mahoney. D: Roman Polanski. CRI [R] 120m. V

Franz 1972 French ★★ Star-crossed love between French mercenary (Brel) and a self-tormented woman. Brel's the whole show. C: Jacques Brel. D: Jacques Brel. DRA 90m.

Frasier the Loveable Lion 1986 *See* **Frasier, the Sensuous Lion**

Frasier, the Sensuous Lion 1973 ★★★ A scientist discovers that he can communicate with a lusty lion living in a Los Angeles wildlife park. Borderline crassness mars the slapstick. (a.k.a. *Frasier the Loveable Lion*) C: Michael Callan, Victor Jory, Katherine Justice. D: Pat Shields. COM 97m.

Fraternity Row 1977 ★★★★ USC fraternity men acted and served as crew in this tragic, true-to-life story of a hazing gone wrong in the '50s. The late Newman was Paul's son. Solid acting in a well-delivered period piece. C: Peter Fox, Gregory Harrison, Scott Newman, Nancy Morgan, Robert Emhardt, Wendy Phillips. D: Thomas Tobin. DRA [PG] 101m.

Fraternity Vacation 1985 ★★ Two vacationing college students show nerdy pal the wild side of Palm Springs. Silly string bikini comedy. C: Stephen Geoffreys, Sheree J. Wilson, Cameron Dye, Leigh McClosky, Tim

Robbins, John Vernon. D: James Frawley. COM [R] 89m. V

Frauds 1993 ★★½ Con artist tries to steal suburban couple's life savings. Tepid black comedy contains a few amusing moments but is generally unsavory. C: Phil Collins, Hugo Weaving, Josephine Byrnes. D: Stephan Elliott. COM [R] 94m. V

Fraulein 1958 ★★★½ German professor's daughter in WWII Berlin aids an escaped American POW. Unconventional wartime tale with innovative casting of Wynter as fraulein. C: Dana Wynter, Mel Ferrer, Dolores Michaels, Maggie Hayes. D: Henry Koster. DRA 98m.

Fraulein Doktor 1969 Italian ★★★½ Based on the true life experiences of an infamous WWI German spy, Anna Maria Lesser. Large-scale war film with strong battle scenes; good Kendall. (a.k.a. *Stamboul Quest* and *Mademoiselle Docteur*) C: Suzy Kendall, Kenneth More, Capucine, James Booth, Alexander Knox, Nigel Green, Giancarlo Giannini. D: Alberto Lattuada. DRA 102m.

Freaked 1993 ★ Tasteless and unfunny comedy about teen trapped in a sideshow in which he and all the other exhibits are the product of horrible experiments by mad scientist. Disgusting, cruel, and boorish. C: Alex Winter, Randy Quaid, Mr. T, Brooke Shields. D: Tom Stern. COM [PG-13] 79m. V

Freakmaker, The 1984 ★★★ In order to create maximum horror at his circus freak show, a mad scientist goes into the laboratory and develops horrific creatures that are part plant, part human being. Typical horror fare. (a.k.a. *Mutations.*) C: Donald Pleasence, Tom Bakier, Michael Dunn. D: Jack Cardiff. HOR 90m. V

Freaks 1932 ★★★★★ A group of circus side-show "anomalies" band together and exact revenge on those who attempt to humiliate and exploit them. Still banned in some countries, suppressed in others for years, this incredible early classic from director of original *Dracula* is one of the most nightmarish and *compassionate* horror films ever made. C: Wallace Ford, Olga Baclanova, Leila Hyams, Roscoe Ates, Harry Earles, Johnny Eck. D: Tod Browning. HOR 66m. V

Freaky Friday 1977 ★★★★ Imaginative fantasy with Harris and Foster as mother/daughter switching personalities for a day. Very amusing as both stars mimic each other's traits with uncanny accuracy. One of the best Disney live-action comedies. C: Barbara Harris, Jodie Foster, John Astin, Patsy Kelly, Dick Van Patten, Kaye Ballard. D: Gary Nelson. FAM/COM [G] 95m. V

Freddie as F.R.O.7 1992 British ★★★ Minor British animated feature reworks James Bond sagas for a frog. Terrific voice work from a distinguished cast, but pretty silly for all but the kids. Voices of Ben Kingsley, Jenny Agutter, Brian Blessed, Nigel Hawthorne, Michael Hordern, Edmund Kingsley, Phyllis Logan, Victor Maddern, Jonathan Pryce, Prunella Scales, Billie Whitelaw. D: Jon Acevski. FAM/COM [PG] 90m. V

Freddy's Dead: The Final Nightmare 1991 ★★½ Promised last entry in the series features Zane as psychologist investigating her charges' nightmares and uncovering her own connection to Freddy. Not bad, with some scary sequences; the climactic battle was originally in 3-D. (a.k.a. *Nightmare on Elm Street 6: Freddy's Dead*) C: Robert Englund, Lisa Zane, Shon Greenblatt, Lezlie Deane, Yaphet Kotto, Roseanne Barr, Johnny Depp, Alice Cooper. D: Rachel Talalay. HOR [R] 96m. V

Free and Easy 1930 ★★★½ Keaton's first talkie is amusing, if uneven backstage look at Hollywood as he tries to make beauty contest winner (Page) into star only to wind up one himself. (a.k.a. *Easy Go*) C: Buster Keaton, Anita Page, Robert Montgomery, Edgar Dearing, Lionel Barrymore, Dorothy Sebastian, Trixie Friganza. D: Edward Sedgwick. MUS 92m. V

Free For All 1949 ★★½ Young inventor invents method for turning water into gasoline, and predictable complications ensue. Mildly amusing fluff. C: Robert Cummings, Ann Blyth, Percy Kilbride, Ray Collins. D: Charles Barton. COM 83m.

Free Ride 1986 ★★★ A young high school pipsqueak, trying to impress his friends, steals a car belonging to the mob. Few surprises but not badly done. C: Gary Hershberger, Reed Rudy, Dawn Schneider, Peter De Luise. D: Tom Trbovich. ACT [R] 92m. V

Free Soul, A 1931 ★★★½ Well-acted but stagy melodrama of boozing lawyer Barrymore defending Gable for murder. Shearer plays Lionel's fast and loose daughter who falls for Clark during the trial. Daring for its time. C: Norma Shearer, Lionel Barrymore, Clark Gable, Leslie Howard, James Gleason. D: Clarence Brown. DRA 95m. V

Free, White and 21 1963 ★★½ A black motel owner (O'Neal) is accused of raping a white civil rights worker (Lund) in the South during the freedom rides era. Ponderous courtroom drama filmed in mock-documentary style. C: Frederick O'Neal, Annalena Lund, George Edgley, Johnny Hicks. D: Larry Buchanan. DRA 104m. V

Free Willy 1993 ★★★½ Can the unhappy kid save the unhappy whale and get adjusted? Kids will love this tearjerker. C: Jason James Richter, Jayne Atkinson, Michael Madsen, Lori Petty. D: Simon Wincer. FAM/DRA [PG] 112m. V

Free Woman, A 1972 German ★★★ After leaving her husband and son, heroine (von Trotta) finds it difficult to cut old ties and begin a new life. Drama negates its points by hammering them home too many times. Trenchant von Trotta is story's saving grace.

C: Margarethe von Trotta, Friedhelm Ptok, Martin Luttge, Walter Sedlmayer. D: Volker Schlondorff. DRA 100m.

Freebie and the Bean 1974 ★★★½ Two outrageous San Francisco cops on a wild chase. Glossy thriller is loud and slick, high on violence and spectacular car chases. Caan and Arkin make an interesting team. C: James Caan, Alan Arkin, Loretta Swit, Jack Kruschen. D: Richard Rush. COM [R] 113m. V

Freedom 1981 ★★★½ Restless teenager (Winningham) leaves a loving home to "find" herself, only to discover the value of what she's left behind. Successful thanks to Winningham, who is thoroughly believable. C: Mare Winningham, Jennifer Warren, Tony Bill, Roy Thinnes, Peter Horton. D: Joseph Sargent. DRA 104m.

Freedom Road 1979 ★★★ Ali is former slave elected to the U.S. Senate. But as an actor, the Greatest is a lightweight, and the power of Howard Fast's inspirational historical novel is diminished by his amateurish performance. C: Muhammad Ali, Kris Kristofferson, Ron O'Neal, Edward Herrmann, John McLiam, Alfre Woodard. D: Jan Kadar. DRA 186m. TVM V

Freejack 1992 ★★ Racer Estevez dies and finds his body transported into the future to harbor the soul of monomaniacal industrialist Hopkins, while bounty hunter Jagger mills about wishing he had chosen a better film in which to make his acting comeback. Silly, brain-dead script. C: Emilio Estevez, Mick Jagger, Rene Russo, Anthony Hopkins, David Johansen, Amanda Plummer. D: Geoff Murphy. SFI [R] 110m. V

Freeway 1988 ★★½ Creepy killer calls a talk radio host while he checks out freeway victims. A nurse whose lover was murdered by this maniac begins pursuing the killer. Predictable, well-intentioned drama based on a series of real-life crimes in Los Angeles. C: Darlanne Fluegel, James Russo, Billy Drago, Richard Belzer, Michael Callan. D: Francis Delia. CRI [R] 91m. V

Freeway Maniac, The 1988 ★ Laughable attempt at a horror film (co-scripted by cartoonist Gahan Wilson) follows an escaped psychopath as he stalks an actress to the set of her new film. Title is meaningless in a film that's so silly it's sometimes surreal. C: Loren Winters, James Courtney. D: Paul Winters. HOR [R] 94m. V

Freeze—Die—Come to Life 1989 ★★★ Unsettling film chronicles the life of a peasant boy and girl in a remote '50s Soviet mining town. Although film won critical acclaim, scenes such as one of a woman drowning kittens give it a raw, disturbing edge that won't be to everyone's taste. C: Pavel Nazarov, Dinara Drukarova, Yelena Popova. D: Vitaly Kanevski. DRA 105m. V

French Cancan 1955 French ★★★★ Renoir's Technicolor homage to his father Auguste's Paris of the 1880s is really an old-fashioned backstage musical about the founding of the Moulin Rouge. Gabin trains a laundry worker to can-can while breaking her heart. Restored and re-released in 1985. (a.k.a. *Only the French Can.*) C: Jean Gabin, Francois Arnoul. D: Jean Renoir. MUS 93m.

French Connection, The 1971 ★★★★★ Tough renegade New York cop Hackman and partner Scheider uncover the trail of an massive overseas heroin ring. The pinnacle of its genre—gritty, fast paced, and action filled. Oscars for Best Picture, Actor, Director, Screenplay, and Editing. C: Gene Hackman, Fernando Rey, Roy Scheider, Tony LoBianco, Marcel Bozzuffi. D: William Friedkin. ACT [R] 102m. V

French Connection II 1975 ★★★½ In this sequel, New York cop Hackman pursues heroin kingpin all the way to Marseille, but is soon addicted to the drug himself. Violent and grim. C: Gene Hackman, Fernando Rey, Bernard Fresson, Jean-Pierre Castaldi, Cathleen Nesbitt. D: John Frankenheimer. ACT [R] 119m. V

French Conspiracy, The 1973 French ★★½ Political thriller, based loosely on notorious real-life Parisian kidnapping of Moroccan leader Ben Barka, with leftist agents and journalists closing in on Volonte (as North African leader). Bloated international project, with a lot of razzle-dazzle. C: Jean-Louis Trintignant, Jean Seberg, Gian Maria Volonte, Roy Scheider, Michel Piccoli. D: Yves Boisset. ACT [PG] 124m.

French Detective, The 1975 French ★★★½ Dark but diverting drama about a tough veteran detective (Ventura) and his cynical, but energetic young sidekick (Dewaere) out to bust a corrupt politician (Lanoux). C: Lino Ventura, Patrick Dewaere, Victor Lanoux, Jacques Serres. D: Pierre Granier-Deferre. CRI 93m. V

French Key, The 1946 ★★½ Private detectives are framed for murder and forced to solve it to save themselves. Thin but passable whodunit. C: Albert Dekker, Mike Mazurki, Evelyn Ankers, John Eldredge, Frank Fenton, Richard Arlen, Byron Foulger. D: Walter Colmes. DRA 64m.

French Lesson, The 1986 ★★★½ A young British woman (Snowden) travels around France, where she learns a few life lessons in romance. Amusing but unoriginal coming-of-age tale, with great scenery. C: Jane Snowden, Alexandre Sterling, Diane Blackburn. D: Brian Gilbert. DRA [PG] 90m. V

French Lieutenant's Woman, The 1981 British ★★★★½ Film-within-a-film follows Streep and Irons as actors having an affair while making a movie about doomed Victorian lovers. Unusual adaptation works well, as the two stories ultimately parallel. Streep and Irons are excellent. Script by Harold Pinter, loosely based on the novel by John Fowles. C: Meryl Streep, Jeremy Irons, Leo McKern, Hilton McRae. D: Karel Reisz. DRA [R] 124m. V

French Line, The 1954 ★★★ Russell was displayed in 3-D original version of this story of a fortune-hunted Texas heiress. Cheerful though thin musical diversion. C: Jane Russell, Gilbert Roland, Arthur Hunnicutt, Mary McCarty, Craig Stevens, Steven Geray. D: Lloyd Bacon. MUS 102m. v

French Postcards 1979 ★★★★ Three American college students travel abroad to study French culture, and find themselves enmeshed in romantic situations. Bubbly comedy with cast of future stars. C: Blanche Baker, Miles Chapin, Debra Winger, Mandy Patinkin, Marie-France Pisier, Jean Rochefort. D: Willard Huyck. COM 92m. v

French Provincial 1974 French ★★★★ Family saga, presented intergenerationally, focuses on hardbitten seamstress Moreau, fey Pisier, and their considerably weaker spouses. Sometimes slow, often demanding, but worth the effort, especially on big screen. C: Jeanne Moreau, Michel Auclair, Marie-France Pisier, Claude Mann, Orane Demazis. D: Andre Techine. DRA 91m.

French Quarter 1978 ★★★ Oddball drama parallels life of early-1900s Storyville hooker with modern-day morality play acted by the same cast. Fontaine plays the fallen woman. More interesting to film critics than to general audiences. C: Bruce Davison, Lindsay Bloom, Virginia Mayo, Alisha Fontaine, Lance LeGault. D: Dennis Kane. DRA [R] 101m. v

French Quarter Undercover 1985 ★★★ A pair of New Orleans cops get involved in a war against terrorists. Taut action and some excellent police work. C: Michael Parks, Bill Holiday. D: Joe Catalanotto. DRA 84m. v

French, They Are a Funny Race, The 1956 French ★★½ Stuffy British military man marries sexy Frenchwoman, and complications result. Comedy king Sturges in last time at bat strikes out with uneven comedy. C: Jack Buchanan, Noel-Noel, Martine Carol, Genevieve Brunet. D: Preston Sturges. COM 83m.

French Way Is, The 1974 *See* **Love at the Top**

French Way, The 1952 French ★★★½ A rare film glimpse of black entertainer Josephine Baker. The owner of a nightclub plays cupid to a pair of young lovers in Paris. Stylized and engrossing, even with weak plot. C: Josephine Baker, Micheline Presle, Georges Marchal. D: Jacques De Baroncelli. DRA 73m.

French Woman, The 1979 ★★ Soft-core porn flick combines political scandal and sexual blackmail. C: Francoise Fabian, Klaus Kinski. D: Just Jaeckin. DRA [R] 97m. v

Frenchie 1950 ★★ Woman (Winters) opens a saloon and plots to avenge the death of her murdered father. Slow, in spite of McCrea as the sheriff. C: Joel McCrea, Shelley Winters, John Russell, John Emery, George Cleveland, Elsa Lanchester, Marie Windsor. D: Louis King. WST 81m.

Frenchman's Creek 1944 ★★★★ After eluding a jaded English nobleman, the beautiful la Fontaine takes up with a French pirate. Lavish, fun, and filling throughout. C: Joan Fontaine, Arturo deCordova, Basil Rathbone, Nigel Bruce, Cecil Kellaway, Ralph Forbes, George Kirby. D: Mitchell Leisen. ACT 113m.

Frenchman's Farm 1987 ★★★½ Stopping at a remote farmhouse, a lost law student realizes that she's caught in a time warp, transported to World War II. An interesting thriller with some engaging suspense. C: Tracey Tainsh, Dávid Reyne, John Meillon, Norman Kaye. D: Ron Way. ACT [PG] 90m. v

Frenzy 1944 *See* **Torment**

Frenzy 1972 British ★★★★½ The Necktie Murderer is loose and stalking the women of London, but police close in on the wrong man (Finch). Hitchcock's most disturbing film has many sensational scenes, and wonderfully dark comic relief. C: Jon Finch, Barry Foster, Barbara Leigh-Hunt, Anna Massey, Alec McCowen, Vivien Merchant, Billie Whitelaw, Jean Marsh. D: Alfred Hitchcock. CRI [R] 116m. v

Fresh 1994 ★★★½ Inner-city coming-of-age film, with a 12-year-old kid (Nelson) splitting his time between family ties, schoolwork, and running errands for the local drug dealer (Esposito). Has a certain low-budget energy that transforms it. Good debut for Yakin. C: Sean Nelson, Giancarlo Esposito, Samuel L. Jackson. D: Boaz Yakin. DRA [R] 112m.

Fresh Horses 1988 ★★ Ringwald and McCarthy played together wonderfully in *Pretty in Pink*, but fail to reprise spark in this gloomy, downbeat tale of well-meaning rich boy obsessed with married teenager from the wrong side of the tracks. C: Molly Ringwald, Andrew McCarthy, Patti D'Arbanville, Molly Hagan, Ben Stiller, Leon Russom. D: David Anspaugh. DRA [PG-13] 105m. v

Fresh Kill 1987 ★★½ Heading west to fulfill his dream of movie stardom, a young Chicago lad finds lots of trouble instead—courtesy of a bunch of drug smugglers he meets along with way. Typical violence that continues throughout. C: Flint Keller, Patricia Parks, Pamela Dixon, Robert Zdar. D: Joseph Merhi. ACT 90m. v

Freshman, The 1925 ★★★★★ Naive college frosh Lloyd longs to play for school football team. By sheer determination, he works his way up from tackling dummy to water boy to Big Game hero. This is one of Lloyd's silent best, a terrific blend of sincere characterization and wonderfully choreographed slapstick. C: Harold Lloyd, Jobyna Ralston, Brooks Benedict, James Anderson, Hazel Keener. D: Sam Taylor, Fred Newmeyer. COM 70m. v

Freshman, The 1990 ★★★★½ Deft comedy of a New York University film student, (Broderick) who inadvertently gets involved with Mafia plot to smuggle endangered animals. Brando is exquisite in self-parody as Godfatherly mob boss who becomes Broderick's benefactor. Bergman's script and direction are delightful. C: Marlon Brando, Matthew Broderick, Bruno Kirby, Penelope Ann Miller, Frank Whaley, B.D. Wong. D: Andrew Bergman. COM [PG] 102m. V

Freud 1962 ★★★ Clift plays the father of psychiatry in his early days in this workmanlike biography. Few insights offered. C: Montgomery Clift, Susannah York, Larry Parks, David McCallum, Susan Kohner, Eileen Herlie. D: John Huston. DRA 120m.

Frida 1984 Mexican ★★★★ Absorbing treatment of life and career of flamboyant Mexican painter and feminist icon Frida Kahlo. Scenes of Kahlo's frenetic life with fellow painter Diego Rivera and revealing self-portraits combine to form a passionate tableau. C: Ofelia Medina, Juan Jose Gurrola, Max Kerlow. D: Paul Leduc. DRA 108m. V

Friday Foster 1975 ★★★½ Fashion photographer by day, avenger by night (Grier) is onto a plot to assassinate several major African-American politicans. Campy fun was inspired by a popular comic strip. Neat cast. C: Pam Grier, Yaphet Kotto, Godfrey Cambridge, Thalmus Rasulala, Eartha Kitt, Jim Backus, Carl Weathers. D: Arthur Marks. ACT 90m. V

Friday the 13th 1980 ★★★½ Influential horror film about teenaged summer camp counselors being systematically slaughtered. Gory, but director Cunningham works up plenty of chills and sympathy for the young victims. C: Betsy Palmer, Adrienne King, Harry Crosby, Kevin Bacon. D: Sean S. Cunningham. HOR [R] 95m. V

Friday the 13th, Part 2 1981 ★★ First sequel to the surprise hit is really just a remake, introducing Jason (whose mom was the killer the first time out) to butcher another camp full of counselors. No surprises, just bloody, methodical murder. C: Betsy Palmer, Amy Steel, John Furey, Adrienne King. D: Steve Miner. HOR [R] 87m. V

Friday the 13th, Part 3 1982 ★ Jason puts on the hockey mask for the first time as he sets out to massacre a new crew of teenagers renting a lake house. More formula repetition; originally filmed in 3-D. C: Dana Kimmell, Paul Kratka, Tracie Savage. D: Steve Miner. HOR [R] 96m. V

Friday the 13th: The Final Chapter 1984 ★ Fourth in the series has absolutely no new twists, aside from the murderous Jason supposedly being put away for good. It's just another predictable, unscary series of murders of oversexed teenagers. C: Crispin Glover, Kimberly Beck, Barbara Howard. D: Joseph Zito. HOR [R] 90m. V

Friday the 13th, Part V: A New Begining 1985 ★★ Has Jason the killer returned from the dead? Opens with a stylish, scary nightmare scene, then plunges into another series of pointless murders and obnoxious characters. C: John Shepard, Melanie Kinnaman, Shavar Ross, Richard Young, Carol Lacatell. D: Danny Steinmann. HOR [R] 92m. V

Friday the 13th, Part VI: Jason Lives 1986 ★★★ The masked slayer climbs from his grave for another round of summer slaughter and Mathews tries to stop him. While story adheres to formula, the script, characters and direction are wittier than usual, making this one of the best of the series. C: Thom Mathews, Jennifer Cooke. D: Tom McLoughlin. HOR [R] 87m. V

Friday the 13th, Part VII: The New Blood 1988 ★ This time, Jason's stable of nubile teenage targets includes a telekinetic girl (Lincoln) who may be able to destroy him with her psychic powers. C: Lar Park Lincoln, Terry Kiser, Susan Blu, Kevin Blair. D: John Carl Buechler. HOR [R] 90m. V

Friday the 13th, Part VIII: Jason Takes Manhattan 1989 ★ He also takes forever; most of this film's student slaughter is set on a cruise ship before finally winding up in the Big Apple (filmed mostly in Canada). C: Jensen Daggett, Kane Hodder, Peter Mark Richman, Scott Reeves, Barbara Bingham, V.C. Dupree. D: Rob Hedden. HOR [R] 100m. V

Friday the 13th, Part IX—Jason Goes to Hell 1993 *See* **Jason Goes to Hell: The Final Friday**

Friday the 13th: The Orphan 1977 ★★½ An abandoned boy goes beserk and gets violent in response to his memories of past abuse. Standard horror item bears no relation to the Jason series. C: Joanna Miles, Peggy Feury. D: John Ballard. HOR 87m. V

Fried Green Tomatoes 1991 ★★★★ An unhappy Southern housewife finds inspiration when she befriends a no-nonsense old Southern lady who tells her a riveting tale of two old friends back in the '20s. Solid Southern charm and satisfying dual story lines. Done to a turn, spicy and nice. C: Kathy Bates, Jessica Tandy, Mary Stuart Masterson, Mary-Louise Parker, Cicely Tyson, Chris O'Donnell, Stan Shaw. D: Jon Avnet. DRA [PG-13] 130m. V

Frieda 1947 British ★★★½ Post-WWII drama of British man bringing home German wife, and the bigotry they endure. Affecting, low-key character study. C: David Farrar, Glynis Johns, Mai Zetterling, Flora Robson. D: Basil Dearden. DRA 98m. V

Friendly Fire 1979 ★★★★ Burnett and Beatty are parents of soldier killed by his own troops in Vietnam in this riveting, based-in-fact drama about a couple's fight to learn the truth about their son's death. C: Carol Burnett, Ned Beatty, Sam Waterston, Timothy Hutton. D: David Greene. DRA 146m. TVM V

Friendly Persuasion 1956 ★★★★★ Beautifully realized adaptation of Jessamyn West's novel about impact of Civil War on family of Indiana Quakers and their vow of pacifism. Simple, timeless, and deeply emotional.

Memorable score by Dmitri Tiomkin. Remade for TV. C: Gary Cooper, Dorothy McGuire, Marjorie Main, Anthony Perkins, Richard Eyer, Robert Middleton. D: William Wyler. DRA 140m. V

Friendly Persuasion 1975 ★★★★ Quaker family aids runaway slaves during Civil War. Remake of 1956 film, with Kiley and Knight admirable as courageous couple who are guided by the teachings of their gentle faith. (a.k.a. *Except for Thee and Me*) C: Richard Kiley, Shirley Knight, Clifton James, Michael O'Keefe, Kevin O'Keefe, Tracie Savage, Sparky Marcus. D: Joseph Sargent. FAM/DRA 100m. TVM

Friends 1971 British ★★ Runaway teenage lovers flee to France's beautiful Camargue region, have a baby, and spend an idyllic year in a secluded cottage before real life intrudes. Romantic Elton John score and lots of soft focus. C: Sean Bury, Anicee Alvina, Pascale Roberts, Sady Rebbot, Ronald Lewis. D: Lewis Gilbert. DRA [R] 101m. V

Friends and Husbands 1983 German ★★★½ The developing friendship between two women becomes mutually destructive. Compelling, well-acted drama is slow paced, but worthwhile. Made in West Germany. C: Hanna Schygulla, Angela Winkler, Peter Striebeck. D: Margarethe von Trotta. DRA 106m.

Friends and Lovers 1931 ★★½ Menjou and Olivier are British soldiers in India, both captivated by sultry Damita (as the unfortunate wife of sinister von Stroheim). Sentimental melodramas was Olivier's first American film (he has fourth billing). C: Adolphe Menjou, Laurence Olivier, Lili Damita, Erich von Stroheim, Hugh Herbert. D: Victor Schertzinger. DRA 68m.

Friends, Lovers & Lunatics 1989 Canadian ★★ Wacky group of acquaintances all arrive at small mountain cabin during the same weekend. Misfired stab at contemporary screwball comedy. (a.k.a. *Crazy House*). C: Daniel Stern, Sheila McCarthy, Deborah Foreman, Elias Koteas. D: Stephen Withrow. COM [R] 87m. V

Friends of Eddie Coyle, The 1973 ★★★★ Authorities coerce aging small-time hood to inform on pals who later track him down. Mitchum's low-key character study highlights powerful gangster drama set in Boston. Based on George V. Higgins novel. C: Robert Mitchum, Peter Boyle, Richard Jordan, Steven Keats, Alex Rocco, Mitchell Ryan. D: Peter Yates. CRI [R] 102m.

Friends of Mr. Sweeney 1934 ★★★ After a bender, a world-weary journalist (Ruggles) improves his character. Endearing, old-fashioned comedy, highlighted by Ruggles. C: Charles Ruggles, Ann Dvorak, Eugene Pallette. D: Edward Ludwig. COM 68m.

Friendship in Vienna 1993 ★★★★ Intelligent, earnest Disney offering about a young Jewish teenager whose best friend's Christian family helps her escape from the Nazis. Sensitively acted, nicely mounted. C: Edward Asner, Stephen Macht, Jenny Lewis, Jane Alexander. D: Arthur Allan Seidelman. DRA 100m.

Friendships, Secrets, and Lies 1979 ★★ Seven sorority sisters convene for last look at sorority house, only to discover a baby's corpse. Whose baby is it? Almost a convention of talented former ingenues. C: Cathryn Damon, Tina Louise, Paula Prentiss, Stella Stevens. D: Ann Zane Shanks, Marlena Laird. DRA 104m. TVM

Fright 1971 British ★★½ Escaped psychopath (Bannen) terrorizes babysitter (George), who's looking after his son in an isolated house. Occasionally tense but just as often exploitative horror drama. C: Susan George, Honor Blackman, Ian Bannen, John Gregson, George Cole, Dennis Waterman. D: Peter Collinson. HOR [PG] 87m. V

Fright Night 1985 ★★★★ Teenager is convinced his neighbor is a vampire. Enlisting the help of friends and a former horror movie actor, he sets out to do battle. Fresh, funny, creepy, and even touching. C: Chris Sarandon, William Ragsdale, Amanda Bearse, Roddy McDowall, Stephen Geoffreys. D: Tom Holland. HOR [R] 105m. V

Fright Night, Part II 1989 ★★½ Occasionally scary and funny but overall disappointing sequel to the 1985 horror hit, with Ragsdale and McDowall returning to battle another squad of ghouls led by Carmen, the sister of the first film's vampire. C: Roddy McDowall, William Ragsdale, Traci Lin, Julie Carmen, Jonathan Gries, Russell Clark, Brian Thompson. D: Tommy Lee Wallace. HOR [R] 108m. V

Frightened Bride 1953 British ★★ An English family confronts its worst fears when one of the sons is convicted of murder. Baffling melodrama. (a.k.a. *The Tall Headlines*) C: Andre Morell, Flora Robson, Mai Zetterling, Michael Denison, Mervyn Johns. D: Terence Young. DRA 75m.

Frightened City, The 1962 British ★★★½ Rival London gangsters have a falling out over shares in a protection racket scheme. Tense melodrama with a gritty, realistic ambiance. C: Herbert Lom, John Gregson, Sean Connery, Alfred Marks, Yvonne Romain. D: John Lemont. CRI 97m.

Frightmare 1974 British ★★ Shocker has little story value beyond presentation of gory murders, following cannibalistic older couple as they slaughter saner family members and other innocents. Gruesome. (a.k.a. *Frightmare II.*) C: Rupert Davies, Sheila Keith, Deborah Fairfax, Paul Greenwood. D: Peter Walker. HOR [R] 86m. V

Frightmare 1983 ★★ Young members of a fan society unearth the body of recently deceased fright-film star. Good setup becomes a rote, gory bore as the corpse comes to life and exacts violent revenge. C: Luca Becovici, Jennifer Starret, Nita Talbot. D: Norman Thaddeus Vane. HOR [R] 84m. V

Fringe Dwellers, The 1986 Australian ★★★½ The Comeaways, an aborigine family, are persuaded by 15-year-old daughter (Nehm) to quit their shantytown and live in white, middle-class suburban enclave. Finely tuned exploration of racism and class prejudice, with engaging debut by Nehm, but facile ending cops out. C: Kristina Nehm, Justine Saunders, Bob Maza, Kylie Belling. D: Bruce Beresford. DRA [PG] 98m. V

Frisco Jenny 1933 ★★★½ Barbary Coast woman (Chatterton, playing Madame X again) gives up baby, decades later finds he's prosecutor at her trial. Chatterton's potent theatrics make hokum work, including only face slap ever to cause an earthquake. C: Ruth Chatterton, Louis Calhern, Helen Jerome Eddy, Donald Cook, James Murray, Hallam Cooley, Pat O'Malley, Harold Huber, J. Carroll Naish. D: William Wellman. DRA 70m.

Frisco Kid, The 1979 ★★★★ In order to make their way West to San Francisco, a Polish rabbi (Wilder) and a taciturn cowhand (Ford) must learn from each other. Lightweight comedy enlivened by two immensely appealing star performances. C: Gene Wilder, Harrison Ford, Ramon Bieri, Val Bisoglio, Penny Peyser. D: Robert Aldrich. COM [PG] 119m. V

Frisco Kid 1935 ★★★★ Typically fast-moving action romp has Cagney on the loose on San Francisco's notorious Barbary Coast. Well-played melodrama of vengeance and mayhem. C: James Cagney, Margaret Lindsay, Ricardo Cortez, Lili Damita, Fred Kohler, George E. Stone, Donald Woods. D: Lloyd Bacon. DRA 77m.

Frisco Sal 1945 ★★ Foster leaves her East Coast home to find her brother's murderer in you know where. Showcase for opera star Foster singing features some great singing. C: Susanna Foster, Turhan Bey, Alan Curtis, Andy Devine, Thomas Gomez, Samuel S. Hinds. D: George Waggner. MUS 94m.

Frisky 1955 Italian ★★★ Sexy Lollobrigida as a precocious young woman chasing the village cop (De Sica) and beating out her rivals breathes life into an otherwise limp story. C: Gina Lollobrigida, Vittorio De Sica, Roberto Risso, Marisa Merlini. D: Luigi Comencini. DRA 98m.

Frog ★★★½ A strange old man adds to his rather bizarre collection of reptiles. But his newest addition, a frog, is actually a prince and the results are quite funny indeed. C: Shelley Duvall, Elliott Gould, Scott Grimes, Paul Williams. D: David Grossman. COM [G] 55m. V

Frogmen, The 1951 ★★★½ Daring WWII Navy underwater demolition teams lay the foundation for assault on a Pacific island occupied by Japanese infantry. Earnest effort, with great underwater photography. C: Richard Widmark, Dana Andrews, Gary Merrill, Jeffrey Hunter, Robert Wagner, Jack Warden. D: Lloyd Bacon. ACT 96m.

Frogs 1972 ★★★½ Ecologically correct, low-budget horror film about snakes, bugs, snapping turtles and, yes, frogs massing against Milland and his family to avenge his destruction of their habitat. Fun, sometimes quite creepy. C: Ray Milland, Sam Elliott, Joan Van Ark, Adam Roarke. D: George McCowan. HOR [PG] 91m. V

From a Far Country: Pope John Paul II 1981 British ★★½ Somewhat fawning biography of the early years of the Polish man (born in 1920) who would become first non-Italian pontiff in 450 years. C: Cezary Morawski, Sam Neill, Christopher Cazenove, Warren Clarke, Lisa Harrow, Maurice Denham, Kathleen Byron. D: Krzysztof Zanussi. DRA 100m. TVM

From Beyond the Grave 1973 British ★★★½ Solid anthology chiller with a strong cast, based on R. Chetwynd-Hayes stories and centering on Cushing's antique shop. (a.k.a. *Creatures*) C: Peter Cushing, Margaret Leighton, Ian Bennen, Donald Pleasence, David Warner, Ian Carmichael. D: Kevin Connor. HOR [PG] 98m. V

From Beyond 1986 ★★★½ Exuberantly gross film tells the story of scientists who lose control of a machine that prevents people from eating one another's brains. A twisted tale, loaded with sickening scenes, and a lot of fun. Based on the novel by H.P. Lovecraft. C: Jeffrey Combs, Barbara Crampton, Ted Sorel, Ken Foree. D: Stuart Gordon. HOR [R] 85m. V

From Hell It Came 1957 ★★★ Voodoo and a strange island witch doctor bring an evil spirit back from beyond—in the shape of a walking tree! Amusing '50s sci-fi. C: Tod Andrews, Tina Carver, Linda Watkins, John McNamara, Gregg Palmer, Robert Swan. D: Dan Milner. SFI 71m.

From Hell to Borneo 1964 ★★★ Montgomery battles criminals to preserve his private island sanctuary. Middling outdoor adventure shot in Philippines. C: George Montgomery, Julie Gregg, Torin Thatcher, Lisa Moreno. D: George Montgomery. ACT 90m. V

From Hell to Heaven 1933 ★★★ *Grand Hotel*-style ensemble drama follows a disparate group of people at a racetrack, each with a different reason for betting the ponies. Classy cavalcade from way back with an effervescent performance by Lombard. C: Carole Lombard, Jack Oakie, Adrienne Ames, Sidney Blackmer. D: Erle Kenton. DRA 67m.

From Hell to Texas 1958 ★★★½ A young cowpoke unintentionally kills a man and flees from a posse led by dead man's vengeful father. Adequate pursuit Western tries to be earnest. C: Don Murray, Diane Varsi, Chill

Wills, Dennis Hopper. D: Henry Hathaway. WST 100m.

From Hell to Victory 1979 French ★★★ Six foreign nationals forced to go different ways by the onset of WWII promise to resume their friendship at war's end. Earnest attempt to address human interest issues in wartime. C: George Peppard, George Hamilton, Horst Buchholz, Sam Wanamaker. D: Hank Milestone. ACT [PG] 100m. V

From Here to Eternity 1953 ★★★★★ Superb adaptation of James Jones' novel about military life in Hawaii before Pearl Harbor bombing. Lancaster's surf-front kiss with Kerr is a classic. Oscars for Best Picture, Director, Screenplay, and Cinematography; also for Reed and Sinatra, both Supporting. Remade for TV. C: Burt Lancaster, Montgomery Clift, Deborah Kerr, Donna Reed, Frank Sinatra, Ernest Borgnine, Jack Warden. D: Fred Zinnemann. DRA 118m. V

From Here to Eternity 1979 ★★★½ Army base in Hawaii on the eve of Pearl Harbor; adapted, like the 1953 film, from James Jones' novel. This version isn't bad; suffers mainly in comparison with earlier powerhouse. C: Natalie Wood, Kim Basinger, William Devane, Steve Railsback, Peter Boyle. D: Buzz Kulik. DRA [PG-13] 120m.

From Hollywood to Deadwood 1989 ★★ When a beautiful young film star is declared missing, a pair of hard-boiled detectives pursue her. C: Scott Paulin, Jim Haynie, Barbara Schock. D: Rex Pickett. CRI [R] 96m. V

From Mao to Mozart: Isaac Stern in China 1980 ★★★★★ Quietly moving account of violinist's visit to Communist China portrays his robust musical genius as well as his virtuoso ability in the classroom, teaching China's best young musicians. Also works as a primer on China's unique culture. Oscar for Best Documentary. C: Isaac Stern, David Golub, Tan Shuzhen. D: Murray Lerner. DOC [G] 84m. V

From Nashville with Music 1969 ★★½ City slickers wind up in country music capital and have wild, wacky adventures. Good music, Nashville color, but amateurish acting and script. C: Marilyn Maxwell, Leo G. Carroll, Gonzalez-Gonzalez, Marty Robbins, Merle Haggard, Buck Owens. D: Eddie Crandall. MUS 87m.

From Noon Till Three 1976 ★★★½ After her affair with a bandit she now believes dead, a widow glorifies him in a novel as a mythic folk hero. Complicated Western satire with a good seriocomic turn by Bronson. C: Charles Bronson, Jill Ireland, Douglas Fowley, Stan Haze, Damon Douglas, Anne Ramsey. D: Frank D. Gilroy. WST [PG] 99m. V

From Pluto with Love 1985 ★★★★½ Anthology of 1941-51 animated cartoons featuring Pluto is a wonderful surprise! Good animation, cute stories make this a must-see for children. FAM/COM 49m. V

From Russia with Love 1963 British ★★★★½ Bond (Connery) is assigned to escort a beautiful Russian defector (Bianchi) with a top secret code machine—but the mission is really a trap by evil organization SPECTRE. A taut thriller with an intense fight between Bond and assassin Shaw aboard the Orient Express. C: Sean Connery, Daniela Bianchi, Lotte Lenya, Pedro Armendariz, Robert Shaw. D: Terence Young. ACT [PG] 118m. V

From the Dead of Night 1989 ★★★½ Nicely done chiller in which a woman is haunted by spirits after near-death experience; it turns out they're deceased souls who feel she should have stayed dead. Creepy and well-acted, too bad it's a little long. Based on Gary Bradner's novel *Walkers*. C: Lindsay Wagner, Bruce Boxleitner, Robin Thomas, Robert Prosky, Diahann Carroll. D: Paul Wendkos. HOR 200m. TVM V

From the Earth to the Moon 1958 ★★ The first moon shot, as adapted from the Jules Verne fantasy. Slow and clunky. For hardcore '50s rocket movie enthusiasts only. C: Joseph Cotten, George Sanders, Debra Paget, Don Dubbins, Patric Knowles. D: Byron Haskin. SFI 100m. V

From the Hip 1986 ★★ Nelson is a young lawyer whose unorthodox courtroom behavior saves Hurt from murder charges at the same time it kills what little entertainment could be salvaged from this painfully bad comedy. C: Judd Nelson, Elizabeth Perkins, John Hurt, Darren McGavin. D: Bob Clark. COM [PG] 112m. V

From the Life of the Marionettes 1980 German ★★★★ Riveting psychological drama of a middle-class businessman's disintegration after he rapes and strangles a prostitute who resembles his nagging wife. Ambiguity surrounding man's rationale for murder may disturb some but is employed effectively. C: Robert Atzorn, Christine Buchegger, Martin Benrath, Heinz Bennent. D: Ingmar Bergman. DRA [R] 104m. V

From the Mixed-Up Files of Mrs. Basil E. Frankweiler 1973 ★★★★ Two misfit children run away from home and hide in NYC's Metropolitan Museum of Art. Charming family comedy with Bergman in cameo role. Based on the award-winning children's book by E. L. Konigsburg. (a.k.a. *The Hideaways*) C: Ingrid Bergman, Sally Prager, Johnny Doran, George Rose, Georgann Johnson, Richard Mulligan, Madeline Kahn. D: Fielder Cook. COM [G] 105m.

From the Terrace 1960 ★★★½ Mainline Philadelphians play with adultery and make too much money. Newman and Woodward turn in static performances; others fare better. Based on O'Hara best-seller. C: Paul Newman, Joanne Woodward, Myrna Loy, Ina Balin, Leon Ames, Barbara Eden, George Grizzard. D: Mark Robson. DRA 144m. V

From This Day Forward 1946 ★★★★ Sentimental but well-made story (told in flashback), of young New York married couple who overcome adversity, unemployment, and wartime separation. Stevens, in his acting debut, and veteran actress Fontaine bring sincerity and realism to roles of husband and wife. C: Joan Fontaine, Mark Stevens, Rosemary DeCamp, Henry Morgan, Arline Judge, Bobby Driscoll, Mary Treen. D: John Berry. DRA 95m.

From Top to Bottom 1933 French ★★½ Slow-moving comedy about a boorish soccer player (Gabin) who tries to improve himself and falls in love with his teacher. C: Jean Gabin, Jeannine Crispin, Michel Simon. D: G.W. Pabst. COM 80m.

Front Page Story 1954 British ★★★½ Editor has tough day, what with unhappy staff, messed-up marriage, murder in the streets. Thank goodness for Hawkins and highly efficient handling. C: Jack Hawkins, Elizabeth Allan, Eva Bartok, Martin Miller, Derek Farr. D: Gordon Parry. DRA 99m.

Front Page, The 1931 ★★★★★ Menjou is conniving Chicago newspaper editor who forces his star reporter O'Brien to cover just one more story in the first of several film adaptations of Hecht/MacArthur play. Fast-moving, witty dialogue sparks this superbly acted comedy classic. Remade as *His Girl Friday*. C: Adolphe Menjou, Pat O'Brien, Mary Brian, Edward Everett Horton, Walter Catlett, Mae Clarke. D: Lewis Milestone. COM 101m. V

Front Page, The 1974 ★★★½ Uneven Billy Wilder remake of 1931 classic film of Chicago newspaper folk. Still funny, with great cast. C: Jack Lemmon, Walter Matthau, Carol Burnett, Susan Sarandon, Vincent Gardenia, David Wayne, Allen Garfield, Austin Pendleton, Charles Durning. D: Billy Wilder. COM [PG] 105m. V

Front Page Woman 1935 ★★★½ Davis and Brent play journalists vying for the scoop in this lively comedy/melodrama with a good share of laughs. C: Bette Davis, George Brent, Winifred Shaw, Roscoe Karns, Joseph Crehan. D: Michael Curtiz. COM 82m.

Front, The 1976 ★★★★½ Pointed, dark comedy about the HUAC Communist witchhunt in the entertainment industry during the '50s. A no-talent (Allen) fronts for various blacklisted TV writers, passing their scripts off as his own. The credits are a who's who of individuals actually blacklisted. C: Woody Allen, Zero Mostel, Herschel Bernardi, Michael Murphy, Andrea Marcovicci. D: Martin Ritt. DRA [PG] 94m. V

Frontier 1935 *See* **Aerograd**

Frontier Alaska 1969 *See* **Joniko and the Kush Ta Ta**

Frontier Gal 1945 ★★★½ Sentimental Western about complications that follow the desperate marriage between an outlaw on the run and a sultry saloon owner. Standard sagebrush yarn with attempts at comedy. C: Yvonne De Carlo, Rod Cameron, Andy Devine, Fuzzy Knight, Andrew Tombes, Sheldon Leonard, Clara Blandick. D: Charles Lamont. WST 84m.

Frontier Hellcat 1966 German ★★★ Third in a series of Westerns, adapted from novels of German writer Karl May, revolving around Apache chief Winnetou (Brice) and the white settlers who come in contact with him. Previous episodes starred Lex Barker and Guy Madison; this one has Granger leading settlers across the Plains. Photographed in Yugoslavia. C: Stewart Granger, Elke Sommer, Pierre Brice, Gotz George. D: Alfred Vohrer. WST 98m.

Frontier Horizon 1939 ★★★ In the wild west, a colony of settlers are set upon by a syndicate of notorious land speculators. But a trio of "mesquiteers" (led by Wayne) come to their rescue. Standard western fare, made better by stars. C: John Wayne, Phyllis Isley (Jennifer Jones). D: George Sherman. WST 55m. V

Frontier Marshal 1939 ★★★½ Sturdy version of the Wyatt Earp-Doc Holliday western legend, culminating in the gunfight at O.K. Corral. Precursor in many ways to John Ford's masterpiece *My Darling Clementine*. C: Randolph Scott, Nancy Kelly, Cesar Romero, Binnie Barnes, John Carradine. D: Allan Dwan. WST 71m.

Frontier Outpost 1950 ★★★ A wrongly arrested lawman puts on a mask to evade the law and track down the real criminals. Slightly above-average Western. C: Charles Starrett, Smiley Burnette, Lois Hall. D: Ray Nazarro. WST 55m.

Frontiersman, The 1938 ★★★ Hopalong Cassidy foils a ruthless gang of rustlers. Good old-time fun. C: William Boyd, George "Gabby" Hayes. D: Lesley Selander. WST 74m. V

Frosty the Snowman 1969 ★★½ Popular animated film about the magical snowman and the children who love him. Okay, but nothing special. C: Jimmy Durante, Jackie Vernon. FAM/COM 30m. V

Frozen Assets 1992 ★ Amazingly bad comedy features Bernsen as bank employee who is transferred to a sperm bank. Several pointless jokes later he meets biologist Long, and film drags on to a predictable finish. C: Shelley Long, Corbin Bernsen, Larry Miller, Dody Goodman, Matt Clark, Jeanne Cooper, Paul Sand, Teri Copley, Gloria Camden, Gerrit Graham. D: George Miller. COM [PG-13] 96m. V

Frozen Dead, The 1966 British ★★ At the end of WWII a crazed scientist (Andrews) froze Nazi leaders. Now he wants to thaw them out and start the Fourth Reich. Solid sci-fi premise. C: Dana Andrews, Anna Palk, Philip Gilbert, Kathleen Breck, Karel Stepanek, Edward Fox. D: Herbert J. Leder. SFI 95m.

Frozen Ghost 1945 ★★ Hypnotist loses

patient in midsession and begins to fear his own powers. Late entry in Universal's *Inner Sanctum* series of the '40s, all starring Chaney. C: Lon Chaney, Evelyn Ankers, Milburn Stone, Douglass Dumbrille, Martin Kosleck, Elena Verdugo. D: Harold Young. HOR 61m.

Frozen Limits, The 1939 ★★★ Wacky group heads for Alaska in pursuit of gold and has amusing adventures. Interesting curio features famous English music hall comedy teams. C: Bud Flanagan, Chesney Allen, Jimmy Nervo, Teddy Knox. D: Marcel Varnel. COM 84m.

Fruit Machine, The 1988 British ★★★★ Two gay teenagers (Charles, Forsyth) witness a gangland shooting, then must run for their lives. Charming British comedy/thriller peopled by three-dimensional characters, for a change. (a.k.a. *Wonderland*) C: Emile Charles, Tony Forsyth, Robert Stephens, Claire Higgins, Robbie Coltrane. D: Philip Saville. CRI 103m. V

F.T.A. 1972 ★★ Taped rendition of Fonda and Sutherland's anti-Vietnam War revue, "F— the Army." Watchable for curiosity value. C: Jane Fonda, Donald Sutherland, Len Chandler, Holly Near, Pamela Donegan, Michael Alaimo. D: Francine Parker. DOC 94m.

Fugitive Among Us 1993 ★★★ Dedicated detective (Roberts) tirelessly hunts down a rapist on the loose. C: Eric Roberts, Peter Strauss, Elizabeth Pena. CRI 90m. V

Fugitive from Justice, A 1940 ★★★½ Speedy gangster story about insurance man trying to keep a highly insured client out of harm's way. Tough, well-plotted crimer. C: Roger Pryor, Lucille Fairbanks, Eddie Foy, Jr. D: Terry Morse. CRI 54m.

Fugitive from Sonora 1943 ★★★½ Twin brothers—one a parolee, the other a parson—battle a gang leader who is terrorizing other parolees. Not bad of its kind, with Barry doing well in his dual role. C: Don "Red" Barry, Wally Vernon, Lynn Merrick. D: Howard Bretherton. WST 57m.

Fugitive Kind, The 1959 ★★★ Hollow screen rendition of Tennessee Williams play features Brando as drifter stuck in small Southern town, having affair with married Magnani. Disappointing plot. TV remake: *Orpheus Descending*. C: Marlon Brando, Anna Magnani, Joanne Woodward, Maureen Stapleton, Victor Jory, R.G. Armstrong. D: Sidney Lumet. DRA 135m. V

Fugitive Lady 1934 ★★★½ A woman takes the fall for her jewel-thief boyfriend, then escapes when the train crashes on the way to prison. Enough plot to fuel three movies, though it takes a while to untangle itself. C: Neil Hamilton, Florence Rice, Donald Cook, William Demarest. D: Al Rogell. CRI 66m.

Fugitive Lady 1951 ★★★ Two women—a dead man's wife and stepsister—are suspects in a suicide that looks distinctly like murder. Slow but handsome mystery. C: Janis Paige, Binnie Barnes, Eduardo Ciannelli, Tony Cepta. D: Sidney Salkow. CRI 78m.

Fugitive Lovers, The 1934 ★★★ Far-fetched romance between escaped convict (Montgomery) and young woman (Evans) who meet on a bus traveling from New York to Los Angeles. Notable for an early appearance by the Three Stooges, here billed as the Three Julians. C: Robert Montgomery, Madge Evans, Nat Pendleton, Ted Healy, C. Henry Gordon, The Three Stooges. D: Richard Boleslawski. COM 84m.

Fugitive, The 1947 ★★★★½ Fonda shines as a priest on the run from a Mexican dictatorship that has outlawed worship. Gripping tale of personal commitment and faith, adapted from a novel by Graham Greene. Remade with the original novel's title, *The Power and the Glory*. C: Henry Fonda, Dolores Del Rio, Pedro Armendariz, J. Carrol Naish, Leo Carrillo, Ward Bond. D: John Ford. DRA 99m. V

Fugitive, The 1993 ★★★★½ Slam-bang action picture based on '60s TV series, with Ford appropriately phlegmatic as Dr. Richard Kimball, convicted of his wife's murder, fleeing Jones, funny and inventive as federal agent pursuer (he won an Oscar as Best Supporting Actor). Stupendous action sequences. C: Harrison Ford, Tommy Lee Jones, Jeroen Krabbe, Sela Ward, Joe Pantoliano. D: Andrew Davis. DRA [PG-13] 131m.

Fulfillment 1993 ★★★½ Romantic melodrama from best-selling LaVyrle Spencer novel about a turn-of-the century farm couple; he's infertile, so they ask his brother to make her pregnant. Good of this kind. C: Cheryl Ladd, Ted Levine, Lewis Smith. D: Piers Haggard. DRA 96m. V

Full Confession 1939 ★★★½ Murderer confesses to priest, who is in a dilemma when the police arrest another man. Melodramatic but gripping plot has had many imitators. Calleia gives a strong performance as the troubled priest. C: Victor McLaglen, Sally Eilers, Joseph Calleia, Barry Fitzgerald, Elizabeth Risdon. D: John Farrow. DRA 73m.

Full Contact 1992 ★★★ Powerful action in the world of back alley kickboxing, where there are really no rules. C: Jerry Trimble, Howard Jackson, Alvin Prouder. D: Rick Jacobson. ACT [R] 96m. V

Full Eclipse 1993 ★★★½ Cop is recruited by group of vigilantes who inject themselves with a serum that turns them into homicidal criminal-hunting werewolves. Twisty horror suspense. C: Mario Van Peebles, Patsy Kensit, Bruce Payne. D: Anthony Hickox. HOR [R] 93m. V

Full Exposure: The Sex Tape Scandals 1989 ★★½ Call girl is murdered after threatening to expose her wealthy clients; two cops seek the killer. Sensationalized drama. C: Jennifer O'Neill, Lisa Hartman, Vanessa Williams, Anthony Denison. D: Noel Nosseck. DRA 95m. TVM V

Full Fathom Five 1990 ★★ Central Americans capture a sub and threaten to nuke Texas to avenge the U.S. invasion of Panama. Intriguing concept of nuclear blackmail by terrorists is wasted on this ill-conceived potboiler. C: Michael Moriarty, Maria Rangel, Michael Cavanaugh, John LaFayette, Todd Field. D: Carl Franklin. DRA [PG] 82m. v

Full Hearts & Empty Pockets 1963 Italian ★★½ Handsome, impecunious young man (Cervi) finds romance in Rome with Christian and Berger. Harmless. C: Linda Christian, Gino Cervi, Senta Berger. D: Camillo Mastrocinque. COM 88m.

Full Metal Jacket 1987 ★★★★ One of the better films on the Vietnam War combat experience follows an Marine photojournalist (Modine) through boot camp, on his first patrols, and into the historic Tet offensive. Gritty, on-the-ground look at the realities of war. C: Matthew Modine, Adam Baldwin, Vincent D'Onofrio, Lee Ermey, Dorian Harewood, Arliss Howard, Kevyn Major Howard, Ed O'Ross. D: Stanley Kubrick. DRA [R] 117m. v

Full Metal Ninja 1989 ★★½ Atmospheric martial arts film about a man called "Eagle" who chases after the criminals who have killed his family and kidnapped his wife. C: Pierre Kirby, Jean Paul, Sean Odell. D: Charles Lee. ACT 90m. v

Full Moon High 1981 ★★★★ High schooler (Arkin) taken to Transylvania by dad (McMahon), who lets him in on dark family secret. Little seen but entertaining werewolf comedy. Good hairy fun. C: Adam Arkin, Ed McMahon, Elizabeth Hartman, Roz Kelly, Bill Kirchenbauer, Kenneth Mars, Joanne Nail, Alan Arkin. D: Larry Cohen. COM [PG] 94m.

Full Moon in Blue Water 1988 ★★★ Predictable story of evil developers scheming to buy waterside bar/restaurant from impoverished owner weakens this comedy's strongest point: the excellent chemistry between Hackman (the owner) and Garr (his long-suffering girlfriend). C: Gene Hackman, Teri Garr, Burgess Meredith, Elias Koteas. D: Peter Masterson. DRA [R] 96m. v

Full Moon in Paris 1984 French ★★★★ Spirited comedy has intelligent, strong-willed young woman left cold by her platonic and sexual involvements with the men in her life. Rohmer's typical confinement of film to small, telling details serves him well here. A delight, as is Ogier's gifted star turn. C: Pascale Ogier, Fabrice Luchini, Tcheky Karyo. D: Eric Rohmer. COM [R] 101m. v

Full of Life 1956 ★★★★ Newlyweds Conte and Holliday move in with groom's father when bride announces she's pregnant. Gentle comedy with wonderful performance by Baccaloni as domineering, soon-to-be grandfather. C: Judy Holliday, Richard Conte, Salvatore Baccaloni, Esther Minciotti. D: Richard Quine. COM 91m. v

Fuller Brush Girl, The 1950 ★★★½ Sequel to *The Fuller Brush Man* puts Lucy in den of thieves, literally, as door-to-door salesrep. Frantic comedy only shows some of Ball's talent. C: Lucille Ball, Eddie Albert, Jeff Donnell, Jerome Cowan, Lee Patrick. D: Lloyd Bacon. COM 85m. v

Fuller Brush Man, The 1948 ★★★½ Fluffy slapstick farce has Skelton as beginning door-to-door salesman getting mixed up in murder. C: Red Skelton, Janet Blair, Don McGuire, Adele Jergens. D: S. Sylvan Simon. COM 93m. v

Fun and Fancy Free 1947 ★★★★ Double bill of Disney animated featurettes. First is okay Bongo (narrated and sung by Dinah Shore) about circus bear falling in love during excursion into countryside. Second is delightful retelling of Jack and the Beanstalk with Mickey Mouse, Donald Duck, and Goofy transported by fast-growing legume into giant's magic kingdom (narrated by Edgar Bergen and Charlie McCarthy). Film is introduced by Jiminy Cricket. Voices of Dinah Shore, Edgar Bergen, Billy Gilbert. D: Jack Kinney, W.O. Roberts, Hamilton Luske, William Morgan. FAM/DRA [G] 73m.

Fun at St. Fanny's 1956 British ★★★½ Witty, though unevenly paced tale of a British headmaster (Emney) who schemes to collect the inheritance of a wealthy student for the school. C: Fred Emney, Cardew Robinson, Vera Day. D: Maurice Elvey. COM 80m.

Fun Down There 1989 ★★★½ A lonely and frustrated young man from upstate New York takes a job in Manhattan, and discovers big city adventure, big city disappointment, and big city love, all in the first week. C: Michael Waite, Nickolas Nagurney. D: Roger Stigliano. DRA 89m. v

Fun in Acapulco 1963 ★★★½ Elvis swivels to a Latin beat in this better than average entry in the Presley series. He's an ex-trapeze artist romancing Andress in photogenic Mexico. Songs include "Bossa Nova Baby." C: Elvis Presley, Ursula Andress, Paul Lukas, Alejandro Rey. D: Richard Thorpe. MUS 97m. v

Fun Loving 1970 *See* **Quackser Fortune Has a Cousin in the Bronx**

Fun on a Weekend 1947 ★★★½ Bracken and Lane play lucky lovers on a weekend fling, who scheme their way into romance and money. Entertaining silliness. C: Eddie Bracken, Priscilla Lane, Tom Conway, Allen Jenkins, Arthur Treacher, Alma Kruger. D: Andrew L. Stone. COM 93m.

Fun with Dick and Jane 1977 ★★★ After Segal loses his job, he and wife Fonda go on a crime spree to make ends meet. Starts off with a bang but premise falters and film ultimately misses intended satirical points. C: Jane Fonda, George Segal, Ed McMahon, Dick Gautier. D: Ted Kotcheff. COM [PG] 95m. v

Funeral for an Assassin ★★★ Morrow is a hired hitman in this thriller set against the horror of apartheid in South Africa. C: Vic Morrow, Peter Van Dissel, Stan Williams. D: Ivan Hall. DRA [PG] 92m. v

Funeral in Berlin 1966 ★★★★ Blue-collar spy Harry Palmer (Caine) goes to Berlin to assist in the defection of a high-ranking Soviet officer. Adaptation of Len Deighton's novel is satisfying, in a dreary sort of way. Follows *The Ipcress File* and followed by *The Billion Dollar Brain.* C: Michael Caine, Eva Renzi, Paul Hubschmid, Oscar Homolka, Guy Doleman. D: Guy Hamilton. DRA 102m. v

Funeral, The 1984 Japanese ★★★★ Sacred Japanese funeral rites are complicated when an affluent family buries its brothel-owning father in three days of funeral preparations. A comic, captivating glimpse into the family politics of contemporary Japan. C: Nobuko Miyamoto, Tsutomu Yamazaki, Kin Sugai. D: Juzo Itami. COM 124m. v

Funhouse, The 1981 ★★★ Four teenagers are trapped overnight in a carnival funhouse, and not all of them are around the next morning to exit. Competently made but awfully familiar. C: Elizabeth Berridge, Cooper Huckabee, Miles Chapin, Largo Woodruff, Sylvia Miles. D: Tobe Hooper. HOR 96m. v

Funland 1989 ★★ Title amusement park is taken over by the Mob—a ticket to trouble if ever there was one! C: David Lander, William Windom, Bruce Mahler, Michael McManus. D: William Vanderkloot. COM [PG-13] 86m. v

Funny About Love 1990 ★★½ Cartoonist Wilder longing for fatherhood tries too hard to have a baby with wife Lahti in this dull comedy. During their separation, he takes up with young sorority sister Masterson. C: Gene Wilder, Christine Lahti, Mary Stuart Masterson. D: Leonard Nimoy. COM [PG-13] 101m. v

Funny Bones 1995 ★★★½ A struggling stand-up comic (Platt) can't escape from his famous father's (Lewis) shadow. Eccentric comedy from the director of *Hear My Song* has many amusing moments, but may be too quirky for some. C: Oliver Platt, Jerry Lewis, Lee Evans, Leslie Caron, Oliver Reed, Ruta Lee. D: Peter Chelsom. COM [R] 128m.

Funny Dirty Little War 1983 Argentine ★★★★ Minor disputes between Marxists and Peronists in Argentine village escalate into a full-blown battle. Witty political satire based on a not-so-funny historical era. C: Federico Luppi, Julio De Grazia, Miguel Angel Sola. D: Hector Olivera. COM 80m. v

Funny Face 1957 ★★★★½ Classic Hepburn/Astaire musical pairing is fey and charming. He's a famous, lionized photographer (based on real-life shutterbug Richard Avedon) and she's a frumpy Greenwich Village bookstore clerk about to be catapulted to fashion stardom. Stylish, sophisticated musical, typical of its period and its director. Terrific Gershwin songs. C: Audrey Hepburn, Fred Astaire, Kay Thompson, Suzy Parker. D: Stanley Donen. MUS 103m. v

Funny Farm, The 1982 Canadian ★★ Young comedian travels from Midwest to Los Angeles, tries to make it as a stand-up comic at L.A. nightclub. Mostly a series of not-so-funny routines. C: Miles Chapin, Eileen Brennan, Jack Carter, Tracy Bregman, Howie Mandel, Marjorie Gross, Lou Dinos, Peter Aykroyd. D: Ron Clark. COM [R] 95m. v

Funny Farm 1988 ★★★½ Chase plays the stereotypical city person—in his case, a NYC sportswriter—who flees to the country for peace and quiet and finds anything but. Uneven, but with some very funny sequences. C: Chevy Chase, Madolyn Smith, Joseph Maher, Jack Gilpin, Brad Sullivan, MacIntyre Dixon. D: George Roy Hill. COM [PG] 101m. v

Funny Girl 1968 ★★★★★ Streisand's sensational film debut. Lavish production of the Broadway hit tells touching story of stage star Fanny Brice's love for doomed gambler Nicky Arnstein. Marvelous score ("People," "Don't Rain on My Parade"). Streisand shared Oscar for Best Actress with Katharine Hepburn—only the second tie in Oscar history. Followed by sequel *Funny Lady.* C: Barbra Streisand, Omar Sharif, Kay Medford, Anne Francis, Walter Pidgeon. D: William Wyler. MUS [G] 155m. v

Funny Lady 1975 ★★★½ Sequel to *Funny Girl* has Streisand as older Brice, embroiled with producer husband Billy Rose (Caan). Some good Kander and Ebb numbers ("How Lucky Can You Get?"). C: Barbra Streisand, James Caan, Omar Sharif, Roddy McDowall, Ben Vereen, Carole Wells. D: Herbert Ross. MUS [PG] 137m. v

Funny Money 1982 ★★½ The comic misadventures of a gang of credit card thieves who steal and use one card too many: one belonging to a mobster. C: Gregg Henry, Elizabeth Daily. D: James Kenelm Clarke. COM 92m. v

Funny Thing Happened on the Way to the Forum, A 1966 ★★★★½ Fabulous, bawdy farce set in ancient Rome, with hilarious Mostel as a wily slave seeking freedom. Wonderful cameo by Keaton, splendid support by Silvers and Crawford, and terrific songs. C: Zero Mostel, Phil Silvers, Buster Keaton, Jack Gilford, Michael Crawford. D: Richard Lester. COM 99m. v

Funnyman 1967 ★★★½ Introspective comic (Bonerz), feels he should be getting more than laughs out of his life. Endearing comedy, low-budgeter is also a sturdy time capsule of late-'60s humor. C: Peter Bonerz, Sandra Archer, Carol Androsky, Larry Hankin, Barbara Hiken, Gerald Hiken. D: John Korty. COM 98m.

Furies, The 1950 ★★★★ A martinet cattle baron and his hard-driving daughter engage in a turbulent power struggle. Ably directed adult Western with Freudian implications. C: Barbara Stanwyck, Walter Huston, Wendell

Corey, Gilbert Roland, Judith Anderson, Beulah Bondi, Thomas Gomez, Albert Dekker, Blanche Yurka, Wallace Ford. D: Anthony Mann. WST 109m.

Furious 1983 ★★★½ Interesting tale of the search for the missing pieces of a coin with mystical powers. Rhee compelling as the student who fights the gang that killed his sister (the first to find the coin), and then his own master, who wants the coin's powers for himself. C: Simon Rhee, Howard Jackson, Arlene Montano. D: Tim Everett. ACT [R] 100m. V

Furious Avenger, The 1976 ★★★½ WWII drama in which a Chinese POW released by the Japanese returns to find his family has been killed by local thugs. Great action sequences. C: Hsiung Fei, Fan Ling. D: Yao Feng Pan. ACT 84m. V

Furious, The 1981 ★★ Bruce Le kung fu flick pits the hero against a malevolent drug dealer. C: Bruce Le. ACT [PG] 90m. V

Further Adventures of Ma and Pa Kettle *See* **Ma and Pa Kettle**

Further Adventures of Tennessee Buck, The 1988 ★★ Alcoholic white hunter (Keith) leads a wealthy young couple on safari in Borneo. Lame adventure yarn lacks humor and genuine thrills. C: David Keith, Kathy Shower, Brant van Hoffman, Sydney Lassick. D: David Keith. DRA [R] 90m. V

Further Adventures of the Wilderness Family, The 1978 *See* **Wilderness Family Part 2, The**

Further Perils of Laurel and Hardy, The 1968 ★★★★ Compilation film features some of the funniest moments from Stan Laurel and Oliver Hardy's silent comedies. Not as good as watching the originals, but still plenty of laughs. C: Stan Laurel, Oliver Hardy, Charley Chase, Max Davidson, James Finlayson. D: Robert Youngson. COM 99m.

Further Up the Creek! 1958 British ★★★½ Whimsical British naval comedy, sequel to *Up the Creek*, follows the adventures of a naive naval officer and his ship (with Howerd replacing Peter Sellers). C: David Tomlinson, Frankie Howerd, Shirley Eaton, Thora Hird, Lionel Jeffries. D: Val Guest. COM 91m.

Fury 1936 ★★★★★ Lang's first American film pulls no punches as it follows an innocent man (Tracy) into the hands of a bloodthirsty lynch mob. Well stocked with unpredictable plot twists and insights into the dark side of the Depression; stands as one of the landmark films of the era. C: Sylvia Sidney, Spencer Tracy, Walter Abel, Bruce Cabot, Edward Ellis, Walter Brennan, Frank Albertson. D: Fritz Lang. DRA 96m. V

Fury at Furnace Creek 1948 ★★★½ A cavalry general, accused of conspiracy with Indians, is defended by his two sons. Interesting plot blends Western and sleuthing to good effect. C: Victor Mature, Coleen Gray, Glenn Langan, Reginald Gardiner, Albert Dekker. D: H. Bruce Humberstone. WST 88m.

Fury at Gunsight Pass 1956 ★★½ Bad guys ride into town, Brian has to stand up to them. Western from B-movie specialist Sears. C: David Brian, Neville Brand, Richard Long, Lisa Davis. D: Fred F. Sears. WST 68m.

Fury at Showdown 1957 ★★½ Derek straps his guns back on to rescue helpless Craig from bad guys. Quickie Western, worth a look for the brash young Adams. C: John Derek, John Smith, Carolyn Craig, Nick Adams. D: Gerd Oswald. WST 75m.

Fury at Smugglers Bay 1963 British ★★★ Shipwrecked pirates blackmail nobleman in Cornish village and menace the region. Adequate but unexceptional sea tale. C: Peter Cushing, Michele Mercier, Bernard Lee, George Coulouris, Liz Fraser. D: John Gilling. ACT 92m.

Fury of Hercules, The 1961 Italian ★★½ Mighty Hercules (Harris) comes to aid of woman (Corey) whose homeland is threatened by a wicked leader. Clichéd swords-and-sandals adventure. C: Brad Harris, Brigitte Corey, Mara Berni, Carlo Tamberlani. D: Gianfranco Parolini. ACT 95m. V

Fury of King Boxer ★★½ Chung socks and chops his way through the deadly Manchus in this period martial arts film. C: Kuo Shu Chung, Wang Yu. D: Ting Shan Si. ACT 85m. V

Fury of the Congo 1951 ★★★ Jungle Jim tangles with narcotics smugglers seeking to enslave friendly natives. Rousing adventure with Weissmuller in familiar surroundings. C: Johnny Weissmuller, Sherry Moreland, William Henry, Lyle Talbot. D: William Berke. ACT 69m.

Fury of the Pagans 1963 Italian ★★½ Tribal chief (Purdom) in ancient Rome seeks to conquer new territory and rescue his sweetheart. Inferior Italian-made costume drama. C: Edmund Purdom, Rossana Podesta, Livio Lorenzon, Carlo Calo. D: Guido Malatesta. ACT 86m.

Fury On Wheels 1971 ★★★½ A race car star (Ligon) risks all with his self-destructive lifestyle, while Hirsch tries to save him. Turgid drama, but great drag race scenes. C: Judd Hirsch, Tom Ligon. ACT [PG] 89m. V

Fury, The 1978 ★★★½ Young man with telekinetic powers (Stevens) is kidnapped, and his father (Douglas) turns to a young woman with similar powers (Irving) to rescue him. De Palma's usual flashy direction and some memorable set pieces help, but the story is still trashy. C: Kirk Douglas, John Cassavetes, Carrie Snodgress, Amy Irving, Fiona Lewis, Andrew Stevens, Charles Durning. D: Brian De Palma. HOR [R] 118m. V

Fuss over Feathers 1954 British ★★★ Citizens rise up to keep the RAF from appropriating their bird sanctuary. Enjoyable comic drama. (a.k.a. *Conflict of Wings*) C: John Gregson, Muriel Pavlow, Keiron Moore. D: John Eldridge. DRA 84m.

Future Cop 1976 ★★★ Seasoned police officer (Borgnine) teams up with a rookie robot (Shannon). Energetic, congenial premise and performance pairing—ultimately became TV series. C: Ernest Borgnine, Michael Shannon, John Amos, John Larch, Ronnie Edwards. D: Jud Taylor. SFI 78m. TVM V

Future Force 1989 ★★★ A copy of the future hunts out the bad guys, both in the police department and on the streets. Gritty performance by Carradine. C: David Carradine, Robert Tessier, Anna Rapagna. D: David A. Prior. CRI [R] 90m. V

Future Hunters 1989 ★★ In the bleak, postholocaust future a young couple searches for their own Holy Grail: an artifact that will change the world. An apocalyptic period piece from the '50s. C: Robert Patrick, Linda Carol, Ed Crick. D: Cirio H. Santiago. SFI [R] 96m. V

Future Shock 1994 ★★★ Compilation of sci-fi shockers, all three about evil medical researchers and their disturbed patients. First stars Schilling as a woman fearful of wolves; second casts Kove as a bookworm hazed by his roommate; and third (best) casts Paxton as a death-obsessed photographer. C: Vivian Schilling, Scott Thompson, Martin Kove, Sam Clay, Bill Paxton, Brion James. D: Eric Parkinson, Matt Reeves, Francis "Oley" Sassone. SFI [PG-13] 93m. V

Future Zone 1990 ★★★½ A boy travels back through time to try to prevent his father's murder. C: David Carradine, Ted Prior. D: David A. Prior. SFI [R] 88m. V

Futurekick 1991 ★★ Cyborgian kickboxer looks the future in the eye and doesn't like what he sees. The usual acrobatics at the expense of everything else. C: Don Wilson, Meg Foster, Christopher Penn. D: Damian Klaus. SFI [R] 80m. V

Futureworld 1976 ★★★½ Two reporters visit a futuristic theme park and discover a plot to clone world leaders. Well-done follow-up to *Westworld*. C: Peter Fonda, Blythe Danner, Arthur Hill, Yul Brynner, Stuart Margolin. D: Richard T. Heffron. SFI [PG] 104m. V

Futz 1969 ★ A farmer falls in love with his pig. Filmed version of controversial '60s off-Broadway play is painful to watch and utterly charmless. Nudity. C: Seth Allen, John Bakos, Mari-Claire Charba, Peter Craig, Sally Kirkland. D: Tom O'Horgan. DRA 92m. V

Fuzz 1972 ★★★ In this offbeat police drama, a detective (Reynolds) leads Boston's 87th Precinct detectives in pursuit of a rapist. Fails to blend comedy and thrills. Based on Evan Hunter story. C: Burt Reynolds, Raquel Welch, Yul Brynner, Jack Weston, Tom Skerritt, Steve Ihnat. D: Richard A. Colla. CRI 92m. V

Fuzzy Pink Nightgown, The 1957 ★★★ Fun comedy features a bleached blonde Russell as a movie star abducted by two incompetent kidnappers. They want ransom money but are frustrated when it's believed their crime is just a publicity stunt. Entertaining nonsense with good pacing. C: Jane Russell, Ralph Meeker, Adolphe Menjou, Keenan Wynn, Fred Clark, Una Merkel. D: Norman Taurog. COM 87m.

G

G-Men 1935 ★★★★ When his buddy is murdered, a fledgling lawyer becomes a government agent and battles the bad guys. Nonstop action and excellent work from Cagney. C: James Cagney, Ann Dvorak, Margaret Lindsay, Robert Armstrong. D: William Keighley. ACT 86m. V

Gable and Lombard 1976 ★ Brolin and Clayburgh try hard to fill the shoes of larger-than-life screen idols Gable and Lombard, but ludicrous writing doesn't help. C: James Brolin, Jill Clayburgh, Allen Garfield, Red Buttons, Joanne Linville, Melanie Mayron. D: Sidney Furie. DRA [R] 131m.

Gabriel over the White House 1933 ★★★½ A corrupt politician becomes President, only to change his ways for the good of the people. An indirect slap at Herbert Hoover, monopolies, and political machines. C: Walter Huston, Karen Morley, Franchot Tone, C. Henry Gordon, Samuel S. Hinds, Dickie Moore. D: Gregory LaCava. DRA 86m. V

Gabriela 1983 Brazilian ★★½ Spin-off from popular Brazilian TV series is a sexy but trite melodrama, with enchanting Gabriela (Braga) gaining employment at a seaside pub and eventually marrying the owner. C: Marcello Mastroianni, Sonia Braga, Antonio Cantafora. D: Bruno Barreto. DRA [R] 105m. V

Gaby 1956 ★★★½ Soldier (Kerr) marries ballerina (Caron); when he's later missing in action, his family disowns her, and she becomes a prostitute. Second, less powerful remake of tearjerker *Waterloo Bridge*. C: Leslie Caron, John Kerr, Sir Cedric Hardwicke, Taina Elg. D: Curtis Bernhardt. DRA 97m.

Gaby—A True Story 1987 ★★★★ Fact-based story of courageous cerebral palsy victim and her dedicated family. Levin plays near-paralyzed patient with discomforting accuracy. Inspiring narrative of strength in the face of tragedy manages to make its point without resorting to sentimentality. C: Liv Ullmann, Norma Aleandro, Robert Loggia, Rachel Levin. D: Luis Mandoki. DRA [R] 115m. V

Gaiety George 1948 *See* **Showtime**

Gaijin 1979 Brazilian ★★★★ The story of a young Japanese woman who, along with hundreds of her compatriots, emigrates to Brazil in the early 1900s to work the coffee plantations. Politically aware film chronicles women's ensuing exploitation. An impressive, emotionally gripping work. C: Kyoko Tsukamoto, Antonio Fargunoes. D: Tizuka Yamasaki. DRA 105m.

Gaily, Gaily 1969 ★★★ Famed Chicago newspaperman Ben Hecht in bio-treatment of his experiences early in century. Shallow but expensively mounted comedy entertains in spots. C: Beau Bridges, Melina Mercouri, Brian Keith, George Kennedy, Hume Cronyn, Margot Kidder. D: Norman Jewison. COM [PG] 107m.

Gal Who Took the West, The 1949 ★★★ Three old men recall an opera singer (De Carlo) who headed west during the 1890s, sparking a rivalry between two brothers. Fair comedy/drama/musical built around the talents of De Carlo. C: Yvonne De Carlo, Charles Coburn, Scott Brady. D: Frederick De Cordova. COM 84m.

Gal Young 'Un 1979 ★★★★ During Prohibition, a young hustler charms a rich widow in an attempt to raise money for a moonshine still. Realistic Florida locations and solid performances from a little-known cast. Based on a story by Marjorie Kinnan Rawlings. C: Dana Preu, David Peck, J. Cameron Smith, Gene Densmore. D: Victor Nunez. DRA 105m. V

Galactic Gigolo 1987 ★ Moronic, low-budget gagfest about an alien who wins a trip to Earth (Connecticut, to be precise) on a game show. Once here, he has his way with a number of women. Definitely a "so bad it's good" entry. C: Carmine Capobianco, Debi Thibeault. D: Gorman Bechard. COM [R] 80m. V

Galaxina 1980 ★★ Filmmakers here tried to lampoon the *Star Wars* genre and fell a galaxy or two short. The late Dorothy Stratten is appealing as a robot. C: Stephen Macht, Dorothy R. Stratten. D: William Sachs. SFI [R] 95m. V

Galaxy Express 1982 Japanese ★★½ Middling animated feature about boy on a quest to find intergalactic choo-choo that promises immortality. Might scare some youngsters. Voices of Corey Burton, Fay McKay, Anthony Pope. D: Taro Rin. FAM/SFI [PG] 91m. V

Galaxy Invader, The 1985 ★★★ An alien spaceship crash-lands in rural America and is discovered by some hostile rednecks who are unaware of their new neighbor's powerful weapons. Interesting premise. C: Richard Ruxton, Faye Tilles. D: Don Dohler. SFI 90m. V

Galaxy of Terror 1981 ★★ Emergency space rescue mission turns into a death ride for astronauts on this doomed rocket ship. A weak *Alien* clone with minimal thrills. (a.k.a. *Mindwarp: An Infinity of Terror* and *Planet of Horrors*) *Forbidden World* followed. C: Edward Albert, Erin Moran, Ray Walston. D: B. D. Clark. HOR [R] 85m. V

Galileo 1973 British ★★★★ Biographical film from Bertolt Brecht play about scientist who challenged the church with his heretical theories of the universe. Well acted by supporting players, but Topol, in title role, chews up the scenery a bit much. C: Topol, Edward Fox, Colin Blakely, Georgia Brown, Clive Revill, Margaret Leighton, John Gielgud, Tom Conti. D: Joseph Losey. DRA [PG] 145m.

Gallagher's Travels 1986 ★★★½ Reporter

and a photographer dodge bullets and crocodiles as they are chased across Australia by an international gang of animal smugglers and poachers. C: Ivar Kants, Joanne Samuel. D: Michael Caulfield. ACT 94m. V

Gallant Bess 1946 ★★★ A Navy man on a Pacific island has his life saved by a military horse, and he gratefully brings the animal home with him after the war. Unexceptional animal picture. C: Marshall Thompson, George Tobias, Jim Davis, Chill Wills. D: Andrew Marton. FAM/DRA [G] 101m.

Gallant Hours, The 1960 ★★★½ Cagney shines in this dignified mosaic of the military life of Admiral William Halsey. Not your standard WWII action film. C: James Cagney, Dennis Weaver, Richard Jaeckel, Ward Costello. D: Robert Montgomery. ACT 116m. V

Gallant Journey 1946 ★★ Misfired labor of love for usually reliable director Wellman, who also produced and co-wrote. Stolid biography of first glider flier, who turns out to suffer from vertigo—oops. C: Glenn Ford, Janet Blair, Charles Ruggles, Henry Travers. D: William Wellman. DRA 85m.

Gallant Lady 1934 ★★★ Favorite '30s theme replayed in this sentimental tale of an unwed mother who has a chance to regain the son she gave up by marrying his widowed, adoptive father—if, that is, she can break up his impending marriage to another. Harding's top-notch acting carries film. Remade in 1938 as *Always Goodbye*. C: Ann Harding, Clive Brook, Dickie Moore. D: Gregory LaCava. DRA 86m.

Gallant Legion, The 1948 ★★★½ Texas Rangers intervene when greedy power brokers attempt to divide the Lone Star State into districts. Competent Republic Western with exciting action. C: William Elliott, Adrian Booth, Joseph Schildkraut, Bruce Cabot, Andy Devine. D: Joseph Kane. WST 88m.

Gallery of Horror 1981 ★ Amateurish production of short stories should be called *Gallery of Tedium*. Episodes involving witchcraft, werewolves, vampires, and zombies invoke unintentional laughs. Several familiar fading cinema faces appear. C: Lon Chaney, John Carradine, Rochelle Hudson. D: David L. Hewitt. HOR 90m. V

Gallipoli 1981 Australian ★★★★½ In 1915, two young Australian men from different backgrounds join the Army and become friends; their relationship is set against the title battle. One of the great films about war, superb in every respect. C: Mel Gibson, Mark Lee, Bill Kerr, Robert Grubb. D: Peter Weir. DRA [PG] 111m. V

Galloping Major, The 1950 British ★★★ Former military officer with a penchant for horse racing mistakenly buys a glue factory candidate rather than a prized steed. Through determination and comic antics, the unwanted nag ends up winning big. Enjoyable stuff for younger audiences. C: Basil Radford, Jimmy Hanley, Janette Scott. D: Henry Cornelius. COM 82m.

Galloping Thru 1932 ★★★ Fair Western about a wrangler (Tyler) out to avenge his father's death. Well handled dramatically. C: Tom Tyler, Betty Mack, Al Bridge. D: Lloyd Nosler. WST 58m.

Gambit 1966 ★★★★ Charming caper film that teams Caine and MacLaine as unlikely thieves in pursuit of priceless sculpture. C: Michael Caine, Shirley MacLaine, Herbert Lom. D: Ronald Neame. CRI 109m. V

Gamble on Love 1986 ★★★ Woman returns to Las Vegas where her father once owned a casino. She discovers that the world that was so much fun in her childhood is filled with danger and romance for her as an adult. C: Beverly Garland, Len Crawford, Gary Wood. D: Jim Balden. DRA 105m. V

Gamble, The 1988 Italian ★★½ An evil countess (Dunaway) takes the wealth of a young man (Modine), and wants him as well. Dunaway dusts off her *Three Musketeers* wardrobe and romps with little success. C: Matthew Modine, Faye Dunaway, Jennifer Beals, Feodor Chaliapin. D: Carlo Vanzina. DRA [R] 108m. V

Gambler from Natchez, The 1954 ★★★ Robertson hunts down the three gamblers who killed his father after a card game. Unoriginal Western set in the mid-19th century. C: Dale Robertson, Debra Paget. D: Henry Levin. WST 88m.

Gambler Returns: The Luck of the Draw, The 1991 ★★★½ A high-stakes poker player (Rogers) races cross-country for a San Francisco game with Teddy Roosevelt. Enjoyable, easy-going fun, thanks to charming cast of country singers and TV veterans. C: Kenny Rogers, Reba McEntire, Gene Barry, Chuck Connors, David Carradine, Brian Keith, Doug McLure, Linda Evans, Mickey Rooney, Hugh O'Brian. D: Dick Lowry. COM 180m. TVM V

Gambler, The 1974 ★★★★ College professor (Caan) is a compulsive gambler with a penchant for self-destruction who falls deeply into debt with the mob. Tough, violent drama; Caan scores with sympathetic portrayal of a total loser. C: James Caan, Paul Sorvino, Lauren Hutton, Morris Carnovsky, Burt Young, James Woods. D: Karel Reisz. CRI [R] 111m. V

Gambler, The 1980 *See* **Kenny Rogers as The Gambler**

Gambler's Choice 1944 ★★★ Two men (Morris, Hayden) who grew up together go different ways—one becoming a crooked gambler and the other a police officer. Well-worn plot centers on their rivalry for Kelly. Reworking of *Manhattan Melodrama*. C: Russell Hayden, Chester Morris, Nancy Kelly, Lee Patrick. D: Frank McDonald. WST 66m.

Gamblers, The 1969 ★★★½ Gambler/con

artist (Gordon) gets taken in by phony financier (Serato) while operating a high-stakes poker game on an ocean cruise. Yugoslavian resort settings add some interest to this smooth international drama. C: Suzy Kendall, Don Gordon, Pierre Olaf, Massimo Serato. D: Ron Winston. DRA 93m.

Gambling House 1950 ★★★ An immigrant gambler (Mature) faces deportation as an undesirable alien after being acquitted of murder. Excessively melodramatic saga with social commentary. C: Victor Mature, Terry Moore, William Bendix. D: Ted Tetzlaff. DRA 80m.

Gambling Lady 1934 ★★★★ Highly enjoyable first teaming of Stanwyck and McCrea. Honest cardsharp marries rich guy, but faces suspicion from his nasty ex-girlfriend (Dodd). Fast, engrossing melodrama, with women's game of 21 a highlight. C: Barbara Stanwyck, Pat O'Brien, Claire Dodd, Joel McCrea. D: Archie Mayo. DRA 66m.

Game for Vultures 1980 British ★★ Rhodesian (Roundtree) rebels against apartheid status quo. Serious subject is shortchanged by bad script stressing melodrama. C: Joan Collins, Richard Harris, Richard Roundtree, Ray Milland, Denholm Elliott. D: James Fargo. DRA 113m. V

Game Is Over, The 1966 French ★★ Typical sleazy Vadim exploitation film, with then-wife Fonda as married woman who prefers bedding her young, handsome stepson rather than her wealthy, older husband. Heavy-handed and obvious. From Zola novel *La Curée*. (a.k.a. *La Curée*) C: Jane Fonda, Peter McEnery, Michel Piccoli. D: Roger Vadim. DRA [R] 96m. V

Game of Danger 1954 British ★★★½ Two young boys accidentally kill a man while playing a game of cops and robbers. British-made melodrama features a unique plot. (a.k.a. *Bang! You're Dead*) C: Jack Warner, Veronica Hurst. D: Lance Comfort. DRA 88m.

Game of Death 1979 ★★★ Mobsters try to blackmail Lee, who takes them on individually. Exciting martial arts action, with a powerhouse, non-stop 20-minute fight at the climax. Kareem Abdul-Jabbar's acting debut. Lee died during filming, and film was finished six years later. C: Bruce Lee, Hugh O'Brian, Colleen Camp, Dean Jagger. D: Robert Clouse. ACT [R] 100m. V

Game of Death, A 1946 ★★★ A lunatic hunter (Barrier) stalks shipwrecked passengers on an isolated island. Modestly effective remake of *The Most Dangerous Game*. C: John Loder, Audrey Long, Edgar Barrier, Jason Robards, Sr. D: Robert Wise. ACT 72m.

Game of Love, The 1990 ★★★½ Young singles flock to Henry's bar searching for love and romance. C: Ed Marinaro, Belinda Bauer, Ken Olin. D: Bobby Roth. DRA 94m. V

Game of Seduction 1985 ★★★ Sexy, adult drama about a professional assassin and suave lady-killer who encounters a woman that can stand up to him on his own terms. C: Sylvia Kristel, Nathalie Delon, Jon Finch. D: Roger Vadim. DRA [R] 81m. V

Game of Survival 1989 ★★½ A dashing interplanetary rebel visits earth to battle for his freedom against the greatest intergalactic warriors. C: Nikki Hill, Cindy Coatman, Roosevelt Miller, Jr. D: Armand Gazarian. SFI 85m. V

Game Show Models 1977 ★★★ Low-budget look at the underbelly of TV game shows. Presence of veteran character actors like Melton and lends some fun to this slapdash attempt at sex comedy. C: John Vickery, Diane Summerfield, Thelma Houston, Sid Melton. D: David Gottlieb. COM 89m.

Game, The 1989 ★★½ A bunch of wealthy men gather for their annual game of hide and seek, using helpless human targets as their prey. Things heat up when the hunted become the hunters. C: Joseph Campanella, Craig Alan, Tadashi Yamashita, Marc Fiorini. D: Cole McKay. ACT 91m. V

Gamekeeper, The 1980 British ★★★½ Year in life of estate gamekeeper in north of England as he wrestles with job and family problems, finding solace in the land and in nature. Realistic and honest, this beautifully shot film owes a lot to cinematographer Chris Menges. C: Phil Askham, Rita May, Andrew Grubb. D: Kenneth Loach. DRA 84m.

Gamera—The Invincible 1966 Japanese ★★★ An atomic blast unearths an enormous flying turtle, propelled by jets on his legs. First entry in a long-running series, featuring the usual Japanese special effects (as well as some additional footage of Americans Dekker and Donlevy). (a.k.a. *Gammera* and *Gammera, The Invincible*) C: Brian Donlevy, Albert Dekker, John Baragrey. D: Noriaki Yuasa. SFI 79m. V

Games Girls Play 1974 ★★½ A wild American teenager attending a posh English boarding school initiates a contest among her friends to determine who can seduce the highest-ranking government official. C: Christina Hart, Jane Anthony, Drina Pavlovic, Ed Bishop. D: Jack Arnold. COM [R] 90m. V

Games of Desire 1968 ★★★ A Swedish ambassador marries Thulin to cover for his homosexuality, and she seeks satisfaction from other men. Dull study of '60s sexual mores, from an international perspective. C: Ingrid Thulin, Claudine Auger, Paul Hubschmid. D: Hans Albin. DRA 90m.

Games, The 1970 British ★★★ Four marathon runners prepare themselves for the 26-mile race at the Rome Olympics. Dull handling of subject matter enlivened only by great race at finale. C: Ryan O'Neal, Michael Crawford, Stanley Baker, Charles Aznavour,

Jeremy Kemp, Sam Elliott. D: Michael Winner. DRA [G] 97m.

Games 1967 ★★★½ Brainy husband and wife have a game-playing marriage that takes a chilling turn. Intricate mystery, memorable Caan. C: Simone Signoret, James Caan, Katharine Ross, Estelle Winwood. D: Curtis Harrington. CRI 100m.

Gamma People, The 1956 British ★★ A scientific ray can either increase a person's intelligence—or generate a crazed killer. Familiar sci-fi. C: Paul Douglas, Eva Bartok. D: John Gilling. SFI 79m. V

Gammera the Invincible *See* **Gamera—The Invincible**

Gammera 1966 *See* **Gamera—The Invincible**

Ganashatru 1989 *See* **Enemy of the People, An**

Gandhi 1982 British ★★★★★ Stimulating biography of the nonviolent lawyer and revolutionary who rises to lead campaign for independence of India after WWII. Unstinting historical spectacle with a memorable performance by Kingsley. Won eight Oscars including Best Picture, Best Actor (Kingsley), Director, and Screenplay. C: Ben Kingsley, Candice Bergen, Edward Fox, John Gielgud, Trevor Howard, John Mills, Martin Sheen, Ian Charleson, Athol Fugard. D: Richard Attenborough. DRA [PG] 187m. V

Gang Busters 1955 ★★★ Film centers on multiple prison breakouts by Healey, a convicted public enemy. Too many clichés sink this routine prison drama (adapted from the radio series of the same name). C: Myron Healey, Don Harvey. D: Bill Karan. DRA 78m.

Gang That Couldn't Shoot Straight, The 1971 ★★★ Misadventures of a bumbling gang of New York hoods. Good cast in so-so adaptation of Jimmy Breslin's best-selling novel. C: Jerry Orbach, Leigh Taylor-Young, Jo Van Fleet, Lionel Stander, Robert De Niro. D: James Goldstone. COM [PG] 96m.

Gang War 1958 ★★★½ Teacher takes on street gang that killed his wife. Well-acted mean streets drama. C: Charles Bronson, Kent Taylor, Jennifer Holden. D: Gene Fowler Jr. ACT 75m.

Gang Wars 1940 ★★ Chinese, African-American, and Puerto Rican gangs duel for control of the big city. Typically violent exploitation affair. (a.k.a. *Devil's Express*) C: Ralph Cooper, Gladys Snyder, Reggie Fenderson. D: Leo Popkin. ACT 60m.

Gang's All Here, The 1943 ★★★½ Garish WWII musical with forgettable soldier in love with chorus girl plot. Made memorable by all-time camp classic musical number "The Lady in the Tutti-Frutti Hat," directed by master Busby Berkeley, featuring Miranda and an army of giant bananas! C: Alice Faye, Carmen Miranda, James Ellison, Charlotte Greenwood, Edward Everett Horton, Benny Goodman. D: Busby Berkeley. MUS 103m.

Gangs, Inc. 1941 *See* **Paper Bullets**

Gangster Boss 1959 French ★★★ Mobsters pursue a meek professor when he comes into possession of a bag of money. Clowning of Fernandel—France's top comedian of the time—saves this. C: Fernandel, Papouf, Gino Cervi. D: Henri Verneuil. COM 100m.

Gangster Story 1960 ★★★½ Tough gangster (Matthau) tries to break away from a crime syndicate after falling in love. Matthau had yet to develop his curmudgeonly charm in this routine crime drama, his sole directing credit to date. C: Walter Matthau, Carol Grace, Bruce McFarlan. D: Walter Matthau. CRI 65m.

Gangster, The 1947 ★★★½ Offbeat psychological film noir follows the violent career of small-time hood to the top of the criminal heap, only to be undone by his own paranoia. Sturdy performances and antislum message help raise thriller above standard fare. C: Barry Sullivan, Belita, Joan Lorring, Akim Tamiroff, Fifi D'Orsay, Shelley Winters. D: Gordon Wiles. CRI 84m. V

Gangster Wars 1981 ★★★ Compilation of miniseries *The Gangster Chronicles*, about three juvenile delinquents who later become crime bosses. Competent examination. C: Michael Nouri, Joe Penny, Markie Post. D: Richard C. Sarafian. CRI 121m. TVM V

Gangsters' Law 1986 ★★½ Ersatz film noir stars Kinski as a manic gangster who successfully dodges the law until he makes one fatal error. C: Klaus Kinski, Maurice Poli, Susy Andersen, Max Delys. D: Siro Marcellini. CRI 89m. V

Gangway for Tomorrow 1943 ★★½ Multiple-plot B-movie focusing on the backgrounds of five war plant workers, told through flashbacks. Arch Oboler's patriotic wartime script may now seem a bit maudlin and dated. C: Margo, John Carradine, Robert Ryan. D: John Auer. DRA 69m.

Ganjasaurus Rex 1987 ★ A green dinosaur emerges from the California mountains and wreaks havoc on mankind. C: Paul Bassis, Dave Fresh, Rosie Jones. D: Ursi Reynolds. SFI 100m. V

Garbage Pail Kids Movie, The 1987 ★★ Popular bubble gum card characters engaged in live-action mindless adventures. C: Anthony Newley, MacKenzie Astin, Katie Barberi. D: Rod Amateau. COM [PG] 87 m. V

Garbo Talks 1984 ★★★½ Dying Bancroft's last desire is to meet her idol, Garbo; her son Silver tries to make it happen. Quirky, uneven, sometimes maudlin, but with good acting. C: Ron Silver, Anne Bancroft, Catherine Hicks, Carrie Fisher, Harvey Fierstein, Hermione Gingold. D: Sidney Lumet. DRA [PG-13] 104m. V

Garde A Vue 1981 French ★★★★ A taut, if talky, drama about an attorney in provincial France being investigated for the rape and murder of two girls. Features four greats of the French cinema. C: Lino Ventura, Michel Serrault, Romy Schneider. D: Claude Miller. CRI 87m.

Garden Murder Case, The 1936 ★★½ Murder by hypnosis is subject of routine Philo Vance mystery. Lowe makes a competent Vance. C: Edmund Lowe, Virginia Bruce, Benita Hume, H. Warner. D: Edwin Marin. CRI 62m.

Garden of Allah, The 1936 ★★★ Silly, contrived story set in Sahara about soul-searching woman (Dietrich) who falls in love with libertine monk (Boyer). Gorgeous, early Technicolor photography. Only Dietrich could look perfect in the middle of a sandstorm. C: Marlene Dietrich, Charles Boyer, Tilly Losch, Basil Rathbone, Joseph Schildkraut, John Carradine. D: Richard Boleslawski. DRA 85m. V

Garden of Delights, The 1970 Spanish ★★ Buñuel protege Saura tells ineffective story of powerful executive reduced to idiocy after an automobile accident, and whose plotting family tries to gain access to his fortune. A cruel parable. C: Jose Luis Lopez Vasquez, Lina Canelejas, Luchy Soto. D: Carlos Saura. DRA [PG] 95m.

Garden of Evil 1954 ★★★ Ex-sheriff and gambler traveling to California stop to help a woman whose husband is trapped in a mine, become trapped themselves by marauding Indians. Competent though melodramatic oater. C: Gary Cooper, Susan Hayward, Richard Widmark, Hugh Marlowe, Cameron Mitchell, Rita Moreno. D: Henry Hathaway. WST 100m.

Garden of the Finzi-Continis, The 1971 Italian ★★★★★ A wealthy, cultured family of Italian Jews ignores the encroaching danger of Mussolini's fascism in '30s Italy, retreating into their beautiful world of privilege. Picturesque photography captures sense of ideal past in this lyrical, thoughtful Oscar winner. C: Dominique Sanda, Helmut Berger, Lino Capolicchio. D: Vittorio De Sica. DRA [R] 95m. V

Garden of the Moon 1938 ★★½ Nightclub owner (O'Brien) fights with bandleader (Payne) over singer (Lindsay). Hackneyed plot gets no help from cast nor score, but some help from Berkeley's numbers. C: Pat O'Brien, Margaret Lindsay, John Payne. D: Busby Berkeley. MUS 94m.

Gardens of Stone 1987 ★★★★ Stateside soldiers during the Vietnam War, on duty at Arlington cemetery and the touching interplay of veteran sergeants and the young privates who are itching for action. Interesting drama makes much of powerful concept. Good chemistry among fine cast. C: James Caan, Anjelica Huston, James Earl Jones, D. B. Sweeney, Dean Stockwell, Mary Stuart Masterson. D: Francis Ford Coppola. DRA [R] 112m. V

Gargoyles 1972 ★★★ Cult-favorite shrieker set in Mexico, where discovery of a monstrous skeleton presages attacks by living, horrible creatures. Genuine frights give way to silliness, but great monster makeup and unusual settings help it along. C: Cornel Wilde, Jennifer Salt. D: B. Norton. HOR 74m. TVM

Garment Jungle, The 1957 ★★★ Unions battle mob in New York's garment industry. Tough, gritty material marred by weak subplots. C: Lee J. Cobb, Kerwin Mathews, Gia Scala, Richard Boone. D: Vincent Sherman. DRA 88m. V

Garnet Bracelet, The 1966 USSR ★★★½ Meticulous, tragic tale of a lowly clerk (Ozeror) who longs for the love of a princess (Shengelayn). Comment, on both the nature of the class system and on love. C: Ariadna Shengelaya, Igor Ozerov, O. Basilashvili. D: Abram Room. DRA 90m.

Garnet Princess, The 1988 ★★ A woman who is puzzled by her family background seeks help from a sleuth, who discovers she's really a princess. C: Jean Le Clerc, Liliane Clune. D: Daniele J. Suissa. DRA 80m. V

Gas 1981 Canadian ★ Catastrophic results of small town forced to endure phony gasoline shortage. Flatulent comedy. C: Donald Sutherland, Susan Anspach, Howie Mandel, Sterling Hayden. D: Les Rose. COM [R] 94m. V

Gas, Food Lodging 1991 ★★★½ A well-intentioned New Mexico truck-stop waitress tries to raise her teenaged daughters. Interesting, highly touted effort that stays earnest and energetic throughout. C: Brooke Adams, Ione Skye, Fairuza Balk, James Brolin. D: Allison Anders. DRA [R] 102m. V

Gas Pump Girls 1979 ★★ Cheesey low-budget item concerns five women who run a gas station, offering extra service on the side. C: Bill Smith, Kirsten Baker, Huntz Hall, Rikki Marin. D: Joel Bender. COM [R] 102m. V

Gas-s-s-s 1970 ★★★★ Gas causing premature aging is unexpectedly released from an Alaskan defense plant, destroying everyone in the world over 30. Hilarious, oddball sci-fi with uneven plotting and many laughs. C: Bud Cort, Cindy Williams, Ben Vereen, Talia Shire. D: Roger Corman. SFI [PG] 90m. V

Gaslight 1940 British ★★★★ First film of Patrick Hamilton play, *Angel Street*, about newlywed Wynyard slowly going insane in a mysterious house. Taut psychological thriller, modestly produced. Worth comparing to more renowned Ingrid Bergman version. (a.k.a. *Angel Street*) C: Diana Wynyard, Anton Walbrook, Frank Pettingell, Robert Newton. D: Thorold Dickinson. DRA 84m.

Gaslight 1944 ★★★★½ Bergman marries Boyer, moves into house where her aunt was murdered. When she begins to hear and see strange events, her sanity is questioned. Atmospheric, effective suspense, with an Oscar-winning Bergman performance. Final confrontation is riveting. Lansbury terrific in film debut as saucy maid. Remake of 1940 film (a.k.a. *The Murder in Thorton Square*). C: Ingrid Bergman,

Charles Boyer, Joseph Cotten, Angela Lansbury, Dame May Whitty. D: George Cukor. DRA 103m. v

Gaslight Follies 1955 ★★ Hodgepodge of classic silent comedy bits; Chaplin, Pickford, et al. C: Charlie Chaplin, Douglas Fairbanks, Mary Pickford, Will Rogers. D: Joseph Levine. COM 110m.

Gasoline Alley 1951 ★★½ Struggles of a young couple trying to make it in the diner business. Popular comic strip stumbled on the way to the big screen. C: Scotty Beckett, Jimmy Lydon, Susan Morrow. D: Edward Bernds. DRA 76m.

Gate of Hell 1953 Japanese ★★★★★ A 12th-century imperial warrior returning from battle relentlessly and tragically pursues a married woman as the spoils of war. Restrained use of color, ahead of its time. Winner of two Oscars, for Best Costume Design and Best Foreign Film. C: Machiko Kyo, Kazuo Hasegawa. D: Teinosuke Kinugasa. DRA 86m. v

Gate, The 1987 ★★★ Two suburban teenagers (Dorff and Tripp) discover a large hole in the ground that leads to Hell. Mildly amusing horror flick, with superior special effects. C: Stephen Dorff, Christa Denton, Louis Tripp. D: Tibor Takacs. HOR [PG-13] 85m. v

Gate II—Return to the Nightmare 1992 ★★½ Tripp (returning from the original) captures a tiny, hellish minion which grants all his wishes—at first. Middling sequel has more emphasis on character than usual and some strong special effects. C: Louis Tripp, Simon Reynolds, Pamela Segall. D: Tibor Takacs. HOR [R] 90m. v

Gates of Heaven 1978 ★★★★ Pet cemetery is focal point of insightful documentary about how people are affected by loss of their pets, and how pet "undertakers" deal with them. Morris' skewed perspective brought him attention as arresting non-fiction filmmaker. D: Errol Morris. DOC 85m. v

Gates of Hell, The 1983 Italian ★ A priest's suicide visits supernatural horrors on a small town. Nauseating gore-for-its-own-sake entry in the early '80s Italian zombie cycle. C: Christopher George, Katherine MacColl, Janet Agren, Carlo de Mejo. D: Lucio Fulci. HOR 90m. v

Gates of Paris 1957 French ★★★★ A lazy, drunken nobody begins to feel important when he hides a killer (Vidal) from the law. Above average French drama, highlighted by comedy, good acting, and direction. Watch for remarkable childrens' reenactment of the crime. C: Pierre Brasseur, Georges Brassens, Henri Vidal. D: Rene Clair. DRA 96m.

Gates of the Night 1950 French ★★★½ French surrealist drama about lovers united after WWII. Written by Jacques Prevert, from his play *La Rendez-Vous.* (a.k.a. *Les Porters de la Nuit*) C: Nathalie Nattier, Yves Montand, Pierre Brasseur, Saturnin Fabre, Raymond Bussieres. D: Marcel Carne. DRA 87m.

Gateway 1938 ★★★ Drama of an Irish immigrant's shipboard encounters with crooks and correspondents. Interesting re-creation of Ellis Island Immigration procedures in otherwise so-so romantic drama. C: Don Ameche, Arleen Whelan, Binnie Barnes, Gilbert Roland, John Carradine. D: Alfred Werker. DRA 73m.

Gathering of Eagles 1963 ★★★★ Newly assigned SAC wing commander (Hudson) has professional and domestic problems as he vigorously prepares his base for peak readiness. Bracing service story of disliked but dedicated colonel well played by Hudson. Excellent aerial photography. C: Rock Hudson, Rod Taylor, Mary Peach. D: Delbert Mann. DRA 115m.

Gathering of Old Men, A 1987 ★★★★½ Exciting social drama with perfect ensemble cast has Widmark as sheriff of Louisiana town who is investigating shotgun murder of notorious racist. Gossett plays leader of elderly black men who take responsibility for the crime. Based on novel by Ernest J. Gaines, author of *The Autobiography of Miss Jane Pittman.* (a.k.a. *Murder on the Bayou*) C: Louis Gossett, Jr., Richard Widmark, Holly Hunter, Joe Seneca. D: Volker Schlondorff. DRA 100m. TVM

Gathering, The 1977 ★★★★ Asner plays a dying man who tries to reconnect with his family during his last Christmas. Stapleton is wonderful as the long-neglected wife. Emmy-winner for outstanding drama. C: Edward Asner, Maureen Stapleton. D: Randal Kleiser. DRA 94m. TVM v

Gathering, Part II, The 1979 ★★★ Widow (Stapleton) has a new romance, which makes her family unhappy. Sequel pales beside original but is still well acted. C: Maureen Stapleton, Efrem Zimbalist, Jr. D: Charles Dubin. DRA 98m. TVM

Gathering Storm, The 1974 ★ Inconsequential and often inept biography of Winston Churchill features Burton in one of his most forgettable films. Complete waste of time, both as history and as entertainment. C: Richard Burton, Virginia McKenna, Robert Hardy, Ian Bannen. D: Herbert Wise. DRA 72m.

Gatling Gun, The 1972 ★★½ Apaches, outlaws, and the U.S. Cavalry scramble to possess a machine gun with a rotating cluster of barrels. Inferior Western offers little excitement. (a.k.a. *King Sun*) C: Guy Stockwell, Woody Strode, Patrick Wayne, John Carradine. D: Robert Gordon. WST [PG] 93m.

Gator 1976 ★★ Moonshiner (Reynolds) is forced undercover to nail sleazy politicians. Herky-jerky sequel to *White Lightning* from first-time director Reynolds. Backwoods chases, little else. C: Burt Reynolds, Jack Weston, Lauren Hutton, Alice Ghostley. D: Burt Reynolds. ACT [PG] 116m. v

Gator Bait 1976 ★★ A Louisiana swamp-woman deals with threats against her family (and virtue) in most aggressive manner. Tawdry, violent offering for exploitation fans. C: Claudia Jennings, Sam Gilman, Doug Dirkson. D: Ferd Sebastian, Beverly Sebastian. ACT [R] 91m. V

Gator Bait II 1988 ★★ Man returns to backwoods Louisiana home with his new, cityborn wife, who must fight off the unwanted advances of some local psychos. C: Jan MacKenzie, Tray Loren, Jerry Armstrong. D: Ferd Sebastian, Beverly Sebastian. ACT [R] 90m. V

Gauguin the Savage 1980 ★★★½ Made-for-TV peek at the demons that drove the great French painter (Carradine). Lacks insight, but full of lush images shot in France and Tahiti. C: David Carradine, Lynn Redgrave, Dame Flora Robson, Michael Hordern, Ian Richardson. D: Fielder Cook. DRA 125m. TVM

Gauntlet, The 1977 ★★★ Las Vegas prostitute (Locke) who is a critical witness in an impending trial is stalked by assassins. A cop (Eastwood) sent to bring her to court fights to save her from good guys and bad. Typically violent Eastwood fare. C: Clint Eastwood, Sondra Locke, Pat Hingle. D: Clint Eastwood. CRI [R] 111m. V

Gawain and the Green Night 1973 British ★★★ Sir Gawain of the Round Table is tested by the invulnerable Green Knight. Imaginative low-budget medieval adventure gets points for trying. C: Murray Head, Nigel Green, Ciaran Madden, Robert Hardy, Davil Leland. D: Stephen Weeks. SFI 93m.

Gay Adventure, The 1953 British ★★★½ Three men board a train and take their seats opposite a young woman—thus begin three fantasies about what her life is like. Cute romantic fairy tale with nice performances, though nothing memorable about slight story. C: Burgess Meredith, Jean-Pierre Aumont, Kathleen Harrison. D: Gordon Parry. DRA 87m.

Gay Bride, The 1934 ★★½ Gold-digging chorus girl (Lombard) wants to marry a mobster. Well-intentioned satire of Hollywood gangster pictures. C: Carole Lombard, Chester Morris, ZaSu Pitts. D: Jack Conway. COM 80m.

Gay Deception, The 1935 ★★★★ A Russian prince, (Lederer) posing as a N.Y. doorman, falls in love with a secretary (Dee) visiting the city. Slim romantic comedy ably handled. C: Francis Lederer, Frances Dee, Akim Tamiroff. D: William Wyler. COM 77m.

Gay Desperado, The 1936 ★★★ Lots of comic stereotypes and goofy characterizations liven up this Western parody. Lupino is an heiress kidnapped by bandit Carrillo and his reluctant cohort, singer Martini. Strange but funny, with energetic musical numbers. C: Nino Martini, Ida Lupino, Leo Carrillo, Mischa Auer. D: Rouben Mamoulian. COM 85m.

Gay Divorcee, The 1934 ★★★★½ Second Astaire/Rogers film has them in leading roles for first time. Slight mistaken-identity plot provides Rhodes with a memorable comedy turn as hired correspondent in divorce action. Stars shine in "Night and Day" dance. Other songs include Oscar-winning "The Continental." C: Fred Astaire, Ginger Rogers, Alice Brady, Edward Everett Horton, Erik Rhodes, Eric Blore, Betty Grable. D: Mark Sandrich. MUS 107m. V

Gay Falcon, The 1941 ★★★ The Falcon's first case, a jewel theft and murder. Pleasing Sanders, as usual. C: George Sanders, Wendy Barrie, Gladys Cooper, Turhan Bey. D: Irving Reis. CRI 67m.

Gay Intruders, The 1946 British ★★★★ Unappreciated general, who has decided to sit out WWII, finds himself pulled back into the world when he is forced to care for six children. A film that's warm and generous of spirit. (a.k.a. *Medal for the General*) C: Godfrey Tearle, Jeanne de Casalis, Morland Graham, John Laurie. D: Maurice Elvey. DRA 100m.

Gay Lady, The 1949 British ★★★ Sassy London stage entertainer's flamboyant lifestyle captures heart of British aristocrat. Colorful costume comedy/drama more entertaining for its look than its story. (a.k.a. *Trottie True*) C: Jean Kent, James Donald, Hugh Sinclair. D: Brian Hurst. DRA 95m.

Gay Nineties, The 1930 *See* **Florodora Girl, The**

Gay Purr-ee 1962 ★★★★ Animated musical will appeal more to adults than children with its sophisticated story of French country cat Musette lured into big city career as fashion model. Good voice work by Garland and Goulet with attractive songs by *Wizard of Oz* writers Harold Arlen and E.Y. Harburg. Voices of Judy Garland, Robert Goulet, Red Buttons, Hermione Gingold. D: Abe Levitow. MUS [G] 85m. V

Gay Sisters, The 1942 ★★★ In order to get her hands on money, bad sibling (Stanwyck) weds wealthy suitor (Brent) while her sisters hang in the background. Routine soap opera plotting, with good acting that fights stodgy dialogue. C: Barbara Stanwyck, George Brent, Geraldine Fitzgerald, Gig Young. D: Irving Rapper. DRA 108m.

Gazebo, The 1959 ★★★½ TV writer (Ford) kills man whom he thinks has been blackmailing his actress wife (Reynolds) with compromising photos and then buries him in their backyard. Herman, the pet pigeon, is the scene-stealer in this able black comedy. C: Glenn Ford, Debbie Reynolds, Carl Reiner. D: George Marshall. COM 100m. V

Geisha, A 1953 Japanese ★★★★½ Two generations of geishas and the methods used to exploit them are explored in Mizoguchi's subtle, sympathetic portrait, a remake of his own 1936 *Sisters of the Gion*. C:

Michiyo Kogure. D: Kenji Mizoguchi. DRA 86m. v

Geisha Boy, The 1958 ★★★★ Jerry as magician who causes catastrophe in Japan. Much better than it sounds, with inventive gags and funny contrast between star and Asian straight men. Suzanne Pleshette's film debut. C: Jerry Lewis, Marie McDonald, Sessue Hayakawa, Suzanne Pleshette. D: Frank Tashlin. COM 98m. v

Gemini Man 1976 ★★ Murphy's invisibility makes him of great use to a top secret government organization trying to stop saboteurs. TV pilot is really a revival of *The Invisible Man*, with a spy backdrop. (a.k.a. *Code Name: Minus One*) C: Ben Murphy, Katherine Crawford. D: Alan Levi. SFI 100m. TVM

Gene Krupa Story, The 1960 ★★★½ Mineo tries valiantly to portray self-destructive drummer Krupa, but is too young for the role. Big-band fans will relish chance to see rare footage of singer Anita O'Day and other Krupa band members. C: Sal Mineo, Susan Kohner, James Darren. D: Don Weis. MUS 101m. v

General Della Rovere 1959 Italian ★★★½ De Sica gives one of his best performances as a petty Genovese crook forced by the Nazis to impersonate a Resistance general. Overlong but engaging. C: Vittorio De Sica, Hannes Messemer, Sandra Milo. D: Roberto Rossellini. DRA 130m. v

General Died at Dawn, The 1936 ★★★★ Idealistic adventurer (Cooper) challenges evil Chinese warlord (Tamiroff) while romancing beautiful spy (Carroll). Exotic sets, sharp characterizations and dab of political philosophy make for atmospheric melodrama of mysterious East. C: Gary Cooper, Madeleine Carroll, Akim Tamiroff, William Frawley. D: Lewis Milestone. DRA 93m. v

General Idi Amin Dada 1974 ★★★★ Documentary about Ugandan dictator had to be approved by Amin himself; despite such a concession, this is still a remarkably vivd portrait of a canny tyrant. D: Barbet Schroeder. DOC 113m. v

General Line, The 1929 Soviet ★★★★½ A poor woman convinces her village to become a cooperative. Eisenstein's last silent film transcends mere propaganda with filmmaking brilliance. Dairy sequence includes one of the most famous montages in cinema history. (a.k.a. *Old and New*) C: Marfa Lapkina, Vasya Buzenkov, Kostya Vasiliev. D: Sergei Eisenstein. DRA 90m.

General Spanky 1936 ★★★ Orphan Spanky organizes a group of kids to defend a plantation against Yankee invaders during the Civil War. Contains too much plot to allow the spontaneity that made the Little Rascals' shorts so wonderful, but worthy of note as the only *Our Gang* feature. C: Spanky McFarland, Billie "Buckwheat" Thomas, Carl "Alfalfa" Switzer, Phillips Holmes. D: Fred Newmeyer, Gordon Douglas. FAM/COM 60m. v

General Suvorov 1941 Soviet ★★★★ Stirring Russian film about the general who defeated Napoleon, at the gates of Moscow. Sturdy wartime historical. C: N.P. Cherkasov-Sergeyev, A. Yachnitsky, M. Astangov, S. Kiligin. D: V.I. Pudovkin, Mikhail Doller. DRA 90m.

General, The 1927 ★★★★★ Silent comedy classic, based on a true Civil War incident, has Keaton driving a stolen train. Wonderful visual gags and great battle scenes, with Keaton deadpan through it all. Highlight: the damaged bridge and the optimistic officer. C: Buster Keaton, Marion Mack, Glen Cavender, Joseph Keaton. D: Buster Keaton. COM v

Generals without Buttons 1938 French ★★★★ Oddball feud between two neighboring towns as viewed through the eyes of the towns' children. A witty and knowing satire; based on the novel *La Guerre des Boutons*, by Louis Pergaud, which won the prestigious French Goncourt Prize. C: Jean Murat, Claude May, Saturnin Fabre, Serge Grave. D: Jacques Daroy. COM 80m.

Generation 1969 ★★★ A young married couple has far out, "natural" ideas about childbirth that drive her stodgy father nuts. Very dated comedy, but with a fine cast. C: David Janssen, Kim Darby, Carl Reiner, Peter Duel, James Coco, Sam Waterston. D: George Schaefer. COM (PG) 104m. v

Generation, A 1954 Polish ★★★★ Wajda's debut film is a hard-hitting political saga about a group of men in Nazi-occupied Warsaw who join the Resistance and become unlikely heroes. A gritty, muscular drama. Look for a very young Roman Polanski. C: Ursula Modrzinska, Tadeusz Lomnicki, Zbigniew Cybulski. D: Andrzej Wajda. DRA 90m. v

Genevieve 1953 British ★★★★★ Delicious comedy about two couples in antique car race. One of the funniest movies about competition ever made with sterling performances by foursome, especially Kendall as zany trumpet-playing fashion model. Famous musical score performed by harmonica virtuoso Larry Adler. C: John Gregsonn, Dinah Sheridan, Kenneth More, Kay Kendall. D: Henry Cornelius. COM 86m. v

Genghis Khan 1965 ★★½ After his father is killed, Mongol leader Genghis Khan sets out for revenge on a rival warlord. Some good action sequences, and great costumes but huge cast of miscast stars, lost in an overblown epic. C: Omar Sharif, Stephen Boyd, James Mason, Eli Wallach, Francoise Dorleac, Telly Savalas, Robert Morley. D: Henry Levin. DRA 124m.

Genius at Work 1946 ★★½ Brown and Carney—a low-budget version of Abbott and Costello—are radio sleuths trying to solve an actual murder. Whodunit comedy unfortunately wastes Lugosi as a butler. Remake of 1937 *Super Sleuth.* C: Wally Brown, Alan Carney, Lionel Atwill, Anne Jeffreys, Bela Lugosi. D: Leslie Goodwins. COM 61m.

Genocide 1982 ★★★★ The Holocaust's unspeakable evils are shown in this worthy addition to historical records. Even insufferable narration by Orson Welles and Liz Taylor does not undermine power of actual film footage, photos, and correspondence. C: Orson Welles, Elizabeth Taylor. D: Arnold Schwartzman. DOC 90m.

Genroku Chusingara, The 1941 *See* **47 Ronin, The**

Gentle Annie 1944 ★★★ Likable rancher adds to her larder by pulling train robberies, to the dismay of the local sheriff. Efficient Western tailored for Main. Based on MacKinlay Kantor novel. C: Donna Reed, Marjorie Main, Harry Morgan. D: Andrew Marton. WST 80m.

Gentle Creature, A 1971 French ★★★★½ A domineering husband (Frangin) must deal with his guilt when his sensitive wife commits suicide. An affecting and subtle drama; based on the novella by Dostoyevsky. (a.k.a. *Une Femme Douce*) C: Dominique Sanda, Guy Frangin, Jane Lobre. D: Robert Bresson. DRA 88m.

Gentle Giant 1967 ★★★½ The film that inspired the *Gentle Ben* television series. A boy and his family raise an orphaned bear cub to maturity and come to terms with the realization that he must be returned to the wild. Simple, appealing children's viewing. C: Dennis Weaver, Vera Miles. D: James Neilson. FAM/DRA 93m. V

Gentle Gunman, The 1952 British ★★★★ Family of IRA sympathizers slowly comes apart after one brother tires of violence and decides he wants peace. Well-made, low-key action with a fine cast. C: Dirk Bogarde, John Mills, Elizabeth Sellars. D: Basil Dearden. ACT 86m.

Gentle Julia 1936 ★★★½ A humorously bratty younger sister (Withers) acts up to keep her older sister (Hunt) from falling for the wrong guy in this amusing family romance. C: Jane Withers, Marsha Hunt, Tom Brown, Hattie McDaniel. D: John Blystone. DRA 63m.

Gentle Rain, The 1966 ★★½ Rio de Janeiro is the meeting place for a pair of social misfits: a frigid socialite (Day) and an architect (George) who has been mute since the accidental death of his girlfriend. Maudlin and slow-moving romantic melodrama. C: Christopher George, Lynda Day. D: Burt Balaban. DRA 110m.

Gentle Sex, The 1943 ★★★ Seven women from different walks of life join Great Britain's war effort during WWII in this interesting propaganda film directed by Leslie Howard. C: Joan Gates, Jean Gillie, Joan Greenwood, Joyce Howard. D: Leslie Howard. DRA 92m.

Gentleman After Dark, A 1942 ★★★ A convicted thief breaks out of prison to ensure his daughter's future by doing away with his blackmailing wife. Sentimental, but offers some decent performances. Remake of 1936's *Forgotten Faces.* C: Brian Donlevy, Miriam Hopkins, Preston Foster. D: Edwin Marin. DRA 77m.

Gentleman at Heart, A 1942 ★★★½ Racketeer (Romero) muscles in on the art gallery of a losing horse bettor (Berle) to reap the benefits of art forgery. Light and breezy gangster comedy with inspired performances. C: Cesar Romero, Carole Landis, Milton Berle. D: Ray McCarey. COM 66m.

Gentleman Bandit, The 1981 ★★★½ True-life mistaken identity story of a Catholic priest (Waite) who was accused of being an armed robber. He's arrested after several eyewitnesses swear he's the man. Good performances; chilling, plausible story. C: Ralph Waite, Jerry Zaks, Estelle Parsons. D: Jonathan Kaplan. DRA 100m. TVM V

Gentleman from Louisiana 1936 ★★★½ At the turn of the century, a young jockey gets mixed up with the wrong crowd and has to prove his honesty and innocence. Not-bad period piece, with realistic costumes and details. C: Edward Quillan, Charles "Chic" Sale, Charlotte Henry, Marjorie Gateson. D: Irving Pichel. CRI 67m.

Gentleman from Nowhere, The 1948 ★★½ A boxer, long thought dead, returns to clear his name with the aid of a detective. Slim pickings. C: Warner Baxter, Fay Baker, Luis Van Rooten. CRI 65m.

Gentleman Jim 1942 ★★★★½ Flynn's the star in this good-natured, entertaining film biography of famous Victorian pugilist Jim Corbett, ably supported by veteran character actors Bond and Hale. Played for laughs. C: Errol Flynn, Alexis Smith, Jack Carson, Alan Hale, William Frawley. D: Raoul Walsh. COM 104m. V

Gentleman's Agreement 1947 ★★★★ Gentile writer Peck poses as a Jew to investigate anti-Semitism in America. Significant Hollywood attempt to deal with prejudice may seem obvious today. Oscars for Best Picture and Director; also to Holm as Supporting Actress. C: Gregory Peck, Dorothy McGuire, John Garfield, Celeste Holm, Anne Revere. D: Elia Kazan. DRA 118m. V

Gentleman's Fate 1931 ★★★ Fair gangster tale of bootleggers during Prohibition, billed as silent star Gilbert's comeback vehicle. C: John Gilbert, Louis Wolheim, Leila Hyams, Anita Page. D: Mervyn LeRoy. CRI 90m.

Gentlemen Marry Brunettes 1955 ★★ Two sisters (Russell, Crain) go to Paris in search of rich husbands. Blatant attempt to capitalize on successful *Gentlemen Prefer Blondes* substitutes Crain for Monroe and inane jokes for genuine wit. C: Jane Russell, Jeanne Crain, Alan Young, Rudy Vallee, Scott Brady. D: Richard Sale. MUS 97m.

Gentlemen Prefer Blondes 1953 ★★★★ Big, colorful musical from popular Broadway show features Monroe and Russell as best friends chasing men and fortunes around the world. Monroe steals the show singing "Diamonds are a Girl's Best Friend." Followed by *Gentlemen Marry Brunettes.* C: Jane Russell, Marilyn Monroe, Charles Coburn, Elliott Reid, Tommy Noonan. D: Howard Hawks. COM 91m. V

Gentlemen's Agreement 1935 British ★★★ Two gentlemen, one rich, one poor, switch places. Trivial comedy, of interest only for Leigh's first starring role. C: Frederick Peisley, Vivien Leigh, Antony Holles. D: George Pearson. COM 71m.

George and Margaret 1940 British ★★★★ A household is turned topsy-turvy by the threat of company in this surprisingly agile farce. C: Marie Lohr, Judy Kelly, Noel Howlett, Oliver Wakefield. D: George King. COM 70m.

George Balanchine's The Nutcracker 1993 ★★★★ Straightforward filming of famed New York City Ballet production. Tchaikovsky's wondrous score is well-served by first-class dancers and orchestra, as Ardolino's camera captures most of the holiday perennial's magic. (a.k.a. *The Nutcracker*) C: Darci Kistler, Damian Woetzel, Kyra Nichols, Macaulay Culkin; narration by Kevin Kline. D: Emile Ardolino. MUS [G] 92m. V

George McKenna Story, The 1986 ★★★½ True story of principal (Washington) who straightens out students of South Central L.A.'s heavily armed, drug-ridden George Washington High School. Riveting drama, realistically acted. C: Denzel Washington, Lynn Whitfield, Akosua Busia, Richard Masur. D: Eric Laneuville. DRA 95m. V

George Raft Story, The 1961 ★★★½ Sensationalized biography of dancer turned actor George Raft's rapid Hollywood ascent. Danton's portrayal reveals Raft's troubled essence. C: Ray Danton, Jayne Mansfield, Barrie Chase, Julie London. D: Joseph Newman. DRA 106m.

George Stevens: A Filmmaker's Journey 1984 ★★★★ George Stevens, Jr.'s splendid tribute to his father, the legendary director of movies such as *Swing Time, Shane, Gunga Din,* and *A Place in the Sun,* with film clips and interviews with friends and colleagues. Footage from Stevens' own home movies rounds out this excellent, loving documentary. D: George Stevens, Jr. DOC 111m. V

George Washington Slept Here 1942 ★★★½ New Yorkers Benny and Sheridan buy historic, falling-down old house in Connecticut and contend with nosy neighbors and other problems. Kaufman/Hart play's a bit dated, but the humor is still intact. C: Jack Benny, Ann Sheridan, Charles Coburn, Hattie McDaniel, Percy Kilbride, Franklin Pangborn. D: William Keighley. COM 91m. V

George White's Scandals 1934 ★★★½ Broadway rival to *The Ziegfeld Follies* gets screen treatment. Same old backstage story, but good production numbers and prime Durante. Faye's film debut. C: Rudy Vallee, Alice Faye, Jimmy Durante, Dixie Dunbar, George White. D: George White, Thornton Freeland, Harry Lachman. MUS 80m.

George White's Scandals 1935 ★★★½ Second in series of loosely plotted revues is notable for screen debut of Powell, the best tap dancer of her time. Faye is charming, as always. (a.k.a. *George White's 1935 Scandals*). C: Alice Faye, James Dunn, Ned Sparks, Eleanor Powell, Lydia Roberti, George White. D: George White. MUS 83m.

George White's Scandals 1945 ★★★ Third, last, and weakest of the Scandals with no originality whatsoever. Davis' clowning and songs such as "Life Is Just a Bowl of Cherries" and the Gershwins' "Liza" help a little. C: Joan Davis, Jack Haley, Margaret Hamilton. D: Felix Feist. MUS 95m. V

Georgia, Georgia 1972 ★★½ Scandinavian slant on interracial relationships, with the beautiful Sands as a black American singer and Benedict as her white photographer lover. Confusing to follow and full of unresolved racial, social questions. Based on story by Maya Angelou. C: Diana Sands, Dirk Benedict. D: Stig Bjorkman. DRA [R] 91m. V

Georgia Peaches, The 1980 ★★★ A Southern woman versed in car repair, her country-singing sister, and their stock car driving friend become federal undercover agents. uneven TV pilot has mix of "good old boy" clichés and crime drama intrigue. COM TVM

Georgy Girl 1966 British ★★★★½ Chronicle of London's mid-'60s youth has an overweight ugly duckling (Redgrave) at a crossroads in her muddled life among groovy friends (Rampling and Bates) and wealthy married suitor (Mason). Excellent performances, keenly observed relationships. A slice-of-life beauty. C: Lynn Redgrave, James Mason, Charlotte Rampling, Alan Bates. D: Silvio Narizzano. COM [R] 100m. V

German Sisters, The 1982 W. German ★★★★ Fascinating and well-done exploration of post-WWII German psyche via story of two sisters, one a political terrorist, the other a journalist. Loosely based on a true story. C: Jutta Lampe, Barbara Sukowa, Rudiger Vogler, Doris Schade, Verenice Rudolph. D: Margarethe von Trotta. DRA 107m.

Germany, Pale Mother 1980 W. German ★★★★½ During WWII, Mattes marries Nazi soldier Jacobi. War, politics, and post-war German life take their toll on this relationship. A daring and well-acted homefront drama that avoids one-dimensional portrayal of the German people. C: Eva Mattes, Ernest Jacobi. D: Helma Sanders-Grahms. DRA 123m.

Germany Year Zero 1947 German ★★★★ Rossellini portrays an utterly unredeemed postwar Germany, as a young boy is so horrified by life that he kills his father and then himself. Starkly pessimistic view of a painful time and place. C: Edmund Moeschke, Ernst Pittschav, Franz Kruger. D: Roberto Rossellini. DRA 87m. V

Germinal 1993 French ★★★★ A 19th-century coal-mining town in provincial France is torn asunder by a rebellious outsider. Emile Zola's novel makes an elaborate social document, dominated by Depardieu as the head of a struggling family. French pop singer Renaud's film debut. C: Gerard Depardieu, Renaud, Miou-Miou. D: Claude Berri. DRA [R] 158m. V

Geronimo 1939 ★★½ When his tribe is forcibly removed to a bleak reservation, an Apache war chief responds with growing bands of renegade raiders. Good story weakened by so-so effects. C: Preston Foster, Ellen Drew, Andy Devine. D: Paul Sloane. WST 89m.

Geronimo 1962 ★★★ Connors turns in a compelling performance as the Native-American renegade in this moderately interesting Western. C: Chuck Connors, Kamala Devi. D: Arnold Laven. WST 101m. V

Geronimo 1993 ★★★½ The turbulent life of the famed Apache leader makes a well-researched (if somewhat dull) TV film. Somewhat inferior to the theatrical feature, *Geronimo: An American Legend*, released at about the same time. C: Joseph Running Fox, Nick Ramus, Michelle St. John. D: Roger Young. WST 100m. TVM V

Geronimo: An American Legend 1993 ★★★½ When his tribe is forcibly removed to a bleak reservation, an Apache war leader heads an increasingly large band of renegade raiders. Capable Western, with commentary on the plight of 19th-century Native Americans. Strong performance by Studi. Not to be confused with the cable TV version of the same story, which premiered simultaneously with this theatrical feature. C: Wes Studi, Jason Patric, Robert Duvall, Gene Hackman. D: Walter Hill. WST [PG-13] 115m. V

Gertrud 1964 Danish ★★★★ A masterpiece of pared-down visual simplicity, Dreyer's final film tells the story of a woman who can't get love from her husband, her younger lover, or her former lover, so she retreats entirely from the world of men. Using long, static takes, Dreyer distills the movie's emotions into spiritually felt essences. A unique viewing experience. C: Nina Pens Røde, Bendt Rothe, Ebbe Røde, Axel Strøbye. D: Carl Dreyer. DRA 116m.

Gervaise 1956 French ★★★★½ A 19th-century Parisian family, struggling to make a living in the laundry business, is destroyed by alocoholism. Emile Zola's French literary classic is brought powerfully to the screen. C: Maria Schell, Francois Perier. D: Rene Clement. DRA 116m. V

Get Back 1991 ★★★½ Ordinary concert film of Paul McCartney's 1989 World Tour, his first in 13 years. Okay souvenir of a terrific show. D: Richard Lester. MUS [PG] 89m. V

Get Carter 1971 British ★★★★ Caine is first-rate as a criminal returning home to avenge gangland murder of his brother. Tautly drawn, provocative English crime drama. Remade as *Hit Man*, with black cast. C: Michael Caine, Ian Hendry, Britt Ekland. D: Mike Hodges. CRI [R] 112m.

Get Charlie Tully 1976 British ★ Emery searches for the location of some desirable bonds through clues tattooed on the rumps of a quartet of women. British sex romp. (a.k.a. *Oooh, You Are Awful*) C: Dick Emery, Derren Nesbitt, Ronald Fraser. D: Cliff Owen. COM [PG] 97m.

Get Christie Love 1974 ★★★ Sexy black female cop goes undercover in L.A. to bust a drug ring. So-so pilot for cult TV series. C: Teresa Graves, Harry Guardino. D: William A. Graham. CRI 100m. TVM V

Get Crazy 1983 ★★★ Gag-splattered satire of troubled New Year's Eve concert includes parodies of famous rock stars (including Mick Jagger and Bob Dylan) and lots of cameos. An energetic mess. C: Daniel Stern, Malcolm McDowell, Gail Edwards, Ed Begley, Jr. COM [R] 98m. V

Get Hep to Love 1944 ★★★ Opera-singing Jean runs away from a mercenary aunt to live with a young married couple. Clichéd story, but a spirited performance by O'Connor provides bright spots. (a.k.a. *It Comes Up Love*) C: Gloria Jean, Donald O'Connor, Jane Frazee. D: Charles Lamont. MUS 71m.

Get on with It 1961 British ★★★ Two dental school graduates attempt to push a new brand of toothpaste. Mild comedy farce starring a pair of refugees from the British *Carry On* series. (a.k.a. *Dentist on the Job*) C: Bob Monkhouse, Kenneth Connor, Shirley Eaton. D: C. Pennington-Richards. COM 88m.

Get Out of Town 1962 ★★½ A reformed gangster returns to his hometown to prove that the death of his brother was murder, not an accident. Weakly written low-budget crime melodrama never gets rolling. C: Douglas Wilson, Jeanne Baird. D: Charles Davis. CRI 62m.

Get Out Your Handkerchiefs 1978 French ★★★★½ Quirky, vibrant comedy has devoted, sacrificing husband (Depardieu) going to great lengths to make a pathetic wife happy, procuring a lover and encouraging a sexual cure for her melancholy. Best Foreign Film Oscar winner delivers laughs at every turn. C: Gerard Depardieu, Patrick Dewaere,

Michel Serrault. D: Bertrand Blier. COM [R] 109m. V

Get Smart, Again! 1989 ★★★ Television hit from '60s is updated with Adams back as Agent 86, fighting nemesis agency KAOS. Most of sitcom cast returns, but this so-so comedy doesn't compare to original series. C: Don Adams, Barbara Feldon. D: Gary Nelson. COM 93m. TVM V

Get to Know Your Rabbit 1972 ★★½ Obscure De Palma comedy features Smothers as social outcast who wants to become a magician. Largely reedited against director's will; the result is a mess with flashes of black humor. C: Tom Smothers, John Astin, Katharine Ross, Orson Welles. D: Brian De Palma. COM [R] 92m. V

Get Yourself a College Girl 1964 ★★★ A vacation resort hotel provides the setting for romance between a music publisher (Everett) and a collegiate songwriter (Mobley). Lightweight plot provides an excuse for dubbed performances by big-name musical performers. C: Chad Everett, Nancy Sinatra, Mary Mobley, The Dave Clark Five. D: Sidney Miller. MUS 88m.

Getaway, The 1972 ★★★★ Bank robbers McQueen and McGraw take it on the lam, leading to a lengthy chase by the police. A showcase for Peckinpah's highly individualized action and violence, heavily based on moody slow-motion shots. Based on a novel by Jim Thompson. C: Steve McQueen, Ali MacGraw, Ben Johnson, Sally Struthers. D: Sam Peckinpah. CRI 123m. V

Getaway, The 1994 ★★½ A master thief (Baldwin) is sprung from jail (on parole secured by political pull) for one last heist; his wife (Basinger) may be double-crossing him. Almost a shot-for-shot remake of the 1972 Peckinpah film of Jim Thompson's novel, but without the same chemistry; a fascinating comparison study in actors, though. C: Alec Baldwin, Kim Basinger, James Woods, Michael Madsen, David Morse, Jennifer Tilly. D: Roger Donaldson. CRI [R] 115m. V

Getting Away With Murder *See* **End of the Game**

Getting Even 1986 ★★ A cast of hams star in this thriller about a killer who threatens to poison Dallas with a fatal gas unless he is paid $50 million. (a.k.a. *Hostage: Dallas.*) C: Edward Albert, Audrey Landers. D: Dwight H. Little. CRI [R] 90m. V

Getting Even with Dad 1994 ★★★½ Or "Home Alone with Dad." A petty thief (Danson) is planning his last job when his son (Culkin) is dropped off for a week. The John Hughes machine rolls in, with his trademark mix of slapstick and silliness; Culkin is again irrepressible. C: Macaulay Culkin, Ted Danson. D: Howard Deutch. COM

Getting Gertie's Garter 1945 ★★★ Marital farce about a husband (O'Keefe) who must retrieve an engraved garter from former flame (McDonald) before his suspicious wife (Ryan) finds out. Takeoff on previous year's *Up In Mabel's Room.* C: Dennis O'Keefe, Marie McDonald, Barry Sullivan, Binnie Barnes. D: Allan Dwan. COM 72m.

Getting Gotti 1994 ★★★ Bracco's notable performance as the crusading prosecutor who tried to put away Mafia chieftain John Gotti carries this movie. Unfortunately, it ends with Gotti being acquitted (although he was subsequently retried and convicted). C: Lorraine Bracco, Anthony John Denison, Kathleen Lasky, August Schellenberg. D: Roger Young. CRI 120m. TVM

Getting It On 1983 ★★★ Facile teen sex comedy focuses on a young nerd using his expensive video equipment to satisfy his voyeuristic tendencies. D: William Olen. COM [R] 96m. V

Getting It Right 1989 ★★½ A virgin in his 30s goes through late rites of passage. Slow-starter rises to satisfying finish. Fine, sweetly comic Redgrave. C: Jesse Birdsall, Helena Bonham Carter, Peter Cook, Lynn Redgrave, Jane Horrocks, John Gielgud. D: Randal Kleiser. COM [R] 101m. V

Getting of Wisdom, The 1980 Australian ★★★★ In Victorian-era Australia, a youngster from the country gets sent to a snobbish girls boarding school in Melbourne. Fowle engagingly plays the talented, feisty girl from the outback who is determined to succeed. Charming, well-acted drama, beautifully photographed. C: Susannah Fowle, Hilary Ryan, Alix Longman. D: Bruce Beresford. DRA 100m. V

Getting Out 1994 ★★★★½ Tough, no-holds-barred portrait of a female convict and her struggle to reenter society when released. De Mornay and Burstyn give knockout performances as the vulnerable parolee and her monster mother, respectively. Based on Marsha Norman's off-Broadway play. C: Rebecca de Mornay, Ellen Burstyn, Robert Knepper, Carol Mitchell-Leon. D: John Korty. DRA 120m. TVM

Getting Over 1980 ★★★ Okay romantic comedy set in the music business casts Daniels as a would-be record producer discovering an enormously talented singer (Hopkins). C: John Daniels, Gwen Brisco, Mary Hopkins. D: Bernie Rollins. COM 108m. V

Getting Physical 1984 ★★½ Young woman religiously pumps iron hoping to compete against champion female body builders. Substandard semidocumentary is nothing special. C: Alexandra Paul, Sandahl Bergman, David Naughton, Robert Wagner. D: Steven Hilliard Stern. DRA 95m. TVM V

Getting Straight 1970 ★★★ Graduate student (Gould) must choose between official college policies and his own set of values. Loosely structured comedy very dated now but Gould still shines. C: Elliott Gould,

Candice Bergen, Jeff Corey. D: Richard Rush. COM [R] 124m.

Getting Wasted 1980 ★★★½ Not bad teen comedy set in a rigid military in the 1960s that gets turned upside down by some closet-hippie cadets. C: Brian Kerwin, Stephen Forst, Cooper Huckabee, Wendy Ratstatter. D: Paul Frizler. COM [R] 98m. V

Gettysburg 1993 ★★★ Over-long, ponderous but well-intentioned re-creation of the pivotal Civil War battle, with brilliantly staged war sequences. Based on Michael Shaara's Pulitzer Prize-winning novel, *The Killer Angels.* C: Tom Berenger, Jeff Daniels, Martin Sheen, Sam Elliott, Maxwell Caulfield, C. Thomas Howell. D: Ronald Maxwell. DRA [PG] 248m.

Ghetto Blaster 1989 ★★ A Vietnam veteran faces off against street thugs to clean up the streets of his town. Appalling title is apt. C: Richard Hatch, R.G. Armstrong, Richard Jaeckel. D: Alan L. Stewart. ACT [R] 86m. V

Ghidrah: The Three-Headed Monster 1965 Japanese ★★★★ Godzilla, Rodan, and Mothra join forces to save Tokyo from an evil monster from Mars. Enjoyable and, at times, clever. One of the best of the genre. C: Yoske Natsuki, Yuriko Hoshi. D: Inoshiro Honda. SFI 85m. V

Ghost 1990 ★★★★ After being murdered, ethereal Swayze tries to protect his mourning girlfriend (Moore) and expose his killer before heading to the Great Beyond. Goldberg won an Oscar for her turn as a wacky, skeptical medium who helps Swayze. Undistinguished plot is redeemed by good performances and terrific special effects. C: Patrick Swayze, Demi Moore, Whoopi Goldberg, Tony Goldwyn. D: Jerry Zucker. DRA [PG-13] 127m. V

Ghost and Mr. Chicken 1966 ★★★ Made-to-order vehicle for fidgety comedian Knotts, as a timid reporter is forced to spend some scary time in a haunted house. He has his fans, and this is for them. C: Don Knotts, Joan Staley, Dick Sargent. D: Alan Rafkin. FAM/COM 90m.

Ghost and Mrs. Muir, The 1947 ★★★★½ Haunting period fantasy about impoverished widow Tierney moving into seaside cottage inhabited by ghost of salty mariner Harrison. Their strange romance is both amusing and moving. Beautifully written by Philip Dunne, from R.A. Dick's novel. C: Gene Tierney, Rex Harrison, George Sanders, Edna Best, Natalie Wood. D: Joseph L. Mankiewicz. DRA 104m. V

Ghost and the Guest 1943 ★★★ Newlyweds think their honeymoon house is haunted, when, in fact, they're sharing it with hoods on the run. Enjoyable B-comedy tingler. C: James Dunn, Florence Rice, Mabel Todd. D: William Nigh. COM 59m.

Ghost Breakers, The 1940 ★★★★ Comedy/horror classic about young woman (delightfully played by Goddard) who inherits a Cuban castle and copes with resident ghouls and zombies as she and sidekick Hope search for treasure. A lot of fun. Remade in 1953 as *Scared Stiff.* C: Bob Hope, Paulette Goddard, Richard Carlson, Paul Lukas, Anthony Quinn. D: George Marshall. COM 85m. V

Ghost Camera, The 1933 British ★★★ Average British mystery about the search for a camera containing a photo that can clear a man of murder. C: Henry Kendall, Ida Lupino, John Mills. D: Bernard Vorhaus. DRA 68m.

Ghost Catchers 1944 ★★★★ Vaudeville comics Olsen and Johnson shine as a pair of nightclub owners hired by a Southern colonel. Before they put on the show they've got to deal with the haunted house next door. Fever-pitched pacing marks one of the comic duo's best films; don't miss Mel Torme's cameo playing drums. C: Ole Olsen, Chic Johnson, Gloria Jean, Martha O'Driscoll, Lon Chaney Jr. D: Edward Cline. COM 67m.

Ghost Chase 1989 ★★ Idiotic comedy about two adolescent filmmakers who inherit a haunted cache of relics and search for cinematic inspiration. C: Jason Lively, Tim McDaniel, Jill Whitlow. D: Roland Emmerich. COM [PG] 89m.

Ghost Chasers 1951 ★★★½ Silly spooks and a high energy level make this story of goofy New Yorkers matching wits with phony clairvoyant one of the better entries in the long-running Bowery Boys series. C: Leo Gorcey, Huntz Hall, William Benedict. D: William Beaudine. COM 69m. V

Ghost Comes Home, The 1940 ★★ Long lost father (Morgan) returns home, much to the embarrassment of his family. Comedy involves their attempts to hide him. C: Frank Morgan, Billie Burke, Ann Rutherford. D: William Thiele. COM 79m.

Ghost Dad 1990 ★★ Feeble comedy casts Cosby as recently dead parent who wants to help his kids from the Great Beyond. Youngsters may enjoy but film is almost entirely devoid of laughs and well beneath Cosby's talents. C: Bill Cosby, Kimberly Russell, Denise Nicholas. D: Sidney Poitier. COM [PG] 84m. V

Ghost Dance 1980 ★★★ Gruesome horror flick starts with the violation of a Native American burial ground, filled with outraged corpses. C: Brian Kerwin, Stephen Forst, Cooper Huckabee, Wendy Ratstatter. D: Paul Frizler. HOR [R] 98m. V

Ghost Dancing 1983 ★★★½ It's farmers and city folk fighting over water rights out West all over again. McGuire plays a gritty old farmer who blows up a pipeline to draw media attention to the destruction of her beloved valley. Good cast, well-meaning drama. C: Dorothy McGuire, Bruce Davison. D: David Greene. DRA 100m. TVM

Ghost Diver 1957 ★★½ A TV star (Craig) and his crew go to the Caribbean to hunt for sunken treasure, and come across more adventure than they can handle. There's action, but the title is a bit misleading: there is no "ghost diver" in the film! C: James Craig, Audrey Totter. D: Richard Einfeld, Merrill White. ACT 76m.

Ghost Fever 1987 ★ Inept comedy features Hemsley and Avalos as two detectives battling a slave-owning ghost haunting Civil War-era home. Director Lee Madden had his real name pulled from this for good reason. C: Sherman Hemsley, Luis Avalos. D: Alan Smithee. COM 86m. V

Ghost Goes West, The 1936 ★★★★ In this charming fantasy/comedy, a nouveau riche American dime store tycoon (Pallette) buys a Scottish castle for his daughter (Parker) complete with a ghost that looks like her boyfriend (Donat, in both roles). Clair's first film in English. C: Robert Donat, Eugene Pallette, Jean Parker, Everly Gregg, Elsa Lanchester. D: Rene Clair. COM 82m. V

Ghost in the Invisible Bikini 1966 ★★ Group of teenagers spend night in supposedly haunted house. Last of bubbleheaded *Beach Party* series. Veteran thespians Karloff, Rathbone, et al do what they can with fluffy material. C: Tommy Kirk, Deborah Walley, Nancy Sinatra, Harvey Lembeck, Basil Rathbone, Boris Karloff, Patsy Kelly, Francis X. Bushman. D: Don Weis. COM 82m.

Ghost in the Machine 1994 ★★★½ An inventive, violent thriller about a serial killer whose electrocution coincides with a freak storm, transforming him into a sort of computer virus. Engaging thriller, with inventive mayhem and wit, but scary and violent for children. C: Karen Allen, Chris Mulkey. D: Rachel Talalay. ACT [R] 98m.

Ghost in the Noonday Sun 1974 British ★★ Slapped-together story of a wacky pirate ship on the high seas, carrying a cast of talented comedians. C: Peter Sellers, Anthony Franciosa, Spike Milligan, Clive Revill, Peter Boyle. D: Peter Medak. COM 95m. V

Ghost Keeper 1980 ★★½ Absurd thriller with three women trapped in a supernaturally possessed hotel during a snowstorm. C: Riva Spier, Murray Ord, Georgie Collins. D: James Makichuk. HOR 87m. V

Ghost of Dragstrip Hollow, The 1959 ★★★ Homeless hot-rodders throw a party in a haunted house. American-International Pictures spoofs its own teenage, horror, and sci-fi genre in a slapdash but lovable film featuring a spirited cast, '50s lingo, and a talking car. C: Jody Fair, Martin Braddock. D: William Hole, Jr. COM 65m.

Ghost of Frankenstein, The 1942 ★★★½ Dr. Frankenstein's son (Hardwicke) picks up where his sibling left off in *Son of Frankenstein*, trying to take some of the fight out of dad's creation by giving the monster a better brain. Creepy atmosphere and Lugosi's second turn as Ygor are highlights of this otherwise stodgy fourth episode in the original Frankenstein series. C: Sir Cedric Hardwicke, Lon Chaney, Jr., Lionel Atwill, Ralph Bellamy, Bela Lugosi. D: Erle C. Kenton. HOR 68m. V

Ghost of St. Michael's, The 1941 British ★★★ Schoolboys in WWII England, evacuated to a Scottish castle, contend with spooks, murder, and German spies in this well-cast British comedy. C: Will Hay, Claude Hulbert, Felix Aylmer, Raymond Huntley, Elliot Mason, Charles Hawtrey. D: Marcel Varnel. COM 82m.

Ghost of the China Sea 1958 ★★★ A Navy ship is stranded in the Pacific without food, supplies, or gasoline during WWII. Standard action drama trots out familiar war movie clichés. C: David Brian, Lynn Bernay. D: Fred Sears. DRA 79m.

Ghost Ship 1953 British ★★★ A young couple buys a yacht that turns out to be haunted by the murder victims of its previous owner. Occasional scares in this otherwise slow-moving British cheapie. C: Dermot Walsh, Hazel Court. D: Vernon Sewell. HOR 69m. V

Ghost Ship, The 1943 ★★★½ Seagoing drama of authority-obsesssed skipper. Story resembles a cross between *The Sea Wolf* and *The Caine Mutiny*; has its share of atmosphere. C: Richard Dix, Russell Wade, Edith Barrett. D: Mark Robson. DRA 69m.

Ghost Story 1975 *See* **Madhouse Mansion**

Ghost Story 1981 ★★★½ Four wealthy, elderly men who share a dark secret gather to swap ghost stories. Perhaps the greatest cast ever assembled for a horror picture. Leisurely pace allows terror to build slowly but fails to generate much suspense. Final movie for Astaire and Douglas. C: Fred Astaire, Melvyn Douglas, Douglas Fairbanks, Jr., John Houseman, Craig Wasson, Patricia Neal. D: John Irvin. HOR [R] 110m. V

Ghost, The 1963 Italian ★★★½ Murdered by his wife and her lover, a man's spirit returns to taunt them. Contrived haunted house story complete with the eerie mansion, strange sounds in the night, and a mysterious housekeeper. Twist ending a plus. C: Barbara Steele, Peter Baldwin. D: Robert Hampton. HOR 96m. V

Ghost Town 1988 ★★★½ Modern sheriff (Luz) tracks a criminal into remote desert village, where he's forced to confront an undead evil gunslinger. Refreshingly unexploitative chiller; more intriguing than scary. C: Franc Luz, Catherine Hickland, Jimmie F. Skaggs. D: Richard Governor. HOR [R] 85m. V

Ghost Town Law 1942 ★★★ High-stepping horse opera, part of the *Rough Riders* series, has Riders confronting killer gang holed up in ghost town. C: Buck Jones, Tim McCoy, Raymond Hatton. D: Howard Bretherton. WST 62m.

Ghost Town Renegades 1947 ★★★½ B-western Larue has field day in this fast-paced good guys versus the bad guys shoot-em-up. C: Lash Larue, Al St. John, Jennifer Holt, Jack Ingram, Terry Frost. D: Ray Taylor. WST 57m. V

Ghost Valley 1932 ★★★ Cowpoke and his ladyfriend have to battle unscrupulous claim jumper who wants their land for the riches in the ground. Competent Western. C: Tom Keene, Merna Kennedy, Mitchell Harris. D: Fred Allen. WST 54m.

Ghost Walks, The 1935 ★★★ A playwright tries to impress a producer with his new murder mystery, only to have it turn into real life. So-so version of familiar plotline. C: John Miljan, June Collyer, Richard Carle. D: Frank Strayer. DRA 69m.

Ghost Warrior 1986 ★★★ Violent tale of ancient samurai, frozen for centuries, revived to cause turmoil in modern-day Los Angeles. C: Hiroshi Fujioka, Janet Julian. D: Larry Carroll. ACT [R] 86m. V

Ghost Writer 1984 ★★★½ Philip Roth helped adapt his own novel for *American Playhouse*, in this story of a writer reminiscing about visiting an older writer many years earlier. Well done. C: Rose Arrick, Claire Bloom, Macintyre Dixon. D: Tristam Powell. DRA 80m. TVM

Ghost Writer 1989 ★★ A slain '60's starlet returns from beyond to investigate her own murder and gets some help from the woman who currently occupies her beach house. C: Judy Landers, Audrey Landers, David Doyle. D: Kenneth J. Hall. COM [PG] 94m. V

Ghostbusters 1984 ★★★★ Rambunctious, big-budget comedy features Murray, Aykroyd, and Ramis as paranormal fumigators trying to clean up Manhattan. Weaver is Murray's possessed love interest, but Moranis steals the show as another haunted New Yorker. Great special effects and one scary marshmallow man! C: Bill Murray, Dan Aykroyd, Harold Ramis, Sigourney Weaver, Rick Moranis, Annie Potts. D: Ivan Reitman. COM [PG] 107m. V

Ghostbusters II 1989 ★★★ Inevitable sequel to original box office smash features Aykroyd, Murray, and Ramis once more battling ghosts worming around the Big Apple. All good jokes on ghostbusting exploited in first film get repeated here, though there are a few original moments. C: Bill Murray, Dan Aykroyd, Sigourney Weaver, Harold Ramis, Rick Moranis, Annie Potts. D: Ivan Reitman. COM [PG] 102m. V

Ghostriders 1987 ★★★ Frightening mix of western and horror as executed outlaws return. C: Bill Shaw, Jim Peters, Ricky Long, Cari Powell, Mike Ammons, Arland Bishop. D: Alan L. Stewart. HOR 85m. V

Ghosts Can't Do It 1990 ★★ Supernatural sex film has beautiful widow (Derek) sampling numerous hunky men in order to pick new body for spirit of dead lover (Quinn). C: Bo Derek, Anthony Quinn, Leo Damian, Don Murray, Julie Newmar. D: John Derek. COM [R] 95m. V

Ghosts—Italian Style 1969 Italian ★★ Loren and Gassman are wasted on this low-octane film about newlyweds who move into a house haunted by a poltergeist. C: Sophia Loren, Vittorio Gassman. D: Renato Castellani. HOR 92m.

Ghosts of Rome 1961 Italian ★★★ Eccentric group of residents of an old house facing the wrecking ball try to find new quarters in various bizarre ways. Crisply directed and interesting. C: Marcello Mastroianni, Belinda Lee, Sandra Milo, Vittorio Gassman. D: Antonio Pietrangeli. DRA 105m.

Ghosts on the Loose 1943 ★★★ The East Side Kids take on a group of Nazi agents (headed by Lugosi) operating out of a "haunted" house. Lesser East Side Kids entry, memorable mainly for an early appearance by Gardner. C: East Side Kids, Bela Lugosi, Ava Gardner. D: William Beaudine. COM 64m. V

Ghoul, The 1933 British ★★★½ Karloff shines as an Egyptologist buried with a valuable stone that brings eternal life. When it's stolen, his corpse rises and goes after the thieves. Nicely made British horror film, with plenty of chills and thrills. C: Boris Karloff, Cedric Hardwicke, Ernest Thesiger, Ralph Richardson. D: T. Hayes Hunter. HOR 77m. V

Ghoul, The 1975 British ★★★½ There's death lurking about Cushing's secluded English manor when people start falling victim to a flesh-eating fiend. Well done and scary. C: Peter Cushing, John Hurt. D: Freddie Francis. HOR 90m. V

Ghoulies 1985 ★★★½ *Gremlins* ripoff does have some fun moments of its own, as a man raises mini-monsters that proceed to kill off his friends. More campy than scary. C: Peter Liapis, Lisa Pelikan, Michael Des Barres, Jack Nance, Peter Risch. D: Luca Bercovici. HOR [PG-13] 81m. V

Ghoulies 2 1987 ★½ Ludicrous sequel brings the creatures to a struggling carnival, where they boost business but also start killing the visitors. Unconvincing, including the little monsters. C: Damon Martin, Royal Dano, J. Downing. D: Albert Band. HOR [R] 89m.

Ghoulies 3—Ghoulies Go to College 1988 ★★ Third in a series of films put the gruesome creatures on a campus for higher learning, mixing comedy with violent horror. C: Kevin McCarthy, Evan MacKenzie, Griffin O'Neal. D: John Carl Buechler. HOR 120m. V

Ghoulies IV 1994 ★ Cheesy sequel is so cheap that the original Ghoulies don't even appear; the story instead focuses on a seductive sorceress, a couple of dwarf creatures, and a young man trying to raise a demon. This is the kind of movie that gives cheap thrills a bad name. C: Peter Liapis, Barbara Alyn Woods, Stacie Randall, Raquel Krelle, Bobby DiCicco. D: Jim Wynorski. HOR [R] 84m.

G.I. Blues 1960 ★★★★ Elvis in the Army, naturally with a guitar. Better than most Presley vehicles. Features "Blue Suede Shoes" and excellent support from Prowse. C: Elvis Presley, Juliet Prowse. D: Norman Taurog. MUS 104m. v

G.I. Executioner, The 1984 ★★★ One more Vietnam-vet-turned-psychotic-vigilante thriller, this time set in picturesque Singapore. C: Tom Kenna, Victoria Racimo. D: Joel M. Reed. ACT [R] 86m. v

G.I. Joe—The Movie 1987 ★★½ Full-length animated cartoon based on the character doll for boys. Joe takes on his archenemy, COBRA, in this one. Parents should be aware of the extreme violence and gender stereotyping. Voices of Don Johnson, Burgess Meredith. D: Don Jurwich. FAM/ACT 90m. v

Giant 1956 ★★★★★ Famed epic of oil barons, class rivalries, and life in Texas, adapted from Edna Ferber's best-seller. Dean, Hudson, and Taylor shine, with excellent supporting cast. Released after Dean's death, this only added to his mythic status. Widescreen visuals lost on video. Oscar for Best Director. C: Elizabeth Taylor, Rock Hudson, James Dean, Carroll Baker, Jane Withers, Chill Wills, Mercedes McCambridge, Sal Mineo. D: George Stevens. DRA [G] 202m. v

Giant Behemoth, The 1959 British ★★★ Some solid thrills as a prehistoric monster leaves its seabed home to wreak havoc on mankind. C: Gene Evans, Andre Morell. D: Eugene Lourie. HOR 80m.

Giant Claw, The 1957 ★ The Air Force must destroy a giant prehistoric bird that terrorizes the U.S. skies. Dead-serious, sci-fi approach contrasts hilariously with one of the most ridiculous monsters in movie history—a comical looking buzzard. A definite "so bad it's good" entry. C: Jeff Morrow, Mara Corday. D: Fred Sears. SFI 76m.

Giant from the Unknown 1958 ★★ An ancient, hulking Spanish conquistador is brought back to life by a bolt of lightning in California, causing much trouble. Sloppy science fiction epic is entertaining, though unintentionally. C: Edward Kemmer, Sally Fraser, Bob Steele. D: Richard Cunha. SFI 77m.

Giant Gila Monster, The 1959 ★★ El cheapo movie about North America's only venomous lizard—increased in size about 10,000 times and terrorizing a small town. Bargain-basement special effects. C: Don Sullivan, Lisa Simone. D: Ray Kellogg. HOR 85m. v

Giant Leeches 1959 *See* **Attack of the Giant Leeches**

Giant of Metropolis, The 1962 Italian ★★★ Set in 10,000 B.C., this offbeat sword-and-loincloth fantasy is about a muscle-bound giant (Mitchell) who must fight the cruel sadist who enslaves a city. C: Gordon Mitchell, Roldano Lupi. D: Umberto Scarpelli. SFI 82m.

Giant Spider Invasion, The 1975 ★ Seasoned B-movie cast thrust into ungodly terror by badly superimposed spiders of enormous scale. The unintentional laughs wear thin very quickly. C: Steve Brodie, Barbara Hale, Leslie Parrish. D: Bill Rebane. SFI [PG] 82m.

Giant Steps 1992 Canadian ★★½ Novice trumpeter (Mahonen) seeks inspiration from a brilliant but troubled pianist (Williams) who eschews money for the sake of his art. Derivative jazz movie defends artistic freedom. C: Billy Dee Williams, Michael Mahonen, Robyn Stevan. D: Richard Rose. DRA 94m. v

Giants of Thessaly, The 1960 Italian ★★½ Jason and his Argonauts voyage in search of the golden fleece battling monsters and evildoers along their way. Predictable, meandering retelling of ancient Greek myth. C: Roland Carey, Ziva Rodann. D: Riccardo Freda. ACT 86m.

Gideon of Scotland Yard 1958 British ★★★ Hawkins is a Scotland Yard inspector who investigates a number of cases during a typical day. "Police procedural" film is an unusual endeavor for legendary Western director Ford. (a.k.a. *Gideon's Day*) C: Jack Hawkins, Dianne Foster, Cyril Cusack. D: John Ford. ACT 91m.

Gideon's Day 1958 *See* **Gideon of Scotland Yard**

Gideon's Trumpet 1980 ★★★★ The story of a Florida convict who, though barely able to read, manages to set a legal precedent entitling every defendant to a lawyer. Fascinating true drama and fine performances by Fonda (the convict) and Ferrer (his lawyer). C: Henry Fonda, Jose Ferrer, John Houseman, Fay Wray, Sam Jaffe. D: Robert Collins. DRA 105m. TVM v

Gidget 1959 ★★★½ The summer adventures of a 16-year-old California girl (Dee). Sunny and wholesome, like its star, this popular surfing beach frolic spawned several sequels and two TV series. C: Sandra Dee, James Darren, Cliff Robertson, Arthur O'Connell. D: Paul Wendkos. FAM/COM 95m. v

Gidget Gets Married 1972 ★★ America's favorite beach bunny (Ellis) settles down as a suburban housewife, but finds the lifestyle boring. Mildly amusing, with a plot that strains credibility a bit. C: Monie Ellis, Michael Burns, Don Ameche, Joan Bennett. D: W. Swackhamer. FAM/COM 73m. TVM

Gidget Goes Hawaiian 1961 ★★½ Sequel gives Gidget (Walley) a hula holiday in Honolulu. Plenty of sunshine and good-natured fun. C: Deborah Walley, James Darren, Michael Callan, Carl Reiner. D: Paul Wendkos. FAM/COM 102m. v

Gidget Goes to Rome 1964 ★★½ The Eternal City looks great, but the series gets kinda jet-lagged. Pleasant teenage romance. C:

Cindy Carol, James Darren, Jessie Royce Landis, Cesare Danova. D: Paul Wendkos. FAM/COM 104m. V

Gidget Grows Up 1970 ★★★½ An adult Gidget (Valentine) starts a relationship with an older man while working at the U.N. in New York. Gets a boost from Lynde's campy performance as a landlord obsessed with old movies. C: Karen Valentine, Edward Mulhare, Paul Lynde. D: James Sheldon. FAM/COM 75m. TVM

Gidget's Summer Reunion 1985 ★★★ Gidget (Richman), now married to longtime beau Moondoggie and working as a travel agent, returns to the beach. Fair pilot for second *Gidget* TV series has no new twists. C: Caryn Richman, Dean Butler. D: Bruce Bilson. FAM/COM 100m. TVM

Gift for Heidi, A 1962 ★★½ Little Swiss girl receives a birthday present of three carved figurines representing Faith, Hope, and Charity. Somewhat maudlin spin-off from Johanna Spyri's famed character should amuse kids. C: Douglas Fowley, Sandy Descher. D: George Templeton. FAM/DRA 71m. V

Gift Horse, The 1952 ★★★½ Against all odds, aging American ship and British crew hold up admirably in battle against Germans at the start of World War II. C: Trevor Howard, Richard Attenborough. D: Compton Bennett. ACT 99m. V

Gift of Love: A Christmas Story, The 1983 ★★★ Adaptation of Bess Streeter Aldrich's short story "The Silent Stars Go By," about the troubles a family goes through at Christmas time. Remick and Landsbury give a lift to this sentimental drama. C: Lee Remick, Angela Lansbury, Polly Holliday. D: Delbert Mann. DRA 100m. TVM

Gift of Love, The 1958 ★★★ Dying Bacall decides to adopt an unusual child (chirpily played by Rudie) so that her taciturn scientist husband (Stack) will have company when she's gone. Sappy remake of the 1946 tearjerker, *Sentimental Journey*. C: Lauren Bacall, Robert Stack, Evelyn Rudie, Lorne Greene. D: Jean Negulesco. DRA 105m.

Gift of Love, The 1978 ★★★½ Osmond plays a struggling housewife circa 1910, trying to buy an expensive Christmas gift for her husband. O. Henry's famous short story, *The Gift of the Magi*, makes charming, albeit sentimental, holiday viewing. C: Marie Osmond, Timothy Bottoms, June Lockhart, David Wayne, James Woods, Bethel Leslie. D: Don Chaffey. FAM/DRA 100m. TVM V

Gift, The 1982 French ★★ A bank employee's retirement is commemorated by his friends in the form of a call girl instructed to behave as a stranger desperately attracted to him. Unsavory premise not given especially charming treatment. C: Pierre Mondy, Claudia Cardinale, Clio Goldsmith. D: Michel Lang. COM [R] 105m. V

Gig, The 1985 ★★★½ Comedy/drama about middle-aged would-be jazz musicians trying to make it big in the Catskills. Frank Gilroy wrote and directed this small independent film, and while it sometimes looks amateurish, it is often entertaining and thought provoking. See before chucking the rat race. C: Wayne Rogers, Cleavon Little. D: Frank D. Gilroy. DRA 95m. V

Gigantis, the Fire Monster 1959 Japanese ★★★ This time, the overgrown reptile engages in combat with something called "Angorous." The loser, another Japanese city. First sequel to *Godzilla* (American distributor was unable to secure rights to the name) features similar rubber-suited scares. (a.k.a. *The Return of Godzilla, Godzilla Raids Again*) C: Hugo Grimaldi, Hiroshi Koizumi. D: Motoyoshi. SFI 78m.

Gigantor: Volumes 1-3 1964 Japanese ★★½ Animated Japanese action/adventure series features toons with names like Inspector Blooper, Jimmy, and Gigantor, an outsize robot crimebuster. Much of the dialogue is wacky, making the goings-on inadvertently funny. But the series is entertaining enough. D: Fred Ladd. FAM/ACT 75m. V

Gigi 1958 ★★★★★ MGM's answer to *My Fair Lady*, adapted from Colette's play about a young girl groomed to be a Parisian courtesan. The stylish score (including "Thank Heaven for Little Girls," "Gigi," and "I Remember It Well"), a literate script, and charming cast helped this sumptuous film win nine Oscars, including Best Picture. C: Leslie Caron, Louis Jourdan, Maurice Chevalier, Herminone Gingold, Isabel Jeans, Eva Gabor. D: Vincente Minnelli. MUS [G] 115m. V

Gigot 1962 ★★★★ Gleason, the Great One, touchingly plays a Parisian deaf mute who comes to the aid of a prostitute and her little girl. Maudlin sentimentality counterbalanced by Gleason's deft Chaplinesque turn and Kelly's sure-footed direction. C: Jackie Gleason, Katherine Kath, Gabrielle Dorziat. D: Gene Kelly. DRA 104m.

Gilda 1946 ★★★★ Steamy drama involves Ford as assistant to casino owner (Macready). When owner disappears, Ford marries his widow (Hayworth), but of course that only means trouble. Hayworth is at her most alluring, overwhelming some of the trite problems of the script. C: Rita Hayworth, Glenn Ford, George Macready. D: Charles Vidor. DRA 110m. V

Gilda Live 1980 ★★★★ Radner takes many of her popular *Saturday Night Live* characters and ups the ante with saltier language. Her Broadway show, captured here by director Nichols, is a valuable record of her marvelous, short-lived, talent. C: Gilda Radner. D: Mike Nichols. COM [R] 90m. V

Gilded Lily, The 1935 ★★★½ Secretary (Colbert) must choose between a titled Englishman (Milland) and poor reporter (MacMurray) she meets in a park. Snappy screwball comedy, one of seven Colbert/MacMurray teamings. C: Claudette Colbert, Fred MacMurray, Ray Milland, C. Aubrey Smith. D: Wesley Ruggles. COM 80m.

Gildersleeve on Broadway 1943 ★★★ Another entry in the series based on the popular radio show offers weak wit in tale of a pharmacist at a convention in New York who inexplicably becomes the object of several women's attentions. C: Harold Peary, Billie Burke, Claire Carleton. D: Gordon Douglas. COM 65m.

Gildersleeve's Ghost 1944 ★★★ Gildersleeve, a nominee for police commissioner, finds himself aided by ghosts. Peary's blustery performance as popular character from the radio show *The Great Gildersleeve* stands out. C: Harold Peary, Marion Martin. D: Gordon Douglas. COM 64m.

Gilligan's Island: The Collector's Edition, Vol. 1 ★★★ A compilation of three episodes from the long-running hit TV series. "Two on a Raft," "Allergy Time," and "Hair Today, Gone Tomorrow." Loaded with laughs as usual. C: Bob Denver, Tina Louise, Alan Hale. COM 90m. V

Gilsodom 1986 ★★★★½ Thirty years after the Korean War, Kim searches for the illegitimate child she bore during war, but the son she finds leads to a troubling conclusion. Deeply moving drama with superb ensemble. C: Kim Ji Mi, Sin Song-Il, Han Ji-Il, Kim Ji-Yong, Lee Sang-A, Kim Jong Sok, Kim Ki Ju. D: Im Kwon-Taek. DRA 97m.

Gimme an "F" 1984 ★ Cheerleader sex comedy concerns bosomy hijinks at tastefully named Camp Beaver View, and plan by foreign investors to take over same. (a.k.a. *T & A Academy 2*) C: Stephen Shellen, Mark Keyloun. D: Paul Justman. COM [R] 100m. V

Gimme Shelter 1970 ★★★★½ Classic rockumentary focuses on the infamous Altamont Speedway concert, which ended tragically. Mixed with painful scenes is superior music footage of the Rolling Stones performing many signature songs, including "Satisfaction" and "Brown Sugar." C: Rolling Stones, Jefferson Airplane. D: David Maysles, Albert Maysles, Charlotte Zwerin. MUS [PG] 91m. V

Gina 1956 *See* **Diamond Hunters**

Ginger Ale Afternoon 1989 ★★ A married couple get involved with their sexy neighbor. A little down and dirty and not for all tastes. C: Dana Anderson, John M. Jackson, Yeardly Smith. D: Rafal Zielinski. COM [R] 88m. V

Ginger and Fred 1986 Italian ★★★★ Aging dancers known for their imitation of the famous dance team of Rogers and Astaire come out of a 40-year retirement to appear on a TV variety show. Sympathetic, vibrant portrait of age enhanced by two glowing leads. C: Giulietta Masina, Marcello Mastroianni, Franco Fabrizi. D: Federico Fellini. DRA [PG-13] 128m. V

Ginger in the Morning 1973 ★★½ Film finds early, pre-stardom Spacek playing a hitchhiker picked up by traveling salesman, who promptly falls in love with her. Minor road movie. C: Sissy Spacek, Monte Markham. D: Gordon Wiles. COM [PG] 90m. V

Giordano Bruno 1973 Italian ★★★½ Sumptuous and provocative biography of the 16th-century philosopher and religious rebel gets beautiful, if self-loving, treatment. C: Gian Maria Volonte, Charlotte Rampling, Hans Christian Blech, Mathieu Carriere. D: Giuliano Montaldo. DRA 115m.

Girl, a Guy, and a Gob, A 1941 ★★★½ A sailor (Murphy) and a blue blood (O'Brien) vie for the affections of a sharp secretary (Ball). Bright comedy owes its quick pacing and gags to the supervision of silent screen great Harold Lloyd. (a.k.a. *The Navy Steps Out*) C: George Murphy, Lucille Ball, Edmond O'Brien, Henry Travers, Franklin Pangborn. D: Richard Wallace. COM 91m. V

Girl Called Hatter Fox, The 1977 ★★★ Concerned doctor (Cox) tries to save the life of an Indian girl possessed by an ancient spirit. One of the wave of movies inspired by *The Exorcist.* (a.k.a. *Lost Legacy*) C: Ronny Cox, Joanelle Romero. D: George Schaefer. HOR 100m. TVM

Girl Can't Help It, The 1956 ★★★★ Cast is terrific in this story of a press agent (Ewell) pressured by a mobster to make Mansfield a star. Classic rock 'n roll score features Gene Vincent, Little Richard, Fats Domino and others; Tashlin's slam-bang direction is on the mark. C: Tom Ewell, Jayne Mansfield, Edmond O'Brien, Julie London. D: Frank Tashlin. COM 99m. V

Girl Crazy 1943 ★★★★½ One of the best Garland/Rooney musicals. A wealthy Easterner (Rooney) is shipped off to a Southwestern college to get his mind off girls, and he falls in love. Paper-thin plot, outstanding Gershwin songs, including "But Not for Me," "Embraceable You," and the Busby Berkeley-directed finale, "I Got Rhythm." C: Mickey Rooney, Judy Garland, June Allyson, Nancy Walker, Guy Kibbee, Tommy Dorsey. D: Norman Taurog. MUS 100m. V

Girl Downstairs, The 1938 ★★★½ Millionaire courts a rich man's daughter, but ends up falling for her maid instead. Dated but charming. C: Franciska Gaal, Franchot Tone, Walter Connolly, Reginald Gardiner, Franklin Pangborn. D: Norman Taurog. COM 73m.

Girl for Joe, A 1951 *See* **Force of Arms**

Girl Friend, The 1935 ★★★½ Easygoing foolishness about a rural writer who wants to take his play to Broadway—and the hustlers who con him by pretending to be producers. C: Ann Sothern, Jack Haley. D: Edward Buzzell. COM 67m.

Girl from Calgary, The 1932 ★★½ A young woman seeking fame in New York gets involved with a notorious producer. Some interesting moments. C: Fifi D'Orsay, Paul Kelly. DRA 60m. V

Girl from Chicago 1932 ★★★ In the deep south, a secret service agent meets up with a young school teacher and they fall in love. An interesting drama from back when. C: Carl Mahon, Starr Calloway, Grace Smith, Frank Wilson, Eugene Brooks. D: Oscar Micheaux. DRA 69m. V

Girl from Hunan 1986 Chinese ★★★½ A young peasant girl, forced into an arranged marriage at 12 discovers passion for the first time at 16, but can't escape the reality and repressions of tradition. Traditional Chinese society graphically represented in a vividly photographed but often predictable drama. C: Na Renhua, Deng Xiaotuang, Zhang Yu. D: Xie Fei. DRA 100m.

Girl from Jones Beach, The 1949 ★★★ Entertaining romance features Reagan as an artist in search of a perfectly proportioned model to improve his drawing abilities. Of course art leads to romance in this competently cheerful comedy. C: Ronald Reagan, Virginia Mayo, Eddie Bracken, Donna Drake. D: Peter Godfrey. COM 78m.

Girl from Lorraine, A 1980 French ★★★★½ Young designer (Baye) moves to Paris in search of steady work but finds only dead ends, harrassment, and broken promises. Scrupulous characterizations and felicitous direction keep this bittersweet exploration of modern city life from cynicism; Baye's perfect performance buoys the whole affair. C: Nathalie Baye, Bruno Ganz. D: Claude Goretta. DRA 107m.

Girl from Manhattan, The 1948 ★★★ Lamour dropped her sarong and took a hike from the Hope/Crosby *Road* pictures to appear in this amusing trifle. She's a New York model who moves into her uncle's Manhattan boarding house, populated with eccentric characters. Funny in spots, but unmemorable. C: Dorothy Lamour, George Montgomery, Charles Laughton, Ernest Truex, Constance Collier, Sara Allgood. D: Alfred Green. COM 81m.

Girl from Mars, The 1991 Canadian ★★★½ The daughter of a politician turns out to be a Martian dispatched to save Earth. Far-fetched cable movie with a conservation theme nevertheless has some enjoyable moments. C: Edward Albert, Eddie Albert. D: Neill Feranley. FAM/SFI 100m. TVM

Girl from Mexico, The 1939 ★★★ The first of the *Mexican Spitfire* series stars Velez as an entertainer hired by ad exec (Woods) to spice up a radio show but whose fiery Latin temperament turns his life—and N.Y.—upside down. Fast-paced fun. C: Lupe Velez, Donald Woods, Leon Errol. D: Leslie Goodwins. COM 71m.

Girl from Missouri, The 1934 ★★★★ An innocent chorus dancer (Harlow) and shrewd girlfriend (Kelly) are on the lookout for marriageable millionaires, but don't want to compromise their virtue in catching one. Lively dialogue and bright performances make this pleasant escapism. (a.k.a. *One Hundred Percent Pure*) C: Jean Harlow, Lionel Barrymore, Franchot Tone, Lewis Stone, Patsy Kelly. D: Jack Conway. COM 72m. V

Girl from Petrovka, The 1974 ★★ Romance between an American correspondent and a young Russian woman. Nothing new, but enjoyable just the same. C: Goldie Hawn, Hal Holbrook, Anthony Hopkins. D: Robert Ellis Miller. COM [PG] 103m. V

Girl from Scotland Yard, The 1937 ★★★ British agent (Morley) is out to stop a mad doctor who is threatening the world with a death ray. Serial-like B-movie features a long airplane chase. C: Karen Morley, Robert Baldwin. D: Robert Vignola. ACT 62m.

Girl from 10th Avenue, The 1935 ★★★ Davis shines in this inferior drama of working girl who sobers up her alcoholic boss only to have his ex-girlfriend try to steal him back. C: Bette Davis, Ian Hunter, Colin Clive. D: Alfred Green. DRA 69m.

Girl-Getters, The 1966 British ★★★★ A womanizing girlie photographer finally meets his match at a seaside resort. Good performances spark this authentic depiction of British youth in the early '60s. (a.k.a. *The System*) C: Oliver Reed, Jane Merrow, Barbara Ferris. D: Michael Winner. COM 79m.

Girl Happy 1965 ★★★ Nightclub owner hires Presley as chaperone for daughter (Fabares) on Fort Lauderdale vacation. Mindless fun, with some snappy songs ("She's Evil," "Wolf Call"). C: Elvis Presley, Shelley Fabares, Harold J. Stone, Nita Talbot, Mary Ann Mobley, Jackie Coogan. D: Boris Sagal. MUS 96m. V

Girl He Left Behind 1956 ★★★ New Army recruit (Hunter) pines for his love (Wood) while in the meantime "becoming a man" through the rigors of basic training. Boy-into-man comedy, with likable leads. C: Tab Hunter, Natalie Wood, Jessie Royce Landis, Jim Backus, Alan King, James Garner. D: David Butler. COM 103m.

Girl Hunters, The 1963 ★★★½ Tough private detective Mike Hammer tangles with killers and mysterious spies while on the trail of his missing secretary/girlfriend. Author Mickey Spillane plays his own fictional creation in violent thriller with fair share of sadism. C: Mickey Spillane, Lloyd Nolan, Shirley Eaton. D: Roy Rowland. CRI 103m.

Girl in a Million, A 1946 British ★★★ A man dumps his nagging wife to seek peace and quiet, then meets a young woman (Greenwood) mute from war trauma, and falls in love with her silence. Modern audiences may find this offbeat British comedy a bit sexist. C: Joan Greenwood, Hugh Williams,

Yvonne Owen, Michael Hordern. D: Francis Searle. COM 81m.

Girl in a Swing, The 1989 U.S. ★★ A young businessman in Amsterdam marries a German woman who turns out to be unstable and a possible murderess. Confusing psychological thriller contains much nudity and violence. C: Meg Tilly, Rupert Frazer. D: Gordon Hessler. CRI [R] 119m. V

Girl in Black Stockings, The 1957 ★★★ Smart, stylish mystery about beautiful women murdered at a remote Utah hotel. Bears a striking resemblance to the plot of *Psycho*, but Koch's film made it to the screen three years earlier than Hitchcock's. C: Lex Barker, Anne Bancroft, Mamie Van Doren. D: Howard Koch. CRI 73m.

Girl in Blue, The 1987 ★★★ Successful lawyer tries to find woman he briefly encountered years ago, and simply can't forget. Romance with mild moments of nudity and sex. (a.k.a. *U-turn*) C: Maud Adams, David Selby, Gay Rowan. D: George Kaczender. COM 103m. V

Girl in Distress 1941 *See* **Jeannie**

Girl in Every Port, A 1928 ★★★½ Two seamen on a world voyage share adventures and compete for women. Entertaining silent comedy, with a grand cast. C: Victor McLaglen, Robert Armstrong, Louise Brooks, William Demarest, Myrna Loy. D: Howard Hawks. COM 62m.

Girl in Every Port, A 1952 ★★ Odd pairing of Bendix and Marx makes for small-scale one-joke comedy. They're Navy men who acquire a racehorse and need a place to stash it—where better than aboard a battleship? Good talents wasted in this mindless caper. C: Groucho Marx, William Bendix, Marie Wilson. D: Chester Erskine. COM 86m. V

Girl in 419 1933 ★★★ Gangster tries to rub out his ex-girlfriend in the hospital, but heroic doctors keep her safe in this rather convoluted thriller. C: James Dunn, Gloria Stuart, David Manners. D: George Somnes, Alexander Hall. CRI 63m.

Girl in His Pocket 1957 French ★★★½ French comedy about a scientist who develops a potion that shrinks people to pocket size, which comes in handy when he needs to hide his lover from his wife. Lightweight zaniness. C: Jean Marais, Agnes Laurent, Genevieve Page. D: Pierre Kast. COM 82m.

Girl in Room 13 1961 ★★½ Private detective (Donlevy) heads for Brazil in search of a murderer, but gets involved with a counterfeiting gang. Glorious Brazilian locations underpin this crime drama. C: Brian Donlevy, Andrea Bayard, Elizabeth Howard. D: Richard Cunha. ACT 97m.

Girl in Room 20 1946 ★★★ A young woman newly arrived in New York takes a job as a nightclub singer and gets involved with some unsavory big city types. Interesting production. C: Geraldine Brock, Shirley Jones, John Hemmings, Myra Hemmings. D: Spencer Williams. DRA 63m. V

Girl in Room 2A 1976 ★★ Fresh out of prison, a young woman moves into a weird old mansion where the furnishings ooze blood. Low level horror. C: Raf Vallone, Daniela Giordano. HOR 83m. V

Girl in the Empty Grave, The 1977 ★★½ Griffith is a small-town sheriff out to catch a murderer. TV pilot for a crime show that never developed is interesting mainly for the familiarity of Griffith playing a rural lawman. Sequel: *Deadly Game*. C: Andy Griffith, James Cromwell. D: Lou Antonio. CRI 100m. TVM

Girl in the Kremlin, The 1957 ★★ A former OSS agent in Russia suspects that presumed dead Stalin is alive and well and living in Greece. The campy presence of Gabor, in a dual role as Stalin's mistress and her sister, highlights this somewhat dated espionage piece. C: Lex Barker, Zsa Zsa Gabor. D: Russell Birdwell. ACT 81m.

Girl in the News, The 1941 British ★★★½ Murder mystery features a strong script and great suspense in tale of a nurse framed for murder. C: Margaret Lockwood, Barry K. Barnes, Emlyn Williams, Roger Livesey. D: Carol Reed. DRA 77m.

Girl in the Painting 1948 British ★★★ Army major finds young German woman suffering from amnesia; the discovery of her past reveals a nest of spies. Average drama with some minor, though predictable twists. (a.k.a. *Portrait from Life*) C: Mai Zetterling, Robert Beatty, Herbert Lom. D: Terence Fisher. DRA 89m.

Girl in the Picture, The 1986 British ★★★ Young people have difficulty forging relationships with the opposite sex in this sweet, enjoyable Scottish feature. Sinclair and Brook as on-again, off-again couple are appealing and cute. Romantic and funny light comedy. C: Gordon John Sinclair, Irina Brook. D: Cary Parker. COM [PG-13] 89m. V

Girl in the Red Velvet Swing, The 1955 ★★★ Mentally unstable millionaire shoots his wife's lover, famous New York architect Stanford White. Fact-based dramatization of a turn-of-the-century scandal lushly re-creates the era, but dramatically sags. C: Ray Milland, Joan Collins, Farley Granger, Cornelia Otis Skinner. D: Richard Fleischer. DRA 109m.

Girl in the Woods 1958 ★★½ A logging town turns a lumberjack (Tucker) into an outcast after he gets involved with two feuding loggers and is falsely accused of robbery. Routine action programmer features several suitably brawny performers, but uninspired scripting and direction. C: Forrest Tucker, Maggie Hayes. D: Tom Gries. ACT 71m.

Girl in White, The 1952 ★★ In turn-of-the-century New York, the first woman to practice medicine in a city hospital fights prejudice of man's world and slum conditions. Ingenuous

Allyson not convincing as intrepid doctor in this dull biography. C: June Allyson, Arthur Kennedy, Gary Merrill, Mildred Dunnock, James Arness. D: John Sturges. DRA 93m.

Girl Most Likely, The 1957 ★★★★ Musicalized update of *Tom, Dick, and Harry*, stars pert soprano Powell, who must select a hubby from a trio of highly eligible bachelors. What's a girl to do? If she's Powell, she'll sing and dance in several witty production numbers staged by Gower Champion before making up her mind. Upbeat and enjoyable Hollywood musical. C: Jane Powell, Cliff Robertson, Keith Andes, Tommy Noonan, Kaye Ballard. D: Mitchell Leisen. MUS 98m. V

Girl Most Likely To . . . , The 1973 ★★★ Joan Rivers co-wrote this black comedy concerning a dowdy college student (Channing) who, following an auto accident and extensive plastic surgery, emerges as a total knockout, and goes on a vengeful rampage against the men who scorned her when she was ugly. Uneven, but Stockard's performance is worth catching. C: Stockard Channing, Ed Asner, Warren Berlinger, Suzanne Zenor, Larry Wilcox, Fred Grandy. D: Lee Philips. COM 74m. TVM

Girl Must Live, A 1941 British ★★★½ Gold-digging chorus dancers carry out their plans to marry well. Engaging comedy. C: Margaret Lockwood, Renee Houston, Lilli Palmer. D: Carol Reed. COM 89m.

Girl Named Sooner, A 1975 ★★★★½ Hearttugger about eight-year-old girl raised by mean-spirited farmwoman grandmother (Leachman, in a movie-stealing role), becomes a ward of the state, and is taken in by a childless couple. Endearing, touching film is beautifully acted. C: Cloris Leachman, Lee Remick, Richard Crenna, Susan Deer, Anne Francis, Don Murray. D: Delbert Mann. FAM/DRA 115m.

Girl Named Tamiko, A 1962 ★★★★ A Eurasian photographer (Harvey) extremely eager to gain U.S. citizenship exploits the affections of an American woman (Hyer), even though he loves the title character (Nuyen). Unique depiction of East/West clash. C: Laurence Harvey, France Nuyen, Martha Hyer, Gary Merrill. D: John Sturges. DRA 110m.

Girl Next Door, The 1953 ★★½ Musical comedy star (Haver) longs for domestic bliss with comic strip artist (Dailey). Clichéd script, bland songs. C: Dan Dailey, June Haver, Dennis Day, Cara Williams, Natalie Schafer. D: Richard Sale. MUS 92m.

Girl of the Golden West, The 1938 ★★★ Horse opera, literally. Saucy and boisterous MacDonald falls for robber (Eddy). Not one of this team's better efforts, with substandard Sigmund Romberg score. C: Jeanette MacDonald, Nelson Eddy, Walter Pidgeon, Buddy Ebsen. D: Robert Z. Leonard. MUS 121m. V

Girl of the Limberlost, A 1990 ★★★★ Fairfield is engaging as young Indiana farmgirl who succeeds in school through her own gumption and belief in herself. This version of much-filmed and eternally popular Gene Stratton Porter novel is an excellent, well-acted production. C: Joanna Cassidy, Annette O'Toole. D: Burt Brinckerhoff. FAM/DRA 115m. TVM V

Girl of the Night 1960 ★★★ A prostitute (Francis) tries to escape her demeaning profession by who undergoing psychoanalysis. Francis' performance redeems this otherwise routine drama. C: Anne Francis, Lloyd Nolan, Kay Medford. D: Joseph Cates. DRA 93m.

Girl on a Motorcycle 1968 British ★ Tale of a married woman who races her motorcycle to meet her lover and finds tragedy on the open road. Flimsy story "fleshed" out with woman's imagination of her carnal reunion. C: Marianne Faithfull, Alain Delon. D: Jack Cardiff. DRA 92m. V

Girl on the Bridge 1951 ★★ Kindly watchmaker (Haas) marries bombshell (Michaels) and ends up caught in a blackmail plot. Yet another Haas B-movie treatise on the ways dangerous women lead innocent old men astray. C: Hugo Haas, Beverly Michaels. D: Hugo Haas. DRA 77m.

Girl on the Late, Late Show, The 1974 ★★★½ The inquiries of a TV producer (Murray) about a faded movie queen (Grahame) lead to a series of murders. Satisfactory mystery set in Hollywood, fortified with appearances by several former film stars in various roles. C: Don Murray, Lorraine Stephens, Bert Convy, Gloria Grahame, Van Johnson, Ralph Meeker. D: Gary Nelson. CRI 104m.

Girl Rush, The 1955 ★★★ Prim and proper museum worker (Russell) inherits a glitzy Las Vegas casino from her gambling father and heads out West to run it. Strained musical, not nearly as good as its star. C: Rosalind Russell, Fernando Lamas, Eddie Albert, Gloria DeHaven. D: Robert Pirosh. MUS 85m.

Girl Rush 1944 ★★★ A vaudeville team (Carney, Brown) pledges to bring women to a California gold rush town. Silly tuner boasts a charming performance by newcomer Mitchum. C: Alan Carney, Wally Brown, Frances Langford, Vera Vague, Robert Mitchum. D: Gordon Douglas. COM 65m. V

Girl Shy 1924 ★★★★ Another variation on Lloyd's earnest young man has the shy character writing a manual on making love. Publisher thinks the tome is a humor book, but Lloyd still finds romance in the end. Climactic chase sequence is one of Lloyd's better slam-bang finishes in this wonderful silent comedy. C: Harold Lloyd, Jobyna Ralston, Richard Daniels, Carlton Griffin. D: Fred Newmeyer, Sam Taylor. COM 65m.

Girl Stroke Boy 1971 British ★★½ Dated '70s sex farce about young man shocking his parents with free-love activities. C: Joan Greenwood, Michael Hordern, Clive Francis, Patrica Routledge. D: Bob Kellett. COM 86m.

Girl, the Gold Watch and Dynamite, The 1981 ★★★ A young couple with a magical gold watch interrupts their wedding to help the bride's mother save her home. MacHale and Purcell assume the lead roles in this sequel to *The Girl, the Gold Watch and Everything*. C: Lee Purcell, Philip MacHale, Burton Gilliam, Jack Elam, Zohra Lampert. D: Hy Averback. FAM/SFI 104m. TVM

Girl, the Gold Watch and Everything, The 1980 ★★★½ Hays inherits a magical gold watch that can stop time, and with girlfriend (Dawber) must keep it out of the clutches of others. TV adaptation of John McDonald's best-seller is a well-paced sci-fi action comedy. C: Robert Hays, Pam Dawber, Jill Ireland, Maurice Evans. D: William Wiard. FAM/SFI 104m. TVM

Girl, The 1986 ★★ A student and an older, married man (Nero) on well-worn path to disaster. Blend of camp and earnest elements. C: Franco Nero, Claire Powney, Christopher Lee. D: Arne Mattsson. CRI 104m. V

Girl Trouble 1942 ★★★½ A N.Y. socialite (Bennett) rents her apartment to a South American playboy (Ameche) in this agreeable comedy about the foibles of the offbeat rich. C: Don Ameche, Joan Bennett, Billie Burke, Frank Craven, Vivian Blaine. D: Harold Schuster. COM 82m.

Girl Who Came Gift-Wrapped, The 1974 ★★★ Valentine is presented to the playboy publisher of a prominent girlie magazine as a birthday gift. Rather predictable, but amusing. C: Karen Valentine, Richard Long, Farrah Fawcett. D: Bruce Bilson. COM 78m.

Girl Who Couldn't Say No, The 1970 Italian ★★★ Doctor (Segal) maintains an on-again, off-again romance with childhood friend (Lisi), who has become a free-spirited, free-love hippie. Fair relationship comedy explores '60s mores. C: Virna Lisi, George Segal, Lila Kedrova, Akim Tamiroff. D: Franco Brusati. COM [PG] 83m.

Girl Who Had Everything, The 1953 ★★½ Taylor plays naive young beauty who falls for her criminal lawyer father's suave, handsome client in this '50s Hollywood melodrama. Powell's her dad; Lamas is the crook. Tedious, at best. Remake of 1931 film *A Free Soul*. C: Elizabeth Taylor, Fernando Lamas, William Powell, Gig Young, James Whitmore. D: Richard Thorpe. DRA 69m. V

Girl Who Knew Too Much 1969 ★★★ When the CIA hires an adventurer (West) to find the killer of a syndicate boss, he discovers that Communists are trying to take over the Mob. Unlike most '60s espionage films, this one takes itself a bit too seriously. C: Adam West, Nancy Kwan. D: Francis Lyon. ACT [R] 96m.

Girl Who Spelled Freedom, The 1986 ★★★★ A teenage Cambodian immigrant comes to the U.S.; though she knows no English she's determined to win the National Spelling Bee. Inspirational true story makes terrific family viewing. Made for the Disney Channel. C: Mary Kay Place, Wayne Rogers, Kieu Chinh. D: Simon Wincer. FAM/DRA 100m. TVM V

Girl with a Pistol, The 1968 Italian ★★★ A young provincial woman (Vitti) is humiliated after being taken advantage of by a cad (Ginffre), and ends up chasing him to England for her revenge. Light sex fluff. C: Monica Vitti, Stanley Baker, Carlo Giuffre, Corin Redgrave. D: Mario Monicelli. COM 100m.

Girl with a Suitcase 1960 Italian ★★★★ Engaging coming-of-age story about a 16-year-old boy's romance with a sexy, wise young woman, his older brother's ex-lover. Marred by some confusions, but enhanced by fine photography of Italian Riviera. C: Claudia Cardinale, Jacques Perrin. D: Valerio Zurlini. COM 96m.

Girl with Green Eyes, The 1964 British ★★★★ Innocent Irish country lass (Tushingham), newly arrived in Dublin, falls in love with cold, callous older man (Finch), who ignores her wisecracking, more sophisticated roommate (Redgrave). Stellar acting makes this adroit, lyrical adaptation of best-selling O'Brien novel a treasure. C: Rita Tushingham, Peter Finch, Lynn Redgrave. D: Desmond Davis. DRA 91m.

Girl with Ideas, A 1937 ★★★★ Former newspaper publisher battles the woman who bought his paper after it libeled her. High-speed screwball comedy. C: Wendy Barrie, Walter Pidgeon, Kent Taylor, Dorothea Kent. D: Sylvan Simon. COM 70m.

Girl with the Hatbox, The 1927 Russian ★★★★ Slapstick à la Russe. Sten plays a poor hatshop worker given a lottery ticket in lieu of her wages. When she wins a fortune, a madcap scramble ensues for possession of the ticket. Gracefully executed Soviet laugh fest compares favorably with best American silent comedies. C: Anna Sten, Vladimir Fogel. D: Boris Barnet. COM 67m.

Girl with the Red Hair, The 1981 Dutch ★★★½ True story of WWII teen who murdered German collaborators is (suprisingly) only moderately gripping. Too deliberate pacing undercuts the drama, and the strange use of color seems excessive. C: Renee Soutendijk, Peter Tuinman, Loes Luca. D: Ben Verbong. DRA [PG] 116m.

Girlfriend from Hell 1990 ★★ When a shy girl becomes possessed by the devil, she suddenly receives the sort of attention she never expected. Low budget. C: Liane Curtis, Dana Ashbrook, James Daughton. D: Daniel M. Paterson. COM [R] 95m.

Girlfriends 1978 ★★★½ A young photographer's life changes after best friend moves out of her apartment. Likable performance by Mayron in uneven but rewarding drama. C: Melanie Mayron, Anita Skinner, Eli Wallach,

Christopher Guest. D: Claudia Weill. DRA [PG] 88m. v

Girls About Town 1931 ★★★½ One of director Cukor's earliest films is a witty look at the war between the sexes. Francis and Tashman are two women who use their skills to manipulate the men in their lives. Saucy fun. C: Kay Francis, Joel McCrea, Lilyan Tashman, Eugene Pallette. D: George Cukor. COM 82m.

Girls' Dormitory 1936 ★★★½ College student (Simon) has a crush on her school's head (Marshall) in this innocent, old-fashioned campus romance. Minor appearance by Tyrone Power helped propell him to stardom. C: Herbert Marshall, Ruth Chatterton, Simone Simon, Constance Collier, Tyrone Power. D: Irving Cummings. DRA 66m.

Girls! Girls! Girls! 1962 ★★½ One of the many vehicles created for Presley; this one has him as a charter boat pilot. Best song: "Return to Sender." C: Elvis Presley, Stella Stevens, Laurel Goodwin, Jeremy Slate. D: Norman Taurog. MUS 98 m. v

Girls in Prison 1956 ★★ Innocent young woman is thrown into female reformatory for bank robbery she didn't commit. Inmates believe she can lead them to the loot. C: Richard Denning, Joan Taylor, Adele Jergens, Jane Darwell, Mae Marsh. D: Edward L. Cahn. ACT 87m. v

Girls in Uniform 1931 *See* **Madchen in Uniform**

Girls Just Want to Have Fun 1985 ★★ A teenager has her heart set on entering a dance contest, but her strong-willed father is against it. Low-octane premise gets plenty of mileage, thanks to likable leads Parker and Hunt, who were practically unknown at the time. C: Sarah Jessica Parker, Lee Montgomery, Jonathan Silverman, Helen Hunt. D: Alan Metter. COM [PG] 90m. v

Girls Nite Out 1983 ★★ A sorority house scavenger hunt turns violent when a psychotic killer stumbles onto the scene. Gruesome suspense. C: Hal Holbrook, Rutanya Alda, Julie Montgomery, James Carroll. D: Robert Deubel. HOR 96m. v

Girls of Huntington House, The 1973 ★★ TV movie set in home for unwed mothers in which Jones is the sympathetic new teacher. Wan effort doesn't do much for subject. C: Shirley Jones, Mercedes McCambridge, Sissy Spacek. D: Alf Kjellin. DRA 74m. TVM v

Girls of Pleasure Island 1953 ★★½ A staunch Briton (Genn) moves his three daughters to an isolated Pacific island to keep them away from men, when 1,500 Marines show up to build an airstrip. Attempt at titillating comedy. C: Alvin Ganzer, Leo Genn, Don Taylor, Elsa Lanchester. D: F. Herbert. COM 95m.

Girls of Summer 1988 *See* **Satisfaction**

Girls of the Night 1959 French ★★★½ A Marseilles priest battles a tough pimp for the souls of a group of prostitutes. Warm and engaging drama holds interest throughout, leading up to a violent climax. C: Georges Marchal, Nicole Berger. D: Maurice Cloche. DRA 114m.

Girls of the Road 1940 ★★★ A governor's daughter, seeking to learn more about the lives of female hoboes, hits the road herself incognito to learn firsthand about their treatment. Interesting B-drama predates the similar and better-known *Sullivan's Travels*. C: Ann Dvorak, Helen Mack, Lola Lane, Ann Doran. D: Nick Grinde. DRA 61m.

Girls of the White Orchid 1983 ★★½ In Japan, a young American woman thinks she's been hired as a nightclub singer. Instead, she finds out that she's a front for a prostitute ring. Hard-boiled and steamy. Engaging, powerful stuff. C: Jennifer Jason Leigh, Ann Jillian. D: Jonathan Kaplan. DRA 96m. TVM v

Girls on Probation 1938 ★★★ An attorney (Reagan) aids and falls in love with a young woman (Bryan) who has gotten into trouble with the law as a victim of circumstance and bad judgment. Warners' B-picture offers historical interest because of Reagan's appearance. C: Jane Bryan, Ronald Reagan, Sig Rumann, Susan Hayward. D: William McGann. DRA 63m.

Girls on the Beach, The 1965 ★★½ A sorority girl promises her sisters she will get the Beatles to perform to pay the bill on their boardinghouse, then has to deliver. Silly teenage beach picture is redeemed by musical performances from the Beach Boys and others. (a.k.a. *Summer of '64*) C: Martin West, Noreen Corcoran, The Beach Boys, Leslie Gore. D: William Witney. COM 80m.

Girls on the Loose 1958 ★★★ A female gang, led by a nightclub owner, stages a payroll robbery, then suffers internal squabbling and fits of conscience. Average crime drama bolstered by spirited "bad girl" performances. C: Mara Corday, Lita Milan. D: Paul Henreid. CRI 78m.

Girls on the Road ★★★ Two young girls pick up a good-looking hitchhiker who may be a serial killer. Gripping. C: Dianne Hull, Kathleen Cody, Michael Ontkean, Ralph Waite. D: Thomas Schmidt. HOR 80m. v

Girls Riot 1988 ★★½ The overseer at a prison for young female delinquents gets her kicks out of abusing her charges—until they begin to fight back. Gruesome revenge tale. C: Angelica Domrose, Jocelyne Boisseau, Cornelia Calwer. D: Manfred Purzer. DRA 100m. v

Girls School Screamers 1986 ★ Seven young women prepare for an estate sale at an old mansion and are set upon by a ghoulish killer. Silly chiller. C: Mollie O'Mara, Sharon Christopher, Vera Gallagher. D: J. P. Finegan. HOR [R] 85m. v

Girls' School 1938 ★★★½ He's no prize—but this guy has the prettiest girl in the girls' school and her teacher both chasing him. Goofy but energetic. C: Anne Shirley, Nan

Grey, Ralph Bellamy. D: John Brahm. COM 71m.

Girls, The 1968 Swedish ★★★½ Actresses in a production of *Lysistrata* try to liberate themselves from their messy home lives. Pretentious comedy/drama makes its feminist pleas too patly—as if the parallel to Aristophanes' play isn't enough. The three leads' acting, however, saves it. C: Bibi Andersson, Harriet Andersson, Gunnar Bjornstrand, Erland Josephson. D: Mai Zetterling. COM 90m.

Girls Town 1959 ★★½ Teen-oriented potboiler has "bad girl" (Van Doren) being sentenced to youth correctional facility. Over-inflated camp entertains now via slang, cult cast, and vintage rock numbers. (a.k.a. *The Innocent and the Damned*) C: Mamie Van Doren, Mel Torme, Paul Anka, Sheilah Graham, The Platters. D: Charles Haas. COM 90m. V

Girls Under Twenty-One 1940 ★★★½ Not-bad story of street-wise gangsters' gals who take tough falls from the life of crime and learn from their mistakes. C: Bruce Cabot, Rochelle Hudson, Paul Kelly. D: Max Nosseck. CRI 64m.

Girls Will Be Boys 1934 British ★★★½ Gender-switching comedy gets light British touch in predictably enjoyable tale of elderly duke who has shut out all women—and the young woman who infiltrates his estate. C: Dolly Haas, Cyril Maude, Esmond Knight. D: Marcel Varnel. COM 70m.

Girly 1969 ★★★ A proper British family seems to be the picture of happiness and health, but underneath it all, they're a sinister lot. Some suspense. C: Vanessa Howard, Michael Bryant, Ursula Howells. D: Freddie Francis. HOR [R] 101m. V

Giro City *See* **And Nothing But the Truth**

Giselle 1965 ★★★★½ Fine film adaptation of classic ballet preserves dazzling artistry of Cuban ballerina Alonso at apex of her career. Not only is her dancing superb, but her acting conveys fine shades of meaning without a word. C: Alicia Alonso, Azari Plisetski, Fernando Alonso. MUS 99m.

Git 1965 ★★★ An orphan runaway teams up with a dog breeder's daughter to train a rescued English setter to be a good hunting dog. Innocuous, child-oriented animal picture. C: Jack Chaplain, Heather North. D: Ellis Kadison. FAM/DRA 90m. V

Give a Girl a Break 1953 ★★★½ Who will get the lead in a new Broadway musical—Reynolds, Wood, or Marge Champion? Pleasant MGM musical notable mainly for Gower Champion's choreography. Songs by Ira Gershwin and Burton Lane. C: Marge Champion, Gower Champion, Debbie Reynolds, Bob Fosse, Helen Wood. D: Stanley Donen. MUS 82m. V

Give 'Em Hell 1954 French ★★★ Involving gangland saga about a tough hood who raises hell with blazing guns and flying fists. This French take on crime movies doesn't achieve American gangster grittiness, but capable cast and astute direction move it along at a quick clip. C: Eddie Constantine, Mai Britt. D: John Berry. CRI 90m.

Give 'em Hell, Harry! 1975 ★★★★ Simple filming of Whitmore's one-man stage tribute to President Harry Truman works, due to the strength of both actor and subject. Proof that great acting alone can be captivating, without special effects or violence (but be advised of Truman's "salty" language). C: James Whitmore. D: Steve Binder. DRA [PG] 102m. V

Give Her the Moon 1970 French ★★★½ Oddball French comedy about an American millionaire (Convy) who tries to woo a French beauty contest winner by moving her entire village to New York. It almost works. (a.k.a. *Les Caprices de Marie.*) C: Philippe Noiret, Bert Convy, Dorothy Marchini, Valentina Cortese. D: Philippe de Broca. COM [G] 92m.

Give Me a Sailor 1938 ★★★ As a gob with a girl in every port, able seaman Hope finds the sailing real smooth. Typical Hope and crew musical comedy. The jokes come fast and the music's easy on the ears. Raye is loads of laughs. C: Martha Raye, Bob Hope, Betty Grable, Jack Whiting. D: Elliott Nugent. MUS 80m.

Give Me Your Heart 1936 ★★★½ Tearjerker starring Francis, queen of the '30s weepies. She's a society woman who hides her past (and her illegitimate child) from her sweetheart, Brent. Elegantly mounted production, good supporting cast but very dated story. C: Kay Francis, George Brent, Roland Young. D: Archie Mayo. DRA 87m.

Give My Regards to Broad Street 1984 British ★★½ Attempt to turn McCartney into movie star fails miserably as thin plot about missing recording keeps getting in the way of the songs. C: Paul McCartney, Bryan Brown, Ringo Starr, Barbara Bach, Linda McCartney, Tracey Ullman, Ralph Richardson. D: Peter Webb. MUS [PG] 109m. V

Give My Regards to Broadway 1948 ★★½ Mediocre musical of vaudevillian (Winninger) determined to stay in show business. Dailey grins interminably. C: Dan Dailey, Charles Winninger, Charles Ruggles, Fay Bainter. D: Lloyd Bacon. MUS 89m.

Give Us this Day 1949 *See* **Salt to the Devil**

Give Us Wings 1940 ★★★ The Little Tough Guys (pale shades of the Bowery Boys) go undercover as pilots for a crooked crop duster. Standard stuff. C: Huntz Hall, Gabriel Dell, Bobby Jordan. D: Charles Lamont. COM 62m.

Given Word, The 1962 Brazilian ★★★★ Two spiritually strong men—a simple farmer and the parish priest—battle over the former's unusual gift of thanks to God. Often mesmerizing if obvious parable of the conflict between different expressions of belief. Cannes Best Film Winner in 1962. C: Leonardo Vilar, Dionizio Azevedo, Gloria Menezes. D: Anselmo Duarte. DRA 98m.

Gizmo 1977 ★★★ Satirical documentary uses old film clips to explore oddball world of inventors. Fun in parts, although it doesn't form much of a whole. D: Howard Smith. DOC [G] 76m. V

Glacier Fox, The 1979 ★★★ A family of wild foxes try to survive their harsh wilderness environment. Filmed in northern Japan. Fascinating and beautifully photographed. D: Koreyoshi Kurahara. DOC [G] 90m. V

Gladiator 1992 ★★ Boxers (Marshall and Gooding, Jr.) get involved in illegal boxing matches. Standard action drama puts all but fight fans down for the count. C: Cuba Gooding, Jr., James Marshall, Robert Loggia, Ossie Davis, Brian Dennehy. D: Rowdy Herrington. ACT [R] 102m. V

Gladiator, The 1938 ★★★ Wimpy college kid drinks magic potion, becomes campus he-man. Brown is an acquired taste. C: Joe E. Brown, June Travis, Dickie Moore. D: Edward Sedgwick. ACT 70m.

Gladiator, The 1986 ★★½ Brother of hit-and-run victim becomes a vigilante in search of the drunk driver who did it in this well-intentioned, but only passably executed drama. C: Ken Wahl, Nancy Allen, Robert Culp. D: Abel Ferrara. DRA 94m. TVM V

Glamorous Night 1937 British ★★½ An opera singer and a Gypsy girl save the throne of a European monarch. Popular stage musical gets okay screen treatment. C: Mary Ellis, Otto Kruger, Victor Jory. D: Brian Desmond Hurst. MUS 65m.

Glamour Boy 1941 ★★★½ Cooper trades on his own experience in this clever comedy about a former child star called upon to groom a hot young actor. Appealing satire. C: Jackie Cooper, Susanna Foster, Walter Abel, Darryl Hickman, William Demerest. D: Ralph Murphy. COM 79m.

Glamour Girl 1947 ★★★½ Grey is a small-town singer whose melodious talents take her to the top when she hits the big city. Slight story is really an excuse to showcase great musical numbers by the Gene Krupa band. C: Gene Krupa, Virginia Grey, Michael Duane. D: Arthur Dreifuss. MUS 68m.

Glass Alibi, The 1946 ★★★½ An unscrupulous man marries a wealthy woman he thinks is dying, but when she recovers he must formulate a more drastic plan. Decent crime drama does well on its small budget. C: Paul Kelly, Anne Gwynne. D: W. Wilder. CRI 70m.

Glass Bottom Boat, The 1966 ★★★½ Entertaining slapstick comedy finds Day as a widow who's hired by scientist (Taylor) to pen his biography. Complications ensue when he puts the moves on her, and she's mistaken for a Russian spy. Silliness amuses due to Tashlin's hilarious set pieces and Day's delightful dithering. C: Doris Day, Rod Taylor, Arthur Godfrey, Paul Lynde, Dom DeLuise. D: Frank Tashlin. COM 110m. V

Glass House, The 1972 ★★★½ In a state prison, a college professor convicted of manslaughter must learn how to survive among the other inmates. Brutal, chilling, and quite realistic drama, based on Truman Capote story. C: Vic Morrow, Billy Dee Williams, Alan Alda, Kristoffer Tabori. D: Tom Gries. ACT 89m. TVM V

Glass Jungle, The 1988 ★★½ In Los Angeles, an innocent cab driver is caught in the crossfire between ruthless terrorists and G-Men. Middling action and some suspense. C: Lee Canalito, Diana Frank, Frank Scala, Mark High. D: Joseph Merhi. ACT 90m. V

Glass Key, The 1935 ★★★½ Loyal sidekick fights adversaries to discover the truth and protect his boss, a politician who's been accused of murder. Early adaptation of Hammett novel. Rich characterizations. C: George Raft, Claire Dodd, Edward Arnold, Ray Milland. D: Frank Tuttle. CRI 80m.

Glass Key, The 1942 ★★★★½ Faithful aide (Ladd) tries to clear his boss, somewhat dishonest politician (Donlevy), of a murder charge. Realistic violence and excellent performances make a particularly stirring version of the Dashiell Hammett novel. Remake of 1935 film of the same name. C: Brian Donlevy, Alan Ladd, Veronica Lake, William Bendix. D: Stuart Heisler. CRI 85m. V

Glass Menagerie, The 1950 ★★★½ First film adaptation of Tennessee Williams' Southern gothic drama about aging belle Amanda Wingfield, her withdrawn, crippled daughter, and her "artistic" son. Film is well cast and aims to do justice to the material but direction fails to establish the all-important fantasy worlds the characters inhabit. C: Gertrude Lawrence, Jane Wyman, Kirk Douglas, Arthur Kennedy. D: Irving Rapper. DRA [PG] 107m.

Glass Menagerie, The 1973 ★★★★½ Hepburn, making her TV acting bow, is triumphant as Amanda Wingfield, in the story of an overbearing mother and her two misfit children. The rest of the ensemble rises to Hepburn's heights, in Tennessee Williams' Southern gothic drama. Williams adapted the play himself for the tube. An exceptional movie experience. C: Katharine Hepburn, Joanna Miles, Sam Waterston, Michael Moriarty. D: Anthony Harvey. DRA 100m. TVM

Glass Menagerie, The 1987 ★★★★ Newman filmed this Tennessee Williams masterwork as a labor of love, and it shows. He draws a deeply emotional performance from Woodward as Amanda Wingfield, while giving the electrifying Malkovich free rein to play Tom. A very worthwhile version of the play. C: Joanne Woodward, Karen Allen, John Malkovich, James Naughton. D: Paul Newman. DRA 134m. V

Glass Mountain, The 1950 British ★★★★½ Drama with music does for opera what *The Red Shoes* did for ballet. Composer (Denison) is obsessed with a young woman who is the inspiration for his work. Beautifully directed with effective performances by members of the La Scala Opera. Worth discovering. C: Valentina Cortese, Michael Denison. D: Henry Cass. MUS 94m.

Glass Slipper, The 1955 ★★★½ The pixieish Caron is charming as a singing Cinderella in this pleasant musical treatment of the fairy tale. Lightweight but well-executed fantasy features exuberant song and dance numbers. C: Leslie Caron, Michael Wilding, Keenan Wynn, Estelle Windwood, Elsa Lanchester. D: Charles Walters. MUS 95m. V

Glass Sphinx, The 1967 Italian ★★ Taylor looks uncomfortable as an archaeologist racing foreign spies to find secret potion in glass sphinx. Acting and production look as plastic as the title prop. C: Robert Taylor, Anita Ekberg. D: Luigi Scattini. ACT 91m.

Glass Tower, The 1957 German ★★★★ Wife is locked away when husband's jealousy gets out of hand. Strong psychological drama with solid (if somewhat overwrought) performances. C: Lilli Palmer, O. E. Hasse, Peter Van Eyck. D: Harold Braun. DRA 92m.

Glass Wall, The 1953 ★★★½ Denied entry into America, immigrant jumps ship and escapes into New York City where he flees authorities before ending up at "glass wall" of the U.N. Some interesting moments of human tragedy in this offbeat drama. C: Vittorio Gassman, Gloria Grahame. D: Maxwell Shane. DRA 80m.

Glass Web, The 1953 ★★★★ When work begins on a TV show about an unsolved slaying, the murderer may be unmasked. Clever crime, drama, with strong performances. C: Edward Robinson, John Forsythe, Kathleen Hughes. D: Jack Arnold. CRI 81m.

Gleaming the Cube 1989 ★★½ Skateboarder (Slater) uses his wits and skills to solve the murder of his brother. Fancy skating stunts barely hoist it over gaping plot holes, but it flies well enough for young skate and Slater fans. C: Christian Slater, Steven Bauer, Ed Lauter. D: Graeme Clifford. DRA [PG-13] 105m. V

Glen and Randa 1971 ★★★ Nuclear holocaust has wiped out most of mankind but teenage survivors search for a long-lost city and fall in love. No-name cast enlivens this interesting premise. C: Steven Curry, Shelley Plimpton. D: Jim McBride. HOR [R] 94m. V

Glen or Glenda 1953 ★★ Trashy pseudo-documentary plea for tolerance of transvestism concerns story of man who wants to wear his fiancée's clothes. Narrated by Lugosi. Often makes "worst movies ever made" lists—but also a camp classic. C: Bela Lugosi, Dolores Fuller, Daniel Davis, Lyle Talbot. D: Edward D. Wood, Jr. DRA [PG] 64m. V

Glengarry Glen Ross 1992 ★★★★ Real estate salesmen hustle to sell their packaged Florida properties. Engrossing film version of David Mamet's noteworthy play. The desperation of the various characters made achingly real in angry vision of the workaday world. Ensemble cast shines, especially Lemmon and Pacino. C: Al Pacino, Jack Lemmon, Ed Harris, Kevin Spacey, Alan Arkin, Alec Baldwin, Jonathan Pryce. D: James Foley. DRA [R] 100m. V

Glenn Miller Story, The 1953 ★★★★ Stewart and Allyson are an appealing couple in this sweet, sanitized biography of the great swing bandleader whose plane disappeared in WWII. Includes such big hits as "String of Pearls." C: James Stewart, June Allyson, Charles Drake, Frances Langford, Louis Armstrong, Gene Krupa. D: Anthony Mann. MUS [G] 113m. V

Glitch 1988 ★ Two young burglars break into a film producer's house and wind up masquerading as filmmakers, just so they can audition dozens of bikini-clad beauties for parts in a new film. Irredeemable Hollywood farce. C: Julia Nickson, Ted Lange, Dick Gautier. D: Nico Mastorakis. COM [R] 88m. V

Glitter Dome, The 1984 ★★★ Joseph Wambaugh mystery about two cops tracking a killer in the film world can't get by on Garner's smooth work or Kidder's odd star turn. C: James Garner, Margot Kidder, John Lithgow, Colleen Dewhurst. D: Stuart Margolin. CRI 95m. TVM V

Glitterball, The 1977 British ★★★½ Bright kiddie film focuses on lost little alien who lands on Earth and the kids who help him get back home. Hey, has Steven Spielberg seen this? C: Ben Buckton, Keith Jayne, Ron Pember, Marjorie Yates. D: Harley Cockliss. FAM/SFI 56m.

Glitz 1988 ★★½ Based on Elmore Leonard's best-seller, this bland mystery centers around the murder of a prostitute. Cast of TV regulars gets points for effort. C: Jimmy Smits, Markie Post. D: Sandor Stern. CRI 96m. TVM V

Global Affair, A 1964 ★★½ A United Nations representative (Hope) becomes the unwilling guardian of an abandoned baby. Average '60s comedy with slightly leering Hope. C: Bob Hope, Yvonne De Carlo, Robert Sterling. D: Jack Arnold. COM 84m. V

Gloria 1980 ★★★½ Ex-gangland moll (Rowlands) flees with unruly Hispanic boy after mobsters kill his parents. A bit long, but an effective crime drama with a gutsy, stand-out performance by Rowlands. Fine New York cinematography. C: Gena Rowlands, Buck Henry. D: John Cassavetes. CRI [PG] 121m. V

Glorifying the American Girl 1929 ★★★★

One of the first talkie revues and the only movie supervised by the great Ziegfeld. Ignore inconsequential plot about chorus dancer resisting marriage and instead relish turns by Cantor, Morgan, Vallee. Famous "first night" sequence uses N.Y. celebrities of the day playing themselves: Texas Guinan, Mayor Jimmy Walker and Irving Berlin. Poor sound a drawback. C: Mary Eaton, Edward Crandall, Eddie Cantor, Helen Morgan, Rudy Vallee, Florenz Ziegfeld, Texas Guinan. D: Millard Webb. MUS 80m. V

Glory 1956 ★★★ Star vehicle for O'Brien as a horse-mad young woman who enters her filly in the Kentucky Derby. Nothing really special; for fans of horse flicks and Margaret O'Brien primarily. C: Margaret O'Brien, Walter Brennan, Charlotte Greenwood. D: David Butler. FAM/DRA 100m. V

Glory 1989 ★★★★★ Breathtaking battle epic on the 54th Massachusetts, the black infantry unit which made history in the Civil War. Broderick is solid as their commander; Washington won Best Supporting Oscar.. C: Matthew Broderick, Denzel Washington, Cary Elwes, Morgan Freeman. D: Edward Zwick. DRA [R] 122m. V

Glory Alley 1952 ★★½ Korean War hero and ex-boxer (Meeker) returns to New Orleans; his attempt to win back his sweetheart (Caron) is complicated by her father (Kasznar), who thinks Meeker was a coward in the boxing ring. Mediocre film enlivened by Armstrong's great jazz interludes. C: Ralph Meeker, Leslie Caron, Kurt Kasznar, Gilbert Roland, Louis Armstrong. D: Raoul Walsh. DRA 79m.

Glory at Sea 1952 British ★★★½ British crew members of a WWII Lend-Lease U.S. destroyer first resent, then grow to admire their new, reluctant skipper. Solid seafaring drama with top-notch acting. C: Trevor Howard, Richard Attenborough, Sonny Tufts, James Donald, Joan Rice. D: Compton Bennett. DRA 100m.

Glory Boy 1972 *See* **My Old Man's Place**

Glory Boys, The 1984 ★★★½ When British intelligence learns that terrorists are targeting a visiting Israeli scientist, they hire a "tracker" to hunt them down. Effective intrique. C: Anthony Perkins, Rod Steiger, Alfred Burke, Joanna Lumley. D: Michael Ferguson. ACT 110m. V

Glory Brigade 1953 ★★★½ During the U.N. police action in Korea, Greeks and Americans join forces as the fighting moves back and forth over the 38th parallel. Watchable war drama with good performances. C: Victor Mature, Alexander Scourby, Lee Marvin, Richard Egan. D: Robert Webb. DRA 82m.

Glory! Glory! 1988 ★★★★ Deft satire of televangelism with Greene marvelous as sex, drugs, and rock 'n' roll singer pulled in (by Thomas) to shore up the show's ratings. Funny and irreverent; a sleeper originally made for cable. C: Ellen Greene, Richard Thomas, James Whitmore, Barry Morse. D: Lindsay Anderson. COM [R] 152m. TVM V

Glory Guys, The 1965 ★★★ Commander dispatches young cavalry officer to lead inexperienced troops in a strike against Sioux. Fair Western burdened with clichés. C: Tom Tryon, Harve Presnell, Senta Berger, James Caan. D: Arnold Laven. WST 112m.

Glory Stompers, The 1967 ★ Violence erupts between feuding bikers when one gang abducts leader of another. Mindless fodder with laughable dialogue and a tepid, perfunctory "love-in." C: Dennis Hopper, Jody McCrea. D: Anthony M. Lanza. ACT 81m. V

Glory Years 1987 ★★★ At their high school reunion, three buddies meet and take off on a "mission" of romance and gambling—all to reclaim their lost youth. Okay comedy. C: George Dzundza, Archie Hahn, Tim Thomerson, Tawny Kitaen, Donna Pescow. D: Arthur Allan Seidelman. COM 150m. V

Glove: Lethal Terminator, The 1978 *See* **Glove, The**

Glove, The 1978 ★★ Routine actioner concerns a jaded bounty hunter pursuing an angry ex-con who lashes out with a steel and leather riot glove at those who put him behind bars. Very violent. (a.k.a. *The Glove: Lethal Terminator*) C: John Saxon, Rosey Grier, Joanna Cassidy, Joan Blondell, Keenan Wynn. D: Ross Hagen. ACT [R] 93m. V

Gnome-Mobile, The 1967 ★★★★ Lumber magnate (Brennan) and two children discover colony of gnomes in a redwood forest and are called upon to protect them from carnival freak-show exploitation. Lively, fanciful Disney comedy at its best. Based on little-known Upton Sinclair children's novel. C: Walter Brennan, Matthew Garber, Karen Dotrice. D: Robert Stevenson. FAM/COM [G] 84m. V

Gnome Named Gnorm, A 1993 ★★★ Young cop (Hall) is amazed to find his new partner's a mythological gnome from beneath the earth. Whimsical fantasy adventure. C: Anthony Michael Hall, Jerry Orbach, Claudia Christian. D: Stan Winston. ACT [PG] 84m. V

Gnomes 1980 ★★½ Film inspired by the illustrations of the Wil Huggen and Rien Poortvliet best-seller about the cunning little creatures who live in the forest and under the earth and spend their days outsmarting humans. Ho-hum for interest value and presentation. FAM/DRA 52m. V

Go Ask Alice 1972 ★★★½ Realistic look at drug use among teenagers, based on book, the actual diary of a teen drug addict. Uneven, perhaps a bit outdated in terms of shock value, but still a must-see for teenagers and concerned parents. C: Jamie Smith-Jackson, Andy Griffith, William Shatner. D: John Korty. DRA 73m. TVM

Go-Between, The 1971 British ★★★★½

Hauntingly romantic costume drama recounts tale of forbidden love as a young boy carries letters back and forth between an upper-class woman and a poor farmer. Strong production benefits from Harold Pinter's lyrical adaptation of L.P. Hartley's novel. C: Julie Christie, Alan Bates, Dominic Guard, Margaret Leighton, Michael Redgrave. D: Joseph Losey. DRA [PG] 116m. v

Go Chase Yourself 1938 ★★★½ Timid bank clerk winds up on the lam with bank robbers, suspected of holdup he had nothing to do with. Fun fluff, featuring popular vaudeville and radio star Penner. C: Joe Penner, Lucille Ball, June Travis, Richard Lane. D: Edward F. Cline. COM 70m.

Go for Broke 1951 ★★★★ A rare look at the highly decorated Japanese-American 442nd Regiment which fought prejudice at home and the Nazis in Europe in WWII. Well acted, with Johnson as the unit's green commander. C: Van Johnson, Warner Anderson, Gianna Canale. D: Robert Pirosh. DRA 90m. v

Go for Gold 1984 ★★★ A young athlete must choose between fame and personal satisfaction. Well acted and often moving. C: James Ryan, Cameron Mitchell. D: Stuart Fleming. DRA 98m. v

Go Into Your Dance 1935 ★★★½ Only screen pairing of husband and wife Jolson and Keeler makes this showbiz story worth seeing. Ordinary plot, but they get to sing two classic Harry Warren songs: "About a Quarter to Nine" and "A Latin From Manhattan." C: Al Jolson, Ruby Keeler, Glenda Farrell, Helen Morgan, Patsy Kelly. D: Archie Mayo. MUS 89m.

Go, Johnny, Go! 1958 ★★½ Deejay (Freed) turns orphan (Clanton) into pop singer matinee idol. Strictly for '50s nostalgia buffs. C: Jimmy Clanton, Alan Freed, Chuck Berry. D: Paul Landres. MUS 75m. v

Go, Man, Go! 1954 ★★★★ Appealing recreation of the development of the Harlem Globetrotters, the comic first all-black basketball team. Poitier is excellent as usual, and cinematographer Howe does a fine job in rare outing as director. A good balance between sports action and personal drama. C: Dane Clark, Pat Breslin, Sidney Poitier. D: James Wong Howe. DRA 82m.

Go Masters, The 1983 Chinese ★★★★ Divisions between China and Japan are played out over 30-year period through strategy game played over decades of war and conflict. Immensely popular film in Asia still moves. First Sino-Japanese coproduction. C: Duan Ji-shun, Rentaro Mikuni. D: Junya Sato. DRA 123m. v

Go Naked in the World 1961 ★★ Borgnine plays father upset that son (Franciosa) is involved with town slut (Lollobrigida). Thick, plodding melodrama. C: Gina Lollobrigida, Anthony Franciosa, Ernest Borgnine. D: Ronald MacDougall. DRA 103m.

Go Tell It on the Mountain 1985 ★★★★ James Baldwin's autobiographical novel serves as the basis for this involving family drama about a youth trying to learn to live with, and get approval from, his strict stepfather. Intelligent drama made for PBS *American Playhouse*. C: Paul Winfield, James Bond III, Olivia Cole, Ruby Dee, Alfre Woodard. D: Stan Lathan. FAM/DRA 100m. TVM v

Go Tell the Spartans 1978 ★★★ A tough major (Lancaster) and his platoon of ne'er-do-well G.I.s and Vietnamese mercenaries build an outpost against the Viet Cong. A straightforward and well-told story, neither antiwar nor flagwaving. C: Burt Lancaster, Craig Wasson, Marc Singer. D: Ted Post. DRA [R] 114m. v

Go West 1940 ★★★½ Three Marx Brothers head West looking for gold, only to discover a railroad company wants the deed to their land. Bright spots include stagecoaches, saloons, and a terrific train chase finale. Not their best, but still fun. C: Groucho Marx, Chico Marx, Harpo Marx, John Carroll, Diana Lewis. D: Edward Buzzell. COM 80m. v

Go West, Young Man 1936 ★★★★ Toned-down vehicle for Mae as movie star touring the tundra who encounters strapping cowhand (Scott). Not West's best, but amusing nonetheless. C: Mae West, Randolph Scott, Warren William, Alice Brady. D: Henry Hathaway. COM 80m. v

Goalie's Anxiety at the Penalty Kick, The 1971 German ★★★★ In this early Wenders effort exploring his favorite theme—existential alienation—a soccer player stops relating to the real world except through the act of killing. Elliptical dialogue and anxiety-ridden atmosphere make this a moody downer. C: Arthur Brauss, Erika Pluhar. D: Wim Wenders. DRA 101m. v

Goat, The 1982 *See* **La Chevre**

Goblin 1993 ★ Bottom-of-the-barrel, homemade horror about a newlywed couple who discover their new home is haunted by a murderous monster. Little to offer but buckets of amateurish gore. C: Jenny Admire, Tonia Monahan, Bobby Westrick, Mike Hellman, Kim Alber. D: Todd Sheets. HOR 75m.

GoBots: Battle of the Rock Lords 1986 ★★ Blatant Tonka Toys animated commercial from Hanna-Barbera with warring Renegades and Gobots and all those caught in between. Electronically altered mishmash of sound effects obscures voices of all-star cast. Voices of Margot Kidder, Roddy Mcdowall, Michael Nouri, Telly Savalas. D: Ray Patterson. FAM/ACT 74m. v

God Bless the Child 1988 ★★★★ Fine social drama about a homeless single mother (Winningham) with a seven-year-old daughter, who can't break out of her impoverished environment no matter how hard she tries. Gripping, occasionally unsettling study doesn't cop out with easy answers and benefits from Winningham's sensitive, multifaceted performance. C: Mare Winningham, Grace Johnston, Dorian Harewood. D: Larry Elikann. DRA 94m. TVM V

God Forgives, I Don't 1969 Italian ★ Derivative spaghetti-Western about a search for missing loot goes nowhere. C: Terence Hill, Bud Spencer. D: Giuseppe Colizzi. WST 101m.

God is My Co-Pilot 1945 ★★★ Air exploits over the Pacific of the distinguished Flying Tigers unit stationed in China during WWII. Earnest, if clichéd drama. C: Dennis Morgan, Raymond Massey, Andrea King, Alan Hale. D: Robert Florey. ACT 90m.

God Is My Partner 1957 ★★½ Brennan is a heartwarming old coot who decides to give away everything he has to get closer to Heaven. Inspirational but labored. C: Walter Brennan, John Hoyt. D: William Claxton. DRA 80m.

God, Man and Devil 1949 Yiddish ★★★ Late example of Yiddish cinema, derived from classic Jacob Gordin play about a wager between God and Satan, a parable about wealth and evil. Downbeat, intermittently effective. C: Michal Michalesko, Gustav Berger, Berta Gersten, Esta Salzman, Max Bozyk, Leon Schachter. D: Joseph Seiden. DRA 100m.

God Told Me To 1977 *See* **Demon**

Godchild, The 1974 ★★★½ Three convicts on the run during the Civil War find themselves serving as guardians for a baby. Umpteenth middling remake of the *Three Godfathers*. C: Jack Palance, Jack Warden, Keith Carradine. D: John Badham. DRA 78m. TVM

Goddess of Love 1960 Italian ★ In ancient times a woman turns to prostitution after her man dies. Dull and pointless. C: Belinda Lee, Jacques Sernas. D: W. Tourjansky. DRA 68m.

Goddess of Love 1988 ★ One of the worst TV movies ever made has *Wheel of Fortune's* letter-turner White playing the Greek goddess Venus in modern-day setting. So terrible, it's worth seeing. C: Vanna White, David Naughton, Little Richard. D: Jim Drake. DRA 100m. TVM

Goddess, The 1957 ★★★★ Stanley is a powerhouse in rare film role (her debut) as Monroe-like actress desperate for love and respect in tawdry Hollywood. Scripted by Paddy Chayefsky with a sometimes heavy hand. C: Kim Stanley, Lloyd Bridges, Betty Holland, Patty Duke. D: John Cromwell. DRA 105m. V

Goddess, The 1960 *See* **Devi**

Godfather, The 1972 ★★★★½ Film that sparked the '70s gangster film revival turns Puzo's potboiler into an operatic epic of Mafia wars. Brilliant performances, evocative Nino Rota score, Coppola's carefully orchestrated violence, and fresh theme made this an instant classic. Oscar-winner for Picture, Screenplay and Actor (Brando). C: Marlon Brando, Al Pacino, James Caan, Diane Keaton, Talia Shire, Robert Duvall. D: Francis Ford Coppola. CRI [R] 175m. V

Godfather, Part II, The 1974 ★★★★★ Relieved of need to be faithful to Puzo novel, Coppola embarks on a sequel with an unusual theme—crime as capitalism—and structure, juxtaposing the youth of Vito Corleone (De Niro) and problems of his son (Pacino) 50 years later as the mob threatens to break apart under Congressional scrutiny. Brilliant supporting cast (especially legendary Strasberg in rare film appearance and playwright Gazzo). Won six Oscars: Picture, Director, Screenplay, Score, Art Direction, Supporting Actor (De Niro). C: Al Pacino, Robert Duvall, Diane Keaton, Robert De Niro, Talia Shire, Lee Strasberg. D: Francis Ford Coppola. CRI [R] 200m. V

Godfather, Part III, The 1990 ★★★★ Autumnal last film of *Godfather* trilogy has a haunting, elegiac tone, but is weakened by near-fatal miscasting of Coppola's daughter. Still, an interesting mix of gangster movie and political thriller (with the Corleones involved with corrupt Vatican bankers), and another masterly performance from Pacino. C: Al Pacino, Diane Keaton, Talia Shire, Andy Garcia, Eli Wallach, Sofia Coppola, Joe Mantegna, George Hamilton, Bridget Fonda. D: Francis Ford Coppola. CRI [R] 161m. V

God's Bloody Acre 1975 ★★½ All's well for three brothers living in seclusion in a remote mountainous region—until a construction crew shows up to build a park there. Violent actioner. C: Scott Lawrence. D: Harry E. Kerwin. ACT 85m. V

God's Country 1946 ★★★ Saddle-sore Western about an innocent man on the run. Partially saved by the presence of brilliant comedian Keaton in the cast. C: Buster Keaton, Robert Lowery, Helen Gilbert. D: Robert Tansey. WST 62m.

God's Country 1985 ★★★★★ Glencoe, Minnesota is the small-town setting for this poignant exploration of people's continuing belief in the American Dream. Malle never sentimentalizes or becomes flippant, and he records real lives with authenticity and flavor. D: Louis Malle. DOC 88m.

God's Country and the Woman 1936 ★★ Notable for being one of the early Technicolor films. Plot revolves around logger who infiltrates his rival's camp and unwittingly falls in love. Melodramatic and slow. C: George Brent, Beverly Roberts. D: William Keighley. DRA 80m.

God's Gun 1980 ★★★ After the local priest is killed, a reformed gunfighter takes on the desperadoes who did it. Solid western action, good cast. C: Richard Boone, Lee Van Cleef, Jack Palance, Leif Garrett. D: Frank Kramer. WST 93m. V

God's Little Acre 1958 ★★★½ Obsessed

poor white Southern farmer (Ryan) tears up his land in futile search for his grandfather's hidden gold. Tamer film version of racy Erskine Caldwell novel, nonetheless has powerful moments and effective performances by energetic cast. C: Robert Ryan, Tina Louise, Aldo Ray. D: Anthony Mann. DRA [PG] 110m. v

Gods Must Be Crazy, The 1984 Botswana ★★★★ Delightful comedy about an African bushman (N!xau) whose chance encounter with a falling Coke bottle leads to unusual clashes with outside world. Engagingly wacky, with an inspired slapstick performance by Weyers. C: N!xau, Marius Weyers, Sandra Prinsloo. D: Jamie Uys. COM [PG] 109m. v

Gods Must Be Crazy II, The 1990 U.S. ★★★ Sequel to original follows African nomadic hunter N!xau, as he goes in search of his children after they are accidentally kidnapped by poachers. Though occasionally funny, this isn't as fresh or original as the first film. C: N!xau, Lena Farugia, Hans Strydom. D: Jamie Uys. COM [PG] 98m. v

Gods of the Plague 1969 German ★★½ One of Fassbinder's early noir-tinged gangster films, this is the story of two small-time hoods whose petty thievery culminates in a supermarket shoot-out. Has touches of his later over-the-top stylings. C: Hanna Schygulla, Margarethe Von Trotta, Harry Baer. D: Rainer Werner Fassbinder. CRI 91m. v

Godsend, The 1979 British ★★★ Cherubic child, left at farm and adopted by family, turns out to be a demon seed sowing death and destruction in her wake. Middling rip-off of *The Omen*. C: Cyd Hayman, Malcolm Stoddard. D: Gabrielle Beaumont. HOR [R] 93m. v

Godson, The 1972 Italian ★★★½ Delon is a contract killer in Paris, on the run from the police and trying to avoid his employers, who also want him dead. Not as many thrills as one would hope. C: Alain Delon, Nathalie Delon, Francois Perier, Cathy Rosier. D: Jean-Pierre Melville. CRI [PG] 103m.

Godspell 1973 ★★★½ Stephen Schwartz's rollicking musical turned the New Testament into soft-rock vaudeville with corny jokes and lovely melodies mixed with parables and preaching. Film uses brilliantly photographed N.Y. locations, but misses the theatrical magic. Hit song: "Day by Day." C: Victor Garber, David Haskell, Lynne Thigpen. D: David Greene. MUS [G] 103m.

Godzilla, King of the Monsters 1956 Japanese ★★★★ Atomic testing thaws the gigantic reptile who then attacks Tokyo for the first time in this manic monster flick. Nifty special effects and laughable dubbing make it a treat for all ages. Greatly inspired by the *Beast from 20,000 Fathoms*. Spawned countless sequels and oversized "thing" movies. Burr filmed his scenes separately, for U.S. release. C: Raymond Burr, Inoshiro Honda, Takashi Shimura. D: Terry Morse. SFI 80m. v

Godzilla 1985 1985 Japanese ★ The Tokyo Destroyer returns, looking cheaper and more tired than ever. Burr reprises his original role in a series of painfully obvious inserts. Mindless remake of the original is best for scale-model buffs only. C: Raymond Burr, Keiji Kobayashi, Ten Tanaka. D: Kohji Hashimoto. SFI [PG] 91m. v

Godzilla on Monster Island *See* **Godzilla vs. Gigan**

Godzilla Raids Again 1959 *See* **Gigantis, the Fire Monster**

Godzilla vs. Biolante 1992 ★½ The ol' granddaddy of rubber monsters is back, fighting a towering and deadly adversary. Don't step on those extras! Campy fun, but not as good as the earlier entries in the series. D: Kazuki Ohmori. SFI [PG] 104m. v

Godzilla vs. Gigan 1972 Japanese ★★★ Godzilla—in his only talking role!—and his new ally Angillus battle space monster Ghidrah and his friend, Gigan, who has a saw blade in his chest. (a.k.a. *Godzilla on Monster Island*) C: Hiroshi Ishikahra, Tomoko Umeda. D: Jun Fukuda. SFI [G] 89m. v

Godzilla vs. Mechagodzilla 1974 Japanese ★★ Godzilla battles his mechanical doppelganger, which was created by a planet of apes seeking total world domination. Not the best from Toho studios. (a.k.a. *Godzilla vs. the Bionic Monster, Godzilla vs. the Cosmic Monster.*) C: Masaaki Daimon, Kazuya Aoyama. D: Jun Fukuda. SFI [G] 80m. v

Godzilla vs. Megalon 1976 Japanese ★ The dregs of the Godzilla series finds our dinosaur hero in cahoots with an automaton to battle Megalon and buzz-saw heavy Gigan. Better than *Son of Godzilla*, but not by much. C: Katsuhiko Sasaki, Hiroyuki Kawase. D: Jun Fukuda. SFI [G] 80m. v

Godzilla vs. Monster Zero 1966 ★★★ Godzilla and Rodan (the big pterodactyl) are kidnapped (airlifted in giant bubbles) and brought to another planet to battle Ghidrah, the three-headed flying monster. More good, clean, monster fun. (a.k.a. *Monster Zero*). C: Nick Adams, Akira Takarada. D: Inoshiro Honda. SFI 92m. v

Godzilla vs. Mothra 1964 French ★★★ This time the big guy, now a full-blown national hero, wrestles with Mothra, the giant moth. Highlights include pretty good special effects and Mothra's strange, diminutive friends. (a.k.a. *Godzilla vs. the Thing*). C: Okira Takarada, Yuriko Hoshi, Hiroshi Koizumi. D: Inoshino Honda. SFI 90m. v

Godzilla vs. the Bionic Monster 1974 *See* **Godzilla vs. Mechagodzilla**

Godzilla vs. the Cosmic Monster 1974 *See* **Godzilla vs. Mechagodzilla**

Godzilla vs. the Sea Monster 1966 Japanese ★★★ The sea monster is a giant shrimp! Former foe Mothra turns up to give Godzilla a hand . . . ah . . . a wing. Hampered by a plot involving human beings. C: Akira Takarada, Toru Watanabe. D: Jun Fukuda. SFI 80m. V

Godzilla vs. the Smog Monster 1972 Japanese ★★★ Ecology-minded Godzilla does his part to clean up the Earth by properly disposing of the title fiend, which was created and nourished by industrial waste. More monster mayhem and bad dubbing. C: Akira Yamauchi, Hiroyuki Kawase. D: Yoshimitu Banno. SFI [G] 85m. V

Godzilla vs. the Thing 1964 *See* **Godzilla vs. Mothra**

Godzilla's Revenge 1969 Japanese ★★½ Like a "Best of" collection of Godzilla clips, strung together by flimsy plot about child dreaming he's playing with Godzilla's son. Loopy attempt to appeal to juvenile market. C: Kenji Sahara, Tomonori Yazaki. D: Inoshiro Honda. SFI [G] 70m. V

Gog 1954 ★★★½ Fathoms below Earth's surface, a top-secret government lab creates a killer computer that gets out of hand. Good use of color, and solid acting. Originally released in 3-D. C: Richard Egan, Constance Dowling, Herbert Marshall. D: Herbert Strock. HOR 85m.

Goha 1958 Tunisian ★★★ Unusual romantic folk tale about a young man, considered town dunce, who actually is bright enough to be romantically involved with the wife of the town wise man. Lush locations, exotic atmosphere. Excellent early work by Cheriff (later Sharif). C: Omar Cheriff, Zina Bourzaiane, Laurro Gazzalo. D: Jacques Baratier. DRA 85m.

Goin' All the Way 1982 ★ A pair of L.A. high schoolers try to make it with the opposite sex. Teen sex comedy doesn't go anywhere a dozen other entries in the genre haven't been before. C: Dan Waldman, Deborah Van Rhyn. D: Robert Freedman. COM [R] 85m. V

Goin' Coconuts 1978 ★★½ Strictly for kids, as thieves go after Marie's necklace in poorly photographed Hawaii. Osmonds' sing sweetly and act gamely but ineptly. C: Donny Osmond, Marie Osmond, Kenneth Mars. D: Howard Morris. FAM/MUS [PG] 96m.

Goin' Down the Road 1970 Canadian ★★★½ Modest story about the misfortunes of a pair of Nova Scotians down on their luck. Low-budget drama features memorable performances. C: Doug McGrath, Paul Bradley, Jayne Eastwood. D: Donald Shebib. DRA [PG] 90m.

Goin' Home 1976 ★★★ Life on the road with youngster and his dog. Rife with stereotypes and clichés as they make their way to California. Kids' stuff. C: Todd Christiansen, Bernard Triche, Kevin Oliver. D: Chris Prentiss. FAM/DRA 97m.

Goin' South 1978 ★★★½ With the noose already around his neck, a ne'er do well (Nicholson) is spared when a spirited young woman agrees to marry him. Raucous and bawdy Western; Steenburgen's impressive debut. C: Jack Nicholson, Mary Steenburgen, Christopher Lloyd, John Belushi, Danny DeVito. D: Jack Nicholson. WST [PG] 109m. V

Goin' to Town 1935 ★★★★ Notorious widow (West) tries to scheme her way into high society. Lots of snappy one-liners, crowned by West's operatic debut in scene from *Samson and Delilah.* C: Mae West, Paul Cavanagh. D: Alexander Hall. COM 71m. V

Going Ape! 1981 ★★ Man will inherit $5 million if he cares for family of orangutans. Moronic monkey business fails to amuse. C: Tony Danza, Jessica Walter, Danny DeVito. D: Jeremy Joe Kronsberg. COM [PG] 87m. V

Going Bananas 1988 ★★ Talking chimp flees to Africa to elude unscrupulous circus owner. Ridiculous comedy; cast apparently has a better time than viewers. C: Dom DeLuise, Jimmie Walker, David Mendenhall, Herbert Lom. D: Boaz Davidson. COM [PG] 95m. V

Going Berserk 1983 Canadian ★★ Sketch comedy amalgam loosely hung on story of man about to wed politician's daughter. Featuring *SCTV* alumni. C: John Candy, Joe Flaherty, Eugene Levy. D: David Steinberg. COM [R] 85m. V

Going for the Gold: The Bill Johnson Story 1985 ★★★½ True story of former Oregon car thief turned downhill skier who boasts he will win a gold medal at 1984 Winter Olympics in Sarajevo. Standard biography of brash athlete. C: Anthony Edwards, Dennis Weaver, Sarah Jessica Parker. D: Don Taylor. DRA 95m. TVM V

Going Hollywood 1933 ★★★★ Sparkling comedy in which straitlaced woman (Davies) abandons her own career to follow singer (Crosby) to Tinseltown, and tries to woo him away from screen siren (D'Orsay). Highly engaging film gently lampoons Hollywood, and features fine songs. C: Marion Davies, Bing Crosby, Fifi D'Orsay, Ned Sparks, Patsy Kelly. D: Raoul Walsh. COM 77m. V

Going Home 1971 ★★½ Obscure Mitchum release about man who goes to jail for stabbing his wife to death while drunk. Movie explores ex-convict's subsequent relationship with his son, who witnessed killing. Performers try hard, but screenplay works against them. C: Robert Mitchum, Jan-Michael Vincent, Brenda Vaccaro. D: Herbert Leonard. DRA [PG] 97m.

Going in Style 1979 ★★★★½ Three elderly gents, bored with their empty lives, decide to pull a bank robbery. Remarkable teaming of Burns, Carney, and Strasberg, and a moving commentary on neglected seniors. Winning, low-key comedy is fine entertainment. C: George Burns, Art Carney, Lee Strasberg. D: Martin Brest. COM [PG] 96m. V

Going My Way 1944 ★★★★½ Priest Crosby brings new life to old-fashioned parish, despite difficulties posed by crusty superior Fitzgerald. Irresistible story expertly handled by McCarey, who won Oscars for Direction and Screenplay. Also Oscars for Crosby, Fitzgerald, the song "Swinging on a Star," and Best Picture. C: Bing Crosby, Barry Fitzgerald, Rise Stevens, Gene Lockhart, Frank McHugh. D: Leo McCarey. DRA 126m. v

Going Places 1938 ★★★ Sporting goods salesrep (Powell) poses as steeplechase jockey. Forgettable, except for song hit "Jeepers Creepers" by Johnny Mercer and Harry Warren, introduced by Armstrong and Sullivan. C: Dick Powell, Anita Louise, Allen Jenkins, Ronald Reagan. D: Ray Enright. MUS 84m.

Going Places 1974 French ★★★½ Comedy of lower-class hooligans Depardieu and Dewaere on a sex and crime spree. This often hilarious look at two marginalized men playing games in a grown-up world put director Blier on the map but may offend some. C: Gerard Depardieu, Patrick Dewaere, Miou-Miou, Jeanne Moreau, Isabelle Huppert. D: Bertrand Blier. COM [R] 117m. v

Going Steady 1958 ★★½ A '50s social drama about teen marriage and its predictable consequences on young lives. Looks its age. C: Molly Bee, Bill Goodwin, Alan Reed, Jr. D: Fred Sears. DRA 90m. v

Going Undercover 1988 ★★ Dim-witted detective loses the heiress he's hired to protect during her European vacation. Witless romp. C: Chris Lemmon, Jean Simmons, Lea Thompson, Viveca Lindfors. D: James Kenelm Clarke. COM [PG-13] 90m. v

Gold 1974 British ★★★ Moore, between James Bond stints, plays the hero of this preposterous adventure tale concerning an evil plot to control worldwide gold prices by taking over a South African mine. Big and a bit silly, but with undeniably impressive action sequences. C: Roger Moore, Susannah York, Ray Milland, Bradford Dillman, John Gielgud. D: Peter Hunt. ACT [PG] 120m. v

Gold Diggers of Broadway 1929 ★★★ Early talkie tells musical tale of three small-town girls who join the chorus of a Broadway show while looking for husbands. Interesting antique. C: Nancy Welford, Conway Tearle, Winnie Lightner, Ann Pennington. D: Roy Del Ruth. MUS 105m.

Gold Diggers of 1933 1933 ★★★★½ Songwriter (Powell) struggles with disapproving wealthy family. Strong cast plays the funny script well. Busby Berkeley production numbers rank with his best: "The Shadow Waltz" with hundreds of violin-wielding dancers and "We're in the Money" with a chorus in Pig Latin. Spawned two sequels. C: Joan Blondell, Warren William, Ruby Keeler, Aline MacMahon, Ginger Rogers, Dick Powell, Guy Kibbee. D: Mervyn LeRoy. MUS 98m. v

Gold Diggers of 1935 1935 ★★★★ First musical directed entirely by Berkeley and second in the "Gold Diggers" series. Weak plot of romantic trystings in New England summer hotel, but big numbers deliver and one of them, "Lullaby of Broadway," (Oscar for Best Song) is Berkeley's best, an astounding tour de force of precision dancing with tragic overtones. C: Dick Powell, Adolphe Menjou, Gloria Stuart, Alice Brady, Glenda Farrell, Frank McHugh, Winifred Shaw. D: Busby Berkeley. MUS 95m.

Gold Diggers of 1937 1936 ★★★ Series winds down with weakest entry; Powell goes from selling insurance to producing Broadway show for his love (Blondell). Weak script and score; Berkeley seems almost to be repeating himself. C: Dick Powell, Joan Blondell, Glenda Farrell, Victor Moore. D: Lloyd Bacon. MUS 100m.

Gold Dust Gertie 1931 ★★★ Olsen and Johnson share a profession—bathing-suit sales reps—and an ex-wife eager to cash in on their salaries. Old-fashioned comedy. C: Ole Olsen, Chic Johnson, Winnie Lightner. D: Lloyd Bacon. COM 66m.

Gold for the Caesars 1964 French ★★ Pseudohistoric spaghetti epic about sweating slaves mining and transporting gold to Rome, with a muscle-bound cast and a handsome out-of-place American star (Hunter). More grist for the late-night B-movie mill. C: Jeffrey Hunter, Mylene Demongeot. D: Andre de Toth. DRA 86m.

Gold Is Where You Find It 1938 ★★★½ Miners drawn by Gold Rush strike pay dirt on California farmland, sparking violent feud. Pleasing Warners Western is aided by good cast and excellent color photography. C: George Brent, Olivia de Havilland, Claude Rains. D: Michael Curtiz. WST 90m.

Gold of Naples, The 1954 Italian ★★★★ Neorealist master De Sica skillfully directs four touching, amusing, and insightful vignettes depicting Neapolitan life. Mangano plays a streetwalker who benefits from a surprising marriage arrangement; Loren is a pizza maker's wife with a roving eye; Toto plays an ineffectual family man; and De Sica is a card shark who's duped by a young boy. The youthful Loren is especially wonderful. C: Sophia Loren, Vittorio De Sica, Toto, Silvana Mangano. D: Vittorio De Sica. DRA 107m.

Gold of the Amazon Women 1979 ★ Adventurerers try to plunder treasure of Amazon queen in contemporary South America. Garbage; sent '50s star Ekberg back into retirement. (a.k.a. *Amazon Women*) C: Bo Svenson, Anita Ekberg, Donald Pleasence. D: Mark L. Lester. ACT 94m. TVM v

Gold Raiders 1951 ★★ Weak Three Stooges Western comedy at less than their best. C: George O'Brien, Sheila Ryan. D: Edward Bernds. COM 56m.

Gold Rush Maisie 1940 ★★½ In the '40s Sothern was an enormous star based on her

Maisie series—her character was a tough cookie with a gooey soft center, and she was the archetypal American girl in the WWII era. Here the plucky poor girl looks for gold in Alaska. C: Ann Sothern, Lee Bowman, Virginia Weidler. D: Edwin Marin. ACT 82m.

Gold Rush, The 1925 ★★★★★ This enduring silent classic is one of the greatest comedies ever made. Chaplin's poignant Little Tramp bravely faces the rigors of the Klondike, while trying to win the heart of a dance-hall artiste. Legendary high points include the Tramp dining on a leather shoe, his dance with two bread rolls, and a cabin precariously poised to fall over a cliff. Not to be missed. C: Charlie Chaplin, Georgia Hale, Mack Swain. D: Charles Chaplin. COM 80m. V

Goldbergs, The 1950 ★★★½ Movie adaptation of the popular radio and TV show about the daily joys and pains of a Bronx family and its matriarch, Molly. Heartwarming and amusing with intimate ensemble playing. (a.k.a. *Molly*) C: Gertrude Berg, Philip Loeb, Eli Mintz, Betty Walker, David Opatoshu, Barbara Rush. D: Walter Hart. COM 83m.

Golden Age of Comedy, The 1957 ★★★★★ The lineup is peerless—Chaplin, Keystone Kops, Harry Langdon, Laurel and Hardy, among others—and hilarious clips follow suit in a hugely entertaining compilation of silent comedy's best moments. C: Stan Laurel, Oliver Hardy, Carole Lombard, Will Rogers. Compiled by Robert Youngson. COM 78m. V

Golden Arrow, The 1936 ★★★ Twist on *It Happened One Night* has phony heiress (Davis) involving a newspaper reporter (Brent) in a marriage of convenience. Light and pleasant. C: Bette Davis, George Brent, Eugene Pallette. D: Alfred Green. COM 68m.

Golden Blade, The 1953 ★★½ Fifties swashbuckler is a minor *Arabian Nights* tale of hero gaining a magic sword, using it to rescue princess from scheming revolutionaries. Typical of its period. C: Rock Hudson, Piper Laurie, Gene Evans. D: Nathan Juran. ACT 81m.

Golden Boy 1939 ★★★½ Poor violinist is forced to give up musical aspirations to become boxer. Hasn't aged well, but Holden in screen debut delivers great performance. Based on Clifford Odets' play. C: William Holden, Barbara Stanwyck, Adolphe Menjou, Lee J. Cobb. D: Rouben Mamoulian. DRA 99m. V

Golden Braid 1990 Australian ★★½ Womanizing watchmaker becomes obsessed almost to the point of insanity with a perfect braid of golden hair he finds hidden away in a drawer. Tedious Australian import has rich cinematography and spurts of unexpected humor, but it's slow going. C: Chris Haywood, Gosia Dobrowolska. D: Paul Cox. DRA 88m.

Golden Child, The 1986 ★★½ In this weak but popular adventure spoof, a pro kid-finder (Murphy) searches for an abducted child with supernatural powers. The oracular parrot (Murphy's guide) has all the good lines. C: Eddie Murphy, Charlotte Lewis, Charles Dance. D: Michael Ritchie. COM [PG-13] 93m. V

Golden Coach, The 1952 Italian ★★★★★ Magnani gives one of her finest performances as the leading lady of an acting troupe touring 18th-century Peru. Highly stylized, amorous comedy is one of the seminal films about the relationship between theater and real life. Renoir's startlingly vivid use of Technicolor, along with his antic direction, make this one of his most joyous movies. C: Anna Magnani, Dante Rino. D: Jean Renoir. COM 103m. V

Golden Demon 1953 Japanese ★★★★ A young man's love for a woman is thwarted by her arranged marriage to a wealthy suitor. Standard story line of this highly acclaimed epic is rescued by vivid portrayal of the power of greed and tradition in medieval Japan. C: Jun Negami, Fujiko Yamamoto. D: Koji Shima. DRA 95m. V

Golden Earrings 1947 ★★★½ Forced on audiences in its time, this is enjoyable, if lesser Dietrich fare. She plays a Gypsy who lends a hand to WWII spy (Milland) when he's hiding out from the enemy. Good mindless fun. C: Ray Milland, Marlene Dietrich. D: Mitchell Leisen. DRA 95m. V

Golden Eighties 1986 French ★★★★ Satirical and cynical musical of love and broken hearts takes place within the sterile milieu of an indoor shopping mall. Episodic development follows various characters through series of botched romances. Interesting, very funny black comedy. (a.k.a. *The Eighties* and *Window Shopping*) C: Delphine Seyrig, Miriam Boyer, Fanny Cottencon, Lio, Pascale Salkin. D: Chantal Akerman. MUS 90m. V

Golden Eye, The 1948 ★★½ Not one of Charlie Chan's stellar outings: weak mystery about played-out gold mine that's suddenly productive again. (a.k.a. *The Mystery of the Golden Eye* and *Charlie Chan and the Golden Eye*) C: Roland Winters, Victor Yung. D: William Beaudine. ACT 69m.

Golden Gate Murders, The 1979 ★★½ Character piece disguised as a slim murder mystery, about detective Janssen and nun York who determine that a priest's suicide was really murder. Good chemistry between the principals saves this average drama. C: David Janssen, Susannah York. D: Walter Grauman. ACT 104m.

Golden Gate 1993 ★★★ An FBI man (Dillon) drove Chen's father to suicide with investigation of his alleged Communist ties, but now he's falling in love with her, and his superior (Kirby) is not happy about it. Plodding but well-intentioned tale of '50s witchhunts. C: Matt Dillon, Joan Chen, Bruno Kirby, Tzi Mah. D: John Madden. DRA [R] 120m.

Golden Girl 1951 ★★★ True story of Civil War entertainer Lotte Crabtree makes fair vehicle for Gaynor. Lots of period songs like "Oh, Dem Golden Slippers." C: Mitzi Gaynor, Dale Robertson, Dennis Day. D: Lloyd Bacon. MUS 108m. V

Golden Gloves Story, The 1950 ★★½ Two fighters' lives are superficially examined through the prism of a championship boxing tournament. C: James Dunn, Dewey Martin. D: Felix Feist. DRA 76m.

Golden Goose, The 1972 ★★★ Weak animated retelling of Grimms' fairy tale about goose that lays golden eggs. Big surprise: Riches don't bring happiness. FAM/DRA 65m. V

Golden Hands of Kurigal 1949 ★★½ Cliffhanger serial isn't helped by reediting into a single film, as government agents battle crime fiend holding archaeologist hostage. C: Kirk Alyn, Rosemary Planche. D: Fred Brannon. ACT 100m.

Golden Harvest 1933 ★★½ A young farmer (Morris) makes good as a commodities trader in Chicago. Scenic but unremarkable drama. C: Richard Arlen, Chester Morris, Genevieve Tobin. D: Ralph Murphy. DRA 72m.

Golden Hawk, The 1952 ★★½ Caribbean swashbuckler details 17th-century alliance between England and Spain in their fight against France. Average Hayden vehicle features Fleming, unofficial queen of '50s adventure films. C: Rhonda Fleming, Sterling Hayden. D: Sidney Salkow. ACT 83m.

Golden Honeymoon, The 1980 ★★★ Set in 1920s Florida, an elderly married couple are momentarily pulled apart when the wife's former beau shows up. Adaptation of Ring Lardner's story is hosted by Henry Fonda. C: James Whitmore, Teresa Wright, Stephen Elliott, Nan Martin. D: Noel Black. DRA 52m. V

Golden Hoofs 1941 ★★★½ One for the whole family, about a young woman who trains horses and falls for a millionaire racehorse breeder. Happily ever after all around. C: Jane Withers, Charles Rogers, Katharine Aldridge. D: Lynn Shores. FAM/DRA 68m.

Golden Horde, The 1951 ★★½ Thirteenth-century Arabian story stands out because central adventurer is a woman (Blyth), who must repel barbarian hordes laying seige to her city. Average costumer. C: Ann Blyth, David Farrar, Richard Egan. D: George Sherman. ACT 77m.

Golden Idol, The 1954 ★★½ Bomba the Jungle Boy recovers a priceless relic. Mundane action. C: Johnny Sheffield, Anne Kimbell. D: Ford Beebe. ACT 71m.

Golden Lady, The 1979 ★★ Action mish-mash sends beautiful gang of women on international adventures of intrigue. Reminiscent of *Charlie's Angels*. C: Christina World, Suzanne Danielle. D: Joseph Larraz. ACT 90m. V

Golden Link, The 1954 British ★★★½ Police detective suspects his own daughter in murder of a neighbor. Okay for its kind. C: Andre Morrell, Thea Gregory, Patrick Holt. D: Charles Sanders. CRI 83m.

Golden Madonna, The 1949 British ★★★ American woman and artist set out to find a missing religious painting. Pleasing romantic comedy/drama, set in Italy. C: Phyllis Calvert, Michael Rennie. D: Ladislas Vajda. COM 88m.

Golden Marie 1956 *See* **Casque D'Or**

Golden Mask, The 1954 British ★★★ Adventurers in Egypt search for golden death mask in above-average action film. C: Van Heflin, Wanda Hendrix. D: Jack Lee. ACT 88m.

Golden Mistress, The 1954 ★ Hunting down voodoo killers: forgettable stuff. C: John Agar, Rosemarie Bowe. D: Joel Judge. ACT 82m.

Golden Needles 1974 ★★½ Assorted characters search for a golden statue bearing seven acupuncture needles with extraordinary powers. Rambling, unoriginal blend of spy thriller and martial arts. (a.k.a. *Chase for the Golden Needles, The*) C: Joe Baker, Elizabeth Ashley, Burgess Meredith, Ann Sothern. D: Robert Clouse. ACT [PG] 92m.

Golden Ninja Invasion ★★½ A fierce gang of ninjas runs wild in an attempt to conquer the world. Violent actioner. C: Leonard West, Stephanie Burd. ACT 90m. V

Golden Rendezvous 1977 ★★½ Gambling ship is captured by hijackers, who threaten to blow it up. Alistair MacLean's novel had much more suspense—and sense—than this. (a.k.a. *Nuclear Terror*) C: Richard Harris, Ann Turkel, David Janssen, Burgess Meredith. D: Ashley Lazarus. ACT 120m. V

Golden Salamander, The 1951 British ★★★½ Adventure story of an English archaeologist (Howard) searching Tunis for site of ancient ruins, but becoming involved with gunrunners and romance instead. Crisp actioner against impressive backdrop. C: Trevor Howard, Anouk Aimee, Herbert Lom. D: Ronald Neame. ACT 96m.

Golden Seal, The 1983 ★★★½ Young boy (Campbell) fights hunters to save the life of a rare golden seal and her pup in Aleutian Islands. Intense story may overwhelm or disturb younger children, but it's beautifully told and lovingly photographed, if rather slow-moving. C: Torquil Campbell, Steve Railsback, Michael Beck, Penelope Milford. D: Frank Zuniga. FAM/DRA [PG] 94m. V

Golden Stallion, The 1949 ★★★ Focus of this amiable Roy Rogers Western is on faithful horse Trigger, who falls in love with a palomino mare. Unbeknownst to both Roy and Trig, the beloved horse is carrying a secret. Two-and four-legged heroes triumph in this hokey but fun Western pleaser. C: Roy Rogers, Dale Evans, Pat Brady. D: William Witney. WST 67m. V

Golden Sun 1984 ★★★ Youthful kung fu enthusiast determines there's something fishy about Bruce Lee's death and sets out to uncover the real story, finding a disturbing conspiracy of silence. Well-done genre item is mainly of interest to kung fu and Lee fans, although the intriguing premise may entice a wider audience. C: Lei Hsiao Lung, Chen Pei Ling. ACT 83m. V

Golden Triangle 1980 ★★ Competing gangs of drug runners battle each other for turf dominance. Violent kung fu action. C: Lo Lieh, Sombat Metanee. D: Lee Lo. ACT 90m. V

Golden Voyage of Sinbad, The 1974 British ★★★★ Sinbad must overcome travails concocted by an evil magician in his quest for the Fountain of Destiny. Good clean fun for children of all ages. Ray Harryhausen (and Caroline Munro) fans will be delighted. Highlight: a magical sword fight. C: John Phillip Law, Caroline Munro, Tom Baker. D: Gordon Hessler. FAM/ACT [G] 104m. V

Golden West, The 1932 ★★★★ Sturdy and touching Zane Grey tale about man who tries to start anew out West. After his death, Indians raise his son. C: George O'Brien, Janet Chandler. D: David Howard. WST 74m.

Goldengirl 1979 ★★½ Anton plays a statuesque runner transformed into an Olympic track star by her scientist father's dangerous experimental drugs. Average fantasy, indifferently handled. C: Susan Anton, Curt Jurgens, Robert Culp, Leslie Caron. D: Joseph Sargent. DRA [PG] 104m. V

Goldenrod 1976 Canadian ★★½ Life and love on the rodeo circuit in Canada in the 1950s. Lo Bianco as crippled champ forced to raise his sons is a pleasure to watch, even if film is so-so. C: Tony LoBianco, Gloria Carlin, Donald Pleasence. D: Harvey Hart. DRA 99m. TVM V

Goldfinger 1964 British ★★★★½ Agent 007 (Connery) fights demented villain Goldfinger (Frobe) who plans to detonate a nuclear bomb inside Fort Knox. From Connery's suave portrayal to Shirly Bassey's hit title song, it's a spy classic. Watch out for Oddjob (Sakata) and his killer hat! C: Sean Connery, Gert Frobe, Honor Blackman, Shirley Eaton. D: Guy Hamilton. ACT [PG] 108m. V

Goldie and the Boxer 1980 ★★½ Runyanesque fodder in which a precocious little girl manages a pug boxer to a comeback. Hackneyed and sugarcoated. C: O.J. Simpson, Melissa Michaelsen, Vincent Gardenia. D: David Miller. DRA 104m. TVM

Goldie and the Boxer Go to Hollywood 1981 ★★★ More kid-centric adventures of charming, articulate little girl and her best friend, a punchy over-the-hill boxer. C: O.J. Simpson, Melissa Michaelsen. D: David Miller. DRA 104m. TVM

Goldstein 1965 ★★½ Strange early Kaufman film, about modern-day reincarnation of Biblical prophet Elijah, wandering the streets of Chicago. Oddball satire based on Martin Buber story, has interesting premise, but doesn't quite work. C: Philip Kaufman, Lou Gilbert, Ellen Madison. D: Benjamin Manaster. COM 85m.

Goldwyn Follies, The 1938 ★★ Disjointed, dismal revue of producer (Menjou) who hires Leeds to judge his work. Scenes of her overpraising mediocre musical numbers are unintentionally funny. Composer George Gershwin died during production, leaving two good songs: "Love Walked In" and "Our Love Is Here to Stay." C: Adolphe Menjou, Andrea Leeds, Kenny Baker, The Ritz Brothers, Vera Zorina, Bobby Clark, Edgar Bergen. D: George Marshall. MUS 115m. V

Golem, The 1937 Czech ★★★★ In 16th-century Prague ghetto, a rabbi creates a clay giant animated by magic to protect the Jews from persecution. But the monster runs amok and can only be overcome by an innocent child. This is Wegener's third *Golem* movie and his best. Expressionistic sets and atmospheric lighting make this a silent classic; influenced many later *Frankenstein* films. C: Paul Wegener. D: Paul Wegener. HOR 80m.

Golgotha 1937 French ★★★ Rarely seen film about the crucifixion of Christ, with dialogue taken verbatim from the New Testament. Film's respectful tone drew large audiences in the '30s, but seems a bit rigid today. C: Harry Baur, Robert Le Vigan, Jean Gabin. D: Julien Duvivier. DRA 97m.

Goliath Against the Giants 1961 Italian ★★½ Muscular leader does battle with evil politicians threatening his kingdom. Silly, comic book swords-and-sandals heroics. C: Brad Harris, Gloria Milland, Fernando Rey. D: Guido Malatesta. ACT 90m. V

Goliath and the Barbarians 1960 Italian ★★½ Rebel leader tries to save Italy as he fights ravaging enemies attacking from the Alps. Lots of bulging biceps and battles in minor spectacle. C: Steve Reeves, Bruce Cabot. D: Carlo Campogalliani. ACT 86m. V

Goliath and the Dragon 1960 Italian ★ Muscular hero endures numerous grueling tests to rescue his country from corrupt political leader. Ridiculous fantasy with awful special effects. C: Mark Forest, Broderick Crawford. D: Vittorio Cottafavi. ACT 87m. V

Goliath and the Vampires 1964 Italian ★★½ Young women are sold into slavery by a vampire ruler. Muscle-and-toga silliness with former Tarzan Scott and robotic monsters. C: Gordon Scott, Gianna Canale. D: Giacomo Gentilomo. ACT 91m. V

Goliath Awaits 1981 ★★ Explorers discover survivors trapped for over 40 years in a sunken ocean liner at the bottom of the sea. Incredible premise sinks this so-so adventure tale. C: Mark Harmon, Christopher Lee, Eddie Albert, John Carradine. D: Kevin Connor. ACT [PG] 110m. TVM V

Gomer Pyle U.S.M.C.—Vol. 1 ★★★ Two episodes from the hit TV series about a dim-witted Marine. Don Rickles guest stars in "My

Buddy—War Hero," while Larry Storch appears in "Wild Bull of Pampas." C: Jim Nabors, Frank Sutton. COM 50m. V

Gomer Pyle U.S.M.C.—Vol. 2 ★★★ Two episodes from the hit TV series about a dim-witted Marine. Jamie Farr guest stars in "Gomer Pyle, P.O.W.," and Pat Morita appears in "The Recruiting Poster." C: Jim Nabors, Frank Sutton. COM 50m. V

Gone Are the Days 1963 ★★★★ Satire of racial stereotypes and prejudices follows a Southern minister's attempts to overthrow a local plantation owner. Though somewhat dated, the satire still hits its mark and performances are wonderful. Based on Davis' Broadway comedy *Purlie Victorious.* C: Ossie Davis, Ruby Dee, Sorrell Booke, Godfrey Cambridge, Alan Alda. D: Nicholas Webster. COM 97m. V

Gone in 60 Seconds 1974 ★★★ An insurance adjuster/car thief is betrayed by his boss and finds himself on the lam with a hot car. Pretty threadbare, except for a spectacular car chase that lasts nearly half the film. Fun but no real story. C: H.B. Halicki, Marion Busia. D: H.B. Halicki. ACT [PG] 97m. V

Gone to Earth 1950 British ★★★ A simple, superstitious young Welsh woman marries a parson, but falls in love with a virile squire. Surprisingly condescending and unsophisticated for a Powell/Pressburger production. (a.k.a. *The Wild Heart*) C: Jennifer Jones, David Farrar, Cyril Cusack, Sybil Thorndike, Edward Chapman, George Cole, Hugh Griffith, Esmond Knight. D: Michael Powell, Emeric Pressburger. DRA 82m.

Gone with the West *See* **Little Moon & Jud McGraw**

Gone with the Wind 1939 ★★★★★ Hollywood entertainment on its grandest scale, adapted from Margret Mitchell's epic novel. Leigh is unforgettable as Scarlett, whose life swirls through the Civil War, Reconstruction, and Rhett Butler (Gable, of course), with superb supporting cast. Fleming received directorial credit, though George Cukor, Sam Wood, and William Cameron Menzies also worked on the David O. Selznick production. The burning of Atlanta and crane shot of wounded Confederate soldiers are iconic moments in American cinema. Won eight Oscars, including Best Picture, Director, Actress (Leigh), and Supporting Actress (McDaniel). C: Clark Gable, Vivien Leigh, Leslie Howard, Olivia de Havilland, Hattie McDaniel, Thomas Mitchell, Butterfly McQueen. D: Victor Fleming. DRA [G] 233m. V

Gong Show Movie, The 1980 ★ Success becomes too much for game show host Barris, unable to escape from the shadow of the infamous Gong Show. Only for the most devoted fans of that 1970's relic. C: Chuck Barris, Jaye P. Morgan, Jamie Farr, Rip Taylor. D: Chuck Barris. COM [R] 89m.

Gonza The Spearman 1986 Japanese ★★★★½ A samurai in 18th-Century Japan must go into exile to save the life of a woman with whom he is accused of having an affair. A powerful classic, beautifully photographed. C: Hiromi Goh, Shima Iwashita. D: Masahiro Shinoda. DRA 126m. V

Good-bye, My Lady 1956 ★★★½ Poor Mississippi farmboy finds and cares for a stray pedigreed dog he must eventually return to its rightful owners. Sentimental film, based on James Street's novel, is brightened by de Wilde's fine performance. C: Walter Brennan, Phil Harris, Brandon de Wilde, Sidney Poitier. D: William Wellman. FAM/DRA [G] 95m. V

Good Companions, The 1933 British ★★★★½ A collection of diverse misfits forms a stage troupe in this utterly magical comedy, from J.B. Priestley's novel. The warm glow of its humanity will keep you grinning long after it ends. Young Gielgud stands out in an expert cast. Remade in 1956. C: Jessie Matthews, Edmund Gwenn, John Gielgud, Finlay Currie. D: Victor Saville. COM 113m.

Good Companions, The 1956 British ★★★½ Musical remake of the 1933 film chronicling the plight of a second-rate theatrical troupe saved by the intervention of a musician, a wealthy benefactor and a young actress. More polished but not quite as entertaining as the original. C: Eric Portman, Celia Johnson, Hugh Griffith, Janette Scott, John Fraser, Joyce Grenfell, Rachel Roberts, Mona Washbourne, Alec McCowen, Anthony Newley. D: J. Thompson. MUS 104m.

Good Dame 1934 ★★ Grifter revels in low life until true love enters the picture. Good cast stymied by routine melodrama. (a.k.a. *Good Girl*) C: Fredric March, Sylvia Sidney, Jack LaRue. D: Marion Gering. DRA 74m.

Good Day for a Hanging 1958 ★★★½ Former lawman (MacMurray) is drafted to capture sheriff's murderer, only to have the townspeople refuse to pass sentence on the roguishly charming killer. Oddball Western tries hard to break out of genre conventions with some success. C: Fred MacMurray, Maggie Hayes, Robert Vaughn. D: Nathan Juran. WST 85m.

Good Day for Fighting *See* **Custer of the West**

Good Die Young, The 1954 British ★★★ Variation of *The Asphalt Jungle* concerns four problem-plagued strangers planning to rob cash-laden mail van. Climactic pursuit through London Underground is highlight. C: Laurence Harvey, Gloria Grahame, Richard Basehart, Margaret Leighton, Joan Collins. D: Lewis Gilbert. ACT 100m.

Good Dissonance Like a Man, A 1977 ★★★★ Fact and fiction blend in this biography of American avant-garde composer Charles Ives. Interesting filmmaking and good performances. C: John Bottoms, Richard Ramos, Sandra Kingsbury. D: Theodore W. Timreck. DRA 60m.

Good Earth, The 1937 ★★★★★ A Chinese farming family is devastated by greed in this faithful adaptation of Pearl S. Buck's classic novel. Rainer won her second consecutive Oscar as the indomitable O-lan; Freund's camerawork was also honored. Locust attack is one among many good special effects. C: Paul Muni, Luise Rainer, Walter Connolly, Jessie Ralph, Keye Luke. D: Sidney Franklin. DRA 138m. V

Good Fairy, The 1935 ★★★★½ Preston Sturges adapted Molnar's play for the screen, lending his sharp wit to this bubbly romantic comedy. The ever-charming Sullavan plays a do-gooder who tries to help up-and-coming lawyer (Marshall) rise to the top of his profession while she's being courted by a rich suitor (Morgan). A high point in '30s comedies. C: Margaret Sullavan, Herbert Marshall, Frank Morgan, Alan Hale, Beulah Bondi, Cesar Romero. D: William Wyler. COM 97m.

Good Father, The 1987 British ★★★★ Hopkins is brilliant as an angry, divorced middle-aged man who decides to get even with his wife for turning his son against him. Bitter look at the war between the sexes. C: Anthony Hopkins, Jim Broadbent, Harriet Walter. D: Mike Newell. DRA [R] 90m. V

Good Fight, The 1983 ★★★½ Well-crafted documentary about Americans fighting in anti-Franco forces during the Spanish Civil War. Interesting, resonant history. D: Mary Dore, Sam Sills, Noel Buckner. DOC 98m. V

Good Fight, The 1992 ★★★★ Standout TV movie concerns a dedicated legal professor (Lahti) who single-handedly battles a tobacco company after her son's closest pal is diagnosed with mouth cancer. Richly nuanced drama boasts an intelligent screenplay and powerful performances. C: Christine Lahti, Terry O'Quinn. D: John David Coles. DRA 91m. TVM V

Good Girl 1934 *See* **Good Dame**

Good Girls Go to Paris 1939 ★★★ Blondell is a waitress who sees the wealthy Curtis as her ticket to the City of Light, even though her heart still longs for professor Douglas. Standard B-movie comedy. C: Melvyn Douglas, Joan Blondell, Alan Curtis, Walter Connolly. D: Alexander Hall. COM 75m.

Good Guys and the Bad Guys, The 1969 ★★★ Formulaic Western comedy about lawman and outlaw who have been lifelong adversaries, but who are now over the hill. C: Robert Mitchum, George Kennedy, David Carradine, Tina Louise, Martin Balsam, John Carradine. D: Burt Kennedy. WST [PG] 91m. V

Good Guys Wear Black 1979 ★★½ Wronged Vietnam platoon leader (Norris) kicks and punches Washington bureaucrats to get at truth. Some good fight scenes keep it going. C: Chuck Norris, Anne Archer, James Franciscus, Dana Andrews, Jim Backus. D: Ted Post. ACT [PG] 96m. V

Good Humor Man, The 1950 ★★★½ Hapless ice cream vendor (Carson) accidentally involved in a holdup is pursued by both police and crooks. He's rescued by kids in the Captain Marvel Club. Good sight gags and swift pace make it enjoyable. C: Jack Carson, Lola Albright, Jean Wallace. D: Lloyd Bacon. COM 79m. V

Good Idea 1975 *See* **It Seemed Like a Good Idea at the Time**

Good Luck, Miss Wyckoff 1979 ★ An innocent schoolteacher is raped in this grim adaptation of William Inge's novel. (a.k.a. *The Sin, The Shaming* and *Secret Yearnings*) C: Anne Heywood, Donald Pleasence, Robert Vaughn, Carolyn Jones, Dorothy Malone. D: Marvin Chomsky. DRA [R] 105m. V

Good Man in Africa, A 1994 ★★ An African presidential candidate (Gossett, Jr.) with British support insists on the murder of a Scottish doctor (Connery). Goofball comedy/drama is a sad misfire for the director of *Driving Miss Daisy*. C: Sean Connery, Louis Gossett, Jr., Diana Rigg. D: Bruce Beresford. COM [R] 95m.

Good Morning, Babylon 1987 Italian ★★★½ Two brothers from Tuscany, stonemasons, come to Hollywood to work on D.W. Griffith's *Intolerance*. Taviani brothers lost their grip in this, their first film in English, even though familiar elements such as magical realism are employed to tell the story. C: Vittorio Taviani, Vincent Spano, Joaquim De Almeida, Greta Scacchi. D: Paolo Taviani. DRA [PG-13] 113m. V

Good Morning, Miss Dove 1955 ★★★½ Sentimental drama about ailing spinster school marm (Jones) whose years of nurturing generations of students are revealed via flashbacks. Although it drips with nostalgia, the emotion is legitimately earned by inspirational story and strong acting throughout. C: Jennifer Jones, Robert Stack, Kipp Hamilton, Chuck Connors, Mary Wickes. D: Henry Koster. DRA 107m.

Good Morning, Vietnam 1988 ★★★★ Williams plays an Armed Forces Radio disk jockey (based on real-life deejay Adrian Cronauer), entertaining troops in Vietnam war zone, circa 1966. Running on sheer adrenaline, Williams' radio comedy is fantastic. C: Robin Williams, Forest Whitaker, Bruno Kirby, Robert Wuhl. D: Barry Levinson. COM [R] 121m. V

Good Morning 1959 Japanese ★★★ Two boys who are admonished to "shut up" after badgering their parents for a TV quite literally refuse to say a word, even "good morning" to their neighbors, which puts neighborhood in an uproar. One of Ozu's most engaging and accessible movies; contains a highly scatological running gag. C: Chishu Ryu, Kuniko Miyake, Masahiko Shimazu, Koji Shidara. D: Yasujiro Ozu. COM 97m.

Good Mother, The 1988 ★★★½ A divorced mother finds misunderstanding along with sexual fulfillment, and must fight for custody of her eight-year-old daughter. Provocative emotional drama. C: Diane Keaton, Liam Neeson, Jason Robards, Ralph Bellamy, Teresa Wright. D: Leonard Nimoy. DRA [R] 106m. v

Good Neighbor Sam 1964 ★★★½ Overlong farce almost saved by Lemmon as married advertising exec pretending to be the husband of a neighbor (Schneider) so she can inherit money. Starts out well, then becomes labored. C: Jack Lemmon, Romy Schneider, Edward G. Robinson, Dorothy Provine. D: David Swift. COM 130m. v

Good News 1930 ★★★ Popular '20s Broadway musical first hit the screen as this stage-bound early talkie. Collegiate plot follows academic troubles of the star quarterback and romantic problems of everybody else. Full of appealing corny innocence and evergreen songs like "Varsity Drag" and "The Best Things in Life Are Free." Remade in 1947. C: Mary Lawlor, Stanley Smith, Bessie Love, Cliff Edwards. D: Nick Grinde, Edgar J. MacGregor. MUS 78m.

Good News 1947 ★★★★½ Second version of '20s campus musical is the cat's meow with clever, funny Comden and Green script, sparkling score and dazzling choreography. Story has Allyson coaching football star Lawford in French so he can score big with vain gold-digger Marshall. Too modest to be a classic musical, just a delicious one. C: June Allyson, Peter Lawford, Joan McCracken, Patricia Marshall, Mel Torme. D: Charles Walters. MUS 95m. v

Good Old Schooldays 1940 *See* **Those Were the Days**

Good Sam 1948 ★★½ The philanthropy of a too-generous department store manager (Cooper) threatens his family's pocketbook and irritates his wife (Sheridan) who wants to build a new house. Some amusing moments. C: Gary Cooper, Ann Sheridan, Ray Collins, Edmund Lowe. D: Leo McCarey. COM 116m. v

Good Soldier Schweik, The 1963 German ★★★★ Satire about military life centers on German draftee during WWI who is nearly killed by his own side. Strong adaptation of a classic Czech novel. C: Heinz Ruhmann, Ernst Stankowski, Ursula Borsodi, Senta Berger. D: Axel Von Ambesser. COM 98m.

Good Son, The 1993 ★★★ Reworking of *The Bad Seed*, about an innocent-looking lad (Culkin) with a taste for violence. Not far enough from today's headlines to be really interesting. C: Macaulay Culkin, Elijah Wood, Wendy Crewson, David Morse. D: Joseph Ruben. DRA [R] 100m. v

Good Sport, A 1984 ★★★½ Low-wattage revamp of *Woman of the Year*, with a sportswriter falling for a chic fashion reporter. Easy-going entertainment. C: Lee Remick, Ralph Waite, Janie Sell, Sam Gray. D: Lou Antonio. COM 104m.

Good, the Bad, and the Ugly, The 1967 Italian ★★★★½ Sequel to Leone's great *A Fistful of Dollars* and *For a Few Dollars More* achieves almost mythic quality as three gunslingers (Eastwood, Wallach, and Van Cleef) search for Civil War gold. Memorable Morricone score was whistled for a generation. C: Clint Eastwood, Lee Van Cleef, Eli Wallach. D: Sergio Leone. WST [R] 161m. v

Good Time Girl 1950 British ★★ Mediocre morality play about modern teen headed down the wrong path until judge tells her a parable. C: Jean Kent, Dennis Price, Herbert Lom, Flora Robson. D: David MacDonald. DRA 81m.

Good Times 1967 ★★★★ Cheery little musical casts Sonny and Cher as themselves, about to make their first movie, acting out Sonny's fantasies of roles they could play. Somewhat in the style of their old TV series, but better. First movie for both Cher and Friedkin. C: Sonny Bono, Cher, George Sanders, Norman Alden. D: William Friedkin. MUS [PG] 91m.

Good to Go 1986 ★★½ A gullible journalist (Garfunkel) is suspected by a police officer bent on capturing a go-go concert murderer. Go-go groups Trouble Funk and Redds & the Boys easily steal the show. (a.k.a. *Short Fuse*) C: Art Garfunkel, Robert Doqui, Harris Yulin, Anjelica Haston. D: Blaine Novak. CRI [R] 87m. v

Good Wife, The 1986 Australian ★★★½ When Neill moves to a small Australian town, Ward eschews her husband for her obsession with the newcomer. Slow-starting drama gets better as it goes; boosted by excellent cast. (a.k.a. *The Umbrella Woman*) C: Rachel Ward, Bryan Brown, Sam Neill. D: Ken Cameron. DRA [R] 92m. v

Goodbye Again 1961 ★★★½ Lush soap opera about a wealthy decorator (Bergman) involved with a much-younger man (Perkins). Still, her heart is set on Montand, a man of her own age and means. Well-acted Françoise Sagan story becomes a real tearjerker about heartache amidst the upper classes in Paris. C: Ingrid Bergman, Anthony Perkins, Yves Montand, Jessie Royce Landis, Diahann Carroll. D: Anatole Litvak. DRA 120m. v

Goodbye Bird, The 1993 ★★★ When a young boy is accused of stealing his school principal's parrot, he must clear his name and find the talkative bird. Good children's fare. C: Cindy Pickett, Christopher Pettiet, Conceita Tomei, Wayne Rogers. D: William Clark. DRA 91m. v

Goodbye Bruce Lee 1982 ★★★ Tribute to the Kung Fu master combines intimate, behind-the-scenes footage along with Lee's last, unfinished action film. C: Bruce Lee. ACT [R] 83m. v

Goodbye Charlie 1964 ★★ Film version of George Axelrod's Broadway play concerns a skirt-chasing mobster named Charlie who dies and is reincarnated as a woman (Reynolds). Plenty of talent on hand, but everyone seems lost. C: Debbie Reynolds, Tony Curtis, Pat Boone, Walter Matthau. D: Vincente Minnelli. COM 117m.

Goodbye, Columbus 1969 ★★★★ Well-directed comedy (from Philip Roth novel) made stars of MacGraw and Benjamin. Poor but bright boy meets Jewish-American princess and they fall in love, over objections of her snobbish parents. Bittersweet coming-of-age film with some very funny moments, including the supermarket check-out scene. C: Richard Benjamin, Ali MacGraw, Jack Klugman. D: Larry Peerce. COM [PG] 105m. V

Goodbye Cruel World 1982 ★★★ Shawn plays a TV anchor who, before committing suicide, films his crazy relatives who drove him to the brink. Funny, offbeat fare. C: Dick Shawn. D: David Irving. COM [R] 90m. V

Goodbye, Franklin High 1978 ★★★ Jock with female and family problems tries to get through an eventful senior year and face the future. Standard but naively engaging. C: Lane Caudell, Ann Dusenberry, Darby Hinton. D: Mike MacFarland. DRA [PG] 94m.

Goodbye Girl, The 1977 ★★★★ Mason is a twice-deserted single mother who reluctantly takes oddball actor Dreyfuss (in an Oscar-winning performance) as roommate. Barbs fly in typical Neil Simon fashion, but somewhere along the way an old-fashioned, teary-eyed romance manages to shine through. C: Richard Dreyfuss, Marsha Mason, Quinn Cummings, Paul Benedict. D: Herbert Ross. COM [PG] 110m. V

Goodbye, Miss 4th of July 1993 ★★★ True-life story of a young Greek immigrant (played by talented Zal) in pre-WWI West Virginia who becomes a heroine during Spanish flu pandemic. Well-meaning but so-so drama. C: Roxana Zal, Louis Gossett, Jr., Chris Sarandon. D: George Miller. FAM/DRA 89m. TVM V

Goodbye, Mr. Chips 1939 U.S. ★★★★★ Donat won the Best Actor Oscar as a reserved British schoolmaster finally finding love with Garson in this marvelous filming of James Hilton's novel. Climactic scene with the boys is a classic example of honorable "heart-tugging." Remade as a musical in 1969. C: Robert Donat, Greer Garson, Paul Henreid, Terry Kilburn, John Mills. D: Sam Wood. DRA 115m. V

Goodbye, Mr. Chips 1969 ★★★½ Flawed remake of classic 1939 film with O'Toole giving one of his best performances as revered schoolteacher in British boys' school. Addition of weak interior monologue songs is a mistake, but Clark is touching as music hall singer, later Mrs. Chips. C: Peter O'Toole, Petula Clark, Michael Redgrave, Sian Phillips. D: Herbert Ross. MUS [G] 151m. V

Goodbye, My Fancy 1951 ★★★ Crawford plays the political career woman in this tepid tale of congresswoman who rekindles romance with former lover when she returns to her college alma mater to receive honorary degree. An intrepid reporter smells scandal, but audience senses soap. C: Joan Crawford, Robert Young, Eve Arden. D: Vincent Sherman. DRA 107m.

Goodbye, New York 1984 U.S. ★★★½ Romance of vacationing American (Hagerty) who is stranded in Israel, joins a kibbutz, and falls in love with Israeli soldier. Unusual locations and charming treatment lift it above norm. C: Julie Hagerty, Amos Kollek. D: Amos Kollek. COM 90m. V

Goodbye, Norma Jean 1975 ★ Exploitative, highly fictionalized, oversexed biography of Marilyn Monroe. Later recut, revised and released as under *Goodbye, Sweet Marilyn.* Tasteless trash. Nudity. C: Misty Rowe, Terence Locke. D: Larry Buchanan. DRA [R] 95m.

Goodbye People, The 1986 ★★★ Strange film about a hot dog vendor (Balsam) who is driven to rebuild his old Coney Island stand. Reed, as his daughter, and Hirsch, as the man who comes into her life, are excellent. Sentimental, offbeat drama. C: Judd Hirsch, Martin Balsam, Pamela Reed, Ron Silver. D: Herb Gardner. DRA [PG] 104m. V

Goodbye Pork Pie 1981 New Zealand ★★★½ Road movie has two mismatched men stealing a car and hitting the highway for adventure while police pursue them. Interesting locations and laid-back attitude make for an enjoyable ride. C: Kelly Johnson, Tony Barry. D: Geoff Murphy. COM [R] 105m. V

GoodFellas 1990 ★★★★½ Scorsese's playful, knowing, and ultraviolent look at the daily life of a hood revolves around ambitious young crook (Liotta) and his rise in the mob. Faithfully rendered period detail, brilliant acting, hyperkinetic direction and mordant, funny script: Pesci won Oscar for Supporting Actor. C: Robert De Niro, Ray Liotta, Joe Pesci, Lorraine Bracco, Paul Sorvino. D: Martin Scorsese. CRI [R] 146m. V

Goodnight God Bless 1987 ★★½ A child who recognizes the face of a murdering psychopath becomes his next target. C: Emma Sutton, Frank Rozelaar Green, Jared Morgan. D: John Eyres. HOR [R] 90m.

Goodnight, Ladies and Gentlemen 1977 Italian ★★★½ Omnibus film strings together several short segments satirizing Italian life, political and otherwise. Somewhat hit-or-miss. C: Senta Berger, Adolfo Celi, Vittorio Gassman, Nino Manfredi, Marcello Mastroianni, Ugo Tognazzi. D: Leo Benvenuti, Luigi Comencini, Piero De Bernardi, Nanni Loy. COM 119m.

Goodnight, My Love 1972 ★★★★ Worthy effort at emulating '40s film noir, with Boone in top form as cynically idealistic private eye. C: Richard Boone, Barbara Bain. D: Peter Hyams. CRI 73m. TVM

Goodnight, Sweet Marilyn 1989 ★★½ Another hypothesis on Marilyn Monroe's death; this one suggests it was a possible mercy killing. C: Paula Lane, Jeremy Slate, Misty Rowe. D: Larry Buchanan. DRA [R] 100m. V

Goof Balls 1987 ★★½ Antics abound in this story of a golf course resort and the wacky director who runs it. C: Ben Gordon, Ron James, John Kozak. D: Brad Turner. COM 89m. V

Goonies, The 1985 ★★★½ A group of misfit children embark on a dangerous adventure to recover hidden treasure. Fast-paced, diverting, but ultimately exhausting kiddie action film; from a story by Steven Spielberg. C: Sean Astin, Josh Brolin, Corey Feldman, Martha Plimpton. D: Richard Donner. ACT [PG] 114m. V

Goose and the Gander, The 1935 ★★½ Slim story about divorcée obsessed with the life of her ex-spouse. C: Kay Francis, George Brent, Genevieve Tobin. D: Alfred Green. DRA 65m.

Goose Girl, The 1967 German ★★★ Adaptation of Grimms' fairy tale about a princess forced to change places with her servant. Would be great for kids, except for the beheading of a horse midway through. C: Rita-Maria Nowotny, Fritz Genschow, Renee Stobrawa, Renate Fischer, Theodor Vogeler. D: Fritz Genschow. DRA 78m.

Gor 1988 ★★★ Cowardly professor is transported to the land of Gor where he does battle with brutal villains. Tired sword-and-sorcery tale, inspired by series of Edgar Rice Burroughs stories, can boast loony performance by Reed. Sequel (*Outlaw of Gor*) features bigger role for Palance. C: Urbano Barbarini, Oliver Reed, Rebecca Ferratti, Jack Palance. D: Fritz Kiersch. SFI 95m. V

Gorath 1963 ★★½ A molten lava meteor is racing through space on a collision course with Earth and scientists have little time to stop it. C: Ryo Ikebe, Akihiko Hirata. D: Inoshiro Honda. SFI 77m. V

Gordon's War 1973 ★★★½ Returning Vietnam vet wages war against Harlem pushers responsible for drug-related death of his wife. Okay vigilante drama with evocative locations. C: Paul Winfield, Carl Lee. D: Ossie Davis. CRI [R] 89m. V

Gore Vidal's Billy the Kid 1989 ★★★★ The roots of the legendary gunslinger get the Vidal treatment in this entertaining western, highlighted by Kilmer's charismatic performance. C: Val Kilmer, Duncan Reghr, Wilford Brimley, Michael Parks, Julie Carmen. D: William A. Graham. WST 100m. TVM V

Gore Vidal's Lincoln 1988 ★★★★½ Masterful TV adaptation of Vidal's long novel spanning Lincoln's White House tenure. Waterson, as Lincoln, and Moore, as his wife, are touchingly human and sympathetic. Heavy but palatable dose of U.S. history. C: Sam Waterston, Mary Tyler Moore, John Houseman, Ruby Dee, Cleavon Little. D: Lamont Johnson. DRA 200m. TVM

Gorgeous Hussy, The 1936 ★★★ Fanciful biography of Peggy Eaton, a controversial figure during Andrew Jackson's administration. Long on sumptuous sets, wardrobe; short on just about everything else. C: Joan Crawford, Robert Taylor, Franchot Tone, Lionel Barrymore, Melvyn Douglas, James Stewart. D: Clarence Brown. DRA 102m. V

Gorgo 1961 British ★★★ Londoners think they're on to something big when they display a large baby sea monster in a circus—until its enormous mother comes to rescue it. Good special effects. Seeing London ravaged by a beast is a nice change. C: Bill Travers, William Sylvester, Vincent Winter. D: Eugene Lourie. SFI 78m. V

Gorgon, The 1964 British ★★★ Living as ordinary villager by day, woman transforms into legendary creature at night, turning those who gaze upon her into stone. Above-average Hammer production. C: Peter Cushing, Christopher Lee, Barbara Shelley. D: Terence Fisher. HOR 83m. V

Gorilla at Large 1954 ★★★★ Murders occur at a tawdry amusement park, and at first it's hard to tell whether a man or a monkey is guilty. Unusual and engrossing mystery, with a killer cast that makes the proceedings believable. C: Cameron Mitchell, Anne Bancroft, Lee J. Cobb, Raymond Burr, Lee Marvin. D: Harmon Jones. DRA 84m.

Gorilla Man, The 1942 ★★½ A flimsy espionage tale set among RAF pilots during World War II, in which Nazi sympathizers attempt to frame a pilot for a series of murders. The title makes no sense. C: John Loder, Ruth Ford. D: D. Lederman. ACT 64m.

Gorilla, The 1939 ★★ The old "the gorilla did it" horror comedy about two dim-witted detectives (The Ritz Brothers) trying to find a murderer in a haunted house owned by Lugosi. Third film version of popular story. C: The Ritz Brothers, Anita Louise, Patsy Kelly, Lionel Atwill, Bela Lugosi. D: Allan Dwan. COM 66m. V

Gorillas in the Mist 1988 ★★★★ The true story of Dian Fossey (Weaver), a naturalist whose efforts on behalf of African mountain gorillas turned to tragedy. Beautifully filmed, with an impressive Weaver. Memorable adventure. C: Sigourney Weaver, Bryan Brown, Julie Harris. D: Michael Apted. DRA [PG-13] 129m. V

Gorky Park 1983 ★★★★ The more Moscow policeman (Hurt) looks into a grisly triple murder, the more he meets resistance. Suspenseful mystery captures the frustrations of an honest cop up against government and business. Based on novel by Martin Cruz Smith. C: William Hurt, Lee Marvin, Brian Dennehy, Joanna Pacula. D: Michael Apted. CRI [R] 127m. V

Gorp 1980 ★★ Summer camp comedy with strong whiffs of drug humor. Not nearly as funny as it thinks it is. C: Michael Lembeck, Dennis Quaid, Philip Casnoff, Rosanna Arquette. D: Joseph Ruben. COM [R] 91m. V

Gospel 1982 ★★★★ Straightforward concert film, starring many top gospel music performers, will leave viewers filled with emotion. D: David Leivick, Frederick Ritzenberg. MUS 92m. V

Gospel According to St. Matthew 1966 Italian ★★★★★ Christ's life is told with striking documentary-like realism, and is strangely respectful coming from a director notorious for radical politics and atheism. Cast of nonprofessional actors adds authenticity. The Virgin Mary is played by Pasolini's mother. C: Enrique Irazoqui, Marcello Morante. D: Pier Paolo Pasolini. DRA 134m. V

Gospel According to Vic, The 1986 British ★★★½ Light comedy about a Catholic school teacher (Conti) who survives a nasty fall. Was it a miracle? Minor but enjoyable. (a.k.a. *Heavenly Pursuits*) C: Tom Conti, Helen Mirren, David Hayman. D: Charles Gormley. COM [PG-13] 92m. V

Gospel Road, The 1973 ★★ Cash tells his own version of the Christ story, country style. Heartfelt but dreary. C: Johnny Cash, June Carter. D: Robert Elfstrom. MUS [G] 62m. V

Gossip Columnist, The 1980 ★★★½ Sordid Hollywood fantasy about gossip columnist who gets the dirt on ambitious movie mogul with political aspirations. Raye a standout. C: Kim Cattrall, Bobby Vinton, Robert Vaughn, Martha Raye. D: James Sheldon. DRA 104m. TVM

Gotcha! 1985 ★★½ Young American college student, studying in Europe, gets involved with an older woman and some tough German spies. Medium spy caper shows some spunk. C: Anthony Edwards, Linda Fiorentino. D: Jeff Kanew. COM [PG-13] 97m. V

Gotham 1988 ★★★½ Detective (Jones) is hired by a rich man to end harassment from his deceased wife (Madsen)—who has reappeared as a ghost. Offbeat, supernatural detective saga is uneven but funny. C: Tommy Lee Jones, Virginia Madsen, Frederic Forrest. D: Lloyd Fonvielle. CRI [R] 93m. TVM V

Gothic 1987 British ★★★ Hallucinatory exploration of the debauchery and nightmares at the gathering of Lord Byron's Swiss villa that inspired Mary Shelley to write *Frankenstein*. Deliriously overwrought but great fun for Russell fans. C: Gabriel Byrne, Julian Sands, Natasha Richardson. D: Ken Russell. HOR [R] 87m. V

Government Agents vs. Phantom Legion 1992 ★★★ There's much at stake when an FBI agent chases a group of criminals hijaking uraniaum. Twelve episodes of series. C: Walter Reed, Mary Ellen Kay, Dick Curtis. ACT 167m. V

Government Girl 1943 ★★★ Government neophyte (Tufts), hired to hasten wartime bomber program, is guided through the bureaucracy by savvy War Department secretary (de Havilland). Directed by screenwriter of the screwball *Bringing Up Baby*. C: Olivia de Havilland, Sonny Tufts, Anne Shirley, Agnes Moorehead. D: Dudley Nichols. COM 94m.

Grace Kelly 1983 ★★½ Wooden film biography of movie star who became real-life princess. Sanctioned by the family, so it's antiseptically tame. C: Cheryl Ladd, Lloyd Bridges, Diane Ladd. D: Anthony Page. DRA 100m. TVM

Grace Quigley 1985 ★★★ Duo of carefree killers (Hepburn and Nolte) murder depressed senior citizens. Potentially daring black comedy. (a.k.a. *Ultimate Solution of Grace Quigley, The*). C: Katharine Hepburn, Nick Nolte. D: Anthony Harvey. COM [PG] 88m. V

Gracie Allen Murder Case, The 1939 ★★★ The original airhead Allen (sans George Burns) plays herself as she helps detective Philo Vance solve the mystery behind a convict's murder. Of course she's more of a hindrance than a help, and that's where the screwball antics come in. Fluffy comic mystery vehicle for the incomparable Gracie. C: Gracie Allen, Warren William, Ellen Drew, William Demarest, H.B. Warner. D: Alfred Green. COM 74m.

Grad Night 1980 ★★ Mindless teen comedy, with jokes based on sex, drinking, and vandalism. C: Joe Johnson, Barry Stoltze. D: John Tenorio. COM [R] 85m. V

Graduate, The 1967 ★★★★★ Sixties romantic comedy classic. Aimless young man, just out of college, is seduced by a middle-aged family friend. Then it gets worse: He falls in love with her daughter. The film made Hoffman a star and won Nichols the Best Director Oscar; Simon & Garfunkel score still sells. C: Anne Bancroft, Dustin Hoffman, Katharine Ross, Murray Hamilton, William Daniels. D: Mike Nichols. COM [PG] 105m. V

Graduation Day 1981 ★ More sequential slaughter of students, this time a high school track team. No scares, just a lot of lethal new uses for athletic equipment. Game-show queen Vanna White has an early acting role. C: Christopher George, Patch Mackenzie, Michael Pataki, Vanna White. D: Herb Freed. HOR [R] 85m. V

Graffiti Bridge 1990 ★★ Sequel to *Purple Rain* has preposterous plot involving an angel. Great soundtrack. C: Prince, Morris Day, Jill Jones. D: Prince. MUS [PG-13] 91m. V

Grambling's White Tiger 1981 ★★½ True

story of white high school quarterback Jim Gregory (Jenner), who enrolls at African-American college seeking a pro football career. Tepid TV-movie hobbled by Olympian Jenner's "acting." Belafonte generates some sparks as coach Eddie Robinson though. C: Bruce Jenner, Harry Belafonte, LeVar Burton, Ray Vitte. D: George Stanford Brown. DRA 98m. TVM V

Grand Canyon 1991 ★★★ In L.A., a disparate group of men and women find common links. Serious contemporary soul searchings; a noble (if ponderous) effort. C: Kevin Kline, Danny Glover, Steve Martin, Mary McDonnell, Mary-Louise Parker, Alfre Woodard. D: Lawrence Kasdan. DRA [R] 134m. V

Grand Central Murder 1942 ★★★ Mystery about an heiress murdered on a private train car and the private eye who seeks her killer. C: Van Heflin, Patricia Dane, Cecilia Parker. D: S. Simon. CRI 73m.

Grand Duel, The 1972 Italian ★★½ A man unjustly charged with murder is protected by an enigmatic gunslinger. Standard, economical spaghetti Western. C: Lee Van Cleef, Peter O'Brian, Marc Mazza. D: Giancarlo Santi. WST [R] 92m.

Grand Highway, The *See* **Le Grand Chemin**

Grand Hotel 1932 ★★★★★ Star-laden melodrama highlighting Garbo as a ballet dancer romanced by jewel thief Barrymore; Crawford as a stenographer with big ideas; and Beery as an overbearing business magnate. Glamorous, influential film won Best Picture Oscar; served as basis for Broadway musical decades later. C: Greta Garbo, John Barrymore, Joan Crawford, Wallace Beery, Lionel Barrymore, Lewis Stone, Jean Hersholt. D: Edmund Goulding. DRA 113m. V

Grand Illusion 1937 French ★★★★★ Poignant examination of the horrors of WWI and of the honor that bound the officers of both sides. Features one of director von Stroheim's most memorable and nuanced performances as a German commandant. Not to be missed. C: Jean Gabin, Pierre Fresnay, Erich von Stroheim. D: Jean Renoir. DRA 111m. V

Grand Isle 1992 ★★★ A 19th-century woman spends an eventful summer in Louisiana and learns a lot about herself. Pretty scenery, sensitive drama. C: Kelly McGillis, Adrian Pasdar, Julian Sands, Ellen Burstyn. D: Mary Lambert. DRA 94m. TVM V

Grand Jury 1977 ★★½ Married couple become dupes in insurance scam. Dull pickings. C: Bruce Davison, Meredith MacRae, Leslie Nielsen. D: Christopher Cain. DRA 100m.

Grand Maneuver, The 1956 French ★★★★½ A Frenchman bets he can seduce a local woman before he leaves for the army, then winds up falling in love. Atmospheric, beautifully rendered romance. (a.k.a. *Les Grands Manoevres*) C: Michele Morgan, Gerard Philipe, Brigitte Bardot, Yves Robert. D: Rene Clair. DRA 104m.

Grand National Night 1953 British ★★½ Upper-crust murder mystery in Great Britain makes dry going. C: Nigel Patrick, Moira Lister, Michael Hordern. D: Bob McNaught. ACT 81m.

Grand Prix 1966 ★★★½ Film follows the cars and loves of racers on the grand prix circuit. Oscars for trend-setting editing and sound. Plenty of noise. C: James Garner, Eva Marie Saint, Yves Montand, Toshiro Mifune. D: John Frankenheimer. ACT 171m. V

Grand Slam 1933 ★★★½ Humorous satire ridiculing the '30s bridge craze has Lucas as a Russian waiter snared into making a fourth during a tournament and promptly proving himself an expert at the game. C: Loretta Young, Paul Lukas, Frank McHugh, Glenda Farrell. D: William Dieterle. COM 67m.

Grand Slam 1968 Italian ★★★½ Entertaining diamond-heist caper throws together a college professor and a gangster who attempt to pull off the perfect crime. Intriguing and suspenseful, with solid international cast. C: Edward G. Robinson, Janet Leigh, Klaus Kinski. D: Giuliano Montaldo. ACT 120m.

Grand Theft Auto 1977 ★★★ Mediocre comedy marks Howard's directorial bow as he and heiress bride are pursued all over L.A. Too many chases and car crashes, but modestly satisfying for genre fans. Howard also co-scripted. C: Ron Howard, Nancy Morgan, Marion Ross. D: Ron Howard. COM [PG] 84m. V

Grand Tour 1992 *See* **Disaster in Time**

Grandma's Boy 1922 ★★★★ Silent comedy charmer of cowardly young man (Lloyd) inspired by tales of heroic grandfather to stand up for his honor. Farce is still funny. It was pasty-faced comedian's first big hit. C: Harold Lloyd, Mildred Davis, Anna Townsend. D: Fred Newmeyer. COM 81m.

Grandma's House 1988 ★★★ Two orphaned adolescents go to live with grandparents, who have a very, very dark side. Okay thriller overcomes familiar ground with original moments. (a.k.a. *Grandmother's House*) C: Eric Foster, Kim Valentine, Ida Lee, Brinke Stevens. D: Peter Rader. DRA [R] 90m. V

Grandmother's House 1988 *See* **Grandma's House**

Grandpa ★★★★ Young Emily learns about living from her grandfather's life and death. Lovely animated short combines graceful visuals, good music—featuring boys' choir—and Peter Ustinov's unique voice as Granpa. FAM/DRA

Grandview, U.S.A. 1984 ★★½ Curtis, a sexy older woman who operates a demolition derby in a small town, becomes attracted to teenager Howell, causing a rift with boyfriend Swayze. Coming-of-age film with lots of adolescent angst and color. C: Jamie Lee Curtis, C. Thomas Howell, Patrick Swayze, Jennifer Jason Leigh, Troy Donahue. D: Randal Kleiser. DRA [R] 97m. V

Grapes of Wrath, The 1940 ★★★★★ Superb adaptation of John Steinbeck's novel about Depression-era Oklahoma dust bowl farmers seeking a better life in California. Oscars for Ford and Darwell as Ma Joad. Fonda's closing speech is unforgettable. Gritty cinematography adds to film's haunting story. Not to be missed. C: Henry Fonda, Jane Darwell, John Carradine, Charley Grapewin, Doris Bowden. D: John Ford. DRA 128m. V

Grass 1925 ★★★★ Cooper and Schoedsack, the adventurous makers of *King Kong*, began their careers making documentaries, and this one is excellent. Here they follow the nomadic Iranian Bakhityari tribe on their annual trek in search of pastures for their herds. Fascinating, beautifully shot landmark documentary. D: Merian Cooper, Ernest Schoedsack, Marguerite Harrison. DOC 70m. V

Grass Is Always Greener Over the Septic Tank, The 1978 ★★★½ Burnett plays humorist Erma Bombeck in uneven comedy based on best-seller about city couple struggling to adapt to suburban life. Sometimes amusing and on target, other times strained. C: Carol Burnett, Charles Grodin. D: Robert Day. COM 98m. TVM V

Grass is Greener, The 1961 ★★★★ Comedy of manners and misbehavior involves Grant and Kerr as a happily married couple who indulge in extramarital dalliances with Simmons and Mitchum. Not as witty as it could be, but still fun to watch. C: Cary Grant, Deborah Kerr, Robert Mitchum, Jean Simmons. D: Stanley Donen. COM [R] 105m. V

Grass Is Singing, The 1981 British ★★★½ Sweltering heat, primitive farm living in the South African bush, and racial paranoia lead settler Black to suffer violent mental breakdown. Wrenching drama taken from Doris Lessing novel, occasionally weakened by intrusive political rhetoric. (a.k.a. *Killing Heat*) C: Karen Black, John Thaw. D: Michael Raeburn. DRA 108m. V

Grasshopper, The 1970 ★★★★ The story of an innocent young woman from Canada and how quickly life turns her into a used-up Las Vegas call girl. Fascinating drama really succeeds, and the chemistry between Bisset and Brown is electric. C: Jacqueline Bisset, Jim Brown, Joseph Cotten, Corbett Monica. D: Jerry Paris. DRA [R] 95m. V

Grateful Dead—Dead Ahead 1980 ★★★★ Legendary band ignites Radio City Music Hall, playing such classics as "On the Road Again" and "Uncle John's Band." MUS 89m. V

Grateful Dead Movie, The 1976 ★★★★ Winning rockumentary on one of the premiere psychedelic bands, San Francisco's Grateful Dead, features trippy animation, concert excerpts, backstage footage, and fan interviews. The Dead's legendary lead guitarist, Jerry Garcia, co-directed, so the selected material reflects an insider's view. Deadheads will love it, and it may help other rock fans see the light. D: Jerry Garcia, Leon Gast. MUS [PG] 131m. V

Grave of the Vampire 1972 ★★★ The offspring of a vampire rape grows up to be a bloodsucker who seeks revenge against his father. Rather ambitious in terms of its story, this low-budget chiller has a nice psychological twist. C: William Smith, Michael Pataki. D: John Hayes. HOR [PG] 95m. V

Grave Secrets: The Legacy of Hilltop Drive 1992 *See* **Grave Secrets**

Grave Secrets 1989 ★★ Soutendijk thinks ghosts are infesting the inn she owns and calls in parapsychologist LeMat to check things out. Largely traditional haunted house story shows some potential, but ultimately fails to distinguish itself. C: Renee Soutendijk, Paul LeMat, David Warner. D: Donald P. Borchers. HOR [R] 90m. V

Grave Secrets 1992 ★★★ Fact-based haunted house thriller about couple (Duke and Selby), whose new home has a life of its own. Toilets flush themselves, ectoplasm drips from the attic, and their daughter hears spirits talking. Some chills, but effective leads can't disguise the fact that this tale has been told better elsewhere. (a.k.a. *Grave Secrets: The Legacy of Hilltop Drive*) C: Patty Duke, David Soul, David Selby, Jonelle Allen. D: John D. Patteson. HOR 94m. V

Graveyard of Horrors 1971 ★★½ Man in mourning for his murdered family accidentally uncovers crazed, skull-stealing scientist. C: John Clark, Titania Clement, Bill Curran. D: Miguel Madrid. HOR 105m. V

Graveyard Shift 1987 ★★½ Vampire cabbie falls for terminally ill music video director. Bizarre genre splicing should interest fans of Italian horror films. C: Silvio Oliviero, Helen Papas, Cliff Stoker. D: Gerard Ciccoritti. HOR [R] 89m.

Graveyard Shift 1990 ★★ Yet another film based on a Stephen King short story that demonstrates why he kept the tale short, with textile mill workers threatened by a monster in the basement. Gets better as it goes along (but only slightly) and looks cheap throughout. C: David Andrews, Kelly Wolf, Brad Dourif. D: Ralph S. Singleton. HOR [R] 89m. V

Graveyard, The 1974 British ★★½ Cat-crazy Turner torments son with deadly results. (a.k.a. *Persecution* and *The Terror of Sheba*). C: Lana Turner, Trevor Howard, Ralph Bates. D: Don Chaffey. HOR [PG] 90m. V

Gravy Train, The 1974 ★★★½ Well-cast, action/comedy of rural brothers (Keach and Forrest) falling into rambunctious life of crime. Above-average B-movie. (a.k.a. *The Dion Brothers*) C: Stacy Keach, Frederic Forrest, Margot Kidder. D: Jack Starrett. COM [R] 96m.

Gray Lady Down 1977 ★★★ Freighter rams nuclear submarine, disabling it, and engineer (Carradine) must perform the rescue. Waterlogged pace and characters get help from decent effects. Christopher Reeves' debut. C: Charlton Heston, David Carradine, Stacy Keach, Ned Beatty. D: David Greene. ACT [PG] 111m. v

Grayeagle 1977 ★★★ A man sets out on a trek to find his daughter, carried off by a brave from a nearby tribe. Plodding, standard Western; John Ford carbon copy. Good script handled with mediocrity. C: Ben Johnson, Iron Eyes Cody, Lana Wood. D: Charles B. Pierce. WST [PG] 104m. v

Grease 1978 ★★★★ Popular filming of the Broadway musical fantasy about teenage life in the '50s has inane plot about shy Newton-John in love with bad boy Travolta. But it also has musical numbers that burst with vitality as performed by ingratiating cast. Hit songs written for film include "Hopelessly Devoted to You," "You're the One That I Want," and title song. C: John Travolta, Olivia Newton John, Stockard Channing, Jeff Conaway, Didi Conn, Eve Arden, Sid Caesar, Joan Blondell, Frankie Avalon. D: Randal Kleiser. MUS [PG] 110m. v

Grease 2 1982 ★★½ Embarrassing sequel to the hit movie picks up at Rydell High in 1961, tracking a different bunch of T-Birds and Pink Ladies. Strictly jayvee compared to the original; only saving grace is attractive performance by Luft. C: Maxwell Caulfield, Michelle Pfeiffer, Adrian Zmed, Lorna Luft, Didi Conn, Eve Arden, Sid Caesar, Tab Hunter, Connie Stevens. D: Patricia Birch. MUS [PG] 115m. v

Greased Lightning 1977 ★★★ The story of Wendell Scott, the first African-American race car driver. Lively cast. C: Richard Pryor, Beau Bridges, Pam Grier, Cleavon Little. D: Michael Schultz. ACT [PG] 96m. v

Greaser's Palace 1972 ★★★½ Satirical takeoff on Christianity has Jesus reappearing as a zoot-suited dude in the Old West, spreading The Word to assorted eccentrics. Wildly uneven, with some irreverant sparkle amidst the tumbleweeds. C: Allan Arbus, Albert Henderson, Luana Anders, George Morgan. D: Robert Downey. COM 91m. v

Great Adventure, The 1952 *See* **Fortune in Diamonds**

Great Adventure, The 1953 Swedish ★★★★½ A pair of Swedish farmboys rescue a wild otter and decide to keep it as a pet. Superbly filmed animal sequences and a fascinating inside look at daily life on a farm through all four seasons. Good family viewing. C: Anders Norberg, Kjell Sucksdorff. D: Arne Sucksdorff. FAM/DRA 73m. v

Great Adventure, The 1975 Italian-Spanish ★★★ Okay boy-and-his-dog story from Jack London novel, with pair struggling to survive in Alaska during the gold rush. Odd mix of European actors with Jack and Joan. C: Jack Palance, Joan Collins, Fred Romer (Fernando Romero), Elisabetta Virgili. D: Paul Elliotts (Gianfranco Baldanello). FAM/ACT 87m. v

Great Alligator, The 1979 Italian ★★½ A monstrous reptile (actually the incarnation of a demon!) lays siege to a tropical resort. The creature looks stiff and mechanical, and so does the movie. C: Barbara Bach, Mel Ferrer, Claudio Cassinelli, Richard Johnson. D: Sergio Martino. HOR 96m. v

Great American Beauty Contest, The 1973 ★★★½ All the melodramatic intrigue you'd like to believe really exists behind the scenes at a big beauty contest. Spicy and knowing social comedy. C: Eleanor Parker, Bob Cummings, Louis Jourdan, Farrah Fawcett. D: Robert Day. COM 74m. TVM

Great American Broadcast, The 1941 ★★★★ Nifty exploration of the origins of radio, circa 1919, with Faye torn between Oakie and Payne. Cameo appearances by Ink Spots, Nicholas Brothers, and the wonderfully weird Wiere Brothers. C: Alice Faye, John Payne, Jack Oakie, Cesar Romero. D: Archie Mayo. MUS 92m.

Great American Bugs Bunny—Road Runner Chase 1979 *See* **Bugs Bunny/Road Runner Movie, The**

Great American Cowboy, The 1974 ★★★★½ Fast-moving documentary on rodeo life follows two performers on the circuit, super-star Larry Mahan and his up-and-coming rival, Phil Lyne. Oscar-winner for Best Documentary Feature. D: Kieth Merrill. DOC [G] 89m. v

Great American Pastime, The 1956 ★★½ Attorney (Ewell) bites off more than he can chew when he agrees to manage his son's little-league team. Amusing suburban comedy. C: Tom Ewell, Anne Francis, Ann Miller. D: Herman Hoffman. COM 89m.

Great American Traffic Jam, The 1980 ★★★ L.A. traffic comes to a frustrating halt when an older woman blazes onto the freeway in umpteenth attempt to earn driver's license. C: Abe Vigoda, Ed McMahon, Lisa Hartman, Rue McClanahan. D: James Frawley. COM 97m. v

Great American Tragedy, A 1972 ★★★★ Kennedy brings great pathos to role of engineer who loses job and must cope with finding a career in advanced middle age. Still stands up. C: George Kennedy, Vera Miles, William Windom, James Woods. D: J. Lee Thompson. COM [PG] 80m.

Great Balloon Adventure, The *See* **Olly, Olly, Oxen Free**

Great Balls of Fire! 1989 ★★★½ The story of Jerry Lee Lewis, the fiery, talented musician who achieved rock 'n' roll greatness in the '50s. Fast-paced and glossy film biography pays much attention to Lewis' personal life. Quaid's good, and Lewis on the soundtrack sounds great. C: Dennis Quaid, Winona Ryder, Alec Baldwin, Lisa Blount. D: Jim McBride. DRA [PG-13] 108m. v

Great Bank Hoax, The 1976 ★★★½ Crime comedy of three bank managers arranging a big robbery to cover up their own embezzlements. Satirical nod to Watergate, still entertains with a sturdy cast and amusing predicaments. (a.k.a. *Shenanigans* and *The Great Georgia Bank Hoax*) C: Richard Basehart, Burgess Meredith, Paul Sand. D: Joseph Jacoby. COM [PG] 89m. V

Great Bank Robbery, The 1969 ★★½ Western spoof of competing would-be bank robbers. Great cast in brainless time passer. C: Zero Mostel, Kim Novak, Clint Walker. D: Hy Averback. COM [PG] 98m.

Great Battle, The 1978 German ★★ Orson Welles narrates a study focusing on the German Panzer Corps' last military action in Tunisia. Multinational jumble features an all-star cast. (a.k.a. *Battleforce* and *Battle of the March Line*) C: Helmut Berger, Samantha Eggar, John Huston, Stacy Keach, Henry Fonda. D: Humphrey Longan. DRA [PG] 97m. V

Great Bear Scare, The 1984 ★★★ Ted E. Bear becomes Bearbank's hero by repelling assorted ghosts; uninspired animation, but may hold some thrills for kids. FAM/ACT 60m. V

Great Big World and Little Children, The 1962 Polish ★★★★ Trio of short science fiction films, all involving children. Kids will love special effects and generous spirit of tales. C: Kinja Sienko, Woychiech Purzynski, Zbigniew Josefowicz. D: Anna Sokolowska. FAM/SFI 102m.

Great Brain, The 1978 ★★★ Somewhat corny family tale about young con artist in the early 1900s. Based on John D. Fitzgerald's celebrated book. C: Jimmy Osmond, James Jarnigan, Len Birman, Pat Delaney. D: Sidney Levin. DRA [G] 82m.

Great British Train Robbery, The 1967 Germany ★★★½ Murky but intriguing true story about mail robbery of train in 19th-century Great Britain. C: Claus Witt, Horst Tappert, Isa Miranda. D: John Olden. ACT 104m.

Great Caruso, The 1951 ★★★★ Highly fictionalized but highly enjoyable biography of the legendary opera singer gives Lanza his best screen role, as he magnificently sings scads of arias and Italian folk songs. Fine support from Blyth as his wife. C: Mario Lanza, Ann Blyth, Jarmila Novotna, Dorothy Kirsten. D: Richard Thorpe. MUS [G] 108m. V

Great Catherine 1968 British ★★ Adaptation of George Bernard Shaw play has English captain visiting royal Russian court of Queen Catherine the Great and causing complications. C: Peter O'Toole, Jeanne Moreau, Zero Mostel, Jack Hawkins. D: Gordon Flemyng. COM 98m.

Great Chase, The 1963 ★★★★ Exciting chase sequences from silent movies are basis for this entertaining compilation; smartly uses chunks of Keaton's action classic, *The General*. C: Buster Keaton, Douglas Fairbanks, Sr., Lillian Gish. COM 79m. V

Great Dan Patch, The 1949 ★★★ Story of a beloved trotting horse and his exceptional career. Nicely done, and horse fans will enjoy the racing scenes. C: Dennis O'Keefe, Gail Russell, Ruth Warrick, Charlotte Greenwood. D: Joseph Newman. DRA 94m.

Great Day 1945 British ★★★½ Documentary-style drama commemorates women's contribution to the British WWII effort by recording a small village's preparation for a visit by Eleanor Roosevelt. Serious, convincing drama. C: Eric Portman, Flora Robson, Isabel Jeans. D: Lance Comfort. DRA 94m. V

Great Day in the Morning 1956 ★★★½ A gambler (Stack) is torn between the lure of gold and the demands of the impending Civil War, as well as between two women (Roman and Mayo). Energetic, entertaining, and beautifully filmed Western drama. C: Virginia Mayo, Robert Stack, Ruth Roman. D: Jacques Tourneur. WST 92m. V

Great Diamond Robbery, The 1953 ★★½ A dim-witted diamond expert (Skelton) is "adopted" by a gang of thieves. Silly comedy with only flashes of Skelton's ebullience. C: Red Skelton, Cara Williams, James Whitmore. D: Robert Z. Leonard. COM 69m.

Great Dictator, The 1940 ★★★★½ The screen's greatest comedian masterfully satirizes Hitler by taking on two roles, a power-mad dictator and an amnesiac Jewish barber who ends up being mistaken for the maniacal leader. Poignant comedy was Chaplin's first full talkie; he later said that if he had known about the concentration camps at the time, he would not have made such a comic treatment of Hitler. A flawed but important film. C: Charlie Chaplin, Paulette Goddard, Jack Oakie, Reginald Gardiner, Billy Gilbert. D: Charles Chaplin. COM [G] 128m. V

Great Escape, The 1963 ★★★★★ The classic POW escape movie combines great casting, story, action and score with a memorable, stunt-filled climax. When Nazis put misfit Allied prisoners into a camp by themselves, a mass breakout ensues. Final chase, capped by McQueen's unforgettable motorcycle ride, is a classic. C: Steve McQueen, James Garner, Richard Attenborough, Charles Bronson, James Coburn, David McCallum, Donald Pleasence. D: John Sturges. ACT [G] 173m. V

Great Escape 2: The Untold Story, The 1988 ★★★ Remake of *The Great Escape*, the '60s classic about prisoners of war who tunnel out of a German war camp. The second half supposedly advances the original story, but the new material in this sequel is unconvincing. See the original. C: Christopher Reeve, Anthony Denison, Judd Hirsch, Donald Pleasence. D: Paul Wendkos, Jud Taylor. ACT [R] 93m. TVM V

Great Expectations 1934 ★★★½ Early screen treatment of Dickens' classic novel about orphan Pip and his unknown benefactor is good in its own right, though it pales next to the 1946 masterpiece. C: Jane Wyatt, Phillips Holmes, George Breakston, Henry Hull. D: Stuart Walker. DRA 100m.

Great Expectations 1946 British ★★★★★ Splendid production based on Dickens novel with Mills perfectly cast as Pip, a penniless orphan staked to an education by secret benefactor. Abounds with wonderful performances and inspired touches. Hunt is superb as the demented Miss Havisham, with Currie a chilling Magwich. From first frame to last, a masterpiece. Oscars for Cinematography and Art Direction. C: John Mills, Valerie Hobson, Martita Hunt, Finlay Currie, Alec Guinness, Jean Simmons. D: David Lean. DRA 118m. V

Great Expectations 1974 U.S. ★★★½ Yet another version of the Dickens classic about a young boy and his mysterious benefactor. Certainly an acceptable remake, with a very capable cast. C: Michael York, Sarah Miles, James Mason, Margaret Leighton, Robert Morley, Anthony Quayle, Rachel Roberts. D: Joseph Hardy. DRA 103m. TVM V

Great Expectations 1981 British ★★★ British miniseries adaptation of the Dickens masterpiece about orphaned Pip and his mysterious benefactor. Literate and involving. C: Gerry Sundquist, Stratford Johns. D: Julian Amyes. DRA 300m. V

Great Flamarion, The 1945 ★★★½ A circus entertainer (von Stroheim) is tricked into murder. Entertaining mystery. C: Erich von Stroheim, Mary Hughes, Dan Duryea. D: Anthony Mann. CRI 78m. V

Great Gabbo, The 1929 ★★ Von Stroheim plays a talented ventriloquist whose ruthless egotism destroys his relationship with a young woman. Von Stroheim's fascinating, as usual, but he can't hold up film's shaky plot and often ridiculous musical numbers. C: Erich von Stroheim, Don Douglas, Betty Compson. D: James Cruze. DRA 94m. V

Great Gambini, The 1937 ★★★ A mind reader (Tamiroff) ferrets out guilt, and begins to foresee an uneasy fate for himself. Entertaining but easy to unravel. C: Akim Tamiroff, Marian Marsh, Genevieve Tobin, William Demarest. D: Charles Vidor. CRI 70m.

Great Garrick, The 1937 ★★★★ Aherne impersonates British theatrical legend David Garrick in this glossy film biography. The highly fictionalized story involves the undoing of Garrick's enormous ego by his fellow thespians. Entertaining production with great cast. Good for family viewing. C: Brian Aherne, Olivia de Havilland, Edward Everett Horton, Lana Turner. D: James Whale. COM 91m.

Great Gatsby, The 1926 ★★★★ First filming of F. Scott Fitzgerald's celebrated novel about elusive millionaire Gatsby, who flirts with '20s Long Island society and loves socialite Daisy Buchanan. This silent version is astutely directed and well acted by a cast of top silent stars. Worth a look. C: Warner Baxter, Lois Wilson, Neil Hamilton. D: Herbert Brenon. DRA

Great Gatsby, The 1949 ★★★½ Middling adaptation of F. Scott Fitzgerald's Roaring '20s novel about enigmatic millionaire (Ladd) who's the talk of Long Island society. First filmed in 1926 and again in 1974. Script plays up love story, weakening Fitzgerald's social drama. C: Alan Ladd, Betty Field, Macdonald Carey, Barry Sullivan, Shelley Winters. D: Elliott Nugent. DRA 92m.

Great Gatsby, The 1974 ★★★½ F. Scott Fitzgerald's classic story of the enigmatic young millionaire and the wealthy social elite of '20s Long Island. Visual splendor of the production tends to overwhelm the elusive story, but it's worth a spin. Oscars for Best Costumes and Score. C: Robert Redford, Mia Farrow, Bruce Dern, Karen Black, Sam Waterston, Lois Chiles. D: Jack Clayton. DRA [PG] 146m. V

Great Gay Road, The 1931 ★★★ Wealthy man, who has been living as a tramp by choice, goes home—only to find himself beset by same kind of problems he'd run away from. Some interesting dialogue, but slow going. C: Stewart Rome, Frank Stanmore, Kate Cutler. D: Sinclair Hill. DRA 88m.

Great Gilbert and Sullivan, The 1953 British ★★★★ Tuneful biography of the gifted operetta composing team offers several excerpts from their best-loved work. Intelligently scripted, with witty characterizations and top-drawer British cast. (a.k.a. *The Story of Gilbert and Sullivan*) C: Robert Morley, Maurice Evans, Eileen Herlie, Peter Finch, Martyn Green. D: Sidney Gilliat. MUS 105m.

Great Gildersleeve, The 1943 ★★★ First movie based on popular radio character had loud-mouthed and rotund Throckmorton P. Gildersleeve (Peary) playing guardian to his niece and nephew while trying to elude marriage-minded Field. Lively and guileless fun. C: Harold Peary, Nancy Gates, Freddie Mercer, Mary Field, Jane Darwell. D: Gordon Douglas. COM 62m.

Great Gleason, The 1987 ★★★★ Glowing pastiche of clips from "The Jackie Gleason Show" and "The Honeymooners," featuring the "Great One's" most beloved characters. COM 90m. V

Great Gundown, The 1975 ★★★ Native American of mixed blood leads bloody raids on outlaw fortification. C: Robert Padilla, Richard Rust, Milila St. Duval. D: Paul Hunt. WST [PG] 98m. V

Great Guns 1941 ★★½ Two loyal retainers (Laurel and Hardy) join the Army when their spoiled charge is drafted—only to discover that he can take care of himself while they suffer under a tough sergeant. Their first comedy for Fox. C: Stan Laurel, Oliver Hardy, Sheila Ryan. D: Monty Banks. COM 74m. V

Great Guy 1937 ★★½ An honest meat inspector campaigns against the crooked meat-packing industry. Sub-standard "clean up the system" Depression-era fare. C: James Cagney, Mae Clarke, James Burke. D: John G. Blystone. DRA 73m. V

Great Hope, The 1954 Italian ★★★½ Intriguing tale of Italian submarine during WWII that picks up survivors of sunken British ship and the camaraderie that ensues. C: Renato Baldini, Lois Maxwell, Folco Lulli, Carlo Bellini. D: Duilio Coletti. DRA 91m.

Great Houdinis, The 1976 ★★★★ Glaser shines in this slick TV biography of the mysterious illusionist, who rose from obscurity to become synonymous with magic. Struthers and Gordon add compelling support as the magician's tortured wife and headstrong mother. C: Paul Michael Glaser, Sally Struthers, Ruth Gordon, Vivian Vance. D: Melville Shavelson. DRA 100m. TVM

Great Hunter, The 1975 Taiwanese ★★ A military captain and his girlfriend search for the men who killed her father. Shrill revenge fantasy is big on over-the-top emotions, but little else. C: Chia Ling, Wang Yu, Hsu Feng. D: Larry Tu. ACT 91m. V

Great Ice Rip-Off, The 1974 ★★½ Dim caper tale about jewel robbery and retired cantankerous cop who tries to foil it. C: Lee J. Cobb, Gig Young. D: Dan Curtis. ACT 72m. TVM

Great Impersonation, The 1942 ★★★½ English nobleman becomes pawn in spy plot, involving German bombmaker who is his identical twin. Interesting twists in this able remake of 1935 spy tingler. C: Ralph Bellamy, Evelyn Ankers, Aubrey Mather. D: John Rawlins. DRA 70m.

Great Impostor, The 1961 ★★★½ Curtis triumphs in the unbelievable life story of amazingly successful con artist Ferdinand Demara, who got away with posing as a doctor, a Trappist monk, a teacher, and a prison warden, among other guises. Uneven, but likable and funny film. C: Tony Curtis, Karl Malden, Raymond Massey, Edmond O'Brien, Gary Merrill. D: Robert Mulligan. DRA 112m. V

Great Jesse James Raid, The 1953 ★★★ Fists fly, bullets blaze in high-strung, hyperbolic taut retelling of famous outlaw's final days. C: Willard Parker, Barbara Payton, Tom Neal. D: Reginald LeBorg. WST 74m.

Great Jewel Robber, The 1950 ★★½ Overwrought British tale about boastful cat burglar. Pedestrian effort. C: David Brian, Marjorie Reynolds, John Archer. D: Peter Godfrey. ACT 91m.

Great John L., The 1945 ★★½ The bittersweet life of celebrated boxer John L. Sullivan, complete with boxing re-enactments. An entertaining, though forgettable, biography. C: Greg McClure, Linda Darnell, Barbara Britton. D: Frank Tuttle. DRA 96m.

Great K&A Train Robbery, The 1926 ★★★★ Silent cowboy superstar Mix plays a railroad detective assigned to bring in the varmints who've been robbing K&A trains. Fast-paced, enjoyable silent Western is one of Mix's best, beautifully photographed against a stunning Colorado backdrop. C: Tom Mix, Dorothy Dwan, William Walling. D: Lewis Seiler. WST 53m.

Great L.A. Earthquake, The 1990 ★★★½ Chaos erupts in Los Angeles when city discovers scientist's long-silenced prediction of imminent great quake. C: Ed Begley Jr., Joanna Kerns, Richard Masur. D: Larry Elikann. ACT 106m. V

Great Lie, The 1941 ★★★★ Sudsy drama with Davis as good girl winning Brent over selfish concert pianist Astor. When he's presumed dead, Bette takes in pregnant Mary and film really starts cooking with dandy confrontation scenes. Astor won the Best Supporting Actress Oscar. C: Bette Davis, Mary Astor, George Brent, Hattie McDaniel. D: Edmund Goulding. DRA 107m. V

Great Locomotive Chase, The 1956 ★★★½ Suspenseful action drama about a train stolen by Union soldiers and the Confederate conductor who pursues them in another. Parker steals movie as Yankee commander; Hunter is his Confederate counterpart. Serious take on true story which was also the inspiration for Keaton's silent comedy *The General.* (a.k.a. *Andrews' Raiders*) C: Fess Parker, Jeffrey Hunter. D: Francis D. Lyon. FAM/DRA 85m. V

Great Love Experiment, The 1982 ★★★½ Cool clique learns a lesson when attempting to transform gawkiest kid at school. C: John Bluthall, Tracy Pollan. D: Claudia Weill. COM 45m. V

Great Lover, The 1931 ★★★ Philandering opera star (Menjou) gets his comeuppance when he falls for a young diva (Dunne) only to be jilted for a younger man. Vintage comedy/drama with entertaining stars. C: Adolphe Menjou, Irene Dunne, Ernest Torrence. D: Harry Beaumont. DRA 72m.

Great Lover, The 1949 ★★★★ Hope blithely wisecracks his way through this entertaining escapade as Boy Scout leader taking his charges aboard a ship where they inadvertently stumble onto a murder plot. Hope is marvelous, and well supported by Fleming. Older kids might enjoy some of the harmless double entendres. C: Bob Hope, Rhonda Fleming, Roland Young. D: Alexander Hall. COM 80m. V

Great Man, The 1956 ★★★ Reporter doing research for memorial show on the life of popular entertainer recently killed in a car accident finds that in real life the "great man" was an ignominious lowlife. Cynical, often bitter look at show business. C: Jose Ferrer, Keenan Wynn, Julie London, Dean Jagger,

Jim Backus, Ed Wynn. D: Jose Ferrer. DRA 92m.

Great Man Votes, The 1938 ★★★★½ Two children (Holden and Wiedler) encourage their father (Barrymore)—an eminent professor taken to drink since his wife's death—to cast the decisive vote in a local election. Warm story; sympathetic performance by Barrymore. C: John Barrymore, Peter Holden, Virginia Weidler, William Demarest. D: Garson Kanin. COM 72m. V

Great Manhunt, The 1950 British ★★★★ An American finds that the leader of European country has been murdered and replaced by a lookalike. Worth watching for the riveting plot alone. (a.k.a. *State Secret*) C: Douglas Fairbanks, Jr., Glynis Johns, Jack Hawkins, Herbert Lom. D: Sidney Gilliat. CRI 97m.

Great Man's Lady, The 1942 ★★★½ Western saga of a pioneer woman who looks back over 10 decades and recalls the love and direction she gave to her husband. Modest family drama told in flashbacks; Stanwyck ages to 100. C: Barbara Stanwyck, Joel McCrea, Brian Donlevy. D: William Wellman. WST 90m.

Great McGinty, The 1940 ★★★★½ Sharply observed political satire of hobo (Donlevy) catapulted into governor's mansion by party machinery. Directorial debut for screenwriter Sturges, with typical bright dialogue and excellent supporting cast, many of whom reappear in director's later films. (Oscar for Best Original Screenplay.) C: Brian Donlevy, Muriel Angelus, Akim Tamiroff, Allyn Joslyn, William Demarest. D: Preston Sturges. COM 82m. V

Great McGonagal 1975 ★★★ Sellers sends up the Royal Family in tale of unemployed man who dreams of becoming United Kingdom's most celebrated poet. C: Peter Sellers, Spike Milligan, Julia Foster. D: Joseph McGrath. COM 95m. V

Great Meadow, The 1931 ★★★ Virginia pioneers in 1777 undertake an arduous mountain journey to establish a settlement in the Kentucky wilderness. Simple narrative with moments of true authenticity. C: John Brown, Eleanor Boardman, Lucille LaVerne, Anita Louise. D: Charles Brabin. WST 78m.

Great Mike, The 1944 ★★★ Affable '40s formula film about eccentric horse trainer who gets one last chance. Vehicle for Erwin, who at time was a top box-office draw. C: Stuart Erwin, Robert Henry, Marion Martin. D: Wallace Fox. COM 70m.

Great Missouri Raid, The 1950 ★★★ Confederate raiders Jesse and Frank James are forced into renegade life by spiteful Army officer. Dim laundering of infamous Western folk legends. C: Wendell Corey, Macdonald Carey, Ellen Drew, Anne Revere, Bruce Bennett. D: Gordon Douglas. WST 83m.

Great Moment, The 1944 ★★½ Puzzling biography of 19th-century Boston dentist pioneering the use of anesthesia can't decide if it's comedy or drama. McCrea is the poor medical student who switches to dentistry when he runs out of funds. One of Sturges' weaker efforts. C: Joel McCrea, Betty Field, Harry Carey, William Demarest, Franklin Pangborn. D: Preston Sturges. DRA 87m. V

Great Mouse Detective, The 1986 ★★★★ Minor Disney animation involves a Sherlock Holmes-like rodent sleuth trying to save England's royal mouse family from the evil Moriarity-like Ratigan. Price is at his villainous best as voice of Ratigan. Great fun for younger audiences and animation fans. (a.k.a. *Adventures of the Great Mouse Detective*) Voices of Vincent Price, Barrie Ingham, Melissa Manchester. D: John Musker, Ron Clements, Dave Michener, Burny Mattinson. FAM/ACT [G] 80m. V

Great Mr. Nobody, The 1941 ★★½ Advertising salesman winds up in hot water when he allows rivals to steal his ideas. Slight comedy, few laughs. C: Eddie Albert, Joan Leslie, Alan Hale, William Lundigan. D: Ben Stoloff. COM 71m.

Great Muppet Caper, The 1981 British ★★★★ The Muppets invade London in a clever jewel heist plot, with Grodin playing bad guy trying to romance Miss Piggy! Full of inventive sequences including bicycle ride and Miss Piggy tap dancing in nightclub production number. Superior family fun. C: The Muppets, Charles Grodin, Diana Rigg, John Cleese, Robert Morley, Peter Ustinov. D: Jim Henson. FAM/COM [G] 95m. V

Great, My Parents Are Divorcing 1992 French ★★★★½ Humor and insight abound in this poignant and heartwarming tale of a group of children in France trying to hold their lives together as their families fall apart. Outstanding acting, especially by the children. C: Patrick Braoude, Clementine Celarie, Patrick Bouchitey. D: Patrick Braoude. DRA 98m.

Great Niagara, The 1974 ★★½ Crippled dad cows two mealy-mouthed sons, who resist following his footsteps, into going over Niagara Falls in barrel. Strong but farfetched. C: Richard Boone, Michael Sacks, Randy Quaid. D: William Hale. DRA 72m. TVM

Great Northfield, Minnesota Raid, The 1972 ★★★½ The James and the Younger gangs plan a far-flung 1876 bank caper that spells disaster. Idiosyncratic, moody Western with a gritty, sordid edge. C: Cliff Robertson, Robert Duvall, Luke Askew, R.G. Armstrong. D: Philip Kaufman. WST [PG] 91m. V

Great O'Malley, The 1937 ★★★★ A mean cop finds redemption in this unapologetically old-fashioned melodrama, featuring a red-hot O'Brien in the title role and a juicy supporting cast. C: Pat O'Brien, Humphrey Bogart, Ann Sheridan, Donald Crisp. D: William Dieterle. DRA 71m.

Great Outdoors, The 1988 ★★½ Candy has plans for a peaceful summer vacation; Aykroyd is the obnoxious in-law who destroys his serenity. Lightweight and silly. C: Dan Aykroyd, John Candy, Stephanie Faracy, Annette Bening. D: Howard Deutch. COM [PG] 91m. v

Great Profile, The 1940 ★★★ The story of the decline of a once-renowned actor who is reduced to performing as an acrobat. The main joy here is in watching Barrymore poke some good-natured fun at his own persona. C: John Barrymore, Mary Hughes, Gregory Ratoff, John Payne, Anne Baxter. D: Walter Lang. DRA 82m.

Great Race, The 1965 ★★★½ Bloated big-budget tribute to silent comedy substitutes excess for imagination as stars try to enliven tale of cross-country car race. Lemmon and Falk come off best as villains of the piece. C: Tony Curtis, Natalie Wood, Jack Lemmon, Peter Falk, Keenan Wynn, Larry Storch, Dorothy Provine, Vivian Vance. D: Blake Edwards. COM 160m. v

Great Ride, A 1978 ★★½ Two young bikers run from both police and homicidal maniac. C: Michael MacRae, Perry Lang. D: Don Hulette. HOR 90m. v

Great Riviera Bank Roberry, The 1979 ★★★★ Based on true story, fascists attempt brilliant scheme to steal millions from French resort-town bank. C: Ian McShane, Warren Clarke, Christopher Malcolm. D: Francis Megahy. ACT 98m. v

Great Rock "n Roll Swindle, The" 1980 British ★★★ Slice of music history in this raucous backstage look at short-lived punk rock sensations, the Sex Pistols. Manager Malcolm McLaren comes across as an outrageous marketing genius. C: Malcolm McLaren, Johnny Rotten, Sid Vicious. D: Julien Temple. DOC 103m. v

Great Rupert, The 1950 ★★★ A family of acrobats down on their luck and headed by Durante are aided by an agile pet squirrel. Sweet family fantasy. C: Jimmy Durante, Terry Moore, Tom Drake. D: Irving Pichel. COM 86m.

Great Santini, The 1979 ★★★★½ A career marine in the peacetime service (it's 1962) takes his natural belligerence out on his family, especially a son who is coming into his own. Wonderful story of family relationships, good Southern setting. Well-paced and insightful with marvelous cast. Excellent. (a.k.a. *The Ace*) C: Robert Duvall, Blythe Danner, Michael O'Keefe. D: Lewis John Carlino. DRA [PG] 116m. v

Great Scout and Cathouse Thursday 1976 ★★★½ Larcenous cowboys team up with addled Indian (Reed) to steal the profits from a big-monied boxing competition. Loud, cartoonish Western/comedy entertains. C: Lee Marvin, Oliver Reed, Robert Culp, Elizabeth Ashley. D: Don Taylor. COM [PG] 102m. v

Great Sinner, The 1949 ★★★½ Moralistic period drama about evils of games of chance, from Dostoyevsky story, "The Gambler." Stellar cast with outstanding Huston performance as Gardner's father fails to raise film above the ordinary. C: Gregory Peck, Ava Gardner, Melvyn Douglas, Walter Huston, Ethel Barrymore. D: Robert Siodmak. DRA 110m.

Great Sioux Massacre, The 1965 ★★★ Chief Crazy Horse leads the slaughter of General Custer's forces at Little Big Horn in 1876. Economical Western told in flashbacks by pair of court-martialed cavalry officers. C: Joseph Cotten, Darren McGavin, Philip Carey. D: Sidney Salkow. WST 91m.

Great Sioux Uprising 1953 ★★½ A former Union soldier faces impending war with Native Americans. Both the facts and the people badly stereotyped. C: Jeff Chandler, Faith Domergue, Lyle Bettger. D: Lloyd Bacon. WST 80m.

Great Skycopter Rescue, The 1982 ★★½ Small town citizen attempts air strikes on violent bikers hired by sleazy entrepreneurs seeking to depopulate the oil-rich hamlet and bleed it dry. C: William Marshall, Aldo Ray, Terri Taylor. D: Lawrence D. Foldes. ACT 96m. v

Great Smokey Roadblock, The 1978 ★★★½ Aging, luckless trucker (Fonda) stays a step ahead of creditors after his rig makes a final cross-country haul. Fonda is miscast in mild, countrified chase flick. (a.k.a. *The Last of the Cowboys*) C: Henry Fonda, Eileen Brennan, John Byner, Susan Sarandon. D: John Leone. ACT [PG] 104m. v

Great Spy Chase, The 1966 French ★★★ Four spies from different countries converge on the same town to try to pry secrets from the widow of a brilliant scientist. Throwaway farce. C: Lino Ventura, Bernard Blair, Francis Blanche, Mireille Darc. D: Georges Lautner. COM 84m.

Great Spy Mission, The 1965 *See* **Operation Crossbow**

Great St. Louis Bank Robbery, The 1959 ★★★ Football hero (McQueen) takes a wrong turn and ends up in a gang of thieves planning to knock over a bank. Crime caper with realistic touches, fine youthful McQueen. C: Steve McQueen, David Clarke, Molly McCarthy. D: Charles Guggenheim, John Stix. ACT 86m.

Great St. Trinian's Train Robbery, The 1966 British ★★½ Late entry in the popular English series has train robbers hiding out at zany female academy. Average comedy for fans of the series. C: Frankie Howerd, Dora Bryan. D: Frank Launder, Sidney Gilliat. COM 90m. v

Great Texas Dynamite Chase, The 1975 ★★½ Two plucky bandits (Jennings, Jonas) take off on a robbery spree. Familiar low-budget entry. Jennings was the 1970 *Playboy* Playmate of the Year. (a.k.a. *Dynamite Women*) C: Claudia

Jennings, Jocelyn Jones, Johnny Crawford. D: Michael Pressman. CRI [R] 90m. v

Great Train Robbery, The 1979 British ★★★★ Connery and Sutherland make an engaging team in this fanciful, stylish thriller about the 19th-century robbery of a moving train. Crichton directed from his own novel, based on a true incident. (a.k.a. *The First Great Train Robbery*) C: Sean Connery, Donald Sutherland, Lesley-Anne Down, Alan Webb. D: Michael Crichton. CRI [PG] 111m. v

Great Victor Herbert, The 1939 ★★★★ Glossy Hollywood biography of the composer features 28 of his songs, many familiar and all finely sung. C: Allan Jones, Mary Martin, Walter Connolly, Lee Bowman. D: Andrew Stone. MUS 91m.

Great Waldo Pepper, The 1975 ★★★★ Charming story of a WWI flying ace who becomes a Midwestern barnstormer and then a stuntman in Hollywood. Little depth, but good color and humor, great stunts. Highly entertaining. C: Robert Redford, Bo Svenson, Susan Sarandon. D: George Roy Hill. DRA [PG] 107m. v

Great Wall, A 1986 ★★★ Chinese-American family faces culture shock when they make a pilgrimage from San Francisco to their homeland after a 30-year absence. A sincere, intriguing, if not always successful, film. C: Peter Wang, Sharon Iwai, Kelvin Han Yee. D: Peter Wang. DRA [PG] 103m. v

Great Wallendas, The 1978 ★★★★ Bridges gives an athletic, inspired performance as the patriarch of The Flying Wallendas, the legendary family of circus high-wire artists. Appealing biography. C: Lloyd Bridges, Britt Ekland, Taina Elg, Cathy Rigby. D: Larry Elikann. DRA 96m. TVM v

Great Waltz, The 1938 ★★★½ Musical biography of composer Johann Strauss is only average drama but lovely to look at and full of his beautiful, lilting waltzes. Oscar for Cinematography. Remade in 1972. C: Luise Rainer, Fernand Gravet, Miliza Korjus, Lionel Atwill. D: Julien Duvivier. MUS 100m. v

Great Waltz, The 1972 ★ Stultifying, unintentionally humorous biography of Viennese composer Johann Strauss. Even the waltzes seem clumsy. Remake of 1938 film. C: Horst Buchholz, Mary Costa, Rossano Brazzi, Nigel Patrick. D: Andrew Stone. DRA [G] 135m.

Great War, The 1959 Italian ★★★½ Pair of Italian ne'er-do-wells caught in WWI do everything in their power to avoid serving in combat but wind up heroes. Flawed but amusing comedy/drama. C: Vittorio Gassman, Alberto Sordi, Silvana Mangano. D: Mario Monicelli. COM 118m.

Great White Hope, The 1970 ★★★★½ Loose dramatization of the life of Jack Johnson, who became the first African-American heavyweight boxing champion of the world in 1910 and drew as much attention for having a white mistress as for his boxing. Powerful version of the Broadway play, and Jones and Alexander are superb. C: James Earl Jones, Jane Alexander, Chester Morris, Hal Holbrook, Moses Gunn. D: Martin Ritt. DRA [PG] 103m. v

Great Ziegfeld, The 1936 ★★★★½ Extravagant MGM production tells life story of fabled producer Florenz Ziegfeld (Powell) and is every bit as overstuffed and entertaining as his own shows were. Powell holds his own against garguantuan production numbers ("A Pretty Girl Is Like A Melody"), real-life Ziegfeld star Brice, and Rainer (Oscar for Best Actress) as Flo's first wife, Anna Held. Oscars for Best Picture and Best Dance Direction. C: William Powell, Myrna Loy, Luise Rainer, Frank Morgan, Fanny Brice, Ray Bolger, Will Rogers, Dennis Morgan. D: Robert Z. Leonard. MUS 177m. v

Greatest Gift, The 1974 ★★★★½ A teenage boy watches his minister father battle corruption in '40s American South. Ably acted and beautifully directed. C: Glenn Ford, Julie Harris. D: Boris Sagal. DRA 100m. TVM

Greatest Love, The 1951 Italian ★★ A somewhat tedious tale of a woman, distraught after her child's death, who tries to find meaning in life by doing good deeds for others. (a.k.a. *Europa '51*) C: Ingrid Bergman, Alexander Knox, Giulietta Masina. D: Roberto Rossellini. DRA 110m.

Greatest Man in the World, The 1980 ★★★ In adaptaton of James Thurber story, unlikable man becomes beloved hero after feat of aeronautic daring. C: Brad Davis, Wiliam Prince, Carol Kane. D: Ralph Rosenblum. DRA 51m. v

Greatest Show on Earth, The 1952 ★★★★★ Extravagant showman DeMille gets to pull out all the stops in this outsize tribute to life under the Big Top. Involving plot includes thrilling circus acts, a spectacular train wreck, a breathtaking high-wire competition, plus all the highs and lows of life on the road. Stellar cast and sure-handed direction make this a superb example of good old-fashioned Hollywood entertainment. Oscars for Best Picture and Best Story. C: Betty Hutton, Charlton Heston, Cornel Wilde, Gloria Grahame, James Stewart, Dorothy Lamour, Emmett Kelly. D: Cecil B. DeMille. DRA 149m. v

Greatest Story Ever Told, The 1965 ★★★½ Jesus, a Nazarene carpenter-rabbi, begins his ministry, gathers followers, performs miracles, is betrayed by Judas Iscariot, and is executed by the Romans in Jerusalem. Long, slow New Testament panorama. C: Max von Sydow, Charlton Heston, Carroll Baker, Angela Lansbury, Sidney Poitier, John Wayne, Jose Ferrer, Claude Rains, Telly Savalas. D: George Stevens. DRA 196m. v

Greatest, The 1977 ★★★ The biography of

Muhammad Ali, considered by many to be the greatest heavyweight boxer of all time. Interesting primarily as an acting forum for the real champ who, appropriately, plays himself. C: Muhammad Ali, Ernest Borgnine, Robert Duvall, James Earl Jones, Paul Winfield. D: Tom Gries. DRA [PG] 100m. V

Greatest Thing That Almost Happened, The 1977 ★★★ Tearjerker about teen basketball star stricken with leukemia who reconciles with his estranged father. C: Jimmie Walker, James Earl Jones, Deborah Allen, Tamu, Valerie Curtin, Kevin Hooks. D: Gilbert Moses. DRA 120m. TVM

Greed 1925 ★★★★★ Dentist's marriage ends in tragedy when his wife's obsession with money she won in lottery prompts his descent to madness. Von Stroheim's silent telling of "money as root of evil" story is still masterful and engrossing. Last scenes shot in Death Valley particularly powerful. Based on novel *McTeague* by Frank Norris. C: Gibson Gowland, ZaSu Pitts, Jean Hersholt, Chester Conklin. D: Erich von Stroheim. DRA 133m. V

Greed in the Sun 1965 French ★★½ Thriller about French truck drivers running contraband in North Africa. Plot careens all over the place while the stark desert vistas remain impressive. C: Jean-Paul Belmondo, Lino Ventura, Reginald Kernan, Andrea Parisy. D: Henri Verneuil. DRA 122m.

Greed of William Hart, The 1948 British ★★½ Grave robbers snatch corpses for an anatomical scientist; when their supply runs low, they begin creating their own. Oft filmed theme receives low-budget outing. (a.k.a. *Horror Maniacs*) C: Tod Slaughter, Henry Oscar, Jenny Lynn. D: Oswald Mitchell. HOR 78m. V

Greedy 1994 ★★★½ Amusing, if overbroad comedy of an obnoxious family gathering to prevent their aging patriarch (Douglas) from giving all his money to his "nurse" (D'Abo). Fox is charming as Kirk's only decent relative. C: Kirk Douglas, Michael J. Fox, Nancy Travis, Olivia D'Abo, Phil Hartman, Ed Begley, Jr. D: Jonathan Lynn. COM [PG-13] 113m. V

Greek Tycoon, The 1978 ★★ Thinly veiled soap opera purporting to be inside story of courtship and marriage of Jackie O. and Aristotle Onassis. Quinn reprises his Zorba the Greek shtick and Bisset practices looking wounded. Video version contains new footage. C: Anthony Quinn, Jacqueline Bisset, Raf Vallone, Edward Albert, Charles Durning. D: J. Lee Thompson. DRA [R] 106m. V

Greeks Had a Word for Them, The 1932 ★★★½ Three young women in Manhattan (Claire, Blondell, and Evans) set their sights on landing rich husbands. Upbeat comedy is innocent fun. C: Joan Blondell, Ina Claire, Madge Evans. D: Lowell Sherman. COM 79m.

Green Archer, The 1961 German ★★★½ Whirlwind action yarn, about masked marksman who becomes people's hero. Based on Edgar Wallace novel. C: Gert Frobe, Karin Dor. D: Jurgen Roland. ACT 95m.

Green Berets, The 1968 ★★½ Vietnam action picture presents WWII-type heroics of American Special Forces. Famous ending features the sun setting in the East. C: John Wayne, David Janssen, Jim Hutton, Aldo Ray, Raymond St. Jacques. D: John Wayne, Ray Kellogg. ACT [G] 141m. V

Green Card 1990 Australian ★★★½ Sedate horticulturalist MacDowell marries passionate Frenchman Depardieu so he can become U.S. citizen and she can get apartment from landlord who will only rent to married couple. Standard romantic fare, but writer/director Weir and his stars bring it off with enormous charm. C: Gerard Depardieu, Andie MacDowell, Bebe Neuwirth, Gregg Edelman, Robert Prosky. D: Peter Weir. COM [PG-13] 107m. V

Green Carnation, The 1960 *See* **Man with the Green Carnation, The**

Green Cockatoo, The 1937 British ★★★ Disappointing adaptation of Graham Greene tale about vaudevillian trying to track down brother's killers. (a.k.a. *Four Dark Hours*) C: John Mills, Rene Ray, Robert Newton. D: William Cameron Menzies. ACT 65m.

Green Dolphin Street 1947 ★★★½ Two sisters (Turner and Reed) living in 19th-century New Zealand, are both romantically interested in the same man, but love is interrupted by earthquakes and tidal waves. Oscar-winning special effects enliven an otherwise standard love story. C: Lana Turner, Van Heflin, Donna Reed, Richard Hart, Frank Morgan, Edmund Gwenn, Dame May Whitty, Reginald Owen, Gladys Cooper. D: Victor Saville. DRA 141m. V

Green-Eyed Blonde, The 1957 ★★½ Poor '50s morality tale about a "good girl" who goes bad. C: Susan Oliver, Tommie Moore, Juanita Moore. D: Bernard Girard. DRA 76m.

Green Eyes 1976 ★★★★ Stinging portrayal by Winfield of a Vietnam War veteran revisiting Saigon to claim his half-Vietnamese son. Sensitively crafted. C: Paul Winfield, Rita Tushingham. D: John Erman. DRA 97m. TVM V

Green Fields 1937 Yiddish ★★★★ Lovely pastoral romance about a wandering Talmud scholar who falls in with a farming family. Beverly is luminous, and a young Bernardi is winning as her kid brother. C: Michael Goldstein, Herschel Bernardi, Helen Beverly, Isidore Casher, Dena Drute, Anna Appel. D: Edgar G. Ulmer, Jacob Ben-Ami. DRA

Green Fire 1954 ★★★½ Romance/adventure set in Colombia and featuring conflicts over love and emerald mines. Energetic adventure sequences and marvelous Grace make it engaging. C: Grace Kelly, Stewart Granger, Paul Douglas. D: Andrew Marton. ACT 100m. V

Green for Danger 1946 British ★★★★½ Compelling tale of a detective searching for a psycho stalking the halls of a British hospital during WWII. A frightening mock operation is the bait he sets to catch the killer. Howard and Sim are superb. C: Alastair Sim, Sally Gray, Trevor Howard. D: Sidney Gilliat. CRI 90m. V

Green Glove, The 1952 ★★½ Former paratrooper (Ford) defies danger in post-WWII Europe to return gem to French church. Twisty thriller never picks up enough speed. C: Glenn Ford, Geraldine Brooks, Cedric Hardwicke. D: Rudolph Mate. ACT 90m. V

Green Goddess, The 1930 ★★★ Three British pilots crash in the far East, where a local tyrant condemns them to death. Early sound feature overplays histrionics, drawing more laughs than suspense. Arliss reprises his 1923 role. C: George Arliss, Alice Joyce, H. B. Warner. D: Alfred Green. DRA 80m.

Green Grass of Wyoming 1948 ★★★½ Follow-up to *Thunderhead—Son of Flicka.* Family of horse breeders are rivals of another clan in the same business. Simply told story that's perfect for younger equestrian fanatics. C: Peggy Cummins, Robert Arthur, Charles Coburn. D: Louis King. FAM/DRA 89m.

Green Grow the Rushes 1951 British ★★½ A civil servant stumbles upon a brandy smuggling operation in a sleepy Kent village in this minor satire. C: Richard Burton, Honor Blackman, Roger Livesey. D: Derek Twist. COM 80m.

Green Hell 1940 ★★★ Treasure hunters in South America, and fun to watch, despite unconvincing jungle sets. C: Douglas Fairbanks, Jr., Joan Bennett, Alan Hale, Vincent Price, George Sanders. D: James Whale. ACT 87m.

Green Horizon, The 1983 ★★½ Stewart plays an old coot living on a piece of undeveloped land in Kenya who must decide whether to provide for his granddaughter's future or save his pristine environment. The always watchable Stewart is a bit at odds with the unsubtle script. (a.k.a. *Afurika Monogatari* and *A Tale of Africa*) C: James Stewart. DRA

Green Hornet, The 1940 ★★★★ Thirteen episodes of legendary serial featuring publisher-turned-superhero and his sidekick, Kato. C: Gordon Jones, Keye Luke. SFI 360m. V

Green Ice 1981 British ★★★ Emeralds are the target for a gang of thieves in this middling, disjointed thriller. C: Ryan O'Neal, Anne Archer, Omar Sharif, John Larroquette. D: Ernest Day. CRI [PG] 115m. V

Green Inferno 1987 ★★★ Hired guns try to silence a wealthy eccentric who pushes South American natives to rebel. C: Richard Yestaran, Didi Sherman, Ceasar Burner. ACT 90m. V

Green Light, The 1937 ★★★ Visionary medic undergoes personal conversion and decides to leave his profession for a more introspective life. Curious drama that philosophizes on life's meaning without scratching the surface. C: Errol Flynn, Anita Louise, Margaret Lindsay, Cedric Hardwicke, Spring Byington. D: Frank Borzage. DRA 85m.

Green Man, The 1957 British ★★★★ Sim has a field day as a mild-mannered man who is actually a professional assassin. Sly black comedy has its amusing moments. C: Alastair Sim, George Cole, Terry-Thomas. D: Robert Day. COM 80m.

Green Man, The 1990 U.S. ★★★ Atmospheric ghost story about lusty English inn owner Finney's encounters with alcohol, women, and the inn's resident specter. Vague and sometimes slow, but not without merit, namely Finney. Adapted from a Kingsley Amis novel. C: Albert Finney, Sarah Berger, Michael Hordern. D: Elijah Moshinsky. HOR 150m. TVM V

Green Mansions 1959 ★★★ Ill-fated romance between forest spirit Hepburn and mortal Perkins in the South American jungle lacks magic of W.H. Hudson's classic. Ferrer (Hepburn's then-husband) stumbles in translating fantastic allegory to the screen. C: Audrey Hepburn, Anthony Perkins, Lee J. Cobb, Sessue Hayakawa. D: Mel Ferrer. DRA 104m. V

Green Pastures, The 1936 ★★★★ All-black film version of Marc Connelly's Pulitzer Prize-winning play tells Old Testament Bible stories using '30s black English. Will be offensive to some, uplifting to others. Stirring performance by Ingram as "De Lawd." C: Rex Ingram, Oscar Polk, Eddie Anderson, Frank Wilson, George Reed. D: William Keighley, Marc Connelly. DRA 93m. V

Green Promise, The 1949 ★★★ A farmer and his four children toil to make a success of their hardscrabble farm. Modest and solemn with Brennan giving one of his reliable performances. C: Marguerite Chapman, Walter Brennan, Natalie Wood. D: William Russell. DRA 93m.

Green Ray 1986 *See* **Summer**

Green Room, The 1978 French ★★★ A despondent widower and survivor, haunted by memories of WWI, builds a shrine to his lost compatriots. Gloomy, rigorous film looks at the obsessive mourning of those left alive; not considered among director's best. C: Francois Truffaut, Nathalie Baye, Jean Daste. D: Francois Truffaut. DRA [PG] 95m. V

Green Scarf, The 1955 British ★★½ Over-the-hill Paris attorney defends blind and deaf murder suspect. Static courtroom drama. C: Michael Redgrave, Ann Todd, Kieron Moore, Leo Genn. D: George O'Ferrall. DRA 96m.

Green Slime, The 1968 Japanese ★★★ Fun space romp where a green slime is oozing over everything and killing all it touches. Neat theme song, too! C: Robert Horton, Richard Jaeckel, Luciana Paluzzi. D: Kinji Fukasaku. HOR [G] 89m. V

Green Wall, The 1970 Peruvian ★★★ First Peruvian feature to reach sizable U.S. audience portrays the life of a city family fighting bureacracy and nature to survive in their new jungle home. An interesting look at a remote corner of the world. C: Julio Aleman, Sandra Riva, Raul Martin, Lorena Duval. D: Armando Robles Godoy. DRA 110m. V

Green Years, The 1946 ★★★ Boy-to-man story of Irish orphan (Stockwell) who's sent to live with his mother's family in Scotland. Stockwell and Coburn (as his great-grandfather) highlight this sentimental drama based on A.J. Cronin's best-seller. C: Charles Coburn, Tom Drake, Hume Cronyn, Gladys Cooper, Dean Stockwell, Jessica Tandy. D: Victor Saville. DRA 127m.

Greene Murder Case, The 1929 ★★★½ Philo Vance unravels a murder on Manhattan's East Side. Powell's second outing as S.S. Van Dine's popular mystery hero is well done, given early sound techniques; Powell is always good. C: William Powell, Florence Eldridge, Jean Arthur, Eugene Pallette. D: Frank Tuttle. DRA 69m.

Greenwich Village 1944 ★★★½ Fluffy, anachronistic musical set in '20s New York, about a serious composer talked into applying his talents to a Broadway revue. Enjoyably corny. C: Carmen Miranda, Don Ameche, William Bendix, Vivian Blaine, Felix Bressart, Tony De Marco, Sally De Marco. D: Walter Lang. MUS 82m.

Greetings 1968 ★★★★ Early De Niro/De Palma feature involves two friends trying to get third buddy away from the draft board while searching for sexual fulfillment in Greenwich Village. Low-budget and very energetic fun from some goofy youngsters destined for bigger things. Followed by sequel of sorts, *Hi, Mom.* C: Jonathan Warden, Robert De Niro, Gerrit Graham. D: Brian De Palma. COM [R] 88m. V

Gregory's Girl 1981 Scottish ★★★★ This fetching romantic comedy achieves its modest goals so well that Scottish director Forsyth gained instant international attention. Simple story has an awkward high school soccer player falling for the team's new female member. Simply delightful. C: Gordon Sinclair, Dee Hepburn, Chic Murray, Jake D'Arcy. D: Bill Forsyth. COM [PG] 91m. V

Gremlins 1984 ★★★½ Boy receives an unusual pet that leads to incredible trouble when he fails to take care of it properly. Spielberg-influenced attempt to combine horror and heartwarming comedy suffers from obvious plotting and violence far too extreme for younger viewers. Still, a plethora of in-jokes helps. C: Zach Galligan, Phoebe Cates, Hoyt Axton, Polly Holliday, Glynn Turman. D: Joe Dante. COM [PG] 106m. V

Gremlins 2—The New Batch 1990 ★★★★ Far superior sequel revolves around gremlins taking over Trump-like tower and hero Galligan's attempt to save the day. Much less violent than original, this relies heavily on gags and parody, coupled with cartoonish plotting and great cameos. C: Zach Galligan, Phoebe Cates, John Glover, Robert Prosky, Robert Picardo, Christopher Lee. D: Joe Dante. COM [PG-13] 106m. V

Grendel, Grendel, Grendel 1982 Australian ★★★★ Animated version of John Gardner's novella looks at *Beowolf* from the monster's point of view. He watches a creature called "man" pillage and attack the world. Though not the best animation, story is still engaging and unusual. Fine allegory for children. Voices of Peter Ustinov, Keith Michell, Arthur Dignam. D: Alexander Stitt. DRA 90m. V

Grey Fox, The 1983 Canadian ★★★★ Farnsworth is appealing as an aging outlaw who abandons stagecoach heists for train holdups. Inspired by silent classic, *The Great Train Robbery.* Witty, affecting, and high-spirited. C: Richard Farnsworth, Jackie Burroughs, Wayne Robson. D: Phillip Borsos. WST [PG] 92m. V

Grey Gardens 1976 ★★★½ Weird, shocking, fascinating documentary about Edith Bouvier Beale, 79, and her daughter, Edie, 57, who are aunt and cousin of Jacqueline Onassis and reside in a filthy, condemned Long Island mansion. A portrait of an eccentric pair of recluses, and it's not a pretty picture. D: David Maysles, Albert Maysles. DOC [PG] 95m.

Greyfriars Bobby 1961 ★★★½ Enjoyable kiddie fare from Disney factory about a Scottish terrier who becomes the pet for an entire Edinburgh neighborhood after the pooch's master passes away. Sweet stuff that will appeal to young audiences. C: Donald Crisp, Laurence Naismith, Alex Mackenzie, Kay Walsh. D: Don Chaffey. FAM/COM 89m. V

Greystoke: The Legend of Tarzan, Lord of the Apes 1983 ★★★★ Tarzan is found in his adopted jungle home, and brought back to Britain. Epic retelling of the Edgar Rice Burroughs legend is visually lush, with fine acting (including Glenn Close's dubbing of MacDowell's voice). C: Christopher Lambert, Andie MacDowell, Ian Holm, Ralph Richardson, James Fox, Ian Charleson. D: Hugh Hudson. DRA [PG] 130m. V

Gridlock 1980 ★★½ Accidental shutdown of L.A. freeways forces stranded motorists into utter chaos. Predictable comedy. C: Desi Arnaz, Jr., John Beck, Shelley Fabares. D: James Frawley. COM 100m. TVM

Grievous Bodily Harm 1988 Australian ★★★ Detective searches for his wife and the man he suspects abducted her. Compelling thriller. C: Colin Friels, John Waters, Bruno Lawrence, Shane Briant. D: Mark Joffe. CRI [R] 136m. V

Griffin and Phoenix: A Love Story 1972 ★★★½ Sentimental TV movie about a couple who know that illness will cut short their lives together. At times touching, but Falk and Clayburgh deserve better. C: Peter Falk, Jill Clayburgh. D: Daryl Duke. DRA 100m. TVM v

Grifters, The 1990 ★★★★ Mother (Huston) and son (Cusack) have little in common save a life of small-time con artistry. But when seductive Bening entices the son to move up to the big time, Huston's possessive jealousy is uncovered. Frank, graphic look at the all-or-nothing world of the hustler. Frears gets dynamic performances from his three stars. C: Anjelica Huston, John Cusack, Annette Bening, Pat Hingle. D: Stephen Frears. CRI [R] 114m. v

Grim Prairie Tales 1990 ★★½ In the Old West, Jones and Dourif swap scary stories (of ill-fated desert travelers, the horrors of bigotry, and a haunted gunfighter) around a campfire. Thoughtful chiller, provides few real scares. C: James Earl Jones, Brad Dourif, William Atherton, Lisa Eichhorn. D: Wayne Coe. HOR [R] 87m. v

Grim Reaper, The 1981 Italian ★ Farrow (Mia's sister) and friends are stranded on a deserted island with a scarred, pickaxe-wielding cannibal. Typical Italian schlock item has plenty of blood and guts but no brains in sight. Grim indeed. C: Tisa Farrow, Saverio Vallone. D: Joe D'Amato. HOR [R] 82m. v

Grip of the Strangler 1958 *See* **Haunted Strangler, The**

Grisbi 1953 French ★★★½ Action-packed gold heist caper set in the Parisian underworld featuring strong role by Gabin. Also a very early look at French superstar, Moreau. Fast-paced and engrossing, with some variations on the caper theme. C: Jean Gabin, Jeanne Moreau, Rene Dary. D: Jacques Becker. CRI 94m.

Grissly's Millions 1944 ★★★½ Above-average '40s B-picture about a murder and ensuing manhunt, with crisp, effective editing. C: Paul Kelly, Virginia Grey, Don Douglas. D: John English. ACT 54m.

Grissom Gang, The 1971 ★★★½ Kidnapped socialite (Darby) falls in love with one of the thugs who abducted her. Some funny moments in violent thriller set in 1931. Remake of *No Orchids for Miss Blandish*. C: Kim Darby, Scott Wilson, Irene Dailey, Tony Musante, Connie Stevens. D: Robert Aldrich. CRI [R] 128m. v

Grizzly 1976 ★★ Blatant ripoff of *Jaws*, though slightly better than many similar films from the same period. Park ranger George leads the hunt for a marauding killer bear that looks somewhat less than terrifying when finally revealed in full. C: Christopher George, Andrew Prine, Richard Jaeckel. D: William Girdler. HOR [PG] 92m. v

Grizzly Adams—The Legend Continues 1990 ★★★ Mountain men and ursine partner protect hamlet from gangster trio. C: Gene Edwards, Link Wyler, Red West. D: Ken Kennedy. DRA 90m. v

Groom Wore Spurs, The 1951 ★★½ A cowpoke actor (Carson), none too steady on his horse, finds trouble in Las Vegas and ex-wife (Rogers) comes to his rescue in court. Marital comedy. C: Ginger Rogers, Jack Carson, Joan Davis. D: Richard Whorf. COM 80m.

Groove Tube, The 1972 ★★★ Low-budget television parody sketch film notable mostly for cast members (Chase and Belzer, among others) who would hit it big elsewhere. At best, this plays like dirty high school humor. C: Ken Shapiro, Lane Sarasohn, Chevy Chase, Richard Belzer. D: Ken Shapiro. COM [R] 75m. v

Gross Anatomy 1989 ★★★ Modine is a medical student who thinks life's one big joke; by the end of the film he's undergone the expected changes thanks to serious-minded doctor Lahti. Strictly by-the-book comedy. C: Matthew Modine, Daphne Zuniga, Christine Lahti, Todd Field. D: Thom Eberhardt. COM [PG-13] 109m. v

Gross Jokes 1985 ★★★½ Rollicking series of comic performances from the L.A. Improv, featuring bright young performers. C: Barry Diamond, Tim Jones, Sheryl Bernstein. D: Bob Williams. COM 53m. v

Grotesque 1987 ★ Low-budget junk wastes good B-movie cast in story of murderous punks who get theirs at the hands of the deformed survivor of the family they've butchered. Grotesque indeed; too bad it's not scary. C: Linda Blair, Tab Hunter, Guy Stockwell. D: Joe Tornatore. HOR [R] 80m. v

Ground Zero 1988 Australian ★★★½ Tense but uneven suspense thriller about a film professional who discovers his father's death may not have been an accident. Intriguing investigation of '50s international nuclear cover-ups. C: Colin Friels, Jack Thompson, Donald Pleasence, Natalie Bate. D: Michael Pattinson, Bruce Myles. DRA [PG-13] 99m. v

Groundhog Day 1993 ★★★★½ Murray is brilliantly inventive as an obnoxious weatherman doomed to replay one of the less glamorous 24 hours of his life as he covers the Groundhog Day festivities in Punxsutawney, PA. Although the plot sounds hopelessly repetitive, it is actually charming and clever as Murray comes to recognize the power of being given a second chance, and a third, and a . . . C: Bill Murray, Andie MacDowell, Chris Elliott. D: Harold Ramis. DRA [PG] 101m. v

Grounds for Marriage 1950 ★★ Ill-advised pairing of Grayson and Johnson as opera star and her doctor ex-husband in saccharine musical. C: Van Johnson, Kathryn Grayson, Barry Sullivan, Lewis Stone. D: Robert Z. Leonard. MUS 91m.

Groundstar Conspiracy, The 1972 Canadian ★★★★ Espionage operative brainwashes scientist to unravel mysterious explosion of top secret space project. Taut but predictable mystery/thriller with added sci-fi touches. C: George Peppard, Michael Sarrazin, Christine Belford. D: Lamont Johnson. ACT 93m. V

Group Marriage 1972 ★★★½ Dated but still entertaining account of "swinging" couples who broaden their ranks, looking to take part in the titular ceremony. The characters are distinguishable (rare in this kind of farce) and the jokes are better than average. C: Victoria Vetri, Claudia Jennings, Aimee Eccles. D: Stephanie Rothman. COM [R] 90m. V

Group, The 1966 ★★★★ Based on Mary McCarthy's best-selling novel of the same title, this film traces the lives of eight women friends through the beginning of WWII. Little more than a high-brow soap opera, but a lot of fun to watch—thanks in large part to a lively and skillful cast. Hackett turns in a particularly fine performance as Dottie. C: Candice Bergen, Joan Hackett, Elizabeth Hartman, Shirley Knight, Joanna Pettet, Jessica Walter, Kathleen Widdoes, Larry Hagman, Hal Holbrook. D: Sidney Lumet. DRA 149m. V

Growing Pains ★★★ Less then perfect paents taught grizzly lessons by son and his ravenously hungry garden. C: Barbara Kellerman, Gary Bond. D: Francis Megahy. HOR 60m. V

Grown Ups 1985 ★★★½ Grodin plays a writer battling every member of his contentious family. Constant bickering is witty, but doesn't add up to a compelling plot. Made-for-cable adaptation of Jules Feiffer play. C: Jean Stapleton, Martin Balsam, Charles Grodin, Marilu Henner. D: John Madden. DRA 106m.

Gruesome Twosome, The 1966 ★★½ Devoted son collects collegiate's scalps to aid his wig-making mother. C: Rodney Bedell, Chris Martel, Gretchen Welles. D: Herschell Gordon Lewis. HOR 75m. V

Grumpy 1930 ★★★ A curmudgeonly old lawyer clears up a diamond heist. Unusual adaptation of the 1913 Broadway hit. (a.k.a. *Cascarrabias*) C: Cyril Maude, Phillips Holmes, Paul Cavanagh, Frances Dade. D: George Cukor, Cyril Gardner. DRA 74m.

Grumpy Old Men 1993 ★★★½ Comedy of an ancient feud between neighbors (Matthau and Lemmon) given new life and real venom when both fall for their new neighbor (Ann-Margret). Familiar chemistry in this fifth teaming of Matthau and Lemmon helps brighten a weak script. C: Walter Matthau, Jack Lemmon, Ann-Margret, Burgess Meredith, Darryl Hannah, Kevin Pollak, Ossie Davis, Buck Henry, Christopher McDonald. D: Donald Petrie. COM [PG-13] 104m. V

Grunt! The Wrestling Movie 1985 ★★ Mock sports "documentary" about fictional Mad Dog Curso, an overenthusiastic wrestler who decapitated his last opponent. Of interest to wrestling fans. C: Jeff Dial, Robert Glaudini. D: Allan Holzman. COM [R] 91m. V

Guadalcanal Diary 1943 ★★★★ Based on Richard Tregaskis' firsthand accounts of the battle against Japanese for strategic base, this WWII classic remains one of the best films on the war in the Pacific. Strong cast and action. C: Preston Foster, Lloyd Nolan, William Bendix, Richard Conte, Anthony Quinn. D: Lewis Seiler. ACT 93m. V

Guardian, The 1984 ★★★½ A tough security guard (Gossett) employs his own violent moral code to keep local hoodlums from well-to-do Manhattan apartment house. Creates some genuine suspense. C: Martin Sheen, Louis Gossett, Jr. D: David Greene. ACT 102m. TVM V

Guardian, The 1990 ★★ Should'a checked those references—Brown and Lowell's new nanny turns out to be an evil Druid who wants to sacrifice their baby to a killer tree. Utterly ridiculous but bizarrely watchable, with a couple of jolting gore scenes. C: Jenny Seagrove, Dwier Brown, Carey Lowell. D: William Friedkin. HOR [R] 92m. V

Guarding Tess 1994 ★★★★ Lighthearted comedy follows unusual love-hate relationship between former first lady and secret service agent assigned to protect her. MacLaine and Cage's crafty characterizations provide a continuous barrage of laughs. C: Nicolas Cage, Shirley MacLaine, Austin Pendleton, Edward Albert, James Rebhorn. D: Hugh Wilson. COM 96m.

Guardsman, The 1931 ★★★★ Exceptionally noteworthy antique film features Lunt and Fontanne—legendary Broadway team for over a quarter century, and happily married for longer than that!—in their only cinematic vehicle. Lunt disguises himself as a handsome Russian to woo his wife and test her fidelity. Witty and charming; a must-see. Remade as *The Chocolate Soldier* and *Lily in Love.* C: Alfred Lunt, Lynn Fontanne, Roland Young, ZaSu Pitts. D: Sidney Franklin. DRA 83m. V

Guendalina 1957 French ★★★★ A young woman meets a student on the Italian Riviera as her parents plan divorce. Tender, insightful look at the joys, pains, and confusion of adolescent love. C: Jacqueline Sassard, Raffaele Mattioli. D: Alberto Lattueda. DRA 95m.

Guerrillas in Pink Lace 1964 ★★ Ludicrous tropical tale about a playboy on the lam from enemy Japanese, accompanied by a bevy of showgirls. Pure hokum. C: George Montgomery, Valerie Varda. D: George Montgomery. COM 96m.

Guess Who's Coming to Dinner 1967 ★★★★ Their daughter's engagement to a black man shakes up her upper-middle-class parents in this predictably soft Hollywood look at race relations. Notable for Tracy's final film appearance, and Oscar-winning work by Hepburn and screenwriter William Rose. C: Spencer Tracy, Katharine Hepburn, Sidney Poitier, Katharine Houghton, Cecil Kellaway, Beah Richards. D: Stanley Kramer. DRA 108m. v

Guess Who's Sleeping in My Bed? 1973 ★★½ Coy but forced comic tale of divorced couple, each remarried, forced to share a house again with their new families. Amusing. C: Dean Jones, Barbar Eden. D: Theodore J. Flicker. COM 90m.

Guest in the House 1944 ★★★ An unstable young woman disturbs the peaceful life of an artist and his family when she comes to visit. Contains implausible plot turns and an over-the-top performance by Baxter. C: Anne Baxter, Ralph Bellamy, Aline MacMahon, Ruth Warrick, Margaret Hamilton, Percy Kilbride. D: John Brahm. DRA 121m. v

Guest, The 1964 British ★★★½ Harold Pinter's play involves a mentally disturbed man and his sadistic brother, who invite a derelict to spend the night in their London house. Theatrical piece emphasizes character interaction. (a.k.a. *The Caretaker*) C: Alan Bates, Donald Pleasence, Robert Shaw. D: Clive Donner. DRA 105m.

Guest Wife 1945 ★★★½ A bachelor borrows his friend's wife so he can fool his boss into thinking he's married. Silly romantic comedy is just another excuse to pair the two stars—and why not? They're swell! C: Claudette Colbert, Don Ameche. D: Sam Wood. COM 88m. v

Guide for the Married Man, A 1967 ★★★½ A rake (Morse) teaches straitlaced husband (Matthau) how to cheat on his wife. Lowbrow comedy hit big when first released. C: Walter Matthau, Robert Morse, Inger Stevens, Lucille Ball, Jack Benny, Polly Bergen, Joey Bishop, Sid Caesar, Art Carney. D: Gene Kelly. COM 91m. v

Guide for the Married Woman 1987 ★★★ A who's-who of TV stars find work in this comedy about a bored married woman, seeking advice on how to cheat on her husband. C: Cybill Shepherd, Charles Frank, Barbara Feldon, Eve Arden. D: Hy Averback. DRA [PG] 100m. TVM v

Guilt of Janet Ames, The 1947 ★★★★ War widow (Russell) seeks the facts behind her husband's death and enlists the help of a journalist in her quest. Engrossing drama of personal growth and discovery, neatly acted by Russell and ensemble. C: Rosalind Russell, Melvyn Douglas, Sid Caesar, Betsy Blair, Nina Foch. D: Henry Levin. DRA 83m.

Guilty? 1956 British ★★★½ A Frenchwoman (Debar) is accused of having murdered a man whom she had rescued from the Nazis in WWII and who had then betrayed her. Thriller features a complex plot, where each answer leads to a new question. C: John Justin, Barbara Laage, Donald Wolfit. D: Edmond T. Greville. CRI 93m.

Guilty as Charged 1932 *See* **Guilty as Hell**

Guilty as Charged 1992 ★★★★ Offbeat black comedy features Steiger as a religious fanatic who executes criminals in his homemade electric chair. Strange, not entirely successful, but edgy enough for cult film devotees. C: Rod Steiger, Lauren Hutton. D: Sam Irvin. COM [R] 95m. v

Guilty as Hell 1932 ★★★ A detective and a reporter set out to prove that a society doctor with an alibi killed his wife. Snappy, audience-pleasing murder yarn. (a.k.a. *Guilty as Charged*) C: Edmund Lowe, Victor McLaglen, Richard Arlen. D: Eric Kenton. CRI 82m.

Guilty as Sin 1993 ★★★ Suave and sleazy defendant (Johnson) hires beautiful lawyer (De Mornay). She's smart, but is she smart enough to learn the truth about her client? Johnson is good. C: Rebecca De Mornay, Don Johnson, Stephen Lang, Jack Warden. D: Sidney Lumet. CRI [R] 120m. v

Guilty by Suspicion 1991 ★★★★½ De Niro turns in a powerful performance as a Hollywood director who refuses to testify against his friends to the House Un-American Activities Committee in the '50s. Winkler admirably avoids melodrama in depicting De Niro's predicament during the blacklist era. C: Robert De Niro, Annette Bening, George Wendt, Patricia Wettig, Sam Wanamaker, Martin Scorsese. D: Irwin Winkler. DRA [PG-13] 105m. v

Guilty Bystander 1950 ★★★ Private eye with morale problem gets new lease on life when he must find kidnappers of his own child. Worth it for Scott. C: Zachary Scott, Faye Emerson, Mary Boland, Sam Levene. D: Joseph Lerner. ACT 92m.

Guilty Conscience, The 1985 ★★★★ Compelling psychological drama about a lawyer debating whether to murder his wife and run off with his younger mistress. Exceptionally fine cast heightens tension. C: Anthony Hopkins, Blythe Danner, Swoosie Kurtz. D: David Greene. DRA 100m. TVM

Guilty Hands 1931 ★★★ D.A. (Barrymore) is determined to protect his daughter from ardent swain (Mobray), even if it means murder. Energetic melodrama from way back seems overly mannered now. C: Lionel Barrymore, Kay Francis, Alan Mowbray, Madge Evans, William Bakewell, C. Aubrey Smith. D: W.S. Van Dyke II. DRA 71m.

Guilty of Innocence: The Lenell Geter Story 1987 ★★★½ In Texas, an African-American man is wrongly imprisoned, and he and his lawyer fight for justice. Solid treatment of true story. C: Dorian Harewood, Dabney Coleman, Paul Winfield. D: Richard T. Heffron. DRA [PG] 95m. v

Guilty of Treason 1949 ★★ Cardinal is convicted of treason in Communist Hungary, and becomes a religious martyr. Too much moralizing, and not enough realistic plot development. C: Charles Bickford, Paul Kelly, Bonita Granville. D: Felix Feist. DRA 86m.

Guilty or Innocent: The Sam Sheppard Murder Case 1975 ★★★★ Decent telling of a true story, about Cleveland osteopath convicted of killing his wife, whose dogged lawyer got him acquitted in a retrial. C: George Peppard, Barnard Hughes. D: Robert Lewis. DRA 150m. TVM

Guilty, The 1947 ★★★ Murder mystery involving twin sisters after same man. Average but engaging. C: Bonita Granville, Don Castle. D: John Reinhardt. ACT 70m.

Guinea Pig, The 1949 *See* **Outsider, The**

Gulag 1984 British ★★★½ By mistake, an American sportscaster is sentenced to a decade of hard labor in a Soviet prison camp. Riveting, brutal and suspenseful. C: David Keith, Malcolm McDowell, David Suchet. D: Roger Young. DRA 120m. TVM V

Gulliver's Travels 1939 ★★★★ Fleischer's animated film of Jonathan Swift's classic novel tells the story of a man cast ashore among the tiny people of Lilliput. Kids will enjoy the story, and adults will appreciate the fine animation. D: Dave Fleischer. FAM/DRA 74m. V

Gulliver's Travels 1977 British ★★ Harris has the only major human role in this (mostly) animated musical film of a normal-size sailor marooned among the pint-size people of Lilliput. Sentimental remake of Fleischer's '39 version. C: Richard Harris, Catherine Schell. D: Peter R. Hunt. MUS [G] 80m. V

Gulliver's Travels Beyond the Moon 1966 Japanese ★★½ Animated feature in which Jonathan Swift's protagonist goes to outer space. Strictly kids' stuff. D: Yoshio Kuroda. FAM/SFI 78m.

Gumball Rally, The 1976 ★★★ Cameo-filled comedy follows a group of manic drivers as they drive pell-mell on a cross-country race. Some funny moments, but repetitive and predictable after awhile. C: Michael Sarrazin, Tim McIntire, Raul Julia. D: Chuck Bail. COM [PG] 107m. V

Gumshoe 1972 British ★★★ Daydreaming bingo parlor owner (Finney) fantasizes about being a Bogart-like private eye, just before he's sucked into a real murder case. Amiable English spoof. C: Albert Finney, Billie Whitelaw, Frank Finlay, Janice Rule. D: Stephen Frears. COM [PG] 85m. V

Gumshoe Kid, The 1989 ★★★ Ivy League-bound teen gets too involved in family's detective business and becomes embroiled in high-stakes intrigue. C: Jay Underwood, Tracy Scoggins, Vince Edwards. D: Joseph Manduke. COM [R] 98m. V

Gun 1968 *See* **Mercenary, The**

Gun Battle at Monterey 1957 ★★½ Hayden can't do much with this pallid horse opera about gunslinger on a mission of vengeance. C: Sidney Franklin, Jr., Sterling Hayden, Pamela Duncan, Lee Van Cleef. D: Carl Hittleman. WST 67m.

Gun Brothers 1956 ★★½ One brother follows the path of righteousness, the other the road to crime in this cardboard western. C: Buster Crabbe, Ann Robinson, Neville Brand, Michael Ansara. D: Sidney Salkow. WST 79m.

Gun Code 1940 ★★★ Good guy battles Old West extortionists. C: Tim McCoy, Ina Guest. WST 70m. V

Gun Crazy 1949 ★★★★½ Minor B-classic, with Cummins and Dall as lovers on the lam. Of all Bonnie and Clyde films, this is one that makes the most explicit link between gunplay and sexuality, giving it sleazy, claustrophobic electricity. Cummins is particularly chilling as carnival trick-shot expert. (a.k.a *Deadly Is the Female*) C: John Dall, Peggy Cummins, Morris Carnovsky. D: Joseph H. Lewis. CRI 87m. V

Gun Duel in Durango 1957 ★★★ Before famous outlaw can go straight, he must kill all his old comrades-in-arms. Seems a bit harsh. C: George Montgomery, Steve Brodie, Bobby Clark. D: Sidney Salkow. WST 73m.

Gun for a Coward 1957 ★★★ Cattle rancher clashes with his two younger brothers, one cowardly and the other ill-tempered. Typical Western, with good cast. C: Fred MacMurray, Jeffrey Hunter, Janice Rule, Chill Wills, Dean Stockwell. D: Abner Biberman. WST 73m.

Gun Fury 1953 ★★★½ Man sets out to rescue his betrothed held hostage by stagecoach robbers. Standard Western perked up by excellent Arizona locations and awesome villains. C: Rock Hudson, Donna Reed, Philip Carey, Lee Marvin. D: Raoul Walsh. WST 83m. V

Gun Glory 1957 ★★★ A retired gunslinger tries to settle down but faces his indignant son, hostile townfolk, and violent showdown with rampant outlaws. Unusual casting in Western star vehicle. C: Stewart Granger, Rhonda Fleming, Chill Wills. D: Roy Rowland. WST 89m. V

Gun Hawk, The 1963 ★★½ Meager Western about notorious bad guy trying to keep young acquaintance from following his example. C: Rory Calhoun, Rod Cameron, Ruta Lee. D: Edward Ludwig. WST 92m.

Gun in Betty Lou's Handbag, The 1992 ★★ When a woman accidently finds weapon, she falsely confesses to high-publicity murder just to get attention. Silly, colorless. C: Penelope Ann Miller, Eric Thal, Alfre Woodard, Cathy Moriarty. D: Allan Moyle. COM 89m. V

Gun in the House, A 1981 ★★½ Woman shoots burglar, then faces legal consequences in formulaic drama. A wasted opportunity. C: Sally Struthers, David Ackroyd. D: Ivan Nagy. DRA 100m. TVM V

Gun Moll 1949 *See* **Jigsaw**

Gun Riders 1970 ★★ Attempt at mythic Western about outsized bad guy and his equally larger-than-life opponent. Overbloated effort falls flat. C: Jim Davis, Scott Brady, John Carradine. D: Al Adamson. WST 98m.

Gun Runners, The 1958 ★★½ Lame, derivative tale of gunrunning in the Florida Keys. C: Audie Murphy, Eddie Albert, Patricia Owens, Jack Elam. D: Don Siegel. ACT 83m.

Gun That Won the West, The 1955 ★★½ Run-of-the-mill Western recounts how the U.S. cavalry used the then-new Springfield rifle to stem Native-American uprisings. A grade-B Western. C: Dennis Morgan, Paula Raymond. D: William Castle. WST 71m.

Gun the Man Down 1956 ★★½ A bitter outlaw is wounded during a robbery and subsequently abandoned by his partners in crime. He seeks revenge, and along the way encounters a very young and nubile Dickinson. So-so Western. (a.k.a. *Arizona Mission*) C: James Arness, Angie Dickinson. D: Andrew McLaglen. WST 78m.

Gun, The 1974 ★★★★ Episodic tale follows one handgun as it tragically touches the lives of several different people. Well written, fast-paced, and acted with depth. C: Stephen Elliott, Jean Bouvier. D: John Badham. CRI 78m. TVM

Guncrazy 1992 ★★★★ Bad girl (Barrymore) and ex-con share their love by embarking on a crime spree, leaving nothing untouched by bullets. Strangely captivating, due in part to always interesting Barrymore. Loosely based on 1949 *Gun Crazy*. C: Drew Barrymore, James Le Gros, Joe Dallesandro, Ione Skye. D: Tamra Davis. ACT [R] 97m. V

Gunfight, A 1971 ★★★ Quirky Western features Cash and Douglas as two washed-up gunfighters who concoct a money-making scheme: they charge the townspeople to see a staged shoot-out. Enjoyable Johnny Cash in his first wide-screen role; also notable as Carradine's film debut. C: Kirk Douglas, Johnny Cash, Jane Alexander, Raf Vallone, Karen Black, Keith Carradine. D: Lamont Johnson. WST [PG] 95m. V

Gunfight at Comanche Creek 1964 ★★★ Ingenious story of thieves who make other outlaws commit robberies, then kill them for the reward. Heavyhanded treatment of interesting premise. C: Audie Murphy, Colleen Miller. D: Frank McDonald. WST 90m.

Gunfight at Dodge City, The 1959 ★★★ Frontier gambler Bat Masterson is elected marshal of a lawless cow town. Stock Western yarn about noted folk hero. C: Joel McCrea, Julie Adams. D: Joseph Newman. WST 81m.

Gunfight at the O.K. Corral 1957 ★★★★ U.S. Marshal of Tombstone, Arizona, Wyatt Earp (Lancaster), his two brothers, and Doc Holliday (Douglas) shoot it out with the Clantons, Johnny Ringo, and the McClowery brothers. Taut, fictional, adult Western with a well-staged climactic gun battle. Exciting score by Dimitri Tiomkin. C: Burt Lancaster, Kirk Douglas, Rhonda Fleming, Jo Van Fleet, John Ireland, Lee Van Cleef. D: John Sturges. WST 120m. V

Gunfight in Abilene 1967 ★★½ A wary ex-Civil War veteran becomes marshal and intervenes when a bitter range war erupts. Minor Western, capably handled. C: Bobby Darin, Emily Banks, Leslie Nielsen, Michael Sarrazin. D: William Hale. WST 86m.

Gunfighter, The 1950 ★★★★½ Peck is perfect as an aging gunfighter who would like to give up the lifestyle but can't get away from young upstarts who want to test their skills. Thoughtful film has become almost clichéd through imitation, but it still stands alone. C: Gregory Peck, Helen Westcott, Millard Mitchell, Karl Malden. D: Henry King. WST 85m. V

Gunfighters, The 1987 Canadian ★★ Three friends take on a crooked land baron in slow-witted Western. C: Art Hindle, Reiner Schoene, George Kennedy. D: Clay Borris. WST [PG] 96m. TVM V

Gunfighters 1947 ★★½ Scott plays a quickdraw killer who resolves never to kill again. Hardly original. C: Randolph Scott, Barbara Britton, Forrest Tucker. D: George Waggner. WST 87m.

Gunfire 1950 ★★ Outlaw gains respect pretending to be one of the James brothers in this movie pretending to be a Western. C: Don Barry, Robert Lowery, Pamela Blake. D: William Berke. WST 60m.

Gunfire 1978 *See* **China 9, Liberty 37**

Gunfire at Indian Gap 1957 ★★ Stick-up artists hold up the stagecoach in this wooden clone. C: Vera Hruba Ralston, Anthony George, George Macready. D: Joseph Kane. WST 70m.

Gung Ho! 1943 ★ Stereotypical grunts dispatch leering Japanese with disturbing gusto in this laughably overwrought WWII propaganda piece. Watch for young Robert Mitchum. C: Randolph Scott, Grace McDonald, Noah Beery, Jr., Robert Mitchum, Sam Levene. D: Ray Enright. ACT 88m. V

Gung Ho 1986 ★★★ When automobile plant shuts down, Keaton convinces Japanese investors to reopen factory. Resulting culture shock on both sides is sometimes amusing, occasionally tasteless. Keaton is fine but the routine material lacks satirical insight. Became a short-lived sitcom. C: Michael Keaton, Gedde Watanabe, George Wendt, Mimi Rogers, John Turturro. D: Ron Howard. COM [PG-13] 111m. V

Gunga Din 1939 ★★★★★ Classic adventure story involves three British military men (Grant, McLaglen, and Fairbanks, Jr.) who carouse, fight, and love in 19th-century India. Jaffe is the water carrier who ultimately saves their skins. Superbly paced and rousing adaptation of Kipling's poem with great talents at their best. C: Cary Grant, Victor McLaglen,

Douglas Fairbanks, Jr., Joan Fontaine, Sam Jaffe. D: George Stevens. ACT 117m. V

Gunman's Walk 1958 ★★★½ Two wild sons (Hunter and Darren) create trouble in the Old West. Director Karlson's focus on character development and psychological insight add scope and dimension to this taut genre Western. C: Van Heflin, Tab Hunter, Kathryn Grant, James Darren. D: Phil Karlson. WST 97m.

Gunmen 1994 ★★★ Lambert and Van Peebles manage a few laughs as smuggler and cop, respectively, feuding and fussing against a drug lord with a large pile of stolen dough in Latin America. Noisy action. C: Christopher Lambert, Denis Leary, Mario Van Peebles. D: Deran Sarafian. ACT [R] 97m. V

Gunmen from Laredo 1959 ★ Tedious tale of posse seeking a killer. Inept. C: Robert Knapp, Jana Davi. D: Wallace MacDonald. WST 67m.

Gunmen of the Rio Grande 1965 Italian ★★½ Wyatt Earp saves a damsel from swindlers. Earp's legend has been better served elsewhere. C: Guy Madison, Madeleine LeBeau. D: Tulio Demicheli. WST 86m. V

Gunn 1967 ★★ Debonair private eye Peter Gunn pursues a gangster's murderer through streets and brothels. Cartoonishly violent and thinly plotted feature version of hit TV series. Mancini score only plus. C: Craig Stevens, Laura Devon, Edward Asner, Helen Traubel. D: Blake Edwards. DRA 94m.

Gunpoint 1966 ★★ Round up the posse and save the kidnapped bargirl: That's the sheriff's job in this fizzle of a Western. C: Audie Murphy, Joan Staley. D: Earl Bellamy. WST 86m.

Gunpowder 1984 ★★½ Interpol agents battle a nefarious fiend seeking to destroy the global economic system. C: David Gilliam, Martin Potter, Anthony Schaeffer. D: Norman J. Warren. ACT 85m. V

Gunrunner, The 1984 Canadian ★★ Costner in an early performance as a bootlegger in 20's Canada who combines gunrunning for Chinese rebels with liquor smuggling. For diehard Costner fans only. C: Kevin Costner, Sara Botsford, Paul Soles. D: Nardo Castillo. DRA [R] 92m.

Guns 1990 ★★ Improbable tale starring Estrada as a gunrunner with an attitude. Principally for Estrada fans. C: Erik Estrada, Dona Spier. D: Andy Sidaris. ACT [R] 95m.

Guns at Batasi 1964 British ★★★★ African rebels threaten violence against British regiment. Tense conflict in '60s Africa with intelligent acting by Attenborough as ramrod sergeant major. C: Richard Attenborough, Jack Hawkins, Mia Farrow, Flora Robson. D: John Guillermin. DRA 103m.

Guns for San Sebastian 1968 ★★★ In 1746, fugitive bandit disguised as priest helps defend poor Mexican villagers against marauding Yaqui Indians. Quinn's star power can't save labored action tale. C: Anthony Quinn, Anjanette Comer, Charles Bronson, Sam Jaffe. D: Henri Verneuil. ACT 111m.

Guns, Girls and Gangsters 1959 ★★★ Van Doren is a Vegas lounge singer who becomes entangled in an armored car heist. Fast and furious entertainment, but ultimately fails to live up to its provocative title. C: Mamie Van Doren, Gerald Mohr, Lee Van Cleef. D: Edward Cahn. ACT 70m.

Guns in the Dark 1947 ★★★ Cowboy, believing he killed his best friend, searches for a way to assuage his guilt. C: Johnny Mack Brown, Claire Rochelle, Syd Saylor. D: Sam Newfield. WST 56m. V

Guns of a Stranger 1973 ★ Adventures of a singing cowboy (Robbins). Absolutely forgettable family fare. C: Marty Robbins, Chill Wills, Dovie Beams. D: Robert Hinkle. WST [G] 91m.

Guns of August, The 1964 ★★★★ Informative documentary, based on Barbara Tuchman's Pulitzer Prize-winning book, analyzes the causes of WWI. Fascinating newsreel and archival material is woven into an important historical document. D: Nathan Kroll. DOC 100m. V

Guns of Darkness 1962 ★★★★ Englishman overseas (Niven) is prompted to act when he feels his own safety and that of his wife is jeopardized by local rebellion. Psychologically interesting drama also pulls off rewardingly tense escape scenes. C: David Niven, Leslie Caron. D: Anthony Asquith. DRA 95m. V

Guns of Fort Petticoat, The 1957 ★★★½ In 1860s Texas, a Confederate soldier disobeys an order to massacre an Indian tribe, then returns home to organize a number of women in soldierly fashion to repulse the imminent Indian revenge assault. Intriguing story line makes entertaining viewing. C: Audie Murphy, Kathryn Grant, Hope Emerson. D: George Marshall. WST 82m. V

Guns of Navarone, The 1961 ★★★★★ British intelligence sends a commando team to destroy huge German gun emplacements threatening Allied ships in the Aegean. Stirring WWII action film memorable for dramatic sets, Oscar-winning effects, and fine performances by Peck, Niven, and Quinn. Sequel: *Force 10 from Navarone*. C: Gregory Peck, David Niven, Anthony Quinn, Stanley Baker, Anthony Quayle, James Darren, Irene Papas, Richard Harris. D: J. Lee Thompson. ACT 157m. V

Guns of the Black Witch 1961 Italian ★★★ Pirate movie has burly buccaneer (Megowan) pursuing villains who murdered his father. Middling adventure romance. C: Don Megowan, Silvana Pampanini. D: Domenico Paolella. ACT 83m.

Guns of the Magnificent Seven 1969 ★★★

Seven professional gunfighters are hired to extricate a Mexican rebel leader from an impregnable government garrison. Okay action Western opens no new horizons for the formula in this second sequel. C: George Kennedy, Monte Markham, James Whitmore. D: Paul Wendkos. WST [G] 106m. V

Guns of the Timberland 1960 ★★ Uninspired tale about the animosity between salt-of-the-earth loggers and staid city dwellers features teen idol Avalon in an early movie role. Other than that, not much to look at. C: Alan Ladd, Jeanne Crain, Gilbert Roland, Frankie Avalon. D: Robert Webb. DRA 91m.

Guns of War 1974 ★★★ During WWII, partisans in Yugoslavia put up stiff and heroic resistance in the face of overwhelming Nazi invaders. Fierce action. D: Zika Mitrovic. ACT 114m. V

Gunsight Ridge 1957 ★★★ McCrea plays a cowhand who leads citizens in ridding a territory of ruthless outlaws. Undistinguished Western with some good acting. C: Joel McCrea, Joan Weldon, Slim Pickens. D: Francis Lyon. WST 85m.

Gunslinger 1957 ★★½ After her marshal husband is bushwhacked, a woman assumes his job and attempts to rid the town of a hired gunslinger. Eccentric Western. C: John Ireland, Beverly Garland. D: Roger Corman. WST 78m. V

Gunsmoke in Tucson 1958 ★★★ Two brothers battle it out in old Arizona. Unpretentious Western features a nice performance by Tucker as the renegade brother. C: Mark Stevens, Forrest Tucker, Gale Robbins. D: Thomas Carr. WST 80m.

Gunsmoke: Return to Dodge 1987 ★★★½ Retired U.S. Marshal Matt Dillon (Arness), wounded after a gun duel, sets out to track down an old nemesis. TV movie with some of the stars reunited from the popular, long-running Western series. Good action, characters, and locales. C: James Arness, Amanda Blake. D: Vincent McEveety. WST 96m. TVM V

Gunsmoke: The Last Apache 1990 ★★★ Marshall Matt Dillon attempts to retrieve his daughter from Apache Indians. Acceptable retread of classic Western *The Searchers*. C: James Arness, Richard Kiley, Michael Learned. D: Charles Correll. WST 100m. TVM

Guru, The 1969 ★★★½ British pop star (York) travels to India for sitar lessons at the feet of a master and meets young woman (Tushingham) on a spiritual odyssey of her own. Dutt splendid as guru. Pleasant but slender story. C: Michael York, Rita Tushingham. D: James Ivory. DRA [G] 112m.

Gus 1976 ★★ When a football-kicking mule takes a bottom-of-the-barrel team to first place, gangsters attempt to kidnap him. Inane Disney slapstick. C: Edward Asner, Don Knotts, Gary Grimes, Tim Conway. D: Vincent McEveety. FAM/COM [G] 96m. V

Guts and Glory: The Rise and Fall of Oliver North 1989 ★★★ Film strives for impartiality in relating the controversial life of North from his rise up the military ranks to his indictment in the Iran-Contra scandal. Over three hours' worth of biography and detail. C: David Keith, Annette O'Toole, Barnard Hughes, Peter Boyle. D: Mike Robe. DRA 200m. TVM

Guy Called Caesar, A 1962 British ★★ Shoddy gangster drama features the usual criminal types running amok and climaxes with a surprise shootout with the coppers. Average. C: Conrad Phillips, George Moon, Maureen Toal. D: Frank Marshall. ACT 62m.

Guy from Harlem 1977 ★★★ Typical tale of vengeance, the Harlem way. Amusing '70s clichés abound, but pretty much of interest only to fans of black exploitation cinema. C: Loye Hawkins, Cathy Davis. D: Rene Martinez, Jr. ACT [R] 86m. V

Guy Named Joe, A 1944 ★★★★ Tracy is superb in this offbeat tale of a deceased WWII pilot who returns to Earth to help a younger pilot (Johnson) run missions and win Dunne, who was once Tracy's girl. At times a bit syrupy, but the talented cast is well worth a little extra sugar. Remade in 1989 as *Always*. C: Spencer Tracy, Irene Dunne, Van Johnson, Ward Bond, Lionel Barrymore, Esther Williams. D: Victor Fleming. DRA 121m. V

Guy Who Came Back, The 1951 ★★★ Douglas plays a former pro-football star who tries to figure out what to do with the rest of his life. Average story line but strong cast kicks things up several notches. C: Paul Douglas, Linda Darnell, Joan Bennett, Zero Mostel. D: Joseph Newman. DRA 91m.

Guyana: Cult of the Damned 1980 Mexican ★★★ Film version of gripping true-life tale of Jim Jones and the Jonestown mass suicide massacre of 1978. Of the two movies released that re-created the tragedy, this one is less satisfying. C: Stuart Whitman, Gene Barry, John Ireland, Joseph Cotten, Bradford Dillman, Yvonne De Carlo. D: Rene Cardona, Jr. DRA 90m.

Guyana Tragedy: The Story of Jim Jones 1980 ★★★★½ Boothe's mesmerizing portrayal of the egomaniacal preacher Jones is the linchpin of this excellent TV drama. Riveting version of events leading to the 1978 massacre at Jonestown. C: Powers Boothe, Ned Beatty, Irene Cara, Veronica Cartwright. D: William Graham. DRA 240m. TVM V

Guys and Dolls 1955 ★★★★ Thoroughly enjoyable adaptation of Damon Runyon's Broadway classic about a gambler who bets that he can win the love of a Salvation Army lady. Despite miscasting of Brando, the musical numbers are all lavishly produced and memorably choreographed. Listen for classics like "Luck Be a Lady" and "Sit Down, You're Rocking the Boat." C: Marlon Brando, Jean Simmons, Frank Sinatra, Vivian Blaine,

Stubby Kaye. D: Joseph L. Mankiewicz. MUS 150m. V

Guyver, The 1992 U.S. ★★★★ Ho-hum college student finds a strange helmet that turns him into this popular Japanese comic book hero. A band of ugly mutants want the helmet for their own evil designs—as does a shady CIA agent (Hamill). Rousing special effects and performances make this U.S.-Japanese film one to watch. C: Mark Hamill, Vivian Wu, Jack Armstrong. D: Screaming Mad George, Steve Wang. ACT [PG-13] 92m. V

Guyver 2: Dark Hero 1994 ★★★½ Our hero discovers alien creatures haunting an archaeological dig and must revert to his armor-clad alter ego to stop them. The sporadic monster battles are fun, though this is too violent for younger audiences—and runs way too long. C: David Hayter, Kathy Christopherson, Christopher Michael, Bruno Gianotta, Stuart Weiss. D: Steve Wang. ACT [R] 124m.

Gymkata 1985 ★ Laughable vehicle for gymnast Thomas, intended to introduce title combo of gymnastics and martial-arts techniques, a trend that lasted for exactly one film. Plot concerns our hero's fight to overthrow military meanies in small European country. C: Kurt Thomas, Tetchie Agbayani. D: Robert Clouse. ACT [R] 89m. V

Gypsy 1937 British ★★½ A Hungarian gypsy (Bouchier) searches for her lion-tamer lover in England. Odd, often laughable romance, with a plot as thick as Bouchier's accent. C: Roland Young, Dorothy "Chili" Bouchier, Hugh Williams. D: Roy William Neill. DRA 77m.

Gypsy 1962 ★★★ Motion picture adaptation of the Broadway hit boasts a magnificent musical score and acting that underwhelms (Russell seems particularly miscast as the overbearing stage mother, Rose). Fortunately Styne and Sondheim's unforgettable songs ("Let Me Entertain You" and "Small World") transcend some of the clumsier moments. C: Rosalind Russell, Natalie Wood, Karl Malden, Paul Wallace, Betty Bruce, Faith Dane. D: Mervyn Le Roy. MUS 143m. V

Gypsy 1993 ★★★★★ Sizzling adaptation of the classic Jule Styne-Stephen Sondheim-Arthur Laurents Broadway musical, with Midler exploding across the screen as the domineering stage mother of stripper Gypsy Rose Lee. Remarkably faithful to original show; infinitely superior to the 1962 version. Interesting comparison, though. Ardolino's final film. C: Bette Midler, Peter Riegert, Cynthia Gibb, Christine Ebersole, Jeffrey Broadhurst, Ed Asner, Michael Jeter, Linda Hart, Andrea Martin. D: Emile Ardolino. MUS 150m. TVM V

Gypsy and the Gentleman, The 1958 British ★★★½ Lusty Gypsy (Mercouri) sets her impassioned sights on an aristocrat, and family money complicates the romance. Colorful, though thickly plotted, entertainment. C: Melina Mercouri, Keith Michell, Patrick McGoohan, Flora Robson. D: Joseph Losey. DRA 107m.

Gypsy Angels 1993 ★★½ A group of beautiful women take off in search of adventure and fun. "Wheel of Fortune's" Vanna White leads the way (in scenes from at least a decade earlier). Just what you'd expect—and plenty of it. C: Vanna White, Richard Roundtree, Gene Bicknell, Tige Andrews, Marilyn Hassett. D: Alan Smithee. ACT [R] 92m. V

Gypsy Colt 1954 ★★★½ A colt is sold to racing interests and taken from its youthful owner. Through faith and courage the loyal nag finds its way back home. Horse twist on old formula makes for nice children's fare. C: Donna Corcoran, Ward Bond, Frances Dee. D: Andrew Marton. FAM/DRA [G] 72m. V

Gypsy Fury 1951 Swedish ★★★ A poor Gypsy woman (Lindfors) attracts the attention of a rich nobleman, who abandons his social rank to marry her. Reasonably charming fable, with fairy-ale ambiance. C: Viveca Lindfors, Christopher Kent, Romney Brent. D: Christian Jaque. DRA 63m.

Gypsy Girl 1966 British ★★★★ Mildly retarded English girl (Mills) falls in love with a Gypsy (McShane), who saves her from being sent away to a home. Beautiful settings, sensitive acting, touching story. (a.k.a. *Sky West and Crooked*) C: Hayley Mills, Ian McShane, Laurence Naismith. D: John Mills. DRA 102m.

Gypsy Moths, The 1969 ★★★★ Three skydiving daredevils touring a small town in Kansas bring romance and tragedy on July 4th holiday. Engaging but ambiguous personal drama with vigorous flying stunts offers revealing look at Midwest. Flawed slightly by uneven pacing. C: Burt Lancaster, Deborah Kerr, Gene Hackman, Bonnie Bedelia. D: John Frankenheimer. DRA [R] 110m.

Gypsy Warriors, The 1978 ★★ Unique story elements can't save this flimsy teledrama. Gypsies aid Army agents (Whitmore Jr., and Selleck) attempting to steal biological warfare secrets from the Nazi's in WWII France. C: Tom Selleck, James Whitmore, Jr., Joseph Ruskin, Lina Raymond. D: Lou Antonio. DRA 77m. V

Gypsy Wildcat 1944 ★★½ Predictable yarn of princess by birth nurtured by Gypsies. Nice costumes, lively dancing, not much else. C: Maria Montez, Jon Hall, Nigel Bruce, Gale Sondergaard. D: Roy Neill. ACT 75m.

H

H-Bomb 1971 ★★★ In the steamy, fetid maelstrom of Indochina, a corrupt Cambodian general teams up with members of Bangkok's mob scene. Their goal: to steal an American H-Bomb. C: Christopher Mitchum, Olivia Hussey. D: P. Chalong. ACT 98m. V

H-Man, The 1959 Japanese ★★½ Radioactive liquid dissolves population into slick, rapidly-reproducing blobs that soon threaten all of Tokyo. C: Yumi Shirakawa, Kenji Sahara, Akihiko Hirata. D: Inoshsiro Honda. SFI 79m. V

Habitation of Dragons, The 1992 ★★★ Typical Horton Foote drama of life in a small Texas town, set in the Depression. Lofty, but despite impressive cast, dreary. C: Brad Davis, Hallie Foote, Horton Foote, Frederic Forrest, Jean Stapleton. D: Michael Hogg. DRA 100m. TVM

Hadley's Rebellion 1982 ★★★ Adolescent angst with O'Neal as an outsider who wants to be a wrestler at a posh Los Angeles boarding school. Well-meaning but somewhat flat. C: Griffin O'Neal, William Devane, Charles Durning. D: Fred Walton. DRA [PG] 96m. V

Hagbard and Signe 1968 ★★★★ Beautifully told Scandinavian tale of star-crossed lovers in the Middle Ages features dramatic Icelandic scenery, spectacularly photographed. C: Gitte Haenning, Oleg Vidov, Gunnar Bjornstrand, Eva Dahlbeck. D: Gabriel Axel. DRA 92m.

Hail! *See* **Hail to the Chief**

Hail 1973 ★★★½ A sharp, often hilarious and constantly provocative look at the Nixon presidency—and what might have occurred had he not resigned over Watergate. (a.k.a. *Hail to the Chief*) C: Richard B. Shull, Dick O'Neil, Dan Resin. D: Fred Levinson. COM [PG] 85m. V

Hail Caesar 1993 ★★ A rock musician (Hall) gets mixed up in political sabotage. Frenetic, noisy farce gets no boost from an obnoxious Hall performance. C: Anthony Michael Hall, Frank Gorshin, Samuel L. Jackson, Robert Downey, Jr., Judd Nelson. D: Anthony Michael Hall. COM [PG] 97m. V

Hail, Hero! 1969 ★★½ Douglas makes his film debut as a young man who signs up for duty in Vietnam even though he's personally against war. Ponderous and dated; of interest as both Douglas' and Strauss' first film. C: Michael Douglas, Peter Strauss, Arthur Kennedy, Teresa Wright. D: David Miller. DRA [PG] 100m. V

Hail, Mafia 1965 ★★★½ Witness to mob violence flees assassins. Adequate European crime melodrama holds interest. C: Henry Silva, Jack Klugman, Eddie Constantine, Elsa Martinelli. D: Raoul Levy. CRI 89m.

Hail the Conquering Hero 1944 ★★★★★ Brilliant Sturges satire about a frail Marine (Bracken) who is rejected for duty because of his hay fever, then assumed to be a war hero by his hometown. Hilarious, on-target comedy takes deadly aim at middle American institutions, especially the mania to create heroes. C: Eddie Bracken, Ella Raines, Raymond Walburn, William Demarest, Franklin Pangborn. D: Preston Sturges. COM 101m. V

Hail to the Chief *See* **Hail**

Hair 1979 ★★★½ "Tribal love rock" musical about Vietnam draft inductee Savage experiencing hippie counterculture before leaving for war. Imaginative approach and zesty Twyla Tharp choreography, but unavoidably dated now. Tuneful score includes "Aquarius," "Good Morning, Starshine," "Frank Mills," etc. C: John Savage, Treat Williams, Beverly D'Angelo, Annie Golden. D: Milos Forman. MUS [PG] 121m. V

Hairdresser's Husband, The 1992 French ★★★ Nostalgic male fantasy of a 12-year-old boy's infatuation with the fully grown, shapely barber he regularly visits. A mixed bag of steamy sensuality. C: Jean Rochefort, Anna Galiena. D: Patrice Leconte. DRA [R] 84m. V

Hairspray 1988 ★★★★ Longtime cult film director (Waters) burst into the mainstream with this cheerfully zany spoof of '60s TV teen dance shows. Eclectic cast scores big as soundtrack consistently delights with oldies, both golden and forgotten. C: Divine, Sonny Bono, Ruth Brown, Deborah Harry, Ricki Lake, Pia Zadora. D: John Waters. MUS [PG] 92m. V

Hairy Ape, The 1944 ★★★ Crude but proud stoker (Bendix) on an oceanliner lusts after rich passenger (Hayward) who, in turn, is fascinated and disgusted by him. Watered-down version of O'Neill's play stays afloat with strong performances. C: William Bendix, Susan Hayward, John Loder. D: Alfred Santell. DRA 90m. V

Half a Hero 1953 ★★½ Marital money problems erupt when writer (Skelton) tries to get his socially ambitious wife (Hagen) to control her spending habits after they move to the suburbs. Low-key comedy. C: Red Skelton, Jean Hagen, Charles Dingle, Mary Wickes, Polly Pergen. D: Don Weis. COM 71m.

Half a Lifetime 1986 ★★★ Four long-time buddies get together for a game of poker and review their lives so far. Sobering, tender and well acted by fine young cast. C: Keith Carradine, Gary Busey, Nick Mancuso, Saul Rubinek. DRA 85m. V

Half a Loaf of Kung Fu 1985 ★★★ When the Sern Chuan bodyguards are charged with safekeeping the priceless Evergreen Jade, they are set upon by legions of ruthless bandits. Ferocious action and heroics by Jackie Chan. C: Jackie Chan. ACT 96m. v

Half a Sixpence 1967 ★★½ Energetic British musical about a draper's assistant who inherits a fortune and tries to ingratiate himself with upper-crust society. Based on H.G. Wells' novel *Kipps*. C: Tommy Steele, Julia Foster, Cyril Ritchard, Grover Dale. D: George Sidney. MUS 145m. v

Half Angel 1951 ★★★ A Decorous nurse (Young) lets her hair down when she sleepwalks, then gets into trouble when she can't remember her amorous encounters. Mild romantic comedy. C: Loretta Young, Joseph Cotten, Cecil Kellaway. D: Richard Sale. COM 77m.

Half-Breed, The 1952 ★★½ A gambler aids Apaches when they are provoked by robber baron into attacking homesteaders. Stereotyped Western. C: Robert Young, Janis Carter. D: Stuart Gilmore. WST 81m. v

Half-Human 1955 Japanse ★★ An oddball experiment in which U.S. actors Carradine and Ankrum are edited into an already existing Japanese movie about the abominable snowman and his offspring. Carradine's voice-over narration is used to tie things together. C: John Carradine, Morris Ankrum. SFI 70m. v

Half Moon Street 1986 ★ Enterprising grad student (Weaver) pays those tuition bills via part-time prostitution; diplomat (Caine) is client. C: Michael Caine, Sigourney Weaver. D: Bob Swaim. DRA [R] 90m. v

Half-Naked Truth, The 1932 ★★★★ A publicity wizard (Tracy) attempts to turn a scheming actress (Velez) into an instant star. Plenty of laughs in a wisecracking comedy with top-notch performances. C: Lupe Velez, Lee Tracy, Eugene Pallette, Frank Morgan. D: Gregory LaCava. COM 75m.

Half of Heaven 1987 Spanish ★★★★½ Intriguing tale of a woman with psychic powers who moves seemingly effortlessly from poverty to great success in business. Finely crafted acting with crisp photography and editing make this a near classic. C: Angela Molina, Margarita Lozano, Fernando Fernan-Gomez. D: Manuel Gutierrez Aragon. DRA 90m. v

Half Shot at Sunrise 1930 ★★★ Straight man Wheeler and funnyman Woolsey play AWOL WWI soldiers enjoying the joie de vivre of Paris while outmaneuvering the MPs. Amusing at times. C: Bert Wheeler, Robert Woolsey, Edna May Oliver. D: Paul Sloane. COM 78m. v

Half Slave, Half Free 1984 ★★★½ A Northern-born free African-American's life changes dramatically when he's grabbed by slave traders and sold into a life of servitude in the 1840s. Compelling; based on true story. (a.k.a. *Solomon Northrup's Odyssey*). C: Avery Brooks, Mason Adams. D: Gordon Parks. DRA 113m. v

Half Slave, Half Free 2 1985 ★★★ Educated, free African-American woman goes south during the Civil War to teach slaves. Calculated to uplift, but ultimately doesn't satisfy. Based on true story. (a.k.a. *Charlotte Forten's Mission: Experiment in Freedom*). C: Melba Moore, Mary Alice, Ned Beatty. D: Barry Crane. DRA 120m. v

Halfway House, The 1943 British ★★★½ Varied group assembles at a quiet country hideaway, where the mysterious host (Johns) and his daughter guide them through life-changing moments. Well-acted ensemble drama, though some stories have more impact than others. C: Mervyn Johns, Glynis Johns, Francoise Rosay, Sally Ann Howes. D: Basil Dearden. DRA 95m.

Hallelujah 1929 ★★★★ Early talkie with all African-American cast portrays life of a field hand who becomes a preacher but is undone by temptation. Historically significant but dated and uncomfortably condescending work. Good musical numbers. C: Daniel L. Haynes, Nina Mae McKinney, William Fountaine. D: King Vidor. MUS 106m. v

Hallelujah, I'm a Bum 1933 ★★★★½ Only early Hollywood musical to deal directly with the Depression casts Jolson as Central Park "mayor" of the hobos in love with young woman (Evans). Sophisticated rhyming couplet dialogue by S.N. Behrman segues seamlessly into Rodgers and Hart songs such as lovely "You Are Too Beautiful." Unusual combination of stylization and realism, way ahead of its time. (a.k.a. *Hallelujah, I'm a Tramp* and *The Heart of New York*) C: Al Jolson, Madge Evans, Frank Morgan, Harry Langdon. D: Lewis Milestone. MUS 82m.

Hallelujah, I'm a Tramp 1933 *See* **Hallelujah, I'm a Bum**

Hallelujah the Hills 1963 ★★★½ New York underground film about two men vying for the affections of the same woman. Playful comedy, cleverly done. C: Peter H. Beard, Martin Greenbaum, Sheila Finn, Peggy Steffans. D: Adolfas Mekas. COM 88m.

Hallelujah Trail, The 1965 ★★★ A cavalry officer, safeguarding a wagon shipment of whiskey bound for thirsty Colorado miners, is harassed by a crusading temperance leaguer, marching tribes, and militiamen. Bumbling, overlong comedy Western. C: Burt Lancaster, Lee Remick, Jim Hutton, Brian Keith, Martin Landau, Donald Pleasence. D: John Sturges. WST 165m. v

Halliday Brand, The 1957 ★★★ Cult director Lewis serves up an offbeat Western about a tyrannical ranch owner whose miserable treatment of both relatives and employees sets off a cycle of revenge. Top-notch cast works hard, but can't surmount the script's shortcomings. C: Joseph Cotten, Viveca Lindfors, Betsy Blair. D: Joseph Lewis. WST 77m.

Halloween 1978 ★★★★★ Carpenter's low-budget classic wrings every possible chill out of its story of a psychopath terrorizing Curtis and her fellow babysitters on Halloween eve. Despite endless imitations (and sequelizations), this movie still has the power to make you scream out loud. C: Jamie Lee Curtis, Donald Pleasence, Nancy Loomis, P.J. Soles. D: John Carpenter. HOR [R] 92m. v

Halloween II 1981 ★★★ Nowhere near as effective as the first film, this is nonetheless a stylish and snappy sequel. Curtis, the only survivor of the original mayhem, is taken to a hospital, where the killer follows to stalk her and decimate the staff. C: Jamie Lee Curtis, Donald Pleasence. D: Rick Rosenthal. HOR [R] 93m. v

Halloween III: Season of the Witch 1982 ★★★ Surprisingly, this sequel abandons repetition of its predecessors for a new Halloween-themed story. A mad toymaker (O'Herlihy) plots to turn the holiday into a real bloodbath with deadly masks, resulting in a minor but cleverly horrific scare show. (a.k.a. *Season of the Witch*) C: Stacey Nelkin, Dan O'Herlihy. D: Tommy Lee Wallace. HOR [R] 98m. v

Halloween 4: The Return of Michael Myers 1988 ★★ After sitting out *Halloween III*, the masked maniac returns to stalk his young niece (Harris) and her teenaged would-be protectors. But the thrill is gone by now; this is just another mechanical, often silly slasher flick. C: Donald Pleasence, Danielle Harris. D: Dwight H. Little. HOR [R] 88m. v

Halloween 5: Revenge of Michael Myers, The 1989 ★ The unstoppable madman hacks his way through another round of mayhem. Includes idiotic cliches, offensive violence, and an insultingly blatant set-up for yet another sequel. C: Donald Pleasence, Danielle Harris, Wendy Kaplan, Ellie Cornell, Don Shanks. D: Dominique Othenin-Girard. HOR [R] 97m.

Halls of Montezuma 1950 ★★★★ WWII leatherneck action as the Marines take on the Japanese in Pacific theater. Solid cast and production. C: Richard Widmark, Jack Palance, Robert Wagner, Karl Malden. D: Lewis Milestone. ACT 113m. v

Hallucination *See* **Hallucination Generation**

Hallucination Generation 1966 ★ Group of American hippies "turn on" in Spain and engage in criminal activities. Inferior nonsense complete with obligatory LSD "trip" scene. (a.k.a. *Hallucination*) C: George Montgomery, Danny Stone. D: Edward Mann. DRA 90m. v

Hambone and Hillie 1984 ★★★ Elderly woman (Gish) is separated from her dog at an airport. But the ever-loyal canine works his way cross-country to reunite with her. No surprises in this average telling of routine story. C: Lillian Gish, Timothy Bottoms, Candy Clark, O.J. Simpson. D: Roy Watts. FAM/DRA [PG] 97m. v

Hamburger Hill 1987 ★★★★ Harrowing, underrated drama (based partially on a real event) about soldiers assigned to capture and defend a virtually impossible position in Vietnam. Vivid and well acted, with moments that drive home the gruesome horrors of war. Not for the squeamish. C: Anthony Barille, Michael Boatman, Michael Dolan, Dylan McDermott, Courtney Vance. D: John Irvin. ACT [R] 104m. v

Hamburger . . . The Motion Picture 1985 ★ With his inheritance hinging on college graduation, a reckless young man enters Burgerbuster University for a degree in fast food management. As awful as it seems. C: Leigh McCloskey, Randi Brooks, Chuck McCann. D: Mike Marvin. COM [R] 90m. v

Hamlet 1948 British ★★★★★ Shakespeare's immortal tragedy, filmed by Olivier on location in Elsinore, Denmark, won Oscars for Best Picture and Actor to Olivier as the doomed prince. A definitive performance and a gripping, totally engrossing film. C: Laurence Olivier, Eileen Herlie, Jean Simmons, Basil Sydney, Stanley Holloway, Felix Aylmer. D: Laurence Olivier. DRA 153m. v

Hamlet 1969 British ★★½ Low-budget, dark, minimalist production of Williamson's successful London hit, unfortunately shot like a play. Speeches have been cut, everyone speaks too fast and sometimes unintelligibly, and supporting cast is mixture of good to terrible (mostly terrible). C: Nicol Williamson, Gordon Jackson, Anthony Hopkins, Judy Parfitt, Marianne Faithful. D: Tony Richardson. DRA [G] 114m. v

Hamlet 1990 ★★★★ Gibson is surprisingly effective as a virile Hamlet in this adaptation of Shakespeare's tragedy. Zeffirelli's direction spotlights action and humor. C: Mel Gibson, Glenn Close, Alan Bates, Paul Scofield, Ian Holm, Helena Bonham Carter. D: Franco Zeffirelli. DRA [PG] 135m. v

Hammer 1972 ★★½ A prizefighter (Williamson) challenges the Mob. Lots of fast action and the mandatory violence, but not much brainpower here. C: Fred Williamson, Bernie Hamilton, Vonetta McGee. D: Bruce Clark. ACT [R] 92m.

Hammerhead 1968 British ★★ U.S. espionage agent chases arch villian. Geeson adds welcome energy to feeble James Bond carbon copy. C: Vince Edwards, Judy Geeson, Diana Dors. D: David Miller. ACT [R] 99m.

Hammersmith Is Out 1972 ★★★ In this adaption of Faust legend, charismatic maniac escapes his confines and creates panic and delight in the people he encounters. Offbeat black comedy with hysterical outbursts. C: Elizabeth Taylor, Richard Burton, Peter Ustinov, Beau Bridges. D: Peter Ustinov. COM [R] 108m. v

Hammett 1982 ★★★ Real-life writer/detective Dashiell Hammett is plunged into the world of his fiction in this clumsy attempt at modern film noir. Even the brilliant Wenders cannot save this studio-savaged clunker. (Coppola is rumored to have reshot much of the film.) C: Frederic Forrest, Peter Boyle, Marilu Henner, Elisha Cook. D: Wim Wenders. CRI [PG] 97m. V

Hand in Hand 1960 British ★★★½ Gentle tale of a young Catholic boy and Jewish girl who become friends, despite parental prejudice, aims to teach children the value of tolerating religious and racial differences. Well intentioned and well done. C: Loretta Parry, Philip Needs, John Gregson, Sybil Thorndike. D: Philip Leacock. FAM/DRA 75m.

Hand of the Night, The 1968 British ★★ A female vampire becomes the object of a man's obsession. Psuedohorror fare, produced without innovation. (a.k.a. *The Beast of Morocco*) C: William Sylvester, Diane Clare, Alizia Gur, Edward Underdown. D: Fredric Goode. HOR 88m.

Hand That Rocks the Cradle, The 1992 ★★★★ Yuppie couple hire nanny, get psycho. Heard-it-before concept gets a terrific, thrillerama production. An entertaining fright ride as De Mornay makes a bid to rule her corner of the world. C: Rebecca De Mornay, Annabella Sciorra, Matt McCoy, Julianne Moore. D: Curtis Hanson. CRI [R] 110m. V

Hand, The 1981 ★★ Stone's first studio production tries to be compellingly intense and winds up looking very silly. Caine plays a cartoonist who loses a hand in an auto accident and finds that the thing is alive and killing people he dislikes. C: Michael Caine, Andrea Marcovicci, Annie McEnroe, Viveca Lindfors. D: Oliver Stone. HOR [R] 105m. V

Handful of Dust, A 1988 British ★★★★ Adapted from Evelyn Waugh's novel set in the '30s, about morally degenerate upper class Brits and their disintegrating marriage. Superb acting, with cameo gem by Huston as individualist lady pilot. Beautiful exterior and interior settings. C: James Wilby, Kristin Scott Thomas, Rupert Graves, Judi Dench, Anjelica Huston, Alec Guinness. D: Charles Sturridge. DRA [PG] 118m. V

Handle with Care *See* **Citizens Band**

Handle with Care 1958 ★★½ Forgettable small-scale drama about an eager law student (Jones) who attempts to solve a real crime while his fellow students labor on a mock grand jury. C: Dean Jones, Joan O'Brien, Thomas Mitchell. D: David Friedkin. DRA 82m.

Handmaid's Tale, The 1990 ★★★ In Margaret Atwood's futuristic feminist morality fable, toxic waste and environmental contamination have reduced fertility and healthy babies are at a premium. A powerful totalitarian regime isolates fertile young women and doles them out as breeders for the ruling elite. An intriguing premise, but ultimately preachy and dull. C: Natasha Richardson, Robert Duvall, Faye Dunaway, Aidan Quinn, Elizabeth McGovern, Victoria Tennant. D: Volker Schlondorff. DRA [R] 109m. V

Hands Across The Border 1944 ★★★½ Roy Rogers, in his uncompromising compassion, comes to the aid of a widow by catching her husband's killer and securing her farm. C: Roy Rogers, Ruth Terry, Trigger. D: Joseph Kane. WST 54m.

Hands Across the Table 1935 ★★★★½ Lombard is wonderful as a fortune-hunting manicurist trying to choose between two beaux. Intelligent comedy scores as a tender love story as well as an uproariously funny tale. C: Carole Lombard, Fred MacMurray, Ralph Bellamy. D: Mitchell Leisen. COM 80m.

Hands of a Murderer 1990 British ★★★ TV-movie continuation of Conan Doyle's tales finds Sherlock Holmes and Dr. Watson once again chasing Moriarty after he narrowly escapes death and purloins top-secret government papers. Woodward is an intriguing Holmes in this well-crafted, intelligent British offering. (a.k.a. *Sherlock Holmes and the Prince of Crime*) C: Edward Woodward, John Hillerman. D: Stuart Orme. DRA 100m. TVM

Hands of a Stranger 1962 ★★★ Routine retelling of *The Hands of Orlac*, in which an injured concert pianist is operated on by a mad doctor and receives the hands of a murderer. From then on, he'd rather strangle than play. C: Paul Lukather, Joan Harvey, Irish McCalla. D: Newton Arnold. HOR 86m. V

Hands of a Stranger 1987 ★★★½ Television adaptation of Robert Daley novel about a police officer whose attraction to a lawyer distracts his search for his wife's rapist. Excellent cast, and first half is particularly gripping. C: Armand Assante, Blair Brown, Beverly D'Angelo. D: Larry Elikann. DRA 179m. V

Hands of Death 1988 ★★½ Ninja pirates spend their time searching for treasure and victimizing anyone foolish enough to try to stop them. Average actioner. C: Richard Harrison, Mike Abbott, Stefan Bredhart, Phil Parker. D: Godfrey Ho. ACT 90m. V

Hands of Orlac, The 1960 British ★★★½ After a concert pianist's hands are crushed, a maniacal doctor fits him with a killer's hands, which act out their own murderous impulses. Although tame by today's standards, some of the horror scenes in this moody thriller are quite chilling. C: Mel Ferrer, Lucile Saint-Simon, Christopher Lee, Donald Pleasence. D: Edmond Greville. HOR 95m.

Hands of Steel 1986 ★★★ A half-man, half-robot goes berserk and tries to kill a scientist who's at work on a crucial project that may save the earth. Harrowing. C: Daniel Greene, John Saxon, Janet Agren, Claudio Cassinelli. D: Martin Dolman. SFI [R] 94m. V

Hands of the Ripper 1971 British ★★★½ Well-made variation on Jack the Ripper story. Here the murderer's traumatized daughter (Rees) goes into trances and carries on dad's work. Shock scenes are plentiful and cast is good, including Porter as sympathetic doctor caught up in the mayhem. C: Eric Porter, Angharad Rees. D: Peter Sasdy. HOR [R] 85m. V

Hands That Picked Cotton ★★★½ A political chronicle of African-Americans in the deep south. An interesting and moving study of the right to vote and all it means. DOC 60m. V

Handy Andy 1934 ★★★½ Will Rogers plays a rural druggist with a stuck-up wife. Amusing star vehicle manages plenty of homespun humor. C: Will Rogers, Peggy Wood, Mary Carlisle, Robert Taylor. D: David Butler. COM 81m.

Handyman, The 1980 Canadian ★★★★ An insecure young man has a doomed affair with a married woman. Lovingly crafted film with sensitive performances should be better known than it is. C: Jocelyn Berube, Andree Pelletier, Jannette Bertrand. D: Micheline Lanctot. DRA 99m.

Hang 'em High 1967 ★★★ The spaghetti-Western returns to the States. Tale of a cow wrangler (Eastwood) who, surviving his own lynching, is driven to search for and kill his attackers. Good cast, good production. C: Clint Eastwood, Inger Stevens, Ed Begley, Pat Hingle. D: Ted Post. WST [PG] 114m. V

Hangar 18 1981 ★★ Tired TV stars fail to enliven this tale of a damaged alien spaceship being hidden by the U.S. government. Silly stuff. C: Darren McGavin, Robert Vaughn, Gary Collins. D: James L. Conway. SFI [PG] 97m. V

Hanged Man, The 1964 ★★½ Man falls for young woman at Mardi Gras, while trailing his pal's killer. Pale, uncompelling remake of *Ride the Pink Horse.* C: Edmond O'Brien, Robert Culp, Vera Miles, J. Carrol Naish. D: Don Siegel. CRI 87m. V

Hangin' with the Homeboys 1991 ★★★★ Interesting independent feature looks at four young pals from the Bronx who journey into Manhattan for a night of thrills and unexpected self-discovery. Wryly intelligent comedy features excellent performances in a promising directorial debut. C: Doug E. Doug, Mario Joyner, John Leguizamo, Kimberly Russell. D: Joseph B. Vasquez. COM [R] 88m. V

Hanging Tree, The 1959 ★★★★ In a Montana gold mining camp, Doc Frail, a gun-toting physician haunted by a guilty past, ministers to a young sightless woman. Solid performances by all in a grave, restrained frontier tale. Scott, in his film debut as a zealous preacher, is a standout. C: Gary Cooper, Maria Schell, Karl Malden, George C. Scott. D: Delmer Daves. WST 108m. V

Hanging Woman, The 1985 ★★★ Decent chiller about Cooper arriving in small town for reading of his deceased aunt's will and discovering zombies. Creepy atmospherics help make up for slow-moving plot. (a.k.a. *Return of the Zombies* and *Beyond the Living Dead*) C: Stan Cooper, Vickie Nesbitt. D: John Davidson. HOR [R] 91m.

Hangman, The 1956 ★★★½ A tough-talking sheriff (Taylor) incurs the wrath of his townspeople for taking the side of an innocent man accused of murder. Solid cast and taut story line. C: Robert Taylor, Tina Louise, Jack Lord. D: Michael Curtiz. WST 86m.

Hangman's House 1928 ★★★½ Troubled romance leads to heartbreak and redemption, with consequences for an entire family. Thin soap opera plot but fine acting and solid direction. Look sharp for young Hollywood nobody John Wayne! C: June Collyer, Larry Kent, Victor McLaglen. D: John Ford. DRA 72m.

Hangman's Knot 1952 ★★★½ Vigilantes ambush homeward-bound Confederate troopers loaded with plundered Union gold. Winning Scott vehicle with fine action and suspense. C: Randolph Scott, Donna Reed, Lee Marvin. D: Roy Huggins. WST 81m.

Hangmen Also Die 1943 ★★★½ Vengeful Germans impose reign of terror over Czechoslovakia after a physician assassinates cruel Gestapo leader Reinhard Heydrich ("the Hangman") in 1942. Compelling WWII propaganda piece, written by Bertolt Brecht.(a.k.a. *Lest We Forget*) C: Brian Donlevy, Walter Brennan, Anna Lee. D: Fritz Lang. DRA 131m.

Hangover Square 1945 ★★★★ Great period atmosphere in well-done suspenser, with detective (Sanders) out to stop a disturbed pianist (Cregar) who's murdering women. Similar to *The Lodger*, with same filmmaking team and leads. Cregar especially good in his last film performance. C: Laird Cregar, Linda Darnell, George Sanders. D: John Brahm. HOR 77m.

Hangup 1974 ★★ Unsatisfying thriller about the evils of drug trafficking. Black exploitation flick notable chiefly as Hathaway's last picture. C: William Elliott, Marki Bey, Michael Lerner. D: Henry Hathaway. CRI 94m.

Hanky Panky 1982 ★★★½ Naive architect (Wilder) is mistaken for a spy and pursued by a slew of international wackos. Comedy thriller with talented cast and crew. C: Gene Wilder, Gilda Radner, Kathleen Quinlan, Richard Widmark. D: Sidney Poitier. COM [PG] 105m. V

Hanna K. 1983 French ★★★ Clayburgh is a Jewish-American lawyer living in Tel Aviv who dumps Byrne, her Zionist boyfriend, for a Palestinian activist. An uneven politicized tour of the region as seen through Clayburgh's conflicted point of view. While some passages are powerful, the politics are rather naive and one-sided. C: Jill Clayburgh, Jean Yanne, Gabriel Byrne. D: Constantine Costa-Gavras. DRA [R] 111m. V

Hannah and Her Sisters 1986 ★★★★★ Allen's mature, masterful look at three sisters in New York and their interconnected lives and loves. Wiest has showiest role as neurotic actress/playwright with self-confidence problem, but everyone here is wonderful, especially Farrow in title role and Allan as her hypochondriac husband in film's funniest sequence. Wise, pungent screenplay by Allen won Oscar, as did Supporting Actor Caine and Supporting Actress Wiest. C: Woody Allen, Mia Farrow, Michael Caine, Dianne Wiest, Barbara Hershey, Lloyd Nolan, Maureen O'Sullivan, Max von Sydow, Sam Waterston, Carrie Fisher. D: Woody Allen. COM [PG-13] 103m. V

Hannah Lee 1953 ★★½ A cafe proprietress falls for a gunfighter in trouble with the town marshal. Old-style Western originally shot in 3-D. (a.k.a. *Outlaw Territory*) C: Macdonald Carey, Joanne Dru, John Ireland. D: John Ireland, Lee Garmes. WST 78m.

Hanna's War 1988 ★★★ Long, labored film chronicles the true exploits of a courageous Hungarian freedom fighter in WWII. Her story is inspiring. C: Ellen Burstyn, Maruschka Detmers, Anthony Andrews, Donald Pleasence, Denholm Elliott. D: Menahem Golan. DRA [PG-13] 148m. V

Hannibal 1960 ★ In order to attack Rome, warrior Hannibal leads his troops and many elephants through dangerous mountain trails. Stiff, dusty and nearly impossible to watch recreation of history. C: Victor Mature, Rita Gam, Gabriele Ferzetti. D: Edgar Ulmer. DRA 103m.

Hannibal Brooks 1969 British ★★★ A British POW dispatched to appropriate a prized elephant from a Munich zoo escapes with it across the Alps during WWII. Patchy comedy/drama with exciting finale. C: Oliver Reed, Michael J. Pollard, Wolfgang Preiss. D: Michael Winner. DRA [PG] 101m.

Hannie Caulder 1972 British ★★★½ With the expertise and companionship of a bounty hunter who teaches her to use a gun, a frontier woman hunts down the three outlaws who sexually assaulted her, killed her husband and burned her home. Unconventional revenge/chase Western with three bumbling miscreants played to the hilt. C: Raquel Welch, Robert Culp, Ernest Borgnine, Jack Elam, Christopher Lee, Diana Dors. D: Burt Kennedy. WST [R] 87m. V

Hanoi Hilton, The 1987 ★★★ War adventure involving POWs in Vietnam, intended to bring attention to their plight. C: Michael Moriarty, Paul LeMat, Jeffrey Jones, Lawrence Pressman, David Soul. D: Lionel Chetwynd. ACT [R] 126m. V

Hanover Street 1979 ★★★½ War is the wrong time for love when American soldier Ford falls for his British nurse Down. Stylish. One of Ford's first starring roles. C: Harrison Ford, Lesley-Anne Down, Christopher Plummer, Alec McCowen. D: Peter Hyams. DRA [PG] 110m. V

Hans Brinker 1979 ★★★½ Musicalized version of children's tale about boy trying to win ice skating race to pay father's doctor's bills. The songs aren't great, but the cast is charming and the European locations are lovely. Good holiday fare for youngsters. C: Eleanor Parker, Richard Basehart, Cyril Ritchard. D: Robert Scheerer. FAM/MUS 103m. TVM

Hans Christian Anderson 1952 ★★★½ Romantic musical biography (very much fictionalized) of the famed storyteller/cobbler (Kaye), centers on a visit to Copenhagen and adventures with a diva of the Royal Copenhagen Ballet. Admirably restrained Kaye and strong score by Frank Loesser. C: Danny Kaye, Jeanmaire, Farley Granger. D: Charles Vidor. MUS 112m. TVM

Hans Christian Andersen's Day Dreamer ★★★ A young boy goes off in search of his favorite fairy tale characters. He finds "The Emperor's New Clothes," "The Ugly Duckling" and many more. A joyful animated treat. FAM/DRA 98m. V

Hansel and Gretel ★★★½ Classic opera version of the beloved fairy tale adventure of two children and an evil witch. Forever charming. C: Brigitte Fassbaender, Edita Gruberova, Hermann Prey. D: August Everding. FAM/MUS 100m. V

Hansel and Gretel 1988 ★★★½ Fine version of the classic fairy tale about two children and a gingerbread house. Enchanting adaptation, exquisite cast. C: David Warner, Cloris Leachman, Hugh Pollard, Nicola Stapleton. D: Len Talen. FAM/DRA 84m. V

Hanussen 1989 German ★★★★½ WWI soldier develops psychic abilities after suffering bullet wound to the head and is tormented by the belief that he can change a grim future. The unusual (and at times incredible) subject matter is effortlessly handled by Brandauer's insightful performance. Last in trilogy, after *Mephisto* and *Colonel Redl*. C: Klaus Maria Brandauer, Erland Josephson. D: Istvan Szabo. DRA [R] 117m. V

Happening, The 1967 ★★★ Retired gangster (Quinn) is kidnapped by group of idealistic rebels hoping to use ransom money to fund their causes. Great cast of newcomers (Dunaway's film debut) saves this comedy/drama from falling apart. C: Anthony Quinn, George Maharis, Michael Parks, Faye Dunaway, Robert Walker, Milton Berle. D: Elliot Silverstein. COM 101m.

Happiest Days of Your Life, The 1950 British ★★★★ Droll comedy about English boys school forced to share space with displaced girl's academy. A delight, thanks to inspired pairing of gifted comic actors Sim and Rutherford. C: Alastair Sim, Margaret Rutherford, Joyce Grenfell. D: Frank Launder. COM 84m.

Happiest Millionaire, The 1967 ★★★½ Sprightly Disney version of the life story of eccentric Philadelphia millionaire Anthony J. Drexel Biddle (MacMurray). Some fine musical numbers and a competent production make for entertaining viewing; the last film personally overseen by Walt. C: Fred MacMurray, Tommy Steele, Greer Garson, Geraldine Page, Gladys Cooper, Lesley Ann Warren, John Davidson. D: Norman Tokar. FAM/MUS [G] 118m.

Happily Ever After 1990 ★★★ Low-grade cartoon feature, saved by famous voices, retells the Snow White story using "dwarfelles" as replacements for the well-known seven little men. Voices of Edward Asner, Phyllis Diller, Carol Channing, Dom Deluise, Zsa Zsa Gabor, Tracey Ullman, Irene Cara. D: John Howley. FAM/DRA [G] 74m.

Happiness 1934 Russian ★★★ Classic silent film depicting Russian folklore story of a villager and his dealings with assorted priests, nuns and others. D: Alexander Medvedkin. COM 69m. V

Happiness Ahead 1934 ★★★½ Bored heiress (Hutchinson) pretends to be poor and finds love with a window-washer (Powell). Typical Depression fantasy with charming songs including "Pop Goes Your Heart," and "Beauty Must Be Loved." C: Dick Powell, Josephine Hutchinson, Frank McHugh, Ruth Donnelly. D: Mervyn LeRoy. MUS 86m.

Happiness Cage, The 1972 *See* **Demon Within, The**

Happiness of Three Women, The 1954 ★★★ To ensure the happiness of local villagers, a fussbudget and a Welsh postman resort to trickery. Small, somewhat dated audience pleaser. C: Brenda de Banzie, Petula Clark, Donald Houston, Patricia Cutts, Eynon Evans. D: Maurice Elvey. COM 79m.

Happy Anniversary 1959 ★★★½ A misunderstanding leads a young girl (Duke) to tell family tales on national TV, embarrassing her happily married parents (Niven and Gaynor). Adult comedy tries a bit too hard, but has its moments—especially Niven kicking the TV. C: David Niven, Mitzi Gaynor, Carl Reiner, Monique Van Vooren, Patty Duke. D: David Miller. COM 81m.

Happy Anniversary 007—25 Years Of James Bond 1987 ★★★½ A fascinating look back at a quarter century of Bond films. Amidst all the clips and memories is a fun-filled meeting of all four stars who played Bond. DOC 59m. V

Happy Birthday, Gemini 1980 ★★★ Film adaptation of Albert Innaurato's play *Gemini*. The psychologically complex story of a boy exploring his sexual identity loses some of its significance in such a big-screen production. C: Madeline Kahn, Rita Moreno, Robert Viharo. D: Richard Benner. DRA [R] 107m. V

Happy Birthday to Me 1981 Canadian ★ Overlong slasher flick, with Anderson as a teenager who may be bumping off her friends. The ads played up the "creativity" of the murders (by shish kebob, motorcycle, etc.), and indeed, they're all the movie has to offer. C: Glenn Ford, Melissa Sue Anderson. D: J. Lee Thompson. HOR [R] 108m. V

Happy Birthday, Wanda June 1971 ★★★½ Kurt Vonnegut-inspired story of an oafish adventurer (Steiger) who returns to his wife after long absence and finds her on the verge of remarrying. Stagy, long-winded black comedy has many outrageous moments. C: Rod Steiger, Susannah York, William Hickey, George Grizzard, Don Murray. D: Mark Robson. COM [R] 105m.

Happy Days 1930 ★★★½ A showboat singer helps out some old chums when she becomes successful in New York. Essentially a filmed revue, with great numbers and screen effects. C: Charles E. Evans, Marjorie White, Richard Keene. D: Benjamin Stoloff. MUS 86m.

Happy Ending, The 1969 ★★ Simmons barely rises above truly dreadful material in soap opera of disillusioned, unhappy wife facing onslaughts of middle age armed with too much booze and not enough to do. C: Jean Simmons, John Forsythe, Lloyd Bridges, Shirley Jones, Teresa Wright, Dick Shawn, Nanette Fabray. D: Richard Brooks. DRA [PG] 112m.

Happy Endings 1983 ★★★ Screenwriter Chris Beaumont draws upon his real-life experience of being a teenage musician forced to raise his younger siblings on his own in this energetic, sentimental story. Gets a bit wet when relatives try to gain custody, but engaging overall. C: Lee Montgomery, Jill Schoelen. D: Jerry Thorpe. DRA 104m.

Happy Ever After 1932 ★★★½ Window cleaners promote a young actress and clear her path to stardom. Amiable comedy made in Germany with English cast. Based on a story by Billy Wilder and Walter Reisch. C: Lilian Harvey, Jack Hulbert, Cicely Courtneidge, Sonnie Hale. D: Paul Martin, Robert Stevenson. COM 86m.

Happy Gigolo—A Man for All Reasons, The 1973 *See* **Happy Gigolo, The**

Happy Gigolo, The 1973 ★ A bellboy takes a very personal interest in the female guests staying in the hotel he works at. A thin premise for a feeble sex comedy. (a.k.a. *The Happy Gigolo—A Man for All Reasons*) C: Peter Ham, Margaret Rose Keil. D: Ilja Nutrot. COM 73m.

Happy Go Lovely 1951 British ★★½ Producer (Nivens) hires dancer (Vera-Ellen) so her boyfriend will invest in show. Routine musical. C: David Niven, Vera-Ellen, Cesar Romero. D: H. Bruce Humberstone. MUS 87m. V

Happy Go Lucky 1943 ★★★½ Martin spends life savings on Caribbean cruise looking for rich husband. Plot's nothing much, but stars are attractive and Hutton a sensation in specialty number "Murder He Says" (by Frank Loesser and Jimmy McHugh). C: Mary Martin, Dick Powell, Eddie Bracken, Betty Hutton, Rudy Vallee. D: Curtis Bernhardt. MUS 81m.

Happy Hooker Goes Hollywood, The 1980 ★★½ Legendary prostitute Xaviera Hollander (Beswick) calls on her professional colleagues to help her save a movie studio from financial ruin. Energetic cast looks lost amidst dull sexual situations and naughty jokes. C: Martine Beswicke, Chris Lemmon, Phil Silvers. D: Alan Roberts. COM [R] 85m. V

Happy Hooker Goes to Washington, The 1977 ★★ In the further adventures of the famous prostitute, Hollander (Heatherton) ends up in D.C. defending her occupation and lifestyle to group of lecherous senators. More dumb sex jokes and crude situations. C: Joey Heatherton, George Hamilton, Ray Walston. D: William A. Levey. COM [R] 86m. v

Happy Hooker, The 1975 ★★★ A solid cast and a knowingly silly script elevate this squeaky-clean adaptation of Xaviera Hollander's once-notorious memoirs. Redgrave plays Hollander, a Dutchwoman who went from being a call girl to a very prosperous N.Y. madam. Followed by two fictional sequels. C: Lynn Redgrave, Jean-Pierre Aumont. D: Nicholas Sgarro. COM [R] 96m. v

Happy Hour 1987 ★★ Scientist invents secret beer ingredient that turns the suds into highly addictive drink, making him a target for international spies. Good cast ends up soused in lowbrow comedy full of juvenile sex jokes and humor. C: Richard Gilliland, Jamie Farr, Tawny Kitaen, Rich Little. D: John De Bello. COM [R] 88m.

Happy Is the Bride 1957 British ★★★ Couple's plans for quiet wedding are waylaid when their parents intervene in the arrangements. A pleasant his-family vs. her-family remake of *Quiet Wedding*. C: Ian Carmichael, Janette Scott, Terry-Thomas, Joyce Grenfell. D: Roy Boulting. COM 84m.

Happy Land 1943 ★★★ Tender family drama about a father who begins to question life when his son dies in WWII. Story not wholly realized since doubts about war aren't fully explored and film slides into support for "what we're doing over there." C: Don Ameche, Frances Dee, Harry Carey, Ann Rutherford, Cara Williams, Dickie Moore. D: Irving Pichel. DRA 73m.

Happy Landing 1938 ★★★½ Entertaining romance-on-ice trifle as Olympic skating champ Henie plays a Norwegian who loses her heart to an American pilot (Ameche) who's crash-landed. Merman's a plus. C: Sonja Henie, Don Ameche, Cesar Romero, Ethel Merman. D: Roy Del Ruth. MUS 102m. v

Happy Mother's Day, Love George 1973 ★★½ Solid cast in middling thriller. A man returns to his boyhood home and uncovers his seriously twisted family background and some gruesome murders. Visually striking but dramatically shaky. (a.k.a. *Run, Stranger, Run*) C: Patricia Neal, Cloris Leachman, Bobby Darin, Ron Howard. D: Darren McGavin. HOR [PG] 90m.

Happy New Year 1974 French ★★★★ A recently paroled convict (Ventura) plots a spectacular jewel robbery on the French Riviera. His plans are sidetracked when he accidentally falls in love with the antiques dealer (Fabian) whose store is next to his intended target. Entertaining mix of comedy, romance, and suspense. (a.k.a. *The Happy New Year Caper*) C: Lino Ventura, Francoise Fabian, Charles Gerard. D: Claude Lelouch. COM [PG] 114m. v

Happy New Year 1987 ★★★½ Two aging crooks plan to rob a local jewelry store but things go hilariously awry. Excellent performances by Durning and especially Falk nearly make up for disjointed story and confusing plot developments. Based on superior French film of same name. C: Peter Falk, Wendy Hughes, Charles Durning, Tom Courtenay. D: John G. Avildsen. COM 86m. v

Happy New Year!, A 1979 Hungarian ★★★ On New Year's Day, a team of men and women engineers meet at a chemical plant for some serious work. Unfortunately, they're all hung over from partying the night before. Funny satire. C: Cecilia Esztergalyos. D: Reszo Szoreny. COM 84m. v

Happy New Year Caper *See* **Happy New Year**

Happy Road, The 1957 ★★½ Cute if uneven comedy about single parents (Kelly and Laage) pursuing their children, who have run away from Swiss boarding school. C: Gene Kelly, Barbara Laage, Michael Redgrave, Bobby Clark. D: Gene Kelly. COM 80m.

Happy Since I Met You 1986 ★★★ An airheaded drama teacher and a struggling actor meet at a party and fall in love. Charming and funny. C: Julie Walters, Duncan Preston, Tracey Ullman, Jim Bowen. COM 55m. v

Happy Thieves 1962 ★★ Debonair thief and companion plan spectacular international robbery. Both Harrison and Hayworth are miscast in poorly scripted European heist caper. C: Rex Harrison, Rita Hayworth, Joseph Wiseman, Alida Valli. D: George Marshall. COM 88m.

Happy Time, The 1952 ★★★★ Playboy photographer Jourdan returns home to French-Canadian family, becoming bad influence for nephew Driscoll and thorn in side of father Boyer. Richly observed comedy/drama from Broadway play, with excellent cast. C: Charles Boyer, Louis Jourdan, Bobby Driscoll, Marsha Hunt. D: Richard Fleischer. DRA 94m.

Happy Together 1989 ★★ Thanks to a mix-up at the dean's office, a nerdy guy winds up sharing a dorm room with a fellow freshman who's much better looking—and female. So-so silliness, with charming stars. C: Patrick Dempsey, Helen Slater. D: Mel Damski. COM [PG-13] 102m. v

Happy Years, The 1950 ★★★★ An energetic adolescent boy struggles to fit into prep school at the turn of the century. Owen Johnson's charming *Lawrenceville Stories* have been transformed into a well-crafted drama. C: Dean Stockwell, Scotty Beckett, Darryl Hickman. D: William Wellman. DRA [G] 110m.

Harakiri 1962 Japanese ★★★★★ Provocative, dramatic view of the traditional Japanese feudal system. A master swordsman (Nakadai), being forced to commit ritual suicide, tells the story of what brought him to this point. Stark, expressive use of wide-screen format, soaring action sequences. Not for the squeamish, though. C: Tatsuya Nakadai, Rentaro Mikuni, Tetsuro Tamba, Shima Iwashita. D: Masaki Kobayashi. ACT 135m. V

Harbor Lights 1963 ★ To call this trash about criminal intrigue a B-movie would be a compliment. The movie's real mystery is what the title has to do with what's happening onscreen. C: Kent Taylor, Jeff Morrow. D: Maury Dexter. ACT 68m.

Harbor of Missing Men 1950 ★★ Thoroughly unremarkable, cheapo flick about a man who accidentally gets caught in a jewel smuggler's web. C: Richard Denning, Barbara Fuller, Steven Geray. D: R. G. Springsteen. ACT 60m.

Hard Act to Follow, A ★★★★ A comprehensive 3-part series that gives ample, delightful coverage of the amazing Buster Keaton and his fabulous career as one of the screen's comic giants. Treat yourself. DOC 156m. V

Hard-Boiled 1992 ★★★★ Leung and Fat are criminal and cop, tied to one another by their pasts. Another memorable explosion of violence from John Woo with some astonishing action setpieces. C: Chow Fat, Tony Leung, Teresa Mo. D: John Woo. ACT 126m.

Hard Boiled Mahoney 1947 ★★½ This installment in the *Bowery Boys* series finds our heroes acting as private eyes as they investigate a crooked fortune-teller. Fairly entertaining blend of comedy and sleuthing. C: Leo Gorcey, Huntz Hall, Gabriel Dell. D: William Beaudine. ACT 64m. V

Hard Choices 1986 ★★★½ Low-budget sleeper with number of surprises. Klenck's solid, believable performance is one of them; she's a social worker who springs juvenile murderer from prison and goes on the lam with him. Tough, inventive film made many 10-Best lists. C: Margaret Klenck, Gary McCleery, John Seitz, John Sayles. D: Rick King. DRA 90m. V

Hard Contract 1969 ★★★½ Coburn stretches as a jet-setting assassin softened by Remick. Speaks out strongly against brutality, but sometimes too preachy. C: James Coburn, Lee Remick, Lilli Palmer, Burgess Meredith, Karen Black. D: S. Pogostin. DRA [PG] 107m.

Hard Country 1981 ★★★ For country-western fans, story of an urban cowboy who falls in love. Actors all blonde and attractive, but nothing really special except maybe music. Basinger's film debut. C: Jan-Michael Vincent, Kim Basinger, Michael Parks, Tanya Tucker, Daryl Hannah. D: David Greene. DRA [PG] 101m. V

Hard Day's Night, A 1964 British ★★★★½ Delightful look at the Beatles on tour makes the most of refreshing, light-hearted rapport between the singers. Slim plot involves Paul and his grandfather. Lester's fast-paced, improvisational style is just right. Beatle fans will scream for wonderful renditions of classic early songs, including "Can't Buy Me Love" and "I Should Have Known Better." C: John Lennon, Paul McCartney, George Harrison, Ringo Starr, Wilfrid Brambell. D: Richard Lester. MUS [G] 90m. V

Hard Driver 1973 *See* **Last American Hero, The**

Hard Drivers 1960 ★★★½ After his parole, an ex-con takes a job as a trucker and vows to go straight. But a shifty boss and some troublemakers keep him in constant temptation. Connery leads a super cast. C: Sean Connery, Stanley Baker, Jill Ireland, Herbert Lom, Patrick McGoohan, David McCallum. D: Cy Endfield. DRA 91m. V

Hard Drivin' 1960 ★★★ In the deep south, a couple of stock car racers go after adventure wherever they can find it—on the race track or off. Action and local color. C: Rory Calhoun, Alan Hale, Connie Hines, John Gentry. D: Paul Helmick. ACT 92m. V

Hard, Fast and Beautiful 1951 ★★★½ Director Lupino (who also makes a cameo appearance) has produced an interesting tale of a mother (Trevor) who pushes her daughter (Forrest) to be a tennis pro. No-nonsense, candid look at relationship dynamics. C: Claire Trevor, Sally Forrest, Carleton Young. D: Ida Lupino. DRA 79m.

Hard Feelings 1981 ★★★★ Troubled young man from suburbia (Marotte) finds understanding and compassion from straight-talking young black urban woman (Woodard). Engaging and intelligent film with good insights into contrasting cultures. C: Carl Marotte, Charlaine Woodard, Grand Bush. D: Daryl Duke. DRA [R] 110m.

Hard Frame 1970 ★★★ An ex-con (Reynolds) arrives at a wine country home, intending to clear his name. Erratic drama is sometimes predictable, but gets by. (a.k.a. *Hunters Are for Killing*) C: Burt Reynolds, Melvyn Douglas, Suzanne Pleshette. D: Bernard Kowalski. DRA 100m. TVM

Hard Knocks 1980 Australian ★★★★ A hard-luck ex-convict, menaced from all sides, tries to straighten out her life. Transcendant acting by Mann as ex-con steals film. C: Tracey Mann, John Arnold, Bill Hunter. D: Don McLennan. DRA 85m.

Hard Knox 1984 ★★ This TV-series pilot, which didn't fly, concerns a Marine who does. A formerly gung-ho aviator (Conrad) must now choose between a boring office job or heading an out-of-control military academy. C: Robert Conrad, Bill Erwin. D: Peter Werner. DRA 90m. TVM V

Hard Man, The 1957 ★★½ Heartthrob Madison plays an honest lawman who falls for the beautiful French widow of a recently murdered rancher. Apart from the attractive leads, a fairly unremarkable, low-key Western outing. C: Guy Madison, Lorne Greene, Valerie French. D: George Sherman. WST 80m.

Hard Nut, The 1991 ★★★★★ Famed Mark Morris Dance Group presents acutely funny adaptation of Tchaikovsky's "The Nutcracker." C: Mark Morris Dance Group. MUS 90m. V

Hard Promises 1992 ★★½ Errant husband discovers he truly loves his wife when he finds out she's divorced him and is going to marry someone else. Familiar theme gets uneven treatment, thanks to less than endearing characters. Needed fewer sparks, more sparkle. C: Sissy Spacek, William Petersen, Brian Kerwin. D: Martin Davidson. COM [PG] 95m. V

Hard Ride, The 1971 ★★★ Vietnam casualty, and former biker, is brought back home by his sergeant, who then discovers that arranging for his funeral is up to him. No name stars in this one, but it's a nice little drama. C: Robert Fuller, Sherry Bain, Tony Russel. D: Burt Topper. DRA [PG] 93m.

Hard Road to Glory, A—The Black Athlete In America ★★★½ A comprehensive look at African American athletes. Narrated by James Earl Jones, this account features track star Jesse Owens and golfer Calvin Peete. Informative and inspiring. C: James Earl Jones. DOC 60m. V

Hard Rock Harrigan 1935 ★★★ Two rival miners get caught in a cave-in. Their only means toward survival is to team up. C: George O'Brien, Irene Hervey, Fred Kohler. D: David Howard. ACT 60m. V

Hard Rock Zombies 1985 ★★½ After her murder, a woman and four rock musicians rise from the grave and perform a special concert. D: Krishna Shah. HOR [R] 90m. V

Hard Target 1993 ★★★★ Van Damme vehicle is glossy update of *The Most Dangerous Game*. Manhunt plot sets up deliriously high decibel action sequences, and Van Damme shines throughout. Hollywood debut of Hong Kong director John Woo. C: Jean-Claude Van Damme, Lance Henriksen, Wilford Brimley. D: John Woo. ACT [R] 97m.

Hard Ticket to Hawaii 1987 ★★★ Buxom narcotics agents incur the wrath of drug runners while conducting an undercover sting in Hawaii. Slick action number for the Playmate set. C: Dona Speir, Hope Marie Carlton, Ronn Moss. D: Andy Sidaris. ACT [R] 96m. V

Hard Times 1975 ★★★★ Quiet street fighter (Bronson) boxes out a living for himself and his hustling manager (Coburn) in Depression-era New Orleans. Enjoyable, but the fight scenes are brutal. May be Bronson's best film. C: Charles Bronson, James Coburn, Jill Ireland. D: Walter Hill. ACT [PG] 97m. V

Hard to Get 1938 ★★★ Depression-era romantic comedy about a down-and-out architect (Powell) working as a gas pump jockey and a millionaire (de Havilland) who stops to get her tank filled. Fun fluff. C: Dick Powell, Olivia de Havilland, Charles Winninger, Bonita Granville. D: Ray Enright. COM 80m.

Hard to Handle 1933 ★★★½ An ad exec/-con artist (Cagney) organizes a get-rich-quick dance marathon in this wisecracking comedy energized by the dynamic presence of its star. C: James Cagney, Mary Brian, Ruth Donnelly. D: Mervyn LeRoy. COM 78m.

Hard to Hold 1984 ★★½ Successful rock star (Springfield) falls for a fiesty school counselor. Good music is only outstanding aspect of this otherwise contrived star vehicle. C: Rick Springfield, Janet Eilber. D: Larry Peerce. DRA [PG] 93m. V

Hard to Kill 1990 ★★½ A righteous cop (Seagal) is left for dead when he slips into a coma, but thanks to the help of a cunning nurse (LeBrock) he is able to fight another day. Seagal fights far better than he acts. C: Steven Seagal, Kelly LeBrock, Frederick Coffin. D: Bruce Malmuth. ACT [R] 96m. V

Hard Traveling 1985 ★★★ In Depression-era California, a farm couple makes the wrong choices in their struggle to survive. Interesting look at how far poverty can push a normally law-abiding person. C: J.E. Freeman, Ellen Geer. D: Dan Bessie. DRA [PG] 99m. V

Hard Way, The 1942 ★★★★ Ruthless Lupino will do whatever it takes to turn naive sister Leslie into a star. Ida's terrific in this hard-edged melodrama that's sometimes preposterous, but always entertaining. Terrific scene with George as aging star sabotaged by Lupino. C: Ida Lupino, Joan Leslie, Jack Carson, Dennis Morgan, Gladys George. D: Vincent Sherman. DRA 109m.

Hard Way, The 1991 ★★★ Spoiled movie actor (Fox), who wants to toughen up his image in a new film, hits the streets with authentic cop (Woods) to develop his character. Occasionally funny banter. C: Michael J. Fox, James Woods, Stephen Lang, Annabella Sciorra, Penny Marshall. D: John Badham. ACT [R] 111m. V

Hardbodies 1984 ★★ Three men suffering from chronic midlife crisis try to get their pacemakers recharged by seeking out bikini-clad women. Ludicrous blending of angst and cleavage. C: Grant Cramer, Gary Wood, Michael Rapport. D: Mark Griffiths. COM [R] 87m. V

Hardbodies 2 1986 ★ Adventures of an American film crew on location on the beaches of Greece—topless beaches, that is. Standard sex comedy, with the requisite ogling characters, and camerawork to match. C: Brad Zutaut, Fabiano Udenio, James Karen. D: Mark Griffiths. COM [R] 89m. V

Hardcase 1971 ★★★½ A mercenary soldier (Walker) comes to the aid of Mexican revolutionaries, only to discover his estranged wife in their company. An oddball Western with a capable cast and intriguing plot. C: Clint Walker, Stefanie Powers, Alex Karras. D: John Llewellyn Moxey. WST 74m.

Hardcase And Fist 1989 ★★★ A cop is jailed for a crime he didn't commit. In jail, he goes after the vicious mobster who masterminded his framing. Effective actioner. C: Ted Prior, Carter Wond, Maureen Lavette. D: Tony Zarindast. ACT [R] 92m. V

Hardcore 1979 ★★★½ Scott portrays a Midwestern Christian fundamentalist trying to find his runaway daughter in L.A.'s seedy porno filmmaking precincts, where he enlists the help of Hubley, a sympathetic young prostitute. Movingly written; terrific acting by Scott. C: George C. Scott, Peter Boyle, Season Hubley. D: Paul Schrader. DRA 108m. V

Harder They Come, The 1973 Jamaican ★★★★ Reggae musical scored a surprise hit in America despite downbeat story of singer turning to crime, then achieving sudden success. Powerful performance by Cliff, exhilarating music. C: Jimmy Cliff, Carl Bradshaw. D: Perry Henzell. MUS [R] 98m. V

Harder They Fall, The 1956 ★★★★ Cynical sportswriter watches as sensitive fighter is exploited by his handlers and comes to realize the true brutality of the sport. A cruel, hard-hitting look at professional sports. Bogie's last film. C: Humphrey Bogart, Rod Steiger, Jan Sterling. D: Mark Robson. DRA 105m. V

Hardhat and Legs 1980 ★★★★ Chauvinistic construction worker becomes involved with a feminist woman who teaches a sex education class. Contrived premise is given surprisingly sophisticated treatment in this delightful comedy written by legendary screenwriting team of Ruth Gordon and Garson Kanin. C: Kevin Dobson, Sharon Gless, Bobby Short. D: Lee Philips. COM 96m. V

Hardly Working 1981 ★★★ Lewis' "comeback" film (which proved to be his last directorial effort) is an occasionally funny, episodic comedy about former clown who tries and fails at various odd jobs. Disjointed and awkward, it still has moments of goofy magic. C: Jerry Lewis, Susan Oliver, Roger C. Carmel. D: Jerry Lewis. COM [PG] 90m. V

Hardware 1990 ★★★ Post-WWIII folks are forced to scavenge—and one finds the remains of a dangerous robot, unaware that it was programmed to destroy. Interesting twists and solid special effects. C: Dylan McDermott, Stacy Travis. D: Richard Stanely. ACT [R] 94m. V

Hardware Wars 1978 ★★★★ Strange and funny short film parodies *Star Wars*, recasting the famed outer space good guys and bad guys with kitchen appliances. Must be seen to be believed. COM 48m.

Hardys Ride High, The 1939 ★★★ First of three Hardy films released in 1939 had Judge Hardy's family believing that they had inherited $1 million, but relieved when they learn it was a mistake since their troubles doubled when their fortunes did. Amiable family entertainment. C: Lewis Stone, Mickey Rooney, Cecilia Parker, Fay Holden, Ann Rutherford. D: George Seitz. COM 80m.

Harem 1985 French ★★ Capable leads and glossy production values can't help shallow plot about a cocky Arab prince (Kingsley) who abducts Kinski and stashes her in his harem. One-dimensional characters don't help either. C: Nastassia Kinski, Ben Kingsley. D: Arthur Joffe. DRA 107m. V

Harem 1986 ★★ Opulent but ultimately silly desert fantasy romance set in the early 1900s with Sharif as the sultan who buys a kidnapped American (Travis) for his harem. Alas, he's no Valentino, and this time the woman's not willing to stay. C: Nancy Travis, Art Malik, Sarah Miles, Omar Sharif, Ava Gardner. D: Billy Hale. DRA 200m. TVM

Harem Girl 1952 ★★½ Ditzy comedienne Davis plays a lowly harem girl who is called upon to impersonate a princess. Thin material forces Davis to rely on her own considerable charm. C: Joan Davis, Peggie Castle. D: Edward Bernds. COM 70m.

Harlan County, U.S.A. 1976 ★★★★½ Stirring documentary account of Kentucky coal miners' strike; Kopple presents union's demands and management's reluctance, but her heart is with struggling workers. Oscar for Best Documentary. D: Barbara Kopple. DOC [PG] 103m. V

Harlem Globetrotters on Gilligan's Island, The 1981 ★★½ The third of Gilligan's comeback TV-movies features his lunatic crew still stuck on that darn island, this time joined by the Globetrotters, a nutty scientist, and a gaggle of slam-dunking robots. So idiotic it's almost funny. C: Bob Denver, Alan Hale, Jr., Jim Backus, Natalie Schafer, Martin Landau, Barbara Bain, The Harlem Globetrotters. D: Peter Baldwin. COM 100m. TVM

Harlem Globetrotters, The 1951 ★★½ The basketball stuntmen show off for the cameras. Amiable but unspectacular film about the lives of these famous hoopsters. C: Thomas Gomez, Dorothy Dandridge. D: Phil Brown. ACT 80m.

Harlem Nights 1989 ★★★ Harlem club proprietors (Murphy and Pryor) fight corrupt cops and Mafiosi invading their turf. All-star cast and good box office results don't reflect the acting and action in Murphy's directorial debut. C: Eddie Murphy, Richard Pryor, Redd Foxx, Danny Aiello, Della Reese, Arsenio Hall. D: Eddie Murphy. COM 115m. V

Harlem Rides the Range 1939 ★★★ A good natured cowboy/gunslinger helps out his girlfriend when her uranium mine goes bust. Some good fun. C: Herbert Jeffrey, Spencer Williams, Clarence Brooks, Tom Southern. WST 58m. V

Harley 1985 ★ Silly prison tale about motorcycle criminal who winds up in a ruthless Texas prison and befriends fellow biker. The motorcycles are more convincing than the actors. C: Lou Diamond Phillips. D: Fred Holmes. ACT [PG] 80m.

Harley Davidson & the Marlboro Man 1991 ★★½ Two gruff and scruffy guys in near future (Rourke and Johnson) rob a bank to save their local hang-out. Just an excuse for the stars to motorcycle, and Redford/Newman they're not. C: Mickey Rourke, Don Johnson, Chelsea Field, Vanessa Williams. D: Simon Wincer. ACT [R] 100m. v

Harlow 1965 ★★★½ Baker, as the glamorous Harlow, is upstaged by Lansbury, who turns in a dynamic performance as Harlow's mother. Too many fictional embellishments are added to already interesting facts. C: Carroll Baker, Peter Lawford, Angela Lansbury, Red Buttons, Martin Balsam, Raf Valloney. D: Gordon Douglas. DRA 125m. v

Harlow 1965 ★★★ Lynley's in past her depth in this biography of silver screen bombshell Jean Harlow. Not as strong as the Carroll Baker version, produced the same year; originally filmed as a live television show, and looks low-tech. C: Carol Lynley, Ginger Rogers, Efrem Zimbalist, Jr., Barry Sullivan. D: Alex Segal. DRA 109m.

Harness, The 1971 ★★★★ Unusually literate adaptation of the John Steinbeck story, set in Salinas Valley's farmland. A shy farmer (Greene) with a sick wife seeks to discover his purpose in life. Sensitive direction and intimate interplay between characters make this a real winner. C: Lorne Greene, Julie Sommars. D: Boris Sagal. DRA 99m. TVM

Harold and Maude 1971 ★★★★½ Huge cult favorite features Cort as a death-obsessed 20-year-old who falls in love with flamboyant senior citizen Gordon. Sick-humored repartee between Cort and mother Pickles has its moments, while Gordon is sheer delight. Soundtrack by Cat Stevens. C: Bud Cort, Ruth Gordon, Vivian Pickles, Cyril Cusack. D: Hal Ashby. COM [PG] 91m. v

Harold Lloyd's World of Comedy 1962 ★★★★★ Many priceless bits from the '20s silent comic genius are included in this delightful compilation, selected by Lloyd himself. C: Harold Lloyd, Bebe Daniels, Mildred Davis. D: Harold Lloyd. COM 94m.

Harold Robbins' the Pirate 1978 ★★★½ Opulent adaptation of bestselling Robbins novel about an Arab prince (Nero) who marries an American beauty (Archer). Filled with all the usual glitz, plus a smattering of Middle East politics. C: Franco Nero, Anne Archer, Olivia Hussey, Christopher Lee, Eli Wallach, Armand Assante. D: Kenneth Annakin. DRA 200m. TVM

Harp of Burma 1956 *See* **Burmese Harp, The**

Harper 1966 ★★★★ Classy and smooth, this rich Newman vehicle follows the jaded private eye as he searches for a missing husband. Strong supporting cast, including some real acting by Wagner. *The Drowning Pool* continues his adventures nine years later. Screenplay by William Goldman. C: Paul Newman, Lauren Bacall, Julie Harris, Shelley Winters, Robert Wagner, Janet Leigh. D: Jack Smight. CRI 121m. v

Harper Valley P.T.A. 1978 ★★★ Based on the popular country song with which the film shares a title. Liberated woman (Eden) is ostracized by her neighbors and then teaches them a few well-needed lessons. Lightweight comedy aims to please. C: Barbara Eden, Nanette Fabray. D: Richard Bennett. COM [PG] 102m. v

Harpy 1970 ★★★★ By focusing on a few offbeat characters living in the desert, this odd little film rises above conventions of the horror genre to deliver some quirky and memorable insights. C: Hugh O'Brian, Elizabeth Ashley. D: Gerald Sindell. HOR 100m. TVM

Harrad Experiment, The 1973 ★★ Liberal-minded college encourages sexual freedom among students. Dated, but fun. Based on best-seller by Robert Rimmer. C: Don Johnson, James Whitmore, Tippi Hedren. D: Ted Post. DRA [R] 88m. v

Harrad Summer 1974 ★★★ Sequel to *The Harrad Experiment*. This time, college students indoctrinated in liberal sex education classes apply their learning outside the lecture hall. Has some sparks. C: Richard Doran, Victoria Thompson, Laurie Walters. D: Steven Stern. DRA [R] 103m. v

Harriet Craig 1950 ★★★★ Crawford is well cast as a control freak who is more interested in perfecting her house and her surroundings than dealing with her family. Interesting remake of *Craig's Wife*. C: Joan Crawford, Wendell Corey, Lucile Watson. D: Vincent Sherman. DRA 94m.

Harry and Son 1983 ★ Conflict between hardhat dad and artsy son degenerates into a tedious succession of shouting matches. Newman overextended himself badly here; Benson is particularly insufferable. Could be better. C: Paul Newman, Robby Benson, Joanne Woodward, Ellen Barkin. D: Paul Newman. DRA [PG] 117m. v

Harry and the Hendersons 1987 ★★★½ Thinking it's dead, normal American family brings home a Bigfoot-type creature they came upon in the woods. Sweet, and good for younger audiences. Oscar for makeup, this later became syndicated sitcom. C: John Lithgow, Melinda Dillon, Lainie Kazan, Don Ameche. D: William Dear. COM [PG] 111m. v

Harry and Tonto 1974 ★★★★★ Heartwarming, singular Oscar-winning performance by Carney in odyssey of elderly man and his cat, who take a cross-country journey and encounter a number of extraordinary people, among them a Native-American medicine man and an old, fondly remembered love. Unforgettable and uplifting; a real treasure. C: Art Carney, Ellen Burstyn, Chief Dan George, Geraldine Fitzgerald, Larry Hagman. D: Paul Mazursky. DRA [R] 110m. v

Harry and Walter Go to New York 1976

★★★ Dispirited, turn-of-the-century vaudeville team heads for the Big Apple and ends up part of bank robbery scheme. Spirited cast and great story are wasted in muddled comedy that tries to capture irreverent spirit of Hope/Crosby *Road* movies. C: James Caan, Elliott Gould, Diane Keaton, Michael Caine, Charles Durning, Lesley Ann Warren. D: Mark Rydell. COM [PG] 123m. V

Harry Belafonte—Global Carnival 1988 ★★★½ A special concert filmed in Zimbabwe. Belafonte performs hits made famous during his long and wondrous career. C: Harry Belafonte. MUS 60m. V

Harry Black and the Tiger 1958 British ★★★ Famed tiger hunter in India romances his friend's wife. Sluggish jungle melodrama with disorienting flashbacks. C: Stewart Granger, Barbara Rush. D: Hugo Fregonese. DRA 107m.

Harry Chapin—The Final Concert 1981 ★★★★ The last concert (before his untimely death in an auto accident) of brilliant Harry Chapin. Features some of his biggest hits like "Cat's in the Cradle," "Taxi" and "Sequel." Wonderfully done and poignant. C: Harry Chapin. MUS 89m. V

Harry Connick, Jr.—The New York Big Band Concert 1993 ★★★★ A special concert that showcases Connick's big band sound. Among the selections are "Sweet Georgia Brown," "Recipe For Love" and plenty more. Excellent. C: Harry Connick, Jr. MUS 60m. V

Harry in Your Pocket 1973 ★★★★ Group of pickpockets try to outdo one another as they engage in series of flamboyant heists. Excellent cast headed by Coburn and Pidgeon do justice to clever script and imaginative, episodical plot twists. C: James Coburn, Michael Sarrazin, Trish Van Devere, Walter Pidgeon. D: Bruce Geller. COM 103m.

Harry Tracy, Desperado 1983 Canadian ★★★½ Law officers in 1901 relentlessly pursue a brazen outlaw who once belonged to the Hole-in-the-Wall Gang. Features an air of authenticity and intense Dern performance. C: Bruce Dern, Helen Shaver, Gordon Lightfoot. D: William Graham. WST [PG] 111m. V

Harry's War 1986 ★★★ A harried taxpayer (Herrmann) decides to wage war on the I.R.S. Occasionally effective, more often overwrought. C: Edward Herrmann, Geraldine Page, Karen Grassle, David Ogden Stiers. D: Keith Merrill. COM [PG] 98m. V

Hart to Hart 1979 ★★★ TV-movie pilot that launched the long-running series. Wagner and Powers star as a globe-trotting couple whose amateur sleuthing solves the mystery behind a friend's untimely death at a spa. Mainly of interest to fans of the series. C: Robert Wagner, Stefanie Powers, Lionel Stander, Roddy McDowall, Jill St. John. D: Tom Mankiewicz. ACT 100m. TVM

Harum Scarum 1965 ★★ Elvis plays a movie star, kidnapped in the Middle East, who gets involved in a political assassination plot while singing "Shake That Tambourine." Enough said. C: Elvis Presley, Mary Ann Mobley, Fran Jeffries, Michael Ansara. D: Gene Nelson. MUS 85m. V

Harvest 1937 French ★★★★★ Two aimless souls find purpose and happiness when they set up house together and farm their own land. Beautiful performances from Gabrio and Demazis distinguish this austere, tender film. C: Fernandel, Gabriel Gabrio, Orane Demazis. D: Marcel Pagnol. DRA 105m. V

Harvey 1950 ★★★★½ Stewart shines in fey comedy about tipsy Elwood P. Dowd and his unusual friendship with invisible six-foot rabbit, "Harvey." Lovely tribute to eccentricity, based on Mary Chase's Pulitzer Prize-winning play. Stage veteran Hull, recreating role of Dowd's sister, won Oscar for Best Supporting Actress. C: James Stewart, Josephine Hull, Peggy Dow, Charles Drake, Cecil Kellaway, Jesse White. D: Henry Koster. COM 104m. V

Harvey Girls, The 1946 ★★★★ It's the demure, ladylike Harvey Girls, led by Garland, vs. the freespirited saloon gals, led by Lansbury, in Wild West musical. Sunny and enjoyable, with musical peak the Oscar-winning "On the Atchison, Topeka and Santa Fe." C: Judy Garland, John Hodiak, Angela Lansbury, Ray Bolger, Virginia O'Brien, Cyd Charisse, Marjorie Main. D: George Sidney. MUS 102m. V

Harvey Middleman, Fireman 1965 ★★★ A small-scale comedy about a gentle firefighter who has problems differentiating his fantasies from real life. Pleasant enough, but it doesn't really amount to much. C: Eugene Troobnick, Hermione Gingold, Patricia Harty, Charles Durning. D: Ernest Pintoff. COM 75m.

Has Anybody Seen My Gal? 1952 ★★★½ An elderly millionaire (Coburn) tests the worthiness of his intended heirs by moving in with them and pretending to be poor. Coburn's delightful performance carries this light, delightful vintage comedy. Watch for James Dean. C: Charles Coburn, Piper Laurie, Rock Hudson, Gigi Perreau. D: Douglas Sirk. COM 89m.

Hasty Heart, The 1949 British ★★★★ Poignant story of wounded Scottish soldier who remains aloof from his fellow hospital inmates. He finally opens up, only to learn that he is dying of a terminal illness. Outstanding performance by Todd in this adaption of John Patrick's play. C: Richard Todd, Ronald Reagen, Patricia Neal. D: Vincent Sherman. DRA 99m.

Hatari! 1962 ★★★★ Milling adventure tale of a group of safari hunters in Africa who capture animals that will be placed in zoos. The hunting thrills perfectly balanced by comic moments. Good fun. C: John Wayne, Elsa

Martinelli, Red Buttons, Hardy Kruger. D: Howard Hawks. ACT 158m. V

Hatchet for the Honeymoon 1974 Italian ★★★ A mad designer takes out his anger at his dead wife by killing young brides. Convoluted, gross shocker is nonetheless visually striking, thanks to Bava's direction. C: Stephen Forsythe, Dagmar Lassander. D: Mario Bava. HOR [PG] 90m. V

Hatchet Man, The 1932 ★★ Story of Chinese immigrant and his efforts to "become American" and avoid conscription in a Chinatown gang looks racist today. Dated and embarrassing, especially casting Caucasians as Asians. C: Edward G. Robinson, Loretta Young, Dudley Digges. D: William Wellman. DRA 74m.

Hatchet Murders, The 1975 *See* **Deep Red**

Hatful of Rain, A 1957 ★★★★ Dramatic story of a junkie is as much about the effect of his addiction on those around him as it is about him. From the play by Michael V. Gazzo. Provocative and finely acted. C: Eva Marie Saint, Don Murray, Anthony Franciosa, Lloyd Nolan. D: Fred Zinnemann. DRA 109m.

Hats Off 1936 ★★★ Undistinguished musical about two press agents (Clarke, Payne). Payne's first starring role. C: Mae Clarke, John Payne, Helen Lynd, Franklin Pangborn. D: Boris Petroff. MUS 70m.

Hatter's Castle 1941 British ★★★ Another examination of the British class system in this tired tale of a poor man trying to become better than he should be. From the well-mined library of A.J. Cronin. C: Deborah Kerr, James Mason, Robert Newton, Emlyn Williams. D: Lance Comfort. DRA 90m.

Hatter's Ghost, The 1982 French ★★★ Hatmaker's nephew is a notorious mass murderer, but uncle refuses to turn him in out of fear. Reworking of Georges Simenon thriller notable for Chabrol's dazzling technique and the talents of a solid cast. C: Michel Serrault, Charles Aznavour, Monique Chaumette. D: Claude Chabrol. DRA 120m.

Haunted 1984 ★★½ A woman (Adams) is haunted by her unknown origins while visiting her adoptive mother. Although the acting is good, Roemer's cloying, overly obvious script kills the tension. An *American Playhouse* production. C: Brooke Adams, John DeVries. D: Michael Roemer. DRA 118m. TVM

Haunted by Her Past 1987 ★★½ Soap opera queen Lucci is helplessly entranced by an infamous murderess whom she happens to closely resemble. A modern-day horror story has a few surprises up its sleeve. C: Susan Lucci, John James. D: Michael Pressman. HOR 96m. TVM

Haunted Gold 1932 ★★★½ Exciting early Wayne, in his first western for Warner, takes on greedy bandits in spooky ghost town. Remake of *The Phantom City*. C: John Wayne. D: Mack Wright. WST 54m. V

Haunted Honeymoon 1940 British ★★★★ Fans of Dorothy Sayers' sleuth Lord Peter Wimsey will delight in this amusing mixture of mystery and marital squabbling, as the newlywed Wimseys (Montgomery, Cummings) try to enjoy their honeymoon—in vain. (a.k.a. *Busman's Honeymoon*) C: Robert Montgomery, Constance Cummings, Leslie Banks, Robert Newton. D: Arthur B. Woods. CRI 83m.

Haunted Honeymoon 1986 ★★½ Wilder and Radner play famous radio actors who try to save Aunt DeLuise (in unfunny drag role) from haunted mansion. This spoof of haunted house movies is probably Wilder's worst outing as writer/director/star. C: Gene Wilder, Gilda Radner, Dom DeLuise, Jonathan Pryce. D: Gene Wilder. COM [PG] 82m. V

Haunted Palace, The 1963 ★★★ Edgar Allan Poe's tale of warlock (Price) returning to New England village. He seeks revenge on descendants of those who burned him alive over a century before. Atmospheric but slow. Remake: *The Resurrected*. C: Vincent Price, Debra Paget, Lon Chaney, Jr., Elisha Cook, Jr. D: Roger Corman. HOR 85m. V

Haunted Ranch 1943 ★★½ When Reno Red is murdered, a rival gang starts spreading a story that his ranch is haunted. C: John "Dusty" King, David Sharpe, Max Terhune. WST 56m. V

Haunted Strangler, The 1958 British ★★★ Unusual mystery tale in which a writer who's researching a strangler executed 20 years before finds himself within the ghostly murderer's reach. A worthwhile genre item. (a.k.a. *Grip of the Strangler*) C: Boris Karloff, Elizabeth Allan. D: Robert Day. HOR 78m. V

Haunted Summer 1988 ★ Drug-taking Romantic poets Byron and Shelley and their female companions debauch themselves on a holiday in Switzerland in 1816. Boring and pointless, Passer's treatment isn't as much fun as Ken Russell's manic version (*Gothic*) of the same story line. C: Phillip Anglim, Laura Dern, Alice Krige, Eric Stoltz. D: Ivan Passer. DRA [R] 106m. V

Haunted, The 1991 ★★★★ Above-average based-on-fact supernatural thriller, with Kirkland giving strong performance as a woman whose family is terrorized by otherworldly forces. Plays fair and realistically, with numerous chilling scenes. C: Sally Kirkland, Jeffrey DeMunn. D: Robert Mandel. HOR 100m.

Haunting Fear 1991 ★★½ A young woman (Stevens) fears being buried alive and turns homicidal. Low-budget nod to Poe's "The Premature Burial," spiced up with nudity and murderous intrigue, gets some spark from B-movie stalwarts in the cast. C: Brinke Stevens, Jay Richardson, Jan-Michael Vincent, Karen Black. D: Fred Olen Ray. HOR 90m. V

Haunting of Julia, The 1976 British ★★★ Eager to start a new life after the death of her daughter, Farrow moves into a house haunted by a moody, juvenile ghost. Okay occult chiller. Based on a story by Peter Straub. C: Mia Farrow, Keir Dullea, Tom Conti. D: Richard Loncraine. HOR [R] 96m. V

Haunting of Morella, The 1991 ★ Ostensible adaptation of an Edgar Allan Poe story, about an executed witch reborn in an innocent girl, is simply an excuse for cheesy cheap thrills and misogynistic exploitation of its actresses. C: Nicole Eggert, David McCallum, Lana Clarkson. D: Jim Wynorski. HOR [R] 82m.

Haunting of Sarah Hardy, The 1989 ★★½ Recently married heiress (Ward) returns to family estate to confront memories of parents' horrible deaths. Standard made-for-TV shocker that showcases beautiful Ward. C: Sela Ward, Michael Woods, Polly Bergen, Morgan Fairchild. D: Jerry London. HOR 92m. TVM V

Haunting Passion, The 1983 ★★★ Romantic ghost story features housewife (Seymour) intrigued by ghostly co-resident of new home. Some heart palpitations; Seymour does fine. C: Jane Seymour, Gerald McRaney. D: John Korty. DRA 98m. TVM V

Haunting, The 1963 ★★★★ Research team investigates a reportedly haunted house. Film adaptation of novel *The Haunting of Hill House* has terrific ensemble acting, placing this several notches above the usual haunted house fare. Some eerie visual and sound effects. C: Julie Harris, Claire Bloom, Richard Johnson, Russ Tamblyn. D: Robert Wise. HOR [G] 112m. V

Haunts 1977 ★★½ A disturbed woman who hallucinates (and sleeps with a goat!) may be responsible for a rash of brutal scissor murders. Strange, disjointed shocker has a creepy feel but becomes too weird for its own good. C: May Britt, Cameron Mitchell, Aldo Ray. D: Herb Freed. HOR [PG] 97m. V

Haunts of the Very Rich 1972 ★★ Seven people each having survived a brush with death, allow themselves to be flown to a mysterious tropical island. Allegorical fantasy à la Sartre's *No Exit.* C: Lloyd Bridges, Cloris Leachman, Edward Asner, Anne Francis, Donna Mills, Robert Reed. D: Paul Wendkos. DRA 72m. TVM V

Havana 1990 ★★ Last days of Batista's freewheeling Cuba, as Castro's rebels begin to take over the countryside. Adulterous love affair between adventurer/cardshark Redford and Cuban society wife Olin lacks sexual tension, and, despite high production values, film is unconvincing and flat. C: Robert Redford, Lena Olin, Alan Arkin. D: Sydney Pollack. DRA [R] 140m. V

Have A Good Funeral, My Friend ★★½ While on the road, a loner passes through a small town where he smells money. But there's danger all around him. C: John Garko, Antonio Villar. WST 90m. V

Have Picnic Basket Will Travel ★★★½ Assorted cartoons starring Yogi Bear, Huckleberry Hound, Augie Doggie and other Hanna-Barbera heroes. The common theme: they're all on vacation. Lots of fun. FAM/COM 90m. V

Have Rocket, Will Travel 1959 ★★½ The Three Stooges are mistakenly locked in a rocket destined for Venus where they meet flamethrowing spiders and practice intergalactic shtick. Warning Stooge fans: Joe de Rita replaces Shemp Howard/Curly Joe. C: Jerome Cowan, Anna Lisa. D: David Rich. COM 76m. V

Having a Wild Weekend 1965 British ★★★½ The Dave Clark Five star in a musical vehicle that allows the '60s rock 'n' rollers to perform some of their hits as they play freelance stuntmen. Although the film shamelessly rides the coattails of earlier Beatles movies, the music will certainly appeal to fans. (a.k.a. *Catch Us If You Can*) C: The Dave Clark Five, Barbara Ferris, Lenny Davidson. D: John Boorman. MUS 91m.

Having Babies 1976 ★★½ Warm and fuzzy TV-movie featuring a stellar '70s cast concerns four couples embarking on natural childbirth via the Lamaze technique. Drama's subject mostly prevails over the corny dialogue. Spawned two sequels and a TV series. C: Adrienne Barbeau, Vicki Lawrence, Linda Purl, Karen Valentine. D: Robert Day. DRA 100m. TVM

Having Babies II 1977 ★★½ This sequel repeats the *Having Babies* multiple-couple formula, only this time the focus includes not only birthing, but young love and adoptive parenting as well. Soapy dramatics culminate with a scene of real twins being born. C: Carol Lynley, Paula Prentiss, Rhea Perlman, Rosanna Arquette. D: Richard Michaels. DRA 100m. TVM

Having Babies III 1978 ★★½ Third installment in this cash cow actually served as the TV-movie pilot for the *Julie Farr, M.D.* series. More high sudsing delivery-room drama on display. C: Susan Sullivan, Patty Duke Astin, Kathleen Beller, Rue McClanahan, Richard Mulligan. D: Jackie Cooper. DRA 100m. TVM

Having It All 1982 ★★ Bi-coastal executive (Cannon) divides her personal time between two husbands. Generally ineffective. C: Dyan Cannon, Barry Newman, Hart Bochner, Sylvia Sidney. D: Edward Zwick. COM 92m. TVM V

Having Wonderful Crime 1945 ★★½ Pair of amateur sleuths (Landis and Murphy) are helped by lawyer friend (O'Brien) when they find themselves embroiled in a case of a missing magician. Low-key comedy/mystery. C: Pat O'Brien, George Murphy, Carole Landis. D: A. Edward Sutherland. COM 70m. V

Having Wonderful Time 1938 ★★★½ Originally a hit on Broadway, this comedy about love and friendship at a Jewish summer resort in the Catskills was transformed into a decidedly unethnic romp wherein Rogers reluctantly falls in love with Fairbanks, Jr. C: Ginger Rogers, Douglas Fairbanks, Jr., Lucille

Ball, Lee Bowman, Eve Arden, Jack Carson. D: Alfred Santell. COM 71m. V

Hawaii 1966 ★★★★ Devout 1820s missionary attempts to westernize natives of Hawaiian Islands. Sweeping adaptation of James Michener epic novel makes for highly watchable entertainment. C: Julie Andrews, Max von Sydow, Richard Harris, Gene Hackman, Carroll O'Connor, Jocelyne LaGarde. D: George Roy Hill. DRA 181m. V

Hawaii Five-O 1968 ★★½ Pilot for the hit series establishes tough cop (Lord) running his pressurized force while attempting to locate a lethal weapon on a Chinese ship. Fun for fans of the series. C: Jack Lord, Nancy Kwan, Leslie Nielsen. D: Paul Wendkos. ACT 100m. TVM

Hawaiians, The 1970 ★★ Disappointing sequel, also based on Michener best seller, continues saga of the settlement of America's Pacific paradise by taking up where 1966 epic *Hawaii* left off (covers 1870-1900). Chen is the only bright spot in otherwise forgettable film. C: Charlton Heston, Geraldine Chaplin, Mako, Tina Chen, Alec McCowen, Keye Luke. D: Tom Gries. DRA [PG] 134m.

Hawk and Castile ★★★ Medieval adventure film, with Cobb out to avenge the murder of his family and the usurping of his throne. C: Jerry Cobb, Mari Real, Tom Griffith, Nurla Forway. ACT 95m.

Hawk Jones 1988 ★★★½ A detective story for children. In fact, all the roles are played by kids, young ones. C: Valiant Du Hart, Charmella Roark. D: Richard Lowry. FAM/ACT 88m. V

Hawk the Slayer 1981 British ★★★ Sword and sorcery epic featuring a good warrior (Terry) fighting his evil older brother (Palance). Comic book characters, but lots of sizzling swordplay. C: Jack Palance, John Terry. D: Terry Marcel. ACT 90m. V

Hawken's Breed 1987 ★★½ A man meets a beautiful Indian woman and he falls in love with her. Over time, he learns that her family had been murdered and he takes off to avenge her. C: Peter Fonda. D: Charles B. Pierce. WST [R] 93m. V

Hawkeye 1988 ★★ A tough cop (Hawkeye), on the beat in Las Vegas, goes after the drug dealing goons who murdered his ex-partner. Fong-style violence and overall rowdiness. C: George Chung, Chuck Jeffreys, Troy Donahue. D: Leo Fong. ACT 90m. V

Hawkins on Murder 1973 ★★★½ Upscale TV-movie pilot for short-lived series has strong actors and an engaging sleuth-in-the-courtroom plotline in which Stewart defends an heiress against multiple murder charges. Classy production and Stewart's graceful presence make this better than average. (a.k.a. *Death and the Maiden*) C: James Stewart, Bonnie Bedelia. D: Jud Taylor. DRA 74m. TVM

Hawks 1988 ★★★ In the hospital with terminal illnesses, a British lawyer and his young American roommate decide to escape and face life full force. C: Timothy Dalton, Anthony Edwards. D: Robert Ellis Miller. COM [R] 105m. V

Hawmps! 1976 ★★½ Army Lieutenant trains Texas soldiers to use camels instead of horses, and balks when Congress demands the beasts be set free in the desert. Cute idea is based on a true incident, but gets repetitive. C: James Hampton, Christopher Connelly. D: Joe Camp. COM [G] 98m. V

Haywire 1980 ★★★½ Based on Brooke Hayward's best-seller, this absorbing TV movie tells of a glamorous family dealt some cruel twists of fate. Robards is satisfyingly on target as producer Leland Hayward, who married actress Margaret Sullavan (Remick). C: Lee Remick, Jason Robards, Deborah Raffin. D: Michael Tuchner. DRA 200m. TVM

Hazard 1948 ★★★ Private detective (Carey), shadowing a professional gambler (Goddard), falls in love with her. Mild, amusing caper. C: Paulette Goddard, Macdonald Carey, Fred Clark. D: George Marshall. COM 95m.

Hazard of Hearts, A 1987 ★★★ Rather improbable Gothic tale by Barbara Cartland about a beautiful young heiress (Bonham-Carter) who is "won" by a dashing aristocrat in a game of cards. Overblown plot verges on the ridiculous, but the first-rate English cast is fun to watch. C: Helena Bonham Carter, Diana Rigg, Edward Fox, Christopher Plummer, Anna Massey. D: John Hough. DRA 96m. TVM

He Is My Brother 1975 ★★★ The hopelessly cuddly Sherman and his friend Rist are shipwrecked and wash up on an island that is a leper colony. Well-intentioned but as leaky as their boat. C: Keenan Wynn, Bobby Sherman, Robbie Rist. D: Edward Dmytryk. DRA 91m.

He Knows You're Alone 1980 ★ This pedestrian chiller was hardly alone in the parade of early '80s slasher films, and offers no distinctions aside from all the victims being brides-to-be and comic relief from Tom Hanks (in his first film). C: Don Scardino, Caitlin O'Heaney. D: Armand Mastroianni. HOR [R] 94m. V

He Laughed Last 1956 ★★★½ Enjoyable spoof of gangster genre about a flapper (Marlow) who inherits a N.Y. crimelord's empire much to the chagrin of her police officer boyfriend. Narrated by Laine, who also sings. C: Frankie Laine, Lucy Marlow, Anthony Dexter. D: Blake Edwards. COM 77m.

He Makes Me Feel Like Dancin' 1983 ★★★★ Jacques D'Amboise, ex-New York City Ballet dancer, spends his time with underprivileged kids, showing them how to express themselves through dance. Lovely, rarely-seen glimpse of a selfless artist. Oscar for Best Documentary. DOC

He Married His Wife 1940 ★★½ McCrea encourages his ex-wife Kelly to marry again so he won't have to pay her alimony, but she wants to remarry him instead. Marital comedy. C: Joel McCrea, Nancy Kelly, Mary Boland, Cesar Romero. D: Roy Del Ruth. COM 83m.

He Ran All the Way 1951 ★★★★ After killing a guard in a holdup, paranoid thug Garfield holes up in Winters' home, taking her unsuspecting family hostage. Tight, subtle thriller with fine performance by Garfield in his last film. C: John Garfield, Shelley Winters, Wallace Ford, Gladys George. D: John Berry. ACT 77m.

He Rides Tall 1964 ★★★½ Sheriff (Young) goes up against lawless gang headed by his stepbrother. Good two-fisted Western, although the usually reliable Duryea as the head bad guy looks rather worn out in this one. C: Tony Young, Dan Duryea. D: R. G. Springsteen. WST 84m.

He Said, She Said 1991 ★★ Slight concept behind this comedy is to tell story of near-breakup of a relationship from the perspective of both parties—first his (Bacon), and then hers (Perkins). Clumsy, uninvolving, and not much fun. C: Kevin Bacon, Elizabeth Perkins, Sharon Stone, Nathan Lane, Anthony LaPaglia. D: Ken Kwapis, Marisa Silver. COM [PG-13] 115m. V

He Stayed for Breakfast 1940 ★★½ This poor man's *Ninotchka* has Communist (Douglas) shooting an American banker in Paris and then seeking refuge in the apartment of the banker's wife (Young), whose decadent capitalist lifestyle weakens the comrade's political mettle. C: Loretta Young, Melvyn Douglas, Una O'Connor. D: Alexander Hall. COM 89m.

He Walked by Night 1948 ★★★★ Great film noir thriller about a killer pursued by two relentless police officers. Top-notch performances (especially by Baseheart) and an exciting chase through the L.A. water canals. Anthony Mann gave uncredited directorial assistance. C: Richard Basehart, Scott Brady, Jack Webb. D: Alfred Werker. CRI 79m. V

He Was Her Man 1934 ★★ A double-crossing safecracker (Cagney) fleeing the mob joins a woman (Blondell) traveling to meet her fisherman fiancé. They fall in love, but Cagney's reluctant to get involved and prepares to leave her. Weak vehicle for talented Cagney and Blondell. C: James Cagney, Joan Blondell, Victor Jory. D: Lloyd Bacon. DRA 70m.

He Who Gets Slapped 1924 ★★★★★ Scientist (Chaney) becomes circus clown after his wife runs off with another man. Under big top, he willingly humiliates himself for audience pleasure, while gradually coming to love bareback rider. Chaney is outstanding in psychologically challenging study of human emotion. Powerful direction in silent classic. C: Lon Chaney, Norma Shearer, John Gilbert. D: Victor Seastrom. DRA 85m.

He Who Must Die 1957 ★★★★ Villagers staging a passion play in Crete after WWI discover that the story of the suffering Christ still has much meaning. Powerful adaptation of the Nikos Kazantzakis novel. C: Melina Mercouri, Pierre Vaneck, Jean Servais. D: Jules Dassin. DRA 122m.

He Who Rides a Tiger 1966 British ★★★ A cat burglar (Bell) with a Jekyll and Hyde personality continues his criminal career upon his release from prison. Routine crime drama. C: Tom Bell, Judi Dench, Paul Rogers. D: Charles Crichton. CRI 103m.

He Who Walks Alone 1978 ★★★½ Compelling biography based on the true story of first African-American elected as Southern sheriff in the 1960s. C: Louis Gossett, Jr., Clu Gulager, Mary Alice. D: Jerrold Freedman. DRA 91m. V

Head 1968 ★★★★ The TV rock group takes on this odd, funny film that's become a cult classic. Nothing makes sense, but director/writer team Rafelson and Nicholson keep surprising the viewer with wild visual gags and imaginative editing. Most interesting as cultural artifact of the '60s. C: The Monkees, Terri Garr, Frank Zappa, Jack Nicholson. D: Bob Rafelson. MUS [G] 86m. V

Head of a Tyrant 1958 Italian ★★ Cheesy biblical epic portraying the Assyrians laying siege to Bethulia. Starlet Corey plays Judith of Bethulia in this uninspired sandals-and-toga outing. C: Massimo Girotti, Isabelle Corey. D: Fernando Cerchio. DRA 83m. V

Head of the Family, The 1970 ★★★½ All the nuances and details, heartaches and hopes of a long-term relationship in trouble. Compelling and sensitive, done the Italian way. C: Leslie Caron, Nino Manfredi. D: Nanni Loy. DRA [PG] 105m. V

Head Office 1986 ★★½ Corporate heads and office staff lock horns over inexperienced worker's promotion to important company post. Uneven material, featherweight comedy. C: Judge Reinhold, Eddie Albert, Jane Seymour, Danny DeVito, Rick Moranis. D: Ken Finkleman. COM [PG-13] 90m. V

Head over Heels 1979 ★★★½ A woman, estranged from her husband, finds her life complicated by the romantic obsession of a former lover. Intriguing comedy/drama entertainingly explores the frustrations of love. Based on Ann Beattie novel. (a.k.a. *Chilly Scenes of Winter*) C: John Heard, Mary Beth Hurt, Peter Riegert, Gloria Grahame. D: Joan Micklin Silver. DRA [PG] 97m. V

Head, The 1959 German ★★ Mad doctor's serum can keep heads of animals and people alive. His assistant kills him and reanimates his head, then transplants a crippled woman's noggin onto a stripper's body. Nicely shot but ridiculous, with laughable attempts at horror. C: Horst Frank, Karin Kernke, Michel Simon, Helmut Schmid. D: Victor Trivas. HOR 92m. V

Headhunter 1988 ★ Supernatural murders

plague Miami; detectives (Lenz, Crawford) encounter voodoo and, ultimately, a fake-looking creature as they try to solve them. Poorly made horror film. C: Kay Lenz, Wayne Crawford. D: Francis Schaeffer. HOR [R] 92m. v

Headin' for Broadway 1980 ★★ Somewhat confused tale of four young people auditioning for their big break on Broadway. C: Rex Smith, Terri Treas, Vivian Reed. D: Joseph Brooks. MUS [PG] 89m.

Heading for Heaven 1947 ★★ Drippy story of how a do-gooder attempts to build an ideal middle-class/middle-income housing development but is hampered by profiteers every step of the way. Overly sentimental. C: Stuart Erwin, Glenda Farrell, Irene Ryan. D: Lewis Collins. DRA 71m.

Headless Ghost 1958 British ★ This unmitigated stinker combines comedy with terror as a group of witless students poke around inside a haunted castle. C: Richard Lyon, Liliane Sottane, Clive Revill. D: Peter Scott. HOR 61m.

Headline Hunters 1955 ★★ Limp remake of *Behind the News* tells the story of an enthusiastic cub reporter who attempts to earn his stripes by investigating big-league criminals. Hardly worth the time. C: Rod Cameron, Julie Bishop, Ben Cooper. D: William Witney. DRA 70m.

Headlines of Destruction 1955 French ★★½ Constantine plays a lawyer whose partner (Darvi) is defending an accused murderer. Potentially gripping plot degenerates into a humdrum melodrama. C: Eddie Constantine, Bella Darvi. D: John Berry. DRA 85m.

Heads 1994 ★★½ It's easy for a newsman to track a demented murderer. All he has to do is keep on trailing a path of decapitated heads. Gruesome. C: Jon Cryer, Jennifer Tilly, Edward Asner. D: Paul Shapiro. COM [R] 102m. v

H.E.A.L.T.H. 1979 ★★★★ Altman's vastly underrated comedy uses a health food convention set in a hot-pink Florida hotel to satirize national-level political "dirty tricks." Highly amusing, ensemble cast, with Bacall, Jackson, and particularly Burnett as comic standouts. C: Carol Burnett, Glenda Jackson, James Garner, Lauren Bacall, Dick Cavett, Alfre Woodard. D: Robert Altman. COM 102m.

Hear Me Good 1957 ★★ Thoroughly inconsequential tale about the trials and tribulations surrounding a rigged beauty pageant. C: Hal March, Joe Ross, Merry Anders. D: Don McGuire. DRA 80m.

Hear My Song 1991 British ★★★★ Hustler (Dunbar) hopes to win back his girlfriend and resurrect his failing Liverpool club by tempting an old favorite (Beatty) to sing. Charming comedy sure to please. C: Ned Beatty, Adrian Dunbar, Shirley Anne Field, David McCallum. D: Peter Chelsom. COM [R] 104m. v

Hear No Evil 1993 ★★½ Young thugs, searching for a stash, menace hearing-impaired woman in her home. *Wait Until Dark* retooling, saved by Matlin's exceptional talents. C: Marlee Matlin, D. B. Sweeney, Martin Sheen. D: Robert Greenwald. CRI [R] 98m. v

Hearing Voices 1990 ★★ A most unusual love triangle: an injured model takes up first with her doctor, then with her doctor's gay lover. Hardly compelling but some moments of interest. C: Erika Nagy, Stephen Gatta. D: Sharon Greytak. DRA 87m. v

Hearse, The 1980 ★ What happens when a innocent young teacher moves into her newly inherited mansion and becomes the target of a murderous hearse? Not much. C: Trish Van Devere, Joseph Cotten. D: George Bowers. CRI [PG] 97m. v

Hearst and Davies Affair, The 1985 ★★★ Glitzy but superficial biography purports to tell of longtime affair between publisher W.R. Hearst and dancer-turned-movie-star Marion Davies. Mitchum gives tired, stolid performance. C: Robert Mitchum, Virginia Madsen, Fritz Weaver. D: David Lowell Rich. DRA 97m. TVM v

Heart 1987 ★★ Has-been boxer pug is on the comeback trail. Poor man's *Rocky* with even poorer production values. C: Brad Davis, Frances Fisher. D: James Lemmo. DRA [R] 96m. v

Heart & Souls 1993 ★★★★ Four wayward souls, inadvertently taken to the Great Beyond before their time, learn the only way they can make peace on earth is by taking over the body of an uptight yuppie. Endearing comedy, highlighted by Downey's funny versatile performance. C: Robert Downey, Jr., Charles Grodin, Alfre Woodard, Kyra Sedgwick, Tom Sizemore, Elizabeth Shue. D: Ron Underwood. COM [PG-13] 104m. v

Heart Beat 1980 ★★ Based on real-life relationship of Beat generation writer Jack Kerouac and his buddy, attractive tough-guy Neil Cassady, who kept leaving his wife to go on the road with Kerouac. Stylish art direction but the story meanders aimlessly. Hardly the definitive Beatnik film. C: Nick Nolte, Sissy Spacek, John Heard, Ray Sharkey. D: John Byrum. DRA [R] 105m. v

Heart Condition 1990 ★★★ This labored comedy is saved by merits of its two stars. Hoskins is bigoted white cop trailing black lawyer Washington. When Washington is killed, his heart is transplanted into Hoskins' chest, while his ghost helps Hoskins find his murderer. C: Bob Hoskins, Denzel Washington, Chloe Webb. D: James Perriott. COM [R] 96m. v

Heart Is a Lonely Hunter, The 1968 ★★★★ Deaf-mute Arkin befriends lonely young Locke (both were Oscar nominees) in this stunningly photographed, sensitive portrait of a small Southern town with more than its share of misfits and bullies. Terrific acting does justice to Carson McCullers' novel. C: Alan Arkin, Sondra Locke, Stacy Keach, Chuck McCann, Cicely Tyson. D: Robert Ellis Miller. DRA [G] 124m. v

Heart Like a Wheel 1983 ★★★★ Fast-paced biography of racecar driver Shirley Muldowney, who struggles against marital discord and sexism to become a racetrack champion. Terrific cast in well-acted character study of a woman's overcoming tough odds. Plenty of car racing thrills. C: Bonnie Bedelia, Beau Bridges, Hoyt Axton. D: Jonathan Kaplan. DRA [PG] 113m. V

Heart of a Champion: The Ray Mancini Story 1985 ★★★½ Gutsy biography of lightweight boxing champion Ray "Boom Boom" Mancini. Modestly affecting father/son drama with ring action choreographed by Sylvester Stallone. C: Robert Blake, Doug McKeon. D: Richard Michaels. DRA 94m. TVM V

Heart of a Nation, The 1943 ★★★½ Charles Boyer narrates the 69-year saga of a Parisian family chronicled from the Franco-Prussian War to the outbreak of WWII. Interesting episodic family narrative. The actual film had to be physically smuggled out of France during the German occupation. C: Louis Jouvet, Raimu, Suzy Prim, Michele Morgan, Charles Boyer. D: Julien Duvivier. DRA 111m.

Heart of Arizona 1938 ★★★½ After being sent to jail on a frame-up, rancher Moorhead is relieved to find that Hopalong Cassidy is fighting to prove his innocence. Good series entry with plenty of B-Western action. C: William Boyd, George "Gabby" Hayes, Natalie Moorhead. D: Lesley Selander. WST 68m.

Heart of Darkness 1994 ★★★★ Great choice of cast and director makes this latest film of Joseph Conrad's novella a success. Roth goes upriver to seek out Malkovich, who has 'gone native' and is now worshipped as a god by local tribes. Dark, scary, and occasionally funny (on purpose). C: Tim Roth, John Malkovich, Isaach de Bankole, James Fox. D: Nicholas Roeg. DRA 120m. TVM V

Heart of Dixie 1989 ★★★ Southern sorority sisters come to terms with civil rights crisis in '50s-going-on-'60s South. Coming-of-age film means well with lovely period details, but suffers from lackluster direction. C: Ally Sheedy, Virginia Madsen, Phoebe Cates, Treat Williams. D: Martin Davidson. DRA [PG] 96m. V

Heart of Glass 1974 German ★★★★ An enigmatic stranger helps residents of a German town rediscover the formula for making red glass, once the village's most famous export. Herzog reportedly hypnotized cast for dream effect in this eerily apocalyptic tale of mass hysteria. C: Josef Bierbichler, Stefan Guttler, Clemens Scheitz. D: Werner Herzog. DRA 93m. V

Heart of Humanity, The 1918 ★★½ Ferocious German hordes mercilessly pound away at Allies in the trenches. WWI propaganda, mainly of historical interest. C: Dorothy Phillips, Erich Von Stroheim. D: Allen Holubar. ACT 133m.

Heart of Midnight 1989 ★★ Emotionally unstable woman (Leigh) inherits sleazy nightclub. Another high excursion into bizarre psychological territory, this time more raunchy than effective. C: Jennifer Jason Leigh, Peter Coyote. D: Matthew Chapman. DRA [R] 93m. V

Heart of New York, The 1933 *See* **Hallelujah, I'm a Bum**

Heart of Paris 1939 French ★★★½ After being acquitted of murdering her lover, Morgan is taken in by sympathetic juror Raimu. This upsets his family's balance, and leads to tragic results. Involving French melodrama with nifty performances from the good ensemble. C: Raimu, Jeanne Provost, Michele Morgan, Gilbert Gil. D: Marc Allegret. DRA 85m.

Heart of Steel 1983 ★★★½ Socially conscious drama of an unemployed steelworker (Strauss) struggling to provide for his family. Excellent script offers compelling characterizations and trenchant political commentary. C: Peter Strauss, Pamela Reed, Barry Primus, John Goodman. D: Donald Wrye. DRA 100m. TVM

Heart of the Golden West 1942 ★★½ When some ranchers are the obvious victims of bogus shipping charges, Roy Rogers comes to their rescue. Good Roy, with nice work by his pals Hayes and Burnette. C: Roy Rogers, Smiley Burnette, George "Gabby" Hayes. D: Joseph Kane. WST 51m. V

Heart of the Matter, The 1954 British ★★★★½ Howard is superb in tragic, powerful story of Sierra Leone law officer who pities his wife but can't love her. He falls for a young woman (Schell) and is blackmailed. Intense adaptation of the classic Graham Greene novel set in 1942. C: Trevor Howard, Elizabeth Allan, Maria Schell, Denholm Elliott. D: George O'Ferrall. DRA 105m.

Heart of the North 1938 ★★★ Canadian Mounties chase after a gang of gold and fur thieves. Early Technicolor processing distinguished this fast-paced action adventure tale. C: Dick Foran, Gloria Dickson, Gale Page. D: Lewis Seiler. ACT 74m.

Heart of The Rio Grande 1942 ★★ Obnoxious young woman who despises her dude ranch vacation signals fake distress call to her father. C: Gene Autry, Smiley Burnette, Fay McKenzie. D: William Morgan. WST 79m. V

Heart of the Rockies 1951 ★★½ Roy Rogers—ably assisted by his faithful horse, Trigger, and dog, Bullet—takes over a major highway construction project. Lots of good Roy music and action. C: Roy Rogers, Penny Edwards, Gordon Jones, Ralph Morgan. D: William Witney. WST 67m. V

Heart of the Stag 1983 New Zealand ★★★½ A triangle consisting of an incestuously linked father and daughter and the farmhand who comes to work on their sheep ranch in New Zealand. Jarring but not exploitative, thanks to terse direction. Violence, profanity; approach with caution. C: Bruno Lawrence, Mary Regan. D: Michael Firth. DRA [R] 94m. v

Heart of the West 1937 ★★★½ When a neighboring rancher causes trouble for Gabriel, cowpoke hero Hopalong Cassidy rides in to save the day. Entertaining B-Western action, enlivened by nifty cattle stampede sequence. C: William Boyd, Jimmy Ellison, George "Gabby" Hayes, Lynn Gabriel. D: Howard Bretherton. WST 63m.

Heart of Tibet—An Intimate Portrait of the 14th Dalai Lama 1992 ★★★★ Fascinating portrait of the Dalai Lama, made during a 1991 trip to Los Angeles. As a spiritual and political leader, he radiates an extraordinary inner calm, visible even on film. DOC 60m. v

Heart to Heart 1978 French ★★★★ The day-to-day lives of ordinary French family seen through the eyes of youngster (Caudry). Warm, buoyant chronicle that leaves a smile. C: Daniel Ceccaldi, Laurence Ligneres, Anne Caudry. D: Pascal Thomas. COM 110m.

Heart Within, The 1957 ★★★★ West Indian native Cameron is a murder suspect solely because he is black. Hemmings comes to Cameron's defense, and Cameron returns the boy's kindness when the real killer surfaces. A keenly felt drama of prejudice and friendship. Cameron and Hemmings are well paired. C: James Hayter, Earl Cameron, David Hemmings. D: David Eady. DRA 61m.

Heartaches 1982 Canadian ★★★½ The comic misadventures of two young women—one forlorn and pregnant, the other just a nut—who become friends when they're thrown off a Toronto-bound bus. Potts and Kidder shine. C: Margot Kidder, Annie Potts, Robert Carradine. D: Donald Shebib. COM [R] 93m. v

Heartbeat 1946 ★★★ Rogers is a pickpocket who falls in love with a diplomat (Menjou) on whom she performs her skills. Polished cast can't overcome flimsy plot. C: Ginger Rogers, Jean-Pierre Aumont, Adolphe Menjou, Basil Rathbone. D: Sam Wood. DRA 102m. v

Heartbeeps 1981 ★★½ Two futuristic robots fall in love in this sometimes sweet, often tedious sci-fi comedy. Tender lead performances. C: Andy Kaufman, Bernadette Peters, Randy Quaid. D: Allan Arkush. COM [PG] 79m. v

Heartbreak Hotel 1988 ★★½ In 1972, the son of a rabid Elvis fan kidnaps The King (Keith) so he can perform for the boy's mother. Farfetched premise, leads to mushy doings. C: David Keith, Tuesday Weld, Charlie Schlatter. D: Chris Columbus. COM [PG-13] 101m. v

Heartbreak House 1986 ★★★ Shaw's play was shortened in this version, which starred Harrison (in one of his last roles) on Broadway, but it's still pretty wordy. Harrison in tour-de-force performance, plays Captain Shotover, the lone man in a household of outspoken women. C: Rex Harrison, Amy Irving, Rosemary Harris. D: Anthony Page. DRA 122m. TVM v

Heartbreak Kid, The 1972 ★★★★ During his honeymoon, a man falls for the beautiful blonde of his dreams, at the expense of his klutzy bride. Offbeat social comedy that is very funny and anxiety-provoking at the same time; a bull's-eye for May's comic wit. The new bride is played by her real-life daughter. C: Charles Grodin, Cybill Shepherd, Jeannie Berlin, Eddie Albert. D: Elaine May. COM [PG] 106m. v

Heartbreak Motel 1975 ★★½ When her car breaks down on a deserted country road, a famous blues singer (Uggams) is kidnapped by a bunch of sadistic hillbillies. It holds your interest. (a.k.a. *Poor Pretty Eddie and Red Neck County*) C: Shelley Winters, Leslie Uggams. HOR 85m. v

Heartbreak Ridge 1986 ★★★½ Standard-issue retelling of the old story of a veteran Marine (Eastwood) preparing his green recruits for realities of combat with the invasion of Grenada. Eastwood is perfect as the aging leatherneck. C: Clint Eastwood, Marsha Mason, Everett McGill, Moses Gunn, Eileen Heckart. D: Clint Eastwood. DRA [R] 130m. v

Heartbreaker 1983 ★★½ Young Hispanic (Allende) battles other neighborhood toughs for the hand of a young WASP (Dunlap) in the midst of Los Angeles gang wars. Potentially interesting material given trite treatment. C: Fernando Allende, Dawn Dunlap. D: Frank Zuniga. DRA [R] 90m. v

Heartbreakers 1984 ★★★★ A successful artist (Coyote) and a success in business (Mancuso) play friends whose careless pursuit of pleasure has dead-ended. Climaxes in an extraordinary scene with artist's model (Wayne) that lays their unhappy, empty lives bare. Strong, stark, compelling drama. C: Peter Coyote, Nick Mancuso, Carole Laure, Carol Wayne. D: Bobby Roth. DRA [R] 98m. v

Heartburn 1986 ★★★ Story of breakup and divorce of food writer and philandering political columnist—based on writer Ephron's failed marriage to Carl Bernstein and her best-selling novel—never seems to gel. Streep and Nicholson try hard, but it's not enough. C: Meryl Streep, Jack Nicholson, Jeff Daniels, Maureen Stapleton, Stockard Channing. D: Mike Nichols. DRA [R] 109m. v

Heartland Reggae 1980 Canadian ★★ 1978 reggae concert in Jamaica, in honor of Haile Selassie's visit; good music. C: Bob Marley and the Wailers, Peter Tosh, Althea Donna. D: J.P. Lewis. MUS 90m. v

Heartland 1979 ★★★★½ Ferrell and Torn triumphant in low-budget sleeper about the real people who won the West. A robust and honest chronicle of the day-to-day struggle faced by ranchers and farmers in rugged

Wyoming, 1910. C: Rip Torn, Conchata Ferrell, Barry Primus, Lilia Skala. D: Richard Pearce. WST [PG] 95m. V

Hearts and Armour 1983 Italian ★★★ Medieval yarn features a woman warrior (De Rossi) loyal to Christian (Edwards), who is destined to kill the Moor she loves. Muddled, but has some spark. C: Tanya Roberts, Barbara DeRossi, Rick Edwards, Leigh McCloskey. D: Giacomo Battiato. ACT 101m. V

Hearts and Minds 1974 ★★★★★ Davis won Best Documentary Oscar for this shattering exploration of American policy in Vietnam and the misguided, often racist ideals that shaped it. An unforgettable viewing experience, assembled with intelligence, irony, and furious compassion. D: Peter Davis. DOC [R] 110m. V

Hearts Divided 1936 ★★½ Another Hearst-financed vanity production for Davies, cast as a young French peasant woman involved with Napoleon's brother (Powell). Slow going musical romance. C: Marion Davies, Dick Powell, Charlie Ruggles, Claude Rains, Edward Everett Horton. D: Frank Borzage. MUS 87m.

Hearts of Darkness: A Filmmaker's Apocalypse 1991 ★★★★½ Brilliant documentary about the making of Francis Ford Coppola's Vietnam masterpiece, *Apocalypse Now*. Fashioned from 60 hours of footage, shot primarily by the director's wife, Eleanor, film chronicles rampant overspending, drugs, Martin Sheen's heart attack, and Brando's temperamental personality. Fascinating insight into filmmaking and Coppola's unique psyche. D: Fax Bahr, George Hickenlooper. DOC [R] 96m. V

Hearts of Fire 1987 ★ Rock 'n' roll rip-off of *The Red Shoes* was a fiasco, released directly to video. Nominal plot has singer (Fiona) rising to fame while torn between mentor (Dylan) and true love (Everett). Dylan's performance is at best self-indulgent. C: Fiona, Rupert Everett, Bob Dylan, Julian Glover. D: Richard Marquand. MUS [R] 96m. V

Hearts of the West 1975 ★★★★½ Sweetheart tribute to old low-budget Westerns features Bridges as would-be novelist who becomes a movie cowboy. Funny and charming; great performance by Arkin as Grade-Z movie director. (a.k.a. *Hollywood Cowboy*) C: Jeff Bridges, Blythe Danner, Andy Griffith, Donald Pleasence, Alan Arkin. D: Howard Zieff. WST [PG] 103m. V

Hearts of the World 1918 ★★★★ Episodic silent saga about a French family separated after outbreak of WWI. Emotional propaganda film made at the behest of the British government. Powerful, with many excellent interludes. C: Lillian Gish, Dorothy Gish, Robert Harron. D: D.W. Griffith. DRA 152m. V

Heartsounds 1984 ★★★★½ Three-handkerchief tale about a doctor's wife (Moore) whose life is changed when her husband (Garner) suffers a series of heart attacks. Adaptation of Martha Weinman Lear's best-seller is as intelligent as it is moving. C: Mary Tyler Moore, James Garner, Sam Wanamaker. D: Glenn Caron Jordan. DRA 135m. TVM

Heartstopper ★★★ Back from the dead vampire doctor terrorizes Pittsburgh. Associates of George Romero worked on this, but the master's touch is sorely needed. C: Kevin Kindlin, Moon Zappa, Tom Savini, John Hall. D: John Russo. HOR 96m.

Heartworn Highways 1981 ★★★★ Pleasant documentary about the then-new wave in country music. Well worth seeing for the performances, especially Coe playing live in a prison in which he was once an inmate. C: Guy Clark, Rodney Crowell, David Allan Coe, Charlie Daniels Band. D: James Szalapski. DOC 92m. V

Heat 1972 ★★★★ *Sunset Boulevard* remake (of sorts) from Andy Warhol factory stars Miles as faded movie queen who takes in studly Dallesandro for sex, sex, and more sex. Feldman is Miles' daughter who further twists the bizarre plot in this delightfully campy feature. C: Sylvia Miles, Joe Dallesandro, Andrea Feldman. D: Paul Morrissey. COM [R] 102m. V

Heat 1987 ★★½ Tough gambler (Reynolds) helps an old flame get even with a gangster rapist. Disorganized star vehicle. C: Burt Reynolds, Karen Young, Peter MacNicol. D: R. M. Richards. ACT [R] 103m. V

Heat and Dust 1982 British ★★★★ A young Englishwoman learns about the past affairs in India of her dead great aunt. Incisively big-budget saga with engaging performances. Screenplay by Ruth Prawar Jhabvala, who wrote the novel. C: Julie Christie, Greta Scacchi, Christopher Cazenove, Julian Glover. D: James Ivory. DRA [R] 130m. V

Heat and Sunlight 1987 ★★★½ A young photographer develops an obsessive relationship with a dancer, then struggles back from the brink after she leaves him. Good performances and emotionally charged story are overshadowed by director/star Nilsson's flashy cinematic style. C: Rob Nilsson, Consuelo Faust. D: Rob Nilsson. DRA 98m. V

Heat of Anger 1972 ★★★½ Feisty Hayward is Cobb's lawyer, defending him in murder trial. Average courtroom drama, later a TV series. C: Susan Hayward, James Stacy, Lee J. Cobb. D: Don Taylor. DRA 74m. TVM

Heat of Desire 1983 French ★★ Ridiculous yarn about a university professor whose career and marriage are destroyed by a young woman who whisks him off for a sin-soaked romp in a Barcelona hotel. Interesting mainly for Dewaere's transformation from a staid intellectual to a take-charge guy. C: Patrick Dewaere, Clio Goldsmith, Jeanne Moreau. D: Luc Beraud. DRA 90m. V

Heat Street 1987 ★★ When punks murder their families and friends two young toughs

her beloved grandfather to be the companion for an infirm young girl. Temple shines in the title role. A wonderful film for children of all ages. Both b&w and colorized versions are available. C: Shirley Temple, Jean Hersholt, Arthur Treacher, Helen Westley. D: Allan Dwan. FAM/DRA 88m. V

Heidi 1952 Swiss ★★★★ This version of Spyri's tale has been updated from 19th-century Switzerland to the 20th century. Good use of Swiss Alpine locations make this remake of the 1937 classic worth watching. Kids will definitely enjoy. C: Elsbeth Sigmund, Heinrich Gretler. D: Luigi Comencini. FAM/DRA 98m. V

Heidi 1968 ★★★½ Competent retelling of Johanna Spyri's children's classic about a young girl (Edwards) who stays with her grandfather in the Swiss Alps. C: Jennifer Edwards, Maximilian Schell, Jean Simmons, Michael Redgrave. D: Delbert Mann. FAM/DRA 105m. TVM V

Heidi 1993 ★★★½ One more go-round for the classic children's tale of Swiss orphan girl who lives in the Alps with her kindly grandfather. The kids will love it, even if they've seen all the other versions. C: Noley Thorman, Jason Robards, Jane Seymour, Lexi Randall, Sian Phillips, Bejamin Brazier, Patricia Neal. D: Michael Rhodes. FAM/DRA 165m. V

Heidi and Peter 1955 Swiss ★★★½ Sequel to the classic story in which the sweet Swiss miss helps her village cope with a catastrophic flood. Good Swiss-produced effort starring many of the principals from the earlier, slightly superior *Heidi* by the same producers. C: Heinrich Gretler, Elsbeth Sigmund, Thomas Klameth. D: Franz Schnyder. FAM/DRA 89m.

Heidi's Song 1982 ★★ Empty retelling of classic Swiss children's story marked by Saturday morning television animation aesthetics, sticky-sweet dialogue, and songs. For younger kids only. Voices of Lorne Greene, Margery Gray, Sammy Davis, Jr. D: Robert Taylor. FAM/MUS [G] 85m. V

Heimat 1984 German ★★★½ Reitz's outsize, uneven 16-hour epic chronicling life in a rural German town between 1919 and 1982 has rich b&w and color camerawork, along with addictive soap opera elements. C: Marita Breuer, Dieter Schaad, Rudiger Weigang. D: Edgar Reitz. DRA 940m.

Heimatlos German ★★★ After her fiancé abandons her in Munich, a small-town girl finds herself homeless and destitute. Contrived, but well acted. C: Marianne Hold, Rudolf Lenz, Peter Weck, Joe Stockel. DRA 95m.

Heiress, The 1949 ★★★★½ Inspired adaptation of Henry James' novel *Washington Square* about a trusting woman (de Havilland) who falls for a fortune-hunting scoundrel (Clift) despite the admonitions of her domineering father. De Havilland won an Oscar for her magnificent performance as an increasingly bitter woman; Aaron Copland won his for Best Score. C: Olivia de Havilland, Montgomery Clift, Ralph Richardson, Miriam Hopkins. D: William Wyler. DRA 115m. V

Heirs of the Vikings, The ★★★ An earnest, if rather slow, documentary about the Norwegian royal family. DOC 80m.

Heist, The 1972 ★★½ An obsessive cop goes overboard in his efforts to prove that an armored car robbery was masterminded by one of the surviving guards. George is good, but too many plot contrivances finally pitch this beyond believability. C: Christopher George, Elizabeth Ashley. D: Don McDougall. ACT 73m. TVM

Heist, The 1979 Italian ★★★ After gangsters engineer theft, cops give chase. Spectacular stunt driving is only plus in this hodgepodge. C: Charles Aznavour, Virna Lisi. D: Sergio Gobbi. CRI 85m.

Heist, The 1989 ★★★ Ex-con Brosnan plots vengeance against former associate who framed him. Unnecessarily complicated but moderately entertaining; okay racetrack atmosphere. C: Pierce Brosnan, Tom Skerritt, Wendy Hughes. D: Stuart Orme. CRI 97m. TVM V

Held Hostage: The Sis and Jerry Levin Story 1991 ★★★ Docudrama based on reporter Jerry Levin's imprisonment in Beirut and his wife's relentless goading of the State Department to negotiate his release. Strong, dedicated cast in high melodrama. C: Marlo Thomas, David Dukes. D: Roger Young. DRA 95m. TVM V

Helen Keller—Separate Views ★★★½ Somewhat unconventional documentary, done in three parts, chronicling the life of Keller; the second part features other famous people (Dwight Eisenhower, Martha Graham, Katharine Cornell) reflecting on Keller's life, and the third part is the Oscar-winning short, "One-Eyed Men Are Kings." DOC 90m. V

Helen Keller: The Miracle Continues 1984 ★★★½ Sequel of sorts to *The Miracle Worker*, with hearing-, speech- and sight-impaired Helen (Winningham) now a college student, trying to cope with her handicaps and demanding relationship with teacher Anne Sullivan Macy (Danner). Good performances but script cops out with pat solutions to complex situations. C: Blythe Danner, Mare Winningham, Perry King, Vera Miles, Jack Warden. D: Alan Gibson. DRA 104m. TVM

Helen Morgan Story, The 1957 ★★½ Fictional account of torch singer Morgan (Blyth) focuses on her alcoholism and romantic troubles and glosses over her talent and career. Studio vehicle all the way. C: Ann Blyth, Paul Newman, Richard Carlson. D: Michael Curtiz. DRA 118m.

Helen of Troy 1955 ★★ Famed story of Helen and Paris and how Trojan War began.

Trivial script reduces lots of costumes and big sets to empty scenes of grandeur. C: Stanley Baker, Rossana Podesta, Brigitte Bardot. D: Robert Wise. DRA 118m.

Hell and High Water 1954 ★★★ Crack team of mercenary sailors on submarine mission bound for Arctic to dismantle enemy plot to start war. Average cold war heroics with fine underwater cinematography. C: Richard Widmark, Bella Darvi, Victor Francen. D: Samuel Fuller. DRA 103m.

Hell Below Zero 1954 ★★½ When Tetzel's father is murdered, she enlists Ladd to find his killer. Sleepy tale set aboard a whaling vessel has neither the excitement of a high seas adventure or the intrigue of a murder mystery. C: Alan Ladd, Joan Tetzel, Stanley Baker. D: Mark Robson. ACT 91m.

Hell Below 1933 ★★★★ Submarine captain (Huston) is pitted against enemy Montgomery in this gripping WWI drama. A spare, tense tale with liberal doses of crowd-pleasing action and romance. C: Robert Montgomery, Walter Huston, Madge Evans, Jimmy Durante, Sterling Holloway. D: Jack Conway. ACT 105m.

Hell Bent for Leather 1960 ★★★½ An innocent drifter is incriminated in a killing by mercenary sheriff. Well-tailored Murphy vehicle. C: Audie Murphy, Felicia Farr, Stephen McNally. D: George Sherman. WST 82m.

Hell Canyon Outlaws 1957 ★★★ A sheriff forced from office goes after the outlaws who have taken over town. Standard "law vs. the lawless" Western shoot-'em-up, but with good performances by Robertson and especially Keith as head outlaw. C: Dale Robertson, Brian Keith, Rosanna Rory. D: Paul Landres. WST 72m.

Hell Comes to Frogtown 1987 ★ Sam Hell (pro wrestler Rowdy Roddy Piper), the only potent male on post-nuclear-holocaust Earth, is assigned procreation duty, but only if he can rescue the women from King Toady and his legion of mutant frogoids. For trash lovers only. C: Roddy Piper, Sandahl Bergman, Rory Calhoun. D: R. J. Kizer, Donald Jackson. SFI [R] 88m. V

Hell Divers 1932 ★★★ Pair of rambunctious Navy fliers compete in love and in the sky. Crowd pleasing service yarn, with good aviation footage. C: Wallace Beery, Clark Gable, Conrad Nagel. D: George Hill. ACT 113m.

Hell Drivers 1958 British ★★★½ Ex-con trucker is sent on a brutal cross-country assignment after his boss learns he knows too much about the company's crooked dealings. Gritty drama features an excellent cast of young up-and-coming British talents. C: Stanley Baker, Herbert Lom, Peggy Cummins, Patrick McGoohan, Jill Ireland, David McCallum, Sean Connery. D: Cy Endfield. ACT 91m.

Hell, Heaven or Hoboken 1958 *See* **I Was Monty's Double**

Hell High 1986 ★★★ A disturbed teacher takes bloody revenge after some students play a near-fatal prank on her. Benefits from atmospheric production, though the characters are obnoxious and the situations sometimes unpleasant. C: Maureen Moony, Christopher Stryker, Christopher Cousins, Millie Prezioso, Jason Brill. D: Douglas Grossman. HOR [R] 84m. V

Hell Hunters 1986 ★★★ Los Angeles is under siege as an old Nazi doctor plots to destroy the city. Will the Nazi hunters get there in time? Do you care? Cheap *Boys from Brazil* rehash features a truly peculiar cast. C: Maud Adams, Stewart Granger, George Lazenby. ACT 98m. V

Hell in Korea 1956 British ★★★ U.N. reconnoitering detachment tries to find a village supposedly held by Chinese Communists. Small-scale military drama focused on the relationships between the men. Caine's screen debut. Based on a book by Max Catto. (a.k.a. *A Hill in Korea*) C: Ronald Lewis, Stephen Boyd, Robert Shaw, Stanley Baker, Harry Andrews, Michael Caine. D: Julian Amyes. DRA 81m.

Hell in the Pacific 1968 ★★★ American Marvin and Japanese Mifune wage a two-man war on a Pacific island in WWII. This allegory substitutes brutality for subtlety with mixed results; still worth a look. C: Lee Marvin, Toshiro Mifune. D: John Boorman. ACT [G] 103m. V

Hell Is a City 1960 British ★★★ In England, a jewel thief (Crawford) breaks out of jail and goes into hiding while the police organize a manhunt. Stirring action effectively handled in documentary style. C: Stanley Baker, John Crawford, Donald Pleasence, Maxine Audley, Billie Whitelaw. D: Val Guest. CRI 98m.

Hell Is for Heroes 1962 ★★★★ Solid, suspenseful WWII tale of McQueen rallying his embattled squadron to hold off a massive German onslaught. Siegel's gut-level direction and an oddball cast (including Fess Parker and Bob Newhart!) make this an unusual entry in the game. C: Steve McQueen, Bobby Darin, Fess Parker, Harry Guardino, James Coburn, Nick Adams, Bob Newhart. D: Don Siegel. ACT 90m. V

Hell Night 1981 ★★ A fraternity initiation turns lethal when the chosen setting is an abandoned mansion stalked by a murderous freak. Competent but resolutely unsurprising stalker film, with horror icon Blair cast as just another screaming would-be victim. C: Linda Blair, Vincent Van Patten, Peter Barton. D: Tom DeSimone. HOR [R] 100m. V

Hell on Devil's Island 1957 ★★½ Inmates of the infamous island prison suffer abominably while working in the island's mines. Unconvincing prison drama, despite a hard-working cast. C: Helmut Dantine, William Talman, Donna Martell. D: Christian Nyby. DRA 74m.

Hell on Earth 1934 German ★★★½ War drama throws five different soldiers—English, German, French, German-Jewish and African-American—in a foxhole. Flashbacks tell each individual's story and how they came together. Dated but well-meaning antiwar drama. C: Georges Peclet, Hugh Douglas, Vladmir Sokoloff. D: Victor Trivas. DRA 64m.

Hell on Frisco Bay 1955 ★★½ A falsely accused policeman is determined to avenge himself on the crime syndicate that framed him. The tough talking is laid on thick in this action-packed film. C: Alan Ladd, Edward G. Robinson, Joanne Dru, William Demarest, Fay Wray, Jayne Mansfield. D: Frank Tuttle. CRI 93m. V

Hell on Wheels 1967 ★★ Race-car driver Robbins falls out with his mechanic brother over girl. Next thing you know, they're trying to kill each other. C: Marty Robbins, John Ashley, Jennifer Ashley, Gigi Perreau, Connie Smith, Robert Dornan, Frank Gerstle. D: Will Zens. DRA 96m. V

Hell River 1975 ★★★ Partisans vs. Nazis in 1941 Yugoslavia. Typical war picture. C: Rod Taylor, Adam West. D: Stole Jankovic. DRA 100m. V

Hell Ship Mutiny 1957 ★★½ A swashbuckling sea captain (Hall) comes to the aid of a South Sea princess after her island paradise is overrun by thieves. Tired plot defeats a cast of fine character actors, but they go down fighting. C: Elmo Williams, Jon Hall, John Carradine, Peter Lorre. D: Lee Sholem. ACT 66m.

Hell Squad 1985 ★ When the State Department is unable to help him, U.S. Ambassador hires nine Vegas showgirls to rescue his son from terrorists. As silly as it sounds. C: Bainbridge Scott, Glen Hartford, Tina Lederman, Marvin Miller. D: Kenneth Hartford. DRA 88m. V

Hell to Eternity 1960 ★★★★ Action-packed biography of WWII hero Guy Gabaldon, who took on the Japanese despite having been raised in a Japanese household. C: Jeffrey Hunter, David Janssen, Vic Damone, Sessue Hayakawa. D: Phil Karlson. DRA 132m. V

Hell Town 1937 *See* **Born to the West**

Hell Town 1985 ★★★ Ex-con turned priest dishes out bitter doses of tough love to several hard-case ghetto parishoners. Preachy pilot was the basis for a short-lived series. Blake's intense though somewhat overbearing lead performance is infused with much-needed conviction. C: Robert Blake, Jeff Corey. D: Don Medford. DRA 100m. TVM

Hell Up In Harlem 1973 ★ After an assassination attempt, a wounded gang lord tries to make a comeback. He needn't have bothered. C: Fred Williamson, Julius W. Harris, Gloria Hendry. D: Larry Cohen. CRI 98m. V

Hell With Heroes, The 1968 ★★★ A smuggler and his girlfriend dupe a pair of air cargo pilots into flying contraband into WWII France. Glossy dimestore heroics, with capable acting. C: Rod Taylor, Claudia Cardinale, Harry Guardino. D: Joseph Sargent. DRA 95m.

Hellbent 1990 ★★ Sleazy, low-budget road movie that pairs drugged-out rocker (Ward) and violence-prone housewife (Levand). C: Phil Ward, Lynn Levand, Cheryl Slean, David Marciano. D: Richard Casey. DRA 90m.

Hellbound: Hellraiser II 1988 British ★★★★ A demented doctor opens the gates of hell again, and Laurence must fight its demons while trying to save her dead father's soul. Superior sequel explores a wider canvas while serving up an even more heaping helping of heart-pounding horror. C: Ashley Laurence, Clare Higgins. D: Tony Randel. HOR [R] 97m. V

Hellcamp 1986 *See* **Opposing Force**

Hellcats of the Navy 1957 ★★★ Adventure in the Pacific with the skipper and crew of a U.S. submarine fighting the Japanese during WWII. Decent action, helped by Davis and Reagan (in their only screen appearance together). C: Ronald Reagan, Nancy Davis. D: Nathan Juran. ACT 82m. V

Helldorado 1946 ★★★ Roy Rogers and his usual entourage take on the bad guys. Lots of hold-your-breath action and snappy music. C: Roy Rogers, George "Gabby" Hayes, Dale Evans. D: William Witney. WST 70m.

Heller in Pink Tights 1960 ★★★½ A traveling theatrical troupe undertakes engagements in 1880s West. Offbeat Western spoof with funny, behind-the-scenes bits. Based on a Louis L'Amour novel. C: Sophia Loren, Anthony Quinn, Margaret O'Brien, Steve Forrest, Eileen Heckart. D: George Cukor. WST 101m. V

Hellfighters 1968 ★★★ Fact-based action-adventure about international oil well firefighters. Watchable fare with good effects and cast; Wayne's character is based on real-life wildcat firefighter "Red" Adair. C: John Wayne, Katharine Ross, Jim Hutton, Vera Miles. D: Andrew V. McLaglen. DRA [G] 121m. V

Hellfire 1948 ★★★½ Oddball, interesting western about a gambler (Elliot) who pledges to build a church after a preacher dies to save his life. C: Wild Bill Elliot, Marie Windsor, Forrest Tucker, Jim Davis. D: R.G. Springsteen. WST 90m.

Hellgate 1952 ★★★½ A 19th-century veterinary doctor (Hayden), falsely accused of aiding a criminal, is sent to a savage prison where he struggles to clear himself. Loosely based on the infamous case of Dr. Mudd—the doctor who treated John Wilkes Booth after he assassinated Lincoln—remake of *The Prisoner of Shark Island* features a solid performance by Hayden. C: Sterling Hayden, Joan Leslie, James Arness. D: Charles Warren. DRA 87m.

Hellhole 1985 ★½ Lurid trash of young woman confined to all-female sanitarium, where the staff is conducting unauthorized experiments in chemical lobotomies. C: Ray

Sharkey, Judy Landers, Mary Woronov, Marjoe Gortner, Edy Williams. D: Pierre de Moro. ACT [R] 95m. V

Hellions, The 1962 British ★★★½ Attempt at a Western set in 19th-century South Africa with Todd as sheriff terrorized by gang of murderers. Well-acted variation on classic *High Noon* motif. C: Richard Todd, Anne Aubrey, Lionel Jeffries. D: Ken Annakin. ACT 87m.

Hellmaster 1992 ★★ Mad scientist experiments on college students, creates superstrong mutants suffering from bad makeup jobs. C: David Emge, John Saxon, Amy Raasch. D: Douglas Schulze. HOR 92m. V

Hello Again 1987 ★★½ One year after her death, Long is brought back to life by her flaky sister Ivey who dabbles in the occult. Long tries her perky best to make the material work, but the premise is merely setup for poorly developed ideas. C: Shelley Long, Corbin Bersen, Judith Ivey, Gabriel Byrne, Sela Ward. D: Frank Perry. COM [PG] 96m. V

Hello, Dolly! 1969 ★★★★ Lavish film adaptation of the Broadway smash, with Streisand as incurable matchmaker Dolly Levi. Music and dance numbers are exuberant, sumptuous large-screen creations. Based on Thornton Wilder's *The Matchmaker*. C: Barbra Streisand, Walter Matthau, Michael Crawford, Marianne McAndrew, Tommy Tune, Louis Armstrong. D: Gene Kelly. MUS [G] 146m. V

Hello Down There 1969 ★★ Silly and empty-headed story involves a family residing in an experimental underwater living space. Notable mostly for an early (and embarrassing) appearance by Richard Dreyfuss. (a.k.a *Sub-A-Dub-Dub*) C: Tony Randall, Janet Leigh, Jim Backus, Roddy McDowall, Richard Dreyfuss. D: Jack Arnold. COM [G] 98m.

Hello, Elephant 1952 Italian ★★ Unsuccessful farce about a royal gift of an elephant to a poor deserving family. Interesting combination of Indian star Sabu and Italian director De Sica, though. (a.k.a. *Pardon My Trunk*) C: Vittorio De Sica, Sabu, Maria Mercader. D: Gianni Franciolini. COM 78m.

Hello, Fred the Beard 1978 Polish ★★★½ Amusing musical comedy about theater's angel who is actually a bank robber. D: Wieslaw Rzeszewski. MUS 98m.

Hello Frisco, Hello 1943 ★★★★ Pleasant period musical. Faye is San Francisco saloon singer in love with social-climbing Payne. Oscar for Best Song: "You'll Never Know." C: Alice Faye, John Payne, Jack Oakie, Lynn Bari. D: H. Humberstone. MUS 98m. V

Hello-Goodbye 1970 British ★★★ Romantic comedy. Crawford is a naive young Englishman who falls in love with a beautiful Frenchwoman who turns out to be the wife of an aristocrat. Unassuming film boasts attractive cinematography. C: Michael Crawford, Curt Jurgens, Genevieve Gilles. D: Jean Negulesco. COM [PG] 107m.

Hello Mary Lou—Prom Night II 1987 Canadian ★★★ Stylish chiller about the spirit of a murdered prom queen returning to wreak vengeance has nothing to do with the first *Prom Night*—and is much the better for it. Schrage is stunning as the evil teen demon. C: Lisa Schrage, Michael Ironside. D: Bruce Pittman. HOR [R] 97m. V

Hello Sister 1933 ★★★ Simple love story about a couple who meet in New York City is more interesting for its filming history than its plot. Erich von Stroheim—legendary for his bizarre perfectionism behind the camera—was the original director, until the studio wrenched it out of his hands and refilmed/reedited much of it for general release. Traces of von Stroheim's eccentricities survived the cutting room floor, however, rendering the picture irresistible to film buffs. C: Alfred Werker, James Dunn, ZaSu Pitts. D: Erich von Stroheim. DRA 62m.

Hello Sucker 1941 ★★★ Two vaudeville veterans decide to go into the talent booking business and fall in love while they promote a slew of eccentric entertainers. Silly screwball comedy enlivened by kooky situations and good cast of character actors. C: Peggy Moran, Tom Brown. D: Edward Cline. COM 60m.

Hellraiser 1987 British ★★★ Popular horror author Barker makes his directorial debut with this intense, gruesome shocker about a woman seduced by her old lover—who's now a skinless zombie for whom she must kill. Uneven but absorbing, with an unusually complex underlying mythology. C: Andrew Robinson, Clare Higgins. D: Clive Barker. HOR [R] 94m. V

Hellraiser III: Hell on Earth 1992 ★★★ Pinhead, a supporting demon from the first two films, takes on a TV newswoman while attempting to secure his power in our dimension. Eschews the Gothic power of its predecessors in favor of Americanized gimmick horror, but gruesomely entertaining nonetheless. C: Terry Farrell, Doug Bradley, Paula Marshall. D: Anthony Hickox. HOR [R] 93m. V

Hell's Angels 1930 ★★★★ The film that launched Harlow is a melodramatic WWI flying adventure with some great aviation photography. This extravagant production features a a clash between two brothers who both desire the same woman, but the air battles steal the show. C: Ben Lyon, James Hall, Jean Harlow, John Darrow. D: Howard Hughes. ACT 129m. V

Hell's Angels Forever 1983 ★★★★ Documentary of legendary motorcycle gang is better than one would expect. You don't really gain sympathy for the bikers but this does give insight on why they do what they do. The Angels authorized the production. D: Richard Chase, Kevin Keating, Leon Gast. DOC [R] 97m. V

Hell's Angels on Wheels 1967 ★★★½ Biker film casts Nicholson as wandering punk joining outlaw motorcycle group, attracting girlfriend of gang leader. Good cast, direction offset meandering story line; made with input from real Hell's Angels. C: Adam Roarke, Jack Nicholson, Sabrina Scharf. D: Richard Rush. ACT 95m. V

Hell's Angels '69 1969 ★★½ Two rich brothers decide to rob a Las Vegas casino with the help of the notorious gang—but don't tell the Angels. A wild pursuit of the criminals ensues. Amusing concept tires quickly. C: Tom Stern, Jeremy Slate, Conny Van Dyke. D: Lee Madden. ACT 97m. V

Hell's Bloody Devils 1970 ★★½ Bikers clash with Las Vegas mobsters and neo-Nazis. Sadistic, bloody action with veteran cast. (a.k.a. *The Fakers* and *Smashing the Crime Syndicate*) C: Broderick Crawford, Scott Brady, John Gabriel, John Carradine. D: Al Adamson. ACT [PG] 92m.

Hell's Brigade—The Final Assault 1980 ★ Clanky, cheapo war film with Palance and other Americans parachuting behind Nazi lines on secret mission. C: Jack Palance, John Jay Douglas, Carlos Estrada. D: Henry Mankewirk. DRA 99m. V

Hell's Crossroads 1957 ★★★ Peaceful Western town is terrorized by members of the infamous James gang, two of whom would like to quit and return to law-abiding life. An old-time shoot-'em-up. C: Stephen McNally, Peggie Castle, Robert Vaughn. D: Franklin Adreon. WST 73m.

Hell's Half Acre 1954 ★★★½ After a long search, a woman finds her missing husband has established a new identity in post-WWII Honolulu. Despite good performances by entire cast, the parts don't gel. C: Wendell Corey, Evelyn Keyes, Elsa Lanchester. D: John Auer. DRA 91m.

Hell's Heroes 1930 ★★★★ A trio of cowhands come upon a dying woman about to give birth, and pledge to look after her baby. Well-done, over-looked version of an oft-filmed story. John Ford remade it himself (the most familiar being 1949's *The Three Godfathers*). C: Charles Bickford, Raymond Hatton, Fred Kohler. D: William Wyler. WST 65m.

Hell's Highway 1932 ★★★★ Unjustly incarcerated convict Dix must revise his scheme for escape from a hellish Southern prison when his brother (Brown) joins him on a chain gang for shooting a man who double-crossed him. Well handled, especially manhunt sequence. C: Richard Dix, Tom Brown, Rochelle Hudson. D: Rowland Brown. CRI 62m.

Hell's Hinges 1916 ★★★★½ A naive preacher's sister wins over a shady roughneck in a wild frontier town. Ground-breaking silent Western still amazes with stark depiction of early Western life. C: William S. Hart, Clara Williams, Jack Standing. D: William S. Hart. WST 65m. V

Hell's Horizon 1955 ★★½ A group of Korean War soldiers attempt to bomb a strategic enemy bridge. Predictable war drama focuses on the relationships between the men. C: John Ireland, Marla English, Hugh Beaumont. D: Tom Gries. ACT 80m.

Hell's House 1932 ★★ An innocent teenager (Durkin) takes the fall for a bootlegger (O'Brien) and is sent to a brutal reform school. Davis—with bleached blonde hair—plays O'Brien's heart-of-gold sweetheart. Assembly line corn. C: Junior Durkin, Pat O'Brien, Bette Davis. D: Howard Higgin. DRA 78m. V

Hell's Island 1955 ★★★½ Down-at-the-heels ex-law officer (Payne), hired to recover a missing ruby, encounters former fiancée (Murphy), for whom he still harbors an unhealthy love. Decent film noir with crackling tough guy dialogue. C: John Payne, Mary Murphy, Francis Sullivan. D: Phil Karlson. ACT 84m.

Hell's Kitchen 1939 ★★★ An ex-con (Fields) tries to straighten out a bunch of kids. Remake of *The Mayor from Hell.* C: Ronald Reagan, Stanley Fields, Margaret Lindsay. D: Lewis Seiler, E. Dupont. DRA 81m.

Hell's Long Road 1963 Italian ★★★½ Costume drama set in ancient Rome deals with a senator trying to remain in the good graces of the insane emperor Nero while carrying on a clandestine romance with a beautiful seductress. Spirited cast and lavish scenic design compensate for the melodramatic story. C: Elena Brazzi, Kay Nolandi. D: Charles Roberti. DRA 89m.

Hell's Outpost 1954 ★★★ Drifter (Cameron) insinuates himself into mining family by claiming to be Korean War buddy of dead son. Fair drama, with likable leads. C: Rod Cameron, Joan Leslie, Chill Wills. D: Joseph Kane. DRA 90m.

Hellstrom Chronicle, The 1971 ★★★★ A visually stunning look at the vast insect world. Oscar for Best Documentary. D: Walon Green, Lawrence Pressman. DOC [G] 90m. V

Hellzapoppin 1941 ★★★★ Olsen and Johnson's stage revue was a precursor of *Laugh-In*, stringing countless gags into zany entertainment. Film begins with studio executive telling the stars that they need a story: "This is Hollywood, we change everything here." C: Ole Olsen, Chic Johnson, Martha Raye, Mischa Auer, Jane Frazee. D: H. Potter. MUS 84m.

Helmut Newton—Frames from the Edge 1991 ★★★ Documentary on controversial photographer, known for his racy nudes and kinky bondage imagery. DOC 95m. V

Help! 1965 British ★★★½ Follow-up to *A Hard Day's Night* adds color, location photography, and millions of dollars to budget. Wild, wacky plot (Ringo has sacred ring stuck on his finger) is unimportant. Great songs and the Fab Four's appeal survive. C: John Lennon, Paul McCartney, George Harrison, Ringo Starr, Leo McKern, Eleanor Bron. D: Richard Lester. MUS [G] 90m. V

Help Me Dream 1981 Italian ★★★★ A romance set to music about American pilot (Franciosa) hidden by an Italian woman (Melato) and her children in their farmhouse during WWII. Inventive, sentimental and quite entertaining, with songs and outstanding choreography of the period. C: Mariangela Melato, Anthony Franciosa, JeanPierre Leaud. D: Pupi Avati. MUS 112m.

Help Wanted: Kids 1986 ★★★ Lonely couple hire a pair of children to be their kids. Inoffensive but nothing special. C: Cindy Williams, Bill Hudson. D: David Greenwalt. COM 104m. TVM

Help Wanted: Male 1982 ★★★ Romantic comedy about a woman (Pleshette) who hires a man to help her get pregnant. Amusing if a tad dated. C: Suzanne Pleshette, Gil Gerard, Bert Convy. D: William Wiard. COM 97m. TVM V

Helsinki Napoli All Night Long 1987 Finnish ★★★½ Various bumblers go through an endless night of dealings, double crosses, and backstabbings. Occasionally lively foray into Sam Fuller land (who shows up periodically): B-movie melodramatics laced with cynical humor and splendid Helsinki locations. C: Kaari Vaananen, Roberta Manfredi, Nino Manfredi, Jean-Pierre Castaldi, Margi Clarke, Melanie Robesson, Samuel Fuller, Eddie Constantine. D: Mika Kaurismaki. DRA 105m.

Helter Skelter 1976 ★★★★½ Manson "family" mayhem, capture, and subsequent trial. Excellent, disturbing production, riveting Railsback. Terrifying adaptation of best-seller by Vincent Bugliosi, prosecutor of the case. Unforgettable. C: George DiCenzo, Steve Railsback, Nancy Wolfe, Marilyn Burns. D: Tom Gries. CRI 119m. TVM V

Helter Skelter Murders, The 1972 ★ Tabloid-like account of the Manson cult's ritualistic slayings. C: Debbie Duff, Brian Klinknett, Phyllis Estes, Paula Shannon. D: Frank Howard. CRI [R] 83m. V

Hemingway's Adventures of a Young Man 1962 *See* **Adventures of a Young Man**

Henderson Monster, The 1980 ★★★ Dark side of genetics experimentation, with Miller as the brilliant scientist and Spielberg as his adversary. Very verbose drama. C: Jason Miller, Christine Lahti, Stephen Collins, David Spielberg. D: Waris Hussein. DRA 94m. TVM V

Hennessy 1975 British ★★ Contrived story of an Irish Republican Army soldier who vows to avenge his murdered family by assassinating the Royal Family and bombing Parliament. Serious politics do not belong with this leaden plot. C: Rod Steiger, Lee Remick, Richard Johnson, Trevor Howard. D: Don Sharp. CRI [PG] 103m.

Henry Aldrich The first film in the Paramount series, *What A Life* (1939), was based on the original play by Clifford Goldsmith. It starred Jackie Cooper as the typical teenage boy in small-town America; two years later Cooper did another Aldrich film. The series proper began later that year with Jimmy Lydon replacing Cooper as the not-terribly-bright teen, a role that he would repeat in ten more comedies.

What A Life (1939)
Life With Henry (1941)
Henry Aldrich for President (1941)
Henry and Dizzy (1942)
Henry Aldrich, Editor (1942)
Henry Aldrich Gets Glamour (1943)
Henry Aldrich Swings It (1943)
Henry Aldrich Haunts a House (1943)
Henry Aldrich, Boy Scout (1944)
Henry Aldrich Plays Cupid (1944)
Henry Aldrich's Little Secret (1944)

Henry Aldrich, Boy Scout 1944 ★★★½ Bumbling Henry (Lydon) leads his scout troop into trouble, resulting in many comical situations and an exciting cliffhanger rescue. Typical series entry with good work from the regular cast members. C: Jimmy Lydon, Charles Smith, Olive Blakeney. D: Hugh Bennett. FAM/COM 66m.

Henry Aldrich, Editor 1942 ★★★★ Henry tries to impress his school chums with his journalism skills but gets in over his head when he's accused of arson to generate stories. The best of the series features an exciting story, particularly good production values (great fire scenes) and standout performances. C: Jimmy Lydon, Charles Smith, Olive Blakeney, Rita Quigley. D: Hugh Bennett. FAM/COM 71m.

Henry Aldrich for President 1941 ★★★★ Henry tries to change his loser image by running for class president of Centerville High. Entertaining first entry in series does an excellent job of introducing the spirited young cast (supported by a bevy of talented character actors). C: Jimmy Lydon, Charles Smith, June Preisser, Mary Anderson, Martha O'Driscoll. D: Hugh Bennett. FAM/COM 73m.

Henry Aldrich Gets Glamour 1943 ★★★½ Henry enters a movie magazine contest and ends up winning a date with a teen starlet. One of the better series films gets to poke fun at Hollywood while providing innocent comical situations for the awkward hero. C: Jimmy Lydon, Charles Smith, John Litel, Olive Blakeney, Diana Lynn. D: Hugh Bennett. FAM/COM 75m.

Henry Aldrich Haunts a House 1943 ★★★ After swallowing a concoction that he believes will give him strength, Henry spends the night in a haunted house. Minor entry in the series suffers from too many contrived plot twists, although cast regulars are still endearing. C: Jimmy Lydon, Charles Smith, Joan Mortimer. D: Hugh Bennett. FAM/COM 73m.

Henry Aldrich Plays Cupid 1944 ★★★½ Dim-witted Henry (Lydon) tries to find his high-school principal a mate so he can get a good grade. Typical B-movie fun. C: Jimmy Lydon, Charles Smith, Diana Lynn, Vera Vague. D: Hugh Bennett. COM 65m.

Henry Aldrich Swings It 1943 ★★★½ Trying to impress his high school music teacher, Henry takes up the violin, leading to calamity when his ordinary instrument is mistaken for a priceless Stradivarius. Solid series entry. C: Jimmy Lydon, Charles Smith, John Litel. D: Hugh Bennett. FAM/COM 64m.

Henry Aldrich's Little Secret 1944 ★★★½ Henry assists a young mother by becoming her lawyer in opposition to his own father's lawsuit. The last in the series is hampered by a strained seriousness, but Lydon carries on in fine style. C: Jimmy Lydon, Charles Smith, Joan Mortimer, John Litel. D: Hugh Bennett. FAM/COM 75m.

Henry and Dizzy 1942 ★★★★ Henry Aldrich and his best pal, the not-too-bright Dizzy Stevens, cavort at the local lake and end up in a wild motorboat chase. One of the best in the series, filled with humorous banter and lively comical action. C: Jimmy Lydon, Charles Smith, Mary Anderson, John Litel. D: Hugh Bennett. FAM/COM 71m.

Henry IV 1985 Italian ★★★ An aristocrat falls on his head and claims to be Emperor Henry IV. His therapist and ex-lover plot to bring him back to sanity; but is he really crazy? Interesting but underdeveloped. C: Marcello Mastroianni, Claudia Cardinale. D: Marco Bellochio. DRA [PG-13] 94m. V

Henry V 1945 British ★★★★★ Olivier opens this version of Shakespeare's play in the Old Globe theater; risky but effective tinkering with the Bard. From there it's a magnificent journey through glory and horror of war. Olivier awarded special Oscar. C: Laurence Olivier, Robert Newton, Leslie Banks, Leo Genn. D: Laurence Olivier. DRA 136m. V

Henry V 1989 British ★★★★★ Young English King Henry consolidates his power by taking on the French, thrashing them soundly at the battle of Agincourt. Bold, resourceful, rousing adaptation of Shakespeare's play with a sterling cast. Branagh's Henry, at the center of it all, is irresistible. C: Kenneth Branagh, Derek Jacobi, Brian Blessed, Alec McCowen, Ian Holm, Robbie Coltrane, Judi Dench, Paul Scofield, Emma Thompson. D: Kenneth Branagh. DRA 138m. V

Henry VIII and His Six Wives 1973 British ★★★★ Adapted from a BBC-TV series and told through flashbacks from Henry VIII's deathbed, this film depicts the king as a lonely man rather than an evil tyrant. Meticulous attention to details of costume and setting, and tour-de-force performance by Michell. C: Keith Michell, Donald Pleasence, Charlotte Rampling, Jane Asher, Lynne Frederick. D: Waris Hussein. DRA [PG] 125m.

Henry, the Rainmaker 1949 ★★½ Eccentric, mild-mannered dad (Walburn) thinks he's come up with a way to control the weather. Low-budget comedy, the first in a short series of B-movies featuring Walburn as a capricious father trying to impress family and friends with his oddball approach to problem solving. Sequel: *Leave It to Henry.* C: Raymond Walburn, Walter Catlett, William Tracy. D: Jean Yarbrough. FAM/COM 64m.

Her Alibi 1989 ★★ Selleck is mystery writer stuck for a new subject when beautiful murder suspect Porizkova catches his interest, and he gets personally involved in her case. A lifeless comedy. C: Tom Selleck, Paulina Porizkova, William Daniels, James Farentino. D: Bruce Beresford. COM [PG] 95m. V

Her Brother 1960 Japanese ★★★½ Slow but moving drama about a dysfunctional family reunited when the son is stricken with tuberculosis. Kishi's performance as the older sister is outstanding. C: Keiko Kishi, Hiroshi Kawaguchi. D: Kon Ichikawa. DRA 98m.

Her Cardboard Lover 1942 ★★★ Sophisticated Shearer hires handsome Taylor to make beau Sanders jealous. Weak, predictable comedy was MGM queen Norma's last film. C: Norma Shearer, Robert Taylor, George Sanders, Frank McHugh. D: George Cukor. COM 93m.

Her First Affair 1947 French ★★★½ Orphaned young woman answers a newspaper romance ad and meets a teacher, who claims to have written the blurb for one of his students. Sweet romantic comedy, with some nice guileless moments. C: Danielle Darrieux, Jacqueline Desmarets, Rosine Luguet, Gabrielle Dorziat. D: Henri Decoin. COM 90m.

Her First Romance 1951 ★★★ A summer camp provides the setting for a budding romance between a precocious girl and her spirited young suitor. Child actress O'Brien's comeback as a grown-up benefits from her infectious charm. C: Margaret O'Brien, Allen Martin, Jr. D: Seymour Friedman. FAM/DRA 73m.

Her Highness and the Bellboy 1945 ★★½ A New York bellboy (Walker) abandons his invalid girlfriend (Allyson) to escort a princess (Lamarr). Hollywood romantic comedy, buoyed by good performances (Lamarr's especially). C: Hedy Lamarr, Robert Walker, June Allyson, Agnes Moorehead. D: Richard Thorpe. COM 112m.

Her Husband's Affairs 1947 ★★★½ Miracle potion created by an oddball inventor is promoted by husband and wife (Tone and Ball) who hope to strike it rich by selling it to a powerful industrialist. Pleasant comedy owes screwy bounce to Ball. C: Lucille Ball, Franchot Tone, Edward Everett Horton. D: S. Sylvan Simon. COM 83m. V

Her Jungle Love 1938 ★★★ Lamour sarong fest, with aviators Milland and Overman crashing on her one-woman island where they're threatened by natural disasters and unnatural villains. Hokey adventure fantasy. C: Dorothy Lamour, Ray Milland. D: George Archainbaud. ACT 81m.

Her Kind of Man 1946 ★★★½ Nightclub chanteuse (Paige) is torn between gangster (Scott) and journalist (Clark). Minor film noir, with some solid singing by Janis. C: Dane Clark, Janis Paige, Zachary Scott. D: Frederick de Cordova. DRA 78m.

Her Life as a Man 1984 ★★★½ Ambitious woman (Douglass) dresses as a man in order to be hired as a sportswriter. Gender-bending plot plays the drag theme for laughs rather than insight; based on a true story. C: Robyn Douglass, Robert Culp, Marc Singer, Joan Collins. D: Robert Ellis Miller. COM 96m. TVM V

Her Lucky Night 1945 ★★★½ Minor musical farce with O'Driscoll following fortuneteller's advice on how to find a man: she buys two movie tickets, then throws one away in the hopes her dream man will find it. The Andrews Sisters perform five numbers. C: The Andrews Sisters, Martha O'Driscoll, Noah Beery, Jr. D: Edward Lilley. MUS 63m.

Her Majesty, Love 1931 ★★★ Bartender (Miller) tries to crash high society. Poor musical enlivened by Fields' famous juggling act, but '20s stage star Miller ill-used here. C: Marilyn Miller, W.C. Fields, Leon Errol. D: William Dieterle. MUS 75m.

Her Man Gilbey 1948 British ★★★½ An English heiress (Ward) finds herself attracted to her manservant (Wilding) during a trip to Geneva, Switzerland. Good cast helps inject much-needed verve in this slow-moving character drama. (a.k.a. *English Without Tears*) C: Michael Wilding, Penelope-Dudley Ward, Lilli Palmer. D: Harold French. DRA 89m.

Her Panelled Door 1951 British ★★★ The stress of London air raids leaves a woman with no memory of her previous life. Drama of self-rediscovery uses predictable amnesia formula. C: Phyllis Calvert, Edward Underdown, Richard Burton. D: Ladislas Vajda. DRA 84m.

Her Primitive Man 1944 ★★★½ An author pretends to be a savage to discredit an anthropologist (Allbritton) and tries to disprove his own theories. Good cast led by spirited Allbritton does much to improve this dizzy farce. C: Robert Paige, Louise Allbritton, Robert Benchley, Edward Everett Horton. D: Charles Lamont. COM 79m.

Her Secret Life 1987 ★★★ Government agent quits quiet schoolteaching job to lead undercover mission in Cuba. Routine espionage caper. (a.k.a. *Code Name: Dancer*) C: Kate Capshaw, Jeroen Krabbe. D: Buzz Kulik. DRA 104m. TVM V

Her Sister's Secret 1946 ★★★½ After a brief romantic affair, a young woman discovers she is pregnant and struggles to deal with her shame. Well-handled melodrama saved from mediocrity by fine cast and no-nonsense direction by cult director Ulmer. C: Nancy Coleman, Margaret Lindsay. D: Edgar Ulmer. DRA 86m.

Her Twelve Men 1954 ★★★½ A dedicated teacher (Garson) at an all-boys' school struggles to inspire her rambunctious students, while romanced by Ryan and Sullivan. Sentimental, predictable vehicle for Greer, who's charming as always. C: Greer Garson, Robert Ryan, Barry Sullivan, James Arness. D: Robert Z. Leonard. DRA 91m.

Herbie Goes Bananas 1980 ★★★ Last of the *Love Bug* films finds Herbie, the Volkswagon with a soul, entered in a Brazilian race. Mild-mannered, empty-headed wackiness abounds. Strictly for youngsters. C: Charles Martin Smith, Cloris Leachman, Harvey Korman. D: Vincent McEveety. FAM/COM [G] 93m. V

Herbie Goes to Monte Carlo 1977 ★★★ Another ride with the "Love Bug" finds Herbie in a heap of trouble after some spies hide a diamond in the automobile. By-the-numbers slapstick for younger viewers. C: Dean Jones, Don Knotts, Julie Sommers. D: Vincent McEveety. FAM/COM [G] 104m. V

Herbie Rides Again 1974 ★★★½ The first sequel to popular film *The Love Bug* features unlikely team of Hayes and Berry on the run in Disney's favorite Volkswagon, while bad guy (Wynn) follows in hot pursuit. Filled with wild slapstick that kids will enjoy. C: Helen Hayes, Ken Berry, Stefanie Powers, Keenan Wynn. D: Robert Stevenson. FAM/COM [G] 88m. V

Hercules 1959 Italian ★★★½ The first of the Italian muscle-man adventures may well be the best. The romantic plot—Hercules (Reeves) undergoes trials before winning the lovely Koscina—enhances the action. C: Steve Reeves, Sylva Koscina. D: Pietro Francisci. ACT [G] 107m. V

Hercules 1983 ★★★ High-tech muscle fest puts the Greek God in a science fiction environment, rescuing kidnapped princess. Ferrigno certainly fits the part. Followed by *Hercules II*. C: Lou Ferrigno, Sybil Danning, Brad Harris, Rossana Podesta. D: Lewis Coates (Luigi Cozzi). ACT [PG] 98m. V

Hercules Against Rome 1960 Italian ★★★ Typical spaghetti mythology with Steel fighting dubbed villains to save lady love from torture. C: Alan Steel, Wandisa Guida. D: Piero Pierott. ACT 87m. V

Hercules Against the Moon Men 1964 Italian ★★½ Steel stars as the muscle-bound Hercules. His mission? To save the people of Samar from the thrall of strange lunar creatures. Mindless fun. C: Alan Steel, Anna-Maria Polani. D: Giacomo Gentilomo. SFI 88m. V

Hercules Against the Sons of the Sun 1963 Italian ★★½ Another campy installment of the Italian strong man series. This time Hercules flexes his muscles in America before it was discovered by Columbus. C: Mark Forest, Anna Pace. D: Osvaldo Civirani. ACT 91m.

Hercules and the Captive Women 1963 Italian ★★★ Against his better judgment, Hercules (Park) is enlisted to foil a plot by the Queen of Atlantis (Spain) to breed a master race. Strange sets and skimpy costumes make this sword-and-sandal epic ideal entertainment for fans of camp. C: Reg Park, Fay Spain. D: Vittorio Cottafavi. ACT 95m. V

Hercules Goes Bananas 1970 *See* **Hercules in New York**

Hercules in New York 1970 ★★½ Greek God becomes a pro wrestler in modern-day N.Y. Strong is alias for Schwarzenegger, who made his film debut in this ludicrous comedy/adventure. (a.k.a. *Hercules Goes Bananas*) C: Arnold Stang, Arnold Strong, Taina Elg. D: Arthur Allan Seidelman. ACT [G] 95m. V

Hercules in the Haunted World 1964 Italian ★★★½ In one of the better sword-and-sandal adventures, Hercules (Park) ventures to the underworld. The action is well paced and exciting, and the imaginative settings enhance this above-average tale. C: Reg Park, Christopher Lee, Leonora Ruffo. D: Mario Bava. ACT [G] 84m. V

Hercules, Samson and Ulysses 1965 Italian ★★½ Three bodybuilders try to outflex each other in cheesy adventure with typical plot of liberating a city from a usurping tyrant. C: Kirk Morris, Richard Lloyd, Enzo Cerusico. D: Pietro Francisci. ACT 85m.

Hercules II 1985 Italian ★★½ Ferrigno returns as muscle-bound hero in silly sequel to his *Hercules*. Certainly the most awesome Hercules, body-wise, but when he opens his mouth, movie deflates. C: Lou Ferrigno, Milly Carlucci. D: Lewis Coates. ACT [PG] 90m. V

Hercules Unchained 1960 Italian ★★★ Reeves is enslaved by black widow queen in campy spear and sandal epic. Steve's in great shape, but movie's flabby. C: Steve Reeves, Sylva Koscina, Primo Carnera. D: Pietro Francisci. ACT [G] 101m. V

Herdsmen Of The Sun 1988 French ★★★★ Feature director Werner Herzog ventured deep into Africa's Sahara and emerged with this moving study of drought and it's horrible effect on humans. Emphasis is on the Wodaabe herdsmen and how they face adversity with courage and dignity. Compelling. D: Werner Herzog. DOC 52m. V

Here Come the Co-eds 1945 ★★★½ Abbott and Costello cause havoc as janitors at an exclusive all-girl school. Too much nonsense and not enough of the comedy team's sizzling patter, although it does include their classic vaudeville routine, "Jonah and the Whale." C: Bud Abbott, Lou Costello, Peggy Ryan, Martha O'Driscoll, Lon Chaney, Jr. D: Jean Yarbrough. COM 87m. V

Here Come the Girls 1954 ★★★½ A naive Hope is made the star of a Broadway musical, unaware that he is becoming embroiled in a murder plot. Funny moments and charming songs enliven this entertaining piece of fluff. C: Bob Hope, Arlene Dahl, Rosemary Clooney, Tony Martin. D: Claude Binyon. COM 100m. V

Here Come the Littles 1985 Luxembourg ★★ Boring, animated kids' feature involves tiny humans with tails who live in the house of a full-sized 12-year-old boy. For fans of the "Littles" book series only; most other children will tune out. D: Bernard Deyries. FAM/COM [G] 76m. V

Here Come the Marines 1952 ★★½ The Bowery Boys enlist by mistake, resulting in a series of military hijinks. Far from the best in the series, but redeemed somewhat by the zany regulars. C: Leo Gorcey, Huntz Hall, Bennie Bartlett. D: William Beaudine. COM 66m.

Here Come the Nelsons 1952 ★★½ Dim-witted, fun family fare about David and Ricky Nelson becoming innocently entangled with gangsters while ad exec Ozzie and housewife Harriet wring their hands. Precursor to popular TV series. C: Ozzie Nelson, Harriet Nelson, David Nelson, Ricky Nelson, Rock Hudson, Sheldon Leonard, Gale Gordon. D: Frederick de Cordova. FAM/COM 76m.

Here Come the Tigers *See* **Manny's Orphans**

Here Come the Waves 1944 ★★★★ Diverting Navy musical has Crosby making fun of his crooner image as singing idol romantically involved with twins, played by Hutton. Good Johnny Mercer/Harold Arlen songs. C: Bing Crosby, Betty Hutton, Sonny Tufts. D: Mark Sandrich. MUS 99m. V

Here Comes Bugs 1991 ★★★½ An assemblage of six Bugs Bunny classic cartoons, including the first of the entire series, entitled "A Wild Hare." FAM/COM 60m.

Here Comes Cookie 1935 ★★★½ When she comes into a small fortune, Gracie Allen turns her father's mansion into a hotel for vaudevillians. Good, zany comedy à la Burns and Allen. C: George Burns, Gracie Allen, Betty Furness. D: Norman Z. McLeod. COM 65m.

Here Comes Elmer 1943 ★★★ Singer Evans is groomed by Pearce to achieve her career goals, and eventually tackles the Big Apple and radio broadcasting. Slight musical comedy, notable mostly for an early appearance by Nat King Cole. C: Al Pearce, Dale Evans, Frank Albertson, Gloria Stuart. D: Joseph Stanley. MUS 74m.

Here Comes Every Body 1973 ★★★ Documentary follows several California encounter groups. Dated and uninspired; narrated by James Whitmore. D: John Whitmore. DOC 110m.

Here Comes Kelly 1943 ★★★ Adventures of lovable brawler who can't hold a job—or keep out of a fight. Some nice, old-style fun. C: Eddie Quillan, Joan Woodbury, Maxie Rosenbloom. D: William Beaudine. COM 65m.

Here Comes Mr. Jordan 1941 ★★★★★ Magical fantasy classic with Montgomery as boxer Joe Pendleton, killed before his time, who is given a new body and identity by heavenly administrator Mr. Jordan (Rains). Plot construction and script are models of invention, winning two Oscars: original story (Harry Segall) and screenplay (Sidney Buchman, Seton I. Miller). Remade in 1978 as *Heaven Can Wait.* C: Robert Montgomery, Evelyn Keyes, Claude Rains, James Gleason, Rita Johnson, Edward Everett Horton. D: Alexander Hall. COM 93m. V

Here Comes Peter Cottontail ★★★ In order to become the number one Easter bunny, Peter Cottontail must rise to the challenge—and confront the notorious bunny villain Evil Irontail. C: Vincent Price. FAM/COM 53m. V

Here Comes Santa Claus 1984 ★★★ When they travel to Santa Claus's enchanting home, a little boy and a little girl meet all their favorite Christmas characters. Season's cheerings for all the young ones. C: Karen Cheryl, Armand Meffre. FAM/DRA [G] 78m. V

Here Comes the Groom 1951 ★★★★ Sentimental but charming film of a reporter (Crosby) returning from Europe who's dead set on reclaiming his true love (Wyman) from her millionaire fiancé (Tone). Capra provides some playful twists on a familiar story—and the brief appearance of Louis Armstrong by itself makes the film worth watching. Oscar-winning song, "In the Cool, Cool, Cool of the Evening." C: Bing Crosby, Jane Wyman, Franchot Tone, Alexis Smith, Anna Maria Alberghett. D: Frank Capra. COM 114m. V

Here Comes the Grump ★★★ A notorious grump is very fond of causing trouble for the beautiful Princess Dawn, her companion Terry and their dog, Bip. The kids will love it. FAM/ACT 60m. V

Here Comes the Navy 1934 ★★★½ Lots of heroic confrontations spice up this comedy/drama about two feuding naval officers (Cagney and O'Brien). C: James Cagney, Pat O'Brien, Gloria Stuart, Frank McHugh. D: Lloyd Bacon. DRA 86m.

Here I Am a Stranger 1939 ★★★★ A wealthy woman tries to come between her son and her heavy-drinking ex-husband. Tender, poignant study of the ups and downs of a prominent family. C: Richard Greene, Richard Dix, Brenda Joyce, Roland Young, Gladys George. D: Roy Del Ruth. DRA 81m.

Here Is My Heart 1934 ★★★ Predictable musical has Crosby as singing star posing as waiter to woo princess (Carlisle). Highlight: "Love Is Just Around the Corner." C: Bing Crosby, Kitty Carlisle, Roland Young. D: Frank Tuttle. MUS 77m.

Here We Go Again 1942 ★★★½ Fibber Magee and Molly meet up with various other radio comics while trekking cross-country. Genial follow-up to *Look Who's Laughing* is a real treat for nostalgia buffs. C: Fibber McGee and Molly (Jim and Marian Jordan), Edgar Bergen (and Charlie McCarthy), Ginny Simms, Harold Peary, Gale Gordon. D: Allan Dwan. COM 76m.

Here We Go Again 1987 ★★★½ Nice educational film about transportation, with Redgrave winning as hostess. C: Lynn Redgrave. DOC 60m. V

Here We Go Round the Mulberry Bush 1968 British ★★★ English teen is repeatedly frustrated in his attempts to score with pretty "birds." Lighthearted but dated '60s sex farce offers likable cast, good songs. C: Barry Evans, Judy Geeson, Denholm Elliott. D: Clive Donner. COM 96m.

Here's George 1932 British ★★★★ Hoping to impress his fiancée's parents, Clarke uses an apartment filled with Rube Goldbergesque inventions to make a big splash. To no surprise, Murphy's Law reigns supreme in this silly and fun slapstick farce. Good energy from cast sparkles the humor. C: George Clarke, Pat Paterson, Ruth Taylor. D: Redd Davis. COM 64m.

Here's Looking At You, Warner Bros. 1991 ★★★★ A lively history of Warner Brothers Studios, including some outtakes that are absolutely hysterical. A real bit of Hollywood history and eminently entertaining in its own right. C: Clint Eastwood, Barbra Streisand, Goldie Hawn, Steven Spielberg. D: Robert Guenette. DOC 108m. V

Heritage of the Desert 1933 ★★★ Vintage tale of a tough-but-good cowhand who becomes a one-man army against a slew of outlaws. A real relic, interesting as Scott's first starring role. Remake of the silent version; based on a Zane Grey novel. C: Randolph Scott, Guinn "Big Boy" Williams, J. Ferrell MacDonald. D: Henry Hathaway. WST 63m.

Heritage of the Desert 1939 ★★★½ A wealthy Easterner (Woods) goes out West to inspect his mine holdings and finds cheating, danger, and love. Solid story is well-developed and action-filled; based on a Zane Grey novel. C: Donald Woods, Evelyn Venable, Russell Hayden. D: Lesley Selander. WST 74m. V

Hero 1992 ★★★½ When Davis is saved from plane crash, Garcia claims it is he who pulled her from the burning wreckage. The real hero, small-time criminal Hoffman, doesn't mind until Garcia gets public recognition. A promising comedy that simply fizzles. C: Dustin Hoffman, Geena Davis, Andy Garcia, Joan Cusack. D: Stephen Frears. COM [PG-13] 116m. V

Hero Ain't Nothin' But a Sandwich, A 1978 ★★★ Inner-city youth gets hooked on drugs, then finds redemption through family love. Overbearing and preachy, but with an air of authenticity. C: Cicely Tyson, Paul Winfield,

Larry B. Scott, Glynn Turman. D: Ralph Nelson. DRA [PG] 107m. V

Hero and the Terror, The 1988 ★★★ Shaken after bringing in a vicious serial killer, rugged cop Norris has to go searching again when the killer escapes. While not a kung fu film, this thriller is actually engrossing at times. C: Chuck Norris, Brynn Thayer, Steve James. D: William Tannen. ACT [R] 97m. V

Hero at Large 1980 ★★★ Out-of-work actor (Ritter) dons superhero costume, and becomes crimefighter "Captain Avenger." Pleasant comedy of errors for those who like Ritter. C: John Ritter, Anne Archer, Bert Convy. D: Martin Davidson. COM [PG] 98m. V

Hero Banker 1971 ★★ Tedious, noisy war movie about Greek partisans battling Nazis. C: John Miller, Maria Xenia. D: George Andrews. DRA 93m. V

Hero of the Year (Top Dog Part 2) 1985 Polish ★★★½ Clever sequel to Falks's *Top Dog* continues earlier film's scathing satire of corruption in Polish society, with a TV personality coping with unemployment. D: Feliks Falks. DRA 101m. V

Hero, The 1972 ★★★ Aging soccer star about to throw a game is brought to his senses by worshipful 10-year-old fan. Harris' sweet but sentimental directorial debut. (a.k.a. *Bloomfield.*) C: Richard Harris, Romy Schneider, Kim Burfield. D: Richard Harris. DRA [PG] 97m. V

Herod the Great 1960 Italian ★ The Biblical king in a simplistic presentation that reduces characters to cardboard cutouts. C: Edmund Purdom, Sylvia Lopez. D: Arnaldo Genoino. DRA 93m.

Heroes 1977 ★★★ Vietnam Vet (Winkler) pursues his dreams during cross-country road trip, gaining new lease on life through accidental meeting with sympathetic woman (Field). Middling vehicle for Winkler. C: Henry Winkler, Sally Field, Harrison Ford. D: Jeremy Paul Kagan. DRA [PG] 97m. V

Heroes Die Young 1960 ★★ Brave Rumanian woman (Peters) leads GIs behind Nazi lines to blow up oil fields. Dull. C: Krika Peters, Scott Borland, Robert Getz, James Strother. DRA 76m. V

Heroes for Sale 1933 ★★★★ Barthelmess endures a lot of suffering in this powerful drama: morphine addiction, labor unrest, unjust imprisonment, and job hunting in midst of Depression. A compelling look at how persistence and endurance could see man and country through hard times. C: Richard Barthelmess, Loretta Young, Aline MacMahon. D: William Wellman. DRA 73m. V

Heroes in Hell 1974 ★★ WWII epic about downed U.S. pilots who hook up with brave partisans and fight behind enemy lines. C: Klaus Kinski, Ettore Manni, Stan Simon, Lars Block. D: Michael Wotruba. DRA 90m.

Heroes of Desert Storm, The 1992 ★★★ Well-intentioned docudrama about U.S. forces in Persian Gulf seems to last longer than the ground war did. Historical curio. C: Daniel Baldwin, Angela Bassett, Marshall Bell, Michael Alan Brooks, William Bumiller, Michael Champion, Maria Diaz. D: Don Ohlmeyer. DRA 93m. TVM V

Heroes of Telemark, The 1965 British ★★★½ Factual WWII adventure of bold Norwegian underground commandos who race against time to blow up German heavy water factory. Large-scale action, good locales. C: Kirk Douglas, Richard Harris, Michael Redgrave, Mervyn Johns, Eric Porter. D: Anthony Mann. ACT 131m.

Heroes of the Hills 1938 ★★★ The Three Mesquiteers devise a penal reform plan to allow good prisoners to work for nearby ranchers. One of the better *Mesquiteer* series entries, with an unusual social message. C: Robert Livingston, Ray Corrigan, Max Terhune. D: George Sherman. WST 55m. V

Heroes Stand Alone 1989 ★ CIA agents race Russkies to a downed U.S. spy plane in Central American jungle. Worth seeing for Dillman's presence. C: Chad Everett, Bradford Dillman, Wayne Grace, Rick Dean, Michael Chieffo, Timothy Wead. D: Mark Griffiths. DRA 85m. V

Heroes, The 1972 Italian ★★½ Colorful gang of thieves plot to steal misplaced military loot. Steiger is wasted in unremarkable caper yarn. C: Rod Steiger, Rod Taylor, Rosanna Schiaffino, Terry-Thomas. D: Duccio Tessari. CRI [PG] 99m.

Heroes Three 1989 ★★★ Competent if uninspired murder mystery, with an American sailor and Chinese detective hunting the man who killed his shipmate. C: Laurens C. Postma, Rowena Cortes, Mike Kelly, Lawrence Tan. D: S.H. Lau. CRI 90m. V

Heroic Adventures of John the Fearless, The 1989 ★★★ Cartoon antics of medieval hero of spotless mien, good for the kiddies. FAM/ACT 80m.

Heroism 1957 *See* **Eroica**

Hero's Island 1962 ★★★ Castaway pirate comes to rescue of widow and her two children struggling to remain on Carolina island in the early 1700s. Costume melodrama boasts colorful action sequences, but falters with weak plotline. C: James Mason, Kate Manx, Neville Brand, Rip Torn, Harry Dean Stanton. D: Leslie Stevens. DRA 94m.

Hers to Hold 1943 ★★★½ Durbin takes a stab at melodrama, but still finds time to sing. She loves pilot (Cotten) who goes to war. Routine, but grown-up child star still charming and not a bad actress. C: Deanna Durbin, Joseph Cotten, Charles Winninger. D: Frank Ryan. MUS 94m.

He's a Cockeyed Wonder 1950 ★★½ A young go-getter who sorts oranges wreaks havoc when he goes into the magic business to impress his girlfriend's executive dad. Rooney's full-tilt performance energizes this slight, shrill screwball farce. C: Mickey Rooney,

Terry Moore, William Demarest. D: Peter Godfrey. COM 77m.

He's Fired, She's Hired 1984 ★★★ When an ad exec is fired, wife takes over and becomes a big success. Charming Karen lifts lukewarm comedy. C: Karen Valentine, Wayne Rogers. D: Marc Daniels. COM 104m. TVM

He's My Girl 1987 ★★ Aspiring musician wins chance at recording contract in Hollywood and his buddy dresses in drag to accompany him. Amateurish comedy. C: T.K. Carter, David Hallyday, Jennifer Tilly. D: Gabrielle Beaumont. COM [PG-13] 104m. V

He's Not Your Son 1984 ★★½ Parents whose child needs heart surgery learn that their baby had been switched with another. Dull soaper. C: Ken Howard, John James, Ann Dusenberry. D: Don Taylor. DRA 104m. TVM

Hester Street 1975 ★★★★ Meticulous recreation of life on New York City's turn-of-the-century Lower East Side frames simple, appealing story of Orthodox Jewish immigrant trying to cope with America. Kane's immigrant is complex, believable. A quiet gem. C: Carol Kane, Steven Keats, Mel Howard. D: Joan Micklin Silver. DRA [PG] 92m. V

Hexed 1992 ★★★ Day-dreaming hotel employee gets involved with model and former arsonist. Strange, but not much more than that. Spencer's debut. C: Arye Gross, Claudia Christian, Adrienne Shelly. D: Alan Spencer. COM [R] 93m. V

Hey Abbott! ★★★ Uncle Miltie hosts this compilation of best moments from A&C's career. Good stuff for Abbott and Costello fans. C: Bud Abbott, Lou Costello, Milton Berle, Phil Silvers, Joe Besser. D: Jim Gates. COM 76m. V

Hey Babu Riba 1986 Yugoslavian ★★★★ Four men recall their own idyllic youth chasing the town beauty and soaking up Esther Williams films in 1953 Belgrade, set against the dissolution of the country's freedoms with Tito's rise to power. Effective interweaving of personal remembrance and political reality. C: Gala Videnovic, Relja Basic, Nebojsa Bakocevic. D: Jovan Acin. DRA 109m. V

Hey Boy! Hey Girl! 1959 ★★★ Prima performs at church bazaar and falls in love with Smith. Bad script, but only film to feature these two great recording stars. Songs include "Autumn Leaves" and "Lazy River." C: Louis Prima, Keely Smith. D: David Rich. MUS 81m.

Hey Cinderella 1970 ★★★½ Cinderella gets the Muppet treatment. Great for kids, but a lot of the jokes are for adults, too. C: The Muppets. D: Jim Henson. FAM/COM 54m. V

Hey Good Lookin' 1982 ★ Ugly, unpleasant Bakshi misfire waxes nostalgic about NYC greasers in the 1950s. Loads of sexual and violent hyperbole without much insight; check out *Heavy Traffic* instead. Voices of Richard Romanus, David Proval, Jesse Welles. D: Ralph Bakshi. DRA 86m. V

Hey, I'm Alive! 1975 ★★★ Two survivors (Asner and Struthers) of a plane crash in the Yukon face peril while awaiting rescue; based on an actual incident. Well acted, but rather tame. C: Edward Asner, Sally Struthers. D: Lawrence Schiller. DRA 74m. TVM V

Hey, Let's Twist! 1961 ★★ Low-budget dance craze musical makes one grateful that all fads come to pass. Joe Pesci's film debut, as an extra. C: Joey Dee, The Starliters, The Peppermint Loungers, Jo Campbell. D: Greg Garrison. MUS 80m.

Hey, Rookie 1944 ★★★ Strictly routine B-movie war musical: worth a look for Miller fans. C: Larry Parks, Ann Miller, The Condos Brothers, Jack Gilford. D: Charles Barton. MUS 77m.

Hey There, It's Yogi Bear 1964 ★★★½ Younger children will enjoy this cartoon feature as TV's Yogi Bear is taken far from his beloved Jellystone Park and into the three rings of a traveling circus. Fairly good animation and engaging story for kids. D: William Hanna, Joseph Barbera. FAM/COM [G] 89m. V

Hi-Di-Hi 1988 British ★★★½ British TV comedy about stuffy prof who takes over holiday camp with predictably farcical results. Not "Fawlty Towers," but amusing. C: Simon Cadell, Paul Shane, ruth Madoc, Jeffrey Holland, Leslie Dwyer. COM 91m.

Hi Diddle Diddle 1943 ★★★ Before a sailor marries his fiancée (Scott), his con artist father wants to gamble back the money lost by the girl's mother (Burke) in a swindle. Convoluted story line, with former silent screen star Negri as Menjou's wife. (a.k.a. *Diamonds and Crime*) C: Adolphe Menjou, Martha Scott, Pola Negri, Billie Burke, June Havoc. D: Andrew L. Stone. COM 72m. V

Hi, Good Lookin' 1944 ★★★ Entertaining musical about an attractive singer (Hilliard) who tries to break into radio. Story takes a back seat to featured performers, making this more of a filmed variety show. First joint appearance of future Mr. and Mrs. Nelson (TV's Ozzie and Harriet). C: Harriet Hilliard, Eddie Quillan, Betty Kean, Roscoe Karns, Ozzie Nelson. D: Edward Lilley. MUS 62m.

Hi, Mom! 1970 ★★★★ De Palma's sequel to *Greetings* features De Niro as would-be pornographer who also bombs buildings. Great satire of late-'60s counterculture with refreshing cinematic technique; in many ways, this is one of De Palma's best and most original efforts. (a.k.a. *Blue Manhattan* and *Confessions of a Peeping John*) C: Robert De Niro, Allen Garfield, Lara Parker, Jennifer Salt. D: Brian De Palma. COM [R] 87m. V

Hi, Nellie! 1934 ★★★ A newspaper's big-time editor (Muni) is demoted to writing lonely hearts column but hopes to regain his status via hot crime racket story. Average star vehicle with Sparks a standout. Similar story done in 1933, called *Advice to the Lovelorn*; remade as *Love is on the Air*, *You Can't Es-*

cape Forever, and *The House Across the Street*. C: Paul Muni, Glenda Farrell, Ned Sparks. D: Mervyn LeRoy. CRI 75m.

Hi-Riders 1977 ★ Young drag-racers duel with middle-aged truckers in story of highway revenge. Aimed at action fans. C: Mel Ferrer, Stephen McNally, Darby Hinton. D: Greydon Clark. ACT 90m. v

Hiawatha 1952 ★★★ The legendary Indian hero (Edwards) tries to bring peace to his people while wooing Minnehaha. Loose adaptation of the famous Longfellow poem, suitable for youngsters. C: Vincent Edwards, Keith Larsen, Yvette Dugay. D: Kurt Neumann. WST 80m.

Hickey & Boggs 1972 ★★★ Two hapless private eyes (Culp and Cosby) have trouble finding missing girl amid death and mayhem. Stylish, violent outing for popular pair, lacks appeal of their *I Spy* teaming. C: Robert Culp, Bill Cosby, Rosalind Cash. D: Robert Culp. ACT [PG] 111m.

Hideaways 1973 *See* **From the Mixed-Up Files of Mrs. Basil E. Frankweiler**

Hidden Agenda 1990 British ★★★½ In Belfast during the tumultuous 1980s, an American activist (McDormand) teams up with a British policeman (Cox) to uncover the truth about a brutal police incident. Tense and tough depiction of a violent place and time. C: Frances McDormand, Brian Cox, Brad Dourif. D: Ken Loach. ACT [R] 108m. v

Hidden City 1988 British ★★★★ Film archivist runs across inexplicable murder footage in secret government videos, investigates with scary results. Convincingly paranoid thriller is an impressive directorial debut for playwright Poliakoff. C: Charles Dance, Cassie Stewart, Alex Norton, Bill Patterson, Tusse Seberg. D: Stephen Poliakoff. HOR 112m. v

Hidden City, The 1950 ★★★½ Bomba the Jungle Boy endears himself to a young princess when he helps restore her sovereignty. Average entry in adventure series strengthened by Sheffield's spirited excitement in the midst of jungle shenanigans. (a.k.a. *Bomba and the Hidden City*) C: John Sheffield, Sue England, Paul Guilfoyle. D: Ford Beebee. ACT 71m.

Hidden Eye, The 1945 ★★★½ Blind detective Duncan McClain (Arnold) uses his highly developed "back-up" senses to track a murderer who deliberately tries to confuse him by leaving false clues. Effective whodunnit, sequel to *Eyes in the Night*. C: Edward Arnold, Frances Rafferty, Ray Collins. D: Richard Whorf. CRI 69m.

Hidden Fear 1957 ★★★ An American cop clears his sister of murder in Copenhagen. Muddled B-movie adventure with attractive location footage. C: John Payne, Alexander Knox, Conrad Nagel. D: Andre de Toth. CRI 83m.

Hidden Fears 1993 ★★★½ Foster witnesses her husband's murder then, years later, confronts the killers with disastrous results. Conventional damsel-in-distress thriller helped by good acting. C: Meg Foster, Frederic Forrest, Bever-Leigh Banfield, Wally Taylor, Marc Macaulay, Patrick Cherry, Scott Hayes. D: Jean Bodon. HOR 90m. v

Hidden Fortress, The 1958 Japanese ★★★★ Humorous "Eastern" has a refined general and two surly farmers escorting an undercover princess to claim her throne during Japan's 16th-century civil war. George Lucas claimed this wonderful adventure as inspiration for *Star Wars*. C: Toshiro Mifune, Misa Uehara. D: Akira Kurosawa. ACT 139m. v

Hidden Gold 1933 ★★★ Cowpoke hero Tom Mix gets in with a group of bandits to learn where they stashed a stolen gold shipment. Early Hollywood action with a notable Western star. C: Tom Mix. D: Lesley Selander. WST 60m. v

Hidden Hand, The 1942 ★★½ On a dark and stormy night, an escapee from a mental institution goes on a killing spree. Scary, but also funny (not necessarily intentionally). C: Craig Stevens, Elisabeth Fraser, Julie Bishop. D: Ben Stoloff. HOR 67m.

Hidden Homicide 1959 British ★★★ A writer (Jones) awakens one morning to discover a dead body by his side and a smoking gun in his hand. Low-budget, somewhat talky murder mystery. C: Griffith Jones, James Kenney, Patricia Laffan. D: Tony Young. CRI 70m.

Hidden Memories—Are You a UFO Abductee? ★ Weird documentary about people who claim to have been abducted by aliens. DOC 90m. v

Hidden Obsession 1992 ★★ Thomas is a newscaster on vacation terrorized by escaped killer. C: Heather Thomas, Jan-Michael Vincent, Nick Celozzi. D: John Stewart. HOR 92m. v

Hidden Room, The 1949 British ★★★★ A doctor holds his wife's lover hostage in a cellar, plotting to torture and kill him. A sadistically pleasurable film. (Retitled *Obsession*.) C: Robert Newton, Sally Gray, Naunton Wayne. D: Edward Dmytryk. CRI 98m.

Hidden, The 1987 ★★★★ L.A. police detective (Nouri) helps offbeat extraterrestrial cop (MacLachlan) track an evil sluglike alien that parasitically enters and takes control of innocent humans, turning them into violent criminals with a taste for heavy metal music. Inventive, energetic, and lots of fun. Christian shines. C: Michael Nouri, Kyle MacLachlan, Claudia Christian, Ed O'Ross. D: Jack Sholder. SFI [R] 98m. v

Hidden II, The 1994 ★★½ The body-hopping alien returns, as does the daughter of the original's cop, teaming with a new alien agent to stop the galactic fiend. What doesn't return is the sense of style, pacing, or any memorable action or horror scenes. C: Raphael Sbarge, Kate Hodge, Jovin Montanaro, Christopher Murphy, Michael Weldon. D: Seth Pinsker. SFI [R] 91m.

Hide and Go Shriek 1987 ★ Someone is murdering the guests at a high school graduation party held overnight in a shuttered furniture store. Can you guess who? C: Brittain Frye, Donna Baltron, George Thomas, Rebunkah Jones, Annette Sinclair. D: Skip Schoolnik. HOR 90m. V

Hide in Plain Sight 1979 ★★★ Fact-based story of a blue-collar worker whose children disappear when their stepfather goes into witness protection program. A straightforward directing debut for Caan. C: James Caan, Jill Eikenberry, Robert Viharo. D: James Caan. DRA [PG] 98m. V

Hide-Out 1934 ★★★ New York gangster Arnold is forced to hide out in country to convalesce from gunshot wound. He learns to appreciate country living from farmer's daughter O'Sullivan. Nice twist on country mouse-city mouse theme. C: Robert Montgomery, Maureen O'Sullivan, Edward Arnold, Mickey Rooney. D: W. S. Van Dyke. CRI 83m.

Hideaway 1995 ★★★ After a near-death experience, a man (Goldblum) experiences psychic flashes of murders-to-come. Good visual effects highlight this confusing adaptation of Dean R. Koontz's novel. C: Jeff Goldblum, Christine Lahti, Alicia Silverstone, Rae Dawn Chong. D: Brett Leonard. SFI [R] 112m. V

Hideous Sun Demon, The 1959 ★ Radiation poisoning plus a dash of sunlight affects nuclear scientist in the most peculiar way: He feels compelled to don a cheap lizard costume. Scientist/lizard Clarke also directed this hilariously awful, no-budget Z-movie. C: Robert Clarke, Patricia Manning, Nan Peterson. D: Robert Clarke. SFI 75m. V

Hideout in the Alps 1938 British ★★★ Despite her criminal family background, a woman falls in love with a cop. This leads to bad blood, climaxing in a wild conclusion in the midst of an Alpine avalanche. Low-level melodrama without much believability. C: June Baxter, Anthony Bushell, Ronald Squire, Margaret Rutherford. D: Bernard Vorhaus. DRA 74m.

Hideout, The 1961 French ★★★½ A Frenchman escapes from the horrors of WWII by passing himself off as crazy and taking refuge in a mental institution. A well-made and diverting story contrasts the insanity of war with mental aberration. C: Marcel Mouloudji, Yves Vincent. D: Raoul Andre. DRA 80m.

Hider in the House 1990 ★★★ An ex-con (Busey), obsessed with a family he barely knows, constructs a secret room in their home. Strong cast tries hard. C: Gary Busey, Mimi Rogers, Michael McKean. D: Matthew Patrick. DRA [R] 109m. V

Hiding Out 1987 ★★★ Young stockbroker on the run from mobsters takes refuge in his cousin's high school. Standard fish-out-of-water story peppered with a few laughs and some action. C: Jon Cryer, Keith Coogan, Annabeth Gish. D: Bob Giraldi. COM [PG-13] 99m. V

Hiding Place, The 1975 ★★★½ Dutch watchmaker (O'Connell) dedicates his life to saving Jews during WWII. Earnest dramatic treatment of an important historical subject. Produced by the Billy Graham Evangelistic Association. C: Julie Harris, Eileen Heckart, Arthur O'Connell. D: James F. Collier. DRA [PG] 145m. V

Higan-Gana 1958 *See* **Equinox Flower**

Higglety Pigglety Pop ★★★½ Excellent operatic version of Maurice Sendak's classic of Jennie, a Sealyham terrier with aspirations to the stage. Superb music may be too difficult for kids, but they'll love the costumes and stage business. MUS 60m. V

High and Dry 1954 British ★★★½ Successful businessman clashes with an eccentric Scottish sea captain when his ragtag ship carrying valuable cargo suffers a series of catastrophes. Douglas stands out in this wry comedy yarn. (a.k.a. *The Maggie*) C: Paul Douglas, Alex Mackenzie. D: Alexander Mackendrick. COM 93m.

High and Low 1962 Japanese ★★★★★ Millionaire acquiesces to kidnapper's demands for an impossibly high ransom. Top-notch suspense film plays on viewers' emotions with ease. Kurosawa's narrative skills create a multilayered crime drama, from an Ed McBain story. C: Toshiro Mifune, Tatsuya Mihashi. D: Akira Kurosawa. CRI 143m. V

High and the Mighty, The 1954 ★★★½ Seminal disaster flick features macho pilot Wayne dealing with lame plane, haunting past, and horde of sensational passengers on troubled flight over the Pacific. Diverting enough, fine cast, but slow and overrated. Adapted by Ernest K. Gann from his novel. C: John Wayne, Claire Trevor, Laraine Day, Robert Stack, Jan Sterling. D: William Wellman. ACT 147m.

High Anxiety 1977 ★★★½ Lesser comedy film pokes fun at Alfred Hitchcock movies through series of obvious gags as Brooks becomes head psychiatrist of San Francisco sanitarium. Good for Brooks' fans. C: Mel Brooks, Madeline Kahn, Cloris Leachman, Harvey Korman, Dick Van Patten. D: Mel Brooks. COM [PG] 94m. V

High-Ballin' 1978 U.S. ★★★½ Small-time independent truckers take on corporate bad-guy rivals out to run them off the road—literally. High-speed adventure suffers from plot holes and over-the-top acting, but the chemistry between Fonda, Reed, and Shaver is infectious. C: Peter Fonda, Jerry Reed, Helen Shaver. D: Peter Carter. ACT [PG] 100m. V

High Barbaree 1947 ★★½ A downed Navy pilot adrift on a raft in the Pacific recalls his past. Rambling WWII melodrama. C: Van Johnson, June Allyson, Thomas Mitchell, Cameron Mitchell. D: Jack Conway. DRA 91m.

High Command, The 1937 British ★★★★ Officer Atwill investigates a murder on African outstation in waning days of the British empire. Superb drama is more than just a crime story; it successfully addresses larger issues of honor, duty, and colonization. C: Lionel Atwill, Lucie Mannheim, James Mason. D: Thorold Dickinson. DRA 90m. V

High Commissioner, The 1968 British ★★ Cold War spy thriller about international diplomacy and intrigue. Plummer is good but the story lacks thrills. (a.k.a. *Nobody Runs Forever*) C: Christopher Plummer, Rod Taylor, Lilli Palmer, Clive Revill, Franchot Tone. D: Ralph Thomas. DRA 93m.

High Cost of Loving, The 1958 ★★½ Just when he learns his wife is pregnant, fretful worker (Ferrer) also discovers that he might lose his job. Satire on the pressures of big-business is confidently acted though predictable. C: Jose Ferrer, Gena Rowlands, Jim Backus, Werner Klemperer. D: Jose Ferrer. COM 87m.

High Country, The 1981 Canadian ★★ An ex-con (Bottoms) and disabled woman (Purl) team up for trek through Canadian Rockies. Action drama. C: Timothy Bottoms, Linda Purl. D: Harvey Hart. DRA [PG] 99m. V

High Crime 1973 Italian ★★½ A narcotics cop squares off against top Mafia brass in Italy. Predictable thriller, compelling scenery. C: Franco Nero, James Whitmore, Fernando Rey. D: Enzo Castellari. ACT 100m. V

High Desert Kill 1990 ★★★ Exciting feature tracks four hunters in the remote desert—then lets a dangerous alien force take over the surveillance. C: Chuck Connors, Anthony Geary, Marc Singer. D: Harry Falk. HOR [PG-13] 100m. TVM V

High Explosive 1943 ★★★½ Morris is a truck driver specializing in nitroglycerin cargo. His girlfriend's younger brother is killed during training, which inspires Morris to fly an explosive load through bad weather. Minor B-movie drama with good action sequences. Similar story used in *The Wages of Fear* and *Sorcerer*. C: Chester Morris, Jean Parker, Barry Sullivan. D: Frank McDonald. DRA 60m.

High Flight 1958 British ★★½ Peacetime students train for jet flying at the RAF college. Propaganda piece focuses on conflict between talented pupil and instructor. C: Ray Milland, Bernard Lee, Kenneth Haigh, Anthony Newley. D: John Gilling. DRA 89m.

High Frequency 1989 Italian ★★★ Two young men, watching a satellite monitor, see a murder committed and try to catch the killer. Interesting attempt at a *Rear Window* update creates some suspense. C: Vincent Spano, Oliver Benny, Ann Canovas. D: Faliero Rosati. CRI 101m. V

High Fury 1947 British ★★★ Two post-WWII newlyweds quarrel over the problems they encounter when they attempt to adopt a war orphan. Carroll is appealing as the young wife. Shot in Switzerland. (a.k.a. *White Cradle Inn*) C: Madeleine Carroll, Ian Hunter, Michael Rennie. D: Harold French. DRA 71m.

High Heels 1972 French ★★★★ Unscrupulous medical intern marries a plain woman to further his career, then falls for her beautiful sister. Sly comedy mixes moral message with sexy shenanigans. (a.k.a *Docteur Popaul* and *Scoundrel in White*). C: Laura Antonelli, Jean-Paul Belmondo. D: Claude Chabrol. COM 100m.

High Heels 1992 Spanish ★★★½ Spain's master of high camp pits a popular, self-absorbed actress mother against her TV newswoman daughter, with the two sharing the mother's former lover and the daughter's present husband. Murder and some laughs ensue in this lesser Almodóvar offering. C: Victoria Abril, Marisa Paredes, Miguel Bose. D: Pedro Almodóvar. DRA [R] 113m. V

High Hell 1958 British ★★½ A mine owner is driven to violence after he learns his wife is carrying on with his partner during a snowbound winter. Suspenseful, despite unappealing characters. C: John Derek, Elaine Stewart, Rodney Burke. D: Burt Balaban. DRA 87m.

High Hopes 1989 British ★★★★½ A seemingly ordinary tale of a working-class couple in London (Davis and Sheen) proves both warmhearted and hilarious. Particularly through the minor characters, Leigh launches a biting and intelligent satire of Thatcherite England. C: Philip Davis, Ruth Sheen, Edna Dore. D: Mike Leigh. COM 110m. V

High Ice 1980 ★★★½ Thrilling suspense yarn about three climbers waiting to be rescued from a mountain ledge. The gripping conflicts among the characters are highly believable. C: David Janssen, Tony Musante, Madge Sinclair, Dorian Harewood. D: Eugene S. Jones. ACT 97m. TVM V

High Infidelity 1964 French ★★★★ Prestigious European cast in short episodes on marital discord. Well crafted, funny, and entertaining directorial anthology. C: Nino Manfredi, Charles Aznavour, Claire Bloom, Monica Vitti, Jean-Pierre Cassel, Ugo Tognazzi. D: Franco Rossi, Elio Petri, Luciano Salce, Mario Monicelli. COM 120m.

High Lonesome 1950 ★★★½ A restless young man wanders into a desert ranch, setting off a stream of mysterious events in which he must prove himself innocent of murder. The mix of mystery and Western elements is deft and well above average. C: John Barrymore, Jr., Chill Wills, Lois Butler, Jack Elam. D: Alan LeMay. WST 81m.

High Mountain Rangers 1987 ★★★½ Forest rangers have their hands full trying to protect their High Sierra paradise from natural and man-made disasters. Robert Conrad shines as director and star, but his script and his two actor sons weaken the overall success of this appealing adventure. C: Robert Conrad, Christian Conrad, Shane Conrad. D: Robert Conrad. ACT 100m. TVM

High Noon 1952 ★★★★★ Classic Western masterpiece with Cooper as retiring, just-married marshal Will Kane, who, unsupported by townsfolk, is obliged to face down a gang of outlaws coming to kill him. Extremely tense, elemental Western won Oscars for Best Actor (Cooper's second), Best Score, and Editing. C: Gary Cooper, Grace Kelly, Lloyd Bridges, Katy Jurado, Thomas Mitchell, Lon Chaney, Jr., Henry Morgan, Lee Van Cleef. D: Fred Zinnemann. WST 111m. V

High Noon, Part II: The Return of Will Kane 1980 ★★½ Retired marshal forces showdown with corrupt lawman who took over his job. Sequel to Oscar-winning Gary Cooper Western. C: Lee Majors, David Carradine, Pernell Roberts. D: Jerry Jameson. WST 96m. TVM V

High Plains Drifter 1973 ★★★★ Highly stylized, early Eastwood directorial effort pays homage to Leone Westerns. A mysterious drifter fights to save a town from gunslingers. Extreme violence appropriate to its genre, with a sparkling supporting turn by Curtis. C: Clint Eastwood, Verna Bloom, Marianna Hill, Billy Curtis. D: Clint Eastwood. WST [R] 106m. V

High Pressure 1932 ★★★★ Fast-talking promoter (Powell) uses hype to sell artificial rubber in this snappy comedy about the sales game. Boiler room scene is a con artist classic. C: William Powell, Evelyn Brent, Frank McHugh, Guy Kibbee. D: Mervyn LeRoy. COM 74m.

High Risk 1981 ★★★ Four Americans, dispirited by inflation and other economic woes, fly to Colombia to rip off a drug lord and have a series of wacky encounters along the way. Ridiculous but sometimes fun. C: James Brolin, Cleavon Little, Bruce Davison, Anthony Quinn, Lindsay Wagner, James Coburn, Ernest Borgnine. D: Stewart Raffill. ACT [R] 91m. V

High Road to China 1983 ★★½ Heiress (Armstrong) hires slovenly WWI flying ace (Selleck) to help locate her missing dad. Biplane stunts and Selleck provide most of the excitement. C: Tom Selleck, Bess Armstrong. D: Brian G. Hutton. DRA [PG] 105m. V

High Rolling in A Hot Corvette 1977 ★★½ A pair of carnies seeking adventurous diversion stumble onto crime and intrigue. C: Joseph Bottoms, Greg Taylor, Judy Davis. D: Igor Auzins. ACT [PG] 82m. V

High School 1968 ★★★★½ A candid documentary look at a Philadelphia school, in which education is essentially an assembly-line product and communications between teachers and students have almost completely broken down. As well-handled as it is bleak. D: Frederick Wiseman. DOC 75m.

High School II 1994 ★★★★★ Documentary filmmaker Wiseman returns to school, this time to an alternative high school in Harlem. A moving examination of social mobility and the pressures that affect inner-city education today. D: Frederick Wiseman. DOC 220m.

High School Caesar 1960 ★★ A spoiled high schooler, suffering from parental indifference, begins cheating and stealing at school. C: John Ashley, Gary Vinson. D: O'Dale Ireland. DRA 75m. V

High School Confidential 1958 ★★ Hopelessly naive tale of undercover cop sent to expose a dope ring at a high school is unintentionally hilarious. Never have so many looked so bad trying to look so cool. C: Russ Tamblyn, Jan Sterling, Mamie Van Doren, Diane Jergens. D: Jack Arnold. DRA 85m. V

High School U.S.A. 1983 ★★ Cast of former TV child stars now grown-ups teaching new generation of rowdy teenagers. Worth watching for its amazing cast. C: Michael J. Fox, Nancy McKeon. D: Rod Amateau. COM 96m. TVM V

High Season 1988 British ★★★½ A photographer residing on the island of Rhodes weathers tourists, her ex-husband, and spies. For this she could have stayed in London! Enjoyable blue-sky to-do. C: Jacqueline Bisset, James Fox, Irene Papas. D: Clare Peploe. COM [R] 95m. V

High Sierra 1941 ★★★★½ A tough ex-con with a soft heart pulls one last robbery and pays the ultimate price. Everything you'd expect from a gangster classic. And this one made Bogart a star. C: Humphrey Bogart, Ida Lupino, Alan Curtis, Arthur Kennedy, Joan Leslie. D: Raoul Walsh. CRI 100m. V

High Society 1955 ★★★ When Sach apparently inherits a fortune, the Bowery Boys go uptown with predictable results. Mediocre entry in the series is known for an Oscar snafu, when it was confused with the MGM musical of the same name and nominated for best original screenplay! C: Leo Gorcey, Huntz Hall, Amanda Blake. D: William Beaudine. MUS 61m.

High Society 1956 ★★★★ Star-studded musical remake of *The Philadelphia Story* with several Cole Porter songs, including "True Love," "You're Sensational," etc. Story of Newport socialite Kelly about to marry the wrong man is pleasantly told, but film lacks imaginative verve of the source material. Musical highlight is Crosby's duet with Sinatra on "Well, Did You Evah?" C: Bing Crosby, Grace Kelly, Frank Sinatra, Celeste Holm, John Lund, Louis Calhern, Louis Armstrong. D: Charles Walters. MUS 107m. V

High Spirits 1988 ★★ Dismal mess features O'Toole as proprietor of haunted Irish castle trying to protect it from American developers Guttenburg and D'Angelo. Confusing and just plain dull. C: Peter O'Toole, Daryl Hannah, Steve Guttenberg, Beverly D'Angelo, Liam Neeson, Peter Gallagher. D: Neil Jordan. COM [PG-13] 99m. V

High Stakes 1989 ★★★ A stripper gets involved with a Wall Street big shot and tries to get her daughter out of trouble with the Mob. Terrific Kirkland. (a.k.a. *Melanie Rose*) C: Sally Kirkland, Robert LuPone, Richard Lynch, Kathy Bates. D: Amos Kollek. CRI [R] 102m. V

High Tension 1936 ★★★ Bubbly romantic

comedy, as an adventure story writer (Farrell) gets involved with one of her subjects, a deep-sea diver (Donlevy). Many laughs, augmented by then-state-of-the-art underwater photography. C: Brian Donlevy, Glenda Farrell. D: Allan Dwan. COM 62m.

High Terrace 1956 British ★★½ A stage star (Maxwell) is suspected of murdering her demanding producer. Low-budget suspense. C: Dale Robertson, Lois Maxwell. D: Henry Cass. CRI 77m.

High Tide 1987 Australian ★★★★ The remarkable Davis triumphs in this unsentimental story of a troubled mother trying to reclaim her abandoned teenaged daughter, who's been raised by her grandmother in a gritty Australian trailer park. No false emotions here, and no easy answers either. C: Judy Davis, Jan Adele, Claudia Karvan. D: Gillian Armstrong. DRA [PG-13] 120m. v

High Tide at Noon 1957 ★★★ The lives and times of lobster fishermen plying the seas off Nova Scotia, focusing on the romance between a fisherman (Sylvester) and a wealthy young woman (St. John). C: Betta St. John, William Sylvester, Michael Craig, Flora Robson, Alexander Knox. D: Philip Leacock. DRA 109m.

High Time 1960 ★★★½ Widowed crooner (Crosby) discovers that the younger generation swings in a whole new way when he returns to college. Mild mix of comedy and music. C: Bing Crosby, Fabian, Tuesday Weld. D: Blake Edwards. MUS 103m.

High Treason 1952 British ★★★½ Three Scotland Yard agents, while avoiding a public panic, must stop a group of anarchists who threaten to disrupt British society by planting bombs in businesses throughout London. Well-directed suspense drama with an almost documentary feel. C: Andre Morell, Liam Redmond. D: Roy Boulting. ACT 93m.

High Velocity 1973 ★★★ Two mercenaries (Vietnam vets) try to free a kidnapped executive from Asian terrorists. Gazzara and Winfield keep the testosterone level high but *Velocity* just runs out of gas. C: Ben Gazzara, Paul Winfield, Britt Ekland, Keenan Wynn. D: Remi Kramer. ACT [PG] 106m. v

High Voltage 1929 ★★★ Painfully obvious tale finds Lombard and Boyd falling in love on bus trip when their coach becomes snowbound in the Sierra Nevada Mountains. Not electric, but vivacious Lombard provides some sparks. C: William Boyd, Owen Moore, Carole Lombard. D: Howard Higgin. DRA 63m. v

High Wall 1947 ★★½ A confessed murderer realizes he has been duped and tries to prove his innocence. Intermittently effective mystery, with reliable Taylor. C: Robert Taylor, Audrey Totter, Herbert Marshall, H. B. Warner. D: Curtis Bernhardt. DRA 99m.

High, Wide, and Handsome 1937 ★★★★ Old-fashioned, tuneful tale of oil driller Scott fighting corruption in 1860s Pennsylvania. Good Jerome Kern/Oscar Hammerstein songs include gorgeous ballad, "The Folks Who Live on the Hill." C: Irene Dunne, Randolph Scott, Dorothy Lamour, Charles Bickford, William Frawley. D: Rouben Mamoulian. MUS 112m.

High Wind in Jamaica, A 1965 British ★★★★ A group of kids captured by pirates throw off the shackles of Victorian morality in this spirited and engaging adventure tale. An overlooked gem. C: Anthony Quinn, James Coburn, Dennis Price, Gert Frobe, Lila Kedrova. D: Alexander Mackendrick. ACT 104m.

Higher and Higher 1943 ★★★★ Sinatramania had reached its height when he made his starring debut in this pleasant Cinderella story about maid turned into debutante. Frank's the thing here, crooning five songs including "A Lovely Way to Spend An Evening" and "I Couldn't Sleep A Wink Last Night'. C: Michele Morgan, Jack Haley, Frank Sinatra, Victor Borge, Mary Wickes, Mel Torme. D: Tim Whelan. MUS 90m. v

Higher Education 1988 ★★ Dull sex farce of innocent boy in first year of college. Sophomoric. C: Kevin Hicks, Lori Hallier, Stephen Black, Richard Monette, Maury Chaykin. D: John Sheppard. COM 83m. v

Higher Learning 1995 ★★★½ Earnest, but simplistic drama set on college campus where racial bigotry runs rampant. Writer/director Singleton (*Boyz N the Hood*) expertly weaves many plot lines, but reduces his characters into the very stereotypes he would like to dispell. In that light, the violent climax doesn't work. C: Omar Epps, Kristy Swanson, Michael Rapaport, Ice Cube, Laurence Fishburne. D: John Singleton. DRA [R] 127m. v

Highest Honor, The 1984 ★★★½ Intelligent if overlong drama of Australian officer Howard and his relationship with Nakamura, his captor. C: John Howard, Atsuo Nakamura, Steve Bisley, Stuart Wilson, Michael Aitkens. D: Peter Maxwell. DRA 99m. v

Highlander 1986 ★★½ Nonsensical fantasy about an immortal race of Scots with nothing better to do than carry on a family feud for eternity. Lambert and Connery try hard, but the script is too silly to allow quality to shine through. Followed by a TV series and two sequels. C: Christopher Lambert, Roxanne Hart, Sean Connery. D: Russell Mulcahy. SFI [R] 110m. v

Highlander II: The Quickening 1991 ★½ The immortal Scots (Lambert and Connery) from *Highlander* return, but wait, they're not Scottish, they're aliens. And rival Ironside is determined to do them harm. Incoherent mess. C: Christopher Lambert, Virginia Madsen, Sean Connery. D: Russell Mulcahy. ACT [R] 90m. v

Highlander: The Final Dimension 1995 ★½ Third in the sci-fi series about two time travellers competing for the power to create illusions. Large budget shows up on screen as high-tech morphing special effects; more power could have gone into the script. C: Christopher Lambert, Mario Van Peebles, Mako, Deborah Unger. D: Andy Morahan. SFI [PG-13] 94m. v

Highly Dangerous 1951 British ★★★½ An American journalist (Clark) accompanies a British scientist (Lockwood) on a secret mission, resulting in pursuit by sinister forces. Well-plotted suspense drama with appealing lead performances. C: Dane Clark, Marius Goring, Margaret Lockwood. D: Roy Baker. CRI 88m.

Highpoint 1984 Canadian ★★ An accountant becomes entangled in a CIA mission. Standard thriller. C: Richard Harris, Christopher Plummer, Beverly D'Angelo, Kate Reid. D: Peter Carter. ACT [PG] 91m. v

Highway Dragnet 1954 ★★★ Low-life crook (Conte) is falsely accused of murder and struggles to prove his innocence. Lurid approach to subject is film's worst and best attribute. First production and writing effort by legendary schlockmeister Corman. C: Richard Conte, Joan Bennett, Wanda Hendrix. D: Nathan Juran. CRI 71m.

Highway 101—Greatest Hits 1987-1990 ★★★ Clip-filled look at acclaimed rock group's career, including "Who's Lonely Now" and "Cry Cry Cry" videos. C: Highway 101. MUS 60m. v

Highway Pickup 1965 French ★★★½ Juicy potboiler follows a gang of crooks conspiring to steal a money-laden safe. Double crosses, murder, and a literally explosive finale pile up in this entertaining story of crime gone terribly wrong. C: Roberto Hossein, Georges Wilson, Jean Sorel. D: Julien Duvivier. CRI 107m.

Highway 61 1992 Canadian ★★★½ Independent road movie involves two misfits traveling the title road from Ontario, Canada to New Orleans. Offbeat fun, with a great soundtrack. C: Don McKellar, Valerie Buhagiar. D: Bruce McDonald. COM [R] 99m. v

Highway 301 1950 ★★★½ A gang of thieves pull a string of robberies, leading cops on a series of high-speed chases. Cheap B-movie takes an appealing, no-nonsense approach to its subject. C: Steve Cochran, Virginia Grey, Robert Webber. D: Andrew Stone. ACT 83m.

Highway to Battle 1960 British ★★★½ A Nazi diplomat in pre-WWII Britain tries to defect and is pursued by Gestapo henchmen. Gripping story hindered by sterile characterizations. C: Gerard Heinz, Margaret Tyzack. D: Ernest Morris. ACT 71m.

Highway to Freedom 1942 *See* **Joe Smith, American**

Highway to Hell 1991 ★★★ Imaginative, engaging horror fantasy, with Lowe venturing into the netherworld to rescue Swanson, who's been kidnapped by a literal cop from hell. Not quite as scary or funny as it might be, but great to look at and fun to watch throughout. C: Patrick Bergin, Chad Lowe, Kristy Swanson. D: Ate DeJong. HOR [R] 94m. v

Highwayman, The 1951 ★★★★ An aristocrat travels byways and back roads of 18th-century England pretending to be a robber to right the injustices of the lower classes. Period, low-budget actioner effectively combines romance and adventure. C: Charles Coburn, Wanda Hendrix, Cecil Kellaway, Victor Jory. D: Lesley Selander. ACT 82m.

Hijack 1973 ★★★ Gambler attempts hijacking scheme to make good on mob debt, but faces bloody complications along the way. C: Adam Roarke, Neville Brand, Jay Robinson. D: Leonard Horn. ACT [R] 90m. v

Hiken Yaburi 1969 Japanese ★★★ Two samurais sharing life journeys encounter corrupt government officials and a string of broken promises in between their many sword-wielding battles. Predictable action-filled samurai adventure. C: Hiroki Matsukata, Kojiro Hongo, Tomomi Iwai. D: Kazuo Ikehiro. ACT 90m.

Hilda Crane 1956 ★★★ Sideways glances begin and gossip erupts when a divorced woman (Simmons) returns to her hometown. Scandal is somewhat outmoded and cliched, but Simmons delivers a fine performance. C: Jean Simmons, Guy Madison, Jean-Pierre Aumont. D: Philip Dunne. DRA 87m.

Hildegarde Withers Detective writer Stuart Palmer created a memorably brisk series of stories and novels featuring Withers, a New York City schoolteacher who finds herself constantly embroiled in mysteries, matching wits with Inspector Oscar Piper of the NYPD. RKO turned out three memorable Withers films, pairing the wry, horse-faced Edna May Oliver with irascible Jimmy Gleason. After Oliver left the studio, they continued the series, first with Gleason and Helen Broderick and then with Gleason and Zasu Pitts.

The Penguin Pool Murder (1932)
Murder on the Blackboard (1934)
Murder on a Blackboard (1934)
Murder on a Honeymoon (1936)
Murder on a Bridle Path (1936)
The Plot Thickens (1936)
Forty Naughty Girls (1937)

Hildur and the Magician 1969 ★★★ Fairy princess kidnapped by a troll swallows a mystical potion that gives her human mortality, though she fondly remembers the enchanted life. Enjoyable for children, but overlong. C: John Graham, Hildur Mahl, Patricia Jordon. D: Larry Jordan. FAM/DRA 95m. v

Hill in Korea, A 1956 *See* **Hell in Korea**

Hill Number One 1951 ★★★½ Early television spiritual tale notable for trademark intensity of a very young James Dean. C: Michael Ansara, James Dean, Ruth Hussey. DRA 57m. TVM v

Hill on the Dark Side of the Moon, A 1983

Swedish ★★★★ Mathematician (Nyroos) and young man (Berggren) fall in love in late 19th-century Sweden. An excellent exposition of the various social and political ramifications of their affair. Strikingly directed, acted, photographed. C: Gunilla Nyroos, Thommy Berggren, Lina Pleijel, Bibi Andersson. D: Lennart Hjulstrom. DRA 105m.

Hill, The 1965 ★★★★½ At a British stockade in WWII Libya, a prisoner dies after harsh punishment and a Royal Army warrant officer (Connery) challenges the staff sergeant responsible. Unusually well acted, shattering drama about military prison discipline. C: Sean Connery, Harry Andrews, Michael Redgrave, Ian Bannen, Ossie Davis. D: Sidney Lumet. DRA 122m.

Hill, The 1988 ★★★ Members of the courageous Bravo Company must fight the war and their own inner demons. C: Terence Knox, Stephen Caffrey, Joshua Maurer. D: Robert Iscove. ACT 93m. V

Hill 24 Doesn't Answer 1955 Israeli ★★★★ Preceding separate ceasefires, four Israeli soldiers are felled outside Jerusalem in the fight for an independent state. Provocative and grisly post-WWII drama, told in lengthy flashbacks. C: Edward Mulhare, Haya Harareet. D: Thorold Dickinson. DRA 102m. V

Hillbilly Bears ★★★½ Animation lovingly captures the sweet lethargy of the Blue Ridge Mountain's Hillbilly Bears. FAM/COM 51m. V

Hillbillys in a Haunted House 1967 ★★½ Two country-western singers en route to Nashville make a stopover in a creepy house and become involved with sinister crooks. Silly sequel to *Las Vegas Hillbillys.* Rathbone's last film. C: Ferlin Husky, Joi Lansing, John Carradine, Lon Chaney, Jr., Basil Rathbone. D: Jean Yarbrough. COM 88m. V

Hills Have Eyes, The 1977 ★★★ Efficiently nightmarish shocker about a family whose camper breaks down in the desert, where they are set upon by a family of savages. Black humor complements the genuine horror in this occasionally brutal story of survival. C: Susan Lanier, Robert Houston, Virginia Vincent. D: Wes Craven. HOR [R] 89m. V

Hills Have Eyes Part II, The 1984 U.S. ★ Amazingly, the original's writer/director Craven was also responsible for this awful follow-up, with a group of young motorcyclists running into conflict with the evil desert dwellers. Too clichéd and ridiculous to be scary. Padded with footage from the first film presented as flashbacks. C: Michael Berryman, John Laughin, Tamara Stafford. D: Wes Craven. HOR [R] 86m. V

Hills of Home, The 1948 ★★★½ Enjoyable film features beloved collie Lassie at fringes of a struggle between a strict father and son who wants to enter medical school. Well-acted story that younger kids will enjoy. C: Edmund Gwenn, Donald Crisp, Tom Drake, Janet Leigh. D: Fred M. Wilcox. FAM/DRA [G] 97m. V

Hills Run Red, The 1966 Italian ★★★ Civil War soldiers execute a series of payroll robberies. Bad dubbing hinders this Italian-produced Western with American actors. Some good action scenes. (a.k.a. *A River of Dollars*) C: Thomas Hunter, Dan Duryea. D: Carlo Lizzani. WST 89m.

Himatsuri 1985 Japanese ★★★★ Cautionary tale about inhabitants of a fishing village who debate whether to build a profit-making tourist park at the cost of their link to nature. Yanagimachi's film boasts stunningly composed visuals and subtle ensemble acting. Considered a modern Japanese classic. (a.k.a. *Fire Festival*) C: Kinya Kitaoji. D: Mitsuo Yanagimachi. DRA 120m. V

Himmo, King of Jerusalem 1987 Israeli ★★★ During 1948 Israeli war, a nurse volunteering for combat ward duty struggles to communicate with quadruple amputee who has also lost eyes and ears. Well-meaning but pretentious drama in the vein of *Johnny Got His Gun.* C: Alona Himchi, Amiram Gavriel, Dov Navon, Amos Lavi, Yossi Graber, Aliza Rosen. D: Amos Guttman. DRA 84m.

Hindenburg, The 1975 ★★★½ Saboteurs carry out the explosion of a Nazi dirigible as it docks at Lakehurst, New Jersey in 1937. Tepid performances but good special effects which won special Oscar. Based on book by Michael M. Mooney. C: George C. Scott, Anne Bancroft, Gig Young, Burgess Meredith. D: Robert Wise. DRA [PG] 126m. V

Hippodrome 1961 German ★★★ German mystery about murders taking place in a European circus. Good Big Top locations and moody atmosphere result in offbeat thriller. C: Gerhard Reidmann, Margit Nunke. D: Herbert Gruber. DRA 96m.

Hips, Hips, Hooray 1934 ★★★ Wheeler and Woolsey, pursued by detectives, enter cross-country race. Broad musical farce benefits from Etting's number, "Just Keep On Doing What You're Doing." C: Bert Wheeler, Robert Woolsey, Thelma Todd, Ruth Etting. D: Mark Sandrich. MUS 68m. V

Hired Gun, The 1957 ★★★ A professional gunslinger (Calhoun) is hired to bring back a woman who was convicted of murdering her husband, and then escaped from prison. However, once he finds her, he realizes she may be innocent. Unusual, but well-done Western. C: Rory Calhoun, Anne Francis, Vince Edwards, Chuck Connors. D: Ray Nazarro. WST 63m.

Hired Hand, The 1971 ★★★★ Drifter seeks to avenge his friend's murder and to reunite with his estranged wife, but she will only take him back as a hired hand. Extravagantly directed but uneven and often rambling Western. C: Peter Fonda, Warren Oates, Verna Bloom. D: Peter Fonda. WST [PG] 93m. V

Hired to Kill 1991 ★★ Violent story of a mercenary who tries to free a prisoner on a far-off island. Nonstop action, preposterous plot twists. C: Brian Thompson, Oliver Reed, George Kennedy, Jose Ferrer. D: Nico Mastorakis. ACT [R] 95m. v
Hired Wife 1940 ★★★★ Efficient secretary (Russell) marries her boss (Aherne) in this featherweight comedy. Thanks to the cast's comic timing, a familiar story grows increasingly funny. C: Rosalind Russell, Brian Aherne, Virginia Bruce, Robert Benchley. D: William Seiter. COM 93m.
Hireling, The 1973 British ★★★★ Class boundaries begin to fall as an upper-class English woman (Miles) and her chauffeur (Shaw) approach intimacy. First-class adaptation of the L.P. Hartley novel, with finely tuned performances. C: Robert Shaw, Sarah Miles, Peter Egan. D: Alan Bridges. DRA [PG] 108m.
Hiroshima, Mon Amour 1959 French ★★★★★ A French actress on location in Hiroshima has an affair with a Japanese architect in this tragic look at the legacy of WWII and the atomic bomb. Deeply felt examination of war and its personal toll for the survivors. Novelist Marguerite Duras wrote the script. C: Emmanuele Riva, Eiji Okada, Stella Dassas. D: Alain Resnais. DRA 91m. v
Hiroshima: Out of the Ashes 1990 ★★★★ The bomb drops on Japan, and its effects are examined through the eyes of survivors. Strong performances, thoughtful telling. Partially based on Michihiko Hachiya's *Hiroshima Diary*. C: Max von Sydow, Judd Nelson, Mako. D: Peter Werner. DRA [PG-13] 98m. TVM v
His Brother's Ghost 1945 ★★★½ Billy "The Kid" Carson and his twin brother scheme to scare bad guys into submission. C: Buster Crabbe, Al St. John, Charles King. D: Sam Newfield. WST 54m. v
His Brother's Wife 1936 ★★½ Glossy melodrama. Woman marries brother of her true love—a brilliant doctor of tropical medicine with an unfortunate weakness for roulette—when she can't have the doctor. Off-screen romance of Stanwyck and Taylor created high box-office interest. C: Barbara Stanwyck, Robert Taylor, Jean Hersholt. D: W.S. Van Dyke II. DRA 90m.
His Butler's Sister 1943 ★★★ Young singer (Durbin) poses as composer's (Tone) servant. Not one of Durbin's best, although her performance of "Nessun Dorma" from Turandot is impressive. C: Deanna Durbin, Franchot Tone, Pat O'Brien. D: Frank Borzage. MUS 94m.
His Double Life 1933 ★★★ Wealthy reclusive painter (Young) finds happiness when he takes over identity of his late valet and marries Gish who's unaware of his true identity. Sentimental adaptation of Arnold Bennett's *Buried Alive*, later remade as much bouncier *Holy Matrimony*. C: Roland Young, Lillian Gish, Montague Love, Lucy Beaumont. D: Arthur Hopkins. COM 67m. v
His Excellency 1952 ★★★ A trade specialist (Portman), who was once a laborer himself, is sent to manage a labor dispute in a small British colony. An interesting glimpse of labor relations. C: Eric Portman, Cecil Parker, Helen Cherry, Susan Stephen. D: Robert Hamer. DRA 84m.
His Fighting Blood 1935 ★★★ Adaptation of James Oliver Curwood story about a Northwest Mountie on an undercover mission. C: Kermit Maynard. WST 65m. v
His First Command 1929 ★★ Boyd (better known from 1934 as Hopalong Cassidy) joins the Army so he can impress a colonel's daughter. Stiff performances and plodding pace doom this early talkie. C: William Boyd, Dorothy Sebastian, Gavin Gordon. D: Gregory La Cava. DRA 61m. v
His First Flame 1926 ★★★★½ Charming story, co-written by Frank Capra, about romance between awkward fireman and a social-climbing woman. C: Harry Langdon, Natalie Kingston. D: Harry Edwards. COM 62m. v
His Girl Friday 1940 ★★★★★ Marvelous reworking of *The Front Page* features Grant as newspaper editor who will do anything to keep star reporter Russell from marrying nice guy Bellamy. Groundbreaking use of overlapping dialogue makes for shower of comic sparks. Hawks' slam-bang direction is terrific, while Grant and Russell take turns outshining each other. Remade as *Switching Channels* in 1988. C: Cary Grant, Rosalind Russell, Ralph Bellamy, Gene Lockhart. D: Howard Hawks. COM 92m. v
His Kind of Woman 1951 ★★★½ Gambler Mitchum is offered $50,000 to leave the U.S. for a year, only to find he's been set up by exiled mob boss Burr. Too long but fairly enjoyable (despite tedious, climatic fight scene) if viewed as a camp piece. Price shines as a slumming actor. C: Robert Mitchum, Jane Russell, Vincent Price, Raymond Burr, Marjorie Reynolds, Jim Backus. D: John Farrow. ACT 120m. v
His Majesty O'Keefe 1953 ★★★½ Lancaster travels to the South Seas and makes a fortune as he teaches the natives entrepreneurial ways. High-energy comedy/adventure. C: Burt Lancaster, Joan Rice, Benson Fong. D: Byron Haskin. COM 92m. v
His Mistress 1984 ★★½ A married tycoon (Urich) falls for seductive company executive. Nice romantic drama. C: Robert Urich, Julianne Phillips. D: David Lowell Rich. DRA 104m. TVM
His Picture In The Papers 1916 ★★★½ Fairbanks must prove his adulthood to his father by getting his photograph in the newspaper. Silent comedy wittily co-scripted by Anita Loos. C: Douglas Fairbanks. D: John Emerson. COM 68m. v
His Prehistoric Past/The Bank 1915 ★★★ Two of the "Little Tramp's" classic silent comedies spotlighting his early genius. C:

Charlie Chaplin, Mack Swain, Edna Purviance. D: Charles Chaplin. COM 54m. V

His Private Secretary 1933 ★★★ Odd comedy with unlikely Wayne playing jet-setting rogue who finally settles down when he meets a preacher's daughter. C: John Wayne, Evalyn Knapp, Natalie Kingston. D: Philip Whitman. COM 60m. V

His Royal Slyness/Haunted Spooks 1919 ★★★ Two Harold Lloyd silent shorts. In "His Royal Slyness," Lloyd pretends to be king; in "Haunted Spooks," he takes up residence in a spooky estate. C: Harold Lloyd, Mildred Davis. D: Alf Goulding. COM 52m. V

His Wife's Lover 1931 Yiddish ★★★★ The first Jewish musical comedy talking picture is film of Yiddish stage hit about famous actor seeking a wife. Sort of Moliere meets the Lower East Side, charming and funny. C: Ludwig Satz, Isidore Casher, Lucy Levine, Lillian Feinman, Michael Rosenberg, Jacob Frank. D: Sidney M. Goldin. COM 80m.

His Woman 1931 ★★ Usually lively Colbert is straitjacketed by a weak script and poor direction as a nurse who falls in love with a boat captain. Cooper is equally inert. Watch them in *Bluebeard's Eighth Wife* instead. C: Gary Cooper, Claudette Colbert, Douglass Dumbrille. D: Edward Sloman. DRA 80m.

History 1987 Italian ★★½ Disappointingly shallow glimpse at how a woman and her children survive during Nazi occupation of Italy. Unfortunately, Comencini's approach is neorealist homage. C: Claudia Cardinale, Lambert Wilson, Francisco Rabal, Andrea Spada, Antonio Degli Schiavi, Fiorenzo Fiorntini. D: Luigi Comencini. DRA 251m.

History Is Made at Night 1937 ★★★★ Romantic triangle leads to revenge, murder, and some grand high seas spectacle as an obsessed steamship owner (Clive) pursues his wife (Arthur) and her lover (Boyer). Unusual, twisty entertainment. Clive stands out. C: Charles Boyer, Jean Arthur, Leo Carrillo, Colin Clive. D: Frank Borzage. DRA 98m. V

History Lessons 1973 W. German ★★★ Bertold Brecht's incomplete novel *The Affairs of Mr. Julius Caesar* gets a daring treatment: Characters in period costume enact the story in modern-day Rome. It doesn't quite work; Straub's overdone distancing effects make less a narrative than a comment on narrative. C: Gottfried Bold, Benedict Zulauf. D: Jean-Marie Straub. DRA 85m.

History Never Repeats—The Best of Split Enz 1987 ★★★½ Features videos covering ten years of the group's celebrated career. Includes "I See Red," and "Dirty Creature." MUS 80m. V

History of Mr. Polly, The 1949 British ★★★★ Mild-mannered shopkeeper (Mills), tired of his business and his wife, leaves both to find simple happiness working in an English inn. Charming adaptation of H.G. Wells' novel, with finely detailed characters and, warm performance by Mills. C: John Mills, Sally Howes, Finlay Currie. D: Anthony Pelissier. COM 96m.

History of the World Part I 1981 ★★★ Scattershot comedy that attempts to parody historical eras from Stone Age to Biblical times to Roman days through slapdash, often scatological humor. Highlights include hilarious "Hitler On Ice" sequence. C: Mel Brooks, Madeline Kahn, Harvey Korman, Gregory Hines, Dom DeLuise, Cloris Leachman, Sid Caesar. D: Mel Brooks. COM [R] 93m. V

History of White People in America, The—Vol. 1 1985 ★★★★ Unique comedy parodies both documentary genre and white middle-class family life. C: Martin Mull, Fred Willard, Mary Kay Place. D: Harry Shearer. COM 48m. TVM V

History of White People in America, The—Vol. 2 1986 ★★★★ Four episodes spoofing white suburbia, including "White Religion," "White Politics," "White Crime," and "White Streets." C: Martin Mull, Mary Kay Place, Fred Willard. D: Harry Shearer. COM 100m. TVM V

Hit 1973 ★★★½ Narcotics agent (Williams) goes after French drug dealers he blames for daughter's death. Suspenseful thriller. C: Billy Dee Williams, Richard Pryor, Gwen Welles. D: Sidney Furie. ACT [R] 135m. V

Hit and Run 1957 ★ An older man (Haas) discovers his wife cheating on him, and takes steps to dispose of her lover. Out-of-gas thriller suffers. C: Hugo Haas, Cleo Moore, Vince Edwards. D: Hugo Haas. DRA [PG] 84m.

Hit and Run 1982 ★★ Two-dimensional drama about a New York cabdriver consumed by memories of a hit-and-run accident that caused his wife's death. C: Paul Perri, Claudia Cron. D: Charles Braverman. DRA 96m. V

Hit Lady 1974 ★★★ A refined assassin (Mimieux) works for a powerful crime syndicate. Nicely produced thriller. C: Yvette Mimieux, Joseph Campanella. D: Tracy Keenan Wynn. DRA 78m. TVM V

Hit List 1989 ★★★ A vengeful family man (Vincent) goes after the cold-blooded Mafia killer who's abducted his son. Fast-moving, hard-edged thriller has solid support from Torn and Henriksen. C: Jan-Michael Vincent, Lance Henriksen, Rip Torn. D: William Lustig. ACT 87m. V

Hit Parade of 1943 1943 *See* **Change of Heart**

Hit the Deck 1955 ★★★ Musical fluff about three sailors on leave in San Francisco. Most memorable for its hit song, "More Than You Know." C: Jane Powell, Tony Martin, Debbie Reynolds, Ann Miller, Vic Damone, Walter Pidgeon. D: Roy Rowland. MUS 114m. V

Hit the Dutchman 1992 ★★★ Interesting gangster epic about the Mob war in NYC that led to the assassination of Dutch Schultz. C: Bruce Nozick, Eddie Bowz, Sally Kirkland, Will Kempe. D: Menahem Golan. CRI [R] 116m. V

Hit the Ice 1943 ★★★★ Abbott and Costello

are news photographers who find themselves unwittingly mixed up with a trio of bank robbers. Some good comedy routines, expertly performed, keep the laughs coming throughout. C: Bud Abbott, Lou Costello, Ginny Simms. D: Charles Lamont. COM 89m. V

Hit the Road 1941 ★★★ The sons of men murdered in a gang war are forced to seek sanctuary on a ranch. Slightly unusual Bowery Boys entry. C: Billy Halop, Huntz Hall, Gabriel Dell, Gladys George. D: Joe May. DRA 61m. V

Hit The Saddle 1937 ★★★ While chasing down cattle rustlers, the Three Mesquiteers temporarily fall under the spell of the enchanting "Rita Cansino," later to be known as Rita Hayworth. C: Robert Livingston, Ray Corrigan, Max Terhune, Rita Cansino. D: Mack V. Wright. WST 60m. V

Hit, The 1985 ★★★½ Hired guns face darkly funny complications as they try to deliver their prey to their mob bosses. C: Terence Stamp, John Hurt, Laura Del Sol, Tim Roth. D: Stephen Frears. COM [R] 97m. V

Hitch-Hiker, The 1953 ★★★★ Considered by many to be Lupino's best directorial effort, this tense thriller recounts the ordeal of two businessmen (O'Brien and Lovejoy) kidnapped by a maniac. C: Edmond O'Brien, Frank Lovejoy, William Talman. D: Ida Lupino. DRA 71m. V

Hitch in Time, A 1978 ★★★½ Scientist invents a time-traveling machine that helps two siblings go back to meet their ancestors. Charming moments spark this cute film for youngsters. C: Michael McVey, Pheona McLellan, Patrick Troughton. D: Jan Darnley-Smith. FAM/SFI 57m.

Hitchcock Collection, The 1987 ★★★★ Packaged as collector's set, contains two features (*The Lady Vanishes* and *The 39 Steps*) and a retrospective chronicling the director's illustrious career. D: Alfred Hitchcock. DRA 200m. V

Hitched 1973 ★★ The misadventures of newlyweds (Field and Matheson) trying to make a go of it in the Old West. Average comedy/Western. C: Sally Field, Tim Matheson, Neville Brand, Slim Pickens, John Fiedler, Denver Pyle. D: Boris Sagal. WST 90m. TVM

Hitcher, The 1985 ★★★★ Young motorist Howell is relentlessly pursued across the American Southwest by hitchhiking serial killer Hauer. Spare, eerie, beautifully shot chiller punctuated by shocking violence and highlighted by Hauer's truly scary performance. C: Rutger Hauer, C. Thomas Howell, Jennifer Jason Leigh. D: Robert Harmon. HOR [R] 97m. V

Hitchhike to Happiness 1945 ★★★ Waiter and struggling writer Pearce is taken under the wing of radio star Evans, who cons a powerful producer into thinking this unknown youngster is a big-name talent. Typical show business schmaltz with no surprises. C: Al Pearce, Dale Evans, Brad Taylor, William Frawley. D: Joseph Santley. DRA 71m.

Hitchhiker's Guide to the Galaxy 1985 ★★★★ British TV movie based on the long-running BBC radio series about a hapless human (Jones), clad only in his bathrobe, forced to wander outer space after escaping Earth's destruction. Hilarious and well made. Based on the popular book by Douglas Adams. C: Simon Jones, David Dixon. D: Alan Bell. SFI 194m.

Hitchhiker's Guide to the Galaxy, Making of, The ★★★ TV special takes viewers behind the scenes of the British radio phenomenon and TV movie. Interesting and informative. SFI V

Hitchhikers, The 1971 ★★ Female hitchhikers steal from anyone who offers to give them a ride. C: Misty Rowe, Norman Klar. D: Ferd Sebastian. ACT [R] 90m. V

Hitler 1962 ★★★ Sensational biography about the Führer's rise and fall. Basehart's performance is intelligent, but not fully realized. C: Richard Basehart, Cordula Trantow, Maria Emo. D: Stuart Heisler. DRA 103m. V

Hitler: A Career 1977 W. German ★★★ An in-depth look at Hitler's rise and fall. Insightful. D: Joachim C. Fest, Christian Herendoerfer. DOC 150m.

Hitler—Dead or Alive 1943 ★★★ A trio of ex-cons set out to kill Hitler for a million-dollar bounty. Intriguing wish-fulfillment propaganda hampered by low-budget, awkward staging. C: Ward Bond, Dorothy Tree, Warren Hymer. D: Nick Grinde. ACT 70m.

Hitler Gang, The 1944 ★★★★ Intriguingly dated drama made for homefront shows rise of German Nazi party under Hitler's direction. Hitler treated as psychopathic criminal in portrait that veers between caricature and on-target biography. Not entirely successful, but unforgettable. C: Robert Watson, Martin Kosleck, Victor Varconi. D: John Farrow. DRA 101m.

Hitler: The Last Ten Days 1973 British ★★★ Guinness is Hitler, ignominiously hiding out in a bunker as the Third Reich falls into shreds. Juxtaposed with actual newsreel footage and voice-over narration. Innovative approach to well-trodden ground. C: Alec Guinness, Simon Ward, Diane Cilento, Eric Porter. D: Ennio de Concini. DRA [PG] 106m. V

Hitler's Children 1943 ★★★★ Examines indoctrination of children into Nazi philosophical and military order. German boy (Holt) becomes Gestapo officer but can't distance himself from childhood sweetheart (Granville) persecuted by Nazis. Immensely popular on first release, now smacks of obvious propaganda. C: Tim Holt, Bonita Granville, Kent Smith, Otto Kruger. D: Edward Dmytryk, Irving Reis. DRA 83m. V

Hitler's Daughter 1990 ★★★½ Frequently chilling cable movie imagines that Hitler had a daughter who sets out to establish the Fourth

Reich in the United States. Far-fetched, but grimly absorbing. C: Patrick Cassidy, Melody Anderson, Veronica Cartwright. D: James A. Contner. DRA [R] 88m. TVM V

Hitler's Hangman *See* **Hitler's Madman**

Hitler's Henchmen 1985 ★★★ Goebbels, Himmler, Borman, and other Nazi leaders are profiled in this probing documentary. DOC 60m. V

Hitler's Madman 1943 ★★★ Chronicles the obliteration of Czech city of Lidice by Germans in retaliation for assassination of sadistic Nazi commander by town's citizens. Based on true story, but plays up sensational and melodramatic elements. (a.k.a. *Hitler's Hangman*) C: John Carradine, Patricia Morison, Alan Curtis. D: Douglas Sirk. DRA 84m.

Hitler's Master Race—The Mad Dream of the S.S. ★★★ Hitler's horrific vision and the role of the S.S. in his plans are the subject of this documentary. DOC V

Hitler's S.S.: Portrait in Evil 1985 ★★★ Two German brothers join notorious brigade of Nazi stormtroopers, witness rise and fall of S.S. through firsthand experience. Average historical drama features an unusual performance by Randall as a nightclub performer. C: John Shea, Lucy Gutteridge, Jose Ferrer, Tony Randall. D: Jim Goddard. ACT 150m. TVM V

Hitman, The 1991 ★★★½ Plenty of high-kicking action as Norris goes undercover in Seattle to dissolve an intricate organized crime ring. C: Chuck Norris, Michael Parks, Alberta Watson. D: Aaron Norris. ACT [R] 94m. V

Hits—Live From London ★★★½ Electric compilation of concert clips, featuring Kid Creole and the Coconuts, Steve Marriot, and the U.K. Subs. C: Various Artists. MUS 52m. V

Hitter, The 1978 ★★★ A boxer, his lady, and a down-and-out promoter are on the run from the mob and the law. Routine action thriller. Typical post-*Superfly* O'Neal fare. C: Ron O'Neal, Adolph Caesar. D: Christopher Leitch. ACT [R] 94m. V

Hittin' The Trail 1937 ★★★ Ritter has to prove that he is a hero, not the Tombstone Kid. C: Tex Ritter. WST 65m. V

Hitting a New High 1937 ★★ Opera diva (Pons) looks uncomfortable in silly musical comedy, surrounded by supporting comics who mug outrageously. Plot at one point has her impersonating African native with singular name of "Oogahunga the Bird-Girl." C: Lily Pons, Jack Oakie, Edward Everett Horton, Lucille Ball, Eric Blore. D: Raoul Walsh. MUS 85m.

Hitwoman: The Double Edge 1993 ★★★½ Soap diva Lucci doubles as a driven FBI agent and the equally obsessed murderer she stalks. C: Susan Lucci, Robert Urich, Michael Woods. D: Stephen Stafford. CRI [R] 92m. TVM V

Hitz 1992 ★★★ The lives of an empathetic judge and a young informant are at stake when a gang member is murdered in the judge's courtroom. C: Elliott Gould, Karen Black, Cuba Gooding, Jr. D: William Sachs. CRI [R] 94m. V

Hi'ya Chum 1943 ★★ Mediocre Ritz Brothers comedy has them running a restaurant, with chaotic results. Scattered musical numbers. C: The Ritz Brothers, Jane Frazee, Robert Paige, June Clyde. D: Harold Young. COM 61m.

H.M. Pulham, Esq. 1941 ★★★★ After a long life of behaving always as society would have him behave, a Boston businessman decides to have some fun. Smart, solid film with outstanding performances. C: Hedy Lamarr, Robert Young, Ruth Hussey, Charles Coburn, Van Heflin, Bonita Granville. D: King Vidor. DRA 120m.

Hoa-Binh 1971 ★★★★ South Vietnamese brother and sister are reduced to begging in the streets until their father returns from the war. Sensitive and emotionally powerful study of life at its most humbling depths wisely avoids injecting politics into the story. C: Phi Lan, Huynh Cazenas, Xuan Ha, Le Quynh. D: Raoul Coutard. DRA 93m.

Hobbit, The 1977 ★★★½ Treacly TV telling of J.R.R. Tolkien's *Lord of the Rings* features Orson Bean as Bilbo and John Huston as Gandlaf. Too cute for its own good, though fantasy-loving children may find a few moments of enjoyment. C: Orson Bean, John Huston. D: Arthur Rankin, Jr. FAM/SFI 76m. V

Hobo's Christmas, A 1987 ★★★ Hughes does another variation on his stock, crusty old man in this Christmas tale of a vagrant who returns to the family he left 20 years before. A so-so story for family holiday viewing, originally shown as a TV movie. C: Barnard Hughes, Gerald McRaney. D: Will Mackenzie. FAM/DRA 94m. V

Hobson's Choice 1954 British ★★★★★ Charming classic about a boot-maker (Laughton) who's desperately opposed when his daughter (de Banzie) decides to wed her father's employee (Mills). Laughton's dazzling performance is a standout. C: Charles Laughton, John Mills, Brenda de Banzie, Prunella Scales. D: David Lean. DRA 102m. V

Hobson's Choice 1983 ★★★½ Remake of father vs. daughter comedy shifts focus to Gless's relationship with husband Thomas as she boosts his confidence in opposition to domineering dad Warden. Folksy and appealing, but earlier version is superior. C: Jack Warden, Sharon Gless, Richard Thomas, Lillian Gish. D: Gilbert Cates. COM 95m. TVM V

Hockey Night 1984 Canadian ★★★½ Good "issue" film for older kids revolves around a girl trying out for an otherwise all-boy's hockey team. Winning performances and honest approach help fill out story. C: Megan Follows, Rick Moranis, Gail Youngs. D: Paul Shapiro. FAM/ACT 77m. V

Hocus Pocus 1993 ★★½ Witches (Midler,

Najimy, and Parker) condemned at Salem, come back centuries later to seek revenge against the teenage descendants of their original accusers. Promising cast tries perhaps too hard. C: Bette Midler, Kathy Najimy, Sarah Jessica Parker. D: Kenny Ortega. COM [PG] 96m. V

Hocus Pocus It's Magic ★★★½ Mystical illusions abound in Dick Cavett-hosted showcase for top magicians, including Mark Wilson and Slydini. C: Dick Cavett. FAM/MUS 97m. V

Hoffa 1992 ★★★ Rough, raw, life and death of the Teamster leader, played to a powerful, harshly realistic turn by makeup-enhanced Nicholson. Mounted on a grand scale, as befits a legend, but Mamet's script disappoints and DeVito's direction falters. C: Jack Nicholson, Danny DeVito, Armand Assante, Kevin Anderson, Robert Prosky. D: Danny DeVito. DRA [R] 140m. V

Hoffman 1970 British ★★★½ Sellers is genuinely creepy as a man who uses blackmail to spend time with a typist. Offbeat film with a strange plot, kept afloat by fine acting. C: Peter Sellers, Sinead Cusack, Jeremy Bulloch. D: Alvin Rakoff. DRA [PG] 116m.

Hog Wild 1980 Canadian ★★½ Silly teen comedy pits the local good guys against nasty motorcycle gang with predictable results. Low-budget production, but with energetic acting. C: Michael Biehn, Patti D'Arbanville, Tony Rosato. D: Les Rose. COM [PG] 97m. V

Holcroft Convenant, The 1985 British ★★★ A deceased Nazi has left a hidden fortune for his son (Caine), who faces all kinds of dangers and intrigue on the way to retrieving it. Intricate thriller, based on the novel by Robert Ludlum. C: Michael Caine, Anthony Andrews, Victoria Tennant, Lilli Palmer. D: John Frankenheimer. ACT 112m. V

Hold Back the Dawn 1941 ★★★★½ Mild-mannered spinster (de Havilland) falls for a rogue (Boyer) who romances her to gain entry into the United States. Moving, witty execution results in a not-to-be-missed romance, with an unusually touching Billy Wilder/ Charles Brackett screenplay. Nominated for an Oscar for Best Picture. C: Charles Boyer, Olivia de Havilland, Paulette Goddard. D: Mitchell Leisen. DRA 115m.

Hold Back the Night 1956 ★★★ A Marine officer stationed in Korea reminisces about a bottle of whiskey that brought him luck in two wars. Competent, watchable war yarn. C: John Payne, Mona Freeman, Peter Graves, Chuck Connors. D: Allan Dwan. DRA 80m.

Hold Back Tomorrow 1955 ★★ A convicted killer asks to spend his last night with a beautiful woman. Preposterous, low-budget melodrama. C: Cleo Moore, John Agar, Harry Guardino. D: Hugo Haas. DRA 75m.

Hold 'Em Jail 1932 ★★½ Two prison inmates (Wheeler and Woolsey) arrange an interprison football game to get on the good side of their pigskin-crazy warden (Kennedy). Typical burlesque. C: Bert Wheeler, Robert Woolsey, Betty Grable, Edgar Kennedy, Edna May Oliver. D: Norman Taurog. COM 65m. V

Hold 'Em Navy 1937 ★★★ Sports film has freshman Naval Academy football player meeting and falling in love with the sweetheart of an upperclassman. Routine sports drama climaxes with football showdown. C: Lew Ayres, Mary Carlisle, John Howard. D: Kurt Neumann. DRA 64m.

Hold 'Em Yale 1935 ★★★ Four con artists wind up taking care of a young heiress and finding her a husband. Damon Runyon's story and colorful characterizations come to life on screen. C: Patricia Ellis, Cesar Romero, Larry Crabbe, William Frawley, Andy Devine. D: Sidney Lanfield. COM 61m.

Hold Everything 1930 ★★★½ A comic decides to pack it in and become a prizefighter. Some good music and lots of boisterous fun, the kind that Brown's famous for. This is the movie that made him a star. C: Joe E. Brown, Winnie Lightner, Georges Carpentier. D: Roy Del Ruth. MUS 78m.

Hold Me, Thrill Me, Kiss Me 1992 ★★★½ Bizarre goings-on in a Southern California trailer park as a young fugitive who's shot his fiancée gets mixed up with a kinky stripper and her animal-loving younger sister. Weirdo characters keep proceedings lively. C: Max Parrish, Adrienne Shelly, Sean Young, Diane Ladd. D: Joel Hershman. COM [R] 93m. V

Hold On! 1966 ★★ Abysmal movie vehicle for British Beatle wannabes has them pursued by NASA so that spaceship can be named for them. C: Peter Noone, Herman's Hermits, Sue Langdon. D: Arthur Lubin. MUS 85m.

Hold That Baby! 1949 ★★½ Laundromat managers (The Bowery Boys) find an abandoned baby who's actually the heir to a huge inheritance. Business as usual for the Bowery Boys. C: Leo Gorcey, Huntz Hall, Billy Benedict, Gabriel Dell, Frankie Darro. D: Reginald LeBorg. COM 64m.

Hold That Blonde 1945 ★★★½ A kleptomaniac (Bracken), told by his psychiatrist to cure his sticky-finger habit by falling in love, ends up attracted to a beautiful jewel thief (Lake). Fluffy fast-paced comedy. C: Eddie Bracken, Veronica Lake, Albert Dekker. D: George Marshall. COM 76m.

Hold That Co-ed 1938 ★★★½ Politics and football come together in this amusing minor musical: good performance by Barrymore as a governor involved with college team. C: John Barrymore, George Murphy, Marjorie Weaver, Joan Davis, Jack Haley. D: George Marshall. MUS 80m.

Hold That Ghost 1941 ★★★★★ One of Abbott and Costello's best comedies with Bud and Lou inheriting haunted castle. Funny-woman Davis gives them top support as professional radio screamer. Highlights include revolving room routine, moving candle gag, and Andrews Sisters singing "Aurora." C: Bud Abbott, Lou Costello, Richard Carlson, Joan Davis, Mischa Auer, Evelyn Ankers, The Andrews Sisters. D: Arthur Lubin. COM 86m. V

Hold That Girl 1934 ★★★½ Investigative reporter Trevor is arrested after going undercover as a nightclub fan dancer. Her embarrassment increases when her nemesis, cop Dunn, bribes trial judge so Trevor will have to perform her seductive dance in the courtroom. Strange but funny sex comedy. C: James Dunn, Claire Trevor. D: Hamilton MacFadden. COM 70m.

Hold That Hypnotist 1957 ★★★ A hypnosis subject (Hall) recalls that in a past life he knew the location of fabulous treasure buried by Blackbeard the Pirate. One of the better Bowery Boys entries. C: Huntz Hall, Stanley Clements, Jane Nigh. D: Austen Jewell. COM 61m.

Hold That Line 1952 ★★★ College student (Hall) discovers supervitamin formula that makes him a football star. Slapstick pigskin comedy and good Bowery Boys fun. C: Leo Gorcey, Huntz Hall, Veda Ann Borg. D: William Beaudine. COM 64m.

Hold the Dream 1986 ★★★ Sequel to author Bradford's *A Woman of Substance*. Not as gripping but still entertaining. Seagrove (lead from first film), reappears as dowager Kerr's heiress granddaughter, who is forced to fight conniving family members to hold on to her grandmother's department stores. C: Jenny Seagrove, Stephen Collins, Deborah Kerr, John Mills, Claire Bloom, Liam Neeson. D: Don Sharp. DRA 195m. TVM V

Hold Your Man 1933 ★★★★ Harlow plays a tough, streetwise woman who falls in love with a con artist (Gable), sticking with him through thick and thin (including a jail term). Both stars shine in this deft mix of comedy and drama. C: Jean Harlow, Clark Gable, Stuart Erwin. D: Sam Wood. DRA 87m. V

Hole in the Head, A 1959 ★★★★ Sinatra is Miami hotel operator struggling to stay afloat, while respectable brother Robinson tries to secure custody of Frank's 10-year-old son Hodges. Touching comedy/drama with strong cast, from Broadway play. Features Oscar-winning song, "High Hopes." C: Frank Sinatra, Eddie Hodges, Edward G. Robinson, Thelma Ritter, Eleanor Parker, Carolyn Jones. D: Frank Capra. COM 121m. V

Hole, The 1964 *See* **Onibaba**

Holes, The 1973 French ★★★ A dark, bizarre tale of street disappearances caused by strange characters living in the sewers of Paris. Solid acting, and at times intriguing, but finally unconvincing. C: Gerard Depardieu, Philippe Noiret. D: Pierre Tchernia. DRA [PG-13] 90m.

Holiday 1930 ★★★★ An offbeat rich girl (Harding) falls for her sister's fiancée (Ames), a lawyer who's reluctant to lead the society life. Witty adaptation of Philip Barry's play, remade in 1938. C: Ann Harding, Robert Ames, Mary Astor, Edward Everett Horton, Hedda Hopper. D: Edward Griffith. COM 96m.

Holiday 1938 ★★★★★ Witty, utterly charming remake of the Philip Barry play about a freethinker (Grant) who takes on the pretensions and hypocrisy of a New York society family. Hepburn is marvelous as a spirited young woman goaded into action by Grant's arrival on the scene. A must-see for fans of *The Philadelphia Story*. C: Katharine Hepburn, Cary Grant, Doris Nolan, Lew Ayres, Edward Everett Horton, Jean Dixon. D: George Cukor. DRA 93m. V

Holiday Affair 1949 ★★★½ Sentimental yuletide romance with Leigh as widow with boy to raise, pursued by two men (Mitchum, Corey). Slight, but charming. C: Robert Mitchum, Janet Leigh, Wendell Corey. D: Don Hartman. DRA 87m. V

Holiday Camp 1948 British ★★★ British vacationers at a summer camp are disrupted by a murderer. Episodic comedy/drama is sparked by winning performances. C: Dennis Price, Flora Robson. D: Ken Annakin. COM 97m.

Holiday for Henrietta 1954 French ★★★★ Engaging comedy about the making of a movie in which the cast and crew begin to confuse film and reality. Clever plot turns, and engaging look at moviemaking make this a thoroughly enjoyable and original film. C: Dany Robin, Hildegarde Neff, Michel Auclair, Michel Roux. D: Julien Duvivier. COM 118m.

Holiday for Lovers 1959 ★★★ A psychiatrist (Webb) and his wife (Wyman), intent on keeping their daughters away from men, take them to South America, where they get into trouble anyway. Innocuous, scenic fun. C: Clifton Webb, Jane Wyman, Jill St. John, Carol Lynley, Paul Henreid. D: Henry Levin. COM 103m.

Holiday for Sinners 1952 ★★½ Colorful backdrop highlights this drama about the lives of four young people in New Orleans for Mardi Gras. C: Gig Young, Janice Rule, Keenan Wynn. D: Gerald Mayer. DRA 72m.

Holiday Hotel 1986 French ★★ Sex farce concerns the amorous adventures of French vacationers. Lang's usual hackneyed look at sexual high jinks. C: Daniel Ceccaldi, Michel Grellier, Guy Marchand, Sophie Barjae. D: Michel Lang. COM 109m. V

Holiday in Havana 1949 ★★½ A young bandleader takes his orchestra to Cuba. Some nice Latin sounds perk up an otherwise bland story. Arnaz and a cast of character pros help. C: Desi Arnaz, Mary Hatcher, Ann Doran, Steven Geray. D: Jean Yarbrough. MUS 73m. V

Holiday in Mexico 1946 ★★★★ Entertaining musical comedy about a musician who romances the wealthy daughter of the ambassador to Mexico (Pidgeon). High-spirited score will lead many a toe to tapping. C: Jane Powell, Walter Pidgeon, Ilona Massey, Roddy

McDowall, Xavier Cugat, Jose Iturbi. D: George Sidney. MUS 127m. ▼

Holiday in Spain 1960 *See* **Scent of Mystery**

Holiday Inn 1942 ★★★★ Crowd pleasing Christmas perennial with evergreen Irving Berlin score tied to slim plot of romantic rivals Astaire and Crosby at latter's inn, open only on holidays. Song gems include "White Christmas," "Easter Parade," "Be Careful, It's My Heart." Redone (sort of), with Crosby again, as *White Christmas* C: Bing Crosby, Fred Astaire, Marjorie Reynolds, Virginia Dale. D: Mark Sandrich. MUS 101m. ▼

Holiday Sing Along With Mitch 1961 ★★★★ Famous bandleader ushers in holiday cheer with subtitled renditions of "Deck the Halls," "Joy to the World," and others. C: Mitch Miller. MUS 50m. ▼

Hollow Boy, The 1989 ★★★½ Young German immigrant tries to have friendships with Jewish neighbors despite his ethnic background. Based on Hortense Calisher short story. C: Alexis Arquette, Jerry Stiller, Kathleen Widdoes. D: Noel Black. DRA 60m. ▼

Hollow Gate 1988 ★★★ Group of trick-or-treaters encounter maniac with flesh-eating canines. C: Katrina Alexy, Richard Dry, J.J. Miller. D: Ray Di Zazzo. HOR 90m. ▼

Hollow Image 1979 ★★★ Successful black woman working in department store fears that she's lost touch with her roots. Above-average drama scores now and then. C: Robert Hooks, Saundra Sharp, Hattie Winston, Morgan Freeman. D: Marvin J. Chomsky. DRA 100m. TVM

Hollow Triumph *See* **Scar, The**

Holly and the Ivy, The 1953 British ★★★½ Small-town English cleric Richardson reminisces about his life and his three grown children over the Christmas season. Quiet, proper British nostalgia based on Wynard Brown play of same name. Good performances. C: Ralph Richardson, Celia Johnson, Margaret Leighton, Denholm Elliott. D: George O'Ferrall. DRA 80m.

Hollywood Boulevard 1936 ★★★½ When former Hollywood star Halliday decides to write his memoirs for a movie magazine, its publication threatens to ruin lives of his family. A sluggish drama. Real enjoyment is looking for cameos of many silent screen stars. C: John Halliday, Marsha Hunt, Robert Cummings, Mae Marsh. D: Robert Florey. DRA 70m.

Hollywood Boulevard 1976 ★★★½ Imaginative spoof of dirt-cheap moviemaking follows an aspiring actress (Rialson) as she encounters various obstacles on the road to stardom. An excellent supporting cast (low-budget veterans all) help put the broad gags across. C: Allan Arkush, Candice Rialson, Mary Woronov, Paul Bartel. D: Joe Dante, Allan Arkush. COM [R] 83m. ▼

Hollywood Canteen 1944 ★★★★ Warner Brothers threw every star on the lot (including Roy Rogers' horse, Trigger) into this tribute to the fighting men of WWII, set in the social club co-founded by Davis and Garfield. Minor plot has Hutton romancing Leslie. Typical grab bag, with more highs than lows. C: Joan Leslie, Robert Hutton, Bette Davis, John Garfield. D: Delmer Daves. MUS 124m. ▼

Hollywood Cavalcade 1939 ★★★★ Lovely romantic musical has Faye starting out in silent-era Hollywood under Ameche's guidance. Full of funny observations and former stars playing themselves; then turns melodramatic, and sad, which doesn't quite work. C: Alice Faye, Don Ameche, J. Bromberg, Al Jolson, Mack Sennett, Buster Keaton, Chester Conklin. D: Irving Cummings. MUS 96m.

Hollywood Chainsaw Hookers 1988 ★★½ A group of beautiful prostitutes hack up their clients. Repetitive and gory parody of the horror genre, a minor cult item for Quigley fans. C: Gunnar Hansen, Linnea Quigley. D: Fred Olen Ray. HOR 90m. ▼

Hollywood Chaos 1989 ★★½ Wannabe star about to get her big break finds herself filming a trouble-plagued movie filled with celebrity impersonators. Silly entertainment. C: Carl Ballantine, Tricia Leigh Fisher. D: Sean McNamara. COM 90m. ▼

Hollywood Cop 1987 ★★★ Hardened police officer gives everything he's got to save youth abducted by the mob. C: Jim Mitchum, David Goss, Troy Donahue. D: Amir Shervan. CRI [R] 101m. ▼

Hollywood Cowboy 1937 ★★★½ Chicago gangsters try to put the muscle on Wyoming ranchers. Fortunately movie star O'Brien is vacationing nearby and uses his B-Western knowledge to foil these outlaws. Fun genre spoof with nice self-parody from O'Brien. (a.k.a. *Wings Over Wyoming*) C: George O'Brien, Cecilia Parker. D: George A. Hirliman. WST 60m.

Hollywood Cowboy 1975 *See* **Hearts of the West**

Hollywood Detective, The 1989 ★★½ A has-been TV actor (Savalas) is caught up in real-life detective case. Savalas spoofs his own *Kojak* series with average results. C: Telly Savalas, Helen Udy, Joe Dallesandro. D: Kevin Connor. COM [PG] 88m. TVM ▼

Hollywood Game, The 1977 *See* **Game Show Models**

Hollywood Ghost Stories 1986 ★★½ John Carradine hosts an "investigation" of that hotbed of paranormal activity: L.A. Hard-hitting reporters such as Elke Sömmer dish out supernatural dirt while sharing time with related horror movie clips. Campy nonsense. C: John Carradine, Elke Sommer. D: James Forsher. HOR 75m. ▼

Hollywood Harry 1986 ★★★½ Likable spoof about a detective who takes his troubled niece to work with him. Succeeds on a modest scale.

(a.k.a *Harry's Machine*) C: Robert Forster, Shannon Wilcox. D: Robert Forster. COM [PG-13] 99m. V

Hollywood High 1977 ★★½ Group of teens party it up in a faded Hollywood legend's odd mansion. C: Marcy Albrecht, Sherry Hardin. D: Patrick Wright. COM [R] 81m. V

Hollywood High, Part 2 ★★ Three young women try to find out why their boyfriends are suddenly ignoring them. C: April May, Donna Lynn, Camille Warner. D: Caruth C. Byrd. COM [R] 86m. V

Hollywood Hot Tubs 1984 ★★½ Teenager gets a job fixing hot tubs of alluring celebrities. C: Edy Williams, Donna McDaniel, Michael Andrew. D: Chuck Vincent. COM [R] 103m. V

Hollywood Hotel 1937 ★★★★ Terrific Busby Berkeley musical has numbers which rely more on cinematic wit and brilliant editing than trademark production values. Oh yes, the plot: Powell's a naive crooner who wins talent contest, sending him to Tinseltown. Hit song: "Hooray for Hollywood." Look for gossip queen Louella Parsons, playing herself. C: Dick Powell, Rosemary Lane, Lola Lane, Ted Healy, Frances Langford, Louella Parsons, Hugh Herbert, Glenda Farrell. D: Busby Berkeley. MUS 109m.

Hollywood in Trouble 1987 ★★½ Middle-aged shop owner tries to realize his dream of making a Hollywood movie and slips up along the way. C: Vic Vallaro, Jean Levine, Pamela Dixon. D: Joseph Merhi. DRA 90m. V

Hollywood Knights, The 1980 ★★★ *Animal House* rip-off focuses on the low-brow hijinks of a '60s high school gang, with an abundance of nudity and sophomoric gross-out jokes. Feature debuts for Pfeiffer and Danza. C: Tony Danza, Michelle Pfeiffer, Fran Drescher. D: Floyd Mutrux. COM [R] 95m.

Hollywood Man 1976 ★★★ His acting days over, man borrows money from the mob to make a film, and soon faces major confrontation with his benefactors. C: William Smith. ACT 90m. V

Hollywood on Trial 1979 ★★★★ House Committee on Un-American Activities' witch-hunts of '50s are the focus of a chilling documentary on the Red Menace. Intriguing footage has been rescued from vaults, giving a many-sided view of this dark period in U.S. history. C: John Huston. DOC 90m. V

Hollywood or Bust 1956 ★★★½ Film buff (Lewis) is desperate to go to Hollywood and meet Anita Ekberg. The belly laughs take a backseat to the musical numbers, and the story finishes a distant third. But this is Martin and Lewis' final movie together, so it's worth a look. C: Dean Martin, Jerry Lewis, Anita Ekberg, Pat Crowley. D: Frank Tashlin. COM 95m. V

Hollywood Party 1934 ★★★½ Thin plot of an actor throwing a lavish Hollywood bash serves as showcase for MGM's biggest and brightest. Some real gems here, including Laurel and Hardy's classic battle with Velez and Durante's song-and-dance specialty. C: Jimmy Durante, Stan Laurel, Oliver Hardy, Lupe Velez, Polly Moran. MUS 68m.

Hollywood Remembers—Gary Coopoer: American Life, American 1991 ★★★½ Clint Eastwood hosts this insightful portrait of "the Coop." DOC 46m. V

Hollywood Retrospectives—Fonda on Fonda ★★★½ Actress Jane Fonda takes us on a journey through her dad Henry Fonda's life and career. C: Henry Fonda. DOC 46m. V

Hollywood Revue of 1929, The 1929 ★★★★½ First of the all-star, no-plot, talkie revues that became very popular—a good one, at that. MGM has spared no expense in presenting their stars, with everything from Crawford doing the Charleston to Gilbert and Shearer in a scene from *Romeo and Juliet*. Introduced the songs "Singin" In the Rain" and "You Were Meant For Me." Rarely shown today. C: Jack Benny, John Gilbert, Norma Shearer, Joan Crawford, Stan Laurel, Oliver Hardy, Bessie Love, Lionel Barrymore, Marion Davies, Buster Keaton. D: Charles Riesner. MUS 130m.

Hollywood Salutes Canadian Animation ★★★★½ Wonderful, award-winning animated shorts including "The Sand Castle," "Neighbors," and "Every Child." COM 57m. V

Hollywood Shuffle 1987 ★★★½ Townsend parodies African-American Hollywood stereotypes in comic tale of one man's attempt to break into the movie business. Uneven but still quite funny and exactly right when it hits the mark; Townsend financed the film with cash advances from credit cards. C: Robert Townsend, Anne-Marie Johnson, Helen Martin. D: Robert Townsend. COM [R] 81m. V

Hollywood Story 1951 ★★★ To solve a 20-year-old murder, a nervy young producer makes a movie about it. Solid melodrama includes high-energy performance by Conte and convincing studio milieu. C: Richard Conte, Julia Adams, Richard Egan. D: William Castle. CRI 77m.

Hollywood Strangler 1982 ★★ Fashion photographer who murders his models meets his match in a woman who works in a magazine store. C: Pierre Agostino, Carolyn Brandt. D: Wolfgang Schmidt. HOR 72m. V

Hollywood Vice Squad 1986 ★ Police help woman find her runaway daughter, who's become a drug-addicted hooker. Unfunny premise for an unfunny movie. C: Trish Van Devere, Ronny Cox, Frank Gorshin, Carrie Fisher. D: Penelope Spheeris. COM [R] 108m. V

Hollywood Zap 1987 ★★½ A young southerner and a game room junkie try to take Tinseltown by storm. C: Ben Frank, Ivan E. Roth, De Waldron, Annie Gaybis. D: David Cohen. COM 85m. V

Hollywood's Children 1987 ★★★★ Former child star Roddy McDowell explores the fascinating and often painful careers of Tinseltown's kids, including interviews with Jackie

Coogan and Spanky McFarland. C: Roddy McDowall. DOC 60m. ▾

Hollywood's New Blood 1988 ★★½ Movie crew journeys from hell to torture youthful thespians. C: Bobby Johnson, Francine Lapense, Martie Allyne. D: James Shyman. HOR 90m. ▾

Holocaust 1978 ★★★★½ Controversial miniseries was accused of homogenizing Nazi atrocities; but stars do solid job of conveying the effects of humanity's greatest crime seen through the fate of one family. Often wrenching, with powerful performances by Streep and Woods. C: James Woods, Meryl Streep, David Warner, Joseph Bottoms, Rosemary Harris, Michael Moriarty, Fritz Weaver. D: Marvin J. Chomsky. DRA 450m. TVM ▾

Holocaust Survivors 1983 ★★★½ In Israel, at the 1981 World Gathering of Holocaust Survivors, a former concentration camp inmate seeks a reunion with the great love of his life. C: Kirk Douglas, Pam Dawber, Chana Eden. D: Jack Smight. DRA 96m. TVM ▾

Holocaust: 2000 1983 ★ The Antichrist (Ward) plans to blow up the world with the unwitting assistance of his father (Douglas), who happens to run a nuclear reactor. Dreadful. (a.k.a. *The Chosen*) C: Kirk Douglas, Simon Ward. D: Alberto De Martino. HOR [R] 101m. ▾

Holy Innocents 1984 Italian ★★★★★ Camus' novelistic account of a peasant family living in '60s Spain is a little-known, uplifting gem. Painterly camerawork, overlapping flashbacks, and a surrealist touch enhance the depiction of a cruel class structure; Landa and Rabal are tremendous. C: Alfredo Landa, Francisco Rabal. D: Mario Camus. DRA [PG] 108m. ▾

Holy Matrimony 1943 ★★★★ Publicity-shy artist (Woolley) returns to his native England to be knighted, and decides to entomb his recently deceased valet as himself in Westminster Abbey. Bright remake of *His Double Life* has wonderful performances. C: Monty Woolley, Gracie Fields, Laird Cregar, Una O'Connor, Franklin Pangborn. D: John M. Stahl. COM 87m.

Holy Terror 1977 *See* **Alice, Sweet Alice**

Hombre 1967 ★★★★ Stagecoach passengers besieged by outlaws are aided by a canny, Indian-bred white man. Literate, tight Western holds interest despite moralizing. From an Elmore Leonard story. C: Paul Newman, Fredric March, Richard Boone, Diane Cilento, Cameron Mitchell, Barbara Rush, Martin Balsam. D: Martin Ritt. WST 111m. ▾

Home Alone 1990 ★★★★ When his family goes to Paris for Christmas and eight-year-old Culkin is accidentally left home alone, he fends off two inept robbers (Pesci and Stern) while learning mysterious neighbor's secret. Culkin brilliantly carries almost all of this heartwarming and riotously funny film. C: Macaulay Culkin, Joe Pesci, Daniel Stern, John Heard, Catherine O'Hara. D: Chris Columbus. COM [PG] 110m. ▾

Home Alone 2: Lost in New York 1992 ★★★ Essentially a remake of first big hit finds Culkin again separated from his family at Christmas. This time he's in New York, running from Pesci and Stern, the bungling burglars of the first film. Has its moments, but not as funny as the original. C: Macaulay Culkin, Joe Pesci, Daniel Stern, Catherine O'Hara, John Heard, Tim Curry, Brenda Fricker, Eddie Bracken. D: Chris Columbus. COM [PG] 120m. ▾

Home and the World, The 1984 Indian ★★★★½ Exquisitely beautiful, gripping tale of a young Indian woman whose husband encourages her to be more liberated, with tragic consequences: She falls in love with her husband's best friend. Based on a novel by Rabindranath Tagore, Ray's film provides an intimate glimpse into life in Bengal at the turn of the century. C: Soumitra Chatterjee, Victor Banerjee, Swatilekha Chatterjee. D: Satyajit Ray. DRA 130m. ▾

Home at Seven 1953 British ★★★★ Clerk, suffering from temporary amnesia, can't prove he's innocent of murder he can't remember committing. Tingling mystery. C: Ralph Richardson, Margaret Leighton, Jack Hawkins. D: Ralph Richardson. CRI 85m.

Home Before Dark 1958 ★★★★ First person story of woman (Simmons) who must not only struggle to maintain her sanity after recovering from a mental breakdown, but contend with her unsympathetic family. Gray, wintry Massachusetts location adds to depressing atmosphere of moving story. C: Jean Simmons, Dan O'Herlihy, Rhonda Fleming. D: Mervyn LeRoy. DRA 136m.

Home Before Midnight 1984 ★★★ A man is arrested for statutory rape after his fourteen-year-old girlfriend's parents discover their romance. C: James Aubrey, Alison Elliot. D: Pete Walker. DRA 115m. ▾

Home Fires Burning 1989 ★★★★ Adapted from a novel by Robert Inman, this trim little jewel of a film offers a charming, evocative portrait of life in Georgia at the end of WWII. Marvelous Hughes; satisfying "feel." C: Barnard Hughes, Sada Thompson, Robert Prosky. D: Glenn Caron Jordan. DRA 100m. TVM

Home for Christmas 1990 ★★★½ Chilly affluent family rediscovers the Christmas spirit, thanks to an aging homeless man. Touching holiday fare. C: Mickey Rooney, Chantellese Kent. D: Peter McCubbin. FAM/DRA 96m. ▾

Home for the Holidays 1972 ★★★ Talented cast in modest little thriller set at Christmastime, with homicidal maniac on the loose at family reunion. C: Eleanor Parker, Sally Field, Jessica Walter, Julie Harris, Walter Brennan. D: John Llewwellyn Moxey. CRI 78m. TVM ▾

Home Free All 1983 ★★★½ A '60s radical searches for substance in the shallow '80s when he reunites with a former compatriot. Appealing, insightful comedy/drama compares two very different decades. C: Allan Nicholls, Roland Caccavo, Lorry Goldman. D: Stewart Bird. COM 92m. V

Home From the Hill 1960 ★★★½ Lengthy soap opera of Southerner Mitchum's troubles with immediate family and bastard son. Tame approach to florid story. C: Robert Mitchum, Eleanor Parker, George Peppard, George Hamilton. D: Vincente Minnelli. DRA 150m. V

Home Front 1987 *See* **Morgan Stewart's Coming Home**

Home in Indiana 1944 ★★★½ Unusual twist on standard horse racing story features a blind filly who makes good in the climactic race. Amiable family fare that horse fanatics will undoubtedly enjoy. C: Walter Brennan, Jeanne Crain, June Haver, Charlotte Greenwood. D: Henry Hathaway. FAM/ACT 103m.

Home in Oklahoma 1946 ★★★½ A small-town newspaper editor (Rogers) teams up with a hot-shot reporter (Evans) to solve the murder of a local rancher. Lots of good, clean fighting and singing, Western-style. C: Roy Rogers, Dale Evans, George "Gabby" Hayes. D: William Witney. WST 72m. V

Home Is the Hero 1959 Irish ★★★ Ex-con returns to family after term in prison and tries to put his life together. Low-key drama features performers from the celebrated Abbey Theatre. C: Walter Macken, Eileen Crowe, Arthur Kennedy. D: Fielder Cook. DRA 83m.

Home Is Where the Hart Is 1988 Canadian ★★ Wealthy 103-year-old man is kidnapped by nurse who wants to marry him, and his 70-year-old twin sons must rescue him. Off-the-wall farce. C: Valri Bromfield, Stephen E. Miller, Martin Mull, Leslie Nielsen. D: Rex Bromfield. COM [PG-13] 94m. V

Home Is Where the Heart Is 1987 *See* **Square Dance**

Home Movies 1979 ★★★½ Nerdy film student (Gordon) consults egomaniacal director (Douglas) on how to deal with life while simultaneously romancing his brother's girlfriend (Allen). Fitfully funny satire lacks focus. C: Keith Gordon, Nancy Allen, Kirk Douglas. D: Brian De Palma. COM [PG] 89m. V

Home of Our Own, A 1975 ★★★½ Based on the life of Father Wasson, inspiring story of an American priest who builds a nurturing home in Mexico for orphan boys. FAM/DRA 100m. V

Home of Our Own, A 1993 ★★★½ Unemployed L.A. mom relocates family to Idaho hamlet and struggles to keep brood together. C: Kathy Bates, Edward Furlong, Soon-Teck Oh. D: Tony Bill. DRA [PG] 90m. V

Home of the Brave 1949 ★★★★ Groundbreaking Hollywood exploration of racism among WWII fighting men (from Arthur Laurents' play) still seems potent for its time, with moving performances by Edwards as black GI and Bridges as his all-too-human buddy. C: James Edwards, Douglas Dick, Steve Brodie, Lloyd Bridges, Frank Lovejoy. D: Mark Robson. DRA 86m. V

Home of the Brave 1985 ★★★★ A fascinating concert film made by performance artist Anderson, who mixes her unconventional music with colorful visuals. Anderson's offbeat sense of humor will appeal to fans but might be offputting to others. C: Laurie Anderson, Adrian Belew, William S. Burroughs. D: Laurie Anderson. MUS 91m. V

Home Remedy 1988 ★★★ Amorous neighbor refuses to allow desperate suburban man to enjoy his much-desired solitude. C: Seth Barrish, Maxine Albert, Richard Kidney. D: Maggie Greenwald. COM 92m. V

Home Sweet Home 1914 ★★★½ The composer of "Home Sweet Home" portrayed in D.W. Griffith's silent melodrama. Life is difficult, but happiness comes via true love (Gish). Typically sentimental, but well told and acted. C: Lillian Gish, Robert Harron, Dorothy Gish. D: D. W. Griffith. DRA 76m.

Home, Sweet Homicide 1946 ★★★½ Thriller about children who solve a murder mystery *and* make a romantic match for their mother. A little comedy, a neatly dispatched whodunit; enjoy. C: Peggy Ann Garner, Randolph Scott, Lynn Bari, Dean Stockwell. D: Lloyd Bacon. CRI 90m.

Home to Stay 1978 ★★½ Spirited adolescent tries to prevent her aging grandfather (Fonda) from being placed in a nursing home. Satisfying adaptation of Janet Majerus' novel *Grandpa and Frank.* C: Henry Fonda, Michael McGuire. D: Delbert Mann. DRA 74m. V

Home Towners, The 1928 ★★★ When a rich man falls for a beautiful young woman half his age, he's told that she's only after his money. Intriguing early talkie. Remade as the 1940 *Ladies Must Live.* C: Richard Bennett, Doris Kenyon, Robert McWade. D: Bryan Foy. DRA 94m.

Homebodies 1974 ★★★★ To save their apartment building from the wrecking ball, senior citizens resort to murder. Well-written, well-acted black comedy makes its point. C: Frances Fuller, Ian Wolfe, Ruth McDevitt. D: Larry Yust. COM 96m. V

Homeboy 1989 ★★★½ Just as he is about to make it big, a dedicated boxer's career and life are put on the line by his unethical manager. C: Mickey Rourke, Christopher Walken, Debra Feuer. D: Michael Seresin. DRA [R] 158m. V

Homeboys 1992 ★ Low-budget exploitation film designed to capitalize on fears about gang violence pits two brothers against each other. Trashy. C: Todd Bridges, Ron Odriozola. CRI 91m. V

Homecoming—A Christmas Story, The 1971 ★★★★ A heartwarming family story that launched the popular TV series *The Waltons.* Neal is top-notch as Olivia Walton, loving wife and mother, raising her large brood during the Depression. C: Patricia Neal, Andrew Duggan, Richard Thomas, Edgar Bergen, Josephine

Hutchinson, Cleavon Little, Dorothy Stickney, Ellen Corby, Andrew Duggan. D: Fielder Cook. DRA 120m. TVM V

Homecoming, The 1973 ★★★★ Powerful drama about a long-estranged son (Jayston) who returns home with his wife (Merchant) to visit his father, uncle, and brothers. An excellent cast re-creates their stage roles in this faithful adaptation of Harold Pinter's play. C: Cyril Cusack, Vivien Merchant, Paul Rogers, Ian Holm, Michael Jayston, Terence Rigby. D: Peter Hall. DRA [PG] 111m.

Homecoming 1948 ★★½ Tedious Hollywood vehicle for glamourous stars Gable and Turner. Told mostly in flashbacks, it's about an arrogant doctor sent to battlefields of WWII who learns all about love and caring in arms of gallant army nurse. They've done better. C: Clark Gable, Lana Turner, Anne Baxter, John Hodiak, Cameron Mitchell. D: Mervyn LeRoy. DRA 113m. V

Homer 1970 ★★ An earnest teenager is caught up in drugs and war protests. Dated generation gap drama. C: Don Scardino, Alex Nicol, Tisa Farrow. D: John Trent. DRA 91m.

Homer & Eddie 1989 ★★★ Belushi and Goldberg in buddy film about retarded man and violence-prone escaped mental patient who hit the road together. No comedy in this grim offering, but stars play surprisingly well together. C: James Belushi, Whoopi Goldberg, Karen Black. D: Andrei Konchalovsky. DRA 100m. V

Homestretch, The 1947 ★★★ An obsessive racehorse enthusiast (Wilde) jeopardizes his marriage by spending far too much time at the track. Exciting location footage of Churchill Downs. C: Cornel Wilde, Maureen O'Hara, Glenn Langan. D: H. Humberstone. DRA 96m.

Hometown Boy Makes Good 1993 ★★★ Medical school dropout-turned-waiter keeps career moves secret and is mistakenly hailed as doctor-hero when he returns to his hometown. C: Anthony Edwards, Grace Zabriskie, Cynthia Bain. D: David Burton Morris. COM 90m. V

Hometown Story 1951 ★★½ A rejected politician blames his defeat on an innocent businessman. Routine drama, heavy-handed script. Small, early role for Monroe. C: Jeffrey Lynn, Donald Crisp, Marjorie Reynolds, Marilyn Monroe. D: Arthur Pierson. DRA 75m. V

Hometown U.S.A. 1979 ★ Not much happens as three teens drive around '50s L.A. in this slow, low-budget *American Graffiti* clone. C: Gary Springer, David Wilson, Brian Kerwin, Sally Kirkland. D: Max Baer. COM [R] 97m. V

Homeward Bound 1980 ★★★★ While spending the summer with his father on his grandfather's vineyard, a terminally ill teenager attempts to heal the rift that separates the three generations. Many emotionally effective moments, thanks to incisive script and fine performances. C: David Soul, Barnard Hughes. D: Richard Michaels. DRA 96m. TVM V

Homeward Bound: The Incredible Journey 1993 ★★★★ Trio of family pets are lost and set out to find their beloved family. Interesting twist on animal cross-country journey home idea features famed voices providing dialogue for live-action creatures. Good use of location and some nice action sequences. Remake of 1963 feature *The Incredible Journey.* Voices of Robert Hays, Kim Greist, Jean Smart, Michael J. Fox, Sally Field, Don Ameche. D: DuWayne Dunham. FAM/ACT [G] 84m. V

Homework 1982 ★★ A teenage boy has his sexual awakening in the arms of an older woman. Awkward sex comedy. C: Joan Collins, Michael Morgan, Wings Hauser, Carrie Snodgress. D: James Beshears. COM [R] 90m. V

Homewrecker 1992 ★★★ Genius unwittingly starts trouble when he invents a female computer that wants to pull the plug on her creator's wife. C: Robby Benson, Sydney Walsh, Kate Jackson. D: Fred Walton. SFI [PG-13] 88m. V

Homicidal 1961 ★★★½ Wacko imitation of *Psycho* is scary fun, with Arliss (a pseudonym for Joan Marshall) as a disturbed nurse who commits a murder and hides out at mansion inhabited by eccentric crew. Some plot twists are predictable, but it's entertaining, nonetheless. C: Jean Arliss, Patricia Breslin, Glenn Corbett, Eugenie Leontovitch. D: William Castle. HOR 87m.

Homicidal Impulse 1992 ★★★ Assistant D.A.'s girlfriend, the D.A.'s niece, kills her uncle to advance her boyfriend's career. C: Scott Valentine, Charles Napier, Vanessa Angel. D: David Tausik. CRI [R] 84m. V

Homicide 1991 ★★★½ Sly Jewish detective (Mantegna) is manipulated into solving an apparent hate crime, then recruited into a secret society of Jewish extremists—or is he? Director/writer Mamet creates crisp, realistic vision of police life, and Mantegna is first-rate. C: Joe Mantegna, W. H. Macy, Natalija Nogulich. D: David Mamet. CRI [R] 100m. V

Homicide Bureau 1939 ★★ No-nonsense cop (Cabot) investigates smalltown hoods. Crime movie includes tiny part for up-and-coming Hayworth. C: Bruce Cabot, Rita Hayworth, Robert Paige. D: C.C. Coleman, Jr. CRI 58m.

Hondo 1953 ★★★★½ Passing through Texas, a cavalry messenger (Wayne) encounters disheartened widow whom he tries to protect from an imminent Apache attack. Outstanding adult Western favors human drama over bloodshed. Page's Oscar-nominated debut. From a Louis L'Amour novel. Filmed in 3-D. C: John Wayne, Geraldine Page, Ward Bond, James Arness. D: John Farrow. WST 84m.

Honey 1981 Italian ★★ A writer (Spaak) forces an editor (Rey) to read her tawdry manuscript about the amorous adventures of the inhabitants of a raucous boardinghouse. Muddled story succeeds neither as soft porn nor art film. C: Clio Goldsmith, Catherine Spaak, Fernando Rey. D: Gianfranco Angelucci. DRA 89m. v

Honey, I Blew Up the Kid 1992 ★★★½ Follow-up to *Honey, I Shrunk the Kids* has scientist (Moranis) accidentally inducing a disastrous growth spurt in his youngest child. Routine special effects and lackluster story development make this sequel a lesser effort than the original, though younger children probably won't mind. C: Rick Moranis, Marcia Strassman, Robert Oliveri, Lloyd Bridges. D: Randal Kleiser. FAM/COM [PG] 89m. v

Honey, I Shrunk the Kids 1989 ★★★★ Moranis is an absentminded scientist who accidentally miniaturizes his children, then desperately tries to get them back to normal. Story takes second place to wonderful special effects as tiny kids battle honeybees and breakfast cereals. Great film for the entire family. C: Rick Moranis, Matt Frewer, Marcia Strassman, Kristine Sutherland. D: Joe Johnston. FAM/COM [PG] 101m. v

Honey Pot, The 1967 ★★★½ A rich misanthrope toys with three former lovers by pretending to be dying, but has the tables turned on him when one of the women ends up really dead. This variation of Ben Jonson's *Volpone* can't decide whether to be a bedroom farce or a murder mystery. Excellent cast. C: Rex Harrison, Cliff Robertson, Maggie Smith, Susan Hayward, Capucine, Edie Adams. D: Joseph L. Mankiewicz. COM 131m. v

Honeybaby 1974 ★★★ Beautiful interpreter (Sands) and urbane adventurer (Lockhart) team up to rescue a politician captured by Mid-East terrorists. Okay black exploitation thriller. C: Calvin Lockhart, Diana Sands. D: Michael Schultz. ACT [PG] 94m. v

Honeyboy 1982 ★★½ Drama follows career struggles of a young boxer (Estrada). Visceral fight footage highlights familiar story. C: Erik Estrada, Morgan Fairchild. D: John Berry. DRA 96m. TVM v

Honeychile 1951 ★★½ Hayseed country woman (Canova) composes a catchy tune, only to see it stolen by unscrupulous music publisher. Usual corn, zany Canova. C: Judy Canova, Eddie Foy, Jr. D: R. Springsteen. COM 90m.

Honeymoon 1947 ★★★ Impulsive 18-year-old (Temple) elopes to Mexico City to marry her corporal fiancé (Madison); when she can't find him, she enlists an American diplomat (Tone) to help. Too cute. (a.k.a. *Two Men and a Girl*) C: Shirley Temple, Franchot Tone, Guy Madison. D: William Keighley. MUS 74m.

Honeymoon 1959 Spanish ★★★ An ex-ballet dancer on her honeymoon is courted by another man. Confused plot and cardboard characters make the dancing the most worthwhile feature. Includes scenes from the fiery ballet, *El Amor Brujo*. C: Anthony Steel, Ludmilla Tcherina. D: Michael Powell. MUS 90m.

Honeymoon Academy 1990 ★★ Slight story about a secret agent (Cattrall) whose new husband has no idea about her career until their action-packed honeymoon. Light comedy. C: Kim Cattrall, Robert Hays, Leigh Taylor-Young. D: Gene Quintano. COM [PG-13] 94m. v

Honeymoon for Three 1941 ★★★ Novelist (Brent) is protected from his female fans by his secretary (Sheridan) who has marriage on her mind. Amusing version of Alan Scott and Georgia Haight's play *Goodbye Again*. C: Ann Sheridan, George Brent, Charlie Ruggles, Jane Wyman. D: Lloyd Bacon. COM 77m.

Honeymoon Hotel 1964 ★★½ Mistaken identities and misunderstandings abound when two bachelors check into a hotel meant for honeymooners. Weak bedroom farce. C: Robert Goulet, Jill St. John, Nancy Kwan, Robert Morse, Elsa Lanchester, Keenan Wynn. D: Henry Levin. COM 89m.

Honeymoon in Bali 1939 ★★★½ A department store manager (Carroll) who doesn't want to marry is pursued by two suitors (MacMurray and Jones) who want to change her mind. Breezy performances move comedy along. (a.k.a. *My Love for Yours*) C: Fred MacMurray, Madeleine Carroll, Allan Jones, Helen Broderick, Akim Tamiroff. D: Edward Griffith. COM 95m. v

Honeymoon in Vegas 1992 ★★★★ Cage is a P.I. who brings lover Parker to Las Vegas to marry her, then loses her to Caan in a poker game. Lots of laughs despite distasteful premise—and Elvis is everywhere. C: James Caan, Nicolas Cage, Sarah Jessica Parker, Pat Morita. D: Andrew Bergman. COM [PG-13] 95m. v

Honeymoon Killers, The 1970 ★★★★ True-crime movie about a gigolo and his overweight sidekick, who romance lonely women and spirit away their savings before murdering them in a variety of terrible ways. This independent picture takes an unswerving look at evil. Filmed in black and white. (a.k.a. *The Lonely Hearts Killers*) C: Shirley Stoler, Tony LoBianco, Mary Jane Higby. D: Leonard Kastle. CRI [R] 103m. v

Honeymoon Machine, The 1961 ★★★½ Likable comedy about a scheming battleship crew using ship's missile-tracking computer to pick winning roulette numbers at a European casino. Energetic cast keeps it light. C: Steve McQueen, Jim Hutton, Paula Prentiss. D: Richard Thorpe. COM 87m. v

Honeymoon Merry-Go-Round 1939 British ★★★½ Honeymooning couple split after first marital spat. The groom is then mistaken for a hockey star and helps lead British team to Olympic victory, winning his bride back in the process. Cute romantic trifle. (a.k.a. *Olympic Honeymoon*) C: Claude Hulbert, Monty Banks, Princess Pearl, Sally Gray. D: Alfred Goulding. DRA 63m.

Honeymoon with a Stranger 1969 ★★★½ A newlywed (Leigh) wakes up to find her husband has disappeared and a stranger has taken his place. Mystery benefits from exotic

Spanish locales. C: Janet Leigh, Rossano Brazzi, Cesare Danova, Barbara Steele. D: John Peyser. DRA 88m. TVM

Honeysuckle Rose 1980 ★★★½ Country music star Nelson finds true love with daughter (Irving) of partner, who objects. Small but charming tale, which will appeal in direct proportion to one's love for country music. (a.k.a. *On The Road Again*) C: Willie Nelson, Dyan Cannon, Amy Irving, Slim Pickens. D: Jerry Schatzberg. MUS [PG] 120m. V

Hong Kong 1951 ★★½ A thief plots to steal a gold treasure from a Chinese orphan girl. Standard heist drama. C: Ronald Reagan, Rhonda Fleming, Nigel Bruce. D: Lewis Foster. CRI 92m.

Hong Kong Affair 1958 ★★½ A visiting American (Kelly) becomes involved with murder and intrigue. Strictly by-the-numbers thriller. C: Jack Kelly, May Wynn, Richard Loo. D: Paul Heard. ACT 79m.

Hong Kong Confidential 1958 ★★★½ American agents in Hong Kong track down a gang responsible for kidnapping an Arabian prince. Solid B-movie crime drama benefits from fast pacing and sympathetic characters. C: Gene Barry, Beverly Tyler, Allison Hayes. D: Edward Cahn. DRA 67m.

Hong Kong Nights 1935 ★★★ A team of special agents cracks down on a powerful Chinese smuggling ring. Rousing action all along the way. C: Tom Keene, Wera Engels, Warren Hymer. D: E. Mason Hopper. ACT 59m.

Honkers, The 1972 ★★★ Egocentric, middle-aged rodeo cowpoke prefers easy women and bucking bulls to domestic life. The modern rodeo circuit is well realized. C: James Coburn, Lois Nettleton, Slim Pickens, Anne Archer. D: Steve Ihnat. WST [PG] 102m.

Honky 1971 ★★★½ Dated story on an interracial high school romance between a black woman (Sykes) and white guy (Nielson). This deliberately modest film handles their problems soberly, but the ending is violent. C: Brenda Sykes, John Nielson, William Marshall, Maia Danziger. D: William Graham. DRA [R] 92m. V

Honky Tonk 1941 ★★★½ On-the-lam gambler Gable meets straight-arrow Turner and her shyster father on a train headed West. Romantic comic Western entertains mainly because of stars' chemistry. Remade for television in 1974. C: Clark Gable, Lana Turner, Frank Morgan, Claire Trevor, Marjorie Main. D: Jack Conway. ACT 105m. V

Honky Tonk 1974 ★★★½ Western romance of suave gambler (Crenna) trying to choose between saloon gal and proper Boston lady. Not up to 1941 original, but engaging nonetheless. C: Richard Crenna, Stella Stevens, Margot Kidder, Will Geer. D: Don Taylor. WST 90m. TVM

Honky Tonk Freeway 1981 ★★½ Mishmash of characters converge in a forgettable comedy about a Florida town's desperate attempts to boost tourism. Slipshod storytelling rarely hits. C: William Devane, Beverly D'Angelo, Beau Bridges, Jessica Tandy, Hume Cronyn, Geraldine Page, Teri Garr. D: John Schlesinger. COM [PG] 107m. V

Honkytonk Man 1982 ★★★ One of director Eastwood's first kinder-and-gentler films tells of an aging country-western artist's swan song, as the alcoholic singer hits the road with his young nephew (Eastwood's son Kyle). Cameos by country-western greats (including Marty Robbins) can't help dull story. C: Clint Eastwood, Kyle Eastwood, John McIntire, Alexa Kenin. D: Clint Eastwood. DRA [PG] 122m. V

Honolulu 1939 ★★★½ Young gets double role of film star and pineapple grower, but film is Powell's, who taps up a storm, even while jumping rope! Plot is numbing, but dance and musical numbers make it enjoyable. C: Eleanor Powell, Robert Young, George Burns, Gracie Allen, Rita Johnson, Sig Ruman, Ruth Hussey. D: Edward Buzzell. MUS 83m. V

Honor Among Thieves 1968 *See* **Farewell Friend**

Honor Among Thieves 1982 ★★★ A mismatched pair try to pull off crime together. Somewhat sluggish. C: Charles Bronson, Alain Delon, Olga Georges-Picot. D: Jean Herman. CRI 93m. V

Honor and Glory 1992 ★★½ A female FBI agent and a spy posing as a TV anchorwoman foil a power-hungry businessman eager to get his hands on nuclear weapons. Predictable martial arts actioner with energetic female protagonists. C: Cynthia Rothrock, Donna Jason, Chuck Jeffreys, Gerald Klein. D: Godfrey Hall. ACT [R] 90m. V

Honor Thy Father 1973 ★★★½ Life on the inside of the Mob, based on Gay Talese book about the life of Joseph Bonanno and his son. TV presentation needs less restrictive development. Merely adequate. C: Joseph Bologna, Raf Vallone, Brenda Vaccaro, Richard Castellano. D: Paul Wendkos. CRI 97m. TVM V

Honor Thy Father and Mother: The True Story of the Menendez Murders 1994 ★★★½ Dramatization of controversial L.A. murder case in which two sons killed their allegedly abusive parents. Surprisingly well-done, but sleazy nevertheless. C: James Farentino, Jill Clayburgh, Billy Warlock, David Beron. D: Paul Schneider. CRI 120m. TVM V

Hooch 1976 ★★★ New York and southern sensibilities collide as gangster tries to get a piece of moonshine action. C: Gil Gerard. D: Edward Mann. CRI [PG] 96m. V

Hooded Terror, The 1938 ★★★ Violent murderers go after earnest government agent. C: Tod Slaughter, George Cuzon, Greta Gynt. D: George King. CRI 70m. V

Hoodlum Empire 1952 ★★★ A young man finds it rough going when he decides not to join the family crime business after being discharged from the military. Distinguished crime drama loosely based on real story. C: Brian Donlevy, Claire Trevor, Forrest Tucker, Vera Ralston. D: Joseph Kane. CRI 98m. V

Hoodlum Priest, The 1961 ★★★★ Murray (who also co-wrote and produced) is clergyman who devotes himself to troubled youth, taking young Dullea under his wing. True story told with conviction. C: Don Murray, Larry Gates, Keir Dullea. D: Irvin Kershner. DRA 101m. V

Hoodlum Saint, The 1946 ★★★ Not even sophisticated Powell can hold together this ho-hum story about con artists running a charity scam. It loses steam when Powell starts developing integrity. C: William Powell, Esther Williams, Angela Lansbury, James Gleason, Lewis Stone. D: Norman Taurog. DRA 91m.

Hoodlum, The 1951 ★★½ A reformed hood finds himself tempted by armored car heist. Decent gangster drama. C: Lawrence Tierney, Allene Roberts. D: Max Nosseck. CRI 61m.

Hoodwink 1981 Australian ★★★★ Based on a true case from Australian crime annals, this prison story revolves around a con game played by a criminal who fakes blindness in hopes of receiving a lighter sentence. Different and intriguing tale that's well told. C: John Hargreaves, Judy Davis, Dennis Miller. D: Claud Whatham. CRI 99m.

Hook 1991 ★★★ Spielberg's big-budget fantasy about adult Peter Pan (Williams) rescuing his own children after their kidnapping by evil Captain Hook (Hoffman). Not much beyond over obvious emotional scenes and showy set pieces. May be too violent for youngest viewers. Tinkerbell Roberts looks as if she's in a different film. C: Dustin Hoffman, Robin Williams, Julia Roberts, Bob Hoskins, Maggie Smith, Charlie Korsmo. D: Steven Spielberg. COM [PG] 142m. V

Hook, Line & Sinker 1969 ★★ When he learns he has only months to live, Lewis runs up a huge credit card debt in a final blowout—then discovers he's not dying after all. Not funny. C: Jerry Lewis, Peter Lawford, Anne Francis. D: George Marshall. COM [G] 91m.

Hook, The 1963 ★★★★ U.S. soldiers fleeing Korea hesitate to carry out the execution of a POW. Discerning examination of wartime moral dilemma. C: Kirk Douglas, Robert Walker, Jr., Nick Adams, Nehemiah Persoff. D: George Seaton. DRA 98m.

Hooked Generation 1969 ★ Murderous drug smugglers kidnap police informers and take them to hideout in the Everglades. C: Jeremy Slate, Willie Pastrano, Steve Alaimo, Socrates Ballis. D: William Grefe. ACT [R] 92m. V

Hooker Cult Murders, The *See* **Pyx, The**

Hooligans, The 1959 ★★★★ Bullfighting is the impossible dream of Spanish youngsters desperate to escape slums. Saura's first film is an accurate and compelling slice of run-down lives, shot on actual locations with an all-amateur cast. C: Manuel Zarzo, Luis Marin, Oscar Cruz. D: Carlos Saura. DRA 90m.

Hoop Dreams 1994 ★★★★★ Brilliant documentary covers five years in the lives of two black Chicago teenagers, both trying to use basketball as a means to escape poverty. Packs a punch as their dreams change, grow, and crumble with the passage of time. Those usually put off by non-fiction films should not deprive themselves the pleasure of seeing this. C: William Gates, Arthur Agee, Sheila Agee, Emma Gates, Gene Pingatore, Isiah Thomas, Spike Lee. D: Steve James. DOC [PG-13] 171m. V

Hooper 1978 ★★★½ Master stuntman (Reynolds) is not ready to be replaced by young upstart (Vincent). Backstage look at movies fills the screen with stunts, and some are clever. The cast seems to be enjoying itself. C: Burt Reynolds, Sally Field, Jan-Michael Vincent, Brian Keith. D: Hal Needham. DRA [PG] 100m. V

Hooray for Love 1935 ★★★★ A young college graduate produces a Broadway musical. Charming story is sparked by the creative artistry of greats like Robinson and Waller. C: Ann Sothern, Gene Raymond, Bill Robinson, Pert Kelton, Fats Waller. D: Walter Lang. MUS 72m.

Hoosier Schoolboy 1937 ★★½ Poor country boy (Rooney) is shown how to rise above his surroundings by kindly schoolteacher (Nagel). Simplistic inspirational tale. C: Mickey Rooney, Anne Nagel, Frank Shields. D: William Nigh. DRA 62m.

Hoosiers 1987 ★★★★ Indiana high school basketball team triumphs in classic underdog story based on real-life incident. Hackman is coach who turns boys into disciplined players; Hopper, as alcoholic father of one of the players, turned in an Oscar-nominated performance. C: Gene Hackman, Barbara Hershey, Dennis Hopper. D: David Anspaugh. DRA [PG] 115m. V

Hootch County Boys, The 1975 ★★½ Backwoods gangsters set the law on wild chase. C: Robert Ridgely, Alex Karras, Dean Jagger. D: Harry Z. Thomason. COM [PG] 90m. V

Hootenanny Hoot 1963 ★★★ Wispy story line about college kids mounting TV show is good enough excuse to offer performances by Johnny Cash, The Brothers Four, and others. Quickly made folk music comedy. C: Peter Breck, Joby Baker, Ruta Lee, Johnny Cash. D: Gene Nelson. MUS 91m.

Hoots Mon! 1939 British ★★★ A London comic gets into a popularity contest with a Scottish female impersonator. Several genuinely funny bits, including real-life variety acts of the time. C: Max Miller, Florence Desmond, Hal Walters. D: Roy William Neill. COM 77m.

Hoover vs. the Kennedys: The Second Civil War 1987 ★★ Historical drama focuses on power struggles between J. Edgar Hoover and JFK and Bobby Kennedy. Uneven, miscast and uninformative exposé was shown on television in two parts. C: Jack Warden,

Nicholas Campbell. D: Michael O'Herlihy. DRA 200m. TVM

Hopalong Cassidy 1935 ★★★½ Clarence E. Mulford's popular genteel cowboy brings six-gun justice to the West in this amiable series opener featuring a white-haired Boyd dressed in black and mounted on his horse, Topper. C: William Boyd, James Ellison, Paula Stone. D: Howard Bretherton. WST 60m.

Hopalong Cassidy Returns 1936 ★★★ The famous cordial cowboy falls for a dance-hall owner in his ongoing struggle against outlaws and rustlers. Good, though relatively violent. C: William Boyd, George "Gabby" Hayes, Gail Sheridan. D: Nat Watt. WST 71m.

Hopalong Cassidy Rides Again 1937 ★★½ Hoppy, dressed in his usual sharp black outfit, goes on a cattle drive and winds up chasing a new bad guy. Lots of solid action for Western lovers. C: William Boyd, George "Gabby" Hayes, Lois Wilde. D: Les Selander. WST 65m.

Hope and Glory 1987 British ★★★★½ Director's autobiographical look at how WWII bombing of London affects a schoolboy and his family. Both comic and touching; Boorman spares not even the smallest detail in his re-creation of '40s England during the Blitz. C: Sarah Miles, David Hayman, Derrick O'Connor, Sammi Davis, Ian Bannen. D: John Boorman. COM [PG-13] 113m. V

Hoppity Goes to Town 1941 ★★★½ Animated feature set in a community of insects, follows their lives as they deal with the threat posed by humans. Pleasant, vividly detailed bug's-eye view of city life. (a.k.a. *Mr. Bug Goes to Town*) D: Dave Fleischer. FAM/DRA 84m. V

Hoppy Serves a Writ 1943 ★★★½ Hopalong Cassidy goes after bunch of toughs at the Texas border. Features youthful Robert Mitchum. C: William Boyd, Andy Clyde, Robert Mitchum, George Reeves. D: George Archainbaud. WST 67m. V

Hoppy's Holiday 1947 ★★★ In Mesa City, Hopalong and California both find themselves in hot water. C: William Boyd, Andy Clyde, Rand Brooks. D: George Archainbaud. WST 60m. V

Hopscotch 1980 ★★★★ A one-time CIA agent (Matthau) revenges himself on his not-so-bright boss by writing a tell-all memoir; the latter responds by desperately trying to squelch its publication. Hilarious, intelligent chase comedy, a fine showcase for the Matthau/Jackson chemistry. C: Walter Matthau, Glenda Jackson, Sam Waterston, Ned Beatty. D: Ronald Neame. COM [R] 102m. V

Horizons West 1952 ★★★ A ruthless rancher clashes with his law officer brother who must bring him to justice. Exaggerated, post-Civil war yarn with plenty of action. C: Robert Ryan, Julia Adams, Rock Hudson, Raymond Burr, James Arness. D: Budd Boetticher. WST 81m.

Horizontal Lieutenant, The 1961 ★★★½ WWII military shenanigans with Hutton as a bumbling Army intelligence officer. Passable service comedy is helped by likable cast. C: Jim Hutton, Paula Prentiss, Miyoshi Umeki, Jim Backus. D: Richard Thorpe. COM 90m. V

Horn Blows at Midnight, The 1945 ★★★½ Amusing comedy/fantasy about angel (Benny) sent down from heaven to destroy Earth with Gabriel's trumpet. Benny used this movie as a running gag, blaming it for end of his film career, but it's not that bad. C: Jack Benny, Alexis Smith, Reginald Gardiner, Guy Kibbee, Margaret Dumont, Franklin Pangborn. D: Raoul Walsh. COM 78m. V

Hornet's Nest 1970 ★★★ Can Hudson and his crew pull off a daring sabotage mission behind enemy lines? Average WWII actioner with a dollop of romance. C: Rock Hudson, Sylva Koscina, Sergio Fantoni. D: Phil Karlson. ACT [PG] 110m. V

Horrible Dr. Hichcock, The 1962 Italian ★★★★ Impressive horror film, dripping with atmosphere and strong sequences. A perverse doctor (Flemyng), who accidentally killed his wife during kinky sex, attempts to restore her years later with new spouse's blood. Also available in lengthier version, *Terror of Dr. Hichcock*, containing more sexual material. Sequel: *The Ghost*. C: Robert Flemyng, Barbara Steele. D: Robert Hampton. HOR 76m. V

Horror at 37,000 Feet 1972 ★★ A group of transatlantic airline passengers are menaced by ancient evil spirits. Begins well, then self-destructs. C: William Shatner, Roy Thinnes, Buddy Ebsen, Tammy Grimes. D: David Rich. HOR 73m. TVM

Horror Chamber of Dr. Faustus, The 1959 French ★★★★ Obsessed plastic surgeon resorts to murder in attempt to graft new face onto his daughter who's been disfigured in car crash. Truly eerie horror drama, graced with breathtaking visual touches. (a.k.a. *Eyes Without a Face* and *Les Yeux sans Visage*) C: Pierre Brasseur, Alida Valli. D: Georges Franju. HOR 88m.

Horror Convention 1976 *See* **Nightmare in Blood**

Horror Express 1972 Spanish ★★★ Cast of genre pros and several genuinely frightening moments propel this horror film. An ancient beast, frozen in ice, thaws out and runs rampant on the Trans-Siberian Railway. C: Christopher Lee, Peter Cushing, Telly Savalas. D: Eugenio Martin. HOR [R] 87m. V

Horror Hospital 1973 British ★★ Morbid, horror/comedy with deformed, demented doctor using clinic as front for his horrific mind-control experiments. Sick tongue-in-cheek humor, not for the squeamish. (a.k.a. *Computer Killers*) C: Michael Gough, Robin Askwith. D: Anthony Balch. COM 91m. V

Horror Hotel 1960 British ★★★½ History

student goes to remote Massachusetts village to research witchcraft for thesis with harrowing results. Very effective use of b&w photography, lighting and shadows, combined with above-average musical score and script. C: Dennis Lotis, Christopher Lee, Betta John. D: John Llewellyn Moxey. HOR [R] 76m. v

Horror Hotel 1976 *See* **Eaten Alive**

Horror House 1969 British ★★ Friends staying in an old mansion are menaced by knife-wielding maniac. Plenty of violence. C: Frankie Avalon, Jill Haworth, Dennis Price. D: Michael Armstrong. HOR [PG] 79m.

Horror Island 1941 ★★★½ Assorted characters search for buried treasure on a fog-shrouded island, and are murdered one by one. Swiftly paced and engaging B-grade thriller. C: Dick Foran, Leo Carrillo, Peggy Moran. D: George Waggner. HOR 60m.

Horror Maniacs 1948 *See* **Greed of William Hart, The**

Horror of Dracula 1957 British ★★★★ Fine retelling of classic Bram Stoker vampire tale, the first and best in the Hammer film series. Lee makes a fiery and ferocious Count Dracula, and Cushing matches his intensity as the indefatigable Van Helsing. Excellent effects and thrilling music score complement this gruesomely fine production. (a.k.a. *Dracula*) C: Peter Cushing, Christopher Lee, Melissa Stribling. D: Terence Fisher. HOR 82m. v

Horror of Frankenstein, The 1970 British ★★★★ A hot-blooded young Baron Frankenstein (Bates) pieces together his ghastly creation—but his gift of life turns into a nightmare. Polished Hammer production features weightlifter Dave Prowse (who later played Darth Vader) as an impressive monster. C: Ralph Bates, Kate O'Mara. D: Jimmy Sangster. HOR [R] 93m. v

Horror of It All, The 1987 ★★★★ Jose Ferrer hosts this excellent compilation of cinema's most terrifying moments, filled with clips and interviews. HOR 60m. v

Horror of Party Beach, The 1964 ★★ Watch out for that ocean dumping—it may come to life and spoil a rockin' beach party. Campy low-budget film that's low on fright, long on laughs. C: John Scott, Alice Lyon, Allen Laurel. D: Del Tenney. HOR 71m. v

Horror Planet 1982 British ★ A female space explorer is attacked by a slimy alien and gives birth to a slimy offspring. Fine cast gets slimed. C: Robin Clark, Jennifer Ashley, Stephanie Beacham. D: Norman J. Warren. SFI [R] 93m. v

Horror Show, The 1989 ★★½ Executed serial killer (James) wages a supernatural reign of terror against cop (Henriksen) and his family. The two leads bring conviction to this grisly story. (a.k.a. *House III*) C: Lance Henriksen, Brion James, Rita Taggart. D: James Isaac. HOR [R] 95m. v

Horrors of the Black Museum 1959 British ★★★½ A crime writer turns to murder in order to spice up his imagination. Gruesome, lurid thriller features classic eyeball-gouging binoculars scene. C: Michael Gough, June Cunningham. D: Arthur Crabtree. HOR 95m.

Horrors of the Red Planet 1965 ★★½ Oz-like epic with astronauts encountering scary aliens and wizard who presides over Mars. C: John Carradine, Roger Gentry, Eve Bernhardt. D: David L. Hewitt. SFI 81m. v

Horse Feathers 1932 ★★★★½ The hallowed halls of Huxley College resound with laughter when the Marx Brothers take over the campus and Dean Groucho uses every means possible to create a winning football team. Superior Marx Brothers hilarity. C: Groucho Marx, Harpo Marx, Chico Marx, Zeppo Marx, Thelma Todd. D: Norman McLeod. COM 68m. v

Horse in the Gray Flannel Suit, The 1968 ★★★½ Ad man (Jones) tries to sell stomach ache remedies while attempting to win his daughter's love via a horse. Cute Disney fare, typical for the studio at that time. Youngsters should enjoy. C: Dean Jones, Diane Baker, Fred Clark, Kurt Russell. D: Norman Tokar. FAM/COM [G] 114m. v

Horse Named Comanche, A 1958 ★★★½ Young indian brave (Mineo) develops a strong attachment to a wild stallion, and tries to claim the horse as his own. Effective Disney adventure with good emotional confrontations. (a.k.a. *Tonka*). C: Sal Mineo, Phil Carey. D: Lewis R. Foster. WST 97m. v

Horse of Pride, The 1980 French ★★★ A turn-of-the-century Breton village from a young boy's point of view. Details of day-to-day peasant life are shown, but the plot is very thin and the story wanders and is finally lost. C: Jacques Dufilho, Bernadette Lesache. D: Claude Chabrol. DRA 118m.

Horse Soldiers, The 1959 ★★★½ John Ford's two-fisted Civil War action film about Yankee cavalrymen behind Rebel lines on a mission to blow up a rail station. Strong leads highlight rugged Western; based on fact. C: John Wayne, William Holden, Constance Towers. D: John Ford. WST 119m. v

Horse, The 1982 Turkish ★★★★ Bitterly realistic film follows the travails of an impoverished father and son on a journey to Istanbul to find employment to pay for the boy's education. D: Ali Ozgenturk. DRA 116m.

Horse Thief, The 1987 Chinese ★★★★ A convicted horse thief and his family struggle to survive as they wander the countryside in search of work. Emotionally affecting period drama, beautifully photographed in Tibet. Subtitled. D: Tian Zhuangzhuang. DRA 88m.

Horse Without a Head, The 1963 ★★★½ Entertaining kiddie caper film about two children who get mixed up with some crooks who've hidden stolen loot in a toy horse. Nice mix of humor and suspense. Fine film for family viewing. C: Leo McKern, Jean-Pierre Aumont, Herbert Lom, Pamela Franklin. D: Don Chaffey. FAM/ACT 89m. v

Horsemasters, The 1961 ★★★½ Funicello is studying horse riding at exclusive European school, where she must learn to get over her fear of toppling during tricky jumps. Standard Disney clichés told in routine fashion, but still good for younger audiences. C: Annette Funicello, Janet Munro, Tommy Kirk, Donald Pleasence. D: William Fairchild. FAM/DRA 85m. v

Horsemen, The 1971 ★★ An Afghanistanian man (Sharif) competes with his father at horsemanship for respect and prestige. May be interesting to polo fans. C: Omar Sharif, Leigh Taylor-Young, Jack Palance. D: John Frankenheimer. DRA [PG] 109m. v

Horseplayer, The 1991 ★★ Painter uses his sister to lure subjects to pose for his paintings. Bizarre yarn. C: Brad Dourif, Sammi Davis. D: Kurt Voss. CRI [R] 89m. v

Horse's Mouth, The 1958 British ★★★★½ Guinness gives tour-de-force performance as crackpot artist who thinks world owes him a living. Slyly satirical script (by star) based on Joyce Cary's novel. Intelligent entertainment. C: Alec Guinness, Kay Walsh, Renee Houston, Mike Morgan. D: Ronald Neame. COM 93m. v

Hospital, The 1971 ★★★★½ Satirical and ultimately fascinating behind-the-scenes look at big city hospital as top doctor Scott tries to overcome depression while coping with bizarre events going on within hospital corridors. Documentary camera style provides disturbingly realistic edge. Oscar to Paddy Chayefsky for screenplay. C: George C. Scott, Diana Rigg, Barnard Hughes, Nancy Marchand, Richard Dysart. D: Arthur Hiller. COM [PG] 103m. v

Hostage 1987 ★★★ It's turn-the-tables time as a planeload of kidnapped passengers revolt against their Arab hijackers. Undistinguished action piece, with good work by vets Hauser and Black. C: Wings Hauser, Karen Black, Kevin McCarthy. D: Hanro Mohr. ACT [R] 94m. v

Hostage 1988 ★★★ A forlorn widow (Burnett) is abducted by teenaged kidnapper. Co-star Hamilton is Burnett's real-life daughter. C: Carol Burnett, Carrie Hamilton, Annette Bening. D: Peter Levin. CRI 100m. TVM

Hostage 1992 ★★★ Aging spy (Neill) wishes his days of dodging bullets and defusing bombs could go on forever. Okay James Bond clone with charming Neill. C: Sam Neill, Talisa Soto, James Fox. D: Robert Young. ACT [R] 100m. TVM v

Hostage: Dallas 1986 *See* **Getting Even**

Hostage Flight 1985 ★★★ Four terrorists skyjack a jetliner and the passengers fight back. Average thriller. C: Ned Beatty, Barbara Bosson, Rene Enriquez. D: Steven Stern. ACT 100m. TVM

Hostage, The 1966 ★★★½ Young boy witnesses a murder before being accidently locked into a moving van driven by the perpetrators. Nifty low-budget thriller, good performances. C: Dan O'Kelly, Harry Dean Stanton, Danny Martins, John Carradine. D: Russell Doughton, Sr. CRI 84m. v

Hostage Tower, The 1980 ★ One of Interpol's most wanted recruits his cronies for an ambitious plot to garner millions in ransom, but finds that no one can be trusted. Decent ensemble cast tries to save film with a comic book plot. C: Peter Fonda, Billy Dee Williams, Keir Dullea, Douglas Fairbanks, Jr., Rachel Roberts, Celia Johnson. D: Claudio Guzman. ACT 105m. TVM v

Hostages 1943 ★★ Paint-by-number drama about the WWII underground has so many brave people doing so many brave things you wonder why the Nazis took so long to lose. C: Luise Rainer, William Bendix, Oscar Homolka, Katina Paxinou, Paul Lukas. D: Frank Tuttle. DRA 88m.

Hostile Guns 1967 ★★★ A federal marshal must hand over a wagonload of criminals to prison authorities. Standard Western fare with familiar cast. C: George Montgomery, Yvonne De Carlo, Tab Hunter. D: R. G. Springsteen. WST 91m. v

Hostile Takeover 1989 ★★★ Meek accountant flips out, holds colleagues hostage, and goes head-to-head with the law. C: David Warner, Michael Ironside, Kate Vernon. D: George Mihalka. ACT [R] 93m. v

Hot Blood 1956 ★★★ The on-again, off-again romance of Gypsies from fighting factions (Russell and Wilde). Quite entertaining, and the dancing and costumes heighten the spectacle. C: Jane Russell, Cornel Wilde, Luther Adler. D: Nicholas Ray. MUS 85m.

Hot Box, The 1972 ★★ Routine look into the inner workings of a women's high security prison. Predictable story line includes gratuitous nudity and offensive language. C: Margaret Markov, Andrea Cagan, Ricky Richardson. D: Joe Viola. ACT [R] 85m. v

Hot Child in the City 1987 ★★★ Young farm woman seeks to avenge her sister's grisly murder in Los Angeles. C: Leah Ayres Hendrix, Shari Shattuck, Geof Prysirr. D: John Florea. CRI 85m. v

Hot Dog . . . The Movie 1984 ★★½ Lame teen comedy about partying goof-offs rallying for the big ski competition. Bits of awesome slope action sandwiched between unfunny, gross humor and raunchiness. C: David Naughton, Patrick Houser. D: Peter Markle. COM [R] 96m. v

Hot Enough for June 1965 *See* **Agent 8 3/4**

Hot Hours 1963 French ★★★ After being stood up at the altar, a woman and her sister go on a therapeutic vacation. The sister tries to romance a rascally stranger, but his interests are with the spurned bride. Unengaging soap opera. C: Liliane Brousse, Francoise

Deldick, Claude Sainlouis, Michele Philippe. D: Louis Felix. DRA 90m.

Hot Ice 1953 British ★★★ Haunted house comic mystery with many charming moments thanks to competent cast. C: John Justin, Barbara Murray, Ivor Barnard. D: Kenneth Hume. COM 65m.

Hot Ice 1974 *See* **Mr. Inside/Mr. Outside**

Hot Lead 1956 ★★ Steiger is unconvincing and forced as a Yankee-hating Southerner who hooks up with a tribe of Sioux at the end of the Civil War so he can continue to kill Northerners. (a.k.a. *Run of the Arrow.*) C: Rod Steiger, Sarita Montiel, Brian Keith, Ralph Meeker, Jay C. Flippen, Charles Bronson. D: Samuel Fuller. WST 85m. V

Hot Lead & Cold Feet 1978 ★★★★ Disney kiddie Western features Dale in triple role as a father and twin sons doing slapstick battle against bad-guy politician (McGavin). Dale is a stitch in this entertaining children's picture. C: Jim Dale, Darren McGavin, Karen Valentine, Don Knotts. D: Robert Butler. FAM/WST [G] 89m. V

Hot Line 1969 *See* **Day the Hot Line Got Hot, The**

Hot Millions 1968 British ★★★★ Ustinov embezzles millions from U.S. corporation via computer. Delightfully larcenous comedy sizzles thanks to Smith's daffy performance, many fine cameos, and a clever screenplay. C: Peter Ustinov, Maggie Smith, Karl Malden, Bob Newhart, Robert Morley, Cesar Romero. D: Eric Till. COM [G] 105m. V

Hot News 1953 ★★ Crusading sportswriter tries to smash gangsters who are infiltrating local athletic organizations. Tired crime story. C: Stanley Clements, Gloria Henry. D: Edward Bernds. DRA 68m.

Hot Paint 1988 ★★★ Crooks steal priceless painting, then have trouble fencing it. Mildly diverting caper. C: Gregory Harrison, John Larroquette. D: Sheldon Larry . COM 96m. TVM

Hot Pepper 1933 ★★★ Two battling marines from *What Price Glory?* (Lowe and McLaglen) head to Latin America to become bootleggers and open a nightclub where they fight over a dancer (Velez). C: Victor McLaglen, Edmund Lowe, Lupe Velez. D: John Blystone. COM 76m.

Hot Potato 1976 ★★½ A wicked Asian criminal abducts a politician's daughter and three bold karate masters swing into action. Filmed on location in Thailand. C: Jim Kelly, George Memmoli. D: Oscar Williams. ACT [PG] 87m. V

Hot Pursuit 1987 ★★½ A college-age couple (Cusack, Gazelle) plan a trip with her parents, but he misses their flight and is soon fighting against all odds to catch up with her. Far from believable, but a few laughs. C: John Cusack, Robert Loggia, Wendy Gazelle. D: Steven Lisberger. COM [PG-13] 93m. V

Hot Resort 1985 ★ Cold sophomoric comedy about horny lackeys at a Caribbean isle hotel. Even the beautiful scenery looks dull. C: Tom Parsekian, Michael Berz, Bronson Pinchot, Daniel Schneider, Frank Gorshin, Marcy Walker. D: John Robins, Tom Parsekian, Michael Berz. COM [R] 92m. V

Hot Rock, The 1972 ★★★★ The perfect crime is thoroughly mangled by incompetent jewel thieves. Breezy caper comedy is consistently entertaining thanks to William Goldman's lively adaptation of Donald E. Westlake's novel. (a.k.a. *How to Steal a Diamond In Four Easy Lessons*) C: Robert Redford, George Segal, Ron Leibman, Paul Sand, Zero Mostel. D: Peter Yates. COM [PG] 105m. V

Hot Rod 1979 ★ Idealistic drag racer vs. corrupt race organizer. Boring. C: Gregg Henry, Robert Culp, Pernell Roberts. D: George Armitage. ACT 97m. TVM V

Hot Rod Gang 1958 ★★½ Speedster fan (Ashley) joins a band of drag racers in order to finance his hot rod mania. Lots of songs. C: John Ashley, Gene Vincent. D: Lew Landers. MUS 72m.

Hot Rod Rumble 1957 ★★ Misfit is falsely accused of murder after a car is forced off the road. Will the true killer be revealed? '50s relic. C: Brett Halsey, Richard Hartunian. D: Leslie Martinson. DRA 79m.

Hot Rods to Hell 1967 ★ A working man (Andrews) rattled by a bad car accident runs into a roaming hot rod gang while attempting to move to the Southwest. Campy B-movie. C: Dana Andrews, Jeanne Crain. D: John Brahm. ACT 92m.

Hot Saturday 1932 ★★★ An innocent shop clerk (Carroll) loses her job when gossip flares up about her relationship with two men (Grant and Scott). Mild romantic comedy. One of Grant's first Hollywood roles. C: Cary Grant, Nancy Carroll, Randolph Scott. D: William Seiter. COM 72m.

Hot Shots! 1991 ★★★★ Goofy parody features Sheen as fighter pilot who storms his way through spoofs of *Top Gun, Dances with Wolves, 9 Weeks*, and the Gulf War among other things. Lots of fun from tongue-in-cheek cast. C: Charlie Sheen, Cary Elwes, Valeria Golino, Lloyd Bridges. D: Jim Abrahams. COM [PG-13] 85m. V

Hot Shots! Part Deux 1993 ★★★½ Sheen returns as fearless (and funny) top-gun pilot, this time outfitted with Rambo-like muscles and a gleefully ridiculous plot about saving kidnapped colleagues from Saddam Hussein. As with the original, the jokes fly faster than the airplanes, though the hit ratio isn't quite as high. C: Charlie Sheen, Lloyd Bridges, Valeria Golino, Richard Crenna. D: Jim Abrahams. COM [PG-13] 89m. V

Hot Spell 1958 ★★★½ The skeletons jump out of the closet when a mother tries to bring her family closer together during a birthday party for her philandering husband. Excellent cast raises this Deep South drama. C: Shirley

Booth, Anthony Quinn, Shirley MacLaine, Eileen Heckart. D: Daniel Mann. DRA 86m.

Hot Spot, The 1990 ★★★ Trouble begins when a used-car salesman (Johnson) gets involved with the boss's wife. Sultry, sexy, and simmering though the plot tends to bog down. C: Don Johnson, Virginia Madsen, Jennifer Connelly. D: Dennis Hopper. CRI [R] 130m. v

Hot Stuff 1979 ★★★½ Undercover cops set up a sting operation to get the goods on the bad guys. Well-etched performances in otherwise middling cops-and-robbers comedy. C: Dom DeLuise, Suzanne Pleshette, Ossie Davis. D: Dom DeLuise. COM [PG] 91m. v

Hot Summer in Barefoot County 1974 ★★½ While looking for moonshine in the backwoods, a policeman comes upon something a lot hotter. Downright sweltering. C: Sherry Robinson, Dick Smith. D: Will Zens. DRA [R] 90m.

Hot Summer Night 1957 ★★★½ Ambitious reporter arranges for interview with dangerous outlaw, soon wishes he hadn't. Interesting low-budget suspenser. C: Leslie Nielsen, Colleen Miller. D: David Friedkin. DRA 86m.

Hot T-Shirts 1979 ★ Exceptionally cheesy (and amusingly dated) farce about a bar owner who saves his establishment from bankruptcy with a series of wet T-shirt contests. C: Ray Holland, Stephanie Lawlor. D: Chuck Vincent. COM [R] 86m.

Hot Times 1974 ★★ High school student sets out for the big city so he can score with a lot of women. Just what you'd expect. Director went on to make much better movies, including *The Big Easy*. C: Henry Cory, Gail Lorber, Amy Farber. D: Jim McBride. COM [R] 80m. v

Hot to Trot 1988 ★½ Goldthwait is inept broker who hits it big after accepting stock tips from horse's mouth only he can hear. Candy is the nag's voice and Coleman is Goldthwait's evil stepfather in this weak time waster. C: Bob Goldthwait, Virginia Madsen, Dabney Coleman. D: Michael Dinner. COM [PG] 83m. v

Hot Tomorrows 1978 ★★★½ Director Brest's first feature is a low-budget black comedy about a young man obsessed with death. Many off-the-wall death gags and a zany final musical number compensate for erratic plotting. C: Ken Lerner, Ray Sharkey, Herve Villechaize, Victor Argo. D: Martin Brest. COM 73m.

Hot Water 1924 ★★★½ A long-suffering husband (Lloyd) gets into trouble while vacationing with his family. Episodic, silent slapstick comedy isn't Lloyd's best, but it's still full of funny routines. Highlight: Car trouble. C: Harold Lloyd, Josephine Crowell, Jobyna Ralston. D: San Taylor, Fred Newmeyer. COM 60m.

Hotel 1967 ★★★ Big, glossy adaptation of Arthur Hailey best-seller focuses on manager of luxurious New Orleans hotel (Taylor), and the tangled lives of his various guests. Lavishly produced precursor to the TV series. C: Rod Taylor, Catherine Spaak, Karl Malden, Melvyn Douglas, Merle Oberon. D: Richard Quine. DRA [PG] 125m. v

Hotel Berlin 1945 ★★★ In the last days of WWII, intrigue and suspense penetrate lives of various guests staying at a grand Berlin hotel. Competent but uninspired working of 1932 classic *Grand Hotel*. C: Helmut Dantine, Andrea King, Raymond Massey, Peter Lorre. D: Peter Godfrey. DRA 98m.

Hotel Colonial 1987 Italian ★★ Man travels to Colombia after brother's suicide, discovers that his sibling's not dead after all. Vapid thriller with talented cast. C: John Savage, Rachel Ward, Robert Duvall. D: Cinzia Torrini. DRA [R] 103m. v

Hotel du Lac 1986 British ★★ Massey plays spinster in mid-life crisis on Swiss holiday where she meets a number of odd hotel guests—among them a man (Elliot) who asks her to marry him. Breathtaking Alpine scenery highlights this film, loosely based on Anita Brookner best-seller. C: Anna Massey, Denholm Elliott. D: Giles Foster. DRA 75m. TVM

Hotel for Women 1939 ★★½ Young gold diggers are coached by an older woman in this decidedly minor comedy/drama. C: Linda Darnell, Ann Sothern, Elsa Maxwell. D: Gregory Ratoff. DRA 83m.

Hotel Imperial 1939 ★★★ Hotel on Austro-Hungarian border plays host to assorted people brought together by advance of Russians in WWI. Uneven production a remake of silent film based on play by Lajos Biro. Remade as *Five Graves to Cairo*. C: Isa Miranda, Ray Milland, Reginald Owen. D: Robert Florey. DRA 67m.

Hotel New Hampshire, The 1984 ★★★½ Fulfilling a longtime fantasy, a teacher, Bridges, buys a hotel for his family which is soon peopled with wacky characters, including a young woman who lives in a bear suit. Quirky adaptation of best-selling John Irving novel. C: Rob Lowe, Jodie Foster, Beau Bridges, Nastassja Kinski, Matthew Modine, Amanda Plummer. D: Tony Richardson. DRA [R] 110m. v

Hotel Paradiso 1966 British ★★★ The licentious plans of a neglected Parisian housewife and her mousy neighbor become a comedy of errors when their tryst is constantly thwarted. Slow costume comedy. C: Alec Guinness, Gina Lollobrigida, Robert Morley, Akim Tamiroff. D: Peter Glenville. COM 96m. v

Hotel Reserve 1944 British ★★★ At a hotel in the south of France during WWII, a suspected spy is caught between Nazis and Nazi hunters. Good adaptation of Eric Ambler thriller, given wan treatment. C: James Mason, Herbert Lom. D: Lance Comfort, Max Greene, Victor Hanbury. DRA 79m. v

Hotel Sahara 1951 British ★★★ During WWII, the owners (Ustinov and De Carlo) of a North African watering hole change their colors whenever a new army takes occupancy. Harmless trifle bounces along via Ustinov's winning performance. C: Yvonne De Carlo, Peter Ustinov. D: Ken Annakin. COM 96m.

Hotel Terminus: The Life and Times of Klaus Barbie 1988 ★★★★★ Absolutely chilling account of notorious Nazi war criminal culminates with his extradition to Israel and trial. One-of-a-kind film uses its extraordinary length—an Ophuls trademark—to draw us into an unbelievable but true story. Well-deserved Oscar for Best Documentary. D: Marcel Ophuls. DOC 267m. v

Hothead 1978 French ★★ Comedy about a carefree soccer player booted from the team, footloose on the streets, and implicated in a rape he didn't commit. Aimless story never quite scores a goal. C: Patrick Dewaere, Jean Bouise, Michel Aumont. D: Jean-Jacques Annaud. COM 98m. v

Hotline 1982 ★★½ A counselor (Carter) at a telephone crisis center takes a call from a psychopathic murderer. Average suspenser. C: Lynda Carter, Steve Forrest. D: Jerry Jameson. CRI 96m. TVM v

H.O.T.S. 1979 ★★ The lusty adventures of two rival college sororities who agree to settle their differences via strip football. Anyway, it's lively. (a.k.a. *T&A Academy*) C: Susan Kiger, Lisa London. D: Gerals Seth Sindell. COM [R] 95m.

Hotshot 1986 ★ Young soccer player tries to get instruction from his idol. Not even footage of the amazing Pele makes this watchable. C: Pele, Jim Youngs, Billy Warlock. D: Rick King. DRA [PG] 90m. v

Houdini 1953 ★★★½ Largely fictionalized biography of famed escape artist re-creates many of his best illusions. Curtis (Brooklyn accent and all) is convincing in otherwise routine film. C: Tony Curtis, Janet Leigh, Torin Thatcher. D: George Marshall. DRA 107m. v

Houghland Murder Case, The *See* **Murder by Television**

Hound-Dog Man 1959 ★★★ Forgettable juvenile romance has Fabian torn between hillbilly (Lynley) and older woman (Moore). C: Fabian, Carol Lynley, Stuart Whitman, Arthur O'Connell, Margo Moore. D: Don Siegel. MUS 87m.

Hound of the Baskervilles, The 1939 ★★★★★ Classic version of the Sherlock Holmes mystery about the effects of the hound's curse on the heirs of a noble British family. This debut teaming of Rathbone and Bruce, setting the standard for all future Holmes-Watson duos, is a pleasure to watch. C: Basil Rathbone, Nigel Bruce, Richard Greene, Wendy Barrie, Lionel Atwill, John Carradine. D: Sidney Lanfield. HOR 80m. v

Hound of the Baskervilles, The 1959 British ★★★★ Cushing ably follows Rathbone's signature performance in this remake of the Sir Arthur Conan Doyle tale of a demonic hound that threatens the life of a Dartmoor baronet. More textured with the supernatural than the 1939 version. C: Peter Cushing, Christopher Lee, Andre Morell. D: Terence Fisher. HOR 86m. v

Hound of the Baskervilles, The 1972 ★★ Conan Doyle classic remade, again, this time for TV. C: Stewart Granger, William Shatner. D: Barry Crane. DRA 73m. TVM

Hound of the Baskervilles, The 1977 British ★ Send-up of Conan Doyle's classic tale falls completely flat, even with Cook as Sherlock Holmes and Moore as Dr. Watson. Great talents wasted. C: Dudley Moore, Peter Cook, Denholm Elliott, Joan Greenwood, Spike Milligan, Jessie Matthews. D: Paul Morrissey. COM 84m. v

Hound of the Baskervilles, The 1983 British ★★★★½ Dashing Sherlock Holmes (Richardson) battles a dreaded curse involving murderous hound from hell. Excellent version of oft-filmed classic. C: Ian Richardson, Donald Churchill, Martin Shaw, Denholm Elliott. D: Douglas Hickox. CRI 101m. TVM v

Hour Before the Dawn 1944 ★★ Lake makes a very unconvincing spy in the WWII star-crossed romance. Even Tone, as her intended victim, looks unconvinced. C: Franchot Tone, Veronica Lake, Binnie Barnes. D: Frank Tuttle. DRA 75m.

Hour of Decision 1957 British ★★½ Reporter's investigation of a columnist's murder leads him to suspect his own wife. Uninspired whodunit with more talk than tension. C: Jeff Morrow, Hazel Court. D: C.M. Richards. CRI 81m.

Hour of Glory 1949 *See* **The Small Back Room**

Hour of the Assassin 1986 ★★ A CIA agent (Vaughn) must try and catch a South American assassin (Estrada) hired by subversive military forces to murder the President. All the trappings of an action film. C: Erik Estrada, Robert Vaughn. D: Luis Llosa. ACT [R] 96m. v

Hour of the Furnaces 1968 ★★★★ Mammoth, incisive documentary relating Argentina's history to Latin America's current political situation. Solanas and Getino are occasionally preachy, but their landmark film is a powerful battle cry for the socialist revolution. D: Fernando Solamas, Octavio Getino. DOC

Hour of the Gun 1967 ★★★★ Even after the O.K. Corral gunfight, Wyatt Earp still has plenty left for the Clanton gang. So he goes a-lookin'. Solid Western that holds your interest. Good Garner outing and Voight's debut. C: James

Garner, Jason Robards, Robert Ryan, Jon Voight. D: John Sturges. WST 88m. V

Hour of the Star, The 1986 Brazilian ★★★★ Unsightly woman from poor village moves to São Paolo to find work, surviving only through her powerful fantasy life. Fascinating character study, observant about Brazil's differences between rural squalor and urban bliss. C: Marcelia Cartaxo, Jose Dumont. D: Suzana Amaral. DRA 96m. V

Hour of the Wolf 1968 Swedish ★★★★ Artist's (von Sydow's) battle with real or imagined demons and the painful attempt of his wife (Ullman) to save him is eerily captured in Bergman's gripping study of evil. Inspired generations of horror directors. C: Liv Ullmann, Max von Sydow, Erland Josephson. D: Ingmar Bergman. DRA 88m. V

Hour of 13, The 1952 ★★★½ In 1890s London, a jewel thief (Lawford) finds he can't fence his loot until an unrelated set of murders is solved, so he gets involved. Good, suspenseful mystery. Remake of 1934's *The Mystery of Mr. X.* C: Peter Lawford, Dawn Addams. D: Harold French. CRI 79m.

Hours of Love, The 1965 Italian ★★ Sex farce makes a case for adultery over faithfulness. Cast notwithstanding, this mediocre little comedy never sustains its invention for more than a few moments at a time. C: Ugo Tognazzi, Emmanuele Riva, Barbara Steele. D: Luciano Salce. COM 89m.

House 1986 ★★★ Snappy mix of horror and humor, with troubled horror novelist Katt encountering even worse trials when he moves into an inherited old house. More special effects than sense, but there's never a dull moment. C: William Katt, George Wendt, Richard Moll, Kay Lenz. D: Steve Miner. HOR [R] 93m. V

House II: The Second Story 1987 ★ Misfired sequel to the successful horror comedy tilts way too far in the direction of laughs—which never come. Wiseguy Gross finds a magic skull in his family's ancestral home, leading to would-be wacky adventures through parallel dimensions. C: Arye Gross, Jonathan Stark, Royal Dano. D: Ethan Wiley. HOR [PG-13] 88m. V

House IV: Home Deadly Home 1991 ★★ Widowed Treas finds herself besieged by both supernatural ghouls and criminal goons in the old house she's inherited. Somewhat improved sequel brings back Katt and, more important, the original balance of chills and comedy. C: Terri Treas, Scott Burkholder, William Katt. D: Lewis Abernathy. HOR [R] 95m. V

House Across the Bay, The 1940 ★★★½ When a convict (Raft) goes to prison, his wife takes up with another man. Sprung from the poky, he goes to reclaim his spouse and exact revenge. Good case gives life to a formula crime drama. C: George Raft, Joan Bennett, Lloyd Nolan, Gladys George, Walter Pidgeon. D: Archie Mayo. CRI 88m. V

House Across the Lake, The 1954 *See* **Heatwave**

House Across the Street, The 1949 ★★★ A reporter finds himself unexpectedly on the trail of a murderer. Good comedy/thriller. C: Wayne Morris, Lanis Paige, James Mitchell. D: Richard Bare. CRI 69m.

House by the Cemetery 1984 Italian ★ Another disgusting piece of gore cinema: a deranged killer living under the house's floorboards terrorizes the residents. C: Katherine MacColl, Paolo Mako. D: Lucio Fulci. HOR 84m. V

House by the Lake, The 1977 Canadian ★★ Woman is brutalized by four thugs in isolated country retreat. Vicious and repellent thriller, alarmingly well-acted. C: Brenda Vaccaro, Don Stroud. D: William Fruet. ACT [R] 89m.

House by the River, The 1950 ★★★½ Devious husband murders his maid and implicates his own brother. Gothic chiller stays effective, though Lang did better. C: Louis Hayward, Jane Wyatt, Lee Bowman. D: Fritz Lang. DRA 88m.

House Calls 1978 ★★★★ A middle-aged doctor (Matthau), recently widowed, reenters world of dating. Enjoyable Matthau/Jackson sparring and a clever supporting cast make this a delightful comedy. C: Walter Matthau, Glenda Jackson, Art Carney, Richard Benjamin. D: Howard Zieff. COM [PG] 98m. V

House Divided, A 1932 ★★★ A hard-bitten, widowed fisherman (Huston) arranges a mail-order bride, but she falls for his son. Interesting antique notable for Wyler's early direction and Huston's powerful performance. C: Walter Huston, Kent Douglas, Helen Chandler. D: William Wyler. DRA 70m.

House in the Woods, The 1957 British ★★★½ Writer and his spouse rent a cottage from an offbeat painter, then learn their strange landlord has killed his own wife and is ready to murder again. Entertaining suspense thriller. C: Ronald Howard, Michael Gough, Patricia Roc, Andrea Trowbridge, Bill Shine, Nora Hammond. D: Maxwell Munden. CRI 60m.

House of Angels 1992 Swedish ★★★★ Pleasant comedy of a small town in Sweden turned upside down when the richest inhabitant leaves his farmland and house to a wayward cabaret performer. Sweet-natured film is sparked by lovely performances. C: Helena Bergstrom, Rikard Wolff, Sven Wollter. D: Colin Nutley. COM [R] 119m. V

House of Bamboo 1955 ★★★★ G.I. Stack goes undercover to infiltrate Ryan's crime ring in post-WWII Tokyo. Intelligent remake of *Street with No Name* is not entirely credible, but always an eyeful. C: Robert Ryan, Robert Stack. D: Samuel Fuller. ACT 102m.

House of Cards 1969 ★★★ While employed

as a tutor in the house of a rich French aristocrat, American expatriot (Peppard) realizes his employer is a neo-Nazi plotting to take over Europe. Excellent international cast, some thrills. C: George Peppard, Inger Stevens, Orson Welles, Keith Michell. D: John Guillermin. DRA [G] 105m. v

House of Cards 1993 ★★★ Strange, almost hypnotic film about a mother (Turner) seeking help for her seemingly autistic daughter. Is she actually a gifted child with unusual powers? Turner tries hard, but, after a strong start, the house tumbles down. C: Kathleen Turner, Tommy Lee Jones, Park Overall, Esther Rolle. D: Michael Lessac. DRA [PG-13] 109m. v

House of Crazies 1972 *See* **Asylum**

House of Dark Shadows 1970 ★★★½ First movie based on hit soap opera *Dark Shadows,* with Frid (like rest of cast) reprising his role as ancient vampire resurrected in modern times and pursuing mortal (Scott). Good makeup and stylish direction elevate this above TV level. Sequel: *Night of Dark Shadows.* C: Jonathan Frid, Grayson Hall, Joan Bennett. D: Dan Curtis. HOR [PG] 98m. v

House of Dracula 1945 ★★★½ This superior sequel to *House of Frankenstein* has a scientist attempting to revive Frankenstein monster (Strange) and Wolf Man (Chaney, Jr.) after becoming infected with the blood of Dracula. Good atmospheric effects and creepy goings on help compensate for story's episodic structure. C: Lon Chaney, Jr., John Carradine, Martha O'Driscoll, Glenn Strange. D: Erle C. Kenton, Onslow Stevens. HOR 67m. v

House of Evil 1971 Mexican ★ Murderous toys dispatch a group of people gathered to claim an inheritance. Karloff (in his last film) only pops in briefly at the beginning and end. Truly awful, with cheap effects and poor acting. C: Boris Karloff. D: Jack Hill, Enrique Vergara. HOR [PG] 80m.

House of Exorcism, The 1975 *See* **Lisa and the Devil**

House of Fear 1939 ★★★½ Mysterious disappearance of corpse after actor is murdered in haunted theater. Sharp showbiz backgrounds, atmosphere, good whodunit. C: William Gargan, Alan Dinehart, Walter King, Dorothy Arnold. D: Joe May. CRI 67m.

House of Fear, The 1945 ★★★½ Supersleuth Holmes and his inimitable sidekick Watson are hot on the trail of a murderer doing in members of a men's club headquartered in a Scottish castle. Very loosely based on "The Five Orange Pips"; one of the slower-paced Rathbone/Bruce efforts. C: Basil Rathbone, Nigel Bruce, Dennis Hoey. D: Roy William Neill. CRI 69m. v

House of Frankenstein 1944 ★★★½ They're all together in this one—Dracula, the Werewolf, and the Creature. Sinister Karloff escapes from prison in quest for revenge on those who sent him there and is joined by all-star monster cast. Compelling and fun. C: Boris Karloff, J. Carrol Naish, Lon Chaney, Jr., John Carradine. D: Erle C. Kenton. HOR 71m. v

House of Games 1987 ★★★★ A psychiatrist (Crouse) appeals to a gambler (Mantegna) to keep him from killing her indebted patient; he agrees on condition that she assist him in a con game. Adaptation is a brilliant study of the contradictions and psychological tricks within such games. Mamet's film directorial debut. C: Lindsay Crouse, Joe Mantegna, Mike Nussbaum, Lilia Skala. D: David Mamet. CRI [R] 102m. v

House of God, The 1979 ★★ Black comedy detailing the daily problems faced by inexperienced doctors interning at a major hospital. Good cast. C: Tim Matheson, Charles Haid, Bess Armstrong, Ossie Davis. D: Donald Wrye. COM [R] 108m.

House of Horrors 1946 ★★½ An angry artist contrives to kill his critics. Minor horror item enhanced by smooth production values. C: Bill Goodwin, Robert Lowery, Virginia Grey. D: Jean Yarbrough. HOR 65m. v

House of Intrigue 1959 Italian ★★★ Espionage drama of spies and double crosses during WWII. Good location photography elevates average thriller. C: Curt Jurgens, Dawn Addams, Folco Lulli. D: Duilio Coletti. DRA 94m.

House of Mystery 1961 British ★★★½ New homeowners learn supernatural history of their nest. Familiar material gets good lean treatment that delivers chills. C: Jane Hylton, Peter Dyneley, Nanette Newman. D: Vernon Sewell. HOR 56m.

House of Numbers 1957 ★★★½ Jail-break film with a twist: replace the imprisoned mobster (Palance) with his spitting-image brother (Palance). Farfetched, but Palance's double role is intriguing enough to sustain interest throughout. C: Jack Palance, Barbara Lang, Harold Stone. D: Russell Rouse. ACT 92m.

House of 1,000 Dolls 1967 British ★★ A small-time magician (Price) hides an alter ego as the head of a bizarre slave trading network. Very low-budget, campy style in a film that might, at least, produce some laughs. C: Vincent Price, Martha Hyer, George Nader. D: Jeremy Summers. HOR 83m. v

House of Ricordi 1956 Italian ★★½ Historical drama covers story behind famed music publishers during the 1700s. Good for music. C: Paolo Stoppa, Roland Alexandre, Marta Toren. D: Carmine Gallone. MUS 117m.

House of Rothschild, The 1934 ★★★★½ Involving and visually stunning re-creation of the affairs and adventures of one of the most powerful families during the Napoleonic wars. Lively cast, especially Karloff as a devious business rival. C: George Arliss, Boris Karloff, Loretta Young. D: Alfred Werker. DRA 88m.

House of Seven Corpses, The 1973 ★★★

In a mansion where seven murders occurred, moviemakers shooting a horror film resurrect an evil spirit. Good low-budgeter. Some humorous touches balance the horror. C: John Ireland, Faith Domergue, John Carradine. D: Paul Harrison. HOR [R] 90m. v

House of Shadows 1983 ★★½ Young woman who suddenly envisions murder from the past grapples with solving mystery without losing her life. C: John Gavin, Yvonne De Carlo. D: Richard Wulicher. HOR [PG] 90m. v

House of Strangers, The 1949 ★★★★ Wealthy banking family is torn apart by the iron-fisted machinations of the father (Robinson), who manipulates each of his four sons for his own gain. C: Edward G. Robinson, Susan Hayward, Richard Conte, Luther Adler. D: Joseph L. Mankiewicz. DRA 101m. v

House of Terror 1972 ★★★ A couple faces deadly complications when they try to steal millions from a haunted home. C: Jennifer Bishop, Arell Blanton, Jacquelyn Hyde. D: Sergei Goncharoff. HOR [PG] 90m. v

House of the Arrow, The 1930 ★★★ When a wealthy French woman is murdered, her niece becomes a suspect in the case as developed by the famous Inspector Hanaud. Suspense is tidy indeed. Remade twice. C: Dennis Neilson-Terry, Benita Hume, Richard Cooper, Stella Freeman. D: Leslie Hiscott. CRI 76m.

House of the Black Death 1965 ★★ An evil, horned sorcerer (Chaney) captures house full of people and blocks rescue attempts by rival warlock (Carradine). Cheap horror offering. C: Lon Chaney, Jr., John Carradine, Andrea King. D: Harold Daniels. HOR 80m.

House of the Living Dead 1978 ★★½ Evil force lurking in South African mansion attacks anything in its path. C: Mark Burns, Shirley Ann Field, David Oxley. D: Ray Austin. HOR [PG] 85m. v

House of the Long Shadows 1982 British ★★★ A camp-fest with a cast of horror movie veterans. Based on the George M. Cohan play, *Seven Keys to Baldpate*, this silly romp follows an author (Arnaz!) who spends the night in haunted house to win a bet. Fun, but with little redeeming value. C: Vincent Price, Christopher Lee, Peter Cushing, John Carradine, Desi Arnaz, Jr. D: Pete Walker. CRI [PG] 96m. v

House of the Rising Sun 1987 ★★★ Cub L.A. reporter happens upon hot story about murder in a trendy brothel. C: John York, Bud Davis, Frank Annese. D: Greg Gold. CRI 86m. v

House of the Seven Gables, The 1940 ★★★½ A ruthless attorney sends his sister's lover away to prison, then pays the price in guilt. Faithful, well-acted adaptation of Hawthorne's classic gothic novel. C: George Sanders, Margaret Lindsay, Vincent Price. D: Joe May. DRA 89m.

House of the Spirits 1993 German ★½ Disappointing, too-literal filming of Isabel Allende's multigenerational epic of a landowning family in Chile. Worth seeing for fabulous cast (especially Close). C: Jeremy Irons, Meryl Streep, Glenn Close, Winona Ryder, Antonio Banderas, Vanessa Redgrave, Armin Mueller-Stahl. D: Bille August. DRA [R] 138m.

House of Usher *See* **Fall of the House of Usher**

House of Wax 1953 ★★★★ Price at his most wicked portrays an insane artist who dips human victims in boiling wax to display as wax figures in museum. The most popular of several 3-D features released in 1953. That's young Charles Bronson as Igor. C: Vincent Price, Frank Lovejoy, Phyllis Kirk, Carolyn Jones. D: Andre de Toth. HOR [PG] 88m. v

House of Women 1962 ★★★ A woman wrongly convicted of robbery is sent to female big house. Cast and rapid pacing help. Routine potboiler. C: Shirley Knight, Andrew Duggan, Constance Ford, Barbara Nichols. D: Walter Doniger. ACT 85m.

House on Carroll Street, The 1987 ★★ Unconvincing tale of woman with "red" sympathies during the McCarthy era, who must convince an FBI agent of a plot to smuggle Nazi war criminals into the U.S. Lots of wasted talent. C: Kelly McGillis, Jeff Daniels, Mandy Patinkin, Jessica Tandy. D: Peter Yates. CRI [PG] 111m. v

House on Garibaldi Street, The 1979 ★★★½ Political thriller dramatizes the 1960 capture in Argentina of Nazi war criminal Adolf Eichmann. Well done, but with lots of oratory. C: Topol, Martin Balsam, Janet Suzman. D: Peter Collinson. DRA 98m. TVM v

House on Greenapple Road, The 1970 ★★★ A philandering wife (Leigh) is murdered and local authorities try to locate her corpse. Above-average pilot for *Dan August* TV series. C: Christopher George, Janet Leigh, Julie Harris, Walter Pidgeon. D: Robert Day. DRA 113m. TVM

House on Haunted Hill 1958 ★★★ Price offers to pay five people $50,000 to spend the night in a haunted house with history of horrific killings. Campy fun, with good twist ending. C: Vincent Price, Carol Ohmart, Richard Long, Elisha Cook, Jr. D: William Castle. HOR 75m. v

House on Marsh Road, The 1959 *See* **Invisible Creature, The**

House on 92nd Street 1945 ★★★★ Excellent newsreel-style drama of scientist employed by the FBI to infiltrate German spy ring in U.S. during WWII. Influential in its use of location photography, and solidly acted by cast of mostly nonprofessionals. Oscar for Screenplay (Charles J. Booth). C: William Eythe, Lloyd Nolan, Signe Hasso, Gene Lockhart, Leo G. Carroll. D: Henry Hathaway. DRA 88m.

House on Skull Mountain 1974 ★★½ Relatives of dead voodoo practitioner gather in creepy mansion for reading of a will. Forgettable black exploitation/horror combo. C: Victor French, Janee Michelle. D: Ron Honthaner. HOR [PG] 85m. V

House on Straw Hill, The 1976 ★★ Sleazy thriller about a writer and his wife involved with a disturbed young woman (Hayden) who goes on a rampage of seduction and murder. Few effective moments. (a.k.a. *Expose*) C: Udo Kier, Linda Hayden, Fiona Richmond. D: James Clarke. HOR [R] 84m. V

House on Telegraph Hill 1951 ★★★ A concentration camp survivor assumes dead woman's identity and discovers she's also inherited a murderous husband. Fairly involving melodrama. C: Richard Basehart, Valentina Cortese, William Lundigan. D: Robert Wise. DRA 93m.

House on the Front Line, The 1963 Soviet ★★★½ During WWII, a Russian woman organizes her colleagues in the post office while waiting for her fiancé's return from combat. Effective drama enhanced by good cast. The usually strong social messages of Soviet films are firmly in place here. C: Larisa Luzhina, Klara Luchko, Vyacheslav Tikhonov. D: Alexandr Galich. DRA 90m.

House Party 1990 ★★★★ Refreshing debut feature for Hudlin involves a group of African-American teens who want to throw a house party. Rappers Kid 'n' Play shine in the leads, with Harris in fine support as parental authority. Followed by two sequels and a television cartoon. C: Christopher Reid, Robin Harris, Christopher Martin, Martin Lawrence, Tisha Campbell. D: Reginald Hudlin. COM [R] 100m. V

House Party 2 1991 ★★★ Lesser sequel to entertaining first feature. Same idea is recycled as Kid 'n' Play turn their attentions to the ultimate pajama party. Gags just don't carry the same vigor the second time around. C: Christopher Reid, Christopher Martin, Tisha Campbell, Queen Latifah, Martin Lawrence. D: Doug McHenry, George Jackson. COM [R] 94m. V

House Party III 1994 ★★★ Third film in series has Kid getting married and Play throwing him a bachelor party. Noisy and silly; getting a bit long in the tooth, but still entertaining. C: Christopher Reid, Christopher Martin, David Edwards, Angela Means, Tisha Campbell, Immature, Betty Lester, Bernie Mac. D: Eric Meza. COM [R] 93m. V

House That Cried Murder, The 1974 ★★★½ An unhinged wife (Strasser) stalks her unfaithful husband and his lover after he cheats on their wedding day. Well-done, intense shocker; only problem is that the low budget really shows. (a.k.a. *The Bride*) C: Robin Strasser, John Beal, Arthur Roberts, Ivy Jean Saraceni. D: Jean-Marie Pelissie. HOR [PG] 85m.

House That Dripped Blood, The 1971 British ★★★★ Four horrific, comic yarns centered around an eerie estate and its new owner. As usual, frightmeisters Lee and Cushing enjoy themselves the most. Best tale is the last. Scripted by *Psycho* author Robert Bloch. C: John Bennett, John Bryans, Denholm Elliott, Peter Cushing, Christopher Lee. D: Peter Duffell. HOR [PG] 101m. V

House That Screamed, The 1970 Spanish ★★★½ Strange goings-on at a wealthy girls' school plagued by grisly murders. Stylish, atmospheric chiller boasts a twisted climax. C: Lilli Palmer, Chistina Galbo. D: Narciso Serrador. HOR [PG] 94m.

House That Vanished, The 1974 ★ A young model (Allan) witnesses the first of a series of rape/murders, but then can't find the house she saw it in. Lots of sex and violence in this predictably trashy thriller. (a.k.a. *Scream & Die*) C: Andrea Allan, Karl Lanchbury, Maggie Walker. D: Joseph Larraz. HOR [R] 95m. V

House That Would Not Die, The 1970 ★★★ Old-fashioned chiller finds woman and her niece moving into haunted house and subjected to supernatural stress. Unremarkable spine tingler. C: Barbara Stanwyck, Richard Egan, Katharine Winn. D: John Llewellyn Moxey. HOR 73m. TVM

House Where Evil Dwells, The 1982 ★★ American couple moves into Japanese house infested by restless spirit of murderous samurai. Violent nonsense isn't helped by laughably transparent "ghosts." C: Edward Albert, Susan George, Doug McClure. D: Kevin Connor. HOR [R] 88m. V

House with an Attic, The 1964 Soviet ★★★ After falling for a young woman, a Russian artist is discouraged from romance by his would-be love's older sister, who disapproves of the man's revolutionary politics. Melodramatic soap opera, loosely adapted from an Anton Chekov story. DRA

House Without a Christmas Tree, A ★★★★ Ten-year-old Lucas cannot convince her emotionally distant, widowed father (Robards) of her need for a Christmas tree. Excellent family entertainment for the holidays. C: Jason Robards, Lisa Lucas. D: Paul Bogart. FAM/DRA 90m. V

Houseboat 1958 ★★★★ Grant is a widower with three children who hires an inexperienced housekeeper (Loren), who quickly wins hearts of kids and eventually Grant as well. Though story is routine, Grant and Loren infuse their romance with charming comic energy. C: Cary Grant, Sophia Loren, Martha Hyer, Harry Guardino. D: Melville Shavelson. COM 110m. V

Houseguest 1995 ★★★ Loudmouth con artist (Sinbad) on the lam hides out in suburban lawyer's dream house, with predictable results. Fans of the popular comic will enjoy this. C: Sinbad, Phil Hartman, Ron Glass, Jeffrey Jones. D: Randall Miller. COM [PG] 108m. V

Household Saints 1993 ★★★★ D'Onofrio wins Ullman in a pinochle game, then surprises his friends and family by marrying her. The result is an uneven, but ultimately moving comedy/drama about Italian-Americans in the '40s, '50s, and '60s, intelligently acted and sensitively directed by Savoca. C: Vincent D'Onofrio, Tracey Ullman, Lili Taylor, Judith Malina, Michael Rispoli, Victor Argo, Michael Imperioli. D: Nancy Savoca. DRA 124m. ▾

Householder, The 1963 U.S.-Indian ★★★½ Newlywed Indian couple faces many comically awkward situations as they struggle to adjust to one another. Low-key humor and compassionate approach are strong points in this slow-moving first effort from award-winning Ivory/Merchant/Jhabvala team. C: Shashi Kapoor, Leela Naidu. D: James Ivory. COM 100m. ▾

Housekeeper, The 1986 *See* **Judgement in Stone, A**

Housekeeper's Daughter, The 1939 ★★★½ Sharp gangster's moll (Bennett), visiting her housekeeper mother, shows pampered son of the household (Hubbard) the ins and outs of crime when they solve a murder myster. Freewheeling comedy, with wild fireworks ending. C: Joan Bennett, Victor Mature, Adolphe Menjou, John Hubbard. D: Hal Roach. COM 79m.

Housekeeping 1987 ★★★★ Two orphaned sisters find their dull lives in '50s rural Idaho revitalized when their eccentric aunt enters the scene. The cast is excellent and the story unfolds with turns both quirky and dark. Based on Marilynne Robinson's book. C: Christine Lahti, Sara Walker. D: Bill Forsyth. COM [PG] 117m. ▾

Housemaster 1938 ★★★ A British boys' school replaces its kindly housemaster with a martinet who alienates the boys to the point of rebellion. Slightly dated comedy still pulls off some real laughs. C: Otto Kruger, Diana Churchill, Phillips Holmes, Joyce Barbour. D: Herbert Brenon. COM 81m.

Housesitter 1992 ★★★ The life and dreamhouse of an architect (Martin) are taken over by a habitual liar (Hawn) who shows up one day posing as his wife. Unoriginal script, but the stars are worth seeing. C: Steve Martin, Goldie Hawn, Dana Delany, Julie Harris, Donald Moffat, Peter MacNicol. D: Frank Oz. COM [PG] 102m. ▾

Housewife 1934 ★★★ Weak, contrived melodrama of writer Brent leaving wife Dvorak for sexpot Davis. One of Bette's lesser efforts. C: Bette Davis, George Brent, Ann Dvorak, Ruth Donnelly. D: Alfred Green. DRA 69m.

Houston Story, The 1956 ★★★ Scheming oil worker finds trouble when he joins a criminal gang that is stealing petroleum. Agreeable B-grade crime melodrama. C: Gene Barry, Barbara Hale, Edward Arnold. D: William Castle. DRA 79m. ▾

Houston, We've Got a Problem 1974 ★★★ Standard docudrama on explosion-wracked flight of Apollo 13 fudges some facts, concentrates on problems suffered by spacecraft's flight controllers rather than the life-threatening (and more interesting) situations facing astronauts themselves. C: Robert Culp, Clu Gulager, Gary Collins, Sandra Dee, Ed Nelson, Sheila Sullivan. D: Lawrence Doheny. DRA 90m. TVM

How Awful About Allan 1970 ★★½ The emotional turmoil of a blind man (Perkins) confined to a mental institution. Misfires despite Perkins. C: Anthony Perkins, Julie Harris, Joan Hackett. D: Curtis Harrington. DRA 90m. TVM ▾

How Do I Love Thee? 1970 ★★ Strained relations between a philosophy professor and his flamboyant, but now elderly and ailing father. Sappy blend of comedy and pathos. C: Jackie Gleason, Maureen O'Hara, Shelley Winters. D: Michael Gordon. DRA [PG] 110m.

How Funny Can Sex Be? 1976 Italian ★½ Eight short episodic treatments of sex, Italian style, with the kind of jokes a Vegas lounge act wouldn't touch. Giannini is amusing, though. C: Giancarlo Giannini, Laura Antonelli, Alberto Lionello. D: Dino Risi. COM [R] 97m. ▾

How Green Was My Valley 1941 ★★★★★ Loving study of Welsh coal miners, as seen through the eyes of child McDowall. Day-to-day life shattered by tragedy has rarely been depicted this well. Well-deserved Oscars for Best Director (Ford), Supporting Actor (Crisp), Art Direction, Cinematography, and Best Picture. C: Walter Pidgeon, Maureen O'Hara, Donald Crisp, Roddy McDowall, Sara Allgood, Barry Fitzgerald, Ann Todd. D: John Ford. DRA 118m. ▾

How I Got Into College 1989 ★★★ College admissions trauma is focus of middling comedy about an ambitionless high schooler who chooses a college just to be near a girl. Satire doesn't carry much bite. C: Anthony Edwards, Corey Parker, Lara Flynn Boyle. D: Steve Holland. COM [PG-13] 87m. ▾

How I Spent My Summer Vacation 1967 ★★½ The adventures of a drifter (Wagner) investigating suspicious death of millionaire. Solid cast, scenic mystery. C: Robert Wagner, Peter Lawford, Walter Pidgeon. D: William Hale. CRI 100m.

How I Won the War 1967 British ★★★★ Off-the-wall antiwar farce finds a reluctant commander and his motley crew charged with turning a North African mine field into an officer's cricket field. Absurd blend of slapstick and black humor, with Lester's crisp direction and right-on, dead-pan performances. Includes a rare Lennon performance. C: Michael Crawford, John Lennon, Jack MacGowran, Michael Hordern. D: Richard Lester. COM 111m. ▾

How Long Can You Fall 1974 *See* **Till Marriage Do Us Part**

How Many Miles to Babylon 1982 ★★★ WWI drama about newly made friends who find themselves placed on opposite ends of a firing squad after one is tried for desertion. Notable mostly for early Day-Lewis performance. C: Christopher Fairbank, Daniel Day-Lewis. D: Moira Armstrong. DRA 106m. V

How Sweet It Is! 1968 ★★★½ Wife lets her hair down when she and hubby take a European vacation. Some very funny moments. C: James Garner, Debbie Reynolds, Paul Lynde, Terry-Thomas. D: Jerry Paris. COM 99m. V

How Tasty Was My Little Frenchman 1971 ★★★ In 1500s, Brazilian natives capture and eat French explorer. With that title, all bets are off: deliberately offensive and bizarrely funny. Comedies don't get much blacker. C: Arduino Colassanti, Maria Magalhaes, Ital Natur. D: Nelson Pereira dos Santos. COM 80m.

How the West Was Won 1962 ★★★★ Sprawling, gargantuan story of Western expansion told through the eyes of one family over three decades. Cast reads like a Who's Who of Hollywood; and most of it is riveting. Only problem: three-screen Cinerama photography's a mess on video. Only one-half of the picture is visible, and that has distracting "seams" through it. The laser disc version shows the whole image, but the splits still appear. C: Caroll Baker, Henry Fonda, Debbie Reynolds, George Peppard, James Stewart, Gregory Peck, John Wayne, voice of Spencer Tracy. D: John Ford, George Marshall, Henry Hathaway. WST [G] 155m. V

How to Be Very, Very Popular 1955 ★★★½ Grable's last film is a rambunctious remake of *She Loves Me Not,* a gangster farce about two belly dancers (Grable and North) who take refuge in a coed dorm after they witness a murder. C: Betty Grable, Robert Cummings, Charles Coburn, Sheree North. D: Nunnally Johnson. COM 89m.

How to Beat the High Cost of Living 1980 ★★ Three suburban housewives consider fighting the '70s recession by ripping off their local shopping plaza. Talented cast tries hard, but is done in by bleak, humorless script. C: Susan St. James, Jane Curtin, Jessica Lange, Richard Benjamin. D: Robert Scheerer. COM [PG] 105m. V

How to Break Up a Happy Divorce 1976 ★★★ Woman tries to rekindle romance with ex-husband by dating handsome playboy and making her ex jealous. Slapstick romantic comedy elevated by appealing cast. C: Barbara Eden, Hal Linden. D: Jerry Paris. COM 78m. TVM V

How to Commit Marriage 1969 ★★½ Marital farce about a couple divorcing just as their daughter gets married. Weak Hope hop with spirited cast. C: Bob Hope, Jackie Gleason, Jane Wyman. D: Norman Panama. COM [PG] 96m. V

How to Frame a Figg 1971 ★★★ Scrupulous schnook Knotts is the unwitting fall guy for a crooked town council. Typical silly Knotts vehicle. C: Don Knotts, Joe Flynn. D: Alan Rafkin. COM [G] 103m.

How to Get Ahead in Advertising 1989 British ★★★ While the premise is certainly original—stressed-out ad exec develops a boil on his shoulder which inexplicably starts to talk!—the comedy never really takes off in this satire of the high-powered world of business. C: Richard E. Grant, Rachel Ward. D: Bruce Robinson. COM [R] 94m. V

How to Make a Monster 1958 ★★½ When studio heads impose a moratorium on monster movies, a mad makeup man uses tainted greasepaint to convince actors they really are the creatures they're portraying. Self-referential horror flick (with color climax) is low-rent fun for fans. C: Robert H. Harris, Walter Reed. D: Herbert L. Strock. HOR 73m. V

How to Make Love to a Negro Without Getting Tired 1989 Canadian ★ Sex comedy about an exploitative Haitian charmer who uses ethnic stereotyping to seduce a slew of Montreal women. Offensive in every way, but it did make some waves among the "art cinema" audience. C: Isaach DeBankole, Maka Kotto. D: Jacques Benoit. COM 97m.

How to Marry a Millionaire 1953 ★★★★ Monroe, Bacall, and Grable are three friends who share strategies as each attempts to land herself a wealthy husband. Dated, but exciting ensemble work makes this still very funny. Remake of *The Greeks Had A Word for Them.* C: Marilyn Monroe, Betty Grable, Lauren Bacall, William Powell. D: Jean Negulesco. COM 96m. V

How to Murder a Rich Uncle 1957 British ★★★½ A poor English nobleman (Patrick) plans to kill off his rich visiting relative (Coburn) in this pleasing black comedy. Michael Caine's film debut. C: Charles Coburn, Nigel Patrick, Wendy Hiller, Anthony Newley. D: Nigel Patrick. COM 80m.

How to Murder Your Wife 1965 ★★★½ Cartoonist (Lemmon) marries Lisi while on a bender, then tries to bump her off. Slick, funny comedy falls apart during courtroom finale. May strike some viewers as sexist. C: Jack Lemmon, Virna Lisi, Terry-Thomas, Eddie Mayehoff, Claire Trevor. D: Richard Quine. COM 119m. V

How to Pick Up Girls! 1978 ★★★ Shy would-be Casanova moves to big city and discovers knack for meeting pretty women. Routine comedy generates some laughs. C: Desi Arnaz, Jr., Bess Armstrong. D: Bill Persky. COM 100m. TVM V

How to Save a Marriage (And Ruin Your Life) 1968 ★★ To salvage his best friend's marriage, a bachelor decides to seduce his buddy's mistress—but targets the wrong woman. Lethargic sex farce limps along. C: Dean Martin,

Stella Stevens, Eli Wallach, Anne Jackson. D: Fielder Cook. COM 108m.

How to Steal a Diamond In Four Easy Lessons 1972 *See* **Hot Rock, The**

How to Steal a Million 1966 ★★★★ Diverting bauble has Hepburn and O'Toole in Paris, mixed up in an art heist. Two charming stars work well together. Excellent support from Boyer, Griffith. C: Audrey Hepburn, Peter O'Toole, Charles Boyer, Eli Wallach, Hugh Griffith. D: William Wyler. COM 127m. V

How to Steal an Airplane 1971 ★★ Plot deals with snatching a jet away from a South American dictator. Listless actioner, appealing Duel. C: Peter Duel, Clinton Greyn, Sal Mineo, Claudine Longet. D: Leslie Martinson. ACT 104m. TVM

How to Stuff a Wild Bikini 1965 ★★ The beach-party antics show signs of wear in this sixth outing. Frankie, separated from Annette on Naval Reserve, turns to a witch doctor to keep her faithful. C: Annette Funicello, Dwayne Hickman, Brian Donlevy, Buster Keaton, Mickey Rooney, Harvey Lembeck. D: William Asher. COM 93m. V

How to Succeed in Business Without Really Trying 1967 ★★★★½ Snappy white-collar musical about ingenious window washer Morse using book to guide him up the corporate ladder. Faithful transcription of Broadway hit is smart and sassy, with fine Frank Loesser songs including "I Believe in You." C: Robert Morse, Michele Lee, Rudy Vallee, Anthony Teague. D: David Swift. MUS 121m. V

How U Like Me Now 1993 ★★★ Independent feature shot in Chicago looks at the world of high fashion models through eyes of a young African-American. Tiny budget and lackluster direction hamper routine story. C: Darnell Williams, Salli Richardson, Daniel Gardner. D: Darryl Roberts. COM [R] 109m. V

Howard Beach: Making a Case for Murder 1989 ★★★ Fact-based drama explores the 1986 case of an African-American man killed in a white section of Queens, New York. Interesting and well-acted story of racial tensions. C: Daniel J. Travanti, William Daniels, Joe Morton. D: Dick Lowry. DRA 100m. TVM

Howard the Duck 1986 ★ Cult comic book character Howard the Duck, blasted from his outer space paradise to Cleveland, becomes an unlikely love interest for Thompson. One of the all-time great bombs. C: Lea Thompson, Jeffrey Jones, Tim Robbins. D: Willard Huyck. COM [PG] 111m. V

Howards End 1992 British ★★★★★ Remarkable, subtle adaptation of E.M. Forster novel, about the conflict between two humanistic sisters whose lives entwine with an ill-fated young clerk and a powerful industrialist. Wonderfully evocative, with exceptional performances by Thompson and Hopkins. Oscars for Best Actress, Screenplay, Art Direction, Set Decoration. C: Emma Thompson, Anthony Hopkins, Helena Bonham Carter, Vanessa Redgrave, James Wilby, Samuel West. D: James Ivory. DRA [PG] 142m. V

Howards of Virginia 1940 ★★½ Historical saga of the Revolutionary War and its impact on a wealthy colonial family. Respectable but dull. C: Cary Grant, Martha Scott, Cedric Hardwicke. D: Frank Lloyd. ACT 117m. V

Howling in the Woods, A 1971 ★★★ While vacationing at isolated Lake Tahoe cabin, a woman is plagued by weird cries of wolves. Routine suspenser. C: Barbara Eden, Vera Miles, Larry Hagman. D: Daniel Petrie. DRA 104m. TVM

Howling, The 1981 ★★★★½ Terrific horror film, with deft comic undertones, in which newswoman Wallace discovers that the psychiatric retreat she's visiting is crawling with werewolves. Packed with chills, in-jokes, and superb Rob Bottin special effects. C: Dee Wallace, Patrick MacNee, Dennis Dugan, John Carradine. D: Joe Dante. HOR [R] 90m. V

Howling II: Your Sister Is a Werewolf 1985 ★★ Inane sequel, set in Transylvania, where a relative of one of the original victims attempts to hunt down the hairy parents of werewolf clan. Tries to mix laughs with gore and fails. C: Christopher Lee, Annie McEnroe, Reb Brown. D: Philippe Mora. HOR [R] 91m. V

Howling III: The Marsupials 1987 ★★ Mora, attempting to atone for the disastrous previous entry, injects some satire into this one. Scientist Otto discovers marsupial werewolves (!) in Australia, while film crewman Biolos falls in love with one. C: Barry Otto, Leigh Biolos, Imogen Annesley. D: Philippe Mora. HOR [PG-13] 93m. V

Howling IV: The Original Nightmare 1988 British ★ Third sequel in the series hews closer to the initial source novel by Gary Bradner—with Windsor and her husband doing battle with a town full of werewolves—but that can't rescue it from listless direction and production values. C: Romy Windsor, Michael T. Weiss, Anthony Hamilton. D: John Hough. HOR [R] 94m. V

Howling V: The Rebirth 1989 ★★ This time, the action takes place in a European castle where one of a dozen or so invited guests is a werewolf. Perfunctory chiller with a notable lack of action, suspense, or interesting characters. C: Victoria Catlin. D: Neal Sundstrom. HOR [R] 99m. V

Howling VI: The Freaks 1991 ★★★ The best of the sequels takes place in a traveling carnival whose sadistic master wants to add a sympathetic werewolf to the attractions. More stylish and intelligent than usual, with a few strong shocks. C: Brendan Hughes, Michelle Matheson, Bruce Martin Payne. D: Hope Perello. HOR [R] 102m. V

Hu-Man 1975 French ★★★½ Offbeat science fiction romance revolves around Stamp, an actor who is manipulated in time by Moreau. Stamp must key into the secret of time travel himself, to overcome Moreau and reunite with his wife. Clever story moves at a neat clip. C: Terence Stamp, Jeanne Moreau. D: Jerome Laperrousaz. SFI 105m.

Huck and the King of Hearts 1993 ★★ Loosely based on Mark Twain's "The Adventures of Huckleberry Finn," this story tells of the adventures of Huck who, in this case, travels along highways instead of rivers. C: Chauncey Leopardi, Dee Wallace Stone, Joe Piscopo. D: Michael Keusch. ACT [PG] 103m. V

Huckleberry Finn 1931 ★★★★ Cast of 1930 film *Tom Sawyer* reunited for Mark Twain's sequel to the original Mississippi boy's adventures. Coogan is featured in title role in an entertaining rendition of the classic story, although the social issues raised in book are watered down considerably. C: Jackie Coogan, Mitzi Green, Eugene Pallette, Jane Darwell. D: Norman Taurog. FAM/DRA 80m.

Huckleberry Finn 1939 ★★★★½ Fine remake of 1931 film with Rooney and Ingram as two runaways traveling on the Mississippi. Doesn't shy away from the tough issues raised by Mark Twain's original story, and a good film to introduce the classic to younger audiences. C: Mickey Rooney, Walter Connolly, William Frawley, Rex Ingram. D: Richard Thorpe, V. FAM/DRA 90m.

Huckleberry Finn 1974 ★★★ Musical version of Twain's story that preceded the later Broadway show. East is Huck and Winfield is Jim but sappy approach to material strips this rendition of any interest. C: Jeff East, Paul Winfield, Harvey Korman, David Wayne. D: J. Lee Thompson. FAM/MUS [G] 118m. V

Huckleberry Finn 1975 ★★★ Dano plays Mark Twain as narrator of the Huck and Jim tale in this remake of the great American novel. Notable mostly for casting of then-popular sitcom stars Howard and Most, as well as some of Howard's siblings. C: Ron Howard, Donny Most, Jack Elam, Merle Haggard, Royal Dano. D: Robert Totten. FAM/DRA 74m. TVM V

Hucksters, The 1947 ★★★ Toothless exposeé of Madison Avenue advertising industry, with exec Gable juggling career and lovers Kerr and Gardner. Well mounted but superficial. C: Clark Gable, Deborah Kerr, Ava Gardner, Sydney Greenstreet, Adolphe Menjou, Keenan Wynn. D: Jack Conway. DRA 116m. V

Hud 1963 ★★★★★ Unethical Texas oil man (Douglas) on hard times turns to roguish son (Newman), who only wants to chase family maid (Neal). Oscars for Douglas and Neal, but Newman steals film with sly performance. Based on Larry McMurtry's *Horseman, Pass By.* C: Paul Newman, Patricia Neal, Melvyn Douglas, Brandon de Wilde. D: Martin Ritt. DRA 112m. V

Hudson Hawk 1991 ★½ Former cat burglar (Willis), rescues friend via daring acts of thievery. Famous flop proves it takes more than a big budget to succeed as action/comedy. Has moments, but they're hard to find amid chaos. C: Bruce Willis, Danny Aiello, Andie MacDowell, James Coburn, Sandra Bernhard. D: Michael Lehmann. ACT [R] 95m. V

Hudson's Bay 1940 ★★★ Muni plays the English navigator and voyager who explored the bay and founded a trading company. Unexceptional biographical drama. C: Paul Muni, Gene Tierney, Laird Cregar, Vincent Price. D: Irving Pichel. DRA 95m.

Hudsucker Proxy, The 1994 ★★★★ The Coen brothers' homage to Preston Sturges and Frank Capra is a vaguely populist comedy about the swift climb of a little guy (Robbins) from mailroom to boardroom, unaware of his manipulation by bad guys. Well acted and handsomely mounted, with oodles of '50s period detail. C: Tim Robbins, Jennifer Jason Leigh, Paul Newman, Charles Durning, John Mahoney, Jim True, Bruce Campbell. D: Joel Coen. COM 111m. V

Hue and Cry 1947 British ★★★½ Crooks use a kiddie news weekly as a means of passing information until a young reader uncovers the subterfuge and leads a gang to apprehend the criminals. Fun, lively comedy with good use of London locations. C: Alastair Sim, Jack Warner, Frederick Piper. D: Charles Crichton. COM 82m.

Huey Long 1985 ★★★★ Unique, fascinating documentary about 1930s Louisiana governor who was one of the most original characters ever to emerge on America's political scene. More classic footage than can be imagined. D: Ken Burns. DOC 88m.

Hugo the Hippo 1975 ★★★½ Fairy tale musical tells the story of how the hippopotamus was saved from extinction in long-ago Zanzibar. Cute fable for young children. Voices of Paul Lynde, Burl Ives, Robert Morley, Marie Osmond. D: William Feigenbaum. MUS [G] 90m. V

Huk 1956 ★★★ Man journeys to the Philippines to avenge his father's murder by marauding guerrillas. Stiffly acted actioner, slightly redeemed by well-staged battle scenes. C: George Montgomery, Mona Freeman. D: John Barnwell. ACT 84m.

Hullabaloo Over Georgie and Bonnie's Pictures 1978 British ★★★ Lighthearted early comedy by the talented Ivory/Merchant/Jhabvala team involves American and British art dealers competing for an Indian rajah's art collection. Well-acted farce. C: Peggy Ashcroft, Victor Banerjee, Larry Pine. D: James Ivory. COM 85m. V

Human Beast, The *See* **La Bete Humaine**

Human Comedy, The 1943 ★★★★ Saroyan won an Oscar for his emotional, slice-of-America story about small-town life during WWII. Wonderful acting, especially by Rooney, keeps sketches from becoming cloying. C: Mickey Rooney, Frank Morgan, Marsha Hunt, Fay Bainter, Darryl Hickman, Donna Reed, Van Johnson. D: Clarence Brown. DRA 118m. v

Human Condition, The—Part One: No Greater Love 1958 Japanese ★★★★½ Young pacifist Kaji finds his ethics compromised by the treatment of POWs in Manchurian mine. First of a trilogy, Kobayashi's epic is a masterpiece times three; here, he lays groundwork for humanist drama and an unyielding depiction of war's horrors. Nakadai (Kaji) is tremendous. C: Tatsuya Nakadai, Michiyo Aratama, Chikage Awashima. D: Masaki Kobayashi. DRA 200m. v

Human Condition, The—Part Two: The Road to Eternity 1959 Japanese ★★★★½ Kaji is one of three survivors after his army unit is nearly wiped out by Russian forces. Middle section of Kobayashi's antiwar epic, like the others, stands on its own, but see all nine hours in order to get the full effect of the director's indictment of Japan's then-rampant nationalism. C: Tatsuya Nakadai, Michiyo Aratama, Kokinji Katsura. D: Masaki Kobayashi. DRA 180m. v

Human Condition, The—Part Three: A Soldier's Prayer 1961 Japanese ★★★★½ After Japan surrenders, Russians capture Kaji and treat him brutally until his escape. Conclusion of this shattering trilogy never blinks in its treatment of its lead character; the final moments are almost too overwhelming. An aptly titled look at of man's inhumanity to man. C: Tatsuya Nakadai, Michiyo Aratama, Yusuke Kawazu, Tamao Nakamura, Chishu Ryu. D: Masaki Kobayashi. DRA 190m. v

Human Desire 1954 ★★★ An adulterous wife (Grahame) tries to convince a railroad engineer (Ford) to help her do away with her husband (Crawford). Stylish film noir, based on Zola's novel *La Bete Humaine.* C: Gloria Grahame, Glenn Ford, Broderick Crawford. D: Fritz Lang. CRI 90m. v

Human Duplicators, The 1964 ★★★½ A race of aliens duplicate humans, thereby making their goal of total world domination more attainable. However, their plan is foiled by . . . love?! Kiel (Jaws in the Bond films) plays the alien leader. Interesting premise, fun to watch. (a.k.a. *Jaws of the Alien*) C: George Nader, Barbara Nichols, Richard Kiel. D: Hugo Grimaldi. SFI 82m. v

Human Experiments 1979 ★★ Terrific opening scene, setting up events that wrongly send Haynes to prison, gives way to sordid, unpleasant horror tale of mad doctor using inmates in sadistic tests. C: Linda Haynes, Geoffrey Lewis, Jackie Coogan. D: Gregory Goodell. HOR [R] 82m. v

Human Factor, The 1975 British ★★ A computer expert (Kennedy) hunts down the terrorists responsible for murdering his family. Gory revenge drama. C: George Kennedy, John Mills, Raf Vallone, Rita Tushingham. D: Edward Dmytryk. ACT [R] 96m. v

Human Factor, The 1979 ★★★ British double agent (Williamson) is forced to go over to the Russians in this surprisingly dreary adaptation by Tom Stoppard of the Graham Greene novel. Good cast. C: Nicol Williamson, Derek Jacobi, Richard Attenborough, Robert Morley, Ann Todd, John Gielgud. D: Otto Preminger. DRA [R] 115m. TVM

Human Feelings 1978 ★★★ Wisecracking God (Walker) orders one of her angels (Crystal) to drive sin from Las Vegas, or else she will destroy the whole town. Silly fantasy borrows from *Oh God,* but doesn't reach the same heights. C: Nancy Walker, Billy Crystal. D: Ernest Pintoff. COM 96m.

Human Highway 1982 ★★½ No-nukes comedy about two gas station attendants (Tamblyn, Young) working near nuclear power plant. Rocker Young co-directed and performs in this off-the-wall effort. Scores high for originality. C: Neil Young, Russ Tamblyn, Dennis Hopper, Sally Kirkland, Dean Stockwell. D: Bernard Shakey, Dean Stockwell. COM 88m.

Human Jungle, The 1954 ★★★½ A new officer takes on gangsters in this day-in-the-life look at a busy police station. Well-paced and absorbing account. C: Gary Merrill, Jan Sterling, Paula Raymond. D: Joseph Newman. CRI 82m.

Human Monster, The 1939 British ★★★½ Benign doctor (Lugosi) moonlights as a vicious insurance swindler, killing London's homeless for their money with the aid of a towering henchman (Walter). Eerie thriller, based on Edgar Wallace's story. (a.k.a. *Dark Eyes of London*) C: Bela Lugosi, Hugh Williams, Greta Gynt. D: Walter Summers. HOR 76m. v

Human Shield, The 1991 ★★ Potboiler has an evil Iraqi officer using the brother of a gung-ho American (Dudikoff) to draw him into a trap. C: Michael Dudikoff, Steve Inwood, Tommy Hinkley. D: Ted Post. ACT [R] 88m. v

Human Side, The 1934 ★★½ After running around with all kinds of women, a big-time entertainment producer tries to return home. Well-intended comedy hits the mark. C: Adolphe Menjou, Doris Kenyon, Charlotte Henry, Reginald Owen. D: Edward Buzzell. COM 60m.

Human, Too Human 1972 ★★★ Documentary shows automobile assembly line employees toiling away. Almost unbearably depressing (Malle cuts between the line and a posh showroom), but technically precise glimpse at the isolation of industrial workers. D: Louis Malle. DOC 77m.

Human Vapor, The 1960 ★★ Astro-man, capable of slipping through keyholes and doors, terrorizes Earthlings. C: Yoshio Tsuchiya, Keiko Sata, Kaoru Yachigusa. D: Inoshiro Honda. SFI 82m. v

Humanoid Defender 1985 ★★ Evil government programs powerful humanoid to kill, but when it refuses, government threatens to terminate it. C: Terence Knox, Gary Kasper, Aimee Eccles. D: Ron Satlof. SFI 94m. V

Humanoids from the Deep 1980 ★ Monsters spawned by pollution rise from the waves to murder men and rape women (both explicitly) in a seaside community. Tacky and sleazy. C: Doug McClure, Ann Turkel, Vic Morrow. D: Barbara Peeters. HOR [R] 83m. V

Humongous 1981 Canadian ★ If a group of young people gets stranded on a deserted island in the movies, you just know there's a half-human murderer waiting to pick them off. That's how it goes in this cheapie, which is the same old thing from beginning to end. C: Janet Julian, David Wallace. D: Paul Lynch. HOR [R] 93m. V

Humoresque 1946 ★★★★½ Streetwise Garfield overcomes slum background to become a concert violinist, thanks to generous contributions of his mercurial patron/love interest (Crawford). Smartly played story avoids clichés; Garfield and Crawford are wonderful, with Levant providing fine comic relief as cynical pianist. Issac Stern played Garfield's violin solos. C: Joan Crawford, John Garfield, Oscar Levant, J. Carrol Naish. D: Jean Negulesco. DRA 126m. V

Hunchback of Notre Dame, The 1923 ★★★★½ Silent adaptation of Victor Hugo's novel features the hideously made-up Chaney as Quasimodo, the bell ringer of Notre Dame who becomes obsessed with gypsy girl Esmeralda. Atmospheric depiction of medieval Paris frames Chaney's compelling performance. Remade in 1939, 1957, and 1982. C: Lon Chaney, Sr., Patsy Ruth Miller, Ernest Torrence, Tully Marshall. D: Wallace Worsley. DRA 95m. V

Hunchback of Notre Dame, The 1939 ★★★★★ Perhaps the finest version of Hugo's story ever done. Laughton's superb performance as the malformed bellringer Quasimodo in love with Esmeralda (O'Hara) dominates a simply marvelous movie. A true classic. C: Charles Laughton, Maureen O'Hara, Cedric Hardwicke. D: William Dieterle. DRA 126m. V

Hunchback of Notre Dame 1957 French ★★★ Least successful adaption of Victor Hugo's classic tale of a crippled bell ringer (Quinn) and the gypsy girl he loves (Lollabrigida). Expansive production lacks emotional substance; Lollabrigida is out of her depth as Esmeralda. C: Anthony Quinn, Gina Lollobrigida, Jean Danet. D: Jean Delannoy. DRA 104m.

Hunchback of Notre Dame, The 1982 ★★★★ Hopkins' Quasimodo is complex and sympathetic, and the other cast members are also excellent in this fine adaptation of the Hugo classic. Re-creation of the cathedral by designer Stoll is the film's centerpiece. (a.k.a *Hunchback*) C: Anthony Hopkins, Derek Jacobi, Lesley-Anne Down, Robert Powell, John Gielgud. D: Michael Tuchner. DRA 150m. TVM V

Hundra 1983 ★★ Leader of a tribe of Amazons seeks revenge against the brutal men who wiped out her followers. Scanty Italian-produced adventure. C: Laurene Landon, John Gaffari, Marisa Casel. D: Matt Cimber. ACT 104m. V

Hundred Hour Hunt 1953 ★★★½ A young woman's life depends on obtaining rare blood type. A departing sailor, a disgraced pugilist, and a fugitive murderer all have the vital fluid in their veins—but can any of them be found in time? Engaging medical drama. (a.k.a. *Emergency Call*) C: Jack Warner, Anthony Steel, Joy Shelton. D: Lewis Gilbert. DRA 92m.

Hungarian Fairy Tale, A 1988 Hungarian ★★★½ Boy who's lost his mother sets out to find dad though fictitious name is on his birth certificate. Allegory of modern-day Eastern Europe, somewhat heavy handed but affecting. Exquisite b&w photography, music from Mozart's *The Magic Flute*. C: Arpad Vermes, Maria Varga, Frantisek Husak. D: Gyula Gazdag. DRA 95m. V

Hunger 1966 Danish ★★★½ Frustrated writer is reduced to physical and spiritual starvation as he awaits an editor's reaction to his work. Sounds ponderous, but director Carlsen and actor Oscarsson save this closely observed study from boredom. C: Per Oscarsson, Gunnel Lindblom, Birgitte Federspiel. D: Henning Carlsen. DRA 100m.

Hunger, The 1983 ★★ When her vampire lover (Bowie) begins deteriorating, ageless vampire Deneuve targets Sarandon as his replacement. A horror film trying not to be one, Scott's glossy style undermines the terror, despite stunning makeup effects. C: Catherine Deneuve, David Bowie, Susan Sarandon. D: Tony Scott. HOR [R] 100m. V

Hungry Hill 1947 British ★★★ Two feuding 19th-century Irish families go through three generations of trouble. So-so period melodrama, based on Daphne du Maurier novel. C: Margaret Lockwood, Dennis Price, Jean Simmons, Eileen Herlie, Siobhan McKenna. D: Brian Hurst. DRA 92m.

Hunk 1987 ★★★½ Dweeb makes a pact with the devil to be gorgeous. Pleasant comedy with wonderful turn by devil Coco. C: John Allen Nelson, Steve Levitt, Deborah Shelton, James Coco, Robert Morse, Avery Schreiber. D: Lawrence Bassoff. COM [PG] 102m. V

Hunt for Red October, The 1990 ★★★★ Soviet submarine commander (Connery) goes AWOL: Is he defecting or about to start WWIII? U.S. intelligence (led by Baldwin) has to figure it out. Fine cast and nifty hardware showcase this adaptation of Tom Clancy's best-seller. *Patriot Games* continued Jack Ryan's story, with Harrison Ford taking over for Baldwin. C: Sean Connery, Alec Baldwin, Scott Glenn, Sam Neill, James Earl Jones. D: John McTiernan. ACT [PG] 135m. V

Hunt for the Night Stalker, The 1991 ★★½ Fact-based drama as two relentless L.A. cops track down serial killer Richard Ramirez. Standard police drama, with some suspense. C: Richard Jordan, Lisa Eilbacher. D: Bruce Seth Green. CRI [R] 95m. V

Hunt the Man Down 1950 ★★★ The clock ticks predictably in this standard yarn about an innocent man accused of murder. This time it's his loyal attorney who must find the real culprit before it's too late. C: Gig Young, Lynne Roberts, Willard Parker. D: George Archainbaud. CRI 68m. V

Hunt, The 1965 Spanish ★★★★ A teenager takes three Spanish Civil War veterans on a rabbit hunt that turns violent. Brilliantly disturbing meditation on the grimness of war, well handled by Spanish director Saura. C: Luis De Pablo, Ismael Merlo, Alfredo Mayo, Jose Maria Prada, Emillio Guiterrez Caba. D: Carlos Saura. ACT 87m. V

Hunted 1988 ★★ Prisoner of war, framed for murder, is persecuted by savage officer. C: Andrew Buckland, Mercia Van Wyk, Ron Smerczak. D: David Lister. ACT 75m.

Hunted Lady, The 1977 ★★½ TV policewoman thriller about an undercover cop (Mills) set up by gangsters. Routine plot. C: Donna Mills, Robert Reed. D: Richard Lang. DRA 100m. TVM V

Hunted Men 1938 ★★★ On the run from the law, a killer (Nolan) winds up hiding out with a friendly, middle-class family, and becomes too close. Compelling thriller, at moments almost sentimental. (a.k.a. *Crime Gives Orders*) C: Lloyd Nolan, Mary Carlisle, Lynne Overman. D: Louis King. CRI 65m.

Hunter, The 1980 ★★½ Bounty hunter McQueen must use all his experience and savvy to continually outsmart fugitives from justice. Based on life story of a real bounty hunter, this muddled tale may be a little too tall in it's retelling. C: Steve McQueen, Eli Wallach, Kathryn Harrold, LeVar Burton. D: Buzz Kulik. ACT [PG] 97m. V

Hunters Are for Killing 1970 *See* **Hard Frame**

Hunter's Blood 1987 ★★½ A group of big-city men hunting bear in the woods wind up being hunted by sadistic hillbillies. Effective, chilling action à la *Deliverance*. C: Sam Bottoms, Kim Delaney, Clu Gulager. D: Robert C. Hughes. ACT [R] 102m. V

Hunters of the Golden Cobra 1982 ★★ When a Japanese military officer steals a golden cobra a few days before the end of WW II, two Americans seek him out. C: David Warbeck, Almanta Suska, Alan Collins. D: Anthony M. Dawson. ACT [R] 95m. V

Hunters, The 1958 ★★★½ A Korean War jet ace (Mitchum) romances the wife of a pilot shot down behind enemy lines—then must rescue him. Passable melodrama with plenty of action aloft. C: Robert Mitchum, Robert Wagner, Richard Egan, Mai Britt. D: Dick Powell. DRA 108m.

Hunting Party, The 1971 ★ When Texas woman in 1890s is abducted and sexually assaulted by desperados, her sadistic husband tracks the culprits, bent on killing them individually. Stellar cast can't redeem excessive violence. C: Oliver Reed, Candice Bergen, Gene Hackman, Simon Oakland. D: Don Medford. WST [R] 108m.

Hurricane 1974 ★★½ A big wind blows a hodgepodge of TV stars across the small screen, to fairly limp disaster extravaganza effects. C: Larry Hagman, Martin Milner, Jessica Walter, Barry Sullivan, Michael Learned, Patrick Duffy, Frank Sutton, Will Geer. D: Jerry Jameson. ACT 78m. TVM V

Hurricane 1979 ★★ Bloated remake of 1937 tropical island adventure. Jumbled story of forbidden love is full of hot air this time out and the big blow comes too late. Island setting is undeniably beautiful in color, however. (a.k.a. *Forbidden Paradise*) C: Jason Robards, Mia Farrow, Max von Sydow. D: Jan Truell. DRA 78m. TVM V

Hurricane Express, The 1932 ★★ Pilot seeks father's murderer in this twelve-part series. C: John Wayne, Tully Marshall, Shirley Grey, Conway Tearle. D: J. P. McGowan. WST 210m. V

Hurricane Island 1951 ★★½ Explorers tramping through Florida jungles encounter evil spirits, lady pirates, and the Fountain of Youth. Unsuccessful amalgam of adventure, horror, and fantasy. C: Jon Hall, Marie Windsor, Marc Lawrence. D: Lew Landers. ACT 70m.

Hurricane Smith 1990 ★★★ Tough Texan (Weathers) takes Australia by storm when he finds his sister has been murdered by a drug czar. Wild stunts and eye-popping nudity follows non-stop as Carl Does Down-Under. C: Carl Weathers, Cassandra Delaney, Tony Bonner. D: Colin Budds. ACT 90m. V

Hurricane, The 1937 ★★★★ Idyllic island existence of lovers Hall and Lamour threatened by adversities human (Massey) and natural (title storm). Archetypal South Seas adventure/romance is great Saturday afternoon fun, and the hurricane at the climax is still impressive. C: Dorothy Lamour, Jon Hall, Mary Astor, C. Aubrey Smith, Raymond Massey, Thomas Mitchell, John Carradine. D: John Ford. DRA 102m. V

Hurried Man, The 1977 French ★★ Unable to control his lust for sex and success, married man self-destructs. C: Alain Delon, Mireille Darc. D: Edouard Malimaro. DRA 91m.

Hurry Sundown 1967 ★★★ An avaricious Georgian plots to expand his land by taking over his cousin's acreage. Het up melodrama with unusual roles for Caine and Fonda. C: Michael Caine, Jane Fonda, John Phillip Law, Diahann Carroll, Robert Hooks, Faye Dunaway, Burgess Meredith, Robert Reed, George Kennedy. D: Otto Preminger. DRA 142m.

Hurry Up, or I'll Be 30 1973 ★★★½ A nebbish despairs as he approaches the big three-O. Low-key, low-budget comedy emphasizes character over laughs. C: John Lefkowitz,

Linda De Coff, Danny DeVito. D: Joseph Jacoby. COM [PG] 87m. V

Husbands 1970 ★★★½ Three middle-aged New Yorkers, shaken by a friend's death, take an impulsive trip to Europe. Strong cast, but Cassavete's improvisational style could use some tightening. C: Ben Gazzara, Peter Falk, John Cassavetes. D: John Cassavetes. DRA [PG] 138m.

Husbands and Lovers 1991 ★ Weak effort in which audience is expected to believe that a husband would love his wife so much that—in order to keep her—he would knowingly allow her to spend time with an abusive lover. C: Julian Sands, Joanna Pacula, Tcheky Karyo. D: Mauro Bolognini. DRA 94m.

Husbands and Wives 1992 ★★★★ A long-married couple's breakup triggers the disintegration of their friends' marriages. Intelligent story, well-played by outstanding ensemble cast; Davis in particular, stands out. C: Woody Allen, Mia Farrow, Judy Davis, Sydney Pollack, Liam Neeson, Juliette Lewis, Lysette Anthony. D: Woody Allen. DRA [R] 107m. V

Husbands, Wives, Money & Murder 1986 ★★½ Suburban couple's afternoon is disrupted when census taker dies in their living room and they have to hide the body before police detective in-law arrives. Oddball comedy more frantic than funny. C: Garrett Morris, Greg Mullavey, Timothy Bottoms. D: Bruce R. Cook. COM 95m. V

Hush . . . Hush, Sweet Charlotte 1965 ★★★★½ A reclusive, aging Southern belle slides into insanity when her conniving cousin shows up and starts yanking skeletons out of the family closet. Excellent follow-up to *What Ever Happened to Baby Jane* with Davis and de Havilland giving it all they've got, and that's plenty. A very chilling gothic shocker. C: Bette Davis, Olivia de Havilland, Joseph Cotten, Agnes Moorehead, Victor Buono, Mary Astor. D: Robert Aldrich. HOR 134m. V

Hussy 1980 British ★★ A hostess/hooker (Mirren) at a London strip club falls for an American (Shea) and both become involved in the drug trade. Mirren can't save it. C: Helen Mirren, John Shea, Murray Salem. D: Matthew Chapman. DRA [R] 95m. V

Hustle 1975 ★★★ Modern film noir about a hardened cop (Reynolds) who suspects that a well-known attorney (Albert) is involved in a prostitute's murder. Cynical and sensational. C: Burt Reynolds, Catherine Deneuve, Ben Johnson, Paul Winfield, Eileen Brennan, Eddie Albert. D: Robert Aldrich. CRI [R] 120m. V

Hustler of Muscle Beach, The 1980 ★★½ New York con artist heads west and falls in love while promoting a slow-witted but determined bodybuilder in a beach contest. Romanticized look at bodybuilding contests, à la *Rocky*. DRA

Hustler, The 1961 ★★★★★ Newman is terrific as pool shark Fast Eddie Felson hustling chumps for small change before he takes a shot at big-timer Minnesota Fats (Gleason). Atmospheric photography won Oscar. 1986 sequel: *The Color of Money*. C: Paul Newman, Jackie Gleason, Piper Laurie, George C. Scott. D: Robert Rossen. DRA 134m. V

Hustling 1975 ★★★★ Strong, tough film about a journalist's exposeé of the prostitution industry in New York City. Fine performances by Remick and Clayburgh; based on Gail Sheehy's book. C: Lee Remick, Jill Clayburgh. D: Joseph Sargent. DRA 96m. TVM V

Hyde Park Corner 1935 ★★★ In Hyde Park Corner, it seems that events of the 18th century are apt to repeat themselves in modern times. Tidy little comedy, based on Walter Hackett's play. C: Gordon Harker, Binnie Hale. D: Sinclair Hill. COM 85m.

Hyper Sapien—People from Another Star 1986 ★★★½ Two teenagers from another solar system run away from home and end up as guests of a Wyoming adolescent. Younger children might enjoy this simple tale of friendship. C: Ricky Paull Goldin, Sydney Penny, Keenan Wynn. D: Peter H. Hunt. FAM/SFI [PG] 94m. V

Hypnotic Eye, The 1960 ★★½ A hypnotist (Bergerac) orders women under his spell to mutilate themselves. Difficult premise; notable primarily for opening segment in which Bergerac tries to hypnotize audience. C: Jacques Bergerac, Merry Anders. D: George Blair. DRA 79m.

Hysteria 1965 ★★★½ An American amnesiac, discharged from a London hospital gets involved in a murder. Psychological thriller gets a bit convoluted, but has real suspense. C: Robert Webber, Lelia Goldoni. D: Freddie Francis. CRI 85m. V

Hysterical 1983 ★★★½ Silly horror spoof has three goofy brothers battling the ghostly inhabitant of a haunted lighthouse. Funnier than it looks, with low-brow laughs. C: The Hudson Brothers, Cindy Pickett, Richard Kiel, Julie Newmar. D: Chris Bearde. COM [PG] 86m. V

I

I Accuse! 1958 British ★★★ Historical drama re-creates 19th-century French scandal of Alfred Dreyfuss, who was accused of treason by anti-Semites. Though Gore Vidal's script handles facts and Ferrer is fine as Dreyfuss, film lacks emotional heart. C: Jose Ferrer, Anton Walbrook, Emlyn Williams, Viveca Lindfors. D: Jose Ferrer. DRA 99m.

I Aim at the Stars 1960 ★★★ Fictionalized story of Werner von Braun, focuses on the Nazi inventor's life in America. Morally lightweight, and unsurprising. C: Curt Jurgens, Victoria Shaw, Herbert Lom. D: J. Thompson. DRA 107m.

I Am a Camera 1955 British ★★★★½ Episodic drama of young British author and fiery dancer in prewar Berlin. Erudite adult treatment that doesn't compromise characters or situations. Based on Christopher Isherwood's autobiographical stories and later remade into Oscar-winning musical *Cabaret.* C: Julie Harris, Laurence Harvey, Shelley Winters, Ron Randell. D: Henry Cornelius. DRA 99m. V

I Am a Dancer 1973 ★★★★ Documentary about acclaimed dancer Rudolf Nureyev covers rehearsals and plenty of duets with Margot Fonteyn. A cut above similar films; broad audience appeal. D: Pierre Jourdan, Bryan Forbes. DOC 90m. V

I Am a Fugitive from a Chain Gang 1932 ★★★★★ A falsely convicted man experiences the inhumanity of a prison chain gang. He escapes and reestablishes normal life until the law once more catches up with him. Powerful and determined drama with still-shocking sequences of brutality. Muni's performance is riveting. C: Paul Muni, Glenda Farrell, Helen Vinson, Preston Foster. D: Mervyn LeRoy. DRA 76m. V

I Am a Thief 1935 ★★★ Intrigue follows a group of passengers competing for possession of precious diamonds aboard a train to Istanbul. Glamorous trappings, ruined by poor plotting. C: Mary Astor, Ricardo Cortez, Dudley Digges. D: Robert Florey. CRI 64m.

I Am My Films: A Portrait of Werner Herzog 1978 ★★★★½ Well-done documentary about a contemporary German director. Herzog, who philosophizes about cinema, discusses his mythic feuds with actor Klaus Kinski, details childhood events, and looks for reasons why he assigns the highest importance to his art. D: Christian Weisenborn, Erwin Keusch. DOC 96m.

I Am the Cheese 1983 ★★★ A teenager (MacNaughton) withdraws from reality after witnessing the deaths of his parents and is treated at a psychiatric hospital. Earnest adaption of Robert Cormier's novel for teens. (a.k.a *Lapse of Memory*) C: Robert MacNaughton, Hope Lange, Don Murray, Robert Wagner. D: Robert Jiras. DRA [PG] 96m. V

I Am the Law 1938 ★★★½ When city government and racketeers enter corrupt partnership, a hard-driving attorney (Robinson) fights back. Robinson's solid lead gives an edge to the routine. C: Edward G. Robinson, Otto Kruger, Wendy Barrie, John Beal. D: Alexander Hall. DRA 83m. V

I Became a Criminal 1947 ★★★★ Thriller about a man who's framed for murder and is dead-set on revenge. Memorable example of British film noir. (a.k.a. *They Made Me a Fugitive*) C: Sally Gray, Trevor Howard, Griffith Jones. D: Alberto Cavalcanti. CRI 78m.

I Beheld His Glory 1978 ★★★ Sincere telling of the story of the Roman centurion who was present at the Crucifixion. Earnest biblical drama. C: George MacReady, Robert Wilson, Thomas Charlesworth. DRA 55m. V

I Believe In You 1952 British ★★★½ Parole officer takes job to heart and helps to reform a juvenile delinquent and a professional criminal. Sentimental but sincere account of life on the downside, marked by some good performances. C: Cecil Parker, Celia Johnson, Lawrence Harvey, Joan Collins. D: Michael Relph, Basil Dearden. DRA 93m.

I Bury the Living 1958 ★★★ Man (Boone) becomes a graveyard caretaker and finds he can control life and death. Unusual horror film has Swiss cheese plot, but neat special effects and a fairly interesting mystery. C: Richard Boone, Theodore Bikel. D: Albert Band. HOR 76m. V

I Can Get It for You Wholesale 1951 ★★★★ Jerome Weidman's novel of rapacious fashion designer stepping over hearts and souls to make it to the top. Hero's sex has been switched, but Hayward's gutsy performance fits refurbished material well. Very entertaining till cop-out ending. C: Susan Hayward, Dan Dailey, Sam Jaffe, George Sanders. D: Michael Gordon. COM 90m.

I Can't Give You Anything But Love, Baby 1940 ★★ Gangster with yen for lyric writing kidnaps composer. Points for originality. C: Broderick Crawford, Peggy Moran, Johnny Downs. D: Albert S. Rogell. MUS 61m.

I Come in Peace 1990 ★★½ Lundgren is a square-jawed cop fighting a bizarre killer from outer space. Prosaic action flick; Lundgren's closing line is a grade-D classic. C: Dolph Lundgren, Brian Benben, Betsy Brantley, Matthias Hues. D: Craig R. Baxley. ACT [R] 92m. V

I Confess 1953 ★★★½ Young priest (Clift) hears the confession of a murderer, but is supected himself. Relatively weak Hitchcock is still superior entertainment. Shot in Quebec City. C: Montgomery Clift, Anne Baxter, Karl

Malden, Brian Aherne, O.E. Hasse. D: Alfred Hitchcock. CRI 95m. V

I Conquer the Sea 1936 ★★ Hurdles set before Newfoundland harpooner as he pursues a disinterested woman. C: Steffi Duna, Dennis Morgan. DRA 67m.

I Could Go on Singing 1963 British ★★★½ In her last film, Garland plays an American singer in England, fighting inner demons as she attempts to win back the affections of her estranged son and his British father. Garland's musical numbers are superbly touching. C: Judy Garland, Dirk Bogarde, Jack Klugman, Aline MacMahon. D: Ronald Neame. MUS 99m. V

I Could Never Have Sex With Any Man Who Has So Little Respect for My Husband 1973 ★★½ Drawn-out title is apropos for this tedious comedy that explores marital infidelity as two couples eye each other during an excursion to the New England shore. Too much dialogue with very little action. C: Carmine Caridi, Lynne Lipton, Cynthia Harris, Andrew Duncan, Dan Greenburg. D: Robert McCarty. COM [R] 86m.

I Cover the War 1937 ★★ A war correspondent (Wayne) is sent to the desert where he tangles with Arab rebels. Typical pulp, of interest to Wayne fans. C: John Wayne, Gwen Gaze, Major Sam Harris, James Bush, Don Barclay. D: Arthur Lubin. DRA 68m.

I Cover the Waterfront 1933 ★★★½ Sensational drama has reporter Lyon romancing Colbert so he can snare her father, a smuggler of illegal immigrants. Fairly lurid in its day, picture is packed with hard-bitten clichés that haven't aged well, though Lyon and Colbert hold audience interest throughout. C: Ben Lyon, Claudette Colbert, Ernest Torrence, Hobart Cavanaugh. D: James Cruze. DRA 70m. V

I Crossed the Line 1966 *See* **Black Klansman, The**

I Deal in Danger 1966 ★★★½ American spy (Goulet) infiltrates the Nazis during WWII by posing as a traitor in this version of the *Blue Light* TV series. Romance with French agent (Carere) adds to the intrigue. C: Robert Goulet, Christine Carere, Donald Harron, Werner Peters. D: Walter Grauman. DRA 89m.

I, Desire 1982 ★★★ Law student and part-time coroner's clerk Naughton becomes obsessed with Hollywood hooker (Stock) who's a vampire. Mild and predictable. C: David Naughton, Dorian Harewood, Brad Dourif, Barbara Stock. D: John Llewellyn Moxey. HOR 104m. TVM

I Died a Thousand Times 1955 ★★★ Competent but unexciting remake of *High Sierra* with Palance as the hard-boiled bank robber on the run from police. Palance is no Bogart, but the supporting cast is top-notch. C: Jack Palance, Shelley Winters, Lori Nelson, Lee Marvin, Earl Holliman. D: Stuart Heisler. CRI 109m. V

I Dismember Mama 1972 ★½ A psycho fresh from the mental ward hacks up mom, then takes up with a nine-year-old. Not very gory, just junk. C: Zooey Hall, Geri Reischel. D: Paul Leder. HOR [R] 88m. V

I Don't Buy Kisses Anymore 1992 ★★★½ Chubby, insecure shoe store owner (Alexander) has romantic designs on sexy researcher (Peeples) but she's only interested in him as a guinea pig for a psychology experiment. Likable, low-key romantic comedy has trouble avoiding clichés but still manages to entertain. C: Jason Alexander, Nia Peeples, Lainie Kazan, Lou Jacobi, Eileen Brennan. D: Robert Marcarelli. COM [PG] 112m. V

I Don't Care Girl, The 1953 ★★½ Musical biography of vaudeville star Eva Tanguay. Features good choreography by legend Jack Cole. C: Mitzi Gaynor, David Wayne, Oscar Levant, Warren Stevens. D: Lloyd Bacon. MUS 78m.

I Don't Want To Talk About It 1994 Argentinian ★★★★ Mysterious man (Mastroianni) woos and weds a 15-year-old girl—who happens to be a dwarf. Unusual love story grows on one as film progresses to its haunting conclusion. C: Marcello Mastroianni, Lusina Brando, Alejandra Podesta. D: Maria Luisa Bemberg. COM [PG-13] 102m. V

I Dood It 1943 ★★★ A bumbling pants presser falls for a movie actress who agrees to marry him only because she wants to make her lecherous boyfriend jealous. Musical remake of Buster Keaton's silent classic *Spite Marriage* benefits from Skelton's endearing charm and nice songs. C: Red Skelton, Eleanor Powell, Richard Ainley, Patricia Dane, Lena Horne. D: Vincente Minnelli. MUS 102m. V

I Dream of Jeannie 1952 ★★½ Biography of American composer Stephen Foster (the third: first was *Harmony Lane*, 1935; and second was *Swanee River*, 1939). Includes many of his well-known ballads, including "Oh Susanna," "Camptown Races," and "My Old Kentucky Home." C: Ray Middleton, Bill Shirley, Muriel Lawrence, Lynn Bari, Louise Beavers, James Kirkwood. D: Allan Dwan. DRA 90m.

I Dream of Jeannie: 15 Years Later 1985 ★★★½ Lively return of '60s TV series finds Eden (with a now uncovered navel) as a suburban homemaker struggling with her desire to be an independent, modern woman. Rogers plays husband. C: Barbara Eden, Wayne Rogers, Bill Daily, Hayden Rorke, MacKenzie Astin, Dori Brenner, Andre De Shields, Dody Goodman. D: William Asher. COM 100m. TVM

I Dream Too Much 1935 ★★★½ Entertaining trifle casts Metropolitan Opera star Pons as a French diva in love with composer Fonda. Features arias from *Rigoletto, Lakme*. Look for Pons' husband, Andre Kostelanetz, as orchestra conductor. C: Lily Pons, Henry Fonda, Eric Blore, Lucille Ball, Osgood Perkins. D: John Cromwell. MUS 90m. V

I Drink Your Blood 1970 ★★ Traveling hippies slip an unwitting elderly man some LSD; for revenge, his grandson turns them into cannibals by selling them rabies-tainted meat pies. Demented. C: Bhaskar, Jadine Wong, Ronda Fultz, George Patterson. D: David Durston. HOR [R] 88m.

I Eat Your Skin 1964 ★★ Novelist visiting Caribbean island falls for daughter of scientist whose experiments are producing cannibalistic zombies. A cult classic. (a.k.a. *Zombies* and *Voodoo Blood Bath*) C: William Joyce, Heather Hewitt, Betty Hyatt Linton, Dan Stapleton. D: Del Tenney. HOR [PG] 82m. V

I Escaped from Devil's Island 1973 ★ Brown and George are convicts who plot to escape from prison island. A Roger Corman special. C: Jim Brown, Christopher George, Paul Richards, Rick Ely, Richard Rust, Jan Merlin. D: William Witney. ACT [R] 89m.

I Escaped from the Gestapo 1943 ★★★½ Nazi group headed by Carradine helps counterfeiter (Jagger) escape from prison so that he can aid the Axis war effort by forging U.S. and foreign currencies. Solid war story. (a.k.a. *No Escape*) C: Dean Jagger, John Carradine, Mary Brian, William Henry, Sidney Blackmer, Ian Keith. D: Harold Young. ACT 75m.

I Found Stella Parish 1935 ★★★ Actress with tarnished past tries to shield her daughter (Jason) from all the dirt. Pulls out the tear-jerking stops. C: Kay Francis, Ian Hunter, Paul Lukas, Sybil Jason, Jessie Ralph, Barton MacLane. D: Mervyn LeRoy. DRA 84m.

I Hate Actors 1986 French ★★★ A Gallic take on Hollywood: Murders confound movie set during production of costume epic. Adapted from Ben Hecht's satirical novel, but made with French crew and actors (look for a quick glimpse of Gerard Depardieu)! C: Jean Poiret, Michel Blanc, Bernard Blier, Michel Galabru, Guy Marchand, Dominique Lavanant. D: Gerard Krawrzyk. COM [PG] 90m.

I Hate Blondes 1981 Italian ★★★★ Ghostwriter (Montesano) of best-selling crime stories gets tangled up with band of burglars who plot their crimes according to plots of his stories. Fast paced and witty, with many cleverly staged sight gags. C: Enrico Montesano, Jean Rochefort, Corinne Clery, Marina Langner. D: Giorgio Capitani. COM 90m. V

I Have A New Master 1951 *See* **Passion for Life**

I Have Seven Daughters 1954 *See* **My Seven Little Sins**

I Heard the Owl Call My Name 1973 ★★★½ A young Anglican priest (Courtenay) learns about life and death when he goes to work among the Indians of an isolated British Columbia reservation. Touching and well handled. C: Tom Courtenay, Dean Jagger, Paul Stanley, Marianne Jones. D: Daryl Duke. DRA 74m. TVM V

I Hired a Contract Killer 1990 Finnish ★★★★ Lowly, lonely clerk (Leaud) hires a hitman to kill him, then meets a woman. Low-key comedy has its moments, and Leaud's hangdog expression is well-utilized, but brevity makes it just another shaggy-dog story. C: Jean-Pierre Leaud, Margi Clarke, Kenneth Colley. D: Aki Kaurismaki. COM 81m.

I, Jane Doe 1948 ★★★ During WWII, Ralston marries an American soldier who disappears. She goes to the U.S., looking for him, and finds him married to someone else. She kills him accidentally, and winds up being defended by his wife. Courtroom drama. (a.k.a. *Diary of a Bride*) C: Ruth Hussey, John Carroll, Vera Ralston, Gene Lockhart, John Howard, John Litel. D: John H. Auer. DRA 85m.

I Killed Einstein, Gentlemen 1970 Czech ★★★★ In the future, women sprout facial hair but can't conceive children thanks to radiation. To restore femininity, time travelers try to alter course of nuclear development by heading to the past to whack Einstein. Strange science fiction parody that runs wild with premise. C: Jiri Sovak, Jana Brezhova. D: Oldrich Lipsky. COM 95m.

I Killed Rasputin 1967 French ★★ Historical picture about the murder of Rasputin, the libertine monk whose hold on Russia's Imperial Court helped lead to downfall of the Czarist regime. Flows like cement, and title character barely shows up at all! C: Gert Frobe, Peter McEnery, Geraldine Chaplin, Robert Hossein. D: Robert Hossein. DRA 95m. V

I Killed That Man 1942 ★★★ Just before his scheduled electrocution, a convict is found dead of poisoning. Quite sharp and sometimes thrilling. C: Ricardo Cortez, Joan Woodbury, Iris Adrian. D: Phil Rosen. CRI 72m.

I Know My First Name Is Steven 1989 ★★★½ Fact-based drama about a youth who was kidnapped at the age of seven and lived in isolation with his captor for seven years before finally escaping back to his family. Well-done film depicts the extraordinary experience of his return. C: Cindy Pickett, John Ashton, Corin Nemec, Ray Walston, Barry Corbin, Arliss Howard. D: Larry Elikann. DRA 200m. TVM

I Know Where I'm Going 1945 British ★★★★½ Determined young woman encounters delays on her way to marry her wealthy fiancé. Magical Scottish atmosphere and Hiller's outstanding lead performance make this simple, expertly crafted romance a delight. C: Wendy Hiller, Roger Livesey, Finlay Currie, Pamela Brown, Valentine Dyall. D: Michael Powell, Emeric Pressburger. COM 91m. V

I Know Why the Caged Bird Sings 1979 ★★★½ Young African-American girl who longs to be a poet grows up in the South, encouraged by her nurturing grandmother. Sentimental but touching film based on Maya Angelou's autobiography. C: Diahann Carroll,

Ruby Dee, Paul Benjamin, Roger E. Mosley, Esther Rolle. D: Fielder Cook. DRA 100m. TVM V

I Like It Like That 1994 ★★★★½ Lisette Linares (Velez) wants to get ahead, and won't let her South Bronx background stop her. Exhilirating, episodic comedy-drama captures its characters and their milieu with razor-sharp precision. Martin's directorial debut. C: Lauren Velez, Jon Seda, Lisa Vidal, Griffin Dunne, Rita Moreno. D: Darnell Martin. DRA [R] 94m. V

I Like Money 1962 British ★★★½ An unscrupulous Parisian city councillor (McKern) hires a scrupulously honest schoolmaster (Sellers) to front for his shady financial dealings. All goes well until the teacher learns he is being duped and decides to turn the tables. Sly satire amuses mostly through the efforts of Sellers; still, he's a much better actor than director. Remake of *Topaze.* C: Peter Sellers, Nadia Gray, Herbert Lom, Leo McKern, Martita Hunt, John Neville, Michael Gough, Billie Whitelaw. D: Peter Sellers. COM 97m.

I Like Your Nerve 1931 ★★½ Romantic comedy trifle has Fairbanks going from meek to manly in Central America, where he wins Young's heart. C: Douglas Fairbanks Jr., Loretta Young, Henry Kolker, Edmund Breon, Boris Karloff. D: William McGann. COM 69m.

I Live for Love 1935 ★★½ Love between an actress and a street singer. Del Rio is the whole show. C: Dolores Del Rio, Everett Marshall, Guy Kibbee, Allen Jenkins, Berton Churchill. D: Busby Berkeley. MUS 64m.

I Live in Fear 1955 ★★★★ When wealthy Mifune decides to sell business and move to Brazil, his potential inheritors try to have him declared mentally incompetent. Intriguing dramatic comedy with strong psychological undertones about societal roles. One of director Kurosawa's lesser-known films. C: Toshsiro Mifune, Eiko Miyoshi, Takashi Shimura. D: Akira Kurosawa. DRA 113m.

I Live My Life 1935 ★★★ Typical comedy puts free spirit Crawford in arms of stuffy archaeologist (Aherne). C: Joan Crawford, Brian Aherne, Frank Morgan, Aline MacMahon, Eric Blore, Arthur Treacher. D: W.S. VanDyke II. COM 92m. V

I Live with Me Dad 1986 ★★ Homeless, alcoholic father whose son is removed to foster care, gives up his vice in order to reclaim his boy. C: Peter Hehir, Haydon Samuels, Rebecca Gibney. D: Paul Maloney. DRA 86m. V

I Lived with You 1933 British ★★★ Lively London family takes in a mysterious roomer and discovers he's a Russian prince in exile. Interesting early showcase for budding stars Lupino and Hawkins. C: Ivor Novello, Ursula Jeans, Ida Lupino, Jack Hawkins. D: Maurice Elvey. DRA 100m.

I Love a Bandleader 1945 ★★★½ During a spell of amnesia, house painter Harris fancies he's a bandleader. Lively songs rise above formula story. C: Phil Harris, Leslie Brooks, Walter Catlett, Eddie Anderson, Frank Sully, Pierre Watkin. D: Del Lord. MUS 70m.

I Love a Mystery 1945 ★★★½ Nutty, convoluted puzzler in which rich pleasure seeker Macready thinks an Oriental sect is after his head to grace their founder's tomb. First of mystery series based on radio show. C: Jim Bannon, Nina Foch, George Macready, Barton Yarborough, Carole Mathews, Lester Matthews. D: Henry Levin. CRI 70m.

I Love a Mystery 1973 ★★ Parody of golden age radio shows involves detectives hired by insurance company trying to find a missing billionaire. C: Ida Lupino, David Hartman, Les Crane, Jack Weston, Terry-Thomas, Hagan Beggs, Don Knotts. D: Leslie Stevens. COM 100m. TVM

I Love a Soldier 1944 ★★½ Strong-willed USO hostess (Goddard) falls for married soldier. Routine wartime soap. C: Paulette Goddard, Sonny Tufts, Beulah Bondi, Mary Treen, Barry Fitzgerald. D: Mark Sandrich. DRA 106m.

I Love Melvin 1953 ★★★½ Enjoyable MGM musical has O'Connor as a photographer's assistant trying to get the picture of his lady love (Reynolds) on the cover of *Look* magazine. Memorable dancing by the two leads. C: Donald O'Connor, Debbie Reynolds, Una Merkel, Allyn Joslyn, Jim Backus, Richard Anderson, Noreen Corcoran. D: Don Weis. MUS 76m. V

I Love My . . . Wife 1970 ★★★ A doctor binges on unfulfilling sexual affairs while his dutiful wife stays home with their newborn baby. Sporadically successful satire, helped considerably by Gould and Vacarro's spirited performances. C: Elliott Gould, Brenda Vaccaro, Angel Tompkins, Dabney Coleman, Joan Tompkins. D: Mel Stuart. COM [R] 95m. V

I Love N.Y. 1987 ★★ Comedy about irate father, skeptical mother, irritated boss, and a Siberian husky. C: Scott Baio, Kelley Van Der Velden, Christopher Plummer. D: Alan Smithee. COM [R] 100m. V

I Love Trouble 1948 ★★★½ Private detective (Tone) tangles with tough guys while searching for missing woman. Reasonably involving mystery. C: Franchot Tone, Janet Blair, Janis Carter, Adele Jergens, Glenda Farrell. D: S. Sylvan Simon. CRI 94m.

I Love You (Eu Te Amo) 1981 Brazilian ★★★ Man and woman get together for fun and games in Rio, and when the passion subsides, they fall in love. Mediocrity saved by the mesmerizing Braga. C: Sonia Braga, Paulo Cesar Pereio. D: Arnaldo Jabor. DRA [R] 104m. V

I Love You Again 1940 ★★★★ Clever screwball comedy with Powell as an amnesia victim living the straight and narrow life and suddenly getting his memory back. Funny, well scripted. C: William Powell, Myrna Loy, Frank McHugh, Edmund Lowe, Donald Douglas. D: W.S. Van-Dyke II. COM 99m. V

I Love You, Alice B. Toklas 1968 ★★★½

Attorney Sellers faces a midlife crises, a badgering mistress and asthma, then turns on, tunes in, and drops out after eating some marijuana-laced cookies. Dated, to be sure, but not without its moments thanks to Sellers' wonderful comic sensibilities. C: Peter Sellers, Jo VanFleet, Leigh Taylor-Young, Joyce VanPatten. D: Hy Averback. COM [R] 93m. V

I Love You, Goodbye 1974 ★★½ Frustrated housewife leaves home to find herself. Modest, with good performance by Lange. C: Hope Lange, Earl Holliman, Michael Murphy, Patricia Smith, Kerry Shuttleton, Brian Andrews. D: Sam O'Steen. DRA 78m. TVM

I Love, You Love 1961 Italian ★★★ An "erotic documentary" that catalogs different styles of romance in the world's capital cities. Straightforward, with rare flashes of inspired wit. C: Marny Trio, Fattini & Cairoli, Don Yada's Japanese Dance Troupe. D: Alessandro Blasetti. DRA 84m.

I Love You Perfect 1989 ★★★★ Dey does fine job as a woman whose life was almost too ideal, stricken with cancer. Predictable script, uncommon performances. C: Susan Dey, Anthony Jon Dennison. D: Harry Winer. DRA 96m. TVM

I Love You, Rosa 1971 Israeli ★★★★ A widow must follow Jewish tradition and marry late husband's surviving brother. However, her new mate presents the ultimate in May-December romances—he's only 11 years old. Sweet romantic comedy about relationships and growth; nice performances by leads. C: Michal Bat-Adam, Gabi Otterman, Yossef Shiloah. D: Moshe Mizrahi. COM 91m.

I Love You to Death 1990 ★★★½ Believe it or not, this black comedy about a wife (Ullman) who tries, without success, to murder her cheating husband (Kline) is based on a true story. Bumbling hired killers are painfully stupid, but Kline is fun to watch. C: Kevin Kline, Tracey Ullman, Joan Plowright, River Phoenix, Keanu Reeves. D: Lawrence Kasdan. COM [R] 97m. V

I Loved a Woman 1933 ★★★ Chicago meatpacker's life is complicated by his socially ambitious wife. Turgid melodrama but Robinson interests nevertheless. C: Edward G. Robinson, Kay Francis, Genevieve Tobin, J.Farrell MacDonald, Robert Barrat. D: Alfred Green. DRA 91m.

I, Madman 1989 ★★★ Bookstore clerk's obsession with supernatural novel brings author to life, then the fireworks, and the loony narrative twists, begin. Ridiculous, illogical, but not dull. C: Jenny Wright, Clayton Rohner, Randall Cook. D: Tibor Takacs. HOR [R] 90m. V

I-Man 1986 ★★★ Bakula, his son (Cramer), and their dog all are endowed with superpowers after sniffing magic gas in TV superhero pilot that might appeal to fans of star's *Quantum Leap* series. C: Scott Bakula, Ellen Bry, Joey Cramer. D: Corey Allen. SFI 96m. TVM

I Married a Centerfold 1984 ★★★ Ad exec pursues his dream lover, who happens to be a men's magazine centerfold. Daly's charm makes this silly fluff almost likable. C: Teri Copley, Timothy Daly, Diane Ladd. D: Peter Werner. COM 100m. TVM V

I Married a Communist 1950 ★★★ A shipping executive with a dubious past is blackmailed by a Communist organizer. Simplistic Cold War propaganda is saved from banality by its fast pace and Ryan's strong portrayal as the harried victim. (a.k.a. *The Woman on Pier 13*) C: Laraine Day, Robert Ryan, John Agar, Thomas Gomez, Janis Carter. D: Robert Stevenson. DRA 73m.

I Married a Monster from Outer Space 1958 ★★★½ Pretty young bride (Talbott) discovers that her virile young hubby is, in fact, not even human! Campy '50s sci-fi fun. C: Tom Tryon, Gloria Talbot, Ken Lynch, John Eldredge, Maxie Rosenbloom. D: Gene Fowler Jr. SFI 78m. V

I Married a Shadow 1982 French ★★★½ Young woman expecting child by man who abandoned her assumes identity of wealthy pregnant woman who was killed in a train wreck. Remake of *No Man of Her Own*, a little overbearing but has its moments. C: Nathalie Baye, Francis Huster, Richard Bohringer, Madeleine Robinson, Guy Trejan. D: Robin Davis. DRA [PG] 110m.

I Married a Vampire 1987 ★★ Small town woman marries urban vampire and goes on a bloodthirsty killing spree driven by revenge and a hunger for blood. C: Rachel Golden, Brendan Hickey. D: Jay Raskin. HOR 85m. V

I Married a Witch 1942 ★★★★½ A victim of the Salem witch hunts returns to haunt descendant of those responsible for burning her at the stake. Imaginative, funny romantic comedy overflows with charm thanks to stellar cast, especially Lake as the sexy witch. C: Fredric March, Veronica Lake, Robert Benchley, Susan Hayward, Cecil Kellaway. D: Rene Clair. COM 77m. V

I Married a Woman 1956 ★★★ Advertising exec (Gobel) can't cope with his job or bombshell wife (Dors). Smarmy sex comedy with amusing bits by Landis and Talbot. C: George Gobel, Diana Dors, Adolphe Menjou, Nita Talbot. D: Hal Kanter. COM 84m. V

I Married an Angel 1942 ★★★ Singing playboy is romanced by a heavenly songstress in this version of the Rodgers and Hart musical. Jeanette and Nelson's last teaming, and the chemistry is still there although many other elements of a good movie are not. Charming songs. C: Jeanette MacDonald, Nelson Eddy, Edward Everett Horton, Binnie Barnes. D: W.S. VanDyke II. MUS 84m. V

I Married Wyatt Earp 1983 ★★½ Unusual

Wild West yarn, with inept Osmond as Earp's Jewish wife, trying to adapt to life with a gunslinger, and having an affair with one of his rivals. Based on a true story, but Osmond isn't strong or convincing enough. C: Marie Osmond, Bruce Boxleitner. D: Michael O'Herlihy. WST 96m. TVM

I Met a Murderer 1939 British ★★★ A fugitive from justice (Mason) joins a novelist on a cross-country auto trip. Twisty plot and good performances make this crime drama. C: James Mason, Pamela Kellino. D: Roy Kellino. CRI 79m.

I Met Him in Paris 1937 ★★★½ Minor comedy with Colbert in Paris, ricocheting romantically between Young, Bowman, and Douglas. Claudette's charm helps a great deal. C: Claudette Colbert, Melvyn Douglas, Robert Young, Lee Bowman, Mona Barrie, Fritz Feld. D: Wesley Ruggles. COM 86m.

I Met My Love Again 1938 ★★★½ A woman leaves small-town life for a more glamorous one, and then regrets it. Typical "woman's picture" of the era. Good cast keeps it moving. C: Joan Bennett, Henry Fonda, Dame May Whitty, Alan Marshal, Louise Platt, Alan Baxter, Tim Holt. D: Arthur Ripley, Joshua Logan. DRA 77m.

I, Mobster 1958 ★★★½ A racket boss (Cochran) recounts his rise to power in front of a Senate Investigating Committee. Slick direction competes with pedestrian scripting and flat performances (especially Milan). C: Steve Cochran, Lita Milan, Robert Strauss, Lili St.Cyr. D: Roger Corman. CRI 80m. V

I, Monster 1972 British ★★ It's business as usual in this *Dr. Jekyll and Mr. Hyde* revamp, as an ambitious scientist turns himself into progressively uglier alter ego. Cast is good but tension is lacking. C: Christopher Lee, Peter Cushing, Mike Raven, Richard Hurndall, George Merritt, Kenneth J. Warren. D: Stephen Weeks. HOR [PG] 74m.

I Never Promised You a Rose Garden 1977 ★★★★ Teenager battles schizophrenia with the aid of her compassionate psychiatrist in this involving true story, mixing sometimes graphic treatment sequences with oddly hallucinatory dream moments. Quinlan, in her film debut, shows great emotional range. C: Bibi Andersson, Kathleen Quinlan, Ben Piazza, Susan Tyrrell, Signe Hasso, Sylvia Sidney. D: Anthony Page. DRA [R] 96m. V

I Never Sang for My Father 1970 ★★★★½ A N.Y. college professor (Hackman) is torn between caring for his difficult elderly father (Douglas) and moving to California to marry. Excellent and emotionally draining. C: Melvyn Douglas, Gene Hackman, Dorothy Stickney, Estelle Parsons. D: Gilbert Cates. DRA [PG] 90m. V

I Only Asked! 1958 British ★★★½ Klutz-ridden military squadron inadvertently quells a revolt in the Mideast, blunders onto a rich cache of oil, and ends up in a harem. Silly and enjoyable lightweight British slapstick. C: Michael Medwin, Bernard Bresslaw, Alfie Bass. D: Montgomery Tully. COM 82m.

I Only Want You to Love Me 1976 German ★★★★½ Trying to escape his domineering parents, young man showers his new bride with expensive gifts, leading to financial ruin and ultimately violence and tragedy. Bleak but fascinating psychological study of one person's downward spiral. C: Vitus Zeplichal, Elke Aberle, Alexander Allerson. D: Rainer Werner Fassbinder. DRA 112m.

I Ought to Be in Pictures 1982 ★★★½ A teenage girl (Manoff) travels from Brooklyn to Hollywood to break into the movies via her screenwriter dad (Matthau). Much to her dismay she finds he's gambling and drinking more than he's writing. So-so Neil Simon trifle is helped by a strong cast. C: Walter Matthau, Ann-Margret, Dinah Manoff, Lance Guest. D: Herbert Ross. COM [PG] 107m. V

I Passed for White 1960 ★★★ Timid, early exploration of racial issues features Wilde as fair-skinned African-American woman seeking a better life by posing as white. She enters troubled marriage with Franciscus, who's unaware of her secret. C: Sonya Wilde, James Franciscus, Pat Michon, Elizabeth Council, Griffin Crafts, Isabelle Cooley. D: Fred M. Wilcox. DRA 93m.

I Posed for Playboy 1991 ★★ Three disparate women pose for *Playboy* to spice up their lives. Tawdry, stale TV effort had extra footage added to get an R rating. C: Lynda Carter, Michele Greene, Amanda Peterson. D: Stephen Stafford. DRA [R] 103m. TVM V

I Promise to Pay 1937 ★★★½ Straitlaced family man has his life turned upside down after he's taken in by slick con artists. Good B-movie has lively pacing and fine performance by Morris as the bewildered innocent surrounded by crooks. C: Chester Morris, Helen Mack, Leo Carrillo, Thomas Mitchell, John Gallaudet, Wallis Clark. D: D. Ross Lederman. DRA 65m.

I. Q. 1994 ★★★★ Cute, clever romantic comedy casts Robbins as lowly mechanic romancing brilliant woman (Ryan), who happens to be Albert Einstein's niece. Matthau is sensational as the gentle genius. C: Tim Robbins, Meg Ryan, Walter Matthau, Gene Saks, Lou Jacobi. D: Fred Schepisi. COM [PG] 96m. V

I Remember Mama 1948 ★★★★½ Charming, beautifully acted series of vignettes from Kathryn Forbes' memoirs of growing up with Norwegian family in San Francisco. Dunne is sturdy center of film as she scrimps, saves, and struggles to keep her family afloat during the Depression. C: Irene Dunne, Barbara Bel Geddes, Oscar Homolka, Philip Dorn, Cedric Hardwicke, Edgar Bergen, Rudy Vallee. D: George Stevens. DRA 134m. V

I Sailed to Tahiti with an All Girl Crew 1968 ★★½ Zany comedy about a wager between two sailors is filled with familiar funny faces, but seems a bit dated now (as does the title). Bare was the director of TV's *Green Acres*. C: Gardner McKay, Fred Clark, Diane McBain, Pat Buttram, Edy Williams. D: Richard Bare. COM 95m.

I Saw What You Did 1965 ★★★ Murderer (Ireland) goes after teenage jokesters (Lane and Garrett) for telephoning people at random and breathily intoning the title: He thinks they really *did* see him kill his wife. Cheap shocker was extremely popular when first released. C: Sara Lane, Andi Garrett, John Ireland, Joan Crawford, Leif Erickson, Patricia Breslin. D: William Castle. HOR 82m.

I See a Dark Stranger 1946 British ★★★★ Irish girl's hatred of British lures her into a WWII plot to aid Nazis. Charming espionage thriller, with good chemistry between Kerr and Howard. (a.k.a *Adventuress, The*) C: Deborah Kerr, Trevor Howard. D: Frank Launder. DRA 98m.

I Sent a Letter to My Love 1981 French ★★★★½ Signoret is caretaker for infirm brother Rochefort. Through personal ads in the newspaper she begins a romantic correspondence, unaware that her pen pal love is actually Rochefort. Sensitive and extremely well-acted tale of love and loss. Signoret is at her finest. C: Simone Signoret, Jean Rochefort, Delphine Seyrig. D: Moshe Mizrahi. DRA [PG] 102m. V

I Shot Jesse James 1949 ★★★½ Fuller makes memorable debut with story of title character Bob Ford (Ireland), whose notoriety chases him across Old West. Film is mostly close-ups, creating suffocating intensity that makes up for minimal gunplay and cheap sets. C: Preston Foster, Barbara Britton, John Ireland, Reed Hadley, J.Edward Bromberg. D: Samuel Fuller. CRI 81m.

I Spit On Your Corpse 1974 ★★ Merciless woman thrives as hired gun for vicious criminal group. C: Georgina Spelvin. D: Al Adamson. ACT [R] 88m. V

I Spit On Your Grave 1973 ★★ Young novelist brutalized while on retreat hunts and tortures each of her attackers. C: Camille Keaton. D: Meir Zarchi. HOR 100m. V

I Spy Returns 1994 ★★★ Kelly Robinson and Alexander Scott are back, this time protecting their offspring—also spies—in Vienna from the depredations of bad guy Hyde. Culp and Cosby bicker like an old married couple, providing the slight story with charm. Mainly for fans of the TV series. C: Robert Culp, Bill Cosby, George Newbern, Salli Richardson, Jonathan Hyde. D: Jerry London. ACT 120m. TVM V

I Stand Condemned 1935 British ★★★ Jealous lover frames his rival as a spy. Slow-moving melodrama with classy, understated performance by youthful Olivier. (a.k.a. *Moscow Nights*) C: Harry Baur, Laurence Olivier, Penelope Dudley Ward. D: Anthony Asquith. DRA 75m. V

I Stole a Million 1939 ★★★½ Cheated by a finance company, a cabdriver (Raft) starts stealing to support his family. Bleak but fascinating film, especially for film noir fans; features a good star cast and a script by novelist Nathanael West. C: George Raft, Claire Trevor, Dick Foran, Victor Jory. D: Frank Tuttle. CRI 76m.

I Take These Men 1983 ★★★ Unhappy wife asks husband for divorce and then wonders what it would be like to be married to other men. Odd cast buoys this amusing trifle. C: Susan Saint James, John Rubinstein, Adam West, Brian Dennehy, Dee Wallace, James Murtaugh. D: Larry Peerce. COM 96m.

I Take This Woman 1940 ★★½ Doctor saves life of suicidal woman, then dedicates himself to her happiness. Ill-fated production saw several directors come and go (without credit), including Joseph von Sternberg. Leave it. C: Spencer Tracy, Hedy Lamarr, Verree Teasdale, Kent Taylor, Laraine Day, Mona Barrie, Louis Calhern, Marjorie Main, Frances Drake, Jack Carson. D: W.S. VanDyke II. DRA 97m.

I Thank a Fool 1962 British ★★ Weird story about a doctor (Hayward) who is convicted of a mercy killing and upon her release from prison is hired by her prosecutor (Finch) to nurse his crazy wife (Cilento). Doesn't work. C: Susan Hayward, Peter Finch, Diane Cilento, Cyril Cusack, Kieron Moore, Athene Seyler. D: Robert Stevens. DRA 100m.

I, the Jury 1982 ★★½ Mike Hammer (Assante) investigates the murder of a friend with his usual shoot-'em-up, bust-'em-in-the-face flair. Testosterone overdose can't hide the film's flaws. Remake of the tamer 1953 version. From the Mickey Spillane novel. C: Armand Assante, Barbara Carrera, Alan King, Laurene Landon, Paul Sorvino. D: Richard T. Heffron. DRA [R] 111m. V

I Vitelloni 1953 Italian ★★★★★ Vibrant look at five young men pursuing pleasure and harboring pipe dreams while floating into an uncertain future in a nondescript Italian seacoast town. Beautifully realized, stunningly photographed film speaks to an aimless postwar generation cast adrift. A masterpiece. (a.k.a. *Vitelloni*) C: Alberto Sordi, Franco Interlenghi, Franco Fabrizi, Leopoldo Trieste. D: Federico Fellini. DRA 104m. V

I Wake Up Screaming 1941 ★★★★ Innocent man accused of murder must prove his claim to an unsympathetic police officer and victim's sister (Grable), with whom he is in love. Fine film noir highlighted by an excellent cast (especially heavies Cook and Cregar) and a satisfying final twist. C: Betty Grable, Victor Mature, Carole Landis, Laird Cregar, William Gargan, Alan Mowbray, Elisha Cook, Jr. D: H. Bruce Humberstone. HOR 82m. V

I Walk Alone 1947 ★★★ Bitter ex-con returns to his old neighborhood, spoiling for trouble. Excellent cast in sappy story. C: Burt Lancaster, Lizabeth Scott, Kirk Douglas, Wendell Corey, Kristine Miller, George Rigaud, Marc Lawrence. D: Byron Haskin. DRA 98m.

I Walk the Line 1970 ★★★½ Tennessee sheriff Peck compromises himself personally and professionally when he gets involved with Weld, the daughter of a moonshiner. Odd drama complemented by Johnny Cash score. C: Gregory Peck, Tuesday Weld, Estelle Parsons, Ralph Meeker, Lonny Chapman, Charles Durning. D: John Frankenheimer. DRA [PG] 95m.

I Walked with a Zombie 1943 ★★★★ Atmospheric tale set in Caribbean about a nurse hired by plantation owner to care for his wife after she sinks into a zombie-like stupor. Well-acted, eerie chiller with dreamlike pacing and darkly moody lighting effects. Very good effort by talented team of Val Lewton and Jacques Tourneur. C: Frances Dee, Tom Conway, James Ellison, Edith Barrett, Christine Gordon, Theresa Harris, James Bell. D: Jacques Tourneur. HOR 69m. V

I Wanna Be a Beauty Queen 1979 ★★★★ Camp treasure deliciously parodies beauty pageants as Divine hosts the "Alternative Miss World" contest. C: Divine, Andrew Logan. D: Richard Gayer. COM 90m. V

I Wanna Hold Your Hand 1978 ★★★★ A group of Beatle fanatics conspire to meet their idols when the Fab Four debuts on *The Ed Sullivan Show*. Zany comedy, acted with incredible verve by fresh young cast, captures the frenzied madness known as Beatlemania. C: Nancy Allen, Bobby DiCicco, Marc McClure, Susan Kendall Newman, Theresa Saldana, Wendie Jo Sperber. D: Robert Zemeckis. COM [PG] 99m. V

I Want a Divorce 1940 ★★★½ Real-life marrieds Powell and Blondell play newlyweds having second thoughts in so-so light comedy. Rare film role for Broadway star Fay. C: Joan Blondell, Dick Powell, Gloria Dickson, Frank Fay, Dorothy Burgess, Jessie Ralph, Harry Davenport, Conrad Nagel. D: Ralph Murphy. COM 75m.

I Want to Keep My Baby 1976 ★★★½ Hemingway plays a pregnant teenager opting for parenthood in this look at a major social issue. Tries for serious understanding, but tends toward the exploitative. C: Mariel Hemingway, Susan Anspach, Jack Rader, Lisa Mordente, Dori Brenner, Vince Baggetta, Rhea Perlman. D: Jerry Thorpe. DRA 100m. TVM

I Want To Live! 1958 ★★★★ True story of Barbara Graham, who was sentenced to death for a murder she didn't commit. Hayward won a well-deserved Oscar for her penetrating portrayal of the accused. Wise carefully slanted the film as an indictment of capital punishment. C: Susan Hayward, Simon Oakland, Virginia Vincent, Theodore Bikel, Wesley Lau. D: Robert Wise. DRA 122m.

I Want What I Want 1972 British ★★★ What he wants is a sex change. But a sudden carnal conundrum makes him stop and think twice. Mildly interesting nonsense. C: Anne Heywood, Harry Andrews, Jill Bennett, Michael Coles, Paul Rogers. D: John Dexter. DRA [R] 97m. V

I Want You 1951 ★★★ Sincere post-Korean War soaper about the impact of the war on an average American family. Talented cast brings the era earnestly to life. C: Dana Andrews, Dorothy McGuire, Farley Granger, Peggy Dow, Robert Keith, Mildred Dunnock, Martin Milner, Ray Collins, Jim Backus. D: Mark Robson. DRA 102m.

I Wanted Wings 1941 ★★★ Rather dated tale of three recruits in training with the Army Air Corps, noteworthy primarily as the debut of Veronica Lake. Oscar for Best Special Effects. C: Ray Milland, William Holden, Wayne Morris, Brian Donlevy, Constance Moore, Veronica Lake, Hedda Hopper. D: Mitchell Leisen. DRA 131m.

I Was a Communist for the FBI 1951 ★★★½ Gritty little counterespionage thriller about man caught between two nations. Made in the midst of the post-WWII Red scare and worth a look. C: Frank Lovejoy, Dorothy Hart, Philip Carey, James Millican. D: Gordon Douglas. DRA 83m.

I Was a Mail Order Bride 1982 ★★½ A young magazine writer (Bertinelli) dates a man to get material for a big article on mail order brides. Unusual role for star; good supporting cast. C: Valerie Bertinelli. DRA

I Was a Male War Bride 1949 ★★★★ After WWII ends, a French officer poses as a woman in order to sail to the States with his American bride. Grant is hilarious in this excellent screwball comedy. C: Cary Grant, Ann Sheridan, Marion Marshall, Randy Stuart, William Neff, Ken Tobey. D: Howard Hawks. COM 105m. V

I Was a Shoplifter 1950 ★★★½ Earnest film with campy title scores with Brady's fine performance as an undercover cop tracking a ring of crooks. Check out Rock Hudson asa department store gumshoe. C: Scott Brady, Mona Freeman, Charles Drake, Andrea King, Anthony Curtis. D: Charles Lamont. CRI 82m.

I Was a Spy 1933 British ★★★½ A nurse is trained to spy on the Germans during WWI. Well-done war espionage story, pulled together by interesting cast, many of whom went on to much bigger things. C: Madeleine Carroll, Conrad Veidt, Herbert Marshall, Gerald du Maurier, Edmund Gwenn, Donald Calthrop, Nigel Bruce. D: Victor Saville. DRA 83m.

I Was a Teenage Boy 1987 *See* **Something Special**

I Was a Teenage Frankenstein 1957 ★★ Classic '50s drive-in fare about a mad doctor who creates a monster out of spare body parts, then sends the brute out to kill. For nostalgia buffs. C: Whit Bissell, Gary Conway, Phyllis Coates, Robert Burton. D: Herbert L. Strock. HOR 72m. V

I Was a Teenage TV Terrorist 1987 ★★ Two cynical teens drive the local cable station nuts with relentless pranks. C: Adam Nathan, Jule Hanlon, Joel Von Ornsteiner. D: Stanford Singer. COM 85m. V

I Was a Teenage Werewolf 1957 ★★★ Low-budget horror film with Landon as high-schooler given serum that's supposed to eliminate a nasty temper but that turns him into a hirsute beast instead. Pure '50s drive-in fare has a few scary moments and a lot of campy nostalgia. C: Michael Landon, Yvonne Lime, Whit Bissell, Vladimir Sokoloff, Guy Williams, Tony Marshall. D: Gene Fowler Jr. HOR 70m. V

I Was a Teenage Zombie 1987 ★★½ A murdered drug pusher (McCoy) comes back to life thanks to some nuclear toxic waste, and seeks revenge on the teenagers who killed him. No-budget exploitation film has campy cult appeal, due mostly to ultrahip soundtrack. C: Michael Ruben, George Seminara, Steve McCoy, Cassie Madden. D: John Elias Michalakias. COM 91m. V

I Was an Adventuress 1940 ★★★½ Jewel thief (Zorina) tries to go straight but gets drawn back into life of crime by her manipulative former cohorts. Lighthearted adventure doesn't fully satisfy but cast makes it highly watchable. C: Vera Zorina, Erich Stroheim, Richard Greene, Peter Lorre, Sig Ruman. D: Gregory Ratoff. COM 81m.

I Was an American Spy 1951 ★★★ Secret agent/singer in the Philippines, uncovering evidence for the war effort against the Japanese. Worldly performance by Dvorak and smoky atmosphere enhances lean script. C: Ann Dvorak, Gene Evans, Douglas Kennedy, Richard Loo, Philip Ahn, Lisa Ferraday. D: Lesley Selander. DRA 85m.

I Was Happy Here 1966 *See* **Time Lost and Time Remembered**

I Was Monty's Double 1958 British ★★★★½ Rousing true WWII story of British diversionary counter-intelligence plot to drive the Germans out of North Africa by recruiting a stage actor to impersonate Field Marshal Bernard Law Montgomery. Top-notch acting by cast in intriguing chase thriller. (a.k.a. *Hell, Heaven or Hoboken*) C: M.E. Clifton-James, John Mills, Cecil Parker, Marius Goring, Michael Hordern, Leslie Phillips, Bryan Forbes. D: John Guillermin. DRA 100m.

I Was Stalin's Bodyguard 1990 ★★★½ Fascinating Russian documentary about the last surviving bodyguard of the notorious Soviet leader. Eerie archival footage and interviews make for engrossing and controversial viewing. D: Semeon Aronovitch. DOC 80m.

I Will Fight No More Forever 1975 ★★★★ Based on true story of Chief Joseph and Nez Perce Indians who tried to escape U.S. government policies by fleeing to Canada. Stark but sturdy. C: James Whitmore, Ned Romero, Sam Elliott, Nick Ramus. D: Richard T. Heffron. DRA 105m. TVM V

I Will, I Will . . . For Now 1976 ★★½ Troubled couple (Gould and Keaton) explore a variety of avenues to get help, including a trip to a very uninhibited sex clinic. Middling but dated satire on relationships in the supposedly free thinking '70s. C: Elliott Gould, Diane Keaton, Paul Sorvino, Victoria Principal. D: Norman Panama. COM [R] 110m. V

I Wonder Who's Killing Her Now 1976 ★★ Loser (Dishy) schemes to get rich by having his wife (Barnes) killed and collecting the insurance. Then he discovers she's not insured. Black comedy's morbid subject and unlikable characters make for strained laughs. C: Bob Dishy, Joanna Barnes, Bill Dana, Vito Scotti. D: Steven Hilliard Stern. COM [PG] 85m. V

Ice 1994 ★★ When married couple steal jewels from Mafia, they become unwittingly involved in mob's internal quarrels. C: Traci Lords, Phillip Troy, Zach Galligan. D: Brook Yeaton. ACT [R] 91m. V

Ice Castles 1979 ★★★ Farm girl becomes an Olympic skating champion and goes on to enjoy a fabulous career until she is blinded in a freak accident. Dazzling skating and good for a cry. C: Lynn-Holly Johnson, Robby Benson, Colleen Dewhurst, Tom Skerritt. D: Donald Wrye. DRA 110m. V

Ice Follies of 1939 1939 ★★★ Extravagant MGM musical-on-ice with silly plot involving rivalry between a theatrical promoter (Stewart) and his movie actress wife (Crawford). Main appeal is seeing the stars stumble around on ice skates while trying to appear carefree. C: Joan Crawford, James Stewart, Lew Ayres, Lewis Stone, Lionel Stander. D: Reinhold Schunzel. MUS 82m.

Ice House 1989 ★★ Man from Texas pursues ex-girlfriend who's gone to Hollywood in search of better things resulting in revelation of unhealed wounds from past. C: Melissa Gilbert, Bo Brinkman, Andreas Manolikakis. D: Eagle Pennell. DRA 81m.

Ice Palace 1960 ★★★ Adaptation of Edna Ferber novel about friendships and conflict between two men set against the 20th-century history of Alaska. Long and predictable. C: Richard Burton, Robert Ryan, Carolyn Jones, Martha Hyer, Ray Danton. D: Vincent Sherman. ACT 143m. V

Ice Pawn 1990 ★★ Corruption behind glittering facade of Olympic Games as seen by American ice skater. C: Paul Cross, Dan Haggerty, Robert Budaska. D: Barry Samson. DRA 120m.

Ice Pirates, The 1984 ★★★ In the future, Earth is starved for water—and whoever has the ice rules! Nifty outer-space pirate spoof. C: Robert Urich, Mary Crosby, John Matuszak, Anjelica Huston, John Carradine. D: Stewart Raffill. ACT [PG] 91m. V

Ice Runner, The 1993 ★★ American spy, caught by Soviets, plans escape from gulag. C: Edward Albert, Victor Wong, Olga Kabo. D: Barry Alan Samson. ACT [R] 114m. V

Ice Station Zebra 1968 ★★★ Agent (McGoohan) tracks Soviet spy, while submarine commander (Hudson) and his Russian counterpart race to the Arctic to retrieve sensitive military info. Some tension, but slow and long-winded overall. Based on Alistair MacLean's novel. C: Rock Hudson, Ernest Borgnine, Patrick McGoohan, Jim Brown, Tony Bill. D: John Sturges. DRA [G] 148m. V

Iceland 1942 ★★★ Skating mixes with patriotism as Henie flirts with Marine corporal (Payne) between toe loops. Outstanding song: "There Will Never Be Another You." C: Sonja Henie, John Payne, Jack Oakie, Felix Bressart, Osa Massen. D: H. Bruce Humberstone. MUS 79m. V

Iceman 1984 ★★★½ What if a Stone Age man was thawed out and brought back to life in, say, 1984? Interesting plot shows the Neanderthal unable to handle life in today's bizarre world. Who can blame him? C: Timothy Hutton, Lindsay Crouse, John Lone, Josef Sommer, David Strathairn. D: Fred Schepisi. HOR 101m. V

Iceman Cometh, The 1973 ★★★★½ Fine filming of O'Neill's classic about saloon habitués and their once-a-year visitor. Ryan, as an embittered idealist, steals the film, which was March's last. C: Lee Marvin, Fredric March, Robert Ryan, Jeff Bridges, Martyn Green, Moses Gunn, Bradford Dillman, Evans Evans. D: John Frankenheimer. DRA [PG] 101m.

Icicle Thief, The 1989 Italian ★★★★ When an Italian director is invited to introduce one of his films on TV, he watches in horror as his masterpiece is invaded by the commercials—literally! Wacky, imaginative satire, with clever visual effects. C: Maurizio Nichetti, Caterina Labini, Heidi Komarek, Renato Scarpa. D: Maurizio Nichetti. COM 90m. V

I'd Climb the Highest Mountain 1951 ★★★½ The new wife of a preacher learns to adapt to life along the back roads of rural Georgia. Pleasant, episodic family drama, has much heart and likable cast, especially Hayward as the resourceful bride. C: Susan Hayward, William Lundigan, Rory Calhoun, Gene Lockhart, Ruth Donnelly, Barbara Bates, Lynn Bari, Alexander Knox. D: Henry King. DRA 88m.

I'd Give My Life 1936 ★★ Young thug who thinks his mother is dead, finds out she's really the governor's wife; tragedy ensues. C: Guy Standing, Frances Drake, Tom Brown. D: Edwin L. Marin. DRA 73m.

I'd Rather Be Rich 1964 ★★★ To comfort her dying grandfather, a rich young woman introduces him to someone who poses as her fiancé—but complications ensue when the old man recovers. Lots of infectious energy and humor and a boisterous Chevalier in fine form. C: Sandra Dee, Maurice Chevalier, Andy Williams, Robert Goulet, Gene Raymond, Charles Ruggles, Hermione Gingold, Allen Jenkins, Rip Taylor. D: Jack Smight. COM 96m.

Idaho 1943 ★★★ Roy Rogers gets involved in a mission to close down a (gasp!) bordello. Some good fun à la Roy and his inestimable entourage. C: Roy Rogers, Smiley Burnette, Virginia Grey. D: Joseph Kane. WST 72m.

Idaho Transfer 1971 ★★ Present day scientists arrive in year 2044 to establish a new world, but instead confront environmental disaster. C: Keith Carradine, Kelley Bohanan, Kevin Hearst. D: Peter Fonda. SFI [PG] 90m.

Ideal Husband, An 1948 British ★★★½ Stagey adaptation of Oscar Wilde comedy of manners with Goddard blackmailing English lord Williams. Lavish costumes by Cecil Beaton. C: Paulette Goddard, Michael Wilding, Diana Wynyard, Hugh Williams, C. Aubrey Smith, Glynis Johns, Michael Medwin. D: Alexander Korda. COM 96m.

Identification Marks: None 1964 Polish ★★★★ Skolimowski (who also wrote, directed, and served as film's art director) is draftee who spends final day of freedom trying to make sense of his aimless life. Skolimowski's real-life wife, Czyzewska, provides several supporting roles. A clever and original film. C: Jerzy Skolimowski, Elzbieta Czyzewska, Tadeusz Mins. D: Jerzy Skolimowski. DRA 76m.

Identification of a Woman 1983 Italian ★★★½ Director without new project has affairs with two women. Interesting misfire explores the sensual side of relationships, without any insights into art or love. C: Thomas Milian, Daniela Silverio, Christine Boisson, Veronica Lazar. D: Michelangelo Antonioni. DRA 130m.

Identity Crisis 1990 ★ Havoc ensues for a rap singer (Van Peebles) when his body is taken over by the spirit of a recently deceased, effeminate fashion designer. Blatant stereotyping dooms this unfunny identity-switching farce. C: Mario Van Peebles, Ilan Mitchell-Smith, Nicholas Kepros, Shelley Burch, Richard Clarke. D: Melvin Van Peebles. COM [R] 98m. V

Identity Unknown 1945 ★★★★ Curious but involving drama features Arlen as a WWII soldier with amnesia who embarks on a cross-country journey to discover his real identity, and encounters Americans with varying perspectives on the war. C: Richard Arlen, Cheryl Walker, Roger Pryor, Bobby Driscoll, Lola Lane. D: Walter Colmes. DRA 70m. V

Idiot, The 1951 Japanese ★★★★ Reworking by director Kurosawa of Dostoyevsky's novel transplants Russian story to postwar Japan as royal family member and his friend share passion for one woman. Dreamlike telling is difficult to follow, but visual beauty makes this worth sticking through. C: Toshiro Mifune, Masayuki Mori, Setsuko Hara, Takashi Shimura, Yoshiko Kuga. D: Akira Kurosawa. DRA 166m. v

Idiot, The 1960 Russian ★★★ Russian adaptation of Dostoyevsky's novel presents story of 18th-century St. Petersburg prince and his romantic foibles. Average production plays like *Cliff Notes* version of what should be a psychologically dense story. C: Julia Borisova, Yuri Yakovlev, N. Podgorny, L. Parkhomenko, R. Maximova, N. Pazhitnov. D: Ivan Pyrlev. DRA 122m.

Idiot's Delight 1939 ★★★★½ Nightclub performer Gable and phony Russian countess Shearer recognize each other at European hotel with the world on verge of WWII. Dated social commentary from Robert E. Sherwood Pulitzer Prize play deals with big ideas, but highlight is Gable's hoofing to "Puttin" on the Ritz." C: Norma Shearer, Clark Gable, Edward Arnold, Charles Coburn, Virginia Grey. D: Clarence Brown. DRA 107m. v

Idol Dancer, The 1920 ★★½ Despite the South Seas locations, this melodrama about a drunken beachcomber who befriends a young woman after she is cast out of her tribe is one of D.W. Griffith's least memorable films. C: Richard Barthelmess, Clarine Seymour, Creighton Hale. D: D.W. Griffith. DRA 105m.

Idol of the Crowds 1937 ★★★½ Entertaining grade B-movie drama stars Wayne as a rural Maine hockey player who makes the pros, and is consequently threatened by gangsters who want him to throw games for profit. A nice change of pace for the Western star. C: John Wayne, Sheila Bromley, Charles Brokaw, Billy Burrud. D: Arthur Lubin. CRI 62m.

Idol, The 1966 ★★ A divorcée and her daughter are seduced by her son's best friend. Pretty trashy '60s drama. C: Jennifer Jones, Michael Parks, John Leyton, Jennifer Hilary, Guy Doleman. D: Daniel Petrie. DRA 107m.

Idolmaker, The 1980 ★★★½ Dramatization of the career of Bob Marcucci, the force behind early rock megastars like Fabian and Frankie Avalon. Good look at inside of music industry, although score fails to capture flavor of era. C: Ray Sharkey, Tovah Feldshuh, Peter Gallagher, Paul Land. D: Taylor Hackford. MUS [PG] 119m. v

If . . . 1969 British ★★★★★ In his film debut, McDowell is a rebellious student at a strict English boarding school who incites his classmates to revolt. Violent, surrealistic, and powerful social commentary. C: Malcolm McDowell, David Wood, Richard Warwick, Robert Swann, Christine Noonan, Arthur Lowe, Mona Washbourne. D: Lindsay Anderson. DRA [R] 111m. v

If a Man Answers 1962 ★★★★ With the help of her mother, a determined young ingenue (Dee) traps a roguish photographer (Darin) into marriage and then resorts to continual trickery to keep him faithful. Spirited battle of the sexes is brightened by clever script and energetic cast. C: Sandra Dee, Bobby Darin, Micheline Presle, John Lund, Cesar Romero, Stefanie Powers, Christopher Knight, Charlene Holt. D: Henry Levin. COM 102m.

Iff Ever I See You Again

If Ever I See You Again 1978 ★ Vanity production. Brooks as a songwriter chasing woman (Hack). Breslin's acting debut. C: Joe Brooks, Shelley Hack, Jerry Keller, Danielle Brisebois, Kenny Karen, Jimmy Breslin. D: Joe Brooks. DRA [PG] 105m. v

If He Hollers, Let Him Go 1968 ★★½ Innocent St. Jacques, convicted of murder, escapes prison and tries to clear his name. Violent. C: Raymond St.Jacques, Kevin McCarthy, Barbara McNair, Dana Wynter, Arthur O'Connell, John Russell, Ann Prentiss, Royal Dano. D: Charles Martin. CRI [R] 106m.

If I Had a Million 1932 ★★★★½ Anonymous millionaire leaves fortune to names picked from telephone book. Entertaining, star-filled anthology film. Best episodes: Old woman turns the tables on old-age home; Laughton and the raspberry; Fields and the road hogs. C: Gary Cooper, George Raft, W.C. Fields, Charles Laughton, Charlie Ruggles, Jack Oakie, Mary Boland, Alison Skipworth. D: James Cruze, H. Bruce Humberstone, Stephen Roberts, William Seiter. COM 83m.

If I Had My Way 1940 ★★★ Crosby vehicle has him taking orphan (Jean) cross-country to her great-uncle (Winninger). C: Bing Crosby, Gloria Jean, Charles Winninger, El Brendel, Allyn Joslyn, Claire Dodd. D: David Butler. MUS 94m.

If I Were Free 1933 ★½ Romantic clunker about man and woman, each in failed marriages, who find each other. Dunne and Brook try to extricate themselves. Based on a John van Druten play. C: Irene Dunne, Clive Brook, Nils Asther, Henry Stephenson, Vivian Tobin, Tempe Pigott, Lorraine MacLean, Laura Hope Crews, Halliwell Hobbes. D: Elliott Nugent. DRA 66m.

If I Were King 1938 ★★★★ Preston Sturges penned this loosely historical but funny take on a duel of wits between French poet Villon (Colman) and Louis XI (Rathbone). Both actors are inspired. C: Ronald Colman, Frances Dee, Basil Rathbone, Ellen Drew, C.V. France, Henry Wilcoxon, Heather Thatcher, Sidney Toler. D: Frank Lloyd. DRA 101m.

If I Were Rich 1933 ★★ Depression-era, British comedy about people waiting for return of good times while fleeing creditors. C: Robert Donat, Wendy Barrie, Edmund Gwenn. D: Zoltan Korda. COM 63m.

If I'm Lucky 1946 ★★★ Crooner Como runs for governor to help radio pals. Remake of 1937's *Thanks a Million*, with a solid supporting cast. C: Vivian Blaine, Perry Como, Harry James, Carmen Miranda, Phil Silvers, Edgar Buchanan, Reed Hadley. D: Lewis Seiler. MUS 79m.

If It's a Man, Hang Up 1975 ★★ Model harrassed by abusive phone calls. C: Carol Lynley, Gerald Harper. DRA 71m.

If It's Tuesday, This Must Be Belgium 1969 ★★★★½ Disparate group of American tourists go on a whirlwind package tour of Europe. Shot on location throughout Europe, this lively, good-natured comedy still bursts with charm and features a bevy of great character actors. C: Suzanne Pleshette, Ian McShane, Mildred Natwick, Murray Hamilton, Sandy Baron, Michael Constantine, Norman Fell, Peggy Cass, Joan Collins. D: Mel Stuart. COM 99m. V

If Looks Could Kill 1991 ★★★ While in Paris with his high school class, ne'er-do-well student Grieco is mistaken for an international spy. Minor caper comedy that goes for the obvious time and again. C: Richard Grieco, Linda Hunt, Roger Rees, Robin Bartlett, Gabrielle Anwar, Roger Daltrey. D: William Dear. COM [PG-13] 89m. V

I.F. Stone's Weekly 1973 ★★★★½ Tom Wicker narrates witty, affectionate documentary about individualistic Washington reporter I.F. Stone. D: Jerry Bruck Jr. DOC 62m.

If Things Were Different 1980 ★★★½ When her husband suffers a nervous breakdown, Pleshette struggles to raise children and rebuild her life by taking job as a TV producer. Credible, well-acted tearjerker. C: Suzanne Pleshette, Tony Roberts, Don Murray, Arte Johnson, Chuck McCann, Dan Shor. D: Robert Lewis. DRA 100m. TVM V

If This Be Sin 1949 British ★★★ Neglected wife Loy is erroneously linked to youthful Greene, and the gossip endangers her marriage with Livesey. Fun fluff. (a.k.a. *That Dangerous Age*) C: Roger Livesey, Myrna Loy, Peggy Cummins, Richard Greene, Elizabeth Allan. D: Gregory Ratoff. COM 98m.

If Winter Comes 1947 ★★★ A discontented husband raises eyebrows in his community when he takes in a young pregnant woman. Sentimental soaper unworthy of its talented cast. C: Walter Pidgeon, Deborah Kerr, Angela Lansbury, Binnie Barnes, Janet Leigh, Dame May Whitty, Reginald Owen. D: Victor Saville. DRA 97m.

If You Can't Say It, Just See It 1991 *See* **Whore**

If You Could Only Cook 1935 ★★★★ Penniless Arthur and tycoon (Marshall) pretend to be servants for a mobster in this lighthearted, fast-paced, funny screwball comedy. C: Herbert Marshall, Jean Arthur, Leo Carrillo, Lionel Stander, Alan Edwards. D: William A. Seiter. COM 70m.

If You Could See What I Hear 1982 Canadian ★★½ Syrupy feature based on the life of Tom Sullivan (Singer) who doesn't let blindness get in his way. Too cheerful to be credible. C: Marc Singer, R.H. Thompson, Sarah Torgov, Shari Harper-Belafonte. D: Eric Till. DRA [PG] 103m. V

If You Knew Susie 1948 ★★★½ Ex-vaudevillian Cantor discovers U.S. government owes him a fortune. Great fun for Cantor fans. C: Eddie Cantor, Joan Davis, Allyn Joslyn, Charles Dingle. D: Gordon Douglas. MUS 90m. V

Igor and the Lunatics 1985 ★★ Small town set upon by crazed cult leader and obedient followers. C: Joseph Eero, Joe Niola, T.J. Michaels. D: Billy Parolini. HOR [R] 79m. V

Ikarie XB 1 1963 *See* **Voyage to the End of the Universe**

Ike: The War Years 1978 ★★★★ Duvall portrays Eisenhower in all his glory commanding Allied forces in Europe and conducting a love affair with Kay Summersby (Remick), his driver. Duvall and Remick are excellent. Originally a miniseries. C: Robert Duvall, Lee Remick, Dana Andrews, J.D. Cannon, Darren McGavin, Paul Gleason, Laurence Luckinbill, Wensley Pithey, Ian Richardson, William Schallert. D: Melville Shavelson, Boris Sagal. DRA 196m. TVM V

Ikiru 1952 Japanese ★★★★½ Downbeat story of widower who finds he has incurable cancer and decides to live his remaining months to the hilt. Kurosawa's extensive use of flashbacks keeps viewer distanced from hero, but truths depicted are valid and heartfelt. C: Takashi Shimura, Nobuo Kaneko, Kyoko Seki, Miki Odagiri. D: Akira Kurosawa. DRA 143m. V

Il Bidone 1955 Italian ★★★★ Crawford is a hardened crook who sees too late the misery he's created. Depressing drama with grim realism replacing Fellini's usual excess. (a.k.a. *The Swindle* and *The Swindlers*) C: Broderick Crawford, Giulietta Masina, Richard Basehart, Franco Fabrizi. D: Federico Fellini. DRA 92m.

Il Girasole 1970 *See* **Sunflower**

Il Ladro di Bambini 1993 Italian ★★★★½ A mother prostitutes her 11-year-old daughter; when the woman is arrested, a softhearted policeman is assigned to take the girl and her younger brother to an orphanage, but the short trip becomes a voyage of caring and recovery. Poignant story, based on a real incident. (a.k.a. *Stolen Children*) C: Enrico Lo Verso, Valentina Scatici. D: Gianni Amelio. DRA 108m.

Il Mare 1962 ★★★★½ Three disparate souls—an alcoholic, an actor, and a woman trying to sell her house—find their lives connecting in an unlikely trio. Careful psychological study of raw human emotion shines under intelligent and sensitive development. Filmed in b&w. C: Umberto Orsini, Francois Prevost, Dino Mele. D: Giuseppe Patroni Griffi. DRA 110m.

I'll Be Home for Christmas 1988 ★★★½

Sentimental Yuletide family drama with Holbrook and Saint as New England couple during WWII, waiting for their soldier sons to come home. C: Hal Holbrook, Eva Marie Saint, Courteney Cox, Peter Gallagher, Nancy Travis, Jason Oliver. D: Marvin Chomsky. DRA 100m. TVM

I'll Be Seeing You 1944 ★★★★ While serving time for manslaughter after accidentally killing her harassing boss, a convict (Rogers) gets a prison furlough. She meets a shell-shocked veteran (Cotten), and a touching relationship ensues. Well-played love story. C: Ginger Rogers, Joseph Cotten, Shirley Temple, Spring Byington, Tom Tully, John Derek. D: William Dieterle. DRA 85m. TVM

I'll Be Yours 1947 ★★★ Musical remake of Preston Sturges comedy *The Good Fairy* with woman (Durbin) helping man (Drake) advance his career by pretending to be married to him. C: Deanna Durbin, Tom Drake, Adolphe Menjou, William Bendix, Franklin Pangborn. D: William A. Seiter. MUS 93m.

I'll Cry Tomorrow 1955 ★★★★½ Riveting biography of singer Lillian Roth and her bout with alcoholism. Brilliant performance by Hayward, who does her own singing, and by Van Fleet as Roth's long-suffering mother. C: Susan Hayward, Richard Conte, Jo VanFleet, Eddie Albert. D: Daniel Mann. DRA 117m. V

I'll Do Anything 1993 ★★★★ Well-observed, often funny comedy about Hollywood, centering on struggling actor (Nolte) as he juggles his career and precocious daughter (Wright). Filmed as a musical, with the songs cut out after negative test screenings. Result holds up surprisingly well. C: Nick Nolte, Wittni Wright, Albert Brooks, Julie Kavner, Joely Richardson, Tracy Ullman. D: James L. Brooks. COM 115m. V

I'll Get By 1950 ★★★ Remake of *Tin Pan Alley* takes backstage look at the music industry during WWII, with Haver as big-band vocalist out to promote music publisher (Lundigan). C: June Haver, William Lundigan, Gloria DeHaven, Dennis Day, Thelma Ritter. D: Richard Sale. MUS 83m.

I'll Give a Million 1938 ★★★ A millionaire "goes underground" as a tramp, telling everyone beforehand that he'll reward acts of kindness, with a fortune. As a result, tramps everywhere are treated with newfound adoration. Pleasant spoof of the Depression years. C: Warner Baxter, Lynn Bari, Jean Hersholt, John Carradine, Peter Lorre. D: Walter Lang. COM 72m.

Ill Met by Moonlight 1957 ★★ During WW II, Cretian partisans and British espionage agents combine forces to capture a German general. Based on a true story. C: Dirk Bogarde, Marius Goring, Cyril Cusack. D: Michael Powell. ACT 104m.

I'll Never Forget What's 'is Name 1967 British ★★★½ A disenchanted director of TV commercials searches for meaning and satisfaction in his life. Intriguing, well-acted comedy/drama makes some strong points about the selling out of modern society. C: Orson Welles, Oliver Reed, Carol White, Harry Andrews, Michael Hordern, Wendy Craig, Marianne Faithful, Peter Graves, Frank Finlay, Edward Fox. D: Michael Winner. COM 99m.

I'll Never Forget You 1951 ★★★★ Fascinating fantasy about Yank (Power) living in modern England whisked to the 1700s where he meets the woman of his dreams (Blyth). Reworking of *Berkeley Square* (1933) makes innovative use of a b&w to color transition. C: Tyrone Power, Ann Blyth, Michael Rennie, Dennis Price, Beatrice Campbell. D: Roy Baker. DRA 90m.

I'll Remember April 1945 ★★½ Pollyannaish singer (Jean) tries to help her father out of a jam in this lightweight mystery. Amusing, even though (or because) Jean can't carry a tune. C: Gloria Jean, Kirby Grant, Samuel S. Hinds, Milburn Stone, Addison Richards, Mary Forbes. D: Harold Young. CRI 63m.

I'll See You in My Dreams 1951 ★★★½ Mundane biography of songwriter Gus Kahn (Thomas) abounds with clichés. Still, there are plenty of vintage songs including "Ain't We Got Fun," "Makin Whoopee," "My Buddy," etc. C: Doris Day, Danny Thomas, Frank Lovejoy, Patrice Wymore, James Gleason. D: Michael Curtiz. MUS 110m. V

I'll Take Romance 1937 ★★½ Vehicle for opera diva Moore casts her as a soprano in Buenos Aires involved with impressario (Douglas). Star warbles arias from *Manon*, *La Traviata*, and *Madama Butterfly*. C: Grace Moore, Melvyn Douglas, Stuart Erwin, Helen Westley, Margaret Hamilton. D: Edward H. Griffith. MUS 85m.

I'll Take Sweden 1965 ★★★ A widowed American oil executive (Hope) stops his daughter (Weld) from romancing a rock musician (Avalon) by relocating to Sweden. But his plan backfires when the intentions of her new boyfriend (Slate) turn out to be less then honorable. Routine sex farce brightened by Hope's presence. C: Bob Hope, Dina Merrill, Tuesday Weld, Frankie Avalon, Jeremy Slate. D: Frederick de Cordova. COM 96m. V

I'll Tell the World 1945 ★★½ Slight comedy with radio disk jockey Tracy rescuing his station's fortunes with a popular show for the lovelorn. If you're dying to hear "Slap Polka" or "Where the Prairie Meets the Sky," it's a must-see. C: Lee Tracy, Brenda Joyce, Raymond Walburn, June Preisser, Thomas Gomez, Howard Freeman, Lorin Raker. D: Leslie Goodwins. COM 61m.

I'll Turn to You 1946 ★★★½ Military pilot wants to dump wife for romantic rendezvous with his wealthy former flame. Agreeably elementary soap opera with some good performances. C: Terry Randall, Don Stannard. D: Geoffrey Faithfull. DRA 96m.

Illegal 1955 ★★★½ Weary, cynical D.A. (Robinson) changes sides and defends racketeer, then switches again to defend former assistant (Foch), endangering them both. Effective remake of *The Mouthpiece* has lawyer on the way down instead of on the way up, but it works just as well. C: Edward G. Robinson, Nina Foch, Hugh Marlowe, Jayne Mansfield, Albert Dekker, Ellen Corby, DeForest Kelley, Howard St. John. D: Lewis Allen. DRA 88m.

Illegal Entry 1949 ★★★★ Duff is convincing as tough U.S. agent out to smash a ring smuggling illegal aliens from Mexico. Taut drama with crisp, no-nonsense tone. C: Howard Duff, Marta Toren, George Brent, Gar Moore. D: Frederick de Cordova. CRI 84m.

Illegally Yours 1988 ★½ A bumbling college student (Lowe) agrees to accept jury duty to help out a childhood flame (Camp) who now stands accused of murder. Frantic but unfunny attempt at screwball comedy falls flat. C: Rob Lowe, Colleen Camp, Harry Carey Jr., Kenneth Mars. D: Peter Bogdanovich. COM 94m. V

Illicit 1931 ★★½ Free-spirited young woman balks at marrying her sweetheart, thinking it will ruin their relationship. Bold for its time, this early talkie is now badly dated, although young Stanwyck is a treat. C: Barbara Stanwyck, James Rennie, Ricardo Cortez, Joan Blondell, Charles Butterworth, Natalie Moorhead. D: Archie Mayo. DRA 81m. V

Illicit Behavior 1992 ★★½ She's a one-woman murder spree in an effort to claim a $2 million inheritance. Sordid stuff. C: Robert Davi, Jack Scalia, Kent McCord, Jenilee Harrison. D: Worth Keeter. CRI [R] 101m. TVM V

Illicit Interlude 1950 *See* **Summer Interlude**

Illumination 1973 Polish ★★★★½ An aptly titled examination of a decent man's personal and professional life, as he studies physics while learning about life and death. Compelling, restrained acting by Latallo, concise directing by Zanussi. C: Stanislaw Latallo, Edward Żebrowski, Małgorzata Pritulak. D: Krzystof Zanussi. DRA 91m.

Illusion Travels by Streetcar 1953 Mexican ★★★½ Two streetcar drivers take beloved vehicle for one final spin around town before it's pulled from fleet. Light Buñuel satire features his usual real-surreal switcheroos, more for effect than meaning. C: Lilia Prado, Carlos Navarro, Domingo Soler, Fernando Soto. D: Luis Buñuel. DRA 90m. V

Illustrated Man, The 1969 ★★★ Drifter (Steiger) searches for time-traveling tattoo artist (Bloom), who etched him from head to foot. His skin designs prompt three bleak sci-fi tales. Nearsighted adaptation of Ray Bradbury's famed fantasy anthology fails to capture writer's imaginative style. C: Rod Steiger, Claire Bloom, Robert Drivas, Jason Evers. D: Jack Smight. SFI [PG] 103m. V

Illustrious Corpses 1976 Italian-French ★★★★½ A man investigates a series of murders of prominent politicians, and finds a mysterious web of conspiracy. Fast-moving, paranoic thriller. C: Lino Ventura, Alain Cuny, Max von Sydow, Marcel Bozzuffi, Fernando Rey, Paolo Bonacelli. D: Francesco Rosi. CRI 110m.

Illustrious Energy 1988 New Zealand ★★★ Two Chinese miners working in New Zealand find the remains of a predecessor. They hope to take his body back home for proper burial, but must confront greedy mine owners. Dry film fails to hold interest. C: Shaun Bao, Harry Ip, Peter Chin, Geeling, Peter Hayden, Desmond Kelly, Heather Bolton. D: Leon Narbey. DRA 100m.

I'm All Right, Jack 1960 British ★★★★½ Satirical look at labor conditions in England with Carmichael working in factory, torn between union leader (Sellers) and employer (Thomas). Sellers' performance is brilliant in well-done social comedy; based on novel by Alan Hackney. C: Ian Carmichael, Terry-Thomas, Peter Sellers, Richard Attenborough, Margaret Rutherford, Dennis Price. D: John Boulting. COM 104m. V

I'm Dancing as Fast as I Can 1982 ★★★½ David Rabe adapted best-selling autobiography by TV journalist Barbara Gordon (Clayburgh) which chronicles her successful career, her Valium addiction,and her excruciating efforts to kick her habit cold turkey. Strong subject and cast, but not as powerful as might be. C: Jill Clayburgh, Nicol Williamson, Dianne Wiest, Daniel Stern, Joe Pesci, Geraldine Page, James Sutorius, Cordis Heard, Richard Masur, Ellen Greene, John Lithgow. D: Jack Hofsiss. DRA [R] 107m.

I'm Dangerous Tonight 1990 ★★ Some stylish touches can't save this disappointing chiller about an evil Aztec garment and a young woman (Amick) who becomes murderous when she dons a dress made from it. Contrived storytelling gets in the way of the scares. Based on a Cornell Woolrich story. C: Anthony Perkins, Madchen Amick, Daisy Hall, R. Lee Ermey, Mary Frann. D: Tobe Hooper. HOR [R] 92m. TVM V

I'm from Missouri 1939 ★★ Fluffy comedy about a Missouri mule breeder making a splash with aristocratic British society. C: Bob Burns, Gladys George, Gene Lockhart, William Henry, George P. Huntley, Judith Barrett, Patricia Morison. D: Theodore Reed. COM 80m.

I'm Gonna Git You Sucka 1988 ★★★★ Goofy parody of '70s black exploitation movies features writer/director/star Wayans as would-be urban hero out to avenge his brother's death. Brimming with great self-mocking cameo appearances, this low-budget comedy keeps the jokes flying. C: Keenen Ivory Wayans, Bernie Casey, Antonio Fargas, Steve James, Isaac Hayes, Jim Brown, Ja'net DuBois, Dawnn Lewis. D: Keenen Ivory Wayans. COM [R] 87m. V

I'm No Angel 1933 ★★★★½ One of West's best has her taming lions (and men) as sideshow entertainer suing Grant for breach of promise. Final courtroom scene caps hilarious movie. C: Mae West, Cary Grant, Edward Arnold, Kent Taylor. D: Wesley Ruggles. COM 88m. v

I'm Nobody's Sweetheart Now 1940 ★★★½ Hoping to grease their professional paths, two rising politicians try to fix up their kids. Though the children initially balk, eventually their hearts give in to the induced romance. Small musical love story with some cute comic moments. C: Dennis O'Keefe, Constance Moore, Helen Parrish. D: Arthur Lubin. MUS 64m.

I'm Still Alive 1940 ★★★½ After a colleague is killed on the job, a movie stuntman splits from his film star spouse rather than retire from his trade. Standard romantic melodrama spiced with terrific movie stunts. C: Kent Taylor, Linda Hayes, Howard da Silva. D: Irving Reis. DRA 72m.

I'm the Girl He Wants to Kill 1974 ★★½ A nail-biting thriller about a woman who becomes the target of a vicious killer after she witnesses one of his murders. C: Julie Sommars, Anthony Steel. DRA 71m. v

I'm the One You're Looking For 1988 Spanish ★★★½ After she's brutally raped, a woman becomes obsessed with her attacker. Disturbing, suspenseful thriller. C: Patricia Adriani, Chus Lampreave, Richard Borras. D: Jaime Chavarri. DRA 85m.

Image of Bruce Lee, The 1978 ★★½ International forgers compete against kung-fu pros in this punch-packed martial arts adventure. C: Bruce Li, Chang Wu Lang, Chang Lei. D: Yeung Kuen. ACT 88m.

Image of Passion 1986 ★★ An ad exec hires a male stripper for a promotional ploy and ends up having an affair with him. Silly and unbelievable but campily funny. C: James Horan, Susan Damante-Shaw, Edward Bell. D: Susan Orlikoff-Simon. DRA 105m. v

Image, The 1991 ★★★ Top-notch cast fights uphill battle in this mediocre effort about a TV news anchor who'll do anything for ratings, and is eventually forced to reevaluate his priorities. Irresistably reminiscent of the much more successful *Network*. C: Albert Finney, John Mahoney, Kathy Baker, Swoosie Kurtz, Marsha Mason. D: Peter Werner. DRA [R] 91m. TVM v

Imagemaker, The 1986 ★★½ Unstable ex-Presidential public relations man claims to possess damaging evidence on his old employer. Dramatic premise; features a game performance by Nouri. C: Michael Nouri, Jerry Orbach, Jessica Harper, Farley Granger. D: Hal Wiener. DRA [R] 93m. v

Images 1972 U.S. ★★★★½ A writer (York) in Ireland struggles to hold herself together while going through phases of madness and lucidity. Sympathetic exploration of mental instability with an excellent performance by York. C: Susannah York, Rene Auberjonois, Marcel Bozzuffi, Hugh Millais, Cathryn Harrison. D: Robert Altman. DRA [R] 101m.

Imaginary Crimes 1994 ★★★★ Keitel gives one of his finest performances as a con man trying to relate to his two teenage daughters. Balk also stands out as the elder girl, an aspiring writer. This neglected gem is worth discovering. C: Harvey Keitel, Fairuza Balk, Kelly Lynch, Vincent D'Onofrio, Elisabeth Moss. D: Anthony Drazan. DRA [PG] 105m. v

Imagine: John Lennon 1988 ★★★½ Saccharin documentary about famed ex-Beatle which emphasizes his pop tunes over his more serious music. A must for fans thanks to numerous home movies of Lennon working and at leisure. D: Andrew Solt. DOC [R] 103m. v

Imitation General 1958 ★★★ Ford plays a WWII sergeant reluctantly impersonating a commanding officer to keep up troop morale. Middling formula comedy. C: Glenn Ford, Red Buttons, Taina Elg, Dean Jones, Kent Smith, Tige Andrews. D: George Marshall. COM 88m.

Imitation of Life 1934 ★★★½ The friendship between a woman (Colbert) and her African-American maid is complicated by the maid's bitter daughter who tries to pass as white. Sentimental first version of Fannie Hurst's best-seller is a well-wrought product of its time. C: Claudette Colbert, Warren William, Rochelle Hudson, Louise Beavers, Fredi Washington, Ned Sparks, Alan Hale, Henry Armetta. D: John M. Stahl. DRA 109m.

Imitation of Life 1959 ★★★★½ Superior soap opera from Fannie Hurst novel with Turner at her best as ambitious actress joining forces with black maid Moore to raise their rebellious daughters. Lush production and excellent performances make this touching and effective. C: Lana Turner, John Gavin, Sandra Dee, Dan O'Herlihy, Susan Kohner, Robert Alda, Juanita Moore. D: Douglas Sirk. DRA 124m. v

Immediate Family 1989 ★★★½ High-powered cast and big emotional moments can't rescue this soap opera about an infertile couple and the pregnant teen whose baby they contract to adopt. Woods, Close, and Masterson outshine the material. C: Glenn Close, James Woods, Mary Stuart Masterson, Kevin Dillon. D: Jonathan Kaplan. DRA [PG-13] 95m. v

Immigrants, The 1978 ★★★ Howard Fast's generation-spanning saga of a poor Italian immigrant at the turn of the century who makes it big in San Francisco. C: Stephen Macht, Sharon Gless, Aimee Eccles, Richard Anderson, Ina Balin, Lloyd Bochner, Kevin Dobson, Roddy McDowall, Pernell Roberts, John Saxon, Susan Strasberg, Barry Sullivan, Yuki Shimoda. D: Alan J. Levi. DRA 200m. TVM

Immoral Charge 1962 British ★★★★ Vicar coming to new church is faced by prejudices of a close-knit community after a surly youth accuses him of making sexual advances. A good portrait of small minds at work in neatly acted drama. (a.k.a. *A Touch of Hell*) C: Anthony Quayle, Sarah Churchill, Andrew Ray. D: Terence Young. DRA 87m.

Immortal Bachelor, The 1979 Italian ★★★ As widow (Vitti) goes on trial for murdering her cheating husband (Giannini), juror (Cardinale) fantasizes that she'd rather have him than her own dull spouse (Gassman). Quartet of top Italian comic actors give it their all. C: Monica Vitti, Giancarlo Giannini, Vittorio Gassman, Claudia Cardinale. D: Marcello Fondato. COM 95m. V

Immortal Battalion, The 1944 ★★★★½ Thoroughly intriguing and stirring WWII tale of how the British army molded its recruits into an effective group of fighters. Solid direction and outstanding performances; a gem. (a.k.a. *The Way Ahead*) C: David Niven, Stanley Holloway, Leo Genn. D: Carol Reed. ACT 89m. V

Immortal Beloved 1994 ★★★★½ Highly effective bio of composer Ludwig van Beethoven (Oldman), focusing on a mysterious letter he wrote to one of three women. Thrilling use of music and loving attention to historical detail (although some music experts strongly disagreed about Rose's interpretation) make this a must for discriminating viewers. C: Gary Oldman, Jeroen Krabbe, Isabella Rossellini, Valeria Golino, Johanna Ter Steege. D: Bernard Rose. DRA [R] 123m. V

Immortal Gentlemen 1935 ★★★½ The Bard himself, William Shakespeare, discusses his work and introduces scenes from his various plays, including *Hamlet, The Merchant of Venice*, and *Romeo and Juliet*. A good introduction to the playwright's work for young viewers. C: Basil Gill, Rosalinde Fuller. D: Widgey R. Newman. DRA 61m.

Immortal Sergeant, The 1943 ★★★½ On patrol in North Africa, a sergeant dies, and a timid corporal (Fonda) is forced to take command. Compelling war drama with a fine cast. C: Henry Fonda, Maureen O'Hara, Thomas Mitchell, Allyn Joslyn, Reginald Gardiner, Melville Cooper. D: John M. Stahl. DRA 91m. V

Immortal Sins 1991 ★★ When a couple inherits an ancient Spanish castle, they fall victim to the spectral temptress who haunts it. C: Cliff DeYoung, Maryam D'Abo. D: Herve Hachuel. HOR 80m. V

Immortal Story, The 1968 French ★★★★½ Welles is a merchant giving life to an old legend when he hires a "wife," then bribes a sailor to sleep with this pretend spouse. Based on Isak Dinesen tale, neatly enhanced by Welles' inventive guidance. Originally made for French television. C: Orson Welles, Jeanne Moreau, Roger Coggio, Norman Eshley, Fernando Rey. D: Orson Welles. DRA 63m.

Immortal, The 1969 ★★★½ Test driver (George) has blood structure that prevents aging and protects him from disease in okay science fiction. Pilot for TV series. C: Christopher George, Jessica Walter, Barry Sullivan, Carol Lynley, Ralph Bellamy. D: Joseph Sargent. SFI 75m. TVM

Immortal Vagabond 1931 German ★★★½ Traveling singer falls for a young woman, though her strict father disapproves. A drowning suicide is thought to be the singer, giving him a chance to secretly reunite with his love. Nicely acted romance. C: Liane Haid, Gustav Frolich, H.A. Schlettow. D: Gustav Ucicky. DRA 70m.

Immortalizer, The 1990 ★★½ A doctor's twisted practice of transplanting elderly clients' brains into the bodies of kidnapped teens goes awry when an unwilling victim escapes and seeks revenge. C: Chris Crone, Clarke Lindsley, Melody Patterson. D: Joel Bender. HOR [R] 96m. V

Impact 1949 ★★★★ Lovers plot the murder of the woman's rich husband, but their plans spin out of control. Film noir gem with clever plot twists and fine Donlevy in a change-of-pace role. C: Brian Donlevy, Ella Raines, Helen Walker, Charles Coburn. D: Arthur Lubin. CRI 111m. V

Impasse 1970 ★★★½ A silly but fair adventure in which Reynolds and friends seek gold that was hidden in the Philippines during WWII. Passable. C: Burt Reynolds, Anne Francis, Vic Diaz, Jeff Corey, Lyle Bettger, Rodolfo Acosta. D: Richard Benedict. ACT 100m.

Impatient Heart, The 1971 ★★★½ A dedicated social worker throws herself into her work in order to avoid her own problems. Drama with fiery, sympathetic performance by Snodgress. C: Carrie Snodgress, Michael Brandon, Michael Constantine, Marian Hailey, Hector Elizondo. D: John Badham. DRA 100m. TVM

Impatient Maiden, The 1932 ★★★ The story of a young, impressionable maid whose romantic fantasies become indistinguishable from reality. Highly interesting film rotates between comedy and drama. C: Lew Ayres, Mae Clarke, Una Merkel, Andy Devine. D: James Whale. COM 72m.

Impatient Years, The 1944 ★★½ Comedy of soldier (Bowman) having trouble adjusting to civilian married life with Arthur. C: Jean Arthur, Lee Bowman, Charles Coburn, Edgar Buchanan, Harry Davenport, Grant Mitchell, Jane Darwell. D: Irving Cummings. COM 91m.

Imperative 1982 German ★★★★ Powell is a math teacher whose conscientious anxieties take him on quest for philosophical truth. Incisive drama, though occasionally weighed down by film's cerebral themes. Fine performance from Powell. C: Robert Powell, Brigitte Fossey, Leslie Caron, Sigfrit Steiner, Matthias Habich. D: Krzysztof Zanussi. DRA 96m.

Imperfect Lady, The 1947 ★★★ Turn-of-the-century story about a member of Parliament who risks his reputation when he falls hard for a pretty ballerina with a shady past. Okay melodrama. C: Teresa Wright, Ray Milland, Cedric Hardwicke, Virginia Field, Anthony Quinn, Reginald Owen. D: Lewis Allen. DRA 97m.

Imperial Venus 1971 French ★★ Napoleon's sister Paolina (Lollobrigida) thirsts for power of her own. Standard costume epic, dulled by many a contrivance. C: Gina Lollobrigida, Stephen Boyd, Raymond Pellegrin, Micheline Presle. D: Jean Delannoy. DRA [PG] 121m. V

Impersonator, The 1961 British ★★½ Man accused of a series of small-town slayings tries to find out who-really-dunit. Minor British suspense film has an unusual resolution but is otherwise unremarkable. C: John Crawford, Jane Griffiths, Patricia Burke, John Salew, Yvonne Ball. D: Alfred Shaughnessy. HOR 64m.

Importance of Being Earnest, The 1952 British ★★★★★ Oscar Wilde's sparkling comedy of manners given elegant production with perfect cast. Redgrave is gentleman of questionable heritage trying to pass Evans' muster for hand of Greenwood. Splendid dialogue, impeccably served. C: Michael Redgrave, Michael Denison, Edith Evans, Margaret Rutherford, Joan Greenwood. D: Anthony Asquith. COM 95m. V

Important Man, The 1961 ★★★★ Hoping for respect from his family, heavy-drinking Mifune buys victory in a mayoral election. His new position fails to gain the veneration he seeks, causing him to go on a drunken rampage. Intelligent character study heightened by Mifune's swaggering performance. C: Toshiro Mifune, Columba Dominguez, Pepito Romay. D: Ismael Rodriguez. DRA 100m.

Imported Bridegroom, The ★★½ Obeying an old custom, a rich Jewish landlord repents for his sins by bidding for a top scholar to be his daughter's husband. When his daughter finds out, however, she must tell him that his plan is too late. C: Avi Hoffman, Annette Miller. D: Pamela Berger. COM 93m. V

Impossible Object 1973 French ★★½ A writer is unable to tell whether his love affair with a beautiful young woman is real or imagined. Solid idea with skillful cast. (a.k.a. *The Story of a Love Story*) C: Alan Bates, Dominique Sanda. D: John Frankenheimer. DRA 110m.

Impossible Spy, The 1987 U.S. ★★★★ Thriller based on the real life of Elie Cohen (Shea), who became a government agent for the Mossad. In Israel he is a quiet family man, but in Syria he poses as a wealthy and well-connected businessman. Well paced and intriguing. C: John Shea, Eli Wallach, Michal Bat-Adam, Rami Danon. D: Jim Goddard. CRI 96m. TVM V

Impossible Voyage, The 1909 French ★★★½ Charming silent adventure from the dawn of movies takes us on the title trek—to the Sun! The primitive special effects are surprisingly effective. D: George Melies. SFI 20m.

Impossible Years, The 1968 ★★ Exasperated father (Niven) falls apart when his older daughter starts to garner attention from the opposite sex. Uneven farce limps along in search of laughs and finds few. C: David Niven, Lola Albright, Chad Everett, Ozzie Nelson, Cristina Ferrare. D: Michael Gordon. COM [G] 92m. V

Impostor, The 1944 ★★★ French convict Gabin escapes, then pretends he's a dead man so he can serve in WWII army. Flag-waving drama with little impact. C: Jean Gabin, Richard Whorf, Allyn Joslyn, Ellen Drew, Peter Van Eyck, Ralph Morgan. D: Julien Duvivier. DRA 95m.

Imposter, The 1975 ★★★ Hecht is hired to serve as a decoy for an official targeted by assassins. Routine intrigue. C: Paul Hecht, Nancy Kelly, Meredith Baxter, Jack Ging, Barbara Baxley, John Vernon, Edward Asner. D: Edward M. Abroms. ACT 78m. TVM

Imposter, The 1984 ★★½ Con artist Geary finagles a job as principal at the school where his former flame teaches, then reforms to fight teen drug abuse. Silly stuff. C: Anthony Geary, Lorna Patterson, Penny Johnson, Billy Dee Williams. D: Michael Pressman. DRA 95mm. TVM V

Impromptu 1991 ★★★★★ Davis gives a bravura performance as cigar-smoking, 19th-century author George Sand who woos shy composer Chopin (Grant) in this delightfully entertaining comedy of manners. Stars get witty, high-spirited support from top-notch script and supporting cast. Broadway director Lapine's debut film. C: Judy Davis, Hugh Grant, Mandy Patinkin, Bernadette Peters, Julian Sands, Emma Thompson. D: James Lapine. DRA [PG-13] 108m. V

Improper Channels 1981 Canadian ★★½ Uncomfortable satire about the horror of bureaucracy run amok shows the frustrating nightmare of parents (Arkin and Hartley) when they are falsely accused of child abuse and lose custody of their five-year-old daughter. Too realistic to be funny. C: Alan Arkin, Mariette Hartley, Sarah Stevens, Monica Parker. D: Eric Till. COM [PG] 91m. V

Improper Conduct 1984 French ★★★★½ Provocative documentary indicts Castro's revolutionary government for savagely restricting civil rights of homosexuals and other minorities. Cuban exiles Nestor Almendros (cinematographer) and Orlando Jiminez-Leal collaborated on the film. D: Orlando Jiminez-Leal. DOC 110m. V

Impulse 1984 ★★½ Tilly returns with her boyfriend (Matheson) to the rural town where she was raised to find that everyone's run amuck after a small earthquake—people are stealing, shooting, screaming, and vandalizing property. Mystifying—but some viewers loved it. C: Tim Matheson, Meg Tilly, Hume Cronyn, Bill Paxton. D: Graham Baker. DRA [R] 91m. v

Impulse 1990 ★★★★ Honest cop (Russell) works undercover as a prostitute and finds her code of honor tested during a murder investigation. Violent, seedy, urban thriller works thanks to Russell's excellent, risk-taking performance and Locke's full-tilt pacing. C: Theresa Russell, Jeff Fahey, George Dzundza, Alan Rosenburg, Robert Wightman. D: Sondra Locke. CRI [R] 109m. v

Impure Thoughts 1986 ★★★½ A fond reminiscence about growing up in the early '60s and attending Catholic school by a group of friends reunited after death. Quirky, nostalgic story manages to amuse as it looks back on a more innocent time. C: Brad Dourif, Lane Davies, Terry Beaver, John Putch. D: Michael A. Simpson. COM [PG] 87m. v

In a Glass Cage 1985 ★★★★ Difficult-to-watch story involving a former Nazi doctor—now confined to an iron lung—who tortured boys for sadistic pleasure while working for the Third Reich. One victim arrives at his ex-tormentor's bedside for psychological revenge. Well made but excruciatingly painful. Definitely not for all tastes. (a.k.a. *Tras el Cristal*) C: Gunter Meisner, David Sust, Marisa Parades. D: Agustin Villaronga. DRA 90m.

In a Lonely Place 1950 ★★★★ While working to clear himself of a murder rap, a jaded Hollywood screenwriter gets involved in a tempestuous love affair. Hard-hitting, sophisticated fare. C: Humphrey Bogart, Gloria Grahame, Frank Lovejoy, Robert Warwick, Jeff Donnell, Martha Stewart. D: Nicholas Ray. CRI 91m. v

In a Moment Of Passion 1993 ★★½ After a series of murders interrupt filming, an aspiring actress wonders if her newly ignited affair with the leading man will also endanger her life. C: Maxwell Caufield, Jeff Conaway, Chase Masterson. D: Zbigniew Kaminski. DRA [R] 100m. v

In a Shallow Grave 1988 ★★½ Weird film about a disfigured, maimed WWII vet (Beihn) who isolates himself back home in Virginia and uses a drifter (Dempsey) as a go-between with his estranged fiancée (Mueller). Very slow, very strange. C: Michael Biehn, Maureen Mueller, Michael Beach, Patrick Dempsey, Thomas Boyd Mason. D: Kenneth Bowser. DRA [R] 92m. v

In a Stranger's Hand 1992 ★★½ Heart-wrenching drama about a mother who begs a witness to help her find her missing child and end the outbreak of child kidnappings in the area. C: Robert Urich, Megan Gallagher, Maria O'Brien. D: David Greene. DRA 93m. v

In a Year of Thirteen Moons 1978 German ★★★★ A troubled transsexual spends her final days trying to avoid humiliation. Fassbinder's bleak study of rejection, alienation, and struggle for identity pulls no punches, from its subject matter to its decidedly final ending. C: Volker Spengler, Ingrid Caven, Gottfried John, Elisabeth Trissenaar, Eva Mattes. D: Rainer Werner Fassbinder. DRA 129m.

In Bed with Madonna 1991 *See* **Truth or Dare**

In Between 1991 ★★ On their way to death, three souls joke about their past life. C: Wings Hauser, Robin Mattson. D: Thomas Constantinides. COM 92m. v

In Broad Daylight 1971 ★★★½ Well-written mystery with Boone as movie star blinded by accident. Convinced that wife is having an affair, he plans to murder her and her lover. C: Richard Boone, Suzanne Pleshette, Stella Stevens, Fred Beir, John Marley, Whit Bissell. D: Robert Day. CRI 73m. TVM

In Broad Daylight 1991 ★★★★ Dennehy gives outstanding performance as evil gunman intimidating small town. Fine script by playwright William Hanley, based on true-life story. C: Brian Dennehy, Cloris Leachman, Marcia Gay Harden, Chris Cooper, John Anderson, Ken Jenkins. D: James Steven Sadwith. DRA 100m. TVM

In Caliente 1935 ★★★½ Musical romance between critic (O'Brien) and Mexican dancer (Del Rio) enlivened by Berkeley production numbers, especially "The Lady In Red," sung by Wini Shaw and Judy Canova. C: Dolores DelRio, Pat O'Brien, Edward Everett Horton, Leo Carrillo, Glenda Farrell. D: Lloyd Bacon. MUS 84m.

In Celebration 1975 British ★★★★ David Storey's down-to-earth play about an English coal miner clashing with his three grown sons is brought boldly to life by director Anderson and excellent cast. C: Alan Bates, James Bolam, Brian Cox, Constance Chapman, Gabrielle Day, Bill Owen. D: Lindsay Anderson. DRA [PG] 110m.

In Cold Blood 1967 ★★★★★ Chilling adaptation of Capote's book features Blake and Wilson as two drifters who slaughter Kansas farming family. Documentary style adds to realistic sense of horror. Strong performances all around in bleakly memorable work. C: Robert Blake, Scott Wilson, John Forsythe, Paul Stewart, Jeff Corey, Will Geer. D: Richard Brooks. CRI [R] 134m. v

In Country 1989 ★★★ An emotionally damaged Vietnam vet (Willis) and his niece (Lloyd) whose father was killed in battle, search for some kind of understanding of war. Well-meaning, with good leads, but script doesn't do justice to story. C: Bruce Willis, Emily Lloyd, Joan Allen, Kevin Anderson, John Terry, Peggy Rea, Judith Ivey, Richard Hamilton, Patricia Richardson, Jim Beaver. D: Norman Jewison. DRA [R] 120m. v

"In" Crowd, The 1988 ★★★½ Breezily entertaining musical, set in the 1960s, follows an amiable group of performers on an *American*

Bandstand-like TV dance show. Good period flavor. C: Donovan Leith, Jennifer Runyon, Bruce Kirby, Joe Pantoliano. D: Mark Rosenthal. MUS [PG] 96m. V

In Dangerous Company 1988 ★★½ A beautiful young woman makes some bad choices where men are concerned. Trash that glitters. C: Tracy Scoggins, Cliff DeYoung, Chris Mulkey, Henry Darrow. D: Ruben Preuss. DRA [R] 92m. V

In Defense of a Married Man 1990 ★★★½ Lawyer (Light) is forced to defend her husband accused of murder. Routine courtroom drama, but well played. C: Jerry Orbach, Judith Light, Michael Ontkean. D: Joel Oliansky. CRI 96m. TVM

In Defense of Kids 1983 ★★★½ A woman lawyer fights for the rights of her troubled young clients. Danner shines in the lead role, although script about neglected youths sometimes resorts to preachiness. C: Blythe Danner, Sam Waterston. D: Gene Reynolds. DRA 104m. TVM

In Enemy Country 1968 ★★½ Complicated action-adventure with Franciosa as an Allied agent fighting Nazis in WWII Europe. C: Tony Franciosa, Anjanette Comer, Guy Stockwell, Paul Hubschmid, Tom Bell, Emile Genest. D: Harry Keller. ACT 107m.

In Fast Company 1946 ★★★ Fair Bowery Boys episode concerning a powerful cab company trying to muscle out its weaker competitors. COM

In for Treatment 1979 Dutch ★★★★ After going to hospital for routine testing, patient learns he is dying of cancer and is sucked into emotionless world of modern medicine. Simply told tale packs a wallop. Heartbreaking and certainly a film many viewers can relate to. C: Marja Kok, Helmert Woudenberg, Frank Groothof, Hans Man Int Veld, Marja Kok, Joop Admiraal. D: Eric Van Zuylen. DRA 99m.

In God We Trust 1980 ★★ Naive monk (Feldman) encounters the evils of society when he leaves the sanctity of the monastery and travels to Hollywood on a fund-raising excursion. Unfunny religious satire. C: Marty Feldman, Peter Boyle, Louise Lasser, Richard Pryor, Andy Kaufman, Wilfrid Hyde-White, Severn Darden. D: Marty Feldman. COM [PG] 97m.

In Harm's Way 1965 ★★★½ Romance and conflicts of WWII U.S. Navy men after the Japanese air raid on Pearl Harbor. Big star cast and numerous subplots in long but entertaining war spectacle. C: John Wayne, Kirk Douglas, Patricia Neal, Henry Fonda, Jill Haworth, Dana Andrews, Burgess Meredith, Franchot Tone. D: Otto Preminger. DRA 165m. V

In-Laws, The 1979 ★★★★ Arkin is dentist involved in series of loony intrigues when he accompanies daughter's future father-in-law Falk on spy mission to Latin America. Gags come fast and furious, with great chemistry between neurotic Arkin and laid-back Falk. C: Peter Falk, Alan Arkin, Nancy Dussault, Michael Lembeck, Ed Begley Jr. D: Arthur Hiller. COM [PG] 103m. V

In Like Flint 1967 ★★½ In his second outing as debonair super-agent, Coburn kicks and smooches his way through spy ring of beautiful women who have kidnapped U.S. President. Still stylish, but dumber than *Our Man Flint*; the antiquated Hefneresque tone is annoying. C: James Coburn, Lee J. Cobb, Jean Hale, Andrew Duggan. D: Gordon Douglas. ACT 114m. V

In Love and War 1958 ★★★ Three inexperienced Marines in the Pacific become hardened by battle. WWII heroics enhanced by striking cast. C: Robert Wagner, Dana Wynter, Jeffrey Hunter, Hope Lange, Bradford Dillman, Sheree North, France Nuyen, Mort Sahl. D: Philip Dunne. DRA 111m. V

In Love and War 1987 ★★★ Movie based on the true story of Navy pilot James B. Stockdale who endured eight years as a Vietnam POW while his wife Sybil (Alexander) worked for his release back in the States. Adaptation of the couple's own book is a sincere effort to champion the plight of Vietnam war veterans. C: Jane Alexander, James Woods, Haing S. Ngor, Richard McKenzie, Concetta Tomei. D: Paul Aaron. DRA 96m. TVM V

In Love with an Older Woman 1982 ★★½ May-December romance has some sparkle but can't shake that seen-it-before feeling. C: John Ritter, Karen Carlson, Jamie Ross, Robert Mandan. D: Jack Bender. COM 100m. V

In Name Only 1939 ★★★★ Grant is wealthy guy stuck in empty marriage with nasty-edged Garner. Enter Lombard, a goofy widowed artist who lightens Grant's personal burdens. Soap opera in a minor key but talented cast lifts this higher than script expectations. C: Carole Lombard, Cary Grant, Kay Francis, Charles Coburn, Peggy Ann Garner. D: John Cromwell. COM 102m. V

In Old Amarillo 1951 ★★★ Ranchers suffering from the double whammy of drought and nefarious doings by evil cattle baron Barcroft are relieved when perennial hero Rogers rides in to save the day. Average Rogers Western, with few shining moments. C: Roy Rogers, Roy Barcroft. D: William Witney. WST 67m.

In Old Arizona 1929 ★★★ The life and times of the fabulous Cisco Kid and his sidekick, Pancho. Although an antique today, this early sound film scored big way back when. Star Baxter won Best Actor Oscar. C: Warner Baxter, Edmund Lowe, Dorothy Burgess. D: Raoul Walsh, Irving Cummings. WST 94m.

In Old Caliente 1939 ★★ A ranch hand seeks to prove his innocence when a ranch's herd mysteriously disappears. C: Roy Rogers, Mary Hart. D: Joseph Kane. WST 54m. V

In Old California 1942 ★★★ A Boston pharmacist hangs out his shingle in Sacramento during the gold rush and crosses paths with the crook who runs the town. Modest Wayne vehicle. C: John Wayne, Binnie Barnes, Albert Dekker, Helen Parrish, Edgar Kennedy. D: William McGann. WST 88m. V

In Old Chicago 1938 ★★★★½ The Great Chicago Fire of 1871 blazes once again in this lavish period drama filled with harrowing action sequences and splendid full-throttle performances. Romantic subplot adds to the emotional heat. Brady's Mrs. O'Leary won her an Oscar. C: Tyrone Power, Alice Faye, Don Ameche, Alice Brady, Andy Devine, Brian Donlevy, Phyllis Brooks, Tom Brown, Berton Churchill, Sidney Blackmer, Gene Reynolds, Bobs Watson. D: Henry King. DRA 95m. V

In Old Kentucky 1935 ★★★½ Rogers is charming in mild, enjoyable country comedy of feuding families. Will's last film. C: Will Rogers, Dorothy Wilson, Bill Robinson, Russell Hardie, Louise Henry, Charles Sellon. D: George Marshall. COM 86m.

In Old Montana 1939 ★★ A grazing area becomes a battleground when sheep and cattle herders once again try to setle an ongoing conflict. C: Fred Scott. WST 65m. V

In Old New Mexico 1945 ★★★ The Cisco Kid and Pancho swing into action to find an old woman's killer. Traditional Sunday-feature Western with rewarding moments. C: Duncan Renaldo, Martin Garralaga, Gwen Kenyon. D: Phil Rosen. WST 62m. V

In Old Santa Fe 1935 ★★★ When a cow wrangler is framed for murder, his good buddies step in and save the day. Of interest as Gene Autry's screen debut. C: Ken Maynard, Evalyn Knapp, H. B. Warner. D: David Howard. WST 62m.

In Our Hands 1982 ★★★★ Musical performances and speeches from celebrity notables highlight this striking documentary, portraying June 1982 antinuclear rally in New York City. C: James Taylor, Carly Simon. DOC 90m. V

In Our Time 1944 ★★★ An Englishwoman and a Polish aristocrat battle to save Poland from Nazi domination. Overtly patriotic soaper is too noble for its own good, but Lupino and Henreid manage to inject sincere moments. C: Ida Lupino, Paul Henreid, Nazimova, Nancy Coleman, Mary Boland, Victor Francen, Michael Chekhov. D: Vincent Sherman. DRA 110m.

In Person 1935 ★★★½ Jaded movie star (Rogers) goes to retreat for rest and meets Brent, who doesn't recognize her. Enjoyable fluff, nicely played. C: Ginger Rogers, George Brent, Alan Mowbray, Grant Mitchell, Samuel S. Hinds, Joan Breslau. D: William Seiter. COM 85m. V

In Praise of Older Women 1978 Canadian ★★½ Hungarian stud (Berenger) recalls a cavalcade of conquests. Some are more interesting than others, though Tom's adorable. C: Tom Berenger, Karen Black, Susan Strasberg, Helen Shaver, Alexandra Stewart. D: George Kaczender. COM [R] 108m. V

In Search of a Golden Sky 1984 ★★ Sincere drama of orphaned children who grow to love their new life in the wilderness under the supervision of their eccentric uncle. C: George Flower, Charles Napier. D: Jefferson Richard. DRA [PG] 94m. V

In Search of Anna 1979 ★★ After being released from prison, a man discovers members from his old gang are after him and that life will never be like it once was. C: Richard Moir, Judy Morris. D: Esben Storm. DRA 91m. V

In Search of Gregory 1970 British ★★½ Two young people have a romance, but only in their fantasies. Far-fetched. C: Julie Christie, Michael Sarrazin, John Hurt, Adolfo Celi, Paola Pitagora. D: Peter Wood. DRA [PG] 90m.

In Search of Historic Jesus 1979 ★★ Docudrama uses the Shroud of Turin to "verify" that Jesus is the Messiah. Poor production values and awkward writing make this an undeserving exploration of a serious subject. C: John Rubinstein, John Anderson, Nehemiah Persoff, Morgan Brittany. D: Henning G. Schellerup. DRA [G] 91m. V

In Search of Noah's Ark 1976 ★★ Documentary follows team of archaeologists out to prove an ancient sailing vessel was in fact, the one Noah used in the great flood. Low-budget production raises some compelling points, but interesting subject matter deserves better treatment. D: James L. Conway. DOC [G] 95m. V

In Search of the Castaways 1962 ★★★½ When his daughter (Mills) is kidnapped, sea captain Chevalier must brave a series of natural disasters before ultimately rescuing her. Good special effects in otherwise average adaptation of Jules Verne tale. Kids will enjoy. C: Hayley Mills, Maurice Chevalier, George Sanders, Wilfrid Hyde-White. D: Robert Stevenson. FAM/ACT [G] 98m. V

In Search of the Perfect 10 1987 ★★ A voyeuristic comedy about the quest for the most captivating women in U.S. C: Andrew Nichols, Michelle Bauer. COM 60m. V

In Self Defense 1993 ★★★ Killer freed on legal technicality hunts for woman whose testimony against him could be devastating. C: Linda Purl, Yaphet Kotto. D: Bruce Seth Green. CRI 94m. V

In Society 1944 ★★★★ Abbott and Costello portray inept plumbers who inadvertently find themselves mistaken for wealthy socialites. Story line is sacrificed for string of howlingly funny burlesque routines including a hilarious rendition of "Floogle Street." C: Bud Abbott, Lou Costello, Marion Hutton, Arthur Treacher, Thomas Gomez, Thurston Hall, Kirby Grant. D: Jean Yarbrough. COM 75m. V

In the Aftermath 1987 ★★★ Post-apocalyptic tale of soldier who dreams of future even bleaker than the decimation that surrounds him. C: Tony Markes, Rainbow Dolan. D: Carl Colpaert. SFI 85m. V

In the Cold of the Night 1990 ★★½ Normal guy is plagued by a recurring nightmare: His unconscious wants to kill a woman he doesn't even know. Puzzler in the *Spellbound* mold. C: Jeff Lester, Adrienne Sachs, David Soul, Tippi Hedren. D: Nico Mastorakis. CRI [R] 112m. V

In the Cool of the Day 1963 British ★★½ Lovers (Fonda and Finch), trapped in unhappy marriages, pine for each other. Meanwhile, the audience goes to sleep. Produced by the venerable John Houseman, who often displayed better judgment. C: Jane Fonda, Peter Finch, Angela Lansbury, Arthur Hill, Constance Cummings. D: Robert Stevens. DRA 89m.

In the Custody of Strangers 1982 ★★★★ Middle-class teenager (Estevez) is thrown in jail for drinking and his parents (real-life dad Sheen and Alexander) fight for his release, fearing the influence of other inmates. Takes a good look at a real problem. C: Martin Sheen, Jane Alexander, Emilio Estevez, Kenneth McMillan, Ed Lauter. D: Robert Greenwald. DRA 100m. TVM V

In the Devil's Garden 1971 British ★★ Perverted killer stalks the campus of an all-girl's English school. Routine suspense. (a.k.a. *Assault* and *The Creepers*) C: Suzy Kendall, Frank Finlay, Freddie Jones, Lesley-Anne Down, James Laurenson, Tony Beckley. D: Sidney Hayers. CRI [R] 89m.

In the French Style 1963 ★★★ An aspiring artist from Chicago (Seberg) goes to Paris and falls in love, but not without some reservations. Trifling romantic drama. C: Jean Seberg, Stanley Baker, Addison Powell, James Leo Herlihy, Philippe Forquet, Claudine Auger. D: Robert Parrish. DRA 105m.

In the Good Old Summertime 1949 ★★★★ Spirited musical updating of *The Shop Around the Corner*, with music store clerk (Garland) falling tunefully in love with a pen-pal who is actually her dreaded boss (Johnson). The two leads make this a delight. C: Judy Garland, Van Johnson, S. Z. Sakall, Spring Byington, Clinton Sundberg, Buster Keaton. D: Robert Z. Leonard. MUS 102m. V

In the Heat of Passion 1992 ★★★ Bored housewife (Kirkland) begins a casual affair with grease monkey (Corri), which leads to murder. Erotic, labyrinthine thriller looks cheap, but holds attention. C: Sally Kirkland, Nick Corri, Jack Carter, Michael Greene. D: Rodman Flender. CRI [R] 86m. V

In the Heat of the Night 1967 ★★★★★ A murder in a small town triggers racial tension between tough, bigoted sheriff and bright African-American detective from up north. Great acting and a strong script make this a classic (and Best Picture Oscar Winner). Steiger's performance won Oscar for Best Actor. Basis for the TV series. C: Sidney Poitier, Rod Steiger, Warren Oates, Lee Grant, Scott Wilson. D: Norman Jewison. CRI 109m. V

In the King of Prussia 1982 ★★★ Based on true story, anti-nuclear activists stand trial for seriously damaging Pennsylvania power plant. C: Martin Sheen, Daniel Berrigan. D: Emile De Antonio. DRA 92m. V

In the Line of Duty: Ambush in Waco 1993 ★★★½ TV movie recounts the FBI's assault on the Davidian cult compound, and dramatizes the events leading up to the tragic climax that shocked the nation. Takes dramatic license, but is still a sincere interesting effort to explain the final chapter of David Koresh's life. C: Tim Daly, William O'Leary, Dan Lauria. D: Dick Lowry. DRA [R] 93m. TVM V

In the Line of Duty: The F.B.I. Murders 1988 ★★★ Fact-based film depicts the notorious 1986 confrontation between the F.B.I. and two killers. Realistic and extremely violent. C: Ronny Cox, Bruce Greenwood, Michael Gross, Doug Sheehan, David Soul, Teri Copley. D: Dick Lowry. CRI 100m. TVM V

In the Line of Fire 1993 ★★★★½ Secret service agent (Eastwood), still wracked with guilt 30 years after witnessing J.F.K. shooting, undergoes emotional turmoil chasing a presidential assassin (Malkovich), gleefully toying with his demons. Taut and chilling, with Malkovich at his psychopathic best. C: Clint Eastwood, John Malkovich, Rene Russo, Dylan McDermott. D: Wolfgang Petersen. CRI [R] 127m. V

In the Matter of Karen Ann Quinlan 1977 ★★★★ Famous case of brain-damaged girl and her parent's fight to let her die naturally given tasteful dramatization with excellent performances. Laurie is particularly good as mother torn between love and conscience. C: Brian Keith, Piper Laurie. D: Hal Jordan. DRA 104m. TVM

In the Meantime, Darling 1944 ★★★ WWII comedy has rich snob (Crain) taught manners and morals by G.I. hubby (Latimore). Look for future director Blake Edwards as Crain's dancing partner. C: Jeanne Crain, Frank Latimore, Eugene Pallette, Mary Nash, Cara Williams, Reed Hadley, Stanley Prager, Gale Robbins. D: Otto Preminger. COM 72m.

In the Mood 1987 ★★★★ True-life story of 15-year-old charmer (Dempsey) who becomes romantically entangled with two women much older than he, eventually marrying one of them. Dempsey's spirited performance keeps fun-filled comedy moving along. Good score, too. C: Patrick Dempsey, Talia Balsam, Beverly D'Angelo, Michael Constantine. D: Phil Alden Robinson. COM [PG-13] 100m. V

In the Mouth of Madness 1995 ★★★★ Bizarre thriller about Stephen King-like novelist whose books literally drive readers mad. When he disappears with his latest manuscript, Neill is called in to investigate, with scary results. Imaginative and nasty. C: Sam Neill, Jurgen Prochnow, Julie Carmen, David Warner, Charlton Heston. D: John Carpenter. HOR

In the Name of Life 1947 U.S.S.R. ★★½ Soviet propaganda from the Cold War era follows three soldiers who become doctors, then blame evil Amerikanskis when groundbreaking medical ideas are stolen. Dull drama, with gruesome scenes of animal dismemberment. C: Victor Kokriakov, Mikhail Kuznetsov, Oleg Zhakov. D: Alexander Zarki, Josef Heifitz. DRA 99m.

In the Name of the Father 1971 Italian ★★★★ Wealthy students at a run-down and autocratic Jesuit boarding school rebel against authority, leading a blasphemous insurrection during school play. Ribald comic assault on society rules and roles, with unique visual style and nice surreal touches. C: Renato Scarpa, Yves Beneyton, Lou Caster, Laura Betti. D: Marco Bellocchio. COM 107m. V

In the Name of the Father 1993 British ★★★★½ Uneven but ultimately moving film based on real events about four men wrongly convicted in an IRA bombing and their battle for freedom. Mostly, though, it's about Day-Lewis' relationship with his father, Postlethwaite, in prison; two superb actors explore one another with an emotional intensity that is majestic to behold. C: Daniel Day-Lewis, Emma Thompson, Pete Postlethwaite, John Lynch, Mark Sheppard, Beatie Edney, Marie Jones. D: Jim Sheridan. DRA 133m. V

In the Name of the Pope King 1977 Italian ★★★★ Vatican City judge (Manfredi) must deal with his son being accused of terrorist activities. Set in 1867, during the battle over papal control, Manfredi's emotional portrayal grounds story in affecting reality. (a.k.a. *Nel Nome del Pape Re*) C: Nino Manfredi, Danilo Mattei, Carmen Scarpitta, Giovannella Grifea, Carlo Bagno. D: Luigi Magni. DRA 105m. V

In the Navy 1941 ★★★★ Early comedy puts Bud and Lou on battleship en route to Hawaii where crooner (Powell) is hiding from photographer (Dodd). Some classic routines (Lou proves that 7 x 13 = 28), songs by Andrews Sisters. Enjoyable nonsense. C: Bud Abbott, Lou Costello, Dick Powell, Andrews Sisters, Claire Dodd. D: Arthur Lubin. COM 85m. V

In the Shadow of Kilimanjaro 1986 ★★½ When drought hits Mt. Kilimanjaro, thirsty baboons are driven into a murderous frenzy and gorge themselves on innocent humans. The simians provide the excitement, the humans the wooden acting. Based on actual events. C: John Rhys-Davies, Timothy Bottoms, Michele Carey, Calvin Jung. D: Raju Patel. ACT [R] 94m. V

In the Shadow of the Stars 1991 ★★★★½ Goes behind-the-scenes at San Francisco Opera Company and finds the stories of the lowly chorus members. Quietly moving, with opera excerpts, it's a successful portrait of dreams and accomplishments. Winner of Best Documentary Oscar. D: Irving Saraf, Allie Light. DOC 93m. V

In the Soup 1992 ★★★ Offbeat comedy of a young writer who teams up with an eccentric gangster who promises to produce his screenplay. C: Steve Buscemi, Seymour Cassel, Jennifer Beals, Will Patton, Jim Jarmusch, Carol Kane, Stanley Tucci. D: Alexandre Rockwell. COM [R] 90m. V

In the Spirit 1990 ★★★ Strange, not entirely successful story about New-Ager Thomas who brings endless problems to married friends May and Falk after murder of local prostitute. Some fun chemistry between Thomas and May, though largely forgettable. C: Marlo Thomas, Elaine May, Peter Falk, Jeannie Berlin, Olympia Dukakis, Melanie Griffith. D: Sandra Seacat. COM [R] 94m. V

In the Summertime 1971 ★★★★ Italian man takes cynical woman under his wing and helps her overcome personal difficulties through his wild daydreaming. A sweet romantic comedy with effervescent performances and wonderful comic turns. C: Renato Paracchi, Rosanna Callegaria. D: Ermanno Olmi. COM 110m.

In the White City 1983 Swiss ★★★★½ Ship mechanic (Ganz) walks around Lisbon with a movie camera, recording his experiences. Tanner's loosely structured approach (he intercuts Ganz's super-8 footage with his wanderings) works beautifully in this exceptional study of alienation. C: Bruno Ganz, Teresa Madruga, Jose Carvalho. D: Alain Tanner. DRA 108m. V

In the Year of the Pig 1969 ★★★★½ Documentary from Vietnam era looks at the conflict, and criticizes U.S. involvement in the war. Riveting real-life drama that refuses to compromise. D: Emile de Antonio. DOC 101m.

In this House of Brede 1975 ★★★½ Rigg plays a London entrepreneur who abandons her successful business to become a Benedictine nun in this touching adaptation of the Rumer Godden novel. Rigg is wonderful. C: Diana Rigg, Judi Bowker, Gwen Watford, Pamela Brown, Denis Quilley. D: George Schaefer. DRA 100m. TVM

In This Our Life 1942 ★★★★½ Searing performance by Davis drives this torrid melodrama about a self-destructive woman who ruins not only her own life, but the lives of those around her—especially that of her sweet-natured sister. Very well done. C: Bette Davis, Olivia de Havilland, George Brent, Dennis Morgan, Charles Coburn, Hattie McDaniel. D: John Huston. DRA 97m. V

In Too Deep 1990 ★★½ Chanteuse and rock star attempt romance despite dangerous, up-hill battle. C: Hugo Race, Santha

Press, Rebekah Elmaloglou. D: Colin South. ACT [R] 106m. v

In Which We Serve 1942 British ★★★★★ Inspirational war drama focuses on a group of naval combat veterans as they recount how their ship was lost to a torpedo. Solid mix of action and drama. Lean's directorial debut. Coward earned a special Oscar for his many contributions. C: Noel Coward, John Mills, Bernard Miles, Celia Johnson, James Donald, Richard Attenborough. D: Noel Coward, David Lean. DRA 115m. v

In Your Face 1977 ★★½ African-American family moves into all-white neighborhood and pays dearly; but motorcycle gang steps in and clears things up. Black exploitation flick doesn't date too well. (a.k.a. *Abar, the First Black Superman*) C: J. Walter Smith, Tobar Mayo, Roxy Young. D: Frank Packard. ACT 90m. v

Inadmissible Evidence 1968 British ★★★½ Williamson reprises his stage role as a lawyer whose unscrupulous ways start to catch up with him both personally and professionally. Stage-bound, but Williamson is riveting. C: Nicol Williamson, Eleanor Fazan, Jill Bennett, Peter Sallis, David Valla, Eileen Atkins. D: Anthony Page. CRI [R] 96m.

Incendiary Blonde 1945 ★★★★½ The rollicking life and times of '20s singing and nightclub star Texas Guinan. Hutton is made for the role and does a superb job throughout. C: Betty Hutton, Arturo de Cordova, Charlie Ruggles, Albert Dekker, Barry Fitzgerald, Mary Phillips, Bill Goodwin. D: George Marshall. DRA 113m.

Inchon 1982 Korean ★ General MacArthur (Olivier) leads Korean War troops in Battle of Inchon. Financed by Reverend Sun Mung Moon's Unification Church, this overbloated, hilariously horrible war epic features Olivier in all-time low. C: Laurence Olivier, Jacqueline Bisset, Ben Gazzara, Toshiro Mifune, Richard Roundtree. D: Terence Young. ACT [PG] 105m.

Incident 1948 ★★★½ Innocent man's uncanny resemblance to a notorious underworld figure results in a savage beating; which leads to exposing the gang to cops, culminating in a bullet-ridden climax. Gritty crime drama with action to spare. C: Warren Douglas, Jane Frazee, Robert Osterloh. D: William Beaudine. CRI 66m.

Incident at Crestridge 1981 ★★★ Silly feminist comedy/Western with Brennan as sheriff trying to oust corrupt mayor. C: Eileen Brennan, Pernell Roberts, Bruce Davison. D: Jud Taylor. COM 104m. TVM

Incident at Dark River 1989 ★★★ Well-meaning but slow environmental drama of Farrell crusading against factory that ruined his daughter's health with toxic waste. C: Mike Farrell, Tess Harper, Helen Hunt, Arthur Rosenberg, Philip Baker Hall, K Callan, Nicolas Coster. D: Michael Pressman. DRA 100m. TVM

Incident at Midnight 1963 British ★★★ Disgraced drug-addicted doctor (Miller) finds redemption when he aids police in nabbing an ex-Nazi drug pusher (Diffring). Preachy, but not without excitement. Based on an Edgar Wallace story. C: Anton Diffring, William Sylvester, Tony Garnett, Martin Miller. D: Norman Harrison. CRI 58m.

Incident at Oglala 1992 ★★★★ Fine documentary attempts to piece together the truth behind events resulting in the arrest of Native American Leonard Peltier for the shooting death of two FBI agents at Pine Ridge Reservation in 1975. Involving throughout. Director Apted also explored these themes in the thriller *Thunderheart*. D: Michael Apted. DOC [PG] 89m. v

Incident at Phantom Hill 1966 ★★★½ Eye-filling Civil War-era Western about the search for hidden gold in Texas. Fast, colorful, and action-packed. C: Robert Fuller, Dan Duryea, Jocelyn Lane, Claude Akins. D: Earl Bellamy. WST 88m.

Incident at Victoria Falls 1991 Belgian ★★★½ King Edward enlists an aging Sherlock Holmes to retrieve a priceless diamond from South Africa. Original running time of four hours cut to two hours for video, resulting in a slightly choppy story. Lee and Macnee are more than competent as Holmes and Watson. C: Christopher Lee, Patrick Macnee, Claude Akins, Richard Todd, Joss Ackland, John Indi, Stephen Gurney, Sunitha Singh, Anthony Fridjhon, Neil McCarthy, Claudia Udi, Jerome Willis. D: Bill Corcoran. CRI 120m.

Incident in San Francisco 1970 ★★★ Journalist (Connelly) investigates case of good samaritan (Kiley) accidentally killing mugger while aiding his victim. Fair pilot for TV series that never happened. C: Richard Kiley, Chris Connelly, Leslie Nielsen, Phyllis Thaxter, John Marley, Ruth Roman, Tim O'Connor, Claudia McNeil. D: Don Medford. CRI 98m. TVM

Incident on a Dark Street 1972 ★★★ Reasonablly well-done law enforcement drama, with Olson out to stop the Mob's drug operation. C: James Olson. D: Buzz Kulik. CRI

Incident, The 1967 ★★★★ Two young thugs (Sheen and Musante) terrorize passengers on NYC subway. Well-done film of an ugly, and unfortunately still timely subject. Sheen's film debut. C: Tony Musante, Martin Sheen, Beau Bridges, Jack Gilford, Thelma Ritter, Brock Peters. D: Larry Peerce. CRI 99m. v

Incident, The 1990 ★★★★ Matthau is perfect as a cagey small-town lawyer in WWII South who finds himself in the hot seat when he defends a German POW accused of murder. Compelling courtroom drama. C: Walter Matthau, Susan Blakely, Robert Carradine, Peter Firth, Barnard Hughes, Harry Morgan, William Schallert. D: Joseph Sargent. DRA 100m. TVM v

Incoming Freshmen 1979 ★★ The raunchy

adventures of a new crop of college students. Junior varsity antics. C: Ashley Vaughn, Leslie Blalock. D: Glen Morgan. COM [R] 84m. V

Inconvenient Woman, An 1991 ★★★½ L.A. tycoon's plan to eliminate his wife's nosey society friend backfires when his mistress decides to blackmail him. Well-made movie adroitly captures the sophisticated debauchery of Dominick Dunne's novel. C: Jason Robards, Jill Eikenberry, Rebecca De Mornay, Peter Gallagher, Roddy McDowall. D: Larry Elikann. DRA 126m. TVM V

Incredible Hulk, The 1977 ★★★ Scientist (Bixby) pops some mean muscles thanks to a radiation leak. Based on the successful Marvel Comic series. Standard action fare, plus lots of pecs, abs, and lats, courtesy of Lou Ferrigno. C: Bill Bixby, Susan Sullivan, Jack Colvin, Lou Ferrigno. D: Kenneth Johnson. ACT 94m. TVM V

Incredible Hulk Returns, The 1988 ★★★ The green manster (Ferrigno) is back, teamed up with that other Marvel Comic staple, the Mighty Thor. Fair thrills. *The Trial of the Incredible Hulk* follows. C: Bill Bixby, Lou Ferrigno, Jack Colvin, Tim Thomerson. D: Nicholas Corea. ACT 100m. TVM V

Incredible Journey of Doctor Meg Laurel, The 1979 ★★★ Sentimental tale of modern doctor (Wagner) returning to practice medicine in Appalachian hometown. She encounters resistance from superstitious residents, led by Wyman as home cure expert. C: Lindsay Wagner, Jane Wyman, Dorothy McGuire, James Woods. D: Guy Green. DRA 143m. TVM V

Incredible Journey, The 1963 ★★★★½ An elderly bull terrier, a Labrador retriever, and a Siamese cat become homesick for their owner and decide to travel across Canada's wildest terrain to return to their master. Heartwarming, action-packed animal adventure should charm children the whole way. Remade as *Homeward Bound: The Incredible Journey*. C: Emile Genest, John Drainie, Tommy Tweed, Sandra Scott. D: Fletcher Markle. FAM/ACT [G] 80m.

Incredible Manitoba Animation 1990 ★★★★ Dazzling array of the best of Canada's famed animated shorts, featuring a bunch of prizewinners. Perfect for animation fans, kids and adults. COM 51m. V

Incredible Master Beggars 1982 ★★ Martial arts' student puts his recent training to use when gangsters kidnap his girlfriend. C: Tan Tao Liang, Ku Feng. ACT 88m. V

Incredible Mr. Limpet, The 1964 ★★★½ An unassuming bookkeeper, obsessed with the sea, falls into the ocean and, to his amazement, turns into a fish. Pleasing comedy/fantasy spotlights the talents of Knotts as it effectively combines animation and live action. Good family fun. C: Don Knotts, Jack Weston, Carole Cook, Andrew Duggan. D: Arthur Lubin. COM [G] 99m. V

Incredible Petrified World, The 1958 ★★ Explorers in a diving bell risk their lives while encountering underwater mountains, volcanoes, etc. Adventurous but slow-moving sci-fi thriller. C: John Carradine, Robert Clarke, Lloyd Nelson, Phyllis Coates. D: Jerry Warren. SFI 78m. V

Incredible Rocky Mountain Race 1977 ★★★ Young Mark Twain (Connelly) challenges rival (Tucker) to cross-country race on horseback. Zany try at mixing comedy with a Western setting. C: Christopher Connelly, Forrest Tucker, Larry Storch, Whit Bissell. D: James L. Conway. COM 100m. TVM V

Incredible Sarah, The 1976 ★★½ Jackson plays famous actress Sarah Bernhardt with exaggerated zest that would have embarrassed even the original. C: Glenda Jackson, Daniel Massey, Yvonne Mitchell, Douglas Wilmer. D: Richard Fleischer. DRA [PG] 83m. V

Incredible Shrinking Man, The 1957 ★★★★★ After floating through a haze of radiation, an average American starts decreasing in size. Suddenly his trip to the basement is fraught with danger from water, cats, and . . . spiders. From the Richard Matheson novel. Outstanding sci-fi, still holds up. C: Grant Williams, Randy Stuart, April Kent, Paul Langton, William Schallert. D: Jack Arnold. SFI 81m. V

Incredible Shrinking Woman, The 1981 ★★★ Remake/parody of *The Incredible Shrinking Man* features Tomlin as housewife who slowly reduces in size after exposure to common household chemicals. Tomlin is fun but heavy-handed satire overshadows comic elements. C: Lily Tomlin, Charles Grodin, Ned Beatty, Henry Gibson. D: Joel Schumacher. COM [PG] 88m. V

Incredible Two-Headed Transplant, The 1971 ★ Incredible is right. Cheapie has mad doctor (Dern) grafting a maniac's head onto the shoulder of a massive, mentally deficient man. Naturally, the new head convinces the old one to go on a rampage. Special effects (and everything else) are inept. C: Bruce Dern, Pat Priest, Casey Kasem. D: Anthony M. Lanza. HOR [PG] 88m. V

Incredibly Strange Creatures Who Stopped Living and Became Mixed up Zombies 1963 ★ Title's a lot more fun than the movie, a melange of horror and rock 'n' roll set at a carnival where the fortune teller turns patrons into disfigured monsters. Color photography is great, but that's about it. Flagg is a pseudonym for director Steckler. C: Cash Flagg, Brett O'Hara, Atlas King, Sharon Walsh, Madison Clarke, Son Hooker. D: Ray Dennis Steckler. HOR 82m. V

Incubus, The 1982 Canadian ★★ Small-town doctor Cassavetes investigates murders in which young women are brutally killed by a creature that may be spawned by a young man's nightmares. Offensive, tacky junk, based on Ray Russell's novel. C: John Cassavetes, Kerrie Keane, Helen Hughes, John Ireland. D: John Hough. HOR [R] 90m. ♥

Indecency 1992 ★★ A gripping thriller about a mentally-fragile woman who becomes entangled in madness, drugs, and thievery when her bosses husband seeks to regain control an advertising agency. C: Jennifer Beals, James Remar, Ray McKinnon. D: Marisa Silver. HOR [PG-13] 88m. TVM ♥

Indecent Behavior 1993 ★★ A cop becomes involved with the wrong women during his investigation of a patient in sex therapy who dies of a drug overdose. C: Shannon Tweed, Gary Hudson. DRA [R] 93m. ♥

Indecent Obession, An 1985 ★★ A weak adaptation of a best-selling Colleen McCullough novel about a group of asylum inhabitants reacting to the Japanese wartime surrender. C: Wendy Hughes, Bill Hunter. D: Lex Marinos. DRA 100m. ♥

Indecent Proposal 1993 ★★★½ Moore and Harrelson are a struggling couple hoping to finance dream home by winning big in Vegas. Enter wealthy Redford, who offers them one million dollars to spend one night with Moore. Intriguing idea given slick treatment; a surefire conversation starter. C: Robert Redford, Demi Moore, Woody Harrelson, Oliver Platt. D: Adrian Lyne. DRA [R] 119m. ♥

Independence 1987 ★★★½ Perry plays town sheriff determined to protect his community from murderer who killed his family years ago. Failed series pilot of some quality takes traditional Western tale of revenge and gives it contemporary spin with energetic writing and editing. C: John Bennett Perry, Isabella Hofman, Sandy McPeak, Macon McCalman, Amanda Wyss, Stephanie Dunnam, Anthony Zerbe. D: John Patterson. WST 100m. ♥

Independence Day 1983 ★★★ Rather strained tale of young photographer in a dead-end town who must choose between the big city and her boyfriend. Well intentioned but erratic film has strong cast, especially Wiest in subplot as abused wife. (a.k.a. *Follow Your Dreams*) C: Kathleen Quinlan, David Keith, Frances Sternhagen, Cliff DeYoung, Dianne Wiest. D: Robert Mandel. DRA [R] 110m. ♥

Indestructible Man, The 1956 ★★½ Freak consequence of an attempted execution gives innocent Chaney superhuman life; not even bazookas can stop him from hunting down those who framed him. Acting doesn't get any worse; great for unintended laughs. C: Lon Chaney, Jr., Marian Carr, Casey Adams, Ross Elliott, Stuart Randall. D: Jack Pollexfen. HOR 70m. ♥

India Song 1975 ★★★★½ While her husband is emissary to India, Seyrig grows bored and depressed. Casual affairs only add to her mental instability. Effective mood piece that achieves a high sense of oppressive ambiance. Seyrig is excellent. C: Delphine Seyrig, Mathiew Carriere. D: Marguerite Duras. DRA 120m.

Indian Agent 1948 ★★★½ Food intended for a Native-American settlement is diverted to gold fields by unscrupulous mine owners. This nearly leads to war, until heroic Holt rides in to settle all scores. Good action in entertaining spin on B-Western formulas. C: Tim Holt, Noah Beery, Jr., Richard Martin, Nan Leslie. D: Lesley Selander. WST 63m.

Indian Fighter, The 1955 ★★★★ Douglas leads a wagon train through hostile Sioux territory. Good and workmanlike, even exciting—but never strays from the expected. C: Kirk Douglas, Walter Matthau, Elsa Martinelli, Walter Abel, Lon Chaney. D: Andre de Toth. WST 88m. ♥

Indian Love Call 1936 *See* **Rose Marie**

Indian Paint 1964 ★★½ The story of an Arikara boy's passage into manhood. Well executed and moving. Star Silverheels played Tonto in TV's *The Lone Ranger*. C: Johnny Crawford, Jay Silverheels, Pat Hogan, Robert Crawford, Jr. D: Norman Foster. WST [G] 91m. ♥

Indian Runner, The 1991 ★★★★ Penn wrote and directed this raw, intense drama about a highway patrol officer and his volatile younger brother, a hell-raiser scarred by his experience in Vietnam. Spiritual moments add further depth and emotion to complement Penn's already heated style, detailing the brothers' inevitable showdown. C: David Morse, Viggo Mortensen, Valeria Golino, Patricia Arquette, Dennis Hopper. D: Sean Penn. DRA [R] 125m. ♥

Indian Scarf, The 1963 German ★★★ Clichéd thriller with weekend guests at country mansion murdered, one by one, with the scarf. C: Heinz Drache, Gisela Uhlen, Corny Collins, Klaus Kinski. D: Alfred Vohrer. CRI 85m.

Indian Summer 1993 ★★★ Young adults suffering premature mid-life crisis return to the summer camp of their youth to seek inner peace in this harmless but predictable comedy. C: Alan Arkin, Matt Craven, Diane Lane, Bill Paxton, Elizabeth Perkins, Kevin Pollak, Vincent Spano. D: Mike Binder. COM [PG-13] 97m. ♥

Indian Tomb, The 1959 German ★★ An architect discovers a lost city in India in this composite of two German films, badly recut and dubbed. (a.k.a *Journey to the Lost City*) C: Debra Paget, Paul Hubschmid, Walther Reyer, Claus Holm, Sabine Bettmann, Rene Deltman. D: Fritz Lang. ACT 97m. ♥

Indian Uprising 1952 ★★½ Cavalry officer tries to mediate between Geronimo and white settlers. As title suggests, things go badly. Typical Native American stereotyping, With requisite cavalry charge. C: George Montgomery, Audrey Long, Carl Benton Reid, Robert Shayne. D: Ray Nazarro. WST 75m. ♥

Indiana Jones and the Last Crusade 1989 ★★★★½ Third film in the series has Jones (Ford) assisting his eccentric father (Connery) in a search for the Holy Grail. Possibly the best of the three films: Connery and Ford are excellent together, and the story, locations, and supporting cast maintain good pace. C: Harrison Ford, Sean Connery, Denholm Elliott, Alison Doody, John Rhys-Davies. D: Steven Spielberg. ACT [PG-13] 126m. V

Indiana Jones and the Temple of Doom 1984 ★★★½ In second film of the series, Jones (Ford), in the Orient before WWII, is inadvertently paired with an American lounge singer (Capshaw) on a quest to save a village from an evil cult. Ford saves a so-so plot; most gratuitously violent of the three adventure films. C: Harrison Ford, Kate Capshaw, Ke Huy Quan, Amrish Puri, Roshan Seth. D: Steven Spielberg. ACT [PG] 118m. V

Indianapolis Speedway 1939 ★★★½ Serviceable remake of the James Cagney race car drama *The Crowd Roars* features Pat O'Brien as the older of two hard-driving brothers. Classic sports drama clichés handled by a capable cast, though not as gripping as the Cagney original. C: Pat O'Brien, Ann Sheridan, John Payne, Gale Page, Frank McHugh, John Ridgely, Regis Toomey. D: Lloyd Bacon. DRA 82m.

Indict and Convict 1973 ★★★½ Good cast enhances mundane mystery as jealous husband (Shatner) faces death penalty for murdering adulterous wife and her lover. C: George Grizzard, Reni Santoni, Susan Howard, Ed Flanders, Eli Wallach, William Shatner, Harry Guardino. D: Boris Sagal. CRI 100m. TVM

Indio 1990 ★★ Marine (Quinn) returns to his roots (the Amazon) and discovers the people and land being pillaged by industrialists. Predictable revenge film with global conscience. Sequel: *Indio 2: The Revolt*. C: Marvin Hagler, Francesco Quinn, Brian Dennehy. D: Anthony M. Dawson. ACT [R] 94m. V

Indio 2: The Revolt 1992 ★ Marine sergeant (Hagler) leads Amazonians against evil developers who are gleefully ravaging the rain forests. Dreadful. C: Marvin Hagler, Grank Cuervo, Dirk Galuba. D: Anthony M. Dawson. ACT [R] 104m. V

Indiscreet 1931 ★★½ Comedy/drama revolves around the affairs and meddling of a tarnished woman (Swanson). No relation to the Cary Grant/Ingrid Bergman classic. C: Gloria Swanson, Ben Lyon, Barbara Kent, Arthur Lake. D: Leo McCarey. DRA 73m.

Indiscreet 1958 ★★★★ Playboy Grant's womanizing comes to a halt when he becomes infatuated with dazzling actress Bergman. Frothy but great fun. Chemistry between Grant and Bergman is delightful. C: Cary Grant, Ingrid Bergman, Cecil Parker, Phyllis Calvert. D: Stanley Donen. COM 100m. V

Indiscreet 1988 ★★½ Suave American diplomat avoids marriage to his lover, a European actress, by pretending he's already married. Remake lacks charm of the original Cary Grant/Ingrid Bergman feature. C: Robert Wagner, Lesley-Anne Down, Maggie Henderson, Robert McBain, Jeni Barnett. D: Richard Michaels. COM 94m. V

Indiscretion of an American Wife 1953 U.S. ★★½ Original 63-minute drama is half-baked tale of married Jones meeting younger lover Clift for last time. Restored version, *Terminal Station*, is 24 minutes longer and somewhat more emotionally complex, but both are turgid and unconvincing. C: Jennifer Jones, Montgomery Clift, Gino Cervi, Richard Beymer. D: Vittorio De Sica. DRA 63m. V

Indochine 1992 French ★★★★ French woman in '30s Indochina (Deneuve) must contend with now-grown adopted Indochinese daughter. Effective use of period detail and political backdrop enhance this historical drama, which received the Oscar for Best Foreign Film. C: Catherine Deneuve, Vincent Perez, Linh Dan Pham, Jean Yanne, Dominique Blanc. D: Regis Wargnier. DRA [PG-13] 155m. V

Indomitable Teddy Roosevelt, The 1983 ★★★★ Story of America's robust 26th President mixes archival footage with historical recreations, and sets it all marching to Sousa music. Entertaining and educational. C: George C. Scott, Bob Boyd. D: Harrison Engle. DOC 93m. V

Inevitable Grace 1994 ★★ Disturbed wife of man obsessed with blondes (Caulfield) winds up in mental institution, run by female doctor with lesbian tendencies (Knights). Self-conscious homage to Hitchcock falls flat. Nicholson is Jack's daughter, making film debut. C: Jennifer Nicholson, Maxwell Caulfield, Stephanie Knights, Tippi Hedren, Samantha Eggar. D: Alex Canawati. CRI 104m.

Infernal Trio, The 1974 ★★★★ Shady attorney is involved with two sisters who he convinces to marry and murder various clients in order to get insurance money. Wicked satire based on true story, thrives on nasty edges and Piccoli's zesty performance. C: Romy Schneider, Michel Piccoli. D: Francis Girod. COM 100m. V

Inferno 1953 ★★★ A beautiful young woman plans to abandon her husband in the desert, then take all his money. Quite compelling and a lot of good suspense. Original film was in 3-D. C: Robert Ryan, Rhonda Fleming, William Lundigan, Henry Hull, Carl Betz, Larry Keating. D: Roy Baker. DRA 83m.

Inferno 1980 Italian ★★★½ Argento's follow-up to *Suspiria* finds the witches' coven relocated to a Manhattan apartment building, where one woman's murder leads her brother to investigate. As usual, director's stylish approach manages to make his tangled script scary. C: Leigh McCloskey, Irene Miracle, Sacha Pitoeff, Alida Valli. D: Dario Argento. HOR [R] 107m. V

Inferno in Paradise 1988 ★★ On the trail of a dangerous pyromaniac, a photographer and firefighter fall in love. C: Richard Young, Betty Ann Carr. D: Ed Forsyth. ACT 115m. ▾

Infested *See* **Ticks**

Infidelity 1987 ★★★ Marital troubles plague "perfect" couple Alley and Horsley in domestic drama that hits every cliché in the book. C: Kirstie Alley, Lee Horsley. D: David Lowell Rich. DRA 104m. TVM

Infinity ★★ An adventure unravels when a retired U.S. naval pilot returns to the scene of his near-death accident in a remote area of the South Pacific. C: Megan Blake, Moises Bertran, Patricia Place. D: Alex Gelman. ACT 90m. ▾

Information Received 1962 British ★★★½ A master safecracker, cooperating with Scotland Yard, infiltrates a gang of criminals. Good dialogue and performances make for a pleasant diversion. C: Sabina Sesselman, William Sylvester, Hermione Baddeley, Edward Underdown. D: Robert Lynn. CRI 77m.

Informer, The 1935 ★★★★★ Classic drama of greed vs. loyalty, based on Liam O'Flaherty novel. McLaglen won the Oscar as Gypo Nolan, a pathetic drunkard informing on his best friend for ocean fare to America during the Irish Rebellion of 1922. Other Oscars received for Direction, Score and Screenplay. C: Victor McLaglen, Heather Angel, Preston Foster, Margot Grahame, Wallace Ford, Una O'Connor, J.M. Kerrigan, Joseph Sauers, Donald Meek. D: John Ford. DRA 91m. ▾

Infra-Man 1976 Hong Kong ★★★★½ Satisfying science fiction nonsense about an oversized superhero who battles a monstrous princess bent on gaining control of the Earth. Ridiculous dubbed dialogue and hilarious special effects make this an unintentional classic of camp. C: Li Hsiu-Hsien, Wang Hsieh, Terry Liu. D: Hua-Shan. SFI [PG] 92m. ▾

Inglorious Bastards 1978 Italian ★★½ WWII adventure about five rogues breaking out of prison and racing to the border. (a.k.a *Counterfeit Commandos*) C: Ian Bannen, Bo Svenson, Fred Williamson, Peter Hooten, Michael Pergolani. D: Enzo G. Castellari. ACT [R] 100m.

Inherit the Wind 1960 ★★★★★ Mesmerizing film version of stage drama based on the 1925 Scopes Trial: Tracy clashes with March over the right of a schoolteacher to teach Darwin's theory of evolution. Superb courtroom drama, fabulous performances. C: Spencer Tracy, Fredric March, Gene Kelly, Florence Eldridge, Dick York, Harry Morgan, Donna Anderson, Elliott Reid, Claude Akins, Noah Beery Jr., Norman Fell. D: Stanley Kramer. DRA 127m. ▾

Inherit the Wind 1988 ★★★½ Inferior remake of Lawrence/Lee play inspired by true-life Scopes trial. Robards plays defender of schoolteacher on trial for teaching Darwin's theory of evolution. Douglas overacts role of Bible-thumping leader of zealous opposition. C: Kirk Douglas, Jason Robards, Jean Simmons, Darren McGavin, Megan Follows, Kyle Secor, John Harkins. D: David Greene. DRA 100m. TVM

Inheritance, The 1947 British ★★★½ A scheming, creepy uncle has designs on ingenue Simmons' fortune. Chills provided mostly by atmospheric photography, Victorian setting, and Simmons' performance. Based on the J.S. Le Fanu novel, *Uncle Silas*. C: Jean Simmons, Derrick DeMarney, Derek Bond, Katina Paxinou, Esmond Knight. D: Charles Frank. DRA 98m.

Inheritance, The 1978 Italian ★★ Except for new daughter-in-law (Sanda) who services him sexually, dying patriarch Quinn disenherits his family. Polished, watchable trash has erotic value. C: Anthony Quinn, Dominique Sanda, Fabio Testi, Adriana Asti. D: Mauro Bolognini. DRA [R] 105m. ▾

Inheritor, The 1989 ★★ Nightmares and unexplained events transpire when a woman returns to her hometown to find some answers to her sister's recent mysterious death. C: Dan Haggerty. D: Brian Savegar. CRI 83m. ▾

Inheritors, The 1984 German ★★ A youngster from a dysfunctional family is easy pickings for neo-Nazi recruitors. Antifascist propaganda. C: Nikolas Vogel, Roger Schauer. D: Walter Bannert. DRA 89m. ▾

Initiation of Sarah, The 1978 ★★★ Young freshman joins sorority run by a witch (Winters) who encourages her to use latent psychic powers to get revenge on her rivals. Not bad, with some effective scenes. C: Kay Lenz, Shelley Winters, Kathryn Crosby, Tony Bill, Morgan Brittany. D: Robert Day. HOR 100m. TVM ▾

Initiation, The 1984 ★★ Obeying a sorority dare, a young woman breaks into a store and discovers there is no way to get out of the nightmare she has entered. C: Vera Miles, James Read. D: Larry Stewart. HOR [R] 97m. ▾

Inkwell, The 1994 ★★★★ Tate is excellent as a shy black kid forced to spend the summer of '76 with overbearing, wealthy relatives on Martha's Vineyard, finding friendship and love in unexpected setting. Part comedy, part drama, film suffers from identity crisis, but works on the strength of the cast. C: Larenz Tate, Joe Morton, Suzanne Douglas, Glynn Turman, Vanessa Bell Calloway. D: Matty Rich. DRA 110m.

Inn of the Damned 1974 Australian ★★★½ Trail of missing vacationers leads an investigator to the ominous hostelry of the title and its even stranger hosts. Sufficiently scary horror film effectively blends chills and humor. C: Judith Anderson, Alex Cord, Michael Craig, Joseph Furst, Tony Bonner, John Meillon. D: Terry Bourke. HOR 118m. ▾

Inn of the Frightened People 1971 British ★★ Suspect in a girl's rape and murder is abducted by victim's parents; they beat him and leave him for dead in the cellar, but his presence drives them to distraction and worse. Aims for psychological tension, but falls short. (a.k.a. *Terror from Under the House*) C: Joan Collins, James Booth, Ray Barrett, Sinead Cusack, Tom Marshall, Kenneth Griffith. D: Sidney Hayers. HOR 89m. V

Inn of the Sixth Happiness, The 1958 ★★★★ Inspiring drama of missionary (Bergman) in '30s China, who leads children to safety through enemy territory. Somewhat drawn out, but beautifully acted by Bergman and Donat (his final film appearance). C: Ingrid Bergman, Curt Jurgens, Robert Donat, Ronald Squire. D: Mark Robson. DRA 158m. V

Inn on the River, The 1962 German ★★★ Killing spree erupts along the docks, thanks to gang of ruthless criminals. Entertaining crime tale, based on Edgar Wallace story. Remake of *The Return of the Frog.* C: Joachim Fuchsberger, Klaus Kinski, Brigitte Grothum, Richard Much. D: Alfred Vohrer. CRI 95m.

Inner Circle, The 1992 ★★★½ Hulce plays simpleminded apparatchik who winds up as personal movie projectionist to Soviet tyrant Stalin. Based on fact. C: Tom Hulce, Lolita Davidovich, Bob Hoskins, Feodor Chaliapin Jr. D: Andrei Konchalovsky. DRA [PG-13] 134m. V

Inner Sanctum 1948 ★★½ A paraplegic woman suspects nurse and husband of conspiring to drive her mad. Thriller with some steamy scenes. C: Charles Russell, Mary Beth Hughes, Lee Patrick, Nana Bryant. D: Lew Landers. CRI 62m.

Innerspace 1987 ★★★★ Comic reworking of *Fantastic Voyage* stars Quaid as experimentally shrunken Navy man injected into hypochondriac Short. High-spirited fun, with Short's physically comedic talents perfectly exploited as he copes with Quaid's presence. Oscar for Best Visual Effects. C: Dennis Quaid, Martin Short, Meg Ryan, Kevin McCarthy, Wendy Schaal. D: Joe Dante. COM [PG] 120m. V

Innocent Affair, An 1948 ★★★ Ad exec (MacMurray) hides identity of his ex-fiancée/client from his wife (Carroll) who gets suspicious and starts harmless fling of her own. Marital misunderstanding comedy. (a.k.a. *Don't Trust Your Husband*) C: Fred MacMurray, Madeleine Carroll, Buddy Rogers, Rita Johnson, Alan Mowbray, Louise Allbritton, Anne Nagel. D: Lloyd Bacon. COM 90m.

Innocent and the Damned, The 1959 *See* **Girls Town**

Innocent Blood 1992 ★★½ Entertaining but uneven combination of comedy and horror; Parillaud is striking as a vampire who preys on the Mob, and Loggia is fun as a mafioso she inadvertently transforms into bloodthirsty monster. C: Anne Parillaud, Robert Loggia, Don Rickles, Anthony La Paglia. D: John Landis. HOR [R] 112m. V

Innocent Bystanders 1973 ★★★ British secret agent (Baker) tries to salvage a fading career by searching for a Russian scientist who's fled Siberia. Fast-paced James Bond knockoff, loaded with violence. C: Stanley Baker, Geraldine Chaplin, Donald Pleasence, Dana Andrews. D: Peter Collinson. ACT [PG] 111m.

Innocent Love, An 1982 ★★★½ Down-to-earth, charming story of a gifted 14-year-old college student who falls for 19-year-old volleyball player (Anderson), whom he tutors in math. McKeon is affecting as the young prodigy. C: Melissa Sue Anderson, Doug McKeon. D: Roger Young. DRA 104m. TVM

Innocent Man, An 1989 ★★★ Contrived prison drama with Selleck, who's framed as a cocaine dealer by cops when they mistakenly raid his home. Abraham has a powerful turn as a hardened con. C: Tom Selleck, F. Murray Abraham, Laila Robins, David Rasche. D: Peter Yates. CRI [R] 113m. V

Innocent Prey 1988 ★★ A woman, who has built a new life, finds herself once again stalked by her obsessive x-husband. C: P.J. Soles, Martin Balsam. D: Colin Eggleston. HOR [R] 88m. V

Innocent Sorcerers 1960 Polish ★★★★ Jazz-playing doctor begins questioning casual lifestyles of fellow band members, as well as goofy antics of his flighty paramour. Engaging human comedy of errors; notable for appearances by future directors Polanski and Skolimowski in leading roles. C: Zbigniew Cybulski, Roman Polanski, Jerzy Skolimowski. D: Andrzej Wajda. COM 91m.

Innocent, The 1976 Italian ★★★★★ Stately, formal tragedy of hedonistic aristocrat (Giannini) who gets his comeuppance at the hands of his ignored wife (Antonelli). O'Neill is surprisingly forceful as Giannini's mistress. Visconti's last film. C: Giancarlo Giannini, Laura Antonelli, Jennifer O'Neill. D: Luchino Visconti. DRA [R] 115m. V

Innocent Victim 1990 British ★★½ A young boy is abducted by a madwoman trying to overcome the memory of her deceased grandchild. Overly complicated drama, fine performances. (a.k.a. *The Tree of Hands*) C: Helen Shaver, Lauren Bacall, Peter Firth, Paul McGann. D: Giles Foster. DRA 100m. V

Innocents in Paris 1953 British ★★★★ Characteristic English tourists meet characteristic Parisians while vacationing in that characteristically French city. Great cast is hilarious. C: Alastair Sim, Ronald Shiner, Claire Bloom, Margaret Rutherford, Claude Dauphin, Laurence Harvey, Jimmy Edwards, Richard Wattis, Louis de Funes, Christopher Lee. D: Gordon Parry. COM 93m.

Innocents, The 1961 British ★★★★★ Superbly atmospheric version of classic Henry James ghost story, *The Turn of the Screw.* Kerr is terrific as 19th-century English governess taking care of two children who may or may not be seeing ghosts at secluded estate. Hair-raising thriller leaves much to the imagination, proving that the power of suggestion can be scarier than buckets of blood. C: Deborah Kerr, Michael Redgrave, Peter Wyngarde, Megs Jenkins, Pamela Franklin, Martin Stephens. D: Jack Clayton. DRA 100m.

Inquest 1931 British ★★½ A mysterious death begins to look suspiciously like murder after a coroner examines the body. Some tingling courtroom action and fair suspense. Remade in 1939. C: Mary Glynne, Campbell Gullan. D: G. B. Samuelson. CRI 95m.

Inquiry, The 1987 Italian ★★★★ Unusual presentation of Christ story has an investigator (Carradine) on the trail of the missing corpse. Pilate (Keitel), tries to sweep everything under the rug. Fine acting and certainly different. C: Keith Carradine, Harvey Keitel, Phyllis Logan. D: Damiano Damiani. DRA 107m. V

Inquisitor, The 1982 French ★★★★ Two-person film revolves around a police interrogator trying to pull a confession out of an accused child molester. Intelligent psychological drama with edgy performances from Ventura and Serrault. C: Lino Ventura, Michel Serrault, Guy Marchand, Romy Schneider. D: Claude Miller. CRI 90m.

Insect Woman 1963 ★★★★ Illegitimate country girl's unhappy life: seduction by stepfather, abuse at factory, rape, prostitution (to care for her child). Strong drama of a woman living by instinct. Disturbing suggestion that the pattern continues from generation to generation. C: Sachiko Hidari. D: Shohei Imamura. DRA 90m. V

Inside Daisy Clover 1965 ★★★ Wood doesn't have enough charisma for this Tinseltown tale of 30-something child actress turned neurotic star inspired by Temple and Garland. After a good start, disintegrates into overwrought soapy clichés. C: Natalie Wood, Robert Redford, Christopher Plummer, Roddy McDowall, Ruth Gordon, Katherine Bard. D: Robert Mulligan. DRA 129m. V

Inside Detroit 1955 ★★★½ Fearless union official O'Keefe takes on gangsters headed by old foe O'Brien, a mobster who wants to seize control of United Auto Workers. Gritty, documentary-style drama. C: Dennis O'Keefe, Pat O'Brien, Margaret Field, Mark Damon. D: Fred M. Sears. DRA 82m.

Inside Job 1946 ★★½ Despite their desire to go straight, married burglars Curtis and Rutherford are blackmailed into performing one last crime, the robbery of the store where they work. C: Preston Foster, Ann Rutherford, Alan Curtis, Jimmy Moss. D: Jean Yarbrough. CRI 65m.

Inside Man, The 1984 ★★★½ Based on true story, enemy agents battle for super-laser in Sweden. C: Dennis Hopper, Hardy Kruger, David Wilson. D: Tom Clegg. DRA 90m. V

Inside Monkey Zetterland 1993 ★★★½ Semiautobiographical farce about struggling screenwriter (Antin), who is overwhelmed by his eccentric family, much the same way this slight material is overwhelmed by Levy's flashy direction. Still promising for a first feature. C: Steven Antin, Patricia Arquette, Sandra Bernhard, Sofia Coppola. D: Jefrey Levy. COM [R] 93m. V

Inside Moves 1980 ★★★★ Affecting drama of two troubled, young disabled men (Morse and Savage), their struggle for self-acceptance, and the young woman (Scarwid) who must come to terms with her own feelings about physical handicaps. A moving film with excellent performances. C: John Savage, David Morse, Diana Scarwid, Amy Wright, Harold Russell. D: Richard Donner. DRA [PG] 113m. V

Inside Out 1975 British ★★★ Unlikely trio (Savalas, Culp, and Mason) will stop at nothing to find a cache of Nazi gold, including breaking a war criminal out of jail. Diverting heist flick. C: Telly Savalas, James Mason, Robert Culp, Aldo Ray, Doris Kuntsmann. D: Peter Duffell. ACT [PG] 98m. V

Inside Out 1986 ★★★ Claustrophobic drama about a man so afraid of being out in public he makes himself a prisoner in his own home. Intriguing premise offers some interesting insight, but is predictably hemmed in. C: Elliott Gould, Howard Hesseman, Jennifer Tilly, Beah Richards, Dana Elcar. D: Robert Taicher. DRA [R] 87m. V

Inside Story, The 1948 ★★★½ Humorous and homely tale of the Great Depression concerns citizens of Vermont town who suddenly discover $1,000 unexpectedly in circulation. Good-natured film is buoyed by winsome performances from Lockhart and Winninger. C: Marsha Hunt, William Lundigan, Charles Winninger, Gail Patrick. D: Allan Dwan. COM 87m.

Inside the Mafia 1959 ★★★½ Lying in wait for a rival boss, a mobster (Mitchell) holds the occupants of a small airport hostage. A semidocumentary approach and decent action sequences provide this thriller with some suspense. C: Cameron Mitchell, Elaine Edwards, Robert Strauss, Jim L. Brown, Ted de Corsia, Grant Richards. D: Edward L. Cahn. CRI 72m.

Inside the Room 1935 British ★★★½ Party at the home of a recently deceased actress comes to the attention of an inspector (Trevor) when guests start dropping like flies. Who's behind these new killings? Good British murder mystery unfolds in time-honored fashion. C: Austin Trevor, Dorothy Boyd. D: Leslie Hiscott. CRI 66m.

Inside the Third Reich 1982 ★★★★½ Adaptation of Albert Speer's autobiography portrays the Nazi inner sanctum in all its banal hideousness; a superb and enormously unsettling presentation. Jacobi's Hitler is the best, but all the performances are tremendous. C: Rutger Hauer, John Gielgud, Derek Jacobi, Maria Schell, Blythe Danner, Trevor Howard. D: Marvin J. Chomsky. DRA 250m. TVM V

Inside the Walls of Folsom Prison 1951 ★★★½ Convict leader Cochran leads revolt against brutal prison warden de Corsia.

Clichéd but forceful. Filmed on location in California's Folsom Prison. C: Steve Cochran, David Brian, Philip Carey, Ted de Corsia. D: Crane Wilbur. ACT 87m.

Insignificance 1985 British ★★★★ Four celebrities—unidentified but clearly representing Albert Einstein, Marilyn Monroe, Joe DiMaggio and Joseph McCarthy—meet in a hotel room on a summer's night in 1950s NYC to ponder fame, relativity, and the Cold War. Well-made and entertaining, with great acting. C: Gary Busey, Tony Curtis, Theresa Russell, Michael Emil. D: Nicolas Roeg. DRA [R] 105m. V

Inspecteur Lavardin 1986 *See* **Inspector Lavardin**

Inspector Calls, An 1954 British ★★★★ Adapation of Priestley play about police inspector (Sim) proving to family members how each was partly to blame for suicide of young female relative. Set in 1912, film version is authentic and beautifully constructed. C: Alastair Sim, Arthur Young, Olga Lindo, Eileen Moore. D: Guy Hamilton. DRA 80m.

Inspector Clouseau 1968 ★★ The infamous French detective (Arkin) tracks the gang responsible for the Great Train Robbery when Scotland Yard begins to suspect they will use the loot to stage an even bigger heist. Arkin tries hard to fill Peter Sellers' shoes but can't in this forgettable comedy. C: Alan Arkin, Delia Boccardo, Frank Finlay, Patrick Cargill, Beryl Reid, Barry Foster. D: Bud Yorkin. COM [G] 94m.

Inspector General, The 1949 ★★★★ Gogol's classic play, *The Government Inspector*, becomes a bright semimusical for Kaye as a simpleton mistaken for important bureaucrat in Eastern European town. Lighthearted fun. C: Danny Kaye, Walter Slezak, Barbara Bates, Gene Lockhart, Alan Hale, John Carradine. D: Henry Koster. COM 102m. V

Inspector Hornleigh 1939 British ★★★ When the Chancellor of the Exchequer is robbed, a couple of mugs (Harker and Sims) must retrieve his stuff. Sims is hilarious, as usual, but the British accents get a bit thick. First of a comedy/drama series (there were three in all), based on the British radio show *Monday Night at Eight.* C: Gordon Harker, Alastair Sim, Miki Hood. D: Eugene Forde. COM 76m.

Inspector Hornleigh on Holiday 1939 ★★★ At a quaint coastal hotel, the great inspector works to solve the murder of another guest. Some genuine laughs and well-handled suspense. C: Gordon Harker, Alastair Sim, Linden Travers. D: Walter Forde. COM 90m.

Inspector Lavardin 1986 French ★★★★ Follow-up to *Cop au Vin* stars Poiret as detective trying to solve bizarre murder of a former lover's husband—the old girlfriend just might be the killer. Whacked-out humor carries this offbeat, cynical comedy nicely. (a.k.a. *Inspecteur Lavardin*) C: Jean Poiret, Jean-Claude Brialy, Bernadette Lafont, Jacques Dacqmine, Jean-Luc Bideau, Hermine Claire, Pierre-Francois Dumeniaud, Florent Gibassier, Guy Louret, Jean Depusse. D: Claude Chabrol. COM 99m.

Inspector Maigret 1958 French ★★★½ When serial killer runs amuk, noted French detective Inspector Maigret (Gabin) goes on the trail. Modest police thriller with a few good twists. (a.k.a. *Woman Bait*) C: Jean Gabin, Annie Girardot, Oliver Hussenot, Jeanne Boitel. D: Jean Delannoy. CRI 110m.

Inspiration 1931 ★★ A young artist's model (Garbo) is wooed by an up-and-coming politician who ignores the dangers her past poses to his future. Luminous Garbo. C: Greta Garbo, Robert Montgomery, Lewis Stone, Marjorie Rambeau, Beryl Mercer. D: Clarence Brown. DRA 74m. V

Instant Justice 1986 Gibraltar ★★ Marine Paré scours the seedy streets of Madrid for the killer of his prostitute sister, enlisting the help of hooker Kitaen and photographer Crook along the way. Cliché-ridden revenge saga with little imagination. (a.k.a. *Marine Issue*) C: Michael Paré, Tawny Kitaen, Peter Crook, Charles Napier, G. Scott Del Amo. D: Craig T. Rumar. ACT [R] 101m. V

Instant Karma 1990 ★★½ Mild comedy about successful television producer's attempts to make his ideal woman love him. C: Craig Sheffer, David Cassidy, Marty Ingels. D: Roderick Taylor. COM [R] 102m. V

Instructor, The 1985 ★★½ Martial arts master teaches eager students about defending honor. C: Bob Chaney, Bob Saal, Lynday Scharnott. D: Don Bendell. ACT 91m. V

Insult 1932 ★★★ After being jailed by superiors, foreign legionnaire (Williams) escapes his cell and saves Gielgud, the son of his accuser (Livesey). Violent though laborious adventure story notable mostly as an early film for future star Gielgud. C: Elizabeth Allan, John Gielgud, Hugh Williams, Sam Livesey. D: Harry Lachman. ACT 79m.

Insurance Man, The 1985 British ★★★½ Kafka-esque story of a factory worker (Hines) who tries to file a disability claim and finds himself in bureaucracy purgatory. Uneven but entertaining. C: Robert Hines, Daniel Day-Lewis, Jim Broadbent, Hugh Fraser, Tony Haygarth. D: Richard Eyre. DRA 77m.

Intent to Kill 1958 British ★★★ Political leader Lom, having barely survived an assassination attempt, journeys to Canada, where the killers plan to finish their work. Mild thriller with some suspenseful moments. C: Richard Todd, Betsy Drake, Herbert Lom, Warren Stevens, Carlo Justini, Alexander Knox, Lisa Gastoni, Jackie Collins. D: Jack Cardiff. ACT 89m.

Interface 1984 ★★★ High-tech game created by college-age computer hacks turns deadly, threatening safety of university community. C: John Davies, Laura Lane. D: Andy Anderson. SFI 94m. v

Interiors 1978 ★★★★ Three daughters of a wealthy businessman must come to terms with their father's remarriage and their mother's suicide. Allen's first serious film owes much to Ingmar Bergman in both look and mental study of characters. Somber and moving. C: Diane Keaton, Geraldine Page, E.G. Marshall, Maureen Stapleton, Kristin Griffith. D: Woody Allen. DRA [PG] 93m. v

Interlude 1957 ★★★ Very minor remake of *When Tomorrow Comes* with Allyson as American who falls in love with composer/conductor (Brazzi), whose wife won't let him go. Even Sirk's ironic touch can't redeem hopelessly clichéd soap opera or make Brazzi convincing. Remade in 1968. C: June Allyson, Rossano Brazzi, Marianne Cook, Jane Wyatt, Francoise Rosay. D: Douglas Sirk. DRA 90m.

Interlude 1968 British ★★★½ Blacklisted orchestra conductor (Werner) has affair with younger woman (Ferris). Engaging romantic trifle offers eye-pleasing scenery and superb classical soundtrack. C: Oskar Werner, Barbara Ferris, Virginia Maskell, Donald Sutherland, Nora Swinburne, Alan Webb, John Cleese. D: Kevin Billington. DRA [PG] 113m.

Intermezzo 1936 Swedish ★★★★ Young pianist (Bergman) falls in love with renowned violinist (Ekman), whose daughter she teaches. Sweet and sentimental in best sense: Bergman's magnetism was such that, when she came to Hollywood, she starred in the 1939 English-language remake. C: Gosta Ekman, Inga Tidblad, Ingrid Bergman, Bullen Berglund. D: Gustav Molander. DRA 88m. v

Intermezzo 1939 ★★★★★ Bergman, in Hollywood debut, is musical protégé and love interest to married violin virtuoso Howard. Classic love story rich with atmosphere, deft direction and top-drawer acting. C: Leslie Howard, Ingrid Bergman, Edna Best, Cecil Kellaway. D: Gregory Ratoff. DRA 70m. v

Internal Affairs 1990 ★★★★ Young Internal Affairs officer Garcia investigates veteran cop Gere, a manipulative smoothie at the center of a sordid corruption ring. Rich in suspense, steamy psychosexual thriller is fertile ground for Gere, whose coolly evil portrayal makes the film. C: Richard Gere, Andy Garcia, Nancy Travis, Laurie Metcalf, Joseph Mazello, Richard Bradford. D: Mike Figgis. CRI [R] 117m. v

International House 1933 ★★★★ Paper-thin but rollicking comedy centering around a hotel gala to introduce a brand-new invention: television. Many popular radio performers of the day, including Rudy Vallee and Cab Calloway, appear, and everyone has a good time, especially the viewer. Fields' risqué one-liners can still make you blush. C: W.C. Fields, Peggy Hopkins Joyce, Stuart Erwin, George Burns, Gracie Allen, Bela Lugosi, Franklin Pangborn. D: A. Edward Sutherland. COM 70m. v

International Lady 1941 ★★★½ Brent, a U.S. agent trying to expose a counterintelligence ring, falls for Massey, an Axis agent who's transmitting coded radio broadcasts to German U-boats. Amusing, if not very deep. C: Ilona Massey, George Brent, Basil Rathbone, Gene Lockhart, Martin Kosleck, Clayton Moore. D: Tim Whelan. ACT 102m.

International Settlement 1938 ★★½ In China during the Japanese invasion, a dashing adventurer gets involved in a gunrunning operation. Fine cast and some highly intricate action add to the fun. C: George Sanders, Dolores Del Rio, June Lang, Dick Baldwin, Leon Ames, John Carradine, Harold Huber. D: Eugene Forde. ACT 75m.

International Squadron 1941 ★★★½ A spoiled young playboy (Reagan) who joins the Air Corps is transformed into an air ace. Unambitious remake of *Ceiling Zero* succeeds at what it attempts. C: Ronald Reagan, James Stephenson, Olympe Bradna, William Lundigan, Joan Perry, Julie Bishop, Cliff Edwards. D: Lothar Mendes. DRA 87m.

International Velvet 1978 British ★★★½ Follow-up to the 1944 *National Velvet* features O'Neal as horse riding Olympic hopeful niece of Newman (in grown-up version of Elizabeth Taylor's original role). Good-looking film, adequately played by cast, though plodding development drags it down a bit. C: Tatum O'Neal, Christopher Plummer, Anthony Hopkins, Nanette Newman. D: Bryan Forbes. FAM/DRA [PG] 126m. v

Internecine Project, The 1974 British ★★★★ A driven businessman (Coburn) is required to murder four partners to keep his end of a bizarre agreement. A refreshingly innovative and stylishly produced story that does not rely on excessive violence to carry the drama. C: James Coburn, Lee Grant, Harry Andrews, Ian Hendry, Keenan Wynn. D: Ken Hughes. DRA [PG] 89m. v

Internes Can't Take Money 1937 ★★★½ First film based on Max Brand's "Doctor Kildare" stories stars McCrea as young intern enlisted by ex-con Stanwyck to help find her missing daughter. Fairly effective mix of medicine and melodrama. (a.k.a. *You Can't Take Money*) C: Barbara Stanwyck, Joel McCrea, Lloyd Nolan, Stanley Ridges, Lee Bowman, Irving Bacon, Pierre Watkin, Charles Lane, Fay Holden. D: Alfred Santell. DRA 77m.

Interns, The 1962 ★★★½ The lives and loves of five recent med school graduates. A hospital full of soap, but moves along with good performances. Sequel: *The New Interns*. C: Michael Callan, Cliff Robertson, James MacArthur, Nick Adams, Suzy Parker, Stefanie Powers, Buddy Ebsen. D: David Swift. DRA 120m. v

Interrogation 1982 Polish ★★★★ After sleeping with a soldier, a nonpolitical actress is tossed behind bars and subjected to brutal questioning about her activities. A brilliant, harrowing presentation of totalitarian Poland, it was banned upon completion and not released until 1991. C: Krystyna Janda, Adam Ferency, Agnieszka Holland. D: Richard Bugajski. DRA 118m.

Interrupted Journey 1949 British ★★½ A writer's fantasies take him back and forth between his married life and a romance with another woman. Intriguing and surreal, if not entirely successful. C: Richard Todd, Valerie Hobson. D: Daniel Birt. DRA 80m.

Interrupted Melody 1955 ★★★★ Moving, well-crafted biography of Australian opera star Marjorie Lawrence (Parker), who struggled to make comeback after she was stricken with polio. Parker does well in the acting department, with dubbed vocals by Met diva Eileen Farrell. C: Eleanor Parker, Glenn Ford, Roger Moore, Cecil Kellaway, Ann Codee, Stephan Bekassy. D: Curtis Bernhardt. DRA 106m.

Intersection 1993 ★★ Soap opera about Gere, forced to choose between wife (Stone, a nice girl for once) and mistress (Davidovich), as he relives his life in flashbacks during auto accident. C: Richard Gere, Sharon Stone, Lolita Davidovich, Martin Landau, David Selby, Jenny Morrison. D: Mark Rydell. DRA [R] 98m. V

Interval 1973 Mexican ★★★ In her final film (which she also produced) Oberon plays a middle-aged woman who falls for a younger man in Mexico where she is trying to escape her past. Slight story and thin characterizations. C: Merle Oberon, Robert Wolders, Claudio Brook, Russ Conway. D: Daniel Mann. DRA [PG] 84m. V

Interview With the Vampire 1994 ★★★★ Stylish, if overlong, adaptation of Anne Rice's celebrated novel. Cruise scores as the Vampire Lestat, whose relationship with the handsome Louis (Pitt) forms the core of this erotic, violent twist on the Dracula legend. C: Tom Cruise, Brad Pitt, Christian Slater, Kirsten Dunst, Stephen Rea, Antonio Banderas. D: Neil Jordan. HOR [R] 120m. V

Intervista 1987 Italian ★★★★ Fellini studies Fellini in this documentary-style picture, which is also a tribute to the glories of Cinecittà, Italy's most famous movie studio. Includes a bittersweet reunion of Mastroianni and Ekberg, who watch their scenes together from *La Dolce Vita*. C: Sergio Rubini, Antonella Ponziani, Maurizio Mein, Paola Liguori, Lara Wendel, Antonio Cantafora, Nadia Ottaviani, Anita Ekberg, Marcello Mastroianni, Federico Fellini. D: Federico Fellini. DRA 108m. V

Intimate Contact 1987 British ★★★★ An upper-class family man (Massey) is infected with AIDS while on a business trip. Difficult subject handled intelligently, with strong performances. C: Claire Bloom, Daniel Massey, Abigail Cruttenden, Mark Kingston, Sylvia Syms. D: Waris Hussein. DRA 140m. TVM V

Intimate Lighting 1965 Czech ★★★★ Following years of separation, two aging musicians reunite for a day of memory and gentle humor at a home in the Czech countryside. Clever comedy of social manners, nicely developed and with fine performances from the ensemble. C: Vera Kresadlova, Zdenek Brezusek, Karel Blazek, Jaroslava Stedra, Jan Vostrcil, Vlastmila Vlkova, Karel Uhlik. D: Ivan Passer. COM 72m.

Intimate Moments 1982 ★★½ Steamy drama about an ultraexclusive French madam who caters to the rich and powerful. More sensual than dramatic. C: Alexandra Stewart, Dirke Altevogt. D: Francois E. Memet. DRA [R] 82m. V

Intimate Obsession 1993 ★★ Frustrated wife gets involved with slippery bartender and finds herself trapped in dangerous games of deception. C: Jodie Fisher, James Quarter, Richard Abbott Booth. D: Lawrence Unger. DRA [R] 80m. V

Intimate Power 1989 ★★★ A young French woman sold into the harem of an Ottoman sultan ultimately bears him a son—who grows up to become a reform-minded political leader. Quite engaging, and based upon a true story. C: F. Murray Abraham, Amber O'Shea. D: Jack Smight. DRA 104m. TVM V

Intimate Stranger 1991 ★★★ Psychotic murders girlfriend while chatting with sex phone operator (Harry). Cat and mouse thriller, with a good turn by Harry. C: Deborah Harry, James Russo, Grace Zabriskie. D: Allan Holzman. CRI [R] 90m. TVM V

Intimate Stranger, The 1956 *See* **Finger of Guilt**

Intimate Strangers 1977 ★★★ Battered wife syndrome is the topic of this superficial drama with an annoying performance by Struthers. Douglas shines in small role of Weaver's father. C: Dennis Weaver, Sally Struthers, Tyne Daly, Larry Hagman, Melvyn Douglas. D: John Llewellyn Moxey. DRA 96m. TVM V

Into the Badlands 1991 ★★★½ Moneygrubbing bounty hunter sparks dark occurrences in three interwoven stories of suspense. Strong performances from well-known players. C: Bruce Dern, Mariel Hemingway, Dylan McDermott, Helen Hunt. D: Sam Pillsbury. ACT [R] 90m. TVM V

Into the Blue 1950 British ★★★ Mildly entertaining comedy set on a yacht captained by Hulbert and Cummings who find stowaway Wilding and can't get rid of him. (a.k.a. *Man in the Dinghy*) C: Michael Wilding, Odile Versois, Jack Hulbert, Constance Cummings, Edward Rigby. D: Herbert Wilcox. COM 83m.

Into the Darkness 1986 ★★ Deranged murderer victimizes famous fashion models. C:

Donald Pleasence, Ronald Lacey. D: Michael Parkinson. CRI 90m. V

Into the Fire 1988 Canadian ★★½ Twisty thriller involving lodge owners (Anspach and Hindle) who hire a naive musician (Montgomery) for murderous scheme. Diverting, if a bit derivative. C: Susan Anspach, Olivia d'Abo, Art Hindle, Lee Montgomery. D: Graeme Campbell. CRI [R] 88m. V

Into the Homeland 1987 ★★★½ A former cop (Boothe) begins investigating the disappearance of his daughter, and confronts a band of white supremacists. Although the plot is predictable, the realistic portrayal of the racists makes this gripping—and unsettling—viewing. C: Powers Boothe, C. Thomas Howell, Cindy Pickett, Paul Lemat. D: Lesli Linka Glatter. ACT 120m. TVM V

Into the Night 1985 ★★★ An average guy's chance encounter with a beautiful jewel smuggler results in both being chased by killers. Spotty comic thriller sports cameos by Hollywood directors; benefits from idea of Michelle Pfeiffer suddenly dropping into a man's life out of nowhere. C: Jeff Goldblum, Michelle Pfeiffer, Richard Farnsworth, Irene Papas. D: John Landis. COM [R] 115m. V

Into the Sun 1992 ★★★ A bratty actor (Hall) trails after a tough fighter pilot (Paré) to prepare for an upcoming film role. Some good aerial bits in an otherwise sorely underproduced film. C: Anthony Michael Hall, Michael Paré, Deborah Moore Maria, Terry Kiser, Lyndon Ashby. D: Fritz Kiersch. COM [R] 101m. V

Into the West 1993 ★★★★ Story about two children running away with a prize horse in the west of Ireland will appeal to parents more than their offspring, due to subtle characterizations and deliberately slow pacing. C: Ellen Barkin, Gabriel Byrne, Ruaidhri Conroy, Colin Meaney. FAM/SFI [PG] 97m. V

Into Thin Air 1985 ★★★★ Burstyn shines as a mother obsessed with the search for a missing teenage son, aided by retired detective Prosky. Their complex relationship fuels this movie and makes it worth seeing. C: Ellen Burstyn, Robert Prosky, Sam Robards, Caroline McWilliams, Nicholas Pryor, John Dennis Johnston. D: Roger Young. DRA 97m. TVM V

Intolerance 1916 ★★★★★ D.W. Griffith's allegorical examination of prejudice in four different eras (Babylon, the last days of Christ, Reformation Europe, and early 20th-century America) and how intolerance tragically affects good-hearted people. Sweeping epic contains some of Griffith's finest visual work, despite dated characterizations. Made by Griffith in response to critics of *The Birth of a Nation*. C: Lillian Gish, Robert Harron, Mae Marsh, Constance Talmadge, Bessie Love, Seena Owen, Alfred Paget, Eugene Pallette. D: D.W. Griffith. DRA 178m. V

Intruder in the Dust 1949 ★★★★ Gripping account of black man wrongly accused of murder in small Southern town. White townsfolk want to string him up, but clear-thinking lawyer and local boy save him. Compelling drama that works as both mystery and study in race relations. Adapted from William Faulkner novel. C: David Brian, Claude Jarman Jr., Juano Hernandez, Porter Hall, Elizabeth Patterson. D: Clarence Brown. DRA 87m. V

Intruder, The 1955 British ★★★ Veteran Hawkins catches member of his former regiment (Medwin) burgling his house. Solidly acted exploration of war's effect on soldiers. C: Jack Hawkins, Hugh Williams, Michael Medwin, Dennis Price, Dora Bryan. D: Guy Hamilton. DRA 84m.

Intruder, The 1961 ★★★★ Shatner plays a hate-monger who travels to various Southern towns inciting riots to protest school integration. Well-executed and authentic. (a.k.a *I Hate Your Guts!* and *Shame*) C: William Shatner, Frank Maxwell, Beverly Lunsford, Robert Emhardt, Leo Gordon, Jeanne Cooper. D: Roger Corman. DRA 80m.

Intruders 1992 ★★★ Masterful movie explores the reasons behind a rash of alien abductions. Packs some genuine thrills. C: Richard Crenna, Mare Winningham, Susan Blakely, Ben Vereen. D: Dan Curtis. SFI 162m. TVM

Invader 1991 ★★★ Tabloid reporter and government agent fight an alien intelligence infiltrating an Air Force base. Rambunctious sci-fi gets away with grand visual effects on a skimpy budget but gets muddled when the script tackles Cold War politics. C: Hans Bachman, A. Thomas Smith, Rich Foucheux, John Cooke. D: Phillip J. Cook. SFI [R] 95m. TVM

Invader, The 1936 *See* **Old Spanish Custom, An**

Invaders from Mars 1953 ★★★★ Boy sees flying saucer descend but nobody believes him; soon aliens are possessing friends, family, and neighbors. Vintage but resonant sci-fi with kid's-eye-view paranoia and satisfyingly strange creatures and effects. Originally shown in 3-D. C: Helena Carter, Arthur Franz, Jimmy Hunt, Leif Erickson. D: William Cameron Menzies. SFI 78m. V

Invaders from Mars 1986 ★★ Remake of 1953 mini-classic about boy whose neighborhood is invaded by aliens isn't bad, but lackluster enough to make one wonder why director Hooper, known for more radiant productions, even bothered. One asset: makeup maestro Stan Winston's wild Martian monster designs. C: Karen Black, Hunter Carson, Timothy Bottoms, Laraine Newman, James Karen, Louise Fletcher, Bud Cort, Jimmy Hunt. D: Tobe Hooper. SFI [PG] 102m. V

Invaders—Volume I 1967 ★★★½ TV series follows a hapless man who witnesses the landing of a UFO and discovers its occupants plan to take over Earth, but cannot convince anyone to believe him. Solid science fiction adventures. C: Roy Thinnes, Diane Baker. SFI 55m. TVM V

Invasion 1966 British ★★★ Creatures from outer space wreak havoc upon a small village in the English countryside. Surprisingly well done and effective on all counts. C: Edward Judd, Yoko Tani, Lyndon Brook, Eric Young, Anthony Sharp, Stephanie Bidmead. D: Alan Bridges. SFI 82m. V

Invasion Earth 2150 A.D. *See* **Daleks—Invasion Earth 2150 A.D.**

Invasion Force 1990 ★★★ When a group of terrorist invaders are parachuted into America, the only "force" that's there to stop them is a film crew—armed with phony guns. Interesting action. C: Richard Lynch, David Shark, Renee Cline. D: David A. Prior. DRA 88m. V

Invasion of Carol Enders, The 1974 ★★½ When a woman is murdered, her spirit takes over the body of a beautiful yong woman. In her new incarnation, she goes about tracking down her murderer. C: Meredith Baxter Birney, Christopher Connelly. HOR 72m. TVM V

Invasion of Johnson County, The 1976 ★★★½ A Wyoming rube befriends a broke Boston socialite and both confront mercenary gunslingers hired by robber barons to illegally seize all land in the region. Plot and action a cut above par. C: Bill Bixby, Bo Hopkins, John Hillerman, Billy Green Bush, Stephen Elliott, Luke Askew. D: Jerry Jameson. WST 100m. TVM

Invasion of Privacy 1992 ★★ Sympathetic journalist (O'Neill) gives ex-con (Benson) a job, unaware that his admiration for her is unhealthy. Stalker yarn with few chills. C: Robby Benson, Jennifer O'Neill, Ian Ogilvy. D: Kevin Meyer. CRI [R] 95m. TVM

Invasion of the Animal People 1962 ★★ An alien army comes to Earth disguised as different animals. Self-conscious sci-fi effort, buoyed somewhat by John Carradine's melodic narration. C: Robert Burton, Barbara Wilson, Sten Gester. D: Virgil Vogel, Jerry Warren. SFI 72m. V

Invasion of the Bee Girls 1973 ★★ Men don't survive their dates with these creatures—but what a way to go. Promising idea fizzles on execution. C: Victoria Vetri, William Smith, Anitra Ford, Cliff Osmond, Wright King, Ben Hammer. D: Denis Sanders. SFI [R] 85m. V

Invasion of the Body Snatchers 1956 ★★★★★ Small-town doctor (McCarthy) discovers his town is being taken over by aliens who make their ugly move when people are asleep. Based on Jack Finney's *The Body Snatchers*. Remade several times, this is still the definitive version and one of the best '50s genre films ever made. Look for Sam Peckinpah in a bit part. C: Kevin McCarthy, Dana Wynter, Larry Gates, King Donovan, Carolyn Jones. D: Don Siegel. HOR 80m. V

Invasion of the Body Snatchers 1978 ★★★★★ Excellent remake of the 1956 classic, updated and relocated to San Fransisco. Lots of chills and some great sound effects. Those are the original's Kevin McCarthy and Don Siegel (director) in cameo roles. C: Donald Sutherland, Brooke Adams, Leonard Nimoy, Jeff Goldblum, Veronica Cartwright. D: Philip Kaufman. HOR [PG] 115m. V

Invasion of the Flesh Hunters 1984 ★★ Serviceman unwittingly brings home a cannibal curse. As a result, he turns his hometown neighbors into flesh-eaters. C: John Saxon. D: Edmondo Amati. HOR [R] 90m. V

Invasion of the Girl Snatchers 1973 ★★ After several young women disappear without a trace, a detective is called in to investigate. His findings point to an alien plot. C: Elizabeth Rush, Ele Grisby, David Roster. D: Lee Jones. SFI 90m. V

Invasion of the Neptune Men 1963 ★★★ Ironsharp, the superhero, dashes through space in order to help conquer a network of interplanetary invaders. C: Sonny Chiba. SFI 82m.

Invasion of the Saucer Men 1957 ★★ Silly campy tale of how hot-rodding teens foil an invasion by little goblins from outer space. More valuable as a '50s cultural artifact than a movie; its grotesque aliens have become emblematic of the whole genre. C: Steve Terrell, Gloria Castillo, Frank Gorshin, Raymond Hatton, Ed Nelson. D: Edward L. Cahn. SFI 69m. V

Invasion of the Space Preachers 1990 ★★½ A preacher from outer space arrives on planet earth. His goal: to steal human souls and broadcast his religious programs over worldwide televison. C: Jim Wolf, Guy Nelson. D: Daniel Boyd. COM 100m. V

Invasion, U.S.A. 1952 ★★ A weird stranger (O'Herlihy) in a New York bar convinces patrons that Communist bomb attack has begun. Highly strung, laughable sci-fi cheapie, courtesy of the Cold War. C: Dan O'Herlihy, Gerald Mohr, Peggie Castle, Phyllis Coates, Noel Neill. D: Alfred E. Green. SFI 74m.

Invasion, U.S.A. 1985 ★★ Retired CIA man (Norris) goes back on the job when deranged Soviet terrorists invade Florida—for starters. Lynch worth watching in otherwise routine Norris outing. C: Chuck Norris, Richard Lynch. D: Joseph Zito. ACT [R] 90m. V

Investigation 1979 French ★★★★ When mill owner is accused of murdering pregnant wife, villagers are less concerned with scrupulous criminal investigation than with its adverse effects on local commerce. Intriguing look at mass psychology under cloak of crime drama. C: Victor Lanoux, Valerie Mairesse, Jean Carmet, Michel Robin. D: Etienne Perier. DRA [R] 116m. V

Investigation of a Citizen Above Suspicion 1970 Italian ★★★★½ Police chief (Volonte) commits murder, plants evidence, and virtually dares his underlings to arrest him. Volonte's tremendous acting and Petri's stunning direction underpin this razor-sharp, bitterly cynical exploration of the abuse of power. Oscar for Best Foreign Film. C: Gian Maria Volonte, Florinda Bolkan, Salvo Randone, Gianni Santuccio, Arturo Dominici. D: Elio Petri. DRA 115m.

Invincible Gladiators, The 1964 ★★★ When his bride is kidnapped by a brutal Queen, a gladiator enlists the aid of Hercules to bring her back. Rough and tumble action, ancient style. C: Richard Lloyd, Claudia Lange, Tony Freeman. D: Robert Mauri. ACT 87m. v

Invincible Six, The 1968 ★★★½ Band of misfit mercenaries protects a besieged desert village, while searching for hidden treasure. Fast-paced action yarn, helped by lively performances and an exotic locale. C: Stuart Whitman, Elke Sommer, Curt Jurgens, Jim Mitchum. D: Jean Negulesco. ACT 96m. v

Invincible Sword, The ★★★ A group of entertainers get together to help one of their own escape from prison. They put their professional skills to work and create an ingenious breakout. C: Wang Yu. ACT 93m. v

Invisible Adversaries 1977 German ★★★ Austrian woman wakes up convinced that outer space intelligence has taken over all human life. Some surreal moments and offbeat ideas, but film never works as a whole. Explicit scenes may not be suitable for sensitive viewers. C: Susanne Widl, Peter Weibel. D: Valie Export. DRA 112m. v

Invisible Agent 1942 ★★★ U.S. agent in WWII has his hands full fighting Nazis who've stumbled across the secret of invisibility. Tired and slow by today's standards, still fun for the younger set. C: Ilona Massey, Jon Hall, Peter Lorre, Cedric Hardwicke. D: Edwin L. Marin. FAM/CRI 83m. v

Invisible Boy, The 1957 ★★★ Classic '50s sci-fi tale about a boy and his robot (Robby from *Forbidden Planet*), mixed up in a strange smuggling case. Dated, but still worth watching. C: Richard Eyer, Diane Brewster, Philip Abbott. D: Herman Hoffman. FAM/SFI 89m. v

Invisible Creature, The 1959 British ★★★ Book critic Wright and his mistress Dorne concoct a plot to murder wife Dainton. Primarily notable for watchdog ghost that puts a stop to the dastardly lovers. (a.k.a. *The House on Marsh Road*) C: Sandra Dorne, Patricia Dainton, Tony Wright. D: Montgomery Tully. CRI 70m.

Invisible Dr. Mabuse, The 1961 German ★★★★½ New York detective, investigating a colleague's death, stumbles on a formula that makes people invisible. Sinister mood throughout heightens the thrill of this neat horror film. (a.k.a. *The Invisible Horror*) C: Lex Barker, Karin Dor, Siegfried Lowitz, Wolfgang Preiss, Rudolf Fernau. D: Harald Reinl. HOR 89m. v

Invisible Ghost, The 1941 ★★½ Lugosi plays a good guy whose wife—believed dead—drives him to commit violent deeds on command. Very weird and often just plain silly low-budget mess. C: Bela Lugosi, Polly Young, John McGuire, Clarence Muse, Terry Walker, Betty Compson. D: Joseph H. Lewis. HOR 64m. v

Invisible Horror, The 1961 *See* **Invisible Dr. Mabuse, The**

Invisible Invaders 1959 ★★★ Alien invaders from the moon inhabit corpses of dead to carry out world takeover attempt. Carradine leads the walking dead, who are ultimately foiled by military man Agar. Not as silly as it sounds. C: John Agar, Jean Byron, Robert Hutton, Philip Tonge, John Carradine, Hal Torey. D: Edward L. Cahn. SFI 67m.

Invisible Kid, The 1988 ★★ Juvenile fantasy involves Underwood as teenager who stumbles onto formula that makes him invisible and subsequently allows him to run amok in a girls locker room. Dumb and sexist. C: Jay Underwood, Karen Black, Wally Ward, Chynna Phillips. D: Avery Crounse. COM [PG] 95m. v

Invisible Man Returns, The 1940 ★★★★ Entertaining and original follow-up to *The Invisible Man*. This time Price is a man wrongly accused of murder who "fades out" to find the real killer. Top-notch stuff. C: Cedric Hardwicke, Vincent Price, John Sutton, Nan Grey, Cecil Kellaway. D: Joe May. ACT 82m. v

Invisible Man, The 1933 ★★★★★ Scientist pays a heavy price for discovering the secret of invisiblity—madness. Precedent-setting film features a standout performance by Raines. Brilliant special effects bring H.G. Wells' tale to life. C: Claude Rains, Gloria Stuart, Una O'Connor, William Harrigan, Dudley Digges, Dwight Frye. D: James Whale. SFI 71m. v

Invisible Maniac, The 1990 ★ A put-upon teacher uses an invisibility formula to stalk and murder his students, making sure to disrobe all the young women in the process. Offensive and cheap. C: Noel Peters, Melissa Moore, Robert R. Ross Jr., Shannon Wilsey, Rod Sweiter. D: Rif Coogan (Adam Rifkin). HOR [R] 85m. v

Invisible Man's Revenge, The 1944 ★★ New serum ingested by killer on the lam renders him invisible. Nothing like the original. C: Jon Hall, Alan Curtis, Evelyn Ankers, Leon Errol, John Carradine, Gale Sondergaard, Ian Wolfe, Billy Bevan. D: Ford Beebe. HOR 77m. v

Invisible Menace, The 1938 ★★½ Murder mystery set at an Army base, with miscast Karloff leading parade of suspects. Standard B-movie whodunit. Remade as *Murder on the Waterfront*. C: Boris Karloff, Marie Wilson, Regis Toomey, Henry Kolker, Eddie Craven,

Eddie Acuff, Charles Trowbridge. D: John Farrow. CRI 55m.

Invisible Monster, The 1950 ★★ Twelve episodes from serial chronicling deranged scientist's attempt to conquer world with invisible fighting force. C: Richard Webb, Aline Towne, Lane Bradford. D: Fred C. Brannon. SFI 167m. V

Invisible Ray, The 1936 ★★★½ Good sci-fi vehicle for the two horror stars casts Lugosi in rare heroic role, trying to help colleague (Karloff), who kills whatever he touches after contact with radioactive meteor. Strong work by two leads and good special effects are highlights. C: Boris Karloff, Bela Lugosi, Frances Drake, Frank Lawton, Beulah Bondi. D: Lambert Hillyer. SFI 80m. V

Invisible Stripes 1939 ★★★½ Ex-con struggles to stay clean while protecting his younger brother from his old gang mates. Effective performances from the A-one cast. C: George Raft, Jane Bryan, William Holden, Flora Robson, Humphrey Bogart, Paul Kelly, Moroni Olsen, Tully Marshall. D: Lloyd Bacon. DRA 82m.

Invisible Woman, The 1940 ★★★½ A wacky prof (Barrymore) turns a chic model (Bruce) invisible in this minor classic of sci-fi comedy. C: John Barrymore, Virginia Bruce. D: Edward Sutherland. SFI 83m. V

Invitation 1952 ★★★½ A wealthy father pays a young man to marry his dying daughter (McGuire). To the young man's surprise, he falls in love with her. If your taste is for syrup, you'll lap it up. C: Van Johnson, Dorothy McGuire, Louis Calhern, Ray Collins, Ruth Roman. D: Gottfried Reinhardt. DRA 84m.

Invitation au Voyage 1983 French ★★★½ Strange but never boring film about incestuous siblings. After sister dies, brother bears her remains in cello case, hoping to revive love of his life. Interesting flourishes carry warped plot, though this one is a matter of individual taste. C: Laurent Malet, Nina Scott, Aurore Clement, Mario Adorf. D: Peter Del Monte. DRA [R] V

Invitation, The 1975 ★★★★ After inheriting his mother's country estate, a simple office worker invites his colleagues over for a garden party. Over the course of the day, different individuals slowly strip away outer camouflage, revealing true nature of their relationships. Highly engaging multicharacter study. C: Jean-Luc Bideau, Francois Simon, Jean Champion. D: Claude Goretta. DRA 100m.

Invitation to a Gunfighter 1964 ★★★★ Civil War veteran's homecoming to New Mexico turns disastrous, leading him to a confrontation with a deranged gun-for-hire. Character-driven Western highlighted by dynamite performances from Brynner and Segal. C: Yul Brynner, George Segal, Janice Rule, Pat Hingle. D: Richard Wilson. WST 92m. V

Invitation To a Wedding 1983 ★★★ Acting royalty bring sparks to mild tale of man who tries to sabotage his best friend's wedding. C: John Gielgud, Ralph Richardson, Paul Nicholas. D: Joseph Brooks. COM [PG] 89m. V

Invitation to Happiness 1939 ★★★½ Rocky romance between society woman (Dunne) and prizefighter (MacMurray). Enjoyable love story, thanks to cast and director. C: Irene Dunne, Fred MacMurray, Charlie Ruggles, William Collier Sr., Eddie Hogan. D: Wesley Ruggles. DRA 95m.

Invitation to Hell 1984 ★★ A middle-class family moves to the suburbs; Lucci is the Welcome Wagon Lady who runs Satan's country club. Craven's unsucessful shot at updating *Faust.* C: Robert Urich, Joanna Cassidy, Susan Lucci, Kevin McCarthy, Patricia McCormack. D: Wes Craven. DRA 96m. TVM V

Invitation to the Dance 1957 ★★★½ Three short films, devised by Kelly, which tell stories entirely in dance and mime. Very uneven, ranging from sophomoric "Ring Around the Rosie" from the play *La Ronde,* to sparkling "Sinbad" finale with Kelly in cartoon Arabian Nights fantasy. C: Gene Kelly, Igor Youskevitch, Claire Sombert, David Paltenghi, Daphne Dale, Claude Bessy, Tommy Rall, Carol Haney, Tamara Toumanova. D: Gene Kelly. MUS 93m. V

Ipcress File, The 1965 British ★★★★½ British spy investigates the Iron Curtain disappearance of scientist. Suspenseful adaptation of Len Deighton novel, highlighted by Caine's witty underplaying and John Barry's zither-tinged score. Sequels: *Funeral in Berlin* and *Billion Dollar Brain.* C: Michael Caine, Nigel Green, Guy Doleman, Sue Lloyd, Gordon Jackson. D: Sidney J. Furie. ACT 107m. V

Iphigenia 1977 Greek ★★★½ Adaptation of classic Greek drama by Euripides about warrior Agamemnon ready to offer up his daughter (Papamoskou) as human sacrifice in exchange for battle victory. Handsome production and nice performance from Papamoskou, though story doesn't fulfill its epic pretensions. C: Irene Papas, Tatiana Papamoskou, Costa Kazakos. D: Michael Cacoyannis. DRA 127m. V

Iran Cowboy 1968 *See* **Fade-In**

Irene 1940 ★★★½ Appealing if dated filming of 1919 Broadway musical hit; a *Cinderella* story of Prince Charming (Milland) romancing poor girl (Neagle). Outstanding song "Alice Blue Gown," filmed in color. C: Anna Neagle, Ray Milland, Roland Young, Alan Marshal, May Robson, Billie Burke, Marsha Hunt, Arthur Treacher, Tommy Kelly. D: Herbert Wilcox. MUS 104m. V

Irezumi: Spirit of Tatoo 1983 ★★★★½ Sensual Japanese drama about a woman who agrees to have her back elaborately tattooed to satisfy her lover's sexual urges. Mesmerizing tale of power and love. Adult themes, nudity. Subtitled. (a.k.a. *Spirit of Tatoo*) C: Masayo Utsunomiya, Tomisaburo Wakayama. D: Yoichi Takabayashi. DRA 88m. v

Irish Eyes Are Smiling 1944 ★★½ Fictitious biography of composer Ernest R. "Mother Machree" Ball (Haymes) showcases 11 turn-of-the-century songs. C: June Haver, Monty Woolley, Dick Haymes, Anthony Quinn, Maxie Rosenbloom, Veda Ann Borg. D: Gregory Ratoff. MUS 90m.

Irish in Us, The 1935 ★★★½ Warner Bros. contract players enliven dim-witted comedy of rival brothers Cagney and O'Brien battling for the hand of De Havilland. C: James Cagney, Pat O'Brien, Olivia de Havilland, Frank McHugh, Allen Jenkins. D: Lloyd Bacon. COM 84m.

Irish Whiskey Rebellion 1972 ★★★ Prohibition-era drama with Irish bootleggers selling to Americans, and sending profits to IRA. Period piece. C: William Devane, Anne Meara, Richard Mulligan, David Groh, Judie Rolin, William Challee, Stephen Joyce. D: J.C. Works. DRA [PG] 93m.

Irishman, The 1978 Australian ★★★★ In the 1920s, an Irish immigrant in the Australian Outback stubbornly refuses to join the mechanical age, thereby jeopardizing his family's livelihood. A compelling story, well filmed and acted. C: Bryan Brown, Michael Craig, Simon Burke, Robin Nevin, Lou Brown. D: Donald Crombie. DRA 108m. v

Irma la Douce 1963 ★★★★ Saucy French soufflé from Broadway musical, without its songs, but not its charm. MacLaine is perfectly cast as Parisian prostitute "protected" by gendarme Lemmon, who tries to keep her for himself through an elaborate disguise. Expert comedy, tastefully risqué. Watch for James Caan. C: Shirley MacLaine, Jack Lemmon, Lou Jacobi, Herschel Bernardi, Joan Shawlee, Hope Holiday, Bill Bixby. D: Billy Wilder. COM 142m. v

Iron and Silk 1991 Chinese ★★★½ American in China makes cross-cultural discoveries, while studying martial arts. Based on the star's true life story. C: Mark Salzman, Pan Qingfu, Jeanette Lin Tsui. D: Shirley Sun. DRA [PG] 94m. v

Iron Curtain, The 1948 ★★★½ Fact-based drama about a Russian official who tries to defect to the West and expose the harshness of Communism. Interesting Cold War souvenir. C: Dana Andrews, Gene Tierney, June Havoc, Berry Kroeger, Edna Best. D: William Wellman. DRA 87m.

Iron Dragon Strikes Back 1984 ★★½ Standard martial arts actioner about a student seeking revenge against those who killed his mentor. Good of this kind. C: Bruce Li. ACT 90m. v

Iron Duke, The 1935 British ★★★ Napoleon's nemesis at Waterloo, the famed "Iron" Duke of Wellington, is portrayed by Arliss in this straightforward and brainy, if fairly undistinguished historical near-epic. Fine performance by a young Emlyn Williams. C: George Arliss, Gladys Cooper, Ellaline Terriss, A.E. Matthews, Emlyn Williams. D: Victor Saville. DRA 88m. v

Iron Eagle 1986 ★★ When the father of a young pilot (Gedrick) is kidnapped, it's up to the son and his tough-as-nails mentor (Gossett) to free him and exact a suitable vengeance on the bad guys. Two sequels followed. C: Louis Gossett Jr., Jason Gedrick, David Suchet, Tim Thomerson. D: Sidney Furie. ACT [PG-13] 117m. v

Iron Eagle II 1988 Canadian ★★ U.S. and Soviet pilots join forces to raid a Middle East missile site. Good aerial footage and little else in this glasnost sequel. Followed by *Aces: Iron Eagle III*. C: Louis Gossett Jr., Mark Humphrey, Stuart Margolin, Maury Chaykin. D: Sidney J. Furie. ACT [PG] 105m. v

Iron Glove, The 1954 ★★★½ An 18th-century Scottish prince (Stapley) tries to capture the British throne. Lighthearted derring-do; Stack does respectably well in a role Vthat cries out for Errol Flynn. C: Robert Stack, Ursula Thiess, Richard Stapley, Charles Irwin, Alan Hale Jr. D: William Castle. ACT 77m.

Iron Horse, The 1924 ★★★★ Epic silent film about the building of the transcontinental railroad. A few too many subplots, but overall a strong early work from Ford, mixing rough-and-tumble characters with top production values. C: George O'Brien, Madge Bellamy, Cyril Chadwick, Fred Kohler, Gladys Hulette, J. Farrell MacDonald. D: John Ford. DRA 119m.

Iron Kiss 1964 *See* **Naked Kiss, The**

Iron Major, The 1943 ★★★½ True story of Frank Cavanaugh (O'Brien), disabled WWI hero and inspirational college football coach. Rousing patriotic drama of one man's triumph over adversity. C: Pat O'Brien, Ruth Warrick, Robert Ryan, Leon Ames. D: Ray Enright. DRA 85m. v

Iron Man, The 1931 ★★★½ Boxer (Ayres) must contend with callous wife (Harlow) who pushes him into the ring to keep her rolling in dough. Standard fight melodrama. Interest now is young Harlow. C: Lew Ayres, Jean Harlow, Robert Armstrong, John Miljan, Eddie Dillon. D: Tod Browning. DRA 73m.

Iron Man, The 1951 ★★★ Coal miner (Chandler) becomes a champion prizefighter to earn money to marry Keyes in mild but somewhat entertaining adaptation of W.R. Burnett's boxing novel. Originally filmed, under same title, in 1931; also filmed as *Some Blondes Are Dangerous* in 1937. C: Jeff Chandler, Evelyn Keyes, Stephen McNally, Joyce Holden, Rock Hudson, Jim Backus. D: Joseph Pevney. DRA 82m.

Iron Mask, The 1929 ★★★★ Elements of Dumas' classics *Three Musketeers* and *The*

Man in the Iron Mask are blended in this robust adventure of a sword-wielding hero fighting for the French monarch. Early talkie holds up well by sheer panache. Fairbanks' swan song to the genre. C: Douglas Fairbanks, Belle Bennett, Marguerite De La Motte, Dorothy Revier. D: Allan Dwan. DRA 138m. V

Iron Maze 1991 U.S. ★★ Japanese developer in Pennsylvania is brutally attacked, and suspects offer different perspectives. Rust-belt variation on *Rashomon*. C: Jeff Fahey, Bridget Fonda, Hiroaki Murakami, J.T. Walsh. D: Hiroaki Yoshida. CRI [R] 105m. V

Iron Mistress, The 1952 ★★★½ Set in 1830s New Orleans, film covers rousing adventures of fighting frontier hero, James Bowie (Ladd), who invented the hunting knife that bears his name. Erratic rendering of life of flamboyant entrepreneur. C: Alan Ladd, Virginia Mayo, Joseph Calleia, Phyllis Kirk. D: Gordon Douglas. WST 110m.

Iron Petticoat, The 1956 ★★★½ Unusual remake of *Ninotchka* casts Hepburn as no-nonsense Russian officer romanced by bodyguard Hope. Odd pairing of two stars actually works. C: Bob Hope, Katharine Hepburn, James Robertson Justice, Robert Helpmann, David Kossoff. D: Ralph Thomas. COM 87m.

Iron Sheriff, The 1957 ★★★ Sheriff Hayden sets out to prove his son didn't commit murder. Offbeat Western, fairly well acted. C: Sterling Hayden, Constance Ford, John Dehner, Kent Taylor, Darryl Hickman. D: Sidney Salkow. WST 73m.

Iron Thunder 1989 ★ Real-life kickboxer Elmore wrote, produced, directed, scored, and starred in this shabby vanity project about a kickboxer's hard rise up the competitive ladder to the championship. C: Anthony Elmore, George M. Young. D: Anthony Elmore. ACT [R] 90m. V

Iron Triangle, The 1988 ★★★ A U.S. serviceman in Vietnam is captured by a Vietcong teen and the two develop a curious, grudging respect for each other. Interesting premise is given dramatic treatment. C: Beau Bridges, Haing S. Ngor, Johnny Hallyday, Liem Whatley. D: Eric Weston. DRA [R] 94m. V

Iron Warrior 1987 ★ Dull dungeons-and-dragons yarn of hulking Ator (O'Keefe), who must battle a powerful villain and his sorceress cohort to restore a beautiful princess to her throne. Just plain awful. Sequel to *Ator, the Fighting Eagle*. C: Miles O'Keefe, Savina Gersak, Tim Lane. D: Al Bradley. ACT [PG-13] 82m. V

Ironheart 1992 ★★ A white slave trader is pursued by a determined cop (Lee) out to avenge his partner's murder. The film alternates between fight scenes and inane nightclub dance numbers. C: Bolo Yeung, Britton Lee, Richard Norton. D: Robert Clouse. CRI 90m. V

Ironmaster 1982 ★★ Violent tale of primitive man who leaves clan and discovers mysterious staff. C: Sam Pasco, Elvire Audray, George Eastman. D: Umberto Lenzi. SFI 98m. V

Ironweed 1987 ★★★★ Fascinating tour-de-force performances by Nicholson and Streep as Depression-era drunks, plagued by their pasts. Haunting film version of William Kennedy's Pulitzer Prize-winning novel. C: Jack Nicholson, Meryl Streep, Carroll Baker, Michael O'Keefe, Diane Venora, Fred Gwynne, Tom Waits, Nathan Lane, James Gammon. D: Hector Babenco. DRA [R] 135m. V

Iroquois Trail, The 1950 ★★★ Historical account of the fight between the Iroquois Indians and the French for the St. Lawrence seaway region. Adaptation of James Fenimore Cooper's *Leatherstocking Tales*. C: George Montgomery, Brenda Marshall, Dan O'Herlihy, Glenn Langan. D: Phil Karlson. WST 85m.

Irreconcilable Differences 1984 ★★★½ Ten-year-old Barrymore sues her parents for divorce. O'Neal and Long shine as the defendants in this middling in-joke comedy about how success in Hollywood can spoil the family. C: Ryan O'Neal, Shelley Long, Drew Barrymore, Sam Wanamaker, Sharon Stone. D: Charles Shyer. COM [PG] 112m. V

Is My Face Red? 1932 ★★★½ Abrasive, abusive Broadway columnist Cortez gets his comeuppance in rapid-fire, modest comedy inspired by gossip legend Walter Winchell. C: Ricardo Cortez, Helen Twelvetrees, Jill Esmond, Robert Armstrong, Sidney Toler, ZaSu Pitts. D: William A. Seiter. COM 66m.

Is Paris Burning? 1966 French ★★★½ During the 1944 liberation of Paris the allies storm the city while the Nazis try to burn it. Understandably, somewhat confusing and rambling, but star cameos add interest. From the best-seller by Larry Collins and Dominique Lapierre; adapted by Gore Vidal and Francis Ford Coppola, among others. C: Jean-Paul Belmondo, Charles Boyer, Leslie Caron, Jean-Pierre Cassel, Alain Delon, Kirk Douglas, Glenn Ford, Yves Montand, Simone Signoret, Robert Stack. D: Rene Clement. DRA 173m. V

Is There Sex After Death? 1971 ★★½ Hit and miss collection of crude and smutty vignettes explores changing sexual morays as it addresses a variety of "clinical" questions. Excessive nudity and graphic descriptions will offend some; others will find sporadic laughs. C: Buck Henry, Marshall Efron, Holly Woodlawn. D: Jeanne Alan Abel. COM [R] 97m. V

Isabel's Choice 1981 ★★★★ Executive secretary (Stapleton) gets frustrated with watching less qualified males climb the corporate ladder in perceptive feminist point of view. Star does well in showing journey of her character toward self-confidence and independence. Grittle comedy/drama livened by top cast. C: Jean Stapleton, Peter Coyote, Richard Kiley. D: Guy Green. DRA 100m. TVM

Isadora 1968 ★★★★ Redgrave's magnificent portrayal of Isadora Duncan, modern dance pioneer and legendary free spirit, is the whole show: A bit long, but what a show! A must-see for Vanessa fans. (a.k.a. *The Loves of Isadora*) C: Vanessa Redgrave, James Fox, Jason Robards. D: Karel Reisz. DRA [PG] 131m. V

Ishi: The Last of His Tribe 1978 ★★★½ In 1910 a San Francisco anthropologist befriends the last of the Yahi Indians, and records his life. Moving and well-handled. True story was also filmed for cable as *The Last of His Tribe.* C: Dennis Weaver, Eloy Casados, Devon Ericson, Joseph Running Fox, Lois Red Elk, Michael Medina. D: Robert Ellis Miller. DRA 150m. TVM

Ishtar 1987 ★★ One of Hollywood's all-time financial disasters features Beatty and Hoffman as fifth-rate songwriters off on the road to Africa for some spy chasing. Though the script is largely uninspired and the film is clearly overpriced, the first half-hour is a riot, and Beatty/Hoffman chemistry is wonderful. C: Warren Beatty, Dustin Hoffman, Isabelle Adjani, Charles Grodin, Jack Weston, Carol Kane. D: Elaine May. COM [PG-13] 107m. V

Island at the Top of the World, The 1974 ★★★ Lesser Disney adaptation of Jules Verne-type tale involves Arctic explorers who stumble across lost Viking colony. Minor adventure tale aimed directly at younger viewers. C: David Hartman, Donald Sinden, Jacques Marin, Mako. D: Robert Stevenson. FAM/ACT [G] 93m. V

Island Claws 1980 ★★ Radioactive waste creates a battalion of giant mutant crabs, which bubble up from the depths to terrorize the Florida coast. Dreary horror features a very phony-looking giant crab. (a.k.a. *Night of the Claw*) C: Robert Lansing, Steve Hanks, Nita Talbot, Barry Nelson. D: Hernan Cardenas. HOR 82m. V

Island in the Sky 1953 ★★★½ A WWII transport plane crash-lands off Greenland and crew stands by for rescue. Suspenseful if clichéd tale of outdoor survival-with a stalwart performance by Wayne. C: John Wayne, Lloyd Nolan, James Arness, Andy Devine, Walter Abel, Allyn Joslyn. D: William Wellman. DRA 109m.

Island in the Sun 1957 ★★★ The beautiful West Indies heat up with racial tension in this awkward dramatization of Alec Waugh's novel. Notable cast, fine photography. C: James Mason, Joan Fontaine, Dorothy Dandridge, Joan Collins, Michael Rennie, Diana Wynyard, John Williams, Stephen Boyd, Harry Belafonte. D: Robert Rossen. DRA 119m. V

Island of Desire 1952 British ★★ Romantic tensions ensue when an Army nurse finds herself stranded with two military men on a lush tropical isle. Sunburned melodrama. (a.k.a. *Saturday's Island*) C: Linda Darnell, Tab Hunter, Donald Gray, John Laurie. D: Stuart Heisler. DRA 103m. V

Island of Doomed Men 1940 ★★★½ Several men are transported to a tiny island and find they are to be slaves for a diabolical plantation owner (Lorre). Lurid melodrama is rather well done. C: Peter Lorre, Robert Wilcox, Rochelle Hudson, George E. Stone, Don Beddoe, Kenneth MacDonald. D: Charles Barton. HOR 67m.

Island of Dr. Moreau, The 1977 ★★★½ Remake of *Island of Lost Souls* (retaining title of H.G. Wells' source novel), with shipwrecked man (York) running afoul of mad scientist (Lancaster) and his "humanimal" creations. Good makeup and production values, but lacks the chills of the original. C: Burt Lancaster, Michael York, Nigel Davenport, Barbara Carrera, Richard Basehart. D: Don Taylor. HOR [PG] 104m. V

Island of Lost Men 1939 ★★½ A young woman (Wong) tries to clear her father's name after he is accused of embezzling government money. Atmospheric mystery boasts a heavyweight cast. Remake of *White Woman.* C: Anna May Wong, J. Carroll Naish, Eric Blore, Ernest Truex, Anthony Quinn, Broderick Crawford. D: Kurt Neumann. CRI 63m.

Island of Lost Souls 1933 ★★★★½ Mad scientist transforms wild animals into monstrous human beings on remote island in creepy, effective adaptation of H.G. Wells' *The Island of Dr. Moreau.* Just as chilling today because of its sinister settings and graphic terror. C: Charles Laughton, Bela Lugosi, Richard Arlen, Kathleen Burke, Leila Hyams. D: Erle C. Kenton. HOR 70m. V

Island of Lost Women 1959 ★★½ Plane crash survivors find their island is also inhabited by a mysterious scientist and his strange daughters. Spooky title given mild treatment. C: Jeff Richards, Venetia Stevenson, John Smith, Diane Jergens, Alan Napier, June Blair. D: Frank Tuttle. HOR 71m.

Island of Love 1963 ★★★½ A failing Greek island's tourist trade skyrockets after an American con artist (Preston) on the run from a mobster (Matthau) promotes it as a legendary isle of love. Routine comedy, but helped by spirited performances and lush travelogue scenery. C: Robert Preston, Tony Randall, Giorgia Moll, Walter Matthau, Betty Bruce, Michael Constantine. D: Morton Da Costa. COM 101m.

Island of Pachyderms, The 1992 French ★★½ Young graffiti artist and budding rap singer dream of escape to title island. Silly, confusing story has spectacular photography and the distinction of being Montand's last movie (he suffered fatal heart attack during shooting). C: Yves Montand, Olivier Martinez, Sekkou Sall, Geraldine Pallhas. D: Jean-Jacques Beineix. DRA 119m.

Island of Procida, The 1952 Italian ★★★½

After killing his philandering wife, a surgeon is imprisoned for 20 years. His personal turmoil comes to an end after he performs emergency surgery on a severely ill child and wins the affections of the patient's older sister. Sudsy Italian soaper. C: Claudio Gora, Carlo Ninchi, Vera Carmi, Franca Marzi, Giulio Donnini, Mario Gallina. D: Mario Cequi. DRA 90m.

Island of Terror 1966 British ★★★½ On a lonely Irish island, a crazed scientist whiles away the hours creating creatures that hunger for human bones. How do they get those bones? They kill, kill, kill! Decent British thriller. C: Peter Cushing, Edward Judd, Carole Gray, Niall MacGinnis. D: Terence Fisher. HOR 90m. V

Island of the Blue Dolphins 1964 ★★★½ Drama about 19th-century brother and sister lost on deserted island. When wild dogs attack, the girl manages to make friends of the beasts. Based on true tale, this occasionally violent film is probably best for older children. C: Celia Kaye, George Kennedy, Ann Daniel, Larry Domasin. D: James B. Clark. FAM/DRA 99m. V

Island of the Burning Doomed 1967 British ★★★ Earth is growing hotter and hotter, courtesy of hostile aliens. Solid British sci-fi thriller features good performances by all. (a.k.a. *Night of the Big Heat*) C: Christopher Lee, Peter Cushing, Patrick Allen, Sarah Lawson, Jane Merrow, William Lucas. D: Terence Fisher. SFI 94m. V

Island of the Doomed 1967 *See* **Man-Eater of Hydra**

Island of the Lost 1968 ★★★ So-so story of anthropologist and family who get shipwrecked on an uncharted island. Has its moments, but no *Swiss Family Robinson*. C: Richard Greene, Luke Halpin, Mart Hulswit, Robin Mattson. D: John Florea, Ricou Browning. FAM/DRA 92m. V

Island Princess, The 1955 Italian ★★★ Love reigns supreme—especially when its object is princess of the Canary Islands. Lavish 16th-century costume drama, with Mastroianni as fleet commander pursuing *all* his interests. C: Marcello Mastroianni, Silvana Pampanini, Gustavo Rojo. D: Paolo Moffa. DRA 98m.

Island Rescue 1951 British ★★★ Niven steals onto a Nazi-occupied island to lead a rescue party for a herd of cows. Johns shines, as usual, in this low-key comedy. (a.k.a. *Appointment with Venus*) C: David Niven, Glynis Johns, George Coulouris, Barry Jones, Kenneth More, Noel Purcell, Bernard Lee, Jeremy Spenser, Anton Diffring. D: Ralph Thomas. COM 87m.

Island Sons 1987 ★★½ After their father disappears, four Hawaiian brothers battle to keep ancient family lineage intact. Note of interest: All the brothers are played by members of the Bottoms family. C: Timothy Joseph, Sam and Ben Bottoms. D: Alan J. Levy. DRA 104m. TVM

Island, The 1962 Japanese ★★★★½ Off the Japanese coast, a struggling family tries to build life for themselves on barren, rocky island. Visually impressive documentary-style camerawork conveys emotional strength of central characters. There's no dialogue, leaving pictures to tell this moving story. C: Nobuko Otowa, Taiji Tonoyama, Shinji Tanaka, Masanori Horimoto. D: Kaneto Shindo. DRA 96m.

Island, The 1980 ★★ A journalist (Caine) finds himself on a Caribbean island populated by sadistic descendants of pirates. Peter Benchley's follow-up to his *Jaws* is poorly plotted, substituting shocks for sense and emotion. C: Michael Caine, David Warner, Frank Middlemass, Don Henderson. D: Michael Ritchie. ACT [R] 114m. V

Island Trader 1970 ★★ Youth's discovery of downed jet filled with gold carries dangerous consequences. C: John Ewart, Ruth Cracknell. D: Howard Rubie. ACT 95m. V

Island Warriors 1986 ★★ Amazon matriarch reigns over island of martial arts masters. C: Ling Young, Yu Fend. D: Au Yeung Chuen. ACT 85m. V

Island Woman 1958 ★★½ Lonely woman sets her sights on sailboat skipper, who is in love with the woman's niece. Unusual cast dances to strains of calypso score. (a.k.a. *Island Women*) C: Marie Windsor, Vincent Edwards, Marilee Earle, Leslie Scott, Maurine Duvalier, George Symonette. D: William Berke. DRA 72m.

Island Women 1958 *See* **Island Woman**

Islands 1984 ★★★½ Contrived but occasionally compelling drama about a former Flower Child and a young rebel who spend revealing summer on remote island. C: Louis Fletcher. D: Rene Bonniere. DRA 55m. V

Islands in the Stream 1977 ★★★½ American sculptor living in Bahamas changes when his three sons arrive at the outbreak of WWII. Based on Hemingway's unfinished novel, sundrenched film version is even less satisfying and more self-absorbed, but Scott's towering performance is worth watching. C: George C. Scott, David Hemmings, Claire Bloom, Susan Tyrrell, Gilbert Roland. D: Franklin J. Schaffner. DRA [PG] 105m. V

Isle of Forgotten Sins 1943 ★★★½ A race to recover lost treasure pits two deep-sea divers (Carradine and Fenton) against a rascally skipper (Toler). Based on director Ulmer's own short story, this odd little intrigue is worth a look. C: John Carradine, Gale Sondergaard, Sidney Toler, Frank Fenton, Rita Quigley, Veda Ann Borg, Rick Vallin, Betty Amann, Tala Birell. D: Edgar G. Ulmer. DRA 82m. V

Isle of Fury 1936 ★★½ A remote South Seas island seems the perfect escape for a fugitive hiding from the law, until he finds that he cannot hide from romance. So-so version of Somerset Maugham's *The Narrow Corner* boasts an early look at Bogart. C: Humphrey Bogart, Margaret Lindsay, Donald Woods, Paul Graetz, Gordon Hart, E.E. Clive. D: Frank McDonald. DRA 60m.

Isle of Lost Ships 1929 ★★★½ A ship comes upon a harbor of empty boats and lands on a remote island where surprises abound. Eerie and atmospheric story with some good suspense. C: Jason Robards, Sr., Virginia Valli. D: Irving Willat. DRA 84m.

Isle of Secret Passion 1986 ★★ In a charming Greek villa, a teacher discovers much-desired romance and thrills. C: Patch MacKenzie, Michael MacRae, Zohra Lampert. DRA 101m. V

Isle of Sin 1960 German ★★ An airplane crashes on deserted island, which causes an understandable degree of tension among those aboard. Choose sides, place your bets, and watch as passengers tear each other apart. C: Christiane Nielsen, Erwin Strahl, Jan Hendriks, Slavo Schwaiger. D: Johannes Kai. DRA 63m.

Isle of the Dead 1945 ★★★★ A cross-section of people in war-ravaged Greece are quarantined on a remote island, where they bide their time waiting for the plague to pass. Well-crafted horror yarn with noteworthy performances and a creepy feel, thanks to Val Lewton's artful touch. C: Boris Karloff, Ellen Drew, Marc Cramer, Katherine Emery, Helene Thimig, Jason Robards. D: Mark Robson. HOR 72m. V

Isn't It Shocking? 1973 ★★★★ Alda is New England police chief puzzled by mysterious deaths of small town's elderly population. Offbeat, funny mystery, stolen by Gordon as woman determined not to follow her friends to the grave. C: Alan Alda, Louise Lasser, Edmond O'Brien, Ruth Gordon, Will Geer, Dorothy Tristan, Lloyd Nolan. D: John Badham. CRI 73m. TVM

Isn't Life Wonderful! 1953 British ★★★½ Turn-of-the-century adventures of a good-natured, heavy-drinking uncle who, when he isn't running a bicycle shop, is helping to patch up various romances. Satisfying family-style fun delivered by a top British cast. C: Cecil Parker, Eileen Herlie, Donald Wolfit. D: Harold French. FAM/COM 83m

Istanbul 1957 ★★½ Hidden diamond treasure lures fortune hunters into adventure and intrigue. Medium Flynn actioner, benefits from musical interlude by Nat King Cole. C: Errol Flynn, Cornell Borchers, John Bentley, Torin Thatcher, Nat King Cole. D: Joseph Pevney. ACT 84m. V

Istanbul 1990 Turkish ★ Bottoms is a reporter in title city who becomes involved with enigmatic Twiggy while researching his familial problems. Confusing and dull plot that goes nowhere in a hurry. C: Timothy Bottoms, Twiggy, Emma Kilberg, Robert Morley. D: Mats Arehn. DRA [PG-13] 88m. V

Istanbul Express 1968 ★★★½ A scientist dies and takes a vital secret with him. Genre Cold War thriller has agent (Barry) and several Communist spies looking for clues on the famous train. C: Gene Barry, John Saxon, Senta Berger, Mary Ann Mobley, Tom Simcox. D: Richard Irving. ACT 94m.

It 1927 ★★★★ It meant sex appeal, and this silent comedy is famous for setting new standards of overt sexuality on the screen. Star and title became synonymous as Bow blazes through story of shopgirl husband-hunting with dollar signs as her guide. A bit tame today, but worth seeing for the fabulous "It"-girl and newcomer Gary Cooper in a bit part. C: Clara Bow, Antonio Moreno, William Austin, Jacqueline Gadsdon. D: Clarence Badger. DRA 72m. V

It 1967 ★★★ A scientist (McDowall) is delighted to find that the statue he brought to life is a bloodthirsty killer. Low-budget shocker is not for the squeamish. (a.k.a. *Curse of the Golem*) C: Roddy McDowall, Jill Haworth, Ernest Clark, Paul Maxwell, Aubrey Richards. D: Herbert J. Leder. HOR 96m.

It Ain't Hay 1943 ★★★½ Damon Runyon story, "Princess O'Hara," turned into funny Abbott and Costello farce as they wrestle with racehorse named Teabiscuit. Track finale is a howl. C: Bud Abbott, Lou Costello, Patsy O'Connor, Grace McDonald, Leighton Noble, Cecil Kellaway, Eugene Pallette, Eddie Quillan. D: Erle C. Kenton. COM 80m.

It All Came True 1940 ★★★½ Mobster (Bogart) on the run lies low in a New York tenement and ends up helping the residents. Fun blend of sweetness and crime plus some nice music. C: Ann Sheridan, Humphrey Bogart, Jeffrey Lynn, ZaSu Pitts, Jessie Busley, Una O'Connor, Grant Mitchell, Felix Bressart. D: Lewis Seiler. DRA 97m.

It Always Rains on Sunday 1947 British ★★★★ Excellent drama insightfully examines working-class London community through the eyes of an escaped criminal hiding out with his former girlfriend. Visually interesting, strong realism. C: Googie Withers, Jack Warner, John McCallum, Edward Chapman, Jimmy Hanley, John Carol, John Slater, Susan Shaw, Sydney Tafler, Alfie Bass, Betty Ann Davies, Jane Hylton, Hermione Baddeley. D: Robert Hamer. DRA 92m.

It Came from Beneath the Sea 1955 ★★★ H-bomb tests rouse a giant octopus from the Pacific to attack San Francisco. Forget the cornball script and watch Ray Harryhausen's stop-motion animated monster. According to movie lore, the mutant cephalopod shows just five tentacles because the budget couldn't cover eight. C: Kenneth Tobey, Faith Domergue, Donald Curtis, Ian Keith. D: Robert Gordon. SFI 80m. V

It Came From Hollywood 1982 ★★★½ Compilation comedy combines footage from bad horror films (including classic *Plan 9 from Outer Space*), along with some good science fiction, and strings them together with narration by famed comic actors. C: Dan Aykroyd, John Candy, Cheech & Chong, Gilda Radner. D: Malcolm Leo, Andrew Solt. COM [PG] 80m. V

It Came from Outer Space 1953 ★★★½ Alien "xenomorphs" who crash-land in the Arizona desert masquerade as local Earthlings to avoid detection. Intelligent sci-fi movie feels somewhat stodgy by modern standards, but still entertaining. Originally in 3-D. C: Richard Carlson, Barbara Rush, Charles Drake, Russell Johnson. D: Jack Arnold. SFI [G] 81m. V

It Came from the Lake *See* **Monster**

It Came Upon the Midnight Clear 1984 ★★★ A New York policeman (Rooney) dies before the holidays but returns to Earth for one more Christmas with his family. Rooney does his best in a routine and predictable affair. C: Mickey Rooney, Scott Grimes, George Gaynes, Elisha Cook. D: Peter H. Hunt. FAM/DRA 96m. TVM V

It Comes Up Love 1944 *See* **Get Hep to Love**

It Conquered the World 1956 ★★ Roger Corman quickie about an alien's efforts to corrupt a scientist into helping it take over Earth. No budget, and it shows. Remake: *Zontar, Thing from Venus*. C: Peter Graves, Beverly Garland, Lee Van Cleef, Sally Fraser. D: Roger Corman. SFI 68m. V

It Could Happen to You 1937 ★★★ At the end of a raucous stag party, a bumbling Madison Avenue honcho discovers the body of a nightclub singer in his car, and his wife must clear his name. Comedy-thriller mixes laughs and suspense well. C: Alan Baxter, Andrea Leeds, Owen Davis, Jr. COM 64m. V

It Could Happen To You 1994 ★★★★ Totally predictable, totally charming romantic comedy stars Cage as a cop who promises a waitress (Fonda) half of his lottery winnings in lieu of a tip. Perez steals the film as Cage's venal wife. Film's working title was *Cop Gives Waitress $2 Million Tip!* C: Nicolas Cage, Bridget Fonda, Rosie Perez. D: Andrew Bergman. COM [PG] 101m. V

It Couldn't Happen Here 1991 ★★½ Pet Shop Boys songs and videos weakly linked by pop duo's fictional journey through England, depicted here as land of eccentricity. C: Pet Shop Boys, Neil Tennant, Chris Lowe. D: Jack Bond. MUS [PG-13] 90m. V

It Grows on Trees 1952 ★★★ A woman is pleasantly surprised to discover that one of the trees in the family yard is blooming currency of rather large denominations. Silly fantasy that served as Irene Dunne's swan song. C: Irene Dunne, Dean Jagger, Richard Crenna, Les Tremayne. D: Arthur Lubin. COM 84m.

It Had to Be You 1947 ★★★½ Breezy romantic comedy with Rogers as perennial near-bride who gets cold feet again, this time with Wilde. C: Ginger Rogers, Cornel Wilde, Percy Waram, Spring Byington, Ron Randell. D: Don Hartman, Rudolph Mate. COM 98m.

It Had to Happen 1936 ★★★½ An Italian-American immigrant (Raft) basks in money and power as he climbs the ladder in the New York political world. Clever cast and sophisticated Russell add spice. C: George Raft, Leo Carrillo, Rosalind Russell, Alan Dinehart, Arline Judge. D: Roy Del Ruth. DRA 79m.

It Happened at Lakewood Manor 1977 ★★½ Unruly ants make life miserable for vacationers at a resort. Grisly film not for the squeamish. (a.k.a. *Ants* and *Panic at Lakewood Manor*) C: Lynda Day George, Robert Foxworth, Myrna Loy, Suzanne Somers, Bernie Casey, Brian Dennehy. D: Robert Sheerer. HOR 100m. TVM V

It Happened at the World's Fair 1963 ★★★ 1962 Seattle fair provides backdrop for typical Presley songfest. This time he's bush pilot involved with Chinese orphan girl. Strictly for Elvisites. Kurt Russell's screen debut. He would play the king himself 17 years later. C: Elvis Presley, Joan O'Brien, Gary Lockwood, Ginny Tiu. D: Norman Taurog. MUS 105m. V

It Happened Here 1966 British ★★★★ An imagined documentary-like tale of a Nazi invasion of Britain. Nurse (Murray), who works for the resistance, discovers cruelty on both sides. Provocative and compelling. Follow-up made in 1974: *It Happened Here Again*. C: Pauline Murray, Sebastian Shaw, Fiona Leland, Honor Fehrson. D: Kevin Brownlow, Andrew Mollo. DRA 95m.

It Happened in Athens 1962 ★★½ Lightweight, campy Mansfield comedy displays her in an array of scanty costumes as she plays an 1896 actress who pledges to marry the winner of the Olympic marathon. C: Jayne Mansfield, Trax Colton, Lili Valenty, Maria Xenia, Bob Mathias, Nico Minardos. D: Andrew Marton. COM 92m.

It Happened in Brooklyn 1947 ★★★½ Unmemorable musical about ambitious Brooklyn performers trying to crack the big-time has two assets: Frank singing "Time After Time," and old pro Durante. C: Frank Sinatra, Kathryn Grayson, Jimmy Durante, Peter Lawford, Gloria Grahame. D: Richard Whorf. MUS 104m. V

It Happened in Flatbush 1942 ★★★½ Ex-ballplayer Nolan gets new lease on life when he is asked to manage Brooklyn club. He whips hostile team into shape and wins devotion of late owner's daughter to boot. By-the-book sports drama, nicely played by cast. C: Lloyd Nolan, Carole Landis, Sara Allgood, William Frawley, Robert Armstrong, Jane Darwell. D: Ray McCarey. DRA 80m.

It Happened on Fifth Avenue 1947 ★★★½ Sentimental hokum with good cast gives Moore plum part of bum who stumbles upon an unoccupied mansion, inviting his friends to live there. C: Don DeFore, Ann Harding, Charlie Ruggles, Victor Moore, Gale Storm, Grant Mitchell. D: Roy Del Ruth. COM 115m.

It Happened One Christmas 1977 ★★★ Misguided remake of classic *It's a Wonderful Life*, with Thomas taking on the Stewart role in sex-switch gimmick that doesn't quite work. C: Marlo Thomas, Wayne Rogers, Orson Welles, Cloris Leachman, Barney Martin, Karen Carlson, Doris Roberts. D: Donald Wrye. DRA 112m. TVM

It Happened One Night 1934 ★★★★★ Classic romantic comedy. Funny, touching tale (based on story by Samuel Hopkins Adams) of spoiled heiress (Colbert) befriended by newsman (Gable) on bus to New York. The quintessential road movie. First film to win all five top Oscars: Picture, Actor, Actress, Director, Screenplay (Robert Riskin). Remade twice, as *Eve Knew Her Apples* and *You Can't Run Away From It*. C: Clark Gable, Claudette Colbert, Walter Connolly, Roscoe Karns, Alan Hale, Ward Bond. D: Frank Capra. COM 105m. V

It Happened to Jane 1959 ★★★★ Charming comedy with social conscience about New England widow (Day) suing large railroad run by Kovaks when her lobster shipment dies en route. Day at her most likable; ditto Lemmon; but it's Kovacs who steals the show. (a.k.a. *Twinkle and Shine*) C: Doris Day, Jack Lemmon, Ernie Kovacs, Steve Forrest, Teddy Rooney, Russ Brown, Mary Wickes, Parker Fennelly. D: Richard Quine. COM 98m.

It Happened Tomorrow 1944 ★★★★ Imaginative, charming comedy/fantasy of reporter (Powell) given newspaper with next day's headlines. He delights in its power until it predicts his own death! C: Dick Powell, Linda Darnell, Jack Oakie, Edgar Kennedy, John Philliber, Edward Brophy, George Cleveland, Sig Ruman, Paul Guilfoyle. D: Rene Clair. COM 84m.

It Happens Every Spring 1949 ★★★★ Chemistry professor Milland discovers a formula that makes baseballs avoid bats, then takes to pitcher's mound for the rest of this clever family comedy. C: Ray Milland, Jean Peters, Paul Douglas, Ed Begley, Ted de Corsia, Ray Collins, Jessie Royce Landis, Alan Hale Jr., Gene Evans. D: Lloyd Bacon. COM 87m. V

It Happens Every Thursday 1953 ★★★★ A couple (Forsythe and Young) move to a small town to run weekly newspaper. Solid comedy/drama works with outrageous plot twists. C: Joseph Pevney, Loretta Young, John Forsythe, Frank McHugh, Edgar Buchanan, Jane Darwell, Dennis Weaver. D: Joseph Pevney. COM 80m.

It Hurts Only When I Laugh 1981 *See* **Only When I Laugh**

It Lives Again 1978 ★★★ Sequel to the cult classic, *It's Alive*, finds the homicidal infant of the original returning to wreck even more murderous havoc when he teams up with two equally destructive pint-size cronies. Gory horror thriller. C: Frederic Forrest, Kathleen Lloyd, John Ryan, John Marley, Andrew Duggan, Eddie Constantine. D: Larry Cohen. HOR [R] 91m. V

It Lives By Night 1974 *See* **Bat People**

It Only Happens to Others 1971 French ★★½ When an affluent couple's child dies, they withdraw from family, friends, and society. Mawkish soap opera improved by talents of Mastroianni and Deneuve. C: Marcello Mastroianni, Catherine Deneuve, Serge Marquand, Dominique Labourier, Catherine Allegret. D: Nadine Trintignant. DRA [PG] 88m.

It Pays to Advertise 1931 ★★★ When he meets the potential love of his life, a mild-mannered youth suddenly turns into a big-business tycoon. Bright and breezy film adaptation of a hit comedy play. Notable also for a late appearance by silent screen legend Louise Brooks. C: Norman Foster, Carole Lombard, Skeets Gallagher. D: Frank Tuttle. COM 66m.

It Rained All Night the Day I Left 1978 ★★★ Desert drama of widow (Kellerman) and her new arrivals (Gossett and Curtis). Strong performances cry for relief from weak script. C: Lou Gossett, Jr., Sally Kellerman, Tony Curtis. D: Nicolas Gessner. DRA 100m. V

It Seemed Like a Good Idea at the Time 1975 Canadian ★★ Lethargic romantic comedy has forlorn husband trying to rekindle love with remarried ex-wife. Early film appearance by Candy as a stumblebum police detective brightens otherwise dull proceedings. (a.k.a. *Good Idea*) C: Anthony Newley, Stefanie Powers, Isaac Hayes, Lloyd Bochner, Yvonne De Carlo, Henry Ramer, Lawrence Dane, John Candy. D: John Trent. COM [PG] 106m.

It Should Happen to You 1954 ★★★★½ Near-classic comedy with Holliday as frustrated New Yorker Gladys Glover, yearning to be famous. When she plasters her name on billboards all over town, things happen! Sparkling script; Holliday's a gem, and Lemmon's charming in his film debut. C: Judy Holliday, Peter Lawford, Jack Lemmon, Michael O'Shea, Vaughn Taylor. D: George Cukor. COM 87m. V

It Shouldn't Happen to a Dog 1946 ★★★ Free-spirited dog bamboozles a meddling reporter and a policewoman. Light and lively family fare features a charming Landis as the policewoman. C: Carole Landis, Allyn Joslyn, Margo Woode, Henry Morgan, Reed Hadley, John Alexander, Jean Wallace, John Ireland. D: Herbert I. Leeds. FAM/COM 70m.

It Stalked the Ocean Floor 1954 *See* **Monster from the Ocean Floor, The**

It Started in Naples 1960 ★★★½ Gable travels to Italy to claim orphaned nephew, but his sexy aunt (Loren) has other plans. Picturesque comedy is pleasantly predictable with

Gable a trifle aged for Loren. C: Clark Gable, Sophia Loren, Vittorio De Sica, Marietto, Paolo Carlini, Claudio Ermelli. D: Melville Shavelson. COM 100m. V

It Started with a Kiss 1959 ★★★ A kiss sold for charity leads to marriage and trouble for a sassy showgirl and an Army officer. Breezy comedy gets most of its sparkle from Reynolds. C: Glenn Ford, Debbie Reynolds, Eva Gabor, Fred Clark, Edgar Buchanan, Harry Morgan. D: George Marshall. COM 104m. V

It Started with a Mouse 1988 ★★★★½ Definitive documentary about the Disney studios, focusing on the Golden Age of animation, 1927-41. Full of rare footage, well-chosen clips and interviews with the pioneers who perfected the art form. Pinocchio fans, in particular, will be thrilled with the in-depth analysis. DOC

It Started with Eve 1941 ★★★★½ Buoyant comedy with Durbin pretending to be Cummings' fiancée so his invalid grandfather Laughton can die happy. Durbin is lovely and subdued here; probably her best film, full of charm and warmth. Remade as *I'd Rather Be Rich.* C: Deanna Durbin, Charles Laughton, Robert Cummings, Guy Kibbee, Margaret Tallichet, Walter Catlett. D: Henry Koster. COM 90m.

It Takes All Kinds 1969 U.S. ★★★ Intrigue about a woman (Miles) who shields a man (Lansing) she has seen kill a sailor in self-defense—but for a price. Engrossing dynamics and machinations highlight this double-crossing drama. C: Robert Lansing, Vera Miles, Barry Sullivan, Sid Melton, Penny Sugg. D: Eddie Davis. CRI 98m.

It Takes Two 1988 ★★★½ Freaking out over his impending marriage, a nervous groom-to-be (Newbern) lets off steam by buying a sexy sports car and taking off for a romantic fling with its even sexier seller. Then the trouble begins. Lively comedy provides enough innocuous fun to be worth a spin. C: George Newbern, Leslie Hope, Kimberly Foster, Anthony Geary. D: David Beaird. COM [PG-13] 79m. V

It! The Terror from Beyond Space 1958 ★★★ Rocketship blasts off from Mars with a stowaway, a reptilian monster who prowls for human snacks. A forerunner of *Alien*, this relic from science fiction's golden age still delivers decent thrills. C: Marshall Thompson, Shawn Smith, Kim Spalding, Ann Doran. D: Edward L. Cahn. SFI 69m. V

Italian Connection, The 1973 U.S.-Italian ★★★ A $6 million heroin heist goes awry,and someone's gotta pay. A New York gang boss puts out contract on a Milanese hood, and the bloodshed begins. Some thrills and chills flesh out a pretty lean script; story is partially dubbed. (a.k.a. *Manhunt*) C: Henry Silva, Woody Strode, Mario Adorf, Luciana Paluzzi, Sylva Koscina, Adolfo Celi. D: Fernando DiLeo. CRI [R] 87m.

Italian Job, The 1969 British ★★★½ From prison, crook masterminds a multimillion-dollar plot to steal a shipment of gold bullion. Caper comedy has some offbeat plot twists and charm. C: Michael Caine, Noel Coward, Maggie Blye, Benny Hill, Tony Beckley, Raf Vallone. D: Peter Collinson. COM [G] 99m. V

Italian Straw Hat, The 1927 French ★★★★★ Marvelous silent comedy about groom whose wedding must be put on hold so he can obtain new straw hat for fickle woman whose chapeau has been devoured by hungry donkey. Gags pile up to great delight in this charming cinematic banquet. C: Albert Prejean, Olga Tchekowa, Alice Tissot. D: Rene Clair. COM 114m. V

Italiano Brava Gente 1965 Italian ★★★½ An international cast stars in this detailed examination of Italian-Russian WWII life, chronicling the tribulations of both soldiers and civilians. Long-winded but interesting. (a.k.a. *Attack and Retreat*). C: Arthur Kennedy, Peter Falk, Tatyana Samoilova, Rafaelle Pisu, Andrea Checchi. D: Giuseppe De Santis. DRA 156m. V

It's a Bet 1935 British ★★★½ Journalist bets rival that he can stay hidden for a month. When his car is used in a crime, the reporter is thought guilty and gets his picture plastered everywhere, making concealment difficult. Cute comedy with neat romantic twist. C: Helen Chandler, Gene Gerrard. D: Alexander Esway. COM 69m.

It's a Big Country 1951 ★★★½ Patriotic tribute to the wonder and diversity.of the U.S. via seven separate vignettes. Some segments are better than others. Anyway, there's no shortage of talent. C: Ethel Barrymore, Keefe Brasselle, Gary Cooper, Nancy Davis, Gene Kelly, Keenan Wynn, Fredric March, Van Johnson, James Whitmore. D: Charles Vidor, Richard Thrope, John Sturges, Don Hartman. DRA 89m.

It's a Bikini World 1967 ★★★ Conceited blowhard (Kirk) can't get to first base with the woman (Walley) he's crazy about so he masquerades as a shy introvert to win her favor. Okay beach party clone could use Frankie and Annette to liven things but does get a boost from an appearance by The Animals. C: Deborah Walley, Tommy Kirk, Bob Pickett, Suzie Kaye, The Gentrys, The Animals. D: Stephanie Rothman. COM 86m.

It's a Bundyful Life 1992 ★★★ Crude, campy version of *It's a Wonderful Life* features crass, guardian angel Kinison showing perennial loser Al Bundy what life would be like had he never been born. Will satisfy fans of the TV show. C: Ed O'Neill, Katey Sagal, Christina Applegate, David Faustino. D: Gerry Cohen. COM 47m. TVM V

It's a Date 1940 ★★★★ Delightful Durbin vehicle has her unwillingly competing with actress mother (Francis) for fame and happiness. Durbin's vocal prowess gets a workout with Schubert's "Ave Maria" and Puccini's

"Musetta's Waltz" from *La Boheme*. (Remake: *Nancy Goes to Rio*.) C: Deanna Durbin, Walter Pidgeon, Kay Francis, Eugene Pallette, Lewis Howard, S.Z. Sakall, Samuel S. Hinds, Cecilia Loftus. D: William A. Seiter. MUS 103m. V

It's a Dog's Life 1955 ★★★★ Bowery bull terrier tells his rags-to-riches story (he wins in fancy dog show) through voice-over narration, in unusual animal yarn. Adapted from Richard Harding Davis story *The Bar Sinister*. Nicely done. C: Jeff Richards, Edmund Gwenn, Dean Jagger, Sally Fraser. D: Herman Hoffman. COM 87m. V

It's a Gift 1934 ★★★★★ Brilliant, unadulterated Fields with just enough of a plot, about henpecked husband tormented by family, friends, neighbors, and Baby LeRoy, to work as a movie. One great gag after another. Remake of 1926 silent Fields flick *It's the Old Army Game*. C: W.C. Fields, Baby LeRoy, Kathleen Howard, Tommy Bupp, Morgan Wallace. D: Norman Z. McLeod. COM 73m. V

It's a Great Feeling 1949 ★★★½ Mild musical spoof of Hollywood is shameless excuse for Warner Bros. stars to make cameo appearances. On view are Gary Cooper, Joan Crawford, Errol Flynn, Danny Kaye, Patricia Neal, Edward G. Robinson, Jane Wyman, and Ronald Reagan, among others. Day has minor role as waitress waiting for big break and sings with a French accent! C: Dennis Morgan, Doris Day, Jack Carson, Bill Goodwin. D: David Butler. MUS 85m. V

It's a Great Life 1943 ★★★½ One of the best *Blondie* series entries has Dagwood buying a horse, then entering a fox hunt. Silly, but fun. (a.k.a. *Blondie and Dagwood—It's a Great Life*) C: Penny Singleton, Arthur Lake, Larry Simms, Hugh Herbert. D: Frank Strayer. COM 75m. V

It's a Joke, Son 1947 ★★★ B-movie comedy takes the bombastic Senator Claghorn (character played by Delmar on Fred Allen radio show, "Allen's Alley,") and puts him in Washington. C: Kenny Delmar, Una Merkel, June Lockhart, Kenneth Farrell, Douglass Dumbrille. D: Ben Stoloff. COM 64m. V

It's a Mad Mad Mad Mad World 1963 ★★★½ Group witnesses gangster Durante's accidental death, then races to recover hidden loot. En route, every disaster that could possibly happen, does. And nearly every comedian known has cameo appearance. Overlong, mammoth indictment of greed proves that, in comedy, bigger is not necessarily better. Talented cast gets buried in expensive debris, except for Merman, who's a vulgar delight. C: Spencer Tracy, Edie Adams, Milton Berle, Sid Caesar, Buddy Hackett, Ethel Merman, Mickey Rooney, Dick Shawn, Dorothy Provine, Phil Silvers, Jonathan Winters, Peter Falk, Jimmy Durante. D: Stanley Kramer. COM [G] 175m. V

It's a Pleasure! 1945 ★★½ Figure skater finds marriage to hockey player is not what it's cracked up to be. Later Henie vehicle. C: Sonja Henie, Michael O'Shea, Bill Johnson, Gus Schilling, Iris Adrian. D: William A. Seiter. DRA 90m.

It's a Wonderful Life 1946 ★★★★★ Perennial family favorite with Stewart as down-on-his-luck Everyman, George Bailey, contemplating suicide. Angel (Travers) shows George the effect his life has had on others in a twilight zone-like sequence with staying power. Capra's first film after returning from duty in WWII is beautifully told and acted, with Reed, Barrymore, and other ensemble members perfectly cast. A financial bust when initially released, now shown on TV at Christmas! C: James Stewart, Donna Reed, Lionel Barrymore, Thomas Mitchell, Henry Travers, Beulah Bondi, Frank Faylen, Ward Bond, Gloria Grahame, H.B. Warner, Frank Albertson, Todd Karns, Samuel S. Hinds. D: Frank Capra. DRA 129m. V

It's a Wonderful World 1939 ★★★★½ Writer (Colbert) joins forces with a fugitive murder suspect (Stewart). Madcap blend of comedy and mystery, packed with laughs from start to finish, thanks to a snappy, gag-laden script. Hilarious. C: Claudette Colbert, James Stewart, Guy Kibbee, Nat Pendleton, Frances Drake, Edgar Kennedy, Ernest Truex, Sidney Blackmer, Hans Conried. D: W.S. Van-Dyke II. COM 86m.

It's Alive! 1974 ★★★½ Low-budget cult hit is a ragged but absorbing shocker about a mutated baby that runs amok, while police try to kill it and its parents attempt to deal with the tragedy. Grisly and offbeat, with some black humor. Followed by *It Lives Again*. C: John Ryan, Sharon Farrell, Andrew Duggan, Guy Stockwell, James Dixon, Michael Ansara. D: Larry Cohen. HOR [PG] 91m. V

It's Alive III: Island of the Alive 1987 ★★★½ Yikes! Third mutant baby shockfest is liveliest of the bunch. This time, crusading daddy (Moriarty) tries to stop society from killing all the monster offspring on an isolated island. C: Michael Moriarty, Karen Black, Gerrit Graham, Laurene Landon. D: Larry Cohen. HOR [R] 91m. V

It's All True 1993 ★★★★½ A look at Orson Welles' unfinished Latin American documentary and how RKO studio politics killed project. Second half, "Four Men on a Raft" shows what Welles was able to shoot, a bold tale of fishermen enduring dangerous waters to protest working conditions. Fascinating throughout. C: Orson Welles. D: Bill Krohn, Myron Meisel, Richard Wilson. DOC 89m. V

It's Always Fair Weather 1955 ★★★★ Three ex-G.I.s, pals during WWII, meet 10 years later to discover some hard truths about friendship. Bittersweet MGM musical with unique blend of charm and cynicism. Some great Kelly-choreographed dance numbers, including one on roller skates. Must be seen in letterbox version, due to split screen gimmick used in two numbers. C: Gene Kelly, Dan Dailey, Michael Kidd, Cyd Charisse, Dolores Gray, Jay C. Flipper. D: Gene Kelly, Stanley Donen. MUS 102m. V

It's Called Murder, Baby 1982 ★★ Faded movie sex queen hires detective to stop blackmailers from sabatoging her climb back to stardom. C: John Leslie, Cameron Mitchell, Lisa Trego. D: Sam Weston. CRI [R] 94m. V

It's Good to Be Alive 1974 ★★★★ A car wreck leaves baseball star Roy Campanella a quadraplegic. With the help of friends and caring doctors he pulls through to lead a rewarding life. True story is helped by a stirring performance from Winfield as Campanella. C: Paul Winfield, Louis Gossett Jr., Ruby Dee, Ramon Bieri, Joe DeSantis. D: Michael Landon. DRA 100m. TVM V

It's Great to Be Young 1946 ★★★ When the new headmaster tries to put an end to the school orchestra, one of the most popular teachers protests. Diverting comedy with excellent work by an able cast (including some big names). C: Leslie Brooks, Jimmy Lloyd, Jeff Donnell. D: Del Lord. MUS 69m.

It's in the Bag 1945 ★★★½ Entrepreneur gets big inheritance and leaves his flea circus in the dust. Zany film comprises a series of inspired gags, including not-to-be-missed confrontion between Allen and his radio nemesis, Benny. (a.k.a. *The Fifth Chair*) C: Fred Allen, Binnie Barnes, Robert Benchley, Sidney Toler, Jack Benny, Don Ameche, Victor Moore, Rudy Vallee, William Bendix. D: Richard Wallace. COM 87m. V

It's in the Blood 1938 British ★★★½ *Walter Mitty*-like story revolves around shy Hulbert, who goes on vacation and through series of mix-ups ends up in the middle of an elaborate jewel theft. Frothy caper film with many fun moments. C: Claude Hulbert, Lesley Brook, James Stephenson. D: Gene Gerrard. CRI 56m.

It's Love Again 1936 British ★★★★ Follow-up to Matthews' successful *Evergreen* is just as good; she plays a chorus-line dancer posing as a socialite. British musical has high spirits and winsome charm. C: Robert Young, Jessie Matthews, Sonnie Hale, Ernest Milton, Robb Wilton, Sara Allgood. D: Victor Saville. MUS 83m.

It's Love I'm After 1937 ★★★★ Witty backstage battle of the sexes with Davis in rare comedy role of actress in jealous rage over co-star hubby Howard's attentions to de Havilland. Diverting fun. C: Bette Davis, Leslie Howard, Olivia de Havilland, Patric Knowles, Eric Blore, Bonita Granville, Spring Byington, Veda Ann Borg. D: Archie Mayo. COM 90m.

It's My Turn 1980 ★★★½ Mother (Clayburgh) doesn't always have time for boyfriend Grodin in this pleasant comedy/drama. Appealing cast makes offbeat story believable. Director's first film. C: Jill Clayburgh, Michael Douglas, Charles Grodin, Beverly Garland. D: Claudia Weill. DRA [R] 91m. V

It's Never Too Late to Mend 1937 British ★★½ An evil wealthy man (Slaughter) plots to gain the attention of a farmer's beautiful daughter, even framing her fiancé. Slaughter's fine performance distinguishes this ultimately dated melodrama. C: Tod Slaughter, Marjorie Taylor, Jack Livesey, Ian Colin. D: David Macdonald. DRA 67m.

It's Never Too Late 1956 British ★★½ Even though the rest of the family considers her frightfully dull, mother sits down and turns out some spicy, successful screenplays. Pleasant enough comedy. C: Phyllis Calvert, Guy Rolfe, Sarah Lawson, Peter Illing, Patrick Barr. D: Michael McCarthy. COM 95m.

It's No Sin *See* **Battle of the Nineties**

It's Not Cricket 1937 ★★★ A cricket widow (Lynne) decides to fight the sport and win back her husband. Cheerful, romantic comedy. C: Claude Hulbert, Henry Kendall, Betty Lynne. D: Ralph Ince. COM 63m.

It's Not Cricket 1949 ★★★ A pair of British soldiers accidentally allow a Nazi spy to escape; he then bedevils them, even after they return to civilian life. Wacky comedy offers some skillful performances. C: Basil Radford, Naughton Wayne, Susan Shaw. D: Alfred Roome. COM 77m.

It's Not the Size That Counts 1974 British ★ Dreadful sequel to the lewd and crude *Percy* continues with the adventures of the man with the transplanted penis. One Percy film was more than enough. (a.k.a. *Percy's Progress*) C: Leigh Lawson, Elke Sommer, Denholm Elliott, Vincent Price, Judy Geeson, George Coulouris, Milo O'Shea. D: Ralph Thomas. COM [R] 90m. V

It's Only Money 1962 ★★★★ Above-average Lewis vehicle where he's a bumbling TV repairman who dreams of being a private eye. He gets his wish but nearly loses his life when he becomes entangled in the search for a long-lost heir. Inventive sight gags and fast-paced direction keep the laughs coming. C: Jerry Lewis, Joan O'Brien, Zachary Scott, Jack Weston, Jesse White, Mae Questel. D: Frank Tashlin. COM 84m.

It's Pat: The Movie 1994 ★★½ Sweeney's unisex character from *Saturday Night Live* makes it to the big screen. Pat finds romance with someone named Chris but can they achieve lasting happiness? What if they get his and hers towels? C: Julia Sweeney, David Foley. COM V

It's Showtime 1976 ★★★★ Lovable collection of movie clips celebrates the contribution of animal performers to the film industry. These pets are very talented, and there's loads of fun for the whole family. COM 86m.

It's Tough to Be Famous 1932 ★★★★ Fairbanks is terrific as a hero manipulated by the press. Slick and stylish comedy/drama captures perfectly the pitfalls of stardom. C: Douglas Fairbanks Jr., Mary Brian, Walter

Catlett, Lilian Bond, Terrence Ray, David Landau. D: Alfred E. Green. COM 79m.

It's Trad, Dad! 1962 *See* **Ring-a-Ding Rhythm**

It's Your Move 1968 Italian ★★★½ Clever European caper comedy with mastermind (Robinson) scheming to rob the local bank by replacing four employees with look-alikes. Fast moving twists and turns. (a.k.a. *Mad Checkmate*) C: Edward G. Robinson, Terry-Thomas, Adolfo Celi. D: Robert Fiz. COM 93m.

Ivan the Terrible, Part One 1944 Russian ★★★★★ Eisenstein's masterful epic, released in two parts, chronicles life and times of Russia's corrupt czar. Made on orders from Joseph Stalin, this first film portrays Ivan's rise to power and subsequent corruption. Enormous in sweep, with stunning camerawork. Excellent Prokofiev score stands on its own. C: Nikolai Cherkassov, Ludmila Tselikovskaya, Serafina Birman. D: Sergei Eisenstein. DRA 96m. V

Ivan the Terrible, Part Two 1946 Russian ★★★★★ Eisenstein's epic picks up with Ivan's return to the throne and his power struggle with new conspiracy. Continuation of one of the great historical films was actually supposed to precede a third part (of which only fragments survive). Shot simultaneously with Part One, politics kept it from release for years. C: Nikolai Cherkassov, Ludmila Tselikovskaya, Serafina Birman. D: Sergei Eisenstein. DRA 88m. V

Ivan 1932 U.S.S.R. ★★★★½ Trio of Soviet workers—all named "Ivan"—perform respective duties in '30s Russia. Each individual stands for different aspect of government's ideals. First sound film for noted Soviet director Dovzhenko; reverberates with powerful images and inventive dialogue. C: Pytor Masokha, Semyon Shagaida. D: Alexander Dovzhenko. DRA 85m.

Ivanhoe 1952 ★★★★ Sir Walter Scott's classic hero leaps onto the screen, valiantly battling for justice in 12th-century England. Very good costume epic breathtakingly recreates the age of knighthood the grand old Hollywood way. C: Robert Taylor, Joan Fontaine, Elizabeth Taylor, Emlyn Williams, George Sanders, Robert Douglas, Finlay Currie. D: Richard Thorpe. ACT 107m. V

Ivanhoe 1982 ★★★★ Spirited TV version of Sir Walter Scott's epic tale admiringly captures all the gusto and excitement of chivalry in 12th-century England. Colorful and very well-done costumer. C: James Mason, Anthony Andrews, Sam Neill, Michael Hordern, Olivia Hussey, Lysette Anthony. D: Douglas Camfield. ACT 142m. TVM V

I've Always Loved You 1946 ★★★½ Lavish costume drama in which a snobbish orchestra conductor (Dorn) does battle with a concert pianist (McLeod). Sumptuous film overflows with beautiful piano masterpieces (Beethoven, Tchaikovsky, Chopin) played by Artur Rubinstein. Restored version brings out the glorious Technicolor. (a.k.a. *Concerto*) C: Philip Dorn, Catherine McLeod, William Carter, Maria Ouspenskaya, Felix Bressart. D: Frank Borzage. DRA 117m. V

I've Heard the Mermaids Singing 1987 Canadian ★★½ A scatterbrained misfit (McCarthy) gets a job at a posh art gallery and becomes very attached to her female boss. McCarthy's effervescent charm is the whole show. C: Sheila McCarthy, Paule Baillargeon, Ann-Marie McDonald, John Evans. D: Patricia Rozema. DRA 82m. V

I've Lived Before 1956 ★★★½ A man thinks he's the reincarnation of a pilot shot down during WWI. Unusual, offbeat little film has its moments. C: Jock Mahoney, Leigh Snowden, Ann Harding, John McIntire, Raymond Bailey. D: Richard Bartlett. DRA 82m.

Ivory Ape, The 1980 ★★½ Slimy promoter captures a white ape for public display, but the ape goes beserk and escapes. Memorable for a showboat performance by Palance. C: Jack Palance, Steven Keats, Cindy Pickett. D: Tom Kotani. HOR 104m. TVM

Ivory Hunter 1951 British ★★★ Mild tale of game warden's attempt to build a nature park at Mt. Kilimanjaro. Filmed documentary style. (a.k.a. *Where No Vultures Fly*) C: Anthony Steel, Dinah Sheridan, Harold Warrender, Meredith Edwards, William Simons. D: Harry Watt. DRA 107m.

Ivory Hunters 1990 *See* **Last Elephant, The**

Ivy 1947 ★★★★ Fontaine excels as a black widow with poisonous desire for wealth and status, until she gets caught in her own web. Solid thriller, with deftly handled finale. Based on Marie Belloc-Lowndes' novel. C: Joan Fontaine, Patric Knowles, Herbert Marshall, Richard Ney, Cedric Hardwicke, Lucile Watson. D: Sam Wood. CRI 99m.

Izzy and Moe 1985 ★★★ Episodic true story of two vaudevillians turned Prohibition agents famous for elaborate disguises used to trap bootleggers. Weak script makes this a disappointment for fans of *Honeymooners* vets Gleason and Carney. C: Jackie Gleason, Art Carney, Cynthia Harris, Zohra Lampert. D: Jackie Cooper. DRA 92m. TVM V

J

J. Edgar Hoover 1988 ★★★ Middling, sanitized drama stars Williams as the man who was emperor of the FBI for almost 50 years. Based on *My 30 Years in Hoover's FBI* by William G. Sullivan and William S. Brown. C: Treat Williams, Rip Torn, David Ogden Stiers, Andrew Duggan, Louise Fletcher. D: Robert Collins. CRI 120m. TVM V

J-Men Forever! 1979 ★★★½ Members of the comedy troupe Firesign Theatre have pieced together clips of old Republic films and added their own wacky dialogue. The plot—what there is of it—involves a special task force committed to stamping out the evils of rock 'n' roll. Inspired lunacy. C: Phil Proctor, Peter Bergman. D: Richard Patterson. COM [PG] 73m. V

Jabberwocky 1977 British ★★½ Director Gilliam's first solo directing effort is a mixed bag of medieval tomfoolery inspired by the Lewis Carroll poem. Innocent Palin struggles to prove his worth so that he can win the hand of his true love. Relies too much on unfunny crudeness for laughs. C: Michael Palin, Max Wall, Deborah Fallender, John Le Mesurier. D: Terry Gilliam. COM [PG] 100m. V

J'Accuse 1919 French ★★★★★ Two men—one refined, one crude—vie for a woman's love during WWI. Director Gance uses this simple tale for emotional pacifist theme, employing actual newsreel footage shot during battles, along with effective use of his trademark split screens. Moving, deeply felt drama, which Gance remade during sound era. C: Sevérin-Mars, Maryse Dauvray, Romuald Joubé. D: Abel Gance. DRA 150m.

J'Accuse 1937 French ★★★★½ Sound remake of 1919 drama follows same story, looking at memories of WWI veteran still haunted by visions of battlefield, and conflict he had over love for one woman. Story still packs an emotional wallop with its strong antiwar message. C: Victor Francen, Jean Max Delaitre, Renee Devillers. D: Abel Gance. DRA 100m. V

Jack and His Friends 1992 ★★½ Inept comedy about two fugitives who take a shoe salesman hostage and sequester themselves at summer retreat. C: Allen Garfield, Judy Reyes, Sam Rockwell. D: Bruce Ornstein. COM 93m. V

Jack and the Beanstalk 1952 ★★★ Bud and Lou get mixed up with a giant in this fantasy; starts out in real world of black and white, then switches to color. Toddlers may like it. C: Bud Abbott, Lou Costello, Buddy Baer. D: Jean Yarbrough. FAM/COM 78m. V

Jack Be Nimble 1994 New Zealand ★★★★★ Riveting horror drama about an orphan (Arquette), who kills his abusive foster parents and sets out to find his long-lost (and psychic) sister. Strong performances (especially Arquette) and stylish direction power this disturbing psychothriller. C: Alexis Arquette, Sarah Smuts-Kennedy, Bruno Lawrence, Tony Barry, Elizabeth Hawthorne. D: Garth Maxwell. HOR [R] 93m.

Jack Frost 1966 USSR ★★★½ Children's film from the Soviet Union about a girl held captive by wicked family. Her savior's head is transformed into a bear's noggin, though noble acts restore his humanity. Nice fairy story for youngsters. C: Aleksandr Khvylya, Natasha Sedykh, Eduard Izotov. D: Aleksandr Rou. FAM/DRA 79m.

Jack Johnson 1971 ★★★★ Excellent documentary about first black American heavyweight boxing champion Jack Johnson, who held the crown from 1908 to 1915. Narrated by Brock Peters. Good jazz score by Miles Davis. D: William Cayton. DOC [PG] 90m.

Jack Kerouac's America 1987 *See* **Kerouac**

Jack Knife Man, The 1920 ★★★★½ Compelling silent drama about a man who tries to reenter civilized society after years of rough exile in a southern colony. C: Fred Turner, Florence Vidor. D: King Vidor. DRA 86m. V

Jack London 1943 ★★★ Loose biography of the life of the great American author, chronicling his rise to national prominence and involvement in several wars. Somewhat dated by wartime anti-Japanese sentiment, but interesting nevertheless. (a.k.a. *The Adventures of Jack London* and *The Life of Jack London*) C: Michael O'Shea, Susan Hayward, Osa Massen, Harry Davenport, Frank Craven, Virginia Mayo. D: Alfred Santell. DRA 92m. V

Jack McCall, Desperado 1953 ★★★ During the Civil War, Southerner (Montgomery) escapes prison to get the man who framed him as a traitor—pursued by Wild Bill Hickok. Plenty of action, but some predictable plotting. C: George Montgomery, Angela Stevens, Jay Silverheels, Douglas Kennedy. D: Sidney Salkow. WST 76m. V

Jack of Diamonds 1967 ★★½ An international jewel thief heads into retirement as his young protégé goes on a crime spree, specializing in stealing gems from famous movie actresses. Passable crime caper. C: George Hamilton, Joseph Cotten, Marie Laforet, Maurice Evans, Carroll Baker, Zsa Zsa Gabor, Lilli Palmer. D: Don Taylor. CRI 105m.

Jack Slade 1953 ★★★ Western chronicles Stevens as the title character: a murderer turned stagecoach shotgun rider and alcoholic. Talented leads outperform the script. C: Mark Stevens, Dorothy Malone, Barton Mac-

Lane, John Litel. D: Harold Schuster. WST 90m.

Jack the Bear 1993 ★★★½ DeVito is affecting in a straight role, as a suddenly single father trying to cope with raising young sons. Interesting dark comic tone but horror movie subplot is distracting. Based on novel by Dan McCall. C: Danny DeVito, Robert Steinmiller, Miko Hughes, Gary Sinise, Julia Louis-Dreyfus. D: Marshall Herskowitz. DRA [PG-13] 110m. V

Jack the Giant Killer 1962 ★★★½ Entertaining story of a young man (Matthews) who battles giants, ogres, and monsters. Kids will enjoy the action and science fiction enthusiasts will enjoy the special effects—Ray Harryhausen's protégé Jim Danforth provided the puppet monsters. C: Kerwin Mathews, Judi Meredith, Torin Thatcher, Walter Burke. D: Nathan Juran. FAM/SFI [G] 95m. V

Jack the Ripper 1960 British ★★★ The notorious madman is butchering victims in London, and an American detective (Patterson) aids Scotland Yard in tracking him down. Gruesome, well-made variation on the oft-dramatized story. C: Monty Berman, Lee Patterson, Eddie Byrne, George Rose, Betty McDowall. D: Robert Baker. HOR 88m. V

Jack the Ripper 1988 ★★★★ Caine plays the Scotland Yard Inspector who originally investigated Jack the Ripper in turn-of-the-century London. In this version he ultimately identifies the famous Whitechapel killer. Director/co-writer Wickes based his speculative conclusion on his own research. Well done. C: Michael Caine, Armand Assante, Ray McAnally, Susan George, Jane Seymour, Lewis Collins, Ken Bones. D: David Wickes. DRA 200m. TVM V

Jackal of Nahueltoro, The 1969 Chilean ★★★★½ Shocking true story involves illiterate Chilean man who slaughters woman and her five children. After imprisonment, the murderer reforms himself into model citizen but still faces wrath of manipulative government forces. Multilayered drama delivers strong indictment against political corruption. C: Nelson Villagra, Shenda Roman, Hector Noguera. D: Miquel Littin. DRA 89m.

Jackals, The 1967 ★★½ Cantankerous miner (Price) must protect his gold stake and his granddaughter against a band of mercenaries. Routine action, notable South African locale. C: Vincent Price, Diana Ivarson, Robert Gunner, Bob Courtney, Patrick Mynhardt. D: Robert D. Webb. ACT 105m.

Jackass Mail 1942 ★★★ Run-of-the-mill comedy about criminal (Beery) turned unlikely hero. One of many Main/Beery pairings. C: Wallace Beery, Marjorie Main, J. Carroll Naish, Darryl Hickman, William Haade, Dick Curtis. D: Norman Z. McLeod. COM 80m.

Jackboot Mutiny 1955 W. German ★★★★ Intriguing re-creation of 1944 attemped assassination of Hitler by German military officials. Stylized acting and uncompromising attitudes create a singular German film about that country's horrifying leader. Definitely worth a look. C: Carl Ludwig Diehl, Carl Wery, Bernhard Wicki, Kurt Meisel. D: G.W. Pabst. DRA 77m.

Jackie Robinson Story, The 1950 ★★★★ Robinson is surprisingly good playing himself in his film biography. Detailing his life in Negro Baseball Leagues to triumphs with Brooklyn Dodgers, this is a straightforward account of racial problems in America and one man's fight against prejudice. C: Jackie Robinson, Ruby Dee, Minor Watson, Louise Beavers, Richard Lane, Harry Shannon, Ben Lessy, Joel Fluellen. D: Alfred E. Green. DRA 76m. V

Jacknife 1989 ★★★★ De Niro is Vietnam vet trying to rescue long-lost buddy Harris from his own inner demons in this wrenching drama that features well-wrought performances, particularly by Baker as the friend's unmarried sister. C: Robert De Niro, Ed Harris, Kathy Baker, Charles Dutton. D: David Jones. DRA [R] 102m. V

Jackpot, The 1950 ★★★½ A surburban man (Stewart) wins radio quiz show cash, complicating his life in unexpected ways. Silly, harmless comedy with always likable star. C: James Stewart, Barbara Hale, James Gleason, Fred Clark, Natalie Wood. D: Walter Lang. COM 87m.

Jack's Back 1988 ★★★ Modern-day Jack the Ripper plys his trade in L.A. Saved by Spader's strong performance, even with too many plot twists. C: James Spader, Cynthia Gibb, Rod Loomis, Rex Ryon. D: Rowdy Herrington. CRI [R] 97m. V

Jackson County Jail 1976 ★★★ Innocent woman (Mimieux) arrested and then raped by police, escapes from jail with the help of another inmate (Jones). Satisfying but unexpected chase film. C: Yvette Mimieux, Tommy Lee Jones, Robert Carradine, Severn Darden, Mary Woronov. D: Michael Miller. ACT [R] 83m. V

Jacksons: An American Dream, The 1992 ★★ The ultimate modern show-biz family saga gets the kid-glove treatment in this tepid biography, over which the family itself had approval. C: Lawrence-Hilton Jacobs, Angela Bassett, Holly Robinson, Billy Dee Williams, Vanessa Williams. D: Karen Arthur. DRA 225m. TVM

Jacob Have I Loved 1988 ★★★★ Early role for Bridget Fonda features her as tomboy who befriends a sea captain and consequently comes out from under her talented twin sister's shadow. Adapted from award-winning children's novel, this is a fine tale for child audiences. C: Bridget Fonda,Jenny Robertson, John Kellogg. D: Victoria Hochberg. FAM/DRA 57m. TVM V

Jacob, Man Who Fought with God 1985 ★★★½ Docudrama re-creation of the biblical story of Jacob. Low-budget production faithfully depicts the Old Testament story. C: Fosco Giacchei, Luisa Della Noce, Jean Mercier. DRA 139m.

Jacob the Liar 1977 East German ★★★★ In midst of bleak life during WWII, Brodsky invents series of stories to provide hope for fellow Jews living in enforced ghetto. Brodsky's poignant lead mixes right amount of drama and comic touches. Oscar nominee for Best Foreign Film. C: Vlastimil Brodsky, Erwin Geschonneck, Manuela Simon, Henry Hubchen, Blanche Kommerell. D: Frank Beyer. DRA 95m.

Jacob Two-Two Meets the Hooded Fang 1977 Canadian ★★★★ Enjoyable childhood tale; a boy finds himself trapped inside a prison for children. Good slapstick and fantasy in fun film for kids, coupled with jabs of humor parents will enjoy. Written by novelist Mordecai Richler. C: Stephen Rosenberg, Alex Karras, Guy L'Ecuyer, Joy Coghill, Earl Pennington, Claude Gail. D: Theodore J. Flicker. FAM/COM [G] 90m. V

Jacobo Timerman: Prisoner Without a Name, Cell Without a Number 1983 ★★★ An Argentine newspaper publisher critical of the government is imprisoned and tortured. Based on a powerful true story, but disappointingly subdued. (a.k.a. *Prisoner Without a Name, Cell Without a Number*) C: Roy Scheider, Liv Ullmann, Sam Robards, David Cryer, Michael Pearlman, Zach Galligan. D: Linda Yellen. DRA 100m. TVM

Jacob's Ladder 1990 ★★★½ Vietnam vet's sanity is pushed to the extreme when he experiences frightful hallucinations; or is he in touch with an otherworldly realm? Dark, moving story looks terrific. C: Tim Robbins, Elizabeth Pena, Danny Aiello, Matt Craven, Bryan Larkin, Pruitt Vince, Jason Alexander. D: Adrian Lyne. DRA [R] 116m. V

Jacqueline 1956 British ★★★ Sentimental and rather dated story of an Irish drunk whose daughter tries to keep him dry and working. C: John Gregson, Noel Purcell, Cyril Cusack. D: Roy Baker. DRA 92m.

Jacqueline Bouvier Kennedy 1981 ★★ Smith is unmemorable in one more mundane movie slobbering over the Kennedys. Plays like a lavish soap opera. C: Jaclyn Smith, James Franciscus, Rod Taylor, Stephen Elliott, Donald Moffat. D: Stephen Gethers. DRA 150m. TVM V

Jacqueline Susann's Once Is Not Enough 1975 ★ Sleazy film of Susann's potboiler about a has-been movie producer (Douglas) who marries a wealthy woman (Smith) so his doting daughter (Raffin) can enjoy the good life. (a.k.a. *Once Is Not Enough*) C: Kirk Douglas, Alexis Smith, David Janssen, Deborah Raffin, George Hamilton, Melina Mercouri, Brenda Vaccaro. D: Guy Green. DRA [R] 121m. V

Jacqueline Susann's Valley of the Dolls 1981 ★★ Unnecessary remake follows the lives of three young women, one of whom is a pill-popping singer. The best that can be said is that it's better than the original. C: Catherine Hicks, Lisa Hartman, Veronica Hamel, David Birney, Jean Simmons, James Coburn, Gary Collins, Bert Convy, Britt Ekland, Carol Lawrence, Camilla Sparv, Denise Hill. D: Walter Grauman. DRA 240m. TVM

Jacques and November 1985 Canadian ★★★★ Offbeat buddy film looks at a film fan dying of cancer who implores his best friend to shoot a movie about his process of dying. Nice balance of humor and pathos, enhanced with good performances. C: Jean Beaudry, Carole Brechetter, Monique Cantin. D: Francois Bouvier, Jean Beaudry. DRA 72m.

Jacques Brel Is Alive and Well and Living in Paris 1975 ★★★ Plotless musical revue consists of 26 songs by Belgian Jacques Brel, from the Off-Broadway hit. Best for fans of the composer or the show. C: Elly Stone, Mort Shuman, Joe Masiell, Jacques Brel. D: Denis Heroux. MUS [PG] 98m.

Jacquot 1991 French ★★★★½ Agnes Varda's documentary tribute to her late husband, director Jacques Demy, mixes interviews with clips from his films to create a loving portrait of Demy's life and work. A unique portrait from a talented and devoted wife. Sheer delight for movie lovers. (a.k.a. *Jacquot de Nantes*) C: Philippe Maron, Edouard Joubeaud, Laurent Monnier, Brigitte de Villepoix, Daniel Dublet. D: Agnes Varda. DOC [PG] 118m. V

Jacquot de Nantes 1991 *See* **Jacquot**

Jade Mask, The 1945 ★★★ Charlie Chan (Toler) attempts to uncover the masked murderers who are behind the killing of an inventor. Late, weak episode of the series. C: Sidney Toler, Mantan Moreland, Edwin Luke, Janet Warren, Edith Evanson, Hardie Albright, Frank Reicher, Alan Bridge, Ralph Lewis. D: Phil Rosen. CRI 66m. V

Jagged Edge 1985 ★★★½ Lawyer Close defends accused wife-killer Bridges, and falls in love with him. Intelligent performances and tense moments outweigh cavernous plot holes and lapses into incredulity. C: Jeff Bridges, Glenn Close, Peter Coyote, Robert Loggia. D: Richard Marquand. CRI [R] 108m. V

Jaguar 1956 ★★½ A former jungle boy (Sabu) raised in Britain begins to doubt his own mental state after being accused of an oilfield murder. B-movie action drama is full of clichés and character stereotypes, but Sabu raises the tone a bit. C: Sabu, Chiquita, Barton MacLane, Jonathan Hale, Mike Connors. D: George Blair. ACT 66m.

Jaguar 1977 Polish ★★★½ Action movie from the Philippines revolves around an apartment security guard who is hired to protect a notorious pornographer. He becomes involved with his boss's lover, leading to disaster. Bleak and violent tale, but well made and enjoyable. D: Gregorz Lasota. ACT 53m. v

Jaguar Lives! 1979 ★★ Kung fu version of a James Bond film, with Lewis as a globetrotting agent busting drug dealers. Some decent fight material lost in over-familiar story. Better cast than the material deserves. C: Joe Lewis, Christopher Lee, Donald Pleasence, Barbara Bach, John Huston. D: Ernest Pintoff. ACT [PG] 91m. v

Jail Bait 1954 ★ A gangster (Farrell) enlists a plastic surgeon to change his appearance. The most professional looking of legendary schlock moviemaker Wood's features, but unfortunately the least entertaining. C: Timothy Farrell, Lyle Talbot, Steve Reeves, Dolores Fuller, Clancey Malone. D: Edward D. Wood Jr. CRI 70m. v

Jail Bait 1972 German ★★★★ Coy and manipulative adolescent (Mattes) becomes involved with an older man, eventually convincing him to murder her father. A bleak portrait of the post-WWII German landscape from director Fassbinder, with seductive performance from Mattes. Not for timid viewers. C: Eva Mattes, Harry Baer, Jorg von Liebenfels, Ruth Drexel, Kurt Raab, Hanna Schygulla. D: Rainer Werner Fassbinder. DRA 99m.

Jail Busters 1955 ★★★ The Bowery Boys get themselves sent to prison to rescue a pal and expose guards giving preferential treatment to a prominent gangster. Main problem is that there isn't enough of the comic interplay between Gorcey and Hall, which is worth seeing. C: Leo Gorcey, Huntz Hall, Bernard Gorcey, Barton MacLane, Anthony Caruso, Percy Helton, David Gorcey, Bennie Bartlett, Murray Alper, Fritz Feld, Lyle Talbot, Henry Kulky. D: William Beaudine. COM 61m.

Jailbird Rock 1988 ★★★ Young woman jailed for killing abusive stepfather seeks salvation in music and dance. C: Robin Antin, Ronald Lacey, Rhonda Aldrich. D: Phillip Schuman. CRI [R] 92m. v

Jailbreakers, The 1960 ★★ Three escaped convicts who are searching for buried loot terrorize an innocent couple in a deserted town. Ho-hum crime drama fails to build suspense or empathy with the leads. C: Robert Hutton, Mary Castle, Michael O'Connell, Gabe Delutri, Anton Stralen. D: Alexander Grasshoff. CRI 64m.

Jailhouse Rock 1957 ★★★★½ Presley's best film, which cemented his image as "rebel with a guitar." He's a convict using music as road to freedom. Terrific Leiber/Stoller songs include "Treat Me Nice," "I Wanna Be Free," and title song exuberantly choreographed by Elvis. C: Elvis Presley, Judy Tyler, Vaughn Taylor, Dean Jones, Mickey Shaughnessy. D: Richard Thorpe. MUS 96m. v

Jakarta 1988 ★★★ A CIA agent, haunted by dreams of his lover who was killed in Jakarta, is drugged and kidnapped—and bound for Jakarta once again. Nice atmospheric action. C: Christopher Noth, Sue Francis Pai, Franz Tumbuan. D: Charles Kaufman. ACT [R] 94m. v

Jake Speed 1986 ★★★½ In this lighthearted adventure, a young woman (Kopins) is aided by a fictional book hero (Crawford) who comes to life to save her abducted sister. A funny and whimsical premise, with well-formed characters. C: Wayne Crawford, Dennis Christopher, Karen Kopins, John Hurt, Leon Ames. D: Andrew Lane. ACT [PG] 93m. v

Jalopy 1953 ★★½ After Sach (Hall) stumbles onto a secret auto fuel formula, the Bowery Boys enter the high-speed world of drag racing. The usual laughs and nonsense, much of it worth the time. C: Leo Gorcey, Huntz Hall, David Gorcey, Bennie Bartlett, Bernard Gorcey, Robert Lowery, Murray Alper, Jane Easton, Richard Benedict. D: William Beaudine. COM 62m.

Jam Session 1944 ★★★★ Dance contest winner Miller falls for screenwriter while almost ruining his career. Slim plot is mere excuse for terrific potpourri of top big band/swing talent doing signature numbers. A jazz fan's dream. C: Ann Miller, Jess Barker, Charles Brown, Eddie Kane, Louis Armstrong, Duke Ellington & His Band, Glen Gray & His Band, Teddy Powell & His Band, Charlie Barnet Orchestra, Nan Wynn. D: Charles Barton. MUS 77m.

Jamaica Inn 1939 British ★★½ Young orphan (O'Hara) involved with cutthroats and assassins in period-locale Cornwall. Hitchcock's adaptation of Daphne du Maurier's gothic novel. Bloated production belongs mostly to Laughton, but this failure was nobody's shining hour. C: Charles Laughton, Maureen O'Hara, Leslie Banks, Robert Newton, Emlyn Williams, Mervyn Johns. D: Alfred Hitchcock. ACT 98m. v

Jamaica Inn 1985 British ★★★½ Innocent (Seymour) becomes involved in intrigue with her dangerous smuggler uncle (McGoohan) in scenic period Cornwall. From the Daphne du Maurier novel. C: Jane Seymour, Patrick McGoohan, Trevor Eve, John McEnery, Billie Whitelaw. D: Lawrence Gordon Clark. DRA 192m. TVM v

Jamaica Run 1953 ★★★ A Caribbean charter boat skipper (Milland) helps Dahl retain possession of a large Jamaican mansion. A jumbled script, but some neat offbeat characters. C: Ray Milland, Arlene Dahl, Wendell Corey, Patric Knowles. D: Lewis Foster. DRA 92m.

Jamboree 1957 ★★★½ Nothing plot involving singers (Carr, Halloway) and their manager (Medford) provides platform for many rock 'n' roll and jazz specialty acts. Highlight: Jerry Lee Lewis singing "Great Balls of Fire." C: Kay Medford, Robert Pastine,

Paul Carr, Freda Halloway, Slim Whitman, Jodie Sands, Frankie Avalon, Fats Domino, Jerry Lee Lewis, Carl Perkins, Lewis Lymon & the Teen Chords, Buddy Knox. D: Roy Lockwood. MUS 71m.

James A. Michener's Dynasty 1976 ★★★½ The trials and tribulations of a pioneer family who head west to Ohio for a new life in the 1820s. TV adaptation of typical Michener historical saga, with strong performances providing the main interest. C: Sarah Miles, Stacy Keach, Harris Yulin, Harrison Ford, Amy Irving. D: Lee Phillips. DRA 96m. TVM

James at 15 1977 ★★★½ Kerwin pines when he realizes his parents' move will take him away from his girlfriend. Pilot for TV series that was one of the first serious attempts to depict the little traumas that make up life as a teenager. C: Lance Kerwin, Linden Chiles, Lynn Carlin, Melissa Sue Anderson, Kate Jackson, Kim Richards. D: Joseph Hardy. DRA 100m. TVM

James Bond The solid-gold Cadillac of series films. Beginning with Sean Connery as Ian Fleming's redoubtable British intelligence agent and ladies' man, continuing through George Lazenby in the underrated *On Her Majesty's Secret Service*, then Roger Moore sleepwalking his way through seven stunt-and-gadget-filled epics, and most recently Timothy Dalton returning the series to its rather more hard-boiled roots, the James Bond films have been top of the line in budgets, casts, and production values. Connery's dry wit still shines brightest, but the *Bond* films can be counted on for spectacle and pace.

On Her Majesty's Secret Service (1969)
Dr. No (1962)
From Russia With Love (1963)
Goldfinger (1964)
Thunderball (1965)
You Only Live Twice (1967)
Diamonds Are Forever (1971)
Live and Let Die (1973)
The Man With the Golden Gun (1974)
The Spy Who Loved Me (1977)
Moonraker (1979)
For Your Eyes Only (1981)
Never Say Never Again (1983)
Octopussy (1983)
A View to a Kill (1985)
The Living Daylights (1987)
License to Kill (1989)

James Dean 1976 ★★★ Tepid dramatized reminiscence of the '50s anti-hero and *Rebel Without a Cause* star, based on memoirs by one of Dean's friends who knew him from his early days in New York until his death in Hollywood. (a.k.a. *The Legend*) C: Stephen McHattie, Michael Brandon, Dane Clark, Meg Foster, Candy Clark, Amy Irving. D: Robert Butler. DRA 99m. TVM V

James Dean Story, The 1957 ★★★ Compilation of uninspiring source material in lethargic documentary of controversial '50s movie actor James Dean (1931-1955). D: George W. George, Robert Altman. DOC 80m. V

James Joyce's Women 1983 ★★★½ Dramatic renderings of the women who populated the great Irish author's pages and his life. Dreamlike and rapturous. Rewarding for Joyce buffs. C: Fionnula Flanagan, Timothy O'Grady, Chris O'Neill. D: Michel Pearce. DRA [R] 89m. V

Jamon Jamon 1993 Spanish ★★★½ Mildly funny social satire, with Javier recruited by Sandrelli to seduce Cruz, who is already pregnant by Molla. Possibly the first film to include nude bullfighting. C: Penelope Cruz, Anna Galiena, Javier Bardem, Stephania Sandrelli, Juan Diego, Jordi Molia. D: Bigas Luna. COM 94m. V

Jane and the Lost City 1987 ★★★ The famous cartoon character from British newspapers is up to her worldwide hijinks once again. Good fun, the British way. C: Maud Adams, Sam Jones, Kirsten Hughes. D: Terry Marcel. COM [PG] 94m. V

Jane Austen in Manhattan 1980 ★★ Two directors fight over the production of a recently unearthed Jane Austen play. Good bits are too infrequent in this rare Merchant/Ivory misfire. C: Robert Powell, Anne Baxter, Michael Wager, Tim Choate. D: James Ivory. DRA 108m. V

Jane Campion Shorts 1988 ★★★ Three short films by the noted director of *The Piano*. They are "Passionless Moments," "Girl's Own Story" and "Peel." D: Jane Campion. COM 49m. V

Jane Doe 1983 ★★★½ Innocent attack victim (Valentine) left for dead; when she survives, she suffers amnesia so she can't identify her attacker. Decent thriller. C: Karen Valentine, William Devane, Eva Marie Saint, David Huffman. D: Ivan Nagy. DRA 96m. TVM V

Jane Eyre 1934 ★★★ First talking picture version of Brontë classic. Creaky but atmospheric interpretation of the romantic tale of the love of estate governess (Bruce) for the enigmatic Mr. Rochester (Clive). Now mainly a curiosity piece. C: Virginia Bruce, Colin Clive, Beryl Mercer, Aileen Pringle, David Torence, Lionel Belmore, Jameson Thomas. D: Christy Cabanne. DRA 67m.

Jane Eyre 1944 ★★★★ Effective, atmospheric adaptation of Charlotte Brontë novel with governess (Fontaine) arriving in gloomy mansion owned by brooding Rochester (Welles). A young Taylor is superb. Film is flawed by Welles' erratic performance, which is sometimes marvelous, sometimes hammy. C: Orson Welles, Joan Fontaine, Margaret

O'Brien, Henry Daniell, John Sutton, Agnes Moorehead, Elizabeth Taylor, Peggy Ann Garner. D: Robert Stevenson. DRA 96m. V

Jane Eyre 1971 British ★★★★ Visually lovely production of Charlotte Brontë classic with Scott a magnificent Rochester, mysterious employer of title character (York). C: George C. Scott, Susannah York, Ian Bannen, Jack Hawkins, Rachel Kempson, Jean Marsh, Nyree Dawn Porter. D: Delbert Mann. DRA 110m.

Jane Eyre 1983 ★★★½ Brontë's gothic tale of the orphan governess who falls in love with her mysterious Yorkshire employer (Dalton). British miniseries version of the classic certainly holds its own against other versions. C: Timothy Dalton, Zelah Clark. D: Julian Amyes. DRA 239m. TVM V

Janie 1944 ★★★½ Saccharine little comedy of teenager (Reynolds) falling for G.I. (Hutton) over papa's (Arnold's) objections. Interesting as a '40s time capsule. Based on Broadway play by Josephine Bentham and Herschel Williams. Sequel: *Janie Gets Married*. C: Joyce Reynolds, Edward Arnold, Ann Harding, Robert Benchley, Robert Hutton, Alan Hale, Hattie McDaniel. D: Michael Curtiz. COM 106m.

Janie Gets Married 1946 ★★★ Okay sequel to *Janie* with perky wife (Leslie) helping ex-soldier (Hutton) adjust to home life. C: Joan Leslie, Robert Hutton, Edward Arnold, Ann Harding, Robert Benchley, Dorothy Malone. D: Vincent Sherman. COM 89m.

Janis 1974 ★★★½ Superficial documentary account makes no mention of anguished spirit of earthy rock singer Janis Joplin. Interviews are interspersed with concert footage; featured songs include "Me and Bobby McGee," "Piece of My Heart," "Mercedes Benz," "Kosmic Blues." D: Di Howard Alk, Seaton Findlay. DOC [R] 96m. V

January Man, The 1989 ★★ Oddball cop turned firefighter (Kline) is asked back onto the force to help solve a puzzling murder case. Respectable cast. C: Kevin Kline, Mary Elizabeth Mastrantonio, Susan Sarandon, Harvey Keitel, Danny Aiello, Rod Steiger, Alan Rickman. D: Pat O'Connor. CRI [R] 97m. V

Japanese War Bride 1952 ★★★★ WWII veteran finds difficulties when he returns home with his new bride—an Asian nurse with whom he fell in love overseas. Intriguing drama realistically captures the mood of '50's America. C: Don Taylor, Shirley Yamaguchi, Cameron Mitchell, Marie Windsor, Philip Ahn. D: King Vidor. DRA 91m.

Jar, The 1984 ★★ A man's normal life ends when he finds a strange jar filled with some embryonic goo that formalizes itself into a horrid killing moster. C: Gary Wallace, Karen Sjoberg. D: Bruce Toscano. HOR 90m. V

Jarrett 1973 ★★★ Investigator (Ford) encounters a suave villain and a phony preacher with a snake dancing niece while attempting to locate priceless biblical scrolls. TV pilot offers a familiar premise, punched up by solid cast. C: Glenn Ford, Anthony Quayle, Forrest Tucker, Yvonne Craig. D: Barry Shear. ACT 72m. TVM

Jason and the Argonauts 1963 British ★★★★ Jason and his sailing crew must conquer numerous mythological beasts on their journey to steal the Golden Fleece. Well done if somewhat standard mythological fare, elevated by Ray Harryhausen's creations and Bernard Herrmann's score. C: Todd Armstrong, Gary Raymond, Nancy Kovack, Honor Blackman, Nigel Green. D: Don Chaffey. FAM/ACT 104m. V

Jason Goes to Hell: The Final Friday 1993 ★ Another gorefest, with Jason dismembered by cops at outset. But his heart beats and glows, hypnotizing the coroner who. . . . Disgusting. Ninth episode in series claims to be the last, but so did several of the previous ones. (a.k.a. *Friday the 13th Part IX—Jason Goes to Hell*) C: John D. LeMay, Erin Gray, Allison Smith. D: Adam Marcus. HOR [R] 89m. V

Jason's Lyric 1994 ★★★½ Yet another reworking of *Romeo and Juliet*, this time set in the ghettos of Houston. Whitaker is excellent as always; his performace alone is worth the price of admission. C: Allen Payne, Jada Pinkett, Forest Whitaker, Bokeem Woodbine, Suzanne Douglas, Treach. D: Doug McHenry. DRA

Jassy 1947 British ★★★ Dark drama of a Gypsy implicated in the violent and untimely death of her husband. Attractively shot and well-acted melodrama set in the 1800s. C: Margaret Lockwood, Patricia Roc, Dennis Price, Dermot Walsh, Basil Sydney, Nora Swinburne. D: Bernard Knowles. DRA 96m.

Java Head 1934 British ★★★★ An English sailor brings his new Chinese bride back to his narrow-minded hometown. Wong's excellent lead performance supplies the keynote for this intelligent period tale. C: Anna May Wong, Elizabeth Allan, Edmund Gwenn, John Loder, Ralph Richardson. D: J. Walter Ruben. DRA 70m. V

Jaws 1975 ★★★★½ A local law officer (Scheider), a scientist (Dreyfuss), and an old salt (Shaw) join forces to capture a great white shark preying on beach vacationers. Biting suspense relieved only by moments of deliberate hilarity. Topflight direction by Spielberg and Oscar-winning John Williams score. Based on a novel by Peter Benchley; and followed by three increasingly dreadful sequels. C: Roy Scheider, Robert Shaw, Richard Dreyfuss, Lorraine Gary, Murray Hamilton. D: Steven Spielberg. ACT [PG] 124m V

Jaws 2 1978 ★★★½ Sole survivor of first shark hunt (Scheider) thinks the toothy trouble is back again, and he's frustrated when everyone around him thinks he's merely shark shocked. Good suspenseful moments and a fine paranoid Scheider deliver gory thrills. C: Roy Scheider, Lorraine Gary, Murray Hamilton, Joseph Mascolo, Jeffrey Kramer, Collin Wilcox. D: Jeannot Szwarc. ACT [PG] 116m. v

Jaws 3 1983 ★★ Shark runs amok in Sea World, threatening all those with any body part near water. Theatrical release was in 3-D, which boosted enjoyment, but now it's mostly just silly. C: Dennis Quaid, Bess Armstrong, Simon MacCorkindale, Louis Gossett Jr., John Putch, Lea Thompson. D: Joe Alves. ACT [PG] 98m. v

Jaws, The Revenge 1987 ★★ That pesky Great White shark is at it again, this time gnoshing on the lovely Bahamas. The fourth to carry the *Jaws* tag, and the worst of the lot. Van Peebles fans might find his turn as a Rastafarian scientist . . . uhm, interesting. C: Lorraine Gary, Lance Guest, Mario van Peebles, Karen Young, Michael Caine. D: Joseph Sargent. ACT [PG-13] 87m. v

Jaws of Justice 1933 ★★★ Stirring tale of a German shepherd in Canada's frozen north. The dog works hard to keep his master and restore civilization in a remote mining town. C: Terry Kazan, Richard Kazan, Lafe McKee. ACT 55m.

Jaws of Satan 1981 ★ Tame, unexciting horror, as a priest (Weaver) tangles with a king cobra possessed by the devil (!) while other snakes run amok elsewhere in town. Visible glass panes protect the actors, but the audience has to fend for themselves. C: Fritz Weaver, Gretchen Corbett, Jon Korkes, Norman Lloyd. D: Bob Claver. HOR [R] 92m. v

Jaws of the Dragon 1980 ★★½ Black Tiger and White Tiger are rival gang leaders involved in a fight to the death. Good martial arts and a lot of huffing and puffing. C: James Name. ACT [R] 96m. v

Jay Leno—The American Dream 1986 ★★★ The "Tonight Show" host is your host here in this look at all kinds of American trophies, including cars, clothes, houses and food. C: Jay Leno. D: Ira Wohl. COM 49m. v

Jayhawkers, The 1959 ★★★½ Antebellum Western about an honest farmer and an ambitious profiteer who grapple for political domination of the state. Florid, unevenly paced fare. C: Jeff Chandler, Fess Parker, Nicole Maurey, Henry Silva, Herbert Rudley. D: Melvin Frank. WST 100m. v

Jayne Mansfield: A Symbol of the '50s 1980 *See* **Jayne Mansfield Story, The**

Jayne Mansfield Story, The 1980 ★★★½ Biography of Monroe wanna-be Mansfield (Anderson), who this movie claims could have been big star. Trite but flashy, with good work by Schwarzenegger as Jayne's bodybuilder husband. (a.k.a. *Jayne Mansfield: A Symbol of the '50s*) C: Loni Anderson, Arnold Schwarzenegger, Raymond Buktenica, G.D. Spradlin. D: Dick Lowry. DRA 100m. TVM v

Jazz Age, The 1929 ★★★½ When his sister runs into trouble, dashing Fairbanks comes to the rescue. Family troubles are compounded when Doug falls for the daughter of his father's worst enemy. Good action and a fun chase highlight this largely silent curio. C: Douglas Fairbanks, Jr., Marceline Day. D: Lynn Shores. ACT 62m.

Jazz Boat 1960 British ★★★ Handyman (Newley) must follow through on his fib about being a criminal. Lightweight study of the British rock 'n' roll subculture features a lively Newley despite a weak caper script. C: Anthony Newley, Anne Aubrey, Lionel Jeffries, David Lodge, Bernie Winters, James Booth. D: Ken Hughes. CRI 90m.

Jazz on a Summer's Day 1959 ★★★★½ Gala record of 1958 Newport Jazz Festival features multitude of big-name talent. Definite must-see for jazz enthusiasts. C: Louis Armstrong, Chico Hamilton, Big Maybelle, Chuck Berry, Gerry Mulligan, Thelonious Monk, Anita O'Day, Mahalia Jackson. D: Bert Stern. DOC 85m. v

Jazz Singer, The 1927 ★★★★ As a movie, this schmaltzy tale of cantor's son (Jolson) determined to be popular singer isn't much. As history, it's indispensable viewing. Introducing the human voice to the screen for the first time, this mostly silent film explodes into brilliance when Jolson starts singing. Songs include "My Mammy," "Toot Toot Tootsie Goodbye," and "Blue Skies." Remade twice. C: Al Jolson, May McAvoy, Warner Oland, Eugenie Besserer, William Demarest, Roscoe Karns. D: Alan Crosland. MUS 89m. v

Jazz Singer, The 1953 ★★★ Earnest if unnecessary remake of the 1927 first talkie replaces Jolson with Thomas as rebellious son determined to sing "Mammy." Careful, tight direction and good support. C: Danny Thomas, Peggy Lee, Mildred Dunnock, Eduard Franz, Tom Tully, Allyn Joslyn. D: Michael Curtiz. MUS 107m. v

Jazz Singer, The 1980 ★ Yet another remake of historic first talkie: Diamond makes his film debut as cantor's son who wants to sing. Only for the star's fans. C: Neil Diamond, Laurence Olivier, Lucie Arnaz, Catlin Adams, Franklyn Ajaye. D: Richard Fleischer. MUS [PG] 115m. v

Jazzband Five, The 1932 German ★★★½ Wrongly accused as accomplice in auto theft committed by Lorre, struggling acrobat Jugo tries to clear herself and reunite with her lover Shall, who owns the stolen car. Good drama with nice performances in this pre-Nazi German crime/romance story. C: Jenny Jugo, Rolf von Goth, Theo Shall, Fritz Klippel. D: Erich Engel. CRI 88m.

J.C. 1971 ★★ The leader of a motorcycle

gang escapes out west to save his father, a religious fanatic who's under fire from the authorities. Unrelenting violence. C: Bill McGaha, Slim Pickens. D: William F. McGaha. ACT [R] 97m. v

JD and the Salt Flat Kid 1978 ★★ On the way to Nashville and singing success, a talented kid gets involved in lots of trouble. C: Jesse Turner, Mickey Gilley, Slim Pickens. D: Alex Grasshoff. COM [PG] 90m. v

J.D.'s Revenge 1976 ★★★ New Orleans student becomes possessed by the spirit of a '30s mobster and goes on a murderous rampage of revenge. Good horror suspense with fine African-American cast. C: Glynn Turman, Joan Pringle, Louis Gossett, Jr., Carl Crudup, James Louis Watkins, Alice Jubert. D: Arthur Marks. HOR [R] 96m. v

Je T'Aime, Je T'Aime 1972 French ★★★★½ Inventive fable of time and memory about despondent individual (Rich) who agrees to travel back in time at behest of two scientists. This works both as great comedy and as intriguing social satire. C: Claude Rich, Olga Georges-Picot, Amouk Ferjac. D: Alain Resnais. COM 91m.

Je Vous Aime 1981 French ★★★½ Deneuve leads a strong cast, playing a woman torn between career and marriage; the whole seems less than the sum of its parts, though. A lukewarm soaper. C: Catherine Deneuve, Jean-Louis Trintignant, Gerard Depardieu. D: Claude Berri. DRA 105m.

Jealousy 1945 ★★★ An innocent physician (Loder), who has taken up with the wife of a prominent writer (Asther), becomes the prime suspect in the man's murder. Interesting but uninvolving attempt to make an American B-film in an arty, European style. C: John Loder, Nils Asther, Jane Randolph, Karen Morley. D: Gustav Machaty. CRI 71m.

Jealousy 1984 ★★★½ Episodic television drama features three separate stories that outline the consequences of what happens when jealousy gets out of hand. The stories vary in quality, while Dickinson displays her versatility in roles ranging from a wealthy sophisticate to a country singer. C: Angie Dickinson, Paul Michael Glaser, David Carradine, Richard Mulligan, Bo Svenson. D: Jeffrey Bloom. DRA 100m. TVM v

Jealousy, Italian Style 1970 *See* **Pizza Triangle, The**

Jean de Florette 1987 French ★★★★ Two bitter farmers (Montand, Auteil) block a spring in an attempt to ruin an unsuspecting newcomer (Depardieu). Splendid scenery and excellent performances help make Berri's adaptation of Marcel Pagnol's novel a superior soap opera. Followed by *Manon of the Spring*. C: Yves Montand, Gerard Depardieu, Daniel Auteuil, Elisabeth Depardieu. D: Claude Berri. DRA [PG] 122m. v

Jeanne Eagels 1957 ★★½ Novak plays the famous '20s Broadway actress. Fair dramatization, but encumbered by Novak's comatose performance. C: Kim Novak, Jeff Chandler, Agnes Moorehead, Gene Lockhart, Virginia Grey. D: George Sidney. DRA 109m.

Jeannie 1941 British ★★★★ Diverting lark about Scottish woman (Mullen) touring Vienna and coming into inheritance. Redgrave steals film as rough Yorkshire salesman who courts her. (a.k.a. *Girl in Distress*) Remade as musical *Let's Be Happy*. C: Michael Redgrave, Barbara Mullen, Wilfrid Lawson, Kay Hammond, Albert Lieven, Edward Chapman, Googie Withers, Rachel Kempson, Ian Fleming. D: Harold French. COM 101m.

Jekyll & Hyde 1990 ★★★ Caine is the doctor with the split personality in this mediocre version of the Robert Louis Stevenson classic. C: Michael Caine, Cheryl Ladd, Joss Ackland, Ronald Pickup, Kim Thomson, Lionel Jeffries, Kevin McNally, Lee Montague. D: David Wickes. HOR 100m. TVM

Jekyll & Hyde . . . Together Again 1982 ★★½ Updating of Robert Louis Stevenson story features Blankfield as scientist with mysterious white powder that changes his personality from normal to monstrous. Though Blankfield is good at physical comedy, leaden satire is largely inept and unfunny. C: Mark Blankfield, Bess Armstrong, Krista Errickson, Tim Thomerson. D: Jerry Belson. COM [R] 87m. v

Jenatsch 1987 Swiss ★★★ After interviewing a geologist about a centuries-old murder, a journalist hallucinates visions of the crime, which wreaks havoc on his everyday life. Interesting idea but unimaginative execution. C: Michael Voita, Christine Boisson, Vittorio Mezzorgiorno, Jean Bouise, Laura Betti, Carole Bouquet. D: Daniel Schmid. CRI 97m.

Jennie Gerhardt 1933 ★★★★½ Turn-of-the-century rags-to-riches weepie, from Dreiser story. Effective vehicle for Sidney who is good, as usual. C: Sylvia Sidney, Donald Cook, Mary Astor, Edward Arnold, Louise Carter, Cora Sue Collins, H.B. Warner. D: Marion Gering. DRA 85m.

Jennifer 1953 ★★★½ Lupino as a caretaker at a mansion where a murder is committed. Occasionally suspenseful drama features an effectively gloomy atmosphere, but limited plot development. C: Ida Lupino, Howard Duff, Robert Nichols, Mary Shipp. D: Joel Newton. CRI 73m.

Jennifer 1978 ★★★ A poor girl (Pelikan) at an exclusive prep school gets back at her tormenting classmates by using her inherited ability to command snakes. A student revenge plot similar to *Carrie*. (a.k.a. *Jennifer the Snake Goddess*) C: Lisa Pelikan, Bert Convy, Nina Foch, John Gavin. D: Brice Mack. HOR [PG] 90m. v

Jennifer: A Woman's Story 1979 ★★★ Montgomery plays the widow of a shipbuilding magnate, engaged in mighty boardroom power struggles while trying to retain control of the business. TV pilot, based on British TV series *The Foundation*, is a showcase for Montgomery. C: Elizabeth Montgomery, Bradford Dillman, Scott Hylands. D: Guy Green. DRA 104m. TVM

Jennifer 8 1992 ★★★ Haunted big-city cop transfers to a sleepy suburb, investigates serial killer who preys on blind women. Implausible thriller has some grisly jolts. C: Andy Garcia, Uma Thurman, Lance Henriksen, Kathy Baker, Graham Beckel, Kevin Conway, John Malkovich. D: Bruce Robinson. CRI [R] 127m. V

Jennifer on My Mind 1971 ★★ Story told in flashbacks of a bored young American couple who meet and fall in love, do drugs in Venice, then come home and do more. An unintentional parody of its own genre. C: Michael Brandon, Tippy Walker, Lou Gilbert, Steve Vinovich, Peter Bonerz, Renee Taylor, Chuck McCann, Barry Bostwick, Jeff Conaway. D: Noel Black. DRA [R] 90m. V

Jennifer the Snake Goddess 1978 *See* **Jennifer**

Jenny 1970 ★★★ A young pregnant woman looks for a husband. Modest weeper gives Alda and Thomas ample opportunity to show off their dramatic acting skills C: Marlo Thomas, Alan Alda, Vincent Gardenia, Elizabeth Wilson. D: George Bloomfield. DRA [PG] 88m. V

Jenny Lamour 1948 French ★★★★ A singer (Delair) thinks she may have killed a producer while fending off his advances; her husband (Blier), finding the body, then becomes a suspect. Jouvet plays the worldly cop on the case. Excellent, atmospheric story, with drama and high suspense. Clouzot's second feature. (a.k.a. *Quai des Orfevres*) C: Suzy Delair, Bernard Blier. D: Henri-Georges Clouzot. CRI 102m.

Jeopardy 1953 ★★½ Flaccid thriller in which wife Stanwyck spends half the film trying to prevent her trapped husband from drowning, then gets kidnapped by psycho killer Meeker. Overly drawn-out suspense. C: Barbara Stanwyck, Barry Sullivan, Ralph Meeker, Lee Aaker. D: John Sturges. CRI 69m.

Jeremiah Johnson 1972 ★★★★½ Authentic wilderness tale of the 1850s as ex-soldier (Redford) decides to become a mountain man and trapper. Simple yet involving story line and meticulous direction result in an engrossing adventure. C: Robert Redford, Will Geer, Stefan Gierasch, Allyn McLerie, Charles Tyner. D: Sydney Pollack. WST [PG] 107m. V

Jeremy 1973 ★★★★ A sensitive teen (Benson) falls in love with a new student at his school (O'Connor). Their romance ends when she must leave New York. Low-key charm with real feelings. C: Robby Benson, Glynnis O'Connor, Len Bari, Leonard Cimino, Ned Wilson, Chris Bohn. D: Arthur Barron. DRA [PG] 90m.

Jericho Fever 1993 ★★★ When terrorists threaten to unleash a deadly worldwide disease, two doctors try and stop them. C: Stephanie Zimbalist, Perry King. CRI [PG-13] 88m. V

Jericho Mile, The 1979 ★★★★ A convict (Strauss) sentenced to life in prison regains his dignity by attempting to become an Olympic miler. Realistic and gripping. C: Peter Strauss, Roger E. Mosley, Brian Dennehy, Ed Lauter. D: Michael Mann. DRA 100m. TVM V

Jerk, The 1979 ★★ A white boy who can't fit in with his adopted black family sets out to find fame and fortune. Martin's first starring role emphasizes his early, broad brand of humor; mainly for diehard fans. C: Steve Martin, Bernadette Peters, Catlin Adams, Mabel King, Richard Ward, Dick Williams, Bill Macy, Jackie Mason. D: Carl Reiner. COM [R] 94m. V

Jerk Too, The 1984 ★★½ A white man raised by black sharecroppers sets out on a cross-country journey to stop his lady love from marrying an aristocrat. Sequel of Steve Martin's film centers on Blankfield's hyperactive clowning with several cameos. C: Mark Blankfield, Ray Walston, Stacey Nelkin, Thalmus Rasulala, Mabel King, Pat McCormick, Gwen Verdon, Jimmie Walker, Martin Mull, Lainie Kazan. D: Michael Schultz. COM 100m. TVM

Jerky Boys, The 1995 ★★★ Complications ensue when the title pranksters use crank phone calls as a way to be sociable. They're no Wayne and Garth, but deft mounting helps the cult radio duo dial up their signature moronic nonsense. Taste gets put on hold. C: John G. Brennan, Kamal Ahmed, Alan Arkin, William Hickey. D: James Melkonian. COM [R] 82m. V

Jerrico, The Wonder Clown *See* **Three Ring Circus**

Jersey Girl 1993 ★★★ A young girl from the Garden State dreams about living the good life across the river in Manhattan. C: Jami Gertz, Molly Price, Star Jasper. D: David Burton Morris. COM [PG-13] 95m. V

Jerusalem File, The 1972 U.S. ★★ American archaeology student finds himself embroiled in a Mid East espionage plot following the Six Day War. Convincing political milieu. C: Bruce Davison, Nicol Williamson, Daria Halprin, Donald Pleasence, Ian Hendry, Koya Yair Rubin. D: John Flynn. DRA [PG] 96m.

Jesse 1988 ★★½ The true story of a heroic nurse (Remick), administering medical treatments to inhabitants of a rural area. TV movie embellishes facts to come up with a story. C: Lee Remick, Scott Wilson, Leon Rippy. D: Glenn Jordan. DRA [PG] 94m. TVM V

Jesse James 1939 ★★★★ Western saga of the ruthless bank robber and his brother Frank is pure entertainment, emphasizing everything a good shoot-'em-up should have, except maybe the truth. Power and Fonda are great as the brothers. Hollywood mythmaking at its lavish best. C: Tyrone Power, Henry Fonda, Nancy Kelly, Randolph Scott, Henry Hull, Brian Donlevy, John Carradine, Jane Darwell. D: Henry King. WST 105m. v

Jesse James Meets Frankenstein's Daughter 1965 ★★ Yes, it's just as tacky as the title suggests, but it's actually Dr. F's *grand*daughter who tangles with the gunslinger, putting the monster's brain in the head of Jesse's sidekick. Bad-film fans just might enjoy it. C: John Lupton, Estelita, Cal Bolder, Steven Geray, Jim Davis. D: William Beaudine. HOR 95m. v

Jesse James vs. the Daltons 1954 ★★½ The rumored son of Jesse James joins the Dalton gang to find out the truth about himself and see if his alleged father is still alive. Western trades on the James name, but offers nothing new. Originally released in 3-D. C: Brett King, Barbara Lawrence, James Griffith, Bill Phipps, John Cliff. D: William Castle. WST 65m.

Jesse James's Women 1954 ★★½ During his career as an outlaw, James finds time for fleeting relations with many women in a Mississippi town. Limp direction undermines an unusual premise. C: Don Barry, Jack Buetel, Peggie Castle, Lita Baron. D: Donald Barry. WST 83m.

Jesse Owens Story, The 1984 ★★★★ Fine biographical drama based on the life of the black track star who won four gold medals in front of Hitler at the 1936 Berlin Olympics. An uncompromising look at Owens' trials and triumphs, pre- and post-Olympics. C: Dorian Harewood, Georg Stanford Brown, Debbi Morgan, Tom Bosley, LeVar Burton, Ronny Cox, Greg Morris, Ben Vereen. D: Richard Irving. DRA 175m. TVM v

Jessica 1962 ★★★ A beautiful young midwife (Dickinson) arrives in a Sicilian village and drives the men crazy; their wives "go on strike" so that she'll go out of business and go home. Picturesque silliness. C: Angie Dickinson, Maurice Chevalier, Noel-Noel, Gabriele Ferzetti, Sylva Koscina, Agnes Moorehead. D: Jean Negulesco. DRA 112m.

Jessi's Girls 1983 ★★★ When her husband is murdered, a woman puts together an all-female gang and they race off to find the culprits. Surprisingly effective. C: Sondra Currie, Regina Carrol. WST [R] 86m. v

Jester, The 1937 *See* **Der Purimshpiler**

Jesus 1979 ★★★½ Life of the biblical founder of Christianity. Sincere but ordinary; shot on location in Israel. C: Brian Deacon, Rivka Noiman, Yossef Shiloah, Niko Nitai, Gadi Roi, David Goldberg. D: Peter Sykes, John Krish. DRA [G] 118m. v

Jesus Christ Superstar 1973 ★★★★ Superstar trendsetting Andrew Lloyd Webber/Tim Rice rock opera based on their Broadway hit looks at last seven days of Christ in an unconventional manner. Filmed on location in the Holy Land. Moving, with striking concept and well sung. Anderson outstanding as Judas. C: Ted Neeley, Carl Anderson, Yvonne Elliman, Barry Dennen, Joshua Mostel, Bob Bingham. D: Norman Jewison. MUS [G] 108m. v

Jesus of Montreal 1989 Canadian ★★★½ Actors stir up controversy when they stage an unorthodox Passion Play. Provocative story is compelling and witty. Heading fine cast, Bluteau gives a haunting performance as Christ-like actor. C: Lothaire Bluteau, Catherine Wilkening, Johanne-Marie Tremblay, Remy Girard, Robert Lepage, Gilles Pelletier. D: Denys Arcand. DRA [R] 119m. v

Jesus of Nazareth 1977 ★★★★ Zeffirelli's painstakingly detailed life of Christ, with Powell charismatic as a Messiah with mesmerizing blue eyes. Hussey is a visually perfect Mary, and Bancroft shines as Mary Magdalene. A visual feast, worth the long sit. C: Robert Powell, Anne Bancroft, James Mason, Laurence Olivier, Rod Steiger. D: Franco Zeffirelli. DRA 371m. v

Jesus Trip, The 1971 ★★★½ Offbeat motorcycle drama as a gang of hoods hides out in a convent to escape from the police. Sounds silly, but manages moments of sincerity and poignancy. C: Tippy Walker, Robert Porter, Billy "Green" Bush, Frank Orsati. D: Russ Mayberry. DRA [PG] 86m. v

Jet Over the Atlantic 1959 ★★★ Panic ensues after a bomb is discovered during transatlantic flight. Solid aviation suspense. C: Guy Madison, Virginia Mayo, George Raft, Ilona Massey. D: Byron Haskin. ACT 92m. v

Jet Pilot 1957 ★★½ American Cold War air ace (Wayne) reforms a Soviet agent (Leigh). Flat, laughable Howard Hughes fiasco took seven years to release. Chuck Yeager performed some of the flying stunts. C: John Wayne, Janet Leigh, Jay C. Flippen, Roland Winters, Hans Conried. D: Josef von Sternberg. DRA [G] 113m. v

Jetsons: The Movie 1990 ★★★ Big-screen adaptation of popular '60s cartoon series suffers from TV animation aesthetics and unnecessary, often weighty messages. Doesn't live up to the clever humor of the original. D: William Hanna, Joseph Barbera. FAM/COM [G] 82m. v

Jeu de Massacre 1967 *See* **Killing Game, The**

Jewel in the Crown 1984 British ★★★★★ Magnificent Emmy award-winning British TV miniseries strikingly depicts personal and political conflicts during the last years of English rule of India. Passionate drama, well acted and beautifully photographed on location. Originally shown in 14 episodes. C: Charles Dance, Susan Woolridge, Art Malik. D: Christopher Morahan, Jim O'Brien. DRA 750m. TVM v

Jewel of the Nile 1985 ★★★½ *Romancing the Stone* sequel has Douglas in pursuit of kidnapped Turner in an okay attempt to leap into Indiana Jones territory. Stars transcend shrill direction; entertaining fare. C: Michael Douglas, Kathleen Turner, Danny DeVito. D: Lewis Teague. ACT [PG] 106m. V

Jewel Robbery 1932 ★★★★ Fast and furious comedy/adventure with wealthy Countess (Francis) being romanced by jewel thief (Powell). Full of snappy repartee, but remarkably similar to Lubitsch classic *Trouble in Paradise*, made the same year. C: William Powell, Kay Francis, Hardie Albright, Helen Vinson, Herman Bing. D: William Dieterle. COM 70m.

Jewish Jester, The 1937 *See* **Der Purimshpiler**

Jewish King Lear, The 1935 Yiddish ★★★ Famous Jacob Gordin play that takes Shakespeare play to turn-of-the-century Vilna, with pious father dividing his fortune among his daughters with disastrous results. Stilted, but of historical interest. C: Maurice Krohner, Fannie Levenstein, Miriam Grossman, Morris Weisman, Janet Paskevitch, Morris Tarlofky. D: Harry Tomashefsky. DRA 86m.

Jewish Luck 1925 Russian ★★★★ Delightful silent comedy of Sholem Aleichem stories about daydreaming Menachem Mendl and his various unsuccessful business ventures. Dream sequence in which he becomes the world's greatest Jewish matchmaker is justly famous. C: Solomon Mikhoels, Tamara Edelheim, T. Khazak, M. Goldblat, Y. Shidlo. D: Alexander Granovsky. COM 100m.

Jezebel 1938 ★★★★½ Willful Southern belle (Davis) loses lover (Fonda) then tries to get him back in pre-Civil War soap opera, giving Davis one of her showiest roles. Whether shocking her friends at a ball dressed in red, or begging Fonda's forgiveness in white, she's brilliant, and deserving of her second Oscar. C: Bette Davis, Henry Fonda, George Brent, Fay Bainter, Margaret Lindsay, Donald Crisp, Spring Byington. D: William Wyler. DRA 105m. V

Jezebel's Kiss 1990 ★★★ Irresistably beautiful woman captivates men of hometown in seemy tale of seduction and blackmail. C: Katherine Barrese, Malcolm McDowell, Meg Foster. D: Harvey Keith. DRA [R] 95m. V

JFK 1991 ★★★★½ Absorbing tale of New Orleans D.A. Jim Garrison's investigation into the Kennedy assassination and his relentless struggle to prove that history's account of this tragedy is different from the actual truth. Star-studded cast accents the drama; lightning quick editing and remarkable cinematography were honored with Oscars. "Director's cut," on video, runs 206m. C: Kevin Costner, Sissy Spacek, Kevin Bacon, Tommy Lee Jones, Laurie Metcalf, Joe Pesci, Donald Sutherland, John Candy, Jack Lemmon, Walter Matthau. D: Oliver Stone. DRA [R] 189m. V

JFK: Reckless Youth 1993 ★★★½ A clear-eyed view of the wild early years of the young man who would become the president. C: Patrick Dempsey, Terry Kinney, Loren Dean, Yolanda Jilot. D: Harry Winer. DRA 182m. TVM V

Jigsaw 1949 ★★★ An assistant district attorney inquires into a series of murders committed by a racist group. Mediocre detective story with a message, notable for surprise celebrity cameos (Dietrich, Garfield, and Henry Fonda, etc.) (a.k.a. *Gun Moll*) C: Franchot Tone, Jean Wallace, Myron McCormick. D: Fletcher Markle. CRI 70m.

Jigsaw 1968 ★★★½ While trying to clear himself of a murder he can't remember, scientist (Dillman) discovers that he may have been drugged with LSD. Good ideas suffer from dizzying '60s pacing and information overload. Remake of *Mirage*. C: Harry Guardino, Bradford Dillman, Hope Lange. D: James Goldstone. ACT 97m.

Jigsaw 1971 ★★★½ A missing persons detective is accused of murder after being discovered in the apartment of a slain diplomat. An exciting chase and an effective performance by Wainwright are the highlights of this pilot for crime series. (a.k.a. *Man on the Move*) C: James Wainwright, Richard Kiley, Vera Miles. D: William Graham. CRI 100m. TVM

Jigsaw Man, The 1983 British ★★★★ British double agent (Caine) defects to the Soviet Union, undergoes plastic surgery and returns unrecognizable to garner secrets in England. Diverting, twisty thriller. C: Michael Caine, Laurence Olivier, Susan George, Robert Powell. D: Terence Young. DRA [PG] 90m. V

Jim Thorpe—All American 1951 ★★★ Biography of famed athlete forced to give up his Olympic medals because he played professional baseball. Lancaster is good in title role, but direction is routine. C: Burt Lancaster, Charles Bickford, Phyllis Thaxter. D: Michael Curtiz. DRA 107m. V

Jimi Hendrix 1973 ★★★★ Well-done documentary probes tragic life of rock star Hendrix with interviews and performance footage. Makes one wonder why no one has attempted a fictional biography of this complex talent. C: Jimi Hendrix. D: Joe Boyd, John Head, Gary Weis. DOC [R] 102m. V

Jimmy and Sally 1933 ★★★½ Trevor bails her go-getting boyfriend (Dunn) out of trouble with gangsters, then helps him with his work as a publicity agent without taking credit. Energetic performances help this nicely paced comedy/drama. C: James Dunn, Claire Trevor. D: James Tinling. COM 68m. V

Jimmy B. & Andre 1980 ★★★½ A Greek restaurant owner in Detroit (Karras) tries to adopt a black child (Yates). Fair drama (based on a true story) centers on the relationship between Karras and the boy. C: Alex Karras, Curtis Yates, Susan Clark, Marge Sinclair. D: Guy Green. DRA 105m. TVM

Jimmy Hollywood 1994 ★★★½ A dreamer

(Pesci) wants to be a movie star; with his buddy (Slater), he cooks up a scheme involving vigilante violence on video that begins to go awry. Abril is fetching as his long-suffering girlfriend. Cute, though slight. C: Joe Pesci, Christian Slater, Victoria Abril, Jason Beghe, John Cothran, Jr. D: Barry Levinson. COM [R] 109m. v

Jimmy the Gent 1934 ★★★½ Offbeat gangster comedy has Cagney pretending to reform for Davis' benefit. Two stars invigorate slight script with machine-gun comic timing. C: James Cagney, Bette Davis, Alice White, Allen Jenkins. D: Michael Curtiz. COM 67m.

Jimmy the Kid 1982 ★★ Poor little rich boy (Coleman) is kidnapped by dizzy crooks who teach him how to be a real kid. Dumb slapstick aimed directly at kids, who are better off elsewhere. Based on a Donald Westlake novel. C: Gary Coleman, Paul LeMat, Ruth Gordon. D: Gary Nelson. FAM/COM [PG] 95m. v

Jinx Money 1948 ★★★ The Bowery Boys find themselves in possession of $50,000 over which a group of poker playing gamblers have been fighting. Murder mystery elements buoy this average series entry. COM

Jinxed! 1982 ★★½ A Las Vegas lounge singer (Midler) teams up with a blackjack dealer (Wahl) to get even with her no-good lover (Torn). Incoherent fiasco, with the men looking uncomfortable and Midler rising above material by sheer comic will. C: Bette Midler, Ken Wahl, Rip Torn. D: Don Siegel. COM [R] 104m. v

Jitterbugs 1943 ★★★ Laurel and Hardy pose as a society matron and a Southern colonel to help Blaine recover family property from gangsters. Better than most of the boys' later films, this one bogs down occasionally in sub-plot. C: Stan Laurel, Oliver Hardy, Vivian Blaine. D: Mal Clair. COM 74m.

Jitters, The 1989 ★ Bizarre adventure, from Chinese fantasy series, about zombie/vampires that can leap tall buildings in a single bound! If weirdness alone has merit, by all means tune in. C: Sal Viviano, Marilyn Tokuda. D: John Fasano. SFI [R] 80m. v

Jivaro 1954 ★★½ Various adventurers search for hidden treasure deep in the Amazon jungle. Beautiful Fleming and a cast of seminotables spice the action. C: Fernando Lamas, Rhonda Fleming, Brian Keith, Lon Chaney, Jr., Rita Moreno. D: Edward Ludwig. ACT 91m.

Jive Turkey 1976 ★ Low-rent fists-and-gunplay shlock. C: Paul Harris, Frank DeKova, Serena. D: Bill Brame. ACT v

Jo Jo Dancer—Your Life Is Calling 1986 ★★½ Pryor wrote, directed and starred in this bleak, autobiographical film about a comic who self-destructs under the influence of drugs and bad judgment. Lots of pain, little laughter; Pryor shortchanges the audience and himself. C: Richard Pryor, Debbie Allen, Carmen McRae, Paula Kelly. D: Richard Pryor. DRA 97m. v

Joan of Arc 1948 ★★★½ Ornate epic of Maid of Orleans (Bergman) assisting the dauphin of France to the throne, then being martyred as heretic. Bergman tries hard, but film's literal rendering of Maxwell Anderson's play has too many dull stretches between the opulently produced battle scenes. C: Ingrid Bergman, Jose Ferrer, Francis L. Sullivan, J. Carrol Naish. D: Victor Fleming. DRA 100m. v

Joan of Ozark 1942 ★★½ Mountain woman (Canova) inadvertently intercepts Nazi carrier pigeon, setting off a wild series of events. Patriotic film with lots of music. (a.k.a. *Queen of Spies*) C: Judy Canova, Joe Brown, Eddie Foy, Jr. D: Joseph Santley. COM 80m.

Joan of Paris 1942 ★★★★½ To help Allied pilots escape the Nazis, a French Resistance leader (Morgan) sacrifices herself. Excellent, absorbing drama with outstanding acting. C: Michele Morgan, Paul Henreid, Thomas Mitchell, May Robson, Alan Ladd. D: Robert Stevenson. DRA 91m. v

Joan of the Angels 1962 Polish ★★★ In 17th-century Poland, a nun is possessed by demons. Religious figures from many faiths try exorcism, but are swallowed up by overwhelming spiritual horror. Intense at times, but ultimately an overblown gothic exercise. (a.k.a. *Mother Joan of the Angels* and *The Devil and the Nun*) C: Lucyna Winnicka, Mieczyslaw Voit. D: Jerzy Kawalerowicz. DRA 101m.

Joanna 1968 British ★★★½ An art student (Waite) new to London joins a fast crowd and gets lessons in life. Donald Sutherland is memorable in a small role. Colorful characters and the London scene bolster thin story. C: Genevieve Waite, Christian Doermer, Donald Sutherland. D: Michael Sarne. DRA [R] 107m.

Jocks 1987 ★ Rag-tag college tennis team tries to take time out from partying and women to win a Las Vegas tournament. Typical exploitation comedy features usual quota of nudity and grossness without any of the laughs. C: Scott Strader, Perry Lang, Mariska Hargitay, Richard Roundtree, Christopher Lee. D: Steve Carver. COM [R] 90m. v

Joe 1970 ★★★½ An executive (Patrick) forms a strange relationship with a bigoted factory worker (Boyle) who helps him search for his daughter, lost among the hippies. Implausible, sometimes violent story made watchable by strong performances. C: Peter Boyle, Dennis Patrick, Audrey Caire, Susan Sarandon. D: John G. Avildsen. DRA [R] 107m. v

Joe and Ethel Turp Call on the President 1939 ★★★½ Silly but pleasant yarn about Brooklyn postman Gargan petitioning the President when he loses his job. From a Damon Runyon short story. C: Ann Sothern,

Lewis Stone, Walter Brennan. D: Robert B. Sinclair. DRA 70m.
Joe Bob Briggs: Bad Girls Go to Hell ★ Brainless housewife runs off to New York after killing her husband and learns what hell really is from group of sadistic sex perverts. Tasteless, demeaning trash from cult sleaze director. So bad it's mesmerizing. COM
Joe Bob Briggs: Deadly Weapons ★★ Porn stars Chesty Morgan and Harry Reems use their God-given talents to wreck havoc on the Mafia in this campy, low-budget sex farce. Sleazy but fun. COM
Joe Butterfly 1957 ★★ Conniving interpreter makes a monkey out of American servicemen stationed in Japan after WWII. Dated military comedy. C: Audie Murphy, Burgess Meredith, Keenan Wynn. D: Jesse Hibbs. COM 90m.
Joe Cocker: Mad Dogs And Englishmen 1971 British ★★★★ Joyful filming of Cocker's 1970 American tour with big band led by Russell, and stellar back-up singers Coolidge and Keys; Linnear leads the choir. Featured songs: "With a Little Help From My Friends," "Darlin" Be Home Soon," "Feelin" Alright." C: Joe Cocker, Leon Russell, Rita Coolidge, Bobby Keys, Claudia Linnear. D: Pierre Adidge. MUS [PG] 119m. V
Joe Dakota 1957 ★★★ Mahoney investigates the death of a Native American friend in a small town. Well-intentioned consciousness-raiser. C: Jock Mahoney, Luana Patten. D: Richard Bartlett. CRI 79m.
Joe Hill 1971 Swedish ★★★ Fictional biography of labor leader Joe Hill chronicles his role as union organizer through eventual execution on trumped-up murder charges. Too sentimental for its own good, this deifies Hill without showing who he really was. Joan Baez sings title song. C: Thommy Berggren, Ania Schmidt. D: Bo Widerberg. DRA [PG] 114m.
Joe Kidd 1972 ★★★ A drifter (Eastwood) stumbles on a feud between the original Mexican settlers and some big American landowners in New Mexico. His decision about who to support is weighted when he falls for Garcia. C: Clint Eastwood, Robert Duvall, John Saxon, Stella Garcia. D: John Sturges. WST [PG] 88m. V
Joe Louis Story, The 1953 ★★★ Real-life boxer Wallace portrays famed heavyweight champion in all-too-standard movie biography. While use of newsreel footage pads out routine story, Wallace's lack of thespian skills ultimately knocks this out of contention. Only surprise is Anita Ellis singing "I'll Be Around." C: Coley Wallace, Paul Stewart. D: Robert Gordon. DRA 88m. V
Joe Macbeth 1955 British ★★★½ Update of Shakespeare's tragedy puts action in '30s underworld, with gangster (Douglas) prodded by wife (Roman) into killing his way up to becoming "king" of organized crime. Film fails because it lacks the moral impact of original. An interesting try, though. C: Paul Douglas, Ruth Roman. D: Ken Hughes. CRI 90m.

Joe Palooka Likable minor '40s Monogram series based on Ham Fisher's comic strip about the life and loves of the boxer Joe Palooka. Joe Kirkwood, Jr., was serviceable as Joe and Leon Erroll was always great fun as his manager and pal, Knobby Walsh. The strip was first filmed, less faithfully, in 1934, with Stu Erwin and Jimmy Durante.

Palooka (1934)
Joe Palooka, Champ (1946)
Fighting Mad (1948)
Joe Palooka in Winner Take All (1948)
Joe Palooka in the Big Fight (1949)
Joe Palooka in the Counterpunch (1949)
Humphrey Takes a Chance (1950)
Joe Palooka in the Squared Circle (1950)
Joe Palooka Meets Humphrey (1950)
Joe Palooka in the Triple Cross (1951)

Joe Palooka 1934 *See* **Palooka**
Joe Palooka, Champ 1946 ★★★ First entry in the series, based on the comic strip, about an affable but simple young fighter who's groomed for big ring success. A little fun, a little nifty action—and Errol, as trainer Knobby Walsh, keeps things moving. Some very famous boxers have cameos, including Joe Louis. C: Leon Errol, Elyse Knox, Joe Kirkwood, Jr. D: Reginald Le Borg. ACT 70m.
Joe Palooka in the Big Fight 1949 ★★★ All the training pays off as Joe goes after the boxing championship and gets involved with gangsters. More series color, with oddball characters straight from the strip. C: Leon Errol, Joe Kirkwood, Jr., Lina Romay. D: Cyril Endfield. ACT 66m.
Joe Palooka in the Counterpunch 1949 ★★½ Further battles—in the ring and in South America—in the life of America's prize pugilist. Audience-pleasing series entry. C: Leon Errol, Joe Kirkwood, Jr., Elyse Knox. D: Reginald Le Borg. ACT 74m.
Joe Palooka in the Squared Circle 1950 ★★★½ Kirkwood returns as the comic book pugster, this time witnessing a Mob killing. The body is nowhere to be found and the press doesn't believe Kirkwood's story. Enjoyable *Joe Palooka* series entry with a good climactic fight scene. C: Joe Kirkwood, Jr., James Gleason, Lois Hall. D: Reginald Le Borg. ACT 63m.
Joe Palooka in Triple Cross 1951 ★★★ The last of the *Joe Palooka* films has Kirkwood and spouse Mager kidnapped by gangsters. The pugilist is told to throw his next

bout—or else! Will Palooka do the right thing? No surprises in this lesser series entry. C: Joe Kirkwood, Jr., James Gleason, Cathy Downs. D: Reginald Le Borg. ACT 60m.

Joe Palooka in Winner Take All 1948 ★★★½ Frawley takes on the role of Kirkwood's trainer, preparing Joe Palooka for that proverbial "big fight." Not much talk but plenty of boxing bravado in this *Rocky* predecessor. C: Joe Kirkwood, Jr., Elyse Knox, William Frawley. D: Reginald Le Borg. ACT 64m.

Joe Palooka Meets Humphrey 1950 ★★★½ Kirkwood leaves the boxing ring to go on his honeymoon, but gets talked into charity brawl with pugilist Coogan. Errol plays dual role as manager of both fighters. Dumb but fun, with good performances. C: Leon Errol, Joe Kirkwood, Jr., Robert Coogan. D: Jean Yarbrough. ACT 65m.

Joe Panther 1976 ★★★½ Oft-filmed idea of Seminole boy (Tracey) who must adapt to white culture. Routine but well-done story for kids. C: Brian Keith, Ricardo Montalban, A. Martinez. D: Paul Krasny. FAM/DRA [G] 110m. V

Joe Smith, American 1942 ★★★ Average guy (Young) is kidnapped by Nazi stooges and tortured for information. Made during the height of WWII, film seems manipulative and transparent. An interesting relic, nonetheless. Remade as *The Big Operator*. (a.k.a. *Highway to Freedom*). C: Robert Young, Marsha Hunt, Darryl Hickman. D: Richard Thorpe. DRA 63m.

Joe Versus the Volcano 1990 ★★½ Millionaire offers fatally ill loser (Hanks) the deal of a lifetime—providing he jumps into a volcano in six months. Director's debut is tired and aimless, although Meg Ryan is pleasantly diverting in three different roles. C: Tom Hanks, Meg Ryan, Lloyd Bridges, Robert Stack, Ossie Davis. D: John Patrick Shanley. COM [PG] 102m. V

Joey 1985 ★★★ An ode to Doo Wop music, as cameo spots by groups like The Limelights and The Silhouettes enliven the story of teenage rocker and alcoholic father. C: Neill Barry, James Quinn. D: Joseph Ellison. MUS [PG] 93m. V

Joey Breaker 1992 ★★½ Cagy waitress convinces successful talent agent to scheme with her. C: Richard Edson, Cedella Marley, Erik King. D: Steven Starr. COM [R] 92m. V

John and Julie 1957 British ★★★½ England is abuzz over the upcoming coronation of the queen, and all the excitement prompts two curious children to run away from home in hopes of attending the ceremonies. Sweet little comedy with a fine cast, including a young Peter Sellers. Great family viewing. C: Colin Gibson, Lesley Dudley, Noelle Middleton, Wilfrid Hyde-White, Constance Cummings. D: William Fairchild. FAM/COM 83m. V

John and Mary 1969 ★★★½ Intriguing examination of the '60s free love lifestyle through a day in the lives of a furniture designer and an art gallery assistant who sleep together and then decide to get to know each other. Low-keyed comedy/drama. C: Dustin Hoffman, Mia Farrow, Michael Tolan, Tyne Daly. D: Peter Yates. COM [PG] 92m.

John and the Missus 1987 ★★★½ In the 1960's, owner of Canadian copper mine fights to protect family and beloved town from government's relocation plans. Often moving political drama. C: Jessica Steen, Timothy Webber, Randy Follett. D: Gordon Pinsent. DRA [PG] 98m. V

John and Yoko: A Love Story 1985 ★★ This hodgepodge of legend, contrivance, and a smattering of fact covers John and Yoko's relationship until his murder in 1980. Helped somewhat by a great Beatles soundtrack. C: Mark McGann, Kim Miyori. D: Sandor Stern. DRA 146m. TVM V

John F. Kennedy: Years of Lighting, Day of Drums 1964 ★★★★★ Highly praised, insightful documentary by U.S. Information Agency on life and death of 35th President (1917-1963). D: Bruce Herschensohn. DOC 85m.

John Goldfarb, Please Come Home 1965 ★★ Loud, leering comedy centered around a downed American pilot's attempt to help an Arab football team defeat Notre Dame to please a buffoonish Middle Eastern king (Ustinov). Screenplay by William Peter Blatty; Notre Dame sued when this came out. C: Richard Crenna, Shirley MacLaine, Peter Ustinov, Jim Backus. D: J. Lee Thompson. COM 96m.

John Henry ★★★½ Entertaining video adaptation of American folksong features Oscar-winning actor Denzel Washington narrating story of the famed "steel-drivin" man." Great for younger audiences. C: Denzel Washington. FAM/DRA V

John Huston: The Man, the Movies, the Maverick 1989 ★★★★★ Documentary about legendary, charismatic American film director Huston, whose career spanned 46 years; his movies include *The Maltese Falcon*, *The African Queen*, *Moby Dick*, *Night of the Iguana*, *The Man Who Would Be King*, and *Prizzi's Honor*. D: Frank Martin. DOC 128m. V

John Loves Mary 1949 ★★★½ Slight but pleasant comedy from Norman Krasna play, with Reagan as soldier who marries best friend's British girlfriend so she can enter the country. Neal's film debut. C: Ronald Reagan, Patricia Neal, Jack Carson, Wayne Morris. D: David Butler. COM 96m.

John Meade's Woman 1937 ★★½ Tedious drama with Larrimore as a country woman who discovers her wealthy husband (Arnold) is stealing land from farmers. C: Edward Arnold, Francine Larrimore, Gail Patrick. D: Richard Wallace. DRA 87m.

John of the Fair 1962 British ★★★½ Adolescent helper of carnival medicine show inherits a royal title, though his wanton uncle will do anything he can to get his hands on the honor. Good period detail of 18th century England gives substance to this amusing historical drama. C: John Charlesworth, Arthur Young, Richard George. D: Michael McCarthy. DRA 63m.

John Paul Jones 1959 ★★ Film biography of America's naval hero. Action and costumes torpedoed by deadly dialogue and stiff direction by Farrow whose daughter Mia makes her film debut. Bette Davis's cameo set adrift. C: Robert Stack, Marisa Pavan, Charles Coburn, Jean-Pierre Aumont, Peter Cushing, Bette Davis. D: John Farrow. DRA 126m. V

John Wesley 1954 British ★★★½ Film biography of Methodist leader portrays Wesley's life from early seminary days through his later years of philosophical development. Produced in association with Methodist church, this sturdy re-creation will please its intended audience. C: Leonard Sachs, Keith Pyott, Curigwen Lewis. D: Norman Walker. DRA 77m.

Johnnie Mae Gibson: FBI 1989 ★★★½ Dynamic Whitfield does fine job as the first African-American female FBI agent. But script hits all the rudimentary TV movie clichés, with no new insights. C: Howard E. Rollins, Jr., Marta DuBois, Richard Lawson. D: Bill Duke. CRI [PG-13] 96m. TVM V

Johnny Angel 1945 ★★★★ A sea captain (Raft), aided by witness (Hasso), tracks down the thieves who killed his father. Somewhat complicated but well-made thriller. C: George Raft, Claire Trevor, Signe Hasso, Hoagy Carmichael. D: Edwin L. Marin. CRI 79m. V

Johnny Apollo 1940 ★★★★ Son of a corporate tycoon falls into life of crime to rebel against his father's hypocritical ways. Absorbing crime drama, highlighted by appealing performances. C: Tyrone Power, Dorothy Lamour, Edward Arnold, Lloyd Nolan. D: Henry Hathaway. CRI 94m. V

Johnny Banco 1967 French ★★½ After stealing $200,000 from a reputed mobster, ghetto dreamer traipses off to sunny Monte Carlo. Clumsy comedy continually falls flat: unfunny actors, stilted situations and dialogue don't help. C: Horst Buchholz, Sylva Koscina. D: Yves Allegret. COM 95m.

Johnny Be Good 1987 ★★ Hall stars as high school athlete who must stave off illegal college recruiters. Muddled morality coupled with witless humor. C: Anthony Michael Hall, Robert Downey, Jr., Uma Thurman. D: Bud Smith. COM [R] 91m. V

Johnny Belinda 1948 ★★★★★ Well-deserved Oscar went to Wyman for her role as hearing- and speech-impaired young woman who gives birth after being raped, despite societal pressures that rain down on her. Ayres is excellent as medical man who also loves her. Good for high school ages. C: Jane Wyman, Lew Ayres, Charles Bickford, Jan Sterling, Agnes Moorehead. D: Jean Negulesco. DRA 103m. V

Johnny Belinda 1982 ★★★½ Remake of the classic 1948 film revamps the story of a deaf-mute woman (Arquette) with an illegitimate baby whose father tries to take him from her. Excellent performances. C: Richard Thomas, Rosanna Arquette, Dennis Quaid, Candy Clark. D: Anthony Harvey. DRA 95m. TVM V

Johnny Bull 1986 ★★★½ A G.I. and his strong-minded Cockney war bride must live with his reluctant parents in a poor Pennsylvania mining town, changing her ideas about America and his about his family. Solid performances and story. C: Jason Robards, Colleen Dewhurst, Peter MacNicol, Kathy Bates. D: Claudia Weill. DRA 100m. TVM V

Johnny Cash: The Man, His World, His Music 1970 ★★★★ Stimulating documentary about famed country music singing star who grew up in poverty in rural Arkansas. Many fine Cash tunes. C: Johnny Cash, June Carter, Bob Dylan. D: Robert Elfstrom. DOC 94m.

Johnny Come Lately 1943 ★★★½ Cagney blusters his way through agreeable comedy about tramp who wanders into town and helps old lady (George) run her newspaper. C: James Cagney, Grace George, Marjorie Main, Hattie McDaniel. D: William K. Howard. COM 97m. V

Johnny Concho 1956 ★★★ A cowardly young man trades on his brother's reputation as a fast gun—until the latter is killed and a gunfighter challenges him. Minor Western with Ol' Blue Eyes an unexpected cowpoke. C: Frank Sinatra, Keenan Wynn, William Conrad, Phyllis Kirk. D: Don McGuire. WST 84m.

Johnny Cool 1963 ★★★★ Young mobster goes on a murder spree to exact revenge. Sizzling crime drama brutally conveys life in the underworld and a killer's vicious mind set. C: Henry Silva, Elizabeth Montgomery, Sammy Davis, Richard Anderson, Jim Backus, Wanda Hendrix, Brad Dexter, Joey Bishop, Marc Lawrence, John McGiver, Mort Sahl, Telly Savalas, Elisha Cook. D: William Asher. CRI 101m.

Johnny Dangerously 1984 ★★★ Gangster spoof features smart-alecky Keaton as mobster battling his nemesis Piscopo in struggle for big-city turf. Loaded with bad one-liners and crude jokes, though Keaton is fun to watch. C: Michael Keaton, Joe Piscopo, Marilu Henner, Peter Boyle, Griffin Dunne, Gynnis O'Connor, Dom DeLuise. D: Amy Heckerling. COM [PG-13] 90m. V

Johnny Dark 1954 ★★★ After Curtis steals the car he's designed from the auto maker who's double-crossing him, he enters it in a big race. The result is some exciting racing footage. C: Tony Curtis, Piper Laurie, Don Taylor, Paul Kelly, Ilka Chase, Sidney Blackmer. D: George Sherman. ACT 85m.

Johnny Doesn't Live Here Any More 1944 ★★★½ Cute wartime farce about young woman's apartment and the many keys that exist for it. (a.k.a. *And So They Were Married*) C: Simone Simon, James Ellison, Minna Gombell, Alan Dinehart, Robert Mitchum, Grady Sutton. D: Joe May. COM 77m.

Johnny Eager 1942 ★★★★ Crusading D.A.'s daughter falls hard for one of the racketeers her father is out to get. Unnecessarily complex plotting, but good atmospherics. Heflin a standout in his Oscar-winning supporting role. C: Robert Taylor, Lana Turner, Edward Arnold, Van Heflin, Robert Sterling, Patricia Dane, Glenda Farrell. D: Mervyn LeRoy. CRI 107m. V

Johnny Got His Gun 1971 ★★★½ Moving antiwar drama concerns a WWI veteran left completely disabled, struggling to communicate his wishes and regain dignity in his life. Trumbo film adaptation of his novel may be uneven at times, but he still poignantly relays his message. C: Timothy Bottoms, Kathy Fields, Marsha Hunt, Jason Robards, Donald Sutherland, Diane Varsi, David Soul, Tony Geary. D: Dalton Trumbo. DRA [PG] 111m. V

Johnny Guitar 1954 ★★★★½ Freudian catfight Western with Crawford as saloon operator and superrighteous McCambridge as lady banker—both in love with the same man. Gripping, imaginative and very entertaining. Two stars have field day in their confrontation scenes. C: Joan Crawford, Mercedes McCambridge, Sterling Hayden, Scott Brady, Ernest Borgnine, John Carradine. D: Nicholas Ray. WST 110m. V

Johnny Hamlet 1972 ★★ Absurd but fascinating attempt to convert Shakespeare's play into a Western. Contours of the original are generally followed, except here the ending is incongruously upbeat. C: Chip Corman, Gilbert Roland. D: Enzo Castellari. WST [PG] 91m.

Johnny Handsome 1990 ★★★ A physically disfigured crook gets a second chance at life when plastic surgery makes him attractive. Intriguing premise slips into standard story of revenge. C: Mickey Rourke, Ellen Barkin, Elizabeth McGovern, Morgan Freeman. D: Walter Hill. CRI [R] 96m. V

Johnny Holiday 1949 ★★★½ Teenage hood struggles to stay on the straight and narrow despite the efforts of his former friends to lead him astray. Honest performances heighten this entertaining, low-budget drama. C: William Bendix, Allen Martin. D: Willis Goldbeck. CRI 92m.

Johnny in the Clouds 1945 British ★★★★★ Stirring, intelligent drama about men stationed at a British airfield during WWII and their personal relationships. A memorable film with stellar performances by a first-rate cast. (a.k.a. *The Way to the Stars*) C: John Mills, Michael Redgrave. D: Anthony Asquith. DRA 109m.

Johnny Nobody 1961 British ★★★½ A priest goes on a puzzling search for clues as to why a drunken writer has turned up dead. Entertaining mystery, made more so by its intriguing religious setting. C: Nigel Patrick, Yvonne Mitchell, Aldo Ray, William Bendix. D: Nigel Patrick. CRI 88m. V

Johnny O'Clock 1947 ★★★½ Roguish high roller's nefarious activities keep him in constant trouble with the police. Solid crime drama with colorful characters and crisp direction. C: Dick Powell, Evelyn Keyes, Lee J. Cobb, Nina Foch, Jeff Chandler. D: Robert Rossen. CRI 95m.

Johnny One Eye 1950 ★★★★ O'Brien hunts down crime pal who betrayed him. Juicy melodrama, played the old-fashioned way, from a Damon Runyan story. Incidentally, title character is a dog. C: Pat O'Brien, Wayne Morris, Dolores Moran. D: Robert Florey. CRI 78m.

Johnny Reno 1966 ★★ A marshal attempts to thwart a lynch mob after a man is charged with murder. Cliché-laden, but also star-filled. C: Dana Andrews, Jane Russell, Lon Chaney, John Agar. D: R.G. Springsteen. WST 83m. V

Johnny Rocco 1958 ★★★ Middling gangster film with a twist: The mob is after a child, who happens to be a mobster's son. Major selling point is a credible performance by the young Eyer. C: Richard Eyer, Stephen McNally, Coleen Gray. D: Paul Landres. CRI 84m.

Johnny Shiloh 1963 ★★★ After his parents are killed, a young man joins up with Confederate army unit led by Keith. Somewhat stagy Disney adventure but kids should enjoy. C: Kevin Corcoran, Brian Keith, Darryl Hickman. D: James Neilson. FAM/DRA 90m. V

Johnny Steals Europe 1932 German ★★★½ Comedy revolves around Piel, who tries to pay off creditors by stealing a horse named Europe, and entering the nag in a big-money race. Fun and energetic comedy, with some nifty acrobatics from Piel (who also wrote and directed). C: Harry Piel, Alfred Abel, Darry Holm. D: Harry Piel. COM 86m.

Johnny Stecchino 1992 Italian ★★★★½ Comic Benigni plays two roles in fast-paced, madcap farce about Mafiosi, mistaken identities, and crooked church leaders. Was biggest box-office hit of all time in Italy, supremely silly and extremely funny. C: Roberto Benigni, Nicoletta Braschi. D: Roberto Benigni. COM [R] 100m. V

Johnny Stool Pigeon 1949 ★★★★ Meaty cops-and-robbers drama about a narcotics agent recruiting a convict to smash a dope ring. Full-blooded characters, a dream cast, and clean, compact direction gives this one steam. C: Howard Duff, Shelley Winters, Dan Duryea. D: William Castle. CRI 76m.

Johnny Suede 1992 ★★★½ Talentless rock 'n' roll wannabe has more success seducing women than he does realizing his dream of becoming a musical legend. Quirky, breezy comedy has more cult appeal than laughs, despite winning performance by Pitt. C: Brad Pitt, Calvin Levels, Alison Moir, Tina Louise. D: Tom DiCillo. COM [R] 97m. V

Johnny Tiger 1966 ★★ A half-Seminole half-white man (Everett) tries to expose others to the unjust plight of native Americans while wrestling with his own mixed identity. Simultaneously overly sympathetic and exploitative. C: Robert Taylor, Geraldine Brooks, Chad Everett. D: Paul Wendkos. DRA 100m. V

Johnny Tremain 1957 ★★★★ Disney's rousing Revolutionary War tale for children involves a silversmith's apprentice caught up in events surrounding birth of America. Based on Esther Forbes' popular novel. Great set pieces and charged-up music make for a highly entertaining film. C: Hal Stalmaster, Luana Patten, Sebastian Cabot. D: Robert Stevenson. FAM/MUS 80m. V

Johnny Trouble 1957 ★★★½ Barrymore's final film is an effective tearjerker about an elderly woman who firmly believes that her long-lost son will return home, despite all evidence to the contrary. C: Ethel Barrymore, Cecil Kellaway, Carolyn Jones, Stuart Whitman. D: John Auer. DRA 80m.

Johnny Vic 1973 ★★★ Hammack is a Native American arrested on a minor charge who escapes from his jail cell and hides out with a sympathetic young woman. Simplistic and self-important drama of alienated angst. C: Warren Hammack, Kathy Amerman. D: Charles Nauman. DRA 90m.

Johnny, We Hardly Knew Ye 1977 ★★★½ Well-crafted movie about John Kennedy's first attempt at political office, a congressional campaign in 1946. Rudd is likable as JFK, and supporting cast is strong. C: Paul Rudd, Kevin Conway, Burgess Meredith. D: Gilbert Cates. DRA 100m. TVM

Johnny Yuma 1966 Spanish ★★ Revenge and double cross are the themes in this sloppy Sergio Leone imitation. C: Mark Damon, Rosalba Neri. D: Romolo Guerrieri. WST 99m.

Johnstown Flood, The 1926 ★★★ Johnstown, Pennsylvania is devastated by flood in this silent disaster film. Amazing special effects and film debut of Janet Gaynor are only real standouts. C: George O'Brien, Florence Gilbert, Janet Gaynor. D: Irving Cummings. DRA 70m.

Join the Marines 1937 ★★★½ When Kelly is ejected from both the police force and Olympic boxing team through series of mix-ups, he enlists in the Marines, hoping to impress fiancée Travis' disapproving father. Kelly and Travis are nice duo in this sweet comic romance. C: Paul Kelly, June Travis, Purnell Pratt. D: Ralph Staub. COM 70m.

Joke of Destiny, A 1984 Italian ★★½ A high-level official is trapped inside his computerized vehicle, and minor problem is treated as a national scandal. Broad farce frequently misses its satiric targets; the wonderful Tognazzi does what he can. C: Ugo Tognazzi, Piera Degli Esposti. D: Lina Wertmuller. COM [PG] 105m. V

Joker is Wild, The 1957 ★★★★ Impressive job by Sinatra as Prohibition-era singer Joe E. Lewis, who ran afoul of the mob. Musical biography/drama features Oscar-winning song "All The Way" by Sammy Cahn and Jimmy Van Heusen. Gets maudlin near end, but worth seeing for Frank. (a.k.a. *All The Way*) C: Frank Sinatra, Mitzi Gaynor, Jeanne Crain, Eddie Albert, Jackie Coogan, Sophie Tucker. D: Charles Vidor. MUS 123m.

Jokers, The 1966 British ★★★★ On a lark, two rich, roguish brothers (Reed, Crawford) scheme to steal the crown jewels of London. Flippant caper comedy/drama provides both thrills and laughs thanks to intelligent plotting and breezy performances. C: Michael Crawford, Oliver Reed, Gabriella Licudi, Harry Andrews, Daniel Massey, Michael Hordern. D: Michael Winner. COM 94m.

Jolly Bad Fellow 1964 British ★★★★ McKern does a wickedly rambunctious turn as a mad professor knocking off his academic rivals with a most unusual poison. Irreverent and macabre, film is in the tradition of British black comedies such as *The Ladykillers.* Plenty of fun. (a.k.a. *They All Died Laughing*) C: Leo McKern, Janet Munro. D: Don Chaffey. COM 94m.

Jolly Paupers 1938 Polish ★★★½ Dzigan and Shumacher are charming as tailor and mechanic who dream up a series of get-rich-quick schemes. Pleasant musical comedy. C: Shimon Dzigan, Yisroel Shumacher, The Warsaw Art Players. D: Zygmunt Turkow, Leon Feannot. MUS 62m. V

Jolson Sings Again 1949 ★★★½ Sequel to *The Jolson Story* once again matches famed musical star's real vocals to Parks' emoting in sentimental account of Jolson's WWII USO tours and near-fatal lung disease. Songs include "Sonny Boy," "Anniversary Song," and "April Showers." C: Larry Parks, Barbara Hale, William Demarest. D: Henry Levin. MUS 96m. V

Jolson Story, The 1946 ★★★★ Parks acts up a storm in entertaining but cliched biography of show biz legend Al Jolson, once billed as "the world's greatest entertainer." Soundtrack uses Jolson's own voice, "Swanee," "Toot Toot Tootsie Goodbye," etc. Keyes' role modeled after Jolson's wife, Ruby Keeler, who refused to have her name used. (Sequel: *Jolson Sings Again.*) C: Larry Parks, Evelyn Keyes, William Demarest. D: Alfred E. Green. MUS 128m. V

Jonah Who Will Be 25 in the Year 2000 1976 Swiss ★★★★ Eight former '60s radicals sort out their lives years later. Involving, original comedy/drama may not be as profound as it thinks it is, but offhand wit, strong acting more than compensate. C: Myriam Boyer, Jean-Luc Bideau. D: Alain Tanner. DRA 110m. v

Jonathan Livingston Seagull 1973 ★★★½ Film version of Richard Bach's popular allegory about a seagull striving to fly right into a perfect world. Fantasy takes wing thanks to heart-soaring photography, supported by Neil Diamond's music. D: Hall Bartlett. FAM/DRA [G] 120m. v

Jonathan Winters on the Ledge ★★★★ Innovative comedian stars in wild variety show, featuring appearances by Martin Mull, Phyllis Diller, Robin Williams, and Milton Berle. C: Jonathan Winters. COM 60m. v

Joni 1979 ★★★ Joni Eareckson plays herself in the story of her struggle to put her life back together after a paralyzing spinal-cord injury, and her concurrent religious awakening. Routine inspiration movie based on Eareckson's book. C: Joni Eareckson, Bert Remsen. D: James F. Collier. DRA [G] 75m. v

Joniko 1969 *See* **Joniko and the Kush Ta Ta**

Joniko and the Kush Ta Ta 1969 ★★★½ After finding a geologist with a broken leg, Alaskan boy overcomes his terror of the Kush Ta Ta (a Native-American spirit of fear) to get help. Beautiful scenery marks this good children's adventure. (a.k.a. *Joniko, Alaska Boy*, and *Frontier Alaska*) C: Tony Tucker Williams, Jimmy Cane. D: Ford Beebe. FAM/ACT 94m.

Jordan Chance, The 1978 ★★★ Failed pilot for TV series casts Burr as ex-con turned lawyer who specializes in proving innocence of wrongly imprisoned defendants. Run-of-the-mill courtroom drama. C: Raymond Burr, Stella Stevens. D: Jules Irving. CRI 104m. TVM

Jory 1972 ★★½ After the wanton slaughter of his father and others, a teenager comes of age. Shot on location in Mexico. C: John Marley, B.J. Thomas, Robby Benson, Linda Purl. D: Jorge Fons. WST [PG] 97m. v

Joseph and His Brethren 1960 ★★ Strictly color-by-numbers retelling of biblical tale about Joseph's woes and triumphs after being cast out by his brothers. Dull stuff aimed at child audiences. C: Marietto, Geoffrey Horne, Belinda Lee. D: Irving Rapper. FAM/DRA 103m. v

Joseph Andrews 1977 British ★★★ Director Richardson tries to repeat his *Tom Jones* triumph by adapting another Fielding novel. Firth is pleasant as servant and later lover to Ann-Margret, but that's not enough; the chemistry ain't there—and it shows. C: Peter Firth, Ann-Margret, Michael Hordern, Beryl Reid, Jim Dale. D: Tony Richardson. COM [R] 98m. v

Josephine Baker Story, The 1991 ★★★½ Whitfield is attractive (and often undressed) in this otherwise standard showbiz biography of the famous black dancer who found stardom by emigrating to France. Nicely mounted. C: Lynn Whitfield, Ruben Blades, David Dukes, Louis Gossett Jr., Craig T. Nelson. D: Brian Gibson. DRA [R] 129m. TVM v

Josette 1938 ★★ Brothers fall for their father's girlfriend—only she isn't. Musical mistaken-identity story. C: Don Ameche, Simone Simon, Robert Young, Bert Lahr, Joan Davis, William Demarest. D: Allan Dwan. MUS 73m.

Josh and S.A.M. 1993 ★★½ Labored comedy/drama about two preteen kids who steal a car and go on the lam after their parents get a divorce. Sort of a *Thelma and Louise* for third graders; pat, slick treatment of potentially interesting situation. C: Joan Allen, Stephen Tobolowsky, Chris Penn, Martha Plimpton. D: Billy Weber. COM [PG-13] 97m. v

Joshua 1976 ★★★ They killed Williamson's mother, so now they're going to pay. Genre revenge Western. C: Fred Williamson, Isela Vega, Brenda Venus, Calvin Bartlett. D: Larry Spangler. WST [PG] 90m. v

Joshua Then and Now 1985 Canadian ★★★½ Engrossing examination of a Jewish writer (Woods) reminiscing about his atypical childhood with his gangster father (Arkin) as well as his unusual marriage into an ultra-WASP family. Arkin's hilarious portrayal of a mobster steals this low-keyed comedy. Based on novel by Mordecai Richler. C: James Woods, Gabrielle Lazure, Alan Arkin, Michael Sarrazin. D: Ted Kotcheff. COM [R] 102m. v

Joshua's Heart 1990 ★★★ Gilbert does well as disturbed woman traumatized by breakup with boyfriend and separation from his son. Manipulative tearjerker. C: Melissa Gilbert, Tim Matheson, Matthew Lawrence. D: Michael Pressman. DRA 96m. TVM

Jour de Fête 1948 French ★★★★★ Exquisite comedy about French postal carrier who longs to emulate American counterparts. Preparing for his village's Bastille Day festivities, he rigs elaborate electronics to improve mail delivery. Tati lets machine-based humor develop organically with hilarious results. (a.k.a. *The Big Day*) C: Jacques Tati, Guy Decomble, Santa Relli. D: Jacques Tati. COM 79m. v

Journey 1977 Canadian ★★ Woman (Bujold) is rescued from drowning by head of a commune in the Canadian wilderness. Her presence causes bad things to happen to everyone around her. Low-voltage offering. C: Genevieve Bujold, John Vernon. D: Paul Almond. DRA 87m. v

Journey Back to Oz 1974 ★★½ Dorothy gets whisked back to Oz, meeting old friends and making new ones. Despite star-dubbed voices, this animated sequel to the classic original is noisy, poorly drawn, and unforgivably dull. Voices of Danny Thomas, Liza Minnelli, Ethel Merman. D: Hal Sutherland. FAM/DRA [G] 88m. v

Journey for Margaret 1942 ★★★★ Child star O'Brien will wrench your heart as homeless survivor of London blitz during WWII. Sentimental but winning. C: Margaret O'Brien, Robert Young, Laraine Day, Fay Bainter. D: W.S. Van Dyke II. DRA 81m. V

Journey from Berlin 1980 ★★★ Surreal story of a woman (Michelson) working through her problems using stream-of-consciousness psychotherapy. Difficult, but rewarding. C: Annette Michelson, Ilona Halberstadt, Yvonne Rainer. D: Yvonne Rainer. DRA 125m.

Journey Into Autumn *See* **Dreams**

Journey into Fear 1942 Canadian ★★★ Welles lost control over this film, despite co-writing, producing, and partially directing it. What's left is confusing story about American bomb expert smuggling arms into Turkey while evading Nazis. Fine turn by Cotten. C: Orson Welles, Joseph Cotten, Delores Del Rio. D: Norman Foster. DRA 69m. V

Journey Into Fear 1975 Canadian ★★ Remake of Orson Welles' 1942 spy melodrama stars Waterston as geologist mixed up with international espionage in Turkey. Stick with the original. C: Sam Waterston, Yvette Mimieux, Zero Mostel, Shelley Winters, Vincent Price, Donald Pleasence. D: Daniel Mann. CRI [R] 103m. V

Journey into Light 1951 ★★★½ A minister reclaims his faith in a Skid Row mission after his wife commits suicide. Film generates some real force, due largely to Hayden's earnest, searching performance. C: Sterling Hayden, Viveca Lindfors, Thomas Mitchell, H. B. Warner. D: Stuart Heisler. DRA 87m.

Journey of Honor 1991 ★★½ Saga of bickering warlords in 17th-century Japan. Bloated story brightened by stunning cinematography. C: David Essex, Kane Kosugi, Christopher Lee, Ronald Pickup, Polly Walker, Toshiro Mifune. D: Gordon Hessler. ACT [PG-13] 107m. V

Journey of Hope 1990 Swiss ★★★★½ Turkish immigrant family arrives in Switzerland with very little and tries to build new lives. Eye-opening glimpse at an alien culture. Oscar for Best Foreign Film. C: Necmettin Cobanoglu, Nur Surer. D: Xavier Koller. DRA [PG] 131m. V

Journey of Natty Gann, The 1985 ★★★★½ In the midst of the Depression, a girl, along with her pet wolf, takes to the road in search of her father. Well-told tale, marked by wonderful photography and attention to period detail. Fine family viewing that will appeal to both adults and children. C: Meredith Salenger, John Cusack, Ray Wise, Lainie Kazan, Barry Miller, Scatman Crothers. D: Jeremy Paul Kagan. FAM/DRA [PG] 101m. V

Journey, The 1959 ★★★ Litvak's trademark direction permeates this ensemble character study of a busload of people stopped at Hungarian border during 1956 uprising. Brynner is intense as Russian major who becomes involved with Kerr. C: Yul Brynner, Deborah Kerr, Jason Robards Jr., Robert Morley, E. G. Marshall, Anne Jackson. D: Anatole Litvak. DRA 125m.

Journey Through Rosebud 1972 ★★★ Well-intentioned recounting of uprising by modern Native Americans in South Dakota. C: Robert Forster, Kristoffer Tabori, Victoria Racimo. D: Tom Gries. WST [PG] 93m. V

Journey to Freedom 1957 ★★ Cold War drama with Communists out to punish a saintly refugee in America. Entertainingly unsubtle. C: Jacques Scott, Genevieve Aumont, Morgan Lane. D: Robert Dertano. DRA 60m.

Journey to Shiloh 1968 ★★★½ The perilous adventures of six young Texans en route to joining the Confederate Army make for an unusual, engrossing antiwar drama. Caan leads an eager, talent-rich cast, which includes a baby-faced Harrison Ford. C: James Caan, Michael Sarrazin, Brenda Scott. D: William Hale. DRA 101m.

Journey to Spirit Island 1992 ★★★★ Native-American teenager Bettina is caught between her love for pop culture vs. her grandmother's traditional beliefs. When tribal burial grounds are bought by unscrupulous real estate interests, Bettina finally takes a stand. Good scenery and performances in this uplifting children's film. C: Bettina, Brandon Douglas, Gabriel Damon, Tarek McCarthy. D: Laszlo Pal. FAM/DRA [PG] 93m. V

Journey to the Beginning of Time 1966 Czech ★★★ Four boys travel back to the time of dinosaurs, after a visit to the New York Museum of Natural History. Fun film for kids and dinosaur fans. C: Vladimir Bejval, Peter Hermann. D: Karel Zeman. FAM/SFI 87m.

Journey to the Center of the Earth, The 1959 ★★★★½ Jules Verne's tale of explorers descending into beautiful but dangerous terrain. Dandy adventure/fantasy creates make-believe world that children of all ages will delight in. Good cast, especially scene-stealer Gertrude the goose! C: James Mason, Pat Boone, Arlene Dahl. D: Henry Levin. FAM/SFI [G] 129m. V

Journey to the Center of Time 1967 ★★ Spaced-out travelers get snagged in a time warp and wind up in the Age of Dinosaurs. Cardboard special effects and plot. C: Scott Brady, Gigi Perreau, Anthony Eisley. D: David L. Hewitt. SFI 82m. V

Journey to the Far Side of the Sun 1969 British ★★★★½ On the other side of the sun, astronauts find a planet that mirrors our own. Solid special effects and good use of color enliven this sci-fi effort. Great ending. Fine for younger audiences. (a.k.a. *Doppelganger*). C: Roy Thinnes, Lynn Loring, Herbert Lom. D: Robert Parrish. SFI [G] 92m. V

Journey to the Seventh Planet 1961 Danish ★★ Scientists battle monsters—and lovely space creatures on the strange planet #7.

Same old, same old. C: John Agar, Greta Thyssen. D: Sidney Pink. SFI 83m. V

Journey Together 1945 British ★★★ Semi-documentary chronicle of American trainee pilots stationed in England during WWII. Clichéd, but dignified and well intended. C: Richard Attenborough, Jack Watling, Edward G. Robinson, Bessie Love. D: John Boulting. DOC 80m.

Journey's End 1930 ★★★½ R.C. Sheriff's controversial play about British troops under fire in WWI receives respectful treatment from director Whale and the British cast. Dated by early sound equipment and stagy acting, but well worth seeing. C: Colin Clive, Ian Maclaren. D: James Whale. ACT 130m.

Joy House 1964 French ★★★ More like a hothouse, with two different men hiding in a gloomy mansion, and their involvement with the women who live there. Slick production values mark this complex mystery. (a.k.a. *The Love Cage*) C: Jane Fonda, Alain Delon, Lola Albright. D: Rene Clement. CRI 98m. V

Joy in the Morning 1965 ★★★ Quiet adaptation of Betty Smith's novel about a newlywed's life and troubles in a small college town, where husband studies law and works overtime. C: Richard Chamberlain, Yvette Mimieux, Arthur Kennedy. D: Alex Segal. DRA [PG] 103m.

Joy Luck Club, The 1993 ★★★★ Two generations of Chinese women tell stories in this three-hanky picture from the Amy Tan bestseller. Cast of unknowns do wonderful job with sprawling narrative in this moving film with flashes of humor. C: Tsai Chin, Kieu Chinh, Ming-Na Wen, Tamlyn Tomita, France Nuyen, Rosalind Chao. D: Wayne Wang. DRA [R] 136m. V

Joy of Living 1938 ★★★½ Penniless playboy (Fairbanks) tries to save rich musical star (Dunne) from grasping family. Okay screwball comedy with music by Jerome Kern doesn't sparkle the way it should. Highlight: the roller rink. C: Irene Dunne, Douglas Fairbanks, Jr., Alice Brady, Guy Kibbee, Lucille Ball, Jean Dixon, Eric Blore. D: Tay Garnett. COM 91m. V

Joy of Sex 1984 ★ Dull teenage sex comedy sticks to formula plotting and typical stereotypes as it chronicles the usual group of vulgar high schoolers in pursuit of carnal satisfaction. Hard-pressed for laughs. C: Michelle Meyrink, Cameron Dye, Christopher Lloyd, Colleen Camp. D: Martha Coolidge. COM [R] 93m. V

Joy Ride 1958 ★★½ Crazed hot-rodders go on a crime spree. Histrionic indictment of juvenile delinquency is indicative of its time, but a novelty today. C: Rad Fulton, Ann Doran, Regis Toomey. D: Edward Bernds. CRI 60m.

Joyless Street, The 1925 German ★★★★ Pre-America Garbo stars in this fascinating look at the grim realities of post-WWI Vienna. She plays a professor's daughter struggling to keep her family fed during hard times. (a.k.a. *The Street of Sorrow*) C: Asta Nielsen, Greta Garbo, Werner Krauss. D: G. W. Pabst. DRA 96m. V

Joyride 1977 ★★½ Four young friends in search of a good time on their way to Alaska soon find themselves swept up into a world of crime. Fair performances by an interestingly odd ensemble cast. C: Desi Arnaz, Jr., Robert Carradine, Melanie Griffith. D: Joseph Ruben. ACT [R] 91m. V

Joyride to Nowhere 1982 ★★½ Two bored young women hit the road and uncover trunkful of cash. C: Leslie Ackerman, Sandy Serrano. D: Mel Welles. ACT [PG] 90m. V

Joysticks 1983 ★ Moronic high jinks abound as an uptight businessman (Baker) struggles to close a video arcade to stop his daughter's descent into juvenile delinquency. Brainless teen comedy offers only nudity and grossness. C: Joe Don Baker, Leif Green. D: Greydon Clark. COM [R] 88m. V

Ju Dou 1991 Chinese ★★★★★ The wife of a cruel mill owner and his nephew enter into a doomed love affair in a repressive Chinese village, circa 1920. A linchpin of the Chinese New Wave, and the film that brought the luminous Gong Li to the world's attention. One of the cinema's most beautiful examples of the use of color. Banned in China. Oscar nomination for Best Foreign Film. C: Gong Li. D: Zhang Yimou. DRA 98m. V

Juarez 1939 ★★★★ Epic bioraphy of Mexican revolutionary (Muni) tells two stories simultaneously, the first dealing with Muni's plot to overthrow Emperor Maximillian (Aherne), the second dominated by Davis as insane Empress Carlotta. Fascinating history lesson given the big-scale treatment. C: Paul Muni, Bette Davis, Brian Aherne, Claude Rains, John Garfield, Gale Sondergaard, Donald Crisp, Gilbert Roland, Louis Calhern. D: William Dieterle. DRA 132m. V

Jubal 1956 ★★★½ Dressed-up Western reworks *Othello*, with newly married rancher (Borgnine) suspicious of cowhand (Ford) after envious odd man out (Steiger) plants suggestions of infidelity. Shakespeare it ain't, but interesting for itself, and especially worth a look if you're familiar with Will's version. C: Glenn Ford, Ernest Borgnine, Rod Steiger, Valerie French, Charles Bronson. D: Delmer Daves. WST 101m. V

Jubilee 1978 British ★★★★ An astrologer transports Queen Elizabeth I to 1970s punk London. Her Majesty's horror and disapproval of "modern" times adds humor even as it legitimates this pointed satire. Some truly provocative insights along with the fun. C: Jenny Runacre, Jordan, Little Nell, Toyah Willcox. D: Derek Jarman. COM 105m. V

Jubilee Trail 1954 ★★★½ Members of wagon train bound for California gold country are plagued by chicanery; upon arrival, sentimental New Orleans singer helps sort out problems of a rancher's wife. Generous entertainment tailored for Ralston by Republic. C: Vera Hruba Ralston, Joan Leslie, Forrest Tucker. D: Joseph Kane. WST 103m. V

Jud 1971 ★★★ Early Vietnam drama about a young veteran facing tremendous difficulties as he tries to readjust to civilian life. C: Joseph Kaufmann, Claudia Jennings. DRA [PG] 80m. V

Jud Suss 1940 German ★★½ Nazi propaganda film involves a Jew who rapes an innocent German woman. Obviously hateful in intent, film was made under supervision of Joseph Goebbels and ordered required viewing for SS guards by Heinrich Himmler. Horrible, yet fascinating, document of Nazi-era best viewed within its historical context. C: Ferdinand Marian, Werner Krauss, Heinrich George, Kristina Söderbaum. D: Veit Harlan. DOC 85m. V

Judas Was a Woman *See* **La Bete Humaine**

Judex 1964 French ★★★★ Remake of old French serial features Pollack as a costumed crime fighter saving a would-be inheritee from the cat-suited Bergé. Gloriously old-fashioned tale of heroes and villains, played with verve and benefiting from wonderful sets and costumes. C: Channing Pollock, Francine Bergé, Michel Vitold. D: Georges Franju. CRI 96m. V

Judge and Jake Wyler, The 1972 ★★★ Failed pilot for TV series gives Davis okay role of eccentric ex-judge who starts a detective agency with help of an ex-con (McClure). Amusing banter makes tolerable entertainment. C: Bette Davis, Doug McClure. D: David Rich. CRI 100m. TVM

Judge and the Assassin, The 1975 French ★★★★ Nineteenth-century courtroom drama explores the relationship between a judge (Noiret) and a child murderer (Galabru); is the man crazy, or lying? Ambitious, absorbing psychological plot. C: Philippe Noiret, Michel Galabru, Isabelle Huppert. D: Bertrand Tavernier. DRA 130m. V

Judge and the Sinner 1964 ★★★½ Judge hoping to aid a juvenile delinquent sentences her to a work program away from her troublesome boyfriend. The judge's trust is put to test when ugly circumstances threaten the girl's rehabilitation. Well-meaning story of youth, though a little overwrought. C: Heinz Ruehmann, Karin Baal, Lola Muthel. D: Paul Verhoeven. DRA 84m.

Judge Dee and the Monastery Murder 1974 ★★★½ Unusual murder mystery set in seventh-century China with Dhiegh as title sleuth. Clever script by Nicholas Meyer, author of *The Seven Percent Solution*. C: Khigh Dhiegh, Mako, Soon-Teck-Oh. D: Jeremy Kagan. CRI 100m. TVM

Judge Hardy and Son 1939 ★★★ Tear-drenched *Andy Hardy* entry has Judge Hardy (Stone) facing possible eviction of poverty-stricken elderly couple as well as his wife's illness. Don't expect a tragic ending. C: Lewis Stone, Mickey Rooney, Cecilia Parker, Fay Holden, Ann Rutherford, Maria Ouspenskaya. D: George Seitz. FAM/DRA 87m.

Judge Hardy's Children 1938 ★★★ When Judge Hardy takes his family to Washington, D.C. on a business trip, the indefatigable Andy woos a diplomat's daughter. Standard *Andy Hardy* series fare. C: Lewis Stone, Mickey Rooney, Cecilia Parker, Fay Holden, Ann Rutherford, Ruth Hussey. D: George Seitz. FAM/COM 78m.

Judge Horton and The Scottsboro Boys 1976 ★★★★ Drama about racial injustice in the South of the '30s, in which a ramrod judge makes sure nine wrongly accused African-Americans get a fair trial for rape. Well acted and even handed. C: Arthur Hill, Vera Miles, Lewis J. Stadlen. D: Fielder Cook. DRA 96m. TVM V

Judge Priest 1934 ★★★★½ Rogers gives his best performance in warm and folksy story of Southern judge up for reelection, based on short stories by Irvin S. Cobb. Only drawback is Fetchit in typically racist role. Remade by Ford as *The Sun Shines Bright*. C: Will Rogers, Tom Brown, Anita Louise, Stepin Fetchit. D: John Ford. COM 81m. V

Judge Roy Bean 1955 ★★★½ Wedding of Old Sam and "Letty Leaves Home," two episodes of western series chronicling life and times of Langtry, Texas's upright justice. C: Edgar Buchanan, Jackie Loughery, Jack Beutel. WST 55m. V

Judge Steps Out, The 1949 ★★★½ A New England judge (Knox) has a midlife crisis and heads for the West Coast where he must ultimately choose between society's standards and his own. Tame by today's standards, but still decent family entertainment. C: Alexander Knox, Ann Sothern, George Tobias. D: Boris Ingster. DRA 91m. V

Judge, The 1949 ★★★ Convoluted B-film about a lawyer whose plot to murder his wife and her lover backfires. Not bad. C: Milburn Stone, Katherine DeMille, Paul Guilfoyle. D: Elmer Clifton. CRI 69m.

Judgment 1990 ★★★★ A small-town Catholic congregation is torn apart when the parents of an altar boy discover that their respected priest has been molesting their son. Fact-based drama with solid performances manages not to exploit subject matter. C: Keith Carradine, Blythe Danner, Jack Warden. D: Tom Topor. DRA [PG-13] 89m. TVM V

Judgment at Nuremberg 1961 ★★★★ Fictionalized reenactment of the 1948 trial of Nazi leaders in wake of WWII crimes. Star-clogged cast dominates sometimes ponderous but important and engrossing drama. Oscars for Schell and screenwriter Abby

Mann. C: Spencer Tracy, Burt Lancaster, Maximilian Schell, Marlene Dietrich, Judy Garland, Richard Widmark, Montgomery Clift. D: Stanley Kramer. DRA 178m. V

Judgment Day 1988 ★★ Vacationing college students visit an isolated town that made a deal with the devil in the 17th century and he's just now returned to settle affairs. Tame, unsurprising supernatural chiller. C: Kenneth McLeod, David Anthony Smith, Monte Markham. D: Ferde Grofe, Jr. HOR 93m. V

Judgment Deferred 1952 British ★★★ Citizens rally when a narcotics smuggler frames one of their friends and get a reporter (Sinclair) to help them investigate. Odd little concept, earnestly produced. C: Hugh Sinclair, Helen Shingler, Abraham Sofaer, Leslie Dwyer, Joan Collins, Harry Locke. D: John Baxter. CRI 88m.

Judgment in Berlin 1988 ★★★½ Courtroom drama with Sheen as American judge called in to decide the fate of East Germans who've hijacked a Polish plane to Berlin. Uneven film, but Sheen's and Penn's performances are class acts. (a.k.a. *Escape to Freedom*) C: Martin Sheen, Sam Wanamaker, Sean Penn. D: Leo Penn. DRA [PG] 92m. V

Judgment in Stone, A 1986 Canadian ★★ Variation on the psychotic domestic help theme, with Tushingham as a violent housekeeper. Adaptation of Ruth Rendell's novel. (a.k.a. *The Housekeeper*) C: Rita Tushingham, Ross Petty. D: Ousama Rawi. CRI 102m. V

Judgment Night 1993 ★★★ After making a wrong turn, four friends drive into a very wrong neighborhood and find they're being hunted by the local berserker (Leary). Emphasis on guns, but the attempt at dramatic content is a plus. Good soundtrack. C: Emilio Estevez, Cuba Gooding, Denis Leary, Stephen Dorff. D: Stephen Hopkins. ACT [R] 110m. V

Judith 1966 ★★★ Austrian Jew (Loren) who survives death camps is determined to hunt down her husband, a war criminal hiding in Israel. Plot and casting make the film. (a.k.a. *Conflict*) C: Sophia Loren, Peter Finch, Jack Hawkins. D: Daniel Mann. DRA 109m. V

Judith of Bethulia 1913 ★★★½ Silent biblical tale of woman who saves her city by offering herself to enemy leader. Not Griffith's finest, but displays maturing storytelling abilities and evolving of his epic format. Interesting viewing for film history buffs. C: Lillian Gish, Dorothy Gish. D: D.W. Griffith. DRA 108m. V

Judo Saga 1965 Japanese ★★★½ Pre-*Karate Kid* story of a young judo trainee who learns the spiritual side of martial arts from master teacher Mifune. Slight story, though well acted. Script by noted director Akira Kurosawa. C: Yuzo Kayama, Toshiro Mifune. D: Seiichiro Uchikawa. ACT 159m.

Judo Showdown 1966 Japanese ★★★ Judo expert saves cop's daughter and learns that a rival is killing opponents for a much-coveted job. Simple plot sets up lots of action, action, action! Martial arts movie fans will get a kick out of this. C: Toshiya Wazaki, ryohei Uchida, Shoichi Hirai. D: Masateru Nishiyama. ACT 87m.

Juggernaut 1974 British ★★★★ A bomb squad expert (Harris) must defuse a bomb on a cruise ship. Unusually suspenseful despite somewhat tired story. All-star cast keeps the pace. C: Richard Harris, Omar Sharif, David Hemmings, Anthony Hopkins, Shirley Knight. D: Richard Lester. ACT [PG] 109m. V

Juggler of Notre Dame, The 1984 ★★★★ Based on a medieval folktale, moving story of nomadic street people whose joint journey transforms them both. Good Christmas fare. C: Carl Carlsson, Patrick Collins, Melinda Dillon. D: Michael Ray Rhodes. FAM/DRA 110m. V

Juggler, The 1953 ★★★★ Auschwitz survivor (Douglas in a moving performance) can't handle transition to peacetime in Israel. Stark and surprisingly un-Hollywood in its honesty. C: Kirk Douglas, Milly Vitale. D: Edward Dmytryk. DRA 86m.

Jugular Wine: A Vampire Odyssey 1994 ★★½ Ambitious, independently made horror film is visually striking but almost completely inert dramatically, with Irons investigating a vampire subculture and finding he can't escape it. C: Shaun Irons, Rachelle Packer, Gordon Capps, Lisa Malkiewicz, Meghan Bashaw. D: Blair Murphy. HOR 97m.

Juice 1992 ★★★★ Tough-minded tale of Harlem youths, with and without futures, whose lives are changed forever by an encounter with a gun. Unsentimental, with frighteningly natural performances by young cast. C: Omar Epps, Jermaine Hopkins, Tupac Shakur. D: Ernest R. Dickerson. CRI [R] 90m. V

Juke Box Jenny 1942 ★★★½ After his boss marries another woman in an alcoholic stupor, record sales manager Murray soothes his employer's spurned fiancée (Hilliard) and turns her into singing sensation. Plenty of musical numbers, and cast provides affable charm. C: Ken Murray, Harriet Hilliard, Don Douglas, Iris Adrian. D: Harold Young. MUS 65m.

Juke Box Rhythm 1959 ★★ European princess (Morrow) jets to New York to buy coronation dress and meets pop singer (Jones). Some fun songs. C: Jo Morrow, Jack Jones, Brian Donlevy, George Jessel. D: Arthur Dreifuss. MUS 81m.

Juke Girl 1942 ★★★½ Reagan is a migrant farm laborer who gets mixed up with Sheridan and murder. Snappy Warners B-film. C: Ann Sheridan, Ronald Reagan, Gene Lockhart, Faye Emerson. D: Curtis Bernhardt. CRI 90m.

Jules and Jim 1961 French ★★★★★ Truffaut's classic adaptation of Henri-Pierre Roché novel traces 20-year relationship between two men, a German Jew (Werner) and a

Frenchman (Serre), and the woman who loves both (Moreau). Masterfully written, acted, and directed, beautiful to look at, and movingly tragic. C: Jeanne Moreau, Oskar Werner, Henri Serre. D: Francois Truffaut. DRA 104m. V

Julia 1977 ★★★★½ Absorbing true story from playwright Lillian Hellman's *Pentimento*. Her life-long friendship with Julia (Redgrave) drew Hellman (Fonda) into WWII resistance movement. Beautifully acted. Won three Oscars: Supporting Actor Robards (as Hellman's companion, Dashiell Hammett), Supporting Actress Redgrave and Adaptation Screenwriter Alvin Sargent. This was also Streep's film debut. C: Jane Fonda, Vanessa Redgrave, Jason Robards, Maximilian Schell, Hal Holbrook, Meryl Streep. D: Fred Zinnemann. DRA [PG] 118m. V

Julia and Julia 1987 Italian ★★★ A woman becomes trapped between two time dimensions (and two men) in what amounts to an oversexed "Twilight Zone" episode. Confused fantasy/drama, notable mostly as an early experiment in high-definition TV. C: Kathleen Turner, Gabriel Byrne, Sting. D: Peter Del Monte. DRA [R] 97m. V

Julia Has Two Lovers 1991 ★★★ Kastner both wrote and stars in this story of a writer trying to spice up her love life. Uneventful treatment of odd-ball premise. C: Daphna Kastner, David Duchovny. D: Bashar Shbib. DRA [R] 87m. V

Julia Misbehaves 1948 ★★★½ Ex-chorus girl (Garson—miscast) visits ex-husband's (Pidgeon) home after nearly 20 years during daughter's wedding preparations. Taylor is stunningly beautiful as daughter. Moderately amusing. C: Greer Garson, Walter Pidgeon, Peter Lawford, Elizabeth Taylor, Cesar Romero. D: Jack Conway. COM 99m. V

Julie 1956 ★★½ Strident wife-in-jeopardy yarn puts Day in clutches of psychopathic hubby (Jourdan). Lacks credibility or true suspense. C: Doris Day, Louis Jourdan, Barry Sullivan. D: Andrew Stone. DRA 99m.

Julie Darling 1982 Canadian ★★ Psychological thriller deals with rape and murder; hurt by disastrous dubbing. C: Maurice Smith, Anthony Franciosa. D: Paul Nicolas. CRI [R] 100m.

Juliet of the Spirits 1965 Italian ★★★★ Ignored wife (Masina) faces her past and her fantasies to come to terms with herself. A stunning succession of images; Fellini's first color film. C: Giulietta Masina, Sandra Milo, Valentina Cortese, Sylva Koscina. D: Federico Fellini. DRA 142m. V

Julietta 1953 French ★★★ Frivolous woman flirts with a handsome lawyer who's engaged to be married. Top cast does what it can with trite material; painless comedy. C: Jean Marais, Jeanne Moreau, Dany Robin. D: Marc Allegret. COM 96m.

Julius Caesar 1953 ★★★★★ One of Hollywood's best Shakespeare adaptations, with stellar cast re-creating the story of political treachery in ancient Rome. Mankiewicz's script and direction infuses this with intelligence. Brando gives passionate performance as Marc Antony. Remade in 1970. C: Marlon Brando, James Mason, Louis Calhern, John Gielgud, Greer Garson, Deborah Kerr, Edmond O'Brien. D: Joseph L. Mankiewicz. DRA 120m. V

Julius Caesar 1970 ★★★ Mixed cast of American and British actors in a straightforward but fairly dull version of Shakespeare's play. Heston is okay as Mark Antony, but Robards is genuinely awful as Brutus. Stick with the Mankiewicz version. C: Charlton Heston, Jason Robards, John Gielgud, Richard Johnson, Robert Vaughn, Richard Chamberlain, Diana Rigg. D: Stuart Burge. DRA [G] 117m. V

Jumbo 1962 *See* **Billy Rose's Jumbo**

Jump into Hell 1955 ★★½ Long, ponderous war film about the French campaign in Indochina. Earnest and well-intentioned. C: Jacques Sernas, Kurt Kasznar. D: David Butler. DRA 93m.

Jumpin' at the Boneyard 1992 ★★★ Two dead-end brothers in the Bronx, one a crack addict, aspire to redemption in this mumbling, gritty, numbing drama, intermittently brought to life by Roth's intense work. C: Tim Roth, Alexis Arquette, Danitra Vance. D: Jeff Stanzler. DRA [R] 107m. V

Jumpin' Jack Flash 1986 ★★½ Computer programer Goldberg networks with secret agent and finds herself embroiled in web of international intrigue. Goldberg's winning performance keeps this lightweight spy comedy hopping. C: Whoopi Goldberg, Stephen Collins, Carol Kane. D: Penny Marshall. COM [R] 98m. V

Jumping Jacks 1952 ★★★½ One of Martin and Lewis' better efforts has them giving up show biz to join the paratroopers. Strongest on physical gags. C: Dean Martin, Jerry Lewis, Mona Freeman. D: Norman Taurog. COM 96m. V

June Bride 1948 ★★★½ Davis is tough woman's magazine editor organizing the perfect June wedding—in December. Montgomery as her sparring partner holds his own in this breezy comedy. C: Bette Davis, Robert Montgomery, Fay Bainter, Tom Tully, Barbara Bates, Mary Wickes. D: Bretaigne Windust. COM 97m. V

June Night 1940 Swedish ★★★ Naive young woman has ill-fated romance with handsome, worldly sailor. Bergman, in her last Swedish film before leaving for Hollywood, lets her personality and grace carry this sudsy love story. C: Ingrid Bergman, Olof Widgren, Gunnar Sjoberg, Marianne Lofgren. D: Per Lindberg. DRA 90m. V

Jungle Assault 1989 ★★ Two soldiers of fortune are given a top-secret mission to disarm a terrorist operation and save a high-ranking military man's deluded daughter. Nothing original here. C: William Smith, Ted

Prior, Maria Rosado. D: David A. Prior. ACT 86m. v

Jungle Book 1942 ★★★★ A boy (Sabu) raised in the jungle uses his wits to survive. Children will enjoy this spirited adaptation of Kipling's classic story, which uses voice-over animal monologues to good effect. Disney produced an animated feature version in the 1960s. C: Sabu, Joseph Calleia, Rosemary DeCamp. D: Zoltan Korda. FAM/DRA 109m. v

Jungle Book, The 1967 ★★★★ Boy-cub Mowgli is befriended by lazy bear Baloo in this popular Disney animated feature, loosely based on Kipling's stories. Easy-going fun, with effective character voices and some jazzy tunes, including "The Bare Necessities." Last cartoon feature supervised by Walt Disney himself. The same company released a live-action follow-up in 1994. Voices of Phil Harris, George Sanders, Sterling Holloway, Louis Prima, Sebastian Cabot. D: Wolfgang Reitherman. FAM/DRA [G] 78m. v

Jungle Bride 1933 ★★★ A shipwrecked trio battle the elements and their fears that one of them is a murderer. C: Charles Starrett, Anita Page, Kenneth Thompson. D: Harry Hoyt. ACT 63m. v

Jungle Cat 1960 ★★★ Disney nature documentary about jaguar in Amazon jungle benefits from great footage, while suffering from pedestrian narration. Kids will enjoy it. D: James Algar. DOC 70m.

Jungle Cavalcade 1941 ★★★ Frank Buck combines best footage from three films: *Bring 'Em Back Alive*, *White Cargo*, and *Fang and Claw*, highlighting his adventurous life as big game hunter. Exciting (though occasionally cruel) scenes of animals on the run. D: Clyde Elliot, Armand Denis, Frank Buck. DOC 77m. v

Jungle Fever 1991 ★★★½ Lee looks at interracial romance, between black architect Snipes and white secretary Sciorra. Promising tale of forbidden love bogs down in politics but noteworthy for the brutally frank subplot about a crack-addicted sibling (Jackson). Turturro provides an immensely appealing performance as a young man searching for love. C: Wesley Snipes, Annabella Sciorra, Spike Lee, Ossie Davis, Ruby Dee, Samuel L. Jackson, Lonette McKee, John Turturro, Anthony Quinn. D: Spike Lee. DRA [R] 135m. v

Jungle Fighters 1961 *See* **Long and the Short and the Tall, The**

Jungle Gents 1954 ★★ Late Bowery Boys entry: While touring Africa, Sach acquires the ability to smell diamonds—literally. Strictly for devotees. COM

Jungle Gold 1944 ★★½ Hilarious serial entry chronicling the exploits of Tiger Woman as she thwarts the invaders of her natural habitat. C: Wallace Grissell, Allan Lane, Linda Stirling. D: Spencer Bennet. ACT 100m.

Jungle Heat 1984 ★★★ Anthropoid mutants hope to feast on adventurous duo searching for pygmies. (a.k.a. *Dances of the Dwarfs*) C: Peter Fonda, Deborah Raffin, John Amos. D: Gus Trikonis. HOR [PG] 93m. v

Jungle Jim in the Forbidden Land 1952 ★★½ Jim is tricked into leading scientists to home of giants. For kids only. C: Johnny Weissmuller, Angela Greene, Jean Willes. D: Lew Landers. ACT 65m.

Jungle Man-Eaters 1954 ★★½ Last *Jungle Jim* effort pits Weissmuller against diamond smugglers. For kids only. C: Johnny Weissmuller, Karin Booth. D: Lee Sholem. ACT 68m.

Jungle Manhunt 1951 ★★ Rams star Waterfield plays—surprise—a football player. Jungle Jim has to help him out when he's stranded in the wild. Pedestrian. C: Johnny Weissmuller, Bob Waterfield, Sheila Ryan. D: Lew Landers. ACT 66m.

Jungle Master, The 1956 ★★½ Hungry animals and angry African natives besiege a group of Britishers hoping to rescue female captive. C: John Kitzmiller, Simone Blondell. D: Miles Deem. ACT 90m. v

Jungle Patrol 1948 ★★ Trapped in the jungles of New Guinea, Allied fliers are treated to a no-holds-barred USO show delivered by a beautiful young singer. Winning words and music in generic wartime story. C: Kristine Miller, Arthur Franz, Ross Ford, Tom Noonan. D: Joe Newman. MUS 71m. v

Jungle Princess, The 1936 ★★★★ Lamour's sarong debut finds her playing a female Tarzan who learns civilized behavior (and singing in English) from an American hunter (Milland). Enjoyably silly adventure, with a fair amount of harmless comedy. C: Dorothy Lamour, Ray Milland, Akim Tamiroff. D: William Thiele. ACT 85m.

Jungle, The 1952 ★★★ Tame safari picture that mixes sci-fi elements with a romantic triangle. C: Rod Cameron, Cesar Romero. D: William Berke. SFI 74m. v

Jungle Warriors 1985 German ★ Fashion models on location in South America decide to take down a drug kingpin. As absolutely silly as it sounds. C: Nina Van Pallandt, Paul L. Smith. D: Ernst Theumer. ACT [R] 96m. v

Jungle Woman 1944 ★★½ Sequel to *Captive Wild Woman* has shrink trying to help ape-woman overcome her penchant for dismembering folks she likes. Pretty tame. C: Acquanetta, Evelyn Ankers. D: Reginald LeBorg. ACT 54m.

Junior 1994 ★★★★ Genial, often amusing comedy in which stoic scientist (Schwarzenegger) allows himself to be impregnated for research purposes, then carries baby to full term. Star's core male audience couldn't accept him in this unusual role, but film works on its own modest terms. Thompson's a dizzy delight as Arnold's love interest. C: Arnold Schwarzenegger, Danny DeVito, Emma

Thompson, Frank Langella, Pamela Reed. D: Ivan Reitman. COM [PG-13] 110m. V

Junior Bonner 1972 ★★★★ Fading rodeo star (McQueen) drifts back to his hometown and finds he must prove his mettle in the arena one more time to help his parents. Infectious comedy/drama with terrific cast and rousing direction. C: Steve McQueen, Robert Preston, Ida Lupino. D: Sam Peckinpah. COM [PG] 101m. V

Junior Miss 1945 ★★★★ Charming, almost plotless teenage turmoil comedy about the struggle between generations from hit Broadway play by Jerome Chodorov and Joseph Fields, adapted from stories by Sally Benson. Garner gives a memorable performance. C: Peggy Ann Garner, Allyn Joslyn, Michael Dunne, Mona Freeman, Mel Torme. D: George Seaton. COM 94m.

Junkman 1982 ★★ Car chase extravaganza about filmmaker whose life is being threatened. Loud, loud, loud. C: H. B. Halicki, Christopher Stone, Susan Shaw. D: H. B. Halicki. ACT [PG] 99m. V

Juno and the Paycock 1930 British ★★½ Tragic tale of an Irish family coping with unrest in Dublin and among the family itself. Decent but dreary, and lacking the usual Hitchcock style. Based on play by Sean O'Casey. C: Sara Allgood, Edward Chapman, Sidney Morgan. D: Alfred Hitchcock. DRA 99m. V

Jupiter's Darling 1955 ★★★½ Big-scale musical about siren (Williams) who trysts with Hannibal (Keel) as distraction to prevent the invasion of Rome. C: Esther Williams, Howard Keel, George Sanders, Marge and Gower Champion. D: George Sidney. MUS 96m. V

Jurassic Park 1993 ★★★★ Dinosaurs on the loose in a theme park. This blockbuster hit has thrilling special effects and a lot of energy. The cast is splendid, especially Goldblum. Oscars for Special Effects and Sound. C: Sam Neill, Laura Dern, Jeff Goldblum, Richard Attenborough, Bob Peck, Martin Ferrero, B. D. Wong. D: Steven Spielberg. ACT [PG-13] 126m. V

Jury of One 1974 French ★★ Even Gabin (as judge) and Loren can't help this derivative melodrama about a mother who goes to excessive lengths to clear her son of a murder charge. (a.k.a. *Verdict*) C: Sophia Loren, Jean Gabin. D: Andre Cayatte. DRA [R] 97m.

Just a Gigolo 1979 West German ★★★½ Briefly appearing in her last film, Dietrich sings the title song in this strange mix of sex and disillusionment where a Prussian war veteran becomes a gigolo in post-WWI Berlin. Unfocused, but captures flavor of the era well. Released in various lengths. C: David Bowie, Sydne Rome, Kim Novak, Maria Schell, Marlene Dietrich. D: David Hemmings. DRA [R] 105m. V

Just Across the Street 1952 ★★★ Good cast buoys minor farce about woman (Sheridan) mistaken for wealthy matron. C: Ann Sheridan, John Lund, Cecil Kellaway. D: Joseph Pevney. COM 78m.

Just an Old Sweet Song 1976 ★★★★ Low-key, tasteful film about a black family from Detroit vacationing in the deep South. Fine performances distinguish this movie; take a look. C: Cicely Tyson, Robert Hooks, Kevin Hooks. D: Robert Miller. DRA 78m. TVM

Just Another Girl on the I.R.T. 1993 ★★★ Fresh, energetic tale about a bright African-American teen who gets pregnant. Tackles a timely topic with verve, but brings it to a hard-to-swallow conclusion. C: Ariyan Johnson, Kevin Thigpen. D: Leslie Harris. DRA [R] 96m. V

Just Around the Corner 1938 ★★★ Shirley Temple feature has America's little darling tap dancing her way into hearts of Depression-weary folk while convincing mean business man to create new jobs. Guaranteed to induce tooth decay, though Temple's dance numbers with Robinson are delightful. C: Shirley Temple, Joan Davis, Charles Farrell, Bill Robinson, Bert Lahr. D: Irving Cummings. MUS 70m. V

Just Before Dawn 1946 ★★★½ One of the best of the *Crime Doctor* series has Dr. Ordway unwittingly used to kill one of his own patients. Dark and brooding B-mystery. C: Warner Baxter, Adelle Roberts. D: William Castle. CRI 66m. V

Just Before Nightfall 1975 French ★★★★ An adulterer murders his mistress, and then confesses to the victim's husband and his own wife. A sly look at middle-class morality, that places appearances over sordid truth. Familiar territory for Chabrol; stunning direction and dialogue. C: Stephane Audran, Michel Bouquet, Francois Perier. D: Claude Chabrol. DRA [PG] 100m.

Just Between Friends 1986 ★★★½ Two women friends unwittingly share the same man—Moore's husband Danson is Lahti's lover. Attempt to wed old-fashioned tearjerker with sophisticated comedy doesn't work, but Lahti's terrific. C: Mary Tyler Moore, Ted Danson, Christine Lahti, Sam Waterston. D: Allan Burns. DRA [PG-13] 110m. V

Just Cause 1995 ★★★ Harvard law professor (Connery) squares off with a corrupt detective (Fishburne) over a Florida death row inmate (Underwood), unjustly convicted. Stylishly directed, but dramatically inert adaptation of John Katzenbach's novel. C: Sean Connery, Laurence Fishburne, Blair Underwood, Kate Capshaw, Ruby Dee, Ed Harris. D: Arne Glimcher. CRI [R] 105m. V

Just for Fun 1963 British ★★ Silly pop musical revolves around teenagers forming political party. Features some almost memorable numbers from the early '60s. C: Mark Wynter, Cherry Roland. D: Gordon Flemyng. MUS 85m.

Just for You 1952 ★★★½ Cheery family musical casts Crosby as Prodigal Father trying to win over son and daughter he's ignored because of Broadway producing career. Wyman is winning, but you can spot the plot development a mile away. C: Bing Crosby, Jane Wyman, Ethel Barrymore, Natalie Wood. D: Elliott Nugent. MUS 104m. V

Just Imagine 1930 ★★★ Man who dies in 1930 is revived in 1980 and can't adapt. Futuristic science fiction musical predicts everything from test-tube babies to electric-eye doors. C: El Brendel, Maureen O'Sullivan, John Garrick. D: David Butler. MUS 102m.

Just Like Us 1983 ★★★ Two young women from opposite sides of the tracks overcome class differences and reach true understanding. C: Jennifer Jason Leigh, Kari Michaelsen. D: Harry Harris. DRA 55m. V

Just Me and You 1978 ★★½ The misadventures of a flighty New Yorker (Lasser) and a staid sales representative (Grodin) lead to romance when they travel cross-country together. Slight character comedy, written by star Lasser, remains in low gear throughout. C: Louise Lasser, Charles Grodin. D: John Erman. COM 100m. TVM V

Just Off Broadway 1942 ★★★½ *Mike Shayne* series entry has Nolan coming to the aid of woman accused of murder. Brisk fun. C: Lloyd Nolan, Marjorie Weaver, Phil Silvers. D: Herbert Leeds. CRI 66m.

Just One Of The Girls 1993 ★★★ Gender chaos erupts when high school boy disguises himself as a girl in order to escape bully. C: Corey Haim, Nicole Eggert, Cameron Bancroft. D: Michael Keusch. COM 94m. V

Just One of the Guys 1985 ★★★½ Predictable film about a girl who poses as a boy to get on school paper, straightens out the school geek, and generally improves life for everyone. Pleasant and light-hearted. C: Joyce Hyser, Clayton Rohner, Billy Jacoby. D: Lisa Gottlieb. COM [PG-13] 100m. V

Just Suppose 1926 ★★★½ Topical silent comedy casts Barthelmess as Prince of Wales visiting New York who falls for American Moran. Dated now, but pleasant, with strong performance by star. C: Richard Barthelmess, Lois Moran, Geoffrey Kerr. D: Kenneth Webb. COM

Just Tell Me What You Want 1980 ★★★½ Long-suffering mistress (MacGraw) finally breaks off with bullheaded corporate head (King) leaving him so miserable that he'll do anything to bring her back. King's comic talents elevate otherwise routine battle of the sexes comedy. Screenplay by Jay Presson Allen, based on her novel. C: Ali MacGraw, Alan King, Myrna Loy (last film), Keenan Wynn, Tony Roberts, Peter Weller. D: Sidney Lumet. COM [R] 114m. V

Just Tell Me You Love Me 1980 ★★ Fun and adventure become profitable when three con artists unleash their talents on unsuspecting wealthy businesspeople. C: Robert Hegyes, Lisa Hartman. D: Tony Mordente. ACT [PG] 90m. V

Just the Way You Are 1984 ★★★★ In an effort to be treated like everyone else, a handicapped musician (McNichol) hides her disability on a trip to the French Alps and ends up finding romance. McNichol's winning performance and beautiful European scenery highlight this engaging comedy/drama. C: Kristy McNichol, Michael Ontkean. D: Edouard Molinaro. COM [PG] 96m. V

Just Tony 1922 ★★★½ Unalloyed Western adapted from a Max Brand story, Tom Mix rescues mistreated horse and makes him his own. Good location photography highlights Mix's loving testimonial to his celebrated horse. C: Tom Mix, Claire Adams. D: Lynn Reynolds. WST 58m.

Just You and Me, Kid 1979 ★★ An octogenarian vaudevillian (Burns) reluctantly comes to the rescue of a runaway teenager (Shields) fleeing a vicious drug dealer. Dreary, slow-paced comedy, despite Burns' charm. C: George Burns, Brooke Shields, Burl Ives, Ray Bolger. D: Leonard Stern. COM [PG] 95m.

Justice Is Done 1950 French ★★★★ A woman (Nollier) is prosecuted for the mercy killing of her lover. Twist: focus is on the jury. Fascinating study of the French judicial system. C: Claude Nollier, Michel Auclair, Valentine Tessier, Jean Debucourt. D: André Cayatte. DRA 105m.

Justin Case 1988 ★★★½ Unsold pilot brings Edwards back to TV with oddball comedy/mystery about ghost of murdered private eye seeking his killers. Okay; not his best. C: George Carlin, Molly Hagan, Douglas Still. D: Blake Edwards. DRA 78m. TVM

Justin Morgan Had a Horse 1972 ★★★ True-life Disney tale of Revolutionary War-era schoolteacher who bred horses prized for their racing abilities. Forgettable material aimed at children. C: Don Murray, Lana Wood, Gary Crosby. D: Hollingsworth Morse. FAM/DRA 91m. V

Justine 1969 ★★★½ The beautiful and enigmatic wife of a wealthy banker influences politics in 1930s Egypt via her passionate affairs. Not much of an adaptation of *The Alexandria Quartet*, but it has style and merit on its own terms. C: Anouk Aimee, Dirk Bogarde, Robert Forster, Anna Karina, Philippe Noiret, Michael York. D: George Cukor. DRA [R] 115m. V

J.W. Coop 1972 ★★★½ Low-key directorial effort by Robertson who plays declining rodeo star, obsessed with winning number-1 rating. Not much story, but richly evocative supporting cast, and vivid rodeo atmosphere give this some merit. C: Cliff Robertson, Geraldine Page, Cristina Ferrare. D: Cliff Robertson. WST [PG] 112m.

K

K-9 1989 ★★★ Nasty cop Belushi is assigned the one partner he can get along with—a dog. But Belushi has met his match and the duo proves to be too much for the bad guys. Lighthearted family comedy is harmless fun. C: James Belushi, Mel Harris, Ed O'Neill. D: Rod Daniel. COM [PG-13] 111m. V

K-9000 1991 ★★ Man's faithful friend turns weapon when a detective and scientist invent a killer canine. C: Chris Mulkey, Catherine Oxenburg. HOR [PG] 96m. V

K2—The Ultimate High 1992 British ★★★ Two climbers ascend world's second highest peak and run into plenty of survival problems. Despite good cinematography it's not always easy to hang on to this adaptation from stage play. C: Michael Biehn, Matt Craven, Hiroshi Fujioka. D: Franc Roddam. ACT [R] 104m. V

Kaddish 1989 ★★★★ Searing indictment of the Nazis' "final solution" as seen through the eyes of a Jewish concentration camp survivor and his son. Enlightening historical documentary took five years to film. D: Steve Brand. DOC 92m. V

Kadoyng 1974 British ★★★½ When business magnates want to destroy beautiful landscapes with a superhighway, a group of children and their outer space companion put a stop to the construction. Entertaining kids' flick. C: Teresa Codling, Adrian Hall, Leo Maguire. D: Ian Shand. FAM/COM 60m.

Kafka 1992 ★★★½ Kafka (Irons) searches the streets of Prague for a friend who mysteriously disappeared. Blends material from the author's works to achieve a frightening, dreamy mood; not a complete success, but very interesting nonetheless. Grey is terrific. C: Jeremy Irons, Theresa Russell, Joel Grey, Ian Holm, Alec Guinness. D: Steven Soderbergh. DRA 100m. V

Kagemusha 1980 Japanese ★★★★★ When warlord dies, underlings substitute a lookalike in his place in hopes of not surrendering power. Great action sequences alternate with contemplative moments in visionary epic from Japanese master. C: Tatsuya Nakadai, Tsutomo Yamazaki. D: Akira Kurosawa. DRA [PG] 159m. V

Kaleidoscope 1966 ★★★ Comedy caper revolving around a flippant cardsharp's scheme to break the bank of every casino in Europe by marking all their decks of cards. Flashy adventure comedy provides only camp appeal as it tries to capture the '60s psychedelic hipness. C: Warren Beatty, Susannah York, Clive Revill, Eric Porter. D: Jack Smight. COM 103m.

Kalifornia 1993 ★★★½ A writer (Duchovny) and photographer (Forbes) on the road researching serial killers unwittingly pick up two dangerous companions. Lewis stands out as the killer's childlike girlfriend. Slow start builds to an explosive climax. C: Brad Pitt, Juliette Lewis, David Duchovny, Michelle Forbes. D: Dominic Sena. CRI [R] 117m. V

Kameradschaft 1931 German ★★★★½ A mine collapse on the French-German border traps French workers; Germans come to the rescue. Powerful view of people brought together in a common cause. C: George Chalia, David Mendaille, Ernest Busch. D: G. W. Pabst. DRA 78m. V

Kamikaze 1983 German ★★½ An unemployed electronics whiz addicted to television invents an electronic gun that allows him to kill TV newscasters he despises. A cadre of famous scientists are brought together to solve the murders. Despite inventive plot, dialogue and performances are disappointing. C: Rainer Werner Fassbinder, Gunther Kaufmann, Brigitte Mira. D: Wolf Gremm. CRI 106m. V

Kamilla 1981 Norwegian ★★★★½ Seven-year-old girl's callous world and hateful parents are contrasted with her friendship with a little boy. A quietly disturbing tale, with shatteringly good acting. C: Nina Knapskog, Vibeke Lokkeberg. D: Vibeke Lokkeberg. DRA 100m.

Kampf um Rom 1969 *See* **Fight for Rome**

Kanal 1956 Polish ★★★★ The second in Wajda's WWII trilogy (after *A Generation,* before *Ashes and Diamonds*) accurately portrays the true story of Polish resistance fighters trapped by Nazis in the sewers of Warsaw. Harrowing subject matter and inventive photography overcome some plot and characterization weaknesses. (a.k.a. *They Loved Life*) C: Teresa Izewska, Tadeusz Janczar. D: Andrzej Wajda. DRA 96m. V

Kandyland 1987 ★ Naive and beautiful erotic dancer (Evenson) learns the ropes from jaded mentor (Bergman). So bad its fun. C: Kim Evenson, Sandahl Bergman, Charles Laulette. D: Robert Allen Schnitzer. DRA [R] 94m. V

Kangaroo 1952 ★★★ Amid the wild splendor of the Australian Outback, a young phony passes himself off as the long-lost heir to a wealthy rancher, then sabotages his scam by falling in love with the rancher's daughter. Good fun and a big-name cast work wonders. C: Maureen O'Hara, Peter Lawford, Finlay Currie. D: Lewis Milestone. WST 84m.

Kangaroo 1986 Australian ★★★★ A disenchanted English writer and his wife relocate to Australia, where he is attracted to a group of quasi-Fascists. Absorbing drama based on the semiautobiographical novel by D.H. Lawrence, with outstanding performances by real-life husband and wife Friels and Davis. C:

Colin Friels, Judy Davis, John Walton. D: Tim Burstall. DRA [R] 105m. v

Kansan, The 1943 ★★★½ A sharpshooting drifter is elected marshal of an untamed town and runs afoul of crooks and corrupt politician. Sturdy, well-paced Western epic. C: Richard Dix, Jane Wyatt, Victor Jory. D: George Archainbaud. WST 79m. v

Kansas 1988 ★★ Nice guy (McCarthy) is victimized by swindler (Dillon). Weak plot, but appealing cast. C: Matt Dillon, Andrew McCarthy, Leslie Hope. D: David Stevens. DRA [R] 111m. v

Kansas City Bomber 1972 ★★★ Welch as roller derby champ in brainless drama with some hair-raising turns. C: Raquel Welch, Kevin McCarthy, Jeanne Cooper, Mary Kay Place, Jodie Foster. D: Jerrold Freedman. DRA [PG] 99m.

Kansas City Confidential 1952 ★★★½ After he quits the police force, a disgruntled man (Foster) puts together an idea—and a crew—for the perfect crime. Provides the meat and marrow of hard-boiled crime, packed with violence and action. C: John Payne, Coleen Gray, Preston Foster. D: Phil Karlson. CRI 98m. v

Kansas City Kitty 1944 ★★½ Faced with the untimely demise of her favorite music publishing company, a young woman turns entrepreneur, buys the business, and fights to keep it alive. Nifty music and peachy fun, with Davis at the lead. C: Joan Davis, Bob Crosby. D: Del Lord. MUS 63m.

Kansas City Massacre 1975 ★★★★ G-Man Melvin Purvis takes on all comers: Pretty Boy Floyd, John Dillinger, and Baby Face Nelson. Knuckles and know-how, with a sense of humor. Better than average TV offering. C: Dale Robertson, Bo Hopkins. D: Dan Curtis. CRI 99m. TVM v

Kansas Cyclone 1941 ★★★½ When outlaws continually rob the Wells Fargo express, Barry goes undercover as a geologist to bring the crime spree to an end. Offbeat Western entertainment and good series entry for Barry. C: Don "Red" Barry, Lynn Merrick, Milt Kibbee. D: George Sherman. WST 57m.

Kansas Pacific 1953 ★★★½ Confederate soldiers attempt to interrupt construction of a railway that spells Union expansion. Interesting historical Western. C: Sterling Hayden, Eve Miller. D: Ray Nazarro. WST 73m. v

Kansas Raiders 1950 ★★ Jesse James joins a group of Rebel raiders during the Civil War. Western fare with heaps of violence and action. C: Audie Murphy, Brian Donlevy, Marguerite Chapman, Tony Curtis. D: Ray Enright. WST 80m.

Kansas Territory 1952 ★★★½ After his brother is killed, Elliot seeks vengeance. When he learns that his sibling was not above reproach, he must come to terms with his brother's true nature. Unusual material for Westerns, nicely played by Elliot. C: Wild Bill Elliott, House Peters, Jr., Peggy Stewart. D: Lewis Collins. WST 64m.

Kaos 1985 Italian ★★★★★ Four Luigi Pirandello tales explore facets of peasant life. Sumptuous photography, natural performances, compelling narratives, and lovely coda about Pirandello himself. Exquisite production. C: Margarita Lozano, Claudio Bigagil, Massimo Bonetti. D: Paolo Taviani, Vittorio Taurani. DRA [R] 188m. v

Kapo 1964 Italian ★★★★ A Jewish girl (Strasberg) saved from death by a Nazi doctor becomes a cruel guard in a concentration camp. Perhaps too melodramatic for intense subject, yet interesting. C: Susan Strasberg, Laurent Terzieff, Emmanuelle Riva. D: Gillo Pontecorvo. DRA 116m.

Karamazov 1931 German ★★★ Early Expressionist telling of Dostoyevsky's classic novel of the famous brothers. Interesting antique may creak a little today, but still worthwhile. (a.k.a. *The Murderer Dmitri Karamazov* and *The Brothers Karamazov*) C: Fritz Kortner, Anna Sten, Fritz Rasp, Bernard Minetti. D: Fyodor Ozep. DRA 100m.

Karate Cop *See* **Slaughter In San Francisco**

Karate Cop 1993 ★★ The last cop and scientist on Earth go on an adventure-packed quest for a secret crystal that has the power to transport them to safety. C: David Carradine, Carrie Chambers. D: Alan Roberts. ACT [R] 100m. v

Karate Cops ★★ A man seeks revenge after the mob kills his best friend. C: Richard Norton, Ronnie Lott, Hidy Ochiai. D: George Chung. ACT 88m. v

Karate Kid, The 1984 ★★★½ Weakling adolescent Macchio is trained by odd jobber Morita to overcome bullies by using martial arts and Eastern philosophy. Admittedly formulaic script presses all the right emotional buttons. Veteran supporting player Morita gets breakout role. C: Ralph Macchio, Noriyuki "Pat" Morita, Elisabeth Shue. D: John G. Avildsen. DRA [PG] 126m. v

Karate Kid, Part 2, The 1986 ★★★ Inevitable and unnecessary sequel takes Macchio and Morita to Okinawa for more martial arts action and tearjerking. Strictly for kids and diehard fans of the first film. C: Ralph Macchio, Noriyuki "Pat" Morita, Nobu McCarthy. D: John G. Avildsen. ACT [PG] 113m. v

Karate Kid, Part 3, The 1989 ★★★ Mentor (Morita) refuses to prepare titler (Macchio) for an upcoming tournament, forcing him to work with a duplicitous trainer. Keeps kicking, but fun of the series running out. C: Ralph Macchio, Noriyuki "Pat" Morita, Robyn Lively, Thomas Ian Griffith. D: John G. Avildsen. DRA [PG] 113m. v

Karate Warrior 1988 ★★ After he is beaten and left for dead by a gangster, Martin must learn martial arts to avenge himself. C: Jared

Martin, Janet Agren, Kim Stuart, Ken Watanabe. D: Larry Ludman. ACT 90m. V

Karen Carpenter Story, The 1989 ★★★½ Musical film biography of pop singer (Gibb) and her fatal struggle with anorexia. Uses real tracks of Karen and brother Richard to good advantage. C: Cynthia Gibb, Mitchell Anderson, Louise Fletcher. D: Joseph Sargent. DRA 100m. TVM

Karma 1986 Swiss ★★★★ After her village is evacuated, circumstances force a South Vietnamese woman to become a prostitute in Saigon. Her wounded husband returns from combat and rejects her before heading back to the war. Slow-moving but keenly acted drama, shot on location in Saigon. C: Tran Quang, Phuong Dwng,Le Cung Bac. D: Ho Quang Minh. DRA 103m.

Katerina Izmailova 1969 USSR ★★★★ In this opera film, backed by a solid Shostakovich score, a wealthy woman has an affair with a laborer, which leads to tragic consequences. Well done and colorful. Opera fans will definitely enjoy. (a.k.a. *Lady Macbeth of the Mtsensk District*) C: Galina Vishnevskaya, Artyom Inozemstsev. D: Mikhail Shapiro. MUS 118m.

Katherine 1975 ★★★★ Interesting study of liberal's pampered daughter Spacek and her transformation into underground radical terrorist. Spacek's expert performance, one of her early gems, is so good that script implausibilities pass unnoticed. (a.k.a. *The Radical*) C: Art Carney, Sissy Spacek, Henry Winkler. D: Jeremy Paul Kagan. DRA 100m. TVM V

Kathleen 1941 ★★★ Low-key comedy casts Temple as matchmaking daughter of widower (Marshall). C: Shirley Temple, Herbert Marshall, Laraine Day. D: Harold S. Bucquet. COM 88m.

Kathy O' 1958 ★★★½ Spoiled Hollywood child star (McCormack) runs out on harried man Duryea, in breezy but second-rate comedy. C: Dan Duryea, Jan Sterling, Patty McCormack. D: Jack Sher. COM 99m.

Katie Did It 1951 ★★★½ Lightweight amusing comedy with Blyth as straitlaced, New England librarian trying to resist persistant lothario (Stevens). Director became noted producer of *The Tonight Show.* C: Ann Blyth, Mark Stevens, Cecil Kellaway. D: Frederick de Cordova. COM 81m.

Katie: Portrait of a Centerfold 1978 ★★ Slick, empty look at the descent of an innocent Texas girl (Basinger) into the sleaziness of Hollywood modeldom and her temptation by men's magazine's offer. Cast of camp icons might rate a look. C: Kim Basinger, Glynn Turman, Vivian Blaine, Dorothy Malone, Fabian, Tab Hunter, Don Johnson. D: Robert Greenwald. DRA 100m. TVM

Katie's Passion 1975 *See* **Keetje Tippel**

Katzelmacher 1969 German ★★★ Exploring mankind's basic fear of the unknown, Fassbinder directs himself as a Greek worker who moves into a poor German suburb and is met with almost universal prejudice. A common theme throughout Fassbinder's work that is more fully explored in his later films. C: Hanna Schygulla, Lilith Ungerer, Elga Sorbas. D: Rainer Werner Fassbinder. DRA 88m.

Kavik the Wolf Dog 1980 ★★★ Another animal returning to master story involves an Alaskan sled dog who travels from Oregon to reunite with his human pal. Ordinary adventure story. C: Ronny Cox, Linda Sorensen, John Ireland, John Candy. D: Peter Carter. FAM/DRA 99m. V

Kaya, I'll Kill You 1969 Yugoslavian ★★★½ After living in peace for 300 years, a quiet Italian town undergoes radical change when troops occupy it during WWII. Disturbing, occasionally sadistic study of life transformed by dire circumstances. C: Zaim Muzaferija, Ugljesa Kojadinovic. D: Vatroslav Mimica. DRA 80m.

Kazablan 1974 Israeli ★★★½ A savvy war veteran (Gaon) vows to keep his old neighborhood from being demolished. Solid musical adaptation of stage show features Gaon reprising his stage role. Sung in English and filmed in Jerusalem. C: Yehoram Gaon, Arie Elias. D: Menahem Golan. MUS [PG] 114m.

Keaton's Cop 1990 ★★ Tedious comedy of the relationship between an ancient ex-mobster and the cop assigned to protect him in a nursing home. C: Lee Majors, Don Rickles, Abe Vigoda. D: Bob Burge. COM [R] 95m. V

Keep 'Em Flying 1941 ★★★½ Raye as twin sisters peps up fast-paced Abbott and Costello service farce with standard romantic subplot of recruit (Foran) adjusting to the Air Force. Highlight: Scene in the diner with Lou and two Marthas. C: Bud Abbott, Lou Costello, Martha Raye, Dick Foran. D: Arthur Lubin. COM 85m. V

Keep It Cool 1958 *See* **Let's Rock!**

Keep, The 1983 ★ Nazi soldiers occupying a Romanian castle uncover a demonic force within its walls; only mysterious stranger Glenn seems to know its secret. More stylish than easily understandable. Based on F. Paul Wilson's novel. C: Scott Glenn, Ian McKellen. D: Michael Mann. HOR [R] 96m. V

Keep Your Powder Dry 1945 ★★★ Three very different young women join the WACS, and learn how to deal with each other. Fair retelling of a familiar story. Nothing new. C: Lana Turner, Laraine Day, Susan Peters, Agnes Moorehead. D: Edward Buzzell. DRA 93m.

Keep Your Seats Please 1936 British ★★★ A cagey young heir believes that his fortune is hidden somewhere in a set of six chairs. Broadly funny idea that plays quite well with this urbane British cast. Filmed many times; best-known version is later Mel Brooks' *The Twelve Chairs.* C: George Formby, Florence

Desmond, Gus McNaughton. D: Monty Banks. COM 82m.

Keeper of the City 1992 ★★★ Ordinary Joe goes on a rampage to wipe out gangsters. Vigilante action drama with lots of bullet and plot holes. C: Louis Gossett, Jr., Peter Coyote, Anthony LaPaglia. D: Bobby Roth. ACT 95m. TVM V

Keeper of the Flame 1942 ★★★★ A journalist (Tracy), assigned to write the story of a much admired, recently deceased American patriot uncovers an ugly secret after befriending his reclusive widow (Hepburn). Fine acting and a worthwhile message. C: Spencer Tracy, Katharine Hepburn, Richard Whorf, Margaret Wycherly. D: George Cukor. DRA 101m. V

Keeper, The 1984 ★★★ Horror spoof features Lee as the ominous head of fancy sanitarium whose patients keep dying mysteriously. C: Christopher Lee, Tell Schreiber, Sally Gray, Ross Vesarian. D: T.Y. Drake. HOR 96m. V

Keepers, The 1958 French ★★★★ A wealthy, troubled young man blames his father for his mother's death, and is committed to an asylum. Frank views of institution's inner workings—picture was actually shot in one—caused a scandal in France upon release; still strong stuff today. C: Jean-Pierre Mocky, Pierre Brasseur, Anouk Aimee, Charles Aznavour. D: Georges Franju. DRA 98m.

Keeping Track 1986 ★★★ Mild thriller about tourists who witness murder on a train, and find themselves holding the bag, which contains $5 million. Decent cast in rather tame effort. C: Michael Sarrazin, Margot Kidder, Ken Pogue. D: Robin Spry. CRI [R] 102m. V

Keetje Tippel 1975 Dutch ★★★★ Poor family in 1880s Holland forces independent daughter into prostitution for support. Superior production values and van der Ven's authentic portrayal lend credence to difficult subject. (a.k.a. *Katie's Passion, Cathy Tippel*) C: Rutger Hauer, Monique van de Ven. D: Paul Verhoeven. DRA 104m. V

Kelly and Me 1957 ★★★ Johnson plays a song-and-dance man who teams up with a dog after his dancing partner leaves him. Tap-dancing canine is certainly a novelty. C: Van Johnson, Piper Laurie, Martha Hyer. D: Robert Z. Leonard. MUS 86m.

Kelly's Heroes 1970 ★★★½ *Dirty Dozen* clone is not as great as its precursor, but fun ensues as crooks led by Eastwood, take on a dangerous assignment to rip off gold behind enemy lines in WWII. Savalas and Rickles are a riot. C: Clint Eastwood, Telly Savalas, Don Rickles, Donald Sutherland. D: Brian G. Hutton. ACT [PG] 143m. V

Kemek 1988 ★★ In spite of the presence of the always watchable Woronov, this tale of an evil chemical tycoon and his mind-altering drug offers some pretty silly suspense. C: David Hedison, Helmut Snider, Alexandra Stewart, Cal Haynes, Charles Mitchell, Mary Woronov. D: Theodore Gershuny. HOR 82m. V

Kennel Murder Case, The 1933 ★★★★½ Apparent suicide at a Long Island dog show may be murder, so detective Philo Vance (Powell) investigates. Intriguing whodunit with Powell suave and appealing in his fourth turn as S.S. Van Dine's sleuth. C: William Powell, Mary Astor, Eugene Pallette. D: Michael Curtiz. CRI 73m. V

Kenny & Co. 1976 ★★★ The story of young boy verging on manhood. Sweet and sensitively handled. C: Dan McCann, Mike Baldwin, Jeff Roth. D: Don Coscarelli. DRA [PG] 90m.

Kenny Rogers as The Gambler 1980 ★★★½ Popular country-western singer made his starring debut in this western tale, based on his hit song. Entertaining vehicle for Rogers; spawned several sequels. (a.k.a. *The Gambler*) C: Kenny Robers, Bruce Boxleitner, Christine Belford, Harold Gould. D: Dick Lowry. WST 94m. TVM V

Kent State 1981 ★★★½ Dramatization of the 1970 clash between Ohio university student protestors and National Guardsmen that left four students dead and nine injured. Unflinchingly intelligent film. Director Goldstone won an Emmy. C: Jane Fleiss, Charley Lang, Talia Balsam, Keith Gordon, Ellen Barkin. D: James Goldstone. DRA 120m. TVM V

Kentuckian, The 1955 ★★★½ After a hard life in Kentucky, a backwoodsman and his son start a new life in Texas. Typical Western fare that holds together largely through Lancaster's charisma. Look for Matthau in his film debut. C: Burt Lancaster, Diana Lynn, Walter Matthau. D: Burt Lancaster. WST 104m. V

Kentucky 1938 ★★★★ Romeo and Juliet win a happy ending in bluegrass country. Walter Brennan won Best Supporting Oscar as Young's aristocratic father. Lush-looking, easygoing drama. C: Loretta Young, Richard Greene, Walter Brennan. D: David Butler. DRA 95m.

Kentucky Fried Movie, The 1977 ★★★★ Consistently wacky collection of parodies that spoof commercials, TV shows, B-movies, kung fu, and porn flicks. Initial laugh-out-loud effort from the screenwriters who went on to create *Airplane* and *Naked Gun*. C: Evan Kim, Bill Bixby, George Lazenby, Donald Sutherland. D: John Landis. COM [R] 85m. V

Kentucky Kernels 1934 ★★★★ Spanky McFarland heads South, with Wheeler and Woolsey, to collect inheritance, getting caught in a Hatfield and McCoy-type feud. One of the team's best films—fast, funny, and full of prime slapstick. C: Bert Wheeler, Robert Woolsey, Spanky McFarland, Noah Beery. D: George Stevens. COM 75m. V

Kentucky Moonshine 1938 ★★★ Trying to

be discovered, the Ritz Brothers pose as hillbillies in this frenetic corn fest; mildly entertaining. C: Tony Martin, Marjorie Weaver, The Ritz Brothers, John Carradine. D: David Butler. MUS 85m.

Kentucky Rifle 1955 ★★ Wagon train must choose beween its guns and a safe passage from the Comanches who threaten it. C: Chill Wills, Lance Fuller, Cathy Downs, Jess Barker, Jeanne Cagney, Sterling Holloway. D: Carl Hittleman. WST 89m. V

Kerouac 1987 ★★★★ Uncommon documentary about beat generation novelist and spokesperson Jack Kerouac. Interviews with friends, clips from his TV talk show appearances, and readings from his works. (a.k.a. *Jack Kerouac's America*) D: Jack Coulter. DOC 73m. V

Kettles in the Ozarks, The 1956 ★★½ Ma takes her brood of children into the backwoods to meet up with their zany uncle (Hunnicutt). Typical madcap Kettle nonsense, with laughs aplenty along the way. C: Marjorie Main, Arthur Hunnicutt, Una Merkel. D: Charles Lamont. COM 81m.

Kettles on Old Macdonald's Farm, The 1957 ★★ In this last entry of the fabulous, long-running *Kettle* series, Ma and Pa (the latter now played by Parker Fennelly) settle in on the fabled farm of nursery rhyme. C: Marjorie Main, Parker Fennelly, Gloria Talbott. D: Virgil Vogel. COM 80m.

Key Exchange 1985 ★★★½ Hesitation abounds when a yuppie New York couple (Masters, Adams) reach the point in their relationship when they're ready to show their commitment by swapping apartment keys. Film adaptation of Kevin Wade's off-Broadway comedy provides ample laughs as it examines the '80s singles' scene. C: Ben Masters, Brooke Adams, Daniel Stern, Danny Aiello. D: Barnet Kellman. COM [R] 96m. V

Key Largo 1948 ★★★★½ In the Florida Keys to pay respects to a dead buddy's family, a war hero tangles with a dangerous mob. Get past the moralizing and enjoy outstanding action delivered by a top-notch cast (particularly Trevor, who nabbed an Oscar). C: Humphrey Bogart, Lauren Bacall, Edward G. Robinson, Claire Trevor, Lionel Barrymore. D: John Huston. DRA 101m. V

Key, The 1934 ★★★½ During the '20s Irish uprising, a resourceful soldier (Powell) working for the British side falls in love with the wife of a British officer (Clive). Saved by Powell and cast. C: William Powell, Edna Best, Colin Clive, Hobart Cavanaugh. D: Michael Curtiz. DRA 69m.

Key, The 1958 British ★★★½ A rather muddled romance about Loren who hands out her room key to WWII naval skippers—for a last chance at romance—before they ship out. Enjoy the action and the star performances. C: William Holden, Sophia Loren, Trevor Howard, Oscar Homolka. D: Carol Reed. DRA 134m. V

Key to Rebecca, The 1985 ★★★½ Painless miniseries adaptation of Ken Follett best-seller pits Soul as a Nazi spy against Robertson, a U.S. counterintelligence agent, in battle for North Africa. Three hours long, but still entertaining. C: Cliff Robertson, David Soul, Season Hubley. D: David Hemmings. ACT 200m. TVM V

Key to the City 1950 ★★★ Two mayors (Gable and Young) meet at a conference in San Francisco, with the usual romantic results. Practiced cast make all the right moves; enjoy. C: Clark Gable, Loretta Young, Frank Morgan, Raymond Burr. D: George Sidney. DRA 101m. V

Key Witness 1960 ★★★ Drawn-out movie about a gang of young hoodlums who terrorize a family to keep the wife off the witness stand. C: Jeffrey Hunter, Pat Crowley, Dennis Hopper. D: Phil Karlson. CRI 82m.

Keys of the Kingdom 1944 ★★★★ Peck is effective missionary in this often engrossing but disjointed drama from A.J. Cronin's novel, set in 19th-century China. McDowall plays Peck as child. Very earnest, and very long. C: Gregory Peck, Thomas Mitchell, Vincent Price, Edmund Gwenn, Roddy McDowall, Cedric Hardwicke. D: John M. Stahl. DRA 137m. V

KGB—the Secret War 1986 ★★ Will a KGB agent defect? Will he give the U.S. computer microchips? Does anyone care anymore? C: Michael Billington, Sally Kellerman, Walter Gotell, Michael Ansara. D: Dwight H. Little. ACT 90m. V

Khartoum 1966 British ★★★ General "Chinese" Gordon (Heston) is besieged in title city by Arab renegades. Heston and Olivier make memorable antagonists, so much so that film is ultimately more talk than action. C: Charlton Heston, Laurence Olivier, Richard Johnson, Ralph Richardson. D: Basil Dearden. ACT 136m. V

Khyber Patrol 1954 ★★ British colonial army in India tangles with insurgents and other dangers at an outpost near the Pakistan border. Everything you'd expect, including the requisite military action and torrid romance. C: Richard Egan, Dawn Addams, Raymond Burr. D: Seymour Friedman. ACT 71m.

Kick or Die 1991 ★ College hires kickboxing champions to protect students from a mad rapist on campus. Honest. C: Kevin Bernhardt. D: Charles Norton. ACT 87m. V

Kickboxer 1989 ★★ Martial arts fans will relish watching Van Damme make mincemeat of the Asian who maimed his brother. Others, beware. C: Jean-Claude Van Damme, Dennis Chan, Denis Alexio. D: Mark DiSalle. ACT [R] 105m. V

Kickboxer 3—The Art of War 1992 ★★ A kickboxer (Mitchell) and his noble master (Chan) journey to Rio for an important bout and come into conflict with a brutal Brazilian gangster. Acceptable shoot-outs and punch-outs. C: Sasha Mitchell. D: Rick King. ACT [R] 92m. v

Kid 1990 ★ Howell comes to town looking for the five men who killed his parents a decade earlier. C: C. Thomas Howell, Sarah Trigger, Brian Austin Green, Dale Dye, R. Lee Ermey. D: John Mark Robinson. ACT [R] 94m. v

Kid Blue 1973 ★★★½ Goofy, off-center Western spoof with Hopper as misfit title character trying to adjust to town life as 20th century arrives. Good supporting cast, especially Johnson and the underrated Purcell, make this bearable. C: Dennis Hopper, Warren Oates, Ben Johnson, Peter Boyle, Janice Rule. D: James Frawley. COM [PG] 100m.

Kid Brother, The 1927 ★★★★★ Silent comedian Lloyd's masterpiece casts him as weakling sibling in all-male family of brutes, as he tries to win carnival performer and prove his virility which, in the end, he does. Hilarious slapstick, but warm and genuine, too. A marvel. C: Harold Lloyd, Jobyna Ralston, Walter James. D: Ted Wilde. COM 82m.

Kid Colter 1985 ★★★★ A boy from the city is abducted by mountain men while visiting his family in the Pacific Northwest. Left for dead, he ~~must fend~~ for himself. Believe it or not, a good family picture in spite of the potentailly lurid plot. C: Jim Stafford, Jeremy Shamos, Hal Terrance, Greg Ward, Jim Turner. D: David O'Malley. FAM/ACT 101m. v

Kid Dynamite 1943 ★★½ Muggs (Gorcey) becomes a prize-fighter. Standard entry in *East Side Kids* series. C: Leo Gorcey, Huntz Hall, Bobby Jordan, Gabriel Dell. D: Wallace Fox. COM 73m.

Kid for Two Farthings, A 1955 British ★★★★ Sweetly nostalgic tale of boy (Ashmore) growing up in Jewish slums of London who finds a one-horned goat he believes is a unicorn, possessed of special powers. Whimsical adaptation by Wolf Mankowitz of his own novel. C: Celia Johnson, Diana Dors, David Kossoff, Jonathan Ashmore, Brenda de Banzie. D: Carol Reed. DRA 96m. v

Kid from Brooklyn, The 1946 ★★★★ Kaye's a milkman who becomes prizefighter in tailor-made remake of Harold Lloyd comedy *The Milky Way*. Not as good as original, but still cheery fun, with strong support from Arden, Stander. C: Danny Kaye, Virginia Mayo, Vera-Ellen, Eve Arden, Lionel Standen. D: Norman McLeod. COM 113m. v

Kid from Left Field, The 1953 ★★★★ Has-been ballplayer (Dailey), now a hotdog vendor, uses his son to help the team win the pennant. Sunny baseball yarn, remade as a TV movie in 1979. C: Dan Dailey, Anne Bancroft, Billy Chapin, Lloyd Bridges. D: Harmon Jones. COM 80m.

Kid from Left Field, The 1979 ★★★½ San Diego Padre batboy (Coleman) passes on the advice of his ex-ball player dad (who works as ballpark hotdog vendor), and leads the team to victory. An amiable remake of the 1953 film. C: Gary Coleman, Robert Guillaume, Tab Hunter, Tricia O'Neil, Ed McMahon. D: Adell Aldrich. FAM/DRA 100m. TVM v

Kid from Not So Big, The 1978 ★★★ Jenny inherits her granddad's newspaper in frontier town, and uses it to foil some swindlers. Family fare. C: Jennifer McAllister, Robert Viharo, Veronica Cartwright, Paul Tulley. D: William Crain. FAM/DRA 87m. v

Kid from Nowhere, The 1982 ★★★½ A young boy with Down's Syndrome tries out for the Special Olympics with the help of his coach and family. Good sentimental drama. C: Beau Bridges, Susan St. James, Loretta Swit. D: Beau Bridges. FAM/DRA 100m. TVM

Kid from Spain, The 1932 ★★★★½ Lavish, immensely entertaining musical casts Cantor as a college dropout in Mexico forced to impersonate matador. Star has a field day in the bullring. The Goldwyn Girls, under direction of Busby Berkeley, score with precision dance routines. Betty Grable, Paulette Goddard, and Lucille Ball appear in chorus. C: Eddie Cantor, Lyda Roberti, Robert Young. D: Leo McCarey. MUS 96m.

Kid Galahad 1937 ★★★★ The archetypal boxing film, with Robinson pushing Morris to fame while losing Davis to his protege pugilist. Warner Brothers melodrama at its best; don't miss the rousing fight scenes. Remade as an Elvis Presley vehicle in 1962. (a.k.a. *The Battling Bellhop*) C: Edward G. Robinson, Wayne Morris, Bette Davis, Humphrey Bogart, Harre Carey. D: Michael Curtiz. ACT 101m. v

Kid Galahad 1962 ★★★½ Presley plays an amateur boxer who'd rather be a mechanic in this musical remake of the 1937 Edward G. Robinson film. One of The King's better efforts. C: Elvis Presley, Gig Young, Lola Albright, Charles Bronson. D: Phil Karlson. MUS 95m. v

Kid Glove Killer 1942 ★★★★ A police scientist (Heflin) probes the suspicious circumstances behind a mayor's murder. Involving little thriller cleverly builds suspense by focusing on its hero's profession. C: Van Heflin, Lee Bowman, Marsha Hunt. D: Fred Zinnemann. CRI 74m.

Kid Millions 1934 ★★★½ Expensive Cantor vehicle casts star as hopeless fool who inherits $77 million and goes to Egypt, where zany characters try to steal the money. Color finale set in Brooklyn ice cream factory is a dilly. C: Eddie Cantor, Ethel Merman, Ann Sothern, George Murphy. D: Roy Del Ruth. MUS 90m. v

Kid, The 1921 ★★★★½ Funny, sentimental first feature for Chaplin; his Little Tramp "adopts" orphan (Coogan). Their adjustments to the world, and each other, are marvelous. Movie made Coogan a major child star. *Addams Family* fans will remember Coogan as TV's Uncle Fester. C: Charlie Chaplin, Jackie Coogan, Edna Purviance. D: Charles Chaplin. COM 60m. V

Kid Vengeance 1977 ★★ When outlaws kill his parents and kidnap his sister, a young cowhand sets out for revenge. A gory, blood-by-the-bucket venture. C: Lee Van Cleef, Jim Brown. D: Joe Manduke. WST 90m. V

Kid Who Loved Christmas, The 1990 ★★★★ Sweet Christmas tale, produced by Eddie Murphy, about an orphan who longs to be with his adopted musician father for the holidays. Engaging performances give this some heart. Sammy Davis, Jr.'s last role. C: Cicely Tyson, Michael Warren, Sammy Davis, Jr., Della Reese, Esther Rolle, Ben Vereen, Vanessa Williams. D: Arthur Allan Seidelman. FAM/DRA 118m. V

Kid with the Broken Halo, The 1981 ★★½ Hoping to earn his angel wings, the ethereal Coleman enters the Earth-bound lives of three troubled families. Overly sentimental and altogether uninspired. C: Gary Coleman, Robert Guillaume, June Allyson. D: Leslie Martinson. FAM/DRA 96m. TVM V

Kid with the 200 I.Q., The 1982 ★★★ A kid genius (Coleman) faces various challenges as the youngest student on a college campus. Standard personal issues tale for children. C: Gary Coleman, Robert Guillaume. D: Leslie Martinson. FAM/DRA 96m. V

Kidco 1983 ★★★ A bunch of precocious kids organize their own corporation—and become wildly successful at it. Based on a true story and presented with captivating charm and good feeling. C: Scott Schwartz, Cinnamon Idles. D: Ronald F. Maxwell. DRA [PG] 104m. V

Kidnap Syndicate 1975 Italian ★★ A rich man (Mason) and a poor man (Merenda) are linked by the abduction of their children. Whatever message this film intends does not come through, but gratuitous violence does. C: James Mason, Valentina Cortese, Luc Merenda. D: Fernando Di Leo. ACT 105m. V

Kidnapped 1934 *See* **Miss Fane's Baby Is Stolen**

Kidnapped 1938 ★★★½ Robert Louis Stevenson's classic winds up as a swashbuckler emphasizing the heroics of an 18th-century Scotsman (Baxter) fighting against British rule. Fast-moving fare. C: Warner Baxter, Freddie Bartholomew, Arleen Whelan, John Carradine. D: Alfred Werker. ACT 90m.

Kidnapped 1960 ★★★ Disney's rendition of the Robert Louis Stevenson classic follows adventures of a young man with recently inherited fortune whose kidnapping is arranged by wicked uncle. Despite strong cast of Britain's better actors, this handsome looking film is surprisingly flat. C: Peter Finch, James MacArthur, Bernard Lee, Peter O'Toole. D: Robert Stevenson. FAM/ACT [PG] 95m. V

Kidnapping of Baby John Doe, The 1988 ★ When a family is faced with a life-or-death decision about their newborn, a doctor and nurse take the law into their own hands to save it. C: Jared Martin, Janet Agren, Kim Stuart, Ken Watanabe. D: Larry Ludman. DRA 90m. TVM V

Kidnapping of the President, The 1980 U.S. ★★★★ Terrorists abduct the President (Holbrook) and hold him hostage as the tension mounts in this sleek and engrossing thriller. C: William Shatner, Hal Holbrook, Van Johnson, Ava Gardner. D: George Mendeluk. ACT [R] 116m. V

Kids Are Alright, The 1979 ★★★★ Rambunctious documentary on rock group The Who depicts the rebellious dash of the band and its spirited music. Interviews, concert footage and history of the band as well as several numbers from *Tommy*, and appearances by Ringo Starr, Tommy Smothers, and Steve Martin. D: Jeff Stein. DOC [PG] 106m. V

Kill and Kill Again 1981 ★★½ A martial artist (Ryan) battles a mad scientist determined to take over the world. Unmemorable sequel to *Kill or Be Killed*. C: James Ryan, Anneline Kriel. D: Ivan Hall. ACT [PG] 100m. V

Kill Baby Kill 1966 Italian ★★★★ A young girl's ghost takes revenge on the citizens of a small town in Transylvania, with a witch and an investigating doctor becoming involved. Beautifully directed chiller, with solid scares and some tongue-in-cheek humor. (a.k.a. *Curse of the Living Dead*) C: Erika Blanc, Giacomo Stuart, Lulli. D: Mario Bava. HOR [PG] 83m. V

Kill Castro 1980 ★★ Rather slow-paced thriller about a fishing skipper whose passenger is actually a CIA agent trying to assassinate Fidel. C: Stuart Whitman, Caren Kaye, Robert Vaughn, Sybil Danning, Albert Salmi, Raymond St. Jacques, Woody Strode. D: Chuck Workman. ACT 90m. V

Kill Cruise 1990 ★★★ Essentially a three-character film about a drunken skipper who reluctantly agrees to take two women on a cruise to Barbados. When the weather turns violent, tempers flare. C: Jurgen Prochnow, Patsy Kensit, Elizabeth Hruley. D: Peter Keglevic. DRA 99m. V

Kill! Kill! Kill! 1972 French ★★½ International agents in relentless pursuit of Italian drug lords. Hard-core violence served up hot and spicy—if you've the stomach for it. C: Jean Seberg, James Mason, Stephen Boyd, Curt Jurgens. D: Romain Gary. ACT [R] 90m.

Kill Line 1989 ★★★½ Better-than-average martial arts vengeance flick has Kim trying to avenge the murder of his brother and family after he returns from jail for a crime he didn't commit. C: Bobby Kim, Michael Parker, Marlene Zimmerman, H. Wayne Lowery, C.R. Valdez. D: Richard H. Kim. ACT 93m. v

Kill Me Again 1990 ★★★ Whalley-Kilmer uses seduction to separate mobsters from their money in the Southwest. Homage to classic film noir and detective flicks is diverting, but shallow. Desert locale is a plus. C: Val Kilmer, Joanne Whalley-Kilmer, Michael Madsen. D: John Dahl. CRI [R] 94m. v

Kill Me if You Can 1977 ★★★★½ True story of the "red light bandit" Caryl Chessman, on death row for 12 years before his 1960 execution. Alda is magnificent, showing rage and calm resolve in equal measure. Mesmerizing. C: Alan Alda, Talia Shire. D: Buzz Kulik. DRA 100m. TVM

Kill or Be Killed 1980 ★★★ Martial artist (Ryan) must fight for his life when a tournament turns out to be staged by an ex-Nazi out for revenge. Lots of action, but (despite the title) little gore; younger martial-arts fans may like it. Sequel: *Kill and Kill Again.* C: James Ryan, Norman Combes, Charlotte Michelle. D: Ivan Hall. ACT [PG] 90m. v

Kill Reflex, The 1989 ★★ Somebody killed Fred's partner, and his higher-ups in the Chicago police don't want him to investigate. C: Fred Williamson, Phyllis Hyman, Maud Adams, Bo Svenson. D: Fred Williamson. ACT 94m. v

Kill Slade 1988 ★★ Dollaghan is supposed to kidnap journalist Brady when she gets too close to the truth about diversion of U.N. food supplies, but the double-crosses and romance pile up fater than the bad dialogue. C: Patrick Dollaghan, Lisa Brady, Anthony Fridjhon, Danny Keogh, Alfred Nowke. D: Bruce McFarlane. ACT 90m. v

Kill the Ninja 1984 ★★ Three rival gangs seek a priceless relic with $2 millon dollars inside it. C: Bob Kim, Karl Sterling, Janet Kim. D: Richard Park. ACT 84m. v

Kill the Umpire 1950 ★★★½ Fans of the sport will enjoy discovering this modestly funny baseball comedy with Bendix as a much maligned umpire who loves the game, hates his job. C: William Bendix, Una Merkel, Ray Collins, William Frawley. D: Lloyd Bacon. COM 78m.

Killbots 1986 *See* **Chopping Mall**

Killcrazy 1989 ★ Mentally ill vets are ambushed on what started out as a camping trip, forced to fight back. C: David Heavener, Danielle Brisebois, Burt Ward, Lawrence Hlton-Jacobs, Bruce Glover, Gary Ownes, Rachelle Carson. D: David Heavener. ACT 94m. v

Killer Bait 1943 *See* **Too Late for Tears**

Killer Bees 1974 ★★½ Schlocky, low-rent thriller with Swanson as wine producer in control of deadly bees swarming over her vineyard. C: Gloria Swanson, Edward Albert, Kate Jackson. D: Curtis Harrington. HOR 78m. TVM

Killer Elephants, The 1976 ★★ When a land baron decides to seize his farm, a young man must go to extremes to protect his family. C: Sung Pa, Alan Yen, Na Yen NA. ACT 83m. v

Killer Elite, The 1975 ★★★ Violent thriller about professional assassin who avenges his own mutilation. High-flying, poetic, late-period Peckinpah may not make much sense but the acting is still great. Gig Young scores as Caan's cynical boss. C: James Caan, Robert Duvall, Arthur Hill, Bo Hopkins. D: Sam Peckinpah. ACT [PG] 124m. v

Killer Fish 1979 Italian ★ The story of killer fish and intrigue in the jungle. Violence and excessive splashing. (a.k.a. *The Deadly Treasure of the Piranha*) C: Lee Majors, Karen Black, James Franciscus, Margaux Hemingway. D: Anthony M. Dawson. ACT [PG] 101m. v

Killer Force 1975 ★★ A security guard guiles his way into a ring of jewel thieves by faking a robbery at his own post. Adequate. C: Peter Fonda, Telly Savalas, Hugh O'Brian, Christopher Lee, Maud Adams. D: Val Guest. ACT [R] 101m. v

Killer Image 1992 ★★ A photographer stumbles onto a conspiracy that includes murder and corrupton in high places. C: John Pyper-Ferguson, Krista Errickson, Michael Ironside, Emmet Walsh. D: David Winning. CRI 97m. v

Killer in Every Corner, A 1974 ★★ Deranged psychcology professor has three students over for a weekend of terror. Will this be on the final? C: Joanna Pettet, Patrick Magee, Max Wall, Eric Flynn. D: Malcolm Taylor. HOR 80m. v

Killer in the Mirror 1986 ★★★★ Jillian scores as good/evil twins, the former taking her rich sister's place after fatal boating accident. Clever remake/combo of two Davis soapers (*A Stolen Life*, *Dead Ringer*) goes both one better with ingenious plot twist two-thirds through movie. C: Ann Jillian, Len Cariou. D: Frank de Felitta. DRA 100m. TVM

Killer Inside Me, The 1976 ★★★½ Keach is terrific in this otherwise average thriller about a small-town sheriff's descent into madness. Based on a Jim Thompson novel. C: Stacy Keach, Susan Tyrrell, Keenan Wynn. D: Burt Kennedy. DRA [R] 99m. v

Killer Instinct 1992 ★★ Bradley and Nozick also brothers who shoot their way to the top of the underworld during Prohibition. C: Christopher Bradley, Bruce Nozick, Rachel York. D: Greydon Clark. CRI [R] 101m. v

Killer Is Loose, The 1956 ★★½ When a policeman accidentally kills a bank robber's wife, the robber seeks revenge. Some chilling moments delivered by an able cast. C: Joseph Cotten, Rhonda Fleming, Wendell Corey. D: Budd Boetticher. CRI 73m.

Killer Klowns from Outer Space 1988 ★★★★ They look like clowns, but these aliens aren't Bozos when it comes to killing off a small town in new and inventive ways. Culty sci-fi with a sense of humor. It works! C: Grant Cramer, Suzanne Snyder, John Allen Nelson. D: Stephen Chiodo. SFI [PG-13] 90m. V

Killer Likes Candy, The 1974 ★★ Someone wants the King of Kafiristan dead, but CIA agent Mathews wants him alive. C: Kerwin Mathews, Marilu Tolo. ACT 86m. V

Killer McCoy 1947 ★★★½ Tough little boxer (Rooney) gets mixed up in murder and the rackets. Punchy little film that gets by largely on the strength of Rooney's believable performance. C: Mickey Rooney, Brian Donlevy, Ann Blyth. D: Roy Rowland. CRI 104m.

Killer Shrews, The 1959 ★★ An unfortunate band of humans are trapped on a remote island, with their wooden compound surrounded by large shrews, the result of science gone amuck. Dogs in shrew costumes are fun to watch. C: James Best, Ingrid Goude, Ken Curtis. D: Ray Kellogg. HOR 70m. V

Killer That Stalked New York, The 1950 ★★½ Police hunt a pair of international diamond smugglers who are carrying smallpox, along with a cache of precious gems into the country. Quality suspense and some excellent action. C: Evelyn Keyes, Charles Korvin, Dorothy Malone. D: Earl McEvoy. CRI 79m.

Killer, The 1989 Hong Kong ★★★★ A professional killer accidentally blinds a singer, then feels responsible for her fate. Astonishing action sequences and some deft tongue-in-cheek humor make this a memorable film, a breakthrough for Woo. C: Chow Yun Fat, Sally Yeh. D: John Woo. ACT [R] 110m. V

Killer With Two Faces 1974 ★★ Mills is terrorized by her boyfriend's identical twin. C: Donna Mills, Ian Hendry, David Lodge, Roddy McMillan. D: John Conway-Scholz. HOR 70m. V

Killers 1988 ★ An attempted coup in southern Africa breeds mayhem and noise. C: Cameron Mitchell, Alicia Hammond, Robert Dix. D: Dwing Miles Brown. ACT 83m. V

Killer's Edge, The 1990 ★★ Can Hauser sacrifice his badge for the man whose life he saved in "Nam?" C: Wings Hauser, Karen Black, Robert Z'Dar. D: Joseph Merhi. ACT 90m. V

Killers from Space 1954 ★★ El cheapo sci-fi picture follows alien creatures kidnapping a human corpse for their own evil designs. Bare-bones script and laughable costumes. C: Peter Graves, James Seay, Barbara Bestar. D: W. Lee Wilder. SFI 71m. V

Killer's Kiss 1955 ★★★ Early Kubrick film is rough-edged story of boxer who romances girl with jealous boss. When she is found murdered, pugilist realizes he's in deep trouble. Standard melodrama gives little hint of Kubrick's later work. C: Frank Silvera, Jamie Smith. D: Stanley Kubrick. DRA 67m. V

Killer's Moon 1984 ★ Deranged murderer escapes from a prison for the criminally insane to attack schoolgirls and campers. C: Anthony Forrest, Tom Marshall. D: Alan Dirkinhsaw. HOR 92m. V

Killers of Kilimanjaro 1959 British ★★★ Railroad building in East Africa leads engineer into love and adventure. Earnest, workmanlike production. C: Robert Taylor, Anthony Newley, Anne Aubrey, Donald Pleasence. D: Richard Thorpe. ACT 91m.

Killers, The 1946 ★★★★½ Memorable film noir expands Hemingway's famous short story about a payroll robbery gone awry. Intense and gripping throughout; marked by an utterly brilliant opening sequence, as the title characters seek out and shoot Lancaster (in his film debut). The script was co-written by John Huston (Hemingway helped a little, too). Remade in 1964. C: Ava Gardner, Edmond O'Brien, Albert Dekker, Burt Lancaster, Sam Levene. D: Robert Siodmak. CRI 105m.

Killers, The 1964 ★★ Two hired killers (Marvin, Cassavetes) learn more than they would like about one of their victims and excessive violence ensues. Now primarily notable for Reagan, atypically cast, in his last film, as a gangster. Based on Ernest Hemingway story. C: Lee Marvin, John Cassavetes, Angie Dickinson, Ronald Reagan. D: Don Siegel. CRI 95m. V

Killing Affair, A 1985 ★★★ The bizarre relationship between a man (Weller) and the woman whose detested husband he has killed is at the center of this strange movie. Good performances help. C: Peter Weller, Kathy Baker. D: David Saperstein. DRA [R] 100m. V

Killing Beach, The 1991 ★★★½ Earnest political thriller about Australian photojournalist (Scacchi) who becomes involved in struggles of Vietnamese boat people encountering racist violence in Malaysia in the '70s. Based on actual events, and intensely serious. (a.k.a. *Turtle Beach*) C: Greta Scacchi, Joan Chen, Jack Thompson. D: Stephen Wallace. DRA [R] 88m. V

Killing Cars 1986 German ★★ Thriller about inventor whose gasoline-free automobile gets Arabs so upset, they try to have him assassinated. C: Jurgen Prochnow, Senta Berger, William Conrad. D: Michael Verhoeven. ACT [R] 104m. V

Killing Device, The 1992 ★ When the government cuts off funding for their research, two weapons scientists decide to use what they know. Wouldn't you? C: Clu Gulager, Antony Alda, Gig Rauch. ACT 93m. V

Killing 'em Softly 1985 Canadian ★★★ Musician (Segal) kills the manager of a rock band, then finds himself romantically involved with singer (Cara)—who's trying to pinpoint the killer to clear her boyfriend. Murder mystery bogs down in too many musical numbers, though Segal and Cara give sound performances. C: George Segal, Irene Cara. D: Max Fischer. CRI 81m. V

Killing Fields, The 1984 British ★★★★½ Moving drama, based on real events, of Cambodian photographer's struggle to survive the genocide that followed rise to power of Pol Pot, and an American journalist's attempts to find and save him. Powerful if a bit overlong. Ngor won Oscar for his performance. C: Sam Waterston, Haing S. Ngor, John Malkovich, Julian Sands, Craig T. Nelson. D: Roland Joffe. DRA [R] 142m. V

·**Killing Floor, The** 1985 ★★★★ A young African-American, just arrived and employed in a Chicago meatpacking plant, finds himself caught in the middle of union-organizing struggle during WWI. Studied and detailed, with surprising subtle beauty. C: Damien Leake, Moses Gunn, Alfre Woodard. D: William Duke. DRA [PG] 118m. V

Killing Game, The 1967 French ★★★★ Struggling comic-book artists devise a murder mystery and act it out with the help of an ultrarich eccentric. Entertaining mystery. (a.k.a. *Comic Strip Hero* and *Jeu de Massacre*) C: Jean-Pierre Cassel, Claudine Auger. D: Alain Jessua. CRI 94m.

Killing Heat 1981 *See* **Grass Is Singing, The**

Killing in a Small Town, A 1990 ★★★ Gripping true-crime shocker gives Hershey the role of a lifetime as a mousy, religious woman who kills her best friend with an ax. This performance is so courageous and so real that what could have been exploitative winds up almost touching. C: Barbara Hershey, Brian Dennehy. D: Stephen Gyllenhaal. CRI [R] 94m. TVM V

Killing Kind, The 1973 ★★★★ Savage is excellent as an ex-con plotting revenge on his lawyer and the woman who accused him of rape. Stylish thriller. C: Ann Sothern, John Savage, Ruth Roman, Luana Anders, Cindy Williams. D: Curtis Harrington. CRI 95m. V

Killing Machine 1984 Spanish ★★★ A Spanish truck driver is swept up in a European labor skirmish while on his final run in Germany. Topical subject indifferently handled; multinational casting strains credibility. C: George Rivero, Margaux Hemingway, Lee Van Cleef. D: Anthony J. Loma. DRA [R] 95m. V

Killing Mind, The 1991 ★★ L.A. cop (Zimbalist) tracks down a dancer's murderer, whom she believes was responsible for a slaying she witnessed as a child. Thriller features interesting heroine. C: Stephanie Zimbalist, Tony Bill. D: Michael Ray Rhodes. CRI 96m. TVM V

Killing of a Chinese Bookie, The 1976 ★★★ To pay off a mob debt, sleazy nightclub owner (Gazzara) is given a murder task. Odd cult favorite. C: Ben Gazzara, Timothy Carey, Seymour Cassel. D: John Cassavetes. CRI [R] 109m. V

Killing of Angel Street, The 1981 Australian ★★★ Neighbors in an Australian town band together to save their homes from unscrupulous developers. Uninspired dramatization of an actual event. C: Liz Alexander, John Hargreaves. D: Donald Crombie. DRA 101m. V

Killing of Randy Webster, The 1981 ★★★★ Classy cast gives weight to story of Holbrook launching an investigation into son's death at hands of Houston police. The performances of Holbrook and his wife (real-life wife Carter) are standouts. C: Hal Holbrook, Dixie Carter, Jennifer Jason Leigh. D: Sam Wanamaker. DRA 90m. TVM V

Killing of Sister George, The 1968 ★★★½ Aging British actress (Reid), in rocky lesbian relationship with York, is distraught when her radio soap character is killed off. From Frank Marcus play. Ferociously acted, but the original was much funnier. C: Beryl Reid, Susannah York, Coral Browne. D: Robert Aldrich. DRA [R] 138m. V

Killing, The 1956 ★★★★ Kubrick's oddly-constructed story of a racetrack holdup. Original and tough, if sometimes hard to follow. C: Sterling Hayden, Coleen Gray, Vince Edwards, Elisha Cook Jr. D: Stanley Kubrick. CRI 83m. V

Killing Time, The 1987 ★★★ A little resort town, known for its tranquil atmosphere, erupts in murder and blackmail. Nest-of-vipers film noir with good action. C: Beau Bridges, Kiefer Sutherland, Wayne Rogers. D: Rick King. CRI [R] 94m. V

Killing Zoe 1994 ★★★½ A bank heist goes wrong, leading to ultraviolence and much profanity. Director Avary was co-author of Quentin Tarantino's *Pulp Fiction*, which this film resembles, but doesn't live up to. C: Eric Stoltz, Julie Delpy, Jean-Hugues Anglade. D: Roger Avary. CRI [R] 96m.

Killjoy 1981 ★★★½ A determined cop (Culp) tracking the murderer of a model (Basinger), finds a host of suspects among a group of hospital professionals. Slick, witty script with some interesting twists. (a.k.a. *Who Murdered Joy Morgan?*) C: Kim Basinger, Robert Culp, Nancy Marchand. D: John Llewellyn Moxey. CRI 96m. TVM V

Killpoint 1984 ★★ A policeman (Fong) and a special agent (Roundtree) join forces and hunt down gunrunners. Unrelentingly violent. C: Leo Fong, Richard Roundtree, Cameron Mitchell. D: Frank Harris. ACT [R] 89m. V

Killzone 1985 ★★ A Vietnam vet suffers flashbacks as a result of brainwashing by the U.S. government years before, goes berserk and starts killing again. C: Ted Prior, David James Campbell, Richard Massery, Fritz Matthews, William Zipp. D: David A. Prior. ACT 86m. V

Kim 1950 ★★★½ Orphaned boy (Stockwell) has adventures in India with British Secret Service agent; from Kipling novel. Stockwell is engaging, but Flynn's physical deterioration is disturbing to see. C: Errol Flynn, Dean Stockwell, Paul Lukas. D: Victor Saville. ACT [G] 113m. V

Kim 1984 ★★★ Kipling's classic of the little Indian boy who joins the British colonial army. O'Toole, as a bald Indian mystic, is a hoot. Good throughout. C: Peter O'Toole, Bryan Brown, John Rhys-Davies. D: John Davies. ACT 150m.

Kind Hearts and Coronets 1949 British ★★★★★ Wickedly funny British comedy. Ambitious, distant relative of aristocratic family (Price) kills off eight relations (all played brilliantly by Guinness!) to get to the title. Witty script by Hamer and John Dighton, adapted from Roy Horniman novel *Israel Rank*. C: Dennis Price, Alec Guinness, Valerie Hobson, Joan Greenwood. D: Robert Hamer. COM 102m. V

Kind Lady 1936 ★★★ Wealthy title character (MacMahon) is blackmailed and held captive by ne'er-do-well Rathbone and pals. Decent thriller, with Rathbone shining above all. From the Edward Chodorov play. Story improved on in the 1951 remake. C: Aline MacMahon, Basil Rathbone, Mary Carlisle. D: George Seitz. CRI 76m.

Kind Lady 1951 ★★★★ This time Barrymore is the rich, aged, kind lady and Evans the sadistic brute trying to separate her from her money. More menacing than original 1936 version. Additional benefit: Edward Chodorov, who wrote the play, helped pen screenplay. C: Ethel Barrymore, Maurice Evans, Angela Lansbury, Betsy Blair, Keenan Wynn. D: John Sturges. CRI 78m.

Kind of Loving, A 1962 British ★★★★ Two young Lancashire factory workers must marry when Ritchie finds herself pregnant. Poignant and skillfully handled. C: Alan Bates, June Ritchie, Thora Hird. D: John Schlesinger. DRA 106m. V

Kindergarten Cop 1990 ★★★½ Arnie goes undercover and ends up teaching a kindergarten class while seeking a drug lord. Formula '90s comedy is a little violent for young kids, but should please others, especially teachers. C: Arnold Schwarzenegger, Penelope Ann Miller, Pamela Reed, Linda Hunt. D: Ivan Reitman. COM [PG-13] 111m. V

Kindred, The 1987 ★★½ Schlocky, derivative horror flick nonetheless has its moments, thanks to confident direction, as a group of young people investigate experiments conducted by the late mother of one of their group and encounter the monstrous results. C: Rod Steiger, Kim Hunter, Amanda Pays. D: Stephen Carpenter, Jeffrey Obrow. HOR [R] 92m. V

King 1978 ★★★½ Long, earnest biography of Dr. Martin Luther King, Jr., with a superb cast. Rare directorial effort for writer Mann. C: Paul Winfield, Cicely Tyson, Ossie Davis, Howard E. Rollins, Jr., Roscoe Lee Browne, Art Evans, Ernie Banks, Cliff De Young. D: Abby Mann. DRA 254m. V

King: A Filmed Record . . . Montgomery to Memphis 1970 ★★★★★ Powerful documentary about slain black civil rights leader and Nobel Prize winner, Rev. Martin Luther King, Jr. Superior, eloquent work. D: Joseph L. Mankiewicz, Sidney Lumet. DOC 153m.

King and Country 1964 British ★★★★½ Adapted from John Wilson's play, this concerns the belief of an Army lawyer (Bogarde) in the innocence of an emotional private (Courtenay) court-martialed for desertion during WWI. Walloping examination of astonishing inequities of wartime brilliantly acted. Not for the squeamish. C: Dirk Bogarde, Tom Courtenay, Leo McKern. D: Joseph Losey. DRA 90m.

King and Four Queens, The 1956 ★★★½ A wrangler looks for money hidden by the husbands of four women and finds himself falling in love with the lovely daughter of a lady sharpshooter. Good, lusty fun and fine acting by a very solid cast led by the king himself (Gable). C: Clark Gable, Eleanor Parker, Jo Van Fleet. D: Raoul Walsh. WST 87m. V

King and I, The 1956 ★★★★★ Rodgers and Hammerstein classic Broadway musical is given the royal screen treatment, sumptuously produced and beautifully cast. Brynner won Oscar re-creating role of the King of Siam who hires widowed English schoolteacher (Kerr) to educate his dozens of children, circa 1904. Kerr is superb, even though her singing voice is dubbed by Marni Nixon. Timeless songs include "Hello, Young Lovers," "Getting to Know You," and "Something Wonderful." C: Yul Brynner, Deborah Kerr. D: Walter Lang. MUS [G] 133m. V

King and the Chorus Girl, The 1937 ★★★½ Engaging comedy of European potentate on a spree in New York, where he finds romance with Blondell. Brisk and winning, with a script co-authored by Groucho Marx. C: Joan Blondell, Fernand Gravet, Edward Everett Horton, Jane Wyman. D: Mervyn LeRoy. COM 94m.

King Arthur, the Young Warlord 1975 ★★★ Before Camelot, Arthur battles the Saxons. Violent film aims at a realistic approach to the medieval period. C: Oliver Tobias, Michael Gothard, Jack Watson, Brian Blessed, Peter Firth. D: Sidney Hayers, Pat Jackson, Peter Sasdy. ACT 90m. V

King Boxer 1990 ★★ Lo has to clean up his martial arts school when it's taken over by bad guys. Violent, even for something like this. C: Lo Lieh, Wang Ping. ACT 106m. V

King Boxers, The 1980 ★★ Kurata fights against evil triads in this martial arts epic. C: Uasuka Kurata, Johnny Nainam. D: Kung Min. ACT 90m. V

King Creole 1958 ★★★½ Elvis in New Orleans as nightclub singer mixed up with organized crime. Attempt to extend singer's acting range is modestly successful. Jones a standout as gangster's moll. Loosely based on Harold Robbins' novel *A Stone for Danny Fisher*. C: Elvis Presley, Carolyn Jones, Dolores Hart, Dean Jagger, Liliane Montevecchi, Walter Matthau. D: Michael Curtiz. MUS 115m. V

King David 1985 ★★★½ Young David (Gere) usurps the power of old King Saul (Woodward) after felling giant Goliath. First half of this biblical tale is well done with Woodward outstanding as Saul, then nosedives when focus shifts to contemporary-sounding Gere. C: Richard Gere, Edward Woodward, Alice Krige. D: Bruce Beresford. DRA [PG-13] 114m. V

King Dinosaur ★ Hilariously shoddy sci-fi film about four scientists sent to explore a new planet in the solar system, where they find the title character and friends. C: Bill Bryant, Wanda Curtis, Patti Gallagher, Douglas Henderson. D: Bert I. Gordon. SFI 63m.

King Elephant 1972 *See* **African Elephant, The**

King in New York, A 1957 British ★★★½ Chaplin's satire of the U.S. in the '50s focusing on McCarthyism and technology. Uneven, but enough flashes of the master comic come through to make it worth watching. First U.S. release in 1973. C: Charlie Chaplin, Dawn Addams, Oliver Johnston, Maxine Audley. D: Charles Chaplin. COM [G] 105m. V

King in Shadow 1956 German ★★★½ In 18th-century Sweden, the young monarch must contend with his own mental instability as well as the machinations of his power-hungry mother. Original Freudian psychodrama costume piece. C: O. Fischer, Horst Buchholz, Odile Versois. D: Harald Braun. DRA 87m.

King Kong 1933 ★★★★★ From Skull Island to the top of the Empire State Building with a big gorilla, this is the classic giant-ape movie. Masterful special effects by Willis O'Brien still look good and the script, hokey as it may seem today, is great fun. C: Fay Wray, Robert Armstrong, Bruce Cabot. D: Merian C. Cooper, Ernest Schoedsack. HOR 105m. V

King Kong 1976 ★★★½ Lavish remake is surprisingly enjoyable, with young Lange (in film debut) as ape's heartthrob. Despite some unintentionally awful dialogue, this stands on its own as an entertaining comic-book epic. Special Oscar for Special Effects. C: Jeff Bridges, Charles Grodin, Jessica Lange. D: John Guillermin. ACT [PG] 135m. V

King Kong Lives 1986 ★ The deep-sleeping Kong gets some TLC from doctor (Hamilton) after his tumble off the World Trade Center. When he awakes to find a Queen Kong being used to help his recovery, all heck ensues. Dreadful sequel to the 1976 remake. C: Brian Kerwin, Linda Hamilton. D: John Guillermin. SFI 105m. V

King Kong vs. Godzilla 1963 Japanese ★★★★ It was inevitable—the two biggest, baddest monsters around mix it up and trash half of Tokyo in the process. Colorful, campy Toho Studios fun. C: Michael Keith. D: Thomas Montgomery, Inoshiro Honda. SFI [PG-13] 90m. V

King Kung Fu 1987 ★ Listen carefully, because this is weird. A karate-trained gorilla is sent to the U.S., where two out-of-work reporters decide to unleash it and then recapture it to get a fake scoop. Only problem: They don't know the gorilla knows kung fu. C: John Balee, tom Leahy, Mazine Gray, Bill Schwartz. D: Bill Hayes. ACT 90m. V

King Lear 1971 British ★★★½ Strong, dense version of Shakespeare's tragedy of the king and his three daughters. Scofield is terrific. C: Paul Scofield, Irene Worth, Jack MacGowran, Alan Webb, Cyril Cusack, Patrick Magee. D: Peter Brook. DRA [PG] 137m. V

King Lear 1983 British ★★★★ Olivier gives a commanding performance as Shakespeare's tortured monarch, who destroys himself and his family when he splits his kingdom between his three daughters. Somewhat stagey but strong physical production truly captures the scope of the tragedy. C: Laurence Olivier, Colin Blakely, John Hurt, Leo McKern, Diana Rigg, Anna Calder-Marshall, Dorothy Tutin. D: Michael Elliott. DRA 158m. V

King Lear 1987 U.S. ★★½ Godard's updated spin on the Bard is a weird filmmaking experiment of lighting, sound, and casting that doesn't quite work. Fascinating for film buffs and Shakespeare fans, though. C: Peter Sellars, Burgess Meredith, Molly Ringwald, Jean-Luc Godard, Woody Allen, Norman Mailer. D: Jean-Luc Godard. DRA [PG] 91m. V

King of Alcatraz 1938 ★★★½ Escapees hijack a passenger ship, and come up against strong-willed sailors Preston and Nolan. Standard gangster film, but has slam-bang pacing and a fine cast. C: J. Carroll Naish, Gail Patrick, Lloyd Nolan, Harry Carey, Robert Preston, Anthony Quinn. D: Robert Florey. CRI 56m.

King of Burlesque 1935 ★★★★ Entertaining backstage musical casts Baxter as down-and-out producer struggling to put on revue with Faye as star. Good songs include "I'm Shooting High" and "Spreading Rhythm Around." Remade as *Hello, Frisco, Hello* with Faye again starring. C: Warner Baxter, Jack Oakie, Alice Faye. D: Sidney Lanfield. MUS 83m.

King of Chinatown 1939 ★★★★ Mobster tries to muscle in on Chinatown, but finds his goons are less than loyal. Fast-paced gangster pic; good performances. C: Anna May

Wong, Sidney Toler, Akim Tamiroff, Anthony Quinn. D: Nick Grinde. CRI 60m.

King of Comedy, The 1982 ★★★★ A crazed fan kidnaps a late-night talk show host to get his shot at stand-up fame. Scorsese wrings edgy comedy from this tale of urban terrorism, with a wonderfully wormy performance from De Niro and an icy one from Lewis. C: Robert De Niro, Jerry Lewis, Sandra Bernhard, Shelley Hack. D: Martin Scorsese. COM [PG] 109m. v

King of Hearts 1967 French ★★★★ Scottish WWI soldier (Bates) arrives in French village left deserted except for local asylum inmates and assorted zoo animals. Obvious parable for war's madness has become a cult classic. Also available in letterbox. C: Alan Bates, Pierre Brasseur, Jean-Claude Brialy, Genevieve Bujold. D: Philippe de Broca. DRA 102m. v

King of Jazz, The 1930 ★★★★ Lavish early talkie revue, in color, with imaginative direction and brilliantly staged numbers. Highlights include Paul Whiteman's rendition of Gershwin's "Rhapsody in Blue," and an early cartoon by Walter Lantz (*Woody Woodpecker*). Bing Crosby made film debut as one of The Rhythm Boys. C: Paul Whiteman, John Boles, Bing Crosby. D: John Murray Anderson. MUS 93m. v

King of Kings 1961 ★★★★½ Intelligent, dignified rendering of Christ's life and works benefits from unobtrusive casting, gorgeous widescreen photography (laser disc format preferable), and a fine performance from Hunter. Easily one of the best Hollywood biblical epics. C: Jeffrey Hunter, Robert Ryan, Rip Torn, Siobhan McKenna, Hurd Hatfield. D: Nicholas Ray. FAM/DRA 168m. v

King of Kings, The 1927 ★★★★½ Stately, silent spectacle tells the story of the life of Christ with the trademark DeMille opulence. The climactic Resurrection scene was shot in early Technicolor. Remade in 1961. C: H.B. Warner, Ernest Torrence, Joseph Schildkraut. D: Cecil B. DeMille. FAM/DRA 115m.

King of Kong Island 1978 Spanish ★ From Spain—a horror picture about mad scientist planting electronic devices in brains of the giant apes of Kong Island in plot for world dominion. Unintentionally funny. C: Brad Harris, Esmeralda Barros. D: Robert Morris. HOR 92m. v

King of Marvin Gardens, The 1972 ★★★★ A quiet, remorseful Nicholson plays touching second fiddle to Dern, as brothers caught in Dern's wild-eyed financial schemes. A haunting examination of desperation and hope, with an explosive performance by Burstyn. C: Jack Nicholson, Bruce Dern, Ellen Burstyn, Julia Ann Robinson. D: Bob Rafelson. DRA [R] 104m. v

King of New York 1990 ★★★½ Cult figure Ferrara's ultraviolent fairy tale of drug king with social conscience (Walken). Highly stylized, crime film features plenty of nudity and brutality. Has its devotees but definitely not for all tastes. C: Christopher Walken, David Caruso, Larry Fishburne, Wesley Snipes. D: Abel Ferrara. CRI [R] 106m. v

King of the Forest Rangers 1946 ★★½ Fun old serial features a forest ranger trying to foil an evil archeologist seeking hidden Indian treasure. C: Larry Thompson, Helen Talbot, Stuart Hamblen. ACT 167m. v

King of the Grizzlies 1969 ★★★ Indian boy raises grizzly cub after baby bear's mother is killed. Years later when both are fully grown, they meet again. Routine Disney yarn, with good use of Canadian wilderness locations. For first-grade audiences and up. C: John Yesno, Chris Wiggins. D: Ron Kelly. FAM/DRA [G] 93m. v

King of the Gypsies 1978 ★★★½ Overheated, lurid yet weirdly compelling, this drama purports to go inside the Gypsy world, chronicling a feud between father and son over who can lay claim to the crown. Roberts smolders, Hirsch embodies sleaze, and Sarandon is a hoot. Based on best-seller by Peter Maas. C: Eric Roberts, Judd Hirsch, Susan Sarandon, Sterling Hayden, Shelley Winters. D: Frank Pierson. DRA [R] 112m. v

King of the Hill 1993 ★★★★½ Young Bradford survives the hardships of Depression-era St. Louis by the sheer power of his fertile imagination, overcoming family strife, class snobbery, and hunger. Gem of a film, with fine period evocation and a superb performance by its child star. Based on A.E. Hotchner's memoir. C: Jesse Bradford, Karen Allen, Jeroen Krabbe, Lisa Eichhorn, Elizabeth McGovern, Spalding Gray. D: Steven Soderbergh. DRA [PG-13] 103m. v

King of the Jungle 1933 ★★★ Jungle man (Crabbe) is brought into civilization. Not a Tarzan movie, but it might as well be. Some lively fun. C: Buster Crabbe, Frances Dee, Sidney Toler. D: H. Bruce Humberstone, Max Marcin. ACT 72m.

King of the Khyber Rifles 1953 ★★½ A half-caste officer (Power) leads British colonial troops in 1857 India. Slow-moving, widescreen adventure. C: Tyrone Power, Terry Moore, Michael Rennie. D: Henry King. ACT 100m.

King of the Kickboxers 1991 ★★ An undercover cop with a grudge (Avedon) infiltrates a movie set where a martial arts star (Blanks) is actually slaying his opponents. Mindless bone-crusher. C: Loren Avedon, Richard Jaeckel, Billy Blanks, Don Stroud. D: Lucas Lowe. ACT [R] 90m.

King of the Mountain 1981 ★★ A mechanic and his gang spend their time racing cars through L.A.'s most treacherous streets. About as compelling as it sounds. C: Harry Hamlin,

Joseph Bottoms, Deborah Van Valkenburgh, Dennis Hopper. D: Noel Nosseck. ACT 92m. V

King of the Pecos 1936 ★★★ Wayne seeks vengeance after his father is murdered by a greedy land baron. Standard Western with young Wayne buoying the proceedings. C: John Wayne, Muriel Evans, Cy Kendall. D: Joseph Kane. WST 54m. V

King of the Roaring Twenties—The Story of Arnold Rothstein 1961 ★★½ Gangster story about the notorious NYC gambler. Janssen miscast in title role of this factually inaccurate, sanitized biography. C: David Janssen, Dianne Foster, Jack Carson, Diana Dors, Mickey Rooney. D: Joseph M. Newman. CRI 106m. V

King of the Rocket Men 1949 ★★★ Can Jeff King and the Rocket Men stop the evil Dr. Vulcan from ruling the world? It takes 12 entertaining episodes to find out. C: Tris Coffin, Mae Clarke, I. Stanford Jolley, Tom Steele. D: Fred C. Brannon. SFI 152m. V

King of the Texas Rangers 1941 ★★½ Football great Baugh is less at home in front of the camera in this serial, playing an ex-grid star turned Texas Ranger, hunting the saboteurs who killed his father. C: "Slingin'" Sammy Baugh, Pauline Moore, Neil Hamlton. D: John English, William Witney. WST 195m. V

King of the Underworld 1939 ★★★ A mob kingpin (Bogart) recruits a reluctant doctor (Francis) to patch him up. Enjoyable, silly melodrama. Remake of *Dr. Socrates*. C: Humphrey Bogart, Kay Francis, James Stephenson. D: Lewis Seiler. CRI 69m.

King of the Wild Stallions 1959 ★★★½ Intelligent steed defends a widow and her young son. Equine-oriented sagebrush yarn will mainly appeal to children. C: George Montgomery, Diane Brewster, Edgar Buchanan. D: R. G. Springsteen. FAM/WST 75m.

King of the Wind 1993 ★★★½ Boy's adventures with his Arabian stallion are given greater heft by this high-powered cast. C: Richard Harris, Glenda Jackson, Jenny Agutter, Navin Chowdhry. D: Peter Duffell. DRA 101m. V

King, Queen, Knave 1974 British ★★★ Weak adaptation of Nabokov novel about a youth who falls for his voluptuous aunt; still, watered-down Nabokov is better than none. Only released on video in the U.S. C: David Niven, Gina Lollobrigida. D: Jerzy Skolimowski. DRA [R] 94m. V

King Ralph 1991 ★★½ After the royal family meets an untimely death, uncouth Las Vegas lounge performer Goodman steps in as only heir to the English throne. And that's about as funny as it gets. Even Goodman couldn't save this one. C: John Goodman, Peter O'Toole, John Hurt, Camille Coduri. D: David S. Ward. COM [PG] 97m. V

King Rat 1965 ★★★★ A compelling, sometimes brutal story of endurance and survival among Allied prisoners in a Japanese POW camp during WWII. Based on the novel by James Clavell. Top performance by Segal. C: George Segal, Tom Courtenay, James Fox, Patrick O'Neal, Denholm Elliott, John Mills. D: Bryan Forbes. DRA 133m. V

King Richard and the Crusaders 1954 ★★ Stiff Crusades epic, with stilted characters and a schoolboy sensibility; interesting mostly for Harrison's performance as Saladin. C: Rex Harrison, Virginia Mayo, George Sanders, Laurence Harvey. D: David Butler. DRA 114m. V

King Solomon's Mines 1937 British ★★★½ Great white hunter Quatermain (Hardwicke) seeks legendary diamond mine in deepest Africa. Worth seeing for Robeson and wild finish. Remade in 1950 and 1985. C: Paul Robeson, Cedric Hardwicke, Roland Young. D: Robert Stevenson. ACT 80m. V

King Solomon's Mines 1950 ★★★★½ Second version of H. Rider Haggard story of search for legendary diamond mine in Africa. This is the ritziest-looking one, with an awfully virile-looking Granger in khaki. C: Stewart Granger, Deborah Kerr, Richard Carlson. D: Compton Bennett, Andrew Marton. ACT 103m. V

King Solomon's Mines 1985 ★★★½ Liveliest version of thrice-told tale has Quatermain (Chamberlain) helping Stone search for her long-lost father and diamond mine. Lots of action. C: Richard Chamberlain, Sharon Stone, Herbert Lom. D: J. Lee Thompson. ACT [PG-13] 101m. V

King Steps Out, The 1936 ★★★★½ Delightful operetta, well suited to Moore's gossamer charm. She's a Viennese dressmaker involved with Emperor Francis Joseph (Tone). Comic Connolly scores as King of Bavaria, "a grease spot on the pages of history." C: Grace Moore, Franchot Tone, Walter Connolly. D: Josef von Sternberg. MUS 85m.

King Sun 1972 *See* **Gatling Gun, The**

Kingdom of the Spiders 1977 ★★★★ One of the best nature-run-amok films, thanks to realistic, intelligent approach to its story of tarantulas massing against humans in Southwest town. Credibly creepy, with a good performance by Shatner. C: William Shatner, Tiffany Bolling, Woody Strode. D: John Cardos. HOR [PG] 90m. V

Kingfisher Caper, The 1976 South African ★★★ A family feud threatens ownership of a South African diamond mine. Well-acted mélange of intrigue and various prurient emotions run amok. C: Hayley Mills, David McCallum. D: Dirk DeVilliers. DRA [PG] 90m. V

Kings and Desperate Men—A Hostage Incident 1983 Canadian ★★ Political terrorists kidnap a radio talk show host and hold him hostage. A thrilling premise—but don't hold your breath. C: Patrick McGoohan, Alexis

Kanner, Andrea Marcovicci, Margaret Trudeau. D: Alexis Kanner. CRI [PG-13] 118m. v

Kings Go Forth 1958 ★★★★ Two WWII footsoldiers (Sinatra, Curtis) are after the same woman (Wood) until they find out that she is the child of an interracial couple. Excellent drama with a timely message. C: Frank Sinatra, Tony Curtis, Natalie Wood. D: Delmer Daves. DRA 109m. v

Kings of the Road 1976 German ★★★★ Two young men drive around aimlessly in the no-man's-land of the East-West Germany divide in this metaphor for the state of decline of postwar Germany. Classical Wenders, full of overpowering images. C: Rudiger Vogler, Hanns Zischler, Lisa Kreuzer. D: Wim Wenders. DRA 176m. v

Kings of the Sun 1963 ★★★ Brynner leads his Mayan tribe from Mexico to Texas, where they reach peaceful settlement with local natives. Offbeat project could have benefited from a better script and more appropriate casting. Filmed in Mexico. C: Yul Brynner, George Chakiris, Shirley Field. D: J. Lee Thompson. ACT 108m.

King's Ransom 1990 ★ Nonsense about a stolen Japanese pearl of great worth, auctioned off at a casino filled with baddies. C: Miles O'Keefe, Dedee Pfeiffer, Christopher Atkins. D: Hugh Parks. ACT 101m.

Kings Row 1942 ★★★★½ Warner Brothers pulled out all the stops in this handsomely mounted melodrama of corruption behind the facade of small-town respectablity. One of Reagan's best performances: superb Erich Korngold score and great William Cameron Menzies sets. C: Ann Sheridan, Robert Cummings, Ronald Reagan, Betty Field, Charles Coburn, Claude Rains, Judith Anderson. D: Sam Wood. DRA 127m.

King's Story, A 1965 British ★★★★ Orson Welles narrates moving this documentary about British King Edward VIII, who abdicated the throne in 1936 to marry American divorcée Wallis Warfield Simpson, thus avoiding a constitutional crisis. C: Orson Welles, Flora Robson. D: Harry Booth. DOC 100m. v

King's Thief, The 1955 ★★★½ When a villainous duke schemes to overthrow Charles II, His Highness calls upon a roguish burglar to foil the plot. Harmless; lushly produced with spectacular costumes. C: David Niven, Ann Blyth, George Sanders, Edmund Purdom, Roger Moore. D: Robert Leonard. DRA 78m. v

King's Vacation, The 1933 ★★★½ A king (Arliss) relinquishes his title to live the peasant life with his ex-wife (Gateson). Agreeable, slightly satirical comedy with fine performances. C: George Arliss, Dudley Digges, Dick Powell, Patricia Ellis, Marjorie Gateson. D: John Adolfi. COM 60m.

King's Whore, The 1990 French ★★★ A seventeenth-century monarch (Dalton) becomes obsessed with a beautiful married woman (Golino). Lush costumes, good cast. C: Timothy Dalton, Valeria Golino, Feodor Chaliapin, Margaret Tyzack. D: Axel Corti. DRA [R] 111m. v

Kinjite: Forbidden Subjects 1989 ★★½ Bronson battles teen prostitution ring in humdrum vigilante flick that's long on gunplay and short on substance. C: Charles Bronson, Juan Fernandez, James Pax. D: J. Lee Thompson. ACT [R] 98m. v

Kipperbang 1982 British ★★½ Schmaltzy recollections of growing up in post-WWII England. Diverting up to a point but its unchecked sentimentality is a bit off-putting. Originally made for British TV, released theatrically in the U.S. in 1984. (a.k.a. *Ptang, Yang, Kippirbang*) C: John Albasiny, Alison Steadman. D: Michael Apted. DRA [PG] 85m. v

Kipps 1941 British ★★★½ Redgrave is charming as shopkeeper who inherits a fortune, then tries to be accepted in high society. Somewhat slow-paced, from H.G. Wells story.(a.k.a. *The Remarkable Mr. Kipps*) C: Michael Redgrave, Diana Wynyard, Phyllis Calvert. D: Carol Reed. DRA 90m. v

Kirlian Witness, The 1978 ★★★ Psychic (Snyder) taps into the energy of a plant that witnessed the murder of her sister. Surprisingly watchable; probably the best ESP/plant flick ever. (a.k.a. *The Plants Are Watching*) C: Nancy Snyder, Ted Laplet, Joel Colodner. D: Jonathan Sarno. CRI 91m.

Kismet 1944 ★★★½ A beggar (Colman) disguises himself as a prince. Filled with romance, adventure, laughs, and Dietrich doing a seethingly sensual turn as a dancer. Filmed twice before; remade as a musical in 1955. C: Ronald Colman, Marlene Dietrich, Edward Arnold, Florence Bates. D: William Dieterle. DRA 100m.

Kismet 1955 ★★★½ Musical Arabian Nights tale based on Broadway hit. Cast tries hard, especially Gray, in gaudy production. Wright/Forrest songs based on themes by classical composer Borodin ("Stranger In Paradise," "And This Is My Beloved," "Baubles, Bangles and Beads"). C: Howard Keel, Ann Blyth, Dolores Gray, Vic Damone, Monty Woolley. D: Vincente Minnelli. MUS 114m. v

Kiss and Be Killed 1991 ★ A knife-wielding psycho destroys a wedding party, killing several. C: Carolne Ludvik, Crystal Carson, Tom Reilly, Chip Hall, Ken Norton, Jimmy Baio. D: Tom Milo. HOR 89m. v

Kiss and Tell 1945 ★★★½ Slight comedy devoted to madcap antics of teenager Corliss Archer (Temple), from Broadway hit. Harmless fluff and one of the few vehicles for teenage Temple that's watchable. C: Shirley Temple, Jerome Courtland, Walter Abel, Robert Benchley. D: Richard Wallace. COM 90m.

Kiss Before Dying, A 1956 ★★★★ Gold-digging Wagner kills one rich sister (Woodward), then romances the other. Effective thriller marred only somewhat by a wan performance from Leith; Wagner's terrific, though. From Ira Levin's novel. Remade in 1991. C: Robert Wagner, Virginia Leith, Jeffrey Hunter, Joanne Woodward, Mary Astor. D: Gerd Oswald. CRI 94m.

Kiss Before Dying, A 1991 ★★ Lackluster thriller, ruined by the double casting of Young as wealthy twin sisters romanced by a murderous cad (Dillon). Stick with the 1956 version of Ira Levin's story. C: Matt Dillon, Sean Young, Max von Sydow, Diane Ladd. D: James Dearden. CRI [R] 95m. V

Kiss Before the Mirror, The 1933 ★★★★ Criminal attorney (Morgan) defending client in crime of passion finds his family life coming to resemble the case at hand. Mixed-genre production sustains interest on several levels—romance, crime, intrigue, even a touch of horror (film was shot on original *Frankenstein* sets!) Project gets full Whale treatment, and high style makes it work despite odd casting. C: Frank Morgan, Paul Lukas, Nancy Carroll, Jean Dixon, Walter Pidgeon. D: James Whale. CRI 67m.

Kiss Daddy Good Night 1987 ★★½ No-frills thriller has alluring downtown girl Thurman seducing, drugging, then robbing older men—except for creepy neighbor, who has a plan of his own. Good film debut for Thurman. C: Uma Thurman, Paul Dillon, Paul Richards, David Brisbin. D: Peter Ily Huemer. CRI [R] 89m. V

Kiss Daddy Goodbye 1988 ★ Bikers kill the father of two kids with telekinetic powers, so they go to the sheriff and help track them down. C: Fabian, Marilyn Burns, Marvin Miller, Jon Cedar. D: Patrick Regan. ACT 81m.

Kiss for Corliss, A 1949 ★★ Teenage tale has Temple making goo-goo eyes at playboy (Niven), who wants nothing to do with her. Last movie for Temple was sequel to fair comedy *Kiss and Tell.* (a.k.a. *Almost a Bride*) C: Shirley Temple, David Niven, Tom Tully. D: Richard Wallace. COM 88m.

Kiss from Eddie, A 1970 *See* **Arousers, The**

Kiss in the Dark, A 1949 ★★ Comic oddity about snooty pianist (Niven) who inherits an apartment house, and turns into a human being managing it. C: David Niven, Jane Wyman, Victor Moore, Broderick Crawford. D: Delmer Daves. COM 87m.

Kiss Me a Killer 1991 ★★½ Use of LA barrio settings can't resuscitate this chestnut about Carmen trying to get boyfriend Beltran to help her kill her older husband. C: Guy Boyd, Robert Beltran, Julie Carmen, Ramon Franco. D: Marcus De Leon. CRI 91m. V

Kiss Me Deadly 1955 ★★★★ P.I. Mike Hammer enmeshed in a labyrinthine plot concerning insane asylum escapee, her roommate, thugs, a dead scientist, and a box containing "the great whatsit." Stylized thriller retains blistering pace and violence of the Mickey Spillane novel. C: Ralph Meeker, Albert Dekker, Paul Stewart, Cloris Leachman. D: Robert Aldrich. CRI 106m. V

Kiss Me Goodbye 1982 ★★★ Sanitized remake of Brazilian *Donna Flor and Her Two Husbands* has widow (Field) about to marry when her dead choreographer husband returns to haunt her. Farce is clearly not Field's forte. Overall, a strained affair. C: Sally Field, James Caan, Jeff Bridges, Paul Dooley, Claire Trevor, Mildred Natwick. D: Robert Mulligan. COM [PG] 101m. V

Kiss Me Kate 1953 ★★★★½ Ebullient filming of Cole Porter Broadway smash preserves brilliant score and witty script about feuding Broadway stars in musical version of Shakespeare's *Taming of the Shrew.* Keel and Grayson are well cast, but picture belongs to Miller, in her best screen role. Highlights include "Too Darn Hot," "So in Love," "From This Moment On." Look for Fosse dancing in latter number. C: Kathryn Grayson, Howard Keel, Ann Miller, Tommy Rall, Keenan Wynn, James Whitmore, Bob Fosse, Bobby Van. D: George Sidney. MUS 109m. V

Kiss Me, Stupid 1964 ★★★★ Las Vegas crooner Martin offers to record a song by nebbish tune smith Walston—but only if he can sleep with his wife. Endearing Novak and lecherous Martin steal the show in this underrated sex farce. C: Dean Martin, Kim Novak, Ray Walston. D: Billy Wilder. COM [PG] 126m. V

KISS Meets the Phantom of the Park 1978 ★ Evil amusment park owner wants to clone rock band KISS as part of an evil plot. Campy fun. C: Gene Simmons, Paul Stanley, Peter Criss, Ace Frehley, Anthony Zerbe, Deborah Ryan, Carmine Caridi, Terry Webster, John Dennis Johnston. D: Gordon Hessler. COM 96m. TVM

Kiss of a Killer 1993 ★★ *Marnie* meets *Looking for Mr. Goodbar* as O'Toole develops promiscuous split persona as result of mstreatment by her mother and then falls into the hands of a serial rapist. C: Annette O'Toole, Eva Marie Saint, Brian Wimmer, Gregg Henry, Vic Polizos. D: Larry Elikann. CRI 93m.

Kiss of Death 1947 ★★★½ Best remembered as film in which Widmark pushes lady in wheelchair down stairs, is actually a skillful semidocumentary about Mature turning against his underworld past to become solid citizen. Widmark in screen debut gives this a perverse energy that otherwise ordinary material lacks. C: Victor Mature, Richard Widmark, Brian Donlevy, Coleen Gray. D: Henry Hathaway. CRI 99m. V

Kiss of the Beast 1990 *See* **Meridian—Kiss of the Beast**

Kiss of the Spider Woman 1985 U.S. ★★★★½ Hurt is gay window decorator who spins tales about his favorite old Hollywood films to maintain sanity for himself and fellow political prisoner Julia in a South American jail. Alternately hallucinatory and starkly real, a very moving, unusual character study. Oscar for Best Actor to Hurt. C: William Hurt, Raul Julia, Sonia Braga. D: Hector Babenco. DRA [R] 119m. V

Kiss Shot 1992 ★★★½ Goldberg plays financially strapped single mother who uses her pool table skills to pay the rent. One-joke comedy is pleasantly diverting, in a script custom-fitted to the talents of the likable star. C: Whoopi Goldberg, Dorian Harewood, Dennis Franz. D: Jerry London. COM [PG] 88m. TVM V

Kiss, The 1929 ★★★★ Garbo's last silent is stylish melodrama of innocent kiss that produces major misunderstanding, culminating in murder and courtroom drama. Also notable as Ayres' film debut in role of young man who receives the well-intentioned peck. C: Greta Garbo, Conrad Nagel, Andres Randolf, Lew Ayres. D: Jacques Feyder. DRA 60m. V

Kiss, The 1988 ★★ Teenager Salenger is understandably put out when her visiting aunt (Pacula) turns out to be a witch who wants to infect her with an evil kiss. Utterly predictable and ludicrously overdirected, though Salenger is appealing. C: Joanna Pacula, Meredith Salenger. D: Pen Densham. HOR [R] 105m. V

Kiss the Blood Off My Hands 1948 ★★½ Hot-tempered Lancaster hides out from murder charges with loving nurturer Fontaine, only to be blackmailed into unlawful behavior by slimy criminal Newton. A melodramatic thriller. C: Burt Lancaster, Joan Fontaine, Robert Newton. D: Norman Foster. CRI 80m.

Kiss the Boys Goodbye 1941 ★★★½ Loose adaptation of Claire Booth play adds songs by Frank Loesser and Victor Schertzinger to story of Southern dancer (Martin) trying to break into movies while sparring with her director. Amiable, with good song, "Sand In My Shoes," sung by Connee Boswell. C: Mary Martin, Don Ameche, Oscar Levant, Virginia Dale. D: Victor Schertzinger. MUS 85m.

Kiss the Girls and Make Them Die 1966 Italian ★★ Suave secret agent uncovers plot to sterilize the entire male population of the world. Lackluster attempt to cash in on the James Bond craze. C: Michael Connors, Dorothy Provine, Terry-Thomas, Raf Vallone. D: Henry Levin. COM 101m.

Kiss the Night 1987 ★★ Stephens plays a prostitute who falls for a client, but finds it harder to leave her profession than she bargained for. C: Patsy Stephens, Warwick Moss, Garry Aron Cook. D: James Ricketson. ACT 99m. V

Kiss the Other Sheik 1965 Italian ★ Arabian wife foils her husband's plan to sell her into slavery. Silly plot; buffoonish performances. C: Marcello Mastroianni, Pamela Tiffin, Virna Lisi. D: Luciano Salce, Eduardo Filippo. COM [PG] 85m.

Kiss Them for Me 1957 ★★★ An unauthorized San Francisco shore leave provides opportunity for lascivious mischief and mayhem for three conniving Navy pilots. Attractive cast can't float this lethargic comedy. C: Cary Grant, Jayne Mansfield, Leif Erickson, Suzy Parker. D: Stanley Donen. COM 105m.

Kisses for My President 1964 ★★★½ Dated comedy tries to show limits of protocol when a woman (Bergen) is elected the first female President of the United States and her husband (MacMurray) becomes the First Spouse. Sometimes it works, sometimes it doesn't. C: Fred MacMurray, Polly Bergen, Arlene Dahl, Eli Wallach. D: Curtis Bernhardt. COM 113m. V

Kissin' Cousins 1964 ★★★ Presley in double role of Air Force officer and his hillbilly cousin feudin "and fightin" over missile base to be built on latter's property. Poor man's *Li'l Abner.* C: Elvis Presley, Arthur O'Connell, Glenda Farrell, Pamela Austin. D: Gene Nelson. MUS 96m. V

Kissing Bandit, The 1948 ★★★ Dull musical romance with Sinatra as shy son of renowned Western "kissing bandit," who tries to fill dad's shoes. Bright spot is "Dance of Fury," with Miller, Montalban, and Charisse. C: Frank Sinatra, Kathryn Grayson, Ann Miller, Ricardo Montalban, Mildred Natwick, Cyd Charisse. D: Laslo Benedek. MUS 102m.

Kissing Place, The 1990 ★★★½ Engrossing thriller about a bereaved mother who kidnaps a boy to replace the son she lost. Her obsessiveness increases as he begins to remember his real family. Baxter-Birney excells in an against-type performance. C: Meredith Baxter-Birney, David Ogden Stiers. D: Tony Wharmby. DRA 88m. TVM V

Kit Carson 1940 ★★★ Frontier Indian scout vies with a Union officer for a woman's affections. Full of action. C: Jon Hall, Lynn Bari, Dana Andrews. D: George Seitz. WST 101m. V

Kitchen Toto, The 1987 ★★★★ A young boy's loyalties are torn between his fellow Kikuyu tribesmen and his British employers during the Mau Mau uprising in Kenya during the 1950s. Powerful story is smoothly directed, with strong performances. C: Edwin Mahinda, Bob Peck, Phyllis Logan. D: Harry Hook. DRA [PG-13] 96m. V

Kitten with a Whip 1964 ★★½ Ann-Margret plays a delinquent with friends who force a staid businessman (Forsythe) to drive them to Mexico. Not as bad as it sounds. C: Ann-Margret, John Forsythe, Patricia Barry. D: Douglas Heyes. DRA 83m.

Kitty 1945 ★★★★ Sharp-tongued street urchin (Goddard) rises in social position with the help of a rake (Milland) in melodramatic

Cinderella story, set in 18th-century England. Goddard is terrific and period details are lovely. C: Paulette Goddard, Ray Milland, Patric Knowles, Reginald Owen, Cecil Kellaway, Constance Collier. D: Mitchell Leisen. DRA 104m.

Kitty Foyle 1940 ★★★½ Rogers won Best Actress Oscar for her portrayal of working-class girl torn between rich and poor suitors. The soapy story doesn't hold up because of poor script and weak supporting cast. C: Ginger Rogers, Dennis Morgan, James Craig, Gladys Cooper. D: Sam Wood. DRA 107m. V

Kitty: Return to Auschwitz 1979 British ★★★★★ Moving documentary about Kitty Hart, death-camp survivor, and her visit to Auschwitz-Birkenau, where she was brought in 1943 at age 16. Haunting, powerful film, made for British TV. A must. C: Kitty Hart. DOC 82m. TVM V

KKK 1974 *See* **Klansman, The**

Klansman, The 1974 ★ Sheriff must face off against Klan landowner fomenting racial trouble in this low-rent potboiler. (a.k.a. *KKK* and *The Burning Cross*) C: Lee Marvin, Richard Burton, Cameron Mitchell, Lola Falana. D: Terence Young. ACT [R] 112m. V

Klondike Annie 1936 ★★★★ San Francisco bad girl (West) goes north and pretends to turn missionary. Good vehicle for Mae benefits from chemistry with McLaglen and song "I'm An Occidental Woman in An Oriental Mood for Love." C: Mae West, Victor McLaglen. D: Raoul Walsh. COM 77m. V

Klondike Fever 1980 ★★ The Alaskan Gold Rush and author Jack London together again. Feature-length adventure glimmers now and then, but tarnished overall by a clichéd script. C: Rod Steiger, Angie Dickinson, Lorne Greene. D: Peter Carter. ACT 106m. V

Klute 1971 ★★★★½ A private investigator (Sutherland) takes up with a call girl (Fonda) who he thinks is involved in a man's disappearance. A solid and compelling character-based thriller crafted with intelligence and beautifully acted. An Oscar-winner for Jane. C: Jane Fonda, Donald Sutherland, Charles Cioffi, Roy Scheider. D: Alan J. Pakula. DRA [R] 114m. V

Klutz, The 1973 French ★★★ Title character is hapless jerk on the way to visit his girlfriend, who finds himself caught up in a robbery and mistaken for wanted criminal. C: Claude Michaud, Louise Portal, Guy Provost. D: Pierre Rose. COM 86m. V

Knack, and How to Get It, The 1965 British ★★★★ Breezy British comedy concerning a shy young school teacher receiving lessons on how to be irresistible to women from his savvy playboy boarder. Fast-moving, hilarious exploration of the battle of the sexes. C: Rita Tushingham, Ray Brooks, Michael Crawford, Donal Donnelly. D: Richard Lester. COM 84m. V

Knave of Hearts 1954 *See* **Lovers, Happy Lovers**

Knickerbocker Holiday 1944 ★★★ Watered-down version of Weill/Anderson musical, set in colonial New York, with Eddy as publisher of controversial literature. Three songs from score survive, including classic "September Song," sung by Coburn. C: Nelson Eddy, Charles Coburn, Constance Dowling, Shelley Winters. D: Harry Brown. MUS 85m.

Knife in the Head 1978 German ★★★★ Man (Ganz) shot in the head during a police raid loses his memory and physical mobility. When arrested for murder, he must defend himself against a political conspiracy. Tense and involving, with remarkable performance by Ganz. C: Bruno Ganz, Angela Winkler, Hans Blech. D: Reinhard Hauff. DRA 113m. V

Knife in the Water 1962 Polish ★★★★★ Young hitchhiker transforms lives of affluent couple who pick him up on their way to weekend sailing vacation. Polanski's debut is a strong, disturbing study of psychological power plays. C: Leon Niemczyk, Jolanta Umecka. D: Roman Polanski. DRA 95m. V

Knight Moves 1993 ★★★½ Chess maestro Lambert, prime suspect in a series of bizarre murders, is taunted by the real killer. Solid cat and mouser. C: Christopher Lambert, Diane Lane, Tom Skerritt. D: Carl Schenkel. CRI [R] 105m. V

Knight Without Armour 1937 British ★★★½ A British spy (Donat) infiltrates a band of revolutionaries in 1913 Russia. Impressive sets and costumes provide this period romance with a solid sense of historical detail. C: Marlene Dietrich, Robert Donat, Irene Vanbrugh. D: Jacques Feyder. DRA 107m. V

Knightriders 1981 ★★★★ An itinerant motorcycle group holds medieval-style fairs, joust on their motorcycles, and dedicate themselves as "knights" to the noble-minded principles of King Arthur's creedo. Odd, but captivating and quite unique. C: Ed Harris, Gary Lahti, Tom Savini, Amy Ingersoll. D: George A. Romero. ACT [R] 145m. V

Knights 1993 ★★★ Another postapocalypse sci-fi action film. A human survivor teams with a cyborg to fight off renegade cyborgs who are terrorizing the few remaining humans on Earth. Competent but uninteresting. C: Kris Kristofferson, Lance Henriksen, Kathy Long, Scott Paulin. D: Albert Pyun. SFI [R] 89m. V

Knights and Emeralds 1986 British ★★★★ A white teenage drummer from a working-class family in northern England stuns his family and friends by consorting with a band of black musicians. Funny and genuine. C: Christopher Wild, Warren Mitchell. D: Ian Emes. DRA [PG] 90m. V

Knights of the City 1985 ★★ When gang members are jailed for fighting, fellow inmate/record executive discovers they're rock 'n' rollers too, and invites them to enter a talent contest. Few surprises in cornball story, except for the graphic violence. C: Nicholas Campbell, Stoney Jackson, Leon Isaac Kennedy. D: Dominic Orlando. ACT [R] 87m. v

Knights of the Round Table 1953 ★★★½ Stalwart Lancelot (Taylor) forced to choose between his love for Guinevere (Gardner) and loyalty to King Arthur. Oft-told story gets lavish MGM treatment. C: Robert Taylor, Ava Gardner, Mel Ferrer. D: Richard Thorpe. ACT 117m. v

Knock on Any Door 1949 ★★★ Intelligent drama features tenement youth accused of murder and the defense lawyer who campaigns to free him. Presented in solid if unexceptional fashion. C: Humphrey Bogart, John Derek, Allene Roberts. D: Nicholas Ray. DRA 100m. v

Knock on Wood 1954 ★★★★ Diverting Kaye comedy with star as ventriloquist whose dummy carries secret documents coveted by a spy ring. Kaye does some funny routines with his wooden co-star, while Zetterling is stunningly beautiful as his love interest. Some of Kaye's best bits. C: Danny Kaye, Mai Zetterling, David Burns. D: Norman Panama, Melvin Frank. COM 103m.

Knockout 1941 ★★★ Melodramatic yarn of a boxer's triumphs and troubles in and out of the ring. Standard. C: Arthur Kennedy, Virginia Field, Anthony Quinn, Cornel Wilde. D: William Clemens. DRA 73m.

Knute Rockne, All American 1940 ★★★★½ This film set the standard for all subsequent Hollywood sports biographies. The focus is on Rockne's (O'Brien's) work developing innovative football maneuvers, and his wholesome outlook on life, although of late much attention has been paid (for obvious reasons) to Ronald Reagan's famous scene as "The Gipper." C: Pat O'Brien, Gale Page, Donald Crisp, Ronald Reagan. D: Lloyd Bacon. DRA 98m. v

Koko: A Talking Gorilla 1977 French ★★★★ Engrossing documentary on education of gorilla who learns to communicate via sign language. Film not only chronicles experiment, but also provides sense of Koko's emotional makeup. D: Barbet Schroeder. DOC 81m. v

Kon-Tiki 1951 ★★★★½ Exciting Oscar-winning documentary of Norwegian anthropologist and adventurer Thor Heyerdahl's 1947 expedition covering 4,300 miles in a primitive balsawood raft across the Pacific Ocean from Peru to Tahiti, demonstrating that ancient Polynesians could have sailed from South America. D: Ben Grauer, Thor Heyerdahl. DOC 73m.

Kongo 1932 ★★★ A paraplegic trader (Huston) turned jungle tyrant hatches a sadistic revenge scheme that is decidedly nasty. Eerie, atmospheric thriller. Remake of *West of Zanzibar*. C: Walter Huston, Lupe Velez, Conrad Nagel. D: William Cowan. DRA 85m. v

Kopek and Broom 1976 *See* **Find the Lady**

Korczak 1990 Polish ★★★★ Sensitive retelling of the Nazi invasion of Poland and the subsequent deportation and murder of children from a Jewish orphanage. Extraordinary performances and photography, including actual period footage, convey horrific events with extreme tenderness and delicacy. D: Andrzej Wajda. DRA 118m. v

Kostas 1979 Australian ★★★ Typically quirky Cox film about a Greek imigrant taxi driver who falls for a wealthy divorcee, and pursues her in London. C: Emmanuel Takis, Wendy Hughes. D: Paul Cox. DRA 88m. v

Kotch 1971 ★★★★½ Lemmon's directorial debut features a warm and humorous performance by Matthau as an aging codger who refuses to be put away by his well-meaning family and instead runs away and, much to the horror of his children, befriends and supports a pregnant unwed mother. Clever and emotionally satisfying. C: Walter Matthau, Deborah Winters, Felicia Farr. D: Jack Lemmon. COM [PG] 114m. v

Kovacs! 1971 ★★★★½ A terrific selection of the best of one of the few real geniuses TV has produced, a startlingly original comic mind who influenced many of the best comics who came after him. C: Ernie Kovacs, Edie Adams. D: Ernie Kovacs. COM 85m. v

Kowloon Assignment 1977 Hong Kong ★★ Chiba plays a comicbook superhero dispatched to crush a drug ring. C: Sonny Chiba. D: Yukio Noda. ACT 93m.

Koyaanisqatsi 1983 ★★★½ Visual tone poem counterposes scenes of great natural beauty with industrial sprawl to hammer home the message that the world is a mess. Philip Glass music and exquisite cinematography works wonders, but this documentary is a bit too self-righteous and, ultimately, condescending. D: Godfrey Reggio. DOC 87m. v

Krakatoa, East of Java 1969 ★★★ Treasure hunters race against time and impending volcanic eruption in chase for loot. Though action-packed and boasting terrific volcano sequence, basic storytelling skills lost in hubbub. (a.k.a. *Volcano*). C: Maximilian Schell, Diane Baker, Brian Keith, Sal Mineo. D: Bernard Kowalski. ACT [G] 101m.

Kramer vs. Kramer 1979 ★★★★★ Self-absorbed advertising executive Hoffman becomes full-time parent to his small son after his wife abandons them. This solid blend of comedy and tearjerking drama, with a strong cast is fulfilling and vastly entertaining. Academy Awards: Best Picture, Actor, Director, Screenplay, Supporting Actress (Streep). C: Dustin Hoffman, Meryl Streep, Jane Alexander, Justin Henry. D: Robert Benton. DRA [PG] 105m. v

Krays, The 1990 British ★★★★ Fascinating tale of ruthless twin brothers (the Kemps) who dominated British underworld in '50s and '60s. Whitelaw is memorably nasty as mother who drove them to success, giving it startling feminist subtext. Powerful but ugly violence may upset some, but film is riveting. C: Gary Kemp, Martin Kemp, Billie Whitelaw, Kate Hardie. D: Peter Medak. CRI [R] 119m. V

Kremlin Letter, The 1970 ★★★ Complicated cold-war thriller about a fake treaty that will cause WWIII if it falls into enemy hands. Huston's dull direction is puzzling. Based on Noel Behn's best-seller. C: Bibi Andersson, Max von Sydow, Richard Boone, Orson Welles, George Sanders, Patrick O'Neal. D: John Huston. CRI [PG] 113m.

Kronos 1957 ★★★½ Entertainingly hokey '50s sci-fi film about giant robot from space, come to Earth to drain our energy supplies. Fun, and a blast from the past. C: Jeff Morrow, Barbara Lawrence. D: Kurt Neumann. SFI 78m. V

Krull 1983 ★★½ Sword and sorcery fantasy of young prince's efforts to save his beautiful fiancée from the hands of Evil. Formula quest story gets highly decorated treatment. C: Ken Marshall, Lysette Anthony, Francesca Annis, Liam Neeson. D: Peter Yates. ACT [PG] 117m. V

Krush Groove 1985 ★★★ The first all-rap musical has little plot to speak of, but solid hip-hop sound track. Hollywood filmmakers' take on life in the Hood is a bit off target, especially compared to strong early '90s entries. C: Blair Underwood, Joseph Simmons, Sheila E. D: Michael Schultz. MUS [R] 95m. V

Kuffs 1992 ★★ When his brother is killed, a most unlikely candidate (Slater) takes over the family security business in an attempt to solve the murder. Odd mix of comedy and action. C: Christian Slater, Tony Goldwyn, Milla Jovovich. D: Bruce A. Evans. ACT [PG-13] 102m. V

Kung Fu 1972 ★★★½ A fugitive Shaolin priest (Carradine) helps a group of oppressed Chinese railroad workers. Asian mysticism grafted onto a classic Western scenario. The pilot for the 1970s TV series. C: David Carradine, Barry Sullivan, Keith Carradine, Keye Luke. D: Jerry Thorpe. ACT 74m. TVM V

Kung Fu Master 1989 *See* **Le Petit Amour**

Kung Fu—The Movie 1986 ★★★ Carradine's return finds the hard-hitting Shaolin priest bent on busting up an opium smuggling ring. Routine plot twists ensue; undistinguished, except for an earnest turn by Lee as a young assassin. Basis for another TV series. C: David Carradine, Kerri Keane, Mako, Brandon Lee. D: Richard Lang. ACT 92m. V

Kuroneko 1968 Japanese ★★★★ Two women, murdered by samurai, haunt their killers. Haunting, hypnotic, but extremely violent tale of revenge. (a.k.a. *The Black Cat*) C: Nobuko Otowa, Kiwako Tachi, Kichiemon Nakamura. D: Kaneto Shindo. HOR 99m.

Kwaidan 1964 Japanese ★★★ Quartet of Lafcadio Hearn ghost stories is more an exercise in atmosphere than thrills. Stylish but distant. The third tale is most eerily successful. C: Rentaro Mikuni, Keiko Kishi. D: Masaki Kobayashi. HOR 160m. V

L

L-Shaped Room, The 1963 British ★★★★ Unwed French mother (Caron) goes to London to have her baby, meeting assorted misfits at run-down boarding house. Sensitive drama with a wonderful performance by Caron. C: Leslie Caron, Tom Bell, Brock Peters, Emlyn Williams. D: Bryan Forbes. DRA 125m.

L.A. Bad 1988 ★★★ Tough Latino teenager learns life lessons during battle against cancer. C: Esai Morales, Chuck Bail, Janice Rule, Carrie Snodgress. D: Gary Kent. FAM/DRA 101m. v

La Balance 1982 French ★★★★ Violent Parisian cops-and-robbers story; small-time pimp (Leotard) and his prostitute girlfriend (Baye) are caught between police and the mob. Baye shines in popular, critically praised thriller. C: Nathalie Baye, Philippe Leotard, Richard Berry. D: Bob Swaim. CRI [R] 102m. v

La Bamba 1987 ★★★★ Earnest, energetic version of the life of '50s Chicano rocker Richie Valens has lots of musical vitality and touches on racial issues he faced. Vigorous performances raise otherwise formulaic biography to higher level. C: Lou Diamond Phillips, Esai Morales, Elizabeth Pena. D: Luis Valdez. DRA [PG-13] 103m. v

La Belle Equipe 1938 *See* **They Were Five**

La Belle Noiseuse 1991 French ★★★★½ A retired artist (Piccoli) is inspired by a beautiful young woman (Beart) to finish a painting he started years before. Challenging, intense study of creativity and passion. C: Michel Piccoli, Jane Birkin, Emmanuelle Beart. D: Jacques Rivette. DRA 240m. v

La Bete Humaine 1938 French ★★★★½ A train engineer (Gabin) plots to murder the husband of a femme fatale (Simon). Gallic forerunner of *Double Indemnity* and countless others, from Emile Zola's novel. Menacing mood is brilliantly sustained by master filmmaker Renoir. (a.k.a. *The Human Beast*, *Judas Was a Woman.*) Remade as *Human Desire* in 1954. C: Jean Gabin, Simone Simon, Julien Carette. D: Jean Renoir. CRI 99m. v

La Boum 1981 French ★★★ A teenager (Marceau) deals with growing up, moving to Paris, and her parents' marital problems. Slight, derivative melodrama, but young star Marceau is the real winner. French box-office smash, followed by *La Boum 2.* C: Claude Brasseur, Brigitte Fossey, Sophie Marceau. D: Claude Pinoteau. DRA 100m. v

La Boum 2 1982 French ★★★ Two years later, young Marceau has her own romantic problems. Virtual carbon copy of first; worth catching for Marceau's unaffected performance. C: Sophie Marceau, Claude Brasseur, Brigitte Fossey. D: Claude Pinoteau. DRA 109m.

L.A. Bounty 1989 ★★★ Former police officer tries to avenge the death of her partner and capture his deranged killer. C: Sybil Danning, Wings Hauser, Henry Darrow. D: Worth Keeter. CRI [R] 85m. v

La Cage aux Folles 1979 French ★★★★½ Elderly gay lovers, proprietors of a drag nightclub in St. Tropez, try to pass as a straight married couple when son of one of them gets engaged. As shrewd a farce as ever filmed wins over audience with hilarious sight gags, uproarious complications and touching performance by Serrault. Highlight is the dinner scene and the soup bowls. Two sequels and a Broadway musical followed. C: Ugo Tognazzi, Michel Serrault, Michel Galabru. D: Edouard Molinaro. COM [R] 91m. v

La Cage aux Folles II 1980 French ★★★ Silly spy farce using characters from the far superior forerunner. Serrault as Italian peasant woman is visually amusing but script is generally witless. C: Michel Serrault, Ugo Tognazzi, Michel Galabru, Gianni Frisonni. D: Edouard Molinaro. COM [R] 101m. v

La Cage aux Folles III: The Wedding 1985 French ★★½ When drag queen Albin (Serrault) receives an inheritance, there's one hitch: he must marry and become a father to receive it. The laughs are few and far between in this third go-round for the St. Tropez gay couple. C: Michel Serrault, Ugo Tognazzi, Michel Galabru, Stephane Audran. D: Georges Lautner. COM [PG-13] 88m. v

La Chene *See* **The Oak**

La Chevre 1982 French ★★★½ Goofball CPA (Richard) teams up with veteran P.I. (Depardieu) to track down missing heiress. Often clumsy farce delivers the laughs; amiable cast helps. American remake, *Pure Luck.* C: Pierre Richard, Gerard Depardieu, Michel Robin. D: Francis Veber. COM 91m. v

La Chienne 1931 French ★★★★½ Disturbing, dark drama about an unhappily married man (Simon) who becomes obsessed with a cold, calculating prostitute (Mareze). Trend-setting use of location and direct sound. Remade as *Scarlet Street.* C: Michel Simon, Janie Mareze. D: Jean Renoir. DRA 95m. v

La Chinoise 1967 French ★★★★ Satirical look at group of Parisian students who form a Maoist commune to experiment with revolutionary theories. Classic Godard theme of rebels vs. the middle class highlighted by several winning performances. C: Anne Wiazemsky, Jean-Pierre Leaud, Michel Semianko. D: Jean-Luc Godard. COM 95m.

La Citta Si Defende 1951 *See* **Four Ways Out**

La Collectioneuse 1971 French ★★★★ Third of Rohmer's Six Moral Tales concerns two older men who share a house in St. Tropez with a sexually liberated young woman and their fight to resist physical temptation. Witty and erotic exploration of human nature. C: Patrick Bauchau, Haydee Politoff. D: Eric Rohmer. DRA 88m.

L.A. Crackdown 1987 ★★★ Valiant youth fights to make a difference in her drug-torn city. C: Pamela Dixon, Kita Harrison, Jeffrey Olsen. D: Joseph Merhi. CRI 90m. V

L.A. Crackdown 2 1987 ★★ West Coast police officer poses as a dancer to trap a maniac who is killing prostitutes. C: Pamela Dixon, Anthony Gates, Cynthia Miguel. D: Joseph Merhi. CRI 90m. V

La Cuisine Polonaise 1991 ★★★★ Polish World War II ace faces trouble from the Communist government when he attempts to settle back home with his foreign wife. D: Jacek Bromski. DRA 108m. V

La Discrete 1990 French ★★★★½ Writer (Luchini) woos seemingly naive waif (Henry) to drop her and get material for a book, but she becomes a formidable adversary in his game. Well acted, with witty, economical writing and directing by Vincent (his first film). C: Fabrice Luchini, Judith Henry, Maurice Garrel. D: Christian Vincent. DRA 96m. V

La Dolce Vita 1960 Italian ★★★★★ Fellini's classic belongs in a time capsule. Society's decline is illustrated in series of vignettes surrounding a disillusioned journalist (Mastroianni). Always engrossing. C: Marcello Mastroianni, Anita Ekberg, Anouk Aimee, Yvonne Furneaux, Lex Barker. D: Federico Fellini. DRA 175m. V

La Femme Infidele 1969 French ★★★★½ A man discovers his wife's infidelity. He murders her lover, and her respect for her husband increases. Brilliant study by Chabrol of the importance of appearances over emotions in middle-class marriages; excellent performances by talented cast. (a.k.a *Unfaithful Wife*) C: Stephane Audran, Michel Bouquet, Maurice Ronet. D: Claude Chabrol. DRA 98m.

La Femme Nikita 1990 French ★★★★ Vicious killer (Parillaud) is reprogrammed as an assassin for a government agency. Stylized, extremely violent thriller pays homage to and betters American action films. Moreau's brief appearance is a gem. American remake, *Point of No Return*. C: Anne Parillaud, Jean-Hugues Anglade, Tcheky Karyo, Jeanne Moreau. D: Luc Besson. CRI [R] 117m. V

La Fiancée du Pirate 1969 *See* **Very Curious Girl, A**

L.A. Goddess 1992 ★★½ Sexy mystery involving a studio head who falls victim to an enticing actress. C: Jeff Conaway, Joe Estevez, Wendy McDonald, Kathy Shower. D: Jag Mundhra. DRA [R] 92m. V

La Gran Fiesta 1987 Puerto Rican ★★★ In 1942 Puerto Rico, the impending U.S. takeover colors final black-tie ball at Old San Juan Casino. Attempt to illuminate little-known area of history shows predictable squabbles among caricatured attendees rather than deeper political implications. C: Daniel Lugo, Miguelangel Suarez, Raul Julia. D: Marcos Zurinaga. DRA 101m.

La Grande Bourgeoisie 1974 ★★★½ True story of man who murders his sister's husband, creating a political brouhaha. Solid performances in a sumptuous production. C: Catherine Deneuve, Giancarlo Giannini, Fernando Rey. D: Mauro Bologmini. CRI 115m.

La Guerre Est Finie 1966 French ★★★★ An aging leftist soldier (Montand) reflects on the Spanish Civil War and realizes his efforts accomplished little. Montand gives a commendable performance in grim, powerful story. C: Yves Montand, Ingrid Thulin, Genevieve Bujold, Michel Piccoli. D: Alain Resnais. DRA 121m.

L.A. Heat 1988 ★★ Brown glowers as a vice cop whose partner has been killed, perhaps by other cops. Lumbering; followed by a sequel, *L.A. Vice*. C: Lawrence Hilton-Jacobs, Jim Brown, Kevin Benton. D: Joseph Merhi. ACT 90m.

La Lectrice 1988 French ★★★★ Woman (Miou-Miou) reading to her boyfriend, imagines herself as the book's heroine—a professional reader who gets caught up in her clients' lives. Light comedy, not as intellectual as it sounds. (a.k.a. *The Reader*) C: Miou-Miou, Christian Ruche, Sylvie Laporte. D: Michel Deville. COM [R] 98m. V

La Mafia 1977 Spanish ★★ Mafia member attempts coup d'etat causing severe repercussions within the organization. C: Alfredo Alcon, Thelma Biral, Jose Slavin. DRA 125m. V

La Main du Diable 1947 *See* **Carnival of Sinners**

La Marseillaise 1938 French ★★★★ Epic story of the Revolution is told in tandem with the story of the French national anthem (La Marseillaise); had political overtones in its day, during Hitler's rise. C: Madeleine Renaud, Paulette Elambert. D: Jean Benoit-Levy. DRA 130m. V

La Maternelle 1932 French ★★★★ Wonderfully emotional, perceptive story of the close relationship between a schoolteacher (Renaud) and her young student, the daughter of a prostitute. Great performances, particularly from the children. C: Madeleine Renaud, Alice Tissot, Paulette Elambert. D: Jean Benoit-Levy. DRA 86m.

La Notte 1961 French ★★★★½ Intimate examination of an eroding marriage over the course of a single day. Claustrophobic atmosphere, focused on noncommumication, is relieved by overwhelmingly honest performances by Mastroianni and Moreau. (Second of trilogy, after *L'Avventura*, C: Jeanne Moreau, Marcello Mastroianni, Monica Vitti. D: Michelangelo Antonioni. DRA [R] 120m.

La Notte Brava 1959 Italian ★★★½ A day in the life of three young Roman men. Gritty depiction of wayward youth enhanced by Pasolini screenplay. (a.k.a. *Night Heat*) C: Laurent Terzieff, Jean-Claude Brialy, Franco Interlenghi. D: Mauro Bolognini. DRA 93m.

La Nuit des Varennes 1982 Italian ★★★★ Tantalizing fantasy puts Casanova and Thomas Paine, among others, together in coach following escape of Louis XVI and Marie Antoinette. Talky, but character interaction is surprising and funny. Wonderful performances all around. C: Marcello Mastroianni, Jean-Louis Barrault, Hanna Schygulla, Harvey Keitel. D: Ettore Scola. DRA [R] 133m. V

La Parisienne 1957 French ★★★★ Frothy Gallic romp with Bardot as the innocent daughter of French premier, tangled up in arranged marriage to Vidal while flirting with older ambassador (Boyer). Bardot reveals unexpected gift for comedy, regrettably seldom used since. C: Brigitte Bardot, Charles Boyer, Henri Vidal. D: Michel Boisrond. COM 85m.

La Passante 1982 French ★★★½ Gentle pacifist murders an ambassador who turns out to be an ex-Nazi. Ambitious drama. Schneider plays two roles in her last film. C: Romy Schneider, Michel Piccoli, Wendelin Werner, Helmut Griem, Maria Schell. D: Jacques Rouffio. CRI 106m. V

La Pelle 1981 Italian ★★ Weak effort tries to be an eye-opening look at U.S. troops in Italy following WWII liberation. Cavani's script and direction are models of how *not* to make a knowing historical treatise. C: Marcello Mastroianni, Burt Lancaster, Claudia Cardinale. D: Liliana Cavani. DRA 131m.

La Petite Bande 1983 French ★★★½ A group of British children run away to France where they save the world from some power-hungry adults. Clever fantasy, told without dialogue, created specifically for children. C: Andrew Chandler, Helene Dassule. D: Michel Deville. FAM/DRA [PG] 91m.

La Prisonniére 1969 French ★★★½ Clouzot's last film is a disturbing tale of a sadomasochistic triangle among photographer, his girlfriend, and rich playboy. Powerful but ugly, with a particularly nasty denouement. C: Laurent Terzieff, Bernard Fresson, Elsabeth Wiener. D: Henri-Georges Clouzot. DRA [R] 104m.

La Ronde 1950 French ★★★★½ Stylish comedy of sexual manners in 19th-century Vienna. Romances of connected characters keep changing, until they're all back as they began. Risque and witty, based on Schnitzler's play of same title; remade as *Circle of Love*. C: Anton Walbrook, Simone Signoret, Simone Simon, Danielle Darrieux, Fernand Gravet, Jean-Louis Barrault, Gerard Philipe. D: Max Ophuls. COM 97m. V

La Salamandre 1971 Swiss ★★★★ Straightforward, entertaining study of the nature of truth, with excellent performances. C: Bulle Ogier, Jean-Luc Bideau, Jacques Denis. D: Alain Tanner. DRA 125m.

La Signora di Tutti 1934 Italian ★★★★½ Italian movie star (Miranda) recalls the circumstances that led to her attempted suicide. Disturbing look at public's fascination with celebrity and the emptiness that often accompanies success. Innovative photography and Miranda's strong performance make this one of Ophuls' best efforts. C: Daniele Amfitheatrof, Isa Miranda. D: Max Ophuls. DRA 89m.

La Soufrière 1977 ★★★★½ The volcano on the island of Guadaloupe is going to blow, prompting the evacuation of all inhabitants save a handful of superstitious villagers. Director Herzog takes his camera and crew to the simmering island to get the story. Bewildering, quirky portrait of human character is marvelously entertaining. Did the volcano erupt? Watch and find out. D: Warner Herzog. COM 30m.

L.A. Story 1991 ★★★½ Frazzled TV weatherman (Martin) falls in love with an English journalist (his then-wife Tennant) and has fling with a flaky young woman (Parker) while observing L.A. Lightweight fantasy has several amusing moments: catch the museum roller-blading sequences. C: Steve Martin, Victoria Tennant, Richard E. Grant, Marilu Henner, Chevy Chase, Patrick Stewart, Sarah Jessica Parker. D: Mick Jackson. COM [PG-13] 98m.

La Strada 1954 Italian ★★★★★ Carnival strongman (Quinn) and his slow-witted companion (Masina) get involved with the new tightrope walker (Basehart) while touring. Simple plot becomes an overwhelmingly emotional experience; the film first brought attention to Fellini, and remains one of his most humane works. Masina is unforgettable. Oscar for best Foreign Language Film. C: Anthony Quinn, Giulietta Masina, Richard Basehart. D: Federico Fellini. DRA 107m. V

La Symphonie Pastorale 1946 French ★★★★ When a young blind girl (Morgan) is taken in by a minister (Blanchar) and his family, both father and son fall in love with her, leading to tragedy. Warm, tender film features a radiant performance by Morgan and sensitive direction. Based on André Gide. C: Pierre Blanchar, Michele Morgan. D: Jean Delannoy. DRA 105m.

La Terra Trema 1947 Italian ★★★★ Gritty, documentary-style, exploration of the life of a Sicilian fisherman, focusing on the back-breaking labor and a corrupt system. Moving story is affectingly acted by nonprofessional cast of Sicilians. D: Luchino Visconti. DRA 160m.

La Traviata 1982 Italian ★★★★★ Sumptuous filming of Verdi's opera, based on Dumas play *La Dame aux Camelias*, about a 19th-century courtesan Violetta (Stratas) and her ill-fated love for Alfredo (Domingo). Brilliantly sung, acted and designed. For novices, a perfect introduction to opera; for buffs, near perfect. C: Teresa Stratas, Placido Domingo, Cornell MacNeil. D: Franco Zeffirelli. MUS [G] 105m. v

La Truite 1982 French ★★★★ Country girl in the business world—the old rags-to-riches story, directed with Losey's usual cool, intelligent eye. Huppert is chilling in the lead. Not for all tastes, but rewarding to those with patience. (a.k.a. *Trout, The*) C:Isabelle Huppert, Jacques Spiesser. D: Joseph Losey. DRA [R] 104m. v

La Viaccia 1962 Italian ★★★½ In 19th-century Florence, a country winemaker's nephew falls in love with a city prostitute, ruining his life and his family's reputation. Standard plot played out against beautiful Tuscan scenery. (a.k.a. *The Lovemakers*) C: Jean-Paul Belmondo, Claudia Cardinale, Pietro Germi. D: Mauro Bolognini. DRA 103m.

L.A. Vice 1989 ★ Brown back to glower again in this sequel to *L.A. Heat.* As though once wasn't enough. C: Lawrence Hilton-Jacobs, Jim Brown, William Smith. D: Joseph Merhi. ACT 90m.

La Vie Continue 1982 French ★★★ Contented housewife must suddenly fend for herself when her husband keels over from a heart attack. The American remake, *Men Don't Leave,* is even better. C: Annie Girardot, Jean-Pierre Cassel, Pierre Dux. D: Moshe Mizrahi. DRA 93m. v

La Vie de Bohème 1993 French ★★★★ A trio of Bohemians drift through Parisian life, from the classic French novel. Kaurismaki's offbeat, crude humor is grounded by sympathy toward his protagonists in this beguiling, spirited romp. Puccini's music is used to great effect. C: Matti Pellonpaa, Andrè Wilms. D: Aki Kaurismaki. DRA 100m. v

La Vie de Chateau, *See* **Matter of Resistance, A.**

La Vie Privee *See* **A Very Private Affair**

L.A. Wars 1994 ★★ L.A. is up for grabs as a mob boss and powerful drug dealer fight to rule the City of Angels. C: Vince Murdocco, Rodrigo Obregon, Mary E. Zilba. D: Tony Kandan. CRI [R] 94m. v

Laboratory 1980 ★★ Small group of creatures from outer space infiltrate Earth, endagering the planet's future. C: Camille Mitchell, Corinne Michaels. SFI 93m. v

Labyrinth 1986 ★★ When teenager (Connelly) learns her brother has been kidnapped by the Goblin King (Bowie), she enters a secret world of mazes and Muppets. *Alice in Wonderland*-like tale is long on dazzling visuals but short on intriguing story and quickly grows tiresome. Third grade and up should enjoy. C: David Bowie, Jennifer Connelly, Toby Froud. D: Jim Henson. SFI [PG] 101m. v

Labyrinth of Passion 1982 Spanish ★★★½ Screwball comedy set in bohemian Madrid, where many love affairs (gay, straight, and bi) are kindled. Almodovar's second feature is uneven, but best scenes reveal his unorthodox talent and growing skill. C: Celia Roth, Imanol Arias, Antonio Banderas. D: Pedro Almodóvar. COM 100m. v

Lacemaker, The 1978 French ★★★½ Working girl Isabelle falls in love with a young aristocrat, who slowly grows disenchanted with her. Woefully trite, despite touching performance by Huppert in one of her first roles. C: Isabelle Huppert, Florence Giorgetti, Yves Beneyton, Anne Marie Duringer. D: Claude Goretta. DRA 108m. v

Lacombe, Lucien 1974 French ★★★★½ Rich, multitextured tale of an opportunistic young layabout who eventually joins the Gestapo during the Occupation, then falls in love with a young Jewish woman. Handsomely mounted, insightfully directed; something to see. Oscar-nominated for Best Foreign Film. C: Pierre Blaise, Aurore Clement. D: Louis Malle. DRA [R] 141m.

Lad: A Dog 1962 ★★★ When a disabled child receives a pet dog, her life takes a turn for the better. Oversentimentalized story doesn't miss a cliché. Strictly for young dog lovers. C: Peter Breck, Peggy McCay, Carroll O'Connor. D: Aram Avakian, Leslie H. Martinson. FAM/DRA [G] 98m.

L'Addition 1985 French ★★★½ Actor (Berry) tries to help shoplifter (Abril) and is rewarded with prison. There, he confronts a cruel jailer (Bohringer). Popular in France, though predictable. C: Richard Berry, Richard Bohringer, Victoria Abril. D: Denis Amar. CRI [R] 85m. v

Ladies and Gentlemen, The Fabulous Stains 1981 ★★★ Punk rock musical features Lane as an aspiring punker touring the country in search of a band. Loud and abrasive, of interest mainly to punk rock fans. Cameos by members of the Clash and the Sex Pistols. C: Diane Lane, Ray Winstone, Peter Donat, David Clennon, Cynthia Sikes, Laura Dern, Christine Lahti. D: Lou Adler. MUS [R] 87m.

Ladies and Gentlemen, the Rolling Stones 1975 ★★★½ Concert film follows Rolling Stones 1975 American tour. No great insights or surprises, but plenty of music. D: Rollin Binzer. MUS [PG] 90m.

Ladies Club, The 1986 ★★★ Victims of rape join forces to avenge themselves against their attackers. Execution of street justice by women uplifting at times. C: Karen Austin, Diana Scarwid, Christine Belford. D: A. K. Allen. ACT [R] 86m. v

Ladies Courageous 1944 ★★★ The WAFs go to war; in this case, they ferry war planes. Workmanlike flagwaver tries almost too hard to pay tribute to the women of WWII. C: Loretta Young, Geraldine Fitzgerald, Diana Barrymore, Evelyn Ankers, Ruth Roman. D: John Rawlins. DRA 88m.

Ladies in Love 1936 ★★★½ Otherwise routine tale of four love-starved young women in Budapest made entertaining by good cast. Bennett shines in typical wisecracking role. C: Janet Gaynor, Loretta Young, Constance Bennett, Don Ameche, Paul Lukas, Tyrone Power. D: Edward Griffith. COM 97m.

Ladies in Retirement 1941 ★★★★ Gripping thriller of housekeeper who tries to save mad sisters from being institutionalized by an evil employer. Lupino's intense performance is one of her best. C: Ida Lupino, Louis Hayward, Evelyn Keyes, Elsa Lanchester. D: Charles Vidor. DRA 92m.

Ladies' Man 1931 ★★½ Dated melodrama of gigolo who falls for the daughter of one of the rich women he preys upon. Powell is reassuringly workmanlike as always, but this one's mostly for movie buffs. C: William Powell, Kay Francis, Carole Lombard. D: Lothar Mendes. DRA 70m.

Ladies' Man 1961 ★★★½ Premise of oddjobber (Lewis) let loose in boarding school for women makes uneven low comedy which star/director also wrote. Former Metropolitan Opera star Traubel plays Jerry's straightwoman/Margaret Dumont type. C: Jerry Lewis, Helen Traubel, Kathleen Freeman. D: Jerry Lewis. COM 106m. V

Ladies of Leisure 1930 ★★★½ Early talkie about prostitute (Stanwyck) who is trying to reform when she meets wealthy man of her dreams. Trite but worth seeing for stars' performances. C: Barbara Stanwyck, Ralph Graves, Lowell Sherman. D: Frank Capra. DRA 98m.

Ladies of the Big House 1931 ★★★½ Sidney is her usual lachrymose self when she and husband are framed for murder and she goes up the river. Stylish tearjerker. C: Sylvia Sidney, Gene Raymond, Louise Beavers, Jane Darwell. D: Marion Gering. DRA 76m.

Ladies of the Chorus 1949 ★★ A small-time chorine (Jergens) fights to keep her naive daughter (Monroe) from making the same mistakes in life and love that she has. A stilted story line and a bad score; Monroe's first role. C: Adele Jergens, Rand Brooks, Marilyn Monroe. D: Phil Karlson. DRA 61m. V

Ladies of the Jury 1932 ★★★½ *Twelve Angry Men* played for laughs, as Oliver turns entire jury around in murder case. She's delightful as always, even if the production itself is a little creaky. C: Edna May Oliver, Jill Esmond, Roscoe Ates. D: Lowell Sherman. COM 65m.

Ladies Should Listen 1934 ★★★ Switchboard operator (Drake) falls in love with caller (Grant) over the wires, then woos him. Fair comedy. C: Cary Grant, Frances Drake, Edward Everett Horton, Ann Sheridan. D: Frank Tuttle. COM 62m.

Ladies They Talk About 1933 ★★★★ An imprisoned female bank robber is reformed when a devoted man helps her find herself. A sad but moving story of a topic rarely covered. Stanwyck is a standout. C: Barbara Stanwyck, Preston Foster, Lillian Roth, Ruth Donnelly. D: Howard Bretherton, William Keighley. DRA 70m. V

L'Adolescente 1979 *See* **Adolescent, The**

Lady and the Highwayman, The 1989 ★★★½ Colorful adventure epic of 17th-century English gentry. Truly superb cast and heightened production values. A real swashbuckler. C: Emma Samms, Oliver Reed, Claire Bloom, Hugh Grant, Michael York, John Mills, Robert Morley. D: John Hough. ACT 100m.

Lady and the Mob, The 1939 ★★★½ Bainter shines in this improbable comedy of bank owner who forms her own gang to fend off mobsters. Brisk bit of cinematic invention. C: Fay Bainter, Lee Bowman, Ida Lupino. D: Ben Stoloff. COM 66m.

Lady and the Monster, The 1944 ★★★ Okay horror film of deceased millionaire's brain possessing the assistant of the scientist keeping it alive. Top-billed Ralston is overshadowed by solid supporting cast. Based on novel *Donovan's Brain*, later remade under that title. C: Vera Ralston, Erich Stroheim, Richard Arlen, Sidney Blackmer. D: George Sherman. HOR 86m.

Lady and the Tramp 1955 ★★★★½ Unpretentious Disney feature cartoon tells charming story of pedigreed cocker spaniel romanced by garrulous mutt. Beautifully drawn and filmed in CinemaScope, with good songs by Peggy Lee and Sonny Burke, including "Bella Notte," "The Siamese Cat Song," and "He's a Tramp." Voices of Peggy Lee, Barbara Luddy. D: Hamilton Luske, Clyde Geronimi, Wilfred Jackson. FAM/MUS [G] 77m. V

Lady Avenger 1989 ★★ Sister swears revenge on brother's killers. Average actioner. C: Peggie Sanders, Tony Josephs, Jacolyn Leeman. D: David De Coteau. ACT [R] 85m. V

Lady Be Good 1941 ★★★★ Bearing no resemblance to the Gershwin Broadway musical, this yarn about squabbling songwriters Sothern and Young is peppered with spunky dance numbers featuring Powell and hundreds of chorus boys and comic bits from Skelton. Highlights include "Fascinatin' Rhythm" finale and Sothern singing "The Last Time I Saw Paris," by Jerome Kern and Oscar Hammerstein II (Oscar for Best Song). C: Eleanor Powell, Ann Sothern, Robert Young, Lionel Barrymore, Red Skelton, Virginia O'Brien, Dan Dailey, Jimmy Dorsey, Orchestra. D: Norman McLeod. MUS 111m. V

Lady Beware 1987 ★★★½ Window dresser (Lane) is stalked by an overzealous admirer who's no dummy. Good thriller, with feminist slant. C: Diane Lane, Michael Woods, Viveca Lindfors. D: Karen Arthur. CRI [R] 108m. V

Lady by Choice 1934 ★★★½ Fan dancer (Lombard) takes in down-and-out Robson and turns her into a respectable lady, hiring her to pose as her mother. Sequel to *Lady for a Day* is practically a remake. Charming, but predictable. C: Carole Lombard, May Robson, Walter Connolly. D: David Burton. DRA 77m. v

Lady Caroline Lamb 1973 British ★★★ Tedious romantic triangle involving title heroine, her husband, and the great Romantic poet Lord Byron (Chamberlain). Envisioned as a vehicle for Miles (Mrs. Bolt at the time), it suffers from uncharismatic lead performances. Some choice moments from excellent supporting cast, however. C: Sarah Miles, Jon Finch, Richard Chamberlain, John Mills, Margaret Leighton, Ralph Richardson, Laurence Olivier. D: Robert Bolt. DRA [PG] 123m. v

Lady Chatterley's Lover 1981 French ★ This version of Lawrence's classic novel has all the right characters—the crippled husband, his cuckolding wife, and the rough-hewn gamekeeper who keeps her satisfied—but no punch. C: Sylvia Kristel, Nicholas Clay. D: Just Jaeckin. DRA [R] 105m. v

Lady Cocoa 1975 ★★ Woman gets out of jail for one day to track down the man who put her there; dreary action film. C: Lola Falana, Gene Washington, Joe Greene. D: Matt Cimber. ACT [R] 93m. v

Lady Consents, The 1936 ★★★ Harding gives Marshall a divorce, but he comes to his senses and realizes how much he really loves his ex-wife. Competent melodrama. C: Ann Harding, Herbert Marshall, Margaret Lindsay. D: Stephen Roberts. DRA 75m.

Lady Dances, The 1934 *See* **Merry Widow, The**

Lady Doctor 1956 Italian ★★★ A Boston physician must conceal her profession when living with her Italian husband's two old-fashioned aunts in Naples. Dated comedy; intermittently humorous. C: Abbe Lane, Vittorio De Sica, Toto. D: Camillo Mastrocinque. COM 90m.

Lady Dracula 1973 ★★★ Moody, '20s-setting horror film about a young girl caught up in the spell of a seductive lesbian vampire. Some real chills, but low budget hampers the movie's pursuit of its own good ideas. Atmosphere is stronger than the tacky makeup effects. C: Cheryl Smith, Lesley Gilb, William Whitton. D: Richard Blackburn. HOR 80m.

Lady Dragon 1992 ★★ When an FBI agent's husband is killed on their wedding day, she takes revenge. Rothrock's nimble physical prowess supplies the main interest. C: Cynthia Rothrock, Richard Norton, Robert Ginty. D: David Worth. ACT [R] 90m. v

Lady Dragon 2 1993 ★★ When her relatives are murdered by terrorists, a young woman (Kothrock) exacts her revenge. C: Cynthia Rothrock, Billy Drago. D: David Worth. ACT [R] 90m. v

Lady Eve, The 1941 ★★★★★ Peerless romantic comedy casts Stanwyck as cardsharp out to fleece naive millionaire (Fonda). When he breaks her heart, she plans an elaborate ruse to get him back. One of the best of its genre with breathtaking wit, wonderful slapstick and two stars at the top of their form. C: Barbara Stanwyck, Henry Fonda, Charles Coburn, Eugene Pallette, William Demarest, Eric Blore. D: Preston Sturges. COM 93m. v

Lady for a Day 1933 ★★★★½ Marvelous sentimental comedy casts Robson as "Apple Annie," street peddler, transformed by friends into a lady when her daughter comes to visit. Heartwarming fable from Damon Runyon story. Remade as *Pocketful of Miracles*. C: May Robson, Warren William, Guy Kibbee, Glenda Farrell. D: Frank Capra. COM 96m. v

Lady for a Night 1942 ★★★ A woman uses her gambling riverboat as a vessel for social climbing only to have her ambitions grounded by murder. Blondell and Wayne are adequate in an otherwise slow potboiler. C: John Wayne, Joan Blondell, Ray Middleton, Blanche Yurka. D: Leigh Jason. CRI 88m. v

Lady Frankenstein 1972 Italian ★ Cotten gets little screen time as Doctor F. in this cheesy variation on the theme. Main character is his daughter (Bey), looking to create a man to satisfy her sexual desires. Tawdry shocker emphasizes cheap sex and violence. C: Joseph Cotten, Mickey Hargitay, Sarah Bey. D: Mel Welles. HOR [R] 84m. v

Lady from Cheyenne 1941 ★★★½ Western romance has schoolteacher (Young) fighting for right to sit on a jury in 1860s Wyoming. Typical studio-inspired conflict, aided by good cast. C: Loretta Young, Robert Preston, Edward Arnold, Gladys George. D: Frank Lloyd. WST 87m.

Lady from Louisiana 1941 ★★ Lottery owner's daughter falls for lawyer out to clean up the town, and that includes her father's business. Predictable and excessive bravado. C: John Wayne, Ona Munson, Ray Middleton. D: Bernard Vorhaus. DRA 83m. v

Lady from Shanghai, The 1948 ★★★★ Opaque but often entertaining mystery/thriller about a seaman who becomes involved with a crippled husband (Sloane) and his scheming wife (Hayworth). Hard to follow thanks to some cutting room butchery, but Welles' direction is full of dazzling tricks, culminating in classic Hall of Mirrors shootout finale. C: Orson Welles, Rita Hayworth, Everett Sloane. D: Orson Welles. CRI 87m. v

Lady from Texas 1951 ★★★½ Broadway character actress Hull almost makes this starring vehicle worthwhile. She's an elderly eccentric Civil War widow who turns a town upside down and the town wants her commited. Middling comedy. C: Josephine Hull, Howard Duff, Mona Freeman. D: Joseph Pevney. COM 77m.

Lady Gambles, The 1949 ★★★½ Somber study of how gambling addiction destroys a marriage. Static film is overwrought despite Stanwyck's fine performance. C: Barbara Stanwyck, Robert Preston, Stephen McNally. D: Michael Gordon. DRA 99m.

Lady Godiva 1955 ★★★ The legend of a young Saxon woman's undraped ride in medieval England is done a disservice in this flatly directed snoozer. Despite its potential, not one of O'Hara's sexiest roles. C: Maureen O'Hara, George Nader, Victor McLaglen. D: Arthur Lubin. DRA 89m.

Lady Godiva Rides Again 1951 British ★★★½ Broad British farce about voluptuous young farm woman (Dors) who wins beauty contest. Great supporting cast makes this fun to watch. Joan Collins' film debut as losing contestant. C: Dennis Price, John McCallum, Stanley Holloway, Diana Dors, Kay Kendall, Alastair Sim. D: Frank Launder. COM 90m.

Lady Grey 1982 ★★ Forgettable showbiz corn about an aspiring country-western singer (Alden) and her struggles to reach the top. C: Ginger Alden, David Allan Coe, Paul Ott. D: Worth Keeter. DRA 111m. V

Lady Has Plans, The 1942 ★★½ Goddard's mistaken for spy in Lisbon. Complicated comedy/drama. C: Paulette Goddard, Ray Milland, Roland Young. D: Sidney Lanfield. COM 77m.

Lady Ice 1973 ★★½ An insurance investigator steals a flawless diamond, then falls for the equally flawless daughter of a mobster. Stellar cast adrift in a rather pointless tale. C: Donald Sutherland, Jennifer O'Neill, Robert Duvall, Patrick Magee. D: Tom Gries. ACT [PG] 93m. V

Lady in a Cage 1964 ★★★½ When wealthy widow gets stuck in her private elevator, she is tormented by hoodlums. Exploitative thriller benefits from Caan's sadistic charm and de Havilland's riveting performance. C: Olivia de Havilland, James Caan, Ann Sothern, Jeff Corey. D: Walter Grauman. CRI 93m. V

Lady in a Jam 1942 ★★★ Screwball comedy has zany heiress (Dunne) obsessed with psychiatrist (Bellamy). Irene's fine, but Ralph's no leading man. C: Irene Dunne, Patric Knowles, Ralph Bellamy, Eugene Pallette. D: Gregory Cava. COM 78m.

Lady in Cement 1968 ★★½ Gumshoe Sinatra searches for killer of the woman wearing the concrete shoes. Pulp '60s detective schlock full of gratuitous violence and sexual teasing—mostly by Welch. Sequel to the 1967 *Tony Rome.* C: Frank Sinatra, Raquel Welch, Dan Blocker, Richard Conte, Lainie Kazan. D: Gordon Douglas. CRI [PG] 93m. V

Lady in Distress 1939 British ★★★½ Offbeat drama about Redgrave, witness to what he thinks is a murder, finding himself increasingly involved with jealous magician and wife. Well acted and unusual. C: Paul Lukas, Sally Gray, Michael Redgrave. D: Herbert Mason. CRI 59m. V

Lady in Question, The 1940 ★★★½ A juror (Aherne) acquits a suspected murderer (Hayworth), then helps her rebuild her shamed life, while hiding her past from his family. Interesting social drama is unusual showcase for Rita. C: Rita Hayworth, Brian Aherne, Glenn Ford. D: Charles Vidor. DRA 81m. V

Lady in the Car with Glasses and a Gun, The 1970 French ★★★½ English secretary (Eggar) encounters disturbing phenomena on road in France. Nervous thriller offers winning performance by Eggar as unsuspecting young woman being "driven" over the edge. C: Samantha Eggar, Oliver Reed, John McEnery, Stephane Audran. D: Anatole Litvak. DRA [R] 105m.

Lady in the Dark 1944 ★★★ Film adaptation of classic Weill/Gershwin Broadway musical—sans almost all the songs!—about psychoanalysis of a career woman with three beaux. Creditable Technicolor production serves primarily as showcase for Rogers. C: Ginger Rogers, Ray Milland, Jon Hall, Warner Baxter, Barry Sullivan, Mischa Auer. D: Mitchell Leisen. DRA 100m.

Lady in the Iron Mask 1952 ★★★ This further adventure of the Three Musketeers has the heroic trio coming to the aid of an imprisoned princess (Medina) who has been replaced by her identical twin. Forgettable swashbuckler, essential only for those bent on seeing every Dumas adaptation. C: Louis Hayward, Patricia Medina, Alan Hale. D: Ralph Murphy. ACT 78m.

Lady in the Lake 1946 ★★★½ P.I. Philip Marlowe investigates numbingly convoluted missing person case. Notable for its gimmicky first-person camera work; the viewer "sees" only what Marlowe sees. An adaptation of Raymond Chandler's novel. C: Robert Montgomery, Audrey Totter, Lloyd Nolan. D: Robert Montgomery. CRI 104m. V

Lady in White 1988 ★★★★½ Youth (Haas) sees the ghost of a young murder victim and in vision can almost identify her killer, who is still at large and at it again. Superior thriller/ghost story with evocative and inspired moments. C: Lukas Haas, Len Cariou, Katherine Helmond. D: Frank LaLoggia. CRI [PG-13] 113m. V

Lady Is Willing, The 1942 ★★★½ Broadway star Dietrich yearns to adopt abandoned baby but legal red tape drives her to marry stuffy pediatrician MacMurray. Tasteful, sleek direction and dependable stars makes this comedy/drama worthwhile. C: Marlene Dietrich, Fred MacMurray, Aline MacMahon. D: Mitchell Leisen. COM 91m. V

Lady Jane 1985 British ★★★★ Romantic, old-fashioned historical epic about the young pawn of political factions who reigned very briefly as England's queen in the 16th century. (An earlier British version was called *Nine Days a Queen.*) Carter and Elwes are very appealing as the leads, backed by a strong supporting cast. C: Helena Bonham Carter, Cary Elwes, John Wood, Michael Hordern, Patrick Stewart. D: Trevor Nunn. DRA [PG-13] 140m. V

Lady Killer 1933 ★★★½ Chased by the law, a mobster hits Hollywood and becomes a movie star. Cagney is tops as the canny wiseguy. Fast, funny, and captivating. C: James Cagney, Mae Clarke, Leslie Fenton, Margaret Lindsay. D: Roy Del Ruth. CRI 77m. V

Lady Killers, The 1955 British ★★★★½ Bumbling gang of thieves, led by Guinness plan a perfect robbery which is thwarted thanks to a little old lady (Johnson). Outstanding black comedy stolen by Johnson, with Sir Alec a close second. A pure delight. C: Alec Guinness, Katie Johnson, Cecil Parker, Herbert Lom, Peter Sellers. D: Alexander Mackendrick. COM 87m. V

Lady L 1965 British ★★½ A celebrated English lady (Loren) reflects on her humble beginnings as a Corsican laundress and how it led to her life in a Parisian brothel and a romantic entanglement with an anarchist criminal. Top stars and elegant scenery are the only appeal of this dull farce. C: Sophia Loren, Paul Newman, David Niven, Claude Dauphin. D: Peter Ustinov. COM 107m. V

Lady Liberty 1972 Italian ★ Embarrassing comedy about an Italian immigrant (Loren) trying to get a big piece of pork through customs. That's right. Your choice. (a.k.a. *Mortadella*) C: Sophia Loren, William Devane, Danny DeVito. D: Mario Monicelli. COM [PG] 95m.

Lady Macbeth of the Mtsensk District 1969 *See* **Katerina Ismaylova**

Lady Mobster 1988 ★★ A female lawyer becomes the voice of the mob, to repay the man who shaped her life. Silly and witless. TV vehicle for Lucci. C: Susan Lucci, Michael Nader, Roscoe Born. D: John Llewellyn Moxey. CRI 94m. TVM V

Lady of Burlesque 1943 ★★★★ Stripper gets mixed up in a murder backstage at burlesque theater. Wisecracking screenplay and gyrating Stanwyck as sleuth do wonders for routine mystery. Based on Gypsy Rose Lee's novel, *The G-String Murders*. C: Barbara Stanwyck, Michael O'Shea, J. Edward Bromberg, Iris Adrian. D: William Wellman. CRI 91m. V

Lady of the Camellias, The 1981 ★★★★½ Unsentimental account of the Paris courtesan Alphonsine Duplessis features Huppert as an earthy peasant who becomes a favored friend of the aristocracy. Stunning sets, costumes, and performances complement an intelligent screenplay. C: Isabelle Huppert, Gian Marie Volonte, Fernando Rey, Bruno Ganz, Yann Babilee. D: Mauro Bolognini. DRA 121m.

Lady of the House 1978 ★★★½ True story of '30s bordello madam Sally Stanford who triumphed over her background and became mayor of Sausalito, California in 1976. Nice work by Cannon, but episodic story is told in bland, antiseptic manner. C: Dyan Cannon, Armand Assante. D: Ralph Nelson, Vincent Sherman. DRA 100m. TVM V

Lady of the Pavements 1929 ★★★★ Cabaret performer (Valez) gets into a marriage of spite to Prussian count (Boyd), who eventually falls for her for real. Griffith's last silent film is a double surprise: It's a light comedy in the Lubitsch vein, and it's actually pretty good, belying tales of the master's decline. C: Lupe Velez, William Boyd, Jetta Goudal, Albert Conti. D: D.W. Griffith. COM 93m.

Lady of the Tropics 1939 ★★★ Lamarr is cast as a half-Eurasian again, this time wooed by Taylor. But when he marries her, she can't get a passport. Little more than the stars to spark this sad tale. C: Hedy Lamarr, Robert Taylor, Joseph Schildkraut. D: Jack Conway. DRA 92m.

Lady on a Train 1945 ★★★★ Nifty comedy/mystery with a couple of songs thrown in as Durbin tries to solve murder on locomotive. Good plotting and wonderful supporting cast. C: Deanna Durbin, Ralph Bellamy, Edward Everett Horton, George Coulouris, Dan Duryea, William Frawley. D: Charles David. COM 93m.

Lady on the Bus 1978 Brazilian ★★★ Frigid wife (Braga) unleashes her passion with strangers she meets on buses. Lots of nudity. C: Sonia Braga, Nuno Leal Maia, Paulo Cesar Pereio. D: Neville D'Almedia. DRA [R] 102m. V

Lady Pays Off, The 1951 ★★★½ Schoolteacher (Darnell) racks up big debts at the tables in Vegas, but casino owner (McNally, playing a good guy for once) lets her pay them off by tutoring his daughter. Fluffy Sirk offering; pleasant, light entertainment. C: Linda Darnell, Stephen McNally, Gigi Perreau. D: Douglas Sirk. DRA 80m.

Lady Possessed 1952 British ★★★ Weird film about mentally unstable woman (Havoc) who is convinced she is supposed to replace dead wife of pianist (Mason). Of course, Hollywood shrinks can solve anything. Trivia note: Kellino was Mason's real-life spouse when film was made. C: James Mason, June Havoc, Pamela Kellino. D: William Spier, Roy Kellino. DRA 87m.

Lady Says No, The 1951 ★★½ Romantic comedy of flighty Caulfield unable to commit to marriage with Niven. C: David Niven, Joan Caulfield. D: Frank Ross. COM 80m.

Lady Scarface 1941 ★★★ Anderson, fresh from her triumph as Mrs. Danvers in *Rebecca*, gets a rare lead as female gangleader in this workaday B-movie crimer. C: Dennis O'Keefe, Judith Anderson, Frances Neal, Eric Blore. D: Frank Woodruff. CRI 69m.

Lady Sings the Blues 1972 ★★★½ Slick biography of jazz great Billie Holiday focuses on her drug problems and miserable love life. Glossy, but utterly untruthful, even insulting at times. Ross sounds nothing like Holiday but her acting is impressive. Pryor is excellent in supporting role. C: Diana Ross, Billy Dee Williams, Richard Pryor. D: Sidney J. Furie. DRA [R] 144m. v

Lady Takes A Chance, A 1943 ★★★★ Charming romantic comedy has city slicker (Arthur) meeting cowboy/rodeo star (Wayne) during bus tour of the West. Two stars connect surprisingly well, with fine comic support from Silvers. C: Jean Arthur, John Wayne, Charles Winninger, Phil Silvers. D: William A. Seiter. COM 86m. v

Lady Takes a Flyer, The 1958 ★★½ Change of pace comedy for Lana casts her and Chandler as competing pilots who fall in love. C: Lana Turner, Jeff Chandler, Richard Denning. D: Jack Arnold. COM 94m.

Lady Takes a Sailor, The 1949 ★★½ Okay comedy of researcher (Wyman) defending her reputation from gossip about naval romance. C: Jane Wyman, Dennis Morgan, Eve Arden. D: Michael Curtiz. COM 99m.

Lady Terminator 1989 ★★ An enemy from the past is hunted down by a anthropology student haunted by a wicked spirit. C: Barbara Constable, Christopher Hart. D: Jalil Jackson. ACT [R] 83m. v

Lady Vanishes, The 1938 British ★★★★★ When Lockwood's traveling companion (Whitty) disappears on moving train, everyone questioned claims she never existed. Hitchock's superb blend of comedy, mystery, romance, and political intrigue makes this one of his early masterpieces. C: Margaret Lockwood, Michael Redgrave, Paul Lukas, Dame May Whitty, Basil Radford, Naunton Wayne. D: Alfred Hitchcock. CRI 96m. v

Lady Vanishes, The 1979 British ★★½ Unnecessary remake of Hitchcock classic with Shepherd inept as heroine looking for lost companion (Lansbury) on train. C: Elliott Gould, Cybill Shepherd, Angela Lansbury, Herbert Lom. D: Anthony Page. CRI [PG] 95m. v

Lady Wants Mink, The 1953 ★★★★ Delightful sleeper comedy with Hussey as fur-obsessed housewife raising her own critters to get a coat. Makes points about consumerism while getting laughs. Animal lovers should be assured there's a happy ending! C: Eve Arden, Ruth Hussey, Dennis O'Keefe, William Demarest. D: William Seiter. COM 92m.

Lady Windemere's Fan 1925 ★★★★★ Superb silent comedy from Oscar Wilde's play about noblewoman mistaking mother, presumed dead, for husband's mistress. Remarkable achievement, considering much of the play's strength comes from witty dialogue. Lubitsch translates it visually—a mark of screen genius. C: May McAvoy, Bert Lytell, Irene Rich, Ronald Colman. D: Ernst Lubitsch. COM 119m. v

Lady with a Dog, The 1960 Russian ★★★½ A married older man on holiday meets an unhappily married young woman. They begin an affair that continues as they both return home to Moscow. Based on short story by Chekhov, the deliberate pace vividly evokes the emotions of the characters. C: Iya Savvina, Alexei Batalov. D: Josif Heifits. DRA 89m. v

Lady with a Lamp, The 1951 British ★★★½ Neagle and husband/director Wilcox turn their attention to Florence Nightingale, pioneering nurse, and her work with British troops during Crimean War. Stately, but by no means dull. C: Anna Neagle, Michael Wilding, Felix Aylmer. D: Herbert Wilcox. DRA 112m.

Lady with a Past 1932 ★★★½ Fast-paced comedy with Bennett as reserved socialite breaking out in rare fashion. Diverting. Done before Hayes censorship code, and it shows. C: Constance Bennett, Ben Lyon, Astrid Allwyn. D: Edward Griffith. COM 80m.

Lady with Red Hair, The 1940 ★★★½ Turn-of-the-century backstage comedy of true romance between leading lady Mrs. Leslie Carter (Hopkins) and impressario David Belasco (Rains). Two stars act with style but script is spotty. C: Miriam Hopkins, Claude Rains, Richard Ainley, Laura Hope Crews. D: Curtis Bernhardt. COM 81m.

Lady without Camellias, The 1953 Italian ★★★★ Story of young actress's rapid rise to and fall from fame. Antonioni caustically examines society's treatment of women through a fascinating glimpse at the movie business. C: Lucia Bose, Andrea Cecchi, Alain Cuny. D: Michelangelo Antonioni. DRA 105m.

Lady without Passport, A 1950 ★★★½ Nicely made drama of Lamarr trying to get out of Havana without papers, not knowing that U.S. government agent (Hodiak) is looking into traffic in illegal aliens. Lewis gives it polish and class. C: Hedy Lamarr, John Hodiak. D: Joseph Lewis. DRA 72m.

Ladybird, Ladybird 1994 British ★★★★½ Impoverished London single mother fights to regain her children from the social agencies that took them away. Rock's devastating performance (her debut) empowers this affecting, downbeat story. It doesn't offer easy answers, and becomes all the more compelling for it. C: Crissy Rock, Vladimir Vega, Sandie Lavelle, Ray Winstone. D: Ken Loach. DRA 102m.

Ladybug, Ladybug 1963 ★★★ A false warning of nuclear attack has lasting effects on schoolchildren and adults in a small rural community. Thoughtful, if somewhat heavy-handed. C: William Daniels, Jane Connell, Richard Hamilton, Kathryn Hays, Estelle Parsons. D: Frank Perry. DRA 84m.

Ladybugs 1992 ★★ Coach Dangerfield, saddled with an inept girl's soccer team, cajoles his fiancé's son, an ace athlete, into a dress and onto the team in the hopes of making it a winner. Brainless comedy can't score a laugh, despite Dangerfield's constant mugging. C: Rodney Dangerfield, Jackée, Jonathan Brandis. D: Sidney J. Furie. COM [PG-13] 91m. V

Ladyhawke 1985 ★★★★ Lush medieval fantasy about lovers (Hauer, Pfeiffer) separated by an evil spell, and how the spell is broken—with help from wisecracking thief Broderick. A satisfying romance, brightened by Broderick's comic patter. C: Matthew Broderick, Rutger Hauer, Michelle Pfeiffer, Leo McKern. D: Richard Donner. ACT [PG-13] 121m. V

Ladykiller 1992 ★★★★ Evidence photographer (Rogers) falls for a man (Shea) she meets through a dating service, but he may be linked to a case she was investigating. Enticing script and a good cast make this suspense drama worthwhile. C: Mimi Rogers, John Shea, Alice Krige. D: Michael Scott. CRI 92m. TVM V

Ladykiller of Rome, The 1961 ★★★★ A seller of antiques is wrongly accused of murder. Fascinating look at the fallibility of police procedure and how "justice" exacts its price—even upon the innocent. DRA

Ladykillers 1988 ★★ A cop (Henner) tries to track down a killer of male strippers. Turnabout mystery yarn lacks compelling thread. C: Marilu Henner, Thomas Calabro, Susan Blakely, Lesley-Anne Down. D: Robert Lewis. CRI 100m. TVM V

Lady's Morals, A 1930 ★★★½ Opera star Moore made her film debut in this heavily fictionalized biography of "Swedish nightingale" Jenny Lind. Arias give star ample opportunity to show off her voice. C: Grace Moore, Reginald Denny, Wallace Beery. D: Sidney Franklin. MUS 75m.

Lafayette 1962 French ★★½ Dull period spectacle about the French diplomat (Le Royer) who aided George Washington (St. John) during the American Revolution. C: Michel Le Royer, Howard St. John, Jack Hawkins, Orson Welles, Vittorio De Sica. D: Jean Dreville. ACT 110m.

Lafayette Escadrille 1958 ★★★½ At the onset of WWI, a young American pilot joins a specially formed squadron of the French air force. Worthy, if corny effort by Wellman, himself a real-life member of the squadron. C: Tab Hunter, Etchika Choureau, David Janssen, Clint Eastwood. D: William Wellman. DRA 93m. V

L'Age d'Or 1930 French ★★★★½ Extremely funny, surreal story of a couple desperately trying to couple while everything and everyone keeps them apart. Co-written by Salvador Dali, banned for years on charges of anticlericism. C: Gaston Modot, Lya Lys, Max Ernst. D: Luis Buñuel. COM 63m. V

Laguna Heat 1987 ★★½ When his partner is murdered, a traumatized private eye (Hamlin) heads home, only to find his former haven devastated by a series of bizarre psychopathic killings. Looks good, but strictly run-of-the-mill suspenser. C: Harry Hamlin, Jason Robards, Rip Torn, Catherine Hicks. D: Simon Langton. ACT 110m. V

Lai Shi: China's Last Eunuch 1988 Cantonese ★★★ Sincere account of a poor child who undergoes castration in hopes of joining the emperor's court. D: Chan Tsi-Liang. DRA 100m. V

Lair of the White Worm, The 1988 British ★★★½ Rousingly bizarre horror fantasy (from Bram Stoker's novel), directed at just the right pitch by Russell. Undermined by no-budget production but highlighted by Donohoe's delicious performance as sardonic, seductive snakewoman who moves into an English estate and terrorizes her neighbors. C: Amanda Donohoe, Hugh Grant, Catherine Oxenberg. D: Ken Russell. HOR [R] 93m. V

Lambada 1990 ★ Math teacher Peck uses dance craze to connect with underprivileged students. Should amuse both teachers and lambada dancers. C: J. Eddie Peck, Melora Hardin, Shabba Doo. D: Joel Silberg. MUS [PG] 104m. V

L'Amour Fou 1968 French ★★★★★ Difficult but brilliant drama about a theater director whose production of a Racine tragedy is beginning to threaten his marriage. Rivette elicits brutally honest performances and finds almost agonizing parallels between theater and life. Long, but it needs to be. A tough film, and a great one. C: Jean-Piere Kalfon, Bulle Ogier, André Labarthe. D: Jacques Rivette. DRA 256m.

Lana in Love 1991 ★★★½ Sweet romance about a forlorn woman who turns to the personals in search of a suitable mate. C: Daphna Kastner, Clark Gregg. COM 89m. V

Lancelot of the Lake 1975 French ★★★★ Age-old story of King Arthur, the knights of the Round Table, and the search for the Holy Grail. In an interesting twist on a familiar plot, Bresson portrays the knights with a cynical realism that contrasts with the splendor of the setting. C: Luc Simon, Laura Duke Condominas, Humbert Balsan, Vladimir Antolek-Oresek. D: Robert Bresson. DRA 85m.

Lancer Spy 1937 ★★★★ WWI espionage story about a British naval officer (George Sanders) who goes undercover to capture German battle plans. Excellent performance by Sanders, with an effective dose of calculated suspense. Voices of Dolores Del Rio, George Sanders, Peter Lorre, Joseph Schildkraut. D: Gregory Ratoff. DRA 84m.

Land Before Time, The 1988 ★★★½ Film from *An American Tale* director follows orphaned dinosaur and his prehistoric pals in their search for new home. Nice animated feature for younger children, though slow pacing will frustrate older viewers. Voices of Helen Shaver, Fred Gwynne, Pat Hingle. D: Don Bluth. FAM/DRA [G] 69m. V

Land of Doom 1984 ★★ A post-nuclear war

survival story barely kept alive by its attractive cast. C: Deborah Rennard, Garrick Dowhen. D: Peter Maris. SFI 87m. V

Land of Faraway, The ★★ Muddled children's fairy tale about lonely boy who learns father is the ruler of fantasy kingdom. In order to claim inheritance, the boy must defeat a wicked knight. Poor production values kill this potentially interesting fantasy. FAM/SFI [PG]

Land of Fury 1954 *See* **Seekers, The**

Land of Promise, The 1975 Polish ★★★★ Turn of the century story of three laborers who overcome ethnic differences and construct a textile factory. Expertly directed. Packs a punch. C: Daniel Olbrychski. D: Andrzej Wajda. DRA 161m. V

Land of Silence and Darkness 1971 Germany ★★★★½ Deaf-blind woman helps those similarly afflicted in this uncompromising documentary. Herzog's remarkably accessible film approaches its subjects without condescension or flippancy. An impressive and educational achievement. D: Werner Herzog. DOC 90m.

Land of the Indians, The 1979 ★★★★½ Harrowing documentary covers history of the Indians in Brazil. Provocative film delves into timely environmental issues. Stunningly photographed. D: Zelito Viana. DOC 102m.

Land of the Minotaur 1977 U.S. ★★ Mad devil worshipers abduct unwary tourists in Greece, and an enraged local priest sets out to rescue them. Unusual, but deadeningly slow. C: Donald Pleasence, Peter Cushing. D: Costa Carayiannis. HOR [PG] 88m. V

Land of the Pharaohs 1955 ★★★½ A camp classic, this epic about the building of the pyramids inspired later epics and was a favorite of Scorsese, Coppola, etc. Famous for its ending and script co-written by William Faulkner. C: Jack Hawkins, Joan Collins, James Robertson Justice. D: Howard Hawks. DRA 104m. V

Land Raiders 1970 ★★½ Sibling rivalry between two brothers is complicated by an Indian uprising. Miscast, but interesting. C: Telly Savalas, George Maharis, Arlene Dahl. D: Nathan Juran. WST 100m.

Land That Time Forgot 1975 British ★★★ WWI submarine surfaces near South Pole and discovers a prehistoric oasis of dinosaurs and ape men. Weak puppet monster effects undo this adaptation of Edgar Rice Burroughs adventure novel. (Sequel: *The People That Time Forgot*) C: Doug McClure, John McEnery, Susan Penhaligon. D: Kevin Connor. SFI [PG] 90m. V

Land Unknown, The 1957 ★★★ Navy crew goes down in uncharted part of Antarctica, where lizards posing as dinosaurs roam. Poor effects hamper this otherwise watchable fantasy. C: Jock Mahoney, Shawn Smith. D: Virgil Vogel. SFI 77m. V

Land Without Music 1936 *See* **Forbidden Music**

Landlord Blues 1987 ★★½ Routine thriller in which a slumlord's victim gets revenge. C: Mark Boone Junior, Richard Litt, Mary Schultz. D: Jacob Burckhardt. DRA 96m. V

Landlord, The 1970 ★★★★ A naive rich kid (Bridges) buys a run-down tenement to turn it into a dream townhouse, but instead finds himself contending with its feisty assortment of urban tenants. Ashby's first film perfectly blends biting social satire with outrageous humor. C: Beau Bridges, Pearl Bailey, Diana Sands, Louis Gossett, Lee Grant. D: Hal Ashby. COM [PG] 113m.

Landru 1962 *See* **Bluebeard**

Landscape in the Mist 1993 Greek ★★★★ Young siblings travel from Greece to Germany in search of their father and learn invaluable life-lessons along the way. Scenic, touching drama suffers just a little from slow pacing. C: Michalis Zeke, Tania Palaiologou. D: Theo Angelopoulos. DRA 126m. V

Landslide 1992 British ★★★ Partial amnesiac (Edwards) who returns to the site of his debilitating car crash to will back memory of the event, finds the townsfolk curiously uncooperative. Okay psychodrama, game acting. C: Anthony Edwards, Tom Burlinson, Melody Anderson. D: Jean-Claude Lord. DRA [PG-13] 95m. V

Lantern Hill 1990 Canadian ★★★★ Originally broadcast as part of PBS *Wonderworks* series, this involves a Depression-era girl whose special gifts help bring her estranged parents back together. Neat blend of reality and fantasy, with fine use of Canadian location. Great for family viewing. Written by L.M. Montgomery, author of *Ann of Green Gables.* C: Sam Waterston, Zoe Caldwell, Colleen Dewhurst. D: Kevin Sullivan. FAM/DRA 112m. V

Larceny 1948 ★★★½ Duryea does a nice turn as a sleazeball who sets out to separate a widow from her money, then falls for her. Ripe thriller potential weighed down by melodrama. C: John Payne, Joan Caulfield, Dan Duryea, Shelley Winters. D: George Sherman. DRA 89m.

Larceny, Inc 1942 ★★★★½ Very funny comedy of three ex-cons who buy luggage store next to bank for one last crime before they go straight. Robinson spoofs his bad-guy image well, and Jackie Gleason has bit part as soda jerk. C: Edward G. Robinson, Jane Wyman, Broderick Crawford, Jack Carson, Anthony Quinn. D: Lloyd Bacon. COM 95m.

Larceny Lane 1931 *See* **Blonde Crazy**

L'Argent 1983 French ★★★★ Tolstoy story of a working man (Patey) caught up in the lies of the wealthy, who is ruined when he behaves as they do. Quiet but damning indictment of hypocrisy and deceit. C: Christian Patey, Sylvie Van Den Elsen, Michel Briguet. D: Robert Bresson. DRA 82m. V

L'Armee des Ombres 1969 French ★★★★½

French Resistance tries to weed out turncoat in their midst. Superb suspenseful drama with no sugarcoating. (a.k.a. *The Army in the Shadows*) C: Lino Ventura, Paul Meurisse, Simone Signoret. D: Jean-Pierre Melville. DRA 140m.

Larry 1974 ★★★★ Well-written true story of man believed retarded who was wrongly committed to mental institution for 26 years. Forrest is memorable in title role. C: Frederic Forrest, Tyne Daly, Katherine Helmond. D: William Graham. DRA 78m.

Las Vegas Hillbillys 1966 ★★ Stage-struck country boy (Husky) inherits a casino but then discovers his gambling palace is really a dilapidated barn. Low-budget comedy has only camp appeal. Sequel: *Hillbillys in a Haunted House.* C: Ferlin Husky, Jayne Mansfield, Mamie Van Doren. D: Arthur C. Pierce. COM 85m. V

Las Vegas Lady 1975 ★ A sexy casino cocktail hostess (Stevens) plots a heist with the help of an enamored security guard (Whitman). Forgettable caper comedy at best. C: Stella Stevens, Stuart Whitman. D: Noel Nosseck. COM 90m. V

Las Vegas Shakedown 1955 ★★★½ Straight-as-an-arrow O'Keefe defies the odds and nefarious Mob types to operate an honest casino. Naive melodrama made more watchable by Vegas backdrop. C: Dennis O'Keefe, Coleen Gray, Charles Winninger. D: Sidney Salkow. DRA 79m.

Las Vegas Story, The 1952 ★★★ Murder mystery about a love triangle involving ex-cabaret singer Russell, her broker husband Price, and ex-flame Mature (a Las Vegas cop). The resulting action drama is thin, with Vegas setting failing to provide much excitement. C: Jane Russell, Victor Mature, Vincent Price, Hoagy Carmichael. D: Robert Stevenson. CRI 88m. V

Las Vegas Weekend 1985 ★★ Computer whiz sets out to conquer Las Vegas casinos. C: Barry Hickey, Jace Damon, Vickie Benson. D: Dale Trevillion. COM 83m. V

Laser Mission 1990 German ★★★ Secret agent (Lee) needs to find laser expert (Borgnine) to keep world-controlling power out of the wrong hands. Actioner greatly benefits from display of Lee's martial artistry. C: Brandon Lee, Debi Monahan, Ernest Borgnine. D: Beau Davis. ACT 83m. V

Laserman, The 1990 ★★★ Madcap farce has Chinese-American chemist (Hayashi), with a secret formula, fending off terrorists, spies, and his Jewish mother. Strained, but diverting. C: Marc Hayashi, Peter Wang, Sally Yeh, Joan Copeland. D: Peter Wang. COM [R] 92m. V

Lassie 1994 ★★★½ "I think that dog's trying to tell us something." Eighth-generation descendant of the original noble canine returns to the big screen, saving family from evil in land dispute in the Shenandoah Valley. Good for the kids. C: Tom Guiry, Richard Farnsworth. D: Daniel Petrie. FAM/DRA [PG] 126m.

Lassie Come Home 1943 ★★★★½ Classic children's film features young McDowall as youngster whose heart is broken when beloved family collie must be sold. Touching without being overly sentimental and perfect family viewing. C: Roddy McDowall, Donald Crisp, Dame May Whitty, Edmund Gwenn, Nigel Bruce, Elsa Lanchester, Elizabeth Taylor. D: Fred M. Wilcox. FAM/DRA [G] 88m. V

Lassiter 1983 ★★★ Jewel thief Selleck is recruited to heist secrets from pre-WWII Nazis. Selleck is okay as a poor man's James Bond. C: Tom Selleck, Jane Seymour, Lauren Hutton, Bob Hoskins. D: Roger Young. ACT [R] 100m. V

Last Action Hero 1993 ★★★ Action comedy in which a kid is sucked into screen action of his favorite hero (Schwarzenegger), and then both are forced to pursue bad guys into the "real world." Well-crafted, but rather cynical and manipulative. C: Arnold Schwarzenegger, F. Murray Abraham, Art Carney, Charles Dance, Robert Prosky, Anthony Quinn, Mercedes Ruehl, Austin O'Brien. D: John McTiernan. ACT [PG-13] 110m. V

Last American Hero, The 1973 ★★★½ North Carolina moonshiner (Bridges) and his fast car outrace the law. Superb performances (especially Bridges) save this stereotypical look at Southern backwoods life. Based on the real-life exploits of stock car racer Junior Johnson. (a.k.a. *Hard Driver*) C: Jeff Bridges, Valerie Perrine, Geraldine Fitzgerald. D: Lamont Johnson, V. DRA [PG] 95m. V

Last American Virgin, The 1982 ★★ Initially perceptive look at teen travails is undermined by crude comedy and cynical ending. Monoson's a sensitive guy who's attracted to new student Franklin, but she falls for his macho friend Antin. C: Lawrence Monoson, Diane Franklin, Steve Antin. D: Boaz Davidson. COM [R] 92m. V

Last Angry Man, The 1959 ★★★½ An old but dedicated doctor (Muni) in a poor Brooklyn neighborhood is made subject of a TV documentary. May be too saccharine at times, but Muni, in his final role, holds things together. Based on Gerald Green's novel. C: Paul Muni, David Wayne, Betsy Palmer. D: Daniel Mann. DRA 100m. V

Last Bastion, The 1992 ★★★½ Behind the scenes look at the last days of WWII, focusing on Roosevelt, Churchill and MacArthur's strategies. Effective use of documentary footage. C: Robert Vaughn, Timothy West. ACT 160m. V

Last Best Year, The 1990 ★★★½ Shameless tearjerker about terminally ill Peters developing friendship with psychologist Moore. Two stars plus exceptional supporting cast lend some dignity to manipulative drama. C: Mary Tyler Moore, Bernadette Peters, Brian Bedford, Dorothy McGuire. D: John Erman. DRA 100m. TVM

Last Blitzkrieg, The 1958 ★½ An anti-Nazi German works with G.I.s in this sloppy, generally unwatchable WWII action-drama. C: Van Johnson, Kerwin Mathews. D: Arthur Dreifuss. DRA 84m.

Last Boy Scout, The 1991 ★★½ Grizzled private eye Willis and dishonored football player Wayans join forces to crack drug and snuff film ring. Fast-paced violence. C: Bruce Willis, Damon Wayans, Chelsea Field. D: Tony Scott. ACT [R] 106m. V

Last Bridge, The 1954 Austrian ★★★★½ During the closing days of WWII, a captured German doctor (Schell) treats her Yugoslav captors—reluctantly at first, but then with growing compassion. A stirring antiwar diatribe, with a bravura performance from Schell. Released in the U.S. in 1957. C: Maria Schell, Bernhard Wicki. D: Helmut Kautner. DRA 95m.

Last Butterfly, The 1991 Czech ★★★★ During WWII, a French collaborator (Courtenay) performs his mime act in Terezin, as part of a Nazi propaganda piece on how well they were treating the Jews. Understandably difficult to watch at times, but well done. C: Tom Courtenay, Brigitte Fossey, Ingrid Held. D: Karel Kachyna. DRA 110m.

Last Call 1990 ★★½ When real estate shark (Katt) gets bamboozled by mobsters, he calls on his old friend (Tweed) to use her seductive charms in a revenge plot. Ostensibly about greed, power, and sex, it's really just about sex. C: William Katt, Shannon Tweed, Stella Stevens. D: Jag Mundhra. DRA [R] 90m. V

Last Call For Murder 1992 ★★½ Thriller with Hendrix and Shattuck as two high-living L.A. women caught in a nightmare of murder and mayhem. C: Anthony Alda, Leah Ayres Hendrix, Shari Shattuck. HOR 90m. V

Last Castle, The *See* **Echoes of a Summer**

Last Challenge, The 1967 ★★★½ Gunslinger turned marshall Ford tries to keep young outlaw Everett from causing trouble in a Western town, with Dickinson as the local saloon owner. Good cast energizes polished but routine Western shoot-out saga. C: Glenn Ford, Angie Dickinson, Chad Everett, Gary Merrill. D: Richard Thorpe. WST 105m.

Last Chance, The 1968 Italian ★★★ Escape yarn follows two men fleeing an Italian internment camp for the sanctuary of Switzerland during WWII. Generally exciting adventure saga. C: Tab Hunter, Michael Rennie, Daniela Bianchi. D: Niny Rosati. DRA 91m.

Last Chase, The 1981 Canadian ★★ Defiant in the face of chronic oil shortages and bans on auto travel, an ex-race car hero zooms across the country, a self-appointed icon of freedom and mobility. C: Lee Majors, Burgess Meredith, Chris Makepeace. D: Martyn Burke. ACT [PG] 101m. V

Last Command, The 1928 ★★★★½ On the verge of the revolution, a Russian officer (Jannings) flees to the U.S., and ends up as a Hollywood actor playing a part with uncomfortable parallels to his own. Excellent performances in a very engaging silent film. Jannings received Oscar for Best Actor. C: Emil Jannings, Evelyn Brent, William Powell. D: Josef von Sternberg. DRA 88m. V

Last Command, The 1955 ★★★½ The final days of knife-fighting pioneer Jim Bowie, who becomes leader at the Alamo in Texas' 1836 struggle for independence from Mexico. Fine battle sequences and historical sweep. C: Sterling Hayden, Anna Maria Alberghetti, Richard Carlson, Ernest Borgnine. D: Frank Lloyd. WST 110m. V

Last Dance 1991 ★★ Five exotic dancers vie for title in nationally-broadcast competition, only to discover a murderer is lurking behind the scenes. C: Cynthia Bassinet, Elaine Hendrix, Kurt T. Williams. D: Anthony Markes. HOR 84m. V

Last Day of the War, The 1969 ★★ Toward the end of WWII, an eminent German scientist flees the Fatherland, pursued by Germans and Americans alike. Yawn. C: George Maharis, Maria Perschy. D: J. A. Bardem. ACT [PG] 95m. V

Last Days of Chez Nous, The 1992 Australian ★★★★ A man (Ganz) finds himself falling for his wife's sister. A warm, intimate film; very non-Hollywood in that, like real life, things don't always work out perfectly. C: Lisa Harrow, Bruno Ganz, Kerry Fox. D: Gillian Armstrong. DRA [R] 96m. V

Last Days of Dolwyn, The 1949 British ★★★½ British society woman at the turn of the century tries to thwart Williams, who has a plan to buy up all the property in a Welsh village where a reservoir is planned. Drama features solid acting (including Richard Burton in his debut), but little excitement. C: Edith Evans, Emlyn Williams, Richard Burton, Hugh Griffith. D: Emlyn Williams. DRA 95m.

Last Days of Frank and Jesse James, The 1986 ★★★ An almost camcorder version of how the James brothers met their end. Interesting primarily for the lead casting of three megastar Nashville music men. C: Johnny Cash, Kris Kristofferson, Willie Nelson. D: William Graham. WST [PG] 97m. V

Last Days of Patton, The 1986 ★★★½ America's toughest WWII general, George S. Patton, wages peace until he succumbs to fatal car crash in Germany in 1945. Subdued and honest rendering of the final hours of "Old Blood and Guts." Well acted by Scott, who reprises his role of the brash military leader. C: George C. Scott, Eva Marie Saint, Richard Dysart. D: Delbert Mann. DRA 146m. TVM V

Last Days of Pompeii, The 1935 ★★★½

Early A.D. gladiator's love for a Christian gets him into big trouble. Thrilling climax of an erupting volcano among the ground-breaking special effects. C: Preston Foster, Basil Rathbone, Dorothy Wilson. D: Ernest B. Schoedsack. DRA 96m. V

Last Days of Pompeii, The 1960 Italian ★★ Musclebound tale of Reeves helping Christian martyrs avoid Roman lions. Can't touch the 1935 Preston Foster/Basil Rathbone version. C: Steve Reeves, Christine Kaufmann. D: Mario Bonnard. ACT 105m.

Last Detail, The 1974 ★★★★½ Shore patrol (Nicholson and Young) escorting young kleptomaniac sailor Quaid to prison decide to give him a taste of life. Profanely funny, it's also a surprisingly soulful drama of friendship and duty. C: Jack Nicholson, Otis Young, Randy Quaid, Michael Moriarty. D: Hal Ashby. DRA [R] 105m. V

Last Dinosaur, The 1977 ★ Boone is an insatiable hunter out to bag the one beast he hasn't stuffed and mounted—a dinosaur. Grade-Z schlock. C: Tom Kotani, Richard Boone, Joan Van Ark. D: Alex Grasshoff. HOR 100m.

Last Dragon, The 1985 ★★½ A martial arts student (Taimak) must confront a video game mogul (Murney) to protect his video deejay (Vanity). Mindless but pleasantly amusing. C: Taimak, Vanity, Chris Murney. D: Michael Schultz. ACT [PG] 109m. V

Last Elephant, The 1990 ★★★½ A writer (Lithgow), a policeman (Jones), and a biologist (Rossellini) join forces to fight the massacre of elephants by ivory hunters in Kenya. Laudable cable effort. (a.k.a. *Ivory Hunters.*) C: John Lithgow, Isabella Rossellini, James Earl Jones. D: Joseph Sargent. DRA 100m.

Last Embrace 1979 ★★★★ A government agent (Scheider) suffers a breakdown after witnessing his wife's murder. Still shaky after leaving the hospital, he starts having doubts: Is he having accidents, or is someone trying to kill him? Early Demme effort owes a real debt to Hitchcock, as well to the screenwriter responsible for some great plot twists. C: Roy Scheider, Janet Margolin, John Glover, Christopher Walken. D: Jonathan Demme. CRI [R] 98m. V

Last Emperor, The 1987 Italian ★★★★★ Spectacular epic about China's last emperor, Pu Yi (Lone), who lives a cloistered life until age three, then must face the harsh realities of life after he's deposed. Direction, screenplay, photography and music combine for a stylized, powerful screen experience. Won 9 Oscars including Best Picture and Director. C: John Lone, Joan Chen, Peter O'Toole, Ryuichui Sakamoto. D: Bernardo Bertolucci. DRA [PG-13] 164m. V

Last Exit to Brooklyn 1990 German ★★★★ Labor tension in a Brooklyn factory in the '50s forms the background for the story of three characters' sexual quests in this adaptation of Hubert Selby, Jr.'s novel. Violent, self-hating, unlikable characters inhabit an ugly urban landscape, making this dark film a somewhat acquired taste. C: Stephen Lang, Jennifer Jason Leigh, Burt Young, Jerry Orbach, Stephen Baldwin, Ricki Lake. D: Uli Edel. DRA [R] 103m. V

Last Flight of Noah's Ark, The 1980 ★★½ Mundane Disney movie about pilot, missionary, two kids, and plane full of critters that crash-lands on island inhabited by two Japanese soldiers still fighting WWII. Boring plot development doesn't help the already contrived story. C: Elliott Gould, Genevieve Bujold, Ricky Schroder. D: Charles Jarrott. FAM/DRA [G] 97m. V

Last Flight Out 1990 ★★½ In the chaotic final hours before the fall of Saigon, a number of Americans and Vietnamese desperately seek safety. Some excitement, but no epic. C: Richard Crenna, James Earl Jones, Haing S. Ngor. D: Larry Elikann. ACT 99m. V

Last Flight, The 1931 ★★★★ After WWI, four G.I.s remain in Paris to heal their psychic and physical wounds. Occasionally lapses into cheap melodrama. Otherwise, a moving and powerful antiwar statement. C: Richard Barthelmess, Helen Chandler, John Mack Brown. D: William Dieterle. DRA 80m.

Last Flight to Hell 1991 ★★★ Mis-matched couple teams up to rescue her drug lord father from abductors. C: Reb Brown, Chuck Connors, Michele Dehne. D: Paul D. Robinson. ACT 94m. V

Last Fling, The 1989 ★★ Before her marriage to a stiff, a beautiful bride wants a one-night stand with a reluctant bachelor. Guess what happens? Charming cast, dark social comedy. C: John Ritter, Connie Sellecca. D: Corey Allen. COM [PG] 95m. V

Last Four Days, The 1977 ★★★ Historical drama probes fascist leader Benito Mussolini's final days. C: Henry Fonda, Rod Steiger, Franco Nero. D: Carlo Lizzani. DRA [PG] 91m. V

Last Frontier, The 1956 ★★★ Ruthless cavalry colonel Preston arrives at a frontier outpost, affecting the lives of those stationed there, including trapper Mature. Interesting performances and well-staged battle scenes shot at night overcome ordinary Western plot. (a.k.a. *Savage Wilderness*) C: Victor Mature, Guy Madison, Robert Preston, James Whitmore, Anne Bancroft. D: Anthony Mann. WST 98m.

Last Game, The 1980 ★ Moving story of student struggling to care for blind and sickly father while pursuing his dream of playing college football. C: Howard Segal, Ed Grady, Joan Hotchkis. D: Martin Beck. DRA 107m. V

Last Gangster, The 1937 ★★★★ Mobster Robinson has a child with an Italian woman before being sent to prison, and upon release searches relentlessly for the son he hopes will be his successor. Smooth MGM film approaches gritty Warner Brothers gangster sagas, with a strong tour-de-force performance by Robinson. C: Edward G. Robinson, James Stewart, Rosa Stradner, Lionel Stander, John Carradine. D: Edward Ludwig. DRA 81m.

Last Gentleman, The 1934 ★★★★ Dying millionaire (Arliss) contends with greedy relatives. Enjoyable farce with strong supporting cast and fun surprise ending. C: George Arliss, Edna May Oliver, Charlotte Henry. D: Sidney Lanfield. COM 80m.

Last Gun, The 1964 ★ Outlaw's chance for serene retirement is jeopardized by his violent past. C: Cameron Mitchell, Carl Moher, Frank Wolff. D: Serge Bergone. WST 98m. V

Last Hard Men, The 1976 ★★½ Former law officer tracks fugitive gang that, bent on rape, abducts his daughter. Appallingly brutal Western, notable mainly for a good cast. C: Charlton Heston, James Coburn, Barbara Hershey, Michael Parks. D: Andrew McLaglen. WST [R] 103m.

Last Hit, The 1993 ★★★½ Sulky professional killer who wants out is given one last job: murder the father of the woman he's falling in love with. Good performances from Brown and Adams in workmanlike thriller. C: Bryan Brown, Brooke Adams, Harris Yulin. D: Jane Egleson. CRI [R] 93m. V

Last Holiday 1950 British ★★★★ Guinness has field day as lonely, terminally ill man having one last fling at a posh English seaside resort. Literate script by novelist J.B. Priestley. C: Alec Guinness, Beatrice Campbell, Kay Walsh, Wilfrid Hyde-White. D: Henry Cass. COM 88m. V

Last Horror Film, The 1984 ★ Would that it were the last *bad* horror film. Psychopathic fan (Spinell) pursues horror star (Munro) to the Cannes Film Festival, slaughtering anyone in his way. Authentic Cannes location shooting gives this ludicrous movie its only trace of professionalism. C: Caroline Munro, Joe Spinell. D: David Winters. HOR [R] 87m. V

Last Hour, The 1991 ★★★½ Cop Paré tries to rescue his ex-wife, who has been kidnapped by a mobster and concealed in an old L.A. office building. Low-budget hostage rescue action drama obviously influenced by *Die Hard*, but still worthwhile. C: Michael Paré, Shannon Tweed, Bobby Di Cicco. D: William Sachs. CRI [R] 85m. V

Last House on the Left, The 1972 ★ A sadistic trio tortures and murders two teenage girls in an old house, then is hunted by one of the girls' fathers seeking revenge. Unrelenting gore and graphic violence mark this repulsive film recommended for fans of the genre only. Loosely based on Bergman's *The Virgin Spring*. C: David Hess, Lucy Grantham, Sandra Cassel. D: Wes Craven. CRI [R] 82m. V

Last Hunt, The 1956 ★★★★ Western focuses on rivalry and partnership between aging buffalo hunters Granger and Taylor. Brooding film with haunting final scenes presaging the end-of-the-West movies of the late '60s. Arguably Brooks' best film. C: Robert Taylor, Stewart Granger, Debra Paget, Lloyd Nolan. D: Richard Brooks. WST 108m. V

Last Hunter, The 1980 ★★★ Stranded in enemy territory during the Vietnam War, a soldier relies on his wits and will to survive. C: David Warbeck, Tisa Farrow. D: Anthony M. Dawson. ACT 97m. V

Last Hurrah, The 1958 ★★★★½ Tracy is magnificent as Frank Skeffington, mayor of Boston, trying to get reelected with outdated methods in savvy filming of the Edwin O'Connor best-seller. Veteran supporting cast and moving script. C: Spencer Tracy, Jeffrey Hunter, Dianne Foster, Basil Rathbone, Pat O'Brien, John Carradine. D: John Ford. DRA 121m. V

Last Hurrah, The 1977 ★★ Boston mayor (O'Connor) tries to get elected one last time in this feeble remake of the 1958 version of Edwin O'Connor's novel. C: Carroll O'Connor, John Anderson, Dana Andrews. D: Vincent Sherman. DRA 110m. TVM

Last Innocent Man, The 1987 ★★★½ Jaded attorney defends accused murderer and unwisely falls for client's ex-wife. Violent story has some real pizzazz. C: Ed Harris, Roxanne Hart, David Suchet. D: Roger Spottiswoode. CRI 114m. TVM V

Last Laugh, The 1924 German ★★★★★ Silent-era classic, told without title cards, of a proud, aging doorman (Jannings) who is unceremoniously demoted. As memorable for Murnau's moody and expressionistic direction as for Jannings' monumental performance; a cinema landmark. C: Emil Jannings, Maly Delschaft. D: F. W. Murnau. DRA 91m. V

Last Light 1993 ★★★½ Death row prisoner and guard form a bond that changes the way both look at the world. C: Kiefer Sutherland, Forest Whitaker, Amanda Plummer. D: Kiefer Sutherland. DRA [R] 104m. V

Last Man on Earth, The 1964 ★★★ Price's performance and creepy, desolate atmosphere are best parts of this erratic story. In a world decimated by plague, the only human left (Price) must constantly fight off vampiric ghouls. Based on Richard Matheson novel *I Am Legend*, later made as *The Omega Man*. C: Vincent Price, Franca Bettoia. D: Sidney Salkow. HOR 86m.

Last Man Standing 1987 ★★★½ Broken down boxer (Wells), trying to adjust to life outside the ring, discovers brutality is not confined within the ropes. Better than average, with violent realism its chief asset. C: Vernon Wells, Franco Columbu, William Sanderson. D: Damian Lee. ACT [R] 92m. V

Last Married Couple in America, The 1980 ★★ Wedded bliss turns into a nightmare for a happily married couple (Segal, Wood) when their relationship is strained by continuing breakups among their friends. Likable cast must endure unlikable script in this sparsely funny sex comedy. C: George Segal, Natalie Wood, Richard Benjamin, Valerie Harper. D: Gilbert Cates. COM [R] 103m. V

Last Message from Saigon 1965 *See* **Operation C.I.A.**

Last Metro, The 1980 French ★★★★ Theatrical troupe in Paris performs during Nazi occupation. Nearly nostalgic view of dark period in French history, but made with Truffaut's accustomed warmth. Nominated for Oscar as Best Foreign Film. C: Catherine Deneuve, Gerard Depardieu, Jean Poiret, Heinz Bennent, Andrea Ferreol. D: Francois Truffaut. DRA [PG] 135m. V

Last Mile, The 1932 ★★★ A frank look at the life of prisoners on death row as some cling to their dignity and others plan their escape. Well-written, tense drama that would have more impact were it not so dated. C: Howard Phillips, Preston Foster, George E. Stone, Noel Madison. D: Sam Bischoff. DRA 69m. V

Last Mile, The 1959 ★★★½ Remake of a classic '30s prison drama, with Rooney leading a takeover of death row before his upcoming execution. Can't match stark tension of the original, but Rooney gives a vivid, believable performance. C: Mickey Rooney, Clifford David, Harry Millard. D: Howard Koch. DRA 81m.

Last Millionaire, The 1934 French ★★★½ Bankrupt kingdom is ruled by a millionaire who issues bizarre proclamations after suffering a blow to the head. Clair satire features many clever touches, but isn't his best work. C: Max Dearly, Renee Cyr, Jose Noguero. D: Rene Clair. COM 90m.

Last Movie, The 1971 ★★ Pretentious mess about an American filmmaker in South America portrays moviemaking as a metaphor for imperialism. Star-director Hopper loses his way completely in incoherent story. C: Dennis Hopper, Julie Adams, Peter Fonda, Kris Kristofferson, Sylvia Miles. D: Dennis Hopper. DRA [R] 108m. V

Last Night at the Alamo 1984 ★★★★ Absorbing character study set in a smoky Houston bar slated for destruction, as sad modern-day cowboys try to save it. Insightful low-budget film is both funny and poignant, with a script by Kim Henkel who also wrote *The Texas Chainsaw Massacre.* C: Sonny Carl Davis, Steve Matilla, Tina Bess Hubbard. D: Eagle Pennell. DRA 82m. V

Last of England, The 1987 ★★★★½ The Fall of the British Empire is documented through the use of home movie footage. Powerful use of sound and montage footage creates a startling if grim personal vision. C: Tilda Swinton, Spencer Leigh. D: Derek Jarman. DOC 87m. V

Last of His Tribe, The 1992 ★★★½ True story of Ishi (Greene), the last member of the ancient Yahi tribe who is brought to San Francisco in the early 1900s by anthropologist Voight, and becomes a virtual prisoner in academia. Middling but earnest scenario doesn't compare to the Dalton Trumbo-scripted 1978 version. C: Jon Voight, Graham Greene, Anne Archer. D: Harry Hook. DRA [PG-13] 90m. TVM V

Last of Mrs. Cheyney, The 1937 ★★★½ Lavish version of the Fredrick Lonsdale play about an American jewel thief in London society. Crawford isn't very comfortable in witty comedy of manners first made as Norma Shearer vehicle in 1929, but film is moderately amusing. C: Joan Crawford, William Powell, Robert Montgomery, Frank Morgan, Jessie Ralph, Nigel Bruce. D: Richard Boleslawski. COM 98m. V

Last of Mrs. Lincoln 1976 ★★★★ After her husband's assassination, Mary Todd Lincoln (Harris) has to deal with poverty and encroaching madness. This version of James Prideaux's Broadway play is made memorable by Harris' towering performance. C: Julie Harris, Robby Benson, Patrick Duffy, Michael Cristofer. D: George Schaefer. DRA 118m. TVM V

Last of Philip Banter, The 1987 ★★★½ Taut psychological thriller. Delusional writer believes a mysterious manuscript foretells his future. C: Tony Curtis, Scott Paulin, Irene Miracle. D: Herve Hachuel. DRA [R] 105m. V

Last of Sheila, The 1973 ★★★★ Intricate murder mystery about rich celebs gathering on Coburn's yacht (named for his dead wife), where they play deadly parlor games. Almost too clever for its own good, but a game cast makes it fun. Script by Anthony Perkins and Stephen Sondheim. C: James Coburn, Dyan Cannon, James Mason, Raquel Welch, Richard Benjamin, Joan Hackett. D: Herbert Ross. CRI [PG] 119m. V

Last of the Buccaneers, The 1950 ★★½ Cheap but well-paced swashbuckler based on the adventures of French pirate Jean Lafitte. For fans of the genre. C: Paul Henreid, Jack Oakie, Mary Anderson. D: Lew Landers. ACT 79m.

Last of the Comanches, The 1952 ★★★ After a battle, Comanche riders pursue the remaining cavalry casualties who find shelter in deserted mission and await rescue. Okay shoot-'em-up. C: Broderick Crawford, Barbara Hale, Lloyd Bridges, Jay Silverheels. D: Andre de Toth. WST 85m.

Last of the Cowboys, The 1978 *See* **Great Smokey Roadblock, The**

Last of the Finest, The 1990 ★★★ Los Angeles undercover cops lose their patience with outdated justice system when one of their own is murdered. Dennehey leads a respectable ensemble in this cops-and-robbers saga. C: Brian Dennehy, Joe Pantoliano, Jeff Fahey. D: John Mackenzie. ACT [R] 106m. V

Last of the Mobile Hot-Shots 1970 ★★½

Cancer-ridden plantation patriarch Coburn marries hooker Redgrave to produce an heir before his death, while a triangle develops with black half-brother Hooks. Mediocre and confused adaptation of Tennessee Williams' *Seven Descents of Myrtle*. C: James Coburn, Lynn Redgrave, Robert Hooks. D: Sidney Lumet. DRA [R] 108m. V

Last of the Mohicans, The 1920 ★★★★ Hawkeye and the title character take on the treacherous French-allied Indian Magua (Beery), who is leading a British colonel's daughters to their father's fort. Exciting silent adaptation of the James Fenimore Cooper novel holds up well. C: Clarence Brown, Wallace Beery, Barbara Bedford, Albert Roscoe. D: Maurice Tourneur. ACT 75m.

Last of the Mohicans, The 1936 ★★★★ Scott is a solid Hawkeye in this adaptation of the James Fenimore Cooper novel about Native Americans who aid colonial settlers during the French-Indian wars. Exciting historical drama, with Cabot a fine villain. C: Randolph Scott, Binnie Barnes, Heather Angel, Hugh Buckler, Bruce Cabot. D: George B. Seitz. ACT 91m. V

Last of the Mohicans, The 1977 ★★★ Hawkeye (Forrest) and Chingachgook tangle with the Hurons during early America's French and Indian War. This made-for-TV adventure does well by the classic James Fenimore Cooper novel on which it's based. C: Steve Forrest, Ned Romero, Andrew Prine, Robert Tessier. D: James L. Conway. ACT 97m. TVM V

Last of the Mohicans, The 1992 ★★★★ James Fenimore Cooper's novel with Day-Lewis as the frontiersman raised by Mohicans who romances a British officer's daughter (Stowe) while fighting for the Mohicans' cause. Mann's attempts at historical accuracy result in a believable and exciting film, despite some very weak dialogue. C: Daniel Day-Lewis, Madeleine Stowe, Russell Means, Wes Studi. D: Michael Mann. ACT [R] 114m. V

Last of the Red Hot Dragons ★★★½ People encounter a dragon that has awakened from a centuries-long hibernation, and it comes to their rescue when they become trapped in an ice cave. Unambitious animated tale is effective children's entertainment. FAM/DRA V

Last of the Red Hot Lovers 1972 ★★½ In an attempt to regain the passion of his youth, a frumpy fish restaurateur (Arkin) attempts a series of romantic tête-à-têtes in his mother's empty apartment. Poor adaptation of a Neil Simon stage farce. C: Alan Arkin, Sally Kellerman, Paula Prentiss, Renee Taylor. D: Gene Saks. COM [PG] 98m. V

Last of the Redmen 1947 ★★★ Saturday matinee version of Cooper's *Last of the Mohicans* with heroic Hawkeye a valiant escort through treacherous 18th-century American wilderness. Entertaining, though not the best adaptation. C: Jon Hall, Michael O'Shea, Evelyn Ankers, Buster Crabbe. D: George Sherman. ACT 79m. V

Last of the Secret Agents?, The 1966 ★ Two bumbling American tourists (Allen, Rossi) in France caught in art heist plot wind up as spies. Flat espionage spoof intended to launch the film career of the comedy team of Allen and Rossi but killed it instead. C: Marty Allen, Steve Rossi, Nancy Sinatra. D: Norman Abbott. COM 90m.

Last of the Ski Bums 1969 ★★★½ Three young adventurers win a small fortune and blow all on an extended skiing holiday. Beautiful location shooting marks this pleasant little surprise. C: Ron Funk, Mike Zuetell. D: Dick Barrymore. ACT [G] 86m.

Last of the Vikings, The 1960 Italian ★★ After their land is pillaged by invaders, Vikings seek revenge. Full of rousing energy, but so badly acted (and dubbed) it inadvertently turns into parody. C: Cameron Mitchell, Edmund Purdom, Isabelle Corey. D: Giacomo Gentilomo. ACT 102m.

Last of the Warriors 1991 ★★½ Valiant friends battle corrupt leader of decimated futuristic empire. C: William Smith, Scott Anderson. D: Lloyd Simandl. SFI 89m. V

Last Outlaw, The 1936 ★★★★½ Amusing, touching Western comedy, with great performance by Carey as gunslinger out of jail after 25 years, returning to a Wild West he doesn't recognize. Low-budget gem well worth discovering. C: Harry Carey, Hoot Gibson, Margaret Callahan. D: Christy Cabanne. COM [R] 72m.

Last Outlaw, The 1994 ★★★ As members of a bandit pack begin to turn up dead, survivors start to suspect each other of the murders. C: Mickey Rourke, Dermot Mulroney. D: Geoff Murphy. WST [R] 90m. TVM V

Last Outpost, The 1935 ★★★★ A British officer (Grant) battles both the Kurds and his feelings for the wife of a soldier of fortune (Rains), to whom he owes his life. Rousing adventure, the *Gunga Din* way. C: Cary Grant, Claude Rains, Gertrude Michael. D: Louis Gasnier, Charles Barton. ACT 70m.

Last Outpost, The 1951 ★★★ Feuding brothers, one a Yankee, the other a Rebel, band together to repel attacking Indians. Set piece redeemed by occasional directorial flourishes. C: Ronald Reagan, Rhonda Fleming, Bruce Bennett. D: Lewis Foster. WST 88m.

Last Page, The 1952 *See* **Man Bait**

Last Party, The 1993 ★★★½ Actor/writer Downey's personal documentary look at the 1992 political conventions. He jumps from Los Angeles to Houston to New York, interviewing just about all the celebrities, politicians, and common men he meets. Scattershot, but lively. C: Robert Downey Jr. D: Mark Benjamin, Marc Levin. DOC 96m. V

Last Picture Show, The 1971 ★★★★★ Bogdanovich and writer Larry McMurtry examine the passing of an American way of life in this artfully assured and elegiac film about the residents of a dying Texas small town. Oscars for Leachman and Johnson; Shepherd's first film. In glorious black and white. Sequel *Texasville* made 20 years later. C: Jeff Bridges, Timothy Bottoms, Ellen Burstyn, Cybill Shepherd, Cloris Leachman, Ben Johnson, Eileen Brennan, Randy Quaid. D: Peter Bogdanovich. DRA [R] 118m. v

Last Plane Out 1982 ★★ The final days of Somoza's regime in Nicarauga—as seen through the eyes of a journalist. Political thriller is taut at times, silly at others. C: Jan-Michael Vincent, Julie Carmen. D: David Nelson. ACT [PG] 98m. v

Last Porno Flick, The 1974 ★ Two daffy cabbies scheme to become Hollywood moguls when the script for a porno movie falls into their laps. Lame low-budget movie is neither sexy nor funny. C: Frank Calcanini, Michael Pataki, Marianna Hill. D: Ray Marsh. COM [PG] 88m.

Last Posse, The 1953 ★★★ Prominent cattle rustler and group of deputies are at odds as they go after holdup bandits. Okay chase Western with surprise ending. C: Broderick Crawford, John Derek, Charles Bickford. D: Alfred Werker. WST 73m.

Last Prostitute, The 1991 ★★ Two '60s teens seek out famous hooker for you-know-what. She's left the life, but that doesn't stop them. Not completely without merit. Adapted from William Borden's play. C: Sonia Braga, Wil Wheaton. D: Lou Antonio. DRA [PG-13] 95m. v

Last Rebel, The 1971 ★ In post-Civil War Missouri, a Confederate veteran tries to prevent wanton lynching of blacks. Namath is—uh—interesting to watch, in a campy kind of way. C: Joe Namath, Jack Elam, Woody Strode, Victoria George. D: Denys McCoy. WST [PG] 89m.

Last Remake of Beau Geste, The 1977 ★★★ Pop-eyed comic Feldman writes, directs, and stars in this uneven spoof of Foreign Legion movies. He's a less-than-dashing desert Legionnaire who bungles his way through confused plot. Added footage of Gary Cooper from original *Beau Geste* doesn't help much. C: Marty Feldman, Ann-Margret, Michael York, Peter Ustinov, James Earl Jones, Trevor Howard, Terry-Thomas. D: Marty Feldman. COM [PG] 85m. v

Last Resort 1986 ★★ When a reserved married man (Grodin) loses his job, he decides to treat his family to a lush tropical resort vacation and unwittingly chooses a spot filled with sex-crazed employees and warring militants. Shrill comedy kills most of its jokes by trying too hard. C: Charles Grodin, Robin Pearson Rose, John Ashton, Jon Lovitz. D: Zane Buzby. COM [R] 84m. v

Last Reunion, The 1980 ★★ A group of WWII soldiers meet in the Philippines for a reunion. Now, more than 30 years after they committed a war crime, an eyewitness is out for revenge. Exceedingly violent. C: Cameron Mitchell, Leo Fong, Chanda Romero. D: Jay Wertz. ACT 98m. v

Last Riders 1990 ★★ Erik hides out from members of his own gang and the police. Watch the bikes go crunch! Violence and profanity. C: Erik Estrada, William Smith, Armand Silvestre, Kathrin Lautner. D: Joseph Merhi. ACT [R] 90m. TVM v

Last Rites 1988 ★★½ Priest (Berenger) with blood ties to the Mafia lovingly protects mob hit witness (Zuniga) via his worldly and otherworldly contacts. Released directly to video. C: Tom Berenger, Daphne Zuniga. D: Donald P. Bellisario. CRI [R] 103m. v

Last Roman, The 1968 German ★★ Rome falls once again in overblown costume epic. Some big names embarrass themselves in new ways. C: Laurence Harvey, Orson Welles, Sylva Koscina, Honor Blackman. D: Robert Siodmak. ACT 92m.

Last Run, The 1971 ★★½ A one-time driver for the syndicate, now comfortably retired in Portugal, goes out on one more job. Interesting cast, particularly Scott, in an average story. C: George C. Scott, Tony Musante, Trish Van Devere, Colleen Dewhurst. D: Richard Fleischer. DRA [PG] 99m.

Last Safari, The 1967 British ★★½ Jaded big game hunter (Granger) leads wealthy couple on his last excursion, and discovers truths he's spent his life ignoring. Melodramatic outing with some good nature photography. C: Stewart Granger, Gabriella Licudi, Johnny Sekka. D: Henry Hathaway. ACT 111m. v

Last Season, The 1987 ★★ Good Samaritan targets yahoo hunters who trash his forest. All hell breaks loose in the finale. C: Christopher Gosch, Louise Dorsey, David Cox. D: Raja Zahr. ACT 90m. v

Last Seduction, The 1994 ★★★★ Fiorentino's sizzling portrayal of man-eating femme fatale charges this modern-day film noir, set in small town near Buffalo, N.Y. Humor alternates with chilling drama, as Linda seduces mild-mannered rube (Berg) and leads him into life of crime. Originally shown on HBO, then released to theatres. By the director of *Red Rock West.* C: Linda Fiorentino, Peter Berg, J.T. Walsh, Bill Pullman. D: John Dahl. CRI [R] 110m. TVM v

Last Slumber Party, The 1987 ★★ Teenagers at slumber party fall prey to vicious murderer. C: Jan Jensen, Nancy Meyer, Joann Whitley. D: Stephen Tyler. HOR 89m. v

Last Starfighter, The 1984 ★★★½ Hapless Earth teenager is recruited via arcade video game to fight in a distant space battle. Breathlessly juvenile sci-fi escapism is surprisingly enjoyable thanks to first-rate cast and pioneering computer-graphics special effects—no model miniatures were built. C: Lance Guest, Robert Preston, Dan O'Herlihy, Catherine Mary Stewart. D: Nick Castle. SFI [PG] 100m. V

Last Summer 1969 ★★★★ Four teenagers spending summer on Fire Island come of age, with tragic consequences. Strong, beautifully acted drama from the Evan Hunter novel, marred by heavy-handed seagull symbolism. Burns is sensational. C: Richard Thomas, Barbara Hershey, Bruce Davison, Cathy Burns. D: Frank Perry. DRA [R] 97m. V

Last Sunset, The 1961 ★★★½ Outlaw Douglas and sheriff Hudson are old enemies thrown together on a drive, with Malone and Lynley as love interests. Peculiar cattle-drive Western with talky Dalton Trumbo script throws in everything from action to incest. C: Rock Hudson, Kirk Douglas, Dorothy Malone, Joseph Cotten, Carol Lynley. D: Robert Aldrich. WST 112m.

Last Supper, The 1976 Cuban ★★★★ A Cuban plantation owner forces 12 slaves to portray the Twelve Apostles at the Last Supper during Easter celebrations, to teach them Christianity. Biting look at Christian hypocrisy as a precursor to the Cuban Socialist revolution; based on a true story. C: Nelson Villagra, Silvano Rey, Laberto Garcia, Jose Antonio Rodriguez. D: Tomas Gutierrez Alea. DRA 110m. V

Last Tango in Paris 1973 French ★★★★½ Brando and Schneider emote their way through explicit love scenes in a film that broke sexual barriers on-screen. He's a recent widower acting out his grief in an obsessive love affair with a younger stranger. Artfully shot, it's both steamy and thought provoking. C: Marlon Brando, Maria Schneider, Jean-Pierre Leaud. D: Bernardo Bertolucci. DRA [R] 129m.

Last Temptation of Christ, The 1988 ★★★ Deeply felt, but controversial look at Christ's life asks the question: What if Christ had doubted himself? The middle section of the film is a fairly traditional telling of events in Christ's life, such as his wanderings in the desert and the raising of Lazarus. The opening and especially the final section, where Christ has a vision of the human life he must give up to be the Savior, are less traditional. Based on the novel by Nikos Kazakantis; with music by Peter Gabriel. C: Willem Dafoe, Harvey Keitel, Barbara Hershey, Harry Dean Stanton, David Bowie, Verna Bloom, Juliette Caton, Irvin Kershner, Barry Miller. D: Martin Scorsese. DRA [R] 164m. V

Last Ten Days, The 1956 German ★★★ In a bunker beneath the shattered streets of war-torn Berlin, Adolf Hitler awaits the end. Poignant study—personally and historically—of the demise of the Third Reich. C: Albin Skoda, Oskar Werner, Lotte Tobisch. D: G. W. Pabst. DRA 113m.

Last Time I Saw Archie, The 1961 ★★★½ Goldbricking Army private (Mitchum) finagles a life of ease for himself and his buddy during the last days of WWII and, despite his chicanery, manages to end up a hero. Likable, mildly funny service comedy. C: Robert Mitchum, Jack Webb, Martha Hyer, France Nuyen. D: Jack Webb. COM 98m.

Last Time I Saw Paris, The 1954 ★★★★ In post-WWII Paris, a writer finds that his marriage to a wealthy American is on the rocks. Adaptation of F. Scott Fitzgerald's *Babylon Revisited* is sleek but familiar, pulled off by great cast. C: Elizabeth Taylor, Van Johnson, Donna Reed, Walter Pidgeon. D: Richard Brooks. DRA 116m. V

Last to Go 1991 ★★★★ Daly breathes new life into old story of a wife deserted by husband for younger woman; she goes for the jugular in this no-holds-barred drama that transcends clichés. C: Tyne Daly, Terry O'Quinn, Annabeth Gish. D: John Erman. DRA 96m. TVM

Last Train From Gun Hill 1959 ★★★★ When his wife is raped and murdered, a U.S. marshal tracks down the man who did it, determined to bring in the suspect. Very suspenseful, culminating in a knockout shoot-'em-up. C: Kirk Douglas, Anthony Quinn, Carolyn Jones, Earl Holliman. D: John Sturges. WST 94m. V

Last Train from Madrid, The 1937 ★★★½ When civil war breaks out in Spain, a diverse group of people tries to flee the country. Combination of *Grand Hotel* and *Stagecoach* is memorable for a better-than-average cast. C: Dorothy Lamour, Lew Ayres, Gilbert Roland, Anthony Quinn, Lee Bowman. D: James Hogan. DRA 77m.

Last Tycoon, The 1977 ★★★★½ De Niro is F. Scott Fitzgerald's '30s Hollywood mogul Monroe Stahr, trying to maintain his empire as his health fails. De Niro's remarkable, restrained performance is the strongest element of this adaptation by Harold Pinter featuring an impressive cast and sensitive direction. C: Robert De Niro, Tony Curtis, Robert Mitchum, Jeanne Moreau, Jack Nicholson, Donald Pleasence, Ray Milland. D: Elia Kazan. DRA [PG] 123m. V

Last Valley, The 1971 British ★★½ At the end of the 30 Years War, a band of warriors goes into a peaceful valley that has entirely avoided bloody conflict. Great scenery eclipses underdeveloped story in beautiful looking bore. C: Michael Caine, Omar Sharif, Florinda Bolkan. D: James Clavell. DRA 126m. V

Last Voyage, The 1960 ★★★½ Luxury ship is crippled after a blast rocks the hull. Dramas abound between characters as they must resolve personal conflicts and find safety before the boat sinks. Special effects are best aspect of this disaster thriller. C: Robert Stack, Dorothy Malone, George Sanders, Edmond O'Brien. D: Andrew L. Stone. DRA 87m. V

Last Wagon, The 1956 ★★★★ A rugged killer wanted by the law safeguards wagon train survivors of an Indian massacre. Competently directed, high-standard Western. C: Richard Widmark, Felicia Farr, Susan Kohner, Tommy Retting. D: Delmer Daves. WST 99m.

Last Waltz, The 1976 ★★★★½ Scorsese's documentary on The Band's farewell concert, which features wonderful guest performances, effectively focuses on the heart of rock 'n' roll and provides an ironic contrast between hyperkinetic interviewer Scorsese and the sedated Band members. C: The Band, Bob Dylan, Neil Young, Joni Mitchell, Van Morrison, Eric Clapton, Neil Diamond, Muddy Waters, Emmylou Harris. D: Martin Scorsese. DOC [PG] 117m. V

Last Warrior, The 1989 ★★★ Japanese soldier and American G.I. fight one-on-one in the South Pacific at the end of World War II. C: Gary Graham, Cary Hiroyuki-Tagawa, Maria Holvoe. D: Martin Wragge. ACT [R] 94m. V

Last Wave, The 1977 Australian ★★★★ In Australia, a lawyer (Chamberlain) gets apocalyptic visions while defending an Aborigine charged with murder. Thoughtful supernatural chiller with great visual effects. C: Richard Chamberlain, Olivia Hamnett. D: Peter Weir. DRA [PG] 103m. V

Last Will of Dr. Mabuse, The 1933 *See* **Testament of Dr. Mabuse, The**

Last Winter, The 1984 Israeli ★★★ Two Israeli women search for their husbands, who have been missing since the Yom Kippur War. C: Kathleen Quinlan, Yona Elian, Stephen Macht. D: Riki Missimoff. DRA [R] 92m. V

Last Wish 1992 ★★★★ Moving drama of terminally ill woman (Stapleton) assisted in suicide by her daughter (Duke). Both actresses excell in difficult roles, and medical profession takes a beating in this true story, based on a memoir by newscaster Betty Rollins. C: Patty Duke, Maureen Stapleton. D: Jeff Bleckner. DRA 100m. TVM

Last Woman on Earth, The 1960 ★ Low-budget nuclear disaster strikes, leaving our heroine in the title predicament. At least she doesn't have to watch this Roger Corman movie, an early writing effort by co-star Edward Wain (actually Robert Towne, of *Chinatown* fame). C: Antony Carbone, Edward Wain, Betsy Jones-Moreland. D: Roger Corman. SFI 71m.

Last Year at Marienbad 1961 French ★★★★ A young man (Albertazzi) at a French resort hotel attempts to revive a relationship with a woman (Seyrig) who doesn't remember their affair. Beautifully photographed, but often confusing art film avoids linear restrictions, and the result is often difficult to follow. C: Delphine Seyrig, Giorgio Albertazzi. D: Alain Resnais. DRA 90m. V

L'Atalante 1934 French ★★★★★ Acknowledged classic of two young lovers aboard barge. Ultraromantic atmosphere, assured direction, presence of Simon, all contribute to sublime example of filmmaking. C: Michele Simon, Dita Parlo, Jean Daste. D: Jean Vigo. DRA 82m. V

Latcho Drom 1994 Romany ★★★★ Unusual documentary about modern-day gypsies covers most of Europe and the Middle East, showing their customs, music, dance, etc. Fascinating to watch and listen to. In the language known as Romany, with English subtitles. D: Tony Gatlif. DOC 97m.

Late Autumn 1960 Japanese ★★★★½ Widow copes with a trio of men who insist on trying to arrange a marriage for her daughter, not understanding that the young woman doesn't necessarily agree with their old-fashioned ways. A quiet, lighthearted drama, reworking many of Ozu's ideas from his *Late Spring*. C: Setsuko Hara, Yoko Tsukasa, Mariko Okada. D: Yasujiro Ozu. DRA 127m.

Late Chrysanthemums 1954 Japanese ★★★★★ To four middle-aged geishas, the future seems bleak indeed. But director Naruse helps us see past the obvious to something humane and hauntingly lovely. This film is a gem waiting to be rediscovered. C: Haruko Sugimura, Yuko Mochizuki, Chikako Hosokawa, Ken Uehara, Sadako Sawamura. D: Mikio Naruse. DRA 101m. V

Late Edwina Black, The 1951 *See* **Obsessed, The**

Late for Dinner 1991 ★★★½ Two men driving from New Mexico to California in 1962 are taken in by a doctor experimenting with cryogenics; they wake up 29 years later and try to pick up their lives. Odd blend of wacky buddy road movie and soul-searching sentiment has its moments but doesn't completely succeed. C: Brian Wimmer, Peter Berg, Marcia Gay Harden, Peter Gallagher. D: W. D. Richter. DRA [PG] 93m. V

Late George Apley, The 1947 ★★★½ Mild satire of Boston society focuses on stuffy family, headed by Colman in an impressive performance. From play by John P. Marquand and George S. Kaufman, adapted from Marquand's novel. C: Ronald Colman, Peggy Cummins, Vanessa Brown, Richard Haydn. D: Joseph L. Mankiewicz. COM 98m.

Late Show, The 1976 ★★★★ Goofball Tomlin hires aging, hard-boiled P.I. Carney to locate her missing cat, and winds up helping him solve the murder of his partner. Both a deft parody of and homage to film noir, highlighted by knowing performances. C: Art Carney, Lily Tomlin. D: Robert Benton. COM [PG] 94m. V

Late Spring 1949 Japanese ★★★★★ Simple tale of widower trying to marry off his daughter is transformed on screen by master director Ozu. Extraordinary chemistry between Hara (daughter) and Ryu (father) enriches this jewel of a film—don't miss it! C:

Chisu Ryu, Setsuko Hara, Jun Usami, Haruko Sugimura. D: Yasujiro Ozu. DRA 107m.

Late Summer Blues 1987 Israeli ★★★ Seven young Israelis gather for one more party after their last exams and before entering the army. Facing being stationed on the Suez Canal, they grow up quickly with the realities of life and death. C: Dor Zweigenbom, Yoav Tsafir, Shahar Segal. D: Renen Schorr. DRA 101m. V

Lathe of Heaven, The 1980 ★★★ This is thinking man's sci-fi—a young man (Davison) undertakes sleep therapy because all his dreams have the habit of coming true. Interesting premise and solid execution. C: Fred Barzyk, Kevin Conway, Bruce Davison. D: David Loston. SFI 105m.

Latin Lovers 1953 ★★ An heiress (Turner) journeys to South America to find true love. Silly romantic drama goes nowhere, but looks good along the way. C: Lana Turner, Ricardo Montalban, John Lund, Louis Calhern, Rita Moreno. D: Mervyn LeRoy. DRA 104m. V

Latino 1985 ★★★½ A Chicano Green Beret fights his conscience as well as the Sandinistas when he is sent to Nicaragua to assist the Contras. Politically heavy-handed drama condemns American involvement in South America. C: Robert Beltran, Annette Cartona, Tony Plana. D: Haskell Wexler. DRA 108m. V

Latitude Zero 1969 Japanese ★★★ Some Western stars add pizzazz to this Japanese undersea adventure in which a gentle race of sea dwellers go to war to prevent an evil power from taking over. From the director of many Godzilla epics; fans and kids will enjoy. C: Joseph Cotten, Cesar Romero, Richard Jaeckel, Patricia Medina. D: Inshiro Honda. SFI [G] 99m.

Lauderdale 1990 ★★ Two guys, a beach, spring break, and bikini-clad co-eds. Not as much fun as the old beach-blanket movies, but still steamy and zany. C: Darrel Guilbeau, Michelle Kemp, Jeff Greenman. D: Bill Milling. COM [R] 91m. V

Laugh for Joy 1960 *See* **Passionate Thief, The**

Laughing Policeman, The 1974 ★★★½ The San Francisco Police Force track a psychopath who machine-gunned a crowded bus. Spicy location thriller and nice chemistry between Matthau and Dern. C: Walter Matthau, Bruce Dern, Louis Gossett, Jr. D: Stuart Rosenberg. ACT [R] 111m. V

Laughing Sinners 1931 ★★★ Salvation Army worker Gable saves nightclub singer Crawford from suicide, then manages to keep her on the straight and narrow until old flame Hamilton shows up. Early pairing of Gable and Crawford is hampered by a confused plot and ending that doesn't ring true. C: Joan Crawford, Clark Gable, Neil Hamilton, Marjorie Rambeau, Guy Kibbee. D: Harry Beaumont. DRA 72m. V

Laughter 1930 ★★★ Follies girl Carroll marries a wealthy, elderly broker, while true love March implores her to forsake money for happiness with him in Paris. Romantic comedy/drama is dated and suffers from early sound staginess. C: Frederic March, Nancy Carroll, Frank Morgan. D: Harry D'Arrast. COM 81m.

Laughter in Paradise 1951 British ★★★★ Clever comedy about rich prankster who leaves fortune to four relatives—provided they carry out fiendishly difficult tasks. Expert cast of British comics makes this wonderfully amusing. C: Alastair Sim, Joyce Grenfell, Hugh Griffith, Fay Compton. D: Mario Zampi. COM 95m.

Laura 1944 ★★★★★ A hard-boiled detective (Andrews) investigates a socialite's murder, and finds himself falling in love with the victim (Tierney). Classic whodunit, with a terrific twist midway through. Brilliant cast of suspects includes Webb as an erudite author and Price as a gigolo. Haunting theme music by David Raskin. From Vera Caspary's novel. C: Gene Tierney, Dana Andrews, Clifton Webb, Vincent Price, Judith Anderson. D: Otto Preminger. CRI 85m. V

Laura Lansing Slept Here 1988 ★★★ Celebrity author (Hepburn) has a bet with her agent that she can't survive with an ordinary family for a week. Star is game but gets little help from script. C: Katharine Hepburn, Karen Austin, Joel Higgins, Nicolas Surovy. D: George Schaefer. COM 100m.

Laurel and Hardy's Laughing 20s 1965 ★★★★½ Tribute to Stan and Oliver's silent work is a joyful compilation of great scenes from their finest shorts. A revelation for those who only know their sound films. Other noteworthy grab bags by Youngson include *Days of Thrills and Laughter*, *The Golden Age of Comedy*, and *When Comedy Was King*. C: Stan Laurel, Oliver Hardy, Charley Chase, James Finalyson. D: Robert Youngson. COM 90m. V

Lavender Hill Mob, The 1950 British ★★★★★ Classic British comedy about shy bank clerk (Guinness) who devises a foolproof scheme to rob a gold shipment, with the help of bumbling accomplices. Marvelous blend of action, adventure, and slapstick comedy, with final chase scene a masterpiece of comic timing. C: Alec Guinness, Stanley Holloway, Sidney James, Alfie Bass. D: Charles Crichton. COM 161m. V

L'Avventura 1960 French ★★★★★ When a pampered heiress disappears during vacation, her friends reexamine their own empty lives. Unique drama put Antonioni on the map; rigorous (and extremely slow) examination of various states of ennui spawned many pale imitations. C: Monica Vitti, Gabriele Ferzetti, Lea Massari. D: Michelangelo Antonioni. DRA 145m. V

Law and Disorder 1974 ★★★½ Disgusted by the rising amount of crime in their area, two blue-collar New Yorkers (O'Connor, Borgnine) decide to do something about it by becoming auxiliary cops. Offbeat social satire starts out as comedy, then veers into serious drama, with mixed results. C: Carroll O'Connor, Ernest Borgnine, Ann Wedgeworth, Karen Black. D: Ivan Passer. COM [R] 103m.

Law and Jake Wade, The 1958 ★★★½ A marshal with a checkered past helps an old friend to escape from jail—only to have his friend turn on him. Solid Western with fine star performances. C: Robert Taylor, Richard Widmark, Patricia Owens. D: John Sturges. WST 87m. V

Law and Order 1932 ★★★½ A top-notch officer, Doc Holliday, and Wyatt Earp team up to rid a wild cow town of the Clantons, who are corrupting the range. Stylish imagining of fabled Western heroes and villains. C: Walter Huston, Russell Hopton, Andy Devine, Walter Brennan. D: Edward Cahn. WST 70m.

Law and Order 1953 ★★★ An outlaw menaces the unruly town of Cottonwood, bringing a law officer out of retirement. Remake of 1932 film. C: Ronald Reagan, Dorothy Malone, Preston Foster. D: Nathan Juran. WST 80m.

Law and Order 1976 ★★★½ Adaptation of Dorothy Uhnak's best-seller about three generations of New York City Irish-American cops. Overlong drama features a good performance by McGavin, and does a decent job of showing that policemen aren't immune to human frailties and weaknesses. C: Darren McGavin, Keir Dullea, Robert Reed, Suzanne Pleshette, Teri Garr. D: Marvin Chomsky. DRA 150m. TVM

Law and the Lady, The 1951 ★★★ Third filming of Fredrick Lonsdale comedy *The Last of Mrs. Cheyney*, with miscast Garson as mischievous jewel thief teamed with Wilding to rob society swells. C: Greer Garson, Michael Wilding, Fernando Lamas, Marjorie Main. D: Edwin Knopf. COM 104m.

Law Is the Law, The 1959 French ★★★½ French customs official helps an Italian friend smuggle contraband over the French-Italian border. Mild comedy has some laughs, courtesy of top comic actors Fernandel and Toto. C: Fernandel, Toto, Mario Besozzi. D: Christian Jaque. COM 103m.

Law of Desire 1986 Spanish ★★★★ Gay filmmaker (Poncela) has enough complications in his life (his sister used to be his brother) and resists getting involved with ardent fan (Banderas). Outrageous comedy thriller revels in its own campy style. Stupendous performance by Maura as a transsexual. C: Eusebio Poncela, Carmen Maura, Antonio Banderas, Bibi Andersson. D: Pedro Almodóvar. COM 100m. V

Law of the Land 1976 ★★★ Sheriff and drifter team up to crack a seamy murder case on the frontier. C: Jim Davis, Don Johnson, Cal Bellini. D: Virgil Vogel. WST 100m. V

Law of the Lawless 1964 ★★★½ Former gunslinger turned circuit-riding judge, must clean up an outlaw-ridden town. Good supporting cast. C: Dale Robertson, Yvonne De Carlo, William Bendix, Bruce Cabot. D: William Claxton. WST 88m.

Law of the Pampas 1944 ★★★ Classic Hopalong Cassidy fare with Happy driving cattle to South America and fighting the local outlaws and his own gaucho foreman. C: William Boyd, Russell Hayden, Sidney Blackmer. D: Nate Watt. WST 54m. V

Lawless Breed, The 1952 ★★★½ Hudson, who turned to crime after his sweetheart was killed, finally stops running and goes to prison; he tries to save his son from following in his footsteps by telling his story. Decent Western occasionally bogs down in too much talk. C: Rock Hudson, Julia Adams, Hugh O'Brian. D: Raoul Walsh. WST 83m.

Lawless Eighties, The 1957 ★★★ Sagebrush yarn finds a gunslinger protecting a traveling clergyman from men in black hats. A good idea turned into an average flick. C: Buster Crabbe, John Smith. D: Joseph Kane. WST 70m.

Lawless Frontier 1935 ★★★ The Duke seeks to avenge the murder of his parents in the early West. Early Wayne, well-done. C: John Wayne, George "Gabby" Hayes, Sheila Terry. D: Robert Bradbury. WST 52m. V

Lawless Land, The 1988 ★★★ An idealistic couple flees the oppresive leader of post-apocalyptic America. C: Nick Corri, Amanda Peterson, Xander Berkeley. D: Jon Hess. SFI [R] 81m. V

Lawless Nineties, The 1936 ★★★ Government man (Wayne) defends the law in wild Wyoming territory, getting help from a moral journalist along the way. C: John Wayne, George "Gabby" Hayes. WST 56m. V

Lawless Range 1935 ★★★ Cowboy (Wayne) protects Pegueno Valley ranchers from merciless raiders. C: John Wayne, Sheila Mannors. D: Robert Bradbury. WST 53m. V

Lawless Street, A 1955 ★★ When his dancehall wife skips off, a hard-boiled marshall lets his responsibilities slide. Doesn't gel. C: Randolph Scott, Angela Lansbury, Warner Anderson, Ruth Donnelly. D: Joseph H. Lewis. WST 78m. V

Lawless, The 1950 ★★½ Journalist tries to defend young Mexican fruit picker against racial injustice in Southern California. Well-meaning, but strained and tepid. C: Gail Russell, Macdonald Carey, Lee Patrick. D: Joseph Losey. DRA 83m.

Lawman 1971 ★★★★ After a few drunken hooligans murder an old man and take over town, a marshal wanders in and finds the town against him. Tightly wrapped and full of violence. An excellent cast (Ryan is a standout) makes this a real winner. C: Burt Lancaster, Robert Ryan, Lee J. Cobb, Robert Duvall, Sheree North. D: Michael Winner. WST [PG] 95m. v

Lawnmower Man, The 1992 ★★½ Research scientist Brosnan uses computer technology to turn a retarded man (Fahey) into a wrathful superbeing. Stephen King lobbied to have his name taken off this unrecognizable adaptation of his short story. Computer-age special effects can't smarten up banal script. C: Jeff Fahey, Pierce Brosnan, Jenny Wright. D: Brett Leonard. SFI [R] 108m. v

Lawrence of Arabia 1962 British ★★★★★ Remarkable epic biography of British officer T.E. Lawrence leading the fight against Turkey in World War I Palestine. O'Toole brilliantly captures the contradictions and characteristics of the title character, and Lean's direction is expansive without sacrificing intelligence. Magnificently photographed. Winner of seven Oscars, including Best Picture and Director. C: Peter O'Toole, Alec Guinness, Anthony Quinn, Omar Sharif, Jack Hawkins, Anthony Quayle, Claude Rains, Arthur Kennedy, Jose Ferrer. D: David Lean. DRA [PG] 216m. v

Laws of Gravity 1991 ★★★½ Three days in the life of two small-time hoods, chronicling their relationships with women as well as their petty thievery. Shoestring budget and cinema verité camera accents seedy Brooklyn neighborhood setting in this absorbing character study. C: Peter Greene, Adam Trese, Edie Falco. D: Nick Gomez. DRA [R] 100m. v

Lawyer Man 1932 ★★★★ Entertaining crime comedy about an ambitious lawyer (Powell) framed for blackmail. Blondell plays his faithful secretary, and they make a great pair. C: William Powell, Joan Blondell, Alan Dinehart, Claire Dodd. D: William Dieterle. COM 72m.

Lazarus Syndrome, The 1979 ★★★★ A surgeon and a former patient try to trap a doctor with a loose grasp of the Hippocratic oath in this predictable but intriguing drama about medical ethics. C: Louis Gossett Jr., E.G. Marshall, Ron Hunter. D: Jerry Thorpe. DRA 90m. v

Lazybones 1925 ★★★★ Jones is an unambitious small-town character who alienates his sweetheart when he adopts her sister's daughter. Surprisingly good dramatic performance by the Western star and Borzage's sentimentally tasteful direction makes this silent film set in the early 1900s a treat. C: Charles Jones, Madge Bellamy, Virginia Marshall. D: Frank Borzage. DRA 79m.

LBJ: The Early Years 1986 ★★★½ Accurate account of Lyndon Baines Johnson (Quaid) from Texas youth in 1934 to his 1963 swearing in as President. Well acted (Lupone as Lady Bird as standout) but story lacks the drama of LBJ's White House years. C: Randy Quaid, Patti LuPone, Pat Hingle. D: Peter Werner. DRA 98m. v

Le Bal 1982 Italian ★★★★ One-of-a-kind mime/dance film, set in the same French ballroom over a 50-year period. Talented cast portrays several characters without a word of dialogue. Portrait of a nation surviving depression, war, and social unrest emerges in this subtle, stylized film. C: Christophe Allwright, Marc Berman, Regis Bouquet, Chantal Capron, Nani Noel. D: Ettore Scola. DRA 112m. v

Le Beau Mariage 1982 French ★★★★ Young woman ends an affair with a married man to find a husband of her own, only to fall in love with a man determined to remain uncommitted. Smart, witty comment on the contradictions of modern love and old-fashioned romance. C: Beatrice Romand, Andre Dussollier, Feodor Atkine. D: Andre Rohmer. DRA [PG] 97m. v

Le Beau Serge 1958 French ★★★★ Convalescent young man (Brialy) returns to his family's village and finds his childhood friend a troubled alcoholic. Perceptive study of city vs. country, as well as the duties of friendship. Considered first film of the French New Wave; also Chabrol's first feature. C: Jean-Claude Brialy, Gerard Blain, Michele Meritz, Bernadette LaFont. D: Claude Chabrol. DRA 97m.

Le Bonheur 1965 French ★★★★ Married man tries to convince his wife he can be devoted to her and his mistress at the same time. A powerful and perceptive morality tale still capable of causing controversy. C: Jean-Claude Drouot, Claire Drouot, Sandrine Drouot. D: Agnes Varda. DRA 87m.

Le Boucher 1969 French ★★★★ Small-town schoolteacher (Audran) wooed by shy butcher (Yanne) discovers he is responsible for a grisly murder. Classic thriller coupled with a complex psychological examination of repression. Strong performances and a great script make this one of Chabrol's finest efforts. C: Stephane Audran, Jean Yanne, Antonio Passallia. D: Claude Chabrol. CRI [PG] 93m. v

Le Cas du Docteur Laurent 1957 French ★★★½ Small town resists attempts by doctor (Gabin) to introduce natural birthing methods to the community. Low-key Gabin adds authority to this lightweight tale. C: Jean Gabin, Nicole Courcel, Sylvia Montfort, Arius Daxely. D: Jean-Paul LeChanois, Jean Orabin. DRA 93m. v

Le Cavaleur 1978 French ★★★½ A concert pianist is easily distracted by the women in his life. Breezy and often amusing comedy is delivered à la mode in amiable De Broca style. (a.k.a. *Practice Makes Perfect*) C: Jean Rochefort, Nicole Garcia, Annie Girardot. D: Phillippe De-Broca. COM 104m. v

Le Caviar Rouge 1985 French ★★ Two KGB spies spend an evening under the watchful eye of their superior, who is trying to determine who double-crossed him. Drama was a vanity project for director/star Hossein (his wife Patou plays other spy). C: Robert Hossein, Candice Patou, Ivan Desny. D: Robert Hossein. DRA [PG] 91m.

Le Complot 1973 French ★★★★ A group of leftist rebels battle Gaulists and police over DeGaulle's decision to pull out of Algeria. Conspiracy thriller maintains taut interest throughout with vivid Franco-Algerian war background. (a.k.a. The Conspiracy) C: Michel Bouquet, Jean Rochefort. D: Rene Gainville. CRI 120m. V

Le Corbeau 1943 French ★★★★½ A small town in France is torn apart by a mysterious poison-pen campaign. A harsh, intelligent study of provincial characters, this thriller was controversial for having been sponsored and financed by the Nazis. Remade in the U.S. as *The Thirteenth Letter.* (a.k.a. The Raven) C: Pierre Fresnay, Ginette Leclerc, Helena Manson. D: Henri-Georges Clouzot. DRA 92m. V

Le Crabe Tambour 1977 French ★★★★½ Trio of sailors (Perrin, Rich, and Dufilho) reminisce about famous captain (Rochefort) with whom they once served. Expertly dovetails many flashbacks with present story; well acted and directed, superbly photographed (by Raoul Coutard). C: Jean Rochefort, Claude Rich, Jacques Dufilho, Jacques Perrin. D: Pierre Schoendoerffer. DRA 120m. V

Le Cri du Hibou 1987 French/Italian ★★★★★ Seemingly harmless voyeurism causes a series of grisly murders. This quiet psychological thriller builds steadily to a powerful climax. One of Chabrol's best, adapted from a Patricia Highsmith novel. C: Christophe Malavoy, Mathilda May, Virginie Thevenet. D: Claude Chabrol. CRI 102m.

Le Dernier Combat 1984 French ★★★½ Stylish fantasy of a postnuclear world without speech, and the attempts of few survivors to pick up the pieces. Notable use of CinemaScope. Besson's directorial debut; people either loved it or hated it. C: Pierre Jolivet, Jean Bouise, Fritz Wepper. D: Luc Besson. SFI [R] 90m. V

Le Doulos 1963 French ★★★★★ An informer wants to rat on the syndicate. Classic French film noir is a spine tingler with the excellent Belmondo leading a splendid cast. Director Melville was a devotee of American gangster films, and it shows. C: Jean-Paul Belmondo. D: Jean-Pierre Mellville. CRI 108m.

Le Feu Follet 1958 *See* **Time to Love and a Time to Die, A**

Le Gai Savoir 1968 France ★★★★ Two militants from another world sit and chat about life on Earth. Great for students of Godard's films, but *Savior* will be a trial for the uninitiated. Made for, but rejected by, French TV. C: Juliet Berto, Jean-Pierre Leaud. D: Jean-Luc Godard. DRA 95m.

Le Gentleman D'Epsom 1962 France ★★★½ Con artist (Gabin) finds it hard to give up his life of leisure. Then a lady comes along and turns his life upside down. Light comedy gets an extra boost from Jean. C: Jean Gabin, Paul Frankeur. COM 83m.

Le Golem: The Lend of Prague 1935 French ★★★★½ In this classic film shot in Czechoslovokia at the onset of WWII, the Jews of Prague use Jewish mysticism and Talmudic legend in an attempt to insulate themselves against persecution and fend off pogroms. Period piece with striking parallels to pre-WWII Prague. C: Harry Baur, Roger Karl, Charles Dorat. D: Julien Duvivier. DRA 96m. V

Le Grand Chemin 1987 French ★★★★ Young boy (Hubert, son of director) comes of age spending summer with relatives while Mom's pregnant; tender tale eschews sentimentality for hard realities of growing up, with wonderful children's performances. American remake, *Paradise.* (a.k.a. *The Grand Highway* C: Anemone, Richard Bohringer. D: Jean-Loup Hubert. DRA 104m. V

Le Joli Mai 1962 French ★★★★½ France is at peace for the first time in 23 years! This documentary about Parisian life at the end of the Algerian war is a classic in its field. Brilliant work from director Marker. D: Chris Marker. DOC 190m.

Le Jouet 1976 French ★★½ A spoiled brat buys a new toy to embarrass his heartless father: a man. Excessively broad comedy, with most of its laughs in bad taste; still superior to U.S. remake, *The Toy.* C: Pierre Richard, Michel Bouquet, Fabrice Greco. D: Francis Veber. COM [PG] 92m.

Le Jour Se Leve 1939 French ★★★★★ Classic film studies trapped killer's reminiscences about how he got where he is. Gabin outstanding as murderer; poet Jacques Prevert's script and Maurice Jaubert's score blended expressively by director Carne. Remade in the U.S. as *The Long Night.* (a.k.a. *Daybreak*) C: Jean Gabin, Jacqueline Laurent, Jules Berry, Arletty. D: Marcel Carne. DRA 85m. V

Le Magnifique 1976 French ★★★½ A spy novelist dreams that he's his own hero, engaging in a series of adventures with next door neighbor Bisset. Amusing though uneven French satire of James Bond movies, with Belmondo perfectly cast in the lead. C: Jean-Paul Belmondo, Jacqueline Bisset. D: Phillippe De Broca. COM 84m. V

Le Mans 1971 ★★★½ McQueen is a racer who overcomes adversity to enter the famous 24-hour Grand Prix endurance race. Lack of dramatic subplot may cause non-racing fans to lose interest, but the authentic Le Mans footage is breathtaking. C: Steve McQueen, Siegfried Rauch, Elga Andersen. D: Lee H. Katzin. DRA [G] 106m. V

Le Million 1931 *See* **Million, The**

Le Petit Amour 1989 ★★½ Middle-aged woman (Birkin) has affair with 15-year-old boy (Demy) obsessed with video game. Intriguing theme. (a.k.a. *Kung Fu Master*) C: Jane Birkin, Mathieu Demy, Charlote Gainsbourg, Lou Doillon. D: Agnes Varda. DRA [R] 80m. v

Le Petit Soldat 1965 French ★★★★ Controversial film about a man with no ideas and the nihilistic youth of Paris. Banned in England for three years, this minor (but occasionally stirring) Godard film looks relatively tame today. A must for fans of the director; others might want to pass. C: Michel Subor, Anna Karina, Henri-Jacques Huet. D: Jean-Luc Godard. DRA 88m.

Le Petit Theatre de Jean Renoir 1969 *See* **Little Theatre of Jean Renoir, The**

Le Plaisir 1951 French ★★★★ A trio of Guy de Maupassant tales about pleasure-induced pain is brought to vivid life by Ophuls, whose trademark camerawork is at its fluid best. French version narrated by Jean Servais; English version by Peter Ustinov. C: Jean Gabin, Danielle Darrieux, Simone Simon, Claude Dauphin. D: Max Ophuls. DRA 97m. v

Le Puritain 1937 French ★★½ Secret cult takes on responsibility of policing morals in society, eventually leading one member (Barrault) to murder a young woman. Once an interesting take on the dangers of extremists in society, but dated. C: Jean-Louis Barrault, Pierre Fresnay, Viviane Romance, Mady Berry. D: Jeff Musso. DRA 87m.

Le Rayon Vert 1986 *See* **Summer**

Le Repos du Guerrier 1962 French ★★★½ Suicidal man is saved by a virtuous young woman—she falls for him and he brings ruin upon her. Brigitte plays the good girl for a change, in this fair tale of obsession. C: Brigitte Bardot, Robert Hossein, James Robertson Justice. D: Roger Vadim. DRA 100m. v

Le Roman d'un Tricheur 1992 *See* **Story of a Cheat, The**

Le Rouge et le Noir 1954 French ★★★★★ Ambitious tutor (Philipe) has affair with mother of children he teaches (Darrieux), then becomes a priest. Picturesque, if not exactly faithful adaptation of Stendal's complex novel has superlative acting and handsome cinematography. C: Gerard Philipe, Danielle Darrieux, Antonella Lualdi. D: Claude Lara. DRA 145m.

Le Samourai 1967 French ★★★★★ Dark, brooding gangster film about a hitman (Delon) filling a contract against his better judment, with cops tracking his every move. Eerie, stylized film has scant dialogue, but uses its soundtrack brilliantly. One of the great crime films. C: Alain Delon, Nathalie Delon, Francois Perier, Cathy Rosier, Jacques Leroy. D: Jean-Pierre Melville. CRI 95m.

Le Secret 1974 French ★★★★ An escaped prisoner (Trintignant) takes writer and wife hostage in the mountains. Tense psychological thriller takes poke at well-meaning liberals who keep falling for the damnedest lies. Subtle and rewarding. C: Jean-Louis Trintignant, Philippe Noiret, Jean-Francois Adam. D: Robert Enrico. CRI 103m.

Le Sex Shop 1973 French ★★★½ Failing bookstore owner (Berri) begins selling pornography and business skyrockets. Silly farce has good comic turns from Romand and Marielle. C: Claude Berri, Juliet Berto, Nathalie Delon, Beatrice Romand, Jean-Pierre Marielle. D: Claude Berri. COM [R] 92m. v

Le Silence Est d'Or 1947 *See* **Man about Town**

Le Voyage en Douce 1980 French ★★★½ Two women go off together away from men, and briefly create an all-purpose relationship—emotional, sexual—for a short time. Unfortunately, DeVille substitutes anecdotes and vignettes for penetrating psychology. C: Dominique Sanda, Geraldine Chaplin. D: Michel Deville. DRA 98m.

Leadbelly 1976 ★★★½ Mosley's terrific in title role of folksinging legend Huddie Ledbetter, who endured years on chain gangs in Texas and Louisiana. C: Roger Mosley, Paul Benjamin, Madge Sinclair. D: Gordon Parks. MUS [PG] 126m.

Leader of the Band 1988 ★★ Oddball music teacher (Landesberg) rallies a ragtag group of misfits and transforms them into a crack high school marching band. Landesberg's performance is flippant, but there are few laughs in this clichéd teen comedy. C: Steve Landesberg, Mercedes Ruehl. D: Nessa Hyams. COM [PG] 90m. v

League of Gentlemen, The 1960 British ★★★★ When a precision Army commander is forced into retirement after 25 years of distinguished service, he decides to use his military skills to stage the perfect bank robbery. Hysterical comedy musters a regiment of laughs thanks to a well-executed screenplay. C: Jack Hawkins, Nigel Patrick, Roger Livesey, Richard Attenborough, Bryan Forbes, Nanette Newman. D: Basil Dearden. COM 115m. v

League of Their Own, A 1992 ★★★★ Nostalgic homage to women's baseball league during WWII, with Davis as the natural athlete who dominates the sport. Strong work from Hanks as alcoholic coach, and Madonna is well used as All-the-Way Mae. High-spirited fun. C: Tom Hanks, Geena Davis, Madonna, Lori Petty, Jon Lovitz, Rosie O'Donnell, David Strathairn, Garry Marshall. D: Penny Marshall. COM [PG] 126m. v

Lean on Me 1989 ★★★★ Freeman gives a vigorous performance as a controversial New Jersey high school principal who cleans up his school and wins the hearts of his students in this formulaic but energetic and engaging version of true story. C: Morgan Freeman, Beverly Todd, Robert Guillaume. D: John G. Avildsen. DRA [PG-13] 109m. v

Leap into the Void 1979 Italian ★★★★★ Very unusual comedy about a judge who plans to drive his mentally ill sister to suicide, as a form of euthanasia. Much more compassionate than it sounds; possibly Bellocchio's warmest film. Brilliantly acted by Piccoli and Aimee. C: Michel Piccoli, Anouk Aimee, Michele Placido. D: Marco Bellocchio. COM 120m.

Leap of Faith 1992 ★★★★ A conning evangelist (Martin) gets stranded in a small Kansas town. When he sets up to bilk the locals, he gets a lesson about faith. A real sleeper, this film is a gentle but canny satire, filled with strong performances. Rock star Meat Loaf does a nice turn as the bus driver. C: Steve Martin, Debra Winger, Lolita Davidovich, Liam Neeson, Lukas Haas. D: Richard Pearce. DRA [PG-13] 110m. v

Learning Curve ★★★½ The fact-based story of Don Castro's career as a motorcycle racer, and the inspiration he drew from his father. C: Roger Gutierrez, Adrianne Valle, Enrique Esparza. D: Tom Naygrow. DRA [PG] 90m. v

Learning Tree, The 1969 ★★★★ Parks adapted his autobiographical novel to the screen, about growing up in black Kansas and coping with racism. Amiable enough and beautifully shot. Inducted into the National Film Registry. C: Kyle Johnson, Alex Clarke, Estelle Evans. D: Gordon Parks. DRA [PG] 107m. v

Lease of Life 1954 British ★★★½ Donat is the dying vicar of a small village parish who tries to raise money so that his daughter can attend a London music school. Donat's strong, moving performance elevates this unevenly scripted British drama. C: Robert Donat, Kay Walsh, Denholm Elliott. D: Charles Frend. DRA 94m.

Leather Boys, The 1963 British ★★★★ Interesting study of motorcycle subculture in England with Campbell as biker who'd rather spend time with his chum (Sutton) than with his wife (Tushingham). Strong homosexual subtext, but nothing overt. C: Rita Tushingham, Colin Campbell, Dudley Sutton. D: Sidney J. Furie. DRA 107m. v

Leather Burners 1943 ★★★ Interesting Hopalong Cassidy adventure in which he uncovers a plot to rustle cattle and hide them in a mine. C: William Boyd, Robert Mitchum. D: Joseph E. Henabery. WST 58m. v

Leather Jackets 1992 ★★ Innocent lovers (Sweeney and Fonda) try to help friend/gang member (Elwes) who's killed a mobster. Low-voltage, urban nightmare; wonderful young cast. C: D. B. Sweeney, Bridget Fonda, Cary Elwes. D: Lee Drysdale. CRI [R] 91m. v

Leather Saint, The 1956 ★★★ Priest Derek dons boxing gloves to raise money for polio victims while reforming alcoholic nightclub singer Lawrence. Overly sentimental drama mixes familiar boxing movie clichés with soap opera elements. C: Paul Douglas, John Derek, Jody Lawrence, Cesar Romero. D: Alvin Ganzer. DRA 86m.

Leatherface: Texas Chainsaw Massacre III 1989 ★★ Yet another attempt to recapture the excitement of the classic original, with the chainsaw gang terrorizing a trio of hapless travelers. Ineffective sequel, not helped by extensive pre-release re-editing, including a ridiculous ending. Contains graphic violence. C: Kate Hodge, Ken Foree, William Butler, R.A. Mihailoff, Viggo Mortensen, Joe Unger. D: Jeff Burr. HOR [R] 82m. v

Leave All Fair 1985 New Zealand ★★★★ John Middleton Murry (Gielgud), widower of New Zealand author Katherine Mansfield, recalls their life together while editing a book of her letters. Birkin plays both the prickly writer and the lover of Murry's publisher. A subtle and evocative drama. C: John Gielgud, Jane Birkin, Feodor Atkine. D: John Reid. DRA 88m. TVM

Leave 'Em Laughing 1981 ★★★½ A Chicago clown (Rooney) and his wife (Jackson), though in sore financial straits, care for dozens of needy children; then he's stricken with terminal cancer. Fact-based story is a solid tearjerker; Rooney is fine. C: Mickey Rooney, Anne Jackson, Red Buttons. D: Jackie Cooper. DRA 103m. TVM v

Leave Her to Heaven 1945 ★★★★ Entertaining melodrama with Tierney as astonishingly beautiful but deadly wife destroying everything she touches, even from the grave. Builds suspense nicely until the neat courtroom climax. C: Gene Tierney, Cornel Wilde, Jeanne Crain, Vincent Price. D: John Stahl. DRA 110m. v

Leave It to Blondie 1945 ★★★ A songwriting contest means trouble for Blondie and Dagwood in this typical series entry. C: Penny Singleton, Arthur Lake, Larry Simms, Marjorie Kent. D: Abby Berlin. COM 75m.

Leaves from Satan's Book 1919 Danish ★★★½ Multilayered silent drama has Satan wreaking havoc in four different eras. Impressive. Early work from Danish master Dreyer borrows heavily from *Intolerence* but lacks its lucidity. (a.k.a. *Blade of Satan's Boy*) C: Helge Nissen, Halvard Hoff, Jacob Texiere. D: Carl Dreyer. DRA 133m.

Leaving Normal 1992 ★★★½ Low-key comedy about a disgruntled cocktail waitress who takes to the road with her mousy friend in search of adventure. Lahti's absorbing performance keeps quirky excursion on the right track. C: Christine Lahti, Meg Tilly, Lenny Von Dohlen. D: Edward Zwick. COM [R] 110m. v

Lecheria De Zacarias, La 1987 Spain ★★★ The hilarious misadventure of two milkmen who fight burglars, the police, and the health inspectors, & husbands. C: Olivia Collins, Sergio Ramos, Cesar Bono. D: Victor Ugalde. COM 92m. v

L'Eclisse 1962 *See* **Eclipse, The**

L'École Buissonière 1951 *See* **Passion for Life**

Leech Woman, The 1959 ★★ Unpersuasive horror tale offers little but good performance by Gray as aging woman who commits a string of murders and drains victims' pituitary fluid, which can rejuvenate her. C: Coleen Gray, Grant Williams. D: Edward Dein. HOR 77m. V

Left for Dead 1978 ★★★ Based on a true story, a wealthy man proves he is innocent of his wife's murder, but discovers all his friends want to see him dead anyway. C: Elke Sommer, Donald Pilon. D: Murray Markowitz. CRI 82m. V

Left Hand of God, The 1955 ★★ In China after WWII, an American aviator poses as a priest to evade a dangerous warlord. Strange and slow moving. C: Humphrey Bogart, Gene Tierney, Lee J. Cobb, Agnes Moorehead, E.G. Marshall. D: Edward Dmytryk. ACT 87m. V

Left-Handed Gun, The 1958 ★★★½ Billy the Kid goes after four hombres who shot his buddy dead. Interesting rendition of Vidal's play. Young Newman makes a fine Billy, although his "method" style may not be to all tastes. C: Paul Newman, Lita Milan, John Dehner. D: Arthur Penn. WST 102m. V

Left-Handed Woman, The 1978 German ★★★★ After forcing her husband to leave her, silent woman withdraws from her family. Extremely demanding, slow-moving study of alienation has rewards for those who stay with it. Exceptional Robby Muller photography. C: Edith Clever, Bruno Ganz, Michel Lonsdale. D: Peter Handke. DRA 119m.

Left Right and Center 1961 British ★★★½ Two political opponents discover mutual attraction. Enjoyable comedy; moneymad Sim gets the biggest laughs. C: Ian Carmichael, Patricia Bredin, Alastair Sim. D: Sidney Gilliat. COM 95m.

Legacy 1975 ★★★ A bored rich woman (Hotchkis) can't find anything to do with her life and slowly loses her grip. Interesting concept; good lead; but finally not compelling. Hotchkis also wrote screenplay from her own play. C: Joan Hotchkis, George McDaniel, Sean Allen. D: Karen Arthur. DRA [R] 90m.

Legacy for Leonette, A 1986 ★★ An innocent young girl is led down a path toward romance, then murder. Low-budget romantic drama. C: Loyita Chapel, Michael Anderson Jr., Dinah Anne Rogers. DRA 100m. V

Legacy of Lies 1992 ★★★ Rogue cop Landau decides to sacrifice himself for his honest policeman son Ontkean when the latter becomes involved in a political scheme while investigating a murder. Script relies on too familiar moral dilemmas and fails to craft three-dimensional characters. C: Michael Ontkean, Martin Landau, Eli Wallach, Joe Morton. D: Bradford May. CRI [R] 94m. V

Legacy, The 1979 ★★★ Creative, scary supernatural death scenes spark this schematic horror film set in a British mansion, where an eccentric family and American guests (Ross and Elliott) find that the inheritance they hope to collect is death. C: Katharine Ross, Sam Elliott, John Standing, Margaret Tyzack, Roger Daltrey. D: Richard Marquand. HOR [R] 100m. V

Legal Eagles 1986 ★★★½ Oddball artist Hannah is suspected of murder. Enter laidback Redford and fiery Winger as warring lawyers who become lovers in this romantic comedy. Stars are no Tracy and Hepburn, but they do manage to make this fairly entertaining. C: Robert Redford, Debra Winger, Daryl Hannah, Brian Dennehy, Terence Stamp. D: Ivan Reitman. COM [PG] 116m. V

Legal Tender 1990 ★★★ The owner of a Venice Beach bar is pressured by the local bank president to add some sexual favors to the interest on a loan. As the corruption gets seedier, a murder threatens to unmask his various scams. C: Robert Davi, Tanya Roberts, Morton Downey, Jr. D: Jag Mundhra. CRI [R] 93m. V

Legend 1986 British ★½ Cruise, the keeper of unicorns in a mythical time and place, must avenge the murder of a unicorn by the Prince of Darkness. A waste of good effects, elaborate make-up, the director's talents, and ultimately, the viewer's time. Curry's not bad, though. C: Tom Cruise, Mia Sara, Tim Curry. D: Ridley Scott. SFI [PG] 89m. V

Legend of Alfred Packer, The 1979 ★★★ Five greenhorns trek into the Colorado Rockies around the turn of the century in fruitless search for a lost gold mine. C: Patrick Dray, Ron Haines. WST [PG] 95m. V

Legend of Big Foot, The 1982 ★★★ Recounting of the Big Foot legend has the hairy beast murdering the population of an out-of-the-way town. C: Stafford Morgan, Katherine Hopkins. D: Bill Rebane. SFI [G] 92m. V

Legend of Billie Jean, The 1985 ★★★ Falsely accused of committing various crimes, a brother and sister escape the police and become modern Texas folk heroes. Okay for what it is. C: Helen Slater, Keith Gordon, Christian Slater. D: Matthew Robbins. ACT [PG-13] 92m. V

Legend of Black Thunder Mountain, The 1979 ★★★ Feature-length kids' pic about the mysterious goings-on at a remote mountain spot. C: Holly Beeman, Steve Beeman, F. A. Milovich. D: Tom Beemer. FAM/ACT [G] 90m. V

Legend of Boggy Creek 1975 ★★★ Horror film in the form of allegedly true documentary about a bigfoot-like creature inhabiting a swamp in Arkansas. What would be grade-Z horror is salvaged by interesting approach featuring "interviews" with witnesses. C: Willie E. Smith, John Nixon. D: Charles B. Pierce. HOR [G] 87m. V

Legend of Earl Durand, The 1986 ★★★½ Oddball western about a boy who's kept isolated from the world because he may have a highly contagious illness. Worth catching. C: Peter Haskell, Martin Sheen, Keenan Wynn, Slim Pickens. D: John D. Patterson. WST [PG] 100m. V

Legend of Frenchie King, The 1971 French

★★ A group of female outlaws get involved with oil at a 19th-century French settlement in New Mexico. Disjointed role-reversal Western, with Bardot and others little more than window dressing. (a.k.a. *The Petroleum Girls* and *The Oil Girls*) C: Brigitte Bardot, Claudia Cardinale, Michael J. Pollard. D: Christian-Jaque. WST [R] 96m. v

Legend of Hell House, The 1973 British ★★★★ Parapsychologists discover that the windowless house they're investigating is truly haunted. Familiar story is genuinely frightening here, thanks to creative horror scenes and a well-plotted script by Richard Matheson (adapting his novel *Hell House*). C: Roddy McDowall, Pamela Franklin, Clive Revill. D: John Hough. HOR [PG] 94m. v

Legend of Hillbilly Johnson 1973 *See* **Who Fears the Devil**

Legend of Jedediah Carver, The 1973 ★★★ Average oater of an iron willed rancher who's abandoned in the desert, fighting native Americans and the brutal heat to save himself. C: De Witt Lee, Joshua Hoffman, Val Chapman. D: De Witt Lee. WST [PG] 90m. v

Legend of Lizzie Borden, The 1975 ★★★★ Blend of fact and fiction about the New England spinster who alledgedly murdered her father and stepmother with an axe. Montgomery is effective in well-written drama that presumes its subject's innocence. C: Elizabeth Montgomery, Ed Flanders, Fionnuala Flanagan. D: Paul Wendkos. DRA 100m. TVM

Legend of Lobo, The 1962 ★★★½ Disney nature picture follows the life of a wolf cub as he matures to adulthood. Interesting for younger audiences and narration is geared toward their understanding. Catchy tunes sung by Sons of the Pioneers. C: Rex Allen. D: James Algar. FAM/DRA [G] 67m. v

Legend of Lylah Clare, The 1968 ★★★½ Cult melodrama with Finch as Hollywood director obsessed with dead movie-star wife, who transforms Novak into her carbon copy. Wildly uneven, sometimes gripping, sometimes laughable. C: Kim Novak, Peter Finch, Ernest Borgnine, Valentina Cortese. D: Robert Aldrich. DRA 130m.

Legend of Nigger Charley, The 1972 ★ Black exploitation goes West, with Williamson as ex-slave on frontier. This atrocious low-budget film misrepresents real historical record of black cowboys and is filled with anachronisms and bad acting. Even worse sequel, *The Soul of Nigger Charley*. C: Fred Williamson, D'Urville Martin, Don Colley. D: Martin Goldman. WST [PG] 98m.

Legend of Sleepy Hollow, The 1979 ★★★ Jeff Goldblum is featured in this retelling of Washington Irving's "Legend of Ichabod Crane and the Headless Horsemen." Minor spook tale for younger audiences. C: Jeff Goldblum, Dick Butkus, Meg Foster. D: Henning Schellerup. FAM/DRA [PG] 100m. TVM v

Legend of Suram Fortress, The 1985 Georgian/Russian ★★★★ When a newly built fortess collapses, a superstitous village offers up a young man for sacrifice. Colorful characterizations and zesty locale work highlight this provocative medieval folk tale. C: Levan Outchanechvili, Zourab Kipchidze. D: Sergei Paradjanov. DRA 89m. v

Legend of the Bayou 1976 *See* **Eaten Alive**

Legend of the Dinosaurs ★★★ A geologist and photographer seek their fortunes by searching for a dinosaur egg in an underwater cave, but unfortunately they come face to face with the parent. Moderately suspenseful horror tale. HOR [PG] 92m. v

Legend of the Eight Samurai 1984 ★★½ A princess, struggling with the loss of her clan and aided only by unseasoned samurai, must battle against warrior phantoms. C: Hiroku Yokoshimaru, Sonny Chiba. D: Haruki Kaduwara. ACT 130m. v

Legend of the Holy Drinker, The 1988 Italian ★★★★ A homeless man (Hauer, who's surprisingly good), haunted by past failures, gets a chance to make good when a stranger gives him money. As with many Olmi films, the silences are often as insightful as any dialogue. Quiet, superior drama. C: Rutger Hauer, Anthony Quayle, Sandrine Dumas. D: Ermanno Olmi. DRA 125m.

Legend of the Lone Ranger, The 1981 ★★ When outlaws bushwhack a company of Texas Rangers, our hero is saved by a wandering Indian, then tames a white mustang and dons a mask to seek retribution. Well-written but poorly acted and violent version of Fran Striker's popular '30s radio and '50s TV hero. C: Klinton Spilsbury, Michael Horse, Christopher Lloyd, Jason Robards. D: William A. Fraker. WST 98m. v

Legend of the Lost 1957 ★★★ Two treasure hunters in the Sahara both make claim to an exotically beautiful slave. Star power and desert photography almost save this uneven jumble. C: John Wayne, Sophia Loren, Rossano Brazzi. D: Henry Hathaway. DRA 109m. v

Legend of the Northwest 1978 ★★★½ A wild dog, who can hold its own against wolves and bears, saves the life of a young girl, but later is hunted by her father who is unaware of the deed. Satisfactory nature/adventure drama is suitable fare for younger viewers. C: Marshall Reed, Denver Pyle. FAM/DRA [PG] 83m.

Legend of the Werewolf 1975 British ★★ Wolfman (Rintoul) kills off clients of the brothel where the girl he loves works; police pathologist (Cushing) sets out to stop him. Unimaginative direction fails to add much to the formula. C: Peter Cushing, Ron Moody, Hugh Griffith, David Rintool. D: Freddie Francis. HOR 90m. v

Legend of the White Horse 1985 U.S. ★★ While traveling through a mythical land, geologist (Lloyd) gets wrapped up with black magic, bad guys, and a magical white horse. Violent and confusing, this poorly made, would-be family film is a complete waste of time. C: Christopher Lloyd, Dee Wallace Stone. D: Jerzy Domaradski. FAM/SFI 91m. v

Legend of the Wolfwoman 1976 ★★½ Cursed ancestry haunts a young woman who can do nothing to stop her cyclical murders. C: Anne Borel, Frederick Stafford. D: R. D. Silver. HOR [R] 84m. v

Legend of Valentino, The 1975 ★★½ Movie does little to illuminate the mysteries surrounding silent-movie idol's life and death. Glossy presentation, okay performances. C: Franco Nero, Suzanne Pleshette, Judd Hirsch, Lesley Ann Warren, Milton Berle. D: Melville Shavelson. DRA 100m. TVM

Legend of Walks Far Woman, The 1980 ★★★ Colin Stuart's novel was adapted as showpiece for Welch's TV debut. The saga of a group of American Indians toward the end of the 19th century as seen through the eyes of an elderly woman (Welch is 102 years old at end). Passable Western adventure. C: Raquel Welch, Bradford Dillman. D: Mel Damski. WST 120m. TVM v

Legend of Wisely 1986 Cantonese ★★★½ Special-effects filled quest to find a priceless stolen Himalayan black pearl. Exotic settings. C: Sam Hui, Teddy Robin Dwan, Ti Lung. D: Teddy Robin Kwan. ACT 100m. v

Legend, The 1976 *See* **James Dean**

Legendary Champions, The 1968 ★★★★ Colorful documentary focusing on heavyweight boxing title-holders from John L. Sullivan to Gene Tunney. Narrated by Norman Rose. D: Harry Chapin. DOC 77m.

Legendary Weapons of Kung Fu 1982 Chinese ★★★ A martial arts master becomes a marked man when he refuses to work for a deadly eunuch. Deadly, indeed. C: Liu Chia-Liang, Fu Sheng. D: Liu Chia-Liang. ACT 110m. v

Legends of the Fall 1994 ★★★★ Sumptuous Western romance puts Ormond in an all-male ranch family, engaged to one brother (Thomas), but attracted to another (Pitt). Hopkins adds a stern father-figure, in this complex story, from Jim Harrison's novella. Should be seen in wide-screen format, if possible, to fully appreciate the Oscar-winning cinematography. C: Brad Pitt, Anthony Hopkins, Aidan Quinn, Julia Ormond, Henry Thomas. D: Edward Zwick. WST [R] 133m. v

Legion of Iron 1990 ★★★ Innocent lovers descend into a brutal underworld ruled by a cruel and envious queen. C: Kevin T. Walsh, Camille Carrigan, Erica Nann, Reggie De Morton. D: Yakov Bentsvi. ACT [R] 90m. v

Legs 1983 ★★★½ Backstage look at what it takes to be a Radio City Music Hall Rockette. Pleasant nonsense enlivened by Broadway star Verdon as jaded choreographer. C: Gwen Verdon, John Heard, Sheree North. D: Jerrold Freedman. DRA 91m. TVM v

Lemon Drop Kid, The 1934 ★★★ Fair version of Damon Runyon tale about reformed racetrack con artist Tracy's past catching up to him. That's Ann Sheridan as "doll" at the track. Compare to the remake with Bob Hope. C: Lee Tracy, Helen Mack, William Frawley, Baby LeRoy. D: Marshall Neilan. COM 71m.

Lemon Drop Kid, The 1951 ★★★★ Good showcase for Hope as a racetrack gangster who owes major bucks. Second, better version of Damon Runyon story; original done in 1934. C: Bob Hope, Marilyn Maxwell, Lloyd Nolan, Jane Darwell, William Frawley. D: Sidney Lanfield. COM 91m. v

Lemon Sisters, The 1990 ★★½ Three female friends must choose between their unhappy lives and their unhappier career as an Atlantic City lounge act. A wonderful cast stranded in half-baked, joke-impaired story. C: Diane Keaton, Carol Kane, Kathryn Grody, Elliott Gould. D: Joyce Chopra. DRA [PG-13] 93m. v

Lemon Sky 1987 ★★★★ A young drifter (Bacon) shakes up his newly married father's household; sort of a Midwestern take on the Greek tragedy of *Phaedra*. Lanford Wilson's play gets a strong production, with fine performances from Bacon and Crouse. C: Kevin Bacon, Lindsay Crouse, Tom Atkins, Kyra Sedgwick. D: Jan Egleson. DRA 90m. TVM

Lemonade Joe 1967 Czech ★★★½ Czech spoof of American Westerns (the hero drinks sweet stuff instead of hard liquor) has its share of laughs, until it runs out of steam midway. C: Carl Fiala, Olga Schoberova, Veta Fialova. D: Oldrich Lipsky. COM 84m.

Lena: My 100 Children 1987 ★★★★½ Lavin plays the Jewish teacher who helped smuggle 100 children out of Poland after WWII. Lavin gives a powerful performance in this movie based on the autobiography of Lena Kuchler-Silberman. C: Linda Lavin, Leonore Harris. D: Ed Sherin. DRA 100m. TVM

Lena's Holiday 1990 ★★★½ Teen from former East Germany making long-awaited trip to L.A. finds chaos, confusion, and culture shock. C: Felicity Waterman, Chris Lemmon, Noriyuki "Pat" Morita. D: Michael Keusch. COM [PG-13] 97m. v

L'Enfant Sauvage 1969 French ★★★★½ True story of boy who is raised in wilderness and who slowly learns to be civilized. Low-key but affecting dramatization, with director Truffaut as boy's patient teacher. Evocative b&w photography, effective use of silent movie tricks like wipes and irises. A gem. (a.k.a. *The Wild Child*) C: Francois Truffaut, Jean-Pierre Cargol. D: Francois Truffaut. DRA [G] 85m. v

L'Enfer 1994 French ★★★½ Man consumed with jealousy may or may not be married to an adulteress. Stylish psychological thriller doesn't pay off, but is intriguing for most of its length. C: Francois Cluzet, Emmanuelle Beart, Nathalie Cardone. D: Claude Chabrol. DRA 100m.

Leningrad Cowboys Go America 1989 Finnish ★★★★ World's worst rock band leaves Finland for disastrous tour of the States. Hilarious deadpan comedy. C: Matti Pellonpaa, Kari Vaananen, Jim Jarmusch. D: Aki Kaurismaki. COM [PG-13] 78m. v

Lenny 1974 ★★★★★ Brilliantly cinematic look at controversial '50s stand-up comic Lenny Bruce's life from the Julian Barry play. Film opens with close-up of a mouth, perfect for story about power of words to offend and/or enlighten. Strong work by Hoffman in title role and Perrine as his sexually liberated wife. Obviously not for the prudish. C: Dustin Hoffman, Valerie Perrine, Jan Miner. D: Bob Fosse. DRA [R] 112m. v

Lenny Bruce—Without Tears 1992 ★★★★ Brilliantly inventive, self-destructive nightclub comic Lenny Bruce, whose hip comedy and scatological monologues brought him notoriety and legal problems in the '60s, is captured in interviews and TV appearances in this important documentary. Bruce's influence on American comedy is discussed by Mort Sahl and Kenneth Tynan. C: Lenny Bruce, Steve Allen, Mort Sahl, Kenneth Tynan. D: Fred Baker. DOC 75m. v

Lensman 1984 Japanese ★★★ Animated sci-fi feature about a boy who uses supernatural powers to defeat evil in the universe. Weak, derivative story line is merely an excuse for Japanese animation tricks, but should please children. C: Kazuyuki Hirokawa. D: Yoshiaki Kawajiri. FAM/SFI 107m. v

Leo the Last 1970 British ★★★ Social commentary focuses on last-of-his-line Italian aristocrat (Mastroianni) long holed up in seedy London mansion who discovers that his neighborhood has become a black ghetto. Uneven but intriguing. C: Marcello Mastroianni, Billie Whitelaw, Calvin Lockhart. D: John Boorman. DRA [R] 103m.

Leolo 1992 Canadian-French ★★★½ An impoverished, maladjusted Montreal family includes a gluttonous father, bodybuilder brother, and central character of a boy who thinks his mother was a tomato! Heavily symbolic, certainly original drama. C: Maxime Collin, Ginette Reno, Roland Blouin. D: Jean-Claude Lauzon. DRA 107m. v

Leon Morin, Priest 1961 *See* **Forgiven Sinner, The**

Leon, the Pig Farmer 1993 ★★★★ Upon discovering he was sired from a sperm bank, a British Jew tracks down his gentile farmer dad. Funny ethnic comedy takes a while to find its bearings, but delivers consistent laughs. C: Mark Frankel, Janet Suzman, Brian Glover, Connie Booth, David DeKeyser, Maryam D'Abo, Gina Bellman. D: Vadim Jean, Gary Sinyor. COM 98m. v

Leona Helmsley: The Queen of Mean 1990 ★★★★ Surprisingly fair film biography of NYC . real estate magnate's wife, her dictatorial reign over hotel employees, and subsequent arrest and conviction for tax evasion. Pleshette makes Helmsley human and the film becomes a funny, touching look at meglomania. C: Suzanne Pleshette, Lloyd Bridges. D: Richard Michaels. DRA 94m. TVM v

Leonard Part 6 1987 ★ Even star Cosby panned this ridiculously unfunny comedy about a retired superspy being forced back into service when a herd of lunatic animals start doing in the U.S. government's top agents. Painful. C: Bill Cosby, Tom Courtenay, Joe Don Baker. D: Paul Weiland. COM [PG] 83m. v

Leonor 1980 French ★ Years after husband buried her, woman rises from the grave. Unfortunate attempt at a horror film, by Luis Buñuel's son. Ullmann and Piccoli have been much better. C: Michel Piccoli, Liv Ullmann. D: Juan Buñuel. HOR 90m. v

Leopard in the Snow 1978 Canadian ★★★ Former race-car driver (Dullea) rescues woman from a snowstorm. He owns a pet leopard. First film production from the publishers of *Harlequin Romances*, and about what you'd expect. C: Keir Dullea, Susan Penhaligon, Kenneth More, Billie Whitelaw. D: Gerry O'Hara. DRA [PG] 89m. v

Leopard Man, The 1943 ★★★★ Are the gruesome killings in a remote New Mexico town the work of an escaped circus leopard or something else? Chills galore in producer Val Lewton's most explicit horror film. Considered quite shocking at the time, and still holds up. Based on Cornell Woolrich novel *Black Alibi*. C: Dennis O'Keefe, Margo, Isabel Jewell. D: Jacques Tourneur. HOR 66m. v

Leopard, The 1963 Italian ★★★★½ Giuseppe di Lampedusa's novel, set during the unification of Italy, about the aging head of a family of Sicilian aristocrats (Lancaster) and how he handles the disappearance of his way of life is given lavish treatment by Visconti. Everything is first-rate; the final banquet scene is justly famous. C: Burt Lancaster, Alain Delon, Claudia Cardinale, Rina Morelli. D: Luchino Visconti. DRA [PG] 205m.

Lepke 1975 ★★★ Petty thief (Curtis) goes for the gold as head of Murder Incorporated. Good Curtis and a surprisingly serious Berle. Worth a look. C: Tony Curtis, Anjanette Comer, Michael Callan. D: Menahem Golan. ACT [R] 110m. v

Leprechaun 1992 ★ Surprise low-budget hit has nothing to offer but its gimmick: an evil leprechaun (Davis) who terrorizes young people on a farm while searching for his stolen gold. Poorly written and directed. C: Warwick Davis, Jennifer Aniston, Ken Olandt, Mark Holton. D: Mark Jones. HOR [PG-13] 91m. v

Leprechaun 2 1994 ★½ A (very) marginal improvement over the original, this is still a tacky horror item in which the ancient little monster attempts to claim a modern teenager as his bride. Cheap and badly plotted. C: Warwick Davis, Shevonne Durkin, Charlie Heath, Sandy Baron, Adam Biesk. D: Rodman Flender. HOR [R] 85m.

Les Amants de Pont Neuf *See* **Lovers on the Bridge.**

Les Biches 1968 French ★★★★ A wealthy older woman (Audran) picks up a young street artist (Sassard). They go to St. Tropez, where the arrival of a smooth architect (Trintignant) causes tension. Typically cool Chabrol treatment of highly charged material; emotions remain in check, adding to story's visceral power. C: Jean-Louis Trintignant, Jacqueline Sassard, Stephane Audran. D: Claude Chabrol. DRA [R] 104m. V

Les Bons Debarras 1978 Canadian ★★★ Teenage girl (Laurier) who lost her father turns to her mother (Tifo) and romanticizes her beyond reason. The performances are memorable, but the script's occasional insights become less frequent as the repetitive story moves toward tragedy. C: Charlotte Laurier, Marie Tifo, Germain Houde. D: Francis Mankiewicz. DRA 115m.

Les Caprices de Marie 1970 *See* **Give Her the Moon**

Les Carabiniers 1963 French ★★★★½ This wildly funny antiwar parable from master auteur Godard hits the spot. Surrender to the director's usual sloganeering and experimental tricks and enjoy! C: Genevieve Galea, Marino Mase. D: Jean-Luc Godard. COM 80m.

Les Choses de la Vie 1970 *See* **Things of Life, The**

Les Comperes 1984 French ★★★½ Two men (Richard, Depardieu) search for runaway son (Bierry) of their ex-lover (Duperey), each believing boy is his son. Entertaining farce, as Richard and Depardieu are effortlessly funny. C: Pierre Richard, Gerard Depardieu, Anny Duperey, Michel Aumont, Stephanie Bierry. D: Francis Veber. COM [PG] 92m. V

Les Deux Anglaises et le Continent *See* **Anne and Muriel**

Les Diaboliques 1954 *See* **Diabolique**

Les Enfants Terribles 1952 France ★★★★½ This adaptation of Cocteau's novel about two enchanted (and doomed) children gets faithful treatment from director Melville. Mystical and beautifully realized film manages not to wallow in its own lyricism. C: Nicole Stephane, Edouard Dermit, Jacques Bernard. D: Jean-Pierre Melville. DRA 107m. V

Les Girls 1957 ★★★★½ Stylish, delightful musical in three parts with story-frame of courtroom libel case dealing with ex-chorus girls' reminiscences of touring with Kelly in Europe. Each dancer recalls the same story differently with uproarious Kendall's version the best. Songs by Cole Porter, including witty "Ladies in Waiting." C: Gene Kelly, Mitzi Gaynor, Kay Kendall, Taina Elg. D: George Cukor. MUS 115m. V

Les Grands Manoevres 1956 *See* **Grand Maneuver, The**

Les Grandes Gueules 1965 ★★★½ A new life awaits two ex-convicts hired as lumberjacks by a naive sawmill owner. Overlong comedy-drama is not without its pleasures. C: Lino Ventura, Bourvil. D: Robert Enrico. DRA 125m. V

Les Miserables 1935 ★★★★½ Satisfying adaptation of Victor Hugo's epic novel features March as Valjean, the convict continually on the run from police inspector Laughton. Sweeping scope, strong period detail. C: Fredric March, Charles Laughton, Cedric Hardwicke, Rochelle Hudson, Frances Drake, Florence Eldridge, Jessie Ralph. D: Richard Boleslawski. DRA 108m. TVM

Les Miserables 1952 ★★★★ Years after his imprisonment for stealing a loaf of bread, Rennie's attempt to lead a new life as a mayor is threatened by relentless detective Newton. Rennie gives a strong performance in this adaptation of the Victor Hugo novel. C: Michael Rennie, Debra Paget, Robert Newton, Sylvia Sidney, Edmund Gwenn. D: Lewis Milestone. DRA 104m.

Les Miserables 1957 French ★★★½ This rather long take on Victor Hugo's classic adventure tale benefits from a tremendous performance by the great Gabin as Jean Valjean. C: Jean Gabin, Daniele Delorme, Bernard Blier. D: Jean-Paul Chanois. DRA 210m.

Les Miserables 1978 ★★★★ Jordan is Victor Hugo's thief who tries to leave his past behind, with Perkins as the policeman who won't let him forget. This TV version of oft-remade tale features lavish staging and Emmy-winning direction. C: Richard Jordan, Anthony Perkins, Cyril Cusack, Claude Dauphin, John Gielgud, Flora Robson, Celia Johnson, Joyce Redman. D: Glenn Caron Jordan. DRA 150m. TVM

Les Parents Terribles 1950 French ★★★★½ Cocteau's play about a haunted family receives a fine cinematic treatment. Marais leads an excellent cast through some treacherous territory. Rather poetic. C: Jean Marais, Yvonne de Bray, Gabrielle Dorziat, Marcel Andre, Josette Day. D: Jean Cocteau. DRA 105m.

Les Porter de la Nuit 1950 *See* **Gates of the Night**

Les Rendezvous D'Anna 1978 ★★★★ Young woman filmmaker journeys across Europe by train and learns about herself through the people she meets. Picaresque, character-driven entertainment; just delightful. Some nudity and adult situations. (a.k.a. *The Meetings of Anna*) C: Aurore Clément, Helmut Griem, Magali Noël. D: Chantal Akerman. DRA 122m. V

Les Tricheurs 1984 ★★★½ Woman tries to break gambler of his self-destructive habit. Not bad, but more interesting for the European locales than for any psychological insights (a.k.a. *The Cheats, Youthful Sinners*). C: Jacques Charrier, Pascale Petit, Andrea Parisy, Jean-Paul Belmondo. D: Marcel Carné. DRA

Les Violins du Bal 1974 ★★★½ Filmmaker decides to tackle the story of how he and his family escaped from Nazi Germany. Clever intercutting between the boy's plight and the director's dilemma sustains pace and maintains interest. C: Michel Drach, Jean-Louis Trintignant, Marie-José Nat. D: Michel Drach. DRA 108m.

Les Visiteurs du Soir 1942 *See* **Devil's Envoy, The**

Les Yeux sans Visage *See* **Faustus, The**

Less than Zero 1987 ★★ Skimpy nihilistic novel by Brett Easton Ellis about privileged teens in the go-go '80s turns into skimpier morality tale about fashion, cocaine, and ennui. Spader and Downey are impressive; the movie never is. C: Andrew McCarthy, Jami Gertz, Robert Downey, Jr., James Spader. D: Marek Kanievska. DRA [R] 98m. V

Lesson in Love, A 1954 Swedish ★★★½ A gynecologist's philandering provokes his wife to leave him for a former flame. Bergman shows an uncharacteristically light touch in this romantic comedy. C: Gunnar Bjornstrand, Eva Dahlbeck, Harriet Andersson. D: Ingmar Bergman. COM 96m. V

Lest We Forget 1943 *See* **Hangmen Also Die**

Let 'Em Have It 1935 ★★★½ Squeaky clean agents of a new organization called the FBI take on the criminal element. Sturdy cops-and-robbers fare that makes for good brisk entertainment. C: Richard Arlen, Virginia Bruce, Alice Brady, Bruce Cabot. D: Sam Wood. CRI 96m. V

Let Freedom Ring 1939 ★★★½ Fairly entertaining Capraesque comedy of idealistic journalist (Eddy) combatting corruption with help of family ghosts. Leads get strong support from rest of cast. C: Nelson Eddy, Virginia Bruce, Victor McLaglen, Lionel Barrymore. D: Jack Conway. COM 100m. V

Let Him Have It 1991 British ★★★★ Gripping tale of feebleminded young hoodlum put to death in England for murder committed by his partner in crime. Based on a true story; told with gritty realism. Courtenay is heartbreaking as the father. C: Chris Eccleston, Paul Reynolds, Tom Courtenay, Tom Bell, Eileen Atkins. D: Peter Medak. DRA [R] 115m. V

Let It Be 1969 British ★★★★ The classic Beatles rockumentary features recording session footage and interviews with the Fab Four. Genius and bitterness are both apparent. C: John Lennon, Paul McCartney, Ringo Starr, George Harrison. D: Michael Lindsay-Hogg. DOC [G] 113m. V

Let It Ride 1989 ★★½ Compulsive bettor (Dreyfuss) finally gets the day he's been waiting for all his life, where no matter what he does he just can't lose, causing untold havoc to his already shaky existence. Unlikable lead character undermines uneven comedy. C: Richard Dreyfuss, Teri Garr, David Johansen, Jennifer Tilly. D: Joe Pytka. COM [PG-13] 91m. V

Let It Rock 1981 W. German ★★ Sleazy promoter plots to transform a little-known performer into a musical icon. C: Dennis Hopper, David Hess, Terrance Robay. D: Roland Klick. DRA 75m. V

Let Joy Reign Supreme 1977 French ★★★★ Noiret is the regency of Philippe, duke of Orleans, in this uneven but generally competent historical drama. (The soundtrack was actually composed by the duke himself.) Lavish direction by Tavernier. C: Philippe Noiret, Jean Rochefort, Jean-Pierre Marielle, Christine Pascal. D: Bertrand Tavernier. DRA 120m.

Let No Man Write My Epitaph 1960 ★★★★ Follow-up to *Knock on Any Door* has Winters as a drug-addicted widow on Chicago's South Side struggling to raise her son (Darren) to be a concert pianist. A tight drama whose only flaw is a rather contrived finale. C: Burl Ives, Shelley Winters, James Darren, Jean Seberg, Ricardo Montalban, Ella Fitzgerald. D: Philip Leacock. DRA 106m.

Let the Balloon Go 1976 ★★★½ Sensitive tale of young crippled boy trying to hold his own in war-torn Australia, circa 1917. C: Robert Bettles, Sally Whiteman. D: Oliver Howes. DRA [G] 92m. V

Let the Good Times Roll 1973 ★★★★ Tuneful '50s rockumentary studies popular rock 'n' rollers of the period. Terrific nostalgia. Fine compilation of concert footage. C: Chuck Berry, Chubby Checker, Bo Diddley, Little Richard, The Five Satins, The Shirelles, The Coasters, Bill Haley and the Comets. D: Bob Abel, Sid Levin. DOC 98m.

Let There Be Light 1945 ★★★★ Somber, moving examination of the plight of battle-fatigue sufferers in an Army hospital. The downbeat subject caused the Pentagon to block public showing of this film for almost 40 years. Strong stuff. D: John Huston. DOC 59m.

Let Us Live 1939 ★★★½ Two men are sentenced to death for crimes they didn't commit, while the fiancée of one (O'Sullivan) struggles to prove their innocence. No big surprises, but dependable formula works like a charm. C: Maureen O'Sullivan, Henry Fonda, Ralph Bellamy. D: John Brahm. DRA 68m.

L'Etat Sauvage (The Savage State) 1978 French ★★★★ Newly liberated country struggles with racism. Intelligent adaptation of Georges Conchon's popular novel. C: Michel Piccoli, Claude Brasseur, Jacques Dutronc. D: Francis Girod. DRA 111m. V

Lethal Games 1990 ★★½ Small town defends itself against toughs sent by organized crime group. C: Frank Stallone, Brenda Vaccaro. D: John Bowen. ACT 83m. V

Lethal Innocence 1991 ★★★½ Inappropriate title for well-meaning drama about Cambodian child refugee who convinces his American foster parents to sponsor his family for immigration to the U.S. Good work by Fricker as U.N. representative. C: Blair Brown, Brenda Fricker, Teresa Wright, Amy Wright. D: Helen Whitney. DRA 90m. TVM

Lethal Lolita—Amy Fisher: My Story 1992 *See* **Amy Fisher: My Story**

Lethal Obsession 1987 ★★★ A pair of tough cops try to stop the endless accumulation of corpses on druglord-seized streets. C: Elliott Gould, Michael York, Tahnee Welch. D: Peter Patzak. CRI [R] 100m. V

Lethal Pursuit 1988 ★★★ Obsessed ex-boyfriend stalks a pop singer (Rapture) and her current lover across the Nevada desert. C: Mitzi Rapture, Blake Bahner, John Wildman. D: Don Jones. ACT [R] 92m. V

Lethal Weapon 1987 ★★★★ Gibson and Glover are police partners tracking L.A. drug dealers. Mucho violence and action, with nice star chemistry between the nut job (Gibson) and the all-American dad (Glover). C: Mel Gibson, Danny Glover, Gary Busey. D: Richard Donner. ACT [R] 110m. V

Lethal Weapon 2 1989 ★★★½ This time the superduo tangle with a hard-core smuggling syndicate. Violence and action aplenty, with a little comic relief courtesy of Pesci's oddball character. C: Mel Gibson, Danny Glover, Joe Pesci. D: Richard Donner. ACT [R] 114m. V

Lethal Weapon 3 1992 ★★★½ Yet another encore for tough cops Gibson and Glover. Now, along with third partner Russo, they're up against a maniac ex-cop. Action-packed fun. C: Mel Gibson, Danny Glover, Joe Pesci, Rene Russo. D: Richard Donner. ACT [R] 118m. V

Lethal Woman 1988 ★ Smarmy, offensive thriller about victims of rape taking over a remote island and turning it into a deathtrap for lecherous men. C: Merete Van Kamp, Robet Lipton, Shannon Tweed, James Luisi. D: Christian Marnham. ACT 96m. V

L'Etoile du Nord 1982 French ★★★ Penniless man (Noiret) kills rich businessman, and gets involved with the dead man's mistress and her mother. Gloomy adaptation of Georges Simenon's novel has long talky sections and some clumsy flashbacks. C: Simone Signoret, Philippe Noiret, Fanny Cottencon. D: Pierre Deferre. DRA [PG] 101m.

Let's Be Happy 1957 British ★★ Musical tale of young woman who inherits Scottish castle. Remake of *Jeannie.* C: Tony Martin, Vera-Ellen. D: Henry Levin. MUS 93m.

Let's Dance 1950 ★★★½ Dancer Hutton enlists aid of former partner Astaire to retake custody of son away from his wealthy grandmother. Unusual pairing of rambunctious Hutton with casual Astaire in one of Fred's least known films. His solos are always worth watching, though. Songs by Frank Loesser. C: Fred Astaire, Betty Hutton, Roland Young, Ruth Warrick. D: Norman McLeod. MUS 112m. V

Let's Do It Again 1953 ★★★ Musical remake of screwball classic *The Awful Truth* puts Wyman and Milland in old Irene Dunne/Cary Grant roles of divorcing couple who try to spoil each other's new romances. Not bad. C: Jane Wyman, Ray Milland, Aldo Ray. D: Alexander Hall. MUS [PG] 95m. V

Let's Do It Again 1975 ★★★★ To raise funds for their fraternal order, two Atlanta workers (Cosby, Poitier) scheme to con two big-time gamblers by turning a pipsqueak (Walker) into a ferocious prizefighter. Fun-filled comedy continues the exploits started in *Uptown Saturday Night.* C: Sidney Poitier, Bill Cosby, Jimmie Walker, John Amos. D: Sidney Poitier. COM [PG] 113m. V

Let's Face It 1943 ★★★½ Wisecracking army private (Hope) gets mixed up with a gang of spies when he plots to meet women by becoming a male escort. Not one of the comedian's funniest, but not bad. C: Bob Hope, Betty Hutton, ZaSu Pitts, Eve Arden. D: Sidney Lanfield. COM 76m.

Let's Get Harry 1986 ★★ An American (Harmon) kidnapped by South American drug lords is rescued by his friends and a wacko mercenary. Outrageously contrived. (a.k.a *The Rescue*) C: Mark Harmon, Michael Schoeffling, Tom Wilson, Glen Frey, Gary Busey, Robert Duvall. D: Alan Smithee. ACT [R] 98m. V

Let's Get Lost 1989 ★★★ Fascinating documentary about jazz trumpeter and drug addict Chet Baker told in interviews with friends, films of his earlier life, and contemporary performances. C: Chet Baker. D: Bruce Weber. DOC 119m. V

Let's Get Tough! 1942 ★★★ Muggs, Glimpy, and the gang tangle with Japanese enemy agents in this fast-moving *East Side Kids* adventure. C: Leo Gorcey, Huntz Hall, Bobby Jordan. D: Wallace Fox. COM 62m. V

Let's Go 1923 ★★★½ Silent social drama with father and son, joint owners of a company, torn between profits and ideals. Could have used words, but facinating. C: Richard Talmadge, Eileen Percy, Tully Marshall. D: Richard Talmadge. DRA 79m. V

Let's Go Navy! 1951 ★★★½ The Bowery Boys join the Navy to track down a gang of bad guys disguised as sailors. One of the best from the troop. C: Leo Gorcey, Huntz Hall, William Benedict. D: William Beaudine. COM 68m.

Let's Hope It's a Girl 1985 Italian ★★★★ Ex-husband returns to his wife and decides to sell part of their estate, outraging the female family members. Seriocomic tale uses black comic moments laced with tragedy to show how women can live without men. The performances (especially the women—Ullmann, Deneuve, Sandrelli) are terrific. C: Liv Ullmann, Philippe Noiret, Catherine Deneuve, Bernard Blier, Stefania Sandrelli. D: Mario Monicelli. DRA 114m.

Let's Kill Uncle 1966 British ★★★ Greedy uncle plots to murder his 12-year-old nephew over an inheritance, but the bratty kid decides he can play that game too. Smirking yarn delivers minor thrills, weak punchline. C: Nigel Green, Mary Badham, Pat Cardi. D: William Castle. CRI 92m.

Let's Make It Legal 1951 ★★★½ Couple calls it quits after 20 years of marriage; their amicable parting is threatened when the wife's (Colbert's) old flame (Scott) comes back into the picture. Good cast is film's main asset. C: Claudette Colbert, Macdonald Carey, Zachary Scott, Robert Wagner, Marilyn Monroe. D: Richard Sale. COM 77m. v

Let's Make Love 1960 ★★★½ Moderately entertaining sex comedy with millionaire (Montand) pretending to be singer-dancer to woo showgirl (Monroe). Plot makes no sense, but Marilyn is charming, as always. Silly but painless. C: Marilyn Monroe, Yves Montand, Tony Randall, Frankie Vaughan. D: George Cukor. COM 118m. v

Let's Make Music 1940 ★★★½ The other Crosby (Bing's brother) plays a bandleader courting a repressed music teacher who doesn't appreciate jazz. Diverting B-musical with script by famed novelist Nathanael West. C: Bob Crosby, Jean Rogers, Elisabeth Risdon. D: Leslie Goodwins. MUS 85m.

Let's Make Up 1954 British ★★½ Okay farce with Neagle pursued by Flynn and Farrar. (a.k.a. *Lilacs In the Spring*) C: Errol Flynn, Anna Neagle, David Farrar, Kathleen Harrison. D: Herbert Wilcox. COM 94m. v

Let's Rock! 1958 ★★★½ Pop singer La Rosa resists pressure to go all the way—into rock, that is. Harmless teen flick with fun numbers including "At the Hop," performed by Danny and the Juniors. (a.k.a. *Keep It Cool*) C: Julius La Rosa, Phyllis Newman, Conrad Janis, Della Reese, Paul Anka. D: Harry Foster. MUS 79m.

Let's Scare Jessica to Death 1971 ★★★★ Young woman with history of delusions retreats to the countryside—where only she sees that locals are vampires. Shuddery, if unresolved, horror is genuinely nightmarish. C: Zohra Lampert, Barton Heyman. D: John Hancock. HOR [PG] 89m. v

Let's Spend the Night Together 1982 ★★½ Vacant, wearisome rockumentary, with highlights from three performances of the Rolling Stones' 1981 concert tour. C: The Rolling Stones. D: Hal Ashby. DOC [PG] 94m. v

Let's Talk About Men 1965 Italian ★★★★ Quintet of self-contained tales (the last ties together the previous four), with Manfredi finding himself at comic cross-purposes with many women. Main treat: Manfredi's winning performances. Follow-up to 1964's *Let's Talk About Women*, made by Ettore Scola. C: Nino Manfredi, Luciana Paluzzi, Margaret Lee. D: Lina Wertmuller. COM [PG] 93m.

Let's Talk About Women 1964 Italian ★★★★ Nine episodes showing how Gassman (who plays different men in each) relates to various women. Hit-or-miss style of comedy has enough amusement—and Gassman's authoritative presence—to score. Followed by Lina Wertmuller's *Let's Talk About Men*. C: Vittorio Gassman, Maria Fiore, Donatella Mauro, Giovanna Ralli. D: Ettore Scola. COM 108m.

Letter from an Unknown Woman 1948 ★★★★★ Brilliant evocation of unrequited love, one of the screen's great tearjerkers. Fontaine is haunting as lonely woman obsessed with concert pianist Jourdan. Great period flair with lush sets and costumes. C: Joan Fontaine, Louis Jourdan, Mady Christians. D: Max Ophuls. DRA 87m. v

Letter from Mama, A 1938 *See* **A Brivele Der Mamen, A**

Letter from Siberia 1957 French ★★★★★ Witty, tongue-in-cheek documentary look at Siberia from various points of view. Director Marker plays around with documentary conventions, questioning the very process of filming "truth." He comes up with both laughs and insight. D: Chris Marker. DOC 60m.

Letter of Introduction, A 1938 ★★★½ Enjoyable tale of stagestruck actress (Leeds) being helped by ham actor (Menjou); she doesn't know, however, that he's her father. C: Adolphe Menjou, Andrea Leeds, Edgar Bergen, Eve Arden. D: John M. Stahl. COM 104m. v

Letter, The 1940 ★★★★½ One of Davis' best films, based on the W. Somerset Maugham story of jilted adulteress who murders her lover, and then claims self-defense. Star makes enigmatic murderess a sympathetic and fascinating tragic heroine. Haunting, stylized photography captures Malaysian atmosphere with stunning symbolic touches. C: Bette Davis, Herbert Marshall, James Stephenson, Gale Sondergaard. D: William Wyler. DRA 96m. v

Letter, The 1982 ★★★ Remick capably plays plantation owner's wife who claims self-defense in murder of her lover. But story seems dated and overheated in this version. Unlike original, haunting mood is never established. C: Lee Remick, Ronald Pickup, Jack Thompson, Ian McShane. D: John Erman. DRA 100m.

Letter to Brezhnev 1985 British ★★★★ Two English girls (Pigg, Clarke) find themselves romantically entangled with two Russian sailors (Firth, Molina) on leave in Liverpool and take unlikely steps to reunite with their military loves when they return to sea. Endearing offbeat romantic comedy charms throughout. C: Peter Firth, Alfred

Molina, Alexandra Pigg, Margi Clarke. D: Chris Bernard. COM [R] 94m. V

Letter to Three Wives, A 1949 ★★★★★ Three women receive letter from a fourth, claiming she has run away with one of their husbands; this triggers flashbacks about each wife's marriage. Mankiewicz won Oscars for Best Writing and Direction for this witty, incisive film with marvelous performances. Best episode is Darnell and P. Douglas, with Thelma and Connie in the kitchen. C: Jeanne Crain, Linda Darnell, Ann Sothern, Kirk Douglas, Paul Douglas, Jeffrey Lynn, Connie Gilchrist, Thelma Ritter. D: Joseph L. Mankiewicz. DRA 103m. V

Letter to Three Wives, A 1985 ★★★ Unnecessary remake of 1949 classic in which three wives try to figure out which husband has deserted her. The TV talent is incapable of the elegant style which gave first film its punch. C: Loni Anderson, Michele Lee, Stephanie Zimbalist, Ann Sothern. D: Larry Elikann. DRA 100m. TVM

Letters from a Dead Man 1986 Russian ★★★★ A dying scientist writes letters to his son in the aftermath of a nuclear war. At times both enlightening and tedious, this film remains a fascinating document of glasnost Soviet filmmaking. C: Rolan Bykov, V. Mikhailov, I. Riklin. D: Konstantin Lopushansky. DRA 87m. TVM

Letters from Frank 1979 ★★★★ When a journalist (Carney) is fired due to old age and new technology, he begins to question the value of his life. Thoughtful, provocative, beautifully acted. Fox's debut. C: Art Carney, Maureen Stapleton, Mike Farrell, Lew Ayres, Margaret Hamilton, Michael J. Fox. D: Edward Parone. DRA 100m. TVM

Letters from My Windmill 1954 French ★★★★ Three stories adapted from Alphonse Daudet's book. Pagnol's last film harkens back to Provençal settings and characters of his earlier triumphs. Deja vu of most enjoyable kind, like spending two hours in an old friend's company. Preston Sturges wrote the subtitles. C: Henri Velbert, Daxely Yvonne, Gamy Rellys. D: Marcel Pagnol. DRA 140m.

Letters from the Park 1988 Spanish ★★★★ Cyrano de Bergerac variation features poetic young man hired by dullard to pen letters to lovely young woman—with predictable boomerang effect. Flavorable romance, set in 1913 Cuba, pumps new life into the oft told tale. C: Victor La Place, Ivonne Lopez, Miguel Paneque. D: Tomas Gutierrez Alea. DRA [R] 85m. V

Letters, The 1973 ★★★½ Superficial three-part soaper of delayed letters lost in mails which are delivered one year late becomes a delicious wallow thanks to juicy performances by old pros Stanwyck, Powell, and Lupino. C: Barbara Stanwyck, Jane Powell, Dina Merrill, Ida Lupino, Leslie Nielsen. D: Gene Nelson, Paul Krasny. DRA 73m. TVM

Letters to an Unknown Lover 1985 British ★★★★ Soldier escapes from Nazi prison camp and is sheltered in France by two sisters who think he's a dead friend. Steady, suspenseful drama. C: Cherie Lunghi, Mathilda May, Yves Beneyton. D: Peter Duffell. DRA 101m. V

Letting Go 1985 ★★★½ Two newly single misfits (Ritter, Gless) meet in a therapy group. Charming stars and good chemistry give this elongated sitcom some snap. C: John Ritter, Sharon Gless. D: Jack Bender. COM 100m. TVM V

Letty Lynton 1932 ★★★ Flirtatious socialite Crawford turns to drastic means to rid herself of determined suitor Asther after she falls for Montgomery. Crawford gives a haughty performance in this vehicle marred by implausible plot turns; adapted from a Marie Belloc Lowndes novel. C: Joan Crawford, Robert Montgomery, Lewis Stone, May Robson, Nils Asther. D: Clarence Brown. DRA 84m.

Leviathan 1989 ★★ The crew of a seabed mining outpost are walking hot lunches for a creature stalking them one by one. Watered-down version of *Alien.* C: Peter Weller, Richard Crenna, Amanda Pays, Daniel Stern. D: George P. Cosmatos. HOR [R] 98m. V

Levy and Goliath 1987 French ★★★ Swiss Hassidic Jew romances Arab beauty while getting mixed up with Parisian drug smugglers. Got that? Oury's attempt to return to ethnic action humor—as exemplified by his *The Mad Adventures of Rabbi Jacob*—is frantic and funny. C: Richard Anconina, Michel Boujenah, Jean-Claude Brialy. D: Gerard Oury. COM 97m.

Lezione de Chimica 1947 *See* **Schoolgirl Diary**

L'Homme au Chapeau Rond 1946 *See* **Eternal Husband, The**

L'Homme Qui Ment 1970 *See* **Man Who Lies, The**

Lianna 1983 ★★★★ Sayles' honest and uncompromising story of an unhappy wife who discovers she is falling in love with her female college professor. Intelligently and sympathetically handled. C: Linda Griffiths, Jane Halloren, Jon De Vries. D: John Sayles. DRA [R] 110m. V

Liar's Club, The 1993 ★★½ Friendships between football buddies become strained when one victimizes a young woman. C: Wil Wheaton, Brian Krause, Soleil Moon Frye. D: Jeffrey Porter. DRA [R] 100m. V

Liar's Edge 1992 ★★★½ A boy prone to violent daydreaming suddenly becomes privy to his new stepfather's murderous relaity. C: Shannon Tweed, David Keith, Christopher Plummer. HOR 97m. V

Liar's Moon 1981 ★★★½ A young star-crossed couple (Dillon and Fisher) marry over their parents' objections. Sympathetic performances hold this slight story together.

Note: Released with two different endings. C: Matt Dillon, Cindy Fisher, Hoyt Axton, Yvonne De Carlo, Broderick Crawford. D: David Fisher. DRA [PG] 106m. v

Libel 1959 British ★★★½ Nobleman accused of being an impostor sues for libel, then finds proving who he is to be more difficult than he expected. Slow-starting drama builds suspense when Bogarde's wife begins to doubt his identity. C: Dirk Bogarde, Olivia de Havilland, Robert Morley, Paul Massie, Wilfrid Hyde-White. D: Anthony Asquith. DRA 100m.

Libeled Lady 1936 ★★★★½ Delicious screwball comedy about socialite (Loy) suing publisher (Tracy) for libel, while he in turn uses Powell and fiancée Harlow to frame his adversary. All four stars are in great form, making sometimes silly script great fun to watch. C: William Powell, Myrna Loy, Spencer Tracy, Jean Harlow. D: Jack Conway. COM 98m. v

Liberace 1988 ★★★ Weaker of two biographies of flamboyant Las Vegas pianist, who died of AIDS in 1987. This sanitized verion glosses over cause of death, and other pertinent facts are skipped altogether. C: Andrew Robinson, John Rubinstein, Rue McClanahan. D: Billy Hale. DRA 100m. TVM

Liberace: Behind the Music 1988 ★★★½ Candid, but glib biography of showman pianist. His death from AIDS is honestly dealt with and Garber does well in those scenes, but movie fails to capture subject's charisma or showmanship. C: Victor Garber, Saul Rubinek, Maureen Stapleton. D: David Greene. DRA 100m. TVM

Liberation of L. B. Jones, The 1970 ★★★ Melodramatic exposeé of bigotry in a Tennessee town. Wyler's swan song has some power but is slow and confused. Adapted by Jessie Hill Ford from his novel. C: Lee J. Cobb, Anthony Zerbe, Roscoe Lee Browne, Lola Falana, Lee Majors, Barbara Hershey. D: William Wyler. DRA [R] 101m. v

Liberty & Bash 1989 ★★★ Two muscle-bound war vets try to rscue their friend from Central American terrorists. Violent. C: Miles O'Keefe, Lou Ferrigno, Mitzi Kapture, Richard Eden, Cheryl Paris, Gary Conway. D: Myrl A. Schreibman. ACT [R] 92m. v

Licence to Kill 1989 British ★★★★ Dalton stars as James Bond, setting out to avenge the assault of a former CIA agent friend whose wife is murdered. Second Dalton installment discards tongue-in-cheek manner of previous Bond films for serious, harder-hitting style. C: Timothy Dalton, Carey Lowell, Robert Davi, Talisa Soto. D: John Glen. ACT [PG-13] 133m. v

License to Drive ★★½ Failure to pass his road test doesn't hinder a determined teen (Haim) from taking his father's car and going on the dream date of his life, but the night's disastrous events just might (make him fail the road test, that is). Innocuous comedy works hard for laughs but runs out of gas. C: Corey Haim, Corey Feldman, Carol Kane, Nina Siemaszko. D: Greg Beeman. COM [PG-13] 90m. v

Lie, The 1990 ★★★ Well-known writer can't stop having affairs with poor young women. Weak script, but a good cast. C: Ben Cross, Stefania Sandrelli, Amanada Sandrelli, Leslie Lyon. D: Giovanni Soldati. DRA 97m. v

Liebelei 1932 Austrian ★★★★★ Young love is destroyed by a thoughtless aristocrat in late 19th-century Vienna. Extremely elegant and wise film by the great Ophuls re-creates a lost world of honor and passion. Not to be missed. C: Magda Schneider, Wolfgang Liebeneiner, Luise Ullrich, Willy Eichberger. D: Max Ophüuls. DRA 85m.

Liebestraum 1991 ★★★ Convoluted tale of an architect who returns home to visit his terminally ill mother and is caught up in old and new scandals, as well as the razing of a historic building. Atmospheric execution. C: Kevin Anderson, Bill Pullman, Pamela Gidley, Kim Novak. D: Mike Figgis. DRA [R] 100m. v

Lies 1983 ★★★½ Enjoyable low-budget thriller has out-of-work actress (Dusenberry) lured into playing the part of heir in an inheritance scheme. Loaded with twists and several genuinely chilling moments. Owes much to *My Name Is Julia Ross*. C: Ann Dusenberry, Bruce Davison, Gail Strickland, Clu Gulager. D: Jim Wheat. CRI [R] 93m. v

Lies Before Kisses 1978 French ★★★½ The wife of a publisher accused of murdering a prostitute puts aside their marital conflicts and fights for her husband's freedom. C: Michel Piccoli, Claude Brasseur, Jacques Dutronc. D: Francis Girod. CRI 111m. v

Lies My Father Told Me 1975 Canadian ★★★★ Nostalgic look at the love of a young Jewish boy (Lynas) for his peddler grandfather (Yadin) in Montreal during the 1920s. Touching family fare. C: Yossi Yadin, Len Birman, Jeffrey Lynas. D: Jan Kadar. FAM/DRA [PG] 102m.

Lies of the Twins 1991 ★★★ Good-twin/bad-twin movie with Quinn as the identical pair, the nicer of whom falls for Rossellini. Predictable thriller. C: Aidan Quinn, Isabella Rossellini, Claudia Christian, Hurd Hatfield. D: Tim Hunter. DRA [R] 95m.

Lieutenant Wore Skirts, The 1956 ★★★½ Slick comedy has Ewell furious with wife (North) when she enlists in the armed forces. Dated, but harmless. C: Tom Ewell, Sheree North, Rita Moreno. D: Frank Tashlin. COM 99m.

Life and Adventures of Nicholas Nickleby, The 1947 *See* **Nicholas Nickleby**

Life and Assassination of the Kingfish, The 1976 ★★★½ Deathbed reminiscences of dynamic Louisiana governor Huey P. Long (Asner). Glosses over some of his checkered career, but overall worthwhile. Asner is superb. C: Edward Asner, Nicholas Pryor, Diane Kagan. D: Robert Collins. DRA 96m. V

Life and Death of Colonel Blimp, The 1943 British ★★★★★ Excellent character study of a British career officer (Livesey) from the turn of the century to WWII. Bittersweet look at aging and obsolescence, insightfully written and directed. Kerr impresses as three different key figures in our hero's life. (a.k.a. *Colonel Blimp*) C: Roger Livesey, Deborah Kerr, Anton Walbrook. D: Michael Powell, Emeric Pressburger. DRA 115m. V

Life and Loves of a Male Stripper, The ★½ Unsuccessful pop singer starts exotic dancing career. Only for beefcake afficionados. C: Rafael, Carl Fuerst, Dennis Landry, Jeff Allen, Troy, Gary Hendricksen. D: John Stagliano. DRA 82m. V

Life and Nothing But 1989 French ★★★★★ WWI survivors, one an officer whose responsibility is to account for France's war dead, and two women searching for signs of their MIA lovers, deal with postwar life. Deeply moving, optimistic study of changing world builds from the personal to the epic. C: Philippe Noiret, Sabine Azema. D: Bertrand Tavernier. DRA 135m. V

Life and Times of Grizzly Adams, The 1975 ★★ Poorly crafted tale of a man who is wrongly pursued by the law and takes refuge in the mountains with his young daughter, where they are befriended by a bear. Sappy nature drama which led to equally forgettable TV series. C: Dan Haggerty, Don Shanks, Lisa Jones. D: Richard Friedenberg. FAM/DRA [G] 96m. V

Life and Times of Harvey Milk, The 1984 ★★★★½ Pioneering documentary of gay rights activist/San Francisco Supervisor Milk who, along with Mayor George Moscone, was assasinated by conservative supervisor Dan White. At once depressing and inspiring, it's an honest portrait of man who galvanized a city, even in death. Oscar for Best Documentary. Narrated by Harvey Fierstein. D: Robert Epstein. DOC 87m.

Life and Times of Judge Roy Bean, The 1972 ★★★½ Legendary self-proclaimed "law west of the Pecos" as seen through the mythmaking machinery of screenwriter John Milius. Oddly comic film recounts Bean legend, including his obsession with actress Lily Langtry. Huston lacks requisite high style to bring off this live-action cartoon Western, but Newman is memorably quirky in title role. C: Paul Newman, Ava Gardner, Victoria Principal, Jacqueline Bisset, Anthony Perkins, Tab Hunter, John Huston, Stacy Keach, Roddy McDowall. D: John Huston. WST [PG] 124m. V

Life and Times of Rosie the Riveter, The 1980 ★★★★½ Engaging, intelligent documentary about WWII female factory workers. Interspersed with newsreel footage and interviews with five women who kept their jobs after the war ended. (a.k.a. *Rosie the Riveter)* C: Wanita Allen, Gladys Belcher. D: Connie Field. DOC 60m.

Life and Times of the Chocolate Killer, The 1988 ★★★ Strange mix of comedy and thriller involving falsely accused "chocolate killer" trying to clear his name. C: Rod Browning, Tabi Cooper, Robert Chapel, Michael D. Roberts. D: Michael Adrian. COM [PG] 75m. V

Life at the Top 1965 British ★★★½ Sequel to *Room at the Top* jumps ahead 10 years as Harvey tries to mend his ways. Sizzling Harvey/Signoret liaison seen in flashbacks, lifts otherwise flat follow-up. C: Laurence Harvey, Jean Simmons, Honor Blackman, Robert Morley. D: Ted Kotcheff. DRA 117m.

Life Begins 1932 ★★★★ A maternity ward is the setting for drama about the problems of nurses and expectant mothers, including convicted murderess Young. Offbeat film based on a Columbia University student play benefits from a fine ensemble cast and intricately woven plot elements. C: Elliott Nugent, Loretta Young, Aline MacMahon, Glenda Farrell. D: James Flood. DRA 71m.

Life Begins at Eight-Thirty 1942 ★★★½ Celebrated actor Woolley becomes an alcoholic; wrecking the life of his daughter (Lupino), he declines to the point where the only job he can get is as a street corner Santa Claus. Weak adaptation of the play *The Light of Heart* by Emlyn Williams. C: Monty Woolley, Ida Lupino, Cornel Wilde, Sara Allgood. D: Irving Pichel. DRA 85m.

Life Begins at Forty 1935 ★★★★ Folksy comedy/drama of small-town editor (Rogers) taking up unpopular cause of man framed for bank robbery. Fine vehicle for star and his witty comments on human nature, all of which still ring true. C: Will Rogers, Rochelle Hudson, Richard Cromwell, Jane Darwell. D: George Marshall. COM 85m.

Life Begins for Andy Hardy 1941 ★★★★ Rooney leaves home for the lights of Manhattan in this Andy Hardy tale. Once in the Big Apple, he learns life has its hard knocks along with the good times. Fairly entertaining series entry; last Andy Hardy outing for co-star Garland. C: Mickey Rooney, Lewis Stone, Judy Garland, Fay Holden, Ann Rutherford. D: George Seitz. FAM/COM 100m. V

Life Begins in College 1937 ★★★½ Crazy college football romp with the irrepressible Ritz Brothers throwing puns and pigskins with abandon. C: Joan Davis, Tony Martin, The Ritz Brothers, Gloria Stuart. D: William Seiter. COM 94m.

Life in the Food Chain 1991 *See* **Age Isn't Everything**

Life in the Pink 1977 *See* **Operation Petticoat**

Life in the Theater, A 1993 ★★★★ Two actors (one a veteran, the other a neophyte) spar and bond in this amusing two-character tour-de-force by David Mamet. Long on atmosphere, short on plot, but a fine vehicle for the stars. C: Jack Lemmon, Matthew Broderick. D: Gregory Mosher. COM 100m. TVM V

Life Is a Bed of Roses 1983 French ★★★★ A dual story, of a rich man and his friends playing at creating a "temple of happiness" at his chateau, in the early '20s. In the '80s, the still unfinished building has become a school, and site of a conference. Beautifully made, with magical sleight-of-hand moments that became the Resnais trademark. C: Vittorio Gassman, Ruggero Raimondi, Geraldine Chaplin. D: Alain Resnais. DRA [PG] 111m.

Life Is a Long Quiet River 1987 French ★★★ Two children are switched at birth—one goes to a poor family, the other to a rich one. Predictable comedy never transcends its subject; some laughs, but not enough. C: Benoit Magimel, Valerie Lalande, Tara Romer. D: Etienne Chatiliez. COM 89m. V

Life Is Beautiful 1979 ★★★½ Lisbon government and resistance both erroneously go after men who, in reality, has taken no political action in either direction. C: Giancarlo Giannini, Ornella Muti. ACT 102m. V

Life Is Sweet 1992 British ★★★★ An exploration of life in the British lower middle class focuses on a complacent food preparer, his longtime wife, and their two extremely opposite, grown twin daughters. Insightfully warm and funny low-key character study. C: Alison Steadman, Jim Broadbent, Claire Skinner, Jane Horrocks, Stephen Rea. D: Mike Leigh. COM [R] 103m. V

Life, Loves and Adventures of Omar Khayyam, The *See* **Omar Khayyam**

Life of Brian 1979 *See* **Monty Python's Life of Brian**

Life of Emile Zola, The 1937 ★★★★½ Imposing biography of 19th-century French author (Muni) who challenged the government during the infamous Dreyfus Affair. Well acted by star, comes to vivid life in courtroom scenes. Oscar-winner for Best Picture, Screenplay, and Supporting Actor Schildkraut. C: Paul Muni, Gale Sondergaard, Joseph Schildkraut, Gloria Holden, Donald Crisp, Morris Carnovsky, Louis Calhern. D: William Dieterle. DRA 110m. V

Life of Her Own, A 1950 ★★★½ Tedious romantic triangles among fashion models, made bearable by supporting work from Dvorak, Calhern, and the smooth professionalism of Cukor's direction. C: Lana Turner, Ray Milland, Tom Ewell, Louis Calhern, Ann Dvorak. D: George Cukor. DRA 108m. V

Life of Jimmy Dolan, The 1933 ★★★★ A boxer (Fairbanks) accidentally kills a reporter and later finds redemption aiding a woman (Young) who runs a children's health center. Swiftly paced, well-done drama. C: Douglas Fairbanks, Jr., Loretta Young, Guy Kibbee, Fifi D'Orsay, Aline MacMahon. D: Archie Mayo. DRA 89m.

Life of Oharu, The 1952 Japanese ★★★★ In 17th-century Japan, a woman (Tanaka) is banished for loving a soldier beneath her class; she gradually falls down the social ladder and ends up a prostitute. Expressive social drama, based on Saikaku's novel, gained Mizoguchi international prominence. C: Toshiro Mifume, Kinuyo Tanaka, Hisako Yamane. D: Kenji Mizoguchi. DRA 146m.

Life of Riley, The 1948 ★★★½ Moderately amusing tale of working man (Bendix) trying to get his daughter hitched to the boss's son. Based on popular radio series, later a popular sitcom. C: William Bendix, James Gleason, Rosemary DeCamp, Beulah Bondi. D: Irving Brecher. COM 87m.

Life of Sin, A 1992 ★★★ Standard prostitution doesn't pay story about a poor girl's career as a high-charging madam. C: Raul Julia, Miriam Colon, Jose Ferrer. D: Efrain Lopez. DRA [R] 112m. V

Life of the Party, The 1937 ★★★½ Modest musical casts Hilliard as singing debutante wooed by two millionaires (Raymond and Penner). Good supporting cast. C: Gene Raymond, Harriet Hilliard, Joe Penner, Ann Miller, Victor Moore, Billy Gilbert, Helen Broderick, Franklin Pangborn, Margaret Dumont. D: William Seiter. MUS 77m.

Life of the Party: The Story of Beatrice 1982 ★★½ Drama of O'Reilly (Burnett) who founded first L.A. recovery clinic for alcoholic women. Miscast Burnett acts dramatic part with petulance against her comic persona. Result is heartfelt but nonetheless one-dimensional. C: Carol Burnett, Lloyd Bridges. D: Lamont Johnson. DRA 100m. TVM

Life of Vergie Winters, The 1934 ★★★ Small-town woman (Harding) rises above malicious gossip in this adaptation of the Louis Bromfield novel. A fine performance by Harding. C: Ann Harding, John Boles, Helen Vinson, Betty Furness. D: Alfred Santell. DRA 82m.

Life on a String 1991 Chinese ★★★★ Blind balladeer devotes his life to music, in hope that he will regain his sight. Powerful fable has breathtaking photography, sure directorial hand. C: Liu Zhong Yuan, Huang Lei. D: Chen Kaige. DRA 107m. V

Life Stinks 1991 ★ High-powered millionaire (Brooks) accepts a bet to give up all his worldly riches and survive on the streets for 30 days. Brooks' attempt to find humor in the subject of homelessness fails miserably. C: Mel Brooks, Lesley Ann Warren, Jeffrey Tambor, Howard Morris. D: Mel Brooks. COM [PG-13] 95m. V

Life Upside Down 1965 French ★★★★ Real estate agent withdraws into himself, losing his job and wife in the process. Banal idea given very amusing treatment. First film by writer/director Jessua is a winner. C: Charles Denner, Anna Gaylor, Guy Jean. D: Alain Jessua. COM 93m.

Life with Blondie 1946 ★★★½ Blondie's dog is kidnapped after it wins pin-up contest. Cute comedy is one of the better entries in the *Blondie* series. C: Penny Singleton, Arthur Lake, Larry Simms, Marjorie Kent. D: Abby Berlin. COM 64m.

Life with Father 1947 ★★★★½ Nostalgic look at turn-of-the-century family life focuses on father's resistance to wife's plans to get him baptized; beautifully modulated performances by Dunne and Powell. Solid adaptation of long-running Broadway play by Howard Lindsay and Russel Crouse; from Clarence Day's stories. C: Irene Dunne, William Powell, Jimmy Lydon, Elizabeth Taylor, ZaSu Pitts. D: Michael Curtiz. COM 118m. V

Life with Henry 1941 ★★★½ Second in Henry Aldrich series has Cooper repeating as bad-luck Henry, this time winning trip to Alaska. C: Jackie Cooper, Leila Ernst, Eddie Bracken, Fred Niblo, Hedda Hopper. D: Ted Reed. COM 80m.

Life with Mikey 1993 ★★★★ Adorable comedy about former child TV star (Fox) now a struggling talent agent, who latches on to a 10-year-old pickpocket with acting potential. Lightweight, but full of showbiz insight. C: Michael J. Fox, Christina Vidal, Nathan Lane, Cyndi Lauper. D: James Lapine. COM [PG] 92m. V

Lifeboat 1944 ★★★★½ After their ocean-liner has been sunk by a German sub in WWII, nine passengers (one of them a Nazi) are left afloat in a lifeboat and kept there for the entire film. Hitchcock's experiment in limited locale builds suspense admirably. Bankhead's remarkable, witty performance as spoiled rich girl tops excellent cast. From a story by John Steinbeck. C: Tallulah Bankhead, John Hodiak, William Bendix, Walter Slezak, Hume Cronyn, Henry Hull, Mary Anderson. D: Alfred Hitchcock. DRA 96m. V

Lifeforce 1984 ★★★ Outer space has a new lifeform—the space vampire, capable of draining a person of all vitality and leaving nothing but a shriveled mass. Good effects, but the story seems to wander. C: Steve Railsback, Peter Firth, Frank Finlay, Mathilda May. D: Tobe Hooper. SFI [R] 100m. V

Lifeguard 1976 ★★★½ Photogenic mood piece about 30-ish beachboy struggling with aging and uncertainties about commitment. Clichéd, but Elliott is appealing. C: Sam Elliott, Anne Archer, Kathleen Quinlan, Parker Stevenson. D: Daniel Petrie. DRA [PG] 96m. V

Lifepod 1993 ★★★ In the twenty-second century, murderer stalks passengers fleeing disaster-pagued luxury space-liner. C: Robert Loggia, Stan Shaw, Ron Silver. D: Ron Silver. SFI 120m. TVM V

Lifespan 1975 ★★★½ Often involving thriller of an American researcher trying to stop secret anti-aging experiments. C: Klaus Kinski, Hiram Keller, Tina Aumont, Fons Rademaker. D: Alexander Whitelaw. DRA 85m. V

Lifetaker 1989 ★★★ Pat tale of betrayed husband plotting revenge on his unfaithful wife. C: Terence Morgan, Lei Dregorn. D: Michael Papas. COM 97m. V

Lift, The 1985 Dutch ★★★ The elevators are killing off the tenants of a new highrise apartment building. Silly premise made worse by shoddy writing; smooth direction makes it passable filler. C: Huub Stapel, Josine Van Dalsum. D: Dick Maas. HOR [R] 95m. V

Lift to the Scaffold 1958 *See* **Frantic**

Light Across the Street, The 1956 French ★★★ For Bardot's legion of fans, another romantic triangle, this one ending up in murder. (a.k.a. *Female and the Flesh*) C: Brigitte Bardot, Raymond Pellegrin. D: Georges Lacombe. DRA 76m.

Light Ahead, The 1939 ★★★★ In a cholera-infected village, two misfits—a handicapped boy and a blind girl—fall in love. Long-lost and then restored, Yiddish-language film retains charm, light touch and ingratiating actors. C: Isidore Cashier, Helen Beverly, David Opatoshu. D: Edgar Ulmer. DRA 94m. V

Light at the Edge of the World, The 1971 Spanish ★★ A Cape Horn lighthouse keeper (Douglas) battles it out with a pirate (Brynner). For dessert, the two dogs fight over shipwrecked Eggar. Exciting at times, but basically absurd. C: Kirk Douglas, Yul Brynner, Samantha Eggar, Fernando Rey. D: Kevin Billington. ACT [PG] 126m. V

Light in the Forest, The 1958 ★★★½ Young man raised by Indians undergoes culture shock when he reenters the white world. Though story is an old one, Disney's treatment makes this a little better than average. Good for younger viewers. C: James MacArthur, Carol Lynley, Fess Parker, Jessica Tandy. D: Herschel Daugherty. FAM/DRA 92m. V

Light in the Jungle, The 1992 ★★★½ Somber, only intermittently absorbing bio of famed doctor Albert Schweitzer and his career in a jungle hospital in Africa. C: Malcolm McDowell, Susan Strasberg, Andrew Davis. D: Gray Hofmeyer. DRA [PG] 91m. V

Light in the Piazza 1962 ★★★★½ Tasty dish of soap, exquisitely produced, with American (de Havilland) in Italy, who tries to marry off her retarded daughter (Mimieux) and then develops a conscience. Heartfelt, sensitively acted drama, with beautiful location photography. C: Olivia de Havilland, Rossano Brazzi, Yvette Mimieux, George Hamilton. D: Guy Green. DRA 101m.

Light of Day 1987 ★★★ Brother and sister (Fox and Jett) in a struggling Cleveland rock band try to keep their lives on track when their mother falls ill. Some good performances in a downbeat story. C: Michael J. Fox,

Gena Rowlands, Joan Jett. D: Paul Schrader. DRA [PG-13] 107m. v

Light Sleeper 1992 ★★★★ Dafoe is a middle-aged drug runner for an upper-class dealer (Sarandon). One of Schrader's more successful examinations of the lives of the down and out, with fine acting. C: Willem Dafoe, Susan Sarandon, Dana Delany, Mary Beth Hurt. D: Paul Schrader. DRA [R] 103m. v

Light that Failed, The 1939 ★★★★ Artist (Colman) struggles with failing sight as he races to finish his portrait of Cockney belle (Lupino), whose over-the-top performance is thrilling to watch. Based on the Kipling novel. C: Ronald Colman, Walter Huston, Ida Lupino, Dudley Digges. D: William Wellman. DRA 97m.

Light Touch, The 1951 ★★★½ A con artist (Granger) woos and uses an innocent woman (Angeli) in his plot to swindle a gangster. Attractive European locations. C: Stewart Granger, Pier Angeli, George Sanders. D: Richard Brooks. CRI 110m.

Light Years 1988 French ★★ Issac Asimov penned this tale of futuristic prince who travels to fantasy world of sex and violence to conquer evil destroying his own land. Poor animation and banal story line kill it. Nudity, violence, and language not for younger audiences. D: Rene Laloux. SFI [PG] 71m. v

Light Years Away 1981 French ★★★½ Howard is a cranky recluse holed up in a deserted filling station in Ireland who befriends drifter Ford while trying to build a flying machine. Low-key drama is mainly a quirky character study. C: Trevor Howard, Mick Ford. D: Alain Tanner. DRA 105m.

Lightblast 1985 ★★½ Weak sci-fi adventure with Estrada as a courageous San Francisco cop trying to stop a mad genius from destroying the world. C: Erik Estrada. D: Enzo Castellari. SFI 89m. v

Lighthorsemen, The 1988 Australian ★★★½ During WWI, Australia's famous Light Horse Brigade meets tragedy in the desert. Outstanding battle sequences beautifully filmed in this true-to-life adventure. C: Jon Blake, Peter Phelps, Tony Bonner. D: Simon Wincer. ACT [PG] 116m. v

Lightning Carson Rides Again 1938 ★★★ Fast-paced western with McCoy as a sheriff trying to locate his missing nephew. C: Tim McCoy, Joan Barclay, Forrest Taylor, Ted Adams. D: Sam Newfield. WST 58m. v

Lightning Incident, The 1991 ★★★ Talented TV star McKeon is trapped in foolish mumbo-jumbo story of psychic mom tryng to save her child from an evil cult. C: Nancy McKeon, Tantoo Cardinal, Elphidia Carrillo, Miriam Colon, Tim Ryan, Polly Bergen. D: Michael Switzer. DRA [R] 90m. v

Lightning Jack 1994 ★ A gunfighter (Hogan) in the Old West teaches his tricks to a deaf-mute black sidekick. Lame spoof, only for die-hard Hogan fans. C: Paul Hogan, Cuba Gooding Jr., Beverly D'Angelo, Pat Hingle, Frank McRae, Roger Daltry. D: Simon Wincer. COM [PG-13] 93m. v

Lightning over Water 1980 ★★★½ Unique if uneasy documentary record of director Nicholas Ray's final months as he struggles with imminent death by cancer and simultaneously hopes to revive his career. C: Wim Wenders, Nicholas Ray. D: Wim Wenders. DOC 91m. v

Lightning Swords of Death 1974 Japanese ★★★½ A disgraced samurai wanders Japan with his infant son in tow; brilliantly choreographed action sequences from start to finish. Very violent; followed by even bloodier action ballet, *Shogun Assassin.* C: Tomisaburo Wakayama, Masahiro Tomikawa. D: Kenji Misumi. DRA [R] 83m.

Lightning, the White Stallion 1986 ★★ When his beloved racehorse is stolen, gambling man (Rooney) does everything he can to save the nag. Listless family film that goes nowhere. C: Mickey Rooney, Isabel Lorca, Susan George. D: William A. Levey. FAM/DRA [PG] 93m. v

Lights! Cameras! Murder! 1989 ★★★ Okay suspense tale of young boy chased by a murderer, after the child accidentally films the crime. C: John Barrett. D: Frans Nel. ACT 89m. v

Lightship, The 1986 ★★★ Three bank robbers attempt to hijack a floating lighthouse captained by pacifist Brandauer, who prevents his crew from fighting back. Offbeat psychological thriller with ill-conceived ending and flamboyant performance by Duvall. C: Robert Duvall, Klaus Maria Brandauer, Tom Bower. D: Jerzy Skolimowski. CRI [PG-13] 87m. v

Like a Turtle on Its Back 1978 French ★★½ Writer's block is subject of this uneven, shallow treatment. Evocative title is the best thing about this earnest but plodding attempt to make sense out of stifled creativity. C: Jean-Francois Stevenin, Bernadette Lafont. D: Luc Beraud. DRA 110m.

Like Father, Like Son 1987 ★★½ When an ancient Indian potion finds its way into the drink of a renowned heart surgeon (Moore), he discovers, much to his horror, that he now inhabits the body of his teen-age son (Cameron) while his son occupies his. Tired body switching formula results in a tedious, laughless comedy. C: Dudley Moore, Kirk Cameron, Margaret Colin, Catherine Hicks. D: Rod Daniel. COM [PG-13] 101m. v

Like Water for Chocolate 1992 Mexican ★★★★ Sensual, fantasy-touched tale about the youngest daughter in a Mexican family who imbues her cooking with her deepest feelings and desires. Adaptation of passionate book by Laura Esquivel is full of suprises. C: Lumi Cavazos, Marco Leonardi. D: Alfonso Arau. DRA [R] 113m. v

Li'l Abner 1940 ★★ Cornpone fest from Al

Capp's hillbilly comic strip with talented cast hiding in ugly makeup. Compare to the 1959 musical version. C: Granville Owen, Martha O'Driscoll, Mona Ray, Buster Keaton. D: Albert Rogell. COM 72m. V

Li'l Abner 1959 ★★★½ Energetic musical based on Al Capp's comic script. Plot has Dogpatch as site for nuclear testing, while Army does bodybuilding experiment involving title character. Tuneful songs, lively choreography. Highlight: The Sadie Hawkins Day Ballet. C: Peter Palmer, Leslie Parrish, Stubby Kaye, Julie Newmar, Stella Stevens. D: Melvin Frank. MUS 114m. V

Lilac Dream 1987 ★★★ Soggy romance of an amnesiac (Rambo) on a desert island, falling in love, and living idyllically til his wife arrives on the scene. C: Dack Rambo, Susan Almgren. DRA 80m. TVM V

Lilacs In the Spring 1954 *See* **Let's Make Up**

Lili 1953 ★★★★½ Magical musical, for youngsters of all ages, involves naive French orphan (Caron) who joins a touring carnival as assistant to a bitter puppet master (Ferrer). It's Lili's relationship with the puppets that provides the enchantment here, highlighted by Oscar-winning song "Hi Lili, Hi Lo," and climactic dream ballet. C: Leslie Caron, Mel Ferrer, Zsa Zsa Gabor, Jean-Pierre Aumont. D: Charles Walters. FAM/MUS [G] 81m. V

Lili Marleen 1981 German ★★★ Marginally talented singer (Schygulla) rockets to fame in Nazi Germany after her hit rendition of title tune. Fassbinder's most expensive, ambitious production, also one of his weakest; it wavers uneasily between cynicism and sentiment. C: Hanna Schygulla, Giancarlo Giannini, Mel Ferrer. D: Rainer Werner Fassbinder. DRA 120m.

Lilies of the Field 1963 ★★★★½ Marvelous inspirational comedy/drama about a black construction worker (Poitier) talked into building a chapel for a determined group of German refugee nuns. Sidney won a Best Actor Oscar for his charming performance. From William E. Barrett's novel. Followed by a television sequel, *Christmas Lilies of the Field*. C: Sidney Poitier, Lilia Skala, Lisa Mann. D: Ralph Nelson. DRA 93m. V

Liliom 1930 ★★★½ Carnival performer in a carnival is killed during a fight, but is allowed to return from heaven for one day to watch over his family. Original inspiration for the musical *Carousel* is a little dated but still has mountains of charm. C: Charles Farrell, Rose Hobart. D: Frank Borzage. DRA 89m.

Lilith 1964 ★★★ A young therapist (Beatty) falls in love with a schizophrenic patient (Seberg). Interesting, not completely successful look at the possible emotional dangers in the doctor-patient relationship. C: Warren Beatty, Jean Seberg, Peter Fonda, Kim Hunter. D: Robert Rossen. DRA 114m. V

Lillian Russell 1940 ★★★ Biography of Gay '90s musical star. Faye sings several period songs ("After the Ball," "The Band Played On"). C: Alice Faye, Don Ameche, Henry Fonda, Edward Arnold. D: Irving Cummings. MUS 127m.

Lily in Love 1984 ★★★ Bland comedy remake of *The Guardsman* as ham actor (Plummer) tests the loyalty of his wife (Smith) by impersonating a younger man. Two stars are wasted. C: Christopher Plummer, Maggie Smith, Elke Sommer, Adolph Green. D: Karoly Makk. COM [PG-13] 104m. V

Lily of Killarney 1935 ★★★ Old-fashioned romance about a rich lord who must give up the ill-bred woman he loves to retain his fortune. C: Gina Malo, John Garrick, Stanley Holloway. D: Maurice Elvey. DRA 82m. V

Lily Tomlin 1986 ★★★★ Behind-the-scenes documentary tracks development of Tomlin's hit Broadway show *The Search for Signs of Life in the Universe*. Rewarding glimpses of Tomlin and collaborator Wagner are of interest to fans. D: Nicholas Broomfield, Joan Churchill. DOC 90m.

Lily Was Here 1989 ★★★ Pregnant teenage runaway bcomes a fugitive from justice. Dull, but earnest problem drama. C: Marion Van Thijn. D: Ben Verbong. DRA [R] 110m. V

Limbo 1972 ★★★ An earnest film that depicts the lives of three women whose husbands are missing in Vietnam. Avoids politics in favor of melodrama. (a.k.a. *Three Women in Limbo*) C: Kathleen Nolan, Kate Jackson, Kate Justice. D: Mark Robson. DRA [PG] 112m.

Limehouse Blues 1934 ★★★½ In London's East End, an Asian thug attempts to leave his possessive girlfriend for a woman with a mysterious past. Slick and contrived. (a.k.a. *East End Chant*) C: George Raft, Jean Parker, Anna May Wong, Eric Blore. D: Alexander Hall. DRA 65m.

Limelight 1952 ★★★★ Historic pairing of Chaplin and Keaton for parts of this sentimental soap opera make it well worth seeing. Story of music hall has-been Charlie's devotion to ballerina (Bloom) is soggy, but touching. Movie wasn't shown in L.A. till 1972, when it won Oscar for Best Score. C: Charlie Chaplin, Claire Bloom, Nigel Bruce, Buster Keaton. D: Charles Chaplin. COM [G] 120m. V

Limit Up 1989 ★★★ Routine Faustian comedy about an aspiring Chicago stock trader (Allen) who makes a pact with the devil (Vance) and gets more than she bargained for. C: Nancy Allen, Dean Stockwell, Brad Hall, Danitra Vance, Ray Charles, Danita Vance. D: Richard Martini. COM [PG-13] 88m. V

L'Immortelle 1962 French ★★★½ Fragmented mystery/love story dominates this often impressive film debut by director Robbe-Grillet who coauthored *Last Year in Marienbad*. Only for French New Wave enthusiasts. C: Jacques Doniol-Valcroze, Françoise Brion. D: Alain Robbe-Grillet. DRA 100m.

Limping Man, The 1953 British ★★★½ After the war, former American serviceman Bridges returns to England to resume his romance with a British actress, and finds himself involved in a murder. Fairly suspenseful British-made mystery let down by hokey ending. C: Lloyd Bridges, Moira Lister, Leslie Phillips, Rachel Roberts, Jean Marsh. D: Charles DeLatour. CRI 76m.

Linda 1993 ★★★ Slick suspense tale of hapy couple (Madsen, Thomas) terrorized by acquaintances during a vacation. C: Virginia Madsen, Richard Thomas, Ted McGinley. D: Nathaniel Gutman. ACT [PG-13] 88m. TVM v

Lindbergh Kidnapping Case, The 1976 ★★★★ Hopkins is superb as Bruno Hauptmann, convicted of kidnapping and murdering the famed aviator's infant son in 1932. Film does a good job of indicting the real criminal here: America's obsession with celebrity. C: Anthony Hopkins, Cliff DeYoung, Joseph Cotten, Martin Balsam. D: Buzz Kulik. DRA 150m. TVM v

Lineup, The 1958 ★★★½ Based on the '50s TV series, this police procedural follows two hired guns looking to retrieve drugs planted on unsuspecting travelers. Skilled direction and real San Francisco locations elevate this routinely plotted B-feature. C: Warner Anderson, Emile Meyer, Eli Wallach. D: Don Siegel. CRI 86m.

Linguini Incident, The 1992 ★★ A Manhattan waitress (Arquette), obsessed with Houdini, schemes to get money to develop her own magic act by robbing the trendy restaurant where she works. Tries too hard, and is neither as hip nor as funny as it thinks it is. C: Rosanna Arquette, David Bowie, Andre Gregory. D: Richard Shepard. COM [R] 99m. v

Link 1986 British ★★★ Trained ape, used as a servant, commits multiple murders at an isolated mansion. Cunning chiller devolves into typical kill-the-teenagers fare in third act. Great circus-of-horrors music by Jerry Goldsmith. C: Terence Stamp, Elisabeth Shue. D: Richard Franklin. HOR [R] 103m. v

Lion Has Seven Heads, The 1970 Conga ★★½ An exploration of imperialist rule in Africa. Intriguing subject frequently falls prey to a lack of focus. C: Jean-Pierre Léaud, Gabriele Tinti. D: Glauber Rocha. DRA 97m.

Lion Has Wings, The 1939 British ★★★ Patriotic docudrama about Britain's Royal Air Force preparedness training for WWII. Good of its kind, but dated. C: Merle Oberon, Ralph Richardson, June Duprez. D: Michael Powell, Brain Hurst, Adrian Brunel. DRA 76m.

Lion in Winter, The 1968 British ★★★★★ A brilliant, complex drama of a royal family. Henry II (O'Toole) gathers his sons and imprisoned queen, Eleanor of Aquitaine (Hepburn in her third Oscar-winning performance) one Christmas to decide succession to the throne. Outstanding performances; Goldman's adaption of his play also won an Oscar, as did Barry's score. C: Peter O'Toole, Katharine Hepburn, Jane Merrow, Anthony Hopkins, Nigel Terry, Timothy Dalton. D: Anthony Harvey. DRA [PG] 134m. v

Lion Is in the Streets, A 1953 ★★★½ A con artist (Cagney) who wins the hearts of the masses is elected governor but ultimately gives in to corruption. Predictable plot is brightened by Cagney's inspired performance. C: James Cagney, Barbara Hale, Anne Francis. D: Raoul Walsh. DRA 88m. v

Lion King, The 1994 ★★★★ Disney's hot streak continues with this animated feature about a cub coming of age in the wild after his evil uncle forces him into exile, sort of a cartoon *Hamlet of the Jungle.* Great animation and the usual excellent voice work. Like *Aladdin, Beauty and the Beast,* and *The Little Mermaid,* winner of Oscars for Best Original Score and Best Song. Voices of Jeremy Irons, James Earl Jones, Matthew Broderick, Whoopi Goldberg. D: Roger Allens, Rob Minkoff. FAM/DRA 87m.

Lion of the Desert 1979 Libyan ★★½ Mussolini (Steiger) continually threatens Libya and the leader of a rebel guerrilla band (Quinn), manages to keep Italian forces at bay. Surprisingly bland war epic. C: Anthony Quinn, Oliver Reed, Rod Steiger, John Gielgud, Irene Papas, Raf Vallone. D: Moustapha Akkad. ACT [PG] 164m. v

Lion, The 1962 ★★★ Predictable drama about a girl who adopts a pet lion in the African bush. Director Cardiff, a former cinematographer, is more successful with beautiful photography than with story. Shot in CinemaScope. C: William Holden, Trevor Howard, Capucine, Pamela Franklin. D: Jack Cardiff. DRA 96m.

Lionheart 1989 ★★★½ During the Middle Ages, homeless children traveling to join Richard the Lionheart's crusade are threatened by Black Prince who wants to sell them as slaves. Entertaining children's film lacks epic scope. C: Eric Stoltz, Gabriel Byrne, Nicola Cowper. D: Franklin J. Schaffner. FAM/ACT 104m. v

Lionheart 1990 ★★ A tough guy (Van Damme) skips out on the Foreign Legion and becomes a professional streetfighter. Any excuse for a fight fest! (a.k.a. *A.W.O.L.* and *Wrong Bet*) C: Jean-Claude Van Damme, Deborah Rennard, Harrison Page. D: Sheldon Lettich. ACT [R] 105m. v

Lion's Share, The 1979 ★★★ Violent gangster film in which an innocent man hapens on stolen loot with tragic results. C: Julio De Grazia, Luisina Brando, Fernanda Mistral, Ulises Dumont, Julio Chevez. ACT 105m. v

Lip Service 1988 ★★★½ Charming character study of an old-fashioned newsman (Dooley) locking horns with a brash newcomer (Dunne) on a local TV news show. C: Griffin Dunne, Paul Dooley. D: W.H. Macy. DRA 67m. v

Lipstick 1976 ★★ A psychopath rapes a beautiful model. After the courts spurn her, she takes matters into her own hands. Horribly violent film with little to redeem it, except for teenage Mariel, in her film debut. C: Margaux Hemingway, Chris Sarandon, Perry King, Anne Bancroft, Mariel Hemingway. D: Lamont Johnson. ACT [R] 88m. v

Lipstick Camera, The 1994 ★★½ Quickie about an aspiring journalist using a camera concealed inside her lipstick to get the story she needs. C: Brian Wimmer, Ele Keats, Terry O'Quinn, Sandahl Bergman, Charlotte Lewis, richard Portnow, Corey Feldman. D: Mike Bonifer. DRA [R] 93m. v

Liquid Dreams 1992 ★★★ In her search to discover her sister's murderer, Daly becomes an erotic dancer in a strip club. Jaded mystery thriller builds little suspense or titillation from its clichéd debauchery. C: Richard Steinmetz, Candice Daly, Barry Dennen. D: Mark Manos. CRI [R] 92m. v

Liquid Sky 1983 ★★★★ An alien invader inhabits the body of a lesbian punker (Carlisle) for the purpose of collecting life-sustaining chemicals that can only be obtained during sex. Very original sci-fi cult comedy is definitely not for all tastes, and especially not for children, but lovers of the avant-garde shouldn't be disappointed. C: Anne Carlisle, Paula Sheppard, Otto Von Wernherr. D: Slava Tsukerman. COM [R] 112m. v

Liquidator, The 1966 British ★★ The Secret Service hires a war hero. A James Bond wanna-be that has its moments, but they're few and far between. C: Rod Taylor, Trevor Howard, Jill St. John. D: Jack Cardiff. ACT 105m.

Lisa 1962 ★★★ WWII is over, but a young Jewish girl is pursued relentlessly by an ex-Nazi. Worth a look for excellent location shooting and intermittent thrills. C: Stephen Boyd, Dolores Hart, Leo McKern, Hugh Griffith, Donald Pleasence. D: Philip Dunne. ACT 112m.

Lisa and the Devil 1975 Italian ★ A woman discovers a mannequin double of herself and gets caught up in satanic horrors at a remote mansion. Convoluted, hokey shocker, particularly confusing in reedited version known as *The House of Exorcism.* (a.k.a. *The House of Exorcism*). C: Telly Savalas, Elke Sommer, Sylva Koscina, Alida Valli. D: Mario Bava. HOR 93m. v

Lisa, Bright and Dark 1973 ★★★½ Teenager (Lenz) suffers nervous breakdown, gets no help from establishment, so her three girlfriends come to the rescue. Depressing drama with good work by Lenz. C: Anne Baxter, John Forsythe, Kay Lenz. D: Jeannot Szwarc. DRA 78m. TVM

Lisbon 1956 ★★★½ A smuggler (producer/director/star Milland) is hired to rescue an American imprisoned behind the Iron Curtain. Highlighted by picturesque locales and Rains' consummate villainy as Milland's boss. C: Ray Milland, Maureen O'Hara, Claude Rains. D: Ray Milland. DRA 90m. v

List of Adrian Messenger, The 1963 ★★★½ Scott searches for the murderer of a wealthy family's heirs. Okay detective yarn with a distracting gimmick: Curtis, Douglas, Lancaster, Mitchum, and Sinatra are disguised in heavy makeup. C: George C. Scott, Clive Brook, Dana Wynter, Herbert Marshall, Tony Curtis, Kirk Douglas, Burt Lancaster, Robert Mitchum, Frank Sinatra, John Huston. D: John Huston. CRI 98m. v

Listen, Darling 1938 ★★★½ Siblings Garland and Bartholomew select a mate (Pidgeon) for widowed mother Astor, instead of her "sensible" choice. Lightweight cutesy musical with wholesome plotting notable mostly for songs sung by young Garland. C: Judy Garland, Freddie Bartholomew, Mary Astor, Walter Pidgeon. D: Edwin L. Marin. MUS 70m. v

Listen to Britain 1942 British ★★★★★ Lyrical documentary short compresses 24 hours of wartime into 20 minutes of cinematic poetry. Very moving. D: Humphrey Jennings. DOC 20m.

Listen to Me 1989 ★★½ Ace high school debater (Cameron) finds that he's out of his league, not only on the podium, but also in love when he enters college. Strained and manipulative plot fails to deliver much in the way of either comedy or drama. C: Kirk Cameron, Jami Gertz, Roy Scheider. D: Douglas Day Stewart. COM [PG-13] 107m. v

Listen Up: The Lives of Quincy Jones 1991 ★★★½ Documentary about influential jazz great Quincy Jones. Footage of Jones at work and interviews with collaborators are informative, but music itself is biggest plus. Must-see for fans of the composer/arranger. D: Ellen Weissbrod. DOC 115m. v

Lisztomania 1975 British ★★½ Rock star Daltrey plays the 19th-century composer in one of director Russel's typically overblown extravaganzas aiming to combine art and satire. Only Nicholas scores as a proto-Nazi Richard Wagner. C: Roger Daltrey, Sara Kestelman, Ringo Starr, Paul Nicholas. D: Ken Russell. DRA 105m. v

Little Annie Rooney 1925 ★★★ Street urchin (Pickford) bands together a scruffy team of waifs to help her avenge her father's murder. Silent film blends elements of comedy, action and melodrama with mixed results. C: Mary Pickford, William Haines. D: William Beaudine. COM 94m. v

Little Ark, The 1972 ★★★★ When severe flooding tears a family apart, two children begin a journey to find their father, (Bikel). Nicely told story for young audiences. C: Theodore Bikel, Philip Frame, Genevieve Ambas. D: James Clark. FAM/DRA [G] 100m.

Little Big Horn 1951 ★★★½ In 1876 Montana, a patrol of the 7th Cavalry, aware that Sioux and Cheyenne nations are massing for major invasion, race to warn General Custer, who refuses to wait for reinforcements and recklessly attacks. Compelling, well-acted, low-budget saga. C: Lloyd Bridges, John Ireland, Marie Windsor. D: Charles Warren. WST 86m. V

Little Big League 1994 ★★★ A 12-year-old (Edwards) inherits a major-league baseball team, the Minnesota Twins, takes over as manager, and teaches everybody a lesson about winning. Sentimental comedy about kids and the great American pastime. C: Jason Robards, Luke Edwards, Timothy Busfield, Dennis Farina, John Ashton, Kevin Dunn, Jonathan Silverman. D: Andrew Scheinman. FAM/COM [PG]

Little Big Man 1970 ★★★★★ The 121-year-old hero of Thomas Berger's historical novel, Jack Crabb (Hoffman), recalls his days raised by Indians, as Wild Bill Hickok's friend, and as the lone white survivor of Custer's Last Stand. Mammoth, high-adventure Western is brilliantly tragic, ironic, and romantic. C: Dustin Hoffman, Faye Dunaway, Chief Dan George, Martin Balsam. D: Arthur Penn. WST 149m. V

Little Boy Lost 1953 ★★★★ Sincere, heart-warming drama detailing man's relationship with orphan who may or may not be the son he lost during WWII. Remarkable performance by eight-year-old Fourcade. C: Bing Crosby, Claude Dauphin, Nicole Maurey. D: George Seaton. DRA 95m.

Little Buddha 1994 Italian/American ★★★½ Is Fonda's and Isaak's little boy the reincarnation of Buddha Gautama? Tibetan monks seem to think so, triggering a wealth of brightly colored flashbacks to sixth-century India and Reeves as an improbable dispenser of wisdom. So loopy it's fascinating. C: Bridget Fonda, Keanu Reeves, Chris Isaak. D: Bernardo Bertolucci. DRA 87m.

Little Caesar 1930 ★★★★½ Robinson became a star in the talkies' first classic gangster movie. Hungry for power and weirdly possessive of his ballroom dancer friend (Fairbanks), Rico is a neurotic blueprint for all the crime kingpins who followed. C: Edward G. Robinson, Douglas Fairbanks, Jr., Glenda Farrell, Sidney Blackmer. D: Mervyn LeRoy. CRI 80m. V

Little Cigars 1973 ★ Ridiculous exploitation film concerning a mob mistress (Tompkins) on the run from her kingpin lover (De Santis). She links up with a gang of midgets, and she and her pint-sized partners stage a string of robberies. The film's absurd premise is the only laugh. C: Angel Tompkins, Billy Curtis, Jerry Murren. D: Chris Christenberry. COM [PG] 92m.

Little Colonel, The 1935 ★★★★ In post-Civil War South, little Shirley Temple manages to reunite her mother (Venable) with estranged grandfather (Barrymore). Filmed in black and white, with final sequence in glorious Technicolor. Nice film for kids, best known for marvelous dance sequence on the stairs between Temple and Bill "Bojangles" Robinson. C: Shirley Temple, Lionel Barrymore, Evelyn Venable, Bill Robinson. D: David Butler. MUS 80m. V

Little Darlings 1980 ★★★ Exploits at a girls' summer camp where two rival campers (McNichol, O'Neal) bet on which one can lose her virginity faster. Odd mix of crude humor and teenage sentimentality hurts the credibility of this too cute comedy, but performances are worth watching. C: Tatum O'Neal, Kristy McNichol, Armand Assante, Matt Dillon. D: Ronald F. Maxwell. COM [R] 95m. V

Little Dorrit 1988 British ★★★★½ Two-part epic employs a huge stellar cast to bring the bleak Dickens classic to the screen. The story of a man and his daughter (Pickering) struggling to survive debtors' prison and her eventual triumph is brilliantly told. Among Guinness' finest work; a tour de force for writer/director Edzard. C: Derek Jacobi, Alec Guinness, Roshan Seth, Sarah Pickering, Miriam Margolyes, Cyril Cusack, Joan Greenwood, Robert Morley. D: Christine Edzard. DRA [G] 360m. V

Little Drummer Girl, The 1984 ★★★ Muddled spy tale of a pro-Palestinian actress recruited to play the part of an Israeli operative. Fine performance by Keaton and the always interesting Kinski. From John Le Carré novel. C: Diane Keaton, Yorgo Voyagis, Klaus Kinski, Sami Frey. D: George Roy Hill. DRA [R] 130m. V

Little Fauss and Big Halsy 1970 ★★ A couple of motorcycle racers (Redford and Pollard) take off on a cross-country adventure. Easygoing road story in the *Easy Rider* mold. C: Robert Redford, Michael J. Pollard, Lauren Hutton, Noah Beery. D: Sidney J. Furie. ACT [R] 97m.

Little Foxes, The 1941 ★★★★½ Greedy Southern family fights and bickers over business deal. Excellent version of Lillian Hellman's play, dominated by Davis as rapacious Regina, desperate to close the deal against opposition of sick husband Marshall. Climactic showdown between the two is memorable. A game cast makes this compelling drama. C: Bette Davis, Herbert Marshall, Teresa Wright, Richard Carlson, Patricia Collinge, Dan Duryea. D: William Wyler. DRA 116m. V

Little Fugitive, The 1953 ★★★★ Believing he has killed his seven-year-old brother, a boy (Andrusco) goes on the lam and winds up at Coney Island. Intriguing and warmly rewarding comedy/drama produced on a low budget with an unprecocious, nonprofessional cast. C: Morris Engel, Ruth Orkin, Richie Andrusco. D: Ray Ashley. DRA 75m.

Little Giant 1946 ★★★½ Abbott and Costello appear as two separate comic performers in this gentle, offbeat comedy about a shy introvert (Costello) who becomes a success selling vacuum cleaners door to door. Plays more for sentiment than laughs. C: Bud Abbott, Lou Costello, Brenda Joyce, Jacqueline Wit, Margaret Dumont. D: William Seiter. COM 91m. V

Little Giant, The 1933 ★★★★ Gentle, winning comedy lets Robinson spoof hs own gangster image, playing a reformed bootlegger trying to mix with high society. C: Edward G. Robinson, Mary Astor, Helen Vinson. D: Roy Del Ruth. COM 74m.

Little Giants 1994 ★★★½ Will the lovable-but-inept Little Giants win the Urbania, Ohio peewee football league tournament? Moranis, O'Neill, and a cast of cute youngsters make one care enough to find out. C: Ed O'Neill, Rick Moranis, Shawna Waldron. D: Duwayne Dunham. COM [PG] 106m. V

Little Girl Who Lives Down the Lane, The 1976 Canadian ★★★★ Chilling thriller has Foster as mysterious girl inhabiting a house with a never-seen father and a basement she is reluctant to show nosy neighbor (Sheen). Unusual plot is not as obvious as it sounds. With a dead-on, creepy performance by Sheen. C: Jodie Foster, Martin Sheen, Scott Jacoby, Alexis Smith. D: Nicolas Gessner. HOR [PG] 90m. V

Little Gloria—Happy At Last 1982 ★★★★½ Gripping, well-acted story of famed custody battle between mother of the eight-year-old Vanderbilt heiress and the child's aunt, Gertrude Whitney (Lansbury). Quartet of older female stars (Davis, Lansbury, Stapleton, and Johns) makes this essential viewing, with Stapleton's warped nanny taking top honors. C: Lucy Gutteridge, Bette Davis, Angela Lansbury, Maureen Stapleton, Glynis Johns, Christopher Plummer, Martin Balsam, Barnard Hughes. D: Waris Hussein. DRA 180m. TVM V

Little House on the Prairie 1974 ★★★★ Pilot for popular TV series based on Laura Ingalls Wilder's stories. In 19th-century America, the Ingalls family (led by Landon) migrates from Wisconsin farm to prairies of Kansas. Sentimental without being sappy, and fine family viewing. Series episodes also available on video. C: Michael Landon, Karen Grassle, Melissa Gilbert. D: Michael Landon. FAM/DRA 98m. TVM V

Little Hut, The 1957 British ★★★ Sexual tensions mount when a husband (Granger), wife (Gardner), and their best friend (Niven) find themselves marooned on a remote tropical island. Too much talk in this well-acted, but too dry comedy. C: Ava Gardner, Stewart Granger, David Niven, Finlay Currie. D: Mark Robson. COM 90m.

Little Kidnappers, The 1953 British ★★★★½ Small but marvelous children's film about two late-19th-century boys (Whiteley and Winter) who kidnap a baby after their stern grandfather denies them a dog. Whiteley and Winter were given special Oscars for their performances. Excellent viewing for children. C: Jon Whiteley, Vincent Winter, Adrienne Corri. D: Philip Leacock. FAM/DRA 95m.

Little Kidnappers, The 1990 Canadian ★★★ Average remake of 1953 original features Heston as grandfather who learns his two charges have taken a baby after he refuses their request for a dog. Appealing performances, but overall not as good as original film. C: Charlton Heston, Bruce Greenwood, Patricia Gage. D: Donald Shebib. FAM/DRA 100m. TVM

Little Lord Fauntleroy 1936 ★★★★ Charming children's film; towheaded Bartholomew is a 19th-century New York boy whisked away to England, where inheritance makes him wealthy British lord. Well done, with good performances by Bartholomew and Smith. Previously made in 1921; redone for TV in 1980. Based on Frances Hodgson Burnett's novel. C: Freddie Bartholomew, C. Aubrey Smith, Guy Kibbee, Dolores Costello, Mickey Rooney, Jessie Ralph. D: John Cromwell. FAM/DRA 102m. V

Little Lord Fauntleroy 1980 ★★★★ Good TV remake stars Schroder as impoverished New York child who becomes the toast of England after he inherits late grandfather's British estate. Schroder carries story well, and Guinness is marvelous as boy's English tutor. C: Ricky Schroder, Alec Guinness, Eric Porter, Colin Blakely, Rachel Kempson. D: Jack Gold. FAM/DRA 98m. TVM V

Little Malcolm 1974 British ★★★ Entertaining, subversive story of three students who instigate a phony revolt pokes fun at counterculture politics. Takes a while to make its point, but strong performances keeps it going. (a.k.a. *Little Malcolm and His Struggle Against the Eunuch.*) C: John Hurt, John McEnery, David Warner. D: Stuart Cooper. DRA 112m. TVM

Little Malcolm and His Struggle Against the Eunuch 1974 *See* **Little Malcolm**

Little Man Tate 1991 ★★★★ Foster's impressive directing debut is a quiet film about a child genius (Hann-Byrd) whose waitress mom wants him to be a regular kid, while a teacher of gifted children (Wiest) wants him to develop his gifts. Warm and provocative. C: Jodie Foster, Dianne Wiest, Adam Hann-Byrd, Harry Connick, Jr. D: Jodie Foster. DRA [PG] 99m. V

Little Man, What Now? 1934 ★★★★ In post-WWI Germany, a young couple copy with poverty and unemployment just when they're about to start a family. Beautifully realized love story, with an excellent performance by Sullavan. C: Margaret Sullavan, Douglass Montgomery, Alan Hale, Mae Marsh, Hedda Hopper. D: Frank Borzage. DRA 91m.

Little Match Girl, The 1987 ★★★ Sentimental version of Hans Christian Andersen tale designed for then-*Cosby Show* sitcom child Pulliam. She plays orphaned child who charms her way into wealthy family during Christmas. Plenty of sap flows throughout, though younger children might enjoy. C: Keshia Pulliam-Knight, William Daniels, John Davies, Hallie Foote, Rue McClanahan. D: Michael Lindsay-Hogg. FAM/DRA 100m. TVM v

Little Men 1940 ★★★½ Average follow-up to *Little Women*, based on book by Louisa May Alcott. Now-adult Jo March (Francis) runs boarding school where ruffian (Lydon) becomes a more refined young man. Somewhat predictable, but not without its moments. Oakie provides nice comic relief. C: Kay Francis, Jack Oakie, George Bancroft, Jimmy Lydon, William Demarest. D: Norman McLeod. FAM/DRA 84m. v

Little Mermaid, The 1989 ★★★★★ Sublime fairy tale with gorgeous animation, beautifully crafted story reminiscent of Disney's Golden Age. Teenage mermaid Ariel falls in love with human, makes pact with witch Ursula to trade her voice for legs. Terrific Ashman/Menken songs include Oscar-winning "Under the Sea," "Part of Your World," and "Kiss the Girl." Carroll is brilliant as the sea witch. Voices of Jodi Benson, Pat Carroll, Samuel E. Wright, Rene Auberjonois. D: John Musker, Ron Clements. FAM/DRA [G] 83m. v

Little Minister, The 1934 ★★★★ Hepburn is perfect as the fiery Gypsy with whom a straitlaced Scottish cleric (Beal) seeks earthly (and earthy) love. He mistakes her for, and she turns out to be, part of the local gentry. Based on a James M. Barrie story. C: Katharine Hepburn, John Beal, Donald Crisp. D: Richard Wallace. DRA 110m. v

Little Miss Broadway 1938 ★★★½ Temple is—what else?—an orphan who becomes the darling of a theatrical boarding house inhabited by Murphy, Durante, and others. Not much on plot, but long on musical numbers and some fun scenes between Temple and Durante. Fine for kids. C: Shirley Temple, George Murphy, Jimmy Durante, Phyllis Brooks, Edna May Oliver. D: Irving Cummings. FAM/MUS 70m. v

Little Miss Marker 1934 ★★★★ Bookie Menjou and his gambling gang succomb to toddler charm when Temple is dropped off as payment for an I.O.U. bet. Delightful, perfect for the youngsters, with Temple at her most adorable. From Damon Runyon short story. Remade three times. C: Shirley Temple, Adolphe Menjou, Dorothy Dell, Charles Bickford. D: Alexander Hall. FAM/COM 80m.

Little Miss Marker 1980 ★★★½ Old Damon Runyon chestnut about bookie Matthau reformed by little girl. Andrews an attractive love interest, but a bland effort. Watch the 1934 original. C: Walter Matthau, Julie Andrews, Sara Stimson, Tony Curtis, Bob Newhart, Lee Grant, Brian Dennehy. D: Walter Bernstein. COM [PG] 142m. v

Little Mister Jim 1946 ★★ A child is cast adrift when his mother dies and father becomes an alcoholic. Weak story matched by weak performances. C: Jackie "Butch" Jenkins, James Craig, Frances Gifford. D: Fred Zinnemann. DRA 92m.

Little Monsters 1989 ★ A young boy (Savage) discovers an obnoxious beast (Mandel) underneath his bed who takes him on an incredible journey into a hideous netherworld. Loud and abrasive comedy is more mean-spirited than funny. C: Fred Savage, Howie Mandel, Ben Savage, Daniel Stern. D: Richard Alan Greenberg. COM [PG] 103m. v

Little Moon and Jud McGraw 1975 ★★★ Misfired attempt at a different kind of western with Caan as an outlaw teaming up with an improbably cast Powers (as a Native-American princess) to get revenge on a small town. (a.k.a. *Gone With the West*). C: James Caan, Stefanie Powers, Sammy David Jr., Aldo Ray. D: Bernard Girard. WST [R] 92m. v

Little Murders 1971 ★★★★ New York City is portrayed as a violent, depressing bastion of urban blight in this black Jules Feiffer comedy that focuses on the attempts of a brassy city woman (Rodd) to marry a reserved photographer (Gould). Hard-edged comedy is bitingly funny and cynical. C: Elliott Gould, Marcia Rodd, Vincent Gardenia, Elizabeth Wilson, Donald Sutherland, Alan Arkin. D: Alan Arkin. COM [PG] 108m. v

Little Nellie Kelly 1940 ★★★★ Bit of George M. Cohan blarney turned into a lovely Garland vehicle as she reconciles family feud caused by grandfather Winninger. Songs include "Singin'" in the Rain." C: Judy Garland, George Murphy, Charles Winninger. D: Norman Taurog. MUS 100m. v

Little Nemo: Adventures in Slumberland 1990 Japanese ★★★½ Based on the beloved Winsor McKay comic strip, this animated feature follows a boy through his dream life into the dangerous world of his nightmares. The animation is excellent, though storytelling is not as powerful as it could be. C: William Hurtz, Mickey Rooney, Rene Auberjonois. D: Misami Hata. FAM/DRA [G] 85m. v

Little Night Music, A 1977 ★★½ Weak film version of Stephen Sondheim's exquisite musical based on Bergman's *Smiles of a Summer Night* about mismatched couples in turn-of-the-century Sweden. Taylor is miscast as charismatic actress who sings "Send In the Clowns," but Rigg shines. C: Elizabeth Taylor, Len Cariou, Diana Rigg, Hermione Gingold, Lesley-Anne Down. D: Harold Prince. MUS [PG] 128m. v

Little Nikita 1988 ★★½ A young California boy discovers that his "typically American" parents are actually Soviet agents. A great idea that somehow doesn't deliver. Nice Poitier, though. C: Sidney Poitier, River Phoenix,

Caroline Kava. D: Richard Benjamin. DRA [PG] 98m. v

Little Ninjas 1992 ★★½ Three black-belt youngsters try to save their friend from the clutches of an evil karate champion. C: Steven Nelson, Jon Anzaldo, Alan Godshaw. D: Emmett Alston. ACT 85m. v

Little Noises 1991 ★★★ Strange account of a loser would-be writer (Glover) who becomes successful when he publishes the poetry of a deaf-mute boy as his own. Intriguing premise, but film never quite comes together. C: Crispin Glover, Tatum O'Neal, Rik Mayall, Tate Donovan. D: Jane Spencer. DRA 91m. v

Little Nuns, The 1965 Italian ★★★½ Pair of convent sisters, plagued by jet noise, go to town to try to resolve matters with the authorities. Story is an amiable and heartwarming tale. C: Catherine Spaak, Sylva Koscina, Amodeo Nazzari. D: Luciano Salce. COM 101m.

Little Old New York 1940 ★★★ Fictionalized biography of Robert Fulton and his invention of the steam engine; entertaining if ordinary romance. C: Alice Faye, Fred MacMurray, Brenda Joyce. D: Henry King. DRA 100m.

Little Orphan Annie 1932 ★★★½ Charming comedy from the popular newspaper comic strip; Green makes a delightful Annie, fending for herself after Kennedy deserts her. C: Mitzie Green, Edgar Kennedy, Buster Phelps, May Robson. D: John S. Robertson. COM 60m. v

Little Prince, The 1974 British ★★★ Antoine de Saint-Exupery's classic fable of an aviator's encounter with a space-traveling child. Highlight: Fosse's snake dance. C: Richard Kiley, Steven Warner, Bob Fosse, Gene Wilder, Donna McKechnie. D: Stanley Donen. MUS [G] 88m. v

Little Princess, The 1939 ★★★★½ Rich daughter of army colonel is forced to work as a servant when her father is reported dead, leaving her penniless. Cinderella story in reverse is one of Temple's best. Moving and lovingly produced. C: Shirley Temple, Richard Greene, Anita Louise, Cesar Romero, Arthur Treacher. D: Walter Lang. DRA 91m. v

Little Rascals, The 1994 ★★ Noisy, disheartening retread of the beloved 1930's kiddie short subjects focuses on Alfalfa's romance with Darla. The original Rascals were irreplaceable. These are the cinematic equivalent of Kleenex. C: Travis Tedford, Bug Hall, Brittany Ashton Holmes, Kevin Jamal Woods. D: Penelope Spheeris. FAM/COM [PG] 82m.

Little Romance, A 1979 ★★★★ An intelligent American girl's blossoming love for an equally smart Parisian boy (Bernard) comes under fire from the adult forces in her life. Charming romantic comedy entertains consistently, with an especially endearing performance by Olivier as a pickpocketing rogue. Oscar for Best Score. C: Laurence Oliver, Diane Lane, Thelonious Bernard, Arthur Hill, Sally Kellerman. D: George Roy Hill. COM [PG] 105m. v

Little Sex, A 1982 ★★ A philandering director of TV commercials (Matheson) finds his pledge of monogamy to his loving wife (Capshaw) is constantly being put to the test. Slow-paced sex comedy offers very little sex or comedy. C: Tim Matheson, Kate Capshaw, Edward Herrmann, John Glover. D: Bruce Paltrow. COM [R] 94m. v

Little Shop of Horrors 1986 ★★★★ Exuberant science-fiction musical puts man-eating plant, Audrey II, in Lower East Side flower shop, tended to by nerd (Moranis). Audrey steals movie, as puppeted by Jim Henson's shop. Martin scores in send-up of sadistic dentist. Greene re-creates stage role of nerd's masochistic girlfriend. From off-Broadway hit, based on Roger Corman's 1960 film. C: Rick Moranis, Ellen Greene, Vincent Gardenia, Steve Martin. D: Frank Oz. MUS [PG-13] 94m. v

Little Shop of Horrors, The 1960 ★★★★ A down-and-out loser working in a plant store lovingly raises a giant man-eating—and talking—plant. Watch for a teenage-looking Jack Nicholson. Showbiz legend has it that this film was made in two days. A campy, fun floral romp. C: Jonathan Haze, Jackie Joseph, Dick Miller, Jack Nicholson. D: Roger Corman. HOR 72m. v

Little Sweetheart 1990 ★★★ Graphic horror film about a little girl obsessed with television and the nightmare world she conjures up. C: John Hurt, Karen Young, Cassie Barasch, Barbara Bosson, James Waterston, John McMartin, Rose Parra, Elie Raab. HOR [R] 93m. v

Little Theatre of Jean Renoir, The 1969 French ★★★★ Three episodes plus a song, each introduced by Renoir, centering around artificiality and contrivance. The final story, about an unconventional menage a trois, is the strongest. Renoir's last film, made for French TV in 1969, then released theatrically. (a.k.a. *Le Petit Theatre de Jean Renoir*) C: Jeanne Moreau, Fernand Sardou, Francoise Arnoul. D: Jean Renoir. DRA 100m. v

Little Thief, The 1989 French ★★★★ An alienated teenager (Gainsbourg) deals with life in post-WWII France by petty theft and dreams of the film world. A wistful tale, based on a Francois Truffaut story—a female counterpart to his *400 Blows* antihero. Gainsbourg is wonderful. C: Charlotte Gainsbourg, Simon De La Brosse. D: Claude Miller. DRA [R] 108m. v

Little Treasure 1985 ★★½ Seeking her lost father in Mexico, a stripper meets up with an American misfit. Together they search for treasure. An odd little story, anchored by Lancaster and a nice job by Danson. C: Margot

Kidder, Ted Danson, Burt Lancaster. D: Alan Sharp. DRA [R] 95m. v

Little Vegas 1990 ★★½ Enterprising gangsters look to re-create Las Vegas in remote trailer park full of oddballs. Quirky comedy has its moments, but talented cast can't sustain an almost nonexistent script. C: Anthony Denison, Catherine O'Hara, Jerry Stiller, Michael Nouri. D: Perry Lang. COM [R] 91m. v

Little Vera 1988 Russian ★★★½ A first from the pre-glasnost Soviet Union: A candid look at disaffected teenagers, particularly the independent, feisty heroine (Negoda), and the effect of the West on life. Famous for nudity and sex—another first from Russia—although Negoda is terrific. C: Natalia Negoda, Andrei Sokolov. D: Vassili Pitchul. DRA 115m. v

Little White Lies 1989 ★★★ Shallow romantic comedy with attractive leads about a detective (Jillian) and a doctor (Matheson) falling in love under assumed identities. C: Ann Jillian, Tim Matheson, Suzie Plakson, Marc McClure. D: Anson Williams. COM 88m. TVM v

Little Women 1933 ★★★★★ Classic version of the Louisa May Alcott novel about four sisters and their varied fortunes during Civil War era. Hepburn is ideally cast as tomboy Jo. Entire film beautifully done with many vivid, moving moments. A delight. C: Katharine Hepburn, Joan Bennett, Frances Dee, Jean Parker, Edna May Oliver, Spring Byington. D: George Cukor. FAM/DRA 116m. v

Little Women 1949 ★★★★ High-gloss version of Louisa May Alcott classic of four impoverished teenage sisters struggling to grow up during hard times. Good, but marred by Allyson's overly cute Jo. C: June Allyson, Peter Lawford, Margaret O'Brien, Elizabeth Taylor, Janet Leigh, Mary Astor. D: Mervyn LeRoy. FAM/DRA 122m. v

Little Women 1978 ★★★½ TV adaptation of Louisa May Alcott's novel about young girls coming of age in 19th-century New England. Veterans McGuire and Garson provide the most sparkling moments in this pilot for an unsuccessful series. C: Meredith Baster Birney, Susan Dey, Eve Plumb, Dorothy McGuire, Robert Young, Greer Garson, William Shatner. D: David Rich. FAM/DRA 200m. TVM

Little Women 1994 ★★★★★ Lovely, faithful rendering of Louisa May Alcott's classic tale of four sisters in Civil War America. Ryder embodies tomboy Jo with restraint and delicacy, Sarandon makes a warm, intelligent Marmee, and Danes excells in her heart-wrenching sickbed scene. Beautifully directed and produced. Matches, if not tops, the 1933 Katharine Hepburn version. C: Winona Ryder, Trini Alvarado, Claire Danes, Kirsten Dunst, Christian Bale, Gabriel Byrne, Susan Sarandon, Samantha Mathis, Mary Wickes. D: Gillian Armstrong. FAM/DRA [PG] 115m. v

Little World of Don Camillo, The 1951 French ★★★ Intermittently amusing comedy about village priest (Fernandel) who cannot abide the election of Communists to local offices. Gentle satire pokes fun at the mix of church and state; carried by Fernandel. Based on Giovanni Guareschi's novel, followed by several sequels. C: Fernandel, Sylvie, Gino Cervi. D: Julien Duvivier. COM 106m. v

Littlest Horse Thieves, The 1976 ★★★★ Solid children's drama from Disney concerning three late-19th-century youngsters who attempt to save ponies that are being mistreated by coal miners. Good use of period detail and English locations in well done film. (a.k.a *Escape from the Dark*) C: Alastair Sim, Peter Barkworth, Maurice Colbourne. D: Charles Jarrott. FAM/DRA 104m. v

Littlest Outlaw, The 1954 ★★★½ After rescuing a mistreated horse from its abusive owner, a young boy escapes with the steed into the countryside. Good children's film from Disney that makes the most of its Mexican locations. C: Pedro Armendariz, Joseph Calleia. D: Roberto Gavaldon. FAM/DRA 73m. v

Littlest Rebel, The 1935 ★★★½ Civil War-era film features Temple as Southern child who tap-dances her way into Union officer Holt's heart, thus saving life of her Confederate father (Boles). Nice moments and good dance sequences. C: Shirley Temple, John Boles, Karen Morley, Bill Robinson, Stepin Fetchit. D: David Butler. MUS 70m. v

Live a Little, Love a Little 1968 ★★½ Photographer Presley moonlights between a conservative publication and a girlie magazine. Odd Elvis vehicle, with only three songs. C: Elvis Presley, Michele Carey, Rudy Vallee, Sterling Holloway, Eddie Hodges. D: Norman Taurog. MUS [PG] 89m. v

Live a Little, Steal a Lot 1975 *See* **Murph the Surf**

Live and Let Die 1973 British ★★★½ James Bond's attempts to crack a Caribbean heroin ring using a voodoo cult as a cover result in a long series of chases. A rather far-fetched Bond (Moore's debut). C: Roger Moore, Jane Seymour, Yaphet Kotto. D: Guy Hamilton. ACT [PG] 121m. v

Live for Life 1967 French ★★★ Television reporter leaves wife for young model. Sudsy follow-up to Lelouch's massively successful *A Man and a Woman* follows the same formula—glossy, slick romance about beautiful people—but only partially succeeds. Good performances from the actors. C: Yves Montand, Annie Girardot, Candice Bergen. D: Claude Lelouch. DRA 130m.

Live From Death Row 1991 ★★★½ When an ambitious talk show host (Cassidy) interviews a serial killer (Davison) on death row, things go wrong when the killer takes her and her staff hostage. Well-acted, if lurid melodrama. C: Bruce Davison, Joanna Cassidy, Art

La Fleur, Calvin Levels. D: Patrick Duncan. DRA 94m. TVM v

Live From Washington It's Dennis Miller 1988 ★★★½ The popular Saturday Night Live comedian in concert, focusing on poitical humor. C: Dennis Miller. D: Paul Miller. COM 60m. v

Live, Love and Learn 1937 ★★★½ Routine fluff given MGM gloss as high society woman (Russell) marries struggling artist (Montgomery) and both struggle to adapt. C: Robert Montgomery, Rosalind Russell, Mickey Rooney, Monty Woolley. D: George Fitzmaurice. COM 78m.

Live Wire 1992 ★★★ An FBI agent (Brosnan) is torn when he discovers that hs wife is having an affair with the Senator he's assigned to protect from a bomb threat. Okay melodrama. C: Pierce Brosnan, Ron Silver, Ben Cross, Lisa Eilbacher. ACT [R] 85m. v

Live Wires 1946 ★★★½ The *Bowery Boys*, in their first adventure, try to bring a cruel gangster (Mazurki) to justice. Fun for kids, a guilty pleasure for the rest of us. C: Leo Gorcey, Huntz Hall, Bobby Jordan, Pamela Blake, Mike Mazurki. D: Phil Karlson. ACT 64m.

Lively Set, The 1964 ★ Young man (Darren) ditches college to race cars. Fast cars, rock 'n' roll, and the opposite sex are the main elements of the familiar formula in this typical '60s teenage comedy. C: James Darren, Pamela Tiffin, Doug McClure. D: Jack Arnold. COM 95m.

Lives of a Bengal Lancer, The 1935 ★★★★ Exciting adventure involving the British colonial army in India. The focus is on macho camaraderie, as heroes (Cooper and Tone) help out the misunderstood son of their colonel (Cromwell). A classic. C: Gary Cooper, Franchot Tone, Richard Cromwell, Guy Standing. D: Henry Hathaway. ACT 110m. v

Livin' Large 1991 ★★★½ Fame and fortune befall a smooth talking black street hipster (Carson) when he accidently becomes a popular TV newscaster. Will success change him? Pointed satire of media figures and the price of fame scores a fair share of laughs. C: Terrence Carson, Lisa Arrindell, Blanche Baker. D: Michael Schultz. COM [R] 95m. v

Livin' the Life 1984 ★★½ Anemic comedy/romance about a man whose fantasies disrupt his life. C: Rupert Everett, Cristina Raines. D: Francis Megahy. COM 83m. v

Living Daylights, The 1987 British ★★★★ In his first outing as Bond, Dalton goes up against phony Soviet defector Krabbe and American loose cannon Baker, conspiring to deal arms. Dalton is terrific as a more modern Bond. C: Timothy Dalton, Maryam d'Abo, Jeroen Krabbe. D: John Glen. ACT [PG] 131m. v

Living Desert, The 1953 ★★★★ Oscar-winning documentary is spectacular look at animal and insect life in the American desert. First of Disney True-Life Adventure series. Worthwhile entertainment. D: James Algar. DOC [G] 73m. v

Living End, The 1992 ★★★★ Two very different HIV-positive men (Dytri and Gilmore) go on a madcap, frantically paced road trip that ultimately ends in tragedy. Absorbingly edgy and uncomfortable examination of homosexuals succeeds largely on account of its frank filmmaking style. C: Mike Dytri, Craig Gilmore, Mary Woronov, Paul Bartel. D: Gregg Araki. COM 85m. v

Living Free 1972 British ★★½ Sequel to *Born Free* continues the adventures of Elsa the lioness, now raising her three cubs in African wilderness. Despite beautiful locations, deadly slow pacing makes this a less-than-adequate follow-up to original story. C: Susan Hampshire, Nigel Davenport. D: Jack Couffer. FAM/DRA 91m. v

Living In a Big Way 1947 ★★★½ Three outstanding dance numbers, choreographed by Kelly and Stanley Donen, greatly improve so-so tale of G.I. (Kelly) married to millionairess (McDonald). C: Gene Kelly, Marie McDonald, Charles Winninger. D: Gregory La Cava. MUS 102m.

Living It Up 1954 ★★★½ Totally reworked version of classic *Nothing Sacred* has Lewis in Carole Lombard's old role of supposedly dying man brought to New York as last-wish publicity stunt designed by aggressive reporter Leigh. Amusing, but uninspired. C: Dean Martin, Jerry Lewis, Janet Leigh, Edward Arnold. D: Norman Taurog. COM 95m.

Living on Tokyo Time 1987 ★★★★½ Cultures clash when a demure Japanese girl (Ohashi) travels to San Francisco and agrees to marry a Japanese-American wannabe rock musician (Nakagawa) so that she can stay in the U.S. Offbeat character comedy explores the humorous side of Japanese and American lifestyles. C: Minako Ohashi, Ken Nakagawa, Mitzie Abe. D: Steven Okazaki. COM [R] 83m. v

Living to Die 1990 ★★★ A no-nonsense former cop is called in to help Las Vegas gambling czar clear himself of a false murder rap. Standard mystery actioner. C: Wings Hauser, Darcy Demoss, Arnold Vosloo, Asher Brauner. D: Wings Hauser. ACT 84m. v

Lizards, The 1963 Italian ★★★★ Small-town loafers never really follow through on half-baked plans for the future. One of director Wertmller's best. Story resembles *I Vitelloni*, but film stands beautifully on its own. C: Toni Petruzzi, Stefano Sattaflores, Sergio Ferranninò, Luigi Barbieri. D: Lina Wertmüller. COM 85m.

Lizzie 1957 ★★★ Tragedy drives a young woman (Parker) to develop multiple personalities. Interesting, but flawed story; adaptation of Shirley Jackson's *The Bird's Nest*. C: Eleanor Parker, Richard Boone, Joan Blondell, Hugo Haas, Johnny Mathis. D: Hugo Haas. DRA 81m.

Lizzies of Mack Sennett, The 1924 ★★★

Compilation of three Sennett shorts featuring legendary Arbuckle, Swain, and Conklin. Silent comedy treat. C: Fatty Arbuckle, Billy Bevan, Mack Swain, Chester Conklin. COM 51m. v

Lloyd's of London 1936 ★★★★ The life of the founder of the prestigious insurance firm (Power) is more interesting than it sounds. An errand boy in the 1700s ends up building a great company but still must spar (with Sanders) for the woman he loves (Carroll). Excellent production. C: Freddie Bartholomew, Madeleine Carroll, Tyrone Power, George Sanders. D: Henry King. DRA 115m.

Loaded Guns 1975 ★★★ Gripping spy adventure features lots of gunplay and action. C: Ursula Andress, Woody Strode, Isabella Biagin. D: Fernando Di Leo. ACT 90m. v

Lobster for Breakfast 1982 Italian ★★★½ Comic study of a toilet salesman focuses on his romances and business dealings. Charming comedy. C: Enrico Montesano, Claude Brasseur, Claudine Auger. D: Giorgio Capitani. COM [R] 96m. v

Lobsterman from Mars 1990 ★ Silly comedy spoofs '50s horror films, with a sleazy Hollywood producer (Curtis) debating whether to purchase a cheesy scare flick about an alien lobster creature terrorizing a sleepy country community. Tongue-in-cheek humor misses its mark. C: Tony Curtis, Deborah Foreman, Patrick MacNee. D: Stanley Sheff. COM [PG] 84m. v

Local Hero 1983 British ★★★★½ An uptight American oil executive (Riegert) experiences a life-affirming transition when he travels to a quirky Scottish town to turn it into an oil refinery site. Refreshingly original comedy surprises and pleases throughout with its engaging characters and unpredictable story turns. C: Peter Riegert, Burt Lancaster, Fulton MacKay. D: Bill Forsyth. COM [PG] 111m. v

Loch Ness Horror, The 1982 ★★★ Divers accidentally rouse the infamous Loch Ness monster and provoke an all-out attack against humans. Average horror suspense. C: Barry Buchanan, Miki McKenzie, Sandy Kenyon. D: Larry Buchanan. HOR [PG] 93m. v

Lock and Load 1990 ★★★ An evil plot is hatched to unleash U.S. commando elite who have been hypnotically programmed to turn into killers. The plan must be stopped at all costs. Average action suspense. C: Jack Vogel, Renee Cline, Jeffrey Smith, William Hathaway-Clark. D: David A. Prior. ACT 88m. v

Lock Up 1989 ★★½ A sadistic warden (Sutherland) with a grudge makes life hell for easygoing convict in this way-below-average Stallone vehicle. Sutherland certainly makes an impression as the demented jailer, though; he does everything but twirl his moustache. C: Sylvester Stallone, Donald Sutherland, Darlanne Fleugel, John Amos. D: John Flynn. ACT [R] 115m. v

Lock Up Your Daughters! 1969 British ★★ Adaptation of Henry Fielding play about three bawdy women who take up with a trio of capricious sailors. Sex farce set in 18th-century England. C: Christopher Plummer, Susannah York, Glynis Johns, Ian Bannen. D: Peter Coe. COM 102m.

Lockdown 1990 ★★★ Framed for a murder he didn't commit, a hard-boiled cop is forced to flee prison and confront the villainous gangster who set him up. OK detective yarn. C: Richard Lynch, Chris De Rose, Joe Estevez, Larry Mintz. D: Frank Harris. ACT [R] 86m. v

Locket, The 1946 ★★★ A strong woman with a disturbing past (Day) destroys the men in her life. Dark and somber atmosphere, but plot lacks direction. C: Laraine Day, Brian Aherne, Robert Mitchum. D: John Brahm. DRA 86m.

Lodger, The 1926 British ★★★★ Hitchcock's first suspense film about a boarder suspected of being a Ripperesque killer in foggy London. Silent thriller is dated but should interest Hitch devotees. Full of the director's trademarks: bungling police, fair-haired women, an innocent man accused, voyeurism, and his first cameo appearance. C: Ivor Novello, Marie Ault. D: Alfred Hitchcock. HOR 65m. v

Lodger, The 1944 ★★★★ New boarding house tenant is suspected of being Jack the Ripper. Tense remake of Hitchcock's silent suspense orginal concentrates on the chills, with Cregar as a convincing heavy. C: Merle Oberon, George Sanders, Laird Cregar, Cedric Hardwicke, Sara Allgood. D: John Brahm. HOR 84m.

Logan's Run 1976 ★★★★ Big-budget sci-fi yarn follows a futuristic cop (York) hunting down people who try to escape from Man's perfect world. Their offense? They've turned 30. Great special effects and sets. C: Michael York, Jenny Agutter, Richard Jordan, Peter Ustinov, Farrah Fawcett-Majors. D: Michael Anderson. SFI [PG] 119m. v

Lois Gibbs and the Love Canal 1982 ★★★★ Absorbing true story of housewife-turned-activist Gibbs (Mason), who petitioned government for relief from chemical pollution in the infamous town near Niagara Falls in the '70s. Mason does well in well-crafted drama. C: Marsha Mason, Robert Gunton, Penny Fuller. D: Glenn Jordan. DRA 95m. v

Lola 1961 French ★★★½ Nightclub singer (Aimee) has to choose between three suitors. Knockout Aimee performance keeps charming but ever-so-slight fairy tale afloat; Demy's first film was tribute to director Max Ophuls. C: Anouk Aimee, Marc Michel, Jacques Harden. D: Jacques Demy. DRA 90m. v

Lola 1971 British ★★★ Middle-aged writer of cheap pornographic novels (Bronson) becomes involved with and ultimately marries a 16-year-old. Adult drama is an uninspired product of '60s social mores, though it features Bronson in offbeat role. (a.k.a. *The Statutory Affair* and *Twinky*) C: Charles Bronson, Susan George, Trevor Howard, Honor Blackman, Robert Morley. D: Richard Donner. DRA [PG] 88m. v

Lola 1982 German ★★★★ An honest, upright commissioner falls in love with a prostitute, not knowing about her background. Update of *The Blue Angel* becomes a strong parable of postwar Germany (and the third part of Fassbinder's trilogy, with *The Marriage of Maria Braun* and *Veronika Voss*). C: Barbara Sukowa, Armin Mueller Stahl, Mario Adorf. D: Rainer Werner Fassbinder. DRA [R] 114m. v

Lola Montes 1955 French ★★★★½ Celebrated circus performer's eventful romantic escapades are recounted in Ophuls' last—and only color—film. Extravagant production features extraordinary use of multiple flashbacks, intricate camera movement, and eye-popping costumes. C: Martine Carol, Peter Ustinov, Anton Walbrook, Oskar Werner. D: Max Ophuls. DRA 110m. v

Lolita 1962 British ★★★★ A middle-aged professor (Mason) marries a woman he doesn't love (Winters) so he can be near her 12-year-old "nymphet" daughter (Lyon). Intense adaptation of then-scandalous Nabokov novel; performances are outstanding, especially Winters'. C: James Mason, Sue Lyon, Shelley Winters, Peter Sellers. D: Stanley Kubrick. DRA 152m. v

Lolly Madonna War, The 1973 *See* **Lolly Madonna XXX**

Lolly Madonna XXX 1973 ★★★½ Well-intentioned rural drama about two feuding families and the rage that's accidently ignited. Falls apart in middle, but has memorable ensemble performances. (a.k.a. *The Lolly Madonna War*) C: Rod Steiger, Robert Ryan, Jeff Bridges, Season Hubley. D: Richard Sarafian. DRA [PG] 103m.

London After Midnight 1927 ★★★½ A vampire stalks unsuspecting London in this silent movie curio. Atmospheric, but damaged by too much comedy relief. Browning remade it in 1935 as *Mark of the Vampire*. C: Lon Chaney. D: Tod Browning. HOR 65m.

London Kills Me 1991 British ★★ Film glamorizes the life of a small-time London drug dealer and thief who wants to get into a new line of business. It's difficult to sympathize with the characters in this superficial film. C: Justin Chadwick, Steven Mackintosh, Fiona Shaw, Brad Dourif. D: Hanif Kureishi. DRA [R] 107m. v

Lone Hand, The 1953 ★★★½ Undercover agent infiltrates a band of outlaws. McCrea delivers the goods in this routine Western. C: Joel McCrea, Barbara Hale, James Arness. D: George Sherman. WST 80m.

Lone Justice 1993 ★★★ Sincere, moderately effective western with Baldwin as gunman on trial for murdering his father. C: Daniel Baldwin, Julia Campbell, Luis Avalos, Chris Cooper, Sean Baca, Taylor Fry. D: Peter Werner. WST [R] 94m. v

Lone Ranger and the Lost City of Gold, The 1958 ★★★½ The Lone Ranger and Tonto search for lost Native American treasure. Entertaining Saturday matinee fare. C: Clayton Moore, Jay Silverheels, Douglas Kennedy. D: Lesley Selander. WST 80m. v

Lone Ranger, The 1956 ★★★½ Legendary masked man and Tonto discover that a greedy rancher is fomenting Indian uprising in hopes of extracting silver from a sacred mountain. Action-packed Western adventure mainly for kids; superior stunts and outdoor photography. C: Clayton Moore, Jay Silverheels, Lyle Bettger, Bonita Granville. D: Stuart Heisler. WST 87m. v

Lone Star 1952 ★★★½ Soldier of fortune finds love and danger during the Texas annexation of Mexico. Large-scale production with real star power. C: Clark Gable, Ava Gardner, Lionel Barrymore, Beulah Bondi, Broderick Crawford, Ed Begley. D: Vincent Sherman. WST 94m. v

Lone Texan 1959 ★★½ War veteran returns to Texas and finds his sheriff brother has gone bad. Interesting premise goes nowhere in this tepid Western. C: Willard Parker, Grant Williams, Audrey Dalton. D: Paul Landres. WST 70m.

Lone Wolf, The Although Louis Joseph Vance's jewel thief with a heart of gold dates back to 1914 and had been the hero of several silent films, he only made his mark as a series figure when Columbia revived him in 1935 with handsome, suave Melvyn Douglas in the role. Three years later, the studio tried Francis Lederer, then settled on Warren William, a former Perry Mason and Philo Vance, for nine quicky mysteries.

The Lone Wolf Returns (1935)
The Lone Wolf in Paris (1938)
The Lone Wolf Spy Hunt (1939)
The Lone Wolf Strikes (1940)
The Lone Wolf Meets a Lady (1940)
The Lone Wolf Takes a Chance (1941)
The Lone Wolf Keeps a Date (1941)
Secrets of the Lone Wolf (1941)
Counter-Espionage (1942)
One Dangerous Night (1943)
Passport to Suez (1943)
The Notorious Lone Wolf (1946)
The Lone Wolf in London (1947)
The Lone Wolf in Mexico (1947)
The Lone Wolf and His Lady (1949)

Lone Wolf and His Lady, The 1949 ★★ Jewel thief-turned-reporter (Randell) is accused of stealing a diamond during the opening of a new museum. Last of the *Lone Wolf* series, and none too soon. C: Ran Randell, June Vincent, William Frawley, Alan Mowbray. D: John Hoffman. CRI 60m.

Lone Wolf in London, The 1947 ★★ The Lone Wolf (Mohr) is once again falsely accused of jewel theft, this time from Scotland Yard's own safe. Reformed burgler series is wearing thin by now. C: Gerald Mohr, Nancy Saunders, Eric Blore. D: Leslie Goodwins. CRI 68m.

Lone Wolf in Mexico, The 1947 ★★½ Reformed burgler (Mohr) helps police track down diamond smugglers south of the border. So-so mystery series entry. C: Gerald Mohr, Sheila Ryan, Eric Blore. D: D. Ross Lederman. CRI 69m.

Lone Wolf in Paris, The 1938 ★★★½ Only reformed thief Michael Lanyard (Lederer) can retrieve crown jewels hijacked by a crooked Grand Duke. Fast-paced *Lone Wolf* caper. C: Francis Lederer, Frances Drake, Walter Kingsford. D: Albert S. Rogell. CRI 66m.

Lone Wolf Keeps a Date, The 1941 ★★½ Michael Lanyard (William), alias The Lone Wolf, helps retrieve stolen money in Havana. Routine mystery. C: Warren William, Frances Robinson, Eric Blore. D: Sidney Salkow. CRI 65m.

Lone Wolf McQuade 1983 ★★★½ A kickboxing Texas Ranger high-tails it to Mexico to rescue his best buddy, daughter, and dog. One of the better kick-and-chop Norris actioners. C: Chuck Norris, David Carradine, Barbara Carrera. D: Steve Carver. WST [PG] 107m. V

Lone Wolf Meets a Lady, The 1940 ★★★ The Lone Wolf (William) comes to the aid of a woman falsely accused of theft and murder. Okay series entry. C: Warren William, Jean Muir, Eric Blore, Victor Jory. D: Sidney Salkow. CRI 71m.

Lone Wolf Returns, The 1935 ★★★½ Expert jewel thief is brought out of retirement by gangsters to pull one last heist. Fine cast and slick production highlight one of the better films in this series. C: Melvyn Douglas, Gail Patrick. D: Roy Neill. ACT 69m.

Lone Wolf Spy Hunt, The 1939 ★★★★ American diplomat is kidnapped by foreign spies for secret military plans. Knockout cast and snappy script deliver the goods in this fast-paced comedy/drama. This is William's first appearance as the Lone Wolf. C: Warren William, Ida Lupino, Rita Hayworth, Virginia Weidler. D: Peter Godfrey. ACT 67m.

Lone Wolf Strikes, The 1940 ★★★½ When an heiress (Perry) loses her prized necklace, former jewel thief (William) and his less-than-honest valet (Blore) come to the rescue. Light and zippy *Lone Wolf* escapade. C: Warren William, Joan Perry, Eric Blore. D: Sidney Salkow. CRI 57m.

Lone Wolf Takes a Chance, The 1941 ★★★ The Lone Wolf (William) gets framed for murder while trying to crack a counterfeit ring. Briskly diverting mystery. C: Warren William, June Storey, Henry Wilcoxon, Eric Blore. D: Sidney Salkow. CRI 76m.

Loneliest Runner, The 1976 ★★★½ Kerwin stars as an Olympic track star who suffered humiliation as a teenager because of his chronic bed-wetting. Landon uses a light touch to direct this movie based on his personal experiences, and also plays the title character as an adult. C: Michael Landon, Lance Kerwin, Brian Keith. D: Michael Landon. DRA 74m. TVM V

Loneliness of the Long Distance Runner, The 1962 British ★★★★★ A jaded young reform-school inmate (Courtenay) is recruited to compete in a race against the students of the local public school. Quintessential '60s British film attacks "the system" as powerfully today as when first released. Brilliant film with brilliant performances. C: Tom Courtenay, Michael Redgrave, Avis Bunnage, Alec McCowen, James Fox. D: Tony Richardson. DRA 104m. V

Lonely Are the Brave 1962 ★★★★ Somber tale of aging cow wrangler (Douglas) rebelling against modern world has not aged well, but Douglas and Matthau as the pursuing marshall give nuanced performances, well worth watching. C: Kirk Douglas, Gena Rowlands, Walter Matthau, Carroll O'Connor, George Kennedy. D: David Miller. WST 107m. V

Lonely Guy, The 1984 ★★★★ Often hilarious Martin vehicle finds him broken up with girlfriend and learning to live without romance. Left-field, deadpan humor makes the most of a slight premise. Adapted by Neil Simon from *The Lonely Guy's Book of Life* by Bruce Jay Friedman. C: Steve Martin, Charles Grodin, Judith Ivey, Robyn Douglass. D: Arthur Hiller. COM [R] 91m. V

Lonely Hearts Killers, The 1970 *See* **Honeymoon Killers, The**

Lonely in America 1993 ★★★ Offbeat comedy of Indian immigrant struggling for success in New York City. C: Ranjit Chowdhry, Adelaide Miller, Robert Kessler, Melissa Christopher, David Toney, Trilok Malik. D: Barry Alexander Brown. COM [PG-13] 96m. V

Lonely Lady, The 1983 ★ Young aspiring screenwriter (Zadora) learns the hard way in wicked Hollywood. Trashy melodrama based on novel by Harold Robbins. C: Pia Zadora, Lloyd Bochner. D: Peter Sasdy. DRA [R] 92m. V

Lonely Man, The 1957 ★★★★ Western outlaw tries to make good and regain the love of his son. Excellent direction and performances redeem unoriginal plot. C: Anthony Perkins, Jack Palance, Elaine Aiken. D: Henry Levin. WST 87m. V

Lonely Passion of Judith Hearne, The 1988 British ★★★★ Smith is brilliant in mood drama of lonely Irish-Catholic spinster in boardinghouse who begins an unlikely relationship with shady American (Hoskins). Based on Brian Moore's novel. C: Maggie Smith, Bob Hoskins, Wendy Hiller. D: Jack Clayton. DRA [R] 120m. v

Lonely Villa, The 1909 ★★★★ Pioneering, silent melodrama of a family trapped in their home burglars. Griffith's use of screen space is very advanced; the drama generates its own shares of thrills, even today. C: Marion Leonard, Mary Pickford, Adele de Garde, Charles Maile, Mack Sennett. D: D.W. Griffith. CRI 10m.

Lonely Wives 1931 ★★★½ Veteran character comedian Horton gets a chance to star in this amusing take on "Dr. Jeckyl and Mr. Hyde", as a mild-mannered lawyer who becomes a lothario at night. C: Edward Everett Horton, Esther Ralston. COM [R] 86m. v

Lonelyhearts 1958 ★★★ An advice columnist (Clift) contacts one of his correspondents (Stapleton) with disastrous results. Great cast in dated adaptation of Nathanael West's classic novel *Miss Lonelyhearts.* Film debut of Stapleton and Donehue. C: Montgomery Clift, Robert Ryan, Myrna Loy, Dolores Hart, Maureen Stapleton. D: Vincent J. Donehue. DRA 104m. v

Lonesome Dove 1990 ★★★★½ Sprawling epic about the twists and turns of Texas cowpunchers herding cattle to Montana. Superb adaptation of Larry MacMurtry's Pulitzer Prize-winning novel. Vivid characterizations, topped by Duvall's convincing performance as a thoughtful, lusty former Texas ranger. C: Robert Duvall, Tommy Lee Jones, Danny Glover, Diane Lane, Robert Urich, Frederic Forrest, Anjelica Huston. D: Simon Wincer. WST 372m. TVM

Lonesome Gun *See* **Stranger on the Run**

Long Absence, The 1962 French/Italian ★★★★ A lonely bistro owner (Valli) think she sees her supposedly dead husband pass by her cafe. She follows the tramp to his home and tries to help him regain his memory. Low-key drama shared Grand Prix award at the Cannes Film Festival. C: Alida Valli, Georges Wilson, Jaques Harden. D: Henri Colpi. DRA 85m.

Long Ago Tomorrow 1971 British ★★★ A bitter young paraplegic (McDowell) begins to soften when he falls in love with a similarly disabled woman (Newman). Tries, but too heavy-handed. (a.k.a. *The Raging Moon*) C: Malcolm McDowell, Nanette Newman, Georgia Brown. D: Bryan Forbes. DRA [PG] 111m. v

Long and the Short and the Tall, The 1961 British ★★★★ During WWII, a British patrol in Malaysia captures a Japanese soldier. Good study of men at war—and how their personalities clash. Top-notch cast. (a.k.a. *Jungle Fighters*) C: Richard Todd, Laurence Harvey, Richard Harris. D: Leslie Norman. DRA 105m.

Long Dark Hall, The 1951 British ★★★½ When a married man is accused of murdering a showgirl, his wife stands by him during the trial which could result in his execution. Average drama comes to life during courtroom scenes. C: Reginald Beck, Rex Harrison, Lilli Palmer. D: Anthony Bushell. DRA 86m.

Long, Dark Night, The 1977 *See* **Pack, The**

Long Day Closes, The 1992 British ★★★★ Touching, autobiographical depiction by director Davies of his working-class childhood in 1950s England. A rich mixture of sound and image makes this a truly memorable film. C: Leigh McCormack, Marjorie Yates, Anthony Watson. D: Terence Davies. DRA [PG] 84m. v

Long Day's Journey Into Night 1962 ★★★★★ Uncompromising, searing adaptation of O'Neill's classic about a disintegrating family at the beginning of the 20th century: an alcoholic brother (Robards), a brother dying of TB (Stockwell), a miserly actor father (Richardson), and a morphine-addicted mother (Hepburn). Riveting all the way through; closing frames are haunting. C: Katharine Hepburn, Ralph Richardson, Jason Robards, Jr., Dean Stockwell. D: Sidney Lumet. DRA 170m. v

Long Duel, The 1967 British ★★★ Old-fashioned adventure concerns charismatic rebel (Brynner) leading revolt against British rule in India. Bland time-killer suffers from lethargic pace and overfamiliar storyline. C: Yul Brynner, Trevor Howard, Harry Andrews, Charlotte Rampling. D: Ken Annakin. DRA 115m.

Long Gone 1987 ★★★★ Sleeper baseball comedy hits solid triple with charming story of minor league team going for championship, headed by dreamer Petersen. Madsen is terrific as team's beauty queen-mascot. C: William L. Petersen, Virginia Madsen, Dermot Mulroney. D: Martin Davidson. COM 112m. TVM v

Long Good Friday, The 1980 British ★★★★½ Powerful, violent modern-day gangster movie has ruthless crime boss Hoskins fighting a turf war in London's underworld. Exciting thriller; only drawback is the sometimes unintelligible English vernacular accents. C: Bob Hoskins, Helen Mirren, Eddie Constantine, Dave King. D: John Mackenzie. CRI [R] 109m. v

Long Goodbye, The 1973 ★★★★ Altman's spoof of Raymond Chandler, with Gould as hard-boiled detective Philip Marlowe. Altman's wacky revisionism undercuts the layered tension of Chandler's original novel, but collection of colorful supporting players keeps things moving. C: Elliott Gould, Nina Van Pallandt, Sterling Hayden. D: Robert Altman. CRI [R] 113m. v

Long Gray Line, The 1955 ★★★★ Melodramatic tale of Irish West Point athletics coach (Power). Standout performances by Power and O'Hara (playing his wife); Ford's direction is tough yet sentimental. C: Tyrone Power, Maureen O'Hara, Ward Bond, Donald Crisp. D: John Ford. DRA 137m. v

Long Hot Summer, The 1958 ★★★★ Vagrant fieldhand Newman strikes up friendship with wealthy Welles, then tries to marry daughter (Woodward). Excellent blending of several William Faulkner works, including *The Hamlet*, with terrific cast. C: Paul Newman, Joanne Woodward, Orson Welles, Angela Lansbury, Lee Remick, Anthony Franciosa. D: Martin Ritt. DRA 117m. v

Long Hot Summer, The 1985 ★★★★½ Lengthy, faithful adaptation of William Faulkner's *The Hamlet* originally filmed in 1958. Johnson is the sexy drifter who makes a play for rich Robards' daughter (Ivey). Excellent cast with Ivey the standout. C: Don Johnson, Jason Robards, Cybill Shepherd, Ava Gardner, Judith Ivey. D: Stuart Cooper. DRA 172m. v

Long John Silver 1955 Australian ★★★½ Colorful sequel to *Treasure Island* that finds the endearingly crabby one-legged pirate (Newton) joining forces again with young Jim Hawkins in search of a fortune in gold. Fine escapist fare. C: Robert Newton, Connie Gilchrist, Kit Taylor. D: Byron Haskin. ACT 106m. v

Long, Long Trailer, The 1954 ★★★½ Honeymooning Ball and Arnaz buy an enormous mobile home. Ball has some lovely slapstick routines, e.g., preparing salad in moving trailer, but film resembles extended sitcom episode. C: Lucille Ball, Desi Arnaz, Marjorie Main, Keenan Wynn. D: Vincente Minnelli. COM 103m. v

Long Lost Father 1934 ★★★½ Barrymore is a father who deserted his daughter long ago but resurfaces to come to her aid when she is implicated in a robbery. Routine script based on G.B. Stern novel unfortunately doesn't Barrymore much to work with. C: John Barrymore, Helen Chandler, Donald Cook, Alan Mowbray. D: Ernest Schoedsack. DRA 63m.

Long Memory, The 1952 British ★★★½ After 12 years behind bars for a murder he did not commit, innocent Mills is released and tries to prove he was framed. Well-told tale, though more melodrama than thriller. Sellars stands out as duplicitous femme fatale. C: John Mills, John McCallum, Elizabeth Sellars. D: Robert Hamer. CRI 91m.

Long Night, The 1947 ★★★ Murderer hides out for night while his girlfriend tries to get him to surrender. Some tense moments, but overall lackluster remake of *Le Jour se Leve*. C: Henry Fonda, Barbara Bel-Geddes, Vincent Price, Ann Dvorak. D: Anatole Litvak. DRA 101m.

Long Ride Home, The 1967 *See* **Time for a Killing, A**

Long Ride, The 1984 *See* **Brady's Escape**

Long Riders, The 1980 ★★★★ Yet another version of the Jesse James saga, this time with real brothers playing the Jameses (Keaches), Youngers (Carradines), Millers (Quaids) and Fords (Guests). Hill's gracefully stylized direction, Ry Cooder's evocative score, and superb acting, particularly by David Carradine and Reed, raise this above the norm. C: David Carradine, Keith Carradine, Robert Carradine, Stacy Keach, James Keach, Randy Quaid, Dennis Quaid. D: Walter Hill. WST [R] 100m. v

Long Ships, The 1964 British ★★ Vikings face off against Moors while searching for mystical bell in this costume action mess. Talented cast goes through the motions without much swash or buckle. C: Richard Widmark, Sidney Poitier, Rosanna Schiaffino, Russ Tamblyn. D: Jack Cardiff. ACT 125m.

Long Summer of George Adams, The 1982 ★★★★ Locomotive driver Garner is put out of business by advent of the diesel engine. Garner and Hackett have special chemistry in this lighthearted homespun yarn. C: James Garner, Joan Hackett, Anjanette Comer. D: Stuart Margolin. DRA 100m. TVM

Long Voyage Home, The 1940 ★★★★½ Adventures of sailors on shore leave. Brilliant drama, adapted from several one-act plays by Eugene O'Neill, features a wonderfully gifted cast. C: John Wayne, Thomas Mitchell, Ian Hunter, Ward Bond, Barry Fitzgerald, Wilfrid Lawson, Mildred Natwick. D: John Ford. DRA 106m. v

Long Walk Home, The 1990 ★★★★½ Outstanding civil rights drama puts human faces on the issues by focusing on two women caught in the Montgomery bus boycott in the '50s. Spacek excells as white suburban matron slowly radicalized by her black maid (Goldberg). Provides new insights into seemingly familiar situations. C: Sissy Spacek, Whoopi Goldberg, Dwight Schultz, Dylan Baker. D: Richard Pearce. DRA [PG] 98m. v

Longest Day, The 1962 ★★★★★ Epic depiction of the Allied invasion of Normandy. The large international cast is exceptional. A true classic. Oscars for Special Effects and Cinematography. Based on Cornelius Ryan's book. C: John Wayne, Rod Steiger, Robert Ryan, Henry Fonda, Robert Mitchum, Richard Burton, Jeffrey Hunter, Sal Mineo, Roddy McDowall. D: Ken Annakin, Andrew Marton, Bernhard Wicki. DRA [G] 183m. v

Longest Yard, The 1974 ★★★★½ Pro-quarterback turned inmate (Reynolds) leads a team of convicts against the champion prison-guard team. Raunchy, tough-edged comedy with Reynolds in top form. Climactic match is a scream. C: Burt Reynolds, Eddie

Albert, Michael Conrad, Bernadette Peters. D: Robert Aldrich. COM [R] 121m. v

Longtime Companion 1990 ★★★★ Follows the fates of a closeknit group of gay New York men and their friends throughout the '80s, from the first faint hints of AIDS to its ultimate devastating ubiquity in their lives. A remarkably uplifting film, one of the first to address the disease. C: Campbell Scott, Bruce Davison, Mark Lamos, John Dossett, Patrick Cassidy, Mary Louise Parker. D: Norman Rene. DRA 100m. v

Look Back in Anger 1959 British ★★★★ Young man (Burton) angry at the world has an affair with his wife's best friend. Adapted from the breakthrough play by John Osborne, the film version retains the powerful, depressing atmosphere and offers excellent performances, but loses the original exhilaration. Remade in 1980 and 1989. C: Richard Burton, Claire Bloom, Edith Evans, Mary Ure, Donald Pleasence. D: Tony Richardson. DRA 99m. v

Look for the Silver Lining 1949 ★★★ Haver stars as '20s Broadway dancer Marilyn Miller in this show biz biography, stolen by Bolger as Miller's Svengali, Jack Donohue. C: June Haver, Ray Bolger, Gordon MacRae. D: David Butler. MUS 100m. v

Look in any Window 1961 ★★ Juvenile delinquency melodrama about a good boy (Anka) driven to a life of crime by his problems at home. Forgettable. C: Paul Anka, Ruth Roman, Alex Nicol, Gigi Perreau. D: William Alland. DRA 87m.

Look Out Sister 1948 ★★★½ Jordan dreams he's on a ranch in the Old West, single-handedly saving the spread from the bankers and winning the woman. All African-American cast shines in this broadly played Western satire. Great music from Louis and his band to boot! C: Louis Jordan, Suzette Harbin, Monte Hawley. D: Bud Pollard. WST 64m. v

Look Who's Laughing 1941 ★★½ Radio star comedy places Bergen and Charlie McCarthy in Fibber and Molly's town of Wistful Vista for some typical squabbling. C: Edgar Bergen, Fibber McGee, Molly McGee, Lucille Ball. D: Allan Dwan. COM 78m. v

Look Who's Talking 1989 ★★★½ Bouncy comedy about a single woman who first gives birth and then begins searching for the perfect father. Willis provides baby's voice-over commentary, the highlight of otherwise routine comedy. C: John Travolta, Kirstie Alley, Olympia Dukakis, George Segal, Bruce Willis. D: Amy Heckerling. COM [PG-13] 96m. v

Look Who's Talking Now 1993 ★ Weak third entry in the comedy series now has high-profile comedy actors speaking the thoughts of dogs. Shut up, already! C: John Travolta, Kirstie Alley, Danny DeVito, Diane Keaton. D: Tom Ropelewski. COM [PG-13] 95m. v

Look Who's Talking Too 1991 ★★ Follow-up to the 1990 hit adds a baby sister (the voice of Roseanne Arnold) to the family. Unfortunately, in their haste to cash in on their first success, the producers forgot to include jokes or a story line this time. C: John Travolta, Kirstie Alley, Olympia Dukakis, Bruce Willis, Roseanne Barr. D: Amy Heckerling. COM [PG-13] 81m. v

Lookalike, The 1991 ★★★½ Young women feverishly searches for daughter she no longer believes is dead. C: Melissa Gilbert, Diane Ladd. DRA 88m. TVM v

Looker 1981 ★★½ Plastic surgeon Finney investigates the mysterious deaths of his beautiful clients, and their association with mega-powerful industrialist Coburn. Interesting premise. C: Albert Finney, James Coburn, Susan Dey, Leigh Taylor-Young. D: Michael Crichton. CRI [PG] 94m. v

Lookin' to Get Out 1982 ★ Tedious comedy about two low-lifes scheming their way into a plush Las Vegas hotel to make a killing at the blackjack table. C: Jon Voight, Burt Young, Ann-Margret. D: Hal Ashby. COM [R] 104m. v

Looking for Love 1964 ★★½ Aspiring singer uses oddball invention to get on Tonight Show so she can sing. Notable only as Carson's one film appearance. C: Connie Francis, Susan Oliver, Jim Hutton, Danny Thomas, Johnny Carson, George Hamilton, Paula Prentiss. D: Don Weis. COM 83m.

Looking for Mr. Goodbar 1977 ★★½ A prim young teacher (Keaton) seeks excitement in singles bars, drugs, and one-night stands, with tragic results. A strong performance by Keaton in a sordid and depressing film. C: Diane Keaton, Richard Gere, William Atherton, Tuesday Weld, Richard Kiley, Tom Berenger. D: Richard Brooks. DRA [R] 136m. v

Looking Forward 1933 ★★★ Depression-era drama concerning a shopkeeper (Stone) who must close his business and fire his loyal staff. Standard tearjerker. Based on play *Service* by Dodie Smith. C: Lionel Barrymore, Lewis Stone, Benita Hume. D: Clarence Brown. DRA 82m.

Looking Glass War, The 1969 British ★★★ Two British Intelligence officers (Richardson and Rogers) recruit an AWOL Polish seaman (Jones) to photograph East German missiles in this tepid Cold War espionage film based on the Le Carre best-seller. C: Christopher Jones, Pia Degermark, Ralph Richardson, Anthony Hopkins. D: Frank Pierson. DRA [PG] 108m. v

Looks and Smiles 1981 British ★★★★ Coming-of-age tale about a frustrated young man (Green) who can't get a break in life. Don't be misled by the title; this is dark and probing and quite good. C: Carolyn Nicholson, Tony Pitts. D: Kenneth Loach. DRA 104m.

Looney, Looney, Looney Bugs Bunny Movie, The 1981 ★★★½ Reedited series of classic Bugs Bunny cartoons takes the wascally wabbit through chase with Yosemite Sam, rescue of Tweety Bird, and on to Hollywood. Acceptable, but the cartoons are better in their original form. Voice of Mel Blanc. D: Fritz Freleng. FAM/COM [G] 80m. v

Loonies on Broadway 1944 *See* **Zombies on Broadway**

Loophole 1980 British ★★★½ English caper film has a money-strapped architect recruited by a crack team of bank robbers to break into a high-security vault. Good cast and production values can't disguise the fact that this is much ado about nothing. (a.k.a. *Break In*) C: Albert Finney, Martin Sheen, Susannah York, Colin Blakely, Jonathan Pryce, Robert Morley. D: John Quested. CRI 105m. v

Loose Cannons 1990 ★★ Dreadful mystery/-buddy picture offers story of no-nonsense cop teamed up with multiple personality detective. Supposedly a comedy, but more like a trip to the dentist's chair. Without anesthesia. C: Gene Hackman, Dan Aykroyd, Dom DeLuise, Ronny Cox, Nancy Travis. D: Bob Clark. COM [R] 94m. v

Loose Connections 1984 ★★★½ Daffy road-trip comedy as feminist must share vehicle with mild-mannered chauvinist on trek to Munich. Unusual story line keeps things from getting predictable. C: Lindsay Duncan, Stephen Rea. D: Richard Eyre. COM [PG] 90m. v

Loose in London 1953 ★★★½ A British Earl is dying, and the closest known living heir turns out to be Sach! The Bowery Boys take on London in one of their better capers. C: Leo Gorcey, Huntz Hall, David Gorcey. D: Edward Bernds. COM 63m.

Loose Screws 1985 ★★ Sex-obsessed teens scheme to make their bawdy fantasies come true. C: Bryan Genesse, Karen Wood, Alan Deveau, Jason Warren. D: Rafal Zielinski. COM 75m. v

Loot 1972 British ★★★½ Adaptation of Joe Orton's play in which two crooks hide their bank-heist takings inside the coffin of one of the robbers' recently departed mother. Fast-paced black-comedy fun from beginning to end. C: Lee Remick, Richard Attenborough, Roy Holder, Milo O'Shea. D: Silvio Narizzano. COM [PG] 102m. v

Lord Jeff 1938 ★★★ Bartholomew is a good kid who falls in with bad crowd and is packed off to military school for rehabilitation. Minor story with predictable plot. C: Freddie Bartholomew, Mickey Rooney, Charles Coburn, Gale Sondergaard. D: Sam Wood. FAM/DRA 78m.

Lord Jim 1965 ★★★½ Epic adaptation of Joseph Conrad novel focuses on English merchant marine officer (O'Toole) committing act of cowardice, and his attempt to atone. Beautiful scenery and great cast, but unfocused themes and needlessly muddled philosophizing. Works best as straight adventure story. C: Peter O'Toole, James Mason, Curt Jurgens, Eli Wallach, Jack Hawkins. D: Richard Brooks. DRA 154m. v

Lord Love a Duck 1966 ★★★½ Offbeat, cult comedy about ambitious high school coed Weld driven to marriage, film stardom, and, when it suits her mood, murder, by high school senior McDowall. Satire of Southern California sends up progressive education, greed, and the idle rich, with some extremely funny bits. Very black comedy indeed, but not to every taste. C: Tuesday Weld, Roddy McDowall, Lola Albright, Martin West, Ruth Gordon, Harvey Korman. D: George Axelrod. COM 104m.

Lord of the Flies 1963 British ★★★★ English schoolboys revert to bloodthirsty savagery when they are marooned on a tropical island. Powerful adaptation of William Golding's classic novel; a frightening commentary on humanity's basic nature. C: James Aubrey, Tom Chapin, Hugh Edwards. D: Peter Brook. DRA 90m. v

Lord of the Flies 1990 ★★★ This color remake of the 1963 film of Golding's novel casts Americans as the stranded schoolboys-turned-savages. Beautifully photographed, but otherwise doesn't compare to its predecessor. C: Balthazar Getty, Christopher Furrh, Danuel Pipoly. D: Harry Hook. DRA [R] 90m. v

Lord of the Rings, The 1978 ★★★ Ineffective adaptation, based on J.R.R. Tolkien's epic fantasy about Middle Earth's inhabitants' quest for a magic ring. Uncomfortable combinatin of live-action and animation. C: Christopher Guard, William Squire, John Hurt. D: Ralph Bakshi. FAM/SFI [PG] 133m. v

Lords of Discipline, The 1983 ★★★½ In 1964, the first black cadet at a prestigious Southern military academy is hazed and brutalized. Senior cadet discovers a quasi-Fascist secret society is responsible. Good performances, though racist sadism threatens to overwhelm story. C: David Keith, Robert Prosky, G. D. Spradlin, Rick Rossovich. D: Franc Roddam. DRA 103m. v

Lords of Flatbush, The 1974 ★★★½ Slight, low-budget comedy about a quartet of punks in '50s Brooklyn. Fun to see proto-stars Winkler and Stallone before they hit it big. C: Perry King, Sylvester Stallone, Henry Winkler, Susan Blakely. D: Stephen Verona, Martin Davidson. COM [PG] 88m. v

Lords of the Deep 1989 ★ Cheap, boring rip-off of director Cameron's infinitely superior *The Abyss* centers on small group of aquanauts trapped below water with psychotic crew chief (Dillman) and supposedly hostile aliens. Don't get your feet wet. C: Bradford Dillman, Priscilla Barnes, Daryl Haney. D: Mary Ann Fisher. SFI 78m. v

Lord's of Treason 1985 *See* **Secret Honor**

Lorenzo's Oil 1993 ★★★★½ Powerful emotional drama about real-life couple (Nolte and Sarandon) who bulldoze their way through the medical establishment literature to find a cure for their son's terminal illness. Sarandon delivers an amazing performance as Lorenzo's mother; Ustinov also scores as a research scientist. Fast paced and engrossing all the way. C: Nick Nolte, Susan Sarandon, Peter Ustinov, Kathleen Wilhoite. D: George Miller. DRA [PG-13] 136m. V

Lorna Doone 1935 British ★★★★ Well-mounted Blackmore romance set in 17th-century England. A farmer is in love with a beautiful woman he thinks is a brigand's daughter. She turns out to be, of course, a kidnapped heiress. C: John Loder, Margaret Lockwood, Victoria Hopper. D: Basil Dean. DRA 89m.

Lorna Doone 1990 British ★★★★ A 17th-century English farmer falls in love with a free-spirited woman he thinks is a brigand's daughter. She turns out to be a kidnapped heiress (of course). Well-mounted romance from the R.D. Blackmore novel. Better than the 1951 remake. C: Clive Owen, Sean Bean, Polly Walker, Billie Whitelaw, Rachel Kempson. D: Andrew Grieve. DRA [PG] 90m. TVM V

Los Amigos 1973 *See* **Deaf Smith and Johnny Ears**

Los Olvidados 1950 Mexican ★★★★★ Uncompromising study of juvenile delinquents in slums of Mexico put Buñuel back on the map after a hiatus of nearly 20 years; a nearly perfect blend of surrealism and ultrarealistic world view. (a.k.a. *The Young and the Damned*) C: Alfonso Mejia, Roberto Cobo, Stella Inda. D: Luis Buñuel. DRA 88m.

Los Tarantos 1964 Spanish ★★★ Romeo and Juliet, flamenco-style: a boy and girl from rival Gypsy clans fall in love, and the inevitable tragedy results. Wondrous dancing and singing can't quite offset sentimentalized story. C: Carmen Amaya, Sara Lezana, Daniel Martin. D: Rovira Beleta. DRA 81m.

Loser Takes All 1956 British ★★★ Scenic comedy with newlyweds (Brazzi and Johns) in Monte Carlo, finding roulette more exciting than each other. Remade as *Strike It Rich* in 1990. C: Rossano Brazzi, Glynis Johns, Robert Morley. D: Ken Annakin. COM 88m.

Losin' It 1982 ★★★ Three fresh-faced teenagers head for Tijuana looking to lose their innocence. Early appearances by Cruise and Long brighten otherwise routine coming-of-age comedy. C: Tom Cruise, Jackie Earl Haley, John Stockwell, Shelley Long. D: Curtis Hanson. COM [R] 104m. V

Losing Isaiah 1995 ★★★½ A world-weary social worker (Lange) adopts an abandoned black infant, but the birth mother (Berry) later seeks custody. Two terrific performances in an effective drama, until the disappointing conclusion. C: Jessica Lange, Halle Beery, David Strathairn, Samuel L. Jackson, Cuba Gooding, Jr., Daisy Eagan, Marc John Jefferies. D: Stephen Gyllenhaal. DRA [R] 108m. V

Loss of Innocence 1961 British ★★★½ English children alone at a French hotel are charmed by an English guest (More). York gives a wonderful performance as a 16-year-old who becomes a woman. Romantic theme; surprise ending. (a.k.a *The Greengage Summer*) C: Kenneth More, Danielle Darrieux, Susannah York. D: Lewis Gilbert. DRA 99m.

Lost 1957 *See* **Tears for Simon**

Lost and Found 1979 ★★★ Romance sizzles for divorced Jackson and widowed Segal, until they spoil it all by getting married. Tumultuous reuniting *Touch of Class* stars begins well, but then loses its sparkle. C: George Segal, Glenda Jackson, Maureen Stapleton, Paul Sorvino, John Candy, Martin Short. D: Melvin Frank. COM [PG] 112m. V

Lost Angel 1943 ★★★★ O'Brien is child genius whose every moment is monitored by scientists. Robbed of her youth, she is taken in by reporter Craig who teaches the girl a few things about spontaneity. Nice story for younger audiences with fine performance by O'Brien. C: Margaret O'Brien, James Craig, Marsha Hunt, Donald Meek, Keenan Wynn. D: Roy Rowland. FAM/DRA 91m.

Lost Angels 1989 ★★★ Horovitz (of Beastie Boys fame) makes a creditable film debut in this muddled drama about a troubled teenager sent to a mental hospital where he meets psychiatrist Sutherland, who has a few loose screws of his own. C: Donald Sutherland, Adam Horovitz, Amy Locane. D: Hugh Hudson. DRA [R] 116m. V

Lost Boundaries 1949 ★★★★ Light-skinned black doctor (Ferrer) is forced to pass for white in order to practice in a conservative New England town. Tasteful look at segregation in the mid-20th century by journeyman director Werker. C: Beatrice Pearson, Mel Ferrer, Richard Hylton. D: Alfred Werker. DRA 99m.

Lost Boys, The 1987 ★★★★ Refreshing updating of the vampire legend mixes horror and humor as the new kid in town begins to notice something strange about the local gang. Imaginative production moves at a killer pace. C: Jason Patric, Corey Haim, Dianne Wiest, Barnard Hughes, Kiefer Sutherland. D: Joel Schumacher. HOR [R] 98m. V

Lost Capone, The 1990 ★★★ Title character is Al's brother, a Nebraska sheriff who must confront Al's crimes and his henchman. Plodding TV gangster film. C: Adrian Pasdar, Ally Sheedy, Eric Roberts. D: John Gray. CRI 92m. TVM V

Lost Command 1966 ★★★★ Gripping account of the French-Algerian guerilla warfare after WWII. Splendid international cast led by Quinn as a peasant turned leader. C: Anthony Quinn, Alain Delon, George Segal, Michele Morgan. D: Mark Robson. ACT 129m. V

Lost Continent, The 1968 British ★★★ Bad-movie buffs should love this bizarre mishmash of conflicting genres, featuring tramp steamers, alcoholic captains, lost civilizations, giant mutated crabs and blood-sucking vines slithering through the Sargasso Sea! Other viewers beware. C: Eric Porter, Hildegard Knef, Tony Beckley. D: Michael Carreras. SFI [G] 89m.

Lost Honeymoon 1947 ★★★ Man (Tone) regains his memory only to discover he has two children! Dependable cast can't do much with trite material. C: Franchot Tone, Ann Richards, Frances Rafferty, Una O'Connor. D: Leigh Jason. DRA 71m.

Lost Honor of Katharina Blum, The 1975 German ★★★★ A woman's life is turned upside down when she spends a night with a man, not knowing he is wanted for treason; she is persecuted by both the press and the police. From Heinrich Boll's novel. Strong attack on both the German police and press focuses on the loss of personal privacy. C: Angela Winkler, Mario Adorf. D: Volker Schlondorff, Margarethe Trotta. DRA 97m. V

Lost Horizon 1937 ★★★★★ Elegant spellbinder of five people who stumble upon Himalayan paradise Shangri-La ruled by Jaffe, where peace prevails and death is unknown. One of the best film fantasies ever made, with unforgettable finale. From the James Hilton novel; remade as musical in 1973. C: Ronald Colman, Jane Wyatt, John Howard, Edward Everett Horton, Margo, Sam Jaffe, H. B. Warner, Thomas Mitchell. D: Frank Capra. DRA 132m. V

Lost Horizon 1973 ★★½ Musical remake of the 1937 classic fantasy-adventure with pilot Finch and small plane passengers crashing into Himalayas where they come upon the idyllic civilization of Shangri-La where no one gets sick, ages, or dies. Good cast hurt by poor score. C: Peter Finch, Liv Ullmann, Sally Kellerman, George Kennedy, Michael York, Olivia Hussey, Bobby Van, Charles Boyer, John Gielgud. D: Charles Jarrott. MUS [G] 143m.

Lost in a Harem 1944 ★★★ Bud and Lou play magicians in this Arabian Nights comedy. More lavish than their other films. C: Bud Abbott, Lou Costello, Marilyn Maxwell, John Conte. D: Charles Riesner. COM 89m. V

Lost in Alaska 1952 ★★½ Abbott and Costello entry, with the boys digging for gold in the Klondike during the 1890s. Ewell gets more laughs than the stars. C: Bud Abbott, Lou Costello, Mitzi Green, Tom Ewell. D: Jean Yarbrough. COM 76m.

Lost in America 1985 ★★★★ Yuppie couple's grand scheme to drop out and tour the country in their Winnebago runs into a hitch when wife loses nest egg in Vegas. Howlingly funny look at the American dream, '80s style. C: Albert Brooks, Julie Hagerty, Garry Marshall. D: Albert Brooks. COM [R] 91m. V

Lost in the Barrens 1991 ★★★½ Friendship and respect are ultimately forged when two boys, one white, one Native American, are lost in the wilderness. C: Graham Greene, Nicholas Shields. ACT 95m. V

Lost in the Stars 1974 ★★★½ Well-meaning adaptation of Weill/Anderson folk opera based on Alan Paton's novel *Cry the Beloved Country*. Stage roots show in this tale of South African preacher searching for his outlaw son, but thrilling score still shines. C: Brock Peters, Melba Moore, Raymond St. Jacques. D: Daniel Mann. MUS 114m.

Lost in Yonkers 1993 ★★★½ During WWII, life changes dramatically for two youngsters when their widowed father must leave them with with their tyrannical grandmother, "simple" aunt, and two-bit-hood uncle. Strong performances enhance Neil Simon's adaptation of his quirky, Pulitzer Prize-winning play. (a.k.a. *Neil Simon's Lost In Yonkers*) C: Richard Dreyfuss, Mercedes Ruehl, Irene Worth, David Strathairn. D: Martha Coolidge. DRA [PG] 114m. V

Lost Legacy 1977 *See* **Girl Called Hatter Fox, The**

Lost Man, The 1969 ★★★ Poitier is a criminal wanted by the police who becomes involved with social worker Shimkus and civil rights leader Freeman, Jr. Uneven remake of *Odd Man Out* features Poitier in an offbeat role, and benefits most from Freeman's performance. C: Sidney Poitier, Joanna Shimkus, Al Freeman, Jr. D: Robert Arthur. DRA [PG] 122m.

Lost Moment, The 1947 ★★★★ American publisher (Cummings) determines lost love letters of famous writer are in Italy and must woo mentally unbalanced (Hayward) who claims to know their location. Interesting, atmospheric drama adapted loosely from Henry James' novella, *The Aspern Papers*. C: Robert Cummings, Susan Hayward, Agnes Moorehead. D: Martin Gabel. DRA 89m. V

Lost One, The 1951 German ★★★ True story of German scientist (Lorre) whose paranoia led him to believe his girlfriend slipped his discoveries to the British during WWII. Actor Lorre does better as an actor than director, but overall not bad. C: Peter Lorre, Karl John, Renate Mannhardt. D: Peter Lorre. DRA 97m.

Lost Patrol, The 1943 ★★★★★ Stranded in the desert, a small group of British soldiers (led by McLaglen) fends off Arab attackers. Top-notch sand saga with taut direction, fine performances (especially Karloff as a pious soldier), and a classic action finale. C: Victor McLaglen, Boris Karloff, Wallace Ford, Reginald Denny, Alan Hale. D: John Ford. ACT 66m. V

Lost Platoon, The 1989 ★★½ A new vampire storyline setting—this time the bloodsuckers are 200-year-old WWII platoon soldiers. C: David Parry, William Knight, Stephen Quadros, Lew Pipes. D: David A. Prior. HOR [R] 91m. V

Lost Samurai Sword, The ★★½ The search for an all-powerful sword brings with it mysticism and danger. C: Tien Pang, Tong Po Wan, Pak Ying, Wang Ping. ACT 90m. V

Lost Squadron, The 1932 ★★★★ Four WWI air force pals become Hollywood stunt pilots in this archetypal "behind-the-scenes" drama. Von Stroheim steals the picture from its romantic leads, playing a tyrannical Prussian movie director. C: Richard Dix, Mary Astor, Erich von Stroheim, Joel McCrea. D: George Archainbaud. ACT 79m.

Lost Weekend, The 1945 ★★★★★ Brilliant, uncompromising study of alcoholism. Milland won much deserved Best Actor Oscar as writer willing to sell his soul for a drink during a three-day binge. Sequence of Ray searching for open pawnshops is harrowing highlight. Other Oscars include Best Picture, Director, and Screenplay (Wilder and Charles Brackett). C: Ray Milland, Jane Wyman, Philip Terry, Howard da Silva. D: Billy Wilder. DRA 101m. V

Lost World 1960 ★★★★ Big-budget epic version of the Arthur Conan Doyle story—this one has a modern expedition trekking to the remote reaches of the Amazon, where they encounter dinosaurs and other ancient lifeforms. Energetic and thrilling. C: Michael Rennie, Jill St. John, David Hedison, Claude Rains, Fernando Lamas. D: Irwin Allen. SFI 98m.

Lost World, The 1925 ★★★★ Silent version of Arthur Conan Doyle's classic tale about a gutsy professor's expedition to a remote area teeming with Jurassic throwbacks, one of which is captured and returned to London. Extremely well done, considering its era. Worth watching. C: Bessie Love, Wallace Beery, Lewis Stone. D: Harry Hoyt. SFI 69m. V

Lots of Luck 1985 ★★★½ Harmless fluff about housewife Funicello winning lottery and finding instant wealth isn't all it's cracked up to be. C: Annette Funicello, Martin Mull, Polly Holliday. D: Peter Baldwin. DRA 88m. TVM V

Lottery Bride, The 1930 ★★½ Operetta with Rudolf Friml score puts MacDonald in unlikely role of a Norwegian maid won by coal miner in a lottery. C: Jeanette MacDonald, John Garrick, Joe E. Brown, ZaSu Pitts. D: Paul Stein. MUS 80m. V

Louisa 1950 ★★★★ Byington is a delight as title character, a lonely grandmother looking for love and shocking her straitlaced son (Reagan). Old pros Coburn and Gwenn make charming suitors. Inspired hit TV sitcom *December Bride*. C: Ronald Reagan, Charles Coburn, Ruth Hussey, Edmund Gwenn, Spring Byington. D: Alexander Hall. COM 90m.

Louisiana Purchase 1941 ★★★★ Funny musical spoof of *Mr. Smith Goes to Washington* casts Hope as naive senator framed by his colleagues. Climax has hero waging filibuster on Senate floor by reading *Gone With the Wind!* Pleasant Irving Berlin score. C: Bob Hope, Vera Zorina, Victor Moore, Irene Bordoni. D: Irving Cummings. MUS 99m. V

Louisiana Story, The 1948 ★★★★½ Lyrical, semidocumentary set in the Louisiana bayous about a young boy following the progress of oil drillers discovering a deposit. Beautiful landscape photography and score by Virgil Thomson. Produced by Standard Oil Company. D: Robert Flaherty. DOC 79m. V

Loulou 1980 French ★★★★ Successful ad exec (Huppert) ends affair with boss, takes up with uncouth, lower-class jerk (Depardieu) who satisfies her sexually. Watch the two stars here, as they define the term "chemistry;" their magnetic performances make up for many script shortcomings. C: Isabelle Huppert, Gerard Depardieu, Guy Marchand. D: Maurice Pialat. DRA 110m. V

Lovable Cheat, The 1949 ★★★½ Strange low-budget comedy with high aspirations casts Ruggles as drunken nobleman eluding his creditors. Based on Honoré de Balzac play. Cast makes it interesting. C: Charlie Ruggles, Peggy Ann Garner, Richard Ney, Alan Mowbray, Buster Keaton. D: Richard Oswald. COM 75m.

Love 1927 ★★★½ Russian woman (Garbo) risks home, health, and happiness when she has an extra-marital affair. Uneven silent adaptation of Tolstoy's classic *Anna Karenina*, which Garbo made again, using the original title, in 1935. That's the version to see. C: Greta Garbo, John Gilbert, George Fawcett. D: Edmund Goulding. DRA 97m.

Love Affair 1939 ★★★★★ Playboy (Boyer) meets sophisticated New Yorker (Dunne) on ocean voyage. They fall in love, plan to meet months later, but fate intervenes. Superb comedy/drama mixes clever repartee with heartbreaking plot twists. Remade twice, as *An Affair to Remember* in 1958, and under original title in 1994. C: Irene Dunne, Charles Boyer, Maria Ouspenskaya, Lee Bowman. D: Leo McCarey. DRA 87m. V

Love Affair 1994 ★★★ Second remake of the 1939 tearjerker updates the premise of two travellers falling in love, then separated by a fateful accident. Stars are attractive; locations are luminous. But the story has been so watered down by now that it's lost all impact. Stick with Boyer/Dunne or Grant/Kerr. C: Warren Beatty, Annette Bening, Katharine Hepburn, Garry Shandling, Pierce Brosnan, Kate Capshaw. D: Glenn Gordon Caron. DRA [PG-13] 107m. V

Love Affair, A: The Eleanor and Lou Gehrig Story 1978 ★★★★ Yankees baseball hero Gehrig (Herrmann) and his wife Eleanor (Danner) meet and marry, then deal with incurable amytropic lateral sclerosis in well-acted drama. Told from Eleanor's point of view, Danner dominates movie with her glowing performance, supported by an unusually interesting cast. Previously filmed as *Pride of the Yankees*. C: Blythe Danner, Edward Herrmann, Patricia Neal, Jane Wyatt. D: Fielder Cook. DRA 96m. TVM V

Love After Love 1994 French ★★★½ Huppert scores as woman involved with married man. Perceptive characterizations, but somewhat talky. C: Isabelle Huppert, Bernard Giraudeau, Hippolyte Giradot, Lio. D: Diane Kurys. DRA 104m.

Love Among the Ruins 1975 ★★★★½ Classy comedy of manners teams two acting legends. Hepburn is "mature" actress sued for breach of promise by young scoundrel. Olivier is the barrister and former lover who takes her case. Literate script, handsome period production. C: Katharine Hepburn, Laurence Olivier, Colin Blakely. D: George Cukor. DRA 100m. V

Love Among Thieves 1987 ★★★½ Hepburn steals jewels to use as ransom save fiancée's life, then teams up with con artist (Wagner) on wild Mexican adventure. Mediocre romantic comedy adventure, but Audrey's sparkle shines through from time to time. C: Audrey Hepburn, Robert Wagner, Jerry Orbach, Samantha Eggar. D: Roger Young. COM 100m. TVM

Love and Anarchy 1974 Italian ★★★★ Naive farmer (Giannini) joins an antifascist group and is ordered to kill Mussolini, but complications arise when he falls in love with prostitute (Melato) in a brothel. Political fable brought Wertmuller worldwide attention. C: Giancarlo Giannini, Mariangela Melato. D: Lina Wertmuller. DRA [R] 108m. V

Love and Bullets 1979 British ★★★ Perfunctory action film has Arizona homicide detective (Bronson) sent to Switzerland to retrieve mobster's girlfriend (Ireland) so she can testify against her boyfriend back in the States. Lesser Bronson vehicle at least has nice scenery. C: Charles Bronson, Rod Steiger, Jill Ireland. D: Stuart Rosenberg. ACT [PG] 95m. V

Love and Death 1975 ★★★★ Slight story line of cowardly Russian soldier in Napoleonic wars is mainly an excuse for Allen's nonstop barrage of philosophical spoofing, including hilarious jabs at Tolstoy, Eisenstein, and Bergman. C: Woody Allen, Diane Keaton, Harold Gould. D: Woody Allen. COM [PG] 85m. V

Love and Fear 1988 Italian ★★★★ Loosely based on Chekhov's *Three Sisters*, this overlong chronicle of sibling rivalries, passions, and disappointments has many effective moments, as well as persuasive acting by Ardant and Scacchi. C: Fanny Ardant, Greta Scacchi, Valeria Golino. D: Margarethe Trotta. DRA 114m.

Love and Hate: A Marriage Made in Hell 1990 Canadian ★★★★ Sordid, well-acted, true tale, about Canadian millionaire (Welsh) who's not above murder to free himself of wife (Nelligan). Gripping drama, with climactic cliffhanger trial. C: Kenneth Welsh, Kate Nelligan, John Colicos. D: Francis Mankiewicz. DRA 153m. TVM V

Love and Larceny 1963 Italian ★★★ Gassman is a swindler with a zest for his work and all its rewards—both monetary and romantic. Dated sex comedy still entertains. C: Vittorio Gassman, Anna Ferrero. D: Dino Risi. COM 94m.

Love and Money 1982 ★★★ Billionaire (Kinski) devises plot to get more money, wrecking the lives of all involved. Oddball drama derails early and never gets back on track. Watch for great director Vidor as a feisty grandpa. C: Ray Sharkey, Ornella Muti, Klaus Kinski, Armand Assante, King Vidor. D: James Toback. DRA [R] 90m. TVM

Love & Murder 1991 ★★ No more or less than the title indicates. C: Todd Waring, Kathleen Lasky. D: Steven Hilliard Stern. HOR [R] 87m. V

Love and Other Sorrows 1989 ★★★ A coming-of-age story centered on a teenage son who must learn to understand himself and his mother's intense loyalty to her children. C: Christopher Collet, Elizabeth Franz. D: Steven Gomer. DRA 60m. TVM

Love and Pain (and the Whole Damn Thing) 1972 French ★★★★ Smith's inspired performance as gawky spinster finding romance with Bottoms on tour of Spain makes this sentimental tearjerker worth watching. C: Maggie Smith, Timothy Bottoms. D: Alan Pakula. DRA [PG] 110m.

Love and the Frenchwoman 1961 French ★★★★ Women go through seven stages of love in life, each represented in a separate vignette. Some episodes may now seem a bit old-fashioned, but film as a whole remains engaging. C: Martin Lambert, Dany Robin, Jean-Paul Belmondo, Annie Girardot. D: Jean Delannoy, Michel Boisrond, Rene Clair, Christian Jaque. COM 143m.

Love at First Bite 1979 ★★★★ Spirited spoof of the Dracula legend finds the count trying to adjust to the urban madness of New York City. Hamilton camps it up delightfully, with strong supporting cast, especially Johnson as the whiny, bug-munching Renfield. C: George Hamilton, Susan St. James, Richard Benjamin, Dick Shawn, Arte Johnson, Sherman Hemsley, Isabel Sanford. D: Stan Dragoti. COM [PG] 96m. V

Love at First Sight 1978 Canadian ★★ Offbeat and off-base comedy about romantic pursuits of a blind man. Very young Aykroyd tries but can't save tasteless screenplay.(a.k.a. *Love is Blind* and *At First Sight*) C: Mary Ann McDonald, Dan Aykroyd. D: Rex Bromfield. COM 90m. V

Love at Large 1990 ★★★ A hapless private eye hired to follow an errant husband finds he himself is being tailed. Confusing mistaken-identity comedy, with typically convoluted story line by writer/director Rudoph. Good performances. C: Tom Berenger, Anne Archer, Elizabeth Perkins, Kate Capshaw. D: Alan Rudolph. COM [R] 97m. V

Love at Stake 1988 ★★★½ Two innocents find themselves on trial for witchcraft—just for laughs. Gag-filled comedy in the spirit of Mel Brooks and *Airplane*. C: Patrick Cassidy, Kelly Preston, Bud Cort, Barbara Carrera. D: John Moffitt. COM [R] 88m. V

Love at the Top 1974 French ★★★ Cassel is a physically impaired author who lives vicariously through romantic advice he provides to pal Trintignant. Empty-headed comedy of money and seduction packs a lot of energy into uninvolving story. (a.k.a. *The French Way Is*) C: Jean-Louis Trintignant, Jean-Pierre Cassel, Romy Schneider, Jane Birkin. D: Michel DeVille. COM [R] 105m. V

Love at Twenty 1962 International ★★★½ Compilation movie from a quintet of international directors features five short films about youthful infatuations. Some segments play better than others, though highlight for movie buffs is *Antoine and Colette*, Francois Truffaut's sequel to *The 400 Blows*. C: Jean-Pierre Leaud, Eleanora Rossi-Drago, Zbigniew Cybulski, Nami Tamura, Marie-France Pisier. D: Francois Truffaut, Renzo Rossellini, Shintaro Ishihara, Marcel Ophuls. DRA 113m.

Love Before Breakfast 1936 ★★★½ Lame-brained yet amusing screwball comedy casts marvelous Lombard as dizzy socialite pursued by Foster and Romero. Fun to watch. C: Carole Lombard, Preston Foster, Cesar Romero. D: Walter Lang. COM 70m.

Love Bug, The 1969 ★★★★ When a Volkswagon bug develops the ability to think for itself, owner (Jones) goes for the wild ride of his life. Pure Disney slapstick that grabs the obvious gag at every possible moment and the results are hilarious. Intended kid audience will love it. C: Dean Jones, Michele Lee, Buddy Hackett. D: Robert Stevenson. FAM/COM 108m. V

Love Butcher, The 1983 ★★½ A persistent newsreporter tries to uncover the bizarre link between a host of murders and a handicapped old man. C: Erik Stern, Kay Neer. D: Mikel Angel. HOR [R] 84m. V

Love by Appointment 1976 ★★½ The lessons to be learned come quickly as two quirky businessmen invest much of their time in a fancy brothel. C: Ernest Borgnine, Robert Alda, Francoise Fabian, Corinne Clery. D: Armando Nannuzzi. ACT 96m. V

Love Cage, The 1964 *See* **Joy House**

Love, Cheat & Steal 1994 ★★★ Lithgow and Roberts are interesting in this passion-filled tale of a million dollar scam. C: John Lithgow, Eric Roberts, Madchen Amick. D: William Curran. DRA [R] 96m. TVM V

Love Child 1982 ★★★ Real-life prison inmate Terry Jean Moore (Madigan) becomes pregnant by prison guard (Bridges) and fights to keep her baby. Better than average. C: Amy Madigan, Beau Bridges, Mackenzie Phillips. D: Larry Peerce. DRA [R] 97m. V

Love Circles 1985 ★★★ A Parisian woman's passion and curiosity are set ablaze as she enters into an affair with a mysterious man. C: John Sibbit, Marie France, Josephine Jacqueline Jones. D: Gerard Kikoine. DRA [R] 84m. V

Love Crazy 1941 ★★★★ Powell will do anything to keep Loy married to him, even pretend he's insane. Madcap screwball comedy with two leads sparring magnificently. Early scene of Powell stuck in elevator is surreal slapstick classic. C: William Powell, Myrna Loy, Gail Patrick, Jack Carson, Florence Bates. D: Jack Conway. COM 100m. V

Love Crimes 1992 ★★ Thriller finds law officer Young going undercover to investigate con artist Bergin, who preys on unsuspecting women by masquerading as fashion photographer. Wooden performances shed little light. C: Sean Young, Patrick Bergin, Arnetia Walker. D: Lizzie Borden. CRI [R] 84m. V

Love Eternal 1943 *See* **Eternal Return, The**

Love Field 1992 ★★★½ Dallas housewife and Kennedy fan (Pfeiffer), devastated by 1963 assassination, travels cross-country to attend Washington funeral. En route, she meets black man (Haysbert) and their lives become entwined. Sensitive, but unconvincing drama; strong performance by Pfeiffer. C: Michelle Pfeiffer, Dennis Haysbert, Stephanie McFadden, Brian Kerwin. D: Jonathan Kaplan. DRA [PG-13] 104m. V

Love Finds Andy Hardy 1938 ★★★½ In this *Andy Hardy* entry, Rooney is caught in the middle of two romances and doesn't know which girl is right for him. Typical shenanigans for the series, with good support from Garland and newcomer Turner. C: Lewis Stone, Mickey Rooney, Judy Garland, Cecilia Parker, Fay Holden, Ann Rutherford, Lana Turner. D: George Seitz. FAM/COM 90m. V

Love Flower, The 1920 ★★★ Silent South Seas melodrama about sailor who discovers desert island inhabited by a young woman and her father who have a terrible secret. C: Richard Barthelmess, Carol Dempster, Anders Randolph. D: D.W. Griffith. DRA 65m.

Love from a Stranger 1937 British ★★★★ When Harding wins the lottery, she's wooed by charming Rathbone, whose demeanor changes considerably once they wed. Fine thriller with Rathbone in his "heavy" heyday. Based on a play by Frank Vosper, which was based on a story by Agatha Christie. Remade in 1947. C: Ann Harding, Basil Rathbone. D: Rowland Lee. CRI 90m.

Love from a Stranger 1947 ★★★½ Sydney falls for and marries debonair gentleman, only to realize his motives might be something other than love. On its own, competent and entertaining, but even then the plot was familiar. Remake of the 1937 version, based on an Agatha Christie story. C: Sylvia Sidney, John Hodiak, John Howard, Isobel Elsom. D: Richard Whorf. CRI 81m. v

Love God?, The 1969 ★★★ Porn publisher turns staid ornithology magazine into girlie rag; now everyone thinks prim editor Knotts is a stud. Formulatic comedy. C: Don Knotts, Anne Francis, Edmond O'Brien. D: Nat Hiken. COM 101m.

Love Goddesses, The 1965 ★★★½ Astute compilation film featuring screen sirens throughout film history. Some clips are far from ideal, but there are delicious moments from classic scenes. D: Saul Turell, Graeme Ferguson. DOC 87m. v

Love Happy 1950 ★★★½ Groucho plays a small role in this moderately amusing late Marx Brothers effort (their last), with Chico and Harpo putting on a musical. Note: Marilyn Monroe has a bit part. Don't be fooled if she's featured on video packaging. C: Chico Marx, Harpo Marx, Groucho Marx, Ilona Massey, Vera-Ellen, Eric Blore, Marilyn Monroe. D: David Miller. COM 85m. v

Love Has Many Faces 1965 ★★ Wealthy matron (Turner) has her hands full with husband (Robertson) and gigolo (O'Brian) in laughable soaper set in Acapulco. Infamous for overbaked dialogue and Lana's many costume changes. C: Lana Turner, Cliff Robertson, Hugh O'Brian, Ruth Roman, Stefanie Powers. D: Alexander Singer. DRA 105m. v

Love Hurts 1989 ★★★ Womanizer Daniels returns home for his sister's wedding to find that his ex-wife and children have moved in with his parents. Slow-moving comedy/-drama about dysfunctional families contains little inspiration and obvious plot devices. C: Jeff Daniels, Judith Ivey, John Mahoney, Cloris Leachman. D: Bud Yorkin. DRA [R] 110m. v

Love in a Fallen City 1984 Cantonese ★★★ Hong Kong in the 1940's is the exotic backdrop for this romance between a wealthy playboy and a young divorcée. C: Chow Yun Fat, Cora Miao. D: Ann Hui. DRA 100m. v

Love in a Taxi 1980 ★★★★ Charming offbeat romantic comedy has Jewish cabby finding drawn to black office worker. Strong characters, endearing performances, and a sincere script. C: Diane Sommerfield, James Jacobs, Earl Monroe. D: Robert Sickinger. COM 90m.

Love in Bloom 1935 ★★★ Minor comedy with Burns & Allen helping songwriter win his lady love. Worth watching for George and Gracie. C: George Burns, Gracie Allen, Joe Morrison, Dixie Lee. D: Elliott Nugent. COM 75m.

Love in Germany, A 1984 German ★★★½ After husband goes to fight in WWII, German woman Shygulla uses Polish P.O.W. Lysak to help with household chores. When they have an affair, resulting scandal enflames entire village. Film starts off well, but second half falters. C: Hanna Schygulla, Marie-Christine Barrault, Armin Mueller-Stahl. D: Andrzej Wajda. DRA [R] 110m. v

Love in Jerusalem 1969 *See* **My Margo**

Love in the Afternoon 1957 ★★★★½ Playboy (Cooper) meets his match in shy gamine (Hepburn). This romantic trifle has the fizz of a champagne cocktail, with age difference between the two leads paying off in a moving finale at train station. Chevalier a gem as Audrey's father. C: Gary Cooper, Audrey Hepburn, Maurice Chevalier. D: Billy Wilder. DRA 130m. v

Love in the City 1953 Italian ★★½ Six-part omnibus film was meant to be neorealist take on several true stories about love in Rome; unfortunately, the best episode is Fellini's contribution, a clearly fictional piece about a reporter. One segment, directed by Lizzani, was cut from foreign release prints for its depiction of prostitution. C: Ugo Tognazzi, Maresa Gallo, Caterina Rigoglioso. D: Michelangelo Antonioni, Federico Fellini, Dino Risi, Carlo Lizzani. DRA 90m.

Love in the Present Tense 1986 ★★★ An ex-model, leading a life of tragedy-induced seclusion, must come to terms with her daughter and the man who influences them both. C: Millie Perkins, Deborah Foreman, Doris Roberts. DRA 97m. v

Love Is a Ball 1963 ★★★½ American adventurer helps matchmaker unite a madcap millionaire and a penniless Duke on the Riviera. Jaunty romantic comedy has strong cast and lush locations, but rather routine scripting. C: Glenn Ford, Hope Lange, Charles Boyer, Ricardo Montalban, Telly Savalas. D: David Swift. COM 111m.

Love Is a Dog from Hell 1987 Belgian ★★★★½ Three-part adaptation of Charles Bukowski stories follows young man from first sexual stirrings, to horrible acne-scarred adolescence, through depraved adulthood. Unusual film alternately sensitive, humorous and shocking. Definitely not for all audiences. (a.k.a. *Crazy Love*) C: Josse DePauw, Geert Hunaerts, Florence Beliard. D: Dominique Deruddere. DRA 90m.

Love Is a Fat Woman 1988 ★★★★½ After tyrannical Argentinean military dictatorship ends, one journalist pries into the hows and whys of his country's terrible past. Fascinating tale of political skullduggery and public amnesia of seemingly unforgettable crimes. C: Elio Marchi, Sergo Poves Campos. D: Alejandro Agresti. DRA 80m.

Love Is a Many Splendored Thing 1955 ★★★★½ First-class love story with Korean War backdrop. Eurasian doctor (Jones) falls for war correspondent (Holden) in Hong

Kong. Their romance builds beautifully to strong, Kleenex-grabbing climax. Title theme song won Oscars, as did costumes. Based on Han Suyin's best-selling memoir. C: William Holden, Jennifer Jones. D: Henry King. DRA 102m. V

Love Is a Racket 1932 ★★★ The life and loves of a theatrical columnist. Considering the cast and director, this comedy/drama is surprisingly drab and stiff. C: Douglas Fairbanks, Jr., Ann Dvorak, Frances Dee, Lee Tracy. D: William Wellman. COM 72m.

Love Is Better Than Ever 1952 ★★★½ Minor MGM musical, with talent agent (Parks) courting dance teacher (Taylor). Unbilled cameo by Gene Kelly. (Release was held up while McCarthy Senate hearings investigated Parks.) C: Elizabeth Taylor, Larry Parks, Josephine Hutchinson. D: Stanley Donen. MUS 81m. V

Love is Blind 1978 *See* **Love at First Sight**

Love Is My Profession 1959 French ★★★½ Classy lawyer Gabin successfully defends young deliquent Bardot on a robbery charge, and she repays him the only way she can, in a steamy affair that leads to tragedy. Controversial in its day, but tame now. The leads are excellent. C: Jean Gabin, Brigitte Bardot, Edwige Feuillere. D: Claude Autant-Lara. DRA 111m.

Love Is Never Silent 1985 ★★★★ Hearing daughter (Winningham) of deaf parents (Frelich, Waterstreet), is caught between her own need for independence and their dependence on her. Wonderful performances by all three leads and a realistic script make this superior drama. C: Mare Winningham, Phyllis Frelich, Cloris Leachman, Sid Caesar. D: Joseph Sargent. DRA 100m.

Love Is News 1937 ★★★ An heiress (Young) plans vengeance on an overly persistant reporter (Power) by announcing their upcoming nuptials—and letting him in for some bad publicity. Remade more successfully in 1948 as *That Wonderful Urge*, also starring Power. C: Tyrone Power, Loretta Young, Don Ameche, Slim Summerville, George Sanders, Jane Darwell, Stepin Fetchit. D: Tay Garnett. COM 78m.

Love Kills 1991 ★★★ Love and loyalty are tested when a wealthy woman falls for someone who may turn out to be her assassin. C: Virginia Madsen, Lenny Von Dohlen, Erich Anderson, Kate Hodge, Jim Metzler. D: Brian Grant. HOR [PG-13] 92m. V

Love Laughs at Andy Hardy 1946 ★★★ After WWII ends, Andy Hardy (Rooney) leaves military and begins college where he chases girls with his pre-war adolescent spirit. A lesser *Andy Hardy* film that put an effective end to the series (though *Andy Hardy Comes Home* briefly revived it in 1958). C: Mickey Rooney, Lewis Stone, Sara Hayden, Bonita Granville. D: Willis Goldbeck. COM 93m. V

Love Leads the Way 1984 ★★★½ Bottoms plays Morris Frank, who trained first seeing-eye dog for the blind. Though a little too sentimental, the good cast overcomes script flaws. Based on Frank's autobiography, *First Lady of the Seeing Eye*. C: Timothy Bottoms, Eva Marie Saint, Arthur Hill, Susan Dey, Patricia Neal. D: Delbert Mann. DRA 99m. TVM V

Love Letters 1945 ★★★★ G.I. convinces fellow soldier (Cotten) to write letters to his girl (Jones) back home, and the plan works. She falls in love with the letter writer, who is not the man who comes home to her (shades of *Cyrano de Bergerac*). Well-acted, gripping drama. C: Jennifer Jones, Joseph Cotten, Anita Louise, Cecil Kellaway, Gladys Cooper. D: William Dieterle. DRA 101m.

Love Letters 1983 ★★★★ Drama of a young woman (Curtis) who discovers among her late mother's correspondence letters from a secret lover, which changes her own outlook on life. Thought-provoking and touching. (a.k.a. *My Love Letters* and *Passion Play*). C: Jamie Lee Curtis, James Keach, Amy Madigan. D: Amy Jones. DRA [R] 88m. V

Love Lottery, The 1954 British ★★½ Comedy with Niven as movie star made prize in international raffle. Humphrey Bogart does uncomfortable cameo. C: David Niven, Peggy Cummins, Herbert Lom. D: Charles Crichton. COM 89m.

Love Machine, The 1972 ★★ A sleazy TV newscaster (Law) uses his boss's wife (Cannon) and others to help him advance. Trashy movie from trashy Jacqueline Susann book. C: John Phillip Law, Dyan Cannon, Robert Ryan, Jackie Cooper. D: Jack Haley, Jr. DRA [R] 108m. V

Love Maneuvers 1935 Polish ★★½ With an arranged marriage threatening their future, two lovers go to unusual lengths to stay together—like switching places with their servants. DRA 67m.

Love Me Deadly 1972 ★ Young woman and her dead lovers. Dud. C: Mary Wilcox, Lyle Waggoner. D: Jacque La Certe. HOR [R] 95m. V

Love Me Forever 1935 ★★★★ Entertaining Moore vehicle has star playing protege of nightclub owner who's jealous of her leading man (Bartlett). Good excuse for Grace to trill her way through Puccini, Verdi, and "Funiculi-Funicula." C: Grace Moore, Leo Carrillo, Robert Allen, Spring Byington. D: Victor Schertzinger. MUS 90m.

Love Me or Leave Me 1955 ★★★★★ One of the best showbiz biographies casts Day as '20s torch singer Ruth Etting, victimized by possessive husband Cagney. Cagney succeeds brilliantly in making unlikeable character human, and Day proves her mettle as an actress. Strong, adult screenplay by Isobel Lennart and Daniel Fuchs. Fuchs' original story won Oscar. New songs include hit "I'll Never Stop Loving You." C: Doris Day, James

Cagney, Cameron Mitchell. D: Charles Vidor. MUS 122m. V

Love Me Tender 1956 ★★★½ Presley made film debut in this Cain and Abel story set in Texas during the Civil War. Elvis seems a bit out of place in period Western, but fans will like it. Features four songs, including title hit. C: Elvis Presley, Richard Egan, Debra Paget. D: Robert D. Webb. MUS 89m. V

Love Me Tonight 1932 ★★★★★ Parisian tailor (Chevalier) romances vain princess (MacDonald) in scintillating musical with grand Rodgers and Hart score ("Isn't It Romantic," "Lover," "Mimi"). Smart and sophisticated, with one of the strongest opening scenes in the history of musicals. C: Maurice Chevalier, Jeanette MacDonald, Charlie Ruggles, Myrna Loy. D: Rouben Mamoulian. MUS 96m.

Love Meetings (Comizi D'Amore) 1964 Italy ★★★ Series of interviews with director as interviewer asking diverse group of people to describe their love histories. D: Pier Paolo Pasolini. DOC 90m. V

Love Nest 1951 ★★★ Mild farce has ex-GI (Lundigan) and wife (Haver) buying apartment house with loony tenants. Nice work by Monroe in early vamp role. C: June Haver, William Lundigan, Frank Fay, Marilyn Monroe, Jack Paar. D: Joseph Newman. COM 84m. V

Love of Jeanne Ney, The 1927 ★★★★ After revolutionary lover kills her bourgeois diplomat father, German woman holes up in Paris and continues the romance, which is threatened by an unscrupulous rogue. Though plot-heavy at points, this German silent film benefits from wonderful visual style. C: Edith Hehanne, Brigitte Helm, Fritz Rasp. D: G.W. Pabst. DRA 113m. V

Love of Three Oranges, The ★★ Moody prince falls in love with three oranges in tis Glyndebourne Festival Opera version of Prokofiev's fantastical opera. C: Ryland Davies, Willard White, Nelly Morpurgo. MUS 120m. V

Love on a Pillow 1962 French ★★★ Suicidal young man becomes revitalized after being taken under loving wing of self-styled sex therapist Bardot. Breezy, though pointless romantic French sex comedy. C: Brigitte Bardot. D: Roger Vadim. COM 102m.

Love on the Dole 1941 British ★★★ Depression-era tale of a London family's struggles. Strong script and solid acting in a familiar story. C: Deborah Kerr, Clifford Evans. D: John Baxter. DRA 100m.

Love on the Ground 1984 French ★★★ Two actresses agree to work on still unfinished play for a rich, mysterious playwright, and complications ensue involving people and relationships that may or may not be part of the play. Rivette's difficult theater vs. film experiment doesn't quite work. C: Geraldine Chaplin, Jane Birkin. D: Jacques Rivette. DRA 126m.

Love on the Run 1936 ★★★½ Gable is a foreign correspondent who travels the globe to court Crawford and becomes involved with international spies. Glossy vehicle for two stars moves quickly from one glamorous locale to the next without much to keep it aloft. C: Clark Gable, Joan Crawford, Franchot Tone, Reginald Owen. D: W. S. Van Dyke II. DRA 80m. V

Love on the Run 1979 French ★★★½ Fifth and last of Truffaut's *Antoine Doinel* films follows Leaud one more time through his role as mixed-up lover. Following divorce, Leaud courts trouble with new amorous adventures. Slight, but pleasing romantic comedy features clips of previous films from series. C: Jean-Pierre Leaud, Marie-France Pisier. D: Francois Truffaut. COM [PG] 90m. V

Love Parade, The 1929 ★★★★½ Lubitsch's first sound film, a naughty tale of Queen of Sylvania (McDonald) and her amorous foreign emissary (Chevalier), sparkles with wit and charm. Lovely score integrated into story in then-daring fashion. Best song: "Dream Lover." Good comic support from Lane and Roth. McDonald's screen debut. C: Maurice Chevalier, Jeanette MacDonald, Lillian Roth, Lupino Lane, Ben Turpin. D: Ernst Lubitsch. MUS 110m.

Love Potion No. 9 1992 ★★★ Two nerdy scientists discover formula that makes them irresistible to the opposite sex. Disjointed, randomly funny comedy. C: Tate Donovan, Sandra Bullock, Mary Mara, Dale Midkiff, Anne Bancroft. D: Dale Launer. COM [PG-13] 97m. V

Love She Sought, The 1990 ★★★★ Retired spinster church teacher (Lansbury) goes to Ireland to meet pen pal she's fallen in love with, only to discover disturbing secret. Touching drama showcases Angela's dramatic talents, with lovely location photography a plus. Based on Hohn Hassler's *A Green Journey*. C: Angela Lansbury, Denholm Elliott, Robert Prosky. D: Joseph Sargent. DRA 100m.

Love Songs 1986 Canadian ★★½ A bisexual rock singer (Lambert) courts an older woman (Deneuve) who is recently separated from her husband. Sophomoric soaper takes itself much too seriously, and becomes bogged down in its own melodramatics. C: Catherine Deneuve, Richard Anconina, Christopher Lambert. D: Elie Chouraqui. DRA 108m. V

Love Story 1970 ★★★ The definitive modern tearjerker. Poor student (MacGraw) meets rich student (O'Neal). They resist class prejudice and marry, only to be thwarted by terminal illness. Immensely popular, with a full-blown emotional payoff. Won Oscar for Best Score. C: Ali MacGraw, Ryan O'Neal, Ray Milland, John Marley. D: Arthur Hiller. DRA [PG] 100m. V

Love Streams 1984 ★★★ Real-life husband and wife Cassavetes and Rowlands are brother and sister in this emotional rollercoaster exploring meaning of love through characters' reflections. Weakened by length and repetitiveness. C: Gena Rowlands, John Cassavetes, Diahnne Abbott. D: John Cassavetes. DRA [PG-13] 122m. v

Love That Brute 1950 ★★★½ Gruff mobster (Douglas) falls for innocent young woman in this amiable Prohibition-era comedy. Remake of *Tall, Dark and Handsome.* C: Paul Douglas, Jean Peters, Cesar Romero, Joan Davis, Keenan Wynn. D: Alexander Hall. COM 85m.

Love Thrill Murders 1971 ★★ Murderous maniac idolized by runaways who do his bidding, unquestioningly. C: Troy Donahue. D: Bob Roberts. COM [R] 92m. v

Love Thy Neighbor 1940 ★★★½ Famous radio feud between Benny and Allen prompted this genial comedy, with songs showing off Broadway's Martin. Will please Jack's fans. C: Jack Benny, Fred Allen, Mary Martin, Eddie Anderson. D: Mark Sandrich. COM 82m.

Love Trap 1976 *See* **Curse of the Black Widow**

Love Under Fire 1937 ★★★½ Against the backdrop of the Spanish Civil War, a hunt is conducted for a valuable necklace stolen by a clever Englishwoman (Young). Convoluted, but the players maintain a delightfully sophisticated front. C: Loretta Young, Don Ameche, Frances Drake, John Carradine. D: George Marshall. DRA 75m.

Love with a Perfect Stranger 1986 ★★ En route to Florence, an American fashion designer meets an enticing Englishman with the expected consequences. Based on a Harlequin romance. C: Marilu Henner, Daniel Massey, Sky Dumont. D: Desmond Davis. DRA 102m. v

Love with the Proper Stranger 1963 ★★★★ Pregnant woman (Wood) seeks help from musician (McQueen) who's reponsible for her condition after one-night stand. Cynical romantic drama and probably Natalie's best performance. Good support from Adams, Bernardi, and Bosley. C: Natalie Wood, Steve McQueen, Edie Adams, Herschel Bernardi, Tom Bosley. D: Robert Mulligan. DRA 100m. v

Love Without Fear 1990 ★★ Film about children with AIDS and how their families cope. DOC 60m. v

Love Without Pity 1990 French ★★ A sometimes pitiless look at relationships and a dismal portrayal of the participants. C: Yvan Attal, Hippolyte Girardot, Jean Marie Rollin. D: Eric Rochant. DRA [R] 94m. v

Love Your Momma 1993 ★★★ Low-budget first film by director Oliver concerns Chicago ghetto matriarch's struggle to keep her family together despite alcoholism, infidelity, teenage pregnancy, and other trials. A laudable effort. C: Carol Hall, Audrey Morgan, Andre Robinson. D: Ruby Oliver. DRA [PG-13] 94m. v

Loved One, The 1965 ★★★★½ Outrageous, scathing black comedy about the business of death and life in Southern California, seen through the eyes of a young Englishman (Morse). Hip adaptation of Evelyn Waugh's 1948 novel is sick humor at its best. C: Robert Morse, Jonathan Winters, Anjanette Comer, Rod Steiger, Milton Berle, John Gielgud, Tab Hunter, Liberace, Roddy McDowall. D: Tony Richardson. COM 122m. v

Loveless, The 1983 ★★★ Affected biker movie in the *Wild One* mode about hoodlums terrorizing a small town in the 1950s. C: J. Don Ferguson, Willem Dafoe. D: Kathryn Bigelow. DRA [R] 85m. v

Lovelines 1984 ★★ Town bully tries to break up romance between his sister and her boyfriend, a student at a rival high school. C: Greg Bradford, Mary Beth Evans, Michael Winslow. D: Rod Amateau. COM [R] 93m. v

Lovely but Deadly 1983 ★★ Young woman tries to track down criminal responsible for brother's drug overdose. C: Lucinda Dooling, John Randolph, Marie Windsor. D: David Sheldon. CRI [R] 95m. v

Lovely to Look At 1952 ★★★★ American funnyman (Skelton) inherits stake in Paris dress shop run by Grayson and Champion. Entertaining MGM musical; vintage Kern songs include "Smoke Gets in Your Eyes" and "I Won't Dance." Fashion show directed by Vincente Minelli. Previously filmed in 1935 as *Roberta.* C: Kathryn Grayson, Red Skelton, Howard Keel, Ann Miller, Marge Champion, Gower Champion, Zsa Zsa Gabor. D: Mervyn LeRoy. MUS 105m. v

Lovely Way to Die, A 1968 ★★★½ When district attorney Wallach assigns detective Douglas to guard a woman accused of murder, he becomes determined to prove her innocence. Plot contains some unexpected elements, and Douglas is likable as the cool, resourceful detective. C: Kirk Douglas, Sylva Koscina, Eli Wallach. D: David Rich. CRI 103m.

Lovemakers, The 1962 *See* **La Viaccia**

Lover Boy 1954 *See* **Lovers, Happy Lovers**

Lover Come Back 1946 ★★★½ Ball shines in amusing trifle about marital jealousy, as Lucy sees red when war reporter (Brent) gets chummy with photographer (Zorina). (a.k.a. *When Lovers Meet*) C: Lucille Ball, George Brent, Vera Zorina, Charles Winninger. D: William Seiter. COM 90m.

Lover Come Back 1962 ★★★★ Day and Hudson are feuding ad execs, trying to steal accounts from each other. Amusing romantic comedy speeds along and is one of team's best, with Randall top-notch as Rock's confidante. C: Rock Hudson, Doris Day, Tony Randall, Edie Adams. D: Delbert Mann. COM 107m. v

Lover, The 1992 French ★★★½ Teenage French girl (March) has torrid affair with older Chinese man (Leung) in '20s Indochina. Well-made adaptation of Marguerite Duras' semiautobiographical novel has an erotic atmosphere, sumptuous photography, and attractive cast. C:

Jane March, Tony Leung. D: Jean-Jacques Annaud. DRA [R] 103m. v

Lover, Wife 1979 *See* **Wifemistress**

Loverboy 1989 ★★½ Nebbishy pizza deliverer finds himself very popular with his clientele of sex-starved Beverly Hills wives. Weak sex farce. C: Patrick Dempsey, Kate Jackson, Barbara Carrera, Kirstie Alley, Carrie Fisher. D: Joan Micklin Silver. COM [PG-13] 98m. v

Lovers 1991 Spanish ★★★★ Young man, betrothed to innocent young woman, begins affair with his widowed landlady. Steamy melodrama, based on a true story from '50s Madrid, works well and features excellent performances, especially Abril as the widow. C: Victoria Abril, Jorge Sanz. D: Vicente Aranda. DRA [R] 105m. v

Lovers and Liars 1980 Italian ★★★ American tourist (Hawn) has romantic liaison with suave Italian banker (Giannini) during her travels. Routine comedy doesn't do much with Hawn's talents. C: Goldie Hawn, Giancarlo Giannini, Claudine Auger. D: Mario Monicelli. COM [R] 96m. v

Lovers and Lollipops 1956 ★★★½ Lonely widow falls in love again, but her daughter disapproves. Charming, mild comedy. C: Ruth Orkin, Lori March, Gerald O'Loughlin. D: Morris Engel. COM 80m.

Lovers and Other Strangers 1970 ★★★★½ Funny, touching comedy about two families converging for swank hotel wedding blends four one-act plays into cohesive movie. Great cast; Diane Keaton's debut. Oscar-winning Best Song, "For All We Know." C: Gig Young, Beatrice Arthur, Bonnie Bedelia, Anne Jackson, Harry Guardino, Richard Castellano, Cloris Leachman, Anne Meara. D: Cy Howard. COM [PG] 106m. v

Lovers, Happy Lovers 1954 British ★★★★ Dark, cynical sex comedy with French cad (Philipe) using British women as ladder to success. Well acted, directed with great style by Clement. Controversial film opened door for similar antiheros. (a.k.a. *Knave of Hearts*, *Lover Boy*) C: Gerard Philipe, Valerie Hobson, Joan Greenwood. D: Rene Clement. COM 103m.

Lovers Like Us 1975 French ★★★½ Two people, each unhappily married, run away, meet and fall in love. French attempt at screwball comedy rests on the enormous charm of its stars. Lovely scenery too. (a.k.a. *The Savage*) C: Catherine Deneuve, Yves Montand. D: Jean-Paul Rappeneau. COM 90m. v

Lovers of Montparnasse, The 1957 French ★★★½ Melodramatic biography of Italian-born painter/sculptor Modigliani; despite persuasive historical look and Philipe's capable performance, a shallow, romanticized tale. (a.k.a. *Montparnasse 19* and *Modigliani of Montparnasse*) C: Gerard Philipe, Lilli Palmer, Anouk Aimee. D: Jacques Becker. DRA 103m.

Lovers of Paris 1957 French ★★★½ Philipe packs up his belongings and moves to the City of Light, where he finds romance in the form of Darrieux. Cute comedy of sexy courtship, with nice chemistry between the duo. (a.k.a. *Pot-bouille*) C: Gerard Philipe, Danielle Darrieux. D: Julien Duvivier. COM 115m.

Lovers of Teruel, The 1962 French ★★★★½ Tcherina is a ballet dancer who finds life and art weaving together when she performs the role of a woman whose misbegotten romance ends tragically. Intriguing story with excellent dance sequences. Tcherina shines in the lead. C: Ludmila Tcherina, Raymond Rouleau. D: Raymond Rouleau. DRA 90m. v

Lovers, The 1958 French ★★★★ Bored rich wife (Moreau) leaves everything to take up with student she picked up the previous night. Malle's first big international success had trouble with the censors in the U.S. originally, now seems relatively tame. Moreau's sensual portrayal of a woman's midlife crisis carries the show. C: Jeanne Moreau, Alain Cuny. D: Louis Malle. DRA 89m. v

Loves and Death of a Scoundrel, The 1956 *See* **Death of a Scoundrel**

Loves and Times of Scaramouche, The 1975 Italian ★★ Irresistible ladies' man meets his match in a bumbling Bonaparte. Resistible farce, broadly played and ill timed. Maccione as Napoleon is funny, but not much else is. (a.k.a. *Scaramouche*) C: Michael Sarrazin, Ursula Andress. D: Enzo Castellari. COM 95m. v

Loves of a Blonde 1965 Czech ★★★★½ Young woman has a brief affair with scoundrel musician. Enraptured, she journeys from her small Czech village to pursue her would-be lover in Prague. Largely nonprofessional ensemble infuses this refreshing comedy/drama with charm. One of the high points of Forman's Czech career. C: Hana Brejchova, Josef Sebanek, Vladimir Pucholt. D: Milos Forman. COM 88m. v

Loves of a Scoundrel, The 1956 *See* **Death of a Scoundrel**

Loves of Carmen, The 1948 ★★★ Spanish military officer Ford is corrupted by his love for Gypsy femme fatale Hayworth in this remake of Bizet's opera *sans* music. What's left is an often corny, melodramatic plot almost solely reliant on Hayworth's charms. C: Rita Hayworth, Glenn Ford, Ron Randell, Victor Jory. D: Charles Vidor. DRA 98m. v

Loves of Edgar Allan Poe, The 1942 ★★★ This biography of the 19th-century American author focuses on his romantic involvements but fails to explore the literary inspirations of a man whose characters were so often wracked with inner turmoil. C: Linda Darnell, John Shepperd, Virginia Gilmore, Jane Darwell. D: Harry Lachman. DRA 67m. v

Loves of Hercules, The 1960 ★★ One of the worst-ever Hercules movies has camp attraction of Mansfield sharing screen with bodybuilder husband Hargitay. Jayne plays dual role of good/bad queen, with atrocious dubbing adding to the unintentional hilarity. (a.k.a. *Hercules vs.Hydra*). C: Mickey Hargitay, Jayne Mansfield. D: Carlo L. Bragagia. SFI 94m. V

Loves of Isadora, The *See* **Isadora**

Loves of Sunya, The 1927 ★★★★ Eastern yogi sets out to right a past wrong by enabling Swanson to envision what life would be like with each of her three suitors. Swanson effectively illustrates the contrasts between very different outcomes in this imaginative silent vehicle. C: Gloria Swanson, John Boles, Anders Randolph. D: Albert Parker. DRA 80m.

Loves of Three Queens, The 1953 Italian ★★½ Three-part film chronicles Genevieve of Brabant, Empress Josephine, and Helen of Troy. Too much story packed into too short a time results in confusing costume drama. C: Hedy Lamarr, Massimo Serato, Cathy O'Donnell. D: Marc Allegret. DRA 90m.

Lovesick 1983 ★★★ Sluggish romantic has happily married psychiatrist (Moore) finding to his horror that he's falling in love with his coquettish new patient (McGovern). Lacks nuance or bite. C: Dudley Moore, Elizabeth McGovern, Alec Guinness, John Huston. D: Marshall Brickman. COM [PG] 94m. V

Lovespell 1979 ★ Wooden version of the classic Tristan and Isolde story is an embarrassment to its talented cast. (a.k.a. *Tristan and Isolde*) C: Richard Burton, Kate Mulgrew, Nicholas Clay, Cyril Cusack, Geraldine Fitzgerald. D: Tom Donovan. DRA 90m. V

Lovey: A Circle of Children, Part II 1978 ★★★★ Alexander reprises her role as teacher of disturbed children in sequel to *A Circle of Children*. Moving, restrained drama matches superior quality of first film. C: Jane Alexander, Ronny Cox, Karen Allen, Danny Aiello. D: Jud Taylor. DRA 100m.

Lovin' Molly 1974 ★★★ Two Texas men (Perkins and Bridges) love the same independent woman (Danner) over a span of 40 years. Truncated adaptation of McMurtry novel *Leaving Cheyenne;* Danner is great. C: Anthony Perkins, Beau Bridges, Blythe Danner, Susan Sarandon. D: Sidney Lumet. DRA [R] 98m. V

Loving 1970 ★★★½ A successful, middle-aged commercial artist (Segal) juggles wife (Saint), mistress (Young), job and housepayments in this ode to the white-collar working man. Main problem is Segal's unsympathetic character. C: George Segal, Eva Marie Saint, Sterling Hayden, Keenan Wynn. D: Irvin Kershner. DRA [R] 90m.

Loving Couples 1980 ★★★ Married couple attempts to spice up their sex life with a little weekend swapping. Teaser premise for rather flat-footed sex comedy. C: Shirley MacLaine, James Coburn, Susan Sarandon, Stephen Collins, Sally Kellerman. D: Jack Smight. COM [PG] 120m. V

Loving in the Rain 1974 French ★★★★ While on vacation with her teenaged daughter, wealthy woman has casual affair with handsome stranger, while daughter discovers her own interest in the opposite sex. Sweet, appealing coming-of-age tale for two generations. C: Romy Schneider, Nino Castelnuovo, Alain David, Benedicte Boucher. D: Jean-Claude Brialy. DRA 90m.

Loving You 1957 ★★★½ Elvis is ideally cast as a country boy promoted into pop star by pushy agent Scott. Presley's second film, and first in color. Songs include "Teddy Bear" and title tune. C: Elvis Presley, Lizabeth Scott, Wendell Corey, Dolores Hart. D: Hal Kanter. MUS 102m. V

Low Blow 1986 ★★ Young women transformed into murderers by cult leader. C: Cameron Mitchell, Troy Donahue, Leo Fong. D: Frank Harris. DRA [R] 90m. V

Low Down Dirty Shame, A 1994 ★★★ Andre Shame (Wayans), a down and out P.I., is hired by Drug Enforcement Agency to find a missing $20 million stash. Genial actioner builds to literally explosive climax in a shopping mall, but Wayans seems out of place as crash-and-smash hero. C: Keenen Ivory Wayans, Charles S. Dutton, Jada Pinkett. D: Keenen Ivory Wayans. ACT [R] 108m. V

Lowell Thomas Remembers—The Roaring Twenties—Vol. 1 ★★ Newsreel clips from 1919 to 1924, including coverage of the women's sufferage movement, prohibition raid, and the first automobiles. DOC 142m. V

Lowell Thomas Remembers—The Roaring Twenties—Vol. 2 ★★ Newsreel headlines covering 1925 to 1929, including coverage of the stock market crash and Lindbergh's flight. DOC 142m. V

Lowell Thomas Remembers—The New Deal—The Thirties ★★ Newsreel headlines from 1930 to 1935, including coverage of Ghandi's activities, Lindbergh's baby snatching, and the repeal of prohibition. DOC 142m. V

Lowell Thomas Remembers—The War Years—The Forties—Vol. 1 ★★ Newsreel clips covering 1940 to 1944, including coverage of Germany's invasion of Russia and the U.S. air raid on Tokyo. DOC 142m. V

Lowell Thomas Remembers—The War Years—The Forties—Vol. 2 ★★ Newsreel clips covering 1945 to 1949, including coverage of WW II and the immediate post-war period. DOC 142m. V

Lowell Thomas Remembers—The Fabulous Fifties ★★ Clips from newsreel headlines covering events from 1950 to 1954, including information on McCarthy's witch hunts, the war in Korea, and the Eisenhower years. DOC 142m. V

Lower Depths, The 1936 French ★★★★★ Gabin is a thief who takes destitute aristocrat under his wing, while saving his lover's kid sister from corrupt authorities. Stylized setting gives weight to this emotionally involving adaptation of the Gorki play, a sordid story of life at its most extreme edges. Gabin's performance is riveting. C: Jean Gabin, Louis Jouvet, Suzy Prim. D: Jean Renoir. DRA 92m. v

Lower Depths, The 1957 Japanese ★★★★½ Kurosawa resets Gorki's play from Moscow to Tokyo, with Mifune as thief with tarnished heart, showing ropes of slum dwelling to magnate who has lost his fortune. Constricted presentation emphasizes desperate situation of characters. Fascinating portrait, though a bit overwritten. C: Toshiro Mifune, Isuzu Yamada. D: Akira Kurosawa. DRA 125m. v

Lower Level 1991 ★★ Security guard, possessed by his attraction for an architect who works in his building, entraps her and her boyfriend after hours. C: Elizabeth Gracen, David Bradley, Jeff Yagher. D: Kristine Peterson. DRA [R] 88m. v

Loyal 47 Ronin 1941 *See* **47 Ronin, The**

Loyalties 1987 Canadian ★★★½ A lonely Englishwoman (Wooldridge) in a small town in northwestern Canada befriends her half-Indian housekeeper (Cardinal). Strong examination of friendship between "wild" and "proper" woman; otherwise familiar marital drama. C: Kenneth Welsh, Tantoo Cardinal, Susan Wooldridge. D: Anne Wheeler. DRA [R] 98m. v

Loyola, The Soldier Saint 1952 Spanish ★★ Valuable biography of founder of Jesuit movement. C: Rafael Duran, Maria Rosa Jiminez. D: Jose Diaz Morales. DRA 93m. v

Lt. Robin Crusoe, USN 1966 ★★★ Stranded Navy pilot Van Dyke comes to the aid of Pacific-isle women. Silly Disney fun should keep kids amused. C: Dick Van Dyke, Nancy Kwan, Akim Tamiroff. D: Byron Paul. FAM/COM [G] 110m. v

Lucas 1986 ★★★★½ Sweet character-driven comedy about a precarious adolescent falling in love. Smartly written teen comedy with insight and sincerity; Haim especially winsome as the title character. C: Corey Haim, Kerri Green, Charlie Sheen, Winona Ryder. D: David Seltzer. COM [PG-13] 100m. v

Lucia 1969 Cuban ★★★★ Episodic film covers three phases (the 1890s, the 1930s, and the 1960s) of Cuba's struggle for independence. A surprisingly subtle and nonjingoistic account of three women and the sexual/political obstacles they have to overcome. One of the finest motion pictures to emerge from Castro's Cuba. C: Raquel Revuelta, Eslinda Nuñez, Adela Legra, Adolfo Liaurado, Ramon Brito. D: Humberto Solas. DRA 155m.

Lucia di Lammermoor 1983 ★★ Italian production of the opera performed at the Metropolitan Opera House in New York City. English subtitles. C: Joan Sutherland, Alfredo Kraus, Pablo Elvira, Paul Plishka. MUS 128m. v

Luciano Pavarotti 1984 ★★★★ With help from the Las Vegas Symphony Orchestra, conducted by Emerson Buckley, the great tenor sings selections from "La Traviata," "La Cioconda," and others. C: Luciano Pavarotti. MUS 77m. v

Lucifer Complex, The 1978 ★★ In South America, Nazi doctors clone duplicates of world leaders including the U.S. President. C: Robert Vaughn, Keenan Wynn, Merrie Lynn Ross, Aldo Ray. D: Kenneth Hartford. HOR 91m. v

Luck Of Ginger Coffey, The 1964 Canadian ★★★★ Irish couple and their daughter immigrate to Canada to find a better life, but he can't seem to hold a job or stop drinking. Scrappy drama with stand-out performance by Shaw. C: Robert Shaw, Mary Ure, Liam Redmond. D: Irvin Kershner. DRA 100m.

Luck of the Irish, The 1937 ★★★★ Financially strapped manor owner mortgages his house to bet everything on a horse in the Grand Steeplechase. Excellent cast is fun to watch in this charming comedy. C: Richard Hayward, Kay Walsh, Niall MacGinnis. D: Donovan Pedelty. COM 80m.

Luckiest Man In The World, The 1989 ★★★½ A brush with death causes ruthless corporate executive to reexamine priorities. Optimistic, ambitious comedy written and directed by playwright Frank D. Gilroy. Well-acted and amusing. C: Philip Bosco, Doris Belack, Joanne Camp. D: Frank Gilroy. COM 82m.

Lucky Day 1991 ★★★½ Retarded woman (Webb) becomes millionaire by winning lottery. When her alcoholic mother (Dukakis) reenters her life, protective sister (Madigan) sees red. Clichéd soap opera benefits from terrific turn by Madigan. C: Olympia Dukakis, Amy Madigan, Chloe Webb. D: Donald Wrye. DRA 96m. TVM

Lucky Devils 1932 ★★★ Stuntman falls for movie extra, but she loves another stuntman. After terrific opening this stiff comedy falters. Good depiction of behind-the-scenes moviemaking. C: William Boyd, Dorothy Wilson, William Gargan, Bruce Cabot. D: Ralph Ince. COM 64m.

Lucky Dube Live in Concert 1993 ★★★ First live performance tape of popular reggae star. C: Lucky Dube. MUS 60m. v

Lucky Jim 1957 British ★★★½ Working-class professor (Carmichael) up against elitist bigotry in British university. Entertaining comedy from Kingsley Amis novel. C: Ian Carmichael, Terry-Thomas, Hugh Griffith. D: John Boulting. COM 91m. v

Lucky Jordan 1942 ★★★ Con artist soldier (Ladd) gets the best of the Nazi agents and gets the lady (Walker) to boot. Ladd adds panache to unbelievable material. C: Alan Ladd, Helen Walker, Marie McDonald, Mabel Paige. D: Frank Tuttle. DRA 84m.

Lucky Lady 1975 ★★ Star trio play bumbling rumrunners in California during Prohibition. Neat, climactic raft chase. C: Liza

Minnelli, Burt Reynolds, Gene Hackman, Geoffrey Lewis, John Hillerman. D: Stanley Donen. COM [PG] 118m. v

Lucky Losers 1950 ★★★ Slip and Satch get jobs as stockbrokers, and Wall Street will never be the same. Wisecracking, silly *Bowery Boys* comedy. C: Leo Gorcey, Huntz Hall, Hillary Brooke, Gabriel Dell, Lyle Talbot. D: William Beaudine. COM 69m.

Lucky Luciano 1974 Italian ★★★ Mundane Italian/French/U.S. co-production details rise and fall of violent American gangster (Volonte). Supposedly plays better (and is somewhat longer) in its original Italian version. C: Gian Maria Volonte, Rod Steiger, Edmond O'Brien. D: Francesco Rosi. CRI [R] 108m. v

Lucky Me 1954 ★★★ Disjointed musical with chorus dancer (Day) trying to crack the big time with the help of a composer (Cummings). Fun cast hampered by clichéd script. C: Doris Day, Robert Cummings, Phil Silvers, Eddie Foy, Jr., Nancy Walker, Martha Hyer. D: Jack Donohue. MUS 100m. v

Lucky Nick Cain 1951 ★★★ While running with a counterfeiting ring, Cain (Raft) is accused of murder. Okay gangster saga doesn't offer anything new. C: George Raft, Coleen Gray, Charles Goldner. D: Joseph Newman. CRI 87m.

Lucky Night 1939 ★★ Noisy screwball with mismatched stars in story of wealthy socialite (Loy) marrying impoverished poet (Taylor). C: Myrna Loy, Robert Taylor, Henry O'Neill, Marjorie Main. D: Norman Taurog. COM 82m.

Lucky Partners 1940 ★★★ Romantic comedy with Colman and Rogers sharing winning lottery ticket. Two stars' charm carries it. C: Ronald Colman, Ginger Rogers, Jack Carson, Spring Byington. D: Lewis Milestone. COM 99m. v

Lucky Star, The 1980 Canadian ★★★★ Jewish boy seeks refuge at a Dutch farm after his parents are seized by the Nazis, and extracts his own revenge against a Nazi officer. Underlying comic elements are allowed to subtly reveal themselves in this sweetly-conceived drama. C: Louise Fletcher, Rod Steiger, Lou Jacobi. D: Max Fischer. DRA [PG] 110m.

Lucky Stiff 1988 ★★★ Overweight, lonely Alaskey thinks his dreams have come true when Dixon makes a play for him. She's actually planning to serve him up as the main course at her next family gathering. Clumsy black comedy, but good Alaskey. C: Joe Alaskey, Donna Dixon, Jeff Kober, Leigh McCloskey. D: Anthony Perkins. COM [PG] 85m. v

Lucky Stiff, The 1949 ★★★ The ghost of a singer (Lamour) has returned to haunt the gangsters who killed her. Or has she? Modestly entertaining comedy-mystery. C: Dorothy Lamour, Brian Donlevy, Claire Trevor. D: Lewis R. Foster. CRI 99m.

Lucky Texan, The 1934 ★★ When one of two mining partners is accused of murder, the team stands to loose all they've gained. C: John Wayne, Barbara Sheldon, George "Gabby" Hayes. D: Robert Bradbury. WST 55m. v

Lucky to Be a Woman 1956 Italian ★★½ A producer (Boyer) and a photographer (Mastroianni) vie for the affections of a free-spirited model/actress (Loren). Rather limp farce, despite the star-power. C: Charles Boyer, Sophia Loren, Marcello Mastroianni. D: Alessandro Blasetti. COM 95m.

Lucrezia Borgia 1993 ★★★ Richard Bonynge conducts orchestra in Australian Opera rendition of famous Donizetti opera. C: Joan Sutherland, Ron Stevens, Richard Allman, Margreta Elkins. MUS 138m. v

Lucy and Desi—Behind the Laughter 1992 ★★★½ Adequate biography of TV dream couple Ball and Arnaz. Desi's womanizing and drinking is emphasized, so story seems slanted in Lucy's favor. Lookalike leads do a decent job imitating two of America's favorite icons. C: Frances Fisher, Maurice Benard. D: Charles Jarrott. DRA [PG] 95m. TVM v

Lucy Gallant 1955 ★★★½ A seamstress (Wyman) becomes a success in the fashion business but fails in her personal life. Superior melodrama with solid acting. C: Charlton Heston, Jane Wyman, Thelma Ritter, Claire Trevor, William Demarest. D: Robert Parrish. DRA 104m.

Lucy's Lost Episodes ★★★ Clips from Ball's TV shows as well as from her appearances on "Toast of the Town," "What's My Line," and other TV shows of the era. C: Lucille Ball. COM 83m. v

Ludmila Semenyaka—Bolshoi Ballerina 1990 ★★★ Clips from the extraordinary ballet dancer's most famous roles. C: Ludmila Semenyaka. MUS 60m. v

Ludwig 1973 Italian ★★★½ Ponderous epic about the demented King Ludwig of Bavaria (Berger). The usually reliable Visconti struggles to lay bare Ludwig's inner torment, but it's no use. Gorgeous to look at, tastefully acted, but staggeringly dull. (Beware the four-hour version!) C: Helmut Berger, Romy Schneider, Trevor Howard, Silvana Mangano. D: Luchino Visconti. DRA [PG] 173m.

Luggage of the Gods! 1983 ★★★ Clone of *The Gods Must Be Crazy* features similar culture-shock satire; some of a jet's cargo falls into the hands of a primitive community. Mild entertainment. C: Mark Stolzenberg, Gabriel Barre, Gwen Ellison. D: David Kendall. COM [G] 78m. v

Luisa Miller 1988 ★★★ The Lyon Opera Orchestra and Chorus, conducted by Marizio Arena, play one of Verdi's less-famous operas. C: June anderson, Taro Ichihara. MUS 150m. v

Luke was There ★★★ Emmy Award-winning story about poor, troubled boy, turned away from crime by sensitive and caring counselor. C: Scott Baio. D: Richard Marquand. DRA 47m. TVM V

Lullaby of Broadway 1950 ★★★½ London musical comedy star (Day) returns to N.Y., unaware her once famous mother has become a down-and-out nightclub singer. Modest musical benefits from strong cast and durable songs ("Just One of Those Things" and the title tune). C: Doris Day, Gene Nelson, Gladys George, S. Z. Sakall, Billy De Wolfe. D: David Butler. MUS 93m. V

Lulu in Berlin 1985 ★★ Interview with Louise Brooks, perhaps best known for her role as Lulu, Germany's most famous fictional siren. DOC 52m. V

Lumière 1976 French ★★★ The lives of four actresses, spotlighting their trials and troubles. Earnest performances are the main recommendation for Moreau's first film as a director as well as a leading lady. C: Jeanne Moreau, Francine Racette, Lucia Bose, Keith Carradine. D: Jeanne Moreau. DRA [R] 101m. V

Luna 1979 ★★★ A neurotic, recently widowed opera singer (Clayburgh) moves to Rome with her son where she attempts to break him of his drug habit. High melodrama marred by silly incestuous overtones. C: Jill Clayburg, Matthew Barry, Veronica Lazar, Fred Gwynne, Alida Valli. D: Bernardo Bertolucci. DRA [R] 144m.

Lunatic, The 1992 ★★ Sexual liaison between tourist, amiable if insane inhabitant of small town, and a third party. C: Reggie Carter, Carl Bradshaw, Julie T. Wallace. D: Lol Creme. COM [R] 93m. V

Lunatics: A Love Story 1992 ★★★½ An introverted paranoid becomes involved with a manic fatalist. Oddball relationship comedy has fine acting and true feelings surfacing in unlikely circumstances. C: Theodore Raimi, Deborah Foreman, Bruce Campbell. D: Josh Becker. COM [PG-13] 87m. V

Lunatics and Lovers 1975 Italian ★★½ Wealthy Mastroianni pretends to be married and must face unwanted companionship when harlot Mori impersonates the nonexistent spouse. A dull and witless effort with cast just going through the motions. C: Marcello Mastroianni, Claudia Mori, Lino Morelli. D: Flavio Mogherini. COM 92m. V

Lunch Wagon 1980 ★★★ Three women set up their mobile canteen at a construction site. Low-budget sex comedy won't strain the brain. (a.k.a. *Lunch Wagon Girls* and *Come 'N Get It*) C: Pamela Bryant, Rosanne Katon, Candy Moore, Rose Marie, Chuck McCann. D: Ernest Pintoff. COM [R] 88m. V

Lunch Wagon Girls 1980 *See* **Lunch Wagon**

Lupe Balazos Spanish ★★ Strange man in town pursued by two sisters. C: Julio Aldama, Lucha Moreno. DRA 70m. V

Lupo 1970 ★★ Conservationist Lupo tries to halt the destruction of his old neighborhood. C: Yuda Barkan, Gabi Amrani, Esther Greenberg. D: Menahem Golan. COM [G] 99m. V

Lure of the Sila 1949 Italian ★★★½ Years after Gassman is wrongly accused of murder, Mangano sets out to vindicate her brother's name. Nicely acted, with interesting performance from Mangano, though story rarely rises above soap opera level. C: Silvana Mangano, Amedeo Nazzari, Vittorio Gassman. D: Duilio Coletti. DRA 72m. V

Lure of the Wilderness 1952 ★★★ A man falsely accused of murder hides out for years in Florida's Okefenokee swamp. Inferior remake of *Swamp Water*. C: Jeffrey Hunter, Jean Peters, Walter Brennan, Jack Elam. D: Jean Negulesco. CRI 92m. V

Lured 1947 *See* **Personal Column**

Lurking Fear 1994 ★★★ Good cast is stranded in an underdeveloped plot of a motley group terrorized in an old church by subterranean monsters. Has little to do with the H.P. Lovecraft story on which it is based, nor is it particularly interesting or scary. Eh. C: Blake Bailey, Ashley Lauren, Jeffrey Combs, Jon Finch, Allison Mackie. D: Courtney Joyner. HOR [R] 81m.

Lust for a Vampire 1970 ★★★ Follow-up to *The Vampire Lovers* takes place in a finishing school for young girls, where lesbian vampire (Stensgaard) turns up to ravish students and teachers alike. Engaging if at times overwrought combo of horror and eroticism. C: Yvette Stensgaard, Ralph Bates, Mike Raven. D: Jimmy Sangster. HOR [R] 92m. V

Lust for Gold 1949 ★★½ A young man ventures to Arizona to search for a gold mine discovered by his grandfather years ago. Okay performances in this typical Western. C: Ida Lupino, Glenn Ford, Gig Young. D: S. Sylvan Simon. WST 90m.

Lust for Life 1956 ★★★★★ Outstanding, engrossing portrayal of Dutch artist Vincent Van Gogh (Douglas). Based on Irving Stone's novel. Anthony Quinn won Oscar for Best Supporting Actor as Van Gogh's closest friend, Gauguin. C: Kirk Douglas, Anthony Quinn, Pamela Brown. D: Vincente Minnelli. DRA 123m. V

Lust in the Dust 1985 ★½ Soldier of fortune (Hunter) searches for gold in New Mexico and gets involved with saloon waitress (Divine). Campy Western spoof is irreverent, outrageous, and none too tasteful. C: Divine, Tab Hunter, Lainie Kazan, Cesar Romero. D: Paul Bartel. COM [R] 85m. V

Lusty Men, The 1952 ★★★½ Competition between rodeo riders (Mitchum and Kennedy) leads to tragedy. Documentary-style photography and a tough performance by Mitchum help to raise this above the routine. C: Susan Hayward, Robert Mitchum, Arthur Kennedy. D: Nicholas Ray. WST 113m. V

Luther 1974 British ★★★½ Keach gives a riveting performance as the priest who sparked the Protestant Reformation in this otherwise unremarkable adaptation of John Osborne's play. C: Stacy Keach, Patrick Magee, Hugh Griffith. D: Guy Green. DRA [PG] 112m.

Luther the Geek 1990 ★★★½ A maniac, obsessed with carnival geekery, terrorizes a family at a remote farmhouse. An often creepy, occasionally silly, effectively atmospheric low-budget shocker. C: Edward Terry, Joan Roth, Stacy Haiduk, J. Jerome Clarke, Thomas Mills. D: Carlton J. Albright. HOR 82m. v

Luther Vandross—Live at Wembley 1989 ★★ London concert performance by famous soul singer. Songs include "She Won't Talk to Me", "Never Too Much", and nine others. C: Luther Vandross. MUS 90m. v

Luv 1967 ★★★ Three New York neurotics search desperately for happiness and fall in and out of love. Cast plays it perfectly, though Murray Schisgal's hit play, with its characters, doesn't translate so perfectly to the screen. C: Jack Lemmon, Elaine May, Peter Falk. D: Clive Donner. DRA 95m. v

Luxury Liner 1948 ★★★½ Pert Powell plays matchmaker for father (Brent) on cruise ship. MGM confection uses stunning Technicolor and star's charm to offset cliched script. The Pied Pipers score with "Yes, We Have No Bananas." C: George Brent, Jane Powell, Lauritz Melchior, Xavier Cugat. D: Richard Whorf. MUS 98m.

Luz—Cama—Accion 1981 Spanish ★★ Chaos produced when a movie production manager rents a mansion to house his in-laws, actresses, and friends. C: Jorge Porcel, Susana Jimenez, Moria Casan. COM 95m. v

Luzia Spanish ★★ When rich landowners murder her parents, young girl seeks revenge. C: Claudia Ohana, Thales Pan Chacon, Jose DeAbreu. D: Fabio Barreto. DRA 112m. v

Lydia 1941 ★★★★ An older woman (Oberon) meets with her four former lovers and reminisces. Interesting remake of *Carnet de Bal* featuring good performances and spectacular costumes. C: Merle Oberon, Edna Oliver, Alan Marshal, Joseph Cotten. D: Julien Duvivier. DRA 104m.

Lydia Bailey 1952 ★★★½ Early 19th-century lawyer visits Haiti on business, becomes involved with native uprising against the ruling French. Ambitious story is glossy and entertaining. C: Dale Robertson, Anne Francis, Juanita Moore. D: Jean Negulesco. ACT 89m.

Lying Lips 1939 ★★ Innocent singer jailed on unfounded murder charge. C: Edna Mae Harris, Robert Earl Jones, Carmen Newsome. D: Oscar Micheaux. DRA 60m. v

M

M ("M") 1931 German ★★★★★ Classic tale of disturbed child murderer (Lorre) hunted down in terrified city. Lorre's magnificent screen debut; Lang's expressionistic visuals enhance stifling atmosphere. Terrifying story has not dated. C: Peter Lorre, Ellen Widmann, Gustav Grundgens. D: Fritz Lang. CRI 95m. V

M 1951 ★★★★ The police and the Mob try and track down a psychopathic child killer. Remake of psychological thriller stands up well beside 1931 German classic. Wayne gives the performance of his career as the murderer. C: David Wayne, Howard da Silva, Luther Adler, Karen Morley. D: Joseph Losey. CRI 88m.

M. Butterfly 1993 ★★★ Tale of misguided passion and espionage in which French diplomat has an affair with Chinese opera singer, not realizing "she" is a he. Based on a true story, David Henry Hwang's Broadway hit suffers in tepid screen adapation in which visual style comes at the expense of energy. C: Jeremy Irons, John Lone. D: David Cronenberg. DRA [R] 101m.

Ma and Pa Kettle Playing the Kettles, a homespun rural couple, Marjorie Main and Percy Kilbride stole *The Egg and I* from the better-known Claudette Colbert and Fred MacMurray, so Universal reasoned, correctly, that they could sustain a series of their own. The result was nine lowbrow, pleasant comedies.

Ma and Pa Kettle (1949)
Ma and Pa Kettle Go to Town (1950)
Ma and Pa Kettle Back on the Farm (1951)
Ma and Pa Kettle at the Fair (1952)
Ma and Pa Kettle on Vacation (1953)
Ma and Pa Kettle at Home (1954)
Ma and Pa Kettle at Waikiki (1955)
Ma and Pa Kettle in the Ozarks (1956)
The Kettles on Old MacDonald's Farm (1957)

Ma and Pa Kettle 1949 ★★★ The poverty-stricken Kettles—Ma, Pa, and 15 young 'uns—come close to losing their home until Pa wins a tobacco slogan contest and the wacky hillbilly family moves into a plush futuristic house. Lots of delightfully silly stuff. (a.k.a. *Further Adventures of Ma and Pa Kettle*) C: Marjorie Main, Percy Kilbride, Richard Long. D: Charles Lamont. COM [G] 75m. V

Ma and Pa Kettle at Home 1954 ★★★½ The Kettles lay it on thick when they try to impress a magazine editor—who may offer one of the kids a college scholarship. Plenty of zany gags and a hysterical closing chase. C: Marjorie Main, Percy Kilbride, Alan Mowbray, Mary Wickes. D: Charles Lamont. COM 81m.

Ma and Pa Kettle at the Fair 1952 ★★½ Ma tries to take a cooking prize at the county fair. Pa's ridiculous horse race tops this one off. C: Marjorie Main, Percy Kilbride, Lori Nelson, James Best, Esther Dale, Russell Simpson, Emory Parnell. D: Charles Barton. COM [G] 78m. V

Ma and Pa Kettle at Waikiki 1955 ★★ The Kettles journey to Hawaii to help out at the family pineapple factory. Not one of the better Kettle offerings. C: Marjorie Main, Percy Kilbride, Lori Nelson, Byron Palmer, Loring Smith, Lowell Gilmore, Mabel Albertson, Esther Dale, Ida Moore. D: Lee Sholem. COM 79m.

Ma and Pa Kettle Back on the Farm 1951 ★★½ When word spreads that there's uranium under the Kettle home, all kinds of con artists try to take over the property. Good series fun. C: Marjorie Main, Percy Kilbride, Richard Long, Meg Randall, Barbara Brown, Ray Collins, Emory Parnell, Peter Leeds. D: Edward Sedgwick. COM 80m. V

Ma and Pa Kettle Go to Town 1950 ★★★½ On a trip to New York, the Kettles encounter some pretty slick crooks, who are no match for these country sharpies! Broadly funny episodes mark this excellent entry. C: Marjorie Main, Percy Kilbride, Richard Long, Meg Randall, Gregg Martell, Charles McGraw, Jim Backus, Elliott Lewis, Bert Freed, Hal March. D: Charles Lamont. COM 70m. V

Ma and Pa Kettle on Vacation 1953 ★★★ On a trip to Paris, Ma and Pa get hooked into dealings with a nest of spies. Absurd situations make for good fun. Catch a young Rita Moreno in this one. C: Percy Kilbride, Marjorie Main, Ray Collins, Bodil Miller, Sig Ruman, Barbara Brown, Oliver Blake, Teddy Hart. D: Charles Lamont. COM 75m.

Ma Barker's Killer Brood 1960 ★★★ Bloodthirsty outlaw Barker recruits her own sons and a slew of notorious gangsters. Grungy crime thriller is redeemed by action and Tuttle's lively lead. C: Lurene Tuttle, Tris Coffin, Paul Dubov, Nelson Leigh, Myrna Dell. D: Bill Karn. CRI 82m.

Mabel and Fatty 1914 ★★★ Three short films by famous comedy team: "He Did and He Didn't," "Mabel and Fatty Viewing the World's Fair at San Francisco," and "Mabel's Blunder." C: Fatty Arbuckle, Mabel Normand. D: Roscoe Arbuckle. COM 61m.

Mac 1993 ★★★ Well-intentioned tale of three Queens brothers who try to go into business for themselves as building contractors during the '50s has lots of emotional acting but little dramatic momentum. C: John

Turturro, Michael Badalucco, Carl Capotorto, Katherine Borowitz, John Amos, Ellen Barkin. D: John Turturro. DRA 118m. v

Mac and Me 1988 ★★½ Saccharine story of handicapped boy befriending lovable lost alien. Derivative of *ET.* C: Christine Ebersole, Jonathan Ward, Katrina Caspary, Lauren Stanley, Jade Calegory. D: Stewart Raffill. SFI [PG] 93m. v

Macabre 1958 ★★★ Frantic doctor fears his kidnapped daughter has been buried alive in local cemetery. Atmospheric but disappointing thriller is best known for the clever gimmick of insuring patrons for $1,000 against death by fright. C: William Prince, Jim Backus, Christine White, Jacqueline Scott, Ellen Corby. D: William Castle. HOR 73m.

Macabre Serenade Spanish ★★ Star is murderous toy maker. Offbeat, to say the least. C: Boris Karloff. D: Juan Ibanez, Jack Hill. DRA 91m. v

Macahans, The 1976 ★★★½ Former *Gunsmoke* marshall Arness is a buckskinned frontier scout leading his family to a new home in Old West. Above-average telefilm was inspired by western epic *How the West Was Won.* Later became a similarly titled TV show. C: James Arness, Eva Marie Saint, Bruce Boxleitner, Richard Kiley, Gene Evans, John Crawford. D: Bernard McEveety. WST 125m. TVM

Macao 1952 ★★★★ Chanteuse Russell falls for wronged good guy Mitchum in this moody melodrama set in Hong Kong. Story takes a backseat to the steamy performances and eerie atmosphere. Worth a look. C: Robert Mitchum, Jane Russell, William Bendix, Gloria Grahame, Thomas Gomez, Philip Ahn. D: Josef Von Sternberg. DRA 80m. v

Macario 1960 Spanish ★★★★½ A Mexican farmer strikes a deal with the devil for the power to heal and, of course, suffers the usual ramifications. Odd retelling of Faustian legend is a classic of its kind. Taken from B. Traven (*The Treasure of the Sierra Madre*) story. C: Ignacio Tarso, Pina Pellicer. D: Roberto Gavaldon. DRA 91m.

Macaroni 1985 Italian ★★★ Lemmon is a WWII vet who pays a nostalgic visit to Italy years after war's end, and hooks up with Mastroianni, the brother of his old love. Treacley sentiment made nearly palatable by two class actors. C: Jack Lemmon, Marcello Mastroianni, Daria Nicolodi, Isa Danieli, Maria Luisa Saniella. D: Ettore Scola. DRA [PG] 104m. v

MacArthur 1977 ★★★ Biographical drama about the controversial American general. Story, which traces MacArthur's career from WWII to the Korean War. Peck turns in a convincing performance. C: Gregory Peck, Dan O'Herlihy, Ed Flanders, Sandy Kenyon, Ivan Boyar, Nicholas Coster. D: Joseph Sargent. ACT [PG] 130m. v

MacArthur's Children 1986 Japanese ★★★½ After WWII, Americans stationed in Japan bring an uneasy cultural clash to people still at odds with their defeat. Original look at postwar Japan, though too many characters mar overall intentions. C: Masako Natsume, Takaya Yamaushi, Yoshiyuka Omori, Shiori Sakura, Uen Watanabe, Juzo Itami. D: Masahiro Shinoda. DRA [PG] 115m. v

Macbeth 1948 ★★★★ Neglected on release, idiosyncratic low-budget adaptation of Shakespeare's tragedy seems more impressive, vibrant today. Welles is commanding in the title role; Nolan miscast as Lady Macbeth. C: Orson Welles, Jeanette Nolan, Dan O'Herlihy, Edgar Barrier, Roddy McDowall, Robert Coote, Erskine Sanford, Alan Napier, John Dierkes. D: Orson Welles. DRA 112m. v

Macbeth 1970 ★★★ Live performance by Bolshoi Ballet, choreographed by Vladimir Vasiliev. C: Bolshoi Ballet, Alexei Fadeyechev, Nina Timofeyeva. MUS 105m.

Macbeth 1971 British ★★★★½ Imaginative adaptation of Shakespeare's drama about a Scottish nobleman driven by ambition to murder. Polanski's relentlessly violent handling of the subject captures the frenzied essence of the original play. C: Jon Finch, Francesca Annis, Martin Shaw, Nicholas Selby. D: Roman Polanski. DRA [R] 139m. v

Macbeth 1987 ★★ Verdi's opera recorded at the Deutsche Opera in Berlin. C: Renato Bruson, Mara Zampieri. MUS 150m.

Machine-Gun Kelly 1958 ★★★½ Bronson has an edgy intensity as famous gangster in quick-moving action picture from the Corman assembly line. Better than average. C: Charles Bronson, Susan Cabot, Barboura Morris, Morey Amsterdam, Wally Campo, Jack Lambert, Connie Gilchrist, Frank DeKova. D: Roger Corman. CRI 84m. v

Machine Gun McCain 1970 Italian ★★★ McCain organizes group to rob Las Vegas casino. Fans of the ever-intense Cassavetes will enjoy watching him chew the scenery in this Italian-made gangster film. C: John Cassavetes, Britt Ekland, Peter Falk, Gabriele Ferzetti, Salvo Randone, Gena Rowlands. D: Giuliano Montaldo. CRI [PG] 94m.

Macho Callahan 1970 ★★★½ Jansen is a wrongly imprisoned Union soldier escaping from custody to track down the mysterious, yellow-shoed stranger who sent him to prison. There's even a one-armed bad guy! Sound familiar? This violent Western is entertaining enough, even if it is similar to TV's *The Fugitive.* C: David Janssen, Lee J. Cobb, Jean Seberg, David Carradine. D: Bernard Kowalski. WST [R] 99m. v

Macho Dancer 1988 Filipino ★★ In order to support his family, mountain boy goes to city where he becomes part of violent world of male strippers and murderers. Disturbing violence. D: Lino Brocka. DRA 136m.

Maciste in Hell 1972 ★★ Warrior follows

executed wife into hell where he struggles with witches, snakes, and eagles. Dubbed in English. C: Kirk Morris, Helene Channel. D: Riccardo Freda. SFI 89m.

Maciste—the Mighty 1960 Italian ★★★ Musclebound superhero (Forest) flexes his biceps against hordes of rampaging Persians. Ancient Egyptian setting is spice in this typical Italian sword-and-sandal flick. C: Mark Forest, Chelo Alonso, Angelo Zanolli, Federica Ranchi. D: Carlo Campogalliani. ACT 87m.

Mack Sennett Comedies—Vol. 1 ★★★ Four of Sennett's best comedies: "The Eyes Have It," "The desperate Scoundrel," "Pride of Pikeville," and "The Cannon Ball." COM 85m. V

Mack Sennett Comedies—Vol. 2 ★ Contains four films including "Fatty and Mabel Adrift" and "Fatty's Tin-Type Tangle." COM 84m. V

Mack, The 1973 ★★★ Pimp (Julien) struggles to rid his Oakland neighborhood of drug dealers. Standard for the genre, brimming with violence and city grit. Very popular when released. C: Max Julien, Don Gordon, Richard Pryor, Carol Speed, Roger E. Mosley. D: Michael Campus. ACT [R] 110m. V

Mack the Knife 1989 ★ Disastrous filming of Brecht/Weill's classic *The Threepenny Opera*, spotlights the title criminal (Julia) and his desire to wed respectable Polly Peachum (Robertson). Millionaire producer Golan assembled a terrific cast, then blew it. C: Raul Julia, Richard Harris, Roger Daltry, Julia Migenes, Rachel Robertson. D: Menaham Golan. MUS [PG-13] 120m. V

Mackenna's Gold 1969 ★★½ When a sheriff gets a treasure map from a dying Indian, all kinds of characters try to steal it. Even the stars don't shine in this clichéd plodder. C: Gregory Peck, Omar Sharif, Telly Savalas, Camilla Sparv, Keenan Wynn, Julie Newmar, Lee J. Cobb, Raymond Massey, Burgess Meredith, Anthony Quayle, Edward G. Robinson, Eli Wallach, Ted Cassidy, Eduardo Crannelli. D: J. Lee Thompson. WST 128m. V

Mackintosh and T.J. 1975 ★★★ Seasoned ranch hand teaches many life lessons to admiring young boy. Resurrection of beloved cowhand Roy Rogers, with songs by Waylon Jennings. C: Roy Rogers, Clay O'Brien, Billy Green Bush, Andrew Robinson, Joan Hackett. D: Marvin Chomsky. WST [PG] 96m.

Mackintosh Man, The 1973 ★★★½ A government agent (Newman) goes to the Big House to flush out a sly, wily Communist spy (Mason). Deftly handled espionage film. Complete with mandatory car chases, fist fights, imprisonment, and escapes. Mason and Newman are consummate pros, as ever. C: Paul Newman, Dominique Sanda, James Mason, Harry Andrews, Ian Bannen, Nigel Patrick, Michael Hordern. D: John Huston. CRI [PG] 100m. V

Macomber Affair, The 1947 ★★★★½ Short story "The Snows of Kilimanjaro" is given the big-budget treatment, as African safari guide Peck falls in love with the wife of a boorish client during hunting expedition. Exceptionally well acted, directed, and scored; literate script delivers one of the finest Hemingway adaptations. C: Gregory Peck, Joan Bennett, Robert Preston, Reginald Denny, Carl Harbord, Jean Gillie. D: Zoltan Korda. DRA 89m.

Macon County Line 1974 ★★★½ Visiting teenage trio is wrongly accused of murdering a small-town sheriff's wife. Violent trash classic was written/produced by Max Baer, Jr. ("Jethro" on TV's *The Beverly Hillbillies*), who plays the sheriff. *Return to Macon County* followed. C: Alan Vint, Cheryl Waters, Max Baer Jr., Jesse Vint, Geoffrey Lewis, James Gammon. D: Richard Compton. DRA [R] 89m. V

Macumba Love 1960 ★★½ American author researches strange religion and becomes involved with voodoo queen. Low-budget silliness shot in Brazil. C: Walter Reed, Ziva Rodann, William Wellman Jr., June Wilkinson, Ruth de Souza. D: Douglas Fowley. DRA 86m.

Mad About Men 1954 British ★★★ Beautiful mermaid Johns switches places with look-alike mortal woman. Romantic and comic complications follow in this mildly diverting English fantasy, a sequel to the more entertaining *Miranda*. C: Glynis Johns, Donald Sinden, Anne Crawford, Margaret Rutherford, Dora Bryan, Noel Purcell. D: Ralph Thomas. COM 90m.

Mad about Music 1938 ★★★★ Movie Star Patrick shuttles daughter Deanna off to Swiss girls' school, where she brags about a fictional father who materializes in the form of Marshall. Entertaining light comedy features knockout version of "Ave Maria" by Durbin. Remade as *Toy Tiger*. C: Deanna Durbin, Herbert Marshall, Gail Patrick, Arthur Treacher, Helen Parrish, Marcia Mae Jones, William Frawley. D: Norman Taurog. COM 98m.

Mad about You 1990 ★★ Daughter caught between millionaire father's desire to have her marry an ivy leaguer and her desire to fool around with a rock 'n' roll musician. C: Claudia Christian, Adam West, Joseph Gian. D: Lorenzo Doumani. COM 92m. V

Mad Adventures of "Rabbi" Jacob, The 1974 French ★★★★ Whirligig farce has the hyperkinetic De Funes playing a bigoted Catholic; mistaken for a hired killer, he's forced to impersonate a rabbi to elude police. Slapstick marathon with a plethora of terrific sight-gags. C: Louis De Funes, Suzy Delair, Marcel Dalio, Claude Giraud, Claude Pieplu. D: Gerard Oury. COM [G] 96m.

Mad at the Moon 1992 ★★ Young woman appeals to husband's half-brother for help when she discovers that the man she's just married is not completely human. C: Mary Stuart Masterson, Hart Bochner, Fionnula Flanagan. D: Martin Donovan. HOR [R] 98m. V

Mad at the World 1955 ★★★ Grief-stricken young father (Brasselle) is out to nail the teenage hoods who injured his baby. Downbeat slum drama tries to be profound, but falls short. C: Frank Lovejoy, Keefe Brasselle, Cathy O'Donnell, Karen Sharpe. D: Harry Essex. DRA 72m.

Mad Bomber, The 1972 ★★★ Tough cop (Edwards) must track down brutal rapist and a paranoid bomber (Connors), who intends to blow up the city. Great cult actors and wildly over-the-top Connors. Cheesy fun. C: Vince Edwards, Chuck Connors, Neville Brand, Hank Brandt. D: Bert I. Gordon. CRI [R] 90m. V

Mad Bull 1977 ★★★ Karras is a skull-thumping pro wrestler who discovers his feminine side after falling in love with Anspach. Goofy romantic drama. C: Alex Karras, Susan Anspach, Nicholas Colasanto, Elisha Cook Jr., Mike Mazurki. D: Walter Doniger, Tracy Walter. DRA 96m. TVM V

Mad Butcher, the 1972 ★★ When a new kind of sausage appears in butcher's shop, people suspect he's responsible for disappearance of young woman from neighborhood. C: Victor Buono, Brad Harris, Karen Field. D: John Zuru. HOR [R] 90m. V

Mad Checkmate 1968 *See* **It's Your Move**

Mad Doctor of Blood Island, The 1969 ★★ Scientist turns his assistant into a plant monster with bloody results. (a.k.a. *Tomb of the Living Dead*) C: John Ashley, Angelique Pettyjohn, Ronald Peary. D: Gerardo De Leon. HOR [PG] 110m.

Mad Doctor of Market Street, The 1942 ★★½ Talented B-movie thespian Atwill plays a demented physician practicing weird experiments on South Sea islanders. Not one of this director's better films. C: Lionel Atwill, Una Merkel, Claire Dodd, Nat Pendleton, Anne Nagel. D: Joseph H. Lewis. HOR 61m.

Mad Doctor, The 1941 ★★★½ Smooth-talking physician marries women for their money, then arranges his own form of quickie divorce. Uneven, but solid filmmaking and Basil's performance make this one worth seeking out. C: Basil Rathbone, Ellen Drew, John Howard, Barbara Jo Allen, Ralph Morgan, Martin Kosleck. D: Tim Whelan. DRA 90m.

Mad Dog *See* **Mad Dog Morgan**

Mad Dog and Glory 1993 ★★★½ Murray lights up film whenever he's on; but that's not enough in this surprisingly flat comedy about a gangster who gives Thurman to a timid police photographer for saving his life. C: Robert De Niro, Uma Thurman, Bill Murray, Kathy Baker, David Caruso, Mike Starr, Tom Towles. D: John McNaughton. COM [R] 97m. V

Mad Dog Coll 1961 ★★½ Polished but forgettable gangster biography follows career of insanely vicious mobster. Catch psycho-specialist Chandler in rare leading role. Gene Hackman, playing a cop, made his film debut here. C: John Davis Chandler, Brooke Hayward, Kay Doubleday, Jerry Orbach, Telly Savalas, Vincent Gardenia. D: Burt Balaban. CRI [R] 86m.

Mad Dog Morgan 1976 Australian ★★★★ Hopper is a 19th-century Australian outlaw, aided by a young Aborigine (Gulpilil, costar of *Walkabout*). Ultraviolent tale is enhanced by tight direction, good performances and atmosphere. (a.k.a. *Mad Dog*) C: Dennis Hopper, Jack Thompson, David Gulpilil, Frank Thring. D: Philippe Mora. ACT 93m. V

Mad Executioners, The 1963 German ★★★ Mad doctors, decapitated women, and a vigilante court set up by a Scotland Yard investigator inhabit this atmospheric but muddled shocker inspired by British mystery writer Edgar Wallace. One of a spate of Wallace-derived, German-lensed thrillers churned out during the mid-'60s. C: Wolfgang Preiss, Harry Riebauer, Rudolph Fernau, Chris Howland. D: Edwin Zbonek. CRI 94m.

Mad Genius, The 1931 ★★★★ Strange puppeteer transforms a boy into a brilliant dancer, vicariously celebrating his triumphs in this bizarre, well-done, *Svengali*-like thriller. Film Students: Note that this film's sets showed ceilings a full decade before Orson Welles was lauded for doing so in *Citizen Kane*. C: John Barrymore, Marian Marsh, Donald Cook, Carmel Myers, Charles Butterworth, Mae Madison, Frankie Darro, Luis Alberni, Boris Karloff. D: Michael Curtiz. DRA 81m.

Mad Ghoul, The 1943 ★★★½ Mad M.D. needing fresh hearts for his longevity experiments, creates zombie assistant to fetch them. Top-notch cast of B-movie vets keep grim, visually static chiller from sinking. C: David Bruce, Evelyn Ankers, George Zucco, Turhan Bey, Charles McGraw, Robert Armstrong, Milburn Stone, Rose Hobart. D: James Hogan. HOR 65m. V

Mad Little Island 1957 British ★★★½ Daffy residents of small Scottish community are up in arms over plans to transform their island into military missile base. English sequel to *Tight Little Island* is amusing enough, but lacks the original's droll charm. (a.k.a. *Rockets Galore!*) C: Jeannie Carson, Donald Sinden, Roland Culver, Noel Purcell, Ian Hunter, Duncan MacRae, Catherine Lacey, Jean Cadell, Gordon Jackson. D: Michael Relph. COM 94m.

Mad Love 1935 ★★★★ Exaggerated performance from Lorre highlights Grand Guignol tale of a demented surgeon who sews the hands of a murderer onto an injured pianist. Impeccably photographed remake of 1924's *The Hands of Orlac* has spawned numerous further remakes. Drake is terrific as the object of Lorre's dark desires. C: Peter Lorre, Frances Drake, Colin Clive, Isabel Jewell, Ted Healy, Sara Haden, Edward Brophy, Keye Luke. D: Karl Freund. HOR 68m. V

Mad Magazine Presents Up the Academy *See* **Up the Academy**

Mad Magician, The 1954 ★★★ Blatant rip-off of Price's earlier *House of Wax* stars Vinnie as deranged wannabe-magician who murders his rivals live, onstage, before unsuspecting audiences. Flat and listless, despite being originally filmed in 3-D. C: Vincent Price, Mary Murphy, Eva Gabor, Patrick O'Neal, John Emery. D: John Brahm. HOR 72m.

Mad Max 1979 Australian ★★★★ A futuristic motorcycle cop (Gibson) seeks revenge for the brutal murders of his wife and child. A squalid but exciting sci-fi version of the venerable "cop turns vigilante" story line. Followed by *The Road Warrior* and *Mad Max Beyond Thunderdome.* C: Mel Gibson, Joanne Samuel, Steve Bisley, Tim Burns. D: George Miller. SFI [R] 93m. ♥

Mad Max 2 1981 *See* **Road Warrior, The**

Mad Max Beyond Thunderdome 1985 Australian ★★★½ Max (Gibson) becomes a gladiator in a post-nuclear-era "Bartertown" run by an evil ruler (Turner) and along the way encounters a self-sufficient tribe of child scavengers. The picture strains for (and sometimes succeeds at) outrageousness. C: Mel Gibson, Tina Turner, Angelo Rossitto, Helen Buday, Rod Zuanic, Bruce Spence. D: George Miller. SFI [PG-13] 107m. ♥

Mad Miss Manton, The 1938 ★★★★ Diverting screwball comedy/mystery with Stanwyck great as a madcap socialite mixed up in murder. Dated, but well done. C: Barbara Stanwyck, Henry Fonda, Sam Levene, Frances Mercer, Stanley Ridges, Vicki Lester, Whitney Bourne, Hattie McDaniel, Penny Singleton, Grady Sutton. D: Leigh Jason. COM 80m. ♥

Mad Mission 3 1984 ★★ In this parody of James Bond films, a man falls from the Eiffel Tower into the Seine and, as a result, becomes involved with an espionage ring. C: Richard Kiel, Tsuneharu Sugiyama. COM 87m. ♥

Mad Monster Party? 1967 ★★★½ Dr. Frankenstein wants to throw his retirement party and invites a horde of famous monsters to his place for the big blowout. Silly animated fare with celebrity voices in the leads; great for kiddie Halloween parties. Voices of Boris Karloff, Phyllis Diller. FAM/COM 94m. ♥

Mad Monster, The 1942 ★★½ Zucco is yet another mad scientist, this one intent on turning Strange into scientifically bred werewolf. Slapdash baloney, even by low-budget '40s horror film standards. C: Johnny Downs, George Zucco, Anne Nagel, Sarah Padden, Glenn Strange, Gordon DeMain. D: Sam Newfield. HOR 72m.

Mad Room, The 1969 ★★★ Stevens is shady companion to wealthy widow Winters, who begins to suspect that Stella's relatives might be a little bit *off* in the head. Bloodier remake of 1941 suspense film *Ladies in Retirement.* The original is superior. C: Stella Stevens, Shelley Winters, James Ward, Carol Cole, Severn Darden, Beverly Garland, Michael Burns. D: Bernard Girard. DRA 92m.

Mad Wax—The Surf Movie 1987 ★★ Surfer uses ancient waxy substance to improve his technique. C: Aaron Napoleon, Marvin Foster, Richard Cram. D: Michael Hohensee. ACT 70m. ♥

Mad Wednesday 1947 ★★★½ Frustrated middle-aged man quits his job and finds new life. Updating of The Freshman has some hilarious moments but is mostly strained. Disappointing between comic geniuses Lloyd and Sturges. (a.k.a. The Sin of Harold Diddlebock) C: Harold Lloyd, Frances Ramsden. D: Preston Sturges. COM 90m. ♥

Madam Satan 1930 ★★★★ One-of-a-kind musical drama about New York elite has silly plot and jaw-dropping production numbers. Denny is a wayward husband and Johnson is his wife, scheming to win him back. C: Kay Johnson, Reginald Denny, Roland Young, Lillian Roth, Elsa Peterson, Tyler Brooke, Boyd Irvin. D: Cecil B. DeMille. MUS 105m. ♥

Madame 1961 French-Italian-Spanish ★★★★ Fizzy, funny fairy tale about Napoleon Bonaparte's laundress (Loren), who'll do anything to join the man she loves at the front. Loren's delightful and so is the film. (a.k.a. *Madame Sans-Gene*) C: Sophia Loren, Robert Hossein, Julien Bertheau. D: Christian-Jaque. COM 104m.

Madame Bovary 1934 French ★★★ Renoir's adaptation of Flaubert's classic novel originally ran for three hours. Unfortunately he was forced to edit for length, and what remains is a confusing tale of romance and adultery in 19th-century France. Some beautiful moments, but these flounder in perplexing development. C: Valentine Tessier, Pierre Renoir, Max Dearly, Daniel Lecourtois, Fernand Fabre. D: Jean Renoir. DRA 102m. ♥

Madame Bovary 1949 ★★★★ Lush adaptation of oft-filmed Flaubert classic features Jones as French libertine whose extramarital affairs lead to destruction. Set pieces, especially a waltz sequence, marvelous; Mason portrays Flaubert in framing sequences. C: Jennifer Jones, James Mason, Van Heflin, Louis Jourdan, Gene Lockhart, Gladys Cooper. D: Vincente Minnelli. DRA 114m. ♥

Madame Bovary 1991 French ★★★½ Story of Flaubert's adulterous, 19th-century heroine is brought to screen yet again. Elegant, elaborate production. C: Isabelle Huppert, Jean-Francois Balmer, Christopher Malavoy, Jean Yanne. D: Claude Chabrol. DRA [PG-13] 130m. ♥

Madame Butterfly 1932 ★★★½ American Navy officer marries a geisha girl, which leads to tragedy. Later filmed version of the Puccini opera is tasteful but predictably static. C: Sylvia Sidney, Cary Grant, Charlie Ruggles, Irving Pichel, Helen Eddy. D: Marion Gering. DRA 86m. ♥

Madame Butterfly 1990 ★★★★ Renowned production of Puccini's opera played by Vienna Philharmonic Orchestra conducted by Herbert von Karajan. C: Placido Domingo, Mirella Freni, Christa Ludwig. MUS 143m. ♥

Madame Curie 1943 ★★★ By-the-numbers

biography of woman who discovered radium suffers from plodding pacing. Garson and Pidgeon, as Madame Curie and husband, add unexpected and welcome romantic chemistry. C: Greer Garson, Walter Pidgeon, Henry Travers, Albert Basserman, Robert Walker, C. Aubrey Smith. D: Mervyn LeRoy. DRA 124m. V

Madame Racketeer 1932 ★★★½ Notorious con woman known as The Countess (Skipworth) undergoes change of heart after her grown daughters unexpectedly reenter her life. Light comedy, crime, and drama are smoothly mixed; features a young George Raft in an early role. C: Alison Skipworth, Richard Bennett, George Raft, Evalyn Knapp, Gertrude Messinger, J. Farrell MacDonald, Robert McWade. D: Alexander Hall, Henry Wagstaff Gribble. COM 71m.

Madame Rosa 1977 French ★★★★½ Madam with heart of gold boards her charges' children to keep afloat. Signoret's stunning performance keeps this sentimental journey from getting maudlin. Oscar for Best Foreign Film. C: Simone Signoret, Samy Youb, Claude Dauphin, Gabriel Jabbour, Theodore Bikel. D: Moshe Mizrahi. DRA 105m. V

Madame Sans-Gene *See* **Madame**

Madame Sin 1962 ★★★½ Davis camps it up as distaff Fu Manchu-like supercriminal out to rule the world via acquisition of nuclear submarine. Handsomely mounted and preposterously enjoyable. C: Robert Wagner, Bette Davis, Catherine Schell, Denholm Elliott. D: David Greene. ACT 91m. V

Madame Sousatzka 1988 ★★ Russian piano teacher in London dotes on young protege with disastrous results. C: Shirley MacLaine, Peggy Ashcroft, Twiggy. D: John Schlesinger. DRA [PG-13] 121m.

Madame X 1929 ★★★ Slow-moving rendition of oft-filmed story. After Chatterton is thrown out of house by cruel husband Stone, she ends up being defended in court years later by the son who has believed his mother dead. A chestnut from the early sound era. Filmed three times as a silent, in 1906, 1916, and 1920, and three times in sound, in 1937, 1966, and 1981. (a.k.a. *Absinthe*) C: Ruth Chatterton, Lewis Stone, Raymond Hackett, Holmes Herbert, Eugenie Besserer, Sidney Toler, Ullrich Haupt. D: Lionel Barrymore. DRA 90m.

Madame X 1937 ★★★½ High gloss and zealous cast marks this version of one woman's tale of love, pain, and redemption. George is the fallen woman who is saved in court by the son who believed her long dead. C: Gladys George, John Beal, Warren William, Reginald Owen, William Henry, Henry Daniell, Phillip Reed, Ruth Hussey. D: Sam Wood. DRA 96m. V

Madame X 1966 ★★★½ The big-bucks version of the oft-filmed soap opera has Turner as the suffering mother tossed out by her husband, then saved from murder charges by her lawyer son years later. Good cast supports Turner as she wallows through her tides of misfortune. C: Lana Turner, John Forsythe, Constance Bennett, Ricardo Montalban, Burgess Meredith. D: David Lowell Rich. DRA 100m. V

Madame X 1981 ★★★½ Television's turn at this familiar story. Here Weld plays the mistreated wife, tossed out by her husband but rescued years later by her son. C: Tuesday Weld, Len Cariou, Eleanor Parker, Robert Hooks, Jerry Stiller, Jeremy Brett, Martina Deignan, Robin Strand, Tom Tully. D: Robert Ellis Miller. DRA 100m. V

Madchen in Uniform 1931 German ★★★★ Classic German early sound film about love relationship between teacher and her pupil in all-girls' school. Antimilitarist point of view and lesbian plot infuriated the Nazis, who forced Sagan into exile. Moving, if dated. Remade in 1958. (a.k.a. *Girls in Uniform*) C: Dorothea Wieck, Hertha Thiele, Emilia Unda. D: Leontine Sagan. DRA 90m. V

Madchen in Uniform 1958 German ★★★½ Schneider falls in love with her teacher (Palmer) at an all-girls' school, with disastrous results. Less frank than the 1931 version, but still effective. C: Lilli Palmer, Romy Schneider, Christine Kaufmann, Therese Giehse. D: Geza Radvanyi. DRA 91m.

M.A.D.D. 1983 ★★ Mourning mother vs. insensitive judicial system in this drama based on true story of Candy Lightner, founder of Mothers Against Drunk Drivers. C: Mariette Hartley, Paula Prentiss, Bert Remsen. D: William Graham. DRA 97m. TVM

Made for Each Other 1939 ★★★★ Lombard and Stewart face an array of trials and tribulations, including sickness, poverty, and meddling relatives. Though material is pure soap, the talented leads and first-rate production add considerable luster. C: Carole Lombard, James Stewart, Charles Coburn, Lucile Watson, Alma Kruger, Esther Dale, Ward Bond. D: John Cromwell. DRA 94m. V

Made for Each Other 1971 ★★★★ Two misfits meet in an encounter group and fall in love. Very funny, heartwarming tale features winning performances from the leads. Taylor and Bologna also wrote the screenplay. C: Renee Taylor, Joseph Bologna, Paul Sorvino, Olympia Dukakis. D: Robert B. Bean. COM [PG-13] 107m.

Made in America 1993 ★★★ Comedy of racial errors ensues when African-American bookstore owner (Goldberg) discovers her teenaged daughter's sperm bank father was a moronic—and white—used car salesman (Danson), who kindles unlikely interracial romance. Embarrassingly witless all around, though supporting player Smith has his moments. C: Whoopi Goldberg, Ted Danson, Will Smith, Nia Long, Jennifer Tilly, Clyde Kusatsu. D: Richard Benjamin. COM [PG-13] 111m. V

Made in Argentina 1986 Spanish ★★ New York-based Argentinian couple return to hometown and consider relocating. C: Luis Barndoni, Marta Bianchi, Leonor Manso. D: Juan Jose Jusid. DRA 90m. V

Made in Heaven 1952 ★★ Domestic bliss of newlyweds disturbed when sexy maid moves in. C: Petula Clark, David Tomlinson, Sonja Ziemann. D: John Paddy Carstairs. COM 90m.

Made in Heaven 1987 ★★★ Young man (Hutton) meets his soul mate (McGillis) in heaven but complications arise and he has to return to Earth to make sure she will fall in love with him in the real world. Weak romantic comedy is too precious, and the myriad cameos (Debra Winger, Neil Young, Tom Petty, among others) are often flat-out weird. C: Timothy Hutton, Kelly McGillis, Maureen Stapleton, Don Murray, Anne Wedgeworth, Debra Winger, Amanda Plummer, Mare Winningham. D: Alan Rudolph. COM [PG] 103m. V

Made in Italy 1967 Italian ★★★½ Franco-Italian co-production covers broad spectrum of people living in Italy—tourists, workers, aristocrats, etc.—each with his or her own separate story. Anthology film hits the mark more often than not. C: Virna Lisi, Anna Magnani, Sylva Koscina, Walter Chiari, Lea Massari, Alberto Sordi, Jean Sorel, Catherine Spaak. D: Nanni Loy. COM 101m.

Made in Paris 1966 ★★★ Love story masquerading as sophisticated continental romance between vivacious fashion buyer Ann-Margret and suave French designer Jourdan. Looks like fluffy French pastry. C: Ann-Margret, Louis Jourdan, Richard Crenna, Edie Adams, Chad Everett. D: Boris Sagal. COM 101m.

Made in USA 1966 ★★★★★ Brilliant, spiky, difficult Godard film, ostensibly a thriller about Karina going to Atlantic City to investigate her lover's death, but really a bizarre rumination on the pervasive influence of American pop culture in France. Hard to see in the U.S. due to rights problems with the source material (a Richard Stark novel which it virtually ignores), but a key film of the '60s. C: Christopher Penn, Adrian Pasdar, Lori Singer. D: Ken Friedman. DRA [R] 82m.

Madeleine 1949 British ★★★½ First-class direction (from epic specialist Lean), cast, and sets elevate oft-told tale of wealthy 19th-century Scottish woman indicted for poisoning her lover. Frustrating climax mars otherwise gripping courtroom drama. C: Ann Todd, Leslie Banks, Elizabeth Sellars, Ivor Barnard. D: David Lean. DRA 101m.

Madeleine 1958 German ★★½ Bartok is a reformed prostitute trying to walk the straight and narrow, meeting resistance every step of the way. Dull German melodrama is poorly done. C: Eva Bartok, Sabina Sesselmann, Ilse Steppat, Alexander Kerst. D: Kurt Meisel. DRA 86m.

Mademoiselle Docteur 1969 *See* **Fraulein Doktor**

Mademoiselle Fifi 1944 ★★★½ French laundress (Simone) on a long coach ride with her social superiors during the Franco-Prussian War, gradually reveals more true character than any of them. Well-produced if erratic costume drama; based on stories by Guy de Maupassant. C: Simone Simon, John Emery, Kurt Kreuger, Alan Napier, Jason Robards Sr., Helen Freeman, Norma Freeman. D: Robert Wise. DRA 69m. V

Madhouse 1974 British ★★★½ Price is a reluctant horror star trying to make new TV series while cast and crew are murdered around him. Mean-minded, bloody British shocker features in-jokes and unusual pairing of terror titans Cushing and Price. Adapted from Angus Hall's novel *Devilday.* C: Vincent Price, Peter Cushing, Robert Quarry, Adrienne Corri, Natasha Payne, Linda Hayden. D: Jim Clark. HOR [PG] 89m. V

Madhouse 1981 ★★ Young woman shocked to discover her twin has become an ugly and violent psychopath. C: Trish Everly, Allison Biggers, Michael MacRae. D: Ovidio G. Assonitis. HOR 90m. V

Madhouse 1990 ★★ Married couple Larroquette and Alley suffer unending torture when their home is invaded by horde of obnoxious houseguests who refuse to leave. Sitcom-level humor pads out this one-joke comedy. C: John Larroquette, Kirstie Alley, Alison LaPlaca, John Diehl, Jessica Lundy, Dennis Miller. D: Tom Ropelawski. COM [PG-13] 90m. V

Madhouse Mansion 1975 British ★★★½ In the late '20s, three English college lads find themselves stranded in a most unusual haunted house. Obscure British chiller gives fresh twists to a very old theme. (a.k.a. *Ghost Story*) C: Marianne Faithfull, Leigh Lawson, Anthony Bate, Larry Dann. D: Stephen Weeks. HOR 90m. V

Madhur Jaffrey's Far Eastern Cooking 1988 ★★★★ Jaffrey takes viewers on tour through Hong Kong, Indonesia, Vietnam, Japan, Korea, and Philippines in search of exciting and typical native foods. DOC 61m.

Madhur Jaffrey's Indian Cookery 1987 ★★★ Step-by-step instructions for eight dishes native to India. DOC 120m.

Madigan 1968 ★★★★½ Dynamic, realistic police thriller about a hard-boiled detective (Widmark) whose service revolver has been stolen by a killer. One of action veteran Seigel's best; complex characterizations, interesting locations, visceral climactic shootout. C: Richard Widmark, Henry Fonda, Harry Guardino, Inger Stevens, James Whitmore, Susan Clark, Michael Dunn, Sheree North. D: Don Siegel. CRI 101m. V

Madigan's Million 1968 ★ IRS agent Hoffman travels to Italy to recover loot stolen from the U.S. Treasury Department. The superstar's first film. C: Dustin Hoffman, Elsa Martinelli, Cesar Romero. D: Stanley Prager. COM [G] 86m. V

Madison Avenue 1962 ★★★½ Andrews is an advertising executive plotting revenge on his ruthless boss in this indictment of corporate savagery. Diverting; a notch above the usual study of interoffice politics. C: Dana Andrews, Eleanor Parker, Jeanne Crain, Eddie Albert, Howard St. John, Henry Daniell. D: H. Bruce Humberstone. DRA 94m.

Madman 1979 Israeli ★ Deranged Israeli soldier (Beck) is determined to kill all the Soviets he can lay his hands on. Your move. C: Michael Beck, F. Murray Abraham, Alan Feinstein, Sigourney Weaver. D: Dan Cohen. ACT [R] 92m. V

Madman 1981 ★ Ax murderer arrives at summer camp for children with the expected results. C: Gaylen Ross, Alexis Dubin. D: Joe Giannone. HOR [R] 89m.

Madness of King George, The 1994 British ★★★★★ After losing the American colonies in 1776, Britain's monarch begins to lose his mind, as well. Stunning treatment of Alan Bennett's play, *The Madness of George III*, with a towering performance by Hawthorne as the distressed title character. Oscar nominations went to Hawthorne and Mirren. Winner of the Academy Award for Best Art Direction. C: Nigel Hawthorne, Helen Mirren, Ian Holm, Amanda Donohoe, Rupert Graves, Rupert Everett. D: Nicholas Hytner. DRA 105m. V

Madonna—Blond Ambition 1990 ★★★ Star on world tour. C: Madonna. MUS 120m. V

Madonna of the Seven Moons 1946 British ★★★★ Calvert is marked by Gypsy curse that forces her to lead a double life. Stilted, unintentionally campy melodrama teeters on the edge of absurdity, but manages to remain entertaining. C: Phyllis Calvert, Stewart Granger, Patricia Roc, Peter Glenville. D: Arthur Crabtree. DRA 88m.

Madonna—The Girlie Show—Live Down Under 1994 ★★ Live performance by star, filmed in Sydney, Australia. C: Madonna. MUS [R] 120m. V

Madonna Truth or Dare 1991 *See* **Truth or Dare**

Madonna's Secret, The 1946 ★★★ Straightforward murder mystery involves identifying the killer of an artist's model. No-frills whodunit. C: Francis Lederer, Gail Patrick, Ann Rutherford, Linda Stirling, John Litel. D: William Thiele. CRI 79m.

Madox 1 / Riding Bean 1993 Japanese ★★ Two popular animated films from Japan. DRA 94m. V

Madrid ★★★ Travelogue of some of city's most beautiful artistic and architectural treasures. DOC 57m. V

Madron 1970 ★★★ Gunslinger Boone accompanies massacre survivor Caron (a nun) on long trek across desert and protects her from attacks by Apaches. Impressive Israeli locations enhance otherwise monotonous Western. C: Richard Boone, Leslie Caron, Paul Smith, Gabi Amrani. D: Jerry Hopper. WST [PG] 90m. V

Madwoman of Chaillot, The 1969 ★★★ Stars overwhelm this adaptation of Jean Giraudoux's play about an eccentric Parisian woman who lives in the glorious past and joins her social inferiors to save Paris from greedy conspirators. Slow-paced, fussy drama laden with fancy scenery and dialogue. C: Katharine Hepburn, Charles Boyer, Claude Dauphin, Edith Evans, John Gavin, Paul Henreid, Oscar Homolka, Margaret Leighton, Giulietta Masina, Nanette Newman, Richard Chamberlain, Yul Brynner, Danny Kaye. D: Bryan Forbes. DRA [G] 132m. V

Mae West 1982 ★★★½ Snappy yet inaccurate biography rewrites life story of seminal screen legend to suit its own glossy agenda. Jillian tries hard in title role. C: Ann Jillian, James Brolin, Piper Laurie, Roddy McDowall. D: Lee Philips. DRA 97m. TVM V

Maestro & the Diva, The ★★★ Strauss performed by Kiri Te Kanawa and the Chicago Symphony Orchestra conducted by Sir Georg Solti. C: Kiri Te Kanawa, Georg Solti, BBC Philharmonic. MUS 118m. V

Maestro's Company, The—Vol. 1 1989 ★★★ An introduction to opera for children using puppets to act out "The Barber of Seville" and La Traviata." C: Renata Tebaldi, Placido Domingo, Joan Sutherland. FAM/MUS 60m. V

Maestro's Company, The—Vol. 2 1989 ★★★ Opera for children using puppets to perform "Rigoletto" and "Hansel and Gretel." C: Renata Tebaldi, Placido Domingo, Joan Sutherland. FAM/MUS 60m. V

Maestros in Moscow ★★★ Mussorgsky, Gershwin, and jazz performed by the Moscow Philharmonic, conducted by Lawrence Leighton Smith and Dmitri Kitayenko. C: Lawrence Leighton Smith, Moscow Philharmonic. MUS 70m. V

Mafia Princess 1986 ★★★½ Autobiography of Antoinette Giancana (Lucci), daughter of long-time Chicago Mafia boss. Curtis gives one of his best performances as Sam Giancana, aging 40 years over the course of the movie. C: Tony Curtis, Susan Lucci, Kathleen Widdoes, Tony DeSantis. D: Robert Collins. DRA 100m. TVM V

Mafia vs. Ninja 1984 ★ Gratuitous Kung-fu violence between above-mentioned groups. Dud. C: Alexander Lou, Silvio Azzolini. ACT 90m. V

Mafu Cage, The 1978 ★★½ Two weird sisters play complicated mind games with one another, by acting out the role of a pet orangutan (named Mafu) and allowing themselves to be caged. Murky feminist allegory. (a.k.a. *My Sister, My Love* and *The Cage*) C:

Lee Grant, Carol Kane, Will Geer, James Olson. D: Karen Arthur. DRA [R] 102m. v

Magdalene 1990 ★★ Baron attacks disinterested lover; when another man comes to protect her, he is targeted as well. C: Steve Bond, Nastassia Kinski, David Warner. D: Monica Teuber. DRA [PG] 89m. v

Magellan Meridian GPS ★★ Guide to navigational tool with ability to track satellites for more accurate plotting. DOC 45m. v

Maggie, The 1954 *See* **High and Dry**

Magic 1978 ★★★ Over time, a ventriloquist becomes obsessed with his dummy, and his dementia turns to murder. Pompous but effective hair-raiser. Adapted by William Goldman from his novel. A fine opportunity to see Hopkins being scary 13 years before *Silence of the Lambs.* C: Anthony Hopkins, Ann-Margret, Burgess Meredith, Ed Lauter. D: Richard Attenborough. HOR [R] 106m. v

Magic Adventure ★★★ Award-winning, animated video based on some of Hans Christian Andersen's tales featuring the mad wind wizard, Captain Crust, and the sultan who won't let kids play with toys. FAM/COM 90m.

Magic Bow, The 1947 British ★★★½ Weak British musical biography focuses on life of famed violinist Paganini. Macho Granger is miscast as talented musician; watch this one for the costumes and music. C: Stewart Granger, Phyllis Calvert, Jean Kent, Dennis Price, Cecil Parker. D: Bernard Knowles. MUS 105m.

Magic Box, The 1951 British ★★★★½ Heartfelt biography focuses on the sad, forgotten life of pioneering Englishman William Friese-Greene, the actual inventor of motion pictures. Episodic drama includes numerous sketches featuring a staggering array of legendary British actors; educational and absorbing. C: Robert Donat, Maria Schell, Margaret Johnston, Robert Beatty, Laurence Olivier, Michael Redgrave, Eric Portman, Glynis Johns, Emlyn Williams, Richard Attenborough, Stanley Holloway, Margaret Rutherford, Peter Ustinov. D: John Boulting. DRA 103m.

Magic Bubble, The 1993 ★★ Magical potion eliminates 40-year old woman's fear of aging and restores her faith in herself. C: Deborah Taper Ringel, Diane Salinger. D: Alfredo Ringel. DRA 90m. v

Magic Carpet, The 1951 ★★★ Exiled caliph's son returns to his homeland to regain throne from evil nobleman. Tepid Arabian Nights hokum, with usually comedic Ball as scrappy heroine. C: Lucille Ball, John Agar, Patricia Medina, Raymond Burr, George Tobias. D: Lew Landers. ACT 84m.

Magic Christian, The 1969 British ★★★ Wealthy Sellers and adopted son Starr give money to strangers just to watch reactions. Based on Terry Southern's novel, this episodic satire works in parts but humor is largely dated. Marvelous cameos—including set pieces by Monty Python cast members—fill out thinner stretches. C: Peter Sellers, Ringo Starr. D: Joseph McGrath. COM [PG] 101m. v

Magic Christmas Tree, The ★★ Boy struggles with giant to save Santa Claus from kidnappers. C: Chris Kroesen, Charles Nix. D: Richard C. Parish. DRA 70m. v

Magic Cloak of Oz, The 1914 ★★ Oz story directed by author of "The Wizard of Oz." D: Frank L. Baum. FAM/DRA 45m. v

Magic Face, The 1951 ★★★ Talented German impersonator murders Adolf Hitler and switches places with him, purposefully pointing Third Reich toward defeat. Adler's not bad as the bogus Führer. C: Luther Adler, Patricia Knight, William L. Shirer, Ilka Windish. D: Frank Tuttle. DRA 89m.

Magic Fire 1956 ★★★ German composer Richard Wagner is profiled in out-of-tune musical biography that ignores best elements of his fascinating real life. Suffers from shabby script, bad color and shallow characterizations; horror icon Peter Cushing appears in rare nonthreatening role. C: Yvonne De Carlo, Carlos Thompson, Rita Gam, Valentina Cortese, Alan Badel. D: William Dieterle. MUS 95m.

Magic Flute, The 1973 Swedish ★★★★½ Bergman's delightful filmed performance of Mozart's great comic opera about a sorcerer who kidnaps the Queen of the Night's daughter. Bergman's direction is sensitive and intelligent, and he's careful not to upstage the performers. C: Ulric Cold, Josef Kostlinger, Irma Urrila, Hakan Hagegard, Elisabeth Erikson. D: Ingmar Bergman. MUS [G] 134m. v

Magic Flute, The 1976 ★★★ Spectacular production of Mozart's opera; Leipzig Gewandhaus Orchestra conducted by Gert Bahner. C: Hermann Christian Plster, Magdalena Falewicz. MUS [G] 169m. v

Magic Flute, The 1982 German ★★ London Philharmonic Orchestra and Chorus, conducted by Bernard Haitink in peformance of Mozart's opera. In German. C: Benjamin Luxon, Felicity Lott. MUS 164m. v

Magic Garden of Stanley Sweetheart, The 1970 ★★½ Directionless '60s college kids turn on, tune in, drop out. A cinematic time capsule though not a very enlightening one. Mostly fun as camp item. C: Don Johnson, Linda Gillin, Michael Greer, Dianne Hull, Holly Near, Victoria Racimo. D: Leonard Horn. DRA [R] 117m.

Magic Kid 1993 ★★ Attempted rescue of uncle, headed for skid row, by niece and nephew. C: Stephen Furst, Ted Jan Roberts, Shonda Whipple. D: Joseph Merhi. DRA [PG] 95m. v

Magic Legend of the Juggler ★★ Juggler discovers sincerity is of greater value than material possessions. C: Barry Dennen, Walter Slezak. FAM/DRA 80m. v

Magic Memories on Ice 1990 ★★★★ Unparalleled figure skating performances by Peggy Fleming, Torvill and Dean, Brian Boitano, and others. MUS 90m. V

Magic Memories on Ice II 1993 ★★★★ Featured skaters include Janet Lynn, Dorothy Hamill, Katarina Witt, and others. MUS 78m. V

Magic of Bing Crosby, The—Part 1 1991 ★★★★ Clips from star's unforgettable performances and interviews with colleagues and friends. DOC 55m.

Magic of Lassie, The 1978 ★★★½ When evil rich guy Roberts can't buy out Stewart's vineyards, he takes beloved family collie instead. Familiar remake of standard *Lassie* formula that benefits from good casting. C: James Stewart, Lassie, Mickey Rooney, Stephanie Zimbalist, Pernell Roberts, Michael Sharrett. D: Don Chaffey. FAM/DRA [G] 100m. V

Magic of the Bolshoi, The 1987 ★★★★ Picture of renowned ballet company through film highlights and contemporary footage. C: Bolshoi Ballet. MUS 60m. V

Magic of the Kirov Ballet, The ★★★★ Scenes from best of company's performances. C: Kirov Ballet. MUS 60m.

Magic on Love Island 1980 ★★★½ On tropical island, tourists seek love and friendship. Loosely based on Shakespeare's "A Midsummer Night's Dream." C: Adrienne Barbeau, Bill Daily. D: Earl Bellamy. DRA 96m. V

Magic Pony, The 1977 ★★★ While guarding his family's wheat field, a boy's encounters with a flying horse provide him with a team of equines to sell and a magic pony of his own. Animated children's film. Voices of Jim Backus, Erin Moran. FAM/DRA [G] 80m.

Magic Show, The 1981 ★★★★ Shari Lewis and Lambchop host an entertaining magic show which features four of the time's most outstanding magicians. They are Mark Wilson, Flip of Holland, Randi and Tomsoni and Company. FAM/COM [G] 60m. V

Magic Snowman, The 1988 ★★★½ A young boy creates a magnificent talking snowman who helps his family through rough times.But when the boy uses the snowman for his own personal gain, he learns a valuable lesson about honesty, integrity and the power of believing. FAM/DRA 85m. V

Magic Sword, The 1962 ★★★½ Young knight (Lockwood) saves a princess after battling a horde of spells conjured up by wizard (Rathbone). Some nice genre spoofing in a fun film for children. Rathbone makes the most of his role. C: Basil Rathbone, Estelle Winwood, Gary Lockwood, Anne Helm. D: Bert I. Gordon. FAM/SFI 80m. V

Magic Town 1947 ★★★★ Clever comedy about an ambitious pollster who finds his lifelong dream of the perfect American town that exactly mirrors the pulse of the country. Trouble brews when word of his discovery leaks out. Bouncy satire of American society entertains throughout. C: James Stewart, Jane Wyman, Kent Smith, Regis Toomey. D: William Wellman. COM 103m. V

Magic Voyage, The 1993 ★★★½ Animated version of Columbus's great discovery, told sweetly through the eyes of an amorous worm and firefly. Voices of Dom Deluise, Corey Feldman, Irene Cara. D: Michael Schoemann. FAM/COM [G] 82m. V

Magic World of Topo Gigio, The 1965 Italian ★★½ Silly film featuring squeaky-voiced mouse puppet who regularly appeared on the old *Ed Sullivan* TV show may appeal to nostalgic baby-boomers. C: Ermanno Roveri, Lgnazio Colnaghi, Frederica Milani, Topo Gigio. D: Luca de Rico. COM 75m.

Magical Mystery Tour 1968 ★★★ The Beatles take a cross-country tour with a group of assorted quirky characters for an unknown destination. Aimless indulgence made at the height of psychedelia, though several musical segments make great pre-MTV music videos. C: The Beatles. MUS 60m. V

Magical Princess Gigi, The ★★ Sweet princess from different world comes to Earth for fun and adventure in this animated video. FAM/ACT 80m. V

Magical Wonderland ★★ Live-action performances of fairy tales including "Hansel & Gretel", "Beauty and the Beast", and others. From Russia. FAM/ACT 90m. V

Magician of Lublin, The 1979 ★★½ Muddled adaptation of fine Issac Bashevis Singer novel stars Arkin as early 20th-century Jewish magician trying to better his life. Good period atmosphere helps to conceal director's heavy-handed touch. C: Alan Arkin, Louise Fletcher, Valerie Perrine, Shelley Winters, Lou Jacobi. D: Menahem Golan. DRA [R] 105m. V

Magician, The 1958 Swedish ★★★★ Mysterious 19th-century magician von Sydow is pitted in contest of faith against coldly rational scientist Bjornstrand. Dark fable with horror film overtones grapples with eternal struggle between illusion and reality. Not one of Bergman's better efforts, but still worthwhile for its cast, craft, and Gothic fairy-tale atmosphere. C: Max von Sydow, Ingrid Thulin, Gunnar Bjornstrand, Bibi Andersson. D: Ingmar Bergman. DRA 101m. V

Magician, The 1973 ★★★½ Smooth, cultivated prestidigitator (Bixby) sidelines as a freelance crimebuster using magic tricks to defeat bad guys. Slick but empty action piece was pilot for short-lived series of the same name. C: Bill Bixby, Keene Curtis, Joan Caulfield, Kim Hunter, Elizabeth Ashley, Barry Sullivan, Signe Hasso, Anne Lockhart. D: Marvin Chomsky. ACT 78m. TVM

Magnate, The 1987 Polish ★★★½ As their beloved fatherland endures the tumultuous first half of the twentieth century, a wealthy German clan spirals toward destruction. D: Filip Bajon. DRA 185m. V

Magnet, The 1951 British ★★★★ Unusually sympathetic portrayal of children at play, presented from a child's perspective. Unique, rewarding essay on childhood fun and innocence, featuring kiddie star William Fox (perhaps better known as James Fox). C: William Fox, Kay Walsh, Stephen Murray. D: Charles Frend. FAM/DRA 78m

Magnetic Monster, The 1953 ★★★ Better-than-average '50s science fiction about a purloined magnetic isotope that threatens humanity as it expands in size and intensity. Entertaining thriller boasts a striking special effects-laden ending. C: Richard Carlson, King Donovan, Jean Byron, Byron Foulger. D: Curt Siodmak. SFI 76m.

Magnificent Ambersons, The 1942 ★★★★★ Masterful screen adaptation of Booth Tarkington novel about the fall of a genteel family unwilling to adapt to the coming age of the automobile. Brilliant; painstakingly controlled directorial achievement. Partly reshot and recut when studio took over film. C: Tim Holt, Joseph Cotten, Dolores Costello, Anne Baxter, Agnes Moorehead, Ray Collins, Richard Bennett, Erskine Sanford. D: Orson Welles. DRA 88m. V

Magnificent Brute, The 1936 ★★★ McLaglen gives a strong performance as the brutish boss of a steel plant who finds himself involved with two women and some stolen loot. A small-scale, but brightly acted piece of work. C: Victor McLaglen, Binnie Barnes, William Hall, Jean Dixon. D: John G. Blystone. DRA 80m.

Magnificent Cuckold, The 1966 Italian ★★★½ Businessman (Tognazzi) and drop-dead gorgeous wife (Cardinale) conduct their own battle of the sexes as each plots to top the other's infidelities. This is a racy sex comedy as only the Italians can do it—good, naughty fun. C: Claudia Cardinale, Ugo Tognazzi, Michele Girardon, Bernard Blier. D: Antonio Pietrangeli. COM 111m.

Magnificent Doll 1946 ★★ Rogers liked to act as well as dance, but she's not up to portraying vivacious First Lady Dolley Madison. Still, the cast for this historical epic includes the dynamic Meredith as President Madison and the suave Niven as Aaron Burr. C: Ginger Rogers, Burgess Meredith, David Niven, Horace McNally, Peggy Wood. D: Frank Borzage. DRA 95m. V

Magnificent Dope, The 1942 ★★★½ Comedic love triangle concerns the unwitting rivalry of a country hick (Fonda) with city slicker (Ameche) over business affairs and the love of Bari. Leading actors are at their most humorous in this pleasantly amusing romp. C: Henry Fonda, Lynn Bari, Don Ameche, Edward Everett Horton, Hobart Cavanaugh, Pierre Watkin. D: Walter Lang. COM 83m.

Magnificent Fraud, The 1939 ★★½ An actor in a fictitious Latin American banana republic is called upon to impersonate the recently assassinated dictator. Standard B-movie, but entertaining. C: Akim Tamiroff, Lloyd Nolan, Mary Boland, Patricia Morison. D: Robert Florey. COM 78m.

Magnificent Kick, The 1980 ★★★ Chronicles life of Wong-Fai-Hung, martial arts master and inventor of "Kick without Shadow," move made famous by Bruce Lee. ACT 90m. V

Magnificent Magical Magnet of Santa Mesa, The 1977 ★★½ An idealistic inventor concocts an energy device to help save mankind, only to have his employers exploit it for money. Innocuous family fluff. (a.k.a. *Adventures of Freddie*) C: Michael Burns, Dick Blasucci, Jane Connell. D: Hy Averback. FAM/COM 76m. TVM

Magnificent Matador, The 1955 ★★★ An over-the-hill matador (Quinn) is concerned about his youthful protégé while trying to understand his own jaded feelings for the sport. Good bullfighting footage. C: Anthony Quinn, Maureen O'Hara, Manuel Rojas, Thomas Gomez, Richard Denning, Lola Albright. D: Budd Boetticher. DRA 94m. V

Magnificent Obsession 1935 ★★★★ Stahl's straightforward treatment of improbable material makes this tearjerker a classic. Taylor is irresponsible playboy who inadvertently costs Dunne her sight, then becomes great surgeon and cures her blindness. Taylor's first major role. Dunne is impressive as always. Remade in 1954. C: Irene Dunne, Robert Taylor, Betty Furness, Charles Butterworth, Sara Haden, Ralph Morgan, Arthur Treacher. D: John M. Stahl. DRA 101m.

Magnificent Obsession 1954 ★★★★ Remake of 1935 melodrama follows plot closely, but with ironic treatment by Sirk turning it into veritable black comedy. Hudson is self-centered rich kid, then is responsible for accident that blinds Wyman. He reforms, cures her blindness against all odds. Catapulted Hudson to stardom. C: Jane Wyman, Rock Hudson, Barbara Rush, Otto Kruger, Agnes Moorehead. D: Douglas Sirk. DRA 108m. V

Magnificent Rebel, The 1962 ★★★½ Surprisingly adult Disney feature (originally aired on Disney's TV show) presents a steely, determined Beethoven, enduring a tortuous life and struggling valiantly against deafness. Sonorous musical passages, photogenic German locations, and a richly brooding performance from Boehm as the great composer. C: Karl Boehm, Ernst Nadhering, Ivan Desny, Gabriele Porks. D: Georg Tressler. DRA 95m.

Magnificent Roughnecks 1956 ★★ Comedians (Carson and Rooney) try working the oil fields and have trouble dealing with a savvy co-worker who's (gasp!) a woman (Gates). Dated premise, but the leads try hard. C: Jack Carson, Mickey Rooney, Nancy Gates, Jeff Donnell. D: Sherman A. Rose. COM 73m.

Magnificent Seven Deadly Sins, The 1971 British ★★★½ This collection of none too subtle comedy sketches has plenty of laughs and a few misfires. Terrific cast makes up for the dry spells. C: Bruce Forsyth, Joan Sims, Roy Hudd. D: Graham Stark. COM 107m.

Magnificent Seven, The 1960 ★★★★½ Seven American gunslingers are hired to protect a Mexican village from bandits. The action is hot and heavy and the cast is quite impressive. Adapted from Kurosawa's *The Seven Samurai*. C: Yul Brynner, Steve McQueen, Eli Wallach, Horst Buchholz, James Coburn, Charles Bronson, Robert Vaughn, Brad Dexter. D: John Sturges. WST 127m. V

Magnificent Seven Ride!, The 1972 ★★★ Third and final sequel to *The Magnificent Seven* concerns a gunslinger who joins the Seven to battle bandits who've abducted his sweet young bride. Series formula is growing stale, but it perks up now and then for some good ol' gritty Western action. C: Lee Van Cleef, Stefanie Powers, Mariette Hartley, Michael Callan, Luke Askew, Pedro Armendariz Jr. D: George McCowan. WST 100m.

Magnificent Sinner 1959 French ★★ The love life of Tsar Alexander II (Jurgens) and his mistress (Schneider) is chronicled against the backdrop of court politics. Slow-paced romantic item. C: Romy Schneider, Curt Jurgens, Pierre Blanchar, Monique Melinand. D: Robert Siodmak. DRA 97m.

Magnificent Yankee, The 1950 ★★★★ Biography of Supreme Court Justice Oliver Wendell Holmes and his caring wife is both an intimate personal drama and an incisive look at the legal system. First-rate acting and touching story line make this a worthy viewing experience. C: Louis Calhern, Ann Harding, Eduard Franz, James Lydon, Philip Ober. D: John Sturges. DRA 80m. V

Magnum Force 1973 ★★★ The second in Eastwood's *Dirty Harry* series of odes to big guns and short, snappy phrases ("Make my day", "Feeling lucky?") is not his best. Harry investigates mob murders implicating someone in his own department. C: Clint Eastwood, Hal Holbrook, Mitchell Ryan, David Soul, Felton Perry, Robert Urich. D: Ted Post. CRI [R] 122m. V

Magus, The 1968 British ★★ Convoluted adaptation of John Fowles multilayered novel details the arrival of English schoolteacher (Caine) on Greek island and attempts by bored, wealthy master-manipulator (Quinn) to govern his fate. C: Anthony Quinn, Michael Caine, Candice Bergen, Anna Karina, Paul Stassino, Julian Glover. D: Guy Green. DRA [PG] 117m.

Mahabharata, The 1989 ★★★★ Nine hours of absorbing theater condensed into six hours of gripping television, tracking gruesome conflict between two factions in ancient India. C: Robert Langdon Lloyd, Bruce Myers, Vittorio Mezzogiorno. D: Peter Brook. DRA 360m.TVM V

Mahler 1974 British ★★★½ Outré biographer Russell focuses on composer Gustav Mahler with his usual overexuberance. Tasteful it's not, but the film's compact classical structure—Mahler's life flashing before his eyes on a train journey—and Russell's flair for provocative images set to music make this one of his better efforts. C: Robert Powell, Georgina Hale, Richard Morant, Lee Montague. D: Ken Russell. DRA [PG] 110m. V

Mahogany 1975 ★★ A model/fashion designer (Ross) achieves success but finds happiness to be as elusive as ever. A notorious misfire, except for Perkins. C: Diana Ross, Billy Dee Williams, Anthony Perkins, Jean-Pierre Aumont, Beah Richards, Nina Foch. D: Berry Gordy. DRA [PG] 110m. V

Maid in Paris 1957 French ★★★ The old romantic tale—a naive country girl sets off for Gay Paree in the hope of finding true love. Slight, harmless story. C: Dany Robin, Daniel Gelin, Marie Daems, Tilda Thamar. D: Gaspard-Huit. COM 84m.

Maid In Sweden 1974 Swedish ★★★ Innocent young rural woman travels to Stockholm and learns all about men. C: Kristina Lindberg, Monika Ekman. D: Floch Johnson. DRA [R] 81m. V

Maid of Salem 1937 ★★★★ Well-executed Colonial drama on the origins of witch-hunting hysteria and how allegations of witchcraft nearly destroyed early Massachusetts communities. Excellent ensemble acting and fascinating subject add considerbly to the appeal of this period piece. C: Claudette Colbert, Fred MacMurray, Louise Dresser, Gale Sondergaard, Beulah Bondi, Bonita Granville, Virginia Weidler, Donald Meek, Harvey Stephens, Edward Ellis. D: Frank Lloyd. DRA 86m.

Maid, The 1991 U.S. ★★★ Wall Street executive Sheen tries to impress French business peer Bisset by becoming her servant. Starts off nicely, but quickly fades into routine and forgettable romantic comedy. C: Martin Sheen, Jacqueline Bisset, Jean-Pierre Cassel, Victoria Shalet, James Faulkner. D: Ian Toynton. COM [PG] 91m. V

Maid to Order 1987 ★★★½ Rich, spoiled Sheedy learns lessons in humility after fairy godmother D'Angelo sends her to work for rich couple Perrine and Shawn. Modern fairy tale has some fun performances and is full of sweet energy. C: Ally Sheedy, Beverly D'Angelo, Michael Ontkean, Valerie Perrine, Dick Shawn, Tom Skerritt. D: Amy Jones. COM [PG] 92m. V

Maid's Night Out 1938 ★★½ Formulaic '30s screwball comedy in which milkman (Lane) mistakes heiress (Fontaine) for a maid. Throw in gossip columnist Hedda Hopper and a fish named Louella, and anything can happen! C: Joan Fontaine, Allan Lane, Hedda Hopper, George Irving, William Brisbane, Billy Gilbert, Cecil Kellaway, Jack Carson. D: Ben Holmes. COM 64m.

Maids of Wilko 1979 Polish ★★★★½ Touching tale of man visiting childhood holiday spot in search of his lost youth. C: Daniel Olbrychski. D: Andrzej Wajda. DRA 111m. V

Maids, The 1975 British ★★★½ Jean Genet's expressionistic play features two scheming, long-winded maids jealous of their glamorous employer. Fine role for Jackson, but the material may leave viewers a bit mystified. C: Glenda Jackson, Susannah York, Vivien Merchant. D: Christopher Miles. DRA [PG] 95m.

Maigret 1988 British ★★½ English TV series pilot features Harris as Parisian police inspector Maigret, a weathered cop investigating the murder of a detective who was also his pal. C: Richard Harris, Patrick O'Neal, Victoria Tennant, Barbara Shelley, Ian Ogilvy, Eric Deacon, Caroline Munro, Andrew McCulloch. D: Paul Lynch. CRI 100m. TVM

Mail Order Bride 1964 ★★★ Meandering plot of this Western finds rowdy, youthful rancher (Dullea) agreeing to marry a widow to mollify his father's best friend. Distinguished by a decent cast and an energetic shoot-'em-up finale. C: Buddy Ebsen, Keir Dullea, Lois Nettleton, Warren Oates, Marie Windsor, Barbara Luna. D: Burt Kennedy. WST 83m.

Mailbag Robbery 1958 British ★★★½ Train heist caper film offers solid suspense, as three thieves plan a complicated robbery. An overlooked, well-crafted piece of work. C: Lee Patterson, Kay Callard, Alan Gifford, Kerry Jordan. D: Compton Bennett. CRI 70m.

Main Attraction, The 1962 ★★ A guitar-strumming vagabond (Boone) wanders through Europe, hooks up with an itinerant circus, and instigates romantic problems within the troupe. Boone's too squeaky-clean, but he tries hard not to be. Shot on location in the British Isles. C: Pat Boone, Mai Zetterling, Nancy Kwan, Yvonne Mitchell, Kieron Moore. D: Daniel Petrie. DRA 90m.

Main Chance, The 1966 British ★★★½ Little-known British item about the planning and execution of a diamond heist. Charmingly eccentric. C: Gregoire Aslan, Tracy Reed, Edward DeSouza, Stanley Meadows. D: John Knight. DRA 60m.

Main Event, The 1979 ★★½ A broke executive (Streisand) "inherits" a down-on-his luck prizefighter (O'Neal) and tries to put him back in the ring for her own financial benefit. Humor is shrill and forced as the two leads antagonize each other until they make love; but they do have some chemistry. Wait for the dynamite disco song Streisand sings over the end credits. C: Barbara Streisand, Ryan O'Neal, Paul Sand, Patti D'Arbanville, Richard Lawson, James Gregory. D: Howard Zieff. COM [PG] 109m. V

Main Street After Dark 1944 ★★★ Unusual movie about an extended family of pickpockets who lose their livelihood because of a city-sponsored anticrime campaign. Snappy cast makes this an interesting drama. C: Edward Arnold, Audrey Totter, Dan Duryea, Hume Cronyn, Selena Royle. D: Edward L. Cahn. DRA 57m.

Main Street to Broadway 1953 ★★★ A stereotypical rags-to-riches showbiz yarn, with a little romance thrown in, but featuring an incredible display of Broadway legends, including Mary Martin, the Barrymores (Lionel and Ethel), Rex Harrison, Helen Hayes, Tallulah Bankhead, Henry Fonda, Shirley Booth, Rodgers & Hammerstein . . . an ongoing parade of dazzling talent. C: Tom Morton, Mary Murphy, Clinton Sundberg, Rosemary Decamp, Lionel Barrymore, Shirley Booth, Rex Harrison, Lilli Palmer, Helen Hayes, Henry Fonda, Tallulah Bankhead, Mary Martin. D: Tay Garnett. DRA 102m. V

Maisie An oddity, an MGM series that didn't benefit from the studio's high-gloss approach. These indifferent comedies feature the generally charming Ann Sothern as Maisie, a wisecracking hoofer whose travels and adventures provide the films with their rather flimsy plots.

Maisie (1939)
Congo Maisie (1940)
Gold Rush Maisie (1940)
Maisie Was a Lady (1941)
Ringside Maisie (1941)
Maisie Gets Her Man (1942)
Swing Shift Maisie (1943)
Maisie Goes to Reno (1944)
Up Goes Maisie (1946)
Undercover Maisie (1947)

Maisie 1939 ★★★½ First entry in the lighthearted comedy series puts wisecracking chorine Sothern on a Wyoming ranch, romancing Young and solving a murder. Most diverting. C: Ann Sothern, Robert Young, Ruth Hussey. D: Edwin L. Marin. COM 74m. V

Maisie Gets Her Man 1942 ★★★ Maisie travels to Chicago and starts up a stage act with hayseed (Skelton). Fine cast of supporting zanies makes this a lot of laughs. C: Ann Sothern, Red Skelton, Leo Gorcey, Pamela Blake, Allen Jenkins, Donald Meek, Walter Catlett, Fritz Feld, Rags Ragland, Frank Jenks. D: Roy Del Ruth. COM 85m.

Maisie Goes to Reno 1944 ★★½ In Reno, Maisie tries to convince a young couple not to divorce. Some nice moments, and a good look at an up-and-coming Ava Gardner. C: Ann Sothern, John Hodiak, Tom Drake, Marta Linden, Paul Cavanagh, Ava Gardner, Bernard Nedell, Donald Meek. D: Harry Beaumont. COM 90m.

Maisie Was a Lady 1941 ★★★ Maisie goes to work for a society family—as their maid. Lots of fun as Maisie sets everybody's life in order. Filled with outstanding supporting talent. C: Ann Sothern, Lew Ayres, Maureen O'Sullivan, C. Aubrey Smith, Edward Ashley, Joan Perry, Paul Cavanagh. D: Edwin Martin. COM 79m.

Maitresse 1976 French ★★★★ Unassuming Depardieu begins a relationship with Ogier, a professional dominatrix. Strange film is absorbing and not overly erotic despite its subject matter. C: Gerard Depardieu, Bulle Ogier, Nathalie Keryan, Roland Bertin. D: Barbet Schroeder. DRA 112m. V

Major and the Minor, The 1942 ★★★★½ Wilder's directorial debut is a wonderfully arch comedy, co-written with Charles Brackett, about a working girl (Rogers) who dresses as a 12-year-old to manage the fare to her hometown and then gets mixed up with military C.O. (Milland) and his boys' academy. The Wilder/Brackett wit is prominently featured and still piquant. C: Ginger Rogers, Ray Milland, Diana Lynn, Rita Johnson, Robert Benchley, Norma Varden. D: Billy Wilder. COM 100m.

Major Barbara 1941 British ★★★★★ Film adaptation of Shaw's poignant intellectual comedy about a rich young woman (Hiller) with lofty ideals who enlists in the Salvation Army to save the world. Although a bit stagebound at times, movie is immortalized by the impassioned performances of Hiller and Harrison. The rest of the brilliant cast represents the cream of the British theater world. Unforgettable. C: Wendy Hiller, Rex Harrison, Robert Morley, Robert Newton, Emlyn Williams, Deborah Kerr. D: Gabriel Pascal. COM 121m. V

Major Dundee 1965 ★★★★ A rough-and-tumble cavalry honcho leads his volunteer band of unsavory soldiers to Mexico to fight against marauding Apaches. Epic-sized Peckinpah adventure that provides nonstop action. C: Charlton Heston, Richard Harris, Jim Hutton, James Coburn, Michael Anderson Jr., Senta Berger, Mario Adorf, Brock Peters, Warren Oates, Slim Pickens, Ben Johnson, R. G. Armstrong, L. Q. Jones. D: Sam Peckinpah. WST 124m. V

Major League 1989 ★★★ Hoping to move baseball franchise to richer opportunities in Miami, owner Whitton hires inept athletes to sabotage Cleveland fan support. Of course, team rallies to victory, led by players Berenger, Sheen, and Bernsen. Sports clichés abound in mildly amusing jock romp. C: Tom Berenger, Charlie Sheen, Corbin Bernsen, Margaret Whitton, James Gammon, Bob Uecker. D: David S. Ward. COM [R] 107m. V

Major League II 1994 ★★★ Sequel has pitcher (Sheen) losing his fastball, Berenger reduced to coaching, and manager (Cammon) in the hospital. Film seems to exist mainly to replay gags from its predecessor, of course, there's a case to be made for that. C: Charlie Sheen, Tom Berenger, Corbin Bernsen, Dennis Haysbert, James Cammon, Omar Epps. D: David S. Ward. COM [PG] 104m. V

Major Payne 1995 ★★★ Predictable comedy about a tough marine (Wayans) stuck in a Virginia boarding school, teaching pre-teen misfits with a super-disciplined approach. Some of Damon's routines are funny, but the film has a sappy, soft center. Loose remake of 1955's *The Private War of Major Benson.* C: Damon Wayans, Orlando Brown, Karyn Parsons. D: Nick Castle. COM [PG-13] 97m. V

Majorettes, The 1987 ★★½ A small town suffers from the murders of its high school majorettes and the assailant remains at large. Some off-beat suspense. C: Sueanne Seamens, Kevin Kindlin, Terrie Godfrey, Mark Jevicky. D: Bill Hinzman. HOR [R] 93m. V

Majority of One, A 1961 ★★★½ Brassy Jewish woman of a certain age (Russell) finds true love with a Japanese widower (Guiness in another tremendous display of range). Leonard Spiegelgass' Broadway play is transferred to the screen with too little finesse, but gets many points for effort. C: Rosalind Russell, Alec Guinness, Ray Danton, Madlyn Rhue. D: Mervyn LeRoy. DRA 149m. V

Make a Wish 1937 ★★ Young vocal prodigy (Breen) is inspired by composer (Rathbone) at a boys' summer camp. Musical has some amusing passages, with a powerful cast of comics. C: Basil Rathbone, Bobby Breen, Leon Errol, Donald Meek. D: Kurt Neumann. MUS 77m. V

Make Haste to Live 1954 ★★★ McGuire is highly credible as a victimized woman whose convict husband has just been released from the pen. Hubby plans to return home to settle the score with those who did him wrong. Better-than-average '50s potboiler, thanks mostly to McGuire's presence. C: Dorothy McGuire, Stephen McNally, Mary Murphy, Edgar Buchanan. D: William A. Seiter. CRI 90m. V

Make Me an Offer 1955 British ★★★ A crazed antiques collector (Finch, in an early role) searches for a priceless vase among the various treasures and fakes on the market. Pleasant send-up of snooty antiques world makes fun of the lengths collectors will go to obtain their coveted objets d'art. C: Peter Finch, Adrienne Corri, Rosalie Crutchley, Finlay Currie. D: Cyril Frankel. COM 88m. V

Make Me an Offer 1980 ★★★½ Sizzling acting and fun script that tells everything you ever wanted to know about Hollywood real estate agents. C: Susan Blakely, Stella Stevens, John Rubinstein. D: Jerry Paris. DRA 97m. TVM V

Make Mine Chartreuse 1987 ★★★ Successful businesswoman and writer of popular fiction fall for each other. C: Joseph Bottoms, Catherine Colvey. D: Jim Kaufman. DRA 80m. V

Make Mine Laughs 1949 ★★ Hour-long RKO feature consists of back-to-back musical numbers as they would be performed in a theater. Interesting for vaudeville fans. C: Frances Langford, Joan Davis, Leon Errol, Ray Bolger, Gil Lamb. D: Richard Fleischer. MUS 64m.

Make Mine Mink 1960 British ★★★★ No, *not* the Doris Day movie. In this hysterical, highly recommended comedy, a former soldier, goofy, gap-toothed Terry-Thomas, heads a motley crew of fur bandits. Once the thieves begin their fleecing operation, the fur flies fast and furious. Avoid the edited tape version. C: Terry-Thomas, Athene Seyler, Hattie Jacques, Billie Whitelaw, Elspeth Duxbury, Jack Hedley. D: Robert Asher. COM 100m. V

Make Mine Music 1946 ★★★ Ten-part Disney production features the voices of the Andrews Sisters, Dinah Shore, and Nelson Eddy, plus music from the Benny Goodman Quartet. Individual segments include "Casey at the Bat," "Peter and the Wolf," and Goodman's swingin' "After You've Gone." Pretentious when it preaches, a joy when it jives. Take your pick. D: Joe Grant. MUS 74m.

Make Room for Tomorrow 1981 France ★★★½ Sweetly affecting tale of engaging family reuniting for patriarch's ninetieth birthday. C: Victor Lanoux, Jane Birkin, Henri Cremieux. D: Peter Kassovitz. COM [R] 104m. V

Make Way for a Lady 1936 ★★★ Shirley becomes a matchmaker for her widowed father (Marshall). Palatable romantic comedy. C: Herbert Marshall, Anne Shirley, Gertrude Michael, Margot Grahame, Clara Blandick, Frank Coghlan Jr. D: David Burton. COM 65m.

Make Way for Tomorrow 1937 ★★★★★ Elderly couple gets the brush-off from their children. Tasteful, right-on-the-money drama about growing old pulls no punches. Exceptional performances from Moore and Bondi and marvelous direction make this a must see. C: Victor Moore, Beulah Bondi, Fay Bainter, Thomas Mitchell, Porter Hall, Barbara Read, Louise Beavers. D: Leo McCarey. DRA 92m.

Make Your Own Bed 1944 ★★ To get the goods on a crooked businessman, detective (Carson) disguises himself as a manservant, with Wyman impersonating a maid for good measure. Labored comedy. C: Jack Carson, Jane Wyman, Alan Hale, Irene Manning, George Tobias, Ricardo Cortez. D: Peter Godfrey. COM 82m.

Making Contact 1985 ★★★ Fatherless boy who develops supernatural powers and brings his toys to life confronts forces of darkness. C: Joshua Morrell, Eve Kryll. D: Klaus Dittrich. HOR [PG] 83m. V

Making It 1971 ★★½ Seventeen-year-old guy has little room in his mind for anything but sex, until he has an experience that makes him rethink his behavior. Some surprisingly good performances. C: Kristoffer Tabori, Joyce Van Patten, Marlyn Mason, Bob Balaban, Lawrence Pressman, Louise Latham, Dick Van Patten. D: John Erman. COM [R] 97m.

Making Love 1982 ★★★ Jackson's marriage to doctor (Ontkean) breaks up when he realizes his love for another man, a handsome writer (Hamlin). Film tries to deal honestly with difficult subject matter, but approach is unfortunately timid. C: Michael Ontkean, Kate Jackson, Harry Hamlin, Wendy Hiller, Arthur Hill. D: Arthur Hiller. DRA [R] 112m. V

Making Mr. Right 1987 ★★★ Miami-based scientist (Malkovich) designs a humanoid robot after his own image, and publicity genius Magnuson is assigned to mass-market the thing. Director Seidelman is at odds with his material here, and creates a brittle comedy. C: John Malkovich, Ann Magnuson, Glenne Headly, Ben Masters, Laurie Metcalf, Polly Bergen. D: Susan Seidelman. COM [PG-13] 95m. V

Making of a Male Model 1983 ★★ A handsome ranch hand (Hexum) is discovered by model agency honcho (Collins) and turned into a hot piece of commercial beefcake. Trite, entertaining trash. C: Joan Collins, Jon-Erik Hexum, Kevin McCarthy, Roxie Roker, Arte Johnson, Ted McGinley, Jeff Conaway. D: Irving J. Moore. COM 100m. TVM

Making the Grade 1984 ★★ A wealthy, spoiled-rotten teen (Nelson) pays an impersonator to stand in for him at his exclusive prep school. Smarmy comedy has few sexually charged laughs—enjoy it for what it is. Includes an appearance by Andrew Dice Clay. C: Judd Nelson, Carey Scott, Dana Olsen, Gordon Jump, Ronald Lacey, Scott McGinnis. D: Dorian Walker. COM 105m. V

Makioka Sisters, The 1985 Japanese ★★★½ Social and political changes in pre-WWII Osaka are seen through the lives of four sisters. Beautifully photographed but often hard-to-follow Japanese drama is worth the effort. C: Keiko Kishi, Yoshiko Sakuma, Sayuri Yoshinaga, Yuko Kotegawa, Juzo Itami. D: Kon Ichikawa. DRA 140m. V

Malaga 1960 British ★★½ Cops-and-robbers tale about a jewel thief and his last job offers some intriguing, offbeat casting. Dandridge's final film. (a.k.a. *Moment of Danger*) C: Trevor Howard, Dorothy Dandridge, Edmund Purdom, Michael Hordern. D: Laslo Benedek. CRI 97m.

Malarek 1989 ★★★½ Maverick journalist struggles to stop police from brutalizing juvenile delinquents. C: Elias Koteas, Kerrie Keane, Michael Sarrazin. D: Roger Cardinal. CRI [R] 105m. V

Malaya 1949 ★★½ Plot of this sturdy WWII drama revolves around Allied attempts to ship rubber supplies out of the Japanese-riddled Pacific. First-rate cast. C: Spencer Tracy, James Stewart, Valentina Cortese, Sydney Greenstreet. D: Richard Thorpe. DRA 98m. V

Malayunta 1986 ★★½ A young and emotionally fragile artist is tormented by a mysterious older couple. Disturbing. C: Federico Luppi, Miguel Angel Sola, Barbara Mujica. DRA 90m. V

Malcolm 1986 Australian ★★★★ Winning, quirky comedy concerns Friels, a dim-witted man who can construct complex mechanical objects, and his outlandish admission to the criminal world. Friels' richly sensitive performance coupled with Tass' sparkling directorial debut make this an unusual but upbeat item. Awarded "Best Picture" by the Australian Film Institute. C: Colin Friels, John Hargreaves, Lindy Davies, Chris Haywood. D: Nadia Tass. COM [PG-13] 86m. V

Malcolm X 1972 ★★★★ Intelligent, thought-provoking portrait of the controversial civil rights activist. Jones does the narration, which was taken from Malcolm's own autobiography. Produced by Marvin Worth and Arnold Perl, who also helped bring the 1992 Spike Lee film to the screen. Voices of James Earl Jones, Ossie Davis. DOC [PG] 92m.

Malcolm X 1992 ★★★★★ Exceptional biography of controversial black activist who rose from petty criminal to political leader. Features riveting, multifaceted performance by Washington and some of Lee's most disciplined and innovative direction. Despite length, it never drags. C: Denzel Washington, Angela Bassett, Albert Hall, Al Freeman Jr., Delroy Lindo, Spike Lee, Theresa Randle, Kate Vernon. D: Spike Lee. DRA [PG-13] 201m. V

Male Animal, The 1942 ★★★★ Witty, engaging James Thurber comedy has university professor (Fonda) too busy standing up for his rights to notice wife (de Havilland) falling into the arms of her former boyfriend (Carson). Later remade as *She's Working Her Way through College*. Thoroughly enjoyable for its ultraclassy cast and hilarious set-pieces, including a send-up of college football rituals. C: Henry Fonda, Olivia de Havilland, Jack Carson, Joan Leslie, Herbert Anderson, Don DeFore, Hattie McDaniel, Eugene Pallette. D: Elliott Nugent. COM 101m.

Male Hunt 1964 French ★★★½ Sassy sex comedy about three men on the make who try at all costs to avoid women with marriage on their minds. But with real-life sibling beauties Deneuve and Dorleac hatching wedding plans, the idea of getting hitched ain't so bad! Lightweight and fun, in a slightly risqué way. C: Jean-Paul Belmondo, Jean-Claude Brialy, Catherine Deneuve, Francoise Dorleac, Marie Laforet. D: Edouard Molinaro. COM 92m.

Male of the Century, The 1975 French ★★★ Berri wrote, directed, and starred in this French sex farce about a paranoid, jealous male chauvinist obsessed with the fear that his wife is having sex with the bank robber holding her hostage. Souflé comedy with occasional flashes of insight into human behavior. C: Juliet Berto, Claude Berri, Hubert Deschamps, Laszlo Szabo, Yves Afonso. D: Claude Berri. COM 90m.

Malibu 1934 *See* **Sequoia**

Malibu 1983 ★★½ Glossy adaptation of William Murray's trash novel about L.A.'s beautiful people, with intertwining stories of life, love, and especially sex on Malibu beach. Superficially engaging, thanks to a large, star-studded cast. But it all begins to pale after the tinsel quotient wears off. C: William Atherton, James Coburn, Susan Dey, Chad Everett, Steve Forrest, George Hamilton, Jenilee Harrison, Ann Jillian, Richard Mulligan, Dyan Cannon, Anthony Newley, Kim Novak, Valerie Perrine. D: E. W. Swackhamer. DRA 200m. TVM

Malibu Beach 1978 ★★ Swinging Californians hit the sand, smoke pot, and make out. You might want to move your blanket. C: Kim Lankford, James Daughton, Susan Player-Jarreau, Stephen Oliver. D: Robert J. Rosenthal. COM [R] 91m. V

Malibu Bikini Shop, The 1985 ★★½ Two brothers inherit a small bikini shop on the beach. Great location, good selection, silly entrepreneurial fun. C: Michael Wright, Bruce Greenwood, Barbara Horan. D: David Wechter. COM [R] 90m. TVM V

Malibu Express 1984 ★★½ Private detective Hinton tries to uncover the culprits in a complicated plot involving blackmail and espionage; however, he's more interested in *Playboy* centerfolds in this neo-soft core film. C: Darby Hinton, Sybil Danning, Art Metrano, Lori Sutton. D: Andy Sidaris. CRI [R] 101m. V

Malibu High 1979 ★ Sleazy tale about a sociopathic high school girl who gets into trouble every which way but loose. Low-rent item should be kept under wraps permanently. C: Jill Lansing, Stuart Taylor, Katie Johnson, Tammy Taylor. D: Irv Berwick. DRA [R] 92m. V

Malice 1993 ★★★★ A dashing doctor (Baldwin) sets up practice in a small New England town, and is soon implicated in a series of brutal rapes and murder. A first-rate thriller. C: Alec Baldwin, Nicole Kidman, Bill Pullman, Peter Gallagher. D: Harold Becker. CRI [R] 106m.

Malice in Wonderland 1985 ★★★½ Glittery but factually confused movie about the archrivalry between Hollywood gossip columnists Hedda Hopper and Louella Parsons. Entertaining, thanks to scenery and stars. C: Elizabeth Taylor, Jane Alexander, Richard Dysart, Joyce Van Patten, Jon Cypher, Leslie Ackerman, Bonnie Bartlett, Thomas Byrd, Rick Lenz, John Pleshette. D: Gus Trikonis. DRA 100m. TVM

Malicious 1974 Italian ★★ Attractive new housekeeper (Antonelli) innocently tempts both father and his 14-year-old son. Erotic farce. (a.k.a. *Malizia*) C: Laura Antonelli, Turi Ferro, Alessandro Momo, Tina Aumont. D: Salvatore Samperi. COM [R] 98m. V

Malizia 1974 *See* **Malicious**

Malone 1987 ★★ Preposterous attempt at espionage has power-crazed Robertson plotting to seize control of the U.S. until former CIA operative Reynolds fortuitously comes along to put a wrinkle in his plans. Ersatz James Bond script offers plenty of action. C: Burt Reynolds, Cliff Robertson, Kenneth McMillan, Scott Wilson, Lauren Hutton. D: Harley Cokliss. ACT [R] 92m. v

Malta Story, The 1953 British ★★½ A British lieutenant (Guinness) on the island of Malta during WWII must forsake love to brave danger. Guinness is good in this competent film about the toll that war exacts. C: Alec Guinness, Jack Hawkins, Anthony Steel, Muriel Pavlow. D: Brian Desmond Hurst. ACT 103m. v

Maltese Bippy, The 1969 ★★½ Movie spin-off of Rowan and Martins *Laugh-In* TV show is a mild send-up of horror movies, featuring haunted houses and all sorts of things that go bump in the night. Decent cast; a must for *Laugh-In* fans. C: Dan Rowan, Dick Martin, Carol Lynley, Julie Newmar, Mildred Natwick, Fritz Weaver, Robert Reed. D: Norman Panama. COM [G] 88m.

Maltese Falcon, The 1931 ★★★★ Sam Spade is on the trail of the elusive and rare bird. Cortez is surprisingly good in a lecherous interpretation of Spade. This is a much sexier *Falcon* than the 1941 classic. Based on Dashiell Hammett's classic detective novel, this was remade in 1936 as *Satan Met a Lady*. (a.k.a. *Dangerous Female*) C: Bebe Daniels, Ricardo Cortez, Dudley Digges, Robert Elliott, Thelma Todd, Una Merkel, Dwight Frye. D: Roy Del Ruth. CRI 80m.

Maltese Falcon, The 1941 ★★★★★ When his private eye partner is set up and murdered, Sam Spade springs into action. As near to perfection in filmmaking as you'll ever see. For that matter, see it more than once. C: Humphrey Bogart, Mary Astor, Peter Lorre, Sydney Greenstreet, Ward Bond, Gladys George, Barton MacLane, Elisha Cook Jr., Lee Patrick, Jerome Cowan. D: John Huston. CRI 100m. v

Mama Dracula 1980 French ★ Vampire (Fletcher) mother has her sons provide virgins for her bloody needs. Intended satire of the vampire genre offers two excellent actresses, but little else. C: Louise Fletcher, Maria Schneider, Marc-Henri Wajnberg, Alexander Wajnberg, Jess Hahn. D: Boris Szulzinger. HOR 93m. v

Mama, There's a Man in Your Bed 1989 French ★★½ Successful French businessman falls in love with his black cleaning woman. Unsubtle farce makes points on racism, prejudice, and the mystery of love. (a.k.a. *Romuald ed Juliet*) C: Daniel Auteuil, Firmine Richard, Pierre Vernier, Maxime Leroux. D: Coline Serreau. COM [PG-13] 111m. v

Mama Turns 100 1979 Spanish ★★★★ A greedy Spanish family battles among themselves during their mother's 100th birthday celebration. Funny film satirizes life under Franco, launching sociopolitical barbs that may miss their mark in the U.S. C: Geraldine Chaplin, Rafaela Aparicio, Fernando Fernan Gomez. D: Carlos Saura. COM 100m. v

Mamas & The Papas, The—Straight Shooter ★★★★ An enthralling and detailed look at one of the definitive musical groups of our times. Footage includes numerous interviews with the group as well as performances of their ht songs. An excellent and informative journey down memory lane. MUS 80m. v

Mama's Dirty Girls 1974 ★★★ Just like Mama, three sisters go out into the world to use men, murder them and take their money. But the tide turns when they run into a genial homicidal maniac. Nifty horror stuff. C: Gloria Grahame, Paul Lambert, Sondra Currie, Candice Rialson, Mary Stoddard. D: John Hayes. HOR [R] 82m. v

Mambo 1954 U.S. ★★★ While struggling for recognition as a dancer, a youthful working woman becomes involved with both a decrepit nobleman and a luckless gambler. The impressive international cast and beautiful Venice settings help maintain a high level of interest in this atypical but affecting romance. C: Silvana Mangano, Michael Rennie, Shelley Winters, Vittorio Gassman, Eduardo Ciannelli, Katherine Dunham. D: Robert Rossen. DRA 94m. v

Mambo Kings, The 1992 ★★★½ Assante brings vigor but not much insight to the role of ambitious Cuban musician in the story of two brothers seeking stardom in New York in the '50s. Banderas is affecting as melancholy younger brother and the music cooks. Based on Pulitzer Prize-winning novel by Oscar Hijuelos. Desi Arnaz plays his own father. C: Armand Assante, Antonio Banderas, Cathy Moriarty, Maruschka Detmers, Desi Arnaz Jr., Celia Cruz, Tito Puente. D: Arne Glimcher. DRA [R] 104m. v

Mame 1974 ★ Wealthy orphan is raised by eccentric aunt yet one more time in this film version of hit Jerry Herman musical based on Lawrence/Lee play, *Auntie Mame*, from Patrick Dennis' autobiographical novel. We love Lucy, but this is sadly, her last feature film. Hold out for version with Rosalind Russell. C: Lucille Ball, Robert Preston, Beatrice Arthur, Bruce Davison, Jane Connell. D: Gene Saks. MUS [PG] 132m. v

Mamele 1938 Polish ★★★½ Yiddish music hall star Picon has a field day as a widower's daughter, forced to play "mamele" (little mother) to help her family survive. Charming oldie. C: Molly Picon, Max Bozyk, Edmund Zayenda. D: Joseph Green, Konrad Tom. MUS 100m. v

Mamma Roma 1962 Italian ★★★★ Early

Pasolini film has Magnani trying to raise her family out of poverty by any means necessary. Very moving, with excellent acting and a sure feel for Roman milieu. C: Anna Magnani, Ettore Garofalo, Franco Citti. D: Pier Paolo Pasolini. DRA 110m.

Mammy 1930 ★★½ Capitalizing on Jolson's trademark song and blackface persona, this stolid Warner Bros. talkie throws together some yarn about backstage gunplay in a minstrel company, with Jolson belting out "To My Mammy," "The Call of the South," and "Let Me Sing and I'm Happy." C: Al Jolson, Lois Moran, Louise Dresser, Lowell Sherman, Hobart Bosworth. D: Michael Curtiz. MUS 84m.

Mam'zelle Pigalle 1956 French ★★½ A schoolgirl (Bardot) develops a mad crush on a sexy singer (Bretonniére) and also manages to get caught up in a counterfeiting ring. Unbelievable plot, but Bardot fans won't care. C: Brigitte Bardot, Jean Bretonniere, Francoise Fabian, Bernard Lancret, Mischa Auer. D: Michel Boisrond. DRA 77m.

Man, a Woman and a Bank, A 1979 Canadian ★★★½ Amusing fluff piece about a $4 million bank robbery boasts sympathetic, humorous lead performances. C: Donald Sutherland, Brooke Adams, Paul Mazursky, Allen Magicovsky, Leigh Hamilton. D: Noel Black. COM [PG] 101m. V

Man About the House, A 1947 British ★★★ Small-time Italian con artist attempts to double-cross the women in the house he resides in. Rather muddy British drama does provide some real suspense. C: Kieron Moore, Margaret Johnston, Dulcie Gray, Guy Middleton. D: Leslie Arliss. DRA 83m.

Man About Town 1939 ★★½ While on tour in England as the head of an acting troupe Benny attempts to make his mark in London society. Energetic musical redeemed by a great cast. C: Jack Benny, Dorothy Lamour, Edward Arnold, Binnie Barnes, Phil Harris, Betty Grable, Monty Woolley, Eddie "Rochester" Anderson. D: Mark Sandrich. MUS 85m.

Man About Town 1947 French ★★½ Insignificant farce from French directing great Clair, with Chevalier in 1906 Paris as a movie director who acts as mentor to young protegé (Derrien). The undubbed U.S. version uses Chevalier's voice-over narration to explicate the action. (a.k.a. *Le Silence Est d'Or*) C: Maurice Chevalier, Francois Perier, Marcelle Derrien, Dany Robin, Raymond Cordy, Paul Olivier. D: Rene Clair. COM 89m.

Man Afraid 1957 ★★★½ A minister (Nader) is forced to protect his family from the enraged father of a teenage boy he accidentally killed while defending his own life. Taut storyline and strong acting. C: George Nader, Phyllis Thaxter, Tim Hovey, Reta Shaw, Martin Milner. D: Harry Keller. DRA 84m.

Man Against the Mob 1988 ★★★ In this TV-movie cum series pilot, an L.A. police detective (Peppard) rounds up his honest cop buddies in an effort to prevent the Chicago Mob from moving to the West Coast. Stylish drama excels at evoking a '40s atmosphere. (Sequel follows.) C: George Peppard, Kathryn Harrold, Max Gail, Barry Corbin, Fredric Lehne, Norman Alden, Stella Stevens. D: Steven Hilliard Stern. CRI 100m. TVM

Man Against the Mob: The Chinatown Murders 1989 ★★½ Second installment finds seasoned detective (Peppard) enlisting upstanding cops to shut down the Chinatown branch of a prostitution ring run by the Mob. Once again, the '40s look and swing era sounds are great. C: George Peppard, Richard Bradford, Charles Haid, Ursula Andress. D: Michael Pressman. CRI 96m. V

Man Alive 1945 ★★★½ O'Brien, presumed dead but very much alive, assumes the role of a ghost to prevent his wife from entertaining new lovers. Sounds silly, but is actually brisk-paced, fairly engaging farce. C: Pat O'Brien, Adolphe Menjou, Ellen Drew, Rudy Vallee, Fortunio Bonanova, Joseph Crehan, Jonathan Hale, Minna Gombell, Jason Robards Sr. D: Ray Enright. COM 70m.

Man Alone, A 1955 ★★★★ Thinking-man's Western concerns an innocent man (Milland) evading a furious lynch mob with the help of local sheriff's daughter, who hides him away. Solid cast and Milland's astute direction (his debut!) make this unique. C: Ray Milland, Mary Murphy, Ward Bond, Raymond Burr, Lee Van Cleef. D: Ray Milland. WST 96m. V

Man and a Woman, A 1966 French ★★★★★ Sentimental tale of love affair between widow (Aimee) and race car driver (Trintignant) became one of the most popular foreign films ever, with intelligent direction and camera work, wonderful star chemistry, and Francis Lai's lush (and catchy) music. Followed by sequel in 1986. Oscar for Best Foreign Film and Best Original Screenplay. C: Anouk Aimee, Jean-Louis Trintignant, Pierre Barouh, Valerie Lagrange. D: Claude Lelouch. DRA 103m. V

Man and a Woman, A: 20 Years Later 1986 ★★★½ Sequel to hit romance picks up story after two decades: Widow is now producer who wants to make film about their affair, which they rekindle after meeting to discuss it. Aimee/Trintignant pairing still strikes sparks. C: Anouk Aimee, Jean-Louis Trintignant, Richard Berry, Marie-Sophie Pochat. D: Claude Lelouch. DRA [PG] 112m. V

Man and Boy 1972 ★★★½ A Civil War soldier (Cosby) and his young son pursue the rustler who's made off with their horse. Although the plot is close to the Italian neorealist classic, *The Bicycle Thief*, the director's touch imparts enough charm and appeal to more than qualify this as harmless family entertainment. C: Bill Cosby, Gloria Foster, Leif Erickson, George Spell, Douglas Turner Ward. D: E.W. Swackhamer. FAM/DRA [G] 98m. V

Man at the Carlton Tower 1961 British ★★ A jewel thief and murderer lurks within the ritzy hallways of London's posh hotel. Good atmosphere and tension in story adapted from a Edgar Wallace mystery. C: Maxine Audley, Lee Montague, Allan Cuthbertson, Terence Alexander. D: Robert Tronson. CRI 57m.

Man at the Top 1975 British ★★★½ The continuing evolution of Joe Compton, focus of theatrical feature *Room at the Top*, which was later made into a British TV series. Current doings grew out of that series and involved Haigh's character Compton in upper-echelon corporate imbroglios. Fairly solid, intriguing update of the original movie. C: Kenneth Haigh, Nanette Newman, Harry Andrews, John Quentin, Mary Maude. D: Mike Vardy. DRA 92m.

Man Bait 1952 U.S. ★★½ Brent plays a bookseller caught up in blackmail—and worse. Light thriller, bolstered by Brent. (a.k.a. *The Last Page*) C: George Brent, Marguerite Chapman, Diana Dors, Raymond Huntley, Peter Reynolds. D: Terence Fisher. CRI 78m.

Man Beast 1955 ★ Grade-Z '50s nonsense about a scientific expedition that sets off to find the Abominable Snowman. Pathetic plot and paltry special effects put this solidly in the "so bad it's good" section. C: Rock Madison, Virginia Maynor, George Skaff, Lloyd Nelson. D: Jerry Warren. SFI 65m. V

Man Behind the Gun, The 1952 ★★★ A cavalry officer (Scott) goes undercover as a teacher to investigate a secessionist rebellion in early California, then falls for a schoolmistress. Scott and the decent supporting cast get top marks for effort in this unoriginal but watchable star vehicle. C: Randolph Scott, Patrice Wymore, Philip Carey, Dick Wesson, Lina Romay. D: Felix E. Feist. WST 82m.

Man Betrayed, A 1941 ★★★ Rather turgid costume melodrama, with Dee caught between a small-town lawyer (Wayne) and her scheming politician father (Ellis). Competently directed and performed, but not very involving. (a.k.a. *Wheel of Fortune*) C: John Wayne, Frances Dee, Edward Ellis, Wallace Ford, Ward Bond, Harold Huber, Alexander Granach. D: John H. Auer. DRA 83m.

Man Between, The 1953 British ★★★★ Intelligent Cold War melodrama with expert Mason as a cynical black marketeer who must end his East/West political fence-sitting after he falls in love. Bloom and Neff lead strong support; fine direction and cinematography create vivid Berlin atmosphere. C: James Mason, Claire Bloom, Hildegarde Neff, Geoffrey Toone. D: Carol Reed. DRA 101m.

Man Called Adam, A 1966 ★★★½ An African-American jazz trumpeter, guilt-ridden over a drink-induced car crash that killed his wife and son, meets a civil rights activist and her faded musician grandfather, and must contend with nasty white booking agent. Downbeat, rambling vehicle for Sammy Davis, Jr. C: Sammy Davis, Jr., Ossie Davis, Cicely Tyson, Louis Armstrong, Frank Sinatra Jr., Mel Torme. D: Leo Penn. DRA 103m. V

Man Called Dagger, A 1967 ★★ Imitation James Bond spy thriller, with secret agent foiling attempt of former Nazi S.S. colonel (Murray) to take over world. Watch for the final fight amid carcasses in meat refrigerator. C: Terry Moore, Jan Murray, Sue Langdon, Paul Mantee, Eileen O'Neill, Maureen Arthur. D: Richard Rush. ACT 86m.

Man Called Flintstone, The 1966 ★★★½ One of the more unusual of the '60s superspy spoofs, with cartoon characters from the Stone Age sitcom encountering the evil Green Goose in Paris. Fred Flintstone is mistaken for an agent (of course!) and kids will enjoy the modest but amusing animated adventures that ensue. D: William Hanna, Joseph Barbera. FAM/COM 87m. V

Man Called Gannon, A 1969 ★★½ A Kansas plains drifter reluctantly takes on a young Easterner as a sidekick and the two help a widow set up barbed wire around her ranch. Game cast tries for this remake of *Man Without a Star*. C: Tony Franciosa, Michael Sarrazin, Judi West, Susan Oliver, John Anderson, Gavin MacLeod. D: James Goldstone. WST [PG] 105m.

Man Called Horse, A 1970 ★★★★½ An English aristocrat in the American West is captured by Indians. In time, he assimilates their culture and becomes their leader. Fascinating for its uncompromising, realistic look at Native American rites and culture. C: Richard Harris, Judith Anderson, Jean Gascon, Manu Tupou. D: Elliot Silverstein. WST [PG] 115m. V

Man Called Peter, A 1955 ★★★★ Gentle biography of Peter Marshall, the Scottish cleric who became chaplain to American senate. Moving story with an excellent characterization by Todd. C: Richard Todd, Jean Peters, Marjorie Rambeau. D: Henry Koster. DRA 117m. V

Man Called Rage, A 1984 ★★★ After a nuclear holocaust, a small group of survivors count on one man (called Rage) to lead them to safety. Engrossingly frightening. C: Conrad Nichols, Stelio Candelli. D: Anthony Richmond. SFI 90m. V

Man Called Sarge, A 1990 ★★★ A group of hapless soldiers—including a bunch of French foreign legion deserters—get into one ridiculous situation after another. A thoroughly entertaining spoof of WWII films. C: Gary Kroeger, Marc Singer, Gretchen German, Jennifer Runyon. D: Stuart Gillard. COM [PG-13] 86m. V

Man Called Sledge, A 1970 Italian ★★½ A small-time outlaw tries to pull the perfect bank heist. Typical spagehtti-Western that's sauced with violence. C: James Garner, Dennis Weaver, Claude Akins, John Marley, Laura Antonelli, Wade Preston. D: Vic Morrow. WST [R] 93m. V

Man Could Get Killed, A 1966 ★★★½ A U.S. businessman, mistaken for a secret agent, gets involved with a sultry adventuress in hunt for smuggled diamonds. Neame tries to keep things light in this spoof, but muddled plotting dampens the fun. Garner, Mercouri, supporting British stalwarts are good. C: Cliff Owen, James Garner, Melina Mercouri, Sandra Dee, Tony Franciosa, Robert Coote, Roland Culver. D: Ronald Neame. ACT 99m.

Man Detained 1961 British ★★★½ Secretary runs with a counterfeiting gang and is soon under suspicion for murder. Tight, trim whodunit is worth a look. C: Bernard Archard, Elvi Hale, Paul Stassino, Michael Coles. D: Robert Tronson. CRI 59m.

Man-Eater of Hydra 1967 West German ★★★ Greek mythology buffs will know that title tells all: Flesh-eating plants menace a mixed-up crew of visitors to remote island. Hokey, unimaginative scripting, but has creepy moments; cast and special effects give it some sense of showmanship. (a.k.a. *Island of the Doomed*) C: Cameron Mitchell, Elisa Montes, George Martin, Kay Fischer, Ralph Naukoff. D: Mel Welles. HOR 88m.

Man-Eater of Kumaon 1948 ★★★ Hunter in the tropics goes after rampaging tiger on the loose. One of Sabu's last films and a bit of a comedown, but solid direction lends more grit and adventure to routine saga than one would expect. C: Sabu, Wendell Corey, Joanne Page, Morris Carnovsky, Argentina Brunetti. D: Byron Haskin. ACT 79m.

Man Escaped, A 1957 French ★★★★★ Meticulous, fascinating study of a WWII French Resistance leader plotting his escape from prison from the Germans. The mesmerizing, dry treatment of the subject by master director Bresson may not be for all tastes but will reward those with patience. C: Francois Leterrier, Charles Le Clainche, Roland Monod. D:Robert Bresson. ACT 102m. V

Man Facing Southeast 1986 Argentine ★★★★ Newly arrived mental hospital patient (Soto) insists he's an alien, and with powers he demonstrates, who can doubt him? Highly original drama allows viewers to read whatever they want into proceedings, greatly enhancing its unnerving quality. Haunting and compelling. C: Lorenzo Quinteros, Hugo Soto, Christina Vcaramuzza. D: Eliseo Subiela. DRA [R] 105m. V

Man for All Seasons, A 1966 British ★★★★★ Scofield is Sir Thomas More, caught in a battle between king and conscience when Henry VIII defies the Pope to form the Church of England. Multiple Oscar-winner, including Best Picture, avoids period spectacle to focus on complex characterizations. Superb cast crowned by Scofield's beautifully nuanced performance. C: Paul Scofield, Wendy Hiller, Leo McKern, Robert Shaw, Orson Welles, Susannah York. D: Fred Zinnemann. DRA 120m. V

Man for All Seasons, A 1988 ★★★★ Heston's courageous attempt to match Paul Scofield's brilliant 1966 performance as Sir Thomas More, political martyr during the reign of Henry VIII, comes off as a qualified success. Robert Bolt's play holds up well with fine support, particularly from Redgrave and Gielgud. C: Charlton Heston, Vanessa Redgrave, John Gielgud, Richard Johnson, Roy Kinnear. D: Charlton Heston. DRA 150m. TVM V

Man Friday 1976 British ★★★ Nice attempt to update Defoe's *Robinson Crusoe* into critique of Western colonialism doesn't quite work. Black sidekick Friday rebels against the white teacher in favor of more liberal principles, with tragic results for Crusoe. Fine acting marred by messy scripting and a heavy-handed finale. C: Peter O'Toole, Richard Roundtree, Peter Cellier, Christopher Cabot. D: Jack Gold. DRA [PG] 109m. V

Man from Atlantis 1977 ★★★ Soggy pilot for series about amphibious humanoid who's persuaded to undertake perilous missions. Endurable thanks to tongue-in-cheek attitude. C: Patrick Duffy, Belinda Montgomery, Art Lund, Victor Buono. D: Lee H. Katzin. SFI 96m. TVM V

Man from Bitter Ridge, The 1955 ★★★½ Attractively shot, suitably paced formula Western as investigator (Barker) looks into charges that sheepherders have been holding up stagecoaches, and finds that a local politician and his killer brothers are behind it all. MacNally, Dehner give entertaining performances. C: Lex Barker, Mara Corday, Stephen McNally, Trevor Bardette. D: Jack Arnold. WST 80m.

Man From Blankley's, The 1930 ★★★½ Drunken aristocrat (Barrymore) wanders into the wrong house and is mistaken for a caterer. Film version of Thomas Asten Guthrie play comes to life through Barrymore's outrageously funny performance. C: John Barrymore, Loretta Young, William Austin. D: Alfred E. Green. COM 67m.

Man From Button Willow, The 1965 ★★★ Animated biography as an undercover agent helps post-Civil War settlers hold onto their land claims. Harmless, bland fodder the kids may enjoy, with a formidable lineup of distinctive vocal talent. Voices of Dale Robertson, Edgar Buchanan. D: David Detiege. FAM/MUS [G] 84m. V

Man from Cairo, The 1953 Italian ★★½ Motley crew in Northern Africa chases after gold, deceiving each other every chance they get. Less than thrilling melodrama, with interesting cast largely wasted. Not one of Raft's more animated performances. C: George Raft, Gianna Maria Canale, Massimo Serato, Irene Papas. D: Ray Enright. DRA 81m.

Man from Clover Grove, The 1974 ★ A nice old man invents and builds toys so he can give them to orphans. Then a toy manufacture comes to town and tries to steal his ideas. An interesting comedy. C: Ron Masak, Cheryl Miller, Jed Allan. COM [G] 96m. V

Man from Colorado, The 1949 ★★★½ A gripping psychological Western, with Civil War colonel (Ford) still killing even after being appointed judge in postwar Colorado. Longtime pal (Holden) must stop him. Implicit statements about WWII vets make for overly facile psychologizing, but Ford and Holden are well matched. C: Glenn Ford, William Holden, Ellen Drew, Jerome Courtland, Edgar Buchanan, Ray Collins. D: Henry Levin. WST 99m. V

Man from Dakota, The 1940 ★★★½ Glamourous Del Rio and salty old Beery in the same movie? Odd, yes, but the result's not half bad. Russian refugee helps two Union soldiers on the lam from Confederate prison during Civil War. Robust if improbable action, with splendid cast. C: Wallace Beery, John Howard, Dolores Del Rio, Donald Meek, Robert Barrat. D: Leslie Fenton. WST 75m.

Man from Deep River, The 1977 ★★★★ On a trip to remote Thailand, a photographer is captured by a primitive native tribe. Initially they torture him, before growing to accept him. Fascinating on all counts. C: Ivan Rassimov. D: Umberto Lenzi. ACT [R] 90m. V

Man from Del Rio, The 1956 ★★★ An uncouth Mexican is enlisted by a scheming saloon owner to help him rule a Western town. Starts well but turns routine, with hammy Quinn and galvanizing Jurado competing for the feistiness sweepstakes. C: Anthony Quinn, Katy Jurado, Peter Whitney, Douglas Fowley, John Larch, Whit Bissell. D: Harry Horner. WST 82m.

Man from Down Under, The 1943 ★★★ Hearty, sentimental Aussie (the always entertaining Laughton, somewhat miscast in Wallace Beery territory) raises two orphans in an awkward, time-spanning saga that veers from flip comedy to boxing melodrama. Carlson is very appealing. C: Charles Laughton, Binnie Barnes, Richard Carlson, Donna Reed, Christopher Severn, Clyde Cook. D: Robert Z. Leonard. COM 103m.

Man from Frisco, The 1944 ★★★½ An ambitious big-city shipbuilder causes contention when he wants to open a factory in a small town, but love helps quiet all the arguments. O'Shea's not ideal star material and film skimps on the action, but smoothly directed hokum anyway. C: Michael O'Shea, Anne Shirley, Dan Duryea, Gene Lockhart, Stephanie Bachelor, Ray Walker. D: Robert Florey. DRA 91m.

Man from Galveston, The 1963 ★★½ A clever frontier lawyer gets his ex-girlfriend off murder charge when he struts his stuff in court. Intended pilot for the *Temple Houston* Western TV series too short and slow for proper character development or plot exposition, which is routine. C: Jeffrey Hunter, Preston Foster, James Coburn, Joanna Moore, Edward Andrews, Kevin Hagen, Martin West, Ed Nelson. D: William Conrad. WST 57m. TVM

Man from God's Country 1958 ★★★ A sheriff who quit the job because he had tired of killing must strap on his guns again when he finds his Civil War buddy under the thumb of another town's crime boss. Well paced, handsomely shot Western suffers from a clichéd plot. C: George Montgomery, Randy Stuart, Gregg Barton, Kim Charney, Susan Cummings. D: Paul Landres. WST 72m.

Man from Hong Kong, The 1975 Australian ★★½ A martial arts expert travels from Hong Kong to Sydney to kick in the face of every thug employed by a nasty drug lord. Plenty of action, some good stunts, but precious little humor or narrative. (a.k.a. *The Dragon Flies*) C: Jimmy Wang Yu, George Lazenby, Ros Spiers, Hugh Keays-Byrne, Rebecca Gilling. D: Brian Smith. ACT [R] 103m.

Man from Laramie, The 1955 ★★★★ When his brother is murdered, a drifting cowpoke sets out for revenge. Top-of-the-line action and great performance by sly pro Stewart. C: James Stewart, Arthur Kennedy, Donald Crisp, Cathy O'Donnell, Alex Nicol, Aline MacMahon, Wallace Ford. D: Anthony Mann. WST 104m. V

Man from Monterey 1933 ★★ Life in rugged California during the early days of settlement there. Featuring John Wayne before he made the big time. C: John Wayne. WST 57m.

Man from Nowhere, The 1937 ★★★ Stick in an unhappy marriage, a weak-willed man realizes that his wife and her mother suddenly believe him dead. He uses the opportunity to start another life! Intriguing and quite funny. C: Pierre Blanchar, Ginette Leclerc. D: Pierre Chenal. COM 98m. V

Man from Planet X, The 1951 ★★★½ A visitor from outer space uses a ray to bewitch a scientist, his daughter, and others in a remote Scottish village after he sees designs of one scheming human. As with his other shoestring budget films, Ulmer tells story well and even manages to be stylish. C: Robert Clarke, Margaret Field, Raymond Bond, William Schallert. D: Edgar G. Ulmer. SFI 70m.

Man from Snowy River, The 1982 Australian ★★★½ An Australian cattle baron hires a young man to work on his ranch. Sweeping in scope, it's based on an Australian epic poem and filled with great scenes of pure natural beauty and astonishing scenes of running horses. The whole family will enjoy this one. C: Kirk Douglas, Tom Burlinson, Sigrid Thornton, Jack Thompson, Terence Donovan. D: George Miller. FAM/DRA [PG] 104m. V

Man from the Alamo, The 1953 ★★★½ A soldier chosen to escape from the Alamo before arrival of Santa Ana's forces in order to warn families is branded a cowardly deserter; he eventually proves himself when he wipes out phony Mexican soldiers who killed his family. Odd script never has soldier deny accusations, but bracing storytelling anyway. C: Glenn Ford, Julia Adams, Victor Jory, Hugh O'Brian, Chill Wills, Jeanne Cooper, Neville Brand. D: Budd Boetticher. WST 79m. V

Man from the Diner's Club, The 1963 ★★★½ A shy credit card company employee (Kaye) okays the application of a bankrupt mob kingpin, and the Runyanesque slapstick begins. Kaye, too determined to kill one with laughter, and Tashlin, master of cartoon stylistics, fight for control of the film and it shows, but Savalas and the hilarious gym routine are highlights. C: Danny Kaye, Martha Hyer, Cara Williams, Telly Savalas, Everett Sloane, George Kennedy. D: Frank Tashlin. COM 96m.

Man from Utah, The 1934 ★★★ A cowboy hero rides into town and finds himself framed for a bank robbery. Good western action brought forth well by young Wayne. C: John Wayne, George "Gabby" Hayes, Polly Ann Young. D: Robert Bradbury. WST 53m. V

Man from Yesterday, The 1932 ★★★½ Despite her remarriage to Boyer, Colbert still carries a torch for first husband (Brook) missing in WWI. Complications occur when the newlyweds encounter Brook on their honeymoon in Switzerland, where he's dying from his war injuries. Strong performances shine through sentimental story. C: Claudette Colbert, Clive Brook, Charles Boyer, Andy Devine, Alan Mowbray. D: Berthold Viertel. DRA 71m.

Man Hunt 1941 ★★★★½ Superb WWII thriller, sharply directed, as a big-game hunter (Pidgeon) misses a chance to assassinate Hitler and later meets up with a helpful lad, a sympathetic prostitute, and several classy but vicious killers. Pidgeon, Bennett, Sanders, McDowall, Carradine are all excellent; and the finale is quite clever. C: Walter Pidgeon, Joan Bennett, George Sanders, John Carradine, Roddy McDowall. D: Fritz Lang. CRI 105m.

Man I Killed, The 1932 *See* **Broken Lullaby**

Man I Love, The 1946 ★★★★½ A world-weary nightclub artist blows into town to visit her sister, and gets involved with both the club owner and a musician. Stunningly directed, compulsively watchable, with tough Lupino at her greatest, slapping around all those weakling men when she gets fed up. C: Ida Lupino, Robert Alda, Bruce Bennett, Andrea King, Dolores Moran, Martha Vickers, Alan Hale. D: Raoul Walsh. DRA 96m. V

Man I Married, The 1940 ★★★★ An American woman marries a German man in 1938, tries to leave with their child when the husband turns Nazi; she's aided by her father-in-law, who has big news for his hateful son. Bennett good, Lederer and Kruger even better in topical, potently scripted and directed yarn. C: Joan Bennett, Francis Lederer, Lloyd Nolan, Anna Sten, Otto Kruger. D: Irving Pichel. DRA 77m.

Man in a Cocked Hat 1959 British ★★★★ An incompetent Foreign Office man is placed in charge of affairs for a tiny, long-forgotten British protectorate. Terry-Thomas is in his element, and Sellers, Walters, Bannen, Mesurier, and Malleson are all able farceurs in broad but frequently amusing film. C: Terry-Thomas, Peter Sellers, Luciana Paluzzi, Thorley Walters, Ian Bannen, John Mesurier, Miles Malleson. D: Jeffrey Dell, Roy Boulting. COM 88m.

Man in Grey, The 1943 British ★★★★ Costumed soap opera has Calvert discovering her husband Mason betraying her with spiteful old school friend Lockwood. Melodramatic histrionics played with gleeful zest. Mason became a star playing cheating spouse. C: Margaret Lockwood, James Mason, Phyllis Calvert, Stewart Granger. D: Leslie Arliss. DRA 116m. V

Man in Half Moon Street, The 1944 ★★★ Walker falls in love with a charming scientist (Asther) whose experiments have enabled him to stop aging—he's 90 years old. Romantic angle provides spark to routine horror story. C: Nils Asther, Helen Walker, Brandon Hurst, Reginald Sheffield. D: Ralph Murphy. HOR 92m.

Man in Hiding 1953 British ★★½ His Hollywood career slipping, Henreid went to England to make this ho-hum yarn about a determined detective out to snare a clever murderer. Supporting cast includes likable British stalwarts, but Fisher's direction and visual style are oddly drab. C: Paul Henreid, Lois Maxwell, Kieron Moore, Hugh Sinclair. D: Terence Fisher. DRA 79m.

Man in Love, A 1987 French ★★★★ While on location for a movie in Rome, a married actor (Coyote) has an affair with his co-star (Scacchi). Adult sexuality dealt with in a thoughtful and extremely sensual manner; Coyote and Scacchi make fine screen lovers. C: Peter Coyote, Greta Scacchi, Peter Riegert, Claudia Cardinale, Jamie Lee Curtis. D: Diane Kurys. DRA [R] 110m. V

Man in Space 1989 ★★★★ Alan Shepard narrates this special produced to coincide with 20th anniversary of the Apollo moon landing, and featuring an overview of the NASA space program. Historic footage and revealing interviews with a number of astronauts make this an absorbing documentary. C: Alan Shepard. DOC 45m. V

Man in the Attic 1954 ★★★½ Remake of *The Lodger*, with Palance entertainingly depraved and hammy as Jack the Ripper, killing women in 19th-century London while he moons over his landlord's daughter in his attic room. Well-handled, punchy melodrama. C: Jack Palance, Constance Smith, Byron Palmer, Frances Bavier, Rhys Williams, Sean McClory, Isabel Jewell, Leslie Bradley. D: Hugo Fregonese. HOR 82m.

Man in the Dark 1953 ★★★ A criminal has brain surgery in order to become a nicer guy, but loses his memory, which proves awfully inconvenient when his former cronies show up wanting to know where he hid their loot. Shot in 3-D. C: Edmond O'Brien, Audrey Totter, Ruth Warren, Ted de Corsia, Horace McMahon. D: Lew Landers. CRI 70m.

Man in the Dinghy 1950 *See* **Into the Blue**

Man in the Glass Booth, The 1975 ★★★★ Excellent adaptation of actor Robert Shaw's play about the capture and prosecution of wealthy Jewish industrialist (Schell) believed to be Nazi Adolf Eichmann. A compelling dramatic exploration of guilt and identity. C: Maximilian Schell, Lois Nettleton, Luther Adler, Lawrence Pressman, Henry Brown, Richard Rasof. D: Arthur Hiller. DRA [PG] 117m.

Man in the Gray Flannel Suit, The 1956 ★★★★ Adaptation of Sloan Wilson's bestseller about corporate postwar America and title character Peck's midlife crisis. Johnson's script and direction add some gloss and melodrama to Wilson's novel, but Peck's performance is superb and veteran cast delivers. C: Gregory Peck, Jennifer Jones, Fredric March, Marisa Pavan, Lee J. Cobb, Keenan Wynn. D: Nunnally Johnson. DRA 153m. V

Man in the Iron Mask, The 1939 ★★★★ Classic story of king of France and his twin brother who teams up with D'Artagnan and the Three Musketeers. Breezy swashbuckler; Hayward fine in dual role. C: Louis Hayward, Joan Bennett, Warren William, Joseph Schildkraut, Alan Hale. D: James Whale. DRA 110m. V

Man in the Iron Mask 1977 ★★★★½ French tyrant imprisons his twin brother (Chamberlain in both roles) in this adaption of Dumas swashbuckler. Excellent entertainment that no family member will be able to resist. C: Richard Chamberlain, Patrick McGoohan, Louis Jourdan, Jenny Agutter, Vivien Merchant, Ian Holm, Ralph Richardson. D: Mike Newell. ACT 103m. TVM V

Man in the Middle 1964 British ★★★ An insane U.S. lieutenant is tried for killing a British sergeant in India at the end of WWII; a lawyer realizes the defendant may be sacrificed for diplomatic relations. Technically smooth, well-acted drama lacks intensity, focus. Interesting Mitchum. C: Robert Mitchum, France Nuyen, Barry Sullivan, Keenan Wynn, Alexander Knox, Trevor Howard. D: Guy Hamilton. DRA 94m.

Man in the Moon, The 1961 British ★★★★ British satire about seemingly average man picked by experimenting scientists as ideal astronaut for the first space flight to moon. Dated drollery-cum-farce is good fun. C: Kenneth More, Shirley Anne Field, Michael Hordern, John Phillips, John Glyn-Jones, Charles Gray, Norman Bird. D: Basil Dearden. COM 99m.

Man in the Moon, The 1991 ★★★★ Touching tale of a young Louisiana girl's love for neighbor, and her older sister who charms him away from her. From the director of *To Kill a Mockingbird*. C: Sam Waterston, Tess Harper, Gail Strickland. D: Robert Mulligan. DRA [PG-13] 99m. V

Man in the Net, The 1959 ★★★ An aspiring artist leaves Madison Avenue for New England to pursue his craft, but when his alcoholic, psychopathic wife vanishes the locals suspect him of foul play. Messy whodunit falls apart long before improbable climax. Jones' flamboyant hysteria is only somewhat better than Ladd's stoicism. C: Alan Ladd, Carolyn Jones, Diane Brewster, Charles McGraw, John Lupton, Tom Helmore. D: Michael Curtiz. CRI 97m.

Man in the Raincoat, The 1957 French ★★★ A timid clarinetist visits a flirty young woman while his wife is away; when she's killed he gets blackmailed and ends up involved with a smuggling ring. Slickly directed, with Fernandel in fine comic form, but overplotted, with humor and grim thrills mixing awkwardly. C: Fernandel, John McGiver, Bernard Blier, Claude Sylvain, Jean Rigaux, Rob Murray. D: Julien Duvivier. CRI 97m. V

Man in the Road, The 1957 British ★★½ Dated Cold War paranoia about nasty Communists who want to get secret formulas out of a poor innocent scientist. Some good directorial touches, and nice acting from Raines and highly professional cast, but situations are just too blah. C: Derek Farr, Ella Raines, Donald Wolfit, Karel Stepanek. D: Lance Comfort. CRI 83m.

Man in the Saddle 1951 ★★★ A vicious large-scale rancher brutalizes his smaller neighbors. One gunfight after another and familiar love triangle. C: Randolph Scott, Joan Leslie, Ellen Drew, Alexander Knox. D: Andre de Toth. WST 87m. V

Man in the Santa Claus Suit, The 1978 ★★★½ Astaire plays eight different characters to help change gloomy lives of three strangers all out to rent Santa Claus suits. Warm fantasy, with Astaire charming, especially when singing "That Once a Year Christmas Day;" almost a holiday favorite. C: Fred Astaire, Gary Burghoff, John Byner, Bert Convy. D: Corey Allen. DRA 96m. TVM V

Man in the Shadow 1957 ★★★½ Welles gives a striking performance as a rancher tyrant who, after he has an underling killed for getting involved with his daughter, must face stalwart Chandler. Somewhat dull visually, with unsubtle script, but potent anyway. C: Orson Welles, Jeff Chandler, Colleen Miller, James Gleason. D: Jack Arnold. WST 80m.

Man In The Silk Hat, The 1983 French ★★★★ A comprehensive look at the life and career of master comic Max Linder, a genius who paved the way for Chaplin, Keaton, Laurel and Hardy and other giants. Tender and informative. C: Max Linder. DOC 99m. V

Man in the Vault 1956 ★★★ A locksmith forced to make keys for a cash-loaded safety deposit box. Shot in both Beverly Hills and Hollywood, capturing both city swank and seamy underside. Unoriginal, fairly predictable but adroitly directed; Ekberg is fun. C: William Campbell, Karen Sharpe, Anita Ekberg, Berry Kroeger, Paul Fix. D: Andrew V. McLaglen. ACT 73m.

Man in the White Suit, The 1951 British ★★★★★ Brilliant dark satire, beautifully handled, with Guinness perfect as an inventor who throws both labor and management into uproar when he creates a textile that never wears out. Superb support from Parker, Thesiger, Hope, Martin, and especially unique, slushy-voiced Greenwood. Justly famous sound effect: Guinness's machine. C: Alec Guinness, Joan Greenwood, Cecil Parker, Michael Gough, Ernest Thesiger, Vida Hope, George Benson, Edie Martin. D: Alexander Mackendrick. COM 84m. V

Man in the Wilderness 1971 ★★★ In the frozen north, a fur trapper is attacked and nearly killed by a giant grizzly. He recovers and seeks revenge. Bloody, man against nature tale. C: Richard Harris, John Bindon, John Huston, Ben Carruthers. D: Richard C. Sarafian. ACT [PG] 105m. V

Man Inside, The 1958 British ★★½ A dapper clerk turned jewel robber is trailed around Europe by a dogged detective, with gem's owner along for the ride. Attractive location shooting and stylish Patrick can't disguise dull plot and direction, so-so Palance, or annoying Newley. C: Jack Palance, Anita Ekberg, Nigel Patrick, Anthony Newley, Sidney James, Donald Pleasence, Eric Pohlmann. D: John Gilling. CRI [PG] 90m.

Man Inside, The 1976 ★★★½ After penetrating an underworld dope ring, a Federal agent finds himself tempted by the chance to make an easy $2 million. Fine acting. C: James Franciscus, Stefanie Powers, Jacques Godin, Len Birman. D: Gerald Mayer. ACT 96m. TVM V

Man Inside, The 1990 U.S. ★★★ A man poses as an arms dealer to find the link between a German official and a foreign general plotting a military coup. Political leaders try to use the newspaper to discredit the hero, so he infiltrates the tabloid. Fast moving, but implausible plotting hurts. C: Jurgen Prochnow, Peter Coyote, Nathalie Baye. D: Bobby Roth. ACT 93m. V

Man Is Armed, The 1956 ★★ Low-budget feature about a failed robbery. Clark, in one of his last leads, looks worried the whole time, perhaps in response to the script. Supporting cast is good. C: Dane Clark, William Talman, May Wynn, Robert Horton, Barton MacLane. D: Franklin Adreon. ACT 70m.

Man Is Not A Bird 1965 Yugoslavian ★★★½ The story of a Serbian engineer who, while installing heavy machinery, falls in love with a sweet young woman. Unfortunately, he's an inept suitor and she falls for someone more attentive. Unusual and tender. C: Eva Ras, Milena Dravic, Janez Urhovec. D: Dusan Makavejev. DRA 80m. V

Man Killer 1933 ★★★½ An undercover man (Powell) agrees to investigate a gambler (Lindsay) in Paris at the behest of a shady private eye (Hohl). Well directed, with Powell's performance adding class and body; good support from Warners' stock company. (a.k.a. *Private Detective 62*) C: William Powell, Margaret Lindsay, Ruth Donnelly, Arthur Hohl, Natalie Moorehead, Arthur Byron. D: Michael Curtiz. CRI 67m. V

Man Like Eva, A 1983 West German ★★★½ A retrospective of the life and career of German filmmaker Werner Fassbinder. It manages to capture the complexity of his life and his work. C: Eva Mattes, Lisa Kreuzer, Charles Regnier, Werner Stocker. D: Radu Gabrea. DOC 92m. V

Man Made Monster 1941 ★★★½ In many ways a model "B" (budget) horror film. Mad doc turns a man with resistance to electricity into a zombie who kills by shocking victims. Efficient storytelling lifts routine aspects of script. Fine cast, with Atwill a delight as the obsessed scientist. C: Lionel Atwill, Lon Chaney Jr., Anne Nagel, Frank Albertson, Samuel S. Hinds, William Davidson, Ben Taggart, Connie Bergen. D: George Waggner. HOR 59m. V

Man Named John, A 1968 Italian ★★★½ Surprisingly compelling documentary on the life of Pope John XXIII, covering not only standard biographical material, but also aspects of his work and his outlook on life. Handled well if not adventurously by Olmi; has good detail. C: Rod Steiger. D: Ermanno Olmi. DOC 94m.

Man of a Thousand Faces 1957 ★★★½ The biography of Lon Chaney Sr., from his humble origins to Hollywood stardom. The irrepressible Cagney is by far the best element. C: James Cagney, Dorothy Malone, Jane Greer, Marjorie Rambeau, Jim Backus, Robert Evans, Roger Smith. D: Joseph Pevney. DRA 122m. V

Man of Aran 1934 British ★★★★★ One of the legendary Flaherty's greatest achievements details the hardships of villagers living on a remote British isle against incredible odds. Historians later showed just how much of this was staged, but one can still marvel at the stark, haunting images and poetic, forceful, slice-of-life dramatics. D: Robert Flaherty. DOC 77m. V

Man of Conflict 1953 ★★ Talky melodrama. Tyrannical industrial executive grooms son to continue the family tradition, but junior converts dad to the ways of love. C: Edward Arnold, John Agar, Susan Morrow, Russell Hicks. D: Hal Makelim. DRA 72m.

Man of Conquest 1939 ★★★★ Solid biography of Sam Houston and his adventures in old Texas, with good Dix in one of his last major pictures. Republic Studios clearly aimed for class in this lavish production, with well-staged action sequences and Western stunts. C: Richard Dix, Gail Patrick, Edward Ellis, Joan Fontaine. D: George Nicholls Jr. WST 105m.

Man Of Destiny 1973 ★★★ A fantasy (from the pen of G.B. Shaw) detaling a rivalry between Napoleon and a rather enigmatic young lady. Light and breezy. C: Stacy Keach, Samantha Eggar. SFI 60m. V

Man of Evil 1944 British ★★★½ Handsomely produced if sometimes rather stodgy Regency melodrama about cruel, hard-drinking Mason nearly ruining sweet young Calvert's chance for happiness. Mason a bit underutilized but his presence is galvanizing; excellent supporting cast makes for fanciful diversion. (a.k.a. *Fanny by Gaslight*) C: Phyllis Calvert, James Mason, Stewart Granger, Wilfrid Lawson, Jean Kent. D: Anthony Asquith. DRA 90m.

Man of Flowers, A 1984 Australian ★★★½ Rather strange comedy/drama about cowed bachelor who loves plants, plays the organ, and pays a model to pose nude. Different and surprisingly involving at times, though it's unsure of itself and runs out of steam. Full of offbeat detail. C: Norman Kaye, Alyson Best, Chris Haywood, Sarah Walker. D: Paul Cox. COM 91m. V

Man of Iron 1956 Italian ★★★★ Cathartic minor triumph for writer/director/star Germi. Amiable railroad engineer's pregnant daughter refuses to marry lover, runs off with another. Running train over a suicide victim brings his world even closer to collapse. Potent realism, full of sad, bitter ironies. (a.k.a. *The Railroad Man*) C: Pietro Germi, Luisa Noce, Sylva Koscina, Carlo Giuffre. D: Pietro Germi. DRA 116m.

Man of Iron 1980 Polish ★★★★½ Excellent sequel to Wajda's *Man of Marble*, realistically portraying struggles in Poland from student reform in 1968 to Solidarity strikes in 1980. Strike leader hassled by government and reporter's smear campaign. Powerfully handled mix of well-acted drama and gripping political documentary. C: Jerzy Radziwilowicz, Krystyna Janda, Marian Opiana. D: Andrzej Wajda. DRA [PG] 140m. V

Man of La Mancha 1972 ★★ Among the worst movies based on a hit Broadway musical ever made. In this case it's the Leigh/Darion/Wasserman retelling of the Don Quixote story, about a deluded Spanish knight defending a prostitute's virtue. Show's best asset is its score. C: Peter O'Toole, Sophia Loren, James Coco, Harry Andrews. D: Arthur Hiller. MUS [PG] 130m. V

Man of Legend 1971 Italian ★★★ A German soldier, mistakenly condemned as a spy in WWI, joins the French Foreign Legion and has an affair with the daughter of a North African rebel commander. Fairly competent cast rolls around in the sand with some panache. C: Peter Strauss, Tina Aumont, Luciana Paluzzi, Massimo Serato. D: Sergio Grieco. DRA [R] 95m. V

Man of Marble 1977 Polish ★★★★★ Moving account of filmmaker Janda tracing life of Radziwilowicz, a single bricklayer who became a champion of the people in '50s Poland. Eye-opening political drama much reviled by Communist Polish authorities, who cut original ending showing Radziwilowicz's fate. Followed by sequel, *Man of Iron*. C: Krystyna Janda, Jerzy Radziwilowicz, Tadeusz Lomnicki, Jacek Lomnicki, Krystyna Zachwatowicz. D: Andrzej Wajda. DRA 160m. V

Man of No Importance, A 1994 British ★★★½ Repressed Irish homosexual bus conductor (Finney) has a crush on the driver and a fixation on Oscar Wilde, culminating in a local stage production of *Salome*, Charming, but a bit fey, so to speak. C: Albert Finney, Brenda Fricker, Rufus Sewell, Michael Gambon, Tara Fitzgerald. D: Suri Krishnamma. COM [R] 98m.

Man of Peace, The 1987 ★★★★ A detailed and compelling biographical study of Pope John Paul II, his life, his work and his visions for the world. Special indeed, and vivid in its views of Rome and St. Peter's. DOC 60m. V

Man of the Forest 1933 ★★★½ After he's framed for murder, a man breaks out of jail—thanks to the aid of his pet mountain lion! Then they set off to find the real killers. Vintage western fare from the old school. C: Randolph Scott, Harry Carey, Buster Crabbe, Verna Hillie. D: Henry Hathaway. WST 62m. V

Man of The Frontier 1936 ★★★ Gene Autry and his friends get on the trail of a notorious grifter who's been setting dynamite to a big irrigation operation. Diverting business from the singing cowboy. C: Gene Autry, Smiley Burnette, Frances Grant. D: B. Reeves Eason. WST 60m. V

Man of the House 1995 ★★★½ Surprisingly charming Disney comedy about an 11-year-old (Thomas) who puts his future step-father (Chase) through numerous trials and tortures. Gratuitous subplot about Mafia hitmen drags movie down, but not out. C: Chevy Chase, Jonathan Taylor Thomas, Farrah Fawcett, George Wendt. D: James Orr. COM [PG] 98m. V

Man of the West 1958 ★★★½ A one-time gunman, since reformed, acquiesces to pull one more bank job as a means to shield innocent people from his ruthless boss. Interesting star vehicle that works hard—and just misses its epic goals. C: Gary Cooper, Julie London, Lee J. Cobb, Arthur O'Connell, Jack Lord, John Dehner, Royal Dano. D: Anthony Mann. WST 100m. V

Man of the World 1931 ★★★★ A once-respected American reporter lives in Paris blackmailing feckless tourists, then falls for the niece of one of them. Atmospheric, sophisticated, adult story, with excellent Powell carrying the show, though Gibson is also fine as his moll. C: William Powell, Carole Lombard, Wynne Gibson, Guy Kibbee, George Chandler. D: Richard Wallace. DRA 71m.

Man of Violence 1971 ★★★ When a group of international bandits steal gold from an Arab sheikdom, they sneak their loot into Europe and violence erupts. C: Michael Latimer, Luan Peters. D: Pete Walker. ACT 107m. V

Man on a String 1960 ★★★★ A Moscow-born U.S. citizen, a famed film producer, doubles as spy for the Soviets. When the CIA catches him, he switches allegiance and spies on Russians in Moscow! Good acting, well-handled action sequences slightly marred by platitudes and an unnecessary romantic triangle. Based on life of Boris Morros. C: Ernest Borgnine, Kerwin Mathews, Colleen Dewhurst, Alexander Scourby, Glenn Corbett. D: Andre de Toth. ACT 92m.

Man on a String 1971 ★★★ Government agent, working undercover, sets out to smash crime ring, discovers himself in midst of Mafia-family war. Movie was meant to revive old '50s action series *Tightrope* but routine rendering of unoriginal plot drained story's energy. C: Christopher George, William Schallert, Joel Grey, Jack Warden, Kitty Winn, Michael Baseleon, Keith Carradine. D: Joseph Sargent. ACT [PG] 73m. TVM V

Man on a Swing 1974 ★★★½ A chief of detectives receives help from a man with ESP in tracking down a sex killer. Clever, potentially interesting variation on formula story builds suspense well but falls apart at the finale. Acting, especially Grey's, is good, however. C: Cliff Robertson, Joel Grey, Dorothy Tristan, Elizabeth Wilson, George Voskovec. D: Frank Perry. CRI [PG] 110m.

Man on a Tightrope 1953 ★★★★ A Czech circus leader wins the respect of his young wife and her rebellious daughter from an earlier marriage when he tries to get company through Iron Curtain. Script has holes, but March is excellent, Kazan's direction suspenseful, and location shooting fine. C: Fredric March, Gloria Grahame, Terry Moore, Cameron Mitchell, Adolphe Menjou, Richard Boone, Robert Beatty. D: Elia Kazan. DRA 105m.

Man on Fire 1957 ★★★½ Small-scale domestic drama stars cast-against-type Crosby as divorced father who refuses to share custody of child with former spouse. C: Bing Crosby, Mary Fickett, Inger Stevens, E. G. Marshall, Malcolm Broderick, Anne Seymour, Richard Eastham. D: Ranald MacDougall. DRA 95m.

Man on Fire 1987 French ★★ Misfired comedy about former spy Glenn reduced to working as bodyguard for spoiled Malle. When she's kidnapped by terrorists, Glenn falls back on old CIA tricks. Talented cast in barely lukewarm satire. C: Scott Glenn, Jade Malle, Paul Shenar, Brooke Adams, Jonathan Pryce, Joe Pesci, Danny Aiello. D: Elie Chouraqui. COM [R] 92m. V

Man on the Eiffel Tower, The 1949 ★★★★ Canny Inspector Maigret (Laughton) stalks a demented murderer (Tone). Tight suspense, deftly handled, based on Simenon novel. Meredith's directorial debut. C: Charles Laughton, Franchot Tone, Burgess Meredith, Robert Hutton, Jean Wallace. D: Burgess Meredith. CRI 97m. V

Man on the Flying Trapeze, The 1935 ★★★★½ The misadventures of a frustrated man, harried on all fronts, who's finally had enough. Hysterically funny Fields, with wonderful supporting cast, and a classic driving scene. C: W. C. Fields, Mary Brian, Kathleen Howard, Grady Sutton, Vera Lewis, Walter Brennan. D: Clyde Bruckman. COM 65m.

Man on the Move 1949 *See* **Jigsaw**

Man on the Outside 1975 ★★★ A retired cop witnesses his son's shooting, then a contract killer abducts his grandson. Top performance by Greene elevates this average effort; pilot for the *Griff* series. C: Lorne Greene, James Olson, Lee H. Montgomery, Lorraine Gary, Brooke Bundy. D: Boris Sagal. ACT 100m. TVM

Man on the Roof 1977 Swedish ★★★★½ When cop is shot by a sniper Stockholm police hunt down the killer. A commanding, meticulous police procedural, full of suspense and action. Based on Maj Sjowall/Per Wahloo novel. C: Gustav Lindstedt, Hakan Serner, Sven Wallter, Thomas Hellberg. D: Bo Widerberg. CRI [R] 110m.

Man on the Run ★★★ After an electronics store is robbed, the police try to find the perpetrator—a murderous high school student. Gripping manhunt. C: Kyle Johnson, James Sikking. D: Herbert L. Strock. CRI 90m. V

Man Outside 1988 ★★★ A dropout lawyer (Logan) and an anthropologist (Quinlan) come together in rural Arkansas. She's attracted to him, even though he's been setup on a child-kidnapping charge. Drab melodrama, with several ex-Band members featured in small roles. C: Robert Logan, Kathleen Quinlan, Bradford Dillman, Levon Helm. D: Mark Stouffer. DRA 97m. V

Man Outside, The 1968 British ★★½ A reclusive loner is falsely accused of kidnapping a neighborhood boy. Interesting. C: Van Heflin, Heidelinde Weis, Pinkas Braun, Peter Vaughan, Charles Gray, Ronnie Barker. D: Samuel Gallu. DRA [G] 98m.

Man-Proof 1938 ★★★ Pidgeon marries socialite Russell, but is also loved by Loy, who is loved by Tone. Star power drives plotless fluff. C: Myrna Loy, Franchot Tone, Rosalind

Russell, Walter Pidgeon, Nana Bryant, Rita Johnson, Ruth Hussey. D: Richard Thorpe. DRA 74m.

Man Stolen 1934 French ★★★ A career woman (Damita) meets kidnapped banker (Garat) and they fall in love on the French Riviera. Early romantic drama by Ophuls. C: Lili Damita, Henry Garat. D: Max Ophuls. DRA 90m.

Man, The 1972 ★★½ Rod Serling's adaptation of Irving Wallace's novel begins with an intriguing premise: The President of the United States is killed accidentally, and his legitimate successor is an African-American senator. Sadly, director Sargent fails to realize the potential of story and cast, settling for a less-than-satisfying cinematic experience. Conceived as a TV movie, but debuted in theaters first. C: James Earl Jones, Martin Balsam, Burgess Meredith, Lew Ayres, William Windom, Barbara Rush, Janet MacLachlan. D: Joseph Sargent. DRA [G] 93m.

Man They Could Not Hang, The 1939 ★★★½ An innocent scientist hanged for murder is reanimated and seeks vengeance. Pretty good Karloff vehicle. C: Boris Karloff, Lorna Gray, Robert Wilcox. D: Nick Grinde. HOR 72m. V

Man to Man 1931 ★★★ A college student (Holmes) must leave school when the administration discovers his father (Mitchell) is in jail for murder. After the old man's pardoned, the two are distrustful of each other until an accident brings them together. Fair, if occasionally forced melodrama. C: Grant Mitchell, Lucille Powers, Phillips Holmes. D: Allan Dwan. DRA 68m.

Man to Man Talk 1958 French ★★★ When his wife becomes pregnant a man must tell his son about the birds and the bees. Banal little piece. (a.k.a *Premier May)* C: Yves Montand, Nicole Berger, Yves Noel. D: Luis Saslavski. DRA 89m.

Man to Remember, A 1938 ★★★½ Told in flashbacks, a recently dead small-town doctor (Ellis) is remembered by his friends, who begin to realize that the simple man they rarely gave a second thought to was a remarkable person. Good-natured drama, refreshingly free of false sentiment. Followed by a sequel, *Career.* C: Anne Shirley, Edward Ellis, Lee Bowman. D: Garson Kanin. DRA 79m.

Man-Trap 1961 ★★★ Crime and adultery bring clamaity to several people in this offbeat yarn of deception and intrigue. Fine cast. C: Jeffrey Hunter, David Janssen, Stella Stevens, Hugh Sanders. D: Edmond O'Brien. DRA 93m.

Man Trouble 1992 ★★ An opera singer (Barkin) hires dog trainer (Nicholson) to protect her against psycho. Unconvincing and flat, although D'Angelo is amusing. C: Jack Nicholson, Ellen Barkin, Beverly D'Angelo, Harry Dean Stanton, Michael McKean, Saul Rubinek, Veronica Cartwright. D: Bob Rafelson. COM [PG-13] 100m. V

Man Under Suspicion 1984 German ★★★½ A defense lawyer takes a provocative case involving violence at a political assembly. Circumspect examination of the seeds of facism drags in spots but is nonetheless compelling. C: Maximilian Schell, Lena Stolze, Robert Aldini, Wolfgang Kieling, Kathrin Ackermann, Reinhard Hauff. D: Norbert Kuckelmann. DRA 126m.

Man Upstairs, The 1958 British ★★★★ An unassuming boarder goes mad and becomes violent. Compelling character study by Attenborough of a depressed man who finally snaps. Solid drama. C: Richard Attenborough, Bernard Lee, Donald Houston, Virginia Maskell. D: Don Chaffey. DRA 88m.

Man Upstairs, The 1992 ★★★½ A jewel thief (O'Neal) on the lam gets more than he bargained for when he hides out in the home of a feisty old lady (Hepburn). By-the-numbers comedy vehicle for the Hollywood grande dame. C: Katharine Hepburn, Ryan O'Neal, Helena Carroll. D: George Schaefer. COM 100m. TVM V

Man Who Broke 1,000 Chains, The 1987 ★★★½ A man wrongly convicted of robbery escapes from a savage chain gang. Hard-hitting episodic TV drama. Based on the autobiographical book by Robert E. Burns which also inspired the classic *I Am a Fugitive from a Chain Gang.* C: Val Kilmer, Charles Durning, Sonia Braga, William Sanderson, Kyra Sedgwick. D: Daniel Mann. DRA 113m. TVM V

Man Who Broke the Bank at Monte Carlo, The 1935 ★★★½ A Russian cabbie in Monaco plans to wipe out the Riviera casino. Urbane Colman sustains breezy tomfoolery. C: Ronald Colman, Joan Bennett, Colin Clive, Nigel Bruce, Montagu Love, Ferdinand Gottschalk. D: Stephen Roberts. COM 66m.

Man Who Came for Coffee, The 1970 Italian ★★★ A libidinous tax-inspector (Tognazzi) visits a boarding house run by three virtuous women whom he successfully woos until he tries to add a fourth to their number, leading (literally) to catastrophically funny denouement. (a.k.a. *Venga Prendere un Caffé da Noi*) C: Ugo Tognazzi, Francesca Romana Coluzzi. D: Alberto Lattuada. COM 98m.

Man Who Came to Dinner, The 1941 ★★★★½ Sparkling comedy from Kaufman Hart play has egocentric critic and radio personality Wooley stranded in Midwest town due to broken hip, bringing chaos to those around him. Kudos to Sheridan as vain actress and Davis in unusual role of mousy secretary. C: Bette Davis, Ann Sheridan, Monty Woolley, Billie Burke, Jimmy Durante, Grant Mitchell, Mary Wickes. D: William Keighley. COM 112m. V

Man Who Changed His Mind, The 1936 *See* **Man Who Lived Again, The**

Man Who Cheated Himself, The 1950 ★★★½ An honorable police officer is led astray. Adequate crime yarn, served by a good cast. C: Lee J. Cobb, Jane Wyatt, John Dall, Terry Frost. D: Felix Feist. CRI 81m.

Man Who Could Cheat Death, The 1959 British ★★★½ Unusual surgery renders a sculptor eternally young. Standard shocker with some grisly moments. C: Anton Diffring, Hazel Court, Christopher Lee, Arnold Marle, Delphi Lawrence. D: Terence Fisher. HOR 83m.

Man Who Could Talk to Kids, The 1973 ★★★½ A social worker tries to help a troubled reclusive teenager. Topical story is above par with excellent casting. C: Peter Boyle, Scott Jacoby, Robert Reed, Tyne Daly. D: Donald Wrye. DRA 73m.

Man Who Could Work Miracles, The 1937 British ★★★★ H.G. Wells short story extended into charming fantasy of shy store clerk (Young) endowed with magical powers. Funny special effects, good supporting cast. C: Roland Young, Ralph Richardson, Edward Chapman, Ernest Thesiger, Joan Gardner, George Zucco, George Sanders. D: Lothar Mendes. COM 82m. V

Man Who Couldn't Walk, The 1964 British ★★★½ A wheelchair-bound jewel thief (Pohlman) hires an ace safecracker (Reynolds) to join his crew in a heist during a convention, but the caper falls apart when Reynolds is captured. Offbeat crime drama, complete with gun-toting mamma. C: Eric Pohlmann, Peter Reynolds. D: Henry Cass. CRI 63m.

Man Who Cried Wolf, The 1937 ★★★½ An actor tries to convince police that he's insane by confessing to several murders, so they won't suspect him of the one he's actually planning. Stone carries this low-budget rendering of a clever concept. C: Lewis Stone, Tom Brown, Barbara Read, Robert Gleckler, Forrester Harvey, Marjorie Main. D: Lewis R. Foster. CRI 66m.

Man Who Dared, The 1933 ★★★½ Good performance by Foster in dramatization of the life of Polish immigrant and Chicago mayor Anton Cermak, who was killed during an assassination attempt on president-elect Franklin Roosevelt. C: Preston Foster, Zita Johann, Joan Marsh, Frank Sheridan. D: Hamilton McFadden. DRA 75m.

Man Who Died Twice, The 1970 ★★★ A man believed dead wanders through Spain and becomes involved with a young woman; flashbacks reveal man's mysterious past. Good cast makes for compelling drama. C: Stuart Whitman, Brigitte Fossey, Jeremy Slate, Bernard Lee, Severn Darden, Peter Damon. D: Joseph Sargent. DRA 100m.

Man Who Fell to Earth, The 1976 British ★★★★ An alien (Bowie) masquerades as a corporate honcho to cover his mission. Wildly original, but viewers may need a road map to follow plot, even with the inclusion of excised footage. C: David Bowie, Rip Torn, Candy Clark, Buck Henry, Bernie Casey. D: Nicolas Roeg. SFI [R] 140m. V

Man Who Finally Died, The 1962 British ★★★★ A man tracing his father's movements in WWII gets involved with espionage agents. Middling thriller with rather complicated plot. C: Stanley Baker, Peter Cushing, Mai Zetterling, Eric Portman, Niall MacGinnis, Nigel Green, Barbara Everest. D: Quentin Lawrence. DRA 100m.

Man Who Had Power Over Women, The 1970 British ★★★ The trials of an ethical London talent agency exec. Broad satiric drama about life and guilt at the top is nicely underplayed by cast. C: Rod Taylor, James Booth, Carol White, Penelope Horner, Charles Korvin. D: John Krish. COM [R] 89m. V

Man Who Haunted Himself, The 1970 British ★★★ A London executive injured in an auto accident finds a double of himself is taking over his life. Slightly overdone thriller. C: Roger Moore, Hildegard Neil, Alastair Mackenzie, Hugh Mackenzie. D: Basil Dearden. SFI [PG] 91m. V

Man Who Knew Too Much, The 1934 British ★★★★ Foreign agents abduct a child to stop her father from exposing their assasination plot. Riveting early Hitchcock suspense with a memorable climax. Remade by Hitchcock in 1956. C: Leslie Banks, Edna Best, Peter Lorre, Nova Pilbeam, Frank Vosper. D: Alfred Hitchcock. CRI 72m. V

Man Who Knew Too Much, The 1956 ★★★★★ An American couple (Stewart and Day) mistakenly get wind of an assassination plot and their son is kidnapped to keep them quiet. Remake of 1934 Hitchcock film is spectacular fun. And, yes, that is Bernard Hermann conducting the orchestra. Song "Que Sera, Sera" won Oscar. C: James Stewart, Doris Day, Brenda De Banzie, Bernard Miles, Alan Mowbray, Daniel Gelin, Christopher Olsen, Reggie Nalder. D: Alfred Hitchcock. CRI [PG] 120m. V

Man Who Lies, The 1970 French ★★★½ An escaped French Resistance fighter (Trintignant) returns to his village to find that no one remembers him and another man (Mistrik) is being honored in his place. Compelling mystery with film noirish twist. (a.k.a. *L' Homme Qui Ment*) C: Jean-Louis Trintignant, Ivan Mistrik, Sylvie Breal. D: Alain Robbe-Grillet. DRA 95m.

Man Who Lived Again, The 1936 British ★★★ A mad scientist tries his hand at brain transplants. Good, tingly Karloff chiller. (a.k.a. *The Man Who Changed His Mind*) C: Boris Karloff, Anna Lee, John Loder, Frank Cellier, Lyn Harding, Cecil Parker. D: Robert Stevenson. SFI 63m. V

Man Who Lived at the Ritz, The 1988 British ★★★½ An artist attempts to insulate himself from the Nazis at the luxurious Parisian hotel. Exciting European locales and a crowd of '40s personalities decorate this rendering of A.E. Hotchner's novel. C: Perry King, Leslie

Caron, Cherie Lunghi, David McCallum, David Robb, Patachou, Mylene Demongeot, Sophie Barjac, Joss Ackland. D: Desmond Davis. DRA 200m. TVM

Man Who Lived Twice, The 1936 ★★★½ A brain transplant gives a killer a new personality. Neat concept makes for fairly efficient thriller. C: Ralph Bellamy, Marian Marsh, Thurston Hall, Isabel Jewell, Nana Bryant, Ward Bond. D: Harry Lachman. SFI 73m.

Man Who Loved Cat Dancing, The 1973 ★★★½ An abused married woman takes off, and falls in with outlaws. Entertaining Western. C: Burt Reynolds, Sarah Miles, George Hamilton, Lee J. Cobb, Jack Warden, Bo Hopkins. D: Richard C. Sarafian. WST [PG] 127m. V

Man Who Loved Redheads, The 1955 British ★★★★ A career diplomat has affairs over the years with women who remind him of his youthful idyll with a beautiful red-haired lady (Shearer). Fine British comedy by Terrence Rattigan, based on his play. C: John Justin, Moira Shearer, Roland Culver, Denholm Elliott, Harry Andrews, Patricia Cutts. D: Harold French. COM 103m.

Man Who Loved Women, The 1977 French ★★★★ Film attempts to uncover the reasons why the lead character falls in love with every woman he meets, and why they respond. Sophisticated light comedy disguises more complex statements about the nature of love. C: Charles Denner, Brigitte Fossey, Nelly Borgeaud, Leslie Caron, Genevieve Fontanel. D: Francois Truffaut. COM 119m. V

Man Who Loved Women, The 1983 ★★★ A modern-day Casanova talks things over with a psychiatrist. Attractive performance by Reynolds, in a sluggish remake of 1977 Truffaut film. C: Burt Reynolds, Julie Andrews, Kim Basinger, Marilu Henner, Barry Corbin, Cynthia Sikes, Jennifer Edwards. D: Blake Edwards. COM [R] 110m. V

Man Who Made Diamonds, The 1937 British ★★ Stiff crime drama about a young laboratory assistant (Madison) who kills a scientist to steal his formula for manufacturing diamonds. C: Noel Madison, James Stephenson, Lesley Brook, George Galleon. D: Ralph Ince. CRI 73m.

Man Who Never Was, The 1956 British ★★★★ Classic spy tale (based on real events) concerning British agents and their efforts to mislead the Germans in Sicily in 1943. Good action with a little romance thrown in. C: Clifton Webb, Gloria Grahame, Robert Flemyng, Josephine Griffin, 600Stephen Boyd. D: Ronald Neame. DRA 103m. V

Man Who Played God, The 1932 ★★★½ A concert pianist (Arliss) loses his hearing but overcomes his ordeal by helping pupils (Davis and Milland). Bathos tailor-made for Arliss, who delivers. Remade as *Sincerely Yours*. C: George Arliss, Bette Davis, Violet Heming, Louise Closser Hale, Donald Cook, Ray Milland. D: John C. Adolfi. DRA 81m.

Man Who Reclaimed His Head, The 1934 ★★★★ A pacifist writer is used and compromised by an unscrupulous politician. Diverting anti-war drama holds interest; fine performance by young Rains. C: Claude Rains, Lionel Atwill, Joan Bennett, Baby Jane, Henry O'Neill, Wallace Ford. D: Edward Ludwig. DRA 80m.

Man Who Saw Tomorrow, The 1981 ★★★★ Dramatic reenactments of the prognostications of Nostradamus, the 16th-century poet, many of whose predictions have come eerily true in subsequent centuries. Welles' resonant narration adds an appropriately awe-inspiring tone. C: Orson Welles. D: Robert Guenette. DRA [PG] 88m. TVM V

Man Who Shot Liberty Valance, The 1962 ★★★★½ A pilgrim lawyer (Stewart) finds fame after outdrawing a vicious outlaw. Ford classic about the making of legends and outliving myths. C: James Stewart, John Wayne, Vera Miles, Lee Marvin, Edmond O'Brien, Andy Devine, Woody Strode, Jeanette Nolan, Ken Murray, John Qualen, Strother Martin, Lee Van Cleef, John Carradine. D: John Ford. WST 122m. V

Man Who Skied Down Everest, The 1981 Japanese ★★★½ Oscar-winning documentary of Japanese skier Yuichiro Miura's obsessive efforts in 1970 to take on the world's highest mountain. English-language version suffers from silly narration. D: Bruce Nyznik. DOC [G] 86m. V

Man Who Talked Too Much, The 1940 ★★★½ Two brothers, a D.A. and a defense lawyer, confront each other at a Mob czar's trial. Snappy courtroom drama. Made before as *The Mouthpiece*, and later as *Illegal*. C: George Brent, Virginia Bruce, Brenda Marshall, Richard Barthelmess, William Lundigan, George Tobias. D: Vincent Sherman. DRA 75m.

Man Who Turned to Stone, The 1957 ★ Mad scientists prey on others for their life energy. Wierd-science film soon turns to granite. C: Victor Jory, Ann Doran, Charlotte Austin, William Hudson, Paul Cavanagh, Jean Willes, Victor Varconi. D: Leslie Kardos. HOR 80m.

Man Who Understood Women, The 1959 ★★★ A brilliant film producer (Fonda) is blind to the needs of his actress-wife (Caron). Uneven, ambiguous intent. C: Leslie Caron, Henry Fonda, Cesare Danova, Myron McCormick, Marcel Dalio, Conrad Nagel. D: Nunnally Johnson. DRA 105m.

Man Who Wagged His Tail, The 1957 Spanish ★★★½ A skinflint slumlord is magically transformed into a hound and must redeem himself in order to be human again. Agreeable fantasy-allegory, filmed in Spain and New York. (a.k.a. *An Angel Passed Over Brooklyn.*) C: Peter Ustinov, Pablito Calvo, Aroldo Tieri, Silvia Marco. D: Ladislao Vajda. COM 91m.

Man Who Wanted to Live Forever, The 1970 ★★★ The new director of a heart-research center owned by a sinister tycoon uncovers a nefarious secret project. Standard medical trailer with a good turn by Ives. C: Burl Ives, Sandy Dennis, Stuart Whitman. D: John Trent. DRA 99m.

Man Who Was Sherlock Holmes, The 1937 German ★★★½ A man mistaken for the famous detective decides to play along and travels to the 1936 Paris Exhibition to uncover a counterfeit stamp ring. Pleasant crime caper with Albers—the "German Clark Gable"—as Holmes. C: Hans Albers, Heinz Ruhmann, Marieluise Claudius. D: Karl Hartl. CRI 80m.

Man Who Wasn't There, The 1983 ★ The wacky misadventures of a federal aide who becomes invisible. Made in 3-D, which is three dimensions too many. Awful. C: Steve Guttenberg, Lisa Langlois, Jeffrey Tambor, Art Hindle, Morgan Hart, Bill Forsythe, Bruce Malmuth, Ivan Naranjo, Clement St. George, Vincent Baggetta. D: Bruce Malmuth. COM 111m. V

Man Who Watched Trains Go By, The 1953 *See* **Paris Express, The**

Man Who Would Be King, The 1975 ★★★★½ Two British soldiers in 1880 India (Caine and Connery) decide to convince the natives of isolated Kafiristan that they are deities. Captivating adventure based on Kipling looks at greed with just the right amount of Huston's dark humor. C: Sean Connery, Michael Caine, Christopher Plummer, Saeed Jaffrey. D: John Huston. DRA [PG] 129m. V

Man Who Would Not Die, The 1975 ★★★ En route to St. Thomas, a boat's captain inadvertantly stumbles onto a crime syndicate and their enormous theft of bonds. Some good action takes you through. C: Dorothy Malone, Keenan Wynn, Aldo Ray. D: Robert Arkless. CRI [PG] 85m. V

Man Who Wouldn't Die, The 1942 ★★★½ Rugged, wisecracking P.I. Mike Shayne (Nolan) tackles extortion and murder at a stately manor. Competent caper mystery; above-par for the series. C: Lloyd Nolan, Marjorie Weaver, Helene Reynolds, Henry Wilcoxon. D: Herbert I. Leeds. CRI [PG] 65m.

Man Who Wouldn't Talk, The 1940 ★★★ A man with a mysterious past declines to defend himself when he's accused of murder. Standard courtroom fare with a dopey climax. C: Lloyd Nolan, Jean Rogers, Onslow Stevens, Eric Blore, Mae Marsh. D: David Burton. DRA 72m.

Man Who Wouldn't Talk, The 1957 British ★★★ A nimble advocate (Neagle) defends a man (Quayle) accused of murder and whose lips are sealed. Improbable courtroom drama. C: Anna Neagle, Anthony Quayle, Zsa Zsa Gabor, Katherine Kath, Dora Bryan. D: Herbert Wilcox. DRA 97m.

Man with a Cloak, The 1951 ★★★½ A mysterious stranger (Cohen) in 1848 New York gets involved with two women (Caron and Stanwyck) and a coveted inheritance. Unusual suspenseful costumer with good acting and a surprise ending. C: Barbara Stanwyck, Joseph Cotten, Louis Calhern, Leslie Caron, Jim Backus, Margaret Wycherly, Joe DeSantis. D: Fletcher Markle. DRA 81m.

Man with a Million 1954 British ★★★½ Mark Twain fable about an American receiving a £1 million note and the ensuing turmoil. Pleasant, well-acted leisurely tale. (a.k.a. *The Million Pound Note.*) C: Gregory Peck, Jane Griffith, Ronald Squire, A. Matthews, Wilfrid Hyde-White, Reginald Beckwith. D: Ronald Neame. COM 90m.

Man with Bogart's Face, The 1980 ★★★½ Plastic surgery transforms a private detective into a dead ringer for Bogie. Homage to hard-boiled genre is escapist mystery/comedy. (a.k.a. *Sam Marlowe, Private Eye*) C: Robert Sacchi, Michelle Phillips, Olivia Hussey, Franco Nero. D: Robert Day. DRA [PG] 106m. V

Man with Connections, The 1970 French ★★★½ A young French soldier tries to use influence to ease his way through the army. Mild, affable service comedy. C: Guy Bedos, Yves Robert, Rosy Varte, Georges Geret, Zorica Lozic. D: Claude Berri. COM [R] 93m.

Man with My Face, The 1951 ★★★ A man's mysterious double impersonates him so well that he himself is branded as an imposter. Interesting premise; execution less interesting. C: Barry Nelson, Lynn Ainley, John Harvey, Carole Mathews. D: Edward Montagne. DRA 86m.

Man with Nine Lives, The 1940 ★★★ Scientist frozen for years in cancer-cure experiment thaws out and runs amock. Good science-fiction hokum, slightly ahead of its time. (a.k.a. *Behind the Door*). C: Boris Karloff, Roger Pryor, Jo Ann Sayers, Stanley Brown, John Dilson, Hal Taliaferro. D: Nick Grinde. SFI 73m.

Man with One Red Shoe 1985 ★★½ Feeble remake of French farce *The Tall Blonde Man with One Black Shoe* about innocent dupe mistaken for an international spy. Hanks is miscast in this Jerry Lewis-style comedy. C: Tom Hanks, Dabney Coleman, Lori Singer, Charles Durning, Carrie Fisher, James Belushi. D: Stan Dragoti. COM [PG] 92m. V

Man with the Balloons, The 1965 Italian ★★½ A jilted businessman (Mastroianni) develops an insane fixation on how much air is required to make a balloon explode. Result isn't as eye-catching as the premise. C: Marcello Mastroianni, Catherine Spaak. D: Marco Ferreri. COM 85m.

Man with the Golden Arm 1955 ★★★★ Chicago poker dealer tries to kick heroin addiction cold turkey. Sinatra's excellent performance enhances this once-sensational drama. Supporting players right on target. C: Frank Sinatra, Eleanor Parker, Kim Novak, Darren McGavin, Arnold Stang, Doro Merande. D: Otto Preminger. DRA 119m. V

Man with the Golden Gun, The 1974 British ★★★½ Bond (Moore) chases hired assassin (Lee) who's stolen a solar energy capsule. Elaborate, global chase scenes and Lee's wonderful villainy compensate for Moore's lack of his predecessor Sean Connery's authority. C: Roger Moore, Christopher Lee, Britt Ekland, Maud Adams, Herve Villechaize. D: Guy Hamilton. ACT [PG] 125m. V

Man with the Green Carnation, The 1960 British ★★★★ Engrossing account of Oscar Wilde's infamous and doomed libel case against the Marquis of Queensbury that led to the writer's downfall and eventual imprisonment. Top performances carry the day. (a.k.a. *The Green Carnation* and *The Trials of Oscar Wilde*) C: Peter Finch, John Fraser, Yvonne Mitchell, Lionel Jeffries, James Mason. D: Ken Hughes. DRA 123m.

Man with the Gun, The 1955 ★★★½ Residents of a small town hire ex-gunslinger (Mitchum) to rid them of outlaws, but they begin to question their decision when he turns out to be just as violent. Suspenseful story kept afloat by Mitchum's steely performance. C: Robert Mitchum, Jan Sterling, Angie Dickinson, Barbara Lawrence, Karen Sharpe, Henry Hull. D: Richard Wilson. WST 83m.

Man with the Power, The 1977 ★★★ Imbued with super powers by his extraterrestrial father, a teacher is recruited as a government agent. Formula movie is decent entertainment. C: Bob Neill, Tim O'Connor, Vic Morrow, Persis Khambatta, Roger Perry, Rene Assa, Noel deSouza. D: Nicholas Sgarro. SFI 120m.

Man with the Transplanted Brain 1972 ★★★½ The brain of a French surgeon (Aumont) is transplanted into a critically injured race-car driver (Carriere) who has been having an illicit affair with the doctor's daughter. Interesting story concentrates on the ensuing moral issues. C: Mathieu Carriere, Jean-Pierre Aumont, Nicoletta Machiavelli. D: Jacques Doniol-Valcroze. SFI 72m.

Man with Two Brains, The 1983 ★★★½ Unhappy scientist (Martin) wants to leave his beautiful but evil wife (Turner) for Spacek. The problem with the latter is—she's only a brain. Entertaining takeoff of '50s sci-fi movies. Watch for the Merv Griffin cameo. Voice of Sissy Spacek. C: Steve Martin, Kathleen Turner, David Warner, Paul Benedict. D: Carl Reiner. COM [R] 91m. V

Man with Two Faces, The 1934 ★★★½ An actor uses disguises to take vengeance against his sister's abusive husband. Entertaining melodrama from this Kaufman/Woollcott play. C: Edward G. Robinson, Mary Astor, Ricardo Cortez, Mae Clarke, Louis Calhern. D: Archie Mayo. DRA 72m.

Man Within, The 1948 *See* **Smugglers, The**

Man Without a Country, The 1973 ★★★★ Philip Nolan joins former vice-president Aaron Burr, who's involved in political intrigue. Excellent character drama about maverick patriotism is based on the Edward Everett Hale classic. Fine performances. C: Cliff Robertson, Beau Bridges, Peter Strauss, Robert Ryan, Walter Abel, John Cullum, Geoffrey Holder, Shepperd Strudwick, Patricia Elliott. D: Delbert Mann. DRA 78m. TVM V

Man Without a Face, The 1993 ★★★ Gibson's directorial debut is a somewhat ponderous tale of a badly scarred teacher and his effect on a lonely young boy whom he tutors. C: Mel Gibson, Margaret Whitton, Fay Masterson, Geoffrey Lewis. D: Mel Gibson. DRA [PG-13] 115m. V

Man Without a Star 1955 ★★★★ A likable drifter (Douglas) takes a young cowpoke (Campbell) under his wing and helps a rancher (Crain) hold on to her land while he romances saloon hostess (Trevor). Good rough 'n' tumble Western is a one-man show for Douglas. C: Kirk Douglas, Jeanne Crain, Claire Trevor, Richard Boone, Jay C. Flippen, William Campbell. D: King Vidor. WST 89m. V

Man/Woman Wanted Poland ★★★ A rare museum painting is stolen and an art historian disguises himself as a museum washerwoman to find it. Some really funny moments. In Polish. D: Stanislaw Bareja. COM 69m. V

Man, Woman and Child 1983 ★★★½ Erich Segal's sentimental story of a family man whose newly orphaned illegitimate son is suddenly thrust into his life. Earnest, well-told domestic drama. C: Martin Sheen, Blythe Danner, Sebastian Dungan, Arlene McIntyre, Craig T. Nelson, David Hemmings. D: Dick Richards. DRA [PG] 100m. V

Manchu Eagle Murder Caper Mystery, The 1973 ★★★½ Several hilarious moments and every corny cliché imaginable pepper this minor detective spoof, with kooky hatchery owner turning deadpan private eye when local milkman is killed. Cast graced by amusing, seasoned character actors; Talbot a standout as victim's widow. Never released theatrically. C: Gabriel Dell, Will Geer, Joyce Van Patten, Anjanette Comer, Jackie Coogan, Huntz Hall, Barbara Harris. D: Dean Hargrove. COM [PG] 80m.

Manchurian Avenger, The 1984 ★★½ A young Asian-American returns home to Colorado from a trip to the Far East. When he discovers his town has been marauded, he goes after the perpetrators. Typical martial arts stuff. C: Bob Kim, Bill Wallace. ACT [R] 87m. V

Manchurian Candidate, The 1962 ★★★★½ Decorated Korean War hero returns home to monstrous mother who maneuvers him to kill her demagogue husband's political rival. Riveting political espionage thriller brilliantly handled by director. High-tension acting by Sinatra. Adapted from Richard Condon's spine-chilling novel. C: Frank Sinatra, Laurence Harvey, Janet Leigh, Angela Lansbury, Henry Silva, James Gregory, Khigh Deigh. D: John Frankenheimer. DRA [PG-13] 127m. V

Mandalay 1934 ★★★★ Steamy, delightful glamourfest, strikingly directed. An ultrachic woman (Francis) abandoned by her gunrunner lover is forced to scheme her way out of Rangoon as a notorious hostess, but is redeemed on a boat to Mandalay by a loving doctor. Great scenes: Kay's entrances at the prefect's office and as "Spot White," and the climactic murder. C: Kay Francis, Lyle Talbot, Warner Oland, Raffaela Ottiano, Ruth Donnelly. D: Michael Curtiz. CRI 65m.

Mandarin Mystery, The 1937 ★★½ Routine, unabsorbing mystery involves a valuable stolen stamp and a killing that somehow took place in a locked room. Unusual casting of diminutive, nervous, fast-talking comic Quillan as brilliant sleuth Ellery Queen. C: Eddie Quillan, Charlotte Henry, Rita Le Roy, Wade Boteler, Franklin Pangborn, George Irving. D: Ralph Staub. CRI 63m.

Mandela 1987 ★★★½ The politics are partisan and the filmmaking is sometimes pedestrian, but Glover and Woodard are compelling in this biography about the South African resistance leader and his struggle against apartheid. C: Danny Glover, Alfre Woodard, John Matshikiza, Warren Clarke. D: Philip Saville. DRA 135m. TVM V

Mandela in America 1990 ★★★★ A comprehensive look at Nelson Mandela's unforgettable tour throughout the United States. Includes interviews with Mandela, President George Bush and many others. DOC 90m. V

Mandela—The Man And His Country 1990 ★★★★ An in-depth study of the factors involved in Nelson Mandela's life—after being released from 27 years in jail. Fascinating portrait of the man who woud become South Africa's first black president. DOC 50m. V

Mandingo 1975 ★ A pre-Civil War plantation contains lust, cruelty and ghastly melodrama in equal doses in this story of a prizefighting slave. Watch for former heavyweight boxing champ Ken Norton in a rare acting role. Followed by a sequel. C: James Mason, Susan George, Perry King, Ken Norton. D: Richard Fleischer. DRA [R] 127m. V

Mandrake 1979 ★★★ When a madman blackmails a tycoon after framing him as responsible for deaths on rollercoasters, it's Mandrake the Magician to the rescue. Acceptable effort brings comic strip hero's antics to the small screen with some panache. C: Anthony Herrera, Simone Griffeth, Ji-Tu Cumbuka, Gretchen Corbett, Peter Haskell, Robert Reed. D: Harry Falk. ACT 100m. TVM

Mandroid 1993 ★★★ Two scientist build a giant of a robot. But one of the scientists steals their invention—and turns it into a killer. A little scary, a little silly. C: Brian Cousins, Jane Caldwell, Michael Dellafemina, Curt Lowers, Patrich Ersgard, Costel Constanin, Robert Symonds. D: Jack Ersgard. SFI 81m. V

Mandy *See* **Crash of Silence**

Maneater 1969 *See* **Shark!**

Maneater 1973 ★★★½ Slightly over-the-top but undeniably entertaining adventure as a crazed trainer sets his tigers onto four vacationing guests. Basehart may be a rude host but he, Gazzara, and good cast sink their teeth into roles in a manner even those hungry cats could respect. C: Ben Gazzara, Sheree North, Kip Niven, Laurette Spang, Richard Basehart, Claire Brennan. D: Vince Edwards. DRA 78m.

Manfish 1956 ★★½ Three men have a falling out while searching for buried treasure in Jamaica. Spiritless melodrama fails to capture the mood and irony of Edgar Allan Poe story *The Gold Bug* which inspired it. C: John Bromfield, Lon Chaney, Victor Jory, Barbara Nichols. D: W. Lee Wilder. DRA 76m.

Manganinnie 1980 Australian ★★★½ Two lost young girls, one white, the other an older Australian Aborigine, try to find their way through the Outback. Concept has merits, as does presentation, with appealing youths and cinematography, but the result is somewhat undramatic and meandering. C: Mawuyul Yanthalawuy, Anna Ralph, Phillip Hinton, Elaine Mangan. D: John Honey. DRA 90m.

Mangler, The 1995 ★★ Almost laughable horror flick in which the villain is—yes—a steam iron, albeit a huge, metal one, terrorizing a New England laundry plant. Adapted from a Stephen King story, but something got lost in the rinse cycle. C: Robert Englund, Ted Levine, Vanessa Pike, Daniel Matmor. D: Tobe Hooper. HOR [R] 105m. V

Mango Tree, The 1977 Australian ★★★½ A 17-year-old (Pate) comes of age in Australia during WWI. Pictorially excellent, with fine music and splendid performances by Helpmann as the town drunk and especially Fitzgerald as the wise grandmother. Important plot developments come far too late, though. C: Christopher Pate, Geraldine Fitzgerald, Robert Helpmann, Gerald Kennedy. D: Kevin Dobson. DRA 92m. V

Manhandled 1949 ★★★ Lamour tries film noir as a secretary who gets involved in a jewel heist and murder while working for a villainous psychiatrist. Convoluted plot, slow direction don't help, but the opening dream sequence is nifty, as is Duryea's signature menace. C: Dorothy Lamour, Dan Duryea, Sterling Hayden, Irene Hervey, Philip Reed. D: Lewis R. Foster. CRI 97m.

Manhandlers, The 1973 ★★ A young woman inherits her dead uncle's massage parlor. She soon realizes that it's a front for some nasty mob business. C: Cara Burgess, Henry Brandon, Judy Brown, Rosalind Miles. D: Lee Madden. DRA [R] 87m. V

Manhattan 1979 ★★★★★ Allen's love song to his favorite city, which has never looked more beautiful in glossy black and white. The story concerns a New York comedy writer's friends and their transitory loves, but it's the romantic mood and Gershwin score that you'll remember. C: Woody Allen, Diane Keaton, Michael Murphy, Mariel Hemingway, Meryl Streep. D: Woody Allen. DRA [R] 95m. V

Manhattan Baby 1983 ★★½ On a trip to Egypt with her parents, a young girl discovers that she has strange powers: she can kill people with her thoughts. Low level horror stuff. C: Christopher Connelly, Martha Taylor. D: Lucio Fulci. HOR 90m. V

Manhattan Madness 1936 *See* **Adventure in Manhattan**

Manhattan Melodrama 1934 ★★★★ Two slum boys grow to adulthood and stay pals although one is a fighting D.A. and the other a sentimental gangster. Hearty '30s entertainment with lively cast and dynamic direction. C: Clark Gable, William Powell, Myrna Loy, Leo Carrillo, Isabel Jewell, Mickey Rooney, Nat Pendleton. D: W. S. Van Dyke II. CRI 94m. V

Manhattan Merry-Go-Round 1937 ★★★ Racketeers take over a recording studio and strong-arm the musical talent into performing. Exceedingly thin plotting, carried mostly by frantic dialect comedians, is excuse for grab-bag revue. Nice to see Calloway, Autry, and others. And DiMaggio sings! C: Phil Regan, Ann Dvorak, Leo Carrillo, James Gleason, Gene Autry, Cab Calloway, Joe DiMaggio. D: Charles Riesner. MUS 80m. V

Manhattan Murder Mystery 1993 ★★★★ The sudden death of a neighbor's wife convinces Keaton there's murder afoot, dragging her neurotic husband (Allen) into an investigation to prove her suspicions. Very funny mystery comedy, livened by Woody's wisecracks and Keaton's hysterical performance. C: Woody Allen, Diane Keaton, Anjelica Huston, Alan Alda. D: Woody Allen. COM [PG] 107m.

Manhattan Project, The 1986 ★★★½ A brilliant teenager breaks into a restricted government plant where he steals enough plutonium to build his own nuclear reactor. Plays fast-and-loose with serious matters, but moves quickly and tingles with suspense throughout. C: John Lithgow, Christopher Collet, Cynthia Nixon, Timothy Carhart, John Mahoney. D: Marshall Brickman. DRA [PG-13] 120m. V

Manhunt for Claude Dallas 1986 ★★★ A fiercely independent mountain man kills two Idaho Fish & Game officers, is hunted and imprisoned, only to escape on Easter Sunday 1986. Fact-based drama. C: Matt Salinger, Claude Akins, Lois Nettleton, Rip Torn, Pat Hingle. D: Jerry London. CRI 93m. TVM V

Manhunt in the Jungle 1958 ★★ An explorer mysteriously disappears in 1928 while searching for an ancient white civilization in the Amazon, so fellow commander sets out to find him. Interesting location shooting. C: Robin Hughes, Luis Alvarez, James Wilson, Jorge Montoro, John B. Symmes. D: Tom McGowan. ACT 79m.

Manhunt: Search for the Night Stalker 1989 ★★★ Based-on-fact movie finds L.A. detectives Frank Salerno and Gil Carrillo tracking serial killer Richard Ramirez, the "Night Stalker." Decent cast does well; some of the details of police work are interesting. C: Richard Jordan, A. Martinez, Lisa Eilbacher, Julie Carmen, Jenny Sullivan. D: Bruce Seth Green. ACT 100m. TVM

Manhunt, The 1986 Italian ★★ A man buys horses, is accosted for trespassing and accused of theft when he tries to water them. Routine chases ensue. The Duke's son and the direction are stiff as a board. C: John Ethan Wayne, Raymund Harmstorf, Henry Silva, Bo Svenson, Ernest Borgnine. D: Larry Ludman. WST [R] 83m. V

Manhunter 1974 ★★★½ Former WWI Marine turns bounty hunter during Great Depression and sets out after bank robbers who murdered his girlfriend. Howard makes a suitable hero in this watchable movie which inspired a TV series. Good period atmosphere. C: Ken Howard, Gary Lockwood, Tim O'Connor, Stefanie Powers. D: Walter Grauman. ACT 78m. V

Manhunter 1983 ★★½ Frank Challenge, a master spy goes off to bust a dangerous and corrupt political ring. Average adventure and characters. C: Earl Owensby. D: Earl Owensby. ACT 92m. V

Manhunter 1986 ★★★★ FBI agent Peterson follows the trail of a vile serial murderer by learning to think like the killer. A truly disturbing thriller, sleekly packaged by Mann. Based on novel *Red Dragon* by Thomas Harris, whose *Silence of the Lambs* character Hannibal Lecter makes a creepy supporting cast appearance. C: William L. Petersen, Kim Greist, Joan Allen, Brian Cox, Dennis Farina, Stephen Lang, Tom Noonan. D: Michael Mann. CRI [R] 120m. V

Manhunter, The 1976 ★★★ A big-game hunter becomes involved with the wife of the bank robbery suspect he's been hired to track through the swampy Louisiana bayou. Competent cast goes through fairly routine paces. C: Sandra Dee, Roy Thinnes, William Smith, David Brian, Madlyn Rhue, Albert Salmi, Al Hirt. D: Don Taylor. ACT 98m.

Mania 1959 *See* **Flesh and the Fiends, The**

Maniac 1934 ★★★ Title doesn't do Esper half justice. An aberration of the Depression era, this unique, extremely low-budget shocker has the title character fill in for a crazed doctor after he kills him. Must be seen to be believed, especially the women's campy catfight with hypo needles. Now now, ladies! C: Bill Woods, Horace Carpenter, Ted Edwards, Phyllis Diller. D: Dwain Esper. HOR 51m. v

Maniac 1963 British ★★★½ An escaped lunatic menaces the neighborhood with a handy blowtorch, and an artist on vacation is just in time for the show! Offbeat psychological thriller has some lurid, unpredictable developments. No masterpiece, but pretty watchable. C: Kerwin Mathews, Nadia Gray, Donald Houston. D: Michael Carreras. HOR 86m. v

Maniac! 1978 ★★ A lunatic tries to blackmail a corrupt millionaire (Whitman) by threatening to kill lots of people, so what does the victim do? Hire a hit man, of course. Some truly frightening sequences amidst a lot of foolishness. (a.k.a. *Ransom*) C: Oliver Reed, Deborah Raffin, Stuart Whitman, Jim Mitchum. D: Richard Compton. ACT [PG] 90m. v

Maniac 1981 ★ A madman dresses up his mannequin collection with scalps from his murder victims. Wouldn't discount wigs have been easier? Intense atmosphere dissipates due to murky, deadening script. Lots of gore. C: Joe Spinell, Caroline Munro. D: William Lustig. HOR [R] 88m. v

Maniac Cop 1988 ★★ A demented cop turns killer on the streets of New York. First in a series, with plenty of violence. C: Tom Atkins, Bruce Campbell, Laurene Landon, Richard Roundtree, William Smith, Sheree North. D: William Lustig. HOR [R] 92m. v

Maniac Cop 2 1991 ★★★½ Superior slasher sequel finds the killer in blue on the loose again in New York City, joining forces with a sex-slayer (Rossi) against another cop (Davi). Clever scripting (by Larry Cohen) and action put this one a couple of notches above the first. C: Robert Davi, Claudia Christian, Bruce Campbell, Laurene Landon, Leo Rossi. D: William Lustig. HOR [R] 88m.

Maniac Cop 3: Badge of Silence 1993 ★★ The title villain contends with crooked cops and corrupt TV newsmen while protecting a comatose policewoman. Some new characters (although Bruce Campbell dropped out on this one), but little new inspiration. C: Robert Davi, Catlin Dulany, Jackie Earle Haley, Caitlin Dulany, Gretchen Becker, Robert Forster. D: William Lustig, Joel Soisson. HOR [R] 86m.

Maniac Warriors 1992 ★ A futuristic clan of raiders venture to Idaho where they intend to annihilate the "lards" (diseased creatures who steal blood). Pretty weird stuff. C: Melanie Kilgour, Thom Schioler. D: Lloyd Simandl. SFI 90m. v

Manifesto 1988 ★★★★½ Bleak yet often hilarious, insightful film, set in the '20s, about bohemian community's interest in political, sexual revolutions, and forces within and outside holding them back. Typical of Makavejev's freewheeling stylistics, fragmented narration, and bold discussion of ideas. Not his best but challenging; more relevant than ever with breakup of Yugoslavia. C: Camilla Soeberg, Alfred Molina, Simon Callow, Eric Stoltz, Lindsay Duncan, Rade Serbedzija, Svetozar Svetkovic, Chris Haywood, Patrick Godfrey, Linda Marlowe, Ronald Lacey. D: Dusan Makavejev. COM [R] 96m.

Manila Calling 1942 ★★★½ An entertainer, a telephone engineer, and a group leader form a guerrilla unit and keep fighting after the Japanese invasion of Mindanao by setting up a shortwave radio station. Script and direction are too flat and "gung ho," but the acting and grim finale are potent. C: Lloyd Nolan, Carole Landis, Cornel Wilde, James Gleason, Martin Kosleck, Ralph Byrd, Elisha Cook Jr., Louis Jean Heydt. D: Herbert J. Leeds. ACT 81m.

Manions of America, The 1981 ★★★★ Chronicle of two families—one British, one Irish—who emigrate to America, focusing on rebellious Irish youth Brosnan and his rise to success. This miniseries contains some soap opera elements, but remains focused and absorbing. C: Pierce Brosnan, Kate Mulgrew, Linda Purl, David Soul. D: Joseph Sargent, Charles S. Dubin. DRA 290m. TVM

Manipulator, The 1971 ★★★ Upon retiring, a Hollywood makeup man kidnaps a beautiful young starlet and takes her to a deserted sound stage. Interstng oddball cast and a story that works. C: Mickey Rooney, Luana Anders, Keenan Wynn. D: Yabo Yablonsky. ACT 91m. v

Manitou, The 1978 ★★ Strasberg is horrified to discover that an ancient Indian shaman's head has sprouted out of her neck. Sure-fire bomb of a plot idea produces a hilariously awful movie; worth a star for laughs. C: Tony Curtis, Susan Strasberg, Michael Ansara, Ann Southern. D: William Girdler. HOR [PG] 104m. v

Mankillers 1987 ★ Twelve female prisoners are hired by the feds to exterminate an agent gone bad. High-concept high-camp film isn't very clever, instead is a waste of time. C: Edd Byrnes, Gail Fisher, Edy Williams, William Zipp. D: David A. Prior. CRI 90m. v

Mannequin 1937 ★★★★ A small-time woman falls for big-time money, as Crawford moves from crook's wife to clotheshorse and then falls in love with shipping tycoon Tracy. Crawford is excessive, but the film a delight nevertheless. C: Joan Crawford, Spencer Tracy, Alan Curtis, Ralph Morgan, Leo Gorcey, Elisabeth Risdon. D: Frank Borzage. DRA 95m. v

Mannequin 1987 ★★½ Possessed by an ancient Egyptian spirit, a store mannequin (Cattrall) comes to life and bewitches the poor schnook (McCarthy) who knows her secret. Weak modern attempt at old-fashioned screwball comedy. Followed by a sequal. C: Andrew McCarthy, Kim Cattrall, Estelle Getty, G. W. Bailey. D: Michael Gottlieb. COM [PG] 90m. v

Mannequin Two: On the Move 1991 ★ Window-dresser's world is rocked when 1,000 year-old mannequin comes to life. Idiotic romantic comedy without a single laugh. C: Kristy Swanson, William Ragsdale, Meshach Taylor, Terry Kiser, Stuart Pankin. D: Stewart Raffill. COM 98m. V

Manny's Orphans 1978 ★★ Out of a job, a coach hires on at an orphanage. To get him out of a financial jam, the kids raise money by betting on themselves during baseball games. Basically, a low-rent version of *The Bad News Bears*. (a.k.a. *Here Come the Tigers*) C: Richard Lincoln, Samantha Grey, James Zvanut, Manny Lieberman. D: Sean S. Cunningham. COM [PG] 92m. V

Manon ★★★★ The New York City Opera rendition of the great opera. Manon, a hot-headed, jealous, selfish woman who gives up love for money. Outstanding production, fabulous Sills. C: Beverly Sills, Henry Price, Richard Fredricks, Samuel Ramey. MUS 152m. V

Manon 1982 ★★★★ The Royal Ballet's rendition of the sad tale of a greedy woman and her heartless approach to love. Excellent and beautiful. C: Jennifer Penney, Anthony Dowell, David Wall, Derek Rencher, Royal Ballet. MUS 120m. V

Manon of the Spring 1987 French ★★★★½ Sequel to *Jean de Florette* has even better characterizations in its story of hunchback's grown-up daughter (Beart) and her effect on the men who ruined her late father. Beart is exquisite, Auteil and Montand outstanding. C: Yves Montand, Emmanuelle Beart, Daniel Auteuil, Hippolyte Girardot, Elisabeth Depardieu. D: Claude Berri. DRA 113m.

Manpower 1941 ★★★★ Two power-line repairmen (Robinson and Raft) vie for a nightclub hostess (Dietrich). Two-fisted, high-voltage melodrama with memorable diner scene. C: Edward G. Robinson, Marlene Dietrich, George Raft, Alan Hale, Walter Catlett, Frank McHugh, Eve Arden. D: Raoul Walsh. DRA 105m.

Man's Best Friend 1985 ★★★ Eight hilarious cartoons featuring Woody Woodpecker, Andy Panda, Cuddles, Strong Nose, Snoozer and friends from the animal kingdom. Lots of fun. D: Walter Lantz, Tex Avery. FAM/COM 51m. V

Man's Best Friend 1993 ★★★½ A killer attack dog, the product of genetic experiments by evil Henriksen, escapes and is adopted by Sheedy with predictable and violent results. Interesting premise receives pedestrian treatment, but with occasional flashes of quirky humor. C: Ally Sheedy, Lance Henriksen, Frederic Lehre, Robert Costanzo. D: John Laha. ACT 87m.

Man's Castle 1933 ★★★★ Poverty-stricken Young moves into macho mug Tracy's East River shanty and together they cope with the Depression. Touching, soulful romance, if a bit dated. Fine performances by the leads. C: Spencer Tracy, Loretta Young, Marjorie Rambeau, Arthur Hohl, Walter Connolly, Glenda Farrell, Dickie Moore. D: Frank Borzage. DRA 66m.

Man's Favorite Sport? 1963 ★★★½ When sports columnist Hudson is entered into a fishing competition, he must somehow hide the fact that he's never gone fishing in his life. Good, slapstick comedy. C: Rock Hudson, Paula Prentiss, John McGiver, Maria Perschy, Charlene Holt. D: Howard Hawks. COM 121m. V

Man's Hope 1939 French, Spanish ★★★★ A Loyalist air squadron during the Spanish Civil War needs a peasant's assistance to take out an enemy bridge. Adapted by Malraux from his novel *Espoir*, the film was shot in Spain during the war and smuggled into France where it wasn't released until 1948. Dramatic combination of actual combat footage and compelling story make a strong anti-war statement. (a.k.a. *Espoir* and *Days of Hope*). C: Majuto, Nicolas Rodriguez, Jose Lado. D: Andre Malraux. DRA 78m.

Mansfield Park 1986 ★★★½ Film version of Jane Austen's novel of a young woman in 18th century England. Stunning locations work and a fine cast make it special. C: Anna Massey, Bernard Hepton, Angela Pleasence. D: David Giles. DRA 261m. V

Mansion of the Doomed 1977 ★★½ Fiendish eye surgeon recruits various "donors" to get fresh eyes for his newly blinded daughter. Low-budget shocks and sockets. C: Richard Basehart, Gloria Grahame, Trish Stewart, Lance Henriksen, Al Ferrara. D: Michael Pataki. HOR 85m.

Manson 1976 ★★★★½ Documentary about cult leader Charles Manson, his "family," and their trial for a series of gruesome murders. Chilling Oscar-nominated documentary looks into the mind of the disturbed, charismatic Manson and the young women who view him as a messiah. DOC [R] 83m. V

Manulescu 1933 ★★★½ A debonair master jewel thief Manulescu (Petrovicz) heads to the Riviera after a spell in jail, only to be nabbed again for his quick fingers. Light drama caper. C: Ivan Petrovicz, Ellen Richter, Mady Christians. D: W. Wolff. DRA 78m.

Manxman, The 1929 British ★★★½ A fisherman presumed dead returns to find his girlfriend involved with his best friend. Austere British romantic-melodrama; Hitchcock's last silent. C: Carl Brisson, Malcolm Keen, Anny Ondra, Randle Ayrton. D: Alfred Hitchcock. DRA 90m. V

Many Faces of Sherlock Holmes, The 1986 ★★★ A compelling study of the super British sleuth, narrated by those who portrayed Holmes (such as the great Basil Rathbone) on film throughout the years. There's even a rare interview with Holmes's creator, Arthur Conan Doyle. A must for Holmes aficianados. DOC 58m. V

Many Happy Returns 1934 ★★★ Allen's father arranges to have Burns marry her, to take her (and her comically destructive ways) as far away as possible. Weak screwball vehicle that tried to capitalize on its stars' popularity. C: Guy Lombardo, Gracie Allen, George Burns. D: Norman McLeod. COM 62m.

Many Happy Returns 1986 ★★★ A middle-class taxpayer (Segal) is stunned when he's hit by an IRS audit. Okay sitcom-style comedy. C: George Segal, Ron Liebman, Helen Shaver. D: Steven H. Stern. COM 104m. TVM

Many Rivers to Cross 1955 ★★★½ A frontier sharpshooter (Parker) sets her sights on a marriage-shy trapper (Taylor). Cheery, energetic Western with a deft blend of action and comedy. C: Robert Taylor, Eleanor Parker, Victor McLaglen, James Arness, Josephine Hutchinson, Rosemary DeCamp. D: Roy Rowland. WST 92m.

Many Thanks to Mr. Atkins 1938 ★★★ A bumbling soldier (Purdell) invents a revolutionary new army tank engine and must then scramble to keep it out of the hands of spies. Fast-paced British farce. C: Reginald Purdell, Claude Holbert, Barbara Greene. D: Roy William Neill. COM 68m.

Map of the Human Heart 1993 British, French, Australian, Canadian ★★★★½ Highly unusual work about an Eskimo who leaves his childhood village and ultimately becomes an airplane pilot. Unexpected developments and often enigmatic approach to material give the film an almost dream-like feel. Great performances from a very talented ensemble cast. C: Jason Scott Lee, Anne Parillaud, Patrick Bergin, John Cusack, Robert Joamie, Annie Galipeau, Jeanne Moreau, Ben Mendelson, Clotilde Courau. D: Vincent Ward. DRA [R] 126m.

Mara Maru 1952 ★★★½ A salvage diver (Flynn) in the Philippines retrieves sunken treasure and battles Burr, who wants it too. Star outing for Flynn. C: Errol Flynn, Ruth Roman, Raymond Burr, Richard Webb, Nestor Paiva. D: Gordon Douglas. ACT 98m.

Mara of the Wilderness 1965 ★★★½ A man tries to "civilize" a young woman bred in the wild North country. Moderately entertaining. C: Adam West, Linda Saunders, Theo Marcuse, Denver Pyle, Sean McClory. D: Frank McDonald. DRA 90m.

Maracaibo 1958 ★★★½ An ace oil-well firefighter battles a conflagration in Venezuela and runs into a former flame. Story wanders a bit but good action sequences. C: Cornel Wilde, Jean Wallace, Abbe Lane, Francis Lederer, Michael Landon. D: Cornel Wilde. ACT 88m.

Marat/Sade (Persecution and Assassination of Jean-Paul Marat Performed by the Inmates of the Asylum of Charenton Under the Direction of The Marquis de Sade) 1966 British ★★★★½ Sade (Magee) directs a "performance" starring French insane-asylum inmates. Brilliant filming of Peter Weiss' revolutionary play; lurid, violent, and profane. Jackson's debut in a starring role. C: Patrick Magee, Clifford Rose, Glenda Jackson, Ian Richardson, Brenda Kempner, Ruth Baker, Michael Williams, Freddie Jones. D: Peter Brook. DRA 115m. V

Marathon 1980 ★★★ A middle-aged married man's yen for a younng runner inspires him to change his jogging habits. Lackluster silliness has some laughs. C: Bob Newhart, Leigh Taylor-Young, Herb Edelman, Dick Gautier, John Hillerman. D: Jackie Cooper. COM 97m. TVM V

Marathon Man 1976 ★★★★ Track star Hoffman is caught in web inadvertently created by spy brother Scheider, involving Nazi Olivier. Powerful thriller with a famous "dentist" scene. Olivier's diamond-district sequence is justifiably considered a classic. Scripted by William Goldman, from his novel. C: Dustin Hoffman, Laurence Olivier, Roy Scheider, William Devane, Marthe Keller, Fritz Weaver. D: John Schlesinger. ACT [R] 125m. V

Marauders, The 1947 ★★★ Boyd and his crusty sidekick Clyde intervene in a battle between a minister and an outlaw in this late Hopalong Cassidy installment, complete with comic book violence and comic relief. WST V

Marauders, The 1955 ★★★ Cattle barons hire gunslingers to force out homesteaders. Adequate Western; familiar theme. C: Dan Duryea, Jeff Richards, Keenan Wynn, Jarma Lewis. D: Gerald Mayer. WST 81m.

Marbella 1985 Spanish ★★★ Caper film has Ekland and boyfriend ripping off tycoon in title resort town. C: Rod Taylor, Britt Ekland. D: Miguel Hermoso. ACT 96m. V

Marcel Duchamp—A Game Of Chess 1963 ★★★★ A compelling look at the life and times of Marcel Duchamp, with special emphasis on his obsessions with art and chess. Intriguing. DOC 56m. V

March Hare, The 1956 British ★★★½ Cummins, the daughter of an Irish manor's new American owners, hires Morgan as a stable groom, unaware that he's the original heir to the estate. Pleasant drama set against beautiful Irish countryside. C: Peggy Cummins, Terence Morgan, Martita Hunt, Cyril Cusack, Wilfrid Hyde-White. D: George More O'Ferrall. DRA 85m.

March of the Wooden Soldiers, The 1934 *See* **Babes in Toyland**

March on Paris 1914 1977 ★★★★ Idiosyncratic, enjoyable fantasy based on the life of a WWI German general who tried to invade Paris but was foiled by a motley group of citizens. Mixture of contemporary and historical scenes, full of non sequiturs. Full title: *March on Paris 1914—of Generaloberst Alexander von Kluck—and His Memories of Jessie Holladay.* C: Wulf Gunther Brandes, Jessie Holladay Duane. D: Walter Gutman. COM 75m.

March or Die 1977 ★★★ Tougher-than-nails French Foreign Legioneer holds down the fort in Africa location. Sullen treatment keeps this one from taking off, despite some compelling elements. C: Gene Hackman, Terence Hill, Max Von Sydow, Catherine Deneuve, Ian Holm. D: Dick Richards. ACT [PG] 106m. V

Marching Out 1988 Poland ★★★★ A study of the violence and confusion that reigned in Poland during the period of 1914-1921. Special emphasis is placed on the nefarious Pilsudski legions. A detailed, interesting look at a time of troubles. In Polish. D: Wincenty Ronisz. DOC 108m. V

Marciano 1979 ★★★ The life of the great Rocky Marciano, the only major prizefighter to retire undefeated, is told in a lightweight vehicle with only moderate punch. C: Tony Lo Bianco, Belinda Montgomery, Vincent Gardenia, Richard Herd. D: Bernard Kowalski. DRA 97m. TVM V

Marco 1973 ★★★ Marco Polo (Arnaz, Jr.) journeys to the Orient, where Kublai Khan (Mostel) offers him the hand of his daughter. Frolicsome attempt to make a musical out of the Polo saga makes good use of Asian locations and lively Mostel. C: Desi Arnaz Jr., Jack Weston, Zero Mostel. D: Seymour Robbie. FAM/MUS [G] 109m. V

Marco Polo 1962 Italian ★★★ Polo saves the daughter of the Great Khan from bandits, and helps overthrow an evil prime minister. Italian-made retelling of the Polo story tries to keep things on a lighthearted level, with Calhoun passable but ordinary in the lead. C: Rory Calhoun, Yoko Tani, Robert Hundar, Camillo Pilotto, Pierre Cressoy, Michael Chow. D: Hugo Fregonese. DRA 90m.

Marco the Magnificent 1965 ★★½ Bloated international attempt to create an epic version of the Polo saga sinks instead. Continuity is thrown to the winds thanks to jagged editing of sequences shot by different crews in different countries. Welles has a small role in heavy makeup, amongst a stellar cast. C: Noel Howard, Horst Buchholz, Anthony Quinn, Omar Sharif, Elsa Martinelli, Akim Tamiroff, Orson Welles. D: Denys De La Patelliere. DRA 100m.

Marcus-Nelson Murders, The 1973 ★★★★½ A police lieutenant aids a black youth falsely charged with murder by unethical cops. Tense police drama introduced Savalas as Kojak, and won Emmy awards for director Sargent and writer Abby Mann. Based on a real-life case. C: Telly Savalas, Marjoe Gortner, Jose Ferrer, Ned Beatty, Allen Garfield, Lorraine Gary, Gene Woodbury, Chita Rivera. D: Joseph Sargent. DRA 148m. TVM

Marcus Welby, M.D. 1969 ★★★½ Old-fashioned doctor Welby suffers a coronary due to compulsive overworking, and consents to hire a young associate who turns out to be as stubborn as he is. Personality contrast makes up the basis for this pilot for the hugely successful TV show. C: Robert Young, James Brolin, Anne Baxter, Peter Duel, Susan Strasberg, Lew Ayres. D: David Lowell Rich. DRA 100m. TVM

Marcus Welby, M.D.: A Holiday Affair 1988 ★★★ Welby, now retired and vacationing in France, woos a divorcée away from a younger man. Veterans Young and Smith play well together, but don't expect much medical activity in this escapist romance. C: Robert Young, Alexis Smith, Craig Stevens, Delphine Forest, Robert Hardy, Betsy Blair. D: Steven Gethers. DRA 100m. TVM

Mardi Gras 1958 ★★★ In New Orleans, a military school cadet (Boone) wins a date with the queen of Mardi Gras (Carere). Pleasant, no-great-shakes musical. C: Pat Boone, Christine Carere, Tommy Sands, Sheree North. D: Edmund Goulding. MUS 107m.

Mardi Gras for the Devil 1993 ★★ Hardened cop (Davi) pursues demonic killer (Ironside), who strikes during carnival in New Orleans. Good supporting cast. C: Robert Davi, Michael Ironside, Lesley-Anne Down. D: David A. Prior. HOR 95m. V

Mardi Gras Massacre 1978 ★ Bottom-of-the-barrel trash about masked fiend who butchers naked women during carnival in New Orleans. Ineptly made, poorly acted, and grossly misogynist. C: Curt Dawson, Gwen Arment. D: Jack Weis. HOR 92m. V

Margaret Bourke-White 1989 ★★★½ Biography of famed *Life* photographer of the '30s, follows her career and her romance with author Erskine Caldwell. Fawcett and Forrest make a handsome couple, though Fawcett is not always convincing as the self-reliant photographer. C: Farrah Fawcett, Frederic Forrest, Mitchell Ryan, David Huddleston, Jay Patterson, Ken Marshall. D: Lawrence Schiller. DRA 105m. TVM

Margaret Mead And Samoa ★★★ Although Margaret Mead said that Polynesian culture is free of stress, Derek Freeman saw things entirely differently. His startling report of aggression and conflict is the basis of this compelling documentary. DOC 51m. V

Margie 1946 ★★★½ A shy '20s high school girl (Crain) tries to romance a handsome French teacher. Nostalgic musical fluff with swell performances, good tunes. C: Jeanne Crain, Glenn Langan, Lynn Bari, Esther Dale, Hobart Cavanaugh, Alan Young, Barbara Lawrence, Conrad Janis. D: Henry King. MUS 94m.

Margin for Error 1943 ★★★½ WWII-era comedy about a Jewish cop (Berle) whose assignment is to guard the German consul in New York. Uneven and dated adaptation of Broadway spoof has a few laughs, but the dialogue is a bit stagy and the direction overbearing. C: Joan Bennett, Milton Berle, Otto Preminger, Carl Esmond, Howard Freeman, Ed McNamara. D: Otto Preminger. COM 74m.

Margin for Murder 1981 ★★★ Mike Hammer investigates the murder of his best friend. Minor but decent effort. C: Kevin Dobson, Charles Hallahan, Cindy Pickett, Donna Dixon. D: Daniel Haller. CRI 95m. TVM V

Margot Fonteyn Story, The 1991 ★★★½ Portrait of one of the world's greatest ballerinas, spanning her forty-year career. Rare footage, candid interviews highlight the film. C: Margot Fonteyn. DOC 93m. TVM

Maria 1987 ★★★½ Interesting portrait of operatic legend Callas, as remembered by friends and colleagues. Great music, of course. C: Maria Callas. D: Tony Palmer. MUS 90m. TVM

Maria Chapdelaine 1949 *See* **Naked Heart, The**

Marianne 1929 ★★★★ Davies in her first sound movie plays a French girl courted by two American doughboys during WWI. Davies' comic flair—complete with fake French accent—translates well to sound in this early talkie with musical sequences. C: Marion Davies, George Baxter, Lawrence Gray, Cliff Edwards, Benny Rubin. D: Robert Z. Leonard. COM 112m.

Marianne and Juliane 1982 German ★★★★ The story of two sisters in West Germany during the 1980s: one an underground political subversive (Sukowa) and the other a feminist editor using more conventional tactics (Lampe). German film analyzes the similarities and differences between them in a way that is richly engrossing. Based on the true story of the Enselin sisters. C: Jutta Lampe, Barbara Sukowa, Rudiger Vogler, Doris Schade, Franz Rudnick. D: Margarethe von Trotta. DRA 106m.

Maria's Day 1984 Hungarian ★★★ After the revolution (in Hungary) of 1848, an aristocratic family tries to come to terms with life. Interesting and thoughtful. In Hungarian with subtitles. D: Judit Elek. DRA 113m. V

Maria's Lovers 1984 ★★★½ Coming home to Pennsylvania after WWII, a young soldier (Savage) suffers a nervous breakdown and faces difficulties in his new marriage. Lush production values and excellent performances lift a lugubrious plot. C: Nastassia Kinski, John Savage, Robert Mitchum, Keith Carradine, Anita Morris, Bud Cort, Karen Young. D: Andrei Konchalovsky. DRA [R] 103m. V

Marie 1985 ★★★★ Spacek plays Marie Ragghianti, a battered divorcée and mother who gets a job on the Tennessee parole board, and can't keep quiet about the corruption she discovers. True story features an impassioned and believable performance by Spacek. C: Sissy Spacek, Jeff Daniels, Keith Szarabajka, Morgan Freeman, John Cullum, Timothy Carhart. D: Roger Donaldson. DRA [PG-13] 113m. V

Marie Antoinette 1938 ★★★★ Shearer plays the Austrian princess who romances a Swedish count (Power) and eventually becomes the queen of France only to lose her head. The film set new standards for lavish budget and costuming at MGM. C: Norma Shearer, Tyrone Power, John Barrymore, Robert Morley, Gladys George, Joseph Schildkraut. D: W.S. Van Dyke II. DRA 149m. V

Marie Antoinette 1955 French ★★★ Morgan plays the woman who rose to prominence in the French court of Louis XVI, whose disdain for the masses led to her beheading. Despite a winning performance by Morgan and handsome staging and costuming, this slow-moving tale lacks a fresh approach to the material. C: Michele Morgan, Richard Todd, Jean Morel. D: Jean Delannoy. DRA 108m.

Marie Galante 1934 ★★★ French woman (Gallian) stuck in the Panama Canal zone becomes entangled with an adventurer (Tracy) as they try to foil an international plot to destroy the famous waterway. Fair drama marked by top-notch performances. C: Spencer Tracy, Ketti Gallian, Ned Sparks, Helen Morgan, Sig Rumann, Leslie Fenton, Jay C. Flippen, Stepin Fetchit. D: Henry King. DRA 88m.

Marigold 1938 British ★★★½ In 1842, a strong-willed young woman (Stewart) defies her family by traveling to Edinburgh to see Queen Victoria, and falls in love with a guard. Early feminist sensibility ably handled. C: Sophie Stewart, Patrick Barr, Phyllis Dare, Edward Chapman. D: Thomas Bentley. DRA 74m.

Marigolds in August 1980 ★★★★ A black gardener (Ntshona), a manual laborer (Kani), and a white poacher (Fugard) are brought together by chance and learn they must work together to solve their problems. Drama oversimplifies the apartheid issue, but is a notable achievement nonetheless. C: Winston Nishona, John Lamo, Athol Fugard. D: Ross Devenish. DRA 87m. TVM

"Marihuana" 1936 ★★ Cautionary tale about a naive girl who attends a wild party, puffs some weed, and presto! turns into a heroin-addicted prostitute. Exploitation film credits factual research to federal, state, and local police. The result is high-camp that's unintentionally funny. C: Harley Wood, Hugh McArthur, Pat Carlyle, Paul Ellis, Dorothy Dehn, Richard Erskine. D: Dwain Esper. DRA 57m. V

Marijuana 1937 *See* **Assassin of Youth**

Marilyn 1963 ★★★½ Documentary on the life of Marilyn Monroe made shortly after her death, with narration by Rock Hudson. Superficial, fan-magazine-style bio has immediacy, but few facts. DOC 83m.

Marilyn Monroe—Beyond the Legend 1985 ★★★★ A real life look at Marilyn, less as a movie star and more as a human being. It includes lots of fascinating footage from her everyday life and interviews with people who knew her well. Gripping and ultimately quite tragic. DOC 60m. V

Marilyn—Say Goodbye to the President 1985 ★★★★ The BBC put together this comprehensive look at the death of superstar actress Marilyn Monroe. All of the suspicions are aired and discussed in depth. DOC 71m. v

Marilyn: The Untold Story 1980 ★★★★ Adaptation of Norman Mailer's biography of Marilyn Monroe features a dynamic, Emmy-nominated performance by Hicks. This version really makes an effort to get behind the myths and look at the traumatic life experiences of Monroe. C: Catherine Hicks, Richard Basehart, Frank Converse, John Ireland, Viveca Lindfors, Jason Miller, Sheree North, Bill Vint, Anne Ramsey. D: John Flynn, Jack Arnold, Lawrence Schiller. DRA 150m. TVM

Marine Issue 1986 *See* **Instant Justice**

Marine Raiders 1944 ★★★ Marines train then hit the beach—and the jungles—at Guadalcanal. Standard RKO flagwaver with consummate heroes (O'Brien, Ryan, and MacLane) and Hussey providing the romantic interest. C: Pat O'Brien, Robert Ryan, Ruth Hussey, Frank McHugh, Barton MacLane. D: Harold D. Schuster. DRA 91m. v

Marines, Let's Go 1961 ★★½ A quartet of soldiers on leave in Tokyo. Poorly constructed Korean war narrative blends comedy with tense battle action. Not the best effort from director Walsh. C: Tom Tryon, David Hedison, Barbara Stuart, William Tyler. D: Raoul Walsh. DRA 104m.

Mario Puzo's "The Fortunate Pilgrim" 1988 ★★★★ Adaptation of Puzo's expansive tale of an Italian immigrant family who try to make a new life for themselves in turn-of-the-century New York. The miniseries elicits a dynamic performance by Loren as family matriarch, while providing authentic atmosphere. C: Sophia Loren, Edward James Olmos, Hal Holbrook, John Turturro, Anna Strasberg, Yorgo Voyagis, Roxann Biggs, Ed Wiley, Mirjana Karanovic, Ron Marquette, Annabella Sciorra. D: Stuart Cooper. DRA 250m. TVM

Marion Rose White 1982 ★★★½ The story of a teenager wrongly committed as retarded to a state asylum in the '30s. Worthy treatment of subject matter. C: Nancy Cartwright, Charles Anderson. D: Joseph Sargent, Robert Day. DRA

Marius 1931 French ★★★★ Engaging study of French working class, which focuses on the son of a Marseilles café owner who gives up his girlfriend in order to go to sea. Humanity of the characters comes through strongly under Korda's realistic direction. First of a trilogy by Marcel Pagnol that later became the musical *Fanny*. C: Raimu, Pierre Fresnay, Charpin, Orane Demazis. D: Alexander Korda. DRA 125m. v

Marjoe 1972 ★★★★ Oscar-winning documentary traces the evangelical career of one-time child prodigy preacher Marjoe Gortner. Cinema verité style captures the electric atmosphere of revival meetings, and vividly demonstrates the effect charismatic Gortner had on worshippers. D: Howard Smith, Sarah Kernochan. DOC [PG] 88m. v

Marjorie Morningstar 1958 ★★★½ Young New York woman aspires to stardom, but after a summer romance settles for contentment as a housewife. Superficial soap opera given stuffy treatment. From Herman Wouk's book. C: Gene Kelly, Natalie Wood, Claire Trevor, Ed Wynn, Everett Sloane, Carolyn Jones. D: Irving Rapper. DRA 123m. v

Mark, I Love You 1980 ★★★½ A widower (Dobson) wages a bitter custody battle with his late wife's parents over his 10-year-old son. Fair effort, based on a real life story, in one of the first explorations of the subject. DRA

Mark of Cain 1986 ★★½ After escaping from an insane asylum, a psychotic passes himself for his twin brother. An old theme given new life. C: Robin Ward, Wendy Crewson, Cynthia Keneluk. D: Bruce Pittman. HOR 90m. v

Mark of the Beast ★★★½ After preparing a video of a public event, two communications students realize that they recorded the assassination of a public figure. Some harrowing happenings and high level excitement. C: James Gordon, Carolyn Guillet. D: Robert Stewart. ACT 90m. v

Mark of the Devil 1972 ★★ An 18th-century European judge (Lom) presides over torture of suspected witches. Notorious in its day for providing vomit bags to audiences, this is certainly unpleasant and graphic. For gore fans. C: Herbert Lom, Olivera Vuco, Reggie Nalder. D: Michael Armstrong. HOR [R] 96m. v

Mark of the Gorilla 1950 ★★½ Jungle Jim (Weissmuller) goes after Nazis who have disguised themselves as gorillas and kidnapped a native princess in their quest for buried gold. Far-fetched action jungle yarn is about average for the series. C: Johnny Weissmuller, Trudy Marshall, Suzanne Dalbert, Onslow Stevens, Selmer Jackson, Robert Purcell, Pierce Lyden. D: William Berke. ACT 68m.

Mark of the Hawk, The 1958 British ★★★ A Western-educated African (Poitier) returns to his homeland as a legislator and finds his nonviolent beliefs tested by racial strife. Engrossing sociopolitical drama. (a.k.a. *Accused*) C: Eartha Kitt, Sidney Poitier, Juano Hernandez, John McIntire. D: Michael Audley. DRA 85m. v

Mark of the Renegade 1951 ★★★½ A Mexican undercover agent in the 1820s (Montalban) is dispatched to prevent villain (Roland) from creating the separate State of California, while romancing Charisse. Interesting view of early California features lavish costuming. C: Ricardo Montalban, Cyd Charisse, J. Carroll Naish, Gilbert Roland. D: Hugo Fregonese. ACT 81m.

Mark of the Scorpion ★★★ After taking a magical ring off the finger of a dead princess, a young man finds himself in one hair-raising episode after another. C: Andy J. Forest, Dannys Cone. ACT 90m. v

Mark of the Vampire 1935 ★★★★ This remake of Browning's 1927 *London After Midnight* combines horror with whodunit as it tells of a family mansion haunted by an undead Count (Lugosi) and his daughter (Borland). Playfully toying with haunted house cliches, the film consistently entertains and surprises. C: Lionel Barrymore, Elizabeth Allan, Bela Lugosi, Lionel Atwill, Carol Borland, Jean Hersholt. D: Tod Browning. HOR 61m. v

Mark of the Whistler 1944 ★★★★ Drifter (Dix) lays claim to an old bank account, leading two men to target him for revenge for a previous dispute their father had over the money. Absorbing mystery from *The Whistler* series, featuring tight plot development and atmospheric direction by Castle. Keeps one guessing right to the end. C: Richard Dix, Janis Carter, Porter Hall, Paul Guilfoyle, John Calvert. D: William Castle. CRI 61m.

Mark of Zorro, The 1920 ★★★★★ First and best of Fairbanks' silent adventure classics, with Doug as the legendary masked man, righting wrongs in 19th-century California. Fabulous duels, grand fun for all ages. Remade in 1940. C: Douglas Fairbanks Sr., Noah Beery, Marguerite De La Motte. D: Fred Niblo. ACT 90m. v

Mark of Zorro, The 1940 ★★★★½ Power is son of an aristocrat in 1820s California who becomes the masked avenger by night. Thrilling swashbuckler, with final duel between Rathbone and Power among the best sword fights ever filmed. C: Tyrone Power, Linda Darnell, Basil Rathbone, Gale Sondergaard, Eugene Pallette, J. Edward Bromberg. D: Rouben Mamoulian. DRA 93m. v

Mark of Zorro, The 1974 ★★★½ The foppish aristocrat (Langella) in 1820s California secretly dons a black mask at night to become the avenging swordsman with his trademark *Z* left as a signature. Presence of veterans Montalban and Roland adds flavor to this good version of the Zorro tale. C: Frank Langella, Ricardo Montalban, Gilbert Roland, Yvonne De Carlo, Louise Sorel, Anne Archer, Robert Middleton. D: Don McDougall. ACT 78m. TVM

Mark, The 1961 British ★★★★ Recently released from prison, a convicted sex offender must adjust to the outside, and the fact that he will be forever haunted and branded as a criminal despite his efforts to reform. Intelligent drama of a timely subject. Fine Whitman in an Oscar-nominated performance. C: Stuart Whitman, Maria Schell, Rod Steiger, Brenda De Banzie, Maurice Denham, Donald Wolfit, Paul Rogers, Donald Houston. D: Guy Green. DRA 127m. v

Mark Twain and Me 1991 Canadian ★★★★ Entertaining Disney production based on true story of young girl who became friends with an elderly Mark Twain. Good family entertainment; Robards' makeup as Twain is uncanny. C: Jason Robards, Talia Shire, R. H. Thomson, Fiona Reid, Amy Stewart. D: Daniel Petrie. FAM/DRA 93m. TVM v

Marked for Death 1990 ★★★ Formulaic action vehicle for Seagal, who portrays ex-DEA man protecting himself and family from evil Jamaican drug dealers. Appearance (and songs) by reggae star Jimmy Cliff and his band buoy the proceedings a bit. C: Steven Seagal, Basil Wallace, Keith David, Tom Wright, Joanna Pacula. D: Dwight H. Little. ACT [R] 93m. v

Marked for Murder 1989 ★★½ Two young employees at a TV station find themselves framed for murder—by their boss. C: Wings Hauser, Renee Estevez, Jim Mitchum. D: Rick Sloane. ACT [R] 88m. v

Marked Woman 1937 ★★★★ Gangster's moll (Davis) turns state's evidence against mob. Tough, gritty crime drama with strong performances. C: Bette Davis, Humphrey Bogart, Lola Lane, Isabel Jewell, Eduardo Ciannelli, Allen Jenkins. D: Lloyd Bacon. CRI 97m. v

Marketa Lazarova 1968 Czech ★★★★ The power of myth and superstition pervades this account of a legendary 13th-century Czech heroine (Vasaryova), set against the backdrop of internecine fighting among feudal lords. Stirring folk tale. C: Magda Vasaryova, Frantisek Velicky, Michal Kozuch. D: Frantisek Vlacil. DRA 180m.

Marksman, The 1953 ★★½ Leaders of a Western town hire an expert with a telescope-sight-equipped gun (Morris) to vanquish cattle rustling murderers. Slow-moving Western. C: Wayne Morris, Elena Verdugo, Frank Ferguson, Rick Vallin. D: Lewis D. Collins. WST 62m.

Marla Hanson Story, The 1991 ★★★ A rising fashion model suffers horrible disfigurement after being slashed in the face, and struggles to make a comeback. Movie is based on real events. C: Cheryl Pollak, Dale Midkiff, Kirk Baltz. D: John Gray. DRA 96m. TVM

Marlene 1986 German ★★★★★ Unusual—to say the least—documentary on film legend Marlene Dietrich by actor Maximilian Schell. Dietrich is only seen in film clips, but is heard on soundtrack being interviewed by Schell—when he can get her to answer his questions. Bewitching, revealing and always reverent of Dietrich's mystique. D: Maximilian Schell. DOC 97m. v

Marlowe 1969 ★★★★ Philip Marlowe (Garner) is hired by a mysterious woman to find her brother, although several people want him to drop the case. Fast-paced adaptation of Raymond Chandler is helped by Garner's self-deprecating wit. C: James Garner, Gayle Hunnicutt, Carroll O'Connor, Rita Moreno, Sharon Farrell, William Daniels, Jackie Coogan, Bruce Lee. D: Paul Bogart. CRI 95m. v

Marnie 1964 ★★★★ Connery tries to get

into the mind of kleptomaniac Hedren to find out why she has a predilection to steal. Unorthodox film for Hitchcock nonetheless has some of his trademarks, and enough intrigue to keep viewers involved. C: Sean Connery, Tippi Hedren, Diane Baker, Martin Gabel, Louise Latham, Bruce Dern. D: Alfred Hitchcock. DRA [PG] 130m. v

Maroc 7 1967 British ★★★ Secret agent (Barry) poses as a safecracker to apprehend a fashion magazine editor (Charisse) who operates a jewel smuggling racket. Scenic Moroccan locations boost otherwise mediocre caper story. C: Gene Barry, Elsa Martinelli, Cyd Charisse, Leslie Phillips. D: Gerry O'Hara. ACT 92m. v

Marooned 1969 ★★½ A ground control chief (Peck) must maintain the sanity of astronauts stranded in space while they wait for a rescue attempt to be launched. Blockbuster sci-fi yarn gets claustrophobic after a while. C: Gregory Peck, Richard Crenna, James Franciscus, David Janssen, Gene Hackman, Lee Grant, Nancy Kovack, Mariette Hartley. D: John Sturges. SFI [G] 134m. v

Marquise of O, The 1976 French ★★★★ During the Franco-Prussian war, an Italian widow rescued from rape finds herself pregnant. Atmospheric 18th-century settings and tender storytelling in this unassuming film. C: Edith Clever, Bruno Ganz, Peter Luhr, Edda Seippel, Otto Sander. D: Eric Rohmer. DRA [PG] 102m.

Marquise, The ★★★★ In 1735, aristocrats gather to celebrate the pending marriage of a duke's son. But a mysterious visitor has some things to say about it all. A sharp comedy delivered in Mr. Coward's inimitable style. C: Diana Rigg, Richard Johnson. COM 55m. v

Marriage, A 1983 ★★★½ A husband (Gitlin) remembers his courtship of high school sweetheart and their marriage as he's about to sign divorce papers. Low-budget drama nicely balances drama and humor. C: Ric Gitlin, Isabel Glasser. D: Sandy Tung. DRA 90m.

Marriage by Contract 1928 ★★★½ Dramatized attack on Judge Ben Lindsey's infamous theory of "companionate marriage" chronicles the unhappiness of a wife whose husband goes out with other women after their celibate honeymoon. Timely in its day, with a strong performance by Miller as the spurned wife. C: Patsy Ruth Miller, Lawrence Gray. D: James Flood. DRA 70m.

Marriage Circle, The 1924 ★★★★½ A comic bonbon in which an amorous bachelor flirts with danger in the form of two married women. Based on Lothar Schmidt's play *Only a Dream*. Lubitsch's genteel handling of the comedic situations of these well-mannered characters soon became known as "the Lubitsch touch." C: Florence Vidor, Monte Blue, Marie Prevost, Creighton Hale, Adolphe Menjou, Harry Myers, Dale Fuller, Esther Ralston. D: Ernst Lubitsch. COM 90m.

Marriage-Go-Round, The 1960 ★★★ Anthropology professor (Mason) finds his marriage imperiled by the arrival of a tall Swedish student (Newmar) who wants to have his baby. So-so adaptation of the Broadway hit delivers some laughs. C: Susan Hayward, James Mason, Julie Newmar, Robert Paige, June Clayworth. D: Walter Lang. COM 98m.

Marriage Is a Private Affair 1944 ★★★ Innocent girl (Turner) marries a soldier before he ships out, and in his absence she begins to seek the company of other men. Slick but empty showcase for Turner, who appears in virtually every scene glamorously gowned and coiffed. C: Lana Turner, James Craig, John Hodiak, Frances Gifford, Hugh Marlowe, Keenan Wynn. D: Robert Z. Leonard. DRA 116m.

Marriage Is Alive and Well 1979 ★★★ Three separate tales of marriage as viewed through the lens of a carefree wedding photographer (Namath). Simplistic sitcom look at marriages and relationships that aims for broad laughs. C: Joe Namath, Jack Albertson, Melinda Dillon, Judd Hirsch. D: Russ Mayberry. COM 97m. TVM v

Marriage Italian Style 1964 Italian ★★★★ Adventures of prostitute (Loren) and longtime lover (Mastroianni), and her attempts to get him to marry her. Pairing of two talented stars makes this film click; inconsequential but funny farce, ably directed by DeSica. C: Sophia Loren, Marcello Mastroianni, Aldo Puglisi, Pia Lindstrom, Vito Moriconi. D: Vittorio De Sica. COM 102m. v

Marriage of a Young Stockbroker, The 1971 ★★★ Stockbroker (Benjamin) becomes tired of his marriage, begins to stimulate himself through adult movies and mindless flirtations. Uneven comedy saved by Benjamin. C: Richard Benjamin, Joanna Shimkus, Elizabeth Ashley, Adam West, Patricia Barry, Tiffany Bolling. D: Lawrence Turman. DRA [PG] 95m.

Marriage of Balzaminov, The USSR ★★★ A Russian Walter Mitty (Vitsin) fantasizes about his life as a great lover, a general and the czar, but settles for marriage in real life to an ugly but rich widow. A bit strained, but an interesting comparison piece alongside Danny Kaye's *The Secret Life of Walter Mitty*. C: Georgiy Vitsin, Lyudmila Shagalova, Ye Savinova. D: Konstantin Voinov. COM 90m.

Marriage of Maria Braun, The 1979 German ★★★★★ Young German woman (Schygulla) advances herself in society during WWII. Metaphor for rise and decline of Germany is engrossing; Schygulla's performance is splendid, and Fassbinder creates a credible dissection of the nature of power. C: Hanna Schygulla, Ivan Desny, Gottfried John, Klaus Lowitsch. D: Rainer Werner Fassbinder. DRA [R] 120m. v

Marriage on the Rocks 1965 ★★★½ After a husband and wife (Sinatra and Kerr) secure a divorce in Mexico, she weds his best friend (Martin). "Rat Pack" taking on marriage leads to complications and misunderstandings, which result in pleasant but vacuous comedy. C: Frank Sinatra, Deborah Kerr, Dean Martin, Cesar Romero, Hermione Baddeley, Tony Bill, Nancy Sinatra, John McGiver, Trini Lopez. D: Jack Donohue. COM 109m.

Marriage Playground, The 1929 ★★★½ Rich expatriate Americans roam Europe looking for love and excitement while their daughter (Brian) stays home, takes care of her siblings, and falls for a kind American (March). Early talkie has good performance as well as historical interest. Adapted from Edith Wharton's *The Children*. C: Fredric March, Mary Brian, Kay Francis. D: Lothar Mendes. DRA 70m.

Marriage: Year One 1971 ★★★ Medical student (Pratt) marries headstrong heiress (Field) then insists that they live on his scant salary. Lightweight sitcom script already seems dated, though Field keeps things lively with a spunky performance. C: Sally Field, Robert Pratt, William Windom. D: William A. Graham. COM 104m. TVM

Married Bachelor 1941 ★★★½ A confirmed bachelor (Young) professes to be an expert on marriage in this predictable but amusing light comedy; Young and Hussey are engaging. C: Robert Young, Ruth Hussey, Felix Bressart, Sheldon Leonard, Sam Levene. D: Edward Buzzell. COM 87m.

Married Couple, A 1969 Canadian ★★★ Documentary-style examination of the disintegrating marriage of a copywriter and his wife. Interest lies in cinema verité approach, but suffers a bit from awkward narrative structure. C: Billy Edwards, Antoinette Edwards. D: Allan King. DRA 96m.

Married Man, A 1983 British ★★★½ A British barrister (Hopkins) cheats on his wife, then finds himself involved in murder. Overlong tale of drama amid British upper crust but Hopkins is always worth seeing. Originally shown as two-part TV miniseries. C: Anthony Hopkins, Ciaran Madden, Lise Hilboldt, Yvonne Coulette, John LeMesurier, Julian Sands. D: John Davies. DRA 190m. TVM V

Married People, Single Sex 1993 ★★ An in-depth look at a few married couples and their temptations regarding extramarital sexcapades. C: Chase Masterson, Josef Pilato, Darla Slavens, Wendi Westbrook. D: Mike Sedan. DRA [R] 90m. V

Married to It 1993 ★★ Three married couples—each a different pair of stereotypes—become friends in this bland Manhattan comedy. Lack of overriding plot kills it from the start. C: Beau Bridges, Stockard Channing, Robert Sean Leonard, Mary Stuart Masterson, Cybill Shepherd, Ron Silver. D: Arthur Hiller. COM [R] 112m. V

Married to the Mob 1988 ★★★★ The widow (Pfeiffer) of a mob hitman (Baldwin) wants to leave the Family, but the mob chief has eyes for her. Modine, as sympathetic FBI agent, is affecting and Pfeiffer enjoys her tough-cookie role, but ganglord Stockwell and jealous wife Ruehl steal the show. C: Michelle Pfeiffer, Matthew Modine, Dean Stockwell, Mercedes Ruehl, Alec Baldwin, Joan Cusack, Charles Napier, Tracey Walter, Al Lewis, Angela De Marco. D: Jonathan Demme. COM [R] 104m. V

Married Woman, A 1964 French ★★★½ Though married to a pilot (LeRoy) Parisianne (Meril) has a lover (Noel) on the side. She becomes pregnant and can't determine which one is the father. The situation provides a premise, not a plot, to explore character but this seems an ordinary outing for Godard, who appears less at home with middle-class subjects than he is with underground issues. C: Macha Meril, Philippe Leroy, Bernard Noel. D: Jean-Luc Godard. DRA 95m. V

Marry Me Again 1953 ★★★½ A woman comes into money while her fighter pilot fiancé (Cummings) is in Korea. Upon his return, he has trouble accepting a potential life of leisure, living off her money. Stylish direction gets plenty of mileage out of the plot. C: Robert Cummings, Marie Wilson, Mary Costa, Jess Barker. D: Frank Tashlin. COM 73m.

Marry Me, Marry Me 1969 French ★★★★ Parisian encyclopedia salesman (Berri) agrees to marry a pregnant woman, then promptly falls in love with an English tutor. Irresistible romantic comedy benefits from the delicate touches of director/writer/star Berri. C: Elisabeth Wiener, Regine, Claude Berri, Luisa Colpeyn. D: Claude Berri. COM [PG] 87m.

Marrying Kind, The 1952 ★★★½ A married couple (Holliday and Ray)—headed for divorce—reminisce about the ups and downs of their marriage. Performances of the two leads prevent comedy laced with sentiment from bogging down. C: Judy Holliday, Aldo Ray, Madge Kennedy, Mickey Shaughnessy, Griff Barnett. D: George Cukor. COM 93m.

Marrying Man, The ★★★½ At end of WWII, a rogue (Baldwin) drives to Las Vegas for one more fling before marriage. He meets gangster Bugsy Siegel's mistress (Basinger), and romantic entanglements ensue. Likable performances by two leads overcome Neil Simon's underwritten plot. C: Kim Basinger, Alec Baldwin, Robert Loggia, Elisabeth Shue, Armand Assante, Paul Reiser, Fisher Stevens. D: Jerry Rees. COM [R] 117m. V

Mars Needs Women 1968 ★★½ Martians arrive on Earth to take five Earth women back with them. Campy, low-budget sci-fi filmed in Texas at least has the sense not to take itself too seriously. C: Tommy Kirk, Yvonne Craig, Byron Lord, Roger Ready, Warren Hammack, Anthony Houston. D: Larry Buchanan. SFI 80m. V

Marshal of Amarillo 1948 ★★★½ "Rocky"

Lane, Waller, and Black Jack the horse run into a gang of outlaws, led by Moore, who are holding a wealthy Easterner and his daughter hostage at a deserted hotel. Action-filled Western. C: Allan "Rocky" Lane, Eddy Waller, Mildred Cole, Clayton Moore. D: Phillip Ford. WST 60m

Marshal of Cedar Rock 1953 ★★★½ Later Allan "Rocky" Lane serial has the Western lawofficer trying to solve a robbery and following a trail that eventually leads to the discovery of a railroad corruption scandal. Fast-paced little Western with nice plot twists. C: Allan Lane, Eddy Waller, Phyllis Coates. D: Harry Keller. WST 54m. V

Marshal of Gunsmoke 1944 ★★★ Standard Ritter mixture of guns and music finds the singing cowboy preventing an outlaw gang from rigging frontier elections. C: Tex Ritter, Russell Hayden, Jennifer Holt. D: Vernon Keays. WST 58m.

Marshal of Mesa City, The 1939 ★★★★ Retired lawman (O'Brien) and reformed gunslinger (Brandon) passing through a dusty Western town decide to stay and take on a dishonest sheriff (Ames). Lots of action and strong story make for an entertaining remake of *The Arizonan.* C: George O'Brien, Henry Brandon, Virginia Vale, Leon Ames. D: David Howard. WST 62m.

Marshal of Reno 1944 ★★★½ Red Ryder (Elliott) and faithful scout Little Beaver (Blake) intervene in a dispute between two frontier towns vying to be the county seat. Elliott's first stab at cartoon cowpoke hero Red Ryder and Hayes' last appearance in the series. C: Bill Elliott, Bobby Blake, Alice Fleming. D: Wallace Grissell. WST 54m.

Marshal's Daughter, The 1953 ★★★ A woman teams with her marshal father to track an outlaw who terrorizes their Western town. Mediocre Western features several action-stopping songs by Anders. Look for several Western veterans in a poker scene. C: Ken Murray, Laurie Anders, Preston Foster, Hoot Gibson. D: William Berke. WST 71m.

Marshmallow Moon 1952 *See* **Aaron Slick from Punkin Crick**

Martha Graham—An American Original In Performance ★★★★ A film comprised of the remarkable Ms. Graham's 3 most memorable performances: "A Dancer's World," "Night Journey" and "Appalachian Spring." Lovely and inspiring—even if you're not a ballet maven. C: Martha Graham. DOC 93m. V

Martha's Attic, Vols. 1-6 ★★★★ Six tapes from Labert's "Kids are People Too" show. Great for the little ones, with songs, stories, puppets and animation. C: Martha Lambert. FAM/COM 60m.

Martial Law 1990 ★★ Carradine pops up in one of his rare big-screen martial arts gigs. Two police officers battle the bad guys with fists and other parts of their anatomy. C: Cynthia Rothrock, David Carradine, Chad McQueen. D: S.E. Cohen. ACT [R] 95m. V

Martial Law 2—Undercover 1991 ★★ Sequel (sans Carradine) sends crack martial arts squad undercover to investigate a swank nightclub that holds martial arts fights to the death. C: Jeff Wincott, Cynthia Rothrock, Paul Johansson. D: Kurt Anderson. ACT [R] 92m. V

Martial Outlaw 1993 ★★★ Two brothers serve as cops. But only one of them operates on the side of the law. C: Jeff Wincott, Gary Hudson, Gary Wood, Richard Jaeckel. D: Kurt Anderson. ACT [R] 89m. V

Martian Chronicles, The 1979 ★★★ Man takes over Mars, but colonization proves problematic. This TV miniseries based on a Ray Bradbury book, has money for its stars, but none left over for special effects. C: Rock Hudson, Roddy McDowall, Bernadette Peters. D: Michael Anderson. SFI TVM V

Martians Go Home 1990 ★★ Song plugger Quaid accidentally brings many Martians flocking to Earth for a visit. Green-around-the gills comedy with subpar jesters cast as aliens. C: Randy Quaid, Margaret Colin, Anita Morris, Barry Sobel, Vic Dunlop, John Philbin. D: David Odell. COM [PG-13] 89m. V

Martin 1978 ★★★★ Young Pennsylvania man believes he may be an 84-year-old Rumanian vampire without fangs who uses razor blades to extract blood. Mixture of horror and social satire is definitely not for those with weak stomachs or hearts. C: John Amplas, Lincoln Maazel, Christine Forrest, Tom Savini. D: George A. Romero. HOR [R] 96m. V

Martin Luther 1953 ★★★ A look at the life of the man who reformed the Catholic church, including his excommunication and his drive toward the Protestant reformation. C: Nial MacGinnis, John Ruddock. DOC 105m. V

Martin Luther King, Jr.: Commemorative Collection 1988 ★★★★ Two outstanding documentaries, each offering a different glimpse of the man and all his incredible efforts and deeds. "In Remembrance Of Martin" chronicles his life and "The Speeches of Martin Luther King" bring his magical words to everlasting life. DOC 115m. V

Martin's Day 1984 Canadian ★★½ Escaped convict (Harris) kidnaps young boy (Henry) and winds up becoming his friend. Canadian film aims to please, but it's hampered by obvious treatment of familiar premise. C: Richard Harris, Lindsay Wagner, James Coburn, Justin Henry, Karen Black, John Ireland. D: Alan Gibson. FAM/DRA 99m. V

Marty 1955 ★★★★½ Lonely, unattractive and single, a Bronx butcher finds he has much in common with a plain young woman he meets at a Saturday night social. Deeply moving and tender story of basic human emotions and relationships. Oscar for Best Actor (Borgnine), Screenplay (Paddy Chayefsky), Picture, Director. C: Ernest Borgnine, Besty

Blair, Joe Mantell, Joe De Santis, Esther Minciotti. D: Delbert Mann. DRA 91m. V

Martyr, The 1976 ★★★½ Dramatization based on life of doctor (Genn) who ran an orphanage in the Warsaw ghetto and was eventually sent to a concentration camp. Often dramatically over the top, but the ghetto scenes are tremendously effective. First West German-Israeli film production. C: Leo Genn, Orna Porat. D: Aleksander Ford. DRA 90m.

Marva Collins Story, The 1981 ★★★★½ A Chicago schoolteacher (Tyson), fed up with an ineffective educational system, starts her own self-funded class for "unteachable" ghetto kids. Strong, Emmy-nominated performance by Tyson in this movie based on a true story. C: Cicely Tyson, Morgan Freeman, Roderick Wimberly, Mashaune Hardy, Brett Bouldin, Samuel Muhammad Jr. D: Peter Levin. DRA 100m. TVM

Marvel Comics Video Library ★★★ All the Marvel Super Heroes are here for the kids in cheaply animated cartoons. Strictly for the younger set. FAM/ACT 60m. V

Marvelous Land of Oz 1981 ★★ Ostensibly a sequel to *Wizard*, this low-budget fantasy takes Dorothy back to Oz. For kids only. C: Children's Theater Company, School of Minneapolis. D: John Clark Donahue. FAM/DRA 104m. V

Marvelous Land of Oz 1988 ★★★ Animated feature with Margot Kidder narrating is based on the second Oz book. Second of four films in series is competent but no *Wizard*. FAM/DRA 90m. V

Marvin and Tige 1983 ★★★ Cassavetes plays an ordinary white man who adopts suicidal 11-year-old African-American boy. Socially conscious soap opera with racial theme. C: John Cassavetes, Gibran Brown, Billy Dee Williams, Fay Hauser. D: Eric Weston. DRA 104m. V

Marvin Gaye 1987 ★★★ Brief documentary on life of late Motown great, with generous helpings of his music. C: Marvin Gaye. MUS 60m. V

Marx Brothers In a Nutshell, The 1990 ★★★★½ Thorough documentary of the reigning comic anarchists of film. Chronicles in depth their rise through vaudeville, their peak as movie stars during the '30s and '40s, and their subsequent years when the comedians went their separate ways to mixed results. DOC 95m.

Mary and Joseph: A Story of Faith 1979 Canadian ★★½ Biblical dramatization of the early years of Mary and Joseph before the birth of Jesus. C: Blanche Baker, Shay Duffin, Jeff East, Colleen Dewhurst, Lloyd Bochner, Paul Hecht, Marilyn Lighstone, Murray Matheson. D: Eric Till. DRA 100m. TVM V

Mary Burns, Fugitive 1935 ★★★½ A gangster's girlfriend (Sidney) finds herself sent to prison for a crime she didn't commit. Polished crime melodrama with Douglas giving a strong performance as Sidney's rescuer. C: Sylvia Sidney, Melvyn Douglas, Pert Kelton, Alan Baxter, Wallace Ford, Brian Donlevy. D: William U. Howard. CRI 84m.

Mary Jane Harper Cried Last Night 1977 ★★★½ A mentally unbalanced mother (Dey) takes out her problems on her young daughter. Dey gives a sincere performance in this troubling exposé of child abuse. C: Kevin McCarthy, Susan Dey, Bernie Casey, Tricia O'Neil. D: Allen Reisner. DRA 104m. TVM

Mary, Mary 1963 ★★★ A man (Nelson) tries to sabotage the romance of his ex-wife (Reynolds) with a film star (Rennie) while she tries to undermine his love interest (McBain) with predictable results. Marital farce has a lot of in-jokes for the literary crowd. Somewhat stagebound adaptation of Jean Kerr's Broadway hit. C: Debbie Reynolds, Barry Nelson, Michael Rennie, Diane McBain, Hiram Sherman. D: Mervyn LeRoy. COM 126m.

Mary, Mary, Blood Mary 1976 ★★ A bisexual vampire (Ferrare) drinks the blood of victims and faces down her vampire father (Carradine). For those who appreciate the limited subgenre of bisexual vampire films. C: Christina Ferrare, David Young, John Carradine. D: Juan Lopez Moctezuma. HOR [R] 95m. V

Mary of Scotland 1936 ★★★★½ Hepburn shines as Mary Stuart, executed for refusing to give up her crown in this historical drama adapted from Maxwell Anderson's play. Outstanding direction from Ford lends proper degree of solemnity, with somber lighting and dense atmosphere. C: Katharine Hepburn, Fredric March, Florence Eldridge, John Carradine, Alan Mowbray, Donald Crisp. D: John Ford. DRA 123m. V

Mary Poppins 1964 ★★★★★ British nanny (Andrews) whose magic changes the lives of two children and their father in 1910 England. Supporting cast is terrific; combination of live action and animation was revolutionary for its time. The best in Disney family viewing. Oscars for Best Actress (Andrews, in her screen debut), Score, and Visual Effects. C: Julie Andrews, Dick Van Dyke, David Tomlinson, Glynis Johns, Ed Wynn, Hermione Baddeley, Arthur Treacher, Reginald Owen. D: Robert Stevenson. MUS [G] 139m. V

Mary, Queen of Scots 1971 ★★★½ The queen of Scotland (Redgrave), locks horns with Queen Elizabeth (Jackson) for control of the English throne. Uneven, often inaccurate script, but great jousting by two leads. C: Vanessa Redgrave, Glenda Jackson, Patrick McGoohan, Timothy Dalton, Nigel Davenport, Trevor Howard, Daniel Massey, Ian Holm. D: Charles Jarrott. DRA [PG] 128m.

Mary Shelley's Frankenstein 1994 ★★★½ British director/star Branagh's vision of this oft-filmed horror story is uneven and self-indulgent, but fascinating, nonetheless. De Niro makes an intelligent, sympathetic monster. His birth scene with a naked Branagh wrestling him in amniotic fluid is an over-the-top camp masterpiece! C: Robert De Niro, Kenneth Branagh, Helena Bonham Carter, Tom Hulce, John Cleese. D: Kenneth Branagh. HOR [R] 128m. v

Mary White 1977 ★★★½ True, inspiring story of young woman who leaves her father's publishing empire behind to find fulfillment. C: Ed Flanders, Kathleen Beller, Fionnula Flanagan. D: Jud Taylor. DRA 100m. TVM v

Maryjane 1968 ★★ An art teacher (Fabian) tries to stop his students' involvement with dope, while he falls under suspicion himself. Uncompelling drug exposé. C: Fabian, Diane McBain, Michael Margotta, Kevin Coughlin, Patty McCormack, Terri Garr. D: Maury Dexter. DRA 104m.

Maryland 1940 ★★★½ Mother (Bainter) objects to her son's plans to follow in his horse trainer father's footsteps. Saddle-sore plot, but good color and fine cast make it run. C: Fay Bainter, John Payne, Walter Brennan, Brenda Joyce. D: Henry King. DRA 92m.

Marzipan Pig, The 1990 ★★★★ Child-oriented animated short about the effects of one animal on another in nature's food chain. Tim Curry narrates this saga focusing on a young candy pig. Voice of Tim Curry. FAM/DRA 30m. TVM v

Masada 1984 ★★★★ General (O'Toole) leads a battalion of Roman warriors against a small group of Jews who make their final stand at the fortress at Masada. Excellent production values and strong performances by O'Toole and Warner (who won an Emmy). C: Peter O'Toole, Peter Strauss, Barbara Carrera. D: Boris Sagal. DRA 131m. TVM

Masala 1993 ★★★★ Quirky comedy exploring life in India, featuring aging woman who believes her television set receives signals from the heavens. C: Saeed Jaffrey. D: Srinivas Krishna. COM 105m. v

Mascara 1987 ★★★½ Detective, his sister, and her significant other slip into seedy Belgian nightlife in search of drag performer's killer. C: Charlotte Rampling, Michael Sarrazin, Derek De Lint. D: Patrick Conrad. CRI [R] 99m. v

Masculine-Feminine 1966 French ★★★★½ Aimless young man finds his niche in left-wing politics after several maturing affairs. One of Godard's most audaciously rewarding films documents mid-'60s generation as "children of Marx and Coca-Cola." Based on a Maupassant story. C: Jean-Pierre Leaud, Chantal Goya, Marlene Jobert, Michel Debord, Catherine-Isbelle Duport. D: Jean-Luc Godard. DRA 103m. v

M*A*S*H 1970 ★★★★★ Doctors at a Korean War mobile army surgical hospital use wisecracks, sex, and sick practical jokes to take their minds off the horrors of war. Altman classic set new standards in black humor. Ring Lardner, Jr., won the Oscar for his screenplay. C: Donald Sutherland, Elliott Gould, Tom Skerritt, Sally Kellerman, Robert Duvall, Rene Auberjonois, Roger Bowen, Gary Burghoff, Bud Cort. D: Robert Altman. COM [R] 115m. v

M*A*S*H—Goodbye, Farewell, Amen 1983 ★★★★ Final episode of popular TV sitcom M*A*S*H (itself based on Oscar-winning film) features cast members celebrating end of Korean War while saying final goodbyes. Worthy series culmination. Individual M*A*S*H episodes also available on casssette. C: Alan Alda, Loretta Swit, Mike Farrell, Harry Morgan, David Ogden Stiers. D: Alan Alda. COM 120m. TVM v

Mask 1985 ★★★★ Cher brings an earthy, spirited quality to role of biker mother who raises deformed son to believe in himself, despite unsettled surroundings. Surprisingly warm and moving. C: Cher, Sam Elliott, Eric Stoltz, Estelle Getty, Richard Dysart, Laura Dern, Harry Carey Jr. D: Peter Bogdanovich. DRA [PG-13] 120m. v

Mask of Dijon, The 1946 ★★★½ No, you can't put it on your hot dog. But von Stroheim's chiller-diller performance as a killer hypnotist with an adulterous wife makes this pungent low-budget mystery very worthwhile, just the same. C: Erich von Stroheim, Jeannie Bates, William Wright, Denise Vernac. D: Lewis Landers. CRI 73m.

Mask of Dimitrios, The 1944 ★★★★½ A Dutch mystery writer (Lorre) visiting Istanbul decides to write a book about criminal Dimitrios Makropoulous (Scott) who's been found dead—but is he? Loyal adaptation of Eric Ambler's novel *A Coffin for Dimitrios* is a marvelous, atmospheric classic of film noir. C: Peter Lorre, Zachary Scott, Sydney Greenstreet, Faye Emerson, Victor Francen, George Toias, Steve Geray, Eduardo Ciannelli, Florence Bates. D: Jean Negulesco. CRI 95m.

Mask of Dust 1954 *See* **Race for Life**

Mask of Fu Manchu, The 1932 ★★★½ Often racy, sometimes silly, but always enjoyable mystery has Stannett and Morley falling into the torture chamber of the diabolical Manchu (Karloff) and his equally devious daughter (Loy, in the last of her Asian roles). C: Boris Karloff, Lewis Stone, Karen Morley, Myrna Loy, Charles Starrett, Jean Hersholt. D: Charles Brabin. CRI [R] 67m. v

Mask of Sheba, The 1970 ★★★ Greedy adventurers hunt for a priceless gold mask in the Ethiopian jungle. Rather clichéd adventure, fun but full of native stereotypes. C: Eric Braeden, Stephen Young, Corinne Camacho, Walter Pidgeon, Inger Stevens, Joseph Wiseman, William Marshall, Christopher Carey. D: David Lowell Rich. ACT 120m.

Mask of the Avenger 1951 ★★★ Hero returns home from war to find his father murdered and dons a black mask to rescue the town from evil governor (Quinn). Swashbuckler gets by, thanks to scene-stealing Quinn. C:

John Derek, Anthony Quinn, Jody Lawrence, Arnold Moss. D: Phil Karlson. ACT 83m.

Mask, The 1961 *See* **Eyes of Hell**

Mask, The 1988 Italian ★★½ Spurned by an actress, a wicked aristocrat disguises himself in elaborate mask and tries again. Despite intriguing fairy-tale overtones, the central character is too vile to be genuinely sympathetic. C: Helena Bonham Carter, Michael Maloney, Feodor Chaliapin, Roberto Herlitzka. D: Fiorella Infascelli. COM 90m.

Mask, The 1994 ★★★★ Stunning special effects drive this slick showcase for the explosive Carrey as a mild-mannered man turned into a wild and crazy cartoon with the help of a magical mask. Highlights include the star's "Cuban Pete" song and dance, and the scene where his dog gets into the mask. C: Jim Carrey, Cameron Diaz, Richard Jeni, Peter Riegert. D: Charles Russell. COM [PG-13] 101m.

Masked Rider, The 1941 ★★★½ South of the border flavor spices up routine Western fare about two cowpokes (Brown and Knight) who find work in Mexican silver mine plagued by bandits. Music by the Guadalajara Trio and the José Cansino Dancers. C: Johnny Mack Brown, Fuzzy Knight, Nell O'Day. D: Ford Beebe. WST 57m.

Masks of Death 1986 ★★★½ Baker Street's master detective comes out of retirement to solve a string of East End murders. Solid mystery. C: Peter Cushing, John Mills, Anne Baxter. D: Roy Ward Baker. CRI 80m.

Masoch 1980 Italian ★★★½ Biography of the infamous writer Sacher-Masoch, whose dominant/submissive relationship with his wife and extramarital adventures led to writings about sexual themes. Tastefully handled, but definitely not for all tastes. C: Paolo Malco, Francesca De Sapio, Fabrizio Bentivoglio. D: Franco Brogi Taviani. DRA 109m.

Masque of the Red Death 1964 ★★★★ A satanic medieval prince (Price) enjoys orgiastic pleasures in his castle while a plague ravages the countryside. Lush photography (by Nicholas Roeg) and English locales make this gothic horror film a visual feast. C: Vincent Price, Hazel Court, Jane Asher, Patrick Magee, Nigel Green. D: Roger Corman. HOR [R] 88m. V

Masque of the Red Death 1989 ★★ Producer Roger Corman's ill-advised remake of his own 1964 classic has its moments, but story of prince (Paul) hiding within his castle as plague ravages the land fails to catch dramatic fire. C: Adrian Paul, Clare Hoak, Patrick MacNee, Tracy Reiner. D: Larry Brand. HOR 83m. V

Masquerade 1965 British ★★★½ A crusty British secret service agent (Hawkins) and an American adventurer (Robertson) are hired by the British government to kidnap the son of a sheik for leverage in their quest for oil. Snazzy spy spoof benefits from great locations and various thrilling adventures. (a.k.a. *Operation Masquerade* and *The Shabby Tiger*). C: Cliff Robertson, Jack Hawkins, Marisa Mell, Michel Piccoli, Bill Fraser, John LeMesurier. D: Basil Dearden. ACT 101m.

Masquerade 1986 Polish ★★★★ Metaphysical intrigue centering on actor who slips between theater spectacle and reality. D: Janusz Kijowski. DRA 102m. V

Masquerade 1988 ★★★½ Lowe woos young, super-rich socialite Tilly for love . . . or money? Revamped old plot spiced up with new twists. Fine performances all around. C: Rob Lowe, Meg Tilly, Kim Cattrall, Doug Savant, John Glover, Dana Delany. D: Bob Swaim. CRI [R] 91m. V

Masquerade in Mexico 1945 ★★★ Banker (Knowles) saves singer (Lamour) from Mexican prison, and asks her to entice bullfighter (De Cordova) away from banker's wife. Musical comedy. Revamp of *Midnight*. C: Dorothy Lamour, Arturo de Cordova, Patric Knowles, Ann Dvorak, George Rigaud, Natalie Schafer, Billy Daniels. D: Mitchell Leisen. MUS 96m.

Masquerader, The 1933 ★★★½ A drugged-out member of Parliament enlists his identical cousin to take his place, which leads to much confusion in their private lives. Tour de force for Colman in a dual role. C: Ronald Colman, Elissa Landi, Halliwell Hobbes, Helen Jerome Eddy. D: Richard Wallace. DRA 78m.

Mass Appeal 1984 ★★★★ An idealistic young seminarian (Ivanek) is assigned to a veteran priest (Lemmon) skilled in the art of clerical politics and pulpit popularity. Excellent blend of comedy and tragedy, and convincing performances mark this Broadway adaptation. C: Jack Lemmon, Zeljko Ivanek, Charles Durning, Louise Latham. D: Glenn Jordan. DRA [PG] 99m. V

Massacre 1934 ★★★ Sioux Indian (Barthelmess) returns to the reservation from college to lead his people against discrimination and oppression. Socially conscious, pro-Native American theme was ahead of its time, though handling is dated now. C: Richard Barthelmess, Ann Dvorak, Dudley Digges, Claire Dodd, Henry O'Neill, Robert Barrat. D: Alan Crosland. WST 70m.

Massacre 1956 ★★★ Gunrunners drive Indians to war with white settlers so they can make a profit on the bloodshed. Western with clichéd dialogue, and an interesting ending that saves the film. C: Dane Clark, James Craig, Marta Roth, Miguel Torruco, Jaime Fernandez. D: Louis King. WST 76m.

Massacre at Central High 1976 ★★★★ New kid in school uses drastic means to stop a gang terrorizing other students. Not just another violent teenage revenge tale. This one's a cut above. C: Derrel Maury, Andrew Stevens, Kimberly Beck, Robert Carradine. D: Renee Daalder. ACT 87m. V

Massacre At Fort Holman ★★½ Union

men seek to regain control of a fort captured by Confederate troops. C: James Coburn, Telly Savalas, Robert Burton. D: Tonino Valerii. WST 91m. V

Massacre In Dinosaur Valley 1985 ★★★ Paleontologist and party hunt for mythological "Valley of the Dinosaur" in dangerous Amazon jungle. C: Michael Sopkiw, Suzanne Carvall, Milton Morris. D: Michael E. Lemick. SFI 98m. V

Massacre in Rome 1973 French ★★★★ A Nazi colonel (Burton) is torn between his humanity and his orders to avenge the death of Nazi soldiers by killing Italian hostages. A priest (Mastroianni) tries to stop him. Emotionally involving drama, based on actual wartime atrocities. C: Richard Burton, Marcello Mastroianni, Leo McKern, John Steiner. D: George Pan Cosmatos. DRA [PG] 103m. V

Massacre River 1949 ★★ When not fighting Indians, cavalry officers skirmish over love interests. Mediocre Western, heap big bore. C: Guy Madison, Rory Calhoun, Johnny Sands, Carole Mathews, Cathy Downs. D: John Rawlins. WST 75m.

Massarati and the Brain 1982 ★★★ A 12-year-old genius assists his soldier-of-fortune uncle in retrieving valuable art from an evil neo-Nazi leader (Lee). Trite movie features some good hammy villainy from the reliable Lee. C: Christopher Lee. FAM/ACT

Massive Retaliation 1985 ★★★ Apocalyptic tale of chaos breaking out in hamlet at the dawn of World War III. C: Jason Gedrick, Tom Bower, Karlene Crockett. D: Thomas A. Cohen. DRA 90m. V

Master Blaster 1987 ★★½ A military game turns lethal when players replace their harmless paint pellets with real bullets. C: Jeff Moldovan, Donna Rosae, Joe Hess. D: Glenn R. Wilder. ACT [R] 94m.

Master Gunfighter, The 1975 ★ Gunslinger (Laughlin) suffers a psychological crisis on the morality of violence while tracking his Indian-murdering father-in-law. Nonetheless he still kills. Based on earlier samurai film, *Goyokin*. C: Tom Laughlin, Ron O'Neal, Lincoln Kilpatrick, Geo Anne Sosa, Barbara Carrera, Victor Campos. D: Frank Laughlin. WST [PG] 121m.

Master Harold and the Boys 1986 ★★★ Amid the brutal and racist society of 1950's South Africa, a young white man befriends two black family servants. Emotion-packed performances. C: Matthew Broderick, John Kani. D: Michael Lindsay-Hogg. DRA 90m. TVM V

Master Killer 1978 ★★ A young man, driven by revenge for the ruthless murder of his family during a Manchu attack, becomes a Shaolin monk and attains the ultimate goal in Kung Fu artistry. C: Liu Chia Hui. D: Liu Chia-Liang. ACT [R] 109m. V

Master Killers, The 1973 ★★ An unworthy son stakes a claim in his late father's estate, inciting the fury of his brother who will stop at nothing to make sure the family's fallen angel gets exactly what he deserves. C: Donald O'Brien, Jason Pai. D: George Bonge. ACT 95m. V

Master Minds 1949 ★★★½ When a toothache gives Sach (Hall) the ability to foretell events, a mad scientist targets his brain for a transplant into an ape man. Hall is in fine form in this enjoyable Bowery Boys romp. C: Leo Gorcey, Huntz Hall, Billy Benedict, Bennie Bartlett, David Gorcey, Gabriel Dell, Alan Napier, Jane Adams, Bernard Gorcey. D: Jean Yarbrough. COM 64m.

Master Ninja ★★½ Daughter's kidnapping forces a father to fight the Chinese mafia. C: Demi Moore, Lee Van Cleef. ACT 90m. V

Master of Ballantrae, The 1953 ★★★½ Flynn battles against his brother and for Bonnie Prince Charlie in medieval Britain. Well-cast, colorful swashbuckler, based on R.L. Stevenson tale. C: Errol Flynn, Roger Livesey, Anthony Steel, Yvonne Furneaux, Beatrice Campbell, Felix Aylmer. D: William Keighley. ACT 89m. V

Master of Ballantrae, The 1984 ★★★★ Fine adaptation of the Robert Louis Stevenson classic about two Scottish brothers fighting for an inheritance and the woman they both love. More faithful to the material than the 1953 Errol Flynn version. C: Michael York, Richard Thomas, John Gielgud, Finola Hughes, Timothy Dalton. D: Douglas Hickox. ACT 150m. TVM

Master of Bankdam, The 1947 British ★★★½ Amiable story follows the fortunes of a family in 19th-century England whose Yorkshire mill is the setting for most of the drama. Historical and comic elements are kept in nice balance, with good performances rounding out a solid production. C: Anne Crawford, Dennis Price, Stephen Murray. D: Walter Forde. DRA 105m.

Master of Dragonard Hill 1989 ★★½ In olde England, a hero fights for the throne and his love. Middling swashbuckler. C: Oliver Reed, Eartha Kitt, Herbert Lom. D: Gerard Kikoine. ACT [R] 92m. V

Master of the House 1925 Danish ★★★★½ A boorish husband's mistreatment of his family leads an elderly nurse to step in to teach him a lesson. Silent classic affords a marvelous seriocomic look at middle-class domestic abuse. C: Johannes Meyer, Astrid Holm, Karin Mellemose. D: Carl Theodor Dreyer. COM 81m. V

Master of the World 1961 ★★★★ Nineteenth-century science fiction caper has Bronson trying to stop a mad scientist (Price) from doing anymore damage in his well-intentioned efforts to end war, which include zapping battleships from his heavily armed flying machine. Inventive and entertaining adaptation of two Jules Verne novels. C: Vincent Price, Charles Bronson, Mary Webster, Henry Hull. D: William Witney. SFI 95m. V

Master of the World 1976 ★★½ Animated adaptation of the Jules Verne tale of a crazed scientist who plans to take control of the world with his new invention. SFI 50m. V

Master Race, The 1944 ★★★★ A German officer (Coulouris) flees the crumbling Nazi empire, but remains in Europe incognito to upset the plans of the occupying Americans. Well-made wartime indictment of the undying obsessive allegiance of Nazi hierarchy. C: George Coulouris, Stanley Ridges, Osa Massen, Lloyd Bridges, Carl Esmond, Morris Carnovsky. D: Herbert J. Biberman. DRA 96m. V

Master Spy 1964 British ★★★½ An asylum-seeking Russian scientist gets a job in a top secret British nuclear research lab but may be a Communist spy. Unexpected plot twists keep this British espionage drama moving forward. C: Stephen Murray, June Thorburn, Alan Wheatley, John Carson. D: Montgomery Tully. DRA 71m.

Master Touch, The 1972 Italian ★★½ Paroled safecracker (Douglas) teams with a trapeze artist in a scheme to steal $1 million from a high-tech safe. Douglas and an international cast from Germany and Italy can't elevate this caper film. C: Kirk Douglas, Florinda Bolkan, Giuliano Gemma, Rene Koldehoff. D: Michele Lupo. ACT [PG] 95m. V

Mastermind 1976 ★★★★ A crack Asian detective (Mostel) is hired to protect a special robot from foreign interests. Mostel shines in this sparkling slapstick homage to *Charlie Chan* films, which sat on the shelf for seven years before its limited theatrical release. C: Zero Mostel, Bradford Dillman, Keiko Kishi, Herbert Berghof, Sorrell Booke. D: Alex March. COM 86m. V

Masterpiece of Murder, A 1986 ★★½ A washed-up detective (Hope) teams with retired international thief (Ameche) to investigate a series of murders and art thefts. Hope's TV "comeback." C: Bob Hope, Don Ameche, Jayne Meadows Allen, Yvonne De Carlo, Anne Francis, Frank Gorshin, Kevin McCarthy, Clive Revill, Stella Stevens, Jamie Farr. D: Charles S. Dubin. COM 100m. TVM

Masters of Menace 1990 ★★½ Law and order take to the road in this adventure about motorcycle gang members who inadvertently break the law and find themselves the targets of a deputy district attorney who seeks to unjustly imprison them. C: David Rasche, Catherine Bach, Ray Baker. D: Daniel Raskov. ACT 97m. V

Masters of the Universe 1987 ★★ He-Man (Lundgren) and archvillain Skeletor (a hammy Langella) battle for magical key. Fantasy yarn may entertain youngsters (there's comic book-type violence); positively mind-numbing for others. C: Dolph Lundgren, Frank Langella, Courteney Cox, James Tolkan, Meg Foster, Christina Pickles, Billy Barty. D: Gary Goddard. ACT 106m. V

Masterson of Kansas 1954 ★★½ Bat Masterson, Doc Holliday, and Wyatt Earp team up to prevent an evil opportunist from inciting an Indian war. Saddle-sore grouping of three legendary Western characters. C: George Montgomery, Nancy Gates, James Griffith, Jean Willes, Benny Rubin. D: William Castle. WST 73m.

Mata Hari 1932 French ★★★★ Dutch-born courtesan becomes world famous for her erotic dances, then spies for Germany before and during WWI. Grandly intricate production, though dated, is generally entertaining with Garbo and company in fine form. C: Greta Garbo, Ramon Novarro, Lionel Barrymore, Louis Stone. D: George Fitzmaurive. DRA 100m. V

Mata Hari 1965 French ★★★½ Moreau plays the notorious Dutch spy, executed for stealing secrets from the French and passing them to the Germans in WWI. Contains more historical details than the Garbo version (1932), but lacks its glossy polish. (a.k.a. *Mata Hari Agent H-21*) C: Jeanne Moreau, Jean-Louis Trintignant, Frank Villard. D: Jean-Louis Richard. DRA 95m.

Mata Hari 1985 ★★★ The story of the notorious WWI German spy. Soft core approach lacks any new story developments, and relies on the eroticism of Kristel. C: Sylvia Kristel, Christopher Cazenove, Oliver Tobias, Gaye Brown. D: Curtis Harrington. DRA [R] 108m. V

Mata Hari Agent H-21 1965 *See* **Mata Hari**

Mata Hari's Daughter 1954 Italian ★★½ Title character tries to pick up the spying business where her mother left off, helping Dutch Indonesians stop the WWII Japanese onslaught. Badly dubbed Italian thriller features dance numbers by ballerina Tcherina. C: Frank Latimore, Ludmilla Tcherina, Erno Crisa. D: Renzo Meruis. DRA 102m.

Matador 1986 Spanish ★★★★ A retired matador (Martinez) encounters a sensual, equally deadly lawyer (Serna) defending his protege (Banderas). Demented black comedy, played absolutely straight—a wicked satire of sex, religion, and bullfighting. C: Assumpta Serna, Antonio Banderas, Nacho Martinez, Carmen Maura, Eva Cobo. D: Pedro Almodovar. COM 102m. V

Match Factory Girl, The 1990 Finnish ★★★★ Pregnant and abandoned by her first lover, a shy woman (Outinen) swears revenge on all who've hurt her. Dark, amusing fable with only six lines of dialogue. Unique. C: Kati Outinen, Elina Salo, Esko Nikkari. D: Aki Kaurismaki. COM 70m. V

Match King, The 1932 ★★★½ A Chicago street-cleaner (William) becomes a millionaire by monopolizing the kitchen match market worldwide and setting up phony businesses. Unusual premise based on a true story, with William showing suave restraint as the ruthless master swindler. C: Warren William, Lili

Damita, Glenda Farrell, Harold Huber, John Wray, Hardie Albright. D: Howard Bretherton, William Keighley. DRA 80m.

Matchless 1967 Italian ★★½ An American journalist (O'Neal) is pursued by the Chinese and then snared by the CIA for espionage work when they discover he has a ring that can make him invisible. As a homage to the James Bond thrillers, it's not bad. C: Patrick O'Neal, Ira Furstenberg, Donald Pleasence, Henry Silva. D: Alberto Lattuada. COM 104m.

Matchmaker, The 1958 ★★★★ While matchmaker tries to find a wife for miserly merchant, she decides she wants him for herself, and Perkins and MacLaine fall for each other as well. Pleasing adaptation of Thornton Wilder stage comedy overcomes its staginess with good performances. Story later remade as the musical *Hello Dolly*. C: Shirley Booth, Anthony Perkins, Shirley MacLaine, Paul Ford, Robert Morse, Wallace Ford. D: Joseph Anthony. COM [R] 101m. V

Matchmaking of Anna, The 1972 Greek ★★★★ A maid (Vaguena) gives up her arranged marriage when her employer doesn't want to let her go and her mother needs her income. Sensitive drama, with social commentary underpinnings. C: Anna Vaguena, Stavros Kalarogiou, Smaro Veaki, Ketty Panou. D: Pantelis Voulgaris. DRA 87m.

Matewan 1987 ★★★★½ Story of the labor struggles in West Virginia during the 1920s that resulted in the massacre of striking coal miners. Director/writer Sayles brings sensitive handling and tremendous attention to detail to this realistic social drama. C: James Earl Jones, Mary McDonnell, William Oldham. D: John Sayles. DRA [PG-13] 100m. V

Matilda 1978 ★★★½ A small-time fight promoter (Gould) tries to make a killing by managing a boxing kangaroo. Occasionally funny and often nicely paced comedy veers toward the "cutesy," but provides light entertainment on a family level. C: Elliott Gould, Robert Mitchum, Harry Guardino, Clive Revill. D: Daniel Mann. FAM/COM [G] 105m. V

Matinee 1993 ★★★½ Tribute to '50s horror king William Castle features Goodman as movie producer premiering new flick *Mant!* ("Half man, half ant!") in Key West during tense week of Cuban missile crisis. Re-creation of Castle's shlock style is terrific. C: John Goodman, Cathy Moriarty, Simon Fenton, Omri Katz, Lisa Jakub, Kellie Martin, Jesse White, Dick Miller, John Sayles. D: Joe Dante. COM [PG] 99m. V

Mating Game, The 1959 ★★★★ IRS official (Randall) falls for farmer's daughter (Reynolds) while her father (Douglas) tries to keep tax records out of his would-be son-in-law's hands. Cute comedy of trials and many errors, nicely played by witty cast. C: Debbie Reynolds, Tony Randall, Paul Douglas, Fred Clark, Una Merkel, Philip Ober, Charles Lane. D: George Marshall. COM 96m. V

Mating of Millie, The 1948 ★★★½ A career woman (Keyes) seeks to marry so she can adopt an orphan. Ford tries to help her find a mate, and they end up falling in love. Heartwarming comedy/drama features agreeable interplay between Ford and Keyes. C: Glenn Ford, Evelyn Keyes, Ron Randell, Willard Parker, Virginia Hunter. D: Henry Levin. DRA 87m.

Mating Season, The 1951 ★★★★ Working-class man's marriage to socialite (Tierney) is jeopardized by the appearance of his mother (Ritter), who is first mistaken for and then poses as his maid. Acid-tongued Ritter elevates this overlooked comedy. C: Gene Tierney, John Lund, Thelma Ritter. D: Mitchell Leisen. COM 101m.

Mating Season, The 1980 ★★★½ Breezy, likable romantic comedy set at a nature resort, where a pair of birdwatchers (Arnaz and real-life hubby Luckinbill) fall in hate, then love. C: Lucie Arnaz, Laurence Luckinbill, Swoozie Kurtz. D: John Llewellyn. COM 100m. TVM V

Matt Helm 1975 ★★★ Smooth private detective (Franciosa) protects a beautiful movie star while he tries to break up an international black market operation. Series pilot has some campy charm. C: Tony Franciosa, Ann Turkel, Gene Evans, Patrick Macnee, Hari Rhodes, James Shigeta, Laraine Stephens, John Vernon, Catherine Bach. D: Buzz Kulik. ACT 78m. TVM

Matt the Gooseboy 1978 ★★★ Enchanting animated interpretation of a Hungarian folktale involving a young boy's rescue of his beloved goose from a greedy landlord. FAM/DRA 77m. V

Mattei Affair, The 1973 Italian ★★★½ Docudrama about an Italian industrialist, his rise to success and his mysterious death. Italian-made drama uses documentary techniques to detail subject and suggest solutions to the mystery. C: Gian Maria Volonte, Luigi Squarizina, Peter Baldwin. D: Francesco Rosi. DRA 118m.

Matter of Cunning, A 1992 ★★½ Nothing will stop a woman's struggle to control an international corporate empire in this battle of the sexes drama. DRA 92m. V

Matter of Days, A 1969 French ★★★½ Set against the Prague/Paris revolts of 1967-68, a young French student (Fruges) must choose between a professor and her actor husband. Standard love story lifted by the historical background. (a.k.a. *A Quelques Jour Prás*) C: Thalie Fruges, Vit Olmer, Philippe Baronnet, Jana Sukova. D: Yves Ciampi. DRA 98m.

Matter of Degrees, A 1990 ★★★ Yuppie guilt overcomes a graduating student with a promising future until he turns to the campus radio station. C: Judith Hoag, John Doe, Arye Gross. D: W.T. Morgan. COM [R] 90m. V

Matter of Dignity, A 1957 Greek ★★½ Emotion-packed drama of a daughter who seeks to save her family after they fall into debt. C: Ellie Lambetti, George Pappas, Eleni Zafirou. D: Michael Cacoyannis. DRA 100m. V

Matter of Innocence, A 1967 British ★★★ A drab woman (Mills) travels to Singapore and is transformed via a romance with a Eurasian (Kapoor). Uneven adaptation of Noel Coward short story. C: Hayley Mills, Trevor Howard, Sashi Kapoor, Brenda de Banzie. D: Guy Green. DRA 102m.

Matter of Life and Death, A 1946 *See* **Stairway to Heaven**

Matter of Life and Death, A 1981 ★★★½ The biography of selfless nurse Joy Ufema who dedicates herself to treatment of the terminally ill. True story gives a plum dramatic role to Lavin, and she makes the most of it. C: Linda Lavin, Salome Jens, Gail Strickland, Ramon Bieri, Tyne Daly. D: Russ Mayberry. DRA 98m. TVM V

Matter of Love, A 1978 ★★ Spouse-swapping at the beach. Forgettable. C: Michelle Harris, Mark Anderson, Christy Neal. D: Chuck Vincent. DRA [R] 87m.

Matter of Morals, A 1961 U.S.A. ★★★ International melodrama chronicles the moral decline of an American financier (O'Neal) after he becomes involved with a woman he meets through his Stockholm bank. Slow but handsome crime story. C: Patrick O'Neal, Maj-Britt Nilsson, Eva Dahlbeck. D: John Cromwell. CRI 98m.

Matter of Principle, A 1984 ★★★ Sincere holiday drama of an overbearing father of eleven children who is forced to discover the true meaning of Christmas when his wife leaves him. C: Alan Arkin, Barbara Dana. D: Gwen Arner. DRA 60m. TVM V

Matter of Resistance, A 1966 French ★★★½ A French housewife (Deneuve) decides to do her part to help the Resistance movement by entertaining soldiers before the D-Day invasion. Light French comedy has its moments, mostly due to charm of Deneuve. (a.k.a *La Vie de Château*) C: Catherine Deneuve, Philippe Noiret, Pierre Brasseur, Mary Marquet, Henri Garcin, Carlos Thompson. D: Jean-Paul Rappeneau. COM 92m.

Matter of Sex, A 1984 ★★★½ True story of eight female employees who wage a hard-fought battle for equal pay and equal promotion opportunities at a Minnesota bank. Film does a good job of depicting the bitter two-year struggle. C: Jean Stapleton, Dinah Manoff, Judge Reinhold, Pamela Putch, Gillian Farrell, Diana Reis, Nancy Beatty. D: Lee Grant. DRA 100m. TVM

Matter of Time, A 1976 ★★½ A hotel maid in Rome (Minnelli) receives advice about living life from a penniless unbalanced countess. Average WWI period piece with an intriguing cast and director. C: Liza Minnelli, Ingrid Bergman, Charles Boyer, Spiros Andros. D: Vincente Minnelli. DRA [PG] 97m. V

Matter of WHO, A 1962 British ★★★½ A detective from the World Health Organization uncovers a plot to take over the oil industry. Terry-Thomas uncharacteristically low keyed in this odd but effective blend of comedy and suspense. C: Terry-Thomas, Alex Nicol, Sonja Ziemann, Guy Deghy, Richard Briers, Carol White, Honor Blackman. D: Don Chaffey. COM 90m.

Matters of the Heart 1990 ★★★ A young musician (Gartin) falls in love with a renowned pianist (Seymour) who is battling cancer. Wonderful performance by Seymour in this old-fashioned weeper. C: Jane Seymour, Christopher Gartin, James Stacy. D: Michael Ray Rhodes. DRA [PG-13] 95m. TVM V

Matusalem 1994 Canadian ★★★★½ Imaginative, funny fantasy about the ghost of an 18th-century pirate (Labreche) who enlists the help of a modern-day kid in his search for a long-lost pardon for his uncle, a fellow pirate. Time travel, sea adventure, and warm wit make this a must for kids and parents alike. C: Marc Labreche, Emile Proullx-Cloutier, Jod Leveille-Bernard, Maxime Collin, Marie-France Monette, Steve Gendron, Jessica Barker. D: Roger Cantin. FAM/ACT TVM

Maurice 1987 British ★★★★ Young Edwardian-era Englishman confronts his own homosexuality when he falls in love with fellow student at Cambridge. Beautifully filmed and sensitively acted, though it does go on too long. Based on E.M. Forster novel. C: James Wilby, Hugh Grant, Rupert Graves, Denholm Elliott, Simon Callow, Billie Whitelaw, Ben Kingsley, Phoebe Nicholls, Barry Foster. D: James Ivory. DRA [R] 139m. V

Maurie 1973 ★★★ True story of Cincinnati basketball star Maurice Stokes (Casey) whose sudden paralysis leads teammates to raise money for medical expenses. Excessively sentimental melodrama tries harder than it needs to for sympathy. C: Bernie Casey, Bo Svenson, Janet MacLachlan, Stephanie Edwards, Paulene Myers, Bill Walker. D: Daniel Mann. DRA [G] 113m.

Mausoleum 1982 *See* **One Dark Night**

Mausoleum 1983 ★ Beautiful Bressée has inherited a family curse, and now she periodically transforms into a murderous demon. Schlocky and silly. C: Bobbie Bresee, Marjoe Gortner, Norman Burton. D: Michael Dugan. HOR [R] 96m.

Maverick 1994 ★★★½ Revives the hit TV series, with Gibson as gambler-charmer Bret Maverick, wooing mystery woman (Foster) while conning and bottom-dealing his way across the Old West. Garner, the original Maverick, watches over the proceedings as fellow gambler. Gibson has a very different presence than Garner, but it works. C: Mel Gibson, Jodie Foster, James Garner, Graham Greene, James Coburn, Alfred Molina, Paul Smith, Geoffrey Lewis. D: Richard Donner. WST 129m.

Maverick Queen, The 1955 ★★★½ A lawman (Sullivan) working undercover in a Western hotel romances a crooked owner (Stanwyck) who is trying to go straight for him. Vibrant Stanwyck and a pretty good story, too. C: Barbara Stanwyck, Barry Sullivan, Scott Brady, Mary Murphy. D: Joseph Kane. WST 90m. V

Max and Helen 1990 U.S. ★★★★ Nazi hunter Simon Wiesenthal (Landau) relates the story of a German Jewish couple (Williams and Krige) separated for 20 years after being placed in concentration camps. Heartbreaking Holocaust drama features a fine performance by Landau. C: Treat Williams, Alice Krige, Martin Landau, Jonathan Phillips, Jodhi May. D: Philip Saville. DRA 94m. TVM V

Max Dugan Returns 1983 ★★★½ An ex-con (Robards) reenters the life of his schoolteacher daughter (Mason) and overwhelms her with gifts to make up for many years' neglect. Neil Simon comedy features good performances by appealing cast. Broderick's debut. C: Marsha Mason, Jason Robards, Donald Sutherland, Matthew Broderick. D: Herbert Ross. COM [PG] 98m. V

Max Fleischer's Koko The Clown Cartoons 1991 ★★★½ Comic antics and cartoon history energize this cartoon animated by the legendary creator of Betty Boop and Popeye. FAM/COM 70m. V

Max Fleischer's Popeye Cartoons ★★★ Popeye enthusiasts will not want to miss these three action-packed cartoons featuring vintage episodes animated by Max Fleischer. FAM/COM 56m. V

Max Havelaar 1976 Dutch ★★★ An officer tries to turn the tide on imperialism in the 19th-century Dutch East Indies. Interesting Dutch-Indonesian production attempts to come to grips with colonial past. C: Peter Faber, Sacha Bulthuis, Elang Mohanad, Adenan Soesilanigrat. D: Fons Rademakers. DRA 167m.

Max Headroom—The Original Story 1986 ★★★ The mysterious birth of the quirky, pompous, and irritating talk show host is revealed. Fans will enjoy it. COM 60m. V

Max, Mon Amour 1986 French ★★½ The phrase "monkeying around" takes on new meaning in this comedy about an unfaithful husband who discovers his wife is having an affair with a chimpanzee. Unusual farce. C: Charlotte Rampling, Victoria Abril, Anthony Higgins. D: Nagisa Oshima. COM 94m. V

Maxie 1985 ★★½ A conservative secretary with lofty ambitions (Close) becomes possessed by the spirit of a fun-loving Roaring '20s flapper. Poorly constructed fantasy-comedy is chiefly a showcase for Close in a dual role. C: Glenn Close, Mandy Patinkin, Ruth Gordon, Barnard Hughes. D: Paul Aaron. COM [PG] 98m. V

Maxie's World—Dancin' & Romancin' 1989 ★★½ Teenager has action-packed adventures at Surfside High. Live animated diversion. FAM/COM 120m. V

Maxie's World—Surfs Up In Surfside 1989 ★★½ Another action-packed animated adventure at Surfside High with teen dream girl making waves at the beach. FAM/COM 120m. V

Maxim Xul 1989 ★★ Powerful killer beast is challenged by professor in this good against evil tale that has more blood than suspense. C: Adam West, Jefferson Leinberger, Mary Schaeffer. D: Arthur Egeli. HOR 100m. V

Maxime 1958 French ★★★ A young millionaire enlists a penniless aristocrat (Boyer) to help him woo his beloved (Morgan)—but the matchmaker falls for her himself. Charm of Boyer and Morgan is chief asset of this dubbed French costumer set in the early 1900s. C: Michele Morgan, Charles Boyer, Arletty, Felix Marten. D: Henri Verneuil. COM 93m.

Maximum Breakout 1991 ★★½ A man and his gang seek revenge for the kidnapping of his girlfriend. Standard. C: Sydney Cole Phillips. D: Tracy Lynch Britton. ACT 93m. V

Maximum Force 1992 ★★ Unholy alliance between an underworld kingpin and the chief of police drives three unorthodox cops undercover. Don't bother. C: Sam Jones, John Saxon, Sherrie Rose. D: Joseph Merhi. CRI [R] 90m. V

Maximum Overdrive 1986 ★★ King made his directorial debut with this mechanical horror film (based on his story "Trucks") about machines turning on humans, and proves better at handling his vehicular villains than the actors they terrorize. C: Emilio Estevez, Pat Hingle, Laura Harrington, Christopher Murvey. D: Stephen King. HOR [R] 97m. V

Maximum Security ★★★ Prisoner takes one step toward freedom when psychiatrist helps him remember the decency of ordinary humanity. Moving prison drama. C: Geoffrey Lewis, Jean Smart. D: Bill Duke. DRA 113m. V

Maximum Thrust 1988 ★★ Thriller romance about a dangerous bodyguard who weakens upon falling in love with the enemy. Lethal love connection. C: Rick Gianasi, Jennifer Kanter, Mizan Nunes. D: Tim Kincaid. SFI 80m. V

May Fools 1990 French ★★★½ A French family gathers to bury its matriarch in May 1968; the family's upheaval is paralleled by concurrent national student unrest. Fascinating and touching. C: Michel Piccoli, Miou-Miou, Michel Duchaussoy, Dominique Blanc, Bruno Carette, Harriet Walter, Francois Berleand, Martine Gautier, Paulette Dubost, Jeanne Herry-le Clerk, Danner Renaud. D: Louis Malle. DRA [R] 105m. V

May Wine 1990 ★★★ Wealthy Boyle enjoys an ongoing sexual romp. Light on plot; some fun moments. C: Joanna Cassidy, Guy Marchand, Lara Flynn Boyle. D: Carol Wiseman. COM [R] 85m. V

Maya 1966 ★★½ TV's former "Dennis the Menace" North stars as young American who teams up with Indian teenager to bring a revered white elephant to a jungle temple. In the process, North must also deal with his big game hunting father. Simpleminded and forgettable. C: Clint Walker, Jay North, I. S. Johar, Sajid Kahn. D: John Berry. FAM/DRA 91m. V

Maya 1982 ★★½ An amorous student and a jealous co-worker cause problems for a fashion design teacher who seeks advice from the Mayan gods. Off-beat drama. C: Berta Dominguez, Joseph D. Rosevich. DRA 114m. V

Maybe Baby 1988 ★★★½ A woman, successful in business at 39, wants to have a baby before time runs out. High-powered cast shines in this comedy/drama. C: Jane Curtin, Dabney Coleman. D: Tom Moore. COM 96m. TVM

Maybe I'll Come Home in the Spring 1970 ★★★½ Disillusioned by the drug-commune culture, a wayward young woman returns home to her family. Compelling generation-gap drama doesn't compromise. First-rate performances. C: Sally Field, Jackie Cooper, Eleanor Parker, David Carradine. D: Joseph Sargent. DRA 74m. TVM V

Mayday at 40,000 Feet! 1976 ★★★ A snowed-in airport and a cold-blooded killer in first class spell danger for the pilot (Janssen) and crew of a crippled 747 airliner. Watchable thrills. C: David Janssen, Don Meredith, Christopher George, Ray Milland, Lynda Day George, Maggie Blye, Marjoe Gortner, Broderick Crawford, Tom Drake, Jane Powell. D: Robert Butler. ACT 120m. TVM

Mayerling 1936 French ★★★★★ Austrian crown prince Rudolf and his 17-year-old lover, Baroness Mary Vetsera, are found shot in the royal hunting lodge, apparent victims of a suicide pact. Superb performances highlight French version of actual romantic tragedy. Remade in 1968. C: Charles Boyer, Danielle Darrieux, Suzy Prim. D: Anatole Litvak. DRA 91m. V

Mayerling 1968 British ★★½ In 1889, the heir to the Hapsburg empire and his commoner mistress end their love through a double suicide in the imperial hunting estate. Ornate historical romance. C: Omar Sharif, Catherine Deneuve, James Mason, Ava Gardner, James Robertson Justice, Genevieve Page. D: Terence Young. DRA 140m.

Mayfair Bank Caper, The 1979 British ★★★ Mild caper film has American ex-con Jordan taking job with securities film for nefarious purposes. Grahame is wonderful as his mother in one of her last film appearances. C: David Niven, Gloria Grahame, richard Jordan, Elke Sommer, Oliver Tobias, Hugh Griffith, Richard Johnson. D: Ralph Thomas. CRI 120m. V

Mayflower Madam 1987 ★★★ Laundered teleplay about Sidney Biddle Barrows, a socialite who operates an infamous call girl service. Elegant Bergen is appropriately cast in true story. C: Candice Bergen, Chris Sarandon, Caitlin Clarke, Chita Rivera. D: Lou Antonio. DRA 93m. TVM V

Mayflower: The Pilgrims' Adventure 1979 ★★★½ Emigrants endure a two-month crossing to become the first English settlers in New England in 1620. Sturdy performance by Hopkins and lovely Agutter's presence highlight period production. C: Anthony Hopkins, Richard Crenna, Jenny Agutter. D: George Schaefer. DRA 97m. TVM

Mayhem 1987 ★ Two losers in Hollywood search for women they lost. Plenty of violence. C: Raymond Martino, Pamela Dixon, Robert Gallo, Wendy MacDonald. D: Joseph Merhi. ACT 90m. V

Mayor of Hell, The 1933 ★★★½ A gangster appointed head of a reform school takes action against poor conditions and maltreatment of boys. Capable star turn for Cagney, with unusual climax. C: James Cagney, Madge Evans, Allen Jenkins, Dudley Digges, Arthur Byron, Frankie Darro, Allen "Farina" Hoskins. D: Archie Mayo. DRA 80m.

Maytime 1937 ★★★★ MacDonald and Eddy are singers in love, though romance is threatened by oppressive husband/mentor (Barrymore). The pair are in top form here, with great musical numbers. C: Jeanette MacDonald, Nelson Eddy, John Barrymore, Herman Bing, Paul Porcasi, Sig Ruman. D: Robert Z. Leonard. MUS 132m. V

Maytime in Mayfair 1949 British ★★★ A chic London dress salon is bequeathed to a playboy, who romances its female manager. Refined fluff enlivened by engaging leads. C: Anna Neagle, Michael Wilding, Peter Graves, Nicholas Phipps. D: Herbert Wilcox. COM 94m.

Maze, The 1953 ★★★½ Great "guilty pleasures" horror story has a newlywed (Carlson) summoned to his ancestral Scottish home where he falls victim to the family curse. Former art director Menzies uses 3-D to good effect. Watch out for the frogman! C: Richard Carlson, Veronica Hurst, Hillary Brooke, Michael Pate, Katherine Emery. D: William Cameron Menzies. HOR 81m.

Maze, The 1983 British ★★★½ Annis is fetching as young woman who meets ghost of her mother's lover in their garden. BBC effort is atmospheric, low-key suspenser. C: Francesca Annis, James Bolam, Sky McCatskill. D: Peter Hammond. CRI 60m. TVM

Mazes and Monsters 1982 Canadian ★★★½ A group of socially withdrawn college students carries their passion for the Dungeons and Dragons game too far. Okay suspenser verges on horror with a fine (and achingly young) Hanks. Wisely, not solely for players of the game. From the Rona Jaffe best-seller. C: Tom Hanks, Wendy Crewson, David Wallace, Chris Makepeace. D: Steven Hilliard Stern. HOR 103m. TVM V

McBain 1991 ★★½ Walken leads band of mercenaries and South American rebels to depose sinister Colombian dictator. Standard shoot-'em-up buoyed slightly by poised dementia of Walken. C: Christopher Walken, Maria Conchita Alonso, Michael Ironside, Steve James, Jay Patterson, T. G. Waites, Victor Argo, Chick Vennera. D: James Glickenhaus. ACT 105m. v

McCabe and Mrs. Miller 1971 ★★★★½ Altman turns Western genre inside out, making a hero out of small-time hustler with the vision to create a town in the Pacific Northwest. Remarkable performance by Beatty, equally well-etched showing by Christie. Magnificently photographed. C: Warren Beatty, Julie Christie, Rene Auberjonois, John Schuck, Bert Remsen, Keith Carradine, Shelley Duvall, Michael Murphy, Hugh Millais. D: Robert Altman. DRA [R] 121m. v

McCloud: Who Killed Miss U.S.A.? 1969 ★★★ A New Mexico U.S. deputy marshal transports a murder witness to New York City, then loses him. Pilot for the popular series. C: Dennis Weaver, Craig Stevens, Diana Muldaur, Mark Richman, Terry Carter, Raul Julia, Shelly Novack, Julie Newmar. D: Richard Colla. DRA 100m. TVM

McConnell Story, The 1955 ★★★½ Life and accidental death of Korean War jet ace. Mawkish but watchable fictional biography of noted Air Force test pilot. C: Alan Ladd, June Allyson, James Whitmore, Frank Faylen. D: Gordon Douglas. DRA 107m. v

McGuffin, The 1985 British ★★★★ Murder results when a curious film critic becomes suspicious of his neighbors. Tribute to Hitchcock suspense thrillers will draw you in early on. C: Charles Dance, Ritza Brown, Francis Matthews, Brian Glover, Jerry Stiller. D: Colin Bucksey. CRI 95m. v

McGuire, Go Home! 1966 British ★★★ A British army officer in 1950s occupied Cyprus tangles with rebel terrorists and falls for an American woman. Energetic action-adventure. C: Dirk Bogarde, George Chakiris, Susan Strasberg, Denholm Elliott. D: Ralph Thomas. ACT 101m.

McHale's Navy 1964 ★★★ The wacky crew of a PT boat contrives to make good on gambling debts. Feature version of popular TV series, complete with slapstick and wisecracks. C: Ernest Borgnine, Joe Flynn, Tim Conway, George Kennedy, Claudine Longet, Bob Hastings, Carl Ballantine, Billy Sands, Gavin MacLeod, Jean Willes. D: Edward Montagne. COM 93m.

McHale's Navy Joins the Air Force 1965 ★★★ Ensign Parker (Conway) is mistaken for an Air Force ace whose blunders result in his repeated advancement in rank. Fair share of snappy dialogue and slapstick. C: Tim Conway, Joe Flynn, Bob Hastings, Ted Bessell, Susan Silo, Henry Beckman, Billy Sands, Gavin MacLeod, Tom Tully, Jacques Aubuchon. D: Edward Montagne. COM 90m. v

McKenzie Break, The 1970 ★★★★ German prisoners at a POW camp in Scotland make a daring escape. Exciting WWII action and fine performances, especially by Keith. C: Brian Keith, Helmut Griem, Ian Hendry, Jack Watson, Patrick O'Connell. D: Lamont Johnson. DRA [PG] 106m.

McLintock! 1963 ★★★★ Slapstick, lusty Western about a tough cattle baron trying to bring his elegant wife back into the fold. Boisterous fun with plenty of Wayne action. C: John Wayne, Maureen O'Hara, Patrick Wayne, Stefanie Powers, Yvonne De Carlo, Chill Wills, Bruce Cabot. D: Andrew V. McLaglen. WST 127m. v

McMasters, The 1970 ★★½ Trouble starts when a black soldier comes home from the Civil War and tries to work in the fields of his former master. Lots of violence, little else. C: Burl Ives, Brock Peters, David Carradine, Nancy Kwan, Jack Palance, John Carradine. D: Alf Kjellin. WST 89m. v

McNaughton's Daughter 1976 ★★½ A saintly missionary charged with murder is prosecuted by a deputy D.A. Pilot for wanna-be TV series. C: Susan Clark, Ricardo Montalban, James Callahan, John Elerick, Vera Miles, Ralph Bellamy, Mike Farrell. D: Jerry London. CRI 100m. TVM

McQ 1974 ★★★ A renegade Seattle cop seeks revenge against the mobster responsible for killing his partner. Action mainly as big John saddles up a green Plymouth. C: John Wayne, Eddie Albert, Diana Muldaur, Colleen Dewhurst, Clu Gulager, Al Lettieri, Julie Adams. D: John Sturges. DRA [PG] 111m. v

McVicar 1980 British ★★★½ Fascinating true story of England's most wanted criminal, John McVicar, who breaks out of prison and eventually reforms. Smartly done and well-acted account, penned by McVicar himself. C: Roger Daltrey, Adam Faith, Cheryl Campbell, Brian Hall, Steven Berkoff. D: Tom Clegg. CRI [R] 111m. v

MD Geist—The Most Dangerous Ever 1986 Japanese ★★★½ Title character in animated tale is a specially crafted fighting machine in orbit exile around its home planet; it must decide whether to save the planet from deadly civil war. Lots of fun and adventure. SFI 45m.

Me and Him 1989 ★ Dunne has many unusual problems after his private part learns how to talk. Fine talents barely survive. C: Griffin Dunne, Ellen Greene, Kelly Bishop, Carey Lowell, Craig T. Nelson, Mark Linn-Baker. D: Doris Dörrie. COM 94m. v

Me and Marlborough 1935 British ★★★½ In 17th-century England, a woman (Courtneidge) disguises herself as a soldier and joins the army to get to the bottom of her innocent husband's conviction for spying. Light costume drama enlivened by the sparkling

Courtneidge. C: Cicely Courtneidge, Tom Walls. D: Victor Saville. DRA 78m.

Me and My Gal 1932 ★★★½ Hard-boiled cop falls for a waitress whose relatives get mixed up with crooks. Fine example of a '30s comedy/drama second feature—cleverly done with crackling dialogue throughout. C: Spencer Tracy, Joan Bennett, Marion Burns, George Walsh, J. Farrell McDonald, Noel Madison. D: Raoul Walsh. COM 78m.

Me and the Colonel 1958 ★★★★ As WWII draws to a close, a Polish Jew who's helping refugees escape clashes with an anti-Semitic colonel. Watchable, heartwarming entertainment with sturdy star performances. C: Danny Kaye, Curt Jurgens, Nicole Maurey, Francoise Rosay. D: Peter Glenville. COM 109m.

Me and the Kid 1993 ★★★½ Two con artists (Aiello and Pantoliano) kidnap a spoiled rich kid (Zuckerman). *Home Alone* meets "The Ransom of Red Chief," in this kid-oriented comedy; highlight is Aiello's fine performance. C: Danny Aiello, Alex Zuckerman, Joe Pantoliano, Cathy Moriarty. D: Dan Curtis. FAM/COM [PG] 97m. V

Me and the Mob 1994 ★★ Naive writer infiltrates the Mafia to write an expose. Truly dreadful attempt to spoof serious mob movies. C: Sandra Bullock, James Lorinz, Tony Darrow, Steve Buscemi. D: Frank Rainone. ACT [R] 89m. V

Me & Veronica 1993 ★★★ The story of two sisters who grow up in a tension-filled home. Later, as adults, they can't escape their past. C: Elizabeth McGovern, Patricia Wettig, Michael O'Keefe. D: Don Scardino. DRA [R] 97m. V

Me, Natalie 1969 ★★★★ Duke gives a heartbreaking performance as an ugly duckling out to conquer New York in this charming comedy/drama. Pacino's film debut. C: Patty Duke, James Farentino, Martin Balsam, Elsa Lanchester, Al Pacino. D: Fred Coe. DRA [PG] 111m.

Mean Dog Blues 1979 ★★½ A drifter unfairly convicted of murder winds up on a prison farm guarded by vicious Dobermans. Well-made penal society drama. C: George Kennedy, Gregg Henry, Kay Lenz, Tina Louise. D: Mel Stuart. CRI [R] 108m. V

Mean Frank & Crazy Tony 1975 Italian ★★★ Hero worship prompts an aspiring thug to emulate his gangster idol. Italian crime yarn, clever at times. C: Lee Van Cleef, Tony Lo Bianco, Jean Rochefort, Jess Hahn. D: Michele Lupo. CRI [R] 92m. V

Mean Johnny Barrows 1976 ★★ Vietnam veteran gets mixed up with syndicate crime lords. Earnest yeoman effort. C: Fred Williamson, Jenny Sherman, Luther Adler, Stuart Whitman, Roddy McDowall, Elliott Gould. D: Fred Williamson. CRI [R] 85m. V

Mean Machine, The 1973 ★ The mob killed his dad, so now he's gonna take his revenge, aided by a busty woman of course. C: Christopher Mitchum, Barbara Bouchet, Arthur Kennedy. CRI 89m.

Mean Season, The 1984 ★★★½ A psychotic killer uses a Miami reporter (Russell) as his means of achieving his 15 minutes of fame. Though essentially a standard catch-me-if-you-can thriller, it does have its moments and deals with the issue of media responsibility. C: Kurt Russell, Mariel Hemingway, Richard Jordan, Richard Masur, Joe Pantoliano. D: Phillip Borsos. CRI [R] 106m. V

Mean Streets 1973 ★★★★½ Breakthrough film for Scorsese, De Niro, and Keitel is gritty urban slice of life. Keitel is a guilt-racked petty racketeer trying to protect crazy, reckless friend DeNiro from loan sharks. Film has edgy nervous energy, great acting and terrific use of pop music, all the trade-marks of a Scorsese movie. C: Robert De Niro, Harvey Keitel, David Proval, Amy Robinson, Richard Romanus, Cesare Danova. D: Martin Scorsese. CRI [R] 112m. V

Meanest Man in the World, The 1940 ★★★★ Fair-minded lawyer (Benny) discovers that cruelty will get him ahead. Funny satire, a perfect vehicle for Jack and his sidekick Rochester (Eddie Anderson). One of Benny's best. C: Jack Benny, Eddie "Rochester" Anderson, Priscilla Lane, Edmund Gwenn. D: Sidney Lanfield. COM 57m.

Meanest Men in the West, The 1976 ★★★★ Two tough varmints who are half brothers go constantly at anyone else in their path. Star cast makes it. C: Charles Bronson, Lee Marvin, Lee J. Cobb, Charles Grodin. D: Samuel Fuller. WST 92m. V

Means and Ends 1985 ★★ Fledgling filmmakers intent on shooting an erotic movie hoodwink small-town citizens into believing the film's a comedy. Ambitious ethical commentary makes up for directorial flaws. C: William Windom, Cyril O'Reilly, Reed Birney, Ken Michelman, Lori Lethin, Doyle Baker, John Randolph, Jack Fletcher, Michael Greene. D: Gerald Michenaud. DRA 105m.

Meantime 1983 British ★★★ Director Leigh, whose films chronicle working-class British life, delves into the dysfunctions and small joys of a marginal London family. Stinging kitchen-sink drama can be depressing, but Leigh's pointed social commentary and on-target characterizations are captivating. Notable for early work from Oldman, Roth, and Molina. C: Marion Bailey, Phil Daniels, Tim Roth, Pam Ferris, Jeff Robert, Alfred Molina, Gary Oldman. D: Mike Leigh. DRA 104m.

Meatballs 1979 Canadian ★★★ Amiable comedy features Murray as summer camp counselor whipping pack of stereotypes into shape, while wooing co-counseler Lynch. Murray dominates every frame, which is definitely for the best. Junior high schoolers will appreciate this the most. C: Bill Murray, Harvey Atkin, Kate Lynch, Russ Banham. D: Ivan Reitman. COM [PG] 93m. V

Meatballs III 1987 ★ A ghostly sex film star helps shy summer camper overcome his carnal naiveté. As bad as bad makeout movies get. C: Sally Kellerman, Patrick Dempsey, Al Waxman, Isabelle Mejias, Shannon Tweed. D: George Mendeluk. COM [R] 95m. V

Mechanic, The 1972 ★★★½ Bronson plays the ultimate killing machine, a super-assassin who must train the next generation. Intense portrayals, but action is for action's sake. C: Charles Bronson, Keenan Wynn, Jan-Michael Vincent, Jill Ireland. D: Michael Winner. ACT [PG] 100m. V

Medal for Benny, A 1945 ★★★★ John Steinbeck tale of small California town hypocrites who capitalize on the death of a local war hero. Moving, incisively written drama with touches of satire and sentiment. C: Dorothy Lamour, Arturo de Cordova, J. Carroll Naish, Mikhail Rasumny, Fernando Alvarado, Charles Dingle, Frank McHugh. D: Irving Pichel. DRA 77m.

Medal for the General 1946 *See* **Gay Intruders, The**

Medea 1970 Italian ★★★½ Euripides' classic tragedy is brought to the screen as a star vehicle for Callas. She plays Jason's wife, whose descent into madness involves killing her own children. Callas is electric. C: Maria Callas, Guiseppi Gentile. D: Pier Paolo Pasolini. DRA 118m.

Medical Story 1975 ★★★★ An idealistic young doctor finds incompetence, cover-ups, and unnecessary surgical procedures among the staff at a famous hospital. Fact-based teleplay by Abby Mann, smartly done. C: Beau Bridges, Jose Ferrer, Claude Akins, Wendell Burton, Shirley Knight, Carl Reiner, Martha Scott, Sydney Chaplin. D: Gary Nelson. DRA 100m. TVM

Medicine Ball Caravan 1971 ★★½ In the summer of 1970, a 150-member troupe tours America on behalf of music, peace, and love. Prosaic direction mars showcase for such stars as B. B. King, Doug Kershaw, and Delaney and Bonnie. C: B. King, Alice Cooper, Delaney, & Bonnie, Doug Kershaw, David Peel. D: Francois Reichenbach. MUS [R] 90m. TVM

Medicine Hat Stallion, The 1977 ★★★½ After his father sells his favorite pony, boy runs off to become Pony Express rider. Nicely TV-made kids' western. C: Leif Garrett, John Quade, Milo O'Shea, Mitchell Ryan, Bibi Besch, charles Tyner, John Anderson. D: Michael O'Herlihy. FAM/ACT 85m. TVM V

Medicine Man 1992 ★★★½ Frenetic biologist (Bracco) reluctantly works for unorthodox scientist (Connery) sequestered deep in Amazon rain forest who's discovered the cure for cancer—then loses it. Noble concept poorly executed, but haunting Goldsmith score and captivating Mexican scenery. C: Sean Connery, Lurraine Bracco, Jose Wilker. D: John McTiernan. DRA [PG-13] 106m. V

Medicine Man, The 1930 ★★½ When a traveling sideshow hits town, its medicine man (Benny) dallies with a local woman who's got trouble at home. Sentimental comedy/drama puts acerbic Benny on his heels. C: Jack Benny, Betty Bronson, E. Alyn Warren. D: Scott Pembroke. COM 66m.

Mediterranean in Flames, The 1972 Greek ★★½ Anti-Nazi resistance fighters in Greece kill and love with equal gusto. C: Costas Precas, Costas Karras. D: Dimis Dadiras. ACT 85m. V

Mediterraneo 1991 Italian ★★★★½ Band of WWII Italian soldiers stranded on Greek island discover the place is paradise; by war's end, they don't want to leave. Picturesque comedy delivers harmless enjoyment. Oscar for Best Foreign Film. C: Diego Abatantuono, Claudio Bigagli, Giuseppe Cederna, Claudio Bisio. D: Gabriele Salvatores. COM [R] 90m. V

Medium Cool 1969 ★★★★ A TV cameraman covering the riots at the 1968 Chicago Democratic Convention detaches himself from the events he's filming as well as from his interpersonal relationships. Realistic, intimate study of people, situations, and involvements. C: Robert Forster, Verna Bloom, Peter Bonerz, Marianna Hill. D: Haskell Wexler. DRA [R] 111m. V

Medium, The 1951 ★★★ Gian-Carlo Menotti's brooding opera about an eccentric medium who accidentally kills her aide. Good acting by Powers enhances unusual tale. C: Marie Powers, Anna Maria Alberghetti, Leo Coleman. D: GianCarlo Menotti. DRA 80m. V

Medusa 1976 ★★½ Who killed the two people found on the yacht, floating in the Aegean? Could it have something to do with a plot to defraud a woman out of her inheritance? C: George Hamilton, Luciana Paluzzi, Cameron Mitchell, Theodore Roubanis. D: Gordon Hessler. CRI 103m. V

Medusa—Dare to Be Truthful 1992 *See* **Dare to Be Truthful.**

Medusa Touch, The 1978 British ★★★ A writer (Burton) can destroy his enemies, real and imagined, by the mere strength of his will. When he's assaulted . . . well, no one's safe. Overemoting Burton and a tremendous supporting cast are squandered on this overblown *Twilight Zone* episode. C: Richard Burton, Lino Ventura, Lee Remick, Harry Andrews. D: Jack Gold. HOR [PG] 109m. V

Meet Boston Blackie 1941 ★★★½ A police inspector can't believe a former thief has gone straight. Successful, entertaining first entry in the nine-year series. Engaging performance by Morris. C: Chester Morris, Rochelle Hudson, Richard Lane, Charles Wagenheim, Constance Worth. D: Robert Florey. CRI 61m.

Meet Danny Wilson 1952 ★★★ An aggressive singer-entertainer becomes successful with help from mobsters. Excellent performance by Sinatra. C: Frank Sinatra, Shelley Winters, Alex Nicol, Raymond Burr. D: Joseph Pevney. DRA 86m. V

Meet Dr. Christian 1939 ★★½ A sagacious small-town doctor helps raise money to build a hospital. First entry in folksy family series. C: Jean Hersholt, Dorothy Lovett, Robert Baldwin, Paul Harvey, Marcia Mae Jones. D: Bernard Vorhaus. FAM/DRA 70m. v

Meet John Doe 1941 ★★★★½ A naive hobo (Cooper) is manipulated by a reporter (Stanwyck) and a corrupt politician (Arnold) to embody the common man in a phony national goodwill drive protesting world conditions. Good characterizations and vivid Capra direction highlight idealistic social commentary. C: Gary Cooper, Barbara Stanwyck, Edward Arnold, Walter Brennan, Spring Byington, James Gleason, Gene Lockhart. D: Frank Capra. DRA 122m. v

Meet Me After the Show 1951 ★★★ Musical love triangle in which singing star suspects that an attractive backer is romancing her husband. Feisty vehicle for Grable. C: Betty Grable, Macdonald Carey, Rory Calhoun, Eddie Albert, Lois Andrews, Irene Ryan. D: Richard Sale. MUS 86m.

Meet Me at the Fair 1953 ★★★ Turn-of-the-century traveling sideshow medicine man harbors an orphan. Engaging outdoor musical. C: Dan Dailey, Diana Lynn, Hugh O'Brian, Carole Mathews, Rhys Williams, Chet Allen, Scatman Crothers. D: Douglas Sirk. MUS 87m.

Meet Me in Las Vegas 1956 ★★★ A ballet star changes the luck of a gambling rancher. Fine dancing sequences highlight musical extravaganza. C: Dan Dailey, Cyd Charisse, Agnes Moorehead, Lili Darvas, Jim Backus, Jerry Colonna, Paul Henreid, Lena Horne, Frankie Laine, Mitsuko Sawamura. D: Roy Rowland. MUS 103m. v

Meet Me in St. Louis 1944 ★★★★★ MGM valentine to Garland improves with each viewing. Based on Sally Benson's short stories, it's a series of sensitive, charming vignettes showing the Smith family during year of St. Louis World's Fair, 1903. Judy performs wonderful Hugh Martin/Ralph Blane songs "The Boy Next Door," "The Trolley Song," and "Have Yourself a Merry Little Christmas." O'Brien won special child actress Oscar. A must for the family. C: Judy Garland, Margaret O'Brien, Lucille Bremer, Tom Drake, Mary Astor, Leon Ames, Marjorie Main, June Lockhart, Harry Davenport. D: Vincente Minnelli. FAM/MUS 114m. v

Meet Me Tonight 1952 *See* **Tonight at 8:30**

Meet Miss Marple 1962 *See* **Murder, She Said**

Meet Mr. Lucifer 1953 British ★★★ The devil schemes to fight the evils of television. Light satire with some amusing moments. C: Stanley Holloway, Peggy Cummins, Jack Watling, Barbara Murray, Joseph Tomelty, Gordon Jackson, Jean Cadell, Kay Kendall, Ian Carmichael. D: Anthony Pelissier. COM 83m.

Meet My Sister 1933 British ★★★ A down-on-his-luck British aristocrat (Mollison) throws his mistress over for an American heiress in this harmless attempt at screwball comedy. C: Clifford Mollison, Constance Shotter, Fred Duprez. D: John Daumery. COM 70m.

Meet Nero Wolfe 1936 ★★★½ First of what was to become only two movie serials starring Rex Stout's rotund dilettante detective. Here, Wolfe solves the mystery of the death of a college president without leaving the comfort of his own home. Enjoyable, well-done mystery. C: Edward Arnold, Joan Perry, Lionel Stander, Victor Jory. D: Herbert Biberman. CRI 73m.

Meet the Applegates 1991 ★★★ Bizarre satire of a family of life-size beetles who travel to the U.S. in human form to make a home in suburbia. Unconventional, weird comedy. (a.k.a. *The Applegates*) C: Ed Begley Jr., Stockard Channing, Dabney Coleman, Bobby Jacoby, Cami Cooper, Glenn Shadix, Susan Barnes, Adam Biesk, Savannah Boucher. D: Michael Lehman. COM 90m. v

Meet the Baron 1933 ★★½ An incompetent bumbler is promoted as the actual Baron Munchhausen. Veteran collection of comedy performers at play. C: Jack Pearl, Jimmy Durante, ZaSu Pitts, Ted Healy & his Stooges, Edna May Oliver. D: Walter Lang. COM 65m.

Meet the Chump 1941 ★★½ A $10 million inheritance, which has been squandered by a nincompoop trustee, is suddenly due the rightful heir. Some funny, frenetic moments in this crazy comedy. C: Hugh Herbert, Lewis Howard, Jeanne Kelly, Anne Nagel, Kathryn Adams, Shemp Howard, Richard Lane. D: Edward Cline. COM 60m.

Meet The Hollowheads 1989 ★★ On another planet in another universe, people live entirely by having all things pumped into homes via tubing. The Hollowheads are a representative family in this swacky civilization. Silly, offbeat fun. C: John Glover, Nancy Mette, Richard Portnow, Matt Shakman, Juliette Lewis, Anne Ramsey. D: Tom Burman. COM [PG-13] 89m. v

Meet the Missus 1937 ★★½ Contest-crazy wife (Broderick) and her put-upon husband (Moore) travel to Atlantic City to compete for the "Happy Noodles Housewives" championship. Minor, quickie comedy. C: Victor Moore, Helen Broderick, Anne Shirley. D: Joseph Santley. COM 65m.

Meet the Navy 1946 British ★★★½ 'Back stage " military musical revue featuring amateur performers recruited from British colonies that toured WWII bases entertaining the troops. No big names, but pleasant vintage song-and-dance entertainment." C: Lionel Murton, Margaret Hurst. D: Alfred Travers. MUS 85m. v

Meet the People 1944 ★★½ To prove she's not stuck-up (*and* to gain a little publicity), a former Broadway star takes a shipyard job. Diverting wartime musical with a charming cast. C: Lucille Ball, Dick Powell, Virginia O'Brien, Bert Lahr, Rags Ragland, June Allyson, Mata & Hari. D: Charles Riesner. MUS 100m.

Meet the Stewarts 1942 ★★★ Wealthy socialite used to luxury weds white-collar working stiff on a budget. Pleasant entertainment. C: William Holden, Frances Dee, Grant Mitchell, Anne Revere, Mary Gordon, Marjorie Gateson, Margaret Hamilton, Don Beddoe. D: Alfred E. Green. COM 73m.

Meeting Venus 1991 British ★★★½ A conductor finds himself in the middle of a politically contentious multinational opera production in Europe. It's a lot more fun than it sounds, in a subtle way. Close is radiant as the diva who beds the conductor. C: Glenn Close, Niels Arestrup, Erland Josephson, Johanna Ter Steege, Jay Sanders, Maria de Medeiros, Ildiko Bansagi. D: Istvan Szabo. DRA [PG-13] 120m. V

Meetings of Anna, The 1978 *See* **Les Rendezvous D'Anna**

Meetings With Remarkable Men 1979 British ★★★½ The religious mystic Gurdjieff wanders throughout Asia and the Middle East seeking enlightenment. Beautiful location filming highlights rather tame effort. Startling and memorable sound track. C: Terence Stamp, Dragan Maksimovic, Mikica Dimitrijevic, Athol Fugard, Warren Mitchell, Gerry Sundquist, Bruce Myers, Natasha Parry, Martin Benson. D: Peter Brook. DRA [G] 110m. V

Megaforce 1982 ★ Elite, state-of-the-art combat team attempt to wrest a small nation from mercenaries. Juvenile action adventure. C: Barry Bostwick, Persis Khambatta, Michael Beck, Edward Mulhare, George Furth, Henry Silva. D: Hal Needham. ACT [PG] 99m. V

Megaville 1991 ★★★ A policeman bravely goes undercover and poses as a dangerous assassin. But the cop himself is being set up. Solid actioner. C: Billy Zane, J.C. Quinn, Grace Zabriskie, Kristen Cloke. D: Peter Lehner. ACT 96m. V

Mein Kampf 1960 Swedish ★★★★ Engrossing compilation of newsreels, presenting the rise and downfall of Nazi Germany. Direct and simply done; a most effective documentary. D: Erwin Leiser. DOC 117m. V

Melanie 1982 ★★★ When a woman is accused of being unfit to raise her child, she fights back to keep her child. Inspiring. C: Glynnis O'Connor, Paul Sorvino, Don Johnson, Burton Cummings. D: Rex Bromfield. DRA [PG] 109m. V

Melanie Rose 1989 *See* **High Stakes**

Melba 1953 British ★★★ Life story of Australian soprano Dame Nellie Melba, the celebrated Victorian opera star. Fairly interesting biography, largely for opera buffs. C: Patrice Munsel, Robert Morley, Sybil Thorndike, Martita Hunt, John McCallum. D: Lewis Milestone. MUS 113m.

Melinda 1972 ★★ An African-American radio personality tracks down his girlfriend's murderers. Unduly violent, sensationalist fare. C: Calvin Lockhart, Rosalind Cash, Vonetta McGee, Paul Stevens, Rockne Tarkington. D: Hugh A. Robertson. ACT [R] 109m.

Melo 1986 French ★★★½ Henry Bernstein's 1920s play about a woman tortured by her unfaithfulness to her lover. Theatrical in presentation, with powerful performances. C: Sabine Azéma, Pierre Arditi, Andre Dussollier, Fanny Ardant, Jacques Dacqmine, Catherine Arditi. D: Alain Resnais. DRA 110m.

Melody 1971 British ★★★ Prepubescent hormones on the rampage, as boy and girl who want to get married face another boy's jealousy. Winsome juvenile leads enhance tale of rebellious adolescents. C: Jack Wild, Mark Lester, Tracy Hyde, Sheila Steafel, Roy Kinnear. D: Waris Hussein. DRA [G] 106m. V

Melody Cruise 1933 ★★★½ Bawdy shipboard musical comedy about a lothario who gets his just desserts but still wins his girl. Ruggles walks away with the show in this wacky comedy-romance. C: Charlie Ruggles, Phil Harris, Helen Mack, Greta Nissen, Chick Chandler, June Brewster. D: Mark Sandrich. MUS 76m. V

Melody for Three 1941 ★★½ Dr. Christian plays matchmaker when he brings together a noted concert conductor and his old flame. Beautiful Wray adds luster to this saga. C: Jean Hersholt, Fay Wray, Walter Woolf King, Schuyler Standish, Irene Ryan. D: Erle C. Kenton. DRA 66m. V

Melody in Love 1978 ★ A woman goes to a tropical island where passion is the exclusive source of entertainment. Guess what happens next? Not for the kiddies. C: Melody O'Bryan, Sasha Hehn. D: Hubert Frank. DRA 90m. V

Melody Master 1941 ★★★ The life and times of composer Franz Schubert, including his disappointments in romance and his fabulous success as a creator of memorable music. Lovely drama, pricesless music. C: Alan Curtis, Ilona Massey, Billy Gilbert, Binnie Barnes. D: Reinhold Schunzel. DRA 60m. V

Melody of Life *See* **Symphony of Six Million**

Melody Ranch 1942 ★★★ Gene Autry returns home and he becomes the sheriff for all. Nice western action and characters. C: Gene Autry, Jimmy Durante, George "Gabby" Hayes. D: Joseph Santley. WST 84m. V

Melody Time 1948 ★★★½ Uneven mix of seven Disney animated musical shorts, highlights being "The Story of Johnny Appleseed" featuring the voice of Dennis Day, and "Pecos Bill" with Roy Rogers and the Sons of the Pioneers. Kids will enjoy the stories while oldtimers will enjoy the music. C: Roy Rogers, Bobby Driscoll, The Andrews Sisters, Frances Langford. D: Clyde Geronimi, Wilfred Jackson, Hamilton Luske, Jack Kinney. FAM/MUS 75m.

Melvin and Howard 1980 ★★★★★ Eccentric billionaire Howard Hughes is felled in a Nevada desert motorcycle accident and hitches a ride to Las Vegas with a feckless laborer, who later finds himself disbelieved when he's mentioned in Hughes' will. An engaging slice of blue-collar Americana, with appealing performances by all concerned. Oscars for Best Supporting Actress (Steenburgen), Best Screenplay (Goldman). C: Paul LeMat, Jason Robards, Mary Steenburgen, Jack Kehoe, Pamela Reed, Dabney Coleman, Charles Napier. D: Jonathan Demme. DRA [R] 95m. V

Melvin Purvis-G-Man 1974 ★★★★ Flashy FBI agent Melvin Purvis chases elusive Midwestern robber/kidnapper George "Machine Gun" Kelly in the early '30s. A bravura performance from Robertson, harking back to old-fashioned gangster films of yore. C: Dale Robertson, Harris Yulin, Margaret Blye, Matt Clark. D: Dan Curtis. CRI 76m. TVM V

Member of the Wedding, The 1952 ★★★★ A sensitive girl comes of age after a friend dies and a brother marries. Stagebound and leisurely paced Carson McCullers Broadway hit is directed with tact and exceptional performances. Film debut for Harris and de Wilde. C: Ethel Waters, Julie Harris, Brandon de Wilde, Arthur Franz, Nancy Gates, James Edwards. D: Fred Zinnemann. DRA 91m. V

Memed My Hawk 1987 British ★★½ A plucky Republican rebel in 1923 Turkey decamps his besieged village with a bumbling feudal tyrant in avid pursuit. Blend of melodrama and comedy in unusual locales. C: Peter Ustinov, Herbert Lom, Denis Quilley, Michael Elphick, Simon Dutton, Leonie Mellinger, Barry Dennen, Siobhan McKenna, T. P. McKenna, Michael Gough. D: Peter Ustinov. DRA [PG-13] 101m.

Memoirs of a Survivor 1981 British ★★ Adaptation of Doris Lessing's fantasy novel about a woman seeking refuge from a blighted future society. Christie's considerable presence brightens this ambitious effort. C: Julie Christie, Christopher Guard, Leonie Mellinger, Debbie Hutchings, Nigel Hawthorne, Pat Keen. D: David Gladwell. DRA 117m.

Memoirs of an Invisible Man 1992 ★★★ Securities analyst Chase becomes a wanted man after an accident renders him invisible. Uneasy blend of thriller and comedy never quite clicks. C: Chevy Chase, Daryl Hannah, Sam Neill, Michael McKean, Stephen Tobolowsky. D: John Carpenter. COM [PG-13] 99m. V

Memorial Day 1983 ★★★★ A chance meeting between a prosperous attorney and his Vietnam war chums triggers unwelcome memories of combat. Courageous film hits the issue on the nose; strong acting by Farrell and Walden. C: Mike Farrell, Shelley Fabares, Bonnie Bedelia, Robert Walden, Edward Herrmann, Bert Remsen. D: Joseph Sargent. DRA 95m. TVM V

Memorial Valley Massacre 1988 ★★ Campers are attacked by psychopath. Lots of blood and gore. C: Cameron Mitchell, Mark Mears, John Kerry, Lisa Lee. D: Robert C. Hughes. HOR [R] 93m. TVM

Memories of a Fairy Godmother 1980 ★★★ Fairy tale characters come to life in a combination of live action and animation. Sweet fantasy adventure for children. C: Rosemary De Camp, Gregg Berger. FAM/DRA 60m. V

Memories of a Marriage 1989 ★★★ During a reunion with his friends, a man finds himself reminiscing about his failed marriage. Tender drama. C: Ghita Norby, Frits Helmuth. D: Kaspar Rostrup. DRA 90m. V

Memories of Me 1988 ★★★ After suffering heart attack, surgeon Crystal attempts to make amends for past with estranged father King, a top Hollywood extra. Nice premise suffers from heavy reliance on sentimental schmaltz and contrived comic bits. Co-written by Crystal, who also produced with King. Directing debut for former television heartthrob Winkler. C: Billy Crystal, Alan King, JoBeth William, Janet Carroll. D: Henry Winkler. COM [PG-13] 103m. V

Memories of Murder 1990 ★★ Woman wakes up one day with no memory—except for visions of a gruesome murder—then discovers someone is stalking her. Easily forgettable thriller. C: Nancy Allen, Robin Thomas, Vanity. D: Robert Lewis. CRI 104m. TVM V

Memories of Underdevelopment 1968 ★★★★★ Young man (Corrieri) is unable to find himself or his political role in postrevolutionary Cuba. Cannily structured "fictional documentary" combines newsreel footage and erotic fantasies to create a subtle, profound indictment of modern man's moral quandary. C: Sergio Corrieri, Daisy Granados. D: Tomas Gutierrez Alea. DRA 97m. V

Memory of Eva Ryker, The 1980 ★★★ Woman seeks the truth about the WWII sinking of the luxury liner on which her mother was a passenger. Wood has a field day as both mother and daughter, but the script leaks a little. C: Natalie Wood, Robert Foxworth, Roddy McDowall, Jean-Pierre Aumont, Mel Ferrer, Ralph Bellamy. D: Water Grauman. DRA 144m.

Memory of Justice, The 1976 German-U.S. ★★★★★ Daring, four-hour plus documentary explores/compares Nazi atrocities during WWII with the French invasion of Algeria and American involvement in Vietnam. The director of the classic *The Sorrow and the Pity* extends his range with shattering impact. D: Marcel Ophuls. DOC [PG] 278m.

Memphis Belle 1990 British ★★★★ An American B-17 crew flies its last bombing mission over Germany. Tense and exciting with a young and able cast. Includes actual war footage; flying scenes were praised by vets for their accuracy. C: Matthew Modine,

Eric Stoltz, Tate Donovan, D. B. Sweeney, Billy Zane, Harry Connick Jr. D: Michael Caton-Jones. DRA [PG-13] 107m. v

Men . . . 1985 German ★★★★½ Jealous husband deliberately becomes roommate of wife's lover. Tender, insightful and raucously funny. Wonderful farce became huge worldwide hit. C: Heiner Lauterbach, Uwe Ochsenknecht, Ulrike Kriener. D: Doris Dörrie. COM 99m. v

Men Against the Sun 1953 British ★★★ Construction supervisor of Mombasa-to-Uganda railroad deals with beauty and the beasts: a missionary doctor (Marshall) and three man-eating lions. African setting raises no temperatures in this pale romantic drama. C: John Bentley, Zena Marshall. D: Brendan J. Stafford. DRA 65m.

Men are Children Twice 1953 British ★★★ Nostalgic comedy about a feud in a Welsh village when the choirmaster chooses a new soloist for the annual production of Handel's *Messiah*. Dated, but performances keep it humming. (a.k.a. *Valley of Song*) C: Mervyn Johns, Clifford Evans, Maureen Swanson, Rachel Roberts. D: Gilbert Gunn. COM 74m.

Men at Work 1990 ★★ When two trash collectors (brothers Estevez and Sheen) find a corpse in the garbage, they end up on trail of a killer. Dumb, but occasionally fun in its own way, with goofy performances by real-life sibling duo. Estevez also directed. C: Charlie Sheen, Emilio Estevez, Leslie Hope, Keith David, Dean Cameron, John Getz, Cameron Dye, John Putch. D: Emilio Estevez. COM [PG-13] 99m. v

Men Don't Leave 1990 ★★★★ When her husband dies suddenly, a young mother (Lange) faces the travails of raising her family and rebuilding her life. Effective, if somewhat clichéd. Cusack gives a strong quirky performance. Remake of *La Vie Continue*. C: Jessica Lange, Arliss Howard, Joan Cusack, Chris O'Donnell, Charlie Korsmo, Kathy Bates, Tom Mason, Jim Haynie. D: Paul Brickman. DRA [PG-13] 115m. v

Men in Her Life, The 1941 ★★★ A beautiful circus rider (Young) becomes a famous ballerina through the efforts of her dance master (Veidt). She marries him while very much remembering her former various love affairs. Entirely unbelievable, old-fashioned melodrama based on Lady Eleanor Smith's novel *Ballerina*. C: Loretta Young, Conrad Veidt, Dean Jagger, Eugenie Leontovich, John Shepperd, Otto Kruger. D: Gregory Ratoff. DRA 90m.

Men In Love 1990 ★★½ When his lover dies, a young man takes his ashes to Hawaii for burial. Along the way, he has a spiritual encounter. Interesting drama. C: Doug Self, Joe Tolbe, Emerald Starr. D: Marc Huestis. DRA 87m. v

Men in War 1957 ★★★½ During the Korean War, a lieutenant (Ryan) leads a platoon of stranded soldiers attempting to reach their battalion's headquarters while a sergeant (Ray) guides his shell-shocked Colonel (Keith) to a field hospital. Gritty, better-than-average war drama. C: Robert Ryan, Aldo Ray, Robert Keith, Vic Morrow, James Edwards, Scott Marlowe, Victor Sen Yung. D: Anthony Mann. ACT 104m. v

Men in White 1934 ★★★½ A young doctor (Gable) is devoted to working with an older surgeon (Hersholt) but engaged to socialite (Loy) who's jealous of her fiancé's work and his nurse (Allan). Film spawned a spate of hospital dramas. Based on Sidney Kingsley's play. C: Clark Gable, Myrna Loy, Jean Hersholt, Elizabeth Allan, Otto Kruger, Wallace Ford, Henry B. Walthall, Samuel S. Hinds. D: Richard Boleslawski. DRA 80m.

Men of Boys Town 1941 ★★★★ The benevolent Father Flanagan continues to straighten out street-tough youths in his refuge for lost boys. Sequel to successful *Boy's Town* is sentimental, but Tracy holds his own alongside good performances all around. C: Spencer Tracy, Mickey Rooney, Bobs Watson, Henry O'Neill, Lee J. Cobb. D: Norman Taurog. DRA 106m. v

Men of Bronze 1977 ★★★½ Documentary on the "Rattlesnake Regiment" of African-American soldiers fighting in WWI. Rare footage and still photos add to the exciting story of a stirring chapter in American history. D: William Miles. DOC 60m. v

Men of Destiny 1942 *See* **Men of Texas**

Men of Respect 1991 ★★ Inept attempt to retell *Macbeth* as a Mafia story. Out, out, damned film! C: John Turturro, Katherine Borowitz, Dennis Farina, Peter Boyle, Rod Steiger, Steven Wright. D: William Reilly. CRI 107m. v

Men of Sherwood Forest 1954 British ★★★ Straightforward adaptation of the English bandit saga lacks the swashbuckling element that enlivened other versions, although Taylor makes an appealing Robin Hood. C: Don Taylor, Reginald Beckwith, Eileen Moore, David Wood. D: Val Guest. DRA 77m. v

Men of Steel 1988 ★★★ Two Canadians, one of French and one of British background, crash land in the frozen north. Working together, they struggle to reach civilization. Interesting symbolism. C: Alan Royal, Robert Lalonde. D: Donald Shebib. ACT [PG] 79m. v

Men of Texas 1942 ★★★ A Northern reporter and his photographer friend travel to the Longhorn state to uncover rumors of a possible rebellion aimed at reviving conflicts from the recent Civil War. Modest low-budget Western adapted by Shumante from his story, *Frontier*. (a.k.a. *Men of Destiny*) C: Robert Stack, Broderick Crawford, Jackie Cooper, Anne Gwynne, Ralph Bellamy. D: Ray Enright. WST 82m.

Men of the Fighting Lady 1954 ★★★½ Pilots on an aircraft carrier during the Korean

War relate their everyday life and death experiences to a writer. Dramatic action footage of dogfights, crashes, and heroics punctuate routine war drama based on stories by James Michener and Cmdr. Harry Burns. C: Van Johnson, Walter Pidgeon, Louis Calhern, Dewey Martin, Keenan Wynn, Frank Lovejoy. D: Andrew Marton. ACT 81m. V

Men of the Sea 1935 ★★★★ An 18th-century British youth (Green) joins Royal Navy for adventure and finds himself rescuing damsels like Lockwood and battling pirates. High-spirited swashbuckler was Reed's first solo effort as director. Filmed in 1935. (a.k.a. *Midshipman Easy*) C: Hughie Green. D: Carol Reed. ACT 77m.

Men of Yesterday 1936 ★★★ Ex-soldiers attending their army reunion relive happy memories and bitter rivalries that haven't cooled. Drama hasn't aged well, but provides a good cross section of British talent. C: Stewart Rome, Sam Livesey. D: John Baxter. DRA 82m.

Men, The 1950 ★★★★½ A paraplegic G.I. (Brando) hospitalized with other war veterans scorns his fiancée (Wright) and struggles against the doctor (Sloane) who forces him to face his physical and emotional challenges. Powerful and sensitive drama notable for its straightforward treatment of sexual themes and as Brando's auspicious screen debut. (a.k.a. *Battle Stripe*) C: Marlon Brando, Teresa Wright, Everett Sloane, Jack Webb. D: Fred Zinnemann. DRA 85m. V

Men with Wings 1938 ★★★½ Aviation drama chronicles the story of two aviators who vie for the affections of the same woman. MacMurray and Milland give top performances. C: Fred MacMurray, Louise Campbell, Ray Milland, Andy Devine, Walter Abel, Virginia Weidler. D: William A. Wellman. DRA 105m.

Men Without Women 1930 ★★★½ Title is a tease, having little to do with this action drama about a submarine sent to the bottom of the sea after a collision and the crew's desperate attempts to escape. Taut, thrilling suspense; many imitators followed. C: Kenneth MacKenna, Frank Albertson, Paul Page. D: John Ford. ACT 77m.

Menace on the Mountain 1970 ★★★½ As the Civil War comes to a close, a father and his young son find themselves in their own war against army deserters. C: Mitch Vogel, Charles Aidman, Albert Salmi, Pat Crowley. ACT 89m. V

Menace, The 1932 ★★½ An ex-con (Byron) with a re-vamped face seeks revenge on his stepmother for framing him. Dull crime drama gets a lift from the presence of Davis as the con's virtuous fiancee. C: Walter Byron, Bette Davis, Natalie Moorhead, H.B. Warner. D: William Neill. CRI 64m.

Menace II Society 1993 ★★★★ A bleak look at inner-city violence, with Turner dragged into a spiral of mayhem by his out-of-control friend (Tate). Well-crafted first feature is spurred by excellent performances by young cast. C: Tyrin Turner, Larenz Tate, Jada Pinkett, Vonte Sweet, Samuel L. Jackson, Charles S. Dutton, Glenn Plummer, Bill Duke. D: Allen &, Albert Hughes. ACT [R] 104m. V

Menendez: A Killing in Beverly Hills 1994 ★★★ Straightforward retelling of the killing of Jose and Kitty Menendez by their sons. Long, but Olmos is memorably evil as the father whose alleged abuse supposedly motivated the killings. C: Edward James Olmos, Beverly D'Angelo, Damian Chapa. D: Larry Elikann. CRI 240m. TVM

Men's Club, The 1986 ★★ A group of men spend an evening together, getting drunk, wrecking the house, visiting prostitutes and otherwise bonding in this pretentious adaptation of Leonard Michaels' spare novel. C: David Dukes, Richard Jordan, Harvey Keitel, Frank Langella, Roy Scheider, Craig Wasson, Treat Williams. D: Peter Medak. DRA 100m. V

Mephisto 1981 Hungarian ★★★★½ Ambitious actor (Brandauer) collaborates with Nazis to advance his theatrical career. Disturbing dissection of effects of totalitarianism features an outstanding Brandauer performance. Based on novel by Klaus Mann. Oscar for Best Foreign Film. C: Klaus Maria Brandauer, Krystyna Janda, Ildiko Bansagi, Karin Boyd, Rolf Hoppe. D: Istvan Szabo. DRA 150m. V

Mephisto Waltz, The 1971 ★★★★ A sickly devil-worshipping concert pianist (Jurgens) has a journalist (Alda) killed so that he can inhabit his body. Everything's okay until the writer's wife (Bisset) begins to catch on. Flashy horror drama has some real scares; even the score is unnerving. C: Alan Alda, Jacqueline Bisset, Barbara Parkins, Curt Jurgens. D: Paul Wendkos. HOR [R] 109m. V

Mercenary Fighters 1988 ★★★ In a developing African country, trouble starts when modern businessmen clash with tribal elders. Violence and some excitement. C: Peter Fonda, Reb Brown, Ron O'Neal, Jim Mitchum. D: Riki Shelach. ACT [R] 93m. V

Mercenary Game, The ★★★ The world's most successful real-life mercenaries tell their stories in this incredible documentary which studies how they train, how much they're paid, and what they really do. DOC 60m. V

Mercenary, The 1968 Italian ★★★ During the Mexican revolution, mercenaries led by Nero assist peasant revolutionaries in keeping control of the mine they've seized. Dusty, violent Italian/Spanish Western. (a.k.a. *A Professional Gun*) C: Franco Nero, Tony Musante, Jack Palance, Giovanna Ralli. D: Sergio Corbucci. WST [PG] 105m.

Merchant of Four Seasons, The 1971 German ★★★★ Fruit-cart vendor slowly unravels in the midst of an unhappy marriage and unrealized dreams. Stark, often brutal, haunting character study. C: Hans Hirschmuller, Irm Hermann, Hanna Schygulla, Karl Sheydt. D: Rainer Werner Fassbinder. DRA 88m. v

Merchant of Venice, The 1974 ★★★★ Shakespeare's tale of the merchant, the money-lender, and the pound of flesh, done with intelligence and grace by Lord Olivier. C: Laurence Olivier. DRA v

Merchants And Masterpieces ★★★½ An intriguing look at those who collect masterpieces of art and the works themselves. Loaded with interesting stories and details about art. Fascinating. DOC 87m. v

Merchants of War 1988 ★★ Two CIA agents, best friends, are sent overseas on an urgent mission and encounter an Islamic terrorist. Low level excitement. C: Asher Brauner, Jesse Vint, Bonnie Beck. D: Peter M. Mackenzie. ACT [R] 100m. v

Merely Mary Ann 1931 ★★★ The popular silent screen duo Gaynor and Farrell reteam in this oft-filmed story of a maid (Gaynor) who falls for a composer (Farrell). Star charisma buoys a familiar plot. C: Janet Gaynor, Charles Farrell. D: Henry King. DRA 72m.

Meridian—Kiss of the Beast 1990 ★★½ While visiting an Italian castle, Fenn becomes caught up between cursed twins—one of whom becomes a beast while making love. Supernatural softcore has a few effective scenes. (a.k.a. *Kiss of the Beast.*) C: Sherilyn Fenn, Malcolm Jamieson, Charlie, Hilary Mason, Alex Daniels. D: Charles Band. HOR [R] 90m. v

Merlin 1992 ★★ A gorgeous young California woman finds out that she's a descendant of Merlin the magician and as a result has special powers. Limited excitement. C: Richard Lynch, Peter Phelps, James Hong, Nadia Cameron. D: Paul Hunt. SFI [PG-13] 112m. v

Merlin and the Sword 1985 ★½ Legend of King Arthur, Excalibur, and Merlin the sorcerer gets a bizarre retelling. A mistake with a good cast. (a.k.a. *Arthur the King*) C: Malcolm McDowell, Candice Bergen, Edward Woodward, Dyan Cannon. D: Clive Donner. ACT 94m. TVM v

Mermaid Forest 1993 Japanese ★★★ Animation spins the tale of Yuta, who has searched the world for a mate and thinks he may have found her in the lovely Mana. Interesting. SFI 55m. v

Mermaids 1990 ★★★★ Comedy/drama set in the early '60s has Ryder trying to come to terms with her oddball mother Cher and her own independence. Very funny, and sweet without being cloying; Ryder has a couple of knockout scenes. C: Cher, Bob Hoskins, Winona Ryder, Michael Schoeffling, Christina Ricci. D: Richard Benjamin. COM [PG-13] 101m. v

Merrill's Marauders 1962 ★★★½ In 1942, an elite U.S. Army unit fights its way across Burma. Tough, graphic war action, heavy on hand-to-hand combat. Chandler's last film. C: Jeff Chandler, Ty Hardin, Peter Brown, Andrew Duggan, Will Hutchins, Claude Akins, John Hoyt. D: Samuel Fuller. ACT 98m. v

Merrily We Go to Hell 1932 ★★½ Great title, poor movie. Soggy drama casts March as a drunken playwright who marries a proper debutante (Sydney). Cary Grant (in his third film) has a bit part. C: Fredric March, Sylvia Sidney, Adrienne Allen. D: Dorothy Arzner. DRA 78m.

Merrily We Live 1938 ★★★½ A family of rich eccentrics hires a chauffeur (Aherne) who turns out to be a writer in disguise and brings their snooty daughter (Bennett) down to earth. A pleasant *My Man Godfrey* imitation. C: Constance Bennett, Brian Aherne, Alan Mowbray, Billie Burke, Bonita Granville, Tom Brown, Ann Dvorak, Patsy Kelly. D: Norman Z. McLeod. COM 90m.

Merry Andrew 1958 ★★★½ A stiff English schoolmaster (Kaye) visits an archaeological dig to unearth ancient statue but becomes a clown in a traveling circus instead when he falls for a beautiful member of the troupe (Angeli). Light musical comedy, enlivened by Michael Kidd's energetic choreography; based on a story by Paul Gallico. C: Danny Kaye, Pier Angeli, Baccaloni, Robert Coote. D: Michael Kidd. MUS 103m.

Merry Christmas, Mr. Lawrence 1983 British ★★★★ In 1942, British soldiers interned in a Japanese POW camp watch as major (Bowie) refuses to conform to the will of the brutal camp commander (Sakamoto). Strong, haunting adult drama with terrific performances from Bowie and Conti. Based on a story by Laurens van der Post. C: Tom Conti, David Bowie, Ryuichi Sakamoto, Takeshi, Jack Thompson. D: Nagisa Oshima. DRA [R] 124m. v

Merry Go Round of 1938 1937 ★★★½ Four vaudevillians raise an orphan (Hodges). Sentimental backstager, nicely hoisted by the cast of old pros. Good songs, too. C: Bert Lahr, Jimmy Savo, Mischa Auer, Billy House, Joy Hodges, Alice Brady. D: Irving Cummings. MUS 87m.

Merry Monahans, The 1944 ★★★ Nostalgic backstage musical about a family of vaudevillians led by Oakie who rekindles romance with his former partner. Likable performances and plenty of period songs. C: Donald O'Connor, Peggy Ryan, Jack Oakie, Ann Blyth, Rosemary De Camp, John Miljan. D: Charles Lamont. MUS 91m.

Merry Widow, The 1925 ★★★★★ Ornate silent version of Franz Lehar's operetta, with famous tunes now serving as the backdrop for von Stroheim's visual pageantry. The plot concerns an impoverished prince romancing a wealthy American widow. Remade twice, in 1934 and 1952. C: Mae Murray, John Gilbert. D: Erich von Stroheim. COM 113m.

Merry Widow, The 1934 ★★★★ A debonair count (Chevalier), ordered to woo a rich widow (MacDonald) for the sake of his bankrupt country ends up falling in love with her. Charming Lehar operetta with smart direction by Lubitsch and new lyrics ny Lorenz Hart. High point is the Grand Ball where the camera follows swirling couples through mirrored hallway. (a.k.a. *The Lady Dances*) C: Maurice Chevalier, Jeanette MacDonald, Una Merkel, Edward Everett Horton, George Barbier, Herman Bing. D: Ernst Lubitsch. MUS 99m. V

Merry Widow, The 1952 ★★★ Lana flounces nicely in the third filming of Franz Lehar's operetta warhorse. No one can sing, but who cares in the era of MGM lip-synching? Stick with Jeanette MacDonald. C: Lana Turner, Fernando Lamas, Una Merkel. D: Curtis Bernhardt. MUS 105m. V

Merry Wives of Windsor 1982 ★★★½ Amiable rendering of Shakespeare's comedy, with Falstaff in love. C: Leon Charles, Gloria Grahame, Valerie Seelie-Snyder, Dixie Tymitz. D: Jack Manning. COM 140m. V

Merton of the Movies 1947 ★★★½ A Hollywood neophyte (Skelton) becomes an overnight sensation in this comedy based on the Kaufman-Connelly Broadway hit. This version is weaker than the previous filmings (1924 and 1932), but Grahame gives a crackling performance as an actress sent to tarnish the new star's image. C: Red Skelton, Virginia O'Brien, Gloria Grahame, Leon Ames, Alan Mowbray, Hugo Haas. D: Robert Alton. COM 82m. V

Mesmerized 1986 British ★★½ Foster is orphan teen married to, and brutalized by, Lithgow. She finally tries hypnotism as a weapon against him. Strange, sometimes incomprehensible drama. (a.k.a. *Shocked*) C: Jodie Foster, John Lithgow, Michael Murphy, Harry Andrews. D: Michael Laughlin. DRA 97m. V

Message from Space 1978 Japanese ★★★ Japanese sci-fi follows the adventures of four young astronauts who respond to a distress signal sent by faraway planet besieged by enemy forces. Unrepentant rip-off of *Star Wars,* from the weird monsters to the talking robots. C: Vic Morrow, Sonny Chiba, Philip Casnoff, Peggy Lee Brennan, Sue Shiomi, Tetsuro Tamba. D: Kinji Fukasaku. SFI [PG] 105m.

Message, The 1977 ★★★ Dramatization of the origins of the Islamic religion, filled with epic scenes of action and color. (a.k.a. *Mohammad, Messenger of God*) C: Anthony Quinn, Irene Papas, Michael Ansara, Johnny Sekka. D: Moustapha Akkad. DRA [PG] 176m. V

Message to Garcia, A 1936 ★★★ During the Spanish-American War, a young Cuban (Stanwyck) helps an American soldier (Boles) on a dangerous mission to find rebel leader. Good, well-mounted adventure, though Missy's Spanish accent takes some getting used to. C: John Boles, Wallace Beery, Barbara Stanwyck, Alan Hale. D: George Marshall. ACT 77m.

Message to My Daughter 1973 ★★★ A troubled young girl comes upon some audio tapes that contain messages for her from her deceased Mom. Interesting drama. C: Bonnie Bedelia, Martin Sheen, King Moody. D: Robert Michael Lewis. DRA 76m. TVM V

Messalina Vs. The Son of Hercules 1964 ★★★ The Romans invade England and enslave Hercules's son. In exchange for his freedom, Hercules agrees to lead the Roman army in their rebellion against the wicked Messalina. Lively. C: Richard Harrison, Lisa Gastoni. D: Umberto Lenzi. ACT 105m. V

Messaline 1952 French ★★★ Felix plays the infamous wife of Emperor Augustus, who leaves her husband to search for "true love" by wandering the streets of Rome as a prostitute. Depiction of ancient Rome's decadence is, well, decadent. C: Maria Felix, Jean Chevrier, Georges Marechal. D: Carmine Gallone. DRA 111m.

Messenger of Death 1988 ★★ Bronson, in a rare gunless role, portrays a journalist investigating the grisly murder of a Mormon family in rural Colorado. Lifeless thriller. C: Charles Bronson, Trish Van Devere, Laurence Luckinbill, Marilyn Hassett, John Ireland. D: J. Lee Thompson. DRA [R] 92m. V

Messenger, The 1987 ★★ Ex-con seeks revenge on Italian drug gang for murder of his wife. C: Fred Williamson, Cameron Mitchell, Sandy Cummings, Christopher Connelly. D: Fred Williamson. ACT [R] 95m. V

Messiah of Evil *See* **Dead People**

Metallica 1983 ★★★ In a distant galaxy, a stalwart civilization organizes an army of robots to storm and capture Earth. Chilling. C: Anthony Newcastle, Sharon Baker, Chris Avran. D: Al Brady. SFI 90m. V

Metalstorm—The Destruction of Jared-Syn 1983 ★ Byron is a futuristic hero out to thwart Earth-destroying plot of title villain. Excruciatingly, hilariously bad science fiction consisting exclusively of stereotypes. Originally shown in 3-D. C: Jeffrey Byron, Tim Thomerson, Kelly Preston, Mike Preston, Richard Moll. D: Charles Band. SFI [PG] 84m. V

Metamorphosis: The Alien Factor 1993 ★★★½ Two teenaged girls, searching for their missing father, encounter horrifying creatures at the lab where he worked. Awkward flashback structure in the first half gives way to genuine scares in the second; great special effects on a low budget. C: Tara Leigh, Tony Gigante, Dianna Flaherty, Katherine Romaine. D: Glenn Takakjian. SFI [R] 98m. V

Meteor 1979 ★★ All-star cast deals with the ultimate threat: a meteor hurtling toward Earth! Disastrous disaster film features a weak script and awful special effects. Don't feel sorry for the planet, feel sorry for the actors. C: Sean Connery, Natalie Wood, Karl Malden, Brian Keith, Henry Fonda. D: Ronald Neame. SFI [PG] 105m. V

Meteor Man 1993 ★★★½ Amiable, meandering comedy about a schoolteacher who is exposed to meteor and acquires superpowers, using them to clean up inner-city neighborhood. Likable. C: Robert Townsend, Marla Gibbs, Robert Guillaume, James Earl Jones, Bill Cosby, Luther Vandross, Sinbad. D: Robert Townsend. COM [PG] 99m. V

Meteor Monster 1957 ★★ When a young boy is exposed to a weird meteorite, he turns into a grotesque, hairy creature and his mother tries to hide him. Not so hot. (a.k.a. *Teenage Monster.*) C: Anne Gwynne, Stuart Wade, Gloria Castillo. D: Jacques Marquette. SFI 73m. V

Metropolis 1926 German ★★★★★ Epic drama of class conflict, set in a futuristic city where wealthy and powerful dwell in glittering skyscrapers while dehumanized workers live underground, toiling anonymously at mammoth machines. Stylized sci-fi spectacle filled with effects and images still unparalleled. Allegedly inspired by director Lang's first glimpse of Manhattan. C: Brigitte Helm, Alfred Abel, Gustav Froelich, Rudolf Klein-Rogge, Fritz Rasp. D: Fritz Lang. SFI 115m. V

Metropolitan 1935 ★★★½ Opera, that is. Legendary baritone Tibbett plays a struggling singer enlisted by a prima donna (Brady) who's forming a company to rival the Met. Good musical numbers help cut through the corn. The first film released by 20th Century-Fox. C: Lawrence Tibbett, Alice Brady, Virginia Bruce, Cesar Romero. D: Richard Boleslawski. MUS 75m.

Metropolitan 1990 ★★★★½ Rich, young preppies at loose ends in New York over Christmas. A well-observed social comedy about class differences, snobbery, and trying to get ahead, wittily played by cast of unknowns. Exceptional debut for writer/director Stillman. C: Carolyn Farina, Edward Clements, Christopher Eigeman, Taylor Nichols, Allison Rutledge Parisi. D: Whit Stillman. DRA [PG-13] 98m. V

Mexicali Rose 1939 ★★★½ Nifty little Western has hero (Autry) and his sidekick (Burnette) investigating the shady dealings of his radio show sponsor. One of Burnette's last outings with Autry. C: Gene Autry, Smiley Burnette, Noah Beery, Luana Walters. D: George Sherman. WST 60m.

Mexican Bus Ride 1951 *See* **Ascent to Heaven**

Mexican Hayride 1948 ★★★½ Bud and Lou search for a lost mine deed in sunny Mexico. Naturally, Costello winds up in a bullfight! Funny outing for the boys, from Cole Porter's musical (minus the songs). C: Bud Abbott, Lou Costello, Luba Malina. D: Charles Barton. COM 77m. V

Mexican Spitfire 1939 ★★★★ First of the immensely popular serial comedies spawned by *That Girl from Mexico* concerned attempts by ex-fiancée (Hayes) and snooty aunt Risdon to break up the marriage of Woods and his fiery Latin bride (Velez). Bright performances and hectic pace conceal a paper-thin plot. C: Lupe Velez, Leon Errol, Donald Woods, Linda Hayes, Cecil Kellaway, Elisabeth Risdon. D: Leslie Goodwins. COM 67m. V

Mexican Spitfire at Sea 1942 ★★★ Vivacious title character (Velez) goes to Hawaii to get her husband (Rogers) an advertising job; loony Uncle Errol comes along for the ride. Frenzied high seas escapade. C: Lupe Velez, Leon Errol, ZaSu Pitts, Charles "Buddy" Rogers. D: Leslie Goodwins. COM 73m.

Mexican Spitfire Out West 1940 ★★★ Carmelita (Velez) threatens divorce so her husband (Woods) will pay more attention to her. Second in the loopy series. C: Lupe Velez, Leon Errol, Donald Woods. D: Leslie Goodwins. COM 76m.

Mexican Spitfire Sees a Ghost 1942 ★★★ When Spitfire & Co. invade a haunted house, it's the ghosts who run from the mayhem. Routine entry in the popular comedy series. Alarmingly, its release was on a double feature bill with Orson Welle's *The Magnificent Ambersons*! C: Lupe Velez, Leon Errol, Charles "Buddy" Rogers, Donald MacBride. D: Leslie Goodwins. COM 70m.

Mexican Spitfire's Baby 1941 ★★★ When Carmelita (Velez) and her husband adopt a war orphan, they're surprised by the results. Another series outing for the zany Spitfire. C: Lupe Velez, Leon Errol, Charles "Buddy" Rogers, ZaSu Pitts. D: Leslie Goodwins. COM 69m.

Mexican Spitfire's Blessed Event 1943 ★★★ Carmelita (Velez) tries to advance her hubby's career by pretending to be the mother of an infant. Lively eighth (and last) Spitfire comedy installment. C: Lupe Velez, Leon Errol, Hugh Beaumont. D: Leslie Goodwins. COM 63m.

Mexican Spitfire's Elephant 1942 ★★★½ The Spitfire (Velez) gets her hands on a glass elephant full of stolen jewels, and smugglers want it back. One of the best in the series; frenetic Velez is very amusing. C: Lupe Velez, Leon Errol, Walter Reed. D: Leslie Goodwins. COM 64m.

MGM's Big Parade of Comedy 1964 ★★★½ Disappointing hodgepodge of clips from funny films mix delights with dross as the scenes fly by, often trimmed down to accommodate annoying narration. Still, a useful guide for the uninitiated. C: Stan Laurel, Oliver Hardy, Buster Keaton, The Marx Brothers, Greta Garbo, Jean Harlow, Clark Gable. D: Robert Youngson. COM 100m. V

MIA—We Can Keep You Here Forever ★ Docudrama makes case that there are still thousands of MIAs in Vietnam. DRA 75m. V

Miami Beach Cops 1993 ★★★ Two veterans look forward to their new jobs as assistant deputies, but some killers come to town and make things tough for them. Solid policing and some excitement. C: Frank Maldonatti, Salvatore Rendino, William Childers, Joyce Geier. D: James R. Winburn. ACT 97m. TVM V

Miami Blues 1990 ★★★ Psychopathic killer (Baldwin) picks up a trusting prostitute (Leigh) and impersonates a macho, world-weary police officer (Ward). Good performances are overwhelmed by violence and tawdriness. C: Fred Ward, Alec Baldwin, Jennifer Jason Leigh, Nora Dunn, Charles Napier. D: George Armitage. CRI [R] 97m. V

Miami Cops 1989 ★★ Typical revenge plot drives this Italian produced shoot-'em-up. Police officer (Roundtree) chases drug trafficker who murdered his father across international borders. C: Richard Roundtree, Michael J. Aronin, Harrison Muller, Dawn Baker. D: Al Bradley. CRI 103m. V

Miami Rhapsody 1995 ★★★½ Young woman (Parker) has second thoughts about marriage when she learns of her family's many infidelities. Intelligent, wry comedy, in the Woody Allen vein. C: Sarah Jessica Parker, Gil Bellows, Mia Farrow, Paul Mazursky, Antonio Banderas, Kevin Pollak, Naomi Campbell. D: David Frankel. COM [PG-13] 95m. V

Miami Vendetta 1987 ★ Low-budget ripoff of "Miami Vice" with Goslins an LAPD detective tracking drug dealers who murdered his best friend. C: Maarten Goslins, Frank Gargani, Sandy Brooke, Barbara Pilavin. D: Stephen Seemayer. CRI 90m. V

Miami Vice 1984 ★★★ Many of the elements that made the TV show a success were set in well-produced pilot. Hunky stars Johnson and Thomas play cops and robbers in the streets of Miami with hot music. C: Don Johnson, Philip Michael Thomas, Saundra Santiago. D: Thomas Carter. CRI 99m. TVM V

Miami Vice 2: The Prodigal Son 1985 ★★★ Crockett and Tubbs chase a bad guy to New York; not enough plot for a full-length movie, but an edgily odd and funny performance by Jillette keeps it interesting. C: Don Johnson, Philip Michael Thomas, Edward James Olmos. ACT 99m. TVM V

Michael Jackson Dangerous—The Short Films 1993 ★★★ Compilation of nine music videos. Aimed at Jackson's fans. C: Michael Jackson. MUS 95m. V

Michael Shayne, Private Detective 1940 ★★★ First in a series of P.I. dramas along the lines of *Mr. Moto* and *Charlie Chan* finds Nolan's sleuth Shayne tracking suspicious cardsharp Weaver. Typical B-picture detective suspense, but worth a look for Nolan's solid pre-Bogart portrayal of a hard-boiled dick. C: Lloyd Nolan, Marjorie Weaver, Joan Valerie, Walter Abel, Elizabeth Patterson, Donald MacBride. D: Eugene Forde. CRI 77m.

Mick Jagger—Running Out of Luck ★★★ Basically a feature length music video with several of Jagger's best songs, ostensibly tied together by his travels in Rio. C: Mick Jagger. MUS [R] 88m. V

Mickey Mouse and Donald Duck Cartoons ★★★★★ Two 82-minute collections of a dozen cartoons each from the vintage Disney years. FAM/COM 82m. V

Mickey Mouse—the Black and White Years, Vol. 1 ★★★★ 34 of the early Disney cartoons in this compilation; a must for anyone seriously interested in American film history. Kids will love it, too. C: Mickey Mouse. FAM/COM 256m.

Mickey One 1965 ★★★★ Beatty scores as an anti-hero, a selfish nightclub comic yearning for a more meaningful life. Pungent, striking comedy-drama, way ahead of its time. A good companion piece to Warren's *Shampoo.* C: Warren Beatty, Alexandra Stewart, Hurd Hatfield, Franchot Tone. D: Arthur Penn. DRA 93m.

Micki + Maude 1984 ★★★½ Moore's wife and mistress are both pregnant and have the same doctor. Tepid comedy teams Moore and Edwards for their first joint effort since *10* and the results are occasionally funny, but often strained. C: Dudley Moore, Amy Irving, Ann Reinking, Richard Mulligan, George Gaynes, Wallace Shawn. D: Blake Edwards. COM 118m. V

Microwave Massacre 1983 ★ Feeble ripoff of classic Roger Corman horror sendups of the '50s, with Vernon as man with a huge appetite who murders and toasts beautiful women. C: Jackie Vernon, Loren Schein, Al Troupe. D: Wayne Berwick. HOR 80m. V

Midas Run 1969 ★★½ British Secret Service man (Astaire) plots gold heist in revenge for being passed over for a knighthood. Astaire is charming, as usual, but the movie hasn't really got the touch. (a.k.a. *A Run on Gold*) C: Fred Astaire, Richard Crenna, Anne Heywood, Ralph Richardson, Cesar Romero, Roddy McDowall. D: Alf Kjellin. ACT [PG] 106m.

Midas Touch, The 1989 Hungarian ★★★★ Cunning political allegory about Hungarian flea market in 1956, where objects are miraculously turned into gold. Clever, biting satire. C: Karoly Eperjes, Barnabas Toth, Judith Pogany. D: Geza Beremenyi. COM 100m. V

Middle Age Crazy 1980 Canadian ★★½ The male midlife crisis is the focus here. Confused, 40-something Dern ditches loyal wife Ann-Margret for an airheaded cheerleader, flashy sports car, and designer duds. In a word: man-o-pause. C: Bruce Dern, Ann-Margret, Eric Christmas, Deborah Wakeham. D: John Trent. DRA [R] 95m. V

Middle Age Spread 1979 ★★★½ Middle-aged college professor is promoted as his personal life crumbles. Fine script and ensemble playing carry this pleasant slice-of-life story. C: Grant Tilly, Dorothy McKegg, Donna Akersten. D: John Reid. DRA 94m.

Middle of the Night 1959 ★★★ Stolid film treatment of Paddy Chayefsky's play about a recently widowed man rejuvenated by the love of a much younger woman. Faithful performances from leads March and Novak and a capable supporting cast. C: Kim Novak, Fredric March, Glenda Farrell, Jan Norris, Lee Grant, Effie Afton, Martin Balsam, Joan Copeland. D: Delbert Mann. DRA 118m.

Middleton Family at the 1939 New York World's Fair, The 1939 ★★½ Minor B-film about family's visit to the legendary '39 Fair. A period piece. C: Marjorie Lord, James Lydon, Ruth Lee, Harry Shannon. DRA 55m. V

Midnight 1939 ★★★★★ Frothy screwball classic in which broke American in Paris (Colbert) pretends to be a baroness to win the love—and money—of aristocrat (Lederer), with lovestruck cabbie (Ameche) threatening to expose her scheme. Truly stellar cast, along with Billy Wilder and Charles Brackett's sparkling script and Leisen's crisp direction; a thoroughly enchanting experience. C: Claudette Colbert, Don Ameche, John Barrymore, Francis Lederer, Mary Astor, Hedda Hopper, Monty Woolley. D: Mitchell Leisen. COM 94m.

Midnight 1989 ★★★ Medium horror about a TV late-night movie hostess (Redgrave) who wants to pull the plug when her staff starts turning up dead. Lynn at least adds a touch of class. C: Lynn Redgrave, Tony Curtis, Steven Parrish, Frank Gorshin, Wolfman Jack. D: Norman Thaddeus Vane. HOR [R] 86m. V

Midnight Angel 1941 ★★★½ Inventor is framed for murder and sentenced to die; he then escapes and searches for real killers. Tense, exciting melodrama. C: Robert Preston, Martha O'Driscoll, Phillip Merivale, Eva Gabor. D: Ralph Murphy. CRI

Midnight Auto Supply 1978 ★★ A cinematic old-age home with nice-guy hot car dealers (operating out of a brothel) donating proceeds to Mexican farm workers. C: Michael Parks, Rory Calhoun, Scott Jacoby, Colleen Camp, Linda Cristal, John Ireland. D: James Polakof. DRA 91m. V

Midnight Cabaret 1988 ★★ Satanic cult seeks young woman to bear Satan's child. You know. C: Laura Carrington, Michael Des Barres, Lisa Hart Carroll. D: Pece Dingo. HOR [R] 93m. V

Midnight Clear, A 1992 ★★★★ Psychological drama about the shifting group dynamics of a bunch of American soldiers during WWII. Top-notch performances, a script chock-full of surprises, and Gordon's able direction make this an insightful morality play about the personal price exacted by war. C: Peter Berg, Kevin Dillon, Arye Gross, Ethan Hawke, Gary Sinise, Frank Whaley, John McGinley, Larry Joshua, Curt Lowens. D: Keith Gordon. ACT [R] 107m. V

Midnight Cop 1989 West German ★★★½ International stars York and Mueller-Stahl add a little class to an otherwise undistinguished thriller. A woman (Fairchild) seeks the help of a cop to save her from trouble, mostly of her own making, in the sleazy world of drugs, prostitution, and crime. C: Armin Mueller-Stahl, Michael York, Morgan Fairchild, Frank Stallone. D: Peter Patzak. CRI [R] 100m. V

Midnight Cowboy 1969 ★★★★★ A young stud decides to become a male prostitute in New York. Anticipating the high life, he instead runs smack into the city's harshest realities. Amazing debut by Voight and one of Hoffman's most vivid portrayals as a sleazy hustler who is Voight's only pal. Oscars for Best Picture and Screenplay. C: Dustin Hoffman, Jon Voight, Sylvia Miles, John McGiver, Brenda Vaccaro, Ruth White. D: John Schlesinger. DRA [R] 113m. V

Midnight Crossing 1987 ★★ Travanti takes blind spouse Dunaway and pal Beatty to find long-sunken stolen loot. Tension inevitably leads to violence. Inane dialogue; obvious development. C: Faye Dunaway, Daniel J. Travanti, Kim Cattrall, Ned Beatty, John Laughlin. D: Roger Holzberg. CRI [R] 96m. V

Midnight Dancer 1987 ★★ Sort of a *Flashdance* in reverse, about a young ballerina (Jeffs) who ends up as stripper against her beter judgment. C: Deanne Jeffs, Mary Regan, Karin Fairfax, Joy Smithers. D: Pamela Gibbons. DRA 97m. V

Midnight Express 1978 ★★★★ As Billy Hayes, an American jailed in Turkey for drug smuggling, Davis suffers every imaginable cruelty. Harrowing and graphic; based on a true story. Oscars for Oliver Stone's screen adaptation and Giorgio Moroder's score. C: Brad Davis, Bo Hopkins, Randy Quaid, John Hurt, Mike Kellin. D: Alan Parker. DRA [R] 121m. V

Midnight Faces 1926 ★★★ Silent with organ music accompaniment added is an antique, haunted house mystery with Bushamm and others stuck in mansion in the bayou. Of historical interest. C: Francis X. Bushman, Jack Perrin, Kathryn McGuire. HOR 72m. V

Midnight Fear 1990 ★ Carradine is a sheriff obsessed with finding a serial killer who skins women alive. For those with a strong stomach. C: David Carradine, Craig Wasson, August West. D: Bill Crain. CRI 90m. V

Midnight Girl 1925 ★★★ Engrossing silent drama in which a Russian singer hopes to make it big in America. Vintage Lugosi before the cape and fangs. C: Lila Lee, Bela Lugosi, Dolores Cassinelli. D: Wilfred Noi. DRA 84m. V

Midnight Hour, The 1986 ★★½ Teen Halloween nonsense has town thrown for a loop when witch's spirit decides it's party time. Silly stuff runs its course. C: Shari Belafonte-Harper, LeVar Burton, Lee Montgomery. D: Jack Bender. COM 97m. TVM V

Midnight Kiss 1993 ★ Undercover cop (Owens) uses herself as bait to trap oversexed vampire. C: Michelle Owens, Michael McMillen, Gregory A. Greer. D: Joel Bender. ACT 85m. V

Midnight Lace 1960 ★★★★ Day receives harassing telephone calls that escalate until she's in physical danger. Well-done thriller, with a good cast giving their all. They can't fill out the slim story, but they do make it fun to watch. Remade for television in 1980. C: Doris Day, Rex Harrison, John Gavin, Myrna Loy, Roddy McDowall. D: David Miller. CRI 108m. V

Midnight Lace 1980 ★★ A society woman is stalked by a fiend no one else believes is real. Spineless remake of the flashy 1960 Doris Day thriller. C: Mary Crosby, Gary Frank, Celeste Holm, Carolyn Jones. D: Ivan Nagy. CRI 100m. TVM

Midnight Madness 1980 ★★ *Animal House* influenced comedy involves pack of clichéd and stereotyped college kids on an all-night scavenger hunt. The resulting mess is a jumbled series of comic scenes that go nowhere in a hurry. Look carefully for a very young Michael J. Fox in his film debut! C: David Naughton, Debra Clinger, Stephen Furst, Michael J. Fox. D: David Wechter, Michael Nankin. COM [PG] 110m. V

Midnight Man, The 1974 ★★ Undercover investigator (Lancaster) passes as ex-con college security guard to solve the mystery of a coed's brutal slaying. Labored whodunit suffers from overcomplicated plot. C: Burt Lancaster, Susan Clark, Cameron Mitchell, Morgan Woodward, Joan Lorring, Ed Lauter, Catherine Bach, Linda Kelsey, Harris Yulin. D: Roland Kibbee, Burt Lancaster. CRI [R] 117m.

Midnight Mary 1933 ★★★½ A low-life moll (Young) is torn between a gangster (Cortez) and the rich man (Tone) she loves. Powerful, brutal crime oldie; Young is very good in a tough role. Story by Anita (*Gentlemen Prefer Blondes*) Loos. C: Loretta Young, Franchot Tone, Ricardo Cortez, Andy Devine, Una Merkel. D: William A. Wellman. CRI 74m.

Midnight Movie Massacre 1988 ★★ Drive-in movie patrons fight tuna-scented monster from outerspace in sendup of '50s horror. Silly. C: Robert Clarke, Ann Robinson. D: Mark Stock. HOR 86m. V

Midnight Run 1988 ★★★★ Surprisingly good chase comedy, as an ex-cop turned bounty hunter (De Niro) apprehends an infuriating bookkeeper (Grodin), who has ripped off the Mob, and tries to deliver him to L.A., but the Mafia, the law, and a competitor are out to get them. Excellent, entertaining chemistry between the stars. C: Robert De Niro, Charles Grodin, Yaphet Kotto, John Ashton, Dennis Farina. D: Martin Brest. COM [R] 125m. V

Midnight Story, The 1957 ★★★ Ex-cop (Curtis) doggedly investigates the unexplained murder of a local priest. Formula detective tale has plenty of ambiance and a strong cast to recommend it. C: Tony Curtis, Marisa Pavan, Gilbert Roland, Ted de Corsia, Kathleen Freeman. D: Joseph Pevney. CRI 89m.

Midnight Warning 1932 ★★★½ Woman whose brother is missing is told by authorities that he never existed! Suspense-filled mystery; filmed again as *So Long at the Fair.* C: William Boyd, Claudia Dell, Henry Hall. D: Spenser Gordon Bennet. DRA 63m.

Midnight Warrior 1989 ★★ A moral TV reporter gets more involved with his stories than is good for his health. Creepy little thriller. C: Bernie Angel, Michelle Berger, Kevin Bernhardt, Lilly Melgar. D: Joseph Merhi. ACT 90m. V

Midnight Witness 1993 ★★ Sleazy exploitation film takes Rodney King-type police action and videotaping as jumping off point for extended chase. C: Paul Johansson, Maxwell Caufield, Karen Moncrieff, Jan-Michael Vincent. D: Peter Foldy. CRI 90m. V

Midnight's Child 1993 ★★ D'Abo is literally an au pair girl from Hell, set on delivering her young charge to the Devil as a bride. Very silly. C: Olivia D'Abo, Marcy Walker, Cotter Smith. D: Colin Bucksey. HOR 89m. V

Midnite Spares 1985 ★★ Man is plunged into the underworld of car theft and chop shop artists when he seeks the gang that kidnapped his father. C: Bruce Spence, Gia Carides, James Laurie. D: Quentin Masters. CRI 90m. V

Midshipman Easy 1935 *See* **Men of the Sea**

Midsummer Night's Dream, A 1935 ★★★ Shakespeare's play of lovers seeking solutions to their problems in the woods at midnight. Broad array of Hollywood talent (led by Cagney) and excellent production values, but there's a looming inconsistency that hurts. C: James Cagney, Dick Powell, Joe E. Brown, Jean Muir, Hugh Herbert, Olivia de Havilland, Frank McHugh, Victor Jory, Mickey Rooney. D: Max Reinhardt, William Dieterle. COM 118m. V

Midsummer Night's Dream, A 1968 British ★★★★ The cast's the thing in the Royal Shakespeare Co.'s take on the Bard's comedy of mortals and fairies, passions and potions. Production more earthy than most; worth comparing to glamorized 1935 Hollywood version. C: Diana Rigg, David Warner, Michael Jayston, Ian Richardson, Judi Dench, Ian Holm, Bill Travers, Helen Mirren. D: Peter Hall. COM 124m. V

Midsummer Night's Sex Comedy, A 1982 ★★★★ Three couples in various stages of their relationships visit the country around 1900. Loose adaptation of Shakespeare and Bergman is also a quirky meditation on Allen's pet themes of sex and death. C: Woody Allen, Mia Farrow, Jose Ferrer, Mary Steenburgen, Tony Roberts, Julie Hagerty. D: Woody Allen. COM [PG] 88m. V

Midway 1976 ★★★ The epic air and sea battle (in 1942) that changed the course of the war against Japan. A little bit of romance (Heston's sailor son) gets in the way, but the presentation of the battle is spectacular. C: Charlton Heston, Henry Fonda, James Coburn, Glenn Ford, Hal Holbrook, Robert Mitchum, Cliff Robertson, Toshiro Mifune, Robert Wagner. D: Jack Smight. DRA [PG] 132m. V

Mighty Barnum, The 1934 ★★★ Hollywood-style biography of circusmeister Barnum: long on glitz and half-truths and short on facts. Still, as fiction it's entertaining enough, and unbridled Beery chews more than a little scenery as good ol' P.T. C: Wallace Beery, Adolphe Menjou, Virginia Bruce, Rochelle Hudson, Janet Beecher, Herman Bing. D: Walter Lang. DRA 87m.

Mighty Ducks, The 1992 ★★★ To make amends for a drunken driving offense, lawyer (Estevez) reluctantly takes a job coaching kiddie hockey team. He proceeds to whip them into shape and onto victory. Not much, but has its moments; a big box-office success that inspired moniker for Disney-owned NHL franchise, and sequel. C: Emilio Estevez, Joss Ackland, Lane Smith, Heidi Kling, Josef Sommer, Joshua Jackson, Elden Ratliff, Shaun Weiss, Matt Doherty. D: Stephen Herek. FAM/DRA [PG] 100m. v

Mighty Jack 1987 ★★½ Animated feature for kids about superheroes fighting against bad guys set on world domination. FAM/ACT 95m. v

Mighty Joe Young 1949 ★★★½ Giant ape is brought from jungle to the big city to star in a nightclub act. *King Kong* knockoff has quality moments, like Joe rescuing kids from a burning orphanage. Oscar-winning special effects by Willis O'Brien. C: Terry Moore, Ben Johnson, Robert Armstrong, Mr. Joseph Young, Frank McHugh. D: Ernest B. Schoedsack. DRA 94m. v

Mighty McGurk, The 1946 ★★½ Yet another boxer-with-heart-of-gold-befriends-orphan-boy yarn; Beery is right in his element. Yes, that's future *Quantum Leap*-er Stockwell as the kid. C: Wallace Beery, Dean Stockwell, Dorothy Patrick, Edward Arnold. D: John Waters. DRA 85m.

Mighty Moose and the Quarterback Kid 1987 ★★★ After School Special type drama about kid who wants to be a photographer in spite of his father's football ambitions for him. His coach has a solution. C: Alex Karras. FAM/DRA 50m. v

Mighty Mouse in the Great Space Chase 1985 ★★★½ Mighty Mouse fights the diabolical feline Harry the Heartless to save the universe. Good animated fun for kids. FAM/ACT 88m. v

Mighty Pawns, The 1987 ★★★ An inner-city teacher turns his kids on to chess as an alternative to the streets. Thoughtful and well done indeed. C: William L. Wallace, Paul Winfield, Alfonso Ribeiro, Terence Knox. D: Eric Laneuville. DRA 58m. TVM v

Mighty Quinn, The 1989 ★★★½ A Jamaican police chief (Washington) discovers that his off-beat friend (Townsend), alleged to have killed a wealthy white man, is probably innocent. Oddball but pleasant comic thriller benefits from high-powered cast, especially Washington. C: Denzel Washington, Robert Townsend, James Fox, Mimi Rogers, M. Emmet Walsh. D: Carl Schenkel. CRI [R] 98m. v

Mighty Treve, The 1937 ★★★½ A youngster is hired to watch over his mean uncle's sheep. When the animals are mysteriously attacked, uncle blames nephew's dog and tries to get rid of it. Sentimental, tasteful family fare. C: Noah Beery Jr., Barbara Reed, Samuel S. Hinds. D: Lewis D. Collins. FAM/DRA 68m.

Migrants, The 1974 ★★★★ Superior TV drama, loaded with talent, paints a bleak portrait of a modern-day migrant family struggling to survive. Adapted by Lanford Wilson from a Tennessee Williams short story. C: Cloris Leachman, Ron Howard, Sissy Spacek, Cindy Williams, Claudia McNeil. D: Tom Gries. DRA 78m. TVM v

Mikado, The 1939 ★★★★ Lush color screen adaptation of Gilbert & Sullivan's ever-popular operetta recounts romantic hijinks in the royal Japanese court. Executed with wit and humor—a pleasing version of the stage original. C: Kenny Baker, John Barclay, Martyn Green, Jean Colin, Constance Wills. D: Victor Schertzinger. MUS 93m. v

Mike's Murder 1984 ★★★ Winger, snooping into brutal murder of drug-dealing friend, finds herself lured into underworld of sex and drugs. Cast is game. Music by Joe Jackson. C: Debra Winger, Mark Keyloun, Darrell Larson, Paul Winfield, Brooke Alderson. D: James Bridges. CRI [R] 109m. v

Mikey 1992 ★★ The Bad Seed revisited, as Mikey causes havoc to anyone around him as he is sent from one foster home to another. Predictable. C: Brian Bonsall, Ashley Laurence, John Diehl, Lyman Ward, Josie Bisset. D: Dennis Dimster. DRA [R] 90m. v

Mikey and Nicky 1976 ★★½ May's sloppy film, edited over a period of *years,* is a run-through for her subsequent *Ishtar* debacle. Here, deficient technical execution nearly destroys the saga of childhood friends who are now penny-ante criminals involved in a Mob hit. Any surviving passion comes from Cassavetes' and Falk's riveting performances. C: Peter Falk, John Cassavetes, Ned Beatty, Joyce Van Patten. D: Elaine May. CRI [R] 105m. v

Milagro Beanfield War, The 1988 ★★★★ Magically realistic tale of a dirt-poor Chicano farmer who won't knuckle under to powerful land developers. A delightful cast and a lot of whimsy with marvelous direction. C: Ruben Blades, Richard Bradford, Sonia Braga, Julie Carmen, James Gammon, Melanie Griffith, John Heard, Daniel Stern, Chick Vennera. D: Robert Redford. DRA [R] 118m. v

Mildred Pierce 1945 ★★★★★ Hard-hitting adaptation of James M. Cain's novel about a housewife who drives her husband away and becomes a successful restaurateur but loses her ungrateful daughter in the process. Film is radiant with sardonic dialogue and fine supporting players. Well-deserved Oscar went to Crawford. C: Joan Crawford, Jack Carson, Zachary Scott, Eve Arden, Ann Blyth, Bruce Bennett. D: Michael Curtiz. DRA 109m. V

Miles Ahead—The Music of Miles Davis 1986 ★★★★½ Tasteful PBS documentary of life and music of great jazz trumpeter Davis. Lots of great music, only wish it could be longer. C: Miles Davis, Bill Evans, John Coltrane, Dizzy Gillespie, Herbie Hancock, George Benson, Bill Cosby. MUS 60m. V

Miles from Home 1988 ★★★½ Rather than let the bank foreclose on their farm, two brothers burn it down and become Reagan-era Robin Hoods in Iowa. Great premise bogs down in melodramatic conflict between brothers. Lively supporting cast (particularly Ivey) adds some spice. C: Richard Gere, Kevin Anderson, Penelope Ann Miller, John Malkovich, Brian Dennehy. D: Gary Sinise. DRA [R] 108m. V

Miles to Go 1986 ★★★★ Clayburgh gives a powerful performance as a victim of terminal cancer, secretly searching for someone to take over her family responsibilities after she's gone. Definitely a cut above the usual "disease of the week" movies. C: Jill Clayburgh, Tom Skerritt, Mimi Kuzyk. D: David Greene. DRA 100m. TVM

Milestones 1975 ★★★★ The lives of several Americans intertwine from coast to coast, as Vietnam vets and an antiwar radical try to cope with war's aftermath. Insightful film features author Grace Paley in prominent role. C: Grace Paley, David C. Stone, John Douglas, Laurel Berger. D: Robert Kramer, John Douglas. DRA 195m.

Milhouse—A White Comedy 1971 ★★★½ Savage documentary-comedy on career of then-President Richard Nixon. Suffers from overkill, but generally funny and disturbing portrait of Nixon as compulsive liar and scoundrel. D: Emile de Antonio. COM 90m. V

Military Secret 1945 U.S.S.R. ★★★★ Soviet agent tries to thwart evil Nazi's plot to kidnap scientist. Solid, well-paced thriller; excellent cinematography. C: Sergei Lukianov, Ivan Malishevsky, Alexi Gribov. D: Vladimir Legoshin. DRA 73m.

Milk Money 1994 ★★★ Okay romantic comedy, with a slightly sleazy premise of three farm boys who go to the big city hoping to see a real live naked woman. Their widower father (Harris) pursues, and eventually they all meet up with a shady lady (Griffith). C: Melanie Griffith, Ed Harris, Malcolm McDowell, Michael Patrick Carter, Brian Christopher, Adam La Vorgna. D: Richard Benjamin. COM

Milkman, The 1950 ★★★ Neophyte dairy delivery boy (O'Connor) learns the business from veteran (Durante). Wholesome comedy with four songs. C: Donald O'Connor, Jimmy Durante, Piper Laurie, Joyce Holden. D: Charles Barton. COM 87m.

Milky Way, The 1936 ★★★★ Silent clown Lloyd, in perhaps his funniest talkie, plays a wimpy milkman who accidentally KOs a boxing champ and is then pursued for ring glory by ruthless promoter Menjou. The scene where Lloyd ducks punches is a comic classic. Later remade as *The Kid from Brooklyn,* with Danny Kaye. C: Harold Lloyd, Adolphe Menjou, Verree Teasdale, Helen Mack, George Barbier, Lionel Stander. D: Leo McCarey. COM [PG] 83m. V

Milky Way, The 1968 French ★★★★½ Surrealist master Buñuel satirizes the history and dogma of the Roman Catholic Church as two men, principals in a seemingly random series of dreamlike visions and parables, wander through France on a religious pilgrimage. Sly, caustic, scathingly heretical, this is a prime example of Buñuel at his mature peak. C: Paul Frankeur, Laurent Terzieff, Alain Cuny, Bernard Verley, Michel Piccoli, Pierre Clementi, Delphine Seyrig. D: Luis Bunuel. DRA 102m. V

Mill on the Floss, The 1937 British ★★½ Disappointing adaptation of George Eliot's powerful novel about a bitter feud between a lawyer and a mill owner whose son and daughter fall in love. Acting is strong and involving, but film lacks dramatic focus, thereby diffusing the rich irony inherent in the book as characters meet their tragic fates. C: Frank Lawton, Victoria Hopper, Fay Compton, Geraldine Fitzgerald, Griffith Jones, Mary Clare, James Mason. D: Tim Whelan. DRA 94m. V

Millennium 1989 ★★ An air safety expert (Kristofferson) meets a woman from the future (Ladd) who can rescue doomed passengers on crashing airplanes, for her own special reasons. Crashes. C: Kris Kristofferson, Cheryl Ladd, Robert Joy, Daniel J. Travanti. D: Michael Anderson. SFI [PG-13] 108m. V

Millennium—Tribal Wisdom and the Modern World 1992 ★★★★½ Five-volume series on ancient tribal rites and wisdom, using folk cultures as lens to examine modern world. Very well done. DOC 600m. TVM V

Miller's Crossing 1990 ★★★★ Highly stylized, violent gangster film, set in small city in '30s, with Byrne as chief aide to embattled city boss Finney, playing all sides against middle. Solid ensemble acting highlights enigmatic story, based on Dashiell Hammett's *The Glass Key*. C: Gabriel Byrne, Albert Finney, Marcia Gay Harden, John Turturro, Jon Polito. D: Ethan and Joel Coen. CRI [R] 115m. V

Million Dollar Baby 1941 ★★★ Poor young woman (Lane) receives a million dollars, which antagonizes her boyfriend (Reagan). Spunky comedy; Robson steals the show as an old lady millionaire. C: Priscilla Lane, Ronald Reagan, May Robson, Jeffrey Lynn. D: Curtis Bernhardt. COM 102m.

Million Dollar Duck 1971 ★★★½ Married couple (Jones, Duncan) own a pet duck who is zapped by radiation and starts laying golden eggs. The new-found riches are used to pay off debts until Feds start getting interested. Standard Disney slapstick that will entertain younger children. (a.k.a. *$1,000,000 Duck*) C: Dean Jones, Sandy Duncan, Joe Flynn, Tony Roberts. D: Vincent McEveety. FAM/COM [G] 92m. TVM v

Million Dollar Kid 1944 ★★★ Wealthy hooligan (Duncan) is reformed by The East Side Kids. Okay entry in the low-budget series. C: Leo Gorcey, Huntz Hall, Johnny Duncan, Gabriel Dell. D: Wallace Fox. COM 65m.

Million Dollar Legs 1932 ★★★★ Wild and crazy Fields stars as president of fictitious country Klopstokia, a wacky duchy with aspirations of winning the gold at the 1932 L.A. Olympics. Top-notch comic cast and zany antics make this a timeless small-scale farce. C: W. C. Fields, Jack Oakie, Susan Fleming, Lyda Roberti, Andy Clyde, Ben Turpin, Dickie Moore, Billy Gilbert, Hugh Herbert. D: Edward Cline. COM 64m.

Million Dollar Legs 1939 ★★★ Amiable-enough campus caper concerns a near bankrupt college whose students buy a racehorse to lift the school out of the red. Cast of up-and-coming stars and Grable's legendary gams (*not* the horse's) distinguish this from lesser, run-of-the-mill college comedies. C: Betty Grable, Jackie Coogan, Donald O'Connor, Buster Crabbe, Peter Lind Hayes, Richard Denning. D: Nick Grinde. COM 65m.

Million Dollar Mermaid 1952 ★★★ Biography of Australian swimming star Annette Kellerman is notable for two spectacular Busby Berkeley water ballets. C: Esther Williams, Victor Mature, Walter Pidgeon, David Brian, Jesse White. D: Mervyn LeRoy. MUS 111m. v

Million Dollar Mystery 1987 ★★★ Just before he dies, Bosley reveals to diner patrons clues to hidden $4 million; mad chase ensues. This clone of *It's a Mad Mad Mad Mad World* was tied in with a real-life treasure-hunt gimmick. C: Eddie Deezen, Penny Baker, Tom Bosley, Rich Hall, Rick Overton. D: Richard Fleischer. COM [PG] 95m. v

Million Pound Note, The 1954 *See* **Man with a Million**

Million, The 1931 French ★★★★½ Clair's classic farce concerns a man who chases all over Paris for his misplaced coat, which contains a winning lottery ticket. Buoyant, utterly charming, and innovative since all the actors sing their lines. Still holds up well today. (a.k.a. *Le Million*) C: Annabella, René Lefèvre, Paul Olivier. D: René Clair. MUS 89m.

Millionaire for Christy, A 1951 ★★★½ Secretary (Parker) sets her romantic sights on a radio personality (MacMurray) who has inherited a fortune. Sassy screwball comedy that's predictable, but fun to watch, nevertheless. C: Eleanor Parker, Fred MacMurray, Richard Carlson, Kay Buckley. D: George Marshall. COM 91m.

Millionaire, The 1931 ★★★ Self-made captain of industry (á la Henry Ford) is told to retire for health reasons, but he just can't stay away. Owes much of its success to Booth Tarkington's dialogue and a grandiloquent performance by Arliss. Clever, appealing light comedy. C: George Arliss, Evalyn Knapp, David Manners, Noah Beery, Florence Arliss, J. Farrell MacDonald, James Cagney. D: John Adolfi. COM 80m.

Millionairess, The 1960 British ★★★ G.B. Shaw's play about the power (and limits) of money is brought to the screen in fits and starts. An extraordinarily beautiful rich lady (Loren) believes everything has a price—until she encounters an Indian M.D. (Sellers), whose love and loyalty can't be bought. Some rewarding moments, although both leads have trouble fleshing out Shaw's humorous yet ironic characters. C: Sophia Loren, Peter Sellers, Alastair Sim, Vittorio De Sica, Dennis Price. D: Anthony Asquith. DRA 90m.

Millions 1991 ★★ Greedy young man tries to romance his way to complete control of the family fortune. C: Lauren Hutton, Billy Zane, Carol Alt. D: Carlo Vanzina. DRA [R] 118m. v

Millions Like Us 1943 British ★★★★ Diverse group of citizens laboring in a British airplane plant learn to overcome their differences and unite for the common good. Top-drawer WWII propaganda tale realistically presents all social classes—a trenchant, engrossing study of life during wartime. C: Eric Portman, Patricia Roc, Gordon Jackson, Anne Crawford, Megs Jenkins, Basil Radford, Naunton Wayne, Irene Handl, Brenda Bruce. D: Frank Launder, Sidney Gilliat. DRA 103m.

Milpitas Monster, The 1980 ★★★ Before the Toxic Avenger there was this creature from a waste dump in California. Silly comedy about mosnter that eats garbage can lids. C: Doug Hagdahl, Scott A. Henderson, Priscilla House, Scott Parker. D: Robert Burrill. COM 80m. v

Milton Berle's Mad World of Comedy 1974 ★★★½ Repackaged TV special with good lineup of comics. For comedy fans. C: Milton Berle, Albert Brooks, Groucho Marx, Flip Wilson, Bob Hope, Don Rickles. COM 70m. v

Mimi 1935 British ★★★ Tune-less *La Boheme* stars Lawrence as the ailing muse to a struggling playwright (Fairbanks). Bumpy vehicle for the stage legend. C: Gertrude Lawrence, Douglas Fairbanks, Jr. D: Paul Stein. DRA 98m.

Min and Bill 1930 ★★★½ Dressler and Beery make a memorable team as a scruffy waterfront couple who fight to keep Dressler's daughter with them rather than allowing her to be placed in a more socially acceptable home. Although a bit static and overly sentimental, this is one landmark, enjoyable early talkie. Dressler copped an Oscar for her work. C: Marie Dressler, Wallace Beery, Dorothy Jordan, Marjorie Rambeau, Frank McGlynn. D: George Hill. DRA 67m. V

Minbo, or the Gentle Art of Japanese Extortion 1994 Japanese ★★★½ Director of *Tampopo* turns his satiric skills to the Japanese Mafia, as Miyamoto plays lawyer hired by luxury hotel to rid itself of the unwanted Yakuza. Huge hit in Japan, but loses something across the Pacific. Director was attacked by the real Yakuza after making this film! C: Nobuku Miyamoto, Akira Takarada. D: Juzo Itami. COM 123m.

Mind Benders, The 1962 British ★★★ Captivating sci-fi involving espionage in the wake of scientific studies on the effects of long-term sensory deprivation. Strong cast of British acting greats. C: Dirk Bogarde, Mary Ure, John Clements, Michael Bryant, Wendy Craig, Edward Fox. D: Basil Dearden. SFI 101m.

Mind, Body and Soul 1992 ★★ Woman is chased by satanic cult after she witnesses them performing human sacrifice. Fortunately, Wings is around to save her. C: Wings Hauser, Ginger Lynn Allen, Jay richardson, Ken Hill, Jesse Kaye, Tami Bakke. D: Rick Sloane. ACT 93m. V

Mind Field 1989 Canadian ★★★ Ironside plays a Montreal cop who starts having hallucinatory episodes and discovers he was part of a botched CIA experiment. Film tries to cover too much; result is muddled spy tale. C: Michael Ironside, Lisa Langlois, Sean McCann, Christopher Plummer, Stefan Wodoslawsky. D: Jean-Claude Lord. DRA [R] 91m. V

Mind Games 1981 *See* **Agency**

Mind Games 1988 ★★★ Couple whose marriage is on rocks are played against one another by deranged psych student who they pick up while on vacation. Typical thriller. C: Edward Albert, Shawn Weatherly, Matt Norero, Maxwell Caufield. D: Bob Yari. ACT 93m. V

Mind of Mr. Soames, The 1970 British ★★★½ Thirty-year-old (Stamp) in lifetime coma is restored to consciousness after undergoing an operation and must immediately gain a lifetime's worth of experience. Unique sci-fi premise is intriguing throughout. C: Terence Stamp, Robert Vaughn, Nigel Davenport, Christian Roberts. D: Alan Cooke. SFI [M/PG] 95m.

Mind Snatchers, The 1972 *See* **Demon Within, The**

Mind Twister 1993 ★★½ With a psychotic killer on the loose, one brave cop steps up and commits himself to finding the murderer before he can strike again. C: Telly Savalas, Suzanne Slater, Richard Roundtree. D: Fred Olen Ray. HOR [R] 87m. V

Mindkiller 1987 ★★★ This experiment has gone haywire! McDonald's brain jumps out of his head and runs around killing people. Send up of the splatter genre is mildly amusing and gory enough for those who like that sort of thing. C: Joe McDonald, Christopher Wade, Shirley Ross, Kevin Hart. D: Michael Krueger. HOR 84m. V

Mindwalk 1991 ★★★½ A group of environmentally concerned professionals talk at length about their concern for ecology. Based on the "New Age" bestseller. C: Liv Ullmann, Sam Waterston, John Heard, Ione Skye. D: Bernt Capra. DRA [PG] 110m. V

Mindwarp 1991 ★★★ Far into the future, an ecological disaster has hit earth, making people live in a sterile protective environment. But a rebellious young woman tries to change things and she suffers as a result. Good effects and nifty sci-fi theme. C: Bruce Campbell, Angus Scrimm, Elizabeth Kent. D: Steve Barnett. SFI [R] 91m. V

Mindwarp: An Infinity of Terror 1981 *See* **Galaxy of Terror**

Mine Own Executioner 1948 British ★★★★ Skilled psychiatrist (Meredith) labors to cure a troubled former POW even as he wrestles with his own private life. Penetrating drama features a strong cast, incisive script, and a few startling visual effects that add up to a compelling viewing experience. C: Burgess Meredith, Dulcie Gray, Kieron Moore, John Laurie. D: Anthony Kimmins. DRA 102m. V

Miners '88 1988 Polish ★★★½ An engrossing account of the Polish miners' strike in August of 1988 which, as we now know, was fundamental to Poland's entire political transformation. Quite well done and loaded with interesting facts. DOC 50m. V

Mines of Kilimanjaro 1987 ★★★ When a distinguished archaeological professor is murdered in Central Africa, his most gifted student sets out to learn what really happened. C: Christopher Connelly, Tobias Hoels, Elena Pompei. D: Mino Guerrini. ACT [PG-13] 88m. V

Mingus 1968 ★★★½ The life and times of Charlie Mingus, the late, great jazz bassist/composer. It's all here; the hot nights, the smokey nightclubs and that great music. C: Charles Mingus. DOC 58m. V

Mini Dragons—Hong Kong ★★★½ An extensive series—in four parts—covering the people, the business and the culture of Hong Kong, Singapore, Taiwan and South Korea. An interesting and comprehensive study of these robust societies. DOC 54m. V

Ministry of Fear 1944 ★★★★ Graham Greene's spy novel set in WWII London is brilliantly transferred to the screen by director Lang. Highly effective thriller finds Milland framed and fighting for his life as he's caught up in a series of complex plot twists. Dynamite cast and Lang's masterful flourishes render this a top-notch espionage drama. C: Ray Milland, Marjorie Reynolds, Carl Esmond, Dan Duryea, Hillary Brooke, Alan Napier, Percy Waram. D: Fritz Lang. DRA 85m.

Ministry of Vengeance 1989 ★★★ When his wife and daughter are murdered by terrorists, a minister leaves the church and vows to avenge his family. C: John Schneider, Ned Beatty, George Kennedy. ACT [R] 96m. v

Miniver Story, The 1950 ★★★ Turmoil and tragedy overshadow dauntless English family after WWII. Disappointing sequel to *Mrs. Miniver*, but there are affecting scenes between Garson and Pidgeon. C: Greer Garson, Walter Pidgeon, John Hodiak, Leo Genn, Cathy O'Donnell, Henry Wilcoxon, Reginald Owen, Peter Finch. D: H. C. Potter. DRA 104m. v

Minnelli On Minnelli 1993 ★★★★ This showcase of the work of director Vincente Minnelli is hosted by his multi-talented daughter, Liza. Minnelli was superb and the evidence of his excellent work is right here. DOC 88m. v

Minnesota Clay 1965 French ★★½ Oddball European Western features Mitchell as an almost blind gunfighter who breaks out of jail to locate the one man who can clear his name—once free, he squares off with his adversaries aided only by his heightened *hearing*. Apart from Mitchell's strong performance, oater takes second place to Sergio Leone's more grandiose spaghetti-Westerns. C: Cameron Mitchell, Georges Riviere, Ethel Rojo, Diana Martin, Anthony Ross. D: Sergio Corbucci. WST 95m. v

Minnie and Moskowitz 1971 ★★★½ Cassavetes' most accessible film. The off-beat flirtation between an educated art curator (Rowlands) and a loony parking-lot attendant (Cassel) makes for a minor, but charming romance. C: Gena Rowlands, Seymour Cassel. D: John Cassavetes. COM [PG] 114m.

Minnie The Moocher 1991 ★★★★ A captivating documentary that shows all the dazzle and glare and excitement of Harlem's classic 30s and 40s nightclubs. Filled with stars so bright, like Waller, Armstrong, Ellington, "Bojangles" Robinson and, as you'd expect by the title, Cab "HideyHideyHo" Calloway. C: Cab Calloway. DOC 55m. v

Minotaur, The 1961 Italian ★★ Cheap sword-and-sandal epic stars gold-medal Olympic decathalete Mathias as the Greek hero Theseus, who must battle a monster that's half-man, half-beast. C: Bob Mathias, Rosanna Schiaffino. D: Silvio Amadio. ACT 92m.

Minute to Pray, a Second to Die, A 1968 Italian ★★★½ Prime spaghetti-Western concerns an epileptic outlaw (Cord) who's being pursued by an assortment of sheriffs, bounty hunters, and other scurvy lawbreakers when all he really wants to do is lie low in mellow Escondido. Vivid color cinematography and an authentic Western atmosphere. C: Alex Cord, Arthur Kennedy, Robert Ryan, Mario Brega, Nicoletta Machiavelli. D: Franco Giraldi. WST [R] 97m. v

Miracle at Moreaux 1986 ★★★½ Hunted by Nazis, a trio of Jewish children is taken in by a nun. Sensitively handled and quietly powerful. C: Loretta Swit, Talya Rubin, Robert Kosoy, Marsha Moreau. D: Paul Shapiro. DRA 55m. TVM v

Miracle Beach 1992 ★★½ Comic twist on the Aladdin story has beach bum Cameron getting everything he wishes from a magic lamp, while the sweet teen genie (Dolenz) falls in love with him. Too formulaic, but likable leads help. C: Dean Cameron, Felicity Waterman, Ami Dolenz. D: Skott Snider. COM [R] 88m. v

Miracle Down Under 1987 ★★★½ This Australian Christmas film involves a stingy and lonely old man whose life changes for the better when a little boy enters his life. Fine holiday viewing for the family. C: Dee Wallace Stone, John Waters, Bill Kerr. D: George Miller. FAM/DRA 106m. v

Miracle in Milan 1951 Italian ★★★★ Young Toto's (Golisano's) eternal optimism gives shantytown residents hope in their rundown surroundings. Intentionally childlike fairy tale exposes political corruption and mistreatment of poor and underprivileged after WWII. C: Francesco Golisano, Paolo Stoppa, Emma Gramatica, Guglielmo Barnabo. D: Vittorio De Sica. DRA 96m. v

Miracle in Soho 1957 British ★★ Romantic fluff about a common London laborer who meets a barmaid on a street corner and falls madly in love with her. Artificial sets and one-dimensional character types squeeze all the charm out of this fairy tale about true love. C: John Gregson, Belinda Lee, Cyril Cusack, Rosalie Crutchley. D: Julian Amyes. DRA 98m.

Miracle in the Rain 1956 ★★★½ Melodrama puts Wyman through the wringer as a woman in love with Johnson during WWII. A trifle soggy, but effective. C: Jane Wyman, Van Johnson, Fred Clark, Eileen Heckart. D: Rudolph Mate. DRA 107m.

Miracle in the Sand 1936 *See* **Three Godfathers**

Miracle in the Wilderness 1991 ★★★ Retreating before U.S. cavalry, Blackfoot Indians kidnap a family of settlers and learn about Christmas. Standard holiday piece. C: Kris Kristofferson, Kim Cattrall. D: Kevin James Dobson. FAM/DRA 88m. TVM v

Miracle Man, The 1932 ★★★ Evangelist pulls an about-face on a pack of criminals who've been exploiting him when he returns them to the path of goodness. Stolid direction and lack of dramatic tension diminish this remake of an earlier silent movie starring Lon Chaney. C: Sylvia Sidney, Chester Morris, Robert Coogan. D: Norman Z. McLeod. CRI 85m.

Miracle Mile 1989 ★★★ L.A. man hearing nuclear war is to begin in 50 minutes, spends predawn hour searching city for his lover before missiles hit. Audacious panic-attack story (largely unfolding in real time) goes from nightmare satire to action thriller through sentimental slop. Not for all tastes. C: Anthony Edwards, Mare Winningham, John Agar, Lou Hancock. D: Steve DeJarnatt. SFI [R] 87m. v

Miracle of Fatima 1952 *See* **Miracle of Our Lady of Fatima, The**

Miracle Of Intervale Avenue, The ★★★★ An intriguing study, based on long-term sociological research, about a once vibrant Jewish community in the Bronx. DOC 65m. v

Miracle of Morgan's Creek, The 1944 ★★★★★ Hysterical wartime comedy about Hutton getting pregnant at all-night party, then trying to recall "who did it." Amazingly daring for its time, now less shocking but still a scream, with witty Sturges script and knockabout farce. Great supporting cast with Demarest and Bracken the standouts. Remade, with many changes, as Jerry Lewis vehicle *Rock-A-Bye Baby.* C: Eddie Bracken, Betty Hutton, William Demarest, Diana Lynn, Brian Donlevy, Akim Tamiroff, Porter Hall, Almira Sessions, Jimmy Conlin. D: Preston Sturges. COM 98m. v

Miracle of Our Lady of Fatima, The 1952 ★★★★ In 1917, outside the small Portuguese village of Fatima, three children see a vision of the Virgin Mary who implores them to spread her word to an unbelieving world. Based on a true incident, this well-told story is excellent family viewing. (a.k.a *Miracle of Fatima*) C: Gilbert Roland, Angela Clark, Frank Silvera, Jay Novello, Sherry Jackson. D: John Brahm. DRA 102m. v

Miracle of the Bells, The 1948 ★★ When a glamorous movie star dies and is returned to her birthplace for burial, a miracle transpires that has the whole town talking. Hardworking cast suffers from sugar shock and inertia—save this one for Christmastime. C: Fred MacMurray, Alida Valli, Frank Sinatra, Lee J. Cobb. D: Irving Pichel. DRA 120m. v

Miracle of the Heart: A Boys' Town Story 1986 ★★★★ Entertaining update of *Boys' Town* films features Carney as former protégé of Father Flanagan battling cold church authorities while trying to help a troubled youth at Christmas time. Nicely acted family film. C: Art Carney, Casey Siemaszko, Jack Bannon, Darrell Larson. D: Georg Stanford Brown. FAM/DRA 96m. TVM v

Miracle of the Hills, The 1959 ★★ Unofficial female mayor of a tiny hamlet has a major run-in with the newly arrived church minister. Bland, unexciting B-Western. C: Rex Reason, Theona Bryant, Jay North, Gilbert Smith, Tracy Stratford, Gene Roth. D: Paul Landres. WST 73m.

Miracle of the White Stallions 1963 ★★½ During WWII, a group of concerned horse lovers smuggle prized Lippizan stallions out of Austria. 825Long stretches of boring dialogue coupled with confused plotting make this a lesser Disney outing. C: Robert Taylor, Lilli Palmer, Curt Jurgens, Eddie Albert, James Franciscus, John Larch. D: Arthur Hiller. FAM/DRA 117m. v

Miracle on Ice 1981 ★★★ *Rocky*-esque formula sports movie recounts 1980 U.S. Olympic hockey team's upset gold-medal victory. Doesn't miss a predictable trick, though hockey footage is pretty exciting. C: Karl Malden, Andrew Stevens, Steve Guttenberg, Jessica Walter. D: Steven Hilliard Stern. DRA 150m. TVM v

Miracle on 34th Street 1947 ★★★★★ Beloved holiday classic of a skeptical child (Wood) who doesn't believe in Santa Claus. Gwenn is "Kris Kringle," Macy's Santa who convinces Wood, as well as a courtroom, that things aren't always what they seem. Marvelous family entertainment; Gwenn won a well-deserved Supporting Actor Oscar. Remade twice, in 1994 and as a TV-movie in 1973. Look for Thelma Ritter as an irate mom in Santaland. C: Maureen O'Hara, John Payne, Edmund Gwenn, Natalie Wood. D: George Seaton. FAM/DRA 96m. v

Miracle on 34th Street 1975 ★★½ Second of three go-rounds for the venerable Yuletide tale casts *Family Affair* co-star Cabot as the lovable old man who may be the real Santa Claus. Buffy and Jody know who he really is. Weakest of the three. C: Sebastian Cabot, Jane Alexander, David Hartman, Suzanne Davidson, Roddy McDowall. D: Fielder Cook. COM 100m. TVM

Miracle on 34th Street 1994 ★★★★ Surprisingly effective remake of 1947 classic with Attenborough as Kris Kringle, a department store Santa, who may or may not be the genuine article. Not quite up to the original, but sweet and charming in its own right. C: Richard Attenborough, Elizabeth Perkins, Dylan McDermott, Mara Wilson. D: Les Mayfield. FAM/DRA [PG] 114m. v

Miracle Rider, The 1934 ★★★ 15 episodes of a classic 30s serial that comes in on Dan'l Boone and follows through to the settlement of Texas. Known as the last film made by long-time Western star Tom Mix. C: Tom Mix, Jean Gale, Jason Robards. D: B. Reeves Eason. WST 300m. v

Miracle, The 1959 ★★★ Young nun falls in love with British soldier during the Napoleonic Peninsular War. Low-octane religious bombast has pageantry but no plausibility. C: Carroll Baker, Roger Moore, Walter Slezak, Vittorio Gassman, Katina Paxinou. D: Irving Rapper. DRA 121m. v

Miracle, The 1991 British ★★★★ Little-known work from the director of *The Crying Game* puts charismatic D'Angelo in a small Irish town, where she becomes the focus of a lonely teenage boy's life. Wistful, lovely to look at. C: Beverly D'Angelo, Donal McCann, Niall Byrne, Lorraine Pilkington. D: Neil Jordan. DRA [R] 100m. v

Miracle Woman, The 1931 ★★★★ In one of her first starring roles, Stanwyck plays an evangelist based on Aimee Semple McPherson who rakes in the dough via fiery tent sermons. Her life becomes complicated when Manners, a blind parishioner, falls for her. Stanwyck's brilliant characterization, together with Capra's astute direction, makes this a worthwhile early talkie. C: Barbara Stanwyck, David Manners, Sam Hardy, Beryl Mercer, Russell Hopton. D: Frank Capra. DRA 90m.

Miracle Worker, The 1962 ★★★★½ Bancroft and Duke are a fiery team in this tough-minded tale of blind, deaf Helen Keller and Annie Sullivan the teacher who broke through to her. Lively adaptation of William Gibson's hit play. Oscars to Bancroft and Duke. Duke played the Sullivan role in 1979 TV remake. C: Anne Bancroft, Patty Duke, Victor Jory, Inga Swenson, Andrew Prine, Beah Richards, Kathleen Comegys. D: Arthur Penn. DRA 107m. V

Miracle Worker, The 1979 ★★★★ Seeing-, hearing-, and speech-impaired, Helen Keller (Gilbert) is taught by teacher-companion Annie Sullivan (Astin) to read, write, and speak (as Patty Duke, Astin played Keller in '62). Excellent TV movie. C: Patty Duke Astin, Melissa Gilbert, Diana Muldaur, Charles Siebert. D: Paul Aaron. DRA 98m. TVM V

Miracles 1986 ★★ *Romancing the Stone* carbon copy about a just divorced couple (Garr and Conti) inadvertently spirited away by a jewel smuggler to a miserable South American country. Veteran comic leads struggle to surmount all the clichés. C: Tom Conti, Teri Garr, Paul Rodriguez, Christopher Lloyd. D: Jim Kouf. COM [PG] 90m. V

Miracles for Sale 1939 ★★ Horrormeister Browning stumbles with this whodunit about a magician who uses his illusionary skills to unmask a murderer. Arch direction, unfocused plotline, and poorly executed magic tricks. C: Robert Young, Florence Rice, Frank Craven, Henry Hull, Lee Bowman. D: Tod Browning. CRI 71m.

Mirage 1965 ★★★★ Peck, practically reprising his amnesiac role from *Spellbound*, finds himself the victim of murder attempts for reasons that escape him. Engaging and slick Hitchcockian thriller with a solid-as-usual Peck. Remade in 1968 as *Jigsaw*. C: Gregory Peck, Diane Baker, Walter Matthau, Kevin McCarthy, Jack Weston, Walter Abel, George Kennedy. D: Edward Dmytryk. CRI 108m. V

Miranda 1948 British ★★★½ Doctor reels in a lovesick, land-loving mermaid while on a fishing trip and then has problems keeping her from his wife. Witty comic fantasy that's nimbly acted by all, especially the charming Johns as the lady with fins. (See *Splash* for a more recent update of this fishy tale.) A sequel followed in 1954, *Mad About Men*. C: Googie Withers, Glynis Johns, Griffith Jones, John McCallum, David Tomlinson, Margaret Rutherford, Maurice Denham. D: Ken Annakin. COM 80m.

Mirror Crack'd, The 1980 British ★★★ Agatha Christie's indefatigable Miss Marple (Lansbury) investigates a murder on a movie set. Timid whodunit stolen by Novak and Taylor as feuding spoiled stars. Best for fans of Lansbury and Christie films. C: Angela Lansbury, Elizabeth Taylor, Rock Hudson, Kim Novak, Tony Curtis. D: Guy Hamilton. CRI [PG] 101m. V

Mirror Has Two Faces, The 1959 French ★★★ Plastic surgery transforms neglected, plain-Jane wife of self-absorbed schoolteacher into the ravishing object of his insane jealousy. Fascinating psychological portrayal of how a profound personal transformation can affect a marriage. C: Michele Morgan, Bourvil, Gerald Oury, Ivan Desny, Elizabeth Manet, Sylvie, Sandra Milo. D: Andre Cayatte. DRA 98m.

Mirror Images 1991 ★★ Sheppard (a real-life *Penthouse* "Pet") portrays twins, one a stripper and the other a repressed housewife. When the nice sister takes a walk on the wild side, a killer appears. Not to be viewed as drama. C: Delia Sheppard, Jeff Conaway, Julie Strain. D: Alexander Gregory Hippolyte. CRI [R] 95m. V

Mirror Images II 1993 ★★★ Identical twin sisters couldn't be more different. When the promiscuous one is murdered, her saintly sister assumes her role to lure her killer. C: Shannon Whirry, Luca Bercovici. D: Gregory Hippolyte. DRA 92m. V

Mirror, Mirror 1991 ★★★ A teenager (Harvest) is seduced by a haunted mirror that bumps off her enemies and others. Derivative but entertaining horror film, with some good scares. Followed by a sequel. C: Karen Black, Rainbow Harvest, Yvonne De Carlo, Kristin Datillo, William Sanderson. D: Marina Sargenti. HOR [R] 104m.

Mirror, Mirror 2: Raven Dance 1994 ★★½ Tacky sequel combines the original's haunted mirror with the old plot about nasty types out to get their hands on a young woman's inheritance. The horrors are hokey and the veterans in the cast are wasted. C: Tracy Welles, Roddy McDowell, Sally Kellerman, Veronica Cartwright, Mark Ruffalo. D: Jimmy Lifton. HOR 91m.

Mirror of Death 1987 ★★ Beaten by her boyfriend, a young woman turns to an occult book for redemption. Quite unusual. C: Julie Merrill, Kuri Browne. D: Deryn Warren. HOR 85m. V

Mirror, The 1975 Russian ★★★★ WWII Soviet life as filtered through director's childhood reminiscences. One of Tarkovsky's most personal, works is experimental on many levels. Includes color and b&w sequences. C: Margarita Terekhova, Philip Yankovsky, Ignat Daniltsev

sev, Oleg Yankovsky. D: Andrei Tarkovsky. DRA 106m. v

Mirrors 1977 ★★★ After her nervous breakdown, a woman and her husband go to New Orleans for some rest. But nightmare of voodoo get in the way of everything. Lots of chills. C: Kitty Winn, Peter Donat. HOR [PG] 89m. v

Mirros 1985 ★★★½ A beautiful dancer meets a handsome, successful reporter. In short time, a romance blossoms, but not without its problems. Soft and sensitive, well played by the cast. C: Timothy Daly, Marguerite Hickey, Keenan Wynn. D: Harry Winer. DRA 99m. v

Misadventures of Merlin Jones, The 1963 ★★½ Kirk is a brilliant college student who dabbles with hypnosis and ESP, which results in a series of sub-par Disney slapstick sequences. Strictly for younger audiences. Followed by a sequel, *The Monkey's Uncle*. C: Tommy Kirk, Annette Funicello, Leon Ames, Stuart Erwin. D: Robert Stevenson. FAM/COM [G] 90m. v

Misadventures of Mr. Wilt, The 1989 British ★★★½ Rhys-Jones is an unhappily married college professor whose wife goes missing—Inspector Smith thinks Jones has done her in. Obvious but still quite funny thanks to Smith and Jones' teamwork. (a.k.a. *Wilt*) C: Griff Rhys-Jones, Mel Smith, Alison Steadman, Diana Quick, Jeremy Clyde. D: Michael Tuchner. COM [R] 93m. v

Mischief 1984 ★★★½ Teenage James Dean fans become friends in this '50s teen sex comedy. C: Doug McKeon, Catherine Mary Stewart, Kelly Preston, Chris Nash. D: Mel Damski. COM [R] 97m. v

Misery 1990 ★★★★ Frustrated romance novelist (Caan) crashes his car in snow and is saved, and then held hostage, by his biggest fan, Bates, a psychotic nurse. Delightfully campy thriller, with genuine chills. Bates won a Best Actress Oscar for her inspired performance. From the Stephen King novel. C: James Caan, Kathy Bates, Richard Farnsworth, Frances Sternhagen, Lauren Bacall. D: Rob Reiner. HOR [R] 107m. v

Misfit Brigade, The 1986 U.S. ★★★ German WWII prisoners are drafted into the military by Nazi forces desperate for troops. Sometimes strangely silly and funny variation on the *Dirty Dozen* theme. (a.k.a. *Wheels of Terror*) C: Bruce Davison, David Patrick Kelly, David Carradine, D. W. Moffett, Jay O. Sanders. D: Gordon Hessler. DRA [R] 99m. TVM v

Misfits of Science 1985 ★★½ Pilot film for short-lived TV series involves four people with unusual extrasensory abilities who fight evil government forces. Strictly by-the-book plotting, dialogue, and characters make this totally forgettable. C: Dean Paul Martin, Kevin Peter Hall, Courteney Cox. D: Dean Zanetos. SFI 96m. v

Misfits, The 1961 ★★★★ Monroe's husband, playwright Miller, penned what ultimately was to be last outing for her and co-star Gable. She plays divorce who befriends group of cowboys; drama is pedestrian but final sequence packed with action. Clift is a standout. C: Clark Gable, Marilyn Monroe, Montgomery Clift, Thelma Ritter, Eli Wallach. D: John Huston. DRA 124m. v

Mishima 1985 ★★★★★ Cinema stylist Schrader's masterpiece is a biographical fantasia on the life and death of Yukio Mishima, Japan's most celebrated post-WWII writer. Visually dazzling film is divided into three sections—scenes of Mishima's youth; brilliant realizations of his stories and novels; and the day in 1970 when he broke into a military post and committed hara-kiri. Sexually charged and violent film is driven along by Philip Glass's propulsive score. Roy Scheider narrates. C: Ken Ogata, Kenji Sawara, Yasosuke Bano, Toshiyuki Nagashima. D: Paul Schrader. DRA [R] 121m. v

Miss A and Miss M 1986 ★★★ During a summer vacation, a young girl becomes close with two visiting schoolteachers. Soon she learns that the women are lesbians. Thoughtful and serious. C: Kika Markham, Jennifer Hilary. DRA 60m. v

Miss Annie Rooney 1942 ★★★ Teenaged Temple plays poor kid who becomes infatuated with rich youth Moore. Innocuous family viewing, in which Temple got her first screen kiss. C: Shirley Temple, William Gargan, Guy Kibbee, Dickie Moore. D: Edwin L. Marin. FAM/DRA 86m. v

Miss Ewa's Follies 1984 Poland ★★★ A little girl runs away so she can bring joy and goodness into the lives of people everywhere. An engaging musical comedy that kids will surely adore. FAM/MUS 158m. v

Miss Fane's Baby 1934 *See* **Miss Fane's Baby Is Stolen**

Miss Fane's Baby is Stolen 1934 ★★½ Inspired by the Lindbergh kidnapping, story hinges on glamorous movie star whose baby is taken hostage and held for ransom. Somewhat involving crime saga with a few comic moments. (a.k.a. *Kidnapped* and *Miss Fane's Baby*) C: Dorothea Wieck, Alice Brady, Baby LeRoy, William Frawley. D: Alexander Hall. CRI 70m.

Miss Firecracker 1988 ★★★★ Bored and lonely in her small Mississippi town, Hunter enters a beauty pageant to get the attention she craves. Clever, very funny satire; Hunter delivers a wonderful recreation of her off-Broadway role; Beth Henley's adapted her own play. Look for cameo by director's wife Christine Lahti. C: Holly Hunter, Mary Steenburgen, Tim Robbins, Alfre Woodard, Scott Glenn. D: Thomas Schlamme. COM [PG] 102m. v

Miss Grant Takes Richmond 1949 ★★★½ Secretary bites off more than she can chew when she crosses swords with the underworld in this comedy/mystery. Talented Ball and great cast make this engaging fluff. C: Lucille Ball, William Holden, Janis Carter, James Gleason, Frank McHugh. D: Lloyd Bacon. COM 88m. V

Miss Julie 1950 Swedish ★★★★½ Fine adaptation of the Strindberg classic has aristocratic Bjork breaking all societal rules by becoming passionately involved with a servant who deeply resents his lot in life. Strong acting and inventive cinematography contribute to film's emotional depth. C: Anita Bjork, Ulf Palme. D: Alf Sjoberg. DRA 90m. V

Miss Mary 1986 Argentine ★★★ Serving as governess for wealthy Argentine family, sexually repressed Christie blossoms in affair with household's eldest son, but their liaison ends tragically. Christie gives intriguing performance in otherwise unexceptional production. C: Julie Christie, Nacha Guevara, Luisina Brando, Iris Marga. D: Maria Luisa Bemberg. DRA [R] 100m. V

Miss Melody Jones 1973 ★★ Young African-American, desperate for money, undresses for wealthy strangers. Nonsense manages to move along. C: Philomena Nowlin, Ron Warden. D: Bill Brame. DRA [PG] 86m. V

Miss President 1935 ★★★½ Feisty heiress doesn't want to marry young executive so she invents another lover. Slow-paced but amiable romantic comedy. C: Lilly Murati, Pal Javor, Ella Gombaszogi. D: Andre Marton. COM 90m.

Miss Right 1981 ★★★ Even though he's got lots of girlfriends, a perfectionist insists that none of them is "Miss Right." Lively. C: William Tepper, Karen Black, Virna Lisi, Margot Kidder, Marie-France Pisier. D: Paul Williams. COM [R] 98m. V

Miss Rose White 1992 ★★★½ In Manhattan during and after WWII, a Polish-Jewish immigrant hides her origins, until her sister, believed dead in Hitler's Europe, arrives. Poignant though slow at times; based on off-Broadway play, *A Shayna Maidel*. C: Kyra Sedgwick, Amanda Plummer, Maximilian Schell, Maureen Stapleton, Milton Selzer. D: Joseph Sargent. DRA [PG] 95m. TVM V

Miss Sadie Thompson 1954 ★★★½ Alluring Hayworth plays the lustful South Seas strumpet Sadie, and Ferrer is the hell-and-damnation clergyman she vamps in this so-so musicalized remake of Somerset Maugham's *Rain*. Hayworth is well worth watching, although the 1932 Joan Crawford version truly sizzles. Originally shot in 3-D. C: Rita Hayworth, Jose Ferrer, Aldo Ray, Charles Bronson. D: Curtis Bernhardt. MUS 91m. V

Miss Susie Slagle's 1945 ★★ Turn-of-the-century comedy about the residents of a medical school boarding house and the trials and tribulations of becoming a doctor or nurse. Mild, inoffensive slice of life. C: Veronica Lake, Sonny Tufts, Joan Caulfield, Lillian Gish, Ray Collins, Billy DeWolfe, Lloyd Bridges. D: John Berry. COM 88m.

Miss Tatlock's Millions 1948 ★★★ A rugged Hollywood stunt man is persuaded to impersonate a dim-witted heir in order to help an attractive heiress inherit what is rightfully hers. Oddball comedy is entertaining once the unusual premise kicks in. C: John Lund, Wanda Hendrix, Monty Woolley, Robert Stack, Ilka Chase, Dorothy Stickney. D: Richard Haydn. COM 101m.

Missile to the Moon 1959 ★★½ Camp fun has scientists and juvenile delinquents battling evil colony of leotard-clad women who rule the moon. Absolutely ludicrous at every level. Made earlier as *Cat Women of the Moon*. C: Richard Travis, Cathy Downs, K. T. Stevens, Tommy Cook. D: Richard Cunha. SFI 78m. V

Missiles from Hell 1958 British ★★½ WWII heroics as Britishers and partisan Poles collaborate to track down a deadly, top-secret Nazi missile device. Standard war adventure has solid cast gamely fielding abrupt plot transitions. C: Michael Rennie, Patricia Medina, Milly Vitale, David Knight, Christopher Lee. D: Vernon Sewell. ACT 72m.

Missiles of October, The 1973 ★★★½ A reenaction of the tension-filled days during October, 1962, when Kennedy's America and the Soviet Union's Khruschev squared off in the Cuban missile crisis. Gripping and realistic. C: William Devane, Ralph Bellamy, Howard Da Silva, Martin Sheen. D: Anthony Page. DRA 155m. V

Missing 1982 ★★★★ True story of American searching for son who disappears in Latin American country, and whose absence may be part of a covert U.S.-backed operation. Crisp, taut and thrilling, with a memorable performance by Lemmon. C: Jack Lemmon, Sissy Spacek, Melanie Mayron, John Shea, Charles Cioffi. D: Constantin Costa-Gavras. DRA [PG] 122m. V

Missing Corpse, The 1945 ★★ A busy newspaper reporter (Bromberg) gets caught up in an unsolved murder case. Extremely low-budget thriller. C: J. Edward Bromberg, Eric Sinclair, Frank Janks, Isabel Randolph, Paul Guilfoyle, John Shay, Lorell Sheldon. D: Albert Herean. CRI 62m.

Missing Evidence 1939 ★★★½ FBI agent falls in love with counterfeiter he's trying to nail. Solid low-budget melodrama. C: Preston Foster, Irene Hervey, Inez Courtney. D: Phil Rosen. DRA 64m.

Missing in Action 1984 ★★½ A former Vietnam POW (Norris) returns years later to rescue American MIAs imprisoned in the jungle. Hard-driving Norris actioner was very popular at the box office. C: Chuck Norris, M. Emmet Walsh, David Tress, James Hong. D: Joseph Zito. ACT [R] 101m. V

Missing in Action 2: The Beginning 1985 ★★ American POW (Norris) plots his own escape from Vietnam. Prequel offers little new, except a few variations on the extremely violent theme. C: Chuck Norris, Soon-Teck Oh, Steven Williams, Bennett Ohta, Cosie Costa. D: Lance Hool. ACT [R] 96m. V

Missing in Action III: Braddock 1988 ★★½ Predictably enough, Braddock returns to Vietnam for some more rescues in the next installment of the saga. Aimed at Norris fans. (a.k.a. *Braddock: Missing in Action III.*) C: Chuck Norris, Aki Aleong, Roland Harrah III. D: Aaron Norris. ACT [R] 104m. V

Missing Juror, The 1944 ★★★½ Taut thriller about a mysterious murderer who methodically bumps off members of a jury that sentenced an innocent man to death. B-movie constraints never jeopardize plot or pace, which develop at a rapid, involving clip. C: Jim Bannon, Janis Carter, George Macready. D: Oscar "Budd" Boetticher, Jr. CRI 66m.

Missing Link, The 1988 ★★★½ A study of pre-historic people, starting from ape-like origins and moving along the chain of development. An altogether sturdy effort that has plenty to interest. C: Peter Elliott, Michael Gambon. D: Carol Hughes. DRA [PG] 92m. V

Missing Ten Days 1941 British ★★★½ Harrison survives a plane crash but forgets fateful events of preceding ten days. Far-fetched, but fast-paced, fun spy thriller. C: Rex Harrison, Karen Verne, C.V. France, Leo Genn. D: Tim Whelan. DRA 77m.

Missing Witnesses 1937 ★★★½ Detective is out to mop up racketeers in NYC. Bustling crime drama is clichéd but entertaining. C: John Litel, Dick Purcell, Jean Dale. D: William Clemens. CRI 60m.

Mission Batangas 1969 ★★½ American flyer (Weaver) tries to stop the Japanese from capturing a Phillipine gold stockpile. Routine WWII actioner. C: Dennis Weaver, Vera Miles, Keith Larsen. D: Keith Larsen. ACT 100m. V

Mission Galactica: The Cylon Attack 1979 ★★ Several episodes from the '70s sci-fi TV series are edited together. Not exactly the formula for success, and it shows. C: Lorne Greene, Lloyd Bridges. D: Vince edwards. SFI [G] 108m. TVM V

Mission Kill 1985 ★★ When his buddy is killed while smuggling arms into Latin America, a man swears revenge. C: Merete Van Kamp, Cameron Mitchell. D: David Winters. ACT [R] 97m. V

Mission Manila 1989 ★★★ When his brother disappears (with a shipment of illegal drugs in his charge), a man combs the slums of Manila in search for him. Harrowing and quite colorful. C: Larry Wilcox, Robin Eisenman, Tetchie Agbayani. D: Peter M. Mackenzie. ACT [R] 98m. V

Mission Mars 1968 ★★ American astronauts on first mission to the Red Planet find it inhabited by decidedly unfriendly occupants. Unimaginative science fiction. C: Darren McGavin, Nick Adams, George DeVries, Heather Hewitt. D: Nick Webster. SFI [G] 87m. V

Mission of Justice 1992 ★★★ Lots of fast and furious martial arts fun as an undercover cop infiltrates the private security force of an evil female politician. C: Jeff Wincott, Brigitte Nielsen, Luca Bercovici. D: Steve Barnett. ACT [R] 95m. V

Mission of the Shark 1991 ★★★★ The USS *Indianapolis* is sunk during WWII, in shark-infested Pacific waters. Graphic, hard-hitting account of a true story. C: Stacy Keach, Richard Thomas, Don Harvey, Bob Gunton, Steve Landesburg, Carrie Snodgress, Andrew Prine, Stacy Keach Sr. D: Robert Iscove. DRA 100m. TVM

Mission Phantom 1979 ★★★ A couple of professional thieves sneak into the Soviet Union and make off with a big hit in diamonds. Then a mad chase across Europe begins, as they rush to sell the goods. Lots of good intrigue throughout. C: Andrew Ray, Ingrid Sholder. D: James Reed. ACT 90m. V

Mission Stardust 1968 Italian ★★½ Scientists encounter aliens infected by unknown disease. Based on popular Perry Rhodan novel, this dubbed feature takes an apathetic approach. C: Essy Persson, Lang Jeffries, John Karelsen, Gianni Rizzo. D: Primo Zeglio. SFI [G] 90m. V

Mission, The 1986 British ★★★★½ Ecstatic, beautifully shot tale of missionaries in 18th-century Brazil, battling mercenary invaders. Gorgeous to look at, and intelligent Oscar-winning cinematography. C: Robert De Niro, Jeremy Irons, Ray McAnally, Aidan Quinn, Ronald Pickup, Liam Neeson. D: Roland Joffe. DRA [PG] 125m. V

Mission To Glory 1980 ★★★ In Old California, Native Americans confront Spanish Conquistadors. Fine cast and nifty action. (a.k.a. *Father Rino Story, The.*) C: Richard Egan, John Ireland, Aldo Ray, Cesar Romero, Ricardo Montalban. D: Ken Kennedy. ACT [PG] 100m. V

Mission to Moscow 1943 ★★★★ Screen adaptation of Joseph Davies' book about life in the USSR provides a fascinating glimpse into the Russian soul circa 1940, simultaneously capturing American attitudes at the time toward their Communist rival. As Davies, the U.S. ambassador to Russia, Huston lends weight and substance to this historical biography, and he's ably assisted by a strong cast. C: Walter Huston, Ann Harding, Oscar Homolka, George Tobias, Gene Lockhart, Frieda Inescort, Eleanor Parker, Richard Travis. D: Michael Curtiz. DRA 123m.

Missionary, The 1982 British ★★★ An innocent missionary (Palin) is sent straight from the heart of Africa to the slums of London to save fallen women. Predictable, mildly amusing comedy scripted by Palin. C: Michael Palin, Maggie Smith, Phoebe Nicholls, Trevor Howard, Denholm Elliott, Michael Hordern. D: Richard Loncraine. COM [R] 86m. V

Mississippi 1935 ★★★★ Running from trouble, Crosby boards Captain Fields' riverboat and becomes the ship singer. Amiable musical featuring delightful Rodgers and Hart score. Fields provides nicely edged comic counterpoint to Crosby's crooning. C: Bing Crosby, W. C. Fields, Joan Bennett, Queenie Smith, Gail Patrick, Claude Gillingwater. D: A. Edward Sutherland. MUS 73m.

Mississippi Blues 1983 ★★★★½ Marvelous documentary by French director Tavernier and American writer Parrish looks at music and people in the American south. A friendly tour, backed up with a terrific soundtrack. D: Bertrand Tavernier, Robert Parrish. DOC 92m. v

Mississippi Burning 1988 ★★★★ FBI agents Hackman and Dafoe investigate murder of civil rights workers in early '60s Mississippi. Provocative, explosive drama, loosely based on fact. Held together by Hackman's subtle but compelling performance as sly Southern law enforcement officer who finds key witness. C: Gene Hackman, Willem Dafoe, Frances McDormand, Brad Dourif, Gailard Sartain. D: Alan Parker. DRA [R] 127m. v

Mississippi Gambler 1953 ★★★ Dapper gambler (Power) with dreams of setting up his own casino in New Orleans must first roll the dice on matters of the heart, even to the point of having to defend his honor and that of the woman he loves. Atmospheric adventure yarn is good escapist fare. C: Tyrone Power, Piper Laurie, Julia Adams, John McIntire, Dennis Weaver. D: Rudolph Maté. ACT 98m.

Mississippi Masala 1992 ★★★½ Expulsion from Idi Amin's Uganda brings an East Indian couple to Mississippi. Conflict arises when their daughter falls in love with a local African-American (Washington). An original, ironic, and, occasionally compelling story of love and racism. C: Denzel Washington, Sarita Choudhury, Roshan Seth, Sharmila Tagore, Charles Dutton, Joe Seneca. D: Mira Nair. DRA [R] 118m. v

Mississippi Mermaid 1969 French ★★★½ Wealthy bachelor (Belmondo) finds bride (Deneuve) through personals. Seemingly surefire acting/directing team has unsure tone: alternates between romance, thrills, and homage to Jean Renoir. Beautifully photographed. C: Jean-Paul Belmondo, Catherine Deneuve, Michel Bouquet, Nelly Borgeaud. D: Francois Truffaut. DRA [PG] 111m. v

Missouri Breaks, The 1976 ★★★ A notoriously big film that failed at the box office. A war begins between Montana ranchers and rustlers. Exceedingly violent Western that hardly puts a talented cast to good use. C: Marlon Brando, Jack Nicholson, Kathleen Lloyd, Randy Quaid, Frederic Forrest, Harry Dean Stanton. D: Arthur Penn. WST [PG] 126m. v

Missouri Traveler, The 1958 ★★★½ Turn-of-the-century Southern ambiance infuses this tale of an orphan (de Wilde) who sets out on his own and supports himself by training horses. Well-meaning (if cloying) Americana; de Wilde is excellent. C: Brandon de Wilde, Lee Marvin, Gary Merrill, Mary Hosford, Paul Ford. D: Jerry Hopper. DRA 104m. v

Missourians, The 1950 ★★★★ Killers seek refuge in a small town and terrorize the gangleader's kinfolk who live there. Tight, low-budget Western packs a mean punch. C: Monte Hale, Paul Hurst, Roy Barcroft, Lyn Thomas. D: George Blair. WST 60m. v

Mistaken Identity 1936 ★★★ Three troublemakers pose as millionaires and get involved in all kinds of misadventures. Enjoyable comedy. C: Evalyn Knapp, Chick Chandler, Billy Gilbert. COM 75m. v

Mister Brown 1972 ★★★½ African-American family moves from Louisiana to L.A. to start their own business. Poignant, low-key drama avoids sentimentality. C: Al Stevenson, Judith Elliotte, Tyrone Fulton. D: Roger Andrieux. DRA 85m.

Mister Buddwing 1966 ★★★½ An amnesia victim (Garner) searches for his past. Slow pacing mars this otherwise compelling, well-acted mystery. C: James Garner, Jean Simmons, Angela Lansbury, Suzanne Pleshette, Katharine Ross. D: Delbert Mann. DRA 100m.

Mister Cory 1957 ★★★ Kid from the Chicago slums becomes a high-rolling gambler, then returns home to parade his wealth. Fast-paced, enjoyable story has a strong cast and Curtis' star chemistry going for it. C: Tony Curtis, Charles Bickford, Martha Hyer, Kathryn Grant. D: Blake Edwards. DRA 92m.

Mister 880 1950 ★★★½ Amiable comedy, based on real characters, concerns an endearing old Manhattan counterfeiter (Gwenn) and the FBI agent (Lancaster) who hunts him down. Gwenn's sterling performance is a winner. C: Dorothy McGuire, Burt Lancaster, Edmund Gwenn, Millard Mitchell, Minor Watson. D: Edmund Goulding. COM 90m.

Mister Hobo 1936 British ★★★½ Hobo Arliss is mistaken for member of aristocratic Rothschild family and begins to lead the life of Reilly. Good ensemble delivers in slick, well-made comedy. C: George Arliss, Gene Gerrard, Patric Knowles, Viola Keats. D: Milton Rosmer. COM 80m.

Mister Johnson 1991 ★★★★ Young black African is destroyed by his own ambition and British contempt for natives when he tries to work his way up to being an Englishman by turning his back on his own people and pledging allegiance to British colonial overlord. Reserved and enigmatic, but emotionally powerful. C: Pierce Brosnan, Edward Woodward, Maynard Eziashi, Beatie Edney. D: Bruce Beresford. DRA [PG-13] 105m. v

Mister Roberts 1955 ★★★★★ Terrific WWII comedy/drama; Fonda shines in title role of bored officer on cargo ship whose malcontent captain (Cagney) refuses his transfer to active duty. Excellent work by Powell in last screen role and Lemmon (Oscar for Best Supporting Actor) as Ensign Pulver. From the Broadway play by Thomas Heggen and Joshua Logan. Sequel: *Ensign Pulver.* C: Henry Fonda, James Cagney, William Powell, Jack Lemmon, Betsy Palmer, Ward Bond, Harry Carey Jr., Ken Curtis. D: John Ford, Mervyn LeRoy. COM 123m. V

Mister Rossi Looks for Happiness ★★★ With a magic whistle in hand, Mr. Rossi can travel through time and space. Fine fun and fantasy for children. FAM/SFI 80m. V

Mister Too Little 1980 ★★★ A poodle and a tiger, the closest of friends, escape from the circus in order to have fun. Charming adventure for children. Voices of Richard Egan, John Ireland, Aldo Ray, Cesar Romero, Ricardo Montalban. D: Ken Kennedy. FAM/DRA 100m.

Mister V 1941 *See* **Pimpernel Smith**

Mistral's Daughter 1984 ★★★★ Adaptation of Judith Krantz's succulent novel chronicles libertene life of painter Keach, whose grown love-child unexpectedly enters the scene. Deliciously trashy soap opera played with gusto. A must for romance fans. C: Stephanie Powers, Lee Remick, Stacy Keach, Robert Urich, Timothy Dalton. D: Douglas Hickox. DRA 390m. TVM V

Mistress 1987 ★★★ After her rich lover passes away, grieving mistress (Principal) realizes she doesn't know how to take care of herself. Minor, harmless diversion. C: Victoria Principal, Don Murray, Joanna Kerns, Alan Rachins. D: Michael Tuchner. DRA 100m. TVM V

Mistress 1992 ★★★ Failed screenwriter (Wuhl) gets chance to direct his dream movie project—just as long as he casts mistresses of his financial backers in key roles. Hit-and-miss comedy never fulfills satirical possibilities of its premise. Good ensemble though. C: Robert Wuhl, Martin Landau, Jace Alexander, Robert De Niro, Danny Aiello, Eli Wallach, Laurie Metcalf, Sheryl Lee Ralph, Jean Smart, Tuesday Knight, Christopher Walken, Ernest Borgnine, Stefan Gierasch. D: Barry Primus. COM [R] 109m. V

Mistress of Atlantis, The 1932 German ★★★½ The island queen leads a life of sin as her empire crumbles. Adventurous, uneven film from master German director Pabst was also filmed in French and English versions. C: Brigitte Helm, John Stuart, Gibb McLaughlin. D: Georg Wilhelm Pabst. DRA 87m.

Mistress Of The Apes 1979 ★★★ When her husband is declared missing, a beautiful New Yorker takes off for the Central African jungles to find him. Okay adventure. C: Barbara Leigh, Garth Pillsbury. D: Larry Buchanan. ACT [R] 88m. V

Mistress of The World 1959 ★★★ Father and daughter scientists are threatened by an evil woman seeking to steal their secret process for saving energy. Interesting. C: Martha Hyer, Sabu, Carlos Thompson. D: William Dieterle. SFI 98m. V

Mistress, The 1953 Japanese ★★★★½ Excellent drama of woman who finds out that her putative husband is really married to someone else. When she falls for medical student, things begin to fall apart. Subtle, low-key tragedy with superb acting. C: Hideko Takamine, Hiroshi Akutagawa. D: Shiro Toyoda. DRA 106m.

Misty 1961 ★★★★ Two children living on the Virginia coastline attempt to tame a wild horse. Nice film for young horse lovers that makes good use of location scenery. Based on Marguerite Henry's popular children's novel *Misty of Chincoteague.* C: David Ladd, Pam Smith, Arthur O'Connell, Anne Seymour. D: James B. Clark. FAM/DRA 91m. V

Misunderstood 1983 ★★★½ Hackman, overwhelmed with grief at wife's death, is blind to his young son's emotional needs. Powerful acting, though film is not completely involving. C: Gene Hackman, Henry Thomas, Rip Torn, Huckleberry Fox. D: Jerry Schatzberg. DRA [PG] 92m. V

Misunderstood 1988 Italian ★★★★ Tragedy reveals to a father (Quayle) the true nature of his two sons, one of whom has been taking the blame for the other's actions. Slow, subtle family drama benefits from workmanlike acting, direction. C: Anthony Quayle, Stefano Colagrande, Simone Gianozzi, Joyn Sharp. D: Luigi Comencini. DRA 101m. V

Mitchell 1975 ★★ Unintentionally hilarious cop picture, with Baker battling mobsters led by Balsam and rich thrill-killer Saxon, while bedding Evans, a high-priced hooker. C: Joe Don Baker, Linda Evans, Martin Balsam, John Saxon, Merlin Olsen, Harold J. Stone. D: Andrew V. McLaglen. CRI [R] 90m. V

Mixed Blood 1985 French ★★ Ensconced in Manhattan's derelict "Alphabet City" on the Lower East Side, the Brazilian head of a posse of youthful heroin dealers (Pera) fights dishonest cops and rival drug pushers to keep her territory. Director Morrissey does with blood what he did with sex in his '70s Warhol pics—he creates an orgy of unjudged violence. C: Marilia Pera, Richard Ulacia, Linda Kerridge, Geraldine Smith. D: Paul Morrissey. DRA 98m. V

Mixed Company 1974 ★★ Comedy with serious undertones about basketball coach (Bologna) who must adapt when his wife adopts abandoned multiracial kids, even though they have three children of their own. Passable as a comedy, but light on its topical social themes. C: Barbara Harris, Joseph Bologna, Tom Bosley, Lisa Gerritsen, Dorothy Shay. D: Melville Shavelson. COM [PG] 109m.

Mixed Nuts 1994 ★ Martin is the head of a

suicide prevention hotline on Christmas Eve Frenetic, ugly farce, with nary a heart or a laugh to recommend it. If you think that suicidal depression is funny, then this one's for you. Hollywood remake of the far less-inhibited French farce *Le Pere Noel Est Une Ordure*. C: Steve Martin, Rita Wilson, Madeline Kahn, Robert Klein, Anthony LaPaglia, Juliette Lewis, Rob Reiner, Adam Sandler, Liev Schreiber, Garry Shandling, Jon Stewart, Parker Posey. D: Nora Ephron. COM [PG-13] 97m. V

Mo' Better Blues 1990 ★★★½ Washington plays a self-destructive trumpet player in overlong jazzfest with excellent music and colorful characters. Features Branford Marsalis' Quartet on soundtrack. C: Denzel Washington, Spike Lee, Wesley Snipes, Giancarlo Esposito, Robin Harris, Joie Lee, John Turturro, Cynda Williams. D: Spike Lee. MUS [R] 129m. V

Mo' Money 1992 ★★ Near vanity production features Damon Wayans (who wrote and produced) as con artist who, along with brother Marlon, gets involved in credit card fraud while trying to romance Dash. Some gratuitous sex jokes and unnecessary violence. C: Damon Wayans, Marlon Wayans, Stacey Dash, Joe Santos, John Diehl. D: Peter Macdonald. COM [R] 91m. V

Moana 1925 ★★★★ Haunting, beautifully photographed, silent semi-documentary, filmed on the South Sea Islands, looks at the daily life of Polynesian fisherman Moana. From the director of the classic *Nanook of the North*, this comes close to equalling its predecessor. D: Robert Flaherty. DOC 85m.

Mob Boss 1990 ★★★ Z-movie maven Ray steps up in class (sort of) with this gangster comedy about inept Deezen taking over his father's mob. Pretty silly. C: Morgan Fairchild, Eddie Deezen, William Hickey, Don Stroud, Stuart Whitman, Mike Mazurki, Brinke Stevens, Jack O'Halloran, Karen Russell, Debra Lamb. D: Fred Olen Ray. CRI 91m. V

Mob Story 1990 ★★★ Vernon is on the run from his former partners in the underworld in this giddy gang spoof. Silly but amusing. C: John Vernon, Al waxman, Margot Kidder, Kate Vernon. D: Gabriel Markiw, Jancario Markiw. COM 98m. V

Mob, The 1951 ★★★ A hard-nosed cop infiltrates the Mob in order to bust their illegal dockyard activities. Crawford is an ideal tough guy, and the stellar supporting cast adds a touch of class to the proceedings. C: Broderick Crawford, Betty Buehler, Richard Kiley, Otto Hulett, Neville Brand, Ernest Borgnine, John Marley, Charles Bronson. D: Robert Parrish. CRI 87m.

Mob War 1989 ★★★ Ambitious but trivial gangster film pits media giant against Mafia. Violent. C: John Christian, Johnny Stumper, David Henry Keller, Jack LaMotta. D: J. christian Ingvordsen. CRI 96m. V

Mobsters 1991 ★★ Slater, Dempsey, Grieco, and Mandylor portray real-life mobsters Lucky Luciano, Meyer Lansky, Frank Costello, and Bugsy Siegel, looking more like kids dressed in their fathers' old suits. Veterans Abraham, Gambon, and Quinn look suitably humiliated. C: Christian Slater, Patrick Dempsey, Costas Mandylor, Richard Grieco, F. Murray Abraham, Michael Gambon, Lara Flynn Boyle, Anthony Quinn, Christopher Penn, Nicholas Sadler. D: Michael Karbelnikoff. CRI [R] 105m. V

Moby Dick 1930 ★★ Bizarre adaptation of Melville's classic whaling adventure includes Bennett as Captain Ahab's love interest—nowhere to be found in the original! Epic tale of Ahab's obsession with the indestructible whale gets lost in plot digressions and Barrymore's outlandish turn as Ahab. Screen this with the 1956 remake and compare. C: John Barrymore, Joan Bennett, Walter Long, Nigel de Brulier, Noble Johnson, Virginia Sale. D: Lloyd Bacon. DRA 75m.

Moby Dick 1956 ★★★★ Compelling remake of Melville's classic tale of Ahab and the great white whale. Peck's performance is outstanding, as is direction by Huston, who also co-wrote screenplay with Ray Bradbury. C: Gregory Peck, Richard Basehart, Leo Genn, Orson Welles, Harry Andrews. D: John Huston. DRA 116m. V

Model and the Marriage Broker, The 1951 ★★★★ Cukor lends his subtle, emotionally charged touch to this seriocomedy about wisecracking marriage broker (Ritter) and her attempts at hooking up lonely people looking for partners. Bittersweet, and most perceptive—and funny—about the ways of the human heart. C: Jeanne Crain, Scott Brady, Thelma Ritter, Zero Mostel, Michael O'Shea, Frank Fontaine, Nancy Kulp. D: George Cukor. COM 103m.

Model Behavior 1982 ★★ Aspiring photographer and his partner take on the modeling world until he falls for one of his subjects. C: Richard Bekins, Bruce Lyons, Cindy Harrel. D: Bud Gardner. DRA 86m. V

Model Shop, The 1969 French ★★★ Celebrated French director Demy set his first American film in the swinging hub of late-'60s L.A., chronicling a day in the life of alienated architect Lockwood, who embarks on a tentative affair with model Aimee. Demy's outsider's view of psychedelic Hollywood is captivating, but the plot is hesitant, so the movie loses its momentum. C: Anouk Aimee, Gary Lockwood, Alexandra Hay, Carole Cole, Severn Darden, Tom Fielding. D: Jacques Demy. DRA [PG] 95m.

Model Wife 1941 ★★★½ Snappy matrimonial comedy concerns two office workers (Blondell and Powell) who marry in secret because their boss objects to Blondell's getting hitched. The leads—previously teamed in the '30s gold-digger musicals—are delightfully funny as they try to keep their marital status under wraps. Sweet-natured farce with lots of laughs. C: Joan Blondell, Dick Powell, Lee Bowman, Charlie Ruggles, Lucile Watson, Ruth Donnelly, Billy Gilbert. D: Leigh Jason. COM 78m.

Moderato Cantabile 1964 French, Italian ★★★★ Theatrical directing great Brook adapts Marguerite Duras' novel in an unadorned, but highly dramatic style. Emotionally rich film boasts striking atmospherics coupled with dynamic performances from Belmondo and especially Moreau, as an isolated married woman obsessed with an unsolved crime. A singular viewing experience. C: Jeanne Moreau, Jean-Paul Belmondo, Didier Haudepin. D: Peter Brook. DRA 95m.

Modern Girls 1986 ★★ Three young women go club-hopping in L.A. A plotless excursion notable for early appearances of Zuniga and Madsen. C: Daphne Zuniga, Virginia Madsen, Cynthia Gibb, Clayton Rohner. D: Jerry Kramer. DRA [PG-13] 82m. V

Modern Love 1990 ★★★ Star Benson also directed, wrote, and produced this family project, with wife DeVito as co-star and their daughter as their daughter. The couple play newlyweds with all the usual problems. Not bad. C: Robby Benson, Karla DeVito, Rue McClanahan, Burt Reynolds, Frankie Valli. D: Robby Benson. COM [NC-17] 110m. V

Modern Problems 1981 ★★½ Bizarre accident gives air traffic controller Chase ability to move objects with brainwaves, and life becomes topsy-turvy, literally and figuratively. Bland and forgettable comedy. C: Chevy Chase, Patti D'Arbanville, Mary Kay Place, Nell Carter. D: Ken Shapiro. COM [PG] 93m. V

Modern Romance 1981 ★★★½ A film editor at loose ends (Brooks) does all he can to drive his sensible girlfriend (Harrold) out of his arms. Not without charms but, like other Brooks films, a little giddy. C: Albert Brooks, Kathryn Harrold, Bruno Kirby, James L. Brooks, George Kennedy. D: Albert Brooks. COM [R] 94m. V

Modern Times 1936 ★★★★★ Marvelous satire of the automated age with Charlie as comic victim of assembly lines and monster machines. Mostly silent, benefiting from beautiful score (including Chaplin's theme song, "Smile"), and charming romance with Goddard, who later became star's real-life wife. Unforgettable final fade-out. C: Charlie Chaplin, Paulette Goddard, Henry Bergman, Chester Conklin. D: Charlie Chaplin. COM [G] 89m. V

Modern World, the—Ten Great Writers ★★★★½ Ten profiles of great modern writers, written by novelist-critic Malcolm Bradbury. Excellent series uses dramatizations, interviews with experts to dissect their work. Kafka and Conrad episodes are particularly striking. DOC 59m. V

Moderns, The 1988 ★★★ Portrayal of the Lost Generation in 1920s Paris life features Carradine as an art forger, his former flame (Fiorentino), and her husband, a sinister art collector (Lone). Good period re-creation, but you know you're in trouble when Hemingway is the most sympathetic character. C: Keith Carradine, Linda Fiorentino, John Lone, Genevieve Bujold, Geraldine Chaplin, Wallace Shawn. D: Alan Rudolph. DRA [R] 126m. V

Modesty Blaise 1966 British ★★ Unfulfilling attempt to two-dimensionalize the comic strip about a supersexy female spy (Vitti). Pop-art visual style is intriguing, but director Losey can't decide if he wants a "comic" spoof or a straightforward adaptation, which results in a filmic mishmash of disjointed scenes. Of mild interest for the presence of Vitti, Bogarde, and Stamp. C: Monica Vitti, Dirk Bogarde, Terence Stamp, Harry Andrews, Michael Craig, Scilla Gabel, Tina Marquand, Clive Revill, Alexander Knox. D: Joseph Losey. COM 119m.

Modigliani of Montparnasse 1957 *See* **Lovers of Montparnasse, The**

Mogambo 1953 ★★★★ A romantic triangle develops in the course of a big game hunt in Kenya. Lurid, zesty remake of *Red Dust*, which also starred Gable. Beautifully made. C: Clark Gable, Ava Gardner, Grace Kelly, Donald Sinden. D: John Ford. DRA 115m. V

Mohammed, Messenger of God 1977 *See* **Message, The**

Mohawk 1956 ★★★ Painter (Brady) gets caught in Colonists vs. Indians crossfire in pre-Revolutionary Boston. Okay actioner. C: Scott Brady, Rita Gam, Neville Brand, Lori Nelson. D: Kurt Neumann. ACT 79m. V

Mole People, The 1956 ★★★ Scientists discover a lost community of albinos who live under Earth's surface and use "mole people" as slaves. Fun, bad sci-fi. C: John Agar, Cynthia Patrick, Hugh Beaumont, Nestor Paiva. D: Virgil Vogel. SFI 78m. V

Molly 1950 *See* **Goldbergs, The**

Molly and Gina 1994 ★★★ Predictable buddy/road movie about two women seeking to avenge the murder of their boyfriends. C: Frances Fisher, Natasha Gregson, Bruce Weitz, Stella Stevens, Peter Fonda. ACT [R] 90m. V

Molly and Me 1945 ★★★★ New maid (Fields) reorders household in previously unconsidered ways. Charming domestic comedy with easy laughs. Woolley and Fields are neatly paired. C: Gracie Fields, Monty Woolley, Roddy McDowall, Reginald Gardiner, Natalie Schafer, Edith Barrett. D: Lewis Seiler. COM 76m.

Molly Maguires, The 1970 ★★★½ Solid, if unremarkable tale of intrigue among Pennsylvania coal miners in 1876, as a group of Irish miners try to form a union, while an Irish newcomer wrestles with his conscience about being an informer. C: Sean Connery, Richard Harris, Samantha Eggar, Frank Finlay. D: Martin Ritt. DRA [PG] 123m. V

Mom 1991 ★★ What's a nice boy to do

when his mom becomes a flesh-eating alien? Silly horror spoof with decent gore effects. C: Mark Thomas Miller, Art Evans, Mary McDonough, Brian James, Stella Stevens, Jeanne Bates, Claudia Christian. D: Patrick Rand. HOR 95m.

Mom and Dad Save the World 1991 ★★ Suburban housewife (Garr) along with husband (Jones) is kidnapped by evil space lord (Lovitz) who is hopelessly infatuated with her. Funny premise is killed by hopelessly amateur production. C: Teri Garr, Jeffrey Jones, Jon Lovitz, Kathy Ireland. D: Greg Beeman. COM [PG] 88m. V

Moment by Moment 1978 ★ Almost legendary disaster casts Tomlin as a wealthy Malibu woman pining for the bikini-clad Travolta. Turgid, unintentionally funny romance sent John's then-rocketing career into a nosedive. C: John Travolta, Lily Tomlin. D: Jane Wagner. DRA [R] 102m.

Moment in Time, A 1986 British ★★★½ Aging widower (Carmichael) finds his romance when he meets attractive Simmons at a health spa. Nicely acted. C: Jean Simmons, Ian Carmichael, John Irvin. DRA 60m.

Moment of Danger 1960 *See* **Malaga**

Mommie Dearest 1981 ★★★ Dunaway chews plenty of scenery in Joan Crawford biography as the ultimate Hollywood two-face: gracious star by day, abusive mother by night. So far over the top it's almost fun to watch. C: Faye Dunaway, Diana Scarwid, Steve Forrest, Howard da Silva. D: Frank Perry. DRA [PG] 129m. V

Mon Oncle 1958 French ★★★★★ Raincoat-clad, pipe-smoking Hulot (Tati) has a hilarious encounter with a gadget-laden modern house. Highlights include the fish fountain, the house's "eyeballs," and a betting game with a lamp post. Entertainingly colorful, warm, and leisurely satire on modernization. Oscar-winning Best Foreign Film. In French with English subtitles. (a.k.a. *My Uncle*) C: Jacques Tati, Jean-Pierre Zola. D: Jacques Tati. COM 126m. V

Mon Oncle Antoine 1971 Canadian ★★★★★ Charming, elegantly directed and written film about boy's growing up in Canadian backwoods with his sympathetic uncle. A superb coming-of-age film. C: Jean Duceppe, Olivette Thibault. D: Claude Jutra. DRA 104m. V

Mon Oncle D'Amerique 1980 French ★★★★½ A textile plant manager (Depardieu) has an affair with an actress (Garcia), and is simultaneously observed by a human behavior analyst (Laborit). Unusual and fascinating, heightened by surreal touches. C: Gerard Depardieu, Nicole Garcia, Roger Pierre, Marie Dubois, Nelly Bourgeaud, Henri Laborit. D: Alain Resnais. DRA [PG] 123m. V

Mona 1986 British ★★★ Slight tale of girl victimized by small-town prejudices after she befriends dying WWI veteran. C: Frank Finlay, Deborah Stokes. DRA 60m. V

Mona Lisa 1986 British ★★★★½ Heart-rending film noir about small-time London thug who drives (and falls in love with) a beautiful, mysterious prostitute. Full of twists and betrayals and a dazzlingly complex performance by Hoskins. C: Bob Hoskins, Cathy Tyson, Michael Caine, Robbie Coltrane. D: Neil Jordan. CRI [R] 104m. V

Mondo Africa ★ Mondo Cane type documentary that purports to show Africa, concentrating on the disgusting and violent. DOC 80m. V

Mondo Cane 1963 ★★★½ Once-shocking documentary looks at global human abnormalities, with an emphasis on the provocative. Fascinating, sometimes silly, with Oscar-nominated hit song, "More." D: Gualtiero Jacopetti. DOC 105m. V

Mondo New York 1988 ★★★ Midnight-film cult classic is a showcase of NYC performance artists, many of them extremely raunchy. Definitely not for kids or the squeamish. C: Joey Arias, Rick Aviles, Charlie Barnett, Joe Coleman, Ann Magnuson, Emilio Cubiero, Karen Finley, Phoebe Legere, Lydia Lunch. DOC 83m. V

Mondo Trasho 1970 ★★ After running over Pearce, heavyweight transvestite Divine stuffs body in her car and drives through Baltimore. First full-length film for cult director Waters suffers from poorly synched sound, cheesy (and obscenity-laced) dialogue, and unending tastelessness—though his fans won't mind. C: Divine, Mary Vivian Pearce, Mink Stole. D: John Waters. COM 95m. V

Mondo World War II—Short Memory ★★★ Also a short film; documentary focusses on homefronts in Europe during the great conflagration. DOC 60m. V

Money for Nothing 1993 ★★★ Cusack is an out-of-work stevedore (in a bizarre piece of casting) who finds a bag containing $5 million in unmarked bills. What he does with the money is supposed to be hilarious, as are the efforts of the cops and mobsters to catch up to him. C: John Cusack, Debi Mazar. COM [R] 90m. V

Money From Home 1953 ★★★ A gambler (Martin) gets a bumbling veterinarian (Lewis) to help him fix a horse race. Middling Martin and Lewis vehicle, originally shot in 3-D (a terrifying notion). C: Dean Martin, Jerry Lewis, Pat Crowley. D: George Marshall. COM 100m.

Money, Money, Money 1962 *See* **Counterfeiters of Paris, The**

Money Movers 1981 Australian ★★★½ Inside job heist goes to pieces in this early Beresford effort. Predictable but entertaining. C: Bryan Brown, Terence Donovan, Tony Bonner, Ed Devereaux, Lucky Gills, Charles Tingwell, Candy Raymond, Alan Cassell. D: Bruce Beresford. DRA 90m. V

Money Pit, The 1986 ★★★ Hanks and Long are a couple determined to construct the perfect home, which naturally turns into a nightmare. Jokes are repetitive and predictable, with none of the wit and style of the similar *Mr. Blandings Builds His Dream House.* C: Tom Hanks, Shelley Long, Alexander Godunov, Maureen Stapleton, Joe Mantegna, Philip Bosco, Josh Mostel. D: Richard Benjamin. COM [PG] 91m. V

Money, The 1975 ★★★½ Ordinary comedy-thriller about desperate young man who pulls off ill-considered kidnapping is transformed by intelligent direction. C: Laurence Luckinbill, Elizabeth Richards, Danny DeVito, Graham Becket. D: Carl Workman. CRI 88m. V

Money to Burn 1973 ★★★½ Aging con (Marshall) cooks up a scheme to export counterfeit money from prison. Old pros Marshall and Natwick make this clever caper work nicely indeed. C: E. G. Marshall, Mildred Natwick, Cleavon Little. D: Robert Michael Lewis. CRI 73m. TVM V

Money Trap, The 1966 ★★★ An impoverished cop (Ford) steals drug money, which leads to murder. Over-baked film noir, of interest as reunion film for *Gilda*'s Ford and Hayworth (effective in a small role). C: Glenn Ford, Elke Sommer, Rita Hayworth, Joseph Cotten, Ricardo Montalban. D: Burt Kennedy. CRI 92m.

Mongrel 1983 ★ Man dreams he's a vicious dog who kills, wakes up and finds the corpses. C: Aldo Ray, Terry Evans. D: Robert A. Burns. HOR 90m. V

Monika 1952 Swedish ★★★★ Minor Bergman tale of young lovers rushing into marriage and parenthood. Charming and tender, if forgettable. (a.k.a. *Summer with Monika*) C: Harriet Andersson, Lars Ekborg. D: Ingmar Bergman. DRA 96m. V

Monique 1970 Italian ★★ Giorgetti is an unbalanced career woman who finds out her husband has been two-timing her. Big mistake. C: Florence Giorgetti, John Ferris. D: Jacques Scandelari. CRI 96m. V

Monitors, The 1969 ★★★ Alien beings invade Earth to rid it of vice, but fun-loving earthlings don't want to reform. Uneven sci-fi satire, via Chicago's fabled Second City troupe. C: Guy Stockwell, Avery Schreiber, Keenan Wynn, Larry Storch, Alan Arkin, Susan Oliver. D: Jack Shea. SFI [PG] 92m.

Monkey Boy 1990 British ★★★½ Surprisingly intelligent horror film about half-human, half-monkey mutant who kills scientists who are experimenting with him, goes on the lam from the lab. C: John Lynch, Christine Kavanaugh, Kenneth Cranham. D: Lawrence Gordon Clark. HOR 104m. V

Monkey Business 1931 ★★★★½ Vintage Marx madness with the boys as ocean voyage stowaways. All four do a hilarious Chevalier imitation to get off boat. Zany fun throughout. Script co-written by noted humorist S.J. Perelman. C: Groucho Marx, Harpo Marx, Chico Marx, Zeppo Marx, Thelma Todd, Ruth Hall, Harry Woods. D: Norman Z. McLeod. COM 77m. V

Monkey Business 1952 ★★★★ Scientist Grant invents potion that rejuvenates anyone who drinks it, and many do after mischievous chimpanzee pours the concoction into a water cooler. In this screwball comedy, gags don't stop as Grant, Rogers, Coburn, and Monroe run at dizzying comic speed under Hawks' zippy direction. C: Ginger Rogers, Cary Grant, Charles Coburn, Marilyn Monroe. D: Howard Hawks. COM 97m. V

Monkey Grip 1982 Australian ★★★½ Single mother becomes involved with a substance-abusing musician. Unflinching contemporary drama; capable, sincere performance by Hazelhurst. C: Noni Hazlehurst, Colin Friels. D: Ken Cameron. DRA 117m. V

Monkey House 1992 ★★★½ Four bizarre tales from the masterful Kurt Vonnegut: "All the King's Horses," "Fortitude," "Euphio Question," and "Next Door." Chills and thrills for all. SFI V

Monkey Hustle 1977 ★★ When expressway threatens ghetto neighborhood, residents work together to stop construction. Good cast can't save weak script, but they try. C: Yaphet Kotto, Rosalind Cash, Rudy Ray Moore, Kirk Calloway, Randy Brooks. D: Arthur Marks. COM [PG] 90m. V

Monkey in the Master's Eye 1972 ★★ Slave becomes martial arts champion. Silly adventury/lowbrow comedy blend. C: Pan Yin Tze, Chin Lung. ACT 92m. V

Monkey in Winter, A 1962 French ★★★★ An encounter with a young man (Belmondo) prompts a reformed alcoholic (Gabin) to look back with fondness and regret on his own youth. Nostalgic journey that treads lightly on sentiment. Gabin and Belmondo are well paired. (a.k.a. *It's Hot in Hell* and *Un Singe En Hiver*) C: Jean Gabin, Jean-Paul Belmondo, Suzanne Flon. D: Henri Verneuil. DRA 104m. V

Monkey Kung Fu ★ A martial arts master tutors a young man in a unique dance-like brand of kung fu. Passable fight sequences, complemented by less-than-adequate acting and a barely visible plotline. C: Chen Mu-Chan, Ssun Jung-Chi. ACT 96m. V

Monkey on My Back 1957 ★★★★ Boxing biography re-creates the true story of fighter Barney Ross, who went from the heights of championship bouts to the depths of drug addiction. Mitchell gives a sincere performance in this thought-provoking account of one person's journey through triumph and tragedy. C: Cameron Mitchell, Paul Richards, Dianne Foster, Jack Albertson, Kathy Garver. D: Andre de Toth. DRA 93m.

Monkey People, The ★★★½ Documentary study of primates, focussing on how much they have in common with people. Interesting, particularly for older children. C: Susan Sarandon. D: Gerard Vienne. DOC 85m. V

Monkey Shines: An Experiment in Fear 1988 ★★★★ Wheelchair-bound student (Beghe) finds that the monkey trained to assist him is literally acting out his darkest impulses. Fascinating, frightening study, confidently written and directed. From Michael Stewart's novel. (a.k.a. *An Experiment in Fear*) C: Jason Beghe, John Pankow, Kate McNeil, Joyce Van Patten, Christine Forrest. D: George A. Romero. HOR [R] 113m. V

Monkey Trouble 1994 ★★½ A young girl (Birch) adopts a cute monkey, not knowing that he has been trained as a pickpocket by evil Keitel. A bit saccharine, but Keitel has some fun. C: Thora Birch, Harvey Keitel, Finster, Mimi Rogers, Christopher McDonald, Kevin Scannell. D: Franco Amurri. COM 95m.

Monkeys, Go Home! 1967 ★★½ Young man uses monkeys as pickers on his olive farm, outraging the locals. Flimsy Disney; Chevalier's swan song. C: Maurice Chevalier, Yvette Mimieux, Bernard Woringer, Clement Harari, Yvonne Constant. D: Andrew V. McLaglen. FAM/COM 101m. V

Monkey's Uncle, The 1965 ★★½ Disney's follow-up to *The Misadventures of Merlin Jones* has college brain (Kirk) conducting sleep experiments with monkeys, then switching to human flying machines. Younger audiences will enjoy the slapstick. C: Tommy Kirk, Annette Funicello, Leon Ames, Frank Faylen. D: Robert Stevenson. FAM/COM 90m. V

Monocacy, the Battle that Saved Washington 1992 ★★★ Documentary recreation of 1864 Shenandoah River campaign of Civil War. For buffs only. DOC 60m. V

Monolith 1993 ★★★ Engaging acting as mystical force lurks below covert government installation. C: Louis Gossett, Jr., John Hurt, Bill Paxton. D: John Eyres. SFI [R] 96m. V

Monolith Monsters, The 1957 ★★★½ Mysterious meteorites appear in desert town, where they keep growing and growing and.... One of the best of the low-budget "aliens are invading us!" flicks. C: Grant Williams, Lola Albright, Les Tremayne. D: John Sherwood. SFI 77m. V

Monsieur Beaucaire 1946 ★★★★ Dandy costume comedy for Hope as French court barber impersonating a nobleman to foil an assassination plot against the king. Holds interest with good jokes, well-paced plot. Youngsters will love it. Based on Booth Tarkington novel. C: Bob Hope, Joan Caulfield, Patric Knowles, Cecil Kellaway, Joseph Schildkraut, Reginald Owen. D: George Marshall. COM 93m. V

Monsieur Hire 1989 French ★★★★ Shy voyeur (Blanc) falls for neighbor (Bonnaire) involved in murder. Captivating tale has strong performances, concise direction, sad (but perfect) ending. Based on a Georges Simenon novel. C: Michel Blanc, Sandrine Bonnaire, Luc Thuillier, Eric Berenger, Andre Wilms. D: Patrice Leconte. CRI [PG-13] 88m. V

Monsieur Verdoux 1947 ★★★★½ Superior black comedy casts star in atypical role of "black widower" Parisian who marries and murders his wives for their money. Considered a bit scandalous when released, but comedy scenes are well done, particularly Charlie's attempts to bump off the indestructible Raye. Probably Chaplin's best sound film. C: Charlie Chaplin, Martha Raye, Isobel Elsom, Marilyn Nash. D: Charles Chaplin. COM 123m. V

Monsieur Vincent 1949 French ★★★★½ The life and times of a 17th-century social worker, St. Vincent de Paul. Fresnay is remarkable in this moving and inspiring biography; exquisite photography. Film won a special Oscar for its stirring accomplishment. C: Pierre Fresnay, Aime Clairiond, Jean Debucourt, Lise Delamare. D: Maurice Cloche. DRA 73m. V

Monsignor 1982 ★★ Unholy mess stars Reeve as WWII-era cleric who manages Vatican business while having an affair with a nun. Each scene adds to the number of unintentional laughs. C: Christopher Reeve, Genevieve Bujold, Fernando Rey, Jason Miller. D: Frank Perry. DRA [R] 121m. V

Monsignor Quixote 1988 British ★★★★ Guinness plays an unassuming priest and Don Quixote descendant who unexpectedly is appointed a monsignor. He and politician McKern commemorate the event by retracing the steps of Guinness' illustrious ancestor. Unusual tale nicely rendered with shining performances. C: Alec Guinness, Leo McKern, Ian Richardson, Philip Stone, Valentine Pelka. D: Rodney Bennett. DRA 118m. V

Monsoon 1953 ★★ American visiting his fiancée in India lusts after her sister in this vapid tale. C: Ursula Thiess, Diana Douglas, George Nader, Ellen Corby. D: Rodney Amateau. DRA 79m.

Monster 1978 ★ Veteran actors star in this horror film about a pollution-spawned aquatic creature that devours residents of a South American town. The beast looks awfully fake, but it's no less convincing than anything else here. (a.k.a. *It Came from the Lake, Monstroid*) C: Jim Mitchum, John Carradine, Philip Carey, Anthony Eisley, Keenan Wynn. D: Kenneth Hartford, Herbert L. Strock. HOR [PG] 77m. V

Monster a Go-Go 1965 ★ Before he discovered the possibilities of gore effects, Lewis made Grade-Z drivel like this tale of a ten-foot-tall monster battling go-go-dancers. Must be seen to be believed. C: Phil Morton, June Travis, Henry Hite, Bill Rebane, Sheldon Seymour. D: Herschell Gordon Lewis. SFI 70m. V

Monster and the Girl, The 1941 ★★★½ Combination gangster and mad-scientist movie, as a woman is forced into prostitution by the Mob and her brother's brain is transplanted into an albino ape! They're not just another dysfunctional family, that's for sure. Energetic B-movie. C: Ellen Drew, Robert Paige, Paul Lukas, Joseph Calleia, George Zucco, Rod Cameron. D: Stuart Heisler. HOR 65m.

Monster Club, The 1981 British ★★½ Writer Carradine interviewing vampire Price in a Transylvanian nightclub is the premise for trio of horror tales, none of which are particularly scary. Lots of rock music on the soundtrack. C: Vincent Price, John Carradine, Donald Pleasence, Stuart Whitman, Richard Johnson, Britt Ekland, Patrick Magee. D: Roy Ward Baker. HOR 104m. v

Monster Dog 1986 ★ Cooper and his band are attacked by a giant mutant German shepherd. Everyone's a music critic. C: Alice Cooper, Victoria Vera. D: Clyde Anderson. HOR [R] 88m. v

Monster Forces of Nature 1993 ★★★ Documentary on the destructive potential of hurricans, volcanoes, earthquakes, floods. Serious and informative. DOC 90m.

Monster from a Prehistoric Planet 1967 Japanese ★★★ Dinosaurs rule Japan as dino-mom goes searching for her house-sized offspring, crushing every plastic tank in her path. Amusing in its own rubbery way. C: Tarrin. D: Haruyasu Noguchi. SFI [PG] 90m. v

Monster from Green Hell 1957 ★★½ An insect experiment gone wrong results in giant wasps flying amok in Africa. '50s sci-fi cheapie has some good camp laughs. C: Jim Davis, Robert E. Griffin, Barbara Turner, Vladimir Sokoloff, Eduardo Ciannelli. D: Kenneth Crane. SFI 71m. v

Monster From the Ocean Floor, The 1954 ★★ Diver discovers giant squid off Mexican coast. Early Roger Corman effort is tame sci-fi/horror outing. (a.k.a. *It Stalked the Ocean Floor* C: Anne Kimball, Stuart Wade, Wyott Ordung. D: Wyott Ordung. SFI 66m. v

Monster High 1989 ★ An alien eats teenagers until they defeat it at basketball. Incredibly silly. C: Dean Iandoli, Diana Frank, David Marriott, D.J. Kerzner. D: Rudiger Poe. SFI 84m. v

Monster in a Box 1992 ★★★★ Like Gray's previous effort, *Swimming to Cambodia*, a single event—this time the writing of his autobiography—is the springboard for reflections about life and death. Gray's ability to laugh at himself and find ironies in the human condition is compelling. C: Spalding Gray. D: Nick Broomfield. COM [PG-13] 90m. v

Monster in the Closet 1986 ★★★★ California reporter and scientist work together to wipe out closet-lurking killer monsters. Bloody good fun in sharp spoof of '50s monster flicks. C: Donald Grant, Denise DuBarry, Claude Akins, Howard Duff, Henry Gibson, Donald Moffat, Paul Dooley, John Carradine, Stella Stevens. D: Bob Dahlin. HOR [PG] 90m. v

Monster Island 1981 Spanish-U.S. ★★½ Jules Verne short story becomes a technically poor tale of shipwreck survivors, tormented by prehistoric creatures and an egotistical madman (Stamp). Stick with *Mysterious Island.* (a.k.a. *Mystery on Monster Island*) C: Terence Stamp, Peter Cushing. D: Juan Piquer Simon. SFI 100m.

Monster Maker, The 1944 ★★ Naish is an evil scientist who develops a formula with which he causes rivals to develop hideous physical deformities. Gross horror film. C: J. Carroll Naish, Ralph Morgan, Wanda McKay, Terry Frost. D: Sam Newfield. HOR 62m. v

Monster of Piedras Blancas, The 1959 ★★½ A monster bearing an uncanny resemblance to the Creature from the Black Lagoon is summoned forth from its cave by a lighthouse keeper, and proceeds to terrorize the seaside. Weak story, but the monster is played by the film's producer! C: Les Tremayne, Forrest Lewis, John Harmon. D: Irvin Berwick. HOR 72m. v

Monster Squad, The 1987 ★★★★ Likable, exciting homage to classic movie monster flicks. Dracula leads his creature cohorts in search of a magic amulet that can grant him world domination, and only a group of savvy, smalltown kids stand in his way. Fast-paced fun. C: Andre Gower, Robby Kiger, Stephen Macht, Duncan Regehr, Tom Noonan. D: Fred Dekker. COM [PG-13] 82m. v

Monster That Challenged the World, The 1957 ★★★½ Outraged killer bugs hatch from prehistoric eggs in California's Salton Sea. Good monster mayhem. C: Tim Holt, Audrey Dalton, Hans Conried, Casey Adams. D: Arnold Laven. HOR [G] 84m. v

Monster, The 1925 ★★★★ Self-parodying silent horror film has mad doctor (Chaney) chewing the scenery as he kidnaps innocent victims for sinister experiments. Good sense of satire in this strange film. C: Lon Chaney, Gertrude Olmstead, Hallam Cooley, Johnny Arthur, Charles Sellon. D: Roland West. HOR 86m.

Monster Walks, The 1932 ★★★½ Reynolds is on the run when evil relative plans to have her murdered and blame killer gorilla. Campy fun. C: Rex Lease, Vera Reynolds, Mischa Auer, Sheldon Lewis. D: Frank Strayer. HOR 59m. v

Monster Zero 1966 *See* **Godzilla vs. Monster Zero**

Monstroid *See* **Monster**

Montana 1950 ★★★½ Okay western stars Flynn as a maverick cowboy, who almost single-handedly opens up the Montana territory. C: Errol Flynn, Alexis Smith, S.Z. Sakall. D: Ray Enright. WST 76m.

Montana 1990 ★★★½ A long-married couple of Montana ranchers go to war against strip miners who are trying to take away their land. Good action and solid drama throughout. C: Gena Rowlands, Richard Crenna, Lea Thompson, Justin Deas, Elizabeth Berridge,

Darren Dalton, Scott Coffey. D: William A. Graham. WST 91m. TVM V

Montana Belle 1952 ★★★ Russell plays Belle Starr, an outlaw who reforms and breaks away from Dalton gang. Pretty good Western with all the expected action sequences. C: Jane Russell, George Brent, Scott Brady, Andy Devine, Forrest Tucker. D: Allan Dwan. WST 81m. V

Montana Mike 1947 *See* **Heaven Only Knows**

Montana Moon 1930 ★★ A socialite (Crawford) defies her father's wishes and marries a cowpoke (Brown). Dull and dated antique. C: Joan Crawford, John Mack Brown, Dorothy Sebastian, Ricardo Cortez, Benny Rubin, Cliff Edwards, Karl Dane. D: Mal St. Clair. WST 89m.

Monte Carlo 1930 ★★★★ A down-on-her-luck countess (MacDonald) must choose between a wealthy prince or a count traveling incognito as a hairdresser. Spun-sugar musical fairy tale floats, thanks to the fabled "Lubitsch Touch." C: Jeanette MacDonald, Jack Buchanan, ZaSu Pitts, Claude Allister, Tyler Brooke. D: Ernst Lubitsch. MUS 90m.

Monte Carlo 1986 ★★★½ Delicious trash features Collins (in her *Dynasty* prime) as a WWII singing spy(!), dallying with men and playing roulette. Insanely silly, but it does keep the attention for more than three hours! C: Joan Collins, George Hamilton, Lisa Eilbacher, Lauren Hutton, Robert Carradine, Malcolm McDowell. D: Anthony Page. DRA 200m. TVM V

Monte Carlo or Bust 1969 *See* **Those Daring Young Men in Their Jaunty Jalopies**

Monte Carlo Story, The 1957 Italian ★★★ Two gold-digging gamblers (De Sica, Dietrich) arrive in "Casino Capital," each thinking the other is wealthy. Two stars don't mix well in predictable comedy. Dietrich seems to be sleepwalking. C: Marlene Dietrich, Vittorio De Sica, Arthur O'Connell, Natalie Trundy. D: Samuel Taylor. COM 99m.

Monte Walsh 1970 ★★★★ Two over-the-hill cowboys are failing in their efforts to keep up with the ever-changing world. Very sensitive—indeed compelling—production of a story that might have turned bleak. Fine performances by the stars. C: Lee Marvin, Jeanne Moreau, Jack Palance, Mitch Ryan, Jim Davis. D: William Fraker. WST [PG] 100m. V

Montenegro 1981 Swedish ★★★★ A bored housewife (Anspach) finds sexual release with one of a group of crude Yugoslav itinerant laborers she meets in a bar. Original and unpredictable, with some outrageous humor. (a.k.a. *Montenegro—or Pigs and Pearls*) C: Susan Anspach, Erland Josephson, Per Oscarsson, John Zacharias. D: Dusan Makavejev. DRA [R] 97m. V

Montenegro—or Pigs and Pearls 1981 *See* **Montenegro**

Monterey Pop 1969 ★★★★½ Historic film of the 1967 rock 'n' roll festival in California was the first of its kind; featuring outstanding performances by some of the biggest names in '60s music. A gem. C: Otis Redding, Jimi Hendrix, Janis Joplin, The Who. D: James Desmond, Barry Feinstein, D.A. Pennebaker, Albert Maysles. MUS 88m. V

Month in the Country, A 1988 British ★★★★ Trying to recover from the horrors of WWI, two veterans retreat to the English countryside. Slow-moving and satisfying. C: Colin Firth, Kenneth Branagh, Natasha Richardson, Patrick Malahide. D: Pat O'Connor. DRA [PG] 92m. V

Montparnasse 19 1957 *See* **Lovers of Montparnasse, The**

Monty Python and the Holy Grail 1975 British ★★★★★ King Arthur and his knights search for the Holy Grail in this bizarre, wildly anachronistic, somewhat violent, and extremely funny parody of the Camelot legend from British TV's *Monty Python* crew. Don't miss that killer bunny! C: Graham Chapman, John Cleese, Terry Gilliam, Eric Idle, Terry Jones, Michael Palin. D: Terry Gilliam, Terry Jones. COM [PG] 90m. V

Monty Python Live at the Hollywood Bowl 1982 British ★★★ Concert film of favorite sketches from cult BBC-TV comedy series *Monty Python's Flying Circus.* Though Python troupe gives this their all, the stagebound antics lack edge of the original broadcasts (which are available on tape). Fans of the troupe may enjoy. C: John Cleese, Graham Chapman, Terry Gilliam, Eric Idle, Terry Jones, Michael Palin, Neil Innes, Carol Cleveland. D: Terry Hughes. COM [R] 78m. V

Monty Python's Flying Circus—Vol. 1 1970 ★★★★ Video includes The Architect's Sketch, The Naughty Chemist, Ministry of Silly Walks, The Piranha Brothers. C: Graham Chapman, John Cleese, Terry Gilliam, Eric Idle, Terry Jones, Michael Palin. D: Ian McNaughton. COM 60m. V

Monty Python's Flying Circus—Vol. 2 1970 ★★★½ Tape includes The Argument Clinic, The Church Police, The Spanish Inquisition, The Semaphore Version of "Wuthering Heights." COM 60m. V

Monty Python's Flying Circus—Vol. 3 1970 ★★★½ Video includes Attilla The Hun, Killer Sheep, Summarize Proust Competition, The Travel Agent Sketch. COM 60m. V

Monty Python's Flying Circus—Vol. 4 1970 ★★★½ Tape includes The Bruce Sketch, The Farming Club, Killer Cars, Sgt. Ducky's Song, Slim Jeans Theatre. COM 60m. V

Monty Python's Flying Circus—Vol. 5 1970 ★★★★ Tape includes Spam Sketch, Gumby Brain Surgery, The Black Eagle, The New Royal Navy, World Forum, The Tobacconist. COM 59m. V

Monty Python's Flying Circus—Vol. 6 1970

★★★★ Tape includes How Not To Be Seen, The Cheese Shop, Dental Appendages, The Exchange and Mart Job Interview. **COM** 58m. **V**

Monty Python's Flying Circus—Vol. 7 1993 ★★★½ Includes Pipe Dreams, Prawn Salad Ltd., Ken Clean-Air-System, The Cheap-Laughs From Next Door, The Rude Butcher. **COM** 60m. **V**

Monty Python's Flying Circus—Vol. 8 1970 ★★★½ Tape includes Behind the 8 Ball, How to Feed A Goldfish, The Lifeboat, The Queen Will Be Watching, Is There? **COM** 58m. **V**

Monty Python's Flying Circus—Vol. 9 1970 ★★★½ Video features Silly Party And Other Favors, Sorry to Interrupt, Book Of The Month Club, Whicker's World, Assaulting A Police Officer. **COM** 60m. **V**

Monty Python's Flying Circus—Vol. 10 1970 ★★★½ Tape includes Blood, Devastation, Death, War, Horror And Other Humorous Events, Pantomime Horses, Army Recruitment Office, The Police Hijacker, Scottish Poetry. **COM** 60m. **V**

Monty Python's Flying Circus—Vol. 11 1970 ★★★½ Video includes Dirty Vicars, Poopy Judges, And Oscar Wilde, Too!, The Dirty Vicar, The Blood Bank, Meet The Gits. **COM** 60m. **V**

Monty Python's Flying Circus—Vol. 12 1970 ★★★½ Tape features Kamikaze Highlanders, The Prejudice Game, Dennis Moore, Spot The Looney. **COM** 60m. **V**

Monty Python's Flying Circus—Vol. 13 1970 ★★★½ Video includes I'm A Lumberjack!, A Spanish Llama Song, Homicidal Barber, The Lumberjack Song, Killer Joke Warfare. **COM** 60m. **V**

Monty Python's Flying Circus—Vol. 14 1970 ★★★½ Includes Chocolate Frogs, Baffled Cats And Other Taste Treats, Confuse-A-Cat, Ltd., The Customs Inspector, Animal Debates, A Legal Crime Ring. **COM** 60m. **V**

Monty Python's Flying Circus—Vol. 15 1970 ★★★½ Video includes Dead Parrats Don't Talk And Other Fowl Plays, Camel Spotting, You're No Fun Anymore, Full Frontal Nudity, Nudes In Art, Hell's Grannies. **COM** 60m. **V**

Monty Python's Flying Circus—Vol. 16 1970 ★★★½ Tape includes A Man With Three Cheeks Or Butt Naught For Me, Flying Sheep, A Man With Three Buttocks, The Marriage Counselor, Boxing For Beliefs. **COM** 60m. **V**

Monty Python's Flying Circus—Vol. 17 1970 ★★★½ Video includes The Upper-Class Twit Competition, Flesh-Eating Vegetarians, Police Proofs, Psychiatric Silliness, Nazi Boarders. **COM** 60m. **V**

Monty Python's Flying Circus—Vol. 18 1970 ★★★½ Tape features Despicable Families, Naughty Complaints And Killer Fruit, The Most Awful Family In Britain Awards, Self-Defense Against Fruit, The Dental Espionage Ring, Sentence Finishers Inc. **COM** 60m. **V**

Monty Python's Flying Circus—Vol. 19 1970 ★★★½ Tape includes Nudge Nudge Wink Wink, Bicycle Repairman, The Milkman Trap, The Queen Victoria Handicap. **COM** 60m. **V**

Monty Python's Flying Circus—Vol. 20 1970 ★★★½ Video includes Pet Ants, Dead Poets & The Mysterious Michael Ellis, The Aspiring Lion Tamer, Gorilla Librarian, Famous Author's Ant Poetry. **COM** 60m. **V**

Monty Python's Flying Circus—Vol. 21 1970 ★★★½ Video includes Scott of the Antarctic, The Long John Silver Impersonator's Soccer Team, A License For Eric The "Alibut, Idiot TV Programmers." **COM** 60m. **V**

Monty Python's Flying Circus—Vol. 22 1970 ★★★½ Video includes Mr. Neutron's Balloonish Bicycle Tour, The Golden Age of Ballooning, Mr. Neutron, The Cycling Tour. **COM** 60m. **V**

Monty Python's Life of Brian 1979 British ★★★★ Born in a manger, harassed by Romans, and condemned to death by a lisping Pontius Pilate, the reluctant messiah's life parallels that of his more notable contemporary. Monty Python's hilarious spoof of biblical epic moviemaking was actually banned in Scotland. (a.k.a. *Life of Brian*) C: Graham Chapman, John Cleese, Terry Gilliam, Eric Idle, Terry Jones, Michael Palin. D: Terry Jones. **COM** **[R]** 94m. **V**

Monty Python's Parrot Sketch Not Included 1990 ★★★½ Video includes Fish-Slapping Dance, The Ministry of Silly Walks, The Argument Clinic. C: Graham Chapman, John Cleese, Terry Gilliam, Eric Idle, Terry Jones, Michael Palin. **COM** 75m.

Monty Python's The Meaning of Life 1983 British ★★★★ Last of the Monty Python films returns to sketch format of the television show in bizarre series of comic vignettes. Birth, life, and death thematically link the sequences, and Jones' restaurant vomit skit with Cleese as obsequious maître d" is a black-humored classic. Not for all tastes, but fans will adore. C: Graham Chapman, John Cleese, Terry Gilliam, Eric Idle, Terry Jones, Michael Palin, Carol Cleveland. D: Terry Jones. **COM** **[R]** 107m. **V**

Mooch Goes To Hollywood 1971 ★★★ An adorable little pooch goes off on a wonderful adventure through Hollywood. Great for kids and fun for adults. Numerous guest cameos. C: Vincent Price, Jill St. John, Jim Backus. D: Richard Erdman. **FAM/COM** 55m. **V**

Moochie of the Little League 1959 ★★★½ Charming Disney tale of a Little Leaguer (Corcoran) helping his team of misfits on to victory. Originally a *Walt Disney Presents* two-parter. C: Kevin Corcoran, Reginald Owen, Frances Rafferty. D: William Beaudine. **FAM/DRA** 90m.

Moon and Sixpence, The 1942 ★★★★ Banker (Sanders) shocks his family by reinventing his life and becoming an artist in Tahiti. Thoughtful, powerful study of the turns one person's life can take. Adapted from Somerset Maugham's novel, which was inspired by the true story of French artist Paul Gauguin. C: George Sanders, Herbert Marshall, Doris Dudley, Eric Blore, Elena Verdugo, Florence Bates, Albert Basserman. D: Albert Lewin. DRA 89m. v

Moon 44 1990 West German ★★ Space cop goes undercover at interplanetary mining operation to defend against corporate sabotage. Sprawling but hollow German sci-fi spectacle barely gets off the launch pad. C: Michael Pare, Lisa Eichhorn, Malcolm McDowell. D: Roland Emmerich. SFI [R] 102m. v

Moon in Scorpio 1987 ★★½ An ocean cruise becomes a trip to terror when some Vietnam veterans' war crimes literally come back to haunt them. Good B-movie cast in mediocre thriller. C: Britt Ekland, John Phillip Law, William Smith. D: Gary Graver. HOR [R] 90m. v

Moon in the Gutter, The 1983 French ★★ Stevedore (Depardieu) searches for his sister's rapist. Pretentious and uninvolving tale of obsession wastes its stars. C: Nastassia Kinski, Gerard Depardieu, Victoria Abril. D: Jean-Jacques Beineix. DRA [R] 125m. v

Moon Is Blue, The 1953 ★★★ Dated adult comedy about a woman who flaunts her virginity in front of eager suitors. Plenty of double entendres and "mature" humor that was risqué in its time but now seems oddly naive. C: William Holden, David Niven, Maggie McNamara, Tom Tully. D: Otto Preminger. COM [PG] 100m. v

Moon Is Down, The 1943 ★★★★ Adapted from John Steinbeck's novel, this multicharacter drama examines the effect of the Nazi invasion on a small Norwegian village. Compelling wartime study. C: Cedric Hardwicke, Henry Travers, Lee J. Cobb, Dorris Bowden, Margaret Wycherly, Peter Van Eyck, William Post, Jr. D: Irving Pichel. DRA 90m.

Moon of The Wolf 1972 ★★★ A werewolf terrorizes a remote section of Louisiana. C: David Janssen, Barbara Rush, Bradford Dillman. D: Daniel Petrie. HOR 73m. TVM v

Moon Over Miami 1941 ★★★★ Three friends head to the warm climate of Miami Beach in hopes of snagging millionaire husbands. Sunny fun, splashy songs. C: Don Ameche, Betty Grable, Robert Cummings, Carole Landis, Charlotte Greenwood. D: Walter Lang. MUS 91m. v

Moon Over Parador 1988 ★★★½ When a South American dictator suddenly dies, look-alike actor Dreyfuss is hired to take his place. Cute idea that never quite lives up to comic potential, though Dreyfuss gives it his best. Braga is great as dictator's mistress. C: Richard Dreyfuss, Raul Julia, Sonia Braga, Jonathan Winters. D: Paul Mazursky. COM [PG-13] 103m. v

Moon Pilot 1962 ★★★ Disney science fiction spoof has reluctant astronaut Tyron contending with chimp and out-of-this-world visitor. Rather dated but still fun family entertainment. C: Tom Tryon, Brian Keith, Edmond O'Brien, Tommy Kirk. D: James Neilson. FAM/SFI 98m. v

Moon-Spinners, The 1964 ★★★★ Hitchcockian suspense á la Disney as a young American woman (Mills) in Crete helps innocent man mixed up with gang of jewel thieves. Former silent star Negri is featured as fence for stolen goods. Decent mystery for Nancy Drew and Hardy Boys fans. C: Hayley Mills, Eli Wallach, Pola Negri, Peter McEnery. D: James Neilson. FAM/DRA 118m. v

Mooncussers 1962 ★★½ A group of pirates lure their victims to shore using false signal lights. Minor kiddie adventure without much suspense or action. C: Oscar Homolka, Kevin Corcoran, Robert Emhardt, Joan Freeman. D: James Neilson. FAM/DRA 85m. v

Moonfleet 1955 ★★★½ Eighteenth-century adventure yarn about a dashing smuggler and a young orphan boy. Colorful swashbuckler, with a high-flying Granger. C: Stewart Granger, Jon Whiteley, George Sanders, Viveca Lindfors, Joan Greenwood, Ian Wolfe. D: Fritz Lang. ACT 89m. v

Moonlight Sonata 1938 British ★★★½ Young woman faces new challenges after marrying into a wealthy Swedish family. Plot plays second fiddle to fine musical numbers by the film's real star, concert pianist Paderewski. Beautiful music. C: Ignace Jan Paderewski, Charles Farrell, Marie Tempest, Barbara Greene, Eric Portman. D: Lothar Mendes. MUS 80m. v

Moonlighter, The 1953 ★★½ Two terrific stars in disappointing, dime-a-dozen western story about a supposed cattle rustler (MacMurray) seeking revenge on the mob that tried to lynch him. Filmed in 3-D. C: Fred MacMurray, Barbara Stanwyck, Jack Elam, Ward Bond. D: Roy Rowland. WST 75m.

Moonlighting 1982 British ★★★★½ A crew of illegal Polish workers in London labor to finish a construction job, while a political crackdown worsens back home. Interesting, poignant drama: Irons is superb. C: Jeremy Irons, Eugene Lipinski, Jiri Stanislav, Eugeniusz Haczkiewicz. D: Jerzy Skolimowski. DRA [PG] 97m. v

Moonlighting 1985 ★★★★ Pilot for popular TV series about a former fashion model (Shepherd) who starts a second career as a detective, partnered by Willis. Great chemistry between Shepherd and Willis spark this witty comic mystery. C: Cybill Shepherd, Bruce Willis, Allyce Beasley. D: Robert Butler. CRI 97m. TVM v

Moonraker 1979 ★★★ James Bond takes on intergalactic tyrant. Some color and fun, but series shows its tired blood. C: Roger Moore, Lois Chiles, Michael Lonsdale, Richard Kiel, Corinne Clery. D: Lewis Gilbert. ACT [PG] 128m. v

Moonrise 1948 ★★★½ After accidentally killing a rival in a bar fight, man (Clark) runs away with loyal girlfriend (Russell) who urges him to surrender to the law. Dark, brooding melodrama set in backwoods moves slowly. C: Dane Clark, Gail Russell, Ethel Barrymore, Allyn Joslyn, Henry Morgan, Lloyd Bridges, Rex Ingram. D: Frank Borzage. CRI 90m. V

Moon's Our Home, The 1936 ★★★½ A movie star (Sullavan) and a novelist (Fonda) enter into a turbulent courtship. Bubbly comic romance, flavored by the fact that the stars had already been married and divorced when they made it. C: Margaret Sullavan, Henry Fonda, Charles Butterworth, Beulah Bondi, Walter Brennan. D: William A. Seiter. DRA 76m. V

Moonshine County Express 1977 ★★★ Moonshiner is murdered; three daughters take over business and hunt dad's killer. Routine. C: John Saxon, Susan Howard, William Conrad, Claudia Jennings. D: Gus Trikonis. COM [PG] 96m. V

Moonstruck 1987 ★★★★ Brooklynite widow Cher is ready to marry earnest bachelor (Aiello) but falls for his brother (Cage) instead. Old-fashioned romantic comedy creaks at times but first-rate ensemble cast, especially Gardenia, saves the day. Cher, Dukakis, and scriptwriter John Patrick Shanley won Oscars. C: Cher, Nicolas Cage, Vincent Gardenia, Olympia Dukakis, Danny Aiello, John Mahoney. D: Norman Jewison. COM [PG] 103m. V

Moontide 1942 ★★★ Roustabout (Gabin) saves a despondent waitress (Lupino) from killing herself, and an attraction develops. Gritty, realistic drama, brightened by the two leads. C: Jean Gabin, Ida Lupino, Thomas Mitchell, Claude Rains, Jerome Cowan, Helene Reynolds, Ralph Byrd, (Victor) Sen Yung, Tully Marshall. D: Archie Mayo. DRA 94m.

Moontrap 1989 ★★★ *Star Trek* actor Koenig finally gets a lead role in this Detroit-made space cheapie. He plays Apollo astronaut who fights hostile breed of shape-changing robot monsters on the moon. Clunky yet watchable. C: Walter Koenig, Bruce Campbell, Leigh Lombardi. D: Robert Dyke. SFI [R] 92m. V

More 1969 Luxembuorg ★★★★ Looking for the meaning of life, a German college student winds up in Paris where he becomes involved in sex, drugs, and rock 'n' roll, psychedelic '60s-style. Interesting, well-acted youth picture, a vivid flashback to its time. C: Mimsy Farmer, Klaus Grunberg, Louise Wenk. D: Barbet Schroeder. DRA 100m. V

More American Graffiti 1979 ★★½ Sequel to *American Graffiti* follows many of original film's characters through four linked stories revolving around hippie era and Vietnam war. Lacks the charm and energy needed as cast just goes through the motions. C: Candy Clark, Bo Hopkins, Ron Howard, Paul Le Mat, MacKenzie Phillips, Charles Martin Smith, Cindy Williams. D: B.W.L. Norton. COM [PG] 111m. V

More Dead Than Alive 1969 ★★★ Trying to escape his outlaw days, a rogue takes a job as a carnival sharpshooter. Title says it all—a medium-caliber Western. C: Clint Walker, Vincent Price, Anne Francis, Paul Hampton. D: Robert Sparr. WST [PG] 101m.

More Milton Berle's Mad World of Comedy 1989 ★★★ Milton Berle hosts variety show combining interviews with clips from performances by Martin and Lewis, Abbott and Costello, and others. C: Terence Knox, Stephen Caffrey. D: Bill L. Norton. COM 89m. V

More Roobarb 1986 ★★★ Fifteen animated episodes featuring fun-loving dog and cat duo. FAM/COM 67m. V

More Than a Miracle 1967 Italian-French ★★★ Intriguing fairy tale about a prince (Sharif) who uses a flying friar (French) to track down his true lady love (Loren). Loren looks stunning, but the film overdoses on whimsy. (a.k.a. *Cinderella, Italian Style, C'era Una Volta*) C: Sophia Loren, Omar Sharif, Leslie French, Dolores Del Rio. D: Francesco Rosi. COM 105m.

More Than a Secretary 1936 ★★★ The old story of a true-blue secretary (Arthur) in love with her boss. Arthur plays it to the hilt, but we've been there before. C: Jean Arthur, George Brent, Dorothea Kent, Lionel Stander. D: Alfred E. Green. COM 77m.

More Than Friends 1979 ★★★½ Uneven comedy about a mis-matched pair (Reiner and Marshall), drawn to marriage despite themselves. Worth seeing for the chemistry of then-married sitcom stars, both now top movie directors. Script by Reiner. C: Rob Reiner, Penny Marshall, Kay Medford, Dabney Coleman, Howard Hesseman. D: Jim Burrows. COM 100m. TVM

More the Merrier, The 1943 ★★★★★ One of the great WWII-era comedies finds love and laughs during the Washington, D.C. housing shortage, as a young woman shares her apartment with two men, a handsome bachelor (McCrea) and an incorrigible matchmaker (Oscar-winner Coburn). Absolutely marvelous romantic comedy; tip-top leads. Remade as *Walk, Don't Run* C: Jean Arthur, Joel McCrea, Charles Coburn, Richard Gaines, Bruce Bennett, Grady Sutton. D: George Stevens. COM 103m. V

More Wild, Wild West 1980 ★★★½ Conrad and Martin once again reprise roles from hit TV series. Here the suave agents are up against weirdo professor Winters. Enjoyable dectective satire. C: Robert Conrad, Ross Martin, Jonathan Winters, Harry Morgan, Rene Auberjonois, Liz Torres, Victor Buono. D: Burt Kennedy. WST 94m. TVM V

Morgan! 1966 British ★★★½ After wife leaves him, an artist (Warner) goes off the deep end and indulges himself in eccentric behavior. Starts off well, but cast of equally nutty characters negates Warner's impact. (a.k.a. *Morgan, a Suitable Case for Treatment*) C: Vanessa Redgrave, David Warner, Robert Stephens, Irene Handl. D: Karel Reisz. COM 93m. V

Morgan, a Suitable Case for Treatment 1966 *See* **Morgan!**

Morgan Stewart's Coming Home 1987 ★★ Cryer is boarding school student who returns home and must cope with parents' political ambitions. Tired comedy. (a.k.a. *Home Front*) C: Jon Cryer, Lynn Redgrave, Nicholas Pryor, Viveka Davis. D: Alan Smithee. COM [PG-13] 96m. V

Morgan the Pirate 1961 Italian ★★★ Highly embellished swashbuckling adventure and romance of real-life pirate Henry Morgan (Reeves), with enough high seas mayhem to sustain interest throughout. C: Steve Reeves, Valerie Lagrange, Lydia Alfonsi, Chelo Alonso. D: Andre de Toth. ACT 93m. V

Morituri 1965 ★★★ WWII naval adventure follows an anti-Nazi German (Brando) tring to stop a shipment of Japanese rubber from reaching German shores. Choppy high-seas action, stays afloat thanks to fascinating Brando. (a.k.a. *Saboteur: Code Name Morituri*) C: Marlon Brando, Yul Brynner. D: Bernhard Wicki. DRA 123m. V

Morning After, The 1974 ★★★★ Van Dyke gives a stunning dramatic performance in this harrowing drama about a business exec with a hidden alchohol problem. C: Dick Van Dyke, Lynn Carlin, Linda Lavin. D: Richard T. Heffron. DRA 78m. TVM

Morning After, The 1986 ★★½ Alcoholic actress (Fonda) prone to blackouts wakes one morning beside a man with a big knife embedded in his chest. Did she do it or is she being framed? C: Jane Fonda, Jeff Bridges, Raul Julia, Diane Salinger, Richard Foronjy. D: Sidney Lumet. CRI [R] 103m. V

Morning Departure 1951 *See* **Operation Disaster**

Morning Glory 1933 ★★★★ Young starstruck woman yearns for success on the Great White Way and earns some hard knocks in the process. Hepburn is enchanting and won her first Oscar for her utterly convincing performance as the eager ingenue. Remade as *Stage Struck* in 1958. C: Katharine Hepburn, Adolphe Menjou, Douglas Fairbanks, Jr., C. Aubrey Smith. D: Lowell Sherman. DRA 75m. V

Moro Affair, The 1986 Italian ★★★★ Fact-based chronicle of the 1978 kidnapping and execution of Italian president-elect Aldo Moro. Uncompromising in scope of questions raised about the notorious crime, with an excellent performance by Volonte as the doomed leader. C: Gian Maria Volante, Margarita Lozano, Mattia Sbragia, Daniele Dublino. D: Giuseppe Ferrara. DRA 110m.

Morocco 1930 ★★★★ Seductive cabaret chanteuse drops a wealthy patron to take up with dashing Foreign Legionnaire. Cooper and Dietrich heat up the screen, and the ending still amazes. Dietrich's Hollywood debut. C: Gary Cooper, Marlene Dietrich, Adolphe Menjou, Francis McDonald, Paul Porcasi. D: Josef von Sternberg. DRA 92m. V

Moron Movies 1986 ★★★ A "guide" to 150 new, often hilarious, uses for everyday items. Some hits, some misses. COM 60m. V

Moron Movies, More ★★★ Picks up where its predecessor left off. Chuckles aplenty. COM V

Morons from Outer Space 1985 British ★★★½ Idiots from another world crash their spaceship in England, where greedy promoter turns them into top rock act. Strange premise delivers hilarious if uneven late-night-type humor. A cult favorite. C: Griff Rhys-Jones, Mel Smith, James B. Sikking, Dinsdale Landen. D: Mike Hodges. COM [PG-13] 78m. V

Mortadella *See* **Lady Liberty**

Mortal Passions 1990 ★ Cheating wife prepares, with an assist from her reluctant lover, to knock off her megarich hubby. Quick, cheapie thriller. C: Krista Errickson, Zach Galligan, Michael Bowen, Sheila Kelley. D: Andrew Lane. CRI [R] 96m. V

Mortal Sins 1990 ★★½ Gumshoe Benben finds the path to a killer leads to the door of a questionable televangelist and his intriguing and beautiful daughter. Rather derivative mystery. (a.k.a. *Dangerous Obsession*) C: Debrah Farentino, Brian Benben, Anthony LaPaglia. D: Yuri Sivo. CRI [R] 85m.

Mortal Storm, The 1940 ★★★★½ When the Nazis' rise to power destroys a teacher's career, daughter (Sullavan) and her lover (Stewart) try to flee political crackdown for safer shores. Heartfelt Hollywood love story compellingly framed by tense realities. Wonderful performances. C: Margaret Sullavan, James Stewart, Robert Young, Frank Morgan, Robert Stack, Bonita Granville, Irene Rich, Maria Ouspenskaya. D: Frank Borzage. DRA 100m. V

Mortal Thoughts 1991 ★★★½ Police suspect a woman of murdering her best friend's brutish husband. Interesting, stylish flashback drama, with a good cast. C: Demi Moore, Glenne Headly, Bruce Willis, John Pankow, Harvey Keitel. D: Alan Rudolph. CRI [R] 104m. V

Mortuary 1981 ★★★ Slasher film set you-know-where gets some juice from Paxton's engagingly unbalanced performance. And, it's certainly a novelty to see *The Waltons* McDonough in a movie like this. Otherwise, pretty lifeless. C: Mary McDonough, Christopher George, Lynda Day George, David Wallace, Bill Paxton. D: Howard Avedis. HOR [R] 91m. V

Mortuary Academy 1988 ★★★ When a couple of star students at the Mortuary Academy learn that their instructors are thieves, they organize a revolt of their fellow classmates. C: Tracy Walter, Lynn Danielson, Christopher Atkins. D: Michael Schroeder. HOR [R] 86m. V

Mosby's Marauders 1966 ★★★½ During the Civil War, a youth joins a group of Confederate raiders and gets the education of a lifetime. Competent cast makes this small effort shine. C: Kurt Russell, James MacArthur, Nick Adams, Peggy Lipton. D: Michael O'Herlihy. DRA 79m. V

Moscow Does Not Believe in Tears 1981 Russian ★★★★ Three sisters from a small Soviet town go to Moscow, where they hope to meet and marry successful men. Russian equivalent of many lightweight Hollywood romances, and familiar material succeeds enjoyably in different setting. Oscar-winner for Best Foreign Film. C: Vera Alentova, Irina Muravyova, Raisa Ryazanova. D: Vladimir Menshov. DRA 145m. V

Moscow Nights 1935 *See* **I Stand Condemned**

Moscow on the Hudson 1984 ★★★★ Williams holds this film together with his superb portrayal of a Russian circus musician who defects while visiting America and suffers through a poignant period of adjustment. Tartly sentimental with an appealing performance from Alonso (her U.S. debut). C: Robin Williams, Maria Conchita Alonso, Cleavant Derricks, Alejandro Rey. D: Paul Mazursky. COM [R] 107m. V

Moscow Peace Festival—Vol. 1 1989 ★★★½ Music and events at the heavy metal rock concert at Moscow's Lenin Stadium. Includes performances by Motley Crue, Ozzy Osbourne and many others. MUS 120m.

Moscow Sax Quintet, The—The Jazznost Tour ★★★ The famed Russian jazz group launched their western swing with this "Jazznost" tour. Entertaining. MUS 62m.

Moses 1975 British ★★½ The story of the great Hebrew leader. The cast is outstanding—unfortunately, far better than the material. C: Burt Lancaster, Anthony Quayle, Ingrid Thulin, Irene Papas. D: Gianfranco DeBosio. DRA [PG] 141m. TVM V

Moses and Aaron 1975 German ★★★★½ Sumptuous filming of Arnold Schoenberg's opera follows the story of the biblical hero and his brother. Shot in a Roman amphitheater, and complemented by sweeping camerawork that heightens the story's drama. Powerfully sung. C: Gunter Reich, Louis Devos. D: Jean-Marie Straub, Daniele Huillet. MUS 105m. TVM

Moshe Dayan: A Portrait ★★★ The life and times of one of Israel's most controversial figures, dealing with Dayan's life from childhood to military command and later political triumphs and failures. DOC 50m. V

Mosquito Coast, The 1986 ★★★★ Scientist Ford moves his family to what proves to be a hostile environment in Central America, following his fanatical need to create an ideal society. Ford is disturbingly convincing in unsettling story of one man's obsession. Based on the novel by Paul Theroux. C: Harrison Ford, Helen Mirren, River Phoenix, Conrad Roberts, Martha Plimpton, Butterfly McQueen. D: Peter Weir. DRA [PG] 119m. V

Most Beautiful Ballets, The 1993 ★★★★ Here are some of the finest ballet presentations ever, featuring some of the greatest performers of our time: Fonteyn, Nureyev and the Kirov Ballet. A must for ballet fans. C: Margot Fonteyn, Kirov Ballet, Rudolf Nureyev. MUS 326m. V

Most Beautiful, The 1944 Japanese ★★★½ Touching drama of Japanese women factory workers during WWII. One of the great director's first films—atypical, but worthy. C: Ichiro Sugai, Takashi Shimura, Takako Irie. D: Akira Kurosawa. DRA 85m.

Most Dangerous Game, The 1932 ★★★★½ Madman (Banks) uses his remote island as a personal game park, hunting human prey captured from ships grounded on a treacherous reef. His newest victim (McCrea) desperately tries to outsmart him. Tense, exciting, and unforgettable action/horror. C: Irving Pichel, Joel McCrea, Fay Wray, Leslie Banks, Robert Armstrong, Noble Johnson. D: Ernest B. Shoedsack. ACT 63m. V

Most Dangerous Man Alive, The 1961 ★★★ After devastating nuclear explosion, a convict develops incredible machine-like capabilities and wreaks havoc on society. Clever combination of gangster and science-fiction movie conventions, played in competent B-movie style. C: Ron Randell, Debra Paget, Elaine Stewart, Anthony Caruso, Gregg Palmer. D: Allan Dwan. ACT 82m.

Most Eligible Bachelor 1982 ★★★ The most confirmed, committed bachelor in the world reaches a point where it's time to pick a lifelong mate. D: Robert Glinski. COM 86m. V

Most Wanted 1976 ★★★ Stack leads a special police unit chasing a psychopathic rapist. Inspired the TV series of the same name. C: Robert Stack, Shelly Novack, Leslie Charleson, Tom Selleck. D: Walter Grauman. CRI 78m. TVM V

Motel Hell 1980 ★★★ Calhoun and Parsons have the best smoked meats in the country; what could their secret recipe be? Answer's not hard to guess, but gruesome, offbeat horror film is spiced with satiric humor and funny performances. C: Rory Calhoun, Paul Linke, Nancy Parsons, Nina Axelrod, Wolfman Jack. D: Kevin Connor. HOR [R] 92m. V

Mother (Okaasan) 1952 Japanese ★★ When her husband comes home from WW II, Masa is unexpectedly given reason to doubt her hopes for a return to normalcy. C: Kinuyo

Tanaka, Kyoko Kagawa, Eiji Okada. D: Mikio Naruse. DRA 98m. v

Mother and the Whore, The 1973 French ★★★★½ Psychosocial study of three people—a student (Leaud), a nurse, and an older woman—involved in a difficult love triangle. Though talky, the film is surprisingly compelling. Explicit themes, for mature audiences only. C: Bernadette Lafont, Jean-Pierre Leaud, Francoise Lebrun, Jacques Renard. D: Jean Eustache. DRA 210m.

Mother Carey's Chickens 1938 ★★★ Hard-working mom (Bainter) makes sacrifice upon sacrifice for the sake of her two "chickens" (Keeler and Shirley). Gushy soap opera that works like a charm. C: Fay Bainter, Anne Shirley, Ruby Keeler, James Ellison, Walter Brennan, Frank Albertson, Virginia Weidler, Ralph Morgan. D: Rowland V. Lee. DRA 82m.

Mother Didn't Tell Me 1950 ★★★½ Psychosomatic illness brings a woman to a doctor, with whom she falls in love. Cute comedy, with an unusually energetic performance from McGuire. C: Dorothy McGuire, William Lundigan, June Havoc, Gary Merrill, Jessie Royce Landis. D: Claude Binyon. COM 88m.

Mother Goose Rock 'n Rhyme 1990 ★★ Mother Goose has disappeared from Rhymeland and Gorden Goose and other rhymeland inhabitants seek her out. C: Bobby Brown, Shelley Duvall, Teri Garr, Cyndi Lauper, Howie Mandel. D: Jeff Stein. FAM/MUS [G] 96m. v

Mother Is a Freshman 1949 ★★★ A widow (Young) and her daughter (Lynn) both set romantic eyes on a college professor (Johnson). Genial campus comedy generates laughs. C: Loretta Young, Van Johnson, Rudy Vallee, Barbara Lawrence, Robert Arthur, Betty Lynn. D: Lloyd Bacon. COM 81m.

Mother Joan of the Angels 1962 *See* **Joan of the Angels**

Mother, Jugs & Speed 1976 ★★★½ Black comedy stars Cosby, Welch, and Hagman as gung ho paramedics trying to rack up patient numbers with total disregard for their welfare. Slam-bang pacing and Hagman's high-energy leering make for a wile ride. C: Bill Cosby, Raquel Welch, Harvey Keitel, Allen Garfield, Larry Hagman, Bruce Davison. D: Peter Yates. COM [PG] 98m. v

Mother Kusters Goes to Heaven 1976 German ★★★★ When a factory worker kills his boss, then commits suicide, his widow (Mira) must contend with liberal activists who want to idolize him as a cultural hero. Cynical Fassbinder satire of leftist ideals is strong in attitude and technique, with a striking performance from Mira. C: Brigitte Mira, Ingrid Caven, Karl-Heinz Bohm, Margit Carstensen, Irm Hermann, Gottfried John. D: Rainer Werner Fassbinder. COM 108m. v

Mother Lode 1982 ★★★ Heston, in film written and produced by son Fraser, plays twins—one good, one bad—pursuing gold in British Columbia. Routine adventure. (a.k.a. *Search for the Mother Lode: The Last Great Treasure*) C: Charlton Heston, Nick Mancuso, Kim Basinger, John Marley. D: Charlton Heston. ACT [PG] 101m. v

Mother of Kings 1976 Polish ★★ Story of impoverished mother and widow in WW II Poland. D: Janusz Zaorski. DRA 126m. v

Mother Teresa 1986 ★★★★ The life and times of the Nobel Peace prizewinner, and her efforts among the poor of Calcutta. Right on the mark. D: Ann Petrie, Jeanette Petrie. DOC 81m. v

Mother Wore Tights 1947 ★★★½ A vaudeville family troupes through life on the performing circuit. Pleasant show business musical, with some fun showcase acts, including the popular Grable. Oscar-winning musical score. C: Betty Grable, Dan Dailey, Mona Freeman, Connie Marshall, Vanessa Brown, Veda Ann Borg. D: Walter Lang. MUS 107m.

Mother's Boys 1993 ★★★ In a startling and effective reversal of typecasting, Curtis is the menacer, a woman who comes back to reclaim her sons a decade after abandoning her family. Yuppie thriller, in the *Hand That Rocks the Cradle* vein, has a certain panache. C: Jamie Lee Curtis, Peter Gallagher, Joanne Whalley-Kilmer, Vanessa Redgrave, Luke Edwards, Colin Ward. D: Yves Robert. ACT 95m. v

Mother's Day 1980 ★★ Sick horror/revenge item about three female campers kidnapped and terrorized by two idiot hulks and their domineering mama. Attempts at black comedy get lost amid unpleasant rape scenes and graphic gore. C: Tiana Pierce, Nancy Hendrickson, Deborah Luce. D: Charles Kaufman. HOR [R] 98m. v

Mothra 1962 Japanese ★★★½ When Tokyo impresario kidnaps six-inch-tall singing twin sisters, they're rescued by their guardian, the colossal caterpillar of the title. Yet another Japanese giant-monster flick; way-out but entertaining. C: Lee Kresel, Franky Sakai, Hiroshi Koizumi, Kyoko Kagawa. D: Inoshiro Honda. SFI 100m. v

Motorama 1991 ★★★½ Depressed rebellious boy steals family car and visits sleaze capitals while attempting to win lottery game. Dark, disturbing satire on America's obsession with greed works for the most part, although weak performance by young Michael hampers overall effectiveness. C: Jordan Christopher Michael, Martha Quinn, Meatloaf, Drew Barrymore. D: Barry Shils. COM [R] 89m. v

Motorcycle Gang 1957 ★ When bikers turns vicious, law tries to clamp down. Grade-Z *Wild One* clone. C: Anne Neyland, John Ashley, Carl Switzer, Raymond Hatton, Edmund Cobb. D: Edward L. Cahn. DRA 78m. v

Motown Time Capsule—The 60's 1986 ★★★ Sampling of some of Motown's finest. Includes songs by Marvin Gaye, The Temptations, Stevie Wonder, The Miracle, and more.

C: The Miracles, Mary Wells, Marvin Gaye. MUS 50m. V

Motown Time Capsule—The 70's 1986 ★★★ Various artists performing some of Motown's all-time greats including "Dancing Machine," sung by the Jackson Five and "Love Hangover," sung by Diana Ross. C: Stevie Wonder, Diana Ross, Smokey Robinson. MUS 50m. V

Motown 25—Yesterday, Today, Forever ★★★ All-star Motown performers in concert hosted by Richard Pryor. Stars include Michael Jackson, Marvin Gaye, and Diana Ross and the Supremes. C: Richard Pryor, Michael Jackson, Marvin Gaye, Stevie Wonder. MUS 130m. V

Mouchette 1966 French ★★★★★ A French country girl's misery-ridden life in an alcoholic family comes to a tragic end when she commits suicide. Sincere and devastating, with a realistic edge provided by cast of non-professional actors. Straightforward storytelling underscores the emotional depth of this rich and moving film. C: Nadine Nortier, Marie Cardinal, Paul Hebert, Marie Susini. D: Robert Bresson. DRA 80m. V

Moulin Rouge 1952 ★★★★1/2 Lavish biography of crippled French artist Toulouse-Lautrec, who fails at romance, but vividly captures Parisian nightlife in his art. Film successfully evokes 19th-century Montmartre and opening cancan sequence is exhilarating. Oscars for Art Direction, Set Decoration, and Costumes. C: Jose Ferrer, Zsa Zsa Gabor, Suzanne Flon, Eric Pohlmann, Christopher Lee, Peter Cushing. D: John Huston. DRA 123m. V

Mountain Family Robinson 1979 ★★1/2 More or less a reworking of *The Wilderness Family*, this virtually plotless film involves happy family living in secluded mountain cabin. Not much here beyond lovely scenery and sappy dialogue. Younger children may like it. C: Robert F. Logan, Susan Damante Shaw, William Bryant, Heather Rattray. D: John Cotter. FAM/DRA [G] 102m. V

Mountain Man 1976 ★★ Galan Clark, with support of President Lincoln, fights to keep what was later to become Yosemite National Park from destruction. C: Denver Pyle, Ken Berry, Cheryl Miller. D: David O'Malley. DRA [G] 96m. V

Mountain Men, The 1980 ★★1/2 Nineteenth-century fur trappers (Heston and Keith) fight off murderous Indians. Weak, violent attempt at sprawling Western epic. C: Charlton Heston, Brian Keith, Victoria Racimo, Stephen Macht, John Glover. D: Richard Lang. WST [PG] 100m. V

Mountain Road, The 1960 ★★1/2 Account of a group of fighter pilots stationed in China during the final days of WWII. War film never quite gets off the ground; a below-average Stewart outing. C: James Stewart, Lisa Lu, Glenn Corbett, Henry Morgan, Frank Silvera, James Best. D: Daniel Mann. ACT 102m.

Mountain, The 1956 ★★★1/2 Brothers (Tracy and Wagner) scale a mountain to reach the wreckage from a plane crash, the younger with bad intentions. Slowly paced, but breathtaking mountain scenery adds tension to perilous journey. C: Spencer Tracy, Robert Wagner, Claire Trevor, William Demarest, Richard Arlen, E.G. Marshall. D: Edward Dmytryk. DRA 105m. V

Mountains of the Moon 1989 ★★★★ The adventures of Sir Richard Burton, who explored the Nile River and other regions of the Middle East during the 1880s. Truly big in scope and quite entertaining. C: Patrick Bergin, Iain Glen, Richard E. Grant, Fiona Shaw, James Villiers, Delroy Lindo. D: Bob Rafelson. DRA [R] 140m. V

Mountaintop Motel Massacre 1983 ★★ Weirdo motel manager attacks guests with knives, appliances, and snakes. C: Bill Thurman, Anna Chappell, Will Mitchell. D: Jim McCullough. HOR [R] 95m. V

Mourning Becomes Electra 1947 ★★★ Soporific, truncated version of Eugene O'Neill's monumental Civil War updating of the Greek tragedy, *The Oresteia*. What passed for "art" in its day is now a bit dull; Russell is good, though, as the murderous Lavinia. C: Rosalind Russell, Michael Redgrave, Katina Paxinou, Raymond Massey, Kirk Douglas. D: Dudley Nichols. DRA 173m.

Mouse and His Child, The 1977 ★★★ Two toy mice find themselves in a junk yard, and must deal with nasty rat rulers. Simplistic, talky children's animation. D: Fred Wolf, Chuck Swenson. FAM/DRA [G] 83m. V

Mouse on the Moon, The 1963 British ★★★★ The flustered Duchess Rutherford tries to get her tiny nation into the space race. Goofy slapstick and happily broad satire rule this entertaining comedy romp, a sequel to *The Mouse That Roared*. C: Margaret Rutherford, Bernard Cribbins, Ron Moody, Terry-Thomas, Michael Crawford. D: Richard Lester. COM 83m.

Mouse That Roared, The 1959 British ★★★★1/2 Wickedly funny satire on international politics as the tiny Duchy of Grand Fenwick declares war on the U.S. so it can lose and get financial relief. Sellers shines in three roles. Based on novel by Leonard Wibberley. C: Peter Sellers, Jean Seberg, David Kossoff, William Hartnell, Leo McKern. D: Jack Arnold. COM 83m. V

Mouth to Mouth 1978 Australian ★★★★ Four bored adolescents, out of work and with no future, turn to theft as a way to find meaning in life. Fresh coming-of-age story, with a zesty cast giving emotional appeal to the material. C: Kim Krejus, Sonia Peat, Ian Gilmour, Sergio Frazetto, Walter Pym. D: John Duigan. COM 95m.

Mouthpiece, The 1932 ★★★★1/2 A young prosecutor, corrupted by success, switches loyalties and starts defending the Mob. Riveting courtroom drama, with excellent performances from a sharp ensemble. C: Warren William, Sidney Fox, Mae Madison, Aline MacMahon, John Wray, Guy Kibee. D: Elliott Nugent, James Flood. DRA 90m.

Move 1970 ★½ "Hip" comedy about a writer of erotica (Gould) who moves to a new apartment and begins confusing reality with his novels. Lousy Gould vehicle. C: Elliott Gould, Paula Prentiss. D: Stuart Rosenberg. COM [R] 90m.

Move Over, Darling 1963 ★★★ Shipwrecked Day, long presumed dead, returns to find her husband remarried. Flat remake of the classic Cary Grant comedy, *My Favorite Wife*, stolen by the wise-cracking Ritter. Started production as *Something's Got to Give* with Marilyn Monroe and Dean Martin. Marilyn was fired, and died soon after. C: Doris Day, James Garner, Polly Bergen, Chuck Connors, Thelma Ritter. D: Michael Gordon. COM 103m.

Movers and Shakers 1985 ★★½ Movie producer Matthau buys rights to sex guide then turns to scribe Grodin for script. Satire of Hollywood system mostly misses the mark. Good premise; good cast unfulfilled. C: Walter Matthau, Charles Grodin, Vincent Gardenia, Tyne Daly, Gilda Radner, Steve Martin, Penny Marshall. D: William Asher. COM [PG] 80m. V

Movie Crazy 1932 ★★★★ A Hollywood newcomer (Lloyd) tries to make it big in pictures. Lloyd portrays a novice's energetic enthusiasm hilariously, and Cummings is good as the love interest. Gags recall Lloyd's best silent work, including a marvelous sequence with a magician's coat. C: Harold Lloyd, Constance Cummings, Kenneth Thomson, Sydney Jarvis, Eddie Fetherstone. D: Clyde Bruckman. COM 84m.

Movie Movie 1978 ★★★★ Comic parody of '30s movies spoofs the double-feature experience. First comes a boxing melodrama, then a Busby Berkeley-type musical. Both are good and as a whole it's a clever and loving tribute to genres gone by and to the moviegoing experience itself. C: George C. Scott, Trish Van Devere, Eli Wallach, Red Buttons, Barbara Harris, Barry Bostwick, Art Carney. D: Stanley Donen. COM [PG] 107m. V

Movie Star's Daughter, A 1979 ★★ Peer pressure affects star's daughter and ultimately enables her to discover the best means to sincere friendships. C: Frank Converse, Marcia Rodd, Trini Alvarado. D: Robert Fuest. DRA 46m. V

Moving 1988 ★★½ When woefully miscast Pryor loses his job, new career opportunities send him moving family from New Jersey to Boise, Idaho. Predictable humor abounds as Pryor engages in unending battle with sadistic movers. C: Richard Pryor, Beverly Todd, Randy Quaid, Dave Thomas, Dana Carvey. D: Alan Metter. COM [R] 89m. V

Moving Out 1985 ★★ When Italian boy's family, living near Melbourne, Australia, decides to move to a new neighborhood, his life becomes unhinged. C: Vince Colosimo. D: Michael Pattinson. DRA 91m. V

Moving Targets 1986 ★★★ Thinking that her past is behind her, a reformed terrorist is pulled back in when her former lover shows up asking for help. Good action sequences. C: Carmen Duncan, Michael Aitkens. D: Chris Langman. DRA 95m. V

Moving Violation 1976 ★★★ Couple goes on the lam after witnessing sheriff's crooked crime. Southern-fried chase film with all the requisite crashes and explosions. C: Stephen McHattie, Kay Lenz, Eddie Albert, Will Geer. D: Charles S. Dubin. ACT [PG] 91m. V

Moving Violations 1985 ★★½ A witlessly wacky traffic school and its denizens. Star Murray tries his hand at wise-guy shtick of big brother Bill. C: John Murray, Jennifer Tilly, Sally Kellerman, Fred Willard, Clara Peller. D: Neal Israel. COM [PG-13] 90m. V

Mowgli's Brothers 1976 ★★★½ MacDowall and Foray are featured voices in this animated retelling of Rudyard Kipling's *Jungle Book* stories. Not as good as Disney version, but still entertaining for younger viewers and fans of animator Jones. FAM/DRA 30m. TVM V

Mozart—A Childhood Chronicle 1976 German ★★★ Documents genius composer's life from childhood through age twenty. Mozart's music comprises the bulk of the soundtrack. D: Klaus Kirschner. DRA 224m. V

Mr. Ace 1946 ★★★ Politician Sidney scams her way into Raft's heart so he'll help launch her career. Routine story with good performances by leads. C: George Raft, Sylvia Sidney, Stanley Ridges, Sara Haden, Jerome Cowan. D: Edwin L. Marin. DRA 84m. V

Mr. & Mrs. Bridge 1990 ★★★½ It's delightful to see Newman and Woodward together, even if it is in this quiet, somewhat stilted tale about an emotionally repressed couple in Depression-era Kansas City. C: Paul Newman, Joanne Woodward, Blythe Danner, Simon Callow, Kyra Sedgwick, Robert Sean Leonard, Austin Pendleton, Lyndon Ashby. D: James Ivory. DRA [PG-13] 127m. V

Mr. and Mrs. North 1941 ★★½ Radio's beloved wisecracking couple (Allen and Post) stumble across corpses in their screen debut. Easygoing comedy paces its laughs, and it's nice to see that Allen can hold her own without George Burns. C: Gracie Allen, William Post, Jr., Paul Kelly, Rose Hobart, Virginia Grey, Tom Conway. D: Robert Sinclair. COM 67m.

Mr. and Mrs. North 1953 ★ Includes "Trained for Murder" and "Million Dollar Coffin," two vintage episodes about the crime-fighting publisher and his wife. CRI 58m. V

Mr. and Mrs. Smith 1941 ★★★★ One of Hitchcock's most unlikely films, about a well-to-do Manhattan couple who constantly quarrel, then discover their marriage is invalid, and they separate—only to find they can't live without each other. Hitch directed as a favor to Lombard, and the result is a workmanlike comedy rather than the hoped-for screwball variety. Lombard and Montgomery's chemistry provide substantial appeal. C: Carole Lombard, Robert Montgomery, Gene Raymond, Jack Carson, Philip Merivale, Betty Compson, Lucile Watson. D: Alfred Hitchcock. COM 93m. V

Mr. Arkadin 1955 Spanish ★★★½ A young woman's lover tries to extort money from her mogul father. Welles more or less reprises his *Citizen Kane* in this dark, yet oddly compelling effort. (a.k.a. *Confidential Report*) C: Orson Welles, Michael Redgrave, Patricia Medina, Akim Tamiroff, Mischa Auer, Katina Paxinou, Robert Arden. D: Orson Welles. DRA 94m. V

Mr. Baseball 1992 ★★★½ Selleck is American ballplayer who ends up on Japanese team, where he quickly becomes persona non grata for his arrogant attitudes. Standard fish out of water comedy is surprisingly appealing, largely due to Selleck's performance. C: Tom Selleck, Ken Takakura, Aya Takanashi, Dennis Haysbert. D: Fred Schepisi. COM [PG-13] 108m. V

Mr. Belvedere Goes to College 1949 ★★★ Belvedere (Webb), the self-absorbed genius of *Sitting Pretty*, embarks on a college degree program and learns there's more to life than books. Some good laughs within formulaic plot. C: Clifton Webb, Shirley Temple, Tom Drake, Alan Young, Jessie Royce Landis, Kathleen Hughes. D: Elliott Nugent. COM 83m.

Mr. Belvedere Rings the Bell 1951 ★★½ Wiseacre Belvedere (Webb), determined to prove that life can be enjoyed at any age, invades an old folks' home and whips his fellow geriatrics into a frenzy of activity. Second *Sitting Pretty* sequel is less engaging than its predecessors. C: Clifton Webb, Joanne Dru, Hugh Marlowe, Zero Mostel, Doro Merande, Billy Lynn. D: Henry Koster. COM 87m.

Mr. Bill Looks Back 1980 ★★★½ Compilation film taken from popular *Saturday Night Live* character revolves around clay character Mr. Bill and his dog Spot as they suffer unending torture from Sluggo and Mr. Hands. Sadistically lighthearted. D: Walter Williams. COM 30m. V

Mr. Billion 1977 ★★★ Mechanic Hill heads west to claim $1 billion inheritance; on the way he must outwit a horde of rogues trying to get the cash themselves. Okay road comedy. C: Terence Hill, Valerie Perrine, Jackie Gleason, Slim Pickens, Chill Wills, William Redfield. D: Jonathan Kaplan. COM [PG] 89m. V

Mr. Blandings Builds His Dream House 1948 ★★★★ Grant, a Manhattan ad exec sick of city life, resettles his family in rural Connecticut, but his "dream house" turns into a homeowner's nightmare. Great fun, with Loy's casting as Grant's spouse just right. C: Cary Grant, Myrna Loy, Melvyn Douglas, Reginald Denny, Sharyn Moffett, Connie Marshall, Louise Beavers, Ian Wolfe, Lurene Tuttle, Lex Barker. D: H.C. Potter. COM 94m. V

Mr. Bug Goes to Town 1941 *See* **Hoppity Goes to Town**

Mr. Cohen Takes a Walk 1936 British ★★★½ Self-made businessman is being pushed into retirement by sons who want to take over. Sweet-tempered, often charming. C: Paul Graetz, Violet Farebrother, Chili Bouchier. D: William Beaudine. COM 81m.

Mr. Deeds Goes to Town 1936 ★★★★★ Classic Capra comedy/drama. Cooper is superb as a naive soul who inherits a fortune and moves to NYC, where everyone's out to exploit him. Arthur's the hard-boiled reporter who dubs him "Cinderella Man," then repents. Capra won second of three Directing Oscars for this. C: Gary Cooper, Jean Arthur, George Bancroft, Lionel Stander, Douglass Dumbrille, Raymond Walburn, Walter Catlett, H.B. Warner. D: Frank Capra. DRA 115m. V

Mr. Denning Drives North 1953 British ★★★½ Driven beyond reason, an airplane builder kills the man blackmailing him and is then tortured by remorse. Gripping murder tale enhanced by talented and solid British cast. C: John Mills, Phyllis Calvert, Eileen Moore, Sam Wanamaker. D: Anthony Kimmins. CRI 93m.

Mr. Destiny 1990 ★★½ Haunted by failure, Belushi's life undergoes miraculous change when he gets to replay failed moment from long-ago baseball game. Whimsical (if obvious) fantasy. C: James Belushi, Linda Hamilton, Michael Caine, Jon Lovitz, Hart Bochner, Rene Russo. D: James Orr. COM [PG-13] 110m. V

Mr. Frost 1990 ★★ An institutionalized mass murderer (Goldblum) comes clean to psychiatrist Baker after three years of silence; he claims to be the Prince of Darkness and his mission is to establish dominion over Earth. Misfired attempt at dark humor, but Goldblum makes an extraordinarily charming Satan. C: Jeff Goldblum, Kathy Baker, Alan Bates. D: Philip Setbon. CRI [R] 92m. V

Mr. Hex 1946 ★★★★ Best of the Bowery Boys. Sach (Hall) develops super-human strength under hynosis, so Slip (Gorcey) turns him into a prize-fighter. A knock-out for the *Boys*. C: Leo Gorcey, Huntz Hall, Bobby Jordan, Gabriel Dell. D: William Beaudine. COM 63m.

Mr. Hobbs Takes a Vacation 1962 ★★★½ Genial family comedy with parents Stewart and O'Hara taking brood for seaside vacation; everything goes wrong, of course. C: James Stewart, Maureen O'Hara, Fabian, John Saxon. D: Henry Koster. COM 116m. V

Mr. Horn 1979 ★★★ Tale of legendary folk hero Tom Horn (Carradine) tracking down Apache warrior Geronimo. So-so Western. C: David Carradine, Richard Widmark, Karen

Black, Jeremy Slate, Enrique Lucero, Jack Starrett. D: Jack Starrett. WST 200m. TVM V

Mr. Hulot's Holiday 1953 French ★★★★★ Comic masterpiece follows adventures of well-meaning bumbler on his beach vacation. First appearance of Tati's now-classic character is one of funniest movies ever made; sequence where he paints his canoe is priceless. Nearly silent; followed by *Mon Oncle.* C: Jacques Tati, Nathalie Pascaud, Michelle Rolla, Valentine Camax, Louis Perrault. D: Jacques Tati. COM 86m. V

Mr. Imperium 1951 ★★★ European king falls for a Hollywood chanteuse (Turner). Old-fashioned comedy/drama/musical hybrid, with Metropolitan Opera baritone Pinza cast as royal Romeo. (a.k.a. *You Belong to My Heart*) C: Lana Turner, Ezio Pinza, Marjorie Main, Debbie Reynolds, Barry Sullivan. D: Don Hartman. COM 87m.

Mr. Inside/Mr. Outside 1974 ★★★½ Diamond smugglers thwarted by two aggressive NYC cops. Good action in otherwise routinely developed story. (a.k.a. *Hot Ice*) C: Hal Linden, Tony Lo Bianco, Phil Bruns, Paul Benjamin. D: William A. Graham. DRA 74m. TVM V

Mr. Jones 1993 ★★½ Psychiatrist (Olin) resists, then succumbs to the advances of her patient (Gere). Is he a crazy guy or just living life to the fullest? Gooey melodrama that charts new territory in implausibility. C: Richard Gere, Lena Olin, Anne Bancroft. D: Mike Figgis. DRA [R] 114m. V

Mr. Klein 1975 French ★★★★ In occupied WWII France, art dealer Delon gouges desperate Jews trying to raise money to escape Nazis; he gets polite justice when he later is mistaken for a Jewish man with his name. Not entirely successful, but still intriguing; Delon is first-rate. C: Alain Delon, Jeanne Moreau, Michael Lonsdale, Juliet Berto, Suzanne Flon. D: Joseph Losey. DRA 123m. V

Mr. Love 1986 British ★★★ Charming comedy of Milquetoast gardener (Jackson) whose 30-year marriage is a lonely sham—but whose funeral is attended by a bevy of luscious women. In flashback it's revealed that Jackson was quite the ladies' man and had the last laugh after all. Agreeable, heartwarming yarn. C: Barry Jackson, Maurice Denham, Donal McCann, Helen Coterill, Julia Deakin, Margaret Tyzack. D: Roy Battersby. COM [PG-13] 91m. V

Mr. Lucky 1943 ★★★★ Slick gambler Grant is determined to con Day out of charity money but instead finds himself falling in love. Vivacious comedy, well played by leads. C: Cary Grant, Laraine Day, Charles Bickford, Gladys Cooper, Alan Carney, Henry Stephenson, Paul Stewart, Kay Johnson, Florence Bates. D: H.C. Potter. COM 100m. V

Mr. Magoo In Sherwood Forest 1974 ★★★★ Mr.Magoo assumes the role of Friar Tuck in this lovable, animated version of Sherwood Forest fun. Voice of Jim Backus. FAM/COM 83m. V

Mr. Magoo—Man of Mystery 1964 ★★★½ Four of Mister Magoo's funniest cartoons. He plays Doctor Watson, Doctor Frankenstein, The Count of Monte Cristo, and Dick Tracy. Voice of Jim Backus. FAM/COM 96m. V

Mr. Magoo—1001 Arabian Nights ★★★½ That delightful curmudgeon is off on the adventure of a lifetime—to fabled old Arabia. Great fun, great character, great voice. (a.k.a. *1001 Arabian Nights*) Voice of Jim Backus. FAM/COM 76m. V

Mr. Magoo's Christmas Carol 1962 ★★★½ The visually impaired Mr. Magoo takes on the role of Ebenezer Scrooge in this animated take on Charles Dickens' classic, "A Christmas Carol." An amusing holiday film for family viewing. Voice of Jim Backus. FAM/COM [G] 53m. TVM V

Mr. Magoo's Story Book 1964 ★★★½ The ubiquitous Mr.Magoo hams it up, starring in animated adaptations of "A Midsummer Night's Dream," "Don Quixote," and "Snow White." Voice of Jim Backus. FAM/COM 113m. V

Mr. Majestyk 1974 ★★★½ Unusual Bronson outing finds our craggy hero playing a dirt-poor watermelon farmer locked in a battle for his land with a Mob hit man. Offers the usual gunplay and macho posturing, coupled with a script that never takes itself too seriously. C: Charles Bronson, Al Lettieri, Linda Cristal, Lee Purcell, Paul Koslo, Alejandro Rey. D: Richard Fleischer. ACT [PG] 103m. V

Mr. Mean ★★★ Mafia chief's former aide comes back to rub out his old boss. Some good insights; lots of violence. DRA V

Mr. Mike's Mondo Video 1979 ★★½ Oddball comedy special starring former Saturday Night Live comic Mr. Mike. C: Michael O'Donoghue, Dan Aykroyd, Jane Curtin, Carrie Fisher. D: Michael O'Donoghue. COM [R] 75m. V

Mr. Mom 1983 ★★★½ When auto exec Keaton loses job, wife Garr goes to work while he takes care of house and kids. Role reversal comedy doesn't explore new ground, but talented comic cast gives fresh aspects to well-worn ideas. Keaton's timing is on the money. C: Michael Keaton, Teri Garr, Martin Mull, Ann Jillian, Christopher Lloyd. D: Stan Dragoti. COM [PG] 92m. V

Mr. Moses 1965 ★★½ Mitchum plays a he-man courting the virginal Baker as they guide an uprooted African tribe to their newly designated home. Decent cast in stereotypical adventure. C: Robert Mitchum, Carroll Baker, Ian Bannen. D: Ronald Neame. ACT 113m.

Mr. Moto Hoping to cash in on the success of their Charlie Chan series, Fox began a series of similar Asian sleuths. Peter Lorre was memorable as John P. Marquand's Japanese intelligence agent (who became more undefined racially as the war approached). The films that resulted are exciting and entertaining, driven mainly by Lorre's cool and ingratiating presence. Unlike Chan, Moto is more than capable of taking the law into his own hands and Lorre gives him a cheerfully amoral underside that presages film noir. Considerably better than the typical series film.

Think Fast, Mr. Moto (1937)
Thank You, Mr. Moto (1937)
Mr. Moto's Gamble (1938)
Mr. Moto Takes a Chance (1938)
Mysterious Mr. Motor (1938)
Mr. Moto's Last Warning (1939)
Mr. Moto In Danger Island (1939)
Mr. Moto Takes a Vacation (1939)
The Return of Mr. Moto (1965)

Mr. Moto in Danger Island 1939 ★★★½ The diminutive detective travels to Puerto Rico to bust up a diamond smuggling operation. Well-plotted B-movie suspense; Lorre's effective, as usual. (a.k.a. *Danger Island*) C: Peter Lorre, Jean Hersholt, Warren Hymer. D: Herbert I. Leeds. CRI 63m.

Mr. Moto Takes a Chance 1938 ★★★ Japanese master-sleuth (Lorre) tries to stop a plot to kill Caucasians in Indochina. Average Moto mystery. C: Peter Lorre, Robert Kent, J. Edward Bromberg, Rochelle Hudson. D: Norman Foster. CRI 63m.

Mr. Moto Takes a Vacation 1939 ★★★½ Master of disguise (Schildkraut) tries to steal priceless Egyptian jewels, but Moto (Lorre) won't let him. Respectable finale for the detective series. C: Peter Lorre, Joseph Schildkraut, Lionel Atwill. D: Norman Foster. CRI 63m.

Mr. Moto's Gamble 1938 ★★★ Inscrutable detective Moto (Lorre) investigates a boxer's mysterious death and uncovers an illegal gambling business behind it. Third entry in the series is pure escapist fun and features a surprising appearance by Charlie Chan's number one son Luke as Moto's humble assistant. C: Peter Lorre, Keye Luke, Dick Baldwin, Lynn Bari, Douglas Fowley, Jayne Regan, Harold Huber. D: James Tinling. CRI 71m. V

Mr. Moto's Last Warning 1939 ★★★½ Japan's answer to Sherlock Holmes tries to thwart Suez Canal plot to cause war between England and France. Good series entry. C: Peter Lorre, Ricardo Cortez, John Carradine, George Sanders. D: Norman Foster. CRI 71m. V

Mr. Muggs Steps Out 1943 ★★★ Amusing *East Side Kids* entry features Muggs (Gorcey) as a rich lady's chauffeur who inadvertently blows the whistle on some socially connected jewel thieves. Low-down humor as the uncouth Kids clash with the uptight upper crust. C: Leo Gorcey, Huntz Hall, Billy Benedict. D: William Beaudine. COM 63m.

Mr. Music 1950 ★★★ Crosby plays songwriter who'd rather play golf; loosely based on Samson Raphaelson play *Accent on Youth.* Highlight: Crosby and Lee dueting on "Life Is So Peculiar." C: Bing Crosby, Nancy Olson, Charles Coburn, Ruth Hussey, Marge Champion, Gower Champion, Peggy Lee, Groucho Marx. D: Richard Haydn. MUS 113m. V

Mr. Nanny 1993 ★★★ Hogan is typecast as an ex-wrestler hired as a bodyguard for an inventor's bratty kids. Weak slapstick is leavened a bit by Hogan's deadpan reactions. C: Hulk Hogan, Sherman Hemsley, Austin Pendleton. D: Michael Gottlieb. COM [PG] 84m. V

Mr. North 1988 ★★★★ During '20s, wealthy Newport social set undergoes whimsical changes after stranger, whose body fires off electrical current, enters community. Sweet fable with a strong cast. John Huston's last film credit (he co-wrote and produced); directed by his son Danny. Based on the autobiographical novel by Thornton Wilder. C: Anthony Edwards, Robert Mitchum, Lauren Bacall, Harry Dean Stanton, Anjelica Huston, Mary Stuart Masterson, Virginia Madsen, David Warner. D: Danny Huston. COM [PG] 92m. V

Mr. Orchid 1948 French ★★★½ French Resistance fighter Noel grows orchids to conceal contraband radio equipment from the Nazis during WWII German occupation. Good suspense holds this little thriller aloft. C: Noel-Noel, Nadine Alari, Jose Arthur. D: Rene Clement. DRA 100m.

Mr. Peabody and the Mermaid 1948 ★★★½ So-so fantasy with Powell as New Englander who "catches" mermaid (Blyth) while fishing, then brings her home. Good Powell but weak script. Based on novel by Greg and Constance Jones. C: William Powell, Ann Blyth, Irene Hervey, Andrea King. D: Irving Pichel. COM 89m. V

Mr. Perrin and Mr. Traill 1948 British ★★★ A generational rivalry erupts between an elderly, conservative schoolteacher and a young instructor when the latter's more progressive methods are championed. Intriguing, well-acted drama that explores the benefits of old and new. C: Marius Goring, David Farrar, Greta Gynt, Raymond Huntley. D: Lawrence Huntington. DRA 90m.

Mr. Potts Goes to Moscow 1953 British ★★★½ Tongue-in-cheek political comedy concerns a sanitary worker who inadvertently purloins highly classified nuclear information and is then considered a traitor. Successful Red-scare send-up with lots of laughs throughout. (a.k.a. *Top Secret*) C: George Cole, Oscar Homolka, Nadia Gray, Wilfrid Hyde-White. D: Mario Zampi. COM 93m.

Mr. Quilp 1975 British ★★★½ Heartless miser (Newley) tries to foreclose on a well-meaning shopowner (Hordern). Okay attempt to turn Dickens' *The Old Curiosity Shop* into another *Oliver!*; unfortunately, it lacks that movie's winning score. (a.k.a. *The Old Curiosity Shop*) C: Anthony Newley, David Hemmings, David Warner, Michael Hordern, Jill Bennett. D: Michael Tuchner. MUS [G] 118m.

Mr. Quincey of Monte Carlo 1933 British ★★★½ Shy bank clerk undergoes radical personality change after inheriting a lot of money. Heady with his newfound wealth, he takes off for Monte Carlo and the allure of gaming tables. Cute minor comedy. C: John Stuart, Rosemary Ames, Ben Welden. D: John Daumery. COM 53m.

Mr. Robinson Crusoe 1932 ★★★★ Fairbanks wagers he can survive by himself on deserted South Seas island. The 50-year-old Fairbanks can still display his famous prowess in this entertaining film for the entire family. C: Douglas Fairbanks, Sr., William Farnum, Earle Browne, Maria Alba. D: Edward Sutherland. FAM/COM 76m. V

Mr. Sardonicus 1961 ★★★★ Creepy, effective "sleeper" thriller about a wealthy nobleman (Rolfe) whose face is permanently frozen in gruesome grin; he hires famous surgeon (Lewis) to treat him, with spine-tingling results. Homolka steals the movie, as a grotesque servant named "Krull." C: Guy Rolfe, Ronald Lewis, Audrey Dalton, Oscar Homolka. D: William Castle. HOR 89m.

Mr. Saturday Night 1992 ★★★ Crystal writes, directs, and stars in fictional life story of shlock comedian whose obnoxious personality plagues him and close associates throughout career. Some interesting backstage humor; and Oscar-nominee Paymer provides nice support. C: Billy Crystal, David Paymer, Julie Warner, Helen Hunt, Jerry Orbach, Ron Silver. D: Billy Crystal. COM [R] 118m. V

Mr. Scoutmaster 1953 ★★★½ Strained comedy about a man (Webb) who dislikes children finding himself scoutmaster to a bunch of Boy Scouts. Kids will appreciate Webb's comic predicament. FAM/COM

Mr. Skeffington 1944 ★★★★½ Effective morality tale casts Davis as a vain society beauty who marries a wealthy man (Rains) for security, only to discover that "no woman is truly beautiful until she is loved." Davis at the peak of her powers here, and Rains is quietly affecting. C: Bette Davis, Claude Rains, Walter Abel, Richard Waring, Jerome Cowan. D: Vincent Sherman. DRA 127m. V

Mr. Skitch 1933 ★★★½ Minor but pleasantly entertaining comedy features Rogers as homespun harried father driving family cross-country to California. Often charming, with some funny bits by co-star Desmond. C: Will Rogers, Rochelle Hudson, ZaSu Pitts, Eugene Pallette. D: James Cruze. COM 70m. V

Mr. Smith Goes to Washington 1939 ★★★★★ Stewart delivers extraordinary performance as idealistic young man appointed U.S. Senator who, with help of savvy assistant (Arthur), exposes corruption in home state. Beautifully crafted Capra Americana with terrific performances and intelligent script. Oscar for best original story. C: James Stewart, Jean Arthur, Claude Rains, Edward Arnold, Guy Kibbee, Thomas Mitchell, Eugene Pallette, Beulah Bondi, Harry Carey. D: Frank Capra. DRA 129m. V

Mr. Superinvisible 1973 Italian, German, Spanish ★★★ Kiddie comedy features Jones as scientist who accidentally comes across secret of invisibility while trying to find a cure for colds. Slapstick humor that's strictly for younger audiences. C: Dean Jones, Ingeburg Schoener, Gastone Moschin. D: Anthony M. Dawson. FAM/COM [G] 91m.

Mr. What's-His-Name 1935 British ★★★★ Pickle magnate Hicks loses memory in train crash, and his new personality opens a hair salon and remarries. Years later he encounters his first wife and his old personality is restored. Interesting twist on old movie amnesia plots, with some clever moments. C: Seymour Hicks, Olive Blakeney, Enid Stamp-Taylor, Garry Marsh. D: Ralph Ince. DRA 67m.

Mr. Winkle Goes to War 1944 ★★★★ When middle-aged, out-of-shape bank clerk Robinson is accidentally drafted during WWII, Army training transforms him. Offbeat comedy benefits from Robinson's boundless energy. C: Edward G. Robinson, Ruth Warrick, Ted Donaldson, Robert Armstrong, Ann Shoemaker, Richard Lane. D: Alfred E. Green. COM 80m. V

Mr. Wonderful 1993 ★★★½ To get out of alimony payments, financially strapped blue-collar worker tries to find a new husband for his ex-wife. Charming chemistry between Dillon and Sciorra make for a winning romantic comedy. C: Matt Dillon, Annabella Sciorra, Mary-Louise Parker, William Hurt, Vincent D'Onofrio, David Barry Gray, Bruce Kirby. D: Anthony Minghella. COM [PG-13] 98m. V

Mr. Wong Monogram's initial entry in the Asian sleuth sweepstakes was a series of fair thrillers starring Boris Karloff as Hugh Wiley's Mr. Wong. Karloff's presence was and remains the main attraction.

Mr. Wong, Detective (1938)
Mystery of Mr. Wong (1939)
Mr. Wong in Chinatown (1939)
The Fatal Hour (1940)
Doomed to Die (1940)

Mr. Wong, Detective 1938 ★★★ Karloff is Asian detective on trail of killer who uses poison gas. Mystery with an unusual twist in first of *Mr. Wong* series, based on character created by writer Hugh Wiley. C: Boris Karloff, Grant Withers, Maxine Jennings, Evelyn Brent. D: William Nigh. CRI 69m. V

Mr. Wong in Chinatown 1939 ★★½ Chinese sleuth (Karloff) investigates the murder of a princess. Third in the series, later remade as a Charlie Chan flick, *The Chinese Ring*. C: Boris Karloff, Grant Withers, Marjorie Reynolds. D: William Nigh. CRI 70m.

Mrs. 'Arris Goes to Paris 1992 ★★★½ A lowly British charwoman (Lansbury) dreams of buying an original Dior gown, and travels to the City of Light to get her wish. Brought to TV, Paul Gallico's wonderful novella loses much of its irony and moving ending, becoming simply a Cinderella vehicle for the ever-charming Lansbury. Not bad, but could have been better. The director is Angela's son. C: Angela Lansbury, Omar Sharif, Diana Rigg. D: Anthony Shaw. COM 100m. TVM

Mrs. Brown, You've Got a Lovely Daughter 1968 British ★★★ This '60s curio features pop band Herman's Hermits performing their hits in the midst of superficial tale about dog racing. Minor, but the boys are cute. C: Herman's Hermits, Stanley Holloway, Mona Washbourne. D: Saul Swimmer. MUS [G] 95m. V

Mrs. Delafield Wants to Marry 1986 ★★★½ A socialite (Hepburn) faces opposition from her family and friends when she becomes engaged to her Jewish doctor (Gould). Vehicle for Kate is pleasant froth; no more, no less. C: Katharine Hepburn, Harold Gould, Denholm Elliott, Kathryn Walker, David Ogden Stiers. D: George Schaefer. COM 100m. TVM

Mrs. Doubtfire 1993 ★★★½ Amusing comedy about a divorced husband (Williams) who disguises himself as a British housekeeper to be near his kids. Surprisingly unclichéd ending and an energetic Williams performance save predictable material. C: Robin Williams, Sally Field, Pierce Brosnan, Harvey Fierstein, Robert Prosky. D: Chriss Columbus. COM [PG-13] 125m. V

Mrs. Mike 1949 ★★★★ City dweller (Keyes) marries Royal Canadian Mountie (Powell) and has to adjust to her new home in the untamed wilderness. Spry romance with nice chemistry between the leads. C: Dick Powell, Evelyn Keyes, J.M. Kerrigan, Angela Clarke. D: Louis King. DRA 99m.

Mrs. Miniver 1942 ★★★★½ Middle-class British housewife and her family show quiet courage in coping with terrors of WWII. Moving, uncomplicated drama of the English fight at home. Won seven Oscars including Best Actress (Garson), Picture, Director, and Supporting Actress (Wright). Sequel: *The Miniver Story*. C: Greer Garson, Walter Pidgeon, Dame May Whitty, Teresa Wright, Reginald Owen, Henry Travers, Henry Wilcoxon, Helmut Dantine. D: William Wyler. DRA 134m. V

Mrs. Parker and the Vicious Circle 1994 ★★★½ Biography of witty, dissolute author Dorothy Parker (Leigh), a member of the famed Algonquin Round Table, who met for lunch and stinging repartee daily during the 1920's and '30's. Film's success depends on one's acceptance of Leigh's controversial performance and accent, and one's feelings for the literary world. C: Jennifer Jason Leigh, Campbell Scott, Matthew Broderick, Andrew McCarthy, Peter Gallagher. D: Alan Rudolph. DRA [R] 125m. V

Mrs. Parkington 1944 ★★★½ Ambitious housekeeper marries rich miner and forces her entry into society. Handsome production of old-fashioned melodrama. C: Greer Garson, Walter Pidgeon, Edward Arnold, Gladys Cooper, Agnes Moorehead, Peter Lawford, Dan Duryea, Lee Patrick. D: Tay Garnett. DRA 124m. V

Mrs. Pollifax—Spy 1971 ★★★ Shy widow Emily Pollifax (Russell), enlisted by the CIA, attempts to solve an international security crisis. Popular character, created by Dorothy Gilman, gets limp screen treatment—mainly because the star wrote the script (under a pseudonym). Russell's last theatrical film. Paging Angela Lansbury for a remake, somebody? C: Rosalind Russell, Darren McGavin, Harold Gould. D: Leslie Martinson. CRI [G] 110m.

Mrs. R's Daughter 1979 ★★★½ TV law drama, focusing on a rape victim's mother (Leachman) and her quest for justice. Those who think of Leachman only as a comedienne will be impressed by her searing performance. C: Cloris Leachman, Season Hubley. D: Dan Curtis. DRA 100m. TVM V

Mrs. Silly 1986 ★★★★ Woman who loses her loved one struggles to redefine herself. Includes a moving performance from Smith. C: Maggie Smith, James Villiers. DRA 60m. V

Mrs. Soffel 1985 ★★★½ In turn-of-the-century Pittsburgh, the repressed wife of a prison warden (Keaton) falls in love with a condemned prisoner (Gibson). Somewhat chilly film, based on a true story, is rescued by fine acting. C: Diane Keaton, Mel Gibson, Matthew Modine, Edward Herrmann, Trini Alvarado. D: Gillian Armstrong. DRA [PG-13] 110m. V

Mrs. Wiggs of the Cabbage Patch 1934 ★★★½ A long-suffering wife (Pitts) overcomes hardships and tries to instill positive attitudes in her large family. Popular melodrama with good Field, ditto Pitts. Remade in 1942. C: W.C. Fields, Pauline Lord, ZaSu Pitts, Kent Taylor, Donald Meek. D: Norman Taurog. DRA 80m. V

Ms. Don Juan 1973 French ★★½ Tasteless sex romp about a female version of the famous lover; a so-so showcase for its star. C: Brigitte Bardot, Maurice Ronet, Robert Hossein, Jane Birkin. D: Roger Vadim. DRA 87m. V

Ms. 45 1981 ★★★★ After she's raped for the second time, a young woman starts murdering every man she comes across. Well done; exceedingly violent. (a.k.a. *Angel of Vengeance*) C: Zoe Tamerlis, Steve Singer, Jack Thibeau, Peter Yellen. D: Abel Ferrara. DRA [PG-13] 82m. V

Much Ado About Nothing 1993 British

★★★★½ Vibrant adaptation of Shakespeare comedy concerning the romantic escapades of two pairs of lovers. Spirited cast enhances this airy production. C: Kenneth Branagh, Emma Thompson, Robert Sean Leonard, Keanu Reeves, Denzel Washington, Michael Keaton, Kate Beckinsale, Brian Blessed. D: Kenneth Branagh. COM [PG-13] 111m. V

Muddy River 1982 Japanese ★★★★½ In postwar Japan, two boys develop a friendship and discover important lessons about life. Simply told and powerful study of youthful camaraderie. C: Nobutaka Asahara, Takahiro Tamura, Yumiko Fujita, Minoru Sakurai, Makiko Shibato. D: Kohei Oguri. DRA [R] 105m.

Mudhoney 1965 ★★★ Hearing-impaired mute Cristiani is saved from leering rednecks by Hopper. Female nudity and smutty humor prevail. Once considered risqué. C: Hal Hopper, Antoinette Christian, John Furlong. D: Russ Meyer. DRA 82m. V

Mudlark, The 1950 ★★★★ Orphan (Ray) sneaks into Windsor Castle and becomes an unlikely friend to Queen Victoria (Dunne), who has led an isolated existence since the death of her husband. Charming drama with good work by all hands. C: Irene Dunne, Alec Guinness, Finlay Currie, Anthony Steel, Andrew Ray, Beatrice Campbell, Wilfrid Hyde-White. D: Jean Negulesco. DRA 99m.

Mugsy's Girls 1985 ★★★ An eccentric house mother watches over her brood in a wild college sorority house. (a.k.a. *Delta Pi*) C: Ruth Gordon, Laura Branigan, Ken Norton. D: Kevin Brodie. COM [R] 87m. V

Multiple Maniacs 1971 ★★ Typical outrageous John Waters blasphemy features transvestite Divine as serial killer who gets detoured by Catholic church en route to another bloodfest. Tasteless, profane, and no-holds-barred sleaze—a real treat for fans of Waters' brand of bizarreness. C: Divine, Edith Massey, Mink Stole. D: John Waters. COM 90m. V

Mummy, The 1932 ★★★★ Cinematographer Freund's directorial debut is a rich, moody tale of an ancient priest buried alive who walks the earth as a modern Egyptian in love with the reincarnation of his eternal sweetheart. A seemingly silly story transformed into resonant horror, thanks largely to Karloff. C: Boris Karloff, Zita Johann, David Manners, Arthur Byron, Edward Van Sloan, Bramwell Fletcher. D: Karl Freund. HOR 72m. V

Mummy, The 1959 British ★★★★ Influential Hammer Studios version of 1932 horror original, with British monster-of-all-trades Lee in hot pursuit of the wife of the 19th-century archaeologist who unearthed him. The first color version of *The Mummy*.. C: Peter Cushing, Christopher Lee, Yvonne Furneaux, Felix Aylmer. D: Terence Fisher. HOR 88m. V

Mummy's Curse, The 1944 ★★ Chaney Jr.'s last performance as the Mummy has the Egyptian monster and his eternal love Ananka unearthed once again in this sequel to *The Mummy's Ghost*. Series may have run its course, relying on wealth of footage from previous Mummy films. Notable for some squeamish moments. C: Lon Chaney, Jr., Peter Coe, Kay Harding, Martin Kosleck. D: Leslie Goodwins. HOR 61m. V

Mummy's Ghost, The 1944 ★★★ Chaney, Jr. revamps his cloth-wrapped creature aided by Carradine in pursuing Princess Ananka, the Egyptian princess reincarnated as a New England college student. Sequel to *The Mummy's Tomb*. C: Lon Chaney, Jr., John Carradine, Barton MacLane, George Zucco. D: Reginald LeBorg. HOR 61m. V

Mummy's Hand, The 1940 ★★★★ Tyler is the bandaged Egyptian Kharis the Mummy, this time with Moran as his romantic prey. Effective horror makes this a cream-of-the-crop *Mummy*. C: Dick Foran, Wallace Ford, Cecil Kellaway, George Zucco, Tom Tyler, Eduardo Ciannelli, Charles Trowbridge. D: Christy Cabanne. HOR 70m. V

Mummy's Tomb, The 1942 ★★★ Sequel to *The Mummy's Hand* with Chaney, Jr. making his Mummy debut and Bey as his sidekick; they travel to America to seek revenge on the men who profaned Princess Ananka's tomb. Recycled footage makes for a rickety horror film, though it was highly successful at the box office. C: Lon Chaney, Jr., Turhan Bey, Dick Foran, Wallace Ford, George Zucco. D: Harold Young. HOR 71m. V

Munchie 1992 ★★★ A little boy finds a magical troll—and it gets him into one problem after another. C: Loni Anderson, Dom De Luise, Andrew Stevens. D: Jim Wynorski. COM [PG] 80m. V

Munchies 1987 ★ *Gremlins* knockoff features Korman as beleaguered parent whose life undergoes turmoil after son's unusual pet goes berserk and multiplies. C: Harvey Korman, Charles Stratton, Nadine Van Der Velde. D: Bettina Hirsch. COM [PG] 83m. V

Munster, Go Home 1966 ★★★ Everyone's favorite family of cuddly monsters treks to England to claim a castle legacy. Nitwit feature film from the popular TV series; mainly for toddlers and baby boomers suffering from attacks of nostalgia (especially if they've wondered what the Munsters would look like in color). C: Fred Gwynne, Yvonne De Carlo, Butch Patrick, Terry-Thomas, John Carradine, Hermione Gingold. D: Earl Bellamy. COM 96m.

Munsters' Revenge, The 1981 ★★ Reunion of '60s sitcom *The Munsters* finds Herman (Gwynne), Grandpa (Lewis) and Lily (DeCarlo) victims of mad scientist who creates art-stealing robots in their images. Slapstick rules this witless outing. C: Fred Gwynne, Yvonne De Carlo, Al Lewis, Sid Caesar, Howard Morris. D: Don Weis. COM 96m. TVM V

Muppet Christmas Carol, The 1992 ★★★½ Charles Dickens' "A Christmas Carol" is recast with Michael Caine as Scrooge and Kermit the Frog as Bob Cratchit. First Muppet film made after Jim Henson's death misses his creative input, though it has its moments. Amiable holiday viewing. C: Michael Caine, Kermit the Frog, Miss Piggy. D: Brian Henson. FAM/DRA [G] 95m. v

Muppet Movie, The 1979 ★★★★ First feature with Jim Henson's Muppets tells how Kermit the Frog travels cross-country, is romanced by Miss Piggy, overcomes bad guys, and succeeds in Hollywood. Utterly charming, with good musical numbers and funny star cameos. Appealing on multiple levels for children and adults. C: Jim Henson, Edgar Bergen, Milton Berle, Mel Brooks, Steve Martin, Muppets. D: James Frawley. FAM/MUS [G] 94m. v

Muppets Take Manhattan, The 1984 ★★★★ Muppet-style parody of show business movie formula finds Henson's cloth creatures taking their college revue to the bright lights of Broadway, where hearts are broken and careers are made. Entertaining, with splashy musical numbers and entertaining star cameos. Perfect for entire family. C: Jim Henson, Elliot Gould, Liza Minnelli, Brooke Shields, Dabney Coleman, Art Carney, James Coco, Joan Rivers, Gregory Hines, Linda Lavin. D: Frank Oz. FAM/MUS [G] 94m. v

Murder! 1930 British ★★★★ Early Hitchcock thriller about an actress on trial for murder and the lone juror who's convinced of her innocence. Neat suspense elements spin out nicely under the hand of the master. C: Herbert Marshall, Nora Baring, Phyllis Konstam, Edward Chapman. D: Alfred Hitchcock. CRI 100m. v

Murder Ahoy 1964 British ★★★★ Christie's plucky Miss Marple (Rutherford) solves a murder aboard a naval ship. Absorbing mystery retains patented Christie whodunit style even though it's not based on any of the author's books. C: Margaret Rutherford, Lionel Jeffries, Charles Tingwell, William Mervyn, Joan Benham, Stringer Davis, Miles Malleson. D: George Pollock. CRI 93m. v

Murder at Midnight 1931 ★★ During a game of charades, a party guest shoots someone with blanks. But it turns out he shot him for real. C: Aileen Pringle, Alice White, Hale Hamilton. DRA 64m. v

Murder at the Baskervilles 1937 ★★★½ Sherlock Holmes investigates the horse-napping of prized steed and the death of a trainer. Fun for the detective's many fans. (a.k.a. *Silver Blaze*) C: Arthur Wontner, Ian Fleming. D: Thomas Bentley. DRA 67m. v

Murder at the Gallop 1963 British ★★★½ Miss Marple's morbid fascination with death leads her to investigate the passing of a rich, elderly eccentric. Morley's presence elevates this otherwise standard whodunit. Based on Christie's *After the Funeral*. C: Margaret Rutherford, Robert Morley, Flora Robson, Charles Tingwell, Duncan Lamont, Stringer Davis, James Villiers, Robert Urquhart. D: George Pollock. CRI 82m. v

Murder at the Vanities 1934 ★★★★ After two backstage murders at the famed New York revue, curmudgeonly detective (McLaglen) goes in search of the showbiz killer. Unusual and fun murder musical with some strange novelty songs, including "Cocktails for Two" and "Sweet Marijuana." C: Jack Oakie, Kitty Carlisle, Carl Brisson, Victor McLaglen, Donald Meek, Gail Patrick. D: Mitchell Leisen. CRI 91m. v

Murder by Death 1976 ★★★★ Cute movie spoof has perfectly cast author Capote inviting world's top detectives to his home to solve a murder. Plenty of self-parodying performances, and tongue-in-cheek tributes make this Neil Simon scripted comedy an enjoyable outing for mystery buffs. C: Peter Sellers, Peter Falk, David Niven, Maggie Smith, James Coco, Alec Guinness, Elsa Lanchester, Eileen Brennan, Truman Capote. D: Robert Moore. COM [PG] 95m. v

Murder by Decree 1979 Canadian ★★★★ Sherlock Holmes mystery features Plummer as the famed detective, assisted by Dr. Watson (Mason) in search of London's notorious murderer, Jack the Ripper. Often violent, consistently intriguing mystery with some surprising twists; neat pairing of Plummer and Mason. C: Christopher Plummer, James Mason, Donald Sutherland, Genevieve Bujold, David Hemmings, Frank Finlay. D: Bob Clark. DRA [PG] 123m. v

Murder by Moonlight 1989 ★★★ In a moon colony, a NASA agent and her Soviet counterpart team up to solve a murder. Kind of silly. C: Julian Sands, Brigitte Nielsen. D: Michael Lindsay-Hogg. CRI [PG-13] 100m.

Murder by Numbers 1989 ★★ Lower-than-low mystery revolving around a killing in the art world. Has definite possibility as a "so bad it's good" candidate. C: Sam Behrens, Jayne Meadows, Shari Belafonte-Harper, Ronee Blakley. D: Paul Leder. CRI [PG-13] 90m. TVM v

Murder By Numbers—Inside the Serial Killers 1993 ★★★★ A no-nonsense documentary on serial killers, their habits and prey. Interviews with killers, their relatives, relatives of victims, psychologists, and some surviving victims. Chilling and fascinating. Narrated by Richard Roth. C: Richard Roth. DOC 116m. TVM v

Murder by Television 1935 ★★½ During a demonstration of a new invention called "television," a professor turns up dead. Is TV, itself, the murderer? Crude mystery, with Lugosi in dual role, sounds more interesting than it is. (a.k.a. *The Houghland Murder Case*) C: Bela Lugosi, June Collyer, George Meeker, Huntley Gordon. D: Clifford Sandforth. CRI 60m.

Murder by the Book 1987 ★★★½ Mystery writer (Hays) using the alter ego of his fictional gumshoe, helps woman (Stewart) solve a murder case involving fake antiques. Unspectacular television movie concentrates on the contrast between the mild-mannered writer and his hard-boiled detective character. C: Robert Hays, Catherine Stewart, Celeste Holm, Fred Gwynne, Christopher Murney. D: Mel Damski. CRI 100m. TVM V

Murder by the Clock 1931 ★★★½ An obsessed woman plants communications device in her grave, just in case she's buried before her time; meanwhile, oddball characters scuttle around pushing bizarre drugs. Peculiar mix of horror and mystery doesn't always work, but offbeat style makes it worth watching. C: William Boyd, Lilyan Tashman, Irving Pichel, Regis Toomey, Blanche Frederici, Sally O'Neil, Lester Vail. D: Edward Sloman. HOR 76m.

Murder, Czech Style 1968 Czech ★★★½ An office worker dreams of killing his young and beautiful spouse after he learns she's been unfaithful. Innovative use of fantasy sequences gives this spoof an interesting comic style. C: Rudolf Hrusinsky, Kyeta Fialova, Vaclav Voska, Vladimir Mensik. D: Jiri Weiss. COM 90m.

Murder Elite 1986 ★★★ A psychotic killer terrorizes a section of British countrysside. C: Ali MacGraw, Billie Whitelaw, Hywel Bennett. D: Claude Whatham. DRA 98m. V

Murder For Sale 1970 ★★½ A secret agent is ordered to stop a terrorist ring from murdering a U.N. official. C: John Gavin, Margaret Lee, Curt Jurgens. D: Renzo Cerrato. ACT [PG] 90m. V

Murder, He Says 1945 ★★★★ A poll taker (MacMurray) looking for a missing co-worker finds unexpected survey participants when he stumbles onto a rural clan of demented killers. Offbeat zaniness with clever moments and genuine laughs. C: Fred MacMurray, Helen Walker, Marjorie Main, Jean Heather, Porter Hall, Peter Whitney, Barbara Pepper, Mabel Paige. D: George Marshall. COM 93m.

Murder in Coweta County 1983 ★★★ Sheriff relentlessly pursues prominent tycoon suspected of murder. Interesting TV movie based on an actual incident in '40s Georgia. From Margaret Anne Barnes' book. C: Johnny Cash, Andy Griffith, Earl Hindman, June Carter Cash. D: Gary Nelson. CRI 96m. TVM V

Murder in Harlem 1935 ★★★ A black night watchman finds the body of a white woman on his rounds. He's framed for the murder and all kinds of trouble ensues. C: Clarence Brooks, Laura Bowman, Dorothy Van Engle. D: Oscar Micheaux. DRA 102m. V

Murder in Mississippi 1990 ★★★★ Three college students/civil rights workers disappear, igniting a major FBI investigation. TV version of the true story which inspired the theatrical feature *Mississippi Burning*. Gripping, faithful drama. C: Tom Hulce, Blair Underwood, Jennifer Grey, CCH Pounder, Josh Charles. D: Roger Young. DRA 200m. TVM

Murder in New Hampshire: The Pamela Smart Story 1992 ★★★ Ripped from yesterday's headlines! Lurid yarn of sexy high school teacher Pamela Smart, who manipulates her teenage lover and pupil to murder her husband. Hunt's icy performance makes this watchable. C: Helen Hunt, Chad Allen, Larry Drake, Howard Hesseman, Ken Howard, Michael Learned. D: Joyce Chopra. DRA 93m. TVM V

Murder in Space 1985 ★★½ Killer stalks spaceship returning from Mars. Colorless suspense tale. C: Wilford Brimley, Arthur Hill, Martin Balsam, Michael Ironside. D: Steven Hillard Stern. CRI 95m. TVM V

Murder in Texas 1981 ★★★★ Fact-based drama of plastic surgeon John Hill (Elliot), who was tried for the murder of his social butterfly wife (Fawcett). Exceptionally well handled and acted. Adapted from *Prescription: Murder*, by Ann Kurth (Hill's second wife). C: Katharine Ross, Sam Elliott, Farrah Fawcett, Andy Griffith, Craig Nelson, Barry Corbin. D: Billy Hale. CRI 200m. TVM V

Murder in the First 1995 ★★★½ After three years in Alcatraz solitary confinement, convict (Bacon) kills a fellow prisoner. Was it his fault, or not? Bacon's strong performance makes it work. Based on a true story. C: Kevin Bacon, Christian Slater, Gary Oldman, Brad Dourif. D: Marc Rocco. DRA [R] 122m. V

Murder in the Music Hall 1946 ★★★ A mysterious killer haunts a music hall, causing suspicion and fear amidst a theatrical troupe. Low-budget murder mystery clicks along just fine. C: Vera Hruba Ralslton, William Marshall, Helen Walker, Nancy Kelly, William Gargan, Ann Rutherford, Julie Bishop. D: John English. DRA 84m.

Murder in the Ring 1971 ★★★ A boxer is framed for murder, and he begins a desperate search for the real killer. (a.k.a. *Ripped Off*) C: Robert Blake, Ernest Borgnine. D: Franco Prosperi. DRA 75m. V

Murder in Thorton Square, The 1940 *See* **Gaslight**

Murder, Inc. 1960 ★★★★ A couple falls into trouble with a powerful crime syndicate and can't get free of its murderous grip. Gritty, fact-based story with Falk turning in a compelling performance as a notorious contract killer. Able supporting cast, potent crime drama. C: Stuart Whitman, May Britt, Henry Morgan, Peter Falk, David J. Stewart, Simon Oakland, Morey Amsterdam, Sarah Vaughan, Joseph Campanella. D: Burt Balaban, Stuart Rosenberg. DRA 103m.

Murder Is My Beat 1955 ★★★ A wrongly accused man hunts for the real killer. Routine B-mystery. C: Paul Langton, Barbara Payton, Robert Shayne, Selena Royle. D: Edgar G. Ulmer. CRI 77m.

Murder Man, The 1935 ★★★★ A hard-bitten reporter (Tracy) finds his regular murder beat disrupted when someone close to him turns up dead. Intriguing mystery, with fine work by Tracy. C: Spencer Tracy, Virginia Bruce, Lionel Atwill, Harvey Stephens, Robert Barrat, James Stewart. D: Tim Whelan. CRI 70m.

Murder Mansion, The 1970 Spanish ★★★ A young couple and a terrified woman they encounter seek shelter in a mysterious house and are terrorized by evil spirits there. Atmosphere triumphs over standard story in this good Spanish production. C: Analia Gade, Evelyn Stewart. D: F.Lara Polop. HOR 84m. V

Murder Masters of Kung Fu 1985 ★★★ An old master teaches all he knows to a fledgling martial artist. C: Yim Nam Hei, Tien Pang. ACT 93m. V

Murder Most Foul 1965 British ★★★★ Obstinate Miss Marple finds herself on jury of a murder trial and must convince her fellow jurors of the accused's innocence. Most entertaining for fans of the genre. The last Rutherford Marple film. From Agatha Christie's novel *Mrs. McGinty's Dead.* C: Margaret Rutherford, Ron Moody, Charles Tingwell, Andrew Cruickshank, Stringer Davis, Francesca Annis, Dennis Price, James Bolam. D: George Pollock. CRI 90m. V

Murder Motel 1974 ★★★ When her fiancé disppears during a vacation, a young woman investigates the hotel he was saying at—and she finds some ghastly goings on. C: Robyn Millan, Derek Francis. D: Malcolm Taylor. HOR 80m. V

Murder My Sweet 1944 ★★★★½ Tough P.I. Philip Marlowe searches for a missing person on the poor side of L.A. and investigates a murder on the rich side of town, only to find there's not much difference. Quintessential film noir. Powell delivers a surprisingly gritty performance. Based on Raymond Chandler's *Farewell My Lovely.* C: Dick Powell, Claire Trevor, Anne Shirley, Otto Kruger, Mike Mazurki. D: Edward Dmytryk. CRI 94m. V

Murder, No Apparent Motive 1984 ★★★ A fascinating study of humans who murder. Utilizes psychology, sociology and actual case studies. C: John Brotherton, Karen Levine. DOC 72m. V

Murder of Mary Phagan, The 1989 ★★★★ Drama details the 1913 Leo Frank case wherein Frank was sentenced to death for murder of a young woman, despite questionable evidence. Buoyed by a stellar cast, with kudos to Lemmon and Spacey. C: Jack Lemmon, Peter Gallagher, Richard Jordan, Robert Prosky, Paul Dooley, Kevin Spacey, Charles Dutton. D: Billy Hale. CRI [PG] 222m. TVM V

Murder on a Honeymoon 1935 ★★★★ Hildegarde Withers (Oliver) investigates an airborne murder on a small plane heading out to beautiful Catalina Island. Clever moments give sparkle to entertaining mystery series entry. C: Edna May Oliver, James Gleason, Lola Lane, Chick Chandler, George Meeker, Dorothy Libaire, Morgan Wallace, Leo G. Carroll. D: Lloyd Corrigan. CRI 74m.

Murder on Flight 502 1975 ★★★ On New York-to-London, flight cast of stars learns one of them is a killer. Standard *Airport*-style disaster film. C: Ralph Bellamy, Polly Bergen, Theodore Bikel, Sonny Bono, Dane Clark, Laraine Day, Fernando Lamas, George Maharis, Farrah Fawcett Majors, Hugh O'Brian, Molly Picon, Walter Pidgeon, Robert Stack. D: George McCowan. DRA 100m. TVM V

Murder on Lenox Avenue 1941 ★★★ When he's dismissed from his position, the ex-leader of Harlem's Better Business League tries to kill his successor. C: Alberta Perkins, Sidney Easton, Alec Lovejoy. D: Arthur Dreifuss. DRA 60m. V

Murder on Line One 1990 ★★ London's streets are terrorized by a murderer who gets his jollies by videotaping his handiwork and watching it over and over. Subpar horror thriller. Reminiscent of *Peeping Tom,* the champ of murderous voyeurism films. C: Emma Jacobs, Peter Blake, Simon Shepherd, Allan Surtees. D: Anders Palm. CRI 103m. V

Murder on the Bayou *See* **Gathering of Old Men, A**

Murder on the Blackboard 1934 ★★★★ When her teaching colleague is found dead, Hildegarde Withers (Oliver) sets her sleuthing friend (Gleason) to uncover the killer. Bright comic winks give added boost to the investigation in this appealing series installment. C: Edna May Oliver, James Gleason, Bruce Cabot, Gertrude Michael, Regis Toomey, Tully Marshall, Edgar Kennedy, Jackie Searle, Fredrik Vogeding, Gustav VonSeyffertitz. D: George Archainbaud. CRI 72m.

Murder on the Midnight Express 1974 ★★★ The fabled train makes its way across Europe with a caravan of wierd characters in count—including a dead body. C: Judy Geeson, James Smilie. D: John Cooper. HOR 70m. V

Murder on the Orient Express 1974 British ★★★★ When a millionaire is murdered aboard the legendary train, it's up to Agatha Christie's dapper detective, Hercule Poirot, to find the killer. It looks great, and the all-star cast is delightful. Oscar to Bergman for Supporting Actress. C: Albert Finney, Lauren Bacall, Martin Balsam, Ingrid Bergman, Jacqueline Bisset, Jean-Piere Cassel, Sean Connery, John Gielgud, Wendy Hiller, Anthony Perkins, Vanessa Redgrave, Rachel Roberts, Richard Widmark. D: Sidney Lumet. CRI [PG] 128m. V

Murder on the Yukon 1940 ★★½ A mountie hero pursues a aring of counterfeiters across the frozen wastes of the north. C: James Newill, Polly Ann Young, Dave O'Brien, Al St. John. D: Louis Gasnier. WST 67m. V

Murder 101 1991 ★★★ Professor rues the day he asks his college class to create the perfect theoretical crime; the assignment ultimately leads to his being set up as prime candidate for the real killing. Good premise, so-so development. C: Pierce Brosnan, Dey Young, Antoni Cerone, Raphael Sbarge, Kim Thomson, J.Kenneth Campbell. D: Bill Condon. CRI [PG-13] 100m. TVM V

Murder Over New York 1940 ★★★½ Chan comes to the Big Apple for a police convention and winds up investigating a murder and a group of saboteurs. MacBride steals the show as a "harried New York detective." C: Sidney Toler, Marjorie Weaver, Robert Lowery, Ricardo Cortez. D: Harry Lachman. CRI 64m. V

Murder Rap 1988 ★★½ A man sets out to investigate his girlfriend's sister's murder, then realizes that he's being framed. C: John Hawkes, Seita Kathleen Feigny. D: Kliff Kuehl. DRA 104m. V

Murder, She Said 1962 British ★★★★ Rutherford plays Christie's Miss Marple for the first of four times, posing as servant to gain access to a home and solve a homicide. Entertaining murder mystery with some good twists. Future Marple Joan Hickson is the crook. Based on *4:50 from Paddington.* (a.k.a. *Meet Miss Marple*) C: Margaret Rutherford, Arthur Kennedy, Muriel Pavlow, James Robertson Justice, Charles Tingwell, Thorley Walters. D: George Pollock. CRI 90m. V

Murder So Sweet 1994 ★★★ Woman's darling boyfriend just may be a serial killer. C: Harry Hamlin, Helen Shaver, K.T. Oslin. D: Larry Peerce. CRI 94m. V

Murder Weapon 1990 ★★ Men face dire consequences when they accept women's invitation to a summer party. C: Lyle Waggoner, Linnea Quigley, Karen Russell. D: Ellen Cabot. HOR 90m. V

Murder with Mirrors 1985 ★★★ Agatha Christie's unassuming Miss Marple (Hayes) has several suspects to choose from when she tries to find out who's trying to kill her friend (Davis) and take her family home. Sole saving grace is unique pairing of legends Hayes and Davis. C: Helen Hayes, Bette Davis, John Mills, Leo McKern, Liane Langland, Dorothy Tutin. D: Dick Lowry. CRI 100m. TVM

Murder Without Motive 1992 ★★★ Intriguing, even-handed look at police brutality in tale of two African American teens shot by undercover cop in New York City. C: Curtis McClaren, Anna Maria Horsford, Carla Gugino. D: Kevin Hooks. DRA 93m. TVM V

Murderer Dmitri Karamazov, The 1931 *See* **Karamazov**

Murderer In The Motel 1983 Spanish ★★★ Tracking down the murderer of a young woman, a detective meets up with the strange owners of a mysterious motel. C: Jose Alonso, Blanca Guerra. D: Luis Mandoki. CRI 99m. V

Murderer Lives at Number 21, The 1942 French ★★★★ Black French comedy-mystery involves a police inspector (Fresnay) who takes on cleric's garb and moves into a boarding house where a suspected serial killer is hiding out. Some unusual touches and a dark sense of humor enrich this offbeat murder film. C: Pierre Fresnay, Suzy Delair, Jean Tissier, Pierre Larquay, Noel Roquevert, Odette Talazac. D: Henri-Georges Clouzot. COM 83m.

Murderers Among Us 1948 German ★★★★ Following end of WWII, a remorseful German doctor who witnessed death camp atrocities must decide whether to testify in war crime tribunals. Moving story of one person's transforming odyssey, and one of Germany's first postwar films to deal with the horrors of the country's Nazi past. C: Hildegard Knef, Ernst Borchert, Arno Paulsen. D: Wolfgang Staudtel. DRA 80m. V

Murderers Among Us: The Simon Wiesenthal Story 1989 ★★★★ True drama of Holocaust survivor Wiesenthal (Kingsley), who dedicates his life to bringing Nazi criminals to justice. Forceful history, superb Kingsley. C: Ben Kingsley, Craig T. Nelson, Renee Soutendijk. D: Brian Gibson. DRA 157m. TVM V

Murderers' Row 1966 ★★½ Second in Matt Helm series (after The Silencers) only has a stylish Lalo Schifrin score in its favor. As Helm, Martin pursues mad Malden, who holds Ann-Margret's inventor dad hostage. Followed by The Ambushers. C: Dean Martin, Ann-Margret, Karl Malden. D: Henry Levin. ACT 108m. V

Murderlust 1986 ★★★ A serial killer has the whole city horrified. C: Eli Rich, Rochelle Taylor, Dennis Gannon. D: Donald M. Jones. DRA 90m. V

Murderous Vision 1991 ★★★ Deranged killer slices off faces of his victims; cop and psychic track him down. Suspense thriller with offbeat premise. C: Bruce Boxleitner, Laura Johnson, Joseph D'Angerio, Glenn Plummer, Beau Starr, Robert Culp. D: Gary Sherman. CRI 93m. TVM V

Murders At Lynch Cross 1985 ★★★ On the British moors, a new hotel is the site of several strange and gruesome murders. Harrowing. C: Jill Bennett, Joanna David, Sylvia Sims. D: Patrick Lau. ACT 60m. TVM

Murders in the Rue Morgue 1932 ★★★½ Lugosi, at his sinister best, is a twisted doctor in turn-of-the-century Paris, trying to cross an ape with a woman and leaving a string of bodies behind him. Gruesome film for its day, based on an Edgar Allan Poe story. Remade many times. C: Bela Lugosi, Sidney Fox, Leon Ames, Brandon Hurst, Arlene Francis. D: Robert Florey. HOR 61m. V

Murders in the Rue Morgue, The 1986 ★★★★ Brutal slaying of a mother and daughter baffles the Parisian police, but not

Edgar Allan Poe's amateur sleuth, C. Auguste Dupin. Exceptional, with a terrific cast and dazzling performance by Scott in the lead. C: George C. Scott, Rebecca de Mornay, Ian McShane, Val Kilmer. D: Jeannot Szwarc. CRI 92m. TVM V

Murders in the Zoo 1933 ★★★★ Gruesome, chilling story about zoologist Atwill, madly jealous of adulterous wife, who uses his trapping skills and some ferocious beasts to exact revenge on her paramours. Original horror film, with good psychotic Atwill. C: Lionel Atwill, Charles Ruggles, Randolph Scott, Gail Patrick, John Lodge, Kathleen Burke. D: A.Edward Sutherland. HOR 64m.

Muriel 1963 French ★★★★ Another of Resnais' memory films examines a widow's reminiscence of her first love, and her stepson's reconsideration of war atrocities committed against a victim named Muriel. Stylized and haunting; a must for Resnais fans. C: Delphine Seyrig, Jean-Pierre Kérien, Nita Klein, Jean-Baptiste Thieree. D: Alain Resnais. DRA 116m. V

Muriel's Wedding 1995 Australian ★★★★ Delightful fairy-tale variation of *The Ugly Duckling,* with Collette as a plain-jane woman who takes a vacation, determined to snare a husband. Breezy, campy, and quite funny. C: Toni Collette, Bill Hunter, Rachel Griffiths. D: P.J. Hogan. COM [R] 105m. V

Murmur of the Heart 1971 French ★★★★½ Recuperating adolescent (Ferreux) and his spirited mother (Massari) take an unexpected turn in their child/parent relationship. Alternately touching and comic satire of French upper classes, though incest theme may disturb some viewers. Lively pacing is enhanced by a wonderful Charlie Parker soundtrack. C: Lea Massari, Benoit Ferreux, Daniel Gelin, Michel Lonsdale. D: Louis Malle. COM [R] 118m. V

Murph the Surf 1975 ★★★★ Florida rogues concoct an outrageous plan to steal a priceless gem from New York's Museum of Natural History. Based on a true story, this caper comedy thrives on sheer energy, topped by a wild chase sequence. (a.k.a. *Live a Little, Steal a Lot*) C: Robert Conrad, Donna Mills. D: Marvin J. Chomsky. ACT [PG] 102m. V

Murphy's Fault 1989 ★★★ Desperate writer tries to survive rollercoaster ride of events involving romance and career. C: Patrick Dollaghan, Anne Curry, Stack Peirce. D: Robert J. Smawley. COM [PG-13] 94m. V

Murphy's Law 1986 ★★★ A tough police officer (Bronson), accused of killing his ex-wife, chases the real murderer while handcuffed to a mouthy streetwalker. Predictably nasty and violent, but a few twists. C: Charles Bronson, Kathleen Wilhoite, Carrie Snodgress, Robert Lyons, Richard Romanus. D: J.Lee Thompson. CRI [R] 101m. V

Murphy's Romance 1985 ★★★½ Divorced mom Field meets and falls in love with older, widowed pharmacist Garner. No great shakes but a cheery change for Field, and Garner turns in a charming, easygoing performance. C: Sally Field, James Garner, Brian Kerwin, Corey Haim. D: Martin Ritt. DRA [PG-13] 107m. V

Murphy's War 1971 British ★★★★ A British sailor (O'Toole) the only survivor of a German U-boat attack, revenges himself. Good combination of character study and action, with another fine performance from O'Toole. C: Peter O'Toole, Sian Phillips, Philippe Noiret, Horst Janson. D: Peter Yates. DRA [PG] 106m. V

Murri Affair 1974 *See* **La Grande Bourgeosie**

Murrow 1985 ★★★½ Travanti plays the legendary newscaster Edward R. Murrow in this surprisingly slow biography. Travanti himself gives a solid performance. C: Daniel J. Travanti, Dabney Coleman, Edward Herrmann, David Suchet. D: Jack Gold. DRA 114m. TVM V

Muscle Beach Party 1964 ★★★½ Controversy rages as the beach is invaded by weightlifters and Don Rickles. Truly weird cast plays it with a straight face. Inspired silliness. C: William Asher, Frankie Avalon, Annette Funicello, Buddy Hackett, Don Rickles, Stevie Wonder, Morey Amsterdam, Dan Haggerty. D: William Asher. COM 96m. V

Music Box 1989 ★★★½ When her father is accused of war crimes during WWII in Hungary, attorney (Lange) defends him at international trial. Political potential takes a backseat to Lange's well-played emotional conflict as she struggles with the possibility of her father's guilt. C: Jessica Lange, Armin Mueller-Stahl, Frederic Forrest, Donald Moffat, Lukas Haas, Cheryl Bruce. D: Costa Gavras. DRA [PG-13] 126m. V

Music for Millions 1944 ★★★½ WWII-era MGM musical about a pregnant war bride (Allyson), an orchestra cellist, who plays and prays for her husband's return. Features wild Durante showstopper, "Umbriago," and fine Iturbi light classical selections. C: June Allyson, Jimmy Durante, Margaret O'Brien, Jose Iturbi, Marsha Hunt. D: Henry Koster. MUS 120m.

Music in Darkness 1948 *See* **Night Is My Future**

Music in My Heart 1940 ★★★ Two singers fall in love during WWII. Slim musical romance gives an early look at the ravishing Hayworth. Songs include Oscar-nominated "It's a Blue World." C: Tony Martin, Rita Hayworth, Eric Blore, Andre Kostelanetz & his orchestra. D: Joseph Santley. MUS 70m. V

Music in the Air 1934 ★★★★ A show business couple's backstage bickering takes a new twist when they use unsophisticated newcomers to make each other jealous. Comic, effervescent fluff with great performances and a wonderful score by Jerome Kern and Oscar Hammerstein. C: Gloria Swanson, John Boles, Douglass Montgomery, June

Lang, Reginald Owen, Al Shean. D: Joe May. MUS 85m.

Music Is Magic 1935 ★★★ Middling musical gamely tries to tune up hackneyed story of two showbiz stars: one on the way up (Faye), and one on the skids (Daniels). Daniels is good in this one, in a role reminiscent of her *42nd Street* turn. C: Alice Faye, Bebe Daniels, Ray Walker. D: George Marshall. MUS 65m.

Music Is My Future 1948 *See* **Night Is My Future**

Music Lovers, The 1971 British ★★★ Russell takes biographical license to new extremes in this overly imaginative depiction of Tchaikovsky's tortured life. Chamberlain and Jackson are game, but the film is overwrought nonsense. C: Glenda Jackson, Richard Chamberlain, Max Adrian, Christopher Gable, Kenneth Colley. D: Ken Russell. DRA [R] 123m. v

Music Man, The 1962 ★★★★½ Preston has a field day recreating his Tony Award-winning performance as charismatic con artist who hoodwinks Iowa town into forming boys' band. Jones plays his nemesis/sweetheart charmingly. Show's script and score are faithfully preserved, with songs including "Trouble," "Trombones, '76" "Till There Was You." C: Robert Preston, Shirley Jones, Buddy Hackett, Hermione Gingold, Paul Ford, Pert Kelton, Ronny Howard. D: Morton Da Costa. MUS [G] 152m. v

Music of Chance, The 1993 ★★★½ Offbeat absurdist trifle about two men (Spader and Patinkin) condemned to work off a gambling debt by building a seemingly pointless wall in the middle of nowhere. Fascinating but difficult, despite an excellent performance by Patinkin. Adapted from Paul Auster's novel. C: James Spader, Mandy Patinkin, M. Emmet Walsh, Charles Durning, Joel Grey. D: Philip Haas. DRA [R] 98m. v

Music Room, The 1963 Indian ★★★★½ After squandering all his money, a dying millionaire uses what's left of his fortune to stage an elaborate concert of Indian music. A wonderful tribute to the joy music brings to everyday life. Director Ray also composed the splendid score. C: Chabi Biswas, Padma Devi, Pinaki Sen Gupta, Tulsi Lahari. D: Satyajit Ray. DRA 95m.

Music Teacher, The 1989 Belgian ★★★½ Retiring opera star turns to coaching but finds his young pupil falling in love with him. Rather prosaic drama, but with Van Dam's terrific singing. C: Jose Van Dam, Anne Roussel, Philippe Volter, Sylvie Fennec, Patrick Bauchau, Johan Leyson. D: Gerard Corbiau. DRA [PG] 100m. v

Musicians in Exile 1990 ★★★½ Hugh Masekela, Quilapayun, Paquito Riviera, and Daniel Ponce are featured in this documentary about the personal struggles, living circumstances, and influences of world music innovators, many of whom now live in exile for political reasons. MUS 75m. v

Mussketeers of Pig Alley & Selected Biograph Shorts 1912 ★★★ Seven classic examples of "one-reel" silent pictures. A must-see for film historians. D: D.W. Griffith. DRA 117m. v

Mussolini and I 1985 ★★★★ Spellbounding performances from a splendid international cast spark this tale of the family conflict and political conspiracy that surrounded the delcine of the Italian Fascist dictator. C: Susan Sarandon, Anthony Hopkins, Bob Hoskins. D: Alberto Negrin. DRA 130m. v

Mutant 1982 *See* **Forbidden World**

Mutant 1983 ★★ Toxic waste turns Southern townspeople into zombie-like monsters who go on a rampage. Professionally made but unexciting chiller, with a decent cast going through the motions. (a.k.a. *Night Shadows*) C: Wings Hauser, Bo Hopkins Jennifer Warrent. D: John Cardos. HOR [R] 100m.

Mutant Hunt 1987 ★★½ Good clashes with evil as a man attempts to stop a troop of killer cyborgs unleashed in New York City by a mad scientist. C: Rick Gianasi, Ron Reynaldi, Taunie Vrenon. D: Tim Kincaid. SFI 90m. v

Mutant Video 1976 ★★★ Belushi and his former comic partner Riley are responsible for the six shorts on this very funny tape. C: Jim Belushi, Bob Riley. COM 60m. v

Mutants in Paradise 1985 ★ Fairy godmother rescues a nerd from mad scientists in this silly comedy. C: Brad Greenquist, Robert Ingham, Anna Nicholas, Edith Massey. COM 78m. v

Mutator 1989 ★ Corporate scientists create lethal mutant cats by mistake. Whoops. C: Brion James, Carolyn Ann Clark, Milton Raphael Murill, Embeth Davidtz. D: John R. Bowey. HOR 84m. v

Muthers, The 1976 ★★½ Tough female prisoners make a daring escape in South American jungle. Plenty of action. C: Jayne Kennedy, Jeanne Bell, Rosanne Katon. D: Cirio H. Santiago. ACT [R] 82m. v

Mutiny on the Bounty 1935 ★★★★★ The classic filming of Nordoff and Hall's novel about the overthrow of the tyrannical Captain Bligh. This truly exquisite film, with superb writing and an outstanding cast (Laughton, as Bligh, is perfect) received a well-deserved Oscar for Best Picture. The remakes don't come close. C: Charles Laughton, Clark Gable, Franchot Tone, Dudley Digges, Donald Crisp, Movita. D: Frank Lloyd. DRA 132m. v

Mutiny on the Bounty 1962 ★★★½ Howard is low-key as Captain Bligh and Brando an offbeat Fletcher Christian in this remake of definitive 1935 film. Beautiful cinematography compensates for slow pacing. Five Oscar nominations, including Best Picture. C: Marlon Brando, Trevor Howard, Richard Harris, Hugh Griffith, Tarita. D: Lewis Milestone. DRA 177m. V

Mutiny on the Western Front Australian ★★★½ Exploration of a little-known episode in WWI, the rebellion by 300,000 Australian and New Zealander volunteers who suffered disproportionately high casualties thanks to incompetence by British and French generals. DOC 90m. V

My American Cousin 1986 Canadian ★★★½ In late 1950s, a summer visit by a charismatic cousin from California brings bittersweet joy to a young Canadian girl. Well-played, heartfelt coming of age story. Sequel: *American Boyfriends.* C: Margaret Langrick, John Wildman, Richard Donat, Jane Mortifee. D: Sandy Wilson. DRA [PG] 94m. V

My Beautiful Laundrette 1985 British ★★★★ Ambitious, young Pakistani immigrant (Warnecke) who runs a laundromat with English lover Day-Lewis, copes with prejudice from both whites and his own people. A stinging political and social satire full of unexpected moments. C: Saeed Jaffrey, Roshan Seth, Daniel Day-Lewis, Gordon Warnecke, Shirley Anne Field. D: Stephen Frears. DRA [R] 94m. V

My Best Friend Is a Vampire 1988 ★★ Knockoff of *Teen Wolf* formula involves high school teenager who has more than the usual amount of adolescent adjustments to cope with after he is bitten by a vampire. Valiant cast. C: Robert Sean Leonard, Evan Mirand, Cheryl Pollak, Rene Auberjonois, Cecilia Peck, David Warner. D: Jimmy Huston. COM [PG] 87m. V

My Best Friend's Girl 1984 French ★★★ Love triangle involves ladies' man (Lhermitte), his current girlfriend (Huppert), and his shy buddy (Coluche). Light farce looks good. C: Coluche Isabelle Huppert, Thierry Lhermitte. D: Bertrand Blier. COM 99m. V

My Bloody Valentine 1981 Canadian ★★½ A pick-ax-wielding murderer visits the small town of Valentine Bluffs on Valentine's night. One of the uglier Halloween-inspired slasher movies. C: Paul Kelman, Lori Hallier, Neil Affleck. D: George Mihalka. HOR [R] 91m. V

My Blue Heaven 1950 ★★★½ Dailey and Grable are showbiz spouses who want to be adoptive parents. Softball dramatics with plenty of music. C: Betty Grable, Dan Dailey, David Wayne, Jane Wyatt, Mitzi Gaynor, Una Merkel. D: Henry Koster. MUS 96m.

My Blue Heaven 1990 ★★★½ A NYC mob informer (Martin) in the FBI's witness protection program is relocated to sunny California, where he's watched over by a Joe Friday-like agent (Moranis). Mildly entertaining, mismatched partners shtick. C: Steve Martin, Rick Moranis, Joan Cusack, Melanie Mayron, Bill Irwin, Carol Kane, William Hickey. D: Herbert Ross. COM [PG-13] 96m. V

My Body, My Child 1982 ★★★★ Ambitious TV movie about abortion, with Redgrave delivering a powerful performance as a pregnant woman who may be carrying a deformed child. Strong support from Albertson, in his last role. C: Vanessa Redgrave, Joseph Campanella, Jack Albertson. D: Marvin J. Chomsky. DRA 100m. TVM

My Bodyguard 1980 ★★★½ New kid in school finds himself the target of a bully, until he hires a tough loner to protect him. Wryly funny, with poignant moments and a "look-at-me" performance by Dillon. Look for Joan Cusack and Jennifer Beals in their debuts. C: Chris Makepeace, Adam Baldwin, Martin Mull, Ruth Gordon, Matt Dillon. D: Tony Bill. DRA [PG] 97m. V

My Boyfriend's Back 1989 ★★★★ Good comedy/drama about a '60s one-hit-wonder singing group, reuniting for a televised comeback. Fine leads make a sparkly appealing threesome. C: Sandy Duncan, Judith Light, Jill Eikenberry. D: Paul Schneider. COM 100m. TVM

My Boyfriend's Back 1993 ★★★ From the grave, that is. He's a zombie, but he's going to take her to the prom just the same. Mild, silly film helped by veteran character actors. (a.k.a. *Johnny Zombie*) C: Tracy Lind, Andrew Lowery. D: Bob Balaban. COM [PG-13] 85m. V

My Breakfast with Blassie 1983 ★★ A crude parody of "My Dinner with Andre," with Kaufman chatting with wrestling champ Blassie about toilets and wrestling with women in a fast-food restaurant. C: Andy Kaufman, Fred Blassie. D: Johnny Legend, Linda Lautrec. COM 60m. V

My Brilliant Career 1979 Australian ★★★★½ A willful young woman chooses education and adventure over love and domesticity, and finds a way to thrive in turn-of-the-century Australia. A visual treat with a heroic central performance by Davis. C: Judy Davis, Sam Neill, Wendy Hughes, Robert Grubb. D: Gillian Armstrong. DRA [G] 101m. V

My Brother Talks to Horses 1946 ★★★ A youngster develops an uncanny ability to communicate with horses, which makes him very popular at the racetrack. Sunny gimmick fades in the home stretch, but amuses long enough. C: Butch Jenkins, Peter Lawford, Beverly Tyler, Edward Arnold, Charlie Ruggles, Spring Byington. D: Fred Zinnemann. COM 93m.

My Brother's Keeper 1949 British ★★★½ Two prisoners escape but are handcuffed together; while on the run, the veteran convict encourages his novice partner to give up criminal life. Standard material boosted by good performances. C: Jack Warner, Jane Hylton, George Cole, Bill Owen, David Tomlinson, Christopher Lee. D: Alfred Roome. DRA 96m.

My Brother's Wedding 1983 ★★★★½ Despite resenting his sibling's upwardly mobile life, a resident of L.A.'s Watts ghetto agrees to be his brother's best man. Powerhouse drama of fraternal rivalry and love, honestly presented. C: Everett Silas, Jessie Holmes, Gaye Shannon-Burnett, Ronnie Bell, Dennis Kemper, Sally Easter. D: Charles Burnett. DRA 115m.

My Champion 1984 ★★★½ An interesting portrait of a marraige between two strong-willed athletes, both marathoners, and how their competitive drives affect them. C: Yoko Shimada, Christopher Mitchum. D: Gwen Arner. DRA 101m. V

My Chauffeur 1986 ★★½ Foreman's troubles with sexist co-workers at limousine service worsen as she excels at her work. Lots of cheap sexual humor and gratuitous female nudity. C: Deborah Foreman, Sam Jones, E.G. Marshall, Sean McClory. D: Daniel Beaird. COM [R] 94m. V

My Childhood 1972 British ★★★★ The first in Douglas' trilogy looks at the world of a British boy living in a rural mining community during WWII, and his relationship with a German POW. Effective drama thrives on the small moments of everyday existence. Followed by *My Ain Folk* and *My Way Home.* C: Stephen Archibald, Hughie Restorick, Jean Taylor-Smith, Karl Fieseler. D: Bill Douglas. DRA 50m.

My Cousin Rachel 1952 ★★★★½ A young householder (Burton) falls in love with his mysterious cousin (de Havilland) while trying to prove that she is a murderess. Atmospheric, romantic mystery makes effective use of settings and perfectly cast leads. Fine adaptation of Daphne du Maurier novel. C: Olivia de Havilland, Richard Burton, Audrey Dalton, John Sutton, Ronald Squire. D: Henry Koster. CRI 98m.

My Cousin Vinny 1992 ★★★½ Good vehicle for Pesci as inexperienced Brooklyn lawyer who ventures to Southern town to defend a young relative on a murder rap. Overlong but often funny farce with fine comic performances, particularly Tomei's witty, Oscar-winning turn as Pesci's self-possessed girlfriend. C: Joe Pesci, Ralph Macchio, Marisa Tomei, Mitchell Whitfield, Fred Gwynne, Austin Pendleton. D: Jonathan Lynn. COM [R] 120m. V

My Darling Clementine 1946 ★★★★★ A beautiful, moving folk epic and director John Ford's distinguished contribution to oft-filmed story of Wyatt Earp (Fonda) tackling vicious Clanton clan with aid of tubercular Doc Holliday (Mature). Fonda is topnotch and Mature never better. Paradigmatic Western classic of friendship and community a tapestry of action, gentle humor, lustrous cinematography, and memorable characterizations. C: Henry Fonda, Linda Darnell, Victor Mature, Walter Brennan, Cathy Downs, Tim Holt, Ward Bond, Alan Mowbray, John Ireland. D: John Ford. WST 97m. V

My Daughter Joy 1950 *See* **Operation X**

My Dear Secretary 1948 ★★★½ Romantic sparring of a novelist (Douglas) and secretary turned best-selling author (Day). Cute comedy, almost stolen by Wynn. C: Laraine Day, Kirk Douglas, Keenan Wynn, Helen Walker, Rudy Vallee. D: Charles Martin. COM 94m. V

My Demon Lover 1987 ★★★ Anytime poor Valentine is turned on by a woman he literally turns into a monster. Little is the girlfriend who finds she's once more fallen for a problem guy. Cute and insubstantial. C: Scott Valentine, Michelle Little, Arnold Johnson, Gina Gallego, Robert Trebor. D: Charles Loventhal. COM [PG-13] 90m. V

My Dinner with Andre 1981 ★★★★ A couple of guys sitting around a dinner table and talking—yet their chat (about subjects great and small) is fascinating. Playing themselves, Shawn (an actor/playwright) and Gregory (a director), are unlikely heroes who make this wide-ranging conversation stimulating. C: Andre Gregory, Wallace Shawn. D: Louis Malle. DRA [PG] 110m. V

My Dog Shep 1946 ★★★ An orphan runs away with his dog, not knowing that he is heir to a sizable fortune. C: Tom Neal, William Farnum, Al St. John, Grady Sutton. D: Ford Beebe. FAM/ACT 70m. V

My Dog the Thief 1969 ★★★ Cute but kleptomaniacal St. Bernard swipes diamond necklace from tough guys, landing his recently acquired owner in hot water. Good, clean family fun. C: Dwayne Hickman, Mary Ann Mobley, Joe Flynn, Elsa Lanchester. D: Robert Stevenson. COM 88m. V

My Dream Is Yours 1949 ★★★½ Show business entrepreneur (Carson) turns an ingenue (Day) into a big-time radio star. Backstage musical-comedy oddly parallels Day's own story; it benefits from lively direction and a terrific dream sequence featuring cartoon star Bugs Bunny. Very enjoyable. C: Jack Carson, Doris Day, Lee Bowman, Adolphe Menjou, Eve Arden, S.Z. Sakall, Franklin Pangborn. D: Michael Curtiz. MUS 101m. V

My Fair Lady 1964 ★★★★★ Landmark Lerner and Loewe musicalization of Shaw's *Pygmalion* comes to screen with almost everything intact, including Harrison (Oscar for Best Actor) as the linguistics expert who bets he can turn Cockney drudge (Hepburn) into a society lady. Lavish film was wildly successful, winning eight Oscars, including Best Picture, Cinematography, Costumes, and Score. C: Rex Harrison, Audrey Hepburn, Stanley Holloway, Wilfrid Hyde-White, Gladys Cooper, Jeremy Brett, Theodore Bikel, Henry Daniell, Mona Washbourne, Isobel Elsom. D: George Cukor. MUS [G] 171m. V

My Family Treasure 1993 ★★ Family film about Stone's trip to find her roots in Russia, in search of an heirloom worth a fortune. C: Dee Wallace Stone, Theodore Bikel, Alex Vincent, Bitty Schram. D: Rolfe Kanefsky. DRA 95m. v

My Father, the Hero 1994 ★★ Silly comedy about a 14-year-old compulsive liar (Heigi), who gets her father (Depardieu) into scrapes while on vacation, by depicting him as her lover, a secret agent. C: Gerard Depardieu, Katherine Heigi, Dalton James, Lauren Hutton, Faith Prince. D: Steve Minor. COM [PG] v

My Father's Glory 1990 French ★★★★ Life in the French countryside, circa 1905, as seen through young boy's eyes. Based on Marcel Pagnol's memoirs; beautiful locations, fine acting highlight rambling narrative. Robert also directed follow-up, *My Mother's Castle.* C: Philippe Caubere, Nathalie Roussel, Didier Pain, Therese Liotard, Julien Caimaca. D: Yves Robert. DRA [G] 110m. v

My Favorite Blonde 1942 ★★★★ Funny espionage comedy with Hope and trained penguin used by spy (Carroll) to transport secret messages. Star in good form here. C: Bob Hope, Madeleine Carroll, Gale Sondergaard, George Zucco. D: Sidney Lanfield. COM 78m. v

My Favorite Brunette 1947 ★★★★ A baby photographer (Hope) falls for Lamour, becomes involved in murder, and gets pursued by gangsters (Lorre and Chaney). Clever spoof of detective films, as Hope glides through troubles with hilarious aplomb. Snappy Hope frolic, great cast. C: Bob Hope, Dorothy Lamour, Peter Lorre, Lon Chaney, Jr., John Hoyt. D: Elliott Nugent. COM 87m. v

My Favorite Spy 1951 ★★★★ U.S. spy chief sends comedian, a look-alike for recently murdered agent, to Tangiers to complete espionage mission. Hilarious Hope hijinks, helped by luminous Lamarr. Have fun. C: Bob Hope, Hedy Lamarr, Francis L. Sullivan, Mike Mazurki, John Archer, Iris Adrian, Arnold Moss. D: Norman McLeod. COM 93m.

My Favorite Wife 1940 ★★★★½ Missing woman (Dunne) returns on the day her husband (Grant) remarries; his embarrassment turns to jealousy when he finds she was shipwrecked with a handsome castaway companion (Scott). Solid gold romantic comedy with 21-carat pairing of Grant and Dunne. C: Cary Grant, Irene Dunne, Gail Patrick, Randolph Scott, Scotty Beckett, Donald MacBride. D: Garson Kanin. COM 88m. v

My Favorite Year 1982 ★★★★ O'Toole (in a delightfully hammy performance) stars as Errol Flynn-like star making a guest appearance on a Sid Caesar-like comedy show in the '50s. Wry, sometimes rambunctious comedy, with Linn-Baker appealing as young writer charged with keeping drunken star sober. Solid supporting performances, especially from Bologna and Kazan. Later adapted into Broadway musical. C: Peter O'Toole, Mark Linn-Baker, Jessica Harper, Joseph Bologna, Bill Macy, Lainie Kazan. D: Richard Benjamin. COM [PG] 92m. v

My First Wife 1984 Australian ★★★★ Tightly focused drama of selfish, work-obsessed disc jockey whose world crumbles when his neglected wife has an affair. Intense, honest, finely acted film. C: John Hargreaves, Wendy Hughes, Lucy Angwin, Anna Jemison. D: Paul Cox. DRA 89m. v

My Foolish Heart 1949 ★★★★ Ideal Hayward showcase. Woman gets pregnant by WWII recruit but doesn't tell him about it; when he's killed she tries to marry quickly to give child a father. Naturalistically handled suds, aided by famous title song and standout support from Keith, Landis. C: Dana Andrews, Susan Hayward, Kent Smith, Lois Wheeler, Jessie Royce Landis, Robert Keith, Gigi Perreau. D: Mark Robson. DRA 98m.

My Forbidden Past 1951 ★★★½ Shady New Orleans woman connives to destroy the marriage of physician who doesn't return her love. Irregularly paced and stodgy period piece highlighted by vigorous performances. C: Robert Mitchum, Ava Gardner, Melvyn Douglas, Janis Carter. D: Robert Stevenson. DRA 81m. v

My Friend Flicka 1943 ★★★★ Warm adaptation of Mary O'Hara novel involves a young man who raises feeble colt despite father's warning that wild horses cannot be tamed. Classic horse story makes for good family viewing. Followed by sequel, *Thunderhead, Son of Flicka.* C: Roddy McDowall, Preston Foster, Rita Johnson, Jeff Corey, James Bell. D: Harold Schuster. DRA 89m. v

My Friend Irma 1949 ★★★½ A dim-witted young woman gets into various misadventures in the Big Apple. Okay comedy from the hit radio series ostensibly stars Wilson, but was stolen by the uproarious film debut of Martin and Lewis. Inspired a sequel, *My Friend Irma Goes West*, and a TV series. C: Marie Wilson, John Lund, Diana Lynn, Dean Martin, Jerry Lewis. D: George Marshall. COM 103m. v

My Friend Irma Goes West 1950 ★★★ Slapdash sequel to popular *My Friend Irma* has the friends (Wilson and Lynn) on a journey to Las Vegas and Hollywood. Supporting duo of Martin and Lewis are thrust to the fore, amid several songs and modest gags. C: John Lund, Marie Wilson, Dean Martin, Jerry Lewis, Corinne Calvet, Diana Lynn, Lloyd Corrigan, Donald Porter, Kenneth Tobey. D: Hal Walker. COM 90m.

My Gal Loves Music 1944 ★★★½ Medicine show con artist passes off assistant as 14-year-old. After she wins singing contest and goes to NYC, trouble brews when bandleader falls for the "kid." Has requisite light touch, and amusing Catlett leads good cast. C: Bob Crosby, Alan Mowbray, Grace McDonald, Betty Kean. D: Edward Lilley. COM 60m.

My Gal Sal 1942 ★★★★ Mature's a songwriter who falls for Hayworth in this love story (set during the Gay '90s), enlivened by colorful production and some fine tunes. Based on Theodore Dreiser's book *My Brother Paul.* C: Rita Hayworth, Victor Mature, John Sutton, Carole Landis, James Gleason, Phil Silvers, Mona Maris, Walter Catlett. D: Irving Cummings. MUS 103m.

My Geisha 1962 ★★★ *I Love Lucy* fans will recognize plot of movie director's wife (MacLaine) trying to convince her husband she's just right for his next movie. Funny at times, though it's a long haul. C: Shirley MacLaine, Yves Montand, Edward G. Robinson, Robert Cummings, Yoko Tani. D: Jack Cardiff. COM 120m. V

My Girl 1991 ★★★½ A 12-year-old girl (Chlumsky) tries to bond with widowed father (Aykroyd) and his girlfriend (Curtis). Honest and touching coming-of-age story. Strong screen debut from Chlumsky and Culkin, as her pal, provides nice support. Note: An onscreen death may upset younger viewers. C: Dan Aykroyd, Jamie Lee Curtis, Macaulay Culkin, Anna Chlumsky, Richard Masur, Griffin Dunne. D: Howard Zieff. COM [PG] 102m. V

My Girl Tisa 1948 ★★★★ Wonderful period piece, set at the turn of the century, deals with the attempts of an immigrant (Palmer) to bring her father over from the home country and aid her boyfriend in his quest to become a lawyer. C: Lilli Palmer, Sam Wanamaker, Akim Tamiroff, Alan Hale, Hugo Haas, Stella Adler. D: Elliott Nugent. DRA 95m. V

My Girl 2 1994 ★★★★ Suprisingly earnest sequel in which Chlumsky decides to find out more about her long-dead mother, and finds first romance with O'Brien. In some ways better than the original. C: Anna Chlumsky, Dan Ackroyd, Jamie Lee Curtis, Austin O'Brien, Richard Masur, Christine Ebersole. D: Howard Zieff. FAM/DRA [PG] 99m. V

My Grandpa Is a Vampire 1994 ★★★ A preteen learns that his grandfather is of the undead variety. Low-brow fun, most of it supplied by "Grampa Munster" Lewis. C: Al Louis, Justin Gocke, Milan Borich, Noel Appleby, Pat Ezison. D: David Blyth. HOR [PG] 90m. V

My Gun Is Quick 1957 ★★ Mike Hammer mystery, with Bray as the detective out to nail a killer. Weak adaptation of Mickey Spillane's hard-boiled novel. C: Phil Victor, Robert Bray, Whitney Blake, Pamela Duncan, Donald Randolph. D: George White. CRI 88m.

My Hero 1 1952 ★★★★ Four funny episodes from Bob Cummings series, including "The Photographer," "Surprise Party," "Oil Land," and "Horsin" Around." C: Robert Cummings, Julie Bishop. COM 100m. V

My Heroes Have Always Been Cowboys 1991 ★★★½ Rodeo star returns home to recover from injuries and rekindle relations with father. Easygoing but predictable, though actual rodeo footage is action-packed. C: Scott Glenn, Kate Capshaw, Ben Johnson, Balthazar Getty, Tess Harper, Gary Busey, Mickey Rooney, Clarence Williams III. D: Stuart Rosenberg. DRA [PG] 106m. V

My Hobo 1963 Japanese ★★★½ A hobo (Kobayashi) who keeps his savings taped to his side, falls for a beggar who passes herself off as A-bomb victim. She steals his money, but all ends well when she invests it successfully. Amusing, realistic Japanese comedy features attractive scenery. C: Keiju Kobayashi, Hideko Takamine, Norihei Miki. D: Zenzo Matsuyama. COM 98m.

My Kidnapper, My Love 1980 ★★★½ Sordid title masks a generally unexploitative movie about the relationship that develops between newsstand owner Stacy and runaway O'Connor in New Orleans. Likable leads help. C: James Stacy, Mickey Rooney, Glynnis O'Connor. D: Sam Wanamaker. DRA 104m. TVM

My Learned Friend 1943 ★★★★ A forger (Johns) vows revenge on those who sent him to prison, including his incompetent lawyer (Hay) and pal (Hulbert). Hay's last film is a well-scripted, often hilarious black comedy, with memorable final scramble across Big Ben. Johns steals it as crazed killer. C: Will Hay, Claude Hulbert, Mervyn Johns. D: Will Hay, Basil Dearden. COM 74m.

My Left Foot 1989 Irish ★★★★½ Day-Lewis won a well-deserved Oscar playing Irish poet Christy Brown, who overcame cerebral palsy to become a noted painter and writer. Gutsy, poignant film biography filled with humor and heart. Best Supporting Actress Oscar went to Fricker for her solid, emotional performance as Brown's mother, but the entire supporting cast (particularly O'Conor as young Brown) is stupendous. C: Daniel Day-Lewis, Brenda Fricker, Ray McAnally, Hugh O'Conor, Fiona Shaw, Cyril Cusack. D: Jim Sheridan. DRA [R] 103m. V

My Life 1993 ★★★½ Multiple-hankie tearjerker as Keaton, dying of cancer, decides to commit his life to videotape for his unborn son. Keaton is effectively subdued. C: Michael Keaton, Nicole Kidman, Bradley Whitford, Queen Latifah, Michael Constantine, Rebecca Shull, Mark Lowenthal. D: Bruce Joel Rubin. DRA 116m. V

My Life As a Dog 1987 Swedish ★★★★ A 12-year-old troublemaker is sent off to live with country relatives; there he learns about life via his own budding adolescence. A wonderfully compelling film, funny and sad, with an excellent cast, especially young Glanzelius. C: Anton Glanzelius, Tomas von Brömssen, Anki Liden. D: Lasse Hallström. DRA [PG-13] 101m. V

My Life to Live 1962 French ★★★★ Both an exploration into the life of prostitute and a celebration of actress Karina (director Godard's wife at the time), this as an observant, intriguing (if dated) look at relationships, presented in documentary fashion. C: Anna Karina, Sady Rebbot, Andre S. Labarthe. D: Jean-Luc Godard. DRA 85m. V

My Life with Caroline 1941 ★★★½ Innocuous comedy coasts by on light-hearted approach and an appealing performance by Colman as a husband who is certain his wife (Lee) is involved with another man. C: Ronald Colman, Anna Lee, Charles Winninger, Reginald Gardiner, Gilbert Roland. D: Lewis Milestone. COM 81m.

My Little Chickadee 1940 ★★★½ Sporadically funny Wild West pairing of Fields and West in a marriage of convenience should have been better, but saloon scenes with W.C. and Mae make it worth catching. Stars co-wrote screenplay, but reportedly did not get along. C: Mae West, W.C. Fields, Joseph Calleia, Dick Foran, Margaret Hamilton, Donald Meek. D: Edward Cline. COM 91m. V

My Little Pony—The Movie 1986 ★★ Cartoon tale of magical ponies who confront a trio of witches bent on destroying them. Despite celebrity voices, this is a poorly animated, simplisticly plotted, and blatantly sexist feature. Voices of Danny DeVito, Madeleine Kahn, Cloris Leachman, Rhea Perlman, Tony Randall. D: Michael Joens. FAM/DRA [G] 87m. V

My Love Came Back 1940 ★★★½ Light romantic comedy about violinist (de Havilland) whose scholarship award raises eyebrows about her relationship to her patron. De Havilland is charming, as is the film, unafraid of its own schmaltz. Has good cast and a lovely waltz montage. C: Olivia de Havilland, Jeffrey Lynn, Eddie Albert, Jane Wyman, Charles Winninger, Spring Byington, Grant Mitchell. D: Curtis Bernhardt. COM 81m.

My Love for Yours 1939 *See* **Honeymoon in Bali**

My Love Letters 1983 *See* **Love Letters**

My Lucky Star 1938 ★★★½ A department store clerk goes to college and falls for store owner's son. Enjoyably silly ice skating musical with fun-loving cast. The "Alice in Wonderland" ice ballet is especially entertaining. C: Sonja Henie, Richard Greene, Cesar Romero, Buddy Ebsen. D: Roy Del Ruth. MUS 90m. V

My Man 1928 ★★★½ Costume shop worker hits it big as singing star. Static part-talkie, a curio treat for Brice fans. Grab bag of songs and comedy includes some of her most famous routines. C: Fannie Brice, Guinn "Big Boy" Williams, Edna Murphy. D: Archie Mayo. COM 99m.

My Man Adam 1986 ★★★ Pizza deliverer Sbarge falls for Hannah (Daryl's real-life sister) and accidentally gets tangled up with a murder. Appealing leads in routine comedy. C: Raphael Sbarge, Page Hannah, Veronica Cartwright, Dave Thomas. D: Roger L. Simon. COM [R] 84m. V

My Man and I 1952 ★★½ Whacked-out melodrama as a Mexican handyman (Montalban), in love with a suicidal taxi-dancer, must contend with his nasty employer and love-starved wife. Likable cast tries hard to put over lumpy script which is lurid and dull at the same time. C: Shelley Winters, Ricardo Montalban, Wendell Corey, Claire Trevor. D: William Wellman. DRA 99m.

My Man Godfrey 1936 ★★★★★ Screwball comedy jewel about wealthy eccentrics hiring a tramp (Powell) as butler, only to discover that appearances can be deceiving. Lombard's dizzy heiress is one of her best creations, while Patrick scores as evil sister. Sparkling script by Morrie Ryskind and Eric Hatch from latter's novel. Beware the 1957 remake. C: William Powell, Carole Lombard, Gail Patrick, Eugene Pallette, Alice Brady, Mischa Auer, Franklin Pangborn. D: Gregory La Cava. COM 95m. V

My Man Godfrey 1957 ★★★ Daffy heiress (Allyson) gets her comeuppance, thanks to an unusual butler (Niven). Misguided update of the 1936 Depression comedy; the story's zing has gone out the window. C: June Allyson, David Niven, Martha Hyer, Jessie Royce Landis. D: Henry Koster. COM 92m. V

My Margo 1969 Israeli ★★★½ A young Israeli woman (Finklestein), who must care for her brothers, sisters and drunken father, has a love affair. Slim plot is basically soap opera, but it offers some good, detailed insights into daily life in Jerusalem. Finklstein is very sensitive and appealing. (a.k.a. *Love in Jerusalem*) C: Levana Finklstein, Avner Hizkyahu, Oded Teomi, Beracha Ne'eman. D: Menahem Golan. DRA 90m.

My Michael 1975 Isreali ★★★ Disappointing but still interesting film adaptation of the Amos Oz novel, about a young woman whose marraige begins to break apart when her fantasy life becomes more interesting than her real one. C: Efrat Lavie, Oded Kotler. D: Dan Wolman. DRA 95m. V

My Mom's Werewolf 1988 ★★★ Blakely starts a romance with a handsome stranger, then odd things happen by the light of a full moon. Silly fun. C: Susan Blakely, John Saxon, John Schuck, Atrina Caspary, Ruth Buzzi, Marcia Wallace, Marilyn McCoo. D: Michael Fischa. COM [PG] 90m. V

My Mother's Castle 1991 French ★★★★½ Follow-up to *My Father's Glory* continues exploration of early 20th-century France through eyes of a small boy on visits to the Provençal countryside with his family. Beautifully told story, with sparkling performances. Based on memoirs of Marcel Pagnol. C: Julien Caimaca, Philippe Caubere, Nathalie

Roussel, Didier Pain, Therese Liotard. D: Yves Robert. DRA [PG] 98m. v

My Name Is Barbra 1965 ★★★★½ Streisand's memorable first TV special, including 23 songs sung exceptionally well. A television milestone. C: Barbra Streisand. D: Dwight Hemion. MUS 60m. v

My Name is Bill W. 1989 ★★★★★ True story of the beginnings of Alcholics Anonymous, focusing on the friendship of Bill Wilson (Woods) and Dr. Robert Smith (Garner), co-founders of AA. Marvelous performances, uplifting drama. One of the best TV movies in years. C: James Woods, James Garner, JoBeth Williams, Fritz Weaver, Gary Sinise. D: Daniel Petrie. DRA 100m. TVM v

My Name Is Ivan 1962 Russian ★★★★ After his family is brutally killed by the Nazis, a young boy spies for the Soviet army behind enemy lines in WWII. Expertly realized and emotionally powerful condemnation of horrors of war. First film by acclaimed Russian director Tarkovsky. (a.k.a. *The Youngest Spy*) C: Kolya Burlaiev, Valentin Zubkov, Ye Zharikov. D: Andrei Tarkovsky. DRA 84m. v

My Name Is Julia Ross 1945 ★★★★ Modestly budgeted but gripping Gothic noir. Unsuspecting woman (Foch) responds to a job ad and winds up imprisoned by sinister family who try to claim she's someone else. Clever and creepy, with an excellent performance by Foch. C: Nina Foch, Dame May Whitty, George Macready, Roland Varno, Anita Bolster, Doris Lloyd. D: Joseph H. Lewis. DRA 65m.

My Name Is Nobody 1974 Italian ★★★½ Team-up of Hill as an enthusiastic fan and his idol, an aging gunman (Fonda) plays out as a spoof of genre conventions and homage to the *Man With No Name* films. Affectionate, if but overlong. Look fast for Western director Sam Peckinpah's inventive cameo—as a name on a cemetary cross. C: Henry Fonda, Terence Hill, Leo Gordon, R. G. Armstrong, Geoffrey Lewis. D: Tonino Valerii. WST 115m. v

My Neighbor Totoro 1988 Japanese ★★★½ Two sisters with an ailing mother are befriended by magical forest creatures, led by rabbit-like Totoro. Charming, gentle, beautifully animated tale for the kids. Voices of Lisa Michaelson, Cheryl Chase. D: Hayao Miyazaki. FAM/DRA [G] 86m. v

My New Gun 1992 ★★★½ Offbeat comedy finds bored housewife Lane dealing with teenaged suitor, while wondering what to do with.38 caliber gun her husband insists on buying her. Straitlaced humor nicely played by good cast. C: Diane Lane, James LeGros, Stephen Collins, Tess Harper, Bruce Altman. D: Stacy Cochran. COM [R] 99m. v

My New Partner 1984 French ★★★½ A cynical, sleazy veteran cop must cope with a sexy, naive, squeaky-clean rookie. Unoriginal but easy to take, sometimes highly amusing. Noiret is excellent and Lhermitte quite appealing. C: Philippe Noiret, Thierry Lhermitte, Regine. D: Claude Zidi. COM [R] 106m. v

My Night at Maud's 1969 French ★★★★ Rohmer's third in his "Six Moral Tales" is a portrait of a straitlaced guy tempted by a less inhibited woman. Subtle, affecting, and beautifully photographed in b&w. C: Jean-Louis Trintignant, Francoise Fabian, Marie-Christine Barrault. D: Eric Rohmer. DRA [PG] 105m. v

My Old Man 1979 ★★★½ Remake of *Under My Skin* adapts Hemingway short story about teenager (McNichol) who helps out her father, small-time horse trainer Oates. Amiable, if uncompelling story. C: Kristy McNichol, Warren Oates, Eileen Brennan, Mark Arnold. D: John Erman. DRA 102m. TVM v

My Old Man's Place 1972 ★★★½ Three Vietnam buddies return home together only to end up in a violent confrontation. Good ensemble of young character actors gives story a sense of immediacy, despite a certain predictability (a.k.a. *Glory Boy*) C: Mitchell Ryan, Arthur Kennedy, William Devane, Michael Moriarty. D: Edwin Sherin. DRA [R] 93m. v

My Other Husband 1985 French ★★★★ Sweetly funny comedy-drama about a woman who juggles two husbands, two families, and two households in Paris. Nicely directed by the underrated Lautner, with a charming performance by Miou-Miou. C: Miou-Miou, Rachid Ferrahe, Roger Hanin, Eddy Mitchell. D: Georges Lautner. DRA 110m.

My Own Private Idaho 1992 ★★★★ Melancholy comedy about friendship between two young male prostitutes in Portland, Oregon-one the mayor's son, the other a vulnerable drifter. Van Sant's attempts to incorporate dialog from Shakespeare's *Henry IV* are less than successful but Phoenix and Reeves hold this together. Black comedy, not for all tastes. C: River Phoenix, Keanu Reeves, James Russo, William Richert, Grace Zabriskie. D: Gus Van Sant. DRA [R] 105m. v

My Pal, the King 1932 ★★★½ Young foreign monarch (Rooney) runs away, and pals up with circus hero (Mix), who comes in handy when nasty prime minister is up to no good. Enjoyable, good-humored Western; something different for cowboy Mix. C: Tom Mix, Mickey Rooney, Paul Hurst, Noel Francis. D: Kurt Neumann. WST 60m.

My Pal Trigger 1946 ★★★★½ Perhaps the definitive Roy Rogers Western. The cowboy hero is unjustly branded a horse thief and he has to bring the real villain (Holt) to justice. Story includes the birth of Roy's horse, racewinner Trigger. First-rate B-Western, with excellent scripting, acting, direction. C: Roy Rogers, Jack Holt. D: Frank McDonald. WST v

My Pal, Wolf 1944 ★★★½ A little girl (Moffett) finds an Alsatian abandoned in a well, and then petitions to keep him when it turns out he's a valuable Army dog. The adorable Moffett is very touching; good supporting adults and restrained direction help stave off sappiness in this tidy girl-and-her-dog story. C: Sharyn Moffett, Jill Esmond, Una O'Connor, George Cleveland. D: Alfred Werker. FAM/DRA 75m.

My Past 1931 ★★★½ Two business partners, one considerably older than the other, both fall for a divorced young actress. Fairly adult soap opera, risqué in that pre-Production Code era way; acting is very good all around, though Lyons and Stone outshine Daniels. C: Bebe Daniels, Ben Lyon, Lewis Stone, Joan Blondell. D: Roy Del Ruth. DRA 83m.

My Pleasure Is My Business 1974 Canadian ★★ Xaviera Hollander, the original "Happy Hooker," stars in a version of her own life story. Sarah Bernhardt she ain't. C: Xaviera Hollander, Henry Ramer, Colin Fox, Kenneth Lynch, Jayne Eastwood. D: Al Waxman. COM [R] 85m.

My Reputation 1946 ★★★★ A widow (Stanwyck) begins dating again too soon, causing gossip, trials and tribulations. Surprisingly effective soap opera, even today, thanks to a great cast playing with conviction. C: Barbara Stanwyck, George Brent, Lucille Watson, Eve Arden, Warner Anderson. D: Curtis Bernhardt. DRA 94m.

My Samurai 1992 ★★½ A young murder witness (John Kallo) tries to elude a band of killers, with the help of his tae kwan do instructor (Lee). Flimsy, youth-oriented action designed as a showcase for Lee's polished fighting skills. C: Julian Lee, Mako, Bubba Smith, Terry O'Quinn. D: Fred Dresch. ACT [R] 87m. V

My Science Project 1985 ★★ Student finds an alien object and tries to pass it off as science experiment; sudden time warps ensue. Hopper is amusing as the science teacher, but no one (and nothing) else is. C: John Stockwell, Danielle Von Zerneck, Fisher Stevens, Raphael Sbarge, Dennis Hopper. D: Jonathan Beteul. SFI [PG] 94m. V

My Seven Little Sins 1954 French ★★★½ An aging rake shelters a young woman who claims to be child of one of his many affairs; but when six more women soon appear, he knows something's up. Pleasant, mild French farce well tailored to Chevalier's screen persona; he also sings two songs. (a.k.a. *I Have Seven Daughters*) C: Maurice Chevalier, Collette Ripert, Paolo Stoppa, Delia Scala. D: Jean Boyer. COM 98m.

My Side of the Mountain 1969 ★★★★ A 13-year-old boy leaves home to carve out a niche for himself in the mountains. Bikel is folksinger who lends a hand when harsh Canadian winter threatens the boy. Engaging adventure tale for children that adults might enjoy as well. C: Ted Eccles, Theodore Bikel, Tudi Wiggins, Frank Perry. D: James B. Clark. FAM/DRA [G] 100m. V

My Sister Eileen 1942 ★★★★ Two sisters move from Ohio to Greenwich Village and the older sister (Russell) becomes writer of stories about their oddball neighbors and friends. Brisk, funny romantic farce, a real showcase for wisecracking Russell. C: Rosalind Russell, Brian Aherne, Janet Blair, George Tobias, Allyn Joslyn, Elizabeth Patterson, June Havoc. D: Alexander Hall. COM 96m.

My Sister Eileen 1955 ★★★★ Musical version of the popular hit about two Midwestern sisters coping with love and wacky visitors to their apartment in bohemian New York neighborhood. Middling score, but game, high-energy performances and plenty of laughs just the same. Fosse has some great moments. C: Betty Garrett, Janet Leigh, Jack Lemmon, Kurt Kasznar, Dick York, Horace McMahon, Bob Fosse. D: Richard Quine. MUS 108m. V

My Sister, My Love 1978 *See* **Mafu Cage, The**

My Six Convicts 1952 ★★★½ A prison psychiatrist develops a relationship with group of convicts, including a safecracker (Mitchell) given chance to prove himself on the outside and a killer (Morgan) who causes problems. Highly appealing cast and realistic setting make it work. C: Millard Mitchell, Gilbert Roland, John Beal, Marshall Thompson, Alf Kjellin, Henry Morgan, Jay Adler, Regis Toomey, John Marley, Charles Buchinsky. D: Hugo Fregonese. DRA 104m.

My Six Loves 1963 ★★★ A Broadway diva (Reynolds) adopts six orphans. Sweet comedy, but too sticky for the more cynically inclined. C: Debbie Reynolds, Cliff Robertson, David Janssen, Eileen Heckart. D: Gower Champion. COM 101m.

My Son Is a Criminal 1939 ★★★ Retiring cop wants son to follow in footsteps, but he ends up on wrong side of the law. Decent, well acted B-picture. C: Alan Baxter, Jacqueline Wells, Gordon Oliver. D: C.C. Coleman Jr. DRA 59m.

My Son John 1952 ★★ One of the most reactionary pieces of Cold War paranoia ever committed to film. Mom and Dad think junior may be (gasp!) a Communist. Performances are good, with Walker great as an edgy son. C: Helen Hayes, Robert Walker, Dean Jagger, Van Heflin, Frank McHugh, Richard Jaeckel. D: Leo McCarey. DRA 122m.

My Son, My Son 1940 ★★★★ Single-parent novelist spoils ungrateful son, who brings tragedy to his childhood girlfriend and tries to seduce the father's lover. Father and son meet again in WWI as correspondent and soldier. Absorbing saga, with Aherne and Hayward splendid as father and son. C: Madeleine Carroll, Brian Aherne, Louis Hayward, Laraine Day, Henry Hull, Josephine Hutchinson, Scotty Beckett. D: Charles Vidor. DRA 115m.

My Son, the Hero 1963 Italian ★★★ Spectacle set in ancient Thebes, and concerning a king, a thief, and a magic helmet. Thin Italian costumer, usually seen poorly dubbed, has a few big laughs and good surprises. C: Pedro Armendariz, Jacqueline Sassard, Antonella Lualdi, Tanya Lopert. D: Duccio Tessari. ACT 111m.

My Song for You 1935 British ★★★ Woman sneaks into opera house to get her pianist "brother" (actually her fiancé) a job in the orchestra, and becomes involved with a tenor who discovers her deception. Watchable British musical has charm. C: Jan Kiepura, Sonnie Hale, Emlyn Williams. D: Maurice Elvey. MUS 75m.

My Stepmother Is an Alien 1988 ★★½ Scientist Aykroyd unknowingly marries space alien Basinger, who's out to find formula of secret ray to save her home planet. High concept science fiction humor strains audience's suspension of disbelief. C: Dan Aykroyd, Kim Basinger, Jon Lovitz, Alyson Hannigan. D: Richard Benjamin. COM [PG-13] 108m. V

My Sweet Charlie 1969 ★★★★½ Duke is white unwed mother hiding out in abandoned rural cottage and joined by black attorney Freeman, also in trouble. Well-acted and very moving drama of a unique friendship. C: Patty Duke, Al Freeman Jr., Ford Rainey, William Hardy. D: Lamont Johnson. DRA [G] 97m. V

My Sweet Little Village 1986 Czech ★★★½ Truck driver tires of working with lovable but half-witted assistant, asks for new partner, but comes to realize how much he needs his friend. Subplots artfully mixed into warm, insightful, slice-of-life Czech comedy/drama, which also offers pointed critique of government meddling. C: Janos Ban, Marian Labuda, Rudolf Hrusinsky, Petr Cedak, Evzen Jegorov. D: Jiri Menzel. DRA 101m. TVM

My Therapist 1984 ★★ Exploitative comedy about a sex therapist, her clients, and her jealous boyfriend. C: Marilyn Chambers. D: Gary Legon. COM 81m. V

My Tutor 1982 ★★ In order to graduate high school, good-looking rich kid (Lattanzi) undergoes French tutoring from sexy teacher (Kaye) who also imparts a different kind of wisdom to her willing pupil. Dumb, if inoffensive, makeout movie that will delight its intended audience. C: Matt Lattanzi, Caren Kaye, Kevin McCarthy. D: George Bowers. COM [R] 97m. V

My 12 Kung Fu Kicks ★ Liang is forced to unveil his secret weapons, Tan Toi, which the filmmakers claim is the ultimate fighting technique. C: Bruce Liang, Ku Feng, Lee Tung Ming, Hon Kwok Tsai. ACT 90m.

My Twentieth Century 1989 Hungarian ★★★★ Beautiful twins in turn-of-the-century Austro-Hungary choose very different paths in life—one becomes a bonne vivante and the other a bomb-throwing anarchist. Magical visuals and magnificent expressionist style, plus a dazzling performance by Segda as both sisters and their mother. C: Dorotha Segda, Oleg Jankovskij, Paulus Manker, Peter Andorai, Gabor Maté. D: Ildiko Enyedi. DRA 92m. V

My Weakness 1933 ★★★★ Saucy musical about a hotel clerk who pretends to be classy socialite so she can woo upscale gent (Ayres). Has ethereal charm and bizarre strange tunes, including "Gather Lip Rouge While You May'! Imaginative highlights include singing gargoyles." C: Lillian Harvey, Lew Ayres, Charles Butterworth, Harry Langdon. D: David Butler. MUS 72m.

My Wicked, Wicked Ways—The Legend of Errol Flynn 1985 ★★★½ Biography based on movie legend Flynn's ribald memoirs features Regehr as the star in boozing, fighting, and romantic modes. Though fast and loose with facts, energetic cast makes this fun to watch. C: Duncan Regehr, Barbara Hershey, Darren McGavin, Lee Purcell, Hal Linden. D: Don Taylor. DRA 142m. TVM V

My Widow and I 1950 Italian ★★★½ A man pretends to be dead so he and his wife can collect insurance. He poses as a brother-in-law, but must watch his former boss make a play for his wife. Black comedy is a bit too talky but has genuine, if rueful, wit; Miranda and especially De Sica (known primarily as a director) are very good. C: Vittorio De Sica, Isa Miranda. D: Carlo L. Bragaglia. COM 81m.

My Wild Irish Rose 1947 ★★½ Blarney-filled film biography of Irish songwriter Chauncey Olcott, and his romances. Irish folk songs and specialty dance acts are plentiful, but the charm wears off early. C: Dennis Morgan, Andrea King, Arlene Dahl, Alan Hale, George Tobias. D: David Butler. MUS 101m.

My Wonderful Life 1990 ★★ Love spoils a woman's plan to climb the social ladder and remain wealthy and famous in this lighthearted comedy. C: Carol Alt, Elliott Gould, Massimo Venturiello. D: Carlo Vanzina. COM [R] 107m. V

Myra Breckinridge 1970 ★ This turkey for the ages, based on Gore Vidal's sensational novel, stars Welch as a transsexual schemer. Lots of past, present and future stars (including Farrah Fawcett and Tom Selleck in their movie debuts) appear in this hugely tasteless satire. C: Mae West, John Huston, Raquel Welch, Rex Reed, Farrah Fawcett, Grady Sutton, Roger C. Carmel. D: Michael Sarne. DRA [R] 100m. V

Mysterians, The 1959 Japanese ★★★★ Aliens attack Earth to kidnap women to repopulate their planet. Straightfaced sci-fi heroics as only the *Godzilla* team could do them, with impressive visuals. C: Kenji Sahara, Yumi Shirakawa, Akihiko Hirata. D: Inoshiro Honda. SFI 85m. V

Mysteries 1984 Dutch ★★★ A beautiful

woman (Kristel) in a resort town becomes the object of a rich foreigner's (Hauer) obsessive desire. Serious and well acted, but the somewhat confusing dialogue is poorly dubbed. C: Rutger Hauer, Sylvia Kristel, Rita Tushingham. D: Paul de Lussanet. DRA 93m. V

Mysterious Avenger, The 1936 ★★★½ Two ranchers, one the Texas Ranger hero's father, accuse each other of rustling, but a third party's responsible. Fairly well done B-Western, with handsome Starrett quite likable; Roy Rogers and the Sons of the Pioneers make a singing appearance. C: Charles Starrett, Joan Perry, Wheeler Oakman, Roy Rogers. D: David Selman. WST 54m.

Mysterious Desperado, The 1949 ★★★½ Cowpoke hero stands in the way of land grabbers who've framed a ranch heir for murder. Suspenseful, balanced B-Western, well-directed by Selander; script has a welcome dash of humor. C: Tim Holt, Richard Martin, Edward Norris. D: Lesley Selander. WST 61m. V

Mysterious Doctor Satan 1940 ★★★½ Ciannelli is clearly having a lot of fun in the title role of this 15-episode serial, trying to take over the world with an army of robots. C: Eduardo Ciannelli, Robert Wilcox, Ella Neal. D: John English. SFI 250m. V

Mysterious Dr. Fu Manchu, The 1929 ★★★ Evil Asian villain uses woman in a trance to avenge himself on British officer whom he feels was responsible for the death of his wife and son during the Boxer Rebellion. Atmospheric, well-directed early talkie benefits from good cast; be prepared for typically dated ethnic bias. C: Warner Oland, Jean Arthur, Neil Hamilton. D: Rowland V. Lee. DRA 80m.

Mysterious Egypt ★★★ Pyramids to the Sphinx. DOC 60m. V

Mysterious House of Dr. C., The 1976 ★★★½ Uneven but lively adaptation of the ballet, *Coppelia*, as dolls have adventures while locked up in the lab of Slezak, who dreams of being a toreador! With fine dancing and the macabre elements of the original toned down, this offbeat, charming mix of live action and animation will please both kids and dance enthusiasts. C: Walter Slezak, Claudia Corday, Terry Thomas. D: Ted Kneeland. MUS 88m.

Mysterious Intruder 1946 ★★★½ Swedish millionaire sets out to acquire rare records made by opera diva Jenny Lind, and the murders begin. Tight installment of *Whistler* series, a good early effort by showman Castle with notable camerawork, excellent Dix. C: Richard Dix, Nina Vale, Regis Toomey, Pamela Blake, Charles Lane, Helen Mowery, Mike Mazurki. D: William Castle. DRA 61m.

Mysterious Island 1961 British ★★★★ Two men escape from a Confederate prison in a hot-air balloon and wind up on an unknown island with Captain Nemo, fighting giant animals and pirates. Very loosely based on the Jules Verne novel, but exciting and entertaining; Ray Harryhausen's special effects are terrific as always. C: Michael Craig, Joan Greenwood, Michael Callan, Gary Merrill, Herbert Lom. D: Cy Endfield. SFI 101m. V

Mysterious Island of Beautiful Women 1979 ★★½ Men marooned on a tropical island are assailed by a tribe of women who seem to have nothing but bikinis in their wardrobes. Some nice and unusual touches. C: Clint Walker, Peter Lawford, Jayne Kennedy. D: Joseph Pevney. SFI 97m. TVM V

Mysterious Lady, The 1928 ★★★½ Garbo stars in silent feature as Russian agent whom unsuspecting Austrian officer Nagel falls for. Average spy drama elevated by Garbo's ethereal presence. C: Greta Garbo, Conrad Nagel, Gustav von Seyffertitz, Albert Pollet, Edward Connelly. D: Fred Niblo. DRA 96m. V

Mysterious Mr. Moto 1938 ★★★½ Private eye Mr. Moto infiltrates League of Assassins by posing as Devil's Island prisoner. Later, as houseboy for gang members, he helps Scotland Yard foil plot to kill rich tycoon. Fast-paced and clever series entry, with Lorre excellent as the Asian hero. C: Peter Lorre, Henry Wilcoxon, Mary Maguire, Erik Rhodes, Harold Huber, Leon Ames, Forrester Harvey. D: Norman Foster. DRA 62m.

Mysterious Mr. Wong, The 1935 ★★★½ Memorable programmer, with Lugosi implausibly but entertainingly cast as crazed Asian seeking the "12 coins of Confucius," which will make him Chinese ruler. Zesty, deliberately silly, well-made actioner. The torture sequence is a camp classic. C: Bela Lugosi, Wallace Ford, Arline Judge, Fred Warren, Lotus Long, Robert Emmett O'Connor. D: William Nigh. DRA 63m. V

Mysterious Rider, The 1933 ★★★ When villain cheats homesteaders out of deposits they've put down on land claims, a cowpoke rides to the rescue. Average Zane Grey Western features appealing Patrick as female lead. WST V

Mysterious Rider, The 1938 ★★★½ Remake of the 1933 film has homesteaders cheated out of land by villain who has them sign claims in invisible ink. Average, competently directed Western with effective casting. C: Sidney Toler, Russell Hayden, Douglas Drumbrille. D: Lesley Selander. WST 72m. V

Mysterious Satellite, The 1956 Japanese ★★★½ The Pairans, who have one eye and look like hormonally developed starfish, disguise themselves as humans to ask for help in exploding burning planet hurtling toward Earth. Decently scripted Japanese sci-fi flick, is unusual in that the aliens aren't enemies. (a.k.a. *The Cosmic Man Appears in Tokyo*; *Space Men Appear in Tokyo*; *Warning from Space*; and *Unknown Satellite Over Tokyo*) C:

Toyomi Karita, Keizo Kawasaki, Isao Yamagata. D: Koji Shima. SFI 87m. v

Mysterious Two 1982 ★★★ Two aliens try to get mankind to send emissaries into space with them. C: John Forsythe, Noah Beery, Vic Tayback, Priscilla Pointer, James Stephens, Robert Englund, Karen Werner, Robert Pine. D: Gary A. Sherman. SFI 97m. TVM v

Mystery Date 1991 ★★★½ Shy young man (Hawke) gets dream date, only to be chased by crooks because of a corpse his brother stuffs in car trunk. Undeniably different spin on teen movie formulas sports some sick moments, but can't sustain black comedy levels throughout. C: Ethan Hawke, Teri Polo, Brian McNamara, Fisher Stevens, B.D. Wong. D: Jonathan Wacks. COM [PG-13] 98m. v

Mystery in Mexico 1948 ★★★ An insurance company investigator searches for missing colleague and finds crime ring. Exciting use of Mexican locations, and Cortez is good as the heavy. C: William Lundigan, Jacqueline White, Ricardo Cortez, Tony Barrett, Jacqueline Dalya, Walter Reed. D: Robert Wise. DRA 66m.

Mystery Island 1981 ★★★½ Nice family film about boys who discover a seemingly abandoned island, not knowing that a retired pirate is there. FAM/ACT 75m.

Mystery Lake 1953 ★★★ Stick with Arne Sucksdorff's nature films. A naturalist (Fenneman—Groucho's *You Bet Your Life* announcer) is unable to find animals at a wild-life reserve until a local woman helps out. Ventriloquist Bergen, sans dummies, is appealing, but dull leads detract from fine documentary footage of animals. C: George Fenneman, Gloria McGough, Edgar Bergen. D: Larry Lansburgh. DRA 64m.

Mystery Liner 1934 ★★★½ Well-spun poverty-row production, as ship with mad captain carries radio-controlled attack device. The bodies pile up, and plot twists take over as identities of killer and detective switch. Don't worry, story ties up well. C: Noah Beery, Astrid Allyn, Cornelius Keefe, Gustav von Seuffertotz, Edwin Maxwell, Ralph Lewis, Zeffie Tilbury. D: William Nigh. DRA 62m. v

Mystery Man, The 1935 ★★★½ After solving a mystery, a Chicago reporter gets a bonus. Celebrating in a big way, he wakes up in St. Louis and winds up solving another crime with a local woman (Doyle). Deliberately modest B-film starts slowly but gains momentum, with Armstrong and Doyle an amusingly punchy pair. C: Robert Armstrong, Maxine Doyle, Henry Kolker. D: Ray McCarey. CRI 65m. v

Mystery Mansion 1983 ★★ Children's film about girl living in Victorian mansion where mysteries revolve around her father, escaped convicts, and dreams. Muddled plot results in a boring film. C: Dallas McKennon, Greg Wynne, Jane Ferguson. D: David E. Jackson. FAM/DRA [PG] 95m. v

Mystery Mountain 1934 ★★ A detective seeks to track down a railroad vigilante. C: Ken Maynard, Sid Saylor. D: Otto Brower. ACT 240m. v

Mystery of Alexina, The 1985 ★★★ Woman teacher in provincial 19th-century France falls for female colleague and is revealed to be a hermaphrodite. Provocative drama based on an actual case. Vuillemin, whose sex is not given, is fine but when all is said and done, movie sheds little light. C: Vuillemin, Valerie Stroh. D: Rene Feret. DRA 84m. v

Mystery of Edwin Drood, The 1935 ★★★★ Atmospheric thriller, adapted from Charles Dickens' unfinished novel, stars Rains as an opium-addicted choirmaster who lusts after his nephew's fiancee. A fine, spine-tingling showcase for Rains. Remade in 1993. C: Claude Rains, Heather Angel, David Manners. D: Stuart Walker. CRI 87m.

Mystery of Edwin Drood, The 1993 British ★★★★ Opium-addicted choirmaster, in love with nephew's fiancée, kills young relative and frames another man, who disguises himself as elderly villager to expose truth. Handsomely made period thriller adds satisfactory resolution to Dickens' unfinished last novel. C: Robert Powell, Michelle Evans, Jonathan Phillips, Rupert Rainsford, Finty Williams, Peter Pacey, Nanette Newman, Freddie Jones, Gemma Craven, Rosemary Leach, Ronald Fraser. D: Timothy Forder. CRI 102m.

Mystery of Kaspar Hauser, The 1980 *See* **Every Man For Himself and God Against All**

Mystery of Marie Roget, The 1942 ★★★ Modest mystery about Parisian singer (Montez) who plots to murder her sister. Loosely based on an Edgar Allan Poe story. (a.k.a. *Phantom of Paris*) C: Maria Montez, Maria Ouspenkaya, Patric Knowles. D: Phil Rosen. CRI 91m.

Mystery of Mr. Wong, The 1939 ★★★ Karloff adds class to what is otherwise a fairly routine mystery about a valuable sapphire which leads to a gem collector's murder during a game of charades. Static filming, but okay story. C: Boris Karloff, Grant Withers, Dorothy Tree, Lotus Long, Morgan Wallace, Holmes Herbert. D: William Nigh. CRI 67m. v

Mystery of Mr. X, The 1934 ★★★★ Maniac released from prison kills one cop for each year he spent in jail. When a jewel thief becomes prime suspect in the crimes, he must hunt down killer himself. Attractively produced thriller has convincing British setting and able cast, led by likable Montgomery. C: Robert Montgomery, Elizabeth Allan, Lewis Stone. D: Edgar Selwyn. CRI 84m.

Mystery of the Dancing Men, The 1985 *See* **Sherlock Holmes: Dancing Men, The**

Mystery of the Golden Eye, The 1948 *See* **Golden Eye, The**

Mystery of the Hooded Horsemen, The 1937 ★★★½ The heroic singing cowboy (Ritter) must unmask a group of villainous hooded horsemen out for gold. Enjoyable B-Western is full of energy. C: Tex Ritter, Iris Meredith, Horace Murphy, Charles King. D: Ray Taylor. WST 59m. V

Mystery of the Million Dollar Hockey Puck, The ★★ A family adventure about two young orphans who get in the way of a diamond smuggling plan. C: Jean Lafleur, Michael MacDonald. D: Jean Lafleur. ACT 88m. V

Mystery of the Riverboat 1944 ★★ Intrigue, murder, and adventure have broken out on a Mississippi riverboat. C: Robert Lowery, Eddie Quillan. D: Henry MacRae. DRA 90m. V

Mystery of the Third Planet ★★ A Russian animated adventure cartoon about a commander, professor, and young girl who try to solve the ultimate mystery as they travel across the galaxies looking for specimens to inhabit their space zoo. FAM/CRI 60m. V

Mystery of the Wax Museum, The 1933 ★★★★½ Sculptor, hideously burned when partner destroys museum for insurance money, returns with new identity, opens horror gallery filled with wax-covered bodies. Classic thriller features haunting use of two-color Technicolor, famous unmasking finale; Farrell a delight as reporter and Atwill superb as demented artist. C: Lionel Atwill, Fay Wray, Glenda Farrell, Frank McHugh. D: Michael Curtiz. HOR 77m. V

Mystery on Bird Island 1954 British ★★★ Four children discover that a bird sanctuary is actually a cover for smugglers, so they report crimes to the police. Inexpensive British quickie made for the kids; nothing special but sprightly storytelling, fairly entertaining. C: Mavis Sage, Jennifer Beach, Nicky Emdett, Alexander Gauge. D: John Haggerty. FAM/ACT 57m.

Mystery on Monster Island *See* **Monster Island**

Mystery Ranch 1932 ★★★½ Intriguing programmer Western as stalwart cow wrangler saves woman from having to marry villain. Enjoyable two-fisted heroics combine with eerily striking visuals in this out-of-the-ordinary oater. C: George O'Brien, Cecilia Parker, Charles Middleton. D: David Howard. WST 56m.

Mystery Street 1950 ★★★½ Swift, deft semidocumentary murder mystery; Montalban seeks murderer of unidentified corpse, with help from Harvard medical school faculty. C: Ricardo Montalban, Sally Forrest, Bruce Bennett, Elsa Lanchester, Marshall Thompson, Jan Sterling. D: John Sturges. DRA 93m.

Mystery Train 1989 ★★★½ Fleabag Memphis hotel is stopping-off point for three different couples over the course of a night. Sex, crime, and mystical visions of Elvis Presley ensue within trio of lightly played stories. Funny in parts, though pretentious around the edges. C: Masatoshi Nagase, Youki Kudoh, Screamin'Jay Hawkins, Cinque Lee, Nicoletta Braschi, Elizabeth Bracco, Joe Strummer, Steve Buscemi. D: Jim Jarmusch. COM [R] 113m. V

Mystic Hour, The 1934 ★★★½ Cheaply made but fast thriller, as a master crook sets a woman up in jewel heist. Her playboy nephew helps both her and his girlfriend, who has an embezzler brother. Busily plotted melodrama features good stunts and lively cliffside finale. C: Montagu Love, Lucille Powers, Charles Middleton. D: Melville DeLay. CRI 63m.

Mystic Pizza 1988 ★★★ Minor summer romance follows three waitresses (Roberts, Gish, and Taylor) who work at a pizza parlor in the small town of Mystic, Connecticut. Cute at times, but overall nothing memorable. C: Julia Roberts, Annabeth Gish, Lili Taylor, Vincent Phillip D'Onofrio, William R. Moses, Adam Storke, Conchata Ferrell. D: Donald Petrie. COM [R] 101m. V

N

Nadia 1984 ★★★ Dazzling Rumanian gymnast Nadia Comaneci competes for a gold medal in 1976 Olympics. Pallid TV biography of magnificent athlete features exciting gymnastics. C: Talia Balsam, Jonathan Banks, Carrie Snodgress. D: Alan Cooke. DRA 99m. TVM V

Nadie Te Quierra Como Yo Spanish ★★ A Spanish drama about a pregnant nun who finds herself alone in the world when everybody looks upon her predicament with disgrace. C: Hilda Aguirre, Andres Garcia. DRA 85m. V

Nadine 1987 ★★★½ Hairdresser Basinger tries to retrieve nude photos of herself from a sleazy photographer but gets into hot water when she witnesses a murder. Basinger and Bridges make an appealing couple, but director lets intriguing plot go down the drain. C: Jeff Bridges, Kim Basinger, Rip Torn, Gwen Verdon, Glenne Headly, Jerry Stiller. D: Robert Benton. COM [PG] 83m. V

Nail Gun Massacre 1986 ★★ A gorish tale of a twisted murderer who takes his victims by nailing them to any surface in sight. C: Rocky Patterson, Ron Queen. D: Bill Lesley. HOR 90m. V

Nails 1992 ★★ Cop (Hopper) seeks violent vengeance against dope peddlers who killed his former partner. Good cast wasted on dull, formula plot. C: Dennis Hopper, Anne Archer, Tomas Milian, Keith David, Cliff DeYoung. D: John Flynn. CRI [R] 96m. V

Nairobi Affair 1986 ★★★ Wildlife photographer Heston has affair with son Savage's ex-spouse Adams in this routine safari drama. Beautiful scenery. C: Charlton Heston, John Savage, Maud Adams, John Rhys-Davies. D: Marvin J. Chomsky. DRA [PG] 95m. TVM V

Nais 1945 French ★★ A hunchback dreams of becoming handsome so that he can win the love of a young country maid in this ordinary French romantic tale. C: Fernandel, Jacqueline Bouvier. D: Marcel Pagnol. DRA 105m. V

Naked 1993 ★★★★ A nihilistic drifter visits his ex-girlfriend in London, sleeps with her roommate and talks metaphysics with a night-watchman, among other aimless doings. Brutally compelling. C: David Thewliss, Lesley Sharp, Katrin Cartlidge, Greg Crutwell, Claire Skinner, Peter Wight. D: Mike Leigh. DRA 131m. V

Naked Alibi 1954 ★★★½ A wrongly fired detective (Hayden) tries to prove his case against a prominent citizen by following the suspect to a Mexican border town. Far-fetched but feisty melodrama has a fine cast and a vividly grim finale. C: Sterling Hayden, Gloria Grahame, Gene Barry, Marcia Henderson, Casey Adams, Chuck Connors. D: Jerry Hopper. CRI 86m.

Naked Among the Wolves 1967 German ★★★★ Powerful, determinedly downbeat drama as WWII concentration camp inmates hide a small boy in a trunk. East German film is sometimes a bit slow and talky, but well-acted and realistic, with fine, stark b&w cinematography. C: Erwin Geschonneck, Fred Delmare, Gerry Wolff, Armin Mueller-Stahl. D: Frank Beyer. DRA 100m.

Naked and the Dead, The 1958 ★★★★ Soldiers fight it out in the Pacific during WWII. Clichéd characterizations mar this adaptation of Norman Mailer's best-selling novel, but it works well nonetheless. C: Aldo Ray, Cliff Robertson, Raymond Massey, William Campbell, Richard Jaeckel, Joey Bishop, Lili St. Cyr, Barbara Nichols. D: Raoul Walsh. DRA 131m. V

Naked Angels 1969 ★★ After recovering from injuries, a motorcycle gang leader seeks to make his attackers pay for what they did to him. C: Jennifer Gan, Richard Rust. D: Bruce Clark. ACT [R] 89m. V

Naked Ape, The 1973 ★★★ Sophomoric adaptation of Desmond Morris's non-fiction study of evolution. Plays like a Playboy article, which fits since that magazine produced it. C: Johnny Crawford, Victoria Principal. D: Donald Driver. COM [PG] 85m.

Naked Cage, The 1986 ★★ A young woman is unjustly imprisoned. Typical jailhouse-brutality piece. C: Shari Shattuck, Angel Tompkins, Lucinda Crosby, Faith Minton, Christina Whitaker, John Terlesky. D: Paul Nicholas. DRA [R] 97m. V

Naked City, The 1948 ★★★★½ A young cop learns a lot from a veteran inspector as they pursue suspects in a woman's murder. Influential thriller combines film noir techniques with realistic New York City location shooting. Exciting manhunt drama won Oscars for Cinematography and Editing. C: Barry Fitzgerald, Howard Duff, Dorothy Hart, Don Taylor, Ted De Corsia. D: Jules Dassin. DRA 96m. V

Naked Civil Servant, The 1975 ★★★★½ The life and times of Quentin Crisp, the outspoken gay British writer who long ago publicly proclaimed his sexuality despite verbal abuse and physical and legal intimidation. Quite powerfully done; excellent Hurt. C: John Hurt. D: Jack Gold. DRA V

Naked Country, The 1993 ★★ A sympathetic drama about a couple who seek to maintain their ranch through good times and hard times. C: John Stanton, Rebecca Gilling. D: Tim Burstall. DRA 90m. V

Naked Dawn, The 1955 ★★★ Firmly handled melodrama about a poor Mexican farmer who helps a crook collect train hold-up money and later plots the robber's death so he can have even more of the loot. Interesting drama is no speedster, but solid Kennedy helps. C: Arthur Kennedy, Betta St. John, Roy Engel, Eugene Iglesias, Charita. D: Edgar G. Ulmer. DRA 82m.

Naked Edge, The 1961 ★★★½ Wife (Kerr) suspects her husband (Cooper) may be a murderer and that she may be next on his list. Fair thriller was Cooper's last film. C: Gary Cooper, Deborah Kerr, Eric Portman, Diane Cilento, Hermione Gingold, Michael Wilding. D: Michael Anderson. CRI 97m. V

Naked Face, The 1984 ★★★½ A psychiatrist (Moore) with a murdered patient is the number one suspect and the killer's next target. Detectives (Gould and Steiger) try to get at the truth. Well-acted murder mystery, but with a few too many red herrings. C: Roger Moore, Rod Steiger, Elliott Gould, Anne Archer, David Hedison, Art Carney. D: Bryan Forbes. CRI [R] 105m. V

Naked General, The 1958 Japanese ★★★½ Biography of the Japanese artist Kiyoshi Yamashita, who declares himself a pacifist in WWII, strips publicly to make his point about the draft and ends up in a mental asylum, with fame as an artist coming later. Interesting story; has some good cynical wit. C: Keiju Kobayashi, Aiko Mimasu, Yasuko Nakada. D: Hiromichi Horikawa. DRA 92m.

Naked Gun, The 1988 ★★★★ Movie incarnation of wacked-out sitcom *Police Squad!* stars Nielsen as a cop watching over the Queen of England during an L.A. visit. Hilarious one-liners and sight gags pile up as Nielsen keeps tongue firmly in cheek. Presley is great fun as love interest. C: Leslie Nielsen, George Kennedy, Priscilla Presley, Ricardo Montalban, O.J. Simpson. D: David Zucker. COM [PG-13] 85m. V

Naked Gun 2 1/2: The Smell of Fear, The 1991 ★★★ So-so follow-up to *The Naked Gun* follows a cop (Nielsen) uncovering a plot by an evil energy conglomerate. As in first film, gags fly by but this time the results run empty all too soon. Reliance on racial stereotypes for easy laughs doesn't help either. *The Naked Gun 33 1/3* followed in 1994. C: Leslie Nielsen, Priscilla Presley, George Kennedy, O.J. Simpson, Robert Goulet, Richard Griffiths. D: David Zucker. COM [PG-13] 85m. V

Naked Gun 33 1/3: The Final Insult 1994 ★★★ Lt. Frank Drebin (Nielsen) is back, this time fighting a terrorist (Ward) and disrupting the Oscars. The material is beginning to wear a little thin on this suit. C: Leslie Nielsen, Priscilla Presley, George Kennedy, O.J. Simpson, Fred Ward, Kathleen Freeman, Anna Nicole Smith, Ellen Greene. D: Peter Segal. COM 82m. V

Naked Heart, The 1949 Canadian ★★★ Three men vie for the attentions of a young woman, fresh out of convent school. Standard love story; filmed also in 1935 and 1983. (a.k.a. *Maria Chapdelaine*) C: Michele Morgan, Kieron Moore, Francoise Rosay, Jack Watling. D: Marc Allegret. DRA 96m.

Naked Hills, The 1956 ★★½ Preachy western about man (Wayne) who deserts his family to search for gold. C: David Wayne, Keenan Wynn, Marcia Henderson, Denver Pyle. D: Josef Shaftel. WST 73m.

Naked Hours, The 1964 Italian ★★★★ A neglected woman (Podesta) indulges her husband's fondness for group sex, and has a brief affair with a young student. Adult story bolstered by good score and camerawork; insightfully written by famed novelist Alberto Moravia. C: Keir Dullea, Rossana Podesta. D: Marco Vicario. DRA [R] 92m.

Naked in New York 1994 ★★★★ A Generation X romantic comedy/drama with Stoltz, charming as always, as a recent college grad and would-be playwright adjusting to life in the big city while trying to keep the passion in an affair with an older woman. Sweet and funny. C: Eric Stoltz, Mary-Louise Parker, Ralph Macchio, Jill Clayburgh, Tony Curtis, Kathleen Turner, Timothy Dalton, Roscoe Lee Browne. D: Daniel Algrant. COM 86m. V

Naked in the Sun 1957 ★★★ Two Native American tribes battle U.S. government agents and slave traders. Craig gives a good performance as Seminole chieftain in this otherwise slow-moving tale. C: James Craig, Lita Milan, Barton MacLane, Tony Hunter. D: R. John Hugh. WST 79m. V

Naked Jungle, The 1954 ★★★★ A South American plantation is overrun by hordes of ferocious red ants. Great local color; lots of excitement; and good chemistry between Heston and Parker as new husband and wife. C: Eleanor Parker, Charlton Heston, Abraham Sofaer, William Conrad. D: Byron Haskin. DRA 95m. V

Naked Killer 1995 Hong Kong ★★★½ First lesbian kung-fu action movie, about female warriors bent on castrating men, then killing them. Tongue-in-cheek style and non-stop action make this something different for chopsocky fans. C: Simon Yam, Chingmy Yau. D: Clarence Fok. ACT 95m.

Naked Kiss, The 1964 ★★★½ A young woman tells of her sordid past after being charged with murder. Dark melodrama. (a.k.a. *Iron Kiss*) C: Constance Towers, Anthony Eisley, Virginia Grey, Betty Bronson, Michael Dante. D: Samuel Fuller. DRA 90m. V

Naked Lunch 1991 Canadian ★★★½ William Burroughs' autobiographical novel comes to psychedelic life in this surreal account of a young writer who, once his wife skips town, gets involved with a lurid bunch who live on drugs. Highly effective; frequently grotesque. C: Peter Weller, Judy Davis, Ian Holm, Julian Sands, Roy Scheider. D: David Cronenberg. DRA [R] 115m. V

Naked Maja, The 1959 ★★★ Rambling but

interesting biography of Francisco Goya, a Spanish peasant who became one of the world's greatest painters. Gardner plays the model who posed for the title painting. C: Ava Gardner, Anthony Franciosa, Amedeo Nazzari, Gino Cervi, Massimo Serato, Lea Padovani. D: Henry Koster. DRA 111m. v

Naked Night, The 1953 *See* **Sawdust and Tinsel.**

Naked Obsession 1991 ★★★ When a respected politician is caught in a house of prostitution, he faces more than a possible scandal—he may be framed for murder. Some good moments, otherwise predictable. C: William Katt, Maria Ford, Rick Dean. D: Dan Golden. DRA [R] 93m. v

Naked Prey, The 1965 ★★★★ Captured by a fierce African tribe, a man (Wilde) is set loose so his captors can hunt him down like a beast. Exciting, tense, and extremely violent; beautifully filmed. C: Cornel Wilde, Gert Van Den Bergh, Ken Gampu. D: Cornel Wilde. DRA 94m. v

Naked Runner, The 1967 British ★★½ WWII vet (Sinatra) is pulled into espionage/assassination plot against his will. Confusing, uncompelling spy story. C: Frank Sinatra, Peter Vaughan, Edward Fox. D: Sidney J. Furie. ACT 104m.

Naked Space *See* **Creature Wasn't Nice, The**

Naked Spur, The 1953 ★★★★½ Magnificent psychological Western about an outlaw (Ryan) being transported back to civilization by a bounty hunter (Stewart), whose posse is torn apart by greed. Majestic Colorado scenery backs up a gripping story (the screenplay was nominated for an Academy Award). Ryan's devious villain is a standout. C: James Stewart, Janet Leigh, Ralph Meeker, Robert Ryan, Millard Mitchell. D: Anthony Mann. WST 93m. v

Naked Street, The 1955 ★★★½ Ganglord (Quinn) gets a hood (Granger) off death row so he can marry the boss's pregnant sister (Bancroft). Far-fetched story gets a potent presentation, with an excellent cast pulling out all stops. C: Farley Granger, Anthony Quinn, Anne Bancroft, Peter Graves, Jerry Paris, Jeanne Cooper. D: Maxwell Shane. DRA 84m.

Naked Tango 1991 ★★★ Three lost souls in '20s Buenos Aires are lured into the dark world of tango dancing. Beautifully moody ambiance, but the story lacks depth; D'Onofrio is woefully miscast. C: Vincent D'Onofrio, Mathilda May, Esai Morales, Fernando Rey, Cipe Lincovski, Josh Mostel, Constance McCashin. D: Leonard Schrader. DRA [R] 90m.

Naked Truth, The 1958 ★★★★ A canny comedy about a tabloid newspaper and the celebrities who go to any lengths to stop it from printing stories about them. (a.k.a. *Your Past is Showing*) C: Peter Sellers, Terry-Thomas, Peggy Mount, Dennis Price. D: Mario Zampi. COM 92m. v

Naked Vengeance 1985 ★★★ A tale of revenge as a woman hunts and brutally kills the men who raped her and murdered her parents. Graphic and tensely violent. C: Deborah Tranelli, Gaz Garas. D: Cirio H. Santiago. DRA [R] 78m. v

Naked Youth 1960 *See* **Cruel Story of Youth**

Nam Angels 1988 ★★ Motorcyclists armed to the teeth go deep into enemy territory to rescue their POW buddies and find a fortune in hidden gold. Lots of action. C: Brad Johnson, Vernon Wells, Kevin Duffis. D: Cirio H. Santiago. ACT [R] 91m. v

Name for Evil, A 1972 ★★★ It looks like a pleasant resort, but the new guests discover that there is evil lurking, and is after them. A tense film. C: Robert Culp, Samantha Eggar. D: Bernard Girard. HOR [R] 74m. v

Name of the Rose, The 1986 Italian ★★★½ A Holmes-like 13th-century monk (Connery) investigates a murder in a monastery. Atmospheric, evocative production focuses on the mystery at the heart of Umberto Eco's wildly popular novel, and skips most of the history. Terrific performances from Connery and Abraham. C: Sean Connery, F. Murray Abraham, Christian Slater, Feodor Chaliapin Jr., William Hickey, Michael Lonsdale. D: Jean-Jacques Annaud. DRA [R] 128m. v

Namu, the Killer Whale 1966 ★★★ Naturalist tames a killer whale, much to the dislike of local fishermen. Simple children's film that develops along predictable lines. C: Robert Lansing, John Anderson, Lee Meriwether, Richard Erdman, Robin Mattson. D: Laslo Benedek. FAM/DRA 89m. v

Nana 1934 ★★★ Emil Zola's classic tale of an aristocratic Parisienne (Sten) degraded by a tragic love affair. A stylish Goldwyn production. Even the fine cinematography by Gregg Toland couldn't make a star out of Sten. C: Anna Sten, Phillips Holmes, Lionel Atwill, Muriel Kirkland, Richard Bennett, Mae Clarke. D: Dorothy Arzner. DRA 89m. v

Nanami, First Love 1968 Japan ★★★½ A complex film, using a dazzling array of flashbacks and dream sequences, about a young man who falls for a model, but cannot truly love her because of the traumatic incidents of his youth. D: Susumu Hani. DRA 104m. v

Nancy Drew—A Haunting We Will Go 1977 ★★ The detective ferrets out the real source of all the ghostly events plaguing her friend. C: Pamela Sue Martin, George O'Hanlon, Bob Crane. D: Jack Arnold. CRI 47m. v

Nancy Drew and the Hidden Staircase 1939 ★★★★ Teenage sleuth (Granville) helps two old ladies figure out strange happenings in huge house. Nancy's best, with charming cast and strong story (from actual ND book *The Hidden Staircase* by Carolyn Keene). C: Bonita Granville, Frankie Thomas, Vera Lewis, Louise Carter. D: William Clemens. CRI 60m.

Nancy Drew, Detective 1938 ★★★★ First

of four entertaining adventures based on Carolyn Keene's juvenile detective stories. Granville is tops as perky teenager determined to solve mystery of rich woman's disappearance. C: Bonita Granville, John Litel, James Stephenson, Frankie Thomas. D: William Clemens. CRI 66m.

Nancy Drew, Reporter 1939 ★★★★ That enterprising mystery Miss (Granville) tries to exhonerate friend accused of murder in zippy, well-plotted juvenile detective story. C: Bonita Granville, John Litel, Frankie Thomas, Mary Lee. D: William Clemens. CRI 68m. V

Nancy Drew—Secret of the Whispering Walls 1977 ★★ Drew investigates those faint voices coming out of the walls, and uncovers a sinister plot behind them. C: Pamela Sue Martin, Jean Rasey, George O'Hanlon. D: Michael Caffey. CRI 47m. TVM V

Nancy Drew—The Mystery of Pirate's Cove 1977 ★★ The detective investigates the strange goings-on in a cove, and uncovers a crime in the process. C: Pamela Sue Martin, William Schallert, George O'Hanlon, Jean Rasey. D: E. W. Swackhamer. CRI 47m.TVM V

Nancy Drew—The Mystery of the Diamond Triangle 1977 ★★ The detective has a puzzle to solve, and behind it is a desperate crime. C: Pamela Sue Martin, Jean Rasey, George O'Hanlon. D: Noel Black. CRI 47m. TVM V

Nancy Drew—The Mystery of the Fallen Angels 1977 ★★ A case in which superstition and fear is used to cover a crime. C: Pamela Sue Martin, William Schallert, George O'Hanlon. D: Noel Black. CRI 47m. TVM V

Nancy Drew—The Mystery of the Solid Gold Kicker 1977 ★★ A precious artifact holds the clues to the mystery the young detective must solve. C: Pamela Sue Martin, William Schallert, George O'Hanlon. D: Andy Sidaris. CRI 47m. TVM V

Nancy Drew, Troubleshooter 1939 ★★★ Pint-sized sleuth (Granville) helps her father try to clear his friend of murder charges. Not up to other entries in series, but still diverting. C: Bonita Granville, John Litel. D: William Clemens. CRI 69m.

Nancy Goes to Rio 1950 ★★★½ Brightly presented MGM musical bonbon, about mother and daughter unknowingly pursuing both the same singing role and the same man. Sothern and Powell deliver appealingly, and Miranda's always a treat. C: Ann Sothern, Jane Powell, Barry Sullivan, Carmen Miranda, Louis Calhern, Fortunio Bonanova, Hans Conried. D: Robert Z. Leonard. MUS 101m. V

Nancy Steel Is Missing 1937 ★★★½ Released criminal met by young woman he kidnapped when she was a baby. She thinks he's her father. Good, tingly melodrama with taut direction and fine cast. C: Victor McLaglen, Walter Connolly, Peter Lorre, June Lang, Jane Darwell, John Carradine. D: George Marshall. DRA 85m.

Nanny, The 1965 British ★★★★ Little boy, home after being institutionalized for two years comes under care of psychotic nanny (Davis) who accidentally killed the boy's sister. Excellent Davis engaged in potent battle of wits in this quietly disturbing horror yarn. C: Bette Davis, Wendy Craig, Jill Bennett, James Villiers, Pamela Franklin, William Dix, Maurice Denham. D: Seth Holt. DRA 93m.

Nanook of the North 1922 ★★★★★ Groundbreaking documentary explores everyday world of Eskimo tribe. Magnificent true-life film is still a model of the form. Narrative soundtrack and music were added in 1939. D: Robert Flaherty. DOC 69m. V

Napoleon 1927 French ★★★★★ Life of the French emperor, culminating in the famed Battle of Waterloo. Magnificent silent masterpiece should be seen on the widest screen possible for the stunning action climax, originally shown on three screens. Restored by British film preservationist Kevin Brownlow in 1981, with a new score by Carmine Coppola, director Francis Ford's father. C: Albert Dieudonne, Antonin Artaud, Pierre Batcheff. D: Abel Gance. DRA 235m. V

Napoleon 1955 French ★★★ The life of the great leader, from young soldier to exile. Filled with screen luminaries and assorted peak moments, but pales beside Gance's 1927 silent giant. C: Orson Welles, Maria Schell, Yves Montand, Erich von Stroheim. D: Sacha Guitry. DRA 115m. V

Napoleon and Samantha 1972 ★★★½ Orphan boy (Whitaker) teams up with Foster (in her movie debut) to trek across Oregon with pet lion in search of benefactor Douglas. Average family movie that younger children will probably enjoy. C: Michael Douglas, Jodie Foster, Johnny Whitaker, Will Geer, Arch Johnson. D: Bernard McEveety. FAM/DRA [G] 91m. V

Narrow Corner, The 1933 ★★★★½ Englishman (Fairbanks) on the lam takes refuge in the East Indies, where he falls in love. An unjustly neglected film of intelligence, maturity, and passion; solid storytelling, marvelous acting. C: Douglas Fairbanks Jr., Patricia Ellis, Ralph Bellamy, Dudley Digges, William V. Mong, Sidney Toler, Henry Kolker, Willie Fung. D: Alfred E. Green. DRA 71m.

Narrow Margin 1990 ★★★½ Remake of 1952 film noir has law enforcer Hackman transporting witness Archer via train to testify at trial. Despite Hackman's usual effortless scene-stealing and terrific climax: it doesn't quite live up to tight, claustrophobic original. C: Gene Hackman, Anne Archer, James B. Sikking, J.T. Walsh, M.Emmet Walsh. D: Peter Hyams. ACT [R] 99m. V

Narrow Margin, The 1952 ★★★★½ Classic B-movie thriller about gangster's widow (Windsor) being transported via train to L.A., the henchman hired to silence her, and the cop (McGraw) determined to protect her. Full of neat plot twists and claustrophobic suspense. Remade in 1990. C: Charles McGraw, Marie Windsor, Gus Forbes. D: Richard Fleischer. CRI 70m. V

Narrow Trail, The 1917 ★★★½ Silent film about an outlaw who captures and tames a wild pinto, but discovers that its markings make the horse easy to identify. C: William S. Hart, Sylvia Bremer. D: Lambert Hillyer. WST 56m. V

NASA—The 25th Year 1987 ★★★ Solid documentary about the first quarter century of the US space program, from Glenn to Armstrong, with the best footage of the flights and the Moon walks. DOC 50m. V

Nashville 1975 ★★★★★ Altman's classic, a tale of the uncomfortable marriage of show business and politics in mid '70s America. Dozens of fascinating characters cross paths as Altman charts the postbreakdown return of a troubled, country singer and the events surrounding her comeback. Oscar for Best Song, "I'm Easy." C: Henry Gibson, Karen Black, Ronee Blakley, Keith Carradine, Geraldine Chaplin, Lily Tomlin, Michael Murphy, Barbara Harris, Ned Beatty, Shelley Duvall. D: Robert Altman. DRA [R] 159m. V

Nashville Beat 1989 ★★★½ Two country cops from Tennessee outfox the street-smart gangs of L.A. C: Kent McCord, Martin Milner. D: Bernard Kowalski. CRI 110m. V

Nasty Girl, The 1990 German ★★★★½ Wonderfully funny and innovative story of a curious young woman (Stolze, in a superb performance) who begins to dig up Nazi "skeletons" in her small town's "closets" and finds many would rather leave them buried. C: Lena Stolze, Monika Baumgartner, Elisabeth Bertram, Hans-Reinhard Muller. D: Michael Verhoeven. DRA [PG-13] 94m. V

Nasty Habits 1977 ★★★ Corruption in a Philadelphia convent is analogy for Watergate. So-so comedy, but snappy cameos make for some fun. C: Glenda Jackson, Melina Mercouri, Geraldine Page, Sandy Dennis, Anne Jackson, Edith Evans. D: Michael Lindsay-Hogg. COM [PG] 92m. V

Nasty Hero 1987 ★★ A car-theft ring is confronted by a gangster whom they framed. C: Robert Sedgwick, Scott Feraco. D: Nick Barwood. ACT [PG-13] 79m. V

Nasty Rabbit, The 1965 ★★★ Russian spies try to destroy U.S. with a diseased rabbit. Would-be spoof with few laughs. (a.k.a. *Spies A Go Go*) C: Arch Hall Jr., Micha Terr, Melissa Morgan, Arch Hall Sr. D: James Landis. COM 88m. V

Natas: The Reflection 1983 ★★★ A reporter in search of a secret comes upon a scene of gore and violence instead. C: Randy Mulkey, Pat bolt. HOR 90m. V

Nate and Hayes 1983 U.S. ★★★½ In the 1800s, heroic adventurer Jones rescues missionary's kidnapped fiancée from pirates. Not exactly a classic swashbuckler, but action-packed feature has plenty of old-fashioned entertainment. C: Tommy Lee Jones, Michael O'Keefe, Max Phipps, Jenny Seagrove. D: Ferdinand Fairfax. ACT [PG] 100m. V

National Exposure 1992 ★★★ All the hysterical, juicy details about the most bizarre of the tabloid stories, from the plastic surgery of celebrities to the money troubles of the Royal Family. COM 50m. V

National Health, The 1973 British ★★★ Send-up of British national health care set among zany hospital staff also has a show-within-a-show spoof of TV hospital soap operas. Some laughs, but all the role doubling becomes more frantic than funny. C: Lynn Redgrave, Eleanor Bron, Donald Sinden, Jim Dale, Bob Hoskins. D: Jack Gold. COM 95m.

National Lampoon Goes to the Movies 1981 ★ Quasi star-studded movie parody piles on the idiot humor in spoofs of cop films, lush romances, and other genres. (a.k.a. *National Lampoon's Movie Madness*) C: Peter Riegert, Diane Lane, Candy Clark, Teresa Ganzel, Ann Dusenberry, Robert Culp, Bobby DiCicco, Fred Willard, Joe Spinell, Mary Woronov, Dick Miller, Robby Benson. D: Henry Jaglom, Bob Giraldi. COM [R] 89m. V

National Lampoon's Animal House 1978 *See* **Animal House**

National Lampoon's Christmas Vacation 1989 ★★★★ Third of National Lampoon's popular *Vacation* movies has the Griswold household preparing for the ultimate dysfunctional family gathering. Well-played idiot humor, with truly demented support from Quaid. Don't miss that squirrel! C: Chevy Chase, Beverly D'Angelo, Randy Quaid, Diane Ladd, John Randolph, E.G. Marshall, Doris Roberts, William Hickey, Juliette Lewis, Johnny Galecki. D: Jeremiah S. Chechik. COM [PG-13] 97m. V

National Lampoon's Class Reunion 1982 ★★ Comic spoof of slasher movies as deranged student outcast reaps revenge on his former classmates at the high school reunion. It's played for laughs but they never come. C: Gerrit Graham, Micheal Lerner, Fred mcCarren, Miriam Flynn. D: Michael Miller. COM [R] 84m. V

National Lampoon's European Vacation 1985 ★★★ The Griswolds play dominoes with Stonehenge as the crudest American tourists ever to hit Europe. The second of three *Vacation* romps sometimes meets its goal of cheap laughs. C: Chevy Chase, Beverly D'Angelo, Jason Lively, Dana Hill, Victor Lanoux. D: Amy Heckerling. COM [PG-13] 94m. V

National Lampoon's Loaded Weapon 1993 ★★★ Take-off of action shoot-em-ups like *Lethal Weapon* has a good cast but the jokes for the most part are predictable and heavy-handed. Best is the spoof of *Basic Instinct*. C:

Emilio Estevez, Samuel L. Jackson, Charlie Sheen, Jon Lovitz, Kathy Ireland, William Shatner. D: Gene Quintano. COM [PG-13] 83m. V

National Lampoon's Movie Madness 1981 *See* **National Lampoon Goes to the Movies**

National Lampoon's Vacation 1983 ★★★★ First in National Lampoon's *Vacation* series has parents (Chase and D'Angelo) driving cross-country for family fun at "Wally World." Accidents and misfortunes pile up, and hilarious idiot humor enforces Murphy's Law. Coca and Candy are great support. C: Chevy Chase, Beverly D'Angelo, Anthony Michael Hall, Imogene Coca, Randy Quaid, Dana Barron, Christie Brinkley. D: Harold Ramis. COM [R] 98m. V

National Velvet 1944 ★★★★★ Family classic of British girl (Taylor) who convinces jockey (Rooney) to train her for Grand National Steeplechase. Engaging throughout, with fine performances and sharply paced direction. Revere, Oscar winner for Best Supporting Actress, is standout as Taylor's mother. Followed 34 years later by sequel *International Velvet.* C: Mickey Rooney, Elizabeth Taylor, Donald Crisp, Anne Revere, Angela Lansbury, Jackie Jenkins, Arthur Treacher. D: Clarence Brown. FAM/DRA [G] 124m. V

Native Land 1942 ★★★★ Dramatization of violations of the Bill of Rights, taken from the Senate's Civil Liberties Commission. Incidents include a farmer who speaks out at an association meeting, and vigilantes who kill sharecroppers. Dramatically unwieldy at times, but potent workers film indicts KKK, land barons, union spies. C: Paul Robeson. D: Leo Hurwitz. FAM/DRA 88m. V

Native Son 1950 ★★★ A young black chauffeur accidentally kills a white woman. Inadequate rendition of Richard Wright's celebrated book (starring the author) ruined by a low budget and poor direction. Decent cast, though. Remade in 1987. C: Richard Wright, Jean Wallace, Gloria Madison, Nicholas Joy. D: Pierre Chenal. DRA 91m. V

Native Son 1987 ★★★½ Sincere but simplistic translation of Richard Wright's novel, about poor young black man in Depression-era Chicago, whose actions, and race, force him into tragic circumstances. Powerhouse cast, but slow going. C: Victor Love, Matt Dillon, Elizabeth McGovern, Geraldine Page, Oprah Winfrey, John Karlen. D: Jerrold Freedman. DRA [PG] 111m. V

Nativity, The 1978 ★★★ Earnest, if dull, rendering of events leading up to the birth of Jesus. C: John Shea, Madeline Stowe, Jane Wyatt. D: Bernard L. Kowalski. FAM/DRA 100m. TVM V

Natural Born Killers 1994 ★★★½ Harrelson and Lewis go on the run as Bonnie-and-Clyde murderers turned into folk heroes by media excesses. Fans of Stone's compelling, if often paranoid, world view will find a lot here. C: Woody Harrelson, Juliette Lewis, Robert Downey, Jr. D: Oliver Stone. CRI

Natural, The 1984 ★★★★ Bernard Malamud's novel, about a star baseball player who gets a chance late in life to redeem himself, seems almost mythological with Redford in the main role. A little full of itself, but entertaining, with poignant Randy Newman score. C: Robert Redford, Robert Duvall, Glenn Close, Kim Basinger, Wilford Brimley, Richard Farnsworth, Barbara Hershey, Darren McGavin. D: Barry Levinson. DRA [PG] 134m. V

Naughty but Nice 1939 ★★★½ Genial Warners nonsense about classical music professor (Powell) who accidentally composes pop hit. Great cast, lots of long-hair music adapted into juke-box ditties. C: Dick Powell, Ann Sheridan, Helen Broderick, Ronald Reagan, ZaSu Pitts, Jerry Colonna, Gale Page. D: Ray Enright. MUS 90m.

Naughty Knights 1971 ★★ Medieval knights, unsure of the meaning of chivalry, battle for more than just the hand of lovely damsels in this raunchy takeoff of *Camelot.* C: Frankie Howard, Graham Crowden, Eartha Kitt. D: Bob Kellett. COM [PG] 94m. V

Naughty Marietta 1935 ★★★★ Vintage Victor Herbert operetta marked impressive debut of MacDonald/Eddy singing team. Jeanette is French princess encountering pirates on the way to America. Big song, "Ah, Sweet Mystery of Life." C: Jeanette MacDonald, Nelson Eddy, Frank Morgan, Elsa Lanchester. D: W.S. Van-Dyke II. MUS [G] 106m. V

Naughty Nineties 1945 ★★★½ Typical Abbott and Costello comedy, set on 1890s riverboat, notable for classic routine, "Who's on First?" C: Bud Abbott, Lou Costello, Alan Curtis, Rita Johnson. D: Jean Yarbrough. COM 76m. V

Navajo 1952 ★★★★ A 7-year-old Navajo boy is taken away from the reservation to be educated and assimilated. He runs away, but when government men get lost chasing him, he saves them. Contrived perhaps, but good intentions shine through; engagingly low-key, nicely photographed and acted. C: Francis Kee Teller, John Michell. D: Norman Foster. WST 70m.

Navajo Joe 1966 Italian ★★½ Low-budget Spanish-Italian Western has sole-survivor (Reynolds) tracking down perpetrators of brutal massacre. Sluggish oater, shot in Spain. C: Burt Reynolds, Aldo Sanbrell, Tanya Lopert, Fernando Rey. D: Sergio Corbucci. WST 89m. V

Navigator, The: A Medieval Odyssey 1988 New Zealand ★★★★ A psychic boy holds the secret to saving his village from the Black Death raging through Europe—by leading them into the future. New Zealand gem. C: Hamish McFarlane, Bruce Lyons, Chris Haywood, Marshall Napier. D: Vincent Ward. SFI [PG] 92m. V

Navy Blue and Gold 1937 ★★★½ Three Annapolis cadets bond during intense military schooling, culminating in famous Army-Navy football game. Actually more of a pigskin movie than anything. Old-fashioned, but endearing. C: Robert Young, James Stewart, Tom Brown, Lionel Barrymore, Billie Burke. D: Sam Wood. ACT 94m. v

Navy Blues 1941 ★★★½ Snappy wartime musical about two gobs (Haley, Oakie) determined to enlist sharpshooter (Anderson) so their unit can win marksmanship contest. Raye runs away with the picture. C: Ann Sheridan, Herbert Anderson, Jack Oakie, Jack Haley, Martha Raye, Jackie Gleason, Jack Carson. D: Lloyd Bacon. MUS 108m.

Navy SEALS 1990 ★★★ Crackerjack military outfit sets out to destroy missiles illegally obtained by terrorists. Military shoot-'em-up keeps the action coming and features a manic Sheen. C: Charlie Sheen, Michael Biehn, Joanne Whalley-Kilmer, Rick Rossovich. D: Lewis Teague. ACT [R] 113m. v

Navy Steps Out, The 1941 *See* **Girl, a Guy, and a Gob, A**

Navy vs. the Night Monsters, The 1966 ★ When walking trees overrun the South Pole, it's up to a stoic Navy officer and a nurse to stop the villainous vegetation. About as bad as it sounds; truly "so bad it's funny." (a.k.a. *The Night Crawlers*) C: Mamie Van Doren, Anthony Eisley, Pamela Mason, Bobby Van. D: Michael Hoey. HOR 90m. v

Nazarin 1958 Mexican ★★★★½ Unfrocked priest Rey emulates life of Christ, suffers the scorn and hypocrisy of others, but ultimately achieves personal salvation. Strong and often moving story, enhanced by Buñel's surreal use of Mexican location. C: Francisco Rabal, Rita Macedo, Marga Lopez, Ignacio Lopez Tarso. D: Luis Bunuel. DRA 100m. v

Nazis, The: Of Pure Blood 1986 ★★½ A bereaved mother (Remick) travels to Germany to unravel the mystery of her son's death only to track down a related mystery having to do with Nazi experiments. Good premise, strong Remick. (a.k.a. *Of Pure Blood*) C: Patrick McGoohan, Lee Remick, Richard Munch. D: Joseph Sargent. DRA 104m. TVM

Nea' 1978 French ★★★ A well-to-do young woman pens a shocking book under a pseudonym. When her identity is maliciously revealed, she takes her revenge in kind. Lightweight, but entertaining comedy/drama. C: Sami Frey, Ann Zacharias, Heinz Bennent. D: Nelly Kaplan. DRA 101m. v

Near Dark 1987 ★★★½ Moody marriage of Western and horror genres, as young Pasdar is seduced by vampire Wright into joining her murderous family of blood drinking nomads. Great cast in stylized film with riveting action sequences. C: Adrian Pasdar, Jenny Wright, Lance Henriksen, Bill Paxton, Jenette Goldstein. D: Kathryn Bigelow. HOR [R] 95m. v

Near Death ★★★★★ Riveting, moving, and often funny documentary about a week in an intensive care unit in a prominent Boston hospital. Director Wiseman had the run of the place, and he got candid stuff that is not to be believed. Six hours long, but never less than fascinating. D: Frederick Wiseman. DOC 360m.

'Neath Brooklyn Bridge 1942 ★★★½ Watchable East Side Kids yarn as the gang shelters a girl when her guardian is killed; they try to find the real killer when one of them is framed. Better than expected: fast-paced, with the raucous gang in fine fettle. C: East Side Kids, Ann Gillis, Noah Beery Jr. D: Wallace Fox. CRI 61m.

'Neath the Arizona Skies 1934 ★★★ Cowhand protects Native-American woman who stands to inherit oil-rich land. Early low-budget Wayne Western has great fisticuffs. C: Sheila Terry, Yakima Canutt, John Wayne. D: Henry Frazer. WST 57m.

'Neath the Canadian Skies 1946 ★★★ A Mountie tries to keep the peace and protect a community during the feverish gold rush of the 1890s. C: Russell Hayden, Inez Cooper. D: B. Reeves Eason. WST 41m. v

Nebo Zowet 1963 *See* **Battle Beyond the Sun**

Necessary Roughness 1991 ★★ Thirty-four-year-old college quarterback fights against meddlesome NCAA types while trying to woo teacher with yen for the gridiron. Unsavory sports comedy trots out stereotypes and sexism in equal proportions. C: Scott Bakula, Robert Loggia, Hector Elizondo, Harley Jane Kozak, Sinbad, Jason Bateman, Kathy Ireland. D: Stan Dragoti. COM [PG-13] 108m. v

Necromancer—Satan's Servant 1988 ★★★ Woman who was brutally attacked makes a deal with the Devil to get her revenge. Eerie and suspensful. C: Elilzabeth Cayton, Russ Tamblyn. D: Dusty Nelson. HOR [R] 90m. v

Necromancy 1972 ★★ Portly satanic priest (Welles) wants a teenager (Franklin) to become a witch. Inept horror film, nadir of former *Citizen Kane*'s career. (a.k.a. *The Witching*) C: Orson Welles, Pamela Franklin, Lee Purcell, Michael Ontkean. D: Bert I. Gordon. HOR [PG] 83m. v

Necropolis 1987 ★★ A witch (Baker) who died three centuries ago comes back to life in New York City, as a bike-riding punk looking for a virgin to sacrifice. A wanna-be stylish horror flick. C: Leeanne Baker, Michael Conte. D: Bruce Hickey. HOR [R] 77m. v

Ned Kelly 1970 British ★★★ Loosely based on the life of the notorious 19th-century Australian criminal. Jagger is good, although movie could have been better. (a.k.a. *Ned Kelly, Outlaw*) C: Mick Jagger, Clarissa Kaye, Mark McManus, Frank Thring. D: Tony Richardson. ACT [PG] 100m. v

Ned Kelly, Outlaw 1970 *See* **Ned Kelly**

Needful Things 1993 ★★★ Atmospheric Stephen King yarn, set in small Maine town, focuses on creepy shop owner who tries to give his customers that little bit extra—with the accompanying horror and devastation one would expect. Nice setup, but this murky business gets old pretty quick. C: Max von Sydow, Ed Harris, Bonnie Bedella, Amanda Plummer. D: Fraser C. Heston. HOR [R] 120m. TVM v

Negatives 1968 British ★★★ Kinky unmarried couple (Jackson and McEnery) like to dress up as historical characters for sex. When photographer (Cilento) enters scene, their unusual games take a new twist. Odd film is mainly redeemed by a good performance from Jackson. C: Peter McEnery, Diane Cilento, Glenda Jackson, Maurice Denham. D: Peter Medak. DRA [R] 99m. v

Negro Soldier 1943 ★★★½ Account of African-American soldiers in WWII. Informative, well-made documentary. D: Frank Capra. DOC 49m. v

Neighbor, The 1993 ★★★½ Steiger in one of his creepier roles as a neighbor who terrorizes a young couple newly arrived to a quiet Vermont town. C: Rod Steiger, Linda Kozlowski, Ron Lea. D: Rodney Gibbons. DRA [R] 93m. v

Neighborhood Thief, The 1983 Spanish ★★★ A light comedy proving once again that there is no honor among thieves, especially the bumbling kind. C: Alfonso Zayas, Alberto Rojas, Angelica Chain. COM 84m. v

Neighbors 1981 ★★★★ Bizarre nightmare comedy features Belushi (in his last film) as mild-mannered suburbanite undergoing radical change when barbarous Aykroyd and sensuous Moriarty move in next door. Over-the-top humor may not appeal to all tastes, but unusual satire has distinctive edge. Belushi is great in against-type role. C: John Belushi, Dan Aykroyd, Cathy Moriarty, Kathryn Walker. D: John G. Avildsen. COM [R] 95m. v

Neil Simon's Broadway Bound *See* **Broadway Bound**

Neil Simon's Lost In Yonkers 1993 *See* **Lost In Yonkers**

Nel Nome del Pape Re 1977 *See* **In the Name of the Pope King**

Nell 1994 ★★★½ An isolated young woman (Foster) with her own language is discovered by Neeson and Richardson, then brought into the outside world. At times threatens to become a human version of *Born Free*, but Jodie's bravura (and Oscar-nominated) performance makes it definitely worth seeing. C: Jodie Foster, Liam Neeson, Natasha Richardson. D: Michael Apted. DRA [PG-13] 122m. v

Nell Gwyn 1935 British ★★★★ Lavish historical romp as Cockney dancer becomes Charles II's mistress, bests the king's reigning favorite by wearing bigger hats. Neagle and Hardwicke have a ball with their roles: Racy costumes and sexual situations outraged censors then, but just play amusingly now. C: Anna Neagle, Cedric Hardwicke, Miles Malleson. D: Herbert Wilcox. DRA 75m.

Nelson Affair, The 1973 ★★★ Period romance of Lord Nelson and Lady Hamilton is hampered by cheap sets and an over-the-top performance from Jackson. Same story fared better in 1941 as *That Hamilton Woman*. C: Glenda Jackson, Peter Finch, Anthony Quayle, Margaret Leighton. D: James Cellan Jones. DRA [PG] 118m.

Nemesis 1993 ★★★ A tough-talking cop in future L.A. battles it out with cyborg criminals. Low budget but some fun. C: Olivier Gruner, Tim Thomerson, Marjorie Monaghan, Brion James, Deborah Shelton, Cary-Hiroyuki Tagawa. D: Albert Pyun. SFI [R] 100m. v

Neon City 1991 ★★★½ A thrilling ride into the future as eight unsavory people on a transport must band together to fend off an attack by futuristic highway robbers. Graphic and violent, but effectively tense. C: Michael Ironside, Vanity, Richard Sanders, Monte Markham, Lyle Alzado. D: Monte Markham. SFI [R] 107m. v

Neon Empire, The 1989 ★★★ Drama about the building of Las Vegas, from a near-ghost town in the desert to the glamorous gambling and show town, by the legendary Bugsy Siegel and Meyer Lansky. C: Ray Sharkey, Martin Landau, Gary Busey, Linda Fiorentino. D: Larry Peerce. DRA [R] 120m. v

Neptune's Daughter 1949 ★★★★ One of Williams' most likable dips in the pool as she plays a swimmer who designs bathing suits and finds romance. Comic subplot benefits from funny Skelton impersonating a polo player. Lively and refreshing. Oscar-winning song "Baby, It's Cold Outside." C: Esther Williams, Red Skelton, Keenan Wynn, Betty Garrett, Ricardo Montalban, Mel Blanc. D: Edward Buzzell. MUS 94m. v

Nervous Ticks 1991 ★★★ A look at modern day America as a young man falls into a series of strange and unnerving situations. C: Bill Pullman, Julie Brown, Peter Boyle. D: Rocky Lang. COM [R] 95m. v

Nest, The 1981 Spanish ★★★★½ Thirteen-year-old Torrent and older widower Alterio scandalize a town when they become romantically involved. Moving drama about hopes and dreams that transcends generations, with delicate performances by the two leads. C: Hector Alterio, Ana Torrent, Luis Politti. D: Jaime De Arminan. DRA [PG] 109m. v

Nesting, The 1980 ★★★ A mystery writer moves into old house, soon discovering it's a former brothel haunted by spirits of murdered prostitutes. Solid little ghost story with Grahame, in her last film, as a ghostly madame. Some chills compensate for deliberate pace. C: Robin Groves, Christopher Loomis, Michael David Lally, John Carradine, Gloria Grahame. D: Armand Weston. HOR [R] 104m. v

Netherworld 1991 ★★½ To learn more about his dead father, a young man visits the old family home in the Louisana bayou, where he uncovers a history of witchcraft. Melodrama with typical thrills and chills. C: Michael C. Bendetti, Denise Gentile, Holly Floria, Anjanette Comer. D: David Schmoeller. HOR [R] 90m. v

Network 1976 ★★★★★ Crisp, crackling and ahead of its time, this tasty satire skewers the way network television news blurs the line between reporting news and creating it. Great performances from Oscar winners Dunaway, Finch, and Straight. Oscar for Best Screenplay to Paddy Chayefsky. C: William Holden, Faye Dunaway, Peter Finch, Robert Duvall, Ned Beatty, Beatrice Straight, Wesley Addy, William Prince. D: Sidney Lumet. COM [R] 122m. v

Neurotic Cabaret 1990 ★★★ An exotic dancer and her friends are driven to extreme measures—kidnapping, blackmail, and even hair weaving—in order to raise money for the filming of a movie. C: Tammy Stones, Edwin Neal, Dennis Worthington. D: John Woodward. COM 84m. v

Neutral Port 1941 British ★★★ British captain's ship is sunk in neutral port, so he steals German supply ship and rams it into Nazi submarine. Wish-fulfillment wartime yarn often played for comedy, but has its suspenseful moments too. Good cast. C: Will Fyffe, Leslie Banks, Yvonne Amaud, Phyllis Calvert. D: Marcel Varnel. ACT 92m.

Neutralizer, The 1974 *See* **Callan**

Nevada 1944 ★★★½ Cow wrangler panning for gold is mistaken for homesteader's killer and nearly lynched; so he falls for dead man's daughter and rounds up bad guys. Decent B-Western has lean, tough, intriguing Mitchum in an early leading role. C: Robert Mitchum, Anne Jeffreys, Guinn Williams, Nancy Gates, Harry Woods. D: Edward Killy. WST 62m.

Nevada Smith 1966 ★★★½ Years-long quest of title character (McQueen) for vengeance on outlaws who murdered his parents. Violent, fitfully successful Western starts off strong, picks up too many subplots. Good performances by leads. Based on a character from Harold Robbins novel *The Carpetbaggers*. C: Steve McQueen, Karl Malden, Brian Keith, Arthur Kennedy, Suzanne Pleshette, Martin Landau. D: Henry Hathaway. WST 135m. v

Nevadan, The 1950 ★★★ Undercover lawman (Scott) searches for man who pilfered a quarter million in gold, while also trying to keep loot out of the hands of an evil rancher. Solid Scott Western features handsome color photography and fine supporting performances. C: Randolph Scott, Dorothy Malone, Forrest Tucker, George Macready, Jock Mahoney. D: Gordon Douglas. WST 81m.

Never a Dull Moment 1943 ★★★★ Madcap Ritz Brothers get mixed up in organized crime, with uproarious results. One of the boys' best farces. If you've never seen or heard of them, grab it. C: Ritz Brothers, Frances Langford, Jack LaRue, Franklin Pangborn. D: Edward Lilley. COM 60m.

Never a Dull Moment 1950 ★★★½ Disappointing comedy with Dunne as city songwriter moving to Wyoming with rancher husband (MacMurray). Two stars don't quite click as a team. Some negative stereotyping of women and Native Americans. Interesting comparison to MacMurray/Colbert *The Egg and I*. C: Irene Dunne, Fred MacMurray, William Demarest, Andy Devine, Gigi Perreau, Natalie Wood, Philip Ober, Ann Doran. D: George Marshall. COM 89m. v

Never a Dull Moment 1968 ★★ Robinson is gangster planning an art heist. Mistaking small-time actor Van Dyke for ruthless hit man, he hires the bumbling comedian to help in the theft. Painfully bad Disney comedy that brings out the worst of a seemingly talented ensemble. C: Dick Van Dyke, Edward G. Robinson, Dorothy Provine, Henry Silva. D: Jerry Paris. FAM/ACT [G] 90m. v

Never Cry Wolf 1983 ★★★★½ Writer (Smith) lives alone in Arctic to study wolf behavior, but learns more about himself. Fascinating character study marked by beautiful photography. Some quick nudity; otherwise perfect family viewing. Based on book by Farley Mowat. C: Charles Martin Smith, Brian Dennehy, Samson Jorah. D: Carroll Ballard. FAM/DRA [PG] 105m. v

Never Forget 1991 ★★★ Angry concentration camp survivor (Nimoy) is challenged by Holocaust denizens to prove that Nazi atrocities really took place. Based on true story, earnest film underscores frightening problem of Holocaust revesionism. C: Leonard Nimoy, Blythe Danner, Dabney Coleman. D: Joseph Sargent. DRA 94m. TVM v

Never Give a Sucker an Even Break 1941 ★★★★½ Hilarious hodgepodge of slapstick gags and wild chases loosely tied to Fields trying to sell a film script to studio. Marx Brothers veteran Dumont also makes a fine foil for Fields. Sometimes chaotic, but ends with classic chase sequence. C: W.C. Fields, Gloria Jean, Leon Errol, Franklin Pangborn, Margaret Dumont. D: Edward Cline. COM 71m. v

Never Give an Inch 1971 *See* **Sometimes a Great Notion**

Never Let Go 1960 British ★★★★ Sellers in fascinating change-of-pace dramatic role as vicious ganglord whose car theft ring is opposed by upright crime victim and by young gang member who goes to cops. Excellent Todd leads fine cast. Well-directed crimer with some brutal film noir moments. C: Richard Todd, Peter Sellers, Elizabeth Sellars, Carol White. D: John Guillermin. DRA 91m. v

Never Let Me Go 1953 ★★★½ Early Cold War drama about an American (Gable) marrying a Russian ballerina (Tierney), then trying to help her defect. Good chemistry between the stars helps. C: Clark Gable, Gene Tierney, Richard Haydn, Kenneth Moore. D: Delmer Daves. DRA 94m. v

Never on Sunday 1960 Greek ★★★★½ When a bookish Yank tries to reform a Greek prostitute he finds he has his hands full. Mercouri gives a vivid star performance in this highly entertaining classic with a catchy Oscar-winning score. C: Melina Mercouri, Jules Dassin, Georges Foundas, Titos Vandis. D: Jules Dassin. DRA 94m. v

Never on Tuesday 1989 ★★★ Standard adolescent nonsense features two bored suburban teenagers who head out for desert jaunt, where they end up stranded. Run-of-the-mill idiot humor, enlivened by strange cameos from brothers Emilio Estevez and Charlie Sheen. C: Claudia Christian, Andrew Lauer, Peter Berg. D: Adam Rifkin. COM [R] 90m.

Never Say Die 1939 ★★★½ Wealthy man (Hope) thinks he has one month to live, marries Raye so she'll inherit his fortune. Modest comedy almost clicks, but moves too slowly for its own good. Co-written by Preston Sturges. C: Bob Hope, Martha Raye, ANdy Devine, Gale Sondergaard, Monty Woolley. D: Elliott Nugent. COM 80m.

Never Say Goodbye 1946 ★★★ Determined child tries to reunite divorcing parents (Flynn, Parker). Routine comedy gives Flynn a chance to be charming and sing a few bars. C: Errol Flynn, Eleanor Parker, Lucile Watson, S.Z. Sakall, Hattie McDaniel. D: James V. Kern. COM 97m. v

Never Say Goodbye 1956 ★★★ Weepy drama of WWII doctor (Hudson) and German wife (Borchers), separated by fate, then reunited by tragedy. Okay remake of *This Love of Ours*. That's Clint Eastwood as Rock's assistant. C: Rock Hudson, Cornell Borchers, George Sanders, David Janssen. D: Jerry Hopper. DRA 96m.

Never Say Never Again 1983 ★★★½ Returning as 007 after a 12-year absence, Connery is, once more, exceptionally watchable as he again takes on villain Brandauer. Bassinger and Carrera are fine additions to gallery of Bond women. A loose remake of *Thunderball*. C: Sean Connery, Klaus Maria Brandauer, Max von Sydow, Barbara Carrera, Kim Basinger, Alec McCowen. D: Irvin Kershner. ACT [PG] 134m. v

Never So Few 1959 ★★★½ In WWII, Americans take command of guerrillas in the Burmese jungle. Well-made combination of combat and romance. Varied, interesting cast, including future stars McQueen and Bronson. C: Frank Sinatra, Gina Lollobrigida, Peter Lawford, Steve McQueen, Paul Henreid, Brian Donlevy, Charles Bronson. D: John Sturges. DRA 125m. v

Never Steal Anything Small 1959 ★★★ Weird comedy/drama about corruption in a longshoreman's union, with ambitious dockworker (Cagney) scheming to win union election. Incidental pleasures and a few laughs can't hoist this mostly unsuccessful amalgam of satire and song. C: James Cagney, Shirley Jones, Roger Smith, Cara Williams, Nehemiah Persoff, Royal Dano, Horace McMahon. D: Charles Lederer. COM 94m. v

Never Take Candy from a Stranger 1961 British ★★★ Delicately handled study of child molestation, as school principal and wife move to new town, where daughter and other girl are abused by elderly pillar of the community. Disbelieving town rallies to old man's defense, but soon regrets it. Quiet, honest drama. C: Gwen Watford, Patrick Allen, Felix Aylmer, Niall MacGinnis. D: Cyril Frankel. DRA 81m.

Never Take No for an Answer 1952 British ★★★½ Italian orphan boy visits tomb of St. Francis with sick donkey. Sentimental but sweetly charming tale. C: Vittorio Manunta, Denis O'Dea, Guido Celano, Nerio Bernardi. D: Maurice Cloche, Ralph Smart. DRA

Never Too Late 1965 ★★★½ Middle-aged O'Sullivan and Ford are expecting; adult daughter Stevens not thrilled. Amusing comedy works on strength of O'Sullivan/Ford chemistry. C: Paul Ford, Connie Stevens, Maureen O'Sullivan, Jim Hutton, Jane Wyatt, Henry Jones, Lloyd Nolan. D: Bud Yorkin. COM 105m.

Never Too Late to Mend 1937 British ★★★ A deranged criminal tries to win the woman he is obsessed with by framing her boyfriend. A stark study of the cirminal mind. C: Tod Slaughter. D: Tod Slaughter. CRI 67m. v

Never Too Young to Die 1986 ★★ Stamos' search for his father's killer leads him to Simmons, an evil hermaphrodite terrorist who, along with Englund, schemes to taint L.A.'s water supply. Saved from the junk heap by Simmons' inspired performance. C: John Stamos, Vanity, Gene Simmons, George Lazenby, John Anderson, Robert Englund. D: Gil Bettman. ACT [R] 97m. v

Never Wave at a WAC 1952 ★★★½ Senator's daughter hopes for cushy Paris commission as a WAC, but ends up with rough job in Arctic testing new textile. Mild but amusing farce, with Russell in good form. Best scene: joining up. C: Rosalind Russell, Marie Wilson, Paul Douglas, Arleen Whelan, Hillary Brooke, Louise Beavers, Frieda Inescort. D: Norman Z. McLeod. COM 87m.

Neverending Story, The 1984 West German ★★★★½ Young boy (Oliver) reads fantasy tale and magically enters land of Fantasia to battle evil forces with a young fighter (Hathaway). Enchanting children's film that adults will also enjoy; of lively story and marvelous special effects. Followed by lesser sequel. Based on best-selling novel by Michael Ende. C: Noah Hathaway, Barret Oliver, Tami Stronach, Moses Gunn. D: Wolfgang Peterson. FAM/SFI [PG] 94m. v

Neverending Story II: The Next Chapter, The 1991 ★★★ When real world proves too stressful, youngster (Brandis) reads himself into fantasy world where he must save a princess. Follow-up to original dream film is violent, with flashes of humor. C: Jonathan Brandis, Kenny Morrison, John Wesley Shipp, Alexandra Johnes. D: George Miller. FAM/SFI [PG] 95m. v

New Adventures of Heidi, The 1978 ★★ The young heroine visits New York in this updating of Johanna Spyri's children's classic. Nice try, but she's better off on her home turf. C: Katy Kurtzman, Burl Ives, John Gavin. D: Ralph Senensky. FAM/DRA 100m. TVM

New Adventures of Pippi Longstocking, The 1988 ★★½ Dashing Pippi comes to the big screen in a treacly musical version of children's classic. Only for small kids. C: Tami Erin, Eileen Brennan, David Seaman Jr., Cory Crow, Dick VanPatten. D: Ken Annakin. FAM/ACT [G] 100m. v

New Adventures of Tarzan, The 1935 ★★ Compilation of '30s *Tarzan* serial, created by Edgar Rice Burroughs' production company, follows vine-swinging hero on search for precious icon. Lesser screen rendition of Tarzan story. C: W. McGaugh, Herman Brix, Ula Holt. D: Edward Kull. ACT 22m. v

New Age, The 1994 ★★ An upscale couple, fed up with their empty lifestyle, looks for spirtual enlightenment, then heads for divorce court. Clumsy satire wastes its talented cast. C: Judy Davis, Peter Weller, Adam West. D: Michael Tolkin. COM [R] 112m.

New Centurions, The 1972 ★★★½ Episodic police drama based on the Wambaugh novel compares experiences of vet cop Scott with upstart rookie Keach. Good story, riveting in parts. C: George C. Scott, Stacy Keach, Jane Alexander, Rosalind Cash, Scott Wilson, Erik Estrada, Clifton James. D: Richard Fleischer. CRI [R] 103m. v

New Faces 1954 ★★★½ Film version of Broadway revue features up-and-comers in variety show of song, dance, and comedy. Fun to see youthful stars in energetic showcase. C: Ronny Graham, Robert Clary, Eartha Kitt, Alice Ghostley, Paul Lynde, Carol Lawrence. D: Harry Horner. MUS 98m. v

New Faces of 1937 1937 ★★★ Thin, poorly paced revue with plot similar to 1967's *The Producers*, as crafty crook (Cowan) tries to produce sure-fire flop so he can pocket investors' money. Ann Miller pops up in the finale. C: Milton Berle, Joe Penner, Jerome Cowan, Parkyakarkus, Harriet Hilliard. D: Leigh Jason. MUS 100m.

New Fist of Fury 1985 ★★ A petty thief masters martial arts and goes off to fight WWII. Classic kung fu action with lots of blood and gore. C: Jackie Chan. D: Jackie Chang. ACT 120m. v

New Gladiators, The 1987 ★ Gladiators battle each other in 21st-century Rome; a sort of return to their ancestral homeland. Merely an excuse to stage one dreadful, excessive violent fight scene after another. C: Jared Martin, Fred Williamson, Howard Ross, Eleanor Gold, Claudio Cassinelli. D: Lucio Fulci. ACT 90m. v

New Interns, The 1964 ★★★ Soap opera sequel to popular *The Interns.* Group of young doctors starting out includes woman-chaser (Callan), after obstetrician (Jones) and bitter slum graduate (Segal). Fun party scene, but otherwise a tongue depressor. C: Michael Callan, Dean Jones, Telly Savalas, Inger Stevens, George Segal, Greg Morris, Stefanie Powers, Lee Patrick, Barbara Eden. D: John Rich. DRA 123m.

New Jack City 1991 ★★★★ Critical acclaim for this hard-rapping, gritty and gutsy thriller about the battle against crack in Harlem. Snipes is razor sharp as the big bad dope lord chased by unconventional narcs. Music by star IceT, 2 Live Crew, and more. C: Wesley Snipes, Ice T, Allen Payne, Chris Rock, Mario VanPebbles, Judd Nelson, Michael Michele, Vanessa Williams, Tracy Camilla Johns. D: Mario Van Peebles. CRI 101m. v

New Kids, The 1984 ★★★ Orphan teens Presby and Loughlin are bullied by new neighbor Spader. Middling drama doesn't do much with premise. C: Shannon Presby, Lori Loughlin, James Spader. D: Sean S. Cunningham. DRA 90m. v

New Kind of Love, A 1963 ★★★½ While in Paris, a reporter (Newman) meets a fashion designer (and real life spouse Woodward) whom he tries to romance. Sweet but slight love story. C: Paul Newman, Joanne Woodward, Thelma Ritter, Eva Gabor, Maurice Chevalier, George Tobias. D: Melville Shavelson. DRA 110m. v

New Land, The 1972 Swedish ★★★★ Good sequel to *The Emmigrants* continues the story as frontier couple searches for gold and encounters hardships in Minnesota. Slow-paced but gripping, sweeping historical saga benefits from fine detail and excellent work from von Sydow and Ullman. C: Max von Sydow, Liv Ullmann, Eddie Axberg, Hans Alfredson, Monica Zetterlund, Per Oscarsson. D: Jan Troell. DRA [PG] 161m. v

New Leaf, A 1971 ★★★ After wealthy Matthau goes broke, he woos ugly duckling millionaire May in effort to get her money. Oddball romantic satire doesn't quite work, though Matthau and May certainly maintain an unusual chemistry. May also wrote and directed. C: Walter Matthau, Elaine May, Jack Weston, George Rose, William Redfield, James Coco. D: Elaine May. COM [G] 102m. v

New Life, A 1988 ★★★½ Well-to-do middle-aged New York couple divorce. Good cast, but material is nothing new. C: Alan Alda, Ann-Margret, Hal Linden, Veronica Hamel, John Shea, Mary Kay Place, David Eisne. D: Alan Alda. COM [PG-13] 104m. v

New Lion of Sonora, The 1970 ★★★ The

grand sweep of "The High Chaparrel" (for which TV series this was the pilot) as the story of the powerful Montoya family begins with Don Domingo assuming the mantle ofleadership. C: Leif Erikson, Gilbert Roland. WST 104m. TVM V

New Moon 1940 ★★★½ Jeanette McDonald/Nelson Eddy musical romance with a great Hammerstein/Romberg score, well sung by the starry-eyed duo. Lighthearted fun. C: Jeanette MacDonald, Nelson Eddy, Mary Boland, George Zucco, H.B. Warner, Grant Mitchell, Stanley Fields. D: Robert Z. Leonard. MUS 106m. V

New Orleans 1947 ★★★½ Forget hackneyed plot about jazz club owner (de Cordova) trying to promote "new" music, and relish classic performances by Armstrong, Herman & Holiday (her only feature film appearance). C: Arturo de Cordova, Dorothy Patrick, Billie Holiday, Louis Armstrong, Woody Herman. D: Arthur Lubin. MUS 89m.

New Wave 1990 *See* **Nouvelle Vague**

New Year's Day 1989 ★★★½ Jaglom directs himself as writer moving back into apartment he's sublet to three women. Typical conversational introspection, some insightful and some painfully self-absorbed. C: Henry Jaglom, Gwen Welles, Maggie Jakobson, Melanie Winter, David Duchovny, Milos Forman, Michael Emil, Irene Moore, Harvey Miller. D: Henry Jaglom. DRA [R] 90m. V

New Year's Evil 1980 ★ During live broadcast of New Year's Eve party, killer knocks off one victim an hour. Another gory holiday-themed slasher rip-off. C: Roz Kelly, Kip Niven, Chris Wallace, Grant Cramer, Louisa Moritz, Jed Mills. D: Emmett Alston. HOR [R] 88m. V

New York, New York 1977 ★★★★½ Scorsese's elaborate, downbeat musical drama has Minnelli and De Niro playing mismatched lovers in the music business during the '40s and '50s. One of Minnelli's best screen performances, and De Niro is riveting as her ambitious partner. Brilliant soundtrack uses period songs mixed with new Kander and Ebb tunes including title song, "And The World Goes Round," and "Happy Endings." C: Robert De Niro, Liza Minnelli, Lionel Stander, Georgie Auld, Mary Kay Place, George Memmoli, Barry Primus, Dick Miller, Diahnne Abbott. D: Martin Scorsese. MUS [PG] 163m. V

New York Ripper 1982 Italian ★ Sick schlock has the Big Apple being terrorized by a maniac who talks like Donald Duck (!) and butchers women. Almost unwatchable. C: Jack Hedley, Almanta Keller, Paolo Malco, Alexandra Delli Colli. D: Lucio Fulci. HOR 85m. V

New York Stories 1989 ★★★½ Three vignettes directed by Three notables—Scorsese ("Life Lessons"), Coppola ("Life Without Zoe"), and Allen ("Oedipus Wrecks")—don't add up to their best material. Worth seeing, if only to argue about which segment works best. C: Nick Nolte, Rosanna Arquette, Steve Buscemi, Julie Kavner, Samantha Larkin, Talia Shire, Giancarlo Giannini, Mae Questal, Woody Allen, Mia Farrow. D: Martin Scorsese, Francis Ford Coppola, Woody Allen. DRA [PG] 126m. V

New York Town 1941 ★★★ Struggling singer (Martin) is torn between rich love (Preston) and true love (MacMurray). Nice cast, trite movie. Mary trills one song only. C: Mary martin, Fred MacMurray, Robert Preston, Akim Tamiroff, Eric Blore. D: Charles Vidor. COM 76m.

New York's Finest 1987 ★ Three prostitutes, fed up with their profession, pose as high society women as they attempt to land millionaire husbands. Lots of nudity. C: Ruth Collins, Jennifer Delora, Scott Thompson Baker, Heidi Paine, Jane Hamilton. D: Chuck Vincent. COM [R] 86m. V

Newlydeads, The 1987 ★★★ A reprise, but with panache and a few twists, of the story of a man who kills his lover when he discovers she is really a he, and then finds all the guests at his wedding ten years later mysteriously being murdered. C: Scott Kaske, Jim Williams, Jean Levine. D: Joseph Merhi. HOR V

Newman's Law 1974 ★★★ Kicked off the force on corruption charges, upright cop Peppard investigates the case on his own. Predictable police film. C: George Peppard, Roger Robinson, Eugene Roche, Abe Vigoda. D: Richard T. Heffron. CRI 98m. V

News at Eleven 1986 ★★★ News anchor Sheen wrestles with downward career slide and personal ethics when he discovers a story about sexual harassment at a local high school. Decent examination of personal journalistic ethics. C: Martin Sheen, Peter Riegert, Barbara Babcock, Sheree J. Wilson. D: Mike Robe. DRA 95m. TVM V

News from Home 1976 French ★★★½ The artistry of Akerman is presented in vignettes of everyday life, seeing fresh but stark beauty in the common, from the New York City subway to a pizzeria. D: Chantal Akerman. DOC 90m. V

Newsfront 1978 Australian ★★★★ Unique tale of newsreel camera crew, led by Hunter, as they chase stories in '40s and '50s. Cleverly constructed yarn effectively combines fiction and actual contemporary newsreel footage. Hunter is terrific. C: Bill Hunter, Gerard Kennedy, Angela Punch, Wendy Hughes, Chris Haywood, Bryan Brown. D: Phillip Noyce. DRA 110m. V

Newsies 1992 ★★ Unlikely Disney musical revolves around 1899 newspaper carriers who go on strike against big New York dailies. Cast sleepwalks through shallow script; overblown song-and-dance numbers don't help. C: Christian Bale, Bill Pullman, Robert Duvall, Ann-Margret, Michael Lerner, Kevin Tighe, Charles Cioffi, David Moscow, Luke Edwards, Max Casella, Jo Ann Harris, Ele Keats. D: Kenny Ortega. FAM/MUS 121m. V

Next Karate Kid, The 1994 ★★ Political

correctness comes to filmmaking, as Morita's newest student is not Ralph Macchio but Swank, the granddaughter of an old war buddy. C: Pat Morita, Hilary Swank. D: Christopher Cain. DRA

Next Man, The 1976 ★★★½ U.N. Saudi Arabian diplomat (Connery), on peace mission to Israel, is targeted for assasination by the woman (Sharpe) he falls in love with. Okay espionage/romance with attractive stars, scenery. (a.k.a. *Double Hit*) C: Sean Connery, Cornelia Sharpe, Albert Paulsen. D: Richard C. Sarafian. DRA [R] 108m. V

Next of Kin 1982 ★★★ Death ensues when a teacher is bequeathed an ominous home for the aged. Australian scarefare. Though unrated, contains nudity and violence. C: Jackie Kerin, John Jarratt, Gerida Williamson, Alex Scott. D: Tony Williams. HOR 90m. V

Next of Kin 1989 ★★★ A cop (Swayze) returns from the streets of Chicago to his roots in the backwoods of Kentucky to avenge his brother's brutal death. Largely a violent action drama but has a good cast and some good ole boy elements like Pollard's menace that give it flavor. C: Patrick Swayze, Liam Neeson, Adam Baldwin, Helen Hunt, Andreas Katsulas, Bill Paxton, Ben Stiller, Michael J. Pollard, Lisa Niemi. D: John Irvin. CRI [R] 109m. V

Next One, The 1983 ★★★ Lonely Barbeau, living on Greek island with son Licht, finds life miraculously changed after enigmatic stranger Dullea appears. Christ allegory suffers from somwhat simplistic approach. C: Keir Dullea, Adrienne Barbeau, Jeremy Licht, Peter Hobbs. D: Nico Mastorakis. SFI 105m. V

Next Stop, Greenwich Village 1976 ★★★★ Director Mazursky wrote this warm, touching evocation of life in Greenwich Village in the '50s. Baker is fine as aspiring Method actor escaping overbearing mother Winters. Colorful support from Greene and Walken. C: Lenny Baker, Shelley Winters, Ellen Greene, Christopher Walken, Lou Jacobi, Mike Kellin, Lois Smith, Dori Brenner, Antonio Fargas, Jeff Goldblum. D: Paul Mazursky. COM [R] 109m. V

Next Time I Marry 1938 ★★★ Enjoyable Lucy must marry working stiff in order to inherit big bucks. C: Lucille Ball, James Ellison. COM 65m. V

Next Time We Love 1936 ★★★½ Sullavan plays a successful actress married to an obscure newsman (Stewart), but wooed by Milland. Terrific chemistry between Jimmy and Margaret elevates this soaper; they would later reteam for the classic *The Shop Around the Corner*. C: Margaret Sullavan, James Stewart, Ray Milland. D: Edward H. Griffith. DRA 87m.

Next to No Time 1958 British ★★★½ Shy engineer (More) must cross Atlantic to close deal on automation system. He gets sales confidence boosted by actress and ship's bartender. Buoyantly directed, with More lots of fun. C: Kenneth More, Betsy Drake, Bessie Love, Harry Green, Patrick Barr, Roland Culver. D: Henry Cornelius. COM 93m.

Next Victim, The 1972 ★★½ Straying wife of an Austrian official hunts down a maniac who slashes the rich. C: George Hilton, Edwige French. D: Sergio Martino. CRI [R] 87m. V

Next Victim, The 1974 British ★★★½ A disabled woman is terrorized by a deranged murderer. Very suspenseful. C: Carroll Baker, T.P. McKenna. D: James Ormerod. HOR 80m. V

Next Voice You Hear, The 1950 ★★★½ Working man hears the voice of God on the radio and the inhabitants of suburban town reverently await celestial forthcoming message. Engrossing allegory narrowly saved from sentimentality by Whitmore's credible performance. C: James Whitmore, Nancy Davis, Lillian Bronson, Jeff Corey. D: William Wellman. DRA 85m. V

Next Year if All Goes Well 1984 French ★★★★ Well-acted farce about a couple with low self-esteem. C: Isabelle Adjani, Thierry Lhermitte. D: Jean-Lous Hubert. COM 95m. V

Ngati 1987 New Zealand ★★★★ A medical school graduate is sent by his father to the New Zealand village where he was born and where mother died. He discovers he's a Maori and stays with villagers as they take over meat preservation plant. Largely nonprofessional cast is sometimes awkward but it's a sincere, finely shot and detailed film. C: Wi Kuki Kaa, Judy McIntosh, Ross Girven, Connie Pewhairangi, Michael Tibble, Oliver Joness, Alice Fraser, Norman Fletcher. D: Barry Barclay. DRA 88m.

Niagara 1953 ★★★★ Wife plots husband's murder while on honeymoon. Effectively done, with beautiful shots of the falls; as well as a young Monroe on the verge of superstardom. C: Marilyn Monroe, Joseph Cotten, Jean Peters, Casey Adams, Don Wilson, Richard Allan. D: Henry Hathaway. DRA 89m. V

Nice Girl? 1941 ★★★½ Deanna develops crush on older man (Tone), while boyfriend (Stack) burns. First "grown-up" vehicle for Durbin, as charming as ever, singing five songs, including "Love At Last." C: Deanna Durbin, Franchot Tone, Walter Brennan, Robert Stack, Robert Benchley. D: William A. Seiter. MUS 95m.

Nice Girl Like Me, A 1969 British ★★★ Orphan escapes aunts by studying languages in Paris; she gets pregnant but passes baby off as someone else's. When the same thing happens in Venice, aunts begin to wonder. Ferris is appealing and film mostly keeps light tone, trying to avoid crassness. C: Barbara Ferris, Harry Andrews, Gladys Cooper, Bill Hinnant. D: Desmond Davis. COM [PG] 91m. V

Nice Girls Don't Explode 1987 ★★★ Horror spoof, as a teenage girl discovers that intimacy with boys makes sparks fly—literally.

Mom keeps extinguisher handy but turns out she suffers from same problem. Good cast, but silly, if cute, idea wears thin. C: Barbara Harris, Michelle Meyrink, William O'Leary, Wallace Shawn, James Nardini. D: Chuck Martinez. COM [PG] 92m. V

Nice Neighbor, The 1979 Hungarian ★★★ Seemingly generous man deceives his neighbors for personal gain. Smartly rendered. C: Laszlo Szabo, Margit Kayka. D: Zsolt Kezdi-Kovacs. DRA 90m. V

Nice Plate of Spinach, A 1976 *See* **What Would You Say to Some Spinach**

Nicholas and Alexandra 1971 British ★★★½ The extravagant life and ultimate downfall of Russia's last royal family. Lots of color and pageantry; fine cast, but quite long and rather slow. C: Michael Jayston, Janet Suzman, Tom Baker, Harry Andrews, Jack Hawkins, Laurence Olivier, Michael Redgrave. D: Franklin J. Schaffner. DRA [PG] 183m. V

Nicholas Nickleby 1947 British ★★★★ Charles Dickens' classic story of a young man safeguarding his family from his despotic uncle and other dangers. Sentimental, handsome production that lovingly re-creates Victorian London. (a.k.a. *The Life and Adventures of Nicholas Nickleby*) C: Derek Bond, Cedric Hardwicke, Alfred Drayton, Bernard Miles, Sybil Thorndike, Stanley Holloway. D: Alberto Cavalcanti. DRA 103m. V

Nick Carter in Prague 1978 *See* **Dinner for Adele**

Nick Carter, Master Detective 1939 ★★★★ Fast-paced Saturday matinee adventure with Pidgeon as super-sleuth trying to crack spy ring before they steal secret airplane plans. Based on stories by Bertram Millhauser & Harold Buckley. C: Walter Pidgeon, Rita Johnson, Henry Hull, Donald Meek. D: Jacques Tourneur. CRI 60m.

Nickel & Dime 1992 ★★★ A young artist will get huge finder's fee, if only he can locate a missing heiress. C: C. Thomas Howell, Wallace Shawn. D: Ben Moses. COM [PG] 96m. V

Nickel Mountain 1985 ★★★★ Unwed pregnant teenager (Langenkamp) is befriended by lonely, overweight diner owner (Cole) in sensitive, modest drama that was over-looked and under-rated on first release. Based on John Gardner's novel. C: Michael Cole, Heather Langenkamp, Patrick Cassidy, Brian Kerwin. D: Drew Denbaum. DRA 88m. V

Nickel Ride, The 1975 ★★★ Small-town L.A. crook (Miller) gets too big for his turf, and the bosses send enforcer (Hopkins) to keep eye on him . . . or to kill him. Harsh look at big-city crime is uneven but has good acting and direction, and doesn't pull its punches. C: Jason Miller, Linda Haynes, Victor French, John Hillerman, Bo Hopkins. D: Robert Mulligan. DRA [PG] 99m.

Nickelodeon 1976 ★★★½ The pioneer period of silent movies is the colorful milieu for this well-acted comedy; it should have been wonderful, but it falls apart in the second half. Ryan O'Neal is a hack film director whose young daughter (Tatum) is the true genius behind the lens. C: Ryan O'Neal, Burt Reynolds, Tatum O'Neal, Stella Stevens, John Ritter, Brian Keith. D: Peter Bogdanovich. COM [PG] 121m.

Nicole 1978 ★★★ Unbelievably wealthy woman's attempts to find happiness lead to great sorrow. C: Leslie Caron, Catherine Bach. D: Itsvan Ventilla. DRA 91m. V

Night after Halloween, The ★★½ A young woman is terrorized by her killer boyfriend in a suspenseful tale. C: Chantal Contouri, Robert Bruning. CRI 90m. V

Night After Night 1932 ★★★½ Dreary romance between speakeasy owner (Raft) and socialite (Cummings), worth sitting through for West's film debut. Speaking most of her own, improvised lines, she bursts into movie, grabs it, and won't let go. C: George Raft, Mae West, Constance Cummings, Wynne Gibson, Roscoe Karns, Louis Calhern, Alison Skipworth. D: Archie Mayo. DRA 73m. V

Night After Night After Night (He Kills) 1970 ★★½ London is once again the haunt of a Jack-the-Ripper style killer, eluding even modern police methods. C: Jack May, Linda Marlowe. CRI 88m. V

Night Alone 1938 British ★★★½ A husband, after a night on the town while his wife's away, wakes up in a strange woman's apartment carrying forged money. If he tries to clear himself of criminal charges, his wife will discover shenanigans. Modest but amusing British comedy lags a bit, but has winning cast. C: Emlyn Williams, Leonora Corbett, Leslie Brook. D: Thomas Bentley. COM 75m.

Night Ambush 1957 British ★★★½ On German-held Crete, British agents and partisans wreak havoc against the occupiers. Superb cast and direction. (a.k.a. *Ill Met by Moon-light*) C: Dirk Bogarde, Marius Goring, David Oxley, Cyril Cusack, Christopher Lee. D: Michael Powell, Emeric Pressburger. ACT 100m. V

Night and Day 1946 ★★★ So-so biography of songwriter Cole Porter is short on fact and long on great music. Grant, clearly not in his element, stars as Porter. Varied cast makes the most of Porter's tunes, but film is unimpressive. C: Cary Grant, Alexis Smith, Monty Woolley, Ginny Simms, Jane Wyman, Eve Arden, Mary Martin. D: Michael Curtiz. MUS 128m. V

Night and Day 1991 France ★★★ A young woman has affairs with two cab drivers on different shifts, until they discover each other's existence. A light and breazy film. C: Guilaine Londez, Thomas Langmann, Francois Negret. D: Chantal Akerman. COM 90m. V

Night and the City 1950 ★★★★ Desperate, shady young man on the run is determined to make his mark. Underrated film noir thriller with artful photography, fascinating array of low-lifes and energetic acting by Widmark. Based on novel by Gerald Kersh. Remade in 1992. C: Richard Widmark, Gene Tierney, Hugh Marlowe, Francis L. Sullivan, Herbert Lom, Mike Mazurki. D: Jules Dassin. CRI 104m. v

Night and the City 1992 ★★★½ A hustling ambulance-chaser tries to give up the law to promote boxing and ends up on the wrong side of just about everyone he encounters. De Niro is a wisecracking marvel with a heart, in what is essentially a downbeat formula story. Remake of a 1951 film noir favorite. C: Robert De Niro, Jessica Lange, Alan King, Jack Warden, Eli Wallach. D: Irwin Winkler. DRA [R] 104m. v

Night Angel 1990 ★★ A demon temptress from hell wants to conquer the world—so naturally, she starts by taking over a fashion magazine. Stylish scenes and effective makeup effects go far to save this silly chiller. C: Isa Andersen, Debra Deuer, Karen Black, Doug Jones. D: Dominique Othenin-Girard. HOR [R] 90m. v

Night Angels 1987 ★★★★ Sum of fragmented parts better than whole, but interesting study of São Paolo streets anyway. Theater director and film actress meet socialite, aging starlet, gay prostitute, sociology student, etc. Barros' impressive first feature difficult but visually intriguing, blurring illusion and reality. DRA

Night at the Opera, A 1935 ★★★★★ Marvelous musical comedy with Marxes in full gear. Snooty world of opera provides a perfect backdrop for Groucho, Chico, and Harpo's insanity as they come to the aid of lovesick, unknown tenor (Jones). Finale is a riot. Maybe the boys' best, though purists prefer *Duck Soup*. C: The Marx Brothers, Kitty Carlisle, Allan Jones, Margaret Dumont, Sig Rumann. D: Sam Wood. COM 84m. v

Night Before, The 1988 ★★★ High school nerd Reeves gets big prom date with dreamy Loughlin after she loses wager to pals. Standard adult comedy. C: Keanu Reeves, Lori Loughlin, Trinidad Silva, Michael Greene. D: Thom Eberhardt. COM [PG-13] 90m. v

Night Breed 1990 ★★★ Choppy but creepy story of young Sheffer, believing he's guilty of a series of murders, discovering he belongs to a hidden tribe of monsters. Highlighted by excellent makeup effects and famed director Cronenberg's performance as the actual killer. C: Craig Sheffer, Anne Bobby, David Cronenberg. D: Clive Barker. HOR [R] 102m. v

Night Brings Charlie, The 1990 ★★½ Suspicions fall upon a disfigured member of the town as a series of horrific murders are discovered; but are attentions misplaced as new terror mounts? C: Kerry Knight, Joe Fishback, Aimee Tenalia. D: Tom Logan. HOR 90m.

Night Call Nurses 1972 ★★★ Unsatisfied nurses perfect their bedside manners on willing patients. Funny and above average; part of series of "Sexy Nurse" flicks directed by schlock king Roger Corman. C: Patti Byrne, Alana Collins, Mittie Lawrence, Dick Miller, Dennis Dugan, Stack Pierce. D: Jonathan Kaplan. COM 85m. v

Night Caller from Outer Space 1965 *See* **Blood Beast from Outer Space**

Night Children 1989 ★★ A Los Angeles parole officer (Kwan), and a police officer (Carradine) join forces to take on a gang leader. Stars are adequate in an otherwise overly violent melodrama. C: David Carradine, Nancy Kwan, Griffin O'Neal. D: Norbert Meisel. CRI [R] 90m. v

Night Club Scandal 1937 ★★★ Doctor kills his wife, then frames her lover for crime. Enjoyable, briskly told B-mystery. C: John Barrymore, Lynne Overman, Louise Campbell, Charles Bickford, Evelyn Brent, Elizabeth Patterson, J. Carroll Naish. D: Ralph Murphy. DRA 70m.

Night Court 1932 ★★★ Evil judge Huston frames innocent young woman to elude investigator Stone. Earnest melodrama partially scripted by fabled New York columnist/producer Mark Hellinger. C: Phillips Holmes, Walter Huston, Anita Page, Lewis Stone, Mary Carlisle, John Miljan, Jean Hersholt. D: W.S. VanDyke II. CRI 90m.

Night Crawlers, The 1966 *See* **Navy vs. the Night Monsters, The**

Night Creature 1979 ★★★ Hemingway-like author Pleasence lives on secluded Southeast Asian island where he develops obsession over deadly jungle cat. So-so human animal fable. (a.k.a. *Out of the Darkness* and *Fear*) C: Donald Pleasence, Nancy Kwan, Ross Hagen. D: Lee Madden. DRA [PG] 83m. v

Night Crossing 1981 British ★★★★ A family of East Germans braves military and political forces by crossing to freedom in the West using a hot air balloon. Based on a true Cold War-era incident; well-acted and intelligent story specifically aimed at younger audiences. C: John Hurt, Jane Alexander, Glynnis O'Connor, Doug McKeon, Beau Bridges, Ian Bannen. D: Delbert Mann. FAM/DRA [PG] 107m. v

Night Digger, The 1971 British ★★★★ Creepy sleeper thriller about psychotic handyman (Clay) on country estate owned by blind woman and her repressed daughter (Neal). Richly atmospheric, well-acted. Adapted by Roald Dahl from Joy Cowley's novel. C: Patricia Neal, Pamela Brown, Nicholas Clay. D: Alastair Reid. HOR [R] 100m.

Night Editor 1946 ★★½ Crooked cop Gargan gets in over his head with Carter. Passable programmer, based on successful radio program. C: William Gargan, Janis Carter, Jeff Donnell, Coulter Irwin. D: Henry Levin. CRI 68m.

Night Eyes 1990 ★★ A security expert/peeping Tom (Stevens) is hired by a jealous husband to record the comings and goings of his wife (Roberts). Plentiful leering, but Robert's fans may enjoy it. Followed by two sequels. C: Andrew Stevens, Tanya Roberts. D: Emilio P. Miraglio. DRA [R] 95m. V

Night Eyes 2 1991 ★★½ Voyeuristic security guard (Stevens) returns, this time becoming involved with his client's wife (Tweed) whom he's supposed to protect. Stronger than the first, thanks to Tweed's alluring performance. C: Shannon Tweed, Andrew Stevens. D: Rodney McDonald. DRA [R] 97m. V

Night Fighters, The 1960 British ★★★½ IRA rebels recruit reluctant Mitchum in a sabotage plot. Good intentions; some good moments. (a.k.a. *A Terrible Beauty*) C: Robert Mitchum, Anne Heywood, Dan O'Herlihy, Cyril Cusack, Richard Harris, Marianne Benet. D: Tay Garnett. DRA 85m.

Night Flight 1933 ★★½ Story of how night flights became standard, despite the dangers. Director/pilot Brown's favorite; from Saint-Exupery's *Vol de Nuit*. DRA

Night Flight from Moscow 1973 French ★★★½ Soviet emissary Brynner defects to the West, taking compromising secrets with him. Elaborate espionage thriller almost gets tangled in its own plot twists. The star cast helps. Based on Pierre Nord's novel *Le 13e Suicide* (a.k.a. *The Serpent*) C: Yul Brynner, Henry Fonda, Dirk Bogarde, Philippe Noiret, Virna Lisi. D: Henri Verneuil. DRA [PG] 113m. V

Night Friend 1987 ★★★ A priest must battle against the pressures of his superiors as he tries to help a high school girl escape from a life of violence, drugs, and prostitution. C: Art Carney, Chuck Shamata, Jayne Eastwood. D: Peter Gerretsen. DRA [R] 94m.

Night Full of Rain, A 1978 Italian ★★★ Wertmuller's first English-language film casts Bergen as feminist photographer married to Italian Communist journalist. Foggy, overintellectualized soap opera brightened a bit by the curiosity of seeing Eikenberry and Tucker before *L.A. Law*. (a.k.a. *End of the World in Our Usual Bed in a Night Full of Rain, The*) C: Giancarlo Giannini, Candice Bergen, Jill Eikenberry, Michael Tucker, Anne Byrne. D: Lina Wertmuller. DRA 104m. V

Night Gallery 1969 ★★★★ Three tales of the supernatural from Rod Serling's TV series. All-star cast in creepy stories narrated by Serling and inspired by equally creepy paintings. Best known as directorial debut of Spielberg (Crawford's segment). C: Roddy McDowall, Ossie Davis, Barry Sullivan, Tom Bosley, George Macready, Joan Crawford, Richard Kiley, Sam Jaffe. D: Boris Sagal, Steven Spielberg, Barry Shear. SFI 95m. TVM V

Night Game 1989 ★★½ Houston law officer Scheider vs. serial killer. Routine crime story. C: Roy Scheider, Karen Young, Richard Bradford, Paul Gleason. D: Peter Masterson. CRI [R] 95m. V

Night Games 1980 ★★½ A sexually troubled housewife (Pickett) finds fulfillment in nighttime trysts with strange men in strange costumes. Bizarre to say the least. C: Cindy Pickett, Joanna Cassidy, Barry Primus, Paul Jenkins. D: Roger Vadim. DRA [R] 100m. V

Night God Screamed, The 1971 ★★½ Revenge is the obsession of a charismatic cult leader convicted of murder. C: Michael Sugich, Jeanne Crain, James Sikking. D: Lee Madden. HOR [PG] 85m.

Night Has a Thousand Eyes 1948 ★★★½ Ex-vaudeville clairvoyant Robinson predicts tragedy for Russell and others. Mysterious fun; adapted from Cornell Wollrich novella. C: Edward G. Robinson, Gail Russell, John Lund, Virginia Bruce, William Demarest. D: John Farrow. DRA 80m.

Night Has Eyes, The 1942 ★★★½ A vacationing teacher (Howard) searches for a friend who has vanished in the Yorkshire moors and encounters a reclusive, shellshocked composer (Mason). Fine performance by Mason highlights an intriguing mystery with boggy atmospherics. (a.k.a. *Terror House*) C: James Mason, Joyce Howard, Wilfrid Lawson, Mary Clare. D: Leslie Arliss. DRA 79m. V

Night Heat 1959 *See* **La Notte Brava**

Night Heaven Fell, The 1958 French ★★★½ Sexpot (Bardot) convinces lover (Boyd) to kill her rich uncle. Good example of Brigitte's appeal. C: Brigitte Bardot, Alida Valli, Stephen Boyd, Pepe Nieto. D: Roger Vadim. DRA 90m.

Night Holds Terror, The 1955 ★★★ Trio on the lam hitch a ride and hold a family hostage. Gets some tension going. C: Jack Kelly, Hildy Parks, Vince Edwards, John Cassavetes, Jack Kruschen, Joel Marston, Jonathan Hale. D: Andrew L. Stone. DRA 86m.

Night in Cairo, A 1933 *See* **Barbarian, The**

Night in Casablanca, A 1946 ★★★½ Mild late Marx Brothers vehicle is low-budget spoof of Bogart's *Casablanca*. Some good scenes, especially Harpo's, as the boys tangle with Nazis looking for missing treasure. C: The Marx Brothers, Lisette Verea, Charles Drake, Lois Collier, Dan Seymour, Sig Ruman. D: Archie Mayo. COM 85m. V

Night in Havana 1957 *See* **Big Boodle, The**

Night in Heaven, A 1983 ★★★ A professor (Warren) goes to a male strip club and finds one of the dancers is her flunking student (Atkins). Unlikely, silly romantic comedy. C: Lesley Ann Warren, Christopher Atkins, Robert Logan, Carrie Snodgress. D: John G. Avildsen. COM [R] 85m. V

Night in the Life of Jimmy Reardon, A 1988 ★★★ High school student (Phoenix) realizes his time in the sun is ending as friends begin preparing for college. Uneven story and mixed bag of performances hamper this coming-of-age film. Adapted by director Richert from his own autobiographical novel. C: River Phoenix, Ann Magnuson, Meredith Salenger, Ione Skye, Louanne, Matthew L. Perry. D: William Richert. COM [R] 95m. V

Night into Morning 1951 ★★½ Grieving for his dead wife and son, professor Milland takes to drink and becomes suicidal. Good Milland in straightforward melodrama. C: Ray Milland, John Hodiak, Nancy Davis, Lewis Stone, Jean Hagen, Rosemary DeCamp. D: Fletcher Markle. DRA 86m.

Night Invader, The 1943 British ★★ English citizen uncovers sabotage by Nazi official. British WWII propaganda. C: Anne Crawford, David Farrar, Carl Jaffe. D: Hebert Mason. DRA 81m.

Night Is Ending, The 1943 *See* **Paris After Dark**

Night Is My Future 1948 Swedish ★★★½ Malmsten is a young pianist blinded in military service whose life is redeemed by love of maid Zetterling. Lesser Bergman, but still Bergman. (a.k.a. *Music Is My Future* and *Music in Darkness*) C: Mai Zetterling, Birger Malmsten, Olof Winnerstrand, Naima Wifstrand, Hilda Borgstrom. D: Ingmar Bergman. DRA 87m. V

Night Key 1937 ★★★ Kindly inventor Karloff is up against thieves who steal his new motion-detection device. Mild thriller. C: Boris Karloff, Warren Hull, Jean Rogers, Hobart Cavanaugh. D: Lloyd Corrigan. DRA 67m.

Night Life of the Gods 1935 ★★½ At the behest of inventor Mobray, statues turn human—but some humans become statues. Slight comic fantasy. C: Alan Mowbray, Florine McKinney. D: Lowell Sherman. COM 74m.

Night Like This, A 1932 ★★½ Irish cop and busybody neighbor join forces to bust gambling ring. Example of one of the Aldwych Repertory stage farces tranferred to the screen in the '20s and '30s, usually with its repertory group intact. C: Ralph Lynn, Tom Walls, Winfred Shotter. D: Tom Walls. COM 72m.

Night Mail 1935 ★★★★ Documentary follows mail train from London to Glasgow. Truly lovely film, with the effective use of W.H. Auden's poetry and composer Benjamin Britten's music. DOC

Night Mayor, The 1932 ★★½ Tracy plays notorious high-living New York mayor Jimmy Walker, who resigned in corruption scandal. Tracy is appropriately fast and nervy; script is rather bland. C: Lee Tracy, Evelyn Knapp, Eugene Pallette. D: Ben Stokoff. DRA 68m.

Night Monster 1942 ★★★½ Nifty grade-B chiller about isolated cripple Morgan, whose doctors are being bumped off by a mysterious stalker that inhabits his rural compound. Ideal cast and surprise twists throughout make this good, creepy fun. C: Irene Hervey, Don Porter, Nils Asther, Lionel Atwill, Leif Erickson, Bela Lugosi, Ralph Morgan. D: Ford Beebe. HOR 80m.

'Night, Mother 1986 ★★★½ Spacek is determined to commit suicide, her mother (Bancroft) tries everything to dissuade her. Based on Marsha Norman's Pulitzer Prize-winning play; claustrophobic and bleak, with fine acting and directing. C: Sissy Spacek, Anne Bancroft. D: Tom Moore. DRA [PG-13] 97m. V

Night Moves 1975 ★★★★★ Tense, extremely intelligent detective tale, with private eye (Hackman) trying to escape his troubled marriage by traveling cross-country to the Florida Keys while searching for a missing teenager (Griffith). Tight script and consummate acting shine under Penn's moody direction. Ending is a real shocker. C: Gene Hackman, Jennifer Warren, Susan Clark, Edward Binns, Harris Yulin, Kenneth Mars, James Woods, Melanie Griffith, Max Gail. D: Arthur Penn. CRI [R] 100m. V

Night Must Fall 1937 ★★★★ Screen adaptation of Emlyn Williams' play about a mysterious psychotic killer masquerading as mild-mannered bellhop. Stagebound but well-done chiller and a tour-de-force for Montgomery. C: Robert Montgomery, Rosalind Russell, Dame May Whitty, Alan Marshal, Kathleen Harrison, E.B. Clive, Beryl Mercer. D: Richard Thorpe. CRI 117m.

Night Must Fall 1964 British ★★★ Brutal axe murderer terrorizes local rural gentry. Intellectual British remake of 1937 psychological drama. From the Emlyn Williams play. C: Albert Finney, Susan Hampshire, Mona Washbourne, Sheila Hancock, Michael Medwin, Joe Gladwin, Martin Wyldeck. D: Karel Reisz. DRA 105m.

Night My Number Came Up, The 1955 British ★★★★½ Edge-of-your-seat suspense film concerns RAF pilot Redgrave's psychic dreams, which may affect the outcome of a seemingly routine flight mission. Taut direction and superlative acting from top-drawer British cast make this an absolutely riveting experience. C: Michael Redgrave, Sheila Sim, Alexander Knox, Denholm Elliott, Ursula Jeans, Michael Hordern, George Rose, Alfie Bass. D: Leslie Norman. DRA 94m.

Night Nurse 1931 ★★★★ A hard-boiled household nurse (Stanwyck) learns of a scheme to do away with her patient's two children for their inheritance. Strong thriller with a snappy script and top acting by the cast. C: Barbara Stanwyck, Ben Lyon, Joan Blondell, Clark Gable, Charles Winninger. D: William Wellman. CRI 73m. V

Night of Adventure, A 1944 ★★★½ Nimble attorney (Conway) tries to avoid scandal while working to clear a man charged with murder who also dallied with a married woman. Crime drama successfully holds attention. C: Tom Conway, Audrey Long, Nancy Gates, Emory Parnell, Jean Brooks, Louis Borell, Edward Brophy, Addison Richards. D: Gordon Douglas. CRI 65m.

Night of Courage 1987 ★★½ Teacher investigates the gang murder of a Hispanic youth. Below-par movie about street-campus violence. C: Barnard Hughes, Daniel Hugh Kelly, Geraldine Fitgerald. D: Elliot Silverstein. CRI 104m.

Night of Dark Shadows 1971 ★ Lousy follow-up to *House of Dark Shadows* lacks Jonathan Frid's popular Barnabas character, as well as scares and style. Story concerns new owner (Selby) of an old mansion becoming possessed by his ancestor who once lived there. (a.k.a. *Curse of Dark Shadows*) C: David Selby, Lara Parker, Kate Jackson, Grayson Hall, John Karlen, Nancy Barrett. D: Dan Curtis. HOR [PG] 95m. V

Night of January 16th, The 1941 ★★½ Sailor who inherits a sizable legacy gets mixed up in a mysterious murder. Chatty mystery. From Ayn Rand's play. C: Ellen Drew, Robert Preston, Nils Asther, Donald Douglas, Rod Cameron, Alice White, Cecil Kellaway. D: William Clemens. CRI 79m.

Night of June 13 1932 ★★★ Eccentrics rally around neighbor charged with murder. Well-handled if episodic melodrama, expertly conceived by Vera Caspary. C: Clive Brook, Lila Lee, Charlie Ruggles, Gene Raymond, Frances Dee, Mary Boland. D: Stephen Roberts. DRA 70m.

Night of Mystery 1937 ★★ Debonair private eye Philo Vance (Richards) prepares to ensnare a cunning murderer who killed off a family piecemeal. Remake of the 1929 *The Greene Murder Case*. C: Grant Richards, Roscoe Karns, Helen Burgess, Ruth Coleman, Elizabeth Patterson, Harvey Stephens, June Martel. D: E.A. Dupont. CRI 66m.

Night of Terror 1933 ★ Insane murderer lurks on the grounds of an elegant manor. Typical B-movie with implausible climax. C: Sally Blane, Wallace Ford, Tully Marshall, Bela Lugosi, George Meeker, Edwin Maxwell, Bryant Washburn. D: Ben Stoloff. HOR 60m.

Night of the Big Heat 1967 *See* **Island of the Burning Doomed.**

Night of the Blood Beast 1958 ★★ Astronaut comes back to Earth with an extraterrestrial embryo. Good premise—dumb execution. (a.k.a. *Creature From Galaxy 27*) C: Michael Emmet, Angela Greene, John Baer, Ed Nelson, Tyler McVey. D: Bernard Kowalski. SFI 65m.

Night of the Blood Monster 1972 British ★★ Political intrigue and witch-hunts plague 15th-century England. Period bloodcurdler. C: Christopher Lee, Maria Schell, Leo Genn, Maria Rohm, Margaret Lee. D: Jess Franco. DRA [PG] 84m.

Night of the Claw 1980 *See* **Island Claws**

Night of the Comet 1984 ★★★½ The same comet that wiped out the dinosaurs does another flyby, taking all but a handful of young humans. Well-done sci-fi thriller with some comic charm. C: Catherine Mary Stewart, Kelli Maroney, Robert Beltran, Geoffrey Lewis, Mary Woronov, Sharon Farrell. D: Thom Eberhardt. SFI [PG-13] 95m. V

Night of the Creeps 1986 ★★★½ Dekker's directorial debut is highly entertaining horror that weaves just about every genre staple (aliens, ax murderers, zombies, heroic teens, etc.) into a coherent and witty homage set on a college campus. C: Jason Lively, Steve Marshall, Jill Whitlow. D: Fred Dekker. HOR [R] 89m. V

Night of the Cyclone 1990 ★★½ An urban flatfoot (Kristofferson) investigating the disappearance of his daughter uncovers a homicide in a lush island paradise. C: Kris Kristofferson, Jeff Meek, Marisa Berenson, Winston Ntshona. D: David Irving. CRI [R] 90m. V

Night of the Demon 1957 *See* **Curse of the Demon**

Night of the Demons 1987 ★ Stylish but empty shocker about partying teens who literally raise hell in a haunted mansion on Halloween night. These obnoxious jerks get exactly what they deserve; after half an hour, you'll be rooting for the demons. C: Cathy Podewell, William Gallo, Mimi Kinkade, Linnea Quigley, Hal Havins. D: Kevin S. Tenney. HOR [R] 87m. V

Night of the Demons 2 1994 ★★★½ Better than the original, thanks to a black-humored approach and some terrific effects, though the formula of excessive gore and gratuitous nudity remains. Catholic school kids accidentally unleash the original's female demon, who proceeds to possess and kill them. C: Johnny Moran, Christi Harris, Merle Kennedy, Jennifer Rhodes, Amelia Kinkade. D: Brian Trenchard-Smith. HOR [R] 95m.

Night of the Eagle 1962 *See* **Burn, Witch, Burn!**

Night of the Following Day, The 1969 ★★★ En route to Paris to visit her father, a young girl (Franklin) is kidnapped by thugs and held for ransom. Middling though sordid thriller is given substance by the powerful cast. C: Marlon Brando, Richard Boone, Rita Moreno, Pamela Franklin, Jess Hahn. D: Hubert Cornfield. CRI [R] 93m. V

Night of the Fox 1990 U.S. ★★ A solid WWII thriller about plot to foil D-Day invasion. C: George Peppard, Deborah Raffin, Michael York, David Birney, John Mills. D: Charles Jarrott. ACT [R] 95m. TVM V

Night of the Generals, The 1967 British ★★★½ During WWII, a German intelligence officer organizes a hunt for a psychopathic Nazi general. Occasionally compelling, occasionally muddled suspense film. C: Peter O'Toole, Omar Sharif, Tom Courtenay, Donald Pleasence, Christopher Plummer, Charles Gray. D: Anatole Litvak. DRA 146m. V

Night of the Grizzly 1966 ★★★ Wyoming rancher (Walker) terrorized by rampaging bear. Average oater filmed in Wyoming. C: Clint Walker, Martha Hyer, Keenan Wynn, Nancy Kulp, Regis Toomey, Jack Elam. D: Joseph Pevney. WST [G] 99m. V

Night of the Hunter 1991 ★★★½ Chamberlain's cast against type as con-artist preacher out to claim stolen money as his own in effective remake of superior 1955 cult classic. C: Richard Chamberlain, Diana Scarwid, Amy Bebout. D: David Greene. CRI 100m. TVM

Night of the Hunter, The 1955 ★★★★½ Stark allegorical narrative about psychotic preacher pursuing his two step-children, who hold the secret to finding $10,000 stolen by their father. Mitchum is spellbinding as phony religious fanatic in Laughton's only outing as director. Uneven in places, but still one of the scariest thrillers ever made. C: Robert Mitchum, Shelley Winters, Lillian Gish, Evelyn Varden, Peter Graves, James Gleason, Billy Chapin, Sally Bruce. D: Charles Laughton. DRA 94m. V

Night of the Iguana, The 1964 ★★★★★ Self-destructive cleric (Burton), now a tour guide at Mexican resort, crosses paths with sexy teenager (Lyon), artist (Kerr), and hotel owner (Gardner). The film's poetry is brilliantly realized under Huston's sure hand. Superior acting by superb cast. From Tennessee Williams play. Won Oscar for Costumes. C: Richard Burton, Deborah Kerr, Ava Gardner, Sue Lyon, James Ward, Grayson Hall, Cyril Delevanti. D: John Huston. DRA 117m. V

Night of the Juggler 1980 ★★½ Former New York police officer (Brolin) pursues the lunatic who snatched his daughter. Improbable, standard thriller sags under the weight of its plotting. Fair quota of car crashes. C: James Brolin, Cliff Gorman, Richard Castellano, Abby Bluestone, Julie Carmen, Mandy Patinkin. D: Robert Butler. DRA [R] 100m. V

Night of the Lepus 1972 ★ Herd of four-foot-tall mutant rabbits terrorize Arizona ranchers. Science-fiction fodder about crazed big bunnies running amok. Must be seen to be believed. C: Stuart Whitman, Janet Leigh, Rory Calhoun, DeForest Kelley, Paul Fix, Melanie Fullerton. D: William F. Claxton. SFI [PG] 88m.

Night of the Living Dead 1968 ★★★★½ Terrifying, groundbreaking horror film (ahead of its time in both gore and social relevance), about a motley group of people taking refuge in an isolated farmhouse from a zombie plague and discovering that their worst enemies are each other. C: Duane Jones, Judith O'Dea, Russell Streiner, Keith Wayne. D: George A. Romero. HOR 95m. V

Night of the Living Dead 1990 ★★★ Unnecessary remake adds color and additional twists to Romero's original, but doesn't improve on it. Still the story retains its basic power, and some of the acting is better than the 1968 version. C: Tony Todd, Patricia Tallman, Tom Towles. D: Tom Savini. HOR [R] 92m. V

Night of the Quarter Moon 1959 ★★ Society blue bloods sponsor a man, then learn his wife had African-American ancestry. Lurid drama sensationalizes miscegenation. (a.k.a. *Flesh and Flame*) C: Julie London, John Drew Barrymore, Nat King Cole, Dean Jones, James Edwards, Anna Kashfi, Agnes Moorehead, Jackie Coogan. D: Hugo Haas. DRA 96m.

Night of the Shooting Stars, The 1982 Italian ★★★★½ Emotional and moving story of citizens in an Italian village near the end of WWII who must choose between the fascists and the approaching Allies. A magical story, simply but delicately told through a six-year-old's eyes. C: Omero Antonutti, Margarita Lozano, Claudio Bigagil, Massimo Bonetti, Norma Martel. D: Paolo Taviani, Vittorio Taviani. DRA [R] 107m. V

Night of the Warrior 1991 ★★★ Eager to keep an athletic nightclub owner (Lamas) competing as a kickboxer, a gangster (Geary) systematically torments his friends and family. Typical action fare, but with more style than usual. C: Lorenzo Lamas, Anthony Geary, Kathleen Kinmont, Arlene Dahl. D: Rafal Zielinski. ACT [R] 96m. V

Night on Earth 1991 ★★★★ Offbeat comedy centers around one-night relationships between five different cab drivers and their various passengers in L.A., Manhattan, Paris, Rome, and Helsinki. Engaging premise benefits from nifty comic ensemble and great score by Tom Waits. C: Winona Ryder, Gena Rowlands, Giancarlo Esposito, Armin Mueller-Stahl, Rosie Perez, Isaach DeBankole, Beatrice Dalle, Roberto Benigni, Paolo Bonacelli, Matti Pellonpaa. D: Jim Jarmusch. COM [R] 128m. V

Night Passage 1957 ★★★★ Outlaw (Murphy) and his gang plan to rob a railroad payroll guarded by his brother (Stewart). Sturdy Western with thrilling gun battle finale. C: James Stewart, Audie Murphy, Dan Duryea, Brandon de Wilde, Dianne Foster. D: James Neilson. WST 90m.

Night Patrol 1985 ★ Wacky hijinks in a police station. *Police Academy* clone is a barrage of bathroom jokes and smutty one-liners. C: Linda Blair, Jayne P. Morgan, Billy Barty, Andrew Dice Clay. D: Jackie Kong. COM [R] 87m. V

Night People 1954 ★★★★ The Russians abduct an American Army corporal in Cold War Berlin, and U.S. Army Intelligence tries to get him back. Smart, suspenseful espionage thriller, ably directed. C: Gregory Peck, Broderick Crawford, Anita Bjork, Rita Gam, Walter Abel, Buddy Ebsen. D: Nunnally Johnson. DRA 93m.

Night Plane from Chungking 1943 ★★★½ Plane bound for India is shot down in China with seven international passengers aboard, one of whom is a deadly Axis agent. Intriguing B-movie handled well. Holds interest. C: Ellen Drew, Robert Preston, Otto Kruger, Steven Geray, Sen Yung, Tamara Geva, Soo Yong. D: Ralph Murphy. ACT 69m.

Night Porter, The 1973 Italian ★★½ Psychosexual drama centering on the accidental reunion between one-time Nazi concentration camp commandant (Bogarde) and his one-time prisoner and s&m partner (Rampling). Offbeat, and definitely not for children; may offend some with its use of the Holocaust as metaphor. C: Dirk Bogarde, Charlotte Rampling, Philippe Leroy, Gabriele Ferzetti, Isa Miranda. D: Liliana Cavani. DRA [R] 117m. V

Night Rhythms 1992 ★ After a night of passion with a fan, a radio personality (Hewitt) awakes to find her murdered. Who's framing him and why? Who cares! The plot is an excuse for gratuitous sex and violence. C: Martin Hewitt, Sam Jones, Deborah Driggs, Delia Sheppard. D: Alexander Gregory Hippolyte. CRI [R] 100m. V

Night Rider, The 1979 ★★★ Wimpy New Orleans lawyer (Selby) dons cape and mask by night to avenge his family's murder and fight for justice. Average swashbuckler reminiscent of *Zorro.* C: David Selby, Percy Rodrigues, Kim Catrall, George Grizzard, Anthony Herrera, Anna Lee, Pernell Roberts. D: Hy Averback. ACT 90m. TVM

Night Runner, The 1957 ★★★ Mental patient (Danton) is released, then runs amuck bent on murder. Violent piece with unsympathetic lead. C: Ray Danton, Colleen Miller, Merry Anders, Eddy Waller. D: Abner Biberman. HOR 79m.

Night School 1981 ★ Awful slasher flick, with especially bad script, about gruesome murders of young women at a Boston college. Ward's first film. C: Leonard Mann, Rachel Ward, Drew Snyder, Joseph R. Sicari, Edward Albert. D: Ken Hughes. HOR [R] 89m. V

Night Shadows 1983 *See* **Mutant**

Night Shift 1982 ★★★★ When Winkler hires new guy Keaton to assist at mortuary night shift, the enterprising employee reorganizes operation as front for prostitution. Truly offbeat premise works thanks to Keaton's adrenaline-charged performance. C: Henry Winkler, Michael Keaton, Shelley Long, Bobby DiCicco, Nita Talbot, Kevin Costner, Vincent Schiavelli. D: Ron Howard. COM [R] 106m. V

Night Slaves 1970 ★★½ Extraterrestrials force small-town citizens to repairing their downed spacecraft. Listless science-fiction jumble. C: James Franciscus, Lee Grant, Scott Marlowe, Andrew Prine, Tisha Sterling, Leslie Nielsen. D: Ted Post. SFI 73m. TVM

Night Song 1947 ★★★ Soapy love story between blind pianist (Andrews) and bored socialite (Oberon) with strong support from Barrymore. It's not every day that one film features Artur Rubinstein, Eugene Ormandy, and Hoagy Carmichael! C: Dana Andrews, Merle Oberon, Ethel Barrymore. D: John Cromwell. DRA 101m.

Night Stalker, The 1971 ★★★★ There's an outbreak of weird murders in Las Vegas and a brash reporter believes they were committed by a vampire. Blends comedy and horror rises way above stereotype. C: Darren McGavin, Carol Lynley, Simon Oakland, Ralph Meeker, Claude Akins. D: John Llewellyn Moxey. HOR 71m. TVM V

Night Strangler, The 1972 ★★★½ Wisecracking journalist (McGavin) follows a lead to Seattle and learns of a series of baffling stranglings in this above-par thriller. Sequel to *The Night Stalker.* C: Darren McGavin, Simon Oakland, Jo Ann Pflug, Richard Anderson, John Carradine, Margaret Hamilton, Wally Cox. D: Dan Curtis. CRI 74m. TVM

Night Sun 1990 Italian ★★★ Italian nobleman in the 18th century refuses to wed a royal concubine and instead becomes a recluse believed to possess supernatural powers. Stern, contemplative morality tale; not for every taste. C: Julian Sands, Charlotte Gainsbourg, Nastassia Kinski, Massimo Bonetti, Margarita Lozano, Rudiger Vogler. D: Paolo Taviani, Vittorio Taviani. DRA 112m. TVM

Night That Panicked America, The 1975 ★★★★ Orson Welles' 1938 Halloween radio broadcast of H. G. Wells' *War of the Worlds* realistically dramatized an invasion of Earth by Martians. This exciting well-made movie offers an authentic recreation of the infamous radio show interspersed with vignettes illustrating its profound effect on many listeners. C: Vic Morrow, Cliff De Young, Michael Constantine, Walter McGinn, Eileen Brennan, Meredith Baxter, Tom Bosley, Will Geer, Paul Shenar, John Ritter. D: Joseph Sargent. DRA 100m. TVM

Night the Bridge Fell Down, The 1983 ★★ Eight people are trapped with a fugitive bank robber on a bridge about to collapse. Irwin Allen disaster movie. C: James MacArthur, Desi Arnaz, Jr., Leslie Nielsen. D: Georg Fenady. DRA 156m. TVM

Night the City Screamed, The 1980 ★★★ Blackout disaster affects the lives of various people. Standard offering with some familiar faces. C: Raymond Burr, Georg Stanford Brown, Robert Culp, David Cassidy, Linda Purl. D: Harry Falk. DRA [PG] 96m. TVM V

Night the Lights Went Out in Georgia, The 1981 ★★★ McNichol and Quaid as sibling country singers? The rest of the movie doesn't get much more plausible as it charts her feeble love affair with Hamill and his scrapes with romantic rivals. C: Kristy McNichol, Mark Hamill, Dennis Quaid, Sunny Johnson, Don Stroud. D: Ronald F. Maxwell. DRA [PG] 112m. V

Night the World Exploded, The 1957 ★★½

impending massive disruption at the Earth's core spells the end of the world. More talk than action in this pretentious science-fiction tale. C: Kathryn Grant, William Leslie, Tris Coffin, Raymond Greenleaf, Marshall Reed. D: Fred F. Sears. SFI 94m.

Night They Killed Rasputin, The *See* **Nights of Rasputin**

Night They Raided Minsky's, The 1968 ★★★★ Young Amish woman in the '20s wants to crash Broadway but winds up as a burlesque stripper on New York's Lower East Side. Ebullient backstage and onstage fun, effectively capturing period charm and seedy milieu. Lahr died during shooting; that's a double in some scenes. C: Jason Robards, Britt Ekland, Norman Wisdom, Forrest Tucker, Harry Andrews, Joseph Wiseman, Denholm Elliott, Elliott Gould, Jack Burns, Bert Lahr. D: William Friedkin. COM [PG] 100m. V

Night They Saved Christmas, The 1984 ★★★★ Three children come to the aid of Santa Claus (Carney) when oil company drilling threatens his North Pole workshop. Entertaining holiday viewing for youngsters; engaging and funny. C: Jaclyn Smith, Art Carney, Paul LeMat, Mason Adams, June Lockhart, Paul Williams. D: Jackie Cooper. FAM/DRA 100m. TVM V

Night They Took Miss Beautiful 1977 ★★½ Terrorists skyjack a Bahamas-bound plane carrying five beauty contestants and a government courier holding a package of deadly biological warfare germs. Standard thriller with a planeload of well-known TV faces. C: Phil Silvers, Stella Stevens, Chuck Connors. D: Robert Michael Lewis. DRA 104m. TVM

Night Tide 1963 ★★★½ Sailor falls for a neurotic carnival woman and becomes convinced she's an evil mermaid in earthly guise. Intersting low-budget fantasy with flashes of creativity. C: Dennis Hopper, Linda Lawson, Gavin Muir, Luana Anders. D: Curtis Harrington. DRA 82m. V

Night Time in Nevada 1948 ★★★ Relatively late entry in Republic's *King of the Cowboys* series; young woman's inheritance is threatened. Tuneful Western. C: Roy Rogers, Andy Devine, Bob Nolan. WST 53m. V

Night to Remember, A 1942 ★★★★½ Very entertaining comedy/mystery, as mystery author (Aherne) and wife (Young) stumble on real-life murder. First-rate performances and good balance between laughs and suspense. C: Loretta Young, Brian Aherne, Sidney Toler, Gale Sondergaard. D: Richard Wallace. COM 91m. V

Night to Remember, A 1958 British ★★★★★ Engrossing, brilliantly directed docudrama detailing the sinking of the luxury liner *Titanic*. Distinguished British cast underplays admirably, creating tight suspense even though the outcome is never in doubt. Based on the best-seller by Walter Lord. C: Kenneth More, David McCallum, Laurence Naismith, Honor Blackman, Jill Dixon, Alec McCowen. D: Roy Ward Baker. DRA 123m. V

Night Train 1940 *See* **Night Train to Munich**

Night Train 1959 Polish ★★★ Young woman has to share a compartment with a taciturn physician on a train with a murderer aboard. Gloomy, tense entry. C: Lucyna Winnicka, Leon Niemczyk, Teresa Szmigielowna, Zbigniew Cybulski. D: Jerzy Kawalerowicz. DRA 90m.

Night Train to Kathmandu, The 1988 ★★★ When their geologist parents move to Asia, suburban adolescents are uprooted from comfortable American lives. After hooking up with a curmudgeon archaeologist, the teens end up searching for a mystical city. Nothing special. C: Pernell Roberts, Eddie Castrodad, Milla Jovovitch, Kavi Raz. D: Robert Wiemer. FAM/DRA 102m. TVM V

Night Train to Munich 1940 British ★★★★½ Carol Reed's triumphant suspense thriller about an English spy masquerading as a Nazi to help rescue a recaptured Czech scientistinventor who holds a critical secret formula. Superior Hitchcockian piece with striking photography and an astute script, based on Gordon Wellesley's *Report on a Fugitive*. (a.k.a. *Night Train*) C: Rex Harrison, Margaret Lockwood, Paul Hernried, Basil Radford, Naunton Wayne, Felix Aylmer, Roland Culver. D: Carol Reed. DRA 93m. V

Night unto Night 1949 ★★★ A scientist (Reagan) with epilepsy and a widow (Lindfors), grieving for her recently dead husband develop a relationship. Well-acted melodrama. C: Ronald Reagan, Viveca Lindfors, Broderick Crawford, Rosemary DeCamp, Osa Massen, Art Baker, Craig Stevens. D: Don Siegel. DRA 85m.

Night Visions 1990 ★★★ A tough cop (Remar) and a psychology grad student join in hunt for serial killer. Psychological thriller has its moments. C: Lori Locklin, James Remar, Penny Johnson, Mitch Pileggi, Jon Tenney, Mark Chapman, Bruce MacVittie. D: Wes Craven. CRI 100m. TVM

Night Visitor 1989 ★★ Teen comedy meets serial-killer thriller. High school student (Rydall) discovers that one of his teachers is a Satan worshipper, and drags retired detective (Gould) into the case. C: Derek Rydall, Allen Garfield, Elliott Gould, Michael J. Pollard, Shannon Tweed. D: Rupert Hitzig. COM 94m. V

Night Visitor, The 1970 ★★★★ Von Sydow, institutionalized for a heinous crime he may or may not have committed, plans his escape and means of revenge. Compelling, quietly spooky thriller with a first-rate cast. C: Max von Sydow, Liv Ullmann, Trevor Howard, Per Oscarsson. D: Laslo Benedek. CRI [PG] 106m. V

Night Walker, The 1964 ★★★★ A rich widow has recurring dreams about her missing husband and his unseen lover. Stanwyck is convincing as the distressed wife in taut psychological thriller, scripted by Robert Bloch. C: Barbara Stanwyck, Robert Taylor, Lloyd Bochner. D: William Castle. HOR 86m. V

Night Warning 1982 ★★ An overprotective aunt (Tyrell) keeps her nephew all to herself by ventilating nosy neighbors. Ultraviolent. C: Jimmy McNichol, Susan Tyrrell, Bo Svenson. D: William Asher. HOR [R] 96m. V

Night Watch 1973 British ★★★½ Taylor, recovering from a breakdown, thinks she's seen a murder but can't prove it. Is she mad? Star vehicle, from Lucille Fletcher play, is well done, if not exactly original. C: Elizabeth Taylor, Laurence Harvey, Billie Whitelaw, Robert Lang. D: Brian G. Hutton. CRI [PG] 100m. V

Night We Never Met, The 1993 ★★★ New York comedy about three renters of time-share apartment and their romantic entanglements. Anderson, Sciorra, and Broderick are well cast, but script gives them nothing more than series of expected sequences to play out. C: Matthew Broderick, Annabella Sciorra, Kevin Anderson, Louise Lasser, Jeanne Tripplehorn, Justine Bateman. D: Warren Leight. COM [R] 98m. V

Night Without Sleep 1952 ★★★ A neurotic (Merrill) thinks he's killed someone. Film noir suspense. C: Linda Darnell, Gary Merrill, Hildegarde Neff, Hugh Beaumont, Mae Marsh. D: Roy Baker. CRI 77m.

Night Without Stars 1951 British ★★★½ A bitter, visually impaired lawyer (Farrar) gets involved in a murder case and is redeemed by love. Solid British suspense. C: David Farrar, Nadia Gray, Maurice Teynac, June Clyde, Gerard Landry. D: Anthony Pelissier. CRI 86m.

Night World 1932 ★★★½ Melodrama set in nightclub frequented by demimonde. Packed with stars from the 30s and before, this pre-Code curiosity piece even has choreography by Busby Berkeley. Fascinating piece of film history. C: Lew Ayres, Mae Clarke, Boris Karloff, Dorothy Revier, Russell Hopton, Clarence Muse, Hedda Hopper, Bert Roach, George Raft. D: Hobart Henley. DRA 56m.

Night Zoo 1987 Canadian ★★★ Offbeat tale of sex and drugs in Montreal, with near-explicit sex and a ridiculous finale in the local zoo. A father and son try to mend old wounds in the midst of the violence of the underworld. C: Roger Le Bel, Gilles Maheu, Lyne Adams. D: Jean-Claude Lauzon. DRA 116m. V

Nightbreaker 1989 ★★★★ U.S. government performs nuclear experiments on military personnel in '50s; research doctor who was there only comprehends the horrific results 30 years later. Son and father Estevez and Sheen play the younger and older doctor. Poignant film; uplifting performances. C: Martin Sheen, Emilio Estevez, Lea Thompson, Melinda Dillon, Joe Pantoliano. D: Peter Markle. DRA 99m. TVM V

Nightcomers, The 1972 British ★★ Distasteful attempt to prequelize Henry James' *Turn of the Screw* has the not-yet-evil children involved with the bizarre affairs of the manor's gardener and housemaid and the murder that follows. If not for Brando, this would be forgotten. C: Marlon Brando, Stephanie Beacham, Thora Hird, Harry Andrews. D: Michael Winner. DRA [R] 96m. V

Nightfall 1956 ★★½ Ray is painter on the lam from both cops and killers, and Bancroft is the model who stays with him. Exciting though small-scale thriller. C: Aldo Ray, Brian Keith, Anne Bancroft, Jocelyn Brando, James Gregory, Frank Albertson. D: Jacques Tourneur. DRA 78m. V

Nightflyers 1987 ★★★ A crew of scientists on board a spaceship are at the mercy of their computer, programmed by a demented woman. Marginally entertaining premise, but the ending is out among the galaxies. C: Catherine Mary Stewart, Michael Praed, John Standing, Lisa Blount, Michael Des Barres. D: T.C. Blake. SFI [R] 88m. V

Night Force 1987 ★★ Low-budget actioner puts "Queen of B's" Blair in Central America with cohorts, trying to liberate U.S. Senator's daughter. Mildly laughable. C: Linda Blair, James Van Patten, Claudia Udy. D: Lawrence D. Foldes. ACT [R] 82m. V

Nighthawks 1981 ★★★★ Cop (Stallone) tracks a psychopathic but brilliant international terrorist (Hauer) through the streets, subways, and discos of New York. European film veteran Hauer joins Yank Stallone in a tautly told and surprisingly well-acted suspense drama. C: Sylvester Stallone, Billy Dee Williams, Lindsay Wagner, Persis Khambatta, Nigel Davenport, Rutger Hauer. D: Bruce Malmuth. CRI [R] 99m. V

Nightingale 1973 *See* **Young Nurses, The**

Nightkill 1980 W. German ★★½ Widow (Smith) and enigmatic shamus (Mitchum) play cat and mouse in a love triangle that leads to murder. Muddled suspenser film has a few bright moments toward the end and pleasing Arizona scenery, but plot is confusing. C: Jaclyn Smith, Mike Connors, James Franciscus, Robert Mitchum, Fritz Weaver. D: Ted Post. CRI [R] 104m. V

Nightlife 1989 ★★½ Modern-day vampire has romantic troubles; should she go for the nice Jewish doctor who runs the blood bank or stick with her old—very old—vampire boyfriend? Mild horror. C: Ben Cross, Maryam D'Abo, Keith Szarabajka, Jessie Cortie, Camille Saviola, Oliver Clark, Glenn Shadix. D: Daniel Taplitz. COM [PG-13] 100m. TVM V

Nightmare 1942 ★★★½ Gambler Donlevy and widow Barrymore are both suspects in her husband's murder, and must track down Nazi spies to clear their names. Decent wartime suspenser. C: Diana Barrymore, Brian Donlevy, Gavin Muir, Henry Daniell, Hans Conried, Arthur Shields. D: Tim Whelan. DRA 81m.

Nightmare 1956 ★★★ New Orleans musician McCarthy is hypnotized into committing murder, then must reconstruct the crime. Able remake of *Fear in the Night*, adapted from Cornell Woolrich's classic thriller. C: Edward G. Robinson, Kevin McCarthy, Connie Russell, Virginia Christine. D: Maxwell Shane. DRA 89m.

Nightmare Alley 1947 ★★★★ Power (ambitious and souless), becomes a conniving carnival barker, but his fortunes soon spiral downward. Power shows more edge than prettiness, aided by marvelous supporting cast (Blondell wonderful!) in a fascinating Jules Furthman script. C: Tyrone Power, Joan Blondell, Coleen Gray, Helen Walker, Taylor Holmes, Mike Mazurki, Ian Keith, Julia Dean. D: Edmund Goulding. DRA 111m.

Nightmare at Bittercreek 1987 ★★½ On a wilderness camping trip, four women and their alcoholic guide are attacked by a survivalist cult. Attempts to be a female *Deliverance*, but result is standard women-in-danger exploitation. C: Lindsay Wagner, Tom Skerritt, Constance McCashin, Joanna Cassidy, Janne Mortil. D: Tim Burstall. DRA [PG-13] 92m. TVM v

Nightmare Before Christmas, The 1993 ★★★★★ Comically gruesome tale of ghoulish Pumpkin King who leaves Halloween land to take over Christmas. Through visually stunning stop-motion animation, great songs, and character voices, the film creates a world audience has never experienced. Voices of Danny Elfman, Chris Sarandon, Catherine O'Hara, William Hickey, Glenn Shadix, Paul Reubens, Ken Page, Ed Ivory. D: Henry Selick. COM [PG] 75m. v

Nightmare Castle 1966 ★★★½ Cult horror star Steele plays dual role in murky, but effective story of mad doctor creating youth serum by draining victims' blood. C: Barbara Steele, Paul Mueller, Helga Line. D: Mario Caiano. HOR 90m.

Nightmare in Badham County 1976 ★★★ Two young women are falsely imprisoned by corrupt country cops. Interesting treatment; lots of lurid action; good cast. C: Deborah Raffin, Lynne Moody, Ralph Bellamy, Chuck Connors, Robert Reed, Della Reese. D: John Llewellyn Moxey. DRA [R] 100m. TVM v

Nightmare in Blood 1976 ★★★½ Low-budget monster comedy where the horror movie star guest at film convention is a real vampire. Clever little parody has lots of genre in-jokes. (a.k.a. *Horror Convention*) C: Jerry Walter, Dan Caldwell, Barrie Youngfellow, Kathleen Quinlan, Kerwin Mathews. D: John Stanley. COM [R] 89m. TVM

Nightmare in Wax 1969 ★★★ Horribly disfigured ex-Hollywood makeup artist Mitchell takes revenge on actors in his wax museum. Great camp fun, with wild Mitchell. C: Cameron Mitchell, Anne Helm, Scott Brady. D: Bud Townsend. HOR 95m. v

Nightmare of Terror *See* **Demons of the Mind**

Nightmare on Elm Street, A 1984 ★★★½ Craven's breakthrough hit tells of suburban teenagers plagued by nightmares about a scarred villain who kills them in their sleep. Imaginative premise generates genuine terror despite sometimes clunky dialogue and occasionally illogical story. C: John Saxon, Ronee Blakley, Heather Langenkamp, Amanda Wyss, Johnny Depp, Robert Englund. D: Wes Craven. HOR [R] 92m. v

Nightmare on Elm Street 2: Freddy's Revenge 1985 ★★★ Dream stalker possesses a teenager who moves into the original heroine's house, intent on using him to create havoc in the real world. Slim story enlivened by stylish effects and serious approach, before Freddy became a jokester. C: Mark Patton, Kim Myers, Robert Rusler, Clu Gulager, Hope Lange, Robert Englund. D: Jack Sholder. HOR [R] 87m. v

Nightmare on Elm Street 3: Dream Warriors 1987 ★★★½ One of the best *Elm Street* sequels is set in a psychiatric hospital, where apparent teen suicides are actually the handiwork of Freddy Krueger. Genuinely scary (with more humor from Freddy), with appealingly varied characters and effects. C: Heather Langenkamp, Patricia Arquette, Larry Fishburne, Priscilla Pointer, Craig Wasson, Robert Englund, John Saxon, Jennifer Rubin. D: Chuck Russell. HOR [R] 96m. v

Nightmare on Elm Street 4: The Dream Master 1988 ★★★ Freddy emerges as wisecracking antihero in this entry, with haphazard script overcome by style. Title refers to Wilcox, who takes on the razor-gloved ghoul after he murders her brother and friends. C: Robert Englund, Lisa Wilcox, Rodney Eastman, Danny Hassel, Andras Jones, Tuesday Knight, Ken Sagoes. D: Renny Harlin. HOR [R] 99m. v

Nightmare on Elm Street 5: The Dream Child 1989 ★★★ This time Wilcox is pregnant, and Freddy seeks reentry into the real world by possessing her unborn child. Formula still works, thanks to imaginative effects and likable teen characters. C: Robert Englund, Lisa Wilcox, Kelly Jo Minter, Erika Anderson, Danny Hassel. D: Stephen Hopkins. HOR [R] 90m. v

Nightmare on the 13th Floor 1990 ★★★½ Gruesome decapitations of guests at a grand Victorian hotel seem to be related to supernatural phenomena. Lightning pace and fine mounting tension. C: Michele Greene, James Brolin, Louise Fletcher, John Karlen, Alan Fudge. D: Walter Grauman. HOR [PG-13] 85m. TVM v

Nightmares 1983 ★★★ Quartet of middling horror stories. A smoker gets the ultimate nicotine fit, a video game fan discovers arcade Zen, a cleric gets chased by a satanic automobile, and (in the best one) boy meets rat. C: Cristina Raines, Emilio Estevez, Lance Henriksen, Richard Masur, Veronica Cartwright. D: Joseph Sargent. HOR [R] 99m. v

Nights of Cabiria 1957 Italian ★★★★★ Fellini's Oscar-winning Best Foreign Film about a gamine prostitute in Rome (Masina) who dreams of respectability and affluence but finds only heartbreak. Extraordinary work with brilliant acting by Masina. Fascinating, bittersweet story is the basis for *Sweet Charity*. (a.k.a. *Cabiria*) C: Giulietta Masina, Francois Perier, Amedeo Nazzari, Dorian Gray. D: Federico Fellini. DRA 111m. v

Nights of Prague 1968 Czechoslovakian ★★★★ Trio of timeless fables set in Prague; Yiddish version of *The Golem* is best of the lot. Haunting and lyrical. C: Jan Klusak, Jana Brezkova. D: Jiri Brdecka, Evald Schorm, Milos Makovek. DRA 92m.

Nights of Rasputin 1960 Italian ★★½ The debauched Russian mystic gains influence over the Tsarina Alexandra. Miscast, labored tale of the "mad monk." (a.k.a. *The Night They Killed Rasputin*) C: Edmund Purdom, Gianna Maria Canale, John Drew Barrymore, Jany Clair. D: Pierre Chenal. DRA 95m. v

Nights of Shame 1961 French ★★★½ Social worker tries to rehabilitate prostitutes in Paris, and is drawn into love and murder. Okay drama helped by splendid Parisian locales. C: Raymond Pellegrin, Giselle Pascal, Philippe Lemaire, Louise Carletti. D: Raoul Andre. DRA 81m.

Nightside 1980 ★★★ Two Los Angeles police officers work the graveyard watch. Predictable night-shift movie with lighthearted acting by veteran McClure. C: Doug McClure, Michael Cornelison. D: Bernard Kowalski. DRA 78m. TVM

Nightwing 1979 ★★½ A cantankerous zoologist (Warner) is obsessed with killing vampire bats in New Mexico. Horror thriller. C: Nick Mancuso, David Warner, Kathryn Harrold, Stephen Macht, Strother Martin. D: Arthur Hiller. HOR [PG] 105m. v

Nightwish 1989 ★★ A professor experimenting with hi students's nightmares turns out to have an even more horrifying agenda. Uneven shocker has some gruesomely effective moments. C: Clayton Rohner, Alisha Das, Jack Starrett, Elizabeth Kaitan. D: Bruce R. Cook. HOR [R] 96m. v

Nijinsky 1980 British ★★★½ Biography of the ballet great (De La Pena) and his love affair with Diaghilev (Bates) is handsome to look at, and Bates is splendid. Irons' film debut. C: Alan Bates, George De La Pena, Leslie Browne, Alan Badel, Colin Blakely, Carla Fracci, Jeremy Irons, Janet Suzman. D: Herbert Ross. DRA [R] 125m. v

Nikki, Wild Dog of the North 1961 ★★★★ Trapper is separated from his loyal canine while hunting in Canadian wilderness. Fresh reworking of familiar plot devices, marked by beautiful use of location. Great family viewing. C: Don Haldane, Jean Coutu, Emile Genest, Uriel Luft. D: Jack Couffer. FAM/DRA [G] 73m. v

9 1/2 Ninjas 1991 ★★★½ Surprisingly entertaining mixture of martial arts film and sex comedy spoof, as Phenicie trains his girlfriend (Gray) to be a ninja, and they wind up fighting bad guys. C: Michael Phenicie, Andee Gray, Robert Fieldsteel. D: Aaron Barsky Worth. ACT [R] 88m. v

9 1/2 Weeks 1986 ★★ Yuppie lawyer (Rourke) draws gallery worker (Basinger) into a sadomasochistic relationship. Most interesting element of the movie was the publicity it got, due to its supposed eroticism. Videocassette version contains some more explicit footage cut before theatrical release. C: Mickey Rourke, Kim Basinger, Margaret Whitton, David Margulies. D: Adrian Lyne. DRA [R] 117m. v

Nine Days A Queen 1936 ★★★½ Tragic tale of Queen Jane, who reigned for only nine days following the death of Henry VII. Historical costume drama. C: Cedric Hardwicke, John Mills, Nova Pilbeam. D: Robert Stevenson. DRA 80m. v

Nine Days of One Year 1964 USSR ★★★½ A Russian nuclear physicist exposed to radiation persists with his work and nearly destroys his private life. Tasteful, well-done drama. C: Aleksey Batlov, Innokentiy Smoktunovskiy. D: Mikhail Romm. DRA 107m.

Nine Girls 1944 ★★★½ Sorority house murder mystery gets by on charm of appealing young cast and B-movie velocity. C: Ann Harding, Evelyn Keyes, Jinx Falkenburg, Anita Louise, Jeff Donnell, Nina Foch, Marcia Mae Jones, Leslie Brooks, Lynn Merrick, Shirley Mills, William Demarest. D: Leigh Jason. CRI 78m.

Nine Hours to Rama 1963 ★★★ Well-intentioned study of the events leading up to assassination of Mahatma Ghandi. Buchholz gives an earnest if uninvolving performance as the killer. Slow-going. C: Horst Buchholz, Jose Ferrer, Robert Morley, Diane Baker, Harry Andrews. D: Mark Robson. DRA 125m.

Nine Lives Are Not Enough 1941 ★★★½ Snappy B-movie mystery has newspaperman (Reagan) on trail of a murderer. Good trooping by supporting cast. C: Ronald Reagan, Joan Perry, James Gleason, Peter Whitney, Faye Emerson, Howard da Silva, Edward Brophy, Charles Drake. D: A. Edward Sutherland. DRA 63m.

Nine Lives of Elfego Baca 1958 ★★½ Following the arrest of a cowhand, an inexperienced deputy must deal with the threat of eighty gunslingers out for blood. C: Robert Loggia, Robert F. Simon, Lisa Montell. D: Norman Foster. WST 78m.

Nine Lives of Fritz the Cat, The 1974 ★★ Toned-down sequel to notorious animation feature follows the hippie feline through more stoned fantasies about his eight other lives. Poorly animated and stuffed with filler material. D: Robert Taylor. COM [R] 77m. v

Nine Men 1943 ★★½ Beleaguered British soldiers battle Mussolini's army in North African desert. Small propaganda film with some tense moments. C: Jack Lambert, Gordon Jackson, Federick Piper. D: Harry Watt. DRA 68m.

976-EVIL 1989 ★★★½ Shy teenager transforms into a Satanic devotee after developing an obsession with a rather unique telephone hot line. Offbeat horror film with some sly comic moments; worth a peek. Directed by *Nightmare on Elmstreet* series star Freddie Krueger (Robert Englund). C: Stephen Geoffreys, Patrick O'Bryan, Sandy Dennis, Jim Metzler, Leslie Deane. D: Robert Englund. HOR [R] 105m. v

976-EVIL II 1991 ★★ The phone line from hell gets some repeat dialing as an imprisoned murderer continues his reign of terror. Gimmicky shocker boasts a few imaginative sequences. C: Debbie James, Rene Assa, Pat O'Bryan, Phil McKeon, Leslie Ryan. D: Jim Wynorski. HOR [R] 92m.

9/30/55 1977 *See* **September 30, 1955**

9 to 5 1980 ★★★★ Trio of mismatched secretaries kidnap their obnoxious, lecherous boss (Coleman) in popular, broadly played comedy. Offbeat role for Fonda; Tomlin shines, and Dolly is delightful—and sings title tune. C: Jane Fonda, Lily Tomlin, Dolly Parton, Dabney Coleman, Henry Jones. D: Colin Higgins. COM [PG] 110m. v

1900 1977 Italian ★★★★ Massive epic follows two friends—one rich, one poor—born on the same day in 1900. Their lives play out against backdrop of Italian history and rise of fascism during WWII. Bertolucci makes skillful use of sumptuous photography and a fine cast, but some judicious cutting might have made it even better. C: Robert De Niro, Gerard Depardieu, Donald Sutherland, Burt Lancaster, Dominique Sanda, Stefania Sandrelli, Sterling Hayden. D: Bernardo Bertolucci. DRA [R] 311m. v

1918 1985 ★★★½ First in a trilogy about life in small Texas town, (followed by prequels, *On Valentine's Day* and *Convicts*), this one examines the effects of the Spanish flu epidemic and the aftermath of WWI. Well-done adaptation of Horton Foote's play, underpinned by good acting. C: William Converse-Roberts, Hallie Foote, Matthew Broderick, Rochelle Oliver, Michael Higgins, Jeanne McCarthy. D: Ken Harrison. DRA 89m. v

1941 1979 ★★ Overblown war comedy finds post-Pearl Harbor Los Angeles frantically preparing for a Japanese invasion. Big production doesn't mean big laughs if they're not in the script. More hectic than funny. C: Dan Aykroyd, Ned Beatty, John Belushi, Treat Williams, Nancy Allen, Robert Stack, Tim Matheson, Toshiro Mifune, Christopher Lee, Warren Oates. D: Steven Spielberg. COM [PG] 120m. v

1969 1988 ★★½ During the Vietnam era, a pair of small-town college chums become New-Left pacifists to avoid entry into the Army. Unreliable, lifeless stab at nostalgia flops, despite a fine cast. C: Robert Downey Jr., Kiefer Sutherland, Bruce Dern, Mariette Hartley, Joanna Cassidy, Winona Ryder. D: Ernest Thompson. DRA [R] 120m. v

1984 1956 British ★★★★ Adaptation of George Orwell's 1949 prophetic book about forbidden lovers, doomed in a dehumanized future totalitarian society. A provocative depiction of a savage police state. C: Edmond O'Brien, Michael Redgrave, Jan Sterling, David Kossoff, Mervyn Johns, Donald Pleasence. D: Michael Anderson. DRA 91m.

92 in the Shade 1975 ★★★ Key West boat captain (Oates) goes to any lengths to stop ambitious rival (Fonda) from starting his own fishing business. Idiosyncratic comedy is a mixed bag of hilarious, off-the-wall humor and sloppy storytelling. C: Peter Fonda, Warren Oates, Margot Kidder, Burgess Meredith, Harry Dean Stanton. D: Thomas McGuane. COM [R] 86m. v

99 River Street 1953 ★★★★ After he's wrongly accused of crime when his spouse turns to robbery, a cabdriver teams up with an actress to battle authorities. Taut, original variation on much used crime movie themes. Acting and direction are first-rate. C: John Payne, Evelyn Keyes, Brad Dexter, Peggie Castle, Ian Wolfe, Frank Faylen. D: Phil Karlson. CRI 83m.

Ninja Academy 1990 ★★ A group of unlikely candidates from all parts of Southern California flock to an irreverent and unconventional ninja school. Goofy blend of comedy and action. C: Will Egan, Kelly Randall, Gerald Okomura. D: Nico Mastorakis. COM 93m. v

Ninja—American Warrior ★★ A ninja druglord vows to destroy the entire DEA. C: Joff Houston, John Wilford. D: Tommy Cheng. ACT 90m.

Ninja Brothers of Blood 1989 ★★½ Seduction, jealousy, and revenge drive members of a gang to violence. C: Fonda Lynn, Marcus Gibson, Brian McClave. D: Raymond Woo. ACT 90m.

Ninja Champion 1986 ★★½ International agents go after jewel thief. Typical martial arts action; not bad. C: Bruce Baron, Pierre Tremblay. ACT 90m. v

Ninja Commandments 1987 ★★½ Stopping at nothing, including killing his master, a ruthless ninja warrior challenges an empire's best warrior to a deadly territorial battle. D: Joseph Lai. ACT 90m. v

Ninja Condors 1987 ★★½ A ninja is assigned to kill the cop who saved him from his father's murderer. Lots of action. C: Alexander Lou, Stuart Hugh. D: James Wu. ACT 90m. V

Ninja Destroyer 1989 ★★½ An emerald mine is the prize the ninjas are vying for. Nonstop action and gore. C: Stuart Smith, Bruce Baron. ACT [R] 92m. V

Ninja in the Claws of the C.I.A. 1983 ★★½ East meets West when KGB and CIA pin their best martial arts masters against each other. C: John Liu. ACT 102m. V

Ninja Massacre 1984 ★★½ A priceless kung fu manual is discovered and fought over. Plenty of diabolical scheming as well as loose flesh and limbs. C: Lo Lieh, Pal Ying. ACT 87m. V

Ninja Phantom Heroes 1987 ★★½ A soldier in the Vietnam War turns against his country, smuggling U.S. arms for his private ninja gang. Typical martial arts action. C: Christine Wells, Glen Carson, George Dickson. D: Bruce Lambert. ACT 90m. V

Ninja Strike Force 1988 ★★ A magical sword, stolen by an evil ninja master, must be retrieved before more clan leaders die. C: Richard Harrison, Geoffrey Ziebart, Gary Carter. D: Joseph Lai. ACT 89m. V

Ninja 3—The Domination 1984 ★★ An aerobics instructor (Dickey) is possessed by the spirit of a killer ninja. Energetic and entirely laughable, exploitation genre hybrid. C: Lucinda Dickey, Jordan Bennett, Sho Kosugi, David Chung. D: Sam Firstenberg. ACT [R] 92m. V

Ninja Thunderbolt 1985 ★★ A woman's ruthless appetite for wealth and power incites ninjas to action. C: Richard Harrison, Jackie Chan, Wang Tao. D: Godfrey Ho. ACT 92m. V

Ninja Turf 1986 ★★ A gang leader turns against his drug dealing boss and must pay the consequences. C: Jun Chong, Bill Wallace, Rosanna King. D: Richard Park. ACT [R] 83m. V

Ninja Vengeance 1992 ★★½ A ninja biker goes against smalltown sentiment to protect a targeted man. C: Craig Boyett, Janet T. Pawlak. D: Karl R. Armstrong. ACT [R] 87m. V

Ninotchka 1939 ★★★★★ Soviet commissar (Garbo) is "Parisized" by playboy (Douglas). Even though topical East vs. West story is outdated, Ninotchka's wickedly funny transformation provides timeless, classy entertainment. Terrific script by Billy Wilder, Charles Brackett, and Walter Reisch. Became Broadway/film musical *Silk Stockings.* C: Greta Garbo, Melvyn Douglas, Ina Claire, Bela Lugosi, Sig Ruman, Felix Bressart, Alexander Granach, Richard Carle. D: Ernst Lubitsch. COM 108m. V

Ninth Circle, The 1961 Yugoslavian ★★★★ Man pushes young Jewish woman into marriage with his Catholic son to shield her from the Nazis. Tragic tale of love and war is a heartbreaker. C: Dusica Zegarac, Boris Dvornik, Ervina Dragman, Branko Tatic. D: France Stiglic. DRA 90m.

Ninth Configuration, The 1979 ★★★★ A psychiatrist and psychopath (Keach) provides a special kind of radical therapy to Vietnam War vets in a government asylum. Offbeat thriller, sometimes harrowing, sometimes darkly funny, and often right on the mark. Numerous edited versions exist (a.k.a. *Twinkle, Twinkle, Killer Kane*) C: Stacy Keach, Scott Wilson, Jason Miller, Ed Flanders, Neville Brand, Moses Gunn. D: William Peter Blatty. DRA 115m. V

Ninth Guest, The 1934 ★★½ Five men and three women are brought together in hotel suite; someone starts bumping them off. Routine stage-bound adaptation of play with ever-so-familiar plot. C: Donald Cook, Genevieve Tobin, Hardie Albright. D: Roy William Neill. CRI 67m.

Ninth Heart, The 1980 Czech ★★★★ A princess is kidnapped by an evil scientist, and a young student rushes to her aid. Fantasy film has splendid wit for all ages. C: Ondrej Pavelka, Julie Juristova, Anna Malova. D: Juraj Herz. FAM/SFI 90m.

Nitti—The Enforcer 1988 ★★★ TV film fictionalizes the life of Frank Nitti, Al Capone's right-hand man. Violent but not well conceived or very interesting. Very bloody and violent. C: Anthony LaPaglia, Vincent Guastaferro, Trini Alvarado, Michael Moriarty. D: Michael Switzer. CRI [PG-13] 95m. V

Nitwits, The 1935 ★★★½ Cigar store proprietors probe murder of music publisher; young Grable is a suspect. Fun song-and-dance vehicle for Wheeler and Woolsey. C: Bert Wheeler, Robert Woolsey, Betty Grable, Fred Keating, Evelyn Brent, Erik Rhodes, Hale Hamilton, Willie Best. D: George Stevens. COM 81m.

No Big Deal 1983 ★★★½ Streetsmart teen Dillon shuttles between juvenile detention and high school, where he tries to make human contact. Predictable but okay story of youthful angst. C: Kevin Dillon, Christopher Gartin, Tammy Grimes, Sylvia Miles. D: Robert Charlton. DRA 94m. V

No Cause For Alarm 1990 *See* **Project: Alien**

No Dead Heroes 1987 ★★½ A green beret soldier caught in the Vietnam jungle falls prey to the manipulations of the KGB and a massive terrorist plot. C: John Dresden, Max Thayer, Dave Anderson. D: J.C. Miller. ACT 87m. V

No Deposit, No Return 1976 ★★★½ Bumbling bad guys are talked into "kidnapping" two lonely rich kids who want to leave stuffy grandfather (Niven) and reunite with mother (Feldon) for Easter holidays. Good cast manages to rise above Disney clichés. Younger audiences may enjoy it. C: David Niven, Darren McGavin, Don Knotts, Herschel Bernardi, Barbara Feldon. D: Norman Tokar. FAM/DRA [G] 115m. V

No Down Payment 1957 ★★★½ Several

couples in suburbia grapple with postwar domestic problems. Excellent cast. C: Joanne Woodward, Jeffrey Hunter, Sheree North, Tony Randall, Cameron Mitchell, Patricia Owens, Barbara Rush, Pat Hingle. D: Martin Ritt. DRA 105m.

No Drums, No Bugles 1971 ★★★½ When a West Virginia farmer's moral principles prevent him from participating in the Civil War, he banishes himself to a Blue Ridge Mountains cave for three years. Tour de force for Sheen. Based on fact. C: Martin Sheen. D: Clyde Ware. DRA [G] 90m. V

No Escape 1936 British ★★★½ Writer bets young man he can keep him hidden for one month; later, young man is apparently murdered. Solid low-budget thriller. (a.k.a. *No Escape/No Exit*) C: Valerie Hobson, Leslie Perrins, Robert Cochran. D: Norman Lee. CRI 85m.

No Escape 1943 *See* **I Escaped from the Gestapo**

No Escape 1953 ★★½ When police suspect them of murder, a couple (Ayres and Steele) must find the real killer. Formula drama. (a.k.a. *City on a Hunt*) C: Lew Ayres, Marjorie Steele, Sonny Tufts, Gertrude Michael. D: Charles Bennett. CRI 76m.

No Escape 1994 ★★★½ In the future, Liotta is exiled to a harsh prison colony. He joins a small, idealistic society headed by Henricksen, then must help defend it. A jungle-bound *Mad Max* knockoff, propelled by great action sequences and Liotta's aggressive charm. (a.k.a. *Prison Colony.*) C: Ray Liotta, Lance Henriksen, Stuart Wilson, Kevin Dillon, Iam McNeice. D: Martin Campbell. SFI [R] 118m.

No Escape/No Exit 1953 *See* **No Escape**

No Escape, No Return 1993 ★★ Three undercover cops are ordered by their captain and the FBI band together to get a druglord. C: Maxwell Caulfield, Dustin Nguyen, Denise Loveday. D: Charles T. Kanganis. ACT [R] 93m. V

No Exit 1962 ★★★★ Three dead people meet in eternity: a cheap hotel room. It is soon apparent that they are each other's hell. Adaptation of Sartre's play is intelligent and chilling. First filmed in 1955. C: Viveca Lindfors, Rita Gam, Morgan Sterne. D: Tad Danielewski. DRA 85m.

No Greater Glory 1934 ★★★★★ A delicate youngster idolizes the tough leader of a local gang; the former's desperate desire to fit in leads to tragedy. Brilliantly realized tale of childhood, with sharp ensemble work and eloquent direction. C: George Breakston, Jimmy Butler, Jackie Searl, Frankie Darro. D: Frank Borzage. DRA 117m.

No Greater Love 1944 USSR ★★★★ When her husband is killed by invading Germans, a Russian woman enlists the aid of friends and goes after a Nazi tank commander. Violent, exciting drama. C: Vera Mertskaya, Anna Smirnova, Peter Aleinikov. D: Federick Emler. DRA 68m. V

No Greater Love Than This 1969 Japanese ★★★★ A nurse goes to work on a secluded island off the Japanese coast, and finds winning over the inhabitants to be no easy matter. Nice slice-of-life story with fine characterizations. C: Fumie Kashiyama, Homare Suguro. D: Kenji Yoshida. DRA 106m.

No Hands on the Clock 1941 ★★★ Newlywed P.I. Morris is so caught up in new case that he has no time for his wife. Thin programmer, watchable for Morris' black-Irish toughness. C: Chester Morris, Jean Parker. D: Frank McDonald. CRI 76m.

No Highway in the Sky 1951 British ★★★★ An aerodynamic engineer (Stewart) has a theory about metal fatigue causing plane crashes. His girlfriend (Johns), and a famous actress (Dietrich) are on the doomed flight that proves his theory. Workmanlike drama, good performances. C: James Stewart, Marlene Dietrich, Glynis Johns, Jack Hawkins, Elizabeth Allan, Kenneth More. D: Henry Koster. DRA 98m.

No Holds Barred 1952 ★★★ Sach suddenly develops physical prowess that turns him into a wrestling pro. Typical Bowery Boys comedy will please fans of the series. C: Leo Gorcey, Huntz Hall, Marjorie Reynolds. D: William Beaudine. ACT 65m.

No Holds Barred 1989 ★★ Charismatic professional wrestler (Hulk Hogan) must defeat a fearsome challenger. Severance is an unlikely love interest. Hulkamaniacs will enjoy the Hollywood treatment. C: Hulk Hogan, Joan Severance, Kurt Fuller, Tiny Lister. D: Thomas Wright. ACT [PG-13] 93m. V

No Leave, No Love 1946 ★★★ Sailors on shore leave typical romantic comedy with Johnson and Wynn. C: Van Johnson, Keenan Wynn, Pat Kirkwood, Guy Lombardo, Edward Arnold, Marie Wilson. D: Charles Martin. COM 119m.

No Limit 1935 British ★★★½ Ukulele-strumming auto mechanic Formby hangs up his wrenches to race horses. Breezy comedy, worth a look primarily for star, who was a jockey before entering show business. C: George Formby, Florence Desmond. D: Monty Banks. COM 80m.

No Longer Alone 1978 ★★★½ Actress Joan Winmill, on the brink of suicide, sees God. Intelligent, subtle film makes good use of flashbacks to reveal the psyche of a tormented woman. C: Belinda Carroll, Roland Culver, James Fox, Wilfrid Hyde White. D: Nicholas Webster. DRA 99m.

No Love for Johnnie 1961 British ★★★★ Intriguing drama of member of Parliament who cares only about getting reelected, with predictably dire results in both his private and professional lives. Good early Finch performance, excellent supporting cast. C: Peter

Finch, Stanley Holloway, Mary Peach, Mervyn Johns, Donald Pleasence, Dennis Price, Oliver Reed. D: Ralph Thomas. DRA 110m. V

No Man Is an Island 1962 ★★★½ True story of lone American sailor left on Guam during WWII, fighting one-man war against Japanese. Engaging. C: Jeffrey Hunter, Marshall Thompson, Barbara Perez. D: John Monks Jr., Richard Goldstone. ACT 114m.

No Man of Her Own 1933 ★★★½ A good woman (Lombard) marries a ne'er-do-well (Gable), and reforms him. Future Mr. and Mrs. Gable in their only film together, provide spark. C: Clark Gable, Carole Lombard, Dorothy Mackaill, Grant Mitchell, Elizabeth Patterson. D: Wesley Ruggles. DRA 81m. V

No Man of Her Own 1950 ★★★½ A pregnant woman (Stanwyck) gets in train wreck and assumes the identity of a dead passenger. Odd mix of film noir and soap opera works on strength of Stanwyck's performance. C: Barbara Stanwyck, John Lund, Jane Cowl, Phyllis Thaxter, Richard Denning, Milburn Stone. D: Mitchell Leisen. DRA 98m.

No Man's Land 1987 ★★★ Young cop goes after the head of a high-class auto-theft ring, then falls for the thief's sister. Okay. C: Charlie Sheen, D.B. Sweeney, Lara Harris, Randy Quaid, Bill Duke, M.Emmet Walsh. D: Peter Werner. CRI [R] 107m. V

No Man's Woman 1955 ★★★½ Serial murderer of independent women is on the loose, so a woman goes on his trail. Snappy story with original premise. C: Marie Windsor, John Archer, Patric Knowles, Nancy Gates, Louis Jean Heydt. D: Franklin Adreon. CRI 70m.

No Mercy 1986 ★★★½ Chicago cop (Gere) heads for the bayous to catch his partner's killer and gets the hots for a woman (Basinger) who "belongs" to the villain. C: Richard Gere, Kim Basinger, Jeroen Krabbe, George Dzundza. D: Richard Pearce. CRI [R] 108m. V

No Minor Vices 1948 ★★½ Romantic triangle has happy marriage of doctor (Andrews) and wife (Palmer) upset by intrusion of artist (Jourdan). C: Dana Andrews, Lilli Palmer, Louis Jourdan, Jane Wyatt, Norman Lloyd, Bernard Gorcey, Beau Bridges. D: Lewis Milestone. COM 96m.

No More Ladies 1935 ★★★½ Wife (Crawford) can't tame playboy husband (Montgomery), so she pretends interest in another man (Tone). Nice character turns, nice lightweight farce. C: Joan Crawford, Robert Montgomery, Charlie Ruggles, Franchot Tone, Edna May Oliver, Gail Patrick. D: Edward H. Griffith. COM 81m.

No More Orchids 1933 ★★★½ Unhappy rich young woman falls for an impecunious man; but her father has other ideas. Standard soaper boasts fine performance from Lombard and a stunning conclusion. C: Carole Lombard, Lyle Tabot, Walter Connolly, Louise Closser Hale, Aubrey Smith. D: Walter Lang. DRA 71m.

No More Women 1934 ★★★½ Ex-servicemen (McLaglen and Lowe) in the deep-sea salvage business brawl over woman boss (Blaine). Good, punchy action comedy. C: Victor McLaglen, Edmund Lowe, Sally Blane, Minna Gombell, Alphonse Ethier, Tom Dugan. D: Albert Rogell. ACT 77m.

No My Darling Daughter 1961 British ★★★½ Comedy of a nice woman (Mills) torn between two suitors, one a playboy layabout, the other an industrious self-made man. Excellent acting keeps it moving. C: Michael Redgrave, Michael Craig, Juliet Mills, Roger Livesey, Rad Fulton, Renee Houston. D: Ralph Thomas. COM 97m.

No Name on the Bullet 1959 ★★★★ A gunfighter (Murphy) is hired to assassinate someone in Western town, but no one knows who the target is. Intelligent, well-crafted, contemplative Western, sparked by coolly detached Murphy. C: Audie Murphy, Charles Drake, Joan Evans, Virginia Grey, Warren Stevens, Edgar Stehli, R. G. Armstrong, Willis Bouchey, Karl Swenson, Charles Watts, Jerry Paris, Whit Bissell. D: Jack Arnold. WST 77m.

No Nukes 1980 ★★★½ Concert film footage of antinuclear power concept boasts electrifying Springsteen. C: Jackson Browne, Crosby, Stills, Nash, John Hall, Gil Scott-Heron, Bonnie Raitt, Carly Simon, Bruce Springsteen, James Taylor, Jesse Young, Jane Fonda. D: Julian Schlossberg, Danny Goldberg, Anthony Potenza. MUS [PG] 93m. V

No One Cries Forever 1985 ★★½ A ruthless mafioso sabotages the efforts of a prostitute trying to go straight. D: Jans Rautenbach. CRI 96m. V

No One Man 1932 ★★½ A socialite (Lombard) finds true meaning of life when forced to choose between selfish playboy (Cortez) and self-sacrificing doctor (Lukas). A rare noncomic role for Lombard. C: Carole Lombard, Ricardo Cortez, Paul Lukas, George Barbier. D: Lloyd Corrigan. DRA 73m.

No Other Love 1979 ★★★½ Two retarded adults meet parental hostility when they fall in love. Tasteful treatment and excellent restrained performances by Kavner and Thomas. C: Richard Thomas, Julie Kavner, Elizabeth Allen, Robert Loggia, Scott Jacoby, Frances McCain. D: Richard Pearce. DRA 100m. TVM

No Place for Jennifer 1951 British ★★★ A child is buffeted between divorcing parents. Reserved, understated treatment keeps it going. C: Leo Genn, Rosamund John, Beatrice Campbell, Guy Middleton. D: Henry Cass. DRA 89m.

No Place Like Home 1989 ★★★★ Surprisingly honest drama of middle-class family forced into ranks of the homeless. Lahti is superb, as always. Interesting treatment of serious problem. C: Christine Lahti, Jeff Daniels, Scott Marlowe, Kathy Bates, CCH Pounder. D: Lee Grant. DRA 100m. TVM

No Place Like Homicide! 1962 British ★★½ Haunted house farce, as a family awaits reading of a will in spooky surroundings. Some real laughs. Remake of 1933 film *The Ghoul*, which was *not* a comedy. (a.k.a. *What a Carve Up!*) C: Kenneth Connor, Sidney James, Shirley Eaton, Donald Pleasence, Dennis Price, Michael Gough. D: Pat Jackson. COM 87m.

No Place to Hide 1981 ★★★ A young woman is the target of a psychopath—no one can say why. Typical chiller; some good moments. C: Mariette Hartley, Keir Dullea, Kathleen Beller. D: John Llewellyn Moxey. DRA [PG] 120m. TVM V

No Place to Land 1958 ★★ Old-fashioned comedy of romantic triangle. C: John Ireland, Mari Blanchard, Gail Russell, Jackie Coogan. D: Albert Gannaway. COM 78m.

No Place to Run 1972 ★★★ A grandfather (Bernardi) and grandson run away together when authorities threaten to terminate older man's custody. A moving story. C: Herschel Barnardi, Scott Jacoby, Larry Hagman, Stefanie Powers. D: Delbert Mann. DRA 78m. TVM

No Prince for My Cinderella 1978 ★★½ Saving the life of a schizophrenic young woman lost in a life of prostitution is the consuming passion for a caring social worker. C: Robert Reed. DRA 100m. TVM V

No Questions Asked 1951 ★★★½ Working-class man (Sullivan) gets into the rackets to make a buck. Efficient crime melodrama aided by good supporting cast. C: Barry Sullivan, Arlene Dahl, Jean Hagen, George Murphy, William Reynolds, Mari Blanchard. D: Harold F. Kress. DRA 81m.

No Regrets for Our Youth 1946 Japanese ★★★★ In the 1930s, after her leftist boyfriend is executed as a spy, a young woman goes to live as a peasant with his parents. One of Kurosawa's most explicitly political films wisely concentrates on individuals; his self-reliant heroine defiantly retains her idealism despite events. C: Setsuko Hara, Takashi Shimura. D: Akira Kurosawa. DRA 110m. V

No Return Address 1961 ★★★½ Man is pushed into committing robbery by avaricious wife; his arrest is only the beginning of his descent into hell. Disturbing melodrama pulls no punches. C: Harry Lovejoy, Alicia Hammond. D: Alexander Grattan. DRA

No Room at the Inn 1950 British ★★★ Malevolent English landlord presses her female tenants into prostitution. Grim melodrama with some script work by Dylan Thomas. C: Freda Jackson, Joy Shelton, Hermione Baddeley. D: Dan Birt. DRA 88m.

No Room for the Groom 1952 ★★★½ Korean vet (Curtis) returns home to find his house filled with his appalling new in-laws. Funny, effective suburban comedy. C: Tony Curtis, Piper Laurie, Spring Byington, Don DeFore, Jack Kelly. D: Douglas Sirk. COM 82m.

No Room to Run 1978 Australian ★★ A concert promoter (Benjamin) plunges into nasty corporate intrigue when he goes on business trip to Australia. C: Richard Benjamin, Paula Prentiss, Barry Sullivan, Noel Ferrier. D: Robert Michael Lewis. DRA 101m. TVM V

No Sad Songs for Me 1950 ★★★★ A terminally ill woman (Sullavan) takes leave of her family, seeing they are provided for financially and emotionally. Ironically, Sullavan was dying as she made it. C: Margaret Sullavan, Wendell Corey, Viveca Lindfors, Natalie Wood, Ann Doran. D: Rudolph Maté. DRA 89m.

No Secrets 1991 ★★ On vacation on an out-of-the-way ranch, three teenagers take in stranger; later discover he's concealing disturbing past. C: Amy Locane, Heather Fairfield, Traci Lind. D: Dezso Magyar. HOR [R] 92m. V

No Sex Please—We're British 1979 ★★ Young bride orders Scandinavian glassware through the mail, but she winds up getting Scandinavian pornography instead—just as her in-laws and husband's employers are arriving. Pretty good filming of funny stage sex farce. C: Ronnie Corbett, Beryl Reed, Ian Oglivy, Susan Penhalgon. D: Cliff Owen. COM 90m.

No Small Affair 1984 ★★★ An awkward adolescent (Cryer) becomes obsessed with singer (Moore), and spends his life savings to trail her around San Francisco. Coming-of-age comedy. C: Jon Cryer, Demi Moore, Jennifer Tilly, George Wendt. D: Jerry Schatzberg. COM [R] 102m. V

No Surrender 1986 British ★★★★ Dark comedy about disastrous New Year's Eve at seedy Liverpool nightclub. New owner has unwittingly booked rival groups for same night—one Irish Protestant, the other Irish Catholic. Mayhem ensues, spurred by an inept magician (Costello) and an IRA assassin (McAnally). C: Michael Angelis, Ray McAnally, Avis Bunnage, Joanne Whalley, Michael Ripper, Elvis Costello, Tom Georgeson. D: Peter K. Smith. COM [R] 100m. V

No-Tell Hotel, The 1984 ★★ Father puts daughter and fiance of whom he disapproves in charge of hotel he owns but intends to burn down. (a.k.a. the *Rosebud Beach Hotel*) C: Fran Drescher, Christopher Lee, Peter Scolari, Colleen Camp. D: Harry Hurwitz. COM [R] 90m. V

No Time for Breakfast 1978 ★★★★ A surgeon's busy schedule leaves her little time for the people in her life; when she learns she may have cancer she does some serious reevaluating. Smart, unsentimental treatment of adult themes; Girardot is superb. C: Annie Girardot, Jean-Pierre Cassel. D: Jean-Louis Bertucelli. DRA V

No Time for Comedy 1940 ★★★★ Sparkling adaptation of S.N. Berhman's drawing-room comedy. Russell and Stewart are a feuding actress/playwright married couple, spouting witty repartee between meals. Dated, but delicious. C: James Stewart, Rosalind Russell, Genevieve Tobin, Charles Ruggles. D: William Keighley. COM 98m.

No Time for Ecstasy 1963 France ★★★½ Young Ukrainian runs off to Spain to fight Franco in the Spanish Civil War; there, he meets an American woman and has a change of heart. Fine romantic drama has devastating finale. C: Peter Van Eyck, Dallah Lavi. D: Jean-Jacques Vierne. DRA 100m.

No Time for Flowers 1952 ★★★ A Prague government worker (Lindfors) falls in love with a secret police agent (Christian) supposedly testing her loyalty. Slight, awkward comedy. C: Viveca Lindfors, Paul Christian, Ludwig Stossel, Manfred Ingor. D: Don Siegel. COM 83m.

No Time for Love 1943 ★★★½ A famous photographer (Colbert) falls for a sandhog (MacMurray) while shooting a tunnel construction project. Interesting milieu, sprightly playing. C: Claudette Collbert, Fred MacMurray, Ilka Chase, Richard Haydn, Paul McGrath, June Havoc. D: Mitchell Leisen. COM 83m.

No Time for Sergeants 1958 ★★★★ Hick (Griffith) is inducted into service and clashes with sergeant (McCormick). Genial and funny, Griffith's best screen work. Based on Ira Levin's Broadway play. C: Andy Griffith, Myron McCormick, Nick Adams, Murray Hamilton, Don Knotts, Jamie Farr. D: Mervyn LeRoy. COM 119m. V

No Time for Tears 1957 British ★★★ Story of a post-WWII British children's hospital and its compassionate director. Sentimental drama. C: Anna Neagle, George Baker, Syliva Sims, Anthony Quayle, Flora Robson. D: Cyril Frankel. DRA 86m.

No Time to Be Young 1957 ★★★ Three troubled young men struggle to grow up. Surprisingly, some good acting. (a.k.a. *Teenage Delinquents*) C: Robert Vaughn, Roger Smith, Merry Anders, Kathy Nolan, Tom Pittman, Dorothy Green. D: David Lowell Rich. DRA 82m.

No Time to Kill 1963 British ★★★ Released from prison, framed ex-con Ireland heads for Sweden to seek vengeance. Okay programmer. C: John Ireland, Ellen Schwiers, Brigitta Anderson. D: Tom Younger. DRA 70m.

No Time to Marry 1938 ★★★½ Two ambitious reporters have finally found the time to get hitched, when she suddenly finds a vital clue in the case he is investigating. Fast paced, snappy romantic comedy. C: Richard Arlen, Mary Astor, Lionel Stander, Virginia Dale. D: Harry Lachman. COM 63M.

No Trace 1950 British ★★★½ Novelist/-broadcaster finds his bright career threatened by a blackmailing figure from his sordid past. Murder and mayhem ensue in this tense thriller with nice twisty ending. C: Hugh Sinclair, Dinah Sheridan, John Laurie, Barry Morse. D: John Gilling. CRI 76m. V

No Trees in the Street 1958 British ★★★ Social drama about denizens of working-class neighborhood, including their relations with small-time hoodlum (Lom) they all fear. Good acting. C: Sylvia Syms, Stanley Holloway, Herbert Lom, Ronald Howard, Joan Miller. D: J.Lee Thompson. DRA 108m.

No Way Out 1950 ★★★★½ Way-ahead-of-its-time drama of racial tensions features Poitier in his film debut as a medical intern treating gangster Widmark and his brother. When the latter dies, Widmark embarks on a bigoted quest for revenge. Searing performances, direction, script. C: Richard Widmark, Sidney Poitier, Linda Darnell, Ruby Dee, Ossie Davis, Stephen McNally. D: Joseph L. Mankiewicz. ACT

No Way Out 1987 ★★★★ Navy officer Costner becomes involved with the mistress of Defense Secretary Hackman, who accidentally kills her. Ensuing cover-up exposes an intricate web of intrigue in this sexy, stylish thriller. Strong performances all around, but Patton is outstanding. Remake of *The Big Clock*. C: Kevin Costner, Gene Hackman, Sean Young, Will Patton, Howard Duff, David Paymer, John DiAquino. D: Roger Donaldson. ACT [R] 114m. V

No Way to Treat a Lady 1968 ★★★½ Black comedy about a theater entrepreneur (Steiger), who strangles middle-aged women as a way of working out his neuroses. Segal is amusing as the cop chasing him. C: Rod Steiger, Lee Remick, George Segal, Eileen Heckart, Murray Hamilton, Michael Dunn, Barbara Baxley, Ruth White, Doris Roberts, David Doyle. D: Jack Smight. COM 108m. V

Noah's Ark 1929 ★★★½ As WWI begins, American O'Brien must give up German love Costello to serve his country. Analogous (?) story of Noah is told in long biblical segment with some spectacular effects. Mostly silent, with some sound. Corny but fun. Shorter version released in '58. C: Dolores Costello, George O'Brien, Noah Beery, Louise Fazenda, Gwynne Williams, Paul McAllister, Myrna Loy. D: Michael Curtiz. DRA 100m.

Nob Hill 1945 ★★★½ Saloon owner Raft falls hard for blue-blood Bennett in 1890s San Francisco. Agreeable musical, with good costumes and color. C: George Raft, Joan Bennett, Vivian Blaine, Peggy Ann Garner, Alan Reed, B.S. Pully, Emil Coleman, Smith & Dale, Rory Calhoun. D: Henry Hathaway. MUS 95m.

Nobody Lives Forever 1946 ★★★½ Crooked Romeo (Garfield) scams wealthy Fitzgerald, then falls in love with her. Good film noir melodrama; sturdy cast. C: John Garfield, Geraldine Fitzerald, Walter Brennan, Faye Emerson, George Coulouris, George Tobias. D: Jean Negulesco. DRA 100m.

Nobody Runs Forever 1968 *See* **High Commissioner, The**

Nobody Waved Goodbye 1965 Canadian ★★★★ Low-key Canadian docu-drama examines problems of Kastner, a troubled young man who is drifting into life of petty crime, and Biggs, the woman he is in a relationship with. A sequel, *Unfinished Business* revisits the real-life couple two decades later. Compelling, well-done social document. C: Peter Kastner, Julie Biggs, Claude Rae, Toby Tarnow, Charmion King, Ron Taylor. D: Don Owen. DOC 80m.

Nobody's Baby 1937 ★★★ Nurses in training are saddled with a baby who belongs to none of them. Light Hal Roach comedy. C: Patsy Kelly, Lyda Robert, Robert Armstrong. D: Gus Meins. COM 67m.

Nobody's Child 1986 ★★★★ Better-than-average TV drama with Emmy-winning performance from Thomas as woman who achieves success in life after 20 years in mental institution. True story, sharply directed by actress Grant. C: Marlo Thomas, Ray Baker, Blanche Baker, Kathy Baker. D: Lee Grant. DRA 100m. TVM

Nobody's Children 1994 ★★★★ Woman tries to adopt Romanian child, encounters many obstacles. Taut, true drama features another fine TV-movie performance from Ann-Margret. C: Ann-Margret, Dominque Sanda, Jay O. Sanders. D: David Wheatley. DRA 100m. TVM

Nobody's Fool 1936 ★★★½ Veteran second banana Horton gets to carry this modestly appealing comedy about a meek Kansas waiter moving to Manhattan where he gets mixed up with gangsters. C: Edward Everett Horton, Glenda Farrell, Cesar Romero. D: Arthur Greville Collins. COM 62m.

Nobody's Fool 1986 ★★★ Oddball Southern romance between stagestruck waitress (Arquette) and lighting designer (Roberts) of visiting theatre company. Script by Beth (*Crimes of the Heart*) Henley. No relation to 1994 Paul Newman film. C: Rosanna Arquette, Eric Roberts, Mare Winningham, Louise Fletcher. D: Evelyn Purcell. COM [PG-13] 107m. V

Nobody's Fool 1994 ★★★★½ Newman's marvelous performance is just one of the pleasures of this luminous character study, with the star cast as a 60-year-old loser trying to put his life in order. Wonderful support from Griffith, Willis, and Tandy (in her final performance). From the novel by Richard Russo. C: Paul Newman, Jessica Tandy, Melanie Griffith, Bruce Willis, Dylan Walsh, Gene Saks, Elizabeth Wilson. D: Robert Benton. DRA [R] 112m. V

Nobody's Perfect 1968 ★★★½ Military comedy of life aboard U.S. Navy submarine in Japan. C: Doug McClure, Nancy Kwan, James Whitmore, David Hartman, Gary Vinson. D: Alan Rafkin. COM 103m.

Nobody's Perfect 1990 Swiss ★★★ A bashful undergrad masquerades as a girl to get next to coed of his dreams. Typical cross-dressing comedy. C: Chad Lowe, Gail O'Grady, Patrick Breen, Kim Flowers, Robert Vaughn. D: Robert Kaylor. COM [PG-13] 90m. V

Nobody's Perfekt 1981 ★★ Three men decide to fight Miami City Hall when their car is wrecked and a legal loophole prevents them from suing. Funny if one hasn't seen many other caper comedies; otherwise, familiar and tired. C: Gabe Kaplan, Alex Karras, Robert Klein, Susan Clark, Paul Stewart, Alex Rocco, Peter Bonerz. D: Peter Bonerz. COM [PG] 95m. V

Nocturna 1981 ★ Dracula (Carradine) is forced by Transylvanian IRS to rent his castle as a disco. Idiotic horror-comedy, hilariously bad. C: Yvonne de Carlo, John Carradine, Nai Bonet, Tony Hamilton. D: Harry Tampa. HOR [R] 82m. V

Nocturne 1946 ★★★★ When a lothario composer is found dead, the police conclude it was suicide, except for detective Warne, who continues his quest for truth, even after being suspended. Solid film noir. C: George Raft, Lynn Bari, Virginia Huston, Joseph Pevney, Myrna Dell. D: Edwin L. Marin. CRI 88m. V

Noises Off 1992 ★★½ Backstage fracas in this adaptation of Michael Frayn's popular play doesn't translate so well to film. Comings and goings of theatrical types involve lots of door slamming and mistaken identities, but humor gets lost along way despite talented comic cast. C: Carol Burnett, Michael Caine, Denholm Elliott, Julie Hagerty, Marilu Henner, Mark Linn-Baker, Christopher Reeve, John Ritter, Nicollette Sheridan. D: Peter Bogdanovich. COM [PG-13] 103m. V

Noisy Neighbors 1929 ★★★½ A group of vaudevillians inherit a Southern plantation and promptly find themselves in the middle of an old-fashioned family feud. Amusing comedy was shot silent; some dialogue added later. C: Eddie Quillan, Alberto Vaughan, Billy Gilbert. D: Charles Reisner. COM 74m.

Nomads 1986 ★★½ Anthropologist Brosnan's unnerving experiences with a group of mysterious street people are relived by psychiatrist Down in this middling chiller, which fails to fully develop its intriguing premise. McTiernan's directorial debut. C: Lesley-Anne Down, Pierce Brosnan, Adam Ant, Anna-Maria Monticelli, Mary Woronov. D: John McTiernan. HOR [R] 91m. V

Nomads of the North 1920 ★★★ A malicious man waits until a woman's fiance is away and tries to force her to repay a debt through marriage to his son. C: Lon Chaney, Lewis Stone, Betty Blythe. D: David M. Hartford. DRA 109m. V

Non-Stop New York 1937 British ★★★★

Lee is witness to murder hiding from killers aboard eye-popping commercial transatlantic airliner. Fast and wild Hitchcock-esque. C: John Loder, Anna Lee, Francis L. Sullivan, Frank Cellier, Desmond Tester. D: Robert Stevenson. DRA 71m.

None But the Brave 1965 ★★★½ After their plane crashes on a remote Japanese-held island, a group of U.S. Marines attempts to forge a fragile peace with the enemy. Flawed but interesting antiwar effort; Sinatra's directorial debut. C: Frank Sinatra, Clint Walker, Tommy Sands, Tony Bill, Brad Dexter, Sammy Jackson, Tatsuya Mihashi, Takeshi Kato. D: Frank Sinatra. DRA 106m. V

None But the Lonely Heart 1944 ★★★½ Notable as screenwriting and directorial debut for playwright Odets, this well-meaning drama features Grant as vagrant who pulls himself together when he learns his mother is dying. Barrymore as the mother won Oscar for Best Supporting Actress. Above-average soap. C: Cary Grant, Ethel Barrymore, Barry Fitzgerald, Jane Wyatt, Dan Duryea, George Coulouris, June Duprez. D: Clifford Odets. DRA 113m. V

None Shall Escape 1944 ★★★★ WWII thriller about Nazi war crimes, prescient in its vision of postwar trials. Unjustly neglected suspense drama is also an effective cautionary tale. Oscar for Best Screenplay. C: Marsha Hunt, Alexander Knox, Henry Travers, Richard Crane, Dorothy Morris, Trevor Bardette. D: Andre de Toth. DRA 85m.

Noon Wine 1985 ★★★★½ Early 20th-century Texas farm family hires hand Skarsgard, who profoundly changes their lives. *American Playhouse* adaptation of a Katherine Anne Porter short story, is a moving, deeply felt drama with strong performances. C: Fred Ward, Lise Hilboldt, Stellan Skarsgard, Pat Hingle. D: Michael Fields. DRA 81m. TVM V

Noose 1950 *See* **Silk Noose**

Noose for a Gunman 1960 ★★★½ Cowpoke is falsely accused of murder and tossed out of town. MacLane shines as evil cattle baron in solid B-Western. C: Jim Davis, Lyn Thomas, Ted de Corsia, Barton MacLane. D: Edward L. Cahn. WST 69m.

Noose Hangs High, The 1948 ★★★½ Abbott and Costello are robbed of $50,000 and try to retrieve it in routine caper that benefits from classic "Mudder, fodder" routine. C: Bud Abbott, Lou Costello, Joseph Calleia, Leon Errol, Cathy Downs, Mike Mazurki, Fritz Feld. D: Charles Barton. COM 77m. V

Noozles—Adventures in Koalawalla Land 1988 ★★½ Two magical stuffed koalas come to life along with their kangaroo and platypus friends. FAM/ACT 120m. V

Noozles—Blinky and Pinky's Excellent Adventure ★★★ Sandy discovers her favorite koala bear can come to life. Perfect for very young children. FAM/ACT 95m. V

Noozles—Fuzzy was a Noozle 1991 ★★★ Stuffed koalas come to life and take their owner Sandy on a magical tour full of adventure. FAM/ACT 95m. V

Noozles—Koala Bear Magic ★★★ Sandy and her magical koala friends take you along on their fun-filled escapades. FAM/ACT 75m. V

Noozles—Nuzzling with the Noozles ★★★ Magical koalas and their young friend Sandy share fun, laughs, and excitement. FAM/ACT 110m.

Nora Prentiss 1947 ★★★½ A nightclub singer (Sheridan) is wooed by doctor (Smith) who commits murder in order to follow her to New York. Stylish, slickly entertaining melodrama. C: Ann Sheridan, Kent Smith, Robert Alda, Bruce Bennett, Rosemary DeCamp. D: Vincent Sherman. DRA 111m.

Norliss Tapes, The 1973 ★★★ A reporter investigates the supernatural. Unsuccessful pilot for horror TV series. C: Roy Thinnes, Angie Dickinson, Claude Akins, Michele Carey, Vonetta McGee, Hurd Hatfield, Don Porter. D: Dan Curtis. HOR 98m. TVM

Norma Rae 1979 ★★★★ Field won her first Oscar playing a blue-collar woman who fights the management of a Southern textiles plant to form a union. It wears its politics on its sleeve, but its heart is in the right place. C: Sally Field, Ron Leibman, Beau Bridges, Pat Hingle, Barbara Baxley, Gail Stickland. D: Martin Ritt. DRA [PG] 114m. V

Norman . . . Is That You? 1976 ★★ Tasteless domestic comedy about a narrow-minded father (Foxx) who discovers his son is gay. Based on the Broadway play. C: Redd Foxx, Pearl Bailey, Dennis Dugan, Michael Warren, Tamara Dobson, Vernee Watson, Jayne Meadows. D: George Schlatter. COM [PG] 91m. V

Norman Loves Rose 1982 Australian ★★★½ Offbeat romance stars Owen as a 13-year-old hopelessly in love with sister-in-law Kane. Affection is returned; then Kane becomes pregnant, by whom she knows not. Oddly sweet comedy, with good kooky Kane. C: Carol Kane, Tony Owen, Warren Mitchell, Myra de Groot. D: Henri Safran. COM [R] 95m. V

Norman Rockwell's Breaking Home Ties 1987 ★★★★ Coming-of-age drama about collegian and his old high school teacher in the 1950s, inspired by Rockwell painting. Nicely mounted, intelligently done. (a.k.a. *Breaking Home Ties*) C: Jason Robards, Eva Marie Saint, Doug McKeon, Erin Gray, Claire Trevor. D: John Wilder. DRA 100m. TVM

Norman's Awesome Experience 1989 ★★ An accident throws a photographer, model, and photo lab worker back into Roman times. C: Tom McCamus, Laurie Patton, Lacques Lussier. D: Paul Donovan. COM [PG-13] 91m. V

Norseman, The 1978 ★★ Viking epic about a young Norseman (Majors) who travels in search of his missing father. Majors first starring role. C: Lee Majors, Cornel Wilde, Mel Ferrer, Jack Elam. D: Charles B. Pierce. ACT [PG] 90m. v

North 1994 ★★★ Potentially saccharine premise is transformed by Reiner's soft touch: Wood thinks his parents take him for granted, so he sets out in search of the perfect family. Surprisingly good, including the many stars in cameo roles. C: Elijah Wood, Jason Alexander, Julia-Louise Dreyfus, Bruce Willis, Jon Lovitz, Kathy Bates. D: Rob Reiner. FAM/COM

North and South 1985 ★★★★ Antebellum adventure features the relationship between a Northern industrial family and their Southern plantation-owning counterparts. They try to maintain their friendship amid the tumult of the approaching Civil War. Based on John Jakes' novel, packs a solid historical punch. C: Patrick Swayze, James Read, Lesley-Anne Down. DRA 561m. TVM v

North Avenue Irregulars, The 1979 ★★★ Young priest (Herrmann) decides to combat neighborhood bookie by turning a group of church ladies into crimefighters. Good idea that quickly deteriorates into mindless Disney-style slapstick. Fine cast is completely wasted. C: Edward Herrmann, Barbara Harris, Susan Clark, Karen Valentine. D: Bruce Bilson. FAM/COM [G] 99m. v

North by Northwest 1959 ★★★★★ Case of mistaken identity has Madison Avenue ad exec Grant on the lam, fleeing evil spies and police in a cross-country odyssey to clear himself. Hard to imagine anyone but devilish, thoroughly charming Grant pulling this off. Mason and Saint are terrific in one of Hitchcock's most dazzling visual treats. Razor sharp script by Ernest Lehman. C: Cary Grant, Eva Marie Saint, James Mason, Leo G. Carroll, Martin Landau, Jessie Royce Landis, Philip Ober, Adam Williams, Josephine Hutchinson, Edward Platt. D: Alfred Hitchcock. CRI 136m. v

North Dallas Forty 1979 ★★★★½ Nolte is a burned-out NFL star battling win-at-any-cost attitude of team management. Davis, in fine film debut, plays his quarterback buddy trying to stay above it all. Fascinating portrait of pain, drugs, and machismo driving athletes, with standout performance by Nolte. C: Nick Nolte, MacDavis, Charles Durning, G.D. Spradlin, Bo Svenson, John Matuszak, Dabney Coleman. D: Ted Kotcheff. COM [R] 119m. v

North of the Great Divide 1950 ★★ Conflict between Oseka Indians and dishonest cannery operator. C: Roy Rogers, Penny Edwards, Gordon Jones. D: William Witney. WST 67m. v

North Sea Hijack 1980 *See* **ffolkes**

North Shore 1987 ★★★ Young surfer goes to Hawaii to ride the big ones and falls in love with his rival's sister. Beautiful Hawaiian surfing scenes make this a great antidote to winter weather. C: Matt Adler, Nia Peeples, John Philbin, Gerry Lopez. D: William Phelps. DRA [PG] 96m. v

North Star, The 1943 ★★★½ Violent WWII propaganda film about Russian villagers fighting off Nazis. Excellent cast; highlight is the sparring between Huston and von Stroheim. (a.k.a. *Armored Attack*) C: Anne Baxter, Dana Andrews, Walter Huston, Ann Harding, Erich von Stroheim, Farley Granger, Walter Brennan. D: Lewis Milestone. ACT 106m. v

North to Alaska 1960 ★★★★ Two turn-of-the-century gold prospectors' difficulties begin when they strike it rich in the Klondike. Expansive, beefy spoof in traditional mold. C: John Wayne, Stewart Granger, Ernie Kovacs, Fabian, Capucine. D: Henry Hathaway. COM 120m. v

Northern Lights 1979 ★★★½ Trenchant study of Scandinavian farmers and farmworkers in 1915 North Dakota trying to organize Nonpartisan League. C: Robert Behling, Susan Lynch, Joe Spano, Henry Martinson. D: John Hanson, Rob Nilsson. DRA 90m. v

Northern Pursuit 1943 ★★★½ Across the frozen wastes of Canada, a Mountie relentlessly hunts down a Nazi pilot. Stirring action and suspense in well-casted effort; Flynn is fine. C: Errol Flynn, Julie Bishop, Helmut Dantine, John Ridgely, Gene Lockhart, Tom Tully. D: Raoul Walsh. DRA 94m. v

Northstar 1986 ★ An astronaut (Evigan) acquires super powers while in outer space, and comes back to fight for truth and justice. Fun space junk. C: Greg Evigan, Deborah Wakeham, Mitchell Ryan, Mason Adams, David Hayward. D: Peter Levin. SFI 78m.

Northville Cemetery Massacre, The 1976 ★★ After bikers are accused of raping young woman who was really raped by cop, they seek revenge. C: David Hyry, Craig Collicott, Carson Jackson. D: William Dear. ACT [R] 81m. v

Northwest Frontier 1959 *See* **Flame Over India**

Northwest Mounted Police 1940 ★★★½ Texas Ranger (Cooper) goes north after fugitive, hooks up with Canadian Mounties. Lusty action film with no shortage of DeMille flair. C: Gary Cooper, Madeleine Carroll, Preston Foster, Paulette Goddard, Robert Preston, George Bancroft, Akim Tamiroff, Lon Chaney Jr., Robert Ryan. D: Cecil DeMille. ACT 125m.

Northwest Outpost 1947 ★★½ Horse operetta has cavalryman Eddy singing through the high Sierras. One of the last collaborations of its kind, unfortunately minus Jeanette MacDonald. C: Nelson Eddy, Ilona Massey, Elsa Lanchester, Joseph Schildkraut. D: Allan Dwan. MUS 91m. v

Northwest Passage 1940 ★★★★★ Stunning Technicolor adventure of colonial hero Robert Rogers (Tracy) and his brave Rangers breaking a trail westward and battling the Native American tribes. Marvelous adventure classic never lets go. Contains Tracy's finest moments as the earthy pioneer hero. C: Spencer Tracy, Robert Young, Walter Brennan, Ruth Hussey, Robert Barrat, Addison Richards. D: King Vidor. ACT 127m. V

Norwood 1970 ★★★ An ex-Marine (Campbell) goes on the road with buddy (Namath), in search of success as a singer. Harmless road movie. C: Glen Campbell, Kim Darby, Joe Namath, Carol Lynley, Pat Hingle, Tisha Sterling, Dom DeLuise. D: Jack Haley Jr. DRA [G] 96m.

Nosferatu 1922 German ★★★★½ Unusual adaptation of Bram Stoker's *Dracula* stars spidery Schreck as perhaps the most frightening incarnation of the famous Count. Intensely creepy, exceptional silent classic that makes later Draculas look like wimps. Remade in 1979. C: Max Schreck, Alexander Granach, Gustav von Wangenheim, Greta Schroeder. D: F.W. Murnau. HOR [PG] 63m. V

Nosferatu the Vampyre 1979 West German ★★★★½ Stunning telling of the story of Count Dracula. Big budget and lavish production values highlight this adaptation of Murnau's classic silent version. Herzog's eerie, witty masterpiece may be the best *Dracula* ever. Kinski's masterful performance evokes both pity and repulsion. C: Klaus Kinski, Isabelle Adjani, Bruno Ganz, Roland Topor. D: Werner Herzog. HOR [PG] 107m.

Nostalghia 1983 USSR ★★★½ Russian writer becomes fascinated by Italian eccentric awaiting the apocalypse. Typically poetic, bleak Tarkovsky. C: Oleg Yankovsky, Dominziana Giordano. D: Andrei Tarkovsky. DRA 130m.

Not a Penny More, Not a Penny Less 1990 British ★★★½ A con artist (Asner) fleeces four men in an insurance scam and they are determined to get revenge. Amusing. Based on Jeffrey Archer bestseller. C: Edward Asner, Ed Begley Jr., Maryam D'Abo, Jenny Agutter, Brian Protheroe, Francis Eric Gendron, Nicholas Jones. D: Clive Donner. COM 200m. TVM

Not as a Stranger 1955 ★★★½ Brilliant medical student, supported through med school by wife, experiences personal and professional troubles. Smooth testimonial to medicine sincerely filmed, but cast too old for roles. Kramer's debut. C: Olivia de Havilland, Frank Sinatra, Robert Mitchum, Charles Bickford, Gloria Grahame, Broderick Crawford, Lee Marvin, Lon Chaney, Henry Morgan, Virginia Christine. D: Stanley Kramer. DRA 136m. V

Not for Publication 1984 ★★★ A reporter (Allen) works on campaign of politically corrupt mayor (Luckinbill) and encounters romantic complications. Modern screwball comedy. C: Nancy Allen, David Naughton, Laurence Luckinbill, Alice Ghostley. D: Paul Bartel. COM [R] 87m. V

Not in Front of the Children 1982 ★★★½ A recent divorcée (Gray) risks losing custody of her children when she moves in with a younger man. Sudsy drama, good Gray. C: Linda Gray, John Getz, John Lithgow, Stephen Elliott, Carol Rossen, Cathryn Damon, George Grizzard. D: Joseph Hardy. DRA 100m. TVM

Not Mine to Love 1969 Israeli ★★★½ Woman asks her ex-boyfriend to watch her child for a few days while she's away. He grapples with his feelings toward her and is soon pushed to the brink. Emotional little film often packs quite a wallop. C: Oded Kotler, Shuy Osherov, Judith Soleh, Misha Asherow. D: Uri Zohar. DRA 90m.

Not My Kid 1985 ★★★★ A teenager's drug use ravages a middle-class family. Superior treatment and excellent cast, particularly Channing. C: George Segal, Stockard Channing, Andrew Robinson, Viveka Davis. D: Michael Tuchner. DRA 97m. TVM V

Not of This Earth 1957 ★★★½ A nurse (Garland) gives a vampire alien (Birch) blood transfusions, while he sneaks around sending Earthlings back to his own planet via a "matter-transformation" device. Silly and clever. Spawned a 1988 remake. C: Paul Birch, Beverly Garland, Morgan Jones, William Roerick. D: Roger Corman. HOR 67m.

Not of This Earth 1988 ★★★ A vampire from outer space touches down to drain the Earth's blood and replenish its own world. Remake of Roger Corman's 1957 film. Lords, in her mainstream debut, provides spark. C: Traci Lords, Arthur Roberts, Lenny Juliano, Rebecca Perle. D: Jim Wynorski. SFI [R] 82m. V

Not of This World 1991 ★★★½ An alien being threatens small town. Amusing sendup of Roger Corman horror quickies of the '50s. Good-natured romp. C: Lisa Hartman, A Martinez, Pat Hingle, Luke Edwards, Michael Greene, Tracey Walter. D: Jon Hess. COM 100m. TVM

Not Quite Human 1987 ★★★ An adventurous inventor creates an android son and sends him to school, where the robot boy strives to blend in. Imaginative Disney feature warms the heart and spawned two sequels. C: Alan Thicke, Joseph Bologna, Jay Underwood, Robyn Lively, Robert Harper. D: Steven Hilliard Stern. FAM/COM 91m. TVM V

Not Quite Human II 1989 ★★★ The robot teenager of *Not Quite Human* finds college life to be exciting and complex. Fun performances make for delightful family fare. Originally shown on Disney Channel. C: Alan Thicke, Jay Underwood, Robin Lively, Greg Mullavey, Katie Barberi. D: Eric Luke. FAM/COM 105m. TVM V

Not Quite Paradise 1984 British ★★★ American medical student goes to work on an Israeli kibbutz for a summer, falls in love with local woman. Rromance enlivened by attractive Israeli scenery. C: Joanna Pacula, Sam Robards, Todd Graff, Kevin McNally. D: Lewis Gilbert. DRA [R] 106m. v

Not So Dusty 1936 British ★★★ Two garbage collectors sort through their work, knowing it contains a valuable book. Slight British comedy. C: Wally Patch, Gus McNaughton, Muriel George. D: Maclean Rogers. COM 69m.

Not So Quiet on the Western Front 1930 British ★★★½ Blowhard cook recalls his days on the front in WWI. Song-and-dance comedy revue is often amusing spoof. C: Leslie Fuller, Mona Goya, Wilfred Temple. D: Monty Banks. COM 50m.

Not Wanted 1949 ★★★½ Thoughtful tale of the struggles of an unwed mother. Daring for its time and well done. C: Sally Forrest, Keefe Brasselle, Leo Penn, Dorothy Adams. D: Elmer Clifton. DRA 94m.

Not with My Wife You Don't! 1966 ★★★½ An Air Force officer (Curtis) is worried about his bored and wandering wife. Typical sex farce is often amusing. C: Tony Curtis, Virna Lisi, George Scott, Carroll O'Connor, Richard Eastham. D: Norman Panama. COM 118m.

Not Without My Daughter 1991 ★★★ Field is an American married to an Iranian, who goes with him to visit his homeland and is shocked when he makes her a virtual prisoner there. Cartoonish Iranians and heavy-handed melodrama make this true story hard to take. C: Sally Field, Alfred Molina, Sheila Rosenthal, Roshan Seth, Sarah Badel, Georges Corraface. D: Brian Gilbert. DRA [PG-13] 106m. v

Notebook on Cities and Clothes 1989 German ★★★★ Unusual portrait of innovative Japanese fashion designer Yohji Yamamoto, culminating in Paris Spring Show at the Louvre. Wenders' probing, stylish direction bears comparison with Yamamoto's striking clothes. D: Wim Wenders. DOC 80m. v

Nothing But a Man 1964 ★★★★½ Groundbreaking story of an African-American railroad worker (Dixon) who encounters more racism than he expects when he moves to the South. Superb acting, intelligent, low-key drama. C: Ivan Dixon, Abbey Lincoln, Julius Harris, Gloria Foster, Martin Priest, Leonard Parker, Yaphet Kotto, Stanley Greene. D: Michael Roemer. DRA 92m.

Nothing But the Best 1964 British ★★★★½ Satire of British upper classes in swinging London, with Bates as a young man on the make who will do anything—even murder—to advance himself. Scathingly funny, and Bates sparkles. C: Alan Bates, Denholm Elliott, Harry Andrews, Millicent Martin, Pauline Delany. D: Clive Donner. COM 99m.

Nothing But the Night 1972 British ★★★ A Scotland Yard inspector (Lee) looks into series of murders committed by orphans who are victims of a cult. Wildly uneven mystery/horror mix. C: Christopher Lee, Peter Cushing, Diana Dors, Georgia Brown, Keith Barron, Fulton Mackay, Gwyneth Strong. D: Peter Sasdy. HOR [PG] 90m.

Nothing But the Truth 1929 ★★★½ Dix is broker Bob Bennett who bets that he can tell absolute truth for 24 hours, no matter what. Great comic premise. Dix not quite as funny as Bob Hope in 1941 version, but still entertaining. Also filmed in 1920. C: Richard Dix, Berton Churchill, Ned Sparks, Helen Kane. D: Victor Schertzinger. COM 78m.

Nothing But the Truth 1941 ★★★★ A stockbroker (Hope) bets a friend he can tell the truth—and nothing but—for 24 hours. Good Hope vehicle. C: Bob Hope, Paulette Goddard, Edward Arnold, Leif Erickson, Helen Vinson, Willie Best. D: Elliott Nugent. COM 90m.

Nothing But Trouble 1944 ★★★½ Relatively weak comedy from the tail end of the classic comic duo's career finds them generating few laughs as a butler and cook who wind up befriending and protecting a visiting child monarch. For aficionados only. C: Stan Laurel, Oliver Hardy. D: Sam Taylor. COM 69m. v

Nothing But Trouble 1991 ★ Chase and Moore are a married couple caught speeding and ending up trapped guests in home of bizarre judge Aykroyd (hidden under pounds of makeup). Aykroyd's directing debut. C: Chevy Chase, Dan Aykroyd, John Candy, Demi Moore. D: Dan Aykroyd. COM [PG-13] 94m. v

Nothing in Common 1986 ★★★★ Hanks shines as a quick-witted workaholic who must help his aging parents through a divorce that leaves him taking care of his estranged father. A comedy that plucks the heartstrings with manipulative glee. Hanks is funny and has a genuine rapport with Gleason. C: Tom Hanks, Jackie Gleason, Eva Marie Saint, Barry Corbin, Bess Armstrong, Sela Ward. D: Garry Marshall. DRA [PG] 119m. v

Nothing Lasts Forever 1984 ★★★½ The futuristic adventures of a would-be artist (Galligan) in New York and on the moon. Peculiar comedy has an original bent, some good stuff. C: Zach Galligan, Apollonia van Ravenstein, Lauren Tom, Dan Aykroyd, Imogene Coca, Eddie Fisher, Sam Jaffe, Paul Rogers, Mort Sahl, Bill Murray, Anita Ellis. D: Tom Schiller. COM [PG] 82m.

Nothing Personal 1980 U.S. ★★ A lawyer (Somers) takes up cause of the baby seals, and falls in love with scientist (Sutherland). Weak screwball comedy. C: Donald Sutherland, Suzanne Somers, Lawrence Dane, Roscoe Lee Browne, Dabney Coleman, Saul Rubinek, John Dehner. D: George Bloomfield. COM [PG] 96m. v

Nothing Sacred 1937 ★★★★½ A small-town woman (Lombard) claims to be dying of radiation poisoning so she can get a trip to

New York City. When a reporter (March) publishes her plight she has trouble on her hands. Hilarious screwball comedy has great pacing, plenty of fun. C: Carole Lombard, Fredric March, Walter Connolly, Charles Winninger, Sig Rumann, Frank Fay. D: William Wellman. COM 75m. V

Nothing Venture 1948 British ★★★ Scientist invents powerful ray gun and soon has crooks on his trail. Rowdy adventure, aimed at kids; unsophisticated, far-fetched fun. C: Peter Artemus, Philip Artemus, Jackie Artemus, Terry Randal. D: John Baxter. FAM/SFI 73m.

Notorious 1946 ★★★★★ Bergman marries Nazi (Rains) to aid the American agent she really loves (Grant). A tale of twisted love makes for one of Hitchcock's most erotically charged films (watch for the longest set of kisses in all of filmdom; each had to be under three seconds to beat the censors). The leads and Konstantin, as the grasping mother, are great but Rains wins acting honors here as the soulful Nazi. C: Cary Grant, Ingrid Bergman, Claude Rains, Louis Calhern, Leopoldine Konstantin, Reinhold Schunzel, Moroni Olsen. D: Alfred Hitchcock. CRI 101m. V

Notorious 1992 ★★ Misguided, updated remake of Hitchcock classic with Shea in Cary Grant role, now a CIA agent trying to stop Cassel from selling arms to the Soviets. C: John Shea, Jenny Robertson, Jean-Pierre Cassel, Marisa Berenson. D: Colin Bucksey. CRI 100m. TVM

Notorious Gentleman 1945 British ★★★★ Rakish playboy (Harrison) works his way through a multitude of attractive women and finally meets his match. Good story, stylish production. (a.k.a. *The Rake's Progress*) C: Rex Harrison, Lilli Palmer, Godfrey Tearle, Griffith Jones, Margaret Johnston, Guy Middleton, Jean Kent. D: Sidney Gilliat. DRA 123m.

Notorious Landlady, The 1962 ★★★½ A tenant (Lemmon) in a London apartment house investigates rumors that the landlady (Novak) is a murderer. Witty, stylish comic mystery. C: Kim Novak, Jack Lemmon, Fred Astaire, Lionel Jeffries, Estelle Winwood, Maxwell Reed. D: Richard Quine. COM 123m.

Notorious Lone Wolf, The 1946 ★★★ Museum jewel theft needs solving in this minor entry in *Lone Wolf* series. C: Gerald Mohr, Janis Carter, Eric Blore, John Abbott, William B. Davidson, Don Beddoe, Adele Roberts, Peter Whitney, Olaf Hytten. D: D.Ross Lederman. DRA 64m.

Notorious Sophie Lang 1934 ★★★½ A gangster's moll helps police nab racketeers. Fast-moving B-film. C: Gertrude Michael, Paul Cavanagh, Alison Shipworth, Leon Errol, Arthur Hoyt. D: Ralph Murphy. DRA 64m.

Nouvelle Vague 1990 French ★★★★ An attractive, wealthy couple (Delon, Giordano) provides the centerpiece for Godard's ruminations on social structures and the cinema. Challenging, difficult, but rewarding. (a.k.a. *New Wave*) C: Alain Delon, Domiziana Giordano, Roland Amstutz, Laurence Cote, Christophe Odent. D: Jean-Luc Godard. DRA 88m. V

Novel Affair, A 1957 British ★★★★ An author (Leighton) writes a best-seller full of sex and finds the novel merging with reality. Witty farce, buoyed by outstanding cast. (a.k.a. *The Passionate Stranger*) C: Ralph Richardson, Margaret Leighton, Patricia Dainton, Carlo Justini, Marjorie Rhodes, Megs Jenkins. D: Muriel Box. COM 83m.

Now About All These Women 1964 *See* **All These Women**

Now and Forever 1934 ★★★½ A jewel thief (Cooper) is charmed by adorable waif (Temple) and decides to go straight. Good for its kind; Temple sweetness the key. C: Gary Cooper, Carole Lombard, Shirley Temple, Sir Guy Standing, Charlotte Granville. D: Henry Hathaway. FAM/DRA 81m.

Now and Forever 1982 Australian ★★★ A woman's marriage breaks apart when her cheating husband is sent to prison on a rape charge. She descends into drugs and desperation. From the novel by Danielle Steele. C: Cheryl Ladd, Robert Coleby, Carmen Duncan, Christine Amor. D: Adrian Carr. DRA [R] 93m. V

Now, Voyager 1942 ★★★★★ Adaptation of Olive Prouty's romantic novel gave Davis one of her best roles as timid spinster who, through psychotherapy, has a physical and emotional metamorphosis. Sterling supporting cast, memorable Max Steiner score, and Bette's bravura performance. C: Bette Davis, Paul Henreid, Claude Rains, Gladys Cooper, Bonita Granville, Ilka Chase, Lee Patrick, Mary Wickes, Janis Wilson. D: Irving Rapper. DRA 118m. V

Now You See Him, Now You Don't 1972 ★★★ Russell returns as college genius from *The Computer Wore Tennis Shoes*. This time he invents invisibility formula and is chased by gangsters who want concoction to pull off big heist. Strictly routine Disney slapstick packed into predictable story, though special effects are good. C: Kurt Russell, Cesar Romero, Joe Flynn, Jim Backus, Ed Begley Jr. D: Robert Butler. FAM/COM [G] 85m. V

Now You See It, Now You Don't 1968 ★★★ An inept art appraiser comes across a possibly forged Rembrandt. Silly, fun farce. C: Jonathan Winters, Luciana Paluzzi. D: Don Weis. FAM/COM 100m.

Nowhere to Go 1958 British ★★★½ Escaped convict Nader takes refuge with aristocrat Smith. Dark crime drama, beautifully photographed, with notable jazz-inflected score by trumpeter Dizzy Reece. C: George Nader, Maggie Smith, Bernard Lee, Geoffrey Keen, Bessie Love. D: Seth Holt. DRA 97m.

Nowhere to Hide 1987 Canadian ★★★ Madigan is forced on the lam after her husband is killed just as he was about to blow the whistle on a crooked defense contractor. No-surprises thriller redeemed only by the presence of Madigan. (a.k.a. *Fatal Chase*) C: Amy Madigan, Daniel Hugh Kelly, Robin MacEachern, Michael Ironside, John Colicos. D: Mario Azzopardi. ACT [R] 90m. V

Nowhere to Run 1978 ★★★★ A man devises a winning blackjack system as part of an elaborate plan to get rid of his wife. Well-done caper film. C: David Janssen, Stefanie Powers, Allen Garfield, Linda Evans, Neva Patterson, John Randolph. D: Richard Lang. CRI 100m. TVM

Nowhere to Run 1993 ★★★ Greedy developers want widow's (Arquette's) ranch, and a sensitive ex-con (Van Damme) is ready to help. Entertaining Van Damme actioner. C: Jean-Claude Van Damme, Rosanna Arquette, Kieran Culkin, Ted Levine, Joss Ackland. D: Robert Harmon. ACT [R] 95m. V

Nuclear Conspiracy 1985 ★★ Wife and friend of mising journalist who was, until his disappearance, investigating transport of nuclear waste, seek him out. C: Birgit Doll, Albert Fortell. D: Rainer Erler. DRA 115m. V

Nuclear Terror 1977 *See* **Golden Rendezvous**

Nude Bomb, The 1980 ★★★ When an evil genius creates a bomb that will destroy the world's clothing, CONTROL Agent 86 (Adams) sets out to stop him. Some minor laughs in reunion film of '60s sitcom *Get Smart.* (a.k.a. *The Return of Maxwell Smart*) C: Don Adams, Andrea Howard, Vittorio Gassman, Dana Elcar, Pamela Hensley, Sylvia Kristel, Norman Lloyd, Rhonda Fleming. D: Clive Donner. COM [PG] 94m. V

Nude in a White Car 1960 French ★★★½ Workmanlike, complex suspense film, set on the Riviera. A man becomes estranged in the lives of two sisters, after one of them seduces him. (a.k.a. *Blonde in a White Car*) C: Marina Vlady, Robert Hossein, Odile Versois, Helena Manson, Henri Cremieux. D: Robert Hossein. CRI 87m.

Nudist Colony of the Dead 1980 ★★ A nudist colony, driven to mass suicide by religious zealots, promises to return and exact its revenge. C: Deborah Lynn, Rachel Latt, Brad Mendelson. D: Mark Pirro. HOR 90m. V

Nudo di Donna 1982 Italian ★★★½ Amusing tale of bookshop owner who falls for the photo of a nude model who (from the rear view) looks suspiciously like his wife. Great shots of Venice and solid comic acting. (a.k.a. *Portrait of a Nude Woman*) C: Nino Manfredi, Eleonora Giorgi, Jean-Pierre Cassel, Georges Wilson. D: Nino Manfredi. COM 112m. V

Nuisance, The 1933 ★★★½ Sleazy shyster Tracy always gets his settlement money. Enter an outraged insurance company trying to get him disbarred. Tracy stands out in this slick comedy/drama. COM

Nukie 1993 ★★ In search of his brother, kindly alien arrives in Africa and is helped by two boys; all are then pursued by U.S. agents who fear extraterrestrial invasion. C: Glynis Johns, Steve Railsback, Ronald France. D: Sias Odendal. SFI [PG] 99m.

Number One 1969 ★★½ Trials of an aging quarterback (Heston). Interesting idea fumbles at the goal line. C: Charlton Heston, Jessica Walter, Bruce Dern, John Randolph, Diana Muldaur. D: Tom Gries. DRA [PG] 105m. V

Number 1 of the Secret Service 1986 ★★ Secret agent pursues evil millionaire bent on murdering other financiers for his own gain. C: Nicky Henson, Richard Todd, Aimi MacDonald. D: Lindsay Shonteff. ACT [PG] 87m.

Number One with a Bullet 1987 ★★★ Mismatched detectives (Carradine and Williams) trail a drug lord. Predictable and uninspired. C: Robert Carradine, Billy Dee Williams, Valerie Bertinelli, Peter Graves, Doris Roberts. D: Jack Smight. CRI [R] 103m. V

Number Seventeen 1932 British ★★★½ A young woman thief helps the police track down her old gang. Hitchcock antique holds up quite well. C: Leon M. Lion, Anne Grey, John Stuart, Donald Calthrop, Barry Jones, Garry Marsh. D: Alfred Hitchcock. DRA 83m. V

Number Six 1962 British ★★ A beauiful young heiress gets herself involved with a gang of murderers. Lukewarm suspense. C: Nadja Regin, Ivan Desny, Brian Bedford, Michael Goodliffe. D: Robert Tronson. DRA 59m.

Numero Deux 1975 French ★★½ A chronicle of the ups and downs of a modern family in a capitalist society. Pretentious but worthwhile. C: Sandrine Battistella, Pierre Dudry, Alexandre Rignault, Rachel Stefanopoli. D: Jean-Luc Godard. DRA 90m. V

Nun and the Sergeant, The 1962 ★★ During the Korean War, a tough sergeant, on a dangerous mission, gets involved with a nun and a little girl. Mediocre war adventure. C: Robert Webber, Anna Sten, Leo Gordon, Hari Rhodes, Robert Easton, Dale Ishimoto, Linda Wong. D: Franklin Adreon. ACT 74m.

Nun, The 1971 French ★★★★½ A poverty-stricken young woman is forced into a convent, where she is tormented by the Mother Superior and other sisters. Cool, intelligent, compelling treatment of the classic Diderot novel; Rivette's direction and Karina's performance are superb. Originally released in 1966; banned in France for several years. C: Anna Karina, Liselotte Pulver, Micheline Presle. D: Jacques Rivette. DRA 130m. V

Nuns on the Run 1990 British ★★★★ Two bumbling crooks (Idle and Coltrane) plan one last heist and retirement in South America, but they botch the job and disguise themselves as nuns to escape. Good fun, with double entendres milked for all they're worth. C: Eric Idle, Robbie Coltrane, Camille Coduri, Janet

Suzman, Doris Hare, Lila Kaye, Robert Patterson. D: Jonathan Lynn. COM [PG-13] 94m. V

Nun's Story, The 1959 ★★★★★ Young woman takes religious vows, serves as a nurse in the Belgian Congo, then has a crisis of faith. Kathryn Hulme's best-selling book is sensitively filmed. Hepburn impressive as nun torn by inner turmoil. C: Audrey Hepburn, Peter Finch, Edith Evans, Peggy Ashcroft, Dean Jagger, Mildred Dunnock, Beatrice Staight, Colleen Dewhurst. D: Fred Zinnemann. DRA 151m. V

Nunsense 1993 ★★ When some of their order suffer food poisoning, other nuns perform musicals to raise money to pay for their care. Based on the long-running off-Broadway play. C: Christine Anderson, Christine Toy, Terri White. D: Dan Goggin. MUS 111m. V

Nunzio 1978 ★★½ A mentally disabled delivery boy from Brooklyn falls in love with a pretty bakery worker. Soft, evocative story, with fine performances. C: David Proval, James Andronica, Tovah Feldshuh, Morgana King, Vincent Russo, Theresa Saldana, Monica Lewis. D: Paul Williams. DRA [R] 87m.

Nurse 1980 ★★★ When her youngest son goes off to college, a widow resumes her nursing career at a big-city hospital. Well played and convincing. C: Michael Learned, Robert Reed, Tom Aldredge, Antonio Fargas. D: David Lowell Rich. DRA 100m. TVM V

Nurse Edith Cavell 1939 ★★ The story of the real-life British army nurse who was accused of espionage by the Germans during WWI. Solid, wrenching drama. C: Anna Neagle, Edna May Oliver, George Sanders, ZaSu Pitts, May Robson. D: Herbert Wilcox. DRA 108m. V

Nurse on Wheels 1963 British ★★★ The adventures of a young nurse who brings her professional talents to a small town. Sharp and pleasant entertainment. C: Juliet Mills, Ronald Lewis, Joan Sims, Noel Purcell, Raymond Huntley, Jim Dale. D: Gerald Thomas. DRA 86m.

Nursemaid Who Disappeared, The 1939 British ★★★½ A kidnapping ring is discovered operating out of an employment agency; the unlikely team of a playwright and detective are soon on the case. Talky thriller makes entertaining fare. C: Arthur Margetson, Peter Coke, Lesley Brook, Coral Browne. D: Arthur V. Woods. CRI 86m.

Nurse's Secret, The 1941 ★★★ When her patient dies, a nurse must solve the murder. Moody mystery. C: Lee Patrick, Regis Toomey, Julie Bishop. D: Noel M. Smith. DRA 65m.

Nutcracker Fantasy 1979 ★★★½ A young girl dreams of a land where a princess is turned into a mouse. Charming animated Japanese production features many cute songs. C: Michele Lee, Melissa Gilbert, Roddy McDowall. FAM/DRA [G] 82m. V

Nutcracker Prince, The 1990 Canadian ★★★ The time-honored children's Christmas tale in a feature-length animated extravaganza. A classic put forth in fine spirit. C: Kiefer Sutherland, Megan Follows, Peter O'Toole, Mike McDonald, Eter Boretski, Phyllis Diller. D: Paul Schibli. MUS [G] 74m. V

Nutcracker, The See **George Balanchine's The Nutcracker**

Nutcracker, The 1977 ★★★★½ A wonderful, rousing version of Tchaikowsky's classic Christmas ballet, starring the amazing Mikhail Baryshnikov. Great for all audiences—and all seasons! C: Mikhail Baryshnikov, Gelsey Kirkland. MUS 78m. V

Nutcracker, The Motion Picture 1986 ★★★½ Pacific Northwest Ballet version of much-loved Tchaikovsky ballet about young Clara and her Christmas dreams. Sticks to original story by E.T.A. Hoffman and greatly benefits from set and costumes designed by children's author Maurice Sendak. C: Hugh Bigney, Vanessa Sharp, Patricia Barker, Wade Walthall, Russell Burnett, Julie Harris, Kent Stowell, Francia Russell. D: Carroll Ballard. MUS 82m. V

Nuts 1987 ★★★½ Courtroom drama about a call girl accused of murder, battling to convince the court of her sanity. Streisand and Dreyfuss act up a storm but the result is stagy and static. Based on the play by Tom Topor. C: Barbra Streisand, Richard Dreyfuss, Maureen Stapleton, Eli Wallach, Robert Webber, James Whitmore, Karl Malden. D: Martin Ritt. DRA [R] 116m. V

Nutty, Naughty Chateau 1964 French ★★½ The madcap happenings among a group of oddballs who live in an ancient castle and wear period clothing. Offbeat, good for a few laughs. C: Monica Vitti, Curt Jurgens, Jean-Claude Brialy, Sylvie, Jean-Louis Trintignant, Francoise Hardy. D: Roger Vadim. COM 100m.

Nutty Professor, The 1963 ★★★★ Funny, well-done twist on Jekyll and Hyde gives Lewis double role as a nerdy chemistry teacher and his suave alter-ego "Buddy Love." Considered Lewis's best film. C: Jerry Lewis, Stella Stevens, Del Moore, Kathleen Freeman, Howard Morris, Elvia Allman, Henry Gibson. D: Jerry Lewis. COM 107m. V

Nyoka and the Lost Secrets of Hippocrates *See* **Nyoka and the Tigerman**

Nyoka and the Tigerman 1942 ★★★ In the heart of equatorial Africa, jungle queen Nyoka and her nemesis, Vultura, try to outfox each other in a search for the ancient tablets of Hippocrates. Enjoyable adventure, edited to feature length from hte serial of the same name. (a.k.a. *Nyoka and the Lost Secrets of Hippocrates*) C: Kay Aldridge, Clayton Moore, William Benedict, Lorna Gray, Charles Middleton. D: William Witney. ACT 100m.

O

O. Henry's Full House 1952 ★★★★ Five of the master's short stories (featuring the heart-warming "Gift of the Magi") brought to film and each introduced by John Steinbeck. Outstanding entertainment. C: Charles Laughton, Anne Baxter, Jeanne Crain, Marilyn Monroe, Fred Allen, Oscar Levant, Jean Peters, Richard Widmark, Farley Granger. D: Henry Hathaway, Howard Hawks, Henry King, Jean Negulesco. DRA 117m.

O Lucky Man! 1973 British ★★★½ Sequel to *If*. . . stars McDowell as coffee sales representative who finds success is a fleeting concept. Rambling social allegory, McDowell good in lead. C: Malcolm McDowell, Rachel Roberts, Ralph Richardson, Alan Price, Helen Mirren. D: Lindsay Anderson. COM [R] 174m. V

O Pioneers! 1992 ★★★ Willa Cather's classic novel adapted for television's Hallmark Hall of Fame. Matriarch (Lange) holds pioneer family together through trials and tribulations in 19th-century Nebraska. Lange gives it her best, but drama never achieves much depth. C: Jessica Lange, David Strathairn, Tom Aldredge. D: Glenn Caron Jordan. DRA [PG] 100m. V

O. S. S. 117—Mission for a Killer 1966 French ★★★ Stafford is American spy á la James Bond, fighting an underground organization bent on world domination. Lacks 007's subtle humor and campy finesse, but offers plenty of the requisite fisticuffs, females, and felons. C: Frederick Stafford, Mylene Demongeot. D: Andre Hunebelle. ACT 84m.

Oak, The 1992 French-Romanian ★★★★ Young Romanian woman's life changes when her father dies suddenly, leaving her at the mercy of corrupt Ceausescu regime. Interesting blend of political satire, road movie and coming-of-age story. (a.k.a. *La Chene*) C: Maia Morgenstern, Razvan Vasilescu. D: Lucian Pintilie. DRA 105m. V

Oasis 1955 French ★★ A one-time aviator meets up with a couple of beautiful women who ply the Sahara with smuggled gold. A little romance and some adventure keeps it going. C: Michele Morgan, Pierre Brasseur, Cornell Borchers. D: Yves Allegret. ACT 84m.

Oasis, The 1984 ★★½ A plane crashes in the Mexican desert and the survivors try to find their way back to civilization. Harrowing and bloody. C: Chris Makepeace, Scott Hylands, Richard Cox, Dori Brenner. D: Sparky Greene. ACT 90m. TVM

Object of Beauty, The 1991 ★★★½ Americans in London (Malkovich and MacDowell) living beyond their means in hotel room try to unload a piece of art to finance extravagances. Unusual, with effective black humor and fine performances, yet story never gels. C: John Malkovich, Andie MacDowell, Lolita Davidovich, Rudi Davies, Joss Ackland. D: Michael Lindsay Hogg. COM [R] 105m. V

Objective, Burma! 1945 ★★★★½ After paratroopers wipe out a key Japanese post in Burma, they must fight through the jungle to make their escape. Excellent—though violent—WWII tale; Flynn and Hull are terrific. Remade as *Distant Drums*. C: Errol Flynn, William Prince, James Brown, George Tobias. D: Raoul Walsh. ACT 142m. V

Obliging Young Lady 1941 ★★½ While her parents go through a messy divorce, a little girl is whisked out of town by a secretary. Lightweight comedy gains stature from sturdy cast. C: Eve Arden, Edmond O'Brien, Ruth Warrick, Franklin Pangborn. D: Richard Wallace. COM 80m.

Oblomov 1980 Russian ★★★★ An aristocrat (Tabakov) trying to avoid life by staying in bed is challenged by an old friend to rejoin the living. Finely acted and directed, especially flashback to Oblomov's youth. Based on novel by Ivan Goncharov. (a.k.a. *A Few Days in the Life of I.I. Oblomov*) C: Oleg Tabakov, Yuri Bogtryev, Elena Soloyei. D: Nikita Mikhalkov. DRA 145m. V

Oblong Box, The 1969 British ★★★ Edgar Allan Poe's story of a man who was buried alive, only to escape and wreak havoc. Tart horror film has its share of frights. C: Vincent Price, Christopher Lee, Hillary Dwyer. D: Gordon Hessler. HOR 91m. V

Obsessed 1989 Canadian ★★ When her son is killed by a hit-and-run driver, a woman becomes obsessed with taking justice into her own hands. Struggles with lackluster story. C: Kerrie Keane, Saul Rubinek, Alan Thicke, Colleen Dewhurst. D: Robin Spry. DRA [PG-13] 100m. V

Obsessed, The 1951 British ★★ A man is accused of killing his wife and he tries to expose the person he says is the real killer. Ordinary mystery with low-level suspense. (a.k.a. *The Late Edwina Black*) C: David Farrar, Geraldine Fitzgerald, Roland Culver. D: Maurice Elvey. CRI 77m.

Obsession 1976 ★★★★ Stylish homage to Hitchcock's masterpiece, *Vertigo*, with Robertson falling in love with woman who looks exactly like wife who was kidnapped 16 years earlier. Stands on its own. Brilliant score by Bernard Herrmann, who also composed Hitch's film. C: Cliff Robertson, Genevieve Bujold, John Lithgow. D: Brian De Palma. DRA [PG] 98m. V

Obsessive Love 1984 ★★½ A reclusive and unbalanced secretary develops an obsession with her favorite soap opera star. She makes herself beautiful and goes to Hollywood with intention of making him hers. Interesting enough. C: Yvette Mimieux, Simon MacCorkindale. D: Steven Stern. DRA 100m. TVM

O.C. & Stiggs 1987 ★★ Two shiftless young teenagers spend their time tormenting a family. Uneven comedy misses the mark. C: Daniel Jenkins, Neill Barry, Paul Dooley, Jane Curtin. D: Robert Altman. COM [R] 109m. V

Occurrence at Owl Creek Bridge, An 1962 ★★★★ Short but intense look at final moments of man shortly to be hung for sabotage. Oscar-winner for Best Short Subject. C: Roger Jacquet, Anne Cornaly. D: Robert Enrico. DRA 29m.

Ocean Drive Weekend 1985 ★★ College kids on vacation spree during the '60s. C: Robert Peacock, Charles Redmond. D: Bryan Jones. COM [PG-13] 98m. TVM

Ocean's Eleven 1960 ★★★½ Crime caper classic mainly because it features the "Rat Pack" (Sinatra, Martin, Davis, Jr., Lawford) in their heydey. Entertaining tale of a group of war buddies out to rob five Las Vegas casinos in a commando-like raid, with a satisfying twist ending. C: Frank Sinatra, Dean Martin, Sammy Davis Jr., Peter Lawford, Angie Dickinson, Joey Bishop. D: Lewis Milestone. CRI 127m. V

Oceans of Fire 1987 ★★½ Trouble is brewing among oil riggers working on an offshore platform. Solid, grinding action, anchored by fine cast. C: Gregory Harrison, Bill Dee Williams, David Carradine. D: Steve Carver. ACT [PG] 93m. TVM V

Octagon, The 1980 ★★★★ Professional bodyguard (Norris) protects woman from ninja assassins. One of Norris's best, spotlighting his martial arts skills. Entertaining. C: Chuck Norris, Karen Carlson, Lee VanCleef. D: Eric Karson. ACT [R] 103m. V

Octaman 1971 ★★ Explorers on expedition in Mexico discover a monstrous man-like octopus. Awful thriller abounds with unintended laughs. C: Kerwin Mathews, Pier Angeli, Jeff Morrow. D: Harry Essex. SFI 79m. V

Octavia 1982 ★★ Escaped con makes friends with abused blind young woman and shows her the realities of the world outside her sheltered home. C: Susan Curtis, Neil Kinsella, Jake Foley. D: David Beaird. DRA [R] 93m.

October 1928 Russian ★★★★½ The Russian Revolution, as re-created through the masterful eyes of Eisenstein. Truly captivating silent epic. (a.k.a. *Ten Days that Shook the World*) C: Nikandrov, N. Popov, Boris Livanov. D: Sergei Eisenstein, Grigori Alexandrov. DRA 103m.

October Man, The 1947 British ★★★ A man with mental problems is arrested and charged with murder, and even he isn't sure about his innocence. Intriguing character study. C: John Mills, Joan Greenwood, Edward Chapman, Joyce Carey. D: Roy Baker. DRA 98m.

October Moth 1959 British ★★ A young man with emotional problems causes a fatal auto accident. Wrenching drama. C: Lee Patterson, Lana Morris. D: John Kruse. DRA 54m.

Octopussy 1983 British ★★★ When a looney Russian general threatens nuclear attack on various NATO forces 007 comes to the rescue. Good special effects and lots of action, but hardly top-drawer Bond. C: Roger Moore, Maud Adams, Louis Jourdan, Steven Berkoff. D: John Glen. ACT [PG] 130m. V

Odd Angry Shot, The 1979 Australian ★★★½ Australian soldiers stationed in Vietnam during war wrestle with their place in it. Good, offbeat blend of humor and seriousness, focusing more on characters than action. C: John Hargreaves, Graham Kennedy, Bryan Brown. D: Tom Jeffrey. DRA 90m. V

Odd Birds 1985 ★★½ An awkward teenage girl dreams about a life of romance and adventure. Provocative and somewhat insightful look at growing up. C: Michael Moriarty, Nancy Lee, Bruce Gray. D: Jeanne Collachia. DRA 87m. V

Odd Couple, The 1968 ★★★★½ Divorcing neatnik Felix Ungar moves in with his great friend, the antineatnik Oscar Madison. A wonderfully funny and intelligent film of Neil Simon's brilliant play. Matthau/Lemon chemistry is golden. C: Walter Matthau, Jack Lemmon, Herb Edelman, Monica Evans, Carole Shelley. D: Gene Saks. COM [G] 106m. V

Odd Job, The 1978 British ★★★ Monty Python veteran Chapman is a business executive who hires Jason to kill him, then changes his mind about dying. Slapstick chases ensue, as Jason doesn't believe Chapman now wants to live. Black comedy that doesn't elicit many yuks. C: Graham Chapman, David Jason, Diana Quick. D: Peter Medak. COM 100m. V

Odd Jobs 1985 ★★½ Five college buddies search for summer jobs, and wind up working for a mob-run moving business. Dumb story, but ongoing laughs from young cast. C: Paul Reiser, Robert Townsend, Scott McGinnis. D: Mark Story. COM [PG-13] 89m. V

Odd Man Out 1947 British ★★★★★ Irish rebel, wounded after a bold stickup and hunted by police, is abetted or obstructed by various Belfast townspeople. Skillfully crafted with extraordinary suspense; unusually powerful. Fugitive's last hours imaginatively rendered. Based on novel by F.L. Green. Remake: *The Lost Man*. C: James Mason, Robert Newton, Kathleen Ryan, Cyril Cusack, Dan O'Herlihy. D: Carol Reed. DRA 111m. V

Odd Obsession 1960 Japanese ★★★½ An old man's marriage to a younger wife is threatened by his possessiveness and impotence, so he promotes her affair with a young doctor. Slow, but fascinating. C: Machiko Kyo, Ganjiro Nakamura. D: Kon Ichikawa. DRA 96m. V

Oddball Hall 1990 ★★½ Curiously flat comedy about four robbers hiding in African village, having to deal with tribal neighbors. C: Don Ameche, Burgess Meredith, Tullio Moneta, Bill Maynard. D: Jackson Hunsicker. COM [PG] 87m. V

Odds Against Tomorrow 1959 ★★★ Three criminals plan a bank job, but racist attitudes intrude. Interesting, downbeat thriller, no-holds-barred performances. C: Harry Belafonte, Robert Ryan, Shelley Winters, Ed Begley, Gloria Grahame. D: Robert Wise. DRA 95m.

Odds and Evens 1978 ★★ Gamblers involved with illegal activity at racetracks and casinos pursued by law enforcement agents. C: Terence Hill, Bud Spencer. D: Sergio Corbucci. COM [PG] 109m.

Ode to Billy Joe 1976 ★★★½ Adapted from popular song by Bobby Gentry, story follows Benson as he flirts with O'Connor, then jumps off the famed Talahatchee Bridge. Not quite successful story of adolescent confusion, though Benson and O'Connor rise above the script. C: Robby Benson, Glynnis O'Connor, Joan Hotchkis. D: Max Baer. DRA [PG] 107m. V

Odessa File, The 1974 British ★★★ A journalist (Voight) trailing a group of neo-Nazis discovers the existence of a document, said to contain the names of ex-Nazis. Lumbering spy saga does have some real cliffhanger episodes, and music by Andrew Lloyd Webber. From the Frederick Forsyth novel. C: Jon Voight, Maximilian Schell, Maria Schell, Derek Jacobi. D: Ronald Neame. DRA [PG] 128m. V

Odette 1950 British ★★★ A beautiful woman works as a spy for the French resistance during WWII. A true story that gets good treatment here. C: Anna Neagle, Trevor Howard, Marius Goring, Peter Ustinov. D: Herbert Wilcox. DRA 100m.

Odongo 1956 British ★★★ A big game hunter runs into trouble and romance in Africa. Spirited adventure. C: Rhonda Fleming, Macdonald Carey. D: John Gilling. ACT 85m.

Odyssey of the Pacific 1982 Canadian ★★½ Three refugees from Cambodia meet up with an eccentric retired railroad engineer (Rooney). Together, they restore an old train engine. Peculiar story that manages some insight. (a.k.a. *The Emperor of Peru*) C: Mickey Rooney, Monique Mercure. D: Fernando Arrabal. DRA 82m. V

Oedipus Rex 1957 Canadian ★★½ Stage-bound presentation (by the Stratford Festival Players) of Sophocles. Well done but lacks cinematic insight. C: Douglas Rain, Douglas Campbell, Eric House, Eleanor Stuart. D: Tyrone Guthrie. DRA 87m.

Oedipus Rex 1967 Italian ★★★★ Extravagant, provocative visuals and Pasolini's left-wing politics alter and update the Greek classic of the king fated to kill his father and wed his mother. Unrated but contains violence and nudity. C: Franco Citti, Silvana Mangano, Alida Valli, Julian Beck. D: Pier Paolo Pasolini. DRA 110m. V

Oedipus the King 1968 British ★★★★ Plummer is the king who fulfills the horrifying prophecy of killing his father and marrying his mother. Filmed in a Greek amphitheater, this is a fine introduction of the Sophocles play for high school audiences. C: Christopher Plummer, Orson Welles, Lilli Palmer, Cyril Cusack, Donald Sutherland. D: Philip Saville. DRA [G] 97m.

Of Flesh and Blood 1962 French ★★★ After stealing engine parts from a jeep, Hossein cheats in a card game and gets his hands broken. Crazed after this maiming, he kills an old woman and must face the consequences. Overplayed histrionics in a violent drama. C: Robert Hossein, Renato Salvatori, Anouk Aimee. D: Christian Marquand. DRA 92m.

Of Human Bondage 1934 ★★★★ Crippled medical student (Howard) becomes obsessed with amoral waitress (Davis). Uneven adaptation of W. Somerset Maugham's novel, famous for Davis' star-making performance: cruel, brutal, and brilliant. C: Leslie Howard, Bette Davis, Frances Dee. D: John Cromwell. DRA 83m. V

Of Human Bondage 1964 British ★★½ Remake of classic W. Somerset Maugham novel about an affluent would-be artist's foolish love for an unrefined waitress. Flimsy disaster; leads miscast. C: Kim Novak, Laurence Harvey, Siobhan McKenna, Robert Morley. D: Kenneth Hughes. DRA 98m. V

Of Human Hearts 1938 ★★★½ The story of a 19th-century preacher and his troubled son. Well-told, well-acted American nostalgia. C: Walter Huston, James Stewart, Gene Reynolds, Beulah Bondi, Guy Kibbee, Charles Coburn, John Carradine. D: Clarence Brown. DRA 100m. V

Of Life and Love 1957 Italian ★★½ Four short tales, three by Pirandello. Touching, sensitive portrayals. C: Anna Magnani, Walter Chiari, Natale Cirino, Turi Pandolfini. D: Aldo Fabrizi, Luchino Visconti, Mario Soldati, Giorgio Pastina. DRA 103m.

Of Love and Desire 1963 ★★ While on assignment in Mexico, an engineer falls in love with the sister of his boss. Curious choice for Oberon, and it stumbles. C: Merle Oberon, Steve Cochran, Curt Jurgens. D: Richard Rush. DRA 97m.

Of Mice and Men 1939 ★★★★½ Fine adaptation of Steinbeck's novella about itinerant ranch hands George (Meredith), cynical yet hopeful, and Lenny (Chaney), his slow-witted friend. Extraordinary performances, espeically Chaney's and Field's. Aaron Copland's brilliant score was his first for Hollywood. C: Lon Chaney Jr., Burgess Meredith, Betty Field, Charles Bickford. D: Lewis Milestone. DRA 107m.

Of Mice and Men 1981 ★★★½ Blake and

Quaid are serviceable as George and Lenny, John Steinbeck's luck-starved protagonists. A workable, if not particularly inspired, version. C: Robert Blake, Randy Quaid, Lew Ayres, Pat Hingle. D: Reza Badiyi. DRA 150m. TVM V

Of Mice and Men 1992 ★★★★ Malkovich transforms himself, while Sinise has the sense of regret and wonder to give George poignance. A beautifully filmed version, with strong supporting performances. C: John Malkovich, Gary Sinise, Sherilyn Fenn, Joe Morton. D: Gary Sinise. DRA [PG-13] 110m. V

Of Pure Blood 1986 *See* **Nazis: Of Pure Blood, The**

Of Stars and Men 1961 ★★★★½ Animated fable looks at humanity's place in the universe. Provides humor and drama in even doses and is a must-see for kids and adults. FAM/DRA

Of Unknown Origin 1983 Canadian ★★★★ Surprisingly taut horror probes the escalating war of nerves between a man and the oversized rat that invades his home and thwarts all his efforts to kill it. Intense direction and Weller's strong performance elevate this film, based on Chauncey G. Parker III's novel *The Visitor.* C: Peter Weller, Jennifer Dale, Lawrence Dane, Kenneth Welsh, Louis Del Grande. D: George P. Cosmatos. HOR [R] 88m.

Off Beat 1985 ★★★ A shy librarian falls for a street tough policewoman. Slight but enjoyable comedy. C: Judge Reinhold, Meg Tilly, Cleavant Derricks, Joe Mantegna, Jacques D'Amboise. D: Michael Dinner. COM [PG] 92m. V

Off Limits 1953 ★★★½ Bantamweight Rooney is managed by Hope while training for Army championship. Silly fun. C: Bob Hope, Mickey Rooney, Marilyn Maxwell. D: George Marshall. COM 89m. V

Off Limits 1987 ★★★ Army agents in the midst of the Vietnam war investigate murders among prostitutes in 1968 Saigon. Macho stars Dafoe, Hines, Ward, and Glenn can't offset overly violent and foulmouthed story with a painfully predictable ending. C: Willem Dafoe, Gregory Hines, Fred Ward, Amanda Pays, Scott Glenn. D: Christopher Crowe. CRI [R] 102m. V

Off on a Comet 1979 ★★ Group of people hurled into space by comet. Loosely based on Jules Verne story. FAM/ACT 52m. V

Off Sides 1984 ★★½ A group of radio disc jockeys take on the police department in a well-publicized football game. Some fun moments. (a.k.a. *Pigs vs. Freaks*) C: Tony Randall, Adam Baldwin, Brian Dennehy, Gloria DeHaven. D: Dick Lowry. COM 100m. TVM

Off the Dole 1935 British ★★★ Formby, aided by real-life wife Beryl, plays ukulele and tracks crooks. Fluffy comedy with music; Formy's second film. C: George Formby, Beryl Formby, Constance Shotter. D: Arthur Mertz. COM 89m.

Off the Mark 1987 ★ Young man troubled by dog thief, spastic muscles in his legs, and inability to secure relationship with young woman, enters Plutonium Man Triathalon in hopes of somehow redeeming himself. C: Mark Neely, Terry Farrell, Jon Cypher. D: Bill Berry. COM [R] 89m. V

Off the Minnesota Strip 1980 ★★★ A young midwestern girl runs away to New York and becomes a prostitute. When she returns home she faces rejection. Downbeat drama, finely layered star performance from Winningham. C: Mare Winningham, Hal Holbrook. D: Lamont Johnson. DRA 105m. TVM

Off the Wall 1982 ★★ A pair of wrongly accused bumblers try to escape from a Tennessee prison. Aptly titled bogus comedy. C: Paul Sorvino, Rosanna Arquette, Patrick Cassidy. D: Rick Friedberg. COM [R] 86m. V

Offence, The 1973 British ★★★★ A British cop (Connery) questions and ends up beating to death an alleged child molester. Connery is powerful as a man whose act of violence leads to a life-changing discovery about his own past. C: Sean Connery, Trevor Howard, Vivien Merchant, Ian Bannen. D: Sidney Lumet. CRI 108m. V

Offering, The 1966 Canadian ★★★½ A Canadian stagehand and a young Chinese opera singer fall in love, only to be separated by politics. Simple, eloquent film was done on minuscule budget. C: Kee Faun, Ratch Wallace. D: David Secter. DRA 80m.

Office Picnic, The 1974 Australian ★★★★ Public service employees share fun and passion at office outing; some lives will never be the same. Touching, humorous film boasts a terrific ensemble. C: John Wood, Kate Fitzpatrick, Phillip Deamer, Patricia Kennedy. D: Tom Cowan. COM 85m.

Officer and a Gentleman, An 1982 ★★★★ A young Naval flight officer (Gere) meets and falls in love with factory worker (Winger). Enormously popular boy-meets-then-loses-then-gets-her-back film. The star performances (including some steamy sex scenes) carry it. Gossett won a well-deserved Best Supporting Actor Oscar. Oscar for Best Song. C: Richard Gere, Debra Winger, David Keith, Louis Gossett Jr. D: Taylor Hackford. DRA [R] 126m. V

Official Story, The 1985 Argentina ★★★★★ Emotionally devastating depiction of the fate of the "disappeared" in Argentina. A mother (Aleandro) fears her adopted daughter's real parents were killed by the repressive regime. Rich and thoughtful examination of the responsibilities and conscience of citizens. Oscar for Best Foreign Film. C: Norma Aleandro, Hector Alterio, Analia Castro. D: Luis Puenzo. DRA 112m. V

Offspring, The 1987 ★ Price brings the only touch of class to this tacky, unpleasant anthology shocker, by narrating tales of vengeance from beyond the grave, including a man who makes a deal to live forever and a Union soldier comfronting murderous Civil War orphans. C: Vincent Price, Clu Gulager, Terry Kiser, Cameron Mitchell. D: Jeff Burr. HOR [R] 99m. V

Oh, Alfie! 1975 British ★★★ The bachelor exploits of a randy Cockney (Price, taking over Michael Caine's role from *Alfie*) land him in a romance with a magazine editor. Minor, predictable sequel. (a.k.a. *Alfie Darling*) C: Alan Price, Jill Townsend, Joan Collins. D: Ken Hughes. DRA 99m. V

Oh, Bloody Life! . . . 1983 Hungarian ★★ Hungarian film follows the deportation of inhabitants from Budapest during Stalin's reign. C: Dorottya Udvaros, Laszlo Szacsvay, Kern Andras. D: Peter Bacso. DRA 115m.

Oh Dad, Poor Dad, Mama's Hung You in the Closet and I'm Feeling So Sad 1967 ★★ An eccentric widow and her son take a tropical vacation, and they take the deceased patriarch with them. Black comedy. C: Rosalind Russell, Robert Morse, Barbara Harris, Hugh Griffith, Jonathan Winters. D: Richard Quine. COM 86m. V

Oh, God! 1977 ★★★★ Mild-mannered grocery store manager Denver (in nice screen debut) is surprised when God—in form of George Burns—tells him to spread message of heavenly goodness. Simple, yet effective comedy doesn't overplay feel-good message. Burns, at his schticky best, is perfectly cast in almighty role. Two sequels followed. C: George Burns, John Denver, Teri Garr, Paul Sorvino. D: Carl Reiner. COM [PG] 104m. V

Oh God! Book II 1980 ★★½ Sequel to *Oh, God!* has Burns reprising Almighty role, once more seeking an Earthbound messenger to proclaim his existence. His choice is sweet child actor Louanne. Follow-up retains the spirit of the original, if not the soul. C: George Burns, Suzanne Pleshette, David Birney Louanne. D: Gilbert Cates. COM [PG] 94m. V

Oh, God! You Devil 1984 ★★★ When a poverty-stricken singer/song writer sells his soul to the Devil in return for success, God enters the picture to lend a divine hand. Burns' double performance both as the Devil and God sparks an otherwise bland effort. C: George Burns, Ted Wass, Ron Silver. D: Paul Bogart. COM [PG] 96m. V

Oh, Happy Day ★★★★ A soulful earful from leading gospel singers in a wonderful and truly inspiring film; singers include the Rev. James Cleveland, Mighty Clouds of Joy, the Clark Sisters, and Shirley Caesar. C: Shirley Caeser, The Mighty Clouds of Joy. MUS 60m. V

Oh, Heavenly Dog! 1980 ★★★★ Third *Benji* film features Chase as detective reincarnated into lovable pooch and in search of his own murderer. Unusual premise nicely played by both human and dog, with Seymour appropriately confused as Chase's girlfriend. Good for both adults and kids. C: Chevy Chase, Benji, Jane Seymour, Omar Sharif, Robert Morley. D: Joe Camp. COM [PG] 104m. V

Oh, Men! Oh, Women! 1957 ★★½ The randy adventures of a hapless psychiatrist who learns that two of his patients are involved with his wife. Dated farce still quite funny. C: Ginger Rogers, David Niven, Dan Dailey, Barbara Rush, Tony Randall. D: Nunnally Johnson. COM 90m.

Oh! Sailor, Behave! 1930 ★★★½ Two American sailors search Naples for a man who has robbed a Navy storehouse. Dated but fun, based on an Elmer Rice play, this rowdy comedy is brimming with good songs. C: Irene Delroy, Charles King, Lowell Sherman, Vivian Oakland, Noah Beery, Sr. D: Archie Mayo. COM 70m. V

Oh! Susanna 1951 ★★ The cavalry get into assorted squabbles, with Indians and among themselves. Turgid Western. C: Rod Cameron, Forrest Tucker, Chill Wills. D: Joseph Kane. WST 90m.

Oh! Those Most Secret Agents 1966 Italian ★★ Another spy spoof. Leave it. (a.k.a. *Worst Secret Agents*) C: Franco Franchi, Ciccio Ingrassia. D: Lucio Fulci. COM 83m.

Oh! What a Lovely War 1969 British ★★★½ World War I set to music. Splashy production is something to see, though some vignettes work better than others. C: Laurence Olivier, John Gielgud, Ralph Richardson, Michael Redgrave, John Mills, Vanessa Redgrave, Dirk Bogarde, Susannah York, Maggie Smith, Jane Seymour. D: Richard Attenborough. MUS [G] 139m.

Oh, What a Night 1992 ★★ Conventional tale of adolescent who moves to new town, forms friendship with high school macho man, and discovers self through experiences with young women and cars. C: Corey Haim, Genevieve Bujold, Robbie Coltrane. COM [PG-13] 93m. V

Oh, You Beautiful Doll 1949 ★★★½ The true story of Fred Fisher, a man who aspired to write opera but achieved success writing popular tunes. Fun evocation of an era. C: June Haver, Mark Stevens, S.Z. Sakall, Charlotte Greenwood. D: John Stahl. MUS 93m.

O'Hara: U.S. Treasury 1971 ★★½ Federal agents move in against a syndicate of dope smugglers. Typical hardnosed crimer, good performances. DRA

O'Hara's Wife 1982 ★★ A widower gets along just fine thanks to help from his wife (as a ghost). Pleasant enough. C: Edward Asner, Mariette Hartley, Jodie Foster. D: William Bartman. DRA [PG] 87m. TVM V

Ohayo 1962 Japanese ★★★★½ Two kids go on a hunger strike when their parents refuse to buy them a TV. Hilarious comedy from master director Ozu hits the spot. Splendid family viewing. C: Koji Shidara, Masahiko Shimazu, Chishu Ryu, Kuniko Miyake. D: Yasujiro Ozu. COM 93m.

OHMS 1980 ★★★ When a rural power company plan to run a major line across farmland, a farmer and an activist unite and fight back. Something for the environmentalists and rather well done. DRA

Oil 1978 Italian ★★ Sahara oil field workers battle danger when their rigs turn into a blazing inferno. Surprisingly unexciting. C: Stuart Whitman, Woody Strode, Ray Milland. D: Mircea Dragan. ACT 95m. V

Oil for the Lamps of China 1935 ★★★★ A representative of an American oil company faces personal and professional problems when he's sent to China. Quality production, first-rate performances. C: Pat O'Brien, Josephine Hutchinson, Jean Muir, Lyle Talbot. D: Mervyn LeRoy. DRA 110m.

Oil Girls, The 1971 *See* **Legend of Frenchie King, The**

Okinawa 1952 ★★½ The story of a U.S. warship's gun crew during the latter days of WWII. Standard war actioner. C: Pat O'Brien, Cameron Mitchell, James Dobson, Richard Denning. D: Leigh Jason. ACT 67m.

Oklahoma! 1955 ★★★★ Enjoyable screen transfer of classic Rodgers and Hammerstein musical Western tells simple story of young woman from country and her two suitors. Gorgeous outdoor photography doesn't mix with stylized musical numbers. But score ("Oh, What a Beautiful Morning," "People Will Say We're In Love," "I Can't Say No," etc.) is well sung and charm of original play shines through. C: Gordon MacRae, Shirley Jones, Gloria Grahame, Gene Nelson, Rod Steiger, Charlotte Greenwood, Eddie Albert. D: Fred Zinnemann. MUS [G] 146m. V

Oklahoma Annie 1951 ★★½ When too many ne'er-do-wells enter her town, feisty deputy (Canova) takes matters into hand. Zany Canova-style fun. C: Judy Canova, John Russell. D: R.G. Springsteen. WST [PG] 90m. V

Oklahoma City Dolls, The 1982 ★★½ Tired of getting one raw deal after another, a group of female factory workers form a football team and take on the corporate big shots. Lively and interesting. C: Susan Blakely, Ronee Blakley. D: E.W. Swackhamer. DRA 104m. TVM

Oklahoma Crude 1973 ★★★½ When a big oil company tries to steal her only oil well, a wildcatter (Dunaway) hires a drifter (Scott) to help. Fine efforts by the leads keep it going. C: George C. Scott, Faye Dunaway, John Mills, Jack Palance. D: Stanley Kramer. WST [PG] 108m. TVM

Oklahoma Kid, The 1939 ★★★ An innocent man is lynched, and his son sets out to even the score. Solid film—somewhat like a gangster epic set out West—pitting good Cagney against bad Bogart. C: James Cagney, Humphrey Bogart, Rosemary Lane, Donald Crisp. D: Lloyd Bacon. WST 82m. V

Oklahoma Territory 1960 ★★½ A cow wrangler takes off to find the man who murdered a local Indian agent. Fair Western. C: Bill Williams, Gloria Talbott. D: Edward Cahn. WST 67m.

Oklahoma Woman, The 1956 ★★ He promises to keep out of trouble, but an ex-con winds up locking horns with a female gunslinger. Low budget Western. C: Richard Denning, Peggie Castle, Cathy Downs. D: Roger Corman. WST 72m.

Oklahoman, The 1957 ★★½ A small town sawbones tries to see that an Indian friend doesn't get cheated out of land. Good McCrea, routine Western. C: Joel McCrea, Barbara Hale, Brad Dexter. D: Francis D. Lyon. WST 80m. V

Old Acquaintance 1943 ★★★½ Friends from childhood continue a rivalry that lasts all their lives. Great performances, good production. C: Bette Davis, Miriam Hopkins, Gig Young, John Loder. D: Vincent Sherman. DRA 110m.

Old and New 1929 *See* **General Line, The**

Old Barn Dance, The 1938 ★★ Classic Autrey western with plenty of shooting and singing. C: Gene Autry, Smiley Burnette, Helen Valkis. D: Joseph Kane. WST 52m. V

Old Bones of the River 1938 British ★★★½ White British teacher in Africa finds himself caught in the middle of civil unrest. Dated but funny farce, left over from the British Empire. A sequel to 1935 *Sanders of the River*. C: Will Hay, Moore Marriott, Graham Moffatt. D: Marcel Varnel. COM 90m.

Old Boyfriends 1979 ★★ In order to more fully understand herself, a woman seeks out all of her old boyfriends. Ineffective drama. C: Talia Shire, Richard Jordan, Keith Carradine, John Belushi. D: Joan Tewkesbury. DRA [R] 102m. V

Old Corral, The 1937 ★★ After chanteuse witnesses murder, she becomes target of Chicago mobsters. C: Gene Autry, Smiley Burnette, Hope Manning. D: Joseph Kane. WST 53m.

Old Curiosity Shop, The 1935 ★★★½ Shopowner Webster, trying to put money away for granddaughter Little Nell (Benson) loses it all, and shop is taken over by avaricious landlord Quilp (Petrie). Competent, though somewhat dark adaptation of Dickens novel. Musical version, *Mr. Quilp*, made in 1975. C: Ben Webster, Elaine Benson. D: Thomas Bentley. DRA 90m.

Old Curiosity Shop, The *See* **Mr. Quilp**

Old Dark House, The 1932 ★★★★ Marooned travelers are forced to stay in a mysterious home. Loaded with bizarre characters, creepy atmosphere. A gem of an antique. C: Boris Karloff, Melvyn Douglas, Charles Laughton, Gloria Stuart. D: James Whale. HOR 71m.

Old Dark House, The 1963 British ★★ Unsuspecting travelers stranded in creepy mansion. Flat remake of the 1932 classic. C:

Robert Morley, Janette Scott, Joyce Grenfell, Tom Poston. D: William Castle. HOR 86m.

Old Dracula 1974 British ★★ Horror spoof has the count surrounded by Playboy Bunnies. Niven does his best with the silly material. (a.k.a. *Vampira*) C: David Niven, Teresa Graves, Peter Bayliss. D: Clive Donner. COM [PG] 89m.

Old English 1930 ★★½ Broker Arliss arranges for his own death for the sake of his grandchildren. Heavy class-conscious drama adapted from John Galsworthy's play. C: George Arliss, Leon Janney, Doris Lloyd, Betty Lawford. D: Alfred E. Green. DRA 85m.

Old Enough 1984 ★★ Two very different teenage girls form a tentative friendship. Low-key comedy that tries hard. C: Sarah Boyd, Rainbow Harvest, Danny Aiello. D: Marisa Silver. COM [PG] 91m. V

Old Explorers 1990 ★★½ Two old men, friends for life, imagine dangerous and exotic adventures they might have had. Good work by the stars, but slow going. C: Jose Ferrer, James Whitmore. D: William Pohland. DRA [PG] 91m. V

Old-Fashioned Way, The 1934 ★★★★½ Fields manages acting troupe performing old melodrama *The Drunkard*. An utter delight, especially Fields' sparring with Baby Leroy and in his unctuous courtliness to women. C: W.C. Fields, Judith Allen, Joe Morrison, Baby LeRoy. D: William Beaudine. COM 74m.

Old Gringo 1989 ★★★½ Culture clash during the Mexican Revolution between an American woman, a fiery rebel general and cynical old American writer, Ambrose Bierce. Epic story is confused, but combined charisma of Fonda, Smits, and Peck make it watchable. C: Jane Fonda, Gregory Peck, Jimmy Smits. D: Luis Puenzo. DRA [R] 120m. V

Old Hutch 1936 ★★★ Near-destitute Beery finds $100,000 but can't spend it without questions being asked. Light-on-its-feet adaptation of the George Kelly comedy, previously filmed in 1920 as *Honest Hutch*, with Will Rogers. C: Wallace Beery, Eric Linden, Cecilia Parker. D: J. Ruben. COM 80m.

Old Ironsides 1926 ★★★★ Adventures of America's earliest merchant ships and their wars with the Barbary pirates. A fascinating and action-packed silent. C: Charles Farrell, Esther Ralston, Wallace Beery. D: James Cruze. ACT 111m. V

Old Maid, The 1939 ★★★★½ Thirty-year rivalry between cousins, as love child of one grows up calling the other one "mother." Unabashed but effective soap opera from Edith Wharton novel, with Davis heartbreakingly good and Hopkins trying to steal her daughter (and the film) to no avail. C: Bette Davis, Miriam Hopkins, George Brent, Jane Bryan, Donald Crisp. D: Edmund Goulding. DRA 96m. V

Old Man and the Sea, The 1958 ★★★★ Lush color photography by James Wong Howe highlights this faithful adaptation of Hemingway's metaphoric tale of an aging fisherman's solitary struggle against nature during a routine fishing trip. Dimitri Tiomkin earned an Oscar for Best Musical Score. C: Spencer Tracy. D: John Sturges. DRA 86m.

Old Mother Riley 1937 British ★★★½ Lucan returns to *Old Mother Riley* series, this time embroiled in a spy caper in Gay Paris, where she's gone to search for her daughter McShane. Offbeat series is funny, with Lucan playing the Irish washerwoman to a tee. C: Arthur Lucan, Kitty McShane, Barbara Everest, Patrick Ludlow. D: Oswald Mitchell. COM 75m.

Old Spanish Custom, An 1936 British ★ Brilliant silent clown Keaton plays a well-to-do ship owner who sails to Spain and is fleeced by spitfire Tovar. For Buster Keaton afficianados. (a.k.a. *The Invader*) C: Buster Keaton, Lupita Tovar, Esme Percy. D: Adrian Brunel. COM 56m. V

Old Yeller 1957 ★★★★ Disney adaptation of Fred Gipson's popular novel about 1860s Texas farm boy (Kirk) who reforms ill-tempered mutt, Old Yeller, who becomes beloved family pet. Well-acted story about life's hard lessons that kids won't forget. Followed by sequel *Savage Sam*. C: Dorothy McGuire, Fess Parker, Tommy Kirk, Kevin Corcoran. D: Robert Stevenson. FAM/DRA [G] 84m. V

Oldest Living Confederate Widow Tells All 1994 ★★★★½ Literate, tasteful adaptation of Allan Gurganus's best-seller chronicling the title character's troubled marriage to a tormented Civil War veteran (Sutherland). Lane is marvelous as the rifle-hating wife and mother; Bancroft plays the same character at age 100. C: Diane Lane, Donald Sutherland, Cicely Tyson, Anne Bancroft, Blythe Danner. D: Ken Cameron. DRA 240m. TVM

Oldest Living Graduate, The 1982 ★★ Conflict between old WW II vet and his son concerning their different feelings about what ought to be done with plot of land owned by family for generations. C: Henry Fonda, George Grizzard, Harry Dean Stanton. D: Jack Hofsiss. DRA 75m. TVM V

Oldest Profession, The 1967 French ★★ Six-part comedy on history of prostitution. Flat and dull, despite several great directors and a bevy of international stars. C: Elsa Martinelli, Jeanne Moreau, Raquel Welch, Jean-Pierre Leaud. D: Franco Indovina, Mauro Bolognini, Philippe DeBroca, Michel Pfleghar. COM 97m. V

Oleanna 1994 ★★★ A college professor (Macy) may or may not have sexually harassed a student (Eisenstadt). Mamet's hit Off-Broadway play reaches the screen virtually intact, but loses most of its power due to static staging, poor technical quality. C: William H. Macy, Debra Eisenstadt. D: David Mamet. DRA [G] 90m.

Oliver! 1968 British ★★★★★ Lionel Bart's musicalization of Charles Dickens' novel, *Oliver Twist*, given splendid film treatment by director Reed. Story of poor orphan boy mixed up with comic gang of pickpockets led by uproarious Moody as Fagin is simply told with catchy songs ("Consider Yourself," "Who Will Buy?," "As Long As He Needs Me"). Onna White's eye-catching choreography and loving period details helped film win six Oscars, including Best Picture and Director. C: Ron Moody, Oliver Reed, Shani Wallis, Mark Lester, Jack Wild. D: Carol Reed. FAM/MUS [G] 145m. V

Oliver and Co. 1988 ★★★★ Disarming, animated and updated version of Dickens' *Oliver Twist*, with a kitten abandoned in New York and taken in by a gang of roving dogs. The quality of the artwork may not quite be up to the usual Disney standard, but the charm of both story and score more than make up for it. Midler's a hoot as the voice of a pampered poodle. C: Voices of Billy Joel, Bette Midler, Cheech Marin, George C. Scott. D: George Scribner. FAM/DRA [G] 72m.

Oliver Twist 1922 ★★★★ Superior silent treatment of Charles Dickens' novel with Chaney a delicious Fagin, leader of a gang of pickpockets who take orphan Oliver (Coogan) in. Remade in 1933, for television in 1982, and most notably in 1948 and 1968. C: Lon Chaney, Jackie Coogan, Gladys Brockwell. D: Frank Lloyd. DRA 77m.

Oliver Twist 1933 ★★ Almost unwatchable, primitive version of Dickens famous story about unfortunate orphan's plight on the mean streets of London. Child actor Moore looks too well-fed for role! C: Dickie Moore, Irving Pichel, Doris Lloyd. D: William Cowen. DRA 77m. V

Oliver Twist 1948 British ★★★★★ Orphan in Victorian London falls in with band of young thieves run by master criminal. Splendid version of Dickens classic expertly brought to screen by Lean with pure reverence. Memorable performance by Guinness, who heads a perfect cast. C: Alec Guinness, Robert Newton, John Davies, Kay Walsh, Anthony Newley. D: David Lean. DRA 116m. V

Oliver Twist 1982 ★★★★ Strong cast, headed by Scott as pick-pocket king Fagin, makes this worthy adaptation of Dickens' tale of poor orphan boy's struggle to find his birthright. 1948 version still reigns, but this one's worth watching, too. C: George C. Scott, Tim Curry, Timothy West, Eileen Atkins, Michael Hordern. D: Clive Donner. DRA 100m. TVM V

Oliver's Story 1978 ★★ Sequel to *Love Story* follows Oliver as he falls in love again, this time with an heiress. Lacks attraction of original; best for those who just have to know what happened next. C: Ryan O'Neal, Candice Bergen, Nicola Pagett, Ray Milland. D: John Korty. DRA [PG] 90m. V

Olivier, Olivier 1993 French ★★★½ A teenage hustler tries to convince a middle-class family he's their son who disappeared several years ago. Intriguing tale examines credibility, identity, and family unity. From the director of *Europa, Europa*. C: Francois Cluzet, Brigitte Rouan, Jean-Francois Stevenin. D: Agnieszka Holland. DRA [R] 110m. V

Olly, Olly, Oxen Free 1978 ★★★ An eccentric woman (Hepburn) takes two lads on hot-air balloon adventure. Vehicle for Hepburn, long on whimsy, short on excitement. Kids may like the airborne sequences. (a.k.a. *The Great Balloon Adventure*) C: Katharine Hepburn, Kevin McKenzie, Dennis Dimster. D: Richard A. Colla. FAM/ACT [G] 83m.

Olympia 1936 German ★★★★★ If one can forget that this document of 1936 Berlin Olympics was intended as Nazi propaganda, then brilliance of direction and athletes' achievements make this must-see viewing. Some prints censored to remove all footage of Hitler, who is prominent in original. D: Leni Riefenstahl. DOC 220m. V

Olympic Honeymoon 1939 *See* **Honeymoon Merry-Go-Round**

Omar Khayyam 1957 ★★★ Campy, moronic, bargain-basement epic about Persian hero (Wilde) in love with Shah's financee (Paget). Must be seen for Sumac's ear-splitting rendition of pop song "The Loves of Omar Khayyam"! (a.k.a. *The Life, Loves and Adventures of Omar Khayyam*) C: Cornel Wilde, Debra Paget, Raymond Massey, John Derek, Yma Sumac. D: William Dieterle. DRA 101m. V

Omega Cop 1990 ★★ Lone cop protects three women and the remains of human civilization after global environmental disaster turns the few remaining people into hoodlums and bandits. C: Adam West, Stuart Whitman, Troy Donahue. D: Paul Kyriazi. ACT [R] 89m. V

Omega Man, The 1971 ★★★★ A lone survivor (Heston) in post-germ war L.A. eludes semihuman zombies out to kill him. A haunting and effective thriller from Richard Matheson's *I Am Legend*. C: Charlton Heston, Rosalind Cash. D: Boris Sagal. SFI [PG] 98m. V

Omega Syndrome 1987 ★★★ Reporter (Wahl) fights back when his young daughter is abducted by terrorists. Unbelievable, by-the-numbers adventure, which failed to turn TV's *Wiseguy* into movie star. C: Ken Wahl, George DiCenzo, Doug McClure, Nicole Eggert. D: Joseph Manduke. ACT [R] 88m. V

Omen, The 1976 ★★★★ The Antichrist is unleashed upon Earth in the form of a five-year-old boy who must be destroyed at the hands of his foster father (Peck). Powerhouse horror smash hit launched numerous sequels and imitators. Oscar for Best Score (Jerry Goldsmith). C: Gregory Peck, Lee Remick, Billie Whitelaw, David Warner. D: Richard Donner. HOR [R] 111m. V

Omen II 1978 *See* **Damien—Omen II**
Omen III—The Final Conflict 1981 *See* **Final Conflict, The**
Omen IV—The Awakening 1991 ★★ The daughter of the Antichrist is now incarnate in a young girl of affluent foster parents headed for the White House. Hellish convolution of mayhem. C: Faye Grant, Michael Woods. D: Jorge Montesi. HOR 97m. TVM V
On a Clear Day You Can See Forever 1970 ★★★½ Lerner/Lane musical with unusual story about reincarnation and ESP brought to screen as Streisand vehicle, with star in dual role of ordinary modern woman and aristocratic 19th-century alter ego. Stylish flashback scenes overwhelm modern story involving psychiatrist (Montand). Strong songs include title tune and "Come Back to Me." Your only chance so far to see Jack and Barbra together. C: Barbra Streisand, Yves Montand, Bob Newhart, Larry Blyden, Jack Nicholson. D: Vincente Minnelli. MUS [G] 129m. V
On an Island with You 1948 ★★★½ Breezy Hawaiian swimfest with Williams as temperamental movie star finding romance on location. Don't miss the water ballet numbers. C: Esther Williams, Peter Lawford, Ricardo Montalban, Jimmy Durante, Cyd Charisse, Xavier Cugat. D: Richard Thorpe. MUS 107m. V
On Any Sunday 1971 ★★★★ Motorcycle enthusiasts will do wheelies over this exciting documentary from the maker of the popular surfing film, *The Endless Summer*. McQueen's involvement adds extra spice. C: Steve McQueen, Mert Lawwill, Malcolm Smith. D: Bruce Brown. DOC [G] 91m. V
On Any Sunday II 1981 ★★★ Second motorcycle documentary lacks the pacing and expert direction of the first. Still, biker fans will enjoy it. C: Don Shoemaker. D: Ed Forsyth. DOC [PG] 90m. V
On Approval 1944 British ★★★★ Remake of 1930 film has a broke duke (Brook) hoping to marry rich woman Lillie. Adaptation of the Frederick Lonsdale play translates well in this dangerously funny tale of high-society shenanigans. Lillie is a delight. C: Beatrice Lillie, Clive Brook, Googie Withers, Roland Culver. D: Clive Brook. COM 80m. V
On Borrowed Time 1939 ★★★★ Heartwarming tale of a grandfather (Barrymore) unwilling to die, who chases and traps Mr. Death (Hardwicke) in an apple tree. Sentimental fable is agreeable slice of Americana. C: Lionel Barrymore, Cedric Hardwicke, Beulah Bondi, Una Merkel. D: Harold S. Bucquet. DRA 99m. V
On Dangerous Ground 1951 ★★★★ Atmospheric film noir has cynical cop (Ryan) getting involved with blind Lupino during manhunt. Both stars very effective in unusual love story. Composer Bernard Herrmann's favorite score. C: Ida Lupino, Robert Ryan, Ward Bond. D: Nicholas Ray. CRI 82m. V
On Deadly Ground 1994 ★ Seagal, in his directorial debut, plays an ex-secret agent who takes on a ruthless oil company executive (Caine) to defend the sacred land of an Eskimo tribe. Ludicrous and preachy action thriller proves that Seagal should stick to acting. C: Steven Seagal, Michael Caine, Joan Chen, John C. McGinley, R. Lee Ermey, Shari Shattuck. D: Steven Seagal. ACT 101m. V
On Dress Parade 1939 ★★★ The Dead End Kids go to military school and get "reformed" in okay programmer that's hard to swallow. (a.k.a. *The Dead End Kids on Dress Parade*) C: Billy Halop, Leo Gorcey, Bobby Jordan, Huntz Hall, Gabriel Dell. D: William Clemens. COM 62m.
On Fire 1987 ★★★ Noble but dull examination of age discrimination with 60ish Forsythe losing his job as arson investigator. C: John Forsythe, Carroll Baker. D: Robert Greenwald. DRA 104m.
On Golden Pond 1981 ★★★★½ Poignant, witty account of daughter's coming to terms with her emotionally cold, 80-year-old father. Tearjerker rises above mere sentimentality to get at the heart of parent-child relationships. Henry Fonda's final screen appearance won him an Oscar in his only film with Jane; Hepburn and author Thompson won Oscars, too. C: Henry Fonda, Katharine Hepburn, Jane Fonda, Dabney Coleman, Doug McKeon. D: Mark Rydell. DRA [PG] 109m. V
On Her Majesty's Secret Service 1969 British ★★★★ James Bond vs. the fiendish Blofeld and his germ warfare. Good action, with Lazenby replacing Connery. C: George Lazenby, Diana Rigg, Gabriele Ferzetti, Telly Savalas. D: Peter H. Hunt. ACT 142m. V
On Moonlight Bay 1951 ★★★½ Musical comedy set in 1917 Indiana of tomboy Day and college kid MacRae's courtship. Nostalgic and saccharine, but still enjoyable. Based on Booth Tarkington's *Penrod* stories. Followed by *By the Light of the Silvery Moon*. C: Doris Day, Gordon MacRae, Mary Wickes, Leon Ames. D: Roy Del Ruth. MUS 95m. V
On My Way to the Crusades, I Met a Girl Who . . . 1968 Italian ★ Tasteless sex comedy about knight Curtis tangling with Vitti's chastity belt. (a.k.a. *The Chastity Belt*) C: Tony Curtis, Monica Vitti, Hugh Griffith. D: Pasquale Campanile. COM [R] 93m.
On Our Merry Way 1948 ★★★½ Odd anthology film with Meredith as roving reporter asking people about their relationships with children. A mixed bag of vignettes, the best of which co-stars Fonda and Stewart. C: Leslie Fenton, Burgess Meredith, Paulette Goddard, Fred MacMurray, Hugh Herbert, James Stewart, Henry Fonda, Dorothy Lamour, Victor Moore. D: King Vidor. COM 107m.
On Our Selection 1932 Australian ★★★½ Early Australian sound film of Outback father managing a ranch and family is an upbeat

comedy, making full use of the local color. Well photographed and acted. C: Bert Bailey, Fred McDonald, Afreda Bevan, Jack McGowan. D: Ken G. Hall. COM 99m.

On Probation 1935 ★★★½ A sleazy politician takes in a down-and-out street urchin to boost his image, and eventually falls in love with her; of course, complications arise. Twisty absorbing crime picture, shot with visual finesse. C: Monte Blue, Lucile Browne, William Blakewell, Barbara Bedford. D: Charles Hutchison. DRA 71m.

On Stage Everybody 1945 ★★★½ Second-string musical with radio-hater Oakie producing show for daughter Ryan. Worth seeing for novelty acts. C: Jack Oakie, Peggy Ryan, Otto Kruger, Julie London. D: Jean Yarbrough. MUS 65m.

On the Air Live with Captain Midnight 1979 ★★★ Rebel with no cause starts illegal broadcasting career in eccentric comedy with bargain-basement feel. (a.k.a. *Captain Midnight*) C: Tracy Sebastian, John Ireland, Dena Dietrich. D: Ferd Sebastian, Beverly Sebastian. COM 93m. V

On the Avenue 1937 ★★★★ Socialite Carroll doesn't like a Broadway revue that caricatures her, but she likes its star (Powell). Spiffy musical with terrific Irving Berlin songs, including "Let's Go Slumming on Park Avenue" and "I've Got My Love to Keep Me Warm." C: Dick Powell, Madeleine Carroll, Alice Faye, The Ritz Brothers, Billy Gilbert, Joan Davis. D: Roy Del Ruth. MUS 89m. V

On the Beach 1959 ★★★★½ Australians wait for inevitable death from post-WWIII radiation while an American submarine sets sail to find signs of life. Thought-provoking anti-war film. Strong performances include Astaire's first purely dramatic role. C: Gregory Peck, Ava Gardner, Fred Astaire, Anthony Perkins. D: Stanley Kramer. DRA 134m. V

On the Beat 1962 British ★★★ Wisdom, Britain's Jerry Lewis, is a moronic Scotland Yard wanna-be posing as a criminal. Comedy that tries too hard. C: Norman Wisdom, Jennifer Jayne. D: Robert Asher. COM 105m.

On the Comet 1970 Czech ★★★★ Czech director Zeman adapts Jules Verne's tale *Hector Servadac* for the screen in this cosmic fantasy of a piece of Earth hurtling through the galaxy, with Earth dwellers on board. Short on sci-fi effects, long on message. Nicely done. C: Emil Horvath Jr., Magda Vasaryova, Frantisek Filipovsky. D: Karel Zeman. SFI 88m.

On the Double 1961 ★★★½ Entertainer Kaye drafted as WWII spy because he resembles British general. Funny, typical Kaye vehicle. Highlight: Danny does Dietrich. C: Danny Kaye, Dana Wynter, Wilfrid Hyde White, Margaret Rutherford, Diana Dors. D: Melville Shavelson. COM 92m.

On the Edge 1986 ★★★½ Earnest, if wan drama about middle-aged runner Dern coming home to reconcile with his father and exorcise old demons. Dern is good, with standard script. C: Bruce Dern, Bill Bailey, John Marley. D: Rob Nilsson. DRA [PG-13,R] 86m. V

On the Fiddle 1961 *See* **Operation Snafu**

On the Isle of Samoa 1950 ★★★ Silly romance of the "Me explorer, you, helpless native girl" variety. C: Jon Hall, Susan Cabot, Raymond Greenleaf. D: William Berke. COM 65m.

On the Line 1984 Spanish ★★★★ A young border guard falls in love with an uneducated Mexican prostitute (Abril). Insightful and moving tale deals with difficulties of policing Mexican immigration into U.S. Abril is the standout in a fine cast. C: David Carradine, Victoria Abril, Sam Jaffe. D: José Luis Boaru. DRA 103m. V

On the Loose 1951 ★★★ Tedious drama of father (Douglas) contending with spoiled, willful daughter. C: Joan Evans, Melvyn Douglas, Lynn Bari. D: Charles Lederer. DRA 78m.

On the Nickel 1980 ★★★½ Offbeat tale of two friends drinking themselves to death on skid row in L.A. Waite and Moffat are credible, but script takes many detours. C: Donald Moffat, Ralph Waite, Penelope Allen. D: Ralph Waite. DRA [R] 96m. V

On the Old Spanish Trail 1947 ★★★½ Roy joins a carnival in order to track down a desperado called "The Gypsy." Lots of neat action and songs. C: Roy Rogers, Jane Frazee, Andy Devine. D: William Witney. WST 75m. V

On the Right Track 1982 ★★★ Orphaned shoeshine boy (Coleman) lives out of train station locker. His ability to accurately predict winning race horses leads to trouble with some bad guys. Simple children's film that stretches thin premise for all it can. C: Gary Coleman, Lisa Eilbacher, Maureen Stapleton. D: Lee Philips. FAM/DRA [PG] 97m. V

On the Riviera 1951 ★★★★ Cheery Kaye musical with star in two roles, as entertainer and French army officer. Clever script shows him off to good advantage; Tierney shines as well. Remake of 1935 *Folies Bergère*. C: Danny Kaye, Gene Tierney, Corinne Calvet, Marcel Dalio. D: Walter Lang. MUS 90m.

On the Road Again 1980 *See* **Honeysuckle Rose**

On the Third Day 1983 ★★½ A mysterious stranger has some shocking news for the school headmaster with whom he is staying. C: Richard Marant, Catherine Schell, Paul Williamson. D: Stanley O'Toole. HOR 101m. V

On the Threshold of Space 1956 ★★★½ Okay drama of astronauts in training takes back seat to fascinating documentary-like sequences showing U.S. space program in its infancy. C: Guy Madison, Virginia Leith, John Hodiak. D: Robert Webb. DRA 98m.

On the Town 1949 ★★★★★ Exhilarating musical tale of three sailors on 24-hour leave in Manhattan during WWII. Groundbreaking use of location footage and perfect ensemble playing contribute to the infectious gaiety. Much of the Broadway score was replaced by new Roger Edens songs, but end result is still terrific. First full directing credit for Kelly and Donen. C: Gene Kelly, Frank Sinatra, Jules Munshin, Vera Ellen, Betty Garrett, Ann Miller. D: Stanley Donen, Gene Kelly. MUS 98m. v

On The Town 1993 ★★★★ A superb Concert performance of this outstanding Bernstein musical. Conducted by Michael Tilson-Thomas. C: Tyne Daly, Thomas Hampson, Frederica Von Stade. MUS 110m.

On the Waterfront 1954 ★★★★★ After his brother is murdered, a misfit longshoreman battles corrupt labor boss to expose union racketeering. Uncompromising dockside drama with forceful performance from Brando and superb "method" characterizations by outstanding supporting cast. Stirring Leonard Bernstein score. Won eight Oscars including Best Actor (Brando), Picture, Director, Supporting Actress (Saint), Story and Screenplay, Cinematography, Art Direction, Editing. C: Marlon Brando, Eva Marie Saint, Karl Malden, Lee J. Cobb, Rod Steiger. D: Elia Kazan. DRA 108m. v

On the Yard 1979 ★★★½ Deadly inmate leader makes life tough for a fellow convict (Heard). Watchable prison fare. C: John Heard, Thomas Waites, Mike Kellin. D: Raphael Silver. CRI [R] 107m. v

On Thin Ice: The Tai Babilonia Story 1990 ★★★½ Okay biography of ice skating's hard-luck case (pre-Tonya Harding), from humble beginnings to her 1980 bid with Randy Gardner for Olympic gold. Exciting skating, so-so drama. C: Rachel Crawford, Charlie Stratton. D: Zale Dalen. DRA 96m. TVM

On Trial 1953 French ★★★ Murky drama of D.A.'s son questioning his father's judgment when he examines years-old conviction of Gelin. C: Madeleine Robinson, Daniel Gelin, Eleonora Drago. D: Julien Duvivier. DRA 70m.

On Valentine's Day 1987 ★★★★ A young southern girl marries a poor fellow. Together they take a room in a boarding house and try to survive. Sensitive, well-acted drama from a screenplay by Horton Foote. (a.k.a. *Story of a Marriage*) C: Hallie Foote, William Converse-Roberts, Matthew Broderick. D: Ken Harrison. DRA [PG] 106m. v

On Wings of Eagles 1986 ★★★½ U.S. employees stationed in Iran are imprisoned, and their billionaire boss (Crenna) hires ex-general (Lancaster) to break them out. TV miniseries has impact, and the stars are good. Adapted from Ken Follett's book based on Ross Perot's experience. C: Burt Lancaster, Richard Crenna, Paul LeMat. D: Andrew McLaglen. ACT 221m. TVM v

On with the Show 1929 ★★★ Theatrical troupe is about to go down the tubes when their show's producer walks out. Because film was made fairly early in sound, doesn't have the visual flair of your typical musical, but engaging nontheless. C: Betty Compson, Louise Fazenda, Joe Brown. D: Alan Crosland. MUS

On Your Toes 1939 ★★★½ Melodramatic tale of backstage mayhem at the ballet only faintly resembles original Rodgers and Hart/George Abbott Broadway show. All the songs are gone, along with the plot. One terrific bit remains: a shortened "Slaughter on Tenth Avenue" ballet, with Zorina dancing Ballanchine's choreography. C: Vera Zorina, Eddie Albert, Frank McHugh, Alan Hale, Donald O'Connor. D: Ray Enright. DRA 94m.

Onassis: The Richest Man in the World 1988 ★★★ The story of the shipping tycoon's life: his financial empire, love affairs, and marriage to Jacqueline Kennedy. Julia is miscast; Quinn and Seymour are fine. (a.k.a. *Richest Man in the World: The Story of Aristotle Onassis*) C: Raul Julia, Jane Seymour, Anthony Quinn. D: Waris Hussein. DRA 120m. TVM v

Once A Hero 1988 ★★ Comic book hero, Captain Justice, fights gang for return of his mother and one of his fans who have been kidnapped. C: Jim Turner, Robert Foster, Caitlin Clarke. D: Claudia Weill. FAM/ACT 74m. TVM

Once a Rainy Day 1968 Japanese ★★★½ Former childhood companions fall in love, much to their guardians' chagrin. Touching, low-key, perceptive drama. C: Michiyo Aratama, Yoko Naito, Ryo Tamura. D: Hideo Onchi. DRA 85m.

Once a Thief 1950 ★★½ A shoplifter falls for an unmitigated cad, who walks off with her money and turns her into the cops. Boy, is she miffed when she gets out of jail! Tacky little potboiler, routinely directed; Havoc and Romero's professionalism can't quite give it class. C: June Havoc, Cesar Romero, Marie McDonald, Lon Chaney, Jr. D: W. Wilder. DRA 88m.

Once a Thief 1965 U.S.; French ★★★½ Ex-con wants to go straight but gets involved with three killers. Hardly original, but directed with zip, and that cast! Delon, Ann-Margret compete engagingly in the sexy sweepstakes; Heflin is sturdy; Palance, Chandler, and Musante are pretty scary. C: Ann-Margret, Alain Delon, Van Heflin, Jack Palance, Davis Chandler, Tony Musante. D: Ralph Nelson. ACT 107m.

Once Around 1991 ★★★½ Timid Hunter blooms when she meets Prince Charming who, to her family's horror, is an obnoxious sales rep (Dreyfuss). Hallstrom does wonders with too-cute script, injecting some real emotion into contrived story. C: Richard Dreyfuss, Holly Hunter, Danny Aiello, Gena Rowlands, Laura San Giacomo. D: Lasse Hallstrom. COM [R] 114m. v

Once Before I Die 1965 ★★★ Motley bunch of U.S. soldiers in the Philippines during WWII try to keep Japan's hands off the turf and their own hands on a beautiful woman (Andress).

Violent, with some tough action scenes, but not especially well directed; nothing new in the plot. C: Ursula Andress, John Derek. D: John Derek. ACT 97m. V

Once Bitten 1985 ★★½ Hutton is game as old vampire seeking out young male virgin blood; Carrey is cute as her prey, and Little flagrantly funny in support. But it's a prurient exercise in adolescent humor all the way. C: Lauren Hutton, Jim Carrey, Cleavon Little. D: Howard Storm. COM [PG-13] 94m. V

Once in a Lifetime 1932 ★★★★ Three vaudevillians pose as bogus vocal coaches to capitalize on Hollywood's talkie revolution in funny farce from George S. Kaufman-Moss Hart play. Pitts is a scream as ditzy studio secretary. C: Jack Oakie, Sidney Fox, Aline MacMahon, ZaSu Pitts. D: Russell Mack. COM 75m.

Once in Paris . . . 1978 ★★★★ Screenwriter Rogers goes to Paris to work, falls for Hunnicutt, and is counseled on *l'amour* by chauffeur Lenoir. Charming comedy/drama written, produced, and directed by playwright Frank D. Gilroy. C: Wayne Rogers, Gayle Hunnicutt, Jack Lenior. D: Frank D. Gilroy. COM [PG] 100m. V

Once Is Not Enough 1975 *See* **Jacqueline Susann's Once Is Not Enough**

Once More My Darling 1949 ★★★½ Cutesy comedy with film star Montgomery pursued by debutante Blyth. Famed stage actress Cowl has supporting role. C: Robert Montgomery, Ann Blyth, Jane Cowl. D: Robert Montgomery. COM 94m.

Once More, With Feeling 1960 British ★★★ Adulterous conductor Brynner is threatened with divorce in strident comedy with few laughs. In her last film, the wonderful Kendall has little to work with. C: Yul Brynner, Kay Kendall. D: Stanley Donen. COM 92m.

Once There Was a Girl 1945 USSR ★★★★ Russian film examines the cost of war for children—little girls Ivanova and Zashipina—who witness the siege of Leningrad during WWII. Introspective drama is slow going, but the children, at nine and five years of age, are remarkable. C: Nina Ivanova, Natasha Zashipina, Ada Voystik. D: Victor Eisimont. DRA 71m.

Once Upon a Crime 1992 ★★ Comic cast together in Europe to scream, run around, and try to solve the murder they find themselves mired in. Loud and abrasive; for SCTV fans only. C: John Candy, James Belushi, Cybill Shepherd, Sean Young, Richard Lewis. D: Eugene Levy. COM [PG] 94m. V

Once Upon a Dead Man 1971 ★★★½ San Francisco police commissioner Hudson investigates bizarre robbery/murder. Nice chemistry between Hudson and Saint James in standard detective yarn. Pilot for *McMillan and Wife* TV series. C: Rock Hudson, Susan St. James, Jack Albertson. D: Leonard Stern. DRA 104m. TVM

Once Upon a Forest 1993 ★★★ Children's feature involves forest animals helping friend who becomes ill after ingesting toxic waste. Good animation, with enjoyable characters and songs, but overly preachy environmental message quickly grows annoying. Younger audiences probably won't mind though. D: Charles Grosvenor. FAM/DRA [G] 71m. V

Once Upon a Honeymoon 1942 ★★★ Strange, badly dated comedy features Grant as radio reporter trying to rescue former burlesque queen Rogers from her marriage to Nazi honcho Slezak. Teeters uneasily between comedy and drama, valuable as WWII-era curio more than anything else. C: Ginger Rogers, Cary Grant, Walter Slezak, Albert Dekker. D: Leo McCarey. COM 116m. V

Once Upon a Horse 1958 ★★★ Pre-*Laugh-In* TV Rowan and Martin are cast as bumbling cattle rustlers in lame Western satire. C: Dan Rowan, Dick Martin, Martha Hyer, Leif Erickson. D: Hal Kanter. WST 85m.

Once Upon a Scoundrel 1977 ★★ Inhabitants of small town seek revenge for disreputable acts committed by dishonest landowner by treating landowner as if he were a ghost. Mostel's last film. C: Zero Mostel, Katy Jurado, Tito Vandis. D: George Schaefer. COM [G] 90m. V

Once Upon a Spy 1980 ★★★ Weak TV pilot for comedy/adventure series has apprehensive computer expert Danson helping government agents foil Lee's plan to conquer the world. C: Ted Danson, Mary Weller, Christopher Lee, Eleanor Parker. D: Ivan Nagy. COM 100m. TVM

Once Upon a Texas Train 1988 *See* **Texas Guns**

Once Upon a Time 1944 ★★★½ Offbeat comedy finds Grant as producer trying to exploit little boy's dancing caterpillar. Not quite as funny as it sounds. C: Cary Grant, Janet Blair, James Gleason. D: Alexander Hall. COM 89m.

Once Upon a Time in America 1984 ★★★★½ Strangely moving, dream-like gangster epic traces rise and fall of partners De Niro and Woods from childhood on Lower East Side through Prohibition to the '50s. Brilliantly acted and well directed sequence by sequence, but film's complex flashback structure undermines it. Leone's last completed film. C: Robert De Niro, James Woods, Elizabeth McGovern, Tuesday Weld. D: Sergio Leone. CRI [R] 227m. V

Once Upon a Time in the West 1969 ★★★★½ Mysterious gunman (Bronson) stalks cold-blooded killer (Fonda), who's interfering with efforts of a widow (Cardinale) to run a future railroad stop. Generally considered to be Italian director Leone's finest, this revisionist Western epic offers striking cinematography, an excellent score, great action, and the most impressively extended opening credits sequence in Spaghetti-Western history. One of the greatest achievements in the genre. C: Charles Bronson, Henry Fonda, Claudia Cardinale, Jason Robards. D: Sergio Leone. WST [PG] 165m. V

Once You Kiss a Stranger 1969 ★★½ Golf pro Burke finds himself "trading murders" with psychopath Lynley in feeble remake of *Strangers on a Train*. C: Paul Burke, Carol Lynley, Martha Hyer. D: Robert Sparr. CRI [PG] 106m.

One Against the Wind 1992 U.S.-Luxembourg ★★★★ Davis is outstanding as Britisher Marty Lindell, who helped organize the escape of Allied soldiers from occupied France during WWII. Strong handling of true story. C: Judy Davis, Sam Neill, Denholm Elliott. D: Larry Elikann. DRA 96m. TVM V

One and Only, Genuine, Original Family Band, The 1968 ★★★½ Brennan is leader of family band that dreams of performing at 1888 Presidential convention in St. Louis. Nothing special, but colorful and full of catchy songs. Look for quick appearance by young Goldie Hawn. C: Walter Brennan, Buddy Ebsen, Lesley Ann Warren, John Davidson, Janet Blair, Kurt Russell, Goldie Hawn. D: Michael O'Herlihy. FAM/DRA 110m. V

One and Only, The 1978 ★★★ Struggling actor Winkler becomes a bleached blond wrestler in witless comedy loosely based on real-life career of Gorgeous George. C: Henry Winkler, Kim Darby, Gene Saks, Herve Villechaize. D: Carl Reiner. COM 98m. V

One Arabian Night 1920 ★★★ Lush, silent recreation of enchanting tale. Musical score. C: Pola Negri, Ernst Lubitsch. D: Ernst Lubitsch. DRA 85m.

One Armed Swordsmen, The 1972 ★★½ A one-armed man commits a murder, and all one-armed men are suspect, so together they track down the real culprit. Interesting spin on old story. CRI 110m. V

One Big Affair 1952 ★★★ Fluffy romance has Keyes and O'Keefe in Mexico, with predictable misunderstandings and reconciliations. C: Evelyn Keyes, Dennis O'Keefe. D: Peter Godfrey. COM 80m.

One Body Too Many 1944 ★★★ Comedy mystery with Haley as insurance salesman accidentally mixed up with missing corpse. Strictly routine. C: Bela Lugosi, Jack Haley, Jean Parker, Blanche Yurka. D: Frank McDonald. COM 75m. V

One Cooks, the Other Doesn't 1983 ★★★ Impoverished Bologna and his new bride share house with his ex-wife and their son. Typical TV sex comedy with loads of innuendo and warmth. C: Suzanne Pleshette, Joseph Bologna, Rosanna Arquette. D: Richard Michaels. COM 96m. TVM V

One Crazy Night 1993 ★★ In 1964 Australia, teenagers become trapped in hotel they've broken into in order to meet the Beatles. C: Noah Taylor, Beth Champion, Willa O'Neill. D: Michael Pattinson. COM [PG-13] 92m. V

One Crazy Summer 1986 ★★★ Repressed cartoonist has series of raucous adventures while vacationing on Nantucket Island. Spirited young cast headed by Cusack helps smooth over rough edges in this uneven but imaginative farce. C: John Cusack, Demi Moore, Bobcat Goldthwait. D: Steve Holland. COM [PG] 94m. V

One Cup of Coffee 1991 *See* **Pastime**

One Dangerous Night 1943 ★★★½ Modest mystery from the *Lone Wolf* series, with detective (Williams) implicated in blackmailer's murder. Entertaining. C: Warren William, Marguerite Chapman, Eric Blore. D: Michael Gordon. CRI 77m.

One Dark Night 1982 ★★★ High schooler Tilly accepts dare to spend night in a mausoleum, little knowing that a recently entombed psychic is not quite deceased and ready to raise the dead. Obvious but well directed, with some lively scares and makeup effects. (a.k.a. *Mausoleum*) C: Meg Tilly, Robin Evans. D: Tom McLoughlin. HOR [PG] 94m. V

One Day in the Life of Ivan Denisovich 1971 British ★★★½ Graphic look at daily life in Siberian labor camp from Solzhenitsyn's novel. Script, direction, photography by Sven Nykvist and Courtenay's performance in the title role are all fine but end result is curiously uninvolving and relentlessly grim. C: Tom Courtenay, Espen Skjonberg. D: Casper Wrede. DRA [G] 105m. V

One Deadly Summer 1983 French ★★★★ Florid, fascinating story of disturbed young woman's quest for man who raped her mother. Adjani's pull-out-the-stops performance won her French equivalent of Academy Award. C: Isabelle Adjani, Alain Souchon, Francois Cluzet, Suzanne Flon. D: Jean Becker. DRA [R] 133m. V

One Desire 1955 ★★★½ Social climber Baxter falls for rake Hudson in period soap opera with strong cast. C: Anne Baxter, Rock Hudson, Julie Adams, Natalie Wood. D: Jerry Hopper. DRA 94m.

One Down Two to Go 1983 ★★½ Kung fu promoter Williamson and fellow tough guys take on thugs who try to fix his tournament. Black exploitation with a capable cast done in by Williamson's lifeless direction. C: Fred Williamson, Jim Brown, Jim Kelly, Richard Roundtree. D: Fred Williamson. ACT [R] 84m. V

One Exciting Adventure 1935 ★★★ Criminal Barnes has a kleptomaniac's affection for other people's baubles, and detectives Mitchell and Pallette must try to break her of her illegal habit in this enjoyable light comedy. C: Binnie Barnes, Neil Hamilton, Paul Cavanagh, Grant Mitchell, Eugene Pallette. D: Ernst L. Frank. COM 70m.

One-Eyed Jacks 1961 ★★★★ Brooding Western follows misadventures of vengeful bandit (Brando), who plans to settle accounts with traitorous ex-partner (Malden) by seducing the man's daughter. Dark psychological undercurrents and beautiful Carmel, California scenery are the prime assets in this overlong character study. C: Marlon Brando, Karl Malden, Katy Jurado, Ben Johnson. D: Marlon Brando. WST 141m. V

One-Eyed Soldiers 1966 ★★ Robertson and Paluzzi look for lost money in Switzerland. Done on the cheap. C: Dale Robertson, Luciana Paluzzi. D: Jean Christophe. DRA 80m. V

One False Move 1992 ★★★★ First-time director Franklin's critically acclaimed crime drama of three L.A. cocaine dealers who flee to a small Arkansas town after a murder. Paxton's portrayal of a local sheriff out to show up the city cops is riveting. C: Bill Paxton, Cynda Williams. D: Carl Franklin. CRI [R] 106m. V

One Flew over the Cuckoo's Nest 1975 ★★★★★ Nicholson gives one of the defining performances of his career, playing a convict who thinks he can beat jail by feigning insanity, but finds the mental institution worse by far. Great cast and visionary direction capture the poignant, rebellious feel of Ken Kesey's novel, without milking it. Swept all five top Oscars: Best Picture, Director, Actor, Actress, Screenplay. C: Jack Nicholson, Louise Fletcher, Brad Dourif, William Redfield, Danny DeVito, Christopher Lloyd. D: Milos Forman. DRA [R] 129m. V

One Foot in Heaven 1941 ★★★★½ Simple, beautifully told story of Methodist minister (March) and wife Scott dealing with changing mores and personal trials in 20th-century small-town America. Wonderful details and heartwarming performances. C: Fredric March, Martha Scott, Beulah Bondi, Gene Lockhart. D: Irving Rapper. DRA 108m.

One Foot in Hell 1960 ★★★½ Somber Western stars Ladd as deputy who blames town for wife's death and seeks revenge. Tries hard, but execution falls short. C: Alan Ladd, Don Murray, Don O'Herlihy, Dolores Michaels. D: James Clark. WST 90m.

One for the Book 1947 *See* **Voice of the Turtle, The**

One Frightened Night 1935 ★★★½ Effective, creepy programmer about greedy relatives waiting avidly for old man Grapewin to distribute his millions among them, till somebody intervenes. C: Charley Grapewin, Mary Carlisle, Arthur Hohl, Wallace Ford. D: Christy Cabanne. DRA 65m. V

One from the Heart 1982 ★★★ Gargantuan, gorgeous musical without much in the way of songs. Estranged couple Forrest and Garr dally with Kinski and Julia. Las Vegas set is phenomenal. C: Frederic Forrest, Teri Garr, Raul Julia, Nastassia Kinski, Lainie Kazan. D: Francis Ford Coppola. MUS [R] 100m. V

One Girl's Confession 1953 ★★½ Sleazy melodrama in which Moore willingly does time after fleecing evil guardian. Low-rent in every department. C: Cleo Moore, Hugo Haas, Glenn Langan. D: Hugo Haas. DRA 74m.

One Good Cop 1991 ★★★ Sentimental cop drama. A harried, caring officer (Keaton) and his wife (Russo) adopt his deceased partner's three daughters. Unfortunately ends with an ordinary action shoot-out. C: Michael Keaton, Rene Russo, Anthony LaPaglia. D: Heywood Gould. CRI [R] 105m. V

One Good Turn 1954 British ★★★½ Cheery British musical with popular song-and-dance man Wisdom as street entertainer who lucks into inheritance. C: Norman Wisdom, Joan Rice. D: John Carstairs. MUS 78m.

One Heavenly Night 1931 ★★★½ Flower girl Laye poses as famous cabaret singer to lure nobleman Boles. Old-time operetta. C: Evelyn Laye, John Boles. D: George Fitzmaurice. MUS 82m.

One Horse Town 1936 *See* **Small Town Girl**

One Hour with You 1932 ★★★★½ Smart, sophisticated musical has married couple Chevalier and MacDonald under a strain when coquette Tobin arrives on the scene. Good example of lighthearted sexuality known as "the Lubitsch Touch." Songs include title tune, "Oh, That Mitzi." C: George Cukor, Maurice Chevalier, Jeanette MacDonald, Genevieve Tobin. D: Ernst Lubitsch. MUS 80m.

One Hundred and One Dalmatians 1961 ★★★★★ Cruella de Vil, a classic Disney villainess, kidnaps dalmatian puppies for her own (gasp!) evil ends. Charming story told from the dogs' viewpoint, with brilliantly presented animation. Superb family entertainment. D: Wolfgang Reitherman, Hamilton Luske, Clyde Geronimi. FAM/DRA [G] 79m. V

One Hundred Men and a Girl 1937 ★★★★½ Enterprising and talented young singer badgers conductor Stokowski so he'll hire her musician father and his cohorts. Ultimate Durbin musical with lots of charm, sentiment, and coloratura chirping. Composer Charles Previn won an Oscar for Best Musical Score. C: Deanna Durbin, Leopold Stokowski, Adolphe Menjou, Alice Brady. D: Henry Koster. MUS 84m.

One Hundred Percent Pure 1934 *See* **Girl from Missouri, The**

100 Rifles 1969 ★★½ Halfbaked Western with Reynolds running guns into Mexico, where he meets unlikely guerrilla Welch. Ex-football hero Brown is third party in triangle. C: Jim Brown, Raquel Welch, Burt Reynolds, Fernando Lamas, Dan O'Herlihy. D: Tom Gries. WST [R] 110m.

One in a Million 1937 ★★★★ Henie's first film cannily casts the Olympic ice-skating champion as an Olympic ice-skating hopeful—and was released in an Olympic year. What film lacks in suspense it makes up for in spectacular skating routines and great supporting cast. C: Sonja Henie, Adolphe Menjou,

Don Ameche, Ned Sparks, Jean Hersholt, The Ritz Brothers. D: Sidney Lanfield. DRA 95m. v

One in a Million: The Ron LeFlore Story 1978 ★★★½ Inspirational true story of Tigers' Leflore (Burton) overcoming his Detroit ghetto childhood and an early prison term for armed robbery to become a major league baseball star. Good performances, standard script. C: LeVar Burton, Madge Siunclair. D: William Graham. DRA 100m. TVM v

One Is a Lonely Number 1972 ★★★★ Van Devere does well in slick story of divorced woman trying to adjust to the single life. Above average. C: Trish Van Devere, Monte Markham, Janet Leigh, Melvyn Douglas. D: Mel Stuart. DRA [PG] 97m.

One Last Fling 1949 ★★★ Flimsy comedy with jealous Smith getting job with husband Scott's company so she can keep tabs on him. C: Alexis Smith, Zachary Scott. D: Peter Godfrey. COM 74m.

One Life *See* **End of Desire**

One Little Indian 1973 ★★★ Lesser Disney feature has AWOL cavalry soldier (Garner) hooking up with Indian boy and a camel as he makes his escape through the desert. Contrived premise doesn't get much help from cliché-ridden script. C: James Garner, Vera Miles. D: Bernard McEveety. FAM/ACT [G] 90m. v

One Magic Christmas 1985 ★★★½ Mother (Steenburgen) has lost her Christmas spirit, so her daughter enlists Santa and guardian angel (Stanton—cast far against type!) to help. Uneven Disney holiday feature veers between overly serious and overly sentimental. C: Mary Steenburgen, Gary Basaraba, Harry Dean Stanton. D: Phillip Borsos. FAM/DRA [G] 88m. v

One Man Force 1989 ★★★ Football great Mutuszak wreaks havoc as a gargantuan Los Angeles drug cop dealing out violent vigilante vengeance to the killers of his former partner. Nothing special. C: John Matuszak, Ronny Cox, Sharon Farrell, Stacey Q. D: Dale Trevillion. CRI [R] 90m. v

One Man Jury 1978 ★★½ Exploitation flick with Palance as cop turned vigilante, on the rampage against sadistic thugs. Low-rent *Dirty Harry*. C: Jack Palance, Christopher Mitchum, Pamela Shoop. D: Charles Martin. ACT [R] 95m. v

One Man Justice 1937 ★★★½ Starrett's arrival in Western town causes concern, as he resembles a man long dead. No matter, he's going to clean up the wayward town anyway. A lot of dust gets kicked up in this boisterous action film. C: Charles Starrett, Barbara Weeks. D: Leon Barsha. WST 59m.

One Man's Journey 1933 ★★★★ Simple country doctor Barrymore would do anything for his patients and is finally rewarded for his unfailing service. Sentimental drama was remade in 1938 as *A Man to Remember*. C: Lionel Barrymore, May Robson, Joel McCrea. D: John S. Robertson. DRA 72m.

One Man's War 1990 British ★★★★½ A crusading physician (Hopkins) speaks out against brutal dictatorship in '70s Paraguay and finds his family persecuted and his son murdered as a result. Compelling factual drama with superb performances. C: Anthony Hopkins, Norma Aleandro, Ruben Blades. D: Sergio Toledo. DRA [PG-13] 91m. TVM v

One Man's Way 1964 ★★★½ Okay film biography of preacher and positive-thinking advocate Norman Vincent Peale. Murray is well-cast as Peale, though the movie tends to portray him as something of a saint. C: Don Murray, Diana Hyland, Veronica Cartwright. D: Denis Sanders. DRA 105m. v

One Million B.C. 1940 ★★★½ Stone Age tribes fight each other and prehistoric creatures. Some great effects; supposedly partially directed by D. W. Griffith. C: Victor Mature, Carole Landis, Lon Chaney Jr. D: Hal Roach, Hal Roach Jr. DRA 80m. v

One Million Years B.C. 1966 British ★★★½ Remake of 1940 prehistoric adventure features marvelous special effects, and made Welch a star. Dialogue is basically grunt and groan, but film offers juvenile fun for all ages. C: Raquel Welch, John Richardson. D: Don Chaffey. DRA 100m.

One Minute to Zero 1952 ★★★ Macho Mitchum, as colonel overseeing evacuation of Americans from Korea, comes up against U.N. representative Blyth in war drama that lapses into standard romance. C: Robert Mitchum, Ann Blyth, Richard Egan. D: Tay Garnett. DRA 105m. v

One More River 1934 ★★★★ Stately, well-acted domestic drama of husband (Clive) bringing divorce suit against unfaithful wife (Wynyard). From John Galsworthy's final novel. C: Diana Wynyard, Colin Clive, Mrs. Patrick Campbell, Jane Wyatt. D: James Whale. DRA 90m.

One More Saturday Night 1986 ★ Screamingly awful comedy from *Saturday Night Live* regulars that supposedly spoofs Minnesota night-life. C: Tom Davis, Al Franken. D: Dennis Klein. COM [R] 96m. v

One More Spring 1935 ★★★★ Depression-era, sunny-side-up comedy has a bevy of hard-on-their-luck characters banding together to fight tough times. Light premise, charming leads. A film that could make anyone forget their troubles. C: Janet Gaynor, Warner Baxter, Walter Woolf King, Jane Darwell, Stepin Fetchit. D: Henry King. COM 86m.

One More Time 1970 ★★ Duo of Lawford and Davis in sequel to their *Salt and Pepper*. This time they inherit English castle when Lawford's twin brother dies. Full of smarmy jokes and racist innuendos. C: Peter Lawford, Sammy Davis Jr. D: Jerry Lewis. COM [PG] 93m.

One More Tomorrow 1946 ★★★ Attractive cast has trouble with weak comedy about rich cad Morgan falling for intellectual magazine chief Sheridan. Loosely based on Philip Barry play, *The Animal Kingdom*. C: Ann Sheridan, Dennis Morgan, Jack Carson, Alexis Smith, Jane Wyman. D: Peter Godfrey. COM 88m.

One More Train to Rob 1971 ★★★ Western twist on *The Count of Monte Cristo*, with Peppard betrayed and jailed for train heist, and returning years later to wreak vengeance. Great idea, average execution. C: George Peppard, Diana Muldaur, John Vernon, France Nuyen. D: Andrew McLaglen. WST [PG] 108m.

One Mysterious Night 1944 ★★★½ Modest, well-constructed *Boston Blackie* mystery with ex-con Morris trying to prove his innocence in theft of priceless diamond. C: Chester Morris, Janis Carter, Richard Lane. D: Oscar Boetticher. CRI 61m.

One New York Night 1935 ★★★½ Country boy Tone goes to the big city to snare a wife but finds murder instead in this involving mystery, with Merkel as the plucky switchboard operator who helps the hero get to the bottom of things. C: Franchot Tone, Una Merkel, Conrad Magel. D: Jack Conway. CRI 71m.

One Night at Susie's 1930 ★★★ Good boy Fairbanks goes up the river to save his girlfriend from a murder rap, followed by plenty of complicated intrigue. Performances are on the corny side, save for Ware, who plays a sweet boardinghouse den mother. C: Billie Dove, Douglas Fairbanks, Jr., Helen Ware, Tully Marshall. D: John Francis Dillon. DRA 85m.

One Night in Lisbon 1941 ★★★½ Standard wartime romantic comedy with crusty American pilot (MacMurray) wooing prim English rose (Carroll). C: Fred MacMurray, Madeleine Carroll, Patricia Morison, Billie Burke. D: Edward Griffith. COM 97m.

One Night in the Tropics 1940 ★★★½ Silly musical romance with Jones and Cummings vying for Kelly while Bud and Lou, in their movie debut, steal the picture. Nice Kern/Fields ballad, "Remind Me." C: Allan Jones, Nancy Kelly, Bud Abbott, Lou Costello, Robert Cummings, Mary Boland. D: A. Sutherland. MUS 82m.

One Night of Love 1934 ★★★★½ Metropolitan Opera star Moore shines as American singer in Italy defying her domineering vocal coach, Carminati. Terrific singing, charming production. Composer Lois Silvers' score won an Oscar. C: Grace Moore, Tullio Carminati, Lyle Talbot, Jessie Ralph. D: Victor Schertzinger. MUS 80m. V

One Night Only! 1984 ★ Sexy college coeds come up with surefire way to pay their tuition fees by posing as prostitutes and staging all-night orgy with football team. Insulting *Risky Business* rip-off. C: Lenore Zann, Jeff Braunstein. D: Timothy Bond. COM [R] 87m. V

One Night With You 1948 British ★★★ Bland British musical casts popular singer Martini as himself, pursued by debutante Roc. C: Nino Martini, Patricia Roc, Bonar Colleano. D: Terence Young. MUS 90m.

One of My Wives Is Missing 1976 ★★★½ Suspenseful mystery has rural cop (Klugman) investigating wealthy man's wife, who disappeared and returned, but may not be whom she claims to be. Based on Robert Thomas' play *The Trap for a Lonely Man*, which was previously filmed as *Honeymoon with a Stranger*, and later for TV as *Vanishing Act*. C: Jack Klugman, Elizabeth Ashley, James Franciscus. D: Glenn Caron Jordan. CRI 100m. TVM V

One of Our Aircraft Is Missing 1941 British ★★★★½ Superior WWII drama of RAF pilots downed in Holland making perilous trip back home. Large cast uniformly excellent in absorbing, edge-of-your-seat adventure. British version runs 102 minutes; some American prints only 82 minutes. C: Godfrey Tearle, Eric Portman, Hugh Williams. D: Michael Powell, Emeric Pressburger. DRA 90m. V

One of Our Dinosaurs Is Missing 1975 ★★★½ While Chinese spy (Ustinov) searches for missing microfilm hidden in a dinosaur bone, British nanny (Hayes) finds it and ends up in unlikely chase through London streets. Minor Disney caper comedy for kids, acted with more verve than expected. C: Peter Ustinov, Helen Hayes, Clive Revill. D: Robert Stevenson. FAM/DRA [G] 101m. V

One of Our Own 1975 ★★★ TV pilot in which hospital administrator/surgeon Peppard battles bureaucracy and disease, in that order. Tries to be realistic, then delivers neat resolutions to all conflicts. C: George Peppard, William Daniels, Louise Ssorel, Strother Martin, Zohra Lampert, Oscar Homolka, Victor Campos. D: Richard Sarafian. DRA 120m. TVM

One on One 1976 ★★★½ Benson co-wrote this rah-rah tale of a hotshot basketball star who learns that playing college ball is not a game. Predictable but diverting. C: Robby Benson, Annette O'Toole, G.D. Spradlin. D: Lamont Johnson. DRA [PG] 100m. V

One Police Plaza 1986 ★★★ TV pilot with Conrad as jaded N.Y. police officer taking on the system to solve woman's murder. Routine. Sequel: *The Red Spider*. C: Robert Conrad, James Olson. D: Jerry Jameson. CRI 104m. TVM

One Potato, Two Potato 1964 ★★★★½ Groundbreaking study of interracial romance between Barrie and Hamilton, which ultimately leads to custody battle with Barrie's ex-husband. Solid performances, honest script with no cop-outs. C: Barbara Barrie, Bernie Hamilton, Richard Mulligan. D: Larry Peerce. DRA 92m.

One Rainy Afternoon 1936 ★★★½ Naive fluff with Lederer causing a major scandal by kissing Lupino in movie theatre. Charming and hopelessly silly. C: Francis Lederer, Ida Lupino, Roland Young, Hugh Herbert. D: Rowland V. Lee. COM 78m. V

One Riot, One Ranger 1994 ★★ Small town marauders controlled in unusual way by Texas Ranger. Pilot for TV series Walker—Texas Ranger. C: Chuck Norris. ACT [PG-13] 96m. TVM V

One Romantic Night 1930 ★★½ Gish plays a princess torn between the prince she should marry and the commoner she loves. The great silent movie star made her talkie debut in this adaptation of Molnar's *The Swan.* Made previously in 1925, and later in 1956, both times as *The Swan.* C: Lillian Gish, Rod La Rocque, Conrad Nagel, Marie Dressler. D: Paul Stein. DRA 71m.

One Russian Summer 1973 Italian ★★ Reed chews the scenery in laughable story of sadistic landowner marked for retribution by former victim McEnery. From Lermontov novel *Vadim.* C: Oliver Reed, John McEnery, Carole Andre. D: Antonio Calenda. DRA [R] 112m. V

One Shoe Makes It Murder 1982 ★★★ Detective hokum somewhat improved by Mitchum's stalwart performance as gumshoe investigating rich Ferrer's errant wife. From Bercovici novel *So Little Cause for Caroline.* C: Robert Mitchum, Angie Dickinson, Mel Ferrer. D: William Hale. CRI 96m. TVM V

One Sings, The Other Doesn't 1977 French ★★★ Well-meaning but shallow feminist tract about two women choosing different paths; one traditional, the other more freewheeling but neither very uninspiring. C: Therese Liotard, Valerie Mairesse. D: Agnes Varda. DRA 105m. V

One Spy Too Many 1966 ★★★½ Two episodes of *Man From U.N.C.L.E.* TV series, spliced together, with Napoleon Solo and Ilya Kuryakin once again saving the world, this time from Torn. Fans, pounce. Others, beware. C: Robert Vaughn, David McCallum, Rip Torn. D: Joseph Sargent. CRI 102m.

One Step to Eternity 1955 French ★★★½ Four women share two things: lover Auclair and death threats against them. Tingling thriller marred by weak ending. C: Danielle Darrieux, Michel Auclair, Corinne Calvet. D: Henri Decoin. CRI 94m.

One Step to Hell 1968 ★★½ Jungle potboiler with Hardin after gang of murderers. Even the African scenery looks cheesy. C: Ty Hardin, Pier Angeli, George Sanders, Rossano Brazzi. D: Sandy Howard. DRA 90m. V

One Summer Love 1976 ★★★ Bridges, released after years in a mental institution, returns home to find his family and is befriended by misfit Sarandon. Good cast, but awash in sticky sentiment. (a.k.a. *Dragonfly*) C: Beau Bridges, Susan Sarandon, Mildred Dunnock. D: Gilbert Cates. DRA [PG] 98m. V

One Sunday Afternoon 1948 ★★★ Stalwart turn-of-the-century dentist Morgan meets flirtatious Paige in slowly-pace musical with forgettable score. Non-musical version made in 1932 with Gary Cooper; also filmed in 1941 as *The Strawberry Blonde.* C: Dennis Morgan, Janis Paige, Dorothy Malone. D: Raoul Walsh. MUS 90m.

One That Got Away, The 1957 British ★★★★½ True WWII story of a captured German pilot duty-bound to escape from the POW camps in which he's interned by the British. Crackerjack suspense thriller with exciting action sequences. C: Hardy Kruger, Colin Gordon. D: Roy Ward Baker. ACT 111m. V

One Third of a Nation 1939 ★★★ Dark Depression-era drama with Sidney as a young woman trapped in a NYC tenement, dallying with landlord Erickson. Talented star, turgid script, but social observations still relevant. C: Sylvia Sidney, Leif Erickson. D: Dudley Murphy. DRA 79m.

1001 Arabian Nights *See* **Mr. Magoo—1001 Arabian Nights**

One Touch of Venus 1948 ★★★½ Amusing, slight story of department store statue of Greek goddess coming to life. From hit Broadway musical by Kurt Weil and Ogden Nash, though the wonderful score has been sharply cut. At least one great song remains: "Speak Low." C: Ava Gardner, Robert Walker, Dick Haymes, Eve Arden. D: William A. Seiter. MUS 82m. V

One-Trick Pony 1980 ★★★ Unsuccessful shot at screen stardom for pop legend Simon. He plays version of himself as a musician having mid-life career and personal crisis. C: Paul Simon, Blair Brown, Rip Torn, Joan Hackett. D: Robert Young. MUS [R] 100m. V

One, Two, Three 1961 ★★★★ In West Germany, a Coke executive peddles his product while trying to keep his boss's daughter from getting hitched to a Communist. Superfunny job by Wilder, I. A. L. Diamond (script), and the inimitable Cagney. C: James Cagney, Arlene Francis, Horst Buchholz, Pamela Tiffin. D: Billy Wilder. COM 110m. V

One Way Passage 1932 ★★★★½ Memorable doomed romance with Powell as condemned convict and Francis as dying socialite having one last fling aboard oceanliner bound. Moving, Oscar-winning story, with marvelous performances. Later made as *'Til We Meet Again.* C: Kay Francis, William Powell, Aline MacMahon, Warren Hymer, Frank McHugh. D: Tay Garnett. DRA 69m.

One Way Pendulum 1965 British ★★★½ Uproariously silly British comedy in swinging '60s style follows the adventures of a family of certified nuts led by dad Sykes, who turns his living room into a construction site. A lot of fun. C: Eric Sykes, George Cole, Julia Foster, Jonathan Miller, Mona Washbourne. D: Peter Yates. COM 90m.

One-Way Street 1950 ★★★ Mason gives his all in this mundane melodrama of doctor stealing gangster's money and his lover. C:

James Mason, Marta Toren, Dan Duryea. D: Hugo Fregonese. DRA 79m.

One Way to Love 1945 ★★★½ Charming B-picture about feuding radio writers on cross-country train ride who discover new material and relationships. C: Chester Morris, Janis Carter, Marguerite Chapman. D: Ray Enright. COM 83m.

One Wild Moment 1981 French ★★★ Flimsy sex comedy of middle-aged widowers on vacation with their nubile daughters. Coarse and obvious. Remade in Hollywood as *Blame It on Rio*. C: Jean-Pierre Marielle, Victor Lanoux, Agnes Soral. D: Claude Berri. COM [R] 88m. V

One Wish Too Many 1956 British ★★★½ Richmond uses a magic marble to get his heart's desire—which, in usual kid fashion, means toys, revenge, and general mayhem. Moral is a bit pat, but this is a charming youngster's fantasy. C: Anthony Richmond, Rosalind Gourgey. D: John Durst. FAM/DRA 55m. V

One Woman or Two 1987 French ★★½ Paleontologist (Depardieu) seeks the missing link, bankrolled by a ditzy philanthropist (Westheimer), discovers fossil remains of the first French woman, and is conned by a greedy Madison Avenue executive (Weaver). Formula remake of *Bringing Up Baby*. C: Gerard Depardieu, Dr. Ruth Westheimer, Sigourney Weaver. D: Daniel Vigne. COM [PG-13] 95m. V

One Woman's Story 1949 British ★★★★ Todd is married to rich man Rains, who can't give his wife the kind of true love she finds with former boyfriend Howard. A believable love story based on H.G. Wells novel. Wonderful performances and Lean's superior direction make it all work. (a.k.a. *Passionate Friendship*) C: Ann Todd, Trevor Howard, Claude Rains. D: David Lean. DRA 95m.

Onibaba 1964 Japanese ★★★★ A mother and daughter survive in medieval Japan by killing warriors to salvage and sell their armor. When a would-be victim seduces her daughter, the mother seeks retribution. A fiercely beautiful and original film. (a.k.a. *The Hole*) C: Nobuko Otawa, Jitsuko Yoshimura, Kei Sato. D: Kaneto Shindo. DRA 103m. V

Onion Field, The 1979 ★★★★★ One of veteran police writer Wambaugh's most compelling and uncompromising dramas. The true story of the psychological collapse of an ex-cop who, disturbed by having seen his partner's murder (and having fled and survived), wrestles with putting his life back together. Savage and Woods are riveting as two very different kinds of survivors. C: John Savage, James Woods, Ronny Cox. D: Harold Becker. CRI [R] 126m. V

Onionhead 1958 ★★★ Routine comedy, similar but inferior to Griffith's *No Time for Sergeants*: this time he joins the coast guard. C: Andy Griffith, Felicia Farr, Walter Matthau. D: Norman Taurog. COM 111m. V

Only Angels Have Wings 1939 ★★★★★ One of Hawks' strongest dramas involves life and loves of South American mail pilots. Many big names, including Grant, Arthur and Barthelmess (along with newcomer Hayworth) back up compelling stories with solid characterizations. C: Cary Grant, Jean Arthur, Richard Barthelmess, Rita Hayworth, Thomas Mitchell. D: Howard Hawks. DRA 121m. V

Only Game in Town, The 1970 ★★★ Strange, miscast version of Frank D. Gilroy's sensitive play. Taylor isn't believable as aging chorus girl in love with pianist Beatty, and though the story is set in Las Vegas, film was shot in Paris, France. C: Elizabeth Taylor, Warren Beatty. D: George Stevens. DRA [PG] 113m.

Only One Survived 1990 ★★★ Title gives it away in routine actioner of four NYC corporate types on fishing trip up the Amazon. ACT

Only the Best 1951 *See* **I Can Get It for You Wholesale**

Only the French Can 1955 *See* **French Cancan**

Only the Lonely 1991 ★★★½ Chicago cop (Candy) who lives with domineering mother (O'Hara), meets mortician's assistant (Sheedy) and must choose between the women. Sweet-natured, with a vivid performances by O'Hara, though lightweight romance doesn't miss a stereotype. C: John Candy, Maureen O'Hara, Ally Sheedy, James Belushi, Anthony Quinn. D: Chris Columbus. COM [PG-13] 105m. V

Only the Strong 1993 ★★ An introduction to the Brazilian fighting style called *capoeira*, which basically looks like gymnastics routines punctuated with roundhouse kicks. Dacascos teaches it to high schoolers so that they can clean up his alma mater with vigilante violence. C: Mark Dacascos, Stacey Travis, Paco Christian Prieto. D: Sheldon Lettich. ACT [PG-13] 125m. V

Only the Valiant 1951 ★★★ Standard cavalry vs. Indians yarn with Peck as officer confronting rebellious troops. Lots of action, little else. C: Gregory Peck, Barbara Payton, Gig Young. D: Gordon Douglas. WST 105m. V

Only Two Can Play 1962 British ★★★★ Lecherous librarian Sellers meets his match in socialite Zetterling. Amusing comedy from Kingsley Amis novel, with sprightly performances. C: Peter Sellers, Mai Zetterling, Virginia Maskell, Richard Attenborough. D: Sidney Gilliat. COM 106m. V

Only Way, The 1970 ★★★½ The story of how the Jews of Nazi-occupied Denmark were aided by their fellow Danes. Filmed in quasidocumentary fashion; quite powerful. C: Jane Seymour, Martin Potter. DRA [G] 86m. V

Only When I Larf 1968 British ★★★ Jokey farce about three con artists fleecing radical African diplomat. Much of its humor has trouble crossing the Atlantic. C: Richard Attenborough, David Hemmings, Alexandra Stewart. D: Basil Dearden. COM [G] 104m.

Only When I Laugh 1981 ★★★★ Perceptive, well-acted comedy/drama, with one of Neil Simon's best scripts. Mason is alcoholic actress desperate to repair her health, career, and relationship with daughter McNichol. Coco and Hackett superb as Mason's neurotic pals. (Hackett won Golden Globe: Best Supporting Actress.) From Simon's play, *The Gingerbread Lady.* (a.k.a. *It Hurts Only When I Laugh*) C: Marsha Mason, Kristy McNichol, James Coco, Joan Hackett. D: Glenn Jordan. COM [R] 120m. v

Only with Married Men 1974 ★★ Woman who wants to remain single dates man interested in marriage. C: David Birney, Michele Lee, Dom De Luise. D: Jerry Paris. COM 74m. TVM v

Only Yesterday 1933 ★★★★ Wonderful, delicately nuanced film debut by Sullavan distinguishes sudsy tale of unwed mother from WWI to onset of The Great Depression. C: Margaret Sullavan, John Boles, Billie Burke, Edna May Oliver, Benita Hume. D: John Stahl. DRA 105m.

Only You 1992 ★★★ After being dumped by his girlfriend, young man finds solace with new face on an exotic beach. Uninteresting and rather blasé romance, artlessly directed by former *Hill Street Blues* star Thomas. C: Andrew McCarthy, Kelly Preston, Helen Hunt. D: Betty Thomas. COM [PG-13] 85m. v

Only You 1994 ★★★½ Pittsburgh schoolteacher (Tomei) runs out on her fiancé, goes to Italy, and meets the man of her dreams, predicted by fortune teller. Lightweight amalgam of *Roman Holliday*, *Moonstruck*, and dozens of other Cinderella stories is carried by lovely locations, Tomei's charm, and Hunt as a voice of reason. C: Marisa Tomei, Robert Downey, Jr., Bonnie Hunt, Fisher Stevens, Joaquim de Almeida. D: Norman Jewison. COM [PG] 108m. v

Oooh, You Are Awful 1976 *See* **Get Charlie Tully**

Open Admissions 1988 ★★★½ Beach is a black student in college due to open admissions policy, but reading at a fourth grade level. Alexander is jaded speech teacher who confronts him in this watered-down version of Shirley Lauro play. Good performances. C: Jane Alexander, Dennis Farina, Estelle Parsons, Michael Beach. D: Gus Trikonis. DRA 96m. TVM

Open All Hours 1983 British ★★★½ A small neighborhood corner store is ruled despotically and hilariously by its avaricious owner. Typical British comedy; quite hysterial at times. C: Ronnie Barker, David Jason, Lynda Baron. COM 85m. v

Open City 1945 Italian ★★★★★ Rossellini's powerful ground-breaking classic defined the harsh look and feel of neorealism. Cowritten by Fellini, the film portrays an Italian city struggling under the fascists in WWII and a leader (Paghero) who emerges from the underground. C: Aldo Fabrizi, Anna Magnani, Maria Michi. D: Roberto Rossellini. DRA 103m. v

Open Doors 1989 Italian ★★★★ Slow-paced but provocative look at fascist Italian legal system with Volante as principled judge struggling to be just in corrupt political environment. Has universal significance despite its focus fascism. Winner of Italian awards for Best Film, Actor, Screenplay, and also many international awards. C: Gian Maria Volonte, Ennio Fantastichini, Renzo Giovampietro. D: Gianni Amelio. DRA [R] 109m. v

Open House 1987 ★★½ A mysterious killer is preying on realtors and their clients. C: Joseph Bottoms, Adrienne Barbeau, Mary Stavin. D: Jag Mundhra. HOR [R] 95m. v

Open Season 1974 Spanish ★★½ Three Vietnam vets go on a sadistic rampage in crude action film. C: Peter Fonda, John Phillip Law, William Holden, Cornelia Sharpe. D: Peter Collinson. ACT [R] 103m. v

Open the Door and See All the People 1964 ★★★½ Elderly twin sisters, one nasty, the other nice, engage in all-out warfare. Oddball comedy. C: Maybelle Nash, Alec Wilder, Charles Rydell. D: Jerome Hill. COM 82m.

Opening Night 1977 ★★★★ An unstable, aging Broadway actress starring in a new play reaches her breaking point when a devoted fan suddenly dies. Lengthy backstage drama superbly acted by Rowlands. C: Gena Rowlands, John Cassavetes, Ben Gazzara, Joan Blondell. D: John Cassavetes. DRA [PG-13] 144m. v

Opera Do Malandro 1987 ★★½ In the slums of Rio, a young smoothie meets up with a Brazilian dreamgirl. C: Edson Celulari, Elba Romalho, Fabio Sabag. D: Ruy Guerra. DRA 108m. v

Operation Amsterdam 1960 British ★★★ Standard thriller, set in 1940, with Dutch patriots trying to get diamonds out of Holland before the Nazis arrive. C: Peter Finch, Eva Bartok, Tony Britton. D: Michael McCarthy. ACT 105m. v

Operation Bikini 1963 ★★★ Twist on typical WWII adventure has teen idols Tab and Frankie wielding grenades as they try to blow up radar equipment before the Japanese get their hands on it. C: Tab Hunter, Frankie Avalon, Eva Six, Scott Brady. D: Anthony Carras. COM 83m.

Operation Bottleneck 1961 ★★½ Low-budget battles in Burma, during WWII, with clutzy cast. C: Ron Foster, Miiko Taka. D: Edward Cahn. ACT 78m.

Operation C.I.A. 1965 ★★★½ Good, early Vietnam actioner, especially interesting in hindsight. Young Reynolds must stop Saigon assassination attempt. (a.k.a. *Last Message from Saigon*) C: Burt Reynolds, Kieu Chinh, Danielle Aubry. D: Christian Nyby. ACT 90m. v

Operation Conspiracy 1957 British ★★★

Hackneyed Red Menace thriller, British style, with Friend as agent protecting nuclear secrets. (a.k.a. *Cloak Without Dagger*) C: Philip Friend, Mary Mackenzie. D: Joseph Sterling. ACT 69m.

Operation Cross Eagles 1969 ★★½ Dime-a-dozen war film with Conte leading attempt to rescue captured American officer. C: Richard Conte, Rory Calhoun, Aili King. D: Richard Conte. ACT 90m. V

Operation Crossbow 1965 ★★★★½ During WWII, a select group of scientist/commandos set out to destroy a secret Nazi missile site. Fine throughout, with a—literally—explosive ending. (a.k.a. *The Great Spy Mission* and *Code Name: Operation Crossbow*) C: George Peppard, Sophia Loren, Trevor Howard, Tom Courtenay, Anthony Quayle, John Mills, Sylvia Syms, Richard Todd, Lilli Palmer. D: Michael Anderson. ACT 116m. V

Operation Daybreak 1976 ★★★½ True WWII story of Czech resistance plot to assassinate Nazi leader Reinhard "Hangman" Heydrich. Suspenseful, but second half falters. C: Timothy Bottoms, Martin Shaw, Joss Ackland, Nicola Pagett. D: Lewis Gilbert. ACT [PG] 102m. V

Operation Disaster 1951 British ★★★★ Outstanding rescue-mission film has 12 sailors trapped in sunken sub, desperately awaiting help. Fine script, exciting pace. (a.k.a. *Morning Departure*) C: John Mills, Helen Cherry, Richard Attenborough, Lana Morris. D: Roy Baker. ACT 102m.

Operation Eichmann 1961 ★★★½ Mildly engrossing story of infamous Nazi death-camp leader Eichmann (Klemperer), pursued after WWII by Israeli activists. C: Werner Klemperer, Ruta Lee, Donald Buke, Barbara Turner. D: R. G. Springsteen. ACT 93m.

Operation Ganymed 1977 German ★★★★ Spacecraft long abandoned in the cosmos crashes to Earth. Psychological survival tale of how the astronauts cope with the ravages of the desert. Sci-fi fans will want to check out this intelligent drama. C: Horst Frank, Dieter Laser, Uwe Friedrichsen. D: Rainer Erler. SFI 126m. V

Operation Haylift 1950 ★★ Corny but true heroics with airforce saving stranded cows in snowstorm. C: Bill Williams, Ann Rutherford, Jane Nigh. D: William Berke. ACT 75m. V

Operation Julie 1985 ★★★ A detective becomes a one-man army against a bunch of drug smugglers. C: Colin Blakely, Lesley Nightingale. D: Bob Mahoney. ACT 100m. V

Operation Kid Brother 1967 Italian ★★ Bottom-of-the-barrel spy story with secret agent defending world's gold supply. Title refers to star Neil Connery, Sean's brother. One of the worst of the Bond rip-offs. (a.k.a. *Secret Agent 00*) C: Neil Connery, Daniela Bianchi. D: Alberto DeMartino. ACT 104m.

Operation Mad Ball 1957 ★★ Misfired attempt at wacky Army comedy has Lemmon et al. planning off-base pleasure-fest. Talented cast. C: Jack Lemmon, Kathryn Grant, Mickey Rooney, Ernie Kovacs. D: Richard Quine. COM 105m.

Operation Manhunt 1954 ★★★½ Second film biography (first was 1948's *The Iron Curtain*) of Soviet defector to Canada Igor Gouzenko (Townes), who is terrorized by Soviet agents who want him dead. Gripping Cold War melodrama shot in a hard-boiled documentary style. Gouzenko himself appears briefly. C: Harry Townes, Irja Jensen, Jacques Aubuchon. D: Jack Alexander. ACT 77m.

Operation Masquerade 1965 *See* **Masquerade**

Operation Mermaid 1963 *See* **Bay of Saint Michel, The**

Operation Nam 1987 ★★★ Vietnam veterans seek to save leader from prison camp. Notable for performance by John Wayne's son. C: John Ethan Wayne, Donald Pleasence, Oliver Tobias. D: Larry Ludman. ACT 85m. V

Operation Pacific 1951 ★★★ A committed WWII submarine captain has a wary approach to command. Tolerable seafaring tale is lean on action and lengthy. C: John Wayne, Patricia Neal, Ward Bond. D: George Waggner. ACT 110m. V

Operation Petticoat 1959 ★★★★ When his submarine appears headed for scrap heap, Commander Grant receives unorthodox support from wheeler-dealer lieutenant (Curtis). Mindless and entertaining fun, with energy bursting in every frame. Later remade as television movie and short-lived sitcom. C: Cary Grant, Tony Curtis, Dina Merrill, Gavin McLeod, Marion Ross, Nicky Blair. D: Blake Edwards. COM 122m. V

Operation Petticoat 1977 ★★½ Battered submarine's crew plans to spruce it up. Remake of 1959 Grant/Curtis film is silly, pointless, pilot for a TV series. (a.k.a. *Life in the Pink*) C: John Astin, Richard Gilliland, Jackie Cooper. D: John Astin. COM 100m. TVM

Operation Secret 1952 ★★★ WWII yarn has Army officer Wilde suspected of treason. Strictly routine. C: Cornel Wilde, Phyllis Thaxter, Karl Malden, Dan O'Herlihy. D: Lewis Seiler. ACT 108m.

Operation Shark Attack 1988 ★★★½ Ron and Valerie Taylor, noted shark authorities, take the viewer on a thrilling tour of Australia's Great Barrier Reef in search of sharks. Compelling, impressive undersea study. DOC 53m. V

Operation Snafu 1961 British ★★½ Silly wartime comedy in which cowards Connery and Lynch accidentally become heroes. One of Sean's worst. (a.k.a. *On the Fiddle* and *Operation Warhead*) C: Alfred Lynch, Sean Connery, Cecil Parker, Stanley Holloway. D: Cyril Frankel. COM 97m.

Operation Snafu 1970 Italian-Yugoslavian

★★½ Falk leads misfit soldiers on special assignment in Sicily during WWII. Derivative war actioner with attempts at humor. C: Peter Falk, Jason Robards, Martin Landau, Nino Manfredi. D: Nanni Loy. COM 97m.

Operation Snatch 1962 British ★★★ Lamebrained WWII satire has Terry-Thomas sent to Gilbraltar to defend it against Nazis. Occasionally amusing. C: Terry-Thomas, George Sanders. D: Robert Day. COM 83m.

Operation St. Peter's 1968 Italian ★★½ Robinson heads gang of art thieves whose ambitious plan is to steal Michelangelo's The Pietá, from the Vatican. Mediocre comedy/adventure. C: Edward G. Robinson, Lando Buzzanca, Jean-Claude Brialy. D: Lucio Fulci. COM 100m.

Operation War Zone 1989 ★★★ Carrying information vital to the war effort, a young American soldier disapepars in the Vietnamese jungle. C: Joe Spinell, Fritz Matthews, David Marriott. D: David A. Prior. ACT 86m. v

Operation Warhead 1961 *See* **Operation Snafu**

Operation X 1950 British ★★★ Robinson plays a possessive father, ruining his daughter's life and his own. B-movie soap opera with star its only major asset. (a.k.a. *My Daughter Joy*) C: Edward G. Robinson, Peggy Cummins, Richard Greene. D: Gregory Ratoff. DRA 79m.

Operator 13 1934 ★★★½ Actress Davies is Union spy during the Civil War, frequently in blackface disguise till she falls for Confederate soldier Cooper. Rather bizarre tale, but certainly never boring. C: Marion Davies, Gary Cooper, Katharine Alexander, Jean Parker, Ted Healy. D: Richard Boleslavsky. DRA 86m.

Operetta 1949 German ★★★★ Celebration of great opera and the professional competition between opera producer Forst and diva Holst. Elegant, well-tuned Bavarian musical features some of opera's most famous scenes and music (played by the Vienna Philharmonic and Vienna State Opera). C: Willy Forst, Maria Holst. D: Willy Forst. MUS 106m.

Opium Connection *See* **Poppy Is Also a Flower**

Opponent, The 1989 ★★★ When a young boxer saves a mafia don's daughter from death, he finds himself involved in organized crime. C: Ernest Borgnine, Daniel Greene, Julian Gemma. D: Sergio Martino. ACT [R] 102m. v

Opportunity Knocks 1990 ★★★ A con artist (Carvey) utilizes his skills as impersonator to finagle his way into a tycoon's home and a young woman's heart while hiding from a hood. Amusing, though predictable vehicle for Carvey, who pulls every vocal and physical trick in his repertoire. C: Dana Carvey, Robert Loggia, Todd Graff, Julia Campbell. D: Donald Petrie. COM [PG-13] 103m. v

Opposing Force 1986 ★★½ Exploitative actioner casts Zerbe as deranged Air Force commander justifying rape of Eichhorn as "training." (a.k.a. *Hellcamp*) C: Tom Skerritt, Lisa Eichhorn, Anthony Zerbe, Richard Roundtree. D: Eric Karson. ACT [R] 99m. v

Opposite Sex (And How to Live with Them), The 1993 ★ Jewish man romances wealthy WASP. Just plain awful romantic comedy and tired gimmick of cast talking directly to camera doesn't help. C: Arye Gross, Courtney Cox, Kevin Pollak, Julie Brown. D: Matthew Meshekoff. COM [R] 87m. v

Opposite Sex, The 1956 ★★★½ Semimusical remake of 1939 classic *The Women* adds men and music to story of gossiping, husband-stealing females, with Allyson getting most of the songs as noble wife who loses her man. Strong supporting cast. C: June Allyson, Joan Collins, Dolores Gray, Ann Sheridan, Ann Miller, Leslie Nielsen, Agnes Moorehead, Charlotte Greenwood, Joan Blondell. D: David Miller. MUS 117m. v

Optimists, The 1973 British ★★★★ Sellers at his most charming dominates sentimental comedy as street performer befriending two urchins. Cute songs by Lionel (*Oliver*) Bart. C: Peter Sellers, Donna Mullane, John Chaffey. D: Anthony Simmons. COM [PG] 110m.

Options 1988 ★★★ A Hollywood agent hacks his way through the African jungles to get exclusive rights to the story of a disowned princess. C: Matt Salinger, Joanna Pacula, John Kant. D: Camilo Vila. COM [PG] 105m. v

Orca—the Killer Whale 1977 ★★ Title character seeks revenge on whale hunter (Harris). Bo's major feature debut. C: Richard Harris, Charlotte Rampling, Bo Derek, Keenan Wynn. D: Michael Anderson. ACT [PG] 92m. v

Orchestra Conductor, The 1980 Polish ★★★★ Exiled Polish conductor (Gielgud) comes home after 50 years to face the music, in more ways than one. Slow-moving but effective showcase for the great actor. C: John Gielgud, Krystyna Janda, Andrzej Seweryn. D: Andrzej Wajda. DRA 101m. v

Orchestra Rehearsal 1979 Italian ★★★½ Minor Fellini allegory depicts life as an orchestra conducted by God. Small in scope, (made for Italian TV), showing only flashes of the master's brilliance. C: Baldwin Baas, Clara Colosimo, Elizabeth Lubi. D: Federico Fellini. DRA [R] 72m.

Orchestra Wives 1942 ★★★½ Glenn Miller and his band are the raison d'être for this modest tale of touring musicians and their neglected spouses. Loaded with great Miller numbers like "Serenade in Blue," "I've Got a Gal in Kalamazoo," etc. C: George Montgomery, Ann Rutherford, The Glenn Miller Orchestra, Carole Landis, Cesar Romero. D: Archie Mayo. MUS 97m. v

Ordeal 1973 ★★★ Rich husband Hill is left in desert with a broken leg by murderous wife Muldaur. Man against nature, with a soap opera twist. C: Arthur Hill, Diana Muldaur. D: Lee Katzin. DRA 74m. TVM

Ordeal by Innocence 1984 ★★½ In a small English village, an American (Sutherland) meets resistance when his doubts about the guilt of a friend executed for murder lead him to investigate. Sub-par adaptation of an Agatha Christie novel; good cast wasted. Score by Dave Brubeck, though. C: Donald Sutherland, Faye Dunaway, Christopher Plummer, Sarah Miles. D: Desmond Davis. CRI [PG-13] 91m. V

Ordeal of Bill Carney, The 1981 ★★★ Fair account of real-life quadraplegic (Sharkey) and his struggle for custody of his children. Slightly maudlin. C: Ray Sharkey, Richard Crenna, Ana Alicia, Vincent Baggetta. D: Jerry London. DRA 96m. TVM V

Ordeal of Dr. Mudd, The 1980 ★★★★ Weaver is outstanding as doctor who innocently treated injured Booth after Lincoln's assassination, then was imprisoned for conspiracy. Interesting, historical sidebar previously filmed as *Prisoner of Shark Island* and as *Hellgate.* C: Dennis Weaver, Susan Sullivan, Richard Dysart. D: Paul Wendkos. DRA 145m. TVM V

Ordeal of Patty Hearst, The 1979 ★★½ Off-the-mark film about kidnapped heiress turned terrorist focuses on FBI investigator (Weaver), instead of Hearst. C: Dennis Weaver, Lisa Eilbacher. D: Paul Wendkos. DRA 156m. TVM

Order of the Black Eagle 1987 ★★★ A high-tech genius finds himself battling vicious neo-Nazi thugs. C: Ian Hunter, Charles K. Bibby, William T. Hicks. D: Worth Keeter. ACT [R] 93m. V

Order of the Eagle 1988 ★★★ A young scout, happening onto a plane crash site, finds computer disks that involve him with international thugs. C: Frank Stallone. D: Thomas Baldwin. ACT 86m. V

Ordered to Love 1960 German ★★★ Weak WWII melodrama about Nazis experimenting on prisoners to breed superrace. C: Maria Perschy, Marisa Mell, Rosemarie Kirstein. D: Werner Klinger. DRA 82m.

Orders Are Orders 1954 British ★★★½ Mild British farce has movie company based at Army camp, with predictable results. Early Sellers at work makes this passable. C: Margot Grahame, Maureen Swanson, Peter Sellers. D: David Paltenghi. COM 78m.

Orders Is Orders 1934 British ★★★★ An obnoxious American director (Gleason) creates havoc for the British army as he tries to make a military drama using real soldiers. Genuinely funny, thanks to Gleason's performance as the "ugly American." Remade in 1954 as *Orders Are Orders.* C: Charlotte Greenwood, James Gleason, Finlay Currie. D: Walter Forde. COM 62m.

Orders, The 1977 Canadian ★★★★ Based-on-fact drama from documentary maker Brault deals with imposition of police state and police abuses in Canada after the radical Liberation Front of Quebec takes hostages. Thoughtful cautionary tale. C: Jean Lapointe, Helene Loiselle, Claude Gauthier. D: Michael Brault. DRA 107m.

Orders to Kill 1958 British ★★★★ Superior WWII spy drama with American Massie sent to Paris to terminate Resistance traitor Albert. Builds suspense admirably. C: Eddie Albert, Paul Massie, Lillian Gish. D: Anthony Asquith. DRA 93m.

Ordet 1955 Danish ★★★★½ Romeo and Juliet from a religious perspective; two French country families clash over their children's romance. Beautiful, deeply moving study of intolerance with shattering climax. C: Henrik Melberg, Emil Hass, Christensen Preben. D: Carl Dreyer. DRA 125m. V

Ordinary Heros 1985 ★★★ Just bfore his departure from Vietnam, a young solider is ambushed and loses his sight. Okay soap opera treatment of a tough subject. C: Doris Roberts, Valerie Bertinelli, Richard Baxter. D: Peter H. Cooper. DRA 105m. TVM V

Ordinary Magic 1993 ★★★ Considered different, a young boy makes friends with a basketball star and a cheerleader—for a most happy ending and proof that being different isn't necessarily bad. C: Glenne Headly, David Fox. ACT 90m. V

Ordinary People 1980 ★★★★★ Redford's directorial debut is sensitive adaptation of Judith Guest's best-selling novel, about reserved WASP family slowly imploding in the wake of a recent tragedy. Strong cast, led by Oscar-winner Hutton as troubled teen. Also Oscar for Best Picture, Director, and Screenplay. C: Mary Tyler Moore, Donald Sutherland, Timothy Hutton, Judd Hirsch, Elizabeth McGovern. D: Robert Redford. DRA [R] 124m. V

Oregon Passage 1957 ★★★ Tame Western with well-intentioned cavalry officer Ericson having Indian troubles. C: John Ericson, Lola Albright, Edward Platt. D: Paul Landres. WST 82m.

Oregon Trail, The 1959 ★★★ Journalist MacMurray covers Indian attacks in 19th-century Oregon. Strictly routine. C: Fred MacMurray, William Bishop, Nina Shipman. D: Gene Fowler Jr. WST 86m.

Oregon Trail, The 1976 ★★★½ TV pilot of pioneer family heading to promised homestead benefits from strong cast; script is familiar. C: Rod Taylor, Blair Brown. D: Boris Sagal. WST 110m. TVM

Orfeo Ed Euridice 1991 ★★★ Gluck's rarely performed opera about a singer travelling to hell to rescue his beloved is modernized with Orpheus now a Presley-like, leather-clad rocker. C: Jochen Kowalski, Gillian Webster. MUS 80m. V

Organization, The 1971 ★★★★ Poitier plays the role of Detective Tibbs from *In the Heat of the Night* for the third and last time. Well-drawn action and good acting in standard tale of cops and vigilantes at war with the narcotics trade. C: Sidney Poitier, Barbara McNair, Sheree North. D: Don Medford. CRI [PG] 107m. V

Organizer, The 1963 Italian ★★★★½ Italian textile workers organize and strike, led by university professor Mastroianni in one of his most compelling performances. Gripping from start to finish. C: Marcello Mastroianni, Annie Girardot, Renato Salvatori. D: Mario Monicelli. DRA 126m.

Orgasmo 1969 *See* **Paranoia**

Oriane 1985 Spanish ★★★ When her aunt dies, a Venezuelan woman returns home from a sojourn in France, and finds herself remembering past experiences of incest. Interesting; well done. C: Doris Wells, Deniela Sliverio, Philippe Rouleau, David Crotto. D: Fina Torres. DRA 88m. V

Origin Of The Lone Ranger, The 1949 ★★★★ Three episodes from the TV series, including the very first one in which the legend of the Lone Ranger is established. C: Clayton Moore, Jay Silverheels, Glenn Strange. WST 75m. V

Original "Dragnet" 1 1953 ★★★ Four classic shows from the original Jack Webb "Dragnet" program, including "The Big Shoplift," "The Big Bank Robbery," "The Big Hit and Run," and "The Big Secret." C: Jack Webb, Ben Alexander. ACT 105m. V

Original Intent 1992 ★★★ A successful lawyer decides to defend a condemned shelter for the homeless—at a great personal cost. C: Kris Kristofferson, Martin Sheen, Candy Clark. D: Robert Marcarelli. DRA [PG] 97m. V

Original Sin 1989 ★★★ Shallow drama has Jillian discovering that father-in-law Heston is Mob king and may have kidnapped her son. DRA

Orion's Belt 1987 Swedish ★★★ A trio of Norwegian adventurers stumble upon a secret Soviet military installation that may threaten their own way of life. C: Helge Jordal, Sverre Anker Ousdal, Hans Ola Sorlie. D: Ola Solum. DRA [PG] 87m. V

Orlando 1993 British ★★★★½ Sprightly, stylish meditation on the nature of gender, based on Virginia Woolf's novel about a young man who lives through several centuries of English history, later as a young woman. Swinton is delightful and knowing, and the film is glorious to look at. C: Tilda Swinton, Billy Zane, Quentin Crisp. D: Sally Potter. DRA [PG-13] 93m. V

Orphan Train, The 1979 ★★★★ Social worker and newspaper photographer lead group of orphans from Manhattan to new home in 19th-century American West. Good period drama marked by good acting and attention to detail. Fine family viewing. C: Jill Eikenberry, Kevin Dobson, Linda Manz. D: William Graham. FAM/DRA 144m. TVM V

Orphans 1987 ★★★★ Hustler Modine brings drunk Finney home, planning to rob him. Instead, Finney takes control of both him and his brother (Anderson). Three brilliant performances in interesting though flawed version of Lyle Kessler play. C: Albert Finney, Matthew Modine, Kevin Anderson. D: Alan J. Pakula. DRA [R] 116m. V

Orphans of the Storm 1921 ★★★★★ Silent epic masterpiece, set at the dawn of the French Revolution, is one of Griffith's finest. The Gishes are Parisian sisters, one of them blind, who were separated at birth. Melodramatic plot, superb performances, and thrilling situations. Highlight: Lillian on the balcony, with Dorothy below, singing. Based on *The Two Orphans*, a 19th-century French play. Also filmed in 1915, 1933, and 1955. C: Lillian Gish, Dorothy Gish, Joseph Schildkraut, Lucille LaVerne. D: D.W. Griffith. DRA 127m. V

Orphans of the Street 1939 ★★★½ What a premise! Orphaned Ryan is booted out of military school, becomes a runaway, then has his trusty dog Ace (played by Skippy) accused of murder! Don't worry, kids, the dog avoids the chair. Lots of fun. C: Tommy Ryan, Robert Livingston, June Storey, Harry Davenport. D: John H. Auer. FAM/DRA 64m.

Orpheus 1949 French ★★★★½ Cocteau's brilliant retelling of the Greek classic in modern France, with unforgettable surreal and poetic imagery. A poet (Marais) joins the "Princess of Death" (Casares) to bring a dead friend back to life. C: Jean Marais, Francois Perier, Maria Casares. D: Jean Cocteau. DRA 95m. V

Orpheus Descending 1990 ★★★★ Italian immigrant Redgrave, married to a small-town Southern invalid, succumbs to drifter Anderson's passion in second superior filming of Tennessee Williams' play (first was *The Fugitive Kind*). Overheated drama but with gutsy, brilliant Redgrave performance. C: Vanessa Redgrave, Kevin Anderson. D: Peter Hall. DRA 117m. TVM V

Orson Welles' Ghost Story 1952 ★★★½ Welles narrates and helped to produce this short supernatural tale, in which a motorist tells of an encounter with mother-and-daughter spirits. Has its moments, but it's of more historical than dramatic interest. C: Orson Welles, Michael Laurence. D: Hilton Edwards. HOR 23m.

Osaka Elegy 1936 Japanese ★★★½ Sad story of a woman condemned and isolated for behavior that would be quite normal indeed if carried out by a man. C: Issuzu Yamada, Kensaku Hara, Eitaro Shindo. D: Kenji Mizoguchi. DRA 75m. V

Oscar 1991 ★★ Stallone, painfully cast against type, plays a gangster who tries—despite the efforts of thugs who surround him—to go legit. Lots of comic cameos (Douglas as his father stands out) and slam-bang pacing compensate pretty well for Stallone's bland performance. C: Sylvester

Stallone, Ornella Muti, Don Ameche, Peter Riegert, Tim Curry. D: John Landis. COM [PG] 109m. V

Oscar, The 1966 ★★ Heartless actor (Boyd) will do anything to win an Academy Award. Hackneyed drama: so bad, it's funny. Singer Bennett actually gives the best performance. Source of the immortal quote: "When you sleep with pigs, you wind up smelling like garbage." C: Stephen Boyd, Elke Sommer, Eleanor Parker, Tony Bennett, Milton Berle, Jill St. John, Ernest Borgnine, Edie Adams. D: Russell Rouse. DRA 119m. V

Oscar Wilde 1960 British ★★★★ Morley does fine job as playwright/novelist and epigrammatist, Wilde, imprisoned for sodomy after sensational trial. Fairly candid film admirably captures his essence. C: Robert Morley, Phyllis Calvert, John Neville, Ralph Richardson. D: Gregory Ratoff. DRA 96m.

O'Shaughnessy's Boy 1935 ★★★★ Terrific re-teaming of Beery and Cooper (*The Champ*) casts the former as a washed-up circus animal trainer trying for reconciliation with the son who was taken from him years ago. Spanky plays Jackie as a toddler. C: Wallace Beery, Jackie Cooper, Spanky McFarland, Sara Haden. D: Richard Boleslawski. DRA 88m.

O.S.S. 1946 ★★★★ Office of Strategic Services agents led by screen idol Ladd, with Fitzgerald as sole female, aim to help Allies by gathering information in war-torn France to use against Nazis. Exciting, engaging spy thriller. C: Alan Ladd, Geraldine Fitzgerald, Patric Knowles. D: Irving Pichel. ACT 107m.

Ossessione 1942 Italian ★★★★★ Magnificent wartime romance, based on James M. Cain's *The Postman Always Rings Twice* (though without permission). Girotti and Calamai fall passionately in love, their only obstacle being her husband. Visconti virtually created neorealism with this influential film. C: Massimo Girotti, Clara Calamai, Juan deLanda. D: Luchino Visconti. DRA 140m. V

Osterman Weekend, The 1983 ★★★½ A TV personality is exploited by the CIA to set up buddies who are said to be KGB members. Impressive cast in Peckinpah's final film, but story is confusing at times. Based on Robert Ludlum's novel. C: Rutger Hauer, John Hurt, Craig T. Nelson, Dennis Hopper. D: Sam Peckinpah. ACT [R] 102m. V

Otello 1982 ★★★★ A rousing, spirited rendition of Verdi's classic opera, delivered by some extraordinary talents. C: Kiri Te Kanawa, Vladimir Atlantov, Piero Cappuccilli. MUS 145m. V

Otello 1987 Italian ★★★★ Shakespeare's classic tale of the tragic Moor destroyed by his own jealousy. Domingo et al are wonderful; a real treat for opera fans. C: Placido Domingo, Katia Ricciarelli, Justino Diaz. D: Franco Zeffirelli. MUS [PG] 123m. V

Otets Soldata 1966 *See* **Father of a Soldier**

Othello 1952 Italian ★★★★ Shakespeare via Welles. Compelling, often brilliant; made over a period of four years in numerous venues. C: Orson Welles, Michael MacLiammoir, Suzanne Cloutier, Robert Coote. D: Orson Welles. DRA 93m. V

Othello 1965 British ★★★★★ Exciting, magnificently cinematic adaptation of Shakespeare's tragedy with Olivier thrilling as the Moor of Venice, wrongly convinced that his innocent wife Desdemona (Smith) is unfaithful. Flawless supporting cast. C: Laurence Olivier, Frank Finlay, Maggie Smith, Joyce Redman, Derek Jacobi. D: Stuart Burge. DRA 166m.

Other Love, The 1947 ★★★½ Stanwyck wrings every tear out of soaper about terminally ill pianist throwing her last days away on wild times, while good doctor Niven loves her from afar. C: Barbara Stanwyck, David Niven, Richard Conte, Maria Palmer. D: Andre deToth. DRA 95m.

Other Lover, The 1985 ★★½ Married publisher Wagner has affair with author Scalia. C: Jack Scalia, Lindsay Wagner. D: Robert Ellis Miller. DRA 96m.

Other Man, The 1970 ★★★½ Neglected wife Hackett falls for gigolo Thinnes. The ever-underrated Hackett makes otherwise trite romance watchable. C: Roy Thinnes, Joan Hackett, Arthur Hill. D: Richard Colla. DRA 99m. TVM

Other Men's Women 1931 ★★★★ Railroad workers Withers and Toomey are best pals, one of whom covets his friend's wife, well-played by Astor. Effective melodrama seethes with pre-Code passions. Cagney and Blondell shine as comic relief. C: Grant Withers, Mary Astor, Regis Toomey, James Cagney, Joan Blondell. D: William Wellman. DRA 70m.

Other People's Money 1991 ★★★★ A zealous Wall Street magnate (DeVito) sets his sights on Peck's small cable and wire firm. But DeVito's slasher tactics are rendered bloodless when he faces Peck's attorney—and daughter—Miller. DeVito steals the show, in a nasty-edged comic tour de farce, adapted from the Jerry Sterner play. C: Danny DeVito, Penelope Ann Miller, Gregory Peck, Piper Laurie, Dean Jones. D: Norman Jewison. COM [R] 101m. V

Other Side of Hell, The 1978 ★★★½ Arkin goes over the top in grim tale of mental patient struggling to be released. C: Alan Arkin, Roger E. Mosley, Morgan Woodward. D: Jan Kadar. DRA 156m. TVM

Other Side of Midnight, The 1977 ★★ A woman (Pisier) uses her guile to rise to top of Hollywood system while planning revenge on the man who seduced her in this Sidney Sheldon drama encompassing eight years, between 1939 and 1947. Sheldon fans may enjoy it. C: Marie-France Pisier, John Beck, Susan Sarandon, Raf Vallone. D: Charles Jarrott. DRA [R] 104m. V

Other Side of Paradise, The 1976 *See* **Foxtrot**

Other Side of the Mountain, The 1975 ★★★½ The true story of Jill Kinmont (Hassett), an outstanding skier with Olympic aspirations until she is paralyzed in a tragic accident. A solid, workmanlike tearjerker. C: Marilyn Hassett, Beau Bridges. D: Larry Peerce. DRA [PG] 102m. v

Other Side of the Mountain (Part 2), The 1978 ★★★½ A continuation of the Jill Kinmont story. After coming to terms with her paralysis, the former skier becomes a teacher and finds love. C: Marilyn Hassett, Timothy Bottoms, Nan Martin. D: Larry Peerce. DRA [PG] 99m. v

Other, The 1972 ★★★★ Thomas Tryon adapted his own novel about twin boys, one seemingly good and the other evil. Deceptively pleasant at first, but builds layer upon layer of tension until a disturbing, blood-freezing finale. C: Uta Hagen, Diana Muldaur, Chris Udvarnoky, Martin Udvarnoky. D: Robert Mulligan. HOR [PG] 100m. v

Other Tomorrow, The 1930 ★★★★ Passionate pairing of Dove and Withers is thwarted by Dove's nasty, jealous husband (Thomson). Dove breathes life into her character and the film. Very effective. C: Billie Dove, Kenneth Thomson, Grant Withers. D: Lloyd Bacon. DRA 64m.

Other Victim, The 1981 ★★★★ Unusual rape theme focusing on the anguish of the victim's husband as he tries to recover some sort of normal life. Devane delivers authentic performance of character with deeply conflicting emotions. C: William Devane, Jennifer O'Neill. D: Noel Black. DRA 96m. TVM

Other Woman, The 1992 ★★ A reporter, suspecting her husband is fooling around, confronts the other woman and finds herself irresistibly attracted to her. Best for fans of Zmed. C: Adrian Zmed, Lee Anne Beaman, Daniel Moriarity. D: Jag Mundhra. CRI [R] 90m. v

Otley 1969 British ★★★ Limp secret agent spoof with Courtenay as bumbling burglar mixed up with spy Schneider. C: Tom Courtenay, Romy Schneider, Alan Badel, James Villiers. D: Dick Clement. COM [PG] 90m.

Our Betters 1933 ★★★½ Amusing trifle from Somerset Maugham is a drawing-room comedy about rich American (Bennett) who marries English lord (Roland). C: Constance Bennett, Gilbert Roland, Charles Starrett, Anita Louise. D: George Cukor. COM 83m.

Our Blushing Brides 1930 ★★★½ Risqué drama with Crawford in typical role of sensible shop assistant seeking rich husband. Star brings vitality to unoriginal plot. C: Joan Crawford, Anita Page, Dorothy Sebastian, Robert Montgomery. D: Harry Beaumont. COM 74m.

Our Daily Bread 1934 ★★★★ Depression era farmers form a successful commune in this populist classic. C: Karen Morley, Tom Keene, John Qualen. D: King Vidor. DRA 74m. v

Our Dancing Daughters 1928 ★★★★ Vivacious Joan dominates definitive Roaring '20s silent as flapper who loses her man to Page, who doesn't want him. Full of party scenes, champagne, and Charlestons. C: Joan Crawford, Johnny Mack Brown, Dorothy Sebastian, Nils Asther, Anita Page. D: Harry Beaumont. DRA 97m. v

Our Family Business 1981 ★★★ Mafia drama covers familiar ground, doesn't say anything new but has some good performances. Was pilot for TV series. C: Sam Wanamaker, Vera Miles, Ray Milland, Ted Danson. D: Robert Collins. DRA 73m. TVM v

Our Father 1985 Spanish ★★★ Spanish cardinal (Rey) leaves Rome for his hometown after a 30-year absence and finds his illegitimate daughter has had a daughter of her own, now entangled with Rey's Marxist brother (Rabal). Fairly grim comedy has ax to grind with Catholicism but meanders too much to be effective. C: Fernando Rey, Francisco Rabal, Victoria Abril, Emma Penella, Amelia de la Torre, Rafaela Aparicio, Lina Canalejas. D: Francisco Regueiro. COM 104m. TVM

Our Gang 1926 ★★★★ 2 of "Our Gang's" classic short films, including "Thundering Fleas" and "Shivering Spooks." Lots of fun for kids and nostalgia for parents. C: Little Rascals. FAM/COM 57m. v

Our Gang Comedies 1939 ★★★ All those loveable little rascals are here, including Spanky, Alfalfa, Buckwheat, Darla and the rest in a series of their funniest films. C: Little Rascals. FAM/COM 53m. v

Our Hearts Were Growing Up 1946 ★★★½ Okay sequel to *Our Hearts Were Young and Gay* with Russell and Lynn involved with bootleggers while at Princeton. C: Gail Russell, Diana Lynn, Brian Donlevy, William Demarest. D: William Russell. COM 83m.

Our Hearts Were Young and Gay 1944 ★★★★ Delightful comedy with Russell and Lynn well matched as chums touring Europe in the 1920s. Based on memoir by Cornelia Otis Skinner. C: Gail Russell, Diana Lynn, Charlie Ruggles, Dorothy Gish, Beulah Bondi. D: Lewis Allen. COM 81m.

Our Hitler 1980 German ★★★★ Unusual portrait of the Third Reich from the perspective of 1980 Germany. The seven-hour collage uses actors, puppets, and documentary footage. Will be spellbinding to some, pretentious to others. C: Heinz Schubert, Peter Kern, Hellmut Lange. D: Hans-Jurgen Syberberg. DOC 420m.

Our Hospitality 1923 ★★★★★ Divine silent comedy may be Keaton's best. Returning to Kentucky, Buster finds himself embroiled in Hatfield-McCoy-type feud between his family and his beloved's. Hysterically funny, with climactic sequence unparalleled in screen comedy. C: Buster Keaton, Natalie Talmadge, Joe Keaton. D: Buster Keaton, Jack Blystone. COM 75m. v

Our Little Girl 1935 ★★★½ While doctor (McCrea) works long hours, wife (Ames) is wooed by neighbor (Talbot). Leave it to perky little Shirley Temple to bring her parents back together. Standard Temple film, dripping with sentimental scenes. C: Shirley Temple, Rosemary Ames, Joel McCrea. D: John J. Robertson. FAM/DRA 65m. v

Our Man Flint 1966 ★★★½ Spoofing James Bond (who spoofs himself pretty well), Coburn is wry title character who stops global conspiracy to control weather. Enjoyable, but never quite as much fun as Coburn seems to be having. Sequel: *In Like Flint.* C: James Coburn, Lee J. Cobb, Gila Golan. D: Daniel Mann. ACT 107m. v

Our Man Flint: Dead on Target 1976 ★★★ Unnecessary revival of James Bond spoof with Danton as lascivious secret agent who'd rather knock off a bottle of champagne than an enemy spy. C: Ray Danton, Sharon Acker. D: Joseph Scanlon. ACT 78m.

Our Man in Havana 1960 British ★★★★ Vacuum cleaner salesman is drafted to spy for his country but nobody tells him how to do it. Uneasy mix of comedy and drama from Graham Greene novel, with Sir Alec in typical top form. C: Alec Guinness, Burl Ives, Maureen O'Hara, Ernie Kovacs, Noel Coward, Ralph Richardson. D: Carol Reed. COM 107m.

Our Man in Marrakesh 1966 *See* **Bang, Bang, You're Dead!**

Our Men in Bagdad 1967 Italian ★★ Cheapo Middle Eastern spy drama with indecipherable plot. C: Rory Calhourn, Roger Hanin, Evi Marandi. D: Paolo Bianchini. DRA 100m.

Our Miss Brooks 1956 ★★★½ Film version of popular TV series gives schoolteacher Arden a love interest (Rockwell) while principal Gordon glowers from the sidelines. Eve is good in a rare leading role. C: Eve Arden, Gale Gordon, Nick Adams, Richard Crenna. D: Al Lewis. COM 85m.

Our Modern Maidens 1929 ★★★½ Sequel to *Our Dancing Daughters* gives fairly risqué look at "modern" relationships as newlyweds Crawford and Fairbanks discover each other's *other* romantic entanglements. Wonderful Art Deco sets give just the right air of formal decadence. C: Joan Crawford, Anita Paige, Douglas Fairbanks, Jr., Rod Larocque. D: Jack Conway. DRA 75m. v

Our Mother's House 1967 British ★★★★ Sensitive drama with children deciding to conceal their mother's death and care for themselves. Then deadbeat father Bogarde shows up. Quirky, insightful, and well acted. C: Dirk Bogarde, Margaret Brooks, Louis Williams. D: Jack Clayton. DRA 105m.

Our Relations 1936 ★★★★ Funny domestic comedy steals its plot from Shakespeare's *Comedy of Errors* as Laurel and Hardy play two sets of twins, one pair sailors, the other henpecked husbands. Lots of mistaken identity twists and slapstick. C: Stan Laurel, Oliver Hardy, Alan Hale, Sidney Toler. D: Harry Lachman. COM 94m. v

Our Silent Love 1969 Japanese ★★★★ Remarkable, poetic drama of hearing-impaired lovers who find little compassion from the woman's father, who looks disfavorably on their relationship and disability. C: Kinya Kitaoji, Keiju Kobayashi. D: Zenzo Matsuyama. DRA

Our Sons 1991 ★★★½ Glossy AIDS drama with stars as mothers of gay couple who meet when one son becomes ill. Julie is fine as a noble parent, but coarse, bigoted, beer-guzzler Ann-Margret walks away with the movie. Some moving, on-target scenes; others simply clichéd. C: Julie Andrews, Ann-Margret, Hugh Grant, Zeljko Ivanek. D: John Erman. DRA 100m. TVM

Our Time 1974 ★★★ Standard coming of age story with Martin and Stevenson in 1950s college romance. (a.k.a. *Death of Her Innocence*) C: Pamela Sue Martin, Parker Stevenson, Betsy Slade. D: Peter Hyams. DRA [PG] 91m. v

Our Town 1940 ★★★★½ The life, times, and people of early-1900s Grover's Corners, New Hampshire. Wilder's Pulitzer Prize-winning play is given a wonderfully poignant treatment, with beautiful Copland music and an exquisite cast. C: William Holden, Martha Scott, Frank Craven, Fay Bainter, Beulah Bondi, Thomas Mitchell. D: Sam Wood. DRA 86m. v

Our Town 1977 ★★★½ TV adaptation of Thornton Wilder's Pulitzer Prize-winning play about the ordinary world of Grover's Corners, New Hampshire. Skillful, well-cast version of the classic drama. C: Ned Beatty, Sada Thompson, Ronny Cox, Robby Benson. D: Franklin Schaffer. DRA 120m. TVM

Our Very Own 1950 ★★★½ Uplifting drama of Blyth discovering she's adopted. Tame today, but sensitively acted. C: Ann Blyth, Farley Granger, Jane Wyatt, Ann Dvorak, Natalie Wood. D: David Miller. DRA 93m.

Our Vines Have Tender Grapes 1945 ★★★★ Affecting story of human devotion among Norwegian farmers in a small Wisconsin town. Kindhearted family movie avoids corniness. Robinson plays against type as compassionate father. C: Edward G. Robinson, Margaret O'Brien, James Craig, Agnes Moorehead. D: Roy Rowland. DRA 106m. v

Our Wife 1941 ★★★½ Drawn-out comedy with Douglas as trumpeter trying to divorce Hussey to marry Drew. Two leads spar well. C: Melvyn Douglas, Ruth Hussey, Ellen Drew, Charles Coburn. D: John Stahl. COM 95m.

Our Winning Season 1978 ★★★ Standard teen drama with track star Jacoby competing for scholarship. C: Scott Jacoby, Deborah Benson, Dennis Quaid. D: Joseph Ruben. DRA [PG] 92m.

Out 1982 ★★★½ Oddball road movie has

hitchhiking Coyote seeking to discover America. The different people he encounters seem familiar—they're played by same cast members. Sometimes diverting, sometimes pretentious. C: Peter Coyote, O-Lan Shepard, Danny Glover. D: Eli Hollander. DRA 88m. V

Out All Night 1933 ★★★½ Okay B-comedy with irrepressible ZaSu as Slim's intended trying to win over his battleaxe mother, Crews. C: ZaSu Pitts, Slim Summerville, Laura Hope Crews, Shirley Temple. D: Sam Taylor. COM 68m.

Out Cold 1989 ★★★½ Timid butcher Lithgow thinks he's murdered his partner by locking him in the freezer; guilty Garr takes advantage. Poorly written black comedy; terrific cast almost pulls it off. C: John Lithgow, Teri Garr, Randy Quaid, Bruce McGill. D: Malcolm Mowbray. COM [R] 91m. V

Out For Blood 1993 ★★★ When an attorney's family is murdered by drug dealers, he takes vengeance into his own hands. C: Don Wilson, Shari Shattuck, Michael De Lano. D: Richard W. Munchkin. ACT [R] 90m. V

Out for Justice 1991 ★★½ Typical Seagal flick where violent action overwhelms interesting story elements. Brooklyn thug (Forsythe) goes ballistic and both the Mob and a streetwise cop (Seagal) chase after him. C: Steven Seagal, William Forsythe, Jerry Orbach, Jo Champa. D: John Flynn. CRI [R] 91m. V

Out of Africa 1985 ★★★★★ An unhappily married Danish woman (Streep) goes with her husband (Brandauer) to Africa. There she falls for an English adventurer (Redford). Excellent period piece portrays unusual human landscape. Oscar winner for Best Picture, Director, Screenplay, Cinematography and John Barry's beautiful, sweeping Musical Score. Loosely based on the life and works of Isak Dinesen. C: Meryl Streep, Robert Redford, Klaus Maria Brandauer. D: Sydney Pollack. DRA [PG] 161m. V

Out of Bounds 1986 ★★ Odd attempt to recast Hall as an action star; he's a guy from the sticks who picks up the wrong bag at L.A. airport and winds up on the run from both drug dealers and the cops. C: Anthony Michael Hall, Jenny Wright, Jeff Kober, Glynn Turman. D: Richard Tuggle. ACT [R] 93m. V

Out of Control 1985 ★ When plane crash strands group of teenagers on remote island it's party time . . . until they encounter local bad guys. Insultingly stupid. C: Martin Mull, Betsy Russell, Claudia Udy. D: Allan Holzman. ACT [R] 78m. V

Out of Darkness 1994 ★★★½ Ross gives a moving performance as a woman recovering from schizophrenia in this episodic, disease-of-the-week movie. The supporting cast is also good, though the script and direction are a bit unfocused. C: Diana Ross, Ann Weldon, Rhonda Stubbins. D: Larry Elikann. DRA 120m. TVM

Out of It 1969 ★★★½ High school comedy about a brain (Gordon) who decides to take on the class jock (Voight). Funny complications ensue. C: Barry Gordon, Jon Voight. D: Paul Williams. COM [PG] 95m.

Out of Order 1984 ★★★ Trapped in an elevator late Friday afternoon, four office workers set about to escape. C: Renee Soutendijk, Gotz George, Wolfgang Kieling. D: Carl Schenkel. ACT [PG] 87m. V

Out of Season 1975 British ★★ A woman and her teenage daughter find themselves vying for the attentions of the woman's old lover—who may be the daughter's father. Dark-toned drama flirts with some provocative ideas. (a.k.a. *Winter Rates*) C: Vanessa Redgrave, Cliff Robertson, Susan George. D: Alan Bridges. DRA [R] 90m. V

Out of Sight 1966 ★★½ Rock 'n' roll comedy thriller, about an unlikely duo who take on agents out to sabotage a music festival. Several real-life rockers even show up. Cartoonish approach is no surprise from animation veteran Weinrib. C: Jonathan Daly, Karen Jensen, Robert Pine. D: Lennie Weinrib. MUS 87m.

Out Of Sight, Out Of Mind 1990 ★★½ Long after seeing her daughter burned alive, a woman "sees" her daughter alive again. C: Susan Blakely, Wings Hauser, Edward Albert. D: Greydon Clark. HOR [R] 94m. V

Out of the Blue 1947 ★★★½ Entertaining lightweight comedy about happily married Brent, who finds himself with an unconscious woman in his apartment and tries to get rid of the "body." The resulting complications are funny and the cast is bright. C: Virginia Mayo, George Brent, Turhan Bey, Ann Dvorak, Carole Landis. D: Leigh Jason. COM [R] 84m. V

Out of the Blue 1980 ★★★★ Sober, downbeat story of an ex-con (Hopper) returning to his wife (Farrell) and rebellious teen daughter (Manz); discord and tragedy, not reconciliation, follow. Intense and affecting, though not for all tastes; Manz is exceptional. C: Linda Manz, Sharon Farrell, Dennis Hopper, Raymond Burr. D: Dennis Hopper. DRA 94m. V

Out Of The Body 1988 ★★½ A man becomes possessed by a spirit that orders him to kill beautiful young women. C: Mark Hembrow, Tessa Humphries. D: Brian Trenchard-Smith. HOR [R] 91m. V

Out of the Dark 1989 ★★★ Phone-sex women are being slaughtered by a clown-masked fiend in this thriller, which has a fun supporting cast and some well-handled moments (especially the first murder). C: Cameron Dye, Lynn Danielson, Tracey Walter, Karen Black, Bud Cort. D: Michael Schroeder. HOR [R] 89m. V

Out of the Darkness 1979 *See* **Night Creature** TVM

Out of the Darkness 1985 ★★★★ Much better than average TV drama about Eddie

Zigo the New York cop who sought and apprehended the infamous Son of Sam. Sheen is intense as the relentless detective. C: Martin Sheen, Hector Elizondo, Matt Clark, Jennifer Salt. D: Jud Taylor. CRI [R] 96m. TVM V

Out of the Fog 1941 ★★★★ Garfield heads a strong cast as a mobster terrorizing innocent fishermen, all the while falling for the daughter of one of his victims, in this atmospheric adaptation of Irwin Shaw's play *The Gentle People.* C: Ida Lupino, John Garfield, Thomas Mitchell, Eddie Albert, Aline MacMahon. D: Anatole Litvak. CRI 93m.

Out of the Past 1947 ★★★★½ Mitchum's a man with a past embroiled in murder and deceit at the hands of a reckless woman and a hood. Masterful brooding film noir with outstanding dialogue and an assured performance by Mitchum. Remade as *Against All Odds.* C: Robert Mitchum, Kirk Douglas, Jane Greer, Rhonda Fleming. D: Jacques Tourneur. CRI 97m. V

Out of the Rain 1990 ★★★ Man and woman vow to transcend small town's drug-induced decay. Passionate performances from leads. C: Bridget Fonda, Michael O'Keefe. D: Gary Winick. DRA [R] 91m. V

Out of the Shadows 1988 British ★★★ Light espionage romantic thriller, with Paul getting caught up with smugglers in Greece. Great scenery. C: Charles Dance, Alexandra Paul, Michael Shannon. D: Willi Patterson. ACT 105m. TVM

Out of This World 1945 ★★★½ All the girls fall for Bracken when he takes up crooning—no surprise, since his singing voice belongs to Bing Crosby. Amusing spoof of fans and stars, with several appearances by other notable singers of the period. C: Eddie Bracken, Veronica Lake, Diana Lynn, Cass Daley. D: Hal Walker. MUS 96m.

Out-of-Towners, The 1970 ★★★½ One disaster after another befalls a hapless Ohio couple (Lemmon and Dennis) on their first visit to NYC. Some truly funny bits, though it tends to bog down in relentlessness. C: Jack Lemmon, Sandy Dennis. D: Arthur Hiller. COM [G] 98m. V

Out on a Limb 1986 ★★★½ Actress MacLaine reflects on her romances and the influence meditation and reincarnation have on her life. The Oscar winner plays herself and she charms and informs. Based on MacLaine's best-seller. C: Shirley MacLaine, Charles Dance, John Heard, Anne Jackson, Jerry Orbach. D: Robert Butler. DRA 160m. V

Out on a Limb 1992 ★★ When his little sister gets in trouble, corporate exec Broderick comes to the rescue in her small hometown. Appealing cast is undone by a forgettable script. C: Matthew Broderick, Jeffrey Jones, Heidi Kling. D: Francis Veber. COM [PG] 83m. V

Out On Bail 1989 ★★★ When a drifter sees a murder committed in a diner, he joins the sheriff in trying to nab the killers. C: Robert Ginty, Kathy Shower, Tom Badal. D: Gordon Hessler. DRA [R] 102m. V

Out West with the Hardys 1938 ★★★½ Andy Hardy and family venture out to sagebrush country to help out a friend and encounter many of the same situations as they do back home. Gently amusing entry in the series, and one of the most popular. C: Lewis Stone, Mickey Rooney, Cecilia Parker, Fay Holden, Ann Rutherford. D: George Seitz. COM 90m.

Outback 1971 ★★★★ Repressed Australian schoolteacher (Bond) degenerates under toughs' influence in the Outback. Interesting character study with some pungent dialogue. (a.k.a. *Wake in Fright*) C: Gary Bond, Donald Pleasence, Chips Rafferty, Sylvia Kay. D: Ted Kotcheff. DRA [R] 99m.

Outback Bound 1988 ★★★ Routine comedy with Californian Mills roughing it in Australian wilderness seeking inherited opal mine. COM

Outbreak 1995 ★★★ Disappointing scientific thriller about the spread of a deadly virus and ex-married researchers's (Hoffman, Russo) efforts to stop it. Treatment of topical subject matter resembles *Jaws* more than *China Syndrome*, to its detriment. C: Dustin Hoffman, Rene Russo, Morgan Freeman, Cuba Gooding Jr., Donald Sutherland, Kevin Spacey. D: Wolfgang Petersen. SFI [R] 125m. V

Outcast 1937 ★★★★ Potent drama casts William as doctor cleared of woman's accidental death, but her sister-in-law won't let it rest, following him to new town. Effective meditation on justice, revenge and mob rule. C: Warren William, Karen Morley, Lewis Stone. D: Robert Florey. DRA 77m.

Outcast of the Islands 1951 British ★★★★½ Howard is a British trader assigned to a tropical island where he falls for a native woman (Kerima). Rejecting society's mores, he sets up a tyrannical rule of his own. Dark drama based on a Joseph Conrad story, intelligently handled by director Reed. C: Ralph Richardson, Trevor Howard, Robert Morley, Wendy Hiller. D: Carol Reed. DRA 102m.

Outcast, The 1953 ★★★½ Fastpaced Western of Derek claiming his inheritance, and opposed by his uncle. C: John Derek, Joan Evans, Jim Davis. D: William Witney. WST 90m. V

Outcast, The 1962 Japanese ★★★★½ Trenchant comment on Japanese class struggle with Ichikawa as schoolteacher concealing his status. Beautifully directed, acted, with shattering climax. C: Shiho Fujimura, Hiroyuki Nagato. D: Kon Ichikawa. DRA 118m.

Outcast, The 1984 ★★½ The story of three brothers with a propensity for murder. C: Ben Dekker, Sandra Prinsloo. HOR 86m.

Outcasts of Poker Flat, The 1952 ★★★½

Four mining-town misfits are stranded in cabin during a snowstorm. Static, uninspired adaptation of Bret Harte story, with some flashy acting by the women. C: Anne Baxter, Miriam Hopkins, Dale Robertson, Cameron Mitchell. D: Joseph Newman. DRA 81m.

Outcasts of the City 1958 ★★★ Turgid war romance of Air Force pilot Hutton in love with German Palmer. C: Osa Massen, Robert Hutton, Maria Palmer. D: Boris Petroff. DRA 61m. V

Outcry, The 1957 Italian ★★★★½ Brilliant post-WWII story of oppositional villagers battling fascist murderers is told in the beautifully composed, emotional style of Italian neorealist cinema. (a.k.a. *Il Grido*) C: Steve Cochran, Alida Valli, Betsy Blair. D: Michelangelo Antonioni. DRA 115m. V

Outer Reach 1981 *See* **Spaced Out**

Outfit, The 1974 ★★★★ Duvall is professional thief forced out of retirement by Mafia hit on his brother in terrific cast of old film noir habitués, crisp direction, and terse and cool performances by Duvall, Baker. C: Robert Duvall, Karen Black, Joe Don Baker, Robert Ryan. D: John Flynn. CRI [PG] 103m.

Outing, The 1987 ★★★ For a lark, teens break into museum at night and incur the wrath of a 3,000-year-old genie. Interesting idea; standard treatment. C: Deborah Winters, James Huston, Danny Daniels. D: Tom Daley. HOR [R] 87m. V

Outland 1981 ★★★ Mediocre space Western borrows its plot from *High Noon* but smartest move was casting reliable Connery as a dogged future law officer who uncovers a criminal conspiracy at a Jupiter mining colony and faces interplanetary gunslingers. C: Sean Connery, Peter Boyle, Frances Sternhagen, James Sikking. D: Peter Hyams. SFI [R] 110m. V

Outlaw And His Wife, The 1917 ★★★½ After he commits a small crime, a farmer and his wife hide out in a remote corner of Iceland. A silent curiosity piece. C: Victor Sjostrom. D: Victor Ssjostrom. DRA 73m. V

Outlaw Blues 1977 ★★★½ Interesting exposé of the country-music business with Fonda as an ex-con whose hit prison song is stolen. Diverting. C: Peter Fonda, Susan St. James, John Crawford, James Callahan. D: Richard T. Heffron. DRA [PG] 101m. V

Outlaw Country 1949 ★★★½ Schizophrenic Western has Lash LaRue fighting himself in a dual role, as good-guy marshal and bad-guy counterfeiter. Great premise and fine execution. C: Lash LaRue, Al St. John, Dan White, House Peters, Jr. D: Ray Taylor. WST 72m.

Outlaw Deputy, The 1935 ★★★½ McCoy is a sheriff imprisoned for siding with bad guys in this effective Western a notch above others of its ilk. C: Tim McCoy, Nora Lane, Bud Osborne. D: Otto Brower. WST 55m.

Outlaw—Josey Wales, The 1976 ★★★★ Eastwood and Phil Kaufman co-directed this complex, classic Western with interesting parallels to Eastwood's later Oscar-winning film *Unforgiven*. Wales (Eastwood) is a farmer turned fugitive in the post-Civil War South who is chased by the law after he avenges the murder of his friends and family. Sequel, *The Return of Josey Wales*. C: Clint Eastwood, Chief Dan George, Sondra Locke. D: Clint Eastwood. WST [PG] 136m. V

Outlaw of Gor 1987 ★ Timid teacher is transported to the planet Gor (again), where he encounters power-mad soothsayer Palance and evil queen Denton. Sequel to *Gor* is even more unimaginative than the original. C: Urbano Barberini, Jack Palance, Rebecca Ferratti. D: John Cardos. ACT [PG-13] 90m. V

Outlaw Territory 1953 *See* **Hannah Lee**

Outlaw, The 1943 ★★★½ Russell stars in this infamous exploitative Western that's surprisingly entertaining. Old Billy the Kid tale holds interest till climactic gunfight, pausing regularly for close-ups of Jane in the hay. C: Jane Russell, Jack Beutel, Walter Huston, Thomas Mitchell. D: Howard Hughes. WST [G] 103m. V

Outlaw Women 1952 ★★★ Town of Las Mujeres is ruled by female gunfighters who keep all menfolk at a distance in this clever subversion of the typical testosterone-laced Western. Fun concept is not enough to sustain an entire film, though the wrap-up is worth a peek. C: Marie Windsor, Richard Rober, Alan Nixon. D: Ron Ormond. WST 76m. V

Outlaw's Daughter, The 1954 ★★½ Stagecoach is robbed and Ryan's accused because her father was a gunfighter. Motley B-Western. C: Bill Williams, Kelly Ryan, Jim Davis. D: Wesley Barry. WST 75m.

Outlaws Is Coming, The 1965 ★★★½ Moe, Larry, and Curley Joe meet Annie Oakley in silly Western comedy which will please Stooges fans. Their last feature. C: The Three Stooges, Adam West, Nancy Kovack, Mort Mills. D: Norman Maurer. COM 89m.

Outlaws of Texas 1950 ★★★ Clyde and Wilson go undercover as outlaws to nab cowhand crook Coates and her band of bank robbers. Competent Western but don't look for a lot of action. C: Whip Wilson, Andy Clyde, Phyllis Coates, Terry Frost. D: Thomas Carr. WST 56m.

Outlaws of the Prairie 1938 ★★★½ Cowpoke king Starrett wants to bust up a band of stagecoach hijackers, with Bob Noland and the Sons of the Pioneers along to provide musical accompaniment. Nicely realized, festive Western. C: Charles Starrett, Donald Grayson, Iris Meredith, Norman Willis. D: Sam Nelson. WST 56m.

Outlaw's Son 1957 ★★★ Outlaw Clark tries to reconcile with son he abandoned long ago.

Mediocre oater with streak of sentimentality. C: Dane Clark, Ben Cooper, Lori Nelson. D: Lesley Selander. WST 89m.

Outpost in Malaya 1952 British ★★★ Feuding marrieds Hawkins and Colbert duke it out at their rubber plantation in remotest Malaya, while the natives threaten rebellion. By-the-books colonial drama. Formerly titled *Planter's Wife.* C: Claudette Colbert, Jack Hawkins. D: Ken Annakin. DRA 88m.

Outpost in Morocco 1949 ★★★ Standard desert adventure, as Raft takes on Arab rebels while carrying on an affair with their leader's daughter. C: George Raft, Marie Windsor, Akim Tamiroff. D: Robert Florey. ACT 92m. V

Outrage 1973 ★★★ New family in a California suburb runs afoul of violent local teen gang until dad (Culp) decides he's mad as hell and isn't going to take it anymore. Variation on *Death Wish* theme has its disturbing moments. C: Robert Culp, Marlyn Mason. D: Richard Heffron. CRI 78m. TVM

Outrage 1986 ★★★★ The trial of a man (Preston) who admits to killing his daughter's murderer becomes an examination of the law itself. Strong courtroom drama, based on Henry Denker's novel, is confidently told, with a powerful cast. C: Robert Preston, Beau Bridges, Burgess Meredith. D: Walter Grauman. DRA 96m. TVM V

Outrage, The 1964 ★★★ Mexican bandit Newman (you read that right) rapes a woman and murders her husband—or did he? Witnesses' stories vary in this semiremake of the Japanese classic *Rashomon.* C: Paul Newman, Claire Bloom, Laurence Harvey, Edward G. Robinson, William Shatner, Albert Salmi. D: Martin Ritt. WST 97m.

Outrageous 1977 Canadian ★★★★ Gay Russell (a female impersonator—his scenes in drag are great) takes up with a pregnant schizophrenic in this funny and sympathetic look at societal outsiders, well acted by the two leads. Sequel *Too Outrageous* followed in 1987. C: Craig Russell, Hollis McLaren. D: Richard Benner. COM [R] 100m. V

Outrageous Fortune 1987 ★★★★ Saucy Midler and ladylike Long are struggling actresses who reluctantly team up to search for the man who tow-timed them both, and become friends along the way. Silly plot involving spies and conspiracies doesn't hinder the two stars, who work well together, attacking the material with comic gusto. C: Bette Midler, Shelley Long, Peter Coyote, Robert Prosky, George Carlin. D: Arthur Hiller. COM [R] 100m. V

Outside Chance 1978 ★★ Since his film *Jackson County Jail* became a cult movie, Miller remade it for TV. Mimieux repeats her role as a prison inmate who can't take the grief and escapes. C: Yvette Mimieux, Royce Applegate. D: Michael Miller. CRI 100m. TVM V

Outside Chance of Maximilian Glick, The 1988 Canadian ★★★★ Good kids' film set in the '60s, with Zylberman as a precocious youngster whose ambitions tend to clash with the traditions of his Jewish family. Nicely observed, with winning performances. C: Saul Rubinek, Jan Rubes. D: Allan Goldstein. FAM/DRA [G] 96m. V

Outside In 1972 ★★ Drama centers on young Larson, who comes home for his father's funeral after ducking the draft and winds up in hot water. (a.k.a. *Red, White, and Busted*) C: Darrell Larson, Heather Menzies, Dennis Olivieri. D: Allen Baron. DRA [R] 90m.

Outside Man, The 1973 ★★★ International cast in story of hired killer on the run from another hired killer. Lots to look at, but little to sink your teeth into. C: Jean-Louis Trintignant, Ann-Margret, Angie Dickinson, Roy Scheider. D: Jacques Deray. CRI [PG] 104m. V

Outside of Paradise 1938 ★★★½ Bandleader (Regan) inherits a castle and travels with his bandmates to Ireland to convert it into a nightclub. Enjoyable, with some snappy musical numbers. C: Phil Regan, Penny Singleton, Bert Gordon. D: John H. Auer. MUS 68m.

Outside the Wall 1950 ★★★½ Ex-con Basehart takes a job that leads him into contact with various shady characters; will he go back to his criminal ways? Well-played crime drama. C: Richard Basehart, Dorothy Hart, Marilyn Maxwell. D: Crane Wilbur. CRI 80m.

Outside These Walls 1939 ★★★½ Former prison newspaper editor (Whalen) tries his hand at the trade outside the Big House, fighting political corruption and other worldly vice. Whalen delivers stand-up performance in this deft drama. C: Michael Whalen, Dolores Costello, Virginia Weidler. D: Raymond B. McCarey. DRA 60m.

Outside Woman, The 1989 ★★★★ Well-made and (surprisingly) fact-based story of a woman (Gless) abandoning her boring Southern small-town existence to help some nice-guy convicts escape from jail. Fine cast and solid storytelling put this one over. C: Sharon Gless, Scott Glenn. D: Lou Antonio. DRA 100m. TVM V

Outsider, The 1949 ★★★★ Country youth Attenborough enters swanky British school that tests his loyalty to his humble background. Multitalented star delivers realistic turmoil of young adulthood. (a.k.a. *The Guinea Pig*) DRA

Outsider, The 1961 ★★★★ Curtis solidly plays true-life hero Ira Hamilton Hayes, a Native American who helped raise the American flag at Iwo Jima. Well-told, effective war drama. C: Tony Curtis, James Franciscus, Bruce Bennett. D: Delbert Mann. DRA 108m.

Outsider, The 1967 ★★★½ Pilot for the '60s series introduces McGavin as an ex-con who's hired as a detective to ferret out an embezzler. McGavin's offbeat character is the chief asset of this mystery. C: Darren McGavin, Anna Hagan, Edmond O'Brien. D: Michael Ritchie. CRI 98m. TVM

Outsider, The 1979 ★★★★ Absorbing drama about a young Irish-American who goes to Ireland expecting to help the IRA, only to find himself exploited for propaganda purposes there. Even-handed, unsentimental storytelling underpinned by evocative location filming (with Dublin doubling for Belfast). C: Craig Wasson, Patricia Quinn, Sterling Hayden. D: Tony Luraschi. DRA [R] 128m. TVM

Outsiders, The 1983 ★★★½ Heavy-handed but well-done telling of S.E. Hinton's novel is less an examination of class conflict among Southwestern youths in the late '60s than a loving homage to Stereophonic sound, Technicolor and CinemaScope. Cast comprises a Who's Who of young male leads of the late '80s. Followed by *Rumble Fish.* C: C. Thomas Howell, Matt Dillon, Ralph Macchio, Patrick Swayze, Rob Lowe, Diane Lane, Emilio Estevez, Tom Cruise, Tom Waits. D: Francis Ford Coppola. FAM/DRA [PG] 91m. V

Outtakes 1976 ★★ Forest Tucker serves as host for smug and smutty series of sketches. Tasteless, vulgar, immature, and amateurish—and those are the good qualities. Great for a bad-movie fest. C: Forrest Tucker. COM 75m. V

Outward Bound 1930 ★★★★ Title doesn't suggest the serious nature of this film, which deals with passengers on an oceanliner who discover that they may be in transit from this world to the next. Howard's first American role. Intriguing adaptation of Sutton Vane's play, remade as *Between Two Worlds* in 1944 and as *The Flight That Disappeared* in 1961. C: Leslie Howard, Douglas Fairbanks Jr., Helen Chandler, Beryl Mercer. D: Robert Milton. DRA 84m.

Over-Exposed 1956 ★★ Moore's a news photographer on the way up who gets involved in blackmail and other intrigue. Most interesting watching her rise to success. C: Cleo Moore, Richard Crenna, Isobel Elsom. D: Lewis Seiler. DRA 80m.

Over Her Dead Body 1991 ★★★½ A man is caught cheating by his wife—who also happens to be his lover's sister! (a.k.a. *Enid Is Sleeping*) C: Elizabeth Perkins, Judge Reinhold, Jeffrey Jones. D: Maurice Phillips. COM [R] 105m.

Over Indulgence 1987 ★★★½ In Kenya, British aristocrats live the good, colonial life—until a murder disrupts the community. C: Elliott Denholm, Holly Aird, Kathryn Pogson. D: Ross Devenish. DRA [R] 95m. V

Over My Dead Body 1942 ★★★½ Amusing vehicle for Berle, who's quite good as a struggling mystery writer who finds himself caught up in a real-life mystery—and on trial himself for murder. Fun plot twists keep the film moving. C: Milton Berle, Mary Hughes, Reginald Denny. D: Malcolm St. Clair. COM 68m.

Over She Goes 1937 British ★★★★ Wood is a retired vaudeville performer who becomes a lord and finds an old girlfriend (Kelly) anxious to reacquaint herself. Accomplished, disarmingly funny comedy. C: John Wood, Claire Luce, Laddie Cliff, Sally Gray, Stanley Lupino. D: Graham Cutts. COM 74m.

Over the Brooklyn Bridge 1983 ★★★ Ethnic comedy once again explores the clash between Jews and gentiles, focusing on restaurateur Gould, his girlfriend Hemingway, and assorted relatives. Saved by good performances. C: Elliott Gould, Margaux Hemingway, Sid Caesar, Shelley Winters. D: Menahem Golan. COM 108m. V

Over the Edge 1979 ★★★★ Dillon makes charismatic debut in troubling drama about parents' inability to connect with their alienated teenagers in a planned suburb. A frighteningly realistic portrayal of the way toward adolescent alienation and rebellion. C: Michael Kramer, Pamela Ludwig, Matt Dillon. D: Jonathan Kaplan. DRA [PG] 95m. V

Over the Hill 1931 ★★★★ Remake of 1920 drama stars silent screen great Marsh as a widow who winds up in the poorhouse. Marsh is magnificent, delivering an elegant performance complemented by artistic b&w photography. C: Mae Marsh, James Kirkwood, Joe Hachey, Tom Conlon. D: Henry King. DRA 87m.

Over-the-Hill Gang, The 1969 ★★★½ Amusing Western comedy, thanks mostly to old-timers in the cast, about former Texas Rangers who reunite to clean up their crime-ridden town. C: Walter Brennan, Pat O'Brien, Edgar Buchanan, Andy Devine, Jack Elam, Gypsy Rose Lee. D: Jean Yarbrough. COM 73m. TVM

Over-the-Hill Gang Rides Again, The 1970 ★★★½ Sequel finds the title group of aging Texas Rangers joined by Astaire as another down-and-outer who pulls himself together to save the day. His terrific performance sparks the whole thing. C: Walter Brennan, Fred Astaire, Edgar Buchanan, Andy Devine, Chill Wills. D: George McCowan. COM 73m. TVM

Over the Moon 1937 British ★★½ Good comic premise, of a young country woman becoming rich thanks to an inheritance, but squandering the money. Harmless fluff, with a great cast; shot in color, though there are some b&w prints. C: Merle Oberon, Rex Harrison, Ursula Jeans. D: Thornton Freeland, William Howard. COM 78m.

Over the Odds 1961 British ★★★½ Flamboyant comedy of Melvyn's estrangement from his wife and new love affair with Cannon, which is complicated by the appearance of his first wife's meddling, obnoxious mother. Silly, excessive fun. C: Marjorie

Rhodes, Glynn Melvyn, Cyril Smith, Esma Cannon. D: Michael Forlong. COM 65m. v

Over the Summer 1985 ★★★½ Sixteen-year-old Hunt spends the summer with her grandparents in their small Southern town in this rare coming-of-age drama told from a female perspective. An unusual film with a melancholy edge. C: Laura Hunt, West Johnson. D: Teresa Sparks. DRA 97m. v

Over the Top 1987 ★★ Trucker (Stallone) wants to win an arm wrestling championship and be with his estranged son. Sly sinks under weight of silly story. C: Sylvester Stallone, Robert Loggia, Susan Blakely. D: Menahem Golan. DRA [PG] 94m. v

Over 21 1945 ★★★★ Winning comedy, from Ruth Gordon play, about mature journalist (Knox) enlisting in army for research purposes, trying wife Dunne's patience. C: Alexander Knox, Irene Dunne, Charles Coburn, Lee Patrick. D: Charles Vidor. COM 102m.

Overboard 1987 ★★★★ Haughty Hawn falls overboard from her yacht and suffers amnesia; woodworker (Russell) pretends he's her husband and brings her home to his ragtag brood. Lighter-than-air star vehicle has great fun with unlikely setup; Hawn and Russell make a great comic duo. C: Goldie Hawn, Kurt Russell, Edward Herrmann, Katherine Helmond, Roddy McDowall. D: Garry Marshall. COM [PG] 112m. v

Overcoat, The 1959 Russian ★★★★½ Nikolai Gogol's story becomes a moving Russian production about a put-upon clerk in Russia who dreams only of a new overcoat; when he gets one, it gives him newfound confidence and security. Short, sweet, and thoroughly engaging. C: Roland Bykov. D: Alexei Batalov. DRA 73m. v

Overdrawn At The Memory Bank 1983 ★★★ A bored bureaucrat watches "Casablanca" so many times, his personality is finally fused onto that of Rick Blaine. C: Raul Julia. SFI 84m. TVM

Overexposed 1990 ★★★ Well-done, weird thriller in which soap star Oxenberg is terrorized by a psychopathic admirer and bizarre recurrent flashbacks. C: Catherine Oxenberg, David Naughton, Jennifer Edwards. D: Larry Brand. CRI [R] 83m. v

Overkill 1987 ★★★ A detective and the brother of a murdered man team up against Japan's dreaded "Yakuza" mobsters. C: Steve Rally, John Nishio, Laura Burkett. D: Ulli Lommel. ACT [R] 81m. v

Overland Mail 1939 ★★★ Pony Express rider Rabdall helps undercover federal agent Joyce smoke out counterfeiters in this routine Western. C: Jack Randall, Vince Barnett, Jean Joyce, Tristram Coffin. D: Robert Hill. WST 51m.

Overland Pacific 1954 ★★★ Railroad agent Mahoney discovers the truth behind a series of attacks by Indians on trains. Solid Western, with good story and action. Expect slightly odd color, due to processing. C: Jock Mahoney, Peggie Castle, Adele Jergens. D: Fred Sears. WST 73m.

Overland Stage Raiders 1938 ★★★½ Wayne and his cronies guard a shipment of gold in this entry in *Three Mesquiteers* Western series. Silent screen legend Brooks makes an unusual Western heroine in her last screen appearance. Film offers both action and tongue-in-cheek humor. C: John Wayne, Ray Corrigan, John Archer. D: George Sherman. WST 55m.

Overland Telegraph 1951 ★★★½ Holt and Martin try to find out who's behind the scheme to keep a telegraph from going through town. Overloaded story line is too heavy on action. Above-average "the phone must get through" Western. C: Tim Holt, Gail Davis, Hugh Beaumont, Mari Blanchard, George Nader. D: Lesley Selander. WST 60m.

Overland Trail 1942 *See* **Trail Riders**

Overlanders, The 1946 Australian ★★★★ A cattle drive across Australia during WWII. Based on actual events, and thoroughly gripping all the way. The cast, starting with Rafferty, is outstanding. C: Chips Rafferty, John Hayward, Daphne Campbell. D: Harry Watt. DRA 91m. v

Overlord 1975 British ★★★★ Examination of the horrors of war through one British soldier's eyes as he undergoes training and eventually lands at Normandy on D-Day. Stirner brings a passionate realism to his role in this beautifully produced, sad drama. C: Brian Stirner, Davyd Harries, Nicholas Ball, Julie Neesam. D: Stuart Cooper. DRA 85m.

Overnight 1986 Canadian ★★★½ Spoof of low-budget filmmaking has its observant, funny moments; Ertmanis plays a serious, self-respecting actor who slums in an X-rated movie for the money. C: Gale Garnett, Victor Ertmanis. D: Jack Darcus. COM 96m.

Overseas 1990 French ★★★★ The pampered lives of three French sisters in Algeria are disrupted when the local people seek independence.A moving lok at chaotic social change. Unrated, nudity, violence. C: Nicole Garcia, Marianne Basler, Brigitte Rouan. D: Brigitte Rouan. DRA 90m. v

Overture to Glory 1940 ★★★½ Drama based on Jewish legend has a cantor (Oysher) abandoning his family to pursue an opera career, but finding nothing but sorrow once he gives up his roots and religion. History gives this film, made at the height of Hitler's reign, added meaning and poignancy. C: Moishe Oysher, Florence Weiss. D: Max Nosseck. DRA 85m. v

Ovide And The Gang 1987 ★★★ Enter the world of Ovide, a wonderful, wacky animated character loved by children around the world. FAM/COM 120m.

Owl and the Pussycat, The 1970 ★★★½ Brassy prostitute (Streisand) makes life miserable for pompous writer Segal who can't help but fall for her. Buck Henry's adaptation of Bill Manoff's play pales beside the classic screwball comedies of the '30s it imitates but still manages a few laughs. C: Barbra Streisand, George Segal, Robert Klein. D: Herbert Ross. COM [PG] 95m. V

Ox-Bow Incident, The 1943 ★★★★½ Stark Western study of innocent cowboys (Andrews, Quinn, and Ford) who become victims of vengeful lynch mob and the effect their murders have on two men (Fonda and Morgan) caught up in the frenzy. Vivid characterizations and uncompromising script compensate for phony-looking sets. Poetic and sobering condemnation of mob violence. C: Henry Fonda, Dana Andrews, Mary Hughes, Anthony Quinn, John Ford, Henry Morgan. D: William Wellman. WST 75m. V

Ox, The 1991 Swedish ★★★½ Oscar-nominated portrait of farm family struggling to survive 1860 Swedish drought/famine. Superb acting, direction, cinematography, but relentlessly depressing. Seems like it goes on for hours! C: Max von Sydow, Liv Ullmann, Erland Josephson, Stellan Skarsgard, Ewa Froling. D: Sven Nykvist. DRA 91m. V

Oxford Blues 1984 ★★★ Likable cast, good locations, and excellent rowing footage carry story of cocky American Lowe, who pursues beautiful Britisher Pays to title college, enrolls, and ultimately proves himself. Essentially *A Yank at Oxford* remade as a traditional youth comedy. C: Rob Lowe, Ally Sheedy, Julian Sands, Amanda Pays. D: Robert Boris. DRA [PG-13] 98m. V

P

Pace That Kills, The 1928 ★★★½ Silent cautionary film about a young rural man who, while searching for his city-living sister, develops a heroin addiction. As expected, campy fun. C: Owen Gorin, Virginia Roye, Florence Turner. DRA 87m. V

Pacific Destiny 1956 British ★★★ True story of a British colonial governor keeping the peace in Pacific islands in the early 20th century. Good acting and handsome locations. C: Denholm Elliott, Susan Stephen, Michael Hordern. D: Wolf Rilla. DRA 97m.

Pacific Heights 1990 ★★★½ A yuppie couple buys their Victorian dream home in a smart section of San Francisco and unwittingly rents part of the house to a psychopath. Good thriller keeps ratcheting up the suspense. Cameo by Melanie's mom Tippi Hedren. Gets violent, though. C: Melanie Griffith, Matthew Modine, Michael Keaton. D: John Schlesinger. DRA [R] 103m. V

Pacific Inferno 1985 ★★★ Two U.S. POWs (Brown, Jackal) in WWII are forced by Japanese captors to search for a cache of silver supposedly hidden by MacArthur. Solid actioner with lush Philippine locations. C: Jim Brown, Richard Jaeckal, Vic Diaz, Timmy Brown. D: Rolf Bayer. ACT 90m. V

Pacific Liner 1939 ★★★ Good actors elevate this story of a cholera outbreak aboard an oceanliner and the doctor who tries to quell it in the face of opposition. C: Chester Morris, Wendy Barrie, Victor McLaglen, Barry Fitzgerald. D: Lew Landers. DRA 75m.

Pack of Lies 1987 ★★★★½ English couple are torn apart when investigators ask them to spy on their best friends, suspected of being Communist agents. Searing performances by Burstyn and Garr in drama that poses interesting questions about truth and loyalty. From Hugh Whitemore's play. C: Ellen Burstyn, Teri Garr, Alan Bates, Sammi Davis. D: Anthony Page. DRA 100m. TVM V

Pack, The 1977 ★★★½ On an island resort, bloodthirsty wild dogs attack humans. Standard horror, well done. (a.k.a. *The Long, Dark Night*) C: Joe Don Baker, Hope Willis, Richard Shull. D: Robert Clouse. HOR [R] 99m. V

Pack Up Your Troubles 1932 ★★★½ Uneven comedy, split in two parts. The first is marvelous fun, as Stan and Ollie cause havoc in WWI army. The second part is sticky nonsense, as they help orphan find relatives. Still worth seeing. C: Stan Laurel, Oliver Hardy, Mary Carr, James Finlayson, Billy Gilbert. D: George Marshall, Ray McCarey. COM 68m. V

Pack Up Your Troubles 1939 ★★★ Wacky WWI farce puts Brothers on the front line as spies. Funny opening. C: The Ritz Brothers, Jane Withers, Lynn Bari, Joseph Schildkraut. D: H. Humberstone. COM 75m.

Package, The 1989 ★★★½ Hackman is responsible for transporting "package" (Jones) from Berlin to D.C.; when he loses him, he realizes his military superiors have their own plans. Despite a predictable climax, thriller moves swiftly, and sparks fly between Hackman and ex-flame Cassidy. C: Gene Hackman, Joanna Cassidy, Tommy Lee Jones, John Heard. D: Andrew Davis. ACT [R] 108m. V

Packin' It In 1982 ★★★½ Unsurprising comedy finds Benjamin and Prentiss moving with their kids from the big bad city to a simple country life—which naturally proves to be anything but simple. Fun cast. C: Richard Benjamin, Paula Prentiss, Tony Roberts, Molly Ringwald. D: Jud Taylor. COM 92m. TVM V

Paco 1976 ★★½ Young boy (Gomez) from South America falls in with his larcenous uncle (Ferrer) who heads up a gang of juvenile thieves. Trite, sluggish drama is definitely no *Oliver Twist*. C: Jose Ferrer, Panchito Gomez, Allen Garfield. D: Robert Vincent O'Neil. CRI [G] 89m. V

Pad and How to Use It, The 1966 ★★½ An introverted classical-music lover plots the seduction of a young woman he meets at a concert. Fairly tame screen adaptation of Peter Shaffer's play *The Private Ear* is more like sitcom than sex romp. C: Brian Bedford, Julie Sommars, James Farentino. D: Brian Hutton. COM 86m.

Paddy 1970 Irish ★★★½ Harassed at home, a Dublin youth escapes through a series of offbeat sexual encounters. Comedy/drama portrays his confusion and dismay through an intriguing story line. C: Milo O'Shea, Des Cave. D: Daniel Haller. COM [PG] 97m. V

Paddy O'Day 1935 ★★★★ Young Irish woman (Withers) searching for her mother in America uses her peppy singing and enthusiastic charm to adapt to the new culture. Plenty of upbeat musical numbers in this congenial drama/comedy. C: Jane Withers, Rita Cansino, Pinky Tomlin, Jane Darwell. D: Lewis Seiler. MUS 73m.

Paddy, the Next Best Thing 1933 ★★★½ Irish papa Connolly pressures older daughter Lindsay to marry a rich man she doesn't love, with plucky younger sister Gaynor coming to the rescue. Likable comedy mostly notable for Gaynor's performance. C: Janet Gaynor, Warner Baxter, Walter Connolly, Harvey Stephens, Margaret Lindsay. D: Harry Lachman. COM 75m.

Padre Padrone 1977 Italian ★★★★½ Sheepherder leaves small village for college—something his overbearing father holds in contempt. Upon returning, he still suffers under his father's emotional yoke. Slow-moving but deeply absorbing drama. Performances of difficult roles are superb. C: Omero Antonutti, Saverio Marioni, Marcella Michelangeli, Fabrizio Forte. D: Vittorio Taviani, Paolo Taviani. DRA 114m. v

Pagan Love Song 1950 ★★★½ Schoolteacher (Keel) moves to Tahiti and mistakes Williams for native woman. A "swim and song" vehicle for Esther, with pretty location footage. C: Esther Williams, Howard Keel, Rita Moreno. D: Robert Alton. MUS 76m. v

Pagan, The 1929 ★★★ Novarro stars in this early sound picture as a singing merchant in love with Polynesian Janis, who's also the apple of Crisp's eye. The two men go head-to-head for her love. About what you'd expect. C: Ramon Novarro, Renee Adoree, Donald Crisp, Dorothy Janis. DRA 83m.

Pagans, The 1958 Italian ★★ The citizens of ancient Rome attempt to defend themselves against invading hordes. Costume drama. C: Pierre Cressoy, Helen Remy, Vittorio Sanipoli. D: Ferrucio Cereo. DRA 80m.

Page Miss Glory 1935 ★★★★ Slick con artist O'Brien enters a beauty contest by mail and has Davies take his place when his entry wins. She becomes the toast of the nation in this clever send-up of American fame and contest culture. C: Marion Davies, Pat O'Brien, Dick Powell, Mary Astor, Frank McHugh. D: Mervyn LeRoy. COM 90m.

Pagemaster, The 1994 ★★★ Young misfit (Culkin) takes refuge in library during thunderstorm, and is transported into cartoon world where classic literature comes to life. Well-intentioned effort to promote the joy of reading is sabotaged by dull story, crude animation. Very young children may like it. C: Macaulay Culkin, Christopher Lloyd, Mel Harris, Ed Begley, Jr., and the voices of Patrick Stewart, Whoopi Goldberg, Leonard Nimoy. D: Maurice Hunt, Joe Johnston. FAM/DRA [G] 75m. v

Pagliacci ★★★★ The great opera of love and art with one of the greatest operatic casts ever. C: Placido Domingo, Teresa Stratas, Juan Pons. MUS 70m. v

Pagliacci, I 1961 Italian ★★★★ An unusually electric live real-time performance of the oepra classic with legendary performers of the past. C: Mario Del Monaco, Gabriella Tucci, Akdo Protti. MUS 75m. v

Paid 1931 ★★★½ Nice young woman learns ruthlessness when she is framed and sent to prison; she comes out plotting vengeance. Interesting early talkie with young Crawford showing star potential. C: Joan Crawford, Kent Douglass, Robert Armstrong, Marie Prevost. D: Sam Wood. DRA 80m.

Paid in Full 1950 ★★★ Feeling responsible for the death of her niece, a woman becomes pregnant even though she knows it will kill her. Formula tearjerker. Carol Channing's cameo is her film debut. C: Robert Cummings, Lizabeth Scott, Diana Lynn, Eve Arden, Frank McHugh. D: William Dieterle. DRA 105m.

Paid to Kill 1954 British ★★★ Oft-told story of man who arranges his own murder and then decides against it is given some new twists. Clark is the failing businessman who makes the deal and then can't call it off. (a.k.a. *Five Days*) C: Dane Clark, Paul Carpenter. D: Montgomery Tully. CRI 70m.

Pain in the A—, A 1974 French ★★★★ While preparing for a hit, Mob assassin Ventura inadvertently helps out pathetic would-be suicide Brel, and gets mixed up in the various hijinks Brel leads him through. Hilarious French-Italian black comedy, remade in America as *Buddy, Buddy*. C: Lino Ventura, Jacques Brel, Caroline Cellier. D: Edouard Molinaro. COM [PG] 90m. v

Paint It Black 1989 ★★★ Murky, pseudo-Hitchcock tale of talented scuptor (Rossovich) who's enslaved by grasping art dealer (Kirkland), until her untimely and mysterious death. Released straight to video. C: Rick Rossovich, Sally Kirkland, Martin Landau, Doug Savant. D: Tim Hunter. CRI [R] 101m. v

Paint Job, The 1993 ★★★½ Patton is terrific as the house painter who becomes romantically involved with his boss' wife and enmeshed in a murderous plot. C: Will Patton, Bebe Neuwirth, Robert Pastorelli. D: Michael Taav. CRI [R] 90m. v

Paint Your Wagon 1970 ★★★½ Mammoth Western musical loosely based on Lerner and Loewe stage show. Two California gold rush prospectors (Marvin, Eastwood) meet Morman woman (Seberg) and share her as their bride. Unusually sexy for this kind of movie, but falters due to overblown production and nonsinger stars (Clint sings!). Songs include "They Call the Wind Maria," "Wandering Star." C: Lee Marvin, Clint Eastwood, Jean Seberg, Harve Presnell, Ray Walston. D: Joshua Logan. MUS [M] 164m. v

Painted Angel, The 1929 ★★★ Small-time chanteuse Dove hits it big and finds herself courted by not one, but two zealous suitors (Lowe and MacFarlane). A few good musical numbers enhance the weak premise. Based on a Fannie Hurst story. C: Billie Dove, Edmund Lowe, J. Farrell McDonald, George MacFarlane. D: Millard Webb. MUS 68m.

Painted Desert, The 1932 ★★★½ A romantic triangle develops between a corrupt banker, a mining engineer, and a young woman embroiled in family feuding. Gorgeous desert photography surmounts wooden acting. Gable's first sound picture. C: William Boyd, Helen Twelvetrees, William Farnum, Clark Gable. D: Howard Higgin. WST 80m. v

Painted Faces 1988 Chinese ★★★½ An interesting look at teheState training of opera singers, from their precocious childhood to stardom in the Peking Opera, with surprising humor and candor. C: Jackie Chan, Yuen Biao. D: Alex Law. DRA 100m. v

Painted Hills, The 1951 ★★★½ Picturesque, familiar Lassie adventure, good for younger audiences. This time, the heroic collie saves her friends from nasty miners. C: Paul Kelly, Bruce Cowling, Gary Gray. D: Harold F. Kress. FAM/DRA [G] 65m. v

Painted Stallion, The 1937 ★★★ An old-fashioned action serial about a mysterious stranger on a painted stallion who leads a wagon train through the perilous passes of the Santa Fe Trail. C: Ray Corrigan, Hoot Gibson. D: Ray Taylor. WST 212m. v

Painted Trail, The 1938 ★★★ Retired lawman Keene returns to his profession when he discovers Mason and Long smuggling goods from Mexico. Not your usual Western clichés, and a good deal of fun, with Keene delivering a strong he-man performance. C: Tom Keene, Eleanor Stewart, LeRoy Mason, Walter Long. D: Robert Hill. WST 50m.

Painted Veil, The 1934 ★★★½ During an epidemic in China, a doctor (Marshall) and his unfaithful wife (Garbo) reconcile their personal problems to assist the victims. Slightly dated but absorbing. Adaptation of Somerset Maugham story; remade as *The Seventh Sin.* C: Greta Garbo, Herbert Marshall, George Brent, Warner Oland. D: Richard Boleslawski. DRA 86m. v

Painting the Clouds with Sunshine 1951 ★★ Second-rate Warner Bros. musical has three gold-digger women looking for rich husbands in the sands of Las Vegas. C: Dennis Morgan, Virginia Mayo, Gene Nelson. D: David Butler. MUS 87m.

Pair of Aces 1990 ★★★½ Kristofferson and Nelson are an odd couple—a cop and a crook—chasing a killer in this laid-back buddy thriller. C: Willie Nelson, Kris Kristofferson, Rip Torn, Helen Shaver. D: Aaron Lipstadt. ACT 94m. v

Paisan 1946 Italian ★★★★★ Timely, lyrical vignettes of wartime Italy. Rossellini offers a harsh and humane view of suffering and the sense of Italy's relief at the demise of fascist rule. Look for the much longer Italian version. C: Carmela Sazio, Gar Moore, Maria Michi. D: Roberto Rossellini. DRA 110m. v

Pajama Game, The 1957 ★★★★½ Joyous musical, with unusual subject of labor dispute in pajama factory. Day shines as union representative in romantic conflict with factory foreman (Raitt). Haney's fine dancing sparks showstoppers "Steam Heat" and "Hernando's Hideway." From Adler and Ross Broadway smash; choreographed by Bob Fosse. C: Doris Day, John Raitt, Carol Haney, Eddie Foy Jr., Reta Shaw. D: George Abbott, Stanley Donen. MUS 101m. v

Pajama Party 1964 ★★★ Fun-loving, wacky American teenagers show a visiting Martian (Kirk) how to live it up American style. Earth girl Funicello falls bouffant-over-heels for the boy from way out of town in this silly *Beach Party* comedy featuring screen legends Dorothy Lamour and Buster Keaton. C: Tommy Kirk, Annette Funicello, Dorothy Lamour, Elsa Lanchester, Harvey Lembeck, Buster Keaton. D: Don Weis. COM 85m. v

Pal Joey 1957 ★★★★ John O'Hara's cynical story of a nightclub heel in love with sweet dancer while selling himself to a wealthy widow is sanitized vehicle for Sinatra. Well-done musical; Rodgers and Hart songs include "The Lady Is a Tramp" and "Where or When." Don't miss Hayworth's striptease. C: Frank Sinatra, Rita Hayworth, Kim Novak. D: George Sidney. MUS 109m. v

Pale Blood 1991 ★★★ Vampiric murders are terrorizing L.A. Which creepy suspect to blame? Woman Detective (Ludwig) attempts to find out in this decent chiller, enlivened by stylish touches and Hauser's fun performance. C: Wings Hauser, Pamela Ludwig, George Chakiris. D: VV Dachin Hsu. HOR [R] 95m. v

Pale Rider 1985 ★★★★ Yet another "man without a name;" this time Eastwood's six-gun mediates between a mining company and independent prosecutors in the California gold rush. Well acted (especially by Moriarty) with director Eastwood really hitting his stride. C: Clint Eastwood, Michael Moriarty, Carrie Snodgress, Christopher Penn. D: Clint Eastwood. WST [R] 116m. v

Paleface, The 1948 ★★★★ One of Hope's better vehicles has him as city coward out West, mistaken for deadly gunslinger. Russell is likable as buxom Calamity Jane. Features Oscar-winning song, "Buttons and Bows." Sequel: *Son of Paleface.* C: Bob Hope, Jane Russell, Robert Armstrong, Iris Adrian. D: Norman McLeod. COM 91m. v

Palermo Connection, The 1991 ★★★ A candidate for mayor of New York gets his eyes opened on the subject of crime while honeymooning in Sicily. An interesting idea that plays well. C: James Belushi, Mimi Rogers. D: Francesco Rosi. CRI [PG-13] 100m. v

Palm Beach 1979 Australian ★★★½ Arty independent features crop of nonprofessional actors in overlapping stories of down-and-outers evading the law and trying to make a dishonest buck. Accomplished and offbeat direction. C: Bryan Brown, John Flaus, Nat Young, Amanda Berry. D: Albie Thoms. DRA 88m. v

Palm Beach Story, The 1942 ★★★★½ Hilarious, screwball farce with Colbert using her looks to ensnare millionaire (Vallee) for the benefit of her husband (McCrea). Train sequence with Ale and Quail Club and surprise ending are classics of madcap comedy. Written and directed by Sturges. C: Claudette Colbert, Joel McCrea, Rudy Vallee, Mary Astor, William Demarest, Franklin Pangborn. D: Preston Sturges. COM 88m. v

Palm Springs Weekend 1963 ★★★ Spring

break is the backdrop for the romantic adventures of youths blowing off steam in the desert. Routine story line; some famous faces. C: Troy Donahue, Connie Stevens, Stefanie Powers, Robert Conrad. D: Norman Taurog. COM 101m. V

Palmy Days 1931 ★★★½ Cantor plays a stooge mixed up in phony spiritualism racket in expensively mounted musical. Early Busby Berkeley dances still effective, but Cantor's blackface routines date badly. Hit song: "My Honey Said Yes, Yes." C: Eddie Cantor, Charlotte Greenwood, Charles Middleton, George Raft. D: A. Edward Sutherland. MUS 77m.

Palombella Rossa 1989 Italian ★★★½ Communist athlete stricken with amnesia receives visits from people he once knew who try to put his pieces back together. Biting poitical satire. C: Nanni Moretti, Mariella Valentini, Silvio Orlando. D: Nanni Moretti. COM 87m. V

Palooka 1934 ★★★★ Durante is at his frantic best, playing the enterprising manager of a country yokel boxer. The one-liners come fast and furious in this adaptation of the popular cartoon "Joe Palooka'; Durante even sings his classic "Inka Dinka Doo." (a.k.a. *Joe Palooka*) C: Jimmy Durante, Stuart Erwin, Lupe Velez, Marjorie Rambeau, Thelma Todd. D: Benjamin Stoloff. COM 80m. V

Pals 1987 ★★½ Ameche and Scott are most enjoyable in this comedy about two trailer-park retirees who rejoice when they come across $3 million in drug money—until its owner returns to take it back. C: George C. Scott, Don Ameche, Sylvia Sidney. D: Lou Antonio. COM 90m. TVM V

Pals of the Pecos 1941 ★★★ *Three Mesquiteers* installment has the avenging good guys guarding a stagecoach business from ne'er-do-wells intent on shutting it down. Solidly acted and directed, but lacks spark. C: Robert Livingston, Bob Steele, Rufe Davis. D: Les Orlebeck. WST 56m.

Pals of the Saddle 1938 ★★★½ Another *Three Mesquiteers* entry with Wayne joining the fray (replacing Robert Livingston) in tale of noxious chemical being exported for evil purposes. Not if Stony, Tucson, and Lullaby can stop it. Superior contemporary Western. C: John Wayne, Ray Corrigan, Max Terhune, Doreen, Mckay. D: George Sherman. WST V

Pan Americana 1945 ★★★ Mediocre offshoot of '40s Good Neighbor Policy is jampacked with Latin-American song-and-dance numbers performed by Carmen Miranda wannabes. American writer (Long) finds man of her dreams (Terry) in Rio. C: Philip Terry, Eve Arden, Robert Benchley, Audrey Long. D: John Auer. MUS 84m.

Panache 1976 ★★★★ Good-looking production in the spirit of *The Three Musketeers*, with title character leading royal guards against Cardinal Richelieu in 17th-century France. Lots of swashbuckling action and color, with a spirited cast. C: Rene Auberjonois, David Healy. D: Gary Nelson. ACT 78m. TVM

Panama Deception, The 1992 ★★★★ A fascinating documentary on American foreign policy in Panama. Particular indictments are leveled at Reagan and Bush re: the 1989 invasion. Elizabeth Montgomery narrates. Winner of a well-deserved Oscar. D: Barbara Trent. DOC 96m. V

Panama Hattie 1942 ★★★ Cole Porter Broadway musical with much of its score cut has Sothern walking (in role created for Ethel Merman) through the title role about a nightclub owner in Panama. C: Ann Sothern, Red Skelton, Rags Ragland, Ben Blue, Virginia O'Brien, Lena Horne, Dan Dailey. D: Norman McLeod. MUS 81m. V

Panama Lady 1939 ★★★½ Lucy sines as mysterous woman who becomes embroiled in dangerous intrigue south of the border. C: Lucille Ball, Evelyn Brent, Allan Lane. D: Jack B. Hively. COM 65m. V

Panama Patrol 1939 ★★★½ Soldiers Ames and Wynters are called away to battle Chinese spies in Panama just as they're about to tie the knot. Substantial B-movie with involving espionage story. C: Leon Ames, Charlotte Wynters, Weldon Heyburn, Adrienne Ames. D: Charles Lamont. ACT 67m.

Panamint's Badman 1938 ★★½ Lawman battles bad guys who prey on stagecoach. C: Smith Ballew, Evelyn Daw, Noah Beery, Sr. D: Ray Taylor. WST 60m. V

Pancho Barnes 1988 ★★★ Bertinelli is terribly miscast in this otherwise average movie about the real-life aviation heroine and hell-raiser. C: Valerie Bertinelli, Ted Wass. D: Richard Heffron. DRA [PG] 150m. TVM

Pancho Villa 1972 Spanish ★★★ Italian spaghetti-Western casts Savalas as a famous Mexican revolutionary, leading an army against an American fort run by an evil military commander (Connors). Tedious adventure is much improved by fast-forwarding to the spectacular climax—two trains crash head on! C: Telly Savalas, Chuck Connors, Clint Walker. D: Eugenio Martin. WST [PG] 90m. V

Panda and the Magic Serpent 1969 ★★★★ Japanese animated adaptation of fairy tale involves young woman who is helped by furry and feathered friends to reunite with love of her life. Amiable story for children that unfolds in lively fashion. D: Robert Tafur. FAM/DRA 78m. V

Pandemonium 1982 ★★½ Teen-slasher spoof has terror stalking Bambi's Cheerleading School. Fun premise; very much a hit-and-miss result. C: Tom Smothers, Carol Kane, Tab Hunter. D: Alfred Sole. COM [PG] 82m. V

Pandora and the Flying Dutchman 1951 British ★★ An American woman (Gardner) visiting Spain falls in love with a sea captain (Mason), only to find he is a ghost—so she dies to be with him forever. So ridiculous even the cast seems embarrassed. C: James Mason, Ava Gardner, Nigel Patrick. D: Albert Lewin. DRA 123m.

Pandora's Box 1928 German ★★★★★ Late silent film in which the legendary Brooks plays Lulu, a classic screen temptress, who drags all the men she meets into a world of moral destruction. Compelling direction. C: Louise Brooks, Fritz Kortner. D: G.W. Pabst. DRA 110m. V

Panhandle 1948 ★★★½ Cameron thinks his gun-toting days are over until Hadley guns down his brother; and now Cameron seeks revenge. Blake Edwards, who plays a member of Hadley's gang, produced and co-wrote this solid Western. C: Rod Cameron, Cathy Downs, Reed Hadley, Anne Gwynne, Blake Edwards. D: Lesley Selander. WST 85m.

Panic Button 1964 ★★½ Needing a surefire, legitimate tax loss, gangster producers set out to make a TV pilot that's bound to fail. Mel Brooks did it better later with *The Producers*, but this energetic production squeaks out some laughs. C: Maurice Chevalier, Eleanor Parker, Jayne Mansfield. D: George Sherman. COM 90m. V

Panic in Echo Park 1977 ★★★ Doctor battles mysterious epidemic and cover-up efforts. Compelling performances. C: Dorian Harwood, Catlin Adams, Ramon Bieri. D: John Llewellyn Moxey. DRA 75m. V

Panic in Needle Park, The 1971 ★★★★ Gritty look at pair of young junkies in love and caught in downward spiral of addiction. Grim drama fueled by raw energy of young Pacino and Winn's poignant performance. C: Al Pacino, Kitty Winn, Alan Vint, Richard Bright. D: Jerry Schatzberg. DRA [PG] 110m.

Panic in the City 1968 ★★★ Low-budget melodrama follows frantic attempts of government agent (Duff) to stop Communist agents from setting off A-Bomb in L.A. Routine potboiler. C: Howard Duff, Linda Cristal. D: Eddie Davis. DRA 97m.

Panic in the Streets 1950 ★★★★ The bubonic plague is carried by gangster to New Orleans, as the authorities search for him. Thrilling drama builds to a rousing climax. Great Louisiana locations. Oscar for story. C: Richard Widmark, Paul Douglas, Barbara Bel Geddes, Jack Palance, Zero Mostel. D: Elia Kazan. DRA 96m. V

Panic in Year Zero! 1962 ★★★½ A man and his family struggle to stay alive and together as the U.S. is consumed by a nuclear attack. Gripping, well acted, and frightening. (a.k.a. *End of the World*) C: Ray Milland, Jean Hagen, Frankie Avalon. D: Ray Milland. SFI 95m. V

Panic on the 5:22 1974 ★★★½ Solid suspense film about three criminals who take a railroad club car full of commuters hostage during rush hour. Sadly, more timely now than it was originally. C: Ina Balin, Bernie Casey, Andrew Duggan. D: Harvey Hart. CRI 78m. TVM V

Panique 1946 French ★★★★ The country that coined the term "film noir" delivers its own moody take on the genre with this downbeat, pessimistic tale of a killer (Bernard) out to ice Simon, who can finger him for the crime. Unexpected turn of events makes this a truly original vision. C: Michele Simon, Viviane Romance. D: Julien Duvivier. CRI 93m. V

Pantaloons 1956 French ★★★ Slight sex comedy features Fernandel as a bon vivant out to seduce innocent women. Nothing spectacular, but inoffensive enough. C: Fernandel, Carmen Sevilla, Christine Carere, Fernando Rey. D: John Berry. COM 95m. V

Panther's Claw, The 1942 ★★★½ Sleuth Thatcher Colt (Blackmer) tries to get to the bottom of murder at an opera company by sorting through backstage and star suspects in this tightly capable, woven whodunit. C: Sidney Blackmer, Byron Foulger, Ricki Vallin. D: William Beaudine. CRI 72m.

Papa's Delicate Condition 1963 ★★★½ Nostalgic turn-of-the-century family comedy/drama with Gleason as hard-drinking patriarch of Texas clan. Slight stuff, but amusing. Oscar for Best Song, "Call Me Irresponsible." C: Jackie Gleason, Glynis Johns, Charlie Ruggles, Laurel Goodwin. D: George Marshall. COM 98m. V

Paper Bullets 1941 ★★★½ Good girl (Woodbury) takes the blame for rich man's hit-and-run and goes to jail, but finds there's more to this crime than meets the eye. Fine, dense melodrama despite minimal budget. (a.k.a. *Gangs, Inc.*) C: Joan Woodbury, Jack La Rue, Alan Ladd, Linda Ware, Vince Barnett, Gavin Gordon, John Archer. D: Phil Rosen. CRI 69m.

Paper Chase, The 1973 ★★★★ Young idealists cope with the pressures of first-year studies at Harvard Law School. Literate, comic tale, with an Oscar-winning turn by king curmudgeon Houseman as school's most feared professor. Based on novel by John Jay Osborne, Jr. C: Timothy Bottoms, Lindsay Wagner, John Houseman. D: James Bridges. DRA [PG] 111m. V

Paper Dolls 1982 ★★★ Would-be exposé of the world of teenage modeling is a real soap opera all the way, with the mothers and agents at least as ambitious as the young models. Basis for a later TV series. C: Joan Hackett, Jennifer Warren, Joan Collins, Daryl Hannah. D: Edward Zwick. DRA 100m. TVM

Paper Gallows 1950 British ★★★½ Overenthusiastic crime writer kills a man to help him flesh out his next novel, leaving his brother, also a writer, to uncover the murder. Fair amount of intrigue and swift action. C: Dermot Walsh, Rona Anderson, John Bentley. D: John Guillermin. CRI 77m.

Paper Hearts *See* **Cheatin' Hearts**

Paper Lion 1968 ★★★★ Enjoyable comedy

based on journalist George Plimpton's book features Alda as writer researching football story by enduring Detroit Lions training camp. Good-natured sports humor even non-football fans will enjoy. Fun cameos by athletes, and surprisingly good work by linebacker Karras as Alda's mentor. C: Alan Alda, Lauren Hutton, Alex Karras. D: Alex March. COM [G] 107m. V

Paper Man 1971 ★★★½ Neat little computer thriller has a programming whiz (Stockwell) crediting fictitious man so college buddies can do credit scam. Then people start to die. Holds attention throughout despite weak script. C: Dean Stockwell, Stefanie Powers. D: Walter Grauman. ACT 73m. TVM

Paper Marriage 1992 ★★★½ Jilted Polish immigrant in England seeking green card convinces petty criminal to marry her. Sweet variation on familiar formula. C: Gary Kemp, Sadie Frost, Joanna Trepechinska, Rita Tushingham. D: Krzysztof Lang. COM 88m. V

Paper Mask 1991 British ★★★★ Hospital orderly seizes opportunity to impersonate a doctor in a frenetic emergency room. Chilling medical thriller keeps adrenaline pumping. Donohoe is outstanding. C: Paul McGann, Amanda Donohoe, Fredrick Treves. D: Christopher Morahan. DRA [R] 105m. V

Paper Moon 1973 ★★★★½ In the midwest of the '30s, a small-time hustler (Ryan) is outconned by a little girl (real-life daughter Tatum). Non-stop excellence; a visual delight and star turn for both O'Neals (Tatum took an Oscar). Kahn is also a hoot—don't miss it! C: Ryan O'Neal, Tatum O'Neal, Madeline Kahn. D: Peter Bogdanovich. COM [PG] 102m. V

Paper Orchid 1949 British ★★★ Newspaper gossip columinst (Hazell) is accused of murdering a thespian and providing the scandal-driven newspaper trade with a hot story. Promises more than it delivers. C: Hugh Williams, Hy Hazell, Sidney James. D: Roy Baker. WST 86m.

Paper, The 1994 ★★★½ An editor (Keaton) of a tabloid newspaper, embroiled in circulation war, tries to break a major scandal story while juggling nasty managing editor (Close) and his very pregnant wife (Tomei). Strong cast, mild material. C: Michael Keaton, Robert Duvall, Glenn Close, Marisa Tomei, Randy Quaid, Jason Robards, Jason Alexander, Spalding Gray, Catherine O'Hara. D: Ron Howard. DRA [R] 110m. V

Paper Tiger 1975 British ★★★ Wild yarns of a British tutor (Niven) about his supposedly adventurous past finally catch up with him when he and young Japanese student (Ando) are kidnapped by terrorists. Saccharine, simplistic action film contains laughable karate sequences to boot. C: David Niven, Toshiro Mifune, Hardy Kruger. D: Ken Annakin. ACT 99m. V

Paperback Hero 1973 Canadian ★★★½ Odd sports/action hybrid has talented hockey player turning to crime after his team can no longer secure financial backing. Offbeat, to be sure, with good performances, but more a curio than a winner. C: Keir Dullea, Elizabeth Ashley. D: Peter Pearson. CRI 93m. V

Paperboy, The 1994 ★★★★★ A divorcee (Paul) returns to her hometown, little knowing that the disturbed youngster next door wants her as his mom—at any price. Taut psychological shocker exceeds expectations, thanks to confident handling and solid acting, especially Marut in the title role. C: Alexandra Paul, Marc Marut, William Katt, Brigid Tierney, Frances Bay. D: Douglas Jackson. HOR [R] 94m.

Paperhouse 1989 British ★★★★½ A young girl finds that her drawings are reflected in her dreams, and that she can alter them for the better—or worse. Intriguing psychological thriller, with some genuinely scary moments and an intelligent approach. Based on Catherine Storr's novel *Marianne Dreams*. C: Charlotte Burke, Elliott Spiers, Glenne Headly, Ben Cross, Gemma Jones. D: Bernard Rose. HOR [PG-13] 93m. V

Papillon 1973 ★★★½ Big-screen adaptation of Henri Charriere's book chronicling "the Butterfly" and his attempts to escape from Devil's Island. McQueen is sweaty and virile and Hoffman suitably lizardy in this overblown but exciting action-adventure. C: Steve McQueen, Dustin Hoffman, Victor Jory. D: Franklin J. Schaffner. ACT [PG] 150m. V

Parachute Battalion 1941 ★★★½ Typical WWII drama focuses on training for title regiment, with the usual assortment of characters and plenty of patriotic fervor. Set apart by some tremendous aerial footage. C: Edmond O'Brien, Nancy Kelly, Robert Preston. D: Leslie Goodwins. DRA 75m.

Parachute Jumper 1933 ★★★½ Lighthearted nonsense about two ex-Marines (Fairbanks, Jr., and McHugh) who become airborne smugglers. Notable primarily for Davis, who helps the heroes to return to the straight and narrow. C: Douglas Fairbanks Jr., Leo Carrillo, Bette Davis, Frank McHugh. D: Alfred Green. CRI 65m.

Parade, The 1984 ★★★½ In a small town making ready for the Fourth of July, a recent ex-con stalks his wife. Taut and compelling. C: Michael Learned, Frederic Forrest, Rosanna Arquette, Geraldine Page. D: Peter Hunt. DRA 100m. TVM

Paradine Case 1947 ★★★ Lawyer (Peck) falls in love with his mysterious client (Valli) at her murder trial. Hitchcock and awesome supporting cast try in vain to bring dull scenario to life. C: Gregory Peck, Alida Valli, Ann Todd, Charles Laughton, Charles Coburn, Ethel Barrymore. D: Alfred Hitchcock. CRI 125m. V

Paradise 1981 ★★½ Adolescent boy and girl are marooned in a desert oasis and fall in love. The sand in this story's shoes isn't from the desert, it's left over from the *Blue Lagoon*. Picture looks great, anyway. C: Willie Aames, Phoebe Cates. D: Stuart Gillard. DRA [R] 96m. V

Paradise 1991 ★★★½ Boy spends summer with mother's friends whose marriage is falling apart after death of their son. Low-key drama is quietly affecting, though it turns sudsy at the end. Enjoyable performance by the youngster Wood. Based on the French film *Le Grand Chemin*. C: Melanie Griffith, Don Johnson, Elijah Wood. D: Mary Agnes Donoghue. DRA [PG-13] 111m. V

Paradise Alley 1978 ★★★ Three brothers (Stallone, Assante, Canalito) pin their hopes for escaping NYC's Hell's Kitchen on Canalito's wrestling talents. Old-fashioned story adequately handled by first-time director Stallone. C: Sylvester Stallone, Lee Canalito, Armand Assante, Frank McRae, Anne Archer, Tom Waits. D: Sylvester Stallone. DRA [PG] 109m. V

Paradise Canyon 1935 ★★★ Federal agent Wayne sniffs out counterfeiters. Not exactly the freshest Western story line, but at least you get the Duke, in an early role. C: John Wayne, Yakima Canutt, Marion Burns, Reed Howes. D: Carl Pierson. WST 55m. V

Paradise for Three 1938 ★★★½ In order to discover how the working class lives, an American businessman takes off for Germany. Odd but pleasant romantic comedy. C: Frank Morgan, Robert Young, Mary Astor, Edna May Oliver. D: Edward Buzzell. COM 75m.

Paradise Hawaiian Style 1966 ★★★½ Reworking of his earlier *Blue Hawaii* casts Elvis as charter pilot with overactive libido. Okay entry in Presley series. C: Elvis Presley, Suzanna Leigh, James Shigeta. D: Michael Moore. MUS 91m. V

Paradise in Harlem 1940 ★★★½ All African-American musical about singer pushed to despair after witnessing murder. Lucky millender and His Orchestra and Juanita Hall Singers provide great fun. C: Frank Wilson, Mamie Smith, Joseph Seiden, Edna Mae Harris. MUS 83m. V

Paradise Isle 1937 ★★★½ Civilization meets natural paradise as Hull falls for islander girl Movita. What the South Seas melodrama lacks in originality, the two leads make up for in intensity as mismatched lovers. C: Movita, Warren Hull, George Pilita, William B. Davidson. D: Arthur Greville Collins. DRA 73m.

Paradise Lagoon 1957 *See* **Admirable Crichton, The**

Paradisio ★★★ Meek academic flees from spies while trying to get dead friend's X-ray glasses into the right hands. C: Arthur Howard, Eva Waegner. COM [R] 82m. V

Parallax View, The 1974 ★★★★½ Investigative reporter Beatty, probing a senator's death, discovers an assassination agency. First-rate paranoid political thriller from director Pakula. Not solely for conspiracy buffs. C: Warren Beatty, Paula Prentiss, William Daniels, Hume Cronyn. D: Alan J. Pakula. CRI [R] 102m. V

Paramount on Parade 1930 ★★★★ Plotless, all-star revue was talkie debut of Paramount's impressive roster of talent. Nostalgia buffs will have a field day. Highlights: Clara Bow cavorting with sailor chorus and Chevalier "Sweeping the Clouds Away." Opening sequence and finale in color. C: Jean Arthur, Clara Bow, Maurice Chevalier, Gary Cooper, Nancy Carroll, Kay Francis, Fredric March, Helen Kane, Jack Oakie, William Powell, Buddy Rogers. D: Dorothy Arzner, Otto Brower, Edmund Goulding, Victor Heerman. MUS 77m.

Paranoia 1969 ★ Misadventures of a seductive widow and the creepy couple she lets stay with her. (a.k.a. *Orgasmo*) C: Carroll Baker, Lou Castel, Colette Descombes. D: Umberto Lenzi. DRA [R] 92m. V

Paranoia 1970 *See* **Quiet Place to Kill, A**

Paranoiac 1963 British ★★★★ Scott is haunted by the presence of her dead brother, which makes her other brother (Reed) try to have her committed. Many twists and turns, not to mention creepiness and gore, in this artistic horror film. C: Janette Scott, Oliver Reed, Liliane Brousse. D: Freddie Francis. HOR 80m.

Parasite 1981 ★ Moore's film debut is a cheapie about a scientist (Glaudini) fighting voracious monsters he's created, one of which is growing inside him. In theaters, 3-D gore was occasionally shocking; on video it's just gross. C: Robert Glaudini, Demi Moore, Luca Bercovici. D: Charles Band. HOR [R] 85m. V

Paratrooper 1953 British ★★★½ Ladd is racked by guilt over having inadvertently caused the death of a comrade and assumes a new identity in the British forces to escape his dark past. Interesting, capable wartime melodrama. Originally titled *The Red Beret*. C: Alan Ladd, Leo Genn, Susan Stephen, Harry Andrews. D: Terence Young. DRA 87m.

Pardners 1956 ★★★½ Plausible remake of same director's *Rhythm on the Range*, with Martin and Lewis having fun out West while their real-life partnership was nearing its end. Plot involves villains out to take over ranch. Scripted by Sidney Sheldon. C: Dean Martin, Jerry Lewis, Lori Nelson, Jackie Loughery, Agnes Moorehead. D: Norman Taurog. COM 90m. V

Pardon Mon Affaire 1977 French ★★★★ A married bureacrat in mid-life crisis tries to romance a beautiful model he meets in a garage. This bright and entertaining comedy is played strictly for laughs with sprightly sophistication. U.S. remake: *The Woman In Red*. C: Jean Rochefort, Claude Brasseur, Guy Bedos, Victor Lanoux. D: Yves Robert. COM [PG] 105m. V

Pardon My French 1951 U.S. ★★★½ Light soufflé with Oberon inheriting French chalet occupied by composer (Henreid) and his brood. C: Paul Henreid, Merle Oberon, Paul Bonifas. D: Bernard Vorhaus. COM 81m.

Pardon My Past 1945 ★★★★ An innocent young rube (MacMurray) is the double of a dissipated playboy, and finds himself saddled with the latter's troubles. Sharp comedy/-drama with a wonderful cast of pros. C: Fred MacMurray, Marguerite Chapman, Akim Tamiroff, William Demarest. D: Leslie Fenton. COM 88m.

Pardon My Rhythm 1944 ★★★ Youth musical has a good spirit, telling of teen queen Jean's attempts to make it as a singer. C: Gloria Jean, Evelyn Ankers, Bob Crosby. D: Felix Feist. MUS 62m.

Pardon My Sarong 1942 ★★★★ Good Abbott and Costello vehicle set in tropical paradise with Bud and Lou as bus drivers mixed up in jewel heist. C: Bud Abbott, Lou Costello, Lionel Atwill, Virginia Bruce, William Demarest. D: Erle C. Kenton. COM 84m. V

Pardon My Trunk 1952 *See* **Hello, Elephant**

Pardon Us 1931 ★★★★ Stan and Ollie in prison. Funny, if a bit padded, spoof of *The Big House* and other cellblock movies. Their feature film debut. C: Stan Laurel, Oliver Hardy, Wilfred Lucas, Walter Long. D: James Parrott. COM 78m. V

Parent Trap, The 1961 ★★★★ Popular juvenile comedy about twins (Mills in a dual role) from broken home meeting accidentally, then hatching scheme to reunite parents (Keith and O'Hara). Agreeable family fun with good trick photography. C: Hayley Mills, Maureen O'Hara, Brian Keith, Joanna Barnes. D: David Swift. FAM/COM 129m. V

Parent Trap II 1986 ★★★½ Popular family classic gets sequel twenty-five years later as grown-up twins (Mills) endure romantic mistaken identities. Cute. Two more frolics followed. Made for cable. C: Hayley Mills, Tom Skerritt, Alex Harvey. D: Ronald F. Maxwell. FAM/COM 95m. TVM

Parent Trap III 1989 ★★★ Hayley competes against herself, as twins, for the affections of attractive, wealthy widower (Bostwick) with triplets of his own. (They're not played by Haley, in a model of restraint!) Series beginning to pall. C: Hayley Mills, Barry Bostwick. D: Mollie Miller. FAM/COM 100m. TVM

Parenthood 1989 ★★★½ Martin plays it relatively straight in this comedy tackling parenthood in a multigenerational family. Good cast steadily directed by Howard doesn't submit to treacle until the very end. C: Steve Martin, Mary Steenburgen, Dianne Wiest, Jason Robards, Rick Moranis, Tom Hulce, Martha Plimpton, Keanu Reeves. D: Ron Howard. COM [PG-13] 124m. V

Parents 1989 ★★★★ When family moves into new home, son begins to suspect his parents are cannibals. First directing effort from actor Balaban is dark-humored satire of family life, marked by alternately nightmarish and cartoonish style. Quaid is particularly creepy as subtly menacing father. Definitely not for all tastes. C: Randy Quaid, Mary Beth Hurt, Sandy Dennis, Bryan Madorsky. D: Bob Balaban. COM [R] 83m. V

Paris After Dark 1943 ★★★½ Well-shot WWII drama, with French doctor (Sanders) living a secret double life as a leader of the French Resistance. Direction provides real sense of authenticity, possibly because Moguy himself had escaped Paris during the occupation. (a.k.a. *The Night Is Ending*) C: George Sanders, Philip VanDorn, Brenda Marshall. D: Leonide Moguy. DRA 85m.

Paris Belongs to Us 1962 French ★★★½ Woman tries to get to the bottom of a young man's suicide and discovers a strange conspiracy. Compelling, if a little slow. C: Betty Schneider, Giani Esposito, Françoise Prévost, Daniel Crohem. D: Jacques Rivette. DRA 140m.

Paris Blues 1961 ★★★★ A pair of jazz musicians (Newman and Poitier) lead an offbeat life on the Left Bank of Paris, where they fall in love with two tourists (Woodward and Carroll). Superb Ellington score and strong performances make this a "must hear." C: Paul Newman, Joanne Woodward, Diahann Carroll, Sidney Poitier, Louis Armstrong. D: Martin Ritt. DRA 98m. V

Paris Calling 1941 ★★★★ During the Nazi invasion of Paris in WWII, a woman begins to suspect that her husband may be a traitor. Story focuses on the French Resistance; somewhat predictable but the performances are great. C: Elisabeth Bergner, Randolph Scott, Basil Rathbone, Gale Sondergaard, Lee J. Cobb. D: Edwin Marin. DRA 95m.

Paris Does Strange Things 1956 *See* **Elena and Her Men**

Paris Express, The 1953 British ★★½ A faithful clerk (Rains) turns embezzler and lights out for Paris and the life of a bon vivant. Intricate story gets increasingly difficult to swallow. (a.k.a. *The Man Who Watched Trains Go By.*) C: Claude Rains, Marta Toren, Marius Goring. D: Harold French. DRA 83m. V

Paris Holiday 1958 ★★★½ Uneven comedy worth seeing for pairing of great French clown Fernandel with American Hope. Plot has Bob on the Seine looking for hot screenplay. Film buffs will enjoy seeing director/writer Sturges in small role. C: Bob Hope, Fernandel, Anita Ekberg, Martha Hyer. D: Gerd Oswald. COM 100m. V

Paris Honeymoon 1939 ★★★½ Pleasant enough musical, with Crosby as Texas millionaire in Paris, torn between two women, one a sophisticate, the other a country girl. C: Bing Crosby, Shirley Ross, Edward Everett Horton, Akim Tamiroff. D: Frank Tuttle. MUS 92m.

Paris in the Month of August 1968 French ★★★½ Clerk and family man (Aznavour)

masquerades as an artist to impress the model (Hampshire) he meets while on vacation in Paris. Breezy comedy is as sweet and light as French pastry. C: Charles Aznavour, Susan Hampshire. D: Pierre Granier-Deferre. COM 94m.

Paris Is Burning 1991 ★★★★½ Powerful documentary about a subculture of male transvestites in NYC who compete, in elaborate costumes and makeup, in "drag balls." For most of them, life revolves around these events. By turns funny and piercingly poignant—beautifully made. D: Jennie Livingston. DOC [R] 76m. V

Paris Model 1953 ★★★ Good cast in anthology of four stories about a Paris original; somewhat less than the sum of its parts. C: Eva Gabor, Tom Conway, Paulette Goddard, Marilyn Maxwell. D: Alfred Green. DRA 81m.

Paris Playboys 1954 ★★ The Bowery Boys fight a spy ring when Sach (Hall) is mistaken for a professor. For diehard fans. C: Leo Gorcey, Huntz Hall, Bernard Gorcey. D: William Beaudine. COM 62m.

Paris, Texas 1984 ★★ A man found wandering in the desert returns home after four years to try to get a fresh start with his wife and son. Cryptic, enigmatic script by Sam Shepard may intrigue some but comes off mostly as pretentious and slow. C: Harry Dean Stanton, Nastassia Kinski, Dean Stockwell. D: Wim Wenders. DRA [R] 145m. V

Paris Trout 1991 ★★★★½ After killing a black mother and daughter over an unpaid debt, racist (Hopper) cannot fathom why he's being charged with a crime. Disturbing portrait of everyday evil in circa 1940s Georgia. Very well handled. Adapted by Pete Dexter from his novel. C: Dennis Hopper, Barbara Hershey, Ed Harris. D: Stephen Gyllenhaal. DRA [R] 99m. V

Paris Underground 1945 ★★★½ Fact-based WWII propaganda drama about two women who, after being captured by Nazis, persist in their resistance work. Resolute flagwaver. Good acting holds interest. C: Constance Bennett, Gracie Fields, George Rigaud. D: Gregory Ratoff. DRA 97m.

Paris—when It Sizzles 1964 ★★★ A screenwriter working on a romantic script in Paris falls in love with his secretary and they act out scenes from his story. Well-intended comedy falls short; excellent cast tries. C: William Holden, Audrey Hepburn, Noel Coward. D: Richard Quine. COM 110m. V

Parisian, The 1931 French ★★★½ Simple, content Frenchman Menjou's American son tries to convince him money is the key to happiness. The charming Menjou turns the tables. Shot in French and English versions. C: Adolphe Menjou, Roger Treville, Redgie Williams, Elissa Landi. D: Jean de la Muir. DRA 63m.

Park Is Mine, The 1985 ★★★ A psychotic Vietnam vet (Jones) takes hostages in NYC's Central Park when his friend is killed. War of bullets ends pointlessly in even bigger shootout. C: Tommy Lee Jones, Helen Shaver, Yaphet Kotto. D: Steven Hilliard Stern. DRA 102m. TVM V

Park Row 1952 ★★★★★ Evans is wonderfully combative as newspaper editor founding N.Y. daily at the end of the 19th century. Energetic, fun, and exciting, a model of the art of making B-movies. C: Gene Evans, Mary Welch, Herbert Heyes. D: Samuel Fuller. DRA 83m.

Parker 1984 ★★★ Freed toy manufacturer hunting for his own kidnappers immerses himself in dangerous intrigue. C: Bryan Brown, Cherie Lunghi. ACT 100m. V

Parking 1985 ★★★ Unusual updated adaptation of the Orpheus myth has Orpheus a rock 'n' roll legend and Eurydice his sculptress lover whom he tries to rescue from the Underworld. Remake of Jean Cocteau's film of the same title is an imperfect, often corny, film. DRA

Parlor, Bedroom and Bath 1931 ★★★ Car accident victim (Keaton) is taken home by driver, then causes further mishaps. Comedy only hints at star's genius. C: Buster Keaton, Charlotte Greenwood, Reginald Denny, Cliff Edwards. D: Edward Sedgwick. COM 75m. V

Parnell 1937 ★★½ Gable is miscast as Irish nationalist leader of the late 1800s, whose career is ruined because of affair with Loy. Ornate costume drama. C: Clark Gable, Myrna Loy, Edna May Oliver, Edmund Gwenn, Donald Crisp, Billie Burke. D: John Stahl. DRA 119m.

Parole, Inc. 1949 ★★★ Racketeers corrupt parole board to get their buddies back on the street. Efficient if routine crime film. C: Michael O'Shea, Evelyn Ankers, Turhan Bey, Lyle Talbot. D: Alfred Zeisler. CRI 71m.

Parrish 1961 ★★ Laughable soaper with virile Donahue as title character living on tobacco plantation with mother (Colbert), fighting owner (Malden) and loving three young women, till tragedy strikes. So badly overacted the film is almost considered a comedy now. C: Claudette Colbert, Troy Donahue, Karl Malden, Dean Jagger, Connie Stevens. D: Delmer Daves. DRA 138m. V

Parsifal 1988 ★★★★ Hans-Jurgen Syberberg directs captivating version of Wagner's opera of ideas. Features Monte Carlo Philharmonic orchestra, conducted by Armin Jordan. Sung in German. C: Armin Jordan, Yvonne Minton. MUS 255m. V

Parson and the Outlaw, The 1957 ★★½ Billy the Kid, forced out of retirement, once again, to avenge the death of a preacher friend. C: Anthony Dexter, Sonny Tufts, Marie Windsor, Buddy Rogers. D: Oliver Drake. WST 71m.

Parson of Panamint, The 1941 ★★★½ Unusual Western has two-fisted minister Terry cleaning up booming mining town. Interesting. C: Charlie Ruggles, Ellen Drew, Phillip Terry, Joseph Schildkraut. D: William McGann. WST 84m.

Part-Time Wife 1961 British ★★ Deadly farce about wife "on loan" to husband's friend. Tedious. C: Anton Rodgers, Nyree Porter, Kenneth Warren. D: Max Varnel. COM 70m.

Part 2, Walking Tall *See* **Walking Tall, Part II**

Parting Glances 1986 ★★★★ Low-budget, intelligent look at gay friendships in New York City, as several men gather to say good-bye to man moving to California. Buscemi stands out as rock performer with AIDS. Unique among gay-themed films in that sexuality takes a back seat to companionship. C: John Bolger, Richard Ganoung, Steve Buscemi. D: Bill Sherwood. DRA 90m. V

Partners 1982 ★★ Straight cop (O'Neal) pretending to be gay in undercover murder investigation takes pointers from homosexual partner (Hurt). Witless. C: Ryan O'Neal, John Hurt, Kenneth McMillan, Robyn Douglass. D: James Burrows. COM [R] 93m. V

Partners in Crime 1973 ★★★ Judge Grant and ex-con Antonio are on the lookout for a cache of stolen valuables in a second unsold pilot for *The Judge and Jake Wyler*. Okay. C: Lee Grant, Lou Antonio, Bob Cummings. D: Jack Smight. CRI [PG] 78m. TVM

Partners of the Plains 1938 ★★★½ Hopalong Cassidy (Boyd) helps a tenderfoot Brit (Gaze) manage her ranch and fend off the nefarious Bridge. One of many in the *Hopalong* series, but this one is a particularly able Western. C: William Boyd, Harvey Clark, Russell Hayden, Gwen Gaza, Hilda Plowright, John Warburton, Al Bridge. D: Lesley Selander. WST 70m.

Parts: The Clonus Horror 1978 ★★★ The government wants to clone the citizenry. Interesting suspenser. (a.k.a. *The Clonus Horror*) C: Tim Donnelly, Dick Sargent, Peter Graves. D: Robert Fiveson. SFI [R] 90m. V

Party Camp 1987 ★★ Boisterous counselor transforms sedate summer camp into relentless party station. C: April Wayne, Billy Jacoby, Kirk Cribb. D: Gary Graver. COM [R] 96m. V

Party Crashers, The 1958 ★★ Juvenile delinquents get their kicks by disrupting parties. Notable mainly for a sad appearance by Farmer, in her last film. C: Mark Damon, Bobby Driscoll, Connie Stevens, Frances Farmer. D: Bernard Girard. CRI 78m.

Party Favors 1987 ★★ Unemployed exotic dancers seek vengeance upon preacher who put them out of business. C: Gail Thackray, Jeanine Winters, Marjorie Miller. D: Ed Hansen. COM 83m. V

Party Girl 1958 ★★★ A mobster loses his girlfriend (Charisse) to a lawyer (Taylor) on a bet. Dramatic retelling of familiar plot is stylized and a little self-conscious but has a cult following. C: Robert Taylor, Cyd Charisse, Lee J. Cobb, John Ireland. D: Nicholas Ray. DRA 99m. V

Party Incorporated 1989 ★★ Widow chips away at IRS debt by throwing parties. C: Marilyn Chambers, Kurt Woodrufff, Christina Veronica. D: Chuck Vincent. COM [R] 80m. V

Party Line 1988 ★ You'll wish you got a busy signal, rather than watch this exploitative yarn about date-seeking singles who wind up dead, not wed. C: Richard Hatch, Shawn Weatherly, Leif Garrett, Richard Roundtree. D: William Webb. HOR [R] 91m. V

Party, The 1968 ★★★½ Sellers stars in Chaplin-like vehicle as Indian actor who accidentally crashes chi-chi Hollywood party, where he innocently induces havoc. Basically a series of good slapstick sequences in one-person showcase; doesn't all work, but what does is very funny. C: Peter Sellers, Claudine Longet, Marge Champion, Denny Miller. D: Blake Edwards. COM 99m. V

Party Wire 1935 ★★★★ Clever comedy about evils of small-town gossip. Arthur terrific as rich guy's girlfriend who falls victim to telephone party line. C: Jean Arthur, Victor Jory, Helen Lowell, Robert Allen. D: Erle Kenton. COM 72m.

Pascali's Island 1988 British ★★★½ On Greek island in the 1900s, a spy (Kingsley) hooks up with Mirren and Dance for an archaeological robbery. Quiet, quirky caper; performances matter more than plot. C: Ben Kingsley, Charles Dance, Helen Mirren. D: James Dearden. CRI [PG-13] 106m. V

Pass the Ammo 1988 ★★★ Frantic spoof of the world of television evangelists, doesn't match the antics of the real thing. Curry tries hard as the phony money-hungry disciple of God. C: Bill Paxton, Linda Kozlowski, Tim Curry, Annie Potts. D: David Beaird. COM [R] 97m. V

Passage Home 1955 British ★★★ Amorous ship's captain Finch gives passenger Cilento the once-over, and sailor Steel protects her honor. It's rough waters for them and us in this predictable but enjoyable drama. C: Anthony Steel, Peter Finch, Diane Cilento, Cyril Cusack, Hugh Griffith. D: Roy Baker. DRA 102m.

Passage, The 1979 British ★★½ During WWII, a Basque (Quinn) leads a scientist and his family to safety with a fanatical Nazi (McDowell) in pursuit. So-so production, but McDowell's over-the-top turn is memorable—to say the least. C: Anthony Quinn, James Mason, Malcolm McDowell, Patricia Neal. D: J. Thompson. ACT [R] 99m.

Passage to India, A 1984 British ★★★★½ In India during the '20s, a young English woman accuses a local doctor of rape. In his last film, Lean fills this adaptation of E.M. Forster's novel with gorgeous color and scenery. Quite spectacular. Oscars went to Ashcroft for Best Supporting Actress and Jarre for Best

Original Score. C: Judy Davis, Victor Banerjee, Peggy Ashcroft, James Fox, Alec Guinness, Nigel Havers. D: David Lean. DRA [PG] 163m. V

Passage to Marseille 1944 ★★★★ A group of French convicts, escaped from Devil's Island, join the fight against the Nazis. Although the flashbacks are a bit of a muddle, the story is strong and the cast excellent. C: Humphrey Bogart, Claude Rains, Michele Morgan, Philip Dorn, Sydney Greenstreet, Peter Lorre. D: Michael Curtiz. ACT 110m. V

Passage West 1951 ★★★½ Outlaws try to shanghai a wagon train led by a kindly minister (O'Keefe) and his devotees. A good story distinguishes this from the usual Western fare. C: John Payne, Dennis O'Keefe, Arleen Whelan, Dooley Wilson. D: Lewis Foster. WST 80m.

Passed Away 1992 ★★★½ A patriarch's funeral brings out the best and worst in the oddball relatives who gather to pay their final respects. Amusing black comedy with very funny cast. C: Bob Hoskins, Jack Warden, William Petersen, Maureen Stapleton. D: Charlie Peters. COM [PG-13] 97m. V

Passenger 57 1992 ★★★½ Antiterrorist (Snipes) finds himself aboard a plane that is hijacked by twisted felon (Payne). Standard story gets entertaining treatment thanks to good Snipes as reluctant hero. C: Wesley Snipes, Bruce Payne, Tom Sizemore. D: Kevin Hooks. ACT [R] 84m. V

Passenger, The 1963 Polish ★★★★★ Director Munk died in a car accident before completing this picture, but what's left is masterful. Shot in a disarmingly realistic, almost documentary manner, story is told in flashback as a former Auschwitz prison guard (Slaska) recounts her relationship with a Polish prisoner (Ciepielewska) at the camp. Brilliant and deeply moving. C: Aleksandra Slaska, Anna Ciepielewska, Marek Walczewski. D: Andrzej Munk. DRA 63m.

Passenger, The 1975 Italian ★★★★ On an assignment in Africa, a jaded TV reporter decides to change identities with a man—who has just died—and gets more trouble than he anticipated. Stylized mood piece that takes its time and manages to be insightful and provocative. C: Jack Nicholson, Maria Schneider. D: Michelangelo Antonioni. DRA [PG] 118m. V

Passing of the Third Floor Back, The 1936 British ★★★★ Mysterious new tenant (Veidt) in run-down boardinghouse befriends his troubled neighbors in this spiritual adaptation of a Victorian novel by Jerome K. Jerome. Veidt's character has a shy, easy manner and gentle sweetness wonderfully appropriate in this role. C: Conrad Veidt, Rene Ray, Frank Cellier, Anna Lee, Cathleen Nesbitt. D: Berthold Viertel. DRA 80m.

Passing, The 1988 ★★★½ Often captivating look at two troubled men whose lives chillingly converge. C: James Plaster, Welton Benjamin Johnson, Lynn Dunn. D: John Huckert. HOR 96m. V

Passing Through 1977 ★★★½ Musician finds frustration and seediness in the recording business and turns to his grandfather and heritage for consolation. Made while director was still a student at UCLA, this thoughtful drama has several memorable performances. C: Nathaniel Taylor, Clence Muse, Pamela Jones. D: Larry Clark. DRA

Passion 1919 ★★★½ Rural French woman charms her way to throne of Louis XV. Strong silent drama with gorgeous costumes. C: Pola Negri, Emil Jannings. D: Ernst Lubitsch. DRA 135m. V

Passion 1954 ★★★ Wilde's family is killed by evil cattle baron, so he tracks and kills bad guys, while police, led by Burr, chase him. Crisp, economical direction by Dwan and lush cinematography by John Alton almost deflect attention from wooden acting and stilted writing in this revenge picture set in old California. C: Cornel Wilde, Yvonne De Carlo, Raymond Burr, Lon Chaney, Jr. D: Allan Dwan. DRA 84m. V

Passion 1982 French ★★★½ Awkward story of filmmaker shooting movie about classical paintings, while fending off questions from his producers. Scant plot is overwhelmed by deluge of cinematic exercises—some confusing and some brilliant. Largely for fans of director Godard. C: Isabelle Huppert, Hanna Schygulla, Michel Piccoli. D: Jean-Luc Godard. DRA [R] 87m.

Passion 1986 Cantonese ★★★½ Told through flashbacks, interesting drama about pair of longtime friends who once vied for the same love interest. C: George Lam, Cora Miao. D: Sylvia Chang. DRA 90m. V

Passion d'Amore 1981 *See* **Passion of Love**

Passion Fish 1992 ★★★★ Sayles mixes comedy and pain in telling story of soap opera star, permanently crippled in a taxi accident, who is taught to cope with life by her nurse, a recovering crack addict. Bravura performances and spicy script. C: Mary McDonnell, Alfre Woodard, David Strathairn. D: John Sayles. DRA [R] 135m. V

Passion for Life 1951 French ★★★½ Sensitive, enthusiastic teacher (Blier) finds his country students embracing his enthusiasm for learning, but their stick-in-the-mud parents are less supportive. An engaging drama. (a.k.a. *Master* and *L'école Buissoniére*) C: Bernard Blier, Juliette Faber, Edouard Delmont. D: Jean-Paul Le Chanois. DRA 94m.

Passion for Power 1985 Spanish ★★★½ Beautiful woman complicates plans as two men attempt to seize control of crime group. C: Hector Suarez, Sasha Montenengro, Manuel Capetillo. ACT 94m. V

Passion in Paradise 1994 ★★★½ Strong cast searches for clues into murder of fabulously wealthy man. C: Armand Assante, Rod Steiger, Mariette Hartley. CRI 94m. V

Passion Island 1943 Mexican ★★★ A Mexican soldier assigned to a remote outpost has to quell rebellion among his troops when their short duty turns into years of war. Interesting period piece. C: David Silva, Isabela Corona, Pituka DeForonda. D: Emilio Fernandez. DRA

Passion of Anna, The 1969 Swedish ★★★★½ Sven Nykvist's photography and the stark Faro Island location enhance Bergman's austere vision of a widow (Ullmann), a widower (von Sydow), and a married couple entangled in each other's lives. Rich and moving. C: Liv Ullmann, Bibi Andersson, Max von Sydow, Erland Josephson. D: Ingmar Bergman. DRA [R] 101m. V

Passion of Beatrice, The 1988 French ★★★ Soldier (Donnadieu) returns from the Hundred Years War to sexually abuse his shy daughter (Delpy). Beautifully directed, but brutal, hard-to-take drama, full of violence and unpleasant characters. (a.k.a. *Beatrice*) C: Bernard Pierre Donnadieu, Julie Delpy, Nils Tavernier. D: Bertrand Tavernier. DRA [R] 128m. V

Passion of Joan of Arc, The 1928 French ★★★★★ The trial and execution of Joan of Arc told almost exclusively in close-ups. Falconetti (in her only film appearance) is staggering as the peasant girl. An unqualified silent masterpiece that instantly and forever established Dreyer as an artistic force. C: Maria Falconetti, Eugene Sylvain, Maurice Schutz. D: Carl Dreyer. DRA 77m.

Passion of Love 1981 Italian ★★★★ Period romance with handsome cavalry officer in love with gorgeous married woman, who finds himself drawn to physically repulsive spinster. Intriguing switch on Beauty and the Beast, poetic and touching. Source for Tony-award-winning Stephen Sondheim musical, *Passion*. (a.k.a. *Passion d'Amore*) C: Bernard Giraudeau, Valeria D'Obici, Laura Antonelli. D: Ettore Scola. DRA 117m. V

Passion of Slow Fire, The 1962 French ★★★½ Complex French drama has a professor (Desailly) accused in the murder of an American student and unable to defend his honor, with tragic results. All the ingredients for a taut, engaging film are here. C: Jean Desailly, Alexandra Stewart, Monique Melinand. D: Edouard Molinaro. DRA 91m.

Passion Play *See* **Love Letters**

Passion to Kill, A 1994 ★★½ California shrink (Bakula) falls for psychotic woman (Field). By-the-numbers low-budget melodrama. C: Scott Bakula, Chelsea Field, Sheila Kelley, France Nuyen. D: Rick King. CRI [R] 93m. V

Passionate Friends 1949 *See* **One Woman's Story**

Passionate Plumber, The 1932 ★★★ To make her lover jealous, a woman (Purcell) hires Keaton to dote upon her. Classic Keaton/Durante antics, and little else, keep this one afloat. (a.k.a. *The Cardboard Lover*) C: Buster Keaton, Jimmy Durante, Irene Purcell. D: Edward Sedgwick. COM 73m.

Passionate Sentry, The 1952 British ★★★★ Cummins falls for a callous St. James Palace guard in this very British comedy replete with dry wit and restrained romance. Characters are a delight, the story crisp and funny. (a.k.a. *Who Goes There?*) C: Nigel Patrick, Peggy Cummins, Valerie Hobson. D: Anthony Kimmins. COM 84m.

Passionate Stranger, The 1957 *See* **Novel Affair, A**

Passionate Thief, The 1960 Italian ★★★★½ Magnani finds herself in the slammer after getting mixed up with two pickpockets and an amorous American in this lively comedy. Fresh and intelligent. (a.k.a. *Laugh for Joy*) C: Anna Magnani, Toto, Ben Gazzara. D: Mario Monicelli. COM 100m. V

Passover Plot, The 1975 ★★★ Very controversial revision of Christian history, with Christ faking his deth as conversion tool and weapon against Romans. C: Harry Andrews, Hugh Griffith, Donald Pleasence. D: Michael Campus. DRA [PG] 105m. V

Passport to Destiny 1944 ★★★ During WWII, a determined scrubwoman (Lanchester) develops a scheme to knock off Hitler. Quite well done. (a.k.a. *Passport To Adventure*) C: Elsa Lanchester, Gordon Oliver, Lloyd Corrigan. D: Ray McCarey. DRA 64m.

Passport to Pimlico 1948 British ★★★★½ Dandy comedy about disgruntled Londoners discovering ancient charter allowing their neighborhood to secede from England. Eccentric leads Holloway and Rutherford romp through this winning fable. C: Stanley Holloway, Margaret Rutherford, Betty Warren, Hermione Baddeley, Basil Radford, Naunton Wayne. D: Henry Cornelius. COM 85m. V

Passport to Suez 1943 ★★★ Lone Wolf (William) visits Egypt to stop Nazi spies from destroying the Suez Canal in standard series entry (Warren's last). Blore's amusing as the Wolf's accomplice. C: Warren William, Ann Savage, Eric Blore. D: Andre De Toth. CRI 71m.

Password Is Courage, The 1963 British ★★★★ True story of British Sergeant Major Charles Coward, whose bold escapes from Nazi prison camps and anti-German actions made him a hero. Exciting action-adventure with a touch of whimsy; Bogarde heads a first-rate cast. C: Dirk Bogarde, Maria Perschy, Alfred Lynch. D: Andrew Stone. ACT 116m.

Past Caring 1985 British ★★★ An aging man is committed to a home for the senile. Powerful at times, but doesn't achieve full potential. Elliot and Williams are fine. C: Denholm Elliott, Emlyn Williams, Connie Booth, Joan Greenwood. D: Richard Eyre. DRA 77m.

Past Midnight 1992 ★★★½ Social worker (Richardson) falls for her patient (Hauer), an ex-con imprisoned for murdering his pregnant wife. Is he the one who is threatening her life? Implausible thriller buoyed by vibrant Richardson. C: Rutger Hauer, Natasha Richardson. D: Jan Eliasberg. CRI [R] 100m. V

Pastime 1991 ★★★★ Sad, funny story of aging minor league pitcher fighting retirement, who takes on teenage rookie as his protégé. Slow, but it pays off. (a.k.a. *One Cup of Coffee*) C: William Russ, Glenn Plummer. D: Robin B. Armstrong. DRA [PG] 95m. V

Pastor Hall 1940 British ★★★★ Incredible film for its day has frank message about the horrors going on in Nazi Germany, with a German minister speaking out against fascism and sent to a concentration camp. A version shot for American audiences features a prologue with Eleanor Roosevelt denouncing Hitler. C: Nova Pilbeam, Seymour Hicks, Wilfred Lawson, Marius Goring. D: Roy Boulting. DRA 97m.

Pat and Mike 1952 ★★★★ Delightful screwball comedy has shy but spunky athlete (Hepburn) being promoted by small-time manager (Tracy) as the Queen of Sports. Ably directed comedy delivers usual punchy chemistry from stars and features many sports star cameos. C: Spencer Tracy, Katharine Hepburn, Aldo Ray, Jim Backus. D: George Cukor. COM 96m. V

Pat Garrett and Billy the Kid 1973 ★★★½ The great bandit team and their violent journey through the American West. Typical Peckinpah: heavy on the blood and gore, light on character. Listen and look for Dylan's fleeting appearance. C: James Coburn, Kris Kristofferson, Richard Jaeckel, Katy Jurado, Bob Dylan, Rita Coolidge. D: Sam Peckinpah. WST [R] 122m. V

Patch of Blue, A 1965 ★★★★ Touching story of blind woman (Hartman) involved with black man (Poitier). Realistic and well acted. Winters won Best Supporting Actress Oscar as Hartman's prejudiced, abusive mother. C: Sidney Poitier, Elizabeth Hartman, Shelley Winters. D: Guy Green. DRA 106m. V

Patchwork Girl of Oz, The 1914 ★★★½ Animated silent adaptation of "The Wizard of Oz," directed by Dorothy's creator himself. D: Frank L. Baum. FAM/DRA 67m. V

Paternity 1981 ★★½ A single man (Reynolds) wants a baby but also wants to stay single, so he hires waitress (D'Angelo) to be the mother. Predictable comedy is directorial debut by stand-up comedian Steinberg. C: Burt Reynolds, Beverly D'Angelo, Norman Fell, Elizabeth Ashley. D: David Steinberg. COM [PG] 94m. V

Pather Panchali 1954 Indian ★★★★½ Classic by legendary filmmaker Ray forms the first part of the "Apu" trilogy. Indian abandoned by his father struggles to survive the extreme poverty of his boyhood in Bengal. Outstanding acting by the Banerjis. Features music by Ravi Shankar. (a.k.a. *The Song of the Road*. C: Kanu Banerji, Karuna Banerji. D: Satyajit Ray. DRA 112m. V

Pathfinder 1987 Norwegian ★★★★ Mythic power carries this tale (based on an old Lapp legend) of how a young boy outwits murderous nomads and saves his peaceful village in ancient Lapland. Harsh, snow-covered locations add to film's brutal feel. Unrated; contains violence, nudity. C: Mikkel Gaup, Nils Utsil. D: Nils Gaup. DRA 88m. V

Paths of Glory 1957 ★★★★★ French colonel in WWI defends three soldiers courtmartialed for cowardice after they fail in an impossible mission ordered by a fanatical general. Brilliantly acted and directed; vivid trench scenes overpoweringly photographed. Plight of three scapegoats is gut-wrenching. C: Kirk Douglas, Ralph Meeker, Adolphe Menjou. D: Stanley Kubrick. DRA 86m. V

Patricia Neal Story, The 1981 ★★★★ True story of actress's recovery from massive stroke, acted with restraint and passion by Jackson as Neal and Bogarde as her writer/husband Roald Dahl. Exceptional script by playwright Robert (*Tea and Sympathy*) Anderson. C: Glenda Jackson, Dirk Bogarde, Mildred Dunnock. D: Anthony Harvey, Anthony Page. DRA 100m. TVM

Patrick 1978 Australian ★★½ In a deep coma, a young murderer still makes his presence felt, psychokinetically. At times effective; mostly predictable. C: Susan Penhaligon, Robert Helpmann. D: Richard Franklin. HOR [PG] 96m. V

Patriot Games 1992 ★★★★ Retired spy (Ford) is pulled back into the agency when he foils an IRA assassination plot. Displeased, they target his family. Slick and brisk action thriller with a fine cast and some spooky imagery. From the Tom Clancy novel. C: Harrison Ford, Anne Archer, Patrick Bergin, James Earl Jones. D: Phillip Noyce. ACT [R] 120m. V

Patriot, The 1986 ★★★ A former Navy SEAL (Henry) is called back into service to foil some nuclear terrorists. Okay thriller, though the action scenes never really take off. C: Gregg Henry, Simone Griffeth, Michael J. Pollard, Jeff Conaway, Leslie Nielsen. D: Frank Harris. ACT [R] 88m. V

Patsy, The 1964 ★★★½ Sly comedy about the efforts of a cynical bunch of Hollywood types who turn bumbling bellhop (Lewis) into a comedy star. Twist of Lewis' typical manic character works better with pathos than with comedy. C: Jerry Lewis, Ina Balin, Everett Sloane, Keenan Wynn, Peter Lorre, John Carradine. D: Jerry Lewis. COM [R] 103m. V

Patterns 1956 ★★★★★ Incisive Rod Serling drama of Ohio executive entangled in boardroom power struggle of New York corporation. Excellent cast. Riveting performance by Begley as older man phased out by younger Heflin. C: Van Heflin, Everett Sloane, Ed Begley, Beatrice Straight, Elizabeth Wilson. D: Fielder Cook. DRA 83m. V

Pattes Blanches (White Paws) 1949 French

★★★★ Compelling adaptation of Jean Anouilh play about wealthy man and bar owner vying for attention of woman in fishing town. C: Suzy Delair, Arlette Thomas, Fernand Ledoux. D: Jean Gremillon. DRA 92m. V

Patti Rocks 1988 ★★★½ Crude young chauvinist visits pregnant girlfriend. Unusual, jarring, with moments of real power. Return of characters from the 1975 *Loose Ends*. C: Chris Mulkey, John Jenkins, Karen Landry. D: David Burton Morris. DRA [R] 86m. V

Patton 1970 ★★★★★ An outstanding biography of the complex, brilliant WWII general Patton and an excellent war drama as well. Scott and Malden are superb. Film was awarded seven Oscars, including Best Picture, Director, Actor (Scott), and Screenplay (by Francis Ford Coppola and Edmund North). (a.k.a. *Patton—Lust for Glory* and *Patton: A Salute to a Rebel.* C: George c. Scott, Karl Malden, Stephen Young, Michael Strong. D: Franklin J. Schaffner. DRA [M/PG] 171m. V

Patty Hearst 1988 ★★★ Adaptation of Hearst's *Every Secret Thing*, her account of her kidnapping by Symbionese Liberation Army is hampered by weird sequences intended to convince us of her brainwashing. Richardson prevails against the odds. C: Natasha Richardson, William Forsythe, Ving Rhames. D: Paul Schrader. DRA [R] 108m. V

Paul and Michelle 1974 British ★★ Young lovers try to plan a life together. Sequel to *Friends*. C: Sean Bury, Anicee Alvina, Keir Dullea. D: Lewis Gilbert. DRA [R] 102m. V

Paul Reiser—Out on a Whim 1988 ★★★ Odd jungle story frames stand-up routines from Reiser and funny friends, comically exploring materialism, health, and authority, etc. C: Paul Reiser, Teri Garr, Elliott Gould, Carrie Fisher. D: Carl Gottlieb. COM 60m. TVM V

Paul Robeson 1977 ★★★★ Jones is marvelous in one-man show chronicling the life of famous singer, actor, and political activist. Stagy and occasionally long-winded, but worth seeing for lead's virtuoso performance. C: James Earl Jones. D: Lloyd Richards. DRA 118m. TVM V

Paula 1952 ★★½ Woman provides speech therapy to a child who was left mute after a car accident. Unknown to both of them, she was the faulty driver. Very tall Young corn. C: Loretta Young, Kent Smith, Alexander Knox. D: Rudloph Mate. DRA 80m.

Pauline at the Beach 1983 French ★★★★ Rohmer's third "Comedies and Proverbs" film is a sly, subtle look at romance as an innocent teenager (Langlet) spends summer at the beach with her sexually more experienced cousin (Dombasle). Smart, realistic look at adult hypocrisy as seen through adolescent eyes. (a.k.a. *Pauline at the Beach*) C: Amanda Langlet, Arielle Dombasle. D: Eric Rohmer. COM [R] 94m. V

Paul's Case 1980 ★★★½ Henry Fonda hosts strong adaptation of Willa Cather story about young worker who attempts to steal his way across class lines. C: Eric Roberts, Michael Higgins, Lindsay Crouse. D: Lamont Johnson. DRA 52m. TVM V

Pawnbroker, The 1965 ★★★★★ Jewish pawnbroker in Harlem haunted by memories of Nazi prison camp atrocities, is forced out of self-imposed isolation by shattering impact of events around him. Staggeringly brilliant performance by Steiger. Important, beautifully made film. C: Rod Steiger, Geraldine Fitzgerald, Brock Peters, Jaime Sanchez. D: Sidney Lumet. DRA 116m. V

Pay or Die 1960 ★★★½ Solid gangster movie about police crackdown on Mafia in early 20th-century Little Italy. Good performances, steady pacing. C: Ernest Borgnine, Zohra Lampert. D: Richard Wilson. DRA 111m.

Payback 1991 ★★★½ Prison escapee sets out to avenge his brother's death but creates mayhem instead by falling in love with a sheriff's daughter. Neat plot twist and nice direction makes for good entertainment. Produced by *Newlywed Game* host Bob Eubanks. C: Corey Michael Eubanks, Don Swayze, Teresa Blake. D: Russell Solberg. ACT [R] 94m. V

Payday 1972 ★★★★½ The underside of life on the road is explored in story of down-and-out country singer Torn who spends his time with drugs, alchohol, and groupies. Torn is mesmerizing in this excellent, little-known film. C: Rip Torn, Ahna Capri, Elayne Heilveil, Cliff Emmich. D: Daryl Duke. DRA [R] 98m. V

Payment Deferred 1932 ★★★★ Meek bank clerk, desperate for money, murders rich relative. Compelling antique with great tension; superlative performance by Laughton at his quirkiest. C: Charles Laughton, Maureen O'Sullivan, Ray Milland. D: Lothar Mendes. DRA 81m.

Payment on Demand 1951 ★★★½ Road to divorce, as Davis/Sullivan marriage collapses. Not one of Davis' best films, but still interesting. C: Bette Davis, Barry Sullivan, Peggie Castle, Jane Cowl, Frances Dee. D: Curtis Bernhardt. DRA 90m.

Payoff 1991 ★★★ Vengeful ex-cop tracks his parents' murderers to Lake Tahoe. Typical rough stuff elevated by cast. C: Keith Carradine, Kim Greist, Harry Dean Stanton, John Saxon. D: Stuart Cooper. CRI [R] 111m. V

P.C.U. 1994 ★★ Tacky, crude comedy about a rebellious dorm fighting off "political correctness" at fictional Port Chester University. Mindless excuse for gross-out jokes; good for late-night goofiness fests. C: Jeremy Piven, Chris Young, Jon Favreau, David Spade, Sarah Trigger, Jake Busey, Jessica Walter, George Clinton. D: Hart Bochner. COM [PG-13] 79m. V

Peacemaker 1990 ★★½ A mass murderer preying on the entire galaxy touches down on Earth—and is chased by a cop from outer space. Exciting premise that falters on execution. C: Robert Forster, Lance Edwards, Hilary Shepard. D: Kevin S. Tenney. SFI [R] 89m. v

Peanut Butter Solution 1985 ★★★½ Pleasant children's film about 11-year-old who investigates hunted house and finds friendly ghosts. C: Mathew Mackay, Siluk Sayeanaay, Helen Hughes. D: Michael Rubbo. ACT 96m. v

Pearl of Death, The 1944 ★★★★ One of the original *Sherlock Holmes* series, the mystery is contrived but the acting is superb. In this adaptation of Sir Arthur Conan Doyle's *The Six Napoleons*, Holmes and Watson are racing to get to the Borgia Pearl before the Creeper (Hatton) can. As always, Rathbone makes a dapper Holmes, and his sidekick Bruce is equally well cast as Watson. C: Basil Rathbone, Nigel Bruce, Evelyn Ankers, Miles Mander. D: Roy William Neill. CRI 69m. v

Pearl of the South Pacific 1955 ★★★ An island paradise is invaded by pearl hunters. Flimsy. C: Virginia Mayo, Dennis Morgan, David Farrar. D: Allan Dwan. DRA 85m. v

Pearl, The 1948 ★★★★ In a small fishing village, a poor Mexican discovers that the fabulous pearl he has found has changed his life—but not, as he had hoped, for the better. Compelling treatment of Steinbeck's story; excellent photography. C: Pedro Armendariz, Maria Marques. D: Emilio Fernandez. DRA 77m. v

Pearls of the Crown 1937 French ★★★★ Historical adventure by director Sacha Guitry is the tale of the seven pearls in an English crown, given to such notables as Napoleon, Henry VIII, and Mary, Queen of Scots. An engaging and witty film best appreciated for cameos of French actors and actresses (Barrault is particularly striking as Napoleon). C: Sacha Guitry, Jacqueline Delubac, Jean-Louis Barrault. D: Sacha Guitry. DRA 121m. v

Peck's Bad Boy 1921 ★★★★ First of several screen versions of this classic about a Midwestern lad born to raise mischief. Young Coogan is delightful, and the production holds up surprisingly well. C: Jackie Coogan, Wheeler Oakman, Doris May. D: Sam Wood. FAM/COM 51m. v

Peck's Bad Boy with the Circus 1938 ★★½ Cline created yet another adventure for Peck (Kelly), a mischievous boy who runs amuck at a circus. Aimed at children, this standard fare now appears hopelessly dated despite a few funny scenes. C: Tommy Kelly, Ann Gillis, Edgar Kennedy, Billy Gilbert. D: Edward Cline. FAM/COM 78m.

Peddlin' In Society 1947 Italian ★★★½ Magnani, magnificent as always, makes and loses a forture on the black market in post-WWII Italy. Well acted drama. C: Anna Magnani, Vittorio de Sica, Virgilio Riento, Laura Gore. D: Genarro Righelli. DRA 90m. v

Pedestrian, The 1974 German ★★★★ German industrialist is exposed as a Nazi monster who helped wipe out a small Greek town. Nimble ensemble cast enable director Schell (in his debut behind the camera) to manipulate themes of guilt and revenge without moralizing. C: Gustav Rudolf Sellner, Peter Hall, Maximilian Schell. D: Maximilian Schell. DRA [PG] 97m. v

Pee-Wee Herman Show, The 1982 ★★★½ Original HBO special which started the award-winning TV series, offering fractured children's entertainment for adults. C: Pee-Wee Herman, Phil Hartman, John Paragon. D: Marty Callner. COM 60m. v

Pee-wee's Big Adventure 1985 ★★★★½ When his beloved bicycle is stolen Pee-wee Herman (Paul Reubens) heads out on a cross-country search to find it. Slam-bang energy radiates throughout this marvelous blend of color, music, and cartoonish comedy. Talents of former animator Burton are perfect match for Reubens' unique sense of humor. Great fun on multiple levels for kids and adults. C: Pee-wee Herman, Elizabeth Daily, Mark Holton, Diane Salinger. D: Tim Burton. COM [PG] 92m. v

Peeper 1975 ★★½ Caine plays a down-and-out British detective in 1947 Los Angeles who's searching for the long-lost daughter of a strange family. Spoof of film noir thrillers delivers the mood more than the laughs. (a.k.a. *Fat Chance*). C: Michael Caine, Natalie Wood, Kitty Winn. D: Peter Hyams. COM [PG] 87m.

Peeping Tom 1960 British ★★★★½ A psychopathic cinematographer is obsessed with filming women's reactions as he is murdering them. Deeply disturbing psychological suspense masterpiece. Gripping, though not for everyone. C: Carl Boehm, Moira Shearer, Anna Massey. D: Michael Powell. DRA 109m. v

Peg o' My Heart 1933 ★★★★ A vibrant young Irish colleen (Davies) is courted by an aging English nobleman. Charming and quaint—good, old-fashioned fun. C: Marion Davies, Onslow Stevens, J. MacDonald, Irene Browne. D: Robert Leonard. COM 89m.

Peg of Old Drury 1936 British ★★★½ Retelling of the real-life romance between 18th-century thespians Peg Woffington and David Garrick. Spirited entertainment. C: Anna Neagle, Cedric Hardwicke, Margaretta Scott, Jack Hawkins. D: Herbert Wilcox. DRA 74m.

Peggy 1950 ★★★½ Two sisters enter a beauty contest at the Rose Bowl parade. Pleasant but lightweight comedy. Cast of old pros and rising stars. C: Diana Lynn, Charles Coburn, Charlotte Greenwood, Rock Hudson. D: Frederick de Cordova. COM 77m.

Peggy Sue Got Married 1986 ★★★★½ At her 25th high school reunion, unhappily married Peggy Sue (Turner) faints, then wakes up as herself in 1961, with her grown-up memory intact. More than a time-travel comedy, film is clever, entertaining, and moving as Turner struggles to change her past. Unusual casting of Cage as goofy husband-to-be. C: Kathleen Turner, Nicolas Cage, Barry Miller, Catherine Hicks, Joan Allen, Kevin O'Connor, Barbara Harris. D: Francis Ford Coppola. COM [PG-13] 103m. V

Peking Express 1951 ★★★ Unremarkable remake of the 1932 *Shanghai Express*, this is the story of a group of people aboard a train in China that's waylaid by criminals. Cotten turns in a fine performance, but Calvet is unconvincing as the mysterious female lead. C: Joseph Cotten, Corinne Calvet, Edmund Gwenn, Marvin Miller. D: William Dieterle. DRA 95m.

Peking Opera Blues 1986 Hong Kong ★★★½ Energetic, amusing action comedy of two women caught up in intrigue in turn of the century China. Full of Hark's patented visual bravura and acrobatics, but the plot is almost indecipherable. C: Sally Yeh, Cherie Chung, Lin Ching-Heai. D: Tsui Hark. COM 104m. V

Pelican Brief, The 1993 ★★★½ Who is murdering Supreme Court justices? Only a law student (Roberts) and journalist (Washington) know. Charismatic stars struggle with an incredible script, adapted from the John Grisham novel. C: Julia Roberts, Denzel Washington, Sam Shepard, John Heard, Tony Goldwyn, Hume Cronyn, John Lithgow. D: Alan J. Pakula. CRI [PG-13] 141m. V

Pelle the Conqueror 1988 Danish ★★★★½ A much-deserved Best Foreign Film Oscar went to this emotional epic of a young boy and his father working as indentured servants for Danish landowners in the 1800s. Memorable, moving performances by Hvenegaard and von Sydow. C: Max von Sydow, Pelle Hvenegaard, Erik Paaske. D: Bille August. DRA [PG-13] 138m. V

Penalty Phase 1986 ★★★★ Stimulating, well-told story of judge who must live with consequences of his decision to release vicious killer because police violated his civil rights. C: Peter Strauss, Melissa Gilbert, Jonelle Allen. D: Tony Richardson. CRI 94m. TVM V

Pendulum 1969 ★★★½ Freed on appeal, a convicted murderer kills the wife of the detective who had arrested him. Tough and hard-hitting. C: George Peppard, Jean Seberg, Richard Kiley. D: George Schaefer. CRI [PG] 106m. V

Penelope 1966 ★★★ Penelope robs her husband's bank of $60,000 to get his attention, but has trouble putting it back. Wood is perky offbeat comedy's main appeal.. C: Natalie Wood, Ian Bannen, Dick Shawn, Peter Falk, Jonathan Winters. D: Arthur Hiller. COM 97m.

Penguin Pool Murder, The 1932 ★★★★ Inspector Gleason gets help and competition on a murder case from teacher Oliver. Nice chemistry between leads in film that launched the short Hildegarde Withers series. Good going. C: Edna May Oliver, James Gleason, Mae Clarke, Robert Armstrong. D: George Archainbaud. CRI 70m.

Penitent, The 1987 ★★½ Weird goings-on in a small town where residents reenact the Crucifixion every year. Julia finds the ritual useful when his friend (Assante) takes to his wife. Strange blend of love triangle and religious fervor. C: Raul Julia, Armand Assante. D: Cliff Osmond. DRA [PG-13] 94m. V

Penitentiary 1979 ★★★½ Brutal tale of framed inmate Kennedy and his battle for respect via the slammer's boxing ring. Fast-paced, furious, and funny. C: Leon Isaac Kennedy, Thommy Pollard, Hazel Spear. D: Jamaa Fanaka. ACT 99m. V

Penitentiary II 1982 ★★ Kennedy must prove himself in prison ring again. Carbon copy sequel to *Penitentiary*. Lacks predecessor's energy and humor, despite the formidable presence of Mr. T. C: Leon Isaac Kennedy, Ernie Hudson, Mr. T., Glynn Turman. D: Jamaa Fanaka. ACT [R] 108m. V

Penitentiary III 1987 ★★½ Kennedy reprises his role as boxer behind bars, this time with the likes of soap star Geary and pro midget wrestler. Better—by only a hair—than *Penitentiary II*. C: Leon Isaac Kennedy, Anthony Geary. D: Jamaa Fanaka. ACT [R] 91m. V

Penn & Teller Get Killed 1989 ★★★ Magicians Penn and Teller go on national television and gleefully discuss murder, which inspires an audience member to go after the pair. Certainly different, but unbridled sick humor is often self-indulgent without being funny. Definitely not for queasy viewers! C: Penn Jillette, Teller, Caitlin Clarke. D: Arthur Penn. COM [R] 90m. V

Penn and Teller's Cruel Tricks for Dear Friends 1988 ★★★½ The magicians of madness are back with a cable special in which they combine astounding feats with sardonic commentary. C: Penn Gillette, Teller. D: Art Wolff. COM 60m. V

Pennies from Heaven 1936 ★★★½ Depression-era bit of schmaltz with songs. Crosby is penniless drifter mixing with orphan girl and her grandfather. Bing sings title tune with singular charm. C: Bing Crosby, Edith Fellows, Madge Evans, Louis Armstrong. D: Norman McLeod. MUS 81m.

Pennies From Heaven 1981 ★★★★ Unusual musical mixes sunny Depression-era songs with a plot about a sheet-music salesman's unhappy marriage and his affair with a schoolteacher. Lavish production numbers and the gloomy story make an uneasy but fascinating combination. Based on a BBC miniseries. C: Steve Martin, Bernadette Peters, Christopher Walken, Jessica Harper. D: Herbert Ross. MUS [R] 107m. V

Penny Princess 1951 British ★★★½ Bogarde is wonderful as the leading man who courts an American shopgirl (Donlan) as she travels to Europe to collect her inheritance (a small principality). The story itself is lightweight but entertaining. C: Dirk Bogarde, Yolande Donlan, Fletcher Lightfoot. D: Val Guest. COM 91m.

Penny Serenade 1941 ★★★★ After Dunne miscarries, she and husband Grant decide to adopt a child in effort to save their marriage. Soap opera material played with compassion by stars. C: Cary Grant, Irene Dunne, Beulah Bondi, Edgar Buchanan. D: George Stevens. DRA 120m. V

Penthouse 1933 ★★★★ The mob uses up a good lawyer—then frames him for murder. Outstanding comedy/drama includes fine performances by Baxter and Loy. Van Dyke went on to direct *The Thin Man* series. C: Warner Baxter, Myrna Loy, Charles Butterworth, Mae Clarke. D: W.S. Van Dyke II. COM 90m.

Penthouse, The 1967 British ★★ Sadistic thieves break into an apartment and shatter bliss of cheating lovers. Disturbing, well acted but unpleasant affair. Definitely not for kids. C: Suzy Kendall, Terence Morgan, Tony Beckley, Martine Beswick. D: Peter Collinson. CRI 96m.

Penthouse, The 1989 ★★ A rich woman (Givens) is held hostage in luxurious apartment by disturbed ex-flame. Thriller puts Givens through more unpleasantness. C: Robin Givens, Robert Guillaume. D: David Greene. CRI 100m. TVM V

People Against O'Hara, The 1951 ★★★½ Defense lawyer with questionable background comes clean to help a client. Intelligent drama with fine Tracy leading a good cast. C: Spencer Tracy, Pat O'Brien, Diana Lynn, John Hodiak. D: John Sturges. DRA 102m.

People Are Funny 1946 ★★★ Antique radio comedy of battling sponsors buoyed by strong cast. C: Jack Haley, Helen Walker, Rudy Vallee, Ozzie Nelson, Art Linkletter. D: Sam White. COM 94m. V

People Next Door, The 1970 ★★★ Suburban couple wrestle with their teenage daughter's drug addiction. Earnest but stilted. C: Deborah Winters, Eli Wallach, Julie Harris, Hal Holbrook, Cloris Leachman. D: David Greene. DRA [R] 93m. V

People That Time Forgot, The 1977 British ★★★½ In 1919, an expedition sets out for an isolated island where three years before colleagues had been left behind. Fair adventure; uneven special effects in sequel to *The Land That Time Forgot.* C: Patrick Wayne, Doug McClure, Sarah Douglas. D: Kevin Connor. DRA [PG] 90m. V

People, The 1972 ★★★½ There's something wrong with the children in the small town where a teacher (Darby) has just been hired. Intriguing, modest sci-fi thriller sneaks up on you and delivers. C: Kim Darby, Dan O'Herlihy, William Shatner, Diane Varsi. D: John Korty. SFI 74m. TVM V

People Under the Stairs 1991 ★★★½ Claustrophobically effective horror film, shot through with humor and social commentary, about poor young boy who breaks into the home of his landlords and finds it to be a house of horrors. McGill and Robie are quite good as the demented duo. C: Brandon Adams, Everett McGill, Wendy Robie. D: Wes Craven. HOR 102m. V

People vs. Jean Harris, The 1981 ★★★★ Fascinating, by-the-transcript re-creation of school headmistress Harris' trial for murder of Scarsdale Diet doctor Herman Tarnower. Burstyn does a fine job in what seems more a televised play than a movie. C: Ellen Burstyn, Martin Balsam, Richard Dysart, Peter Coyote. D: George Schaefer. DRA 147m. TVM V

People Will Talk 1935 ★★★ An older couple are determined to get their daughter's failing marriage back on track. Ruggles and Boland provide the laughs in this otherwise minor comedy. C: Mary Boland, Charles Ruggles, Leila Hyams, Dean Jagger. D: Alfred Santell. COM 67m.

People Will Talk 1951 ★★★★½ Literate, thought-provoking comedy/drama about a doctor (Grant) who believes in treating patients, not diseases. Mankiewicz's witty script is well-served by the sparkling cast. C: Cary Grant, Jeanne Crain, Walter Slezak, Hume Cronyn, Finlay Currie. D: Joseph L. Mankiewicz. COM 110m. V

People's Hero 1987 Chinese ★★ Robbery gone wrong turns into hostage situation. C: Ti Lung, Tony Leung. D: Yee Tung-Shing. CRI 82m. V

Pepe 1960 ★ Hollywood's attempt to cash in on Cantinflas casts him as a Mexican peasant coming to Tinseltown and meeting positive mob of stars. C: Cantinflas, Dan Dailey, Shirley Jones. D: George Sidney. COM 157m.

Pepe Le Moko 1937 French ★★★★½ Gabin is charming gangster Le Moko, hiding out in the notorious Casbah district of Algiers and blowing his cover when he romances a beautiful woman. Atmospheric pre-noir film remains a classic. Remade in U.S. the next year as *Algiers.* C: Jean Gabin, Mireille Balin, Gabriel Gabrio. D: Julien Duvivier. DRA 95m. V

Pepi, Luci, Bom 1980 Spanish ★★★½ Young woman caught growing a marijuana plant decides to revenge herself on the arrogant cop in question by seducing his girlfriend. Debut film by Almodovar is the first in his series of off-the-wall sex romps. C: Carmen Maura, Felix Rotaeta. D: Pedro Almodovar. COM 86m. V

Pepper and His Wacky Taxi 1972 ★★★ Father of four starts cab company. Self-styled zaniness. C: John Astin, Frank Sinatra, Jr., Jackie Gayle, Allan Sherman. D: Alex Grasshof. COM 81m. V

Peppermint Rose 1992 ★★★½ Twelve-year-old Rose Richards visits the fantasy land of Peppermint Rose, where she must find a magical flower. Charming fun. FAM/SFI 25m. V

Peppermint Soda 1977 French ★★★★ Two

adolescent sisters try to cope with pain of their parents' separation while exploring their own growing maturity. Refreshingly unsentimental autobiographical coming-of-age story, bolstered by honest performances. C: Eleanore Klarwein, Odile Michel. D: Diane Kurys. DRA 97m. V

Percy and Thunder 1993 ★★★½ Former prizefighter (Jones) grooms a potential champion (Vance) while a crime syndicate tries to corrupt him. Standard boxing tale given punch and stature from an outstanding cast. C: James Earl Jones, Courtney B. Vance, Billy Dee Williams, Gloria Foster, Zakes Mokae. D: Ivan Dixon. DRA 100m. TVM V

Percy's Progress 1974 *See* **It's Not the Size That Counts**

Perfect 1985 ★★½ *Rolling Stone* reporter (Travolta) falls in love with the aerobics guru (Curtis) he intends to destroy in his article. Sleek and flashy, but not much above the neck. Appealing stars deserve better. C: John Travolta, Jamie Lee Curtis, Laraine Newman, Marilu Henner. D: James Bridges. DRA [R] 120m. V

Perfect Bride, The 1991 ★★½ A young woman with a history of violence and dementia, torments her fiancé's sister. Forced thriller. C: Sammi Davis, Kelly Preston. D: Terrence O'Hara. DRA [R] 95m. TVM V

Perfect Couple, A 1979 ★★★★½ A computer-dating service matches a repressed middle-aged antiques dealer with a free-spirited rock singer—and romance blossoms. Altman makes premise work with likable, unpredictable characters and a charmingly easy attitude throughout. C: Paul Dooley, Marta Heflin, Titos Vandis. D: Robert Altman. COM [PG] 110m. TVM

Perfect Crime, The 1978 ★★½ Someone is killing the top executives in a corporate empire and Scotland Yard wants to know why. C: Joseph Cotten, Anthony Steel, Janet Agren. D: Aaron Leviathan. ACT 90m. V

Perfect Family 1992 ★★ Knockoff of *The Stepfather*, with O'Neill and kids meanced by unknown nut in their own household. C: Bruce Boxleitner, Jennifer O'Neill, Juliana Hansen, Shiri Appleby, Joanna Cassidy. D: E.W. Swackhamer. DRA 92m. V

Perfect Friday 1970 British ★★★★ A disgruntled assistant bank manager plots with a millionairess and her weirdo husband to rip off the bank. Nimble heist comedy, thanks to breezy direction and plot twists. C: Stanley Baker, Ursula Andress, David Warner. D: Peter Hall. COM [R] 94m.

Perfect Furlough, The 1958 ★★★½ A soldier stationed in the Arctic wins a dream furlough to Paris. Has its bright moments, thanks to a quality cast. C: Tony Curtis, Janet Leigh, Keenan Wynn, Elaine Stritch. D: Blake Edwards. COM 93m. V

Perfect Gentlemen 1978 ★★★½ Prison widows (Bacall and Dennis) hire retired crook (Gordon) to help them rob bank in amusing heist comedy written by Nora Ephron. The female leads get high comedy marks all around. C: Lauren Bacall, Ruth Gordon, Sandy Dennis. D: Jackie Cooper. COM 100m. TVM

Perfect Harmony 1993 ★★★★ Restricted private school for boys undergoes turmoil when black students enter in the '50s. Disney cable feature intelligently presents historical and very human subject to younger audiences. C: Peter Scolari, Darren McGavin, Catherine Mary Stewart. D: Will Mackenzie. FAM/DRA 93m. TVM V

Perfect Marriage, The 1946 ★★★½ Married couple begins squabbling incessantly after 10 years of marriage. One-note and repetitive, but the stars are charming. Same premise as *The Awful Truth*, but nowhere near that classic. C: David Niven, Loretta Young, Eddie Albert, Charles Ruggles. D: Lewis Allen. COM 87m. V

Perfect Match, The 1987 ★★★½ A man and woman meet through the personals and pretend to be everything they're not. Routine relationship comedy elevated by charm of two leads. C: Marc McClure, Jennifer Edwards, Diane Stilwell. D: Mark Deimel. COM [PG] 92m. V

Perfect People 1988 ★★★★ A middle-aged couple try everything from diets to plastic surgery to escape the doldrums. Pointed, humorous satire on what "perfection" means. C: Lauren Hutton, Perry King. D: Bruce Green. COM 100m. TVM

Perfect Specimen, The 1937 ★★★ A wealthy woman sees to it that her grandson grows up in a very sheltered environment. But when he falls in love . . . ! Odd little comedy, interesting Flynn. C: Errol Flynn, Joan Blondell, Hugh Herbert, Edward Everett Horton, May Robson. D: Michael Curtiz. COM 97m.

Perfect Strangers 1945 *See* **Vacation from Marriage**

Perfect Strangers 1950 ★★★½ Two jurors on a murder case fall in love. Good cast; sharp writing. C: Ginger Rogers, Dennis Morgan, Thelma Ritter, Margalo Gillmore. D: Bretaigne Windust. CRI 88m.

Perfect Strangers 1985 ★★★½ A three-year-old boy (Stockley) witnesses an assassin (Rijn) commit a crime, and then the man falls in love with the boy's mother. There are some suspenseful scenes before this promising plot runs out of steam. (a.k.a. *Blind Alley*) C: Anne Carlisle, Brad Rijn, John Woehrle, Matthew Stockley. D: Larry Cohen. CRI [R] 91m. V

Perfect Tribute, The 1991 ★★★★ Southern teenager searches in Washington for her wounded brother during the Civil War and meets a melancholy President Lincoln. Touching family entertainment. C: Jason Robards, Lukas Haas, Campbell Scott. D: Jack Bender. FAM/DRA 100m. TVM

Perfect Victims 1988 ★★½ Cop goes after psycho model-killer. Bloody and predictable. C: Deborah Shelton, Clarence Williams III. D: Shuki Levy. CRI [R] 100m. V

Perfect Weapon, The 1991 ★★½ When Korean gangsters murder a martial arts instructor, they fail to consider effect on his American pupil (Speakman). Standard revenge/martial arts yarn with Speakman fast as lightning, but very frightening. C: Jeff Speakman, John Dye, Mako. D: Mark DiSalle. ACT [R] 85m. V

Perfect Witness 1989 ★★★½ Man who witnessed a mob rubout fears for his life after threats and agrees to testify only after pressure from the government. This HBO film builds to a harrowing finale. C: Brian Dennehy, Stockard Channing, Aidan Quinn. D: Robert Mandel. CRI [R] 104m. TVM V

Perfect Woman, The 1949 British ★★★ Screwball British comedy in which a mad scientist tries to improve upon women by making a female robot. The scientist's niece (Roc) masquerades as the robot with comic results. C: Patricia Roc, Stanley Holloway, Miles Malleson. D: Bernard Knowles. COM 89m.

Perfect World, A 1993 ★★★★ Costner plays a convict who kidnaps a child in '60s Texas, instigating massive manhunt, led by Eastwood. Thoughtful action drama notable for solid, charismatic performances. C: Kevin Costner, Clint Eastwood, Laura Dern, T.J. Lowther. D: Clint Eastwood. DRA [PG-13] 138m. V

Perfectly Normal 1991 Canadian ★★½ Weird comedy about average guy and overbearing restauranteur who open an eatery featuring opera-singing staff. Slow-moving; not as quirky as premise suggests. C: Robbie Coltrane, Michael Riley, Deborah Duchene. D: Yves Simoneau. COM [R] 106m. V

Performance 1970 British ★★★★ Seeking refuge from the law, a criminal hides out with a rock star and becomes wrapped up in his life. Intriguing psychological drama has a wide cult following. Jagger's great. C: James Fox, Mick Jagger, Anita Pallenberg. D: Donald Cammell, Nicolas Roeg. DRA [R] 104m. V

Perfume 1991 ★★★ Five friends who grew up together start a fragrance business. Story of friendship vs. ambition has some effective moments. C: Cheryl Francis Harrington, Kathleen Bradley Overton, Shy Jefferson, Lynn Marlin. D: Roland S. Jefferson. DRA 98m. V

Perfumed Nightmare, The 1977 Filipino ★★★★ An enthusiastic young Filipino (Tahimuk) is quickly disillusioned by modern Paris in this disarming comedy of errors. Small classic delivers the goods. C: Kidlat Tahimik, Dolores Santamaria. D: Kidlat Tahimik. COM 93m. V

Peril 1985 French ★★★ A guitar teacher's contact with a rich family leads to sexual attraction and murder. A self-conscious attempt at a New Wave visual style. C: Michel Piccoli, Nicole Garcia, Christophe Bohringer. D: Michel Deville. CRI 100m. V

Perilous Holiday 1946 ★★★★ Mexican counterfeiters make mischief for O'Brien, who is investigating the case. A surprisingly suspenseful tale with some clever comic touches. C: Pat O'Brien, Ruth Warrick, Alan Hale, Edgar Buchanan. D: Edward Griffith. CRI 89m.

Perilous Journey, A 1953 ★★½ Lackluster story of a ship of women who have set out for the California gold rush in search of mates. The acting is so-so, although there are a few laughs. C: Vera Ralston, David Brian, Scott Brady, Virginia Grey. D: R. G. Springsteen. WST 90m.

Perils of Gwendoline 1985 French ★★ Good production design and ample female nudity can't arouse this limp French hybrid of *The Perils of Pauline* and *Raiders of the Lost Ark*. Story (as if it mattered) concerns nubile young woman (Kitaen) leaving convent to search for her long-lost father. C: Tawny Kitaen, Brent Huff, Bernadette LaFont. D: Just Jaeckin. ACT [R] 88m. V

Perils of Pauline, The 1947 ★★★★ Nifty, unassuming musical biography of Pearl White (Hutton), heroine of silent cliff-hangers, is also a tribute to the genre. Tuneful Frank Loesser songs and zesty star make this genial entertainment. C: Betty Hutton, John Lund, Constance Collier, William Demarest. D: George Marshall. MUS 96m. V

Perils of Pauline, The 1967 ★★½ Saccharine tale in which two childhood sweethearts (Boone and Austin) search for one another through a series of predictable trials and tribulations. C: Pat Boone, Terry-Thomas, Pamela Austin. D: Herbert Leonard, Joshua Shelley. DRA 99m.

Perils of the Darkest Jungle 1944 ★★ Dull cliffhanger pits Tiger Woman against oil-company bad guys. C: Linda Stirling, Allan Lane, George Lewis, Duncan Renaldo. D: Spencer Gordon Bennet. ACT 196m. V

Period of Adjustment 1962 ★★★★½ Based on a play by Tennessee Williams, a romantic comedy about two couples, one recently married (Hutton and Fonda), and another (Franciosa and Nettleton) that's having marital difficulties. Director Hill coaxes fine comic performances out of his talented cast. Worth seeing. C: Anthony Franciosa, Jane Fonda, Jim Hutton, Lois Nettleton. D: George Roy Hill. COM 111m. V

Permanent Record 1988 ★★★★ The suicide of a popular teen (Boyce) stuns his school and devastates his best friend (Reeves), who's always lived in the shadow of his classmate's "ideal" life. Powerful, thought-provoking teen drama. C: Alan Boyce, Keanu Reeves, Michelle Meyrink. D: Marisa Silver. DRA [PG-13] 92m. V

Permission to Kill 1975 British ★★★ Cold War drama about a British intelligence officer (Bogarde) trying to keep an exiled government official from returning home behind the

Iron Curtain. Dark espionage adventure. C: Dirk Bogarde, Ava Gardner, Bekim Fehmiu, Timothy Dalton, Frederic Forrest. D: Cyril Frankel. DRA [PG] 96m. V

Perri 1957 ★★★★ Disney nature film combines live-action footage with voice-over narration showcasing the life of a squirrel through the seasons. Well-done movie that grammar school kids will enjoy. Based on book by Felix Salten. D: N. Kenworthy, Jr., Ralph Wright. FAM/DRA [G] 75m.

Perry Mason Warners managed four snappy Perry Masons, with Warren William playing Erle Stanley Gardner's indomitable defense attorney as a bit of a lounge lizard. The series declined a bit after William departed, with the next two films, starring Ricardo Cortez and Donald Woods, respectively, only managing moderate success. Of course, it fell to Raymond Burr and television to achieve the definitive Mason.

The Case of the Howling Dog (1934)
The Case of the Curious Bride (1935)
The Case of the Lucky Legs (1935)
The Case of the Velvet Claws (1936)
The Case of the Black Cat (1936)
The Case of the Stuttering Bishop (1937)

Perry Mason Returns 1984 ★★★★ Ace attorney Perry Masson defends beloved secretary Della Street after she is accused of slaying her new boss. A most welcome return. C: Raymond Burr, Al Freeman, Jr., Barbara Hale. D: Ron Satlof. CRI 95m. TVM V

Perry Mason: The Case of the Lost Love 1987 ★★★½ Burr returns as the detective he once popularized on TV, now defending the husband of a former flame he hasn't seen in years. Result transcends the mere revival of an old TV show, with a nifty twist at the end. C: Raymond Burr, Barbara Hale, William Katt. D: Ron Satlof. CRI 98m. TVM V

Persecution 1974 *See* **Graveyard, The**

Persona 1966 Swedish ★★★★½ Premiere teaming of director Bergman and actress Ullman in a complex psychological study. A star becomes mute and begins to switch personalities with the nurse (Andersson) caring for her in a rural cottage. Thick and nuanced; a rewarding though difficult film. C: Bibi Andersson, Liv Ullmann, Gunnar Bjornstrand. D: Ingmar Bergman. DRA 83m. V

Personal Affair 1954 British ★★ A schoolteacher becomes the prime murder suspect when his student disappears. An exasperating yawner. C: Gene Tierney, Leo Genn, Glynis Johns. D: Anthony Pelissier. CRI 82m.

Personal Best 1982 ★★★★ Track star finds herself torn between her coach and a lesbian teammate, who becomes her lover. Running has never been shot more lovingly; homosexual themes handled with wit and intelligence. C: Mariel Hemingway, Scott Glenn, Patrice Donnelly. D: Robert Towne. DRA [R] 124m. V

Personal Choice 1989 *See* **Beyond the Stars**

Personal Column 1947 French ★★★½ Ball is superb as a chorus-line dancer asked by the London police to lure a serial killer, who finds his female victims through the personal ads. Although the comic moments work well, the mystery itself often strains credibility. (a.k.a. *Lured*) C: Lucille Ball, George Sanders, Charles Coburn, Alan Mowbray, Boris Karloff. D: Douglas Sirk. CRI 102m.

Personal Foul 1987 ★★★★ Traveling buddies (Morse and Arkin) strain their friendship when they both become enamored of Duff. Offbeat road comedy occasionally drags, but rings true-to-life, bolstered by heartwarming performances. C: David Morse, Adam Arkin, Susan Duff. D: Ted Lichtenfeld. COM 92m.

Personal Property 1937 ★★★½ Taylor and Harlow radiate star quality and sex appeal in this comedy about an American woman who falls in love with her bailiff. Nothing substantial, but some clever scenes; a remake of *The Man in Possession.* C: Jean Harlow, Robert Taylor, Una O'Connor, Reginald Owen. D: W.S. Van Dyke II. COM 85m. V

Personal Services 1987 British ★★★★ An unassuming British woman inadvertently becomes a madam and finds herself excelling in her new job. Bawdy examination of the prostitution business, with wonderful performance by Walters and a frank approach to its subject matter. Inspired by real-life story of Cynthia Payne. C: Julie Walters, Alec McCowen, Danny Schiller. D: Terry Jones. COM [R] 104m. V

Personals, The 1983 ★★★★ Charming slice-of-life comedy follows misadventures of divorced man (Schoppert) trying to spice up his romantic life by placing personal ad in local newspaper. Realistic and amusing; independently shot in Minneapolis. C: Bill Schoppert, Karen Landry, Paul Eiding. D: Peter Markle. COM 90m. V

Persons in Hiding 1939 ★★★ Loosely based on the adventures of Bonnie and Clyde, this film features a deliciously wicked heroine who takes up with a gang of criminals. A competent if uninspired film. C: Patricia Morison, J. Carroll Naish, Lynne Overman, William Henry, Helen Twelvetrees, William Frawley. D: Louis King. CRI 71m.

Pet Sematary 1989 ★★½ Adaptation of Stephen King's best-seller about doctor's obsession with burial ground that can bring back the dead, suffers from unwieldy inclusion of too many of the novel's subplots and a lack of interesting characterizations. C: Dale Midkiff, Fred Gwynne, Denise Crosby. D: Mary Lambert. HOR [R] 103m. V

Pet Sematary II 1992 ★ Sequel to the box-office hit abandons original's logic (and ultimately its own), going mostly for repulsive gore and laughable plot, centering on the young Furlong's discovery of the burial ground and horrors that result. C: Edward Furlong, Anthony Edwards, Clancy Brown. D: Mary Lambert. HOR [R] 102m. V

Pete Kelly's Blues 1955 ★★★★ Set in Kansas City during Prohibition, this stylish film pays homage to jazz, gin, gangsters, and the men and women who made the '20s roar. A weak story line, but the soundtrack, which features Lee and Ella Fitzgerald, is a knockout. C: Jack Webb, Janet Leigh, Edmond O'Brien, Peggy Lee, Lee Marvin, Jayne Mansfield, Ella Fitzgerald. D: Jack Webb. DRA 95m. V

Pete 'n' Tillie 1972 ★★½ Romantic comedy about a cynical bachelor (Matthau) who marries Burnett, descends into melodrama half-way through. Based on Peter De Vries' novel *Witch's Milk*. C: Walter Matthau, Carol Burnett, Geraldine Page, Barry Nelson, Rene Auberjonois. D: Martin Ritt. DRA [PG] 100m. V

Peter and Paul 1981 ★★★½ Inspirational Biblical story of the followers of Christ after the Crucifixion, spreading the infant religion through the Roman Empire. Focuses on Peter (Foxworth) and Paul (Hopkins, in a fine performance). C: Anthony Hopkins, Robert Foxworth, Raymond Burr, Jose Ferrer, Jean Peters, Eddie Albert. D: Robert Day. DRA 200m. TVM

Peter And The Wolf And Other Tales 1982 ★★★★ Innovative versions of classic stories, including "The Ugly Duckling" and "Beware of the Jabberwock." Lovely blend of music and poetry. C: Ray Bolger, Jake Hathcock, Ray Dawe. D: Dan Bessie. FAM/DRA 82m. V

Peter Grimes 1981 ★★★★ Colin Davis conducts excellent royal Opera House production of Benjamin Britten's operatic masterwork. C: Jon Vickers, Heather Harper, Norman Bailey. MUS 90m. V

Peter Gunn 1989 ★★★ Vintage TV crime series is resuscitated with a new cast in this mundane tale of P.I. Gunn (Strauss) torn between the Mob and a corrupt police force. Script by Edwards. Classic title music by Henry Mancini. C: Peter Strauss, Barbara Williams, Jennifer Edwards, Pearl Bailey. D: Blake Edwards. CRI 100m. TVM V

Peter Ibbetson 1935 ★★★★½ Based on a novel by George du Maurier, a romantic fantasy of best friends separated as children who overcome tremendous obstacles to reunite in the afterlife. Cooper is particularly memorable as the lovelorn architect in search of Harding. A cult favorite often praised by surrealist writers like André Breton and Luis Buñuel, it still has the power to charm. C: Gary Cooper, Ann Harding, John Halliday, Ida Lupino. D: Henry Hathaway. DRA 88m.

Peter Pan 1953 ★★★★ Disney turns Barrie's tale of Neverneverland, Captain Hook and the mischievous Peter into an elaborate cartoon sure to delight most youngsters. Tinker Bell (drawn as a combination of Audrey Hepburn and Marilyn Monroe) steals the picture. Voices of Bobby Driscoll, Kathryn Beaumont, Hans Conreid. D: Hamilton Luske, Glyde Geronimi, Wilfred Jackson. FAM/ACT 77m. V

Peter Pan 1960 ★★★★½ Martin flies into the hearts of young and old alike as the boy who won't grow up in this entrancing TV version of James Barrie's Broadway musical hit. Catchy score by Moose Charlap, Carolyn Leigh, Jule Styne, Comden & Green. We defy anyone not to clap their hands to save Tinker Bell! C: Mary Martin, Cyril Ritchard. D: Vincent Donohue. FAM/MUS 100m. TVM V

Peter Rabbit and the Tales of Beatrix Potter 1971 *See* **Tales of Beatrix Potter, The**

Peter's Friends 1993 British ★★★★ Old theater friends gather for weekend reunion at British house, leading to set pieces revolving around romance, heartbreak, and talk, talk, talk. Witty adult comedy. Scripted by co-star Rudner and husband Martin Bergman. C: Kenneth Branagh, Emma Thompson, Rita Rudner, Stephen Fry. D: Kenneth Branagh. COM 102m. V

Petersen 1974 Australian ★★ Confused tale that stars Thompson as an extremely unlikable protagonist trapped in an unhappy marriage. Some social commentary. C: Jack Thompson, Jacki Weaver, Joey Hoenfels, Amanda Hunt. D: Tim Burstall. DRA [R] 97m.

Pete's Dragon 1977 ★★★ To escape drudgery of life with foster parents, an eight-year-old boy dreams up cartoon dragon only he can see. Unusually clumsy blend of live action and animation from Disney is hampered by mundane script and hammy acting. Strictly for kids. C: Helen Reddy, Jim Dale, Mickey Rooney, Red Buttons, Shelley Winters. D: Don Chaffey. FAM/DRA [G] 128m. V

Petit a Petit 1969 French ★★★½ Anthropologist/filmmaker Rouch gives African dignitaries a chance to study the "primitive" peoples of Paris in this humorous satire of anthropological films. Very funny, even though it runs out of gas towards the end. C: Damoure Zika, Lam Ibrahim Dia, Illo Gaoudel, Safi Faye. D: Jean Rouch. DOC 105m.

Petit Con 1984 French ★★★½ Movie version of the French comic strip about a rich teenage boy (Brieux) who drops out and pursues girls. Amusing Gallic satire. C: Guy Marchand, Caroline Cellier, Bernard Brieux. D: Gerard Lauzier. COM [R] 90m. V

Petite Sirene, La (The Little Mermaid) 1985 ★★★ Classic tale of a poor little rich girl who dreams of having some friends and fun in her life. C: Philippe Leotard, Laura Alexis, Evelyne Dress. D: Roger Andrieux. DRA 104m.

Petrified Forest, The 1936 ★★★★½ On the lam from their latest job, a group of gangsters hole up in an Arizona cafe. Davis and Howard are superb, as is Bogart's bold characterization. A major film with a splendid cast.

C: Leslie Howard, Bette Davis, Humphrey Bogart. D: Archie Mayo. DRA 83m. v

Petroleum Girls, The 1971 *See* **Legend of Frenchie King, The**

Petticoat Fever 1936 ★★★ Okay screwball about a lonely Arctic-based weatherman (Montgomery) who madly pursues Loy when she and her husband crashland their plane near his post. It's refreshing to see the woman shown as the level-headed part of the equation, but the script is tepid. C: Robert Montgomery, Myrna Loy, Reginald Owen, Winifred Shotter. D: George Fitzmaurice. COM 81m.

Petulia 1968 ★★★★½ A divorced doctor (Scott) gets involved far too deeply with a fascinating but troubled woman (Christie). Captivating comedy/drama with fine performances, and '60s San Francisco never looked better. C: Julie Christie, George C. Scott, Richard Chamberlain, Shirley Knight, Joseph Cotten. D: Richard Lester. DRA [R] 105m. v

Peyton Place 1957 ★★★★½ Delightfully juicy soap opera based on Grace Metalious' popular novel explores what lurks under the whitewashed surface of a New England town. Great cast pulls out all the stops, helped by Franz Waxman's score. Later a prime-time TV soap opera. Movie sequel: *Return to Peyton Place.* C: Lana Turner, Hope Lange, Arthur Kennedy, Lloyd Nolan, Lee Philips, Russ Tamblyn, Betty Field, Diane Varsi. D: Mark Robson. DRA 157m. v

Phaedra 1962 U.S.-French-Greek ★★★½ A Greek shipping magnate's new wife (Mercouri) has an affair with her step-son (Perkins). Depressing but effective updating of Euripides tragedy, *Hippolytus.* C: Melina Mercouri, Anthony Perkins, Raf Vallone. D: Jules Dassin. DRA 115m.

Phantasm 1979 ★★★½ Wild horror fantasy throws conventional storytelling to the winds, piling one giggly shock onto another as young Baldwin encounters a sinister mortician, killer dwarves, and a flying, bloodsucking steel ball. Not especially coherent, but tremendously energetic. C: Michael Baldwin, Bill Thornbury, Reggie Bannister. D: Don Coscarelli. HOR [R] 88m. v

Phantasm II 1988 ★★★ Le Gros and Bannister track evil Tall Man (Scrimm) across the country, encountering all manner of horrors as they go. More polished than the original, and thus lacking some of its anything-goes appeal, but often scary and funny nonetheless. C: James LeGros, Reggie Bannister, Angus Scrimm. D: Don Coscarelli. HOR [R] 97m. v

Phantasm III: Lord of the Dead 1994 ★★★½ Coscarelli's outlandish formula still works, as Bannister teams with some unlikely allies to rescue Baldwin from the sinister, otherworldly Scrimm. Has its lapses (including some misconceived humor) but also plenty of genuine shocks. C: Reggie Bannister, Michael Baldwin, Angus Scrimm, Gloria Lynne Henry, Kevin Connors. D: Don Coscarelli. HOR [R] 91m.

Phantom Empire 1989 ★★★ Affectionate parody of old serials and '50s sci-fi films. Group of scientists stumbles onto lost city ruled by buxom queen. C: Sybil Danning, Russ Tamblyn, Ross Hagen, Jeffrey Combs. D: Fred Olen Ray. COM [R] 85m. v

Phantom Lady 1944 ★★★★★ Extremely suspenseful tale about a man (Curtis) unjustly accused of murdering his wife. His secretary (Raines) takes it upon herself to find the real killer to save him from the electric chair. The psychological insight makes this film a must-see. C: Franchot Tone, Ella Raines, Alan Curtis, Thomas Gomez, Elisha Cook, Jr. D: Robert Siodmak. CRI 87m.

Phantom Light, The 1935 British ★★★ Set in Wales, this low-budget thriller is long on atmosphere, if short on sophisticated technique. Harker turns in a strong performance as a lighthouse keeper who confronts a boatload of wreckers intent on mischief. C: Binnie Hale, Gordon Harker, Ian Hunter. D: Michael Powers. DRA 75m.

Phantom of Liberty, The 1974 French ★★★★ Series of surreal vignettes examining various ironies and contradictions of everyday life. The dinner party scene is unforgettable. Strange, funny, and disconnected—a film that revels in the bizarre. C: Jean-Claude Brialy, Michel Piccoli, Monica Vitti. D: Luis Buñuel. COM 104m. v

Phantom of Paris *See* **The Mystery of Marie Roget**

Phantom of Paris, The 1931 ★★★ There are a few wonderful surprises in this otherwise ordinary tale of an illusionist accused of murdering the father of the woman he loves. Although the plot is confusing, there are some striking twists. Based on the Gaston Leroux novel. C: John Gilbert, Leila Hyams, Lewis Stone, Jean Hersholt. D: John Robertson. DRA 73m.

Phantom of Terror, The 1970 *See* **Bird with the Crystal Plumage**

Phantom of the Mall—Eric's Revenge 1989 ★★½ When her boyfriend burns to death in a mysterious fire, a young woman tries to get on with her life—but some force is stopping her. C: Morgan Fairchild, Kari Whitman, Jonathan Goldsmith. D: Richard Friedman. HOR [R] 91m. v

Phantom of the Opera 1943 ★★★★ Remake of the silent classic, with the deformed phantom (Rains) again unleashing his reign of terror on the Paris Opera House while pursuing a singer (Foster). Fine revamped horror, with a notable musical score. Oscars for art direction and lush color cinematography. C: Claude Rains, Susanna Foster, Nelson Eddy, Edgar Barrier. D: Arthur Lubin. HOR 93m. v

Phantom of the Opera 1989 ★★½ Yet another version of the classic horror story, as a disfigured composer/voice teacher haunts a Parisian opera house. This time the overtone is decidedly bloody. C: Robert Englund, Jill Schoelen, Alex Hyde-White. D: Dwight H. Little. HOR [R] 93m. V

Phantom of the Opera, The 1925 ★★★★½ Classic silent melodrama, with flourishes of horror, has Chaney as the mysterious phantom haunting a Parisian opera house. Plenty of innovative surprises, including two-strip Technicolor sequences. Chaney is brilliant as the lovesick monster. Remade several times; was also the basis for the popular Broadway show. C: Lon Chaney, Mary Philbin, Norman Kerry. D: Rupert Julian. HOR 86m. V

Phantom of the Opera, The 1962 British ★★★ British horror factory Hammer Studios takes its turn with the oft-filmed Gaston Laroux thriller about a scarred composer (Lom) who's obsessed with a fledgling diva (Sears). Some real shocks. C: Herbert Lom, Heather Sears, Thorley Walters, Edward DeSouza. D: Terence Fisher. HOR 84m.

Phantom of the Opera, The 1983 ★★★★ Opulent TV version of the oft-filmed horror tale features a marvelously hammy performance by Schell as the masked opera aficionado who'll stop at nothing to promote his favorite singer (the stunningly beautiful Seymour). Very entertaining indeed. Not based on the Broadway show. C: Maximilian Schell, Jane Seymour, Michael York. D: Robert Markowitz. HOR 100m. TVM

Phantom of the Paradise 1974 ★★★½ A scarred songwriter (Finley) seeks revenge on a duplicitous record company honcho (Williams) in this flashy, funny takeoff on the classic Gaston Leroux story, *Phantom of the Opera*. Flamboyant and melodramatic rock musical, with an entertaining cast. C: Paul Williams, William Finley, Jessica Harper. D: Brian De Palma. COM [PG] 92m. V

Phantom of the Ritz 1990 ★★ A disfigured killer haunts a rock-and-roll club. Lackadaisical variation on the classic horror story suffers from too much soul-searching, too little phantom. C: Peter Bergman, Deborah Van Valkenburgh, Russell Curry, Joshua Sussman. D: Allen Plone. HOR [R] 88m. V

Phantom of the Rue Morgue 1954 ★★★ Ineffective, by-the-numbers variation on *Murders in the Rue Morgue*, with a wildly overacting Malden controlling a murderous gorilla. Originally filmed in 3-D, with negligible effects. C: Karl Malden, Claude Dauphin, Patricia Medina, Steve Forrest, Allyn Ann McLerie. D: Roy Del Ruth. HOR 84m.

Phantom President, The 1932 ★★½ Conventional Rodgers and Hart score does little to animate this lifeless musical about a presidential candidate (Cohan) whose girlfriend (Colbert) is wooed by a slick look-alike (also played by Cohan). C: George M. Cohan, Claudette Colbert, Jimmy Durante, Sidney Toler. D: Norman Taurog. MUS 80m.

Phantom Ship 1937 ★★★ A cruise ship is found drifting off the coast of Africa. Her sails are set but there's not a trace of anyone. Based on a true story. C: Bela Lugosi, Shirley Grey. D: Denison Clift. HOR 61m. V

Phantom Strikes, The 1939 British ★★★★ Low-budget thriller about a man who dons clever disguises to outwit the police and kill a notorious criminal. Some fine moments and a touch of humor make this a well above-average suspense tale. (a.k.a *The Gaunt Stranger*) C: Wilfrid Lawson, Sonnie Hale, Alexander Knox, Louise Henry. D: Walter Forde. CRI 58m.

Phantom Tollbooth, The 1970 ★★★★ Young boy steps into tollbooth and enters the Land of Wisdom where numbers battle letters. Unusual mixture of live action and animation based on Norton Juster's popular children's book. Entertaining, but story line could confuse some younger viewers. Originally released in Japan in 1986, the American version is narrated by Dudley Moore. (a.k.a. *Adventures of Milo in the Phantom Tollbooth, The*) C: Butch Patrick. D: Levitow Jones. FAM/DRA [G] 90m.

Phantom Treehouse, The 1984 ★★★ Two kids enter a colorful strange world through a treehouse in the swamps. FAM/SFI 76m. V

Phar Lap 1984 Australian ★★★★ Uplifting story of Australia's greatest race horse told with wit, intelligence, and feeling. Race photography is top-notch. C: Tom Burlinson, Martin Vaughan, Judy Morris. D: Simon Wincer. FAM/DRA [PG] 107m. V

Phase IV 1975 ★★★½ Unusual sci-fi thriller about a colony of brainy ants that run amuck in the desert and are confronted by a pair of bumbling scientists (Davenport and Murphy). C: Nigel Davenport, Lynne Frederick, Michael Murphy. D: Saul Bass. SFI 86m. V

Phenix City Story, The 1956 ★★★½ Honest attorney-general (Kiley) goes up against a corrupt, drug-ridden town. A violent but gripping drama, based on a true story. C: Richard Kiley, Edward Andrews, Kathryn Grant, John McIntyre. D: Phil Karlson. CRI 100m.

Phffft! 1954 ★★★★ Lovely chemistry between Holliday and Lemmon brightens this sardonic look at marriage from point of view of divorcing couple; did they make a mistake? Screenplay by George Axelrod. C: Judy Holliday, Jack Lemmon, Jack Carson, Kim Novak. D: Mark Robson. COM 91m. V

Philadelphia 1993 ★★★★ Well-meaning film about a lawyer with AIDS (Hanks) who sues his former firm for discrimination. Hollywood's first big-budget film to tackle AIDS directly is earnest and memorably acted. Hanks won the Oscar for Best Actor. C: Tom Hanks, Denzel Washington, Jason Robards, Antonio Banderas, Mary Steenburgen, Ron Vawter, Robert Ridgley, Charles Napier. D: Jonathan Demme. DRA 122m. V

Philadelphia Experiment, The 1984 ★★★½ Time-travel romance of WWII sailor finding himself in 1980s. Tame fun. C: Michael Pare, Nancy Allen. D: Stewart Raffill. DRA [PG] 101m. V

Philadelphia Experiment 2, The 1993 ★★½ A mad scientist sends stealth bomber back in time to Nazis; after they win WWII, Johnson has to go back in time and straighten things out. Interesting premise slips into an ordinary action film. C: Brad Johnson, Marjean Holden. D: Stephen Cornwall. ACT [PG-13] 98m. V

Philadelphia Story, The 1940 ★★★★★ Brilliant, giddy screwball comedy centers on a Main Line society family's preparation for wedding and bright, headstrong bride's (Hepburn's) cold feet. Sparkling, top-notch comedy with Hepburn, Stewart, and Grant in rare form. Later set to music in *High Society*. Stewart's only Best Actor Oscar. C: Cary Grant, Katharine Hepburn, James Stewart, Ruth Hussey, Roland Young, Virginia Weidler. D: George Cukor. COM 112m. V

Phillip Marlowe—Finger Man 1983 ★★★ Private Eye Marlowe goes head to head against a brutal drug ring. C: Powers Boothe, Gayle Hunnicutt, Ed Bishop. D: Peter H. Hunt. ACT 54m. TVM V

Phillip Marlowe: Smart-Aleck Kill 1983 ★★★ Private Eye must solve the case of a movie star who's found murdered the night before a big premiere. C: Powers Boothe, Michael Shannon, Liza Ross. D: Peter H. Hunt. ACT 53m. TVM

Philo Vance S.S. Van Dine's foppish amateur sleuth has the distinction of being the only series detective to be portrayed in competing films by three different series, beginning his film life at Paramount with William Powell in three titles, then being done by Basil Rathbone at MGM, and Warren William at Warners. None of these films is particularly distinguished, but Powell's *Vance* mystery with Warners, *The Kennel Murder Case*, is one of the best series mysteries of the '30s, thanks largely to Michael Curtiz's sinuous direction. The character ended up at Poverty Row studio PRC in 1947 for three quickies.

The Canary Murder Case (1929)
The Greene Murder Case (1929)
Bishop Murder Case (1930)
Benson Murder Case (1930)
The Kennel Murder Case (1933)
The Dragon Murder Case (1934)
Casino Murder Case (1933)
The Garden Murder Case (1936)
Night of Mystery (1937)
The Gracie Allen Murder Case (1939)
Calling Philo Vance (1940)
Philo Vance Returns (1947)
Philo Vance's Gamble (1947)
Philo Vance's Secret Mission (1947)

Philo Vance Returns 1947 ★★★★ Clever, low-budget thriller stars William Wright as the dapper detective Philo Vance. One of Vance's better silver-screen efforts. C: William Wright, Terry Austin, Leon Belasco. D: William Beaudine. CRI 64m.

Philo Vance's Secret Mission 1947 ★★★★½ Top-drawer mystery stars Curtis as Philo Vance, the suave detective/hero who goes undercover as a technical advisor for a detective magazine with his girlfriend (Ryan), but can't prevent the publisher being murdered. Worth seeing. C: Alan Curtis, Sheila Ryan, Tala Birell. D: Reginald Borg. CRI 58m.

Phobia 1980 Canadian ★★ Nonsensical tale of a psychiatrist whose phobic patients are being serially murdered. Cast tries. C: Paul Michael Glaser, Susan Hogan, John Colicos. D: John Huston. CRI [R] 90m. V

Phoenix The Warrior 1988 ★★★ Female barbarians (far in the future) fight each other for control of the earth. C: Persis Khambatta, Kathleen Kinmont. D: Robert Hayes. SFI 90m. V

Phone Call from a Stranger 1952 ★★★½ Merrill stars as the sole survivor of a plane crash who visits the victims' families. Nothing more than a series of vignettes, and yet wonderful performances by Davis and Winters make it worthwhile. C: Bette Davis, Shelley Winters, Gary Merrill, Michael Rennie, Keenan Wynn. D: Jean Negulesco. DRA 96m. V

Phone Call, The 1989 ★★ An otherwise happy family man calls a sex phone line, but he misdials and winds up talking to a man who's crazy for revenge—against him. C: Michael Sarrazin, Ron Lea, Linda Smith. DRA 95m. V

Photographer, The 1975 ★★★ A photogrpaher snaps and starts to kill off his models—in excessively brutal ways. C: Michael Callan, Isabel Sanford. D: William Byron Hillman. DRA [PG] 94m. V

Physical Evidence 1989 ★★½ An-ex cop (Reynolds) accused of a killing is defended by a lawyer (Russell) who is hindered by his not remembering anything about the alleged crime. She also falls in love with him, muddying the waters even more. Dull script further weakened by Russell. C: Burt Reynolds, Theresa Russell, Ned Beatty. D: Michael Crichton. CRI [R] 99m. V

Piaf 1981 ★★★½ The life, times and sounds of France's great chanteuse. Complex portrait does not shy away from her penchant for self-destruction. D: Jane Lapotaire. MUS 114m. V

Piaf—The Early Years 1974 U.S. ★★ The facts of Piaf's early life—she was raised in a brothel and both lost and recovered her sight—are almost too far-fetched for any film. Unfortunately, this one plays up the melodrama to a clichéd pitch. Although made in 1974, *Piaf* was not released in the U.S. until 1982. C: Brigitte Ariel, Pascale Christophe, Guy Trejan. D: Guy Casaril. DRA [PG] 104m.

Piano for Mrs. Cimino, A 1982 ★★★★ A feisty widow (Davis), declared unfit to control a fortune, fights back. One of the best of a string of TV movies starring the veteran actress. C: Bette Davis, Penny Fuller, Keenan Wynn, George Hearn. D: George Schaefer. DRA 100m. V

Piano, The 1993 ★★★★ At the turn of the century, a mute pianist (Hunter) is sent to New Zealand as a mail-order bride for Neill, but she feels a special kinship with Brit expatriate/honorary Maori Keitel. The heroine is cold and enigmatic and the story has some reverse sexism, but there is exceptional acting from all, and stunning cinematography. Be warned, though; there is one scene of real violence. Film garnered three Oscars: Hunter (Best Actress), Paquin (Best Supporting), and Screenplay. C: Holly Hunter, Harvey Keitel, Sam Neill, Anna Paquin. D: Jane Campion. DRA [R] 121m. V

Picasso Summer, The 1969 ★★½ Married art fanatics (Finney, Mimieux) take to European roads to find their favorite artist. Good performances and scenery can't mask the void at the center of the story, which fails to hold interest. Inspired by a Ray Bradbury story. C: Albert Finney, Yvette Mimieux. D: Serge Bourguignon. DRA [PG] 90m.

Picasso Trigger 1989 ★★★ Spy looks for murderer in Hawaii, with occasional sidestops for sex, violence and scenery. Sleek but average adventure sequel to *Hard Ticket to Hawaii.* C: Steve Bond, Dona Speir, John Aprea. D: Andy Sidaris. ACT [R] 99m. V

Piccadilly Jim 1936 ★★★★ Sparkling comedy about the romantic quests of a son and his father. Adaptation of a story by P.G. Wodehouse uses its London setting to great advantage. C: Robert Montgomery, Madge Evans, Frank Morgan, Eric Blore, Billie Burke. D: Robert Z. Leonard. COM 100m.

Pick-up Artist, The 1987 ★★★ Young womanizer Downey pursues Ringwald and is shocked when she doesn't respond. Downey is tiring but Ringwald is striking in a thankless role. C: Molly Ringwald, Robert Downey, Jr., Dennis Hopper, Danny Aiello, Mildred Dunnock, Harvey Keitel, Vanessa Williams. D: James Toback. COM [PG-13] 81m. V

Pickle, The 1993 ★★½ Hollywood director examines his life and the state of his career as he agrees to make a horror movie about a giant, rampaging pickle. Cynical comedy attempts to satirically spear the film business, but doesn't have enough bite. C: Danny Aiello, Dyan Cannon, Shelley Winters, Little Richard. D: Paul Mazursky. COM [R] 103m. V

Pickles Make Me Cry 1988 Chinese ★★★ Offbeat comedy of a young Asian couple tangling with a tough chinese gang in NYC. D: Peter Chow. COM 85m.

Pickpocket 1963 French ★★★★ Young unemployed man begins picking pockets on the Parisian metro and becomes irresistibly attracted to theft. Fascinating portrayal of obsession narrated by the pickpocket in flashbacks from prison. C: Martin Lassalle, Marika Green, Pierre Leymarie, Jean Pelegri. D: Robert Bresson. DRA 75m. V

Pickup on 101 1972 ★★½ An unlikely trio—a college student (Warren), an unemployed musician (Sheen), and a homeless drifter (Albertson)—become friends and traveling companions. Slight story never seems to hit its stride. (a.k.a. *Where the Eagle Flies*) C: Jack Albertson, Lesley Ann Warren, Martin Sheen, Michael Ontkean. D: John Florea. DRA [PG] 93m. V

Pickup on South Street 1953 ★★★★½ FBI agents pursue a pickpocket (Widmark) who has unintentionally stolen some top secret microfilm. Agents are hunting Communist sympathizers, giving a political twist to the action. Absolutely absorbing suspense thriller. C: Richard Widmark, Jean Peters, Thelma Ritter, Richard Kiley. D: Samuel Fuller. CRI 81m. V

Pickwick Papers 1985 ★★★ An animated rendition of Dicken's classic tale of the members of the Pickwick Club. FAM/ACT 72m.

Pickwick Papers, The 1952 British ★★★★ Well-made adaptation features many of the high points from Dickens' novel as jolly Mr. Pickwick and his friends look for adventure. Director Langley captures Dickens' sly humor as well as the flavor of 19th-century England. C: James Hayter, James Donald, Hermione Baddeley, Kathleen Harrison, Hermione Gingold. D: Noel Langley. DRA 109m. V

Picnic 1956 ★★★★½ Screen version of William Inge's Pulitzer Prize-winning play about seductive drifter who arouses passions of a small Kansas town's women and falls for his college chum's girlfriend. Powerful rendering of American life with fine supporting performances. C: William Holden, Rosalind Russell, Kim Novak, Betty Field, Cliff Robertson, Arthur O'Connell, Susan Strasberg. D: Joshua Logan. DRA 113m. V

Picnic at Hanging Rock 1975 Australian ★★★★ Eerie turn-of-the-century tale about a teacher and group of young schoolgirls who take off on a picnic outing and disappear. Beautifully shot and richly atmospheric suspense. C: Rachel Roberts, Dominic Guard, Helen Morse, Jacki Weaver. D: Peter Weir. DRA [PG] 110m. V

Picnic On The Grass 1960 French ★★★½ Impressionistic tale from master director about scientist running for president of Europe who falls in love with young rural woman. Dreamlike pleasure. C: Paul Meurisse, Catherine Rouvel, Fernand Sardou. D: Jean Renoir. DRA 90m. V

Picture Bride 1994 ★★★★ Handsome low-budget drama about Kudoh, the bride in an arranged marriage to a Hawaiian planter circa 1915, whose only acquaintance with him is a

20-year-old photo. When she gets to the islands, she gets an unpleasant surprise. Inventive, well-acted independent feature. C: Youki Kudoh, Akira Takayama, Cary-Hiroyuki Tagawa, Tamlyn Tomita, Toshiro Mifune, Yoko Sugi. D: Kayo Hatta. DRA 98m.

Picture Mommy Dead 1966 ★★ A young girl (Gordon) witnesses the death of her mother in a fire and becomes possessed by her spirit. When her father (Ameche) remarries, the girl and her new stepmother begin fighting in this depressingly silly horror film. C: Don Ameche, Martha Hyer, Zsa Zsa Gabor, Susan Gordon. D: Bert I. Gordon. HOR 85m. V

Picture of Dorian Gray, The 1945 ★★★★ Oscar Wilde story of vain, handsome young Victorian gentleman whose self-portrait ages while he remains youthful. Discerning, elegant presentation of ominous subject. Sanders winning as foppish cad. Won Oscar for Cinematography. Remade as *Dorian Gray*. C: George Sanders, Hurd Hatfield, Donna Reed, Angela Lansbury. D: Albert Lewin. DRA 101m. V

Picture of Dorian Gray, The 1973 ★★★½ An updated version of Wilde's story of the young man who stays young forever—while his portrait ages. C: Nigel Davenport, Shane Briant, Charles Aidman. D: Glenn Jordan. HOR 129m. V

Picture Show Man, The 1977 Australian ★★★ Sweet Australian comedy based on the real-life attempts of rival picture show troupes to bring movies to the bush in the '20s. At times heavy-handed, the film too often depends on nostalgia for the early days of movies. C: Rod Taylor, John Meillon, John Ewart. D: John Power. COM [PG] 99m.

Picture Snatcher 1933 ★★★★ Strange little gem about a photographer (Cagney) who snaps a forbidden image—a woman in the electric chair. Fast-paced blend of comedy and suspense. C: James Cagney, Ralph Bellamy, Alice White. D: Lloyd Bacon. CRI 77m.

Piece of the Action, A 1977 ★★★½ Poitier (who also directed) and co-star Cosby as con artists who sidestep jail by volunteering to work with underprivileged children. Third Poitier and Cosby teaming showcases their easy chemistry in funny comedy which occasionally spouts unnecessary preachy messages. C: Sidney Poitier, Bill Cosby, James Earl Jones, Denise Nicholas. D: Sidney Poitier. COM [PG] 135m. V

Pied Piper, The 1942 ★★★★ A man (Woolley) who hates kids helps a group of them escape from the Nazis in occupied France. Absolutely compelling. Nominated for an Oscar for Best Picture. C: Monty Woolley, Roddy McDowall, Otto Preminger, Anne Baxter, Peggy Ann Garner. D: Irving Pichel. DRA 86m.

Pied Piper, The 1972 British ★★★½ Children's classic features a mysterious piper whose music mesmerizes the rats of Hamelin. Plague and the Middle Ages seem terrifyingly real in Demy's horror movie about infestation. C: Donovan, Donald Pleasence, Michael Hordern, Jack Wild, Diana Dors, John Hurt. D: Jacques Demy. HOR [G] 90m.

Pierrot le Fou 1965 French ★★★★ New Wave classic tells of two fugitives—he from his wife, she from mobsters—whose lives intersect. Innovative and improvisational: Belmondo and Karina's chemistry is riveting. C: Jean-Paul Belmondo, Anna Karina, Jean-Pierre Leaud. D: Jean-Luc Godard. CRI 110m. V

Pigeon That Took Rome, The 1962 ★★ A U.S. soldier (Heston) in WWII Rome uses pigeons as couriers to Allied troops. Lame-brained service comedy is strictly for the birds. C: Charlton Heston, Elsa Martinelli, Harry Guardino. D: Melville Shavelson. COM 101m.

Pigs 1984 ★★★★ Gritty tale of squatters sharing the same rundown space in Dublin has a dark fascination. Poverty is never romanticized in this idiosyncratic look at a group of people on the fringes of society. DRA

Pigs, The 1992 ★★★ The police are called in to try and put an end to a dope smuggling ring. C: Boguslaw Linda. D: Wladyslaw Pasikowski. DRA 108m. V

Pigs vs. Freaks 1984 *See* **Off Sides**

Pigskin Parade 1936 ★★★½ Garland's first major film is a musical comedy about the joys of college football. Campy songs and some good acting. C: Stuart Erwin, Judy Garland, Patsy Kelly, Jack Haley, Betty Grable. D: David Butler. MUS 93m.

Pilgrimage 1933 ★★½ Mawkish tale of an old woman who regrets encouraging her son to enlist in WWI to prevent his marriage and then travels to France to see his grave. Even the strong character study of the mother doesn't provide enough relief from melodrama. C: Henrietta Crosman, Heather Angel, Norman Foster. D: John Ford. DRA 95m.

Pillars of Society 1936 German ★★★★ Adapted from an Ibsen play, Sirk's fascinating portrait of a bourgeois family does a wonderful job of uncovering hypocrisy and complacent attitudes; the psychological undercurrents build to a satisfying crescendo. C: Heinrich George, Maria Krahn, Horst Teetzmann, Albretch Schoenhals. D: Douglas Sirk. DRA 82m.

Pillars of the Sky 1956 ★★½ Unremarkable Western about an Army officer (Chandler) and a missionary (Marshall) determined to bring about peace between the cavalry and the Indians. C: Jeff Chandler, Dorothy Malone, Ward Bond. D: George Marshall. WST 95m.

Pillow Talk 1959 ★★★★½ Cute, entertaining battle of the sexes comedy with Rock and Doris unknowingly sharing a party line. Two stars do this kind of stuff very well, supported by peerless Ritter and Randall. Spiffy production—lavish sets, costumes and, oh, those fashions! Oscars for story and screenplay. C:

Doris Day, Rock Hudson, Tony Randall, Thelma Ritter. D: Michael Gordon. COM 102m. V

Pillow to Post 1945 ★★ Predictable WWII comedy about a young girl (Lupino) who pretends to have married a soldier in order to rent a hotel room is more irritating than entertaining. C: Ida Lupino, Sydney Greenstreet, William Prince, Ruth Donnelly. D: Vincent Sherman. COM 92m.

Pimpernel Smith 1941 British ★★★★ Adaptation of *The Scarlet Pimpernel* believably translates that classic into a WWII tale. Howard is superb as professor zealously rescuing scientists from the Nazis. (a.k.a. *Mister V.*) C: Leslie Howard, Mary Morris, Francis Sullivan. D: Leslie Howard. DRA 122m. V

Pin 1988 Canadian ★★★★ A doctor uses a medical mannequin as a way to communicate with his children; after he and his wife die in an accident, their son believes that "Pin" is alive. Unusual, absorbing, well-acted psychothriller, from Andrew Neiderman's novel. C: David Hewlett, Cyndy Preston, John Ferguson, Terry O'Quinn, Helene Udy. D: Sandor Stern. HOR [R] 103m. V

Pin Up Girl 1944 ★★★★ A chorus dancer on the verge of stardom pretends to be a secretary to be close to the man she loves. Typical Grable Technicolor nonsense, but with fun musical numbers. Raye belts out a tune or two with gusto. C: Betty Grable, Joe E. Brown, Martha Raye, John Harvey. D: Bruce Humberstone. MUS 83m. V

Pinchcliffe Grand Prix 1981 ★★★ A brilliant inventor matches wits against an evil man during the famous Pinchcliffe Grand Prix. FAM/ACT [G] 88m. V

Pink Cadillac 1989 ★★★ Semientertaining chase movie has bail-bond bounty hunter (Eastwood) protecting the wife (Peters) of the guy he's chasing. C: Clint Eastwood, Bernadette Peters, Timothy Carhart, William Hickey. D: Buddy Van Thorn. CRI [PG-13] 121m. V

Pink Floyd—The Wall 1982 ★★★½ Youth grows up to become rock star, but is unfeeling and unconnected. Based on Pink Floyd's 1979 LP; striking, but grim and surreal, including the animation. C: Phyllis Diller, Slim Pickens, Terri Berland, Brad Cowgill. D: Mike MacFarland. DRA [R] 90m. V

Pink Jungle, The 1968 ★★★ Implausible but entertaining story of photographer (Garner) and model (Renzi) who become involved in jewel-smuggling scheme in South America. Likable, despite confusing sequences and tired plot devices. C: James Garner, Eva Renzi, George Kennedy, Michael Ansara. D: Delbert Mann. ACT 104m.

Pink Panther, The 1964 ★★★★½ In this wacky and very funny comedy, Clouseau, the cinema's most inept detective, attempts to find out who stole a fabulous pink diamond. Sellers is hilarious; fine support by Niven as the thief and Capucine as Clouseau's wife (and Niven's lover). First in long series. C: Peter Sellers, David Niven, Capucine, Robert Wagner, Claudia Cardinale. D: Blake Edwards. COM 113m. V

Pink Panther Strikes Again, The 1976 British ★★★★ Hilarious fourth *Panther* sequel finds the now-insane Chief Inspector Dreyfus (Lom) out to destroy bumbling underling Clouseau (Sellers) and the rest of the world. Outrageous plot is bolstered by an assortment of sidesplitting gags. Don't miss the opening credits. C: Peter Sellers, Herbert Lom, Colin Blakely, Lesley-Anne Down. D: Blake Edwards. COM [PG] 110m. V

Pinky 1949 ★★★★ Ground-breaking tale of a black woman (Crain) in the South who complicates her life by passing as white. Fine acting and a moving script. C: Jeanne Crain, Ethel Barrymore, Ethel Walters. D: Elia Kazan. DRA 102m. V

Pinocchio 1940 ★★★★★ One of Disney's finest retells Carlo Collodi tale of wooden puppet Pinocchio. With conscience Jiminy Cricket at his side, Pinocchio sets off on series of misadventures. Masterful animation, unforgettable sequences and Oscar for Best Song, "When You Wish Upon a Star." Some sections may be too frightening for youngest viewers, but otherwise superior family entertainment. Voices of Dick Jones, Cliff Edwards. D: Ben Sharpsteen, Hamilton Luske. FAM/MUS [G] 88m. V

Pinocchio 1968 ★★★★ Fabled story receives innovative treatment in magical performance by Prague Maionette Theater. FAM/COM 73m. V

Pinocchio 1977 ★★★½ Spirited performances add zest to musical adaptation of classic tale. C: Danny Kaye, Sandy Duncan. FAM/MUS [G] 76m. V

Pinocchio and the Emperor of the Night 1987 ★★ Follow-up of famous tale sends real-life boy Pinocchio and wooden cricket pal on series of adventures. Weak animation, clichéd storytelling, and dubious moral teachings (Pinocchio saves friends with lies!) make this a questionable choice for younger viewers. D: Hal Sutherland. DRA [G] 91m. V

Pinocchio in Outer Space 1964 French-U.S. ★ Parents might wish he'd stay there after watching this badly dubbed cartoon about the puppet touring the galaxy. Voices of Arnold Stang, Jess Cain. D: Ray Goosens. FAM/DRA 90m. V

Pinocchio's Christmas 1980 ★★★★ Geppetto grows concerned after Pinocchio elopes with another young puppet during the Christmas season. Puppet animation, with help from Alan King and George S. Irving. D: Jules Bass. FAM/COM 50m. V

Pinocchio's Storybook Adventures 1979 ★★★ Pinochio helps ill puppeteer by staging show of his own, starring the Three Carpenters, the Magic Elf, the Lost dog, and others. Blends animation and live-action. FAM/COM [G] 80m. v

Pioneer Builders *See* **The Conquerors**

Pipe Dreams 1976 ★★★ African-American couple tries to jumpstart its marriage by moving to Alaska to work on the pipeline. Knight's acting debut. C: Gladys Knight, Barry Hankerson. D: Stephen Verona. DRA [PG] 89m. v

Pippi Goes on Board 1975 ★★ Pippi Longstocking, she of red hair and piercing vocal chords, joins sea captain father for shipboard adventures. Annoying and badly dubbed kids' film. C: Inger Nilsson, Par Sundberg, Margot Trooger. D: Olle Hellbom. FAM/DRA [G] 84m. v

Pippi in the South Seas 1974 ★★ Brave Pippi and friends try to save her father from a gang of cruel pirates. C: Inger Nilsson, Par Sundberg, Maria Persson. D: Olle Hellbom. FAM/DRA [G] 99m. v

Pippi Longstocking 1974 ★★ Popular Swedish children's heroine based on Astrid Lindgren books entered movies in this simplistic, badly dubbed, and often shrill production—characteristics which mark entire series. Here red-haired Pippi is introduced, leading friends through tiresome antics. For undiscriminating youngsters. C: Inger Nilsson, Par Sundberg. D: Olle Hellbom. FAM/ACT [G] 99m. v

Pippi Longstocking—New Adventures of, The 1988 ★★ Bad Swedish films of this red-haired brat aren't bad enough: Americans must duplicate the formula. Here Pippi runs circles around adults with zany antics that will delight youngsters and terminally pester parents. C: Tami Erin, Eileen Brennan, Dick Van Patten. D: Ken Annakin. FAM/COM [G] 100m. v

Pippi On The Run 1977 ★★ Pippi battles the odds in all-out effort to retrieve her wandering friends. C: Inger Nilsson, Par Sundberg, Maria Persson. D: Olle Hellbom. FAM/DRA [G] 99m. v

Pippin 1981 ★★★½ Straightforward video transfer of Broadway show about Charlemagne's son and his search for the meaning of life. Fosse's razzle-dazzle staging and talented cast almost put it over. Rivera and Raye are standouts. C: Ben Vereen, William Katt, Martha Raye, Chita Rivera. D: Bob Fosse. MUS 110m. TVM v

Piranha 1978 ★★★½ Dante's directing debut is amusingly self-conscious and frequently exciting *Jaws* rip-off. Dillman and Menzies accidentally unleash killer piranha into a river and then race them downstream toward a summer camp and resort. Witty screenplay by John Sayles. C: Bradford Dillman, Heather Menzies, Kevin McCarthy, Keenan Wynn. D: Joe Dante. HOR [R] 90m. v

Piranha II: The Spawning 1982 Italian ★★ Cameron, making his first feature, actually manages to wring a few chills out of this sequel's laughable premise: a tropical resort besieged by flying killer fish. Unrelated to the original, except by title. C: Tricia O'Neil, Steve Marachuk. D: James Cameron. HOR [R] 88m. v

Pirate Movie, The 1982 Australian ★★ When Joe Papp turned Gilbert and Sullivan's *The Pirates of Penzance* into a modern Broadway hit, the producers of this rip-off version decided to do a little pirating of their own. Result is silly update of original operetta about a band of silly pirates. C: Kristy McNichol, Christopher Atkins. D: Ken Annakin. MUS [PG] 98m. v

Pirate, The 1948 ★★★★½ Stylish musical reworking of S.N. Behrman play casts Kelly as circus clown pretending to be an infamous pirate so Garland will fall for him. Wonderful Cole Porter songs ("Mack the Black," "Be a Clown"), with amusing comic scenes and great dancing by Kelly and the fabulous Nicholas Brothers. C: Judy Garland, Gene Kelly, Walter Slezak, Gladys Cooper. D: Vincente Minnelli. MUS 102m. v

Pirates 1986 French ★★★ Matthau is a scoundrel pirate who plunders many ships in effort to obtain an Aztec throne. Lots of flash, lots of costumes, lots of action but little coherence in colorfully overblown mess. C: Walter Matthau, Damien Thomas, Richard Pearson. D: Roman Polanski. COM [PG-13] 117m. v

Pirate's Fiancée 1969 *See* **Very Curious Girl, A**

Pirates of Blood River, The 1962 British ★★½ Greedy pirates menace the Huguenots in this violent and heavy-handed adventure tale, redeemed only by spectacular action sequences. C: Kerwin Mathews, Glenn Corbett, Christopher Lee, Oliver Reed. D: John Gilling. ACT 87m.

Pirates of Capri, The 1949 ★★ Filmed in Italy, this confused adventure tale features a group of Neapolitans who rebel against their evil oppressor. Violent and silly. (a.k.a. *Captain Sirocco*) C: Louis Hayward, Binnie Barnes, Alan Curtis. D: Edgar Ulmer. ACT 94m.

Pirates of Dark Water, The—The Saga Begins 1991 ★★★½ Animated space feature from maker of "An American Tail." Delivers thrills for young action lovers. FAM/SFI 90m. v

Pirates of Penzance, The 1983 ★★★★ Joe Papp's popular Broadway version of Gilbert and Sullivan operetta, brought to screen with Lansbury added to original cast. Wonderful sets by Elliot Scott and fresh orchestrations bring new verve to the material; Kline's Pirate King is a standout. C: Kevin Kline, Angela Lansbury, Linda Ronstadt, George Rose, Rex Smith. D: Wilford Leach. MUS [G] 112m. v

Pirates of the Coast 1961 ★★★ Daring Spanish navy man seeks vengeance after escaping from cruel prison. C: Lex Barker, Estella Blain. D: Domenico Paolella. ACT 102m. v

Pistol for Ringo, A 1966 Italian ★★½ Spaghetti-Western starring Wood as the tough Texan who takes on hooligans from south of the border. Lots of action, but little else. C:

Montgomery Wood, Fernando Sancho. D: Duccio Tessari. WST 97m.

Pistol—The Birth of a Legend, The 1990 ★★★½ The life, career, and untimely death of basketball legend "Pistol" Pete Maravich. Well done. C: Adam Guier, Nick Benedict. D: Frank C. Schroeder. DRA [G] 104m. v

Pit and the Pendulum 1961 ★★★★★ Striking entry in the Corman/Poe series, with Price terrific as the son of an Inquisition torturer descending into madness and carrying on dad's work. Builds deliberately to some truly scary scenes. C: Vincent Price, John Kerr, Barbara Steele, Luana Anders, Antony Carbone. D: Roger Corman. HOR 80m.

Pit and the Pendulum, The 1991 ★★★★½ *Re-Animator* director Gordon expands the Edgar Allan Poe story into a graphic, sometimes black-humored exploration of the horrors of the Inquisition, with Torquemada (vividly portrayed by Henriksen) overseeing gruesome tortures while fighting his own romantic desires. C: Lance Henriksen, Rona De Ricci, Jonathan Fuller, Jeffrey Combs, Tom Towles. D: Stuart Gordon. HOR [R] 97m.

Pit, The 1981 ★★½ Opressed autistic boy teams up with scary critters to punish nasty hometown. C: Sammy Snyders. HOR 96m. v

Pitfall, The 1948 ★★★★ A family man gets into a whole lot of trouble when he has an affair. A tight, tough noir tale. C: Dick Powell, Lizabeth Scott, Jane Wyatt, Raymond Burr. D: Andre de Toth. DRA 88m. v

Pittsburgh 1942 ★★★½ A coal and steel miner's ambition cause him to lose his woman to another man. Leisurely paced, standard love triangle. Top cast helps. C: Marlene Dietrich, John Wayne, Randolph Scott, Frank Craven. D: Lewis Seiler. DRA 92m. v

Pixote 1981 Brazilian ★★★★½ Brazilian Babenco's U.S. film debut is a graphic, gruesome look at the lives of street children in the slums of Rio. Forced into crime and prostitution at an early age, violence and abuse are the only realities they know. Stellar performances by da Silva and Pera. C: Fernando Ramos da Silva, Marilia Pera. D: Hector Babenco. DRA 127m. v

Pizza Triangle, The 1970 Italian ★★★★ Absorbing satire about two men (Mastroianni and Giannini) who compete for the attention of the same woman (Vitti). The photography is lovely, and the performances top-notch. (a.k.a. *Jealousy, Italian Style* and *A Drama of Jealousy*) C: Marcello Mastroianni, Monica Vitti, Giancarlo Giannini. D: Ettore Scola. COM [R] 99m.

P.K. and the Kid 1985 ★★★½ Engaging story of a young girl (Ringwald) who flees her abusive home and hops a ride with a man (LeMat) heading to California for the annual arm-wrestling championship. Quirky characters enliven an otherwise ordinary plot. C: Paul LeMat, Molly Ringwald, Alex Rocco. D: Lou Lombardo. DRA [PG-13] 90m. v

Place for Lovers, A 1969 Italian-French ★ Unbelievably bad soap opera about a dying American divorcee (Dunaway) in a torrid affair with an Italian engineer (Mastroianni). Marcello's incomprehensible accent complements Faye's sonnambulistic acting. C: Faye Dunaway, Marcello Mastroianni. D: Vittorio De Sica. DRA [R] 90m.

Place in the Sun, A 1951 ★★★★½ A poor, ambitious young man (Clift) is caught between two women (glamorous, wealthy Taylor, frumpy, poor Winters), and is eventually accused of murdering Winters. Brilliant adaptation of Dreiser's *An American Tragedy* won six Oscars: Best Director, Screenplay, Score, Cinematography, Costumes, and Editing. C: Montgomery Clift, Elizabeth Taylor, Shelley Winters, Raymond Burr. D: George Stevens. DRA 122m. v

Place of One's Own, A 1945 British ★★★½ Stylish Edwardian ghost story about a couple who buy an old house. Lockwood becomes possessed by the spirit of the former owner, who was murdered. Based on a novel by Osbert Sitwell. C: James Mason, Margaret Lockwood, Barbara Mullen, Dennis Price. D: Bernard Knowles. DRA 92m.

Place of Weeping 1986 ★★★½ Low-budget film made by South Africans about apartheid in South Africa. Although the moviemaking is sometimes heavy-handed, this story of a woman who fights apartheid is serious, dramatic, and worthwhile. C: James Whylie, Gcini Mhlophe, Charles Comyn. D: Darrell Roodt. DRA [PG] 88m. v

Places in the Heart 1984 ★★★★½ Solid melodrama about a Depression-era Texas woman who must learn to fend for herself when her husband is killed. Manipulative, but enjoyably so, featuring strong support from Malkovich and Glover. Oscars for Best Actress (Field's 2nd), Screenplay. C: Sally Field, Lindsay Crouse, Ed Harris, Amy Madigan, John Malkovich, Danny Glover. D: Robert Benton. DRA [PG] 113m. v

Plague Dogs, The 1982 ★★★★ Canines used as lab animals escape from their imprisonment and are hunted down by scientists. Unusual and very affecting animated feature based on novel by Richard Adams. May be too intense for younger children. D: Martin Rosen. FAM/DRA 99m.

Plague of the Zombies, The 1966 British ★★★½ Boasting some spectacularly eerie photography, this zombie thriller is absorbing despite a sometimes illogical plot. A Cornish mine owner begins using the local undead to work his tin mine with disastrous results. C: Andre Morell, Diane Clare, Brook Williams. D: John Gilling. HOR 90m.

Plague, The 1978 Canadian ★★★½ Grim, thought-provoking but slow-moving adaptation of Albert Camus' novel, about doctor confronting the existential dilemmas posed by epidemic of bubonic plague. C: Daniel Pilon, Kate Reid, Celine Lomez. D: Ed Hunt. DRA [PG] 88m. v

Plain Clothes 1988 ★★★ Eccentric comedy about cop Howard masquerading as a high school student to solve the murder of which his brother's been accused. Offbeat supporting cast is more memorable than shaky plot. C: Arliss Howard, George Wendt, Suzy Amis, Diane Ladd, Robert Stack. D: Martha Coolidge. COM [PG] 98m. v

Plainsman, The 1937 ★★★★ A Cecil B. DeMille extravaganza that plays fast and loose with Western conventions and historical fact. Abe Lincoln, George Custer, and Calamity Jane all appear in this gloriously outlandish epic, but Cooper steals the show as Wild Bill Hickok. C: Gary Cooper, Jean Arthur, James Ellison, Charles Bickford. D: Cecil B. DeMille. WST 113m. v

Plan 9 from Outer Space 1959 ★ Traditionally cited as the worst movie ever made—what more can we add? Fey aliens try to conquer Earth by reviving the dead. When Lugosi died during production, director Wood replaced him in most of his scenes with a non-look-alike covered in a cape. Unintentionally hilarious. C: Tor Johnson, Lyle Talbot, Bela Lugosi, Vampira Criswell. D: Edward D. Wood Jr. SFI 78m. v

Planes, Trains & Automobiles 1987 ★★★½ A buttoned-down executive (Martin), trying to get home for Thanksgiving, plays the straight man to a raucous curtain-ring salesman (Candy) when they are forced to travel together. Hilarious performances save this one-joke movie. C: Steve Martin, John Candy, Laila Robins, Michael McKean, Kevin Bacon. D: John Hughes. COM [R] 93m. v

Planet of Blood 1966 *See* **Queen of Blood**

Planet of Horrors 1981 *See* **Galaxy of Terror**

Planet of the Apes 1967 ★★★★½ The mother of them all. Astronauts land on a strange world where human beings are the slaves of apes. Fantastic, shocking sci-fi, co-scripted by Rod Serling and Michael Wilson, with an unforgettable ending. Makeup designer Chambers received a special Oscar. C: Charlton Heston, Roddy McDowall, Kim Hunter, Maurice Evans. D: Franklin J. Schaffner. SFI [G] 112m. v

Planet of the Vampires 1965 Italian ★★★½ Seeking missing colleagues, astronauts land on a mysterious planet dominated by strange vampire-like creatures. Good, though predictable. (a.k.a. *Terror In Space*; *The Demon Planet*; and *Space Mutants*) C: Barry Sullivan, Norman Bengell, Angel Aranda. D: Mario Bava. SFI 86m. v

Plants Are Watching, The 1978 *See* **Kirlian Witness, The**

Platinum Blonde 1931 ★★★★½ Fast-paced, clever comedy about a poor reporter (Williams) who marries a society girl (Harlow) only to rebel against her lifestyle. Although Harlow made her name with this fine movie, it is Williams who steals the show in his final film appearance. C: Jean Harlow, Loretta Young, Robert Williams. D: Frank Capra. COM 86m. v

Platoon 1986 ★★★★½ A harrowing account of the American infantry in Vietnam, from the point of view of a young soldier (Sheen); the firefight scene may be one of the most intense on film. As a perfect showcase for Stone's heavy-handed style, the film won Oscars for Best Picture, Director, Editing and Sound. C: Tom Berenger, Willem Dafoe, Charlie Sheen, Forest Whitaker. D: Oliver Stone. DRA [R] 120m. v

Platoon Leader 1988 ★★ Weak *Platoon* clone about hardened soldiers in Vietnam and recently arrived young lieutenant. C: Michael Dudikoff, Robert F. Lyons, Michael De Lorenzo. D: Aaron Norris. DRA [R] 97m. v

Play Dirty 1968 British ★★★½ Run-of-the-mill WWII drama in which Caine leads a group of British ex-cons into North Africa to attack German supplies. Despite its predictable plot, the surprise ending hammers home the antiwar message nicely. C: Michael Caine, Nigel Davenport, Nigel Green, Harry Andrews. D: Andre de Toth. ACT [M/PG] 117m.

Play It Again, Sam 1972 ★★★★ Allen adapted his own play to the screen about a film buff who seeks advice and solace in his love life from the ghost of Humphrey Bogart. Keaton's first film with Allen. Leisurely paced, but very funny. C: Woody Allen, Diane Keaton, Tony Roberts, Jerry Lacy, Susan Anspach. D: Herbert Ross. COM [PG] 85m. v

Play It As It Lays 1972 ★★★½ Prototypical feminist tract, with a terrific performance from Weld as the downtrodden wife of a successful film director (Perkins). C: Tuesday Weld, Anthony Perkins, Tammy Grimes, Adam Roarke. D: Frank Perry. DRA [R] 99m.

Play It Cool 1962 British ★★ With virtually no plot, this film promotes the virtues of rock 'n' roll and of helping out one's friends. Well below average. C: Billy Fury, Michael Anderson, Jr., Dennis Price, Richard Wattis, Anna Palk. D: Michael Winner. DRA 82m.

Play Misty for Me 1971 ★★★★½ The request of an obsessive woman (Walter) for a song turns the life of a deejay (Eastwood) into a nightmare. Walter gives the performance of a lifetime. Eastwood's directorial debut reflects his mentor Siegel's action style and bears comparison to *Fatal Attraction*. C: Clint Eastwood, Jessica Walter, Donna Mills. D: Clint Eastwood. CRI [R] 103m. v

Play Nice 1992 ★★★ Cop chases a serial killer, whose victims are all men accused of sexually abusing children. Interesting concept dulled by mediocre production values. C: Ed O'Ross, Michael Zand. D: Teri Treas. CRI [R] 90m. v

Playboy of Paris 1930 ★★★ Inheriting $1 million doesn't change Chevalier's day job—he's still a waiter—but it does allow him to live an extravagant nightlife. Chevalier is magnificent, but the rest of the cast can't quite hold its own in this featherweight tale. C: Maurice Chevalier, Frances Dee, Dorothy Cristy, Eugene Pallette. D: Ludwig Berger. DRA 79m.

Playboy of the Western World 1972 Irish ★★★★½ Christy Mahon (Raymond) wins Irish town over with boasts of patricide in entertaining satire. One warning, though: Thick Irish accents may frustrate some viewers. Based on J.M. Synge's classic play. C: Gary Raymond, Siobhan McKenna, Elspeth March. D: Brian Desmond Hurst. COM 96m. V

Playboys, The 1992 ★★★½ Irish tale set in the '50s, about a headstrong woman who causes a local scandal when she has a baby out of wedlock and won't say who the father is. Lightweight but charming, lovingly played by delightful cast. C: Albert Finney, Aidan Quinn, Robin Wright, Milo O'Shea. D: Gillies MacKennon. DRA [PG-13] 113m. V

Player, The 1992 ★★★★½ Stylish comedy/drama about a young movie producer (Robbins) who starts getting threats from a mysterious screenwriter. A dark, satirical pageant of contemporary Hollywood manners and morals, built on a strong script, wicked humor, and great direction. So full of star cameos that some well-known actors were miffed at being left out. C: Tim Robbins, Greta Scacchi, Fred Ward, Whoopi Goldberg, Peter Gallagher. D: Robert Altman. DRA [R] 124m. V

Players 1979 ★★ Tennis pro (Martin) scores "love" when he falls for a rich man's mistress (MacGraw). Poorly acted soaper killed Dino's son's career before it started; did nothing for Ali's, either. C: Ali MacGraw, Dean-Paul Martin, Maximilian Schell, Steve Guttenberg. D: Anthony Harvey. DRA [PG] 120m. V

Playful Little Audrey ★★★½ A collection of cartoons starring Little Audrey, the mischievous scamp of comic books. Great fun for kids. FAM/COM V

Playgirl 1954 ★★½ Winters stars as the girl next door who falls in love with nightlife and takes up with gangsters. Don't expect any surprises. C: Shelley Winters, Barry Sullivan, Gregg Palmer. D: Joseph Pevney. DRA 85m.

Playgirl Killer 1966 ★★ When a painter's models tire of holding a pose, he kills them. Trash thriller with some unintentional laughs. (a.k.a. *Decoy for Terror*) C: William Kerwin, Jean Christopher, Neil Sedaka. D: Erick Santamaria. CRI 86m. V

Playing for Time 1980 ★★★★½ Gripping drama about women prisoners recruited to play music for orchestra in Auschwitz while others are marched to the gas chambers. Tough, unsentimental film, with strong script by Arthur Miller. A multiple Emmy winner. C: Vanessa Redgrave, Jane Alexander, Maud Adams, Viveca Lindfors, Shirley Knight, Melanie Mayron, Marisa Berenson. D: Daniel Mann. DRA 143m. TVM V

Playing the Game 1931 *See* **Touchdown!**

Playmates 1972 ★★★★ Entertaining movie about a pair of pals (Alda and McClure) who each begin dating the other's ex-wife. Lively romantic comedy that revels in its own plot twists. C: Alan Alda, Connie Stevens, Doug McClure, Barbara Feldon. D: Theodore Flicker. COM [R] 78m. TVM V

Playroom 1990 ★★ Archaeologist and friends fall victim to a murderous spirit while on a dig in an ancient tomb. Jokey horror film is neither scary nor funny, with characters too cardboard to elicit much sympathy. (a.k.a. *Schizo*) C: Christopher McDonald, Lisa Aliff. D: Manny Coto. HOR [R] 87m. V

Playtime 1967 French ★★★★ Tati's Mr. Hulot is a unique character in French comedy. In this third film in the trilogy (*Mr. Hulot's Holiday, Mon Oncle*) he is a bumbling victim of civilization, who fights vainly to keep an appointment on the other side of Paris. Filled with hilarious sight and sound gags. C: Jacques Tati, Barbara Dennek. D: Jacques Tati. COM 108m. V

Plaza Suite 1971 ★★★★ In this adaptation of a very funny Neil Simon play, Matthau stars in three separate vignettes, each taking place in the same swanky New York hotel room. Amusing if mild entertainment. C: Walter Matthau, Maureen Stapleton, Barbara Harris, Lee Grant. D: Arthur Hiller. COM [PG] 115m. V

Please Believe Me 1950 ★★★½ Pleasant enough tale of shipboard romance. Kerr is wonderful as a British heiress who has inherited land in America and is wooed by a trio of opportunistic men. C: Deborah Kerr, Robert Walker, James Whitmore, Peter Lawford, Spring Byington. D: Norman Taurog. COM 87m.

Please Don't Eat the Daisies 1960 ★★★★ Slick, pleasant domestic comedy from Jean Kerr's autobiographical look at life as a drama critic's wife. Good supporting cast, especially Paige as Broadway diva. Day croons title song and sighs a lot. Became '60s TV series. C: Doris Day, David Niven, Janis Paige, Spring Byington. D: Charles Walters. COM 111m. V

Please Turn Over 1960 British ★★★ Adolescent girl writes a steamy roman á clef that reveals the secrets of friends and family. Based on Basil Thomas' play *Book of the Month*, the film is amusing but tame. C: Ted Ray, Jean Kent, Leslie Phillips. D: Gerald Thomas. COM 86m.

Pleasure Garden, The 1925 British ★★½ Hum-drum silent backstage fable about two chorus dancers would be completely forgotten today if it weren't the director's first film, shot in Germany. C: Virginia Valli, Carmelita Geraghty, Miles Mander. D: Alfred Hitchcock. DRA 75m.

Pleasure of His Company, The 1961 ★★★ Charmer arrives for his daughter's wedding and wreaks havoc with his ex-wife's life. The movie is uneven, and lacks the necessary vigor despite a top-notch cast. C: Fred Astaire, Lilli Palmer, Debbie Reynolds, Tab Hunter. D: George Seaton. COM 115m.

Pleasure Seekers, The 1964 ★★★ Musical numbers enhance this tale of three girls seeking fun and romance in Madrid. A likable production. C: Ann-Margret, Pamela Tiffin, Tony Franciosa, Carol Lynley, Gene Tierney, Brian Keith, Gardner McKay. D: Jean Negulesco. MUS 107m.

Plenty 1985 ★★★★ A British woman, who fought for the French resistance in WWII, returns home to discover the rest of life is a disappointment. Talky but affecting adaptation of David Hare's play, with spiky Streep performance. C: Meryl Streep, Charles Dance, Tracey Ullman, John Gielgud, Sting, Sam Neill. D: Fred Schepisi. DRA [R] 119m. v

Plot Against Harry, The 1989 ★★★★ Quirky, intelligent comedy about a con-man (Priest), just out of prison, trying to adjust to his new life on New York City's streets. Filmed in 1969, but not released until 20 years later, to critical acclaim. C: Martin Priest, Ben Lang, Maxine Woods. D: Michael Roemer. COM 80m. v

Plough and the Stars, The 1936 ★★½ Sean O'Casey's play is not wellserved by this stiff film adaptation. Foster is good as the Irish revolutionary whose political commitment threatens his marriage, but the entire effort seems lifeless and overlong. C: Barbara Stanwyck, Preston Foster, Barry Fitzgerald, Una O'Connor. D: John Ford. DRA 78m.

Ploughman's Lunch, The 1984 British ★★★★½ Career-obsessed radio reporter plays both ends against the middle in trying to get ahead while handling sensitive material during Falklands war. Tough stuff, smartly handled. C: Jonathan Pryce, Tim Curry, Rosemary Harris, Frank Finlay. D: Richard Eyre. DRA [R] 107m. v

Plumber, The 1980 Australian ★★★½ A demented local plumber destroys the home of a perplexed couple. Tense, offbeat black comedy was Peter Weir's first feature; a must for his fans. C: Judy Morris, Ivar Kants, Robert Coleby, Candy Raymond. D: Peter Weir. COM 76m. v

Plunder of the Sun 1953 ★★★ Contemporary treasure hunters compete for buried Aztec fortune in Mexico. Capable intrigue with interesting locales. C: Glenn Ford, Diana Lynn, Patricia Medina. D: John Farrow. DRA 81m.

Plunder Road 1957 ★★★½ Modest crime caper is something of a sleeper surprise. Engrossing film about an ingeniously plotted $10 million robbery is enlivened by sharp performances and atmospheric photography. C: Gene Raymond, Jeanne Cooper, Wayne Morris, Elisha Cook, Jr. D: Hubert Cornfield. CRI 72m. v

Plunderers, The 1948 ★★½ Desperados and the Cavalry team up against attacking Indians. Standard Western action. C: Rod Cameron, Ilona Massey, Forrest Tucker. D: Joseph Kane. WST 87m.

Plunderers, The 1960 ★★★ An outlaw gang harrasses peaceful folk of a frontier town. Pretty good Western yarn. C: Jeff Chandler, John Saxon, Dolores Hart, Marsha Hunt. D: Joseph Pevney. WST 93m.

Plymouth Adventure, The 1952 ★★★★ Chronicle of Pilgrim's transatlantic voyage in the Mayflower. Expert Hollywood history lesson has good cast and genuine excitement, despite those silly outfits. Oscar winner for Best Special Effects. C: Spencer Tracy, Gene Tierney, Van Johnson, Leo Genn, Lloyd Bridges. D: Clarence Brown. DRA 105m.

Poacher's Daughter, The 1960 Irish ★★★ A tenderhearted young woman reforms her roguish boyfriend. Good acting by Harris highlights mildly affecting Irish lark. (a.k.a. *Sally's Irish Rogue*) C: Julie Harris, Harry Brogan, Tim Seeley, Marie Keen. D: George Pollock. COM 74m.

Pocket Money 1972 ★★★ You'd think Marvin and Newman would strike sparks, but the comedy is pretty soggy in tale of dim cowpoke and con artist buddy running a scam with a shady cattle baron. C: Paul Newman, Lee Marvin, Strother Martin, Christine Belford. D: Stuart Rosenberg. COM [PG] 100m. v

Pocketful of Miracles 1961 ★★★½ Damon Runyon's sentimental yarn about a Broadway gambler (Ford) who transforms an apple vendor (Davis) into a socialite for a day. High Capra corn is colorful and hard to resist. Ann-Margret's feature debut has her in very good company. C: Bette Davis, Glenn Ford, Hope Lange, Arthur O'Connell, Thomas Mitchell, Peter Falk, Ann-Margret. D: Frank Capra. COM 138m. v

Poetic Justice 1993 ★★★ Singleton's followup to *Boyz 'n' the Hood* is a road picture that pairs Jackson, a would-be poet, and Shakur, a postal worker, as they try to escape the dangers of the 'hood for a vacation with friends in Oakland. Well-intentioned, if predictable; with poetry by Maya Angelou. C: Janet Jackson, Tupac Shakur, Tyra Ferrell, Regina King. D: John Singleton. DRA [R] 109m. v

Poil de Carotte 1932 French ★★★ A young boy is driven to suicide by his overbearing mother. Some stylish scenes highlight dated French pastoral drama. C: Harry Baur, Robert Lynen, Catherine Fontenay. D: Julien Duvivier. DRA 80m. v

Point Blank 1967 ★★★★ Shot and abandoned by his wife's gangland lover, an L.A. gangster (Marvin) sets out on a course of bloody revenge. Violent thriller with lurid style all its own. Compelling. C: Lee Marvin, Angie Dickinson, Keenan Wynn, Carroll O'Connor. D: John Boorman. ACT 89m. v

Point Break 1991 ★★★ Waves of action when a gang of surfers led by a guru-like adrenalin junkie (Swayze) robs banks for fun and profit. A green FBI agent (Reeves) infiltrates the group and is drawn into a nonstop, if improbable, series of thrill-filled adventures. C: Patrick Swayze, Keanu Reeves, Gary Busey, Lori Petty. D: Kathryn Bigelow. ACT [R] 120m. V

Point of Impact 1993 ★★★ A Miami Customs agent blamed for partner's death quits and becomes body guard to drug smuggler's girlfriend—but job is just cover for his search for the real killer. Lots of violence and action. C: Michael Pare, Michael Ironside, Barbara Carrera. D: Bob Misiorowski. CRI [R] 96m. V

Point of No Return 1993 ★★★ A U.S. government agency transforms street urchin (Fonda) into an assassin. Glossy American remake of popular French actioner *La Femme Nikita*. Fonda is exciting to watch and Keitel is good, but second version fails to top the previous one. C: Bridget Fonda, Gabriel Byrne, Dermot Mulroney, Anne Bancroft, Harvey Keitel. D: John Badham. ACT [R] 109m. V

Point, The 1971 ★★★★½ Wonderful children's morality fable tells story of round-headed boy who is born in a land where everyone and everything is topped with a point. Nicely animated feature, marked by fine score and wise storytelling. Original narration by Dustin Hoffman was later redone by Alan Thicke, and again by Ringo Starr. D: Fred Wolf. FAM/DRA 74m. TVM V

Pointed Heels 1930 ★★★ Backstage love triangle centers on a beautiful musical comedy star. Moderate, predictable melodrama. C: William Powell, Fay Wray, Helen Kane, Richard "Skeets" Gallagher. D: A. Edward Sutherland. DRA 62m.

Poison Ivy 1985 ★★½ Summer camp movie packed with fresh-faced stars. Fox is cool counselor chasing camp nurse McKeon, while various romances and hijinks abound. Unremarkable excursion with talented ensemble. C: Michael J. Fox, Nancy McKeon. D: Larry Elikann. COM 97m. TVM V

Poison Ivy 1992 ★★½ Barrymore is a bad teen who seduces Gilbert into becoming her best friend, then moves into her house and shakes up the whole family. Lurid, sordid stuff; takes itself far too seriously. C: Drew Barrymore, Sara Gilbert, Tom Skerritt. D: Andy Ruben. DRA [R] 91m. V

Poison Pen 1941 British ★★★ A malicious letter writer causes conflict among inhabitants of a village. Capable small drama with nice touches. C: Flora Robson, Robert Newton, Ann Todd. D: Paul L. Stein. DRA 66m.

Poker Alice 1987 ★★★½ Easy-going western vehicle for Liz casts her as a card sharp who wins a whorehouse during a poker game. Attractive stars combine well with the clever script. C: Elizabeth Taylor, George Hamilton, Tom Skerritt, Richard Mulligan. D: Arthur Allan Seidelman. WST 100m. TVM V

Police 1985 French ★★★½ A rugged cop falls for a suspect while on the trail of Tunisian drug traffickers. Depardieu is effective in this taut, well-handled thriller; highly successful in France. C: Gerard Depardieu, Sophie Marceau. D: Maurice Pialat. DRA 113m. V

Police Academy 1984 ★★★½ Large and varied comic cast adds spark to dumb but likable comedy about hijinks among a group of misfits undergoing police training. Inventive comedy recycled its jokes through series of five sequels. C: Steve Guttenberg, G. W. Bailey, Kim Cattrall. D: Hugh Wilson. COM [R] 96m. V

Police Academy 2: Their First Assignment 1985 ★★½ The wacky trainees have somehow graduated; they take their bumbling brand of law enforcement to the streets. The inspiration is already running low, but some of the actors (particularly human sound effects machine Winslow) get a few laughs. C: Steve Guttenberg, Bubba Smith, David Graf. D: Jerry Paris. COM [PG-13] 87m. V

Police Academy 3: Back in Training 1986 ★ With this, the series descended to lame slapstick and stayed there, with cast and filmmakers just going through the motions. Here, the comic cops return to the Academy to take charge of trainees. C: Steve Guttenberg, Bubba Smith, David Graf, Michael Winslow, Marion Ramsey. D: Jerry Paris. COM [PG] 83m. V

Police Academy 4: Citizens on Patrol 1987 ★ This time the gang sets up neighborhood watch program; too bad reinforcements weren't called in to provide this exhausted franchise with some new jokes. A couple of chuckles. C: Steve Guttenberg, Bubba Smith, Michael Winslow, David Graf, Tim Kazurinsky, Sharon Stone. D: Paul Maslansky. COM [PG] 88m. V

Police Academy 5: Assignment Miami Beach 1988 ★ Original stars abandoned ship for this one, leaving the supporting cast to flounder through another round of stupid jokes that Miami Beach locations (where Gaynes is receiving a retirement award) can't save. C: Bubba Smith, George Gaynes, G. W. Bailey, David Graf. D: Alan Myerson. COM [PG] 90m. V

Police Academy 6: City Under Siege 1989 ★ Comedy franchise continues, with wacky cops taking on criminal gang who use circus-style techniques. C: Bubba Smith, David Graf, Michael Winslow, Leslie Easterbrook, Marion Ramsey. D: Peter Bonerz. COM [PG] 84m. V

Police Force 1985 Hong Kong ★★★★ A cop must protect a government witness against a drug lord. The impressively choreographed comic shtick makes this a good introduction to Chan's very charming screen persona. (a.k.a. *Jackie Chan's Police Story* and *Police Story*.) C: Jackie Chan, Brigette Lin. D: Jackie Chan. ACT 85m. TVM V

Police Squad!—Help Wanted 1982 ★★★★ Compilation of cult television show that never saw high ratings, but developed a rabid audience following. Whacked-out stories follow misadventures of police captain Frank Drebin (Nielsen) and cohorts. *More Police Squad!* followed. Show was ultimately basis for popular *Naked Gun* movie series. C: Leslie Nielsen, Alan North. D: Jim Abrahams. COM 75m. TVM V

Polly 1989 ★★★★ Ebullient musical remake of the 1960 Disney film, from Eleanor Porter's story, stars Pulliam as an optimistic orphan trying to change the life of her tight-lipped aunt (Rashad). New Alabama locale and mostly black cast really work, with a strong assist from Allen's choreography and rousing songs. C: Keshia Knight Pulliam, Phylicia Rashad, Celeste Holm, Brock Peters, Dorian Harewood, Butterfly McQueen. D: Debbie Allen. MUS 100m. TVM

Polly of the Circus 1932 ★★½ Silly melodrama about a stuffy minister (Gable) falling for a naughty high-wire circus performer (Davies). Both stars are miscast. C: Clark Gable, Marion Davies, C. Aubrey Smith. D: Alfred Santell. DRA 69m.

Pollyanna 1920 ★★★★★ In one of her classic "America's Sweetheart" roles, Pickford plays Pollyana, the ever-glad daughter of a missionary who charms everyone in her life. Sentimental, but lightened with laughs and Pickford's glow. A classic from the silent era. Remade by Disney in 1960. C: Mary Pickford, Katherine Griffith, Herbert Ralston, Helen Jerome Eddy. D: Paul Powell. FAM/DRA 60m. V

Pollyanna 1960 ★★★★★ Sweethearted young orphan (Mills) goes to live with miserable aunt (Wyman) and ends up spreading joy throughout small town. Fine blend of sentiment and humor that never overplays either quality. Snappy direction and good performances make this winning family entertainment. C: Hayley Mills, Jane Wyman, Richard Egan, Karl Malden, Adolphe Menjou, Agnes Moorehead. D: David Swift. FAM/DRA [G] 134m. V

Poltergeist 1982 ★★★★½ Steven Spielberg produced (and, some say, helped direct) this scary, exciting and visually entertaining ghost story, in which a suburban California family are set upon by spirits that abduct their youngest daughter. Powerhouse special effects and a sneaky sense of humor. C: Craig T. Nelson, JoBeth Williams, Dominique Dunne. D: Tobe Hooper. HOR [PG] 115m. V

Poltergeist II: The Other Side 1986 ★★★ The Freelings have moved to a new house in a new town, but the nasty spirits aren't giving up their pursuit of little O'Rourke. Sequel does little more than recycle the original story, but it has its moments, thanks largely to creepy Beck. C: JoBeth Williams, Craig T. Nelson, Heather O'Rourke, Zelda Rubinstein. D: Brian Gibson. HOR [PG-13] 92m. V

Poltergeist III 1988 ★★ Repetitious, completely unnecessary follow-up has O'Rourke going to stay with aunt and uncle in high-tech building where evil lurks in mirrored hallways. Lacks thrills and logic; sole bright spot is O'Rourke who died shortly before its release. C: Tom Skerritt, Nancy Allen, Heather O'Rourke, Zelda Rubinstein. D: Gary A. Sherman. HOR [PG-13] 104m. V

Polyester 1981 ★★★★ Outrageous transvestite Divine plays a suffering housewife who's saved by the man of her dreams (Hunter). Waters' first semi-mainstream film is often gross but high-spirited and weirdly amusing. (Flashing numbers on screen were for "odorama" gimmick used in the theatrical release, providing scratch 'n sniff scents ranging from pleasant to revolting.) C: Divine, Tab Hunter, Edith Massey, Mink Stole. D: John Waters. COM [R] 86m. V

Pom-Pom Girls 1976 ★★½ Rambunctious teens spark up their aimless lives with pranks, parties and promiscuity. Airheaded comedy slightly redeemed by good-natured cast and mildly entertaining antics. C: Robert Carradine, Jennifer Ashley, Lisa Reeves. D: Joseph Ruben. COM [PG] 90m. V

Pontiac Moon 1994 ★★★ A rural science teacher (Danson) takes his son on road journey to discover the meaning of life. Cloying, sentimental mood piece almost saved by its cast. But when Danson starts singing "Cheek to Cheek," that's all folks. C: Ted Danson, Mary Steenburgen, Ryan Todd, Cathy Moriarty. D: Peter Medak. COM [PG-13] 108m. V

Pony Express 1953 ★★★½ Wild Bill Hickok and Buffalo Bill Cody establish westward mail routes in the 1860s. Spirited Western action with historical flavor. C: Charlton Heston, Rhonda Fleming, Jan Sterling, Forrest Tucker. D: Jerry Hopper. WST 101m. V

Pony Express Rider, The 1976 ★★★½ Out-of-the-ordinary oater recounts how Peterson becomes a Pony Express messenger in 1861 to find his father's murderer. Fast-paced film features readily recognizable Western character actors and is recommended as wholesome family entertainment. C: Stewart Peterson, Henry Wilcoxon, Buck Taylor, Maureen McCormick. D: Robert Totten. WST [G] 100m. V

Pony Soldier 1952 ★★★½ Royal Canadian Mounties intervene to prevent an Indian uprising. Fast-paced though familiar open-air action, with Power effectively stalwart. C: Tyrone Power, Cameron Mitchell, Robert Horton. D: Joseph Newman. WST 82m.

Pool of London 1951 British ★★★ A seafaring smuggler gets entangled in a murder web. Imaginative cop thriller with fine London docks locations. C: Bonar Colleano, Susan Shaw, Renee Asherson, Max Adrian. D: Basil Dearden. DRA 86m.

Poor Cow 1967 British ★★★ While her criminal husband is in jail, a young London mother romances his best friend. A good performance by White highlights a striking tale of lower-class mores. C: Carol White, Terence

Stamp, John Bindon, Malcolm McDowell. D: Kenneth Loach. DRA 104m.

Poor Little Rich Girl 1936 ★★★★ Whirlwind musical finds young Shirley running away from home, hooking up with vaudeville duo (Haley and Faye), and fixing up widowed father (Whalen) with Stuart. Singing, dancing, and pathos fill every frame in a simple, but entertaining mix. Fine for kids. C: Shirley Temple, Alice Faye, Frank Haley. D: Irving Cummings. MUS 72m. V

Poor Little Rich Girl: The Barbara Hutton Story 1987 ★★½ Fawcett wears all kinds of fancy clothes but otherwise this biography of troubled Woolworth heiress is dull and conventional. C: Farrah Fawcett, James Read, Kevin McCarthy, Burl Ives. D: Charles Jarrott. DRA 98m. TVM V

Poor Pretty Eddie and Red Neck County 1975 *See* **Heartbreak Motel.**

Poor White Trash II 1975 ★★ Insane Vietnam Vet, returns to boondocks home and makes life murderously miserable for everyone. (a.k.a. *Scum of the Earth*) C: Gene Ross, Ann Stafford. D: S.F. Brownrigg. HOR [R] 90m. V

Popcorn 1991 ★★★ Overly complex tale of multiple murders occurring at a fright film festival. Opening dream sequence is the highlight. Perhaps best remembered for its ad line: "Buy it in a bag. Go home in a box."! C: Jill Schoelen, Tom Villard, Dee Wallace Stone, Tony Roberts, Ray Walston. D: Mark Herrier. HOR [R] 93m. V

Pope Joan 1972 British ★★ A woman (Ullmann) disguised as a man becomes Pope in this far-fetched drama, unworthy of its high-powered cast. (a.k.a. *The Devil's Imposter*) C: Liv Ullmann, Keir Dullea, Jeremy Kemp, Olivia de Havilland, Maximilian Schell, Trevor Howard, Franco Nero. D: Michael Anderson. DRA [PG] 132m.

Pope Must Diet, The 1991 British ★★½ After computer error elevates ecclesiastic Coltrane to head of Catholic Church, the new pope finds himself on the run from mobsters. Silly farce. Originally called *The Pope Must Die* until public outrage forced title change. C: Robbie Coltrane, Beverly D'Angelo, Herbert Lom, Alex Rocco, Paul Bartel. D: Peter Richardson. COM [R] 90m. V

Pope of Greenwich Village, The 1984 ★★★ It's a contest to see who can overact most, but Roberts is the clear winner in this feverish thriller about small-timers trying to rip off New York mob. Bungled adaptation of Vincent Patrick's witty novel builds to a boil, but goes nowhere. C: Eric Roberts, Mickey Rourke, Daryl Hannah, Geraldine Page. D: Vincent Patrick. CRI [R] 120m. V

Popeye 1980 ★★ Cartoon sailor (Williams) woos Olive Oyl (Duvall) while battling bad guys. Live-action realization of popular Fleischer Brothers animated series boasts top production names, but is uninspired and often pointless. C: Robin Williams, Shelley Duvall, Ray Walston, Paul L. Smith, Paul Dooley. D: Robert Altman. FAM/COM [PG] 114m. V

Popi 1969 ★★★½ In New York's Puerto Rican ghetto, a resourceful, slightly off-the-wall widower seeks a better life for his two sons. Lustrous performance by Arkin highlights well-done ethnic comedy/drama. C: Alan Arkin, Rita Moreno. D: Arthur Hiller. DRA [G] 115m. V

Poppy 1936 ★★★★ A free-spirited carnival drummer cheats country yokels while his daughter falls for the mayor's son. Overly subplotted farce, but conniving Fields is a delight. C: W. C. Fields, Rochelle Hudson, Richard Cromwell. D: A. Sutherland. COM 75m.

Poppy Is Also a Flower, The 1966 ★★ Ian Fleming story about drug smugglers. Cameos by an international cast cannot save this limp antidrug tale. (a.k.a. *Opium Connection*) C: Senta Berger, Stephen Boyd, E.G. Marshall, Trevor Howard, Marcello Mastroianni, Angie Dickinson, Rita Hayworth, Yul Brynner. D: Terence Young. DRA [PG] 105m. V

Porgy and Bess 1959 ★★★★ George Gershwin's classic folk opera about the poor residents of Catfish Row and a crippled beggar's love for a wayward girl. Oscar-winning score arrangements by Andre Previn and Ken Darby highlight the lavish production by Samuel Goldwyn, with standout African-American cast. C: Sidney Poitier, Dorothy Dandridge, Pearl Bailey, Sammy Davis, Jr., Brock Peters, Diahann Carroll. D: Otto Preminger. MUS 138m.

Pork Chop Hill 1959 ★★★½ In spite of fierce opposition, American forces take a vital hill in Korea. Brutal action and fine performances mark this distinguished war drama. Milestone also directed *All Quiet on the Western Front* (in 1930). C: Gregory Peck, Harry Guardino, Rip Torn, George Peppard. D: Lewis Milestone. DRA 98m. V

Porky's 1981 Canadian ★★★½ Mindless comedy about misadventures of lusty teens in '50s Florida. Broad, tasteless humor, but many scenes are undeniably hilarious and it's certainly superior to its countless rip-offs. Followed by two sequels. C: Dan Monahan, Mark Herrier, Wyatt Knight, Roger Wilson, Kim Cattrall. D: Bob Clark. COM [R] 94m. V

Porky's 2: The Next Day 1983 Canadian ★★½ More plot and slightly less raunch than the first time, with the gang rallying to rout a corrupt, meddlesome preacher and the KKK. Not as funny as the original, but the characters are a bit more humanized and likable. C: Dan Monahan, Wyatt Knight, Mark Herrier, Roger Wilson. D: Bob Clark. COM [R] 95m. V

Porky's Revenge 1985 ★ The original film's portly villain returns to make trouble for our heroes. Half-baked script and direction, with cast that looks distinctly older than high school age. C: Dan Monahan, Wyatt Knight, Tony Ganios, Kaki Hunter. D: James Komack. COM [R] 95m. v

Porridge 1979 *See* **Doing Time**

Port of Call 1948 Swedish ★★★ Ingmar Bergman's tale, set in a harbor slum, about an ostracized young woman reformed by a sailor's love. Slender early effort by the master. C: Nine Christine Jonsson, Bengt Eklund. D: Ingmar Bergman. DRA 100m. v

Port of New York 1949 ★★★ U.S. Customs agents set out to crack a drug-smuggling case. Standard crime melodrama shot in New York. Brynner's feature debut. C: Scott Brady, Richard Rober, K.T. Stevens, Yul Brynner. D: Laslo Benedek. DRA 86m.

Port of Seven Seas 1938 ★★★★ The Marseilles waterfront is the setting for story of a romance between a young woman and a sailor. Capable cast does well in moving, early version of Marcel Pagnol's *Fanny*. C: Wallace Beery, Frank Morgan, Maureen O'Sullivan, Jessie Ralph. D: James Whale. DRA 81m.

Port of Shadows 1938 French ★★★★½ An army deserter (Gabin) falls for a young woman (Morgan) involved with a group of shady characters. Moody, fatalistic melodrama conveys the dark mood of prewar France; banned by the Nazis during their occupation. C: Jean Gabin, Michele Morgan, Michele Simon. D: Marcel Carne. DRA 91m.

Portia on Trial 1937 ★★★ An attorney deftly employs her courtroom abilities to even the score for earlier wrongs done to her. Competent tearjerker. C: Walter Able, Frieda Inescort, Neil Hamilton, Heather Angel, Ruth Donnelly. D: George Nicholls, Jr. DRA 85m.

Portnoy's Complaint 1972 ★★ Adaptation of Philip Roth's best-seller about a hung-up urban Jewish boy's difficult relationship with his mother. Excellent Karen Black and little else in this cinematic misfire. C: Richard Benjamin, Karen Black, Lee Grant. D: Ernest Lehman. DRA 101m. v

Portrait from Life 1948 *See* **Girl in the Painting**

Portrait in Black 1960 ★★★ A millionaire's wife (Turner) plots to murder him with help of his doctor (Quinn). Convoluted variation of the classic *Postman Always Rings Twice* should have spent as much care on the script as it does on the star's costumes! C: Lana Turner, Anthony Quinn, Sandra Dee, Lloyd Nolan, Richard Basehart, John Saxon. D: Michael Gordon. CRI 112m.

Portrait of a Nude Woman 1982 *See* **Nudo di Donna** TVM

Portrait of Jennie 1948 ★★★★ Struggling artist (Cotten) finds inspiration in a mysterious young woman (Jones) who ages every time they meet. A Hollywood life, death and art fantasy; well done version of a far-fetched story. Oscar for special effects. C: Jennifer Jones, Joseph Cotten, Ethel Barrymore, Lillian Gish. D: William Dieterle. DRA 86m. v

Portrait of the Artist as a Young Man, A 1979 ★★★★ Film of James Joyce's first novel about the passage to adulthood of young Stephen Dedalus in early-1900s Ireland, and his examination of his faith. Thoughtful and entertaining. C: Bosco Hogan, T. McKenna, John Gielgud, Rosaleen Linehan, Maureen Potter, Niall Buggy, Brian Murray. D: Joseph Strick. DRA [PG] 98m. v

Portrait, The 1993 ★★★★ An artist (the younger Peck) returns home to paint a portrait of her aging parents (Bacall and Peck senior). Sensitive and intelligent family drama from Tina Howe's play *Painting Churches*, with fascinating chemistry between Peck father and daughter. C: Gregory Peck, Lauren Bacall, Cecilia Peck. D: Arthur Penn. DRA 89m. TVM v

Poseidon Adventure, The 1972 ★★★★½ Passengers on a capsized oceanliner struggle to survive. First of the all-star disaster pictures of '70s. Script holes plugged by terrific storyline, Oscar-winning special effects, and stars' sincerity. Based on the novel by Paul Gallico. Sequel: *Beyond the Poseidon Adventure*. C: Gene Hackman, Ernest Borgnine, Red Buttons, Carol Lynley, Roddy McDowall, Stella Stevens, Shelley Winters, Jack Albertson. D: Ronald Neame. ACT [PG] 117m. v

Positively True Adventures of the Alleged Texas Cheerleader-Murdering Mom, The 1993 ★★★★½ Based on true story, this made-for-cable feature involves high school cheerleader's mother who tries to have daughter's rival bumped off. Self-parodying approach to material satirizes both subject and TV film format. Good, biting humor played with relish by fine ensemble. C: Holly Hunter, Beau Bridges, Swoosie Kurtz. D: Michael Ritchie. COM [R] 99m. TVM v

Posse 1975 ★★★½ When U.S. marshal tries to turn the capture of a train robber into a personal political crusade the outlaw becomes an underdog case. An intelligent and probing Western that goes beyond the usual shoot-'em-up. C: Kirk Douglas, Bruce Dern, Bo Hopkins. D: Kirk Douglas. WST [PG] 94m. v

Posse 1993 U.S. ★★★½ Old West posse composed largely of African-Americans vs. evil sheriff and racist cronies. Traditional story told from different point of view, with exciting moments. C: Mario Van Peebles, Stephen Baldwin, Charles Lane, Tiny Lister, Blair Underwood, Melvin Van Peebles. D: Mario Van Peebles. WST [R] 113m. v

Posse from Hell 1961 ★★½ A gunfighter hunts down four escaped desperados who killed his friend. Routine Western with its share of violence. C: Audie Murphy, John Saxon, Zohra Lampert, Vic Morrow. D: Herbert Coleman. WST 89m.

Possessed 1931 ★★★★ Factory worker

(Crawford) gets ahead in the world by sleeping with rich lawyer (Gable). Above average, well-paced soap opera with leads teamed to excellent effect. C: Joan Crawford, Clark Gable, Wallace Ford, Skeets Gallagher. D: Clarence Brown. DRA 78m. V

Possessed 1947 ★★★★ Unrequited love and murder result as madness overcomes a woman who marries her boss. Heavy-duty film noir with subtle handling of mental illness. Intelligent performance from Crawford in complex role. C: Joan Crawford, Van Heflin, Raymond Massey, Geraldine Brooks. D: Curtis Bernhardt. CRI 110m. V

Possession 1981 French ★ Aggressively weird but incoherent horror fantasy (further hampered by extensive cutting for U.S. release), has Adjani mating with slime monster, to the consternation of hubby Neill. C: Isabelle Adjani, Sam Neill, Heinz Bennent. D: Andrzej Zulawski. HOR [R] 79m. V

Possession of Joel Delaney, The 1972 ★★★½ The spirit of a deceased Puerto Rican—who used to behead women—possesses the body of a Manhattan divorcée (MacLaine)'s younger brother (King). Slow-motion, off-beat horror film with a memorable exorcism scene. C: Shirley MacLaine, Perry King, Michael Hordern. D: Waris Hussein. HOR [R] 105m. V

Postcards from the Edge 1990 ★★★★ Witty, acerbic tale of Hollywood actress who cleans up her own drug problem in rehab, then tries to cope with the movie business, an unfaithful lover, and a competitive mother without falling off the wagon. Entertaining adaptation of Carrie Fisher's scathingly funny novel, highlighted by flamboyant comic performances from Streep (who does her own singing) and MacLaine. C: Meryl Streep, Shirley MacLaine, Dennis Quaid, Gene Hackman. D: Mike Nichols. COM [R] 101m. V

Postman Always Rings Twice, The 1946 ★★★★½ Betrayal follows when a streetwise drifter and an unfaithful wife conspire to kill her husband. Garfield and Turner play down smoldering sexuality for the censors with meaningful looks and dialogue laced with double entendres. Compelling tale of guilt and retribution. From James M. Cain's book. Remade in 1981. C: Lana Turner, John Garfield, Cecil Kellaway, Hume Cronyn. D: Tay Garnett. CRI 113m. V

Postman Always Rings Twice, The 1981 ★★★½ Housewife (Lange) and loner (Nicholson), blinded by lust, scheme to murder her husband. Somber remake of the 1946 film is more explicit but strangely less steamy. Good leads. Adapted by David Mamet from the James M. Cain novel. C: Jack Nicholson, Jessica Lange, John Colicos, Michael Lerner. D: Bob Rafelson. CRI [R] 121m. V

Postmark for Danger 1955 British ★★ An artist suspects foul play after his reporter brother dies. Mediocre murder mystery. C: Terry Moore, Robert Beatty, William Sylvester. D: Guy Green. DRA 84m.

Pot Carriers, The 1962 British ★★½ A sensitive young man feels demeaned by prison routine. Peculiar British comedy/-drama. C: Ronald Fraser, Paul Massie, Carole Lesley, Dennis Price. D: Peter Graham Scott. DRA 84m.

Pot Luck 1936 British ★★★ The staff of a department store help a Scotland Yard Inspector retrieve a stolen Chinese vase. Not bad comic actioner; Walls and Lynn were a popular screen duo for years, and you can see why. C: Tom Walls, Ralph Lynn, Robertson Hare, Diana Churchill. D: Tom Walls. CRI 71m.

Potbouille 1957 *See* **Lovers of Paris**

Potemkin *See* **Battleship Potemkin**

Pourquoi Pas! 1979 French ★★★★ Three misfits experiment successfully with a ménage á trois until a fourth sexual partner is included. Attractive, unique French comedy/drama is alternately moving and funny. (a.k.a. *Why Not!*.) C: Sami Frey, Mario Gonzalez, Christine Murillo, Coline Serreau. COM 93m.

P.O.W. The Escape 1988 *See* **Behind Enemy Lines**

Powaqqatsi 1988 ★★★½ Visually stunning, aurally hypnotic documentary follow-up to the superior *Koyaanisqatsi* is a mosaic of global images, focusing on third-world cultures. This time, the effect is more sleep-inducing than intended. Soundtrack by Philip Glass. D: Godfrey Reggio. DOC [G] 97m. V

Powder River 1953 ★★½ A gunslinger elected town marshal learns who killed his friend. Minor Western. C: Rory Calhoun, Corrine Calvet, Cameron Mitchell. D: Louis King. WST 78m.

Power 1986 ★★★½ Hard-hitting satire about the world of political consultants, features Gere as slick operator, up against his folksy mentor Hackman. Story ends predictably but still a smart, savvy tale. C: Richard Gere, Julie Christie, Gene Hackman, Kate Capshaw, Denzel Washington, E.G. Marshall, Beatrice Straight. D: Sidney Lumet. COM [R] 111m. V

Power and the Glory, The 1933 ★★★½ A ruthless industrial titan rises to the top from modest beginnings. Flashback drama is an intriguing character study. C: Spencer Tracy, Colleen Moore, Ralph Morgan, Helen Vinson. D: William Howard. DRA 76m.

Power of One, The 1992 ★★★½ *Rocky* meets apartheid in this slick, but entertaining story of a white South African boxer (Dorff) willing to fight black challengers to achieve integration. Freeman steals the film as the hero's trainer. C: Stephen Dorff, Morgan Freeman, Armin Mueller-Stahl, John Gielgud. D: John G. Avildsen. DRA [PG-13] 111m. V

Power, The 1968 ★★★ A scientist tries to control a powerful evil force. Stimulating science-fiction thriller. C: George Hamilton, Suzanne Pleshette, Richard Carlson, Yvonne De Carlo. D: Byron Haskin. SFI 109m.

Powwow Highway 1989 ★★★½ Two Native Americans—one activist, one pacifist—encounter racism while driving beat-up Buick on road trip to sister's home. Well-intentioned film suffers from conventional villains, though ensemble gives material some heart. C: Gary Farmer, A. Martinez, Amanda Wyss. D: Jonathan Wacks. COM [R] 91m. V

Practically Yours 1944 ★★★ A pilot presumed dead returns to find himself engaged to a young woman who accidentally intercepted his message of love. Silliness put over by terrific cast. C: Claudette Colbert, Fred MacMurray, Gil Lamb, Robert Benchley. D: Mitchell Leisen. COM 90m.

Practice Makes Perfect 1978 *See* **See Le Cavaleur**

Prancer 1989 ★★★½ Father (Elliot) tries to cope with mounting financial difficulties while young farm girl (Harrell) cares for injured reindeer she is convinced belongs to Santa. Slow to start and occasionally too cute for its own good, but eventually settles into heartwarming family feature for holidays. C: Sam Elliott, Rebecca Harrell, Cloris Leachman. D: John Hancock. FAM/DRA [G] 110m. V

Pray for Death 1985 ★★★ When a Japanese (Kosugi) moves to Texas to open a restaurant, he encounters violent resistance from local hoods—until he unleashes his heretofore suppressed deadly ninja training! Well-crafted action punctuates this cartoon-like crime yarn. C: Sho Kosugi, James Booth, Donna Kei Benz, Kane Kosugi. D: Gordon Hessler. ACT [R] 93m. V

Prayer for the Dying, A 1987 British ★★½ An IRA assassin wants out, but a change of careers, at this point, isn't so easily done. Overwrought drama, less than perfect casting, leave many questions. C: Mickey Rourke, Bob Hoskins, Alan Bates. D: Mike Hodges. DRA [R] 108m. V

Prayer of the Rollerboys 1991 ★★ In dismal future L.A., Haim searches for brother by joining the Rollerboys, a gang of rollerblading Nazi punks led by Collet, who may be descendant of Hitler. About as bad as it sounds. Good skating though. C: Corey Haim, Patricia Arquette, Christopher Collet. D: Rick King. ACT [R] 120m. V

Predator 1987 ★★★½ A SWAT team battles an invisible alien killer while on a rescue mission in the dense Latin American jungle. Good action after slow start. C: Arnold Schwarzenegger, Carl Weathers, Elpidia Carrillo, Bill Duke. D: John McTiernan. ACT [R] 107m. V

Predator 2 1990 ★★★½ The intergalactic hunter is back, targeting the restive citizens of L.A. in 1997. Only one cop (Glover) stands in its way. Energetic, explosive but unworthy follow up to *Predator*. Glover is no Schwarzenegger! C: Danny Glover, Gary Busey, Ruben Blades, Maria Conchita Alonso. D: Stephen Hopkins. ACT [R] 105m. V

Prehysteria! 1993 ★★½ Youngster comes upon a miniaturized *Tyrannosaurus rex* that he tries to keep as a pet. Dinosaur take on *E.T.* formula suffers from stock plotting and below-average special effects. Young dinosaur fans probably won't mind. C: Brett Cullen, Austin O'Brien, Samantha Mills, Colleen Morris. D: Albert Band. FAM/SFI [PG] 86m. V

Prelude to a Kiss 1992 ★★★½ A young couple falls in love and marry very quickly; almost immediately the husband starts to notice bizarre changes in his wife. Fantasy about true nature of love has fine performances, though Lucas' play makes difficult transition to screen. C: Alec Baldwin, Meg Ryan, Kathy Bates, Ned Beatty, Patty Duke. D: Norman Rene. COM [PG-13] 106m. V

Prelude to Fame 1950 British ★★★½ A musical child prodigy is pushed to fame and finds disappointment. Well-produced drama, based on an Aldous Huxley story. C: Guy Rolfe, Kathleen Byron, Kathleen Ryan, Jeremy Spenser. D: Fergus McDonnell. DRA 78m.

Premature Burial, The 1962 ★★★ Adaptation of Edgar Allan Poe chiller concerns a medical student, buried alive, who returns to exact revenge. Low-budget Gothic ghoulishness, the Roger Corman way. C: Ray Milland, Hazel Court, Richard Ney. D: Roger Corman. HOR 81m. V

Premonition, The 1975 ★★★ When a young girl vanishes in the South, her adoptive parents turn to parapsychology for help, leading to supernatural intrigue. Low-budget production boasts evocative location shooting and creepy atmospherics. C: Sharon Farrell, Richard Lynch, Jeff Corey. D: Robert Allan Schnitzer. HOR [PG] 94m. V

Preppie Murder, The 1993 ★★ Sordid drama detailing the murder of Jennifer Levin by Robert Chambers, who claimed he accidentally strangled her during rough sex. C: William Baldwin, Lara Flynn Boyle, Danny Aiello. D: John Herzfeld. CRI 100m. TVM V

Presenting Lily Mars 1943 ★★★½ A stage-struck singer aspires to make it big on Broadway. Routine story enlivened by glorious Garland. C: Judy Garland, Van Heflin, Fay Bainter, Richard Carlson, Spring Byington. D: Norman Taurog. MUS 105m. V

President's Analyst, The 1967 ★★★★½ Cult favorite features Coburn as secret psychiatrist to Commander in Chief. When he leaves position, Coburn is subject of mad and merry chase by horde of demagogues and agents. Wonderfully offbeat satire runs through rapid comic pace with terrific cast enlivening razor-sharp script. C: James Coburn, Godfrey Cambridge, Severn Darden. D: Theodore J. Flicker. COM 100m. V

President's Lady, The 1953 ★★★½ Adaptation of Irving Stone's historical romance about Andrew Jackson's love affair with a previously married woman. Good rustic costume drama boasts an able cast and appealing story. C: Charlton Heston, Susan Hayward, John McIntire, Fay Bainter. D: Henry Levin. DRA 96m.

Presidio, The 1988 ★★★½ Strong stars wasted in routine story of a laid-back San Francisco cop (Harmon) dealing with his former commander (Connery) in a murder investigation on a military base. Their mutual dislike is enhanced when the cop falls for the Army officer's daughter (Ryan). C: Sean Connery, Mark Harmon, Meg Ryan, Jack Warden. D: Peter Hyams. CRI [R] 97m. V

Press for Time 1966 British ★★½ A government minister sends his inept grandson to work as a journalist in a provincial seaside town. Capable British comedy with the star effective in three roles. C: Norman Wisdom, Angela Browne, Derek Bond. D: Robert Asher. COM 102m.

Pressure Point 1962 ★★★★ Psychosociodrama of early '60s featuring Poitier as prison psychologist trying to get to the roots of the hatred harbored by Nazi convict Darin. Deft direction creates real tension. Based on true story. C: Sidney Poitier, Bobby Darin, Peter Falk. D: Hubert Cornfield. DRA 88m. V

Presumed Innocent 1990 ★★★★ A married attorney (Ford) is under suspicion when a colleague he has become infatuated with (Scacchi) is murdered. Excellent cast in a taut, compelling adaptation of Scott Turow's bestseller. C: Harrison Ford, Brian Dennehy, Raul Julia, Bonnie Bedelia, Paul Winfield, Greta Scacchi. D: Alan J. Pakula. CRI [R] 127m. V

Pretender, The 1947 ★★★½ By mischance a ruthless financier finds himself the intended victim of the hitman he hired. Taut suspense, well played. C: Albert Dekker, Catherine Craig, Linda Stirling. D: W. Wilder. DRA 69m.

Pretty Baby 1978 ★★★½ Malle caused a scandal with this story of photographer in turn-of-the-century New Orleans, shooting pictures of prostitutes and falling in love with one hooker's prepubescent daughter (Shields). Lushly photographed by Sven Nyqist. C: Keith Carradine, Susan Sarandon, Brooke Shields, Antonio Fargas. D: Louis Malle. DRA [R] 109m. V

Pretty Boy Floyd 1960 ★★½ The FBI tracks down the '30s Oklahoma bank robber. Standard Hollywood historical crime fiction with vigorous acting by Ericson. C: John Ericson, Barry Newman, Joan Harvey. D: Herbert Leder. DRA 96m.

Pretty in Pink 1986 ★★★★ Poor girl and rich boy test whether love can triumph over high school. Appealing and very popular—both the movie and its star. C: Molly Ringwald, Jon Cryer, Andrew McCarthy, Harry Dean Stanton, Annie Potts, James Spader. D: Howard Deutch. COM [PG-13] 96m. V

Pretty Maids All in a Row 1971 ★★★½ Intriguing black comedy about a lecherous high school guidance counselor (Hudson) who seduces female students, then murders them. Runs out of steam, but Rock's performance is one of his best. Script by Gene (*Star Trek*) Roddenberry. C: Rock Hudson, Angie Dickinson, John David Carson, Telly Savalas, Barbara Leigh. D: Roger Vadim. CRI [R] 92m.

Pretty Poison 1968 ★★★★ An eccentric arsonist (Perkins) recruits a sexy teenager (Weld) for a bizarre plot that heats up. Fine performances and an excellent script make for absorbing black comedy. C: Anthony Perkins, Tuesday Weld, Beverly Garland. D: Noel Black. COM [R] 89m.

Pretty Smart 1987 ★★ Charming performance by Arquette is one of the few redeeming features of this chaotic, low-grade comedy about shenanigans among girls' school students in the Greek Isles. C: Tricia Leigh Fisher, Patricia Arquette, Dennis Cole. D: Dimitri Logothetis. COM [R] 84m. V

Pretty Woman 1990 ★★★★ Ruthless business magnate (Gere) hires hooker (Roberts) to be his companion during an important week of takeover negotiations. Slowly, his Cinderella makes him see the light. A true star turn by Roberts and slick direction by old pro Marshall disguise unsavory premise with breezy comedy and romantic fantasy. C: Richard Gere, Julia Roberts, Ralph Bellamy, Jason Alexander, Laura San Giacomo, Hector Elizondo. D: Garry Marshall. COM [R] 89m. V

Prey of the Chameleon 1991 ★★★ Mental ward escapee and murderer (Zuniga) takes on identities of her victims. Who will she be next? Intriguing thriller. C: Daphne Zuniga, James Wilder, Alexandra Paul, Don Harvey. D: Fleming Fuller. DRA [R] 91m. V

Prey, The 1980 ★ Group of young campers are the prey and a subhuman creature is the predator in this tiresome shocker, which contains the absolute minimum of plot and dialogue required to make a horror film. C: Debbie Thurseon, Steve Bond, Jackie Coogan. D: Edwin Scott Brown. HOR [R] 80m. V

Price of Fear, The 1956 ★★½ A hit-and-run driver (Oberon) covers up her crime and her life spirals into danger. Ill-conceived melodrama. C: Merle Oberon, Lex Barker, Charles Drake. D: Abner Biberman. DRA 79m.

Priceless Beauty 1988 Italian ★★★½ Guilt-ridden ex-rock star gets another chance at happiness when he finds a genie in a lamp. Game, fun fantasy. C: Christopher Lambert, Diane Lane. D: Charles Finch. DRA [R] 94m. V

Prick Up Your Ears 1987 British ★★★★ The life of British playwright Joe Orton gets a tart, clear-eyed telling with sure-handed direction by Frears. Oldman makes a marvelous transformation as the cheeky Orton, but Molina steals the film as his jealous lover. C: Gary Oldman, Alfred Molina, Vanessa Redgrave, Wallace Shawn. D: Stephen Frears. DRA [R] 111m. V

Pride and Prejudice 1940 ★★★★★ Respectable adaptation of Jane Austen comedy of manners about a stubborn young 19th-century woman sparring with a wealthy man she hates for his pride. Excellent performances loaded with satisfying moments. Spirited entertainment. C: Laurence Olivier, Greer Garson, Mary Boland, Maureen O'Sullivan, Edna May Oliver, Edmund Gwenn. D: Robert Z. Leonard. DRA 118m. V

Pride and Prejudice 1985 British ★★★★ Five sisters in 19th-century England hunt husbands. The result is an interesting BBC adaptation of Jane Austen's novel of manners. C: Elizabeth Garvie, David Rintoul. D: Cyril Coke. DRA 226m. TVM V

Pride and the Passion, The 1957 ★★ Hopelessly miscast Sinatra is Spanish peasant who steals cannon from British commander Grant in midst of Napoleonic wars. Incredibly wasted talents—including love interest Loren—and overblown production makes for either bad movie or great silly camp, depending on viewer tastes. C: Cary Grant, Frank Sinatra, Sophia Loren, Theodore Bikel. D: Stanley Kramer. DRA 132m. V

Pride of St. Louis, The 1952 ★★★½ Biography of St. Louis pitching star Dizzy Dean, who retired after an injury and became a popular sports commentator. Modest, sentimental biography about an extraordinary character. C: Dan Dailey, Joanne Dru, Richard Crenna. D: Harmon Jones. DRA 93m. V

Pride of the Marines 1945 ★★★★ Garfield plays Marine Al Schmid, a real-life WWII hero who killed two hundred Japanese soldiers and was later blinded by a grenade blast. Touching, well-done movie chronicles Schmid's journey into darkness, and has first-rate ensemble playing along with Garfield's dynamic characterization. C: John Garfield, Eleanor Parker, Dane Clark. D: Delmer Daves. DRA 119m.

Pride of the Yankees, The 1942 ★★★★½ Fine biography of Lou Gehrig, first baseman for the New York Yankees and known as the "Iron Man" of baseball, who died of a rare muscle-wasting disease. Homespun Cooper is ideal as sports great Gehrig in tender American saga. Memorable farewell speech. C: Gary Cooper, Teresa Wright, Babe Ruth, Walter Brennan, Dan Duryea. D: Sam Wood. DRA 128m. V

Priest 1995 British ★★★★ A gay priest (Roache) in Liverpool parish discovers that his superior is having an affair with their housekeeper. Well-acted study of personal needs vs. religious responsibility. Includes graphic gay bedroom scene. C: Linus Roache, Tom Wilkinson, Cathy Tyson, Robert Carlyle. D: Antonia Bird. DRA [R] 97m.

Priest of Love 1981 British ★★★★ English author D.H. Lawrence battles his tempestuous wife, censors, and tuberculosis in his last years. Distinguished biographical drama directed with intelligence and sensitivity. C: Ian McKellen, Janet Suzman, Ava Gardner, Penelope Keith, John Gielgud, Sarah Miles. D: Christopher Miles. DRA [R] 125m. V

Primary 1960 ★★★★ Compelling documentary of the 1960 Wisconsin presidential primary—JFK versus Hubert Humphrey. Pioneering cinema-verite film captures the tension of the high-stakes political battle, while letting in plenty of personality, too. D: Richard Leacock, Robert Drew. DOC 60m.

Primary Motive 1992 ★★★½ Sometimes involving, sometimes contrived political thriller pits campaign aide against boss' corrupt opponent who's golden in the eyes of the gullible public. C: Judd Nelson, Justine Bateman, Richard Jordan, Sally Kirkland, John Savage. D: Daniel Adams. DRA [R] 93m. V

Prime Cut 1972 ★★★½ Nasty gangster film with professional killer Marvin sent to Kansas City to rein in renegade Hackman. (Previous attempt ended with assassins turned into sausages.) Sick, sour humor of film is redeemed by well-crafted performances of Marvin and Hackman. Spacek's debut. C: Lee Marvin, Gene Hackman, Angel Tompkins, Sissy Spacek. D: Michael Ritchie. CRI [R] 86m. V

Prime of Miss Jean Brodie, The 1969 ★★★★½ Maggie Smith won an Oscar for her portrayal of an eccentric '30s Edinburgh schoolmistress who influences her young charges irresponsibly. Astonishingly realized character drama adapted from Muriel Spark's novel. C: Maggie Smith, Robert Stephens, Pamela Franklin, Gordon Jackson, Celia Johnson. D: Ronald Neame. DRA 116m. V

Prime Risk 1984 ★★½ Novice thieves tangle with terrorists out to ruin the U.S. monetary system. Low-interest account. C: Toni Hudson, Lee Montgomery. D: W. Farkas. DRA [PG-13] 98m. V

Prime Suspect 1992 British ★★★★★ Terrific crime drama mini-series stars Mirren as Chief Inspector Jane Tennison, who takes over a serial murder investigation despite gender prejudice. Great acting all around, building to a sizzling climax. Originally shown in four parts. Followed by two sequel series. C: Helen Mirren, Tom Bell, Zoe Wanamaker. D: David Drury. CRI 240m. TVM V

Prime Suspect 2 1993 British ★★★★½ Jane Tennison returns, this time to investigate the murder of a black girl whose corpse is discovered years after the crime. Exploration of racial tensions both on the force and in London in general is well-handled, with Mirren superb as Jane. Second of three mini-series to date. C: Helen Mirren, Tom Bell, David Thewlis. D: David Drury. CRI 240m. TVM V

Prime Suspect 3 1994 ★★★★½ Detective Chief Inspector Jane Tennison (Mirren) returns in another exceptionally intelligent and tough-minded police procedural. Mirren is riveting as always, this time involved in a case that takes her into an underground world of pedophilia and child sexual abuse. Well-written, acted, and directed. C: Helen Mirren, Tom Bell, Peter Capaldi, David Thewlis. D: David Drury. CRI 240m. TVM

Primo Baby 1992 ★★★½ A ward of the state is sent to live with an oddball widowed rancher and his wheelchair-bound son. Quirky comedy/drama. C: Duncan Regehr, Janet Laine Green. D: Eda Lever Lishman. COM 97m. V

Primrose Path, The 1940 ★★★½ Poor young woman falls for an ambitious hard worker. Absorbing poor-side-of-town soap opera. Good Joel and Ginger. C: Ginger Rogers, Joel McCrea, Marjorie Rambeau. D: Gregory Cava. DRA 93m. V

Prince and the Pauper, The 1937 ★★★★½ Adventure and trouble ensue when identical lads, one a prince and the other a London street urchin, change places. Based on Twain's novel, this rip-roaring film is filled with action, color, and charm. Flynn et al are captivating. C: Errol Flynn, Billy Mauch, Bobby Mauch, Claude Rains, Alan Hale. D: William Keighley. COM 117m. V

Prince and the Pauper, The 1962 ★★★ Remake of the Twain story about look-alikes swapping places has some charm and adventure, but it pales beside the 1937 Flynn version. C: Guy Williams, Laurence Naismith, Donald Houston, Sean Scully. D: Don Chaffey. COM [G] 93m. V

Prince and the Pauper, The 1978 *See* **Crossed Swords**

Prince and the Showgirl, The 1957 ★★★★ During 1912 coronation of George V, American showgirl Monroe is romanced by Carpathian prince Olivier against beautiful English setting. Fun in parts, slow in others, and interesting screen chemistry between two costars. C: Marilyn Monroe, Laurence Olivier, Sybil Thorndike. D: Laurence Olivier. COM 117m. V

Prince of Bel Air 1986 ★★½ Southern California hunk (Harmon) shows why so many women have crushes on the poor man. Flimsy vehicle for Harmon and Alley; they keep it going surprisingly well. C: Mark Harmon, Kirstie Alley, Robert Vaughn. D: Charles Braverman. COM [R] 95m. TVM V

Prince of Darkness 1987 ★★½ Carpenter manages to wring few chills out of convoluted plot about a priest, a physics professor and his students who are trying to stop the rebirth of Satan in a church basement via a canister of foul liquid. C: Donald Pleasence, Lisa Blount, Jameson Parker. D: John Carpenter. HOR [R] 102m. V

Prince of Foxes 1949 ★★★½ A medieval adventurer tangles with a powerful tyrant. Handsomely mounted costume epic, splendidly photographed on location. C: Tyrone Power, Wanda Hendrix, Orson Welles, Katina Paxinou. D: Henry King. ACT 107m.

Prince of Pennsylvania, The 1988 ★★★½ Off-beat look at generation-gap conflict between a rebellious youth (Reeves) and his father (Ward). Uneven, but worth a look for Keanu's charismatic performance. C: Keanu Reeves, Fred Ward, Bonnie Bedelia, Amy Madigan. D: Ron Nyswaner. COM [R] 87m. V

Prince of Pirates 1953 ★★★ Prince turns pirate to fend off the mighty Spanish Armada. Entertaining, seafaring costume piece with a fast pace. C: John Derek, Barbara Rush. D: Sidney Salkow. ACT 80m.

Prince of Players 1955 ★★★½ Biography of famous Shakespearean actor Edwin Booth, older brother of Lincoln's assassin, John Wilkes Booth. Worthwhile entertainment via Burton's fine acting and Moss Hart's screenplay. C: Richard Burton, Maggie McNamara, Raymond Massey, Charles Bickford, Eva Le Gallienne. D: Philip Dunne. DRA 102m.

Prince of The City 1981 ★★★★½ Fascinating (if long) drama depicts true story of New York narcotics cop whose testimony exposed corruption in his department but devastated the lives of his closest friends. Williams shines in the lead role. C: Treat Williams, Jerry Orbach, Richard Foronjy. D: Sidney Lumet. CRI [R] 167m. V

Prince of Tides, The 1991 ★★★½ When his sister attempts suicide, a South Carolina teacher (well-played by Nolte) comes to New York to consult with her psychiatrist (Streisand), and dredges up his own horrific family memories. Effective film of Pat Conroy's novel, though not as intense as the book. Streisand seems to be everywhere at once. C: Nick Nolte, Barbra Streisand, Blythe Danner, Kate Nelligan, Jeroen Krabbe, Melinda Dillon. D: Barbra Streisand. DRA [R] 132m. V

Prince Valiant 1954 ★★★½ Classic cartoon hero comes to life fighting for good in Camelot. Some nice color. C: James Mason, Janet Leigh, Robert Wagner, Debra Paget, Sterling Hayden, Victor McLaglen. D: Henry Hathaway. FAM/DRA 100m. V

Princess and the Goblin, The 1993 British ★★★½ Animated fairy tale based on George MacDonald children's story about a princess whose kingdom is threatened by evil goblins. Excellent voice work by Bloom and Ackland. C: Joss Ackland, Claire Bloom, Roy Kinnear, Sally Ann Marssh, Rik Mayal, Peggy

Mount, Peter Murrya, Victor Spinetti. D: Jozsef Gemes. FAM/SFI 111m. v

Princess and the Pirate, The 1944 ★★★½ An imposter is pursued by a ruthless pirate. Wacky costume action-comedy is an enjoyable Hope fest. C: Bob Hope, Virginia Mayo, Walter Slezak, Walter Brennan. D: David Butler. COM 94m. v

Princess Bride, The 1987 ★★★★ Delightful comic adventure spoofs swashbucklers as a young hero (Elwes) rescues his beloved (Wright) from clutches of evil prince Sarandon, and meets some wonderfully eccentric characters along the way. Adapted by William Goldman from his novel. C: Cary Elwes, Robin Wright, Mandy Patinkin, Chris Sarandon, Christopher Guest, Wallace Shawn, Andre the Giant. D: Rob Reiner. COM [PG] 98m. v

Princess Caraboo 1994 ★★★★½ Disarming fantasy stars Cates as a shipwrecked princess in 19th-century England. Is she faking? Children and the young at heart will fall for this underrated gem. Kline shines in a small role as a dotty butler. C: Phoebe Cates, Stephen Rea, Kevin Kline, Jim Broadbent. D: Michael Austin. COM [PG] 96m. v

Princess Comes Across, The 1939 ★★★½ A young Brooklyn woman, posing as a princess, finds love on an oceanliner and gets involved in a murder mystery. Delightfully zany Lombard comedy. C: Carole Lombard, Fred MacMurray, Douglass Dumbrille, Alison Skipworth, William Frawley. D: William Howard. COM 76m.

Princess Daisy 1983 ★★★ Young woman member of the Russian royal family puts money and power before love until she sees the emptiness of her life. Based upon Judith Krantz's best-selling novel. It's trash, but it's fun trash. C: Merete Kamp, Lindsay Wagner, Paul Michael Glaser, Robert Urich, Claudia Cardinale, Ringo Starr. D: Waris Hussein. DRA 188m. TVM v

Princess of the Nile 1954 ★★ An Egyptian princess leads her nation in war against invaders. Campy costume story. C: Debra Paget, Jeffrey Hunter, Michael Rennie. D: Harmon Jones. ACT 71m.

Princess O'Rourke 1943 ★★★ An ace pilot (Cummings) discovers his fiancée (de Havilland) is of royal blood. Cheerful wartime comedy. C: Olivia de Havilland, Robert Cummings, Charles Coburn, Jack Carson, Jane Wyman, Gladys Cooper. D: Norman Krasna. COM 94m.

Princess Yang Kwei Fei 1955 Japanese ★★★★★ Chinese emperor falls in love with lowly maid. Mizoguchi's first color film has spectacular photography, and a charming love affair at its center.(a.k.a. The *Empress Yank Kwei Fei*) C: Machiko Kyo, Masayuki Mori. D: Kenji Mizoguchi. DRA 91m. v

Princess Tam Tam 1935 French ★★★★ A tribal African woman (Baker) is discovered, nurtured by a writer, and then poses as an exotic princess in this charming take-off of *Pygmalion*. Rare film appearance by the legendary Follies Bergere star features some high-stepping musical numbers. C: Josephine Baker, Albert Prejean, Germaine Aussey, Robert Arnoux. D: Edmond T. Greville. MUS 77m. v

Principal, The 1987 ★★★ Troublemaking school principal is assigned the district's most dangerous high school. Like a Western set in the modern inner city, has enough action to keep you watching, but not much else. C: James Belushi, Louis Gossett, Jr., Rae Dawn Chong. D: Christopher Cain. DRA [R] 112m. v

Prison 1988 ★★★ Spirit of an electrocuted warden haunts penitentary. Visually striking, with some solid scares. C: Lane Smith, Chelsea Field. D: Renny Harlin. HOR [R] 102m. v

Prison Stories: Women on the Inside 1991 ★★★ Compelling trilogy of tales about female convicts marred by uneven acting and directing. C: Penelope Spheeris, Rae Dawn Chong, Lolita Davidovich, Annabella Sciorra. D: Donna Deitch, Joan Micklin Silver. CRI 90m. TVM v

Prisoner of Honor 1991 British ★★★★ Volatile moment in French history—the Dreyfus affair—is dramatized in better than average style, examining the injustice and anti-Semitism that surrounded the case. C: Richard Dreyfuss, Oliver Reed, Peter Firth. D: Ken Russell. DRA [PG] 90m. TVM v

Prisoner of Second Avenue, The 1975 ★★★½ Shrill, hilarious Neil Simon comedy stars Lemmon as unemployed business executive on verge of nervous breakdown. Bancroft is wife trying to boost morale before Lemmon completely cracks. Look for Sylvester Stallone and F. Murray Abraham in small parts. C: Jack Lemmon, Anne Bancroft. D: Melvin Frank. COM [PG] 99m. v

Prisoner of Shark Island, The 1936 ★★★★½ Baxter plays real-life Dr. Samuel Mudd, sentenced to life in prison after innocently treating the injured John Wilkes Booth after Lincoln's assasination. Carradine is a cruel guard in this well-acted historical drama. C: Warner Baxter, Gloria Stuart, Claude Gillingwater, John Carradine. D: John Ford. DRA 95m.

Prisoner of Zenda, The 1937 ★★★★★ A medieval commoner pretends to be his cousin, the kidnapped king of a small European monarchy; his troubles really begin when he falls for his cousin's wife, the queen. Non-stop action, color, and a fabulous cast (led by the always superb Colman and lovely Carroll) in one of the finest swashbucklers ever filmed. C: Ronald Colman, Madeleine Carroll, Douglas Fairbanks, Jr., Raymond Massey, Mary Astor. D: John Cromwell. ACT 102m. v

Prisoner of Zenda, The 1952 ★★★½ Remake of 1937 classic offers grand sets, colorful costumes, and a cast of notables, but doesn't have the same power as its more famous predecessor. C: Stewart Granger, Deborah Kerr, Jane Greer, Louis Calhern, James Mason. D: Richard Thorpe. ACT 100m. v

Prisoner of Zenda, The 1979 ★★½ Sellers plays a Cockney cabbie who covers for his double, the king of Ruratanian. Slapstick is laid on with a trowel, but results are mostly unfunny. C: Peter Sellers, Lynne Frederick, Lionel Jeffries, Elke Sommer. D: Richard Quine. COM [PG] 108m. v

Prisoner, The 1955 British ★★★★ Guinness is a cardinal under arrest in a totalitarian country who suffers brutal interrogation and brainwashing at the hands of Hawkins. Brilliant performances from and powerful chemistry between the two leads. C: Alec Guinness, Jack Hawkins. D: Peter Glenville. DRA 91m. v

Prisoner Without a Name, Cell Without a Number 1983 *See* **Jacobo Timmerman: Prisoner Without Name, Cell Without a Number**

Private Affairs 1990 Italian ★ Romantic intrigues abound amidst the confines of Italian design firm. Cast runs through embarrassing rings in witless sex farce. C: Kate Capshaw, David Naughton, Giuliana deSio. D: Francesco Massaro. COM 83m. v

Private Affairs of Bel Ami, The 1947 ★★★★ Elegant rogue uses friends and important women for his own ruthless ends, leaving a trail of victims. Literate and exacting narrative of heartless climb to fame. Based on Guy de Maupassant story. C: George Sanders, Angela Lansbury, Ann Dvorak, Frances Dee. D: Albert Lewin. DRA 112m. v

Private Benjamin 1980 ★★★★ After husband Brooks dies unexpectedly, his grieving widow, the much-pampered Hawn, joins military. Through series of entertaining lessons, she goes from princess to mean, lean, fighting machine at the hands of priceless D.I. Brennan. Fine showcase for Hawn (who also produced). C: Goldie Hawn, Eileen Brennan, Armand Assante, Robert Webber. D: Howard Zieff. COM 110m. v

Private Detective 62 1933 *See* **Man Killer**

Private Duty Nurses 1971 ★★ Three Florence Nightingales provide lots of tender loving care to their patients. Second entry in director's "Sexy Nurse" series. C: Kathy Cannon, Joyce Williams, Pegi Boucher. D: George Armitage. COM [R] 80m. v

Private Eyes, The 1980 ★★½ Knotts and Conway are bumbling Scotland Yard detectives who must protect a girl after her parents are murdered. Overdoes silly humor without much effect; kids will enjoy the slapstick antics though. C: Tim Conway, Don Knotts, Trisha Noble. D: Lang Elliott. FAM/COM [PG] 97m. v

Private Files of J. Edgar Hoover, The 1977 ★★★½ Schlocky but perversely entertaining biography of FBI kingpin from his early years through his final paranoid days. Eclectic cast provides historical histrionics in this extremely campy and occasionally downright bizarre film. C: Broderick Crawford, Dan Dailey, Jose Ferrer, Rip Torn. D: Larry Cohen. DRA [PG] 111m. v

Private Function, A 1984 British ★★★★ During the strict food rationing in post-WWII England, a timid podiatrist (Palin) and his domineering wife (Smith) harbor a blackmarket pig to be slaughtered in celebration of Princess Elizabeth's marriage. Smith's attempt to slaughter the pig is a hilarious spoof of Lady Macbeth. A very black comedy. C: Michael Palin, Maggie Smith, Denholm Elliott. D: Malcolm Mowbray. COM [R] 96m. v

Private Hell 36 1954 ★★★★ Effective crime drama about two cops who keep some recovered stolen money, and then suffer from guilt. Siegel directs with smart pacing; Lupino also co-wrote and co-produced. C: Ida Lupino, Steve Cochran, Howard Duff. D: Don Siegel. CRI 81m. v

Private Lessons 1981 ★★ Horny, virginal teenager is left alone with voluptuous maid. Routine sexual initiation flick, this time with *Emmanuelle* films star Kristel as the maid. C: Sylvia Kristel, Howard Hesseman, Eric Brown. D: Alan Myerson. COM [R] 87m. v

Private Life of Henry VIII, The 1933 British ★★★★★ Truly spectacular film of life of 16th-century king of England, from sharp direction to great writing and performances. Laughton's brilliant portrayal won him the Best Actor Oscar. C: Charles Laughton, Binnie Barnes, Robert Donat, Elsa Lanchester, Merle Oberon. D: Alexander Korda. DRA 90m. v

Private Life of Sherlock Holmes, The 1970 ★★★★½ A different take by Wilder on legend of famed sleuth. Holmes' cerebral gifts are portrayed as defense mechanism against certain character elements—including his cocaine addiction. Neatly acted, with a fine score and beautiful photography. C: Robert Stephens, Colin Blakely, Genevieve Page, Irene Handl, Christopher Lee. D: Billy Wilder. DRA [PG] 125m. v

Private Lives 1931 ★★★★ Shearer and Montgomery shine in Noel Coward's comedy of manners about a bickering couple who are still in love. Sparkling cast and direction keeps this classic fresh. C: Norma Shearer, Robert Montgomery, Una Merkel, Reginald Denny. D: Sidney Franklin. COM 84m. v

Private Lives of Elizabeth and Essex, The 1939 ★★★★ Historically inaccurate but dramatically gripping costume drama of the power struggle and romance between the Earl of Essex and Queen Elizabeth I. Davis shines through the ornate scenery in her first of two tries as the "Virgin Queen" (the title of the other movie). Based on Maxwell Anderson's verse drama *Elizabeth the Queen*. (a.k.a. *Eliza-*

beth the Queen) C: Bette Davis, Errol Flynn, Olivia de Havilland, Donald Crisp, Vincent Price. D: Michael Curtiz. DRA 106m. v

Private Matter, A 1992 ★★★★ In 1962 a young pregnant woman learns that she has been taking the birth-defect-causing drug thalidomide. She decides to have an abortion, and is publicly condemned by right-to-lifers. A compelling, intelligent film, with fine Spacek, based on the true story of Sherri Finkbine. C: Sissy Spacek, Aidan Quinn, Nanette Fabray. D: Joan Micklin Silver. DRA [PG-13] 89m. TVM v

Private Navy of Sgt. O'Farrell, The 1968 ★ There's no hope for this tasteless comedy about a WWII sergeant (Hope) trying to "recruit" beautiful women for his outfit, and winding up with a harridan (Diller) by mistake. C: Bob Hope, Phyllis Diller, Jeffrey Hunter, Gina Lollobrigida. D: Frank Tashlin. COM [G] 92m.

Private Parts 1972 ★★★½ Runaway teen (Ruymen) takes up residence in her aunt's flop house and becomes involved with kinky photographer (Ventantonio), one of many oddball tenants. Perverse but genuinely compelling cult classic mixes sex and violence with dark humor. C: Ann Ruymen, Lucille Benson, Laurie Main, John Ventantonio. D: Paul Bartel. HOR [R] 86m. v

Private Resort 1985 ★★ Bunch of young swingers let loose when they go to a resort hotel. Sophomoric sex comedy. C: Rob Morrow, Johnny Depp, Hector Elizondo. D: George Bowers. COM [R] 82m. v

Private School 1983 ★ Cates and her boyfriend Modine work out their relationship surrounded by all kinds of sex plays. The cast is better than the crude script. C: Phoebe Cates, Matthew Modine, Michael Zorek. D: Noel Black. COM [R] 89m. v

Private War of Major Benson, The 1955 ★★★ A crusty military officer (Heston) gets valuable lessons from grammar school students in a soft-hearted comedy which should have been funnier. Loosely remade in 1995 as *Major Payne.* C: Charlton Heston, Julie Adams, William Demarest, Sal Mineo. D: Jerry Hopper. FAM/COM 105m.

Private Wars 1993 ★★½ War hero turned psychopath trains troops in Vietnam. Utterly violent; questionable entertainment. C: Michael Champion, Holly Floria, Michael De Lano, Stuart Whitman, Steve Railsback. D: John Weidner. ACT [R] 90m. v

Private Worlds 1935 ★★★½ This story of two mental health professionals (Boyer and Colbert) and the challenges they face working at a psychiatric hospital was heavy-duty drama for its time. Material has aged somewhat, but story and performances still worth watching. C: Claudette Colbert, Charles Boyer, Joan Bennett, Joel McCrea. D: Gregory Cava. DRA 84m.

Privates on Parade 1984 British ★★★½ A troop of drag singers and dancers in a British entertainment unit tours South East Asia during the late '40s with an oblivious, straitlaced commander (Cleese). Bleak satire, laced with high comedy. C: John Cleese, Denis Quilley, Nicola Pagett, Patrick Pearson. D: Michael Blakemore. COM [R] 107m. v

Prize Fighter, The 1979 ★★ Dimwitted boxer (Conway) managed by a wiseguy promoter (Knotts) in '30s. Weak gags and half-hearted slapstick amounts to forgettable kiddie comedy. C: Tim Conway, Don Knotts, David Wayne, Robin Clarke. D: Michael Preece. FAM/COM [PG] 99m. v

Prize of Arms, A 1961 British ★★★★ Crooks hatch a plot to steal a military payroll. Well-played thriller that holds tension start to finish. C: Stanley Baker, Tom Bell, Helmut Schmid. D: Cliff Owen. DRA 105m.

Prize of Gold, A 1955 British ★★★★ During Berlin airlift following end of WWII, thieves plot to filch a load of gold bullion. Nicely developed intrigue, with effective suspense and good cast. C: Richard Widmark, Mai Zetterling, Nigel Patrick. D: Mark Robson. DRA 98m.

Prize Pulitzer: The Roxanne Pulitzer Story, The 1989 ★★½ A sordid, superficial tale tells one side of a divorce among the wealthy. High-flown dross, based on true story. C: Perry King, Chynna Phillips. D: Richard A. Colla. DRA 95m. TVM v

Prize, The 1963 ★★★★ Nobel Prize-winning author in Stockholm gets entangled in espionage plot to abduct a noted scientist. Lively fun in Hitchcock tradition. From Irving Wallace novel. C: Paul Newman, Elke Sommer, Edward G. Robinson, Diane Baker. D: Mark Robson. DRA 136m. v

Prizefighter and the Lady, The 1933 ★★★½ Pugilist Baer makes his screen debut as a boxer who falls for mobster's girlfriend Loy. Cliché-ridden, but entertainingly so; helped by cameos of some of Baer's boxing colleagues. (a.k.a. *Every Woman's Man*) C: Myrna Loy, Max Baer, Otto Kruger, Walter Huston. D: W. S. Van Dyke II. DRA 102m.

Prizzi's Honor 1985 ★★★★½ Huston is perfect director to film Richard Condon's darkly funny tale of Mafia families at work and play. Nicholson and Turner are inspired as amorous assassins. Anjelica Huston justly won Oscar for supporting performance as Nicholson's ardent pursuer; and Hickey is hilarious as aging Don. C: Jack Nicholson, Kathleen Turner, Anjelica Huston, Robert Loggia, William Hickey, John Randolph. D: John Huston. CRI [R] 130m. v

Problem Child 1990 ★★ Ritter and Yasbeck want to adopt, but wind up with tiny terror Oliver, who seems determined to destroy their lives. Potentially funny idea is undermined by unpleasant characters. C: John Ritter, Michael Oliver, Jack Warden. D: Dennis Dugan. COM [PG] 81m. V

Problem Child 2 1991 ★★ Attempt to double the laughs by giving the title character an equally hellacious little sister. Flat, with humor even baser than the first time around. C: John Ritter, Michael Oliver, Jack Warden, Laraine Newman. D: Brian Levant. COM [PG-13] 91m. V

Prodigal, The 1955 ★★★½ Hollywood biblical tale of Hebrew farmer who falls in love with pagan priestess. Good cast in rambling story that bears little resemblance to any accounts in the Bible. C: Lana Turner, Edmund Purdom, James Mitchell, Louis Calhern, Neville Brand. D: Richard Thorpe. DRA [PG] 113m. V

Producers, The 1968 ★★★★★ Brooks' classic (for which he won Best Screenplay Oscar) about shady producer Mostel luring timid accountant Wilder into a plot to oversell shares in surefire flop musical and make off with the profits. One hilarious scene after another, climaxing with unforgettable "Springtime for Hitler" musical sequence; the two leads are brilliantly funny. C: Zero Mostel, Gene Wilder, Kenneth Mars, Dick Shawn, Christopher Hewett, Estelle Winwood. D: Mel Brooks. COM 88m. V

Professional, A 1968 *See* **Mercenary, The**

Professional Soldier 1936 ★★★½ Hired thug McLaglen kidnaps royal youngster Bartholomew; then friendship develops between them. Routine material with nice lead performances. Adapted from Damon Runyon tale. C: Victor McLaglen, Freddie Bartholomew, Gloria Stuart, Constance Collier. D: Tay Garnett. DRA 78m.

Professional, The 1994 ★★★ Plant-loving recluse (Reno), actually a professional killer, is hired by young Portman to avenge her murdered family. Extremely violent, uninvolving melodrama from the director of *La Femme Nikita*, C: Jean Reno, Gary Oldman, Natalie Portman, Danny Aiello. D: Luc Besson. CRI [R] 112m. V

Professional, The—Golgo 13 ★★★ Cult Japanese cartoon involves professional killer and his highly stylized, extremely violent adventures. Strictly for genre fans and definitely *not* for younger viewers. ACT V

Professionals, The 1966 ★★★★ When a wealthy rancher's wife is kidnapped by Mexican desperadoes, he hires a quartet of tough guys to get her back. Super action combined with a quality cast. C: Lee Marvin, Burt Lancaster, Robert Ryan, Woody Strode, Jack Palance, Claudia Cardinale. D: Richard Brooks. WST [PG] 117m. V

Professor Beware 1938 ★★★ Lesser Lloyd comedy about Egyptologist who believes himself to be reincarnated. C: Harold Lloyd, Phyllis Welch, William Frawley, Etienne Girardot, Raymond Walburn, Lionel Stander. D: Elliott Nugent. COM 87m.

Program, The 1993 ★★½ Cliché-ridden gridiron yarn of young bucks suffering the bruises and pressures of big-time college football. Bone-crushing action should please football fans during the off-season. C: James Caan, Halle Berry, Kristy Swansón, Craig Sheffer. DRA [R] 115m. V

Project A-Ko 1986 Japanese ★★★ Japanese animated feature for adults about teenagers with various supertype powers confronting an alien spaceship hurtling toward Earth. Different. SFI 86m. V

Project: Alien 1990 ★★★ Rival newshounds try to uncover the truth behind conspiracy cloaking an apparent UFO crash in Norway. Incongruously lighthearted treatment undermines serious theme. (a.k.a. *No Cause For Alarm*) C: Michael Nouri, Maxwell Caulfield, Darlanne Fluegel, Charles Durning. D: Frank Shields. SFI [R] 92m. V

Project M7 1953 British ★★★½ Scientist at secluded lab is developing an amazing new aircraft, unaware that one of his colleagues is a nefarious spy. Small but entertaining thriller. C: Phyllis Calvert, James Donald, Robert Beatty, Herbert Lom. D: Anthony Asquith. DRA 86m.

Project: Shadowchaser 1992 ★★ Coarse composite of *Die Hard* and *The Terminator* and every action cliché in between; terrorists led by unstoppable robot invade high-rise hospital and hold president's daughter hostage. (Originally called *Shadowchaser*) C: Martin Kove, Meg Foster, Frank Zagarino, Joss Ackland. D: John Eyres. SFI [R] 97m. V

Project X 1987 ★★★½ When assigned duty in bio-experiment lab, Airman (Broderick) becomes attached to the main subject, a chimp. When he discovers chimp is slated for experiment from which he won't return, he wants to set him free. Likable yarn with engaging performances. C: Matthew Broderick, Helen Hunt, Bill Sadler. D: Jonathan Kaplan. DRA [PG] 107m. V

Projectionist, The 1971 ★★★½ Movie projectionist imagines himself a superhero while watching the films he shows. Somewhat hit-and-miss comedy, but inventive use of old film clips and loopy humor help film over slower moments. Dangerfield's screen debut. C: Chuck McCann, Ina Balin, Rodney Dangerfield. D: Harry Hurwitz. COM [PG] 85m. V

Prom Night 1980 Canadian ★★ Six years after the death of a little girl, teens who were at the scene of the crime are being bumped off. Typically ghastly. C: Leslie Nielsen, Jamie Lee Curtis, Casey Stevens. D: Paul Lynch. HOR 91m. V

Prom Night II 1987 *See* **Hello Mary Lou**

Prom Night III: The Last Kiss 1990 U.S. ★★ Mary Lou, the prom queen from hell, returns to seduce a high school suitor while she spreads her murderous evil. Campier (and schlockier) than predecessors, but somewhat redeemed by sense of style and humor. C: Tim Conlon, Cyndy Preston, Courtney Taylor. D: Ron Oliver, Peter Simpson. HOR [R] 97m. v

Prom Night IV: Deliver Us From Evil 1992 Canadian ★★ Series returns to mad slasher mode, with partying teens stalked by demonic priest in an isolated mansion. Inventive direction can't disguise the thinness and predictability of the material. C: Alden Kane, Joy Tanner. D: Clay Borris. HOR [R] 95m. v

Promise at Dawn 1970 U.S. ★★★½ Fictionalized account of author Roman Gary's childhood has mom Mercouri showing her son the world while pursuing her acting career. Mercouri dominates zestfully. C: Melina Mercouri, Assaf Dayan, Francois Raffoul. D: Jules Dassin. DRA [PG] 101m.

Promise Her Anything 1966 ★★½ Porn filmmaker agrees to take care of his neighbor's baby. Random funny moments, but delightful supporting cast has little to do. C: Warren Beatty, Leslie Caron, Bob Cummings, Hermione Gingold, Lionel Stander, Keenan Wynn. D: Arthur Hiller. COM 98m. v

Promise, The 1978 ★★ After a car wreck, a woman receives a new face through plastic surgery. Her boyfriend, who believes she's dead, falls for her new identity. Over-the-top tearjerker holds nothing back. C: Kathleen Quinlan, Stephen Collins, Beatrice Straight. D: Gilbert Cates. DRA [PG] 97m. v

Promise, The 1986 ★★★★★ A swinging single man (Garner) must take care of his schizophrenic brother (Woods) because of a death-bed pledge to their mother. Great acting, writing, and direction make this as memorable as the similar *Rain Man.* Emmys for Actor (Woods), Supporting Actress (Laurie), and Best TV Movie. C: James Garner, James Woods, Piper Laurie, Peter Michael Goetz, Alan Rosenberg. D: Glenn Jordan. DRA 100m. TVM

Promised a Miracle 1992 ★★★★ Believing their diabetic son divinely healed, a deeply religious couple discontinue his insulin injections and face manslaughter charges when he dies. Deeply disturbing. Based on true story presented in Larry Parker's *We Let Our Son Die.* C: Rosanna Arquette, Judge Reinhold. D: Steven Gyllenhaal. DRA [PG-13] 94m. TVM v

Promised Land 1988 ★★★½ Haunting, but underdeveloped tale of small-town angst and post-high school stress, as experienced by two high school friends: one a star athlete, the other a dreamy loser. Features a fiery, complex performance by Ryan. C: Jason Gedrick, Kiefer Sutherland, Meg Ryan, Tracy Pollan. D: Michael Hoffman. DRA [R] 110m. v

Promises in the Dark 1979 ★★★★ Underrated weepie about a terminal cancer patient (Beller) and her therapeutic effect on her doctor (Mason). Both actresses score high on the "Kleenex meter." C: Marsha Mason, Kathleen Beller, Ned Beatty, Susan Clark. D: Jerome Hellman. DRA [PG] 115m. v

Promises! Promises! 1963 ★★ Two married couples meet on a cruise and swap mates. Generally unpleasant sex comedy, famous at the time for Mansfield's nude scene. C: Jayne Mansfield, Marie McDonald, Tommy Noonan, Mickey Hargitay, Fritz Feld. D: King Donovan. COM 90m. v

Promoter, The 1952 British ★★★★ Guinness is a poor kid who, through hard work and a little craftiness, hits it big. Entertaining, very clever comedy with fun lead by Guinness and script by Eric Ambler. (a.k.a. *The Card*) C: Alec Guinness, Glynis Johns, Valerie Hobson, Petula Clark. D: Ronald Neame. COM 89m. v

Proof 1991 Australian ★★★★★ Offbeat, eerie drama about a blind photographer who begins a friendship with a working-class youth (Crowe) and introduces him to his mistress for sinister reasons. Stunning to look at, superbly written and directed; a darkly funny film. C: Hugo Weaving, Genevieve Picot, Russell Crowe. D: Jocelyn Moorhouse. DRA [R] 90m. v

Prophecy 1979 ★ Promising horror story about Foxworth and Shire investigating pollution-spawned mutants in Maine is rendered laughable by listless direction and unconvincing monsters. C: Talia Shire, Robert Foxworth, Armand Assante, Richard Dysart, Victoria Racimo. D: John Frankenheimer. HOR [PG] 103m. v

Prospero's Books 1991 British ★★½ Pretentious, impressionistic adaptation of Shakespeare's *The Tempest.* Visually ambitious (and loaded with nudity), but style doesn't compensate for the rest. C: John Gielgud, Michael Clark, Michel Blanc, Erland Josephson. D: Peter Greenaway. DRA [R] 126m. v

Prostitute 1980 British ★★★ A British prostitute relocates to London and faces unending harassment from law officials. Slice-of-life drama uses documentary style presentation for its familiar message. C: Eleanor Forsythe, Kate Crutchley, Kim Lockett, Nancy Samuels. D: Tony Garnett. DRA 96m.

Protector, The 1985 ★★½ Tough cops who know martial arts go after drug ring. The usual. C: Jackie Chan. D: James Glickenhaus. ACT [R] 94m. v

Protocol 1984 ★★★ Hawn is a D.C. cocktail waitress who saves Mideast bigwig's life and is rewarded with government job. She subsequently gets involved with international shenanigans, and concludes with an uplifting speech. Starts off well, but satire fizzles. C: Goldie Hawn, Chris Sarandon, Richard Romanus, Gail Strickland. D: Herbert Ross. COM [PG] 93m. v

Prototype X29A 1992 ★★★ In 21st-century postnuclear-war L.A., Cyborg killers hunt human mutants who can interract with computers. Odd sci-fi effort with plenty of violence. C: Brenda Swanson. SFI [R] 98m. V

Proud and Profane, The 1956 ★★★★ Attractive WWII romance, with Kerr as a prim war widow falling for a rugged Marine (Holden) on a Pacific tour of duty. Dependable stars pull this one through. C: William Holden, Deborah Kerr, Thelma Ritter. D: George Seaton. DRA 111m.

Proud Men 1987 ★★★ Acrimony and alienation endure between a cattle baron (Heston) and his estranged son (Strauss), despite their awkward efforts to come together. Nice work by cast; otherwise routine. C: Charlton Heston, Peter Strauss, Belinda Belaski. D: William Graham. DRA 94m. TVM V

Proud Ones, The 1956 ★★★½ Western sheriff must overcome handicaps when outlaws threaten his town. Good action tale; a fun ride to the inevitable showdown. C: Robert Ryan, Virginia Mayo, Jeffrey Hunter, Walter Brennan. D: Robert Webb. WST 94m. V

Proud Rebel, The 1958 ★★★★½ Civil War vet Ladd and his mute son (Ladd's real-life son) work on de Havilland's farm while Ladd seeks doctor's help. Excellent cast makes for superior drama; fine family viewing. C: Alan Ladd, Olivia de Havilland, Dean Jagger, Cecil Kellaway. D: Michael Curtiz. DRA 99m. V

Providence 1976 British ★★★½ Dying novelist Gielgud imagines his last work with family members as characters. Offbeat concept; sometimes confusing story line; but with enjoyable cinematic puzzles. C: Dirk Bogarde, John Gielgud, Ellen Burstyn, David Warner, Elaine Stritch. D: Alain Resnais. DRA [R] 104m. V

Provoked 1989 ★★½ Police can't find man held hostage by thugs. His wife vows vengeance. She gets some heavy metal—the kind that goes bang. No more thugs. Ultracheapie is almost funny. C: Cindy Maranne, McKeiver Jones III, Harold Wayne Jones. D: Rick Pamplin. ACT 90m. V

Prowler, The 1951 ★★★★ Cop Heflin investigates burglary, becomes involved with victim Keyes, then plans her husband's murder. Bleak, gripping, moody melodrama with riveting performances. Suspenseful to the end. C: Van Heflin, Evelyn Keyes. D: Joseph Losey. DRA 92m.

Prudence and the Pill 1968 British ★★★½ Silly sex comedy features Niven as frustrated spouse who replaces his wife's birth control pills with aspirin. Witty cast given tame material. C: Deborah Kerr, David Niven, Robert Coote, Irina Demick. D: Fielder Cook, Ronald Neame. COM [R] 98m.

Psych Out 1968 ★★½ Throwaway comic curio, valuable only for its depiction of '60s hippies and for appearances by soon-to-be famous Nicholson, Dern, Stockwell, and Jaglom. C: Susan Strasberg, Jack Nicholson, Dean Stockwell, Bruce Dern. D: Richard Rush. COM 95m. V

Psychic 1991 ★★★ Psychic (Galligan), cursed with a direct line to the mind of a serial killer, must find him to save himself. Thriller stays on the surfac. C: Zach Galligan, Catherine Mary Stewart, Michael Nouri. D: George Mihalka. CRI [R] 95m. V

Psycho 1960 ★★★★★ A desperate thief (Leigh) finds refuge in the quiet, Bates Motel, unaware she is now in even greater danger from its disturbed young owner (Perkins). Classic that inspired all of those inferior remakes taps on the essential Hitchcock themes (guilt, mother love, and sexual repression) in a gloriously dark and funny manner. Memorable score from Bernard Hermann, and script from the Robert Bloch novel, but the real star is the director. C: Anthony Perkins, Janet Leigh, Vera Miles, John Gavin, Martin Balsam. D: Alfred Hitchcock. HOR [R] 109m. V

Psycho 2 1983 ★★ Norman (Perkins) leaves prison and returns to the scene of his crimes. The lights of the Bates Motel go on again but it's all pretty vacant. Fair attempt to cash in on the early '80s horror craze makes you appreciate the orginal even more. C: Anthony Perkins, Vera Miles, Meg Tilly, Robert Loggia. D: Richard Franklin. HOR [R] 113m. V

Psycho 3 1986 ★★★ Norman's having mother trouble again. Second sequel is more spoof than horror; Perkins' first directing gig. C: Anthony Perkins, Diana Scarwid, Jeff Fahey, Roberta Maxwell. D: Anthony Perkins. HOR [R] 96m. V

Psycho IV: The Beginning 1991 ★★★ Norman Bates is invited to share his memories of Mom with a radio talk-show host. Hitchcock's writer Joseph Stefano returns for this "prequel," but it's all pretty threadbare. C: Anthony Perkins, Henry Thomas, Olivia Hussey. D: Mick Garris. HOR [R] 96m. TVM V

Psycho Killer *See* **Flesh and the Fiend, The**

Psychopath, The 1966 British ★★★½ Serial killer leaves little dolls as clues for pursuing detectives. Efficient crime thriller with some nifty scares; scripted by *Psycho* author Robert Block. C: Patrick Wymark, Margaret Johnston, John Standing. D: Freddie Francis. HOR 83m.

Psychotic 1975 *See* **Driver's Seat, The**

PT 109 1963 ★★★ Young Jack Kennedy as a PT-boat commander and war hero in the South Pacific. Not much action; more a tribute to JFK. C: Cliff Robertson, Robert Culp, Ty Hardin, James Gregory. D: Leslie Martinson. DRA 140m. V

Ptang, Yang, Kippïrbang 1982 *See* **Kipperbang**

Puberty Blues 1981 Australian ★★★½ Two Australian teens struggle with adolescent turmoil as they strive to master their surfing. Typical story told atypically from female perspective. C: Nell Schofield, Jad Capelja, Geoff Rhoe. D: Bruce Beresford. DRA [R] 86m. V

Public Affair, A 1962 ★★★ Politician goes after unscrupulous collection agencies. Uninvolving drama has competent performances. C: Myron McCormick, Edward Binns, Harry Carey, Jr. DRA 71m. V

Public Cowboy No. 1 1937 ★★★ When modern-day rustlers use airplanes and trucks to steal cattle, singing cowpoke Autry saves the day. Offbeat, enjoyable material for the B-Western star. C: Gene Autry, William Farnum. WST 60m. V

Public Enemy, The 1931 ★★★★½ Two kids from the tenements bootleg and murder their way to power within the mob. Consistently powerful—stunning, in fact; the prototypical gangster film. C: James Cagney, Jean Harlow, Eddie Woods, Beryl Mercer, Mae Clarke. D: William Wellman. CRI 84m. V

Public Enemy's Wife 1936 ★★★★ Obsessively jealous over spouse Lindsay, mobster Romero escapes from prison; FBI agent Baxter enlists Lindsay's help to recapture him. Ensemble gives entertaining crime drama its grit. C: Pat O'Brien, Margaret Lindsay, Robert Armstrong, Cesar Romero. D: Nick Grinde. CRI 69m.

Public Eye, The 1992 ★★★½ A 1940s crime scene photographer (Pesci) becomes entangled with femme fatale (Hershey). Effective evocation of period atmosphere as seen by real-life shutterbug Weegee. C: Joe Pesci, Barbara Hershey, Stanley Tucci, Jerry Adler, Jared Harris. D: Howard Franklin. CRI [R] 99m. V

Public Hero No. 1 1935 ★★★½ FBI agents do their best to break up a notorious gang. A good attempt, though not always successful, to blend crime drama with lighthearted romantic humor. C: Lionel Barrymore, Jean Arthur, Chester Morris, Joseph Calleia. D: J. Ruben. CRI 91m.

Public Pigeon No. One 1957 ★★★ Skelton is mild-mannered cafeteria worker who inadvertently gets involved with and ultimately brings down a bunch of gangsters. Highly predictable comedy. C: Red Skelton, Vivian Blaine, Janet Blair, Allyn Joslyn. D: Norman McLeod. COM 79m.

Pulp 1972 ★★★½ A writer of cheap detective fiction (Caine) is hired by a Hollywood star with an alleged gangster past (Rooney) to ghostwrite his autobiography. Some amusing moments in this satire of crime films, with a fun performance by Rooney. C: Michael Caine, Mickey Rooney, Lionel Stander, Lizabeth Scott. D: Mike Hodges. CRI [PG] 95m. V

Pulp Fiction 1994 ★★★★½ Kaleidoscopic portrait of assorted drug addicts, gangsters and other oddballs is a tour de force for both cast and director. Pungent dialogue shares equal time with graphic violence, which may turn off some viewers. Tarantino and Roger Avary won an Academy Award for Best Original Screenplay (known in film circles as the *Citizen Kane* Consolation Prize, for movies too daring to win Best Picture). The movie also won the Palme D'Or at the Cannes Film Festival. And Travolta, in his comeback performance, shows that he still can dance! C: John Travolta, Uma Thurman, Samuel L. Jackson, Bruce Willis, Harvey Keitel, Ving Rhames, Tim Roth, Amanda Plummer. D: Quentin Tarantino. DRA [R] 160m. V

Pulse 1988 ★★★ Ordinary electrical appliances go (inexplicably) haywire and attack the suburban family which once mastered them. Uneven sci-fi/horror flick with just enough hair-raising chills to warrant a viewing. C: Joey Lawrence, Cliff DeYoung, Roxanne Hart. D: Paul Golding. HOR [PG-13] 90m. V

Pump Up the Volume 1990 ★★★★ Lonely high schooler creates a sensation when he starts a pirate radio station that invigorates his classmates and angers the strait-laced school officials. Surprisingly substantial teen drama with winning performances by Slater and Mathis. C: Christian Slater, Ellen Greene, Annie Ross, Samantha Mathis. D: Allan Moyle. DRA [R] 105m. V

Pumping Iron 1977 ★★★½ Documentary on men's bodybuilding, featuring Arnold Schwarzenegger, Lou Ferrigno, and others. Compelling study of fierce competitors. C: Arnold Schwarzenegger, Lou Ferrigno, Mike Katz. D: George Butler, Robert Fiore. DOC [PG] 85m. V

Pumping Iron II: The Women 1985 ★★★★ Interesting look at the distaff side of professional bodybuilding. Contest between ultramasculine Bev Francis, more feminine Rachel McLish is the focus of this surprisingly entertaining documentary. Sequel to the 1977 film, which focused on the men. D: George Butler. DOC 107m. V

Pumpkin Eater, The 1964 British ★★★½ A weary mother of eight (Bancroft) discovers that her third husband (Finch) is having an affair. Dreary, overlong slice-of-life drama saved by superb acting, especially by Bancroft, and a great script by Harold Pinter. Adapted from a novel by Penelope Mortimer. C: Anne Bancroft, Peter Finch, James Mason, Cedric Hardwicke, Maggie Smith. D: Jack Clayton. DRA 110m.

Pumpkinhead 1988 ★★★ Special effects master Winston made impressive directing debut with this chiller about a farmer who raises a legendary demon to avenge the death of his son-and lives to regret it. Evocative story with strong performances and a terrific monster. C: Lance Henriksen, Jeff East, John DiAquino. D: Stan Winston. HOR [R] 87m. V

Pumpkinhead II: Blood Wings 1994 ★★★

Flashy but empty-headed sequel turns the original's compelling mythology into the same old sequential murder formula, as the title demon rises to avenge murders both old and new. Stylish photography and a good creature still can't quite save this material. C: Ami Dolenz, Andrew Robinson, Steve Kanaly, J. Trevor Edmond, Soleil Moon Frye. D: Jeff Burr. HOR [R] 88m.

Punchline 1988 ★★★ A look at the lives of ambitious stand-up comics, offstage and on. Field seems miscast, though Hanks dazzles as manic, self-destructive comedian with lacerating wit. Behind-the-scenes story is strictly clichéd. C: Sally Field, Tom Hanks, John Goodman, Mark Rydell. D: David Seltzer. DRA [R] 123m. V

Punisher, The 1990 ★★½ After mobsters kill his family, distraught cop Lundgren exacts bloody revenge. Violent action thriller sunk by leaden acting (excepting Gossett) and brainless script. Based on Marvel Comics character. C: Dolph Lundgren, Louis Gossett, Jr., Jeroen Krabbe, Kim Miyori. D: Mark Goldblatt. ACT [R] 92m. V

Punk Rock Movie, The 1979 ★★★ A documentary on the punk rock movement traces its origins to the '70s at England's Roxy. For afficianados. DOC 86m. V

Puppetmaster 1989 ★★½ Parapsychologists at a deserted inn run into murderous living puppets. Okay horror, with decent effects but a pedestrian story. Followed by several sequels. C: Paul LeMat, Irene Miracle. D: David Schmoeller. HOR [R] 90m. V

Puppetmaster II 1990 ★ Another team of investigating scientists, another series of puppet attacks—and this time their undead master joins the fun. Lifeless sequel, with surprisingly unexciting effects. C: Elizabeth MacLellan, Collin Bernsen, Steve Welles. D: David Allen. HOR [R] 90m. V

Puppetmaster III: Toulon's Revenge 1991 ★★★ Second follow-up is best of the series, flashing back to the puppets' creator taking on the Nazis in WWII. Covers more ground than its predecessors, with colorful use of lenses and inventive effects. C: Guy Rolfe, Richard Lynch, Ian Abercrombie. D: David Decoteau. HOR [R] 86m. V

Puppetmaster 4 1993 ★★★ The lethal playthings become good guys this time, helping another team of young scientists fight off new tiny terrors. Creative direction breathes some life into a tired franchise; shot back-to-back with *Puppetmaster 5*. C: Gordon Currie, Chandra West, Jason Adams, Guy Rolfe. D: Jeff Burr. HOR [R] 81m.

Puppetmaster 5 1994 ★★★ The puppets, their human protector, bad guys who want their secret, and some evil creatures all converge, for one of the series' more convoluted entries. Fairly well filmed, but enough already. C: Gordon Currie, Chandra West, Ian Ogilvy, Teresa Hill, Nicholas Guest. D: Jeff Burr. HOR [R] 80m.

Puppetoon Movie, The 1987 ★★★★½ Compilation film combines best work from '30s and '40s shorts of visionary puppet animator George Pal. A real treat for animation buffs. D: Arnold Leibovit. FAM/COM 80m. V

Pure Country 1992 ★★ Strait makes an unfortunate acting debut playing a country star who decides to chuck his singing career so he can be a regular guy again. Even duller than it sounds. C: George Strait, Lesley-Ann Warren, Isabel Glasser. D: Christopher Cain. DRA [PG] 113m. V

Pure Hell of St. Trinian's, The 1961 British ★★★ Wacky British girls accidentally set their school ablaze, then must entertain offers from strange men to rebuild. Opposite sex, upper-crust English equivalent of the Bowery Boys has its moments, but may be more entertaining for the Anglophile. C: Cecil Parker, Joyce Grenfell, George Cole. D: Frank Launder. COM 94m. V

Pure Luck 1991 ★★ When wealthy client's daughter disappears, detective Glover and goofy sidekick Short try to find her in Mexico. Short's antics are the entire film, while Glover just gives wearied looks. C: Martin Short, Danny Glover, Sheila Kelley, Sam Wanamaker. D: Nadia Tass. COM [PG] 100m. V

Purgatory 1988 ★★ Tourists unjustly jailed, then attacked. Women in chains, international style. C: Tanya Roberts, Julie Pop, Hal Orlandini. D: Ami Artzi. ACT [R] 90m. V

Purple Gang, The 1960 ★★★ Prohibition-era saga focuses on a gang of young crooks encroaching on the status quo mobsters. Standard cops and robbers; watchable but forgettable. C: Barry Sullivan, Robert Blake, Elaine Edwards, Marc Cavell. D: Frank McDonald. CRI 85m.

Purple Heart, The 1944 ★★★½ During WWII, flyer (Andrews) and crew are shot down over Japan and tried as war criminals. Solid performances and engaging story line outweigh the obvious propaganda angle. C: Dana Andrews, Farley Granger, Sam Levene, Richard Conte. D: Lewis Milestone. DRA 99m. V

Purple Hearts 1984 ★★ At a Vietnam field hospital, a Navy medic finds romance with a nurse. Slim story with a hokey twist. C: Cheryl Ladd, Ken Wahl, Stephen Lee, David Harris. D: Sidney J. Furie. DRA [R] 115m. V

Purple Mask, The 1955 ★★★½ In 19th-century France, Curtis fights the good fight as if he were the Scarlet Pimpernel: He's a brave swashbuckler when donning the titular disguise, but acts the foppish dandy when not. Diverting fluffy costumer with a game Curtis. C: Tony Curtis, Gene Barry, Angela Lansbury, Dan O'Herlihy. D: H. Humberstone. DRA 82m.

Purple Noon 1960 French ★★★★ Marvelous nail-biter has Delon plotting the elimination of his roguish friend Ronet so that he may take over his life. Finely tuned thriller with a wonderful turn by Delon. From Patricia Highsmith's *The Talented Mr. Ripley*. C: Alain Delon, Marie Laforet, Maurice Ronet. D: Rene Clement. DRA 115m.

Purple People Eater 1988 ★★★½ Minor fun based on Sheb Wooley's novelty song involves an outer-space creature who lands in suburbs and becomes part of a garage band. Low-budget and routine, though it has its moments. Cute cameos by Little Richard, Chuck Berry, and Wooley himself. C: Ned Beatty, Shelley Winters, Neil Patrick Harris, Chubby Checker, Little Richard. D: Linda Shayne. FAM/COM [PG] 91m. v

Purple Plain, The 1954 British ★★★★ During WWII, an airman (Peck) loses his nerve and crashes his plane in Burma, giving him plenty of time to pull himself together. Superb against-the-odds adventure based on Eric Ambler novel with Peck doing a standout job in essentially a one-role film. C: Gregory Peck, Bernard Lee, Win Than, Maurice Denham. D: Robert Parrish. DRA 100m. v

Purple Rain 1984 ★★★½ Prince made his film debut with this semiautobiographical study of an aspiring black rocker struggling to make it. Dynamic concert footage shares space with sexist dramatic scenes. Song score won Oscar. C: Prince, Apollonia Kotero, Morris Day, Olga Karlatos. D: Albert Magnoli. MUS [R] 113m. v

Purple Rose of Cairo, The 1985 ★★★★ A lonely waitress (Farrow) who finds escape in the movies during the Depression, starts a scandal when a character in one of them walks off the screen and into her life. Allen's skillful direction keeps it sweet without cloying, but the ending is tough. C: Mia Farrow, Jeff Daniels, Danny Aiello. D: Woody Allen. COM [PG] 84m. v

Pursued 1947 ★★★½ Tough veteran of the Spanish-American War (Mitchum) goes after those who murdered his father. A fine cast in a neat, taut story. C: Teresa Wright, Robert Mitchum, Judith Anderson, Dean Jagger. D: Raoul Walsh. WST 101m. v

Pursuit of the Graf Spee 1956 British ★★★★ A German battleship is targeted by the British navy. Effective, patriotic docudrama, from a famed directing team. Final battle climax is worth waiting for. C: John Gregson, Peter Finch, Anthony Quayle, Patrick Macnee. D: Michael Powell, Emeric Pressburger. ACT 119m. v

Pursuit to Algiers 1945 ★★★½ Holmes and Watson protect a prince aboard a steamer bound for Algiers. Middling *Sherlock Holmes* adventure, but Rathbone and Bruce still manage to make it entertaining. Not based on an Arthur Conan Doyle story. C: Basil Rathbone, Nigel Bruce, Margorie Riordan. D: Roy William Neill. CRI 61m. v

Pushed to the Limit 1991 ★★ A pro wrestler (Lesseos) moonlighting as a Las Vegas performer enters a deadly fighting competition to get closer to the crimelord responsible for her brother's murder. Stilted acting; looks like a homemade production. C: Mimi Lesseos, Verrel Reed, Henry Hayshi, Greg Ostrin. D: Michael Mileham. ACT [R] 90m. v

Pushover 1954 ★★★★ Mobster's moll draws honest cop into web of robbery and murder. Familiar territory, but a well-tailored cut above most. First major role for Novak put her on the map. C: Fred MacMurray, Kim Novak, Phillip Carey, Dorothy Malone, E.G. Marshall. D: Richard Quine. CRI 88m. v

Puss in Boots 1988 ★★★½ Christopher Walken narrates this tale of clever feline who provides his master with the good life by conning a king. Good fare for youngest audiences. C: Christopher Walken, Jason Connery. D: Eugene Marner. FAM/DRA [G] 96m. v

Putney Swope 1969 ★★★ When all-white Madison Avenue advertising firm is taken over by blacks, TV commercials take on new demeanor. Funny in its time, though satire has withered through years. Commercial parodies by Brooks, Abel, and Fargas still hold clever moments. C: Arnold Johnson, Pepi Hermine, Allen Garfield, Mel Brooks. D: Robert Downey. COM [R] 88m. v

Pygmalion 1938 British ★★★★★ Loverly adaptation of Shaw's comedy of manners involving a Cockney flower girl (Hiller) transformed into a lady by phonetics expert (Howard). Two leads give definitive performances. Brittle, witty screenplay by playwright won Oscar. Source for Broadway musical *My Fair Lady*. C: Leslie Howard, Wendy Hiller, Wilfrid Lawson, Marie Lohr. D: Anthony Asquith. COM 96m. v

Pyrates 1991 ★★ Young man and woman fall in love and find that their sexual encounters produce sparks—the kind that cause actual fires. Off-the-wall comedy with real-life marrieds in the lead. C: Kevin Bacon, Kyra Sedgwick. D: Noah Stern. DRA [R] 98m. v

Python Wolf 1988 ★★½ The C.A.T. Squad, a group of anti-terrorist specialists, track down a no-good smuggler. Some nifty hardware, but it can't overcome the stilted acting and weal script. Sequel to *C.A.T. Squad*. C: Jack Youngblood, Patricia Charbonneau, Barry Corbin. D: William Friedkin. ACT [R] 93m. TVM v

Pyx, The 1973 Canadian ★★★½ A cop (Plummer), investigating the murder of a prostitute (Black), finds himself deluged with suspects—among them, members of a satanic cult. Engaging melding of sci-fi, horror/occult, and thriller genres manages to overcome the underlying dreariness of the story. (a.k.a. *The Hooker Cult Murders*) C: Karen Black, Christopher Plummer, Donald Pilon. D: Harvey Hart. HOR [R] 111m. v

Q

Q 1982 ★★★ Energetic if typically uneven Cohen film about prehistoric flying creature terrorizing Manhattan. Monster material is fun, but Moriarty owns the movie as moody ne'er-do-well who discovers the beast's nesting place and uses the information to get ahead. C: David Carradine, Michael Moriarty, Richard Roundtree, Candy Clark. D: Larry Cohen. HOR [R] 92m. V

Q & A 1990 ★★★ A dirty cop (Nolte) kills a drug dealer and pleads self defense, but Assistant D.A. (Hutton) gets new evidence from a pusher (Assante) who is dating his ex-girlfriend. Convoluted, violent thriller that even intelligent direction can't save. C: Nick Nolte, Timothy Hutton, Armand Assante, Patrick O'Neal. D: Sidney Lumet. CRI 132m. V

Q Planes 1939 *See* **Clouds Over Europe**

Quackser Fortune Has a Cousin in the Bronx 1970 Irish ★★★★½ Wilder is mild-mannered Irish dung dealer, happy selling manure as fertilizer. When he meets American student Kidder, his quiet life suddenly hits series of unexpected changes. Charming and original romantic comedy, with excellent performances by two leads. (a.k.a. *Fun Loving*) C: Gene Wilder, Margot Kidder. D: Waris Hussein. COM [R] 88m. V

Quadrophenia 1979 British ★★★★ Inspired by album by The Who, film captures gritty, pre-Beatles London and the battles between Mods and Rockers, gangs who defined early '60s English youth movement. C: Phil Daniels, Mark Wingett, Sting. D: Franc Roddam. DRA [R] 115m. V

Quai des Orfevres 1948 *See* **Jenny Lamour**

Quality Street 1937 ★★★★ A woman (Hepburn) pretends to be her own niece to regain the love of a man who's been away for 10 years. Lovely period romance, from James Barrie's play, makes a perfect vehicle for young Hepburn. C: Katharine Hepburn, Franchot Tone, Fay Bainter, Eric Blore, Estelle Winwood. D: George Stevens. COM 87m. V

Quantrill's Raiders 1958 ★★½ Civil War saga of the legendary outlaw gang's storming of a Kansas arsenal. Substandard fare with too many lapses into the bad acting realm, only partially rescued by a thrifty running time. C: Steve Cochran, Diane Brewster, Leo Gordon. D: Edward Bernds. DRA 68m.

Quarantine 1990 ★★★ During a plague epidemic a ruthless senator wields absolute power in McCarthy-type hearings that weed out dissidents and other "infected" citizens. Intriguing mix of metaphors-political, sci-fi and AIDS, but hobbled by a low budget. C: Beatrice Boepple, Garwin Sanford, Jerry Wasserman. D: Charles Wilkinson. SFI [R] 92m. V

Quare Fellow, The 1962 Irish ★★★★½ McGoohan, a novice prison guard assigned death row duty, must come to terms with his conflicted feelings about the inmates' imminent execution. Minus the gallows humor of the Brendan Behan play, the script is a bit somber, but overall, it remains an effective and moving work. C: Patrick McGoohan, Sylvia Syms, Walter Macken. D: Arthur Dreifuss. DRA 85m.

Quarterback Princess 1985 ★★★ High school girl (Hunt) is elected homecoming queen but also tries out for the boys' varsity football team. Real-life story gets dull treatment. C: Helen Hunt, Don Murray, Barbara Babcock. D: Noel Black. FAM/DRA 96m. TVM V

Quartet 1981 British ★★★★½ A young wife (Adjani), left alone in Paris when her husband is jailed, is taken in by an English couple, and then seduced by the bohemian husband (Bates). Sad tale of manipulative human relationships, with brilliant acting and outstanding production values. C: Alan Bates, Maggie Smith, Isabelle Adjani, Anthony Higgins. D: James Ivory. DRA 101m. V

Quebec 1951 ★★½ Historical saga, circa 1830, revolving around a puppet governor, his wife, and the object of her affection, a dashing rebel. Dull melodrama with some excellent footage of the province. C: John Barrymore Jr., Corinne Calvet, Barbara Rush, Patric Knowles. D: George Templeton. DRA 85m.

Queen Bee 1955 ★★★★ A power-crazed matriarch (Crawford) will stop at nothing to control the lives of those in her Southern mansion. Main attraction is the perfect pairing of star and role, but the Tennessee Williams-like characters help carry this melodrama a long way as well. C: Joan Crawford, Barry Sullivan, Betsy Palmer, John Ireland, Fay Wray, Tim Hovey. D: Ranald MacDougall. DRA 95m.

Queen Boxer 1982 ★★ After her family is enslaved, a kickboxer goes after the perpetrators. Typical blood and violence. C: Judy Lee, Peter Yang Kwan. ACT 92m. V

Queen Christina 1933 ★★★★½ Drama of Swedish queen who refuses political marriage and abdicates in 1654, then leaves the country (in male disguise) and falls in love with the ambassador of Spain. Spellbinding performance from Garbo in one of her finest films; she and Gilbert generate extraordinary passion. C: Greta Garbo, John Gilbert, Ian Keith, Lewis Stone, C.Aubrey Smith. D: Rouben Mamoulian. DRA 97m. V

Queen Kelly 1928 ★★★★ An innocent young woman leaves her convent, is corrupted through association with her decadent aunt, and winds up in a brothel. Unfinished silent film, famous for its presence in Swanson's *Sunset Boulevard* as the movie Norma

Desmond shows her gigolo boyfriend. Worth seeing for its own ornate splendor, though it may seem overdone to some. C: Gloria Swanson, Seena Owen, Walter Byron. D: Erich von Stroheim. DRA 96m. v

Queen Margot 1994 French ★★★★ The court of Catherine de Medicis is the backdrop for epic historical romance inspired by the Dumas novel. Adjani and Lisi act up a storm as rivals for power amidst glorious trappings. Sometimes confusing, gorgeous to look at, but extremely violent. C: Isabelle Adjani, Virna Lisi, Daniel Auteuil, Jean-Hugues Anglade. D: Patrice Chereau. DRA [R] 143m. v

Queen of Blood 1966 ★★★½ Hopper and his space-traveling buddies bring their exciting find to earth: a space vampire. Fascinating sci-fi/horror (with effects "borrowed" from Russian sci-fi classic *Planet of Storms*), but can drag at times. (a.k.a. *Planet of Blood*) C: John Saxon, Basil Rathbone, Judi Meredith, Dennis Hopper. D: Curtis Harrington. SFI 81m. v

Queen of Destiny 1938 *See* **Sixty Glorious Years**

Queen of Hearts 1989 British ★★★½ An Italian immigrant family struggles in strange, unsympathetic London after WWII. Director Amiel's film debut is a witty, tender-hearted comedy/fantasy, beautifully shot and acted by charming cast. C: Vittorio Duse, Joseph Long, Anita Zagaria, Eileen Way, Vittorio Amandola, Ian Hawkes, Tat Whalley. D: Jon Amiel. DRA [PG] 112m. v

Queen of Outer Space 1958 ★★★ The lonely women of the all-female planet Venus intercept an Earth spaceship filled with virile men. Campy sci-fi adventure is a bad-film classic, with a now-legendary performance from Zsa Zsa. C: Zsa Zsa Gabor, Eric Fleming, Laurie Mitchell, Patrick Waltz. D: Edward Bernds. SFI 79m. v

Queen of Spies 1942 *See* **Joan of Ozark**

Queen of the Mob 1940 ★★★½ G-men track down a criminal mom and her felonious brood. Blistering cops-and-robbers tale, loosely based on the hunt for Ma Barker and her sons. Sure to delight anyone who enjoys a b&w crime story. C: Ralph Bellamy, Jack Carson, Blanche Yurka, Richard Denning. D: James Hogan. CRI 61m.

Queen of the Stardust Ballroom 1975 ★★★★ A lovely, unusual, musical romance between a newly widowed matron and an unattractive, married mailman who meet at a NY ballroom. Stapleton's and Durning's performances are marked by sensitivity and depth. Source for the Broadway musical, *Ballroom.* C: Maureen Stapleton, Charles Durning, Michael Brandon, Charlotte Rae. D: Sam O'Steen. MUS 100m. TVM v

Queenie 1987 ★★★ Sequel to landmark *Roots* miniseries wallows in sentimentality and phony Hollywood touches that make it ring false, as it follows story of African-American woman who rises from slavery. C: Mia Sara, Kirk Douglas, Martin Balsam, Claire Bloom, Topol, Joel Grey, Sarah Miles, Gary Cady, Joss Ackland. D: Larry Peerce. DRA 233m. TVM v

Queens Logic 1991 ★★★½ Old friends come home to Queens for a wedding. Another recycling of *The Big Chill* theme with some funny situations and a fine young cast. C: Kevin Bacon, Linda Fiorentino, John Malkovich, Joe Mantegna, Ken Olin, Tony Spiridakis, Tom Waits, Chloe Webb, Jamie Lee Curtis, Ed Marinaro. D: Steve Rash. DRA [R] 113m. v

Quelques Jour Prás, A 1969 *See* **Matter of Days, A**

Quentin Durward 1955 ★★★½ Title character (Taylor) dutifully does his uncle's bidding for a fair maiden's hand in 15th-century France, only to be swept off his feet by her. Fun swashbuckler, based on Sir Walter Scott's novel. Plenty of color and action. C: Robert Taylor, Kay Kendall, Robert Morley, George Cole, Alec Clunes, Duncan Lamont, Marius Goring. D: Richard Thorpe. DRA 101m.

Querelle 1983 German ★★ A homosexual sailor explores the underbelly of society amidst drug dealers and killers in the French port of Brest. Fassbinder's final film is an overwrought, stylized mess. Based on novel by Jean Genet. C: Brad Davis, Franco Nero, Jeanne Moreau. D: Rainer Werner Fassbinder. DRA [R] 106m. v

Quest for Fire 1982 French ★★★★½ An Ice Age tribe loses its source of fire in a battle, and three members go looking for more, confronting danger along the way. Entertaining and riveting at times. Anthony Burgess created a special language for the film, and Desmond Norris developed body movement and gestures for the actors. Costumes won an Oscar. C: Everett McGill, Rae Dawn Chong, Ron Perlman. D: Jean-Jacques Annaud. DRA [R] 100m. v

Quest for Love 1971 British ★★★★ After a freak accident, a young scientist finds himself in a not-altogether-different dimension where he discovers the meaning of love. Entertaining and effective mixture of sci-fi and romance. From John Wyndham's *Random Quest.* C: Tom Bell, Joan Collins, Denholm Elliott, Laurence Naismith. D: Ralph Thomas. SFI 90m. v

Quest, The 1985 *See* **Longest Drive**

Quest, The 1986 Australian ★★★ Youngster (*E.T.* star Thomas) discovers an unusual creature while prowling through a hidden graveyard in Australia. Bland children's film riddled with predictable characters and situations. C: Henry Thomas, Tony Barry, Rachel Friend, Tamsin West. D: Brian Trenchard-Smith. FAM/DRA [PG] 94m.

Question of Adultery, A 1959 British ★★½ Shallow presentation of the serious issues involved in artificial insemination. Many furrowed brows, but no sign of much going on behind them. (a.k.a. *The Case of Mrs. Loring*) C: Julie London, Anthony Steel, Basil Sydney,

Donald Houston, Anton Diffring, Andrew Cruickshank. D: Don Chaffey. DRA 86m.

Question of Faith 1993 ★★★½ A married woman (Archer) is diagnosed with terminal cancer, and fights back using alternative therapies; Sam Neill plays her noble husband. Three-hankie movie, sparked by great performances. Based on a true story. C: Anne Archer, Sam Neill, Frances Lee McCain, James Tolkan. D: Stephen Gyllenhaal. DRA 90m. TVM V

Question of Guilt, A 1978 ★★★ A partying divorcée (Weld) is accused of killing her child. Leibman excellent, but the film is slow paced and only average TV fare. C: Tuesday Weld, Ron Leibman, Peter Masterson, Alex Rocco. D: Robert Butler. DRA 100m. TVM V

Question of Honor, A 1980 ★★★ Gazzara excellent as principled police officer informing on his fellow cops, and being deceived by wily politician (Vaughn). Solid cast works well together, but the pacing is slow and the plot predictable. Based on *Point Blank* by Sonny Grosso and Phillip Rosenberg. C: Ben Gazzara, Paul Sorvino, Robert Vaughn, Tony Roberts. D: Jud Taylor. DRA 134m. TVM

Question of Love, A 1978 ★★★★ Compelling film that includes first-rate performances by Rowlands and Alexander as a lesbian couple involved in a child custody suit. Sensitive and relevant portrayal of a relationship, and serious treatment of the issues involved. C: Gena Rowlands, Jane Alexander, Ned Beatty, Clu Gulager. D: Jerry Thorpe. DRA 90m. V

Question of Silence, A 1983 Dutch ★★★★ Three women who have never met are tried for murdering the same man. Emotional courtroom drama used effectively as an insightful feminist commentary on the controlling position held by men in contemporary society. C: Cox Habbema, Nelly Frijda, Henriette Tol. D: Marleen Gorris. DRA [R] 92m. V

Quick and the Dead, The 1987 ★★★½ When a homesteading family is attacked, a mysterious young gunslinger comes to their aid; an attraction soon develops between him and the wife. Well done, smartly taken from the Louis L'Amour novel. C: Sam Elliott, Kate Capshaw, Tom Conti, Kenny Morrison. D: Robert Day. WST 91m. TVM V

Quick and the Dead, The 1995 ★★ A gunslinger (Stone) swaggers into a western town called Redemption, causing havoc among its inhabitants. Poor script could have used some "redemption." C: Sharon Stone, Gene Hackman, Leonardo DiCaprio, Gary Sinise, Woody Strode, Russell Crowe. D: Sam Raimi. WST [R] 103m. V

Quick Before It Melts 1964 ★★ Comedy about lonely researchers in the Antarctic and their scheme to lure women to their compound. Unfunny drivel only for those who love American '60s nonsense movies. A shameful waste of a decent title. C: George Maharis, Robert Morse, Anjanette Comer, James Gregory, Yvonne Craig, Doodles Weaver, Howard St.John, Michael Constantine. D: Delbert Mann. COM 98m.

Quick Change 1990 ★★★ Clever, fast-paced comedy about trio of bank robbers, headed by Murray, who pull off a complicated heist but then fail to find a way out of Manhattan. Enjoyable and very funny. C: Bill Murray, Geena Davis, Randy Quaid, Jason Robards, Philip Bosco, Phil Hartman. D: Howard Franklin, Bill Murray. COM [R] 89m. V

Quick Gun, The 1964 ★★ Standard Murphy Western in which hero defends a town against outlaws. Done many times and much better; for die-hard Murphy fans only. C: Audie Murphy, Merry Anders, James Best, Ted de Corsia, Frank Ferguson, Raymond Hatton. D: Sidney Salkow. WST 87m. V

Quick, Let's Get Married 1964 ★ Confusing and poorly filmed story of a madam (Rogers) and traveling con artist (Milland) tricking a naive prostitute (Eden) into marriage. Notable only as Gould's inauspicious film debut. (a.k.a. *Seven Different Ways*) C: Ginger Rogers, Ray Milland, Barbara Eden, Michael Ansara, Walter Abel, Elliott Gould. D: William Dieterle. COM 96m. V

Quick Millions 1931 ★★★½ A truck driver (Tracy), tired of being the low man on the totem pole, sets out to become a feared and powerful mobster. Solid, fast gangster drama; young Tracy's mesmerizing performance is reason enough for viewing. C: Spencer Tracy, Marguerite Churchill, Sally Eilers, Robert Burns, John Wray, George Raft. D: Rowland Brown. CRI 72m.

Quicksand 1950 ★★★½ Suspenseful drama about an auto mechanic (Rooney) who helps himself to $20 from the cash register in order to woo a woman (Cagney). Tense, atmospheric, with chilling Lorre, and good Rooney. C: Mickey Rooney, Jeanne Cagney, Barbara Bates, Peter Lorre, Taylor Holmes, Wally Cassell. D: Irving Pichel. DRA 79m. V

Quicksand: No Escape 1992 ★★★★ Ordinary guy (Matheson) sinks into a black hole of evil when he meets sleazy shamus (Sutherland). Terrific Sutherland; some serious thrills. C: Donald Sutherland, Tim Matheson, Jay Acovone, Timothy Carhart, Felicity Huffman, John Finn. D: Michael Pressman. DRA [PG-13] 93m. TVM V

Quicksilver 1986 ★★ Follows the lives of bicycle messengers, one a failed stockbroker, who pedal like maniacs through three different cities. Exciting stunt work, but where's the story? Energetic music by Roger Daltry and Ray Parker, Jr. C: Kevin Bacon, Jami Gertz, Paul Rodriguez, Rudy Ramos. D: Tom Donnelly. DRA [PG] 101m. V

Quiet American, The 1958 ★★★½ Murphy effective as naive American diplomat assigned to Saigon in this pro-American adaptation of Graham Greene's novel. Redgrave chilling as the cynical Englishman. Don't expect a political thriller, but enjoy it as a tight, classic murder mystery. C: Audie Murphy, Michael Redgrave,

Claude Dauphin, Giorgia Moll, Bruce Cabot. D: Joseph L. Mankiewicz. CRI 120m.

Quiet Cool 1986 ★★ A police officer (Remar) joins forces with a teenager (Howard) to nail psycho marijuana farmer Cassavetes (son of John). Mind-numbing shoot-'em-up actioner. C: James Remar, Daphne Ashbrook, Adam Coleman Howard, Nick Cassavetes. D: Clay Borris. ACT [R] 80m. v

Quiet Day in Belfast, A 1984 ★★½ Kidder portrays twin Irish Catholic lasses, one of whom is in love with a British soldier. Naive portrayal of the Northern Ireland situation fails both as a political statement and a love story, but does try. C: Barry Foster, Margot Kidder. D: Milad Bessada. DRA 88m. v

Quiet Earth, The 1985 New Zealand ★★★★ Small sci-fi stunner from New Zealand has a scientist realizing that every other life form on Earth has been wiped out—and one of his experiments may be the cause. Thought-provoking and riveting. C: Bruno Lawrence, Alison Routledge, Peter Smith. D: Geoff Murphy. SFI [R] 91m. v

Quiet Fire 1991 ★★½ No-budget no-brainer action film stars Jacobs fleeing from sleazy senatorial candidate bent on eliminating all who know about his dubious past. Entertaining of its kind, but nothing special. C: Lawrence Hilton-Jacobs, Lance Lindsey, Karen Black, Robert Z'Dar. D: Lawrence Hilton-Jacobs. ACT 100m. v

Quiet Little Neighborhood, A Perfect Little Murder, A ★★★½ Light comedy about an off-center homemaker who overhears her neighbors plot a murder. When the police don't believe her, she decides to play amateur detective. Few surprises, yet charming. COM

Quiet Man, The 1952 ★★★★★ John Ford's brawling Irish comedy/drama about complications that arise when a tempestuous colleen, her earthy brother, and local villagers gain the favor of an American prizefighter who comes home to Ireland to claim his family farm. Rollickingly bright romp won Ford the Oscar for Best Director. C: John Wayne, Maureen O'Hara, Barry Fitzgerald, Victor McLaglen, Mildred Natwick, Ward Bond. D: John Ford. DRA 129m. v

Quiet Place to Kill, A 1970 Italian ★ Woman helps her ex-husband conceal his involvement in his second wife's accidental death—but if it's an accident why conceal it? Uninspired acting and a muddled script. (a.k.a. *Paranoia*) C: Carroll Baker, Jean Sorel, Marina Coffa. D: Umberto Lenzi. DRA 90m. v

Quiet Please, Murder 1942 ★★★★ A counterfeiter (Sanders) forges a priceless Shakespeare folio and replaces it with the original. Unique and nifty thriller/mystery, well handled all around. About as much mayhem as you are ever likely to see in a library. C: George Sanders, Gail Patrick, Richard Denning, Sidney Blackmer, Lynne Roberts, Kurt Katch, Minerva Urecal, Theodore Eltz. D: John Larkin. CRI 70m.

Quiet Victory: The Charlie Wedemeyer Story 1988 ★★★★ True story of star athlete stricken by Lou Gehrig's disease who went on to become a successful coach. Intelligently handled, inspiring. C: Pam Dawber, Michael Nouri, Bess Meyer, Peter Berg, James Handy, Dan Lauria, Gracie Harrison. D: Roy Campanella II. DRA 100m. TVM

Quiet Wedding 1941 British ★★★★½ When a young couple decide to marry, their preparations and their families turn out to be more than they can bear. Sly and sophisticated comedy, the British way. Remade in 1957 as *Happy Is the Bride*. A sequel of sorts followed in *Quiet Weekend*. C: Margaret Lockwood, Derek Farr. D: Anthony Asquith. COM 63m.

Quiet Weekend 1948 British ★★★½ The proper and somewhat loony family from *Quiet Wedding* returns. This time their peaceful country holiday is disturbed by extremely strange people. Disappointing sequel, but still worth a view for fans of the original. C: Derek Farr, Frank Cellier, Marjorie Fielding. D: Harold French. COM 83m.

Quigley Down Under 1990 ★★★ A self-possessed sharpshooter moves to Australia and takes a job under a wealthy landowner. Their relationship quickly sours and violence ensues. Pretty pictures wrapped in a thin plot. C: Tom Selleck, Laura San Giacomo, Alan Rickman. D: Simon Wincer. WST [PG-13] 121m. v

Quiller Memorandum, The 1966 British ★★★★ American spy (Segal) infiltrates a resurgent Nazi group in Berlin circa 1960. Intelligent, strong espionage thriller with a perfectly handled cast. Adapted by Harold Pinter. C: George Segal, Alec Guinness, Max VonSydow, Senta Berger. D: Michael Anderson. DRA 103m. v

Quintet 1979 ★★½ Altman's portrait of a frozen city of the future, where a game of life-and-death is played just to pass the time. Newman is at a loss, and before long so is the viewer. C: Paul Newman, Bibi Andersson, Fernando Rey, Vittorio Gassman, David Langton. D: Robert Altman. DRA [R] 118m. v

Quiz Show 1994 ★★★★★ 1950's TV quiz show, "21," secretly gives out answers to its most popular contestant (Fiennes). Now it's up to a government agent (Morrow) to prove it. True-life scandal was the inspiration for this intelligent, expertly crafted drama that says much about American ethics, manners, and morals. C: John Turturro, Ralph Fiennes, Rob Morrow, David Paymer, Paul Scofield. D: Robert Redford. DRA [PG-13] 124m. v

Quo Vadis? 1951 ★★★★ In ancient Rome, one of Nero's commanders (Taylor) falls in love with Christian (Kerr), endangering both their lives. Huge epic is long, but full of action and spectacle, with good cast of big names. C: Robert Taylor, Deborah Kerr, Peter Ustinov, Leo Genn. D: Mervyn LeRoy. DRA 171m. vQuo Vadis?

R

Ra Expeditions, The 1971 Norwegian ★★★★ Engrossing documentary narrated by Heyerdahl, about his attempt to re-create ancient transatlantic crossing in a papyrus boat. Sequel to *Kon-Tiki*, gripping every nautical mile. Voices of Thor Heyerdahl, Roscoe Lee Browne. D: Lennart Ehrenborg. DOC [G] 93m.

Rabbit, Run 1970 ★★½ Plodding adaptation of celebrated Updike novel about a former high school athlete (Caan) who spends the rest of his life making himself, his wife, and everyone else in his Pennsylvania town miserable. C: James Caan, Carrie Snodgress, Anjanette Comer, Jack Albertson, Melodie Johnson, Carmen Matthews, Henry Jones, Nydia Westman, Josephine Hutchinson, Ken Kercheval, Arthur Hill. D: Jack Smight. DRA [R] 94m.

Rabbit Test 1978 ★★ Bathroom humor and star cameos fill this dismal comedy about the first pregnant man. Crystal looks embarassed, and Rivers' direction (her debut) is inept. C: Billy Crystal, Alex Rocco, Joan Prather, Roddy McDowall. D: Joan Rivers. COM [PG] 86m. V

Rabbit Trap, The 1959 ★★★½ Borgnine intelligently portrays a workaholic who reforms when his boss, frighteningly portrayed by Rickles, calls him in from a vacation for a trivial assignment. From a TV play by J.P. Miller, the pace is deliberate but characterizations are finely etched. C: Ernest Borgnine, David Brian, Bethel Leslie, Kevin Corcoran, June Blair, Jeanette Nolan, Don Rickles. D: Philip Leacock. DRA 72m.

Rabid 1977 Canadian ★★★ Botched plastic surgery leaves Chambers suffering from infectious madness that soon spreads across the country. Cronenberg's effect is strong, gruesome stuff, with chilling storytelling overcoming low-budget limitations. C: Marilyn Chambers, Frank Moore, Joe Silver, Patricia Gage, Susan Roman, Howard Ryshpan. D: David Cronenberg. HOR [R] 90m. V

Rabid Grannies 1989 ★★★ Two elderly sisters celebrate their birthdays by inviting relatives to a party, and then devouring them, thanks to a rabies inducing gift from a devil-worshipping nephew. Extremely gory, but has satiric bite. C: Danielle Daven, Anne Marie Fox, Jack Mayar. D: Emmanuel Kervyn. HOR [R] 89m. V

Race for Life 1954 British ★★ Conte as the "driven" race-car driver determined to take on all the fast tracks of Europe, over his wife's objections. Formula film of little interest, even on the track. (a.k.a. *Mask of Dust*) C: Richard Conte, Mari Aldon, George Coulouris, Peter Illing, Alec Mango, Meredith Edwards. D: Terence Fisher. ACT 68m.

Race for Your Life, Charlie Brown 1977 ★★★½ Charles Schultz's *Peanuts* gang heads off to summer camp and enters a dangerous white-water raft race. Stock plot, mildly ambling animated children's feature. C: Peanuts Gang. D: Bill Melendez. FAM/COM [G] 76m. V

Race Street 1948 ★★★½ Club owner Raft agrees to help cops penetrate group of extortionist thugs who murdered Raft's best pal. Low-budget crime drama builds tension nicely. Raft gives nifty performance. C: George Raft, William Bendix, Marilyn Maxwell, Frank Faylen, Henry Morgan, Gale Robbins. D: Edwin Marin. CRI 79m.

Race to the Yankee Zephyr 1981 Australian ★★½ Neither the good guys (Wahl and Pleasence), nor the bad guy (Peppard), nor the film ever get up to speed in this tale of a race to recover a WWII treasure lost at sea. (a.k.a. *Treasure of the Yankee Zephyr*) C: Ken Wahl, Lesley Ann Warren, Donald Pleasence, George Peppard, Bruno Lawrence, Grant Tilly. D: David Hemmings. ACT 108m. V

Race With the Devil 1975 ★★ While on vacation in secluded area, two couples witness deadly Satanic cult ritual and must try to outrun pursuing pack of Beelzebub's buddies. A combination of horror and chase movie clichés without much terror between the two. C: Peter Fonda, Warren Oates, Loretta Swit, Lara Parker, R. Armstrong. D: Jack Starrett. HOR [PG] 88m. V

Racers, The 1955 ★★½ Routine slice of life looks at automobile racers on the European circuit. No stock cars, but plenty of stock clichés. Despite talented cast, this one quickly runs out of gas. C: Kirk Douglas, Bella Darvi, Gilbert Roland, Lee J. Cobb, Cesar Romero. D: Henry Hathaway. DRA 112m. V

Rachel and the Stranger 1948 ★★★★ Wilderness farmer (Holden) realizes love for his wife (Young) when an appealing drifter (Mitchum) notices her. Entertaining Western romance strengthened by star performances. C: Loretta Young, William Holden, Robert Mitchum, Tom Tully. D: Norman Foster. DRA 93m. V

Rachel Papers, The 1989 British ★★★★ Touching story of a British computer nerd who woos a beautiful young American woman with the help of his PC. Fletcher and Skye give scintillating performances and the direction plumbs the bittersweet depths of unrequited love. Director's first film, adapted from Martin Amis novel. C: Dexter Fletcher, Ione Skye, Jonathan Pryce, James Spader. D: Damian Harris. DRA [R] 92m. V

Rachel, Rachel 1968 ★★★★★ Sexually repressed schoolteacher Woodward lives with overbearing mother in small Connecticut town. Slowly she reaches out to the world beyond her home and cautiously undergoes awakening of identity. Deeply moving film, with superb performance by Woodward. Directorial debut for her husband, Paul Newman. C: Joanne Woodward, James Olson, Kate Harrington, Estelle Parsons, Geraldine Fitzgerald. D: Paul Newman. DRA [R] 102m. v

Rachel River 1987 ★★★ Minnesota woman tries to cope with keeping family together and running radio station in the sticks. Some appealing moments; otherwise, it crawls. C: Zeljko Ivanek, Pamela Reed, Craig Nelson, James Olson, Viveca Lindfors. D: Sandy Smolan. DRA [PG-13] 88m. v

Racing Fever 1964 ★ All-wet story of speedboat racer out to avenge the death of a friend. C: Joe Morrison, Charles Martin, Maxine Carroll, Barbara Biggart. D: William Grefe. ACT 80m.

Racing With the Moon 1984 ★★★★ Two small-town buddies experience romance and heartbreak while biding their time before WWII enlistment. Penn and Cage are wonderfully teamed in a film that re-creates time and place with loving accuracy. McGovern and Kane are great in support. C: Sean Penn, Elizabeth McGovern, Nicolas Cage, John Karlen, Carol Kane. D: Richard Benjamin. DRA [PG] 108m. v

Rack, The 1956 ★★★★ Newman gives a multifaceted performance as a former Korean War POW, brainwashed by his captors and now on trial for treason. Pidgeon convincing in this courtroom drama, adapted from a TV play by Rod Serling. C: Paul Newman, Wendell Corey, Walter Pidgeon, Edmond O'Brien, Anne Francis, Lee Marvin, Cloris Leachman. D: Arnold Laven. DRA 100m.

Racket Busters 1938 ★★★½ When gangster Bogart decides to infiltrate trucking industry, clean-cut driver Brent wants nothing to do with criminal activities. Good cast makes the most of this otherwise routine crime drama. C: George Brent, Humphrey Bogart, Gloria Dickson, Allen Jenkins, Walter Abel, Henry O'Neill, Penny Singleton. D: Lloyd Bacon. CRI 71m.

Racket Man, The 1944 ★★★ Mobster reformed by Army stint becomes undercover agent fighting wartime black market. Effective though dated melodrama. C: Tom Neal, Hugh Beaumont, Jeanne Bates, Larry Parks. D: D. Ross Lederman. DRA 65m.

Racket, The 1951 ★★★★ Mitchum is a police captain who maintains his integrity despite pressure from all sides to give in to powerful gangster Ryan. Intriguing look at political and legal corruption, marked by antagonistic chemistry between Mitchum and Ryan. C: Robert Mitchum, Robert Ryan, Lizabeth Scott, William Conrad. D: John Cromwell. CRI 88m. v

Racketeer, The 1929 ★★★ Gangster helps a woman's boyfriend in his musical career in exchange for her promise to marry him. Trite premise handled as well as possible, but Lombard's star quality already evident. C: Carole Lombard, Robert Armstrong, Hedda Hopper. D: Howard Higgin. DRA 68m. v

Racquet 1979 ★ A tennis pro (Convy) seduces women in order to finance his dream tennis court. Diluted imitation of *Shampoo*. C: Bert Convy, Edie Adams, Lynda Day George, Phil Silvers. D: David Winters. DRA [R] 89m. v

Rad 1986 ★★½ Off-road bicycle racers prepare for the big competition. Same old story, different sport, but the race scenes are exciting. C: Bart Connor, Talia Shire, Jack Weston, Bill Allen. D: Hal Needham. ACT [PG] 94m. v

Radio Days 1986 ★★★★½ This warm, funny nostalgic piece about the days when radio was a part of everyone's life is one of Allen's least cyncial movies. Allen narrates this '40s story about his family in Queens and their favorite radio personalities. C: Mia Farrow, Dianne Wiest, Danny Aiello, Jeff Daniels, Tony Roberts, Diane Keaton. D: Woody Allen. COM [PG] 96m. v

Radio Flyer 1992 ★★ Surrealistic movie about two boys trying to escape their abusive stepfather via their Radio Flyer wagon. Good performance, beaten by an odd, weak script; Tom Hanks is the uncredited narrator. C: Lorraine Bracco, John Heard, Elijah Wood. D: Richard Donner. DRA [PG-13] 114m. v

Radio On 1979 British ★★★½ After his brother is murdered, British disc jockey hits the road to find the mysterious killer. Some intriguing moments, though film never gels. Terrific soundtrack includes songs by David Bowie, Devo, Kraftwerk, and Lene Lovich. C: David Beames, Lisa Kreuzer, Sting. D: Chris Petit. DRA 101m.

Radioactive Dreams 1986 ★★★ Postnuclear-holocaust comedy about two men who emerge from a fallout shelter after 15 years of reading nothing but detective novels. The surreal juxtaposition of their hard-boiled point of view and the bleak ruins of civilization can't carry the entire film. C: John Stockwell, Michael Dudikoff, Lisa Blount, George Kennedy. D: Albert Pyun. SFI [R] 94m. v

Radioland Murders 1994 ★★½ Murder and mayhem reigns supreme at a new radio network's premiere broadcast in 1939. Frenetic, not very funny farce with an attractive cast doing its best. C: Mary Stuart Masterson, Brian Benben, Ned Beatty, Scott Michael Campbell, Michael Lerner, Christopher Lloyd. D: Mel Smith. COM [PG] 112m. v

Radium City 1987 ★★★★ Documentary about the young women factory workers of Ottawa, Illinois, who painted radium on clock faces and were slowly poisoned. Effective and unsettling. D: Carole Langer. DOC 110m.

Raffles 1930 ★★★★ Finding life outside the force unchallenging, ex-police officer Colman takes to jewel theft as pleasant diversion. Delightful version of a much-filmed story. Colman leads the way in a film brimming with wit. C: Ronald Colman, Kay Francis, Bramwell Fletcher, Frances Dade, David Torrence, Alison Skipworth. D: Harry D'Arrast, George Fitzmaurice. DRA 72m.

Raffles 1940 ★★★ Niven plays the cop-turned-jewel thief in this bland remake of the 1930 original based on E.W. Hornung's popular novel *The Amateur Cracksman.* Despite good cast, the story never takes off. C: David Niven, Olivia de Havilland, Dudley Digges, Dame May Whitty, Douglas Walton, Lionel Pape. D: Sam Wood. CRI 72m.

Rage 1966 U.S. ★★ Ford plays a hard-drinking doctor in a Mexican village who must race for help or else succumb to rabies. Preposterous story, labored acting. C: Glenn Ford, Stella Stevens, David Reynoso, Armando Silvestre, Ariadna Welter. D: Gilberto Gazcon. DRA [PG] 103m.

Rage 1972 ★★½ A rancher is driven to kill when his son dies from poison gas accidentally sprayed from an Army helicopter. Scott's performance, in his directorial debut, seems distracted and perfunctory. C: George C. Scott, Richard Basehart, Martin Sheen, Barnard Hughes. D: George C Scott. DRA 100m. V

Rage 1980 ★★★★ Enlightening look at a rapist who goes through intensive rehabilitation. Tough, but well-done. C: David Soul, James Whitemore, Yaphet Kotto, Vic Tayback, Craig T. Nelson. D: William A. Graham. DRA 100m. TVM V

Rage and Honor 1993 ★★★ A concerned high school teacher (Rothrock) teams up with an Australian cop (Norton) to take on an L.A. drug lord. Mercilessly slow-paced action saga. C: Cynthia Rothrock, Richard Norton. D: Terence H. Winkless. ACT [R] 90m. V

Rage at Dawn 1955 ★★★ After his wife is gunned down by bank-robbing outlaws, Scott saddles up his horse, loads his gun, and gathers up a posse for a little revenge. B-Western action with no surprises. C: Randolph Scott, Forrest Tucker, Mala Powers, J.Carroll Naish, Edgar Buchanan. D: Tim Whelan. WST 87m. V

Rage in Harlem, A 1991 ★★★★ A woman (Givens) with a load of stolen gold is chased through a sharply evoked Harlem of the '50s. Good adaptation of Chester Himes' story with a strong cast, some laughs, and some violence. C: Forest Whitaker, Gregory Hines, Robin Givens, Danny Glover, Badja Djola. D: Bill Duke. CRI [R] 110m. V

Rage in Heaven 1941 ★★★ Downbeat, intricate story of a man going insane and plotting the murder of his relatives. Adapted from James Hilton's novel. Ambitious film misses, but Montgomery is good. C: Robert Montgomery, Ingrid Bergman, George Sanders, Lucile Watson, Oscar Homolka, Philip Merivale, Matthew Boulton. D: W.S. VanDyke II. DRA 83m.

Rage of Angels 1983 ★★★½ Smart and ultra-ambitious lawyer fights her way to professional prominence. Glitzy and entertaining, the Sidney Sheldon way. C: Jaclyn Smith, Ken Howard, Armand Assante, Ron Hunter. D: Buzz Kulik. DRA 192m. TVM V

Rage of Angels: The Story Continues 1986 ★★½ Further adventures of Sidney Sheldon's power lawyer (Smith) and her professional and personal entanglements. Glittery soap opera with a good cast, especially Lansbury. C: Jaclyn Smith, Ken Howard, Michael Nouri, Susan Sullivan, Brad Dourif, Angela Lansbury, Mason Adams. D: Paul Wendkos. DRA 200m. TVM

Rage of Honor 1986 ★★★ A narcotics cop (Kosugi) journeys to South America to hunt down those responsible for his partner's death. Wearisome revenge saga, redeemed only by Kosugi's skilled fighting technique. C: Sho Kosugi, Robin Evans, Lewis Van Bergen. D: Gordon Hessler. ACT [R] 92m. V

Rage of Paris, The 1938 ★★★½ Darrieux is delightful as the beautiful woman her friends try to marry off to a rich man, only to find she falls in love with him anyway. Witty comedy with class, and a brief early role for Mary Martin. C: Danielle Darrieux, Douglas Fairbanks Jr., Mischa Auer, Louis Hayward. D: Henry Koster. COM 78m. V

Rage of the Buccaneers, The 1962 Italian ★★ Spirited hokum as good-hearted pirates spar with evil landlubbers, and everyone overacts. (a.k.a. *The Black Buccaneer*) C: Ricardo Montalban, Vincent Price, Giulia Rubini, Liana Orfei. D: Mario Costa. ACT 88m.

Rage of the Master 1975 ★★½ Martial artists on the move, this time in China during the Ching dynasty. The usual wallops, with moments of fun. C: Ng Ming Tsai, Tiger Yang. ACT 100m. V

Rage to Live, A 1965 ★★ Pleshette badly miscast as woman still interested in having affairs after she marries. Satiric irony of John O'Hara novel missing from poor adaptation and some scatterbrained performances. C: Suzanne Pleshette, Bradford Dillman, Ben Gazzara, Peter Graves, Bethel Leslie, James Gregory. D: Walter Grauman. DRA 101m.

Raggedy Ann and Andy 1979 ★★ The two popular dolls star in a dull movie. Essentially a commercial for Raggedy Ann and Andy toys, syrupy songs and too-cute characters fill a badly animated feature aimed at kiddie consumers. Voices of Didi Conn, Mark Baker. D: Richard Williams. FAM/MUS [G] 85m. V

Raggedy Man 1981 ★★★★ Divorced small-town Texas phone operator Spacek struggles to support her children during WWII. When soldier Roberts enters her life, her world is permanently changed. A small gem of a film, with remarkable performance by Spacek. Directed by her husband, Jack Fisk. C: Sissy Spacek, Eric Roberts, William Sanderson, Tracey Walter, Sam Shepard, Henry Thomas. D: Jack Fisk. DRA [PG] 94m. v

Raging Bull 1980 ★★★★★ The story of prizefighter Jake Lamotta, who lived by his fists both in and out of the ring. A wrenching, powerful film; much more than a fine boxing epic. Oscar-winner De Niro leads a superlative cast and Scorsese's direction is masterful. Brilliant editing by Thelma Schoonmaker also won an Oscar. C: Robert De Niro, Cathy Moriarty, Joe Pesci, Frank Vincent, Nicholas Colasanto, Theresa Saldana. D: Martin Scorsese. DRA [R] 129m. v

Raging Moon, The 1971 *See* **Long Ago Tomorrow**

Raging Tide, The 1951 ★★ Predictable story about falsely accused man on the run. Cast caught in the undertow. Adapted by Ernest K. Gann from his novel. C: Richard Conte, Shelley Winters, Stephen McNally, Charles Bickford. D: George Sherman. DRA 93m.

Ragman's Daughter, The 1972 British ★★★★ Wonderful, seldom-seen film about a burglar (Rouse) who falls in love with young woman (Tennant) who lives in the apartment he's casing. Directorial debut shows real control. Worth looking for. C: Simon Rouse, Victoria Tennant, Patrick O'Connell, Leslie Sands. D: Harold Becker. DRA 94m.

Rags to Riches 1986 ★★★ Television pilot film revolves around dilemmas faced by millionaire Bologna after he adopts six girls. His sharp-edged image softens as life grows into series of cutie-pie adventures. C: Joseph Bologna, Bill Maher. D: Bruce Seth Green. COM 96m. v

Ragtime 1981 ★★★★ Glimpses of American life in the early 20th century provide the backdrop to the central story of a black ragtime musician's fight against racism for simple justice. A colorful but somewhat disjointed distillation of E.L. Doctorow's novel; Cagney's last film appearance. C: James Cagney, Elizabeth McGovern, Howard Rollins Jr., Mary Steenburgen, Brad Dourif, Kenneth McMillan, Moses Gunn. D: Milos Forman. DRA [PG] 156m. v

Raid on Entebbe 1976 ★★★★ Drama of the 1976 hijacking of an airliner in Uganda and its subsequent rescue by Israeli commandos. Excellent version of a true story, with good action sequences and terrific cast. (a.k.a. *Entebbe: Operation Thunderbolt*) C: Peter Finch, Charles Bronson, Horst Buchholz, Martin Balsam. D: Irvin Kershner. ACT 113m. TVM v

Raid on Rommel 1971 ★★★ During the North African campaign in WWII, a British officer (Burton) leads released POWs on a raid. An unexceptional war piece; try to spot the stock desert footage from *Tobruk* and other films. C: Richard Burton, John Colicos, Clinton Greyn, Wolfgang Preiss. D: Henry Hathaway. ACT 98m. v

Raid, The 1954 ★★★★ Intriguing Civil War drama about Confederate prisoners who escape a New England jail and plan revenge on nearby Vermont town. Bancroft and Rettig excellent as defenders of the town. C: Van Heflin, Anne Bancroft, Richard Boone, Lee Marvin, Tommy Rettig, James Best, Peter Graves, Claude Akins. D: Hugo Fregonese. ACT 83m.

Raiders of Atlantis ★★★ The fabled continent rises in the Caribbean, and nuclear battles erupt. Exciting, with some fun special effects. C: Christopher Connelly. D: Roger Franklin. SFI 100m. v

Raiders of the Buddhist Kung Fu 1984 ★★★ Nat Kit, the Manchu leader, and the Buddhist Wong Lung battle over who will rule China. Classic martial arts excitement. ACT 40m. v

Raiders of the Lost Ark 1981 ★★★★★ The original in the Indiana Jones series by Spielberg and Lucas. Archaeologist/adventurer Ford sets out on an incredible adventure to save the world's most famous treasure from the Nazis. Thrilling, inventive, funny, and so action-packed it takes the breath away. C: Harrison Ford, Karen Allen, Paul Freeman, Ronald Lacey, John Rhys-Davies, Denholm Elliott. D: Steven Spielberg. ACT [PG] 116m. v

Raiders, The 1952 ★★★½ Rancher (Conte) fights judge who heads gang of land grabbers. Sharp script and effective use of the California scenery. (a.k.a. *Riders of Vengeance*) C: Richard Conte, Viveca Lindfors, Barbara Britton, Hugh O'Brian, Richard Martin, William Reynolds. D: Lesley Selander. WST 80m.

Raiders, The 1963 ★★★½ Culp and Keith lead a strong cast in saga about railroaders vs. cattle ranchers. Sweeping vistas, good treatment of familiar story. C: Robert Culp, Brian Keith, Judi Meredith, James McMullan, Alfred Ryder, Simon Oakland. D: Herschel Daugherty. WST 75m.

Railroad Man, The 1956 *See* **Man of Iron**

Railroaded 1947 ★★★★ Ireland is a sadistic mobster out to get Ryan—if only he can keep cop Beaumont out of his way. Intelligent and tightly controlled crime picture with sharp performances. Suspense holds up right to the end. C: John Ireland, Sheila Ryan, Hugh Beaumont, Jane Randolph. D: Anthony Mann. CRI 72m. v

Rails Into Laramie 1954 ★★★ When outlaws threaten railway expansion into Laramie, it's up to Payne to put an end to the nefarious deeds. Standard B-Western plot that runs through the expected paces. C: John Payne, Mari Blanchard, Dan Duryea, Joyce MacKenzie, Barton MacLane, Lee Van Cleef. D: Jesse Hibbs. WST 81m.

Railway Children, The 1970 British ★★★★ Family's serene life is shattered when father is wrongly imprisoned. His three children combine forces to set him free. Good-looking, well-done period piece from England, based on popular children's novel by E. Nesbit. C: Dinah Sheridan, Bernard Cribbins, William Mervyn, Jenny Agutter. D: Lionel Jeffries. FAM/DRA [G] 104m. v

Railway Station Man, The 1992 British ★★★★ An Irish widow with a rebellious son falls for the quiet American who is restoring the town railway station. Magical re-teaming of Christie and Sutherland in this quietly powerful tale. Beautiful location photography. It will hook you. C: Julie Christie, Donald Sutherland, John Lynch, Frank MacCusker, Mark Tandy. D: Michael Whyte. DRA 93m. TVM v

Rain 1932 ★★★★ When fiery hussy meets stiff-necked preacher on remote Pago Pago, something's got to give. Crawford terrific as untamed tramp Sadie Thompson from the story by Somerset Maugham. Good work all around. C: Joan Crawford, Walter Huston, William Gargan, Guy Kibbee. D: Lewis Milestone. DRA 91m. v

Rain Makers, The 1951 French ★★★½ Short anthropological documentary focuses on rainmaking rituals among the Songhay peoples of Niger. A dated but interesting ethnographic document. D: Jean Rouch. DOC 35m.

Rain Man 1988 ★★★★½ Aggressive con artist on the skids discovers he has autistic brother who inherited the family fortune. Modest tale of human connection overcoming cynicism and greed. Cruise is surprisingly good, but is overshadowed by Hoffman's Oscar-winning bravura performance. Oscars for Best Picture, Director, and Screenplay as well. C: Dustin Hoffman, Tom Cruise, Valeria Golino, Jerry Molden. D: Barry Levinson. DRA [R] 134m. v

Rain or Shine 1930 ★★★½ Capra antique about a manager trying to save a failing circus owned by his girlfriend. Stars rarely filmed stage luminary Cook. C: Joe Cook, Louise Fazenda, Joan Peers, Dave Chasen, William Collier Jr., Tom Howard. D: Frank Capra. DRA 92m.

Rain People, The 1969 ★★★★ A pregnant Long Island housewife (Knight) decides to leave her boring life and hit the road. She picks up a simpleminded ex-football player, played with depth by Caan. Coppola wrote and directed this thoughtful, ambitious character study. C: James Caan, Shirley Knight, Robert Duvall, Marya Zimmet, Tom Aldredge. D: Francis Ford Coppola. DRA [R] 102m. v

Rain Without Thunder 1992 ★★★ Heavy-handed allegory about the dangers of government encroachment into the private lives of citizens. A young woman and her mother are imprisoned in a frightening futuristic America that forbids abortion. C: Betty Buckley, Jeff Daniels, Frederic Forrest, Graham Greene, Linda Hunt, Carolyn McCormick, Austin Pendleton, Alyssa Rallo, Ali Thomas, Steve Zahn, Robert Jones. D: Gary Bennett. DRA 87m.

Rainbow 1978 ★★ Painful attempt to recount Judy Garland's youthful rise to stardom, up to *The Wizard of Oz*. McArdle, famous as Broadway's *Annie*, is not up to the challenge, and the story wavers. Cooper, who knew Garland well, should have known better. C: Andrea McArdle, Don Murray, Piper Laurie, Martin Balsam, Michael Parks, Jack Carter, Donna Pescow. D: Jackie Cooper. DRA 100m. TVM v

Rainbow Drive 1990 ★★★ Tangerine Dream score and Weller's presence try to lift this steamy cop drama above its cable TV roots. Story of officer investigating multiple murders in Hollywood and a possible cover-up never takes off. Based on a Roderick Thorp novel. C: Peter Weller, Sela Ward, Bruce Weitz. D: Bobby Roth. CRI [R] 93m. v

Rainbow Island 1944 ★★★ After landing in the tropics, a crew of merchant marines start chasing the local women, who are led by perennial movie island dweller Lamour. Bland songs and the expected contrivances rule this ultimately minor and dated musical. C: Dorothy Lamour, Eddie Bracken, Gil Lamb, Barry Sullivan, Anne Revere, Olga San Juan, Elena Verdugo, Yvonne De Carlo, Reed Hadley, Marc Lawrence. D: Ralph Murphy. MUS 97m.

Rainbow Jacket, The 1954 British ★★★½ A jockey (Owen) barred from racing, teaches his protégé (Edmonds) the tricks of the trade. Formulaic story gets lift from exciting race sequences. C: Kay Walsh, Bill Owen, Fella Edmonds, Robert Morley, Willfrid Hyde-White, Honor Blackman. D: Basil Dearden. ACT 99m.

Rainbow 'Round My Shoulder 1952 ★★ Humdrum story of starstruck young woman whose dreams of becoming an actress are blocked by disapproving grandmother. Guess who wins. Flat tunefest. C: Frankie Laine, Billy Daniels, Charlotte Austin, Ida Moore, Arthur Franz, Barbara Whiting, Lloyd Corrigan. D: Richard Quine. MUS 78m.

Rainbow, The 1989 British ★★★★ Young and innocent school teacher (Davis) learns about life and love from an older, worldly woman (Donohoe). Mature, interesting adaptation of the D.H. Lawrence novel, surprisingly subtle—for this director. C: Sammi Davis, Amanda Donohoe, Paul McGann, Christopher Gable, David Hemmings, Glenda Jackson, Ken Colley. D: Ken Russell. DRA [R] 104m. v

Rainbow Trail, The 1925 ★★★½ A young cowhand (Mix) rescues his uncle from an outlaw siege in desolate Paradise Valley. Spunky retelling of Zane Grey adventure. Good Mix. C: Tom Mix, Anne Cornwall, George Bancroft, Lucien Littlefield, Mark Hamilton, Vivien Oakland. D: Lynn Reynolds. WST 58m.

Raining Stones 1993 British ★★★★½ Incisive comedy/drama about an unemployed man who needs money to buy communion dress for his daughter, and gets mixed up with local mobsters as a result. As usual, Loach is on target in his view of the British working class. C: Bruce Jones, Julie Brown, Ricky Tomlinson, Tom Hickey, Gemma Phoenix, Jonathan James, Mike Fallon. D: Ken Loach. COM 90m.

Rainmaker, The 1956 ★★★★ A 1913 swindler (Lancaster) claims he can bring rain to a drought-ravaged Kansas town, and in the meanwhile romances unmarried local woman (Hepburn). Talky but pleasing fare. From N. Richard Nash's stage play. C: Burt Lancaster, Katharine Hepburn, Wendell Corey, Lloyd Bridges, Earl Holliman. D: Joseph Anthony. DRA 121m. V

Rains Came, The 1939 ★★★ When uppercrust Loy travels to India with her husband, she unexpectedly falls in love with local doctor Power. Trite romance, with Power woefully miscast. Excellent natural disaster special effects, though, which won an Oscar. Later remade as *The Rains of Ranchipur.* C: Myrna Loy, Tyrone Power, George Brent, Brenda Joyce, Nigel Bruce, Maria Ouspenskaya, Joseph Schildkraut, Laura Hope Crews. D: Clarence Brown. DRA 104m.

Rains of Ranchipur, The 1955 ★★★ Turner, the wife of an English official, causes a scandal when she falls in love with Indian physician Burton. Lush production can't lift story above its soap opera plot. Remake of *The Rains Came.* C: Lana Turner, Richard Burton, Fred MacMurray, Joan Caulfield, Michael Rennie, Eugenie Leontovich. D: Jean Negulesco. DRA 104m.

Raintree County 1957 ★★★★ A Southern belle in Civil War times suffers disillusionment with all the men she knows. Epic *Gone With the Wind* clone has Taylor leading a fine cast of notables. Long, but impressive, with superb music. C: Elizabeth Taylor, Montgomery Clift, Eva Marie Saint, Lee Marvin. D: Edward Dmytryk. DRA 175m. V

Raise the Red Lantern 1991 China ★★★★★ An educated concubine adapts to life as rich man's fourth wife in Yimou's powerful, but well-paced drama on the role of women in '20s China, with a stunning performance by Gong Li. A masterpiece of composition and color. C: Gong Li, Ma Jingwu, He Caifei, Cao Cuifeng, Jin Shuyuan. D: Zhang Yimou. DRA [PG] 125m. V

Raise the Titanic! 1980 British ★★ A group of scientists and treasure hunters struggle to raise the famed sunken ship. Tremendous cast struggles to raise film to a watchable level, and they fail. C: Jason Robards, Richard Jordan, Anne Archer, Alec Guinness. D: Jerry Jameson. ACT [PG] 112m. V

Raisin in the Sun, A 1961 ★★★★½ Struggling black Chicago family wants to break away from their confining existence by moving into a white neighborhood. Stagebound but uniformly excellent performances and sharp dialogue. Based on play by Lorraine Hansberry. C: Sidney Poitier, Claudia McNeil, Ruby Dee, Louis Gossett, Jr. D: Daniel Petrie. DRA 128m. V

Raisin in the Sun, A 1989 ★★★★ Strong, emotional version of Lorraine Hansberry's play about a '50s African-American family trying to cope with move to an all-white neighborhood. Glover brings dignity and fire to his role. C: Danny Glover, Esther Rolle, Starletta DuPois. D: Harold Scott. DRA 177m. TVM V

Raising Arizona 1987 ★★★★ The Coen brothers hit their stride with this outrageous comedy, quite a contrast to their chilling *Blood Simple* brimming with hilarious gags and striking camerawork. Cage and Hunter shine as a young couple (he's a reforming criminal, she's a cop) who can't have children so he kidnaps one of a set of quintuplets. C: Nicolas Cage, Holly Hunter, Trey Wilson, John Goodman, William Forsythe, Randall Cobb. D: Joel Coen. COM [PG-13] 94m. V

Raising Cain 1992 ★★½ Psychologist, with the aid of his twin brother, kidnaps children for psychological experiments conducted by their father. Lithgow plays all three family members. Wildly over-the-top thriller is a tour de force for Lithgow. C: John Lithgow, Lolita Davidovich, Steven Bauer, Frances Sternhagen, Gregg Henry, Tom Bower, Mel Harris. D: Brian De Palma. CRI [R] 91m. V

Raising the Wind 1961 British ★★½ Students at an English music conservatory outdo each other in being odd (in a British sort of way). Frolicsome but forgettable. C: James Robertson Justice, Leslie Phillips, Sidney James, Paul Massie, Kenneth Williams. D: Gerald Thomas. COM 91m.

Rake's Progress, The 1945 *See* **Notorious Gentleman**

Rally 'Round the Flag, Boys! 1958 ★★★½ Fifties comedy has suburban town flexing its muscle to prevent a missile base from moving in next door. Newman and Woodward are effective foils in this funny adaptation of Max Shulman's best-seller. C: Paul Newman, Joanne Woodward, Joan Collins, Jack Carson, Dwayne Hickman, Tuesday Weld, Gale Gordon. D: Leo McCarey. COM 106m.

Ramblin' Man 1979 ★★ Two good ol' boys, moseying around innocently in country-music mecca Nashville become involved in the kind of blackmail plot only TV writers can dream up. Decent acting, though. Pilot for TV series. (a.k.a. *Concrete Cowboys*) C: Tom Selleck, Jerry Reed, Morgan Fairchild. D: Burt Kennedy. ACT [R] 100m. TVM V

Rambling Rose 1991 ★★★★ Charmingly bucolic tale of sexually precocious young woman who comes to work for wealthy family and has a comically unsettling effect on all of its members. Ladd and Dern were first mother and daughter Oscar nominees. C:

Laura Dern, Robert Duvall, Diane Ladd, Lukas Haas. D: Martha Coolidge. DRA [R] 115m. V

Rambo: First Blood, Part II 1985 ★★★ Steroid-injected, blockbuster sequel to the quieter, smaller *First Blood.* Stallone goes to Cambodia searching for American MIAs. Even the presence of always-reliable Crenna doesn't help much. Jungle action sometimes enjoyable, but acting and script are never quite believable. C: Sylvester Stallone, Richard Crenna, Charles Napier, Julia Nickson. D: George P. Cosmatos. ACT [R] 95m. V

Rambo III 1988 ★★★ Rambo defeats Soviet forces in Afghanistan in order to free friend (Crenna). No-brainer action picture that manages to excite in spite of itself. C: Sylvester Stallone, Richard Crenna, Marc de-Jonge, Kurtwood Smith. D: Peter Macdonald. ACT [R] 102m. V

Ramona 1936 ★★★ In old California, a young Indian peasant (Ameche) sweeps the daughter of a Spanish landowner off her feet. Trite story line helped by good period detail, fine Ameche. C: Loretta Young, Don Ameche, Kent Taylor, Pauline Frederick, Jane Darwell, Katherine DeMille. D: Henry King. WST 90m.

Rampage 1963 ★★ The wife of a big game-hunter falls for their guide (Mitchum). Mitchum's menace saves it, barely. Great Elmer Bernstein score. C: Robert Mitchum, Elsa Martinelli, Jack Hawkins, Sabu, Cely Carillo, Emile Genest. D: Phil Karlson. DRA 98m.

Rampage 1992 ★★★ The defense for vicious serial killer wants him declared legally insane, but prosecutor (Biehn) wants to prove the murderer was in complete control. Violent treatment gets in way of "victim's rights" theme. C: Michael Biehn, Alex McArthur, Nicholas Campbell, Deborah van Valkenburgh. D: William Friedkin. CRI [R] 92m. V

Ramparts of Clay 1971 French ★★★½ Realistic portrayal of both a country (Tunisia) and a young woman coming of age, as she becomes a leader of her village's workers when they strike against a powerful company. Slow going at times, but rewarding. C: Leila Schenna. D: Jean-Louis Bertucelli. DRA [PG] 85m. V

Ramrod 1947 ★★★ Lake is a ruthless cattle rancher fighting with her father (Ruggles) until sheep farmer McCrea brings romance into her life. Tepid blend of B-Western formulas and romance film. C: Veronica Lake, Joel McCrea, Arleen Whelan, Donald Crisp, Charles Ruggles. D: Andre deToth. WST 94m. V

Ran 1985 Japanese ★★★★½ Magnificently choreographed battles and moments of penetrating character exploration give massive scope to Kurosawa's acclaimed Japanese version of *King Lear.* A warlord in the 1500s faces the tragedy of an empire torn asunder by his sons' greed and selfish ambitions. Highlighted by Harada's ferocious performance as a vengeful woman. C: Tatsuya Nakadai, Akira Terao, Mieko Harada. D: Akira Kurosawa. DRA [R] 160m. V

Ranch, The 1988 ★★★ A failed executive inherits a broken-down ranch amd turns it into a fancy health spa. Some good fun. C: Andrew Stevens, Gary Fjellgard, Lou Ann Schmidt, Elizabeth Keefe. D: Stella Stevens. COM [PG-13] 90m. V

Rancho Deluxe 1975 ★★★★ Two latter-day cowhands—one white, one Native American—rustle cattle, then run ragged from inept deputies. Droll postmodern Western, scripted by popular novelist Tom McGuane, spoofs genre conventions with affection. Bridges shines amid talented cast. Jimmy Buffet—who provided music—has bit part. C: Jeff Bridges, Sam Waterston, Elizabeth Ashley, Charlene Dallas, Clifton James, Slim Pickens, Harry Dean Stanton, Richard Bright, Patti D'Arbanville, Jimmy Buffett. D: Frank Perry. COM [R] 93m. V

Rancho Notorious 1952 ★★★½ While searching for his girlfriend's murderer, a cowhand takes up with a captivating saloon singer. All the elements are there—including Dietrich in Western garb—but plot is subordinate to the stars. C: Marlene Dietrich, Arthur Kennedy, Mel Ferrer, Lloyd Gough, Jack Elam, George Reeves. D: Fritz Lang. WST 89m. V

Random Harvest 1942 ★★★★½ A shell-shocked WWI vet (Colman) marries entertainer (Garson), then forgets about her after accident leaves him an amnesiac. He returns to his wealthy family to recover, but is reunited with Garson when she contrives to be hired as a secretary. Stirring feature, extremely well acted. Based on the James Hilton story. C: Ronald Colman, Greer Garson, Philip Dorn, Susan Peters. D: Mervyn LeRoy. DRA 127m. V

Randy Rides Alone 1934 ★★★½ It's up to law official Wayne to find out who robbed the pony express. Fairly entertaining B-Western with good performance from the Duke. C: John Wayne, George "Gabby" Hayes, Alberta Vaughan. D: Henry Frazer. WST 53m. V

Rangers of Fortune 1940 ★★★★ Three bandits just a step ahead of Mexican posse, stop in a Texas town long enough to protect an old man and his daughter. Satisfying change-of-pace Western directed with flair. C: Fred MacMurray, Albert Dekker, Gilbert Roland, Patricia Morison, Dick Foran, Joseph Schildkraut. D: Sam Wood. WST 80m.

Ransom *See* **Maniac!**

Ransom 1956 ★★★ After his son is kidnapped, a business magnate (Ford) debates whether he should pay ransom or use other means to rescue the boy. Overplayed drama with few gripping moments. C: Glenn Ford, Donna Reed, Leslie Nielson. D: Alex Segal. DRA 109m.

Ransom for a Dead Man 1971 ★★★★ Falk stars as Columbo, everyone's favorite rumpled detective, in a clever story about a high-powered lawyer (Grant) who kills her husband, using her own faked kidnapping as an alibi. Very entertaining. C: Peter Falk, Lee Grant, John Fink, Harold Gould, Patricia Mattick, Paul Carr. D: Richard Irving. CRI 100m. TVM

Rape & Marriage: The Rideout Case 1980 ★★★½ Based on true story of Oregon woman who accused her husband of rape; he claimed it was impossible for a husband to rape his wife. Intriguing legal questions well handled by above-average cast. C: Mickey Rourke, Linda Hamilton, Rip Torn, Eugene Roche. D: Peter Levin. DRA 96m. TVM V

Rape of Love 1979 French ★★★ Serious but didactic study of the process by which a woman deals with sexual assault. Sensitive acting and direction, despite a graphic opening gang rape scene. Unrated; contains violence, nudity, and profanity. C: Nathalie Nell, Alain Foures. D: Yannick Bellon. DRA 117m. V

Rape of Richard Beck, The 1985 ★★★★ Taut police drama about a hardened cop (Crenna) who is brutally raped. He catches the culprits, but his believable transformation (Crenna's Emmy-winning performance) into a sensitive guy is the real interest. C: Richard Crenna, Meredith Baxter Birney, Pat Hingle, Frances McCain, Cotter Smith, George Dzundza, Joanna Kerns. D: Karen Arthur. DRA 100m. TVM V

Rape Squad, The 1974 ★★★½ Fast-moving story of a group of women who exact vengeance on rapist freed on a technicality. Brutal, unpleasant action drama. (a.k.a. *Act of Vengeance*) C: Jo Ann Harris, Peter Brown, Jennifer Lee, Steve Kanaly, Lada Edmund Jr. D: Bob Kelljan. DRA [R] 90m. V

Rapid Fire 1992 ★★★½ Brandon Lee (son of Bruce) becomes the target of mobsters after witnessing a gangland murder. Not bad action, chock full of chops, kicks, and bullets. Capable Lee, though Bruce's charisma wasn't inherited. C: Brandon Lee, Powers Boothe, Nick Mancuso, Raymond J. Barry. D: Dwight H. Little. ACT [R] 95m. V

Rappin 1985 ★★ Rap music retread of old story line about good guy (Van Peebles) who wants to go straight, but his felonious friends and a corrupt society won't let him. Limp break dancing concoction that falls flat. C: Mario Van Peebles, Tasia Valenza, Charles Flohe, Harry Goz. D: Joel Silberg. MUS [PG] 92m. V

Rapture 1965 French ★★★½ Gozzi is sheltered daughter of former judge Douglas. Her sedate life changes radically after she becomes involved with Stockwell, a crook on the lam. Though drama doesn't hit every note, core relationship receives sensitive and effective treatment. C: Melvyn Douglas, Dean Stockwell, Patricia Gozzi, Gunnel Lindblom, Leslie Sands. D: John Guillermin. DRA 104m.

Rapture, The 1991 ★★★ A bored telephone operator is sexually self-indulgent until she becomes a fundamentalist Christian, marries happily, and has a child. When her husband dies, she waits for a sign from God. Overblown film sometimes tries too hard. C: Mimi Rogers, Patrick Bauchau, David Duchovny, Will Patton. D: Michael Tolkin. DRA [R] 100m. V

Rapunzel ★★★½ Olivia Newton-John narrates fairy tale about a young woman whose long hair allows a prince to climb up to her rescue from the tower in which she's imprisoned. Simple animated fare that's fine for younger audiences. C: Olivia Newton-John. FAM/DRA

Rare Breed, The 1966 ★★★½ Sparks fly when a determined woman takes her English bull to St. Louis for breeding with American longhorns. Some fun in a different Western angle. The cast is terrific. C: James Stewart, Maureen O'Hara, Brian Keith, Juliet Mills. D: Andrew V. McLaglen. WST 97m. V

Rascal 1969 ★★★½ Enjoyable Disney adaptation of Sterling North's autobiographical novel about his boyhood friendship with a racoon. Typically engaging Disney tale. C: Steve Forrest, Bill Mumy, Pamela Toll, Bettye Ackerman, Elsa Lanchester, Henry Jones. D: Norman Tokar. FAM/DRA [G] 85m.

Rascals and Robbers—The Secret Adventures 1982 ★★★½ New adventures based on the Mark Twain characters, who join the circus and outsleuth a con artist. Engaging story, good circus activity. C: Patrick Creadon, Anthony Michael Hall, Anthony Zerbe, Anthony James, Ed Begley Jr., Cynthia Nixon. D: Dick Lowry. FAM/DRA 95m. TVM V

Rascals, The 1981 French ★★★½ Youths' misadventures at Catholic school; film focuses on one mischievious youngster and his encroaching adulthood. Thoughtful, with some good laughs. C: Bernard Brieux, Thomas Chabral, Pascale Rocard. D: Bernard Revon. COM [R] 93m. V

Rashomon 1951 Japanese ★★★★★ Kurosawa's masterpiece about four different views of the same violent crime. The film became a symbol for the subjectivity and relative nature of truth and has lent it's name to the language. Mifune is haunting as the vicious 12th-century rapist/bandit. U.S. remake: *The Outrage*. Oscar for Best Foreign Film. C: Toshiro Mifune, Machiko Kyo, Masayuki Mori, Takashi Shimura. D: Akira Kurosawa. DRA 83m. V

Rasputin 1985 Russian ★★★★ Fascinating biography of the "mad monk" who manipulated the czar's family before the Russian Revolution. Released after much tampering and years of censorship by the Soviets. Unrated; contains nudity, violence. C: Alexei Petrenko, Anatoly Romashin, Velta Linei, Alice Freindlikh. D: Elem Klimov. DRA 107m. V

Rasputin and the Empress 1932 ★★★★ In last days of Czarist Russia, mystic "mad monk" gains influence over Tsarina Alexandra after supposedly curing her son's hemophilia. Ambitious drama with impressive production values and a romanticized look at Russia before communism. Only film featuring all three Barrymores. C: John Barrymore, Ethel Barrymore, Lionel Barrymore, Ralph Morgan, Diana Wynyard, Tad Alexander, C.Henry Gordon, Edward Arnold, Jean Parker. D: Richard Boleslawski. DRA 123m. V

Rasputin—the Mad Monk 1966 British ★★★½ Historically inaccurate but entertaining film biography features Lee as the holy man with mesmerizing powers who controls the court of Russia's last Tzar. Lee's performance manages to rise above the script. C: Christopher Lee, Barbara Shelley, Richard Pasco, Francis Matthews. D: Don Sharp. DRA 92m.

Rat Pfink and Boo Boo 1966 ★ Deliriously wretched low, low-budget parody of *Batman* about a rock singer and his servant who lead double lives as crime fighters. Pure bliss for lovers of bad movies. Film's strange title is thanks to incompetent credit designer who misspelled "and"! C: Carolyn Brandt, Vin Saxon, Titus Moede. D: Ray Dennis Steckler. ACT 72m. V

Rat Race, The 1960 ★★★★ Garson Kanin's adaptation of his own play about a musician (Curtis) and a dancer (Reynolds) who each come to New York seeking fame. Charming leads, energetic production. C: Tony Curtis, Debbie Reynolds, Jack Oakie, Kay Medford, Don Rickles, Joe Bushkin. D: Robert Mulligan. COM 105m.

Ratboy 1986 ★★ Locke (who also directed) is a window dresser who—after finding half-boy, half-rat—tries to crack showbusiness. Weak humor and offensive stereotyping prevail in this underdeveloped satire. Made with help from production company of Locke's then-paramour, Clint Eastwood. C: Sondra Locke, Robert Townsend, Christopher Hewett, Gerrit Graham, Louie Anderson, Bill Maher, Sharon Baird. D: Sondra Locke. DRA [PG-13] 104m. V

Ratings Game, The 1984 ★★★½ Fun TV spoof about a businessman who invents a bogus ratings service to instantly make any lame show he produces a hit. Charmingly crooked DeVito, solid supporting cast in this keen satire. C: Danny DeVito, Rhea Pearlman, Gerrit Graham, Kevin McCarthy, Whitney Bain. D: Danny DeVito. COM 102m. TVM V

Rationing 1944 ★★★★ Beery has fun as the town butcher who has to implement wartime rationing over the objections (and seductions) of the townspeople. Well-scripted and still resonant. C: Wallace Beery, Marjorie Main, Donald Meek, Gloria Dickson, Henry O'Neill, Connie Gilchrist. D: Willis Goldbeck. COM 93m.

Raton Pass 1951 ★★★½ Morgan and Neal are a married couple who duke it out over controlling interests in a cattle ranch. Standard material, played with some flair by the leads. C: Dennis Morgan, Patricia Neal, Steve Cochran, Scott Forbes, Dorothy Hart. D: Edwin L. Marin. WST 84m.

Rats, The *See* **Deadly Eyes**

Rats, The 1955 German ★★★★ Through crushing series of events, a new mother living in post-WWII Berlin is forced to give up her newborn to a woman who has always longed for a baby of her own. A moving and intelligent drama for adult viewers. C: Maria Schell, Curt Jurgens. D: Robert Siodmak. DRA 91m.

Rattle of a Simple Man, The 1964 British ★★★½ On a bet, a shy bachelor spends the night with a sexy cabaret singer. Good-natured English sex comedy, with wonderful Cilento. C: Harry H. Corbett, Diane Cilento, Thora Hird, Michael Medwin. D: Muriel Box. COM 91m. V

Rattlers 1976 ★★ Courageous zoologist and photographer try to find out why rattlesnakes are suddenly attacking humans without provocation. Standard low-budget film whose effectiveness depends largely on how much you already fear slithery reptiles. C: Sam Chew, Elizabeth Chauvet. D: John McCarley. HOR 82m. TVM V

Raubfischer in Hellas 1960 *See* **As the Sea Rages**

Ravagers 1979 ★ Apolcalyptic story set in futuristic postnuclear 1992 has a motley crew of survivors going against a gang. Don't bother. C: Richard Harris, Ann Turkel, Ernest Borgnine, Art Carney, Anthony James, Woody Strode, Alana Hamilton. D: Richard Compton. SFI [PG] 91m. TVM

Raven, The 1935 ★★★★ A doctor with a passion for Poe keeps a roomful of torture devices on hand for guests. Thrilling, action-packed treat. Karloff is the doctor's unwitting sidekick and great company to Lugosi's sick surgeon. C: Boris Karloff, Bela Lugosi, Irene Ware, Lester Matthews, Samuel S. Hinds. D: Lew Landers. HOR 62m. V

Raven, The 1943 *See* **Le Corbeau**

Raven, The 1963 ★★★★ Ribald teaming of horror vets Karloff and Price as battling 15th-century magicians, with Lorre as the title bird-man being knocked around between them. Silly fantasy with some welcome frivolity and interesting special effects. Has nothing to do with Poe poem. C: Vincent Price, Boris Karloff, Peter Lorre, Hazel Court, Jack Nicholson. D: Roger Corman. HOR 86m. V

Raven's End 1970 Swedish ★★★★ During 1930s, young author must sort out personal problems as well as those of his boozing father and depressive mother. Heavy Swedish drama with some unique perspectives on old themes. C: Thommy Berggren, Keve Hjelm, Emy Storm. D: Bo Widerberg. DRA 100m. TVM

Ravine, The 1969 Italian ★★½ Bland story of a WWII soldier (McCallum) infatuated with the sniper he has been sent to kill. Slow-going. C: David McCallum, Nicoletta Machiavelli, John Crawford, Lars Loch. D: Paolo Cavara. ACT 97m.

Ravishing Idiot 1965 French ★★ A bank clerk (Perkins) is recruited by the Soviets to steal NATO secrets. Silly and pointless. C: Anthony Perkins, Brigitte Bardot. D: Edouard Molinaro. COM 99m. v

Raw Deal 1948 ★★★★ After being sprung from prison, vengeful O'Keefe goes after gangster Burr, who framed him. Some taut moments and great use of b&w photography in this moody crime drama. C: Dennis O'Keefe, Claire Trevor, Marsha Hunt, Raymond Burr, John Ireland. D: Anthony Mann. CRI 79m.

Raw Deal 1986 ★★½ Secret agent moles his way into the Mob. Typical Schwarzenegger blood and guts. C: Arnold Schwarzenegger, Kathryn Harrold, Sam Wanamaker, Paul Shenar, Ed Lauter, Darren McGavin. D: John Irvin. ACT [R] 90m. v

Raw Edge 1956 ★★★ The ranch hands have their eyes on the boss' wife, so they plot to kill him. Surprisingly bland. C: Rory Calhoun, Yvonne De Carlo, Mara Corday, Rex Reason, Neville Brand. D: John Sherwood. WST 76m.

Raw Force 1981 ★★ Gruesome escapade about traveling American karate club encountering gang of Asian cannibals. Pointless. C: Cameron Mitchell, Geoffrey Binney. D: Edward Murphy. ACT [R] 90m. v

Raw Meat 1973 British ★★★½ Juicy tale of people-snatching cannibals thriving beneath the London underground. Not for the faint-hearted. C: Donald Pleasence, David Ladd, Sharon Gurney, Christopher Lee, Norman Rossington, Clive Swift. D: Gary Sherman. HOR [R] 87m.

Raw Wind in Eden 1958 ★★★ Wealthy couple crash-land on a deserted island, and the wife falls for the pilot. Okay romantic adventure. C: Esther Williams, Jeff Chandler, Rossana Podesta, Carlos Thompson, Rik Battaglia. D: Richard Wilson. DRA 89m.

Rawhead Rex 1987 ★ An ancient pagan god erupts from the underworld in the form of a big rubber monster that terrorizes an Irish town. Clive Barker adapted his own story, but disowned the result. For bad film fans. C: David Dukes, Kelly Piper, Ronan Wilmot. D: George Pavlou. HOR [R] 103m. v

Rawhide 1938 ★★½ Famed New York Yankee Lou Gehrig stars in unlikely role of Western rancher suffering at the hands of outlaws. Ballew is the sharp lawyer who rides in to save the day. An intriguing film curiosity, despite amateur performances. C: Smith Ballew, Lou Gehrig, Evalyn Knapp. D: Ray Taylor. WST 58m.

Rawhide 1951 ★★★★ Villains take over a stagecoach depot and hold everyone hostage until the law rides in to save the day. Action-packed Western with good character roles and terrific climax. Remake of 1935's crime film *Show Them No Mercy*. (a.k.a. *Desperate Siege*) C: Tyrone Power, Susan Hayward, Hugh Marlowe, Dean Jagger, Edgar Buchanan. D: Henry Hathaway. WST 86m. v

Rawhide Trail, The 1958 ★★ Story of pioneers who must prove they were not involved in assisting Indians who attacked their fellow settlers. C: Rex Reason, Nancy Gates, Richard Erdman, Ann Doran. D: Robert Gordan. WST 67m.

Rawhide Years, The 1956 ★★★½ Curtis gives an athletic and unaccented performance as a gambler charged with murder, who escapes prison to clear himself. Solid support from Kennedy and Demarest. C: Tony Curtis, Colleen Miller, Arthur Kennedy, William Demarest, William Gargan. D: Rudolph Maté. WST 85m.

Ray Bradbury Chronicles: The Martian Episodes 1993 ★★★★ Out-of-this-world thrills in stories based on Bradbury's popular book *The Martian Chronicles*. Well acted and scary. C: David Carradine, Ben Cross, John Vernon, Hal Linden, David Birney. SFI 100m. TVM

Raymie 1960 ★★★½ Charmingly told story of a boy's determined pursuit of an elusive barracuda. Ladd is wonderful. C: David Ladd, Julie Adams, John Agar, Charles Winninger, Richard Arlen, Frank Ferguson, Ray Kellogg. D: Frank McDonald. FAM/DRA 72m.

Razorback 1983 Australian ★★★ Harrison confronts enormous wild boar ravaging Australian outback. Mulcahy (in his directorial debut) makes dubious material work with spare, scary style, though the stunning visuals lose some impact on video. C: Gregory Harrison, Arkie Whiteley, Bill Kerr, Chris Haywood. D: Russell Mulcahy. HOR [R] 95m. v

Razor's Edge, The 1946 ★★★★ Glossy adaptation of W. Somerset Maugham's philosophical story of faithless young American soldier who survives WWI and searches for truth and salvation. Earnest version of hard-to-film book is long and rambling; but well acted. Oscar for Best Supporting Actress (Baxter). Remade in 1984. C: Tyrone Power, Gene Tierney, Anne Baxter, Clifton Webb, Herbert Marshall. D: Edmund Goulding. DRA 146m. v

Razor's Edge, The 1984 ★★½ Murray tries to get serious in Somerset Maugham tale of WWI-era man searching for truth and meaning in life. Not up to the original. C: Bill Murray, Theresa Russell, Catherine Hicks, Denholm Elliott, James Keach. D: John Byrum. DRA [PG-13] 129m. v

R.C.M.P. & the Treasure of Genghis Khan 1948 ★ Canadian mounties search for ancient treasure, foil crime ring. Forgettable. (a.k.a. *Dangers of the Canadian Mounted*) C: Jim Brannon, Virginia Belmont, Anthony

Warde, Dorothy Granger. D: Fred Brannon, Yakima Canutt. ACT 100m.

Re-Animator 1985 ★★★★ Ambitious medical student experiments in bringing the dead back to life, with horrific results. Directed with gusto, gleeful black humor and lots of gore by Gordon. Sharp performances, especially Combs'. Based on an H.P. Lovecraft story. C: Jeffrey Combs, Bruce Abbott, Barbara Crampton, David Gale. D: Stuart Gordon. HOR [R] 86m. V

Reach for Glory 1963 British ★★★½ During WWII, a group of British teens form their own social structure, replete with hard and fast rules of behavior, ultimately leading to tragedy for one member. A small, intriguing coming-of-age tale. C: Harry Andrews, Kay Walsh, Oliver Grimm, Michael Anderson Jr., Martin Tomlinson, Alexis Kanner. D: Philip Leacock. DRA 89m.

Reach for the Sky 1956 British ★★★½ True story of Douglas Bader, the WWII flying ace who had no legs. Good inspirational drama. C: Kenneth More, Muriel Pavlow, Alexander Knox, Sydney Tafler, Nigel Green. D: Lewis Gilbert. ACT 123m. V

Reaching for the Moon 1931 ★★½ Inebriated business magnate Fairbanks is torn between good intentions of servant Horton and bad intentions of gold-digging Daniels. Depression-era comedy. C: Douglas Fairbanks Sr., Bebe Daniels, Edward Everett Horton, Bing Crosby. D: Edmund Goulding. COM 66m. V

Reaching for the Sun 1941 ★★★½ When a backwoods fisherman goes to work on a Detroit assembly line to earn enough money for an outboard motor, he meets a nice city woman, too. Film's low key is the right tone and the result is a modestly enjoyable city/country romance. C: Joel McCrea, Ellen Drew, Eddie Bracken, Albert Dekker, Billy Gilbert, George Chandler. D: William Wellman. COM 90m. V

Reader, The 1988 *See* **La Lectrice**

Ready to Wear 1994 ★★★★ Sprawling Altman's-eye-view of the fashion world, set in Paris. While not the masterpiece the director's fans were waiting for, film does have a drop-dead cast, stylish visuals, and glamor for days. Originally titled *Pret-a-Porter*, which is "ready to wear" in French. C: Kim Basinger, Sophia Loren, Marcello Mastroianni, Tim Robbins, Julia Roberts, Anouk Aimee, Tracey Ullman, Forest Whitaker, Sally Kellerman, Linda Hunt, Lauren Bacall, Stephen Rea, Danny Aiello, Teri Garr. D: Robert Altman. COM [R] 132m. V

Ready, Willing and Able 1937 ★★½ An aspiring actress impersonates a famous star to land a role. Undistinguished musical has one bright spot: the "Too Marvelous For Words" dance on a giant typewriter. C: Ruby Keeler, Lee Dixon, Allen Jenkins, Louise Fazenda, Carol Hughes, Ross Alexander, Winifred Shaw, Teddy Hart. D: Ray Enright. MUS 95m.

Real American Hero, A 1978 ★★½ After three *Walking Tall* features, real-life Tennessee sherrif Buford Pusser gets depicted again in a made-for-TV drama about fighting local moonshiners. Violent and corny. C: Brian Dennehy, Forrest Tucker, Brian Kerwin, Ken Howard. D: Lou Antonio. DRA 100m. TVM V

Real Genius 1985 ★★★½ Of all the teen science comedies of the mid-'80s, this one has the most brains and the most laughs. Kilmer and Jarret are college science stars who discover their professor (Atherton) is exploiting them and decide to turn the tables. C: Val Kilmer, Gabe Jarret, Michelle Meyrink, William Atherton. D: Martha Coolidge. COM [PG] 106m. V

Real Glory, The 1939 ★★★★ After the Spanish-American War a small group of American soldiers helps a Filipino village. Relentless action includes a cholera epidemic, a dynamited dam, ravaging ants and a love interest for Cooper. Fine cast; vintage Hollywood excitement. C: Gary Cooper, David Niven, Andrea Leeds, Reginald Owen, Kay Johnson, Broderick Crawford, Vladimir Sokoloff, Henry Kolker. D: Henry Hathaway. DRA 96m. V

Real Life 1979 ★★★★ Over-the-top humor written, directed by, and starring Brooks as sleazy documentary filmmaker chronicling life of "typical" family. Before finishing, both Brooks' career and lives of subject family (headed by Grodin) are ruined. Gleefully demented satire, played to manic perfection under Brooks' sharp eye. C: Albert Brooks, Charles Grodin, Frances McCain, J.A. Preston. D: Albert Brooks. COM [PG] 99m. V

Real McCoy, The 1993 ★★★ A world-class thief (Basinger) is saddled with a klutzy partner (Kilmer), forced by the Mob into pulling a job she doesn't want. Handsome stars have too little to do in this fair comic thriller. C: Kim Basinger, Val Kilmer, Terence Stamp. D: Russell Mulcahy. CRI [PG-13] 106m. V

Real Men 1987 ★★ Belushi is undercover CIA operative who recruits novice Ritter to poise as dead agent so elaborate enemy plot can be foiled. Nifty premise gets swallowed up. C: James Belushi, John Ritter, Barbara Barrie, Bill Morey. D: Dennis Feldman. COM [PG-13] 86m. V

Reality Bites 1994 ★★★½ A smart, 20-something woman (Ryder) juggles a low-level job in TV and the two men (Hawke, Stiller) who are after her. Pleasant, old-fashioned romantic comedy updated with brand names and modern music; Ryder is wonderful, as usual. C: Winona Ryder, Ben Stiller, Ethan Hawke, Janeane Garofalo, Swoosie Kurtz, Joe Don Baker, John Mahoney, Steve Zahn. D: Ben Stiller. COM 98m. V

Really Weird Tales 1987 ★★★½ Three stories of comic horror, originally done by HBO, features SCTVeterans Short, Candy, and

O'Hara. Short is lounge singer who endures strange party; Candy plays con artist fleecing small town; O'Hara is product of orphanage, now endowed with killer love. Has its moments, the best of which are O'Hara's. C: John Candy, Catherine O'Hara, Martin Short. D: Paul Lynch. COM 85m. TVM V

Reap the Wild Wind 1942 ★★★★ Period adventure concerning two battling ship salvagers who vie for a strong-willed Georgia siren. Impressive DeMille entertainment with stirring undersea sequences. Special Effects Oscar for mechanical giant squid. C: Ray Milland, John Wayne, Paulette Goddard, Robert Preston, Susan Hayward. D: Cecil B. DeMille. DRA 123m. V

Rear Window 1954 ★★★★★ Bored, wheelchair-bound photographer (Stewart) spies on neighbors, to the horror of his girlfriend (Kelly). One day, he thinks he witnesses a murder, but nobody believes him. Stewart gives a fascinating performance in this classic Hitchcock, adapted from a Cornell Woolrich story. C: James Stewart, Grace Kelly, Wendell Corey, Thelma Ritter, Raymond Burr. D: Alfred Hitchcock. CRI [R] 112m. V

Rearview Mirror 1984 ★★★ Lunatic escaped convict hijacks a woman's car and they are both chased by the law through South Carolina countryside. Beck is very scary and Remick is very scared in this okay thriller. C: Lee Remick, Tony Musante, Michael Beck, Jim Antonio, Don Galloway, Ned Bridges. D: Lou Antonio. DRA 100m. TVM

Reason to Live, a Reason to Die, A 1974 Italian, French, German, Spanish ★★½ A Union colonel enlists the aid of seven condemned men in retaking a Missouri fort captured by Confederates. Uneven European-made Western. C: James Coburn, Telly Savalas, Bud Spencer, Robert Burton. D: Tonino Valerii. WST [PG] 92m. V

Rebecca 1940 ★★★★★ Young woman (Fontaine) marries mysterious, brooding widower (Olivier) with a past. Adaptation of Daphne du Maurier's gothic classic is a haunting tale of misguided passion. Anderson steals the show as the jealous housekeeper. Hitchcock's first American film won Oscar for Best Picture. C: Laurence Olivier, Joan Fontaine, George Sanders, Judith Anderson. D: Alfred Hitchcock. CRI 104m. V

Rebecca of Sunnybrook Farm 1917 ★★½ Pickford as the sparkling orphan heroine of the Kate Wiggins novel, sent to live with her flinty spinster aunts. Routine silent showcase for Pickford. C: Mary Pickford, Eugene O'Brien, Daw, Helen Jerome Eddy. D: Marshall Neilan. FAM/DRA 71m. V

Rebecca of Sunnybrook Farm 1938 ★★★½ Bearing no resemblance to the classic children's book, a talented child (Temple) is turned into radio darling by mentor (Scott). There's also time for a dance number between Temple and Robinson. Standard Temple vehicle. C: Shirley Temple, Randolph Scott, Jack Haley, Bill Robinson. D: Allan Dwan. FAM/DRA [G] 80m. V

Rebel 1986 Australian ★★ Drab musical drama about an American Army deserter in WWII who seeks the help of an Australian nightclub singer. Dillon is all wrong in this overdone misfire. C: Matt Dillon, Debbie Byrne, Bryan Brown, Bill Hunter. D: Michael Jenkins. MUS [R] 93m. V

Rebel in Town 1956 ★★★★ After his brother accidentally kills a boy, an ex-Confederate soldier tries to squelch resulting tensions in a small Western town. Taut psychological story that handles unusual premise with grace. Good cast makes story work. C: John Payne, Ruth Roman, J.Carroll Naish, Ben Cooper, John Smith. D: Alfred Werker. WST 78m.

Rebel Love 1985 ★★½ Overly mannered love story of a Confederate spy and Yankee widow. Tries too hard, misses. C: Jamie Rose, Terence Knox, Fran Ryan, Carl Spurlock. D: Milton Bagby Jr. DRA [R] 84m. V

Rebel Rousers 1967 ★★★ Psycho Dern stages a drag race with pregnant Ladd as first prize. Terrific low-budget camp for bad-movie mavens features talented cast of future stars gleefully overacting. Nicholson's wardrobe is unforgettable! C: Cameron Mitchell, Jack Nicholson, Bruce Dern, Diane Ladd, Harry Dean Stanton. D: Martin B. Cohen. DRA [R] 80m. V

Rebel Without a Cause 1955 ★★★★½ Alienated teenager finds love and friendship but runs afoul of parents, juvenile delinquents, and police. Prototype '50s-generation movie is somewhat dated but remains forceful. Sensitive performances from Dean, Wood, and Mineo. C: James Dean, Natalie Wood, Sal Mineo, Jim Backus, Corey Allen, Edward Platt, Dennis Hopper, Nick Adams. D: Nicholas Ray. DRA 111m. V

Rebellion 1967 Japanese ★★★★ Period Japanese tale about 18th-century shogun overlord whose power is challenged by young man who refuses to follow tradition and give up his wife. Fierce and bloody story of pride and prejudices, marked by good cast and well-staged sword fights. C: Toshiro Mifune, Takeshi Kato, Yoko Tsukasa. D: Masaki Kobayashi. ACT 120m.

Rebels, The 1979 ★★★½ A young American colonist (Stevens) fights in the Revolutionary War and encounters the Founding Fathers. Fair sequel to John Jakes' *The Bastard*, with a diverse cast, anchored by William Conrad's narration. Followed by *The Seekers*. C: Andrew Stevens, Don Johnson, Doug McClure, Richard Basehart, Joan Blondell, Tom Bosley, Macdonald Carey, Gwen Humble, Kim Cattrall, Kevin Tighe, Robert Vaughn, Anne Francis, Peter Graves. D: Russ Mayberry. DRA 200m. TVM V

Reckless 1935 ★★★ Glamorous dancer

forsakes her agent to wed wealthy alcoholic. Hackneyed backstage melodrama wastes stellar cast. Contrary to myth, MGM did make some lemons, and this was one of them. C: Jean Harlow, William Powell, Franchot Tone, May Robson, Rosalind Russell, Allan Jones, Mickey Rooney. D: Victor Fleming. DRA 96m. V

Reckless 1984 ★★★½ Straightlaced coed (Hannah) is attracted to guy from the gritty side of town. Honest look at class-snobbery, with solid performances by up-and-comers. Strong sexual content. C: Aidan Quinn, Daryl Hannah, Kenneth McMillan, Cliff DeYoung, Lois Smith. D: James Foley. DRA [R] 93m. V

Reckless Disregard 1984 ★★½ Poorly staged courtroom drama based on defamed doctor's lawsuit against *60 Minutes* correspondent Dan Rather. Flat, unsympathetic treatment. C: Tess Harpêr, Leslie Nielsen, Ronny Cox, Kate Lynch. D: Harvey Hart. DRA 92m. TVM V

Reckless Moment, The 1949 ★★★★½ Tense, layered excitement as a sympathetic murderer (Bennett) becomes the victim of a blackmailer (Mason). Well-crafted suspense. Grab it. C: James Mason, Joan Bennett, Geraldine Brooks, Henry O'Neill, Shepperd Strudwick. D: Max Ophuls. DRA 82m. V

Reckoning, The 1969 British ★★★½ A bitter businessman (Williamson) returns to his English village where his father lies sick and dying. He is determined to settle an old score with the villagers. Excellent performances and an interesting, offbeat story. C: Nicol Williamson, Rachel Roberts, Paul Rogers, Ann Bell. D: Jack Gold. DRA [R] 111m.

Red 1994 *See* **Trois Couleurs: Rouge**

Red Alert 1977 ★★★★ Crackling suspense about computers going haywire at a nuclear power plant. Adaptation of Harold King's novel, *Paradigm Red*, is a good issue drama that doesn't sacrifice excitement. C: William Devane, Michael Brandon, Adrienne Barbeau, Ralph Waite. D: William Hale. ACT 95m. TVM V

Red and the Black, The 1957 French ★★★★ Young man's climb up the social ladder in 19th-century France, first through religion, then career and romance. Movie adaptation of Stendal's novel is an intelligent adult drama, played with care and polish in all-around classy production. C: Gerard Philipe, Michelle Morgan, Danielle Darrieux. D: Claude Autant-Lara. DRA 134m. V

Red and the White, The 1968 Hungarian ★★★★ Epic portrayal of the civil war between the Bolshevik Red Army and the counterrevolutionary "Whites" in central Russia in 1918. Stirring, thoughtful, and thoroughly engaging. D: Miklos Jancso. DRA 92m. V

Red Badge of Courage, The 1951 ★★★★½ During the Civil War, a young man joins the Union Army, flees under fire but eventually returns. A literate and highly personalized meditation on cowardice, courage, and manhood; a fine adaptation of Stephen Crane's classic novel. Remade for TV in 1974. C: Audie Murphy, Bill Mauldin, Royal Dano, John Dierkes, Arthur Hunnicutt. D: John Huston. DRA 70m. V

Red Balloon, The 1956 French ★★★★★ Sublime children's classic about a French boy who is followed around Paris by a red balloon. Told largely without dialogue, it's a touching allegory for young people about loss and rebirth—with an ending that is both beautiful and exhilarating. C: Pascal Lamorisse, Roger Jacquet. D: Albert Lamorisse, Robert Enrico. FAM/DRA 34m. V

Red Beard 1965 Japanese ★★★★ Sprawling film centers on relationship between ambitious young intern and arrogant but brilliant doctor at a badly run-down health clinic. A nearly perfect combination of expert acting and direction, along with extraordinary physical production. C: Toshiro Mifune, Yuzo Kayama. D: Akira Kurosawa. DRA 185m. V

Red Dawn 1984 ★★½ Red, as in Commie menace; Dawn, as in when they invade Smalltown U.S.A.; mindless, as in one not necessary for viewing. Violent and subtle as a tank. For fans of teens-save-the-world genre only. C: Patrick Swayze, C. Thomas Howell, Lea Thompson, Charlie Sheen. D: John Milius. ACT [PG-13] 114m. V

Red Desert 1964 French, Italian ★★★★ A housewife (Vitti) slips into depression as she comes to grips with her dead-end marriage and her bleak surroundings. Antonioni effectively uses desolate locations to parallel and bring feeling to the woman's turmoil. C: Monica Vitti, Richard Harris. D: Michelangelo Antonioni. DRA 120m. V

Red Dust 1932 ★★★★½ Jungle plantation foreman (Gable) romances classy wife (Astor) of engineer (Raymond), despite the sultry presence of another woman. Zesty interplay between Harlow and Gable creates steamy jungle romance. For the love of mud, grab it. Remade as *Mogambo*. C: Clark Gable, Jean Harlow, Mary Astor, Donald Crisp, Gene Raymond, Tully Marshall, Willie Fung. D: Victor Fleming. ACT 83m. V

Red Garters 1954 ★★★½ Cowboy musical casts pop star Clooney as saloon dancer wooed by both Carson and Mitchell. Inventive use of stylized sets and dynamic choreography. C: Rosemary Clooney, Jack Carson, Guy Mitchell, Pat Crowley, Gene Barry, Cass Daley, Frank Faylen, Buddy Ebsen. D: George Marshall. MUS 91m. V

Red-Headed Stranger 1987 ★★★ It's not enough that the town preacher has a naughty wife. Now he has to deal with a bunch of marauders. Somewhat turgid drama adapted from Willie's record (!) that never gets itself going. Fairchild trashes herself with an abominable performance. C: Willie Nelson, Morgan Fairchild, Katharine Ross, Royal Dano, R. G. Armstrong. D: William Wittliff. WST [R] 109m. V

Red-Headed Woman 1932 ★★★½ Gold-digging shopgirl (Harlow) marries her boss (Morris) but can't crash society. Brassy entertainment with sizzling Harlow in engaging Anita Loos story. C: Jean Harlow, Chester Morris, Una Merkel, Lewis Stone, May Robson, Leila Hyams, Charles Boyer. D: Jack Conway. DRA 81m. V

Red Heat 1988 ★★★ Soviet police officer and his American counterpart go after drug lord. Interesting Moscow location shots; old story. C: Arnold Schwarzenegger, James Belushi, Peter Boyle, Ed O'Ross. D: Walter Hill. ACT [R] 106m. V

Red, Hot and Blue 1949 ★★★½ A chorus dancer (Hutton) unknowingly gets involved with comic crooks. Cole Porter's Broadway romp comes to the screen with a new plot and most of its score missing, but musical theatre fans should pounce on the chance to see the author of *Guys & Dolls* (Loesser) on screen. C: Betty Hutton, Victor Mature, William Demarest, June Havoc, Frank Loesser. D: John Farrow. MUS 84m.

Red Hot Tires 1935 ★★★ Auto racer (Talbot) goes to jail for killing another driver during a race, escapes and races in South America under a pseudonym while girlfriend (Astor) works to clear him. Average B-action melodrama with a lot of racing footage. C: Lyle Talbot, Mary Astor, Roscoe Karns, Frankie Darro. D: D. Ross Lederman. ACT 61m.

Red House, The 1947 ★★★★ Robinson plays a taciturn farmer obsessed with a guilty secret involving an ominous old house in the woods. Suspenseful thriller with sturdy acting. C: Edward G. Robinson, Lon McCallister, Judith Anderson, Rory Calhoun. D: Delmer Daves. DRA 95m. V

Red Inn, The 1951 French ★★½ A monk (Fernandel) discovers that inn proprietors are robbing and murdering travelers who stop for the night. Bizarre blend of comedy and brutal murder. C: Fernandel, Francoise Rosay, Carette, Gregoire Aslan, Marie-Claire Olivia. D: Claude Autant-Lara. COM 100m.

Red Kiss 1985 French ★★★★ Engaging tale of a French teenager of the '50s torn between belief in her parents' leftist views and her love for an older, apolitical American. Valandrey is appealing as the young woman caught between love and conscience. (a.k.a. *Rouge Baiser*) C: Charlotte Valandrey, Lambert Wilson, Marthe Keller, Gunter Lamprecht. D: Vera Belmont. DRA 110m. V

Red Lanterns 1965 Greek ★★★★ A quasi-sociological study of five prostitutes, working for a madam in the Greek port city of Piraeus, and how they got into the profession. Greek-made film takes a psychological perspective, without offering any moral judgements. C: Jenny Karezi, George Foundas, Mary Chronopoulou. D: Vassilis Georgiades. DRA 85m.

Red Line 7000 1965 ★★★½ Chronicle of American racing set, focusing on the romances, jealousies, and tragedies. Disjointed drama maintains a brisk pace due to excellent race footage, though keeping track of romantic subplots is a difficult task. C: James Caan, Laura Devon, Gail Hire, Charlene Holt, John Crawford. D: Howard Hawks. ACT 110m. V

Red Lion 1969 Japanese ★★★ A lowly groom, posing as a military officer in feudal Japan, winds up leading a rebellion against oppression in his village. Mifune is irrepressible as the reluctant revolutionary, but the film plods. C: Toshiro Mifune, Shima Iwashita. D: Kihachi Okamoto. DRA 115m. V

Red Mountain 1951 ★★★½ Confederate officer (Ladd) tries to stop mercenary outlaw Quantrill (Ireland), who seeks to establish his own empire. Good Western manages to retell the saga of Quantrill's Raiders from a slightly different perspective. C: Alan Ladd, Lizabeth Scott, John Ireland, Arthur Kennedy. D: William Dieterle. WST 84m.

Red Planet Mars 1952 ★★ Cold War sentiment extends into outer space as Earthlings get messages from the cosmos—perhaps even from God. Interesting artifact of its period. C: Peter Graves, Andrea King, Marvin Miller, Herbert Berghof, House Peters. D: Harry Horner. SFI 87m. V

Red Pony, The 1949 ★★★★ Young man is given a colt; he grows attached to the horse, but faces heartache when it runs away. Warm adaptation of John Steinbeck's novel, marked by good performances and wonderful Aaron Copland orchestral score. Later remade for television with Henry Fonda. C: Myrna Loy, Robert Mitchum, Peter Miles, Louis Calhern. D: Lewis Milestone. FAM/DRA 89m. V

Red Pony, The 1973 ★★★★ Terrific TV remake of the 1949 classic, with Fonda marvelous as the father of a young boy who has grown attached to his pet horse. From John Steinbeck's novella. Lovingly produced and beautifully cast. C: Henry Fonda, Maureen O'Hara, Ben Johnson, Clint Howard, Jack Elam, Richard Jaeckel. D: Robert Totten. FAM/DRA 100m. TVM

Red Riding Hood 1988 ★★★½ Isabella Rossellini narrates this musical children's video of young girl who encounters big bad wold while en route to her grandmother's house. Average telling of well-known story. C: Craig T. Nelson, Rocco Sisto, Isabella Rossellini. FAM/MUS [G] 84m. TVM V

Red River 1948 ★★★★★ Hard cattle men forge the Chisholm Trail as an empire-building father vows to kill his son should they meet again. Brilliant landmark Western. Superbly acted and directed. Memorable action, photography and climax. C: John Wayne, Montgomery Clift, Walter Brennan, Joanne Dru, John Ireland, Coleen Gray. D: Howard Hawks. WST 133m. V

Red River Valley 1941 ★★★½ Roy tries to get the goods on a gambler who has conned the townspeople out of money for a new reservoir. Early Rogers B-Western boosted by good music, including performances by the Sons of the Pioneers (Rogers' former musical group). C: Roy Rogers, George "Gabby" Hayes, Sally Payne, Gale Storm. D: Joseph Kane. WST 62m.

Red Rock West 1993 ★★★★ Four murderers out-trick each other in ingeniously plotted tribute to classic film noir. Nothing is what it appears to be in this stylish thriller by a clever suspense director to keep watching in years to come. First shown on cable, then released to theatres. C: Nicolas Cage, Dennis Hopper, Lara Flynn Boyle, J.T. Walsh. D: John Dahl. CRI [R] 110m. V

Red Rope, The 1937 ★★★½ Hero interrupts his honeymoon to investigate mysterious murders of ranchers. Interesting Western/mystery with fast action and plot twists. C: Bob Steele, Lois January, Forrest Taylor. D: S. Roy Luby. WST 56m.

Red Roses for the Führer 1969 *See* **Code Name, Red Roses**

Red Scorpion 1989 ★ Grunting Lundgren plays a Soviet spy dispatched to Africa to assassinate a rebel leader. Sleep-inducing. C: Dolph Lundgren, M. Emmet Walsh, Al White, T. P. McKenna, Carmen Argenziano, Brion James, Alex Colon. D: Joseph Zito. ACT [R] 100m. V

Red Shoes, The 1948 British ★★★★★ Classic ballet film mixes melodramatic tale of dancer torn between her art and the man she loves with stunning photography and vivid use of color. Brilliant set piece title ballet is justly famous. Two Oscars for score, art direction. C: Emeric Pressburger, Anton Walbrook, Marius Goring, Moira Shearer, Robert Helpmann. D: Michael Powell. MUS 133m. V

Red Skies of Montana 1952 ★★★ Action drama about heroic lives of forest firefighters. Breathtakingly exciting fire sequences. C: Richard Widmark, Jeffrey Hunter, Constance Smith, Richard Boone, Richard Crenna, Charles Buchinsky. D: Joseph M. Newman. ACT 89m.

Red Sky at Morning 1970 ★★★★ Two teenagers fall in love during WWII. Small, sensitive coming-of-age film. Beautifully acted and rewarding. C: Richard Thomas, Catherine Burns, Desi Arnaz, Jr., Richard Crenna, Claire Bloom. D: James Goldstone. DRA [PG] 112m.

Red Sonja 1985 ★★½ Woman warriors vs. the bad queen. Typical sword action. C: Brigitte Nielsen, Arnold Schwarzenegger, Sandahl Bergman, Paul Smith. D: Richard Fleischer. ACT [PG-13] 89m. V

Red Sorghum 1987 Chinese ★★★★½ A rural wheat field is the scene of love, violence and death in Yimou's powerful, epic fantasy of Chinese village life from the '20s through Japanese occupation in WWII. Brimming with pathos, rich in character, and masterfully photographed and directed. C: Gong Li, Jiang Wen, Ji Cun Hua. D: Zhang Yimou. DRA 95m. V

Red Stallion in the Rockies, The 1949 ★★★ Ranchers hunt a wild horse that's raiding their corrals. Colorado Rockies provide beautiful backdrop to this animal drama. C: Arthur Franz, Wallace Ford, Ray Collins, Jean Heather, Leatrice Joy. D: Ralph Murphy. WST 85m.

Red Stallion, The 1947 ★★★ A boy (Donaldson) hopes that the foal he raised to be a racehorse can save his grandma's ranch from foreclosure. Beautiful outdoor photography and exciting animal scenes. C: Robert Paige, Noreen Nash, Ted Donaldson, Jane Darwell. D: Lesley Selander. DRA 82m. V

Red Sun 1971 Italian, French, Spanish ★★★★ An Arizona outlaw steals a rare Japanese samurai sword and is pursued by samurai determined to get it back. Intriguing idea delivered by a swell international cast. C: Charles Bronson, Ursula Andress, Toshiro Mifune, Alain Delon, Capucine. D: Terence Young. WST [PG] 115m. V

Red Tent, The 1969 Italian, Russian ★★★★ Survival drama based on true story of fateful blimp expedition to the North Pole in 1928. Plenty of excitement and game cast. C: Sean Connery, Claudia Cardinale, Hardy Kruger, Peter Finch. D: Mikhail Kalatozov. ACT [G] 121m. V

Red, White, and Busted 1972 *See* **Outside In**

Redhead and the Cowboy, The 1950 ★★½ A saloon dancer turned Confederate courier (Fleming) mistakes cowhand (Ford) for a Southern spy. Plenty of action. C: Glenn Ford, Rhonda Fleming, Edmond O'Brien, Morris Ankrum. D: Leslie Fenton. WST 82m.

Redhead from Wyoming, The 1952 ★★★½ Dance-hall queen (O'Hara) rustles cattle on the side, but her feelings for the sheriff cause her to waiver between the law and the lawless. Feisty O'Hara gives it kick. C: Maureen O'Hara, Alexander Scourby, Alex Nicol, Jack Kelly, William Bishop, Dennis Weaver. D: Lee Sholem. WST 80m.

Reds 1981 ★★★★½ Remarkable story of John Reed (Beatty), famed journalist who covered the Russian Revolution, and his love for the unconventional Louise Bryant (Keaton). Outstanding cast; interesting narrative technique intercutting real-life interviews with fictional recreation and production values on an epic scale. Dominant, charismatic performance from Beatty, who won the Oscar for his directing. So did the cinematography and Stapleton (Supporting Actress). C: Warren Beatty, Diane Keaton, Edward Herrmann, Jerzy Kosinski, Jack Nicholson, Maureen Stapleton, Nicolas Coster, Gene Hackman, William Daniels. D: Warren Beatty. DRA [PG] 195m. V

Reefer Madness 1936 ★★ Good kids take a puff of the demon weed and descend into the lower depths, leading to self-destruction! Camp classic was originally designed to warn viewers about the dangers of marijuana, but histrionic presentation and delightfully bad acting make for unintentionally funny viewing. (a.k.a. *Tell Your Children* and *The Burning Question*) C: Dave O'Brien, Dorothy Short, Lillian Miles, Kenneth Craig. D: Louis Gasnier. COM 64m. V

Ref, The 1994 ★★★½ Dark comedy of a dysfunctional family held hostage by a thief (Leary) at Christmas, who ends up caught in the middle of their multiple feuds and neuroses. Biting, often bleak film is hilarious, aided by solid performances. C: Denis Leary, Judy Davis, Kevin Spacey, Glynis Johns, Robert J. Steinmiller, Jr., Raymond J. Barry, Richard Bright. D: Ted Demme. COM [R] 93m. V

Reflecting Skin, The 1991 British ★★★ Youngster believes his neighbor, an attractive young widow, is a vampire. No one buys it, of course, least of all his brother, who starts an affair with her. Strange, artistic stunner; not for everyone. C: Viggo Mortensen, Lindsay Duncan, Jeremy Cooper. D: Philip Ridley. DRA [R] 98m. V

Reflection of Fear, A 1972 ★★★½ A disturbed young girl may have an alter ego responsible for criminal acts and murder. Psychological mystery, with handsome photography and a first-rate cast. C: Robert Shaw, Mary Ure, Sally Kellerman, Sondra Locke, Signe Hasso. D: William A. Fraker. DRA [PG] 90m. V

Reflections in a Golden Eye 1967 ★★★ Lurid tale of a warped, closeted homosexual army captain (Brando) married to an adulteress (Taylor); from the superior Carson McCullers novel. High-tone trash. C: Elizabeth Taylor, Marlon Brando, Julie Harris, Brian Keith, Robert Forster. D: John Huston. DRA 108m. V

Reflections of Murder ★★★★ A teacher (Waterson) has so incensed his wife and mistress that they scheme to murder him. When dead, his presence is felt more than before. Gem of a chiller with fresh twists; good American remake of the French classic *Diabolique*. C: Tuesday Weld, Joan Hackett, Sam Waterston, Lucille Benson, Michael Lerner, Lanie Kermin. D: John Badham. CRI 97m. V

Reform School Girl 1957 ★ Hot-rodding weasel runs over pedestrian, blames killing on his girlfriend, she's sent to reformatory. Standard '50s women-in-prison fare. C: Gloria Castillo, Ross Ford, Edward Byrnes, Ralph Reed, Sally Kellerman. D: Edward Bernds. ACT 72m. V

Reform School Girls 1986 ★★½ Another innocent runs afoul of the penal system in this broad spoof of female penitentiary cliches. Witless cast includes the world's oldest teenager (Williams) and former Warhol star Ast. C: Linda Carol, Wendy O. Williams, Pat Ast, Sybil Danning. D: Tom DeSimone. ACT [R] 94m. V

Reformer and the Redhead, The 1950 ★★★ Staid mayoral candidate (Powell) tries to keep a rein on unpredictable girlfriend (Allyson) lest his reputation suffer. Disorganized comedy tends to get very wacky. C: June Allyson, Dick Powell, David Wayne, Cecil Kellaway, Ray Collins. D: Norman Panama, Melvin Frank. COM 90m.

Regal Cavalcade 1935 ★★★½ The 25-year reign of King George V of England is chronicled through the journeys of a penny. Interesting idea (penny buying coronation program, in the pocket of a soldier, etc.). (a.k.a. *Royal Cavalcade.*) C: Hermione Baddeley, Esme Percy, John Mills, C.M. Hallard. D: Thomas Bentley, Herbert Brenon, Norman Lee, Walter Summers, Will Kellino, Marcel Varnel. DRA 100m.

Regarding Henry 1991 ★★★½ Brain injury has soulless lawyer rebuilding his life and discovering formerly unfelt humanity. Sedately done, good performances, though potential power isn't fully realized. C: Harrison Ford, Annette Bening, Bill Nunn, Mikki Allen, Donald Moffat. D: Mike Nichols. DRA [PG-13] 107m. V

Regenerated Man, The 1994 ★★★ A scientist, forced by bad guys to swallow some of his own chemicals, transforms into a monster that kills criminals. Homage to '50s B-movies adds gruesome special effects—and not much else to the old formula. C: Arthur Lundquist, Cheryl Hendricks, Andrew Featherolf, Greg Sullivan, Pete DeLorenzo. D: Ted A. Bohus. HOR [R] 92m.

Reilly: The Ace of Spies 1984 British ★★★★ Actual pre-Bond spy Reilly (Neill) steals valuable information from under Russian noses circa 1900, and, of course, beds the enemy. British espionage series is intelligent and atmospheric. Great Neill. C: Sam Neill, Sebastian Shaw, Jean-anne Crowley, Leo McKern. D: Jim Goddard. DRA 80m. V

Reincarnation of Peter Proud, The 1975 ★★★½ A murdered man's soul returns in Sarrazin's body, causing havoc. Max Ehrlich's novel makes a reasonably suspenseful thriller. C: Michael Sarrazin, Jennifer O'Neill, Margot Kidder. D: J. Lee Thompson. HOR [R] 104m. V

Reivers, The 1969 ★★★★½ In early 20th-century South, youngster goes on cross-country road trip with roguish adult McQueen. Based on novel by William Faulkner (and narrated by Burgess Meredith), this ambling comedy makes the most of episodic format, marvelously showcasing unique side of American life. Terrific performance by McQueen. C: Steve McQueen, Sharon Farrell, Will Geer, Michael Constantine. D: Mark Rydell. COM [PG] 107m. V

Relentless 1989 ★★★ L.A. serial killer (Nelson) frustrates the cops assigned to capture him. Standard thriller with convincing Nelson. C: Judd Nelson, Robert Loggia, Leo Rossi, Meg Foster. D: William Lustig. CRI [R] 92m. V

Relentless 2: Dead On 1991 ★ Violent sequal aims to show the effects serial killer from original *Relentless* had on victims who survived. C: Leo Rossi, Ray Sharkey, Meg Foster. D: Michael Schroeder. CRI [R] 93m. V

Reluctant Astronaut, The 1967 ★★½ A coward (Knotts) goes through rigorous astronaut training, despite his fears and phobias. Juvenile comedy has a good supporting cast, but is recommended mainly for those who enjoy watching Knotts do his trademark shtick. C: Don Knotts, Leslie Nielsen, Joan Freeman, Arthur O'Connell, Jesse White. D: Edward Montagne. COM 101m.

Reluctant Debutante, The 1958 ★★★★½ Two old world parents (Kendall and Harrison) have to present their thoroughly modern daughter to society. Stars were happily married to each other in real life and it shows. Exquisite; one of Minnelli's best comedies. Kendall wins top acting honors here. C: Rex Harrison, Kay Kendall, John Saxton, Sandra Dee, Angela Lansbury. D: Vincente Minnelli. COM 94m. V

Reluctant Dragon, The 1941 ★★★★½ Humorist Benchley receives a behind-the-scenes tour of the Walt Disney Studios, interspersed with Disney cartoons. A rare and entertaining opportunity to see some of Disney's early animators and voice actors at work. Includes title cartoon short. C: Robert Benchley. D: Alfred Werker. COM 72m.

Remains of the Day 1983 ★★★★★ Merchant/Ivory gem about an emotionally repressed butler (Hopkins), his unquestioning loyalty to the man and manor he serves, and his relationship with a headstrong housekeeper (Thompson). As expected, visually impeccable, and Hopkins is positively brilliant in a role that would crush most actors. From the Kazuo Ishiguro novel. C: Anthony Hopkins, Emma Thompson, Christopher Reeve, James Fox, Hugh Grant. D: James Ivory. DRA [PG] 134m. V

Remarkable Andrew, The 1942 ★★★★ The ghost of President Andrew Jackson (Donleavy) helps a young man (Holden) in his quest for small-town justice. Sleeper comedy casts a warm, modest glow. Script by Dalton Trumbo. C: William Holden, Brian Donlevy, Ellen Drew. D: Stuart Heisler. COM 80m.

Remarkable Mr. Kipps, The 1941 *See* **Kipps**

Remarkable Mr. Pennypacker, The 1959 ★★★ The story of a turn-of-the-century scoundrel (Webb) who has two different large families. Uneven adaptation of Broadway play; Webb gives his usual fussy performance. C: Clifton Webb, Dorothy McGuire, Charles Coburn, Ray Stricklyn, Jill St. John, Ron Ely, David Nelson. D: Henry Levin. COM 87m.

Rembrandt 1936 British ★★★★½ Biography of the great Dutch painter of the 17th century. Laughton shows good restraint in the title role of this beautifully mounted film biography. Fine drama has all the richness of Rembrandt's paintings. C: Charles Laughton, Elsa Lanchester, Gertrude Lawrence, Edward Chapman, Roger Livesey, Marius Goring. D: Alexander Korda. DRA 84m. V

Remember the Night 1940 ★★★★½ Touching, well-acted comedy/drama, with a script by Preston Sturges. Shoplifter (Stanwyck) spends court's Christmas recess in the custory of prosecutor (MacMurray). Their travels to his hometown and her subsequent transformation provide excellent holiday viewing. C: Barbara Stanwyck, Fred MacMurray, Beulah Bondi, Elizabeth Patterson, Sterling Holloway. D: Mitchell Leisen. COM 94m.

Remembrance 1982 British ★★★½ Grim study of a group of sailors and their last 24 hours in England before setting sail. Modern allegory for the decline of the British empire presents an unattractive contemporary landscape dotted with seedy discos, drinking, sex, and violence. Dank doings. C: John Altman, Al Ashton, Sally Jane Jackson, Gary Oldman. D: Colin Gregg. DRA 117m.

Remo Williams: The Adventure Begins 1985 ★★★½ NYC cop (Ward) a novice in a supersecret agency, must cope with a wise, wisecracking Korean teacher (Grey). Enjoyable, lighthearted adventure/spy yarn with an exciting fight sequence on the Statue of Liberty, highlighted by Ward and Grey's repartee. Based on the *Destroyer* books by Richard Sapir and Warren Murphy. C: Fred Ward, Joel Grey, Wilford Brimley, Kate Mulgrew. D: Guy Hamilton. ACT [PG-13] 121m. V

Remote 1993 ★★★½ A 13-year-old electronics prodigy makes trouble with his collection of "toys." Some nasty stuff that has a real bite to it. C: Chris Carrara, Jessica Bowman, John Diehl. D: Ted Nicolaou. SFI [PG] 80m. V

Removalists, The 1975 Australian ★★★½ Two cops almost kill an abusive husband while helping his wife retrieve furniture, then strike a deal with him so he won't talk. Uneven adaptation of Australian stage play about abuse of sex and power by authority. C: John Hargreaves, Peter Cummins, Kate Fitzpatrick. D: Tom Jeffrey. DRA 88m.

Renaissance Man 1994 ★★★★ DeVito gets sacked from his advertising job, starts temping. His first assignment, teaching English to nearly illiterate Army enlistees, is a success thanks to his off-the-wall teaching methods. Amusing entertainment, largely thanks to DeVito and Hines. C: Danny DeVito, Gregory Hines, Ed Begley, Jr., James Remar, Cliff Robertson, Lillo Brancato, Stacey Dash, Kadeem Hardison. D: Penny Marshall. COM 129m.

Renaldo and Clara 1978 ★★½ At its original length of nearly five hours, this was intolerable Dylan self-indulgence, intercut with concert footage of 1976's Rolling Thunder Revue. Some prints now run only 122 minutes, with mostly the songs left. That version should be of interest to fans of 1970's folk-rock. C: Bob Dylan, Sara Dylan, Sam Shepard, Ronnie Hawkins, Ronee Blakley, Joni Mitchell, Joan Baez, Arlo Guthrie, Roberta Flack. D: Bob Dylan. MUS [R] 292m/122m.

Rendez-vous 1985 French ★★★½ A promiscuous actress (Binoche) becomes involved in a kinky sexual underground inhabited by sex show performer (Wilson) and director (Trintignant). Unsettling French study of demimonde lifestyles is simultaneously riveting and repellent. C: Juliette Binoche, Lambert Wilson, Wadeck Stanczak, Jean-Louis Trintignant. D: Andre Techine. DRA 82m. v

Rendezvous 1935 ★★★½ Newspaper puzzle editor (Powell) is disappointed with his desk assignment during WWI, until he manages to crack an espionage ring. Uneasy blend of war intrigue and comedy has moments, plus ever-reliable Powell. C: William Powell, Rosalind Russell, Binnie Barnes, Lionel Atwill, Cesar Romero. D: William U. Howard. DRA 91m.

Rendezvous with Annie 1946 ★★★ WWII vet (Albert) tries to prove that his wife's baby is the result of his secretly going AWOL nine months earlier. Postwar comedy has promising premise, colorful supporting cast, and some laughs. C: Eddie Albert, Faye Marlowe, Gail Patrick, Phillip Reed, C. Aubry Smith, Raymond Walburn, William Frawley. D: Allan Dwan. COM 89m.

Renegade Girls 1974 *See* **Caged Heat**

Renegade Ranger 1938 ★★★ Texas Ranger (O'Brien) helps townspeople stop a crooked, land-grabbing politician. Good O'Brien outing features an early Hayworth and good Western music. C: George O'Brien, Rita Hayworth, Tim Holt. D: David Howard. WST 60m.

Renegades 1930 ★★★ Baxter and Beery desert the Foreign Legion, then meet up with Loy in atypical role of sultry femme fatale. Antique curio has some robust action sequences to recommend it. C: Warner Baxter, Myrna Loy, Noah Beery, Bela Lugosi. D: Victor Fleming. ACT 84m.

Renegades 1989 ★★★ A Lakota Indian (Phillips) and a young Philadelphia cop (Sutherland) are thrown together in the search for a band of criminals. As in most police buddy movies, they don't get along but begin to depend on each other when the action gets hot. C: Kiefer Sutherland, Lou Diamond Phillips, Jami Gertz, Rob Knepper. D: Jack Sholder. CRI [R] 105m. v

Renfrew of the Mounties James Newill starred in this short-lived series of hour-long B-movies about the square-jawed, red-coated Renfrew, hero of a kids' radio series. He sang heartily and fought criminals north of the border, but the series may seem a bit antique today.

Renfrew of the Royal Mounted (1937)
On the Great White Trail (1938)

Reno 1939 ★★★ In Reno's early days, young lawyer takes advantage of Nevada's lenient laws to make city the divorce capital, while simultaneously neglecting his wife and sowing the seeds of his own divorce. Interesting historical drama. C: Richard Dix, Gail Patrick, Anita Louise, Laura Hope Crews. D: John Farrow. WST 73m.

Rent-a-Cop 1988 ★ A tart with a heart of gold (Minnelli) is an eyewitness to a fatal drug bust which threatens to end a cop's (Reynolds) career. This turkey almost ended theirs. C: Burt Reynolds, Liza Minnelli, Richard Masur, Dionne Warwick, Robby Benson. D: Jerry London. ACT [R] 96m. v

Rent Control 1981 ★★★½ A writer (Spiner)—abandoned by his wife—tries to get a rent-controlled apartment in Manhattan, while becoming involved in a newspaper's attempt to pin a murder charge on a Senator. Low-budget comedy marked by a witty script, along with good performances. C: Brent Spiner, Elizabeth Stack, Leonard Melfi. D: Gian L. Polidoro. COM 95m.

Repeat Performance 1947 ★★★★ On New Year's Eve, a remorseful stage star gets a chance to relive the previous year. Engrossing film noir features sensational Basehart. C: Louis Hayward, Joan Leslie, Tom Conway, Benay Venuta, Richard Basehart, Virginia Field. D: Alfred L. Werker. DRA 93m.

Repentance 1988 Russian ★★★½ Political intrigue accompanies disinterment of the body of a city father in Soviet Georgia. Intriguing if uneven Russian-made indictment of how Stalin-influenced repression smothered the individuality of rural Soviet states. C: Avtandil Mukharadze, Zeinab Botsvadze. D: Tenghiz Abuladze. DRA [PG] 157m. v

Repo Man 1983 ★★★★ Almost indescribable comedy involves young man (Estevez) persuaded to take job repossessing cars who becomes involved with various eccentrics and dead aliens in a car trunk. Unique style and solid lineup of character actors give this one its juice. A cult classic. C: Emilio Estevez, Harry Dean Stanton, Vonetta McGee, Olivia Barash, Tracey Walter. D: Alex Cox. COM [R] 92m. v

Report to the Commissioner 1974 ★★★½ Rookie cop (Moriarty) becomes a fall guy when he accidentally kills an undercover cop at the home of a drug dealer. Exposé of police department cover-ups survives shaky plot turns. Intriguing cast, including Gere in his film debut. C: Michael Moriarty, Yaphet Kotto, Susan Blakely, Hector Elizondo, Tony King, Richard Gere. D: Milton Katselas. DRA [PG] 113m. v

Repossessed 1990 ★★½ Low-grade *Exorcist* spoof has Blair as housewife taken over by an evil spirit and Nielsen as exorcist. A few honest laughs from off-color humor. C: Linda Blair, Ned Beatty, Leslie Nielsen, Anthony Starke. D: Bob Logan. COM [PG-13] 89m. V

Reptilicus 1962 ★★ Danish-filmed attempt at a giant monster movie features one of the least convincing movie creatures ever, a prehistoric beast that regenerates from an unearthed hunk of flesh. Awful, but good for laughs. C: Carl Ottosen, Ann Smyrner, Mimi Heinrich, Asbjorn Andersen, Marla Behrens. D: Sidney Pink. SFI 90m.

Repulsion 1965 British ★★★★★ Emotionally unstable woman (Deneuve) goes to pieces when left alone in her sister's apartment. Polanski's study in sexual repression is unforgettable. Minimal dialogue, visual imagery, and Deneuve's physicality dominate. A horror classic. C: Catherine Deneuve, Ian Hendry, Yvonne Furneaux. D: Roman Polanski. HOR 105m. V

Requiem for a Gunfighter 1965 ★★★ Mistaken for a judge, gunslinger (Cameron) decides to play along to ensure conviction of bad guy. Familiar cast. C: Rod Cameron, Stephen McNally, Mike Mazurki, Olive Sturgess, Tim McCoy, John Mack Brown, Bob Steele, Lane Chandler, Raymond Hatton. D: Spencer C. Bennet. WST 91m.

Requiem for a Heavyweight 1962 ★★★★ A washed-up fighter (Quinn) attempts to find a job after his misguided boxing career ends. Feature version of *Playhouse 90* TV drama packs a powerful punch in its indictment of corruption in the fight game. C: Anthony Quinn, Jackie Gleason, Mickey Rooney, Julie Harris. D: Ralph Nelson. DRA 100m.

Rescue, The 1988 ★★ Teenage sons of captured Navy Seals rescue them when government won't. Threadbare, flagwaving nonsense. C: Kevin Dillon, Christina Harnos, Marc Price, Charles Haid, Edward Albert. D: Ferdinand Fairfax. ACT [PG] 97m. V

Rescuers, The 1977 ★★★★ Entertaining Disney feature about two mice who found a rescue society, then save girl from kidnappers who are after a diamond. Newhart and Gabor do terrific lead voices and supporting cast is excellent. Animation fans of all ages will enjoy. Followed by *The Rescuers Down Under*. C: John Lounsbery, Art Stevens, Bob Newhart, Eva Gabor, Geraldine Page, Joe Flynn, Jeanette Nolan, Pat Buttram, Jim Jordan, John McIntire. D: Wolfgang Reitherman. FAM/DRA [G] 77m. V

Rescuers Down Under, The 1991 ★★★★ Sequel to *The Rescuers* finds mice Newhart and Gabor taking their rodent rescue society to Australia, where they help young boy plagued by villainous elder. Animation is not quite up to standards of original, but story is still a treat and characters are delightful. Voices of Bob Newhart, Eva Gabor, George Scott, John Candy, Tristan Rogers, Adam Ryen, Frank Welker. D: Hendel Butoy, Mike Gabriel. FAM/DRA [G] 77m. V

Reserved for Ladies 1932 British ★★★½ A London waiter (Howard) poses as a prince in the Austrian Tyrol to be worthy of upper-class Allan. First British-made directorial effort by Korda is a remake of the 1927 *Service for Ladies*. Witty comedy is now a tad dated, but still holds up. C: Leslie Howard, George Grossmith, Benita Hume, Elizabeth Allan, Cyril Richard, Merle Oberon. D: Alexander Korda. COM 71m.

Reservoir Dogs 1992 ★★★★½ Impressive debut by writer/director Tarantino. Witty, violent ensemble piece about conflict among thieves after aborted jewel robbery. Inventive use of limited resources (filmed mostly in an abandoned warehouse-garage), and terrific acting. However, violence is extremely graphic and may be upsetting. C: Harvey Keitel, Tim Roth, Michael Madsen, Chris Penn, Steve Buscemi, Lawrence Tierney. D: Quentin Tarantino. CRI [R] 100m. V

Resistance 1994 Australian ★★★½ Tribal woman (Jones) leads rebellion against military coup. Stunning photography is strong point of this rambling look at political tensions on the Australian outback. C: Helen Jones, Lorna Lesley, Stephen Leeder, Robyn Nevin. D: Paul Elliot, Hugh Keays-Byrne. DRA 112m.

Rest in Pieces 1987 ★ A demonic cult wreaks havoc in an old Spanish mansion when a young woman who's inherited the place comes to claim it. Lots of blood. C: Scott Thompson Baker, Lorin Jean, Dorothy Malone. D: Joseph Braunstein. HOR 90m. V

Rest Is Silence, The 1960 German ★★★½ A young man tries to prove that his uncle murdered his father. Clever German updating of *Hamlet* incorporates many references to the original. C: Hardy Kruger, Pete Von Eyck, Ingrid Andree, Adelheid Seeck, Rudolf Forster, Boy Gobert. D: Helmut Kautner. DRA 106m.

Resurrected, The 1991 ★★★ Gratifyingly serious and faithful adaptation of H.P. Lovecraft's *The Case of Charles Dexter Ward*, with Sarandon attempting to continue his ancestor's attempts to raise the dead. Often creepy, though multiple flashback structure is a distracting drawback. C: John Terry, Jane Sibbett, Chris Sarandon. D: Dan O'Bannon. HOR [R] 108m. V

Resurrection 1980 ★★★★ Thoughtful, moving tale of woman who emerges from deadly auto accident with the ability to heal others with her touch. Provocative tale of faith and spirituality, with a terrific cast. C: Ellen Burstyn, Sam Shepard, Roberts Blossom, Eva LeGallienne. D: Daniel Petrie. DRA [PG] 102m. V

Resurrection of Zachary Wheeler, The 1971 ★★★ Reporter (Nielsen) stumbles onto a top-secret medical clinic in New Mexico where a senator has been taken after a car crash. Odd sci-fi mystery. C: Angie Dickinson, Bradford Dillman, Leslie Nielsen. D: Bob Wynn. SFI [G] 100m. v

Retreat, Hell! 1952 ★★★½ During the Korean War, a massive Chinese offensive sends a unit of Marines into retreat. Standard war drama. C: Frank Lovejoy, Richard Carlson, Russ Tamblyn, Anita Louise. D: Joseph H. Lewis. DRA 95m. v

Retribution 1988 ★★★ After surviving suicide attempt, Lipscomb discovers he's been possessed by restless soul who's bent on bloody revenge. More emphasis on characterization here than usual, though there are plenty of shocking moments as well. C: Dennis Lipscomb, Leslie Wing, Suzanne Snyder, Hoyt Axton. D: Guy Magar. HOR [R] 107m. v

Return 1988 ★★ Questioning her grandfather's mysterious passing, woman hooks up with man whose forays into the occult may provide answers. So-so handling of good idea. C: Karlene Crockett, John Walcutt, Lisa Richards, Frederic Forrest, Anne Lloyd Francis. D: Andrew Silver. DRA [R] 78m. v

Return from the Sea 1954 ★★★½ Seaman (Brand) and waitress (Sterling) meet and fall in love in San Diego, then put wedding on hold while he serves in Korea. Low-key romance benefits from well-layered performance by Sterling. C: Jan Sterling, Neville Brand, John Doucette, Paul Langton, John Pickard. D: Lesley Selander. DRA 80m.

Return from Witch Mountain 1978 ★★★★ Disney's sequel to *Escape to Witch Mountain* features Lee and Davis as villains who kidnap a youngster with unusual powers (Eisenman) but for different purposes: Lee hungers for world power while Davis wants quick wealth. Well-played family entertainment. C: Bette Davis, Christopher Lee, Ike Eisenman. D: John Hough. FAM/DRA [G] 93m. v

Return of a Man Called Horse, The 1976 ★★★★ A former captive of the Sioux returns from his home in England to help them confront white settlers and the U.S. Army. Powerful, intelligent sequel. C: Richard Harris, Gale Sondergaard, Geoffrey Lewis, William Lucking. D: Irvin Kershner. WST [PG] 125m. v

Return of a Stranger 1961 British ★★★½ A paroled psychopath returns to stalk a former victim (Stephen) and her husband (Ireland). Creepy British suspense thriller packs plenty of tension, and features taut direction. C: John Ireland, Susan Stephen, Cyril Shaps, Timothy Beaton. D: Max Varnel. DRA 63m.

Return of Dr. Mabuse, The 1961 German ★★★½ Inspector (Frobe) teams with FBI agent (Barker) and reporter (Lavi) to stop a master criminal from attacking a nuclear reactor using zombie-like slaves. Silly but fun madman-on-the-loose plot. C: Gert Frobe, Lex Barker, Daliah Lavi. D: Harald Reinl. DRA 88m.

Return of Dr. X, The 1939 ★★★ A scientist revives zombie doctor (Bogart), who must kill to maintain his blood supply. Silly mad doctor horror movie gets boost now from fun of seeing Bogart as a zombie. C: Humphrey Bogart, Rosemary Lane, Dennis Morgan, John Litel, Huntz Hall, Wayne Morris. D: Vincent Sherman. HOR 62m.

Return of Dracula, The 1958 ★★★½ The nefarious count masquerades as a refugee artist in sunny California while devastating the locals with his lethal charms. Remarkably well-put-together film considering the small budget. C: Francis Lederer, Norma Eberhardt, Ray Stricklyn, Jimmie Baird. D: Paul Landres. HOR [PG] 77m. v

Return of Fist of Fury 1977 ★★½ Bruce Le, shows off his martial arts stuff in tale of gut-wrenching violence. C: Bruce Le. ACT 88m.

Return of Frank James, The 1940 ★★★★ Frank James (Fonda) seeks revenge against man who killed his brother. Excellent sequel to *Jesse James* features strong performance by Fonda and atmospheric direction. C: Henry Fonda, Gene Tierney, Jackie Cooper, John Carradine. D: Fritz Lang. WST 92m. v

Return of Godzilla, The 1959 *See* **Gigantis, the Fire Monster**

Return of Jafar, The 1994 ★★★½ Animated, direct-to-video sequel to the Disney favorite *Aladdin* brings back the villainous Jafar to exact his revenge on the young hero and Princess Jasmine. Subsequently shown on the tv series. Entertaining, but inferior to the first film—visually, in particular. Voices of Jason Alexander, Dan Castellaneta, Liz Callaway, Gilbert Gottfried, Jonathan Freeman. D: Toby Shelton, Tad Stones, Alan Zaslove. FAM/COM [G] 66m. TVM v

Return of Jesse James, The 1950 ★★★½ Petty outlaw (Ireland) finds that he can successfully pretend to be Jesse James, until the remaining members of the James gang find out. Low-budget Western benefits from a light touch and the persuasive Ireland. C: John Ireland, Ann Dvorak, Henry Hull, Hugh O'Brian, Reed Hadley. D: Arthur Hilton. WST 75m.

Return of Jimmy Valentine, The 1936 ★★★ A reward is offered to find a notorious old safecracker, and the search leads to a small town and some scheming nemeses. Interesting B-movie mystery. C: Roger Pryor, Charlotte Henry, Robert Warwick, Edgar Kennedy. D: Lewis D. Collins. DRA 67m.

Return of Martin Guerre, The 1984 French ★★★★½ A soldier (Depardieu) returns to his wife and village in France in the 1500s seemingly a better person and husband. Soon his very existence is questioned in a trial claiming he is an imposter. Gripping plot and solid acting. Remade in the U.S. as *Sommersby.* C: Gerard Depardieu, Nathalie Baye, Roger Planchon. D: Daniel Vigne. DRA 111m. v

Return of Maxwell Smart, The 1980 *See* **Nude Bomb, The**

Return of Monte Cristo, The 1946 ★★★½ The nephew of the famous count gets imprisoned on Devil's Island in order to keep him from claiming the inheritance of Monte Cristo. Costumer pales next to original Dumas tale, but swashbuckling action keeps things interesting and enjoyable. C: Louis Hayward, Barbara Britton, George Macready, Una O'Connor, Henry Stephenson. D: Henry Levin. ACT 91m.

Return of Mr. Moto, The 1965 British ★★½ The Japanese detective returns to investigate the murder of a British executive by an evil international syndicate trying to corner the oil market. Far-fetched attempt to update Mr. Moto, with Silva miscast. C: Henry Silva, Terrence Longdon, Suzanne Lloyd, Marne Maitland, Martin Wyldeck. D: Ernest Morris. DRA 71m.

Return of Peter Grimm, The 1945 ★★★½ After his death, patriarch (Barrymore) returns to earth to reconcile matters with his family. Stagy melodrama foreshadows *It's a Wonderful Life.* Barrymore stands out with a dependably blustery performance. C: Lionel Barrymore, Helen Mack, Edward Ellis, Donald Meek, Allen Vincent. D: George Nicholls Jr. DRA 83m. v

Return of Rin Tin Tin, The 1947 ★★★½ Psychologically traumatized boy (Blake) is happy only when in the presence of Rin Tin Tin. He fights to keep dog when the owners come to retrieve him. Good children's story focuses on the therapeutic aspects of dogs, with exciting action scenes. C: Bobby Blake, Donald Woods, Rin Tin Tin, Claudia Drake, Gaylord Pendleton, Earl Hodgins. D: Max Nosseck. DRA 65m. v

Return of Spinal Tap, The 1992 ★★★ Reunion of *This is Spinal Tap* cast further chronicles life of England's notorious (and fictional) heavy metal band. Has some amusing moments, but lacks satirical originality of Rob Reiner's pseudodocumentary. C: Harry Shearer, Michael McKean, Christopher Guest. COM 110m. v

Return of Superfly, The 1990 ★★½ Ex-drug dealer Priest (now played by Purdee) returns to U.S. and finds he's on wrong side of the law and his old drug dealing pals. Tired *Superfly* sequel; for diehard fans only. C: Nathan Purdee, Margaret Avery, San Jackson. D: Sig Shore. ACT [R] 94m. v

Return of Swamp Thing 1989 ★★★ Comic-book camp humor reigns in thinly plotted follow-up that once again pits the Man of Muck against his old enemy, Dr. Arcane. At least they spent more bucks on monster costumes this time. A short-lived TV series followed. C: Dick Durock, Heather Locklear, Louis Jourdan, Sarah Douglas, Joey Sagal. D: Jim Wynorski. SFI [PG-13] 87m. TVM v

Return of the Alien's Deadly Spawn *See* **The Deadly Spawn**

Return of the Ape Man 1944 ★★½ Mad scientist (Lugosi) attempts to revive a Neanderthal man by means of a transplanted brain. Campy performances spice up this low-budget horror movie, which even has the ancient ice man wearing long johns! C: Bela Lugosi, John Carradine, George Zucco, Judith Gibson. D: Phil Rosen. HOR 51m. v

Return of the Bad Men 1948 ★★★½ An ex-sheriff (Scott) settles in Oklahoma, where he takes on a who's who of Western outlaws: the Sundance Kid, Billy the Kid, the Daltons, and Youngers. Ryan stands out as a dastardly Sundance. C: Randolph Scott, Robert Ryan, Anne Jeffreys, George "Gabby" Hayes, Jacqueline White. D: Ray Enright. WST 90m. v

Return of the Boomerang 1970 *See* **Adam's Woman**

Return of the Chinese Boxer 1974 ★★ Battle royale between samurai and ninja warriors. C: Jimmy Wang Yu, Lung Fei. D: Jimmy Wang Yu. ACT 93m. v

Return of the Dragon 1973 Hong Kong ★★★½ Gangsters lean on Chinese restaurant owners in Rome. Bruce Lee comes to the rescue; fight scenes with Chuck Norris are classics. Lee's last-released film. C: Bruce Lee, Chuck Norris, Nora Miao. D: Bruce Lee. ACT [R] 91m. v

Return of the Fly, The 1959 ★★★½ Son of an insane scientist tries to vindicate his father's memory, but winds up repeating his mistakes. Price and good special effects make this an adequate sequel. Followed by *Curse of the Fly.* C: Vincent Price, Brett Halsey. D: Edward L. Bernds. SFI 80m. v

Return of the Jedi, The 1983 ★★★★ Conclusion of *Star Wars* trilogy portrays final showdown between Rebel Alliance and the Empire in tumultuous tri-level battle on a jungle moon, in space, and in Luke Skywalker's personal duel with Darth Vader. Yet pacing lumbers when it should soar, and the big climax is merely a grand rerun of the first film's finale. An eye-filling, satisfactory wrap-up, but still a step below predecessors *Star Wars* and *The Empire Strikes Back.* C: Mark Hamill, Harrison Ford, Carrie Fisher, Billy Dee Williams. D: Richard Marquand. SFI [PG] 132m. v

Return of the Killer Tomatoes 1988 ★★½ In a world where tomatoes are banned, mad scientist Astin plans to conquer the world by creating human/tomato hybrids. Slicker but just as silly as original *Attack of the Killer Tomatoes,* though Mistal is endearing as a tomato-girl. Sequel: *Killer Tomatoes Strike Back.* C: Anthony Starke, George Clooney, Karen Mistal, John Astin. D: John De Bello. COM [PG] 99m. v

Return of the King 1979 ★★★★ Third of the animated J.R.R. Tolkien trilogy about Hobbits in Middle Earth. Quite entertaining. Voices of Orson Bean, John Huston, William Conrad,

Roddy McDowall. D: Jules Bass. FAM/DRA 98m. TVM V

Return of the Living Dead, The 1985 ★★★½ Directorial debut of screenwriter O'Bannon is wild half-parody of Romero's *Living Dead* films, with zombies terrorizing medical supply house workers and punks in nearby cemetery. One of the few films of this type that's genuinely frightening and funny. C: Clu Gulager, James Karen, Don Calfa. D: Dan O'Bannon. HOR [R] 86m. V

Return of the Living Dead: Part II 1988 ★★½ Disappointing sequel suffers from lack of real wit and standard characters fleeing from rampaging zombies, then revived by mysterious gas. Still works up a few chills and laughs, mostly thanks to returning Karen and Mathews. C: James Karen, Thom Mathews, Marsha Dietlein, Dana Ashbrook, Philip Bruns. D: Ken Wiederhorn. HOR [R] 89m. V

Return of the Living Dead 3 1993 ★★★½ Lurid, witty horror film in which Edmond revives his girlfriend (Clarke) by unwittingly turning her into a flesh-craving zombie. Surprisingly inventive black comedy with a punch. C: J. Trevor Edmond, Mindy Clarke, Sarah Douglas, Kent McCord. D: Brian Yuzna. HOR [R] 96m. V

Return of the Magnificent Seven 1966 ★★★½ They're back! the same seven heroes are this time out to save a group of kidnapped farmers. It almost works like its predecessor. C: Yul Brynner, Robert Fuller, Warren Oates, Claude Akins. D: Burt Kennedy. WST 97m. V

Return of the Musketeers, The 1989 British ★★★½ Dumas's Musketeers reunite after twenty years when Queen (Chaplin) and her lover cause new trouble. Rehash of successful series formula, and why not? More swashbuckling fun. Dumas' *Twenty Years Later*. Third in the trilogy. C: Michael York, Oliver Reed, Frank Finlay, C. Thomas Howell, Kim Cattrall, Richard Chamberlain, Geraldine Chaplin, Christopher Lee. D: Richard Lester. ACT [PG] 103m. V

Return of the Pink Panther, The 1975 British ★★★½ Once again, a diamond is stolen, and once again, inept Inspector Clouseau is the only man for the job. Not all the gags are gems in third sequel, but enough of them work to make this occasionally uproarious entertainment. C: Peter Sellers, Christopher Plummer, Catherine Schell, Herbert Lom. D: Blake Edwards. COM [G] 113m. V

Return of the Rat, The 1929 British ★★★½ After his marriage to Jeans crumbles, the notorious Rat (Novello) returns to a life of crime, falls for a barmaid, and must dodge his ex-wife's vengeful lover. Final installment of British *Rat* series was originally filmed as a silent, with sound added later. C: Ivor Novello, Isabel Jeans. D: Graham Cutts. CRI 84m.

Return of the Secaucus Seven, The 1981 ★★★★½ Surprisingly beguiling sleeper about seven college friends who get together for a reunion weekend. Made on a shoestring, it has wit, warmth, and intelligence and sparked independent film revolution of the 1980s. C: Mark Arnott, Gordon Clapp, Adam Lefevre, Maggie Renzi, David Strathairn. D: John Sayles. DRA [R] 100m. V

Return of the Soldier, The 1981 British ★★★½ Shell-shocked WWI soldier (Bates) has no memory of the years before the war. He tries to forge a new life on the homefront. Interesting psychological premise and first-rate cast. C: Alan Bates, Julie Christie, Glenda Jackson, Ann-Margret. D: Alan Bridges. DRA 101m. V

Return of the Tall Blond Man With One Black Shoe, The 1975 French ★★★ The stumbling, baby-faced violinist (Richard) is mistaken for a spy in this sequel. This time the head spy wants him killed. Not as funny as the original, but the master comic milks a few guffaws from his pratfalls and misadventures. C: Pierre Richard, Mireille Darc, Jean Rocheforty. D: Yves Robert. COM 81m. V

Return of the Texan 1952 ★★★ Widower (Robertson) returns to the ranch where he grew up and gets embroiled in a battle with landowner (Boone). Average homesteader Western. C: Dale Robertson, Joanne Dru, Walter Brennan, Richard Boone, Robert Horton. D: Delmer Daves. WST 88m.

Return of the Vampire, The 1943 ★★★ Dracula (under another name, for legal reasons) returns to, of all places, London during the WWII blitz, with another horror standby, the Werewolf, also making an appearance. Commonplace and predictable. C: Bela Lugosi, Frieda Inescort, Nina Foch, Miles Mander. D: Lew Landers, Kurt Neumann. HOR 63m. V

Return to Boggy Creek 1977 ★★ The Bigfoot-like monster returns as the title says, but now he's a nice creature who rescues some children threatened by a hurricane. Inoffensive but unexciting, this unofficial sequel to *Legend of Boggy Creek* was followed by a genuine follow-up, *Boggy Creek II*. C: Dawn Wells, Dana Plato, Louis Belaire. D: Tom Moore. HOR [G] 87m. V

Return to Eden 1987 Australian ★★½ Philosophy student falls in love with her tutor, but he can't or won't respond. Posturing and slow, with pseudosophisticated discussions galore. C: Rebecca Gilling, James Reyne, Wendy Hughes. D: Karen Arthur. DRA 259m. V

Return to Horror High 1987 ★★ Ambitious low-budget affair, with a film crew making a movie about gory high school murders caught up in a bunch of real slayings. Never really takes off due to slack direction. C: Vince Edwards, Alex Rocco, Brendan Hughes, Lori Lethin. D: Bill Froehlich. HOR [R] 95m. V

Return to Mayberry 1986 ★★★★ Fans of television sitcom *The Andy Griffith Show* will enjoy this reunion film. Griffith returns to his small home town to run for sheriff, but finds his opponent is former deputy Barney Fife (Knotts). Gathering of many series originals adds sentiment and nostalgia. C: Andy Griffith, Ron Howard, Don Knotts, Jim Nabors, Aneta Corseaut, Jack Dodson, George Lindsay, Betty Lynn. D: Bob Sweeney. FAM/COM 96m. TVM V

Return to Oz 1985 ★★★ Live action sequel to the classic; Dorothy finds Oz in the hands of evil rulers and works with forces of good to set things straight. Okay effort, enhanced by Will Vinton's Claymation effects. C: Nicol Williamson, Jean Marsh, Fairuza Balk, Piper Laurie, Matt Clark. D: Walter Murch. FAM/DRA [PG] 109m. V

Return to Paradise 1953 ★★★ Soldier of fortune (Cooper) settles on a Polynesian island, where he falls for a native woman (Haynes). Slight romance, good Cooper. C: Gary Cooper, Roberta Haynes, Barry Jones. D: Mark Robson. DRA 100m. V

Return to Peyton Place 1961 ★★★ More hubbub in the little town full of secrets finds a visiting author trying to pry loose some juicy scandals. There's plenty to be found in this sequel, though it lacks notoriously zestful relish of original. C: Carol Lynley, Jeff Chandler, Eleanor Parker, Mary Astor, Robert Sterling, Luciana Paluzzi, Brett Halsey, Gunnar Hellstrom, Tuesday Weld, Bob Crane. D: Jose Ferrer. DRA 123m. V

Return to Salem's Lot, A 1987 ★★★ Cohen's quirky approach enlivens this sequel (barely related to Stephen King-based original), in which Moriarty and son discover vampires in their home town. More witty than scary, especially when it explores the bloodsuckers' lifestyle. C: Michael Moriarty, Ricky Addison Reed, Samuel Fuller, Andrew Duggan, Evelyn Keyes, June Havoc, Ronee Blakely. D: Larry Cohen. HOR [R] 101m. V

Return to Snowy River 1988 Australian ★★★½ When the girl he loves gets engaged to an unsavory man, a young Australian cattleman prepares to fight. Stilted effort is enlivened by exquisite photography, especially those fabulous running horses. Sequel of sorts to *The Man from Snowy River*. C: Tom Burlinson, Sigrid Thornton, Brian Dennehy, Nicholas Eadie. D: Geoff Burrowes. WST [PG] 99m. V

Return to the Blue Lagoon 1991 ★★ A mother, her daughter, and an orphaned boy are marooned on a desert island and the kids teach each other about sex. Still pretty, still dumb. C: Brian Krause, Milla Jovovich, Lisa Pelikan. D: William A. Graham. DRA [PG-13] 102m. V

Return to Two Moon Junction 1994 ★★★ A famous model (Clarke) throws it all away to return to her sleepy Southern hometown. Glossy but dull. C: John Clayton Schafer, Louise Fletcher, Mindy Clarke. D: Farhad Mann. DRA [R] 96m. V

Reuben, Reuben 1983 ★★★★ An inebriate poet (Conti), coasting on his reputation through the college lecture circuit, falls for a student (McGillis). Charming, eccentric comedy, inspired by the works of humorist Peter DeVries. McGillis' film debut. C: Tom Conti, Kelly McGillis. D: Robert Ellis Miller. COM [R] 101m. V

Reunion 1932 British ★★★★ A poor British officer (Rome) must pawn his valuables to attend a gathering in London—where he is to give a speech about hope and self-sufficiency. Rome gives a nicely underplayed performance in this ironic study of honor during the Depression. C: Stewart Rome, Antony Holles. D: Ivar Campbell. DRA 60m.

Reunion 1936 ★★★ Townspeople honor retiring doctor (Hersholt) by staging a reunion of some of the 3,000 children he delivered, including a set of quintuplets (the Dionne Quintuplets). Sequel to *The Country Doctor* features good performance by Hersholt. C: Jean Hersholt, Rochelle Hudson, Helen Vinson, Slim Summerville. D: Norman Taurog. DRA 80m.

Reunion in France 1942 ★★★ Parisian woman discovers that her French patriot boyfriend may be a Nazi collaborator, and she takes up with an American flyer eluding the Gestapo. Interesting pairing of Crawford and Wayne fuels this dated WWII romance. C: Joan Crawford, John Wayne, Philip Dorn, Reginald Owen. D: Jules Dassin. DRA 100m. V

Reunion in Reno 1951 ★★★½ A nine-year-old girl asks Reno lawyer if she can divorce her parents, and a hearing is held to find reason why. Young Perreau is a charmer in this fluffy, enjoyable comedy/drama. C: Mark Stevens, Peggy Dow, Gigi Perreau, Frances Dee, Leif Erickson. D: Kurt Neumann. DRA 79m.

Reunion in Vienna 1933 ★★★★ Ex-duke, now a cabdriver (Barrymore), is reunited with former love (Wynyard) by her psychiatrist husband (Morgan). Sophisticated romance, from Robert E. Sherwood play, boasts a wonderful, comic performance from Barrymore. C: John Barrymore, Diana Wynyard, Frank Morgan, May Robson. D: Sidney Franklin. COM 98m.

Reveille With Beverly 1943 ★★★½ Radio star (Miller) puts on a show for the troops. Modest musical gets a boost from jazz greats in cameo roles, including Frank Sinatra, Count Basie, Duke Ellington, and the Mills Brothers. C: Ann Miller, William Wright, Franklin Pangborn, Larry Parks. D: Charles Barton. MUS 78m.

Revenge *See* **Blood Feud**

Revenge 1990 ★★★ Costner, Quinn, and Stowe in triangle that turns violent. The story is chilly but the love scenes with Costner and

Stowe are hot. C: Kevin Costner, Anthony Quinn, Madeleine Stowe, Sally Kirkland. D: Tony Scott. ACT [R] 123m. V

Revenge of Fist of Fury ★★½ Various kung fu experts meet to pay homage to the late great Bruce Lee. Blood galore. ACT V

Revenge of Frankenstein, The 1958 British ★★★★ Under a new identity, Dr. Frankenstein (Cushing) transplants his hunchback servant's brain into a monster, with the help of a medical student. Excellent sequel to *The Curse of Frankenstein* builds to an ending with a real jolt. C: Peter Cushing, Francis Matthews, Eunice Gayson, Michael Gwynn, Lionel Jeffries, John Welsh. D: Terence Fisher. HOR 91m.

Revenge of General Ling 1938 *See* **Wife of General Ling, The**

Revenge of the Creature 1955 ★★★ The Creature from the Black Lagoon resurfaces, but much to his dismay, as scientific case study at Florida's Marine Land. Clint Eastwood's film debut as a lab tech. Originally released in 3-D. C: John Agar, Lori Nelson, John Bromfield, Nestor Paiva, Clint Eastwood. D: Jack Arnold. HOR 82m. V

Revenge of the Innocents 1986 *See* **South Bronx Heroes**

Revenge of the Nerds 1984 ★★★½ Erratic but sometimes hilarious comedy about fraternity of misfits and losers who take on the cool jocks on their college campus. Predictable story is exuberantly goofy and likable. Followed by sequel. C: Robert Carradine, Anthony Edwards, Curtis Armstrong, Julie Montgomery. D: Jeff Kanew. COM [R] 89m. V

Revenge of the Nerds 2: Nerds in Paradise 1987 ★ Triumphant geeks travel to Ft. Lauderdale where they once again run up against the jocks. Sequel has few surprises, even for those who haven't seen the original. C: Robert Carradine, Curtis Armstrong, Courtney Thorne-Smith, Ed Lauter. D: Joe Roth. COM [PG-13] 89m. V

Revenge of the Nerds 3: The Next Generation 1992 ★★ Made-for-TV continuation of *Revenge of the Nerds* saga reunites cast members, now older but still geeky, as they watch next generation of socially inept brains enter all-nerd institute of high learning and low comedy. Few laughs. C: Robert Carradine, Ted McGinley, Curtis Armstrong, Morton Downey Jr. D: Roland Mesa. COM 93m. TVM V

Revenge of the Ninja 1983 ★★★ Retired master ninja (Kosugi) battles a former rival who is running a heroin smuggling operation. Above-average martial arts action may appeal to general audiences, despite Kosugi's atrocious accent. Violence. Sequel to *Enter the Ninja*; followed by *Ninja III*. C: Sho Kosugi, Keith Vitali, Virgil Frye, Arthur Roberts. D: Sam Firstenberg. ACT [R] 90m. V

Revenge of the Ninja Warrior ★★½ Noble ninja confronts bad ninja. For fans. ACT V

Revenge of the Pink Panther 1978 ★★½ The formula's starting to run out of steam in the fifth sequel, but Sellers' Inspector Clouseau is still occasionally funny. Plot concerns his apparent murder and efforts to track down the culprits who think they've killed him. C: Peter Sellers, Herbert Lom, Robert Webber, Dyan Cannon. D: Blake Edwards. COM [PG] 99m. V

Revenge of the Teenage Vixens from Outer Space 1985 ★★★ Space aliens invade Earth, sample the male populace, and exact revenge when the Earthlings fail to satisfy. Silly attempt at space farce has its moments. C: Lisa Schwedop, Howard Scott. COM 83m. V

Revengers, The 1972 ★★½ A rancher (Holden) vows revenge against the killers of his family, enlisting convicts to help him track the culprits in Mexico. Holden, Borgnine and Hayward's strong performances can't totally hide a predictable script; Hayward's last film. C: William Holden, Ernest Borgnine, Susan Hayward, Woody Strode, Roger Hanin, Rene Koldehoff. D: Daniel Mann. WST [PG] 112m.

Revenue Agent 1950 ★★★½ IRS agent (Kennedy) goes undercover to smash a plot by Stevens to avoid taxes by smuggling $1 million in gold dust to Mexico. Low-budget, documentary-style crime drama maintains high-wire tension. C: Douglas Kennedy, Jean Willes, Onslow Stevens. D: Lew Landers. CRI 72m.

Reversal of Fortune 1990 ★★★★½ Fascinating and outrageously funny dark comedy about true story of Claus Von Bulow, tried for the attempted murder of his rich wife, told from her point-of-view. Irons' wicked wit and Silver's (as Alan Dershowitz) crackling legal chatter makes it a seductively engaging film. C: Glenn Close, Jeremy Irons, Ron Silver, Annabella Sciorra, Uta Hagen, Fisher Stevens. D: Barbet Schroeder. COM [R] 109m. V

Revolt at Fort Laramie 1957 ★★★½ Outbreak of the Civil War causes rift at Army fort, with the commander having to choose between duty as an officer and loyalty to the South. Above average B-Western does well with its interesting premise. C: John Dehner, Frances Helm, Gregg Palmer, Don Gordon, Robert Keys. D: Lesley Selander. WST 73m.

Revolt in the Big House 1958 ★★★½ Racketeer kingpin stages a prison break with fellow inmates, who are unaware he considers them expendable. Well-done, low-budget prison drama. C: Gene Evans, Robert Blake, Timothy Carey, John Qualen. D: R. G. Springsteen. ACT 79m.

Revolt of Job, The 1984 Hungarian ★★★★★ Stunning film about Jewish couple and their non-Jewish adopted child facing the Holocaust. Warm family scenes are powerfully juxtaposed with stark threat of violence. A must-see. C: Ferenc Zenthe, Hedi Temessy. D: Imre Gyongyossy, Barna Kabay. DRA 98m. V

Revolt of Mamie Stover, The 1956 ★★★½ Banished from San Francisco, saloon girl (Russell) sets up profitable shop in wartime Hawaii. Fairly tame lowlife drama benefits from Russell's charm. C: Jane Russell, Richard Egan, Joan Leslie, Agnes Moorehead, Jorja Curtright, Jean Willes, Michael Pate. D: Raoul Walsh. DRA 92m.

Revolt of the Mercenaries 1964 ★★½ A daring mercenary (Sanmartin) aids a duchess (Mayo) in her war with her greedy neighbor (Lorenzon), but not without a series of double crosses. Great costumes. C: Virginia Mayo, Conrado Sanmartin. D: Piero Costa. ACT 102m.

Revolution 1985 ★★ Clumsily told story of American revolution, with Pacino miscast as Brooklyn-accented Yankee soldier. Lots of sweep but this one should have been swept out the door. C: Al Pacino, Donald Sutherland, Nastassja Kinski, Joan Plowright, Annie Lennox. D: Hugh Hudson. DRA [PG] 125m. V

Revolutionary, The 1970 ★★★★ Campus rebel (Voight) allows himself to be drafted, then goes AWOL to aid radical bomber (Cassel) in his attempt to kill an antilabor judge. Well-written character study that refuses to take sides, and presents various contradictory points of view. C: Jon Voight, Jennifer Salt, Seymour Cassel, Robert Duvall. D: Paul Williams. DRA [PG] 100m.

Reward, The 1965 ★★ A posse receives reward money, then members greedily turn against each other. Study of greed against a Western backdrop. C: Max von Sydow, Yvette Mimieux, Efrem Zimbalist Jr., Gilbert Roland, Emilio Fernandez, Henry Silva, Rodolfo Acosta. D: Serge Bourguignon. WST 92m.

Rhapsody 1954 ★★★½ A rich and beautiful young woman (Taylor) has affairs with two prominent classical musicians. Love triangle benefits from a good performance by Taylor and exquisite music. C: Elizabeth Taylor, Vittorio Gassman, John Ericson, Louis Calhern, Michael Chekhov. D: Charles Vidor. DRA 115m. V

Rhapsody in August 1991 Japanese ★★★ Grandmother who survived bombing of Nagasaki at end of WWII relates her terrible story to extended family. Gere, playing Japanese-American grandson, is shunted to relatively minor role despite star billing. Well-meaning but shallow drama a lesser effort from director Kurosawa. C: Sachiko Murase, Richard Gere, Hisashi Igawa, Narumi Kayashima. D: Akira Kurosawa. DRA [PG] 98m. V

Rhapsody in Blue 1945 ★★★★ Better than average biography of composer George Gershwin, whose glamorous life and untimely death did not have to be drastically changed to fit Hollywood standards. Presence of Gershwin's real-life pal Levant adds authority, as does complete version of title work. Rare footage of pianist/singer Scott also a highlight. C: Robert Alda, Joan Leslie, Alexis Smith, Oscar Levant, Charles Coburn, Julie Bishop, Albert Basserman, Morris Carnovsky, Herbert Rudley, Rosemary DeCamp, Paul Whiteman, Hazel Scott. D: Irving Rapper. MUS 142m. V

Rhinestone 1984 ★★ Dolly tries to win a bet by teaching Sly to sing country. If that sounds like a reasonable premise to you, go for it. C: Dolly Parton, Sylvester Stallone, Richard Farnsworth, Ron Liebman. D: Bob Clark. COM [PG] 111m. V

Rhino! 1964 ★★★½ Animal doctor (Culp) goes on the trail of a rare white rhino, and is double-crossed by big game hunter (Guardino). Family jungle adventure with good African animal footage. C: Robert Culp, Harry Guardino, Shirley Eaton, Harry Mekela. D: Ivan Tors. ACT 91m.

Rhinoceros 1974 ★★ Uneven film adaptation of Ionesco's landmark absurdist play, about a man turning into a rhinoceros (without aid of make-up). Fine cast in a pickle, reuniting the stars of *The Producers*. C: Zero Mostel, Gene Wilder, Karen Black. D: Tom O'Horgan. DRA [PG] 101m.

Rhodes 1936 British ★★★½ Biographical drama of imperialist Cecil Rhodes (Huston), whose explorations changed the face of Africa. Dated British drama may surprise viewers with its supportive depiction of Rhodes' actions. (a.k.a. *Rhodes of Africa*) C: Walter Huston, Oscar Homolka, Basil Sydney, Frank Cellier, Peggy Ashcroft, Renne De Vaux, Bernard Lee, Ndanisa Kumalo. D: Berthold Viertel. DRA 91m.

Rhodes of Africa 1936 *See* **Rhodes**

Rhubarb 1951 ★★★★ The eccentric owner of a Brooklyn ball club bequeaths his team to his pet cat, whose presence at games leads the team to glory. Lively farce, and the cat gives a great performance. C: Ray Milland, Jan Sterling, Gene Lockhart, William Frawley, Elsie Holmes, Leonard Nimoy, Taylor Holmes. D: Arthur Lubin. COM 95m.

Rhythm on the Range 1936 ★★½ Ranchhand (Crosby) romances wealthy Easterner (Farmer). Western musical comedy features Bing's crooning and the terrific debut of brassy Raye. Remade as *Pardners*. C: Bing Crosby, Frances Farmer, Bob Burns, Martha Raye, Lucile Watson, Samuel S. D: Norman Taurog. MUS 85m.

Rhythm on the River 1940 ★★★★ Songwriters (Crosby and Martin) tire of ghosting for composer (Rathbone) and end up falling in love. Breezy comedy makes the most of its plot and songs, and Crosby and Martin really click. Delightful. C: Bing Crosby, Mary Martin, Basil Rathbone, Oscar Levant, Oscar Shaw, Charley Grapewin, William Frawley. D: Victor Schertzinger. MUS 92m. V

Rich and Famous 1981 ★★★½ Remake of *Old Acquaintance*. Lifelong rivalry and friendship between two women, each of whom has many ups and downs. Some witty moments, but the material is only middling. C: Jacqueline Bisset, Candice Bergen, David Selby, Hart Bochner. D: George Cukor. DRA [R] 117m. v

Rich and Strange 1932 British ★★★½ A battling husband and wife decide to seek adventure in an around-the-world cruise. Offbeat comedy/drama is an unusual early effort from Hitchcock; worth seeing. C: Henry Kendall, Joan Barry, Betty Amann, Percy Marmont. D: Alfred Hitchcock. DRA 83m. v

Rich in Love 1993 ★★★½ A charming teenager tries to maintain balance in her zany family. Some wonderful elements in an uneven story. C: Albert Finney, Jill Clayburgh, Kathryn Erbe, Kyle MacLachlan, Piper Laurie, Ethan Hawke, Suzy Amis, Alfre Woodard. D: Bruce Beresford. COM [PG-13] 105m. v

Rich Kids 1979 ★★★½ Two young New Yorkers (Alvarado and Levy) form a friendship that helps them through divorces of their parents. Solid study of the effects of divorce, realistic performances. C: Trini Alvarado, Jeremy Levy, John Lithgow, Kathryn Walker. D: Robert M. Young. DRA [PG] 97m. v

Rich Man, Poor Girl 1938 ★★★★ A wealthy young businessman (Young) tries to prove his love to secretary (Hussey) by moving in with her eccentric family. Frothy comedy knockoff of *You Can't Take It With You* benefits from good cast. C: Robert Young, Lew Ayres, Ruth Hussey, Lana Turner, Rita Johnson, Don Castle, Guy Kibbee. D: Reinhold Schunzel. COM 70m.

Rich Man's Folly 1931 ★★½ An obsessed ship-building magnate (Bancroft) treats his family ruthlessly, alienating his son and daughter. Modernization of Charles Dickens' *Dombey and Son.* C: George Bancroft, Frances Dee, Robert Ames, Juliette Compton. D: John Cromwell. DRA 80m.

Rich People 1929 ★★★½ Blaming wealth for her parents' divorce, Bennett spurns society fiancée (Ames) for an insurance salesman (Toomey) whose pride won't allow him to marry into money. Early talkie is a well-made vehicle for Bennett. C: Constance Bennett, Regis Toomey, Robert Ames. D: Edward H. Griffith. DRA 75m.

Rich, Young and Pretty 1951 ★★★½ A young American woman (Powell) meets her long-lost French mother (Darrieux) while vacationing in Paris, and also finds romance. Frothy MGM musical, with sparkling Powell. C: Jane Powell, Danielle Darrieux, Wendell Corey, Vic Damone, Fernando Lamas, Marcel Dalio, Una Merkel, Richard Anderson. D: Norman Taurog. MUS 95m. v

Richard 1972 ★★★★ A young man (Resin) succeeds in politics through plastic surgery and brainwashing—forced watching of Nixon speeches. Clever, low-budget, pre-Watergate Nixon satire includes a good cast of veterans in support, and has some eerily prophetic moments. C: Richard M. Dixon, Dan Resin, Lynn Lipton, Mickey Rooney, John Carradine, Paul Ford, Vivian Blaine. D: Lorees Yerby. COM [G] 83m.

Richard Pryor Here and Now 1983 ★★ Stand-up concert unintentionally showcases comic in his decline. Often difficult film to watch. Language and subject matter may offend some viewers. C: Richard Pryor. D: Richard Pryor. COM [R] 83m. v

Richard Pryor Live and Smokin' 1971 ★★ Uneventful Richard Pryor concert film marked by some of his lesser comedy routines. Viewers with easily offended sensitivities should steer clear. C: Richard Pryor. D: Michael Blum. COM [R] 47m.

Richard Pryor—Live in Concert 1979 ★★★★½ Pryor in his prime gives his musings on the foibles of life, liberty, and the pursuit of happiness. Loud and raunchy—and extremely funny. Pryor's razor wit never sharper. Language and subject matter may offend some viewers. C: Richard Pryor. D: Jeff Margolis. COM 78m. v

Richard Pryor Live on the Sunset Strip 1982 ★★★★ In his first performance after accidentally setting himself on fire while freebasing cocaine, Pryor tells that story with the same nasty edge he gives everything else. This is Pryor doing what he does best. C: Richard Pryor. D: Joe Layton. COM [R] 82m. v

Richard III 1955 British ★★★★½ Gripping, intricately staged version of Shakespeare's play about ruthless, hunchbacked prince who seized British throne in 15th century. Finely crafted performance by Olivier, with able support from Gielgud, Richardson, and Bloom. C: Laurence Olivier, John Gielgud, Ralph Richardson, Claire Bloom, Cedric Hardwicke. D: Laurence Olivier. DRA 138m. v

Richard's Things 1980 British ★★ Woman grieving over husband's death finds herself lured into bed by the dead man's mistress. Not that much fun. C: Liv Ullmann, Amanda Redman, Tim Smith, Elizabeth Spriggs, David Markham. D: Anthony Harvey. DRA [R] 104m. v

Richest Girl in the World, The 1934 ★★★★ Tired of suitors who are after her money, a rich woman (Hopkins) poses as a secretary to ensure that her next boyfriend (McCrea) will love her for herself. Old theme shines like new thanks to an Oscar-nominated script by Norman Krasna. C: Miriam Hopkins, Joel McCrea, Fay Wray, Reginald Denny, Henry Stephenson. D: William A. Seiter. COM 76m.

Richest Man in the World 1988 *See* **Onassis: The Richest Man in the World**

Richie Rich 1994 ★★★½ Diverting family fare stars Culkin as the world's richest tot, subject to the schemes of greedy Larroquette. Slick, expensively produced, but suffers from weak writing and a curiously bland performance from Culkin. C: Macaulay Culkin, John Larroquette, Edward Herrmann, Christine Ebersole, Jonathan

Hyde, Michael McShane, Reggie Jackson. D: Donald Petrie. FAM/COM [PG] 95m. v

Rickshaw Man, The 1960 Japanese ★★★★½ Early 20th-century rickshaw driver (Mifune) becomes surrogate father to a rich boy, but class differences result in his eventual abandonment. Mifune gives an eloquent performance in this tragic drama about social castes. C: Toshiro Mifune, Hideko Takamine, Hiroshi Akutagawa. D: Hiroshi Inagaki. DRA 98m.

Ricochet 1991 ★★★★ Sharp story line, tightly acted leads, and lots of suspense power this thriller about a crazy convict (Lithgow) out to get the then-rookie cop (Washington) who put him away. C: Denzel Washington, John Lithgow, Ice T. D: Russell Mulcahy. CRI [R] 110m. v

Riddle of the Sands, The 1979 British ★★★ In 1901, two British pleasure sailors (MacCorkindale and York) discover a German plot to invade England. Solid spy thriller that's also good to look at. C: Simon MacCorkindale, Michael York, Jenny Agutter, Alan Badel. D: Tony Maylam. DRA 102m. v

Ride a Wild Pony 1976 Australian ★★★★ Two children—poor boy who needs transportation to school and polio-stricken rich girl undergoing therapy—compete for ownership of horse in 18th-century Australia. Interesting children's film that regards moral conflict with sensitivity and compassion for both sides. C: Michael Craig, John Meillon, Robert Bettles, Eva Griffith. D: Don Chaffey. FAM/DRA [G] 86m. v

Ride Back, The 1957 ★★★★ An American lawman (Conrad) and the murderer he tracks down in Mexico (Quinn) must help each other survive the return trip. Taut, well-played psychological Western. C: Anthony Quinn, Lita Milan, William Conrad, Ellen Monroe, Louis Towers. D: Allen Miner. WST 79m.

Ride Clear of Diablo 1954 ★★★½ Hero seeks the help of gunslinger to avenge the murder of his family. Good, twisty Murphy vehicle. C: Audie Murphy, Dan Duryea, Susan Cabot, Abbe Lane, Russell Johnson, Jack Elam. D: Jesse Hibbs. WST 80m.

Ride 'Em Cowboy 1942 ★★★½ Abbott and Costello at work on Wild West dude ranch in good vehicle; solid songs help, especially Fitzgerald singing "A Tisket A Tasket." C: Bud Abbott, Lou Costello, Dick Foran, Anne Gwynne, Johnny Mack Brown, Ella Fitzgerald, Douglass Dumbrille. D: Arthur Lubin. COM 82m. v

Ride Him, Cowboy 1931 ★★★ Wayne saves a horse accused of killing a rancher, then tries to catch the bank robber who really committed the crime. Early Wayne B-Western features good action scenes, and is a remake of the 1926 silent, *The Unknown Cavalier.* C: John Wayne. WST 55m. v

Ride Lonesome 1959 ★★★½ In order to bring in his wanted brother, a bounty hunter captures a desperado and uses him as bait. Typical Western with gripping moments of moderate suspense. C: Randolph Scott, Karen Steele, Pernell Roberts, James Best, Lee Van Cleef, James Coburn. D: Budd Boetticher. WST 73m. v

Ride on Vaquero 1941 ★★★½ The Cisco Kid (Romero) tries to catch kidnappers who are using his name in their activities, while romancing dancer (Hughes). Last episode in the *Cisco Kid* series starring Romero. C: Cesar Romero, Mary Beth Hughes, Lynne Roberts. D: Herbert I. Leeds. WST 64m.

Ride, Ranger, Ride 1936 ★★★ Texas Ranger (Autry) goes undercover to stop Indians from looting Army ammunition. Good Autry vehicle. C: Gene Autry, Smiley Burnette, Kay Hughes, Monte Blue. D: Joseph Kane. WST 56m. v

Ride, Tenderfoot, Ride 1940 ★★★½ Heir to a meatpacking plant (Autry) locks horns with a rival owner (Storey) while finding romance with her sister (Lee). Autry vehicle benefits from witty dialogue and plenty of songs. C: Gene Autry, Smiley Burnette, June Storey. D: Frank McDonald. WST 65m.

Ride the High Country 1962 ★★★★★ Peckinpah's finest and Scott's swan song is about a couple of retired lawmen hired to transport a big gold shipment. Introspective character piece with good casting and gorgeous photography works exceptionally well. Hartley's debut. C: Randolph Scott, Joel McCrea, Mariette Hartley, Edgar Buchanan. D: Sam Peckinpah. WST 93m. v

Ride the High Wind 1967 South African ★★★½ Pilot (McGavin) crash-lands in Southwest African desert, gets involved with a couple seeking gold bullion left in a wagon from the Boer War. Greed, sexual treachery, and desert desperation mark this action picture. C: Darren McGavin, Maria Perschy. D: David Millin. DRA 77m.

Ride the Pink Horse 1947 ★★★★ During a fiesta in a New Mexico village, a man tries to blackmail a mobster. Highly suspenseful film noir thriller. C: Robert Montgomery, Wanda Hendrix, Thomas Gomez, Andrea King, Fred Clark, Art Smith, Rita Conde, Grandon Rhodes. D: Robert Montgomery. CRI 101m.

Ride the Wild Surf 1964 ★★★½ Young adventurers go to Hawaii for fun, surfing, and romance. Light and breezy, great surfing. Above-average beach fling. C: Fabian, Tab Hunter, Barbara Eden, Anthony Hayes, Jim Mitchum. D: Don Taylor. COM 101m. v

Ride to Glory *See* **Deserter, The**

Ride to Hangman's Tree, The 1967 ★★★ Two reformed outlaws (Lord and Galloway) believe that their old partner (Farentino) is robbing stagecoaches. By-the-numbers Western, interesting cast. C: Jack Lord, James Farentino, Don Galloway, Melodie Johnson, Richard Anderson, Robert Yuro. D: Al Rafkin. WST 90m.

Rider of Death Valley 1932 ★★★★ Mix helps Wilson reclaim her father's desert gold mine, against the opposition of two badmen. Well-staged action scenes make good use of bleak desert settings; excellent production values lift this well above the average. C: Tom Mix, Lois Wilson. D: Albert Rogell. WST 76m.

Rider on the Rain 1970 French ★★★★½ Woman kills the man who raped her and mysterious witness (Bronson) pursues her. Fine thriller á la Hitchcock, with many twists and table turnings. Probably Bronson's best (and most uncharacteristic) film. C: Charles Bronson, Marlene Jobert, Jill Ireland, Annie Cordy. D: Rene Clement. CRI [PG] 119m. V

Riders in the Sky 1949 ★★★½ Autry tries to rescue a friend framed for murder by a crooked gambler (Livingston), who has the town in his grasp. Later Autry features a good villainous performance by Livingston and more action than the usual Autry film. C: Gene Autry, Gloria Henry, Pat Buttram, Mary Beth Hughes, Robert Livingston. D: John English. WST 69m.

Riders of Destiny 1933 ★★★ An undercover agent (Wayne) helps some ranchers recover their water rights. B-Western, chiefly interesting for seeing very early Wayne. C: John Wayne, Cecilia Parker, George "Gabby" Hayes. D: Robert Bradbury. WST 52m. V

Riders of the Badlands 1941 ★★★½ Starrett plays a dual role as a ranger sentenced to hang for the crimes of a look-alike outlaw. Good gunplay and action scenes in this B-Western, notable mainly for a sidekick role by musical star Edwards. C: Charles Starrett, Russell Hayden, Cliff "Ukelele Ike" Edwards, Ilene Brewer. D: Howard Bretherton. WST 58m.

Riders of the Black Hills 1938 ★★★½ The Three Mesquiteers try to rescue a favored thoroughbred kidnapped just before a rich horse race. Exciting train robbery highlights enjoyable B-movie horse opera. C: Bob Livingston, Ray Corrigan. D: George Sherman. WST 61m.

Riders of the Deadline 1943 ★★★ Texas Ranger Hopalong Cassidy goes undercover to break a smuggling ring. Above-average entry in Cassidy series. C: William Boyd, Andy Clyde, Jimmy Rogers, Robert Mitchum. D: Lesley Selander. WST 47m. V

Riders of the Desert 1932 ★★★ Hero tracks the money stolen in a stagecoach robbery. B-Western features a good cliff shoot-out. C: Bob Steele, Al "Fuzzy" St. John, George "Gabby" Hayes. WST 57m. V

Riders of the Purple Sage 1925 ★★★★½ Silent western classic with Mix as a lawman in search of his kidnapped sister. Terrific photography, thrilling story. Remade in 1931 and 1941, but this version's the best. From a Zane Grey novel. C: Tom Mix, Beatrice Burnham, Warner Oland. D: Lynn Reynolds. WST 56m.

Riders of the Range 1949 ★★★ Hero tries to keep rancher's ne'er-do-well brother on the straight and narrow. Holt B-Western, nicely done. C: Tim Holt, Richard Martin, Jacqueline White. D: Lesley Selander. WST 60m. V

Riders of the Rockies 1938 ★★★ Routine B-Western with Ritter and cronies accused of being cattle rustlers. C: Tex Ritter, Louise Stanley, Charles King. D: Robert Bradbury. WST 56m. V

Riders of the Storm 1988 British ★★½ Vietnam vets (Hopper and Pollard) use electronic know-how to disrupt right-wing TV broadcasts. Hopper and Pollard make interesting weirdo team but film's offbeat elements (including drag queen presidential candidate) never gel. (a.k.a. *The American Way*) C: Dennis Hopper, Michael J. Pollard, Eugene Lipinski, James Aubrey. D: Maurice Phillips. COM [R] 92m. V

Riders of the Whistling Skull 1937 ★★★½ Best of the *Three Mesquiteers* B-Western series with Livingston, Corrigan, and Terhune out to stop outlaws from robbing ancient Incan gold. C: Bob Livingston, Ray Corrigan, Max Terhune. D: Mack V. Wright. WST 60m. V

Riders of Vengeance 1952 *See* **Raiders, The**

Ridin' Down the Canyon 1942 ★★★½ Standard Roy Rogers Western in which he helps government foil outlaws trying to steal WWII ponies. Rogers croons four songs with the Sons of the Pioneers. C: Roy Rogers, George "Gabby" Hayes, Linda Hayes. D: Joseph Kane. WST 54m.

Ridin' for Justice 1932 ★★★ Cowpoke (Jones) known for his prowess with women gets mixed up in murder investigation. Average B-Western. C: Charles "Buck" Jones, Mary Doran. D: D. Ross Lederman. WST 61m.

Riding Bean 1989 Japanese ★★★ In this Japanese animated feature for adults, a courier unjustly accused in a kidnapping sets out to prove his innocence. Highly creative. DRA 46m. V

Riding High 1950 ★★★½ Damon Runyon's horseracing yarn, a remake of Capra's *Broadway Bill*, is okay fluff, expertly played by Crosby as owner of underdog colt. C: Bing Crosby, Coleen Gray, Charles Bickford, Margaret Hamilton, Frances Gifford, James Gleason, Raymond Walburn, William Demarest, Ward Bond, Clarence Muse, Percy Kilbride, Gene Lockhart, Douglass Dumbrille. D: Frank Capra. WST 112m.

Riding on Air 1937 ★★★ Routine comedy of radio invention that controls airplanes, with Brown hamming it up, as usual. C: Joe E. Brown, Guy Kibbee, Florence Rice, Vinton Haworth. D: Edward Sedgwick. COM 58m. V

Riding the Sunset Trail 1941 ★★★½ Keene plays cowboy out to solve murder mystery in routine oater with exciting chase finale. C: Tom Keene, Betty Miles, Frank Yaconelli, Sugar Dawn. D: Robert Tansey. WST 56m.

Riding the Wind 1942 ★★★ Formula Western with Holt as leader of ranchers trying to protect their water rights. C: Tim Holt, Ray Whitley, Mary Douglas. D: Edward Killy. WST 60m.

Riding Tornado, The 1932 ★★★ McCoy is hired hand falling for ranch owner Grey in routine Western romance. C: Tim McCoy, Shirley Grey, Wallace MacDonald. D: D. Ross Lederman. WST 64m.

Riding West 1944 ★★½ Greedy gamblers try to stop hero Starrett from starting Pony Express route. Tepid. C: Charles Starrett, Arthur Hunnicutt, Shirley Patterson. D: William Berke. WST 58m.

Riff Raff 1992 British ★★★½ A working-class Brit tries to shed his disreputable past. Unflinching tale of contemporary struggles, peppered with black humor. Genuine and brash. C: Jimmy Coleman, George Moss. D: Ken Loach. COM 96m. V

Riffraff 1935 ★★★½ Tragedy and comedy follow a cannery worker (Harlow), who falls for a big-talking fisherman and union member (Tracy) and eventually finds her way into prison. Snappy dialogue. C: Jean Harlow, Spencer Tracy, Una Merkel, Joseph Calleia, Victor Kilian, Mickey Rooney. D: J. Walter Ruben. DRA 89m. V

Rififi 1954 French ★★★★★ Marvelously entertaining, influential film about jewel heist and the quarreling thieves who perpetrate it. Climax is 25-minute robbery sequence that's a marvel of editing—and totally silent. Based on Auguste LeBreton's novel. (a.k.a. *Du Rififi Chez des Hommes*) C: Jean Servais, Carl Mohner, Marie Sabouret. D: Jules Dassin. CRI 116m. V

Rififi in Tokyo 1963 French ★★★ So-so bank heist film about aging criminal trying to round up others to help him. Has absolutely nothing to do with 1954 classic, *Rififi.* C: Karl Boehm, Michel Vitold, Charles Vanel, Eiji Okada, Keiko Kishi, Barbara Lass, Yanagi. D: Jacques Deray. CRI 89m.

Right Cross 1950 ★★★½ Average boxing flick with prizefighter Montalban vying with sportswriter Powell for Allyson's affections. Hits the soapsuds midway and never recovers. C: June Allyson, Dick Powell, Lionel Barrymore, Ricardo Montalban, Marilyn Monroe. D: John Sturges. DRA 90m.

Right Hand Man, The 1986 Australian ★★★ Life becomes tough for a couple of greenhorns in turn-of-the-century Australia when their father dies. Hiring a new driver only complicates matters in slow-moving drama. C: Rupert Everett, Hugo Weaving, Catherine McClements, Arthur Dignam. D: Di Drew. DRA [R] 101m. V

Right of the People, The 1986 ★★½ Wooden fable of gun control in a small town; they want to openly bear their arms. Makes its point, but at the expense of putting the viewer to sleep. The fine cast deserves better. C: Michael Ontkean, Jane Kaczmarek, Billy Dee Williams, John Randolph, M. Emmet Walsh, Jamie Jackson, Joanne Linville. D: Jeffrey Bloom. DRA 100m. TVM

Right of Way 1983 ★★★ Jimmy and Bette, in their first (and only) film together, play a married couple deciding to kill themselves. Downbeat subject and a dull script, but those two make it worth a look, at least. C: James Stewart, Bette Davis, Melinda Dillon. D: George Schaefer. DRA 102m. TVM V

Right Stuff, The 1983 ★★★★ Kaufman's sprawling, stately look at training of first astronauts. Terrific performances overall, but more cerebral and brilliant than emotional. Watch for amazing special effects by independent filmmaking veteran Jordan Belson. Oscar for Best Score. Based on best-seller by Tom Wolfe. C: Sam Shepard, Scott Glenn, Ed Harris, Fred Ward, Barbara Hershey, Charles Frank. D: Philip Kaufman. DRA [PG] 193m. V

Right to Love, The 1931 ★★★★ Chatterton plays both mother and illegitimate daughter in superior soap opera with spiritual twist. Working as a missionary, daughter feels connection to mother, half a world away. Star pulls the stops out. C: Ruth Chatterton, Paul Lukas, David Manners. D: Richard Wallace. DRA 79m.

Right to the Heart 1942 ★★★ Silly trifle of wealthy Allen being disowned by family and winding up as aspiring prizefighter. C: Brenda Joyce, Joseph Allen, Jr., Cobina Wright, Jr. D: Eugene Forde. DRA 74m.

Rikki and Pete 1988 Australian ★★★ Brother and sister eccentrics make their own way in the Outback with quirky Ausralian style. Goofball charm gets it far enough. C: Stephen Kearney, Nina Landis, Tetchie Agbayani, Bill Hunter. D: Nadia Tass. COM 103m. V

Rim of the Canyon 1949 ★★★½ Autry plays dual father/son role in solid B-Western. As the son he tries to recover stolen loot from escaped outlaws jailed by his father 20 years earlier. C: Gene Autry, Nan Leslie, Thurston Hall, Denver Pyle. D: John English. WST 70m. V

Ring-a-Ding Rhythm 1962 British ★★★ Producers Shapiro and Douglas put on variety show. Loose excuse for appearances by early rock 'n' roll performers, none of whom are in top form.(a.k.a. *It's Trad, Dad!*) C: Helen Shapiro, Craig Douglas, Felix Felton, Arthur Mullard, John Leyton, Chubby Checker, Del Shannon, Gary Bonds, Gene Vincent, Gene McDaniels, Acker Bilk, Temperance Seven. D: Richard Lester. COM 78m.

Ring Around the Clock 1953 Italian ★★★½ Amusing political satire about a broken town clock and its use as a pawn in a power struggle between democrats, Communists, and the clergy. Well-handled idea, perhaps best appreciated by those with an interest in Italian politics. C: Patrizia Mangano, Nando Burno,

Lauro Gazzolo. D: Paolo W. Tamburella. COM 88m.

Ring of Bright Water 1969 British ★★★½ McKenna and Travers reprise roles from *Born Free*, playing two naturalists who face many challenges while raising a wild otter. Well-made attempt to capture earlier film's magic mainly proves that lions are more entertaining movie animals than otters. C: Bill Travers, Virginia McKenna, Peter Jeffrey, Jameson Clark. D: Jack Couffer. FAM/DRA [G] 109m. V

Ring of Fire 1961 ★★ A Sheriff (Janssen) is held hostage by three fugitives. Film notable for harrowing forest fire climax. C: David Janssen, Joyce Taylor, Frank Gorshin, Joel Marston, Doodles Weaver. D: Andrew L. Stone. ACT 91m.

Ring of Spies 1964 British ★★★½ Intriguing but slow-paced drama based on true story of English suburban spies, known as the Portland ring, and their eventual discovery.(a.k.a. *Ring of Treason*) C: Bernard Lee, William Sylvester, Margaret Tyzeck. D: Robert Tronson. DRA 90m.

Ring of Terror 1962 ★ Bottom of the barrel shocker, with fraternity pledge (Mather) mixed up with corpses as part of initiation rite. C: George Mather, Esther Furst, Austin Green, Joseph Conway. D: Clark Paylow. DRA 72m. V

Ring of Treason 1964 *See* **Ring of Spies**

Ringside 1949 ★★★½ Sentimental boxing yarn with concert pianist (Barry) taking to the ring when brother (Brown) is blinded in fixed fight. Obvious, but entertaining. C: Don Barry, Tom Brown, Sheila Ryan. D: Frank McDonald. DRA 68m. V

Rio Bravo 1959 ★★★★½ A big law officer recruits four unlikely deputies in a stand-off against outlaws attempting to break a killer out of jail. Underrated, enduring Western entertainment skillfully done by all. A classic! C: John Wayne, Dean Martin, Ricky Nelson, Angie Dickinson, Walter Brennan, John Russell, Claude Akins. D: Howard Hawks. WST 140m. V

Rio Conchos 1964 ★★★★ Exciting Western set after the Civil War with shipment of 2,000 rifles stolen from Army by ex-Confederates who want to continue the war. Good action sequences. C: Richard Boone, Stuart Whitman, Tony Franciosa, Jim Brown. D: Gordon Douglas. WST 107m. V

Rio Grande 1950 ★★★★ A post-Civil War cavalry officer and his raw recruit son clash as their troop fights hostile Apaches. Highly dramatic, epic Western, with outstanding action and locales. Last of Ford's cavalry trilogy, after *Fort Apache* and *She Wore a Yellow Ribbon*. C: John Wayne, Maureen O'Hara, Ben Johnson, Harry Carey Jr., Victor McLaglen, Claude Jarman Jr., Chill Wills. D: John Ford. WST 105m. V

Rio Grande Raiders 1946 ★★½ Brothers drive for rival stagecoach companies. Minor B-Western. C: Sunset Carson, Linda Stirling, Bob Steele. D: Thomas Carr. WST 56m.

Rio Lobo 1970 ★★★½ A Civil War Yankee colonel tracks down stolen gold and unmasks a turncoat. Light humor and sharp dialogue highlight big action Western. Last movie for Hawks. C: John Wayne, Jorge Rivero, Jennifer O'Neill, Jack Elam, Chris Mitchum. D: Howard Hawks. WST [G] 105m. V

Rio Rita 1929 ★★★½ Early sound musical spectacular with great dancing, good clowning from Broadway stars Wheeler and Woolsey, and a ridiculous plot about a Texas Ranger stalking outlaws. Musical numbers in primitive color. Remade in 1942, with Abbott and Costello. C: Bert Wheeler, Robert Woolsey, John Boles, Bebe Daniels. D: Luther Reed. MUS 135m.

Rio Rita 1942 ★★★½ Second filming of Broadway musical makes amusing Abbott and Costello outing with Bud and Lou roping Nazis on dude ranch. First version starred Wheeler and Woolsey in 1929. C: Bud Abbott, Lou Costello, Kathryn Grayson, John Carroll, Tom Conway, Barry Nelson. D: S. Sylvan Simon. COM 91m. V

Riot 1969 ★★½ The prison kind, with inmates torturing guards, etc. Gratuitously ugly and brutal film, with Hackman's solid performance the only reason to view it. C: Jim Brown, Gene Hackman, Ben Carruthers, Mike Kellin, Gerald O'Loughlin. D: Buzz Kulik. ACT [PG] 97m. V

Riot in Cell Block 11 1954 ★★★★ Powerful, low-budget look at prison conditions and inmates' violent attempt to change them. Impressive, no-frills documentary-like technique. C: Neville Brand, Emile Meyer, Frank Faylen, Leo Gordon, Robert Osterloh. D: Don Siegel. ACT 80m. V

Riot on Sunset Strip 1967 ★★ When police officer Ray's daughter gets involved with drug culture, he starts one-man vendetta of violence on title street. Silly, exploitational melodrama. C: Aldo Ray, Mimsy Farmer, Michael Evans, Laurie Mock, Tim Rooney, Bill Baldwin. D: Arthur Dreifuss. ACT 85m.

Ripping Yarns—Vol. 1 1988 ★★★★ Originally broadcast on BBC television, this loopy parody features ex-Monty Python player Michael Palin in series of comic episodes satirizing British periods and society. Palin takes on his different parts with zest, making for an unusual and quite funny historical romp. C: Michael Palin, Gwen Watford, Ian Oglivy, Roy Kinnear. D: Alan Bell. COM [PG] 90m. TVM V

Riptide 1934 ★★★★ Lush, overbaked soap opera, with American (Shearer) marrying English noble (Marshall), then carrying on with Montgomery. Not believable for a minute, but fun to watch, with outrageous costumes and over-the-top acting. C: Norma Shearer, Robert Montgomery, Herbert Marshall, Skeets Gallagher, Ralph Forbes, Lilyan Tashman, Helen Jerome Eddy. D: Edmund Goulding. DRA 90m. V

Rise Against the Sword 1966 Japanese ★★★ Mediocre samurai film with Mifune as chief of warrior tribe in conflict with feudal lord. Quite violent, but Mifune excels, as usual. C: Toshiro Mifune, Makoto Sato. D: Hiroshi Inagaki. ACT 101m.

Rise and Fall of Legs Diamond, The 1960 ★★★★ Fast, clever and ultimately poignant story of slick killer Diamond (Danton), a man incapable of giving love, but very good at dealing death. Boetticher brings the same panache and black humor to the gangster film that he did to the Western. Excellent supporting cast and stunning b&w cinematography. C: Ray Danton, Karen Steele, Elaine Stewart, Jesse White, Simon Oakland, Robert Lowery, Warren Oates. D: Budd Boetticher. CRI 101m. V

Rise and Fall of the Third Reich, The 1968 ★★★★ This outstanding documentary—a compilation of newsreel footage—provides a riveting, detailed chronology of Germany's Nazi movement and its horrors. DOC 120m. V

Rise and Rise of Michael Rimmer, The 1970 British ★★★½ A young advertising exec quickly climbs the British political ladder all the way to the top. Broad, farcical satire is typically British, with interesting bits of Monty Python-type humor from Cleese and Chapman. C: Peter Cook, Denholm Elliott, Ronald Fraser, Vanessa Howard. John Cleese Graham Chapman. D: Kevin Billington. COM [R] 94m.

Rise and Shine 1941 ★★★½ Not-too-bright football hero Oakie is kidnapped by rival team in amusing nonsense with outstanding cast. Adapted from James Thurber's *My Life and Hard Times*. C: Jack Oakie, Linda Darnell, George Murphy, Walter Brennan, Sheldon Leonard, Donald Meek, Ruth Donnelly, Milton Berle, Donald MacBride, Raymond Walburn. D: Allan Dwan. DRA 93m.

Rise of Louis XIV 1966 French ★★★ Rossellini made this biography for French TV as a part of a historical series. Richly detailed but slow account of the life of King Louis XIV. C: Jean-Marie Patte, Raymond Jourdan. D: Roberto Rossellini. DRA [G] 100m. V

Rise of the Moon, The 1957 Irish ★★★½ Famed Abbey Players perform three Irish short stories in well-acted, but static film. C: Cyril Cusack, Maureen Connell, Noel Purcell, Frank Lawton, Jimmy O'Dea. D: John Ford. DRA 81m.

Rising Damp 1980 British ★★★½ Boardinghouse landlord (Rossiter) has his hands full trying to seduce tenant. Amusing, if somewhat coarse feature-length version of popular British TV series. C: Leonard Rossiter, Frances de la Tour, Don Warrington, Christopher Strauli. D: Joe McGrath. COM 96m.

Rising Sun 1993 ★★★ A veteran detective (Connery) and his young partner (Snipes) investigate a murder committed during a party at a Japanese conglomerate's lavish L.A. headquarters. Slick and predictable, with stereotypical characters of various ilks. Based on the novel by Michael Crichton. C: Sean Connery, Wesley Snipes, Harvey Keitel, Mako. D: Philip Kaufman. CRI [R] 129m. V

Risk 1994 ★★★½ A struggling NY artist (Sillas) picks up a disturbed young man (Ilku), and begins a romance with violent undertones. Good performances spark a somewhat trite story. C: Karen Sillas, David Ilku, Molly Price. D: Deirdre Fishel. DRA 85m.

Risk, The 1960 British ★★★★ Dynamic thriller about scientist (Cushing) who's invented a cure for plague, then pursued by rival governments. Momentum never lets up in entertaining adventure. C: Tony Britton, Peter Cushing, Ian Bannen, Virginia Maskell, Donald Pleasence. D: Roy Boulting, John Boulting. ACT 81m.

Risky Business 1983 ★★★★ What could have been another prurient teen sex comedy is instead a sharp, perceptive satire. Cruise became a star playing slightly repressed teen, and DeMornay is terrific as a call girl who convinces him to turn his house into a bordello while his parents are away. Director's debut. C: Tom Cruise, Rebecca De Mornay, Curtis Armstrong, Bronson Pinchot, Raphael Sbarge, Joe Pantoliano, Nicholas Pryor, Richard Masur. D: Paul Brickman. COM [R] 99m. V

Rites of Summer 1987 *See* **White Water Summer**

Ritz, The 1976 ★★★½ A loser (Weston) plans to inherit profitable garbage business, but when he starts getting death threats, he must hide out in a gay bathhouse. Humor hasn't aged well, though slam-bang farce provides some laughs. C: Jack Weston, Rita Moreno, Jerry Stiller, F. Murray Abraham, Treat Williams. D: Richard Lester. COM [R] 91m. V

River Changes, The 1956 ★★★★ Fascinating propaganda piece about river changing course, putting villagers under jurisdiction of Communist country which ruins their lives. One-dimensional, but gripping. C: Rossana Rory, Harald Maresch. D: Owen Crump. DRA 91m.

River Lady 1948 ★★★ De Carlo runs Mississippi riverboat, with casino as lure for rich men she intends to ruin. Fairly trite melodrama does have some good action sequences. C: Yvonne De Carlo, Dan Duryea, Rod Cameron, Helena Carter, Lloyd Gough, Florence Bates. D: George Sherman. DRA 78m.

River Niger, The 1978 ★★★½ African-American family furthers their knowledge of themselves and world, based on 1972 Broadway play. Notable mostly for strength of cast. C: James Earl Jones, Cicely Tyson, Glynn Turman, Lou Gossett Jr. D: Krishna Shah. DRA [R] 104m. V

River of Dollars, A 1966 *See* **Hills Run Red, The**

River of No Return 1954 ★★★½ After rescuing Calhoun and Monroe from near drowning, Mitchum is double-crossed by Calhoun and left to defend Monroe and his young son against an Indian uprising. Neat premise and gorgeous locations, but relatively unexciting drama despite cast. C: Robert Mitchum, Marilyn Monroe, Rory Calhoun, Tommy Rettig. D: Otto Preminger. DRA 91m. V

River of Unrest 1937 British ★★★½ Irish vs. British struggle forms backdrop for Romeo and Juliet-type romance as Loder kills the brother of his lover (Cellier) by mistake. Undistinguished acting mars good idea. C: John Lodge, John Loder, Antoinette Cellier. D: Brian Desmond-Hurst. DRA 70m.

River Rat, The 1984 ★★★½ Wrongly imprisoned ex-con (Jones) returns home after 13 years in jail, and tries to establish a relationship with his daughter (Plimpton). Good, workmanlike cast, stuck with a fair but minor script. C: Tommy Lee Jones, Nancy Lea Owen, Brian Dennehy, Martha Plimpton. D: Tom Rickman. DRA [PG] 93m. V

River Runs Through It, A 1992 ★★★★ Graceful if somewhat plodding story of two very different brothers growing up in pre-WWI Montana, bonded by their love of fly fishing. Beautifully photographed, movie is triumph of thoughtful moviemaking over mediocre acting. C: Craig Sheffer, Brad Pitt, Tom Skerritt, Emily Lloyd, Brenda Blethyn. D: Robert Redford. DRA [PG] 124m. V

River, The 1951 Indian ★★★★★ Renoir's masterpiece about three young women growing up in British colonial India. Simple, life-affirming story and lyrical photography have made this a classic. Based on the novel by Rumer Godden. C: Patricia Walters, Nora Swinburne, Arthur Shields, Radha. D: Jean Renoir. DRA 99m. V

River, The 1961 Indian ★★★½ A timid fisherman dreams of finding work by the sea, instead of his river, but dares not venture from his home. Quiet, simple story. C: Niranijan Ray, Janash Muknerii, Sandhya Ray, Ruma Gangaly. D: Rajen Tarafder. DRA 105m.

River, The 1984 ★★★½ A farm family contends with flood waters threatening their land. Well-intended drama goes overboard in making heroes out of its characters—they seem more mythic than real. C: Sissy Spacek, Mel Gibson, Shane Bailey, Scott Glenn. D: Mark Rydell. DRA [PG-13] 124m. V

River Wild, The 1994 ★★★★ A major departure for Streep as a mom whose family whitewater rafting trip turns into a battle for survival when they encounter a charming psycho (Bacon) on the river. Rousing action sequences carry the day. C: Meryl Streep, Kevin Bacon, David Strathairn, Joseph Mazzello, John C. Riley. D: Curtis Hanson. ACT [PG-13]

River's Edge 1987 ★★★★ Bleak, nihilistic yet restrained tale of suburban teens so jaded that they can't react when a friend shows them the dead body of the girlfriend he murdered. A definitive and frightening look at disengaged teens struggling to give meaning to their world. C: Crispin Glover, Keanu Reeves, Ione Skye, Daniel Roebuck, Dennis Hopper. D: Tim Hunter. DRA [R] 99m. V

River's Edge, The 1957 ★★★½ Bank robber Milland takes farmer Quinn hostage on journey to Mexico. Milland's bitter performance is one of his best, but unfortunately the film loses steam halfway through. C: Ray Milland, Anthony Quinn, Debra Paget, Byron Foulger. D: Allan Dwan. CRI 87m.

River's End 1931 ★★★★ Bickford plays a double role as a fugitive who impersonates the Canadian Mountie who dies during his manhunt. Suspenseful action piece, well played. Originally done as a silent film in 1920, and also remade in 1940. C: Charles Bickford, Evelyn Knapp, Zasu Pitts. D: Michael Curtiz. WST 75m.

River's End 1940 ★★★½ Fugitive (Morgan) assumes the identity of the law officer who dies accidentally while pursuing him in fair remake of 1931 drama. (a.k.a. *Double Identity*) C: Dennis Morgan, George Tobias, Elizabeth Earl, Victor Jory. D: Ray Enright. WST 69m.

Road Back, The 1937 ★★★ Sequel to *All Quiet on the Western Front*, following problems of German soldiers trying to readjust to civilian life after WWI. Whale tried to make a strong anti-war statement, but under Nazi pressure the studio re-edited and diluted it. Still very very interesting. C: Richard Cromwell, John King, Slim Summerville, Andy Devine, Barbara Read, Louise Fazenda, Noah Beery Jr., Lionel Atwill. D: James Whale. DRA 97m.

Road Games 1981 Australian ★★★½ Trucker (Keach) and hitchhiker (Curtis) track down a serial killer who preys on female hitchers. Twists keep things interesting. Don't expect Hitchcock, despite homages. C: Stacy Keach, Jamie Lee Curtis, Marion Edward, Grant Page. D: Richard Franklin. CRI [PG] 100m. V

Road House 1948 ★★★ Strange little film noir with Lupino as singer who comes between Widmark and Wilde, who are already sworn enemies. Becoming obsessed, Widmark tries to frame ex-con Wilde for other crimes. Strong cast undone by awkward script and direction. C: Ida Lupino, Cornel Wilde, Celeste Holm, Richard Widmark, O.Z. Whitehead, Robert Karnes. D: Jean Negulesco. CRI 95m. V

Road House 1989 ★★ Roadhouse bouncer/philosophy student Swayze cleans up Missouri town run by Gazzara. Violent action, best for Swayze fans. Lynch does the best she can with the thankless role as Swayze's most ardent admirer. C: Patrick Swayze, Kelly

Lynch, Sam Elliott, Ben Gazzara. D: Rowdy Herrington. ACT [R] 123m. V

Road Runner Chase *See* **Runner Movie, The**

Road Scholar 1993 ★★★★ Hilarious tour of the U.S., guided by poet and radio commentator Andrei Codrescu. Starts out as a visit to the scenes of Kerouac's *On the Road* but quickly gets much loopier. Very funny, if a bit too glib for its own good at times. C: Andrei Codrescu. D: Roger Weisberg. COM 81m.

Road Show 1941 ★★★½ Two sane inmates of mental hospital escape and join a traveling circus. Quirky comedy is charming at times, slow at others. Co-written by silent-era star Harry Langdon. C: Adolphe Menjou, Carole Landis, John Hubbard, Charles Butterworth, Patsy Kelly, George Stone. D: Hal Roach, Gordon Douglas, Hal Roach Jr. COM 87m.

Road to Bali 1952 ★★★★ Hope, Crosby, and Lamour in color for the first and only time as the boys contend with cannibals and jungle animals in their pursuit of Lamour. Very funny, with star cameos—Bogart's a stand-out. C: Bob Hope, Dorothy Lamour, Bing Crosby, Murvyn Vye. D: Hal Walker. COM 91m. V

Road to Denver, The 1955 ★★★ Tepid Western of good brother Payne risking all to help no-good black sheep Cobb. C: John Payne, Lee J. Cobb, Skip Homeier, Mona Freeman, Ray Middleton, Lee Van Cleef, Andy Clyde, Glenn Strange. D: Joseph Kane. WST 90m.

Road to Glory, The 1936 ★★★½ Episodic WWI drama set in France, with March and Baxter as doomed soldiers. Morose, plodding at times, but well acted. C: Fredric March, Warner Baxter, Lionel Barrymore, June Lang, Gregory Ratoff, Victor Kilian. D: Howard Hawks. DRA 95m.

Road to Hong Kong, The 1962 ★★★ The Road Series comes to a lumbering halt in dull escapade involving spies and space travel. Lamour has a small role here, as herself, while Peter Sellers does a funny cameo. C: Bob Hope, Bing Crosby, Joan Collins, Dorothy Lamour, Robert Morley. D: Norman Panama. COM 92m. V

Road to Life 1932 Russian ★★★★ Excellent early Soviet talkie dramatizes then-current social problem of children left homeless after the Bolshevik Revolution. Though somewhat melodramatic, it is an interesting piece of Soviet propaganda. C: Mikhail Zharov, Maria Gonta, Tzyvan Kyrla. D: Nikolai Ekk. DRA 101m.

Road to Morocco 1942 ★★★★ One of the best of the Road movies, with Hope sold into slavery by Crosby, then both fall for princess Lamour. Silly stuff but very amusing. Bing gets to croon a good ballad, "Moonlight Becomes You." C: Bing Crosby, Dorothy Lamour, Bob Hope, Dona Drake, Anthony Quinn, Vladimir Sokoloff, Monte Blue, Yvonne De Carlo, Jerry Colonna. D: David Butler. COM 82m. V

Road to Reno, The 1938 ★★★ Unusual mixture of screwball comedy with Western drama as cowpoke (Scott) refuses to let wife (Hampton) divorce him. C: Randolph Scott, Hope Hampton, Glenda Farrell. D: S. Sylvan Simon. COM 72m.

Road to Rio 1947 ★★★★ The boys in Brazil. Crosby and Hope have a field day helping Lamour out of evil aunt's (Sondergaard's) clutches. The Andrews Sisters even pop up to put over a hit song, "You Don't Have to Know the Language." C: Bing Crosby, Bob Hope, Dorothy Lamour, Gale Sondergaard. D: Norman McLeod. COM 100m. V

Road to Singapore 1940 ★★★½ First movie in long-running Road series sets up the formula: Hope's wisecracks, Crosby's crooning, Lamour's sarong. Not as funny as some of the ones that followed, but worth seeing. C: Bing Crosby, Dorothy Lamour, Bob Hope, Charles Coburn, Judith Barrett, Anthony Quinn, Jerry Colonna. D: Victor Schertzinger. COM 84m. V

Road to Utopia 1945 ★★★★½ Probably the best Road picture, with Hope and Crosby in Alaska, looking for lost gold mine and finding saloon singer Lamour, who does a nice job with "Personality." Funny sight gags, great sled scenes, and a good script. C: Bing Crosby, Bob Hope, Dorothy Lamour, Hillary Brooke, Douglass Dumbrille. D: Hal Walker. COM 90m. V

Road to Wellville, The 1994 ★★½ Hopkins runs an unusual health spa in turn-of-the-century Michigan, where Broderick is subjected to enemas, salt scrubs, and vats of yogurt. Lovingly produced, but ultimately tasteless comedy, attempting to spoof America's obsession with health fads. C: Matthew Broderick, Anthony Hopkins, Bridget Fonda, Dana Carvey, John Cusack. D: Alan Parker. COM [R] 117m. V

Road to Zanzibar 1941 ★★★½ Lukewarm trek for Hope and Crosby as they tromp through jungle in search of diamond mine. Some good animal gags. C: Bing Crosby, Bob Hope, Dorothy Lamour, Una Merkel, Eric Blore. D: Victor Schertzinger. COM 92m. V

Road Warrior, The 1981 Australian ★★★★½ Hyperdynamic sequel to original *Mad Max* finds brooding ex-cop Gibson reluctantly drawn into battle between peaceful gasoline manufacturers and bike-riding barbarians. Vivid characterizations, jaw-dropping stunts, influential costume designs add up to the best of action cinema. (a.k.a. *Mad Max 2*) *Mad Max Beyond Thunderdome* followed. C: Mel Gibson, Bruce Spence, Vernon Wells, Mike Preston, Virginia Hey. D: George Miller. ACT [R] 96m. V

Roadblock 1951 ★★★ Predictable B-movie film noir with standard plot of insurance investigator involved with corrupt, greedy woman. C: Charles McGraw, Joan Dixon, Lowell Gilmore, Louis Jean Heydt, Milburn Stone. D: Harold Daniels. CRI 73m.

Roadhouse Murder, The 1932 ★★★½ B-mystery with intriguing premise. Reporter (Linden) frames himself for murder so he can write series for paper; but plan backfires. Routinely acted and scripted, but entertaining nonetheless. C: Eric Linden, Dorothy Jordan, Bruce Cabot. D: Walter Ruben. CRI 77m.

Roadhouse Nights 1930 ★★★½ Roadhouse singer (Morgan) tries to protect an old boy-friend from the wrath of the club's gangster owner. The performances are better than the script, but it's still a treat for Morgan fans. Jimmy Durante's film debut. C: Helen Morgan, Charles Ruggles, Jimmy Durante. D: Hobart Henley. CRI 68m.

Roadie 1980 ★★★ Meat Loaf stars as a road crew member on a quest with a never-ending rock 'n' roll show tour. Lowbrow humor reigns supreme here. Packed with music cameos ranging from Roy Orbison to Alice Cooper. C: Meat Loaf, Kaki Hunter, Art Carney, Gaillard Sartain, Alice Cooper, Blondie, Roy Orbison, Hank Williams Jr., Ramblin Jack Elliot. D: Alan Rudolph. MUS [PG] 105m. V

Roaming Lady 1936 ★★★½ Slick action piece with Wray as stowaway heiress getting involved with aviator Bellamy's secret mission, and both getting captured by Chinese revolutionaries. Absurd, but entertaining. C: Fay Wray, Ralph Bellamy, Thurston Hall. D: Albert S. Rogell. ACT 68m.

Roaring Twenties, The 1939 ★★★★ Home from the Great War, a young New Yorker joins a band of bootleggers. In short time he rises to the top of the crime world. Unrelenting action and engaging performances. Entertaining! C: James Cagney, Priscilla Lane, Humphrey Bogart, Gladys George, Jeffrey Lynn. D: Raoul Walsh. ACT 106m. V

Rob Roy, the Highland Rogue 1953 ★★ Historical Disney epic features 18th-century Scottish rebel (Todd) who leads people in battle against King George. Stagy production and painfully stiff dialogue make a boring costume drama. C: Richard Todd, Glynis Johns, James Robertson Justice, Michael Gough. D: Harold French. FAM/DRA 81m. V

Robber Symphony, The 1937 British ★★★½ Enigmatic, surrealistic story of pianist Feher and his mother getting mixed up with crooks after loot is hidden in their piano. Told with minimum of dialogue and maximum of expressionistic tricks, to mixed effect. For the curious. C: George Graves, Magda Sonja, Hans Feher. D: Friedrich Feher. DRA 136m.

Robbers of the Range 1941 ★★★ Rancher (Holt) is framed for murder by railroad company coveting his land. Passable B-Western. C: Tim Holt, Virginia Vale, Ray Whitley, Emmet Lynn. D: Edward Killy. WST 61m.

Robber's Roost 1955 ★★★½ It's cattle rustlers vs. honest ranchers in fair Western with good production values, from Zane Grey novel. C: George Montgomery, Richard Boone, Bruce Bennett, Warren Stevens, Peter Graves, Sylvia Findley. D: Sidney Salkow. WST 82m.

Robbery 1967 British ★★★★ Reasonably suspenseful dramatization of famous Royal Mail train robbery of 1963. Builds steam steadily till exciting chase finale. C: Stanley Baker, Joanna Pettet, James Booth, Frank Finlay, Barry Foster. D: Peter Yates. CRI 113m. V

Robe, The 1953 ★★★½ Biblical epic of Roman centurion's conversion to Christianity is often dull and uninspired, though Simmons is lovely and Mature's character spawned a sequel *Demetrios and the Gladiators.* Popular first film in CinemaScope loses much on small screen. C: Richard Burton, Jean Simmons, Victor Mature, Michael Rennie. D: Henry Koster. DRA 133m. V

Robert A. Heinlein's The Puppet Masters 1994 ★★★★ UFO lands in Iowa and starts taking over the minds of all who come close to it. Chilling sci-fi, with an expert performance by Sutherland as a CIA agent out to stop the alien menace. Heinlein's classic previously "inspired" the 1958 quickie, *The Brain Eaters.* C: Donald Sutherland, Eric Thal, Julie Warner, Yaphet Kotto. D: Stuart Orme. SFI [R] 109m. V

Roberta 1935 ★★★★ American football hero Scott inherits his aunt's fashion salon in Paris. Ridiculous plot doesn't stop Astaire and Rogers from seizing Jerome Kern's wonderful songs and dancing themselves silly. Highlights include "I Won't Dance," "I'll Be Hard to Handle," "Let's Begin," and Dunne's renditions of "Smoke Gets In Your Eyes" and "Yesterdays." Remade in 1952 as *Lovely to Look At.* C: Irene Dunne, Fred Astaire, Ginger Rogers, Randolph Scott. D: William A. Seiter. MUS 106m. V

Robin and Marian 1976 British ★★★★ A middle-aged Robin Hood (Connery) returns from the Crusades to find life has passed him by. Melancholy, bittersweet romance with Maid Marian (Hepburn) highlights this quiet, revisionist view of a legend. C: Sean Connery, Audrey Hepburn, Robert Shaw, Richard Harris, Nicol Williamson, Denholm Elliott, Ronnie Barker. D: Richard Lester. DRA 112m. V

Robin and the Seven Hoods 1964 ★★★★ Diverting musical casts Sinatra as gangster Robin Hood in Chicago during Prohibition. Best of the Rat Pack movies has them high-stepping their way through good Jimmy Van Heusen/Sammy Cahn songs ("My Kind of Town," "Style"). Crosby's a standout; look for cameo by Edward G. Robinson. C: Frank Sinatra, Dean Martin, Sammy Davis Jr., Bing Crosby, Peter Falk. D: Gordon Douglas. MUS 123m. V

Robin Hood 1922 ★★★★ Silent swashbuckler casts Fairbanks as the rambunctious lord of Sherwood Forest, who robs from the rich . . ., well, you know. Marvelous action sequences makes this an entertaining version, second only to Flynn's. C: Douglas Fairbanks, Sr., Wallace Beery, Enid Bennett, Alan Hale. D: Allan Dwan. ACT 110m.

Robin Hood 1973 ★★★½ Disney's animated version of Robin Hood legends reworks story with forest animals. Robin is typecast as fox battling evil wolf Sheriff of Nottingham for freedom in Sherwood Forest. Average by usually high Disney standards, though there's enough action, comedy, and music here to entertain younger audiences. Voices of Brian Bedford, Phil Harris, Monica Evans, Peter Ustinov, Terry Thomas, Andy Devine, Roger Miller, Pat Buttram. D: Wolfgang Reitherman. FAM/MUS 83m. V

Robin Hood 1991 ★★★½ The likable rogue (Bergin) and his merry men steal from the rich and give to the poor once again in this familiar but watchable version of the swashbuckling tale. A theatrical feature that went straight to TV in the U.S. C: Patrick Bergin, Uma Thurman, Jeroen Krabbe, Jurgen Prochnow. D: John Irvin. ACT 116m. TVM V

Robin Hood: Men in Tights 1993 ★★★ Mel Brooks' lampoon of Robin Hood aims more at Kevin Costner than Errol Flynn. Elwes plays the Prince of Thieves, leading his goofy band guided by Brooks' patented formula of repetitive (if often obvious) jokes. C: Cary Elwes, Tracey Ullman, Richard Lewis, Dom Deluise, Isaac Hayes, Mel Brooks. D: Mel Brooks. COM [PG-13] 105m. V

Robin Hood of El Dorado, The 1936 ★★★½ Flashy, fictionalized biography of Mexican bandit Joaquin Murietta (Baxter), who becomes a bandit to avenge his wife's death. C: Warner Baxter, Ann Loring, Margo, Bruce Cabot, J. Naish. D: William Wellman. WST 86m.

Robin Hood: Prince of Thieves 1991 ★★★½ Retelling of the classic tale with Costner as the rebel hero and Freeman as a misplaced Moor. Rickman is the show stealer as the Sheriff of Nottingham. C: Kevin Costner, Morgan Freeman, Mary Elizabeth Mastrantonio, Christian Slater, Alan Rickman. D: Kevin Reynolds. ACT [PG-13] 144m. V

Robin of Texas 1947 ★★★★ Outstanding Autry musical Western casts Gene as owner of ranch, victimized by bank robbers. Benefits from good action sequences and star's easygoing charm. C: Gene Autry, Lynne Roberts, Sterling Holloway. D: Lesley Selander. WST 71m. V

Robinson Crusoe 1952 *See* **Adventures of Robinson Crusoe, The**

Robinson Crusoe on Mars 1964 ★★★★ Superior science fiction recasts Defoe story into space travel tale as astronaut is stranded on Mars, with only his moneky, encountering alien "Friday." Beautifully photographed in Death Valley. C: Paul Mantee, Vic Lundin, Adam West. D: Byron Haskin. SFI 109m.

Robocop 1987 ★★★★ Brain of slain Detroit police officer is implanted in powerful robot body, creating a computerized supercop who solves his own murder-and finds his corporate creators implicated. Wickedly smart, ultraviolent action sci-fi, but what makes it a winner is acid satire of big business and media culture, plus misfit melancholy of its cyborg hero. C: Peter Weller, Nancy Allen, Ronny Cox, Kurtwood Smith. D: Paul Verhoeven. SFI [R] 103m. V

Robocop 2 1990 ★★★ Plot-crammed follow-up pits Robocop against a drug cult, a stronger rival cyborg, and his amoral corporate creators. Despite thrill-a-minute pace, overwhelming cynicism and brutality make this far less enjoyable than the original. C: Peter Weller, Nancy Allen, Daniel O'Herlihy, Belinda Bauer, Tom Noonan, Gabriel Damon. D: Irvin Kershner. SFI [R] 117m. V

Robocop 3 1993 ★★ Cyborg cop has to defend the downtrodden when a Japanese magnate sends Torn to clean up Detroit for corporate gain. The popular *Robocop* film became the basis for a syndicated TV series. C: Robert John Burke, Nancy Allen, Rip Torn, Jill Hennessy, CCH Pounder. D: Fred Dekker. ACT [PG-13] 105m. V

Robot Jox 1991 ★★★ Future superpowers settle disputes through duels between huge, robot-like fighting machines. Flaccid storyline pits champion U.S. robot pilot against Russian nemesis. Moderately entertaining cheapie. C: Gary Graham, Paul Koslo, Anne-Marie Johnson. D: Stuart Gordon. SFI [PG] 85m. V

Robot Wars 1993 ★★ The makers of *Robot Jox* didn't spend much time on the script of this sketchy follow-up. When bad guys hijack nation's only mega-robot, hotshot pilot locates a spare and the two giants clash. Sparse but okay David Allen special effects. C: Don Michael Paul, Barbara Crampton, James Staley. D: Albert Band. SFI [PG] 106m. V

Rocco and His Brothers 1960 Italian ★★★★ Family of brothers, who are rivals in love and business, and their mother leave the countryside for the urban life in Milan. Brilliantly complex, if at times slow-moving, character study. C: Alain Delon, Renato Salvatori, Annie Girardot, Claudia Cardinale. D: Luchino Visconti. DRA 175m. V

Rock-a-Bye Baby 1958 ★★★½ Film star with illegitimate triplets asks high school admirer Lewis to take care of them. Loose remake of classic *Miracle of Morgan's Creek*, in Lewis's inimitable manic style. C: Jerry Lewis, Marilyn Maxwell, Connie Stevens, Baccaloni, Reginald Gardiner, James Gleason, Hans Conried. D: Frank Tashlin. COM 103m.

Rock-a-Doodle 1992 ★★★ Rooster tired of crowing around the barnyard heads to Las Vegas, where he becomes an Elvis for the poultry set. Flashy animated kids' feature is packed with songs, but skimps on plot development and interesting characters. C: Glen Campbell, Christopher Plummer, Phil Harris, Sandy Duncan, Charles Nelson Reilly, Ellen Greene. D: Don Bluth. FAM/MUS 90m. v

Rock All Night 1957 ★★½ Strange, low-budget Corman film casts the diminuitive Miller as bartending hero fighting two murderers who have taken nightclub patrons hostage. C: Dick Miller, Russell Johnson, Jonathan Haze, Abby Dalton, The Platters, Robin Morse. D: Roger Corman. MUS 63m. v

Rock & Read ★★★★ Learn-to-read video for kids has exciting music and graphics that encourages youngsters to interract and sing along. Highly innovative, progressive, and intelligent. FAM/MUS 29m. v

Rock & Rule 1983 ★★★½ Sorcery adventure, fully animated with a sound track by rock stars like Deborah Harry, Cheap Trick, Earth, Wind & Fire, and Lou Reed. Not much plot, but good animation and music. Voices of Don Francks, Paul Le Mat, Susan Roman, Sam Langevin, Catherine O'Hara. D: Clive Smith. MUS 85m. v

Rock Around the Clock 1956 ★★★½ Nostalgic look at early days of American rock 'n' roll scene with performances by some of the innovators. Slim plot about band's career problems is unimportant. Songs include "See You Later Alligator," "The Great Pretender," and title tune. Remade as *Twist Around the Clock*. C: Bill Haley, The Comets, The Platters, Tony Martinez, & his Band, Freddie Bell, & His Bellboys, Alan Freed, Johnny Johnston. D: Fred F. Sears. MUS 77m.

Rock 'n' Roll High School 1979 ★★★½ Ramones fan Soles leads her friends (and ultimately, her favorite band) against rock music-hating principal Woronov. Energetic low-budget comedy bursting with funny gags and hard-driving music. C: P. J. Soles, Vincent Van Patten, The Ramones. D: Allan Arkush. COM [PG] 93m. v

Rock, Rock, Rock! 1956 ★★★½ Low-budget teen flick about Weld's desire for a strapless prom dress. Campy look at '50s mores, with some vintage rock 'n' roll performances, including Frankie Lymons' rendition of "I'm Not a Juvenile Delinquent." Weld's film debut. C: Tuesday Weld, Alan Freed, Frankie Lymon, Chuck Berry, Fats Domino. D: Will Price. COM 78m. v

Rocket Gibraltar 1988 ★★★ Tragicomedy about large clan coming together for patriarch's birthday, each arriving with problems to solve. Culkin's first film. C: Burt Lancaster, Suzy Amis, John Glover, Bill Pullman. D: Daniel Petrie. DRA [PG] 100m. v

Rocket Ship X-M 1950 ★★★½ A space mission to the lunar surface winds up exploring Mars instead. Fifties-era special effects make this one interesting. C: Lloyd Bridges, Osa Massen, Hugh O'Brian, John Emery. D: Kurt Neumann. SFI 77m. v

Rocket to Nowhere 1962 Czechoslovakian ★★★★ Diverting children's fantasy, as robotic spacehip saves alien children from their ravaged world. Good special effects, charming atmosphere. C: Jiri Vrstala, Eva Hrabetova. D: Jindrich Polak. FAM/SFI 73m.

Rocketeer, The 1991 ★★★★ Ordinary guy (Campbell) becomes Nazi-battling superhero after a high-tech (for the '30s) jet pack lands in his hands. Entertaining adventure in the Saturday matinee mold with a great performance by Connelly. Good family viewing. C: Bill Campbell, Jennifer Connelly, Alan Arkin, Timothy Dalton, Paul Sorvino, Ele Keats. D: Joe Johnston. ACT [PG] 109m. v

Rockets Galore! 1957 *See* **Mad Little Island**

Rocking Horse Winner, The 1949 British ★★★★ When a young boy learns he can select racetrack winners while mounted on an old rocking horse his mother's greed spells calamity. Solid production of D.H. Lawrence short story despite lapses into sentimental pathos. C: Valerie Hobson, John Howard Davies, John Mills, Ronald Squire. D: Anthony Pelissier. DRA 91m. v

Rocky 1976 ★★★★½ Down-and-out palooka has impossible dream, gets just one chance—and beats all the odds. Blockbuster catapulted writer/star Stallone to fame in similar fashion. Very simply, this is a film that anyone can love. Oscars for Best Picture, Direction, and Editing. C: Sylvester Stallone, Talia Shire, Burt Young, Carl Weathers, Burgess Meredith, Thayer David. D: John G. Avildsen. DRA [PG] 125m. v

Rocky 2 1979 ★★★½ Rocky Balboa struggles to get another chance against champ Apollo Creed. After the genuine class of the original, series settles in for the long haul. Nevertheless, keeps punching and does fine here. C: Sylvester Stallone, Talia Shire, Burt Young, Carl Weather, Burgess Meredith. D: Sylvester Stallone. ACT [PG] 120m. v

Rocky 3 1982 ★★★ Clubber Lang (Mr. T) challenges Rocky and beats him senseless. Rocky gets one-time rival Creed to train him for the rematch. Fun wearing thin now, but Stallone keeps punching. C: Sylvester Stallone, Talia Shire, Mr. T, Hulk Hogan. D: Sylvester Stallone. ACT [PG] 100m. v

Rocky 4 1985 ★★ Boxer Rocky Balboa comes out of retirement after his friend, Apollo Creed is killed in the ring by super Commie Ivan Drago (Lundgren). Guess what happens? More of the same, with James Brown's musical number the show-stopping highlight. C: Sylvester Stallone, Dolph Lundgren, Carl Weathers, Talia Shire. D: Sylvester Stallone. DRA [PG] 91m. v

Rocky 5 1990 ★★½ A brain-damaged Rocky trains a protégé, real-life pugilist Tommy "The Duke" Morrison, and then must return to the ring, one last time, to fight the cocky youngster. Dopey, punch-drunk sequel. C: Sylvester Stallone, Talia Shire, Sage Stallone, Tommy Morrison, Thunder Wolf, Jeff Langton. D: John Avildsen. DRA [PG-13] 104m. V

Rocky Horror Picture Show, The 1975 British ★★★★ Stuffy young couple (Sarandon and Bostwick) with car trouble will never be the same after a night in a spooky old house with the anything-goes gang from Transylvania. Cult classic horror spoof has fabulous cast and music. Utterly unique. C: Tim Curry, Susan Sarandon, Barry Bostwick, Richard O'Brien, Charles Gray, Patricia Quinn, Meat Loaf. D: Jim Sharman. MUS [R] 106m. V

Rocky Mountain 1950 ★★★½ Confederate officer (Flynn) joins forces with Northern troops to fight Indians. Civil War drama offers some tremendous action set pieces. C: Errol Flynn, Patrice Wymore, Scott Forbes, Slim Pickens, Sheb Wooley, Yakima Canutt. D: William Keighley. WST 83m.

Rocky Mountain Mystery 1935 ★★★ Unusual comic whodunit set at a western radium mine, with Scott as stalwart cowboy turned detective. Presence of famed stage actress Mrs. Leslie Carter seems a bit gratuitous. (a.k.a. *The Fighting Westerner*) C: Randolph Scott, Leslie Carter, Willie Fung. D: Charles Barton. WST 63m. V

Rodan 1957 Japanese ★★★½ Two mutant pterodactyls emerge from mountain and menace Tokyo. Early Japanese giant-monster horror film, one of the first of its kind in color and still entertaining. C: Kenji Sawara, Yumi Shirakawa, Akihiko Hirata, Akio Kobori. D: Inoshiro Honda. SFI 74m. V

Roe vs. Wade 1989 ★★★★ Gripping, well-made TV film chronicles the story behind the Supreme Court case that led to the legalization of abortion. Controversial and well played. C: Holly Hunter, Amy Madigan, Terry O'Quinn, Kathy Bates. D: Gregory Hoblit. DRA 92m. TVM V

Roger & Me 1989 ★★★★½ Wiseacre documentary follows its director's efforts to speak personally with General Motors chairman Roger Smith: Moore wants to ask Smith why he closed down a Michigan factory, and threw the entire city of Flint out of work. A mighty escapade, both acerbic and touching. D: Michael Moore. DOC [R] 87m. V

Rogue Cop 1954 ★★★½ Undercover cop Taylor joins underworld to find brother's murderer. Good cast pumps some energy into standard melodrama. C: Robert Taylor, Janet Leigh, George Raft, Steven Forrest, Anne Francis, Vince Edwards. D: Roy Rowland. CRI 92m.

Rogue Song, The 1930 ★★★½ Famed baritone Tibbett appears to good advantage in this antique Franz Lehar operetta, as a good-hearted thief romancing a Russian princess.If Laurel and Hardy's appearances seem a bit tacked on, it's because they were. C: Lawrence Tibbett, Catharine Dale Owen, Judith Voselli, Nance O'Neil. D: Lionel Barrymore. MUS 115m.

Roll of Thunder, Hear My Cry 1978 ★★★½ Preteen girl in '30s Mississippi struggles with adolescence while her family copes with hard times and racism. Nothing new, but competent storytelling. C: Claudia McNeil, Janet MacLachlan, Rockne Tarkington, John Cullum, Morgan Freeman, Lark Ruffin. D: Jack Smight. DRA 115m. TVM V

Roll on Texas Moon 1946 ★★★½ Rogers plays peacemaker between feuding sheepherders and cattle ranchers in typical star vehicle, with lively mix of action, songs, and Trigger. C: Roy Rogers, George "Gabby" Hayes, Dale Evans. D: William Witney. WST 67m. V

Roll, Wagons, Roll 1939 ★★★½ Singing cowboy Ritter escorts wagon train through Indian territory, toward Oregon. Average western with Tex's crooning of "Oh, Susannah" is a highlight. C: Tex Ritter, Nelson McDowell, Muriel Evans. D: Al Herman. WST 52m. V

Rollerball 1975 ★★★★½ Science fiction about the ups and downs of futuristic, violent sport, a combination roller derby, professional hockey, and American Gladiators. Provocative, but violent. C: James Caan, John Houseman, Maud Adams, John Beck, Moses Gunn. D: Norman Jewison. SFI [R] 128m. V

Rollercoaster 119m ★★★ An amusement park saboteur (Bottoms) is the target of a police manhunt, spearheaded by Segal. Tedious thriller opens with an exciting disaster sequence, then goes downhill. Shown in theatres with "Sensurround;" seats shook, which kept one awake, at least. C: George Segal, Timothy Bottoms, Richard Widmark, Henry Fonda, Susan Strasberg. D: James Goldstone. ACT [PG] 119m. V

Rolling Stones, The: In the Park ★★★½ Concert film of the Rolling Stones performing in London's Hyde Park, in 1969. Highlights include Jagger reading Shelley. MUS 58m. V

Rolling Thunder 1977 ★★★½ Vietnam veteran (Devane) falls into the world of violent vengeance when his family is brutally murdered. Starts out as a probing look at post-traumatic stress disorder, then slips into a standard vigilante film with some graphic violence. Jones steals the show. C: William Devane, Tommy Lee Jones, Linda Haynes, James Best, Dabney Coleman. D: John Flynn. ACT [R] 99m. V

Rollover 1981 ★★★ A wealthy woman (Fonda) and her banker (Kristofferson) fall in love during highly irregular financial intrigues which threaten the U.S. economy. Uneven thriller makes no sense, but is still fun to watch, in spots. Cronyn steals the film as a banking baddie. C: Jane Fonda, Kris Kristofferson, Hume Cronyn, Martha Plimpton. D: Alan J. Pakula. DRA [R] 118m. v

Roman Holiday 1953 ★★★★★ Wyler's lushly romantic fable chronicles an oppressed Princess (Hepburn) as she runs away to have a night on the town in Rome and falls in love with a cynical reporter (Peck), changing his life forever. Hepburn's dazzling debut won her an Oscar; Peck has never been better. Simply marvelous. C: Audrey Hepburn, Gregory Peck, Eddie Albert, Tullio Carminati. D: William Wyler. COM 118m. v

Roman Scandals 1933 ★★★★ Entertaining musical hodgepodge loosely tied together by Cantor dreaming himself back in time to ancient Rome. Includes good Busby Berkeley numbers, a funny chariot chase spoof of *Ben-Hur* and a rare screen appearance by singing star Etting. C: Eddie Cantor, Ruth Etting, Alan Mowbray, Edward Arnold, Lucille Ball, Marjorie Main. D: Frank Tuttle. MUS 92m. v

Roman Spring of Mrs. Stone, The 1961 ★★★★ Sadly adrift when her husband dies, a middle-aged actress (Leigh) finds adventure in Rome, via an affair with a disreputable young man (Beatty). Sparked by terrific performances. Based on a Tennessee Williams story. C: Vivien Leigh, Warren Beatty, Lotte Lenya, Jill St. John. D: Jose Quintero. DRA 104m. v

Romance 1930 ★★★½ Romantically experienced opera star (Garbo) has affair with young curate (Gordon). A bit sudsy, but Garbo is marvelous. C: Greta Garbo, Lewis Stone, Gavin Gordon, Elliott Nugent, Florence Lake, Clara Blandick. D: Clarence Brown. DRA 78m. v

Romance and Riches 1937 *See* **Amazing Adventure**

Romance of Rosy Ridge, The 1947 ★★★ Mediocre post-Civil War yarn has Mitchell opposed to Johnson's wooing of daughter Leigh (her film debut). C: Van Johnson, Thomas Mitchell, Janet Leigh, Marshall Thompson. D: Roy Rowland. DRA 105m.

Romance of the Rio Grande 1929 ★★★½ Prodigal son Baxter vies with evil uncle for grandfather's affection and inheritance. Star's flair compensates for rather predictable script. C: Warner Baxter, Mary Duncan, Antonio Moreno. D: Alfred Santell. DRA 95m.

Romance on the High Seas 1948 ★★★★ Day scored big in her screen debut as singer hired by socialite Paige to impersonate her on cruise. Catchy Cahn/Styne score features hit song "It's Magic." Highly enjoyable. C: Jack Carson, Janis Paige, Don DeFore, Doris Day, Oscar Levant, S.Z. Sakall, Fortunio Bonanova, Eric Blore, Franklin Pangborn. D: Michael Curtiz. MUS 99m. v

Romancing the Stone 1984 ★★★★ Shy romance novelist Turner travels to Columbia looking for her kidnapped sister, where she teams up with a charming rogue (Douglas). Stars' engaging performances, witty script, and breakneck pace make this a winner. Followed by hit sequel *Jewel of the Nile*. C: Kathleen Turner, Michael Douglas, Danny DeVito, Alfonso Arau. D: Robert Zemeckis. ACT [PG] 106m. v

Romanoff and Juliet 1961 ★★★½ Stage-bound political satire with Shakespeare's star-crossed lovers' plot transferred to Cold War world, with ambassadors' children falling in love. Amusing, with some slow stretches. C: Peter Ustinov, Sandra Dee, John Gavin, Akim Tamiroff, Rik Nutter. D: Peter Ustinov. COM 103m.

Romantic Comedy 1983 ★★★ Moore is half of a famed playwriting duo, trying to resist his attraction for his partner (Steenburgen). Bernard Slade's Broadway comedy would have been fun in 1933: It's now hopelessly out of date, but the nice cast tries. C: Dudley Moore, Mary Steenburgen, Frances Sternhagen, Ron Leibman. D: Arthur Hiller. COM [PG] 103m. v

Romantic Englishwoman, The 1975 British ★★★★★ Brilliant, electrifying comedy/drama of triangle between novelist Caine, wife Jackson, and houseguest Berger. Scintillating dialogue by Tom Stoppard; masterful direction and acting. C: Michael Caine, Glenda Jackson, Helmut Berger, Beatrice Romand, Michel Lonsdale. D: Joseph Losey. COM 117m. v

Rome Adventure 1962 ★★★½ A bookish young American (Pleshette) finds romance on her holiday in Rome with an architect (Donahue) and a casanova (Brazzi). Well done, if a bit soupy; Max Steiner's score is the highlight. C: Troy Donahue, Angie Dickinson, Rossano Brazzi, Suzanne Pleshette, Constance Ford, Chad Everett, Al Hirt. D: Delmer Daves. DRA 119m. v

Rome Express 1932 British ★★★★ Clever mystery with assorted types on European express train, mired in blackmail and murder. Slightly dated, but influential, as first of the "strangers on trains" genre. C: Conrad Veidt, Esther Ralston, Harold Huth, Gordon Harker, Donald Calthrop, Joan Barry, Cedric Wicke, Frank Vosper, Hugh Williams. D: Walter Forde. CRI 94m.

Rome Wants Another Caesar 1974 Italian ★★★½ Picturesque, but dramatically static story of ancient Rome during and immediately following the reign of Julius Caesar. Made for Italian TV. C: Daniel Olbrychsky, Hiram Keller. D: Miklos Jancso. DRA 100m.

Romeo and Juliet 1936 ★★★½ Howard and Shearer are really too old to play Shakespeare's star-crossed lovers and, frankly, not good enough for the verse. Barrymore has a splendidly hammy bit as Mercutio and Oliver is good as the Nurse, but even the sumptuous production (including Agnes

DeMille choreography) can't disguise disappointing results. C: Norma Shearer, Leslie Howard, John Barrymore, Edna May Oliver, Basil Rathbone, C. Aubrey Smith, Andy Devine, Reginald Denny, Ralph Forbes. D: George Cukor. DRA 126m. v

Romeo and Juliet 1954 British ★★★★ Shakespeare's famed romantic tragedy of young, doomed lovers features Harvey and Shentall in the title roles, with introduction by Gielgud. Great production, well-acted. Shot in location in Italy. C: Laurence Harvey, Susan Shentall, Flora Robson, Mervyn Johns. D: Renato Castellani. DRA 138m. v

Romeo and Juliet 1966 British ★★★½ A must for balletomanes, this filmed record of legendary dance pair Fonteyn and Nureyev is an important artistic document. But much of their stage magic can't be captured on screen. C: Margot Fonteyn, Rudolf Nureyev, Royal Ballet. D: Paul Czinner. DRA 124m. v

Romeo and Juliet 1968 British/Italian ★★★★★ Much-loved Zeffirelli adaptation of Shakespeare play benefits from the daring casting of actual teenagers Whiting, then 17, and Hussey, then 15, in title roles, adding fresh qualities. Wonderful to look at and handsomely done all around. Narrated by Sir Laurence Olivier. Oscars for Cinematography and Costumes. C: Olivia Hussey, Leonard Whiting, Michael York, Milo O'Shea. D: Franco Zeffirelli. DRA 138m. v

Romeo is Bleeding 1994 ★★½ Cop (Oldman) is assigned spy duty: his subject, a ruthless lady mobster (Olin). Black comedy or over-the-top film noir? Visually fascinating either way, though its slickness may seem dated. Olin is riveting. C: Lena Olin, Gary Oldman, Annabella Sciorra, Juliette Lewis, Roy Scheider, David Proval, Will Patton. D: Peter Medak. CRI [R] 108m.

Romero 1989 ★★★★ Julia is haunting and impassioned as real-life Salvadoran priest who put his religious beliefs to practice and his life on the line to protest human rights' injustices in his country. Often compelling. C: Raul Julia, Richard Jordan, Ana Alicia, Eddie Velez. D: John Duigan. DRA 105m. v

Romper Stomper 1993 Australian ★★★★½ Violent, brutally realistic portrait of neo-Nazi skinhead and his gang. Difficult to watch, but undeniably powerful, all the more so for Wright's refusal to make obvious moral points. C: Russell Crowe, Daniel Pollock, Jacqueline McKenzie, Alex Scott. D: Geoffrey Wright. DRA [R] 85m. v

Romuald ed Juliet 1989 *See* **Mama, There's a Man in Your Bed**

Rooftops 1989 ★★★ Anemic "pop" musical about a white teenage boy in love with a Hispanic girl. Obvious rip-off of *West Side Story*, from the same director, but it doesn't have either the score or the style of the original. C: Jason Gedrick, Troy Beyer, Tisha Campbell. D: Robert Wise. MUS [R] 95m. v

Rookie of the Year 1993 ★★★½ Predictable comedy about a boy who breaks his arm, then develops a major-league fastball and is signed by the hapless Chicago Cubs. C: Thomas Ian Nicholas, Gary Busey, Dan Hedaya, Daniel Stern. D: Daniel Stern. COM [PG] 103m. v

Rookie, The 1990 ★★★ Overused formula of experienced cop (Eastwood) with wet-behind-the-ears new partner (Sheen) is reprised yet again for no discernible reason. Oddball supporting cast including Julia, Braga, and Flynn Boyle is of some interest. C: Clint Eastwood, Charlie Sheen, Raul Julia, Sonia Braga, Lara Flynn Boyle. D: Clint Eastwood. CRI [R] 121m. v

Room at the Top 1959 British ★★★★½ Classic drama of a social climber. Harvey jilts faithful lover Signoret to marry the boss's daughter. Potent social commentary with superb cast. Signoret won Best Actress Oscar. Neil Paterson won for Best Screenplay. Sequels: *Life at the Top, Man at the Top*. C: Laurence Harvey, Simone Signoret, Heather Sears, Hermione Baddeley. D: Jack Clayton. DRA 115m. v

Room for One More 1952 ★★★★ Charming, sentimental comedy with Grant and Drake as childless couple adopting unwanted children. Stars make the sugar palatable. (a.k.a. *The Easy Way*) C: Cary Grant, Betsy Drake, Lurene Tuttle, George Winslow, John Ridgely. D: Norman Taurog. COM 98m.

Room Service 1938 ★★★★ Three struggling Broadway producers try to con hotel management so they can stay in their unpaid-for room. Though Marx Brothers are squeezed into format of conventional play, this is an amusing romp, with good support by Ball. Later remade as musical *Step Lively*. C: Marx Brothers, Lucille Ball, Ann Miller, Frank Albertson. D: William A. Seiter. COM 78m. v

Room with a View, A 1986 British ★★★★ Merchant/Ivory production of E.M. Forster novel about young Englishwoman's awakening to life on trip to Florence has humor, longing, and lovely design, though juvenile lovers seem miscast. Thoughtful and elegant. Oscar for screenplay and costumes. C: Maggie Smith, Helena Bonham Carter, Denholm Elliott, Julian Sands, Daniel Day-Lewis. D: James Ivory. DRA 117m. v

Roommates 1995 ★★★½ Cranky, but lovable grandfather (Falk) moves in with his doctor grandson (Sweeney). Contrived, but amusing comedy. Falk has some wonderful moments in what his perhaps his best screen work to date. From a novel by Max Apple. C: Peter Falk, D. B. Sweeney, Ellen Burstyn, Julianne Moore. D: Peter Yates. COM [PG] 109m. v

Rooney 1958 British ★★★½ Irish sanitation worker Gregson, avoiding marriage, is befriended by invalid Fitzgerald in quaint comedy with more than its share of blarney. C: John Gregson, Muriel Pavlow, Barry Fitzgerald, June Thorburn. D: George Pollock. COM 88m.

Rooster Cogburn 1975 ★★★ A crusty U.S. marshal and a spinsterish missionary pursue the outlaws who killed her father. The well-intentioned teaming of two screen giants is the main virtue of this derivative attempt to cast *The African Queen* as a Western. C: John Wayne, Katharine Hepburn, Anthony Zerbe, Strother Martin. D: Stuart Millar. WST [PG] 107m. V

Rootin' Tootin' Rhythm 1937 ★★★★ Lighthearted Autry Western with star and sidekick Burnette involved in mistaken identity mix-up with outlaw robbers. One of Autry's best. C: Gene Autry, Smiley Burnette, Monte Blue. D: Mack V. Wright. WST 53m. V

Roots 1977 ★★★★★ One of the best miniseries, is based on author Alex Haley's research into his family's past. Story follows family fortunes beginning with 18th-century abduction to America and enslavement of African Kunte Kinte, through horrific trials as well as joys and triumphs, until finally, Kunte Kinte's grandson attains his freedom. Epic and excellent. C: Ed Asner, Lloyd Bridges, LeVar Burton. D: David Greene. DRA 540m. TVM V

Roots: The Next Generation 1978 ★★★★½ Alex Haley's family history continues, from freeing of Kunte Kinte's grandson, Chicken George, through Civil War times and into the 20th century, culminating in Haley's own birth in 1921. A grand family saga. C: Georg Stanford Brown, Olivia de Havilland, Henry Fonda, Avon Long, Lynne Moody. D: John Erman. DRA 480m. TVM V

Roots of Heaven, The 1958 ★★★ Failed symbolic drama of white adeventurer in Africa, trying to save the elephants. Overall, doesn't quite work, but the intentions are clear, and Flynn stands out in the cast. From Romain Gary's novel. C: Errol Flynn, Juliette Greco, Trevor Howard, Eddie Albert, Orson Welles, Herbert Lom, Paul Lukas. D: John Huston. DRA 131m.

Rope 1948 ★★★★ Two young killers (Dahl and Granger) invite their family and friends to a party but don't tell them about the dead body. Coolly macabre affair, based on the '20s Leopold-Loeb murders, is one of Hitchock's more daring experiments (shot in eight separate 10 minute takes). A must see for Hitchcock enthusiasts. C: James Stewart, John Dall, Farley Granger, Cedric Hardwicke, Joan Chandler, Constance Collier. D: Alfred Hitchcock. CRI [PG] 81m. V

Rosalie 1937 ★★★★ Lavish musical with silly plot of football hero (Eddy) involved in romance with princess (Powell). Some wonderful Cole Porter songs, including "In the Still of the Night," and phenomenally gaudy production numbers make this fun viewing. C: Eleanor Powell, Nelson Eddy, Frank Morgan. D: W.S. Van Dyke II. MUS 125m. V

Rosalie Goes Shopping 1989 ★★★★ A German-born Arkansas housewife (Sagebrecht) becomes a shopaholic, then devises a plan to avoid the bills. Off-beat sleeper makes satiric points about materialism, credit cards and marriage with wit and charm. C: Marianne Sagebrecht, Brad Davis, Judge Reinhold. D: Percy Adlon. COM [PG] 94m. V

Rosary Murders, The 1987 ★★½ Priest (Sutherland) is tormented by his oath of confidentiality after hearing the confession of a murderer who kills priests and nuns. Good dialogue, thanks to coscripter Elmore Leonard. Premise borrowed from the superior *I Confess.* C: Donald Sutherland, Charles Durning, Belinda Bauer, Josef Sommer. D: Fred Walton. CRI [R] 105m. V

Rose and the Sword, The 1985 *See* **Flesh + Blood**

Rose Marie 1936 ★★★½ Mountie (Eddy) is torn between quest for fugitive and love for fugitive's sister. Quaint Victor Herbert operetta makes good vehicle for Nelson and Jeanette, but songs like "Indian Love Call" evoke ridicule by today's standards. (a.k.a. *Indian Love Call*) C: Jeanette MacDonald, Nelson Eddy, Reginald Owen, James Stewart. D: W.S. Van Dyke. MUS 112m. V

Rose Marie 1954 ★★★½ Attractively filmed remake of Victor Herbert's Canadian Mountie operetta with Keel as law enforcer trying to tame spirited Blyth. Somewhat stodgy and inevitably dated. C: Ann Blyth, Howard Keel, Fernando Lamas, Bert Lahr, Marjorie Main, Joan Taylor, Ray Collins. D: Mervyn LeRoy. MUS 119m. V

Rose of Cimarron 1952 ★★★ Run-of-the-mill Western drama with Powers seeking revenge for the murder of her Cherokee foster parents. C: Jack Beutel, Mala Powers. D: Harry Keller. WST

Rose of Washington Square 1939 ★★★★ Thinly disguised Fanny Brice story with Broadway star (Faye) hopelessly in love with no-good husband (Power). Entertaining mix of nostalgia and soap opera, with Jolson stealing the picture as Faye's loyal producer. C: Tyrone Power, Alice Faye, Al Jolson, William Frawley, Horace McMahon, Moroni Olsen. D: Gregory Ratoff. MUS 86m. V

Rose Tattoo, The 1955 ★★★★½ Earthy Sicilian widow in Gulf Coast town finally gives up mourning when wooed by muscular, boisterous truck driver. Bravura Oscar-winning performance by Magnani in distinctive adaptation of Tennessee Williams play. Theatrical in tone and acted with authority. Oscar for Cinematography. C: Anna Magnani, Burt Lancaster, Marisa Pávan, Ben Cooper, Virginia Grey, Jo Van Fleet. D: Daniel Mann. DRA 116m. V

Rose, The 1979 ★★★★ Janis Joplin-like singer rises from clubs to concert stardom, but falls apart because of drugs and manipulative manager. Midler's film debut is wrenching, though the story itself is tough to swallow at times. C: Bette Midler, Alan Bates, Frederic Forrest. D: Mark Rydell. DRA [R] 134m. v

Roseland 1977 ★★★★ Three vignettes about the various lonelyhearts who congregate at New York's fabled dance hall. An interesting premise, at times quite beautifully done. C: Teresa Wright, Lou Jacobi, Geraldine Chaplin, Helen Gallagher. D: James Ivory. DRA [PG] 103m. v

Rosemary 1958 German ★★★ Lurid drama of German prostitute blackmailing wealthy businessman in post-WWII Frankfurt. Based on a true story. C: Nadja Tiller, Peter Van Eyck, Gert Frobe, Mario Adorf, Carl Raddatz. D: Rolf Thiele. CRI 99m.

Rosemary's Baby 1968 ★★★★★ Young woman (Farrow) moves with her husband into a new apartment, where he falls in with a coven of witches who intend for her to bear the devil's child. Genuinely horrifying chiller (based on Ira Levin's novel) builds unbearable tension; cast (including Best Supporting Actress Oscar-winner Ruth Gordon) is first-rate. C: Mia Farrow, John Cassavetes, Ruth Gordon, Sidney Blackmer, Maurice Evans, Ralph Bellamy. D: Roman Polanski. HOR [R] 137m. v

Rosencrantz and Guildenstern Are Dead 1990 ★★★ Stoppard directed his own hilarious play and came up with this dawdling, overly literal film, which lacks the stage version's magical sense of wordplay and absurdity. C: Gary Oldman, Tim Roth, Richard Dreyfuss. D: Tom Stoppard. COM [PG] 117m. v

Rosie 1967 ★★★½ Updated, gender-switched reworking of Shakespeare's *King Lear*, with Roz as a madcap millionairess whose children try to get her committed. Not bad, but inherently depressing: Kind of like *Auntie Mame* in a strait-jacket. C: Rosalind Russell, Sandra Dee, Brian Aherne, Audrey Meadows, James Farentino. D: David Lowell Rich. DRA 98m.

Rouge Baiser 1985 *See* **Red Kiss**

Rough Cut 1980 ★★★½ Down is the Scotland Yard bait meant to catch infamous jewel thief (Reynolds) in light caper comedy with attractive stars, weak script. C: Burt Reynolds, Lesley-Anne Down, David Niven, Timothy West. D: Don Siegel. CRI [PG] 112m. v

Rough Night in Jericho 1967 ★★★ An otherwise meek stagecoach driver confronts a villain and throws him out of town. Ho-hum. C: Dean Martin, George Peppard, Jean Simmons, Slim Pickens. D: Arnold Laven. WST 104m. v

Rough Riders' Roundup 1934 ★★★ Rogers and the Riders help mining town against no-good foreman (Meeker). Not one of Rogers' better efforts. C: Roy Rogers, Raymond Hatton, Lynn Roberts. D: Joseph Kane. WST 60m. v

Rough Waters 1930 ★★★½ Thieves take old sailor and his little girl hostage. It's up to canine superstar Rin-Tin-Tin to save them in entertaining juvenile fare. C: Rin Tin Tin, Lane Chandler, Jobyna Ralston. D: John Daumery. FAM/ACT 53m.

Roughshod 1949 ★★★½ Well-crafted Western about two outlaws mistaken for revenge-mad villains by unstable farmer. C: Robert Sterling, Claude Jarman, Jr., Gloria Grahame, Jeff Donnell, John Ireland, Myrna Dell, Martha Hyer. D: Mark Robson. WST 88m.

Round Midnight 1986 U.S. ★★★★½ Tribute to jazz performers focuses on real-life sax legend Gordon (in a stunning acting debut) as alcoholic American in Paris befriended by fan Cluzet. Features spontaneous improvisations with jazz great Herbie Hancock (Oscar for Best Score) and many astute insights on the creative spirit. C: Dexter Gordon, Francois Cluzet, Sandra-Reaves Phillips, Lonette McKee, Herbie Hancock, Martin Scorsese. D: Bertrand Tavernier. MUS [R] 132m. v

Round Up, The 1966 Hungarian ★★★★½ Eerily beautiful film about violence set during a Hungarian revolt against the Austrians in the middle 1800's, depicted in a highly stylized, almost dance-like manner; Jansco constantly moves camera in sinuous patterns that add to the musical quality. Much nudity and brutality. Not to *all* tastes, but brilliant. (a.k.a. *The Hopeless Ones* and *The Poor Outlaws*) C: Janos Gorbe, Tibor Molnar. D: Miklos Jancso. DRA 90m.

Rounders, The 1965 ★★★½ Modest, amusing comedy Western with Fonda and Ford well cast as aging cattle wranglers causing mayhem in small town as they try to handle a difficult horse. C: Glenn Ford, Henry Fonda, Sue Anne Langdon, Hope Holiday, Chill Wills, Edgar Buchanan, Kathleen Freeman. D: Burt Kennedy. WST 85m. v

Roundup Time in Texas 1937 ★★★½ Autry delivers herd of horses to diamond hunter brother in Africa, with jewel thieves in pursuit. Western star in Tarzan locale produces unusual results. C: Gene Autry, Smiley Burnette, Maxine Doyle. D: Joseph Kane. WST 54m. v

Roustabout 1964 ★★★½ Drifter (Elvis) seeks work at Stanwyck's carnival and grows up in the process. One of the better Presley musicals with Barbara lending strong support. Songs include "Little Egypt." C: Elvis Presley, Barbara Stanwyck. D: John Rich. MUS 101m. v

Rover Dangerfield 1991 ★★★½ Comic Las Vegas canine, who looks and sounds like the film's writer and producer, comedian Rodney Dangerfield, goes from bright lights to rural living and can't adjust. Animated feature combines a strange mix of adult and child humor; fun, but definitely not for all tastes. Voices of Rodney Dangerfield, Susan Boyd, Dana Hill. D: Jim George. FAM/COM [G] 74m. v

Roxanne 1987 ★★★★ Martin wrote this

witty, intelligent update of *Cyrano de Bergerac* as a prodigiously proboscised fire chief (Martin) who pens love letters to a visiting astronomer (Hanna) on behalf of a tongue-tied fireman (Rossovich) but then falls for her himself. Charming and satisfying. C: Steve Martin, Daryl Hannah, Rick Rossovich, Shelley Duvall. D: Fred Schepisi. COM [PG] 107m. v

Roxie Hart 1942 ★★★½ Rogers plays 20s publicity hungry dancer who murders her boyfriend in raucous comedy which sometimes tries too hard and suffers from exhaustion by its climax. Based on Nunnally Johnson play and source for Bob Fosse musical, both titled *Chicago*. C: Ginger Rogers, Adolphe Menjou, George Montgomery, Lynne Overman, Nigel Bruce, Phil Silvers, Spring Byington, Iris Adrian, George Chandler. D: William Wellman. COM 75m.

Royal Affair, A 1950 ★★★½ Chevalier is king of an unnamed country, arriving in Paris to sign a treaty, but he winds up spending most of his energy romancing a French senator's wife (and also his mistress). Amusing bit of puff pastry, with charming star. C: Maurice Chevalier, Annie Ducaux, Sophie Desmarets, Alfred Adam. D: Marc Gilbert Sauvajon. COM 100m.

Royal Affairs in Versailles 1954 French ★★★½ Dull, but star-studded Gallic history lesson with Guitry as King Louis XIV. Episodic court intrigue plot serves as excuse for cast to impersonate Molière, Marie Antoinette, etc. Retitled *Affairs in Versaille*. C: Claudette Colbert, Orson Welles, Jean-Pierre Aumont, Edith Piaf, Gerard Philipe, Jean Marais, Sacha Guitry, Micheline Presle, Daniel Gelin, Danielle Delorme. D: Sacha Guitry. DRA 152m.

Royal Family of Broadway, The 1930 ★★★★ Colorful family of actors try to convince their youngest to devote life to stage, rather than marriage. Thinly disguised lampoon of the Barrymores, from George S. Kaufman-Edna Ferber play, with stunning turns by March as John and Claire as Ethel. C: Fredric March, Ina Claire, Mary Brian, Henrietta Crossman, Charles Starrett, Arnold Korff, Frank Conroy. D: George Cukor, Cyril Gardner. COM 82m.

Royal Flash 1975 British ★★★★ Fast-paced swashbuckling adventure with McDowell and Reed involved in Prussian intrigue. Tongue-in-cheek style overplayed at times, but often ingratiating. C: Malcolm McDowell, Alan Bates, Florinda Bolkan, Oliver Reed, Britt Ekland, Lionel Jeffries, Tom Bell, Alastair Sim, Michael Hordern, Joss Ackland, Christopher Cazenove, Bob Hoskins. D: Richard Lester. ACT [PG] 98m.

Royal Game, The 1960 *See* **Three Moves to Freedom**

Royal Hunt of the Sun, The 1969 British ★★★½ Earthbound version of superior Peter Shaffer play about Spanish explorer Pizarro's quest for Incan gold at expense of natives. C: Robert Shaw, Christopher Plummer, Nigel Davenport, Michael Craig, Leonard Whiting, James Donald. D: Irving Lerner. ACT [G] 118m.

Royal Mounted Patrol, The 1941 ★★★ Mounties struggle to keep order in the Canadian forest, fighting lunatic lumberjack. Film is low-budget, action is routine. (a.k.a. *Giants A'Fire*) C: Charles Starrett, Russell Hayden. D: Lambert Hillyer. ACT 59m.

Royal Scandal, A 1945 ★★★½ Arch comedy about Catharine the Great (Bankhead) and her insatiable appetite for athletic officers. Those with a taste for camp may find this amusing. C: Tallulah Bankhead, Charles Coburn, Anne Baxter, William Eythe, Vincent Price, Mischa Auer. D: Ernst Lubitsch, Otto Preminger. COM 94m.

Royal Wedding 1951 ★★★★ Astaire and Powell play brother/sister dance team visiting England during wedding of then-Princess Elizabeth to Philip Mountbatten. Good Lerner/-Lane score includes "Too Late Now" and showstopping "How Could You Believe Me When I Said I Love You When You Know I've Been a Liar All My Life." Astaire's famous dance on the walls and ceiling to "You're All the World for Me" is a must-see. C: Fred Astaire, Jane Powell, Keenan Wynn. D: Stanley Donen. MUS 93m. v

R.P.M. 1970 ★★ Liberal college prez allows police to raid a radical campus newspaper office in order to save the school. From Erich Segal script, a confused and cloying echo of the '60s. C: Anthony Quinn, Ann-Margret, Gary Lockwood, Paul Winfield. D: Stanley Kramer. DRA [R] 90m. v

Ruby 1977 ★★★½ Above-average drive-in horror film is actually set at a drive-in, where a young woman (Baldwin) becomes a murdered gangster's vehicle of supernatural revenge. Decent mix of scares and humor boasts some good murderous setpieces. C: Piper Laurie, Stuart Whitman, Roger Davis, Janit Baldwin. D: Curtis Harrington. HOR [R] 85m. v

Ruby 1992 ★★½ Aiello is fine as small-timer Jack Ruby, who stepped way out of his league to become historic figure. Stiff not always believable film makes broad hints about conspiracies but never follows up. C: Danny Aiello, Sherilyn Fenn, Arliss Howard, Joe Cortese, Marc Lawrence. D: John Mackenzie. DRA [R] 111m. v

Ruby Gentry 1952 ★★★½ Impoverished Ruby (Jones) marries a rich man (Malden) when her lover (Heston) rejects her. Overbaked soap opera offers guilty pleasure for fans of romance novels. C: Jennifer Jones, Charlton Heston, Karl Malden. D: King Vidor. DRA 82m. v

Ruby in Paradise 1993 ★★★★ A young rural woman pulls up stakes and embarks on a journey of self-discovery that takes her to a Florida tourist town. Not terribly profound, but sweet and atmospheric. C: Ashley Judd, Todd Field, Bentley Mitchum, Allison Dean. D: Victor Nunez. DRA [R] 115m. v

Ruby's Dream 1982 *See* **Dear Mr. Wonderful**

Rude Awakening 1989 ★★½ Two perfectly preserved hippies (Marin and Roberts) experience culture shock when they return to yuppified '80s America. Silly without being funny as one-joke premise quickly burns itself out. C: Cheech Marin, Eric Roberts, Julie Hagerty, Robert Carradine. D: Aaron Russo. COM [R] 100m. v

Rudy 1993 ★★★ True story of a kid who wants to play football for Notre Dame and will stop at nothing to realize his dream. Sort of a *Rocky* for losers, by the director of *Hoosiers*. C: Sean Astin, Ned Beatty, Charles S. Dutton, Lili Taylor, Jason Miller, Robert Prosky, Jon Favreau. D: David Anspaugh. DRA [PG] 113m. v

Rudyard Kipling's The Jungle Book 1994 ★★★★ Disney recycles Kipling's tale of a boy raised by animals, this time as live-action film that captures much of original's sense of wonder. Lee is a charismatic Mowgli. Filmed before, in 1942 (with Sabu), and by Disney in 1967 as animated feature. C: Jason Scott Lee, Cary Elwes, Lena Headey, John Cleese. D: Stephen Sommers. FAM/DRA [PG] 108m. v

Rue Cases Ngres 1984 *See* **Sugar Cane Alley**

Ruggles of Red Gap 1935 ★★★★★ Laughton is wonderful as straitlaced English butler forced to travel to Wild West as valet to Ruggles and Boland. Delightful "fish out of water" comedy from Harry Leon Wilson novel is one of Hollywood's best. Great cast, especially Pitts. Previously filmed in 1918, 1923. Remade as *Fancy Pants* in 1950. C: Charles Laughton, Mary Boland, Charlie Ruggles, ZaSu Pitts. D: Leo McCarey. COM 90m. v

Rules of the Game, The 1939 French ★★★★★ Renoir's tour-de-force satire on the foibles of the ruling class. Film portrays a weekend in the country with sex-obsessed aristocrats on the eve of WWII. Funny and affecting. C: Marcel Dalio, Nora Gregor, Mila Parely, Jean Renoir, Gaston Modot, Julien Carette. D: Jean Renoir. COM 105m. v

Ruling Class, The 1972 British ★★★★½ British Earl dies suddenly and insane offspring (O'Toole)—who's convinced he's Christ, then Jack the Ripper—inherits title, sending relatives scurrying. Maniacal satire on British society with fanatically funny performance by O'Toole. Doesn't entirely succeed, but a determined comic roller coaster. C: Peter O'Toole, Alastair Sim, Arthur Lowe, Harry Andrews, Coral Browne, Michael Bryant, Carolyn Seymour, Nigel Green, William Mervyn, James Villiers. D: Peter Medak. COM [PG] 154m. v

Rumble Fish 1983 ★★★½ Interesting b&w experiment by Coppola, based on S.E. Hinton novel about troubled youths trying to cope on their own. Dreamy, moody tale may be too leisurely and arty for some. C: Matt Dillon, Mickey Rourke, Diane Lane, Dennis Hopper. D: Francis Ford Coppola. DRA [R] 94m. v

Rumor of War, A 1980 ★★★★ Stirring movie, the first to address Vietnam, is based on the best-selling memoir by journalist Philip Caputo. A naive youth is transformed into a bitter, battle-scarred veteran court-martialed for murder. C: Brad Davis, Keith Carradine, Michael O'Keefe, Stacy Keach. D: Richard T. Heffron. DRA 106m. v

Rumpelstiltskin 1986 ★★★ Filmed fairy tale of woman (Irving) who spins straw into gold after appearance of mysterious Rumpelstiltskin (Barty); years later, she must guess his name or lose her first-born child. Uninvolving, routine version of oft-told story. Directed by Irving's brother (and featuring her mom in supporting role). C: Amy Irving, Billy Barty, Clive Revill, Priscilla Pointer. D: David Irving. FAM/DRA [G] 84m. v

Run 1991 ★★ Student (Dempsey) is pursued by mobsters and crooked cops after accidentally killing a gangster's son. Standard chase movie. C: Patrick Dempsey, Kelly Preston. D: Geoff Burrowes. ACT [R] 91m. v

Run for Cover 1955 ★★★½ Ex-convict (Cagney) becomes sheriff in odd Western drama with strong cast and weak script. C: James Cagney, Viveca Lindfors, John Derek, Jean Hersholt, Ernest Borgnine. D: Nicholas Ray. WST 93m.

Run for Your Money, A 1949 British ★★★★ Welsh miners, in London during rugby match for one day, have an exhilirating spree. Delightful comedy, with terrific British cast. Slight, but winning. C: Donald Houston, Meredith Edwards, Moira Lister, Alec Guinness, Hugh Griffith, Joyce Grenfell. D: Charles Frend. COM 83m.

Run on Gold, A *See* **Midas Run**

Run Silent, Run Deep 1958 ★★★★ Emotions run high aboard a U.S. submarine in the Pacific during WWII. Powerful psychological interplay between rival officers (Gable and Lancaster), with outstanding star performances. Based on a novel by Commander Edward L. Beach. C: Clark Gable, Burt Lancaster, Jack Warden, Brad Dexter. D: Robert Wise. DRA 93m. v

Run, Stranger, Run 1973 *See* **Happy Mother's Day, Love George**

Run Wild, Run Free 1969 British ★★★½ British mute boy (Lester) develops love for white colt in slow-moving, but touching children's film. C: John Mills, Mark Lester, Sylvia Syms, Gordon Jackson, Bernard Miles, Fiona Fullerton. D: Richard Sarafian. FAM/DRA [G] 100m.

Runaway 1984 ★★ Police tracker (Selleck) hunts down dangerous robots. Rocker Gene Simmons is good as the villain, but the effects are more special than the plot. C: Tom Selleck, Cynthia Rhodes, Gene Simmons, Kirstie Alley. D: Michael Crichton. SFI [PG-13] 100m. V

Runaway Bus, The 1954 British ★★★½ Diverting, British comedy with fogbound airport passengers involved in robbery chase on bus. Rutherford steals film as disgruntled matron; Howard's film debut. C: Frankie Howard, Margaret Rutherford, Petula Clark. D: Val Guest. COM 80m. V

Runaway Train 1985 ★★★★ Two escaped cons (Voight, Roberts) hide out in a train only to discover there is no engineer. Beautiful Alaskan background, terrific performances, and some great imagery make a gripping, adventure. Based on a script by Akira Kurosawa. C: Jon Voight, Eric Roberts, Rebecca De Mornay, Kyle Heffner. D: Andrei Konchalovsky. DRA [R] 111m. V

Runaways, The 1986 *See* **South Bronx Heroes**

Runestone, The 1991 ★★★½ When an archaeologist uncovers the title relic and brings it home, he becomes transformed into a murderous monster. Above-average chiller with engaging writing and characterizations, plus some real scares. C: Peter Riegert, Joan Severance, William Hickey, Alexander Godunov. D: Willard Carroll. HOR [R] 105m. V

Runner Stumbles, The 1979 ★★½ A small-town priest is accused of murdering the young nun with whom he was believed to be infatuated. Ponderous rendering of potentially intriguing material based on Milan Stitt's play. Van Dyke is woefully miscast in an otherwise tasteful rendering of sensitive material. C: Dick Van Dyke, Kathleen Quinlan, Maureen Stapleton, Ray Bolger, Tammy Grimes, Beau Bridges. D: Stanley Kramer. DRA [PG] 109m. V

Running Against Time 1990 ★★★ Time traveler goes back to 1963 to prevent assassination of President Kennedy and botches up history even worse. Despite grand premise, this is inconsequential sci-fi drama. C: Robert Hays, Catherine Hicks, Sam Wanamaker. D: Bruce Seth Green. SFI [PG] 93m. TVM V

Running Man, The 1987 ★★★½ In the grim near future, convicts are pursued by assassins for the entertainment of TV gameshow audiences—those who live go free. Lavish production; based on Stephen King's novel. C: Arnold Schwarzenegger, Maria Conchita Alonso, Yaphet Kotto, Richard Dawson. D: Paul Michael Glaser. SFI [R] 101m. TVM V

Running Mates 1992 ★★★ Harris is bachelor presidential candidate who ends up in romance with journalist Keaton. The catch: they're ex-high school classmates and she always ignored him. Silly romantic fluff. C: Diane Keaton, Ed Harris, Ed Begley, Jr. D: Michael Lindsay-Hogg. COM [PG-13] 88m. V

Running on Empty 1988 ★★★★ Radicals from the '60s, still on the run from the FBI for political bombing, must deal with teen son's musical talent and craving for a normal life. Interesting, unusual story, with terrific performances (especially Lahti and Phoenix). C: Christine Lahti, River Phoenix, Judd Hirsch, Martha Plimpton. D: Sidney Lumet. DRA [PG-13] 117m. V

Running Scared 1986 ★★★½ Unconventional Chicago cops (Hines, Crystal) try to get one last bust so they can retire to Key West. Lots of laughs (especially from Crystal) and plenty of action including a car chase on the el tracks. C: Gregory Hines, Billy Crystal, Steven Bauer, Darlanne Fluegel, Joe Pantoliano, Dan Hedaya. D: Peter Hyams. CRI [R] 108m. V

Running Target 1956 ★★★ Four escaped convicts are chased by overzealous sheriff and his posse; tension between posse members adds to tension of the film. C: Doris Dowling, Arthur Franz, Richard Reeves, Myron Healey, James Parnell. D: Marvin Weinstein. ACT 83m.

Running Wild 1927 ★★★½ Fine silent showcase for Fields casts him as a mild-mannered sap who completely changes character after a bout with hypnotism. Very amusing. C: W.C. Fields, Mary Brian, Claude Buchanan, Marie Shotwell. D: Gregory La Cava. COM 68m.

Running Wild 1973 ★★★★ Free-lance photographer (Merrill) becomes involved in liberation of mistreated horses. Though story is old, treatment is fresh and highlighted by Merrill's engaging performance. Beautiful locations make an effective backdrop. C: Lloyd Bridges, Dina Merrill, Pat Hingle, Gilbert Roland. D: Robert McCahon. FAM/DRA [G] 102m. V

Rush 1991 ★★★★ Unique and moody drug film in which a young woman agent (Leigh) is drawn by a veteran but strung out narc (Patric) into violence, addiction, and an affair. Patric's performance is outstanding; classic rocker Allman plays a seedy pusher; and guitar legend Clapton provides a great blues score. Excellent debut for director. C: Jason Patric, Jennifer Jason Leigh, Sam Elliott, Max Perlich, Gregg Allman. D: Lili Fini Zanuck. CRI [R] 120m. V

Russia House, The 1991 ★★★½ English publishing agent (Connery) becomes entangled in espionage when he follows up on a manuscript sent by Russian (Pfeiffer). Beautiful to look at, nice touches, low-key suspense. Scripted by Tom Stoppard from the John Le Carré novel. C: Sean Connery, Michelle Pfeiffer, Roy Scheider, James Fox, Klaus Maria Brandauer, John Mahoney. D: Fred Schepisi. DRA [R] 124m. V

Russians Are Coming! The Russians Are Coming!, The 1966 ★★★★ A Soviet submarine runs aground offshore of New England village and local residents run amok anticipating invasion. Madcap situation comedy that works thanks to a talented cast, including Arkin as befuddled Soviet sailor and great work from Winters. C: Carl Reiner, Eva

Maria Saint, Alan Arkin, Brian Keith, Jonathan Winters. D: Norman Jewison. COM 126m. V

Rustlers of Devil's Canyon 1947 ★★★ Lane tries to make peace between ranchers and farmers in mundane Western. Young sidekick Blake, playing Indian boy, later became Robert Blake, star of *Baretta* TV series. C: Allan Lane, Bobby Blake, Martha Wentworth. D: R. G. Springsteen. WST 58m.

Rustlers' Rhapsody 1985 ★★★ Parody of '40s "B" Westerns features a singing movie cowpoke (Berenger). While this re-creates formula nicely jokes are 40 years too late. C: Tom Berenger, G. W. Bailey, Marilu Henner, Andy Griffith, Fernando Rey, Sela Ward, Patrick Wayne. D: Hugh Wilson. COM [PG] 88m. V

Ruthless People 1986 ★★★★½ Absolutely hilarious farce about young couple Reinhold and Slater kidnapping Midler as revenge against her conniving husband DeVito—who doesn't want her back. One funny plot twist follows another in outrageous black comedy, brightly directed and brilliantly played. C: Danny DeVito, Bette Midler, Judge Reinhold, Helen Slater, Anita Morris, John Coleman. D: Jim Abrahams, David Zucker, Jerry Zucker. COM [R] 93m. V

Rutles, The 1978 ★★★★½ Eric Idle, of Monty Python fame, created this mock documentary of The Rutles, a phenomenal '60s rock group with uncanny satirical parallels to The Beatles. Great nasty fun, with razor wit zealously slashing through Beatles history. Ex-Fab Four member George Harrison makes a cameo appearance. C: Eric Idle, Neil Innes, Mick Jagger, Paul Simon, John Belushi, Gilda Radner. D: Eric Idle, Gary Weis. COM 90m. V

Ryan's Daughter 1970 British ★★★½ Lushly filmed romantic triangle set in Ireland, with tempestuous Miles suffering the consequences of affair with British soldier (Jones) despite marriage to gentle schoolteacher (Mitchum). Gorgeous production values overwhelm trifling central story. Mills won a supporting Oscar as the village idiot. Oscar also for Cinematography. C: Robert Mitchum, Trevor Howard, Sarah Miles, Christopher Jones, John Mills. D: David Lean. DRA [PG] 176m. V

S

Sabata 1970 Italian ★★★ Minor spaghetti-Western with gambler (Van Cleef) employed by swindlers to pull off $100,000 robbery. C: Lee Van Cleef, William Berger, Franco Ressel, Linda Veras, Pedro Sanchez. D: Frank Kramer. WST [PG] 107m.

Sabotage 1936 British ★★★★ Woman (Sidney) suspects her husband (Homolka) is not what he seems in this suspense thriller about a dangerous secret agent operating undercover in England. Heightened atmosphere and crackling tension played to the hilt under Hitchcock's trademark direction. C: Sylvia Sidney, Oscar Homolka, John Loder, Desmond Tester. D: Alfred Hitchcock. DRA 76m. v

Saboteur 1942 ★★★★ Classic, quirky man-on-the-run thriller follows the cross-country flight of a wartime factory worker accused of arson and murder. Numerous flourishes including the climactic showdown atop the Statue of Liberty. C: Robert Cummings, Priscilla Lane, Norman Lloyd, Otto Kruger, Alan Baxter. D: Alfred Hitchcock. CRI [PG] 108m. v

Saboteur: Code Name Moritur *See* **Morituri**

Sabra 1970 French ★★★ Arab/Israeli conflict fuels mediocre tale of police officer Tamiroff trying to trick Dayan into betraying his country. Reissued as *Death of a Jew.* C: Akim Tamiroff, Assaf Dayan, Jean Claudio. D: Denys de la Patalliere. CRI 98m.

Sabrina 1954 ★★★★½ Hepburn, the daughter of a rich family's chauffeur, returns from Paris to find she's Cinderella and two Prince Charmings are wooing her. Refreshing, classy comedy from Samuel Taylor play *Sabrina Fair.* Bogart shows surprising flair for sophisticated banter. C: Humphrey Bogart, Audrey Hepburn, William Holden, John Williams, Martha Hyer. D: Billy Wilder. COM 113m. v

Sacco and Vanzetti 1970 French ★★★½ Dramatization of famous prosecution/execution of innocent immigrants. Cheap production and bad dubbing diminish impact, but overall it's a fairly accurate portrayal of the facts. C: Gian Maria Volonte, Riccardo Cucciolla, Milo O'Shea, Cyril Cusack. D: Giuliano Montaldo. DRA [PG] 120m. v

Sacketts, The 1979 ★★★½ After the Civil War, three adventurist brothers take off on an epic journey through the West. Based on two L'Amour novels. Fine casting and many heads above usual TV fare. C: Sam Elliott, Tom Selleck, Jeff Osterhage, Glenn Ford, Ben Johnson, Gilbert Roland, Jack Elam, Mercedes McCambridge, Slim Pickens. D: Robert Totten. WST 200m. TVM v

Sacred Ground 1983 ★★½ Trouble starts with mountain man and Apache woman's marriage and is further compounded when he settles his family on a holy Paiute burial ground. Their situations don't totally engage. C: Tim McIntire, Jack Elam, Serene Hedin, Mindi Miller. D: Charles B. Pierce. WST [PG] 100m. v

Sacred Hearts 1985 British ★★★½ Disturbed Mother Superior (Massey) makes her fellow sisters' lives a living hell in WWII British convent. Predictable, if well-acted melodrama. C: Anna Massey, Katrin Cartlidge, Oona Kirsch, Fiona Shaw, Anne Dyson, Gerard Murphy, Murray Melvin. D: Barbara Rennie. DRA 95m.

Sacred Music Of Duke Ellington, The 1982 ★★★★ This collection of Ellington concerts, including guest appearances by Tony Bennett and Phyllis Hyman, are priceless. A must see for jazz fans. MUS 90m. v

Sacrifice, The 1986 Swedish ★★★★★ A thoughtful, if difficult treatment of one man's determination to save his family from nuclear destruction. Typifies the Soviet director's breathtaking command of imagery and spiritual themes, aided by Bergman's cinematographer Sven Nykvist. Not for everyone, but rewarding. Tarkovsky's final film. C: Erland Josephson, Susan Fleetwood, Valerie Mairesse. D: Andrei Tarkovsky. DRA [PG] 145m. v

Sacrilege 1988 ★★ Behind the sacred walls of a convent, a nun and nobleman fall in love. C: Myriem Roussel, Alessandro Gassman. D: Luciano Odorisio. DRA 104m. v

Sad Horse, The 1959 ★★★½ Wymore's prize horse suffers depression when separated from its best friend, a dog. Canine-equestrian love story, diverting for the youngsters, cloying for adults. C: David Ladd, Chill Wills, Rex Reason, Patrice Wymore. D: James B. Clark. FAM/DRA 78m.

Sad Sack, The 1957 ★★★ Popular service comedy, inspired by comic strip, with Lewis causing mayhem in the Army. Star's slapstick turns often misfire here. C: Jerry Lewis, Phyllis Kirk, David Wayne, Peter Lorre. D: George Marshall. COM 98m. v

Sadat 1992 ★★★½ Biography of the life and times of Egyptian president Anwar Sadat, focusing on his crusade for peace in the troubled Middle East and eventual assassination. Exceptional, if only for marking a rare TV foray into Third World politics. C: Louis Gossett, Jr., Madolyn Smith, John Rhys-Davies. D: Richard Michaels. DRA [PG] 191m. TVM v

Saddle the Wind 1958 ★★★½ Standard Western with good guy (Taylor) shooting it out with bad brother (Cassavetes). Some good acting sparks bland script. C: Robert Taylor, Julie London, John Cassavetes, Donald Crisp, Charles McGraw, Royal Dano. D: Robert Parrish. WST 84m.

Saddle Tramp 1950 ★★★½ Heartwarming

family Western with McCrea adopting four tykes while fighting outlaws. C: Joel McCrea, Wanda Hendrix, John McIntire, John Russell, Ed Begley, Jeanette Nolan, Antonio Moreno. D: Hugo Fregonese. FAM/WST 77m.

Sadie McKee 1934 ★★★★ Rags-to-riches melodrama of maid (Crawford) who flees domestic servitude for the promise of New York City, where she works her way through a succession of wealthy beaux. Crawford carries the film almost single-handedly, though the male leads do help a bit. C: Joan Crawford, Franchot Tone, Gene Raymond, Edward Arnold, Esther Ralston, Leo G. Carroll, Akim Tamiroff, Gene Austin. D: Clarence Brown. DRA 93m. v

Sadie Thompson 1928 ★★★★ First and best of four versions of the W. Somerset Maugham play about a woman with a past (Swanson) who torments an uptight minister (Barrymore) on the island of Pago Pago. A silent classic; the final 10 minutes were lost, now reconstructed with stills and titles. Remade as *Rain* (Joan Crawford), *Dirty Gertie From Harlem*, and *Miss Sadie Thompson* (Rita Hayworth). C: Gloria Swanson, Lionel Barrymore, Raoul Walsh. D: Raoul Walsh. DRA 97m. v

Sadist, The 1963 ★★★ An unbalanced thug menaces three innocent customers at a roadside gas station. Tidy second feature with a convincing performance by Hall, Jr., and interesting photography. C: Arch Hall, Jr., Helen Hovey, Richard Alden, Marilyn Manning. D: James Landis. DRA 95m. v

Safe at Home 1962 ★★½ Young baseball player lies to his buddies about his friendship with N.Y. Yankee stars, then must produce the pros when fabrications get out of hand. Stock and severely dated juvenile fantasy, notable mostly for stiff cameos by ballplayers Mantle and Maris. C: Mickey Mantle, Roger Maris, William Frawley, Patricia Barry, Don Collier, Bryan Russell. D: Walter Doniger. FAM/DRA 83m. v

Safe Passage 1995 ★★★½ Middle-class family is torn asunder when tragedy strikes. Sarandon's perceptive portrayal of a world-weary housewife keeps this from sinking into soap opera oblivion. C: Susan Sarandon, Sam Shepard, Nick Stahl, Robert Sean Leonard, Marcia Gay Harden, Sean Astin. D: Robert Allan Ackerman. DRA [PG-13] 97m. v

Safecracker, The 1958 British ★★★ Tedious tale of expert safecracker (Milland) freed from prison to help country during WWII. Long buildup with bland payoff. C: Ray Milland, Barry Jones, Jeannette Sterke, Ernest Clark, Melissa Stribling, Victor Maddern. D: Ray Milland. ACT 96m.

Safety Last 1923 ★★★★★ Terrific silent slapstick farce about a shy man (Lloyd) trying to get ahead in big business. Features the classic highwire ledge sequence, still amazing to watch, with Lloyd seemingly suspended over a bustling city street. P.S.: He did his own stunts. C: Harold Lloyd, Mildred Davis. D: Fred Newmeyer, Sam Taylor. COM 78m. v

Saga Of Death Valley 1939 ★★½ Rancher confronts a greedy gang. Typical Rogers vehicle. C: Roy Rogers, Gabby Hayes. WST 60m. v

Saga of the Vagabonds 1964 Japanese ★★★½ Uneven samurai soap opera with noble Tsurata joining forces with Mifune's bandits to clear his name. Some stirring action sequences. C: Koji Tsuruta, Toshiro Mifune, Misa Uehara, Takashi Shimura. D: Toshio Sugie. ACT 115m.

Sahara 1943 ★★★★ Sergeant (Bogart) in charge of American and British armored crewmen marooned in the desert manages to outmaneuver the Germans. Fine WWII drama with excellent action and strong supporting performances. C: Humphrey Bogart, Bruce Bennett, Lloyd Bridges, Rex Ingram, Dan Duryea. D: Zoltan Korda. ACT 97m. v

Sahara 1983 ★★ Romantic 1920-period adventure follows a young woman who replaces dead father in a car race across the North African desert, then is carried off by a dashing sheik. Forced silliness harks back to Valentino and '20s serials. C: Brooke Shields, Lambert Wilson, Horst Buchholz, John Mills. D: Andrew V. McLaglen. DRA [PG] 111m. v

Said O'Reilly to McNab 1938 *See* **Sez O'Reilly to McNab**

Saigon 1948 ★★½ Three war buddies, stationed in Vietnam, are offered small fortune to help in robbery. Tame action drama, with stars at their worst. C: Alan Ladd, Veronica Lake, Luther Alder, Douglas Dick, Wally Cassell, Morris Carnovsky. D: Leslie Fenton. ACT 94m.

Saigon Commandos 1988 ★★ Saigon's military police force must defeat a crooked gang of heroin dealers and shady politicians who are plotting to infiltrate a government weakened by war in the streets. C: Richard Young, John Allen Nelson. D: Clark Henderson. ACT [R] 87m. v

Sail a Crooked Ship 1962 ★★★½ A gang of thieves take advantage of a naive naval officer (Wagner) to use his ship for bank heist. Light, amusing comedy with plenty of slapstick, vintage Kovacs. C: Robert Wagner, Ernie Kovacs, Dolores Hart, Carolyn Jones, Frankie Avalon. D: Irving S. Brecher. COM 88m. v

Sailor Beware 1951 ★★★★ Martin and Lewis join the Navy in this entertaining frolic, with some of their best routines. Hutton makes a cameo appearance in this remake of her 1942 debut film, *The Fleet's In*. Watch closely for James Dean. C: Dean Martin, Jerry Lewis, Corinne Calvert, Robert Strauss, Betty Hutton. D: Hal Walker. COM 108m.

Sailor Who Fell from Grace with the Sea 1976 British ★★★½ In its day considered shocking this story of a widow's passionate affair with a seaman is still fairly graphic. Trouble comes when the woman's troubled son gets wind of the romance. A slow but handsome film—definitely for adults. Loosely adapted from the novel by Yukio Mishima. C: Sarah Miles, Kris Kristofferson, Jonathan Kahn, Margo Cunningham. D: Lewis John Carlino. DRA [R] 108m. v

Sailors Three 1940 *See* **Three Cockeyed Sailors**

Saint, The Although it was Louis Hayward who first played Leslie Charteris' sophisticated freelance do-gooder in 1938's *The Saint in New York*, it was George Sanders who made Simon Templar his own, with five adventure-mysteries driven by his dry wit. Stage actor Hugh Sinclair played the character twice after Sanders departed to play the Falcon. Of course, Roger Moore launched his career as Templar with a popular British TV series, which also enjoyed a considerable cult following in the States.

The Saint in New York (1938)
The Saint Strikes Back (1939)
The Saint in London (1939)
The Saint's Double Trouble (1940)
The Saint Takes Over (1940)
The Saint in Palm Springs (1941)
The Saint's Vacation (1941)
The Saint Meets the Tiger (1943)
The Saint's Girl Friday (1954)

Saint in London, The 1939 ★★★½ Urbane detective (Sanders) travels to England where a daffy heiress (Gray) helps him ferret out counterfeiters. Entertaining entry in series. C: George Sanders, David Burns, Sally Gray, Henry Oscar. D: John Paddy Carstairs. CRI 72m. v

Saint in New York, The 1938 ★★★★ First, and best, of series with Hayward well cast as detective hired to murder gangland bosses. Faithful adaptation of original Leslie Charteris novel. C: Louis Hayward, Kay Sutton, Sig Rumann, Jonathan Hale, Frederick Burton, Jack Carson. D: Ben Holmes. CRI 71m. v

Saint Jack 1979 ★★★★ Perceptive comedy/drama about a charming opportunist (Gazzara) in 1972 Singapore. Perhaps the best Bogdanovich film since his *Last Picture Show*, *Paper Moon* heyday. From Paul Theroux's novel. C: Ben Gazzara, Denholm Elliott, Joss Ackland. D: Peter Bogdanovich. COM [R] 110m. v

Saint Joan 1957 ★★★½ Overly ambitious filming of the story of Joan of Arc (Seberg), the 15th-century teenager who was burned for heresy after having led the French troops to victory. Graham Greene wrote the script from Bernard Shaw's play, but Seberg's inexperience (in her debut) hurts the overall effect. C: Jean Seberg, Richard Widmark, Richard Todd, Anton Walbrook, John Gielgud, Harry Andrews. D: Otto Preminger. DRA 90m. v

Saint of Fort Washington, The 1993 ★★★½ The daily struggles of two homeless friends—one down and out (Glover) and the other schizophrenic (Dillon)—are detailed in this drama with a conscience. Gritty but not harrowing. Dillon measures up to a demanding role. C: Danny Glover, Matt Dillon, Rick Aviles, Nina Siemaszko, Ving Rhames, Joe Seneca. D: Tim Hunter. DRA 108m. v

Saint Strikes Back, The 1939 ★★★★ Suave British detective Simon Templar (Sanders) helps a woman trap robbers who framed her policeman father. Well-done private eye yarn, part of series based on the character created by Leslie Charteris. Sanders' first. C: George Sanders, Wendy Barrie, Jonathan Hale, Barry Fitzgerald. D: John Farrow. DRA 127m. v

Saint Takes Over, The 1940 ★★★½ Sanders helps a friendly cop (Hale) clear himself of a bribery charge. Average as far as Saint mysteries go, but the witty script helps. C: George Sanders, Jonathan Hale, Wendy Barrie, Paul Guilfoyle, Morgan Conway, Robert Emmett Keane. D: Jack Hively. CRI 69m.

Saint's Double Trouble, The 1940 ★★★ Routine entry in mystery series has Sanders in double role of debonair detective and the jewel thief for whom he's mistaken. C: George Sanders, Helene Whitney, Jonathan Hale, Bela Lugosi. D: Jack Hively. CRI 56m. v

Saint's Girl Friday, The 1954 British ★★★ Hayward returns to the role he originated 16 years earlier in tedious tale of detective out to avenge his ex-girlfriend's murder. Last in the series. C: Louis Hayward, Naomi Chance, Sidney Tafler, Charles Victor. D: Seymour Friedman. CRI 68m.

Saint's Vacation, The 1941 ★★★½ Entertaining entry in series gets WWII espionage twist as Sinclair tracks down music box with secret codes before it gets in Germany's hands. C: Hugh Sinclair, Sally Gray, Arthur Macrae, Cecil Parker, Leueen McGrath, Gordon McLeod. D: Leslie Fenton. CRI 60m. v

Sal of Singapore 1929 ★★★½ Partial talkie with Haver as young woman of questionable morality entrusted with baby found by seaman (Hale) in lifeboat. Interesting antique melodrama starts out silent, then finds its voice in last half hour. C: Phyllis Haver, Alan Hale, Fred Kohler. D: Howard Higgin. DRA 70m.

Salaam Bombay! 1988 Indian ★★★★ On the streets of Bombay, thieves, addicts, and prostitutes educate a young boy (Syed) in the ugliness of poverty as he struggles to return to his country home. Director Nair for her first feature, cast real street children in this gripping but sad work with an accomplished visual style. C: Shafiq Syed, Raghubir Yadav, Aneeta Kanwar, Hansa Vithal, Chand Sharma, Nana Patekov. D: Mira Nair. DRA 113m. v

Salamander, The 1981 U.S. ★★ Cautionary

tale about Italian neo-Fascist coup d'état and an intelligence colonel's efforts to thwart it. Locations and pageant of stars help this otherwise poor effort based on the Morris West novel. C: Franco Nero, Anthony Quinn, Martin Balsam, Sybil Danning, Claudia Cardinale. D: Peter Zinner. DRA 101m. V

Salem's Lot: The Miniseries 1979 ★★★★ Early Stephen King TV-movie adaptation is one of the best, tautly told with a good cast. The setting is a small Maine town haunted by vampires that are combatted by an author (Soul) and young man (Kerwin). Also available in a shorter, more violent version known as *Salem's Lot: The Movie.* C: David Soul, James Mason, Lance Kerwin, Bonnie Bedelia, Lew Ayres, Reggie Nalder. D: Tobe Hooper. HOR [PG] 184m. TVM V

Salem's Lot: The Movie 1979 *See* **Salem's Lot: The Miniseries**

Saleslady 1938 ★★★ Tawdry melodrama with heiress (Nagel) marrying beneath her, then regretting it. C: Anne Nagel, Weldon Heyburn, Harry Davenport. D: Arthur Greville Collins. DRA 65m.

Salesman 1969 ★★★ Intriguing but often smarmy documentary follows door-to-door Bible salesmen on their rounds. D: Albert and David Maysles. DOC 90m.

Sallah 1965 Israeli ★★★★ Clever satire of the immigration of a North American Jew (Topol) to Israel with his wife and children in 1949, and his various schemes to assimilate and secure decent housing for his family. Topol portrays a wonderfully three-dimensional character, warts and all. C: Chaim Topol, Geula Noni, Gila Almagor, Arik Einstein. D: Ephraim Kishon. COM 105m. V

Sally and Saint Anne 1952 ★★★½ Sugary comedy of daughter (Blyth) believing her prayers to title saint will keep her family from being evicted. Cute and naive. C: Ann Blyth, Edmund Gwenn, Hugh O'Brian, Jack Kelly, King Donovan. D: Rudolph Maté. FAM/COM 90m.

Sally, Irene and Mary 1938 ★★★½ Predictable, but entertaining musical about young women trying to break into show business. Davis and Durante steal film with their spirited comedy routines. C: Alice Faye, Tony Martin, Fred Allen, Joan Davis, Marjorie Weaver, Gregory Ratoff, Jimmy Durante, Louise Hovick. D: William A. Seiter. MUS 72m.

Sally of the Sawdust 1925 ★★★½ The hobo guardian of a child who's really a society tot tries to reunite her with her grandparents. Sweet but sentimental silent vehicle for Fields. Remade with the same star as *Poppy.* Includes a rare film appearance (especially without partner/wife Lynn Fontanne) by theatre star Lunt. C: W.C. Fields, Carol Dempster, Alfred Lunt, Erville Alderson. D: D.W. Griffith. COM 91m. V

Sally's Irish Rogue 1960 *See* **Poacher's Daughter, The**

Salome 1953 ★★★½ Uneven embellishment of Biblical tale with Hayworth as lascivious daughter of Herod in love with John the Baptist (Granger). It's a long wade through, but Rita's Dance of the Seven Veils almost makes the wait worthwhile. C: Rita Hayworth, Stewart Granger, Charles Laughton, Judith Anderson, Cedric Hardwicke, Basil Sydney. D: William Dieterle. DRA 103m. V

Salome, Where She Danced 1945 ★★★ Campy costumer, full of laughs, about an exotic dancer (De Carlo), suspected of espionage, who takes flight to Old West. Deliberately silly plot, and ridiculously bad acting made this Mata Hari-type actioner an instant cult classic. C: Yvonne De Carlo, Rod Cameron, David Bruce, Walter Slezak, Albert Dekker, Marjorie Rambeau, J. Edward Bromberg. D: Charles Lamont. DRA 90m.

Salome's Last Dance 1989 British ★★★ Dandy, playwright, and wit Oscar Wilde is entertained one evening in a brothel by prostitutes performing his forbidden play *Salome.* Unrelentingly excessive debauchery, the Ken Russell way. C: Glenda Jackson, Stratford Johns, Nickolas Grace, Imogen Millais-Scott, Douglas Hodge. D: Ken Russell. DRA [R] 89m. V

Salsa 1988 ★★ Car mechanic (Rosa, one of the many ex-members of Puerto Rican pop phenomenon Menudo) fixes autos by day while dancing to salsa music by night. Hot music can't hide the lack of a plot. Choreographed by Kenny Ortega (*Dirty Dancing*). Strictly for fans. C: Robby Rosa, Rodney Harvey, Magali Alvarado, Miranda Garrison. D: Boaz Davidson. MUS [PG] 96m. V

Salt Lake Raiders 1950 ★★★ Run-of-the-mill Western with a cowpoke trying to clear himself of murder charge. C: Allan "Rocky" Lane, Eddy Waller, Roy Barcroft, Martha Hyer. D: Fred C. Brannon. WST 60m.

Salt of the Earth 1953 ★★★★½ Excellent drama of striking New Mexico mineworkers, written and directed by Hollywood blacklist victims (Michael Wilson, Biberman). Union members' wives prove to be true heroines. Many memorable dramatic confrontations in stirring story, way ahead of its time. C: Juan Chacon, Rosaura Revueltas, Will Geer, Mervin Williams. D: Herbert J. Biberman. DRA 94m. V

Salt to the Devil 1949 British ★★★½ Tragic tale of Italian immigrant family in Depression-era New York. Grim but poignant story suffers mainly from British production out of step with subject matter. (a.k.a. *Give Us This Day*) C: Sam Wanamaker, Lea Padovani. D: Edward Dmytryk. DRA 120m.

Salty O'Rourke 1945 ★★★★ Schoolteacher (Russell) tries to convert racetrack veteran (Ladd) to the straight and narrow path in charming comedy with better-than-average script. C: Alan Ladd, Gail Russell, William Demarest, Stanley Clements, Bruce Cabot, Spring Byington. D: Raoul Walsh. COM 99m.

Salute 1929 ★★★½ Lively football yarn

with two brothers playing for rival Army/Navy teams. Unfortunate appearance by Fetchit in demeaning, racist role may offend modern sensibilities. C: George O'Brien, William Janney, Frank Albertson, Helen Chandler, John Wayne, Stepin Fechit. D: John Ford, David Butler. DRA 83m.

Salute of the Juggler, The 1990 *See* **Blood of Heroes, The**

Salvador 1985 ★★★½ A brash American foreign correspondent (Woods) covers civil-war-torn El Salvador. Based on co-scriptor Richard Boyle's own journalistic experiences. Film is preachy but forceful, and Woods is terrific. C: James Woods, James Belushi, John Savage, Elpedia Carrillo, Kara Glover. D: Oliver Stone. DRA [R] 123m. V

Salvador Dali—A Soft-Self Portrait 1977 ★★★½ A made-for-French-television close-up look at the artistic process of Surrealist Salvador Dali. Narrated by Orson Welles, this documentary is a must see for fans of eccentricity. C: Orson Welles. DOC 60m. V

Salvage Gang, The 1972 ★★★½ Modest, charming tale of four youngsters trying to raise money to repair their father's broken saw. FAM/DRA

Salvatore Guiliano 1962 Italian ★★★½ A Sicilian Mafia chieftan is gunned down in public, and his life then flashes before his (and our) eyes. Sort of a "marinara" version of *Citizen Kane*, but frequently effective. From a true story. Remade as *The Sicilian*. C: Pietro Cammarata, Frank Wolff. D: Francesco Rosi. CRI 125m.

Salzburg Connection, The 1972 ★★½ An American lawyer vacationing in Austria tangles with international spies. Film adaptation of Helen MacInnes' best-seller, with attractive locales and annoying camera tricks. C: Barry Newman, Anna Karina, Klaus Maria Brandauer, Karen Jensen. D: Lee H. Katzin. DRA [PG] 93m. V

Sam Kinison Live! 1988 ★★★ Religion, sex, and politics are among the topics controversial comic Kinison touches on in this energetic performance at L.A.'s Roxy Theatre. C: Sam Kinison. D: Walter C. Miller. COM 50m. TVM V

Sam Marlowe, Private Eye 1980 *See* **Man with Bogart's Face, The** TVM

Sam Whiskey 1969 ★★★½ A gambler (Reynolds) is hired by a thief's widow (Dickinson) to recover sunken gold. Diverting western comedy, helped immensely by Burt's charm. C: Burt Reynolds, Angie Dickinson, Clint Walker, Ossie Davis. D: Arnold Laven. WST [PG] 96m.

Samantha 1992 ★★½ A light comedy about a young woman who on her 21st birthday decides to travel around and find herself. C: Martha Plimpton, Dermot Mulroney, Mary Kay Place, Ione Skye. D: Stephen La Rocque. COM [PG] 101m. V

Samaritan: The Mitch Snyder Story 1986 ★★★★ Depiction of Vietnam vet and ceaseless Washington activist Snyder (Sheen), focusing on his political crusade against homelessness that ended his own tragic death. Excellent all-around effort, especially Sheen's. C: Martin Sheen, Cicely Tyson, Roxanne Hart, Joe Seneca, Stan Shaw, James Avery, Conchata Ferrell. D: Richart T. Heffron. DRA 90m. TVM V

Same Time, Next Year 1978 ★★★★ Alda and Burstyn are couple—married to others—who meet annually for 26 years in long-term affair. Entertaining episodic film, based on popular play, mildly satirizes quarter century of American culture. Excellent performances by two leads undergoing numerous character transformations. C: Ellen Burstyn, Alan Alda. D: Robert Mulligan. COM [PG] 119m. V

Sammy and Rosie Get Laid 1987 British ★★★ British woman and East Indian man living in London experience renewed problems with their open marriage when husband's diplomat father arrives from India. A compelling look at the erosion of traditions. Intelligent and thoughtful. Discriminating viewers should note film's frank sexuality. C: Shashi Kapoor, Claire Bloom, Ayub Kahn Din, Frances Barber, Roland Gift. D: Stephen Frears. COM 97m. V

Sammy Going South 1963 *See* **Boy Ten Feet Tall, A**

Sammy, the Way-Out Seal 1962 ★★★½ Mumy (of TV's *Lost in Space*) plays a young boy who tries to keep a seal for a pet. Though hampered by one-note premise, humorous situations are energetic enough to raise it above sitcom level. C: Robert Culp, Jack Carson, Billy Mumy, Patricia Barry, Michael McGreevey. D: Norman Tokar. FAM/COM 89m. V

Sam's Son 1984 ★★★½ Landon's melodramatic autobiographical study of young athlete's relationship with wistful father. Wallach has some fine moments. C: Eli Wallach, Anne Jackson, Timothy Murphy, Hallie Todd, Alan Hayes, Jonna Lee, Michael Landon. D: Michael Landon. DRA [PG] 104m. V

Samson 1961 Italian ★ Samson, the hulking spiritual leader, strives to restore peace to his land via his rippling pecs. Only for those who love awful acting, dubbing, costumes, and sets. C: Brad Harris, Brigitte Corey, Alan Steele, Serge Gainsbourg. D: Gianfranco Parloni. ACT 90m.

Samson and Delilah 1949 ★★★★ A grand biblical epic, reenacting the Old Testament tale with added doses of Hollywood romance as Delilah (Lamarr) plots an elaborate vengeance upon the rebellious Samson (Mature) who scorned her love. Not one of DeMille's more spectacular spectacles, but still quite entertaining. C: Victor Mature, Hedy Lamarr, George Sanders, Angela Lansbury, Henry Wilcoxon, Olive Deering, Fay Holden. D: Cecil B. DeMille. DRA 128m. V

Samson and Delilah 1984 ★★★ Biblical

hero noted for his great strength is betrayed by his treacherous lover. Competent version of the familiar story. The big guy gets clipped and brings the house down. C: Antony Hamilton, Belinda Bauer, Max von Sydow, Jose Ferrer, Victor Mature. D: Lee Philips. DRA 95m. TVM V

Samurai Cowboy 1993 ★★½ An urban Japanese man sets out for the American countryside to fulfill his dream of becoming a cowboy. C: Hiromi Go, Robert Conrad. D: Michael Keusch. DRA 101m. V

Samurai from Nowhere 1964 Japanese ★★½ Warrior (Nagato) rescues woman from evil nobleman who pursues them for the rest of the movie. Low-budget Japanese film should appeal to martial arts fans. C: Isamu Nagato, Testuro Tamba, Shima Iwashita. D: Seiichiro Uchikawa. ACT 93m.

Samurai 1—Musashi Miyamoto 1955 Japanese ★★★ A defeated Samurai's spirit is broken until a loving woman and Buddhist priest rebuild his faith. First episode of "samurai" trilogy. C; Toshiro Mifune, Kaoru Yachigusa. D: Hiroshi Inagaki. DRA 92m. V

Samurai 2—Duel at Ichijoji Temple 1955 Japanese ★★½ A Samurai warrior confronts and defeats his enemies. C: Toshiro Mifune, Tsurata Koji. D: Hiroshi Inagaki. DRA 102m. V

Samurai 3—Duel at Ganryu Island 1956 Japanese ★★½ A lifelong enemy battles with a Samurai expert in an amazing struggle of swords and punches. C: Toshiro Mifune, Koji Tsurata. D: Hiroshi Inagaki. ACT 102m. V

San Antonio 1945 ★★★½ A dance-hall entertainer of easy virtue (Smith) reforms for love of straight-shooter Flynn. Typical and well done. C: Errol Flynn, Alexis Smith, S. Z. Sakall, Victor Francen, Florence Bates, John Litel, Paul Kelly. D: David Butler. WST 107m. V

San Antonio Kid, The 1944 ★★★ Elliott helps ranchers keep their land from outlaws in weak entry of the *Red Ryder* Western series. C: Bill Elliot, Bobby Blake, Alice Fleming. D: Howard Bretherton. WST 59m.

San Antonio Rose 1941 ★★★½ Entertaining B-musical/Western with Frazee and Arden as hostesses of rival roadhouses. Popular songs include title tune, "Hi Neighbor," and "The Hut Sut Song." C: Jane Frazee, Robert Paige, Eve Arden, Lon Chaney, Jr., Shemp Howard. D: Charles Lamont. MUS 63m.

San Demetrio, London 1947 ★★★ Dated war story of British merchant marine ship damaged at sea and crew's efforts to salvage it. Melodramatic propaganda was popular in its day. C: Walter Fitzgerald, Mervyn Johns, Ralph Michael, Robert Beatty. D: Charles Frend. DRA 76m.

San Diego, I Love You 1944 ★★★★ Delightful, modest comedy of inventor (Horton) and his family journeying to San Diego to sell Pop's latest: a collapsible life raft. Allbritton's a joy as spunky daughter. C: Jon Hall, Louise Allbritton, Edward Everett Horton, Eric Blore, Buster Keaton, Irene Ryan. D: Reginald LeBorg. COM 83m.

San Francisco 1936 ★★★★½ Dandy costume epic with enterprising saloon owner (Gable) who becomes the Svengali of an opera singer (MacDonald) in Barbary Coast yarn that culminates in spectacular earthquake finale. Sight of Jeanette chirping like loon among the ruins is camp classic. Tracy does fine job as sympathetic priest. C: Clark Gable, Jeanette MacDonald, Spencer Tracy, Jack Holt, Jessie Ralph, Ted Healy, Shirley Ross, Al Shean. D: W.S. Van Dyke II. DRA 116m. V

San Francisco Story, The 1952 ★★★½ Wealthy mine owner (McCrea) vows to get rid of corrupt San Francisco politician (Blackmer) in sturdy melodrama with good performances. C: Joel McCrea, Yvonne De Carlo, Sidney Blackmer, Florence Bates. D: Robert Parrish. DRA 80m.

San Quentin 1937 ★★★★ Warden (O'Brien) falls for convict Bogart's sister (Sheridan) in muscular prison drama with three strong leads compensating for predictable script. C: Pat O'Brien, Humphrey Bogart, Ann Sheridan, Veda Ann Borg, Barton MacLane. D: Lloyd Bacon. DRA 70m.

San Quentin 1946 ★★★ Typical good convicts vs. bad story with Tierney trying to stop prison revolt. Mundane and no relation to 1936 film with same name. C: Lawrence Tierney, Barton MacLane, Marian Carr, Harry Shannon, Carol Forman, Richard Powers. D: Gordon Douglas. DRA 66m.

Sanctuary 1961 ★★ A Southern belle (Remick) is torn between respectable life and fun in a brothel. Over-heated, over-plotted adaptation of two novels by William Faulkner (*Sanctuary*, *Requiem for a Nun*). C: Lee Remick, Yves Montand, Bradford Dillman, Odetta. D: Tony Richardson. DRA 100m.

Sand 1949 ★★★½ Satisfying horse drama of prize colt lost in railroad accident, enjoying newfound freedom, till owner tries to recapture him. Best for animal lovers and juveniles. (a.k.a. *Will James' Sand*) C: Mark Stevens, Rory Calhoun, Coleen Gray, Charley Grapewin. D: Louis King. FAM/DRA 78m.

Sand And Blood 1987 French ★★ Bullfighting provides a metaphor for a matador's and doctor's intense love for one another. D: Jeanne Labrune. DRA 101m. V

Sand Castle, The 1960 ★★★★ Unusual fantasy about two neglected children building sand castle on beach, then inhabiting it in animated dream sequence. Captures secret world of youngsters in disarming manner. C: Barry Cardwell, Laurie Cardwell, George Dunham, Alec Wilder. D: Jerome Hill. FAM/SFI 67m.

Sand Fairy, The 1993 ★★★½ The sand fairy is a wonderful and wise friend who opens up a magical world of enchantment for children. Nice adventure. FAM/DRA [PG] 139m. V

Sand Pebbles, The 1966 ★★★★½ Revolution-torn China of the '20s is the backdrop for the political and romantic awakening of a cynical American sailor (McQueen) as he falls in love with an idealistic schoolteacher (Bergen). Drama on a grand scale, highlighted by McQueen's performance—the best of his career—which earned the actor his only Oscar nomination. C: Steve McQueen, Richard Attenborough, Richard Crenna, Candice Bergen, Mako. D: Robert Wise. DRA 179m. v

Sandakan 8 1974 Japanese ★★★ A heartbreaking drama of a young Japanese woman who is forced to prostitute her body in order to pay off her family's debts. C: Kinuyo Tanaka, Komaki Kurihara. D: Kei Kumai. DRA [R] 121m. v

Sanders of the River 1935 British ★★★★ The adventures of a British colonial officer posted in Africa. Stunning location shooting helps this antique, as do performances by Banks and especially Robeson. Zesty and colorful. The character of Sanders was later seen during the '60s in *Sanders (Death Drums Along the River)* and *Coast of Skeletons.* (a.k.a. *Bosambo*) C: Paul Robeson, Leslie Banks, Nina Mae McKinney, Robert Cochran. D: Zoltan Korda. DRA 86m. v

Sandflow 1937 ★★★½ Jones plays cowpoke trying to atone for his father's sins. Well-made B-Western with clever plot and good action sequences. C: Buck Jones, Lita Chevret, Bob Kortman. D: Lesley Selander. WST 58m.

Sandlot, The 1993 ★★½ Sandlot baseball team takes on board the clutzy new kid on the block and tangles with strange monstrous dog behind the outfield fence. Uninvolving exercise in boyhood nostalgia. C: Tom Guiry, Mike Vitar, Patrick Renna, James Earl Jones, Karen Allen. D: David Mickey Evans. FAM/DRA [PG] 90m. v

Sandpiper, The 1965 ★★★ Limp soap opera with Taylor and Burton as adulterous couple shot against pretty seascapes. Painfully predictable, but haunting Oscar-winning theme song, "The Shadow of Your Smile." C: Elizabeth Taylor, Richard Burton, Eva Marie Saint, Charles Bronson, Robert Webber. D: Vincente Minnelli. DRA 117m. v

Sands of Iwo Jima 1949 ★★★★½ Superb Wayne performance as a battle-hardened WWII Marine Corps sergeant who leads his squad in fierce combat on a Japanese-held volcanic island. Tough, realistic war action is well staged. C: John Wayne, John Agar, Adele Mara, Forrest Tucker, Richard Jaeckel. D: Allan Dwan. DRA 109m. v

Sands of the Kalahari 1965 British ★★★★ A plane crashes in the wilderness, leaving passengers to struggle against nature and themselves. Stirring tale of survival in the desert, with a fine ensemble cast. C: Stuart Whitman, Susannah York, Stanley Baker, Harry Andrews, Theodore Bikel. D: Cy Endfield. DRA 119m.

Sandu Follows the Sun 1965 Russian ★★★½ Allegorical children's film chronicles Russian boy's journey "following the sun" as he encounters Good and Evil on the streets of Moscow. Sometimes affecting, but often too symbolic. (a.k.a *Man Following the Sun*) C: Nika Krimnus, Tatyana Bestayeva. D: Mosei Kalik. FAM/DRA 66m.

Sandwich Man, The 1966 British ★★★½ Series of comic improvisations built around Bentine, a man hired to wear an advertising board, wandering through London, encountering eccentric strangers. Mostly silent, sometimes quite funny, with stellar cast of British comics. C: Michael Bentine, Dora Bryan, Diana Dors, Stanley Hollowey, Wilfrid Hyde-White, Ron Moody, Anne Quayle, Terry Thomas, Norman Wisdom. D: Robert Hartford-Davis. COM 95m.

Sandy Gets Her Man 1940 ★★★ Fair comedy is one of series featuring cute two-year-old. This time Baby Sandy is caught in funding rivalry between police and fire departments. C: Paul Smith, Stuart Erwin, Una Merkel, Baby Sandy, Edgar Kennedy, William Frawley. D: Otis Garrett. COM 74m.

Sanjuro 1962 Japanese ★★★★½ Kurosawa samurai film has master swordsman (Mifune) help a group of warriors seeking revenge on the clan that has kidnapped a comrade in 19th-century Japan. Though a lesser version of its prequel *Yojimbo*, film has a sly sense of humor, and Mifune excels as the stony-faced hero. C: Toshiro Mifune, Tatsuya Nakadai, Yuzo Kayama. D: Akira Kurosawa. ACT 96m. v

Sans Soleil 1982 French ★★★★★ A world traveler writes letters to an unknown woman. A witty and whimsical essay on the nature of memory; a brilliant film. D: Chris Marker. DOC 100m. v

Sansho the Bailiff 1954 Japanese ★★★★★ Classic Japanese drama tells mythic tale of 11th-century family's degeneration. Mizoguchi's visual style is extraordinary as dream-like sequences alternate with harrowing realism. A magnificent work of cinematic art. (a.k.a. *The Bailiff*) C: Kinuyo Tanaka, Yoshiaki Hanayagi, Kyoko Kagawa, Eitaro Shindo. D: Kenji Mizoguchi. DRA 132m. v

Santa Claus Conquers the Martians 1964 ★★ Jealous aliens from the Red Planet abduct Kris Kringle and two Earth children to help them solve their kid's addiction to television. Very low-budget fantasy as silly as it sounds; a midnight-movie classic. C: John Call, Leonard Hicks, Vincent Beck, Donna Conforti, Pia Zadora. D: Nicholas Webster. SFI 81m. v

Santa Claus, The Movie 1985 ★★½ When evil toy manufacturer (Lithgow) tries to undermine Santa Claus, sweet-natured elf (Moore) saves his employer and spirit of Christmas. Film's look achieves magical qualities, but script doesn't. Intended for family viewing, though some parents may object to mild swearing. C: Dudley Moore, John Lithgow, David Huddleston, Burgess Meredith, Judy Cornwell, Jeffrey Kramer, Christian Fitzpatrick, Carrie Heim. D: Jeannot Szwarc. FAM/DRA [PG] 112m.

Santa Clause, The 1994 ★★★★½ Jolly, charming Christmas fable for the '90s casts Allen as divorced father who, through a series of mishaps, literally becomes the fat man in the red suit. Imaginative, funny. Destined to become a holiday classic. C: Tim Allen, Judge Reinhold, Wendy Crewson, Eric Lloyd, Mary Gross. D: John Pasquin. FAM/COM [PG] 95m. V

Santa Fe Passage 1955 ★★★½ Wagon train carrying rifles to Santa Fe is threatened by Apaches, and a man (Payne) must protect it while courting the cargo's owner (Domergue), who's part Indian herself. Good performances and an honest look at prejudices underpin this solid Western. C: John Payne, Faith Domergue, Rod Cameron, Slim Pickens. D: William Witney. WST 70m.

Santa Fe Stampede 1938 ★★★½ Wayne and cowboy cronies help aged prospector recover his claim from wicked Mason in entertaining entry of *The Three Mesquiteer* series. C: John Wayne, LeRoy Mason, Ray Corrigan, Max Terhune. D: George Sherman. WST 58m. V

Santa Fe Trail 1940 ★★★ In pre-Civil War days, cavalry officer Jeb Stuart (Flynn) is charged with bringing in the abolitionist John Brown. Action-packed pseudohistorical film is filled with battles and romance, and a solid cast of old pros. C: Errol Flynn, Olivia de Havilland, Raymond Massey, Ronald Reagan, Alan Hale, Guinn Williams, Van Heflin. D: Michael Curtiz. WST 110m. V

Santa Sangre 1990 Italian ★★★★ Controversial cult director Jodorowsky's surreal fantasy of a Mexican circus has a boy (played at different ages by director's two sons) helping his armless mother commit vile acts. Though not to every taste this strange, visually arresting film will truly interest those in search of a new cinematic experience. C: Axel Jodorowsky, Blanca Guerra, Guy Stockwell. D: Alejandro Jodorowsky. DRA [R] 120m. V

Santee 1973 ★★★½ Boy is adopted by the bounty hunter (Ford) who murdered his father. Thought-provoking western, good production. C: Glenn Ford, Michael Burns, Dana Wynter. D: Gary Nelson. WST [PG] 93m. V

Santiago 1956 ★★★½ Old adversaries (Ladd and Nolan) must work together as they run illegal guns to Cuba during Spanish-American War. Typical story of a cynic regaining his values is strengthened by sparring of leads. C: Alan Ladd, Rossana Podesta, Lloyd Nolan, Chill Wills, Paul Fix, L.Q. Jones, Frank DeKova. D: Gordon Douglas. ACT 93m.

Sap from Syracuse, The 1930 ★★★½ Minor musical with Rogers as shipboard heiress involved with unfortunate Oakie, pretending to be celebrated engineer. Rogers is charming, but plot is leaky. C: Jack Oakie, Ginger Rogers. D: A. Edward Sutherland. MUS 68m.

Sapphire 1959 British ★★★★ British detective yarn about Scotland Yard's investigation into murder of black music student who had been passing for white. Effective and suspenseful with fine soundtrack. C: Nigel Patrick, Yvonne Mitchell, Michael Craig, Paul Massie, Bernard Miles, Earl Cameron, Rupert Davies, Yvonne Buckingham. D: Basil Dearden. CRI 92m.

Saps at Sea 1940 ★★★½ A stressful job at a horn factory drives Ollie to a vacation in a small boat with Stan. Out of the frying pan and into the fire, with comedy greats Laurel and Hardy. Fair comedy from the duo finds most of its laughs coming in the first half. C: Stan Laurel, Oliver Hardy, James Finlayson, Ben Turpin, Richard Cramer. D: Gordon Douglas. COM [G] 57m. V

Saraband 1948 British ★★★★ Memorable romantic drama of wife of future King George I falling in love with dashing commoner (Granger). Beautifully produced, well acted. (a.k.a. *Saraband for Dead Lovers*) C: Stewart Granger, Joan Greenwood, Flora Robson, Francoise Rosay, Frederick Valk, Peter Bull, Anthony Quayle, Michael Gough, Megs Jenkins, Christopher Lee. D: Basil Dearden. DRA 95m.

Saraband for Dead Lovers 1948 *See* **Saraband**

Saracen Blade, The 1954 ★★★½ Unintentionally funny period drama of 13th-century knight (Montalban) avenging his father's death. Quite entertaining, but for all the wrong reasons. C: Ricardo Montalban, Betta St. John, Rick Jason, Carolyn Jones, Whitfield Connor. D: William Castle. DRA 76m.

Sarafina! 1992 U.S. ★★★★ A defiant schoolteacher (Goldberg) helps her students understand the injustices of apartheid in '70s South Africa and inspires an optimistic young girl (Khumalo) to fight the system in this film version of the stage musical. Uplifting Soweto music translates beautifully to the screen. Worthwhile, though occasionally violent. C: Whoopi Goldberg, Leleti Khumalo, Miriam Makeba, John Kani, Mbongeni Ngema. D: Darrell James Roodt. MUS [PG-13] 99m. V

Sarah and Son 1930 ★★★½ Chatterton gives stirring performance in mother-love saga of widow hiring lawyer to search for lost child. C: Ruth Chatterton, Fredric March, Doris Lloyd, Philippe de Lacy. D: Dorothy Arzner. DRA 76m.

Sarah, Plain and Tall 1991 ★★★★½ New England schoolteacher (Close) arrives in 1910 Kansas to teach the children of a widower (Walken). Wholesome, uplifting, and totally winning. C: Glenn Close, Christopher Walken, Lexi Randall, Margaret Sophie Stein, Jon De Vries, Christopher Bell. D: Glenn Jordan. DRA [G] 98m. TVM V

Saratoga 1937 ★★★★ Clever romantic racetrack comedy of a slick gambler/bookie (Gable) embroiled in a mad love/hate relationship with sheltered Harlow, whose father is a horse breeder. Splendid last performance from Harlow, who died before completion of the film and was replaced by doubles. C: Clark Gable, Jean Harlow, Lionel Barrymore, Frank Morgan, Walter Pidgeon, Una Merkel, Cliff Edwards, George Zucco, Hattie MacDaniel, Margaret Hamilton. D: Jack Conway. COM 92m. V

Saratoga Trunk 1945 ★★★ Adaptation of Edna Ferber novel with Bergman as New Orleans-born Creole returning to exact her revenge on antagonistic townsfolk. Ingrid's too nice, Cooper's too stiff, and the movie's too long. C: Gary Cooper, Ingrid Bergman, Flora Robson, Jerry Austin, John Warburton, Florence Bates. D: Sam Wood. DRA 135m.

Sardinia: Kidnapped 1968 Italian ★★★½ Moderately suspenseful thriller, with Nero out to rescue a kidnapped friend from Sardinian bandits. C: Franco Nero, Charlotte Rampling. D: Gianfranco Mingozzi. ACT 110m.

Sartana's Here . . . Trade Your Pistol For A Coffin 1970 Italian ★★½ A soldier of fortune with an eye for fine women gets involved with gold robbers. C: George Hilton, Charles Southwood. D: Anthony Ascot. ACT 92m. V

Sartre by Himself (Sartre Par Lui Meme) 1979 French ★★★½ An in-depth study of the leading French existentialitist philosopher, including extensive discussions with Jean-Paul Sartre himself. DOC 190m. V

Saskatchewan 1954 ★★★½ A Canadian Mountie (Ladd) helps Winters recover from savage Indian ambush, and gets involved with politics and misunderstandings between Canadian soldiers, peaceful Cree Indians, and violent Sioux. Some athletic sequences, but fairly predictable. Notable for actually distinguishing different Indian tribes. C: Alan Ladd, Shelley Winters, J. Carroll Naish, Hugh O'Brian, Robert Douglas, Richard Long, Jay Silverheels. D: Raoul Walsh. DRA 87m.

Satan Bug, The 1965 ★★★½ Insane millionaire (Basehart) theatens L.A. with vials of a killer virus; government agent (Maharis) tries to stop him. Sci-fi thriller builds steadily to an exciting helicopter chase climax. C: George Maharis, Richard Basehart, Anne Francis, Dana Andrews. D: John Sturges. SFI 114m.

Satan Killer, The 1993 ★★★ A serial killer is on the loose and murders the fiance of the investigator charged with his capture. C: Steve Sayre, Billy Franklin, James Westbrook. D: Stephen Calamari. HOR 90m. V

Satan Met a Lady 1936 ★★½ Dreadful version of Dashiell Hammett's *The Maltese Falcon*, changing the black bird to a ram's horn. Interesting mainly for Davis' performance and as a point of comparison to the far superior *Maltese Falcon* of 1941. C: Bette Davis, Warren William, Alison Skipworth, Arthur Treacher, Winifred Shaw, Marie Wilson, Porter Hall. D: William Dieterle. CRI 75m. V

Satan Never Sleeps 1962 ★★½ Missionary priests (Holden, Webb) in 1949 China battle the Communists. Uneasy mix of sentiment and politics. Director McCarey's (*Going My Way*) last film. (a.k.a. *Flight From Terror, The Devil Never Sleeps*) C: William Holden, Clifton Webb, France Nuyen, Robert Lee. D: Leo McCarey. DRA 126m.

Satanic Rites of Dracula, The 1973 ★ Inauspicious finale for Hammer Films' *Dracula* series really stretches for a new angle: This time the Count attempts to decimate the human race with deadly bacteria! (a.k.a. *Count Dracula and His Vampire Bride.*) C: Christopher Lee, Peter Cushing, Michael Coles. HOR [R] 88m. V

Satan's Black Wedding 1974 ★★ Lush title for an ultra-cheap horror flick about a man's search for his missing sister and a monastery full of the undead. Production values are low, low, low, but at least it's short. C: Greg Braddock, Ray Miles, Lisa Milano, Barrett Cooper. D: Philip Miller. HOR [R] 62m. V

Satan's Cheerleaders 1977 ★★½ Drive-in camp about a busload of cheerleaders trying to flee their devil-worshipping captors. Docile spine-tingler just misses going bust. C: Kerry Sherman, John Ireland, Yvonne De Carlo, John Carradine. D: Greydon Clark. HOR [R] 92m. V

Satan's Satellites 1958 ★★ A Martian (Nimoy) who helps Earthlings fend off invading space aliens. Adolescent science-fiction byproduct of the 1952 Republic serial *Zombies of the Stratosphere.* C: Judd Holdren, Aline Towne, Wilson Wood, Lane Bradford, Leonard Nimoy. D: Fred Brannon. SFI 70m. V

Satanwar 1979 ★★★ It's war between God and the Devil. And man is caught right in the middle. C: Bart La Rue, Sally Schermerhorn, Jimmy Drankovitch. HOR 95m. V

Satisfaction 1988 ★★ Bateman fronts pop garage band that's trying to make it big as they spend summer in resort town. Neeson adds the only touch of class. (a.k.a. *Girls of Summer*) C: Justine Bateman, Liam Neeson, Trini Alvarado, Britta Phillips, Julia Roberts, Scott Coffey. D: Joan Freeman. MUS [PG-13] 93m. V

Saturday Night and Sunday Morning 1960 British ★★★★★ Working-class rebel (Finney) thumbs his nose at authority and carries on affairs with older, married woman (Roberts) and conventional girl (Field), whom he gets pregnant. Brilliant; first and best-made of several '60s "angry young men" films from Britain. C: Albert Finney, Shirley Anne Field, Rachel Roberts, Norman Rossington. D: Karel Reisz. DRA 90m.

Saturday Night Fever 1977 ★★★★½ Effective character study about an egocentric

Brooklynite (Travolta) growing weary of buddies and nightly rituals, before ultimately facing up to life's realities with his dance partner (Gorney). Gritty story with honest performances, edgy direction, and some definitive disco dancing from Travolta. Great Bee Gees soundtrack. Film available in both R and PG versions. C: John Travolta, Karen Lynn Gorney, Barry Miller, Donna Pescow. D: John Badham. MUS [PG,R] 118m. V

Saturday the 14th 1981 ★★ Parody of *Friday the 13th* films finds couple (Benjamin and real-life spouse Prentiss) moving into new abode, where horror lurks behind every door. Witless spoof with all the expected jokes. C: Richard Benjamin, Paula Prentiss, Severn Darden, Jeffrey Tambor. D: Howard R. Cohen. COM [PG] 91m. V

Saturday's Children 1940 ★★★★ Well-acted comedy/drama with Garfield as struggling inventor tricked into marriage by Shirley. Lovingly adapted from Maxwell Anderson play, previously filmed in 1929 and 1935 (latter as *Maybe It's Love*). C: John Garfield, Anne Shirley, Claude Rains, Lee Patrick, George Tobias, Roscoe Karns, Dennis Moore, Elisabeth Risdon. D: Vincent Sherman. COM 101m.

Saturday's Island 1952 *See* **Island of Desire**

Saturday's Millions 1933 ★★★½ Odd football drama with Young as college hero struggling to support himself while rich girlfriend does nothing to help him. Heartfelt, but clichéd. C: Robert Young, Leila Hyams, John Mack Brown, Andy Devine. D: Edward Sedgwick. DRA 76m.

Saturn 3 1980 British ★★½ Deep below the surface of one of Saturn's moons, 2 scientists (Douglas, Fawcett) work to create food for starving Earth. Life is peachy until a visitor from Earth (Keitel) creates life form that could kill them all. Interesting premise runs out of air. C: Farrah Fawcett, Kirk Douglas, Harvey Keitel, Douglas Lambert. D: Stanley Donen. SFI [R] 90m. V

Saul and David 1968 ★★★ Biblical story of young David of Judea, his dealings with King Saul, his slaying of Goliath, and more. Visually splendid family treat. C: Norman Woodland, Giannie Garko, Lyz Marquez. FAM/DRA 120m. V

Savage Abduction 1973 ★★★ Two young girls are kidnapped by a biker gang and sold into white slavery. C: Tom Drake, Amy Thomson, Stephen Oliver. D: John Lawrence. HOR [R] 84m. V

Savage and Beautiful 1984 ★★★★ Exquisite wildlife documentary with enthralling footage of lions and elephants in Africa, polar bears in the Arctic, and whales off the coast of Patagonia. Outstanding. C: Donald Sutherland. DOC 60m. V

Savage Attraction 1984 ★★ A 16-year-old is blackmailed into marrying ex-Nazi. Potentially intriguing true story gets sloppy, disjointed treatment. (a.k.a. *Hostage* and *Hostage: The Christine Maresch Story*) C: Kerry Mack, Ralph Schicha. D: Frank Shields. ACT [R] 93m. V

Savage Beach 1989 ★★ Feds discover lost WWII gold on isolated island and deal with villains who want it for themselves. Sub-par sequel to *Picasso Trigger*. C: Dona Spier, Hope Marie Carlton, Bruce Penhall, John Aprea. D: Andy Sidaris. ACT [R] 94m. V

Savage Bees, The 1976 ★★★½ A swarm of killer African bees attacks New Orleans during Mardi Gras. Tidy, predictable chiller a notch above par. C: Ben Johnson, Michael Parks, Horst Buchholz, Gretchen Corbett. D: Bruce Geller. ACT 90m. V

Savage Dawn 1985 ★★★ In a small western town, an ex-Green Beret takes on a gang of savage bikers. C: George Kennedy, Karen Black, Richard Lynch. D: Simon Nuchtern. ACT [R] 102m. V

Savage Guns, The 1962 United States ★★★ American gunslinger (Basehart), trying to retire after being wounded, settles in Mexico after the Civil War, but is hounded by bandits. Somewhat offbeat Western, but hackneyed plot. C: Richard Basehart, Don Taylor, Alex Nicol. D: Michael Carreras. WST 84m.

Savage Hunger, A 1984 ★★½ When their plane crashes in remote Mexico, a group of survivors are faced with cannibalism. C: Chris Makepeace, Scott Hylands, Anne Lockhart. D: Sparky Greene. ACT 90m. V

Savage Innocents, The 1959 Italian ★★★★ Uneven, but original study of Eskimo life, with Quinn giving a solid performance as a native struggling to survive in the wilderness. Stunning photography, intelligent direction. C: Anthony Quinn, Yoko Tani, Peter O'Toole, Marie Yang, Anna May Wong. D: Nicholas Ray. DRA 110m.

Savage is Loose, The 1974 ★★ Marooned for years on a desert island, an incestuous relationship develops between a scientist's companionless son and his mother. The Oedipus complex is revisited, without much pizzazz. C: George C. Scott, Trish Van Devere, John David Carson, Lee H. Montgomery. D: George C. Scott. ACT [R] 114m. V

Savage Island 1985 U.S. ★★ Female reformatory in the tropics. Badly reedited version of *Escape From Hell*. Standard. C: Nicholas Beardsley, Linda Blair, Anthony Steffen, Ajita Wilson, Christina Lai, Leon Askin. D: Edward Muller. ACT [R] 74m. V

Savage Justice 1988 ★★ Ex-Green Beret and mistreated woman team up in Southeast Asia to take on revolutionaries who killed her parents. Violent, nudity-packed escapism. C: Julia Montgomery, Steven Memel. D: Joey Romero. ACT 90m. V

Savage Lust 1993 ★★★ When they get lost on the road on a rainy night, a group of teenagers discover a mysterious, coffin-filled mansion. C: William Russell, Jennifer Delora, Clark Tufts. D: Jose Ramon Larraz. HOR 90m. V

Savage Messiah 1972 British ★★★½ Sculptor Henri Gaudier (Antony) falls in love with an older woman (Tutin). Visually impressive, stylized portrait of the artist; fans of director Russell's florid technique will be pleased. C: Dorothy Tutin, Scott Antony, Helen Mirren. D: Ken Russell. DRA [R] 100m. V

Savage Nights 1993 French ★★★★ An intense, autobiographical film about a sexually insatiable HIV-positive cameraman in a bisexual triangle. Powerful, almost histrionic. Collard died from AIDS two days before his film won four Césars (French equivalent of the Oscar). C: Cyril Collard, Romane Bohringer, Carlos Lopez, Corine Blue, Claude Winter, Rene-Marc Bini, Maria Schneider. D: Cyril Collard. DRA 126m.

Savage Pampas 1966 Spanish ★★★ Mutiny on the range, as fort commander (Taylor) tries to keep his squadron from deserting to the gang of a bandit (Randall). Sturdy, but a bit slow. C: Robert Taylor, Ron Randall, Ty Hardin, Rosenda Monteros. D: Hugo Fregonese. WST 100m.

Savage Sam 1963 ★★★ When three children are kidnapped by tribe of local Native Americans, beloved pet pooch Savage Sam comes to their rescue. Simple-minded sequel to *Old Yeller* has plenty of action-driven plot but lacks depth. C: Brian Keith, Tommy Kirk, Kevin Corcoran, Dewey Martin. D: Norman Tokar. FAM/DRA 103m. V

Savage Streets 1983 ★★½ Schoolmates seek revenge against a gang of raping murdering bums. Unduly violent vigilante yarn with Blair miscast as a girl next door. C: Linda Blair, John Vernon, Robert Dryer, Linnea Quigley. D: Danny Steinmann. ACT [R] 93m. V

Savage, The 1952 ★★★ White man (Heston), raised by Sioux, must fight his loved ones. Ahead of its time, in that story focuses on the Sioux point of view, but heavy-handed script weakens it. C: Charlton Heston, Susan Morrow, Peter Hanson, Joan Taylor, Ted de Corsia. D: George Marshall. WST 95m.

Savage, The 1975 *See* **Lovers Like Us**

Savage Weekend 1980 ★★½ A weekend of fun turns into nightmare of death and destruction for a group of partygoers. C: Christopher Allport, James Doerr, Marilyn Hamlin. D: John Mason Kirby. HOR [R] 88m. V

Savage Wilderness 1956 *See* **Last Frontier, The**

Savannah Smiles 1982 ★★★★ Runaway poor little rich girl (Andersen) hides out in car that belongs to a pair of robbers. Crooked duo demand ransom, but soon come to love child. Unlikely but cute story that develops with fresh comic twists. Co-star Miller also wrote script. C: Mark Miller, Donovan Scott, Bridgette Andersen, Peter Graves. D: Pierre DeMoro. FAM/COM [PG] 104m. V

Save Me 1993 ★★★ Timeless tale of greed gone rampant and the price that evil-doers must pay. C: Harry Hamlin, Lysette Anthony, Olivia Hussey. D: Alan Roberts. DRA [R] 90m. V

Save the Tiger 1973 ★★★★ A misguided businessman (Lemmon) tries to hang tough in the dog-eat-dog clothing manufacturing world in this look at the American rat race. Lemmon received a well-deserved Best Actor Oscar for his gritty performance. C: Jack Lemmon, Jack Gilford, Laurie Heineman, Patricia Smith. D: John G. Avildsen. DRA [R] 100m. V

Saving Grace 1986 ★★★½ Down-to-earth Pope (Conti) tries to balance bureaucratic duties of his position with the secular world and flees to the Italian countryside to get in touch with real people. Enjoyable, light fluff. C: Tom Conti, Fernando Rey, Giancarlo Giannini, Edward James Olmos. D: Robert M. Young. COM [PG] 112m. V

Sawdust and Tinsel 1953 Swedish ★★★★★ An international triumph that drew attention to writer/director Bergman. A circus owner leaves his mistress to reconcile with his wife; when she turns him away, he finds the mistress has a new lover. Mature, poetic, splendidly acted. (a.k.a. *The Naked Night*) C: Harriet Andersson, Åke Gronberg, Gunnar Bjornstrand. D: Ingmar Bergman. DRA 95m. V

Saxon Charm, The 1948 ★★★★ Interesting backstage story of demonic Broadway producer and the lives he destroys. Light comedian Montgomery is miscast in lead role, but film boasts witty script, good supporting cast. C: Robert Montgomery, Susan Hayward, John Payne, Audrey Totter, Harry Morgan, Cara Williams, Harry Von Zell, Heather Angel. D: Claude Binyon. DRA 88m.

Say Amen, Somebody 1983 ★★★★½ Documentary features the wonders of gospel music, spotlighting careers of "Mother" Willie Mae Ford Smith and "Professor" Thomas Dorsey. A beautiful showcase of glorious gospel. C: Willie Mae Ford Smith, Thomas A. Dorsey, Sallie Martin. D: George Nierenberg. DOC [G] 100m. V

Say Anything . . . 1989 ★★★★ Teenaged wise guy Cusack inexplicably finds himself falling in love with class brain Skye, who is devoted to her widowed father Mahoney. Enjoyable, unusually intelligent adolescent romance, marked by Cusack's engaging performance. C: John Cusack, Ione Skye, John Mahoney, Lili Taylor, Loren Dean. D: Cameron Crowe. COM [PG-13] 100m. V

Say Goodbye, Maggie Cole 1972 ★★★½ Newly widowed research scientist (Hayward) returns to general practice in a Chicago ghetto. Earnest, well-handled medical drama; Hayward's touching swan song. C: Susan Hayward, Darren McGavin, Michael Constantine, Beverly Garland. D: Jud Taylor. DRA 73m. TVM V

Say Hello to Yesterday 1971 British ★★

Middle-aged woman has an affair with a twenty-ish Romeo (Whiting). Groovy London soaper; Simmons looks out of place. C: Jean Simmons, Leonard Whiting, Evelyn Laye. D: Alvin Rakoff. DRA [PG] 91m. v

Say It with Music 1932 British ★★★ Minor British musical with bandleader Payne playing himself, in sentimental tale of friend's plane crash and struggle with amnesia. C: Jack Payne, Percy Marmont, Joyce Kennedy. D: Jack Raymond. MUS 69m.

Say It with Songs 1929 ★★★½ Musical tearjerker with Jolson pulling out all the stops as radio singer sent to prison on a bum rap. Songs include "Little Pal," "I'm in Seventh Heaven," and "Used to You." C: Al Jolson, Davey Lee, Marian Nixon, Holmes Herbert, Kenneth Thompson, Fred Kohler, Frank Campeau, John Bowers. D: Lloyd Bacon. MUS 85m.

Say One for Me 1959 ★★½ Show-biz priest (Crosby) looks out for naive chorus girl (Reynolds). Very attractive cast, caught in a sentimental musical. C: Bing Crosby, Debbie Reynolds, Robert Wagner, Ray Walston, Stella Stevens (debut). D: Frank Tashlin. MUS 119m.

Say Yes 1986 ★★ A man has to get married within 24 hours if he's to inherit a fortune. Silly comedy gets needed lift from Winters. C: Lissa Layng, Art Hindle, Jonathan Winters, Logan Ramsey. D: Larry Yust. COM [PG-13] 87m. v

Sayonara 1957 ★★★★½ Lush, well-acted tale of forbidden love between American soldiers and Japanese women during the Korean War lets Brando play a stalwart romantic lead. Excellent Oscar-winning support from both Buttons and Umecki as doomed couple. Title song by Irving Berlin. Based on a James Michener novel. C: Marlon Brando, Ricardo Montalban, Miiko Taka, Miyoshi Umeki, Red Buttons, James Garner. D: Joshua Logan. DRA 147m. v

Scalawag 1973 ★★½ Douglas's directorial debut is an odd blend of *Treasure Island* and *Oliver!*, about a peg-legged pirate (Douglas) searching for treasure with the help of two youngsters (Lester, Down). The drunken parrot gives the best performance. Watch for Danny DeVito C: Kirk Douglas, Mark Lester, Lesley-Anne Down, Neville Brown. D: Kirk Douglas. FAM/DRA [G] 93m.

Scalpel 1978 ★★★ A plastic surgeon (Lansing) crafts his disappeared daughter's face onto another woman so that he can collect her inheritance. Interesting premise, marred by faulty direction and violent, sometimes tasteless situations. (a.k.a. *False Face*) C: Robert Lansing, Judith Chapman, Arlen Dean Snyder. D: John Grissmer. DRA [PG] 95m. v

Scalphunters, The 1968 ★★★½ A fur trapper acquires a slave who is much smarter and better educated than he. Middling comedy; superior cast. C: Burt Lancaster, Shelley Winters, Ossie Davis, Telly Savalas, Armando Silvestre, Nick Cravat, Dabney Coleman. D: Sydney Pollack. COM 102m. v

Scalps 1983 ★★★ A brutal rancher tries to abduct a beautiful comanche woman, who escapes and plots revenge. C: Karen Wood, Albert Farley, Beny Cardosa. D: Werner Knox. WST [R] 90m. v

Scam 1992 ★★★ A con artist picks the wrong mark—he winds up blackmailing her, with deadly results. Some good action and atmosphere. C: Christopher Walken, Lorraine Bracco. D: John Flynn. DRA [R] 100m. v

Scandal 1989 ★★★★ This reenactment of the sensational '60s Profumo Affair concerns a showgirl's notorious, news-making dalliances with heads of state and the country's uppercrust that shocked British society. Engaging, compelling entertainment. C: John Hurt, Joanne Whalley-Kilmer, Bridget Fonda, Ian McKellen. D: Michael Canton-Jones. DRA [R] 105m. v

Scandal in a Small Town 1989 ★★★ Turgid melodrama in which fallen woman (Welch) in small town instigates court case against anti-Semitic high school teacher. Vibrant star tries too hard to be "noble." C: Raquel Welch, Christa Denton, Peter Van Norden, Ronny Cox. D: Anthony Page. DRA 100m. TVM v

Scandal in Paris, A 1946 ★★★★ Lighthearted, enjoyable adventure casts Sanders as French thief conniving his way into job as prefect of police. Based on a true story. (a.k.a. *Thieves' Holiday*) C: George Sanders, Signe Hasso. D: Douglas Sirk. CRI

Scandal in Sorrento 1957 ★★★ Bumbling police chief (De Sica) is pursued by a woman (Loren) who wants to make her fiance jealous. Sex farce wastes its two stars, but the Italy location footage looks great. C: Sophia Loren, Vittorio De Sica, Lea Padovani. D: Dino Risi. COM 92m.

Scandal Sheet 1952 ★★★★ Well-constructed thriller with Crawford as editor who accidentally kills his ex-wife, then has to encourage his star reporter's investigation of the murder. Based on Samuel Fuller novel. (a.k.a. *The Dark Page*) C: Broderick Crawford, Donna Reed, John Derek, Rosemary DeCamp, Henry O'Neill, Henry Morgan. D: Phil Karlson. CRI 82m.

Scandal Sheet 1985 ★★★½ Hard-hearted supermarket tabloid publisher (Lancaster) gets hold of a story that could ruin innocent lives. Acerbic press room intrigue, fine Lancaster. C: Burt Lancaster, Pamela Reed, Robert Urich, Lauren Hutton. D: David Lowell Rich. DRA 100m. TVM

Scandalous 1984 ★★ A TV journalist framed for murder tangles with a pair of con artists. Frenetic black comedy slapstick wastes Gielgud. C: Robert Hays, John Gielgud, Pamela Stephenson, Jim Dale. D: Rob Cohen. COM [PG] 93m. v

Scandalous 1988 ★★★ A young Duke runs

out of money. Desperate, he ties in with some international intriquers to get some. C: Albert Fortell, Lauren Hutton, Ursula Karven. D: Robert W. Young. ACT 90m. v

Scandalous John 1971 ★★★ Annoying Disney comedy with Keith hamming it up as ranch owner refusing to sell his property to land developer. C: Brian Keith, Michele Carey, Rick Lenz, Harry Morgan, Alfonso Arau. D: Robert Butler. COM [G] 113m. v

Scanner Cop 1994 ★★★★ Nicely conceived and executed marriage of cop-movie standards with the scanner mythology; here, a psychically gifted officer (Quinn) must use his repressed powers to stop a madman who's orchestrating cop killings. C: Daniel Quinn, Darlanne Fluegel, Richard Lynch, Richard Grove, Mark Rolston. D: Pierre David. SFI [R] 93m.

Scanners 1981 Canadian ★★★★ Medically spawned supertelepaths split into warring factions: the good, who try to deal with their powers, and evil, who exploit them shamelessly. Ambitious sci-fi shocker with some strong moments, particularly the notorious exploding-head scene. C: Jennifer O'Neill, Stephen Lack, Patrick McGoohan. D: David Cronenberg. HOR [R] 102m. v

Scanners II—The New Order 1991 Canadian ★★★ In this sequel, good scanner (Hewlett) takes on a corrupt police official attempting to rule with a corps of scanners he controls. Well done and generally well acted, this better-than-average sequel nonetheless loses some of the freshness of the original. C: David Hewlett, Deborah Raffin, Yvan Ponton, Isabelle Mejias, Raoul Trujillo. D: Christian Duguay. HOR [R] 104m. v

Scanners III—The Takeover 1992 Canadian ★★★½ A scanner (Komorowska) goes crazy thanks to experimental cure and plots to send her mind-controlling vibes over TV airwaves. Second sequel is actually an improvement over its predecessor, thanks to high-powered filmmaking style with a heavy dash of sardonic humor. C: Liliana Komorowska, Valerie Valois, Steve Parrish. D: Christian Duguay. HOR [R] 101m. v

Scapegoat, The 1959 British ★★★½ Botched adaptation of Daphne du Maurier novel with Guinness in dual role of innocent British gentleman on Parisian holiday duped into helping French look-a-like commit murder. Muddled script, choppy editing. Davis gives bizarre performance as Guinness' evil, drug-crazed mother. C: Alec Guinness, Bette Davis, Nicole Maurey, Irene Worth, Peter Bull, Pamela Brown, Geoffrey Keen. D: Robert Hamer. CRI 92m.

Scar, The 1948 ★★★ To evade the police, a killer assumes the identity of his doctor. (a.k.a. *Hollow Triumph*) C: Paul Henreid, Eduard Franz, Joan Bennett. D: Steve Sekely. HOR 83m. v

Scaramouche 1952 ★★★★½ Eighteenth-century nobleman (Granger) seeks to avenge the death of his friend in this colorful adventure tale. Sterling cast and rousing action make this one of the very best swashbucklers ever. Big fun for all. C: Stewart Granger, Eleanor Parker, Janet Leigh, Mel Ferrer. D: George Sidney. ACT 118m. v

Scaramouche 1975 *See* **Loves and Times of Scaramouche, The**

Scaramouche 1976 ★★★½ A prince in 18th Century France gets involved in a plot to assassinate Napoleon. C: Ursula Andress, Michael Sarrazin. D: Enzo Castellari. COM 82m. v

Scarecrow 1972 ★★★★ Road movie of two homeless men, an ex-con (Hackman) and a drifter (Pacino), who travel across America together was a Best Film winner at the Cannes Film Festival. This neglected sleeper, filmed on location in Detroit, has a realistic look and great performances. C: Gene Hackman, Al Pacino, Dorothy Tristan, Eileen Brennan, Ann Wedgeworth. D: Jerry Schatzberg. DRA [R] 112m. v

Scarecrow in a Garden of Cucumbers 1972 ★★★½ Cult camp musical stars ex-Warholite/transvestite Woodlawn as Broadway hopeful "Eve Harrington" (name from classic *All About Eve*) encountering bizarre New Yorkers, also with famous character names. Virtually plotless string of in-jokes; Bette Midler sings the soundtrack. C: Holly Woodlawn, Tally Brown, David Margulies. D: Robert J. Kaplan. MUS 82m.

Scarecrows 1988 ★★★★ A small group of soldiers gone AWOL with stolen money parachute into a deserted farm, where they're terrorized by murderous, living scarecrows. Prosaic story line is enlivened by scary direction, with strong use of visuals and sound effects. C: Ted Vernon, Michael Simms, Richard Vidan. D: William Wesley. HOR [R] 80m. v

Scared Stiff 1953 ★★★★ Scott inherits spooky Caribbean mansion, then makes it even stranger by inviting Lewis, Martin, and Miranda to stay there. Amusing remake of *The Ghost Breakers* with Jerry and Carmen making memorable team. C: Dean Martin, Jerry Lewis, Lizabeth Scott, Carmen Miranda, Dorothy Malone. D: George Marshall. COM 108m. v

Scared Stiff 1987 ★★ Various unfortunate victims are stranded in a southern mansion haunted by an evil slave trader's ghost. Lacks suspense and surprises, with a villain who's scarier in flashbacks as a human than with the rubber monster makeup he wears in the present. Utterly generic horror item. C: Andrew Stevens, Mary Page Keller. D: Richard Friedman. HOR [R] 85m. v

Scared Straight 1972 ★★★★ Peter Falk hosts this documentary about young delinquents getting the low-down on life of crime from the prisoners in a maximum security lock-up. Chilling truth packs a punch more than ever. C: Peter Falk. D: Arnold Shapiro. DOC 122m. V

Scared to Death 1981 ★★ A monster spawned by DNA experiment gone awry stalks Los Angeles, with a detective (Stinson) attempting to track it down. Decent initial premise quickly falls into predictable B-movie routine. Followed by semisequel *Syngenor.* C: John Stinson, Diana Davidson. D: William Malone. HOR [R] 93m. V

Scarface 1932 ★★★★★ Loosely based on life of Al Capone, this is the gangster movie that set the standard in the '30s, with wonderfully id-driven performance by Muni, countered equally by Raft as his rival. Made before the production code, has material not seen in later gangster epics. C: Paul Muni, Ann Dvorak, George Raft, Boris Karloff, Karen Morley, Vince Barnett, Osgood Perkins. D: Howard Hawks. CRI [PG] 93m. V

Scarface 1983 ★★★½ De Palma's updated version of the gangster classic follows a Cuban refugee in Miami who becomes a cocaine kingpin. Excess is this movie's middle name, in everything from acting to length. Very violent. C: Al Pacino, Steven Bauer, Michelle Pfeiffer, Mary Elizabeth Mastrantonio, Robert Loggia. D: Brian De Palma. CRI [R] 170m. V

Scarface Mob, The 1962 ★★★½ Brisk, satisfying gangster yarn of Eliot Ness vs. Al Capone. Originally the pilot for *The Untouchables* TV series. C: Robert Stack, Keenan Wynn, Barbara Nichols, Pat Crowley, Neville Brand, Bruce Gordon. D: Phil Karlson. CRI 102m. TVM

Scarlet and the Black, The 1983 ★★★★ During WWII, an Irish priest gives aid to fugitive Allied POWs at Vatican City and becomes a Nazi target himself. Well-acted, based on a true story. Peck's first TV venture. C: Gregory Peck, Christopher Plummer, John Gielgud, Raf Vallone. D: Jerry London. DRA 145m. TVM V

Scarlet Buccaneer, The *See* **Swashbuckler**

Scarlet Camellia, The 1965 Japanese ★★★ Violent revenge drama with Iwashita vowing to murder all of her promiscuous mother's lovers before her ailing father dies. Interesting premise, but poorly acted and directed. C: Shima Iwashita, Yoshi Kato. D: Yoshitaro Nomura. CRI 117m.

Scarlet Claw, The 1944 ★★★★½ Sherlock Holmes (Rathbone) and Watson (Bruce) try to unravel gruesome murders in French-Canadian town. Clever, atmospheric, and exciting; the best of the series. C: Basil Rathbone, Nigel Bruce, Paul Cavanagh, Kay Harding. D: Roy William Neill. CRI 74m. V

Scarlet Clue, The 1945 ★★★ WWII-themed Charlie Chan mystery, with Chan (Toler) out to stop murderous spies after top-secret radar plans. Lightweight entry, with plenty of comic relief. C: Sidney Toler, Benson Fong, Mantan Moreland, Helen Deveraux, Robert Homans, Virginia Brissac, Jack Norton, Stanford Jolley, Janet Shaw. D: Phil Rosen. CRI 65m. V

Scarlet Coat, The 1955 ★★★½ Static Revolutionary War-era drama with patriot (Wilde) becoming double agent, joining the British to expose traitor Benedict Arnold. Good photography and cast help. C: Cornel Wilde, Michael Wilding, George Sanders, Anne Francis, Bobby Driscoll. D: John Sturges. DRA 101m.

Scarlet Dawn 1932 ★★★ Post-Revolution costume drama about a Tsarist officer forced to flee Russia with his maid (Carroll). Magnificent production design and charming leads make the most of the tepid script. C: Douglas Fairbanks, Jr., Nancy Carroll. D: William Dieterle. DRA 76m. V

Scarlet Empress, The 1934 ★★★★★ Von Sternberg cast his favorite and frequent collaborator Dietrich as the strong-willed Queen of Russia, Catherine the Great, who overthrows her imbecile husband Peter to lead the nation. Historically accurate it ain't, but in style and effect it's absolutely first-rate. Dietrich's daughter, Maria Sieber, plays Catherine as a young girl. C: Marlene Dietrich, John Lodge, Louise Dresser, Sam Jaffe, C. Aubrey Smith. D: Josef von Sternberg. DRA 105m. V

Scarlet Letter, The 1926 ★★★★★ Superb silent adaptation of Nathaniel Hawthorne's classic novel about a woman (Gish) marked as an adultress in 18th-century Salem. Lillian's luminous performance and terrific use of close-ups make this a powerful example of the silent era's artistry. Remade several times, including a 1995 version. C: Lillian Gish, Lars Hanson, Henry B. Walthall. D: Victor Seastrom. DRA 80m.

Scarlet Letter, The 1934 ★★★ Comedienne Moore is out of her depth as Hawthorne's Hester Prynne, branded an outcast for bearing a child out of wedlock. Sound remake of the 1926 Lillian Gish vehicle is overshadowed by its superb predecessor. C: Colleen Moore, Hardie Albright, Henry B. Walthall, Alan Hale. D: Robert G. Vignola. DRA 70m. V

Scarlet Letter, The 1973 German ★★★★ Another version of Nathanial Hawthorne's tale of Puritanical hypocrisy, as Hester Prynne (Berger) endures the public shame of adultery. Wenders' film is a moody, intelligent study of suffering that makes the most of production limitations; Colonial New England is effectively portrayed in a German production filmed in Spain. C: Senta Berger, Lou Castel, Hans-Christian Blech. D: Wim Wenders. DRA 90m. V

Scarlet Pages 1930 ★★ Ludicrous soap opera with attorney (Ferguson) unknowingly defending her own daughter in murder trial. Overacted by underwhelming cast. C: Elsie Ferguson, John Halliday, Marion Nixon. D: Ray Enright. DRA 65m.

Scarlet Pimpernel, The 1935 British ★★★★ British dandy (Howard) moonlights as swashbuckling liberator of innocent victims of French Revolution. Marvelous costume adventure with strong cast. C: Leslie Howard, Merle Oberon, Raymond Massey, Nigel Bruce. D: Harold Young. ACT 98m. V

Scarlet Pimpernel, The 1982 ★★★★ Classic story of rescuer (Andrews) of French nobility during the Revolution gets terrific treatment in this made-for-TV adaptation. Exciting and lush production with superb McKellen and Seymour. C: Anthony Andrews, Jane Seymour, Ian McKellan, James Villiers. D: Clive Donner. DRA 142m. TVM V

Scarlet Street 1945 ★★★★★ Hypnotic film noir with superb cast has married Robinson falling for Bennett, then getting roped into art scam that leads to murder. Dark and disturbing, holds interest till exciting surprise ending. C: Edward G. Robinson, Joan Bennett, Dan Duryea, Margaret Lindsay, Rosalind Ivan. D: Fritz Lang. CRI 103m. V

Scarred 1983 ★★½ A teenaged mother is forced into prostitution to take care of her baby. C: Rose-Marie Turko, Jennifer Mayo, Jackie Berryman. D: Rosemarie Turko. ACT [R] 85m. V

Scars of Dracula 1970 British ★★★½ A young man stumbles upon Dracula's castle and is killed by the Count. Victim's brother and girlfriend soon arrive to search for him. Some chilling sequences sit uneasily alongside exploitative ones, but generally a good entry in Hammer's *Dracula* series. C: Christopher Lee, Dennis Waterman, Jenny Hanley, Christopher Matthews. D: Roy Ward Baker. HOR [R] 92m. V

Scary Tales ★★★★ Compilation of Disney cartoons featuring b&w shorts *Skeleton Dance* and *Haunted House*, along with Donald Duck classics *Donald's Lucky Day* and *Duck Pimples*. Halloween fun for kids and animation buffs. FAM/DRA 43m. V

Scattergood Baines 1941 ★★★½ Folksy comedy with Kibbee as nosy owner of small-town hardware store. First of a series, based on the radio program. C: Guy Kibbee, Carol Hughes. D: Christy Cabanne. COM 69m.

Scavenger Hunt 1979 ★★½ The relatives and servants of a deceased wealthy man are pitted against time and one another in a scavenger hunt competition to inherit a vast fortune. Strained comedy with a talented cast. C: Richard Benjamin, James Coco, Scatman Crothers, Ruth Gordon. D: Michael Schultz. COM [PG] 117m. V

Scavengers 1987 ★★ A bird-watcher gets mixed up in a mission involving American and Russian intelligence operatives. Inept satire action piece doesn't fly. C: Kenneth Gilman, Brenda Bakke, Crispin De Nys. D: Duncan McLachlan. DRA [PG-13] 94m. V

Scene of the Crime 1949 ★★★½ Tight film noir, with Johnson as police officer investigating fellow cop's murder. Well scripted. C: Van Johnson, Arlene Dahl, Gloria DeHaven, Tom Drake, Leon Ames. D: Roy Rowland. CRI 94m.

Scene of the Crime 1987 French ★★★★ A provincial mother (Deneuve) and son (Giraudi) are manipulated by an escaped convict (Stanczak) in this sleek, sexy thriller featuring earthy, nuanced performances from Deneuve and Darrieux, backed by artful photography and direction. C: Catherine Deneuve, Danielle Darrieux, Wadeck Stanczak, Nicholas Giraudi, Victor Lanoux. D: Andre Techine. CRI 90m. V

Scenes from a Mall 1991 ★★★ Allen, cast miles against type, is a California hedonist spending wedding anniversary with wife Midler at shopping mall. Worth seeing for unusual leads. C: Bette Midler, Woody Allen. D: Paul Mazursky. COM [R] 87m. V

Scenes from a Marriage 1973 Swedish ★★★★★ Superbly reformatted Swedish TV drama is a penetrating, intimate examination of disintegrating marriage. Stunningly directed marital portrait by Bergman, with excellent acting by Ullmann and Josephson. C: Liv Ullmann, Erland Josephson, Bibi Andersson. D: Ingmar Bergman. DRA [PG] 168m. V

Scenes from a Murder 1972 Italian ★★½ A killer stalks a beautiful actress. Inadequate chase thriller. C: Telly Savalas, Anne Heywood, Giorgio Piazza, Osvaldo Ruggeri. D: Alberto DeMartino. DRA 91m. V

Scenes from the Class Struggle in Beverly Hills 1989 ★★★ Anarchy rules in a game of bed hopping amidst "beautiful people," including fading sitcom star and her ghostly husband. Not nearly as funny as it wants to be, but wild work from eclectic cast keeps this moving. C: Jacqueline Bisset, Ray Sharkey, Mary Woronov, Robert Beltran, Ed Begley, Jr., Wallace Shawn, Paul Mazursky. D: Paul Bartel. COM [R] 103m. V

Scenes from the Goldmine 1987 ★★½ A beautiful young songwriter falls in love with the lead singer of a band. But he's more interested in fame than in her. C: Catherine Mary Stewart, Caremon Dye, Steve Railsback. D: Marc Rocco. DRA [R] 99m. V

Scent of a Woman 1992 ★★★★ A poor high school student (O'Donnell) becomes the after-school caretaker for a cantankerous and blind ex-military officer (Pacino), which somehow ends up including a wild weekend in Manhattan. A fireworks performance from a vibrant Pacino won him an Oscar, after eight nominations. Inspired by the 1975 Italian film *Profumo di Donna*. C: Al Pacino, Chris O'Donnell, James Rebhorn, Gabrielle Anwar, Philip S. Hoffman, Bradley Whitford, Richard Bradford, Ron Eldard. D: Martin Brest. DRA [R] 137m. V

Scent of Green Papaya 1994 Vietnamese ★★★★ First Vietnamese film ever released in the United States is a potent, evocative drama of a young servant woman who falls in love with the young master of the house in Saigon in early '50s. Handsome, low-key film is a remarkable debut for director Tran. C:

Tran Nu Yen-Khe, Lu Man San, Truong Thi Loc, Nguyen Anh Hoa, Vuong Hoa Hoi, Tran Ngoc Truong. D: Tran Anh Hung. DRA 104m.

Scent of Mystery 1960 ★★★ Englishman (Elliott) on vacation in Spain gets mixed up in murder. Routine mystery was first to use "Smell-o-Vision" gimmick in theaters, hitting audiences with odors to "enhance" their viewing. (a.k.a. *Holiday in Spain*) C: Denholm Elliot, Peter Lorre, Beverly Bentley, Paul Lukas, Leo McKern, Diana Dors, Elizabeth Taylor. D: Jack Cardiff. CRI 125m.

Schindler's List 1993 ★★★★★ Spielberg's powerful, heartfelt story of WWII entrepreneur Oskar Schindler (Neeson), whose profiteering operations made him the unexpected savior for over 1,000 Jewish factory workers. Stark, often brutally realistic Holocaust drama, shot in black and white, with a marvelous, enigmatic performance by Neeson. Winner of seven Oscars including Best Picture, Director, and Adapted Screenplay. Shattering and unforgettable. C: Liam Neeson, Ben Kingsley, Ralph Fiennes, Embeth Davidtz, Caroline Goodall, Jonathan Sagalle. D: Steven Spielberg. DRA [R] 195m. V

Schizo 1990 *See* **Playroom**

Schizoid 1980 ★★ The patients of a therapist (Kinski) are being gruesomely murdered by a mysterious psychotic. Gore galore with nary a plot in sight. Saved from obvious by the imaginative casting of Kinski. C: Klaus Kinski, Marianna Hill, Donna Wilkes, Christopher Lloyd, Flo Gerrish. D: David Paulsen. CRI [R] 89m. V

Schlock 1973 ★★★½ Loving send-up of Roger Corman-type horror cheapies, focusing mainly on an unruly Bigfoot. Landis' directorial debut contains a few of his later trademarks, many film in-jokes. (a.k.a. *Banana Monster*) C: Saul Kahan, Joseph Piantadosi, Eliza Garrett, John Landis. D: John Landis. HOR [PG] 78m. V

School Daze 1987 ★★★½ Mixed-up comedy about an African-American college and various struggles between fraternities, townies, and intraracial strife. Some marvelous musical sequences, and interesting dramatic performances but sidetracked by subplots and an uneasy combination of fantasy and reality. C: Larry Fishburne, Giancarlo Esposito, Tisha Campbell, Ossie Davis, Spike Lee, Julian Eaves, Jane Toussaint. D: Spike Lee. COM [R] 114m. V

School for Scoundrels 1960 British ★★★★ Perennial loser (Carmichael) learns the ways of the world, and how to beat them, at Sim's "College of One-upmanship." Jaunty British comedy with expert cast. C: Alastair Sim, Terry-Thomas, Ian Carmichael, Janette Scott, Dennis Price. D: Robert Hamer. COM 94m.

School for Secrets 1946 British ★★★ Inventors of radar suddenly find themselves in real combat action. Terrific cast in uneasy mix of comedy, drama, and documentary. C: Ralph Richardson, Raymond Huntley, Richard Attenborough. D: Peter Ustinov. DRA 108m.

School Spirit 1985 ★ A randy teenage boy dies in an automobile accident, then returns to Earth as a randy teenage ghost. Dreadful sex comedy. C: Tom Nolan, Elizabeth Foxx, John Finnegan, Larry Linville. D: Alan Holleb. COM [R] 90m. V

School Ties 1992 ★★★½ A Jewish student (Fraser) on a football scholarship at an exclusive boys prep school faces vicious anti-Semitism. Earnest attempt to look at an important question is well done, if obvious. C: Brendan Fraser, Matt Damon, Chris O'Donnell, Andrew Lowery. D: Robert Mandel. DRA [PG-13] 110m. V

Schoolgirl Diary 1947 Italian ★★★½ Wealthy student (Valli) tries to ensnare chemistry professor (Checchi) in heavy-handed drama, well acted by stars. (a.k.a. *Lezione di Chimica*) C: Alida Valli, Irasema Dilian, Andrea Checchi. D: Mario Mattoli. DRA 95m.

Scissors 1991 ★★½ Jumbled thriller has damsel-in-distress (Stone) thinking she's losing her mind—or is someone making her think that? Convoluted plot gets tangled; Railsback outshines Stone in a dual role that is unfortunately tangential to the story line. C: Sharon Stone, Steve Railsback, Ronny Cox, Michelle Phillips. D: Frank De Felitta. CRI [R] 105m. V

Scorchers 1992 ★★½ Sultry Southern story set on the Louisiana bayou explores dysfunctional marriages and quirky small-town folk. Tilly stars as a wife whose husband is cheating on her, and who befriends celibate newlywed Lloyd. Corny attempt at capturing unusual people has an interesting cast, but little else. C: Faye Dunaway, Denholm Elliot, James Earle Jones, Emily Lloyd, Jennifer Tilly. D: David Beaird. DRA [R] 81m. TVM V

Scorchy 1976 ★★ Stevens is seriously miscast as a cop who goes undercover to land a drug lord. Sex and violence for its own sake. C: Connie Stevens, Cesare Danova, William Smith, Marlene Schmidt. D: Howard Hikmet Avedis. DRA [R] 100m. V

Score 1973 ★★ An insatiable couple turns to their neighbors for sexual satisfaction. C: Claire Wilbur, Calvin Culver, Lynn Lowry. D: Radley Metzger. COM [R] 89m. V

Scorpio 1973 ★★★½ Capable spy thriller finds operatives (Lancaster and Delon) cat and mousing in exciting world of espionage. Generally satisfying. C: Burt Lancaster, Alain Delon, Gayle Hunnicutt, Paul Scofield, John Colicos. D: Michael Winner. ACT [PG] 114m. V

Scotch on the Rocks 1954 British ★★★½ A handful of Scots rebel against excessive road tax, pointing out that the road is unusable. Quiet, understated humor in the best British tradition. (a.k.a. *Laxdale Hall*) C: Ronald Squire, Kathleen Ryan, Raymond Huntley, Sebastian Shaw. D: John Eldridge. COM 77m.

Scotland Yard Hunts Dr. Mabuse 1963 German ★★★½ Spirit of departed, demonic doctor enters body of psychiatrist (Kinski). Fair series entry misses Lang's direction, but the performances have a definite edge. C: Peter Van Eyck, Werner Peters, Sabine Bethmann, Klaus Kinski. D: Paul May. CRI 90m.

Scotland Yard Investigator 1945 ★★★½ Team of French thieves try to steal the Mona Lisa from its WWII site in England's National Gallery. Unassuming caper film, expertly cast. C: C. Aubrey Smith, Erich von Stroheim, Stephanie Bachelor, Forrester Harvey, Doris Lloyd, Eva Moore. D: George Blair. CRI 68m.

Scotland Yard's Chamber of Crime 1992 ★★★ The 11 tales of murder and thievery offered here were among the most notorious in Britain during the 19th century. Sensationalistic hodgepodge, fun for crime buffs. DOC 55m. V

Scott of the Antarctic 1948 British ★★★½ Absorbing, downbeat depiction of doomed South Pole expedition. Excellent British cast and clever use of trick photography. C: John Mills, Derek Bond, Kenneth More, Christopher Lee. D: Charles Frend. DRA 110m. V

Scoundrel in White 1972 *See* **High Heels**

Scoundrel, The 1935 ★★★★ Jaded, selfish writer/publisher (Coward) abuses everyone. When he dies, his spirit tries to redeem itself in sophisticated comedy/drama that's clever, witty, and slightly pretentious. Coward excells in first starring film role. Oscar for Best Original Story. C: Noel Coward, Julie Haydon, Stanley Ridges, Martha Sleeper, Ernest Cossart, Eduardo Ciannelli, Alexander Woollcott, Lionel Stander. D: Ben Hecht, Charles MacArthur. COM 78m.

Scout, The 1994 ★★½ NY Yankees talent scout (Brooks) discovers a brilliant talent (Fraser) with severe emotional problems. Erratic baseball comedy/drama starts out as a home run, but winds up a foul ball. C: Albert Brooks, Brendan Fraser, Dianne Wiest, Anne Twomey. D: Michael Ritchie. COM [PG-13] 101m. V

Scream & Die 1974 *See* **House that Vanished, The**

Scream and Scream Again 1970 British ★★★½ A deranged physician (Price) borrows body parts from living subjects to create zombie-like humanoids. Though bogged down by too much (and too familiar) plot, the three principals do have fun. C: Vincent Price, Christopher Lee, Peter Cushing. D: Gordon Hessler. HOR [M/PG] 95m. V

Scream, Blacula, Scream! 1973 ★★★ Marshall reprises his role as the modern-day African-American vampire looking for blood in L.A. Suffers from the law of diminishing returns that applies to most sequels, but does have both chilling and funny moments. C: William Marshall, Pam Grier, Michael Conrad, Richard Lawson. D: Bob Kelljan. HOR [PG] 96m. V

Scream Bloody Murder 1972 ★★½ When he loses his hand, a man replaces it with a hook—which becomes a very convenient murder weapon. C: Fred Holbert, Leigh Mitchell. D: Robert J. Emery. HOR [R] 90m. V

Scream Dream 1989 ★★½ A flashy heavy metal rocker is fired from her band, so she turns to an occult group to get revenge. C: Melissa Moore, Nikki Riggens, Michelle Uber. D: Donald Farmer. HOR 80m.

Scream for Help 1986 ★★ A young girl tries to convince others her stepfather is plotting to murder her mother. Formulaic paranoia thriller falls into the hilariously bad category. C: Rachael Kelly, David Allen Brooks, Marie Masters. D: Michael Winner. CRI [R] 95m. V

Scream of Fear 1961 British ★★★★ Low-budget, effective thriller with Strasberg as crippled heiress who sees her missing father's corpse in the strangest places. (a.k.a. *Taste of Fear*) C: Christopher Lee, Susan Strasberg, Ronald Lewis, Ann Todd. D: Seth Holt. DOC 81m. V

Scream, Pretty Peggy 1973 ★★★½ Scary matriarch (Davis) terrorizes the new housekeeper (Allen), in an old house full of blood-curdling secrets. Good late-career Davis hair-raiser. C: Bette Davis, Ted Bessell, Sian Barbara Allen. D: Gordon Hessler. HOR 78m. TVM

Screwballs 1983 ★ Oversexed high school teens make life miserable for repressed homecoming queen. Just as intelligent and meaningful as it sounds. C: Peter Keleghan, Linda Speciale, Alan Daveau, Linda Shayne. D: Rafal Zielinski. COM [R] 80m. V

Scrooge 1935 British ★★★½ Faithful but stodgy adaptation of Dickens' *A Christmas Carol* with Hicks an adequate Scrooge, visited by three ghosts on Christmas Eve in an attempt to save his soul. C: Seymour Hicks, Donald Calthorp, Mary Glynne, Maurice Evans. D: Henry Edwards. DRA 70m. V

Scrooge 1951 *See* **Christmas Carol, A**

Scrooge 1970 British ★★★½ Musical based on Dickens' *A Christmas Carol*, with likable performance by Finney as Ebenzer Scrooge, Victorian skinflint visited by three ghosts on Christmas eve. Score has one good song: "Thank You Very Much." C: Albert Finney, Alec Guinnesse, Edith Evans, Kenneth More, Lawrence Naismith, Michael Medwin, David Collings, Gordon Jackson, Roy Kinnear, Kay Walsh. D: Ronald Neame. MUS [G] 118m. V

Scrooged 1988 ★★★ Noisy, unpleasant modernization of *A Christmas Carol* with Murray as despicable TV honcho visited by comic ghosts on Christmas eve. Some funny bits but eclectic cast, full of guest cameos, goes overboard. C: Bill Murray, Karen Allen, John Forsythe, John Glover, Bobcat Goldthwait, David Johansen, Carol Kane, Robert Mitchum, Alfre Woodard. D: Richard Donner. COM [PG-13] 101m. V

Scrubbers 1982 British ★★★ British reform school drama, with young York and various other female inmates trying to cope with pathos of life behind bars. Grim, well-acted but monotonous. C: Chrissie Cotterill, Amanda York, Elizabeth Edmonds, Kate Ingram. D: Mai Zetterling. DRA [R] 93m. V

Scruffy 1980 ★★★ Adventures of a young orphan and his dog. Very sweet animated tale. FAM/DRA 60m. TVM V

Scruples 1981 ★★★½ Prime-time soap opera, based on Judith Krantz's best-selling novel of sex and sin in Beverly Hills. Run-of-the-mill, sugared fantasy of life among the rich and fictional; glamorous and slick. C: Shelley Smith, Priscilla Barnes, Dirk Benedict, James Darren, Vonetta McGee, Laraine Stephens, Robert Peirce, Roy Thinnes, Jessica Walter, Brett Halsey. D: Robert Day. DRA 100m. TVM V

Scudda Hoo! Scudda Hay! 1948 ★★½ Given his choice, a farmer's son finds his two mules far more interesting than women. Basic romance with little to distinguish it . . . if you don't count a glimpse of young Marilyn Monroe. C: June Haver, Lon McCallister, Walter Brennan, Anne Revere, Natalie Wood. D: F. Hugh Herbert. COM 95m.

Scum of the Earth 1975 *See* **Poor White Trash II**

Sea Bat, The 1930 ★★½ In Mexico, rival fishermen set off to kill a giant, deadly stingray. Chilling sea suspense. C: Raquel Torres, Charles Bickford, Niles Asthur. D: Wesley Ruggles. ACT 74m.

Sea Chase, The 1955 ★★★ German sea captain (Wayne) pilots an outlaw freighter laden with strange cargo from Australia to Germany during WWII. Weirdly improbable seafaring romance/melodrama. C: John Wayne, Lana Turner, Tab Hunter, David Farrar, Lyle Bettger, James Arness, Dick Davalos. D: John Farrow. DRA 117m. V

Sea Devils 1937 ★★★ In between ice patrol voyages, these U.S. Coast Guardsmen drink, fight, and run after women. Nice interplay between old pros McLaglen and Foster in this seafaring tale. C: Victor McLaglen, Preston Foster, Ida Lupino, Donald Woods, Helen Flint, Gordon Jones. D: Ben Stoloff. ACT 88m.

Sea Devils 1953 British ★★★½ Brisk, entertaining swashbuckler, with Hudson tangling with British spy De Carlo during the Napoleonic wars. Walsh keeps it perking nicely. C: Yvonne De Carlo, Rock Hudson, Maxwell Reed, Denis O'Dea, Michael Goodliffe, Bryan Forbes. D: Raoul Walsh. ACT 91m. V

Sea Fury 1958 British ★★★ Friendship of tugboat captain (McLaglen) and mate (Baker) is threatened by their love for beautiful woman (Paluzzi). Romantic triangle hoisted by fine performances, exciting seagoing action. C: Stanley Baker, Victor McLaglen, Luciana Paluzzi, Gregoire Aslan, Francis de Wolff, Percy Herbert, Rupert Davies, Robert Shaw. D: Cy Endfield. ACT 72m. V

Sea Gull, The 1968 British ★★★½ Chekov's play about simmering emotions on a 19th-century Russian estate. Excellent performances and a well-done British effort that's just a little too slow. C: James Mason, Vanessa Redgrave, Simone Signoret, David Warner, Harry Andrews, Eileen Herlie, Denholm Elliott. D: Sidney Lumet. DRA [G] 141m.

Sea Gypsies, The 1978 ★★★★ Widower takes two daughters and freelance photographer on world sailing voyage, but they're shipwrecked on the Aleutian Islands. Lots of plot packed into entertaining family film; nifty look at seldom-seen part of the world. C: Robert Logan, Heather Rattray, Mikki Jamison-Olsen, Shannon Saylor, Cjon-Damitri Patterson. D: Stewart Raffill. FAM/DRA 102m. V

Sea Hawk, The 1940 ★★★★★ Queen Elizabeth I (Robson) relies on pirate (Flynn) to destroy Spanish Armada and save England. Top-flight swashbuckler with unparalleled Flynn, exciting action, great color. Fiery, full-rigged adventure. Grab it. Memorable score by Erich Wolfgang Korngold. C: Errol Flynn, Brenda Marshall, Claude Rains, Donald Crisp, Flora Robson, Alan Hale, Henry Daniell. D: Michael Curtiz. ACT 128m. V

Sea of Grass, The 1947 ★★★½ Unusual Tracy/Hepburn drama has two stars on opposite sides of a farmer vs. ranchers conflict in Midwest. Story sags in places; not one of the team's best. C: Katharine Hepburn, Spencer Tracy, Melvyn Douglas, Phyllis Thaxter, Robert Walker, Edgar Buchanan, Harry Carey. D: Elia Kazan. DRA 133m. V

Sea of Lost Ships 1953 ★★½ When a ship strikes an iceberg, the Coast Guard must rescue it. Gritty, realistic action with a documentary feel. C: John Derek, Wanda Hendrix, Walter Brennan, Richard Jaeckel. D: Joseph Kane. ACT 85m.

Sea of Love 1989 ★★★★ Pacino and Barkin make sparks as a cop falling in love with his key suspect in a serial murder case. Excellent thriller, with great writing by Richard Price and soulful performance by Pacino. C: Al Pacino, Ellen Barkin, John Goodman, Michael Rooker, William Hickey. D: Harold Becker. CRI [R] 113m. V

Sea Shall Not Have Them, The 1955 British ★★½ After a WWII British bomber goes down in the North Sea, the race is on to find the surviving crew. Sleepy, often melodramatic yarn which too frequently resorts to annoying flashbacks. C: Michael Redgrave, Dirk Bogarde, Anthony Steel, Nigel Patrick. D: Lewis Gilbert. ACT 97m. V

Sea Wall, The *See* **This Angry Age**

Sea Wife 1957 British ★★★ Shipwrecked strangers fall in love on a deserted island while waiting to be rescued, but unbeknownst to him, she's a nun. Moderate castaway story gets a helpful boost from the fun of watching Collins portray a nun. C: Richard Burton, Joan Collins. D: Bob McNaught. DRA 82m.

Sea Wolf, The 1941 ★★★★½ Cruel freighter Captain (Robinson) tyrannizes crew and unexpected passengers (Knox, Garfield, Lupino) rescued from a shipwreck. Excellent, brooding adaptation of the Jack London adventure novel. Splendid cast. C: Edward G. Robinson, John Garfield, Ida Lupino, Alexander Knox, Gene Lockhart, Barry Fitzgerald, Stanley Ridges. D: Michael Curtiz. ACT 90m. v

Sea Wolf, The 1993 ★★ Sea captain (Bronson) rescues shipwreck survivors (Reeve and Stewart) then keeps them virtual hostages. Bland adaptation of Jack London's classic novel, with cast looking marooned. C: Charles Bronson, Christopher Reeve, Catherine Mary Stewart, Marc Singer, Clive Revill, Len Cariou. D: Michael Anderson. ACT 93m. v

Sea Wolves, The 1980 British ★★★½ In India during WWII, a group of retired British soldiers attack a German radio transmitter. Rousing adventure and lots of fun with a cast of luminaries. C: Gregory Peck, Roger Moore, David Niven, Trevor Howard. D: Andrew V. McLaglen. ACT [PG] 122m. v

Sealed Cargo 1951 ★★★½ Canadian fishing boat captain (Andrews) takes on the Nazis in a small Newfoundland village. Outstanding cast goes a long way in this gripping WWII melodrama. C: Dana Andrews, Carla Balenda, Claude Rains, Philip Dorn, Onslow Stevens, Skip Homeier. D: Alfred L. Werker. ACT 90m.

Seance on a Wet Afternoon 1964 ★★★★½ Marvelously spooky, ultimately gut-wrenching drama of a demented spiritualist (Stanley) involved in a kidnapping. From the novel by Mark McShane. Stanley's superb performance won the NY Film Critics Award, but she lost the Oscar to Julie Andrews in *Mary Poppins*. C: Kim Stanley, Richard Attenborough, Patrick Magee, Nanette Newman. D: Bryan Forbes. DRA 115m. v

Seapower 1981 ★★★½ Film follows the development of naval warfare from the turn of the century. Fairly comprehensive documentary includes previously unseen footage. DOC 109m. v

Search and Destroy 1988 ★★★ A small town is the setting for a war between police SWAT teams and terrorists fighting for control of a biochemical laboratory. C: Stuart Garrison Day, John Christian, Kosmo Vinyl. D: J. Christian Inbvordsen. ACT [R] 90m. v

Search for Signs of Intelligent Life in the Universe, The 1991 ★★★★½ Lily Tomlin's multiple personalities come out to play, amuse, and enlighten in this film version of her one-woman Broadway show. Stand-up, performance art, or social commentary? All three, and awfully funny. C: Lily Tomlin. D: John Bailey. COM 106m. v

Search for the Mother Lode: The Last Great Treasure 1982 *See* **Mother Lode**

Search, The 1948 ★★★★ At the end of WWII, a G.I. (Clift) cares for a concentration-camp child (Jandl) in Berlin while his mother searches frantically for the boy. Unabashed tearjerker teeters on the edge of hypersentimentality, but is saved by its pseudodocumentary style. C: Montgomery Clift, Ivan Jandl, Aline MacMahon, Jarmila Novotna, Wendell Corey. D: Fred Zinnemann. DRA 105m. v

Searchers, The 1956 ★★★★★ Ford's exemplary classic Western with Wayne as a bitter Texan in a ruthless five-year search for his niece, abducted and assimilated by Indians. Stark, flinty saga of hate, pursuit, and revenge. Magnificently crafted, much imitated film. C: John Wayne, Jeffrey Hunter, Vera Miles, Ward Bond, Natalie Wood, Harry Carey, Jr. D: John Ford. WST 119m. v

Searching for Bobby Fischer 1993 ★★★★½ Strong, sensitive coming-of-age picture focuses on chess prodigy with confused parents and two opinionated, antagonistic mentors (Kingsley, Fishburne). Amazingly pumps excitement into what is, after all, a board game. Ideal family entertainment. C: Joe Mantegna, Max Pomeranc, Joan Allen, Ben Kingsley, Laurence Fishburne, Michael Nirenberg, Robert Stephens, David Paymer. D: Steven Zaillian. FAM/DRA [PG] 110m. v

Searching Wind, The 1946 ★★★½ Adventures of an American diplomat in Europe during the tumultuous 1930s. Excellent production of a solid story based on the Lillian Hellman play. C: Robert Young, Sylvia Sidney, Ann Richards, Douglas Dick, Dudley Digges. D: William Pieterle. DRA 108m.

Seas Beneath, The 1931 ★★★★ When submarine commander O'Brien romances Lessing, a German spy, he opens the door to her brother, who navigates an enemy ship out to destroy the Americans. Tense direction from Ford and some great action sequences give this war drama grit. C: George O'Brien, Marion Lessing, Mona Maris, Walter C. Kelly. D: John Ford. ACT 99m.

Seaside Swingers 1965 British ★★ Young British beach resort workers prepare for the big summer talent show. Lame goofball comedy/musical the London swingin " '60s way." C: John Leyton, Mike Sarne, Freddie and the Dreamers, Ron Moody, Grazina Frame. D: James Hill. MUS 94m. v

Season for Assassins 1971 ★★★ When Rome is plagued by gangs of young hoodlums, a police inspector rises to the occasion. C: Martin Balsam, Joe Dallesandro. ACT 102m. v

Season of Dreams 1987 *See* **Stacking**

Season of Fear 1989 ★★★ A young man, visiting his estranged father, becomes entangled romantically with his step-mother. C: Michael Bowen, Ray Wise, Clare Wren. D: Douglas Campbell. ACT [R] 89m. v

Season of Passion 1959 Australian ★★★½ A couple of mill workers venture into the city every year for a liaison with the same two women. Interesting study of men and women and the relationships they weave. Australian production, based on Ray Lowler's play *Summer of the 17th Doll*. C: Anne Baxter, John

Mills, Angela Lansbury, Ernest Borgnine, Janette Craig. D: Leslie Norman. DRA 93m.

Season of the Witch 1976 ★★½ A housewife gets involved with a satanic cult and winds up accosted by a demon. C: Jan White, Ray Lane, Anne Muffly. D: George A. Romero. HOR [R] 89m. V

Season of the Witch 1982 *See* **Halloween III: Season of the Witch**

Sebastian 1968 British ★★½ British counterintelligence agent gets involved in big-time espionage. Engaging but uneven. C: Dirk Bogarde, Susannah York, Lilli Palmer, John Gielgud, Margaret Johnston, Nigel Davenport. D: David Greene. DRA 100m.

Second Best 1994 ★★★½ Lonely Welsh postmaster (Hurt) tries to adopt an orphan boy. Sentimental character study compromised by star's weak accent and good looks. C: William Hurt, Chris Cleary Miles, John Hurt, Jane Horrocks. D: Chris Menges. DRA [PG-13] 105m. V

Second Best Bed 1937 British ★★½ Governmental functionary, considered a real family man, is accused of having an affair. Charming and well-played comedy. C: Tom Walls, Jane Baxter, Veronica Rose. D: Tom Walls. COM 74m.

Second Best Secret Agent in the Whole Wide World 1965 British ★★★ Bumbling secret agent (Adams) must stop Russians from perfecting an anti-gravity machine. Enjoyably silly James Bond spoof. C: Tom Adams, Veronica Hurst, Peter Bull. D: Lindsay Shonteff. COM 96m.

Second Chance 1953 ★★½ A gambler's girl (Darnell) and a loser of a prizefighter (Mitchum) meet in Mexico while they're both running away from their lives. Dark, brooding and effective. C: Robert Mitchum, Linda Darnell, Jack Palance, Reginald Sheffield. D: Rudolph Maté. DRA 82m. V

Second Chance 1980 ★★½ A woman marries young, has children and 18 years later, files for divorce. Drab, but earnest marital drama. C: Susannah York, Ralph Bates. D: Richard Handford. DRA 270m. TVM V

Second Chorus 1940 ★★★ Two musicians (Astaire and Meredith) make a play for the same woman (Goddard). Best for the music and dancing. C: Fred Astaire, Paulette Goddard, Artie Shaw & Orchestra, Burgess Meredith. D: H.C. Potter. MUS 90m. V

Second Fiddle 1939 ★★★ Big-time promoter (Power) wants all of America to fall in love with his young budding starlet (Henie). Meanwhile, he falls in love with her himself. Story's okay, but you'll love Irving Berlin's music! C: Sonja Henie, Tyrone Power, Rudy Vallee, Edna May Oliver, Lyle Talbot. D: Sidney Lanfield. COM 86m. V

Second Honeymoon 1937 ★★★ After his divorce, an ex-husband (Power) plays all kinds of games in order to get his wife (Young) back. Charming cast and pleasant story. C: Tyrone Power, Loretta Young, Stuart Erwin, Claire Trevor, Lyle Talbot. D: Walter Lang. COM 79m.

Second Mrs. Tanqueray, The 1952 British ★★ When his beloved wife passes on, a Victorian gentleman marries a woman with a scandalous reputation. Enjoyable characters but precious little action. C: Pamela Brown, Hugh Sinclair, Ronald Ward, Virginia McKenna. D: Dallas Bower. DRA 75m.

Second Serve 1986 ★★★★ A male doctor becomes a female tennis star after a sex-change operation. True story of transsexual Renee Richards (Redgrave) may not be to everyone's taste, but Vanessa scores brilliantly over the middling script. C: Vanessa Redgrave, Martin Balsam, Louise Fletcher. D: Anthony Page. DRA 100m. TVM

Second Sight 1989 ★ Private detective (Larroquette) relies on psychic (Pinchot) to solve crime. Cast of TV refugees should feel at home in this; film plays like overlong witless sitcom. C: John Larroquette, Bronson Pinchot, Bess Armstrong, Stuart Pankin. D: Joel Zwick. COM [PG] 85m. V

Second Time Around, The 1961 ★★★½ Widow (Reynolds) settles in Arizona and becomes sheriff of a small town, where she must cope with a couple of tireless suitors (Griffith and Forrest). Gentle Western with comedy. C: Debbie Reynolds, Andy Griffith, Steve Forrest, Juliet Prowse, Thelma Ritter, Isobel Elsom. D: Vincent Sherman. COM 99m.

Second Victory, The 1992 ★★ British occupation forces in postwar Austria investigate the mysterious murder of one of their own. Somewhat forced attempt at suspense. C: Max Von Sydow, Anthony Andrews, Renee Soutendijk, Birgit Doll. D: Gerald Thomas. ACT 95m. V

Second Wind 1989 ★★★ A married man, searching for something, becomes obsessed with jogging. C: Lindsay Wagner, James Naughton. DRA [PG] 93m. V

Seconds 1966 ★★★★ Disturbing science fiction-like film about a mysterious and sinister organization that provides new lives and identities to those willing to pay the high price. Hudson is excellent as one of the organization's victims. Striking camerawork. C: Rock Hudson, Salome Jens, John Randolph, Will Geer, Jeff Corey, Murray Hamilton, Wesley Addy. D: John Frankenheimer. DRA 106m.

Secret Admirer 1985 ★★★½ An anonymous love letter finds its way into the hands of various teenagers, causing predictable mix-ups. As far as teen fodder goes, not half-bad, with capable cast. C: C. Thomas Howell, Lori Loughlin, Kelly Preston, Fred Ward. D: David Greenwalt. COM [R] 98m. V

Secret Agent 1936 British ★★★★ Offbeat Hitchcock offering mixes humor and thrills, as a pair of British secret agents (Gielgud and Carroll) pretend to be married as they hunt a spy. Lorre's bizarre performance stands out, as the comical but malevolent General. Based on a W.S. Maugham story. C: John Gielgud, Madeleine Carroll, Robert Young, Peter Lorre. D: Alfred Hitchcock. CRI 84m. V

Secret Agent 00 *See* **Operation Kid Brother**

Secret Beyond the Door 1948 ★★★★ Tense drama of the growing suspicion of a wife (Bennett) that the gloomy husband she has hurriedly married (Redgrave) is a murderer owes much to Hitchcock. Great use of moody gothic atmosphere, weakened somewhat by pat psychology. C: Joan Bennett, Michael Redgrave, Anne Revere, Barbara O'Neill. D: Fritz Lang. CRI 99m. V

Secret Bride, The 1935 ★★★ After secretly marrying the governor's daughter, a state Attorney General learns that his new father-in-law has criminal connections. Top-quality tension and fine acting. C: Barbara Stanwyck, Warren William, Glenda Farrell, Grant Mitchell, Arthur Byron. D: William Dieterle. DRA 64m.

Secret Ceremony 1968 British ★★★½ Two women strike up a conversation on a bus and decide to live together as mother (Taylor) and daughter (Farrow) in a gothic London mansion but their plan is complicated by the arrival of the young woman's stepfather. Twisted plot and twisted characters make this an acquired taste. C: Elizabeth Taylor, Mia Farrow, Robert Mitchum, Pamela Brown. D: Joseph Losey. DRA [R] 109m. V

Secret Diary of Sigmund Freud, The 1984 ★★½ Comedy based on the early life and theories of Dr. Freud (Cort). Fine cast used mainly as targets for psychoanalytical jokes, which aren't terribly funny. C: Bud Cort, Carol Kane, Klaus Kinski, Marisa Berenson, Carroll Baker, Dick Shawn. D: Danford B. Greene. COM [PG] 129m. V

Secret Fantasy 1982 ★★★½ A frustrated man finally finds the woman of his dreams. C: Laura Antonelli, Lando Buzzanca. COM [R] 88m. V

Secret File on J. Edgar Hoover, The 1993 ★★★½ This controversial documentary focuses on Hoover's reputed homosexuality and his blackmailing JFK into putting Lyndon Johnson on the 1960 presidential ticket. Includes many eyewitness accounts and previously suppressed documents. Fascinating fare. DOC 60m. V

Secret Four, The 1940 British ★★ After their friend is murdered, three young men engage in a hapless plot to destroy the Suez Canal. Quality performances but the story is a stretch. C: Hugh Sinclair, Griffith Jones, Francis L. Sullivan, Frank Lawton, Anna Lee. D: Walter Forde. ACT 79m.

Secret Friends 1992 British ★★½ A man (Bates) sits on a train and fantasizes nasty things about his wife and mistress. Bates is always watchable, but the flashbacks and time jumps get confusing. From Dennis Potter's novel *Ticket to Ride*. C: Alan Bates, Gina Bellman, Tony Doyle, Frances Barber. D: Dennis Potter. DRA 97m.

Secret Fury, The 1950 ★★★★ Mystery person tries to drive a woman (Colbert) mad to prevent her from getting married. First-rate suspense delivered by first-rate cast. C: Claudette Colbert, Robert Ryan, Jane Cowl, Paul Kelly, Vivian Vance, Philip Ober. D: Mel Ferrer. DRA 86m. V

Secret Games 1992 ★★ A man (Hewitt) helps an unhappily married woman live out her fantasies at a Beverly Hills brothel for "frustrated" women but then develops a dangerous fixation on her. Not for children. C: Martin Hewitt, Michele Brin, Delia Sheppard, Bill Drago. D: Alexander Gregory Hippolyte. DRA [R] 100m. V

Secret Games—The Escort 1993 ★★½ A lonely performance artist calls an escort service; introduced into a dark world of erotic misadventures, he soon finds only his art will save him. Kinky, silly, film. C: Martin Hewitt, Marie Leroux, Amy Rochelle. D: Alexander Gregory Hipolyte. DRA [R] 83m. V

Secret Garden, The 1949 ★★★★ Best version of oft-filmed Frances Hodgson Burnett's classic. O'Brien reigns in this production as the shy English orphan who finds a magical garden on her uncle's property. The final scene in color is equally magical. C: Margaret O'Brien, Herbert Marshall, Dean Stockwell, Gladys Cooper, Elsa Lanchester. D: Fred M. Wilcox. FAM/DRA [G] 92m. V

Secret Garden, The 1987 ★★★½ Jacobi's hammy performance as the loveless uncle of an orphan (James) upsets the balance of an otherwise lovely production, the third version of Francis Hodgson Burnett's children's novel. Some beautiful English countryside footage. Film was shot in 1987 but not released until 1992. C: Gennie James, Barret Oliver, Jadrien Steele, Michael Hordern, Billie Whitelaw, Derek Jacobi. D: Alan Grint. FAM/DRA 100m. TVM V

Secret Garden, The 1993 ★★★★ Haunting, gorgeously photographed take on the Hodgson Burnett classic, is the fourth film version. A little too reserved, nevertheless this version makes one care for the lonely orphan girl who finds a hidden garden. Lovely for older children. C: Maggie Smith, Kate Maberly, Heydon Prowse, Andrew Knott. D: Agnieszka Holland. FAM/DRA [G] 102m. V

Secret Heart, The 1946 ★★★ Young girl (Allyson) mourns her late father and despises her stepmother. Cast excels in this downbeat melodrama. C: Claudette Colbert, Walter Pidgeon, June Allyson, Lionel Barrymore, Robert Sterling, Patricia Medina, Marshall Thompson. D: Robert Z. Leonard. DRA 97m.

Secret Honor 1985 ★★★★½ Richard Nixon (Hall) goes berserk, and the camera is rolling.

Altman's edge is put to good use in this darkly funny look at Tricky Dick through a liberal artist's eyes. From Hall's one-man show. (a.k.a. *Lord's of Treason*) C: Philip Baker Hall. D: Robert Altman. COM 90m. V

Secret Ingredient 1990 ★★★ An ancient monastery comes up with a secret recipe for a fantastic new brandy. C: Rick Rossovich, Catherine Hicks, Gary Kroeger. D: Slobodan Shijan. COM 95m. V

Secret Invasion, The 1964 ★★★½ British Intelligence places five convicted criminals behind Nazi lines in WWII Yugoslavia. Their objective: commando raids. Intriguing idea that works despite low budget. C: Stewart Granger, Mickey Rooney, Raf Vallone, Henry Silva, Edd Byrnes, Mia Massini. D: Roger Corman. ACT 95m.

Secret Life of an American Wife, The 1968 ★★★ A housewife (Jackson), questioning her sexual allure, poses as a prostitute and seduces her husband's friend. Suburban comedy tries to hit the same (albeit older) nerve as *The Graudate*, but fails. Fine cast tries its darndest, though. C: Walter Matthau, Anne Jackson, Patrick O'Neal, Edy Williams. D: George Axelrod. COM [R] 97m. V

Secret Life of Walter Mitty, The 1947 ★★★★ One of Kaye's best as he brings to life James Thurber's classic daydreaming book editor who's in for the adventure of his life when his farfetched fantasies begin to come true. Bouncy musical numbers add to the fun. C: Danny Kaye, Virginia Mayo, Boris Karloff, Fay Bainter. D: Norman McLeod. COM 110m. V

Secret Mission 1942 British ★★★ British Intelligence officers sneak into occupied France to learn about Nazi defenses. Fine British cast makes the most of this good WWII action epic. C: Hugh Williams, James Mason, Roland Culver, Carla Lehmann, Michael Wilding, Herbert Lom, Stewart Granger. D: Harold French. ACT 82m.

Secret Obsession 1988 ★★★½ Complicated tale of an estranged father and son who meet up with each other years later. Good performances. C: Julie Christie, Ben Gazzara, Patrick Bruel. D: Henri Vart. DRA [PG] 82m. V

Secret of Blood Island, The 1965 British ★★ A female secret agent is parachuted into Japanese POW camp. Those who enjoy violence and gore will find this one entertaining. C: Barbara Shelley, Jack Hedley, Charles Tingwell, Patrick Wymark. D: Quentin Lawrence. ACT 84m.

Secret of Convict Lake, The 1951 ★★★ In 19th-century California, a group of convicts bust out of prison and hide in a community of women settlers. Interesting story and good performances. C: Glenn Ford, Gene Tierney, Ethel Barrymore, Zachary Scott, Ann Dvorak, Jeanette Nolan, Ruth Donnelly. D: Michael Gordon. DRA 83m.

Secret of Dorian Gray, The *See* **Dorian Gray**

Secret of Dr. Kildare, The 1939 ★★★½ The physician is trying to help a young woman overcome psychosomatic blindness, while convincing old Dr. Gillespie to take some time off. Fine entry in this ongoing series. C: Lew Ayres, Lionel Barrymore, Lionel Atwill, Laraine Day, Helen Gilbert, Nat Pendleton, Sara Haden, Samuel S. Hinds, Emma Dunn, Grant Mitchell, Walter Kingsford, Alma Kruger, Nell Craig. D: Harold S. Bucquet. DRA 84m.

Secret of Madame Blanche, The 1933 ★★★ After her husband kills himself, Dunne gives up her newborn child and spirals downward into a life of degradation. Years later, when her grown son Walton is charged with murder, Dunne takes the rap. Well-worn clichés dominate minor melodrama. C: Irene Dunne, Lionel Atwill, Phillips Holmes, Douglas Walton, Una Merkel, C. Henry Gordon, Jean Parker. D: Charles Brabin. DRA 83m.

Secret of My Success, The 1987 ★★★ Hoping to make it big in business, bright-eyed mail clerk (Fox) bounds up corporate ladder of Manhattan firm. Though Fox gives his usual energetic best, script relies on standard situations and uncomfortable sexual humor for laughs. C: Michael J. Fox, Helen Slater, Richard Jordan, Margaret Whitton. D: Herbert Ross. COM [PG-13] 110m. V

Secret of NIMH, The 1982 ★★★½ Brilliantly animated adaptation of Robert C. O'Brien's prize-winning book is the tale of widowed mouse Mrs. Frisby seeking help from underground network of hyperintelligent rats. Gorgeous to look at, but a mite slowly paced; may lose some children's attention. Voices of Elizabeth Hartman, Derek Jacobi, Dom DeLuise, John Carradine, Peter Strauss. D: Don Bluth. FAM/DRA [G] 84m. V

Secret of Roan Inish, The 1994 ★★★★½ Charming children's film about a 10-year-old girl who goes in search of her brother in the islands off western Ireland, and finds him living with the seals. Lovely writing, direction, and performances from the kids. C: Mick Lally, Eileen Colgan, John Lynch, Jeni Courtney, Richard Sheridan, Cillian Byrne. D: John Sayles. FAM/DRA [PG] 103m.

Secret of Santa Vittoria, The 1969 ★★★½ During the German occupation, a little Italian village tries to hide over a million bottles of wine from the Nazis. Overlong but charmingly funny. Based on the Robert Crichton novel. C: Anthony Quinn, Anna Magnani, Virna Lisi, Hardy Kruger, Sergio Franchi, Renato Rascel, Eduardo Ciannelli, Giancarlo Giannini, Valentina Cortese. D: Stanley Kramer. COM 140m.

Secret of the Blue Room 1933 ★★★½ Atwill owns a mysterious castle where three people were murdered 20 years before. Now Stuart asks three potential suitors to spend a night in the blue room where the slaughter took place. Good creepy fun in an entertaining little horror picture. Remade as *The Missing Guest* and *Murder in the Blue Room.* C: Lionel Atwill, Gloria Stuart, Paul Lukas, Edward Arnold, Onslow Stevens, William Janney. D: Kurt Neumann. HOR 66m.

Secret of the Golden Eagle, The 1991 ★★★ An explorer and his young companion try to beat out a team of thugs for a rare and valuable statue. C: Michael Berryman, Brandon McKay, Robert Moon. D: Cole McKay. ACT 90m. V

Secret of the Ice Cave, The 1990 ★★★ A group of youngsters try to unearth the treasured secret of the ice cave. C: Sally Kellerman, Michael Moriarty, David Mendenhall. D: Radu Gabrea. ACT [PG-13] 106m. V

Secret of the Incas 1954 ★★★½ Rival adventurers go all out in their search for rare Inca treasures. Quality cast and suspenseful, fast-moving story. C: Charlton Heston, Robert Young, Nicole Maurey, Thomas Mitchell, Glenda Farrell, Yma Sumac. D: Jerry Hopper. ACT 101m.

Secret Of The Seal, The 1992 ★★★½ A little Italian boy discovers a rare seal and her cubs in this charming animated tale. FAM/DRA 60m.

Secret of the Telegian, The 1961 Japanese ★★★★ Scientist dabbling in teleportation has his invention stolen by soldier, who uses it to kill fellow platoon members and nab gold. Interesting combination of crime and science fiction from Japan. (a.k.a. *The Telegian*) C: Koji Tsuruta, Yumi Shirakawa, Akihiko Hirata. D: Jun Fukuda. CRI 85m.

Secret of the Whistler 1946 ★★★½ A woman believes that her husband (Dix) is trying to murder her in this entry in the ongoing *Whistler* series. Excellent suspense enhanced by the mood of lurking danger. C: Richard Dix, Leslie Brooks, Mary Currier, Michael Duane, Mona Barrie, Ray Walker. D: George Sherman. DRA 65m.

Secret of Yolanda, The 1982 ★★½ A deaf-mute is the object of two men's affections in this soft-core potboiler. (a.k.a *Ahava Ilemeth*) C: Aviva Ger, Asher Zarfati, Shraga Harpaz. DRA 90m. V

Secret Passions 1989 ★★★ A young couple try to make the most of a dark and sinister past in this soapy romance. C: Susan Lucci, John James, Finola Hughes. D: Michael Pressman. DRA 95m. TVM

Secret Places 1985 British ★★★½ Two young girls form a special friendship that is crushed with the onset of WWII. Tender, thoughtful, and sensitive approach to youth and understanding. C: Marie-Theres Relin, Tara MacGowran, Claudine Auger, Jenny Agutter. D: Zelda Barron. DRA [PG] 98m. V

Secret Policeman's Other Ball, The 1982 British ★★★★ Concert film of two Amnesty International fundraisers features musical performances by Sting, Eric Clapton, and Jeff Beck among others, with comedy by ex-Monty Python and Goon Show cast members. Doesn't quite capture spirit of live performances, though some moments do shine. C: John Cleese, Peter Cook, Michael Palin, Graham Chapman, Terry Jones, Pete Townshend, Sting, Eric Clapton. D: Julian Temple, Roger Graef. MUS [R] 101m. V

Secret Scrolls (Part I) 1968 Japanese ★★★ Mifune is a 17th-century samurai warrior trying to collect three scrolls which could bring down a government and instigate rebellion. Though idea is intriguing, film is heavy on talk and light on action. Sequel followed. C: Toshire Mifune, Koji Tsuruta. D: Hiroshi Inagaki. ACT 106m.

Secret Scrolls: Part II 1968 Japanese ★★★ Mifune continues his search in ancient Japan for potentially dangerous secret scrolls, which have been split by the family that possesses them. Lots of swordplay in this sequel, but film makes little sense without seeing *Part I.* C: Toshiro Mifune, Koji Tsuruta, Nobuke Otawa. D: Hioshi Inagaki. ACT 106m.

Secret Service of the Air 1939 ★★★ Government agents hot on the trail of smugglers. Fine, fast moving action that hops along like a Saturday morning serial. C: Ronald Reagan, John Litel, Ila Rhodes, James Stephenson, Eddie Foy, Jr., Rosella Towne. D: Noel Smith. ACT 61m.

Secret Six, The 1931 ★★★½ Gangster bootleggers go up against businessmen and nosy reporters. Good old-fashioned crime film with lots of action delivered by a star-laden cast. C: Wallace Beery, Lewis Stone, Clark Gable, Jean Harlow, Johnny Mark Brown, Ralph Bellamy, Marjorie Rambeau, John Miljan. D: George Hill. CRI 83m.

Secret War of Harry Frigg, The 1968 ★★ After five generals are captured behind enemy lines, a sullen private (Newman) is recruited to mastermind their rescue. Lackluster humor and gaps in general logic deflate the comic potential of this tired farce. C: Paul Newman, Sylva Koscina, Andrew Duggan, Tom Bosley, John Williams, Vito Scotti, James Gregory. D: Jack Smight. COM 110m. V

Secret Weapon 1942 ★★★★ Sherlock Holmes mystery as WWII propaganda has the British sleuth battling Nazis and arch-nemesis Professor Moriarty (Atwill) for a wartime invention. Brisk entry in series, complete with multiple disguises and witty banter. (a.k.a. *Sherlock Holmes and the Secret Weapon*) C: Basil Rathbone, Nigel Bruce, Lionel Atwill. D: Roy William Neill. CRI 68m. V

Secret World 1969 French ★★ Young man develops an intense crush on his uncle's mistress (Bisset). This one is a bit too full of itself. C: Jacqueline Bisset, Giselle Pascal, Pierre Zimmer, Marc Porel, Jean-Francois Maurin. D: Robert Freeman. DRA [PG] 94m.

Secret Yearnings 1979 *See* **Good Luck, Miss Wyckoff**

Secrets 1971 ★★½ Melodrama concerns parents and their daughter learning of each other's sexual encounters over the course of a day. Bisset's fleeting nude scene seems to be film's raison d'etre. C: Jacqueline Bisset, Per Oscarsson, Shirley Hopkins, Robert Powell, Tarka Kings, Martin C. Thurley. D: Philip Saville. DRA [R] 85m. V

Secrets 1977 ★★★ Young British woman is the sad and innocent victim of frequent misunderstandings. Tender and well played. C: Susan Blakely, Roy Thinnes, Joanne Linville, John Randolph, Melody Thomas, Anthony Eisley, Andrew Stevens. D: Paul Wendkos. DRA 100m. TVM

Secrets of the Lone Wolf 1941 ★★★ Crooks confuse the Lone Wolf, a debonair jewel thief (Warren William), with his valet (Blore), whom they use in their plans to make a big heist. Well done and funny with Blore—a classic Milquetoast of the screen—hoisted into thug status. C: Warren William, Ruth Ford, Roger Clark, Victor Jory, Eric Blore, Thurston Hall, Fred Kelsey, Victor Kilian. D: Edward Dmytryk. DRA 67m.

Secrets of Women 1952 Swedish ★★★½ Several women in a summer house spend their time confiding to each other about their relationships and experiences with men. Good work by the tireless Bergman. C: Anita Bjork, Karl Arne Homsten, Eva Dahlbeck, Gunnar Bjornstrand. D: Ingmar Bergman. DRA 114m. V

Sect, The *See* **Devil's Daughter, The**

Seduced 1985 ★★★ States attorney Harrison becomes entangled with ex-girlfriend Shepherd after her wealthy husband is murdered. Okay standard romantic thriller. C: Gregory Harrison, Cybill Shepherd, Mel Ferrer, Adrienne Barbeau. D: Jerrold Freedam. DRA 94m. TVM V

Seduced and Abandoned 1964 Italian ★★★★ Sex farce involving a Lothario, his fiancée, and her younger sister, whom he impregnated. Effective, often hilarious film derives many of its laughs by toppling stereotypical macho behavior. Fans of cinematic Italian humor will have a ball. C: Stefania Sandrelli, Saro Urzi. D: Pietro Germi. COM 118m. V

Seducers, The *See* **Death Game**

Seduction of Joe Tynan, The 1979 ★★★ Title senator (Alda), young and ambitious, nearly destroys his marriage and morals when he discovers the lure of power. Well-meaning drama with a conscience rings a little hollow as well as naive. Scripted by Alda. C: Alan Alda, Barbara Harris, Meryl Streep, Rip Torn. D: Jerry Schatzberg. DRA [R] 107m.

Seduction of Mimi, The 1972 Italian ★★★★½ Mimi (Giannini), a dim and stubborn Sicilian, bumbles his way through various sexual encounters and political situations. Brilliant turn by the star in this typical, darkly humorous Wertmuller saga. Guilty, politically incorrect laughter is still being heard over his sex scene with a massively obese woman. C: Giancarlo Giannini, Mariangela Melato, Agostina Belli, Elena Fiore. D: Lina Wertmuller. COM [R] 89m.

Seduction, The 1981 ★★ Glamorous news anchor (Fairchild) is stalked by a fan (Stevens) in this thriller that shoots for sensationalism but winds up more campy than scary. Fairchild's screen debut. C: Morgan Fairchild, Michael Sarrazin, Vince Edwards, Andrew Stevens. D: David Schmoeller. DRA [R] 103m. V

See Here, Private Hargrove 1944 ★★★½ The adventures of an utterly green Army recruit. Lots of wonderful, zany fun mixed well with genuine tenderness. The cast is great. Sequel is *What Next, Corporal Hargrove?* C: Robert Walker, Donna Reed, Keenan Wynn, Robert Benchley, Bob Crosby, Grant Mitchell. D: Wesley Ruggles. COM 100m.

See How She Runs 1978 ★★★★★ Superb, well-rounded story of a middle-aged divorcee (Woodward) who challenges herself to train for the Boston Marathon. Woodward's performance won an Emmy. A true champion. C: Joanne Woodward, John Considine, Lissy Newman, Barnard Hughes. D: Richard T. Heffron. DRA 100m. TVM V

See No Evil 1971 British ★★★★ Young blind woman (Farrow) discovers that a murderer has been stalking her. Well-done and chilling to the bone. (a.k.a. *Blind Terror*) C: Mia Farrow, Dorothy Alison, Robin Bailey. D: Richard Fleischer. HOR [PG] 90m. V

See No Evil, Hear No Evil 1989 ★★ Comedy team of Wilder and Pryor in barren effort about seeing-impaired man and hearing-impaired man who team up when they're wrongly accused of murder. Nothing added to lame premise, Wilder and Pryor resort to caricatures of earlier comic glory. C: Richard Pryor, Gene Wilder, Joan Severance, Kevin Spacey. D: Arthur Hiller. COM [R] 103m. V

See You in the Morning 1989 ★★★ Parents and children must all make adjustments when Bridges and Krige tie the knot, each for the second time. Well-intentioned, warm, though sometimes clichéd romantic comedy. C: Jeff Bridges, Alice Krige, Farrah Fawcett, Drew Barrymore, Lukas Haas. D: Alan J. Pakula. DRA 119m. V

Seedpeople 1992 ★ A man revisits his hometown and discovers that alien pods have zombified the residents, transforming some into hideous creatures. Shameless ripoff of *Invasion of the Body Snatchers* isn't helped by astonishingly fake rubber monsters. C: Sam Hennings, Andrea Roth, Dane Witherspoon, David Dunard, Holly Fields, Bernard Kates. D: Peter Manoogian. HOR [R] 87m. V

Seekers, The 1954 British ★★★½ A British family emigrates to look for a new life in 1820 New Zealand. More earnest than epic.

(a.k.a. *Land of Fury*) C: Jack Hawkins, Glynis Johns, Noel Purcell, Laya Raki, Tony Erstich. D: Ken Annakin. DRA 90m. v

Seems Like Old Times 1980 ★★★ Sitcom premise finds attorney (Hawn) trying to build life with new husband (Grodin), while fending off unwanted attention from still-pining ex-spouse (Chase). Good cast livens Simon's uninvolving script, but unbelievable conclusion ultimately does them in. C: Goldie Hawn, Chevy Chase, Charles Grodin, Robert Guillaume. D: Jay Sandrich. COM [PG] 101m. v

Seize the Day 1986 ★★★★½ Acutely observed character study from the Saul Bellow novel stars Williams as a lost and lonely 40ish man hustled out of love and money, confronting a society that just doesn't care. Wonderful performances. C: Robin Williams, Joseph Wiseman, Jerry Stiller, Glenne Headly. D: Fielder Cook. DRA 93m. TVM v

Seizure 1974 Canadian ★★½ Frid's family and friends are puppets in the hands of evil uninvited guests who force them to engage in life-threatening party games. Incomprehensible chiller notable mainly as Stone's directorial debut. C: Jonathan Frid, Martine Beswick, Christina Pickles, Herve Villechaize. D: Oliver Stone. HOR [PG] 93m. v

Self-Defense 1989 ★★ Armed citizens protect themselves from thugs when police stage devastating strike. C: Tom Nardini, Brenda Bazinet, Jeff Pustil. D: Paul Donovan. ACT [R] 83m. v

Sellout, The 1952 ★★★ A journalist (Pigeon) wants to blow the lid off his corruption-laden burg, but the sheriff (Gomez) has other ideas. Watchable though not very original thriller/drama stolen by the heavy. C: Walter Pidgeon, John Hodiak, Audrey Totter, Paula Raymond, Cameron Mitchell, Karl Malden, Everett Sloane, Thomas Gomez. D: Gerald Mayer. DRA 83m.

Semi-Tough 1977 ★★★★ Two professional football players (Reynolds and Kristofferson) vie for the affection of the owner's daughter. Rude and crude locker room-type humor hits and misses, but the jabs at American trends still land solidly. Extremely diverting. C: Burt Reynolds, Kris Kristofferson, Jill Clayburgh, Robert Preston, Bert Convy, Lotte Lenya, Roger Mosley, Richard Masur, Carl Weathers, Brian Dennehy. D: Michael Ritchie. COM [R] 108m. v

Seminole 1953 ★★★½ Fresh out of West Point, a cavalry officer (Hudson) shows unique understanding toward Florida's independent-minded Seminole Indians. A thoughtful, intelligent Western. C: Rock Hudson, Barbara Hale, Anthony Quinn, Richard Carlson, Hugh O'Brian, Russell Johnson, Lee Marvin, James Best. D: Budd Boetticher. WST 87m.

Senator Was Indiscreet, The 1947 ★★★½ In order to fuel his aspirations for the presidency, a senator hires a press agent in this entertaining satire. C: William Powell, Ella Raines, Peter Lind Hayes, Hans Conried. D: George S. Kaufman. COM 81m. v

Send Me No Flowers 1964 ★★★★ Funny, inventive farce with Day married to hypochondriac (Hudson) who, convinced he's going to die, enlists friend (Randall) to find new husband for Doris. Lynde is a scream as cemetery salesman, his best film performance. C: Rock Hudson, Doris Day, Tony Randall, Paul Lynde, Clint Walker. D: Norman Jewison. COM 100m. v

Sender, The 1982 British ★★★½ A hospitalized amnesiac (Ivanek) wreaks telepathic mayhem and causes his doctor (Harrold) to experience nightmarish visions. Pulp premise is handled with more style and intelligence than usual, with good acting and special effects. C: Kathryn Harrold, Zeljko Ivanek, Shirley Knight, Paul Freeman. D: Roger Christian. HOR [R] 92m. v

Senior Week 1988 ★★ Two high school seniors face unforseen obstacles in attempt to enjoy fun week in Florida. C: Michael St. Gerard, Devon Skye, Leesa Bryte. D: Stuart Goldman. COM 97m. v

Seniors, The 1978 ★★ Ambitious and lusty college students (Quaid et al.) open a sex clinic and make millions. Occasionally offensive. C: Jeffrey Byron, Gary Imhof, Dennis Quaid, Priscilla Barnes. D: Rod Amateau. COM [R] 87m. v

Sensations 1945 ★★★ Essentially a variety show displaying some fine musical, dance, and comedy acts of the era. The Hi-Di-Ho Man's song and Powell's dance number inside a pinball machine are the highlights. Sure to satisfy those thirsting for nostalgia. (a.k.a. *Sensations of 1945*) C: Eleanor Powell, Dennis O'Keefe, C. Aubrey Smith, Eugene Pallette, W.C. Fields, Cab Calloway, Sophie Tucker. D: Andrew L. Stone. MUS [R] 86m. v

Sensations of 1945 *See* **Sensations**

Sense and Sensibility 1986 ★★★ Strong BBC adaptation of Jane Austen's masterpiece about two sisters searching for contentment. C: Irene Richard, Tracey Childa. D: Rodney Benett. DRA 174m. TVM v

Sense of Freedom, A 1978 ★★★ Racketeer with a record a mile long is shuttled from one institution to another. Compelling drama handled with heightened sensitivity. C: David Hayman, Alex Norton, Jake D'arcy. D: John Mackenzie. DRA 81m. v

Senso 1955 Italian ★★★★½ Fascinating 19th-century drama follows romance between a Venetian countess (Valli) and a rugged Austrian officer (Granger) played out against Austria's evacuation of Italy. Rich Technicolor scenery and a marvelous operatic score; splendid performances. (a.k.a. *Wanton Contessa* and *The Wanton Countess*) C: Alida Valli, Farley Granger, Massimo Girotti. D: Luchino Visconti. DRA 115m. v

Sensual Man, The 1974 Italian ★★ Grim "comedy" about a libidinous Italian man frustrated because his new wife won't respond to his amorous advances. C: Giancarlo Giannini, Rossana Podesta. D: Marco Vicario. COM [R] V

Sensualita 1952 Italian ★★★ Two men mix it up for the very best of reasons: They're rivals for the affections of a highly sensual young woman (Rossi-Drago). Very entertaining indeed! (a.k.a. *Barefoot Savage*) C: Eleonora Rossi-Drago, Amadeo Nazzari, Marcello Mastroianni, Francesco Liddi, Corrado Nardi. D: Clemente Fracassi. DRA 72m.

Sensuous Nurse, The 1979 Italian ★★ Greedy relatives hire sexy nurse for their ailing rich uncle, hoping she'll give him a heart attack so they can inherit his fortune. Typical Italian sex farce. C: Ursula Andress, Jack Palance, Duilio Del Prete, Mario Pisu. D: Nello Rossati. COM [R] 79m. V

Sensuous Vampires 1978 *See* **Vampire Hookers**

Sentimental Journey 1946 ★★★½ Terminally ill actress (O'Hara) adopts a little girl so that her husband won't be alone when she's gone. A real sob story that makes for a good and cleansing cry. C: John Payne, Maureen O'Hara, William Bendix, Cedric Hardwicke, Glenn Langan, Mischa Auer, Connie Marshall. D: Walter Lang. DRA 94m.

Sentinel, The 1977 ★★★ Solid lineup of veteran actors and stars-to-be in sometimes grotesque horror tale of woman taking up residence in a brownstone populated by evil spirits. C: Cristina Raines, Martin Balsam, Chris Sarandon, Jose Ferrer, John Carradine. D: Michael Winner. HOR [R] 92m. V

Separate But Equal 1991 ★★★★½ Excellent docudrama of youthful lawyer Thurgood Marshall (Poitier) arguing Supreme Court decision *Brown* vs. *Board of Education*, which outlawed segregation in public schools. Poitier's vivid performance is matched by Lancaster as opposing counsel and Kiley as Chief Justice Earl Warren. C: Sidney Poitier, Burt Lancaster, Richard Kiley. D: George Stevens, Jr. DRA [PG] 193m. TVM V

Separate Peace, A 1973 ★★½ Adaptation of John Knowles novel of an East Coast boarding school has seven students coping with the onset of WWII and their own adulthood. Coming-of-age tale never really hits its mark. C: John Heyl, Parker Stevenson, William Roerick, Peter Brush. D: Larry Peerce. DRA [PG] 104m. V

Separate Tables 1958 ★★★★★ Masterfully constructed character drama, with several lonely people in small seaside hotel discovering secrets and hurting each other. Niven won Oscar for Best Actor, and Hiller won for Best Supporting Actress. Originally two one-act plays by Terence Rattigan. C: Burt Lancaster, Rita Hayworth, David Niven, Deborah Kerr, Wendy Hiller, Gladys Cooper. D: Delbert Mann. DRA 98m. V

Separate Vacations 1986 ★★½ Loving wife (Dale) gets the kids and an icy holiday; naughty hubby (Naughton) gets to ogle women in steamy Mexico. He can't get arrested, while she (surprise!) has an affair. One-joke romantic comedy. C: David Naughton, Jennifer Dale, Mark Keyloun, Lally Cadeau. D: Michael Anderson. COM [R] 94m. V

Separate Ways 1981 ★★★ Racecar driver's marriage hits the skids after his bored wife (Black) has an affair with a younger man (Naughton). Very good cast, but its just another marital infidelity potboiler. C: Karen Black, Tony LoBianco, David Naughton, Arlene Golonka. D: Howard Avedis. DRA [R] 92m. V

September 1987 ★★★ Dreary film of Farrow trying to stop Stritch from selling summer home, while dealing with marital infidelity. Allen's homage to Chekhov with everyone talking, nothing happening, and Stritch the only highspot of comic relief. C: Denholm Elliott, Mia Farrow, Elaine Stritch, Sam Waterston, Jack Warden, Dianne Wiest. D: Woody Allen. DRA [PG] 82m. V

September Affair 1950 ★★★½ Two musicians having an adulterous affair are mistakenly reported dead in a plane crash; their unexpected freedom leads to unanticipated challenges. Quality melodrama features lovely Italian scenery. C: Joseph Cotten, Joan Fontaine, Francoise Rosay, Jessica Tandy, Robert Arthur. D: William Dieterle. DRA 105m. V

September Gun 1983 ★★★ An aging, tired gunslinger takes on an unfamiliar job: protect a nun and her Apache orphans. Familiar sagebrush yarn, saved by Preston's considerable charm. C: Robert Preston, Patty Astin, Geoffrey Lewis, Sally Kellerman, David Knell, Jacques Aubuchon, Christopher Lloyd. D: Don Taylor. WST 94m. TVM V

September 30, 1955 1977 ★★★★ An Arkansas youth (Thomas) obsessed with James Dean cannot cope with his death in this insightful look at the profound attachment of some fans to the stars they worship. Thomas and Benson are convincing in this subtle, intelligent drama. Quaid's debut. (a.k.a. *9/30/55*) C: Richard Thomas, Susan Tyrrell, Deborah Benson, Lisa Blount, Tom Hulce, Dennis Quaid, Dennis Christopher, Collin Wilcox, Mary Kai Clark. D: James Bridges. DRA [PG] 107m. V

Sequoia 1934 ★★★ Young woman who lives near a primeval forest provides tender loving care for all kinds of animals. Routine story elevated by extraordinary sequences with deer, mountain lions, and other wild animals. (a.k.a. *Malibu*) C: Jean Parker, Russell Hardie, Samuel S. Hinds, Paul Hurst. D: Chester Franklin. FAM/DRA 73m.

Serafino 1970 French ★★★ After taking advantage of his naive cousin, Celentano is kicked out of the army. Coming into a good-sized inheritance, the lusty French rogue takes his money and runs off with a prostitute. Ribald comedy has more energy than laughs. C: Adriano Celentano, Ottavia Piccolo, Saro Urzi, Francesca Romana Coluzzi. D: Pietro Germi. COM [PG] 94m. TVM

Serenade 1956 ★★½ Vineyard worker becomes preeminent opera singer and the object of desire of two elegant women. Another rags-to-riches tale with a significant bonus in the voice of the fabulous Lanza. From James M. Cain novel. C: Mario Lanza, Joan Fontaine, Sarita Montiel, Vincent Price, Joseph Calleia, Vince Edwards. D: Anthony Mann. MUS 121m. V

Serenade for Two Spies 1966 Italian ★★★ James Bond spoof stars Lange as an undercover agent who pilfers a dangerous laser from the wrong hands. Lass joins the shenanigans as Lange's romantic interest. Lots of chases and gadgets but few laughs. C: Helmut Lange, Tony Kendall, Barbara Lass. D: Michael Pfleghar. COM 90m.

Sergeant Deadhead 1965 ★★½ Army man (Avalon) exchanges personalities with a chimpanzee during a space mission snafu. Silly astronaut comedy, despite a high-flying supporting cast. C: Frankie Avalon, Deborah Walley, Eve Arden, Cesar Romero, Buster Keaton, Gale Gordon, Harvey Lembeck. D: Norman Taurog. MUS 89m.

Sergeant Jim 1962 Yugoslavian ★★★★ African-American WWII soldier Kitzmiller is shot down behind enemy lines and is befriended by two war orphans. Together they run from the approaching German army. A small but emotionally engaging drama. (a.k.a. *Sergeant Jim—American, Soldier and Gentleman*) C: John Kitzmiller, Evelyne Wohlfeiler, Tugo Stiglic. D: France Stiglic. DRA 82m.

Sergeant Jim—American, Soldier and Gentleman 1962 *See* **Sergeant Jim**

Sergeant Madden 1939 ★★½ Policeman is brokenhearted when his son becomes a gangster. Interesting and sentimental melodrama with good work by Beery and supporting cast. C: Wallace Beery, Tom Brown, Alan Curtis, Laraine Day, Fay Holden, David Gorcey, Etta McDaniel, Horace McMahon. D: Josef von Sternberg. DRA 82m.

Sergeant Matlovich vs. the U.S. Air Force 1978 ★★★★ Mature, well-written TV drama about a homosexual officer's court struggle to remain in the armed forces. Dourif excels in the title role. C: Brad Dourif, Marc Singer, Frank Converse, William Daniels, Rue McClanahan. D: Paul Leaf. DRA 100m. TVM V

Sergeant Rutledge 1960 ★★★★ Heroic African-American cavalry man is wrongly accused of rape and murder. Excellent, underrated courtroom drama, directed by John Ford, benefits from solid ensemble cast and suspenseful flashback sequences. C: Jeffrey Hunter, Woody Strode, Constance Towers, Juano Hernandez, Willis Bouchey. D: John Ford. DRA 112m. V

Sergeant Ryker 1968 ★★★ A soldier (Marvin) is accused and tried for treason during the Korean War. Passable courtroom drama buoyed by fine acting, especially the low-key Marvin and energetic Dillman. Based on the made-for-TV movie *The Case Against Sergeant Ryker*. C: Lee Marvin, Bradford Dillman, Vera Miles, Peter Graves. D: Buzz Kulik. DRA 85m. V

Sergeant, The 1968 ★★½ At a U.S army base in France, 1952, the title character (Steiger) develops a sexual obsession with a young private (Law). Surprisingly routine. C: Rod Steiger, John Philip Law. D: John Flynn. DRA [R] 107m.

Sergeant York 1941 ★★★★½ True-life story of the unassuming, straightforward Tennessee farmer who became a hero in WWI France. Heartworming Americana, extraordinarily well told. Cooper (who took the Oscar) and Max Steiner's music are delightful. C: Gary Cooper, Walter Brennan, George Tobias, Ward Bond, Noah Beery, Jr., June Lockhart. D: Howard Hawks. DRA 134m. V

Sergeants 3 1962 ★★★ Joked-up remake of the classic adventure *Gunga Din* twists the original story of three friends in the British army into a vehicle for Sinatra and pals, known as "The Rat Pack." Stick with Cary & Co. C: Frank Sinatra, Dean Martin, Sammy Davis, Jr., Peter Lawford, Joey Bishop, Ruta Lee. D: John Sturges. COM 112m.

Serial 1980 ★★★½ Slice of wacky life, California style, complete with goofy fashions, bizarre religious cults, inane self-help groups, and marital infidelity. May seem a bit dated, but on the mark (and overlooked) when originally released. C: Martin Mull, Tuesday Weld, Sally Kellerman, Tom Smothers. D: Bill Persky. COM 90m. V

Serial Mom 1994 ★★★★½ Only John Waters (*Hairspray*) could have made this loony comedy about the perfect suburban housewife (Turner) who has a darker sideline in murder. Of course, she only kills people who are rude, but her family is getting suspicious. Hilarious satire, sparked by Turner's off-the-wall performance. C: Kathleen Turner, Sam Waterston, Ricki Lake, Matthew Lilliard, Scott Wesley Morgan, Walter MacPherson, Justin Whalin, Mink Stole, Traci Lords. D: John Waters. CRI [R] 93m.

Serpent and the Rainbow, The 1987 ★★★★½ Wade Davis' nonfiction book about Haitian voodoo becomes an effective supernatural thriller, with anthropologist (Pullman) running afoul of black magic and real zombies. Gets a boost from location shooting and authentic-sounding voodoo lore. Violent, but strikingly effective. C: Bill Pullman, Cathy Tyson, Zakes Mokae, Paul Winfield. D: Wes Craven. HOR [R] 98m. V

Serpent Island 1954 ★★ Pair of sailors battle for exotic woman's affections on dangerous tropical island. C: Sonny Tufts, Rosalind Hayes. ACT 63m. V

Serpent of Death, The 1989 ★★★ Young researcher's archeological dig unleases wicked curse locked in a statue. C: Jeff Fahey, Camilla More, Peiros Focas. D: Anwar Kawadri. ACT [R] 97m. v

Serpent's Egg, The 1978 German ★★★ An American trapeze artist (Carradine) finds himself stuck in Germany during Hitler's rise. The director's angst here seems more like nastiness. Bizarrely cast misfire, for Bergman devotees only. C: Liv Ullmann, David Carradine, Gert Frobe, James Whitmore. D: Ingmar Bergman. DRA [R] 119m. v

Serpico 1973 ★★★★★ An idealistic New York cop (Pacino, in one of his best roles), a whiz at undercover work, finds himself taking on the entire police department in an effort to root out corruption. Gritty and tough, the kind of film Lumet does with style and feeling. C: Al Pacino, John Randolph, Jack Kehoe, Biff McGuire, Barbara Eda-Young, Tony Roberts. D: Sidney Lumet. CRI [R] 130m. v

Servant, The 1963 British ★★★★★ A scheming manservant (Bogarde) begins to control the life of his jaded wealthy employer (Fox) in this grim, arresting drama scripted by Harold Pinter (who has a small cameo). A dark commentary on a perverse and sordid society. C: Dirk Bogarde, James Fox, Sarah Miles, Wendy Craig. D: Joseph Losey. DRA 112m. v

Servants of Twilight, The 1991 ★★★½ Efficient little thriller about detective (Greenwood) protecting youngster and his mother from religious fanatics who think the child's the antichrist. Realistically told, with downplayed supernatual elements and a genuinely surprising ending. C: Bruce Greenwood, Belinda Bauer, Grace Zabriskie. D: Jeffrey Obrow. HOR [R] 96m. v

Service De Luxe 1938 ★★ Woman starts an all-inclusive service business that does whatever its clients desire. Silly comedy that plays along and provides a few smiles. C: Constance Bennett, Vincent Price, Charles Ruggles, Mischa Auer, Joy Hodges, Helen Broderick. D: Rowland V. Lee. COM 85m.

Sesame Street: Big Bird in China 1987 ★★★½ A young Asian child leads Big Bird and faithful dog Barney through China in search of the mystical phoenix. A fine festival of Chinese culture for the kids and adults alike. Big Bird even learns a few words of Chinese. C: Big Bird, Barkley the Dog. D: Jon Stone. FAM/COM 75m. v

Sesame Street: Big Bird in Japan ★★★½ Big Bird and Barney are separated from their tour bus in Japan. Their ensuing adventures teach them much about Japanese customs and tradition. Informative for all. FAM/COM

Sesame Street Presents Follow That Bird 1985 ★★★ Going through an identity crisis, TV's Big Bird leaves the *Sesame Street* show and joins up with some real birds. Fun for the kids and an interesting cast. (a.k.a. *Follow that Bird*) C: Sesame Street Gang, Sandra Bernhard, John Candy, Chevy Chase, Joe Flaherty. D: Ken Kwapis. FAM/COM [G] 89m. v

Set-Up, The 1949 ★★★★½ A has-been prizefighter (Ryan) refuses to take a dive. Bleak but fascinating look at boxing and the human condition. Screenplay is sharp, acting (particularly Ryan's) is superb. One of the best boxing films ever made. C: Robert Ryan, Audrey Totter, George Tobias, Alan Baxter. D: Robert Wise. DRA 72m. v

Seven 1979 ★★★½ Tough-guy (Smith) assembles crimefighting team to nab gangsters plaguing Hawaii. Sexy, violent adventure and one of the better Sidaris pics. C: William Smith, Barbara Leigh, Guich Koock, Art Metrano, Martin Kove. D: Andy Sidaris. ACT [R] 106m. v

Seven Against the Sun 1968 South African ★★★ During WWI, one South African army unit is chosen to combine their talents and confuse advancing Italian troops by airing phony radio broadcasts. Average war drama. C: Gert van den Bergh, John Hayter, Brian O'Shaughnessy, Elizabeth Meyer. D: David Millin. DRA 115m.

Seven Alone 1974 ★★★ When their parents are killed, a 13-year-old boy leads his six siblings across Oregon Trail in 1840s America. Plenty of crises develop along route, but nothing too surprising in mundane outing aimed at child audiences. Based on a true story. C: Dewey Martin, Aldo Ray, Anne Collins, Dean Smith. D: Earl Bellamy. FAM/DRA [G] 97m. v

Seven Angry Men 1955 ★★★ John Brown and his family fight to end the evils of slavery in pre-Civil War America. Effective historical drama and a riveting portrayal by Massey. C: Raymond Massey, Debra Paget, Jeffrey Hunter, James Best, Dennis Weaver, Dabbs Greer, Ann Tyrrell. D: Charles Marquis Warren. DRA 90m.

Seven Beauties 1976 Italian ★★★★½ A two-bit Italian thief turned soldier will do anything to survive a Nazi prison camp, including seducing the cruel female commandmant. Controversial blend of politics and comedy distinguishes Wertmueller's masterful dark vision of moral corruption. C: Giancarlo Giannini, Fernando Rey, Shirley Stoler. D: Lina Wertmuller. DRA [R] 115m. v

Seven Blows of the Dragon 1973 ★★★ Solid martial arts film, set in medieval times and based on the Chinese novel *All Men Are Brothers*. The range of weaponry goes from swords and spears to fists of fury. C: David Chiang. ACT [R] 79m. v

Seven Brides for Seven Brothers 1954 ★★★★★ Sublime MGM period musical set in Oregon with fur trapper (Keel), deciding to marry and inspiring six roustabout brothers to do the same. Lilting score, delightful performances and brilliant Michael Kidd choreography, with Russ Tamblyn a standout. Highlight: the barn-raising sequence. Loosely based on

Stephen Vincent Benet short story. C: Howard Keel, Jane Powell, Jeff Richards, Russ Tamblyn, Tommy Rall. D: Stanley Donen. MUS [G] 102m. V

Seven Brothers Meet Dracula, The 1974 British ★★★½ Dracula-hater Van Helsing (Cushing) takes a slow boat to China and, with an assist from some kung fu fighters, battles the vampires. Delightfully crazy! The original, longer version, entitled *Legend of the Seven Golden Vampires*, is crazier still. C: Peter Cushing, David Chiang, Julie Ege, Robin Stewart, Shih Szu, John Forbes-Robertson. D: Roy Ward Baker. HOR [R] 72m. V

7 Capital Sins 1961 French ★★★★ Entertaining grab-bag of short films directed by new wave masters, each inspired by a different "deadly" sin. Best are de Broca's "Gluttony" and Vadim's "Pride." C: Eddie Constantine, Jean-Louis Trintignant, Marina Vlady, Jean-Pierre Aumont. D: Sylvain Dhomme, Eugene Ionesco, Max Douy, Édourd Molinaro, Phillipe de Broca, Jacques Demy, Jean-Luc Goddard, Roger Vadim, Claude Chabrol. COM 113m.

Seven Chances 1925 ★★★★★ A shy man (Keaton) learns he has one day to find a wife in order to inherit a fortune; next thing he knows he is being chased by an army of would-be brides. A hilarious, inventive mastaerpiece of silent comedy. C: Buster Keaton, T. Roy Barnes, Snitz Edwards, Ruth Dwyer, Frankie Raymond. D: Buster Keaton. COM 60m.

Seven Cities of Gold 1955 ★★½ An 18th-century Spanish expedition moves north from Mexico into California in an effort to spread religion and find gold. A good-looking, exciting adventure. C: Richard Egan, Anthony Quinn, Jeffrey Hunter, Rita Moreno, Michael Rennie. D: Robert D. Webb. ACT 103m. V

Seven Daring Girls 1960 German ★★ Seven female students from a posh Swiss school are stranded on an island with renegade gold-seekers. Implausible idea that never gets going. C: Jan Hendricks, Adrian Hoven, Ann Smyrner, Dorothee Glocklen. D: Otto Meyer. DRA 62m.

Seven Days in May 1964 ★★★★ Taut political thriller has a right-wing U.S. general (Lancaster) planning a military coup in order to sabotage the attempts by the President (March) to make peace with the Soviets. Intelligent drama with spellbinding intrigue in a script by Rod Serling. C: Burt Lancaster, Kirk Douglas, Fredric March, Ava Gardner, Edmond O'Brien, Martin Balsam, George Macready, John Houseman. D: John Frankenheimer. DRA 118m. V

Seven Days' Leave 1942 ★★★ To cash in on his inheritance, a G.I. (Mature) must find a bride during his week-long furlough. Slim musical comedy gets by on Lucy's personality and Les Brown and His Band of Renown. C: Lucille Ball, Victor Mature, Harold Peary, Ginny Simms, Peter Lind Hayes, Arnold Stang, Ralph Edwards. D: Tim Whelan. MUS 87m. V

Seven Days to Noon 1950 British ★★★★½ British atomic scientist threatens to blow up London as a protest against nuclear development. Effective suspense that leaves viewers on the edge of their seats. C: Barry Jones, Olive Sloane, Andre Morell, Sheila Manahan, Hugh Cross, Joan Hickson. D: John Boulting. ACT 93m.

Seven Deadly Sins 1952 ★★★ Seven episodes, all individually introduced, the seven biggies: sloth, lust, etc. Intriguing look at a fascinating subject. Well done and highly entertaining. C: Michele Morgan, Françoise Rosey, Gerard Philipe, Isabelle Miranda. D: Eduardo De Filippo, Jean Dreville, Yves Allegret, Roberto Rossellini. DRA 127m.

Seven Deaths in the Cat's Eye 1973 Italian ★★½ Yet another chiller about hopeful heirs to a big inheritance being bumped off, this time at a Scottish castle that may be haunted by a cat creature. Been there, done that. C: Jane Birkin, Anton Diffring, Serge Gainsbourg, Venantino Venantini. D: Anthony M. Dawson (Antonio Margheriti). HOR [R] 86m. V

Seven Dials Mystery, The 1981 ★★★½ Youthful guests at the estate of a tycoon and his wife plan a prank on a sleeping guest—who then fails to awake. Light mood buoys this overlong British-made Agatha Christie mystery. C: Cheryl Campbell, Harry Amdrews, John Gielgud. D: Tony Wharmby. CRI 110m. TVM V

Seven Different Ways 1964 *See* **Quick, Let's Get Married**

7 Doors of Death 1983 Italian ★★★★ A hotel once owned by a satanist becomes a conduit for zombies and other horrors to invade our dimension. Superior Italian gore film, thanks to stylish direction and some genuinely chilling scenes. (a.k.a. *The Beyond*) C: Katherine MacColl, David Warbeck, Sarah Keller, Tony Saint John, Veronica Lazar. D: Lucio Fulci. HOR [R] 89m.

Seven Doors to Death 1944 ★★ As the law wrongfully closes in on him, a youthful architect must evade prosecution by finding real perpetrator of crime. C: Chick Chandler, June Clyde. D: Elmer Clifton. CRI 70m. V

7 Faces of Dr. Lao 1963 ★★★★ A Chinese carnival owner and his troupe of miracle workers change lives in a small 19th-century Western town. Pleasant fantasy; Randall is wonderful in seven different roles. C: Tony Randall, Barbara Eden, Arthur O'Connell, John Ericson. D: George Pal. SFI 101m. V

Seven Hills of Rome, The 1958 ★★★ When a singing star (Lanza) chases his girlfriend to Eternal City, new romance blooms. Glorious location photography steals the show, even from Lanza's powerhouse voice. The script comes in a distant third. C: Mario

Lanza, Peggie Castle, Marisa Allasio. D: Roy Rowland. MUS 104m. v

Seven Hours to Judgment 1988 ★★½ A murder victim's crazed widower (Liebman) targets the judge (Bridges) who freed the killers in this forceful but implausible revenge tale. C: Beau Bridges, Ron Leibman, Julianne Phillips, Reggie Johnson. D: Beau Bridges. DRA [R] 90m. v

Seven Indignant 1985 ★★½ During the 1941 Japanese occupation of China, a group of warriors tries to uncover a sacred Chinese treausre, which elite Chinese warrior group must defend. C: Kwok Chun Yan, Kong Hoi. ACT 90m. v

Seven Little Foys, The 1955 ★★★★ Hope plays famed vaudevillian Eddie Foy, whose family act headlined across the country. Bob is touching as father fighting to retain custody of his children. Musical numbers include tap-dancing Cagney, reprising his role of George M. Cohan from *Yankee Doodle Dandy*. C: Bob Hope, Milly Vitale, George Tobias, Billy Gray, James Cagney. D: Melville Shavelson. MUS 95m. v

Seven Magnificent Gladiators, The 1984 ★★ TV's Incredible Hulk plays warrior trying to protect Roman town from destruction. C: Lou Ferrigno, Sybil Danning, Brad Harris. D: Bruno Mattei. ACT [PG] 86m. v

Seven Men from Now 1956 ★★★★ When his wife is killed in a bank robbery, a settler (Scott) devotes his life to hunting down the murderers. First-rate Western with plenty of action and good performances. First collaboration between Scott and Buetticher. C: Randolph Scott, Gail Russell, Lee Marvin, Walter Reed, John Larch, Donald Barry. D: Budd Boetticher. WST 78m.

Seven Miles from Alcatraz 1943 ★★½ A couple of cons escape from Alcatraz and wind up tangling with Nazi spies at their hideout spot. Jailbirds turn into heroes in this solid little wartime suspense film. C: James Craig, Bonita Granville, Frank Jenks, Cliff Edwards. D: Edward Dmytryk. ACT 127m. v

Seven Minutes in Heaven 1986 ★★★★ Teenagers find first love in this nicely done, small-scale comedy-drama. Very appealing cast—though the bubblegum music score has to go. C: Jennifer Connelly, Byron Thames, Maddie Corman, Alan Boyce Polly Draper. D: Linda Feferman. DRA [PG-13] 88m. v

Seven Minutes, The 1971 ★★★½ Courtroom drama centering on a pornographic book, the people who read it, and the effect it had on them. As drama, Russ Meyers' only "serious" film is pure silliness; great cast helps a lot, though. From the Irving Wallace best-seller. C: Wayne Maunder, Marianne McAndrew, Philip Carey, Yvonne De Carlo, Jay C. Flippen, Edy Williams, John Carradine, Harold Stone. D: Russ Meyer. DRA [PG] 116m.

711 Ocean Drive 1950 ★★★ Bookmakers and racketeers mix it up with the law. Powerful little crime story that features a knockout finale shot on location at Hoover Dam. C: Edmond O'Brien, Joanne Dru, Otto Kruger, Bert Freed. D: Joseph M. Newman. CRI 102m.

Seven Percent Solution, The 1976 ★★★★½ Superior Sherlock Holmes tale. The great detective consults Sigmund Freud in hopes of being cured of his cocaine addiction, and the two join forces on a case. Imaginative, witty synthesis of fact and fiction, sleuthing and psychiatry, with numerous great performances. C: Nicol Williamson, Alan Arkin, Vanessa Redgrave, Robert Duvall, Laurence Olivier, Joel Grey, Samantha Eggar, Jeremy Kemp. D: Herbert Ross. DRA [PG] 113m. v

Seven Samurai, The 1954 Japanese ★★★★★ A 16th-century farming community seeks protection from outlaws by hiring a cadre of swordsmen in Hurasawa's much-imitated, never-equaled class. Regarded as *the* samurai film, with powerful human drama as well as gripping battle scenes, it was remade in 1960 as *The Magnificent Seven*. Available in several versions of varying length. C: Toshiro Mifune, Takashi Shimura, Yoshio Inaba, Ko Kimura, Minoru Chiaki. D: Akira Kurosawa. DRA 208m. v

Seven Sinners 1940 ★★★★ A cabaret performer (Dietrich) gets under the skin of John Wayne and every other man in the South Seas. Breezy romantic comedy made eminently watchable by its two stars. Remade in 1950 as *South Sea Sinner*. C: Marlene Dietrich, John Wayne, Albert Dekker, Broderick Crawford, Mischa Auer. D: Tay Garnett. COM 83m. v

Seven Sweethearts 1942 ★★★ Six lovesick sisters must try to get their eldest sibling (Hunt) married so they can tie the knot themselves. Minor MGM musical, loosely based on *Pride and Prejudice*. C: Kathryn Grayson, Van Heflin, S.Z. Sakall, Marsha Hunt. D: Frank Borzage. MUS 98m.

Seven Thieves 1960 ★★★★ Snappy caper film, with Robinson and Steiger leading group in casino rip-off. Smooth and professional, with a tangy twist ending. C: Edward G. Robinson, Rod Steiger, Joan Collins, Eli Wallach, Alexander Scourby. D: Henry Hathaway. CRI 102m. v

Seven-Ups, The 1973 ★★★½ Tough cop (Scheider) leads group of colleagues in ex officio work to get rid of bad guys when lenient courts don't. Plenty of action, not much brains. C: Roy Scheider, Tony LoBianco, Bill Hickman, Richard Lynch. D: Philip D'Antoni. CRI [PG] 109m. v

Seven Waves Away 1957 *See* **Abandon Ship!**

Seven Women 1966 ★★★½ In the war-torn China of 1935, an isolated mission staffed by American women is besieged by bandits. Good acting and excellent production; John Ford's last film. C: Anne Bancroft, Sue Lyon, Margaret Leighton, Flora Robson, Mildred Dunnock. D: John Ford. ACT 87m.

Seven Year Itch, The 1955 ★★★★ A married man (Ewell) is tempted to play with upstairs neighbor (Monroe) while his wife is away on summer vacation. Amusing sex comedy from George Axelrod play. Marilyn's comic timing is deft here and the famous subway grating scene established her permanently as a cultural icon. C: Marilyn Monroe, Tom Ewell, Evelyn Keyes, Sonny Tufts. D: Billy Wilder. COM 105m. V

Seventeen 1940 ★★★★ Midwestern youth copes with the wonders, discoveries, and agonies of adolescence. A charming film and young Cooper is great. Based on the Booth Tarkington novel. C: Jackie Cooper, Betty Field, Otto Kruger, Richard Denning, Peter Lind Hayes, Betty Moran, Ann Shoemaker, Norma Nelson. D: Louis King. DRA 78m.

1776 1972 ★★★★ History and Broadway join forces for a musical depicting the birth of the United States, dramatizing the efforts of Adams, Franklin, and Jefferson to persuade congressional opponents to sign Declaration of Independence. Fine family fare, entertaining and historically honest, with good dramatic moments between numbers. C: William Daniels, Howard da Silva, Ken Howard, Donald Madden, Ron Holgate, David Ford, Blythe Danner, Roy Poole, Virginia Vestoff, John Cullum. D: Peter H. Hunt. MUS [G] 141m.

Seventeenth Bride, The 1984 ★★★½ Affecting World War II story of Jewish woman in Czechoslovakia who escapes concentration camps by marrying unlikable man. C: Lisa Hartman. D: Israeli Nadav Levitan. DRA 91m. V

Seventh Cavalry 1956 ★★★½ Accused of cowardice, an officer (Scott) tries to right his reputation by attempting to retrieve General Custer's body after the battle of the Little Big Horn. Superior Western fare sparked further by the cast. C: Randolph Scott, Barbara Hale, Jay C. Flippen, Jeanette Nolan, Frank Faylen. D: Joseph H. Lewis. WST 75m. V

Seventh Coin, The 1993 ★★★ Mild action film for kids, with a teenage American tourist meeting an Arab kid who is a petty thief and both of them getting mixed up with O'Toole who's searching for rare coin. O'Toole's performance is hilariously over-the-top and the kids are pleasant. C: Peter O'Toole, Alexandra Powers, John Rhys-Davis. FAM/DRA [PG-13] 92m. V

Seventh Continent, The 1968 Czech ★★★½ Two children of different races decide to create their own island paradise of multicolored youngsters, and try to expand their utopian dreams to the world of adults. A nice animated parable for kids. C: Iris Vrus, Tomislav Pasaric. D: Dusan Vukotic. FAM/DRA 84m.

Seventh Cross, The 1944 ★★★★ Smart and suspenseful thriller of seven escapees from a Nazi concentration camp and their efforts to avoid capture. Tracy wonderful as a cynic whose shared ordeal allows him to recover his faith in humanity. C: Spencer Tracy, Signe Hasso, Hume Cronyn, Jessica Tandy, Felix Bressart, Agnes Moorehead, George Macready, Kaaren Verne, George Zucco. D: Fred Zinnemann. DRA 111m. V

Seventh Heaven 1927 ★★★★★ Classic silent romance, with Gaynor as a Parisian gamine who needs the help of sewerman Farrell. Lovingly photographed and scored. Gaynor won the very first Best Actress Oscar for this and two other 1927-28 performances: *Sunrise* and *Street Angel*. C: Janet Gaynor, Charles Farrell, David Butler. D: Frank Borzage. DRA 119m.

Seventh Heaven 1937 ★★★ Poor Parisienne finds true love with her boastful and charming new boyfriend in this remake of the hit silent version of 1927. The story remains excellent, but you're better off with the original. C: Simone Simon, James Stewart, Jean Hersholt, Gregory Ratoff, Gale Sondergaard, J. Edward Bromberg, John Qualen. D: Henry King. DRA 102m.

Seventh Seal, The 1957 Sweden ★★★★★ Bergman's masterpiece is a deeply moving examination of death and religious disillusionment. A dispirited 14th-century knight (von Sydow) returns from the Crusades to a country ravaged by the Black Plague. Playing a game of chess with Death in which the stakes are the knight's own life, he searches for the meaning of that life. Stunning b&w cinematography complements this profound work. C: Max von Sydow, Gunnar Bjornstrand, Bibi Andersson. D: Ingmar Bergman. DRA 96m. V

Seventh Sign, The 1988 ★★★ Husband (Biehn) and pregnant wife (Moore) take on mysterious boarder (Prochnow), who proves to be a supernatural agent with designs on their unborn baby. Has some striking moments, but this supernatural drama is played very low-key. C: Demi Moore, Michael Biehn, Jurgen Prochnow, Peter Friedman. D: Carl Schultz. HOR [R] 97m. V

Seventh Veil, The 1947 British ★★★★ When a brilliant concert pianist (Todd) loses her mind, a psychiatrist (Lom) tries to cure her through hypnosis. Outstanding British melodrama delivered by first-rate cast. This was Mason's big breakthrough film. C: James Mason, Ann Todd, Herbert Lom, Hugh McDermott. D: Compton Bennett. DRA 91m. V

Seventh Victim, The 1943 ★★★★½ Naive young woman (Hunter) searching in New York for her missing sister becomes involved with sister's devil-worshipping "friends." Considered by many to be early horror producer Val Lewton's best work, this expertly crafted, unsettling classic hasn't lost any of its nightmarish potency. C: Tom Conway, Kim Hunter, Jean Brooks, Hugh Beaumont. D: Mark Robson. HOR 70m. V

7th Voyage of Sinbad, The 1958 ★★★★½ When an evil magician (Thatcher) shrinks a princess (Grant), her beau, Sinbad (Mathews) searches for the egg that can restore her. Wonderful fantasy yarn, with stand-out Ray Harryhausen effects and fine score by music maestro Bernard Herrmann. C: Kerwin Mathews, Kathryn Grant, Richard Eyer, Torin Thatcher. D: Nathan Juran. FAM/ACT [G] 94m. v

Severance 1988 ★★ Former flight ace must protect estranged daughter from seedy and dangerous life. C: Lou Liotta, Lisa Wolpe. D: David Max Steinberg. ACT 93m. v

Severed Arm, The 1973 ★★ Mining cave-in survivors cut off a comrade's arm for food, and then get bumped off one by one. Mystery/horror film is neither mysterious nor horrifying—just low-budget. C: Deborah Walley, Paul Carr, David G. Cannon, Roy Dennis. D: Thomas S. Alderman. HOR [R] 92m. v

Severed Head, A 1971 British ★★★★ Unfaithful husband (Holm) is shocked by the news that his wife (Remick) is having an affair of her own. Clever black comedy about sexual permissiveness. Wickedly tart script by Frederic Raphael, from Iris Murdoch's novel. C: Ian Holm, Lee Remick, Richard Attenborough, Claire Bloom. D: Dick Clement. COM [R] 96m.

Severed Ties 1992 ★★½ Cluttered shocker about young scientist's experiments in limb regeneration, and his mother's attempts to exploit his discovery. Some good effects, but silly plot might have been better played for laughs. C: Oliver Reed, Elke Sommer, Garrett Morris. D: Damon Santostefano. HOR [R] 95m. v

SEX 1920 ★★ Silent production, with a musical accompaniment, of a sexy actress whose flirtacious ways lead to her downfall. C: Louise Glaum, William Conklin. D: Fred Niblo. DRA 94m. v

Sex and Buttered Popcorn 1989 ★★★★ Ned Beatty narrates highly entertaining documentary about classic exploitation films of '30s and '40s. Many hilarious film clips and fascinating interviews with early sleaze producers. C: Ned Beatty. D: Sam Harrison. COM [R] 70m. v

Sex and the Single Girl 1964 ★★★½ Girly magazine editor (Curtis) tries to bed beautiful psychologist (Wood) in this sex farce loosely based on the Helen Gurley Brown book of the same name. Star-studded cast lends some, but not much, dignity to the lively silliness. C: Natalie Wood, Tony Curtis, Lauren Bacall, Henry Fonda, Mel Ferrer, Fran Jeffries. D: Richard Quine. COM 110m. v

Sex, Drugs, Rock & Roll 1991 ★★★★ Film version of in-your-face performance artist Bogosian's one-man stage show, featuring ten assorted unpleasant characters. Not for all tastes, but worth a whirl for the downtowners. From the director of *Henry: Portrait of a Serial Killer*. C: Eric Bogosian. D: John McNaughton. DRA [R] 96m. v

Sex Kittens Go to College 1960 ★ A professor (Van Doren) causes a brouhaha when it's discovered she was once a stripper. Title may be the best part. (a.k.a. *The Beauty and the Robot*) C: Mamie Van Doren, Tuesday Weld, Mijanou Bardot, Louis Nye, Martin Milner, Mickey Shaughnessy, Pamela Mason, "Woo Woo" Grabowski, Jackie Coogan, John Carradine. D: Albert Zugsmith. COM 94m.

sex, lies, and videotape 1989 ★★★★½ A repressed young wife discovers that her husband is sleeping with her sister when his mysterious college pal (who videotapes women's intimate revelations) arrives and shakes everything up. Soderbergh's incisive first film is a modern-day morality play with a brilliant cast. Won Best Picture Award at Cannes, and Spader won Best Actor. C: James Spader, Andie MacDowell, Laura San Giacomo, Peter Gallagher. D: Steven Soderbergh. DRA [R] 100m. v

Sex Machine, The 1976 ★ In the 21st century, a scientist brings together the world's greatest lovers so he can harness the energy they generate. See, high school science is important after all. C: Agostine Belli. COM [R] 80m. v

Sex on the Run 1978 ★★ Playful affairs abound in this period comedy following the adventures of an amorous Casanova look-alike (Curtis). C: Tony Curtis, Marisa Berenson, Sylva Koscina, Britt Ekland. D: Francois Legrand. COM 88m. v

Sex Pistols—Great Rock 'n' Roll Swindle 1980 British ★★★★ Semidocumentary offers a dark glimpse into the lives and loves of one of rock 'n' roll's most notorious and greatest bands, The Sex Pistols. At times sordid, at times fascinating, this gritty movie is not for the faint of heart. C: Sex Pistols, Malcolm McLaren. D: Julien Temple. MUS 105m. v

Sex Through a Window 1973 ★★ Sexploitation film is as seedy looking as its subject, as a news reporter-turned-voyeur shoots a television "exposé," so to speak. Written by Michael Crichton. (a.k.a. *Extreme Close-Up*) C: James McMullan, Kate Woodville. D: Jeannot Szwarc. DRA [R] 81m. v

Sex with a Smile 1976 Italian ★★ Inept, unsatisfying Italian sex comedy made up of five bawdy vignettes. C: Marty Feldman, Edwige Fenech, Sydne Rome, Dayle Haddon. D: Sergio Martino. COM [R] 95m. v

Sexpot 1988 ★★ Woman marries rich men then bumps them off to inherit their fortunes. Old-as-the-hills premise; average execution. C: Troy Donahue, Joyce Lyons, Jack Carter. D: Chuck Vincent. COM [R] 95m. v

Sextette 1978 ★★ Former Hollywood sex goddess's marriage to a much younger man (Dalton) is interrupted by the endless parade of her previous husbands. West (in her last film) gives an incredible cast the octogenarian once-over. More of a curiousity than a movie. C: Mae West, Timothy Dalton, Tony Curtis, Ringo Starr, George Hamilton, Alice Cooper, Rona Barrett, George Raft, Keith Moon, Walter Pidgeon, Dom DeLuise, Regis Philbin. D: Ken Hughes. COM [PG] 91m. V

Sexton Blake and the Hooded Terror 1938 British ★★½ The leader of a gang of dangerous criminals turns out to be a well-respected multimillionaire. Another hard-hitting entry in the *Sexton Blake* series. C: George Curzon, Tod Slaughter, Greta Gynt. D: George King. CRI 70m.

Sez O'Reilly to McNab 1938 British ★★★½ Mahoney is a business magnate who avoids American jails by fleeing to Scotland, where he hides out in Fyffes' home. The love/hate relationship between the friends makes for some exasperated humor. A cute comedy. (a.k.a. *Said O'Reilly to McNab*) C: Will Mahoney, Will Fyffe. D: William Beaudine. COM 83m.

Sgt. Pepper's Lonely Hearts Club Band 1978 ★★ All-star cast uses myriad Beatles's songs to tell the story of how Sgt. Pepper's Lonely Hearts Club Band saves Heartland from Mean Mr. Mustard. Garish color, hideous sets, famous names and sheer musical horror dominate every frame. Must be seen to be believed. C: Peter Frampton, The Bee Gees, George Burns, Frankie Howard, Donald Pleasence, Sandy Farina, Dianne Steinberg, Billy Preston, Steve Martin. D: Michael Schultz. MUS [PG] 111m. V

Shabby Tiger, The 1965 *See* **Masquerade**

Shades of Love: Champagne for Two ★★ A young woman is torn between love and career. Much ado about hardly anything. DRA V

Shades of Love: Echoes in Crimson ★★½ Art world striver is shaken when an old lover returns to her life. DRA V

Shades of Love: Lilac Dream 1987 ★★★ When an amnesiac washes up on the shore of an island retreat, a lonely woman nurses him back to health, and they share a life of bliss until his past presents itself. Enjoyable romantic mystery. C: Dack Rambo, Susan Almgren. D: Marc Volzard. DRA 83m. V

Shades of Love: The Ballerina and the Blues ★★★ Ambitious young ballerina becomes involved with a noisy blues musician who uses the same warehouse practice space. Colorful romance. DRA V

Shades of Love: The Garnet Princess ★★★ Private detective informs young woman that she is descended from royalty and she is actually a princess. Far-fetched, fun romantic fare. DRA 80m. V

Shadow Between, The 1932 British ★★★½ After wrongly being sent to prison, Tearle is joined behind bars by spouse O'Regan, who has committed a crime so her husband won't be alone. Intriguing spin on prison movie formulas with some nice performances. C: Godfrey Tearle, Kathleen O'Regan. D: Norman Walker. CRI 86m.

Shadow Box, The 1980 ★★★★ Sad, well-cast drama of three terminally ill patients and their families at an experimental retreat, from Michael Cristofer's Pulitizer Prize-and Tony Award-winning play. Fine acting from Woodward and Sidney. C: Joanne Woodward, Christopher Plummer, Robert Urich, Valerie Harper. D: Paul Newman. DRA 96m. TVM V

Shadow Dancing 1988 ★★★ A tempestuous woman's spirit possesses a young dancer. C: Nadine Van Der Velde, John Colicos, Christopher Plummer. D: Lewis Furey. DRA [PG] 100m. V

Shadow Force 1992 ★★★ Detective investigating the murder of two coworkers discovers a plot to assassiante important U.S. law enforcement officials. C: Dirk Benedict, Bob Hastings, Jack Elam. D: Darrell Davenport. ACT 90m. V

Shadow Hunter 1992 ★★½ When L.A. policeman tries to track down a killer who has escaped into the desert, he gets caught in a web of mystical illusion and becomes the hunted himself. Ambitious thriller, some suspense. C: Scott Glenn, Angela Alvarado, Robert Beltran. D: J.S. Cardone. ACT [R] 98m. V

Shadow in the Sky 1951 ★★★ A soldier still in shock from WWII leaves an institution and moves in with his sister. Poignant and moving. C: Ralph Meeker, Nancy Davis, James Whitmore, Jean Hagen, Gladys Hurlbut. D: Fred M. Wilcox. DRA 78m.

Shadow Killers ★★½ A lady Ninja is hired by a wealthy businessman to save his kidnapped child. Action-packed adventure featuring a climatic Ninja battle. C: Barbara Watson, Daniel Wells. D: Tommy Cheng. ACT 90m. V

Shadow Man 1975 ★★★ High-class thief who's a master of disguise plans to steal the rare Treasure of the Knights Templar. Good suspense and some nifty tricks. Nicely done. C: Gert Frobe, Gayle Hunnicutt, Josephine Chaplin. ACT [PG] 89m. V

Shadow of a Doubt 1943 ★★★★★ Average, small-town family welcomes beloved Uncle Charlie (Cotten) home for a visit, where his niece (Wright) begins to suspect he's a murderer. One of Hitchock's finest thrillers, with suspense coming from danger in mundane setting. Script co-written by playwright Thornton Wilder. C: Teresa Wright, Joseph Cotten, Macdonald Carey, Patricia Collinge, Henry Travers, Hume Cronyn. D: Alfred Hitchcock. CRI 108m. V

Shadow of Chikara, The ★★★½ A Confederate army officer and a young orphan girl prospect for diamonds in Arkansas. Unusual premise that's brought off nicely. WST V

Shadow of China, The 1991 ★★★★ International intrigue as young man grapples for position and romance in Hong Kong. Gripping, thrillingly filmed adaptation of Japanese novel "Snakehead." C: John Lone, Vivian Wu, Sammi Davis. D: Mitsuo Yanagimachi. DRA [PG-13] 100m. V

Shadow of Fear 1956 British ★★ Woman

discovers her mysterious stepmother killed her father—and now she's about to kill her! Typical suspense film with little to distinguish it. (a.k.a. *Before I Wake*) C: Mona Freeman, Jean Kent, Maxwell Reed, Hugh Miller, Gretchen Franklin. D: Albert S. Rogell. DRA 76m.

Shadow of the Eagle 1932 ★★½ Russian envoy in 18th-century Venice is ordered to kidnap a princess and falls in love with her instead. A period piece adventure with nice work by swashbuckler Greene. C: John Wayne, Dorothy Gulliver, Walter Miller. D: Ford Beebe. ACT 226m. V

Shadow of the Law 1930 ★★★★ After being jailed for murder, Powell breaks out and changes his identity. However, his new life is threatened by the very woman he helped out during his original crime. An involved and complicated plot-twister, with some energetic performances by leads. C: William Powell, Marion Shilling, Paul Hurst. D: Louis Gasnier, Max Marcin. DRA 69m.

Shadow of the Thin Man 1941 ★★★★ Fourth film in the husband-and-wife detective series has Nick and Nora tracking down a racetrack murderer. Method-acting guru Stella Adler makes a rare film appearance in this witty, stylish film. C: William Powell, Myrna Loy, Barry Nelson, Donna Reed, Sam Levene. D: W.S. Van Dyke II. CRI 97m. V

Shadow of the Wolf 1993 Canadian ★★★ Young, proud Eskimos (Phillips and Tilly) struggle to survive the hostilities of both nature and the white man in the Arctic circa 1930. Careful and visually stunning melodrama with good work by Phillips. C: Lou Diamond Phillips, Toshiro Mifune, Jennifer Tilly, Donald Sutherland. D: Jacques Dorfman. ACT [PG-13] 108m. V

Shadow on the Sun 1988 *See* **Beryl Markham: A Shadow on the Sun**

Shadow on the Wall 1950 ★★½ When she witnesses the murder of her stepmother, a little girl goes into shock. Good, tight murder mystery with psychological overtones. C: Ann Sothern, Zachary Scott, Nancy Davis, Gigi Perreau, Barbara Billingsley, Kristine Miller. D: Patrick Jackson. DRA 84m.

Shadow on the Window, The 1957 ★★ Three young hooligans break into a house, murder a man, and hold his daughter (Garrett) hostage. Typical suspense story marked by occasional violence. C: Phil Carey, Betty Garrett, John Barrymore, Jr., Corey Allen, Jerry Mathers. D: William Asher. DRA 73m.

Shadow Play 1986 ★★½ A writer (Stone), suffering from prolonged grief for her dead boyfriend, is visited by his spirit—or is she delusional? Predictable, weak horror chiller. C: Dee Wallace Stone, Cloris Leachman, Ron Kuhlman, Barry Laws. D: Susan Shadburne. HOR 98m. V

Shadow Riders, The 1982 ★★★½ Two brothers on a desperate search for family members who were kidnapped by Confederate soldiers. Solid L'Amour oater, well played throughout. C: Tom Selleck, Sam Elliott, Ben Johnson, Katharine Ross. D: Andrew V. McLaglen. WST [PG] 96m. TVM V

Shadow, The 1937 ★★★ Crimefighting scientist adopts a new identity (the Shadow) in order to triumph over evil in general, and the notorious Black Tiger in particular. Good action serial that remains popular today. C: Rita Hayworth, Charles Quigley, Marc Lawrence, Marjorie Main. D: Charles C. Coleman, Jr. CRI 59m.

Shadow, The 1994 ★★★ "Who knows what evil lurks in the hearts of men?" Baldwin does, as Lamont Cranston, a wealthy playboy who is the title superhero. Snazzy, fun filming of old radio serial is helped immeasurably by Lone, as the villain. C: Alec Baldwin, John Lone, Penelope Ann Miller, Peter Boyle, Tim Curry, Ian McKellan, Jonathan Winters. D: Russell Mulcahy. CRI

Shadow World 1983 ★★½ Animated adventure about an ordinary boy who transforms himself into an intergalactic crime fighter. Okay action tale for kids. FAM/ACT 77m. V

Shadowlands 1993 British ★★★★ Literate tearjerker from Broadway play about the romance of writer/theologian C.S. Lewis (Hopkins) with outspoken American (Winger). Beautifully acted. C: Anthony Hopkins, Debra Winger. D: Richard Attenborough. DRA [PG] V

Shadows 1960 ★★★★½ Ray dates light-skinned African-American Goldoni, until he discovers she's black. Cassavetes' directorial debut is American independent cinema verité at its best. A must for the director's fans and anyone interested in stretching a bit. C: Hugh Hurd, Lelia Goldoni, Ben Carruthers, Anthony Ray, Rupert Crosse. D: John Cassavetes. DRA 87m.

Shadows and Fog 1992 ★★★ A milquetoast hides in an unnamed city from society crazies and serial killer. Allen's attempt to recall Kafka and silent German film expressionism doesnt quite come off, despite an all-star cast. C: Woody Allen, Kathy Bates, John Cusack, Mia Farrow, Jodie Foster, Fred Gwynne, Julie Kavner, Madonna, John Malkovich, Kate Nelligan, Donald Pleasence, Lily Tomlin. D: Woody Allen. COM [PG-13] 86m. V

Shadows in the Storm 1989 ★★★ In the woods, unemployed man falls for dangerous woman. Intriguing and well acted. C: Ned Beatty, Mia Sara. D: Terrell Tannen. ACT [R] 90m. V

Shadows of Forgotten Ancestors 1964 Russian ★★★½ Deep in the pre-Revolution Russian countryside, an old peasant faces the end of a life that's brought nothing but tragedy. Absorbing and powerful film from the Soviet Union. C: Ivan Mikolaichuk, Tatiana Bestaeva, Larisa Kadochnikova. D: Sergei Paradjanov. DRA [R] 99m. V

Shadowzone 1989 ★★★ Dreaming becomes the gateway to another dimension, as experiments in sleep prove fatal for band of researchers. No snoozing in this low-budget sci-fi thriller. C: David Beecroft, Louise Fletcher, Shawn Weatherly, James Hong, Miguel Nunez, Lu Leonard, Frederick Flynn. D: J.S. Cardone. SFI [R] 89m. v

Shaft 1971 ★★★★ Breakthrough action film with an African-American hero: a private eye who must track down a Harlem gangster's kidnapped daughter. Fast and furious, with a lot of style and a smashing score by Isaac Hayes. Followed by sequel two. C: Richard Roundtree, Moses Gunn, Charles Cioffi, Antonio Fargas. D: Gordon Parks. CRI [R] 98m. v

Shaft in Africa 1973 ★★★½ Detective Shaft is forced into service by an African leader who wants to end a modern-day slave trading ring. Last and least entertaining in the *Shaft* cycle, but it still packs a pretty good punch. C: Richard Roundtree, Frank Finlay, Vonetta McGee, Neda Arneric, Cy Grant, Jacques Marin. D: John Guillermin. ACT [R] 112m.

Shaft's Big Score! 1972 ★★★ Shaft returns in sequel that has gangsters on his trail, while he tries to find out who murdered his friend. Not as tight as the original but a memorable chase ending. C: Richard Roundtree, Moses Gunn, Drew Bundini Brown, Joseph Mascolo, Kathy Imrie, Wally Taylor, Joe Santos. D: Gordon Parks. CRI [R] 105m. v

Shag, The Movie 1989 ★★★★ When one of their own decides to get married, a group of Southern high school coeds decide to head for one last hurrah at Myrtle Beach. Cute period comedy, set in summer of 1963, with Cates providing a winning lead performance and getting good support from Fonda, Gish, and Hannah. C: Phoebe Cates, Bridget Fonda, Annabeth Gish, Page Hannah, Robert Rusler, Tyrone Power, Jr. D: Zelda Barron. COM [PG] 96m. v

Shaggy D.A., The 1976 ★★★½ Sequel to Disney's *The Shaggy Dog* features district attorney (Jones) falling victim to ancient curse that changes him into a sheep dog. Lots of star cameos mainly fill time in slapstick comedy for kiddies. C: Dean Jones, Suzanne Pleshette, Tim Conway, Keenan Wynn. D: Robert Stevenson. FAM/COM [G] 90m. v

Shaggy Dog, The 1959 ★★★ Youngster (Kirk) finds an ancient ring which magically transforms him into a sheep dog, much to the dismay of his befuddled parents (MacMurray, Hagen). Disney comedy suffers from slow script that can't match energetic slapstick. Two sequels, *The Shaggy D.A.* and *Return of the Shaggy Dog*. C: Fred MacMurray, Jean Hagen, Tommy Kirk, Annette Funicello, Tim Considine, Kevin Corcoran. D: Charles Barton. FAM/COM [G] 101m. v

Shaka Zulu 1968 ★★★½ British miniseries reedited into film about Zulu king Shaka and his battles with British colonialists in the 1800s. Engrossing historical drama. C: Robert Powell, Edward Fox, Fiona Fullerton, Trevor Howard, Christopher Lee. D: Willian C. Faure. DRA 300m. TVM v

Shake Hands with the Devil 1959 ★★★ A mild-mannered Dublin physician is, in reality, the violent leader of the IRA. A political muddle, but captures the turbulence of '20s Ireland—and quite convincing as entertainment. C: James Cagney, Don Murray, Dana Wynter, Glynis Johns, Michael Redgrave, Cyril Cusack, Sybil Thorndike, Richard Harris. D: Michael Anderson. ACT 110m. v

Shake, Rattle and Rock 1956 ★★★½ Square adults try to put the kibosh on hip youngsters and their way-out music, but rock 'n' roll prevails. Unintentionally campy humor makes this dated comedy fun, as do appearances by Fats Domino and Turner. C: Lisa Gaye, Sterling Holloway, Fats Domino, Joe Turner, Tommy Charles, Margaret Dumont. D: Edward L. Cahn. MUS 76m. v

Shakedown 1988 ★★ Undercover cop and thrill-seeking lawyer try to bust open police corruption ring. Pointless and violent. C: Peter Weller, Sam Elliott, Patricia Charbonneau, Blanche Baker, Antonio Fargas, Richard Brooks. D: James Glickenhaus. CRI [R] 96m. v

Shakedown, The 1959 British ★★★½ London blackmailer takes photos of prominent people in compromising situations. Fine performances give it strength. C: Terence Morgan, Hazel Court, Donald Pleasence, Bill Owen. D: John Lemont. DRA 92m.

Shakes the Clown 1992 ★★ Cult comedy about an alcoholic clown (Goldthwait) framed for murder. Plenty of strange bits and Brown deliriously cast against type as Goldthwait's mistress, but ultimately it's all just bizarre. C: Bobcat Goldthwait, Julie Brown, Paul Dooley. D: Bobcat Goldthwait. COM [R] 87m. v

Shakespeare Wallah 1965 Indian ★★★★ A young woman (Kendal) traveling through postcolonial India with a threadbare British Shakespeare company falls in love with an aristocratic Indian (Kapoor). Worthwhile, moving drama on a small scale. C: Shashi Kapoor, Felicity Kendal, Geoffrey Kendal, Laura Liddell. D: James Ivory. DRA 120m. v

Shakiest Gun in the West, The 1968 ★★★½ Nebbish dentist (Knotts) leaves his home in 1860s Philadelphia for life in Western frontier, where he inadvertently becomes both a gunfighter and lover. Amusing remake of *The Paleface* that both adults and kids will enjoy. C: Don Knotts, Barbara Rhoades, Jackie Coogan, Donald Barry. D: Alan Rafkin. COM 101m. v

Shaking the Tree 1991 ★★½ Lives and loves of four Chicago school chums as they teeter on the brink of adulthood. Will they make it into the world of grown-ups? Another old-friends-hanging-out movie, with low-key atmosphere. C: Arye Gross, Gale Hansen, Doug

Savant, Courteney Cox, Ron Dean, Nathan Davis. D: Duane Clark. DRA [PG-13] 97m. v
Shakma 1990 ★★★ Young players of a "Dungeons and Dragons"-style game are terrorized by a vicious experimental baboon. Admittedly unique variation on slasher standards has some strong shocks, but ultimately manages to be predictable and unbelieveable at the same time. C: Roddy McDowall, Christopher Atkins, Amanda Wyss, Ari Meyers, Robb Morris. D: Hugh Parks, Tom Logan. HOR [R] 101m. v
Shalako 1968 British ★★★½ In 1880 New Mexico, an elite European hunting expedition runs into a band of hostile Apaches. From a Loais L'Amour novel. C: Sean Connery, Brigitte Bardot, Stephen Boyd, Jack Hawkins. D: Edward Dmytryk. WST [PG] 113m. v
Shall We Dance 1937 ★★★★ Ballet dancer (Astaire) and musical comedy star (Rogers) pretend they're married. Slim plot with grand Gershwin songs ("They All Laughed," "They Can't Take That away From Me," "Let's Call the Whole Thing Off") makes good vehicle for star team. C: Fred Astaire, Ginger Rogers, Eric Blore, Edward Everett Horton, Ann Shoemaker, Jerome Cowan, Harriet Hoctor. D: Mark Sandrich. MUS 116m. v
Shallow Grave 1987 ★★ Killer pursues four college vacationers after they witenss his murderous deed. C: Tony March, Lisa Stahl, Tom Law. D: Richard Styles. HOR [R] 90m. v
Shaman, The 1987 ★★ Fiendish shaman shops for successor. C: Michael Conforti, Elvind Harum, James Farkas. D: Michael Yakub. HOR [R] 88m. v
Shame 1968 Swedish ★★★★★ Heartrending, erudite examination of the toll exacted by war on humanity. Husband and wife concert muscians von Sydow and Ullmann flee to a secluded island hoping to avoid the horrors of a civil war, but ultimately, they cannot escape. A pessimistic, difficult work and one of Bergman's triumphs, with powerful cinematography enhancing the awesome dramatic achievement. C: Liv Ullmann, Max von Sydow, Gunnar Bjornstrand, Sigge Furst, Birgitta Valberg, Hans Alfredson. D: Ingmar Bergman. DRA 103m. v
Shame 1988 Australian ★★★ Furness, a one-woman wrecking crew (and lawyer!) on a motorcycle arrives in an Australian Outback town where women are mistreated, to put it mildly. Feminist/biker angle is the freshest aspect of this *Mad Max* wannabe. C: Deborra-Lee Furness, Tony Barry, Simone Buchanan, Gillian Jones. D: Steve Jodrell. ACT [R] 95m. v
Shame 1992 ★★★ Female lawyer (Donohoe) on a motorcycle goes on the rampage in a small town that has been mistreating women. Effective remake of the 1988 Australian film. C: Amanda Donohoe, Dean Stockwell, Dan Gauthier, Fairuza Balk. D: Dan Lerner. ACT 100m. TVM v
Shameless Old Lady, The 1965 French ★★★★ Poor old woman lives alone, in squalor, until things suddenly change. Wonderful character study and outstanding work by the cast, Sylvie in particular. C: Sylvie, Malka Ribovska, Victor Lanoux, Etienne Bierry. D: Rene Allio. DRA 94m.
Shaming, The 1979 *See* **Good Luck, Miss Wyckoff**
Shampoo 1975 ★★★★ Observant comedy/-satire of hairdresser (Beatty) and his many romantic entanglements captures period with mix of cynicism, warmth, wit. Marvelous ensemble cast, with Grant winning Supporting Actress Oscar. C: Warren Beatty, Julie Christie, Goldie Hawn, Lee Grant, Jack Warden, Carrie Fisher. D: Hal Ashby. COM [R] 112m. v
Shamrock Hill 1949 ★★★½ Ryan uses a beloved hilltop to share her tales of leprechauns to local children. This tradition is threatened when real estate baron Litel buys up the property to build himself a new TV station. Cute little musical that youngsters will enjoy. C: Peggy Ryan, Ray McDonald, John Litel. D: Arthur Dreifuss. MUS 70m.
Shamus 1973 ★★★½ P.I. Reynolds finds himself embroiled in a '40s-style mystery plot involving missing gems, arms dealing, and murder. So fast-paced and action-packed that the silliness is nearly unnoticeable. Good mindless entertainment. C: Burt Reynolds, Dyan Cannon, Giorgio Tozzi, John Ryan. D: Buzz Kulik. CRI [PG] 106m. v
Shane 1953 ★★★★★ Homesteader family is intimidated by a mob of cattlemen. To the rescue comes a mysterious, capable, stranger. A simply outstanding, stately Western that like all classics stays as sharp as ever over the years. C: Alan Ladd, Jean Arthur, Van Heflin, Jack Palance, Brandon de Wilde, Ben Johnson, Edgar Buchanan, Emile Meyer, Elisha Cook, Jr. D: George Stevens. WST 117m. v
Shanghai 1935 ★★★ The romance of an American tourist (Young) and a Chinese-Russian businessman (Boyer) is doomed because of "racial differences." Melancholy drama, strong stuff in its day. C: Charles Boyer, Loretta Young, Warner Oland. D: James Flood. DRA 75m.
Shanghai Cobra, The 1945 ★★½ Chan (Toler) investigates a series of suspicious deaths by snake bite. Lesser entry in the *Charlie Chan* series lacks suspense. C: Sidney Toler, Benson Fong, Mantan Moreland, Walter Fenner, James Cardwell, Joan Barclay, James Flavin, Addison Richards. D: Phil Karlson. CRI 64m.
Shanghai Express 1932 ★★★★★ Dietrich is notorious prostitute Shanghai Lily in wonderfully strange von Sternberg drama with a bevy of passengers, including Lily's ex-lover, traveling on the Shanghai Express through a China beset by civil unrest. Deliciously decadent romance. Remade as *Peking Express*. C: Marlene Dietrich, Anna May Wong, Warner Oland, Clive Brook, Eugene Pallette, Louise

Closser Hale. D: Josef von Sternberg. DRA 82m. v

Shanghai Gesture, The 1941 ★★★★ Weird later von Sternberg offering has a Chinese gambling-parlor owner (Munson) confronting the Brit (Huston) who fathered her daughter years before and is now meddling in her business. Brooding and sardonic. C: Gene Tierney, Walter Huston, Victor Mature, Ona Munson, Albert Bassermann, Eric Blore, Mike Mazurki. D: Josef von Sternberg. DRA 106m. v

Shanghai Surprise 1986 ★ When opium bound for hospitalized patients in 1937 is stolen, a missionary (Madonna!) hires a rogue (Penn) to find it. If you can buy Madonna as a missionary, you might like this movie. C: Sean Penn, Madonna, Paul Freeman. D: Jim Goddard. DRA [PG-13] 93m. v

Shaolin Devil: Shaolin Angel 1977 ★★★ When several great swordsmen get killed, a search begins for the devil agent responsible for the foul deeds. Twisty plot sustains the kung fu action. C: Chen Sing. ACT 90m. v

Shaolin Drunk Fighter ★★½ Kung fu fighters avenge the murder of the master of the Shaolin temple. Plenty of action. ACT v

Shaolin Executioner 1982 ★★½ The Manchus and the Shaolin warriors do battle over the powerful Shaolin temple. Gore and violence and lots of kung fu action. C: Chen Kuan-Tai, Lo Lieh. D: Liu Chia-Liang. ACT 104m. v

Shaolin Temple Strikes Back 1972 ★★½ Defenders of the Shaolin temple fight barbarian invaders. Violent kung fu revenge tale. C: Chan Chien Chang, Sho Kosugi. D: Joseph Kuo. ACT 90m. v

Shaolin Traitor 1982 ★★½ Tale of traitorous intrigue experiments with the number of ways a man can die. Grisly martial arts film with impressive martial arts displays. C: Carter Wong, Ling-Feng Shangkuan. ACT 90m. v

Shaolin vs. Lama 1984 ★★ The Shaolin masters run up against Tibetan monks in this otherwise standard kung fu film. D: Lee Tso Nan. ACT 90m. v

Share Out, The 1962 British ★★ Scotland Yard investigators go out full force to destroy a notorious syndicate of blackmailers. Good action and nimble police work. C: Bernard Lee, Patrick Cargill, Alexander Knox, Moira Redmond. D: Gerard Glaister. ACT 62m.

Shark! 1969 ★★★ American gunrunner in the Sudan meets up with unsavory divers seeking gold in shark-infested waters. Gobs of gore mark this average adventure story. Fuller disowned final version. (a.k.a. *Maneater*) C: Burt Reynolds, Barry Sullivan, Arthur Kennedy, Silvia Pinal. D: Samuel Fuller. ACT [PG] 93m. v

Shark Hunter, The 1984 ★★★ Man must get rid of gangsters before obtaining riches hidden in plane wreck. C: Franco Nero, Mike Forrest, Jorge Luke. D: Enzo Castellari. ACT 92m. v

Shark River 1953 ★★★ Civil War veteran tries to smuggle accused comrade to safety. Gripping cinematography. C: Steve Cochran, Carole Mathews, Warren Stevens. D: John Rawlins. ACT 80m. v

Sharks' Treasure 1975 ★★½ Rival divers vie for sunken booty in shark infested waters. Routine adventure saga with that special Wilde touch. Best for shark lovers. C: Cornel Wilde, Yaphet Kotto, John Neilson, Cliff Osmond. D: Cornel Wilde. DRA [PG] 96m. v

Sharky's Machine 1981 ★★★½ A vice cop (Reynolds) gets involved with an expensive prostitute (Ward) while chasing her boss. Overlong, with unconvincing romance. Otherwise, this is one of Burt's better action efforts, though very violent. Based on a novel by William Diehl. C: Burt Reynolds, Rachel Ward, Vittorio Gassman, Brian Keith, Charles Durning, Bernie Casey, Henry Silva. D: Burt Reynolds. CRI [R] 122m. v

Sharma and Beyond 1984 ★★ Ambitious fantasy writer first rejoices then squirms after discovering lover is idol's daughter. C: Suzanne Burden, Robert Urquhart, Michael Maloney. D: Brian Gilbert. DRA 85m. v

Shatter *See* **Call Him Mr. Shatter**

Shattered 1991 ★★★½ Weird thriller of wealthy husband Berenger, injured in a car accident and suffering from amnesia, who begins to suspect his wife has tried to kill him. Updated film noir has bizarre premise and psychological ambitions that aren't always realized. C: Tom Berenger, Bob Hoskins, Greta Scacchi, Corbin Bernsen, Joanne Whalley-Kilmer. D: Wolfgang Petersen. DRA 103m. v

Shawshank Redemption, The 1994 ★★★★ Maine banker (Robbins), wrongfully convicted for murder, is sent to Shawshank State Prison, where he encounters fellow inmate Freeman. Terrific performance from two leads and a pungent script make this superior drama. Based on a novella by Stephen King, in a change-of-pace. C: Tim Robbins, Morgan Freeman, James Whitmore, Bob Gunton. D: Frank Darabont. DRA [R] 142m. v

She 1935 ★★★ Cambridge professors journey to a lost Antarctic city where, as legend has it, the queen (Gahagan) will not die until she finds true love. Fascinating, well-done fantasy. C: Lansing C. Holden, Helen Gahagan, Randolph Scott, Helen Mack, Nigel Bruce, Gustav von Seyffertitz. D: Irving Pichel, Lansing C. Holden. SFI 95m.

She 1965 British ★★★½ Often filmed tale of H. Rider Haggard's Eternal Woman (Andress), her quest for peace, and the search for her reincarnated lover. Mindless fun. Sequel: *The Vengeance of She.* C: Ursula Andress, John Richardson, Peter Cushing, Christopher Lee. D: Robert Day. SFI 106m.

She 1983 ★ Yet another remake of Haggard's classic fantasy tale of an immortal queen (Bergman), dressed up in *Road War-*

rior garb and completely unrecognizable. C: Sandahl Bergman, David Goss, Quin Kessler, Harrison Muller. D: Avi Nesher. SFI 90m. V

She and He 1967 Italian ★★★ Poet Harvey (who also produced this) falls in love with the spirited Koscina. Their personalities continually clash, for he is more reserved and she sparks with sexual energy. Strictly soap opera material in unimaginative love story. C: Laurence Harvey, Sylva Koscina. D: Mauro Bologini. DRA 110m.

She-Beast, The 1966 Italian ★★½ A sultry English tourist (Steele) discovers she harbors within her the soul of a long-dead Transylvanian witch, then behaves bizarrely. Fun, in that dreadful sort of way, and sure to please Steele fans. C: Barbara Steele, John Karlsen, Ian Ogilvy, Jay Riley. D: Michael Reeves. HOR [PG] 74m. V

She Came to the Valley 1977 ★★½ In Texas, a hardy pioneer woman gets emmeshed in political struggle during Spanish-American War. C: Ronee Blakley, Dean Stockwell, Scott Glenn. D: Albert Band. WST [PG] 90m. V

She Couldn't Say No 1952 ★★ An ultrarich oil baroness (Simmons) returns to her Arkansas birthplace and doles out loads of cash to its citizenry, upsetting the town's balance. Goofy premise, but a flat movie. Simmons tries though. (a.k.a. *Beautiful but Dangerous*) C: Robert Mitchum, Jean Simmons, Arthur Hunnicutt, Wallace Ford. D: Lloyd Bacon. DRA 89m. V

She Couldn't Take It 1935 ★★★½ Deceased millionaire's family is outraged when an ex-con (Raft) is appointed trustee of the estate. Unusual mix of screwball comedy and gangster movie works well, especially when Bennett and Raft are squabbling. (a.k.a. *Woman Tamer*) C: Constance Bennett, George Raft, Billie Burke, Walter Connolly, Lloyd Nolan. D: Tay Garnett. COM 75m.

She Creature, The 1957 ★★ When a low-rent Dr. Mesmer coaxes an evil entity out of his lovely hypnotized assistant, all heck breaks loose. Pretty terrible, with some horrendous acting, but master makeup man Paul Blaisdell's full-figured creation is quite striking. C: Marla English, Tom Conway, Chester Morris, Ron Randell, Frieda Inescort, Cathy Downs, El Brendel, Jack Mulhall, Frank Jenks. D: Edward L. Cahn. HOR 77m.

She Dances Alone 1981 U.S. ★★★ Young film director (Cort) makes a documentary film on the life of the great ballet dancer Nijinsky. A unique film; Nijinsky's daughter, Kyra, is riveting. C: Kyra Nijinsky, Bud Cort, Patrick Dupond, Sauncey Le Sueur, Max von Sydow. D: Robert Dornhelm. DRA 87m.

She Demons 1958 ★★ An insane Nazi doctor hides on an island and conducts disfiguring experiments on the local women until he's interrupted by a meddlesome threesome. Cheap and boring, the '50s way. C: Irish McCalla, Tod Griffin, Victor Sen Yung, Rudolph Anders, Gene Roth. D: Richard B. Cunha. HOR 68m. V

She-Devil 1990 ★★★ Disappointing comedy from Fay Weldon's novel with slovenly housewife (Barr) enjoying revenge on wayward husband and mistress (Streep). Meryl is marvelous as selfish romance novelist. C: Meryl Streep, Roseanne Barr, Ed Begley, Jr., Linda Hunt, Sylvia Miles, Bryan Larkin. D: Susan Seidelman. COM [PG] 99m. V

She Didn't Say No! 1962 British ★★★ Young Irish widow has five illegitimate children, all by different fathers. Rich and bawdy, and broadly entertaining. C: Eileen Herlie, Perlita Nielson, Wilfred Downing, Joan O'Hara. D: Cyril Frankel. COM 96m.

She Done Him Wrong 1933 ★★★★½ Gay '90s saloon keeper goes sweet on the undercover cop who's trying to get the goods on her. Fun-filled, zesty classic with superb work by West and Grant. This is the one in which Mae invites Cary to "come up and see me sometime." C: Mae West, Cary Grant, Gilbert Roland, Noah Beery, Owen Moore. D: Lowell Sherman. COM 65m. V

She Freaks 1967 ★★ Circus oddities punish woman for betraying their employer. C: Claire Brennan, Lee Raymond, Lynn Courtney. D: Byron Mabe. HOR 87m. V

She Goes to War 1929 ★★★ Determined young woman plays an active part in WWI. Highly entertaining, and a compelling piece of Hollywood history. Partial sound. C: Eleanor Boardman, John Holland, Edmund Burns. D: Henry King. COM 87m.

She Got What She Asked For 1964 *See* **Yesterday, Today and Tomorrow**

She Loves Me Not 1934 ★★★★ After witnessing a Mob murder, a young female nightclub entertainer (Hopkins) hides out at a men's college. A lot of good nonsense with a lot of good music—and a superbly talented cast. Based on the Howard Lindsay play. Remade as *True to the Army* and *How to Be Very, Very Popular.* C: Bing Crosby, Miriam Hopkins, Kitty Carlisle, Lynne Overman, Henry Stephenson, George Barbier, Warren Hymer. D: Elliott Nugent. MUS 83m.

She Married Her Boss 1935 ★★½ Secretary (Colbert) marries her boss (Douglas) and finds her life different in a variety of ways. Excellent cast makes the most out of a feeble script. C: Claudette Colbert, Melvyn Douglas, Edith Fellows, Michael Bartlett, Raymond Walburn, Jean Dixon. D: Gregory La Cava. COM 90m.

She Waits 1971 ★★ Woman marries widower (McCallum) and they move into an old house, where she is possessed by the ghost of his first wife. Pedestrian story is beneath the talents of director and cast; result is mediocre. Made for TV. C: Patty Duke, David McCallum, Lew Ayres, Beulah Bondi, Dorothy McGuire. D: Delbert Mann. HOR 74m. TVM V

She Wolf 1987 ★★ Beautiful woman turns into vicious werewolf under the full moon. C: Anne Borel, Frank Stafford. HOR 80m. V
She Wore a Yellow Ribbon 1949 ★★★★★ About to leave active service, an aging career cavalryman refuses to leave his men when Indians mass for attack. Vintage Ford Western with a layered performance from Wayne. Oscar for Photography. Second of Ford's Cavalry trilogy. C: John Wayne, Joanne Dru, John Agar, Ben Johnson, Harry Carey, Jr., Victor McLaglen, Mildred Natwick, George O'Brien. D: John Ford. WST 103m. V
Sheba Baby 1974 ★★½ Female private eye rights the wrongs leveled against her rich father's loan company. Poorly written, directed actioner has less sex and violence than usual for Grier fans. C: Pam Grier, Austin Stoker, Rudy Challenger, Dick Merrifield. D: William Girdler. ACT [PG] 90m. V
Sheena 1984 ★★ Orphaned British child is raised by an African tribe to be their beautiful protectress. Campy jungle adventure, based on a comic strip. Despite the source, it's not for kids. C: Tanya Roberts, Ted Wass, Donovan Scott, Elizabeth of Toro. D: John Guillermin. ACT [PG] 117m. V
Sheep Has Five Legs, The 1954 French ★★★★ An ancient vintner is visited by his quintuplet sons. Mainly a vehicle for French comedian Fernandel, who manages to pull off the six roles quite well. Its off-the-wall humor translates well. Try it on a Francophobe. C: Fernandel, Françoise Arnoul. D: Henri Verneuil. COM 92m. V
Sheepman, The 1958 ★★★★ Two sheepherders (Ford and Nielsen) fight it out constantly—over their flocks and over the woman they both love (MacLaine). Nicely done comic Western. C: Glenn Ford, Shirley MacLaine, Leslie Nielsen, Mickey Shaughnessy, Edgar Buchanan. D: George Marshall. WST 85m.
Sheer Madness 1984 German ★★★★ Beautifully filmed, intelligent exploration of relationship between two women, one an academic and the other despondent artist. C: Hanna Schygulla, Angelea Winkler. D: Margarethe Von Trotta. DRA 105m. V
Sheik, The 1921 ★★★½ A sophisticated British woman (Ayres) falls madly in love with an Arab sheik (Valentino). The film that launched Valentino into the stratosphere of stardom is dated but still enjoyable, if only to witness the star's appeal. Sequel: *Son of the Sheik.* C: Rudolph Valentino, Agnes Ayres, Adolphe Menjou, Walter Long, Lucien Littlefield, George Waggner. D: George Melford. DRA 79m. V
Sheila Levine Is Dead and Living in New York 1975 ★★★ Jewish single woman (Berlin) contemplates suicide when her boyfriend jilts her. Misfire adaptation of Gail Parent's novel. C: Jeannie Berlin, Roy Scheider, Rebecca Dianna Smith. D: Sidney J. Furie. COM [PG] 113m.
She'll Be Wearing Pink Pajamas 1984 British ★★★½ Eight women forge strong bonds as they persevere through arduous survival course. Moving performances. C: Julie Walters, Anthony Higgins, Jane Evers. D: John Goldschmidt. COM 90m. V
Shell Seekers, The 1993 ★★★★ Sturdy adaptation of Rosamunde Pilcher's novel; Lansbury is moving as recently widowed Englishwoman widow coming to terms with loneliness and trouble with her grown children. C: Angela Lansbury, Christopher Bowen, Michael Gough, Patricia Hodge, Irene Worth, Anna Carteret. D: Waris Hussein. DRA [PG] 94m. TVM V
Sheltering Sky, The 1990 ★★★½ Adaptation of Paul Bowles' novel has American couple Winger and Malkovich and companion Scott drifting through '40s Africa seeking adventure and passion. Brilliant desert photography but weak development of three central characters. Bowles' complicated work is brought to the screen only with difficulty. C: Debra Winger, John Malkovich, Campbell Scott, Jill Bennett, Timothy Spall, Eric Vu-An. D: Bernardo Bertolucci. DRA [R] 139m. V
Shenandoah 1965 ★★★★ The tale of a Virginia family and how their reluctant involvement in the Civil War causes heartbreak in their lives. Very sturdy and earnest. The performances, in particular Stewart's, are quite good. Later became musical. C: James Stewart, Doug McClure, Glenn Corbett, Patrick Wayne. D: Andrew V. McLaglen. WST 105m. V
Shenanigans 1958 *See* **Captain's Table, The**
Shepherd Girl, The 1965 Hong Kong ★★★ Feng is a young woman whose father is deeply in debt. A wealthy interloper offers to pay off these accounts if Feng will marry him, though an impoverished suitor risks his life to earn the money. Lackluster Hong Kong soaper. C: Julie Yeh Feng, Kwan Shan, Chu Mu. D: Lo Chen. DRA 105m.
Shepherd of the Hills 1941 ★★★★ Ozark mountain man (Wayne) vows to kill the father who deserted him, then lives to regret it. Stirring, well-acted drama from Harold Bell Wright short story, with a fine performance from the Duke that helped establish him as a front-rank star. His first color film. C: John Wayne, Betty Field, Harry Carey, Beulah Bondi, Marjorie Main. D: Henry Hathaway. WST 98m.
Shepherd of the Hills, The 1964 ★★★ Remake of the 1941 film. A nice retelling of a wonderful story; but the earlier version is far richer in content and in cast. (a.k.a. *Thunder Mountain*) C: Richard Arlen, James W. Middleton, Sherry Lynn, James Collie. D: Ben Parker. DRA 110m.
Shepherd of the Ozarks 1942 ★★★ Down-home fun with Hollywood's Weaver family involves a pilot who bails out near the clan's mountain home. After a trip to the big town,

the Weavers mistakenly believe a battle re-creation is the real thing. Dated hayseed humor. C: Leon Weaver, Frank Weaver, June Weaver, Marilyn Hare, Frank Albertson. D: Frank McDonald. COM 70m.

Sheriff of Cimarron 1945 ★★★½ After wrongly being arrested, gunslinging B-Western hero Sunset Carson busts out of jail and meets up with the outlaw gang that set him up. Plenty of action sequences fill out the standard plot. C: Sunset Carson, Linda Stirling, Jack Ingram, Riley Hill. D: Yakima Canutt. WST 56m.

Sheriff of Fractured Jaw, The 1959 British ★★★½ A proper Englishman (More) becomes the unlikely sheriff of a Wild West town. Entertaining fish-out-of-water tale. C: Kenneth More, Jayne Mansfield, Henry Hull, Bruce Cabot, Robert Morley. D: Raoul Walsh. COM 103m. V

Sherlock Holmes It has been said that Arthur Conan Doyle's Victorian sleuth is the most filmed fictional character of all time; some 20 different actors have played Holmes on TV and film. But to many the portrait of Holmes and Watson that endures is that of Basil Rathbone and Nigel Bruce in the 14 films made at Fox and Universal between 1939 and 1946. As long as the films stuck close to the source, as in *The Adventures of Sherlock Holmes* and *The Hound of the Baskervilles*, they were superior entertainment. But as they drifted away from the original, they relied more and more on the not inconsiderable charms of Rathbone's sonorous line readings and Bruce's bumbling befuddlement. Serious Holmesians will also want to see the Granada TV series with Jeremy Brett, perhaps the most faithful adaptations yet, which are becoming available on tape in the U.S.

The Hound of the Baskervilles (1939)
The Adventures of Sherlock Holmes (1939)
Sherlock Holmes and the Voice of Terror (1942)
Sherlock Holmes and the Secret Weapon (1942)
Sherlock Holmes in Washington (1943)
Sherlock Holmes faces Death (1943)
Sherlock Holmes and the Spider Woman (1944)
The Scarlet Claw (1944)
The Pearl of Death (1944)
The House of Fear (1945)
The Woman in Green (1945)
Pursuit to Algiers (1945)
Terror by Night (1946)
Dressed to Kill (1946)

Sherlock Holmes, Adventures of, The ("Copper Beeches") 1985 British ★★★★ A young governess is alarmed when her employee makes her cut off her lovely hair. Then, a creepy message brings Holmes on the case. Offbeat and eerie fun. C: Jeremy Brett, David Burke. CRI 55m. V

Sherlock Holmes, Adventures of, The ("Final Problem") 1986 ★★★★ The *Mona Lisa* is stolen from the Louvre in Paris. Holmes is soon on the case and matching wits with the brilliant "Napoleon of Crime." Intriguing change of pace for the master sleuth. C: Jeremy Brett, David Burke. D: Ken Grieve. CRI 55m. TVM V

Sherlock Holmes, Adventures of, The ("Greek Interpreter") 1985 ★★★★ Mycroft hires brother Sherlock when he is baffled by a strange request from a mysterious Greek interpreter. Low-key mystery is not without its rewards. C: Jeremy Brett, David Burke. D: Alan Grint. CRI 55m. TVM V

Sherlock Holmes, Adventures of, The ("Red Headed League") 1986 ★★★★½ Holmes is alerted to a strange ad that calls for redheaded men to join a private league. When the league is dissolved under mysterious circumstances, Holmes looks into the murky business. Offbeat story helps make this one of the better entries in the new series. C: Jeremy Brett, David Burke. D: Paul Annett. CRI 55m. TVM V

Sherlock Holmes, Adventures of, The ("Resident Patient") 1986 ★★★★ When a Russian father and son disappear after consultation with a doctor, all points lead toward the doctor's nervous benefactor. Enter Holmes. Solid performances boost slight story. C: Jeremy Brett, David Burke. D: John Bruce. CRI 55m. TVM V

Sherlock Holmes and the Prince of Crime 1990 *See* **Hands of a Murderer**

Sherlock Holmes and the Secret Weapon 1942 *See* **Secret Weapon**

Sherlock Holmes and the Spider Woman 1944 ★★★½ Has Holmes met his match in the infamous Sondergaard? One of the better entries in the Rathbone *Holmes* series, in which victims are driven to suicide after being bitten by spiders. C: Basil Rathbone, Nigel Bruce, Gale Sondergaard, Dennis Hoey, Mary Gordon, Arthur Hohl, Alec Craig. D: Roy William Neill. CRI 62m. V

Sherlock Holmes and the Voice of Terror 1942 ★★★½ Holmes (Rathbone) and Watson (Bruce) try to uncover the identity of a radio broadcaster spreading Nazi propaganda across England. The first of the Universal series transports the 19th-century detective to the WWII era, but works otherwise. C: Basil Rathbone, Nigel Bruce, Evelyn Ankers, Reginald Denny, Thomas Gomez, Henry Daniell. D: John Rawlins. CRI 65m. V

Sherlock Holmes—Baskerville Curse,The ★★ Sherlock Holmes and loyal assistant Dr. Watson are on a murderer's trail in cheesy adaptation of A. Conan Doyle's *The Hound of Baskervilles*. Low-grade animation and gross simplification of story make a weak retelling of classic mystery. FAM/CRI v

Sherlock Holmes, Casebook of, The ("Creeping Man") ★★★★ The daughter of a professor is shocked to see a dark, hunchbacked figure at her window. Holmes soon finds the mysterious figure to be a different kind of nightmare. Intriguing, often eerie mystery. C: Jeremy Brett, Edward Hardwicke. CRI 50m. v

Sherlock Holmes, Casebook of, The ("Disappearance of") ★★★★½ A beautiful woman has seemingly disappeared from the face of the earth. Holmes is baffled in what is one of his most frustrating cases. Quiet, probing look at the dark side of the master sleuth. CRI v

Sherlock Holmes, Casebook of, The ("Illustious Client") ★★★★ Holmes takes his own life into his hands when he locks horns with a diabolical Austrian baron and the man's strange young fiancée. Unusual look at the sleuth succeeds admirably. CRI v

Sherlock Holmes, Casebook of, The ("Problem of Thor Bridge") ★★★★ A governess is charged with murdering her employer's wife. When he disappears, under mysterious circumstances, Holmes is on the case. Twisty mystery makes for good fun. CRI v

Sherlock Holmes, Casebook of, The ("Shoscombe Old Place") ★★★★½ Facing financial ruin, an English lord trains his prize horse for a run in the championship stakes. A body and the return of an enemy ruins his plans. Holmes takes on one of his most sordid cases. Dicey and enertaining. CRI v

Sherlock Holmes: Dancing Men, The 1985 ★★★½ Early installment in the Sherlock Holmes series with Jeremy Brett has Holmes involved with breaking a secret code. (a.k.a. *The Mystery of the Dancing Men*) C: Jeremy Brett, David Burke. D: John Bruce. CRI 52m. v

Sherlock Holmes Faces Death 1943 ★★★★½ Fourth in Universal's *Sherlock Holmes* series, based on Doyle's "The Musgrave Ritual." Great eerie atmosphere and tightly knit story line of string of murders at a military veterans' home—sure to satisfy. C: Basil Rathbone, Nigel Bruce, Hillary Brooke, Milburn Stone. D: Roy William Neill. CRI 68m. v

Sherlock Holmes in Washington 1943 ★★★½ This WWII picture pits Holmes against Nazi spies searching for crucial microfilm. Some subtle laughs thanks to Dr. Watson, and Rathbone is masterful as always. C: Basil Rathbone, Nigel Bruce, Marjorie Lord, Henry Daniell, George Zucco. D: Roy William Neill. CRI 71m. v

Sherlock Holmes, Return of, The ("Abbey Grange") 1990 ★★★★ When a mean English lord is murdered, all clues point to his beautiful Australian wife, but Holmes isn't so sure she's the culprit. Intriguing stew of twists and turns. C: Jeremy Brett, David Burke. D: Paul Annett. CRI 55m. v

Sherlock Holmes, Return of, The ("Bruce Partington") ★★★★ When a top secret submarine disappears, threatening to cause an international crisis, Mycroft Holmes brings brother Sherlock on the case. Tense, intriguing caper. CRI v

Sherlock Holmes, Return of, The ("Empty House") 1990 ★★★★ Holmes locks horns with the evil Colonel Moran in this case of murder. Holmes makes unexplained reappearance after being thought dead. Good, sinister fun. C: Jeremy Brett, David Burke. D: John Bruce. CRI 55m. v

Sherlock Holmes, Return of, The ("Man With the Twisted Lip") 1990 ★★★★ When Holmes goes undercover to look for an aristocrat who has disappeared he finds the man is living the life of a beggar. Strange tale of deceit. C: Jeremy Brett, David Burke. D: David Carson. CRI 55m. v

Sherlock Holmes, Return of, The ("Musgrave Ritual") 1990 ★★★★½ Aristocrat hires Holmes to get to the bottom of the strange happenings at his country manor. Spooky fun abounds in one of the finer Holmes stories. C: Jeremy Brett, David Burke. D: Ken Grieve. CRI 55m. v

Sherlock Holmes, Return of, The ("Priory School") ★★★★ The 10-year-old son of a wealthy duke has disappeared from a select public school. Holmes looks into this peculiar "kidnapping." Intriguing mystery is full of twists and turns. C: Jeremy Brett, David Burke. D: Alan Grint. CRI 55m. v

Sherlock Holmes, Return of, The ("Second Stain") 1991 ★★★★ A missing letter turns up and throws light on a mysterious death in the family, but Holmes has his doubts about the letter's validity. Classic tale gets fine treatment. C: Jeremy Brett, David Burke. D: Derek Marlowe. CRI 55m. v

Sherlock Holmes, Return of, The ("Six Napoleons") 1991 ★★★★ Napoleonic busts are found broken at the scenes of several recent break-ins. A even stranger robbery brings Holmes on the case. Odd, entertaining mystery. C: Jeremy Brett, David Burke. D: Paul Annett. CRI 55m. v

Sherlock Holmes, Return of, The ("Wisteria Lodge") ★★★★ After being alerted to the strange events at a run-down vacationing lodge, Holmes pays a visit only to find the owner has been murdered. Pleasingly wry. CRI v

Sherlock Holmes: Scandal in Bohemia 1985 ★★★½ Brett stars as the brilliant detective, adopting multiple ingenious disguises in this above-average entry in the British *Sherlock Holmes* series. C: Jeremy Brett, David Burke. D: Paul Annett. CRI 52m. v

Sherlock Holmes' Smarter Brother 1978 *See* **Adventure of Sherlock Holmes' Smarter Brother, The**

Sherlock Holmes, Solitary Cyclist, The 1985 ★★★★ Holmes becomes a tracker to trace the clues in a boarding school murder. Fine countryside setting and eerie atmosphere make up for rather slight story. C: Jeremy Brett, David Burke. D: John Bruce. CRI 52m. V

Sherlock Holmes: The Speckled Band 1985 ★★★★ Holmes is alerted to a mysterious death in a Surrey mansion. There he comes face-to-face with the "speckled band," a deadly snake. Dry, amusing entry. C: Jeremy Brett, David Burke. D: David Carson. CRI 52m. V

Sherlock, Jr. 1924 ★★★★★ Incomparable silent comedy, perhaps Keaton's best. Buster's a projectionist who is so fascinated with the mystery movie on the screen that he jumps right into it! Movie's influence can be seen in such films as *Purple Rose of Cairo* and *Pennies from Heaven*. C: Buster Keaton, Kathryn McGuire, Ward Crane. D: Buster Keaton. COM 45m.

Sherman's March 1986 ★★★★½ One-of-a-kind documentary features director McElwee, equipped with camera on shoulder, searching for romance as he retraces path of Sherman's march through South. Sweetly naive and droll, each of McElwee's loves puts her unique stamp on proceedings. Followed by *Time Indefinite*. D: Ross McElwee. DOC 155m. V

She's Back 1989 ★★★ Murdered woman returns from beyond and forces husband to help find criminals who did her in. Witty performances. C: Carrie Fisher, Robert Joy, Matthew Cowles. D: Tim Kincaid. COM [R] 89m. V

She's Back on Broadway 1953 ★★★ Okay tuner about a fading movie star (Mayo), making a comeback on Broadway in a show directed by her ex-lover (Cochran). C: Virginia Mayo, Steve Cochran, Gene Nelson, Patrice Wymore. D: Gordon Douglas. MUS 95m.

She's Dressed to Kill 1979 ★★½ The new line of a fashion designer (Parker) is being displayed by the most fabulous models, who are also being murdered one at a time. Average (but good-looking) thriller. (a.k.a. *Someone's Killing the World's Greatest Models*) C: Eleanor Parker, Jessica Walter, John Rubinstein, Corinne Calvet. D: Gus Trikonis. CRI 98m. TVM V

She's Gotta Have It 1986 ★★★★ Spike Lee's debut feature revolves around independent woman Johns, with three very different boyfriends trying to win her affections. Lee's invigorating style and casts' winning performances make great entertainment. A family affair: Lee's dad did music, sister costarred, and brother did opening photo montage. C: Tracy Camilla Johns, Tommy Hicks, John Canada Terrell, Spike Lee, Raye Dowell, Bill Lee. D: Spike Lee. COM [R] 84m. V

She's Having a Baby 1988 ★★★½ Bacon narrates a husband's unsure adventures in marriage and impending fatherhood as tale of his life with McGovern unfolds over course of film. Domestic comedy propelled by likable performances. C: Kevin Bacon, Elizabeth McGovern, Alec Baldwin, William Windom, Paul Gleason. D: John Hughes. COM [PG-13] 106m. V

She's in the Army 1942 ★★★½ WWII homefront film portrays the lives and loves within a group of female ambulance drivers. Borg is a former singer who falls for captain (Talbot) while undergoing her training from drill instructor Gleason. Cute wartime comedy with some nice performances. C: Lucille Gleason, Veda Ann Borg, Lyle Talbot. D: Jean Yarbrough. COM 63m.

She's Out of Control 1989 ★★ When adolescent daughter (Dolenz) begins dating, widowed father (Danza) realizes what he put so many fathers through when he was a teen. Expanded sitcom material with no fresh ideas and barely a laugh. C: Tony Danza, Catherine Hicks, Wallace Shawn, Ami Dolenz. D: Stan Dragoti. COM [PG] 97m. V

She's Working Her Way Through College 1952 ★★½ When a burlesque queen decides to get a higher education, she puts the entire college into an uproar. Good fun mixed with nice music. Remake of *The Male Animal*. C: Virginia Mayo, Ronald Reagan, Gene Nelson, Don DeFore, Phyllis Thaxter, Patrice Wymore, Roland Winters. D: H. Bruce Humberstone. MUS 101m.

Shield For Murder 1954 ★★½ Detective falls in with a bunch of crooks and gets involved in murder. Action-packed, hard-boiled account of a good guy who turns bad. C: Edmond O'Brien, John Agar, Mara English, Carolyn Jones, Claude Akins. D: Edmond O'Brien, Howard Koch. CRI 80m.

Shifting Sands 1918 ★★★½ Early silent melodrama about struggling artist wrongful jailed for prostitution after she shuns her landlord's amorous advances. Excellent Swanson. C: Gloria Swanson, Joe King, Lillian Langdon. DRA 60m. V

Shillingbury Blowers, The 1980 British ★★ Young upstart (Nedwell) comes to a small British village and tries to update the town band. Enjoyable but slow going. C: Trevor Howard, Robin Nedwell, Diane Keen, Jack Douglas, Sam Kydd, John LeMesurier. D: Val Guest. MUS 82m.

Shinbone Alley 1971 ★★★½ Animated version of Broadway musical about relationship between literate cockroach archie and wayward pussycat mehitabel. Too sophisticated for kids, but musical comedy fans may like it. Based on characters from Don Marquis book. C: Eddie Bracken, Carol Channing. D: John Wilson, David Detiege. MUS [G] 83m. V

Shine On, Harvest Moon 1944 ★★★½ The lives, loves, trials, and triumphs of vaudeville entertainers Nora Bayes and Jack Norworth. A diverting musical with sprightly numbers. The final sequence, filmed in color, is a true highlight. C: Ann Sheridan, Jack Carson, Dennis Morgan, Irene Manning, S.Z. Sakall, Marie Wilson, Step Brothers. D: David Butler. MUS 112m.

Shining Hour, The 1938 ★★★½ Trouble starts when a farmer brings home his new wife, a nightclub dancer. A muddle of a story, that somehow manages to shine through the efforts of a cast of Hollywood notables. C: Joan Crawford, Margaret Sullavan, Robert Young, Melvyn Douglas, Fay Bainter, Allyn Joslyn. D: Frank Borzage. DRA 80m. V

Shining Season, A 1979 ★★★½ When track star John Baker (Bottoms) is diagnosed with a terminal illness, he decides to spend the remainder of his life coaching a girls' track team. A decent illness-of-the-week special (keep tissues handy), based on a true story. C: Timothy Bottoms, Allyn Ann McLerie, Rip Torn, Connie Forslund, Mason Adams. D: Stuart Margolin. DRA 100m. TVM V

Shining Star 1975 *See* **That's the Way of the World** TVM

Shining, The 1980 ★★★★ A writer (Nicholson) vacationing with his family at an isolated hotel develops a murderous case of cabin fever. Film version of Stephen King's novel turned off some of the book's fans with its simplifications of the story, but it succeeds splendidly as an exercise in chilly Kubrick-created style. C: Jack Nicholson, Shelley Duvall, Danny Lloyd, Scatman Crothers, Joe Turkel. D: Stanley Kubrick. HOR [R] 144m. V

Shining Through 1992 ★★ In this misguided update of a WWII anti-Nazi spy thriller, young woman (Griffith) has an affair with her boss (Douglas), a U.S. spy, and convinces him to send her to Berlin on espionage work. A wildly improbable plotline and bad accents make this picture unintentionally funny. C: Michael Douglas, Melanie Griffith, Liam Neeson, John Gielgud. D: David Seltzer. DRA [R] 133m. V

Shinobi Ninja, The 1984 ★★ Koga ninja survivor must stop ninja warriors bent on destroying Japan. C: Tadashi Yamashita, Eric Lee. D: Luk Chuen. ACT 103m. V

Ship Ahoy 1942 ★★★½ An ocean liner is Puerto Rico-bound, with plenty of sunny MGM talent on the passenger list. Highlights include Powell's tapping, Red's mugging, the Tommy Dorsey Orchestra with Buddy Rich, and a skinny young singer named Sinatra. All aboard. C: Eleanor Powell, Red Skelton, Bert Lahr, Virginia O'Brien, Tommy Dorsey, Jo Stafford, Frank Sinatra. D: Edward Buzzell. MUS 95m. V

Ship of Fools 1965 ★★★★½ Katharine Anne Porter's novel of a symbolic ocean voyage shortly before WWII interweaves several stories with fascinating characters. Brilliantly acted; only drawback is heavy-handed social commentary, mostly involving Nazi (Ferrer). Leigh's last film. Oscars for Best Art Direction and Cinematography. C: Vivien Leigh, Oskar Werner, Simone Signoret, Jose Ferrer, Lee Marvin, George Segal, Elizabeth Ashley, Michael Dunn. D: Stanley Kramer. DRA 149m. V

Ship of the Condemned Women, The 1963 Italian ★★★ A wrongly convicted woman is being shipped with other female convicts to an island prison. However, with a little detective work by her attorney, the real killer is uncovered. Uninvolving story of murder and mutiny. C: Ettore Manni, May Britt, Tania Weber. D: Raffaello Matarazzo. DRA 95m.

Ship That Died of Shame, The 1955 British ★★★★ British wartime buddies purchase their old gunboat and go into business for themselves as smugglers. They have a great time . . . until their ship refuses to cooperate. Melodramatic, moralistic tale with standout cast. C: Richard Attenborough, George Baker, Bill Owen, Virginia McKenna, Roland Culver, Bernard Lee, Ralph Truman. D: Basil Dearden. ACT 91m.

Shipbuilders, The 1943 British ★★½ British shipbuilding magnate has problems with workers, unions, and suppliers. Interesting look at a world gone by. C: Clive Brook, Morland Graham, Nell Ballantyne. D: John Baxter. DRA 89m.

Shipmates Forever 1935 ★★★ Admiral is heartbroken when his son rejects the Navy and becomes a singer instead. Nice song and dance but thin on plot. C: Dick Powell, Ruby Keeler, Lewis Stone, Ross Alexander, Eddie Acuff, Dick Foran, John Arledge. D: Frank Borzage. MUS 124m. V

Shipwrecked 1991 Norwegian ★★★★ Shipwrecked cabin boy marooned on deserted island where nasty pirate has buried his booty. Excellent action entertainment for young and old. C: Stian Smestad, Gabriel Byrne. D: Nils Gaup. ACT [PG] 91m. V

Shiralee, The 1957 British ★★★ Faced with an unfaithful wife, an Australian man takes his five-year-old daughter on the road for adventure. Interesting look at a father-daughter relationship. Filmed beautifully on location. C: Peter Finch, Elizabeth Sellars, Dana Wilson, Rosemary Harrys, Tessie O'Shea, Sidney James, George Rose. D: Leslie Norman. DRA 99m.

Shirley Valentine 1989 U.S. ★★★★ A bored, middle-aged British woman (Collins), goes on a life-changing trip to Greece. Repeating her role from London and Broadway stages, Collins creates a winning character in an engaging and very personable comedy; she was nominated for an Oscar. C: Pauline Collins, Tom Conti, Alison Steadman, Julia McKenzie. D: Lewis Gilbert. COM 108m. V

Shmenges, The—The Last Polka 1984 ★★★★ Life and times of two Polka-playing brothers from fictional Leutonia. Oddball delight. C: John Candy, Eugene Levy, Catherine O'Hara. D: John Blanchard. COM 54m. TVM V

Shoah 1985 French ★★★★★ Monumental documentary chronicling the Holocaust, mostly through interviews with the victims and their Nazi persecutors. Long, but worth every minute; this is filmmaking at its most powerful and most important. D: Claude Lanzmann. DOC 570m. V

Shock 1946 ★★★½ Killer psychiatrist (Price) has a special treatment in mind for the witness to the murder who unknowingly comes to him as a patient. Not that shocking but Price makes a marvelous villain. C: Vincent Price, Lynn Bari, Frank Latimore, Anabel Shaw. D: Alfred L. Werker. CRI 70m. V

Shock Corridor 1963 ★★★★ As his cover, a journalist (Breck) acts mad to investigate a murder inside an insane asylum, and gradually finds himself really becoming unhinged. Textured b&w photography and realistically acted inmates make this caustic psychodrama a pulp classic. C: Peter Breck, Constance Towers, Gene Evans, James Best, Hari Rhodes. D: Samuel Fuller. CRI 101m. V

Shock 'em Dead 1990 ★★ A young nerd makes a deal with the devil to win rock 'n' roll stardom, but guess what? There are gruesome strings attached. A few amusing moments, but largely familiar horror fare. C: Traci Lords, Aldo Ray, Try Donahue. D: Mark Freed. HOR [R] 94m. V

Shock! Shock! Shock! 1987 ★★ Deranged slasher and outer space smugglers collide, wreaking multilevel havoc. C: Brad Isaac, Cyndy McCrossen, Alan Rickman. D: Arn McConnell. HOR 60m. V

Shock to the System, A 1990 ★★★½ After accidentally killing a homeless man, an advertising executive (Caine) commits murder when he is overlooked for a promotion. This is a satisfying small-scale thriller that indicts ruthless corporate competition. Riegert, Kurtz, and Caine are excellent. C: Michael Caine, Elizabeth McGovern, Peter Riegert, Swoosie Kurtz, Will Patton. D: Jan Egleson. CRI [R] 88m. V

Shock Treatment 1981 ★★ Sequel to the insanely successful *Rocky Horror Picture Show*. This time, supernerds Janet and Brad (Harper and DeYoung) are trapped in a kind of game show hell. The director and some of the cast return, but the magic just isn't there. C: Jessica Harper, Cliff De Young, Richard O'Brien, Patricia Quinn. D: Jim Sharman. MUS [PG] 95m. V

Shock Waves 1977 ★★½ Bizarre horror yarn involving a demented Nazi scientist (Cushing), his creations (aquatic zombies), and the unfortunate innocents who cross their path. Not as outrageous as it sounds. C: Peter Cushing, Brooke Adams, John Carradine. D: Ken Wiederhorn. HOR [PG] 90m. V

Shocked 1986 *See* **Mesmerized**

Shocker 1990 ★★½ Executed mass murderer lives beyond his death, possessing both people and electrical devices. Starts out good and scary, but takes a wrongheaded turn into dumb comedy at the 40-minute mark and goes down the tubes. C: Michael Murphy, Peter Berg, Cami Cooper, Mitch Pileggi. D: Wes Craven. HOR 111m. V

Shocking Miss Pilgrim, The 1947 ★★★ Feminist (Grable) in 19th-century Boston is tamed by her employer (Haymes). Middling tuner, notable for putting Grable in long skirts. Fine Gershwin songs. C: Betty Grable, Dick Haymes, Anne Revere. D: George Seaton. MUS 85m.

Shockproof 1949 ★★★½ When a parole officer (Wilde) falls in love with a parolee (Knight), she takes him down the road to serious trouble. Interesting cast in story by Samuel Fuller. C: Cornel Wilde, Patricia Knight, John Baragrey, Esther Minciotti, Howard St. John. D: Douglas Sirk. DRA 79m.

Shoemaker and the Elves, The 1967 German ★★★½ German rendition of the beloved children's classic retells the story of an impoverished shoemaker and how a group of enchanted little people change his life overnight. A good one for younger viewers. C: Nora Minor, Ado Reigler, Heini Gobel. D: Erich Kobler. FAM/DRA

Shoes of the Fisherman, The 1968 ★★½ A Russian Pope (Quinn) labors to end the possibility of global atomic warfare and starvation in China. Stellar cast can do little to save this overblown epic. A sluggishly directed adaptation of Morris L. West's best-selling novel. C: Anthony Quinn, Laurence Olivier, Oskar Werner, David Jansen, Leo McKern, John Gielgud. D: Michael Anderson. DRA [G] 152m. V

Shoeshine 1946 Italian ★★★★★ Two street urchins eke out survival in Nazi-occupied Italy. Their attempts at black marketeering result in tragedy. A fabulous, harrowing, and riveting effort by the masterful De Sica, this Italian film justifiably received a special Oscar, before Hollywood awarded prizes for Best Foreign Film. C: Rinaldo Smerdoni, Franco Interlenghi, Aniello Mele, Bruno Ortensi, Pacifico Astrologo. D: Vittorio De Sica. DRA 93m.

Shogun 1980 U.S. and other countries ★★★★½ A shipwrecked British sailor (Chamberlain) becomes the first Western samurai when a Japanese samurai warrior takes him under his wing. Lavish, smash hit miniseries colorfully re-creates feudal Japan. Emmy-winner was based on James Clavell's novel. One warning: Video copies are drastically shortened. C: Richard Chamberlain, Toshiro Mifune, Yoko Shimada, Frankie Sakai. D: Jerry London. ACT 124m. TVM V

Shogun Assassin 1980 Japanese ★★★★ Executioner with growing son searches all of Japan for the killer of his wife. Extreme violence and dazzling action in this superior martial arts adventure, expertly edited from Japanese series *Sword of Vengeance*. Wild ride, head and shoulders above most in the genre. C: Tomisaburo Wakayama, Masahiro Tomikawa, Lamont Johnson, Marshall Efron. D: Kenji Misumi, Robert Houston. ACT [R] 89m. V

Shogun's Ninja 1983 ★★½ Two ancient ninja families struggle for superiority, as one commander searches for the dagger that

holds the secret of ninja. Okay martial arts actioner. C: Henry Sanada, Sonny Chiba. D: Noribumi Suzuki. ACT 115m. v
Shoot 1976 Canadian ★★ When a group of hunters decide they want human prey, they stalk another group of hunters, who don't find the game much fun and decide to retaliate. A weak attempt at an antigun *Deliverance.* C: Cliff Robertson, Ernest Borgnine, Henry Silva, Helen Shaver. D: Harvey Hart. DRA [R] 98m. v
Shoot It Black, Shoot It Blue 1974 ★★½ Violent police officer must face the music after his brutal attack on purse snatcher shows up on film. C: Michael Moriarty. DRA [R] 93m. v
Shoot the Living Pray for the Dead 1973 ★★★ Brutal western about gangster and guide who battle for stolen treasure in Mexico. C: Klaus Kinski. D: Joseph Warren. WST 90m. v
Shoot the Moon 1981 ★★★★ The 15-year marriage between a writer (Finney) and his placid wife (Keaton) disintegrates as they lock horns and rage at each other. Brilliant leading performances and occasional astute observations. C: Albert Finney, Diane Keaton, Karen Allen, Peter Weller. D: Alan Parker. DRA [R] 124m. v
Shoot the Piano Player 1960 French ★★★★ A once-successful concert pianist (Aznavour) is now reduced to playing in a Parisian dive. His former life is revealed in comic and violent flashbacks. There are some great visual jokes, and Aznavour's bemused ennui as the world comes tumbling down around him is stunning. C: Charles Aznavour, Marie Dubois, Nicole Berger, Michele Mercier. D: François Truffaut. DRA 92m. v
Shoot to Kill 1988 ★★★★ Poitier ends a 10-year screen absence playing a tough FBI agent working with a mountain guide (Berenger) to track a killer through the rugged Pacific Northwest. Priceless moment: Poitier facing down a 10-foot grizzly bear. C: Sidney Poitier, Tom Berenger, Kirstie Alley, Clancy Brown. D: Roger Spottiswoode. ACT [R] 109m. v
Shootfighter: Fight to the Death 1993 ★★★ Lifelong rivals wage a martial arts battle that has no rules and escalates into extreme violence. Exciting, brutal actioner. C: Bolo Yeung, Martin Kove, Edward Albert, Maryam D'Abo. D: Pat Alan. ACT [R] 94m. v
Shooting Elizabeth 1992 ★★★ When his obnoxious wife disappears, disgruntled husband must clear his name of "murder" he only wished he could commit. C: Jeff Goldblum, Mimi Rogers. D: Baz Taylor. COM [PG-13] 96m. v
Shooting Party, The 1984 British ★★★★ Erudite gentleman (Mason) hosts a weekend shooting party in turn-of-the-century England that brings out the worst in each of the guests. Fine acting and a deft script make this an engaging comedy of manners. C: James Mason, John Gielgud, Dorothy Tutin, Edward Fox, Cheryl Campbell, Gordon Jackson. D: Alan Bridges. COM 108m. v
Shooting Stars 1985 ★★ Unemployed t.v. crime fighters take dangerous jobs as real-world private investigators. C: Billy Dee Williams, Parker Stevenson, Edie Adams. D: Richard Lang. ACT 96m. v
Shooting Straight 1930 ★★★½ Gambler Dix takes on the guise of an evangelist after he is wrongly accused of murder. He ends up romancing a minister's daughter, which ultimately changes his life. Stale plot, but well played Western drama. C: Richard Dix, Mary Lawlor, James Neill. D: Geroge Archainbaud. WST 72m.
Shooting, The 1967 ★★★½ Super-young Nicholson stars as a gun for hire in this offbeat revenge western-culminating in a surprisingly effective climax. C: Millie Perkins, Jack Nicholson, Will Hutchins, Warren Oates. D: Monte Hellman. WST [G] 82m. v
Shootist, The 1976 ★★★★★ The Duke's last—and most poignant—role, as a legendary gunslinger dying of cancer. He just wants to end his days in peace, but his violent reputation always precedes him. Highly entertaining, from the director of *Dirty Harry.* C: John Wayne, Lauren Bacall, Ron Howard, James Stewart, Richard Boone, Hugh O'Brian. D: Don Siegel. WST [PG] 100m. v
Shop Around the Corner, The 1940 ★★★★★ Story of two shopclerks unwittingly writing love letters to each other glows with beautifully written characters, sparkling dialogue, and superb performances; a special joy for Christmas viewing. Remade as *In the Good Old Summertime* and source for Broadway musical, *She Loves Me.* Based on Nikolaus Laszlo's play, *Parfumerie.* C: Margaret Sullavan, James Stewart, Frank Morgan, Joseph Schildkraut, Felix Bressart, William Tracy. D: Ernst Lubitsch. COM 100m. v
Shop at Sly Corner, The 1946 *See* **Code of Scotland Yard**
Shop on Main Street, The 1965 Czech ★★★★★ As the Germans invade Czechoslovakia during WWII, a rough carpenter shelters an elderly Jewish woman from persecution. Oscar-winning Best Foreign Film is a critically acclaimed, poignant fable with superior acting and sensitive direction. C: Josef Kroner, Ida Kaminska, Han Slivkova, Frantisek Holly, Martin Gregor. D: Jan Kadar, Elmar Klos. DRA 128m. v
Shopworn 1932 ★★★ Waitress (Stanwyck) in love with a millionaire gets framed and sent up the river by his scheming mother. Routine melodrama, enlivened by feisty Stanwyck. C: Barbara Stanwyck, Regis Toomey, ZaSu Pitts, Clara Blandick. D: Nick Grinde. DRA 72m.
Shopworn Angel 1928 ★★★½ A hardened showgirl (Carroll) meets up with a young and innocent soldier (Cooper) who's about to go off to war. They fall for each other and her

gentler side emerges. Nicely done soap opera and a fascinating look at young Cooper. C: Nancy Carroll, Gary Cooper, Paul Lukas, Emmett King. D: Richard Wallace. DRA 82m.

Shopworn Angel, The 1938 ★★★★ Remake of the 1928 story of a tough dancer and a young soldier, this time featuring an excellent pairing of Sullavan and Stewart in the lead roles; they get solid support from the rest of the cast. C: Margaret Sullavan, James Stewart, Walter Pidgeon, Hattie McDaniel, Sam Levene, Nat Pendleton. D: H.C. Potter. DRA 81m. V

Short Circuit 1986 ★★½ Lightning-zapped robot comes alive, and hides out with friend (Sheedy) while inventor (Guttenburg) and sidekick (Stevens) go on mad chase for the talking hardware. Dumb comedy younger kids might enjoy; beware endless product plugs and obscenities. C: Ally Sheedy, Steve Guttenberg, Fisher Stevens, G.W. Bailey, Austin Pendleton. D: John Badham. COM [PG] 98m. V

Short Circuit 2 1988 ★★ Talking robot (Number 5) returns with Indian scientist (Stevens) in empty-headed chase from toy manufacturers and bad guys. Lots of silly slapstick will turn off adults; reliance on obscenities makes this questionable for children too. C: Fisher Stevens, Michael McKean, Cynthia Gibb, Jack Weston. D: Kenneth Johnson. COM [PG] 112m. V

Short Cuts 1993 ★★★★ Nine Raymond Carver short stories are woven into an epic narrative of miscommunication between the sexes in Southern California. Persons and events flow into one another in a dazzling tapestry. The director's cynical view of human nature may put some viewers off. C: Tim Robbins, Julianne Moore, Anne Archer, Matthew Modine, Madeleine Stowe, Lily Tomlin, Peter Gallagher, Jack Lemmon, Lyle Lovett. D: Robert Altman. DRA [R] 189m. V

Short Eyes 1977 ★★★★½ Child molester "Short Eyes" (Davison) gets what's coming to him from his disgusted fellow inmates. Gripping, graphic, violent film from Pinero's acclaimed play was shot in the Tombs, the former NYC prison. Powerful acting. C: Bruce Davison, Jose Perez, Nathan George, Don Blakely. D: Robert M. Young. DRA [R] 100m. V

Short Fuse 1986 ★★ Washington, D.C. journalist framed for ghetto murder hunts down real killer. (a.k.a. *Good to Go*) C: Art Garfunkel, Robert Doqui, Harris Yulin. D: Blaine Novak. CRI [R] 91m. V

Short Grass 1950 ★★★½ After going into exile thanks to Ankrum's nefarious doings, Cameron returns to his ranch to win back the land that he rightfully owns. Good Western action that culminates in a great fight sequence. C: Rod Cameron, Cathy Downs, Johnny Mack Brown, Morris Ankrum. D: Lesley Selander. WST 82m.

Short Time 1990 ★★★½ Unlikely comedy premise finds cop (Coleman), mistakenly diagnosed as terminally ill, trying to get offed on duty so his family can collect benefits. Potentially tasteless, but Coleman's acerbic demeanor actually rises above script and occasionally makes it work. C: Dabney Coleman, Matt Frewer, Teri Garr, Barry Corbin, Joe Pantoliano. D: Gregg Champion. COM [PG-13] 97m. V

Shot at Dawn 1934 German ★★★★ Lorre and Odemar are thieves who conspire with jeweler Salfner to pull off a robbery. Despite an abundance of mix-ups and complicated plot twists, the crime finally is pulled off. An intriguing and action-packed German gangster film, with neat Lorre performance. C: Heinz Salfner, Ery Bos, Karl Ludwig Diehl, Fritz Odemar, Peter Lorre. D: Alfred Zeisler. CRI 73m.

Shot in the Dark, A 1964 ★★★★½ Second entry in *Pink Panther* series features inept detective Sellers trying (despite his best efforts) to discover if Sommer is guilty of murdering her lover. One great farcical sequence follows another in wonderfully choreographed series of comic escapades. Director Edwards and Sellers are at their best. C: Peter Sellers, Elke Sommer, George Sanders, Herbert Lom. D: Blake Edwards. COM [PG] 103m. V

Shotgun 1955 ★★½ A deputy sheriff avenges a brutal murder. Routine but violent Western love triangle. C: Sterling Hayden, Zachary Scott, Yvonne De Carlo, Guy Prescott, Angela Greene. D: Lesley Selander. WST 81m. V

Shout 1991 ★★ On-the-run Travolta is hired as musical muse and reforming angel for '50s juvenile delinquents' school, where he ruffles all the right feathers. String of rock film stereotypes held together by Travolta's appeal. C: John Travolta, James Walters, Heather Graham, Richard Jordan, Linda Fiorentino, Scott Coffey, Glenn Quinn, Frank von Zerneck, Michael Bacall. D: Jeffrey Hornaday. MUS [PG-13] 90m. V

Shout, The 1980 British ★★★★ A shabby madman eccentric convinces a married couple that he can kill by shouting. Sinister and gripping tale with provocative undercurrents. C: Alan Bates, Susannah York, John Hurt, Robert Stephens, Tim Curry. D: Jerzy Skolimowski. DRA [R] 88m. V

Show Boat 1936 ★★★★½ Landmark Kern/-Hammerstein musical, with Morgan re-creating role of mulatto leading lady of Mississippi show boat, forced by southern codes to quit. Robeson's singing of "Old Man River" is a stirring high point. Previously filmed in 1929, and redone again in 1951. Originally based on Edna Ferber novel. C: Irene Dunne, Allan Jones, Helen Morgan, Paul Robeson, Charles Winninger, Hattie McDaniel. D: James Whale. MUS 113m. V

Show Boat 1951 ★★★★ Lavish remake of musical, with Grayson and Keel as ill-fated lovers meeting on Mississippi show boat. Powerful story deals with racism in moving fashion through Gardner's performance as mulatto Julie. Sublime songs include "Old Man River," "Make Believe," "Bill," and "Can't Help Lovin' Dat Man Of Mine." C: Kathryn Grayson, Ava Gardner, Howard Keel, Joe E. Brown, Marge Champion, Gower Champion, Agnes Moorehead, William Warfield. D: George Sidney. MUS 115m. v

Show Business 1944 ★★★ The lives and times of four fast friends, all vaudeville players. Good fun and great music. A must for fans of the irrepressible Cantor. Followed by *If You Knew Susie*. C: Eddie Cantor, Joan Davis, George Murphy. D: Edwin L. Martin. MUS 92m. v

Show Goes On, The 1937 British ★★ Poor female millworker becomes a star singer. A turn at drama by Britain's great comedienne Fields. The story plods along. C: Gracie Fields, Owen Nares. D: Basil Dean. DRA 93m.

Show of Force, A 1990 ★★★ Reporter (Irving) at a Puerto Rico TV station thinks the FBI has killed two political extremists in an effort to keep the country's moderate government from toppling. Explosive material, based on fact. Solid cast, although Garcia isn't in it much. C: Amy Irving, Robert Duvall, Andy Garcia, Lou Diamond Phillips. D: Bruno Barretto. DRA 93m. v

Show-Off, The 1946 ★★★½ Right after he gets married, an inept young man nearly ruins his brother-in-law's business. Some truly funny situations and an early showpiece for Skelton. C: Red Skelton, Marilyn Maxwell. COM 83m. v

Show People 1928 ★★★★½ Silent comedy classic gives Davies her best role as innocent hopeful who arrives in Hollywood to become a serious actress, but winds up in comedy. Full of witty insight into the business of making movies. Guest-star cameos include Charlie Chaplin and director Vidor. C: Marion Davies, William Haines, Del Henderson, Polly Moran. D: King Vidor. COM 82m. v

Show Them No Mercy! 1935 ★★★ After kidnappers strike, Federal agents relentlessly track them down. Lots of good, hard-boiled excitement. Remade Western-style as *Rawhide*. C: Rochelle Hudson, Cesar Romero, Bruce Cabot, Edward Norris, Edward Brophy, Warren Hymer. D: George Marshall. CRI 76m. v

Showdown 1973 ★★★½ When a gang of outlaws starts to prey on his town, a sheriff learns that the gang leader is his old friend. Middling Western that does its job. C: Rock Hudson, Dean Martin, Susan Clark. D: George Seaton. WST [PG] 99m. v

Showdown 1993 ★★½ A band of retired mobsters are disenchanted when a gang of bandit bikers set up operations in town, so they hire a martial arts expert to clean things up. Best gag: the town's name—Sanctuary. C: Werner Hoetzinger, Richard Lynch, Michelle McCormick. D: Leo Fong. ACT [PG-13] 92m. v

Showdown at Abilene 1956 ★★★ Disillusioned Civil War veteran (Mahoney) returns home and becomes the town's new sheriff. Solid Western loaded with good action. C: Jock Mahoney, Martha Hyer, Lyle Bettger, David Janssen, Grant Williams. D: Charles Haas. WST 80m.

Showdown at Boot Hill 1958 ★★★★ Early venture for Bronson features him as U.S. marshal who can't collect a bounty when no one will identify the body of a murderer he's killed. Interesting stab at psychological introspection within Western format, and solid performance from Bronson. C: Charles Bronson, Robert Hutton, John Carradine, Carole Mathews. D: Gene Fowler, Jr. WST 71m. v

Showdown At The Equator 1983 ★★ Kung Fu experts battle it out at the equator. C: Bruce Liang, Lo Lieh. D: Kwan Ching Liang. ACT 95m. v

Showdown at Williams Creek 1991 Canadian ★★★½ In the Montana Territory, a strange young gold prospector is put on trial for the brutal murder of an old man. Based on a real occurrence and played quite well. C: Tom Burlinson, Donnelly Rhodes. D: Allan Kroeker. WST [R] 97m. v

Showdown in Little Tokyo 1991 ★★ An L.A. cop (Lundgren) takes on the Chinese Mafia to get revenge for the brutal murder of his parents. Lots of kickboxing, but not much else. C: Dolph Lundgren, Brandon Lee, Carey-Hiroyuki Tagawa, Tia Carrere. D: Mark L. Lester. ACT [R] 80m. v

Showdown, The 1940 ★★½ When his brother is murdered, a trail boss goes after the culprits. Good suspense in a taut Western format. C: William Boyd, Russell Hayden, Britt Wood. D: Howard Bretherton. WST 65m. v

Showtime 1948 British ★★★ Greene is a show business impresario who tries to rebuild his career after being wounded during WWI. Based on life of British music hall producer George Edwards. Good cast can't overcome poorly staged musical numbers. (a.k.a. *Gaiety George*) C: Richard Greene, Ann Todd. D: George King, Freddie Carpenter, Leontine Sagan. MUS 90m.

Shredder Orpheus 1989 ★★½ A campy horror film about a group of rockers who battle the devil in the depths of hell with a guitar and a skateboard. C: Jesse Bernstein, Vera McCaughan. D: Robert McGinley. HOR 88m. v

Shrieking, The 1991 ★★ A group of raucous bikers push around two supernatural sisters and end up paying for their bad behavior. C: Keith Carradine, Gary Busey, cott Glenn, Dan Haggerty. D: Leo Garen. HOR [PG] 93m. v

Shrike, The 1955 ★★★★ Stark drama of a Broadway director driven crazy by his cruel, neurotic wife (Allyson, cast against type). Ferrer repeats as star and director in this transcription of the Pulitzer Prize-winning Joseph Kramm play. Effective, except for the changed, upbeat ending. C: Jose Ferrer, June Allyson, Joy Page, Ed Platt. D: Jose Ferrer. DRA 88m.

Shrimp on the Barbie, The 1990 ★★½ Marin is Mexican waiter in Australia trying to help wealthy Samms with problems caused by her father. Cheech doesn't do drug jokes! Alan Smithee is pseudonym for real director, who pulled name off film. C: Cheech Marin, Emma Samms, Vernon Wells, Terence Cooper, Jeanette Cronin, Carole Davis, Bruce Spence. D: Alan Smithee. COM [PG-13] 87m. V

Shrunken Heads 1994 ★★★½ Off-the-wall—and wildly uneven—marriage of comic-book horror and East Side Kids homage, with three young murder victims transformed in to the crimefighting title creatures. Hard to take seriously, but also hard to dislike. Director is the brother of composer Danny Elfman, who contributes a musical theme. C: Aeryk Egan, Becky Herbst, Meg Foster, Julius Harris, A.J. Damato. D: Richard Elfman. HOR [R] 86m.

Shut My Big Mouth 1942 ★★★ Hapless young man ventures out West and winds up involved with a group of bandits. Typical madcap adventures with Brown the center of lots of laughs. C: Joe E. Brown, Adele Mara, Victor Jory, Fritz Feld, Lloyd Bridges, Forrest Tucker, Pedro de Cordoba. D: Charles Barton. COM 71m.

Shy People 1987 ★★★½ New York photojournalist (Clayburgh) and daughter look for their roots in Louisiana swamp country. Provocative and, poignant culture clash, with excellent cast, especially Hershey and fine bayou cinematography. C: Jill Clayburgh, Barbara Hershey, Martha Plimpton, Mare Winningham, Merritt Butrick, John Philbin, Don Swayze. D: Andrei Konchalovsky. DRA [R] 119m. V

Sibling Rivalry 1990 ★★½ After sister convinces bored Alley to have extramarital affair, Alley is horrified when new lover dies in bed. C: Kirstie Alley, Bill Pullman, Carrie Fisher, Jami Gertz, Sam Elliott, Ed O'Neill. D: Carl Reiner. COM [PG-13] 88m. V

Sicilian Clan, The 1969 French ★★★★ The aging head of a French crime family (Gabin) plans one last jewel heist, abetted by eager young thief with grandiose ideas (Delon) he brings in to help. Solid caper film, despite some loose ends. C: Jean Gabin, Alain Delon, Lino Ventura, Irina Demick, Amedeo Nazzari, Sydney Chaplin. D: Henri Verneuil. CRI [PG] 121m.

Sicilian Connection, The 1974 ★★★½ Lurid, dangerous dealings of a band of notorious opium traders. A lot of excitement and relentless action. C: Ben Gazzara, Silvia Monti, Fausto Tozzi. ACT [R] 100m. V

Sicilian, The 1987 ★★★ Ponderous, confusing chronicle of Salvatore Giuliano (Lambert), who took money from Italy's Big Three—the Church, the State, and the Mob—to fund Sicily's secession from mother Italy. Extensive cutting hurts film, adapted from Mario Puzo novel. Director's cut available on video and worth another half-star. C: Christopher Lambert, Terence Stamp, Barbara Sukowa, Joss Ackland, John Turturro. D: Michael Cimino. CRI [R] 146m. V

Sid and Nancy 1986 ★★★½ In London's '70s punk scene, the strange relationship of the Sex Pistols' Sid Vicious and his girlfriend, Nancy Spungen, is explored. Documentary-like details of the couple's life make them sympathetic. Tour de force performances by Oldman and Webb. C: Gary Oldman, Chloe Webb, Drew Schofield, David Hayman. D: Alex Cox. DRA [R] 111m. V

Siddharta and the City 1973 *See* **Adversary, The**

Siddhartha 1973 ★★★ Herman Hesse's story of a young Indian fellow who embarks upon a journey to find the meaning of existence. Thoughtful and pensive. Best primarily for the breathtaking location photography by Sven Nykvist. C: Shashi Kapoor, Simi Garewal, Romesh Shama, Pinchoo Kapoor, Zul Vellani, Amrik Singh. D: Conrad Rooks. DRA [R] 95m.

Side Out 1990 ★★★ Law student (Howell) gets involved in a beach volleyball tournament while trying to help an ex-star (Horton) pay his bills. Fans of the sport will enjoy this one. C: C. Thomas Howell, Peter Horton, Harley Jane Kozak, Christopher Rydell. D: Peter Israelson. DRA [PG-13] 100m. V

Side Show 1981 ★★★½ A young budding circus star seeks glamour and stardom. Instead, he finds himself the object of a psycho's murderous plan. C: Lance Kerwin, Anthony Franciosa, Red Buttons. D: William Conrad. DRA 98m. V

Side Street 1929 ★★★ While investigating a gang of bootleggers, a determined police officer learns his brother is running the gang, forcing him to choose between law and familial loyalty. Standard studio crime drama. CRI

Side Street 1949 ★★★½ Small-time thief (Granger) gets in over his head with some big-time mobsters. Lots of crime action, including a super car chase. C: Farley Granger, Cathy O'Donnell, James Craig, Paul Kelly, Jean Hagen, Paul Harvey. D: Anthony Mann. DRA 83m. V

Side Street Angel 1937 British ★★★½ Wealthy Williams takes a bad turn when he falls in with a group of thieves, but is saved from a life of crime by hotel operator Brook. Romantic comedy with gangster backdrop; nicely played by ensemble. C: Hugh Williams, Lesley Brook, Henry Kendall, Reginald Purcell, Phyllis Stanley, Madeleine Seymour, Edna Davies. D: Ralph Ince. COM 63m.

Sidekicks 1994 ★★★ Young boy who worships Chuck Norris dreams himself into a film starring his action hero doing battle with well-muscled bad guy (Piscopo). Somewhat novel approach, as Norris spoofs himself, but few real surprises. C: Chuck Norris, Beau Bridges,

Mako, Joe Piscopo. D: Aaron Norris. FAM/ACT [PG] 100m.

Sidewalk Stories 1989 ★★★★ Unusual, virtually silent look at homelessness in New York's Greenwich Village, as a street person looks after an abandoned tot. A charming, lovely little movie, reminiscent of Chaplin's classics. C: Charles Lane, Nicole Alysia, Sandye Wilson, Darnell Williams. D: Charles Lane. DRA [R] 97m.

Sidewalks of London 1938 British ★★★★ Middle-aged street entertainer (Laughton) falls in love with a young singer (Leigh) who uses him up and breaks his heart. Outstanding star performances and truly entertaining. Released in England as *St. Martin's Lane.* C: Charles Laughton, Vivien Leigh, Rex Harrison, Tyrone Guthrie. D: Tim Whelan. DRA 85m. V

Sidewalks of New York 1931 ★★★½ Wealthy landlord (Keaton) tries to help his tenement residents when he falls in love with one of them. Game talkie starring effort by the silent comedy genius. C: Buster Keaton, Anita Page, Cliff Edwards. D: Jules White, Zion Meyers. COM 70m. V

Siege at Red River, The 1954 ★★½ In the thick of the Civil War, a Confederate agent works his way behind enemy lines before making a daring break for the South. Typical action film. C: Van Johnson, Joanne Dru, Richard Boone, Milburn Stone, Jeff Morrow. D: Rudolph Maté. WST 81m.

Siege of Firebase Gloria, The 1988 ★★½ Vastly outnumbered, a detachment of U.S. Marines fight desperately to hang on to a remote Vietnamese hilltop. Blood and guts galore. C: Lee R. Ermey, Wings Hauser, Albert Popwell. D: Brian Trenchard-Smith. ACT [R] 95m. V

Siege of Punchgut 1960 *See* **Four Desperate Men**

Siege of the Saxons 1963 British ★★½ As soon as King Arthur falls ill, Saxons plot his overthrow, and are thwarted by a mysterious but loyal outlaw. Fair swashbuckler action and good color. C: Janette Scott, Ronald Lewis, Ronald Howard, John Laurie, Mark Dignam. D: Nathan Juran. ACT 85m.

Sierra Baron 1958 ★★½ Nineteenth-century California landowners are beseiged by rustlers trying to steal their property. Beautiful location scenery strengthens this Western. C: Brian Keith, Rick Jason, Rita Gam, Mala Powers, Steve Brodie. D: James B. Clark. WST 80m.

Sierra Sue 1941 ★★★½ Autry sings his way through an investigation of poisoned cattle and realizes a chemical spray is behind the bevy of sick and dying bovines. Offbeat B-Western benefits from modern setting and a neat plane crash climax. C: Gene Autry, Smiley Burnette. D: William Morgan. WST 64m.

Siesta 1987 ★★ A stuntwoman (Barkin) suffering from amnesia finds herself in Spain involved in a mystery which may include murder. A nonsensical plot and choppy MTV-style direction muddy the proceedings. The Iberian-flavored score is excellent. Music by Miles Davis. C: Ellen Barkin, Gabriel Byrne, Jodie Foster, Martin Sheen, Grace Jones, Julian Sands, Isabella Rossellini, Alexi Sayle. D: Mary Lambert. DRA [R] 98m. V

Sign o' the Times 1987 ★★★½ Fans of the rock singer formerly known as Prince will enjoy this concert film, taken from performances in Minnesota and the Netherlands. C: Prince, Sheila E., Sheena Easton, Dr. Fink. D: Prince. MUS [PG-13] 85m. V

Sign of Four, The 1983 ★★★★½ A beautiful woman is sent a pearl on each anniversary of the mysterious death of her father. One of Sherlock Holmes' greatest cases is handled with grace. Good fun. C: Ian Richardson, Donald Churchill. D: Desmond Davis. CRI 97m. V

Sign of the Cross, The 1932 ★★★★ No-punches-pulled epic of Roman Empire under mad, nasty Emperor Nero (played to fine turn by Laughton), fiddling away while debauchery rules and Christians are tossed to the lions. Colbert has some sexy scenes as Poppaea. A bit dated, but still impressive. C: Fredric March, Elissa Landi, Claudette Colbert, Charles Laughton, Ian Keith, Vivian Tobin, Nat Pendleton, Joe Bonomo. D: Cecil B. DeMille. DRA 118m.

Sign of the Pagan 1954 ★★½ When Atilla the Hun (Palance) tries to conquer the Romans, a noble centurion (Chandler) does his best to fight back. Overblown historical epic. C: Jeff Chandler, Jack Palance, Ludmilla Tcherina, Rita Gam. D: Douglas Sirk. ACT 92m.

Sign of Zorro, The 1960 ★★½ Disney's *Zorro* television series was recut to create this action feature. Zorro defends the defenseless against an evil official in what amounts to a series of poorly connected set pieces. Watchable in parts, but too confusing to sustain interest. C: Guy Williams, Henry Calvin, Gene Sheldon, Romney Brent. D: Norman Foster, Lewis R. Foster. FAM/ACT [G] 89m. V

Signatures of the Soul 1987 ★★★½ Peter Fonda hosts this interesting documentary on the history of tattoos in cultures around the globe, including the U.S. today. Eye-opening, informative and different. C: Peter Fonda. DOC 60m. V

Silas Marner 1985 British ★★★★ Beautifully acted filming of George Eliot's novel about a reclusive miser (Kingsley) and his redemptive love for a child. See *Simple Twist of Fate.* C: Ben Kingsley, Jenny Agutter, Patrick Ryecart. D: Giles Foster. DRA 92m. V

Silence 1973 ★★★ When a young autistic boy (Flanders) is lost in the wilderness, his family and the authorities go all out to rescue him. Sensitively handled and well done. (a.k.a. *Crazy Jack and the Boy*) C: Will Geer,

Ellen Geer, Richard Kelton, Ian Flanders. D: John Korty. DRA [G] 99m. v

Silence Has No Wings 1971 Japanese ★★★★ After bringing a rare butterfly to class, a student is humiliated by his teacher. The story then details how this insect flew through Japan before ending up in the child's hands. A nice allegory for older children, thoughtfully rendered. C: Mariko Kaga, Fumio Watanabe, Hiroyuki Nagato. D: Kazuo Kuroki. FAM/DRA 103m.

Silence Like Glass 1990 ★★★½ Two young women discover solace from fatal illness in newfound friendship with each other. Sentimental, but effective. C: Jami Gertz, Martha Plimpton, George Peppard, Rip Torn. D: Carl Schenkel. DRA [R] 102m. v

Silence of Dean Maitland 1934 Australian ★★½ Clergyman sires an illegitimate child, then murders his lover's father and frames another man for the crime. A complex melodrama that must have been shocking at the time. C: John Longdon, Charlotte Francis. D: Ken G. Hall. DRA 95m.

Silence of Dr. Evans, The 1973 Russian ★★★ A scientist tries to prolong human life span, but is challenged by aliens from another world who believe Earth is a primitive society. Heavy-handed symbolism overwhelms this Russian science fiction film. C: Sergei Bondarchuk, Zhanna Bolotova. D: Budimir Metalnikov. SFI 90m.

Silence of the Lambs, The 1991 ★★★★½ A terrifying version of Thomas Harris' novel about a rookie FBI agent (Foster) assigned to persuade a jailed master criminal (Hopkins) into assisting with the capture of a rampaging serial killer. Combination of taut direction and superlative acting by the leads make the picture highly effective. Oscars for Best Picture, Actor, Actress, Director, and Screenplay. C: Jodie Foster, Anthony Hopkins, Scott Glenn, Ted Levine, Anthony Heald, Brooke Smith, Diane Baker. D: Jonathan Demme. CRI [R] 118m. v

Silence of the North 1981 Canadian ★★★ This is the true story of an independent woman who chooses to live on her own in the Canadian outback. Except for Burstyn's tough-minded performance and great nature scenery, this film is undistinguished. C: Ellen Burstyn, Tom Skerritt, Gordon Pinsent, Jennifer McKinney. D: Allan Winton King. DRA [PG] 94m. v

Silence, The 1963 Swedish ★★★★ Two disparate sisters (one a lesbian, the other a single mother of a 10-year-old boy) spend time together in a hotel, confronting their inner desires. Stunningly acted, heavily symbolic drama may be tough going for those not accustomed to Bergman's cinematic vision. Conclusion of director's "faith trilogy", after *Through a Glass Darkly* and *Winter Light*. C: Ingrid Thulin, Gunnel Lindblom, Hakan Jahnberg. D: Ingmar Bergman. DRA 95m. v

Silencer, The 1992 ★★ Avenging hired killer uncovers prostitution ring as she struggles to keep her former boyfriend out of her head. Busy biker action thriller. C: Lynette Walden, Chris Mulkey, Morton Downey Jr. D: Amy Goldstein. ACT [R] 85m. v

Silencers, The 1966 ★★★ First of four Matt Helm adventures has the womanizing secret agent (Martin) trying to stop an evil madman (Buono) from blowing up a nuclear test site. Best of the series, with strong support from Stevens. C: Dean Martin, Stella Stevens, Victor Buono, Robert Webber, Cyd Charisse. D: Phil Karlson. ACT 102m.

Silent Call, The 1961 ★★ When they are separated, a dog journeys across the country to find his young master. The idea is engaging, but loses steam in this tepid production. C: Gail Russell, Roger Mobley. D: John Bushelman. DRA 63m.

Silent Conflict 1948 ★★★ A good friend of Hopalong Cassidy (Boyd) is hypnotized by a mysterious medicine man into stealing gold and then to kill him. C: William Boyd, Rand Brooks, Andy Clyde. D: George Archainbaud. WST 60m.

Silent Dust 1949 British ★★★ Believing his son to be dead in WWII action, a baron grieves and builds a memorial. Then his son turns up alive. A solid little melodrama. C: Sally Gray, Stephen Murray, Nigel Patrick. D: Lance Comfort. DRA 82m.

Silent Enemy, The 1958 British ★★★½ British Navy frogmen fight their German counterparts in the Mediterranean during WWII. Best for its excellent underwater battle sequences. C: Laurence Harvey, Dawn Addams, John Clements, Michael Craig. D: William Fairchild. ACT 92m. v

Silent Fall 1994 ★★★½ An autistic boy (Faulkner) witnesses the murder of his parents. Dreyfuss is the psychiatrist who trys to pry the truth from his frightened patient. Good performances keep up the suspense, until unbelievable plot twists take over. C: Richard Dreyfuss, Linda Hamilton, Ben Faulkner, John Lithgow, Liv Tyler. D: Bruce Beresford. DRA [R] 102m. v

Silent Madness 1984 ★★½ A psychotic killer escapes from the asylum and returns to the sorority house where he committed his first murders years ago. C: Belinda Montgomery, Viveca Lindfors, David Greenan. D: Simon Nuchtern. HOR [R] 93m. v

Silent Motive 1992 ★★★ A beautiful and talented screenwriter suddenly realizes that several film industry murders follow the plots of her films. Good work by Thirtysomething star Wettig. C: Patricia Wettig, Edward Asner, Mike Farrell. HOR 90m. v

Silent Movie 1976 ★★★½ Uneven tribute to silent comedy has only one word of spoken dialogue (given to mime Marceau). Pirandelloish plot concerns Brooks' attempt to produce silent movie in the 1970s. Some sequences extremely funny (such as Reynolds in the shower). C: Mel Brooks, Marty Feldman, Dom DeLuise, Bernadette Peters, Sid Caesar, Burt Reynolds, James Caan, Liza Minnelli, Paul Newman, Marcel Marceau. D: Mel Brooks. COM [PG] 88M. v

Silent Night, Deadly Night 1984 ★★ First Jason and Freddy . . . now Santa! Yes, good old St. Nick gets the low-budget horror treatment as a psychopath (Wilson) dons a Santa suit and goes on an axe-swinging spree. Film made headlines (and angered parents) with its cheesy Xmas ad campaign. C: Lilyan Chauvan, Gilmer McCormick. D: Charles Sellier, Jr. HOR [R] 92m. v

Silent Night, Deadly Night (Part II) 1987 ★★ A lame continuation (made up mainly of footage from the previous film shown in handy "flashback" form) with another evil ersatz Santa hefting a razor sharp axe. C: Eric Freeman, James L. Newman, Elizabeth Cayton, Jean Miller. D: Lee Harry. HOR [R] 88m. v

Silent Night, Deadly Night (Part III—Better Watch Out!) 1989 ★★½ Heeee's back—but this time, Santa's a victim! Competently made installment has grown-up killer from the previous film chasing after a young blind woman, with whom he has a psychic link. Not as gory as first two. C: Samantha Scully, Bill Moseley, Richard Beymer, Robert Culp. D: Monte Hellman. HOR [R] 90m. v

Silent Night, Deadly Night (Part IV—The Initiation) 1990 ★★★½ Completely unrelated to the earlier killer-Santa series entries (and better than all of them), this gruesome film pits a reporter (Hunter) against a modern witches' coven. Frequently scary and sprinkled with gross-out effects. C: Maud Adams, Keith Hunter, Allyce Beasley, Tommy Hinkley, Clint Howard. D: Brian Yuzna. HOR [R] 86m. v

Silent Night, Deadly Night (Part V—The Toy Maker) 1991 ★★½ Just like the title says: An evil toymaker and his twisted son create toys that kill their young owners. No plot compared to earlier installments. Gory and grisly. C: Jane Higginson, William Thorne, Tracy Fraim, Mickey Rooney, Keith Hunter. D: Martin Kitrosser. HOR [R] 90m. v

Silent Night, Lonely Night 1969 ★★★½ Two middle-aged misfits meet on Christmas Eve at a New England lodge. Sensitive, well-acted adaptation of Robert Anderson's play. C: Lloyd Bridges, Shirley Jones, Carrie Snodgress, Cloris Leachman. D: Daniel Petrie. DRA 98m.

Silent One, The 1986 ★★ Polynesian youth has a mystical relationship with a sea turtle. Exquisite underwater photography makes this film memorable. C: Teb Malese, George Henare. D: Yvonne Mackay. DRA [PG] 96m. v

Silent Partner, The 1978 Canadian ★★★★ Bank teller (Gould) runs afoul of a robber (Plummer) when he decides to scoop up some loot for himself. Uncompromising script, skillfully performed: an offbeat suspenseful production. C: Elliott Gould, Christopher Plummer, Susannah York, John Candy. D: Daryl Duke. CRI [R] 103m. v

Silent Passenger, The 1935 British ★★ Noted British detective clears a man of a murder charge. Based on characters created by British mystery writer Dorothy Sayers. Anemic story and middling production values. C: John Loder, Peter Haddon, Mary Newland, Austin Trevor, Donald Wolfit, Aubrey Mather. D: Reginald Denham. DRA 75m.

Silent Rage 1982 ★★★½ Chuck is the small-town sherrif with a black belt in martial arts and a genetically engineered psychopath (Libby) on his hands. Nonsensical plot, but fun to watch. C: Chuck Norris, Ron Silver, Steven Keats, Toni Kalem, William Finley, Brian Libby, Stephen Furst. D: Michael Miller. ACT [R] 105m. v

Silent Rebellion 1982 ★★★ After a long life in the new world, an elderly Greek man and his son return for a visit to the old country. C: Telly Savalas, Keith Gordon, Michael Constantine. D: Charles S. Dubin. DRA 90m. v

Silent Running 1972 ★★★★ Dern is charged with protecting Earth's last surviving flora and fauna, preserved in a space ship—until he gets the order to destroy it! Imaginative sci-fi effort, directed by the special effects whiz behind *2001* and *Close Encounters*. C: Bruce Dern, Cliff Potts, Ron Rifkin, Jesse Vint. D: Douglas Trumbull. SFI [G] 90m. v

Silent Tongue 1994 ★★½ Pulitzer Prize-winning playwright Shepard wrote and directed this odd Western. Bates sends his half-Native-American daughter to Harris' son Phoenix, but after she dies in childbirth Harris kidnaps her sister as a replacement. Film is heart-felt, but confusing. Phoenix's last completed film. C: Richard Harris, Alan Bates, River Phoenix, Dermot Mulroney. D: Sam Shepard. WST [PG-13] 98m. v

Silent Victim 1992 ★★★ A young pregnant housewife is the victim of a cruel husband. To make things worse, national pro-choice and pro-life activists start to us her for their own ends. C: Michele Greene, Kyle Secor, Ely Pouget. D: Menahem Golan. DRA [R] 116m. v

Silent Witness 1985 ★★ After a woman (Bertinelli) and her husband accidentally witness a barroom rape in which her husband's brother is a participant, the woman struggles with whether or not to reveal this family crime. Inferior made-for-TV movie. C: Valerie Bertinelli, John Savage, Chris Nash, Melissa Leo. D: Michael Miller. CRI [R] 97m. TVM v

Silk 1986 ★★★ A beautiful, brainy detective gets in the middle of a ring of heroin smugglers. C: CEC Verrell, Bill Laughlin, Fred Bailey. D: Ciro H. Santiago. ACT [R] 84m. v

Silk Noose, The 1950 British ★★★★ Reporter Landis stumbles onto the story of her career when she accidentally uncovers a murderous gang of counterfeiters run by Calleia and Patrick. Entertaining and intense study of the criminal underworld, with good performances. (a.k.a. *Noose*) C: Carole Landis, Joseph Calleia, Stanley Holloway, Nigel Patrick. D: Edmond T. Greville. CRI 76m.

Silk Road, The 1992 Chinese ★★★ This epic set in 11th-century China chronicles the adventures of a youth who falls in love with a princess. In the highly stylized Eastern tradition, movie features opulent sets and costumes and well-executed battles. C: Koichi Sato, Toshiyuki Nishida, Tsunehiko Watase, Anna Nakagawa. D: Junya Sato. DRA [PG-13] 99m. V

Silk Stockings 1957 ★★★★ Entertaining if dated musical version of *Ninotchka*, with frigid Soviet emissary (Charisse) transformed by American movie producer (Astaire) into warm, loving woman. Cole Porter score includes lovely ballad "All of You." Some terrific dance numbers, and great comic support from Paige and Lorre. C: Fred Astaire, Cyd Charisse, Janis Paige, Peter Lorre. D: Rouben Mamoulian. MUS 117m. V

Silk 2/Circle of Fear 1990 ★★ Tough woman cop stamps out crime in Honolulu. Hawaiian settings help this female actioner. C: Monique Gabrielle, Peter Nelson, Jan Merlin, Maria Clair. D: Cirio H. Santiago. ACT [R] 163m. V

Silkwood 1983 ★★★★½ Hard-living woman who labors at nuclear facility finds courage and political acumen when she discovers she and her coworkers are being needlessly exposed to excess radiation. Thriller that manages to be a character study, with terrific ensemble work. Streep a standout. C: Meryl Streep, Kurt Russell, Cher, Craig T. Nelson, Fred Ward, Josef Sommer. D: Mike Nichols. DRA [R] 131m. V

Silver Blaze *See* **Murder at the Baskervilles**

Silver Bullet 1985 ★★½ A small town is terrorized by a vicious, animal-like killer . . . but only when the moon is full. Some suspense, but town takes so long to come to its senses that there's a credibility strain. Half-baked effort, based on Stephen King's *Cycle of the Werewolf*. C: Corey Haim, Gary Busey, Everett McGill, Terry O'Quinn. D: Daniel Attias. HOR [R] 95m. V

Silver Chalice, The 1954 ★★½ The trials and tribulations of a Greek sculptor (Newman) who winds up designing the chalice used by Christ at the Last Supper. Stultifying religious epic was Newman's first film, which he apologized for in a famous newspaper ad years later, when it was shown on TV. C: Paul Newman, Virginia Mayo, Jack Palance, Pier Angeli. D: Victor Saville. DRA 144m. V

Silver City 1951 ★★★ When a farmer and his daughter find ore, an assayer helps them protect it. Good cast and plenty of color and action. C: Edmond O'Brien, Yvonne De Carlo, Richard Arlen, Gladys George, Barry Fitzgerald. D: Byron Haskin. WST 90m.

Silver City 1983 Australian ★★★ Polish refugees crowd into Australia after WWII, with special emphasis on a pair of lovers who meet in an internment camp. An interesting and emotional film that holds one's interest throughout. C: Gosia Dobrowolska, Ivar Kants, Anna Jemison, Steve Bisley. D: Sophia Turkiewicz. DRA [PG] 110m. V

Silver City Raiders 1943 ★★★ When Ingram starts land-grabbing in the Old West, Hayen stops him through action, laughs, and a few musical numbers. Mildly entertaining but forgettable B-Western outing. C: Russell Hayden, Bob Wills, Jack Ingram. D: William Berke. WST 55m.

Silver Cord, The 1933 ★★★★ A strong-willed matriarch (Crews) gets resistance from her new daughter-in-law (Dunne), which tears the family in two. Superbly acted version of the Sidney Howard play. C: Irene Dunne, Laura Hope Crews, Joel McCrea, Frances Dee. D: John Cromwell. DRA 74m.

Silver Dollar 1932 ★★★ Poor farmer ventures to Colorado, where he finds gold and strikes it rich. Based on the life of H.A.W. Tabor, who helped build Denver into a major city. Robinson is effective in this solid biographical adventure. C: Edward G. Robinson, Bebe Daniels, Aline MacMahon, Robert Warwick, Jobyna Howland. D: Alfred E. Green. WST 84m.

Silver Fleet, The 1945 British ★★★ In Holland during WWII, a shipbuilder plans to blow up a Nazi U-boat. Slow at times, but otherwise filled with excellent wartime suspense. Richardson is fine. C: Ralph Richardson, Googie Withers, Edmond Knight. D: Vernon Campbell Sewell, Gordon Wellesley. ACT 77m.

Silver Horde 1930 ★★★½ In this early career break, McCrea stars as Alaskan fishery operator who overcomes difficulties raised by rival Gordon. His romantic life is also complicated when wealthy Arthur intrudes on McCrea's romance with dance hall entertainer Brent. Routine material, bolstered by good action sequences. C: Evelyn Brent, Joel McCrea, Jean Arthur. D: George Archainbaud. DRA 76m.

Silver Lode 1954 ★★½ A man accused of murder fights to prove his innocence. Good little hard-boiled Western, with plenty of action and violence. C: John Payne, Lizabeth Scott, Dan Duryea, Dolores Moran. D: Allan Dwan. WST 80m. V

Silver on the Sage 1939 ★★★½ Boyd uncovers a plot by a pair of desperado twins, who use their casino as a front for a cattle rustling operation. Entertaining *Hopalong Cassidy* series entry, with a nice blend of action and comedy. C: William Boyd, Russell Hayden, George "Gabby" Hayes, Ruth Rogers. D: Lesley Selander. WST 66m.

Silver River 1948 ★★★ The rise and fall of a gambling scoundrel. A real hodgepodge of events that's ultimately saved by Errol and Ann. C: Errol Flynn, Ann Sheridan, Thomas

Mitchell, Bruce Bennett, Tom D'Andrea, Barton MacLane, Monte Blue. D: Raoul Walsh. WST 109m. V

Silver Spurs 1943 ★★½ Outlaw murders a wealthy landowner to take over of his oil holdings, but Roy Rogers catches up with him. A good, action-filled Western with Roy up to standard. C: Roy Rogers, Phyllis Brooks, Smiley Burnette, John Carradine. D: Joseph Kane. WST 60m. V

Silver Streak 1976 ★★★★ On cross-country train trip passengers (Wilder, Pryor, and Clayburgh) get mixed up with murderers (McGoohan and Walston), leading to wild climax at Chicago's Union Station. Fine mix of comedy and suspense that's well played by very funny ensemble. First of Pryor and Wilder's many screen pairings. C: Gene Wilder, Jill Clayburgh, Richard Pryor, Patrick McGoohan, Ned Beatty, Ray Walston, Scatman Crothers, Clifton James, Richard Kiel. D: Arthur Hiller. COM [PG] 113m. V

Silver Trails 1948 ★★★ Meeker is a land grabber whose nefarious turns are ultimately undone by Wakely and his sidekick Taylor. Typical minor B-Western material with all the prerequisite characters and sequences. C: Jimmy Wakely, Christine Larson, George Meeker. D: Christy Cabanne. WST 53m.

Silver Whip, The 1953 ★★½ Bandits prey on a stagecoach line. Good action in this Western and a fine young, up-and-coming cast. C: Dale Robertson, Rory Calhoun, Robert Wagner, Kathleen Crowley, Lola Albright. D: Harmon Jones. WST 73m.

Silverado 1985 ★★★★ Modern Western about four gunfighters teaming up to clean up a frontier town. Fast moving, well made with some genuinely funny moments. Perhaps too violent for some kids. C: Kevin Kline, Scott Glenn, Kevin Costner, Danny Glover, John Cleese, Rosanna Arquette, Brian Dennehy, Linda Hunt. D: Lawrence Kasdan. WST 132m. V

Simchon Family, The 1969 Israeli ★★★½ Government bureaucrat tries to elevate himself and his family's social standing by installing the clan in a plush condominium that is well beyond their means. Some cute moments in this comedy adapted from a popular Israeli radio series. C: Meir Margalit, Shoshana Barnea, Oded Kotler. D: Yoel Zilberg. COM 88m.

Simon 1980 ★★½ Scientists brainwash their colleague into believing he's from another planet. Intriguing idea that has its fun moments, but the some serious world-saving satire waters down the comedy. C: Alan Arkin, Madeline Kahn, Austin Pendleton, Fred Gwynne. D: Marshall Brickman. COM [PG] 90m. V

Simon and Laura 1956 British ★★★★ Married TV personalities (Finch, Kendall), whose show trumpets them as "divinely happy," can't stand each other off-screen. Lively sparring of the two fine stars generates wicked fun. C: Peter Finch, Kay Kendall, Maurice Denham. D: Muriel Box. COM 91m.

Simon Bolivar ★★★½ The tale of Latin America's famed revolutionary, Simon Bolivar, and his victorious fight for liberation from the Spaniards. C: Maximilian Schell, Rosanna Schiaffino. WST 120m.

Simon, King Of The Witches 1971 ★★ A contemporary warlock's occult activitites, which include human sacrifice, threaten innocents around him. C: Andrew Prine, Brenda Scott, George Paulsin. D: Bruce Kessler. HOR [R] 89m.

Simon of the Desert 1965 Mexican ★★★★★ Religion gets a roasting in this savage, brilliant satire about a possible lunatic who camps out on a pinnacle to talk to God. Bunuel's known for his surreal, visionary fables, and this is one of his bravest and best. C: Claudio Brook, Silvia Pinal, Enrique Alvarez Felix. D: Luis Bunuel. COM 65m. V

Simple Case of Money, A 1952 French ★★★ Wrong lottery numbers are published in a newspaper, which causes a bizarre cast of characters to make claims for big money. A one-gag French farce. C: Gaby Morlay, Jean Brochard, Jacques Baumer, Bernard Lajarrige. D: Andre Hunebelle. COM 82m.

Simple Justice 1989 ★★½ Justice is ironically served when two murderous thieves are themselves slain by an unknown. C: Cesar Romero, Doris Roberts, John Spencer. D: Deborah Del Prete. ACT [R] 91m.

Simple Men 1992 ★★★½ Offbeat tale of two mismatched brothers searching for their long lost father. Dryly humorous. C: Robert Burke, William Sage, Karen Sillas, Elina Lowensohn. D: Hal Hartley. DRA [R] 105m.

Simple Story, A 1978 French ★★★★ A middle-aged woman (Schneider) re-examines her life after having an abortion. Sensitive topic gets suitably restrained treatment, with a fine performance by Schneider. C: Romy Schneider, Bruno Cremer, Claude Brasseur. D: Claude Sautet. DRA 110m. V

Simple Truth 1986 ★★ A receptionist falls in love with the owner of the company. Some poignancy. C: Nancy Morgan, Brad Maule, Lyle Waggoner. DRA 100m. V

Simple Twist of Fate, A 1994 ★★★½ Uneven attempt to update George Eliot's classic novel, *Silas Marner*, stars Martin as reclusive miser whose life is altered by young girl who becomes his ward. Gentle, touching, but should have been funnier. C: Steve Martin, Alana Austion, Gabriel Byrne, Catherine O'Hara. D: Gillies MacKinnon. COM [PG-13] 110m. V

Sin of Harold Diddlebock, The 1947 *See* **Mad Wednesday**

Sin of Madelon Claudet, The 1931 ★★★★ Hayes made her mark (and earned an Oscar for Best Actress) in this unabashed tearjerker about a young woman who becomes a thief to support her out-of-wedlock infant. Terribly dated, but worth it for Hayes' exceptional performance. C: Helen Hayes, Lewis Stone, Neil Hamilton, Robert Young, Cliff Edwards, Jean Hersholt, Marie Prevost, Karen Morley. D: Edgar Selwyn. DRA 76m. V

Sin Takes a Holiday 1930 ★★★½ To save boss MacKenna from unwanted nuptials, loyal employee Bennett agrees to marriage of convenience. Enter kindly Rathbone, who teaches Bennett her self-worth. Now she must decide what she really wants. Simple soap opera is greatly improved by good performances. C: Constance Bennett, Kenneth MacKenna, Basil Rathbone, Zasu Pitts. D: Paul L. Stein. DRA 81m.

Sin, The 1979 *See* **Good Luck, Miss Wyckoff**

Sinai Commandos 1968 ★★★ A group of Israeli commandos set out to destroy Arab radar installations at the onset of the June 1967 war. Good action sequences, including some real combat footage. C: Robert Fuller. D: Raphael Nussbaum. ACT [PG] 99m. V

Sinatra 1992 ★★★★ Up-and-down life of the famed pop singer/actor gets unique TV film treatment. Not your typical soap-and-schmaltz, but a well-written, well-cast drama which uses Frank's recordings (lip-synched by Casnoff) to grand effect. Produced by Nancy Sinatra. C: Philip Casnoff, Marcia Gay Harden, Olympia Dukakis, Joe Santos, Rod Steiger. D: James Sadwith. MUS 250m. TVM V

Sinbad and the Eye of the Tiger 1977 British ★★★½ The hero sailor (Wayne) romances a beautiful princess (Seymour) but first has to save her brother from a terrible curse. Special effects by Ray Harryhausen. Good for kids. C: Patrick Wayne, Jane Seymour, Taryn Power, Margaret Whiting, Patrick Troughton. D: Sam Wanamaker. ACT [G] 113m. V

Sinbad Of The Seven Seas 1989 ★★ Evil magic and danger await Sinbad and a young prince who join forces against a wizard in an effort to save a princess. Sinbad on steroids. Crude and violent. C: Lou Ferrigno, John Steiner, Cork Hubbert. D: Enzo Castellari. ACT [PG-13] 90m.

Sinbad the Sailor 1947 ★★★★ The great mythical mariner sets off to locate the lost treasure of Alexander the Great. Enormously colorful period swashbuckler, with a first-class cast. C: Douglas Fairbanks, Jr., Maureen O'Hara, Anthony Quinn, Walter Slezak. D: Richard Wallace. ACT 117m. V

Since You Went Away 1944 ★★★★½ Colbert plays the matriarch of a family coping with WWII on the homefront in good-willed, patriotic, well-produced drama. Temple's a bit cloying but rest of cast makes this sentimental tearjerker well worth seeing. Oscar for Max Steiner's score. C: Claudette Colbert, Jennifer Jones, Joseph Cotten, Shirley Temple, Monty Woolley, Hattie McDaniel, Agnes Moorehead, Craig Stevens, Keenan Wynn, Nazimova, Robert Walker, Lionel Barrymore. D: John Cromwell. DRA 172m. V

Sincerely, Violet 1987 ★★★ A wily professor adopts an eccentric alter-ego after being caught stealing historical documents and winds up falling in love with her captor. C: Simon MacCorkindale, Patricia Phillips. DRA 80m.

Sincerely Yours 1955 ★ Liberace, then a TV heartthrob, made his film debut in one of the worst movies ever made. He's a concert pianist out to help others, and woo Malone. One of those instances of so bad, it's funny. Remake of *The Man Who Played God.* C: Liberace, Joanne Dru, Dorothy Malone, William Demarest, Richard Eyer. D: Gordon Douglas. MUS 115m. V

Sing 1989 ★★ Strange pack of '50s stereotypes plugged into '80s movie about Brooklyn high school students competing in a song/-dance contest. Some good numbers. C: Lorraine Bracco, Peter Dobson, Jessica Steen, Louise Lasser, George DiCenzo, Patti La Belle. D: Richard Baskin. MUS [PG-13] 97m. V

Sing As We Go 1934 British ★★★★ When she loses her job, a young millworker fills in at various industrial positions. A star vehicle for the great Ms. Fields and lots of fun. C: Gracie Fields, John Loder, Stanley Holloway. D: Basil Dean. COM 80m.

Sing, Baby, Sing 1936 ★★★ A boozed-up Shakespearean superactor becomes infatuated with a nightclub singer. Quality cast and fabulous music! C: Alice Faye, Adolphe Menjou, Gregory Ratoff, Ted Healy, Patsy Kelly, Tony Martin. D: Sidney Lanfield. MUS 87m.

Sing, Cowboy, Sing 1937 ★★★½ Tex Ritter leads a wagon train, sings a few ditties and stops a horde of plundering thieves in this comic B-Western. Support by former silent clowns St. John, Pollard, and Conklin add to the easy laughs. C: Tex Ritter. WST 60m. V

Sing, You Sinners 1938 ★★★ Carefree family parades their racehorse from track to track. Lots of good fun and an earful of great Crosby tunes. C: Bing Crosby, Fred MacMurray, Donald O'Connor, Elizabeth Patterson, Ellen Drew, John Gallaudet. D: Wesley Ruggles. MUS 88m.

Singin' in the Rain 1952 ★★★★★ Widely heralded as the best movie musical of all time, this buoyant satire of the advent of talkies gets better with each viewing. Perfect script about silent acting team having difficulties with transition to sound is studded with classic numbers including Kelly's title dance, O'Connor's hysterical "Make 'Em Laugh," and the grand fantasy "Broadway Melody" production number. Top-notch support from Hagen as nasal-voiced star and Charisse as stunning dancer in finale. C: Gene Kelly, Debbie Reynolds, Donald O'Connor, Jean Hagen, Cyd Charisse, Millard Mitchell, Rita Moreno. D: Gene Kelly, Stanley Donen. MUS [G] 102m. V

Singing Blacksmith 1938 ★★★½ Filmed version of popular Yiddish theater piece involves the domestic woes of blacksmith Oysher and his spouse Riselle. An interesting look at a vanished art form. Watch for a very young Herschell Bernardi playing Oysher's character in a flashback sequence. C: Miriam Riselle, Florence Weiss, Moishe Oysher. D: Edgar G. Ulmer. DRA 95m.

Singing Fool, The 1928 ★★★ When his young son dies, a successful singer's career starts to fall apart. The story is too sentimental, but Jolson is a singing/dancing dynamo. Sequel to *The Jazz Singer*. C: Al Jolson, Betty Bronson, Josephine Dunn, Arthur Housman, Davey Lee, Edward Martindel, Helen Lynch, Robert Emmett O'Connor. D: Lloyd Bacon. DRA 101m.

Singing Kid, The 1936 ★★★ Famed singing star loses his voice, goes to the country to recover. Jolson vehicle features fine musical guest stars, top-notch Harburg-Arlen songs. C: Al Jolson, Sybil Jason, Edward Everett Horton. D: William Keighley. MUS 85m.

Singing Nun, The 1966 ★★½ Overly sentimental and unintentionally campy story of real-life nun (Reynolds) torn between the church and her music career after her recording of "Dominque" is an unlikely chart buster. Packed with uplifting scenes. C: Debbie Reynolds, Ricardo Montalban, Greer Garson, Agnes Moorehead, Chad Everett, Katharine Ross, Ed Sullivan, Juanita Moore, Tom Drake. D: Henry Koster. FAM/DRA 98m. ▾

Singing Princess, The 1967 Italian ★★★½ The third version of this animated Italian film, orginally made in 1949, features the voice of Julie Andrews as the princess who runs from a cruel sheik to the arms of a dashing minstrel. Pleasant, tuneful affair for kids and adults. British version dubbed in 1952. Voices of Julie Andrews, Howard Marion-Crawford. D: Anton Gino Domeneghini. FAM/MUS 76m. ▾

Single Fighter 1978 ★★ A martial arts master must seek out and bring to justice World War II traitors who helped the Japanese. C: Tu Chiang. D: Lee Chin-Chuan. ACT [R] 79m. ▾

Single Room Furnished 1968 ★ A dim-witted woman (Mansfield) abandoned after she becomes pregnant, decides to become a hooker. Released after her death, film only reveals how talentless she was. C: Jayne Mansfield, Dorothy Keller, Fabian Dean, Billy M. Greene, Terri Messina, Martin Horsey, Walter Gregg. D: Matteo Ottaviano. DRA 93m. ▾

Single Standard, The 1929 ★★★½ Society woman (Garbo) flouts convention by having an affair with a dissolute artist (Asther). Gorgeous Garbo makes gold out of a by-the-numbers silent romance. C: Greta Garbo, Nils Asther, John Mack Brown. D: John S. Robertson. DRA 73m. ▾

Single White Female 1992 ★★½ A newly single yuppie (Fonda) shares her fabulous N.Y. apartment with an apparently innocuous roommate (Leigh), who begins to assume her personality and exhibit nasty behavioral traits. Not for the squeamish. C: Bridget Fonda, Jennifer Jason Leigh, Steven Weber, Peter Friedman, Stephen Tobolowsky, Frances Bay, Rene Estevez, Ken Tobey. D: Barbet Schroder. HOR [R] 107m. ▾

Singles 1992 ★★★½ Episodic tale about young singles living on fringes of Seattle grunge culture of early '90s. Good acting bolsters an uneven script; great soundtrack by top Seattle-based bands. C: Bridget Fonda, Matt Dillon, Campbell Scott, Kyra Sedgwick, Sheila Kelley, Jim True, Bill Pullman, James LeGros, Devon Raymond. D: Cameron Crowe. COM [PG-13] 99m. ▾

Singleton's Pluck 1984 British ★★★ A tenacious farmer must find a way to deal with delays and unexpected events while trying to deliver his holiday geese to market. C: Ian Holm, Penelope Wilton. D: Richard Eyre. DRA 89m. ▾

Sinister Journey 1948 ★★½ Three eccentric friends sign up for railroad jobs in an effort to uncover the cause of numerous suspicious accidents. C: William Boyd, Andy Clyde, Rand Brooks. D: George Archainbaud. WST 58m.

Sink the Bismarck! 1960 British ★★★★ High seas thrills (historically accurate), as the British Navy targets the dreaded Nazi battleship. Fast moving, with a very entertaining (and explosive) climax. C: Kenneth More, Dana Wynter, Carl Mohner, Laurence Naismith, Geoffrey Keen, Karel Stepanek. D: Lewis Gilbert. ACT 97m. ▾

Sinners 1989 ★★ A man cheats on his wife and becomes target practice for his lover's brother whose favorite hobby is blowing up cars. C: Joey Travolta, Joe Palese, Lou Calvelli. D: Charles Kanganis. COM 90m. ▾

Sinner's Holiday 1930 ★★½ Fairground barker falls for a young woman who works nearby, but her brother is trying to frame him. An old gem, and James Cagney's first film. C: Grant Withers, Evalyn Knapp, James Cagney, Joan Blondell, Lucille LaVerne, Noel Madison. D: John G. Adolfi. DRA 60m.

Sinners in the Sun 1932 ★★★ A woman is torn between riches and true romance. Lombard is always good, and her performance in this mediocre material proves it. Grant, in his second film, has a small part as a society bon vivant. C: Carole Lombard, Chester Morris, Adrienne Ames, Walter Byron, Alison Skipworth, Cary Grant. D: Alexander Hall. DRA 70m.

Sins 1985 ★★★ A woman advances her fashion career—at the expense of others along the way. Lively comeuppance soaper. C: Joan Collins, Timothy Dalton, Catherine Mary Stewart, Gene Kelly. D: Douglas Hickox. DRA 336m. TVM ▾

Sins of Desire 1992 ★★½ Woman goes undercover as a nurse in a sex clinic after her sister, a former patient, dies mysteriously. Torrid mystery thriller. C: Delia Sheppard, Jay Richardson, Jan-Michael Vincent, Tanya Roberts. D: Jim Wynorski. DRA 90m. V
Sins of Dorian Gray, The 1982 ★ A woman stays eternally young while her video screen test ages. Attempt at updating Oscar Wilde's classic story comes off as misconceived and laughable, despite some genre veterans in the cast. C: Anthony Perkins, Joseph Bottoms, Belinda Bauer, Olga Karlatos. D: Tony Maylam. HOR 95m. TVM V
Sins of the Fathers 1986 German ★★★ Epic story of the effects of WWII on a German family. Talented cast. C: Burt Lancaster, Julie Christie, Bruno Ganz, Dieter Laser, Tina Engel, Martin Benrath, Cyrielle Claire, Katharina Thalbach, Christian Doermer. D: Bernhard Sinkel. DRA 200m. TVM
Sins of the Night 1993 ★★½ An ex-con turned insurance investigator looks into a claim by an erotic dancer. He falls under her spell and into degradation. Lurid potboiler. C: Deborah Shelton, Nick Cassavetes. CRI [R] 82m. V
Sioux City Sue 1946 ★★★ Talent scouts "discover" Gene Autry . . . but trick the singing cowboy into becoming the voice of a crooning donkey! Plenty of fun and good music. C: Gene Autry, Lynne Roberts, Sterling Holloway. D: Frank McDonald. MUS 69m. V
Siren of Bagdad 1953 ★★ When a sultan is deposed, a traveling magician comes to the rescue to get him reinstated. Lots of silly stuff that provides occasional laughs. C: Paul Henreid, Patricia Medina, Hans Conried, Charlie Lung. D: Richard Quine. ACT 77m.
Sirens 1994 ★★★★½ Neill is memorable as Australian artist Norman Lindsey, famous for his erotic works, visited by a minister (Grant), who wants to save him from his bohemian lifestyle. But who saves whom? A witty, warm film with lovely acting and smart direction. C: Hugh Grant, Tara Fitzgerald, Sam Neill, Elle Macpherson, Portia de Rossi, Kate Fischer. D: John Duigan. DRA [R] 94m.
Sirocco 1951 ★★★★ Solid performance from Bogie; he's a tough-talking gunrunner in '20s Syria, who finds himself caught in a standoff between police and terrorists. C: Humphrey Bogart, Marta Toren, Lee J. Cobb, Everett Sloane, Zero Mostel. D: Curtis Bernhardt. ACT 111m. V
Sister Act 1992 ★★★★ A Las Vegas lounge singer (Goldberg) accidentally sees a gang hit and has to go into the witness protection program, masquerading as a nun in a convent. Funny idea and likable performers, with exhilarating musical numbers as Whoopi whips the church choir into shape. Manipulative, but it works. Followed by a sequel. C: Whoopi Goldberg, Maggie Smith, Harvey Keitel, Kathy Najimy, Mary Wickes. D: Emile Ardolino. COM [PG] 100m. V
Sister Act 2: Back in the Habit 1993 ★★★ Sequel to the hit comedy puts everyone's favorite lounge singer (Goldberg) back in the habit as a teacher of underprivileged children. Saved by the star's energy. C: Whoopi Goldberg, Kathy Najimy, Barnard Hughes, Mary Wickes, James Coburn, Michael Jeter, Sheryl Lee Ralph. D: Bill Duke. COM [PG] 106m. V
Sister Kenny 1946 ★★★ Life story of the Australian nurse who helped pioneer treatment—and ultimately the cure for polio. Efficient, well-played film biography. Russell is solid. C: Rosalind Russell, Alexander Knox, Dean Jagger, Beulah Bondi. D: Dudley Nichols. DRA 116m. V
Sister, Sister 1982 ★★★ The uncomfortable reunion of three sisters ultimately leads them to reconsider their family history. Solid acting by Carroll, Cash, and Cara, and an evocative script make this made-for-TV movie a rewarding viewing experience. C: Diahann Carroll, Rosalind Cash, Irene Cara, Paul Winfield, Dick Williams, Robert Hooks, Christopher John, Diana Douglas, Albert Powell. D: John Berry. DRA 100m. TVM V
Sisterhood, The 1988 ★★½ In the year 2021, women are helplessly oppressed by a male-dominated society and their only hope for freedom lies in the special power and strength of a select group of maidens. C: Rebecca Holden, Chuck Wagner, Lynn-Holly Johnson. D: Cirio H. Santiago. SFI [R] 75m. V
Sisters 1973 ★★★★ Early horror effort from director De Palma is an in-your-face shocker about reporter (Salt) witnessing a murder and tangling with one of two separated Siamese twins (Kidder). Plenty of surprises and stylish touches. C: Margot Kidder, Jennifer Salt, Charles Durning, Barnard Hughes, Bill Finley, Lisle Wilson. D: Brian De Palma. HOR [R] 92m. V
Sisters of Death 1978 ★★½ Six high school girls are mysteriously invited to an eerie reunion on the anniversary of a tragic accident in which one of their schoolmates was killed. C: Claudia Jennings, Arthur Franz. HOR [PG] 87m. V
Sisters, The 1938 ★★★★ Handsome period soap opera in which Davis finds philandering husband (Flynn) too much to handle in turn-of-the-century San Francisco. Nice chemistry between stars. C: Errol Flynn, Bette Davis, Anita Louise, Ian Hunter, Donald Crisp, Beulah Bondi, Jane Bryan, Lee Patrick. D: Anatole Litvak. DRA 99m. V
Sitting Bull 1954 ★★ After Custer and his men are vanquished at the Little Bighorn, a cavalry officer tries to reason with Chief Sitting Bull. Plodding and ineffective Western. C: Dale Robertson, Mary Murphy, J. Carroll Naish, Iron Cody, John Litel. D: Sidney Salkow. WST 105m. V

Sitting Ducks 1980 ★★★½ Two men (Emil and Norman) steal a bundle of cash from the Mob and hide out in Miami, where they take up with a couple of women who aren't what they seem. Sharp, smart, engaging comedy. C: Michael Emil, Zack Norman, Patrice Townsend, Irene Forrest. D: Henry Jaglom. COM [R] 88m. V

Sitting in Limbo 1986 ★★★½ Four African-American teenagers try to make sense of their confused lives in Montreal. Fine low-budget feature takes a rarely seen dignified approach to teenage issues. C: Pat Dillon, Fabian Gibbs, Sylvie Clarke, Debbie Grant. D: John N. Smith. DRA 96m. V

Sitting Pretty 1933 ★★★ A couple of hard-working songwriters (Oakie and Haley) make it to the big time . . . in Hollywood! Fascinating antique filled with big smiles and wonderful music. C: Ginger Rogers, Jack Oakie, Jack Haley, Thelma Todd, Gregory Ratoff, Lew Cody. D: Harry Joe Brown. MUS 85m.

Sitting Pretty 1948 ★★★★ Model middle-class suburbanites (O'Hara and Young) need a nanny for their three spoiled kids. Justifiably famous comedy, with Webb at his appealing prissiest as Lynn Belvedere, and some sharp observations about postwar America. Adapted from Gwen Davenport novel *Mr. Belvedere*; Webb starred in four sequels. C: Robert Young, Maureen O'Hara, Clifton Webb, Richard Haydn, Louise Allbritton, Ed Begley. D: Walter Lang. COM 84m.

Situation Hopeless—But Not Serious 1965 ★★★ Guinness is lonely German lunatic who holds American flyers Redford and Connors prisoner in his cellar, long after World War II ends. Quirky comedy remains grounded and claustrophobic. C: Alec Guinness, Michael Connors, Robert Redford, Anita Hoefer, Mady Rahl, Paul Dahlke. D: Gottfried Reinhardt. COM 97m.

Six Bridges to Cross 1955 ★★½ Thief (Curtis) gets big break leading $2.5 million robbery. Decent caper, loosely based on Brinks heist; somewhat too glittery for its Boston gangland milieu. Mineo's debut. C: Tony Curtis, Julia Adams, George Nader, Sal Mineo, Jay C. Flippen. D: Joseph Pevney. CRI 96m.

Six Degrees of Separation 1993 ★★★½ A charlatan (Smith), posing as the son of Sidney Poitier, finagles his way into NYC society, and once unmasked, reveals unwelcomed truths about the upper class. Fine debut by Smith, an Oscar-nominated performance by Channing, and good use of locations highlight this uneven adaptation of the John Guare play. C: Stockard Channing, Donald Sutherland, Will Smith, Mary Beth Hurt, Bruce Davison. D: Fred Schepisi. DRA [R] 112m. V

Six Gun Law 1962 ★★★ Appropriately set in Tombstone, Arizona, a stubborn lawyer refuses to give up on his defense of an innocent rancher accused of bank robbery. C: Robert Loggia, James Dunn, Lynn Bari. D: Christian NYBY. WST 77m.

Six of a Kind 1934 ★★★ George and Gracie and Mary and Charlie motor across country. Inspired, episodic nonsense, second of several teamings of Boland and Ruggles. C: W.C. Fields, George Burns, Gracie Allen, Charlie Ruggles, Mary Boland, Alison Skipworth. D: Leo McCarey. COM 62m.

Six Pack 1982 ★★½ Country singer Rogers made his acting debut here as stock car racer who adopts six orphans after he catches them stripping his car. Rogers couldn't be any stiffer in this contrived and saccharine comedy. C: Kenny Rogers, Diane Lane, Erin Gray, Barry Corbin. D: Daniel Petrie. FAM/COM [PG] 108m. V

Six Shootin' Sheriff 1938 ★★ Framed by outlaws and unjustly maligned, Trigger Martin returns to town for revenge. C: Ken Maynard, Marjorie Reynolds, Walter Long. D: Harry Fraser. WST 59m. V

633 Squadron 1964 British ★★½ Pilots in England during WWII prepare to bomb a factory in Norway that's supplying fuel to the Nazis. This British adventure is long on self-importance, and short on punch. C: Cliff Robertson, George Chakiris, Maria Perschy, Harry Andrews. D: Walter Grauman. ACT 102m. V

Six Weeks 1982 ★★★ Politico tries to help a young girl dying of leukemia and falls in love with her mother. Old-fashioned tearjerker with good performances from the two leads. C: Dudley Moore, Mary Tyler Moore, Katherine Healy, Shannon Wilcox. D: Tony Bill. DRA 107m. V

Sixteen Candles 1984 ★★★★ Ringwald's a teenager with problems: her parents forget her 16th birthday, nerdy Hall is chasing her, and her dream guy doesn't know she's alive. Charming adolescent comedy revels in goofy sense of humor and sweet performances. Ringwald's lead is a winner. C: Molly Ringwald, Anthony Michael Hall, Paul Dooley, Justin Henry, Michael Schoeffling, John Cusack. D: John Hughes. COM [PG] 93m. V

'68 1988 ★★ Hungarian restaurateur undergoes family difficulties during '60s antiwar era in San Francisco. Political focus eclipses thin character development. C: Eric Larson, Robert Locke, Neil Young, Sandor Tecsi, Terra Vandergaw. D: Steven Kovacks. DRA [R] 99m.

Sixty Glorious Years 1938 British ★★★½ Neagle is Queen Victoria in stately follow-up to *Victoria the Great*. Soporific pomp, but Dame Anna is exquisite and properly regal. Technicolor and costumes almost make it worthwhile. (a.k.a. *Queen of Destiny*) C: Anna Neagle, Anton Walbrook, C. Aubrey Smith, Walter Rilla, Charles Carson. D: Herbert Wilcox. DRA 95m.

Sizzle 1981 ★★★ Flapper in Prohibition-era Chicago. Florid melodrama gives Anderson a chance to kick up her heels, but the title especially applies when Uggams is on screen as a speakeasy chanteuse. C: Loni Anderson, John

Forsythe, Leslie Uggams, Roy Thinnes. D: Don Medford. DRA 100m. TVM V

Sizzle Beach, U.S.A. 1986 ★★ Brainless beach jiggle flick. Costner's first film (his scenes shot in 1974). C: Terry Congie, Leslie Brander, Roselyn Royce, Kevin Costner. D: Richard Brander. COM 90m. V

Skateboard Kid, The 1993 ★★½ A skateboarding misfit finds a ticket of acceptance when he comes across a magical talking skateboard that assures him of competition success. C: Timothy Busfield, Bess Armstrong, Cliff De Young. D: Larry Swerdlove. COM [PG] 83m. V

Skeeter 1994 ★★ A lethal strain of mosquitos has risen from the fumes of a toxic pool of water and offers little hope for escape. C: Tracy Griffith, Jim Youngs, Charles Napier. D: Clark Brandon. SFI [R] 90m.

Sketch Artist 1992 ★★ A police sketch artist (Fahey) finds himself in a delicate situation when a murder witness identifies his wife as a suspect. Disappointing effort without the requisite tension a thriller needs. C: Jeff Fahey, Sean Young, Drew Barrymore, Frank McRae, Tcheky Karyo, James Tolkan, Charlotte Lewis. D: Phedon Papamichael. CRI [R] 89m. TVM V

Sketches of a Strangler 1978 ★★ A demented art student combines his passions for murder and art, resulting in the gruesome deaths of unsuspecting streetwalkers. C: Allen Goorwitz, Meredith MacRae. D: Paul Leder. HOR 91m. V

Ski Patrol 1990 ★★ Pseudozany antics abound in mindless tale of sex and slapstick swirling around ski patrol. Same creative team produced *Police Academy* films, which should come as no surprise. C: Roger Rose, T.K. Carter, Paul Feig, Martin Mull, Ray Walston, Corby Timbrook. D: Richard Correll. COM [PG] 91m. V

Ski School 1990 ★★ Ski bums compete against uptight ski instructors on the slopes and in bed. Indifferently executed sex comedy, easy to take late at night. C: Dean Cameron, Patrick Labyorteaux, Ava Fabian. D: Damian Lee. ACT [R] 89m. V

Skidoo 1968 ★★½ Reformed mobster (Gleason) is tapped by gang to perform one last hit. Sprawling comedy, straining to be "hip," doesn't know how to use its talented cast. C: Jackie Gleason, Carol Channing, Frankie Avalon, Mickey Rooney, Groucho Marx, Fred Clark, Peter Lawford. D: Otto Preminger. COM [PG] 98m.

Skier's Dream 1988 ★★½ A modern day "Walter Mitty" story centering around a bored executive and his love for thrilling sports adventures. C: John Eaves, Ian Boyd. ACT 75m.

Skin Deep 1989 ★★★ Self-indulgent writer Ritter lives booze-ridden, runaround life that he's constantly bemoaning yet can't stop himself from wallowing in. Episodic plotting sets up some real knee-slappers. C: John Ritter, Vincent Gardenia, Alyson Reed, Julianne Phillips, Chelsea Field. D: Blake Edwards. COM [R] 102m. V

Skin Game 1971 ★★★½ Two con artists pull all kinds of jobs in one Western town after another. Fast-moving and quite funny at times. C: James Garner, Louis Gossett Jr., Susan Clark, Edward Asner. D: Paul Bogart. COM [PG] 102m. V

Skin Game, The 1931 British ★★ Talky drama from John Galsworthy's play about feuding neighbors. Wobbly early effort feels like Hitch is on training wheels. C: Edmund Gwenn, Jill Esmond, John Longden. D: Alfred Hitchcock. DRA 86m. V

Skinned Alive 1990 ★★ A psychotic family traveling cross-country is literally taking the skin off human backs to keep up their stock of custom leather clothing. C: Mary Jackson, Scott Spiegel, Susan Rothacker. D: Jin Killough. HOR 90m.

Skippy 1931 ★★★½ Towheaded, pie-faced little Cooper befriends derelict Coogan; together they try to buy a dog license. Searingly sentimental, though Cooper's performance is never false. Based on Percy Crosby's popular comic strip. Taurog won Oscar for Best Director. Sequel: *Sooky.* C: Jackie Cooper, Robert Coogan, Mitzi Green, Jackie Searl, Willard Robertson, Enid Bennett, Donald Haines. D: Norman Taurog. FAM/DRA 85m.

Skirts Ahoy! 1952 ★★★ Three military WAVEs seek romance and musical thrills while on shore. Unassuming romantic comedy that does little with *On the Town* gender flip. C: Esther Williams, Joan Evans, Vivian Blaine, Barry Sullivan, Keefe Brasselle, Debbie Reynolds, Bobby Van, Billy Eckstine. D: Sidney Lanfield. MUS 109m. V

Skokie 1981 ★★★★ Demonstrations by Illinois Nazis in 1977 pit a Jewish concentration camp survivor (Kaye, in his final film) against a defender of free speech (Rubinstein). Engrossing, hard-hitting drama. Kaye's fine dramatic performance gets outstanding support from the very talented cast. C: Danny Kaye, John Rubinstein, Kim Hunter, Lee Strasberg, Brian Dennehy, Eli Wallach, Carl Reiner. D: Herbert Wise. DRA [PG] 125m. TVM V

Skull, The 1965 British ★★★ The skull of the Marquis de Sade turns two old-timers to quivering jelly. Never dull, thanks to Lee's scenery chewing. C: Peter Cushing, Patrick Wymark, Christopher Lee, Nigel Green, Jill Bennett, Michael Gough, George Coulouris, Patrick Magee. D: Freddie Francis. HOR 83m. V

Skullduggery 1970 ★★★ A rugged explorer (Reynolds) and an anthropologist (Clark) fall in love while discovering the "missing link" in New Guinea. Intermittently fun adventure tale can't decide whether it's a spoof or for real. C: Burt Reynolds, Susan Clark, Roger C. Carmel. D: Gordon Douglas. DRA [PG] 105m.

Sky Above Heaven 1964 French ★ French navy tracks UFO. Amateur time. The English-dubbed version may provide a laugh or two. C: Andre Smagghe, Jacques Monod, Marcel Bozzufi. D: Yves Ciampi. DRA 107m.

Sky Above, The Mud Below, The 1961 French ★★★★ Intelligent, Oscar winning documentary looks at the daily lives of poor villagers in Dutch New Guinea. Thought-provoking film is very educational. D: Pierre-Dominique Gaisseau. DOC 92m.

Sky Dragon, The 1949 ★★ Conclusion of the Charlie Chan series best left to devotees, with Chan investigating $250,000 theft on airliner over the Pacific. C: Ronald Winters, Keye Luke, Mantan Moreland, Noel Neill, Tim Ryan, Iris Adrian, Elena Verdugo, Milburn Stone, Lyle Talbot, John Eldredge. D: Lesley Selander. CRI 64m.

Sky Is Gray, The 1980 ★★★★ Toung African-American boy from rural Louisiana takes an eye-opening journey to the dentist with his mother. Sensitive, thoughtful look at prejudice, set in the '40s. Based on an Ernest Gaines story. C: Olivia Cole, James Bond III, Margaret Avery, Cleavon Little. D: Stan Lathan. DRA 46m. TVM V

Sky West and Crooked 1966 *See* **Gypsy Girl**

Skyjacked 1972 ★★★ A passenger airline is hijacked to Moscow. Medium speed all-star adventure melodrama. C: Charlton Heston, Yvette Mimieux, James Brolin, Jeanne Crain, Walter Pidgeon, Leslie Uggams. D: John Guillermin. ACT [PG] 100m. V

Skylark 1941 ★★★★ After five years of marriage to career-driven Milland, Colbert needs a fling; Aherne is ardent suitor. Fastball romantic comedy, not as daffy as it might be but watchable and enjoyable. C: Claudette Colbert, Ray Milland, Brian Aherne, Binnie Barnes, Walter Abel, Ernest Cossart, Grant Mitchell. D: Mark Sandrich. COM 94m.

Skylark 1993 ★★★½ Follow-up to popular television film *Sarah, Plain and Tall* continues adventures of Maine woman (Close) transplanted to Kansas. Early 20th-century period piece with fine ensemble details daily life well. C: Glenn Close, Christopher Walken, Lexi Randall, Christopher Bell, Margaret Sophie Stein, Jon DeVries. D: Joseph Sargent. FAM/COM [G] 98m. TVM V

Skyline 1983 Spanish ★★★½ Spanish magazine photographer moves to New York to make his name. Story is familiar but often ingratiating. Mostly in Spanish, with some English. C: Antonio Resines, Susana Ocana. D: Fernando Colomo. DRA 84m. V

Sky's the Limit, The 1937 British ★★ Song-and-dance man (Buchanan) also designs airplanes. Musical, with British prewar overtones, is a showcase for Buchanan's comedy. C: Jack Buchanan, Mara Loseff, William Kendall. D: Lee Garmes. MUS 78m.

Sky's the Limit, The 1943 ★★★★ Flyer (Astaire), on leave, falls for Leslie but has to return to war. Relatively thin Astaire, but his elegant "One for My Baby" and stirring "My Shining Hour" are worth infinite re-viewings. C: Fred Astaire, Joan Leslie, Robert Benchley, Robert Ryan. D: Edward H. Griffith. MUS 89m. V

Slacker 1991 ★★★★ Rambling account of aimless dwellers in Austin, Texas simply follows characters at leisurely pace, letting them ramble on various topics ranging from J.F.K. assassination theories to Madonna. Unusual, engaging look at life. Well acted by cast of nonprofessionals. D: Richard Linklater. COM [R] 97m. V

Slam Dance 1987 ★ L.A. underground artist/illustrator (Hulce) is wrongly accused of murdering a club kid (Madsen). Trying hard to evoke a trendy atmosphere, the director lets the drama fall flat on its face. C: Tom Hulce, Mary Elizabeth Mastrantonio, Virginia Madsen, Harry Dean Stanton, Millie Perkins, Adam Ant. D: Wayne Wang. CRI [R] 99m. V

Slander 1956 ★★★½ Johnson plays a TV personality crucified by scandal sheet. Overly earnest melodrama. C: Van Johnson, Ann Blyth, Steve Cochran, Marjorie Rambeau, Richard Eyer. D: Roy Rowland. DRA 81m.

Slap Shot 1977 ★★★★ When his minor league hockey team can't break losing streak, boisterous coach Newman encourages his rag-tag athletes to play dirty. Outrageous humor, peppered by cheerful use of obscenities, and Newman's zestful performance. Language may offend. C: Paul Newman, Michael Ontkean, Lindsay Crouse, Jennifer Warren, Strother Martin. D: George Roy Hill. COM [R] 123m. V

Slapstick of Another Kind 1984 ★★★ Double roles for Lewis and Kahn as both wealthy parents and their ugly alien twins. Spotty and rather grotesque adaptation of Kurt Vonnegut's novel *Slapstick* makes an unlikely vehicle for Lewis. C: Jerry Lewis, Madeline Kahn, Marty Feldman, Jim Backus, Pat Morita. D: Steven Paul. COM [PG] 82m. V

Slaughter 1972 ★★½ Vietnam vet (Brown) single-handedly takes on the mob to avenge the murder of his family. Violent, all-too-familiar revenge movie. Followed by *Slaughter's Big Rip-Off.* C: Jim Brown, Stella Stevens, Rip Torn. D: Jack Starrett. ACT [R] 92m. V

Slaughter 1986 ★ A psycho mistakes people for livestock and butchers them accordingly. Not so far-fetched given today's headlines, but the film is still awful. C: David McCallum, Linda Gray. D: Burt Brinckerhoff. HOR 91m. V

Slaughter Day 1977 ★★½ Via short wave radio, a resourceful thief anonymously recruits ex-cons for a robbery, but an innocent woman ruins his plans. C: Rita Tushingham, Micheal Hausserman, Fredrick Jaeger. D: Peter Patzak. ACT [R] 87m. V

Slaughter High 1986 ★★★ Five years after high school graduation, Marty the nerd is back—this time his a killer. C: Caroline

Munro, Simon Scuddamore, Sally Cross. D: George Dugale. HOR [R] 90m. v

Slaughter in San Francisco 1981 Hong Kong ★★½ Cop (Wong) uses fists and feet to avenge the murder of his partner. Abysmal martial arts bore made in 1973 but released eight years later to capitalize on Norris' blossoming fame. For die-hard, hard-core Chuck fans only. (a.k.a. *Karate Cop*) C: Don Wong, Chuck Norris, Sylvia Channing, Robert Jones. D: William Lowe. ACT [R] 87m. v

Slaughter of the Innocents 1993 ★★★ When a special agent is charged with finding the killer of small children, he enlists the aid of his young son, a computer genius. C: Scott Glenn, Jesse Cameron-Glickenhaus, Zitto Kazann. D: James Glickenhaus. ACT [R] 114m. v

Slaughter on Tenth Avenue 1957 ★★★★ Assistant D.A. vs. NYC waterfront mobsters. Tightly constructed crime melodrama; Matthau fine as snarly racketeer. Famous title ballet score by Richard Rodgers. C: Richard Egan, Jan Sterling, Dan Duryea, Julie Adams, Walter Matthau, Sam Levene, Charles McGraw, Mickey Shaughnessy. D: Arnold Laven. CRI 103m.

Slaughterhouse-Five 1972 ★★★★ Well-done, if difficult adaptation of Vonnegut's novel about a man who becomes "unstuck" in time and can travel back and forth throughout his own life. From the director of "The Sting." C: Michael Sacks, Ron Leibman, Valerie Perrine. D: George Roy Hill. DRA 104m. v

Slaughter's Big Rip-Off 1973 ★★ Sequel to *Slaughter* finds Brown once again beating up on the Mafia, this time avenging the death of a friend. Substandard, tedious action, but it's kind of fun to see McMahon as a mob boss. C: Jim Brown, Ed McMahon, Brock Peters, Don Stroud. D: Gordon Douglas. ACT [R] 92m. v

Slave Girls from Beyond Infinity 1987 ★★★ Slaves from distant universe escape prison and land in world ruled by murderous hunter. Funny spoof of B-movies; plenty of gags. C: Elizabeth Cayton, Cindy Beal, Brinke Stevens. D: Ken Dixon. COM [R] 80m.

Slave Ship 1937 ★★★★ 19th-century ship captain (Baxter) wants to stop slave trading, but his crew won't let him. Rooney shines in the comic relief role of cabin boy. Strong, full-rigged adventure yarn. C: Warner Baxter, Wallace Beery, Mickey Rooney, George Sanders, Jane Darwell, Elizabeth Allan, Joseph Schildraut. D: Tay Garnett. ACT 92m.

Slave, The 1971 *See* **Fable, A**

Slavers 1978 German ★★ Sleepy yarn features Milland as a cruel slave trader in 19th-century Africa. A little action, a little melodrama, a lot of bad script. Viewer sympathizes for the veteran cast. C: Trevor Howard, Ron Ely, Britt Ekland, Ray Milland, Cameron Mitchell. D: Jurgen Goslar. DRA [R] 102m. v

Slaves of New York 1989 ★½ Trendy collection of short stories by Tama Janowitz makes a stultifying hodge-podge showing life in Manhattan's downtown punk/performance art community. About as amusing as sludge. A rare misfire from the Merchant/Ivory team. C: Bernadette Peters, Chris Sarandon, Mary Beth Hurt, Mercedes Ruehl. D: James Ivory. COM [R] 125m. v

Sleep My Love 1948 ★★★½ Ameche plots to drive wife Colbert insane, but Cummings is an unforeseen obstacle. Terrific cast handles somewhat verbose script, from a Leo Rosten novel. C: Claudette Colbert, Robert Cummings, Don Ameche, Hazel Brooks, Rita Johnson, George Coulouris, Keye Luke, Raymond Burr, Ralph Morgan. D: Douglas Sirk. DRA 97m.

Sleep of Death 1979 ★★★ A young nobleman pursues a mysterious, beautiful woman who appears as an old hag by night. Bizarre murders ensue. Understated, well-told supernatural film based on a J. Sheridan Le Fanu story. C: Brendan Price, Marilu Tolo, Patrick Magee, Curt Jurgens. D: Calvin Floyd. HOR 90m. v

Sleep With Me 1994 ★★★ Two friends compete for the same woman's love in a mediocre "Generation X" comedy. The three leads are charming, but the film covers too-familiar ground. C: Eric Stolz, Meg Tilly, Craig Sheffer, Quentin Tarantino. D: Rory Kelly. DRA [R] 86m. v

Sleepaway Camp 1983 ★★ This camp-conveniently located in deep, dark woods-is a real killing ground. Raw, violent and pointless. C: Mike Kellin, Jonathan Tiersten, Felissa Rose. D: Robert Hiltzik. HOR [R] 90m. v

Sleepaway Camp 2—Unhappy Campers 1988 ★★★ Frighteningly funny followup, with campers being done in by a nutzo counselor. Cast features rocker Bruce Springsteen's younger sister Pam. C: Pamela Springsteen, Renee Estevez, Brian Patrick Clarke. D: Michael A. Simpson. HOR [R] 82m. v

Sleepaway Camp 3—Teenage Wasteland 1989 ★ A camp for troubled youth is visited by a psychotic killer who's got a permanent cure for the teens' problems. No new twists here as the by-the-numbers body count piles up. C: Pamela Springsteen, Tracy Griffith, Micahel J. Pollard. D: Michael A. Simpson. HOR [R] 80m. v

Sleeper 1973 ★★★★★ Allen is a 1973 nebbish frozen and reawakened 200 years later, where he inadvertently ends up leading revolt against monolithic government. High-pitched comedy blends hysterical mix of snappy dialogue and sight gags, backed by jumping Dixieland jazz score. Allen and Keaton's on-screen chemistry is effervescent. C: Woody Allen, Diane Keaton, John Beck, Mary Gregory. D: Woody Allen. COM [PG] 88m. v

Sleeping Beauty 1959 ★★★★ Visually splendid animation bolsters slim story of title heroine put to sleep by evil fairy Maleficent's curse. Sometimes too derivative of earlier Disney triumphs, but dragon battle finale is sensational. Voices of Eleanor Audley, Mary Costa. D: Clyde Geronimi. FAM/DRA [G] 75m. v

Sleeping Beauty 1988 ★★★½ Morgan Fairchild reads the beloved fairy tale about a sleeping princess who is saved from an evil spell thanks to the work of a brave prince. Average material for younger audiences. C: Morgan Fairchild, Tahnee Welch, Nicholas Clay, Slyvia Miles. FAM/DRA 90m. v

Sleeping Car Murder, The 1965 *See* **Sleeping Car Murders, The**

Sleeping Car Murders, The 1965 French ★★★★ Montand and Signoret try to solve the murder of a young woman on the Marseilles-to-Paris overnight train. Brain teaser very much in the style of Hollywood's '40s detective thrillers, only not as frenetic. Costa-Gavras' directorial debut. (a.k.a. *The Sleeping Car Murder*) C: Simone Signoret, Yves Montand, Pierre Mondy, Jean-Louis Trintignant, Jacques Perrin, Michel Piccoli, Catherine Allegret, Charles Denner. D: Costa-Gavras. CRI 90m.

Sleeping Fist, The ★★★ Young man masters new form of kung fu so he can save his girlfriend from a gang of thugs. Okay martial arts action. ACT

Sleeping Tiger, The 1954 British ★★★½ Psychiatrist Knox takes his charge, parolee Bogarde, home to wife Smith, setting up a dangerous triangle. Heated melodrama but Bogarde is marvelous. "Terence Hanbury" was blacklisted director Joseph Losey. C: Alexis Smith, Alexander Knox, Dirk Bogarde, Hugh Griffith, Patricia McCarron, Billie Whitelaw. D: Terence Hanbury, Joseph Losey. DRA 89m. v

Sleeping with the Enemy 1991 ★★★★ An abused wife (Roberts) fakes her own death, but psychopathic husband pursues and finds her. Unconvincing thriller serves as showcase for Roberts. C: Julia Roberts, Patrick Bergin, Kevin Anderson, Elizabeth Lawrence, Kyle Secor. D: Joseph Ruben. DRA [R] 99m. v

Sleepless in Seattle 1993 ★★★★ Seattle-based widower (Hanks) is pressured by 10-year-old son to advertise for wife on call-in radio show, which is heard by Ryan in Baltimore. Despite obstacles, the rest is inevitable. Winning, refreshingly sentimental comedy uses pop standards and charming actors to offset predictable script. C: Tom Hanks, Meg Ryan, Bill Pullman, Ross Malinger, Rosie O'Donnell, Rob Reiner, Gaby Hoffmann, Rita Wilson. D: Nora Ephron. COM [PG] 105m. v

Sleepwalk 1986 ★★★ When a computer typesetter translates rare Chinese scriptures, she finds them amazingly similar to her current life. C: Ann Magnuson, Suzanne Fletcher, AKO, Dexter Lee. D: Sara Driver. DRA [R] 78m. v

Sleepwalkers *See* **Sleepwalkers**

Slender Thread, The 1965 ★★★½ A well-off white woman (Bancroft) overdoses on pills and then calls a crisis center, where she receives a telephone rescue from a black student (Poitier) until proper help can reach her. Bravura acting by Bancroft and Poitier. C: Sidney Poitier, Anne Bancroft, Telly Savalas, Steven Hill, Edward Asner, Dabney Coleman. D: Sydney Pollack. DRA 98m. v

Sleuth 1972 ★★★★½ Stylish, entertaining comedy/thriller with bravura performances from Olivier and Caine as game-playing mystery writer and his wife's lover. Plot teases audiences with surprise twists and red herrings. From Anthony Shaffer's play. C: Laurence Olivier, Michael Caine. D: Joseph L. Mankiewicz. COM [PG] 139m. v

Slight Case of Murder, A 1938 ★★★★ With repeal of Prohibition, gangster Robinson tries to go legit but his old cronies—and their corpses!—keep getting in the way. Sharp black comedy that avoids sentiment. Adapted from play by Damon Runyon and Howard Lindsay; remade as *Stop, You're Killing Me.* C: Edward G. Robinson, Jane Bryan, Allen Jenkins, Ruth Donnelly, Willard Parker, John Litel, Edward Brophy, Harold Huber. D: Lloyd Bacon. COM 85m.

Slightly Dangerous 1943 ★★½ Small-town waitress Turner gets herself and hometown boyfriend in trouble when she poses as daughter of New York magnate. Flimsy premise never quite gels into a credible plot. C: Lana Turner, Robert Young, Walter Brennan, Dame May Whitty, Eugene Pallette, Florence Bates, Alan Mowbray, Bobby Blake. D: Wesley Ruggles. COM 94m.

Slightly Honorable 1939 ★★★½ Wacky murder mystery stars O'Brien and Crawford as law partners attempting to break up crime ring—but one of them isn't quite as he appears. Odd mixture of comedy and melodrama, worth seeing for Arnold as Mob boss, and brief appearances by Arden. C: Pat O'Brien, Edward Arnold, Broderick Crawford, Eve Arden. D: Tay Garnett. COM 83m. v

Slightly Pregnant Man, A 1976 ★★★½ Imagine the shock of a fellow (Mastroianni) who discovers that he is pregnant! C: Marcello Mastroianni, Catherine Deneuve. D: Jacques Demy. COM [PG] 92m. v

Slightly Scarlet 1955 ★★★½ Fleming and Dahl play sisters on opposite sides of the law, each involved with hoodlum Payne, who switches sides himself. Fair crime thriller, though sometimes tough to follow. C: John Payne, Arlene Dahl, Rhonda Fleming, Kent Taylor, Ted de Corsia. D: Allan Dwan. CRI 99m. v

Slipper and the Rose, The 1976 British ★★★ Musical version of *Cinderella*, with Craven as the oppressed young heroine and Chamberlain as the stalwart Prince. Airy production, with lots of singing and dancing. Songs by Richard M. and Robert B. Sherman. C: Richard Chamberlain, Gemma Craven, Annette Crosbie, Michael Hordern, Margaret Lockwood, Christopher Gable, Kenneth More,

Edith Evans. D: Bryan Forbes. FAM/MUS [G] 128m.

Slipping Into Darkness 1988 ★★★ An ex-biker discovers retarded brother has been murdered and vows revenge. C: Michelle Johnson, John Di Aquino, Neill Barry. D: Eleanor Gaver. ACT [R] 87m. V

Slipstream 1989 British ★★ Vicious winds batter the Earth as tough guy (Paxton) confronts an evil bounty hunter (Hamill). Overblown. C: Bill Paxton, Bob Peck, Mark Hamill, Kitty Aldridge, Eleanor David, F. Murray Abraham, Ben Kingsley, Robbie Coltrane. D: Steven M. Lisberger. SFI [PG-13] 92m. V

Slither 1973 ★★★½ Comic caper about marginal characters seeking lost loot in California. Intermittently funny road movie, with Caan fine as a dim car thief and Kellerman delicious as a kook. Occasionally violent, otherwise easy to take, with a quirky script. C: James Caan, Peter Boyle, Sally Kellerman, Louise Lasser, Allen Garfield, Richard B. Shull. D: Howard Zieff. COM [PG] 97m. V

Slithis 1979 ★★½ Out of a nuclear waste pollution pile slithers a horrible, scaley monster. C: Alan Blanchard, Judy Motulsky. D: Stephen Traxler. SFI [PG] 86m. V

Sliver 1993 ★★ A book editor (Stone) moves into a NYC apartment building with history of mysterious deaths. Tenants keep dying, and the major suspects are a writer (Berenger) and the building's landlord (Baldwin). Overheated sex scenes fail to make this film either erotic or a thriller. C: Sharon Stone, William Baldwin, Tom Berenger, Martin Landau. D: Phillip Noyce. CRI [R] 106m. V

Sloane 1984 ★★★ When his girlfriend is kidnapped by thugs, a martial arts instructor journeys to the Philippines to find her. C: Robert Resnick, Debra Blee, Raul Aragon. D: Dan Rosenthal. ACT 95m. V

Slow Burn 1986 ★★★ Weary cop tries to solve friction between Mafia and Chinese gangs. Lackluster performances and uninspired production. C: Eric Roberts, Beverly D'Angelo, Henry Gibson, Dan Hedaya. D: Matthew Chapman. CRI [R] 92m. TVM V

Slow Dancing in the Big City 1978 ★★½ Hard-boiled New York journalist (Sorvino) falls for pretty but ill ballerina (Ditchburn). Sorvino does what he can with clichéd role. Script is shameless in its tearjerking efforts. C: Paul Sorvino, Anne Ditchburn, Nicolas Coster, Anita Dangler, Hector Mercado. D: John G. Avildsen. DRA [PG] 101m. TVM

Slow Motion 1980 *See* **Every Man for Himself**

Slugger's Wife, The 1985 ★★½ A baseball bum (O'Keefe) chases after a sultry singer (De Mornay). Perhaps Neil Simon's weakest script, written for the screen with nary a laugh. C: Rebecca De Mornay, Michael O'Keefe, Martin Ritt, Randy Quaid. D: Hal Ashby. COM [PG-13] 105m. V

Slugs 1987 ★★ The slimy garden pests become flesh-eating killers thanks to toxic waste, and no amount of salt can stop them. A few effective gross-outs can't save this dumb shocker, with a noticeably European supporting cast. C: Michael Garfield, Kim Terry, Philip Machale. D: Juan Piquer Simon. HOR [R] 90m. V

Slumber Party '57 1976 ★★ Young women at slumber party take turns recounting their first times. Goofy, untitillating sex scenes. Memorable only for early appearance by then unknown Debra Winger. C: Noelle North, Bridget Hollman, Debra Winger, Will Hutchins. D: William A. Levey. COM [R] 89m. V

Slumber Party Massacre, The 1982 ★ Boys meet girls . . . boys and girls have a sleepover . . . sicko killer crashes the party with a high-speed drill. Skip this and call the coroner. C: Michele Michaels, Robin Stille, Michael Villela. D: Amy Jones. HOR [R] 77m. V

Slumber Party Massacre II 1987 ★★ Same idea as first installment, but the killer is a rock 'n' roll ghost whose guitar comes equipped with a drill. C: Crystal Bernard, Kimberly McArthur, Juliette Cummins, Patrick Lowe, Heidi Kozak, Atanas Ilitch. D: Deborah Brock. HOR [R] 90m. V

Small Back Room, The 1949 British ★★★★ Scientist is an unappreciated recluse until a WWII emergency presents him with a test of courage. Finely wrought character study, from a famed directing team. Very well done. (a.k.a. *Hour of Glory*) C: David Farrar, Jack Hawkins, Kathleen Byron. D: Michael Powell, Emeric Pressburger. DRA 106m.

Small Change 1976 French ★★★★½ The director follows the rich and diverse adventures of an interlocking group of children in a French town. Highly rewarding movie captures the innocence and joy of being a child. A seminal work from a director wonderfully attuned to the marvels of childhood. C: Geory Desmouceaux, Philippe Goldman, Claudio Deluca, Frank Deluca, Richard Golfier, Laurent Devlaeminck. D: François Truffaut. DRA [PG] 104m. V

Small Sacrifices 1989 ★★★★ Fawcett's riveting performance makes this true-crime story of Diane Downs, modern Medea-killer of three kids, superior drama. Warning: it's uncompromising and ultimately depressing. C: Farrah Fawcett, Ryan O'Neal, John Shea. D: David Greene. DRA 159m. TVM V

Small Town Girl 1936 ★★★ Gaynor snares playboy Taylor into a marriage proposal when he's drunk, then has to do it all over again after he sobers up. Middling comedy; Gaynor comes through in lightweight role. (a.k.a. *One Horse Town*) C: Janet Gaynor, Robert Taylor, Binnie Barnes, Lewis Stone, Andy Devine, James Stewart. D: William Wellman. COM 108m.

Small Town Girl 1953 ★★★★ Granger is caught in remote Connecticut speed trap and falls for judge's daughter (Powell). Loose musical remake of 1936 MGM comedy, somewhat hampered by stiff leads and silly script. As Broadway star, Miller taps away with picture. C: Jane Powell, Farley Granger, Ann Miller, Fay Wray, Billie Burke. D: Leslie Kardos. MUS 94m. v

Small Town in Texas, A 1976 ★★½ Bottoms returns home from a prison stretch to avenge his framing and cuckolding by crooked lawman (Hopkins). Silly and violent, with more portent and car wrecks than it needs. C: Timothy Bottoms, Susan George, Bo Hopkins, Art Hindle. D: Jack Starrett. DRA [PG] 95m. v

Small World of Sammy Lee, The 1963 British ★★★ Petty London hood Newley can't pay off his gambling debts. Authentic melodrama. C: Anthony Newley, Julia Foster, Robert Stephens, Wilfrid Brambell. D: Ken Hughes. DRA 107m.

Smallest Show on Earth, The 1957 British ★★★★ Gentle British comedy concerning the efforts of a married couple to restore a dilapidated movie house they've inherited. Nostalgic, loving tribute to motion pictures, especially silents. Endearing performances by Sellers and Rutherford. C: Bill Travers, Virginia McKenna, Margaret Rutherford, Peter Sellers. D: Basil Dearden. COM 81m. v

Smart Money 1931 ★★★½ Robinson is a barber who hits it big gambling, then loses it all. Robinson is charming, with able support from Cagney; story tends toward obviousness as it nears climax. C: Edward G. Robinson, James Cagney, Margaret Livingstone, Evalyn Knapp, Noel Francis. D: Alfred B. Green. DRA 90m.

Smash Palace 1981 New Zealand ★★★½ Retired race car driver (Lawrence) kidnaps his 7-year-old daughter when his wife begins an adulterous affair. Well-acted character study that builds up steam throughout. C: Bruno Lawrence, Anna Jemison, Greer Robson, Keith Aberdein. D: Roger Donaldson. DRA 100m. v

Smash-Up, the Story of a Woman 1947 ★★★★ A drunken ex-singer (Hayward) is trapped in an unhappy marriage; effective melodrama, distinguished by Hayward's star-making performance. C: Susan Hayward, Lee Bowman, Marsha Hunt, Eddie Albert. D: Stuart Heisler. DRA 103m. v

Smashing the Crime Syndicate 1970 *See* **Hell's Bloody Devils**

Smashing the Money Ring 1939 ★★½ Reagan is Secret Service agent uncovering counterfeiting ring at sea. Third in a series; okay of its kind. C: Ronald Reagan, Margot Stevenson, Eddie Foy, Jr., Joe Downing, Charles D. Brown. D: Tery Morse. DRA 57m.

Smashing Time 1967 ★★★ Two ugly ducklings try to break into the mod London world of low fashion and "high" music business. Tushingham and Redgrave make a rambunctious, but ultimately exhausting comedy team. Each is better alone in other films (*A Taste of Honey, Georgy Girl*). C: Rita Tushingham, Lynn Redgrave, Michael York. D: Desmond Davis. COM 96m.

Smile 1975 ★★★★ Delicious satire of beauty pageants puts spotlight on California teenage contest as behind-the-scenes calamity contrasts with onstage hokum. Bright cast of newcomers and terrific work by Kidd as cynical choreographer. C: Bruce Dern, Barbara Feldon, Michael Kidd, Colleen Camp, Annette O'Toole, Melanie Griffith. D: Michael Ritchie. COM [PG] 113m. v

Smile Jenny, You're Dead 1974 ★★½ A private investigator, working on solving the murder of his falls in love with his prime suspect. C: David Janssen, Andrea Marcovicci, John Anderson, Jodie Foster. D: Jerry Thrope. DRA 99m. TVM v

Smiles of a Summer Night 1955 Swedish ★★★★★ One of Bergman's few comedies, and a masterpiece. Several mismatched couples share weekend at country estate of aging actress in love with a married lawyer. Sexy, lyrical, and ultimately moving. Source for Stephen Sondheim musical, *A Little Night Music*. C: Ulla Jacobsson, Eva Dahlbeck, Margit Carlquist, Harriet Andersson, Gunnar Bjornstrand. D: Ingmar Bergman. COM 108m. v

Smiley 1957 Australian ★★★ Petersen is title character, a preadolescent boy who'll do almost anything to get a bicycle. Coasting family entertainment, bolstered by adult supporting roles. C: Ralph Richardson, John McCallum, Chips Rafferty, Reg Lye. D: Anthony Kimmins. FAM/COM 97m.

Smiley Gets a Gun 1959 Australian ★★½ Sequel to *Smiley* has title character trying to stay out of mischief so he can earn himself a rifle. Standard follow-up. C: Sybil Thorndike, Keith Calvert, Bruce Archer, Chips Rafferty, Margaret Christensen. D: Anthony Kimmins. FAM/COM 89m.

Smilin' Through 1932 ★★★★ Victorian fantasy/romance takes wing when a young woman is forbidden to marry by her uncle, whose bride was accidentally killed on their wedding night 50 years earlier. Lavish production, good for a satisfying cry. Franklin's 1922 version starred Norma Talmadge; the film was remade in 1941. C: Norma Shearer, Fredric March, Leslie Howard, O.P. Heggie, Ralph Forbes. D: Sidney Franklin. DRA 100m. v

Smilin' Through 1941 ★★★½ Remake of successful 1932 fantasy/romance feels more remote. Strong performance by Aherne as uncle looking back over several generations. C: Jeanette MacDonald, Gene Raymond, Brian Aherne, Ian Hunter, Francis Robinson, Patrick O'Moore. D: Frank Borzage. DRA 100m. v

Smiling Lieutenant, The 1931 ★★★★ Rakish guardsman is assigned to princess visiting Vienna. Second marvelous film version (first with sound) of popular Oscar Straus operetta *The Waltz Dream* given sly, voluptuous treatment by top-notch filmmakers. Chevalier heads charming cast. C: Maurice Chevalier, Claudette Colbert, Miriam Hopkins, Charles Ruggles. D: Ernst Lubitsch. MUS 102m.

Smith! 1969 ★★★½ Farmer (Ford) helps a Native American man accused of murder. Well-intentioned, well-acted Disney drama. C: Glenn Ford, Nancy Olson, Keenan Wynn, Warren Oates, Chief Dan George. D: Michael O'Herlihy. FAM/DRA [G] 112m. V

Smithereens 1982 ★★★½ Modest portrait of a Lower East Side young woman (Berman) trying to make it in the punk-rock world. First film directed by Seidelman (*Desperately Seeking Susan*) shows real talent, but suffers from low-budget blues. Still worth seeing. C: Susan Berman, Brad Rinn, Richard Hell, Roger Jett. D: Susan Seidelmann. DRA [R] 90m. V

Smoke 1970 ★★★ Future director Howard (billed here as "Ronny Howard") stars as a young boy who befriends a German shepherd when life with his new stepfather becomes too difficult. Uninvolving story for children that doesn't miss a canine movie cliché. C: Ron Howard, Earl Holliman, Andy Devine. D: Vincent McEveety. FAM/DRA 89m. TVM V

Smokescreen 1990 ★★★ Man meets his dreamgirl, but has to deal with her pushy and belligerent boyfriend. C: Dean Stockwell, Kim Cattrall, Matt Craven, Kim Coates. DRA [R] 91m. V

Smokey and the Bandit 1977 ★★★★ Good-natured, mindless highway shenanigans abound as a southern driver (Reynolds) runs beer from Texas to Atlanta, with a sheriff (Gleason) in hot pursuit. The plot is basically a handy excuse for stunts and car wrecks, whipped up into an energetic frenzy. Just good ol' "fun at the movies." Followed by two sequels. C: Burt Reynolds, Sally Field, Jackie Gleason, Jerry Reed, Mike Henry, Paul Williams, Pat McCormick. D: Hal Needham. COM [PG] 96m. V

Smokey and the Bandit, Part 2 1980 ★★½ Reynolds returns as the driver trying to outwit the sheriff (Gleason). This time he's hired to transport an expectant elephant to her new home. C: Burt Reynolds, Jackie Gleason, Jerry Reed, Dom DeLuise, Sally Field, Paul Williams, Pat McCormick, John Anderson. D: Hal Needham. COM [PG] 101m. V

Smokey and the Bandit III 1983 ★ While transporting a giant plastic shark cross-country, a trucker (Reed) is chased by a vulgar sheriff (Gleason). Disasterous second sequel to the popular Burt Reynolds comedy, with Burt making an uncomforable cameo at the end. Originally shot with Gleason as both sheriff and trucker, but Reed was brought in after previews. C: Jackie Gleason, Jerry Reed, Paul Williams, Colleen Camp, Pat McCormick. D: Dick Lowry. COM [PG] 88m. V

Smoky 1946 ★★★★ A family's devotion to a spirited, free-roaming horse. Second of three filmed versions of Will James novel is solid, colorful family entertainment. Fine David Raksin score. Filmed previously in 1933, and subsequently in 1966. C: Fred MacMurray, Anne Baxter, Burl Ives, Bruce Cabot, Esther Dale, Roy Roberts. D: Louis King. FAM/DRA 87m.

Smoky Mountain Christmas, A 1986 ★★★½ Country-western musical variation on *Snow White* puts Dolly in charge of seven ultra-cute orphans. Holiday pudding—mighty sweet, with more than a few lumps. Six songs by Parton keep it toe-tapping, though. C: Dolly Parton, Lee Majors, Anita Morris, Bo Hopkins. D: Henry Winkler. MUS 100m. TVM V

Smooth as Silk 1948 ★★★½ When his fiancée dumps him, attorney plans to bump off her new boyfriend. Tightly constructed formula thriller; fast-paced suspense. C: Kent Taylor, Virginia Grey, John Litel. D: Charles Barton. DRA 64m.

Smoothtalker 1992 ★★★ Police drama about an officer, who gets distracted when his ex-wife, the prosecuting attorney fora falsely-charged suspect, becomes the target of the real killer. C: Joe Guzaldo, Stuart Whitman, Sydney Lassick. D: Tom Milo. DRA [R] 89m. V

Smorgasbord 1983 *See* **Cracking Up**

Smugglers' Cove 1948 ★★★ The Bowery Boys trek out to Long Island to confront a band of Naziesque smugglers. Middle-period entry in series, no sillier than the others. C: Leo Gorcey, Huntz Hall, Gabriel Dell, Billy Benedict, David Gorcey, Bennie Bartlett, Martin Kosleck, Paul Harvey, Amelita Ward. D: William Beaudine. COM 66m. V

Smugglers, the 1948 British ★★ Attenborough is cowardly lad who supplies smugglers for his guardian. Feeble adaptation of Graham Greene novel. (a.k.a. *The Man Within*) C: Michael Redgrave, Jean Kent, Joan Greenwood, Richard Attenborough, Felix Aylmer. D: Bernard Knowles. DRA 86m.

Smurfs and the Magic Flute, The 1983 ★★ Popular little blue people move from bad TV cartoons to bad feature cartoon. Here they suffer dance fever every time a magic flute sends music through the air. Terminally cute, bare minimum story, grade-Z animation techniques. Strictly for undiscerning children. FAM/COM 74m. V

Smurfs, The 1987 ★★★½ Six animated episodes of the happy-go-lucky wee ones include "Gargamel's Giant", "Smurfliplication" "The Pussywillow Pixies", "The Whole Smurf and Nothing but the Smurf", "Man in the Moon", "The Gargoyle of Quarrel Castle". Wholesome viewing for the kids. FAM/COM 90m. V

Snafu 1945 ★★★ Family in turmoil after their darling son returns from the military transformed into a lean, mean fighting machine. Unmemorable domestic comedy with some occasional laughs. C: Robert Benchley, Vera Vague, Conrad Janis, Nanette Parks, Janis Wilson, Marcia Mae Jones, Kathleen Howard, Jimmy Lloyd, Enid Markey, Eva Puig. D: Jack Moss. COM 82m.

Snake Eater 1989 ★★ A tough cop (Lamas) takes on the backwoods clan who killed his parents and kidnapped his sister. Lots of fights and fireballs, missing only a coherent story and character development. C: Lorenzo Lamas, Larry Csonka, Ron Palillo. D: George Erschbamer. ACT [R] 89m. v

Snake Eater 2—The Drug Buster 1990 ★★★ Lamas is back and taking out the trash—a group of vicious drug lords. More action, a touch more story than the first. C: Lorenzo Lamas, Michele Scarabelli. D: George Erschbamer. ACT [R] 93m. v

Snake Eater 3—His Law 1992 ★★★ Lamas kicks biker booty as he avenges a family whose daughter was attacked by a biker gang. C: Minor Mustain, Lorenzo Lamas, Tracy Cook. D: George Erschbamer. ACT [R] 109m. v

Snake Fist Fighter 1981 ★★½ Female Kung-Fu fighter uses the feared "snake fist" in this action-packed martial arts film. C: Jackie Chan, Cheung Lung. D: Chin Hsin. ACT [R] 82m. v

Snake in the Eagle's Shadow—2 1983 ★★½ Three martial arts experts form an impressive team and knock out their foes. Typical martial arts action. C: Wang Tao, Cheng Shing. D: Chang Shinn. ACT 89m. v

Snake Pit, The 1948 ★★★★½ Uncompromising drama of woman (de Havilland) who has nervous breakdown, and is committed to mental institution. Brilliantly acted by star, full of harrowing episodes. Look for classic overhead shot of writhing inmates. C: Olivia de Havilland, Mark Stevens, Leo Genn, Celeste Holm, Glenn Langan. D: Anatole Litvak. DRA 108m. v

Snapdragon 1993 ★★½ Bauer plays a cop who investigates a series of murders where men are dying shortly after having sex. Anderson is lovely as the "Snapdragon" and the sex scenes are steamy. C: Steven Bauer, Chelsea Field. D: Worth Keeter. CRI [R] 96m. v

Snapper, The 1993 British ★★★★ The eldest, unmarried daughter of working-class Irish family announces she's pregnant, throwing her entire clan into state of turmoil. A warm and humorous look at everyday life in Ireland, deftly directed. From the author of *The Commitments*.) C: Tina Kellegher, Colm Meaney, Ruth McCabe, Colm O'Byrne, Pat Laffan. D: Stephen Frears. COM 90m. v

Snatched 1973 ★★★ Three women must fend for themselves when one of their husbands refuses to give the kidnappers a 3 million dollar ransom fee. C: Leslie Nielsen, Barbara Parkins, robert Reed. D: Sutton Roley. DRA [R] 73m. TVM v

Sneakers 1992 ★★★★ Well-done, high-tech spook fest about a computer hacker (Redford) forced to use his skills against a former friend. C: Robert Redford, Dan Aykroyd, Ben Kingsley, Mary McDonnell, River Phoenix, Sidney Poitier, David Strathairn. D: Phil Alden Robinson. CRI [PG-13] 125m. v

Sniper's Ridge 1961 ★★½ Just before Americans pull out of Korea, an American captain goes into battle once more, hoping to become hero. Small but ambitious war-action film. C: Jack Ging, Stanley Clements, John Goddard, Douglas Henderson. D: John Bushelman. DRA 61m.

Snoopy, Come Home 1972 ★★★★ *Peanuts*-sized road movie finds Snoopy taking bird companion Woodstock on the highway in search of adventure, ultimately learning there's no place like home. Second animated feature for Charles Schultz's popular characters offers nice moral lesson for kids, coupled with good music and humor. C: Chad Webber, David Carey, Stephen Shea. D: Bill Melendez. FAM/COM [G] 80m. v

Snow—The Movie 1990 ★★ Coming-of-age comedy with plenty of good times and fancy trick skiing sequences. C: David Argue, Lance Curtis. D: Robert Gibson. COM 90m. v

Snow Treasure 1967 ★★ True story about a group of Norwegian children who risk Nazi persecution in order to save their national treasure from the Germans. C: James Franciscus. ACT [G] 96m. v

Snow White 1988 ★★★½ Diana Rigg is the Evil Queen in this tale of young woman who is taken in by seven dwarfs, then is rescued by handsome prince after falling under spell of poisoned apple. Acceptable version of much-loved fairy tale. C: Diana Rigg, Sarah Patterson. FAM/DRA 85m. v

Snow White and the Seven Dwarfs 1937 ★★★★★ Snow White runs away from her evil stepmother, who is plotting to kill her, meets seven little men who live in the forest and a prince. The first Disney animated feature and still the best. A timeless masterpiece of the animator's art. Voices of Adriana Caselotti, Harry Stockwell. FAM/DRA [G] 83m. v

Snow White and the Three Stooges 1961 ★★ Silly update of the fairy-tale with Moe, Larry, and Curly Joe substituting for Seven Dwarfs. Ice-skating fans may want to take a look at 1960 Olympic gold medalist Heiss. C: Three Stooges, Patricia Medina, Carol Heiss, Buddy Baer. D: Walter Lang. COM 108m. v

Snowball Express 1972 ★★★ When Manhattan family inherits run-down Colorado ski lodge, they overcome financial difficulty and some slapstick mayhem to make the hotel a success. By-the-numbers Disney humor. C: Dean Jones, Nancy Olson, Harry Morgan, Keenan Wynn. D: Norman Tokar. FAM/COM [G] 93m. v

Snowbeast 1977 ★★ A luxious ski resort falls under siege by a bizarre snow monster.

C: Bo Svenson, Yvette Mimieux. D: Herb Wallerstein. HOR 96m. V

Snowblind 1989 ★★★ Murder paralyzes a ski resort in this well-acted thriller. C: Don Johnson, Deborah Raffin, Suzy Chaffe. DRA 98m. V

Snows of Kilimanjaro, The 1952 ★★½ A writer in Africa (Peck) is haunted by past love and career successes. While the leads labor nobly, references to Africans as "the white man's burden" seem painfully antiquated. Hemingway disavowed this bloated Hollywood adaptation of his short story. C: Gregory Peck, Susan Hayward, Ava Gardner, Leo G. Carroll. D: Henry King. DRA 117m. V

So Big 1953 ★★★½ Third filming (previously made in 1925 and 1932) of sprawling Edna Ferber novel, with Wyman as self-sacrificing schoolteacher turned cabbage farmer. Melodramatic doings; sensitive performances. C: Jane Wyman, Sterling Hayden, Nancy Olson, Steve Forrest, Martha Hyer, Tommy Rettig. D: Robert Wise. DRA 101m.

So Dark the Night 1946 ★★★½ Jean Renoir meets Raymond Chandler in this detective story about ace Paris investigator Geray vacationing in French countryside, untangling web of murders and more trapped than he knows. Famous B-suspenser given extra verve by director Lewis. C: Steven Geray, Micheline Cheirel, Eugene Borden, Ann Codee, Egon Brecher, Helen Freeman. D: Joseph H. Lewis. CRI 71m.

So Dear to My Heart 1948 ★★★★ Nostalgic animal story, nicely served, with farm boy (Driscoll) determined to send black sheep to State Fair. Animation sequences make this satisfying family fare. C: Burl Ives, Beulah Bondi, Bobby Driscoll, Luana Patten, Harry Carey. D: Harold Schuster. FAM/DRA 84m. V

So Ends Our Night 1941 ★★★★ Anti-Nazi German refugees are on the run among the great capitals of Europe during World War II. Sterling adaptation of Erich Maria Remarque's novel *Flotsam*. C: Fredric March, Margaret Sullavan, Glenn Ford, Erich von Stroheim. D: John Cromwell. DRA 117m. V

So Evil My Love 1948 ★★★ Wicked artist Milland worms his way into widow's home and heart. Victorian costumer aiming for *Dorian Gray*-like quality. C: Ray Milland, Ann Todd, Geraldine Fitzgerald, Leo G. Carroll, Raymond Huntley, Martita Hunt, Hugh Griffith. D: Lewis Allen. DRA 109m.

So Fine 1981 ★★★ When college professor (O'Neal) gets dragged into clothing business by father (Warden) he inadvertently starts national rage by designing clear-bottomed jeans. Unlikely satire starts off well but quickly degenerates into one constantly repeated gag. C: Ryan O'Neal, Jack Warden, Mariangela Melato, Richard Kiel. D: Andrew Bergman. COM [R] 91m. V

So Goes My Love 1946 ★★★½ Loy lands eccentric inventor Ameche and they set up house together. Pleasant, not-quite-screwball comedy. C: Myrna Loy, Don Ameche, Rhys Williams, Bobby Driscoll, Richard Gaines, Molly Lamont. D: Frank Ryan. COM 88m.

So I Married An Axe Murderer 1993 ★★★ Chilling laughs abound when Myers begins to suspect that his "dream woman" may be responsible for leaving a trail of murdered husbands across the country. C: Mike Myers, Brenda Fricker, Nancy Travis, Amanda Plummer, Phil Hartman, Anthony La Paglia. D: Thomas Schlamme. COM [PG-13] 93m. V

So Long at the Fair 1950 British ★★★½ Young Englishwoman Simmons and brother Tomlinson arrive in Paris for the 1889 Expo; when he vanishes overnight, only Bogarde believes her story. Slight suspenser given substance by Simmons. C: Jean Simmons, Dirk Bogarde, David Tomlinson, Honor Blackman, Cathleen Nesbitt, Felix Aylmer, Andre Morell, Betty Warren. D: Terence Fisher, Anthony Darnborough. DRA 90m.

So Proudly We Hail! 1943 ★★★½ Army nurses serve at Bataan, dressing wounds and falling in love. Well-meaning war melodrama with relatively unglamorized stars and some authentic background. C: Claudette Colbert, Paulette Goddard, Veronica Lake, George Reeves, Sonny Tufts, Barbara Britton, Walter Abel. D: Mark Sandrich. DRA 126m. V

So Red the Rose 1935 ★★★½ As Civil War ends, Sullavan and family await the return of Confederate soldier Scott. Closely examined Southern melodrama rather small and static for its saga-like framework. Fine cast. C: Margaret Sullavan, Walter Connolly, Randolph Scott, Elizabeth Patterson, Janet Beecher, Robert Cummings, Dickie Moore. D: King Vidor. DRA 82m.

So This Is London 1930 ★★★ Sprightly role for Rogers as an American industrialist who gets a lesson in foreign relations when his youngster falls for child of his British counterpart. Based on George M. Cohan's play, and remade in 1939. C: Will Rogers, Irene Rich, Maureen O'Sullivan. D: John G. Blystone. COM 92m.

So This Is Love ★★½ Musical biography of opera star Grace Moore. Nice color and '20s costumes, but Grayson walks through this one. C: Kathryn Grayson, Merv Griffin, Walter Abel, Rosemary DeCamp, Jeff Donnell. D: Gordon Douglas. MUS 101m.

So This Is New York 1948 ★★★★ After World War I a small-town Indiana couple (Morgan and Grey) visit the Big Apple hoping to find a mate for the sister of one of them. Funny, deadpan take on flapper-era Gotham adapted from Ring Lardner's *The Big Town*. C: Henry Morgan, Rudy Vallee, Bill Goodwin, Hugh Herbert, Leo Gorcey, Virginia Grey, Dona Drake. D: Richard Fleischer. COM 79m.

So This Is Paris 1954 ★★★ Three American sailors spend their leave in Paris falling in love, adapting to local customs, and aiding war refugees. Snappy musical, with lovely De Haven, passable Curtis. C: Tony Curtis, Gloria DeHaven, Gene Nelson, Corinne Calvet, Paul Gilbert, Allison Hayes, Mara Corday. D: Richard Quine. MUS 96m.

So This Is Washington 1943 ★★★ Radio comics Goff and Lauck tell Washington politicians how to run the country. Wartime hoo-ha. C: Chester Lauck, Norris Goff. D: Ray McCarey. COM 64m.

So Well Remembered 1947 British ★★★½ Mills is well-intentioned mill-town newspaperman who tries to help his community, but is thwarted by grasping wife Scott. Dark and heavy-handed. Best performance: Howard as alcoholic doctor. C: John Mills, Martha Scott, Trevor Howard, Patricia Roc, Richard Carlson, Ivor Barnard. D: Edward Dmytryk. DRA 114m.

So Young, So Bad 1950 ★★★½ Sympathetic psychiatrist Henreid attempts to help youngsters at girls' reformatory who are abused by authorities. Decent, well-structured melodrama. Henreid also starred in the male variation on this theme, *For Men Only*, the following year. C: Paul Henreid, Catherine McLeod, Grace Coppin, Cecil Clovelly, Anne Francis, Rosita Moreno, Anne Jackson, Enid Pulver. D: Bernard Vorhaus. DRA 91m.

Soapdish 1991 ★★★½ Uneven comedy takes backstage look at soap operas with leading lady (Field) having trouble keeping her personal miseries separate from her character's. Strong supporting cast and some funny situations. C: Sally Field, Kevin Kline, Robert Downey Jr., Cathy Moriarty, Whoopi Goldberg, Elisabeth Shue, Carrie Fisher, Garry Marshall. D: Michael Hoffman. COM [PG-13] 97m. V

S.O.B. 1981 ★★★★ Blake Edwards' brutal satire of Tinseltown. Producer plans to salvage his failed movie by having his wife (Andrews), a family musical star, bare her breasts on film. Somewhat autobiographical story is uneven, but often hilarious. Holden's last film. C: Julie Andrews, William Holden, Richard Mulligan, Robert Preston, Robert Vaughn, Loretta Swit, Shelley Winters. D: Blake Edwards. COM [R] 121m. V

Society 1992 ★★½ Teenager (Warlock) has always felt out of place in his rich, pampered surroundings, but has no idea just how "different" his friends and family are. Uneven but intriguing horror-mystery that explodes in slimy special effects at the end. C: Billy Warlock, Devin De Vasquez. D: Brian Yuzna. HOR [R] 99m. V

Sodom and Gomorrah 1963 Italian ★★★ A big-budget Italian epic that recounts in gaudy detail the rise and fall of the Bible's loosest cities. The able cast and no-nonsense direction provide an engrossing and enjoyable depiction of sin and mayhem. C: Stewart Granger, Pier Angeli, Stanley Baker, Anouk Aimee, Rossana Podesta, Claudia Mori. D: Robert Aldrich. DRA 148m. V

Sofia 1948 ★★★ Cold War spy film, with Raymond fighting Soviets in Turkey. Good, solid example of espionage thriller from the immediate postwar era. C: Gene Raymond, Sigrid Gurie, Patricia Morison, Mischa Auer. D: John Reinhardt. DRA 82m.

Soft Skin, The 1964 ★★★★ Modest Truffaut love triangle about an airline attendant (Dorleac) involved with a married man (Desailly). Routine material, elevated by a master. C: Francoise Dorleac, Jean Desailly, Nelly Benedetti. D: Francois Truffaut. DRA 120m. V

Soggy Bottom USA 1984 ★★ Wild chases and madcap antics enliven this parody about a sheriff and his moonshining cousin who get into trouble with the law. C: Don Johnson, Lois Nettleton, Ben Johnson. D: Theodore J. Flicker. COM [PG] 96m. V

Solar Crisis 1993 ★★★ Space station threatened by dangerous sunspots. Solid acting, big budget, worth a look. C: Charlton Heston, Jack Palance, Tim Matheson, Peter Boyle. SFI [PG-13] 111m. TVM V

Solaris 1971 Russian ★★★½ A government psychologist investigates a series of space station deaths which lead him into the supernatural realm. A cult favorite. C: Natalya Bondarchuk, Donatas Banionis, Yuri Jarvet, Vladislav Dvorzhetsky. D: Andrei Tarkovsky. SFI [PG] 167m. V

Soldier Blue 1970 ★★½ A division of the U.S. cavalry is attacked by Indians. In revenge, the cavalry stages a horrific raid on an Indian village. Stilted moralizing and excessive violence is difficult to watch. C: Candice Bergen, Peter Strauss, Donald Pleasence, John Anderson. D: Ralph Nelson. WST [PG] 105m. V

Soldier in the Rain 1963 ★★★★ Odd-couple friendship blooms between two Army staff sergeants, slack-jawed McQueen and genius Gleason. Adapted from William Goldman novel, comedy/drama leans heavily on sentiment. Weld is utterly delightful, and poignant Mancini theme is memorable. C: Jackie Gleason, Steve McQueen, Tuesday Weld, Tony Bill, Tom Poston, Ed Nelson. D: Ralph Nelson. DRA 88m. V

Soldier of Fortune 1955 ★★★★ Gable is a gun for hire, employed by Hayward to find her husband, kidnapped by the "Red" Chinese. 1950s anti-Communist paranoia is laid on a bit thick, but Hong Kong locations look great—as do both of the stars. C: Clark Gable, Susan Hayward, Michael Rennie, Gene Barry. D: Edward Dmytryk. ACT 96m. V

Soldier of Orange 1979 Dutch ★★★★ The lives of a group of rich Dutch university students are drastically changed by the 1940 German occupation. This emotionally powerful movie was a breakthrough for the director. C: Rutger Hauer, Jeroen Krabbe, Derek De

Lint, Susan Penhaligon, Edward Fox. D: Paul Verhoeven. DRA [R] 144m. v

Soldier, The 1982 ★ Tough CIA operative (Wahl) must stop terrorists from doing nasty things with the unhealthy amount of plutonium they have stolen. Unappealingly violent thriller. C: Ken Wahl, Klaus Kinski, William Prince, Alberta Watson. D: James Glickenhaus. ACT [R] 90m. v

Soldier's Fortune 1991 ★★ Soldier of fortune (Gerard) calls on his war specialist friends to help him rescue his kidnapped daughter. By-the-numbers movie making at its blandest. C: Gil Gerard, Charles Napier, Dan Haggerty. D: Arthur N. Mele. ACT [R] 96m. v

Soldier's Home 1977 ★★★½ Henry Fonda hosts this Ernest Hemingway story of a soldier who comes home after WWI to discover that he grew up, but his hometown stayed the same. C: Richard Backus, Nancy Marchand. D: Robert M. Young. DRA 41m.

Soldiers Of Music 1990 ★★★ Grand maestro goes home to Russia to conduct soaring works by Tchaikovsky, Shostakovich, Dvorak, and Prokoviev. C: Mstislav Rosstropovich. MUS 90m. v

Soldier's Revenge 1990 ★★½ A Vietnam fighter, treated as a traitor upon returning from war, reenters in order to rescue the woman he loves and save her battle-torn country. C: John Savage, Maria Socas. D: David Worth. ACT 92m. v

Soldier's Story, A 1984 ★★★★ A black officer's murder in a '40s Southern military outpost sets off a compelling drama about racism as well as an absorbing murder mystery adapted from a Pulitzer Prize-winning play by Charles Fuller. Brilliant ensemble acting and sharp direction make this somewhat stagey story exciting. C: Howard E. Rollins Jr., Adolph Caesar, Dennis Lipscomb, Art Evans, Denzel Washington. D: Norman Jewison. CRI [PG] 101m. v

Soldier's Tale, A 1988 ★★★½ Touching story of a beautiful woman (Basler) who stands accused of being a Nazi collaborator in WWII France. Byrne is the British soldier who loves and tries to protect her. C: Gabriel Byrne, Marianne Basler, Judge Reinhold, Paul Wyett. D: Larry Parr. DRA [R] 96m. v

Soldiers Three 1951 ★★★½ Three British officers fight side by side and with each other in 19th-century India. *Gunga Din*-type tale often played for laughs. C: Stewart Granger, Walter Pidgeon, David Niven, Robert Newton, Cyril Cusack, Greta Gynt, Robert Coote, Dan O'Herlihy. D: Tay Garnett. ACT 87m.

Sole Survivor 1984 ★★½ An airplane crash survivor struggles to stay alive. C: Anita Skinner, Kurt Johnson. D: Thom Eberhardt. ACT [R] 85m. v

Solid Gold Cadillac, The 1956 ★★★★ Holliday, as bird-voiced but fearless shareholder, brings a giant corporation to its knees. Entertaining adaptation by Abe Burrows of Kaufman/Teichmann Broadway comedy. As tycoon, Douglas plays off Holliday better than anyone. Costume designer Jean Louis won an Oscar. C: Judy Holliday, Paul Douglas, Fred Clark, John Williams, Arthur O'Connell, Hiram Sherman, Neva Patterson, Ray Collins. D: Richard Quine. COM 99m.

Solo 1983 ★★ Amusing and heartwarming adventur of a hitchhiking woman who transforms the quiet, alienated lives of a father and son living in New Zealand. C: Vincent Gill, Perry Armstrong. D: Tony Williams. ACT [PG] 90m. v

Solomon and Sheba 1959 ★★★½ Biblical vixen (Lollobrigida) gets virtuous king (Brynner) all steamed up in entertaining biblical hokum with lavish sets and thousands of extras. C: Yul Brynner, Gina Lollobrigida, George Sanders, Marisa Pavan. D: King Vidor. DRA 139m. v

Solomon Northrup's Odyssey *See* **Half Slave, Half Free**

Sombrero Kid, The 1942 ★★ Man struggles to prove a number of lawmen innocent of crimes committed by outlaws. C: Don Barry. WST 70m. v

Some Call It Loving 1972 ★ Weird attempt to transpose Sleeping Beauty fairy tale to ultra-groovy L.A. in the early '70s. C: Zalman King, Carol White, Tisa Farrow, Richard Pryor. D: James B. Harris. DRA 103m. v

Some Came Running 1958 ★★★★ A G.I. and failed writer (Sinatra) returns to uncertain future in his small Illinois hometown. Strong melodrama with excellent performances, especially by MacLaine and Martin as a dying drunk. C: Frank Sinatra, Dean Martin, Shirley MacLaine, Martha Hyer, Arthur Kennedy. D: Vincente Minnelli. DRA 137m. v

Some Kind of Hero 1982 ★★½ Pryor is good in serious role about a Vietnam vet who finds his world changed when he gets out of POW camp. Based on novel by James Kirkwood. C: Richard Pryor, Margot Kidder, Ray Sharkey, Ronny Cox. D: Michael Pressman. DRA [R] 97m. v

Some Kind of Wonderful 1987 ★★★½ Tomboy (Masterson) falls in love with her best friend (Stoltz), but he's chasing a rich girl (Thompson) who's part of the snob crowd. Insightful and endearing look at high school life. The three leads are very good. C: Eric Stoltz, Lea Thompson, Mary Stuart Masterson. D: Howard Deutch. DRA [PG-13] 93m. v

Some Like It Cool 1978 ★★½ Impotent Casanova hires stand-in (Curtis) to keep his reputation as a lover intact. Average sex frolic. (a.k.a. *Casanova & Co.* C: Tony Curtis, Britt Ekland, Marisa Berenson, Sylva Koscina. D: Francois Legrand. COM [R] 89m. v

Some Like It Hot 1959 ★★★★★ After witnessing a 1920s gang slaying, unemployed musicians Curtis and Lemmon don frocks and join a Florida-bound all-woman band, featuring lead singer Monroe. One of the great comedies, exquisitely timed, flawlessly performed and underpinned by Wilder's perfect script (co-written by I.A.L. Diamond) and excellent direction. Well-earned Oscar to Orry-Kelly for Costumes. Final line is justly famous. C: Jack Lemmon, Tony Curtis, Marilyn Monroe, Joe B. Brown, George Raft, Pat O'Brien, Mike Mazurki. D: Billy Wilder. COM 121m. V

Somebody Has to Shoot the Picture 1990 ★★★★ Pulitzer Prize-winning photographer (Scheider) takes on his toughest assignment—capturing the final days of a death row prisoner. Tension in this film develops from the nerve-wracking stays of execution and resumptions of the countdown. C: Roy Scheider, Bonnie Bedelia, Robert Carradine, Andre Braugher, Arliss Howard. D: Frank Pierson. CRI [R] 104m. TVM V

Somebody Up There Likes Me 1956 ★★★★½ Life of middleweight boxing champion Rocky Graziano (Newman) from his beginnings as a NYC hoodlum to his eventual triumph in the ring. Gritty, realistic fight movie with outstanding performances (debut for McQueen and Loggia). Ruttenberg's cinematography won an Oscar. C: Paul Newman, Pier Angeli, Everett Sloane, Eileen Heckart, Sal Mineo, Robert Loggia, Steve McQueen. D: Robert Wise. DRA 97m. V

Someone Behind the Door 1971 French ★★½ Amnesiac (Bronson) gets radical treatment from neurosurgeon (Perkins), a therapy which includes instructions to murder. Melodramatic thriller. C: Charles Bronson, Anthony Perkins, Jill Ireland. D: Nicolas Gessner. CRI [PG] 95m. V

Someone Like You ★★ Aspiring songwriter decides to research love in order to write song about it. Silly comedy. C: Jim Bonfield, Rena Davonne, Amy Tribbey, Donna Peretti, Michael Wais, Erin Casimir, Kelley McAuliffe. D: Jim Meyers. COM 90m. V

Someone to Love 1987 ★★★ Henry Jaglom's investigation of romance takes place at a party in a theater. A group of actors tell the camera and each other how they're seeking (and usually not finding) emotional fulfillment. Typically eclectic Jaglomian "home movie." Welles offers pithy touching insights in his last screen appearance. C: Henry Jaglom, Andrea Marcovicci, Sally Kellerman, Orson Welles, Michael Emil, Oja Kodar, Dave Frishberg, Stephen Bishop, Ronee Blakley, Kathryn Harrold, Monte Hellman, Jeremy Kagan, Miles Kreuger. D: Henry Jaglom. DRA [R] 111m. V

Someone to Watch Over Me 1987 ★★★½ In this visually stylish thriller, a married cop from Queens (Berenger) is assigned to protect a rich Manhattan woman (Rogers) whose life has been threatened. Of course he falls for Rogers, which complicates an already dangerous situation. Reasonably gripping movie, enhanced by excellent musical score. C: Tom Berenger, Mimi Rogers, Lorraine Bracco, Jerry Orbach. D: Ridley Scott. CRI [R] 106m. V

Someone's Killing the World's Greatest Models 1979 *See* **She's Dressed to Kill**

Something About Amelia 1984 ★★★★½ Shocking, expertly acted story focuses on a teenager (Zal) who accuses her clean-cut father (Danson) of sexual abuse. Don't let this searing drama's TV pedigree keep you away: It's a pioneer in its field. Beautifully written by William Hanley. Zal won an Emmy for her performance. C: Ted Danson, Roxana Zal, Glenn Close, Oliva Cole. D: Randa Haines. DRA 100m. TVM

Something for Everyone 1970 ★★★★ Wickedly funny black comedy about a sexually voracious young man (York) who attempts to seduce all family and staff members (male and female) in a bankrupt Countess's villa. C: Michael York, Angela Lansbury, Anthony Corlan, Jane Carr. D: Harold Prince. COM [R] 112m. V

Something for the Birds 1952 ★★★½ Capraesque comedy about young Neal trying to save bird sanctuary in nation's capital. Overly whimsical, but Gwenn is winning as ubiquitous engraver and Mature is surprisingly appealing. C: Patricia Neal, Victor Mature, Edmund Gwenn, Larry Keating. D: Robert Wise. COM 81m.

Something for the Boys 1944 ★★★½ Blaine's Old South plantation becomes home base for service wives. Loose adaptation of Cole Porter wartime musical that's easy to take, with Silvers and young Perry Como in fine form. C: Carmen Miranda, Michael O'Shea, Vivian Blaine, Phil Silvers, Sheila Ryan, Perry Como, Glenn Langan, Cara Williams, Thurston Hall. D: Lewis Seiler. MUS 85m.

Something in the Wind 1947 ★★★ Durbin is a singing disk jockey who's mistakenly believed to be the paramour of elderly millionaire. Amusing minor musical showcase for Durbin and O'Connor. C: Deanna Durbin, Donald O'Connor, Charles Winninger, Helena Carter. D: Irving Pichel. MUS 89m.

Something Is Out There 1977 *See* **Day of the Animals**

Something of Value 1957 ★★★★ Documentary-like drama based on the novel by Robert Ruark about the bloody Mau Mau uprising in Kenya that threatened the lives of British settlers. Hudson and Poitier are boyhood friends whose relationship is threatened by the violence. Gripping and well handled. C: Rock Hudson, Dana Wynter, Sidney Poitier, Wendy Hiller. D: Richard Brooks. DRA 113m. V

Something Special 1987 ★★★½ Oddball comedy/fantasy about adolescent Segall convincing herself she'd rather be a boy; her wish magically comes true, and she renames herself Willy. More delicately and humorously handled than subject suggests. (a.k.a. *Willy Milly* and *I Was a Teenage Boy*) C: Pamela

Segall, Patty Duke Astin, Eric Gurry, John Glover. D: Paul Schneider. COM [PG-13] 90m. v

Something to Live For 1952 ★★★ Alcoholics Anonymous veteran Milland falls for needy alcoholic Fontaine, but won't leave his wife. Romantic melodrama wih pale overtones of *Lost Weekend* has inescapable seen-it-all-before feel. C: Joan Fontaine, Ray Milland, Teresa Wright, Douglas Dick, Rudy Lee. D: George Stevens. DRA 89m.

Something to Sing About 1937 ★★½ Manhattan bandleader Cagney goes west to conquer Hollywood. Bland moviebiz satire, with Cagney's feet the most active part of the picture. (a.k.a. *Battling Hoofer*) C: James Cagney, Evelyn Daw, William Frawley, Mona Barrie. D: Victor Schertzinger. MUS 89m. v

Something Wicked This Way Comes 1983 ★★★½ A shady carnival sets up tents outside a small American town, and helps the inhabitants live their dreams—but their payment is hell! A few surprises but disappointing, even though author Ray Bradbury wrote the script. C: Jason Robards, Jonathan Pryce, Diane Ladd, Royal Dano. D: Jack Clayton. SFI [PG] 94m. v

Something Wild 1986 ★★★★ Yuppie (Daniels) gets picked up by mystery woman (Griffith), who takes him on life-changing road trip. Her ex-husband (Liotta) provides a violent turn of events. Offbeat approach, good performances, and terrific soundtrack. C: Jeff Daniels, Melanie Griffith, Ray Liotta, Margaret Colin, Tracey Walter. D: Jonathan Demme. COM [R] 116m. v

Sometimes a Great Notion 1971 ★★★½ A feisty Oregon logging family refuses to go along with a labor strike. Intriguing moments and an electrifying, Oscar-nominated performance from Jaeckel. Based on the novel by Ken Kesey. (a.k.a. *Never Give an Inch*) C: Paul Newman, Henry Fonda, Lee Remick, Michael Sarrazin. D: Paul Newman. DRA [PG] 115m. v

Sometimes They Come Back 1991 ★★★★ A high school teacher (Matheson) revisits his hometown, where his brother was killed. The death still haunts him—as do the ghosts of the kids responsible, who also died with his brother. Based on a Stephen King story. C: Tim Matheson, Brooke Adams, Robert Hy Gorman, William Sanderson, Chris Demetral. D: Tom McLoughlin. HOR 97m. TVM v

Somewhere I'll Find You 1942 ★★★½ War correspondents in love during WWII. So-so story, but Gable and Turner strike sparks. C: Clark Gable, Lana Turner, Robert Sterling, Patricia Dane, Reginald Owen, Lee Patrick, Rags Ragland, Van Johnson. D: Wesley Ruggles. DRA 117m. v

Somewhere in Sonora 1933 ★★★ Wayne plays cowboy who infiltrates gang planning to rob his girlfriend's father's silver mine. Remark of 1927 Ken Maynard western. C: John Wayne, Marceline Day, Paul Fix, Henry B. Walthall, Ralph Lewis. D: Mack V. Wright. WST 57m. v

Somewhere in the Night 1946 ★★★ Amnesiac veteran Hodiak gradually recovers his identity—and the memory of his criminal career. Early, lesser Mankiewicz feature. C: John Hodiak, Nancy Guild, Lloyd Nolan, Richard Conte, Josephine Hutchinson, Fritz Kortner, Sheldon Leonard, Whit Bissell, Jeff Corey, Henry Morgan. D: Joseph L. Mankiewicz. DRA 108m.

Somewhere in Time 1980 ★★★ A lonely playwright (Reeve) falls in love with an ancient portrait of an actress, then travels back through time to meet his beloved. Beautiful to look at, if not particularly deep. C: Christopher Reeve, Jane Seymour, Christopher Plummer, Teresa Wright. D: Jeannot Szwarc. DRA [PG] 103m. v

Sommersby 1993 U.S. ★★★★ Soldier (Gere) returns to hometown from Civil War a changed man, so changed that wife (Foster) begins to doubt his identity. Moving love story with both leads giving sensitive performances. Remake of French film, *The Return of Martin Guerre.* C: Richard Gere, Jodie Foster, Bill Pullman, James Earl Jones. D: Jon Amiel. DRA [PG-13] 114m. v

Son-In-Law 1993 ★★½ Hipper-than-thou Shore shapes up his drab college friend (Gugino), then goes with her to visit family farm for Thanksgiving. Mindless fun, for the under-25 crowd. C: Pauly Shore, Carla Gugino, Lane Smith. D: Steve Rash. COM [PG-13] 96m. v

Son of a Badman 1949 ★★ Masked cattle rustler, pursued by U.S. marshal, is actually a prominent local doctor whose father was lynched. Western quickie (six-day production) shot alongside *Son of Billy the Kid*, with same cast. C: Lash La Rue, Al "Fuzzy" St. John, Noel Neill, Michael Whalen. D: Ray Taylor. WST 64m.

Son of Ali Baba 1952 ★★★½ High-spirited Arabian Nights adventure follows Ali Baba, Jr., (Curtis) in quest to save beautiful princess and recover treasure. Good cast and colorful production. C: Tony Curtis, Piper Laurie, Susan Cabot, Victor Jory, Hugh O'Brian. D: Kurt Neumann. ACT 75m. v

Son of Belle Starr 1953 ★★½ Another quick rip-off of Western outlaw legend, not halfway as watchable as its mother. C: Keith Larsen, Dona Drake, Peggie Castle, Regis Toomey. D: Frank McDonald. WST 70m.

Son of Captain Blood 1962 Italian ★★ Flynn, the real life son of Errol, plays his finctional son, a brave and handsome pirate like his dad. C: Sean Flynn, Ann Todd, Alessandra Panaro, Jose Nieto. D: Tulio Demicheli. ACT 90m. v

Son of Dracula 1943 ★★★★ Chaney plays the bloodsucker "Count Alucard" ("Dracula" spelled backward), doing his thing down South. Atmospheric with some genuine chills.

C: Lon Chaney Jr., Robert Paige, Louise Allbritton, Frank Craven. D: Robert Siodmak. HOR 78m. ▾

Son of Flubber 1963 ★★★ Sequel to *The Absent Minded Professor* finds professor (MacMurray) inventing gravity-defying formula. Everyone wants a piece of the action, which sends the cast on series of goofy chases. Not much in either story or special effects departments, though younger audiences may enjoy. C: Fred MacMurray, Nancy Olson, Keenan Wynn, Tommy Kirk. D: Robert Stevenson. FAM/COM [G] 105m. ▾

Son of Frankenstein 1939 ★★★★½ Outstanding third installment in the original Frankenstein series. The Doctor's son (Rathbone) moves in to the family mansion and tries to revive his father's creation. Karloff is superb in his last appearance as "The Monster," and Lugosi is at the top of his form as "Ygor." C: Basil Rathbone, Boris Karloff, Bela Lugosi, Lionel Atwill, Josephine Hutchinson, Donnie Dunagan. D: Rowland V. Lee. HOR 99m. ▾

Son of Fury 1942 ★★★ In pre-Victorian England, Power is cheated by uncle Sanders, bolts to Pacific island to plot vengeance, and meets Tierney. Good-looking costume drama with decidedly cosmopolitan Tierney. Filmed again as *Treasure of the Golden Condor*. C: Tyrone Power, Gene Tierney, George Sanders, Frances Farmer, Roddy McDowall, Kay Johnson, John Carradine, Elsa Lanchester, Harry Davenport, Dudley Digges, Ethel Griffies. D: John Cromwell. DRA 98m. ▾

Son of Godzilla 1969 Japanese ★★★ Father and son (?!) join forces to do in giant insects threatening the Earth. Campy fun. C: Tadao Takashima, Akira Kubo. D: Jun Fukuda. SFI 84m. ▾

Son of Kong, The 1933 ★★★ Follow up to *King Kong* is a letdown as explorer Denham (Armstrong) returns to Skull Island and finds big daddy's offspring. Hurried production is saved by humor and animator Willis J. O'Brien's mastery. C:. Robert Armstrong, Helen Mack, Victor Wong, John Marston. D: Ernest B. Schoedsack. SFI 70m. ▾

Son of Lassie 1945 ★★★ Collie and master shot down over Nazi Germany. Hokey sequel, with Lawford and best friend definitely in the wrong place at the wrong time. C: Peter Lawford, Donald Crisp, June Lockhart, Nigel Bruce, William Severn, Leon Ames, Fay Helm, Donald Curtis, Nils Asther, Terry Moore. D: S. Sylvan Simon. FAM/DRA [G] 100m. ▾

Son of Paleface 1952 ★★★★ Hope returns to the Western arena he shot to bits four years earlier in *Paleface* and scores again as the timid dentist who's mistaken for a deadly gunfighter. Addition of Rogers as the gunslinger everyone mistakes Hope for adds to the laughs. C: Bob Hope, Jane Russell, Roy Rogers, Douglass Dumbrille, Iron Eyes Cody. D: Frank Tashlin. COM 95m. ▾

Son of the Morning Star 1991 ★★★★½ General Custer's definitive battle at the Little Bighorn. An outstanding film that's laced with drama, action and a real sense of being there. C: Gary Cole, Rosanna Arquette, Terry O'Quinn, David Strathairn, Dean Stockwell, George American Horse, Rodney A. Grant, Stanley Anderson. D: Mike Robe. WST [PG-13] 186m. TVM ▾

Son of the Pink Panther 1993 ★★★ Benigni is son of the bumbling Clouseau, and the apple doesn't fall far from the tree. In search of a kidnapped Middle Eastern princess, he manages to demolish everything in his path with consummate ineptitude. Labored work from Edwards, saved by Benigni's wacky charm. C: Roberto Benigni, Herbert Lom, Robert Davi, Claudia Cardinale. D: Blake Edwards. COM [PG] 115m. ▾

Son of the Sheik 1926 ★★★★ Dandy silent Valentino vehicle casts him in the double role of a desert seducer and noble rescuer of Banky. Almost as good as its predecessor, *The Sheik*. Rudy's last film. C: Rudolph Valentino, Vilma Banky. D: George Fitzmaurice. ACT 72m. ▾

Son of Zorro 1947 ★★ Serial pits offspring of the masked swordsman against bandits who prey on poor ranchers. C: George Turner, Peggy Stewart, Francis MacDonald, Roy Barcroft. WST 164m. ▾

Song is Born, A 1948 ★★★½ Mild-mannered musicologist (Kaye) is pounced on by gangster's moll (Mayo) in genial remake of better *Ball of Fire*. True stars are the big bands led by Goodman, Armstrong, Hampton, and Dorsey. C: Danny Kaye, Virginia Mayo, Hugh Herbert, Steve Cochran, Felix Bressart, Benny Goodman, Louis Armstrong, Charlie Barnet, Lionel Hampton, Tommy Dorsey. D: Howard Hawks. COM 113m. ▾

Song O' My Heart 1929 ★★★ Irish tenor McCormack looks after the orphaned chilren of the woman who broke his heart. Beautiful music in melodrama tailor-made for McCormack. Nineteen-year-old O'Sullivan brought to America from Dublin by director Borzage for her screen debut. C: John McCormack, Alice Joyce, Maureen O'Sullivan, John Garrick, Andres De Segurola. D: Frank Borzage. MUS 91m. ▾

Song of Arizona 1946 ★★½ Roy helps save Gabby's ranch while performing eight songs. C: Roy Rogers, Dale Evans, Gabby Hayes. D: Frank McDonald. WST 68m. ▾

Song of Bernadette, The 1943 ★★★★½ Moving religious film that's never cloying or sanctimonious. Tells true story of peasant girl (Jones) who sees vision of Blessed Mother in 19th-century France, outraging the organized church. Jones won Oscar for sweet, straightforward performance. C: Jennifer Jones, Charles Bickford, Vincent Price, Lee J. Cobb. D: Henry King. DRA 156m. ▾

Song of Freedom 1936 British ★★★½ A London longshoreman turned opera singer learns he's an African prince and goes home to assist his oppressed tribe. Unusual showcase for Robeson, whose splendid singing overshadows the story. C: Paul Robeson, Elizabeth Welch, Esme Percy. D: J. Elder Wills. MUS 80m. v

Song of Love 1947 ★★ Stately but dull biography of Clara Schumann (Hepburn) and her composer husband Robert, and their friend Johannes Brahms. Sluggish and uninspired; Hepburn is the only standout. C: Katharine Hepburn, Paul Henried, Robert Walker, Henry Daniell, Leo G. Carroll, Gigi Perreau, Tala Birell, Henry Stephenson, Else Janssen. D: Clarence Brown. DRA 121m. v

Song of Nevada 1944 ★★★½ Familiar Roy Rogers oater with all the gang (including Dale and Trigger) along to battle a band of criminals terrorizing the Nevada frontier. Everything you'd expect including singing, riding, and shoot-'em-ups. C: Roy Rogers, Dale Evans, Mary Lee, Thurston Hall. D: Joseph Kane. WST 60m. v

Song of Norway 1970 ★ Dreadful biography of composer Edvard Grieg, from stage operetta, that mutiliates his melodies and soaks his story in syrup. C: Florence Henderson, Toralv Maurstad, Christina Schollin, Edward G. Robinson. D: Andrew L. Stone. MUS [G] 143m. v

Song of Russia 1943 ★★★½ Fascinating, sympathetic look at Russian-American relations during WWII casts Taylor as a U.S. conductor in love with a Russian pianist (Peters). C: Robert Taylor, Susan Peters, John Hodiak, Robert Benchley. D: Gregory Ratoff. DRA 107m.

Song of Songs 1933 ★★★½ Conflict, anguish, and despair await a country maid in 19th-century Germany who must abandon the sculptor she loves to marry his patron—a lecherous nobleman. Formula romance/melodrama distinguished by Dietrich's magnetic persona. C: Marlene Dietrich, Brian Aherne, Lionel Atwill, Alison Skipworth, Hardie Albright, Helen Freeman. D: Rouben Mamoulian. DRA 90m. v

Song of Texas 1943 ★★★★ Perfect for Roy Rogers fans, this entertaining Western has plenty of songs, but still manages a fast-paced wagon race with our hero trying to win back an illegally taken cattle ranch. C: Roy Rogers, Barton MacLane, Pat Brady, Sheila Ryan. D: Joseph Kane. WST 53m. v

Song of the Buckaroo 1939 ★★★ A Robin Hood of the range decides to give up his stagecoach-robbing ways and go straight, but his villainous gang has other plans. Ritter and his songs are the main appeal of this otherwise routine Western. C: Tex Ritter, Jinx Falkenberg, Mary Ruth, Tom London, Frank LaRue, Charles King, Bob Terry. D: Al Herman. WST 55m.

Song of the Islands 1942 ★★★½ Bubbly Technicolor musical fruit basket about a Romeo and a Juliet in Hawaii. The silly score is half the fun. Fine trouping. C: Betty Grable, Victor Mature, Jack Oakie, Thomas Mitchell, Billy Gilbert. D: Walter Lang. MUS 75m. v

Song of the Open Road 1944 ★★★ Child star (Powell) runs away to raise tomatoes on a failing farm cooperative. Musical non-plot provides fertile ground for sporting supporting cast, including Fields and Bergen (with Charlie McCarthy, of course). Powell's film debut. C: Jane Powell, W.C. Fields, Edgar Bergen, Bonita Granville, Sammy Kaye & His Orchestra. D: S. Sylvan Simon. MUS 93m.

Song of the Road, The 1983 *See* **Pauline at the Beach**

Song of the Sierra 1947 *See* **Springtime in the Sierras**

Song of the South 1946 ★★★★½ Live-action/animation Disney classic full of delightful Uncle Remus stories featuring tricky Br'er Rabbit and sly Br'er Fox. First-rate entertainment for children and adults alike. "Zip-a-Dee-Do-Dah" won Oscar for Best Song. C: Ruth Warrick, James Baskett, Bobby Driscoll, Luana Patten, Lucile Watson, Hattie McDaniel, Glenn Leedy. D: Wilfred Jackson, Harve Foster. FAM/MUS [G] 94m.

Song of the Thin Man 1947 ★★★½ Nick and Nora Charles (Powell and Loy) return in this sixth and final *Thin Man* picture. The couple's witty interaction is still dry and effervescent as they investigate a murder set in the Gotham nightclub milieu. C: William Powell, Myrna Loy, Keenan Wynn, Dean Stockwell, Gloria Grahame. D: Edward Buzzell. CRI 87m. v

Song of the Trail 1936 ★★½ Maynard is clever cowpoke who saves Hayes from cardsharps, woos Brent. C: Kermit Maynard, Gabby Hayes, Fuzzy Knight, Wheeler Oakman, Evelyn Brent, Andrea Leeds. D: Russell Hopton. WST 60m. v

Song Remains the Same, The 1976 ★★★ Sluggish '70s concert footage and *very* '70s fantasy interludes make this Led Zeppelin concert movie an entertaining flashback to the glory days of the heavy metal superstars. C: Led Zeppelin. MUS [PG] 136m. v

Song to Remember, A 1945 ★★★½ In this hokey Hollywood biography of Chopin (Wilde), color and spectacle prevail over plotting and characterization. Muni and Oberon are worth watching. C: Cornel Wilde, Paul Muni, Merle Oberon, Stephen Bekassy, Nina Foch, George Coulouris, Sig Arno. D: Charles Vidor. DRA 113m. v

Song Without End 1960 ★★★ Bogarde stars in film biography of composer Franz Liszt. Great score won an Oscar, but lavish sets overshadow the everyday story. George Cukor took over film's direction after Charles Vidor died in middle of production. C: Dirk Bogarde, Capucine, Genevieve Page, Patricia

Morison, Ivan Desny, Martita Hunt, Lou Jacobi. D: Charles Vidor, George Cukor. MUS 130m. V

Songwriter 1984 ★★★½ Country-western superstar (Nelson) needs help from a former partner (Kristofferson) when he takes on a troubled, talented protege (Warren). Entertaining musical is a fine vehicle for the likeable Nelson. Kris's tunes were nominated for an Oscar. C: Willie Nelson, Kris Kristofferson, Lesley Ann Warren, Melinda Dillon, Rip Torn. D: Alan Rudolph. MUS [R] 94m. V

Sons 1991 ★★★ Vietnam vets are upset when their sons consider joining the military. Surprisingly earnest low-budget drama. C: Tom Taylor, Perry Moses, Steve Barbey, Charie Perry. D: Steven Miller. DRA 80m. V

Sons and Lovers 1960 British ★★★★★ Film adaptation of D.H. Lawrence's novel set in 1910 England, about a sensitive, artistic young man who is urged by his mother to make good away from their grim coal-mining town—and in so doing comes to grips with love and life. Expertly directed, engrossing film, with powerful performances by all. Oscar for Best Cinematography. C: Trevor Howard, Dean Stockwell, Wendy Hiller, Mary Ure, Heather Sears, William Lucas, Donald Pleasence, Ernest Thesiger. D: Jack Cardiff. DRA 103m.

Sons and Mothers 1967 Russian ★★½ Heavy-handed drama chronicles the hardships faced by a Russian widow with her six children, one of whom will grow up to be Lenin, struggling through the turbulent late 1800s. Clumsy biography is marred by extremely biased political slant. C: Yelena Fadeyeva, Rodion Nakhapetov. D: Mark Donskoy. DRA 95m.

Sons of Adventure 1948 ★★★★ When a Western movie star is murdered on the set, a stuntman turns sleuth to prove that his buddy isn't the killer. Interesting look behind-the-scenes of a movie set gives special insights into the role of the stuntman. C: Lynne Roberts, Russell Hayden, Gordon Jones. D: Yakima Canutt. CRI 60m.

Sons of Katie Elder, The 1965 ★★★★ Fun on the range as a frontier mother's strapping sons join together to avenge her death. One of the Duke's better efforts. C: John Wayne, Dean Martin, Martha Hyer, Earl Holliman, James Gregory, George Kennedy. D: Henry Hathaway. WST 122m. V

Sons of the Desert 1933 ★★★★½ One of the team's best features, with both Laurel and Hardy lying to their wives so they can go to lodge convention. No romantic subplots, no musical interludes. Just Stan and Ollie at their funniest. C: Stan Laurel, Oliver Hardy, Charley Chase, Mae Busch. D: William A. Seiter. COM 86m. V

Sons of the Pioneers 1938 ★★★½ Gabby Hayes, the sheriff of a small town, calls on Roy Rogers to deal with a group of pillaging outlaws. Good adventure thanks to hero Roy. C: Roy Rogers, George "Gabby" Hayes. D: Joseph Kane. WST 53m. V

Sooner or Later 1978 ★★ Now that she has her guitar hero convinced she's 16, should a 13-year-old tell him? Sleazy, unfunny comedy. C: Denise Miller, Rex Smith, Judd Hirsch, Barbara Feldon, Morey Amsterdam, Lynn Redgrave. D: Bruce Hart. COM 100m. V

Sophia Loren: Her Own Story 1980 ★★★½ True story of an Italian waif growing into an international movie star makes a fair bio, with a twist: Its subject plays both herself and her own mother! Too long, but has its moments. C: Sophia Loren, John Gavin, Rip Torn, Armand Assante. D: Mel Stuart. DRA 145m. TVM V

Sophie's Choice 1982 ★★★★ A Polish Catholic woman tries to deal with her horrific WWII past. Streep's incandescent, Oscar-winning performance and Nestor Almedros' rich cinematography hold the movie together. C: Meryl Streep, Kevin Kline, Peter MacNicol, Rita Karin. D: Alan J. Pakula. DRA [R] 150m. V

Sophie's Place 1969 *See* **Crooks and Coronets**

Sophisticated Gents, The 1981 ★★★★½ Assorted members of a black social club gather for a reunion. Excellent cast and script make this memorable drama; from John A. Williams' novel, *The Junior Bachelor Society*. C: Bernie Casey, Rosey Grier, Robert Hooks, Ron O'Neal, Paul Winfield, Alfre Woodard, Beah Richards. D: Harry Falk. DRA 200m. TVM V

Sophisticated Ladies ★★★½ Film version of hit Broadway revue features the extraordinary music of Duke Ellington, conducted by Merce Ellington. Terrific mix of tap and modern dance; dancer Gregg Burge won a Tony. MUS V

Sorcerer 1977 ★★★ Fugitives in South America sign up to drive an unstable explosive over a rough road to help quell a raging oil fire. Visually stunning remake of *The Wages of Fear*, but oddly flat and unexciting. C: Roy Scheider, Bruno Cremer, Francisco Rabal, Amidou, Ramon Bieri. D: William Friedkin. DRA [PG] 122m. V

Sorcerers, The 1967 British ★★½ Fountain-of-youth experiments, conducted by an elderly couple trained in scientific research, involve dominating the wills of wholesome young people. Minor thriller aims to please. C: Boris Karloff, Catherine Lacey, Ian Ogilvy, Elizabeth Ercy, Susan George. D: Michael Reeves. HOR 87m.

Sorceress 1982 ★★ Voluptuous twins struggle to keep their clothes on while using magical powers to battle supernatural foes. Sluggish action/fantasy shows plenty of skin. C: Leigh Harris, Lynette Harris, Bob Nelson. D: Brian Stuart. ACT [R] 83m. V

Sorority Babes in the Slimeball Bowl-O-Rama 1987 ★★★ The young women take it off and take on a little monster at a local shopping mall. Campy with its own sense of humor about itself. C: Linnea Quigley, Michelle Bauer, Andas Jones, John Wildman. D: David DeCoteau. HOR [R] 80m. v

Sorority Girl 1957 ★★ A disturbed college student is cast out from her sorority and takes it out on everyone within striking distance in this ineptly told tale of Eisenhower-era rebellion. C: Susan Cabot, Dick Miller, Barbara Crane, Fay Baker. D: Roger Corman. DRA 62m. v

Sorority House 1939 ★★★★ Daughter of a small-town grocer learns that to be accepted on campus she must pretend to be something she's not. Entertaining melodrama provides a delightful look at student life during the '30s. C: Anne Shirley, James Ellison, Barbara Read, Helen Wood, J.M. Kerrigan. D: John Farrow. DRA 64m.

Sorority House Massacre 1986 ★ Low-budget chiller is one big cliché, as a sorority girl (O'Neill) who stays behind with some housemates on a weekend, only to be terrorized by a slasher who's connected to her past. C: Angela O'Neill, Wendy Martel, Pamela Ross, Nicole Rio. D: Carol Frank. HOR [R] 74m.

Sorority House Massacre 2 1992 ★ An abandoned house is taken over by sorority girls whose only purpose is to be slaughtered by a mysterious killer. For exploitation fans. C: Robyn Harris, Melissa Moore. D: Jim Wynorski. HOR 80m. v

Sorrow and the Pity, The 1970 Swiss ★★★★★ Monumental documentary of French involvement in WWII is a classic of its kind; consists mostly of interviews and historical footage. Not a dull moment in its four-hour-plus length. D: Marcel Ophuls. DOC 260m. v

Sorrowful Jones 1949 ★★★½ Bookie (Hope) uses little girl to handicap horses. Okay remake of *Little Miss Marker*, with very good interplay between Hope and Ball. C: Bob Hope, Lucille Ball, William Demarest, Mary Jane Saunders, Bruce Cabot, Thomas Gomez. D: Sidney Lanfield. COM 88m. v

Sorry, Wrong Number 1948 ★★★★ Thanks to a bad phone connection, a petulant, shrewish invalid (Stanwyck) overhears a murder plot, then begins to realize she's the victim. Effective melodrama from radio play, with tremendous performance from Stanwyck. Remade for TV in 1989. C: Barbara Stanwyck, Burt Lancaster, Wendell Corey, Ed Begley, William Conrad. D: Anatole Litvak. CRI 89m. v

Sorry, Wrong Number 1989 ★★★ Remake of the 1948 thriller about a bed-bound woman terrorized by a strange phone call that may mean murder. Sorry, wrong actress! Durable suspense tale gets by okay, but Anderson can't fill Barbara Stanwyck's sheets. C: Loni Anderson, Patrick MacNee, Hal Holbrook, Carl Weintraub. D: Tony Wharmby. CRI 100m. TVM v

S.O.S. Iceberg 1933 ★★★★ Breathtaking action in the frozen Arctic as a team of explorers put their lives in danger attempting to recreate an ill-fated expedition. Gripping adventure sequences, filmed mostly in Greenland, highlight this effective drama. C: Rod La Rocque, Leni Riefenstahl, Sepp Rist. D: Tay Garnett. ACT 77m.

S.O.S. Titanic 1979 ★★★★ The 1912 sinking of the legendary oceanliner is told in the style of an airport disaster movie. A little hackneyed, but otherwise very well done, as acts of heroism and bravery accompany the infamous ill-fated voyage. C: David Janssen, Cloris Leachman, Susan St.James, David Warner. D: William Hale. DRA 98m. TVM v

Soul Man 1986 ★★ In order to get into Harvard Law school, white student (Howell) pretends he's black to receive minority scholarship. He falls for African-American classmate, and has his consciousness raised. Shallow premise results in even more shallow, somewhat offensive film. C: C. Thomas Howell, Rae Dawn Chong, James Earl Jones, Leslie Nielsen, James B. Sikking. D: Steve Miner. COM [PG-13] 101m. v

Soul of Samurai ★★ Two warriors search for the essence of Kung Fu and find blood, terror and bad dubbing. C: Kong Pun, Miu Tin, Kong Ching Ching. ACT 90m. v

Soul of the Beast 1923 ★★★★ Charming, offbeat silent film about circus elephant who protects Bellamy from unwanted advances of Beery. C: Madge Bellamy, Cullen Landis, Noah Beery, Sr. DRA 77m. v

Souls at Sea 1937 ★★★★ A 19th-century intelligence officer on a secret antislavery mission saves himself during a sea tragedy and is court-martialed for cowardice. He-men Cooper and Raft buoy this adventure with plenty of two-fisted action. C: Gary Cooper, George Raft, Frances Dee, Olympe Bradna, Henry Wilcoxon, Harry Carey, Robert Cummings, Joseph Schildkraut, George Zucco, Virginia Weidler. D: Henry Hathaway. ACT 92m.

Soultaker 1990 ★★ Tedious fantasy/suspense film about souls of nice young couple, separated from their bodies in car crash, with only an hour to get to hospital and rejoin them. C: Joe Estevez, Vivian Schilling, Gregg Thomsen. D: Michael Rissi. HOR [R] 90m. v

Sound and the Fury, The 1959 ★★★½ Film version of Faulkner's classic story of a Southern family fallen on hard times. Brynner is miscast as stern uncle; screenplay works hard to capture spirit of the book. C: Yul Brynner, Joanne Woodward, Margaret Leighton, Stuart Whitman, Ethel Waters, Jack Warden, Albert Dekker. D: Martin Ritt. DRA 115m.

Sound and the Silence, The 1993 Canadian ★★★ Long, meticulous but undramatic retelling of life of Alexander Graham Bell. C: Brenda Fricker, John Bach, Ian Bannen, Vanessa Baughan, Elizabeth Quinn. D: John Kent Harrison. DRA 186m. v

Sound of Fury, The 1951 ★★★½ An amoral

criminal (Bridges) draws a regular Joe (Lovejoy) into a career of petty larceny and kidnapping. Taut, exiting suspense yarn. C: Frank Lovejoy, Lloyd Bridges, Richard Carlson, Katherine Locke. D: Cy Endfield. CRI 92m. v

Sound of Music, The 1965 ★★★★★ Superb family musical from Rodgers and Hammerstein show. The true story of Maria von Trapp (Andrews), governess for the seven children of an Austrian captain (Plummer), and the family's escape from the Nazis is charming, beautifully photographed, and winningly played. Taste and skill turned a saccharine Broadway musical into a deserved phenomenon. Songs include "My Favorite Things," "Climb Every Mountain," "Do Re Mi," and title tune. Winner of five Oscars including Best Picture, Director. C: Julie Andrews, Christopher Plummer, Eleanor Parker, Peggy Wood, Richard Haydn. D: Robert Wise. FAM/MUS 175m. v

Sound of Trumpets, The 1961 Italian ★★★★½ Young man from rural Italy gets job with Milan firm and must adjust to life in the city. Neatly detailed comedy with exquisite blend of affection and satire. (a.k.a. *Il Posto* or *The Job*) C: Sandro Panzeri, Loredana Detto, Tullio Kezich. D: Ermanno Olmi. COM 90m.

Sound Off 1952 ★★★ Entertainer Rooney gets drafted, but can't fight his urges to perform and romance a WAC. Simpleminded musical comedy helped by Rooney's sparky energy. C: Mickey Rooney, Anne James, John Archer, Sammy White. D: Richard Quine. MUS 83m.

Sounder 1972 ★★★★½ By presenting the lives of a black sharecropping family in the 1930s South in a heroic, positive light, socially conscious Ritt made film history. When the father (Winfield) is jailed unjustly, the mother (Tyson) and son (Hooks) keep the family together. C: Cicely Tyson, Paul Winfield, Kevin Hooks, Carmen Mathews. D: Martin Ritt. DRA [G] 105m. v

Sounder, Part Two 1976 ★★★★½ Continues uplifting story of Louisiana sharecropper's family maintaining their integrity during the Depression. Warm, wonderful family entertainment. C:Harold Sylvester, Ebony Wright, Taj Mahal, Annazette Chase. D: William A. Graham. DRA [G] 98m.

Sourdough 1977 ★★★ Mountain man's journey through the wilds of Alaska. Visually breathtaking. C: Gil Perry, Charles Brock, Slim Carlson, Carl Clark. D: Martin J. Spinelli. ACT 94m. v

South Beach 1992 ★★½ Two football stars turned bon vivant Miami detectives have their easygoing lives disrupted by a mysterious woman. Interesting cast in a thriller with real sand in its shoes. C: Fred Williamson, Gary Busey, Vanity, Peter Fonda. D: Fred Williamson. DRA [R] 93m. v

South Bronx Heroes 1986 ★★★ Two children escape from a pornographer and get an unconventional cop to crack the crime ring. Could have been better. (a.k.a. *The Runaways* and *Revenge of the Innocents*) C: Mario Van Peebles, Brendan Ward, Megan Van Peebles. D: William Szarka. ACT [R] 105m. v

South Central 1992 ★★★★ L.A. gang member gets his attitude turned around in prison and comes out, hoping to save his son from making the same mistakes. Tough-minded and effective. C: Glenn Plummer, Byron Keith Minns, Carl Lumbly, Christian Coleman. D: Steve Anderson. DRA [R] 99m. v

South of Pago Pago 1940 ★★½ Dated pirate movie has cast in tropics searching for pearls while simultaneously trying to quell revolution of the indigenous population. Routine. C: Victor McLaglen, Jon Hall, Frances Farmer, Gene Lockhart. D: Alfred E. Green. ACT 97m. v

South of St. Louis 1949 ★★★½ Three post-Civil War ranch partners have a falling out over women, money, land, and running guns. Good casting, lots of fast-paced action, but an otherwise unremarkable Western. C: Joel McCrea, Alexis Smith, Zachary Scott, Dorothy Malone. D: Ray Enright. WST 88m. v

South Pacific 1958 ★★★½ Rodgers and Hammerstein's romantic musical of WWII nurse (Gaynor), stationed on Pacific island, falling for French planter (Brazzi) until racial prejudice intervenes. Superb songs like "Some Enchanted Evening" or "Bali Hai." Warning: strange experiments with color filters cause cast to turn purple during certain musical numbers. Do not adjust your set! C: Rossano Brazzi, Mitzi Gaynor, John Kerr, Ray Walston, Juanita Hall, France Nuyen, Tom Laughlin. D: Joshua Logan. MUS 150m. v

South Riding 1938 British ★★★½ Adaptation of Winifred Holtby's novel about a Yorkshire schoolmistress who uncovers corrupt local officials and dallies with a dejected country gentleman. Sturdy, old-fashioned storytelling with a persuasive depiction of British provincial living. C: Ralph Richardson, Edna Best, Edmund Gwenn, Ann Todd. D: Victor Saville. DRA 84m. v.

South Sea Woman 1953 ★★★½ A rugged Marine romances a Pacific island woman and brawls with his buddy during WWII. Boisterous, uneven comedy of love and war. C: Burt Lancaster, Virginia Mayo, Chuck Connors, Arthur Shields, Paul Burke. D: Arthur Lubin. COM 99m.

Southern Comfort 1981 ★★★½ A squad of National Guardsmen get caught in a bayou full of trouble as they face down armed locals. Thrilling and well directed, but occasionally muddled. C: Keith Carradine, Powers Boothe, Fred Ward, T.K. Carter. D: Walter Hill. ACT [R] 105m. v

Southern Yankee, A 1948 ★★★★ Skelton

remakes Keaton's silent classic *The General* and fares quite well as a klutzy bellboy who finds himself in the heart of Confederate territory as a spy. And why shouldn't he? The best gags were contributed by Keaton himself. C: Red Skelton, Brian Donlevy, Arlene Dahl, George Coulouris, Lloyd Gough, John Ireland, Charles Dingle, Joyce Compton. D: Edward Sedgwick. COM 91m. V

Southerner, The 1945 ★★★★½ Director Renoir's tender study, adapted from George Sessions' novel, of poor tenant farmer in the South, struggling to sustain his family despite overpowering conflicts. Evocative outdoor drama, rich in detail and emotion. C: Zachary Scott, Betty Field, Beulah Bondi, J. Carroll Naish, Norman Lloyd. D: Jean Renoir. DRA 91m. V

Southside 1-1000 1950 ★★★½ An FBI agent pursues counterfeiters. Earnest film noir, with a terrific performance from King. C: Don Defore, Andrea King, George Tobias, Barry Kelley. D: Boris Ingster. CRI 73m.

Soylent Green 1973 ★★★★ Heston stars as a future cop who discovers what the City's favorite food is really made of, while investigating a murder. Robinson's last film. Compelling—if bleak—probably not for the kids. C: Charlton Heston, Edward G. Robinson, Leigh Taylor Young, Chuck Connors. D: Richard Fleischer. SFI [PG] 97m. V

Space Camp 1986 ★★ Kids at a NASA training camp blast off into trouble. Regrettable effort. C: Kate Capshaw, Lea Thompson, Kelly Preston, Larry B. Scott, Leaf Phoenix, Tate Donovan, Tom Skerritt. D: Harry Winer. SFI [PG] 115m. V

Space Children, The 1958 ★★★ An illusory alien being mind-controls nuclear scientists' children into sabotaging a missile test site. Entertaining low-budget science fiction, with an antiwar message. C: Michel Ray, Peggy Webber, Adam Williams, Jackie Coogan, Johnny Washbrook. D: Jack Arnold. SFI 69m.

Space Firebird 1982 ★★★ Japanese animated film follows the flight of a bird-monster who is wreaking havoc on several planets. Idealistic farce. SFI 103m. TVM V

Space Men Appear in Toyko 1956 *See* **Mysterious Satellite, The**

Space Mutants 1965 *See* **Planet of the Vampires**

Space 1999: Alien Attack 1979 ★★★ The crew of moon base Alpha (led by Landau) face down vicious aliens in this version of the cult British TV series. Solid effects and production. C: Martin Landau, Barbara Bain. D: Lee H. Katzm. SFI 109m. TVM V

Space 1999: Journey Through Black Sun 1982 ★★★ The crew of moon base Alpha (led by Landau and Bain) on a trip that could destroy them all. From the cult British TV series. C: Martin Landau, Barbara Bain. SFI 92m. TVM V

Space 1999—Vol. 1—Voyager's Return 1975 ★★★ When the long-lost Voyager probe is discovered, the crew of Moonbase Alpha has to act fast to stop the errant spacecraft in its path of destruction. Okay sci-fi, from the British TV series. C: Martin Landau, Barbara Bain. D: Bob Kellett. SFI 60m. TVM V

Space Ninja—Sword of the Space Ark 1981 ★★½ Warrior pilot returns home to find his planet crumbling under a twisted emperor's reign of terror. Low-octane sci-fi. D: Bunker Jenkins. SFI 75m. V

Space Raiders 1983 ★★★ Space travelers are pursued throughout the galaxy by an evil adversary. Passable *Star Wars* retread, from the legendary house of Corman cut and paste. (a.k.a. *Star Child*) C: Vince Edwards, David Mendenhall, Patsy Pease, Luca Bercovici. D: Howard R. Cohen. SFI [PG] 84m. V

Space Vampires 1967 *See* **Astro-Zombies**

Space Zombies 1967 *See* **Astro-Zombies**

Spaceballs 1987 ★★ Mel Brooks parody uses *Star Wars*, as an excuse for endless series of obvious one-liners and moldy visual jokes. Moranis, Rivers, Candy, and Brooks seem amused by their on-screen antics, even if audience isn't. C: Mel Brooks, John Candy, Rick Moranis, Bill Pullman, Daphne Zuniga. D: Mel Brooks. COM [PG] 97m. V

Spaced Invaders 1990 ★★ After getting transmission of Orson Welles "War of the Worlds" radio show, space people invade Earth and surprise small town residents. One overblown joke that drags on and on. C: Douglas Barr, Royal Dano, Ariana Richards, Kevin Thompson, Jimmy Briscoe, Tony Cox, Debbie Lee Carrington, Tommy Madden. D: Patrick Read Johnson. COM [PG] 100m. V

Spaced Out 1981 British ★★ Spaceship of female aliens takes four Earthlings hostage to discover the differences between men and women. Unfunny sex comedy parody. (a.k.a. *Outer Reach*) C: Barry Stokes, Tony Maiden, Glory Annen, Michael Rowlatt, Ava Cadell, Kate Ferguson, Lynne Ross. D: Norman J. Warren. COM [R] 84m.

Spacehunter: Adventures in the Forbidden Zone 1983 Canadian ★ A hunter (Strauss) rescues lovely ladies from a disfigured captor in a futuristic toxic wasteland. Watching it could be toxic. C: Peter Strauss, Molly Ringwald, Ernie Hudson, Andrea Marcovicci. D: Lamont Johnson. SFI [PG] 90m. V

Spaceman in King Arthur's Court, The 1979 *See* **Unidentified Flying Oddball, The**

Spaceship, The *See* **Creature Wasn't Nice, The**

Spanish Affair 1958 Spanish ★★½ An interpreter in Madrid falls for a visiting American architect. Travelogue scenery dominates this genre romance. C: Richard Kiley, Carmen Sevilla, Jose Guardiola, Jesus Tordesillas. D: Don Siegel. DRA 95m.

Spanish Gardener, The 1956 British ★★★★ Film adaptation of A.J. Cronin's novel about a

British diplomat in Spain who envies the burgeoning relationship between his son and their gardener. Penetrating and well-acted human drama, exquisitely filmed. C: Dirk Bogarde, Maureen Swanson, Jon Whiteley, Cyril Cusack, Bernard Lee, Michael Horden. D: Philip Leacock. DRA 95m. v

Spanish Main, The 1945 ★★★½ Caribbean adventure as a swashbuckling Dutch pirate romances the fiancée of an unscrupulous Spanish viceroy. Slightly inflated, colorful sea saga to delight one and all. C: Paul Henreid, Maureen O'Hara, Walter Slezak, Binnie Barnes. D: Frank Borzage. ACT 100m. v

Sparkle 1976 ★★★½ Rise and fall of Supremes-like singing group in '60s features McKee as small-time singer who becomes international sensation. Slickly produced film is thin on story but Curtis Mayfield musical numbers are entertaining and McKee gives a fine performance. C: Philip Michael Thomas, Irene Cara, Lonette McKee, Dwan Smith, Mary Alice, Dorian Harewood, Tony King. D: Sam O'Steen. COM [PG] 100m. v

Spartacus 1960 ★★★★½ A slave leader (Douglas) foments a revolt against the oppressive Roman ruling class. Muscular direction and sterling performances from the large cast make this one of Hollywood's best Biblical epics. Restored letterbox version contains footage missing from the original theatrical release. Oscars for Supporting Actor (Ustinov), Art Direction, Costume Design, and Cinematography. C: Kirk Douglas, Laurence Olivier, Jean Simmons, Tony Curtis, Charles Laughton, Peter Ustinov, John Gavin. D: Stanley Kubrick. DRA [PG-13] 185m. v

Spasms 1982 Canadian ★★ Trophy hunter (Reed) is on the same wavelength as a deadly giant snake he encounters on a hunt. Fonda is the psychologist who has to get to the bottom of it all. Good luck! C: Peter Fonda, Oliver Reed, Kerrie Keane, Al Waxman. D: William Fruet. HOR [R] 92m. v

Spawn of the North 1938 ★★★★ American salmon fishermen in 1890s Alaska fight to protect their fisheries from encroaching Russian pirates. Stirring, well-tailored adventure yarn with a star-studded cast. Remade as *Alaska Seas*. C: George Raft, Henry Fonda, Dorothy Lamour, Louise Platt, John Barrymore, Akim Tamiroff, Lynne Overman. D: Henry Hathaway. ACT 110m.

Speak Easily 1932 ★★★★ Early talkie features Keaton as a bumbling professor who inherits a theatrical troupe trying to crash Broadway. Excellent gags; wonderful supporting cast. C: Buster Keaton, Jimmy Durante, Ruth Selwyn, Thelma Todd, Hedda Hopper, Sidney Toler. D: Edward Sedgwick. COM 82m. v

Special Agent 1935 ★★★½ A detective impersonating a journalist (Brent) pursuades a bookkeeper (Davis) to get the goods on a mobster. Agreeable, crusading crime buster. C: Bette Davis, George Brent, Ricardo Cortez, Jack LaRue, Henry O'Neill. D: William Keighley. DRA 78m.

Special Day, A 1977 ★★★★½ A morose homosexual (Mastroianni) and a lonely housewife (Loren) meet on the day Hitler's army invades Rome. Lovely character study gains political resonance as it progresses to a moving ending. Don't miss this chance to catch these occasional co-stars at the top of their form. C: Marcello Mastroianni, Sophia Loren. D: Ettore Scola. DRA 106m. v

Special Delivery 1977 ★★★½ After he robs a bank, a Vietnam veteran (Svenson) has to contend with a ditzy artist (Shepherd) and killers tracking the loot. Entertaining escapism with complex plot turns. C: Bo Svenson, Cybill Shepherd, Michael Gwynne, Tom Atkins. D: Paul Wendkos. ACT [PG] 99m. v

Special Investigator 1936 ★★ Lawyer who specializes in defending mobsters decides to join the Justice Department after his G-man brother is murdered during an FBI raid. Action piece switches from crime drama to Western, failing to generate much excitement in either milieu. C: Richard Dix, Margaret Callahan. D: Louis King. ACT 61m.

Specialist, The 1975 ★★★ Lawyer West falls for beautiful Capri, unaware she's been hired to kill him. C: Ahna Capri, John Anderson, Adam West, Alvy Moore. D: Howard Hikmet Avedis. ACT [R] 93m. v

Specialist, The 1994 ★★½ Woman wants revenge on the drug dealers who killed her parents, so she hires Stallone to do the job. Overused plot from dozens of low-budget actioners is grafted on to big-budget explosions, chases and stars. The shower scene with Sly and Sharon is a classic of narcissistic kitsch. C: Sylvester Stallone, Sharon Stone, James Woods, Rod Steiger, Eric Roberts. D: Luis Llosa. ACT [R] 120m. v

Spectre of the Rose 1946 ★★★★ An offbeat theatrical story of a deranged ballet dancer who almost kills his wife, features a witty, literate script and some campy fun performances. Very original—people either love it or hate it. C: Judith Anderson, Michael Chekhov, Ivan Kirov, Viola Essen. D: Ben Hecht. DRA 90m. v

Speechless 1994 ★★★½ Speechwriters for rival political candidates fall in love. Keaton and Davis try hard, but their scenes together don't work as well as the subordinate campaign humor. Close, but no cigar. C: Michael Keaton, Geena Davis, Christopher Reeve, Bonnie Bedelia. D: Ron Underwood. COM [PG-13] 98m. v

Speed 1936 ★★★ Early Stewart vehicle casts him as nervy test-car driver. One of eight features he made in 1936. C: James Stewart, Wendy Barrie, Una Merkel, Ted Healy. D: Edwin L. Marin. ACT 70m.

Speed 1994 ★★★★ L.A. police have a nasty problem: there's a bus on the freeway rigged with explosives set to go off if it slows below 50 mph. Reeves gives a nicely gauged performance as the SWAT officer on the case. Taut and suspenseful, with excellent effects—it won two Oscars for Sound and Sound Editing. The premise was actually borrowed from a Japanese thriller, *Bullet Train*. C: Keanu Reeves, Dennis Hopper, Sandra Bullock. D: Jan DeBont. ACT 90m. ▾

Speed Zone! 1989 ★★ Group of zanies engage in cross-country motor race, trying to outwit each other and sheriff (Boyle). *Cannonball Run* zest missing here and much comic talent goes to waste. C: Peter Boyle, Donna Dixon, John Candy, Eugene Levy, Tim Matheson, John Candy, Smothers Brothers, Matt Frewer, Joe Flaherty, Shari Belafonte, Art Hindle, John Schneider, Jamie Farr. D: Jim Drake. COM [PG] 96m. ▾

Speedway 1968 ★★★ Singing racecar driver (Presley) develops a crush on Sinatra, cast as (of all things) an inspector for the IRS! Dim-witted Presley vehicle runs low on gas. C: Elvis Presley, Nancy Sinatra, Bill Bixby, Gale Gordon. D: Norman Taurog. MUS 94m. ▾

Spellbinder 1988 ★★ A lawyer (Daly) is obsessed with a lovely woman (Preston)—who is a member of a Satanic cult that wants her back in the fold. Shallow plot with an ending you can see coming from the main credits. C: Timothy Daly, Kelly Preston, Rick Rossovich, Audra Lindley. D: Janet Greek. HOR [R] 99m. ▾

Spellbound 1945 ★★★★ A kindly psychiatrist (Bergman) works to uncover severe childhood trauma of fellow doctor (Peck) after he's been framed for murder. Surreal Salvador Dali-designed dream sequences explore psychic landscapes in this fascinating psychological whodunit. C: Ingrid Bergman, Gregory Peck, Leo G. Carroll, Michael Chekhov, Rhonda Fleming. D: Alfred Hitchcock. CRI 111m. ▾

Spellcaster 1991 ★★ TV contest winners are invited to a remote castle to claim a six-figure prize. Once there, the screaming starts. Horrifically dull. C: Adam Ant, Richard Blade, Gail O'Grady. D: Rafal Zielinski. HOR [R] 83m. ▾

Spencer's Mountain 1963 ★★★ Simplistic tale of Wyoming landowner (Fonda) who never quite can fulfill the promise of new house for his family. Script too slight to carry thin drama, though performances aren't bad. Based on novel by Earl Hamner, Jr.; later served as inspiration for popular television series *The Waltons*. C: Henry Fonda, Maureen O'Hara, James MacArthur, Donald Crisp, Wally Cox, Veronica Cartwright, Victor French. D: Delmer Daves. FAM/DRA 118m. ▾

Spetters 1980 Dutch ★★★ Dutch teenage pranks and ambitions dominate this tale of pubescent sex and motorcycle racing. Disconnected story with standout performances from Hauer and Soutendijk. Contains overt sexuality. The title means "grease spatterings." C: Hans VanTongeren, Toon Agterberg, Renee Soutendijk, Rutger Hauer. D: Paul Verhoeven. DRA [R] 100m. ▾

Sphinx 1980 ★★½ As she searches for a lost tomb, Egyptologist (Down) encounters more than just old dead bodies. Superior production values and slew of great actors can't breathe life into this mummified thriller. C: Lesley-Anne Down, Frank Langella, Maurice Ronet, John Gielgud, John Rhyse Davies. D: Franklin J. Schaffner. DRA [PG] 118m. ▾

Spider and the Fly, The 1949 British ★★★½ At the outbreak of WWI, the unlikely team of a Sûreté inspector and Parisian safecracker engage in a desperate hunt for vital enemy documents. Thrilling espionage suspense melodrama; fine ensemble acting. C: Guy Rolfe, Nadia Gray, Eric Portman, Maurice Denham, James Hayter, Arthur Lowe. D: Robert Hamer. DRA 87m.

Spider-Man (The Amazing Spider-Man) 1977 ★★★ Marvel comics superhero in adequate adaptation that concentrates on the origins of his unique powers. Not as fresh and witty as the comic, but clever effects and lively action. C: Nicholas Hammond, David White, Michael Pataki, Hilly Hicks, Lisa Eilbacher, Thayer David, Jeff Donnell. D: E.W. Swackhamer. ACT 94m. TVM ▾

Spider, The 1958 *See* **Earth vs. the Spider**

Spider Woman, The 1944 ★★★★½ It's elementary, my dear Watson, this is one of the best Sherlock Holmes movies. The Baker Street sleuth is baffled by mysterious suicides linked to spider bites. Sondergaard makes a suitably slithery villainess. C: Basil Rathbone, Nigel Bruce, Gale Sondergaard. D: Roy William Neill. CRI 62m. ▾

Spiderman: The Deadly Dust 1978 ★★★ A group of brilliant college students build a nuclear device and Spiderman must step in to prevent mass destruction. Good live action *Spiderman* adventure. C: Nicholas Hammond, Michael Pataki. D: Ron Satlof. SFI 92m. TVM

Spiderman Vol. 1 ★★★ Two episodes of the '70s TV series. Solid production values bring Marvel's #1 hero to life. ACT ▾

Spiderman Vol. 2 ★★★ Two episodes of the '70s TV series feature a superhero whose powers comes from a spider's bite. Energetically acted and produced. ACT ▾

Spider's Stratagem, The 1970 ★★★★ A small town behaves with suspicious antagonism to a man searching for information about his dead father, who used to live there. Hypnotic mystery works, thanks to Bertolucci's bravura direction. C: Giulio Brogi, Alida Valli, Tino Scotti. D: Bernardo Bertolucci. DRA 100m. ▾

Spies 1928 German ★★★★★ Silent espionage classic, with secret agent (Fritsch) pitted against a wheelchair-bound arch villain (Klein-Rogge). Entertaining, seat-of-your-pants suspense doesn't need to make a sound. (a.k.a.

Spione). C: Rudolph Klein-Rogge, Willy Fritsch, Gerda Maurus. D: Fritz Lang. CRI 90m. v

Spies A Go Go 1965 *See* **Nasty Rabbit, The**

Spies Like Us 1985 ★★★ Government employees (Chase and Aykroyd) in over their heads on mission in Afghanistan where they cause international shenanigans. Starts off well, but loses its road picture map. Many cameos, including one by Bob Hope who was in funnier *Road* movies than this. C: Chevy Chase, Dan Aykroyd, Steve Forrest, Donna Dixon, Bruce Davison. D: John Landis. COM [PG] 103m. v

Spinout 1966 ★★★ Yet another Elvis as racecar driver musical (see *Speedway*)! This one has former Donna Reed daughter, future *Coach* wife Fabares as Presley's amore. Weak songs; for Elvisites. C: Elvis Presley, Shelley Fabares, Diane McBain, Una Merkel. D: Norman Taurog. MUS 90m. v

Spinster, The *See* **Two Loves**

Spione *See* **Spies**

Spiral Staircase, The 1946 ★★★★½ Spine-tingling suspense thriller of a deaf-mute servant (beautifully acted by McGuire) being stalked by a killer in a spooky house. Based on Ethel Lina White's novel *Some Must Watch*. C: Dorothy McGuire, George Brent, Ethel Barrymore, Kent Smith. D: Robert Siodmak. DRA 83m. v

Spiral Staircase, The 1975 British ★★★ Remake of superb 1946 film stars Bisset as a mute servant threatened by a homicidal maniac. Based on E.L. White's novel *Some Must Watch*. A milder version of the original. C: Jacqueline Bisset, Christopher Plummer, Sam Wanamaker, Mildred Dunnock, John Phillip Law. D: Peter Collinson. CRI 89m. v

Spirit of Crazy Horse, The ★★★★ Intriguing documentary follows the Native-American Sioux of South Dakota and their efforts to preserve their legacy. This disturbing look at American history should not be missed. Excellent educational fare for the children. DOC v

Spirit of St. Louis, The 1957 ★★★★ Stewart delivers a strong performance as the youthful Lindbergh in the story of flyer's daring solo flight across Atlantic. Able direction and script by Wilder. C: James Stewart, Patricia Smith, Murray Hamilton, Marc Connelly. D: Billy Wilder. DRA 137m. v

Spirit of Tatoo 1983 *See* **Irezumi: Spirit of Tatoo**

Spirit of the Beehive 1973 Spanish ★★★½ An isolated peasant girl (Torrent) watches Boris Karloff in *Frankenstein* and, fascinated by the tale, wanders off to find the monster, whom she believes to be real. This intriguing spin on the Frankenstein legend features an outstanding performance by Torrent. C: Fernando Fernan Gomez, Teresa Gimpera, Ana Torrent, Isabel Telleria. D: Victor Erice. DRA 95m. v

Spirit of the Dead 1972 *See* **Asphyx**

Spirit of the Eagle 1990 ★★ Mountain man (Haggerty) saves the day when his son is kidnapped. Deadly slow pace kills any potential entertainment in this pack of wilderness film clichés. C: Dan Haggerty, William Smith. D: Kathleen Phelan. FAM/DRA [PG] 93m. v

Spirits of the Dead 1968 French-Italian ★★★★ Three short films, each inspired by an obscure Edgar Allan Poe story. Fellini's, with Stamp, is the best. Vadim's tale of obsessed brother/sister (Jane and Peter) is overheated, but memorable. Well worth sampling. C: Brigitte Bardot, Alain Delon, Jane Fonda, Peter Fonda, Terence Stamp. D: Roger Vadim, Louis Malle, Federico Fellini. HOR [R] 117m.

Spiritual Kung Fu 1978 ★★★ Kung fu gods give a young warrior private lessons, enabling him to defeat his enemies. Plenty of action. C: Jackie Chan. ACT 97m. v

Spite Marriage 1929 ★★★★ Clever comedy from the great stone face Keaton finds him marrying an actress he's fallen head over heels for. But she's marrying him only to get revenge on her true love who's jilted her. Silent classic may not be one of Keaton's best but still provides ample slapstick humor. C: Buster Keaton, Dorothy Sebastian, Edward Earle, Leila Hyams. D: Edward Sedgwick. COM 70m. v

Spitfire 1934 ★★★★ A backwoods Ozark mountain woman involved in faith healing falls for a married engineer. Hopelessly elegant Hepburn plays against type in winsome melodrama adapted from Lula Vollmer's play; some memorable scenes. C: Katharine Hepburn, Robert Young, Ralph Bellamy, Sidney Toler. D: John Cromwell. DRA 88m. v

Spitfire 1942 British ★★★★ WWII biography of visionary inventor R.J. Mitchell, who created the Spitfire, the tactically superior Allied fighter plane that served in the Battle of Britain. Howard and Niven are fine in gallant, action-packed true story, with exciting aerial photography. (a.k.a. *The First of the Few*) C: Leslie Howard, David Niven, Rosamund John, Roland Culver. D: Leslie Howard. DRA 89m. v

Spittin' Image 1983 ★★ Girl lost in woods falls under tutelage of tobacco-chewin' mountian fellow. C: Sharon Barr, Karen Barr. ACT 92m. v

Splash 1984 ★★★★ Hanks is bored bachelor who falls in love with mermaid Hannah, whom he ultimately must protect when scientists and military try to capture her. Cute romantic comedy with some clever twists and nice performances: Hannah's lobster-eating sequence is inspired. C: Daryl Hannah, Tom Hanks, John Candy, Eugene Levy. D: Ron Howard. COM [PG] 109m. v

Splatter University 1984 ★ Nubile college students keep having their study sessions and sexual interludes interrupted by knife-wielding maniac. Lots of blood and guts but no brains. C: Francine Forbes, Ric Randig, Cathy LaCommare. D: Richard Haines. HOR [R] 79m. v

Splendor in the Grass 1961 ★★★★ Adolescent adjustment problems plague Wood and Beatty in sensitive drama scripted by playwright William Inge. Their romantic awakening is beautifully handled, but last half hour becomes melodramatic. C: Natalie Wood, Warren Beatty, Pat Hingle, Audrey Christie, Sandy Dennis, Barbara Loden. D: Elia Kazan. DRA 124m. V

Split 1990 ★★ One man holds the key to safety when outer space androids fight for control of the planet. C: Timothy Dwight, Joan Bechtel, John Flynn. D: Chris Shaw. SFI 85m. V

Split Second 1992 U.S. ★★½ Futuristic bounty hunter searches for alien monster responsible for killing his partner and terrifying all of London. Lackluster, poorly executed *Blade Runner* rip-off. C: Rutger Hauer, Kim Cattrall, Neil Duncan, Michael J. Pollard. D: Tony Maylam. SFI [R] 90m. V

Splitface 1945 *See* **Dick Tracy**

Splitting Heirs 1993 U.S. ★★★ When down-and-out Idle discovers he's really heir to a lordship, he tries to wrest title from phony duke Moranis. Ridiculous humor filled with puns, sight gags, and silly contrivances. C: Rick Moranis, Eric Idle, Barbara Hershey, Catherine Zeta Jones, John Cleese. D: Robert Young. COM [PG-13] 87m. V

Spoilers, The 1930 ★★★ Gold prospectors in Alaska battle corrupt politicians who are pillaging prosperous gold claims. First sound version of popular Gold Rush Western (filmed twice as a silent, in 1914 and 1923) was a successful vehicle for Cooper. Features the de rigeur barroom fight. C: Gary Cooper, Kay Johnson, Betty Compson, William "Stage" Boyd. D: Edwin Carewe. WST 85m.

Spoilers, The 1942 ★★★★ Two adventurers (Wayne, Scott) after gold in the Yukon fight over claims and a saloon hostess (Dietrich). Fourth version of the classic Western boasts plenty of two-fisted action, including the signature barroom fight, along with charismatic, top cast. Possibly the best of the five versions filmed—so far. C: Marlene Dietrich, Randolph Scott, John Wayne, Margaret Lindsay, Harry Carey. D: Ray Enright. WST 104m. V

Spoilers, The 1955 ★★★½ Fifth version of Rex Beach's saga of claim jumpers in the Klondike again highlighted by a furious barroom brawl. C: Anne Baxter, Jeff Chandler, Rory Calhoun, Barbara Britton, Raymond Walburn. D: Jesse Hibbs. WST 84m.

Spontaneous Combustion 1989 ★ Crushingly mediocre horror fest; with unnecessary government conspiracy gimmick; about humans suddenly bursting into flames (supposedly fact-based). C: Brad Dourif, Cynthia Bain, William Prince, Melinda Dillon. D: Tobe Hooper. HOR 97m. V

Spook Buster 1946 ★★★ The Bowery Boys battle demons and a zany mad scientist after forming their own ghost extermination service, in what seems to be a '40s warmup for 1984's *Ghostbusters*. Average approach to this material was better served in the Boy's own later *Ghost Chasers*. COM V

Spook Who Sat By the Door, The 1973 ★★ Black CIA agent, fed up with racist put-downs by fellow operatives, trains street youths in undercover methods, then unleashes them on white communities. Poorly executed exploitative action flick. C: Lawrence Cook, Paula Kelly, Janet League, J.A. Preston, Paul Butler. D: Ivan Dixon. ACT [PG] 102m. V

Spookies 1985 ★★ Aged alchemist collects bodies hoping to revive his unconscious wife. C: Felix Ward, Dan Scott, Alec Nemser. D: Thomas Doran. HOR [R] 85m. V

Spooks Run Wild 1941 ★★★½ The East Side Kids run afoul of Nardo (Lugosi), a sinister caped villain. Lugosi pokes fun at his own persona in this horror-comedy prototype of the popular Monogram series. C: Bela Lugosi, Eastside Kids. D: Phil Rosen. COM 64m. V

Sporting Blood 1931 ★★★½ Energetic horse-racing yarn about a mishandled Thoroughbred and his latest owner, a tough gambler determined to win the Kentucky Derby despite threats from gangsters who want to fix the race. Early roughneck Gable in top form. C: Clark Gable, Ernest Torrence, Madge Evans, Lew Cody, Marie Prevost, J.Farrell MacDonald. D: Charles Brabin. ACT 82m.

Spot 1975 *See* **Dogpound Shuffle**

Spotlight Scandals 1943 ★★★★ Vaudeville comic convinces a goofy Midwestern barber to team up with him in order to get back to New York, then discovers his new partner is bringing him the stardom he's always wanted. Pleasant mix of comedy and drama works, thanks to the talents of its two leads, both veteran vaudvillians. C: Billy Gilbert, Frank Fay, Bonnie Baker. D: William Beaudine. MUS 79m.

Spread Eagle 1950 *See* **Eagle and the Hawk, The**

Spring Break 1983 ★★ 'Tis the season once again, and hordes of hormone-hopping students arrive in Ft. Lauderdale to par-taay! Predictably moronic. C: David Knell, Steve Bassett, Paul Land. D: Sean S. Cunningham. COM [R] 101m. V

Spring in Park Lane 1948 British ★★★★ While disguised as a diamond broker's household servant, a penniless English lord (Wilding) falls for his employer's niece (Neagle). Clever humor marks tasteful comedy of mistaken identity and romance. Sparkling fun from Alice Duer Miller's play. C: Anna Neagle, Michael Wilding, Tom Wallis, Marjorie Fielding, Nicholas Phipps, Josephine Fitzgerald. D: Herbert Wilcox. COM 100m.

Spring Meeting 1941 British ★★★ A penniless widow in Ireland is anxious for her son to wed the daughter of her former sweetheart. Reserved adaptation of Norman Lee's eccentric theatrical comedy. C: Enid Stamp-Taylor, Michael Wilding, Basil Sydney, Sarah Churchill, Nova Pilbearn, Margaret Rutherford. D: Walter C. Mycroft. COM 93m.

Spring Parade 1940 ★★★★ Decorative period froth about a singing baker's helper (Durbin) in Austria who falls in love with a waltz composer (Cummings). Charming escapism. C: Deanna Durbin, Robert Cummings, Mischa Auer, Henry Stephenson, Butch & Buddy, Anne Gwynne. D: Henry Koster. MUS 89m.

Spring Shower 1932 Hungarian ★★★★ Forced to leave her village after she becomes pregnant out of wedlock, a Hungarian peasant girl finds the only place willing take her in is a Budapest bordello. Striking visuals and keen direction highlight this early French/Hungarian melodrama. C: Annabella. D: Paul Fejos. DRA

Spring Symphony 1986 ★★★½ Chronicle of the romance between leading pianist Clara Wieck and major 19th-century German composer Robert Schumann. Very melodic biography, with Kinski appealing in the lead. C: Nastassia Kinski, Herbert Gronemeyer. D: Peter Schamoni. MUS [PG-13] 102m. V

Spring, The 1989 ★★½ Two archeologists, hot on trail of the fountain of youth, face hidden evil along the way. C: Dack Rambo, Shari Shattuck, Gedde Watanabe. D: John D. Patterson. ACT 110m. V

Springfield Rifle 1952 ★★★½ A Union officer-agent poses as a turncoat to uncover a traitor involved in the theft of government weapons. Plenty of espionage in this Civil War Western. C: Gary Cooper, Phyllis Thaxter, David Brian, Lon Chaney, Paul Kelly, Phil Carey, Guinn Williams. D: Andre de Toth. WST 93m. V

Springtime in the Rockies 1942 ★★★★ A leggy singer's romance with her Broadway stage partner runs hot and cold. Archetypal, splashy studio musical features great numbers from Miranda and the Harry James Band. C: Betty Grable, John Payne, Carmen Miranda, Cesar Romero. D: Irving Cummings. MUS 90m. V

Springtime in the Sierras 1947 ★★★ Songs by the Sons of the Pioneers highlight this otherwise routine Western with Rogers and his old pal Devine teaming up to stop a local rancher from shooting animals out of season. Good action, fair story. (a.k.a. *Song of the Sierra*) C: Roy Rogers, Jane Frazee, Andy Devine. D: William Witney. WST 54m. V

Springtime on the Volga 1961 Russian ★★★ Infatuated with a ballet dancer, a Moscow optician pretends to be a cook so he can travel with the troupe. Slight film, mixing comedy and drama is most interesting for its insight into cultural differences. C: Mira Koltsava, D. Agafonova. D: Veniamin Dorman. DRA 75m.

Spy in Black, The 1939 British ★★★★ During WWI in Scotland amid espionage duplicity, a German navy spy and a British counterspy fall in love. Textured romance between unlikely lovers and cold-blooded intrigue woven entertainingly. C: Conrad Veidt, Sebastian Shaw, Valerie Hobson, June Duprez. D: Michael Powell. DRA 82m. V

Spy Smasher 1942 ★★★½ Twelve episodes from intriguing serial about hero waging brave battle against Nazis. C: Kane Richmond, Marguerite Chapman, Sam Flint. D: William Witney. ACT 215m. V

Spy Who Came In from the Cold, The 1966 ★★★★ Burton gives one of his greatest performances as a cynical over-the-hill Cold War agent. His portrayal of a broken man who helplessly observes his world coming apart at the seams is galvanizing. Fine supporting cast and tight direction make this adaptation one of the best of its kind. C: Richard Burton, Claire Bloom, Oskar Werner, Peter Van Eyck, George Voskovec, Sam Wanamaker. D: Martin Ritt. DRA 110m. V

Spy Who Loved Me, The 1977 ★★★★½ Superior, ultralavish James Bond spy extravaganza in which 007 (Moore, at his best) goes up against suave villain (Jurgens) who plans to rule the world from his undersea fortress. Action-packed sequences topped by Bond's encounters with giant, steel-toothed nemesis "Jaws" (Kiel). C: Roger Moore, Barbara Bach, Curt Jurgens, Richard Kiel, Caroline Munro. D: Lewis Gilbert. ACT [PG] 125m. V

Spymaker—The Secret Life of Ian Fleming 1990 British ★★★ Fictionalized exploits of undercover agent Fleming (Connery, Sean's son), the creator of James Bond. Attempts to capture the action propelled pacing and dry wit of the Bond films, but succeeds only sporadically. C: Jason Connery, Kristin Scott Thomas, Joss Ackland, David Warner, Patricia Hodge. D: Ferdinand Fairfax. ACT 96m. TVM V

S.P.Y.S. 1974 ★★½ Two incompetent CIA agents incur wrath of their own agency and the KGB. Funny performances from Gould and Sutherland. C: Donald Sutherland, Elliott Gould, Zouzou. D: Irvin Kershner. COM [PG] 87m. V

Square Dance 1987 ★★★★ Young girl comes of age at a snail's pace in this likable but lagging tale of heroine's move from strict grandfather's custody to more freewheeling life with mother. Saved by strong cast. (a.k.a. *Home Is Where the Heart Is.*) C: Jason Robards, Jane Alexander, Winona Ryder, Rob Lowe. D: Daniel Petrie. DRA [PG-13] 112m. V

Square Jungle, The 1955 ★★★ A young boxer (Curtis) battles his way to the championship. Everything you'd expect from a prizefighting yarn. C: Tony Curtis, Pat Crowley, Ernest Borgnine, Paul Kelly, Jim Backus. D: Jerry Hopper. DRA 86m.

Square Ring, The 1955 British ★★½ A motley group of individuals pin their hopes and bankrolls on the outcome of a boxing match. For fight enthusiasts and TV trivia buffs, who'll enjoy seeing pre-*Dynasty* Collins. C: Jack Warner, Kay Kendall, Joan Collins, Robert Beatty, Bill Owen, Maxwell Reed. D: Michael Relph, Basil Dearden. DRA 73m.

Square Shoulders 1929 ★★★ Petty thief who returns home to find his wife dead and his son running wild decides to change his life in order to make sure the boy stays on the straight-and-narrow. Early melodrama of only marginal interest, mostly for its mixing of sound and silent scenes. C: Junior Coghlan, Louis Wolheim. D: E. Mason Hopper. DRA 60m. V

Squaw Man, The 1931 ★★★★ DeMille's sound remake of a silent he directed in 1918 and 1914 is an early interracial romance between a British aristocrat (Baxter) and a Native American (Velez). Touching and unusually restrained, for this director. C: Warner Baxter, Lupe Velez, Eleanor Boardman, Charles Bickford, Roland Young. D: Cecil B. DeMille. DRA 105m.

Squeeze Play 1979 ★ Small-town battle of the sexes is settled on the softball field. Vulgar comedy swings and misses. C: Jim Harris, Jenni Hetrick, Rick Gitlin, Al Corley. D: Samuel Weil. COM [R] 92m. V

Squeeze, The 1987 ★★ Con artist (Keaton) in trouble after fetching mysterious black box for ex-wife. Gangsters want the package, a shrunken head. Runaround comedy deteriorates into messy and uninteresting slapstick sequences. C: Michael Keaton, Rae Dawn Chong, Meat Loaf, Ronald Guttman. D: Roger Young. COM [PG-13] 102m. V

SSSSSSS 1973 ★★★ A deranged doctor uncovers a method of changing young men into cobras. Up-to-scale reptilian shocker, with skillful makeup work. C: Strother Martin, Dirk Benedict, Heather Menzies, Richard B. Shull, Tim O'Connor, Jack Ging. D: Bernard L. Kowalski. HOR [PG] 99m.

St. Benny the Dip 1949 ★★★½ Con artists evade police by masquerading as priests. Predictable comedy with top-notch cast has good share of laughs. (a.k.a. *Escape If You Can*) C: Dick Haymes, Nina Foch, Roland Young, Lionel Stander, Freddie Bartholomew. D: Edgar G. Ulmer. COM 80m. V

St. Elmo's Fire 1985 ★★★ A group of just-graduated college friends face trials and tribulations in the real world. Pointless melodrama, but the actors—especially Lowe, Moore, and Estevez—turn in surprisingly good performances. C: Rob Lowe, Demi Moore, Andrew McCarthy, Judd Nelson, Ally Sheedy, Emilio Estevez, Mare Winningham. D: Joel Schumacher. DRA 110m. V

St. Louis Blues 1958 ★★★★ Musical bio of famed black composer W.C. Handy. Forget the fictionalized story; sit back and enjoy the wonderful cast, performing vintage songs. C: Nat "King" Cole, Eartha Kitt, Pearl Bailey, Ruby Dee, Cab Calloway, Ella Fitzgerald, Mahalia Jackson. D: Allen Reisner. MUS 93m.

St. Louis Kid 1934 ★★★½ Star vehicle for Cagney has him cast as a hot-headed trucker who gets involved in a dispute involving dairy farmers. Lighthearted action comedy, and Cagney is welcome anytime. C: James Cagney, Patricia Ellis, Allen Jenkins, Robert Barrat, Addison Richards. D: Ray Enright. COM 67m.

St. Valentine's Day Massacre, The 1967 ★★ Bullets fly and bodies pile up in umpteenth version of famed Roaring '20s gangland massacre. Lots of violence, and hammy acting. C: Jason Robards, George Segal, Ralph Meeker, Jean Hale, Frank Silvera, Bruce Dern. D: Roger Corman. ACT 100m. V

Stablemates 1938 ★★★ A boozy veterinarian grooms a plucky young jockey for horseracing fame. Well-directed sentiment with both stars expertly turning on the waterworks at appropriate moments. C: Wallace Beery, Mickey Rooney, Arthur Hohl, Margaret Hamilton, Minor Watson, Marjorie Gateson. D: Sam Wood. DRA [G] 89m.

Stacking 1987 ★★★½ Fame and fortune await a teenage girl and a drunken family friend who attempt to construct a mechanical hay stacker in 1954 rural Montana. Multilayered lead performances distinguish this rite-of-passage tale. (a.k.a. *Season of Dreams*) C: Christine Lahti, Frederic Forrest, Megan Follows, Peter Coyote. D: Martin Rosen. DRA [PG] 111m. V

Stage Door 1937 ★★★★★ Scintillating ensemble comedy with histrionic society newcomer (Hepburn) and wisecracker (Rogers) unlikely roommates at theatrical boarding house. Funny, touching, and full of great performances, including Collier's pretentious acting coach and Leeds' depressed ingenue. Has Hepburn's signature line "The calla lillies are in bloom again." C: Katharine Hepburn, Ginger Rogers, Adolphe Menjou, Andrea Leeds, Lucille Ball, Eve Arden, Ann Miller. D: Gregory LaCava. COM 92m. V

Stage Door Canteen 1943 ★★★½ During WWII a GI and a canteen hostess fall in love at the famed New York Armed Forces center. Pleasant wartime entertainment with cameos and musical numbers by a huge roster of stars. C: Cheryl Walker, William Terry, Lon McCallister, Edgar Bergen, Harpo Marx, Katharine Hepburn, Helen Hayes. D: Frank Borzage. MUS 132m. V

Stage Fright 1950 ★★★½ Actress (Wyman) pretends to be maid of star (Dietrich) to clear fugitive boyfriend (Wilding) of backstage murder. Film sounds great on paper but misfires, due to slow pacing and predictable finish. Marlene sings Cole Porter gem, "The Laziest Gal in Town." C: Marlene Dietrich, Jane Wyman, Michael Wilding, Richard Todd, Alastair Sim, Sybil Thorndike. D: Alfred Hitchcock. DRA 110m. V

Stage Struck 1957 ★★★½ An ambitious

young actress is determined to carve out a career on the Broadway stage. Luminous Strasberg in well-realized theatrical atmosphere. Remake of 1933 Katherine Hepburn Starrer, *Morning Glory*. C: Henry Fonda, Susan Strasberg, Joan Greenwood, Christopher Plummer. D: Sidney Lumet. DRA 95m. v

Stage to Thunder Rock 1964 ★★★ A sheriff is forced to arrest the family of desperados that brought him up. Impressive supporting cast of veteran character actors work to make the most of this Technicscope Western. C: Barry Sullivan, Marilyn Maxwell, Lon Chaney, Scott Brady, John Agar, Keenan Wynn, Allan Jones. D: Wiliam F. Claxton. WST 82m.

Stagecoach 1939 ★★★★★ Landmark Western of incompatible passengers traveling on same stagecoach through uncharted Indian territory. Complex characters fuse with remarkable action sequences. Standouts in brilliant cast include Wayne, Trevor, and Supporting Actor Oscar-winner Mitchell as alcoholic doctor. Remade twice. C: Claire Trevor, John Wayne, Andy Devine, John Carradine, Thomas Mitchell, Louise Platt, George Bancroft, Donald Meek, Berton Churchill. D: John Ford. WST 96m. v

Stagecoach 1966 ★★★½ Inferior retread of 1939 classic substitutes color photography for adequate script and cast. Still, there's enough life in the old story of stagecoach passengers fighting Indians (and each other) to make this fairly entertaining. C: Ann Margret, Alex Cord, Red Buttons, Michael Connors, Bing Crosby, Bob Cummings, Van Heflin, Slim Pickens, Stefanie Powers, Keenan Wynn. D: Gordon Douglas. WST 115m.

Stagecoach 1986 ★★★ Country-fied version of classic Western with Nashville stars trying to act story of stagecoach travelers en route to Arizona. Weak script and clumsy action sequences. Newley is so out of place here, he comes off best. C: Willie Nelson, Kris Kristofferson, Johnny Cash, Waylon Jennings, Elizabeth Ashley, Anthony Newley, Tony Franciosa. D: Ted Post. WST 95m. TVM v

Stagecoach Buckaroo 1942 ★★★½ Noble lawman goes after a ruthless gang of stagecoach robbers. Standard Western contains all the elements of a good oater, including a few range songs, but it is mostly the heroics of Brown and the antics of Knight that make it work. C: Johnny Mack Brown, Fuzzy Knight, Neil O'Day, Herbert Rawlinson. D: Ray Taylor. WST 58m.

Stagecoach to Dancers' Rock 1962 ★★ Five travelers struggle for their lives after they're abandoned by the stagecoach taking them to Arizona. Average Western drama rarely rises above the clichéd. C: Warren Stevens, Martin Landau, Jody Lawrance, Judy Dan. D: Earl Bellamy. WST 72m.

Stagecoach To Denver 1946 ★★★½ Brave Red Ryder discovers nasty plot hatched by "respected" man. Well-paced fun. C: Allan Lane, Bobby Blake, Martha Wentworth. D: R.G. Springsteen. WST 56m. v

Staircase 1969 ★★★ Two talented stars are unconvincing as a squabbling homosexual couple; mediocre version of the stage play. C: Rex Harrison, Richard Burton, Cathleen Nesbitt. D: Stanley Donen. COM [R] 100m.

Stairway to Heaven 1946 British ★★★★★ Seriously injured after a bail-out, a pilot under surgical anesthesia is caught in a netherworld between the next life and Earth and pleads for his life before a celestial tribunal. Formidable original fantasy—entertains both technically and dramatically. A dazzling film. (a.k.a. *A Matter of Life and Death*) C: David Niven, Kim Hunter, Raymond Massey, Roger Livesey, Robert Coote, Marius Goring, Richard Attenborough. D: Michael Powell, Emeric Pressburger. DRA 104m.

Stakeout 1987 ★★★★ While cops keep an eye on the house of an escaped convict's lover, one of them falls in love with her. Excellent blending of humor, action, and romance, plus great chemistry between principals make this a superior, although overly violent, action-comedy. C: Richard Dreyfuss, Emilio Estevez, Aidan Quinn, Madeleine Stowe. D: John Badham. ACT [R] 115m. v

Stakeout on Dope Street 1958 ★★★ Three youths dream of a lavish future after finding a briefcase full of heroin—unaware that the mobsters who lost it are after them. Effective morality crime tale. C: Yale Wexler, Jonathan Haze, Morris Miller, Abby Dalton, Herschel Bernardi. D: Irvin Kershner. CRI 83m.

Stalag 17 1953 ★★★★★ WWII prisoners of war struggle to survive harsh confines, using bitter humor and escape plots as weapons. Outstanding comedy/drama features top-notch cast led by Oscar-winner Holden as cynical sergeant suspected by other prisoners of being Nazi informant. C: William Holden, Don Taylor, Otto Preminger, Robert Strauss, Harvey Lembeck, Peter Graves, Neville Brand, Sig Rumann. D: Billy Wilder. DRA 120m. v

Stalin 1992 ★★★½ Duvall is a master, but he can't master a script cloned from molasses. Still, an intriguing portrait of monstrous dictator that makes him seem almost human. C: Robert Duvall, Julia Ormond, Jeroen Krabbe, Maximilian Schell, Joan Plowright. D: Ivan Passer. DRA 177m. TVM v

Stalker 1979 Russian ★★★ In this highly intellectual tale we follow a guide through a forbidding, desolate tract known as the "Zone." This long and punishingly slow film nonetheless delivers strong acting and a powerful cumulative storyline. C: Alexander Kaidanovsky, Nikolai Grinko, Anatoli Solonitsin, Alice Friendlich. D: Andrei Tarkovsky. DRA 160m. v

Stalking Danger 1986 ★★½ Government antiterrorist squad uses high-tech gadgetry to thwart baddies hell-bent on assassinating top officials. High expectations are not met by this mediocre effort. (a.k.a. *C.A.T. Squad*) C: Joseph Cortese, Stephen W. James, Patricia Charbonneau. D: William Friedkin. ACT [PG] 97m. V

Stalking Moon, The 1969 ★★★ Woman and her child are terrorized by her Apache husband after they take refuge with an army scout. Fine performances and some chillingly effective scenes help lift this well-mounted but slow-paced Western a notch above average. C: Gregory Peck, Eva Marie Saint, Robert Forster, Noland Clay, Russell Thorson, Frank Silvera. D: Robert Mulligan. DRA [G] 109m. V

Stalking the President 1992 ★★★ Little known facts and unseen footage behind the presidential assassinations. A fair introduction for the uninitiated. DOC 50m. V

Stamboul Quest 1934 ★★★½ Germany's ace double agent, Anna Maria Lesser, outwits British intelligence in WWI Turkey and falls for an American med student. Thrilling true story of espionage and romance, done with flair. C: Myrna Loy, George Brent, Lionel Atwill, C.Henry Gordon, Mischa Auer. D: Sam Wood. DRA 88m.

Stamboul Quest 1969 *See* **Fraulein Doktor**

Stammheim 1986 West German ★★★★ Striking West German drama painstakingly re-creates the infamous Baader-Meinhof trial, trying to find some insight into terrorism. Thought-provoking, though a little too politically biased. C: Ulrich Tukur, Affolter Therese, Wagner Sabine, Kremer Hans. D: Reinhard Hauff. DRA 107m.

Stamp of a Killer 1989 ★★★ Cop becomes obsessed with finding and stopping brutal serial killer. Standard action drama only slightly redeemed by Smit's intense performance. C: Judith Light, Jimmy Smits, Rhea Perlman. DRA [PG] 95m. TVM V

Stand and Deliver 1988 ★★★½ This is the true-life story of an East L.A. high school teacher who inspires his barrio students to academic excellence. Olmos' riveting performance makes this relatively low-budget film an edifying entertaining underdog drama. C: Edward James Olmos, Lou Diamond Phillips, Rosana de Soto, Andy Garcia. D: Ramon Menendez. DRA [PG] 103m. V

Stand by for Action 1942 ★★★ An arrogant Navy officer tangles with a gruff career Navy man aboard an outmoded destroyer. Thoughtful WWII sea saga. C: Robert Taylor, Brian Donlevy, Charles Laughton, Walter Brenan, Marilyn Maxwell, Henry O'Neill. D: Robert Z. Leonard. ACT 109m.

Stand by Me 1986 ★★★★ In the '50s, four preteen boys head for the woods to retrieve a dead boy's corpse. Coming-of-age drama focuses on themes of friendship and manhood with a nimble and amusing touch. Lead actors are terrific. Based on Stephen King's short story "The Body." C: Wil Wheaton, River Phoenix, Corey Feldman, Jerry O'Connell, Kiefer Sutherland, Richard Dreyfuss. D: Rob Reiner. DRA [R] 87m. V

Stand-In 1937 ★★★★ Playful satire about pompous efficiency expert dispatched to save financially shaky Hollywood studio. Howard (the expert) and Blondell (the stand-in) are perfection; Bogart's a riot as alcoholic producer in love with one of his stars. C: Leslie Howard, Humphrey Bogart, Joan Blondell, Alan Mowbray, Jack Carson. D: Tay Garnett. COM 91m. V

Stand-In, The 1985 ★★½ Action gangster film parody that's more strange than funny. C: Robert Zagone, Danny Glover. D: Robert Zagone. ACT 87m. V

Stand, The 1994 ★★★½ Long (like the book) but effective adaptation of Stephen King's epic about survivors of a germ warfare accident that wipes out most of the U.S. Good guys, led by Sinise and Dee, face off against the forces of Satan (Sheridan) on the outskirts of what is left of Las Vegas. Violent and grim, yet often witty. C: Gary Sinise, Molly Ringwald, Jamey Sheridan, Miguel Ferrer, Rob Lowe, Ruby Dee. D: Mick Garris. DRA 360m. TVM V

Stand Up and Cheer 1934 ★★★ Depression-era musical revolves around Baxter fulfilling duties in new government post as Secretary of Amusement. Brimming with disjointed and dated set pieces, most notable of which is Shirley Temple's star-making "Baby Take a Bow." Of historical interest only. C: Warner Baxter, Madge Evans, James Dunn, John Boles, Shirley Temple. D: Hamilton McFadden. MUS 69m. V

Stand Up and Fight 1939 ★★★ As America expands westward, the railroad supersedes the stagecoach. Plenty of fisticuffs in this spirited Western. C: Wallace Beery, Robert Taylor, Florence Rice, Charles Bickford, Charley Grapewin, Selmer Jackson. D: W.S. Van-Dyke II. WST 97m.

Standing Room Only 1944 ★★★ A hotel room shortage in Washington, D.C., forces a man and his secretary to work as servants in a home. Moderately amusing wartime comedy. C: Fred MacMurray, Paulette Goddard, Edward Arnold, Hillary Brooke, Roland Young, Anne Revere. D: Sidney Lanfield. COM 83m.

Standing Tall 1978 ★★★ In Montana, a rancher and his wife are victimized by a notorious and grabber. C: Linda Evans, Chuck Connors, Robert Forster. D: Harvey Hart. WST 100m. TVM V

Stanley & Iris 1990 ★★½ A recently widowed bakery worker (Fonda) meets an oddball loner (De Niro) and discovers that he is illiterate. As she teaches him to read, they gradually fall in love. This well-meaning tract is undermined by an unconvincing story and its own star power. C: Jane Fonda, Robert De

Niro, Swoosie Kurtz, Martha Plimpton. D: Martin Ritt. DRA [PG-13] 107m. v

Stanley and Livingstone 1939 ★★★★ *New York Herald* journalist Henry M. Stanley is sent to Africa in 1871 to find missionary-explorer David Livingstone. Fact-based adventure with a fine, low-key performance by Tracy. Thoughtful, entertaining historical saga. C: Spencer Tracy, Nancy Kelly, Walter Brennan, Charles Coburn, Cedric Hardwicke. D: Henry King. DRA 101m. v

Star! 1968 ★★★½ Lavish, lengthy musical biography of British and Broadway stage star Gertrude Lawrence is episodic rags-to-riches tale, focusing on star's eccentric behavior and inability to find lasting love. Andrews and Massey are terrific, both cast against type. The production numbers are well done. (a.k.a. *Those Were the Happy Times*) C: Julie Andrews, Richard Crenna, Michael Craig, Daniel Massey, Robert Reed. D: Robert Wise. MUS [G] 172m. v

Star Chamber, The 1982 ★★★ A principled yet frustrated judge (Douglas) is recruited by a ring of vigilante magistrates who administer their version of justice (they hire hit men!) when criminals get off on technicalities. Decent performances mired in a ridiculous premise. C: Michael Douglas, Hal Holbrook, Yaphet Kotto, Sharon Gless. D: Peter Hyams. DRA [R] 109m. v

Star Child 1983 *See* **Space Raiders**

Star Crystal 1985 ★ Astronauts discover asteroid chunk containing human-devouring alien creature. The rock gives the best performance. C: C. Jutson Campbell, Faye Bolt. D: Lance Lindsay. SFI [R] 93m. v

Star Dust 1940 ★★★½ A football player and a starstruck young woman, hoping to break into movies, are discovered by a Hollywood talent scout. Entertaining, lightweight hokum. C: Linda Darnell, John Payne, Roland Young, Charlotte Greenwood, William Gargan, Mary Beth Hughes, Mary Healy, Donald Meek. D: Walter Lang. DRA 85m.

Star 80 1983 ★★★★ A naive young woman, Dorothy Stratton (Hemingway), is promoted into a *Playboy* centerfold by her driven, husband, and finally murdered by him. Disturbing, downbeat film, brilliantly acted and directed, is a difficult study of sleaze and stardom. Fosse's last film. C: Mariel Hemingway, Eric Roberts, Cliff Robertson, Carroll Baker, Roger Rees, David Clennon, Josh Mostel, Sidney Miller, Jordan Christopher, Keenen Ivory Wayans, Stuart Damon, Ernest Thompson. D: Bob Fosse. DRA [R] 102m. v

Star Fairies 1985 ★★½ Based on the Tonka Toy characters; the Star Fairies can grant every wish. Sticky-sweet animated film, aimed at very young children. FAM/DRA 40m. TVM v

Star for a Night 1936 ★★★ Three grown children overemphasize their achievements to their blind mother to convince her they're all a bigger success than they really are. Standard melodrama helped by strong performances. C: Claire Trevor, Jane Darwell, Arline Judge, Evelyn Venable, Dean Jagger. D: Lewis Seiler. DRA 76m.

Star in the Dust 1956 ★★★ Townspeople oppose a sheriff's efforts to maintain law and order. Family Western with interesting cast. C: John Agar, Mamie VanDoren, Richard Boone, Leif Erickson, Coleen Gray, James Gleason. D: Charles Haas. WST 80m.

Star Is Born, A 1937 ★★★★½ Young woman from a farm (Gaynor) journeys to Hollywood where her career rises as alcoholic movie star husband's (March) falls. Classic Tinseltown soap opera with pungent script and poignant work by both stars. Remade twice. Special Oscar for color photography. C: Fredric March, Janet Gaynor, Adolphe Menjou, May Robson, Lionel Stander, Franklin Pangborn. D: William Wellman. DRA 112m. v

Star Is Born, A 1954 ★★★★★ Restored, superb remake of 1937 film, turned into showcase for Garland at peak of her powers. She and Mason play Hollywood couple, her career on the rise, his falling apart. Judy's acting matches her full-throttled renditions of "The Man That Got Away," "Born in a Trunk," etc. Mason is heartrending as an alcoholic, aging matinee idol. Must be seen in restored version which pieces together footage cut during first release. C: Judy Garland, James Mason, Charles Bickford, Jack Carson, Tom Noonan. D: George Cukor. MUS [PG] 150m. v

Star Is Born, A 1976 ★★★ Classic Hollywood story of two stars in love, one on the upswing, the other doomed to self-destruction, is updated and transferred to the rock music world. As such, it works on its own terms with dynamic musical numbers that present Streisand singing at her best. Not so her acting here. Kristofferson is outclassed sonically, but does well in dramatic scenes. C: Barbra Streisand, Kris Kristofferson, Gary Busey, Paul Mazursky. D: Frank Pierson. DRA [R] 140m. v

Star Knight 1992 Spanish ★ Medieval knights do battle with time-traveling space ship. Spanish-produced action-fantasy embarrasses talented cast. C: Klaus Kinski, Harvey Keitel, Fernando Rey. D: Fernando Colomo. SFI [PG-13] 91m. v

Star Maker, The 1939 ★★★½ Vaudeville impresario Gus Edwards makes stars out of gifted kids. Hollywood studio biography pleases handily with numerous songs. C: Bing Crosby, Louise Campbell, Laura Hope Crews, Ned Sparks, Ethel Griffies, Billy Gilbert. D: Roy DelRuth. MUS 94m.

Star of Midnight 1935 ★★★ A witty lawyer (Powell) must solve his own case when he is framed for murder. Okay clone of the *Thin Man* series. C: William Powell, Ginger Rogers, Paul Kelly, Gene Lockhart, Ralph Morgan,

Leslie Fenton, J.Farrell MacDonald. D: Stephen Roberts. CRI 90m. v

Star Packer, The 1934 ★★★½ A gang of outlaws make trouble for a small western town. Good early Wayne showing. C: John Wayne, Yakima Canutt, Verna Hillie. D: Robert Bradbury. WST 53m. v

Star Quest ★★½ Android fights to free herself from evil military regime she was created to serve. Medium sci-fi. C: Tracy Davis, Hans Bachman. D: Phillip Cook. SFI [PG] 90m. v

Star Said No, The 1951 *See* **Callaway Went Thataway**

Star Spangled Girl 1971 ★★★ Quaint, hopelessly dated comedy of Doris Day-type conservative young woman (Duncan) being romanced by two Dustin Hoffman-type liberal young men (Roberts, Susman). From Neil Simon's play. C: Sandy Duncan, Tony Roberts, Todd Susman. D: Jerry Paris. COM [G] 92m. v

Star Spangled Rhythm 1942 ★★★★ Story line about a Paramount Studios doorman who tells his sailor son he's a bigshot producer serves as a vehicle for a star-studded variety extravaganza held for Navy servicemen. Numerous stars appear in Paramount hoopla, including Alan Ladd, Eddie Anderson, Paulette Goddard, Betty Hutton, Bob Hope, and more. Lighthearted wartime fun. C: Bing Crosby, Ray Milland, Bob Hope, Veronica Lake, Dorothy Lamour, Susan Hayward, Dick Powell, Mary Martin, Alan Ladd, Paulette Goddard, Cecil B. DeMille, Arthur Treacher, Preston Sturges. D: George Marshall. MUS 99m.

Star, The 1952 ★★★½ Middling look at Hollywood star on the skids trying to make comeback. Davis' drunken scene with an Oscar is terrific, but most of movie is obvious melodrama. C: Bette Davis, Sterling Hayden, Natalie Wood, Warner Anderson, Minor Watson, June Travis. D: Stuart Heisler. DRA 89m. v

Star Trek—Episode 1: The Cage 1966 ★★★★ Pilot episode for the cult TV show, including long-lost color footage. A classic. C: William Shatner, Leonard Nimoy, Deforest Kelley, George Takei, Michelle Nichols, James Doohan, Walter Koenig. SFI 64m. v

Star Trek—Episode 2: Where No Man Has Gone Before 1966 ★★★½ The Enterprise leaves the known galaxy and discovers real danger. SFI 51m. v

Star Trek—Episode 3: The Corbomite Manuever 1966 ★★★½ Confronted by a menacing alien spaceship, Kirk must play a desperate gamble: will it succeed? SFI 51m. v

Star Trek—Episode 4: Mudd's Women 1966 ★★★ The first of two episodes featuring the funny, fast-talking con man Harry Mudd (he also appears in "I, Mudd"). Here he is introduced, along with three unusually beautiful women. SFI 51m. v

Star Trek—Episode 5: The Enemy Within 1966 ★★★ After a transporter accident, Kirk splits into the two opposite halves of his personality, and good must confront evil. SFI 51m. v

Star Trek—Episode 6: The Man Trap 1966 ★★★½ A dangerous alien comes aboard the Enterprise, and the entire crew is in danger. SFI 51m. v

Star Trek—Episode 7: The Naked Time 1966 ★★★★ In one of the most entertaining episodes, a strange (and highly contagious) virus infects the Enterprise's crew, bringing out fascinating reactions. SFI 51m. v

Star Trek—Episode 8: Charlie X 1966 ★★★½ The Enterprise rescues a 17 year-old boy, a survivor of a spaceship crash years ago, whose lack of social skills becomes a threat to the crew. SFI 51m. v

Star Trek—Episode 9: Balance of Terror 1966 ★★★½ An alien spaceship has destroyed four Federation outposts, and the Enterprise goes after it. SFI 51m. v

Star Trek—Episode 10: What Are Little Girls Made Of 1966 ★★★½ The Enterprise answers a distress call from a Dr. Korby, a long-lost scientist (and Nurse Chapel's fiancé). SFI 51m. v

Star Trek—Episode 11: Dagger of The Mind 1966 ★★★½ On an inspection trip to the penal colony Tantalus, Kirk and ship psychologist Helen Noel are threatened by a mad genius. SFI 51m. v

Star Trek—Episode 12: Miri 1966 ★★★★ Kirk and McCoy discover a planet where all the adults have died and only children survive, and are caught in a desperate race against time to find out why. SFI 51m. v

Star Trek—Episode 13: The Conscience of the King 1966 ★★★★ While a company of actors visits the Enterprise, people start dying mysteriously. Could their leader be the notorious murderer Kodos? SFI 51m. v

Star Trek—Episode 14: The Galileo Seven 1966 ★★★½ After their shuttlecraft crashes, Spock and six other crew members struggle to repair it and rejoin the Enterprise. SFI 51m. v

Star Trek—Episode 15: Court Martial 1966 ★★★½ Kirk is tried for murder, and it's up to Spock to save him. SFI 51m. v

Star Trek—Episode 16: The Menagerie, Parts I and II 1966 ★★★★ Spock is court-martialled for mutiny when he hijacks the Enterprise and kidnaps his former commander, Captain Pike. SFI 102m. v

Star Trek—Episode 17: Shore Leave 1966 ★★★★ The Enterprise crew finds the perfect planet for shore leave. But they quickly learn to be careful for what they wish for. One of the wittiest episodes of the series. SFI 51m. v

Star Trek—Episode 18: The Squire of Gothos 1966 ★★★½ Kirk confronts an egomaniacal alien who sees the Enterprise as a new toy. SFI 51m. v

Star Trek—Episode 19: Arena 1966 ★★★½ Kirk is abruptly taken from the Enterprise and forced to fight a large alien reptile, as part of an alien study of Good and Evil. SFI 51m. v

Star Trek—Episode 20: The Alternative Factor 1966 ★★★½ The Enterprise takes a passenger, not realizing that his double has also boarded—and that they could destroy the universe. SFI 51m. v

Star Trek—Episode 21: Tomorrow Is Yesterday 1967 ★★★½ The enterprise accidentally falls back in time to the 20th century, and a U.S. Air Force pilot thinks it's a UFO. SFI 51m. v

Star Trek—Episode 22: Return of the Archons 1967 ★★★½ Kirk and Spock try to rescue zombie-like humans, on a planet with strange leaders, before they become zombies themselves. SFI 51m. v

Star Trek—Episode 23: A Taste of Armageddon 1967 ★★★★ The ultimate clean war: Kirk and Spock find themselves caught in a battle between two planets who fight by computer, and simply assign people to die as casualties. An effective, unusual anti-war statement. SFI 51m. v

Star Trek—Episode 24: Space Seed 1967 ★★★★ The enterprise picks up a group of genetically-engineered supermen, led by the brilliant but dangerous Khan, and Kirk must confront the threat they pose. *Star Trek II: The Wrath of Khan*, continues the story begun here. SFI 51m. v

Star Trek—Episode 25: This Side of Paradise 1967 ★★★★ What the Enterprise crew expects to be a barren planet turns out to be a lush wonderland; unfortunately, appearances can be deceiving. SFI 51m. v

Star Trek—Episode 26: The Devil in the Dark 1967 ★★★★ The Enterprise is sent to investigate the deaths of several miners on the tunnels of Janus VI, and discover a strange alien creature. A classic. SFI 51m. v

Star Trek—Episode 27: Errand of Mercy 1967 ★★★½ Kirk and Spock find themselves fighting the Klingons, until a being from another civilization intervenes. SFI 51m. v

Star Trek—Episode 28: The City on the Edge of Forever 1967 ★★★★ Kirk and Spock travel back in time to find McCoy, and Kirk falls hopelessly in love. Joan Collins guest stars. SFI 51m. v

Star Trek—Episode 29: Operation-Annihilate 1967 ★★★½ An alien force has driven Kirk's brother, and the rest of the population of planet Deneva, insane. It's up to Kirk and the Entrprise crew to investigate. SFI 51m. v

Star Trek—Episode 30: Catspaw 1967 ★★★★ On a strange planet, Sula and Scotty are turned into zombies, and Kirk must battle the tricks and illusions of Korob and Sylvia to save them. The perfect Halloween episode. SFI 51m. v

Star Trek—Episode 31: Metamorphosis 1967 ★★★½ While transporting a sick diplomat, their shuttle crashes, and Kirk, Spock, and McCoy find themselves trapped on a planet with a famous explorer—who had been thought dead for a century. SFI 51m. v

Star Trek—Episode 32: Friday's Child 1967 ★★★★ Kirk, Spock, and McCoy are forced to rescue an unwilling princess when they get caught up in clan politics on Capella IV. "McCoy" has some great lines. SFI 51m. v

Star Trek—Episode 33: Who Mourns for Adonis 1967 ★★★★ The last of the ancient Greek gods captures the Enterprise and demands only one thing: worship. SFI 51m. v

Star Trek—Episode 34: Amok Time 1967 ★★★★ Spock must return to Vulcan to satisfy the Vulcan mating urge. An important episode, explaining a great deal about Spock's Vulcan background. Written by Theodore Sturgeon. SFI 51m. v

Star Trek—Episode 35: The Doomsday Machine 1967 ★★★½ After rescuing a disabled ship, Kirk is trapped there while its captain commandeers the Enterprise in a suicidal quest for revenge. SFI 51m. v

Star Trek—Episode 36: Wolf in the Fold 1967 ★★★★ On an alien planet, women are being murdered—and Scotty is the chief suspect! Is he really Jack the Ripper? SFI 51m. v

Star Trek—Episode 37: The Changeling 1967 ★★★½ A warning story of technology run amok, as Kirk must outwit Nomad, a computer determined to eliminate all "imperfect" beings. SFI 51m. v

Star Trek—Episode 38: The Apple 1967 ★★★½ The Enterprise is threatened by Vaal, of Gamma Triangui: VI. SFI 51m. v

Star Trek—Episode 39: Mirror, Mirror 1967 ★★★★ After a transporter accident, Kirk, McCoy, and Uhura wind up in a parallel universe—on an Enterprise of ruthless pirates (including a bearded Spock!). SFI 51m. v

Star Trek—Episode 40: The Deadly Years 1967 ★★★★ A deadly, "fast-aging" disease strikes the members of a landing party, and McCoy must race time to find a cure. SFI 51m. v

Star Trek—Episode 41: I, Mudd 1968 ★★★★ The lovable rogue, Harry Mudd is back; this time he gets the Enterprise crew mixed up with a group of androids. Priceless. SFI 51m. v

Star Trek—Episode 42: The Trouble With Tribbles 1968 ★★★★ One of the most famous and light-hearted episodes, as Kirk must deal with political troubles, Klingons, and a bunch of adorable little furballs known as Tribbles. SFI 51m. v

Star Trek—Episode 43: Bread and Circuses 1968 ★★★½ Kirk, Spock, and McCoy go to investigate a planet, and find a starship captain corrupted by power in a society which has taken the ideas of TV ratings and gladiatorial combats to new extremes. SFI 51m. v

Star Trek—Episode 44: Journey to Babel 1968 ★★★★ Spock's parents are among a group of diplomats aboard the Enterprise; when his father becomes ill, Spock is torn between conflicting loyalties. June Wyman guest stars, as Spock's mother. SFI 51m. V

Star Trek—Episode 45: A Private Little War 1968 ★★★½ Kirk falls, first to the bite of a deadly animal, and then under the spell of the woman who cures him. SFI 51m. V

Star Trek—Episode 46: The Gamesters of Triskelion 1968 ★★★½ Kirk, Uhura, and Chekov are snatched by aliens and turned into slaves, fighting for their lives. This episode was even spoofed by the Simpsons. SFI 51m. V

Star Trek—Episode 47: Obsession 1968 ★★★★ Kirk gets a second chance to confront an alien cloud creature that he'd faced years earlier; but are his feelings of guilt clouding his thinking? SFI 51m. V

Star Trek—Episode 48: The Immunity Syndrome 1968 ★★★½ In an early look at the possibilities of biological warfare, the Enterprise must confront an enormous, single-celled creature which is threatening the universe. SFI 51m. V

Star Trek—Episode 49: A Piece of the Action 1968 ★★★★ The Enterprise finds a planet which has modelled itself on American gangster society, circa 1920s, and gets entangled in a planetary gang war. Kirk's driving lesson is a classic. SFI 51m. V

Star Trek—Episode 50: By any Other Name 1968 ★★★★ Virtually the entire Enterprise crew is turned in dehydrated blocks by a group of aliens, and those remaining must find a way to retake control of the ship. SFI 51m. V

Star Trek—Episode 52: Patterns of Force 1968 ★★★★ In a frightening look at history repeating itself, Kirk and the Enterprise find a planet run by Nazis. SFI 51m. V

Star Trek—Episode 53: The Ultimate Computer 1968 ★★★★ An unstable genius uses the Enterprise to test the latest version of his supercomputer, and refuses to recognize any possible flaws—even if they may destroy the ship. SFI 51m. V

Star Trek—Episode 54: The Omega Glory 1968 ★★★½ On the planet Omega IV, Kirk tries to deal with people who live a thousand years, a dangerous virus, and a ghost ship. SFI 51m. V

Star Trek—Episode 55: Assignment: Earth 1968 ★★★½ Having traveled back in time, Kirk meets a being who says he's an alien who must save the Earth. Teri Garr has an early appearance. SFI 51m. V

Star Trek—Episode 56: Spectre of the Gun 1968 ★★★½ After a misunderstanding with an alien civilization, Kirk, Spock, McCoy, Scotty and Chekov find themselves reliving the shoot-out at the O.K. Corral—as participants. SFI 51m. V

Star Trek—Episode 57: Elaan of Troyius 1968 ★★★½ Kirk falls to the charms of the princess Elaan, while the Enterprise transports her to her wedding. SFI 51m. V

Star Trek—Episode 58: The Paradise Syndrome 1968 ★★★½ Suffering from amnesia, Kirk settles down, marries, and joins a Native-American-like culture, while Spock tries to find him and deal with the threat of an oncoming asteroid. SFI 51m. V

Star Trek—Episode 59: The Enterprise Incident 1968 ★★★½ Kirk seems to have snapped, when he orders the Enterprise into Romulan space; but when they are captured, Spock falls for the Romulan captain! SFI 51m. V

Star Trek—Episode 60: And The Children Shall Lead 1969 ★★★★ The Enterprise reaches the planet Triacus to find all the adult colonists dead. But do the rescued children know something about the mysterious deaths? SFI 51m. V

Star Trek—Episode 61: Spock's Brain 1969 ★★★½ Spock's brain is suddenly and mysteriously stolen by an alien woman. Will Kirk and McCoy be able to get it back? SFI 51m. V

Star Trek—Episode 62: Is There In Truth No Beauty? 1969 ★★★★ An alien ambassador comes on board the Enterprise, accompanied by a jealous telepath who is his only intermediary with outsiders. Diana Muldaur, who later appeared in Star Trek: The New Generation, guest stars. SFI 51m. V

Star Trek—Episode 63: The Empath 1969 ★★★★ Aliens decide to use McCoy and Kirk for medical research, but an "empath" gets involved, leading to an amazing conclusion. SFI 51m. V

Star Trek—Episode 64: The Tholian Web 1969 ★★★½ Kirk disappears; disaster is averted when his will is read. SFI 51m. V

Star Trek—Episode 65: For The World Is Hollow And I Have Touched the Sky 1969 ★★★½ An entire world is threatened by the threat of collision with an asteroid, and Kirk must find a way to save it. SFI 51m. V

Star Trek—Episode 66: Day of The Dove 1969 ★★★½ The Enterprise crew learns the danger of violence, as an evil alien incites them to fight Klingons and feeds off their hatred. Also, the only episode where a female Klingon appears. SFI 51m. V

Star Trek—Episode 67: Plato's Stepchildren 1969 ★★★★ A cynical, telepathic group of aliens take Kirk, Spock, Uhura, and Nurse Chapel prisoner and use them for their own entertainment. SFI 51m. V

Star Trek—Episode 68: Wink of an Eye 1969 ★★★½ The leader of a planet plans to use Kirk as a stud, to revive her dying people. SFI 51m. V

Star Trek—Episode 69: That Which Survives 1969 ★★½ A deadly female alien abducts Kirk, McCoy, and Sulu from the Enterprise. SFI 51m. V

Star Trek—Episode 70: Let That Be Your Last Battlefield 1969 ★★★½ The Enterprise becomes the site for a battle between a half-white, half-black man, and his half-white, half-black opponent. A good example of social commentary in science fiction. SFI 51m. V

Star Trek—Episode 71: Whom Gods Destroy 1969 ★★★½ A criminally insane genius takes over an asylum; when the Enterprise investigates, he turns himself into a double of Kirk. Will his mad scheme work? SFI 51m. V

Star Trek—Episode 72: The Mark of Gideon 1969 ★★★½ Beaming back to the Enterprise, Kirk finds himself on an empty ship, alone with an alien woman trying to seduce him. But, where is everybody? SFI 51m.

Star Trek—Episode 73: The Lights of Zetar 1969 ★★★½ Scotty finds romance, but an alien energy force threatens the woman he loves. SFI 51m. V

Star Trek—Episode 74: The Cloud Minders 1969 ★★★½ The Enterprise gets caught up in the cause of oppressed miners, known as Troglytes. SFI 51m. V

Star Trek—Episode 75: The Way To Eden 1969 ★★★★ Galactic hippies are detrmined to reach the planet of "Eden"—even if they have to take over the Enterprise. The scene of Spock joining them in an impromptu jam (on Vulcan harp) is a must-see. SFI 51m. V

Star Trek—Episode 76: Requiem for Methuselah 1969 ★★★★ Kirk, Spock, and McCoy meet a man who may have been Leonardo Da Vinci, as well as other famous humans throughout time. SFI 51m. V

Star Trek—Episode 77: The Savage Curtain 1969 ★★★★ Famous figures from the past, including Abraham Lincoln, help Kirk and Spock fight evil aliens. SFI 51m. V

Star Trek—Episode 78: All Our Yesterdays 1969 ★★★½ Spock goes back in time and finds a happy life as a primitive man—but he still has to rescue Kirk. SFI 51m. V

Star Trek—Episode 79: Turnabout Intruder 1969 ★★★★ A vengeful woman from Kirk's past takes over his body—and control of the Enterprise. SFI 51m. V

Star Trek: The Motion Picture 1980 ★★★ Starship *Enterprise* seeks out a strange force threatening the balance of the universe. Stodgy, reverential approach to cast and special effects results in a slow-moving but modestly compelling first voyage. C: William Shatner, Leonard Nimoy, DeForest Kelley, Stephen Collins, Persis Khambatta. D: Robert Wise. SFI [G] 145m. V

Star Trek II: The Wrath of Khan 1982 ★★★★½ Film series hits its stride as crew of Starship *Enterprise* battles Khan (Montalban), an old foe from the original series. Full-throttled sci-fi adventure that even non-Trekkies will love. C: William Shatner, Leonard Nimoy, DeForest Kelley, Ricardo Montalban, James Doohan. D: Nicholas Meyer. SFI [PG] 113m. V

Star Trek III: The Search for Spock 1984 ★★★½ *Enterprise* crew struggles to save a synthetically created planet, one that might have the power to resurrect a dead Vulcan. Terrific story, effects, and villainous Klingons. C: William Shatner, DeForest Kelley, James Doohan, George Takei, Walter Koenig, Nichelle Nichols, Christopher Lloyd. D: Leonard Nimoy. SFI [PG] 105m. V

Star Trek IV: The Voyage Home 1986 ★★★★ Superior *Trek* adventure has principal crew members traveling back in time to 20th-century San Francisco on a mission to save the world with the help of two "borrowed" humpbacked whales. Perfect blending of comedy, adventure, effects, and cast chemistry. Also available in special director's edition. C: William Shatner, Leonard Nimoy, DeForest Kelley, Catherine Hicks. D: Leonard Nimoy. SFI [PG] 119m. V

Star Trek V: The Final Frontier 1989 ★★★ *Enterprise* is hijacked by messianic Vulcan in search of galactic Heaven. Heavy metaphysical story premise demands more serious approach than it receives; character chemistry is all this one has going for it. C: William Shatner, Leonard Nimoy, DeForest Kelley, James Doohan, Walter Koenig, Nichelle Nichols, Laurence Luckinbill. D: William Shatner. SFI [PG] 107m. V

Star Trek VI: The Undiscovered Country 1991 ★★★★ Having negotiated peace between arch-enemy Klingons, *Enterprise* crew members are then accused of murdering the key peace negotiator. Great whodunit approach to action-packed story results in excellent (alleged) final adventure for original *Trek* cast. C: William Shatner, Leonard Nimoy, DeForest Kelley, James Doohan, Walter Koenig, Kim Cattrall, Christopher Plummer. D: Nicholas Meyer. SFI [PG] 110m. V

Star Trek Generations 1994 ★★★★ Captain Kirk meets Picard, as two crews of the Enterprise unite to battle the inevitable mad scientist (McDowell). Seventh voyage might be a bit confusing for non-Trekkies, but builds up to warp speed for exciting climax. C: Patrick Stewart, William Shatner, Malcolm McDowell, Jonathan Frakes, Whoopi Goldberg, Brent Spiner, Michael Dorn, James Doohan, Walter Koenig, LeVar Burton. D: David Carson. SFI [PG] 110m. V

Star Trek 25th Anniversary Special 1991 ★★★½ Original cast members join "The Next Generation" in a highlight show commemorating the 25th anniversary of the hugely popular television and film series. Interesting compilation includes bloopers and behind-the-scenes footage. C: William Shatner, Leonard Nimoy, DeForest Kelly, George Takei, James Doohan, Walter Koenig. D: Gene Roddenberry. SFI V

Star Wars 1977 ★★★★★ With help from a wizard-knight, a space pirate, two robots, and the Force, Luke Skywalker (Hamill) fights to save the universe—and a princess—from Darth Vader (Prowse, with James Earl Jones' voice). Incredibly exciting, influential achievement created a special effects renaissance and revolutionized the science fiction adventure genre. Seven Oscars for technical excellence. Sequels: *The Empire Strikes Back* and *Return of the Jedi.* C: Mark Hamill, Harrison Ford, Carrie Fisher, Peter Cushing, Alec Guinness, David Prowse, Anthony Daniels. D: George Lucas. SFI [PG] 121m. V

Star Witness 1931 ★★★★ Gangsters threaten a family that witnessed their crime. Strong crime melodrama with good acting, fast pace. C: Walter Huston, Sally Blane, Chic Sale, Frances Starr, Grant Mitchell, Edward Nugent, Ralph Ince, Dickie Moore. D: William Wellman. CRI 68m.

Starbirds 1982 ★★½ Starfighters struggle to save the Earth from alien invaders. Medium animated sci-fi. FAM/SFI 75m. TVM V

Starchaser—Legend of Orin, The 1985 ★★★ When the future world is threatened by an evil dictator, a young boy must save the day. Entertaining animated sci-fi. SFI 107m. TVM V

Starcrash 1979 Italian ★ Space adventurers are recruited to prevent universe from being destroyed by evil galactic maniac. Ludicrous Italian-produced sci-fi space opera. (a.k.a. Stella Star) C: Marjoe Gortner, Caroline Munro, Christopher Plummer, David Hasselhoff. D: Lewis Coates. SFI [PG] 92m. V

Stardust Memories 1980 ★★★½ A famous director spends an agonizing film festival weekend fending off fans, critics, and sycophants. Good, though self-indulgent: Numerous Fellini movie references play more like rip-offs than tributes. Sharon Stone film debut. C: Woody Allen, Charlotte Rampling, Jessica Harper, Tony Roberts, Daniel Stern. D: Woody Allen. COM [PG] 91m. V

Stargate 1994 ★★★½ Space captain (Russell) and archeologist (Spader) explore strange planet which resembles ancient Egypt. Clichéd but beautifully designed. Davidson certainly makes an impression as a transvestite sun god. C: James Spader, Kurt Russell, Jaye Davidson. D: Roland Emmerich. SFI [PG-13] 125m. V

Starlift 1951 ★★★½ Warner Brothers stars visit Travis Air Base to entertain troops on their way to Korea. Nearly plotless variety show, with cameos and acts by James Cagney, Doris Day, Virginia Mayo, Gary Cooper, Jane Wyman, and many others. C: Janice Rule, Dick Wesson, Ron Hagerthy, Richard Webb. D: Roy Del Ruth. MUS 103m.

Starlight Hotel 1988 New Zealand ★★★★ Involving story about odd-couple friendship between troubled kid and combat-fatigued WWI veteran in Depression-era Australia. C: Peter Phelps, Greer Robson, Marshall Napier, Alice Fraser. D: Sam Pillsbury. DRA [PG] 94m. V

Starlight Slaughter 1976 *See* **Eaten Alive**

Starman 1984 ★★★★ Grieving widow (Allen) is visited by extraterrestial being (Bridges), who assumes dead husband's form. Unusual action romance, with Bridges giving remarkable performance as alien learning about human life and love. C: Jeff Bridges, Karen Allen, Charles Martin Smith, Richard Jaeckel. D: John Carpenter. SFI [PG] 115m. V

Stars and Bars 1988 ★★½ Comic misfire, with Day-Lewis out of place as a Britisher in U.S., amazed at barbaric customs and rude behavior. Nothing he encounters is as rude as this movie! C: Daniel Day-Lewis, Martha Plimpton, Harry Dean Stanton, Joan Cusack. D: Pat O'Connor. COM [R] 94m. V

Stars and Stripes Forever 1952 ★★★ Standard Hollywood musical biography gives high-gloss fictional treatment to life of march composer John Philip Sousa. Routine story of personal triumph is filled out by rousing musical score. C: Clifton Webb, Robert Wagner, Ruth Hussey, Debra Paget, Finlay Currie. D: Henry Koster. MUS 89m. V

Stars in My Crown 1950 ★★★★ Post-Civil War small town is positively influenced by an enigmatic minister (McCrea). Enjoyable, big-hearted drama with a fine McCrea performance. C: Joel McCrea, Ellen Drew, Dean Stockwell, Ed Begley. D: Jacques Tourneur. DRA 89m. V

Stars Look Down, The 1939 British ★★★★ Coal miner's son (Redgrave) runs for Parliament in order to improve the lot of his people. From the best-selling novel by A.J. Cronin. Thought-provoking, realistic social drama has a lot of power. C: Michael Redgrave, Margaret Lockwood, Edward Rigby, Emlyn Williams. D: Carol Reed. DRA 103m. V

Starship Invasions 1977 Canadian ★ Ufologist is abducted by aliens, then helps them deal with nasty intergalactic neighbors. Waste of time and talent. C: Robert Vaughn, Christopher Lee, Daniel Pilon, Helen Shaver, Henry Ramer, Victoria Johnson. D: Ed Hunt. SFI [PG] 89m. V

Starstruck 1982 Australian ★★★½ A working-class teenager hustles and promotes his cousin to rock stardom. Feisty musical comedy satirizes media hype and Hollywood musicals. C: Jo Kennedy, Ross O'Donovan, Pat Evison, Margo Lee, Max Cullen, John O'May. D: Gillian Armstrong. MUS [PG] 95m. V

Start Cheering 1938 ★★★½ Cheerful, funny musical about a Hollywood star (Starrett) who goes back to college. Durante's antics steal the show. C: Charles Starrett, Joan Perry, Jimmy Durante, Walter Connolly, The Three Stooges, Louis Prima. D: Albert S. Rogell. MUS 78m.

Start the Revolution Without Me 1970 ★★★★ Two sets of twins (Sutherland and Wilder) mixed at birth. One set is raised rich, the other poor, and both meet under bizarre circumstances during French Revolution. Merry mayhem twists mistaken identity plot into knots, with one of Wilder's best comic performances. C: Gene Wilder, Donald Sutherland, Hugh Griffith, Jack MacGowran, Billie Whitelaw. D: Bud Yorkin. COM [PG] 91m. v

Starting Over 1979 ★★★★ After divorcing Bergen, Reynolds tries new romance with Clayburgh but has hard time getting ex-wife out of his mind. Great performances mark this appealing, wry comedy. C: Burt Reynolds, Jill Clayburgh, Candice Bergen, Charles Durning, Frances Sternhagen, Austin Pendleton. D: Alan J. Pakula. COM [R] 105m. v

State Fair 1933 ★★★★ Romance, prize pigs, and pie contests abound as a rural farm family attends the annual state fair. Nice slice of pastoral Americana, with good acting and folksy atmosphere. C: Janet Gaynor, Will Rogers, Lew Ayres, Sally Eilers, Norman Foster, Louise Dresser, Victor Jory, Frank Craven. D: Henry King. MUS 96m.

State Fair 1945 ★★★★ Sunny lollipop of a musical about what happens to Iowa farm family during state fair. Attractive leads, sturdy supporting players, and charming Rodgers and Hammerstein songs, including Oscar-winning "It Might As Well Be Spring." Remade in 1962. C: Jeanne Crain, Dana Andrews, Dick Haymes, Vivian Blaine, Charles Winnninger, Fay Bainter, Donald Meek, Frank McHugh. D: Walter Lang. MUS 100m. v

State Fair 1962 ★★½ Tired remake of Rodgers and Hammerstein musical with Ann-Margret only standout in mediocre cast. String of vignettes of Iowa family at state fair has lost all of its charm. Even the animals look lackluster. C: Pat Boone, Bobby Darin, Pamela Tiffin, Ann-Margret, Alice Faye, Tom Ewell, Wally Cox. D: Jose Ferrer. MUS 118m. v

State of Grace 1990 ★★★★ Irish police officer returns to New York to confront some old friends gone bad. This type of ethnic character drama, spiced with gangster violence, has been done much better, but explosive performances help mask story weaknesses. C: Sean Penn, Ed Harris, Gary Oldman, Robin Wright, John C. Reilly. D: Phil Joanou. DRA [R] 144m. v

State of Siege 1972 French ★★★★ Costa-Gavras' controversial film about an American technical expert in police procedures who is abducted and assassinated in Uruguay. Provocative political thriller involves U.S. covert operations in Latin America. C: Yves Montand, Renato Salvatori, O.E. Hasse, Jean-Luc Bideau. D: Costa-Gavras. DRA 120m. v

State of the Union 1948 ★★★★ When Tracy decides to run for President, his estranged wife (Hepburn) becomes his outspoken conscience. Part thought-provoking and amusing political intrigue and part screwball comedy. Hepburn's sharpness and Tracy's consternation are perfect foils. C: Spencer Tracy, Katharine Hepburn, Angela Lansbury, Van Johnson, Adolphe Menjou, Lewis Stone, Raymond Walburn, Margaret Hamilton. D: Frank Capra. DRA 122m. v

State of Things, The 1983 German ★★½ A movie crew remakes Roger Corman's *The Day the World Ended* in Portugal. This Corman tribute and, to a lesser extent, insider's view of moviemaking is confused. C: Allen Garfield, Samuel Fuller, Paul Getty III, Roger Corman, Patrick Bauchau. D: Wim Wenders. DRA 120m. v

State Secret 1950 *See* **Great Manhunt, The**

State's Attorney 1931 ★★★★ A colorful district attorney defends his boyhood chum, now a prominent mobster. Stirring courtroom drama, with a provocative performance by Barrymore. C: John Barrymore, Helen Twelvetrees, William Boyd, Ralph Ince. D: George Archainbaud. DRA 81m. v

Station Six-Sahara 1964 British ★★½ Desert oil workers get hot and bothered when a woman gets stuck on their patch of sand. Predictable, sweaty doings. C: Carroll Baker, Peter Van Eyck, Ian Bannen, Denholm Elliott. D: Seth Holt. DRA 99m.

Station West 1948 ★★★★ Lawman (Powell) tries to find the murdering outlaws responsible for a string of gold thefts. Fine adaptation of Luke Short story, full of pungent, witty dialogue. C: Dick Powell, Jane Greer, Tom Powers, Raymond Burr, Agnes Moorehead. D: Sidney Lanfield. WST 92m. v

Stationmaster's Wife, The 1977 German ★★★★ Beautiful, unfaithful wife tantalizes and torments her working-class husband in pre-WWII Germany. Fascinating Fassbinder film is slow but effective drama. Subtitles. C: Kurt Raab, Elisabeth Trissenaar, Udo Kier, Volker Spengler. D: Rainer Werner Fassbinder. DRA 111m. v

Statue, The 1971 British ★★½ Famed diplomat (Niven) suffers embarrassment when his wife (Lisi) sculpts a 20-foot nude statue of him. Tasteless change of pace for the very classy Niven. C: David Niven, Virna Lisi, Robert Vaughn. D: Rod Amateau. COM [R] 84m. v

Statutory Affair, The 1971 *See* **Lola**

Stavisky 1974 French ★★★★½ Handsomely mounted, icily intelligent film about the famous con artist who swindled investors in '30s France and brought down the Socialist government. Gorgeous to look at and listen to (Sondheim did the score), but also thoughtful and provocative. C: Jean-Paul Belmondo, Charles Boyer, Francois Perier, Anny Duperey, Michel Lonsdale, Gerard Depardieu. D: Alain Resnais. CRI [PG] 117m. v

Stay As You Are 1978 French ★★★ Middle-aged Lothario learns his teenage lover may be his own daughter. Lurid potboiler for Mastroianni and Kinski. C: Marcello Mastroianni, Nastassia Kinski, Francisco Rabal, Monica Randal. D: Alberto Lattuada. DRA 105m. v

Stay Hungry 1976 ★★★★ Rich southern misfit (Bridges) gets mixed up with bodybuilders in this modest comedy/drama that benefits from its now high-powered cast. Schwarzenegger is surprisingly charming. Based on Charles

Gaines' novel. C: Jeff Bridges, Sally Field, Arnold Schwarzenegger, R.G. Armstrong. D: Bob Rafelson. COM [R] 102m. V

Stay Tuned 1992 ★★ A married couple (Ritter and Dawber) get zapped inside an infernal television and must interfuse with satirical video netherworld. Title's funny idea quickly gets strained. Ritter and Dawber just look confused. C: John Ritter, Pam Dawber, Eugene Levy, Salt'n Pepa. D: Peter Hyams. COM [PG] 89m. V

Stay Tuned For Murder 1988 ★★★ A beautiful TV reporter gets into big trouble when she investigates a corrupt attorney and his political connections. C: Tery Reeves-Wolf, Christopher Ginnaven, B.J. Hardin. D: Gary W. Jones. DRA 92m. V

Staying Alive 1983 ★★ Sequel to *Saturday Night Fever* has Tony Manero (Travolta) quitting the disco floors of Brooklyn for the Broadway stage. Songs and hungry atmosphere of predecessor are missing, and Sly's misguided direction really dooms it. C: John Travolta, Cynthia Rhodes, Finola Hughes, Steve Inwood. D: Sylvester Stallone. MUS [PG] 96m. V

Staying Together 1989 ★★★★ Quirky, idiosyncratic comedy about three brothers in a small town, each trying to emerge from shadow of strong-willed father after his death. Pleasantly surprising performances. C: Sean Astin, Stockard Channing, Dermot Mulroney, Tim Quill. D: Lee Grant. DRA [R] 91m. V

Stealing Heaven 1988 British ★★★★ A true story of the medieval lovers Abelard and Héloise: he, a clergyman and she, an aristocrat who must confront religious and social authority in their quest for romance. An erotic, intelligent drama. C: Kim Thompson, Derek de Lint, Denholm Elliott, Kenneth Cranham, Rachel Kempson. D: Clive Donner. DRA [R] 116m. V

Stealing Home 1988 ★★★ At loose ends, a ne'er-do-well comes home for the funeral of the older woman who changed his life. Foster is fine, but otherwise this is maudlin melodrama. C: Mark Harmon, Jodie Foster, William McNamara, Blair Brown, Harold Ramis, Jonathan Silverman, Richard Jenkins, John Shea, Thatcher Goodwin. D: Steven Kampmann, Will Aldis. DRA [PG-13] 98m. V

Steamboat Bill, Jr. 1928 ★★★★½ Keaton's silent classic of a shy weakling, out to prove his mettle on a steamboat helmed by his father. Full of the deadpan genius's comic invention, building to the knock-out cyclone sequence. C: Buster Keaton, Ernest Torrence, Marion Byron. D: Charles F. Riesner. COM 71m. V

Steamboat 'Round the Bend 1935 ★★★★ Eccentric riverboat captain (Rogers) tries to prove the innocence of an accused murderer. Atmospheric, folksy drama builds steam to grand chase climax. Rogers's last film, released posthumously. C: Will Rogers, Anne Shirley, Eugene Pallette, Stepin Fetchit. D: John Ford. DRA 96m.

Steaming 1985 British ★★★½ A group of British women gather in a London bathhouse for steamy and steaming gab sessions. Good performances boost a slightly stagy production in director Losey's final film. C: Vanessa Redgrave, Sarah Miles, Diana Dors, Patti Love. D: Joseph Losey. DRA [R] 102m. V

Steel 1980 ★★★ Management battles labor as construction workers race to finish a skyscraper before deadline. Fast-paced action with virile heroics. C: Lee Majors, Jennifer O'Neill, Art Carney, George Kennedy. D: Steve Carver. ACT [PG] 100m. V

Steel Arena 1972 ★★★ The ups, downs, and dangers of professional stunt car racing. C: Dusty Russell, Gene Drew. D: Mark L. Lester. ACT [PG] 99m.

Steel Dawn 1987 ★★★ In the savage, not-too-distant future, a loner (Swayze) must save a young woman (Niemi) and her perky son from a maurauding villain (Zerbe). Sort of *Mad Max* meets *Shane*, but not as strong as either of those. C: Patrick Swayze, Lisa Niemi, Anthony Zerbe, Christopher Neame. D: Lance Hool. ACT [R] 100m. V

Steel Fisted Dragon 1982 ★★½ When his mother is brutally murdered a martial arts expert seeks revenge. C: Steve Lee, Johnny Kongkong. ACT [R] 85m. V

Steel Helmet, The 1951 ★★★★ The bloody outbreak of the Korean War forces a tough American sergeant to confront deep-seated notions of courage and heroism. Compact wartime melodrama carries a wallop. C: Gene Evans, Robert Hutton, Steve Brodie, James Edwards, Richard Loo, Sid Melton. D: Samuel Fuller. ACT 84m.

Steel Magnolias 1989 ★★★★ Women customers at Parton's beauty parlor bond together during illness of Field's daughter. Sentimental but entertaining picture benefits from all-star cast, with MacLaine and Roberts the standouts. From Robert Harling's off-Broadway play. C: Sally Field, Dolly Parton, Shirley MacLaine, Daryl Hannah, Olympia Dukakis, Julia Roberts, Tom Skerritt, Sam Shepard. D: Herbert Ross. DRA [PG] 116m. V

Steel Trap, The 1952 ★★★½ Time is running out for a conscience-stricken assistant bank manager trying desperately to return the $500,000 he stole from his employer's vault—before the theft is discovered. Suspenseful drama. C: Joseph Cotten, Teresa Wright, Jonathan Hale, Walter Sande. D: Andrew L. Stone. CRI 85m.

Steele's Law 1991 ★★½ Chicago undercover cop helps FBI bring down gaggle of Texas desperados. Even Williamson can't save this violent action thriller from mediocrity. C: Fred Williamson, Bo Svenson, Phyllis Cicero. D: Fred Williamson. ACT [R] 90m. V

Steelyard Blues 1973 ★★★★ Nutsy, nonconformism comedy with Fonda, Sutherland, and Boyle joining forces to salvage a neglected airplane. Shouldn't work, but it does. Boyle steals it. (a.k.a. *The Final Crash*) C: Jane Fonda, Donald Sutherland, Peter Boyle, Howard Hesseman, John Savage. D: Alan Myerson. COM [PG] 93m. v

Stella 1989 ★★½ Mother (Midler) sacrifices herself for her out-of-wedlock daughter (Alvarado) in remake of classic 1937 weepie. Arbitrary updating and the change of Stella's marital status doesn't work. Midler tries valiantly to stay afloat, despite the weak script. C: Bette Midler, John Goodman, Trini Alvarado, Stephen Collins, Marsha Mason, Ashley Peldon. D: John Erman. DRA [PG-13] 109m. v

Stella Dallas 1937 ★★★★½ Vulgar Stanwyck, estranged from stuffy husband (Boles), sacrifices her own happiness for daughter (Shirley) in saga of mother love. One of Barbara's best performances—flamboyant, yet heartfelt—makes this top-notch soap opera. From Olive Higgins Prouty novel; remade in 1990 as *Stella*. C: Barbara Stanwyck, John Boles, Anne Shirley, Barbara O'Neil, Alan Hale, Tim Holt, Marjorie Main. D: King Vidor. DRA 110m. v

Step Lively 1944 ★★★★ A sharpie theatrical producer beset by money troubles struggles to get his show on the stage. Entertaining musical is a lively remake of *Room Service*. C: Frank Sinatra, George Murphy, Adolphe Menjou, Gloria DeHaven. D: Tim Whelan. MUS 86m. v

Stepfather, The 1987 ★★★★ Pleasant looking, middle-class maniac butchers his new wife and kids when they fail to live up to his notion of the ideal family. Gruesome premise is given darkly brilliant treatment, thanks to top-notch script and O'Quinn's performance as All-American psycho dad. C: Terry O'Quinn, Jill Schoelen, Shelley Hack. D: Joseph Ruben. HOR [R] 89m. v

Stepfather II 1989 ★★½ Psychotic stepdad tries to pass himself off as marriage counselor as he continues his search for the perfect family. Disappointing follow-up to excellent original, slightly redeemed by O'Quinn's creepy nice-guy portrayal. C: Terry O'Quinn, Meg Foster, Jonathan Brandis. D: Jeff Burr. HOR [R] 93m. v

Stepfather 3—Father's Day 1991 ★★ Evil stepdad from Hell is more determined than ever to have the perfect family, no matter how much killing it takes. Bears almost no resemblance to infinitely superior original. Relentlessly gory. C: Robert Wightman, Priscilla Barnes, Season Hubley. D: Guy Magar. HOR [R] 109m. v

Stepford Wives, The 1975 ★★★★ Connecticut housewives are being replaced with more compliant robotic models by their husbands; can our heroines escape their fate? Entertaining gothic shocker from a script by William Goldman. C: Katharine Ross, Paula Prentiss, Peter Masterson, Nanette Newman, Patrick O'Neal, Tina Louise, Dee Wallace, William Prince. D: Bryan Forbes. HOR [PG] 115m. TVM

Stephen King's Golden Years 1991 ★★★½ After being exposed to toxins, elderly lab janitor begins to grow younger, then is pursued by strange government officials. Creepy, well-made miniseries ultimately disappoints due to muddled, abrupt conclusion. C: Keith Szarabajka, Felicity Huffman, Frances Sternhagen, Ed Lauter. HOR 232m. TVM v

Stephen King's It 1990 ★★★ Group of adults, all from the same town, return home to confront an evil force that terrorized them long ago. Excellent cast and engaging first half, but falls apart during the final showdown. C: Tim Reid, Richard Thomas, John Ritter, Annette O'Toole, Dennis Christopher, Harry Anderson. D: Tommy Lee Wallace. HOR 193m. TVM v

Stephen King's Sleepwalkers 1992 ★★★½ Mother/son pair of shape-shifting sleepwalkers invade a midwestern town, looking for young virgins to sustain them. Stephen King's original screenplay is not one of his better stories, but fine special effects help a lot. (a.k.a. *Sleepwalkers*) C: Brian Krause, Madchen Amick, Alice Krige. D: Mick Garris. HOR [R] 91m. v

Stepmonster ★★★ Young boy discovers his new stepmother is a real, live monster. Lighthearted family horror/comedy doesn't always work, but tries. C: Alan Thicke, Corey Feldman, Edie McClurg, John Astin. D: Jeremy Stanford. FAM/COM [PG-13] 86m. v

Stepmother, The 1971 ★★ Twisty, cheap thriller about homicide between near relatives, with delusions of Hitchcockian grandeur. Best for hard-core Claudiaphiles. C: Alejandro Rey, John Anderson, Katherine Justice, John D. Garfield, Marlene Schmidt, Claudia Jennings, Duncan McLeod. D: Hikmet Avedis. CRI [R] 94m. v

Steppenwolf 1974 ★★★ Herman Hesse's novel, an existential fable, ultimately cannot be translated to film, but this is an interesting try. C: Max von Sydow, Dominique Sanda, Pierre Clementi, Carla Romanelli. D: Fred Haines. DRA [R] 105m. v

Stepping Out 1991 ★★★ In this dated but pleasant musical, a tap-dancing teacher (Minnelli) leads her clumsy students from ineptness to dazzling finesse to let them shine in a big "show-stopping" finale. C: Liza Minnelli, Shelley Winters, Bill Irwin, Ellen Greene, Julie Walters, Robyn Stevan, Jane Krakowski, Sheila McCarthy, Andrea Martin, Carol Woods. D: Lewis Gilbert. MUS [PG] 113m. v

Sterile Cuckoo, The 1969 ★★★★ A lonely, neurotic college student eager for her first sexual experience sets her sights on a naive, shy freshman. Winsome, sensitive performance by Minnelli in a moving story of young love. C: Liza Minnelli, Wendell Burton, Tim McIntire. D: Alan J. Pakula. DRA [PG] 107m. v

Steve Allen's Golden Age of Comedy 1986 ★★★★ A wonderful look at TV's early days of glorious comedians and non-stop laughter. Appearances by Johnny Carson, Mel Brooks, the Muppets and more make this loads of fun. C: Steve Allen. D: Anthony Potenza. COM 50m. V

Steve Martin Live! 1980 ★★★ The first Martin concert on home video has the star performing most of his best routines. Watch for David Letterman and Henny Yongman. C: Steve Martin, David Letterman, Henny Youngman. D: Carl Gottlieb. COM 60m. V

Stevie 1978 British ★★★★ Famed British poet Stevie Smith (Jackson) talks with her old maiden aunt (Washborne) for almost two hours, elaborating on the life experiences that would inform her work. That's all, folks, but two old pros make it almost mesmerizing. C: Glenda Jackson, Mona Washbourne. D: Robert Enders. DRA [PG] 102m. V

Stewardess School 1986 ★ The trials and tribulations of nubile young women yearning to earn their "wings." One-joke comedy. C: Brett Cullen, Mary Cadorette, Donald Most, Sandahl Bergman, Sherman Hemsley, Judy Landers. D: Ken Blancato. COM [R] 84m. V

Stick Up, The 1987 ★★★ A naive young American sets out to see the world in the mid-1930's, he falls victim to unlimited schemes at the hands of a swindler. C: David Soul, Pamela McMyler, Johnny Wade. D: Jeffrey Bloom. COM 101m.

Stickfighter 1989 ★★★ A repressive Spanish governor in the Philippines has his comeuppance when a stickfighting expert arrives on the scene. C: Dean Stockwell, Roland Dantes, Nancy Kwan. D: Luis Nepomuceno. ACT [PG] 102m.

Sticks Of Death 1984 ★★★ After his grandson is shot by thugs, an old man teaches the boy the ancient lethal art of the "sticks of death." C: Roland Dantes, Rosemarie Gil. D: Ava C. Caparas. ACT 90m.

Sticky Fingers 1988 ★★★ Oddball comedy about two wacky women who come into possession of a suitcase loaded with drug money. Attractive cast, plenty of manic energy, ho-hum story. C: Melanie Mayron, Helen Slater, Danitra Vance, Eileen Brennan, Carol Kane. D: Caitlin Adams. COM [PG-13] 97m. V

Stigma 1972 ★★ An island settlement, and a member of its rank, an ex-con ex-med student (Thomas), must cope with the aftermath of past sexual excesses when the scourge of venereal disease follows. Thomas does decently, but the medical scenes may disturb some viewers. C: Philip Michael Thomas, Richard Geisman, Edwin Mills. D: David E. Durston. DRA [R] 77m. V

Still Life 1987 ★★★ A psycho has an awful habit of making sculptures out of his murder victims. C: Michael York, Donald Pleasence, Edwige Frenech. D: Ruggero Deodato. HOR 95m.

Still Not Quite Human 1992 ★★★ The third film in Disney Channel's *Not Quite Human* series continues zany collegiate adventures of captivating robot boy and his inventor-father. It is as entertaining as its predecessors. C: Alan Thicke, Jay Underwood, Christopher Neame, Betsy Palmer, Adam Philipson. D: Eric Luke. FAM/COM 84m. TVM V

Still of the Night 1982 ★★★ Confusing mystery/thriller imitates Hitchcock with little skill as Streep plays art gallery worker who may have killed one of Scheider's psychotherapy patients. Writers lost track of their own plotline. C: Roy Scheider, Meryl Streep, Jessica Tandy, Joe Grifasi, Josef Sommer. D: Robert Benton. CRI [PG] 91m. V

Stilts, The 1984 Spanish ★★★★ Middle-aged teacher falls for a beautiful young woman, and his world is crushed when she begins to love someone else. Provocative, honest story of a love triangle from great Spanish director Saura. C: Laura Del Sol, Fernando Gomez, Francisco Rabal, Antonio Banderas. D: Carlos Saura. DRA 95m. V

Sting of the Dragon Masters 1974 ★★★ Deadly female kung fu artist returns to wreak havoc on all challengers to her reign. Violent martial arts action adventure. C: Angela Mao, Jhoon Rhee, Carter Huang. D: Huang Feng. ACT [R] 96m. V

Sting, The 1973 ★★★★½ In Roaring '20s Chicago, two con artists (Newman and Redford) set out to "sting" a sophisticated gangster (Shaw) who had their partner killed. Enjoyable nostalgia shows a great script, direction, and chemistry between the leads. Film won seven Oscars, including Best Picture, Director, and Screenplay. Marvin Hamlisch's Oscar-winning musical adaptation helped contribute to the revival of interest in Scott Joplin's ragtime melodies. Followed by a sequel. Knockout musical score. C: Paul Newman, Robert Redford, Robert Shaw, Charles Durning, Ray Walston, Eileen Brennan, Harold Gould. D: George Roy Hill. COM [PG] 129m. V

Sting II, The 1983 ★★½ If you can accept Gleason and Davis in the same roles played by Newman and Redford in the original 1973 hit, then by all means, watch this. Garr is the main asset of this dull boxing-scam comedy. C: Jackie Gleason, Mac Davis, Karl Malden, Teri Garr, Oliver Reed. D: Jeremy Paul Kagan. COM [PG] 102m. V

Stir Crazy 1981 ★★★½ Two losers from New York on their way to California are sidetracked in small town and mistakenly sent to prison for robbing a bank. Wilder and Pryor are the main reasons to watch, as the plot wears so thin it disappears. C: Gene Wilder, Richard Pryor, Georg Stanford Brown, JoBeth Williams. D: Sidney Poitier. COM [R] 114m. V

Stocks and Blondes 1984 ★★★ A beautiful woman seduces wealthy married men—and then blackmails them for a fortune. C: Veronica Hart, Leigh Wood. D: Arthur Greenstands. DRA [R] 79m.

Stolen Babies 1993 ★★★½ Moore (in an Emmy-winning dramatic performance) plays the sinisterly charming proprietor of an illegal adoption ring. Absorbing drama. C: Lea Thompson, Mary Tyler Moore, Kathleen Quinlan. D: Eric Laneuville. DRA 100m. TVM

Stolen Children 1993 *See* **Il Ladro di Bambini**

Stolen Face, A 1952 British ★★★½ Odd little film about an obsessed plastic surgeon who transforms a convict to look like the woman of his dreams. Interesting drama, pulled off by solid cast. C: Lizabeth Scott, Paul Henreid, Andre Morell, Susan Stephen, Mary Mackenzie, John Wood. D: Terence Fisher. DRA 72m.

Stolen Hours, The 1963 ★★ The classic Bette Davis tearjerker *Dark Victory* gets watered down into an annoying hairpuller as Hayward battles a brain tumor, this time in a contemporary British setting. Susan tries hard, but the script is terminal. C: Susan Hayward, Michael Craig, Diane Baker. D: Daniel Petrie. DRA 100m. V

Stolen Kisses 1968 French ★★★★ Third installment of Truffaut's autobiographical Antoine Doinel series follows his hero (Leaud) from a dishonorable discharge and series of affairs to finally settling down—for good? Gently amusing and touching, this minor work remains thoroughly engaging. C: Jean-Pierre Leaud, Delphine Seyrig, Michel Lonsdale, Claude Jade. D: Francois Truffaut. DRA [R] 90m.

Stolen Life, A 1946 ★★★★ Bette plays twin sisters after the same man (Ford) in satisfying soaper. Starts slow, but when one sister dies and the other takes her place, film takes off. Loosely remade by Bette 20 years later as *Dead Ringer*. C: Bette Davis, Glenn Ford, Dane Clark, Walter Brennan. D: Curtis Bernhardt. DRA 107m. V

Stone Boy, The 1984 ★★★★½ A young Montana farm boy (Presson) accidentally kills his older brother, a tragedy that tears at all the remaining members of the family and places the boy in a personal limbo. Carefully structured, shattering story, with outstanding performances. C: Robert Duvall, Jason Presson, Glenn Close, Frederic Forrest. D: Christopher Cain. DRA [PG] 93m. V

Stone Cold 1991 ★★ Football star Bosworth strikes some cool poses playing an undercover cop out to bust notorious biker gang. Gratuitous, ultraviolent extravaganza. C: Brian Bosworth, Lance Henriksen, William Forsythe, Arabella Holzbog. D: Craog R. Baxley. ACT [R] 90m. V

Stone Fox 1987 ★★★½ Boy enters dogsled race to save the farm of his grandpa (Ebsen). Will he beat the local boy who's never lost a race? Conventional tale of triumph based on John Reynolds Gardiner's children's book. C: Buddy Ebsen, Joey Cramer, Belinda Montgomery, Gordon Tootoosis. D: Harvey Hart. FAM/ACT 96m. TVM V

Stone Pillow 1985 ★★★½ A homeless woman (Ball) is aided by an inexperienced social worker (Zuniga) in this social-issue-of-the-week TV movie. Lucy's surprisingly effective performing in grim drama. C: Lucille Ball, Daphne Zuniga, William Converse Roberts, Susan Batson. D: George Schaefer. DRA 100m. TVM

Stoned Age, The 1994 ★★★½ The '70s nostalgia kick continues with this tale of a high school student in search of heavy metal music, fast cars, and cheap thrills. Mildly amusing. (a.k.a. Tack's Chicks) C: Michael Kopelow, Bradford Tamm, China Kantner. D: James Melkonian. COM TVM

Stones for Ibarra 1988 ★★★★ An American couple in Mexico make discoveries about themselves, against a panoramic background. Lush and inviting, though a bit long. C: Glenn Close, Keith Carradine, Alfonso Arau, Jorge Cervera Jr., Trinidad Silva, Angie Porres. D: Jack Gold. DRA 100m. TVM

Stones of Death 1988 ★★ When some townspeople find a cave filled with dead bodies, a horrible chain of violent events begins. C: Tom Jennings, Terry McKay, Zoe Carides. D: James Bogle. HOR [R] 90m. TVM

Stooge, The 1953 ★★★★ A mean-spirited pop singer (Martin) underestimates the contribution of his comic partner (Lewis) to his success. Something different from Martin and Lewis resonates today with autobiographical overtones. Fans of the popular duo will find this fascinating. C: Dean Martin, Jerry Lewis, Polly Bergen. D: Norman Taurog. DRA 100m. V

Stoogemania 1985 ★★★ Lonely misfit (Mostel) finds happiness in his obsession with *The Three Stooges*. Wobbly comedy-drama gets a boost from generous helping of vintage clips. C: Josh Mostel, Sid Caesar, Melanie Chartoff. D: Chuck Workman. COM [PG] 83m. V

Stop! Look! and Laugh! 1960 ★★★½ Compilation of *Three Stooges* comedy routines, interspersed with new material featuring ventriloquist Paul Winchell and kid's show host Bolton. Enjoyable Saturday morning smorgasbord; snobs stay away. C: The Three Stooges, Paul Winchell, Officer Joe Bolton, The Marquis Chimps. D: Jules White. FAM/COM 78m. V

Stop Making Sense 1984 ★★★★½ Terrific rock concert film, with the Talking Heads, led by David Byrne, making their film debut (the group would later star in *True Stories*). Demme's masterful direction makes this something special for music fans. C: Talking Heads. D: Jonathan Demme. MUS 99m. V

Stop! or My Mom Will Shoot 1992 ★★ Can

Stallone do comedy—intentionally? Watch this story about an L.A. policeman and his domineering mother (Getty) who interferes with his work and love life, and decide for yourself. C: Sylvester Stallone, Estelle Getty, JoBeth Williams, Roger Rees. D: Roger Spottiswoode. COM [PG-13] 87m. V

Storm and Sorrow 1992 ★★½ Hot-shot American mountain climber (Singer) joins team scaling Russia's Pamir Mountains. Standard mountaineering adventure with usual cliffhanging dangers and near-fatal close calls. C: Lori Singer, Todd Allen. ACT 96m. V

Storm Boy 1976 ★★½ A young Australian boy makes friends with an aborigine and a pelican. C: Peter Cummins, David Gulpilil. D: Henr Safran. DRA 90m.

Storm Center 1956 ★★★ Well-meaning story of a small-town librarian (Davis) becoming involved in censorship when a book on Communism is banned. Dull treatment of potentially provocative material. C: Bette Davis, Brian Keith, Kim Hunter. D: Daniel Taradash. DRA 85m.

Storm in a Teacup 1937 British ★★★★ Reporter (Harrison) in a Scottish town turns the mayor's poor treatment of a dog-owning old lady (Allgood) into a cause celebre. Sharp, clever comedy; Harrison and Leigh make fine sparring partners. C: Rex Harrison, Vivien Leigh, Sara Allgood, Cecil Parker. D: Victor Saville, Ian Dalrymple. COM 87m. V

Storm Warning 1951 ★★★ Rogers's up in arms when her sweet kid sister (Day) marries a Klu Klux Klan member. So-so drama trivializes a sensitive subject, but Doris is surprisingly good. C: Ginger Rogers, Doris Day, Ronald Reagan, Steve Cochran. D: Stuart Heisler. DRA 93m.

Stormquest 1987 ★★½ An Amazon queen reigns over a society of women. When one of them is discovered to have a male lover, she's sentenced to death, while a group of men try to save. C: Brent Huff, Kai Baker, Linda Lutz. D: Alex Sessa. ACT 90m.

Stormy Monday 1988 British ★★★½ Stylish film depicts culture clash between a rich, corrupt American (Jones) and a world-weary but honest jazz club owner (Sting), with a woman (Griffiths) as the pawn in the middle. Ambiance is somewhat hampered by clumsy plot. C: Melanie Griffith, Tommy Lee Jones, Sting, Sean Bean. D: Mike Figgis. DRA [R] 93m. V

Stormy Weather 1943 ★★★★½ One of the "specialty" musicals assembled during segregation in the movie industry is a showcase of outstanding African-American talent strung together with a thread of a story line. Horne is the standout, performing the title song. C: Lena Horne, Bill Robinson, Cab Calloway, Fats Waller, Dooley Wilson, Eddie Anderson. D: Andrew L. Stone. MUS 78m. V

Story Lady, The 1991 ★★★½ When a retired schoolteacher (Tandy) achieves fame reading children's stories on public-access TV, big business and media hype take over. Tandy's performance makes it wonderful. C: Jessica Tandy, Ed Begley Jr., Stephanie Zimbalist, Charles Durning. D: Larry Elikann. DRA [G] 100m. TVM V

Story of a Cheat, The 1992 Chinese ★★★ The multitalented Sacha Guitry tells the story of a reformed cardsharp in pantomime, with voice-over narration. (a.k.a. *Le Roman d'un Tricheur*) C: Gong Li, Lei Lao Sheng, Liu Pei Qi, Ge Zhi Jun, Ye Jun, Yang Liu Xia. D: Zhang Yimou. DRA [PG] 100m.

Story of a Love Story, The 1973 *See* **Impossible Object**

Story of a Marriage 1987 *See* **On Valentine's Day**

Story of a Three-Day Pass, The 1967 French ★★★★ An African-American soldier gets three-day leave while stationed in France. He heads to Paris, where he engages in a whirlwind affair with a French woman. Poignant look at interracial romance, with sweet performances by leads. C: Harry Baird, Christian Marin, Pierre Doris, Nicole Berger. D: Melvin VanPebbles. DRA 87m. V

Story of Adele H, The 1975 French ★★★★½ Increasingly delusional daughter of Victor Hugo follows the British soldier who spurned her, trying to convince him of her love. Adjani is wonderful as the haunted, obsessive Adele. Exquisite, lyrical film is one of Truffaut's best. C: Isabelle Adjani, Bruce Robinson, Sylvia Marriott, Reubin Dorey, Joseph Blatchley, M. White. D: Francois Truffaut. DRA [PG] 97m. V

Story of Alexander Graham Bell, The 1939 ★★★★ Lavishly produced biography of famous inventor Bell (the role with which Ameche was forever associated), who brought us the telephone. Young plays the young deaf woman Bell marries. Smooth, satisfying entertainment. C: Don Ameche, Loretta Young, Henry Fonda, Charles Coburn, Spring Byington, Gene Lockhart, Polly Young. D: Irving Cummings. DRA 97m.

Story of Boys and Girls, The 1991 Italian ★★★★ At a sumptuous banquet celebrating their children's impending marriage, two disparate families come into conflict. Sharp, wry, funny look at human behavior, superbly directed. C:Lucretia della Rovere, Valeria Bruni Tadeschi, Davide Bechini. D: Pupi Avati. COM 92m. V

Story of Danny Lester, The 1949 *See* **Bad Boy**

Story of Dr. Wassell, The 1944 ★★★★ Cooper shines as the Navy physician hero stationed in Java during WWII. True story, from the book by James (*Goodbye, Mr. Chips*, *Lost Horizon*) Hilton. Shows another side of the usually flamboyant DeMille. C: Gary Cooper, Laraine Day, Signe Hasso, Dennis O'Keefe. D: Cecil B. DeMille. DRA 140m.

Story of Drunken Master, The 1987 ★★★

Wild master Sung and his kung-fu gang take on the notorious Billy Chan. C: Yang Pan Pan, Chi Sa Fu, Yuan Hsiao Tien. ACT 90m.

Story of Esther Costello, The 1957 British ★★★ Melodramatic tale of a blind, mute, and deaf girl (Sears) who's adopted by a wealthy woman (Crawford) and is exploited shamelessly. Tailor-made Crawford star vehicle. C: Joan Crawford, Rossano Brazzi, Heather Sears, Lee Patterson, Fay Compton, Bessie Love, Ron Randell. D: David Miller. DRA 103m.

Story of 15 Boys, The 1990 ★★★½ Fifteen boys are cast ashore on a desert island. Instead of becoming savages, the boys learn trust and their experiences help them grow into men. Animated film is based on the Jules Verne novel Two Years Vacation. Good viewing for the kids. FAM/ACT 80m. TVM V

Story Of G.I. Joe, The 1945 ★★★★½ From the pen of war correspondent Ernie Pyle, the exploits of the common fighting man, the foot soldier of WWII, in the Italian campaign. Superior wartime drama, with magnificent performances by Meredith (as Pyle) and by Mitchum as an ordinary soldier. C: Burgess Meredith, Robert Mitchum, Freddie Steele, Wally Cassell, Jimmy Lloyd. D: William Wellman. ACT 109m.

Story of Gilbert and Sullivan, The 1953 *See* **Great Gilbert and Sullivan, The**

Story Of Gosta Berling, The 1924 ★★★½ A drunken clergyman is banished from the church. He meets up with a beautiful, sweet woman (Garbo) who saved him. Silent classic was Greta's star-making role. C: Greta Garbo, Lars Hansel, Ellen Gederstrom. D: Mauritz Stiller. DRA 85m.

Story of Louis Pasteur, The 1936 ★★★★½ Oscar for Best Actor went to Muni for his incisive, absorbing portrayal of the French scientist who combated a number of deadly diseases (including rabies) and developed the process that came to be called pasteurization. Additional Oscar for Best Original Story and Screenplay. C: Paul Muni, Josephine Hutchinson, Anita Louise, Donald Woods, Fritz Leiber, Porter Hall. D: William Dieterle. DRA 85m. V

Story of Mankind, The 1957 ★★ Simplistic "history of civilization" plays like a high-school pageant put on by Hollywood stars. So bad, you've just got to see it. Sample treat: Harpo Marx as Sir Isaac Newton! C:Ronald Colman, Vincent Price, Hedy Lamarr, Groucho, Harpo and Chico Marx, Virginia Mayo, Agnes Moorehead, Charles Coburn, Cedric Hardwicke. D: Irwin Allen. DRA 100m.

Story of Qiu Ju, The 1992 Chinese ★★★★★ A Chinese peasant woman (Gong Li) won't take no for an answer as she seeks recompense after her husband is beaten by village chief. Emotionally rewarding, engrossing film from the director of *Raise the Red Lantern.* Gong Li is unforgettable. C: Gong Li, Lei Lao Sheng, Liu Pei Qi. D: Zhang Yimou. DRA [PG] 100m. V

Story of Robin Hood and His Merrie Men, The 1952 ★★★½ Disney's live-action Robin Hood (animated version followed in 1973) benefits from talented cast that lifts story above routine script. Todd is title character, battling evil Sheriff of Nottingham (Finch). Fun in its own right. C: Richard Todd, Joan Rice, Peter Finch. D: Ken Annakin. FAM/DRA [PG] 84m. V

Story of Ruth, The 1960 ★★ Film version of the Bible story of heroine's faith and allegiance runs far afield of original material. Whither it goest, it's hard to follow. C: Elana Eden, Stuart Whitman, Tom Tryon, Peggy Wood. D: Henry Koster. DRA 132m. V

Story of Seabiscuit, The 1949 ★★★ Horse trainer (Fitzgerald) drives title nag on to become racetrack champ. Fitzgerald's the best part of otherwise commonplace racing film. C: Shirley Temple, Barry Fitzgerald, Lon McCallister, Rosemary DeCamp. D: David Butler. FAM/DRA 93m.

Story of Sin 1990 ★★★ The story of a young woman, following her path from innocence to adulthood and ultimate self-sacrifice. In Polish. C: Timothy Dwight, Joan Bechtel, John Flynn. D: Chris Shaw. DRA 85m. V

Story of Temple Drake, The 1933 ★★★ Faulkner's shocking novel, *Sanctuary*, was sanitized, retitled, and fashioned into a star vehicle for the talented Hopkins, as Southern flapper/playgirl Temple Drake. Dated, but interesting to compare with the more daring 1961 Lee Remick version. C: Miriam Hopkins, Jack LaRue, William Gargan. D: Stephen Roberts. DRA 70m.

Story of Three Loves, The 1953 ★★★★ Three romances are recalled by ocean voyagers in this mixed bag, with a terrific cast. Douglas and Angeli share a circus affair, and Shearer plays a doomed ballerina in a retread of *The Red Shoes.* Best is Minnelli's "Mademoiselle," with Caron, Granger and Barrymore in tale of a boy magically transformed into his governess's suitor. C: Pier Angeli, Moira Shearer, Leslie Caron, Ethel Barrymore, Kirk Douglas, Farley Granger, James Mason, Agnes Moorehead. D: Vincente Minnelli, Gottfried Reinhardt. DRA 122m.

Story of Vernon and Irene Castle, The 1939 ★★★★ In their last film together for RKO, Fred and Ginger appear as the celebrated ballroom dancers the Castles. Very pleasant musical biography with more than enough of Astaire's and Rogers' marvelous singing and dancing to appeal to all their fans. C: Fred Astaire, Ginger Rogers, Edna May Oliver, Walter Brennan. D: H.C. Potter. MUS 93m. V

Story of Will Rogers, The 1952 ★★★★ Simple, straightforward and refreshingly faithful bio of political pundit, stage and screen star Rogers (portrayed by his son). Wyman shines as his patient wife. C: Will Rogers, Jr., Jane Wyman, Carl Benton Reid, James Gleason, Eddie Cantor. D: Michael Curtiz. DRA 109m.

Story of Women, The 1988 French ★★★★ Events (based on reality) of the life of a woman who was charged with performing abortions in France during the Nazi occupation. Her punishment: the guillotine. Intense and well done; Huppert is positively splendid. C: Isabelle Huppert, Francois Cluzet, Marie Trintignant. D: Claude Chabrol. DRA 110m. v

Story on Page One, The 1959 ★★★★ An adulterous wife (Hayworth) and her lover (Young) stand trial for the murder of her husband. Standard courtroom drama, elevated by Rita's impressive performance. C: Rita Hayworth, Gig Young, Anthony Franciosa, Mildred Dunnock. D: Clifford Odets. DRA 123m.

Storyville 1992 ★★½ A political star on the rise (Spader) discovers some unsavory family secrets. Spader, Whalley-Kilmer, and Robards are superb, but the script isn't. C: James Spader, Joanne Whaley-Kilmer, Jason Robards, Charlotte Lewis, Michael Parks. D: Mark Frost. DRA [R] 112m. v

Stowaway 1936 ★★★★ Shipboard orphan (Temple) ingratiates herself with millionaire (Young). Before film ends, Temple fixes Young up with Faye, sings many songs (one in Chinese!) and gets adopted by the happy couple. Predictable, but one of Temple's better features, with fine performances that don't overplay the sentiment. C: Robert Young, Alice Faye, Shirley Temple. D: William A. Seiter. FAM/DRA 86m. v

Straight Out of Brooklyn 1991 ★★★★ Young man living in the Brooklyn projects thinks a violent crime will solve his problems. Earthy and gritty; made for peanuts and looks it, though this lends an intriguingly raw emotional feeling to the film. C: George T. Odom, Ann Sanders, Lawrence Gilliard Jr., Mark Malone. D: Matty Rich. CRI [R] 83m. v

Straight Talk 1992 ★★★½ Fresh-from-the-country Parton is hired by a Chicago radio station to host its call-in advice show, where her plain-talking advice makes her a hit. Good supporting cast and charming Parton make it fun, if not exactly believable. C: Dolly Parton, James Woods, Griffin Dunne, Teri Hatcher, Jerry Orbach, Jay Thomas. D: Barnet Kellman. COM [PG] 91m. v

Straight Through the Heart 1983 German ★★★★ Offbeat first feature for Dorrie, about the troubled relationship between a distraught young woman and a repressed middle-aged dentist. C: Beate Jensen, Sepp Bierbichler, Gabrielle Litty, Nuran Filiz. D: Doris Dorrie. DRA 91m.

Straight Time 1978 ★★★★½ Tough tale of criminal recidivist who runs afoul of his parole officer and returns to life of crime. Great supporting performances surround Hoffman's memorable depiction of the amoral criminal. Based on Edward Bunker's *No Beast So Fierce.* C: Dustin Hoffman, Theresa Russell, Harry Dean Stanton, Gary Busey, M. Emmet Walsh. D: Ulu Grosbard. CRI [R] 114m. v

Straight to Hell 1987 ★ Awful spoof of spaghetti-Westerns falls solidly into the "Wow, how bad could that cast be—whoops!" category. Amusing, in a backwards way. C: Joe Strummer, Dick Rude, Dennis Hopper, Elvis Costello, Grace Jones, Pogues. D: Alex Cox. COM [R] 86m. v

Straightline 1992 ★★½ Muscle-bound private eye is hired to find creep turning street kids into racist maniacs. Ridiculous combination of social drama and head-banging violence; tailor-made for Mr. T.'s menacing, cartoonish presence. C: Mr. T., Alex Amini, Sean Roberge, Ron Ryan. D: George Mihalka. ACT 95m. v

Strange Affair of Uncle Harry, The 1945 *See* **Uncle Harry**

Strange And Deadly Occurrence, The 1974 ★★★ When they move into a beautiful new country home, a couple come under the spell of horrible spirits. C: Vera Miles, Robert Stack, L.Q. Jones. D: John Llewellyn Moxey. HOR 74m.

Strange Awakening, The 1958 *See* **Female Fiends**

Strange Bedfellows 1964 ★★★ A squabbling married couple (Hudson, Lollobrigida) must fake domestic bliss so hubby can get a job promotion. By-the-numbers comedy, but stars' enormous charm carries it through. C: Rock Hudson, Gina Lollobrigida, Gig Young, Terry-Thomas. D: Melvin Frank. COM 98m.

Strange Behavior 1981 New Zealand ★★★½ Shocker about a rash of murders in a Midwestern town, directed with a grisly sense of the absurd. (a.k.a. *Dead Kids*) C: Michael Murphy, Louise Fletcher, Fiona Lewis, Dan Shor. D: Michael Laughlin. HOR [R] 98m. v

Strange Brew 1983 ★★★ Bob and Doug MacKenzie (Moranis and Thomas—from their SCTV skit) outwit(?) an evil brewmeister fooling with the recipe at a local brewery. Dull in spots, but overall pretty good, eh? C: Rick Moranis, Dave Thomas, Rick Moranis, Max von Sydow, Paul Dooley. D: Dave Thomas, Rick Moranis. COM [PG] 91m. v

Strange Cargo 1940 ★★★ A boatload of escapees from Devil's Island led by Gable are influenced by Christ-like stranger (Hunter). Offbeat combination of adventure and mysticism, with good performances. C: Joan Crawford, Clark Gable, Ian Hunter, Peter Lorre, Albert Dekker, Eduardo Ciannelli. D: Frank Borzage. DRA 105m. v

Strange Case of Dr. Jekyll And Mr. Hyde, The ★★★★½ Outstanding version of the Robert Louis Stevenson tale of the brilliant doctor who drugs himself into an evil, grotesque figure. Palance is marvelous in one of his best roles. C: Jack Palance, Leo Genn, Oscar Homolka, Billie Whitelaw. D: Charles Jarrott. HOR 128m.

Strange Case Of The End of Civilization As We Know It 1993 ★★★ The great grandson of Sherlock Holmes (Cleese) solves a major matter of international intrigue. C: John Cleese, Connie Booth, Arthur Lowe. D: Joseph McGrath. COM 55m.

Strange Interlude 1932 ★★★ Shortened version of O'Neill's Pulitzer Prize-winning play where characters' thoughts are heard in voice-overs. A woman whose husband has a tainted family history enlists a friend to give her a child. Shearer is outstanding. C: Norma Shearer, Clark Gable, May Robson, Maureen O'Sullivan, Robert Young, Ralph Morgan, Henry B. Walthall, Mary Alden. D: Robert Z. Leonard. DRA 101m. V

Strange Invaders 1983 ★★★★ Space aliens who took over a Midwestern town in the '50s are finally found and pursued by survivors on invasion. Terrific homage to '50s science fiction "paranoia" films aided by fine performances and tongue-in-cheek script. C: Paul LeMat, Nancy Allen, Diana Scarwid, Louise Fletcher. D: Michael Laughlin. SFI [PG] 94m. V

Strange Lady in Town 1955 ★★★½ A confident doctor (Garson) must overcome 19th-century prejudice in Santa Fe. Grand slice of western pie for Garson, who delivers her signature brand of Mrs. Miniver, Medicine Woman. C: Greer Garson, Dana Andrews, Cameron Mitchell, Nick Adams. D: Mervyn LeRoy. WST 112m.

Strange Love of Martha Ivers, The 1946 ★★★★ Powerful melodrama of an embittered, dominating woman (Stanwyck) unable to leave her weak husband (Douglas, in screen debut) because of a dark secret in her past. Things come to a head when her ex-boyfriend hits town. C: Barbara Stanwyck, Kirk Douglas, Lizabeth Scott, Van Heflin, Judith Anderson. D: Lewis Milestone. DRA 116m. V

Strange Skirts 1941 *See* **When Ladies Meet**

Strange Tales/Ray Bradbury Theatre 1986 ★★★½ An anthology of award-receiving stories from the modern expert of science fiction and fantasy. D: Douglas Jackson. SFI 90m. V

Strange Woman, The 1946 ★★★½ Title character (Lamarr) seduces men, betrays husbands and generally misbehaves in this deliciously trashy costume soaper from Ben Ames Williams' best seller. Fine fun for Lamarr fans. C: Hedy Lamarr, George Sanders, Gene Lockhart, Louis Hayward, Hillary Brooke. D: Edgar G. Ulmer. DRA 100m.

Strangeness, The 1985 ★★★ Deep within the earth miners accidently unleash a horrid creature, causing mass destruction. C: Dan Lunham, Terri Berland. D: David Michael Hillman. HOR 90m.

Stranger Among Us, A 1992 ★★½ A NYC cop (Griffith) goes undercover in a closed Hasidic community to find the murderer of one of its members. Griffith is quite believable as a cop, but less so as an Hasidic woman. C: Melanie Griffith, Eric Thal, John Pankow, Tracy Pollan, Mia Sara. D: Sidney Lumet. CRI [PG-13] 109m. V

Stranger From Venus 1959 ★★★½ Into the English countryside falls a powerful, mysterious alien—with whom the fate of humankind sits. C: Patricia Neal, Helmut Dantine, Derek Bond. D: Burt Balaban. SFI 120m.

Stranger in My Arms 1959 ★★★ Adaptation of Robert Wilder's novel about a Korean War widow (Allyson) who opposes her mother-in-law (Astor) by falling for her dead husband's friend (Chandler). Classic soap opera performed by pros. C: June Allyson, Jeff Chandler, Sandra Dee, Charles Coburn, Mary Astor, Peter Graves, Conrod Nagel. D: Helmut Kautner. DRA 88m.

Stranger In Paso Bravo, A 1973 ★★½ When his wife and daughter are murdered, a cowboy seeks revenge. C: Anthony Steffen. D: Salvator Rosso. WST 97m.

Stranger Is Watching, A 1982 ★★★ Deranged Torn has a special hiding place underneath NYC's Grand Central Station and it's just perfect for his abductees (Mulgrew and Von Schreiber). Thriller with a good turn by Torn, but routine, despite attempts at being shockingly lurid. Based on Mary Higgens Clarke best-seller. C: Kate Mulgrew, Rip Torn, James Naughton. D: Sean S. Cunningham. CRI [R] 98m. V

Stranger on Horseback 1955 ★★★ The old story about one lone man (McCrea) fighting a town to bring a criminal to justice. *High Noon* it ain't. From a Louis L'Amour novel. C: Joel McCrea, John McIntire, Kevin McCarthy. D: Jacques Tourneur. WST 66m.

Stranger on My Land 1988 ★★★½ Feds try to take Vietnam vet's land to build a missile base, but he resists. Middling drama. C: Tommy Lee Jones, Dee Wallace Stone, Ben Johnson, Pat Hingle, Terry O'Quinn. D: Larry Elikann. DRA 100m. TVM V

Stranger on the Prowl 1953 Italian ★★★ A man wanted for murder and a wounded boy join forces to evade the police. As usual, Muni adds texture and tension. Made in Italy. C: Paul Muni, Vittorio Manunta, Joan Lorring, Aldo Silvani. D: Joseph Losey. CRI 82m.

Stranger on the Run 1967 ★★★★ An ex-con (Fonda) is pursued by lawmen into the desert while trying to deliver a message from his imprisoned friend. Taut, well-directed thriller, with a good script by veteran TV writer Reginald (*12 Angry Men*) Rose. (a.k.a. *Lonesome Gun*) C: Henry Fonda, Michael Parks, Anne Baxter, Dan Duryea, Sal Mineo. D: Don Siegel. CRI 97m. TVM

Stranger on the Third Floor 1940 ★★★½ After a convicted criminal is sentenced to death, the reporter who provided the damning testimony begins to second-guess himself when a similar series of crimes sweeps through the city. Nifty crime thriller, with some terrific cinematic flourishes adding to the suspense. C: John McGuire, Margaret Tallichet, Charles Waldron, Elisha Cook Jr., Peter Lorre. D: Boris Ingster. CRI 64m. V

Stranger Than Paradise 1984 ★★★★ Style over substance is the key to this successful independent film vaguely about a cool New Yorker whose uncool cousin from Hungary joins him and a friend on a road trip. Often slow and cryptic, but definitely original. C: John Lurie, Eszter Balint, Richard Edson, Cecilla Stark. D: Jim Jarmusch. COM 90m. V

Stranger, The 1946 ★★★★½ Knock-out thriller about fugitive Nazi Welles living in quiet Connecticut town. G-Man Robinson trails him, while fianceé Young slowly discovers his true identity but can't make herself turn him in. Great performances. C: Orson Welles, Loretta Young, Edward G. Robinson, Richard Long. D: Orson Welles. DRA 95m. V

Stranger, The 1967 Italian-French ★★★★ Skillfull adaptation of Albert Camus's existential novel about a man divorced from society. Mastroianni's finest hour, all the more impressive because the original material had been deemed unfilmable. C: Marcello Mastroianni, Anna Karina, Bernard Blier. D: Luchino Visconti. DRA 105m.

Stranger Who Wore a Gun, The 1953 ★★★ An honest man learns that the stranger who saved his life is a stagecoach bandit. Shot in 3-D, action sequences are choreographed for special effects and fall flat on the screen. C: Randolph Scott, Claire Trevor, George Macready, Lee Marvin, Ernest Borgnine. D: Andre DeToth. WST 83m. V

Stranger Within, The 1974 ★ Suburban housewife starts acting very strangely after becoming pregnant by a sinister force. Slapdash, rip-off of *Rosemary's Baby* demeans talented cast. C: Barbara Eden, George Grizzard, Joyce VanPatten, David Doyle, Nehemiah Persoff. D: Lee Philips. HOR 78m. TVM

Stranger's Gold ★★½ Vigilante ride small town of corruption and greed. C: John Garko, Antonio Vilar. WST 90m.

Stranger's Hand, The 1954 British ★★★★ Graham Greene twister about a British espionage officer abducted by foreign agents while on the way to meet his young son in Venice. A jaw-clenching suspense thriller with first-rate acting. C: Trevor Howard, Alida Valli, Richard Basehart, Eduardo Ciannelli, Richard O'Sullivan, Stephen Murray. D: Mario Soldati. DRA 86m.

Strangers in Good Company 1991 Canadian ★★★★ Group of women on bus trip are stranded in the Canadian wilderness and pass time talking about their lives, hopes, and dreams. Beguiling dialogue makes up for plotlessness. C: Alice Diablo, Constance Garneau, Winifred Holden, Cissy Meddings, Mary Meigs, Catherine Roche, Michelle Sweeney, Beth Webber. D: Cynthia Scott. DRA [PG] 100m. TVM

Strangers in Love 1932 ★★★ A mild-mannered man tries impersonating his cruel twin brother. March has a field day playing both siblings in this very well-acted comic drama. C: Fredric March, Kay Francis. D: Lothar Mendes. DRA 76m.

Strangers in Paradise 1986 ★★ A man has himself frozen to avoid life under Hitler only to be revived forty years later by a dictatorial crazed man who uses him to control rebellious youths. C: Ulli Lommel. D: Ulli Lommel. HOR 81m. V

Strangers in the City 1962 ★★★½ A family of Puerto Ricans retrench in New York City and attempt to adjust to new customs. Frequently compelling if uneven tale. C: Robert Gentile, Camilo Delgado, Kenny Delmar. D: Rick Carrier. DRA 80m. V

Strangers in the House 1949 French ★★★★ Club of young petty thieves must deal with blackmail and murder after they run someone down during a drunken spree. Fascinating drama thoughtfully explores the alienation of French teenagers during WWII. C: Raimu, Andre Reybas. D: Henri Decoin. DRA 95m.

Strangers Kiss 1984 ★★★½ In 1955 a shady promoter produces a low-budget movie starring his girlfriend, then gets jealous of her off-camera relationship with her co-star. Offbeat, intricate tale. C: Peter Coyote, Victoria Tennant, Blaine Novak, Dan Shor, Richard Romanus, Linda Kerridge. D: Matthew Chapman. DRA [R] 94m.

Strangers May Kiss 1931 ★★★½ Complex melodrama about can't-win-for-losing Shearer following her faithless love, reporter Hamilton, across the globe but unable to win him. Enjoyable adaptation of Ursula Purrott's novel, with fine leads. C: Norma Shearer, Robert Montgomery, Neil Hamilton, Marjorie Rambeau, Jed Prouty, Henry Armetta, Irene Rich. D: George Fitzmaurice. DRA 85m. V

Strangers on a Train 1951 ★★★★★ When a psychopath meets up with a tennis celebrity, he suggests that each one murder the other's least favorite person. His words start a fascinating chain of murderous events. This is Hitchcock in his finest element, complete with a murder reflected in a pair of eye glasses and a runaway carousel. C: Farley Granger, Robert Walker, Ruth Roman, Leo G. Carroll, Patricia Hitchcock. D: Alfred Hitchcock. CRI 101m. V

Stranger's Return, The 1933 ★★★★ City woman (Hopkins) returns to her grandfather's farm, where she falls in love with a married man (Tone). Absorbing tale; fine work by the very appealing Hopkins. C: Miriam Hopkins, Lionel Barrymore, Franchot Tone, Beulah Bondi. D: King Vidor. DRA 89m.

Strangers, The *See* **Voyage to Italy**

Strangers: The Story of a Mother and Daughter 1979 ★★★★ A lonely old woman (Davis) reunites with her estranged daughter (Rowlands)

in this perceptive, unusually strong TV drama. Perhaps Davis's best "aged" performance; it won her an Emmy. C: Bette Davis, Gena Rowlands. D: Milton Katselas. DRA 100m. TVM V

Strangers When We Meet 1960 ★★★½ A wealthy architect falls in love with lonely neighbor and they begin a torrid affair, even though they are both married to others. High gloss soap opera adapted by Evan Hunter from his own novel. C: Kirk Douglas, Kim Novak, Ernie Kovacs, Barbara Rush, Walter Matthau. D: Richard Quine. DRA 117m. V

Strangler of the Swamp 1945 ★★★½ The vengeful ghost of a hanged man seeks human sacrifices from a small village. Low-budget thriller, a remake of the director's German *Fahman Maria*, is sparked by some stylish touches. C: Rosemary La Planche, Blake Edwards, Charles Middleton. D: Frank Wisbar. HOR 60m. V

Strangler of the Swamp 1946 ★★ When an innocent man is hanged for a crime, his ghost comes back to take revenge. Cheap horror flick, memorable only for the rare acting appearance of director Edwards. C: Rosemary La Planche, Blake Edwards, Charles Middleton, Robert Barrat. D: Frank Wisbar. HOR 60m.

Strangler, The 1964 ★★★½ Mother-obsessed man (Buono) gives the Boston Strangler a run for his neckties. A sturdy, low-budget knock-off of *Psycho*. C: Victor Buono, David McLean, Ellen Corby, Jeanne Bates. D: Burt Topper. HOR 89m. V

Strapless 1990 British ★★★★ An American doctor (Brown) caught in a troubled marriage, reconsiders her life when her vacationing younger sister (Fonda) visits. Strong story of emotional crossroads, played with verve by excellent cast. C: Blair Brown, Bruno Ganz, Bridget Fonda, Hugh Laurie. D: David Hare. DRA [R] 103m. V

Strapped 1993 ★★★ In order to free his pregnant girlfriend, a young man from a drug-ridden ghetto must provide the police with evidence that could get his best friend in trouble. C: Michael Biehn, Kia Joy Goodwin. D: Forest Whitaker. DRA [R] 102m. V

Strategic Air Command 1955 ★★★½ The least impressive of the Stewart/Mann collaborations, this glossy production follows pro baseball player Stewart as he is redrafted during the Cold War to help the SAC with its new long-range bombers. C: James Stewart, June Allyson, Frank Lovejoy, Barry Sullivan. D: Anthony Mann. DRA 114m. V

Stratton Story, The 1949 ★★★★ True story of White Sox pitcher Monty Stratton, who lost a leg in a hunting accident, but returned to the game. Inspirational and moving. Writer Morrow won an Oscar. The real Stratton was a technical advisor on the film. C: James Stewart, June Allyson, Frank Morgan, Agnes Moorehead, Bill Williams. D: Sam Wood. DRA 106m. V

Straw Dogs 1971 ★★★★½ A mild-mannered professor (Hoffman) in a backwater English village becomes feral when the locals rape his wife and threaten his home. Slow, steady buildup to the last reel's unremitting and disturbing violence. Pekinpah's darkest and most cynical dissection of violence. C: Dustin Hoffman, Susan George, Peter Vaughan, T.P. McKenna, Peter Arne, David Warner. D: Sam Peckinpah. ACT 116m. V

Strawberry and Chocolate 1993 Cuban ★★★★ Charming comedy/drama about an unlikely friendship, between a Cuban communist (Cruz) and a gay intellectual (Perrugoria). Appealing light tone. Oscar nominee for Best Foreign Film. C: Jorge Perrugoria, Vladimir Cruz. D: Tomas Gutierrez Alea, Juan Carlos Tabio. COM [R] 110m.

Strawberry Blonde, The 1941 ★★★★ Turn-of-the-century dentist (Cagney) muses about his infatuation with stunningly beautiful woman (Hayworth) after marrying bland but loving girl next door (de Havilland). Sentimental period drama brought to life by Cagney. C: James Cagney, Olivia De Havilland, Rita Hayworth, Alan Hale, Jack Carson, George Tobias. D: Raoul Walsh. DRA 100m. V

Strawberry Roan, The 1948 ★★★★ Remake of 1933 film stars Autry as a horse-lover defending his steed against vengeful Holt, who wants to see the animal turned into glue for injuring his son. Never has a man fought so valiantly for the love of a horse. Nice family picture. C: Gene Autry, Gloria Henry, Jack Holt, Dick Jones. D: John English. FAM/DRA 79m.

Stray Dog (Nora Inn) 1949 Japanese ★★★★★ In this imaginative, powerful transposition of film noir to post-WWII Japan, a detective (Mifune) tracks his stolen pistol and a murderer. A lesser-known milestone in Japanese cinema. C: Toshiro Mifune, Takashi Shimura, Keiko Awaji, Isao Kimura. D: Akira Kurosawa. DRA 122m. V

Strays 1992 ★★ A vicious population of cats destroys a young couple's dream home. C: Kathleen Quinlan, Claudia Christian. D: John McPherson. HOR [R] 83m. V

Streamers 1983 ★★★★½ Riveting story about paratroopers in barracks on eve of Vietnam War, and the tensions in their relationships that finally burst into ugly violence. Brilliantly acted, directed. Adapted by David Rabe, from his play. C: Matthew Modine, Michael Wright, Mitchell Lichtenstein, David Alan Grier, Guy Boyd, George Dzundza. D: Robert Altman. DRA [R] 118m.

Street Angel 1928 ★★★★½ A young woman (Gaynor) seeks refuge in a traveling circus, where she gets involved with a struggling artist (Farrell). Classic silent romance, visually stunning, with great performances from both Farrell and Gaynor (who won an Oscar for three 1927-28 performances: this,

Sunrise, and *Seventh Heaven*). C: Janet Gaynor, Charles Farrell. D: Frank Borzage. DRA 102m.

Street Asylum 1990 ★★½ A police officer seeks to save a group of anit-crime fighters whose bodies have been implanted with a deadly device. C: Wings Hauser, G. Gordon Liddy, Sy Richardson. D: Gregory Brown. HOR 94m.

Street Crimes 1992 ★★ Street lord incites rampant gang warfare, ruiing a cops efforts to convince gang kids to resolve their differnces in a boxing ring. C: Dennis Farina, Max Gail, Mike Worth. D: Stephen Smoke. ACT [R] 94m. V

Street Fighter 1994 ★★★ Julia's last screen performance, as power-mad General M. Bison, steals this mundane actioner inspired from the video game. C: Jean-Claude Van Damme, Raul Julia, Simon Callow, Wes Studi. D: Steven E. de Souza. ACT [PG-13] 101m. V

Street Fighter's Last Revenge, The 1979 ★★½ Martial arts fighter is hired to stop the underworld's plot to steal the formula for a synthetic heroin substitute developed by a pharmaceutical manufacturer. C: Sonny Chiba, Sue Shiomi. ACT [R] 80m.

Street Girls 1975 ★★ Desperate father penetrates the underworld of prostitution to track down runaway daughter. Sordid. C: Carol Case, Christine Souder. D: Michael Miller. ACT [R] 77m. V

Street Hunter 1990 ★ Former cop turned urban mercenary wages bloody war against drug dealers. Abundant, wretched excess. C: Steve James, Reb Brown. D: John A. Gallagher. ACT [R] 96m. V

Street Knight 1993 ★★½ Ex-cop uncovers evil group of killers while investigating a series of gang murders. Typically brutal, violent cop action thriller with few redeeming qualities. C: Jeff Speakman. D: Albert Magnoli. ACT [R] 90m. V

Street Music 1981 ★★★★ A young couple (Daily and Breeding) living in a rundown hotel help its elderly residents fight for their home and dignity in this well-observed, heartfelt drama. Shot on-location in San Francisco's appropriately seamy Tenderloin district. C: Elizabeth Daily, Larry Breeding, Ned Glass, Marjorie Eaton. D: Jenny Bowen. DRA [R] 88m. V

Street of Chance 1942 ★★★★½ Early film noir is edgy drama of amnesiac (Meredith) reconstructing his increasingly disturbing past. Based on Cornell Woolrich's novel *The Black Curtain*, this superbly expressive psychological drama sweeps the viewer along on a turbulent ride. C: Burgess Meredith, Claire Trevor, Sheldon Leonard, Frieda Inescort. D: Jack Hively. DRA 74m.

Street Scene 1931 ★★★★½ Brilliantly nuanced study of immigrant residents in a New York City tenement has Sidney desperate to escape. Fine social-issue tale from early Hollywood and Vidor, master of subtle human dramas. Elmer Rice adapted his own Pulitzer Prize-winning play; the Newman score is a classic. C: Sylvia Sidney, William Collier Jr., David Landau, Estelle Taylor, Beulah Bondi. D: King Vidor. DRA 80m. V

Street Smart 1987 ★★★½ A struggling magazine journalist (Reeve) fictionalizes an expose of NYC pimps/prostitutes, with deadly consequences. True story should have been a sizzling thriller, but it crawls instead of runs. Freeman's brilliant performance as a lowlife pimp makes it worth watching, though. C: Christopher Reeve, Kathy Baker, Morgan Freeman, Mimi Rogers. D: Jerry Schatzberg. DRA [R] 97m. V

Street Soldiers 1991 ★★½ When a bunch of punks and assorted young ruffians take over the streets, a band of martial artists determined to take them back. Gruesome, bloody, and violent. C: Jun Chong, Jeff Rector, David Homb, Johnathan Gorman. D: Lee Harry. ACT [R] 98m. V

Street with No Name 1948 ★★★★ Documentary-style thriller about undercover cop (Stevens) infiltrating ruthless mob headed by sadistic killer (Widmark). Taut, fact-based script and good cast led by Widmark's slimy, hammy performance overrides some plodding moments in this otherwise strong film noir gem. C: Mark Stevens, Richard Widmark, Lloyd Nolan, Barbara Lawrence, Ed Begley, Donald Buka. D: William Keighley. DRA 91m. V

Streetcar Named Desire, A 1951 ★★★★★ Superb transcription of Tennessee Williams play about ethereal spinster (Leigh) in battle to the finish with earthbound brother-in-law Brando. Overt sexuality of the original had to be toned down, but most of play's power comes through, thanks to brilliant performances by Brando and Leigh (Best Actress Oscar). Oscars also went to Malden and Hunter. Can be seen in restored version, with four extra minutes of suggestive material. C: Marlon Brando, Vivien Leigh, Kim Hunter, Karl Malden. D: Elia Kazan. DRA [PG] 122m. V

Streetcar Named Desire, A 1984 ★★★★ Effective remake of Tennessee Williams classic with Ann-Margret as faded southern belle, Blanche DuBois, on a collision course with brute brother-in-law Stanley Kowalski (Williams). Ann's acting is impressive and her physical attributes give extra dimension to role. C: Ann-Margret, Treat Williams, Beverly D'Angelo, Randy Quaid, Rafael Campos, Erica Yohn. D: John Erman. DRA 124m.

Streets 1990 ★★★ A crazed cop preys on runaways in sunny Southern California. A surprisingly good Applegate and realistic depiction of street life are undermined by cheapness and tired thriller plot. C: Christina Applegate, David Mendenhall, Ed Lottimer. D: Katt Shea Ruben. CRI [R] 86m. V

Streets of Fire 1984 ★★★½ After rock star (Lane) is kidnapped by ruthless bikers, her rebellious ex-boyfriend (Paré) is hired to bring her back alive. Dreamy visual style, along with energetically moody rock score, nearly compensates for script weaknesses in this deadpan takeoff on '50s teen flicks. C: Michael Pare, Diane Lane, Rick Moranis, Amy Madigan, Willem Dafoe, Rick Moranis, Lee Ving, Ed-Bagley Jr. D: Walter Hill. DRA [PG] 93m. v

Streets of Gold 1986 ★★★½ A Soviet emigree (Brandauer) who sacrificed a champion boxing career for religious freedom in America trains two Brooklyn pugs (Snipes and Pasdar) for the Olympics in upbeat drama with a *Rocky* feel. Brandauer brings much-needed weight to this film. C: Klaus Maria Brandauer, Adrian Pasdar, Wesley Snipes. D: Joe Roth. DRA [R] 94m. v

Streets of Laredo 1949 ★★★½ Holden and Bendix are outlaws who give up their gunfighting ways to become respectable Texas Rangers, and then must rope in former crony Carey. A solid remake of the 1936 *Texas Rangers*, this Western owes much to Holden's gritty presence. C: Macdonald Carey, William Holden, William Bendix, Mona Freeman. D: Leslie Fenton. WST 92m.

Streetwise 1985 ★★★★½ A stark and riveting documentary look at children who live—and work—on the streets of Seattle. Occasional moments of natural humor, but the underlying tone is one of dismay for the dim reality of life in America's cities. An outstanding film. D: Martin Bell. DOC 92m. v

Strictly Ballroom 1993 Australian ★★★★ Brash young Australian challenges the traditions of competitive ballroom dancing, and is challenged in turn by young woman who wants to partner him. Delightfully loony, energetic, and romantic. C: Paul Mercurio, Tara Morice, Bill Hunter, Barry Otto, Pat Thompson, Gia Carides, Peter Whitford. D: Baz Luhrmann. COM [PG] 94m. v

Strictly Business 1991 ★★★½ A savvy mailroom worker hitches his career hopes on an up-and-coming young executive who needs his hip expertise in catching a budding actress. Better than you'd expect, with engaging performances. C: Tommy Davidson, Joseph C. Phillips, Halle Berry. D: Kevin Hooks. COM [PG-13] 83m. v

Strictly Dishonorable 1931 ★★★★ Musical version of Preston Sturges' Broadway hit, remade in 1951, has Lukas as love-'em-and-leave-'em opera star who reforms for the love of Fox. Rapid-fire comic timing and some memorable characters make this a wonderful old-fashioned delight of a comedy. C: Paul Lukas, Sidney Fox, Lewis Stone. D: John M. Stahl. MUS 94m.

Strictly Dishonorable 1951 ★★★½ Real-life opera star Pinza courts Southern farmer Leigh in this juicy musical comedy, a pleasurable but inferior remake of the 1931 version. C: Ezio Pinza, Janet Leigh, Millard Mitchell, Gale Robbins. D: Melvin Frank, Norman Panama. MUS 86m.

Strike 1924 Russian ★★★★ Silent semi-documentary account of factory workers' revolt in 1912 Russia. Masterfully directed (Eisenstein's debut). C: Grigori Alexandrov, Maxim Strauch. D: Sergei Eisenstein. DRA 82m. v

Strike It Rich 1990 ★★ A junior exec (Lindsay) takes an expensive Monte Carlo honeymoon to get in good with his boss. Stars bet all on a limp script (from Graham Greene's novella *Loser Takes All*), and lose their shirts. C: Robert Lindsay, Molly Ringwald, John Gielgud. D: James Scott. COM [PG] 87m. v

Strike Me Pink 1936 ★★★ Broadway star Cantor as a demure tailor who becomes a brash amusement park manager to prove his mettle, tangling with the Mob in the process. Not one of Cantor's best efforts. Look out for the marvelous but out-of-place Merman. C: Eddie Cantor, Ethel Merman, Sally Eilers, Parkyakarkus, William Frawley, Brian Donlevy. D: Norman Taurog. MUS 100m.

Strike Up the Band 1940 ★★★½ Wholesome leaders of a teen swing band compete for a radio spot in this lively musical with vibrant tunes and nostalgic charm, a follow-up to the Rooney/Garland winner *Babes in Arms*. Highlighted by typically overwhelming camerawork from reigning musical king Berkeley. C: Mickey Rooney, Judy Garland, Paul Whiteman, June Preisser, William Tracy, Larry Nunn. D: Busby Berkeley. MUS 120m.

Striking Distance 1993 ★★ Pennsylvania river cop (Willis), haunted by his failure to apprehend the murderer who killed his father, is confronted by a series of similar murders. Overheated thriller, with exciting opening car chase. C: Bruce Willis, Sarah Jessica Parker, Dennis Farina, Robert Pastorelli. D: Rowdy Herrington. ACT [R] 102m. v

Stripes 1981 ★★★½ Immensely popular, familiar military comedy with Murray and buddy Ramis enlisting because they have nothing better to do and discovering life in fatigues isn't like the TV ads. Oates and Candy provide additional comic relief. C: Bill Murray, Harold Ramis, Warren Oates, P.J. Soles, Sean Young, John Candy, John Larroquette. D: Ivan Reitman. COM 105m. v

Stripped to Kill 1987 ★★★½ An undercover cop (Lenz) poses as a stripper to catch a killer obsessed with knocking off exotic dancers. Tawdry, exploitative premise is handled surprisingly well by B-movie master Corman. Sequel: *Stripped to Kill II*. C: Kay Lenz, Greg Evigan, Norman Fell, Pia Kamakahi. D: Katt Shea Ruben. ACT [R] 88m. v

Stripped to Kill II—Live Girls 1989 ★★ Sequel to effective stripper/slasher exploitation flick throws in an ESP plot twist but drowns in gore and sleaze. C: Maria Ford, Ed Lottimer, Karen Mayo Chandler, Birke Tan, Debra Lamb. D: Katt Shea Ruben. ACT [R] 83m. v

Stripper, The 1963 ★★★½ Stranded in her old home town, a stripper (Woodward) takes a good hard look at her life when a young man (Beymer) declares his love for her. The performances are much better than the script, which was based on a play by William Inge, *A Loss of Roses*. Woodward's part was originally written for Marilyn Monroe! C: Joanne Woodward, Richard Beymer, Claire Trevor, Carol Lynley. D: Frank J. Schaffner. DRA 95m. v

Stroke of Midnight 1990 ★★½ Cinderella-inspired story of high-powered designer (Lowe) on a search for new model, not realizing that his novice shoe designer (Grey) is the one he's looking for. Fairy tale pretensions are just that. C: Rob Lowe, Jennifer Grey, Andrea Ferreol. D: Tom Clegg. DRA [PG] 105m. v

Stroker Ace 1983 ★★ A woman-chasing race car driver (Reynolds) is sponsored by a fried-chicken company that emblazons his car with the motto "Fastest Chicken in the South." Weak down-home comedy, but may appeal to sentimental Burt and Loni fans. C: Burt Reynolds, Ned Beatty, Jim Nabors, Loni Anderson, Parker Stevenson. D: Hal Needham. COM [PG] 96m. v

Stromboli 1950 Italian ★★★½ An Italian fisherman's wife (Bergman) on a volcanic island yearns for a more exciting life. Slow-moving, early example of neo-realism is more notable for its behind-the scenes scandal of Ingrid leaving her husband (and American stardom) for the director than for anything on screen. Also available in an expanded director's cut (107m.). C: Ingrid Bergman, Mario Vitale, Renzo Cesana. D: Roberto Rossellini. DRA 81m. v

Strong Man, The 1926 ★★★★ WWI soldier (Langdon) arrives home after the war and searches for his romantic pen pal. Harry's best comedy, full of poignant touches. Capra's feature film debut. C: Harry Langdon, Priscilla Bonner, Gertrude Astor. D: Frank Capra. COM 78m. v

Stronger Than Fear 1950 *See* **Edge of Doom**

Strongest Man in the World, The 1975 ★★★½ The third of Disney's Medfield College comedies has Russell and his pals cooking up a mysterious formula that gives humans super strength. Battle is soon joined by rival cereal companies for possession of the secret. Children should enjoy this silly send-up of superhyped cereal claims. C: Kurt Russell, Joe Flynn, Eve Arden, Cesar Romero, Phil Silvers, Dick VanPatten, Harold Gould, James Gregory. D: Vincent McEveety. FAM/COM [G] 92m.

Stroszek 1977 German ★★★★ Three German outcasts emigrate to America in search of fame and riches, and wind up in Wisconsin. Wryly funny, sometimes tragic study of broken dreams. C: Bruno S., Eva Mattes, Clemens Scheitz. D: Werner Herzog. DRA 108m. v

Stuck On You! 1983 ★★½ The angel Gabriel is sent down to Earth to reconcile a handsome couple. Professor Irwin Corey uninspired here. Negligible story takes back seat to negligees. C: Irwin Corey, Virginia Penta, Mark Mikulski. D: Herz Samuel. COM [R] 88m.

Stud, The 1978 British ★★ A nightclub manager sleeps with his employer's wife, then works his way up the social, corporate and sexual ladder. Soft-core trash, acted with histrionics by Joan Collins from script by sister Jackie. C: Joan Collins, Oliver Tobias, Sue Lloyd, Mark Burns, Walter Gottell, Emma Jacobs. D: Quentin Masters. DRA [R] 95m.

Student Nurses, The 1970 ★★★ The first and best of the series of five *Nurse* movies, this one about the lives and loves of four student nurses in their last year of school. A low-budget Corman production, but better than most. C: Elaine Giftos, Karen Carlson, Brioni Farrell, Barbara Leigh. D: Stephanie Rothman. COM [R] 89m. v

Student Prince in Old Heidelberg, The 1927 ★★★★½ A prince (Navarro) meets a barmaid (Shearer) in this glittering, silent version of Sigmund Romberg's operetta. Lovely score, now background music, complements that delicious Lubitsch touch. Remade in 1954. C: Norma Shearer, Ramon Navarro, Jean Hersholt. D: Ernst Lubitsch. COM 105m. v

Student Prince, The 1954 ★★★ Fair adaptation of popular operetta about a prince (Purdom, whose singing is gloriously dubbed by Mario Lanza) who falls in love with a barmaid (Blyth) but gives her up to fulfill his royal duties. Also filmed in 1919 and 1927. C: Ann Blyth, Edmund Purdom, John Ericson, Louis Calhern, Edmund Gwenn. D: Richard Thorpe. MUS [G] 107m. v

Student Teachers, The 1973 ★★★ Comings and goings at a large high school, where '60s freedom has invaded the halls in the way of sex, drugs, and rock 'n' roll. Followed by a sequel. C: Susan Damante, Brooke Mills, Bob Harris, Brenda Sutton, Dick Miller. D: Jonathan Kaplan. COM [R] 79m. v

Study in Terror, A 1966 British ★★★★ Sherlock Holmes takes on Jack the Ripper in this clash of Victorian England's twoi biggest legends. Successful execution of an intriguing idea, though Doyle purists may not approve. C: John Neville, Donald Houston, Anthony Quayle, Judi Dench. D: James Hill. CRI 94m. v

Stunt Man, The 1980 ★★★★½ Terrific behind-the-scenes tale about escaped convict hiding out as stunt man on a movie location who begins to confuse moviemaking with reality. Dazzling performances and great stuntwork. O'Toole is wildly charismatic as bullying director. C: Peter O'Toole, Steve Railsback, Barbara Hershey, Chuck Bail, Allen Goorwitz, Adam Roarke, Alex Rocco, Sharon Farrell, Philip Bruns. D: Richard Rush. DRA [R] 129m. v

Subject Was Roses, The 1968 ★★★★½

Adaptation by Frank Gilroy of his Pulitzer Prize-winning play about a WWII vet (Sheen) who comes home to find his parents' marriage crumbling. A modern, richly observed tale of a family struggling to come to terms with profound changes. Albertson received an Oscar for his touching performance. C: Patricia Neal, Jack Albertson, Martin Sheen, Don Saxon, Elaine Williams, Grant Gordon. D: Ulu Grosbard. DRA [G] 107m.

Submarine Command 1951 ★★★½ Submarine captain Holden is guilt-ridden over causing two comrades' deaths at the close of WWII, and so he tries to atone in the Korean War. On-land psychological battle much more intriguing than lackluster undersea action. C: William Holden, Nancy Olson, William Bendix, Don Taylor. D: John Farrow. DRA 87m.

Submarine Seahawk 1959 ★★½ On the eve of a big naval engagement with the Japanese, an inexperienced young man is made captain of a vitally important submarine. Plenty of action. C: John Bentley, Brett Halsey, Wayne Heffley. D: Spencer G Bennet. DRA 83m.

Submarine X-1 1968 British ★★★½ Caan is incompetent captain of WWII miniature submarine trying to make up for past mistakes. Good work from Caan but film takes unoriginal approach, and action scenes are tedious. C: James Caan, Rupert Davies, David Summer, William Dysart, Norman Bowler. D: William Graham. DRA [G] 89m.

Submarine Zone *See* **Escape to Glory**

Submission 1980 ★★½ A pharmacist, out of romantic circulation for a while, rediscovers her sensuality when she hires a young clerk for her shop. Some fun and a lot of lust. C: Franco Nero, Lisa Gastoni. D: Salvatore Samperi. DRA [R] 110m. V

Subspecies 1991 ★★½ Transylvanian brothers duel for control over supernatural family talisman. Effectively atmospheric setting and frightening encounters can't compensate for murky script and hollow performances. C: Michael Watson, Laura Tate, Anders Hove, Michelle McBride, Irina Movila, Angus Scrimm. D: Ted Nicolaou. HOR [R] 90m. V

Subterraneans, The 1960 ★★★½ Slick look at the beatnik subculture, from the Jack Kerouac novel. Nothing like the gritty book, but entertaining in its own right. Great use of jazz greats like Gerry Mulligan, Carmen McRae and Art Pepper. C: Leslie Caron, George Peppard, Janice Rule, Jim Hutton. D: Ranald MacDougall. DRA 89m.

Suburban Commando 1991 ★★★½ Space alien (Hogan) moves in with neurotic suburban family, causing them nothing but havoc while he enjoys the good life. Deliberately dumb humor actually works in this star vehicle for professional wrestler Hulk Hogan. Kids will definitely enjoy the cartoonish nonsense. C: Hulk Hogan, Christopher Lloyd, Shelley Duvall, Larry Miller. D: Burt Kennedy. FAM/SFI [PG] 90m. V

Subway 1985 French ★★★½ A Parisian punk (Lambert) escapes the authorities and finds refuge deep in the city's metro system, where he encounters a weird subculture of people living there. Stylish thriller, with a great look and New Wave sound; people tend to either love this or hate it. C: Isabelle Adjani, Christopher Lambert, Richard Bohringer. D: Luc Besson. CRI [R] 103m. V

Subway in the Sky 1959 German ★★★½ Johnson is a military medic in post-WWII Berlin running from drug-trafficking charges, and Neff is the concerned nightclub performer who tries to help him. Well-done crime melodrama. C: Van Johnson, Hildegarde Neff, Katherine Kath, Cec Linder, Albert Lieven, Edward Judd. D: Muriel Box. CRI [R] 85m.

Success 1979 *See* **American Success Company, The**

Successful Calamity, A 1932 ★★★½ Rich father Arliss convinces family he's broke so spoiled-rotten kids will learn to pull their own weight. Fluffy but engaging comedy much indebted to Arliss's light comic touch. C: George Arliss, Mary Astor, Evalyn Knapp, Grant Mitchell, David Torrence, William Janney, Hardie Albright, Randolph Scott, Leon Waycoff. D: John G. Adolfi. COM 72m.

Such a Gorgeous Kid Like Me 1973 French ★★★½ Con artist (Lafont, who's delightful) dupes budding sociologist into springing her from prison, then suckers him. Truffaut's touch is too light, making this black comedy more innocuous than witty. C: Bernadette Lafont, Claude Brasseur, Charles Denner, Guy Marchand, Philippe Leotard. D: Francois Truffaut. COM [R] 98m.

Such Good Friends 1971 ★★★½ Acerbic look at NY society friendships uses Luckinbill's minor surgery as the catalyst for revelations which his wife (Cannon) takes badly. Good cast, witty script, but sometimes tasteless (like the seduction scene between Cannon and Coco). C: Dyan Cannon, James Coco, Jennifer O'Neill, Ken Howard, Nina Foch, Louise Lasser, Laurence Luckinbill, Burgess Meredith. D: Otto Preminger. COM [R] 100m.

Sucker, The 1966 French ★★★½ Crime comedy has dopey Bourvil unwittingly transporting drugs and heisted jewels from Naples to Bordeaux when a gangster (De Funes) lends him his Cadillac. Consistently amusing foreign co-production with hilarious performances from both leads. C: Bourvil, Louis de Funes. D: Gerard Oury. COM 101m.

Sudan 1945 ★★★½ Cult star Montez is Queen Khemmis masquerading as a peasant to find her father's killer and elude the nefarious Zucco. She'd aided by Hall and Devine. A romantic desert B-movie adventure. C: Maria Montez, Jon Hall, Turhan Bey, Andy Devine,

George Zucco, Robert Warwick. D: John Rawlins. DRA 76m.

Sudden Danger 1955 ★★★ Crime melodrama has Elliott investigating murder of businesswoman, with all clues pointing to her blind son (Drake). Intriguing drama keeps the pressure on. C: Bill Elliott, Tom Drake, Beverly Garland, Lucien Littlefield, Minerva Urecal, Lyle Talbot, Frank Jenks. D: Hubert Cornfield. CRI 85m.

Sudden Fear 1952 ★★★½ A playwright (Crawford) learns that her husband is planning to kill her, and devises a scheme to fend him off. Clever and nasty. If you like this, try *Deathtrap*. C: Joan Crawford, Jack Palance, Gloria Grahame, Bruce Bennett, Touch Connors, Virginia Huston. D: David Miller. CRI 110m.

Sudden Fury 1975 Canadian ★★★½ Hogan is sinister husband who takes revenge on unsupportive wife by leaving her for dead after a car crash. Hennessey comes to Rowan's aid in this suspenseful melodrama. C: Dominic Hogan, Gay Rowan, Dan Hennessy. D: Brian Damude. DRA [PG] 95m.

Sudden Impact 1983 ★★★½ Fourth "Dirty Harry" adventure finds Harry (Eastwood) tracking vengeance seeking woman (Locke), out to kill thugs who raped her and her sister. May make the day for Eastwood fans, but the pacing is sometimes slow and the violence gratuitous. C: Clint Eastwood, Sondra Locke, Pat Hingle, Bradford Dillman. D: Clint Eastwood. ACT [R] 117m. V

Sudden Terror 1970 British ★★★ Lester is a mischievous boy who witnesses an African leader's murder, but can't convince adults. Capable suspense-drama. (a.k.a. *Eyewitness*) C: Mark Lester, Lionel Jeffries, Susan George, Tony Bonner. D: John Hough. DRA 91m. V

Suddenly 1954 ★★★★ Sinatra stars in an offbeat role as a ruthless assassin who invades a small-town family's house on the route of a presidential motorcade. A fine thriller, withheld from distribution for several years after Kennedy assassination, at Sinatra's insistence. C: Frank Sinatra, Sterling Hayden, James Gleason, Nancy Gates. D: Lewis Allen. DRA 77m. V

Suddenly, It's Spring 1947 ★★★ Husband-and-wife lawyers (MacMurray and Goddard) plan to divorce but have second thoughts, causing some consternation to their prospective new mates. Pleasant low-key comedy. C: Paulette Goddard, Fred MacMurray, Macdonald Carey, Arleen Whelan, Lillian Fontaine. D: Mitchell Leisen. COM 87m.

Suddenly, Last Summer 1959 ★★★★ Gripping drama of fierce matriarch (Hepburn), her institutionalized niece (Taylor), and the neurosurgeon (Clift) trying to help his patient remember the circumstances behind her cousin's death. Based on the Tennessee Williams play. C: Elizabeth Taylor, Katharine Hepburn, Montgomery Clift, Mercedes McCambridge, Albert Dekker. D: Joseph L. Mankiewicz. DRA 114m. V

Suddenly, Last Summer 1992 ★★★½ Second filming of Tennessee Williams' overheated southern gothic tale, dealing with lobotomies, cannibalism, and other would-be scandalous matters. Towering performances by Smith, Richardson make it palatable; Lowe's no Montgomery Clift, though. C: Maggie Smith, Natasha Richardson, Rob Lowe. D: Richard Eyre. DRA 95m. TVM

Sudie and Simpson 1990 ★★★★ Friendship between a young white girl and an older African-American man accused of child molestation in the rural South during WWII. Strong emotional pull. Based on Sara Flanigan Carter's novel. C: Louis Gossett Jr., Sara Gilbert. D: Joan Tewkesbury. DRA 95m. TVM V

Suds 1920 ★★★½ One of Pickford's first adult roles, as a laundrywoman in love with a customer who inexplicably disappears. Silent drama's plenty soapy itself, but charming. C: Mary Pickford, Albert Austin. D: John Dillon. DRA 67m.

Suez 1938 ★★★★ Glossy, epic "biography" of French inventor Ferdinand de Lesseps (Power), whose dream it was to build the canal. Young and Annabella are his romantic dilemma. Beautifully produced with sweeping action. C: Tyrone Power, Loretta Young, Annabella, Henry Stephenson, Maurice Moscovich, Joseph Schildkraut, Sidney Blackmer, J.Edward Bromberg, Sig Ruman, Nigel Bruce, Miles Mander, George Zucco, Leon Ames. D: Allan Dwan. DRA 104m.

Sugar Cane Alley 1984 French ★★★★ On the Caribbean isle of Martinique in the '30s, a young boy, orphaned at 11, joins his grandmother at work on a sugar plantation. A moving and highly memorable film. (a.k.a. *Rue Cases Ngres*) C: Darling Legitimus, Garry Cadenat. D: Euzhan Palcy. DRA [PG] 107m. V

Sugar Hill 1994 ★★★ Snipes plays one of two Harlem drug-dealing brothers, intent on finding other means of support. Well-intentioned look at drug culture makes an only adequate vehicle for the riveting Snipes. C: Wesley Snipes, Michael Wright, Clarence Williams III, Leslie Uggams, Theresa Randle. D: Leon Ichaso. DRA [R] 123m. V

Sugarbaby 1987 German ★★★½ In Munich, an overweight mortician decides to seduce a handsome young subway worker. Some nice moments, from the creators of *Bagdad Cafe* and *Rosalie Goes Shopping*. (a.k.a. *Zuckerbaby*) C: Marianne Sagebrecht, Eisi Gulp. D: Percy Adlon. DRA 86m. V

Sugarland Express, The 1974 ★★★★½ A couple on the lam drive to Sugarland, Texas to find their son, and become the subject of a media circus. Exhilirating comedy/drama was the director's first full-fledged theatrical film. Hawn's sensational as the somewhat dim-witted, but strong-willed mother. C: Goldie Hawn, Michael Sacks, William Atherton, Ben Johnson. D: Steven Spielberg. COM [PG] 109m. V

Suicide Club, The 1988 ★★½ Bored rich kids' favorite pasttime is seeing how close they can come to killing themselves. Hemmingway, equally bored and rich, is the new kid in the clique. Cold thriller focuses on decadence. C: Mariel Hemingway, Robert Joy, Madeleine Potter, Lenny Henry. D: James Bruce. CRI [R] 90m. V

Suicide Squadron 1941 *See* **Dangerous Moonlight**

Sullivans, The 1944 ★★★★ Poignant, skillfully played true story of the Sullivan family, who lost five courageous sons in WWII. Downbeat film but wonderfully done. C: Anne Baxter, Thomas Mitchell, Selena Royle, Ward Bond, Bobby Driscoll, Addison Richards. D: Lloyd Bacon. DRA 111m.

Sullivan's Travels 1941 ★★★★★ Successful comedy director (McCrea) wants his next film to be a Depression drama, so he pretends to be penniless hobo. As he and his partner (Lake) discover, the plight of the homeless is no laughing matter. Or is it? Sturges' perceptive script is a drama and satire and more pertinent today than ever. C: Joel McCrea, Veronica Lake, Robert Warwick, William Demarest, Eric Blore, Robert Greig, Jimmy Conlin, Al Bridge, Franklin Pangborn, Porter Hall. D: Preston Sturges. COM 91m. V

Summer 1986 French ★★★★½ Difficult young woman (Riviere) abandoned by her friends is forced to take summer holiday alone. A polished, exquisitly focused gem typical of Rohmer's films, this is one of the best. (a.k.a. *Le Rayon Vert* and *The Green Ray*) C: Marie Riviere, Lisa Heredia, Vincent Gauthier, Beatrice Romand. D: Eric Rohmer. DRA [R] 98m. V

Summer and Smoke 1961 ★★★½ The repressed sexual yearnings of a single woman (Page) burst forth when a handsome doctor (Harvey) moves into small Southern town. Somewhat melodramatic, stage-bound adaptation of Tennessee Williams' play; the cast plays it to the hilt. C: Geraldine Page, Laurence Harvey, Una Merkel, John McIntire, Pamela Tiffin, Rita Moreno, Thomas Gomez, Earl Holliman, Casey Adams, Lee Patrick. D: Peter Glenville. DRA 118m. V

Summer Fantasy 1984 ★★½ Teenager hits California beach, intent on becoming the first female lifeguard on the sandy turf where aging hunk (Shackelford) reigns supreme. Sort of a feminist *Baywatch*. Typical bikini-clad doings. C: Ted Shackelford, Julianne Phillips, Michael Gross, Dorothy Lyman. D: Noel Nosseck. DRA 100m. TVM V

Summer Heat 1987 ★★★ Ignored by her farmer husband (Edwards), a lonely and bored wife (Singer) sets her gaze on a drifter (Abbott) and quickly finds herself involved in a heated affair. Predictable, but with some steam. C: Lori Singer, Anthony Edwards, Bruce Abbott, Kathy Bates. D: Michie Gleason. DRA [R] 80m. V

Summer Holiday 1948 ★★★★ Charming musical version of the 1935 film, *Ah Wilderness!*, with an appealing Rooney playing a young man coming of age in a small American town at the turn of the century (he played the younger brother in 1935). Colorful, funny, and poignant. C: Mickey Rooney, Walter Huston, Frank Morgan, Agnes Moorehead, Butch Jenkins, Selena Royle, Marilyn Maxwell, Gloria DeHaven, Anne Francis. D: Rouben Mamoulian. MUS 92m. V

Summer Holiday 1963 British ★★★ Yates' directorial debut stars several British pop stars from the early '60s, meeting on a bus and traveling through Europe. Low-key, pleasant amusement, featuring some good numbers and some great scenery. C: Cliff Richard, Lauri Peters, David Kossoff, Ron Moody, The Shadows, Melvyn Hayes, Una Stubbs, Teddy Green, Jeremy Bulloch. D: Peter Yates. MUS 107m.

Summer House, The 1993 British ★★★★ England 1959: Headey is about to marry the shmoe next door when mysterious Moreau comes to rescue her. Moreau and Plowright have delightful scene-stealing duels, with the audience winning. Slender premise results in a charming character comedy. C: Jeanne Moreau, Joan Plowright, Julie Walters, Lena Headey, David Threlfall, Maggie Steed, John Wood. D: Waris Hussein. COM 82m.

Summer Interlude 1950 Swedish ★★★½ A ballerina obsesses about the time she fell in love with a young innocent—who died tragically—while her present lover tries to help her. Interesting drama shows some early flexing of the Bergman muscles. (a.k.a. *Illicit Interlude* and *Summerplay*) C: Maj-Britt Nilson, Alf Kjellin. D: Ingmar Bergman. DRA 95m. V

Summer Job 1988 ★ College kids at a summer resort. Mindless sex comedy. C: Sherrie Rose, Fred Boudin, Dave Clouse. D: Paul Madden. COM [R] 92m. V

Summer Lovers 1982 ★★★ Take one man and two women. Add the hot summer and a Greek island. Voilá, a plot. Silly but good-looking production follows the ensuing ménage á trois. C: Peter Gallagher, Daryl Hannah, Valerie Quennessen, Barbara Rush. D: Randal Kleiser. DRA [R] 98m. V

Summer Magic 1963 ★★★½ Widowed woman (McGuire) brings her family to Maine, where they live rent free in home provided by Ives. Snippy rich cousin nearly ruins it all, but happiness inevitably prevails in this lightweight Disney comedy. Remake of *Mother Carey's Chickens*. C: Hayley Mills, Burl Ives, Dorothy McGuire, Deborah Walley, Eddie Hodges, Darren McGavin, Una Merkel. D: James Neilson. FAM/DRA [G] 100m. V

Summer Night, with Greek Profile, Almond Eyes and Scent of Basil 1987 Italian ★★½ Enraged by political terrorists who have no respect for the environment, a conservationist launches a counterterror campaign to teach them a lesson. Oddball comedy. C: Mariangela Melato, Michele Placido, Roberto Herlipzka, Massimo Wertmuller. D: Lina Wertmuller. COM 94m. V

Summer of '42 1971 ★★★★ Classic date movie of its time tells a wistful coming-of-age story set in rural America, during WWII. Teenage boy (Grimes) pursues a lonely war bride (O'Neill) while Michel Legrand's persistant theme swells in the background. Sequel: *Class of '44.* C: Jennifer O'Neill, Gary Grimes, Jerry Houser, Oliver Conant. D: Robert Mulligan. DRA [PG] 102m. V

Summer of My German Soldier 1978 ★★★★ A young Jewish woman living in Georgia during WWII meets an escaped German POW and the two find an unlikely romance. Sympathetic handling of an unusual relationship; Rolle won Emmy for supporting role as family housekeeper. C: Kristy McNichol, Bruce Davison, Esther Rolle, Michael Constantine. D: Michael Tuchner. DRA 100m. V

Summer of '64 1965 *See* **Girls on the Beach, The**

Summer Place, A 1959 ★★★½ A group of vacationers in a resort town experience adultery and teenage heartbreak. Sap flows freely in this dated, but highly entertaining tale of bittersweet love conquering all. Dee and Donahue were catapulted to stardom, and the theme song became a major pop hit. C: Richard Egan, Dorothy McGuire, Sandra Dee, Arthur Kennedy, Troy Donahue, Constance Ford. D: Delmer Daves. DRA 130m. V

Summer Rental 1985 ★★★ A harried air traffic controller (Candy) takes his family on a well-deserved vacation to Florida where they must put up with annoying visitors. Mainly a showcase for Candy's talents. C: John Candy, Karen Austin, Richard Crenna, Rip Torn. D: Carl Reiner. COM [PG] 87m. V

Summer School 1987 ★★★½ A gym teacher (Harmon) is forced to teach remedial English to delinquents during summer school, the joke being he's something of a delinquent himself and doesn't want to be there any more than the students do. Fast and light. C: Mark Harmon, Kirstie Alley, Robin Thomas, Dean Cameron. D: Carl Reiner. COM [PG-13] 98m. V

Summer School Teachers 1975 ★★★ Sequel to *Student Teachers* that follows the lives of three student teachers. It being summer, they can now wear short skirts and bathing suits. C: Candice Rialson, Pat Anderson, Rhonda Leigh-Hopkins, Dick Miller. D: Barbara Peeters. COM [R] 87m. V

Summer Solstice 1981 ★★★★ An aging artist (Fonda) enjoys his final years with his longtime wife (Loy). Bittersweet romance with fine performances by the two leads. One of Fonda's final appearances. C: Henry Fonda, Myrna Loy. D: Ralph Rosenblum. DRA 75m. TVM V

Summer Stock 1950 ★★★★ Agreeable "let's put on a show" musical with Gene, Gloria, and Phil putting it on in Judy's barn. Charming, but forgettable till Garland's sensational "Get Happy" finale. C: Judy Garland, Gene Kelly, Gloria De Haven, Eddie Bracken, Marjorie Main, Phil Silvers. D: Charles Walters. MUS 110m. V

Summer Storm 1944 ★★★★ Frustrated Russian farmer's wife (Darnell) engages in multiple affairs. Surprisingly effective adaptation of Chekhov short story, "The Shooting Party," is beautifully photographed and scored. C: George Sanders, Linda Darnell, Edward Everett Horton, Sig Ruman. D: Douglas Sirk. DRA 106m.

Summer Story, A 1988 British ★★★★ In the summer of 1902 a London lawyer (Wilby) vacations in the English countryside where he meets a farmer (Stubbs). Though class differences threaten the relationship, the two still fall in love. Quiet romance that develops with strength, featuring excellent lead performances. Based on John Galsworthy story "The Apple Tree." C: Imogen Stubbs, James Wilby, Ken Colley, Sophie Ward, Susannah York. D: Piers Haggard. DRA [PG-13] 97m. V

Summer Wishes, Winter Dreams 1973 ★★★★½ Poor title for an exceptional drama, about a middle-aged suburban matron (Woodward) dealing with aging, loss, childhood memories, and her inability to express emotion. Bergmanesque in its technique, and quite affecting. Features two marvelous performances from Woodward and Sidney. C: Joanne Woodward, Martin Balsam, Sylvia Sidney. D: Gilbert Gates. DRA [PG] 93m. V

Summer with Monika *See* **Monika**

Summerdog 1978 ★★★ After a vacationing family rescues a dog, the dog turns around and returns the favor—several times over! Fun and laughter for moms, dads, and all the kids. C: James Congdon, Elizabeth Eisenman. D: John Clayton. FAM/DRA [G] 88m. V

Summerplay 1950 *See* **Summer Interlude**

Summertime 1955 ★★★★½ Middle-aged midwestern spinster (Hepburn) on tour of Venice, discovers romance with married shopowner (Brazzi). Poignant, charming, enormously entertaining, due to Hepburn's subtle performance and glorious location photography. From Arthur Laurents' play *The Time of the Cuckoo.* C: Katharine Hepburn, Rossano Brazzi, Isa Miranda, Darren McGavin. D: David Lean. DRA 99m. V

Summertree 1971 ★★★ College student (Douglas) doesn't want to fight in the Vietnam War. Interesting, topical drama, with a fine cast, weakened by a muddy script. C: Michael Douglas, Jack Warden, Brenda Vaccaro, Barbara Bel Geddes. D: Anthony Newley. DRA [PG] 88m.

Sun Also Rises, The 1957 ★★★★ Hemingway's classic tale of disillusioned expatriates in Europe between the two world wars. Power and Gardner star as the two star-crossed lovers, but Flynn steals the show with his memorable portrayal of a drunkard with a death wish. Riveting. C: Tyrone Power, Ava Gardner, Mel Ferrer, Errol Flynn, Eddie Albert, Gregory Ratoff, Juliette Greco, Marcel Dalio, Henry Daniell, Bob Cunningham, Danik Patisson, Robert Evans. D: Henry King. DRA 129m.

Sun Comes Up, The 1949 ★★★★ Bitter war widow (MacDonald, in her last film) retreats from society, but is cheered by a boy with a dog named Lassie. Above-average vehicle for America's favorite collie. C: Jeanette MacDonald, Lloyd Nolan, Claude Jarman, Jr., Lewis Stone, Dwayne Hickman. D: Richard Thorpe. FAM/DRA 93m.

Sun Shines Bright, The 1953 ★★★★½ Very effective remake of *Judge Priest.* An honest southern judge (Winninger), up for reelection, must battle the persistent prejudices of his constituents. Charming, skillful slice-of-life drama was director Ford's personal favorite. C: Charles Winninger, Arleen Whelen, Slim Pickens, John Russell, Milburn Stone, Stepin Fetchit, Jane Darwell. D: John Ford. DRA 90m. V

Sun Valley Serenade 1941 ★★★★ Romantic complications arise when the manager (Payne) of a band leader (Miller) agrees to chaperon a pert Norwegian refugee (Henie). Great Miller songs, with Henie skating on black ice in famous finale. Slight, lighthearted musical. C: Sonja Henie, John Payne, Glenn Miller, Milton Berle, Lynn Bari, Joan Davis, Dorothy Dandridge, Nicholas Brothers. D: H.Bruce Humberstone. MUS 86m. V

Sunburn 1979 ★ It's the audience that gets burned watching this unfunny farce about an insurance detective (Grodin) paying Fawcett-Majors to pretend she's his wife on Mexican investigation. Attempt to make movie star of the then-Charlie's Angel failed. C: Farrah Fawcett-Majors, Charles Grodin, Art Carney, Joan Collins. D: Richard C. Sarafian. COM [PG] 94m. V

Sunday, Bloody Sunday 1971 British ★★★★★ Love triangle with a handsome, caddish young bisexual (Head) at its center and Jackson and Finch as the woman and man who both have the misfortune to love him. Strong adult drama, with crackerjack performances. Stylishly produced. C: Glenda Jackson, Peter Finch, Murray Head, Peggy Ashcroft. D: John Schlesinger. DRA [R] 110m. V

Sunday Dinner for a Soldier 1944 ★★★½ Impoverished family, living on a houseboat, scrimps and saves so they can entertain a soldier (Hodiak). Warm drama generates a real glow. C: Anne Baxter, John Hodiak, Charles Winninger, Anne Revere, Chill Wills, Bobby Driscoll. D: Lloyd Bacon. DRA 86m.

Sunday in New York 1963 ★★★½ An innocent young woman arrives in NY to find love. Routine sex farce from Norman Krasna's play makes a nice vehicle for fresh, charming Fonda. C: Jane Fonda, Cliff Robertson, Rod Taylor, Robert Culp. D: Peter Tewksbury. COM 105m.

Sunday in the Country, A 1984 French ★★★★½ On a day in 1910, an aging French impressionist painter is visited at his rural estate by members of his family. A gorgeous, compelling study of the nature of relationships. C: Louis Ducreux, Sabine Azema, Michel Aumont. D: Bertrand Tavernier. DRA [G] 94m. V

Sundays and Cybele 1962 French ★★★★★ The ravages of post-war France are dramatized with devastating force in tale of a traumatized soldier (Kruger) and orphan (Gozzi). Won Oscar for Best Foreign Film; a must-see. C: Hardy Kruger, Patricia Gozzi, Nicole Courcel. D: Serge Bourguignon. DRA 110m. V

Sundown 1941 ★★★ A young local woman (Tierney) helps the British to fend off Nazi influence in WWII Africa. Outlandish story gets fine production, with exciting battle scenes. Oscar-nominated for cinematography, sets and score. C: Gene Tierney, Bruce Cabot, George Sanders, Harry Carey, Dorothy Dandridge (early appearance). D: Henry Hathaway. ACT 90m. V

Sundown, The Vampire in Retreat 1991 ★★★ Unsuspecting family wanders into desert town and finds itself in the middle of war between feuding cowrustling vampires. Screwball blending of comedy and horror in Western setting nearly works, but is undone by muddled climax. C: David Carradine, Morgan Brittany, Bruce Campbell, Jim Metzler, Maxwell Caulfield, Deborah Foreman, M.Emmet Walsh, John Ireland, John Hancock, Dabbs Greer, Bert Remsen. D: Anthony Hickox. HOR [R] 104m.

Sundowners, The 1960 ★★★★½ Fine film of a nomadic family of sheep drovers struggling for a home of their own in '20s Australia. Warm, sensitive family drama, beautifully acted. C: Deborah Kerr, Robert Mitchum, Peter Ustinov, Glynis Johns, Dina Merrill, Michael Anderson Jr. D: Fred Zinnemann. FAM/DRA 133m. V

Sunflower 1970 Italian ★★★½ Loren searches throughout Russia for her missing husband (Mastronianni), who disappeared there during WWII, fifteen years earlier. Plot stretches credibility at times, but drama prevails thanks to Loren's performance. (a.k.a. *Il Girasole*) C: Sophia Loren, Marcello Mastroianni, Ludmilla Savelyeva, Anna Carena. D: Vittorio De Sica. DRA [G] 101m.

Sunny 1930 ★★★½ A circus performer (Miller) falls for a rich young man—will love conquer all? Creaky oldie retains interest as a record of the Broadway star (recreating one of her hits); the charming Jerome Kern score helps, too. C: Marilyn Miller, Lawrence Gray, Joe Donahue, Mackenzie Ward, O.P. Heggie. D: William A. Seiter. MUS 81m.

Sunny Side Up 1929 ★★★★ Run-of-the-mill plot about a poor young woman (Gaynor) in love with a wealthy man (Farrell) is the only drawback of this nifty early sound musical. Charming performances, good songs by DeSylva-Brown-Henderson. C: Janet Gaynor, Charles Farrell, Jackie Cooper. D: David Butler. MUS 115m.

Sunrise 1927 ★★★★★ Remarkable silent tragedy focuses on a poor farmer (O'Brien) who plots to kill his wife (Gaynor). Poignant, magnificently photographed. Gaynor's heartbreaking portrayal helped win her Oscar for this and two other films (*Seventh Heaven, Street Angel*). C: Janet Gaynor, George O'Brien. D: F.W. Murnau. DRA 110m.

Sunrise at Campobello 1960 ★★★★ Bellamy gives tour-de-force performance as Franklin Delano Roosevelt in film version of popular Tony Award-winning Broadway play that chronicled Roosevelt's early life and onset of his crippling polio. Garson is superb as Eleanor Roosevelt. C: Ralph Bellamy, Greer Garson, Hume Cronyn, Jean Hagen. D: Vincent J. Donehue. DRA 144m. V

Sunset 1988 ★★ Real-life cowboy star Tom Mix (Willis) works with Wyatt Earp (Garner) to solve a Hollywood murder mystery. Promising premise is ruined by the heavy-handed, raucous script and direction. Garner's easygoing charm is the only formidable asset. C: Bruce Willis, James Garner, Malcolm McDowell. D: Blake Edwards. COM [R] 107m. V

Sunset Boulevard 1950 ★★★★★ Towering drama with comic overtones as silent screen has-been Norma Desmond (Swanson) tries for comeback with help of gigolo/screenwriter (Holden). Gloria's uncanny performance verges on self-parody, as does former silent director von Stroheim's. Full of classic scenes including "waxworks" bridge party, Norma's return to the studio, and the demented star's final descent down the stairs. Oscars for Screenplay, Score. Source for Andrew Lloyd Webber's 1994 musical. C: Gloria Swanson, William Holden, Erich von Stroheim, Nancy Olson. D: Billy Wilder. DRA 100m. V

Sunset Heat 1992 ★★½ Ex-drug dealer turned photographer (Pare) returns to his old L.A. stomping ground and runs afoul of his ex-friend (Hopper), a maniacal drug kingpin. Glossy sleaze, but with some excellent performances. C: Dennis Hopper, Michael Pare, Adam Ant, Little Richard. D: John Nicolella. DRA [R] 94m. TVM V

Sunshine Boys, The 1975 ★★★★½ Matthau and Burns are the title characters, feuding ex-vaudevillians who attempt to reunite for TV special. Funny vehicle for two pros won Burns Supporting Actor Oscar. Perhaps most effective film from a Neil Simon play. C: Walter Matthau, George Burns, Richard Benjamin, Lee Meredith. D: Herbert Ross. COM [PG] 102m. V

Sunstroke 1992 ★ Seymour goes in search for her missing daughter which leads to a fugitive-like lifestyle. Substandard excuse for emoting. C: Jane Seymour, Steve Railsback, Don Ameche. D: James Keach. DRA [R] 90m. TVM V

Super Brother 1990 ★★½ The benign leader of a group of oppressed people is arrested—and that's when serious trouble starts. Some nice work, particularly from the aging Strode. C: Woody Strode. DRA [R] 90m. V

Super Mario Bros. 1993 ★★ Movie version of popular video game follows game character plumbers (Hoskins, Leguizamo) plunged into dark underworld, led by snake-tongued bad guy (Hopper). Confusing, ultimately boring film is long on stunning visuals, but desperately in need of a plot. C: Bob Hoskins, Dennis Hopper, Samantha Mathis, Richard Edson, Fiona Shaw. D: Rocky Morton, Annabel Jankel. FAM/ACT [PG] 104m. V

Super Seal 1977 ★★★½ When a seal pup is injured, a little girl finds it and brings it home for "adoption," a deed which has numerous ramifications in her household. Pleasant little family number made better with a few old faces. C: Foster Brooks, Sterling Holloway, Sarah Brown. FAM/DRA 95m. V

Super, The 1991 ★★★½ New York slumlord (Pesci) is every tenant's nightmare, who gets his comeuppance when he's sentenced to live in one of his own decrepit buildings. Pesci's great.. C: Joe Pesci, Madolyn Smith-Osborne, Ruben Blades, Stacey Travis. D: Rod Daniel. COM [R] 86m. V

Supercarrier 1988 ★★ When a Soviet jet invades U.S. airspace, a number of American top guns are charged with escorting it out. Typical TV fare—no more, no less. C: Robert Hooks, Richard Jaeckel, Paul Gleason. D: William Graham. ACT 90m. TVM V

Superchick 1973 ★★ By day she's just another flight attendant. By night she's a sexy black belt in karate who's always searching for excitement—of all kinds. C: Joyce Jillson, Louis Quinn, Thomas Reardon, John Carradine. D: Ed Forsyth. ACT [R] 94m. V

Superdad 1973 ★★ Crane plays every child's nightmare, a father who wants to prove to daughter Cody he's hip to younger generation. Entering into competitions with future son-in-law (Russell), Crane fails at every turn. So does this miserable comedy. C: Bob Crane, Kurt Russell, Barbara Rush, Joe Flynn. D: Vincent McEveety. FAM/COM [G] 94m. V

Superfly 1972 ★★★½ New York drug lord wants to score one more big deal before calling it quits. Influential, ultraviolent black exploitation film keeps the blood pumping thanks to charismatic performance by O'Neal and superb score by Curtis Mayfield. C: Ron O'Neal, Carl Lee, Sheila Frazier, Julius W. Harris, Charles McGregor. D: Gordon Parks Jr. ACT [R] 93m. V

Superfly T.N.T. 1973 ★ Ex-pusher expatriate Superfly (O'Neal) becomes involved with the struggles of an African politician (Browne). O'Neal directed this bomb of a sequel which has none of the energy or grit of the 1st *Superfly*. Followed by *The Return of Superfly*. C: Ron O'Neal, Roscoe Lee Browne, Sheila Frazier, Robert Guillaume, Jacques Sernas, William Berger, Roy Bosier. D: Ron O'Neal. ACT [R] 87m. V

Supergirl 1984 British ★★½ Attempt to continue the Superman franchise falls short with dull adventure about Man of Steel's cousin. Slater is good-looking but one-dimensional. Dunaway is a campy delight as a witch with a magic wand that resembles a dead chicken. C: Faye Dunaway, Helen Slater, Peter O'Toole, Brenda Vaccaro. D: Jeannot Szwarc. SFI [PG] 105m. V

Superman and the Mole Men 1958 ★★★½ TV's first Superman (Reeves) takes on pint-sized "Mole Men" up from the depths of the Earth. This was the premiere episode of the '50s TV series. Great acting in dated production. C: George Reeves, Phyllis Coates, Jeff Corey, Walter Reed, J.Farrell MacDonald. D: Lee Sholem. SFI 59m. V

Superman—The Movie 1978 ★★★★½ Intelligent, spectacular treatment of Superman legend traces the Man of Steel's origins from his exile from Krypton to his early life with Ma and Pa Kent, and finally on to Metropolis where he fights a neverending battle for truth, justice, etc., while masquerading as a mild-mannered reporter. Lavish effects, excellent all-star cast, and perfect seriocomic tone make this production soar. C: Christopher Reeve, Margot Kidder, Marlon Brando, Gene Hackman, Ned Beatty, Jackie Cooper, Marc McClure, Glenn Ford, Valerie Perrine, Phyllis Thaxter, Jeff East, Trevor Howard, Susannah York. D: Richard Donner. ACT [PG] 143m. V

Superman 2 1980 ★★★★ Outstanding follow-up to first big-budget treatment of Superman story, using plot thread from original involving three evil villains from Superman's home planet out to destroy the Man of Steel and take over Earth. Captures the excitement, action, and most of the endearing charm of the original. C: Christopher Reeve, Margot Kidder, Gene Hackman, Ned Beatty, Jackie Cooper, Clifton James, Terence Stamp. D: Richard Lester. ACT [PG] 127m. V

Superman 3 1983 ★★★ Series slips the third time out when dastardly executive (Vaughn) persuades computer whiz (Pryor) to help bring down the Man of Steel. Inappropriate humor cheapens the story, although Reeve remains in good form, especially in scenes where Superman confronts his evil twin. C: Christopher Reeve, Richard Pryor, Annette O'Toole, Jackie Cooper, Robert Vaughn, Margot Kidder. D: Richard Lester. ACT [PG] 125m. V

Superman 4: The Quest for Peace 1987 ★★★ Cheap look and overly cartoonish performances nearly cripple this fourth Superman adventure. However, interesting antinuclear story, along with Superman's battles with Nuclear Man and Reeve's sincere portrayal help restore some dignity. C: Christopher Reeve, Gene Hackman, Jackie Cooper, Marc McClure, Mariel Hemingway, Margot Kidder. D: Sidney J. Furie. ACT [PG] 90m. V

Superstar: The Life and Times of Andy Warhol 1991 ★★★★ A compelling documentary detailing the artist's existence in virtually every area: his work, his ideas, and his influence. Some really nifty moments and a treasure for pop art freaks. C: Tom Wolfe, Sylvia Miles, David Hockney, Taylor Mead, Dennis Hopper. D: Chuck Workman. DOC 87m.

Superstorms ★★★★ An exploration into the wonders of weather at its very worst. Hurricanes, cyclones, tornadoes, and other natural phenomena are studied and watched from all angles. Truly fascinating and naturally astounding. DOC

Support Your Local Gunfighter 1971 ★★★★ Con artist (Garner) attempts to swindle a small mining town by passing off his dopey sidekick (Elam) as a notorious gunslinger. As in earlier *Support Your Local Sheriff*, Garner and rest of cast shine in well-scripted, satirically funny send-up of classic Westerns. C: James Garner, Suzanne Pleshette, Jack Elam, Harry Morgan, John Dehner, Joan Blondell, Dub Taylor, Ellen Corby, Henry Jones, Marie Windsor, Dick Curtis, Chuck Connors, Grady Sutton. D: Burt Kennedy. COM [G] 92m. V

Support Your Local Sheriff 1969 ★★★★½ Quick-witted drifter (Garner) winds up sheriff of mining town and uses his brains rather than his guns to keep the peace. Hilarious Western spoof respects the genre while sending it up, thanks to clever script and excellent performances by Garner and a bevy of great character actors. C: James Garner, Joan Hackett, Walter Brennan, Harry Morgan, Jack Elam, Bruce Dern, Henry Jones, Gene Evans. D: Burt Kennedy. COM [G] 92m. V

Suppose They Gave a War and Nobody Came? 1970 ★★½ Tensions mount between a small southern town and the nearby military base. Oddball comedy/drama keeps shifting gears, doesn't get too far. (a.k.a. *War Games*) C: Tony Curtis, Ernest Borgnine, Brian Keith, Don Ameche, Suzanne Pleshette. D: Hy Averback. COM [PG] 113m. V

Sure Thing, The 1985 ★★★★ College student (Cusack) and antagonistic coed (Zuniga) share cross-country trip to meet their respective mates, but complications develop. Predictable but engaging road movie with intelligent script (loosely based on *It Happened One Night*) and charming actors. C: John Cusack, Daphne Zuniga, Anthony Edwards, Tim Robins, Viveca Lindfors, Nicollette Sheridan. D: Rob Reiner. COM [PG-13] 94m. V

Surf Nazis Must Die 1987 ★ In post-earthquake-devasted L.A., a gang of sadistic surfers headed by "Adolf" and "Eva" turn the beach into a bloodbath until challenged by "good" vigilantes. From the folks who brought you *Toxic Avenger*, another entry in the "so bad it's good" category. C: Barry Brenner, Gail Neely. D: Peter George. COM [R] 83m. V

Surf Ninjas 1993 ★★ Two surfer kids (Reyes and Cowan) inherit a South Seas island, and then must fight off evil martial-arts guys led by Nielsen. So bad it's good. C: Leslie Nielsen, John Karlen, Nicolas Cowan. D: Neal Israel. COM [PG] 87m. V

Surfacing 1984 ★ Urban teen lost in the North Woods looks for her missing father. Movie barely makes sense; instead, relies heavily on liberal doses of sex and violence. C: Joseph Bottoms, Kathleen Beller, R.H. Thompson. D: Claude Jutra. DRA 90m. V

Surprise Package 1960 British ★★★ Suave mob boss, on the lam in Greece, wants to buy crown jewels from exiled king (Coward). Synthetic yet amusing comedy gives high-carat cast plenty of chances to shine, if not sparkle. C: Yul Brynner, Mitzi Gaynor, Noel Coward, Barry Foster. D: Stanley Donen. COM 100m. V

Surrender 1987 ★★ Two misfits (Field, Caine) discover each other while bound and gagged during a robbery. Plot of this unfunny farce goes downhill from there. Field's talents are better served in drama. C: Sally Field, Michael Caine, Steve Guttenberg, Peter Boyle, Julie Kavner. D: Jerry Belson. COM [PG] 95m. V

Surrogate, The 1984 Canadian ★★★½ The woes of a husband (Hindle) to his hypersexy wife (Tweed) bring them to radical therapist (Laure), and then all sorts of twisty, kinky mayhem ensues. Erotic thriller with some bite and enough energy and wit to sustain interest. C: Art Hindle, Carole Laure, Shannon Tweed, Michael Ironside, Jim Bailey. D: Don Carmody. CRI [R] 100m. V

Surviving the Game 1994 ★★★½ Yet another reworking of *The Most Dangerous Game*, with hunters tracking Ice-T in the Pacific Northwest, only to have their quarry turn on them. Lifted by effective direction. C: Ice T., Rutger Hauer, F. Murray Abraham, Charles S. Dutton, Gary Busey, John C. McGinley, Jeff Corey. D: Ernest Dickerson. ACT 96m.

Survivors, The 1983 ★★ After being fired by his boss' parrot, Williams meets Matthau in an unemployment line, finds himself on the Mob's hit list, and then joins a survivalist group in New Hampshire to protect himself. Star pairing doesn't really work, but is interesting. C: Walter Matthau, Robin Williams, Jerry Reed, James Wainwright, Kristen Vigard, Anne Pitoniak, John Goodman. D: Michael Ritchie. COM [R] 102m.

Susan and God 1940 ★★★½ A selfish socialite (Crawford) takes up religion and alienates her family and friends, until she learns how to practice what she preaches. Strong performances mark the drama; from Rachel Crothers' play. C: Joan Crawford, Fredric March, Ruth Hussey, John Carroll, Rita Hayworth, Nigel Bruce, Bruce Cabot, Rose Hobart, Rita Quigley, Marjorie Main, Gloria De Haven. D: George Cukor. DRA 115m. V

Susan Lenox: Her Fall and Rise 1931 ★★★½ When her bullying father tries to force her into an unwanted marriage, farmgirl Garbo runs away to big city and into Gable's arms. Melodrama inspired by two very hot stars who play well together. C: Greta Garbo, Clark Gable, Jean Eric Hersholt, John Miljan, Alan Hale. D: Robert Z. Leonard. DRA 77m. V

Susan Slade 1961 ★★★½ McGuire shines in the role of a woman pretending to be the mother of her illegitimate grandchild. Effective suds. C: Dorothy McGuire, Troy Donahue, Connie Stevens, Lloyd Nolan. D: Delmer Daves. DRA 116m.

Susan Slept Here 1954 ★★★½ Harmless comedy about a screenwriter (Powell) taking interest in spunky young woman (Reynolds). Funny narration by an animated Oscar opens film. C: Dick Powell, Debbie Reynolds, Anne Francis. D: Frank Tashlin. COM 98m. V

Susannah of the Mounties 1939 ★★★½ After her parents are killed in Indian attack, perennial orphan Temple is adopted by Canadian mountie (Scott), then sets down to make peace between whites and local Native Americans. Conventional Temple story develops with no surprises but fans will enjoy. C: Shirley Temple, Randolph Scott, Margaret Lockwood, Victor Jory. D: William A. Seiter. FAM/DRA 79m. V

Suspect 1987 ★★★★ Public defender (Cher), representing a deaf homeless veteran (Neeson) in murder case, finds an unlikely ally in flirtatious juror Quaid. Though the plot occasionally bends logic, some neat suspense tricks and Cher's credible performance make this very watchable. C: Cher, Dennis Quaid, Liam Neeson, John Mahoney, Philip Bosco. D: Peter Yates. CRI [R] 101m. V

Suspicion 1941 ★★★★ After marrying a dashing but enigmatic man (Grant), a young woman (Fontaine) starts to believe that he may well be a murderer. Some vintage Hitchcock along the way as he sets up a truly dire situation. Fontaine won her Oscar for this performance, and all the talent is superb. Based on the novel *Before the Fact*, by Francis Iles (a pseudonym for Anthony Berkeley Cox). C: Cary Grant, Joan Fontaine, Cedric Hardwicke, Nigel Bruce. D: Alfred Hitchcock. CRI 99m. V

Suspicion 1987 British ★★★ Remake of Hitchcock's 1941 thriller sends Curtin on a wild ride, convinced her husband (Andrews) is out to kill her. Ineffectual thriller suffers from a miscast Curtin, although the rest of the cast does well. C: Anthony Andrews, Jane Curtin, Jonathan Lynn, Michael Hordern. D: Andrew Greive. CRI 97m. TVM V

Suspiria 1977 Italian ★★★★ American ballet dancer enrolls in European dance school, unaware it's really a witch's coven. Italian director Argento earned his cult status with this effectively eerie horror romp filled with bravura camera flourishes and splashy gore. Harper captures the right balance of innocence and terror. C: Jessica Harper, Stefania Casini, Joan Bennett, Alida Valli, Flavio Bucci, Udo Kier. D: Dario Argento. HOR [R] 92m. V

Suture 1994 ★★★★ Fascinating, somewhat abstract thriller about a man stalking his supposedly identical twin; the major difference between them is that one is black, the other white. Hypnotic, difficult, but ingenious film. CRI

Suzy 1936 ★★★½ Dancer (Harlow) gets involved in intrigue in Europe during WWI and falls for flying ace (Grant) in this bit of fluff. Harlow (dubbed) and Grant both sing "Did I Remember." Dorothy Parker was one of the scriptwriters. C: Jean Harlow, Franchot Tone, Cary Grant, Lewis Stone, Benita Hume. D: George Fitzmaurice. DRA 93m. V

Svengali 1931 ★★★★ Vintage drama of a young singer (Marsh) molded by an obsessive teacher (Barrymore) into a star, via hypnosis. Fascinating, with a magnetic performance by Barrymore at the height of his powers. There have been numerous remakes and imitations. C: John Barrymore, Marian Marsh, Donald Crisp. D: Archie Mayo. DRA 82m. V

Svengali 1983 ★★★ Gifted singer (Foster) rises to the top due to her mentor's hypnosis. So-so rock music updating of the old story is dominated by O'Toole's exaggerated performance. C: Peter O'Toole, Jodie Foster, Elizabeth Ashley, Holly Hunter. D: Anthony Harvey. MUS 100m. TVM V

Swamp Thing 1981 ★★★½ Campy adaptation of comic book hero tells how scientist (Wise) accidently turns himself into a walking, talking hunk of slime, but still remains able to woo his girlfriend (Barbeau) while battling an evil rival (Jourdan). Entertaining mix of action and humor, with creepy makeup effects. C: Louis Jourdan, Adrienne Barbeau, Ray Wise, David Hess. D: Wes Craven. ACT 91m. V

Swamp Water 1941 ★★★½ A fugitive from justice (Brennan), hiding out in the Georgia swamplands, pursuades a man (Andrews) to help him clear his name. Renoir's first American film is fascinating and well-acted. Remade as *Lure of the Wilderness*, with Brennan repeating his role. C: Dana Andrews, Walter Brennan, Anne Baxter, Walter Huston, John Carradine. D: Jean Renoir. DRA 90m.

Swan Lake 1967 ★★★★ Two of ballet's finest, Nureyev (who choreographed) and Fonteyn, perform Tchaikovsky's classic tale of a prince in search of his princess. Dance fans will be delighted. C: Margot Fonteyn, Rudolf Nureyev. MUS 113m. V

Swan Princess, The 1994 ★★★★ Animated musical, suggested by *Swan Lake*, focuses on romance between Prince Derek and Princess Odette, who is transformed into a swan by the evil magician, Rothbart. Gorgeous animation and tuneful songs make this the best of recent Disney imitations. Voices of Jack Palance, Howard McGillin, Liz Callaway, John Cleese, Steven Wright, Sandy Duncan, Michelle Nicastro. D: Richard Rich. FAM/MUS [G] 90m. V

Swan, The 1956 ★★★½ In 1910 Hungary a princess (Kelly) finds herself caught between the affections of a prince (Guinness) and a commoner (Jourdan). Minor romantic comedy based on Molnar play. Kelly's last picture before she became a real-life princess. Earlier versions of story were made in 1925, and as *One Romantic Night* in 1930. C: Grace Kelly, Alec Guinness, Louis Jourdan, Agnes Moorehead. D: Charles Vidor. DRA 111m. V

Swanee River 1939 ★★★½ Ameche stars as songwriter Stephen Foster in mediocre drama that tends to sugarcoat his life. Nice Technicolor photography of Southern landscape and peppy musical numbers save the film. C: Don Ameche, Al Jolson, Andrea Leeds, Felix Bressart, Russell Hicks. D: Sidney Lanfield. MUS 84m.

Swann in Love 1984 French ★★★½ Exquisitely photographed adaptation of Proust's *Remembrance of Things Past* has an elegant Irons falling for a heartless courtesan (Muti) in 19th-century Paris. Resonant performance from Muti, though film itself rings hollow. Cinematography by Sven Nykvist. (a.k.a. *Un Amour de Swann*) C: Jeremy Irons, Ornella Muti, Alain Delon, Fanny Ardant. D: Volker Schlondorff. DRA [R] 110m. V

Swarm, The 1978 ★★ All-star cast (six Oscars among them) gets stung in this swollen disaster extravaganza of killer bees terrorizing Houston. Laughable special effects. Oscar-nominated for Best Costumes. C: Michael Caine, Richard Widmark, Henry Fonda, Olivia de Havilland, Patty Duke Astin, Lee Grant, Katharine Ross, Richard Chamberlain. D: Irwin Allen. ACT [PG] 116m. V

Swashbuckler 1976 ★★ Two pirates (Shaw,

Jones) try to rid Jamaica of its evil ruler. Scattered attempt to re-create old-style adventure films may leave you feeling Flynn-flammed. (a.k.a. *The Scarlet Buccaneer*) C: Robert Shaw, James Earl Jones, Peter Boyle, Genevieve Bujold, Beau Bridges. D: James Goldstone. ACT [PG] 101m. V

Swedenhielms 1935 Swedish ★★★★ A dedicated Swedish scientist (Ekman) strives for a Nobel Prize. Intelligent drama offers well-realized detailed portrait of tension between work and family, and features Bergman at age 20. C: Gosta Ekman, Hakan Westergren, Ingrid Bergman, Kann Swanstrom. D: Gustaf Molander. DRA 90m. V

Swedish Wedding Night 1965 Swedish ★★★ Strange melodrama featuring drunken revelations and intrigues at the wedding feast of butcher Kulle and his young bride Schollin. C: Jarl Kulle, Lena Hansson, Christina Schollin, Edvin Adolphson. D: Ake Falck. DRA 95m.

Sweeney Todd, the Demon Barber of Fleet Street 1980 ★★★★★ Video version of Stephen Sondheim's brilliant Broadway musical/opera faithfully preserves disturbing story of the vengeful barber (Hearn) and loony pie shop owner (Lansbury) who join forces with gruesome results. Magnificent melodies, lyrics, performances. Highlights: "Pretty Women," "A Little Priest." Sweeney's story previously inspired a low-budget British horror movie, in 1939 (*The Demon Barber of Fleet Street*). C: Angela Lansbury, George Hearn. D: Harold Prince. MUS 150m. TVM V

Sweepstakes Winner 1939 ★★★ Formula comedy of waitress Wilson who wins a fortune, loses it, and then wins even bigger. Wilson is charming but the premise is strained. C: Marie Wilson, Johnie Davis, Allen Jenkins. D: William McGann. COM 59m.

Sweet Adeline 1935 ★★★½ Bubbly musical about flirtatious Dunne and her true love songwriter Woods, is set in her pop's Jersey beer hall. Great score by Jerome Kern and Oscar Hammerstein. C: Irene Dunne, Donald Woods, Hugh Herbert, Ned Sparks, Joseph Cawthorn, Louis Calhern, Winifred Shaw. D: Mervyn LeRoy. MUS 88m. V

Sweet and Sour 1964 French ★★★½ Funny, well-intentioned send-up of the art film cult, with a group of cineastes paying homage to their Gallic masters. Best appreciated by lovers of French New Wave cinema. C: Guy Bedos, Jean-Pierre Marielle, Sophie Daumier. D: Jacques Baratier. COM 93m.

Sweet Bird of Youth 1962 ★★★★½ Censored version of Tennessee Williams' play still bites thanks to magnificent Page (re-creating her Broadway performance) as the washed-up movie star involved with the hometown stud. Newman, Torn, and Sherwood also stand out repeating their stage roles. C: Paul Newman, Geraldine Page, Shirley Knight, Ed Begley, Rip Torn, Mildred Dunnock, Madeleine Sherwood, Philip Abbott, Corey Allen. D: Richard Brooks. DRA 120m. V

Sweet Bird of Youth 1989 ★★★ Faded actress (Taylor) visits hometown of young stud (Harmon) who hopes she'll get him into movies and they descend into a haze of alcohol, drugs, and sex. Sincere but turgid TV version of Williams' classic. C: Elizabeth Taylor, Mark Harmon, Rip Torn, Valerie Perrine, Kevin Geer, Michael Wilding Jr. D: Nicolas Roeg. DRA [R] 95m. TVM V

Sweet Charity 1968 ★★★★½ Bittersweet, dynamic musical from Broadway hit with MacLaine well cast as hard-luck dance hall hostess trying for happiness with junior executive (McMartin). Fosse's hyperkinetic camerawork (in his film directorial debut) gets out of hand occasionally, but musical numbers ("Big Spender," "If They Could See Me Now," etc.) are exciting and story is emotionally involving. Based on Fellini's *Nights of Cabiria*. C: Shirley MacLaine, John McMartin, Ricardo Montalban, Sammy Davis Jr., Chita Rivera, Paula Kelly, Stubby Kaye, Ben Vereen. D: Bob Fosse. MUS [G] 148m. V

Sweet Country 1986 ★★½ An American couple gets caught up in political intrigue while living in Chile after the 1973 coup. Well-meaning drama struggles with a talky script. C: Jane Alexander, Franco Nero, Joanna Pettet, Irene Papas, Randy Quaid, Jean-Pierre Aumont. D: Michael Cacoyannis. DRA [R] 150m. V

Sweet Devil 1937 British ★★★ Silly comedy about business partners Howes and Kendall both wooing secretary Gillie. Pleasant and dumb. C: Bobby Howes, Jean Gillie, William Kendall. D: Rene Guissart. COM 79m.

Sweet Dreams 1985 ★★★★ Conventional telling of story of country singer Patsy Cline has power and heart, thanks to gritty, realistic performances by Lange and Harris as embattled couple. C: Jessica Lange, Ed Harris, Ann Wedgeworth, David Clennon. D: Karel Reisz. DRA [PG-13] 130m. V

Sweet 15 1990 ★★★★ The birthday celebration of a young Hispanic girl (Montana) falls under a cloud when family faces possible deportation of father. Intriguing issue drama, originally broadcast on public television, with solid performances and script. C: Karla Montana, Panchito Gomez, Susan Ruttan. D: Victoria Hochberg. FAM/DRA 120m. TVM V

Sweet Hearts Dance 1988 ★★★½ High school sweethearts (Sarandon and Johnson) find that their marriage has become stale in contrast to friends starting new relationships. Well acted, with an interesting cast of secondary characters in engaging subplots about friendships and commitments. C: Don Johnson, Susan Sarandon, Jeff Daniels, Elizabeth Perkins. D: Robert Greenwald. DRA [R] 101m. V

Sweet Kill 1970 *See* **Arousers, The**

Sweet Liberty 1986 ★★★ Chaos erupts in a small New England town when a crass Hollywood crew invades to film a novel by wholesome local professor (Alda), who struggles to maintain artistic integrity. Mildly humorous, the film never achieves the bittersweet insight it seeks. C: Alan Alda, Michael Caine, Michelle Pfeiffer, Bob Hoskins, Lise Hilboldt, Lillian Gish, Timothy Carhart. D: Alan Alda. COM [PG] 107m. V

Sweet Lorraine 1987 ★★★★ Sweet indeed is this story about the Lorraine, a classic Catskills resort in what might be its final season. Stapleton and Alvarado bring humanity and compassion to this understated and refreshingly cheerful drama. C: Maureen Stapleton, Trini Alvarado, Lee Richardson, John Bedford Lloyd, Giancarlo Esposito. D: Steve Gomer. DRA [PG-13] 91m. V

Sweet November 1968 ★★★★ Underrated comedy/drama with Dennis as a free spirit who takes up and discards a new boyfriend each month. Complications develop when November's man (Newley) insists on breaking the pattern. Sandy's a charmer. C: Sandy Dennis, Anthony Newley, Theodore Bikel. D: Robert Ellis Miller. COM 114m.

Sweet Perfection 1990 ★ Flimsy sex comedy about beauty contest, which features the hook: Who will be named "Perfect Woman'?" C: Stoney Jackson, Anthony Norman McKay, Liza Crusat, Titiana Tumbtzen. COM 90m. V

Sweet Rosie O'Grady 1943 ★★★½ Grable stars in this charming musical as an 1880s Brooklyn showgirl affecting high-society airs to lure British duke Gardiner. Ex-lover, reporter Young, is determined to pierce her facade. Previously made as *Love Is News* (1937), and subsequently as *That Wonderful Urge* (1948). C: Betty Grable, Robert Young, Adolphe Menjou, Reginald Gardiner, Virginia Grey, Phil Regan. D: Irving Cummings. MUS 74m.

Sweet Sea 1985 ★★★½ An animated tale for children on a large scale, as the forces of Good and Evil fight it out in an undersea battle. Call it a meaningful fantasy or an arresting allegory: Either way, it's something of value for young and old. FAM/ACT 30m. TVM V

Sweet Smell of Success 1957 ★★★★½ Hard-hitting exposé of gossip columnists and press agents stars Lancaster as merciless scribe whose sister is his only soft spot. Curtis gives a fine performance as desperate press agent cooperating with Lancaster, against his better judgment. Powerful, harsh drama. C: Burt Lancaster, Tony Curtis, Marty Milner, Sam Levene, Barbara Nichols. D: Alexander Mackendrick. DRA 97m. V

Sweet Sugar 1972 ★★½ Sexy chain gang women working on a sugar planation rebel against their cruel enslavers and take to the swamps. Typical "women in bondage" exploitation fare. C: Phyllis Elizabeth Davis, Ella Edwards, Pamela Collins. D: Michel Levesque. ACT [R] 90m. V

Sweet Sweetback's Baadasssss Song 1971 ★★★★ Violent black pimp uses all of his street-wise savvy to elude capture after he kills two cops for doing in a black militant. Visually exciting and controversial black exploitation film. C: Melvin Van Pebbles, Rhetta Hughes, Simon Chuckster, John Amos. D: Melvin Van Pebbles. DRA [R] 90m. V

Sweetheart of the Campus 1941 ★★★ Jazz band tries to save a financially strapped college. Sprightly, tune-filled nonsense; tapster Keeler's last starring role. C: Ruby Keeler, Ozzie Nelson, Harriet Hilliard. D: Edward Dmytryk. MUS 67m.

Sweethearts 1938 ★★★★ Backstage musical of husband-and-wife (MacDonald and Eddy) stars with little time for romance in hurly-burly of showbiz. Flavorful dance and music; winning leads. C: Jeanette MacDonald, Nelson Eddy, Frank Morgan, Ray Bolger. D: W.S. VanDyke. MUS 115m. V

Sweetie 1989 Australian ★★★½ Two sisters with personality disorders quarrel and bond during their struggle for independance from their parents. Disturbing character study. Uneven, but notable as the first film from the director of *The Piano.* C: Genevieve Lemon, Karen Colston. D: Jane Campion. DRA [R] 97m. V

Swept Away 1975 Italian ★★★★★ When her yacht sinks, an arrogant Milanese aristocrat is shipwrecked with her Communist Sicilian deckhand. In short time, the snobbish woman becomes completely dependent upon—and slavishly in love with—the firebrand. A fascinating, enthralling study of personal and political relationships. A gem from Wertmuller, with brilliant work by Giannini and Melato. (a.k.a. *Swept Away . . . by an Unusual Destiny in the Blue Seas of August*) C: Giancarlo Giannini, Mariangela Melato. D: Lina Wertmuller. DRA [R] 116m. V

Swept Away . . . by an Unusual Destiny in the Blue Seas of August 1975 *See* **Swept Away**

Swimmer, The 1968 ★★★★ Lancaster is an introspective suburbanite who "swims home" via his Connecticut neighbors' backyard pools; at each stop we learn something new about him. Unfailingly watchable and sharply evocative. Based on a John Cheever story. C: Burt Lancaster, Janet Landgard, Janice Rule, Tony Bickley, Marge Champion, Kim Hunter. D: Frank Perry. DRA [PG] 94m. V

Swimming to Cambodia 1987 ★★★★ Gray adapted his one-man show to the screen, a monologue outwardly about his trip to Thailand during the shooting of *The Killing Fields*, but really about the search for one's self. An acquired taste, but worth it. C: Spalding Gray. D: Jonathan Demme. COM 85m. V

Swindle, The 1955 *See* **Il Bidone**

Swindlers, The 1955 *See Il Bidone*

Swing High, Swing Low 1937 ★★★★ Red-hot jazz and Lombard battle low-down blues and the bottle for the soul of a trumpet player (MacMurray) in this solid comedy/drama with a top-flight cast. Previously made as *The Dance of Life* and subsequently as *When My Baby Smiles at Me*. C: Carole Lombard, Fred MacMurray, Charles Butterworth, Jean Dixon, Dorothy Lamour. D: Mitchell Leisen. DRA 95m. V

Swing It, Professor 1937 ★★★½ Funny premise has classical-minded music professor (Tomlin) discovering the delights of jazz through late-night excursions among the hepcats. C: Pinky Tomlin, Paula Stone. D: Marshall Neilan. MUS 62m.

Swing Kids 1993 ★★★ Rebellious youth in the Third Reich ignore Hitler by dancing to forbidden American swing music. Silly notion, yet poses a few interesting questions about grace under pressure. C: Robert Sean Leonard, Christian Bale, Frank Whaley, Barbara Hershey, Kenneth Branagh. D: Thomas Carter. DRA [PG-13] 110m. V

Swing Parade of 1946 1946 ★★★ Singer (Storm) tries to save nightclub threatened with closure by her boyfriend's father. Slim plot leaves plenty of room for the entertaining novelty numbers from Boswell, Storm, and the Stooges. C: Gale Storm, Phil Regan, The Three Stooges, Will Osborne & Orchestra, Connee Boswell. D: Phil Karlson. MUS 74m.

Swing Shift 1984 ★★★½ Jumbled account of life on the WWII homefront follows a group of women who take factory jobs while husbands are overseas. Production develops the women's characters (Lahti stands out) but neglects the men's, resulting in an interesting but unbalanced story. C: Goldie Hawn, Kurt Russell, Christine Lahti, Ed Harris, Fred Ward, Holly Hunter. D: Jonathan Demme. DRA [PG] 100m. V

Swing Time 1935 ★★★★★ Top of the line Astaire/Rogers, with Fred in love with Ginger, but engaged to Furness. Classic Kern/Fields songs, including Oscar-winning "The Way You Look Tonight." Best dance number: "Waltz in Swing Time." C: Fred Astaire, Ginger Rogers, Victor Moore, Helen Broderick, Eric Blore, Betty Furness. D: George Stevens. MUS V

Swing Your Lady 1938 ★★★ Wrestling promoter (Bogart) arranges match between his protege (Pendleton) and a female fighter. Goofy comedy generates laughs, though Bogart seems out of place. C: Humphrey Bogart, Nat Pendleton, Frank McHugh, Penny Singleton, Frank McHugh, Ronald Reagan. D: Ray Enright. MUS 77m.

Swinger, The 1966 ★★★½ Ann-Margret is a wholesome small-town writer who pitches racy pieces to puzzled sex-magazine editor Franciosa by pretending they're autobiographical. Clever satire makes the most of the star's charms *and* intelligence. C: Ann-Margret, Tony Franciosa, Robert Coote, Horace McMahon, Nydia Westman. D: George Sidney. COM 81m.

Swinging Cheerleaders, The 1974 ★★ Lively sideline lovelies encourage excitement in the stands and elsewhere. Routine sex romp. C: Colleen Camp, Cheryl Smith. D: Jack Hill. COM [R] 90m. V

Swinging Wives 1979 ★ They're wives and they're lovers. Enough said. C: Gale Mayberrie, Ron James. COM [R] 84m. V

Swiss Family Robinson 1940 ★★★★ First movie version of Johann Wyss' novel features patriarch (Mitchell) leading his family to victory over nature and buccaneers after they are shipwrecked on uninhabited isle. Family film with good performances, a bit darker than Disney's later take. Narrated by an unbilled Orson Welles. C: Thomas Mitchell, Edna Best, Freddie Bartholomew, Tim Holt, Terry Kilburn. D: Edward Ludwig. FAM/DRA [G] 93m.

Swiss Family Robinson 1960 ★★★★★ Family shipwrecked on a deserted island thrives by their own ingenuity, but their idyllic home is endangered when pirates threaten. Alternating turns of humor, excitement, and drama, make this Disney adventure grand family entertainment. Inventive set design, too. Based on Johann Wyss' novel. C: John Mills, Dorothy McGuire, James MacArthur, Janet Munro. D: Ken Annakin. FAM/DRA [G] 126m. V

Swiss Miss 1938 ★★★½ Two hapless salesmen (Laurel and Hardy) take over a hotel in the Swiss Alps, creating chaos but providing Ollie the opportunity to fall in love. Setting and story push this comedy to better than average. C: Stan Laurel, Oliver Hardy, Della Lind, Eric Blore. D: John G. Blystone. COM 97m. V

Switch 1991 ★★½ The old "switching bodies" shtick is exhausted in this somewhat sexist comedy about a womanizer (King) killed by his lovers who returns to life in a woman's body (Barkin). Barkin is great. C: Ellen Barkin, Jimmy Smits, JoBeth Williams, Lorraine Bracco, Tony Roberts, Perry King. D: Blake Edwards. COM [R] 104m. V

Switching Channels 1988 ★★½ Dismal update of *His Girl Friday* with Turner as TV network co-anchorwoman trying to quit job, but ex-husband Reynolds won't let her. C: Kathleen Turner, Burt Reynolds, Christopher Reeve, Ned Beatty, Henry Gibson. D: Ted Kotcheff. COM [PG] 108m. V

Swoon 1992 ★★★ Overly arty and surrealistic film examines homophobia behind famous Leopold-Loeb murder case of the '20s. Director's debut. C: Daniel Schlachet, Craig Chester, Ron Vawter, Michael Kirby, Michael Stumm. D: Tom Kalin. DRA [R] 95m. V

Sword and the Dragon 1960 Russian ★★★½ The epic tale of a mythical leader of old Russia. Extraordinary special effects. C: Boris Andreyen, Andrei Abrikosov. D: Alexander Ptushko. ACT 81m. v

Sword and the Rose, The 1953 ★★★★ Mary Tudor (Johns) uses guile to woo brave knight (Todd)—but nasty duke (Gough) attempts to sabotage the romance. Fine period detail gives realistic feel to Disney historical family drama. Based on novel *When Knighthood Was in Flower.* Filmed in England. C: Richard Todd, Glynis Johns, James Robertson Justice, Michael Gough. D: Ken Annakin. FAM/DRA [PG] 92m. v

Sword and the Sorcerer, The 1982 ★★★ Dethroned, sword-wielding prince goes up against evil king and his wizard to rescue fair damsel. Standard warrior vs. diabolical magician story slightly redeemed by good-natured Horsley and better than average sorcery effects. C: Lee Horsley, Kathleen Beller, Simon MacCorkindale, George Maharis. D: Albert Pyun. SFI [R] 100m. v

Sword in the Desert 1949 ★★★½ WWII Jewish refugees are smuggled to Palestine by ship. Provides some good suspense-filled moments. Not bad. C: Dana Andrews, Marta Toren, Stephen McNally, Jeff Chandler, Philip Friend. D: George Sherman. ACT 100m.

Sword in the Stone, The 1963 ★★★½ Animated tale of King Arthur as boy named Wart, learning about life from wizard Merlin. Crudely drawn Disney feature isn't up to studio's standard. Highlight is magic duel between Merlin and Madame Mim. Based on first part of T.E. White's *The Once and Future King.* C: Ricky Sorenson, Sebastian Cabot, Karl Swenson, Junius Matthews. D: Wolfgang Reitherman. FAM/SFI [G] 75m.

Sword of Doom 1967 Japanese ★★★ A samurai elder takes in a young firebrand and teaches him the secrets of samurai life—including knowledge of the martial arts. Quite rousing, with great work by the indomitable Mifune. C: Tatsuya Nakadai, Toshiro Mifune. D: Kihachi Okamoto. ACT 120m. v

Sword of Lancelot 1963 British ★★★ A swashbuckler extravaganza, featuring the romantic triangle among King Arthur, Sir Lancelot, and Lady Guinevere. The action stays on full blast and the adventure is first-rate. C: Cornel Wilde, Jean Wallace, Brian Aherne, George Baker. D: Cornel Wilde. ACT 115m. v

Sword of Monte Cristo, The 1951 ★★★ A mysterious masked heroine battles a nefarious government stooge for a sword that promises great wealth to its owner. Standard action-adventure yarn. C: George Montgomery, Paula Corday, Berry Kroeger, William Conrad. D: Maurice Geraghty. ACT 80m. v

Sword of the Valiant 1982 British ★★★ Sir Gawain (O'Keeffe) must solve a riddle or be killed by the Green Knight (Connery). Elaborate re-telling of ancient tale gets off to good sword & sorcery start. C: Miles O'Keeffe, Sean Connery, Leigh Lawson, Trevor Howard, Peter Cushing. D: Stephen Weeks. ACT [PG] 101m. v

Swordkill 1984 ★★★½ A Japanese samurai (Fujioka), frozen since the 16th century, is defrosted in contemporary Los Angeles and continues seeking his kidnapped wife. Fujioka nicely blends determination and confusion in this silly but oddly watchable primitive man vs. modern science drama. C: Hiroshi Fujioka, John Calvin, Janet Julian, Charles Lampkin, Frank Schuller, Bill Morey, Andy Wood. D: J. Larry Carroll. DRA 80m.

Swordsman, The 1948 ★ Cop (Lamas) uses not only his saberwielding skills, but also his extra-sensory perception to crack a burglary/murder case. Wait, there's more: He's also Alexander the Great reincarnated. Mindless meld of genres fails to entertain on any level. C: Larry Parks, Ellen Drew, George Macready, Edgar Buchanan. D: Joseph H. Lewis. CRI 81m.

Sybil 1977 ★★★★½ Engrossing, true-life psychological drama with Fields giving a tour de force performance as a young woman with 17 separate personalities. Woodward brings warm authority to role of her psychiatrist. Superior, disturbing drama. C: Joanne Woodward, Sally Field, Brad Davis, Martine Bartlett, Jane Hoffman, William Price. D: Daniel Petrie. DRA 122m. v

Sylvester 1984 ★★★½ A headstrong young equestrian is determined to compete against high-society rivals. Predictably heart-tugging at times, but also involved with more adult concerns. C: Richard Farnsworth, Melissa Gilbert, Michael Schoeffling, Constance Towers. D: Tim Hunter. FAM/DRA [PG] 104m. v

Sylvia 1986 New Zealand ★★★★ David delivers a high-calibre performance in real-life account of 1940s New Zealand educator Sylvia Ashton-Warner, who fought prejudice and bureaucracy to teach Maori children with her unorthodox methods. Uplifting drama based on Ashton-Warner's books *Teacher* and *I Passed This Way.* C: Eleanor David, Nigel Terry, Tom Wilkinson, Mary Regan. D: Michael Firth. DRA [PG] 99m. v

Sylvia and the Ghost 1945 *See* **Sylvia and the Phantom**

Sylvia and the Phantom 1945 ★★★½ Supernatural fantasy of French youngster (Joyeux) visited on her birthday by multiple ghostly incarnations of a French nobleman. Cute. (a.k.a. *Sylvia and the Ghost*) C: Odette Joueux, Jacques Tati, Francois Perier. D: Claude Autant-Lara. FAM/DRA 97m. v

Sylvia Scarlett 1935 ★★★★ A wanted down-and-out con artist (Gwenn) and his daughter (Hepburn, disguised as a boy), go on the lam and join the road show of a Cockney (Grant). Grant and Hepburn's first pairing is an entertaining comedy/drama that hints at the fun to come in their three subsequent films together. The film was a major failure when released, but has fared better in retrospective showings. C: Katharine Hepburn, Cary Grant, Brian Aherne, Edmund Gwenn. D: George Cukor. COM 94m. V

Symphonie Pastorale 1948 French ★★★★★ Compelling adaptation of Gide's tragic novel *Two Symphonies* features Morgan as an uneducated, blind orphan who ignites passion in a married pastor (Blanchar) and his son (Desailly). Morgan received a well-earned Best Actress award at Cannes. An unforgettable film. C: Michele Morgan, Pierre Blanchar, Lino Noro, Jean Desailly. D: Jean Delannoy. DRA 105m.

Symphony for a Massacre 1965 French ★★½ Four gangsters plan to split a fortune in drugs until one of them decides to kill his cohorts and abscond with the goods. Average revenge tale. C: Michel Auclair, Claude Dauphin, Jose Giovanni, Charles Vanel, Jean Rochefort. D: Jacques Deray. CRI 115m.

Symphony of Living 1935 ★★★ True story of over-the-hill musician who unknowingly tutors his musically gifted grandson, the pawn in an ugly custody battle. Truth is stranger than fiction. C: Evelyn Brent, Al Shean. D: Frank Strayer. DRA 75m.

Symphony of Six Million 1932 ★★★ A young doctor (Cortez) is forced to operate on his beloved (Dunne). Triple-hankie medical soaper, from Fannie Hurst's novel, features Max Steiner's first full musical score. (a.k.a. *Melody of Life*) C: Ricardo Cortez, Irene Dunne, Gregory Ratoff. D: Gregory La Cava. DRA 94m.

Synanon 1965 ★★★½ Drama about drug addicts trying to cope is set in Synanon House, a real-life California rehab center. Cameos by actual patients enhance the film's sharp realism. Unflinchingly honest for its day. C: Chuck Connors, Stella Stevens, Alex Cord, Richard Conte, Eartha Kitt, Edmond O'Brien, Chanin Hale, Alejandro Rey. D: Richard Quine. DRA 107m.

Syngenor 1990 ★★ The creature from *Scared to Death* returns in multiples, creating mayhem in a corporate lab. Mostly ineffective horror film, though *Re-Animator*'s Gale devours the scenery entertainingly. C: Starr Andreeff, Mitchell Laurence, David Gale, Charles Lucia, Riva Spier. D: George Elanjian, Jr. HOR [R] 98m.

System, The 1966 *See* **Girl-Getters, The**

T

T&A Academy 1979 *See* **H.O.T.S.**
T&A Academy 2 1984 *See* **Gimme an "F"**
T Bone N Weasel 1992 ★★ Two inept criminals (Hines and Lloyd) try to scam some not-so-naive smalltown folks. An uphill battle. C: Gregory Hines, Christopher Lloyd, Ned Beatty. D: Lewis Teague. COM 94m. TVM V
T-Men 1947 ★★★★½ Two Treasury agents (O'Keefe and Ryder) go undercover to expose a counterfeiting ring in this trenchant examination of how far good guys will go to catch bad guys. Vividly styled, with gritty voice-over narration and expressionistic lighting. Tops. C: Dennis O'Keefe, June Lockhart, Alfred Ryder. D: Anthony Mann. CRI 93m. V
Table for Five 1983 ★★★★ Guilt-ridden over his role as estranged father, divorced dad (Voight) takes his three children on a Mediterranean cruise in hopes of reconciliation. Solid domestic story avoids sap thanks to a heartfelt performance from Voight. Some strong language, but otherwise a nice family film. C: Jon Voight, Richard Crenna, Marie-Christine Barrault, Millie Perkins, Roxana Zal, Kevin Costner. D: Robert Lieberman. DRA 122m.
Tabu 1931 ★★★★ Unusual mix of documentary and fictional narrative, mostly silent, depicts the doomed romance between a Tahiti fisherman (Matahi) and a seductive woman whom the locals insist is cursed. Beautiful photography won Oscar. C: Anna Chevalier, Matahi. D: F.W. Murnau. DRA V
Tack's Chicks 1994 *See* **Stoned Age, The**
Taffin 1987 British ★★★ When Irish industrialists threaten to turn small town's soccer field into a chemical waste dump, citizens plead with tough bill collector for help. Brosnan is good but meandering story packs little wallop. C: Pierce Brosnan, Ray McAnally, Alison Doody, Jeremy Child. D: Francis Megahy. DRA [R] 96m. V
Tai-Pan 1986 ★★★ Saga of a greedy industrialist (Brown) in 19th-century Hong Kong. Rocky, condensed screen adaptation of James Clavell's monumental novel. C: Bryan Brown, Joan Chen, Kyra Sedgwick, John Stanton. D: Daryl Duke. DRA [R] 127m. V
Take a Giant Step 1959 ★★★½ Young African-American man tries to adapt to a world of intolerance and indifference. Earnest, well-acted adaptation of Louis E. Peterson's play. C: Johnny Nash, Rubby Dee, Frederick O'Neal, Beah Richards, Estelle Hemsley. D: Philip Leacock. DRA 100m.
Take a Hard Ride 1975 ★★½ In this violent, Italian produced shoot-'em-up, cattle hand (Brown) and his scruffy band of misfits are stalked by a merciless bounty hunter as they attempt to deliver a bag of loot to the proper authorities. Good cast can't overcome muddled script. C: Jim Brown, Lee Van Cleef, Fred Williamson, Catherine Spaak, Dana Andrews. D: Anthony M. Dawson. ACT [PG] 103m. V
Take a Letter, Darling 1942 ★★★★ High-powered executive Russell hires MacMurray to masquerade as her secretary/fiancée to mollify her clients' jealous wives, with predictable results. Well-crafted office comedy with sizzling dialogue. C: Rosalind Russell, Fred MacMurray, Constance Moore, Robert Benchley, Macdonald Carey. D: Mitchell Leisen. COM 93m.
Take Down 1978 ★★★½ A high school English teacher (Herrmann) unwillingly takes on the job of wrestling coach and inspires his students in spite of himself in this funny, engaging sports story which blends humor and sentiment. C: Edward Herrmann, Kathleen Lloyd, Lorenzo Lamas. D: Kieth Merrill. COM 96m. V
Take Her by Surprise 1967 Canadian ★★½ Nasty suspense tale has thug Negri hiring a sex criminal (Beckett) to murder his wife (Armstrong), with some unpleasant twists. (a.k.a. *Taken By Surprise* and *Violent Love*) C: Paul Negri, Nuel Beckett, Joan Armstrong. D: Rudi Dorn. CRI 80m.
Take Her, She's Mine 1963 ★★★½ Stewart is charming as a harassed father trying to cope with his hippie daughter (Dee). Meadows is his staid wife in this innocent, lively family comedy. C: James Stewart, Sandra Dee, Audrey Meadows, Robert Morley. D: Henry Koster. COM 98m.
Take Me Out to the Ball Game 1949 ★★★★ Breezy musical about early days of baseball, with four ingratiating leads and tuneful score. Esther is surprisingly good, and stays out of the pool for most of the movie. C: Gene Kelly, Frank Sinatra, Esther Williams, Jules Munshin, Betty Garrett. D: Busby Berkeley. MUS 90m. V
Take Me to Town 1953 ★★★½ A singer with a shady past (Sheridan) hides out in a lumber camp and falls for a preacher (Hayden) with three kids. Genial vehicle for the delightful Sheridan. C: Ann Sheridan, Sterling Hayden, Lee Patrick, Philip Reed. D: Douglas Sirk. COM 81m.
Take One False Step 1949 ★★★★ Powell is a college professor whose dinner with an old love (Winters) leads to a false murder charge against him, and his determined quest to find the killer. Film combines comedy and genuine thrills. C: William Powell, Shelley Winters, James Gleason, Marsha Hunt. D: Chester Erskine. CRI 94m.
Take the Money and Run 1969 ★★★★ Allen wrote/directed/starred in this pseudo-documentary about an incompetent crook, chronicling his youth, his sentence on a Southern chain gang, and his life on the run.

Exploits the clichés of crime/prison dramas while allowing Allen's own brand of humor to shine. C: Woody Allen, Janet Margolin, Marcel Hillaire. D: Woody Allen. COM [PG] 85m. V

Take this Job and Shove It 1981 ★★★ Taking its cue from Johnny Paycheck's hit song, film follows an executive (Hays) who returns to his backwoods hometown to modernize the local brewery, but ends up organizing the workers instead. The working man's *Wall Street.* C: Robert Hays, Art Carney, Barbara Hershey, David Keith. D: Gus Trikonis. COM [PG] 100m. V

Taken By Surprise 1967 *See* **Take Her By Surprise**

Taking Care of Business 1990 ★★★½ When an escaped small-time con (Belushi) finds a high-powered ad man's (Grodin) notebook, he takes over his life and ends up being better at it than the executive. Slow start, but picks up steam toward the end. C: James Belushi, Charles Grodin, Anne DeSalvo, Veronica Hamel, Mako. D: Arthur Hiller. COM [R] 108m. V

Taking of Beverly Hills, The 1991 ★★½ Ruthless football team owner angers his star quarterback when he attempts to loot all of Beverly Hills by creating a bogus chemical spill. Kooky premise gets blitzed way before halftime, although Wahl injects some flair. C: Ken Wahl, Matt Frewer, Harley Jane Kozak, Robert Davi. D: Sidney J. Furie. ACT [R] 96m. V

Taking of Pelham One Two Three, The 1974 ★★★★½ Ruthless thugs hijack New York subway train and demand $1 million for their terrified passenger hostages. Excellent urban thriller with plenty of suprises and lots of nail-biting action. Shaw as the head crook and Matthau as beleagured subway security officer lead an outstanding cast. C: Walter Matthau, Robert Shaw, Martin Balsam, Hector Elizondo, Earl Hindman. D: Joseph Sargent. ACT [R] 102m. V

Taking Off 1971 ★★★★½ A father (Henry) and mother (Carlin) trying to find their runaway hippie daughter (Heacock) experience a few new adventures of their own that change their dull suburban lives forever. Czech director Forman's first American film is a stunner. C: Lynn Carlin, Buck Henry, Linnea Heacock, Audra Lindley. D: Milos Forman. DRA [R] 93m.

Tale of Africa, A 1983 *See* **Green Horizon, The**

Tale of Four Wishes, A ★★★½ Animated tales of a family in which a young girl learns life's lessons from her wise grandfather. C: Ricky Nelson, Tracey Gold. D: Nick Bosustow. FAM/DRA 45m. V

Tale of Ruby Rose, The 1987 ★★★★ A Depression-era Australian mountain woman (Jurisic) living off the land with her husband and son leaves home on a journey of self-discovery. Absorbing portrait of an unusual heroine. C: Melita Jurisic, Chris Haywood. D: Roger Sholes. DRA [PG] 101m. V

Tale of Springtime, A 1989 French ★★★★ A lonely philosphy teacher (Teyssedre) finds herself pursued by a student's father, in this small-scale, charming comedy/drama. Rohmer's films are an acquired taste; it may move too slowly for some. First of the director's projected "Tales of the Four Seasons." C: Anne Teyssedre, Hugues Quester, Florence Darel. D: Eric Rohmer. COM 112m. V

Tale of Two Cities, A 1935 ★★★★★ Definitive screen version of Dickens' tale of the French Revolution has lavish epic scope and memorable performances. The understated Colman is perfect in dual roles: as Sydney Carton, a lawyer who sacrifices himself on the guillotine, and as Charles Darnay, the underground fighter whose life is saved. C: Ronald Colman, Elizabeth Allan, Edna May Oliver, Reginald Owen, Basil Rathbone, Blanche Yurka. D: Jack Conway. DRA 128m. V

Tale of Two Cities, A 1958 British ★★★½ Accurate adaptation of events surrounding Dickens' version of the storming of the Bastille. Bogarde cuts a less romantic figure than Colman in 1935 version but Pleasance makes good in small part as spy. C: Dirk Bogarde, Dorothy Tutin, Cecil Parker, Stephen Murray, Christopher Lee, Donald Pleasence. D: Ralph Thomas. DRA 117m. V

Tale of Two Cities, A 1980 ★★★½ A workmanlike presentation of Dickens' classic tale of love, honor, and courage during the French Revolution (here in its seventh film version), but be sure to catch Colman's definitive 1935 rendition. C: Chris Sarandon, Peter Cushing, Kenneth More, Barry Morse, Flora Robson, Billie Whitelaw. D: Jim Goddard. DRA 216m. TVM V

Tale of Winter, A 1992 ★★★★ A vacationing hairdresser (Very) becomes pregnant after a brief liaison with a hotel cook. Sentimental romance benefits from expert direction, lovely performances. Second of Rohmer's "Tales of the Four Seasons." C: Charlotte Very, Frederic Van Den Driessche. D: Eric Rohmer. DRA 114m.

Talent for the Game 1991 ★★★ Sports fans may enjoy meager, formula tale about down-and-out baseball scout who discovers a hot young pitcher, only to see the unscrupulous team owner exploit him. C: Edward James Olmos, Lorraine Bracco, Jamey Sheridan. D: Robert M. Young. DRA [PG] 91m. V

Tales from the Crypt 1972 British ★★★★ Excellent anthology about five people in a mysterious cave who have their futures foretold by a sinister keeper. Brisk pace and surprisingly good performances make this stand out from other films of its kind. C: Ralph Richardson, Peter Cushing, Joan Collins, Patrick Magee. D: Freddie Francis. HOR [PG] 92m. V

Tales from the Crypt 1989 ★★★★ Classic tales of eerie happenings and the downright macabre. Some good fun and nifty effects. Based on stories by William M. Gaines, from E.C. Comics. C: Bill Sadler, Mary Ellen

Trainer, Larry Drake. D: Richard Donner. HOR 81m. ▼

Tales from the Crypt 1990 ★★★½ Videotape series of episodes from the popular HBO cable series presents stories from the classic EC horror comics, produced by some of Hollywood's biggest names. The episodes, which usually deal with some sort of supernatural revenge, feature solid casts, gruesome special effects, and a mix of up-and-coming directors, including some established actors (Arnold Schwarzenegger, Michael J. Fox, etc.) making their debuts behind the camera. Overall high quality. C: Lea Thompson, Amanda Plummer, M. Emmet Walsh. D: Howard Deutch. HOR 87m. ▼

Tales From the Crypt Presents Demon Knight 1995 ★★★ Hit TV series was inspiration for this clever, appropriately gruesome tale of assorted misfits hounded by supernatural forces in a New Mexico brothel. The skeletal Crypt Keeper is on hand to serve as host/narrator. C: Billy Zane, William Sadler, Jada Pinkett, Brenda Bakke, Dick Miller, C.C.H. Pounder. D: Ernest Dickerson, Gilbert Adler. HOR [R] 93m. ▼

Tales from the Crypt II 1973 *See* **Vault of Horror**

Tales From the Darkside: The Movie 1990 ★★★½ Uneven horror anthology, with stories told by an imprisoned boy to a cannibal (Harry), trying to stall the dinner bell. Bizarre twist on Arabian Nights includes three tales. Last, about a promise to a magical gargoyle, is best. C: Deborah Harry, Matthew Lawrence, Christian Slater, William Hickey, Robert Klein, Rae Dawn Chong. D: John Harrison. HOR [R] 93m. ▼

Tales of Beatrix Potter, The 1971 British ★★★★ Handsome ballet film, with members of Britain's Royal Ballet Company presenting their version of the classic children's stories. Dance fans will enjoy it. (a.k.a. *Peter Rabbit and the Tales of Beatrix Potter*) D: Reginald Mills. FAM/MUS [G] 90m. ▼

Tales of Hoffman 1951 ★★★★ Offenbach's opera tells three episodes of doomed love in the title character's life. Wonderful music, beautiful photography. The directors' follow-up to *The Red Shoes* is a real treat for opera fans. A 118-m. version had previously been circulated in the U.S. C: Moira Shearer, Robert Rounseville, Leonide Massine, Robert Helpmann. D: Michael Powell, Emeric Pressburger. MUS 127m. ▼

Tales of Manhattan 1942 ★★★★½ A coat that changes the lives of its wearers is passed from character to character in this engrossing drama/comedy/thriller. Film unfolds in five episodes, some better than others, but generally splendid writing, expert photography, and interesting characters make this a supremely rewarding experience. C: Charles Boyer, Rita Hayworth, Henry Fonda, Ginger Rogers, Charles Laughton, Edward G. Robinson, Ethel Waters, Paul Robeson, Thomas Mitchell, Cesar Romero, George Sanders. D: Julien Duvivier. DRA 118m.

Tales of Robin Hood 1951 ★★★ Run-of-the-mill hero takes from rich, gives to the poor. Told with less finesse than some Sherwood Forest films, but still entertaining. C: Robert Clarke, Mary Hatcher, Paul Cavanagh. D: James Tinling. DRA 60m.

Tales of Terror 1962 ★★★½ Uneven but generally successful anthology based on Edgar Allan Poe tales: a woman is murderously possessed by her daughter; cuckolded husband walls up his wife and her lover; a devious hypnotist gets his comeuppance. Fairly true to the source, with last segment the best. C: Vincent Price, Peter Lorre, Basil Rathbone, Debra Paget. D: Roger Corman. HOR 90m. ▼

Tales of the Uncanny 1932 ★★★★½ Early German talkie with Wegener confined to a mental institution for murder and inspiring revolt among his fellow patients. Brilliant Expressionistic cinematography highlights this dark psychological drama. C: Paul Wegener. D: Richard Oswald. DRA 80m.

Tales of the Unexpected 1991 ★★½ An anthology of four half-hour stories in the *Alfred Hitchcock Presents* mold, none very chilling or unexpected. The best is a humorous episode in which a parrot exposes an unfaithful spouse. C: Arthur Hill, Don Johnson, Samantha Eggar, Sharon Gless, Dick Smothers. D: Paul Annett. DRA 107m. ▼

Talion 1966 *See* **Eye for an Eye, An**

Talisman, The 1966 ★★½ Romero is an Indian who spares the life of a white woman (Hawkins), who is then ravished by white men. Romero exacts a grisly revenge in this gory Western. C: Ned Romero, Linda Hawkins. D: John Carr. WST 93m.

Talk of the Town, The 1942 ★★★★ Unusually intelligent comedy, with a fugitive from justice (Grant) hiding out in the house of supreme court nominee (Colman), under the protection of a kindly landlady (Arthur). Bogs down somewhat, but witty script tackles tough subjects of law and honor. C: Jean Arthur, Ronald Colman, Cary Grant, Glenda Farrell. D: George Stevens. COM 118m. ▼

Talk Radio 1989 ★★★★ A few days in the life of an obnoxious but fascinating radio personality, who turns his self-hatred into venom aimed at his audience. Bogosian is electrifying and Stone's visual style makes this feature film from the off-Broadway play crackle. C: Eric Bogosian, Alec Baldwin, Ellen Greene. D: Oliver Stone. DRA [R] 100m. ▼

Talkin' Dirty After Dark 1992 ★★ Backstage at comedy club a young comedian (Lawrence) looks for his chance. Potty humor and tasteless stereotyping in what turns out to be a showcase for popular entertainer Lawrence. C: Martin Lawrence, John Witherspoon, Phyllis Stickney. D: Topper Carew. COM 89m. V

Talking Walls 1985 ★★ A sociology student examines human sexuality by secretly videotaping couples in an L.A. motel. Rather lowbrow, but Danning's legions of fans might find it worth a peek. C: Stephen Shellen, Marie Laurin, Barry Primus, Sybil Danning. D: Stephen Verona. DRA 85m. V

Tall Blond Man with One Black Shoe 1972 French ★★★★ When hapless innocent is mistaken for a notorious spy, he becomes everyone's target. Silly and most enjoyable in the French way. C: Pierre Richard, Bernard Blier, Jean Rochefort. D: Yves Robert. COM [PG] 89m. V

Tall, Dark and Handsome 1941 ★★★½ Love story of '20s mobster Romero and his reluctant sweetheart, straight arrow Gilmore, is a good-natured comedy. Remade as *Love That Brute.* C: Cesar Romero, Virginia Gilmore, Charlotte Greenwood, Milton Berle, Sheldon Leonard, Stanley Clements, Marc Lawrence, Frank Jenks. D: H. Humberstone. COM 78m.

Tall Guy, The 1990 British ★★★½ An American actor in London (Goldblum) plagued by hay fever, a horrible job, and a languishing love life falls for the nurse (Thompson) giving him allergy shots. Goldblum seems out of place in this decidedly British comedy, but Thompson fans: Alert! C: Jeff Goldblum, Emma Thompson, Rowan Atkinson, Geraldine James. D: Mel Smith. COM [R] 92m. V

Tall Headlines, The 1953 *See* **Frightened Bride**

Tall in the Saddle 1944 ★★★½ Loner cowpoke Wayne is caught up in a fatal feud. Nice Western action and that great Wayne-Bond-Hayes chemistry keep things cooking. C: John Wayne, Ella Raines, Ward Bond, George "Gabby" Hayes. D: L. Edwin Marin. WST 79m. V

Tall Men, The 1955 ★★★★ Satisfying drama, though perhaps not up to director Walsh's usual high standard. This is a tale of brother cattle drivers Gable and Mitchell, their various adventures and romantic rivalry. Good cast and cinematography. C: Clark Gable, Jane Russell, Robert Ryan, Cameron Mitchell. D: Raoul Walsh. WST 122m. V

Tall Story 1960 ★★★½ College basketball hero (Perkins) is pursued by a perky student (Fonda). Frivolous adaptation of Howard Lindsay-Russel Crouse play, of interest mainly as Jane's film debut. C: Anthony Perkins, Jane Fonda, Ray Walston. D: Joshua Logan. COM 91m. V

Tall T, The 1957 ★★★½ After they rob a stagecoach, a trio of outlaws are hunted down by a very clever ranch owner. Plenty of action and a good dose of closing violence in this taut Western thriller based on an Elmore Leonard story. C: Randolph Scott, Richard Boone, Maureen O'Sullivan. D: Budd Boetticher. WST 78m. V

Tall Tale: The Unbelievable Adventures of Pecos Bill 1995 ★★★½ Genial, episodic Disney family film about a boy who is aided by mythological heros Pecos Bill (Swayze), John Henry (Brown), and Paul Bunyan (Platt). C: Patrick Swazye, Oliver Platt, Roger Aaron Brown, Nick Stahl, Scott Glenn, Stephen Lang. D: Jeremiah Chechik. FAM/ACT [PG] 98m. V

Tall Timbers 1937 Australian ★★★½ Battles over love and money divide timber companies in New South Wales in this interesting Australian drama. Worth seeing. C: Shirley Ann Richards, Frank Leighton, Frank Harvey. D: Ken. G. Hall. DRA 85m. V

Tamango 1959 French ★★★ Unusual drama of a slave ship en route to Cuba, and the rebellion brewing against the Dutch captain Jurgens, who's in love with slave Dandridge. C: Dorothy Dandridge, Curt Jurgens, Jean Servais. D: John Berry. DRA 98m. V

Tamarind Seed, The 1974 ★★★★ A widowed British government worker (Andrews) vacationing in Barbados becomes romantically involved with a KGB agent (Sharif) and the resulting intrigue takes them around the world. Handsome production, star power, and solid direction do wonders for the script. C: Julie Andrews, Omar Sharif, Anthony Quayle, Sylvia Sims. D: Blake Edwards. CRI 123m. V

Taming of the Shrew, The 1929 ★★★½ Early sound version of Shakespeare's battle of the sexes. Famous Hollywood couple Pickford and Fairbanks don't sizzle as warring lovers in their only co-starring roles. Hotter 1967 version starred Elizabeth Taylor and Richard Burton. C: Mary Pickford, Douglas Fairbanks. D: Sam Taylor. COM 93m. V

Taming of the Shrew, The 1967 U.S. ★★★★ Real life spills onto the screen in this bawdy adaptation of Shakespeare's comedy. Spitfire Taylor tamed by flamboyant Burton with plenty of witty repartee to keep it lively. Entertaining for both general audiences and fans of the Bard. C: Elizabeth Taylor, Richard Burton, Michael Hordern, Natasha Pyne, Michael York, Cyril Cusack. D: Franco Zeffirelli. COM 126m. V

Tamlin 1972 *See* **Devil's Widow, The**

Tammy and the Bachelor 1957 ★★★ Too-cute story of a backwoods girl (Reynolds) who falls in love with a pilot (Nielsen) she's nursed back to health after he's injured in a plane crash. Title song sung by Reynolds went to the top of the charts. (a.k.a. *Tammy*) C: Debbie Reynolds, Walter Brennan, Leslie Nielsen, Mala Powers, Fay Wray, Mildred Natwick. D: Joseph Pevney. COM 89m. V

Tammy and the Doctor 1963 ★★½ Sweet country girl Tammy (Dee) is romanced by a young doctor (Fonda, in his film debut) in this slip of a movie. C: Sandra Dee, Peter Fonda, Macdonald Carey, Beulah Bondi, Adam West. D: Harry Keller. COM 88m. V

Tammy Tell Me True 1961 ★★★½ Second Tammy movie, now with Dee as the title character, this time in college setting. Episodic, all-American teenage tale is too cute for its own good, but sometimes amusing. C: Sandra Dee, John Gavin, Beulah Bondi. D: Harry Keller. COM 97m.

Tampico 1944 ★★★ Commander of U.S. supply ship (Robinson) must counter a band of Nazi spies. Effective though routine WWII espionage drama. C: Edward G. Robinson, Lynn Bari, Victor McLaglen. D: Lothar Mendes. DRA 75m.

Tampopo 1987 Japanese ★★★★½ Winning comedy about food with main plot concerning a widow's success upon discovering the secret of perfect noodles, thanks to truck driver's assistance. Spoof of spaghetti-Westerns often interrupted by short, madcap vignettes, all with culinary themes. C: Ken Watanabe, Tsutomu Yamakazi, Nobuko Miyamoto. D: Juzo Itami. COM 114m. V

Tangled Destinies 1932 ★★★★ Psychological drama of passengers on a grounded plane and the revelation that one of them is a murderer. A small, contained drama with plenty of human insight. Wonderful. C: Lloyd Whitlock, Doris Hill, Glenn Tryon, Vera. D: Frank M. Strayer. DRA 64m.

Tango & Cash 1989 ★★★ Stallone and Russell are two L.A. police detectives, framed by a drug lord, who join forces to clear their names. Standard Buddy/Cop movie has lots of action and a few funny gags, but nothing that hasn't been done before, with better talent. C: Sylvester Stallone, Kurt Russell, Teri Hatcher, Jack Palance. D: Andrei Konchalovsky. CRI [R] 104m. V

Tango Bar 1988 Puerto Rican ★★★★ A tango dancer flees her native Argentina to escape the military junta. A decade later she returns and meets up with her one-time dancing partner. Interesting combination of dance and politics. C: Raul Julia, Valeria Lynch. D: Marcos Zurinaga. MUS 90m. V

Tanya's Island 1981 Canadian ★★★½ A mistreated young woman indulges in escape fantasy. She imagines herself on a tropical island, where her love interest is an ape. Quite peculiar and worth a look. C: D.D. Winters, Richard Sargent, Don McCleod. D: Alfred Sole. DRA 82m. V

Tap 1989 ★★★★ A former tap-dancing child wonder (Hines) returns from prison and must decide whether to return to dancing or the easy money of crime. Serious drama, but soars with tap dancing by some of the all-time great practitioners. C: Gregory Hines, Suzanne Douglas, Sammy Davis Jr., Savion Glover. D: Nick Castle. COM [PG-13] 110m. V

Tap Roots 1948 ★★★★ As the Civil War looms, Mississippi landowner Bond leads a faction of Southerners trying to stay neutral. Offbeat historical drama mixes in various love affairs and political intrigues. Shot on-location, with inevitable echoes of *Gone With the Wind.* C: Van Heflin, Ward Bond, Susan Hayward, Boris Karloff, Julie London. D: George Marshall. DRA 109m.

Tapeheads 1989 ★★★½ A mild-mannered video virtuoso (Robbins) is talked into making music videos by an irritating swindler (Cusack) who wants to make money and impress women. Goofy, offbeat comedy; cult potential. C: John Cusack, Tim Robbins, Doug McClure, Connie Stevens. D: Bill Fishman. COM [R] 93m. V

Taps 1981 ★★★½ Cadets at a military school barricade themselves and take on the real Army, rather than be shut down. Drama runs out of steam, but is noteworthy for early appearances by Cruise and Penn. C: Timothy Hutton, George C. Scott, Ronny Cox, Sean Penn, Tom Cruise. D: Harold Becker. DRA [PG] 118m. V

Tarantula 1955 ★★★★ Scientist's new growth formula creates a giant spider that escapes from the lab to terrorize a small community. Better than average horror thriller; very entertaining with convincing special effects. C: John Agar, Mara Corday, Leo G. Carroll. D: Jack Arnold. HOR 81m. V

Taras Bulba 1962 ★★★½ In 16th-century Russia a cossack firebrand leads peasants in revolt. Lots of action, color, and an excellent score, based on Gogol's story. C: Tony Curtis, Yul Brynner, Christine Kaufmann. D: J.Lee Thompson. DRA 125m. V

Tarawa Beachhead 1958 ★★★½ Complex WWII drama of patriotic Marine Mathews who has doubts about his commander (Danton) but stays loyal, even after they return home. Insightful observation of soldier's psychology. C: Kerwin Mathews, Julie Adams, Ray Danton. D: Paul Wendkos. DRA 77m.

Target 1985 ★★★ Disappointing spy thriller about a young man who learns his father is an ex-CIA agent after his mother is kidnapped. Despite a good cast and director, the predictable plot and poorly written screenplay detract from one's involvement in the story. C: Gene Hackman, Matt Dillon, Gayle Hunnicutt. D: Arthur Penn. CRI [R] 117m. V

Target: Embassy 1972 *See* **Embassy**

Target for Today ★★★★½ Superb quasi-documentary treatment of an RAF bombing run over Germany. Truly rousing, and the well-deserved winner of a special Academy Award. DOC V

Targets 1968 ★★★★½ Superbly acted thriller about a Vietnam veteran (O'Kelly) who carefully shoots lots of innocent bystanders, finally facing off against an aging horror-movie star (Karloff, in a brilliant performance). Impressive debut for Bogdanovich. C: Boris Karloff, Tim O'Kelly, Nancy Hsueh, James Brown. D: Peter Bogdanovich. CRI [PG] 90m. V

Tarka the Otter 1986 ★★★★ The story of a lovable little otter doing otter-type things like searching for otter-type food. Nice fun for kids. FAM/DRA 91m. V

Tarnished Angels, The 1958 ★★★★½ Faulkner's steamy novel *Pylon* is faithfully translated under Sirk's expert direction, relating the sexual tensions among a band of aerial daredevils and a bedraggled local reporter (Hudson) fascinated with their lifestyle. C: Rock Hudson, Dorothy Malone, Robert Stack, Jack Carson, Troy Donahue. D: Douglas Sirk. DRA 91m.

Tars and Spars 1946 ★★★½ A Coast Guard hero's girlfriend thinks he's a phony. Shipshape Jule Styne-Sammy Cahn musical features stage star Drake in a rare film performance, and Caesar in his hysterical movie debut. C: Alfred Drake, Janet Blair, Sid Caesar, Marc Platt. D: Alfred E. Green. MUS 88m.

Tarzan "Me Tarzan, you Jane." Has there been any series of films so loved, so parodied as the ones based on Edgar Rice Burroughs' vine-swinging man in a loin cloth? Although Burroughs' books about an English nobleman raised by great apes in the African jungle were first filmed in 1918 with Elmo Lincoln, Tarzan finally found his filmic home at MGM in 1934, and his best-known embodiment in Olympic swim champ Johnny Weissmuller. Maureen O'Sullivan played Jane, and MGM production values gave the first films in the series real class, especially the 1934 *Tarzan and His Mate*. Other Olympians also tried their hand at Tarzantics—Buster Crabbe, Herman Brix (who would become Bruce Bennett), and decathlete Glenn Morris. Weissmuller kept at it, moving to RKO, until 1949. After that, the role was filled by a succession of brawny guys.

Tarzan of the Apes (1918)
Tarzan, the Ape Man (1932)
Tarzan the Fearless (1933)
Tarzan and His Mate (1934)
New Adventures of Tarzan (1935)
Tarzan Escapes (1936)
Tarzan's Revenge (1938)
Tarzan and the Green Goddess (1939)
Tarzan Finds a Son! (1939)
Tarzan's Secret Treasure (1941)
Tarzan's New York Adventure (1942)
Tarzan Triumphs (1943)
Tarzan's Desert Mystery (1943)
Tarzan and the Amazons (1945)
Tarzan and the Leopard Woman (1946)
Tarzan and the Huntress (1947)
Tarzan and the Mermaids (1948)
Tarzan's Magic Fountain (1949)
Tarzan and the Slave Girl (1950)
Tarzan's Peril (1951)
Tarzan's Savage Fury (1952)
Tarzan and the She-Devil (1953)
Tarzan's Hidden Jungle (1955)
Tarzan and the Lost Safari (1957)
Tarzan's Fight for Life (1958)
Tarzan and the Trappers (1958)
Tarzan's Greatest Adventure (1959)
Tarzan, the Ape Man (1959)
Tarzan the Magnificent (1960)
Tarzan Goes to India (1962)
Tarzan's Three Challenges (1963)
Tarzan and the Valley of Gold (1966)
Tarzan and the Great River (1967)
Tarzan and the Jungle Boy (1968)
Tarzan's Jungle Rebellion (1970)
Tarzan's Deadly Silence (1970)
Tarzan, the Ape Man (1981)
Greystoke: The Legend of Tarzan, Lord of the Apes (1984)
Tarzan in Manhattan (1989)

Tarzan and His Mate 1934 ★★★½ Jane attempts to create a home for herself and Tarzan in the jungle while her jilted fiancé returns, wanting to be led to the elephant graveyard. Good production values and risqué innuendoes make this innocent fun. C: Johnny Weissmuller, Maureen O'Sullivan, Neil Hamilton. D: Cedric Gibbons, Jack Conway. DRA 91m. V

Tarzan and the Amazons 1945 ★★★½ Tarzan, Jane, and Boy encounter a lost tribe of strange Amazon women whose gold is coveted by a team of archaeologists. Good action and all the expected jungle thrills. C: Johnny Weissmuller, Brenda Joyce, Johnny Sheffield, Henry Stephenson, Maria Ouspenskaya. D: Kurt Neumann. ACT 76m.

Tarzan and the Leopard Woman 1946 ★★★½ Tarzan seems at a loss when faced with the exotic charms and murderous deeds of leopard priestess Acquanetta in this amusing jungle drama. Cheta the Chimp adds his own charm. C: Johnny Weissmuller, Brennda Joyce, Johnny Sheffield, Acquanetta. D: Kurt Neumann. ACT 72m.

Tarzan and the Mermaids 1948 ★★★½ The ape-man must save his native friends enslaved by ruthless pearl thieves posing as jungle gods. Vigorous Tarzan adventure with fine cinematography. C: Johnny Weissmuller, Brenda Joyce, Linda Christian. D: Robert Florey. ACT 68m.

Tarzan Escapes 1936 ★★★½ Tarzan is captured by a hunter who wants to put him up for exhibition in England. Energetic, entertaining, and surprisingly violent for its time. C: Johnny Weissmuller, Maureen O'Sullivan, John Buckler, Benita Hume. D: Richard Thorpe. DRA 95m. V

Tarzan Finds a Son 1939 ★★★ Tarzan and Jane come upon the a crashed plane; inside is a child whom they take for their own. One of the classics in the sturdy series. C: Johnny Weissmuller, Maureen O'Sullivan, Johnny Sheffield, Frieda Inescort, Laraine Day. D: Richard Thorpe. ACT 83m. V

Tarzan in Manhattan 1989 ★★ Jungle man (Lara) arrives in 1989 NY to rescue Cheetah from scientists and meets a cab-driver named

Jane (Crosby). Casting of the muscular male model as title character was one of film's few good ideas. C: Joe Lara, Kim Crosby, Tony Curtis, Jan-Michael Vincent. D: Michael Schultz. ACT 100m. TVM

Tarzan of the Apes 1918 ★★★ First silent film version of the Edgar Rice Burroughs novel is pretty good, though Lincoln is hardly one's visual image of the title character. Well worth a peek for curiosity's sake. C: Elmo Lincoln, Enid Markey. D: Scott Sidney. ACT 55m. V

Tarzan, the Ape Man 1932 ★★★★ The first talking *Tarzan* film and first Weissmuller entry is generally considered *the* Tarzan flick. Quite entertaining, lots of color and action. Swimming champ Weissmuller does fine as man raised by apes who becomes a force for Good in the jungles of Central Africa. C: Johnny Weissmuller, Maureen O'Sullivan, C. Aubrey Smith. D: W.S. Van Dyke. ACT 104m. V

Tarzan, the Ape Man 1981 ★★ Bo Derek and husband John do a campy sendup of the original Tarzan Tale, with the emphasis on slow motion eroticism. C: Bo Derek, Richard Harris, Miles O'Keeffe. D: John Derek. DRA [R] 112m. V

Tarzan the Magnificent 1960 British ★★★★ Tarzan treks through the jungle, trying to bring a murderer to justice. Outstanding entry in the long-running series; impressive Scott and terrific location footage really put it over. C: Gordon Scott, Jock Mahoney, Betta St. John, John Carradine. D: Robert Day. ACT 88m.

Tarzan Triumphs 1943 ★★★½ Our favorite vine-swinger battles Nazis. Topical entry in the jungle adventure series features a very patriotic Cheetah. Good going. C: Johnny Weissmuller, Frances Gifford, Johnny Sheffield. D: William Thiele. ACT 78m.

Tarzan's Greatest Adventure 1959 British ★★★★ Tarzan searches for an old nemesis and his murderous gang who are out to plunder a hidden diamond mine. Excellent large-scale Tarzan story filled with action, splendid African locales, and a pre-Bond Connery. C: Gordon Scott, Anthony Quayle, Sara Shane, Sean Connery. D: John Guillermin. ACT 88m.

Tarzan's New York Adventure 1942 ★★★½ Mean circus men kidnap Tarzan's Boy, so the jungle man follows them to the big city. Lively change of locale, including a scene on the Brooklyn Bridge, sets this entertaining entry apart from the rest. C: Johnny Weissmuller, Maureen O'Sullivan, Johnny Sheffield, Virginia Grey, Charles Bickford. D: Richard Thorpe. DRA 71m. V

Tarzan's Secret Treasure 1941 ★★★ Tarzan fights off a band of explorers in search of gold. Concisely told but melodramatic at times. C: Johnny Weissmuller, Maureen O'Sullivan, Johnny Sheffield, Reginald Owen, Barry Fitzgerald. D: Richard Thorpe. DRA 81m. V

Task Force 1949 ★★★★ An admiral (Cooper) struggles to get the U.S. government to accept aircraft carriers as strategic defense tools. Solid war story, outstanding battle scenes. C: Gary Cooper, Jane Wyatt, Walter Brennan, Wayne Morris. D: Delmer Daves. ACT 116m. V

Taste for Killing, A 1992 ★★★ College boys (Bateman and Thomas) spend a working summer on an offshore oil rig with Biehn, and find themselves being blackmailed for a murder it *appears* they committed. A thriller with too many contrivances, but saved by Biehn's good bad-guy. C: Michael Biehn, Jason Bateman, Henry Thomas. D: Lou Antonio. DRA [R] 87m. V

Taste of Fear 1961 *See* **Scream of Fear**

Taste of Honey, A 1961 British ★★★★½ Tony Richardson's adapation of Shelagh Delaney's hit play about an unattractive young woman who becomes pregnant by an African-American sailor and is nurtured by her homosexual friend. Bittersweet, deeply drawn narrative is splendidly acted and memorable. C: Rita Tushingham, Robert Stephens, Dora Bryan, Murray Melvin. D: Tony Richardson. DRA 100m. V

Taste the Blood of Dracula 1970 British ★★½ Dracula pits the children of three families against their fathers to avenge the death of a wizard. Not as stylish as others of this genre. Horror veteran Lee is not in the film long enough to save it. C: Christopher Lee, Geoffrey Keen, Gwen Watford. D: Peter Sasdy. HOR 91m. V

Tatie Danielle 1991 French ★★★½ A nasty old woman ruins life for her good-guy nephew by moving in with him. Black screwball comedy with wonderfully vicious Chelton. C: Tsilla Chelton, Catherine Jacob, Isabelle Nanty, Neige Dolsky. D: Etienne Chatiliez. COM [PG-13] 115m. V

Tattoo 1981 ★★ A deranged tattoo artist (Dern) abducts a supermodel (Adams) to ply his inky trade on her flawless skin. Not for kids; might work as antitattoo publicity. C: Bruce Dern, Maud Adams, Leonard Frey. D: Bob Brooks. DRA [R] 122m. V

Tawny Pipit 1944 British ★★★★ In WWII England an entire village is affected when a pair of rare songbirds are discovered nesting in a local meadow. Charming, genteel comedy. C: Charles Saunders, Bernard Miles. D: Bernard Miles. COM 85m.

Taxi! 1932 ★★★★ Cagney battles opposing cab drivers, dance marathoners and his girl—*and* he speaks Yiddish, and dances, too. What more could you want? A delightful action comedy. C: James Cagney, Loretta Young, George Stone, Dorothy Burgess, Guy Kibbee. D: Roy Del Ruth. COM 70m.

Taxi Blues 1990 Russian ★★★★ The odd, super-charged "friendship" between a lout of a Moscow cabdriver and a Jewish musician with a drinking problem. Quite fascinating indeed with the two central characters mirroring the modern evolution of Russia. C: Piotr

Mamonov, Piotr Zaitchenko, Vladimir Kachpour. D: Pavel Lounguine. DRA 110m. V

Taxi Driver 1976 ★★★★★ Cabbie Travis Bickle (De Niro), harboring inexpressible frustrations, cruises aimlessly through the scum of NYC until he finds Shepherd, who becomes his reason to live and his inspiration to kill. Scorsese's harrowing portrait of the city as nightmare. Violent, ugly, yet as compelling as a ten-car pileup. You talkin' to me? C: Robert DeNiro, Cybill Shepherd, Harvey Keitel, Peter Boyle, Jodie Foster, Albert Brooks. D: Martin Scorsese. DRA [R] 113m. V

Taxing Woman, A 1987 Japanese ★★★★½ A young agent for Japan's internal revenue service matches wits with a cagey businessman whose constant mission is to cheat the government. A bright, intelligent, thoroughly charming comedy. C: Nobuko Miyamoto, Tsutomo Yamazaki. D: Juzo Itami. COM 127m. V

Taxing Woman's Return, A 1990 Japanese ★★★★ The tireless Japanese revenue agent makes a second foray against tax scammers. This time she's up against a syndicate of baddies involved in a real estate con. Funny and well done. C: Nobuko Miyamoto, Rentaro Mikuni. D: Juzo Itami. COM 127m. V

Taza, Son of Cochise 1954 ★★★ Warring Apache chief Geronimo tries to turn the son of a dead chief against the white man. Pro-Native American Western with good battle scenes. Followed by *Broken Arrow*. C: Rock Hudson, Barbara Rush, Gregg Palmer. D: Douglas Sirk. WST 79m.

Tchao Pantin 1985 French ★★★★ A former police officer meets a young Arab who gets him involved with drug smugglers. Dark and compelling. C: Coluche, Richard Anconnia, Philippe Leotard. D: Claude Berri. DRA 100m. V

Tea and Rice 1964 Japanese ★★★★ Japanese woman's arranged marriage leads to unhappiness so she convinces her niece to rebel against her parents' similar plans. Absorbing drama effectively explores Japanese customs. C: Shin Saburi, Michiyo Kogure, Koji Tsurata. D: Yasujiro Ozu. DRA 115m.

Tea and Sympathy 1956 ★★★★ Kerr is outstanding as headmaster's wife in boys' school, reaching out to troubled student whose manhood is in question. What was once daring drama seems a bit tame by today's standards, but the performances still ring true. From Robert Anderson play. C: Deborah Kerr, John Kerr, Leif Erickson, Edward Andrews, Darryl Hickman. D: Vincente Minnelli. DRA 123m. V

Tea for Two 1950 ★★★½ Lilting musical from Broadway's *No, No, Nanette*, with Broadway hopeful (Day) betting uncle she can say no to any question for a weekend. Silly, but pleasant fluff, with hit songs "I Want to Be Happy" and title tune. C: Doris Day, Gordon MacRae, Gene Nelson, Eve Arden, Billy De Wolfe, S. Z. Sakall. D: David Butler. MUS 98m. V

Teacher and the Miracle, The 1961 Italian ★★★½ A man is devastated by the death of his son, who had persuaded him to attend art school. Good soap opera with satisfactory acting. C: Eduardo Nevola, Marco Paolette. D: Aldo Fabrizi. DRA 88m.

Teacher, The 1974 ★★★½ Coming-of-age action thriller involves an older woman's affair with a younger man to whom she teaches the facts of life, while they're stalked by a psychotic killer. Junky but entertaining. C: Angel Tompkins, Jay North, Anthony James, Marlene Schmidt. D: Hikmet Avedis. CRI [R] 97m. V

Teachers 1984 ★★★ Social satire chronicles struggle of dedicated inner-city teachers against unthinking bureaucracy. Implausible, but does supply a few laughs. C: Nick Nolte, JoBeth Williams, Judd Hirsch, Ralph Macchio, Lee Grant, Richard Mulligan, Morgan Freeman. D: Arthur Hiller. COM [R] 106m. V

Teacher's Pet 1958 ★★★★ Old pro newsman (Gable) tangles with journalism teacher (Day) in engaging romantic comedy, stolen by Young as Clark's rival for Doris's affection. C: Clark Gable, Doris Day, Gig Young, Mamie Van Doren. D: George Seaton. COM 120m. V

Teahouse of the August Moon, The 1956 ★★★★½ Faithful adaptation of popular, Tony Award-winning Broadway play about an Army captain (Glenn Ford) sent to postwar Okinawa to bring democracy and recovery to the island. Brando has great comic turn as interpreter but Paul Ford stands out as blundering Colonel. C: Marlon Brando, Glenn Ford, Machiko Kyo, Eddie Albert, Paul Ford. D: Daniel Mann. COM 124m. V

Teamster Boss: The Jackie Presser Story 1992 ★★★½ The story of Jackie Presser, Jimmy Hoffa's tough-talking, hard-stomping successor as leader of the union. Typical film bio elevated by Dennehy's bullheaded performance. C: Brian Dennehy, Jeff Daniels, Maria Conchita Alonso, Eli Wallach, Robert Prosky, Tony Lo Bianco. D: Alastair Reid. DRA [R] 111m. TVM V

Tears and Laughter: The Joan and Melissa Rivers Story 1994 ★★★★ The Rivers women hold up well playing themselves in this account of the turmoil that struck their family in the late 1980s: Joan didn't replace Carson, her own late-night show was a bomb, and her husband committed suicide. Focus is on a mother and daughter who can't get along and is surprisingly effective. C: Joan Rivers, Melissa Rivers, Dorothy Lyman, Mark Kiely. D: Oz Scott. DRA 120m. TVM V

Tears for Simon 1957 British ★★★★ Police swing into action in manhunt for child's kidnappers. Intricate, adroit police work highlights semidocumentary, offbeat crime tale. (a.k.a. *Lost*) C: David Farrar, David Knight, Julia Arnall. D: Guy Green. CRI 91m. V

Teckman Mystery, The 1954 British ★★★½

Author (Justin) writing the biography of supposedly dead war hero (Medwin) discovers he's alive and his own life is in jeopardy. Fast-moving espionage mystery, well plotted and entertaining. C: Margaret Leighton, John Justin, Michael Medwin, Meier Tzelniker. D: Wendy Toye. ACT 89m.

Teen Witch 1989 ★★½ It's not hormones, it's witchcraft. A shy 16-year-old finds out she's a descendant of Salem witches and uses her powers to capture a cute boyfriend and get back at her teachers. Cute idea. C: Robyn Lively, Dan Gauthier, Joshua Miller, Dick Sargent. D: Dorian Walker. COM [PG-13] 94m. V

Teen Wolf 1985 ★★ Fox is the only reason to watch this dreadful movie about a runt on a high school basketball team whose social life improves when he starts growing hair in strange places and developing a bad overbite. Followed by a sequel. C: Michael J. Fox, James Hampton, Scott Paulin, Susan Ursitti. D: Rod Daniel. COM [PG] 92m. V

Teen Wolf Too 1987 ★★ Lame sequel to *Teen Wolf* has Fox's cousin (Bateman) suffering the family affliction. Collapses without Michael J. Fox. C: Jason Bateman, Kim Darby, John Astin, Paul Sand. D: Christopher Leitch. COM [PG] 95m. V

Teenage Delinquents 1957 *See* **No Time to Be Young**

Teenage Exorcist 1993 ★★★ With that title, you know what you're in for, as Deezen is pressed into service ridding Stevens of evil spirits. Likably schlocky mix of haunted-house shenanigans and goofy humor lacks real inspiration, but isn't nearly as bad as it could have been. C: Eddie Deezen, Brinke Stevens, Robert Quarry, Jay Richardson, Tom Shell. D: Grant Austin Waldman. HOR 86m.

Teenage Monster *See* **Meteor Monster**

Teenage Mutant Ninja Turtles—The Movie 1990 ★★★ Sewer-dwelling reptilian comic book superheroes use martial arts to aid a perky television reporter in solving a Manhattan crime spree. Good news: Jim Henson's nifty turtle costumes. Bad news: inane dialogue and plot. Bottom line: TMNT fans won't care. C: Judith Hoag, Elias Koteas. D: Steve Barron. FAM/COM [PG] 95m. V

Teenage Mutant Ninja Turtles 2: The Secret of the Ooze 1991 ★★½ Evil Shredder battles the pizza-munching heroes as they discover the source of their power. More of the same, only worse. Strictly mindless violence, plus pseudo-rapper Vanilla Ice! C: Paige Turco, David Warner, Ernie Reyes Jr. D: Michael Pressman. FAM/COM [PG] 88m. V

Teenage Mutant Ninja Turtles III 1993 ★★ The high-kicking superturtles are whisked back in time to feudal Japan, where they encounter real Ninja warriors, along with unaccountable references to *Wayne's World*. Less violent than the two previous TMNT features, but even worse as far as pointless plot. C: Elias Koteas, Paige Turco, Stuart Wilson, Sab Shimono. D: Stuart Gillard. FAM/COM [PG] 95m. V

Telefon 1977 ★★★★ Crackling suspense drama about a KGB agent (Bronson) sent to stop deranged agents from blowing up U.S. defense bases. C: Charles Bronson, Lee Remick, Donald Pleasence, Tyne Daly. D: Don Siegel. ACT [PG] 102m. V

Telegian, The 1961 *See* **Secret of the Telegian, The**

Telephone, The 1987 ★★ Goldberg sued to keep this film from release, so beware.She's a psycho actress who can't find work or an answer to her problems. C: Whoopi Goldberg, Elliott Gould, John Heard. D: Rip Torn. COM [R] 96m. V

Tell It to the Judge 1949 ★★★½ Lawyer (Russell) up for a judgeship can't decide whether to reunite with her skirt-chasing ex-husband (Cummings). Cornball farce depends mainly on star power. C: Rosalind Russell, Robert Cummings, Gig Young, Marie McDonald. D: Norman Foster. COM 87m. V

Tell Me a Riddle 1980 ★★★½ Reclusive dying woman attempts a reconciliation with her family. Talkative but moving, intelligent drama about tenuous relationships. Fine acting by Kedrova. C: Melvyn Douglas, Lila Kedrova, Brooke Adams. D: Lee Grant. DRA [PG] 94m. V

Tell Me Lies 1968 British ★★½ Ponderous film version of an experimental play denouncing U.S. involvement in Vietnam. Best left for fans of stage wizard Brook. C: Glenda Jackson, Paul Scofield, Kingsley Amis, Peggy Ashcroft, Stokely Carmichael. D: Peter Brook. DRA 118m.

Tell Me That You Love Me, Junie Moon 1970 ★★★★ Depressing, yet uplifting story of three emotional/physical cripples who band together: epileptic (Howard), facially scarred woman (Minnelli), and a lame homosexual (Moore). Could be Liza's best, least affected, performance. From Marjorie Kellogg's novel. C: Liza Minnelli, Ken Howard, Robert Moore, James Coco, Kay Thompson. D: Otto Preminger. DRA [PG] 112m..

Tell Them Willie Boy Is Here 1969 ★★★★ Set in 1909, story follows sheriff hunting down young Native American who killed in self-defense. Well-crafted screenplay, first-rate performances, and sensitive direction make this sometimes self-conscious issue drama gripping. C: Robert Redford, Katharine Ross, Robert Blake, Susan Clark, Barry Sullivan. D: Abraham Polonsky. CRI [PG] 98m. V

Tell Your Children 1936 *See* **Reefer Madness**

Temp, The 1993 ★★★ Hutton plays an office worker whose life is made easier by temporary secretary (Boyle) until she turns homicidal. Thriller starts off well, then goes into amazingly silly tailspin. C: Timothy Hutton, Lara Flynn Boyle, Faye Dunaway, Oliver Platt. D: Tom Holland. CRI [R] 99m. V

Tempest 1928 ★★★½ Based on Alexander Puskin's novel about 18th-century Russian empress Catherine the Great, who fends off a peasant uprising. Bloated costume epic about old Russia; elaborate production. C: John Barrymore, Camilla Horn, Louis Wolheim, George Fawcett. D: Sam Taylor. DRA 148m. V

Tempest 1959 Italian ★★½ Russian ensign, dismissed from the service of Catherine the Great, becomes involved in a movement to overthrow her. Overblown Italian/French costume melodrama has trouble keeping its act together. C: Silvana Mangano, Van Heflin, Viveca Lindfors, Geoffrey Horne, Agnes Moorehead, Vittorio Gassman. D: Alberto Lattuada. DRA 125m.

Tempest 1982 ★★★½ Update of Shakespeare's play with a burned-out architect (Cassavetes) who takes his daughter (Ringwald) to Greece, hoping to make a fresh start in life, only to have his past impinge nevertheless. Lively cast can't overcome ponderous story and misfired attempts at sorcery, but Ringwald's performance is exceptional. C: John Cassavetes, Gena Rowlands, Susan Sarandon, Vittorio Gassman, Raul Julia, Molly Ringwald. D: Paul Mazursky. DRA [PG] 140m. V

Tempter, The 1974 Italian ★★½ Ludicrous Italian rip-off of *The Exorcist* deals with a crippled woman who is the reincarnation of witch burned at stake centuries ago. Unpleasant and silly. C: Carla Gravina, Mel Ferrer, Arthur Kennedy, Alida Valli. D: Alberto De Martino. HOR [R] 96m. V

Temptress, The 1926 ★★★★ Garbo plays title role of a woman who proves to be a curse to those who love her. Her magnetic presence makes this silent romance much more than the claptrap it could have been. C: Greta Garbo, Antonio Moreno, Lionel Barrymore. D: Fred Niblo. DRA 117m.

10 1980 ★★★★ Moore became a star in this frothy sex comedy about a middle-aged composer risking his relationship with Andrews to chase after a mystery woman (Derek). Bo's cornrow hairdo and impressive physique caused a sensation at the time. C: Dudley Moore, Bo Derek, Julie Andrews, Robert Webber. D: Blake Edwards. COM [R] 122m. V

Ten Cents a Dance 1931 ★★★ Dance hall hostess (Stanwyck) falls for the wrong guy. Frowsy melodrama, but Stanwyck stays on her feet via fine, tough performance. C: Barbara Stanwyck, Ricardo Cortez, Monroe Owsley. D: Lionel Barrymore. DRA 80m.

Ten Commandments, The 1923 ★★★★ Silent, original version of the better-known 1956 epic (also done by DeMille). Film is split between the Biblical tale of Moses leading the Jews out of Egypt and a modern-day, parallel story (a la *Intolerance*). Period spectacle sequences stand out, including the parting of the Red Sea, in early two-color Technicolor. C: Theodore Roberts, Richard Dix, Leatrice Joy, Nital Naldi, Estelle Taylor. D: Cecil B. DeMille. DRA 146m. V

Ten Commandments, The 1956 ★★★★★ The extraordinary tale of Moses, the Hebrews, and their arduous journey out of bondage in Egypt is told by DeMille with immense power and scope. The Oscar-winning effects include the peerless parting of the Red Sea and the cast is a list of Hollywood's finest. DeMille's remake of his own 1923 silent is one of his supreme efforts. C: Charlton Heston, Yul Brynner, Anne Baxter, Edward G. Robinson, Yvonne De Carlo, Debra Paget, Cedric Hardwicke, Nina Foch, Martha Scott, Judith Anderson. D: Cecil B. DeMille. DRA [G] 219m. V

Ten Days that Shook the World 1928 *See* **October**

Ten Days Wonder 1972 French ★★★½ Perkins falls for Jobert, who just happens to be the new wife of his father (Welles). Flawed but intriguing mystery, based on an Ellery Queen story. C: Orson Welles, Anthony Perkins, Marlene Jobert, Michel Piccoli. D: Claude Chabrol. CRI [PG] 101m. V

Ten From Your Show of Shows 1973 ★★★★★ Once one understands that the poor technical quality comes from the Kinescope process, this collection of 10 sketches from the legendary 1950's TV series is hard to top for sheer comic brilliance. Watching Caesar, Coco, et. al. spoofing silent movies, *From Here to Eternity*, big business, *This is Your Life*, etc. is pure joy. Personal favorite: the clock! C: Sid Caesar, Imogene Coco, Carl Reiner, Howard Morris, Louis Nye. D: Max Liebman. COM 92m. V

Ten Little Indians 1965 British ★★★½ A group of people trapped in an Alpine village are murdered one by one. Second filmed version of Christie's novel lacks the visual appeal of *And Then There Were None*, but still suspenseful, thanks to Dame Agatha. C: Hugh O'Brian, Shirley Eaton, Fabian, Leo Genn, Stanley Holloway, Wilfrid Hydee White, Daliah Lavi. D: George Pollock. CRI 90m. V

Ten Little Indians 1975 ★★★ Agatha Christie's oft-filmed whodunit puts 10 strangers, including a murderer, in a remote setting; this time it's Iran. Great cast helps a weak script adaptation. C: Oliver Reed, Elke Sommer, Herbert Lom, Richard Attenborough, Charles Aznavour, Stephane Audran. D: Peter Collinson. CRI 98m. V

Ten Little Indians 1989 ★★ Third remake of Agatha Christie's famed *And Then There Were None* puts the nine victims (and one murderer) on an African safari. Weakest of the bunch. C: Donald Pleasence, Frank Stallone, Brenda Vaccaro, Herbert Lom. D: Alan Birkinshaw. CRI [PG] 98m. V

Ten North Frederick 1958 ★★★★ A man (Cooper) is urged into local politics by his ambitious wife (Fitzgerald), and finds comfort in the arms of a younger woman (Parker). Fine performances enhance strong family drama of May-September love, political machinations, survival of the fittest. Based on John O'Hara's novel. C: Gary Cooper, Diane Varsi, Suzy Parker, Geraldine Fitzgerald, Stuart Whitman, Barbara Nichols. D: Philip Dunne. DRA 102m.

Ten Seconds to Hell 1959 ★★★ German bomb disposal professionals in Berlin (Chandler and Palance) vie for the affections of the same woman (Carol). Vacant postwar melodrama. C: Jeff Chandler, Jack Palance, Martine Carol. D: Robert Aldrich. DRA 93m.

Ten Tall Men 1951 ★★★½ Reckless adventures of Foreign Legionnaires involving harem women and attacking Riffs. Good action that doesn't take itself seriously. Energetic performance by Lancaster. C: Burt Lancaster, Jody Lawrence, Gilbert Roland, Kieron Moore. D: Willis Goldbeck. ACT 97m.

Ten Thousand Bedrooms 1957 ★★½ In Rome, a lecherous hotel magnate (Martin) tries to seduce a family of daughters. Martin's first film without Lewis, and not so hot. C: Dean Martin, Anna Maria Alberghetti, Eva Bartok, Walter Slezak, Paul Henreid, Jules Munshin. D: Richard Thorpe. COM 114m.

Ten Tigers of Shaolin 1986 ★★½ Another martial arts hoopdeedoo with the usual damage to the human anatomy. C: Bruce Leung. D: Wei Hui Feng. ACT 90m. V

Ten to Midnight 1983 ★★ In zeal to catch woman-killing psychotic, a hardbitten cop (Bronson) plants evidence on suspect, which gets him kicked off force. After his daughter is victimized, he begins his own pursuit. Non-Bronson fans note: This is an extremely violent reworking of *Death Wish* formula. C: Charles Bronson, Andrew Stevens, Lisa Eilbacher, Wilford Brimley. D: J. Lee Thompson. ACT [R] 100m. V

Ten Who Dared 1960 ★★ Dull action/adventure story deals with expedition to chart the Colorado river and conflicts within the group of explorers. Relentlessly slow pace and unfocused direction. C: Brian Keith, John Beal, James Drury, R.G. Armstrong. D: William Beaudine. ACT 92m. V

Tenant, The 1976 French-U.S. ★★★★ A nebbish leases an apartment once rented by a suicidal man. Director Polanski casts himself in the lead, which pays off. Haunting, somewhat perplexing, but an ultimately rewarding thriller. C: Roman Polanski, Isabelle Adjani, Shelley Winters, Melvyn Douglas, Jo Van Fleet. D: Roman Polanski. HOR [R] 125m. V

Tender Comrade 1943 ★★★ Plodding drama of Rogers forming an all-female commune while the spouses are away, fighting WWII. Interesting only because, years later, the film was used by HUAC as an example of Communist influence in Hollywood. The script was co-written by Dmytryk and Dalton Trumbo, both blacklisted in the 1950's. C: Ginger Rogers, Robert Ryan, Ruth Hussey, Patricia Collinge, Kim Hunter, Jane Darwell. D: Edward Dmytryk. DRA 102m. V

Tender Cousins 1983 *See* **Tendres Cousines**

Tender Is the Night 1962 ★★★½ Film version of F. Scott Fitzgerald's novel about wealthy American psychiatrist (Robards, Jr.) who marries disturbed patient (Jones) in 1920s Europe. Characters' self-destructive traits leave them unsympathetic. C: Jennifer Jones, Jason Robards, Jr., Joan Fontaine, Tom Ewell, Jill St. John. D: Henry King. DRA 146m.

Tender Loving Care 1973 ★★½ At the local hospital, a trio of young nurses makes a variety of people feel better. C: Donna Desmond, Leah Simon, Anita King. D: Don Edmonds. COM [R] 72m.

Tender Mercies 1983 ★★★★½ A country singer hits bottom, then rebuilds his life with the love of a good woman in this low-key but effective drama, featuring an Oscar-winning performance by Duvall. Oscar for Best Screenplay. C: Robert Duvall, Tess Harper, Allan Hubbard, Betty Buckley. D: Bruce Beresford. DRA [PG] 93m. V

Tender Trap, The 1955 ★★★★ Confirmed bachelor (Sinatra) is trapped into wedlock by Reynolds. Breezy, very attractive comedy with excellent support from Holm and Wayne. Terrific title tune helps, too. C: Frank Sinatra, Debbie Reynolds, Celeste Holm, David Wayne, Carolyn Jones. D: Charles Walters. COM 116m. V

Tenderfoot, The 1932 ★★★½ Simple cow wrangler travels to New York to back flagging Broadway show and tangles with gangsters. Excellent comedy vehicle for Brown as a naif lost in a world of guile. C: Joe E. Brown, Ginger Rogers, Lew Cody, George Chandler. D: Ray Enright. COM 70m.

Tendres Cousines 1983 French ★★★ Growing up in the French countryside, two cousins share some experiences with life and love. Charming and heartfelt. (a.k.a. *Tender Cousins*) C: Thierry Tevini, Anja Shute. D: David Hamilton. COM [R] 90m. V

Tennessee Champ 1954 ★★★½ Religious prizefighter tries to reform his corrupt boss. Good acting enhances standard fight yarn. C: Shelley Winters, Keenan Wynn, Earl Holliman. D: Fred Wilcox. DRA 73m.

Tennessee Johnson 1942 ★★★★ President Lincoln's assassination catapults Vice President Andrew Johnson (Heflin) into office, where his battles with Congress lead to his impeachment and near ousting in 1868. Outstanding performance by Heflin in earnest, glossy historical biographical drama. C: Van Heflin, Lionel Barrymore, Ruth Hussey, Marjorie Main, Charles Dingle, Regis Toomey. D: William Dieterle. DRA 103m.

Tennessee's Partner 1955 ★★★½ Friendship between a frontier gambler and a drifter, who become involved with double-crossers and a gambling queen. Offbeat Western with superior cast and good action; based on a Bret Harte story. C: John Payne, Rhonda Fleming, Ronald Reagan, Coleen Gray. D: Allan Dwan. WST 87m. V

Tension 1949 ★★★½ Chemist (Basehart) learns his wife (Totter) is having an affair and plots to murder her lover; when the lover is killed by someone else, Basehart finds himself the prime suspect anyway. Suspenseful, with occasional (not necessarily unwelcome) lulls. C: Richard Basehart, Audrey Totter, Cyd Charisse, Barry Sullivan. D: John Berry. CRI 95m.

Tension at Table Rock 1956 ★★★ Wanted gunslinger redeems himself by taming wild Western town. Cliché-laden and derivative cow wrangler yarn with soap opera trimmings. C: Richard Egan, Dorothy Malone, Cameron Mitchell, Angie Dickinson. D: Charles Warren. WST 93m. V

Tenth Avenue Angel 1948 ★★ Plucky young woman (O'Brien) tries to better the lives of everyone around her. Glum city twist on *Pollyanna* does nothing for O'Brien. C: Margaret O'Brien, Angela Lansbury, George Murphy, Phyllis Thaxter. D: Roy Rowland. FAM/DRA 74m.

Tenth Man, The 1988 ★★★★ Rich lawyer gives his possessions to fellow inmate who agrees to take his place in front of Nazi firing squad; after war, lawyer ends up a servant in his former home, now owned by the dead inmate's family. Stylish handling of moral ambiguities. Based on Graham Greene story. C: Anthony Hopkins, Kristin Scott Thomas, Derek Jacobi, Cyril Cusack, Paul Rogers. D: Jack Gold. DRA 99m. TVM V

Tenth Month, The 1979 ★★★ A middle-aged woman faces single motherhood. Earnest issue drama, change-of-pace role for comedy veteran Burnett. From the Laura Z. Hobson novel. C: Carol Burnett, Keith Michell, Dina Merrill. D: Joan Tewkesbury. DRA 130m. TVM V

Tenth Victim, The 1965 Italian ★★★★ Futuristic chiller about legalized murder games. Attention-grabbing cult classic that actually has something to say about society's fascination with violence. C: Marcello Mastroianni, Ursula Andress, Elsa Martinelli. D: Elio Petri. SFI 92m. V

Tenting Tonight on the Old Camp Ground 1943 ★★★ Brown's attempts to finish a new road for the stagecoach keep getting sabotaged by a rival determined to establish his own route to win a lucrative mail contract. Nothing new in this typical Western, but production's energy makes it enjoyable. C: Johnny Mack Brown, Tex Ritter, Jennifer Holt, Lane Chandler. D: Lewis D. Collins. WST 59m.

Teorema 1968 Italian ★★ An irresistible stranger (Stamp) sleeps with every member of an Italian household. Is he Christ, or the devil? Incomprehensible fiasco from great director Pasolini is tasteless and pretentious, but undeniably fascinating. Scenes with Mangano screaming into the camera were famous for causing audiences to scream with laughter! C: Terence Stamp, Silvana Mangano, Laura Betti, Massimo Girotti. D: Pier Paolo Pasolini. DRA 98m. V

Tequila Sunrise 1988 ★★★ Overlong, glitzy Hollywood melodrama about former drug dealer and cop who fight for the same woman. Big budget can't really hide film's weaknesses. Pointless, despite talented cast and writer/director Towne. C: Mel Gibson, Michelle Pfeiffer, Kurt Russell, Raul Julia. D: Robert Towne. CRI [R] 116m. V

Teresa 1951 ★★★★ Confused WWII G.I. (Ericson) marries Italian woman (Angeli) and brings her home to New York, where she is assailed by bigotry. Well-observed, cautious, and sensitive film about social problems. C: Pier Angeli, John Ericson, Patricia Collinge, Peggy Ann Garner, Ralph Meeker. D: Fred Zinnemann. DRA 102m.

Term of Trial 1963 British ★★★★ Feckless British schoolmaster (Olivier) browbeaten by his wife (Signoret) rebuffs the advances of a 16-year-old student (Miles) who charges him with sexually assaulting her. Intelligent, workmanlike performance by Olivier and fine acting by all highlight somber narrative with a subtle twist. C: Laurence Olivier, Simone Signoret, Sarah Miles, Terence Stamp, Hugh Griffith. D: Peter Glenville. DRA 113m.

Terminal Bliss 1992 ★★ Obnoxious rich kid and down-to-earth best friend come to loggerheads over new girl in town. Drama tries to condemn decadence, even as it glorifies it in this gaudy mess. C: Timothy Owen, Luke Perry, Estee Chandler. D: Jordan Alan. DRA [R] 94m. V

Terminal Entry 1987 ★★½ Teenage hackers accidentally access a terrorist computer network and unknowingly instruct villains to destroy targets in the U.S. Interesting idea ruined by clumsy execution of the material. C: Edward Albert, Yaphet Kotto. D: John Kincade. CRI [R] 95m.

Terminal Island 1973 ★★ At a brutal California island jail, death-row inmates stage a breakout. Typical violence and overall unpleasantness. C: Phyllis Davis, Don Marshall, Barbara Leigh, Tom Selleck. D: Stephanie Rothman. DRA [R] 88m. V

Terminal Man, The 1974 ★★★ A mentally unstable scientist (Segal) has computer-controlled regulators installed in his head; when they fail, he goes murderously berserk. Well made; good performances; based on Crichton's compelling novel. C: George Segal, Joan Hackett, Richard Dysart, Jill Clayburgh. D: Mike Hodges. SFI [PG] 107m.

Terminal Velocity 1994 ★★★ Top ex-KGB agent (Kinski) tolerates wise-cracking skydiving instructor (Sheen) during deadly mission to retrieve stolen Russian bullion. Lamebrained actioner seems to have been written before perestroika. Some good daredevil air stunts, though. C: Charlie Sheen, Nastassja Kinski, James Gandolfini, Christopher McDonald. D: Deran Sarafian. ACT [PG-13] 102m. v

Terminator, The 1984 ★★★★½ An unstoppable, death-dealing android, sent back from the 21st century to assassinate a young woman, is pursued by a futuristic soldier who must stop him. Inventive effects and heart-stopping action are its most obvious assets, but it's the compelling emotional story that really makes this work. C: Arnold Schwarzenegger, Michael Biehn, Linda Hamilton, Paul Winfield. D: James Cameron. SFI [R] 108m. v

Terminator 2—Judgment Day 1991 ★★★★½ Sequel to 1982 hit involves Schwarzenegger returning to save heroine (Hamilton) and her son (Furlong), who is destined to save the world, from an evil terminator. Spectacular, state-of-the-art special effects and some tremendous action sequences help it keep pace with the original. C: Arnold Schwarzenegger, Linda Hamilton, Edward Furlong, Robert Patrick, Joe Morton. D: James Cameron. SFI [R] 139m. v

Terms of Endearment 1983 ★★★★★ Wonderful story of mother/daughter relationship as mother (MacLaine) tries to understand her own life while dealing with her dying daughter (Winger). The definitive four-hankie movie. Oscars for Best Picture, Director, Actress (MacLaine), Supporting Actor (Nicholson), and Screenplay. C: Shirley MacLaine, Debra Winger, Jack Nicholson, John Lithgow, Jeff Daniels, Danny DeVito, Bonnie Bedelia. D: James L. Brooks. DRA [PG] 130m. v

Terrible Beauty, A 1960 *See* **Night Fighters, The**

Terrible Joe Moran 1984 ★★★★½ Former boxing great (Cagney), now an invalid, tries to tie up the loose ends of his life. Cagney's only TV movie and his distinguished swan song; worthy support from Carney and Barkin. C: James Cagney, Art Carney, Ellen Barkin, Peter Gallagher. D: Joseph Sargent. DRA 100m. TVM

Terror at London Bridge 1985 *See* **Bridge Across Time**

Terror at the Opera 1991 Italian ★★★★ Creepy Italian horror film about violent, mysterious murders taking place at opera house during avant-garde production of *Macbeth*. Attention to mood and tone, and disturbing, frightening images make this a memorable thriller. Contains graphic violence. C: Cristina Marsillach, Ian Charleson, Urbano Barberini. D: Dario Argento. HOR [R] 107m. v

Terror By Night 1946 ★★★½ Sherlock Holmes (Rathbone) guards a valuable gem on a Scotland-bound train, and must solve a series of murders while on board. Cheap sets, but the whodunit elements and reliable cast make for a more than satisfactory mystery. C: Basil Rathbone, Nigel Bruce, Alan Mowbray. D: Roy Neill. CRI 60m.

Terror from Under the House 1971 *See* **Inn of the Frightened People**

Terror House 1942 *See* **Night Has Eyes, The**

Terror House 1972 ★★ A young woman (Gillin) takes a vacation, and winds up in a spooky old house. For its time, original in its take on cannibalism, but still not very good. C: Linda Gillin, Arthur Space, John Neilson. D: Bud Townsend. HOR [PG] 98m. v

Terror in a Texas Town 1958 ★★★½ A Swedish sailor (Hayden) returns to his father's Texas farm and tangles with a greedy land-grabbing oil baron (Cabot). Well-done, offbeat film with an exciting finale. C: Sterling Hayden, Sebastian Cabot, Carol Kelly. D: Joseph Lewis. WST 80m.

Terror in Beverly Hills 1990 ★★ An ex-marine tracks down terrorists who've abducted the President's daughter. What's worse, the lead bad guy already has a grudge against him. Pretty ridiculous. C: Frank Stallone, Cameron Mitchell. D: John Meyers. ACT 88m.

Terror in Space 1965 *See* **Planet of the Vampires**

Terror in the Aisles 1984 ★★★½ Clipfest tribute to horror films delivers a bunch of shocks from dozens of the best. Well worth sampling, despite annoying on-screen intros from Allen and Pleasence (who were both then screamfest favorites). C: Nancy Allen, Donald Pleasence. D: Andrew J. Kuehn. DOC [R] 85m. v

Terror in the Forest *See* **Forest, The**

Terror of Mechagodzilla 1978 Japanese ★★★ A surprisingly grim sci-fi flick about a mechanical monster, re-created for villains, to get rid of Godzilla once and for all. Colorful and often unintentionally funny. For fans only. C: Katsuhiko Sasaki, Tomoko AI. D: Inoshiro Honda. SFI 89m. v

Terror of Rome Against the Son of Hercules 1960 ★★ Blood and gore as Roman gladiators strive to eviscerate each other. C: Mark Forrest, Marilu Tolo. D: Mario Caiano. ACT 100m.

Terror of Sheba, The 1974 *See* **The Graveyard**

Terror of Tiny Town, The 1938 ★ Yep, folks, here it is! The world's only all-midget musical Western, now universally regarded as one of the worst movies of all time. Worth a look, a laugh—then rewind, fast! C: Billy Curtis, Yvonne Moray, Little Billy. D: Sam Newfield. MUS 63m. v

Terror Stalks the Class Reunion 1992 ★★ Homecoming is marred by a psychotic class member. Unremitting violence. C: Kate Nelligan, Jennifer Beals. D: Clive Donner. DRA 95m.

Terror, The 1963 ★★ Trail of a vanished woman leads a young man (Nicholson) to an eerie Baltic castle overseen by a sinister baron (Karloff). Roger Corman quickie shot over a long weekend. C: Boris Karloff, Jack Nicholson, Sandra Knight. D: Roger Corman. HOR 81m. V

Terror Train 1980 Canadian ★★½ A psychotic killer knocks off victims having a costume party on a train. Less-than-original story is helped by a stylish look and one interesting gimmick: the killer takes (and wears) each victim's costume as he goes. C: Ben Johnson, Jamie Lee Curtis, Hart Bochner, David Copperfield. D: Roger Spottiswoode. HOR [R] 97m. V

Terror Within, The 1989 ★★½ Scientists in an underground lab are the only survivors of a plague that has turned the populace into murderous zombies. Generic mutant/monster film. C: Andrew Stevens, Starr Andreeff, Terri Treas, George Kennedy. D: Thierry Notz. SFI [R] 95m. V

Terror Within II, The 1992 ★ Hero fights more mutants in futuristic wastelands while another group of underground scientists have similar problems. Unexciting sequel adds nothing to the original. C: Andrew Stevens, Stella Stevens, Chick Vennera. D: Andrew Stevens. HOR [R] 89m. V

Terrornauts, The 1967 British ★ Alien creatures hold a building and its residents hostage, transporting the entire structure to their planet. Lame material is further hampered by poor production values. Based on a novel by Murray Leinster. C: Simon Oates, Zena Marshall, Charles Hawtrey. D: Montgomery Tully. SFI 77m. V

Tess 1980 French ★★★★★ Beautiful adaptation of Thomas Hardy's novel stars Kinski as a 19th-century British woman ruined by her marriage to an aristocrat. Hardy's condemnation of society remains a powerful study of human foibles, with breathtaking Kinski providing a sympathetic lead. Well-earned Oscars for Cinematography, Costumes, and Art Direction. C: Nastassia Kinski, Peter Firth, John Bett. D: Roman Polanski. DRA [PG] 180m. V

Tess of the Storm Country 1960 ★★½ The daughter (Gaynor) of a retired ship's master falls in love but various troubles, including rumors of her being an unwed mother, crop up. Old-fashioned soap opera, buoyed by Gaynor. Adapted from Grace Miller White's novel; remade in 1961. C: Diane Baker, Jack Ging, Lee Philips. D: Paul Guilfoyle. DRA 84m.

Test Pilot 1938 ★★★★ Lives and loves of those death-defying airmen and their experimental flying machines. The plot is a vehicle to plop its huge stars into one film. Surprisingly it works, with fits of comedy to keep things moving. C: Clark Gable, Myrna Loy, Spencer Tracy, Lionel Barrymore, Marjorie Main. D: Victor Fleming. DRA 118m. V

Testament 1983 ★★★★ Aftermath of nuclear annihilation and its day-by-day effect on a small California town. Restrained doomsday personal drama with an exceptionally touching performance by Alexander. C: Jane Alexander, William Devane, Roxana Zal, Ross Harris, Lukas Haas. D: Lynne Littman. DRA [PG] 90m. V

Testament 1988 British ★★½ Twenty years after Ghanian dictator Kwame Nkrumah was overthrown by a military coup, a TV interview with Werner Herzog emerged which sought to shed light on the past. Equal parts fiction and documentary. C: T. Rogers. D: John Akomfrah. DOC 80m.

Testament of Dr. Mabuse, The 1933 German ★★★★ Fritz Lang's tale of an archcriminal who masterminds his empire of crime from an insane asylum. Controversial during the Nazi era, this German film is stylish and entertaining. (a.k.a. *The Last Will of Dr. Mabuse* and *The Crimes of Dr. Mabuse*) C: Rudolf Kleine Rogge, Otto Wernicke, Gustav Diesl. D: Fritz Lang. CRI 120m. V

Testament of Orpheus 1962 French ★★★★½ Cocteau's final effort is an autobiographical, fantastical reverie. Complex and demanding, but fascinating. C: Jean Cocteau, Edouard Dermit, Jean-Pierre Leaud, Henri Cremieux. D: Jean Cocteau. DRA 79m.

Tevye 1939 ★★★★ During the Russian pogroms, a Jewish milkman (Schwartz) must contend with the possibility that his daughter may marry a gentile. Splendid Yiddish film production based on Sholom Aleichem story is well acted and beautifully staged. Later turned into the musical *Fiddler on the Roof.* C: Maurice Schwartz, Rebecca Weintraub, Miriam Riselle. D: Maurice Schwartz. DRA 96m. V

Tex 1982 ★★★★ Two young brothers in the Southwest, their mother dead and their father absent, try to get along while fending for themselves. Amiable young-adult drama based on S.E. Hinton's best-seller, honestly rendered and well acted by Dillon. C: Matt Dillon, Jim Metzler, Meg Tilly, Ben Johnson, Emilio Estevez. D: Tim Hunter. DRA [PG] 102m. V

Texas 1941 ★★★★ Two Confederate veterans (Holden and Ford) plan to set up a cattle business in Texas after the Civil War, but things don't quite work out that way. Star vehicle with plenty of action and a sometimes hilarious script. C: William Holden, Glenn Ford, Claire Trevor, George Bancroft. D: George Marshall. ACT 94m. V

Texas Across the River 1966 ★★★½ Comedy/Western about a gun-happy wanderer who befriends a sexually frustrated Spanish nobleman. Engaging cast delivers good gags that poke fun at Westerns, but not as funny as it thinks it is. C: Dean Martin, Alain Delon, Joey Bishop, Rosemary Forsyth, Peter Graves. D: Michael Gordon. COM 101m. V

Texas Carnival 1951 ★★½ Good cast can't save tired tuner about a poor performer (Skelton) mistaken for a millionaire. Proof that not all MGM musicals were *Singin' in the Rain*! C:

Red Skelton, Esther Williams, Howard Keel, Ann Miller, Keenan Wynn. D: Charles Walters. MUS 77m. V

Texas Chainsaw Massacre, The 1974 ★★★★ Terrifying cult hit about a group of people who discover a demented family that eats and sells human flesh. Low budget adds to the film's harshly gritty, creepy tone. Not as violent as sequels, but more frightening. C: Marilyn Burns, Gunnar Hansen. D: Tobe Hooper. HOR [R] 84m. V

Texas Chainsaw Massacre, The—Part 2 1986 ★★ Chainsaw family opens a rolling grill, featuring its usual surprising ingredient, while an ex-ranger is obsessed with revenge against them. Silly, and attempts at black humor fall flat. Contains more graphic violence than original. C: Dennis Hopper, Caroline Williams, Bill Johnson, Jim Siedow. D: Tobe Hooper. HOR 95m. V

Texas Chainsaw Massacre—A Documentary—Family Portrait ★★½ The people who created the cult horror classic discuss its making, which was sometimes as horrifying as what occurs on screen. Clearly a labor of love. DOC

Texas Guns 1988 ★★★½ A young boy foils a daring train robbery planned by a cagy group of geezers. Light and breezy and lots of fun. (a.k.a. *Once Upon a Texas Train.*) C: Willie Nelson, Richard Widmark, Angie Dickinson. D: Burt Kennedy. WST TVM V

Texas Lady 1955 ★★★ Wild West newspaper editor (Colbert) tries to expose cattle rustlers. Routine western; Colbert's class spurs it. C: Claudette Colbert, Barry Sullivan. D: Tim Whelan. WST 86m. V

Texas Ranger, The 1931 ★★★★ Ranger discovers he may be pursuing the wrong culprits when he travels to a town in the midst of a homesteader war to arrest a murderous gang of cattle rustlers. Good old-fashioned Western action dominates in this early talking shoot-'em-up. C: Buck Jones, Carmelita Geraghty. D: D. Ross Lederman. WST 65m.

Texas Rangers, The 1936 ★★★★ When three outlaws go their separate ways, two of them reform and become Texas Rangers (MacMurray and Oakie). Well done, detailed, fact-based Western history. Remade as *Streets of Laredo.* Followed by *The Texas Rangers Ride Again.* C: Fred MacMurray, Jack Oakie, Jean Parker, Lloyd Nolan. D: King Vidor. WST 95m.

Texas Rangers, The 1951 ★★★ Gunplay ensues when Texas Rangers clash with a gang of outlaws. Meandering Western with plenty of shoot-outs. C: George Montgomery, Gale Storm, Jerome Courtland. D: Phil Karlson. WST 74m.

Texas Stampede 1939 ★★★½ Dedicated lawman comes to the rescue when cattlemen and sheepherders begin feuding over water rights. Solid Western action overcomes mundane plotting and clichéd characters. C: Charles Starrett, Iris Meredith. D: Sam Nelson. WST 57m. V

Texas Terror 1935 ★★★½ Early Wayne oater finds him a lawman on the run when he thinks he's murdered his closest buddy—that is, until he discovers who's really to blame. Fast-paced, low-budget Western, especially fun for the Duke's fans. C: John Wayne, George "Gabby" Hayes, Lucille Brown, Yakima Canutt. D: Robert Bradbury. WST 58m. V

Texasville 1990 ★★★½ Larry McMurtry's sequel to *The Last Picture Show* features same cast, wonderfully weatherbeaten. But even amazing performance by Bridges can't leaven slow-moving drama. C: Jeff Bridges, Cybill Shepherd, Annie Potts, Timothy Bottoms, Cloris Leachman, Randy Quaid, Eileen Brennan, William McNamara. D: Peter Bogdanovich. DRA [R] 126m. V

Thank God, It's Friday 1978 ★★ Idiotic disco musical; only highlight is Summer's Oscar-winning song, "Last Dance." C: Donna Summer, Valerie Landsburg, Jeff Goldblum, Debra Winger, Lionel Ritchie. D: Robert Klane. MUS [PG] 90m. V

Thank Heaven for Small Favors 1965 French ★★ Down-and-out French aristocrat comes to the conclusion that God wants him to rob church charity boxes instead of going to work. Unusual black comedy from France may offend rather than amuse. C: Bourvil. D: Jean-Pierre Mocky. COM 84m.

Thank You All Very Much 1969 British ★★★★ Pregnant by her first love, a London student considers abortion then keeps her baby. Moving, substantive narrative of unwed motherhood. C: Sandy Dennis, Ian McKellen, Eleanor Bron, John Standing. D: Waris Hussein. DRA [PG] 105m.

Thank You, Mr. Moto 1938 ★★★★ John P. Marquand's cunning Asian sleuth hunts for a map to ancient treasure. Sharp B-movie expertly played by Lorre. Best of the series of eight. C: Peter Lorre, Pauline Frederick, Sidney Blackmer, Sig Rumann, John Carradine. D: Norman Foster. CRI 67m.

Thank Your Lucky Stars 1943 ★★★★ Eddie Cantor and his taxi-driving twin plan a Warner Brothers WWII all-star musical extravaganza. Enjoyable, with stars poking fun at themselves. C: Dennis Morgan, Joan Leslie, Humphrey Bogart, Bette Davis, Olivia de Havilland, Errol Flynn, John Garfield, Ida Lupino, Ann Sheridan. D: David Butler. MUS 130m. V

Thanks a Million 1935 ★★★★ Popular singer (Powell) runs for governor. Crisp and entertaining songfest. Allen stands out as a wisecracking campaign manager. Remade as *If I'm Lucky.* C: Dick Powell, Ann Dvorak, Fred Allen, Patsy Kelly. D: Roy Del Ruth. MUS 87m.

Thanks for Everything 1938 ★★★½ Madison Avenue promoters package a "Mr. Average American." Punchy, satirical comedy lampoons the world of advertising. C: Adolphe Menjou, Jack Oakie, Jack Haley, Arleen Whelan. D: William A. Seiter. COM 70m.

Thanksgiving Day 1990 ★★★★½ Screwball family has a lot to cope with when the patriarch (Curtis) drops dead—during Thanksgiving dinner. Very entertaining black comedy features Moore's best comic performance since *The Mary Tyler Moore Show.* C: Mary Tyler Moore, Tony Curtis, Joseph Bologna, Sony Bono. D: Gino Tanasescu. COM 100m. TVM V

Thanksgiving Promise, The 1986 ★★★½ Entire Bridges clan (including unbilled Jeff) acts up a storm in this sentimental holiday tale about a boy's pet goose being primed for the carving board. Pleasing, made-for-cable fare. C: Beau Bridges, Lloyd Bridges, Jordan Bridges, Dorothy Dean Bridges, Millie Perkins, Ed Lauter, Jason Bateman. D: Beau Bridges. FAM/DRA 100m. TVM

Thark 1932 British ★★★½ Heir to an old baronial manor stays there overnight to demonstrate it isn't haunted. Hysterically funny farce filmed with the original stage team of the Ben Travers play. C: Tom Walls, Ralph Lynn, Mary Brough, Evelyn Bostock. D: Tom Walls. COM 79m.

That Certain Age 1938 ★★★ Wholesome young singer (Durbin) falls for suave journalist (Douglas), leaving her boyfriend (Cooper) to organize their upcoming amateur show. Cloying, clean-cut musical for the whole family. Songs by Jimmy McHugh. C: Deanna Durbin, Melvyn Douglas, Jackie Cooper, Irene Rich. D: Edward Ludwig. MUS 95m.

That Certain Feeling 1956 ★★★★ Smart, snappy Hope comedy casts him as an artist ghosting for a nationally syndicated cartoonist. Eva's charming, Pearlie Mae sings two songs, and *Lil'l Abner* creator Al Capp does a funny cameo. C: Bob Hope, Eva Marie Saint, George Sanders, Pearl Bailey, Al Capp, Jerry Mathers. D: Norman Panama, Melvin Frank. COM 103m.

That Certain Summer 1972 ★★★★ A divorced homosexual (Holbrook) must tell his 13-year-old son about himself. Ground-breaking TV film seems a little tame now, but good acting and writing carry it through. C: Hal Holbrook, Martin Sheen, Hope Lange, Scott Jacoby. D: Lamont Johnson. DRA 74m. TVM

That Certain Woman 1937 ★★★½ Gangster's widow (Davis) tries to go straight by marrying a rich good-for-nothing (Fonda) who then abandons her. She has a baby, endures scandal, and reunites with her husband. Contrived mother love drama saved by steely Davis. Remake of silent *The Trespasser.* C: Bette Davis, Henry Fonda, Donald Crisp, Anita Louise. D: Edmund Goulding. DRA 96m. V

That Championship Season 1982 ★★½ 24th annual reunion of a winning high-school basketball team becomes a night of rancor and recriminations. Stage-bound adaptation of Jason Miller's Pulitzer-Prize-winning play, with hammy acting, overblown emotions. Playwright's directing debut (a mistake). C: Robert Mitchum, Bruce Dern, Stacy Keach, Martin Sheen, Paul Sorvino. D: Jason Miller. DRA [R] 110m. V

That Cold Day in the Park 1969 ★★★ A sexually repressed eccentric (Dennis) invites a young man into her home, and doesn't let him leave. Psychodrama (emphasis on psycho) is lumbering and not all that disturbing. Early Altman. C: Sandy Dennis, Michael Burns, Susanne Benton. D: Robert Altman. DRA [R] 106m. V

That Dangerous Age 1949 *See* **If This Be Sin**

That Darn Cat 1965 ★★★★ Feline gets involved in FBI espionage in Disney family yarn. Sounds ridiculous, but movie works, due to funny visual gags and ingratiating cast. Highlight: Cat goes to the movies. C: Hayley Mills, Dean Jones, Dorothy Provine, Roddy McDowall, Elsa Lanchester, William Demarest. D: Robert Stevenson. FAM/COM [G] 116m. V

That Forsythe Woman 1949 ★★★ Period soap opera, with cold married woman (Garson) having illicit affair with Young, her niece's fiancé. Shallow, unconvincingly acted adaptation of Galsworthy's classic novel *The Man of Property*, from *The Forsythe Saga.* C: Errol Flynn, Greer Garson, Walter Pidgeon, Robert Young, Janet Leigh. D: Compton Bennett. DRA 112m. V

That Funny Feeling 1965 ★★½ Mistaken-identity comedy about a maid (Dee) who doesn't know that the new man in her life is really her boss. So-so romantic nonsense, with Sandra and Bobby trying very hard to be Doris and Rock. C: Sandra Dee, Bobby Darin, Donald O'Connor, Nita Talbot. D: Richard Thorpe. COM 93m.

That Girl From Paris 1936 ★★★★ Opera star (Pons, who else?) poses as a jazz singer to stay in America. Bright, breezy mixture of classical and popular tunes. Lily's best movie. C: Lily Pons, Jack Oakie, Gene Raymond, Mischa Auer, Lucille Ball. D: Leigh Jason. MUS 105m. V

That Hagen Girl 1947 ★★ Odd story of a drifter (Reagan) and a small-town girl (Temple) who may or may not be his illegitimate daughter. Reagan claimed to regret making it. C: Ronald Reagan, Shirley Temple, Rory Calhoun. D: Peter Godfrey. DRA 83m.

That Hamilton Woman 1941 ★★★★½ Love and scandal overtake Lord Nelson, Britain's 18th-century naval hero, and Lady Hamilton. A fine effort (Churchill's favorite) with super performances by real-life lovers, Olivier and Leigh. C: Vivien Leigh, Laurence Olivier, Alan Mowbray, Sara Allgood, Gladys Cooper. D: Alexander Korda. DRA 125m. V

That Kind of Woman 1959 ★★★★ Loren

gives one of her better, early performances as a woman torn between a handsome but penniless soldier (Hunter) and an older, wealthy gentleman (Sanders). Predictable, but quite entertaining. C: Sophia Loren, Tab Hunter, George Sanders, Keenan Wynn, Jack Warden. D: Sidney Lumet. COM 92m.

That Lady 1955 ★★★½ Costumer profiles the famed Princess of Eboli (de Havilland), who gets on the King's bad side when she falls in love with a commoner (Roland). Don't miss your chance to see Olivia in an eye patch. Lavish historical drama; Scofield's film debut. C: Olivia de Havilland, Gilbert Roland, Paul Scofield. D: Terence Young. DRA 100m.

That Lady in Ermine 1948 ★★★ Ancestors emerge from portraits to help European noblewomen in distress in a mythical kingdom. Uninspired musical comedy is mildly entertaining. C: Betty Grable, Douglas Fairbanks Jr., Cesar Romero, Reginald Gardiner. D: Ernst Lubitsch, Otto Preminger. MUS 89m.

That Man From Rio 1964 French ★★★½ Pilot-adventurer thwarts treacherous thieves in a global hunt for a fabulous Brazilian treasure. Amiable takeoff on spy films, with Belmondo's athleticism a high point. C: Jean-Paul Belmondo, Francoise Dorleac, Jean Servais, Adolfo Celi. D: Phillippe DeBroca. ACT 114m. V

That Midnight Kiss 1949 ★★★★ In Lanza's auspicious movie debut, he plays a singing truckdriver spotted by an heiress (Grayson) who wants to be an opera singer. Schmaltz thickens a thin plot, but great for music fans and lovers of wonderful singing. C: Kathryn Grayson, Mario Lanza, Jose Iturbi, Ethel Barrymore, Keenan Wynn, Jules Munshin. D: Norman Taurog. MUS 98m. V

That Night 1957 ★★★½ Overworked television writer (Beal) suffers a heart attack, and his family stands by him during his recovery. Honest small case history holds interest. C: John Beal, Augusta Dabney, Shepperd Strudwick, Rosemary Murphy. D: John Newland. DRA 88m.

That Night 1993 ★★½ Two young lovers (Lewis and Howell) in the '50s and their 10-year-old friend (Dushku) watch as their world falls apart when Lewis becomes pregnant. Overstated, adaptation of Alice McDermott's novel. C: Juliette Lewis, C. Thomas Howell, Eliza Dushku, Helen Shaver. D: Craig Bolotin. DRA [PG-13] 89m.

That Night in Rio 1941 ★★★½ Nightclub performer is hired to assume the identity of his double, a European nobleman, whose wife presents unforeseen complications. Snappy musical is a good-looking and good-sounding farce of mistaken identities. Miranda is well placed. C: Alice Faye, Don Ameche, Carmen Miranda, S. Z. Sakall, J. Carroll Naish. D: Irving Cummings. MUS 90m.

That Obscure Object of Desire 1977 Spanish ★★★★½ A wealthy man has a new girlfriend, but she won't sleep with him. A farce of thwarted libido done as only Buñuel could: This was his last film. Pierre Louy's novel has also been filmed as *The Devil is a Woman*, *La Femme et le Pantin*, and *The Female*. (a.k.a. *Cet Obscur Objet du Désir*) C: Fernando Rey, Carole Bouquet, Angela Molina. D: Luis Bunuel. COM [R] 100m. V

That Sinking Feeling 1979 Scottish ★★★★ Director Forsyth's brand of low-key, quirky humor carries his first movie about a group of bored Glasgow youths who decide to steal and then have difficulty getting rid of a shipment of stainless steel sinks. Funny and charming. C: Robert Buchanan, John Hughes, Billy Greenlees. D: Bill Forsyth. COM [PG] 82m. V

That Touch of Mink 1962 ★★★½ In this he vs. she comedy, corporate raider Grant's limousine splashes Day with mud. She accosts him in his office, he charms her, she acquiesces, he takes her to Bermuda.... Frolicsome fare with winning performances and witty dialogue. C: Cary Grant, Doris Day, Gig Young, Audrey Meadows. D: Delbert Mann. COM 99m. V

That Uncertain Feeling 1941 ★★★½ Hypocondriac socialite jeopardizes her marriage by becoming involved with an eccentric live-in pianist. Stylish screwball Lubitsch comedy; Meredith walks away with the show. C: Merle Oberon, Melvyn Douglas, Burgess Meredith, Alan Mowbray, Eve Arden. D: Ernst Lubitsch. COM 86m. V

That Wonderful Urge 1948 ★★★½ Vengeful heiress evens the score against journalist who's been writing mean articles about her. Pleasing romantic comedy with top cast. Remake of *Love Is News*. C: Tyrone Power, Gene Tierney, Arleen Whelan, Reginald Gardiner. D: Robert Sinclair. COM 82m.

That'll Be the Day 1973 ★★★★ Discontented British youth (Essex) leaves his family, works at humdrum employment, then opts for rock stardom. Intelligent, realistic, and inventive pop music odyssey. Followed by *Stardust*. C: Ringo Starr, Keith Moon, David Essex, Rosemary Leach. D: Claude Whatham. DRA [PG] 87m. V

That's Dancing 1985 ★★★½ Enjoyable assembly of big-screen dancing contains recent material overlooked by the *That's Entertainment* films, but somehow lacks those two films polish. Still a must for dancing and musical fans. C: Gene Kelly, Sammy Davis Jr., Mikhail Baryshnikov, Liza Minnelli, Ray Bolger. D: Jack Haley Jr. MUS 105m. V

That's Entertainment 1974 ★★★★½ Compilation of the cream of MGM musical catalog hosted by some of the studio's former stars (even though Taylor wasn't a hoofer or singer) is an uncredited homage to producer Arthur Freed. Wonderful entertainment for everyone. C: Fred Astaire, Bing Crosby, Gene Kelly, Peter Lawford, Liza Minnelli, Donald O'Connor, Debbie Reynolds, Mickey Rooney, Frank Sinatra, James Stewart, Elizabeth Taylor. D: Jack Haley, Jr. MUS 122m. V

That's Entertainment, Part 2 1976 ★★★★ Hosted by Kelly and Astaire, this sequel to the MGM clipfest doesn't have quite the excitement of its predecessor, mostly because the best numbers were already taken. But it does have the Irving Berlin music missing from the first and some great comedy bits, including the Marx Brothers. Followed by *That's Entertainment III* in 1994. C: Fred Astaire, Gene Kelly. D: Gene Kelly. MUS [G] 133m. V

That's Entertainment 3 1994 ★★★★ More MGM musical highlights, with hosts Kelly, Horne, Miller, and Rooney providing nostalgic introductions. No movie with Garland, Sinatra, and Astaire could be bad. C: Gene Kelly, Lena Horne, Mickey Rooney, Ann Miller. MUS

That's Life! 1986 ★★★★ Comedy/drama of the middle-age crisis of a man (Lemmon) and the patience of his stoic wife (Andrews) with his unbearable behavior despite her private dread of her upcoming biopsy result. Excellent performances strike a perfect (and difficult) balance. C: Jack Lemmon, Julie Andrews, Sally Kellerman, Robert Loggia. D: Blake Edwards. COM [PG-13] 102m. V

That's My Boy 1951 ★★★ Dino's employed to teach spastic Jerry how to play football. Strident comedy makes too few touch-downs. A treat for Martin and Lewis fans; others, watch out. C: Dean Martin, Jerry Lewis, Ruth Hussey, Marion Marshall, Eddie Mayehoff, Polly Bergen. D: Hal Walker. COM 98m.

That's the Spirit 1945 ★★★ Dead entertainer returns as an angel to explain to his wife that he didn't desert her and to give his daughter. a career boost. Ponderous fantasy musical with good songs and an excellent gag by Keaton. C: Peggy Ryan, Jack Oakie, June Vincent, Gene Lockhart, Andy Devine, Arthur Treacher, Irene Ryan, Buster Keaton. D: Charles Lamont. MUS 93m.

That's the Way of the World 1975 ★★ Behind-the-scenes look at music business involves recording studio that suffers under control of organized crime. Music by group Earth, Wind and Fire is the standout. (a.k.a. *Shining Star*) C: Harvey Keitel, Ed Nelson, Bert Parks. D: Sig Shore. COM [PG] 100m. V

Theatre of Blood 1973 British ★★★½ Third-rate actor takes revenge on critics who gave him bad reviews, murdering them in ways inspired by Shakespeare's plays. Price is terrific, well supported by the charming Rigg. A wickedly funny horror comedy, marred only by the lagging pace. C: Vincent Price, Diana Rigg, Robert Morley, Ian Hendry, Coral Browne, Michael Hordern, Diana Dors, Milo O'Shea. D: Douglas Hickox. HOR 105m. V

Theatre of Death 1967 British ★★★★ Well-produced and acted chiller centering on a Grand Guignol-style theater in Paris, where horrific murders are happening for real. Lee is fun as the catty director who might be the killer. (a.k.a. *Blood Fiend*) C: Christopher Lee, Julian Glover, Lelia Goldoni, Jenny Till, Evelyn Laye. D: Samuel Gallu. HOR [PG] 89m.

Theatre Royal 1943 British ★★★★ Pleasant British comedy mixes song, comedy, and a taste for the old vaudeville stage as a prop man maneuvers to keep a local music hall revue open. Thin on story, but an entertaining look at a charming milieu. C: Bud Flanagan, Chesney Allen. D: John Baxter. COM 101m.

Their Only Chance 1975 ★★★ Young man (Hoddy) shows older rancher (Mahoney) his ability to relate with to animals. Amiable, if forgettable, nature film. C: Jock Mahoney. D: David Siddon. FAM/DRA 84m. V

Thelma & Louise 1991 ★★★★½ Superlative action drama with knockout performances by Sarandon and Davis as two women, unsatisfied with their lives, who go on vacation together and accidentally become wanted criminals. Powerful, emotional, and highly entertaining. Oscar went to Callie Khouri for her dynamite screenplay. C: Susan Sarandon, Geena Davis, Harvey Keitel, Brad Pitt, Timothy Carhart. D: Ridley Scott. DRA [R] 127m. V

Them! 1954 ★★★★ Classic science fiction thriller about giant ants who take over the sewers of a community near the Mojave Desert. Terrific special effects and an exciting climax make this a tremendously enjoyable monster classic. C: James Whitmore, Edmund Gwenn, Joan Weldon, James Arness. D: Gordon Douglas. SFI 93m. V

Theodora Goes Wild 1936 ★★★★ Librarian (Dunne) pens a sizzling best-seller about small-town scandals and falls for a suave New York illustrator (Douglas). Excellent entrée into comedy for the versatile Dunne in charming madcap farce based on a Mary McCarthy story. C: Irene Dunne, Melvyn Douglas, Thomas Mitchell, Spring Byington. D: Richard Boleslawski. COM 94m.

There Goes My Heart 1938 ★★★½ Runaway heiress (Bruce) poses as a shopgirl, and a reporter (March) on her trail discovers her identity. Zippy but derivative stereotypical comedy for the era. C: Fredric March, Virginia Bruce, Patsy Kelly, Alan Mowbray, Nancy Carroll. D: Norman McLeod. COM 84m.

There Goes the Neighborhood 1992 ★★★ Locals go after treasure under a neighborhood house. Middling comedy. C: Jeff Daniels, Catherine O'Hara, Hector Elizondo, Rhea Perlman, Judith Ivey. D: Bill Phillips. COM [PG-13] 88m. V

There Must Be a Pony 1986 ★★★½ A Hollywood legend (Taylor) with a history of mental instability falls in love with a mysterious man (Wagner). Pure soap opera, but well-done. Liz's best performance in years. C: Elizabeth Taylor, Robert Wagner, James Coco, Chad Lowe. D: Joseph Sargent. DRA 100m. TVM

There Was a Crooked Man 1970 ★★★★ Intriguing Western about friendship between a convicted robber in prison and a reform-minded warden who suspects he's planning an escape. Talky script is compensated by sparkling direction and polished performances by Fonda and Douglas. C: Kirk Douglas, Henry Fonda, Hume Cronyn, Warren Oates, Burgess Meredith. D: Joseph L. Mankiewicz. WST [R] 123m. v

There Was an Old Couple 1967 USSR ★★★★ Elderly Russian couple decide to live with their daughter when their farmhouse burns down, but when they discover she's abandoned her alcoholic husband and daughter, they move in with them instead. Unusual, but moving drama. C: Ivan Marin, Vera Kuznetsova, Grigoriy Martynyuk. D: Grigory Chukhray. DRA 103m.

There's a Girl in My Soup 1970 British ★★★ Womanizing TV star (Sellers) is caught off guard by a screwball beatnik (Hawn) in this sex comedy that never really goes anywhere. C: Peter Sellers, Goldie Hawn, Tony Britton, Diana Dors. D: Roy Boulting. COM [R] 95m. v

There's Always a Woman 1938 ★★★★ New District Attorney (Douglas) turns over his detective agency to his investigator wife (Blondell) and soon the couple sets out to solve the same murder. Appealing cast in deft mix of mystery and comedy á la Nick and Nora Charles. C: Joan Blondell, Melvyn Douglas, Mary Astor. D: Alexander Hall. COM 82m.

There's Always Tomorrow 1956 ★★★½ Businessman (MacMurray) with bratty children and selfish wife (Bennett) is discontented until he encounters old flame (Stanwyck). Thoughtful soap opera with excellent performances. C: Barbara Stanwyck, Fred MacMurray, Joan Bennett, William Reynolds. D: Douglas Sirk. DRA 84m.

There's No Business Like Show Business 1954 ★★★½ Overlong but flamboyant Irving Berlin songfest, with silly plot about show business family headed by Merman and Dailey. Sons Ray and O'Connor get mixed up with the priesthood and Monroe, respectively. Some flashy numbers, best of which is Marilyn's "Heat Wave." C: Ethel Merman, Dan Dailey, Donald O'Connor, Marilyn Monroe, Johnny Ray, Mitzi Gaynor. D: Walter Lang. MUS 117m. v

Therese 1986 French ★★★★ A young nun bears a love for Christ that is highly romantic. Based on a true story; offers a fascinating view of convent life. Enormously powerful and evocative. C: Catherine Mouchet, Aurore Prieto. D: Alain Cavalier. DRA 90m. v

Therese Raquin *See* **The Adulteress**

These Are the Damned 1962 British ★★★½ Violent gang of motorcycle thugs clash with scientists when radioactive children are discovered sealed in a cliff cave. Confusing blend of delinquent youth gangs and science fiction. Downbeat, hard, and strangely compelling. (a.k.a. *The Damned*) Sequel is *Children of the Damned*. C: Macdonald Carey, Shirley Field, Viveca Lindfors, Oliver Reed. D: Joseph Losey. ACT 96m.

These Thousand Hills 1959 ★★★½ Young cow wrangler (Murray) becomes a wealthy rancher and learns his friend is cattle rustler. Spotty Western laden with subplots; dependable acting. Based on novel by A.B. Guthrie, Jr. C: Don Murray, Richard Egan, Lee Remick, Stuart Whitman. D: Richard Fleischer. WST 96m.

These Three 1936 ★★★★½ Spiteful little girl spreads malicious lie that destroys the lives of her two schoolmistresses. Expurgated but compelling rendition of Lillian Hellman's play *The Children's Hour*, later remade by director Wyler under that name. Excellent performances, particularly by Granville. C: Miriam Hopkins, Merle Oberon, Joel McCrea, Alma Kruger, Bonita Granville, Margaret Hamilton, Walter Brennan. D: William Wyler. DRA 93m. v

These Wilder Years 1956 ★★★½ Complications arise when a steel tycoon (Cagney) tracks down his illegitimate son and becomes involved with the director of an orphanage (Stanwyck). Sentimental soap opera off the beaten track for Cagney. That's a young Michael London in the pool room. C: James Cagney, Barbara Stanwyck, Walter Pidgeon, Betty Keim. D: Roy Rowland. DRA 91m.

They All Come Out 1939 ★★★½ Insightful drama with a documentary feel examines prison rehabilitation of convicts who decide to go straight. Realistic drama poignantly portrays this unusual struggle. C: Rita Johnson, Tom Neal, Bernard Nedell. D: Jacques Tourneur. DRA 70m.

They All Died Laughing 1964 *See* **Jolly Bad Fellow**

They All Kissed the Bride 1942 ★★★½ An executive and a journalist out to discredit her organization fall in love. Bland romantic comedy, but with a top-notch cast. C: Joan Crawford, Melvyn Douglas, Roland Young, Billie Burke. D: Alexander Hall. COM 85m.

They All Laughed 1981 ★★★ Several New York City private detectives find romance while working on various cases. Vague, insubstantial curiosity with few chuckles. Stratten was murdered shortly after production. C: Audrey Hepburn, Ben Gazzara, John Ritter, Colleen Camp, Dorothy Stratten. D: Peter Bogdanovich. COM [PG] 115m. v

They Are Not Angels 1948 French ★★★★ Stirring war drama focuses on squadron of French paratroopers stationed in England as they prepare for the invasion of Nazi-occupied France. Realistic characters and intense attention to detail keep this riveting throughout. C: Pierre Blanchar, Raymond Bussieres, Jean Wall. D: Alexandre Esway. ACT 130m.

They Call Me Bruce 1982 ★★½ A recent

Asian immigrant (Yune) with a resemblance to the martial arts idol and a clumsiness mistaken for kung fu mastery becomes something of a crime-fighting hero. Funniest for viewers who have watched serious martial arts movies, and know the details being spoofed. C: Johnny Yune, Ralph Mauro, Pam Huntington, Margaux Hemingway. D: Elliot Hong. COM [PG] 88m. v

They Call Me MISTER Tibbs! 1970 ★★★ Tame sequel to *In the Heat of the Night* involves detective who investigates the murder of a young woman while trying to clear a friend's name. Poitier is surprisingly dull this time around, not helped by the predictable plot. C: Sidney Poitier, Barbara McNair, Martin Landau. D: Gordon Douglas. CRI [PG] 108m. v

They Call Me Trinity 1971 Italian ★★★½ Genial satire of spaghetti-Westerns involves gunslingers who try to save a settlement from marauding cattle rustlers. Loaded with sight gags and wisecracks. Sequel: *Trinity Is Still My Name*. C: Terence Hill, Bud Spencer, Farley Granger. D: E. B. Clucher. COM [G] 110m. v

They Came From Within 1975 Canadian ★★★½ Cronenberg's first feature is an offbeat tale of sexually transmitted parasites that make everyone in a community hyper-sexual. Outrageous black humor and graphic violence, which have become the director's trademark. C: Paul Hampton, Joe Silver, Lynn Lowry, Barbara Steele. D: David Cronenberg. SFI [R] 87m. v

They Came to a City 1944 British ★★½ Several people between two worlds imagine their ideal Utopias while outside the gates of a strange city. Well acted and written but offbeat and uncinematic. C: John Clements, Googie Withers, Raymond Huntley, Renee Gadd. D: Basil Dearden. SFI 78m.

They Came to Blow Up America 1943 ★★★½ FBI agent of German heritage subverts a gang of Nazi saboteurs in deep cover in the United States. Taut, well-done spy-counterspy WWII yarn with good acting, but dated propaganda. C: George Sanders, Anna Sten, Ward Bond. D: Edward Ludwig. ACT 73m.

They Came to Cordura 1959 ★★★½ Soldier (Cooper) with a shady past accepts assignment in Mexico during WWI and gets involved with a lady of dubious virtue (Hayworth) he meets along the way. Entertaining character study (albeit glib) with a distinctly Western flavor. C: Gary Cooper, Rita Hayworth, Van Heflin, Tab Hunter. D: Robert Rossen. WST 123m. v

They Died With Their Boots On 1941 ★★★★ Big, splashy Western epic about life of General Custer, from West Point cutup to the Battle of Little Bighorn. Not very accurate, but splendid entertainment. C: Errol Flynn, Olivia de Havilland, Arthur Kennedy, Anthony Quinn. D: Raoul Walsh. WST 141m. v

They Drive by Night 1940 ★★★★ Two truck driving brothers run afoul of a crooked boss and his sexy, murderous wife. Standout cast, given terrific dialogue, shines in this compelling melodrama. C: George Raft, Ann Sheridan, Ida Lupino, Humphrey Bogart. D: Raoul Walsh. CRI 96m. v

They Flew Alone 1942 *See* **Wings and the Woman**

They Gave Him a Gun 1937 ★★★★ Embittered WWI veteran (Tone) turns to crime against the wishes of his war buddy (Tracy). Compelling moral tale with fine acting and a good script. C: Spencer Tracy, Gladys George, Franchot Tone. D: W. S. Van Dyke II. DRA 94m.

They Got Me Covered 1943 ★★★ Routine Hope comedy with lots of one-liners, colorful supporting players, and the ubiquitous Lamour in this spy romp set in Washington, D.C. C: Bob Hope, Dorothy Lamour, Lenore Aubert, Otto Preminger. D: David Butler. COM 93m. v

They Had to See Paris 1929 ★★★★½ Oklahoma garage owner strikes it rich when he discovers oil and his wife insists they use their new-found wealth to visit Paris. Early Will Rogers talkie wonderfully displays his down-home wit and disdain for pretentiousness and insincerity. An amusing comedy throughout. C: Will Rogers, Irene Rich. D: Frank Borzage. COM 96m.

They Knew What They Wanted 1940 ★★★★ Complications ensue when a California vintner takes a waitress as his mail-order bride. Top drama with expert acting and fine production values. Based on Sidney Howard's play. The musical *The Most Happy Fella* was based on this movie. C: Carole Lombard, Charles Laughton, William Gargan, Harry Carey, Frank Fay. D: Garson Kanin. DRA 96m. v

They Learned About Women 1930 ★★★ Would you believe, with that title, this is a *baseball* musical! Enjoyable early talkie songfest about ball-playing song-and-dance men. Remade in 1949 as *Take Me Out To the Ballgame*. C: Joseph T. Schenck, Gus Van, Bessie Love. D: Jack Conway, Sam Wood. MUS 81m. v

They Live 1988 ★★★★ Arriving in L.A., a young wanderer discovers plot by aliens to control humans through TV advertising. Witty sci-fi spoof of yuppie culture runs out of gags before it's over. C: "Rowdy" Roddy Piper, Keith David, Meg Foster. D: John Carpenter. SFI [R] 95m. v

They Live by Night 1949 ★★★★½ Pair of young lovers with criminal pasts are forced into becoming fugitives from justice during the Depression. Powerhouse crime drama, refreshingly free of clichés; the cast excels with strong characterizations. From Edward Anderson's novel *Thieves Like Us*; later remade as a film of that name. C: Farley Granger, Cathy O'Donnell, Howard da Silva, Jay C. Flippen. D: Nicholas Ray. CRI 95m. v

They Loved Life 1956 *See* **Kanal**

They Made Me a Criminal 1939 ★★★½

Boxer believes he committed murder, flees to a California farm, where he's befriended by delinquents. Entertaining fare with fine acting by Garfield. Remake of *The Life of Jimmy Dolan.* C: John Garfield, Claude Rains, May Robson, Huntz Hall, Leo Gorcey, Gabriel Dell, Ann Sheridan. D: Busby Berkeley. DRA 92m. v

They Made Me a Fugitive 1947 *See* **I Became a Criminal**

They Met in Bombay 1941 ★★★½ Two jewel thieves on the run team up and fall in love. Star power elevates ordinary romantic-comedy-chase-action film. C: Clark Gable, Rosalind Russell, Peter Lorre, Jessie Ralph. D: Clarence Brown. ACT 93m. v

They Might Be Giants 1971 ★★★★ A retired jurist (Scott) is convinced he's Sherlock Holmes and is joined in a mock adventure by a family-appointed psychiatrist—Dr. Mildred Watson (Woodward). Wacky, enjoyable fantasy fable with superb performances by the leads. C: Joanne Woodward, George C. Scott, Jack Gilford, Lester Rawlins. D: Anthony Harvey. COM [G] 98m. v

They Only Kill Their Masters 1972 ★★★½ When a woman is found dead on the beach, investigator (Garner) finds himself on the trail of a Doberman pinscher. Complex mystery suffers because suspense is too casually handled, but the cast is worth watching. C: James Garner, Katharine Ross, Hal Holbrook, Harry Guardino, June Allyson, Tom Ewell, Peter Lawford. D: James Goldstone. CRI [PG] 98m. v

They Passed This Way 1948 *See* **Four Faces West**

They Saved Hitler's Brain 1963 ★★ Neo-Nazis flourish on the island of Mandoras, thanks to Hitler's pickled head, still living in what looks like a large mayonnaise jar. Brain-dead horror film, actually two bad movies (one shot in 1955, the other 1962) put together, with sometimes hilarious results. C: Walter Stocker, Audrey Claire, John Holland. D: David Bradley. HOR 74m. v

They Shall Have Music 1939 ★★★ Samuel Goldwyn's try at popularizing classical music features Heifetz as "pied piper" to youngsters at music school for the deprived. The story is sentimental nonsense, but the music is fine. C: Joel McCrea, Jascha Heifetz, Andrea Leeds, Gene Reynolds, Marjorie Main, Walter Brennan. D: Archie Mayo. MUS 101m. v

They Shoot Horses, Don't They? 1969 ★★★★½ Brutal, uncompromising study of desperation in the Depression, seen through a grueling dance marathon. Fonda is unforgettable; together the claustrophic set and brilliant cast create an atmosphere of unrelenting gloom. Young won Best Supporting Actor Oscar as venal master of ceremonies. Based on a novel by Horace McCoy. C: Jane Fonda, Michael Sarrazin, Susannah York, Gig Young, Red Buttons, Bonnie Bedelia, Bruce Dern, Allyn Ann McLerie. D: Sydney Pollack. DRA [PG] 121m. v

They Still Call Me Bruce 1987 ★★ No improvement nor relation to its predecessor. This time Yune tries to find the G.I. Joe who saved his life back in Korea, and returns the favor by helping an orphan. C: Johnny Yune, David Mendenhall, Pat Paulsen, Joey Travolta, Robert Guillaume. D: Johnny Yune, James Orr. COM [PG] 91m. v

They Were Expendable 1945 ★★★★½ First-rate action drama about American PT boat crews fighting losing battle against Japanese forces in the Philippines. Director Ford does an excellent job of authentically re-creating, and gorgeously filming, the atmosphere and time period. C: Robert Montgomery, John Wayne, Donna Reed, Jack Holt, Ward Bond. D: John Ford. ACT 135m. v

They Were Five 1938 French ★★★★ Unemployed quintet of Parisians win the lottery and decide to use the money to open a restaurant. French melodrama movingly portrays the desperation and hardship brought on by the Depression. (a.k.a. *La Belle Equipe*) C: Jean Gabin, Charles Vanel, Viviane Romance. D: Julien Duvivier. DRA 78m.

They Were Sisters 1945 British ★★★½ The tribulations of three loyal sisters and their dissimilar lives and marriages. Ensemble melodrama well acted and refreshingly done. C: Phyllis Calvert, James Mason, Hugh Sinclair. D: Arthur Crabtree. DRA 110m.

They Who Dare 1953 British ★★★½ Allied commando raiders during WWII undertake a daring mission to dynamite German-held airfields on the island of Rhodes. Exciting war yarn, well acted, plenty of action. C: Dirk Bogarde, Denholm Elliott, Akim Tamiroff. D: Lewis Milestone. ACT 101m.

They Won't Believe Me 1947 ★★★★½ After car wreck, harried husband (Young) comes up with the perfect plan to kill his wife, with the help of scheming Greer and Hayward. Tense film noir thriller about lowlifes in wrong places, packed with crackling performances and a terrific twist before it's all over. C: Susan Hayward, Robert Young, Jane Greer, Rita Johnson. D: Irving Pichel. CRI 95m. v

They Won't Forget 1937 ★★★★½ Political aims take precedence over due process in a murder case involving a man accused of killing a high school student (Turner, in her first major role) in a small Southern town. Taut direction marks this powerful high-voltage drama. Well written, intricately plotted, and expertly acted. C: Claude Rains, Gloria Dickson, Otto Kruger, Lana Turner, Elisha Cook Jr. D: Mervyn LeRoy. DRA 95m.

They're a Weird Mob 1966 Australian ★★★ Mishaps of an Italian reporter who relocates to Australia. Hodgepodge comedy from the novel by Nino Culotta. C: Walter Chiari, Clare Dunne, Chips Rafferty, Alida Chelli. D: Michael Powell. COM 109m. v

They're Playing With Fire 1984 ★★½ Professor entices student into bed and then into a murder scheme. Low-budget lust and some violence. C: Eric Brown, Sybil Danning, Andrew Prine. D: Howard Hikmet Avedis. DRA [R] 96m. V

Thief 1981 ★★★½ Caan plays sympathetic professional thief struggling for survival against all odds. Moody photography and taut direction, but material is shallow and the caper unsatisfying. Pulsating score by Tangerine Dream. Mann's debut film. C: James Caan, Tuesday Weld, Willie Nelson, James Belushi. D: Michael Mann. CRI [R] 123m. V

Thief of Bagdad, The 1924 ★★★★ Outlandish, elaborate and quite entertaining silent spectacle, with dashing Fairbanks as thief in love with a princess. Stunning Arabian Nights scenery and special effects that, for the period, are astounding. Remade three times. C: Douglas Fairbanks, Julanne Johnston, Anna May Wong, Charles Belcher. D: Raoul Walsh. ACT 155m. V

Thief of Bagdad, The 1940 British ★★★★★ Sumptuous, exciting adaptation of Arabian Nights tale: Wily youth (Sabu) constantly outwits evil magician while helping restore fallen king to rightful throne. Rousing fantasy mixes grand sets, glorious music, superb direction, and energetic cast. Great for entire family. Much-deserved Oscars for Cinematography, Art Direction and Special Effects. C: Sabu, John Justin, June Duprez, Conrad Veidt. D: Ludwig Berger, Tim Whelan, Michael Powell. FAM/DRA 106m. V

Thief of Bagdad, The 1978 British-French ★★★ Story of a beggar boy, blinded prince and magic lamp gets dusted off for this attractively produced, effective TV version. C: Peter Ustinov, Roddy McDowall, Kabir Bedi, Frank Finley, Terence Stamp. D: Clive Donner. ACT 100m. TVM V

Thief of Baghdad 1961 Italian ★★½ Retelling of classic legend has Reeves in search of the blue rose that will permit him to marry the princess. Despite creative use of color, the director leaves out the passion and intrigue that made earlier versions so magical. C: Steve Reeves, Giorgia Moll, Arturo Dominici. D: Arthur Lubin. DRA 90m. V

Thief of Hearts 1984 ★★★ A cat burglar (Bauer) uses information he reads in stolen diaries to seduce a woman (Williams) whose house he has robbed. Stylish, but strangely uninvolving, considering the enticing premise. C: Steven Bauer, Barbara Williams, John Getz, David Caruso. D: Douglas Day Stewart. DRA [R] 101m. V

Thief of Paris, The 1967 French ★★★★ Young heir (Belmondo) is duped out of his inheritance, turns to crime and becomes an accomplished thief. Overpowering comedy/drama and social commentary with solid acting and good production values. C: Julien Guiomar, Jean-Paul Belmondo. COM 119m.

Thief of Venice, The 1952 ★★½ Eighth-century Venetian tavern owner joins forces with naval officer to foil the plans of a Turkish marauder to take over the city. Epic costume melodrama offers a host of exciting battle scenes, but little in the way of plot. C: Maria Montez, Paul Christian, Massimo Serato. D: John Brahm. DRA 91m.

Thief Who Came to Dinner, The 1973 ★★★ A computer hacker (O'Neal) becomes a jewel thief in Houston high society. Initially amusing, then lumbering crime comedy. Ryan's no Cary Grant, and film suffers accordingly. C: Ryan O'Neal, Jacqueline Bisset, Warren Oates, Jill Clayburgh. D: Bud Yorkin. COM [PG] 105m. V

Thieves Fall Out 1941 ★★★ Novice businessman sets out to save his abducted grandmother. Cast carries mild script. C: Eddie Albert, Joan Leslie, Alan Hale, Anthony Quinn. D: Ray Enright. DRA 72m.

Thieves' Holiday 1946 *See* **Scandal in Paris, A**

Thieves Like Us 1974 ★★★★½ Robert Altman's tale of three convicts after their escape from a Midwestern prison camp in the 1930s. Moving performances by Carradine and Duvall highlight wonderfully directed film based on Edward Anderson's novel. Remake of *They Live by Night*. C: Keith Carradine, Shelley Duvall, John Schuck, Louise Fletcher. D: Robert Altman. CRI [R] 123m. V

Thin Blue Line, The 1988 ★★★★★ A cop was shot to death in Dallas in 1977, and according to this film—and director Morris—an innocent man was convicted of the crime. Morris made such a powerful case with this documentary that it led to the release of the convicted man. D: Errol Morris. DOC 101m. V

Thin Ice 1937 ★★★★ Incognito nobleman (Power) falls for an ice skating teacher (Henie) at an Alpine resort. Wonderful ice ballets and enjoyable musical numbers enhance lighthearted fairy tale romance. C: Sonja Henie, Tyrone Power, Arthur Treacher, Joan Davis, Alan Hale. D: Sidney Lanfield. MUS 80m. V

Thin Line, The 1967 Japanese ★★★★ Japanese couple must live with the torment that the husband has accidently murdered his best friend's wife. Effective melodrama powerfully portrays the culture's regard for honor and integrity. C: Keiju Kobayashi, Michiyo Aratama, Tatsuya Mihashi, Akiko Wakabayashi. D: Mikio Naruse. DRA 102m.

Thin Man, The *The Thin Man* was not originally intended as a series. MGM paired William Powell (a former Philo Vance) and Myrna Loy as the sprightly sleuthing couple Nick and Nora Charles for a typically high-class adaptation of Dashiell Hammett's novel. But the success of the film led to another and another, and eventually there were six of the delightful mystery-comedy efforts. Unlike most mystery series, the *Thin Man* films had "A" budgets, good actors and writers, and the usual MGM production values. The care taken with them shows in every frame, but it's Powell and Loy's chemistry that really makes the films zing.

The Thin Man (1934)
After the Thin Man (1936)
Another Thin Man (1939)
Shadow of the Thin Man (1941)
The Thin Man Goes Home (1944)
Song of the Thin Man (1947)

Thin Man Goes Home, The 1944 ★★★★ Nick Charles (Powell) takes his wife Nora (Loy) and their infant son for a vacation respite at his parents' rural home but the inevitable murder occurs once they get there. Typically entertaining and witty *Thin Man* entry plays up the comic chemistry between the two principals. C: William Powell, Myrna Loy, Lucile Watson, Gloria De Haven, Ann Revere, Harry Davenport. D: Richard Thorpe. CRI 102m. v

Thin Man, The 1934 ★★★★★ One of filmdom's most popular series began in this smashing adaptation of a Dashiell Hammett mystery. Powell and Loy brought screwball comic timing to a straightforward mystery. Nick and Nora Charles track an inventor's killer. The wisecracking, tender relationship of the tipsy husband and wife was a disarming novelty. And of course, there's Asta. Fine viewing with older children. Five sequels followed. C: William Powell, Myrna Loy, Maureen O'Sullivan, Nat Pendleton, Cesar Romero, Porter Hall. D: W.S. Van Dyke. CRI 90m. v

Thin Red Line, The 1964 ★★★ A raw private (Dullea) and a hardened sergeant (Warden) clash during a decisive 1943 battle in which allies recapture Guadalcanal from the Japanese. Realistic battle scenes but standard war yarn based on James Jones' novel. C: Keir Dullea, Jack Warden, Kieron Moore. D: Andrew Marton. ACT 99m.

Thing Called Love, The 1993 ★★★★ Bogdanovich continues his exploration of the underside of the American Dream with this tasteful, restrained character study of four would-be country stars adrift in Nashville. Phoenix is particularly effective as a cool songwriter. Unfairly neglected film received minimal release. C: River Phoenix, Samantha Mathis, Dermot Mulroney, Sandra Bullock. D: Peter Bogdanovich. DRA [PG-13] 116m. v

Thing, The 1951 ★★★★½ Suspenseful sci-fi thriller involving scientific researchers in Arctic who dig up and defrost an alien creature that turns out to be an unstoppable predator. Unusually creepy for a genre picture of its type, thanks to skillful direction and air of genuine mystery. C: Kenneth Tobey, Margaret Sheridan, Douglas Spencer, James Arness. D: Christian Nyby. SFI 80m. v

Thing, The 1982 ★★★★ Carpenter's terrifying and graphically violent remake of the '50s classic (about an Antarctic research center terrorized by an alien) is nerve-wracking study of paranoia. Suspenseful and genuinely frightening from beginning to end. C: Kurt Russell, Wilford Brimley, Richard Dysart, Richard Masur. D: John Carpenter. SFI [R] 108m. v

Things Change 1988 ★★★★ A change for Mamet—a comedy. An Italian shoemaker (Ameche) hired to take the fall for a mobster is taken to Lake Tahoe by an errand boy (Mantegna) to enjoy one last weekend of pleasure. Old-fashioned idea, but well realized. C: Don Ameche, Joe Mantegna, Robert Prosky, J.J. Johnson. D: David Mamet. COM [PG] 105m. v

Things of Life, The 1970 French ★★★½ A man looks over his life with regret and nostalgia while recuperating from a car crash. A wife and mistress wait in the wings for his recovery. Potentially sappy story helped considerably by strong work from the stars. (a.k.a. *Les Choses de la Vie*) C: Michel Piccoli, Romy Schneider, Lea Massari. D: Claude Sautet. DRA 90m. v

Things to Come 1936 British ★★★★ Eerily prophetic look at humankind's future, predicting world war in 1940, followed by disease, revolution, and space travel. Ambitious, imaginative drama with magnificent futuristic art design. Adapted from the H.G. Wells novel. C: Raymond Massey, Cedric Hardwicke, Ralph Richardson, Ann Todd. D: William Cameron Menzies. SFI 92m. v

Think Big 1990 ★★½ Brothers Paul and Paul are truckers hauling hazardous waste to Southern California, with a bright-eyed stowaway who's sneaked aboard for the ride. Inoffensive but forgettable. C: Peter Paul, David Paul, Martin Mull, Claudia Christian. D: Jon Turteltaub. COM [PG-13] 86m. v

Think Fast, Mr. Moto 1937 ★★★½ Japanese detective (Lorre) travels to China in pursuit of stolen gems. Lorre's first stab at the bespectacled sleuth makes for an entertaining, fast-paced mystery. C: Peter Lorre, Virginia Field, Sig Rumann. D: Norman Foster. CRI 66m.

Thinkin Big' 1986 ★★ Spring break on the gulf coast of Texas, with all those nubile bodies romping. Harmless teen comedy with peekaboo nudity and hints of teenage angst. C: Bruce Anderson, Kenny Sargent, Randy Jandt. D: S.F. Brownrigg. COM [R] 96m. v

Third Alibi, The 1961 British ★★★½ Modest but effective thriller about a man plotting to murder his wife with the aid of his mistress/sister-in-law (Griffiths). Terrific twist ending. C: Laurence Payne, Patricia Dainton, Jane Griffiths. D: Montgomery Tully. CRI 68m.

Third Day, The 1965 ★★★½ Amnesia victim (Peppard) is accused of murder and he has no idea why or how he might have done it. Solid mystery with better-than-average cast. C: George Peppard, Elizabeth Ashley, Roddy McDowall, Arthur O'Connell, Mona Washbourne, Herbert Marshall. D: Jack Smight. DRA 119m.

Third Degree Burn 1989 ★★★½ Private eye (Williams) is hired to look after Madsen by her husband (Masur). Williams is then seduced by Madsen and led into a complicated murder plot against her spouse. Modern attempt at film noir doesn't quite work, given a weak script, but not for lack of trying. C: Treat Williams, Virginia Madsen, Richard Masur. D: Roger Spottiswoode. CRI 97m. TVM V

Third Finger, Left Hand 1940 ★★★½ No-nonsense fashion magazine executive (Loy) wears a phony wedding ring to keep away men, but one guy (Douglas) is undeterred. Both leads have had better scripts, but who cares? They're delightful together. C: Myrna Loy, Melvyn Douglas, Lee Bowman. D: Robert Z. Leonard. COM 96m.

Third Generation, The 1979 German ★★★★ Band of well-to-do German terrorists find their activities keep backfiring, in more ways than one. Technically a comedy, and one of director Fassbinder's best (and darkest) films. C: Eddie Constantine, Hanna Schygulla. D: Rainer Werner Fassbinder. COM 111m.

Third Key, The 1956 British ★★★★ Scotland Yard chief (Hawkins) and his green assistant (Stratton) are on the trail of safecrackers in this nifty British mystery with effective surprise ending. C: Jack Hawkins, John Stratton, Dorothy Alison. D: Charles Frend. DRA 96m.

Third Man on the Mountain 1959 ★★★★ Young man (MacArthur) joins mountain-climbing team ascending the Matterhorn. Good Disney coming-of-age story that benefits from location shooting and thoughtful casting. MacArthur's real-life mom Helen Hayes makes cameo appearance. C: James MacArthur, Michael Rennie, Janet Munro, Herbert Lom. D: Ken Annakin. FAM/DRA [G] 106m. V

Third Man, The 1949 British ★★★★★ Writer (Cotten) searches post-WWII Vienna for his friend, Harry Lime, (Welles) who may or may not be dead. A terrific film noir, with cynical insights about the victims of war, a memorable zither score, and an incredible sewer chase scene. Oscar for Cinematography. Written by Graham Greene. C: Orson Welles, Joseph Cotten, Alida Valli, Trevor Howard. D: Carol Reed. CRI 100m. V

Third Secret, The 1964 British ★★★ Routine mystery has patient (Boyd) pursuing his psychiatrist's murderer. C: Stephen Boyd, Jack Hawkins, Richard Attenborough, Diane Cilento. D: Charles Crichton. CRI 103m.

Third Time Lucky 1950 British ★★★ Preachy drama about the evils of gambling with jaded Walsh using naive Johns as his good luck charm. C: Glynis Johns, Dermot Walsh. D: Gordon Parry. DRA 91m.

Thirteen at Dinner 1985 ★★★★ Hercule Poirot (Ustinov) investigates the murder of a British nobleman, and tries to differentiate the man's real widow from a cagey impersonator. British TV movie based on Agatha Christie's *Lord Edgware Dies*, with Dunaway stealing the show both as the theatrical wife and her would-be imitator. C: Peter Ustinov, Faye Dunaway, David Suchet, Lee Horsley. D: Lou Antonio. CRI 91m. TVM V

13 Ghosts 1960 ★★★ Sporadically fun combination of spooks and spoofery, with a family inheriting a mansion inhabited by a dozen ghosts who want to add another to their number. Some good moments; some dull stretches. Movie audiences were given "ghost viewers" through which they could see or not see the spooks. C: Charles Herbert, Donald Woods, Martin Milner, Jo Morrow, Margaret Hamilton. D: William Castle. HOR 88m. V

Thirteen Hours By Air 1936 ★★★½ Mixed bag of passengers on transcontinental flight must endure hijacking, murder, and romance. Capable melodrama with stalwart cast. C: Fred MacMurray, Joan Bennett, ZaSu Pitts, John Howard, Ruth Donnelly. D: Mitchell Leisen. DRA 80m.

13 Lead Soldiers 1948 ★★★ Bulldog Drummond (Conway) finds the title toys, which provide a clue to the whereabouts of buried treasure. Okay series entry. C: Tom Conway, Maria Palmer, Helen Westcott, John Newland. D: Frank McDonald. DRA 64m.

13 Rue Madeleine 1946 ★★★★ Four American spies search for a Nazi missile site in occupied France. Absorbing espionage tale, told in semidocumentary style. Good Cagney. C: James Cagney, Annabella, Richard Conte, Frank Latimore, Sam Jaffe. D: Henry Hathaway. ACT 95m. V

Thirteen, The 1937 U.S.S.R. ★★★★ Russian cavalry soldiers and their captain's wife are stranded in the desert. Well-crafted Soviet-made adventure film, loosely inspired by American movie, *The Lost Patrol*. C: Ivan Novoseltsev, Helen Kuzmina, Alexander Christyakov. D: Mikhail Romm. ACT 86m.

Thirteen Women 1932 ★★★½ A half-Japanese, half-Indian woman (Loy) exacts revenge on the racist college sorority members who ostracized her. Entertaining, overheated oldie; Loy is wonderful. C: Myrna Loy, Irene Dunne, Ricardo Cortez, Florence Eldridge. D: George Archainbaud. CRI 73m.

Thirteenth Guest, The 1932 ★★★★ 13 guests reconvene for dinner 13 years after their host dropped dead during repast. Now there's a hooded murderer looking for dessert! Old story holds up fine, thanks to a great ending and vibrant Ginger in one of her first roles. C: Ginger Rogers, Lyle Talbot. D: Albert Ray. CRI 69m.

13th Letter, The 1951 ★★★½ Residents of a small town are plagued by poison pen letters. Talkative, but still suspenseful puzzler. An absorbing remake of the French film *Le Corbeau.* C: Linda Darnell, Charles Boyer, Michael Rennie, Judith Evelyn. D: Otto Preminger. DRA 85m. v

Thirty Day Princess 1934 ★★★½ Amusing comedy about an actress (Sidney) impersonating ailing princess on one month tour of America. Preston Sturges co-wrote the screenplay for this pleasant jaunt. C: Sylvia Sidney, Cary Grant, Edward Arnold. D: Marion Gering. COM 75m.

35 Up 1993 British ★★★★½ Emotionally honest sequel to *28 Up* follows its subjects as they stand on the brink of middle age, capturing their reflections of years past. Sweeping epic of human life is just as powerful as its predecessor. D: Michael Apted. DOC 128m. v

30 Foot Bride of Candy Rock, The 1959 ★★★ A mild-mannered inventor (Costello) accidentally enlarges his wife (Provine) in this harmless comedy; may appeal to youngsters. Lou's only starring role without Abbott. C: Lou Costello, Dorothy Provine, Gale Gordon. D: Sidney Miller. COM 75m. v

30 Is a Dangerous Age, Cynthia 1968 British ★★★½ Struggling nightclub pianist (Moore) makes one last attempt to win fame, fortune, and the woman he loves. Talented star registers laughs, despite lumpy script. C: Dudley Moore, Eddie Foy Jr., Suzy Kendall. D: Joseph McGrath. COM 85m. v

39 Steps, The 1935 British ★★★★½ Innocently involved Canadian visitor (Donat) searches for spies while on the run from cops who think he's a murderer. Carroll is the woman he gets handcuffed to along the way. Lots of great comic wit mixed in with the trademark Hitchcock suspense. Although remade twice, this is the best of the lot. C: Robert Donat, Madeleine Carroll, Lucie Mannheim, Godfrey Tearle, Peggy Ashcroft. D: Alfred Hitchcock. CRI 81m. v

39 Steps, The 1959 British ★★★ Remake of the 1935 Hitchcock classic, with More as an innocent man caught in a web of espionage and murder. Pale shadow of its predecessor, although the stars are charming. C: Kenneth More, Taina Elg, Brenda deBanzie, Barry Jones. D: Ralph Thomas. DRA 93m.

Thirty-Nine Steps, The 1979 British ★★★½ Second remake of Hitchock spy classic about pair (Powell and Dotrice) on the run from deadly agents. Colorful, and fairly suspenseful, but the original still on top. C: Robert Powell, David Warner, Eric Porter, Karen Dotrice, John Mills. D: Don Sharp. ACT [PG] 98m. v

Thirty Seconds Over Tokyo 1944 ★★★★ Jingoistic war film details the planning involved in the first bombing run over Japan during WWII. Gripping, gritty, and sparse, its documentary style is mesmerizing. Scripted by HUAC blacklisted Dalton Trumbo. C: Spencer Tracy, Van Johnson, Robert Walker, Phyllis Thaxter, Robert Mitchum. D: Mervyn LeRoy. DRA 139m. v

36 Fillette 1988 French ★★★★ An adolescent French girl tries to exercise her budding sexuality while on a seaside vacation with her family. Charming, sensitive comedy with some winning performances and keen satire. (The title comes from a dress size!) C: Delphine Zentout, Etienne Chicot, Olivier Parniere, Jean-Pierre Leaud. D: Catherine Breillat. COM 88m. v

36 Hours 1964 ★★★½ Clever WWII espionage drama follows a captured American spy (Garner) who has been brainwashed by the Nazis into thinking the war is over. Nifty premise, keeps churning. C: James Garner, Eva Marie Saint, Rod Taylor. D: George Seaton. ACT 115m. v

Thirty-Six Hours to Kill 1936 ★★★½ Fair crime-comedy about a wanted gangster (Fowley) unable to redeem winning sweepstakes ticket. Witty dialogue, but unfortunately some of the stereotyped humor now appears racist. (a.k.a. *Thirty-Six Hours to Live*) C: Brian Donlevy, Gloria Stuart, Douglas Fowley. D: Eugene Forde. COM 65m.

Thirty-Six Hours to Live 1936 *See* **Thirty-Six Hours to Kill**

Thirty Two Short Films About Glenn Gould 1993 Canadian ★★★★ The brilliant, reclusive concert pianist's life is interpreted/documented in an unusual potpourri of short subjects. Inventive, as expected, but uneven. Gould's own performances, featuring the compositions of J.S. Bach, enliven the soundtrack. D: Francois Girard. DOC 93m. v

This Above All 1942 ★★★★ Moving wartime drama of doctor's daughter (Fontaine) falling for deserter (Power) who is challenged to prove his bravery. Dated, but well done. C: Tyrone Power, Joan Fontaine, Thomas Mitchell, Nigel Bruce, Gladys Cooper, Sara Allgood. D: Anatole Litvak. DRA 110m.

This Angry Age 1958 French-U.S.-Italian ★★½ Family of farmers in Indochina struggle against the sea for their livelihood. Stars from three different countries act in seven different styles in this muddled, sporadically interesting drama. (a.k.a. *The Sea Wall*) C: Anthony Perkins, Silvana Mangano, Alida Valli, Richard Conte, Jo Van Fleet. D: Rene Clement. DRA 111m.

This Boy's Life 1993 ★★★★ Mother just barely making it in Eisenhower era Seattle marries hard-drinking martinet, who comes to blows with her teen son. Engrossing and hard-edged tale of self-realization in an abusive household, based on Tobias Wolff's autobiographical book. C: Robert De Niro, Ellen Barkin, Leonardo Di Caprio, Jonah Blechman. D: Michael Caton-Jones. DRA [R] 115m. v

This Can't Be Love 1994 ★★½ Elderly movie stars (Hepburn and Quinn) finally realize they're attracted to one another, after a 50-

year feud. Bumpy TV vehicle for one of America's most admired stars. C: Katharine Hepburn, Anthony Quinn, Jason Bateman, Jami Gertz. D: Anthony Harvey. COM 100m. TVM

This Could Be the Night 1957 ★★★ Comedy about a straitlaced shoolteacher (Simmons) who becomes gangster's secretary and falls for his young associate (Franciosa). Rhinestone romance sparkles well enough. C: Jean Simmons, Paul Douglas, Anthony Franciosa, Joan Blondell, ZaSu Pitts. D: Robert Wise. COM 105m. V

This Day and Age 1933 ★★★★ Unusual (for director DeMille) social drama about high school boys taking the law into their own hands when mobster (Bickford) kills a neighborhood tailor. Powerful stuff, well handled. C: Charles Bickford, Judith Allen, Richard Cromwell, Eddie Nugent. D: Cecil B. DeMille. DRA 85m.

This Earth Is Mine 1959 ★★★½ The California wine industry, circa 1930s, is the backdrop for a fair melodrama, notable for fine work from Simmons and Rains. Rock is the archtypical field hand working his way up the vines, so to speak. C: Rock Hudson, Jean Simmons, Dorothy McGuire, Claude Rains. D: Henry King. DRA 125m.

This Green Hell 1936 British ★★★★ A mild-mannered clerk (Rigby) gets into train crash, winds up with amnesia, and assumes the heroic identity of a fictional character from his son's bedtime stories. Imaginative, clever low-budget farce. C: Edward Rigby. D: Randall Faye. COM 71m.

This Gun for Hire 1942 ★★★★ Hard-edged dramatization of Graham Greene's thriller *A Gun for Sale*, about the taking of revenge for a double-cross. Ladd (in the performance that made him a star) and Lake (in her first major screen role) are unforgettable as a professional killer and his girlfriend. C: Alan Ladd, Veronica Lake, Robert Preston, Laird Cregar. D: Frank Tuttle. DRA 81m. V

This Happy Breed 1947 British ★★★½ Stagy, but well-acted saga of a British family between the two World Wars. Rambling, quintessentially British drama, beautifully acted. Johnson is lovely. From Noel Coward play. C: Robert Newton, Celia Johnson, John Mills, Kay Walsh, Stanley Holloway. D: David Lean. DRA 110m. V

This Happy Feeling 1958 ★★★½ A pert secretary (Reynolds) thinks she's in love with an aging sophisticate (Jurgens), but that doesn't explain why she feels the way she does whenever his handsome young neighbor (Saxon) is around. Charming Reynolds outing. Great supporting cast. C: Debbie Reynolds, Curt Jurgens, John Saxon, Alexis Smith, Estelle Winwood, Mary Astor, Troy Donahue. D: Blake Edwards. COM 92m. V

This Is Elvis 1981 ★★★★ The King performs a spectacular array of his greatest hits in a specially filmed documentary. A must for fans. C: Elvis Presley. D: Malcolm Leo, Andrew Solt. DOC [PG] 144m. V

This Is My Affair 1937 ★★★★ Period adventure about an under cop (Taylor) implicated in assassination of President McKinley. Effective melodrama with Stanwyck lending strong support as nightclub singer in love with Taylor. C: Barbara Stanwyck, Robert Taylor, Victor McLaglen, Brian Donlevy, John Carradine. D: William Seiter. DRA 101m. V

This Is My Life 1992 ★★★★ Single mother moves her two children from Queens to Manhattan in pursuit of her dream—becoming a stand-up comic. Warmly comedic with some sharp edges; light but enjoyable. C: Julie Kavner, Samantha Mathis, Gaby Hoffmann, Carrie Fisher, Dan Aykroyd. D: Nora Ephron. COM [PG-13] 94m. V

This Is My Street 1964 British ★★½ Tawdry soap opera about a housewife (Ritchie) carrying on with her mother's lodger. C: Ian Hendry, June Ritchie, Annnette Andre. D: Sidney Hayers. DRA 94m.

This Is Spinal Tap 1984 ★★★★ You'll never look at another concert movie the same way again after viewing this hilarious send-up. This "rockumentary" follows the tribulations of a once-popular English band and mocks every rock 'n' roll cliché in the process. C: Michael McKean, Christopher Guest, Harry Shearer, Rob Reiner. D: Rob Reiner. COM [R] 93m. V

This Is the Army 1943 ★★★★ Film version of famed wartime musical revue hangs a vintage Irving Berlin score onto a slim plotline of WWI soldiers reuniting to entertain WWII troops. Irving himself pops up to sing "Oh, How I Hate to Get Up in the Morning." Fans of actors-turned-politicians will enjoy seeing Murphy play Reagan's father. C: George Murphy, Joan Leslie, Ronald Reagan, Kate Smith, Frances Langford, Irving Berlin. D: Michael Curtiz. MUS 121m. V

This Is the Life 1933 British ★★★½ English music-hall stars Harker and Hale portray teahouse owners who inherit a fortune from uncle, who, unbeknownst to them, was involved in the Mob. Thin comedy with likable performances. C: Gordon Harker, Binnie Hale. D: Albert de Courville. COM 78m.

This Is the Life 1935 ★★★½ Refreshing comedy musical, with child star Withers as a performing orphan who runs away from her cruel managers, taking up with a kindly fugitive (McGuire). Withers' natural appeal carries it. C: Jane Withers, John McGuire. D: Marshall Neilan. MUS 63m.

This Is the Life 1944 ★★★ Energetic minor musical about a teen singer (Foster) with a crush on an older man (Knowles) and pursued by a young G.I. (O'Connor). Adapted from a play by Sinclair Lewis (the novelist) and Fay Wray (yes, King Kong's girlfriend). C: Donald

O'Connor, Patric Knowles, Peggy Ryan, Susanna Foster. D: Felix Feist. MUS 87m.

This Is the Night 1932 ★★★½ A randy bachelor (Young) with his eye on a married woman (Todd) gets an actress (Damita) to pose as his wife, and trap the woman's husband (Grant). Minor marital farce with charming players, sophisticated air. C: Lily Damita, Charlie Ruggles, Roland Young, Thelma Todd, Cary Grant. D: Frank Tuttle. COM 78m.

This Island Earth 1955 ★★★★ Top scientists lured into using their talents to save an alien civilization. Good '50s special effects and performances. C: Jeff Morrow, Rex Reason, Faith Domergue. D: Joseph M. Newman. SFI 86m. V

This Land Is Mine 1943 ★★★ A shy French schoolteacher (Laughton) finds his heroic destiny when the Nazis overrun his town. Interesting wartime propaganda. The show is all Laughton's. C: Charles Laughton, Maureen O'Hara, George Sanders, Walter Slezak, Una O'Connor. D: Jean Renoir. DRA 103m. V

This Love of Ours 1945 ★★½ Sappy love story about a couple reunited after 12 years. No one can suffer like Oberon can suffer, except maybe the viewer. Luckily Rains is around to run interference. C: Merle Oberon, Charles Korvin, Claude Rains, Sue England. D: William Dieterle. DRA 90m.

This Madding Crowd 1964 Japanese ★★★★ Absorbing story of traditional vs. modern-day Japanese customs as professor/author (Morishige) visits backward fishing village outside of Tokyo and learns about its inhabitants. C: Hisaya Morishige. D: Yuzo Kawashima. DRA 101m.

This Man in Paris 1939 British ★★★ Sequel to *This Man Is News* puts reporter (Barnes) in the City of Light, trying to catch a counterfeit money gang. Okay, but doesn't soar like the first. C: Barry K. Barnes, Valerie Hobson, Alistair Sim, Edward Lexy, Garry Marsh. D: David MacDonald. COM 86m.

This Man Is Mine 1934 ★★★½ Woman defends marriage against homewrecker. We say, "You want him, take him." Try again, Irene. C: Irene Dunne, Ralph Bellamy, Constance Cummings, Kay Johnson. D: John Cromwell. DRA 76m.

This Man Is Mine 1946 British ★★★★ Warm, moving WWII drama with British family taking in Canadian soldier for the Yuletide holiday. C: Glynis Johns, Hugh McDermott, Nova Pilbeam. D: Marcel Varnel. DRA 103m.

This Man Is News 1938 British ★★★★ Zippy comedy/mystery with newsman (Barnes) unjustly accused of jewel theft. Sim's performance is a comic gem. Sequel: *This Man in Paris.* C: Barry Barnes, Valerie Hobson, Alastair Sim. D: David MacDonald. COM 77m.

This Man Must Die 1970 French ★★★★½ Obsessed with revenge, a father (Duchaussoy, in a searing performance) goes after the hardened villain (Yanne) who killed his young son in a hit-and-run accident. Outstanding story and acting, with exquisite photography. Chabrol at his best. C: Michael Duchaussoy, Jean Yanne, Caroline Cellier. D: Claude Chabrol. DRA [PG] 112m. V

This Man's Navy 1945 ★★★½ Sentimental Navy tale with old salt (Beery) taking young recruit (Drake) under his wing. Easy to take, with good performances. C: Wallace Beery, Tom Drake, James Gleason, Jan Clayton. D: William Wellman. DRA 100m.

This Modern Age 1931 ★★★★ Stylish vehicle for Crawford casts her as an American debutante reunited with her mother in Paris, who turns out to have a "blemished" reputation, which rubs off on Joan. Entertaining picture pours on the suds with no apology. C: Joan Crawford, Neil Hamilton, Marjorie Rambeau. D: Nick Grinde. DRA 76m.

This Property Is Condemned 1966 ★★★½ A stranger (Redford) is sent to small town to lay off railroad workers. While staying at a boarding house, he becomes object of the affections of a young woman (Wood). Beautifully filmed melodrama, adapted from Tennessee Williams' one-act play. C: Natalie Wood, Robert Redford, Charles Bronson, Kate Reid, Mary Badham. D: Sydney Pollack. DRA 109m. V

This Savage Land 1968 ★★★½ Absorbing homesteader drama with pioneer (Sullivan) and family contending with ornery ex-Confederate soldiers. Great Scott as one of the Rebs. Originally made for television as part of *The Road West* series. C: Barry Sullivan, Glenn Corbett, Kathryn Hays, George C. Scott. D: Vincent McEveety. WST [G] 98m. TVM

This Side of Heaven 1934 ★★★ Screwball comedy about a nutty family rallying to defense of patriarch (Barrymore) when he's framed for embezzlement. Enjoyable loopiness. C: Lionel Barrymore, Fay Bainter, Mae Clarke, Tom Brown, Mary Carlisle, Una Merkel. D: William K. Howard. COM 76m.

This Sporting Life 1963 British ★★★★½ Powerful, realistic study of tough Yorkshire coal miner (Harris) who becomes professional rugby star but whose personal life is a torment of violence and unrequited love. C: Richard Harris, Rachel Roberts, Alan Badel, Colin Blakely. D: Lindsay Anderson. DRA 134m. V

This Thing Called Love 1941 ★★★★ Expertly played marital farce with newlyweds (Russell, Douglas) deciding to give their marriage a three month, platonic trial run. The stars make it shine. C: Rosalind Russell, Melvyn Douglas, Binnie Barnes, Allyn Joslyn, Lee J. Cobb. D: Alexander Hall. COM 98m.

This Week of Grace 1933 British ★★★½ Nice comedy vehicle for Fields casts her as a maid given free rein over duchess' mansion. Thin script carried by star's charm. C: Grace Fields. D: Maurice Elvey. COM 92m.

This Wine of Love 1948 Italian ★★★½ Uneven opera film from Donizetti's *L'Elisir D'Amore* is notable for rare screen appearance of legendary Gobbi. Plot concerns outrageous flirt (Corradi) wooed by a young man with a love potion. Terrible lip-synching compromises the otherwise fine performances. C: Nelly Corradi, Loretta Di Lelio, Tito Gobbi. D: Mario Costa. DRA 75m.

This Woman Is Dangerous 1952 ★★★½ A lady mobster (Crawford) goes blind and finds romance with her doctor. All in a day's work for Joan. Grab it. C: Joan Crawford, Dennis Morgan, David Brian. D: Felix Feist. DRA 100m.

Thomas Crown Affair, The 1968 ★★★★ Rich but bored McQueen plans the perfect robbery, while efficient, gorgeous insurance investigator (Dunaway) tries to probe his involvement. Instead she succumbs to his charm. Slick entertainment (the heist is thrilling to watch) is engaging throughout. Song "The Windmills of Your Mind" won Oscar. C: Steve McQueen, Faye Dunaway, Paul Burke. D: Norman Jewison. DRA [R] 102m. V

Thomasine & Bushrod 1974 ★★★ Black exploitation film casts Julien and McGee as Bonnie and Clyde-type couple, robbing banks across Texas in 1911. Okay, but no better. C: Max Julien, Vonetta McGee, George Murdock, Glynn Turman. D: Gordon Parks Jr. ACT [PG] 95m.

Thorn Birds, The 1983 ★★★★½ Massive miniseries from Colleen McCullough's novel about Australian family and the priest whose fortunes affect it. Involving throughout, but opening three hours are superb, thanks to Stanwyck's brilliant performance as matriarch lusting for youthful Chamberlain. Other standouts include Kiley, Simmons, and Plummer. C: Richard Chamberlain, Rachel Ward, Barbara Stanwyck, Jean Simmons, Christopher Plummer, Richard Kiley, Mare Winningham, Piper Laurie, Bryan Brown, Philip Anglim. D: Daryl Duke. DRA 486m. TVM V

Thoroughbreds Don't Cry 1937 ★★★½ Mickey and Judy's first film together is an entertaining racetrack yarn about a jockey conned into shady deals, helped by singing friend. C: Judy Garland, Mickey Rooney, Sophie Tucker, C. Aubrey Smith, Frankie Darro. D: Alfred E. Green. DRA 80m. V

Thoroughly Modern Millie 1967 ★★★½ Diverting, if overlong, musical set in the '20s with flappers (Andrews, Moore) in danger of being sold to white slavery ring by landlady (Lillie). First two thirds are terrific with snappy numbers and great cast (Channing almost steals movie). Then falls apart with a messy chase scene. Still, a crowd pleaser. C: Julie Andrews, James Fox, Mary Tyler Moore, Carol Channing, Beatrice Lillie, John Gavin. D: George Roy Hill. MUS [G] 138m. V

Those Calloways 1965 ★★★★ Keith leads his family in attempt to build bird sanctuary despite constant trouble from local officials and big business interests. Nice combination of nature and family drama, coupled with gentle Disney humor. Keith's performance is wonderfully eccentric. C: Brian Keith, Vera Miles, Brandon de Wilde, Walter Brennan, Ed Wynn, Linda Evans. D: Norman Tokar. FAM/DRA [PG] 130m. V

Those Daring Young Men in Their Jaunty Jalopies 1969 British ★★★½ Okay comedy adventure of high-stakes car race from London to Monte Carlo during the '20s. Some bits funny, but much of the slapstick falls flat. (a.k.a. *Monte Carlo or Bust*) C: Tony Curtis, Susan Hampshire, Terry-Thomas, Gert Frobe, Peter Cook, Dudley Moore. D: Ken Annakin. COM [G] 125m. V

Those High Grey Walls 1939 ★★★ Average prison drama about a doctor (Connolly) sent up the river for treating sick criminal. C: Walter Connolly, Onslow Stevens. D: Charles Vidor. DRA 81m.

Those Lips, Those Eyes 1980 ★★★★ Fresh, poignant coming-of-age story casts Hulce as a stagehand in a 1950s operetta summer stock company, learning the ropes from the hammy leading man (Langella). Theatre buffs will lap it up, but one wishes Frank had a stronger singing voice. C: Frank Langella, Tom Hulce, Glynnis O'Connor, Kevin McCarthy. D: Michael Pressman. MUS [R] 107m. V

Those Magnificent Men in Their Flying Machines 1965 ★★★★½ Highly entertaining slapstick adventure with aviators around the world competing in air race, circa 1910. Highlights include Frobe trying to fly plane by reading manual and Thomas as gleeful saboteur. C: Stuart Whitman, Sarah Miles, James Fox, Alberto Sordi, Robert Morley, Gert Frobe, Jean-Pierre Cassel, Terry-Thomas, Benny Hill. D: Ken Annakin. COM [G] 138m. V

Those Redheads From Seattle 1953 ★★★½ Modest musical with engaging cast follows mother (Moorehead) and four flame-haired daughters on the move to Alaska during the gold rush. C: Rhonda Fleming, Gene Barry, Agnes Moorehead, Teresa Brewer. D: Lewis Foster. MUS 90m.

Those Were the Days 1934 British ★★★½ Gay '90s comedy about a British magistrate (Hay) trying to keep his son out of the local music hall. Some delightful musical numbers and authentic period detail make this worth watching. C: Will Hay, Iris Hoey. D: Thomas Bentley. COM 80m.

Those Were the Days 1940 ★★★½ Turn-of-the-century period comedy with Holden reminiscing about his days as a college student, wooing a judge's daughter to beat minor jail rap. Creaks a bit now, but Holden's charm and energy are still fresh. (a.k.a. *Good Old Schooldays* and *At Good Old Siwash*) C: William Holden, Bonita Granville, Ezra Stone, Judith Barrett. D: J. Reed. COM 76m.

Those Were the Happy Times 1968 *See* **Star!**

Thousand and One Nights, A 1945 ★★★★ Diverting Arabian Nights fantasy with Wilde as a rather mature Aladdin. Good matinee fare—lively and pretty to look at. C: Cornel Wilde, Evelyn Keyes, Phil Silvers, Adele Jergens. D: Alfred Green. MUS 93m.

Thousand Clowns, A 1965 ★★★★ An unemployed and free-spirited TV writer (Robards) must join the mainstream to keep custody of his streetwise 12-year-old nephew. Robards, Balsam (Oscar for Best Supporting Actor), Harris, and Daniels reprise their stage roles of Gardner's hit Broadway ode to noncomformity. C: Jason Robards, Barbara Harris, Martin Balsam, Barry Gordon, William Daniels. D: Fred Coe. COM 118m. V

Thousand Eyes of Dr. Mabuse, The 1960 German ★★★½ Dedicated detective (Frobe) must vanquish the insidious criminal Dr. Mabuse, who has come back to life and is on the loose again, in this, the third part of Lang's trilogy. Effectively chilling. C: Dawn Addams, Peter Van Eyck, Gert Frobe. D: Fritz Lang. CRI 103m.

Thousand Mile Escort ★★★½ Threatened by warlords and natural catastrophes, a group of Chinese peasants try to make a life for themselves. Quite moving and inspiring. DRA V

Thousand Pieces of Gold 1991 ★★★★ Chinese woman sold as prostitute in 19th-century America manages to escape her fate and create a new life for herself. Spirited and compassionate historical tale. C: Dennis Dun, Rosalind Chao, Chris Cooper. D: Nancy Kelly. DRA [PG-13] 105m. V

Thousands Cheer 1943 ★★★½ MGM's try at the studio all-star wartime entertainment extravaganza. An officer's daughter (Grayson) puts together a show to win the heart of a soldier (Kelly). Of course plot is just an excuse for some high-powered numbers by Metro talent, best of which is Lena's "Honeysuckle Rose." C: Gene Kelly, Kathryn Grayson, Judy Garland, Mickey Rooney, Red Skelton, Eleanor Powell, Lena Horne, Frank Morgan. D: George Sidney. MUS 126m. V

Thrashin' 1986 ★ Youth new to L.A. finds he must battle a nasty gang of street skaters. Juvenile from beginning to end. For skateboarding fans only. C: Josh Brolin, Robert Rusler, Pamela Gidley. D: David Winters. ACT [PG-13] 93m. V

Threat, The 1949 ★★★★ Vindictive killer (McGraw) escapes from prison and, intent on getting even with those who prosecuted him, kidnaps a policeman, the district attorney, and a singer who testified against him. Suspenseful, well-acted B-movie with lots of action. C: Charles McGraw, Michael O'Shea, Virginia Grey. D: Felix Feist. CRI 65m.

Three 1967 Yugoslavian ★★★½ Young rakes touring Europe meet vivacious English girl and make tenuous pact to keep relations with her platonic. Slight, but well-acted, romantic drama from Irwin Shaw short story. C: Bata Zivojinovic. D: Alexander Petrovic. DRA 79m.

Three Amigos! 1986 ★★★ Cowboy matinee idols (Martin, Chase, Short) are hired by Mexicans to rid their town of bad guys. The townspeople are under the—mistaken—impression that the Amigos are as brave in real life as they are on screen. In fact, they're idiotic. C: Steve Martin, Chevy Chase, Martin Short. D: John Landis. COM [PG] 103m. V

Three Avengers, The 1964 Italian ★★★ Two kung fu masters and a young Chinese American open up a martial arts school. Typical of the genre. C: Alan Steel, Mimmo Palmara. D: Gianfranco Parolini. ACT 97m. V

Three Blind Mice 1938 ★★★½ Three girls from Midwest hit New York, looking for rich husbands. Expert fluff, often reworked since. C: Loretta Young, Joel McCrea, David Niven, Pauline Moore, Jane Darwell. D: William A. Seiter. COM 75m.

Three Brave Men 1957 ★★★½ Courageous courtroom drama in semidocumentary style about a navy worker (Borgnine) suspended for suspected Communist affiliation. Milland scores as lawyer determined to get him reinstated. C: Ray Milland, Frank Lovejoy, Ernest Borgnine, Nina Foch, Dean Jagger. D: Philip Dunne. DRA 88m.

Three Brothers 1980 Italian ★★★★ Title characters come home to their childhood village when they hear that their mother has died. Engrossing, sensitive, and well handled. C: Philippe Noiret, Charles Vanel, Michele Placido, Andrea Ferreol. D: Francesco Rosi. DRA [PG] 113m. V

Three Caballeros, The 1945 ★★★★ Cult Disney cartoon, crammed with amazing imagery. Donald Duck, Jose Carioca, and Panchito tour Latin America as part of '40s Good Neighbor Policy. Impressive mix of live action with animation, plus catchy songs. May be too sophisticated for younger children. C: Aurora Miranda, Carmen Molina, Dora Luz, Sterling Holloway, Clarence Nash. D: Norman Ferguson. FAM/ACT [G] 71m. V

Three Came Home 1950 ★★★★½ Harrowing account, based on a true story, of civilian American and British POWs interned by the Japanese in Asia during WWII. Surprisingly even-handed treatment of captors and captured, with Colbert and Hayakawa turning in superb performances. C: Claudette Colbert, Patric Knowles, Florence Desmond, Sessue Hayakawa. D: Jean Negulesco. DRA 106m.

Three Cases of Murder 1954 British ★★★½ Trio of unrelated thrillers, with two winners: "In the Picture," about a painting coming to life; and "Lord Mountdrago," about a politician (Welles) inclined toward murder. C: Wendy Toye, George O'Ferrall, Alan Badel, John Gregson, Orson Welles. D: David Eady. DRA 99m.

Three Cheers for the Irish 1940 ★★★½ Cheery bit of fluff about New York Irish cop (Mitchell) outraged when daughter (Lane) falls for a Scotsman. C: Thomas Mitchell, Dennis Morgan, Priscilla Lane, Alan Hale, Virginia Grey. D: Lloyd Bacon. COM 100m.

Three Cockeyed Sailors 1940 British ★★★½ Amusing British wartime comedy about a trio of drunken sailors accidentally overpowering a Nazi battleship. (a.k.a. *Sailors Three*) C: Tommy Trinder, Claude Hulbert, Michael Wilding. D: Walter Forde. COM 86m.

Three Coins in the Fountain 1954 ★★★★ Glossy, well-mounted soap opera about three visitors to Rome (Peters, McGuire, and McNamara) and their three different wishes for romance. Good cast, lovely location footage, Oscar-winning title song. C: Clifton Webb, Dorothy McGuire, Jean Peters, Louis Jourdan, Maggie McNamara, Rossano Brazzi. D: Jean Negulesco. DRA 102m.

Three Comrades 1938 ★★★★½ Three ex-soldiers (Taylor, Tone, Young) struggle together through the upheavals of post-WWI Germany until one is killed in a street riot and their devoted companion (Sullavan) dies of TB. Erich Maria Remarque's story, as co-scripted by F. Scot Fitzgerald and Edward Paramore is a sad and sentimental ode to friendship. C: Robert Taylor, Margaret Sullavan, Franchot Tone, Robert Young. D: Frank Borzage. DRA 99m. V

Three-Cornered Moon 1933 ★★★★ Screwball delight about a family of impoverished eccentrics trying to beat the Depression without really trying. Early comedy has been imitated often since. C: Claudette Colbert, Richard Arlen, Mary Boland, Wallace Ford, Lyda Roberti. D: Elliott Nugent. COM 77m.

Three Crowns of the Sailor 1984 ★★★★ Weird comic thriller about sailor stranded ashore; lots of strange camera angles combined with tongue-in-cheek writing. Very well done, though not to all tastes. C: Jean-Bernard Guillard, Philippe Deplanche, Jean Baudin, Nadege Clair, Lisa Lyon. D: Raul Ruiz. COM 117m.

Three Daring Daughters 1948 ★★★½ Three sisters plot to stop their mother (MacDonald) from remarrying. Pleasant musical comedy. C: Jeanette MacDonald, Jose Iturbi, Elinor Donahue, Ann Todd, Jane Powell. D: Fred M. Wilcox. COM 115m. V

Three Days of the Condor 1975 ★★★★ Mere chance keeps CIA researcher (Redford) from his office the day all his co-workers are murdered by unknown assassins. He realizes he's being stalked (by hit man von Sydow) and gets help from a stranger (Dunaway). Thriller packs a punch. C: Robert Redford, Faye Dunaway, Cliff Robertson, Max von Sydow, John Houseman. D: Sydney Pollack. DRA [R] 118m. V

Three Faces East 1930 ★★★ Underrated early talkie about a British minister's household being infiltrated by double agents during WWI. Sleek Connie's just great. Remade as *British Intelligence*. C: Constance Bennett, Erich von Stroheim. D: Roy Del Ruth. DRA 71m.

Three Faces of Eve, The 1957 ★★★★ Woodward's bravura performance as a schizophrenic housewife with three distinct personalities is the main reason to see this true-life psychological drama. Joanne won Best Actress Oscar. C: Joanne Woodward, David Wayne, Lee J. Cobb. D: Nunnally Johnson. DRA 95m. V

Three Faces West 1940 ★★★ Strange hybrid of Western and WWII drama about a group of Austrian refugees heading to a new life in Oregon. The Duke leads 'em. Not entirely successful, but interesting wartime product. C: John Wayne, Sigrid Gurie, Charles Coburn. D: Bernard Vorhaus. WST 92m. V

3:15 1986 ★★½ High school gang member (Baldwin) tries to quit, but gangleader won't let him. Decent cast squandered on cliché-ridden teen action film. Fans of B-queen Foreman may find it entertaining. C: Adam Baldwin, Deborah Foreman, Rene Auberjonois. D: Larry Gross. ACT [R] 86m. V

Three for the Road 1987 ★★½ Pretty but obnoxious senator's daughter (Green) is escorted to reform school by handsome but duty-bound senator's aide (Sheen). Contrived humor has a few moments. C: Charlie Sheen, Kerri Green, Alan Ruck, Sally Kellerman. D: Bill L. Norton. COM [PG] 98m. V

Three for the Show 1955 ★★★ A married musical comedy star (Grable) is stunned when her supposedly dead first husband returns. Minor musical version of play *Too Many Husbands*, with Jack Cole's choreography its strongest asset. C: Betty Grable, Marge Champion, Gower Champion, Jack Lemmon. D: H.C. Potter. MUS 93m.

Three Fugitives 1989 ★★★½ Fresh out of prison, master thief (Nolte) plans to go straight but walks into a robbery and is kidnapped by nervous triggerman (Short) who blackmails him into helping him and his daughter. Starts brightly, but chemistry fails. Adaptation of French Veber's own *Les Fugitifs*. C: Nick Nolte, Martin Short, Sarah Roland Doroff, James Earl Jones. D: Francis Veber. COM [PG-13] 96m. V

Three Godfathers 1936 ★★★★ Trio of gruff outlaws find abandoned infant in the desert. Warm, winning Western with fine performances from Stone, Morris, and Brennan. (a.k.a. *Miracle in the Sand*) C: Chester Morris, Lewis Stone, Walter Brennan, Irene Hervey. D: Richard Boleslawski. WST 82m.

Three Godfathers, The 1948 ★★★★½ Ford's take on familiar yarn about three renegades finding a baby in the wilderness. Sentimental, but an effective change of pace for Wayne. Beautiful location photography. Based on a Peter B. Kyne story. C: John Wayne, Pedro Armendariz, Harry Carey Jr., Ward Bond, Mae Marsh. D: John Ford. WST 103m. V

Three Guys Named Mike 1951 ★★★ Strident comedy with stewardess (Wyman) courted by three eligible bachelors. Story by Sidney Sheldon. C: Jane Wyman, Van Johnson, Barry Sullivan, Howard Keel. D: Charles Walters. COM 90m.

Three Hats for Lisa 1965 British ★★★½ Two English working-class men (Brown, James) help Italian film star (Hardy) steal three English hats for her collection. Sprightly musical nonsense with attractive photography and pleasant songs. C: Joe Brown, Sophie Hardy, Sidney James, Una Stubbs, Peter Bowles. D: Sidney Hayes. MUS 99m.

Three Hours 1944 French ★★★½ Aumont gives moving performance as French WWII soldier who goes AWOL to visit girlfriend, then spends rest of film searching for her. Originally shot in 1940. C: Jeane-Pierre Aumont, Betty Bovy, Corinne Luchaire. D: Leonide Morguy. DRA 85m.

Three Hours to Kill 1954 ★★★★ Gripping Western with Andrews as a man unjustly accused of murder and given chance by lynch mob to find the real killer. Fascinating story, well done. C: Dana Andrews, Donna Reed, Dianne Foster, Stephen Elliott, Carolyn Jones. D: Alfred Werker. WST 77m.

Three Husbands 1950 ★★★ Three men receive letters from dead Lothario claiming he had an affair with one of their wives. But which of the three wives has strayed? Comic twist on superior *Letter to Three Wives* manages to entertain well enough. C: Eve Arden, Ruth Warrick, Howard DaSilva, Billie Burke, Emlyn Williams. D: Irving Reis. COM 78m.

Three in One 1956 Australian ★★★½ Interesting group of three short, neorealist films dealing with economic insecurity. Best is the first about Australian miners confronted with body of unknown pauper who died in their town. Second deals with wood stolen by poor workers freezing to death, while third involves couple hesitant to marry because of financial woes. C: John McCallum, Edmund Allison, Jerome Levy, Leonard Thiele, Joan Landor, Brian Viary. D: Cecil Holmes. DRA 90m.

Three in the Attic 1968 ★★★½ The big stud on campus finds the tables turned when the three girls he's been bedding discover his unfaithfulness and decide to teach him a lesson by making him a sexual prisoner. Spicy premise and sexy performances keep it lively. C: Christopher Jones, Judy Pace, Yvette Mimieux. D: Richard Wilson. COM [R] 92m. V

Three in the Cellar 1970 *See* **Up in the Cellar**

Three Into Two Won't Go 1969 British ★★★ Mid-life crisis drama about an aging businessman (Steiger) involved in affair with sexy hitchhiker (Geeson), who confronts his staid wife (Bloom). Strong cast lifts it. C: Rod Steiger, Claire Bloom, Judy Geeson, Peggy Ashcroft. D: Peter Hall. COM [R] 93m.

Three Is a Family 1944 ★★★★ Middle-aged man is consigned by his nagging wife to the role of house-husband in an apartment full of frantic family and friends. Funny domestic comedy loaded with laughs. C: Fay Bainter, Marjorie Reynolds, Charlie Ruggles, Helen Broderick, Hattie McDaniel. D: Edward Ludwig. COM 81m.

Three Little Girls in Blue 1946 ★★★★ Turn-of-the-century Atlantic City is the appealing backdrop for lavish musical about three sisters (Blaine, Haver, and Vera-Ellen) in search of rich husbands. Pleasant escapism, with good songs, including "You Make Me Feel So Young." C: June Haver, Vivian Blaine, Vera-Ellen, George Montgomery, Celeste Holm. D: H. Humberstone. MUS 90m.

Three Little Words 1950 ★★★★ Astaire and Skelton make a surprisingly effective team in this bright MGM musical biography of songwriters Kalmar and Ruby. Entertaining story of team's rivalries and misunderstandings refrains from sentiment or melodrama. Songs are good and cast is tops. C: Fred Astaire, Vera-Ellen, Red Skelton, Arlene Dahl, Keenan Wynn, Gloria DeHaven, Debbie Reynolds. D: Richard Thorpe. MUS 102m. V

Three Lives of Thomasina, The 1963 ★★★★ Fanciful tale of Scottish cat with rejuvenatory powers and the girl who loves it. Beautifully photographed English locations. Charming. Based on a Paul Gallico story. C: Karen Dotrice, Patrick McGoohan, Susan Hampshire, Matthew Gerber. D: Don Chaffey. FAM/DRA [PG] 97m. V

Three Men and a Baby 1987 ★★★★ Popular American remake of a French hit about three confirmed bachelors (Danson, Selleck, Guttenberg) who find a baby on their doorstep and must figure out how to bathe, bottle, and burp it. Entertaining fun. Followed by *Three Men and a Little Lady*. C: Tom Selleck, Steve Guttenberg, Ted Danson, Nancy Travis, Margaret Colin, Philip Bosco, Celeste Holm. D: Leonard Nimoy. COM [PG] 102m. V

Three Men and a Cradle 1985 French ★★★★ Three irresponsible Gallic playboys grow up when one of them acquires an infant. Cute, clever comedy was a huge hit in France, becoming inspiration for the American remake, *Three Men and a Baby*. C: Roland Giraud, Michel Boujenah, Andre Dussolier. D: Coline Serreau. COM 106m. V

Three Men and a Little Lady 1990 ★★★½ Sequel to *Three Men and a Baby* finds the three dads rallying to keep "their" baby when the mother (Travis) wants to marry and move to England. Not quite up to the first, but close. C: Tom Selleck, Steve Guttenberg, Ted Danson, Nancy Travis, Robin Weisman. D: Emile Ardolino. COM [PG] 100m. V

Three Men from Texas 1940 ★★★★½ Best of the *Hopalong Cassidy* Westerns, with

Hopalong (Boyd) becoming a Texas Ranger to protect the Mexican border from an evil villain (Ankrum). Prime Saturday matinee fare, full of action with liberal touches of humor. C: William Boyd, Russell Hayden, Andy Clyde, Morris Ankrum, Esther Estrella. D: Lesley Selander. WST 70m.

Three Men on a Horse 1936 ★★★★ Snappy farce about a meek clerk (McHugh) with an uncanny ability to pick winning racehorses. Blondell stands out from an overall good cast as a wisecracking gangster's moll. Good screen adaptation of the Broadway hit. C: Frank McHugh, Sam Levene, Joan Blondell, Teddy Hart, Guy Kibbee. D: Mervyn Le Roy. COM 96m. V

Three Moves to Freedom 1960 German ★★★½ Art smuggler (Jurgens) and ballerina (Bloom) are captured by the Nazis in murky melodrama with talented cast. (a.k.a. *The Royal Game*) C: Curt Jurgens, Claire Bloom. D: Gerd Oswald. DRA 104m.

Three Musketeers, The 1921 ★★★½ Fairbanks is in top form as the neophyte Musketeer D'Artagnan in this handsome, silent version of Dumas's classic novel. C: Douglas Fairbanks, Sr., Leon Barry, Eugene Pallette. D: Fred Niblo. ACT 120m.

Three Musketeers, The 1935 ★★½ Antique version of Dumas swashbuckler about three French swordsmen who team up to defend the Queen's honor. Not the best of the *Musketeers* bunch. C: Walter Abel, Paul Lukas, Margot Grahame. D: Roland V. Lee. ACT 90m. V

Three Musketeers, The 1939 ★★★★ Sprightly musical version of Dumas adventure features the popular comedy team of The Ritz Brothers cavorting as the title characters. Charming, entertaining frolic. C: The Ritz Brothers, Don Ameche, Binnie Barnes, Lionel Atwill. D: Allan Dwan. MUS 73m. V

Three Musketeers, The 1948 ★★★½ Middling version of the Dumas swashbuckler classic has its ups and downs (Kelly's witty athleticism is a major up, but his dramatic ability is a definite down). Beautifully produced, though. C: Gene Kelly, June Allyson, Lana Turner, Van Heflin, Angela Lansbury, Robert Coote, Frank Morgan, Vincent Price, Keenan Wynn, Gig Young. D: George Sidney. ACT 125m. V

Three Musketeers, The 1974 British ★★★★½ Big, splashy, colorful remake of Dumas' classic swashbuckler, about a young man (York) determined to join the Musketeers. Director Lester spices up the action with plenty of sight gags, witty dialogue and a breakneck pace. Terrific cast and top-notch production values make this the most entertaining of all remakes. C: Michael York, Raquel Welch, Faye Dunaway, Oliver Reed, Frank Finlay, Christopher Lee, Geraldine Chaplin, Charlton Heston, Jean-Pierre Cassel. D: Richard Lester. ACT [PG] 105m. V

Three Musketeers, The 1993 ★★★ Sutherland, Platt, and Sheen are the trio of sword-wielding heroes, joined by upstart O'Donnell. Stuffed with slapstick and phony swagger, this version of Dumas' oft-filmed novel is merely glossy star vehicle in fancy costumes. Curry's wicked Richelieu and DeMornay's luminous Lady DeWinter make up for a lot. C: Kiefer Sutherland, Charlie Sheen, Chris O'Donnell, Oliver Platt, Tim Curry, Rebecca De Mornay. ACT [PG] 105m. V

Three Nights of Love 1969 Italian ★★½ Anthology showcase for the physical charms and acting abilities of star Spaak. All three tales are highly suggestive; the first, about Catherine's dalliance with priest (Law) in hospital, may cause some to take offense. C: Catherine Spaak, John Phillip Law. D: Luigi Comencini, Renato Castellani, Franco Rossi. DRA 112m.

3 Ninjas 1992 ★★★½ Three young boys trained in ninja techniques by their grandfather foil a kidnap plot. Action-packed fun for the whole family. C: Michael Treanor, Max Elliott Slade, Chad Power, Rand Kingsley. D: Jon Turteltaub, Victor Wong. FAM/ACT [PG] 87m. V

Three Ninjas Kick Back 1994 ★★ The little menaces return to fight Evil and encourage viewing children to behave like monsters. For kids from solidly furnished homes. C: Victor Wong, Max Elliott Slade, Sean Fox, Evan Bonifant, Caroline Junko King. D: Charles T. Kanganis. ACT [PG] 99m. V

Three Nuts in Search of a Bolt 1964 ★★ To find a cure for their phobias without emptying their wallets, three zanies hire an actor to emote their problems to a psychiatrist and relay the results back to them. Crazy comedy features scantily clad Van Doren. C: Mamie Van Doren, Tommy Noonan, Ziva Rodann, Paul Gilbert. D: Tommy Noonan. COM 80m. V

Three O'Clock High 1987 ★★★ A school newspaper assignment proves life threatening for a hapless reporter when the new student he must interview turns out to be a violent psychotic. Humorous teen version of *High Noon*. C: Casey Siemaszko, Anne Ryan, Richard Tyson, Jeffrey Tambor. D: Phil Joanou. COM [PG-13] 90m. V

Three of Hearts 1993 ★★★½ Sensitive story of a lesbian (Lynch) who hires a gigolo (Baldwin) to woo and then dump her former girlfriend (Fenn), but unforseen relationships confuse her plan. A witty depiction of modern relationships. C: William Baldwin, Kelly Lynch, Sherilyn Fenn, Joe Pantoliano. D: Yurek Bogayevicz. DRA [R] 105m. V

Three on a Couch 1966 ★★ To free his psychiatrist girlfriend (Leigh) to go to Paris with him, a man (Lewis) tries to solve the problems of her patients. Strained Lewis vehicle. C: Jerry Lewis, Janet Leigh, Mary Ann Mobley, Gila Golan, Leslie Parrish. D: Jerry Lewis. COM 109m.

Three on a Match 1932 ★★★½ Low-budget, gripping melodrama about three reunited friends and the different paths their lives take. Davis has only a small part. Dvorak gets most of the dramatic stuff, and she's quite good. C: Ann Dvorak, Joan Blondell, Bette Davis, Warren William, Humphrey Bogart, Glenda Farrell. D: Mervyn LeRoy. DRA 64m. v

Three Ring Circus 1954 ★★★ Martin and Lewis go under the big top, with silly results. Funniest scene: Jerry and the bearded lady. (a.k.a. *Jerrico, The Wonder Clown*) C: Dean Martin, Jerry Lewis, Joanne Dru, Zsa Zsa Gabor, Elsa Lanchester. D: Joseph Pevney. COM 103m.

Three Sailors and a Girl 1953 ★★½ The title characters conspire to put on a Broadway show. Songs by Sammy Cahn and Sammy Fain. Good-natured tuner. C: Jane Powell, Gordon MacRae, Gene Nelson, Sam Levene. D: Roy Del Ruth. MUS 95m.

Three Secrets 1950 ★★★★ Expert soap opera about three women (Parker, Neal, Roman) anxiously awaiting word as to whose child survived plane wreck. Smooth flashback drama, good performances. C: Eleanor Parker, Patricia Neal, Ruth Roman. D: Robert Wise. DRA 98m.

Three Sisters 1974 British ★★★★½ Distinguished British cast does well with Chekhov's moody comedy/drama about three improverished siblings and their desire to move to Moscow. Basically a filmed play, but an outstanding example of that genre. C: Jeanne Watts, Joan Plowright, Louise Purnell, Derek Jacobi. D: Laurence Olivier. DRA 165m.

Three Smart Girls 1936 ★★★★½ Jim-dandy musical about three daughters of divorced parents trying to squelch Dad's remarriage to a scheming gold-digger. Durbin (in her feature debut) is delightful, so much so that her part was beefed up during filming. Songs include "Someone To Care For Me." Followed by sequel, *Three Smart Girls Grow Up*. C: Deanna Durbin, Charles Winninger, Binne Barnes, Alice Brady, Ray Milland, Mischa Auer. D: Henry Koster. MUS 84m. v

Three Smart Girls Grow Up 1939 ★★★★ Helpful sibling (Durbin) tries to unravel her older sisters' love lives in this sunny sequel to *Three Smart Girls* that's just as good as its predecessor. Deanna sings several songs, including hit "Because." C: Deanna Durbin, Charles Winniger, Nan Grey, Helen Parrish, Robert Cummings. D: Henry Koster. MUS 90m. v

Three Sovereigns For Sarah 1985 ★★★★ A woman tries to clear her name and the names of her dead sisters after they are convicted of witchcraft in Salem. Intriguing tale of justice in the face of hysteria, with Redgrave both steely and compassionate. C: Vanessa Redgrave, Phyllis Thaxter, Kim Hunter. D: Philip Leacock. DRA 152m. TVM

Three Stooges Go Around the World in a Daze, The 1963 ★★★½ The Stooges help Phileas Fogg's great-grandson repeat his ancestor's feat of traveling the globe in 80 days. High-spirited, comic updating of the Jules Verne novel makes a fine outing for the trio. C: The Three Stooges, Jay Sheffield, Joan Freeman. D: Norman Maurer. COM 94m. v

Three Stooges in Orbit, The 1962 ★★½ The Three Stooges vs. Martians. Funny space slapstick. C: The Three Stooges, Emil Sitka. D: Edward Bernds. COM 87m.

Three Stooges Meet Hercules, The 1962 ★★★ Time-traveling, toga-clad Stooges venture back to 961 B.C., where they meet Hercules and a Siamese-twin Cyclops. Stooge fans will "nyuk" it up. C: The Three Stooges, Quinn Redeker, Vicki Trickett. D: Edward Bernds. COM 89m. v

Three Strangers 1946 ★★★★ Unusual tale of three people (Greenstreet, Fitzgerald, Lorre) who meet by chance and form alliance over cursed sweepstakes ticket. Memorable, moody drama creates haunting atmosphere. Good star trio. C: Sydney Greenstreet, Geraldine Fitzgerald, Peter Lorre. D: Jean Negulesco. DRA 92m.

3:10 to Yuma 1957 ★★★★½ Classic Western suspense film, with farmer (Heflin) holding outlaw (Ford), awaiting train that will take latter to prison. Ford plays mind games throughout, hoping his gang will spring him. Taut, brilliantly acted, and well written. C: Van Heflin, Glenn Ford, Felicia Farr. D: Delmar Daves. WST 92m. v

Three the Hard Way 1974 ★★★★ Psychotic racist (Robinson) plans to eliminate African-Americans by tainting the water supply with a race specific poison. Brown, Williamson, and Kelly join forces to stop him. Nonstop action minus gore make this thriller a stand-out. C: Jim Brown, Fred Williamson, Jim Kelly, Jay Robinson. D: Gordon Parks, Jr. ACT 93m. v

Three Violent People 1956 ★★★½ Action-packed Western stars Heston as a rancher fighting villainous carpetbaggers trying to steal his land after the Civil War. Interesting relationship is explored between rancher and wife who has a dark secret in her past. C: Charlton Heston, Anne Baxter, Gilbert Roland, Tom Tryon, Forrest Tucker, Elaine Stritch. D: Rudolph Mate. WST 100m. v

Three Wise Fools 1946 ★★★½ Plucky little girl (O'Brien) sets out to win the hearts of three curmudgeons. All-stops-out sentiment, tailor-made for the child star. C: Margaret O'Brien, Lionel Barrymore, Lewis Stone, Edward Arnold, Thomas Mitchell, Jane Darwell, Cyd Charisse. D: Edward Buzzell. FAM/COM 90m.

Three Wise Girls 1931 ★★★ Hayseed (Harlow) hits the big town and has to wise up fast. Genial programmer, fine early Harlow. C: Jean Harlow, Mae Clark, Marie Prevost. D: William Beaudine. COM 66m.

3 Women 1977 ★★★★½ Controversial, heavily symbolic story of roommates (Spacek, Duvall), with the former slowly assuming the latter's persona. Rule's role as older woman involved with the other two defies explanation. An enigmatic Altman masterpiece. C: Sissy Spacek, Shelley Duvall, Janice Rule. D: Robert Altman. DRA [PG] 125m.

Three Women in Limbo 1972 *See* **Limbo**

3 Worlds of Gulliver, The 1960 ★★★★ Jonathan Swift's tale of a sailor who is a giant in one land, doll-sized in another, makes an effective fantasy adventure for kids of all ages. Terrific special effects, evocative Bernard Herrmann score. C: Kerwin Matthews, Jo Morrow, Lee Patterson. D: Jack Sher. FAM/DRA 100m. V

Threepenny Opera, The 1931 German/American ★★★★½ In the sinister underworld, the notorious Mack the Knife runs his gang of murderers and thieves. A fabulous commingling of German impressionism and the artistry of Brecht, Weill, and Lenya. Outstanding. C: Rudolf forster, Carola Neher, Reinhold Schunzel. D: Georg Wilhelm Pabst. MUS 113m. V

Threesome 1994 ★★★½ Boyle, Baldwin, and Charles are thrown together as dormmates in college, develop a romantic triangle. Gay character's coming-out is handled with intelligence and the leads are appealing, but the writing overall is uneven. C: Lara Flynn Boyle, Stephen Baldwin, Josh Charles, Alexis Arquette, Martha Gehman, Mark Arnold, Michele Matheson. D: Andrew Fleming. COM [R] 93m. V

Threshold 1981 Canadian ★★★★ Engrossing, prophetic medical drama about the first artificial heart recipient (Winningham). Not released in the U.S. until 1983, when Barney Clark made headlines with the real-life procedure. Winningham is excellent. C: Donald Sutherland, Jeff Goldblum, Mare Winningham. D: Richard Pearce. DRA [PG] 97m. V

Thrill of a Romance 1945 ★★★½ Williams plays a swimming star doing her patriotic duty by entertaining newly "civilianized" soldier (Johnson). Formula swim-and-song vehicle for Esther stays charmingly afloat. Outstanding song: "I Should Care." C: Van Johnson, Esther Williams, Spring Byington, Lauritz Melchior, Tommy Dorsey. D: Richard Thorpe. MUS 105m. V

Thrill Of It All, The 1963 ★★★★ One of the better Day comedies, with wife (Doris) of doctor (Garner) thrust in national spotlight as star of TV commercials. Some hilarious jabs at advertising, television, and marriage. C: Doris Day, James Garner, Arlene Francis. D: Norman Jewison. COM 108m. V

Throne of Blood 1961 Japanese ★★★★★ Macbeth as samurai via the master Kurosawa. Intensely gripping, with a powerful Mifune as the Macbeth character. His death by a volley of arrows is a film icon. C: Toshiro Mifune, Isuzu Yamada, Takashi Shimura. D: Akira Kurosawa. DRA 108m. V

Through a Glass Darkly 1962 Swedish ★★★★★ Upon her release from a mental hospital, a woman vacations with her family on a remote island. A gripping look at madness, with Bergman at the top of his powers. Foreign-language film Oscar-winner. C: Harriet Andersson, Gunnar Bjornstrand, Max von Sydow. D: Ingmar Bergman. DRA 91m. V

Through Days and Months 1969 Japanese ★★★½ Depressing, but well-acted, drama of a young Japanese woman (Iwashita) pursued by two men who are equally unworthy of her. C: Shima Iwashita, Jin Nakayama, Koji Ishizaka, Masayuki Mori. D: Noboru Nakamura. DRA 98m.

Throw Momma From the Train 1987 ★★★½ Inspired by Hitchcock's *Strangers on a Train*, a timid university student (DeVito) conspires to murder the venal wife of his college teacher (Crystal) in exchange for the favor of killing his own intolerable mother. Black comedy deftly handled by director DeVito. C: Danny DeVito, Billy Crystal, Anne Ramsey. D: Danny DeVito. COM [PG-13] 88m. V

Thumbelina 1970 ★★★½ Low-budget, but entertaining, live-action version of Hans Christian Andersen fairy tale with Garner as tiny maiden kidnapped by evil toad. C: Shay Garner, Pat Morell, Bob O'Connell. D: Barry Mahon. FAM/DRA 62m.

Thumbelina 1994 ★★★½ Bluth (*An American Tail*) adapts Hans Christian Andersen's tale of a girl, "no bigger than your thumb" and her adventures in the real world after she is kidnapped by a toad and must find her way home to her fairy prince. Nice animation, fine for kids, with a sweet Barry Manilow score. Voices of Jodi Benson, Carol Channing, Charo, Gino Conforti, Barbara Cook. D: Don Bluth, Gary Goldman. FAM/DRA [G] 94m. TVM V

Thunder Bay 1953 ★★★★ Vigorous action-adventure tale about oil driller (Stewart) battling shrimp fishermen in a Louisiana bay. Magnificent wide-screen photography, and a script that holds interest. C: James Stewart, Joanne Dru, Dan Duryea, Gilbert Roland. D: Anthony Mann. ACT 102m. V

Thunder in the City 1937 ★★★★ One of Robinson's better comic turns puts him in England, huckstering new metal known as Magnelite. Fun to watch Eddie play off staid British actors like Richardson. C: Edward G. Robinson, Nigel Bruce, Luli Deste, Ralph Richardson, Constance Collier. D: Marion Gering. DRA 86m. V

Thunder in the East 1953 ★★½ A gunrunner (Ladd) tries to take advantage of India's newfound independence, but gets caught up in the struggle. Good cast in a stilted but entertaining actioner. C: Alan Ladd, Deborah Kerr, Charles Boyer, Corinne Calvet. D: Charles Vidor. ACT 98m.

Thunder in the Sun 1959 ★★½ A Basque beauty (Hayward) finds herself the object of three men's affections during an 1850s wagon train journey to California. Hayward struggles with her accent, sometimes amusingly. C: Susan Hayward, Jeff Chandler, Jacques Bergerac, Carl Esmond. D: Russell Rouse. WST 81m.

Thunder Mountain 1935 ★★★½ Rugged Western about a gold rush prospector (O'Brien) swindled by barkeeper (Wallace). Exciting action sequences. Based on Zane Grey novel. C: George O'Brien, Morgan Wallace. D: David Howard. WST 68m.

Thunder Mountain 1964 *See* **Shepherd of the Hills, The**

Thunder on the Hill 1951 ★★★★ Unusual mystery about a nun (Colbert) trying to clear a woman of a murder charge. Well-played, thoughtful drama saddled with an inappropriate title. Try it. C: Claudette Colbert, Ann Blyth, Robert Douglas, Gladys Cooper. D: Douglas Sirk. DRA 84m.

Thunder Road 1958 ★★★½ Cult favorite is a murky drama about Kentucky moonshiners, who battle gangsters and the law. Features a strong performance by Mitchum (who also wrote, produced, and sings the title tune very well!) and interesting setting. C: Robert Mitchum, Gene Barry, Keely Smith, James Mitchum. D: Arthur Ripley. CRI 92m. V

Thunder Rock 1944 British ★★★★½ Lovely, ethereal tale of disillusioned journalist (Redgrave) sojourning in isolated lighthouse, visited by ghosts of drowned immigrants. Moving and uplifting, with a wonderful cast. C: Michael Redgrave, Barbara Mullen, James Mason. D: Roy Boulting. DRA 90m.

Thunder Trail 1937 ★★★½ Satisfying Western with better-than-average plot of brothers (Roland, Craig) separated by outlaw (Bickford), who kills their father and raises one of them as his own. From Zane Grey novel. C: Gilbert Roland, Charles Bickford, Marsha Hunt, J. Carrol Naish. D: Charles Barton. WST 58m. V

Thunderball 1965 British ★★★★½ James Bond must stop the evil SPECTRE before they blow up Miami. Fourth entry is pretty routine; remade in 1983 as *Never Say Never Again*, also with Connery. C: Sean Connery, Claudine Auger, Adolfo Celi. D: Terence Young. ACT [PG] 130m. V

Thunderbirds Are Go 1966 ★★★½ Imaginative children's science fiction feature from cult British TV series with all-marionette cast. The Thunderbirds are 21st-century spacemen on life or death mission to Mars. Remarkably exciting, addictive stuff. C: The Tracy Brothers. SFI 92m. V

Thunderbolt 1929 ★★★½ Early gangster drama about the redemption of a fugitive from justice (Bancroft). Interesting oldie helped enormously by von Sternberg's directorial stamp. C: George Bancroft, Fay Wray, Richard Arlen, Tully Marshall. D: Josef von Sternberg. CRI 91m.

Thunderbolt and Lightfoot 1974 ★★★★ Offbeat action drama features one of Eastwood's most underrated performances as Vietnam veteran who teams up with drifter Bridges to pull a heist, only to find themselves in competition with two other robbers. Cimino's directorial debut is fast-paced fun. C: Clint Eastwood, Jeff Bridges, Geoffrey Lewis. D: Michael Cimino. CRI [R] 114m. V

Thundercloud 1950 *See* **Colt .45**

Thunderhead—Son of Flicka 1945 ★★★½ Continuation of the boy and his horse saga begun in *My Friend Flicka*. Family film not as good as the first, but still sunny. C: Roddy McDowall, Preston Foster, Rita Johnson. D: Louis King. FAM/DRA [R] 78m. V

Thunderheart 1992 ★★★★ Young FBI agent Kilmer, who is part Sioux, is sent to a Sioux reservation to investigate a murder and learns about himself in the process. Well-done suspense with exquisite South Dakota location photography. C: Val Kilmer, Sam Shepard, Fred Ward. D: Michael Apted. DRA [R] 119m. V

Thunderhoof 1948 ★★★½ Overheated but fascinating Western drama borrows from Greek tragedy *Phaedra* in its tale of an older man (Foster), young wife (Stuart), and adopted son (Bishop) involved in a romantic triangle while pursuing a wild colt. C: Preston Foster, Mary Stuart, William Bishop, Thunderhoof. D: Phil Karlson. WST 77m.

Thundering Herd, The 1933 ★★★½ Scott and Crabbe are out to foil evil Beery's plan to steal buffalo hides from settlers in robust pioneer Western. From a Zane Grey novel. C: Randolph Scott, Judith Allen, Buster Crabbe, Noah Beery. D: Henry Hathaway. WST 62m. V

Thundering Mantis, The ★★½ Rival martial arts gangs; one of them specializes in the particularly ruthless thundering mantis style. Nonstop violence. ACT V

Thursday's Game 1974 ★★★★½ Sparkling comedy about two middle-aged misfits (Wilder, Newhart) who play poker weekly. Sprightly dialogue by James L. Brooks (*Broadcast News*) and a terrific cast make for exceptionally fun viewing. C: Bob Newhart, Gene Wilder, Ellen Burstyn, Cloris Leachman, Nancy Walker, Valerie Harper, Rob Reiner. D: Robert Moore. COM [PG] 100m. TVM V

THX 1138 1971 ★★★½ Lucas' first film is set in a grim future of underground cities where everything and everyone is controlled by computers. Two lovers unite to challenge the machine masters. Lucas expanded one of his student projects to make this interesting thriller. C: Robert Duvall, Donald Pleasence, Don Pedro Colley. D: George Lucas. SFI [PG] 88m. V

. . . tick . . . tick . . . tick . . . 1970 ★★★ A black sherrif (Brown) comes to a southern town, and tensions run high. Medium thriller knock-off of *In the Heat of the Night* benefits from March's crusty performance as the community's mayor. C: Jim Brown, George Kennedy, Fredric March, Don Stroud. D: Ralph Nelson. DRA [PG] 100m.

Ticket to Heaven 1981 ★★★★ Powerful indictment of religious cults, as a healthy college student (Mancuso) is gradually transformed into an emaciated, brainwashed member of a Moonie-like organization. Mancuso is terrific. C: Nick Mancuso, Saul Rubinek, Meg Foster, Kim Cattrall. D: Ralph L. Thomas. DRA [PG] 107m. V

Ticket to Tomahawk, A 1950 ★★★½ Fluffy comedy/Western about stagecoach operators conspiring to derail rival train line. A pleasantly entertaining excursion. Look for Marilyn Monroe as chorus girl in Dailey's big dance number. C: Dan Dailey, Anne Baxter, Rory Calhoun. D: Richard Sale. WST 90m.

Tickle Me 1965 ★★★ Cowhand (Presley) at a women-only dude ranch doesn't have a hard time finding romance. Presley seems to be enjoying himself—and you might, too. C: Elvis Presley, Jocelyn Lane, Julie Adams. D: Norman Taurog. MUS 90m. V

Ticks 1993 ★★★★½ Genuinely creepy and often gruesome horror film about city kids running into mutated, bloodthirsty insects (and some human villains) on a camping trip. No real surprises, but the killer bugs deliver the scary goods. (a.k.a. *Infested*) C: Peter Scolari, Rosalind Allen, Ami Dolenz, Seth Green, Virginya Keehne. D: Tony Randel. HOR [R] 83m.

Tiger and the Flame, The 1955 Indian ★★★★ Compelling Indian drama with Mehtab as Hindu queen leading revolt against British rule. First Indian film done entirely in Technicolor. C: Mehtab, Modi, Sohrab Modi, Ulhas. D: Sohrab M. Modi. DRA 97m.

Tiger and the Pussycat, The 1967 Italian-U.S. ★★★ Leering sex comedy casts Gassman as a Neopolitan businessman pursued by an American playgirl (Ann-Margret). Energetic cast can't save tired script. C: Ann-Margret, Vittorio Gassman, Eleanor Parker. D: Dino Risi. COM 105m. V

Tiger Bay 1959 British ★★★★ Mills plays a misfit child who witnesses murder, then is kidnapped by the criminal (Buchholz). Complex, fascinating thriller with good performance by Hayley in her first major role. C: John Mills, Horst Buchholz, Hayley Mills. D: J. Lee Thompson. DRA 105m. V

Tiger in the Smoke 1956 British ★★★½ Thieves search London for missing loot which they suspect has been hidden by a little girl. Interesting melodrama tries for something different, often succeeds. C: Donald Sinden, Murial Pavlow, Tony Wright, Bernard Miles. D: Roy Baker. DRA 94m.

Tiger Makes Out, The 1967 ★★★ A lowly mailman rebels against society by kidnapping a suburban matron and holding her prisoner. Adaptation of Murray Schisgal's play *The Tiger* features husband-and-wife team Wallach and Jackson in tailor-made roles. Dustin Hoffman makes an early career appearance in bit part of a beatnik. C: Eli Wallach, Anne Jackson, Bob Dishy, David Burns, Charles Nelson Reilly. D: Arthur Hiller. COM 94m.

Tiger Shark 1932 ★★★★ Pungent drama of a Portuguese fisherman (Robinson) who takes in a destitute young woman, marries her, but fears losing her to his best friend. Features great location footage, an excellent Robinson performance, and that patented Hawks pacing. C: Edward G. Robinson, Richard Arlen, Zita Johann, J. Carrol Naish. D: Howard Hawks. DRA 80m.

Tiger Town 1983 ★★★★ Good-natured baseball film involves *Kramer vs. Kramer* star Henry as young boy who helps fading Detroit Tiger (Scheider) achieve one last success. Solid performances and avoidance of cheap sentiment give warmth to this Disney feature. C: Roy Scheider, Justin Henry. D: Alan Shapiro. FAM/DRA 76m. V

Tiger vs. Dragon 1986 ★★ The Hungry Tiger fights the Crazy Dragon in Chinese boxing. Typical. ACT 88m. V

Tiger Walks, A 1964 ★★★★ Unusual drama about girl (Franklin) who takes on small-minded townspeople in defense of tiger that escapes from traveling circus. Cast of veteran character actors and tough-minded script provide a biting edge not normally seen in Disney family films. C: Brian Keith, Vera Miles, Pamela Franklin, Sabu. D: Norman Tokar. FAM/DRA 88m. V

Tiger Warsaw 1988 ★ He bumped off his dad and left town; now he's clean and sober and back home to start over. But nobody wants him around; you won't either. C: Patrick Swayze, Piper Laurie, Lee Richardson. D: Amin Chaudhri. DRA [R] 92m. V

Tigers in Lipstick 1979 Italian ★★★ European sex romp features four ravishing actresses (Andress, Antonelli, Kristel, Vitti) prowling after men in seven separate episodes. Fun, but hardly a feminist movie. (a.k.a. *Wild Beds*) C: Ursula Andress, Laura Antonelli, Sylvia Kristel, Monica Vitti. D: Luigi Zampa. COM [R] 83m. V

Tiger's Tale, A 1987 ★★½ Improbable fluff about a high school student (Howell) who has an affair with his ex-girlfriend's mom (Ann Margaret), who ends up pregnant. Adolescent fantasy material played without much attention to reality. Directed by Kirk Douglas' son. C: Ann-Margret, C. Thomas Howell, Charles Durning, Kelly Preston. D: Peter Douglas. DRA [R] 97m. V

Tight Little Island 1949 British ★★★★★ Whiskey-laden shipwreck off the coast of small Scottish island causes local uproar. High-spirited, terrific, British comedy with champagne performances and wonderful flavor. A gem. (a.k.a. *Whisky Galore!*) Followed by sequel: *Mad Little Island*. C: Basil Radford, Joan Greenwood, James Justice, Jean Cadell, Gordon Jackson, John Gregson. D: Alexander Mackendrick. COM 82m.

Tight Shoes 1941 ★★★★ Modest, winning

comedy concerns a corrupt politician (Crawford) whose tight shoes lead to disaster. Snappy fun from Damon Runyon story. C: Broderick Crawford, Binnie Barnes, John Howard, Anne Gwynne. D: Albert Rogell. COM 68m.

Tight Spot 1955 ★★★★½ Rogers has agreed to testify against her mobster boyfriend, so now the hoods want her dead. A great paranoid crime film, with excellent lead performances, terrific plot twists, and tense, claustrophobic direction. C: Ginger Rogers, Edward G. Robinson, Brian Keith, Lorne Greene. D: Phil Karlson. CRI 97m. V

Tightrope 1984 ★★★½ Eastwood is terrific in this engrossing thriller about homicide investigator who begins to identify with the sex crime perpetrator he pursues. Disturbingly compelling, with intriguing performance by Bujold as woman with secrets of her own. C: Clint Eastwood, Genevieve Bujold, Alison Eastwood, Jennifer Beck. D: Richard Tuggle. CRI [R] 115m. V

Tiki Tiki 1971 ★★★★ Offbeat, hilarious combo of live action and animation takes footage from a Russian kiddie film, *Dr. Abolit*, and incorporates it into a tale about a simian Hollywood studio head (K.K., or King Kong) anxious to make film with an "all-people" cast. Funny and imaginative spoof; for both adults and kids. C: Barrie Baldaro, Peter Cullan, Joan Stuart. D: Gerald Potterton. FAM/COM 71m.

'Til We Meet Again 1940 ★★★ Terminally ill woman (Oberon) falls in love with death row criminal (Brent) on ship bound for San Francisco. Good remake of classy tearjerker *One Way Passage*. C: Merle Oberon, George Brent, Pat O'Brien, Geraldine Fitzgerald, Binnie Barnes, Eric Blore. D: Edmund Goulding. DRA 99m.

Till Death Us Do Part 1991 ★★★½ Courtroom drama chronicles famed Los Angeles D.A. Vincent Bugliosi's case against Alan Palliko and his mistress for the murder of his wife. Diverting, with solid performances. Bugliosi was the prosecutor of Charles Manson and author of *Helter Skelter*. C: Treat Williams, Arliss Howard, Rebecca Jenkins. D: Yves Simoneau. CRI [R] 93m. TVM V

Till Marriage Do Us Part 1974 Italian ★★★ On their wedding night, a young couple learn that they are brother and sister, causing some really serious sexual complications. Silly and, at times, downright funny. (a.k.a. *Dio Mio, Come Sono Caduto in Basso* and *How Long Can You Fall?*) C: Laura Antonelli, Alberto Lionello, Michele Placido. D: Luigi Comencini. COM 97m. V

Till the Clouds Roll By 1946 ★★★★ Star-studded biography of Broadway composer Jerome Kern is completely fictitious, but that hardly matters when MGM's top roster of talent is on hand. Highlights include Lena's medley from *Show Boat*, Judy's "Look For the Silver Lining." C: Robert Walker, Van Heflin, Lucille Bremer, Judy Garland, Kathryn Grayson, Lena Horne, Tony Martin, Dinah Shore, Frank Sinatra, June Allyson, Angela Lansbury, Cyd Charisse. D: Richard Whorf. MUS 123m. V

Till the End of Time 1946 ★★★½ Three WWII servicemen return home to face adjustment problems. Modest soap opera benefits from McGuire's sensitive portrayal of recent war-widow being wooed by Madison. Title song (from Chopin's Polonaise in A-flat Major) was a big juke-box hit. C: Dorothy McGuire, Guy Madison, Robert Mitchum, Bill Williams. D: Edward Dmytryk. DRA 105m. V

Till There Was You 1990 U.S. ★★ Harmon's expectations of a frolicsome time with his brother on a remote tropical island are put on hold when his brother is murdered and Harmon has to solve the crime. Mainly for fans of spectacular island cinematography. C: Mark Harmon, Deborah Unger, Jeroen Krabbe. D: John Seal. CRI [R] 95m. V

Till Tomorrow Comes 1962 ★★★½ Japanese soap opera about a blind girl during WWII, desperate to have surgery that may restore her sight. Well acted, but trite. C: Aru Kagirl, Ashita Aru Kagiri. D: Shiro Toyodo. DRA 113m.

Till We Meet Again 1944 ★★★ French nun (Britton) helps American pilot (Milland) flee the Nazis. Standard WWII romantic adventure. C: Ray Milland, Barbara Britton, Walter Slezak. D: Frank Borzage. DRA 88m.

Tillie and Gus 1933 ★★★★ Two retired cardsharps (Fields, Skipworth) return home to help favorite niece and nephew gain family inheritance by winning boat race. Forget the plot and enjoy W.C.'s first encounter with arch-nemesis Baby LeRoy! C: W.C. Fields, Alison Skipworth, Baby LeRoy, Edgar Kennedy. D: Francis Martin. COM 58m.

Tillie's Punctured Romance 1914 ★★★½ First comedy feature is a disjointed silent antique, telling tale of naive Dressler falling into con man Chaplin's clutches. Charlie's cast against type here, which doesn't help, but film's worth seeing for its historical value. C: Marie Dressler, Charlie Chaplin, Mabel Norman, The Keystone Kops. D: Mack Sennett. COM 73m. V

Tim 1979 Australian ★★★★ Unusual Australian love story about middle-aged woman who falls in love with her gardener, an attractive, mildly retarded young man. Delicate material is wonderfully handled because of its sensitive portrayals. Slight but very affecting romance. C: Piper Laurie, Mel Gibson. D: Michael Pate. DRA 94m. V

Time After Time 1979 ★★★★ Imaginative "what if" movie puts science fiction pioneer H.G. Wells in pursuit of Victorian serial killer Jack the Ripper. Chase lands them both in modern-day America, via Wells' time machine. Romance between Wells (McDowell) and shy bank teller (Steenburgen) who befriends him is charming. C: Malcolm McDowell, Mary Steenburgen, David Warner. D: Nicholas Meyer. SFI [PG] 112m. V

Time Bandits 1982 British ★★★½ An English boy accompanies pack of dwarves, traveling through history via holes in the universe. Somewhat muddled comedy, from several Monty Python alumni, but eye-popping visuals provide some amazement. Children may get confused. C: Sean Connery, Shelley Duvall, John Cleese, Katherine Helmond, Ian Holm, Michael Palin, Ralph Richardson, David Warner. D: Terry Gilliam. COM [PG] 116m. V

Time Bomb 1961 French ★★½ Average French suspense has shipowner (Jurgens) trying to blow up his own vessel to collect insurance money. Tick-tock, boys. C: Curt Jurgens, Mylene Demongeot, Alain Saury. D: Yves Ciampi. DRA 92m.

Time Flyer 1986 *See* **Blue Yonder, The**

Time for Dying, A 1971 ★★★★ Unusual Western about hero worship recounts adventures of farm boy (Lapp) who wishes to become a gunslinger, encountering several Wild West figures along the way. Well written. C: Richard Lapp, Anne Randall, Audie Murphy, Victor Jory. D: Budd Boetticher. WST 87m.

Time for Killing, A 1967 ★★½ Bandy-legged Civil War melodrama casts Ford as Union Captain feuding with Confederate Major (Hamilton) over the heart of lady fair (Stevens). Needs reinforcements. (a.k.a. *The Long Ride Home*) C: Glenn Ford, Inger Stevens, George Hamilton. D: Phil Karlson. WST 88m.

Time, Gentlemen, Please? 1953 ★★★½ A British town, known for its order and neatness, tries to get rid of its one unsightly citizen (Byrne). Terrific concept survives uneven treatment. C: Eddie Byrne, Hermione Baddeley, Jane Barrett, Raymond Lovell. D: Lewis Gilbert. COM 79m.

Time Guardian, The 1989 Australian ★★½ Two men from the future travel through time to the present where they battle cyborgs in the Australian desert. Atmospheric adventure, undone by dialogue and confusing plot, despite some impressive special effects. C: Tom Burlinson, Nikki Coghill, Dean Stockwell, Carrie Fisher. D: Brian Hannant. SFI [PG] 95m. V

Time Indefinite 1992 ★★★★★ Sad, sometimes amusing self-portrait by documentary maker McElwee (*Sherman's March*) about his impending marriage and relationship with his elder relatives. Quirky, sometimes repetitive, but never boring. D: Ross McElwee. DOC 117m. V

Time Limit 1957 ★★★★ Taut Korean war drama about American officer accused of committing treason while imprisoned in POW camp. Excellent courtroom climax. Adapted from Henry Denker play. C: Richard Widmark, Richard Basehart, Dolores Michaels, June Lockhart, Rip Torn, Martin Balsam. D: Karl Malden. DRA 96m.

Time Lost and Time Remembered 1966 British ★★★½ British housewife (Miles), married to older man, becomes dissatisfied with her life. Sensitive, well-shot drama. (a.k.a. *I Was Happy Here*) C: Sarah Miles, Cyril Cusack, Julian Glover. D: Desmond Davis. DRA 91m.

Time Machine, The 1960 ★★★★½ A British inventor (Taylor) journeys forward in time to find man has evolved into a placid race of people enslaved by vicious neanderthals called Morlocks. Highly entertaining treatment of the H.G. Wells story, won an Oscar for its special effects. C: Rod Taylor, Yvette Mimieux, Alan Young, Sebastian Cabot. D: George Pal. SFI [G] 103m. V

Time of Indifference 1964 Italian ★★½ Ruthless con man (Steiger) infiltrates a wealthy Italian family fallen on hard times. Fine cast in a rather muddled drama. C: Rod Steiger, Claudia Cardinale, Shelley Winters, Paulette Goddard. D: Francesco Maselli. DRA 84m. V

Time of The Gypsies 1990 Hungarian ★★★½ A young Gypsy boy is growing up, and accordingly, his people teach him the ways of the Gypsy life. Long but generally effective; filmed in the Romany language. (a.k.a. *Dom Za Vesanje*) C: Davor Dumjovic, Bora Todorovic, Ljubica Adzovic. D: Emir Kusturica. DRA [R] 136m. V

Time of the Roses 1970 ★★★½ Futuristic, Orwellian tale of a 21st-century filmmaker trying to depict the 1970s and distorting history in the process. Interesting comment on how humankind regards the past, but suffers from pretentiousness. C: Ritva Vespa, Arto Tuominen. D: Risto Jarva. DRA

Time of Their Lives, The 1946 ★★★★ Two Revolutionary patriots (Costello, Reynolds), mistaken for traitors, turn up as ghosts 200 years later to clear their name. Underrated, delightful surprise. One of Abbott and Costello's best. C: Bud Abbott, Lou Costello, Marjorie Reynolds, Binnie Barnes, John Shelton, Gale Sondergaard. D: Charles Barton. COM 82m. V

Time of Your Life, The 1948 ★★★ Saloon sage (Cagney) tries to help the various down-on-their-luck patrons of his favorite waterfront dive. Uneasy mix of realism and whimsey, adapted from the prizewinning stage play by William Saroyan. C: James Cagney, William Bendix, Wayne Morris, Jeanne Cagney, Broderick Crawford. D: H. C. Potter. DRA 109m. V

Time Out for Love 1961 French ★★★½ Sensitive drama of American woman (Seberg), living in Paris, falling victim to smooth-talking Frenchman (Ronet). Captivating Seberg. C: Jean Seberg, Maurice Ronet, Micheline Presle. D: Jean Valere. DRA 91m. V

Time Out for Rhythm 1941 ★★★½ Ambitious singer (Lane) tries to get on a radio show. Forget about plot—catch this for vintage Three Stooges routines, Miller's tap specialty, and fine trouping all around. C: Rudy Vallee, Ann Miller, Rosemary Lane, The Three Stooges. D: Sidney Salkow. MUS 75m.

Time Runner 1992 Canadian ★★ A man from the future—when the Earth is battling aliens—falls through hole in space and arrives in 1990s America. Can he prevent the future war? Familiar plot not enhanced by wooden acting. C: Mark Hamill, Rae Dawn Chong. D: Michael Mazo. SFI [R] 90m. v

Time Slip 1981 Japanese ★★★½ Contemporary Japanese soldiers are transported back to samurai days. Effective battle scenes highlight strange mixture of action/adventure and science fiction, with an unusual ending. C: Sonny Chiba, Isao Natsuki, Miyuki Ono. D: Kosei Saito. SFI 139m.

Time, the Place and the Girl, The 1946 ★★★½ Song-and-dance team tries to persuade an opera star to back a Broadway show. Good songs and game cast make for pleasant viewing. C: Dennis Morgan, Jack Carson, Janis Paige, S.Z. Sakall, Florence Bates. D: David Butler. MUS 105m.

Time to Die, A 1991 ★★★★½ Crime photographer Lords catches a cop committing murder and holds the only evidence. C: Robert Miano, Jesse Thomas, Nitchie Barrett, Traci Lords, Richard Roundtree, Jeff Conaway. D: Charles Kanganis. DRA [R] 90m. v

Time to Kill 1942 ★★★½ Hard-boiled detective Michael Shayne goes after rare-coin counterfeiters. Tough-guy Nolan is in fine form. C: Lloyd Nolan, Ralph Byrd, Heather Angel. D: Herbert Leeds. CRI 61m.

Time to Love and a Time to Die, A 1958 ★★★½ Depressing but well-told story of a dissolute playboy's final 24 hours as he searches for a reason not to commit suicide. Scripted by the director, adapted from the 1933 novel by Drien La Rochelle. (a.k.a. *Le Feu Follet, The Fire Within* and *Will O' the Wisp*) C: John Gavin, Lilo Pulver, Jock Mahoney, Don DeFore, Kennan Wynn. D: Douglas Sirk. DRA 133m. v

Time Travelers, The 1964 ★★★½ Imaginative science fiction yarn about time traveling scientists whose visit to the future can have profound affects on the past. Skillful, thought provoking. C: Preston Foster, Philip Carey, Merry Anders, John Hoyt. D: Ib Melchior. SFI 82m. v

Time Walker 1982 ★★ Archaeologist unwittingly releases an alien being that had been entombed with King Tut and extraterrestrial mummy mayhem ensues. Egyptians had the right idea: Bury it! C: Ben Murphy, Nina Axelrod, Kevin Brophy. D: Tom Kennedy. SFI [PG] 86m. v

Time Without Pity 1956 British ★★★★ Drunken father (Redgrave) has 24 hours to save his son from execution. Suspenseful drama that tries to build a case against capital punishment. C: Michael Redgrave, Alec McCowen, Ann Todd, Peter Cushing, Leo McKern, Joan Plowright. D: Joseph Losey. DRA 88m.

Timebomb 1991 ★★★ When an amnesiac (Biehn) realizes he's the target of assassins, he kidnaps psychologist (Kensit) to help him restore his memory. Offbeat melding of sci-fi and spy genres; but Kensit and Biehn are a good pairing. C: Michael Biehn, Patsy Kensit, Tracy Scoggins, Robert Culp. D: Avi Nesher. ACT 96m. v

Timecop 1994 ★★★ Van Damme is sent back through time to catch a corrupt cop (a histrionic Silver) who is trying to change the future by manipulating the past. Expect the usual van Dammage. C: Jean-Claude Van Damme, Ron Silver, Mia Sara, Gloria Reuben, Bruce McGill, Jason Schombing. D: Peter Hyams. ACT

Timerider 1983 ★★ A motorcycle racer (Ward) and his 1980s-era bike are transported back to the Wild West where he has to fight for survival. Interesting premise falls flat. C: Fred Ward, Belinda Bauer, Peter Coyote. D: William Dear. SFI [PG] 94m. v

Times Square 1980 ★★ Teenage runaways (Alvarado, Johnson) try to crack into the music business while hanging out on 42nd Street. Title area looks about as unrealistic as when Ruby Keeler tried the same thing! Most interesting for its introduction of the talented Alvarado, and the energetic "new wave" soundtrack. C: Trini Alvarado, Robin Johnson, Tim Curry, Peter Coffield, Herbert Berghof. D: Alan Moyle. MUS [R] 111m. v

Timetable 1956 ★★★½ Modest suspense tale of insurance investigator (Stevens) assigned to look into robbery which he himself committed. Effective moments. C: Mark Stevens, King Calder, Felicia Farr. D: Mark Stevens. DRA 79m.

Tin Drum, The 1979 German ★★★★★ In '20s Germany a little boy stops growing to protest the rise of Nazism. A truly extraordinary film with powerful, utterly unique imagery. The cast is excellent, especially young Bennent; Charles Aznavour's cameo is quite moving as well. Winner of the Oscar for Best Foreign Film. C: David Bennent, Mario Adorf, Angela Winkler. D: Volker Schlondorff. DRA [R] 141m. v

Tin Men 1987 ★★★½ After their Cadillacs collide, two unscrupulous aluminum-siding salesmen (Dreyfuss, DeVito) seek revenge and battle for customers in 1963 Baltimore. Levinson raises movie above simple vendetta by keeping the characters sympathetic. C: Richard Dreyfuss, Danny Devito, Barbara Hershey. D: Barry Levinson. COM [R] 112m. v

Tin Pan Alley 1940 ★★★★ Immensely enjoyable songfest for Grable and Faye, cast as two chorus girls in love with the same composer (Payne). Oakie steals the show as Payne's partner. Remade as *I'll Get By*. C:

Alice Faye, Betty Grable, John Payne, Jack Oakie, The Nicholas Brothers. D: Walter Lang. MUS 94m. V

Tin Star, The 1957 ★★★★½ Rookie sheriff (Perkins) enlists aid of grizzled bounty hunter (Fonda) to clean up frontier town. Exciting Western with solid script and superb performance from Fonda. C: Henry Fonda, Anthony Perkins, Betsy Palmer, Neville Brand. D: Anthony Mann. WST 93m. V

Tingler, The 1959 ★★★½ Weird, often funny horror film with Price as scientist discovering strange growth on patients' spines that's caused by fear and can only be cured by screaming. Film was famous for theater gimmick of seats wired with buzzers to simulate "electric shocks." C: Vincent Price, Judith Evelyn, Darryl Hickman. D: William Castle. HOR 82m.

Tintorera 1978 British ★ Fishermen troll for sharks and women in this soft-core *Jaws* ripoff. An exercise in gore and nudity. C: Susan George, Hugo Stiglitz. D: Rene Cardona, Jr. ACT [R] 91m. V

Tip on a Dead Jockey 1957 ★★★ Ex-pilot (Taylor) becomes smuggler, and also falls in love. Good crimer. C: Dorothy Malone, Robert Taylor, Gia Scala. D: Richard Thorpe. CRI 99m.

Tipp-Off Girls 1938 ★★★½ Fast-paced B-movie gangster picture with G-man (Nolan) trying to bust truck hijackers. C: Lloyd Nolan, Mary Carlisle, J. Carroll Naish, Harvey Stephens, Roscoe Karns. D: Louis King. CRI 64m.

TISH 1942 ★★½ Busybody spinster (Main) tries to run her relatives' lives for them. Comic misfire. C: Marjorie Main, ZaSu Pitts, Aline MacMahon. D: S. Sylvan Simon. COM 84m.

Titanic 1953 ★★★★ Passengers on the ill-fated oceanliner deal with personal problems till the ship hits an iceberg. Shipshape soap opera with good cast and gripping climax. Ritter as bridge-playing widow is a standout. C: Clifton Webb, Barbara Stanwyck, Robert Wagner, Richard Basehart, Thelma Ritter, Brian Aherne. D: Jean Negulesco. DRA 98m.

Titfield Thunderbolt, The 1953 British ★★★★½ Prime farce as villagers hijack their beloved rural rail line before the powers that be can close it. Charming cast, pretty color photography. C: Stanley Holloway, George Relph, Naunton Wayne, John Gregson, Edie Martin, Hugh Griffith. D: Charles Crichton. COM 84m.

T.N.T. Jackson 1974 ★★★ When her brother is declared missing in Hong Kong, a martial arts expert goes looking for him. Some good action. C: Jeanne Bell, Stan Shaw, Pat Anderson. D: Cirio Santiago. ACT [R] 73m. V

To All My Friends On Shore 1971 ★★★½ Father must deal with news of son's incurable illness. Above average with solid acting by Cosby. C: Bill Cosby, Gloria Foster. D: Gilbert Cates. DRA 75m. TVM V

To Be a Crook 1967 French ★★★½ Four French toughs attempt to kidnap a movie star, but abduct her stand-in instead. Amusing caper comedy has two endings: the original French version is tragic, while the American version is happy. (a.k.a. *Une Fille et Des Fusils*) C: Jean-Pierre Kalfon, Amidou Ben Messoud, Pierre Barouth. D: Claude Lelouch. CRI 93m.

To Be or Not to Be 1942 ★★★★½ Wonderful WWII comedy with Benny and Lombard as stars of Polish theater company using their acting skills to confound the Nazis. Manages to find humor in desperate situations with intelligence and uncanny style. Benny's takeoff on Hamlet is a classic. Remade in 1983. C: Jack Benny, Carole Lombard, Robert Stack, Lionel Atwill, Felix Bressart, Sig Ruman. D: Ernst Lubitsch. COM 102m. V

To Be or Not to Be 1983 ★★★★ Brooks and Bancroft play husband and wife stars of Polish theater troupe during Nazi occupation, trying to act their way out of the country. Brooks' take on classic Lubitsch film is well-crafted comedy with many warm moments. Zany highlight: opening duet of "Sweet Georgia Brown," in Polish! C: Mel Brooks, Anne Bancroft, Charles Durning, Tim Matheson, Jose Ferrer, James Haake, Christopher Lloyd. D: Alan Johnson. COM [PG] 107m. V

To Catch a Killer 1992 ★★★★ Fact-based saga about police efforts to nail party clown/serial killer John Wayne Gacy. Dennehy's creepy and intimidating portrayal of evil incarnate is reason enough to watch this well done procedural. Significantly shortened for video. C: Brian Dennehy, Michael Riley, Margot Kidder, Meg Foster. CRI 186m. TVM V

To Catch a Thief 1955 ★★★★½ A debonair jewel thief (Grant) tries to reform, but the rich American he's falling for (Kelly) suspects he may still be in business. Thoroughly charming thriller with extravagant dollops of comedy, gorgeous French Riviera locations, and all the great Hitchcockian touches. Photography won an Oscar. C: Grace Kelly, Cary Grant, Jessie Royce Landis. D: Alfred Hitchcock. DRA 103m. V

To Dance with the White Dog 1993 ★★★★½ A lonely widower (Cronyn) is befriended by a stray canine who may be possessed by his dead wife's spirit. Loving, tender drama with beautiful work by Tandy and Cronyn, in their next-to-last film together. One of the few films to handle bereavement in an intelligent, honest manner. C: Hume Cronyn, Jessica Tandy, Christine Baranski, Esther Rolle. D: Glenn Jordan. DRA 100m. TVM V

To Die For 1989 ★ Once again, ancient vampires are on the loose in modern-day Los Angeles. This time Dracula, calling himself Vlad Tepish, pursues an attractive realtor. Lackluster attempts at intrigue and terror fall flat. C: Brendan Hughes, Sydney Walsh, Amanda Wyss. D: Deran Sarafian. HOR [R] 94m. V

To Die For 2—Son of Darkness 1991 ★★ An improvement on the original that nonetheless gets tangled up in too many extraneous characters and subplots for its own good. Main story is of a good vampire (Hughes) who romances a woman and tangles with evil brother. Has its moments. C: Rosalind Allen, Steve Bond, Scott Jacoby. D: David F. Price. HOR [R] 95m. v

To Dorothy a Son 1956 *See* **Cash on Delivery**

To Each His Own 1946 ★★★★½ Unwed mother (de Havilland) loses son to another, then spends rest of life hovering around him. Classy, wonderfully acted soap opera won de Havilland her first Oscar. Final scene guaranteed to draw tears. C: Olivia de Havilland, John Lund, Mary Anderson, Roland Culver, Philip Terry. D: Mitchell Leisen. DRA 122m.

To Forget Venice 1979 ★★★★ Two gay couples (one male, one female) discover the meaning of life while caring for a dying opera singer. Somewhat talky, but this effective drama treats its characters as three-dimensional people, not stereotypes. C: Erland Josephson, Mariangela Melato, Elenora Giorgi, David Pontremoli. D: Franco Brusati. DRA 110m. v

To Have and Have Not 1945 ★★★½ During WWII, an American boat captain wages war against Nazi agents on Martinique. A moody, shadowy, sexy thriller with good performances by all. Notable as Bogie/Bacall duet debut. C: Humphrey Bogart, Lauren Bacall, Walter Brennan, Hoagy Carmichael. D: Howard Hawks. ACT 101m. v

To Hell and Back 1955 ★★½ The story of Audie Murphy, the most decorated American infantry soldier of WWII. High point is Murphy, who plays himself quite nicely. C: Audie Murphy, Marshall Thompson, Charles Drake. D: Jesse Hibbs. ACT 106m. v

To Kill a Clown 1972 ★★★ A disturbed Vietnam vet (Alda) terrorizes a married couple on a remote island. Interestingly odd mix of thrills and politics. C: Alan Alda, Blythe Danner, Heath Lamberts. D: George Bloomfield. DRA [R] 104m. v

To Kill a Mockingbird 1962 ★★★★★ In a small Southern town during the Depression, a soft-spoken lawyer (Peck) defends an innocent African-American man accused of rape while trying to protect his children (Badham and Alford) from the hatred and racism ignited by the trial. Outstanding family drama. Oscars for Best Actor, Screenplay, Art Direction and Sets; also nominated for Best Picture. Based on Harper Lee's novel. C: Gregory Peck, Mary Badham, Philip Alford, Brock Peters, Robert Duvall. D: Robert Mulligan. DRA 129m. v

To Kill a Priest 1988 U.S.-French ★★★½ A Polish policeman (Harris) plots to kill a politically active priest (Lambert). Earnest drama, inspired by the true story of Father Jerzy Popieluszko, asassinated in 1984. C: Christopher Lambert, Ed Harris, Joanne Whalley, David Suchet, Joss Ackland. D: Agnieska Holland. DRA [R] 117m. v

To Kill With Intrigue 1985 ★★★ Seeking revenge after his family is butchered, young kung fu master perfects totally new techniques. Chillingly violent. C: Jackie Chan. ACT 107m. v

To Live 1994 Chinese ★★★★½ Thirty years of Chinese history are recounted through the eyes of gambler and his stoic wife. Magnificent performances and an insightful script show the effect of politics on everyday lives. Another gem from director of *Raise the Red Lantern.* C: Gong Li, Ge You. D: Zhang Yimou. DRA 129m. v

To Live and Die in L.A. 1985 ★★★½ Treasury agents on the trail of a cold-blooded counterfeiter. Agents aren't particularly likable, and neither is film, though it has a great car chase sequence. C: William L. Petersen, Willem Dafoe, John Pankow, John Turturro. D: William Friedkin. CRI [R] 114m. v

To Love Again 1980 ★★★ On a college campus, a middle-aged professor finds herself falling in love with an affable campus handyman. Good work by Redgrave and a gentler Dennehy. C: Lynn Redgrave, Brian Dennehy, Conchata Ferrell. D: Joseph Hardy. DRA 96m. v

To Paris With Love 1955 British ★★★ British widower (Guinness) and son (Gray) play matchmaker for each other during vacation in the City of Light. Pleasant romantic diversion. C: Alec Guinness, Odile Versois, Vernon Gray. D: Robert Hamer. COM 78m. v

To Please a Lady 1950 ★★★½ Star-watchers will want to see rare pairing of Stanwyck as tough journalist with Gable as stock car racer. Routine action story, but there's nothing routine about these two. C: Clark Gable, Barbara Stanwyck, Adolphe Menjou. D: Clarence Brown. DRA 91m. v

To Protect and Serve 1992 ★★★ A big-city police department battles crime without and corruption within. Fairly typical; spiced with excitement. C: C. Thomas Howell, Richard Romanus, Joe Cortese. D: Eric Weston. DRA [R] 93m.

To Sir with Love 1967 British ★★★★ Poitier is inexperienced teacher of underprivileged teenagers in '60s London. Inspiring, somewhat predictable comedy/drama with Sidney likable in lead role. Contains hit title song, sung by Lulu. Based on E.R. Braithwaite's novel. C: Sidney Poitier, Judy Geeson, Christian Roberts, Suzy Kendall, Lulu. D: James Clavell. DRA 105m. v

To Sleep With a Vampire 1985 ★★½ A vampire and a stripper form an unusual relationship over the course of a night. Remake of *Dance of the Damned,* right down to the dialogue. Fairly well acted and directed, but the original's still better. C: Scott Valentine, Charlie Spradling, Ingrid Vold, Stephanie Hardy. D: Adam Friedman. HOR [R] 104m.

To Sleep With Anger 1990 ★★★★ Los Angeles couple's life starts to fall apart when an old friend comes to town and moves in. Menacingly subtle performance by Glover energizes story. C: Danny Glover, Paul Butler, Mary Alice, Carl Lumbly. D: Charles Burnett. DRA [PG] 102m. V

To the Devil A Daughter 1976 British ★★★½ Priest turned satanist (Lee), has plans for a young woman (Kinski) to bear the devil's child. Nicely handled, occasionally explicit Gothic chiller, with good performances by Lee and Widmark. (a.k.a. *Child of Satan*) C: Richard Widmark, Christopher Lee, Honor Blackman, Denholm Elliott, Nastassia Kinski. D: Peter Sykes. HOR [R] 93m. V

To the Ends of the Earth 1948 ★★★★½ Government agent (Powell) will stop at nothing to track down worldwide narcotics ring. Riveting, ruthlessly edited actioner with grand climax. C: Dick Powell, Signe Hasso, Ludwig Donath. D: Robert Stevenson. DRA 109m.

To the Lighthouse 1983 British ★★★ Virginia Woolf's story of a couple whose hidden marital desperation makes itself apparent on a vacation. Unfortunately, neither author's wit nor perception comes across in this stiff and lifeless version. C: Rosemary Harris, Michael Gough. D: Colin Gregg. DRA 115m. TVM V

To the Shores of Tripoli 1942 ★★½ Wealthy gent (Payne) makes transition to rugged Marine in standard service drama that never really heats up. C: John Payne, Maureen O'Hara, Randolph Scott, Nancy Kelly, Iris Adrian. D: H. Bruce Humberstone. ACT 86m. V

To the Victor 1948 ★★½ Potentially gripping drama of French Nazi collaborators standing trial for war crimes gets little help from the cast. C: Dennis Morgan, Viveca Lindfors, Victor Francen, Bruce Bennett, Dorothy Malone. D: Delmer Daves. DRA 100m.

Toast of New Orleans, The 1950 ★★★½ Fresh from the Bayou Lanza is groomed by urbane Niven for an operatic career and enjoys a storybook romance with soprano Grayson. Watch for Lanza/Grayson hit "Be My Love" sung refulgently. Slim plot filled in by musical score. C: Kathryn Grayson, Mario Lanza, David Niven. D: Norman Taurog. MUS 98m. V

Toast of New York, The 1937 ★★★★ Fictionalized biography of "Jubilee Jim" Fisk (Arnold) a post-Civil War Wall Street millionaire whose manipulation of the market leads to his assassination. Grant plays his best friend and Farmer shines in a small part. Good entertainment that's aged well. C: Edward Arnold, Cary Grant, Frances Farmer, Jack Oakie. D: Rowland Lee. DRA 109m. V

Tobacco Road 1941 ★★★½ Oddly lighthearted film version of Erskine Caldwell story about Southern poor folks and dislocated families. The book was toned down in Broadway adaptation, and even more for Hollywood, but picture has merit on its own terms nevertheless. C: Charley Grapewin, Marjorie Rambeau, Gene Tierney, William Tracy, Elizabeth Patterson, Dana Andrews. D: John Ford. DRA 84m.

Tobruk 1966 ★★★ A motley crew of British officers and Jewish refugees set out to destroy Nazi fuel supplies in North Africa. Typical WWII action film occasionally hits higher levels. C: Rock Hudson, George Peppard, Nigel Green, Guy Stockwell. D: Arthur Hiller. ACT 110m. V

Toby Tyler 1959 ★★★½ Corcoran (from television's *Mickey Mouse Club*) stars as fantasy-living kid who runs away from home to join the circus, where he befriends humans and animals. Amiable fluff showcases cute acts. C: Kevin Corcoran, Henry Calvin, Gene Sheldon. D: Charles Barton. FAM/DRA [G] 93m. V

Today We Live 1933 ★★★ The lives of a sophisticate (Crawford) and three soldiers become entangled during WWI. Fine stars and director do their best with stodgy script, co-written by William Faulkner (based on one of his short stories.) C: Joan Crawford, Gary Cooper, Robert Young, Franchot Tone. D: Howard Hawks. DRA 113m. V

Todd Killings, The 1971 ★★★½ Psychodrama follows hepcat (Lyons) down his path of drug use, rape, and murder. Lurid, chilling yarn supposedly based on actual events works best as a study of young and handsome evil. (a.k.a. *A Dangerous Friend*) C: Richard Thomas, Barbara Bel Geddes, Gloria Grahame, Edward Asner. D: Barry Shear. CRI [R] 91m. V

Together 1981 Italian ★★★½ Two London mutes find happiness together in a secret, silent world, but tragedy intervenes. Dark, experimental, but earnest attempt to tell a different kind of love story. C: Jacqueline Bisset, Maximilian Schell, Terence Stamp. D: Armenia Balducci. DRA [R] 91m. V

Together Again 1944 ★★★½ Widowed mayor's wife (Dunne) of New England town hires big-city sculptor (Boyer) to immortalize her deceased husband. Charming romantic comedy with wonderfully charismatic stars. C: Irene Dunne, Charles Boyer, Charles Coburn. D: Charles Vidor. COM 100m.

Together Brothers 1974 ★★★½ Violent, but well-written story of five black youths taking justice into their own hands when a friendly policeman is murdered. C: Anthony Wilson, Ahmad Nurradin, Glynn Turman. D: William Graham. ACT [PG] 94m.

Tokyo Joe 1949 ★★½ An American nightclub owner returns to Japan after WWII to find his ex-wife and child. Bogart as nightclub owner? Well, it doesn't work this time anyway. Not his best. C: Humphrey Bogart, Florence Marly, Sessue Hayakawa, Alexander Knox. D: Stuart Heisler. DRA 88m. V

Tokyo Olympiad 1966 Japanese ★★★★½

Stunningly photographed documentary about triumphs and defeats occurring during the 1964 Tokyo Olympics. Even non-sports fans will find this exhilirating. Make sure you see the restored 1984 version, and not the hacked-to-ribbons 93-minute cut. D: Kon Ichikawa. DOC 170m. v

Tokyo Pop 1988 ★★★★ Rock star wannabe (Hamiliton) moves to Japan and clashes with the culture. Funny, fizzy musical comedy, charmingly performed by Hamilton (daughter of Carol Burnett). C: Carrie Hamilton, Yutaka Tadokoro, Tajji Tonoyama. D: Fran Rubel Kazui. MUS [R] 99m. v

Tokyo Story 1953 Japanese ★★★★★ Classic drama from Japanese master Ozu explores old age and the indifference of youth as elderly parents (Ryu, Higashiyama) visit their children in Tokyo, only to be ignored. Wonderful performances, fine script. C: Chishu Ryu, Chieko Higashiyama, So Yamamura, Haruko Sugimura, Setsuko Hara. D: Yasujiro Ozu. DRA 139m. v

Tom and Jerry: The Movie 1993 ★★ Popular MGM cat and mouse from '40s receive voices and social cause in this musical cartoon film. Now homeless, former foes Tom and Jerry become friends while helping girl escape from unhappy life. Heavy-handed story, really awful songs, and average animation make this entirely forgettable. Voices of Dana Hill, Charlotte Rae, Henry Gibson, Rip Taylor. D: Phil Roman, Richard Kind. FAM/COM [G] 84m. v

Tom and Viv 1994 ★★★★ Disturbing, beautifully acted portrait of marriage between poet T.S. Eliot (Dafoe) and his emotionally disturbed wife (Richardson). From Michael Hastings' play. C: Willem Dafoe, Miranda Richardson, Tim Dutton, Rosemary Harris. D: Brian Gilbert. DRA [PG-13] 125m. v

Tom Brown's School Days 1940 ★★★★ Episodic, delightful story of a Victorian boys' prep school, from Thomas Hughes's novel. Bartholomew is quite affecting in the title role. Remade in 1951. C: Freddie Bartholomew, Cedric Hardwicke, Gale Storm, Jimmy Lydon. D: Robert Stevenson. FAM/DRA 86m. v

Tom Brown's Schooldays 1951 British ★★★★ Impeccably cast filming of Thomas Hughes's novel about a young lad causing trouble in a high-toned, Victorian all-boys school. As good as the 1940 version (and an interesting comparison piece). C: John Howard Davies, Robert Newton, Diana Wynyard, James Hayter. D: Gordon Parry. FAM/DRA 93m. v

Tom, Dick and Harry 1941 ★★★★½ Delightful romantic comedy with Rogers choosing among beaus. Which one should she marry? Sparkling dialogue and acting; Paul Jarrico received an Oscar nomination for his screenplay. Remade as *The Girl Most Likely*. C: Ginger Rogers, George Murphy, Alan Marshal, Burgess Meredith, Phil Silvers. D: Garson Kanin. COM 86m. v

Tom Horn 1980 ★★★ An ex-cavalry scout runs into serious trouble when he becomes a bounty hunter. An oddly fascinating misfire with McQueen in his next-to-last role. C: Steve McQueen, Linda Evans, Richard Farnsworth. D: William Wiard. WST [R] 90m. v

Tom Jones 1963 British ★★★★★ Rollicking, captivating adaptation of Henry Fielding novel set in 18th-century England. Finney is marvelous in title role of lusty black sheep with questionable past and uncertain future. Delightful performances from Griffith, Evans, and Redman, whose eating scene with Finney is bawdy highlight; nothing sedate or stodgy here. Winner of four Oscars: Best Picture, Director, Screenplay, and Score. C: Albert Finney, Susannah York, Hugh Griffith, Edith Evans, Joyce Redman, Diane Cilento, Joan Greenwood, David Warner. D: Tony Richardson. COM 127m. v

Tom Sawyer 1930 ★★★½ Enjoyable adaptation of Mark Twain classic about a 19th-century boyhood in rural Missouri. Deliberate retelling of Tom's adventures with Coogan and Green well-suited to their roles. C: Jackie Coogan, Mitzi Green, Junior Durkin, Jackie Searle, Clara Blandick. D: John Cromwell. FAM/DRA 86m. v

Tom Sawyer 1973 ★★½ Whitaker is Mark Twain's mischievous antihero causing trouble for Aunt Polly (Holm) and ultimately running into trouble with evil Injun Joe (Oates). Simplistic, musical retelling of children's classic benefits from location shooting but suffers from sanitized story and annoying songs. C: Johnnie Whitaker, Celeste Holm, Warren Oates, Jodie Foster. D: Don Taylor. FAM/DRA [G] 99m. TVM v

Tom Thumb 1958 ★★★★ Five-inch-tall tp, (Tamblyn) is kidnapped by goofy crooks (Terry-Thomas and Sellers) for their own ill use. Tamblyn turns tables on the pair, which leads to their capture. Oscar-winning special effects from Puppetoon creator George Pal enliven this charming family musical. C: Russ Tamblyn, June Thorburn, Peter Sellers, Terry-Thomas, Jessie Matthews. D: George Pal. FAM/DRA [G] 92m. v

Tomb of Ligeia 1965 ★★★★½ Spine-chilling horror, from the Edgar Allan Poe story, casts Price as a nobleman obsessed with his dead wife. Last and one of the best of Corman/Price's series of Poe movies. Proof that a horror movie can be restrained, tasteful, and STILL scare you to death! C: Vincent Price, Elizabeth Shepherd, Richard Johnson. D: Roger Corman. HOR 81m. v

Tomb of the Living Dead 1969 *See* **Mad Doctor of Blood Island**

Tombstone 1993 ★★★ The shootout at the O.K. Corral remade as the Bloods vs. the Crips. Wyatt Earp (Russell), Doc Holliday (Kilmer), and company take on the West's first crime syndicate, headed by Boothe and Biehn, in this wildly overblown Western. Entertaining, though there's more hot air than hot lead. C: Kurt Russell, Val Kilmer, Michael Biehn, Powerss Boothe, Robert Burke, Dana Delany, Sam Elliott, Stephen Lang, Terry O'Quinn. D: George Pan Cosmatos. WST [R] 127m. V

Tombstone Canyon 1935 ★★½ Routine Western with hero and his horse, Tarzan, on trail of a murderer. C: Ken Maynard, Sheldon Lewis. WST 60m. V

Tommy 1975 British ★★★★ Flamboyant exhibition of The Who's rock opera about a boy (Daltrey)—deaf, dumb, and blind after witnessing his father's murder—who becomes a pinball virtuoso. Lots of cameos and great music. C: Roger Daltrey, Ann-Margret, Oliver Reed, Elton John, Eric Clapton, Keith Moon, Tina Turner, Jack Nicholson. D: Ken Russell. MUS [PG] 111m. V

Tommyknockers, The 1993 ★★★★ Aliens take over a small New England town in powerful movie based on Stephen King's popular book. C: Jimmy Smits, Marg Helgenberger, Traci Lords, Joanna Cassidy. D: John Power. SFI [R] 120m. TVM V

Tomorrow 1971 ★★★★ Lonely laborer cares for and eventually falls in love with pregnant woman whose husband has left her. Beautiful; low-key drama features one of Duvall's most touching performances. C: Robert Duvall, Olga Bellin, Sudie Bond, Richard McConnell. D: Joseph Anthony. DRA [PG] 102m. V

Tomorrow and Tomorrow 1932 ★★★½ Chatterton gives strong performance as housewife who can't resist her attraction to suave scientist (Lukas). Very good in its day. C: Ruth Chatterton, Robert Ames, Paul Lukas, Harold Minjir. D: Richard Wallace. DRA 80m.

Tomorrow at Ten 1964 British ★★★½ Kidnapped boy is trapped in unknown location with bomb set to go off. When the kidnapper is killed, a massive search starts. Effective thriller, builds to suspenseful climax. C: John Gregson, Robert Shaw, Alec Clunes. D: Lance Comfort. DRA 80m.

Tomorrow Is Forever 1946 ★★★ Wife (Colbert) suspects that the Austrian scientist (Welles) her second husband (Brent) hired is really her first husband supposedly killed 20 years earlier during WWI. Melodramatic tearjerker based on Gwen Bristow's novel, carried along by steady performances. C: Claudette Colbert, Orson Welles, George Brent, Lucile Watson, Natalie Wood. D: Irving Pichel. DRA 105m. V

Tomorrow the World 1944 ★★★★ WWII tale of teacher (March) adopting German nephew, then discovering the young boy is a vicious Nazi. Provocative drama, very timely adaptation of Broadway hit. C: Fredric March, Betty Field, Agnes Moorehead. D: Leslie Fenton. DRA 86m.

Tomorrow We Live 1936 British ★★★ Modest WWII patriotic drama of French townspeople aiding British spy caught in enemy territory. Sturdy enough. (a.k.a. *At Dawn We Die*) C: Godfrey Tearle, Haidee Wright, Renee Gadd, Sebastian Shaw. D: Manning H. Haynes. DRA 72m.

Toni 1935 French ★★★★½ Early example of neorealism tells gripping tale of violence surrounding Italian worker (Blavette) in love with girl who marries another. Filmed in town where the story it's based on actually happened, with many villagers playing themselves. Powerfully disturbing drama. C: Charles Blavette, Celia Montalvan, Jenny Helia, Max Dalban. D: Jean Renoir. DRA 90m. V

Tonight and Every Night 1945 ★★★½ Lively musical about London chorus girls enduring the blitz with a patriotic "show must go on" attitude. Gorgeous Rita and glorious Technicolor. C: Rita Hayworth, Janet Blair, Lee Bowman, Marc Platt. D: Victor Saville. MUS 92m. V

Tonight at 8:30 1952 British ★★★½ Classy compiliation of three Noel Coward one-act plays, each an entertaining example of his sophisticated comic style. (a.k.a. *Meet Me Tonight*) C: Valerie Hobson, Nigel Patrick, Jack Warner, Kay Walsh, Martita Hunt, Stanley Holloway. D: Anthony Pelissier. DRA 81m.

Tonight We Raid Calais 1943 ★★★½ Sturdy WWII tale of British soldier behind Nazi lines, trying to sabotage French munitions plant. Above-average flag waver. C: Annabella, John Sutton, Lee J. Cobb, Beulah Bondi, Blanche Yurka. D: John Brahm. ACT 70m.

Tonight We Sing 1953 ★★★★ Classical music fans will enjoy this film biography of impressario Sol Hurok. Musical performances include Peters in arias from *La Traviata* and *Madame Butterfly*, Pinza in an excerpt from *Faust*, Stern, Rubinstein, etc. And they sound just wonderful! C: David Wayne, Ezio Pinza, Roberta Peters, Anne Bancroft, Isaac Stern, Jan Peerce. D: Mitchell Leisen. MUS 109m.

Tonka 1958 *See* **Horse Named Comanche, A**

Tons of Trouble 1956 British ★★★½ Silly, offbeat English comedy somehow works, with Hearne as a building maintenance supervisor overly attached to apartment house boilers nick-named "Mavis" and "Ethel." C: Richard Hearne, William Hartnell, Austin Trevor, Joan Marion. D: Leslie Hiscott. COM 77m.

Tony Draws a Horse 1951 British ★★★ Parents split on what to do when their precocious eight-year-old boy draws an anatomically correct sketch of a horse. This often clever English comedy is right up Freud's alley. C: Cecil Parker, Anne Crawford, Derek Bond. D: John Carstairs. COM 90m. V

Tony Rome 1967 ★★★½ Sinatra plays seedy, tough private eye hired by wealthy man to guard his wayward daughter. Frank delivers the punch in okay detective yarn. C: Frank Sinatra, Jill St. John, Richard Conte,

Gena Rowlands. D: Gordon Douglas. DRA 110m. v

Too Beautiful for You 1991 French ★★★★ A man's comfortable life, including his marriage to a beautiful woman, starts to crumble when he falls head over heels for his plain-Jane secretary. Modest comedy with nice personal touches; Depardieu makes things interesting. C: Gerard Depardieu, Josiane Balasko, Carole Bouquet. D: Bertrand Blier. COM [R] 91m. v

Too Busy to Work 1939 ★★★½ A vagabond tries to locate his wife and reclaim former domestic life. Will Rogers gives good, moving performance in in this remake of his silent smash. C: Jed Prouty, Spring Byington, Ken Howell, George Ernest. D: Otto Brower. COM 65m.

Too Far to Go 1979 ★★★★ Literate, perceptive portrait of decaying marriage, from 17 John Updike short stories. Moriarty and Danner are brilliant, in a rare film that does full justice to their talents. Close's debut. C: Blythe Danner, Michael Moriarty, Kathryn Walker, Ken Kercheval, Glenn Close. D: Fiedler Cook. DRA 100m. TVM

Too Hot to Handle 1938 ★★★★ Screwball comedy gem with savvy Gable and buddy Pigeon as gung-ho newsreel photographers who both become smitten by tough-edged flyer, Loy. Frantic pace and snappy dialogue make this a laugh-filled treat. C: Clark Gable, Myrna Loy, Walter Pidgeon. D: Jack Conway. COM 108m. v

Too Hot to Handle 1976 ★★½ A young woman (who just happens to be a ruthless contract killer) gets involved in a war against the Mob. Violence and more violence. C: Cheri Caffaro, Sharon Ipale, Corinne Calvet. D: Don Schain. ACT [R] 86m. v

Too Late Blues 1962 ★★★½ A jazz musician/singer is exploited by agents, clubs, and his girlfriend. Uneven melodrama, worth seeing both for Darin and as an early, atypical Cassavetes film. C: Bobby Darin, Stella Stevens, John Cassavetes, Vince Edwards. D: John Cassavetes. MUS 100m.

Too Late for Tears 1943 ★★★½ Film noir about a husband and wife who reveal their true colors when they discover a bag of stolen loot. Black, moody crimer features characteristically crunchy Duryea. (a.k.a. *Killer Bait*) C: Lizabeth Scott, Don DeFore, Dan Duryea, Arthur Kennedy. D: Byron Haskin. CRI 98m. v

Too Late the Hero 1969 ★★ On a small Pacific island, British and American forces battle the Japanese. Solid cast lifts an otherwise undistinguished effort. C: Michael Caine, Cliff Robertson, Henry Fonda, Ian Bannen, Harry Andrews, Denholm Elliott. D: Robert Aldrich. ACT [PG] 133m. v

Too Many Crooks 1958 British ★★★ Average British farce about bumbling thieves attempting a kidnapping. Delightful Terry-Thomas keeps it moving. C: Terry-Thomas, George Cole, Brenda DeBanzie. D: Mario Zampi. COM 85m. v

Too Many Girls 1940 ★★★★ Sprightly college musical about four young men hired to keep an eye on heiress (Ball). Good Rodgers and Hart score from their Broadway show includes "I Didn't Know What Time It Was," and Miller does some terrific tapping. Lucy and Desi met while making this one. C: Lucille Ball, Richard Carlson, Eddie Bracken, Ann Miller, Desi Arnaz, Frances Langford. D: George Abbott. COM 85m. v

Too Many Husbands 1940 ★★★½ Oft-adapted W. Somerset Maugham play about a happily married woman (Arthur) discovering her first husband, thought dead, is alive. Lighthearted comedy casts terrific threesome who make the most of it. C: Jean Arthur, Fred MacMurray, Melvyn Douglas, Harry Davenport. D: Wesley Ruggles. COM 84m.

Too Many Parents 1936 ★★★½ Sincere, but slow-paced drama about boys in military school, one of whom is driven to despair by his father's indifference. C: Buster Phelps, George Ernest, Billy Lee, Howard C. Hickman, Frances Farmer. D: Robert F. McGowan. DRA 73m.

Too Much Harmony 1933 ★★★ Broadway star (Crosby) discovers talent and romance in a small town. Pleasant musical features the song "Thanks." C: Bing Crosby, Jack Oakie, Judith Allen, Ned Sparks. D: A. Edward Sutherland. MUS 76m.

Too Much, Too Soon 1958 ★★★½ Fascinating Hollywood bio of actress Diana Barrymore (Malone), whose career was cut short by her self-destructive behavior. Flynn is outstanding as her dissipated dad (and his real-life drinking buddy), John. C: Dorothy Malone, Errol Flynn, Efrem Zimbalist, Jr. D: Art Napoleon. DRA 121m.

Too Outrageous! 1987 ★★★ A female impersonator must decide between success and art; hackneyed sequel to the much fresher *Outrageous!*. Choice tidbits from Russell's act far outshine the plot line. C: Craig Russell, Hollis McLaren. D: Richard Benner. COM [R] 100m.

Tootsie 1982 ★★★★★ Unemployed actor (Hoffman) disguises himself as actress, and finds work and success. Delicious comedy has a lot to say about sexual identity. Hoffman's performance is one of his best, making alter ego Dorothy Michaels a credible character in her own right. Lange won Supporting Actress Oscar as Dustin's co-star/object of affections, while Garr and unbilled Bill Murray lend fine support as befuddled friends. C: Dustin Hoffman, Jessica Lange, Teri Garr, Dabney Coleman, Charles Durning, Bill Murray, Sydney Pollack. D: Sydney Pollack. COM [PG] 116m. v

Top Banana 1954 ★★★★ A burlesque star makes the move to television. Stage-bound transfer of Broadway hit survives now mostly as evidence of Silvers' talent and as a record of burlesque days. C: Phil Silvers, Rose Marie, Danny Scholl. D: Alfred Green. **COM** 100m.

Top Fights of Kung Fu ★★★ An assemblage of kung fu specialists fight it out for some kind of glory. Just what you'd expect. **ACT V**

Top Gun 1986 ★★★½ Romantic military fantasy centering around the blooming affair between cocky young fighter pilot (Cruise) and his sultry teacher (McGillis). Pounding soundtrack and frenetic editing make it resemble an extended music video; terrific dog-fight scenes make for effective Navy recruitment tool. Oscar for Best Song. C: Tom Cruise, Kelly McGillis, Val Kilmer, Anthony Edwards. D: Tony Scott. **ACT [PG]** 110m. **V**

Top Guns: The Real Story ★★★½ A look at the naval base called "Fightertown, USA," where jet pilots are trained. Quite interesting, especially the graduate "assignment," a flight over Libya. **DOC** 68m. **V**

Top Hat 1935 ★★★★★ Quintessential Fred and Ginger. Crackerjack Irving Berlin score; well-written mistaken-identity plot; sterling support from Broderick, Horton, and Rhodes; and sumptuous sets provide their best film with some of their finest dancing. Songs include "Cheek to Cheek," "Isn't It a Lovely Day," and "Top Hat, White Tie and Tails." C: Fred Astaire, Ginger Rogers, Edward Everett Horton, Helen Broderick, Eric Blore, Erik Rhodes. D: Mark Sandrich. **MUS** 99m. **V**

Top o' the Morning 1949 ★★★ Sentimental musical malarkey about a crooner (Crosby) searching for Ireland's Blarney Stone. Another pleasant shamrock via the *Going My Way* pairing of Crosby and Fitzgerald. C: Bing Crosby, Barry Fitzgerald, Ann Blyth, Hume Cronyn. D: David Miller. **MUS** 100m.

Top Secret 1953 *See* **Mr. Potts Goes to Moscow**

Top Secret 1984 ★★★½ The originators of *Airplane!* take on Elvis flicks and spy movies, as rock star (Kilmer), touring Europe, is pressed into service against Nazis. Spirited cast helps a film whose anything-for-a-gag approach has a satisfying success rate. C: Val Kilmer, Lucy Gutteridge, Omar Sharif, Peter Cushing. D: Jim Abrahams, David Zucker, Jerry Zucker. **COM [PG]** 90m. **V**

Top Secret Affair 1957 ★★★ A magazine publisher (Hayward) tries to discredit a political appointee (Douglas) but ends up falling in love instead. Diverting comedy is a change of pace for the two stars. Adapted from John P. Marquand's novel *Melville Goodwin, U.S.A.*. C: Susan Hayward, Kirk Douglas, Jim Backus, Paul Stewart. D: H.C. Potter. **COM** 100m.

Top Speed 1930 ★★★½ Musical comedy, with Brown as a downtrodden clerk pretending to be millionaire and entering in yacht race, using girlfriend's father's boat. Clever dialogue was considered quite daring at time of release. C: Joe E. Brown, Bernice Claire, Jack Whiting, Frank McHugh. D: Mervyn LeRoy. **MUS** 80m.

Topaz 1969 ★★★½ Mutual interest in Soviet spy activity in Cuba brings together American and French intelligence agents seeking information. Lesser Hitchcock is still intriguing and entertaining with its share of thrills. C: John Forsythe, Frederick Stafford, Dany Robin, Michel Piccoli, Philippe Noiret. D: Alfred Hitchcock. **DRA [PG]** 126m. **V**

Topaze 1933 ★★★★ Barrymore is brilliant as timid French schoolteacher duped by wealthy businessman into crooked scheme. Charming comedy/satire from Marcel Pagnol play. C: John Barrymore, Myrna Loy, Albert Conti. D: Harry D'Arrast. **DRA** 127m. **V**

Topeka 1953 ★★★½ Low-budget Western with superior script casts Elliott as renegade hired by town to get rid of bandits. On-target oater. C: Wild "Bill" Elliott, Phyllis Coates, Rick Vallin, John James. D: Thomas Carr. **WST** 69M.

Topkapi 1964 ★★★★★ Delicious caper film with appealing international cast as an oddball team of thieves who plot to rob an Istanbul museum. Witty and thrilling. Dassin lets his wife (Mercouri) rule the film, but you won't mind at all. Based on Eric Ambler's novel *The Light of Day*. C: Melina Mercouri, Peter Ustinov, Maximilian Schell, Robert Morley. D: Jules Dassin. **CRI** 122m. **V**

Topper 1937 ★★★★½ Classic screwball comedy casts Grant and Bennett as sophisticated, wealthy socialites who have only one problem—they're dead. Young is outstanding as the meek businessman they befriend as ghosts. Spawned two sequels, a TV series, and a TV movie remake. C: Constance Bennett, Cary Grant, Roland Young, Billie Burke. D: Norman McLeod. **COM** 97m. **V**

Topper Returns 1940 ★★★★ Inspired second sequel to *Topper* casts Blondell as ghostly murder victim who tries to solve her own death. Terrific supporting cast, witty script. C: Joan Blondell, Roland Young, Carole Landis, Billie Burke, Patsy Kelly, Eddie Anderson. D: Roy Del Ruth. **COM** 87m. **V**

Topper Takes a Trip 1940 ★★★½ Good first sequel to *Topper* brings ghostly Marian Kirby (Bennett) back again, sans hubby. She proceeds to addle Topper (Young) some more, this time the Riviera. C: Constance Bennett, Roland Young, Billie Burke, Franklin Pangborn. D: Norman McLeod. **COM** 80m. **V**

Tops Is The Limit 1936 *See* **Anything Goes**

Tor—Mighty Warrior 1964 ★★½ A medieval village besieged by a bunch of toughs is rescued by the even tougher Tor. Served up with violence aplenty. C: Joe Robinson, Bella Cortez, Harry Baird. D: Antonio Leonuiola. **ACT** 94m. **V**

Tora! Tora! Tora! 1970 U.S. ★★★½ The

historic attack on Pearl Harbor, offering viewpoints from the Americans and the Japanese. Includes events leading up to December 7, but memorable primarily for an outstanding re-creation of the strike itself. C: Toshiro Mifune, Martin Balsam, Jason Robards, Joseph Cotten, Tatsuya Mihashi, E. G. Marshall. D: Richard Fleischer. ACT 144m. V

Torch Song 1953 ★★★½ Tough Broadway musical star (Crawford) is softened by romance with blind pianist (Wilding). Ridiculous, over-the-top soap opera has much to offer camp afficionados, including Joan's big dance number—in blackface. C: Joan Crawford, Michael Wilding, Marjorie Rambeau, Gig Young. D: Charles Walters. DRA 90m. V

Torch Song Trilogy 1988 ★★★★ Fierstein's breakthrough Broadway play about gay life and love is enjoyable and funny. His first starring role as well. C: Harvey Fierstein, Anne Bancroft, Matthew Broderick, Brian Kerwin. D: Paul Bogart. DRA [R] 120m. V

Torchy Blane This series showcased Warner Brothers stalwarts Glenda Farrell and Barton MacLane in seven films about Blane, a wisecracking, crime-busting reporter and her nemesis, Lt. McBride. The films are engagingly snappy in the usual Warners' urban crime and comedy vein. The other two films in the series, with Lola Lane and Jane Wyman, respectively, were less successful.

Smart Blonde (1936)
Fly-Away Baby (1937)
Adventuress Blonde (1937)
Blondes at Work (1938)
Torchy Blane in Panama (1938)
Torchy Gets Her Man (1938)
Torchy Blane in Chinatown (1939)
Torchy Runs for Mayor (1939)
Torchy Plays With Dynamite (1939)

Torment 1944 Swedish ★★★★½ A young couple is harassed by a cruel Latin teacher. Dark, brooding, and evocative, with a superb script by a young Ingmar Bergman. (a.k.a. *Frenzy*) C: Mai Zetterling, Stig Jarrel, Alf Kjellin. D: Alf Sjoberg. DRA 90m. V

Torn Apart 1990 ★★★½ A Jewish man falls for an Arab woman he grew up with in Israel, despite cultural and political obstacles. Interesting romance, though the obviously American actors drain ethnicity from characters. Good use of Israeli locations. C: Adrian Pasdar, Cecilia Peck, Barry Primus. D: Barry Markowitz. DRA [R] 95m. V

Torn Between Two Lovers 1979 ★★★½ Wealthy Remick takes vacation and meets a divorced architect. Now she must reassess her own marriage as she is drawn to the newcomer. Remick floats it. C: Lee Remick, Joseph Bologna, George Peppard. D: Delbert Mann. DRA 100m. TVM V

Torn Curtain 1966 ★★★½ A famous American scientist shocks the free world when he "defects" to East Germany. Not top Hitchcock, but sparked by the screen chemistry between Newman and Andrews. C: Paul Newman, Julie Andrews, Lila Kedrova, Ludwig Donath. D: Alfred Hitchcock. DRA [PG] 125m. V

Torpedo Alley 1953 ★★★½ Fine submarine drama about ex-Navy flyboy (Stevens) on dangerous submarine mission. Solid action, good romantic subplot. C: Dorothy Malone, Mark Stevens, Charles Winninger. D: Lew Landers. ACT 84m. V

Torpedo Run 1958 ★★ Prowling Japanese waters, an American submarine sinks an enemy aircraft carrier. Plenty of action, but a waterlogged script. C: Glenn Ford, Ernest Borgnine, Diane Brewster. D: Joseph Pevney. ACT 96m. V

Torrent, The 1926 ★★★★ Garbo made her sizzling American debut in this silent melodrama, about a poor singer becoming a famous opera diva after being jilted by a wealthy man. C: Greta Garbo, Ricardo Cortez, Gertrude Olmstead. D: Monta Bell. DRA 68m.

Torrid Zone 1940 ★★★★½ Richly entertaining comic actioner about romantic entanglement of a feisty Central American plantation manager (Cagney). Splendid star power, punchy script. C: James Cagney, Ann Sheridan, Pat O'Brien, Andy Devine. D: William Keighley. DRA 88m.

Torso Murder Mystery, The 1940 British ★★★ Inaccurately titled spy melodrama about an evil double agent (Cabot) trying to peddle British submarine plans to the Germans. Improbable script kept going by the swift pace. (a.k.a. *Traitor Spy*) C: Bruce Cabot, Marta Labarr, Tamara Desni, Romilly Lunge. D: Walter Summers. DRA 70m.

Tortilla Flat 1942 ★★★★½ A tale of the intertwining lives of colorful characters in a poor little California fishing village. This absolute gem of a film, based on Steinbeck's novel, brings together superb direction and writing, and exquisite performances by an all-star cast. Morgan is downright captivating. C: Spencer Tracy, Hedy Lamarr, John Garfield, Frank Morgan. D: Victor Fleming. DRA 100m. V

Torture Garden 1968 British ★★★ Carnival psychic Dr. Diablo (Meredith) sees into the future via four horrifying tales. The best is last, about the spirit of Edgar Allan Poe. Solid shocker anthology, written by Robert (*Psycho*) Bloch. C: Jack Palance, Peter Cushing, Beverly Adams, Burgess Meredith. D: Freddie Francis. HOR 93m. V

Total Exposure 1991 ★★★½ When a photographer (Hubley) is set up for the murder of a model, she hires shamus (Nouri) to find the real killer. Entertaining, twisty thriller with enough freshness to cancel out its clichés and a game Nouri doing an admirable job with a tired character. C: Michael Nouri, Jeff

Conaway, Deborah Driggs. D: John Quinn. CRI [R] 96m. V

Total Recall 1990 ★★★★ In the 21st century, a man discovers his memories have been artificially implanted, and goes in search of his real identity. The Oscar-winning special effects are outstanding, and there's much gratuitous violence. High-tech chills and thrills. C: Arnold Schwarzenegger, Rachel Ticotin, Sharon Stone, Ronny Cox. D: Paul Verhoeven. SFI [R] 113m. V

Toto le Héros 1991 *See* **Toto the Hero**

Toto the Hero 1991 Belgian ★★★★ Segments from the life of a fellow named Thomas. As a boy he dreamed of greatness, but his adulthood has been one of absolute run-of-the-mill mediocrity. Fascinating, funny at times, and truly poignant. (a.k.a. *Toto le Héros*) C: Michel Bouquet, Mireille Perrier, Jo DeBacker, Peter Bohlke. D: Jaco Dormael. DRA [PG-13] 90m. V

Touch and Go 1986 ★★★ An egotistical Chicago hockey star (Keaton) gets romantically involved with single mom Alonzo after her son tries to mug him. Good performances, despite a violent conclusion. C: Michael Keaton, Maria Conchita Alonso, Ajay Naidu, Maria Tucci. D: Robert Mandel. COM [R] 101m. V

Touch of Class, A 1973 ★★★★ Stylish romantic comedy as London married man (Segal) tries to have a minor affair with Jackson but falls in love. Plot isn't much, but sparring scenes between two stars are terrific. Jackson won her second Best Actress Oscar. C: George Segal, Glenda Jackson, Paul Sorvino, Hildegard Neil. D: Melvin Frank. COM [PG] 103m. V

Touch of Evil 1958 ★★★★★ Mexican narcotics investigator (Heston) and his new American bride (Leigh) are caught up in a murder investigation headed by the unstable police chief (Welles) of a trashy border town. Welles uses high, impact musical score and baroque visual style to create a thrilling, outrageous mystery. Note famous long traveling shot that opens film. C: Charlton Heston, Orson Welles, Janet Leigh, Marlene Dietrich, Akim Tamiroff, Joseph Calleia. D: Orson Welles. CRI 108m. V

Touch of Hell, A 1962 *See* **Immoral Charge**

Touch of Larceny, A 1959 British ★★★★ Lighthearted British comedy of a naval officer (Mason) deliberately framing himself as traitor so he can sue for slander. Sounds improbable, but works, thanks to a masterful cast and expert script. C: James Mason, George Sanders, Vera Miles, Oliver Johnston. D: Guy Hamilton. COM 93m.

Touch, The 1971 ★★★★ Interesting study of human relations features Andersson falling for a Jewish-American archeologist (Gould), despite her marriage to a doctor (Von Sydow). Fine performances by leads, and knowing direction and dialogue by Ingmar Bergman give this love triangle a sophisticated edge. C: Elliott Gould, Bibi Andersson, Max von Sydow. D: Ingmar Bergman. DRA [R] 112m. V

Touchdown! 1931 ★★★½ Entertaining football story, with Arlen as a ruthless coach who will do anything to win, even jeopardize the lives of his players. (a.k.a. *Playing the Game*) C: Richard Arlen, Peggy Shannon, Jack Oakie, Regis Toomey. D: Norman McLeod. DRA 79m.

Touched by Love 1980 ★★★ Sentimental drama of cerebral palsy patient and her pen-pal relationship with Elvis Presley. Based on true story. Moving, well played. C: Deborah Raffin, Diane Lane, Michael Learned, Mary Wickes. D: Gus Trikonis. DRA [PG] 95m. V

Tough Guy 1936 ★★★½ Rich kid (Cooper) runs away from home because his father won't let him keep Rin-Tin-Tin, and winds up mixed up with gangsters. Fast-paced boy/dog adventure. C: Jackie Cooper, Joseph Calleia, Rin Tin Tin, Jr. D: Chester M. Franklin. DRA 76m.

Tough Guys 1986 ★★★½ Elderly ex-cons (Lancaster and Douglas) try to adjust to life outside and find limited opportunities in contemporary world. Funny setup consistently works, thanks to good-natured hamming and chemistry of stars. C: Burt Lancaster, Kirk Douglas, Charles Durning, Alexis Smith, Dana Carvey, Eli Wallach. D: Jeff Kanew. COM [PG] 103m. V

Tough Guys Don't Dance 1987 ★★★½ Norman Mailer's venture into James Cain territory features O'Neal as failed, alcoholic writer who can't remember the previous night and now has a fresh tattoo and a dead body on his hands. Weirdness swirls throughout this troubled mystery. Mailer's moody direction is not quite right, though good performances overcome his blunders. C: Ryan O'Neal, Isabella Rossellini, Wings Hauser. D: Norman Mailer. CRI [R] 110m. V

Tour of Duty 1987 ★★★ Our fighting forces in Vietnam. It's all here, from the initial "advisers" to the Tet offensive and more. A rouser well told. C: Terence Knox, Stephen Caffrey, Stan Foster, Joshua Maurer. D: Bill L. Norton. ACT 93m. V

Tour of Duty II—Bravo Company ★★ The further adventures of our fighting forces in Southeast Asia. More guts, more glory. Let's bring 'em home already! ACT TVM V

Tous Les Matins du Monde *See* All the Mornings of the World

Tout Va Bien 1973 French ★★★½ Fonda plays American reporter in France, covering riot and takeover by French factory workers who have imprisoned their bosses. Political tract benefits from Jane's expert performance. C: Jane Fonda, Yves Montand, Vittorio Caprioli. D: Jean-Luc Godard. DRA 95m.

Tovarich 1937 ★★★★ A Russian nobleman and his wife wind up in Paris as penniless servants. Dated, but charming comedy from Robert E. Sherwood play benefits immensely from Colbert/Boyer chemistry. C: Claudette Colbert, Charles Boyer, Basil Rathbone, Anita Louise. D: Anatole Litvak. COM 98m.

Toward the Unknown 1956 ★★★½ Muscular airforce drama with test pilot (Holden) trying to redeem himself after a costly blunder. Not bad. C: William Holden, Lloyd Nolan, Virginia Leith, James Garner. D: Mervyn LeRoy. ACT 115m.

Tower of Evil *See* **Horror on Snape Island**

Tower of London 1962 ★★★ Insane British monarch Richard III (Price) rules with a bloody hand. Medium remake of the 1939 horror classic (in which Price had a supporting role). Price essayed the role a third time in one segment of *Theatre of Blood.* C: Vincent Price, Michael Pate, Joan Freeman. D: Roger Corman. HOR 79m. v

Tower of London, The 1939 ★★★½ With help of faithful, demented executioner (Karloff), evil Richard III (Rathbone) tortures enemies to death as he struggles to maintain the throne of England. Lavish, although somewhat stodgy costume drama with unsettling scenes of torture and effectively hammy performances by principals. C: Basil Rathbone, Boris Karloff, Barbara O'Neil, Vincent Price, Leo G. Carroll. D: Rowland Lee. HOR 93m. v

Towering Inferno, The 1974 ★★★ The world's tallest skyscraper bursts into flames trapping swank party guests on the top floor. Terrific cast in memorable '70s outfits help to make this the Cadillac of disaster pictures. Never much of a nail-biter, but who cares with all those stars. Break out the marshmallows. C: Steve McQueen, Paul Newman, William Holden, Faye Dunaway, Fred Astaire, Richard Chamberlain, Jennifer Jones, Robert Wagner. D: John Guillermin, Irwin Allen. ACT [PG] 165m. v

Town Like Alice, A 1956 British ★★★★ British women suffer at the hands of Japanese in Malaysian prison camps during World War II. Tough and tense. Based on Nevil Shute's novel. Retitled: *Rape of Malaza.* C: Virginia McKenna, Peter Finch. D: Jack Lee. DRA 117m. v

Town on Trial 1956 British ★★★½ Police inspector (Mills) investigates a killing in London suburb loaded with suspects. Murder mystery distinguished by fine cast, interesting atmosphere. C: John Mills, Charles Coburn, Derek Farr, Alec McCowen. D: John Guillermin. DRA 96m.

Town That Dreaded Sundown, The 1976 ★★★ Fact-based horror film about the unsolved case of the "Phantom Killer," who preyed on the citizens of a small town in 1946. Decent cast plays second fiddle to the explicit, sometimes sadistic murder scenes. C: Ben Johnson, Andrew Prine, Dawn Wells. D: Charles Pierce. HOR [R] 90m. v

Town Without Pity 1961 ★★★★ When a young woman is raped in a postwar German village, three G.I.s are accused of the crime. Douglas shines in this armed services version of *Anatomy of a Murder.* Flawed, but engrossing. Title song was a pop hit. C: Kirk Douglas, E. G. Marshall, Robert Blake, Christine Kaufmann. D: Gottfried Reinhardt. DRA 105m.

Toxic Avenger, The 1985 ★★★ Anything goes, gross-out horror/comedy revels in bad taste and schlocky filmmaking, telling story of put-upon New Jersey nerd transformed by toxic waste into a monstrous hero. Full of exploitative elements, but still undeniably fun at times. C: Andree Maranda, Mitchell Cohen, Jennifer Baptist. D: Michael Herz, Samuel Weil. HOR [R] 83m. v

Toxic Avenger—Part II, The 1989 ★ Toxie travels to Japan to take on the evil corporation wreaking havoc in his peaceful hometown. Dreadful sequel with the same brand of cheesy humor as the original—only this time it's not funny. Authentic Japanese locations are an asset. C: Ron Fazio, John Altamura, Phoebe Legere, Rick Collins. D: Michael Herz, Lloyd Kaufman. HOR [R] 96m. v

Toxic Avenger—Part III, The: The Last Temptation of Toxie 1989 ★★½ The chairman of Apocalypse Inc. turns out to be the devil, leading the Avenger into temptation and another round of sophomoric humor. Lowbrow fun powered by cheerful irreverence and a constant series of gross-out special effects. C: Ron Fazio, Phoebe Legere, Rick Collins, Lisa Gaye. D: Michael Herz, Lloyd Kaufman. HOR [R] 102m. v

Toy Soldiers 1984 ★★ College student (Miller) joins mercenary Little in his effort to rescue children of a war-ravaged Latin American country. Dopey action film with a couple of nice sequences, but little else. C: Jason Miller, Cleavon Little, Rodolfo DeAnda, Terri Garber. D: David Fisher. ACT [R] 85m. v

Toy Soldiers 1991 ★★★ Prep schoolers show they're not pushovers when they are taken hostage by thugs who want their drug lord released from prison. Lame plot, but good handling and fine acting put it over. C: Sean Astin, Wil Wheaton, Keith Coogan, Andrew Divoff, Louis Gossett Jr., Denholm Elliott. D: Daniel Petrie. ACT [R] 104m. v

Toy, The 1982 ★★½ Broke writer (Pryor) hired by rich man (Gleason) as "toy" for pampered son. The son learns that friends can't be bought. Simplistic message no substitute for story development and ignorance of racial issues. C: Richard Pryor, Jackie Gleason, Scott Schwartz, Ned Beatty. D: Richard Donner. COM [PG] 107m. v

Toys 1992 ★★½ Daffy siblings (Williams and Cusack) try to keep their late father's toy factory from being taken over by militaristic Gambon. Overproduced, unwieldly comic fantasy has sumptuous visuals and some very funny moments, but suffers from an undisciplined script. C: Robin Williams, Michael

Gambon, Joan Cusack, Robin Wright, Donald O'Connor, Jack Warden. D: Barry Levinson. COM [PG-13] 121m. V

Toys in the Attic 1963 ★★★½ Bloodless version of Lillian Hellman play about a man and his new bride returning home to his manipulative spinster sisters. Hiller comes off best in uneven cast including scenery chomping Page. C: Dean Martin, Geraldine Page, Yvette Mimieux, Wendy Hiller, Gene Tierney. D: George Roy Hill. DRA 90m. V

Traces of Red 1992 ★★ Weak erotic thriller featuring Belushi and Goldwyn as Palm Beach cops on the trail of a serial killer. A failed modern film noir not bad if seen as a sort of film fashion show. C: James Belushi, Lorraine Bracco, Tony Goldwyn. D: Andy Wolk. CRI [R] 105m. V

Track of the Cat 1954 ★★½ Period drama of California backwoods family menaced by deadly cougar. Slow-moving, heavy with symbolism. C: Robert Mitchum, Teresa Wright, Tab Hunter, Diana Lynn, Beulah Bondi. D: William Wellman. DRA 102m.

Track 29 1988 British ★★½ Woman with unfulfilling marriage to toy-train nut disturbed by young man claiming to be her son. Confusing and ineffective. C: Theresa Russell, Gary Oldman, Christopher Lloyd, Colleen Camp, Sandra Bernhard. D: Nicolas Roeg. DRA [R] 90m. V

Trade Winds 1938 ★★★½ March, a classy detective who suspects Bennett of murder, chases her around the world. Charming and suspenseful. C: Fredric March, Joan Bennett, Ralph Bellamy, Ann Sothern, Thomas Mitchell. D: Tay Garnett. CRI 90m.

Trader Horn 1931 ★★★★ Dated but still-exciting tale of trader in jungle among hostile Africans. Early talkie actually shot in Africa. C: Harry Carey, Edwina Booth, Duncan Renaldo. D: W. S. Van Dyke II. ACT 120m. V

Trading Mom 1994 ★★ After magically dispensing with their mother, three children go to the "Mommy Market" to try out three wacky alternatives, all played by Spacek. Grotesque comic misfire. What can you say about a movie in which Andre the Giant gives the best performance, while Spacek gives the three worst of her career! C: Sissy Spacek, Anna Chlumsky, Maureen Stapleton, Andre the Giant. D: Tia Brelis. COM [PG] 82m. V

Trading Places 1983 ★★★★ Aykroyd and Murphy are at their comic peak as a snooty preppie and a street bum who have their lives switched—and turned upside down—by the former's scheming bosses (Bellamy and Ameche). Lots of laughs, and a memorable supporting cast. C: Dan Aykroyd, Eddie Murphy, Ralph Bellamy, Don Ameche, Denholm Elliott, Jamie Lee Curtis. D: John Landis. COM [R] 118m. V

Traffic 1972 French ★★★ M. Hulot tries to get a model car-trailer from France to the Netherlands; some funny stuff early on, but slows down later on. C: Jacques Tati, Maria Kimberly, Marcel Fraval. D: Jacques Tati. COM [PG] 89m.

Tragedy of a Ridiculous Man 1982 Italian ★★★ Bertolucci tries his hand at existential drama—about manufacturer whose son may be victim of political kidnapping—but winds up with disjointed, confusing tale. C: Ugo Tognazzi, Anouk Aimee, Laura Morante. D: Bernardo Bertolucci. DRA [PG] 117m. V

Tragedy of Flight 103, The: The Inside Story 1990 British ★★★★ Real-life story of plane that was downed over Lockerbie, Scotland by terrorist bomb. Told in chilling detail; provocative docudrama spares no one. C: Ned Beatty, Peter Boyle, Vincent Gardenia. D: Leslie Woodhead. DRA [PG] 89m. TVM V

Trail of Robin Hood 1950 ★★★½ Evil big company tries to drive a small Christmas tree seller out of business, so Rogers and friends save the day. Unusual Yule Western was Rogers' last in color; entertaining, with many in-jokes for genre fans. C: Roy Rogers, Penny Edwards, Gordon Jones, Jack Holt. D: William Witney. WST 67m. V

Trail of the Lonesome Pine 1936 ★★★½ Arrival of the railroad proves a catalyst for feud between two families. Dated but well acted and beautifully filmed. C: Sylvia Sidney, Henry Fonda, Fred MacMurray, Fred Stone, Beulah Bondi, Spanky McFarland, Nigel Bruce. D: Henry Hathaway. DRA 102m.

Trail of the Pink Panther 1982 ★★½ *Citizen Kane*-like *Pink Panther* film revolves around TV reporter investigating death of Inspector Clouseau. Made after death of series star Peter Sellers, this exploits unused footage from previous *Pink Panther* films as memory flashbacks. However, poor construction sabotages attempts at both tribute and entertainment. C: Peter Sellers, David Niven, Herbert Lom, Richard Mulligan, Robert Wagner, Capucine, Harvey Korman. D: Blake Edwards. COM [PG] 97m. V

Trail Riders 1942 ★★★ Part of Range Busters series, in which the heroic group tries to capture bank robbers who killed the local marshal. Average going. (a.k.a. *Overland Trail*) C: John King, David Sharpe, Max Terhune. D: Robert Tansey. WST 55m. V

Trail Street 1947 ★★★ Bat Masterson aids Kansas townfolk in struggle against crooked land barons in this average Western. C: Randolph Scott, Anne Jeffreys, Robert Ryan, George "Gabby" Hayes. D: Ray Enright. WST 84m. V

Train Goes East, The 1949 Russian ★★★★ In this Soviet comedy, two unmarried train passengers flirt, mistakenly believing each other to be wed. Their trip takes some wild turns, including a strange donkey ride. Inventive slapstick makes this a winner. C: Lydia Dranovskaya, Leonid Gallis, M. Yarotskaya. D: Yuri Raizman. COM 83m.

Train of Events 1952 British ★★★ British train crash is told and retold, from viewpoint of four different passengers. Uneven, episodic precursor of disaster films. C: Jack Warner, Gladys Henson, Joan Dowling, Peter Finch. D: Sidney Cole. ACT 88m. v

Train Robbers, The 1973 ★★★ A widow bargains with some shady gunfighters who assist her in a search for her dead husband's cache of stolen gold. Kennedy Western soft pedals most of the way. Few shoot-outs topped by twist at the climax. C: John Wayne, Ann-Margret, Rod Taylor, Ben Johnson, Ricardo Montalban. D: Burt Kennedy. WST [PG] 92m. v

Train, The 1965 ★★★★½ Thrilling WWII drama set in Paris during Nazi occupation. French resistance fighters, led by Lancaster, try to stop Germans from taking art treasures out of France. Unusual subject matter, taut script, superb cast. C: Burt Lancaster, Paul Scofield, Jeanne Moreau, Michel Simon. D: John Frankenheimer. ACT 133m. v

Traitor Spy 1940 *See* **Torso Murder Mystery, The**

Tramplers, The 1966 Italian ★★½ Son returns to the post-Civil War South and finds his domineering father is a vigilante preserving antebellum values. He and his younger brother join his father's pursuers. Meandering story that's filled with mindless violence. C: Joseph Cotten, Gordon Scott, Jim Mitchum, Franco Nero. D: Albert Band. WST 105m. v

Trancers 1985 ★★★★ L.A. cop Jack Deth (Thomerson) comes back from the future to capture a criminal who escaped from his time into ours. Well done, but heavy on the violence.(a.k.a. *Future Cop*) C: Tim Thomerson, Helen Hunt, Art LaFleur. D: Charles Band. SFI [PG-13] 76m. v

Trancers II—The Return of Jack Deth 1991 ★★ Thomerson reprises his role as an L.A. cop from future—this time fighting zombies. Tepid follow-up to *Trancers*. C: Tim Thomerson, Helen Hunt, Megan Ward. D: Charles Band. SFI [R] 85m. v

Trancers III—Deth Lives 1992 ★★★★ Deth (Thomerson) hunts down his toughest Trancers yet in this third action-packed installment. Thomerson has fun as the stoic L.A. cop from the future. C: Tim Thomerson, Melanie Smith, Andrew Robinson, Helen Hunt. D: C. Courtney Joyner. SFI [R] 83m. v

Transatlantic 1931 British ★★★ Mysteries on an oceanliner. Lightweight, but strong camera work. C: Pete Murray, June Thorburn, Malou Pantera. D: Ernest Morris. DRA 63m.

Transatlantic Merry-Go-Round 1934 ★★★ Benny leads radio troupe caught up in a murder case on an oceanliner. Awkward blend of comedy, mystery, and production numbers. C: Jack Benny, Nancy Carroll, Gene Raymond, Patsy Kelly, The Boswell Sisters. D: Benjamin Stoloff. COM 90m. v

Transatlantic Tunnel 1935 British ★★½ Futuristic sets only thing noteworthy in otherwise unmemorable tale about conflict during the building of a tunnel from England to America. C: Richard Dix, Leslie Banks, Madge Evans, George Arliss, Walter Huston. D: Maurice Elvey. SFI 70m. v

Transformers, The 1986 ★ Big names provide voices for this cheap cartoon, based on popular toy line. The Transformers defend universe against an evil planet (Orson Welles, in one of his last and most appalling credits). Extreme violence and some vulgarities make this a questionable choice for intended child audience. C: Orson Welles, Robert Stack, Leonard Nimoy, Eric Idle. D: Nelson Shin. FAM/SFI [PG] 86m. v

Transylvania 6-5000 1985 ★★ Tabloid reporters (Goldblum and Begley, Jr.) travel to the legendary land of monsters and tangle with a nutty scientist (Bologna). Weak attempt at spoofing horror movies offers a great cast, if not a great script. C: Jeff Goldblum, Joseph Bologna, Ed Begley Jr., Carol Kane, Jeffrey Jones, John Byner, Geena Davis. D: Rudy DeLuca. COM [PG] 93m. v

Trapeze 1956 ★★★½ Three-ring love triangle between crippled trapeze artist (Lancaster) and his star replacement (Curtis) who vie for Lollobrigida's attention. Aerial triple somersaults add punch to this circus drama. C: Burt Lancaster, Tony Curtis, Gina Lollobrigida, Katy Jurado. D: Carol Reed. DRA 105m. v

Trapped in a Submarine 1931 British ★★★½ Action-packed sea drama involves a British submarine patrolling Chinese coast, when it's accidentally hit by a cargo ship. Valiant turns are taken as crew tries to escape before sinking to ocean bottom. Some good suspense in this episodic thriller. C: John Batten, James Enstone, Edward Gee, John Hunt. D: Walter Summers. ACT 63m.

Trapped in Paradise 1994 ★★½ Two crooks on the lam find themselves in the wholesome village of Paradise, Pa., where they try to rob a bank with the help of their shy brother (Cage). Mediocre comedy, too jovial for its own good, wastes the talents of its three stars. C: Nicolas Cage, Dana Carvey, Jon Lovitz, Florence Stanley, Donald Moffat, Madchen Amick. D: George Gallo. COM [PG-13] 111m. v

Trapped in Silence 1986 ★★★★ Effective performances mark this psychological drama about a disturbed man (Sutherland) who refuses to speak and the psychiatrist (Mason) determined to help him. Skillful change of pace for Mason. C: Kiefer Sutherland, Marsha Mason, Ron Silver, John Mahoney. D: Michael Tuchner. DRA 100m. TVM v

Tras el Cristal 1985 *See* **In a Glass Cage**

Trauma 1993 ★★★★ Argento's first full American-made feature casts his daughter as a young woman who witnesses her parents' murder and teams with a recovering addict to find the killer. More restrained than the director's usual work, but inventive and scary nonetheless. C: Christopher Rydell, Asia Argento, Piper Laurie, Frederic Forrest, Laura Johnson. D: Dario Argento. HOR [R] 104m.

Traveling North 1988 Australian ★★★★ Manipulative but engaging story about curmudgeonly retiree who marries a divorcée and finds happiness, only to discover a bad heart will limit his time with her. C: Leo McKern, Julia Blake. D: Carl Schultz. DRA [PG-13] 97m. V

Traveling Saleslady 1935 ★★★½ Enjoyable piffle about rebellious daughter (Blondell) of toothpaste magnate who hawks liquor-flavored toothpaste of her own. Blondell carries the show. C: Joan Blondell, Glenda Farrell, William Gargan, Hugh Herbert. D: Ray Enright. COM 63m.

Travels With My Aunt 1972 ★★★★ Smith and McCowen make a delicious pair in story of stiff young man on a European trip with anarchic aunt. Excellent performances although story may be too slow for some. From Graham Greene book. Oscar for Best Costumes. C: Maggie Smith, Alec McCowen, Robert Stephens. D: George Cukor. DRA [PG] 109m. V

Treachery Rides the Range 1936 ★★★½ Foran overcomes evil buffalo hunters while helping Stone travel the road West. In the process he also makes peace with local Cheyenne tribe, whose chief is played by athletic great Jim Thorpe. Routine B-Western action with some good kicks. C: Dick Foran, Paula Stone, Craig Reynolds, Monte Blue. D: Frank McDonald. WST 56m.

Treasure at the Mill 1957 British ★★★½ Searching for treasure buried by ancestor, Palmer ventures to an old mill. Unfortunately nasty Ruddock is also after the loot, but mill owners help Palmer. Kid-sized action film with some entertaining moments for younger viewers. C: Richard Palmer, John Ruddock, Hilda Fenemore, Merrilyn Pettit. D: Max Anderson. FAM/ACT 60m.

Treasure Island 1934 ★★★★ Young lad (Cooper) finds adventure and danger on treasure hunt with Long John Silver (Beery). Sumptuous production values highlight spirited telling of Stevenson's classic. Beery is all scene-stealing swagger, leading cast of MGM's finest. C: Wallace Beery, Jackie Cooper, Lewis Stone, Lionel Barrymore, Nigel Bruce. D: Victor Fleming. FAM/DRA 105m. V

Treasure Island 1950 ★★★★ Young Jim Hawkins (Driscoll) contends with pirates as they search for buried gold in thoroughly satisfying Disney version of Stevenson classic (although it changes original ending). Newton's hammy performance as Long John Silver is a delight. Perfect for all ages. C: Bobby Driscoll, Robert Newton, Basil Sydney, Walter Fitzgerald. D: Byron Haskin. FAM/DRA [G] 96m. V

Treasure Island 1989 ★★★★★ Marvelous retelling of Stevenson's adventure tale involves boy whose treasure map leads to danger with pirate Long John Silver (Heston). Wonderful talents, Caribbean locations invigorate story. Heston's son Fraser was writer/producer/director. C: Charlton Heston, Christian Bale, Oliver Reed, Christopher Lee. D: Fraser Heston. FAM/DRA [PG] 132m. TVM V

Treasure of Lost Canyon, The 1952 ★★★ Kid finds treasure, causing problems for everyone involved. Powell is top-notch, but otherwise this one's humdrum. C: William Powell, Julia Adams, Rosemary DeCamp. D: Ted Tetzlaff. ACT 82m.

Treasure of Matecumbe 1976 ★★★ Two youngsters go off in search of secret treasure somewhere in the Florida Keys. Of course bad guys are on their heels, wanting the loot. Overlong children's adventure that runs out of steam. C: Robert Foxworth, Joan Hackett, Peter Ustinov. D: Vincent McEveety. FAM/ACT [G] 104m. V

Treasure of San Gennaro, The 1966 Italian ★★½ Guardino and Berger plot to steal treasure of Naples' patron saint. Dull and poorly dubbed. C: Nino Manfredi, Senta Berger, Harry Guardino. D: Dino Risi. CRI 102m.

Treasure of the Golden Condor 1953 ★★½ Wronged nobleman must live on the run while trying to reclaim his fortune. Run-of-the-mill period costume drama. Remake of *Son of Fury*. C: Cornel Wilde, Constance Smith, Fay Wray, Anne Bancroft, Leo G. Carroll. D: Delmer Daves. DRA 93m.

Treasure of the Sierra Madre, The 1948 ★★★★½ Three misfits join forces and prospect for gold in Mexico. Much heralded, adventure-packed tale of greed—and the glitter that blinds. Superb local flavor and outstanding performances, particularly by Oscar-winner Walter Huston. C: Humphrey Bogart, Walter Huston, Tim Holt, Bruce Bennett. D: John Huston. ACT 124m. V

Treasure of the Yankee Zephyr 1981 *See* **Race to the Yankee Zephyr**

Tree Grows in Brooklyn, A 1945 ★★★★½ Precocious girl in turn of the century Brooklyn tries to surmount her working-class upbringing in marvelous adaptation of Betty Smith's novel. Child actress Garner is heartbreaking (and won a special Oscar), while McGuire is memorable as downtrodden mother. Dunn won Supporting Oscar as alcoholic father. C: Dorothy McGuire, Joan Blondell, James Dunn, Peggy Ann Garner, Lloyd Nolan. D: Elia Kazan. FAM/DRA 128m. V

Tree of Hands, The 1990 *See* **Innocent Victim**

Tree of Wooden Clogs, The 1978 Italian ★★★★½ The story of peasant families who work on an estate in Italy around the turn of the century. Sedate in pace and exquisitely beautiful. C: Luigi Ornaghi, Francesca Moriggi, Omar Brignoli. D: Ermanno Olmi. DRA 185m. V

Tree We Were Hurting, The 1986 Greek ★★★★ While on holiday on the Island of Chilos, two Greek boys cut open a tree to remove the gum inside. Their actions lead to unhappy consequences in a sensitive and often funny coming-of-age film. Beautiful scenery enhances story. C: Yannis Avdeliodis, Nicos Mioteris, Marina Delivoria, Takis Agoris, Demos Avdeliodis. D: Demos Avdeliodis. DRA 76m.

Tremors 1989 ★★★★ The citizens of a small desert town come under siege by giant sandworms that suck victims into the ground. Terrific, old-fashioned creature feature mixes real scares with tongue-in-cheek humor; likable cast is supported by excellent monster effects. C: Kevin Bacon, Fred Ward, Michael Gross, Reba McEntire. D: Ron Underwood. HOR [PG-13] 96m. V

Trenchcoat 1983 ★★½ A mystery writer (Kidder) in Malta finds herself immersed in the real thing. Haphazard comedy/thriller; the star manages some engaging silliness. C: Margot Kidder, Robert Hays. D: Michael Tuchner. COM [PG] 91m. V

Trespass 1992 ★★★★ Two cops hear of a king's ransom waiting to be taken from an abandoned warehouse. They didn't hear about the nasty drug dealers who inhabit the place too. Solid, tense entertainment from action-crazed director Hill. C: Bill Paxton, Ice T, William Sadler, Ice Cube. D: Walter Hill. ACT [R] 101m. V

Trespasser, The 1929 ★★★½ Early Swanson talkie has her scorned by her rich fiancé after he gives in to parental disapproval. Bruised but not broken, Swanson goes to work for an attorney. Soapsudsy melodrama and good campy fun. C: Gloria Swanson, Robert Ames, Purnell Pratt, William Holden. D: Edmund Goulding. DRA 91m.

Trial 1955 ★★★½ Youngster is accused in murder, but turns out to be pawn in political plot involving Communist witchhunt. Thoughtful courtroom drama. From Don Mankiewicz's novel. C: Glenn Ford, Dorothy McGuire, John Hodiak, Arthur Kennedy, Katy Jurado. D: Mark Robson. CRI 105m.

Trial by Jury 1994 ★★★ Whalley-Kilmer is a juror on big case involving Mob chief; the bad guys want her dead. D.A. Byrne wants her alive. C: William Hurt, Joanne Whalley-Kilmer, Armand Assante, Gabriel Byrne. D: Heywood Gould. CRI

Trial of Joan of Arc 1965 French ★★★★ This account of the trial and burning at the stake of France's young saint concentrates on psychological aspects that weigh on Joan of Arc during her persecution. Taken from the actual trial record, this is a gripping realization of the legendary historical event. C: Florence Carrez, Jean-Claude Fourneau, Marc Jacquier, Roger Honorat. D: Robert Bresson. DRA 65m.

Trial of Lee Harvey Oswald, The 1977 ★★★★ Speculative courtroom drama posits what might have happened if the accused killer of JFK had reached trial. Unusual, well-researched drama, with a fine performance by Pleshette in the title role. C: John Pleshette, Ben Gazzara, Lorne Greene, Marisa Pavan. D: David Greene. DRA 192m. TVM V

Trial of Mary Dugan, The 1929 ★★★★ After her lover is killed, murder suspect (Shearer) is defended by attorney Stone. When he suddenly leaves the case, Shearer's brother Hackett takes over and uncovers the surprising truth. A tense and well-acted courtroom drama. Remade in 1941. C: Norma Shearer, Lewis Stone, H.B. Warner, Raymond Hackett. D: Bayard Veiller. DRA 113m.

Trial of the Catsonville Nine, The 1972 ★★★★ Historical moment—trial of anti-war activists who raided a draft office and burned files in 1968—reenacted in thoughtful if plodding fashion. From Daniel Berrigan's play. C: Gwen Arner, Ed Flanders, Barton Heyman. D: Gordon Davidson. DRA [PG] 85m. V

Trial of the Incredible Hulk, The 1989 ★★★ Regular cops try to take in the green one after an outburst. Does the Hulk need Perry Mason? Not with those muscles. In this one he teams up with another Marvel Comic character, Daredevil. Interesting variation for the green muscleman. *The Death of the Incredible Hulk* follows. C: Bill Bixby, Lou Ferrigno, Rex Smith. D: Bill Bixby. ACT 100m. TVM V

Trial, The 1963 French ★★★★ Moody, brooding, and artful version of Kafka tale of man on trial for unspecified crime. Performances and Welles' direction are excellent. C: Anthony Perkins, Jeanne Moreau, Romy Schneider, Elsa Martinelli, Orson Welles. D: Orson Welles. DRA 115m. V

Trials of Oscar Wilde, The 1960 *See* **Man with the Green Carnation, The**

Tribes 1970 ★★★★ Drill sergeant roughs up a long-haired draftee during Vietnam; energetic and entertaining tale of generational clash, with lessons learned on both sides. C: Darren McGavin, Jan-Michael Vincent, Earl Holliman. D: Joseph Sargent. DRA [G] 90m. TVM V

Tribute 1980 Canadian ★★★½ Lemmon was Oscar-nominated for this sentimental tale of an obnoxious ad exec who has cancer and tries to make peace with alienated son. C: Jack Lemmon, Robby Benson, Lee Remick, Colleen Dewhurst. D: Bob Clark. DRA [PG] 125m. V

Tribute to a Bad Man 1956 ★★★★ An unscrupulous land owner (Cagney) will do anything to keep his property. Trenchant western gives Jimmy one of his better, latter-day roles. C: James Cagney, Don Dubbins, Irene Papas, Vic Morrow. D: Robert Wise. WST 95m. V

Trick or Treat 1986 ★★★ A put-upon teen resurrects a dead rocker to exact revenge on bullies, but finds the rocker has bigger, frightening plans. There are fun touches throughout in this heavy metal/horor combo. Actor Smith's directorial debut. C: Marc Price, Tony Fields, Lisa Orgolini, Ozzy Osbourne, Gene Simmons. D: Charles Martin Smith. HOR [R] 97m. V

Trilogy of Terror 1975 ★★★★ Way-above-average horror film is an anthology casting Karen Black in three different stories, all well written and directed. She plays a seductress, a withdrawn schoolteacher, and in classic final segment, a woman terrorized by a vicious, living African doll. C: Karen Black, Gregory Harrison. D: Dan Curtis. HOR 78m. TVM V

Trio 1950 British ★★★★ Three Somerset Maugham short stories: "The Verger," "Mr. Knowall," and "Sanatorium." All are beautifully acted (note performances of James Hayter, Nigel Patrick, John Laurie, and Finlay Currie especially) and a treat to watch. C: Kathleen Harrison, Anne Crawford, Nigel Patrick, Jean Simmons, Michael Rennie. D: Ken Annakin, Harold French, James Hayter. DRA 88m. V

Trip, The 1967 ★★½ Late-'60s drug movie about a TV director who experiments with LSD. Psychedelic relic with good, campy humor. C: Peter Fonda, Susan Strasberg, Bruce Dern, Dennis Hopper. D: Roger Corman. DRA 85m. V

Trip to Bountiful, The 1985 ★★★★½ Elderly woman escapes constrictive home of son to visit long-lost town where she was a girl. Blithe and winning, with Oscar-winning performance by Page. C: Geraldine Page, John Heard, Rebecca De Morney. D: Peter Masterson. DRA [PG] 107m. V

Triple Cross 1967 French ★★ A British petty thief agrees to spy for the Germans—then becomes a double agent. Occasionally interesting, but altogether too long. C: Christopher Plummer, Yul Brynner, Romy Schneider, Trevor Howard. D: Terence Young. ACT 126m. V

Tripoli 1950 ★★½ Marines battle Barbary pirates in 1805. Stale costume action film. C: John Payne, Maureen O'Hara, Howard da Silva. D: Will Price. ACT 95m.

Tristan and Isolde 1979 *See* **Lovespell**

Tristana 1970 French-Spanish ★★★★★ Title character (Deneuve) must fend off the attentions of her lecherous guardian (Rey), while being romanced by Nero. Superb, thought-provoking drama from a brilliant director takes an old story, and makes it fresh through symbolism and a wry sense of humor. C: Catherine Deneuve, Fernando Rey, Franco Nero. D: Luis Bunuel. DRA 98m. V

Triumph of Hercules, The 1964 Italian ★★½ Bicep-bulging hero, evil rulers, and downtrodden slaves—all poorly dubbed. You get the idea. C: Dan Vadis, Moira Orfei, Pierre Cressoy. D: Alberto De Martino. ACT 90m.

Triumph of the Spirit 1989 ★★★½ A Jewish prize fighter (Dafoe) during WWII must use his fists to escape death in a German concentration camp. Gripping, but depressing drama from a true story was filmed on location in Auschwitz. C: Willem Dafoe, Edward James Olmos, Robert Loggia. D: Robert M. Young. DRA [R] 121m. V

Triumph of the Will 1935 German ★★★★★ The Nazi Nuremberg rallies of 1934. A darkly captivating testament to the insidious power of propaganda on film. Utterly enthralling, bizarre, and, in retrospect, terrifying. D: Leni Riefenstahl. DRA 110m. V

Triumphs of a Man Called Horse 1983 U.S. ★★★ Third film about Englishman (Harris) captured by Sioux who grew to become one of them. His half-Indian son (Beck) helps defend tribe from white settlers. Last and weakest of the series. C: Richard Harris, Michael Beck. D: John Hough. DRA [PG] 86m. V

Trog 1970 British ★★ An ancient creature goes on a rampage. No, we don't mean Miss Crawford, though her wooden acting gives the title monster a run for his money. Sadly, Joan's last film. C: Joan Crawford, Michael Gough, Kim Braden. D: Freddie Francis. HOR [PG] 91m. V

Troika 1969 ★★★½ Wildly offbeat look at the movie business features Hobbs (who also wrote and directed) discussing everything from concessions to box office to artistic ideals with a directing colleague. Surreal curio of '60s psychedelic era and quite funny at times. C: Fredric Hobbs, Richard Faun, Nate Thurmond. D: Frederic Hobbs, Gordon Mueller. DOC [R] 89m.

Trois Couleurs: Blanc 1994 French ★★★★½ Second film in Kieslowski's tricolor trilogy is a bittersweet rags-to-riches comedy/drama, with Zamachowski seeking revenge on ex-wife Delpy after she divorces him and takes everything he's got. Black comedy is stylish, witty, and ultimately moving. (a.k.a. *Three Colors: White, White.*) C: Zbigniew Zamachowski, Julie Delpy, Janusz Gajos, Jerzy Stuhr, Juliette Binoche, Florence Pernel. D: Krzysztof Kieslowski. DRA [R] 89m.

Trois Couleurs: Rouge 1994 French ★★★★★ Third installment brings Kieslowski's trilogy to a masterful conclusion, with characters from the previous two films making cameo appearances. Drama focuses on a model (Jacob) whose boyfriend is away and how she interacts with a judge who likes to eavesdrop on phone conversations. A stunning film about personal morality and how it is altered by circumstance. (a.k.a. *Red*) C: Irene Jacob, Jean-Louis Trintignant, Frederique Feder, Jean-Pierre Lorit, Juliette Binoche, Julie Delpy. D: Krzysztof Kieslowski. DRA 99m.

Trojan Horse, The 1962 Italian ★★★ Tedious retelling of Homer's epic. Only notable for costumes and sets. C: Steve Reeves, John Barrymore, Jr., Hedy Vessel. D: Giorgio Ferroni. DRA 105m.

Trojan Women, The 1971 Greek ★★★½ Star-studded version of Greek tragedy by Euripides puts female survivors of Trojan War on bloodied battleground, mourning their loss and bemoaning their future. Static, often hard to take, but Hepburn's Hecuba is riveting. C: Katharine Hepburn, Irene Papas, Genevieve Bujold, Vanessa Redgrave. D: Michael Cacoyannis. DRA [PG] 105m. v

Troll 1986 ★★★ Apartment dwellers are turned into mythic creatures by a little girl who's possessed by a troll. Intermittently entertaining fantasy/horror film. Trivia note; now-Senator Bono gets transformed into a plant. C: Michael Moriarty, Shelley Hack, Noah Hathaway, Jenny Beck, Sonny Bono. D: John Carl Buechler. SFI [PG-13] 83m.

Troll II 1992 ★ A vacationing family is terrorized by stunted monsters in the town of Nilbog (get it?), with dialogue and situations that are jaw-droppingly ludicrous. So bad it's good. C: Michael Stephenson, Connie McFarland. D: Drago Floyd. HOR [PG-13] 94m. v

Troll in Central Park, A 1994 ★★★★ Pleasant animated film has troll who's too nice being exiled from troll world to NYC, where he meets and befriends a lonely little girl. Good for the kids. C: Cloris Leachman. D: Don Bluth. FAM/DRA

Tron 1982 ★★★★ A brainy computer jock (Bridges) finds himself trapped inside a computer world, fighting for his life in a video game. Eye-popping effects, combining computer animation and live action. Enjoyable Sci-fi. C: Jeff Bridges, Bruce Boxleitner, David Warner. D: Steven Lisberger. SFI [PG] 95m. v

Troop Beverly Hills 1989 ★★½ Wealthy-but-bored Beverly Hills mom (Long) runs daughter's girl scout troop with Rodeo Drive style. Laughs take a hike in soft satire of consumerism. C: Shelley Long, Craig T. Nelson, Mary Gross, Stephanie Beacham. D: Jeff Kanew. COM [PG] 105m. v

Tropic of Desire 1983 ★★★ In Key West for a little "work," a gigolo gets involved in one affair after another. Best element in the film is the oddball cast. C: Matt Collins, Eartha Kitt, Pat Carroll. DRA 87m. v

Trottie True 1949 *See* **Gay Lady, The**

Trouble Along the Way 1953 ★★★ Sentimental tale of a rugged, unorthodox football coach at a rural parochial school trying to prove he's a worthy father. Some funny moments mixed with campus religion. C: John Wayne, Donna Reed, Charles Coburn, Marie Windsor. D: Michael Curtiz. DRA 110m. v

Trouble Bound 1992 ★★½ Ex-con (Madsen) and waitress (Arquette) take to the road after running afoul of mobsters. Doesn't quite work as either an offbeat thriller, or an off-the-wall comedy, but is saved by Arquette's fine performance. C: Michael Madsen, Patricia Arquette, Seymour Cassel. D: Jeffrey Reiner. CRI [R] 90m. v

Trouble Brewing 1939 British ★★★½ VAfter winning a bundle at the racetrack, Formby learns his payoff is counterfeited cash. Investigating the source leads him to a crooked group run by Formby's own employer. A clever little caper comedy. C: George Formby, Googie Withers, Gus McNaughton, Garry Marsh. D: Anthony Kimmins. COM 87m.

Trouble in Mind 1985 ★★★½ Fascinating, futuristic melodrama about an ex-cop's relationship with a gang of homeless kids. Sometimes infuriatingly vague, but full of atmospheric touches. C: Kris Kristofferson, Lori Singer, Keith Carradine, Genevieve Bujold, Joe Morton, Divine. D: Alan Rudolph. DRA [R] 111m. v

Trouble in Paradise 1932 ★★★★★ One of the all-time great comedies stars Hopkins and Marshall, as two competitive jewel thieves who fall in (and out) of love while trying to fleece wealthy Francis. Daring and risque for its time—a prime example of "the Lubitsch Touch." C: Herbert Marshall, Miriam Hopkins, Kay Francis, Edward Everett Horton. D: Ernst Lubitsch. COM 83m.

Trouble in Paradise 1988 ★★★½ Snooty woman (Welch) and earthy sailor bicker and bond when they are marooned on a tropical island. Welch is a good sport in this otherwise light-weight version of *Swept Away*. C: Raquel Welch, Jack Thompson. D: Di Drew. COM 92m. TVM v

Trouble in Store 1953 British ★★★ Adventures of mild-mannered department store clerk. Wan comedy. C: Norman Wisdom, Margaret Rutherford, Moira Lister. D: John Carstairs. COM 85m. v

Trouble in Sundown 1939 ★★★½ When outlaws muscle in on a bank owner and foreclose on innocent farmers, one uprighteous individual puts a stop to the dirty dealings and wins the banker's daughter in the process. Standard B-Western action with some good moments. C: George O'Brien, Rosalind Keith, Ray Whitley, Chill Wills. D: David Howard. WST 60m.

Trouble in Texas 1937 ★★★ Ritter to the rescue, singing and punching out bad buys in simple story built around a series of rodeo robberies. Average fare. C: Tex Ritter, Rita Hayworth, Yakima Canutt. D: Robert Bradbury. WST 60m. v

Trouble Makers 1948 ★★★ Average Bowery Boys caper in which the gang investigates a hotel murder by posing as employees. C: Leo Gorcey, Huntz Hall, Gabriel Dell, Billy Benedict. D: Reginald LeBorg. COM 69m.

Trouble Preferred 1949 ★★★½ Officers Knudsen and Roberts leave their desk jobs and prove themselves equal to male partners when they rescue a would-be suicide. Pre-feminist twist on the usual B-crime movie formula is a good police drama ahead of its time. C: Peggy Knudsen, Lynne Roberts, Charles Russell, Mary Bear. D: James Tinling. CRI 63m.

Trouble With Angels, The 1966 ★★★½ Two adolescent misfits (Mills, Harding) terrorize nuns at girls' academy, with Mother

Superior (Russell) glaring throughout. Episodic movie's attempts at comedy often misfire, but cumulative effect is surprisingly moving. Recommended for older children. Sequel: *Where Angels Go . . . Trouble Follows.* C: Rosalind Russell, Hayley Mills, June Harding, Marge Redmond, Mary Wickes. D: Ida Lupino. FAM/COM 112m. V

Trouble With Dick, The 1987 ★ A science fiction writer finds it hard keeping his writing separate from his real life. Boring. C: David Clennon, Susan Dey, Jack Carter. D: Gary Walkow. COM [R] 86m. V

Trouble With Girls, The 1969 ★★★½ Period musical casts Presley as the main attraction of a touring medicine show. Unusual Elvis vehicle flopped on first release, but is now a pleasant surprise. C: Elvis Presley, Marlyn Mason, Sheree North, Vincent Price. D: Peter Tewksbury. MUS [G] 104m. V

Trouble With Harry, The 1955 ★★★★ A little boy (Jerry Mathers, "the Beaver") finds a body in the woods, which rather rattles his little Vermont town. Another side of Hitchcock: whimsicality laced with delicious black humor. MacLaine's debut. C: Edmund Gwenn, John Forsythe, Shirley MacLaine, Mildred Natwick, Mildred Dunnock. D: Alfred Hitchcock. DRA [PG] 100m. V

Trout, The 1982 *See* **La Truite**

Truck Turner 1974 ★★★½ Tough-as-nails African-American bounty goes up against all kinds of evil. Hayes' score is tops. C: Isaac Hayes, Yaphet Kotto, Alan Weeks. D: Jonathan Kaplan. ACT [R] 91m. V

True Believer 1989 ★★★★½ Former '60s radical lawyer (Woods) has traded ideals for money-making cases, but wide-eyed clerk (Downey, Jr.) persuades him to take on the cause of a wrongly convicted Asian prisoner. Intriguing drama of personal rebirth, crossed with suspenseful courtroom sequences. Woods' performance is riveting. C: James Woods, Robert Downey Jr., Yuji Okumoto, Margaret Colin. D: Joseph Ruben. CRI [R] 103m. V

True Colors 1988 ★★★½ In early days of WWII, a French woman exhorts her community to battle against Hitler. Well-done and quite moving. C: Noni Hazelhurst, John Waters, Patrick Ryecart. D: Pina Amenta. DRA 160m. V

True Colors 1991 ★★★½ Two law school buddies go in different directions after college: one to the Justice Department, the other to elective office, via sleazy practices. Good acting, formulaic plot. C: John Cusack, James Spader, Imogen Stubbs, Mandy Patinkin, Richard Widmark. D: Herbert Ross. DRA [R] 111m. V

True Confession 1937 ★★★ Lombard is cockeyed rich girl who confesses to murder she didn't commit, setting plot in motion in this fast, lightweight comedy. C: Carole Lombard, Fred MacMurray, John Barrymore, Una Merkel, Edgar Kennedy. D: Wesley Ruggles. COM 85m.

True Confessions 1981 ★★★★ Police detective in '40s L.A. must solve a murder that takes him to the upper echelons of the Catholic Church—and to his brother, a powerful priest. Quiet but effective, though story is occasionally confusing. Based on the infamous "Black Dahlia" case. C: Robert DeNiro, Robert Duvall, Charles Durning, Ed Flanders, Burgess Meredith. D: Ulu Grosbard. CRI [R] 108m. V

True Game of Death 1973 ★★★½ An examination of the mystery behind the death of kung fu legend Bruce Lee. Quite an amazing story. C: Bruce Lee, Shou Lung. DOC 90m. V

True Grit 1969 ★★★★★ A one-eyed, drunken old federal marshal is hired by a plucky girl to track and capture her father's murderer while a Texas Ranger tags along to collect the reward. Wayne won Oscar for Best Actor for his extraordinary performance in this bittersweet, wonderful action-packed Western based on Charles Portis' novel where an odd threesome forms a reluctant bond. C: John Wayne, Glen Campbell, Kim Darby, Robert Duvall, Dennis Hopper. D: Henry Hathaway. WST [G] 128m. V

True-Heart Susie 1919 ★★★★ A small-town innocent (Gish) overcomes tragedy to win the heart of her beloved (Harron). Charmingly romantic silent comedy/drama from way back when; its unpretentious honesty will strike many as especially refreshing today. C: Lillian Gish, Bobby Harron, Wilbur Higby, Loyola O'Connor, George Fawcett. D: D.W. Griffith. DRA 75m.

True Identity 1991 ★★★ British comedian Henry does his best in typically lightweight Disney comedy, playing a black actor who hides out from a Mob boss by disguising himself as a white man. Predictable, but a good showcase for Henry. C: Lenny Henry, Frank Langella, Charles Lane, Andreas Katsulas. D: Charles Lane. COM [R] 93m. V

True Lies 1994 ★★★★ *Terminator* team of Schwarzenegger and Cameron reunite for this tale of an antiterrorist expert juggling his work with an equally arduous struggle to keep his marriage afloat. Well-done comedy thriller is a change of pace for both, but there's still plenty of action. C: Arnold Schwarzenegger, Jamie Lee Curtis, Tom Arnold, Bill Paxton, Eliza Dusku, Grant Heslov, Karina Lombard, Art Malik. D: James Cameron. ACT [R]

True Love 1989 ★★★★ Italian-American wedding in the Bronx, with both bride and groom having second thoughts. Fresh, funny take on familiar material. Final reception sequence is both hilarious and heartbreaking. C: Annabella Sciorra, Ron Eldard, Aida Turturro. D: Nancy Savoca. DRA [R] 104m. V

True Romance 1993 ★★½ Violent, slick film about a movie-obsessed loser (Slater) and his ex-callgirl wife (Arquette), who go on the lam with a suitcase full of cocaine. Many star cameos. Written by Quentin Tarantino. C: Christian Slater, Patricia Arquette, Dennis Hopper, Val Kilmer, Gary Oldman, Brad Pitt, Christopher Walken. D: Tony Scott. DRA [R] 119m. v

True Stories 1986 ★★★½ David Byrne leads stylized tour of mythical Texas town as quirky locals prepare for their annual "Day of Specialness." Deliberately offbeat and colorful, its alternately eccentric and condescending. Great soundtrack by Talking Heads. C: David Byrne, John Goodman, Swoosie Kurtz, Spalding Gray. D: David Byrne. COM [PG] 111m. v

True Story of Jesse James, The 1957 ★★★ Wagner makes a pale James, but film vitalized by offbeat style. C: Robert Wagner, Jeffrey Hunter, Hope Lange, Agnes Moorehead, John Carradine. D: Nicholas Ray. WST 92m.

True Story of Lynn Stuart, The 1958 ★★★ Undercover housewife poses as tough gangster moll to capture criminals. Not as exciting as it sounds. C: Betsy Palmer, Jack Lord, Barry Atwater. D: Lewis Seiler. CRI 78m.

True to Life 1943 ★★★½ Cute comedy about radio soap opera writer who moves in with "normal" family and borrows their chitchat for the dialogue in this show. C: Mary Martin, Franchot Tone, Dick Powell, Victor Moore, William Demarest. D: George Marshall. COM 94m.

Truly Madly Deeply 1991 British ★★★½ After her boyfriend dies, a young woman enters deep depression—until he returns as a ghost. Nice performances; genuinely romantic. C: Juliet Stevenson, Alan Rickman, Bill Paterson. D: Anthony Minghella. COM [PG] 107m. v

Truman Capote's Trilogy 1969 ★★★★½ Wonderfully acted omnibus film combines three Capote short stories and a terrific cast of performers. Capote narrates the third story himself. C: Mildred Natwick, Susan Dunfee, Maureen Stapleton, Geraldine Page, Truman Capote. D: Frank Perry. DRA [G] 100m.

Trunks of Mr. O.F., The 1932 German ★★★★½ When trunks labeled "O.F." arrive in a small German village, rumors fly as to their ownership. Inventive reporter Lorre creates fictional owner to satisfy residents' curiosity. Crisp satire with good comic turns by Lorre. Later retitled *Build and Marry* after severe cuts by Nazi censors. (a.k.a. *Build and Marry*) C: Alfred Abel, Peter Lorre, Harald Paulsen, Hedy Kiesler. D: Alexis Granowsky. COM 80m.

Trust 1991 ★★★★ An angry, abused young man and abandoned young woman meet and fall in love in this engaging off-kilter comedy. Better than average with ultradry humor, not for all tastes. C: Adrienne Shelly, Martin Donovan, Merritt Nelson. D: Hal Hartley. COM [R] 105m. v

Trust Me 1989 ★★★ A greedy gallery owner (Ant) plots the death of a talented artist (Packer) so his paintings will increase in value. Satire of the modern art world has some sharp and witty edges. C: Adam Ant, David Packer, Talia Balsom, Joyce Van Patten. D: Bobby Houston. COM [R] 104m. v

Truth About Spring, The 1965 British ★★★ Romantic story about teen's first crush. Slot but enjoyable; aimed at younger viewers. C: Hayley Mills, John Mills, James MacArthur, Lionel Jeffries. D: Richard Thorpe. DRA 102m.

Truth About Women, The 1958 British ★★★ A suave bounder (Harvey) uses women like Kleenex in this uneven, episodic comedy-drama. Catch it for Cilento's performance. C: Laurence Harvey, Julie Harris, Diane Cilento, Mai Zetterling, Eva Gabor. D: Muriel Box. COM 98m.

Truth About Youth, The 1930 ★★★★ Manners is spurned by chanteuse Loy, who prefers rich, older lovers. Things don't improve when Young also ignores Manners' amour for the more experienced Tearle. Interesting drama and risqué for its time. Previously filmed in 1915. C: Loretta Young, David Manners, Conway Tearle, J. Farrell Macdonald, Myrna Loy. D: William A. Seiter. DRA 62m.

Truth or Dare 1991 ★★★★ Compelling documentary of pop singer Madonna on tour, focusing on her backstage relationship with family and crew. Though commissioned by Madonna, the film captures many unflattering moments. Non-fans may still find it rough going. (a.k.a. *In Bed with Madonna* and *Madonna Truth or Dare*) C: Madonna. D: Alek Keshishian. DOC [R] 118m. v

Tsar's Bride, The 1966 USSR ★★★★ Stately Soviet drama, based on 1899 Rimsky-Korsakov opera and the 1849 play of the same name. A woman is selected to marry the fearsome Tsar, but one of his bodyguards loves her too; intrigue and tragedy follow. C: Raisa Nedashkovskaya, Natalya Rudnaya, Otar Koberidze. D: Vladimir Gorikker. MUS 95m. v

Tuck Everlasting 1980 ★★★★ Fantasy story of a family that suffers neither pain, aging, nor even death. Charmingly done, especially for children. C: Margaret Chamberlain, Paul Flessa, Fred Keller. D: Frederick Keller. FAM/DRA 100m. v

Tucker—The Man and His Dream 1988 ★★★★½ True story of automobile designer (Bridges) whose revolutionary ideas were suppressed by Detroit auto industry and D.C. politicians. Unappreciated during first release, this spiffy comedy/drama is as sleek and elegantly designed as Tucker's cars. Well acted, especially by Landau as Bridges' reluctant partner. C: Jeff Bridges, Joan Allen, Martin Landau, Frederic Forrest, Mako, Dean Stockwell, Lloyd Bridges. D: Francis Ford Coppola. DRA 111m. v

Tucson Raiders 1944 ★★★½ First *Red Ryder* film for Elliot has him stopping wanton Governor Wanton from overtaking the territory. Funny and exciting B-Western with good comic support from Hayes. Don't miss future *In Cold Blood* star Bobby (Robert) Blake as sidekick "Little Beaver." C: "Wild" Bill Elliott, Robby (Robert) Blake, George "Gabby" Hayes, Alice Fleming. D: Spencer G. Bennett. WST 55m.

Tuff Turf 1985 ★★★½ New kid in the valley becomes target of thuggish classmates at his new high school—and finds ways to fight back. Above-average action, but silly story. C: James Spader, Kim Richards, Paul Mones, Matt Clark. D: Fritz Kiersch. ACT [R] 113m. V

Tugboat Annie 1933 ★★★★ Dressler's and Beery's chemistry outshines material in aimless but enjoyable tale of tugboat operator and her heavy-drinking spouse. C: Marie Dressler, Wallace Beery, Robert Young, Maureen O'Sullivan. D: Mervyn LeRoy. DRA 87m.

Tulsa 1949 ★★★★ Hayward throws everyone else aside when she gets caught up in wildcat oil-drilling while trying to hang on to her land. Engaging action drama. C: Susan Hayward, Robert Preston, Pedro Armendariz, Chill Wills, Ed Begley. D: Stuart Heisler. DRA 90m. V

Tumbledown Ranch in Arizona 1941 ★★★ Part of the Range Busters series: A college student (King) hits his head during a rodeo and dreams about adventures in the Wild West. Solid series entry. WST 60m. V

Tumbleweeds 1925 ★★★★★ Classic silent western about a cowboy making his way west to win the woman of his dreams. Gorgeous outdoor photography, memorable action sequences. C: William S. Hart, Barbara Bedford. D: King Baggot. WST 81m. V

Tuna Clipper 1949 ★★½ To prove his manhood and help a friend, a young man (McDowall) becomes tuna fisherman. Lightweight story, competently executed. C: Roddy McDowall, Elena Verdugo, Ronald Winters, Dickie Moore. D: William Beaudine. DRA 79m.

Tune In Tomorrow 1990 ★★★★ Radio soap opera writer (Reeves) becomes attracted to sexy aunt Hershey while getting swept up in kooky adrenaline of boss/mentor Falk. Wildly energetic comedy set in '50s New Orleans; great cast and Wynton Marsalis score keep oddball plot moving forward. Based on a novel by Mario Vargas Llosa. C: Barbara Hershey, Keanu Reeves, Peter Falk. D: Jon Amiel. COM [PG-13] 90m. V

Tune, The 1992 ★★★★ Cartoon chronicles the ups and downs, dreams, and realities of a musician seeking success. Fascinating throughout, with wonderful songs. D: Bill Plympton. MUS 80m. V

Tunes of Glory 1960 British ★★★★½ Captivating comic drama that pits two soldiers with contrasting styles against each other as they climb through the ranks. Guinness is superb. From James Kennaway's novel. C: Alec Guinness, John Mills, Susannah York, Kay Walsh, Dennis Price. D: Ronald Neame. COM 106m. V

Tunnel of Love, The 1958 ★★★½ Happily married suburban couple Day and Kelly want to adopt a child but face miles of bureaucratic red tape. Nicely played by leads. C: Doris Day, Richard Widmark, Gig Young, Gia Scala. D: Gene Kelly. COM 98m. V

Tunnelvision 1976 ★★½ Crude sketch comedy compiliation speculates on what TV might be like in the 21st century. The appearances of Chase, Newman, et al. are disappointingly brief in this uneven comic stew. Film debut for many of the now familiar faces in the cast. C: Howard Hesseman, Phil Proctor, James Bacon, Betty Thomas, Chevy Chase, William Schallert, Laraine Newman, Ron Silver. D: Neal Israel, Brad Swirnoff. COM [R] 67m. V

Turk 182! 1985 ★★★ Unbelievable comedy about an injured fireman's younger brother (Hutton) who becomes famous spraying grafitti in "artistic protest." C: Timothy Hutton, Robert Urich, Kim Cattrall, Robert Culp. D: Bob Clark. COM [PG-13] 98m. V

Turkey Time 1933 British ★★★ Trouble brews on vacation when pals Walls and Lynn meet winsome Hyson. Walls nearly forgets about his fiancée, but all is saved when Lynn starts wooing Hyson. Cute in parts but humor is dated. C: Tom Walls, Ralph Lynn, Dorothy Hyson, Robertson Hare. D: Tom Walls. COM 73m.

Turkish Delights 1973 ★★★½ Love blooms between an offbeat sculptor and a young woman from a straitlaced family. They enjoy life until she's felled by a brain tumor. A peculiar tale, well told in its own way. C: Monique Van De Ven, Rutger Hauer. D: Paul Verhoeven. DRA [R] 100m. V

Turn Back the Clock 1989 ★★★★ Woman gets chance to start life afresh—with surprising results in this unheralded but vivacious and entertaining comedy. C: Connie Sellecca, Wendy Kilbourne. D: Larry Elikann. DRA 100m. TVM

Turn of the Screw, The 1989 ★★★ Competent adaptation of Henry James' classic novel (previously filmed as *The Innocents*) about children pursued by evil spirits in a British mansion, and a governess (Irving) trying to protect them. C: Amy Irving, David Hemmings, Balthazar Getty, Nicole Mercurio. D: Graeme Clifford. HOR 60m. TVM V

Turn of the Screw, The 1992 British ★★ A nanny (Kensit) presides over two young orphans and fends off ghosts. An updated setting (the '60s) and story retains its basic power, but there's little to justify another telling of this classic tale. C: Patsy Kensit, Stephane Audran, Julian Sands, Marianne Faithful. D: Rusty Lemorande. HOR 95m. V

Turnabout 1940 ★★½ Husband and wife switch personalities when they encounter a magic figurine. Rattle-brained comedy is funny in spots, even with the poor quality of the voice dubbing/switching. From Thorne Smith's (*Topper*) novel. C: Carole Landis, John Hubbard, Mary Astor, Adolphe Menjou. D: Hal Roach. COM 83m.

Turner & Hooch 1989 ★★½ Clean freak detective (Hanks), assigned murder case where only living witness is perennially drooling canine named Hooch. Unlikely duo solves crime, while stretching to breaking point already strained premise. C: Tom Hanks, Mare Winningham, Craig T. Nelson. D: Roger Spottiswoode. COM [PG] 99m. V

Turning Point, The 1952 ★★★½ Cop (O'Brien) and reporter (Holden) clash while investigating police and government corruption. Fast-paced, modest crime drama with good cast. C: William Holden, Edmond O'Brien, Alexis Smith, Ed Begley, Carolyn Jones. D: William Dieterle. CRI 85m.

Turning Point, The 1977 ★★★★ Exceptional soap opera as retired dancer (MacLaine) rekindles friendship—and rivalry—with prima ballerina (Bancroft) when former's daughter begins ballet career of her own. Intelligent Arthur Laurents script; dance sequences feature Baryshnikov, Browne, and many American Ballet Theatre stars. C: Anne Bancroft, Shirley MacLaine, Mikhail Baryshnikov, Leslie Browne, Tom Skerritt. D: Herbert Ross. DRA [PG] 119m. V

Turtle Diary 1986 British ★★★★ Jackson and Kingsley make an intriguing pair in this low-key but engaging film about two lost souls who discover each other while trying to free giant turtles from the London zoo. Scripted by Harold Pinter. C: Glenda Jackson, Ben Kingsley, Richard Johnson, Michael Gambon. D: John Irvin. DRA [PG] 96m. V

Tuttles of Tahiti, The 1942 ★★★★ Laughton is in rare form as the father of a family living in the South Seas and relishing the relaxed lifestyle. Leisurely, entertaining story. C: Charles Laughton, Jon Hall, Peggy Drake. D: Charles Vidor. DRA 91m. V

Twelfth Night 1956 USSR ★★★★ Russian version of Shakespeare's comedy about mistaken identity and young love is short, but well done and amusing. Good score, too. C: Katya Luchko, Anna Larionova, Vadim Medvediev, M. Yanshin. D: Y. Fried. COM 54m.

12 Angry Men 1957 ★★★★½ One man stands up to 11 other jurors; they just want to convict the teenager accused of murder and go home, but Fonda wants to think about it first. Enthralling ensemble acting, taut script, fine direction (Lumet's debut). Only flaw is a rather predictable structure, stemming from its roots as live TV drama. C: Henry Fonda, Lee J. Cobb, Ed Begley, E.G. Marshall, Joseph Sweeney, Jack Warden, Jack Klugman, Martin Balsam, Robert Webber, John Fiedler, George Voskovec. D: Sidney Lumet. DRA 95m. V

Twelve Chairs, The 1970 ★★★★ Stylish, frantic fable about a penniless Russian count (Moody) enlisting the aid of a thief (Langella) in search for scattered family chairs, one of which contains priceless jewels. Sometimes hilarious, sometimes overwrought, always amusing. C: Ron Moody, Frank Langella, Dom DeLuise, Mel Brooks. D: Mel Brooks. COM [G] 94m. V

Twelve-Handed Men of Mars, The 1964 Italian ★★★★ Instead of conqueriing Earth, a quartet of Martians become enamored with the planet and take up residence in various private and public professions. An engaging Italian-made science fiction parody. Early film score for noted composer Morricone. C: Paolo Panelli, Carlo Croccolo, Enzo Garinei, Alfredo Landa. D: Franco Castellano. COM 95m.

Twelve Months 1984 ★★½ Child is recognized by spirit from each month of the year despite troubles provided by evil stepmother. Children's fantasy runs through initial premise over and over without sustaining much interest. FAM/DRA 65m. TVM V

Twelve O'Clock High 1949 ★★★★½ An American bomber squadron, based in England during WWII, deals with the unrelenting pressure of combat. Excellent drama of war and its effect on human beings. Outstanding Peck leads a most impressive cast, especially Jagger (Supporting Actor Oscar). C: Gregory Peck, Hugh Marlowe, Gary Merrill, Dean Jagger. D: Henry King. DRA 136m. V

12 Tasks of Asterix, The ★★★½ Gallic heroes Asterix and Obelix fight their way through tangles of Roman bureaucracy in this animated parody of the 12 labors of Hercules. Lovers of the French comic strip are not the only ones who will enjoy this fast-paced, fanciful romp. D: Rene Gosscinny, Albert Underzo. FAM/COM 80m.

Twentieth Century 1934 ★★★★★ Classic screwball battle of the sexes. Manic Broadway producer (Barrymore) makes Lombard a star; she leaves him and he spends long train ride trying to get her back. Hyperactive, hilarious script by Hecht and McArthur features memorable confrontations between the two stars. C: John Barrymore, Carole Lombard, Walter Connolly. D: Howard Hawks. COM 91m. V

Twenty Bucks 1993 ★★★½ Intriguing comedy/drama follows a $20 bill on its odyssey from hand to hand in NYC starting at a cash machine. Offbeat premise, competently executed. C: Linda Hunt, David Rasche, George Morfogen, Sam Jenkins, Brendan Fraser, Gladys Knight, Elisabeth Shue, Steve Buscemi, Christopher Lloyd, Melora Walters, Diane Baker, Spalding Gray, William H. Macyedding. D: Keva Rosenfeld. DRA [R] 91m. V

28 Up 1985 British ★★★★½ A cross-section of British society is interviewed at seven-year intervals by Apted, who has intercut the resulting footage into a fascinating documentary of young promise, lost dreams. Followed by *35 Up*. D: Michael Apted. DOC 133m. V

Twenty-Four Hours to Kill 1965 British ★★★ Rooney is tough to swallow as airline purser who accidentally gets caught up in modestly suspenseful smuggling plot. C: Mickey Rooney, Lex Barker, Walter Slezak. D: Peter Bezencenet. CRI 92m.

20 Million Miles to Earth 1957 ★★★½ Monster from Venus winds up in Italy, causing havoc. Typical movie sci-fi gets a boost from special effects wizard Ray Harryhausen. C: William Hopper, Joan Taylor. D: Nathan Juran. SFI 82m. V

Twenty Million Sweethearts 1934 ★★★½ Powell wants a career in radio but doesn't realize it will cost him his happiness. Some beautiful ballads but basically flimsy. Remake: *My Dream is Yours.* C: Dick Powell, Ginger Rogers, Pat O'Brien, The Mills Brothers. D: Ray Enright. MUS 89m.

20 Mule Team 1940 ★★½ Well-executed drama of miners hauling borax across the desert and dealing with romance and rivals for their claim. Baxter's debut. C: Wallace Beery, Leo Carrillo, Marjorie Rambeau, Anne Baxter. D: Richard Thorpe. WST 84m.

29th Street 1991 ★★★★ A winning lottery ticket proves unlucky for its winner, a beleaguered New Yorker who has trouble getting along with his hapless father. Character comedy draws laughs from its low-key approach. C: Danny Aiello, Anthony LaPaglia, Lainie Kazan. D: George Gallo. COM [R] 101m. V

Twenty-One 1991 British ★★★½ Nonjudgemental coming-of-age story of a young British woman (Kensit) dealing with love and sex. The film incorporates monologues on how she sees things, which doesn't always work. Frankness about sex and drugs will appeal to some, but may offend others. C: Patsy Kensit, Jack Shepherd, Patrick Ryecart. D: Don Boyd. DRA [R] 92m. V

21 Days Together 1938 British ★★★½ Early pairing of Leigh and Olivier casts them as illicit lovers with only three weeks together before he stands trial for murder. The stars generate plenty of sparks. C: Vivien Leigh, Laurence Olivier, Hay Petrie, Leslie Banks. D: Basil Dean. DRA 75m.

21 Hours at Munich 1976 ★★★★ Outstanding TV re-creation of 1972 Olympics crisis in which athletes were killed in a terrorist attack. Fine cast, literate script. C: William Holden, Shirley Knight, Franco Nero, Anthony Quayle. D: William A. Graham. DRA 100m. V

21 Up 1976 British ★★★★★ Third in a series documenting the lives of various subjects at seven-year intervals. This one finds the group entering adulthood with high expectations but limited resources. Provocative, well-thought-out, and often amusing. *28 Up* and *35 Up* followed. D: Michael Apted. DOC 120m.

27th Day, The 1957 ★★★½ Aliens, wishing to colonize Earth, give five people give lethal capsules to kill everyone off; naturally, the evil commies want to use this power to destroy the U.S. Can they be stopped? Solid example of Cold-War SF. From John Mantley's novel. C: Gene Barry, Valerie French, George Voskovec. D: William Asher. DRA 75m.

20,000 Leagues Under the Sea 1954 ★★★★★ Grand Disney adventure, based on Jules Verne's novel. Hardy sailor (Douglas), scientist (Lukas), and cohort (Lorre) are picked up at sea by a futuristic submarine, captained by a unstable genius (Mason). Oscar-winning special effects, fine performances, and exhilarating action provide glorious entertainment for the entire family. C: Kirk Douglas, James Mason, Paul Lukas, Peter Lorre. D: Richard Fleischer. FAM/DRA [G] 127m. V

20,000 Pound Kiss, The 1963 British ★★★½ Short British mystery mixes murder and blackmail in a complex plot, based on an Edgar Wallace story. Not as heavy as it sounds. C: Dawn Addams, Michael Goodliffe, Richard Thorp. D: John Moxey. CRI 57m.

20,000 Years in Sing Sing 1933 ★★★★ Original hard-boiled prison drama, with Davis the woman who gives up everything for tough but intriguing Tracy. Stalwart and well played. Remade as *Castle on the Hudson.* C: Spencer Tracy, Bette Davis, Arthur Byron, Lyle Talbot, Louis Calhern. D: Michael Curtiz. CRI 81m.

23 Paces to Baker Street 1956 ★★★½ When a blind playwright (Johnson) overhears murder plans, he tries to stop the crime. Very entertaining mystery has nothing to do with Sherlock Holmes, despite its title. C: Van Johnson, Vera Miles, Cecil Parker, Estelle Winwood. D: Henry Hathaway. CRI 103m.

Twice Around the Daffodils 1962 British ★★★ Slim comedy about nurse in tuberculosis clinic who is target of patients' libidinous interest. C: Juliet Mills, Donald Sinden, Donald Houston, Jill Ireland, Nanette Newman. D: Gerald Thomas. COM 89m.

Twice in a Lifetime 1985 ★★★★½ A middle-aged, married man (Hackman) falls for a barmaid (Ann-Margret), and decides to divorce his wife (Burstyn), disrupting the rest of their grown family. What could have been hackneyed is instead a surprisingly profound comment on responsibility versus personal need. Madigan is brilliant as Hackman's enraged daughter. C: Gene Hackman, Ann-Margret, Ellen Burstyn, Amy Madigan, Ally Sheedy, Brian Dennehy. D: Bud Yorkin. DRA [R] 111m. V

Twice-Told Tales 1963 ★★★½ Adaptation of three Hawthorne tales, including drastically reduced version of "House of Seven Gables." Interesting of its kind, with some genuine thrills. C: Vincent Price, Sebastian Cabot, Mari Blanchard, Brett Halsey. D: Sidney Salkow. DRA 120m. V

Twice Upon a Time 1983 ★★★★ When depraved desperadoes endanger dream worlds, a gang of goofy good guys save the day. Unusual animated feature uses cut-out figures and sophisticated humor to tell loopy story.

Animation fans and older children will appreciate. George Lucas executive produced. C: Lorenzo Music, Marshall Efron, Hamilton Camp. D: John Korty, Charles Swenson. FAM/ACT [PG] 75m. v

Twilight for the Gods 1958 ★★★ A group of misfits must struggle to survive when their ship sinks en route to Mexico. Standard soap-and-sea story, from a novel by Ernest K. Gann. C: Rock Hudson, Cyd Charisse, Arthur Kennedy, Leif Erickson. D: Joseph Pevney. DRA 120m.

Twilight People 1983 *See* **Beasts**

Twilight Story, The 1962 Japanese ★★★½ Desperate to support her mother, a woman turns to prostitution, then meets and falls in love with an unhappily married man. Well-acted tale of tragic love, though many expected buttons are pushed. C: Hiroshi Akutagawa, Fujiko Yamamoto, Masao Oda. D: Shiro Toyoda. DRA 150m.

Twilight Women 1953 British ★★★★ Jackson runs a boardinghouse that's really a front for an illegal adoption ring. She pushes her residents' babies, fooling innocent victims. Hard-edged and intense crime drama that never flinches. (a.k.a. *Women of Twilight*) C: Freda Jackson, Rene Ray, Lois Maxwell, Joan Dowling. D: Gordon Parry. CRI 89m.

Twilight Zone—The Movie 1983 ★★★½ Top-flight directors give the classic TV series big screen treatment in special-effects-laden trilogy. Tragedy struck production with death of actor Vic Morrow and two Asian child actors during chopper stunt in the Landis segment. Third segment, directed by George (*Road Warrior*) Miller worth watching. C: Vic Morrow, Scatman Crothers, Kevin McCarthy, John Lithgow. D: John Landis, Steven Spielberg, Joe Dante, George Miller. SFI [PG] 101m. v

Twilight Zone—Treasures of the Twilight Zone ★★★★ Four of the best episodes from Serling's classic '60s TV series, including the pilot. SFI v

Twilight's Last Gleaming 1977 U.S.-German ★★★ World War III is imminent when a deranged general captures a missile base, demanding the U.S. apologize for its Vietnam policy. Good cast hoists lengthy, moralistic script, from Walter Wager's novel *Viper Three*. C: Burt Lancaster, Richard Widmark, Melvyn Douglas, Paul Winfield, Joseph Cotten, Charles Durning, Vera Miles. D: Robert Aldrich. DRA [R] 146m. v

Twin Peaks 1990 ★★★★½ Pilot for a groundbreaking, bizarre TV series from David Lynch and Mark Frost about FBI Special Agent Cooper (Maclachlan) searching for killer of dual-natured high school student Laura Palmer (Lee) in small Pacific Northwest town. Part mystery, part soap opera, and part tongue-in-cheek parody. A cult classic. C: Kyle MacLachlan, Lara Flynn Boyle, Michael Ontkean, Piper Laurie, Joan Chen, Sherilyn Fenn. D: David Lynch. DRA 113m. TVM v

Twin Peaks: Fire Walk With Me 1992 ★★★ Movie "prequel" that followed TV series sets up events leading to murder of Laura Palmer. Just as strange and moody as the original, but with less of the foreboding ambience. Fans won't mind, though. C: Sheryl Lee, Ray Wise, Kyle MacLachlan, David Bowie. D: David Lynch. DRA [R] 134m. v

Twin Sisters of Kyoto 1964 Japanese ★★★½ Believing she was kidnapped as a baby, a young woman learns she has a twin sister from whom she was separated at birth because of an ancient superstition. Their meeting ultimately leads to sticky romantic entanglements. Intriguing Japanese drama. C: Shima Iwashita, Seiji Miyaguchi, Teruo Yoshida. D: Noboru Nakamura. DRA 107m.

Twinkle and Shine 1959 *See* **It Happened to Jane**

Twinky 1971 *See* **Lola**

Twins 1988 ★★★★ Schwarzenegger and DeVito meet as adults and learn that they are twin brothers born of a haywire genetic experiment. Once united, they proceed to share adventures. Some nice touches, and more warmth than slapstick. C: Arnold Schwarzenegger, Danny DeVito, Kelly Preston, Chloe Webb. D: Ivan Reitman. COM [PG] 107m. v

Twins of Evil 1971 ★★★½ A vampiric count transforms one of two beautiful twins into a bloodsucker, and a witch-hunter (Cushing) must determine which one's been victimized and destroy her. Effectively sexy and scary; the Collinsons were *Playboy*'s first twin Playmates. C: Peter Cushing, Madeleine Collinson, Mary Collinson. D: John Hough. HOR [R] 86m. v

Twist and Shout 1984 Danish ★★★½ Wistful coming-of-age story, set in 1963 Denmark, with two teenage boys caught up in Beatlemania while coping with dysfunctional families and the pangs of first love. Well-acted. C: Adam Tonsberg, Lars Simonsen, Camilla Soeberg. D: Bille August. DRA [R] 99m. v

Twist Around the Clock 1961 ★★★½ Fun rock & roll numbers combine with silly plot of a booking agent (Cronin) trying to turn Checker into a star. Lively musical capitalizes on the early '60s dance craze. C: Chubby Checker, Dion, The Marcels, John Cronin, Mary Mitchell. D: Oscar Rudolph. MUS 86m.

Twist of Sand, A 1968 British ★★½ Former submarine commander leads smugglers on foray to find diamonds. C: Richard Johnson, Honor Blackman, Jeremy Kemp, Roy Dotrice. D: Don Chaffey. ACT [G] 90m.

Twist, The 1976 French ★★½ An American writer (Dern) is torn between an upper-crust socialite (Audran) and a free-spirit (Ann-Margret). Good cast, but the script could have used more of the trademark Chabrol wit. (a.k.a. *Folies Bourgeoises*) C:

Bruce Dern, Stephane Audran, Ann-Margret, Jean-Pierre Cassel, Curt Jurgens, Charles Aznavour. D: Claude Chabrol. COM 105m. V

Twisted 1992 ★ A psychopathic youngster (Slater) locks horns with disturbed babysitter (Smith). Stagy, slow-moving thriller, finally released six years after production, thanks to presence of Slater. Mercedes Ruehl also has small early part. C: Lois Smith, Christian Slater, Tandy Cronyn, Dina Merrill. D: Adam Holender. HOR 87m. V

Two Bits 1994 ★★★½ It's the Depression and the title 25 cents is what a kid needs to get into the local movie palace. Offbeat, intriguing drama, with workmanlike performances from Pacino and Mastrantonio. C: Al Pacino, Mary Elizabeth Mastrantonio, Gerlando Barone, Patrick Borriello, Andy Romano. D: James Foley. DRA

Two Bright Boys 1939 ★★★½ Orphan Cooper inherits a Texas oil field. His would-be benefactor Dinehart wants the property for himself, but fellow child star Bartholomew helps Cooper keep what is rightfully his. A nice pairing of kid actors make this an entertaining children's adventure. C: Jackie Cooper, Freddie Bartholomew, Melville Cooper, Alan Dinehart. D: Joseph Santley. FAM/DRA 70m.

Two Colonels, The 1963 Italian ★★★ Maggio and Pidgeon, opposing but friendly WWII military leaders, take turns capturing each other while stationed in a small town, but ultimately unite forces to fight Nazis. Stereotypes abound in predictable situations. C: Toto, Walter Pidgeon, Seilla Gabel. D: Steno. DRA 90m.

Two Daughters 1961 Indian ★★★★ A pair of stories by Nobel Prize-winner Tagore. The first deals with an orphan and a mailman; the second with a young man who rejects his arranged marriage. Beautifully adapted and directed by the masterful Ray. C: Anil Chatterjee, Chandana Bannerjee, Soumitra Chatterjee. D: Satyajit Ray. DRA 114m. V

Two English Girls 1972 French ★★★★ Before WWI, a young Frenchman visits England and falls in love with two enchanting English sisters. A rolling, moving, tender, fascinating film from Truffaut. (a.k.a. *Les Deux Anglaises et le Continent*) C: Jean-Pierre Leaud, Kika Markham, Stacey Tendeter. D: Francois Truffaut. DRA 130m. V

Two Evil Eyes 1991 Italian ★★½ Team-up of two horror masters, each adapting Poe stories, is disappointing, but both segments have their moments. First tale has scheming couple using hypnosis to get their hands on an inheritance. Second features Keitel (amusingly over the top) as crime photographer losing his mind. C: Adrienne Barbeau, Harvey Keitel, Sally Kirkland, Martin Balsam, E.G. Marshal. D: George Romero, Dario Argento. HOR [R] 121m. V

Two Eyes, Twelve Hands 1958 Indian ★★★★ Jail guard who believes in the good of all humankind sets up six inmates to work on nearby farm. When he is killed in an accident, the prisoners realize the good he has done. Sincere and well-acted drama. C: Shri V. Shantaram, Sandhya. D: Shri V. Shantaram. DRA 124m.

Two-Faced Woman 1941 ★★★½ Not-bad screwball comedy about a wife who poses as her flamboyant twin sister to test husband's affections. Notorious, though, as Garbo's first flop and last film, prematurely ending her career. Greta does seem out of place as she swims, rides and dances the "Chica-Choca." C: Greta Garbo, Melvyn Douglas, Constance Bennett, Roland Young, Ruth Gordon. D: George Cukor. COM 94m. V

Two-Fisted Sheriff 1937 ★★★½ When Lane is wrongly accused of murder, range rider Starrett tries to find the real killer. Lane's escape from jail doesn't help his case, but Starrett doggedly pursues the truth. Good B-Western mystery with plenty of action. C: Charles Starrett, Bruce Lane, Alan Sears. D: Leon Barsha. WST 58m.

Two Flags West 1950 ★★★ Weak Civil War drama not quite salvaged by strong battle sequence at conclusions. C: Joseph Cotten, Linda Darnell, Jeff Chandler, Cornel Wilde. D: Robert Wise. DRA 92m.

Two for the Road 1967 ★★★★★ Stylish, unique look at marriage; Hepburn and Finney reminisce about their years of falling in and out of love. Never confusing, always insightful, graced with sublime star performances and gorgeous location footage. C: Audrey Hepburn, Albert Finney, Eleanor Bron, William Daniels, Claude Dauphin. D: Stanley Donen. DRA 112m. V

Two for the Seesaw 1962 ★★★★ Hoping to recharge boring life, lawyer Mitchum moves from Omaha to New York City. There he becomes involved with eccentric MacLaine, who shows him life in different vein. Two-character comedy, adapted from popular play, gets plenty of laughs from leads. C: Robert Mitchum, Shirley MacLaine. D: Robert Wise. COM 109m. V

Two for Tonight 1935 ★★★ Struggling songwriter (Crosby) bets he can write a show for Broadway star (Todd) in seven days. Pleasing tuner, nice cast. C: Bing Crosby, Joan Bennett, Thelma Todd, Mary Boland. D: Frank Tuttle. MUS 61m.

Two Girls and a Sailor 1944 ★★★★ Fine MGM musical with insignificant plot about a sailor (Johnson) and his amorous involvement with two singing canteen managers (Allyson and DeHaven). Vastly entertaining. C: Van Johnson, June Allyson, Gloria De Haven, Jose Iturbi, Jimmy Durante, Lena Horne, Virginia O'Brien, Gracie Allen. D: Richard Thorpe. MUS 125m. V

Two Girls on Broadway 1940 ★★★ Love

triangle involving sisters chasing the same guy. Standard musical, elevated by Blondell's pizzazz. C: Lana Turner, George Murphy, Joan Blondell. D: S. Simon. MUS 71m.

Two Great Cavaliers, The 1973 ★★★ A lone Ming warrior fights off the entire Manchurian army with lots of hard heels and flailing wrists. C: Chen Shing, Mao Ying. D: Yeung Ching Chen. ACT 95m. V

Two Gun Lady 1956 ★★½ Uninspired Western about female sharpshooter who tries to bring her father's murderer to justice. C: Peggie Castle, Marie Windsor, William Talman. D: Richard Bartlett. WST 75m.

Two Guys From Milwaukee 1946 ★★★½ Upbeat comedy about sassy cabbie, who helps acclimate European prince to American ways. Slight but fun. C: Dennis Morgan, Jack Carson, Joan Leslie, Janis Paige, S.Z. Sakall. D: David Butler. COM 90m.

Two Guys From Texas 1948 ★★★½ Two show-biz types temporarily mislocated on a Texas ranch. Amusing musical, featuring—it's true—sharp guest appearance by Bugs Bunny. C: Dennis Morgan, Jack Carson, Dorothy Malone, Forrest Tucker. D: David Butler. MUS 86m.

Two Hundred Motels 1971 ★★★½ Frank Zappa's visualization of his unique musical style features ex-Beatle Starr taking a tour of indescribable ocular freak show. Though certainly original, film grows hard on the eyes after awhile. Zappa's music is excellent throughout. C: Frank Zappa, Theodore Bikel, Ringo Starr, Keith Moon. D: Frank Zappa, Tony Palmer. MUS [R] 98m. V

Two in the Shadow 1968 Japanese ★★★½ After accidentally causing a traffic fatality, a motorist eases guilt by financially assisting out his victim's widow. The two become romantically involved, but when they witness a similar traffic accident everything changes. Soap opera plotting is bolstered by nice performances. C: Yuzo Kayama, Yoko Tsukasa, Mitsuko Mori. D: Mikio Naruse. DRA 108m.

Two Jakes, The 1990 ★★★½ Sequel to *Chinatown* finds Nicholson involved with Keitel, the other "Jake," whose extramarital activities leads to land-grabbing conspiracy by unscrupulous oil interests. Complex series of plot twists make no sense unless you've seen the brilliant original. Look for the anachronistic cash machine in background! C: Jack Nicholson, Harvey Keitel, Meg Tilly, Madeleine Stowe, Eli Wallach. D: Jack Nicholson. CRI [R] 137m. V

Two Kouney Lemels 1966 Israeli ★★★★ Bourstein, in a dual role, plays a hopeless klutz and a wealthy individual who both face impending nuptials in this slam-bang, hundred-mile-an-hour farce. The first film for this popular Israeli character thrives on its unrestrained comic energy. C: Mike Bourstein, Rafael Klatchkin, Jermain Unikovsky. D: Israel Becker. COM 120m.

Two-Lane Blacktop 1971 ★★★★ Two guys (Taylor and Wilson) driving southwest in a souped-up '55 Chevy make a racing bet with middle-aged man (Oates) in new GTO that escalates into an obsession for all concerned. Cult film has some riveting stretches, and fine work by Oates. C: James Taylor, Warren Oates, Laurie Bird. D: Monte Hellman. DRA [R] 101m.

Two Little Bears, The 1961 ★★½ Odd comedy about man who discovers his children can turn themselves into bears. Lightweight. C: Eddie Albert, Jane Wyatt, Soupy Sales. D: Randall Hood. COM 81m.

Two Lives of Mattias Pascal, The 1985 Italian ★★★★ After jilting his fiancée, Mastroianni heads to Monte Carlo, where he wins big. He helps himself to a suicide victim's ID and uses his newly acquired money to reinvent his life. A very funny black comedy. C: Marcello Mastroianni, Flavio Bucci, Laura Morante, Laura Del Sol, Caroline Berg, Andrea Ferreol, Bernard Blier. D: Mario Monicelli. COM 125m.

Two Living, One Dead 1964 British ★★★½ After a colleague is killed in a robbery, Travers is cited for heroism while McGoohan is treated with disdain. But when layers are peeled away, Travers is not all he appears to be. Some good moments in a routine crime drama. C: Virginia McKenna, Bill Travers, Patrick McGoohan, Dorothy Alison. D: Anthony Asquith. CRI 92m.

Two Loves 1961 ★★½ Meandering soaper about a spinster teacher (MacLaine) in New Zealand who is shocked by the local morals—and tempted. MacLaine looks as uncomfortable as her character. (a.k.a. *The Spinster*) C: Shirley MacLaine, Lawrence Harvey, Jack Hawkins. D: Charles Walters. DRA 100m.

Two Men and a Girl 1947 *See* **Honeymoon**

Two Minute Warning 1976 ★★★ An insane gunman, at large in a crowded football stadium, must be caught before it's too late. Flabby thriller may be enjoyable for gridiron fans. This is the original theatrical version. The version usually used for commercial broadcasts was re-edited and revised for TV. C: Charlton Heston, John Cassavetes, Martin Balsam, Beau Bridges, David Janssen, Gena Rowlands, Walter Pidgeon. D: Larry Peerce. CRI [R] 115m. V

Two Moon Junction 1988 ★★★½ Energetic and delightful trash about rich nymphet (Fenn) who runs off with muscled carnival worker (Tyson) while her grandmother (Fletcher) and law official (Ives) try to stop her. Zestfully silly acting makes this deliberately campy story pure cheesecake cinema. C: Sherilyn Fenn, Richard Tyson, Louise Fletcher, Burl Ives, Kristy McNichol. D: Zalman King. DRA [R] 104m. V

Two Mrs. Carrolls, The 1947 ★★★ Sad

story of a deranged artist who paints his wives as the Angel of Death and then murders them. Offbeat Bogey in his looney mode. Stanwyck shows why she's tops. C: Humphrey Bogart, Barbara Stanwyck, Alexis Smith, Nigel Bruce. D: Peter Godfrey. DRA 99m. v

Two Mrs. Grenvilles, The 1987 ★★★★ Outstanding adaptation of Dominick Dunne's roman a clef about the 1955 Woodward slaying. Ann-Margret shines as the woman with a shady past, accused of killing her society husband (Collins), as does Colbert as her stoic mother-in-law. Full of high-kitsch touches and high-gloss melodrama. C: Ann-Margret, Claudette Colbert, Stephen Collins, Elizabeth Ashley, John Rubinstein. D: John Erman. DRA 200m. TVM

Two Mules for Sister Sara 1969 ★★★★ Unlikely combo of Eastwood and MacLaine actually makes for bright chemistry in tale of mercenary aiding eccentric nun in gunrunning scheme. C: Clint Eastwood, Shirley MacLaine. D: Don Siegel. DRA [PG] 105m. v

Two of a Kind 1983 ★★ Angels bet Lord that humanity can redeem itself, then put all their chips on bank robber Travolta and crooked teller Newton-John. Strong cast has little to do. Inane dialogue and situations are nearly impossible to watch. C: John Travolta, Oliver Newton-John, Charles Durning, Oliver Reed, Beatrice Straight. D: John Herzfeld. COM [PG] 87m. TVM v

Two of Us, The 1968 French ★★★★½ Moving comic drama about gruff anti-Semite in rural France who becomes guardian of a young Jewish boy from Paris during WWII. Touching and beautifully performed and directed. C: Michel Simon, Alain Cohen, Luce Fabiole. D: Claude Berri. COM [R] 86m. v

Two Rode Together 1961 ★★★ When Comanches capture a group of soldiers, an Army commander and a U.S. marshal team up to get them back. A forced Ford effort, meant to recapture spirit of *The Searchers.* C: James Stewart, Richard Widmark, Linda Cristal, Shirley Jones, Andy Devine. D: John Ford. WST 109m. v

Two Seconds 1932 ★★★½ A convicted murderer reviews his life in the moments before the electric chair does its job. Solid crime drama, fine Robinson. C: Edward G. Robinson, Vivienne Osborn, J. Carrol Naish, Preston Foster, Guy Kibbee. D: Mervyn LeRoy. DRA 68m.

Two Sisters From Boston 1946 ★★★½ Two young women that find work—and a world they never imagined—in a Bowery saloon. Airy, entertaining musical. C: Kathryn Grayson, June Allyson, Lauritz Melchior, Jimmy Durante, Peter Lawford. D: Henry Koster. MUS 112m.

2001: A Space Odyessy 1968 British ★★★★★ Visual, mystical epic based on Arthur C. Clarke book traces man's history from the Stone Age to the Space Age, culminating in two astronauts' Jupiter mission, where they contend with their homicidal computer, HAL. Audiences either love it or are confused, but everyone agrees it was important. Oscar for Best Special Effects. Followed by *2010.* C: Keir Dullea, William Sylvester, Gary Lockwood. D: Stanley Kubrick. SFI [G] 139m. v

2010: The Year We Make Contact 1984 ★★★★ A joint U.S./Soviet mission seeks to discover what happened to the earlier *Discovery* mission. Follow-up to *2001,* not nearly as mystical, but still highly watchable. Sometimes it's better to leave things unexplained. C: Roy Scheider, John Lithgow, Helen Mirren, Keir Dullea. D: Peter Hyams. SFI [PG] 106m. v

2,000 Maniacs 1964 ★★½ Two carloads of Northern vacationers are terrorized in a Southern town that rises every 100 years to avenge Civil War atrocities. Early gore film has a novel premise and some tacky charm, but the squeamish and discriminating need not bother to attend. C: Connie Mason, Thomas Wood, Jeffrey Allen. D: Herschell Gordo Lewis. HOR 75m. v

2020 Texas Gladiators 1984 ★ In a wasteland future, three gladiators battle a horde of sadists for control of fuel. Sound familiar? cheap, quick *Road Warrior* knock-off devoid of any originality. C: Al Cliver, Harrison Muller. D: Kevin Mancusco. ACT 92m. v

2000 Year Old Man, The ★★★★ Twenty-five minutes of animated madness as an ancient Eathling reminisces about a time when life was more primitive. Classic Mel Brooks/-Carl Reiner comedy that never grows old. COM

Two Tickets to Broadway 1951 ★★★ Simplistic musical about earnest performers trying to get shot on national television variety show. Amiable enough, with good songs. C: Tony Martin, Janet Leigh, Gloria de Haven, Eddie Bracken, Ann Miller. D: James Kern. MUS 106m. v

Two Way Stretch 1960 British ★★★★½ Fast and funny farce about three convicts who break out of jail to rob a maharajah and then break back in again—all in the same night. Superb comedic turns by cast make this a classic of its type. C: Peter Sellers, Wilfrid Hyde-White, Liz Fraser. D: Robert Day. COM 84m. v

Two Weeks in Another Town 1962 ★★★ A trouble-stricken actor (Douglas) and director (Robinson) join forces on a low-budget Italian shoot, fraught with difficulties. Disappointing follow-up to the same director's *The Bad and The Beautiful* suffers from a poor script, and near-fatal miscasting of Charisse in the female lead. From Irwin Shaw's novel. C: Kirk Douglas, Edward G. Robinson, Cyd Charisse, Claire Trevor, George Hamilton. D: Vincente Minnelli. DRA 107m. v

Two Weeks with Love 1950 ★★★ Reynolds as teen on vacation with parents in the Catskills, trying her hand at romance. Engaging score helps. C: Jane Powell, Ricardo Montalban, Louis Calhern, Ann Harding, Debbie Reynolds, Carleton Carpenter. D: Roy Rowland. COM 93m. V

Two Women 1961 Italian ★★★★½ Devastating story, set in WWII Italy, of mother (Loren) seeking refuge for herself and her adolescent daughter, as they survive bombings, lack of food and shelter, etc. Loren's Oscar-winning performance is breathtaking as film builds irrevocably to tragic climax. C: Sophia Loren, Jean-Paul Belmondo, Eleanora Brown, Raf Vallone. D: Vittorio De Sica. DRA 99m. V

Two Wondrous Tigers 1979 ★★ *The Magnificent Seven* minus five and a decent budget, as a kung fu master dares to stand up to the martial arts-practicing gang terrorizing his village. Standard chopsocky. C: John Chang. D: Wilson Tong. ACT 87m. V

Two Worlds of Jennie Logan, The 1979 ★★★½ After buying an old house, Wagner finds an ancient dress in the attic. She tries it on and presto! She takes a trip back in time. Clever idea, so-so presentation. C: Lindsay Wagner, Linda Gray, Marc Singer. D: Frank De Felitta. DRA 99m. TVM V

Two Years Before the Mast 1946 ★★½ Weak tale of man who goes undercover to expose physical abuse of sea-going workers. C: Alan Ladd, Brian Donlevy, William Bendix, Howard da Silva, Barry Fitzgerald. D: John Farrow. DRA 98m.

Tycoon 1947 ★★★ Muscular drama about a railroad contractor (Wayne) in conflict with his employer (Hardwicke) over construction of tracks through the Andes Mountains. Good action sequences. C: John Wayne, Larraine Day, Cedric Hardwicke, Judith Anderson, James Gleason, Anthony Quinn. D: Richard Wallace. ACT 128m. V

Typhoon 1940 ★★★½ Two sailors come upon a beautiful shipwreck survivor (Lamour) who's been living by herself on a remote tropical island. Breezily entertaining and romantic, if a bit implausible, and pleasant to watch. C: Dorothy Lamour, Robert Preston, Lynne Overman, J. Carroll Naish, Jack Carson. D: Louis King. COM 70m.

U

U-turn 1987 *See* **Girl in Blue, The**

U2: Rattle and Hum 1988 ★★★ Entertaining, fairly ambitious documentary feature about the popular rock band, mixing grainy, b&w offstage footage with concert scenes in color. Non-fans will find the best moments occur outside the arenas. C: U2. D: Phil Joanou. MUS [PG-13] 99m. V

UFO—Contact UFO: Alien Abductions ★★★ Interviews with people who claim to have had real-life close encounters. Interesting and at times chilling. SFI V

UFO: Top Secret ★★★ Docudrama probes military's relationship with extraterrestrials. Has man already made contact? Provoking, but way out. SFI V

UFOria 1980 ★★★★ Ditsy supermarket cashier (Williams) says she's received a message from outer space and a country singer lookalike (Ward) and a crooked evangelist (Stanton) are just two of the assorted lunatics who are ready to believe her. Funny, low-budget UFO spoof, and Williams is delightful. C: Cindy Williams, Harry Dean Stanton, Fred Ward, Harry Carey Jr. D: John Binder. SFI [PG] 92m. V

UFO'S: It Has Begun ★★ Low-budget docudrama about Man/Alien contacts through the years. Tired rehash of tabloid headlines. SFI V

UFO'S: The Hidden Truth ★★ Is there anybody out there? Low-budget docudrama looks for clues. Finds little. SFI V

Ugetsu 1953 Japanese ★★★★½ In 16th-century Japan, two peasants leave their homes and families to seek their fortunes, only to be confronted by ghosts and, ultimately, the death of their dreams. Beautifully crafted mix of supernatural and morality themes is a classic of Asian fantasy. C: Machiko Kyo, Masayuki Mori, Kinnyo Tannka, Sakae Ozawa. D: Kenji Mizoguchi. DRA 96m. V

Ugly American, The 1963 ★★★½ Ineffectual American Ambassador (Brando) to small Asian country mismanages every political problem he faces. Cold War relic shows its age, though Brando still interests. C: Marlon Brando, Sandra Church, Pat Hingle, Eiji Okada. D: George Englund. DRA 120m. V

Ugly Dachshund, The 1966 ★★½ Married dog trainers (Jones, Pleshette) specialize in dachshunds but face new challenges with Great Dane that wants to fit in with his smaller canine relatives. Contrived nonsense packed with sub-par pooch gags in Disney slapstick. Strictly for younger children. C: Dean Jones, Suzanne Pleshette. D: Norman Tokar. FAM/COM 93m. V

UHF 1989 ★★★ Music parodist Yankovic makes his starring debut as a nebbish who inherits a struggling TV station and manages to turn it around. Minimal story and erratic comedy, but some of the sketches are side-splitting. C: "Weird" Al Yankovic, Victoria Jackson, Kevin McCarthy, Michael Richards. D: Jay Levey. COM [PG-13] 97m. V

Ulisse 1955 *See* **Ulysses**

Ulterior Motives 1992 ★★★ Low-budget vehicle for wanna-be action star Griffith casts him as a P.I. who takes on the Yakuza and other enemies while protecting reporter Keller. Not bad, with more plot twists than usual. C: Thomas Ian Griffith, Mary Page Keller, Joe Yamanaka, Ellen Crawford. D: James Becket. CRI [R] 90m. V

Ultimate Solution of Grace Quigley, The 1985 *See* **Grace Quigley**

Ultimate Teacher, The 1992 Japanese ★★★ Okay Japanese animation feature finds the title character taking a job at the ultimate problem school and whipping violent students into shape. Typical mix of colorful graphics, humor, and violence. SFI 60m. V

Ulysses 1955 Italian ★★★½ Homer's epic poem becomes a would-be epic movie, with Douglas in the heroic lead, encountering challenges on the way home from the Trojan War. Intelligent historical drama, with solid performances; Ben Hecht and Irwin Shaw were among the scriptwriters. (a.k.a. *Ulisse*) C: Kirk Douglas, Silvana Mangano, Anthony Quinn, Sylvie, Rossana Podesta, Jacques Dumesnil. D: Mario Camerini. DRA 104m. V

Ulysses 1967 ★★★ Film adaptation of James Joyce's unfilmmable stream-of-consciousness masterpiece. Interesting direction, surreal imagery and memorable dream sequences, but never forms coherent whole. C: Barbara Jefford, Milo O'Shea, Maurice Roeves, T.P. McKenna, Martin Dempsey, Sheila O'Sullivan. D: Joseph Strick. DRA 140m. V

Ulzana's Raid 1972 ★★★½ After an especially brutal Apache attack, an Indian fighter who's seen better days teams up with a green young Army officer to gain revenge. Gripping though violent and somewhat distressing character piece. C: Burt Lancaster, Bruce Davison, Jorge Luke, Richard Jaeckel, Joaquin Martinez, Lloyd Bochner. D: Robert Aldrich. WST [R] 103m. V

Umberto D 1952 Italian ★★★★★ One of De Sica's greatest films (and his personal favorite), with a wrenching performance by Battisti as a former government employee struggling with life and love while living in Rome on an insufficient pension. Heartbreaking and always honest. C: Carlo Battisti, Maria Pia Casilio, Lina Gennari. D: Vittorio De Sica. DRA 89m. V

Umbrella Woman, The 1986 *See* **Good Wife, The**

Umbrellas of Cherbourg, The 1964 French

★★★★ Unusual love story, completely sung. Young heroine (Deneuve) marries another when her lover (Castelnuovo) goes off to war and she finds herself pregnant. After the war, Castelnuovo returns. Lovely Michel Legrand score includes "I Will Wait for You" and "Watch What Happens." Slight, but beguiling. C: Catherine Deneuve, Nino Castelnuovo, Anne Vernon, Marc Michel. D: Jacques Demy. MUS 90m. V

Un Amour de Swann 1984 *See* **Swann in Love**

Un Carnet De Bal 1938 French ★★★★½ Rich, lonely widow (Bell) sifting through girlhood memories finds dance program from fondly remembered ball and goes in search of her youth. Bittersweet, romantic drama with stellar cast. Winner of several international film awards. C: Marie Bell, Francoise Rosay, Louis Jouvet, Harry Baur. D: Julien Duvivier. DRA 109m.

Un Chien Andalou 1928 French ★★★★ Buñuel's best-known film, made in collaboration with Salvador Dali, is a powerful, disturbing expedition into the surreal, with numerous bizarre visions (including the notorious eye-slicing scene). Not for all tastes, but fascinating. C: Simone Mareull, Pierre Batcheff, Jaime Miravilles. D: Luis Buñuel. DRA 17m. V

Un Coeur en Hiver 1992 French ★★★★ A middle-aged violin restorer (Auteuil) who has never opened up to women falls for young violinist (Beart). Unusual study of a man who cannot love, colored by superlative performances and sublime chamber music by Ravel. C: Daniel Auteuil, Emmanuelle Béart, André Dussollier. D: Claude Sautet. DRA 105m. V

Un Soir Sur La Plage 1961 *See* **Violent Summer**

Unbearable Lightness of Being, The 1988 ★★★½ Screen adaptation of Milan Kundera's novel stars Day-Lewis as doctor who flits between young wife (Binoche) and sophisticate (Olin), while trying to avoid encroaching government oppression in Prague in 1968. Though well acted and lushly photographed (especially the notorious sex scenes), film has an oddly hollow ring. C: Daniel Day-Lewis, Juliette Binoche, Lena Olin, Derek De Lint, Erland Josephson, Daniel Olbrychski, Donald Moffat. D: Philip Kaufman. DRA [R] 171m. V

Unbeaten 28, The 1983 ★ This time it's a whole passel of kung fu champs whose mettle is tested by a squad of criminals. Unfortunately more doesn't mean better in this martial arts malarkey. C: Meng Fei, Lisa Chang, Lung Sikar. D: Joseph Kuo. ACT 88m. V

Unbelievable Truth, The 1990 ★★★½ An ex-con (Burke) returns to his home town, disrupting it. Quirky comedy/drama suffers from inconsistency of tone, but has some wonderful moments. C: Adrienne Shelly, Robert Burke. D: Hal Hartley. COM [R] 90m. V

Unborn, The 1991 ★★★ When Adams consults an oddball doctor for help with her repeated miscarriages, she finds herself pregnant with an evil and invincible creature. Subject matter makes otherwise ordinary horror flick extra creepy. C: Brooke Adams, Jeff Hayenga, James Karen, Jane Cameron. D: Rodman Flender. HOR [R] 85m. V

Unborn II, The 1994 ★★★ A pregnant young woman accompanies her fiance back to his ancestral home and discovers that his family are vampires that feed on fetuses! Admittedly unique twist on horror traditions unfortunately winds up more silly than scary. C: Norman Moses, Tina Ona Paukstelis, John Kishline, Flora Coker, Midred Nierras. D: Wrye Martin, Barry Poltermann. HOR [R] 82m.

Uncertain Glory 1944 ★★★ Wartime star vehicle for Flynn casts him as a criminal who, when given a chance to do the right thing, nobly sacrifices himself for the French cause. Shallow melodrama entertains nonetheless. Lukas is excellent as policeman. C: Errol Flynn, Jean Sullivan, Paul Lukas, Lucile Watson, Faye Emerson, Douglass Dumbrille, Dennis Hoey, Sheldon Leonard. D: Raoul Walsh. ACT 102m.

Uncle Buck 1989 ★★★★ Family black sheep (Candy) tries to prove himself by taking care of his brother's children during a three-day weekend. Genial, family-oriented slapstick comedy, with outstanding interplay between Candy and tot Culkin. C: John Candy, Amy Madigan, Gaby Hoffmann, Macaulay Culkin. D: John Hughes. COM [PG] 100m. V

Uncle Harry 1945 ★★★★ Hitchcockian thriller about a man (Sanders), manipulated by his obsessive, hypochondriac sister (Fitzgerald) who can't abide his relationship with another woman (Raines). Involving story, strong acting. (a.k.a. *The Strange Affair of Uncle Harry*) C: George Sanders, Geraldine Fitzgerald, Ella Raines. D: Robert Siodmak. DRA

Uncle, The 1966 British ★★½ Modest comedy/drama about a young boy who begins to grow up when he finds out he's an uncle. Slight but endearing. C: Rupert Davies, Brenda Bruce, Robert Duncan, William Marlowe. D: Desmond Davis. COM 87m.

Uncle Tom's Cabin 1970 French ★★★ Harriet Beecher Stowe's novel about slavery and the underground railroad is reworked with an international cast and setting (Yugoslavia instead of Kentucky). Not bad, but poorly dubbed, overly sentimental story doesn't really land itself to internationalization. C: Herbert Lom, John Kitzmiller, O. W. Fisher. D: Geza Radvanyi. DRA [G] 120m.

Uncle Tom's Cabin 1987 ★★★★ More contemporary revision of Stowe's novel has tougher violence, but also more interesting characterizations that capture sense of human brutality and possibility for redemption. Rashad surprisingly effective. C: Avery Brooks, Kate Burton, Bruce Dern, Paula Kelly, Phylicia Rashad, Kathryn Walker, Edward Woodward,

Frank Converse, George Coe, Albert Hall. D: Stan Lathan. DRA 110m. TVM V

Uncle Vanya 1972 USSR ★★★½ Chekhov's masterpiece of human frailty and yearning is given a stagy and flawed production, but the thoughtful, rousing performances make it worthwhile. C: Innokenty Smoktunovsky, Sergei Bondarchuk, Vladimir Zeldin, Irina Kupchenko. D: Andrei Mikhalkov Konchalovsky. DRA [G] 110m. TVM

Uncommon Valor 1983 ★★★½ Retired veteran soldier Hackman takes pack of down-and-out warriors to Vietnam to find his son, missing in action. Great acting makes this surprisingly effective. C: Gene Hackman, Robert Stack, Fred Ward, Reb Brown, Randall Cobb, Patrick Swayze. D: Ted Kotcheff. ACT [R] 105m. V

Unconquered 1947 ★★★½ Frontier action-adventure epic has American colonist hero (Cooper) fighting English and Indians and yearning for spunky indentured servant, played to hilt by gorgeous Goddard. Explosive, fast-paced action sequences, lavish production values, exciting cast. C: Gary Cooper, Paulette Goddard, Howard da Silva, Boris Karloff, Cecil Kellaway, Ward Bond, Katherine DeMille, C. Aubrey Smith, Porter Hall, Mike Mazurki. D: Cecil B. DeMille. ACT 146m.

Undead, The 1957 ★★★½ A modern-day prostitute time-travels to the Middle Ages, where she's accused of being a witch. Early Corman schlock-shocker has its moments, some of them unintentionally humorous. C: Pamela Duncan, Richard Garland, Allison Hayes, Billy Barty. D: Roger Corman. HOR 75m.

Undefeated, The 1969 ★★★ Just after the Civil war, a Union colonel (Wayne) and a Confederate colonel (Hudson) join forces to fight Mexican general. Routine star vehicle lacks sparkle. C: John Wayne, Rock Hudson, Tony Aguilar, Roman Gabriel, Bruce Cabot, Lee Meriwether, Ben Johnson, Merlin Olsen, Marian McCargo. D: Andrew V. McLaglen. DRA [G] 119m. V

Under Capricorn 1949 British ★★½ Subpar Hitchcock melodrama set in 19th-century Australia involves Bergman, wife of convict turned millionaire Cotten, turning to drink; arrival of her cousin Wilding further complicates matters. Of course, even so-so Hitchcock can be better than none at all. Based on the novel by Helen Simpson. C: Ingrid Bergman, Joseph Cotten, Michael Wilding, Margaret Leighton, Cecil Parker. D: Alfred Hitchcock. DRA 117m. V

Under Cover 1987 ★★ Narcotics detective (Leigh) and police officer (Neidorf) go undercover into the world of drug dealers to find the pusher/cop-killer who murdered Neidorf's friend. The whole thing lacks distinction. C: David Neidorf, Jennifer Jason Leigh, Barry Corbin, Kathleen Wilhoite, David Harris. D: John Stockwell. ACT 95m. V

Under Fire 1983 ★★★★ Nolte, Hackman, and Cassidy play journalists caught up in Nicaragua's 1979 civil war. A gutsy thriller with a steamy romantic triangle subplot and terrific performances. C: Nick Nolte, Gene Hackman, Joanna Cassidy, Ed Harris. D: Roger Spottiswoode. ACT 100m. V

Under Mexicali Stars 1950 ★★★½ Contemporary Western, with the bad guys using choppers instead of horses to transport their stolen goods. Allen is stalwart as modern cow wrangler hero. C: Rex Allen, Dorothy Patrick, Roy Barcroft, Buddy Ebsen. D: George Blair. WST 67m.

Under Milk Wood 1973 British ★★★ Dylan Thomas' fantasy Welsh village of Llareggub is brought to life in this spotty adaptation that gets help from star casting, including Burton, as Narrator, and O'Toole as Captain Cat. C: Richard Burton, Elizabeth Taylor, Peter O'Toole, Glynis Johns, Victor Spinetti, Vivien Merchant. D: Andrew Sinclair. DRA 90m. V

Under My Skin 1950 ★★★ Uneven drama about the devotion of a young boy to his crooked jockey father (Garfield). Loosely based on a Hemingway story about the racing business. No sprinter, but hangs in there. C: John Garfield, Micheline Presle, Luther Adler, Orley Lindgren, Noel Drayton. D: Jean Negulesco. DRA 86m.

Under Nevada Skies 1946 ★★★½ Good Rogers oater, complete with songs from the Sons of the Pioneers. Plot concerns a missing map to a rich uranium deposit. Lots of action, exciting chases. C: Roy Rogers, Dale Evans, George "Gabby" Hayes. WST 68m.

Under Pressure 1935 ★★★½ Tale of rival tunnel-digging crews, with McLaglen and Bickford as the combative crew bosses. Atmospheric photography and gritty direction boosts predictable melodrama. C: Edmund Lowe, Victor McLaglen, Florence Rice, Marjorie Rambeau. D: Raoul Walsh. DRA 72m. V

Under-Pup, The 1939 ★★★½ Musical comedy about struggles of musically talented young woman from wrong side of tracks (Jean) who gets scholarship to exclusive summer camp and is snubbed by rich teenagers. Corny, but satisfying. C: Gloria Jean, Robert Cummings, Nan Grey, Beulah Bondi, Virginia Weidler, Margaret Lindsay, C. Aubrey Smith, Billy Gilbert. D: Richard Wallace. MUS 81m.

Under Satan's Sun 1987 *See* **Under the Sun of Satan**

Under Siege 1992 ★★★★ Seagal plays a Navy Seal finishing his military stint as a cook on a battleship marked for hijacking by Jones, a CIA agent gone bad. Very violent and very enjoyable, with nonstop action. C: Steven Seagal, Tommy Lee Jones, Gary Busey, Erika Eleniak, Patrick O'Neal. D: Andrew Davis. ACT [R] 103m. V

Under Suspicion 1992 ★★★½ A sleazy detective (Neeson), who specializes in less-than-ethical divorce cases, must rely on his investigative wits when he is the main suspect in his own wife's murder. Watchable modern film noir suffers slightly from one too many plot twists and a leisurely pace, but hold on for a nifty, nail-biting climax. C: Liam Neeson, Laura Sàn Giacomo, Kenneth Cranham, Alphonsia Emmanuel, Stephen Moore. D: Simon Moore. CRI [R] 99m. V

Under Ten Flags 1960 ★★★ WWII naval action drama told from viewpoint of German commander cleverly eluding capture by British warships hot on his trail. Suspenseful, involving. C: Van Heflin, Charles Laughton, Mylene Demongeot, John Ericson, Cecil Parker, Liam Redmond, Alex Nicol. D: Duilio Coletti. ACT 92m.

Under the Biltmore Clock 1985 ★★★½ A 1920s flapper (Young) gets more than she bargained for when she tries to marry into a wealthy family. Delightful adaptation of F. Scott Fitzgerald's short story, "Myra Meets His Family." C: Sean Young, Lenny Von Dohlen, Barnard Hughes. D: Neal Miller. COM 90m. TVM V

Under the Boardwalk 1989 ★ Venice Beach surfers and San Fernando Valley interlopers undergo sub-Shakespearean crises when two members of these opposing factions become star-crossed lovers. Teenaged-aimed comedy. C: Richard Joseph Paul, Danielle Van Zerneck, Sonny Bono, Roxana Zal, Tracey Walter, Keith Coogan. D: Fritz Kiersch. COM [R] 102m. V

Under the Cherry Moon 1986 ★★ Ego-fest for rock star Prince features him as gigolo wooing rich Scott-Thomas while her father tries to halt romance. Directed by Prince, with clumsy staging and laughably amateurish acting. Plenty of facades and posing but no substance. C: Prince, Jerome Benton, Kristin Scott Thomas, Steven Berkoff, Francesca Annis, Emmanuelle Sallet. D: Prince. COM [PG-13] 98m. V

Under the Gun 1988 ★★½ Another movie about unsuitable companions—a police officer (Jones) bent on avenging the death of his brother, and a lawyer (Williams)—who must to work together. Fast-paced but predictable. C: Sam Jones, Vanessa Williams, John Russell, Michael Halsey, Nick Cassavetes. D: James Sbardellati. ACT [R] 90m. V

Under the Rainbow 1981 ★ When detective (Chase) investigates spy case involving Nazis and Japanese, he encounters the little people playing Munchkins in *The Wizard of Oz.* Painfully dismal comedy without an iota of humor, Chase sinks to incredible career depths. C: Chevy Chase, Carrie Fisher, Eve Arden, Adam Arkin, Billy Barty. D: Steve Rash. COM [PG] 97m. V

Under the Red Robe 1937 British ★★★★ Well-made swashbuckler stars Veidt as heroic soldier-of-fortune working against his will for the sinister Cardinal Richelieu (Massey) to uncover Huguenot plot. Annabella co-stars as love interest. Entertaining costume drama, lots of action. C: Conrad Veidt, Raymond Massey, Annabella, Romney Brent. D: Victor Seastrom. ACT 82m. V

Under the Roofs of Paris 1930 French ★★★★½ Early French talkie uses clever mix of silent and sound techniques in wonderful telling of simple story of three lovers. A beautifully acted film, directed with a light, sure touch. Exquisite. C: Albert Prejean, Pola Illery, Gaston Modot. D: Rene Clair. DRA 92m. V

Under the Sun of Rome 1949 Italian ★★★½ Gritty, neorealistic look at a group of post-WWII Roman adolescents, focuses on one youth (Blando). An ambitious film; the episodic plot works well, but flawed by romantic subplot. A good example of postwar Italian cinema. C: Oscar Blando, Liliana Mancini, Francesco Golisano. D: Renato Castellani. DRA 100m.

Under the Sun of Satan 1987 French ★★★½ Heavily stylized account of country priest Depardieu, who cannot abide his own imagined sins and faces temptation from various characters, one of whom may be Satan in disguise. Intense exploration of faith will engross some and leave others cold; but Depardieu's performance is undeniably strong. (a.k.a. *Under Satan's Sun*) C: Gerard Depardieu, Sandrine Bonnaire. D: Maurice Pialat. DRA 98m. V

Under the Tonto Rim 1947 ★★★ Stagecoach driver is out for revenge after his coach is held up and another driver is killed. Briskly paced B-Western. C: Tim Holt, Nan Leslie, Richard Martin, Richard Powers. D: Lew Landers. WST 61m.

Under the Volcano 1984 ★★★★½ Uncompromising character study of British diplomat (Finney, in superb Oscar-nominated performance), whose life has become one long alcoholic bender. Death symbols cropping up throughout film, set in Mexico on eve of WWII, grimly foreshadow the ending. Exceptional piece of work. Based on the novel by Malcolm Lowry. C: Albert Finney, Jacqueline Bisset, Anthony Andrews, Katy Jurado. D: John Huston. DRA [R] 109m. V

Under the Yum Yum Tree 1963 ★★★½ If it weren't for likable Lemmon playing a lecherous landlord chasing Lynley, this sex comedy might be offensive. As it is, it's mildly enjoyable. C: Jack Lemmon, Carol Lynley, Dean Jones, Edie Adams, Paul Lynde. D: David Swift. COM 110m.

Under Two Flags 1936 ★★★★ Tragic cafe girl (Colbert) saves her true love (Colman) and band of French legionnaires from murderous desert tribesman. Lavishly produced adaptation revival of popular novel (made twice before as a silent film), with superb action sequences, dashing Colman, and a cast of thousands. C: Ronald Colman, Claudette Colbert, Victor McLaglen, Rosalind Russell,

Gregory Ratoff, Nigel Bruce, Herbert Mundin, John Carradine, J. Edward Bromberg. D: Frank Lloyd. ACT 96m.

Under Western Skies 1938 ★★★ Rogers is very good in his first feature film as a young congressman fighting to get waterpower for his drought-ravaged constituency. His song, "Dust," got an Oscar nomination. C: Roy Rogers, Smiley Burnette, Carol Hughes. D: Joseph Cane. WST 67m. V

Undercover Blues 1993 ★★ Turner and Quaid are utterly wasted in this weary farce of secret agents involved in post-Cold War intrigue while caring for their baby. C: Kathleen Turner, Dennis Quaid, Park Overall, Tom Arnold. D: Herbert Ross. CRI [PG-13] 100m. V

Undercover Man, The 1949 ★★★★ U.S. Treasury agent (Ford) gets the goods on a Capone-like gangster and gets him convicted for tax evasion. Suspenseful, convincingly realistic drama. C: Glenn Ford, Nina Foch, James Whitmore, Barry Kelley, Howard St. John. D: Joseph H. Lewis. CRI 85m.

Undercurrent 1946 ★★★ A woman (Hepburn) marries dreamy, ultrarich man (Taylor), and soon suspects he may not be an upstanding gentleman. More melodrama than thriller; best for devoted Hepburn fans. C: Katharine Hepburn, Robert Taylor, Robert Mitchum, Edmund Gwenn, Marjorie Main, Jayne Meadows. D: Vincente Minnelli. CRI 111m. V

Undergound 1941 ★★★★ WWII action drama of two German brothers, one (Lynn) a soldier loyal to Hitler and the other (Dorn) an anti-Nazi conspiring to aid the Allies. Fine acting and vivid plot. C: Jeffrey Lynn, Philip Dorn, Kaaren Verne, Mona Maris, Frank Reicher, Martin Kosleck. D: Vincent Sherman. ACT 95m.

Underground Agent 1942 ★★★½ Government agent investigates fascist snooping at top-secret defense plant. Basic WWII espionage thriller helped by good cast. C: Bruce Bennett, Leslie Brooks, Frank Albertson. D: Michael Gordon. DRA 70m.

Undertow 1949 ★★★ Drama about ex-racketeer (Brady) falsely accused of murdering a former associate. Well put together, though predictable. Effective Brady. Look for a youthful Rock Hudson in a small role. C: Scott Brady, John Russell, Dorothy Hart, Peggy Dow, Bruce Bennett, Gregg Martell. D: William Castle. CRI 71m.

Underwater! 1955 ★★ Howard Hughes produced this soggy tale of scuba-diving treasure hunters mainly as a showcase for Russell, but Mansfield's presence is a distraction. C: Jane Russell, Gilbert Roland, Richard Egan, Jayne Mansfield. D: John Sturges. ACT 99m. V

Underworld 1927 ★★★★ Groundbreaking crime film follows a gangster (Bancroft), fighting to stay on top in the Chicago underworld. This riveting silent film set the style for many gangster pictures that came after. Stylish and exciting. C: George Bancroft, Evelyn Brent, Clive Brook, Larry Semon. D: Josef von Sternberg. CRI 75m.

Underworld U.S.A. 1961 ★★★½ The Mob and the FBI are at war, and a loner (Robertson) out to avenge his father's brutal murder gets caught in the middle. Violent, but visually effective piece. C: Cliff Robertson, Dolores Dorn, Beatrice Kay, Robert Emhardt, Larry Gates, Richard Rust. D: Samuel Fuller. CRI 99m. V

Une Femme Douce 1971 *See* **Gentle Creature, A**

Une Fille et Des Fusils 1967 *See* **To Be a Crook**

Unearthly Stranger, The 1964 British ★★★ A beautiful alien falls in love with the man whose research project (a time-space formula) she was dispatched to Earth to destroy. Modestly produced science fiction film has some surprisingly effective moments. C: John Neville, Gabriella Licudi, Philip Stone, Jean Marsh. D: John Krish. SFI 75m.

Unexpected Guest 1946 ★★★½ Woman and her five relatives inherit a ranch. When the relatives start dropping like flies it's Hopalong Cassidy to the rescue. Suspenseful B-Western. C: William Boyd, Andy Clyde, Rand Brooks, Una O'Connor. D: George Archainbaud. WST 59m. V

Unfaithful, The 1947 ★★★★ Sheridan shines in drama of straying wife who kills lover and must cover up the crime. Remake of *The Letter*, with Sheridan taking an interesting approach. Fine supporting cast, too. Catch it. C: Ann Sheridan, Lew Ayres, Zachary Scott, Eve Arden, Steven Geray, John Hoyt. D: Vincent Sherman. DRA 109m.

Unfaithfully Yours 1948 ★★★★★ Paranoid orchestra conductor (Harrison) is convinced his wife (Darnell) is having an affair. He fantasizes revenge and murder as he conducts three hilariously appropriate pieces of classical music. Clever, funny film, with an outstanding comedic performance by Harrison. Remade in 1984. C: Rex Harrison, Linda Darnell, Rudy Vallee, Barbara Lawrence, Kurt Kreuger, Lionel Stander. D: Preston Sturges. COM 105m.

Unfaithfully Yours 1984 ★★★ Coarse remake of Preston Sturges's semi-classic stars Moore as an orchestra conductor who, convinced that his wife (Kinski) is having an affair, plots his revenge. C: Dudley Moore, Nastassja Kinski, Armand Assante, Albert Brooks. D: Howard Zieff. COM [PG] 96m. V

Unfinished Business 1941 ★★★ Opera singer (Dunne) bounces between the man she loves (Foster) and his brother (Montgomery), whom she marries. Uneven comedy/drama showcase for the very appealing star. C: Irene Dunne, Robert Montgomery, Preston Foster, Eugene Pallette. D: Gregory La Cava. COM 96m.

Unfinished Dance, The 1947 ★★★ Minor vehicle for child star O'Brien casts her as a star-struck balletomane whose obsession with a dancer (Charisse) leads to a near-tragic climax. Sentimental drama, with good dance sequences. Thomas's film debut. C: Margaret O'Brien, Cyd Charisse, Karin Booth, Danny Thomas. D: Henry Koster. DRA 101m.

Unfinished Journey of Robert F. Kennedy, The 1969 ★★★★½ Thoughtful, moving personal study of crusading politician and U.S. Attorney General as seen through the eyes of friends, family and associates. D: Mel Stuart. DOC 75m. TVM

Unfinished Symphony, The 1953 Australian ★★★½ Impoverished, unknown composer Franz Schubert tries to finish his symphony while wooing a princess. Better-than-average biography; divine music. C: Martha Eggerth, Hans Yaray, Helen Chandler, Ronald Squire. D: Willy Forst. DRA 84m.

Unforgiven 1992 ★★★★½ Poetic anti-Western attacks the glorification of violence as an ex-killer comes back for one last hit. Quirky dialogue and great acting bring an excellent screenplay to life. Winner of four Oscars, including Best Picture, Best Director, and Best Supporting Actor (Hackman). C: Clint Eastwood, Gene Hackman, Morgan Freeman, Richard Harris, Jaimz Woolvett, Frances Fisher. D: Clint Eastwood. WST [R] 130m. V

Unforgiven, The 1960 ★★★★ Great acting, and great direction from Huston, lift this Western above the competition. Hepburn plays the central character in the film, treated as one of their own by the Native Americans and coveted by two separate groups of Texas settlers. C: Burt Lancaster, Audrey Hepburn, Audie Murphy, Lillian Gish. D: John Huston. WST 125m. V

Unguarded Hour, The 1936 ★★★½ Suspense thriller about a blackmailed woman (Young) forced to keep the truth about a murder to herself or risk losing her husband. Nice twisty plot and good cast. C: Loretta Young, Franchot Tone, Lewis Stone, Roland Young, Jessie Ralph, Dudley Digges, Henry Daniell, Aileen Pringle. D: Sam Wood. CRI 90m.

Unguarded Moment, The 1956 ★★½ A school teacher (Williams) is blackmailed by disturbed pupil and his equally unstable father. Swimming star Williams is in dry-dock and she does fine, though the story could have used a splash of something. C: Esther Williams, George Nader, John Saxon, Edward Andrews, Les Tremayne, Jack Albertson. D: Harry Keller. DRA 95m.

Unholy Partners 1941 ★★★½ Shaky alliance between newspaper publisher (Robinson) and mobster (Arnold) is threatened. Good tug-of-war drama, and these two sure can handle it. Day is terrific, too, as Robinson's secretary. Intriguing. C: Edward G. Robinson, Edward Arnold, Laraine Day, Marsha Hunt, William Orr, Don Beddoe, Walter Kingsford. D: Mervyn LeRoy. DRA 94m.

Unholy, The 1988 ★★★ Cross plays a priest assigned to exorcise a New Orleans church. Eerie and intriguing horror film, it sets up a classic showdown, but doesn't quite deliver. C: Ben Cross, Hal Holbrook, Trevor Howard, Ned Beatty. D: Camilo Vila. HOR [R] 105m. V

Unholy Three, The 1925 ★★★★ A ventriloquist (Chaney) enlists a circus muscleman and midget to form a crime gang. Offbeat silent thriller, with strong performances. Remade as a talkie in 1930 (also with Chaney, in his only post-silent movie appearance). C: Lon Chaney, Victor McLaglen, Harry Earley, Mae Busch, Matt Moore. D: Tod Browning. CRI 86m.

Unholy Three, The 1930 ★★★½ Remake of Chaney's own 1925 silent. A ventriloquist who commits robberies with circus cohorts has his conscience pricked when an innocent man is arrested for his crimes. A tour de force by the multitalented Chaney. C: Lon Chaney, Lila Lee, Elliott Nugent, Harry Earles, John Miljan, Ivan Linow. D: Jack Conway. DRA 72m.

Unholy Wife, The 1957 ★★ Young woman (Dors), out to murder her wealthy husband, kills the wrong man. Boy, is she in trouble. Could have been better. C: Rod Steiger, Diana Dors, Tom Tryon, Beulah Bondi. D: John Farrow. DRA 94m. V

Unidentified Flying Oddball 1979 ★★★★ Mark Twain's story, *A Connecticut Yankee in King Arthur's Court*, with a 20th-century twist: The Yankee is an astronaut. Excellent family entertainment has good guys (Arthur, Gawain, astronaut) triumphing over bad guys (Mordred and Merlin). Imaginative, well-worked special effects. Time travel fun. (a.k.a. *The Spaceman in King Arthur's Court*) C: Dennis Dugan, Jim Dale, Ron Moody, Kenneth More. D: Russ Mayberry. COM [G] 92m. V

Uninvited, The 1944 ★★★★½ Must-see for fans of great ghost stories. Russell plays a woman haunted by her dead mother, who then involves Milland and Hussey in the chilling mystery. Truly bloodcurdling. C: Ray Milland, Ruth Hussey, Donald Crisp, Gail Russell, Cornelia Skinner, Dorothy Stickney, Barbara Everest, Alan Napier. D: Lewis Allen. HOR 98m. V

Union Depot 1932 ★★★★ A busy, bustling train station brings together all sorts of people, including a hustler (Fairbanks) and a chorus dancer, (Blondell). Great ensemble acting with scads of subplots. Forerunner of modern airport/hotel dramas is lively, energetic, and wittily scripted. All aboard. C: Douglas Fairbanks Jr., Joan Blondell, Guy Kibbee, Alan Hale, David Landau, Frank McHugh. D: Alfred Green. DRA 75m.

Union Pacific 1939 ★★★★½ McCrea is the brawny hero in this blockbuster action Western about the building of the first transcontinental railroad. Strong narrative enlivened by great action sequences involving Indians on the warpath, the U.S. cavalry, and a railroad chase and wreck. McCrea, Stanwyck, DeMille—what are you waiting for? Hop on. C: Barbara Stanwyck, Joel McCrea, Robert Preston, Akim Tamiroff, Brian Donlevy, Anthony Quinn, Lynne Overman, Evelyn Keyes, Fuzzy Knight, J.M. Kerrigan, Stanley Ridges, Regis Toomey. D: Cecil B. DeMille. WST 135m.

Union Station 1950 ★★★½ A blind woman is kidnapped, with planned ransom drop at Chicago's railroad terminal. Kidnapper gets away, and manhunt ensues. Suspense thriller is not the most believable, but Bettger and Fitzgerald keep it going. C: William Holden, Nancy Olson, Barry Fitzgerald, Jan Sterling, Allene Roberts, Lyle Bettger. D: Rudolph Maté. DRA 80m. v

Universal Soldier 1992 ★★★ Van Damme and Lundgren star as military androids constructed from deceased soldiers in this entertaining action flick with a touch of sci-fi. The two remember that, when alive, they were mortal enemies, and continue their feud. C: Jean-Claude Van Damme, Dolph Lundgren, Ally Walker, Ed O'Ross, Jerry Orbach, Leon Rippy, Tico Wells, Ralph Moeller. D: Roland Emmerich. ACT [R] 102m. v

University of Life 1941 Russian ★★★★ Young Maxim Gorky frequents shipyards to get a taste of worker's life. Thoughtful, often brutal film based on Gorky's memoirs. C: N. Valbert, S. Kayukov, N. Dorokhin. D: Mark Donskoy. DRA 90m.

Unknown Satellite Over Tokyo 1956 *See* **Mysterious Satellite, The**

Unknown World 1951 ★★ Scientists attempt to escape nuclear destruction by tunneling to the center of the Earth via a mechanical mole device called the Cyclotram. Underachiever, but not exactly a bore, dig? C: Bruce Kellogg, Marilyn Nash, Victor Kilian, Jim Bannon. D: Terrell O. Morse. SFI 86m. v

Unlawful Entry 1992 ★★★½ A security specialist/cop/psychopath (Liotta) has a crush on Russell's wife (Stowe), and will stop at nothing to have her. Slick production and a fine cast highlight this often implausible thriller. A tighter script would have helped. C: Kurt Russell, Ray Liotta, Madeline Stowe, Roger E. Mosley, Ken Lerner, Deborah Offner. D: Jonathan Kaplan. CRI [R] 110m. v

Unman, Wittering and Zigo 1971 British ★★★★ Unusual, creepy mystery about a schoolteacher at a boys' school (Hemmings) who discovers his immediate predecessor was murdered by his students . . . and that he might be next. More than just a weird title, this well-photographed, witty, cleverly written sleeper deserves a wider audience. C: David Hemmings, Carolyn Seymour, Douglas Wilmer, Hamilton Dyce, Anthony Haygarth, Donald Gee. D: John Mackenzie. DRA [PG] 102m.

Unmarried Woman, An 1978 ★★★★½ In this compassionate and romantic comedy that made a star out of Clayburgh, a New York housewife, abandoned by her husband, finds that she can survive quite well without him. C: Jill Clayburgh, Alan Bates, Michael Murphy, Cliff Gorman. D: Paul Mazursky. COM [R] 124m. v

Unnameable, The 1988 ★ H.P. Lovecraft story about indescribable evil haunting an old mansion becomes a generic film about college students falling victim one by one to a not-very-mysterious monster. Clichéd plotting results in tedium. C: Charles King, Mark Kinsey Stephenson, Alexandra Durrell, Laura Albert. D: Jean-Paul Ouellette. HOR [R] 87m. v

Unnameable II, The 1992 ★★ Student takes up with ancient monster's beautiful alter ego while her beastly half goes on a bloody rampage. Better than its predecessor, with a few decent scares, but lacks the dread of the Lovecraft stories that inspired it. C: John Rhys-Davies, Mark Kinsey Stephenson, Maria Ford, David Warner. D: Jean-Paul Ouellette. HOR [R] 104m. v

Unnatural Causes 1987 ★★★★ Riveting drama about U.S. government's attempt to cover up effects of Agent Orange chemical on Vietnam vets. Excellent and mature portrayals of the people who worked to make the government accountable. C: John Ritter, Alfre Woodard, Patti LaBelle, John Sayles. D: Lamont Johnson. DRA 96m. TVM v

Unremarkable Life, An 1989 ★★½ The title is appropriate in this slow-moving tale of elderly sisters still arguing over petty squabbles that have consumed their lives. C: Patricia Neal, Shelley Winters, Mako, Rochelle Oliver. D: Amin Q. Chaudhri. DRA [PG] 97m. v

Unsane 1982 Italian ★★½ Drab plot—Franciosa plays a man who is dogged by repeated death threats—somewhat enlivened by exciting camera work and attractive visuals. Only for those who like their movies gory. C: Anthony Franciosa, John Saxon, Daria Nicolodi, John Steiner. D: Dario Argento. HOR [PG] 91m. v

Unseen, The 1945 ★★½ Wealthy family's governess (Russell) discovers her job entails solving an eerie mystery as well as childcare. Premise is interesting, but the ending is flawed. C: Joel McCrea, Gail Russell, Herbert Marshall, Phyllis Brooks, Isobel Elsom, Norman Lloyd. D: Lewis Allen. HOR 81m.

Unsettled Land 1988 ★★ Young Palestinians must struggle for control of their land in the '20s Middle East; viewers must struggle to pay attention. C: Kelly McGillis, John Shea, Arnon Zadok, Christine Boisson. D: Uri Barbash. DRA [PG] 109m. v

Unsinkable Molly Brown, The 1964 ★★★★ Reynolds works almost too hard as Molly, a backwoods young woman who overcomes poverty, prejudice, and the sinking of the *Titanic* to become the richest woman in Denver in the late 1800s. Based on the Broadway musical. C: Debbie Reynolds, Harve Presnell, Ed Begley. D: Charles Walters. MUS 128m. V

Unsuspected, The 1947 ★★★★ Dapper, silken-tongued radio personality (Rains) gets away with murder and plans to press his luck in this tense film noir. Caulfield is good as his vulnerable, unsuspecting niece. C: Claude Rains, Joan Caulfield, Audrey Totter, Constance Bennett, Hurd Hatfield, Michael North. D: Michael Curtiz. DRA 103m.

Untamed 1929 ★★★½ An uncouth heiress (Crawford) travels to New York to learn some social skills, and falls for a penniless man (Montgomery) en route. Crawford's first talkie is a fairly routine romance, but she gets by just fine, even getting to sing and dance the "Chant of the Jungle." C: Joan Crawford, Robert Montgomery, Ernest Torrence. D: Jack Conway. DRA 88m.

Untamed 1940 ★★½ Brave doctor (Milland) faces an epidemic and a blizzard in the far frozen north. Against-all-odds adventure tries hard. Remake of 1926 Clara Bow film *Mantrap*. C: Ray Milland, Patricia Morison, Akim Tamiroff, William Frawley, Jane Darwell, Esther Dale. D: George Archainbaud. WST 83m.

Untamed 1955 ★★★½ Love among the Zulus, as a feisty Irish heroine (Hayward) follows her man (Power) to Africa, where she sparks a lot of squabbling and colorful action sequences. Utterly ridiculous, and utterly entertaining. C: Tyrone Power, Susan Hayward, Agnes Moorehead, Richard Egan, Rita Moreno, John Justin. D: Henry King. ACT 111m.

Untamed Heart 1993 ★★★½ Tomei's effervescent performance as diner waitress attracted to shy, odd busboy (Slater) is the best reason to see this well-meaning, but contrived romance. C: Christian Slater, Marisa Tomei, Rosie Perez, Kyle Secor, Willie Carson. D: Tony Bill. DRA [PG-13] 104m. V

Until September 1984 ★★★ An American stranded in Paris (Allen) finds herself falling in love with a married banker. Romance with a lovely Parisian setting, more of a postcard than a movie. C: Karen Allen, Thierry Lhermitte, Christopher Cazenove, Nitza Saul. D: Richard Marquand. DRA [R] 96m. V

Until the End of the World 1991 ★★★½ Dommartin and Hurt team up to travel the world in order to solve an enigmatic puzzle, encountering bizarre characters along the way. Cryptic, arty mystery with deadpan sense of humor. C: William Hurt, Solveig Dommartin, Sam Neill, Max von Sydow, Jeanne Moreau, Rudiger Vogler. D: Wim Wenders. DRA [R] 158m. V

Until They Sail 1957 ★★★½ Four sisters in New Zealand are involved in bittersweet wartime romances and foul play. Above-average, well-cast soap opera, based on a story by James Michener. Intriguing sister ensemble. C: Paul Newman, Joan Fontaine, Jean Simmons, Sandra Dee, Piper Laurie, Charles Drake, Patrick Macnee, Dean Jones. D: Robert Wise. DRA 95m. V

Untouchables, The 1987 ★★★★½ G-man Eliot Ness and his small band of deputies bring notorious Chicago crime boss Al Capone to justice. Superb direction, acting, and dialogue make this a modern gangster classic. Connery's Oscar-winning performance as a veteran street cop, and the train station shoot-out are spectacular. C: Kevin Costner, Sean Connery, Charles Martin Smith, Andy Garcia, Robert De Niro, Richard Bradford. D: Brian De Palma. CRI [R] 119m. V

Unvanquished, The 1957 *See* **Aparajito**

Up Against the Wall 1991 ★★★½ Inner-city youth gets chance to escape harsh home environment for a school in the suburbs, but finds drugs and violence there as well. Somewhat effective, when it isn't sermonizing. C: Marla Gibbs, Stoney Jackson, Catero Colbert. D: Ron O'Neal. DRA [PG-13] 103m. V

Up for the Cup 1950 British ★★½ Remake of popular 1931 film about a Yorkshireman who comes to London for sporting finals. Good slapstick farce, the British way. C: Albert Modley, Mai Bacon, Helen Christie. D: Jack Raymond. COM 76m.

Up From the Beach 1965 ★★★★ A G.I. (Robertson) tries to assist French civilians liberated from the Nazis after D-Day. Effective WWII drama puts the emphasis on human relationships, not battles. C: Cliff Robertson, Irina Demick, Red Buttons, Marius Goring. D: Robert Parrish. DRA 99m.

Up Front 1951 ★★★ Wayne and Ewell play live action versions of cartoonist Mauldin's weary and wise G.I.s Willie and Joe, in this WWII comedy set in Italy. Some fun. C: David Wayne, Tom Ewell, Marina Berti, Jeffrey Lynn, Richard Egan. D: Alexander Hall. COM 92m.

Up in Arms 1944 ★★★★ In his film debut, Kaye plays a hypochondriac who's drafted and accidentally smuggles his girlfriend aboard his Pacific-bound troopship. Pleasant Kaye shenanigans with lots of good music, fine Dinah. C: Danny Kaye, Dana Andrews, Constance Dowling, Dinah Shore, Virginia Mayo. D: Elliott Nugent. MUS 105m. V

Up In Central Park 1948 ★★½ A reporter (Haymes) works to expose a crooked politician in turn-of-the-century New York, while his lady love (Durbin) seizes every opportunity to sing. Sigmund Romberg Broadway musical proves to be a weak vehicle for the charming Durbin. C: Deanna Durbin, Dick Haymes, Vincent Price. D: William A. Seiter. MUS 88m.

Up in Mabel's Room 1944 ★★★½ An old flame (Patrick) shows up, complicating the life of a happily married man (O'Keefe) who wants to keep the evidence of the former relationship from his wife (Reynolds). Bedroom farce with some very funny moments and good trooping by O'Keefe. C: Dennis O'Keefe, Marjorie Reynolds, Gail Patrick, Mischa Auer, Charlotte Greenwood, Lee Bowman. D: Allan Dwan. COM 76m.

Up in Smoke 1978 *See* **Cheech and Chong—Up in Smoke**

Up in the Cellar 1970 ★★★½ Unstable college freshman (Stern) plots to get even with his school president (Hagman) by seducing the man's wife, daughter, and mistress. Dated, but witty screenplay has some genuinely funny bits. (a.k.a. *Three in the Cellar*) C: Wes Stern, Joan Collins, Larry Hagman, Judy Pace. D: Theodore Flicker. COM [R] 92m. V

Up Periscope 1959 ★★★ Garner stars as Navy lieutenant transferred to submarine duty. Typical of the slew of WWII movies made during this period, where sailors contemplate life as their destinies gravitate toward a violent climax. Competent but routine. C: James Garner, Edmond O'Brien, Andra Martin, Alan Hale, Carleton Carpenter, Frank Gifford. D: Gordon Douglas. ACT 111m. V

Up the Academy 1980 ★★ Sophomoric teen comedy, set in an all boys' military school, features a predictable mix of gross-out humor and sexual situations. (a.k.a. *Mad Magazine Presents Up the Academy*) C: Ron Leibman, Wendell Brown, Ralph Macchio. D: Robert Downey. COM [R] 88m. V

Up the Creek 1984 ★★★½ Above-average youth comedy assembles the usual gang of losers, jocks, and preppies for a spirited raft race. Cheerful, spirited comedy with plenty of laughs and some striking whitewater footage. C: Tim Matheson, Jennifer Runyon, Stephen Furst, Dan Monahan. D: Robert Butler. COM [R] 95m. V

Up the Down Staircase 1967 ★★★★½ Excellent drama about young idealistic New York City schoolteacher (Dennis) learning to cope with the system while trying to educate her students. Intelligent, captivating story; a great job by Dennis and all concerned. Adapted from Bel Kaufman's popular book. Memorable. C: Sandy Dennis, Patrick Bedford, Eileen Heckart, Ruth White, Jean Stapleton, Sorrell Booke, Roy Poole, Ellen O'Mara. D: Robert Mulligan. DRA 124m. V

Up the River 1930 ★★★½ Ex-con (Bogart) is lent a helping hand by two pals (Tracy and Hymer) who break out of prison to be at his side. Enjoyable comedy notable for its teaming of future superstars Bogart (in his second film role) and Tracy (in his first). C: Spencer Tracy, Claire Luce, Warren Hymer, Humphrey Bogart, William Collier Sr. D: John Ford. COM 92m.

Up The River 1938 ★★★½ Fair remake of 1930 Bogart/Tracy film, with Preston Foster and Tony Martin in those roles. The leads are less charismatic (though who wouldn't be?), but the script still holds up. C: Preston Foster, Tony Martin. D: Alfred Werker. COM 75m.

Up the Sandbox 1972 ★★★½ Streisand is in top form dramatically in an atypical role as a frustrated housewife/mother in New York, who finds release in strange daydreams. Wildly uneven, with Castro fantasy the highlight. C: Barbra Streisand, David Selby, Jane Hoffman, John C. Becher, Jacobo Morales, Iris Brooks. D: Irvin Kershner. COM [R] 98m. V

Up to His Ears 1965 French ★★★★ Depressed millionaire (Belmondo) contacts a paid assassin to kill him and end his troubles, then changes his mind after he meets a voluptuous stripper (Andress). Problem is, he can't call the assassin off. Twisty, fast-moving comedy full of slapstick. C: Jean Belmondo, Ursula Andress, Maria Pacome, Valerie Lagrange, Jess Hahn. D: Philippe de Broca. COM 94m.

Up to the Neck 1933 British ★★★½ Bank clerk inherits a fortune, quits his job and tries his hand at big-time theater producing. Creaky comedy has its share of laughs. C: Ralph Lynn, Winifred Shotter. D: Jack Raymond. COM 73m.

Upperworld 1934 ★★★★ Social-climbing wife (Astor) ignores her wealthy husband (William) and he finds consolation with a young burlesque star (Rogers). Stylish romantic melodrama is entertaining and well-acted. C: Warren William, Mary Astor, Ginger Rogers, Dickie Moore, Andy Devine, J. Carroll Naish, Mickey Rooney, Sidney Toler. D: Roy Del Ruth. DRA 72m. V

Uptown Angel ★★½ Young black woman struggles to better herself despite problems and pressures at home and in her neighborhood. Familiar, earnest drama. C: Caron Tate, Cliff McMullen, Gloria Davis Hill. D: Joy Shannon. DRA 90m. V

Uptown Saturday Night 1974 ★★★½ Con artists (Poitier and Cosby) try to retrieve stolen lottery ticket from godfatherly gangster (Belafonte). Caper comedy misses right pace, though performances are fun. Pryor's supporting role steals the show. Two sequels, *Let's Do It Again* and *A Piece of the Action*, followed. C: Sidney Poitier, Bill Cosby, Harry Belafonte, Flip Wilson, Richard Pryor. D: Sidney Poitier. COM [PG] 104m. V

Uranus 1991 French ★★★½ A great cast is the chief asset of this complicated drama, set in a French village after WWII where various groups vie for power. Avoids taking political sides, which weakens dramatic thrust, but there are many vivid scenes. C: Philippe Noiret, Gerard Depardieu, Jean-Pierre Marielle, Michel Blanc, Gerard Desarthe. D: Claude Berri. DRA [R] 100m. V

Urban Cowboy 1980 ★★★★ Steamy romance between Texas oil worker (Travolta)

and a strong young woman (Winger), played out against the backdrop of dancing and mechanical bull riding at a country-western nightclub. Packed with music, film tries hard to present a slice-of-life portrait of American "manhood." Based on Aaron Lathom's magazine articles. C: John Travolta, Debra Winger, Scott Glenn, Madolyn Smith. D: James Bridges. DRA [PG] 132m. v

Urga 1992 *See* **Close to Eden**

Used Cars 1980 ★★★★ Russell is a used-car sales rep who refuses to let his boss (Warden) lose his lot to his evil twin brother (also Warden)—even after the old guy dies. Hilarious exercise in often appalling taste is pulled off by sharp cast and energetic filmmaking. C: Kurt Russell, Jack Warden, Gerrit Graham, Frank McRae, Deborah Harmon. D: Robert Zemeckis. COM [R] 111m. v

Used People 1992 ★★★½ Jewish widow finds herself being romanced by Italian widower, who has secretly loved her for two decades. Ethnic comedy clash with pleasant cast and obvious stereotypes drive humorous situations. C: Shirley MacLaine, Kathy Bates, Jessica Tandy, Marcello Mastroianni, Marcia Gay Hayden, Sylvia Sidney. D: Beeban Kidron. COM [PG-13] 116m. v

Utah 1945 ★★★ Ranch foreman (Rogers) persuades new owner, a musical comedy star (Evans), not to cash in the spread to finance a show. Rogers and Evans make it work, as usual. C: Roy Rogers, Dale Evans, George "Gabby" Hayes. D: John English. WST 55m. v

Utopia 1950 French ★★½ Duo inherits an island paradise that's uranium-rich. Last film pairing of Laurel and Hardy is above-average comedy, though below average for them. (a.k.a. *Atoll K*, *Robinson Crusoeland*, and *Escapade*) C: Stan Laurel, Oliver Hardy, Suzy Delair, Max Elloy. D: Leo Joannon. COM 83m. v

Utu 1983 New Zealand ★★★ A Maori tribesman goes on the warpath after the British army kills his family. Violent; impact is undermined by stereotyping. C: Anzac Wallace, Bruno Lawrence, Tim Elliott, Kelly Johnson. D: Geoff Murphy. CRI [R] 104m. v

Utz 1993 British-German-Italian ★★★★ A Polish baron (Mueller-Stahl) becomes obsessed with collecting German porcelain figures and hiding them from the Communist regime. Bittersweet comedy/drama makes a prime showcase for its marvelous star. C: Armin Mueller-Stahl, Brenda Fricker, Peter Riegert, Paul Scofield. D: George Sluizer. DRA 94m. v

V

V 1983 ★★★★ Outstanding TV sci-fi about seemingly human-like aliens winning political power on Earth, but resisted by rebels led by Singer. Excellent special effects bolster a powerful story. Followed by *V: The Final Battle.* C: Marc Singer, Faye Grant, Michael Durrell, Jane Badler, Robert Englund. D: Kenneth Johnson. **sfi** 180m. **tvm v**

Vacation From Marriage 1945 British ★★★★½ When ordinary British married couple go off to separate wartime duties, their dull lives are sparked by extramarital romances which change their outlooks on life, and each other. Great fun and wonderfully acted. Oscar for Best Screenplay. (a.k.a. *Perfect Strangers*) C: Robert Donat, Deborah Kerr, Glynis Johns, Ann Todd, Roland Culver, Elliot Mason. D: Alexander Korda. **com** 92m.

Vagabond 1985 French ★★★★½ Harsh, unsentimental, and ultimately moving account of young drifter Bonnaire—for whom life on the road is anything but blissful freedom—and the people she meets during her travels. Varda's screenplay and direction are beautifully straightforward and unstinting. C: Sandrine Bonnaire, Macha Meril, Stephane Freiss, Elaine Cortadellas. D: Agnes Varda. **dra** 105m. **v**

Vagabond King, The 1930 ★★★½ Romantic take on the life of free-spirited medieval poet François Villon. Earliest musical version based on excerpts from Friml's operetta, after several silents. C: Dennis King, Jeanette MacDonald, O.P. Heggie. D: Ludwig Berger. **mus** 104m.

Vagabond King, The 1956 ★★★½ Hollywood musical extravaganza of Rudolf Friml's popular operetta about medieval vagabond poet and lover François Villon. Wonderful music. C: Kathryn Grayson, Oreste, Rita Moreno, Cedric Hardwicke, Walter Hampden, Leslie Nielsen. D: Michael Curtiz. **mus** 86m.

Vagabond Lady 1935 ★★★ The sons of a wealthy department store owner fall for his private secretary (Venable). Pleasant romantic comedy. C: Robert Young, Evelyn Venable, Reginald Denny. D: Sam Taylor. **dra** 75m.

Vagabond Lover, The 1929 ★★★ An orchestra conductor/singer (Vallee) pretends to be a rich producer in this early talkie, starring the then-most popular recording star. Of interest mainly to nostalgia buffs and the curious. C: Rudy Vallee, Sally Blane, Marie Dressler. D: Marshall Neilan. **mus** 69m. **v**

Vagrant, The 1992 ★★½ A wimpy executive (Paxton) buys a house only to be harassed by homeless man who used to live there. Offbeat, satiric misfire. C: Bill Paxton, Michael Ironside, Marshall Bell, Mitzi Kapture, Colleen Camp, Stuart Pankin. D: Chris Walas. **com [R]** 91m. **v**

Valachi Papers, The 1972 Italian ★★★ Notorious gangster (Bronson) turns informer on the Mob. Violent film version of Peter Maas' fact-based bestseller about the Mafia. C: Charles Bronson, Lino Ventura, Jill Ireland, Joseph Wiseman, Walter Chiari, Amedeo Nazzari. D: Terence Young. **dra [PG]** 125m.

Valdez Horses, The *See* **Chino**

Valdez Is Coming 1971 ★★★★ Thoughtful Western as a law officer (Lancaster) is pitted against vicious landowner who oppresses the locals. The fact that Lancaster's character is both Mexican and American spices up the straightforward plot. C: Burt Lancaster, Susan Clark, Jon Cypher, Barton Heyman, Richard Jordan, Frank Silvera, Hector Elizondo. D: Edwin Sherin. **wst [PG]** 90m. **v**

Valentino 1977 ★★★ Russell's overblown bio of the legendary silent film romantic idol suffers from miscasting of ballet great Nureyev in the title role. This Rudy doesn't do that Rudy justice. C: Rudolf Nureyev, Leslie Caron, Michelle Phillips, Carol Kane. D: Ken Russell. **dra [R]** 127m. **v**

Valhalla 1989 Danish ★★★½ Two children of humankind follow the God of Thunder and an evil demigod to Valhalla. Violent, often grotesque animated film is more for adults than kids. Based on Danish comic strip. C: Stephen Thorne, Allan Corduner, Suzanne Jones, Alexander Jones, Michael Elphick, John Hollis, Mark Jones. D: Peter Madsen. **dra** 88m.

Valiant Is the Word for Carrie 1936 ★★★★½ One of the all-time great weepers, unjustly obscure, stars George as a long-suffering, childless woman who dedicates herself to caring for orphans. Women will love it, but most men will shrug their shoulders. Send them to a football game, ladies, and get out the Kleenex! C: Gladys George, John Howard, Harry Carey, Arline Judge. D: Wesley Ruggles. **dra** 110m.

Valiant, The 1929 ★★★★ Drifter Muni commits murder and is sentenced to the electric chair, but finds a way to redeem himself while in jail. Grim, often fascinating melodrama was Muni's first feature. C: Paul Muni, Marguerite Churchill, Edith Yorke. D: William K. Howard. **dra** 66m.

Valley Girl 1983 ★★★½ Minor teenage romance with Romeo and Juliet premise features punk rocker Cage falling for San Fernando Valley resident Foreman. Fresh take on age-old idea, with good performances by leads. Camp and Forest have some amusing moments as Foreman's aging hippie parents. C: Nicolas Cage, Deborah Foreman, Colleen Camp, Frederic Forrest, Elizabeth Daily, Lee Purcell, Michelle Meyrink. D: Martha Coolidge. **com [R]** 95m. **v**

Valley of Decision, The 1945 ★★★★ Effective period soap opera, with a maid (Garson) falling in love with the scion (Peck) of the wealthy family responsible for the deaths of her father and brother. Superb cast, stuffed with terrific MGM character actors. Based on the novel by Marcia Davenport. C: Greer Garson, Gregory Peck, Donald Crisp, Lionel Barrymore, Preston Foster, Gladys Cooper, Reginald Owen, Dan Duryea, Jessica Tandy. D: Tay Garnett. DRA 111m. v

Valley of Gwangi 1969 ★★½ Cowpokes O'Connolly and Franciscus happen onto hidden valley where dinosaurs roam; they try to capture one to exploit for money. Entertaining, especially the monster effects. Based on Willis O'Brien's story. C: James Franciscus, Gila Golan, Richard Carlson, Laurence Naismith, Dennis Kilbane. D: James O'Connolly. WST [G] 95m. v

Valley of Hunted Men 1942 ★★★ Escaped Nazi uses name of good-citizen German refugee so he can steal from American plant. Weird entry in *Three Mesquiteers* series suffers from too much flag waving. C: Bob Steele, Tom Tyler, Jimmie Dodd. D: John English. DRA 60m.

Valley of Song 1953 *See* **Men Are Children Twice**

Valley of the Dolls 1967 ★ All-time trash classic, from Jacqueline Susann's best-seller, tells ludicrous tale of three women on roller-coaster ride of fame, fortune, drugs, suicide, incurable diseases, etc. Filled with laughable dialogue. Hayward as veteran Broadway star provides only touch of class. C: Barbara Parkins, Patty Duke, Sharon Tate, Susan Hayward. D: Mark Robson. DRA [PG] 123m. v

Valley of the Kings 1954 ★★★ An archeologist (Taylor) on an Egyptian dig becomes distracted by his partner's wife (Parker). Okay romance with excellent location footage. C: Robert Taylor, Eleanor Parker, Carlos Thompson, Kurt Kaznar. D: Robert Pirosh. DRA 86m.

Valley of the Sun 1942 ★★★ Western restaurant owner (Ball) gets involved in a plan to counter a thieving government agent. Dusty intrigue, stolen by good supporting cast. C: Lucille Ball, James Craig, Cedric Hardwicke, Dean Jagger, Billy Gilbert, Antonio Moreno. D: George Marshall. WST 84m. v

Valley, The 1972 French ★★★ Pink Floyd score was key attraction—and is one of key assets—of this dated but well-shot chronicle of hippie types in New Guinea. Full title of this early effort from Schroeder is *The Valley Obscured by Clouds*. D: Barbet Schroeder. DRA 106m. v

Valmont 1989 French ★★★★ Third film version of de Laclos' novel *Les Liasons Dangereuses*. Forman's take, using younger actors, is lighter and perhaps more likable, but for the same reasons loses some of the original's edge. Bening's first major role. Previously filmed in 1959 and 1988. Remade in 1981 as *Jacqueline Susann's Valley of the Dolls*. C: Colin Firth, Annette Bening, Meg Tilly, Fairuza Balk, Sian Phillips, Jeffrey Jones, Henry Thomas. D: Milos Forman. DRA [R] 137m. v

Vamp 1986 ★★★ Makepeace plays a college kid out for some kicks, but he gets more than he bargains for with a female vampire (Jones). The movie's flippant take on the classic horror concept is mildly engaging. C: Chris Makepeace, Sandy Baron, Robert Rusler, Dedee Pfeiffer, Gedde Watanabe, Grace Jones. D: Richard Wenk. HOR [R] 93m. v

Vampira 1974 *See* **Old Dracula**

Vampire Bat, The 1933 ★★★½ Mad doctor (Atwill) searching for a "blood substitute" to appease demands of a supernatural bat commits rampant murder in a small town. Energetic horror film from back when, with better-than-usual cast. C: Lionel Atwill, Melvyn Douglas, Fay Wray, Dwight Frye. D: Frank Strayer. HOR 63m. v

Vampire Happening, The 1971 ★★ Silly German bloodsucker comedy has actress (Dagermark) inheriting the vampiric tendencies of her grandmother. Gimmicky, but not very funny or sexy, despite occasional orgy scenes. C: Betty Williams, Thomas Hunter, Ivor Murillo. D: Freddie Francis. HOR [R] 90m. v

Vampire Hookers 1978 ★ A vampire (Carradine) oversees a bevy of beautiful bloodsuckers who lure unsuspecting victims to his lair. Cheesy cheapie. (a.k.a. *Sensuous Vampires*) C: John Carradine, Karen Stride, Lenka Novak. D: Cirio H. Santiago. HOR [R] 82m. v

Vampire Lovers, The 1970 ★★★ A lesbian vampire (Pitt) descends upon a small town and feasts on the blood of young women. The excitement is sub-par but unusual sensuality distinguishes film. Based on story "Carmilla" by Sheridan Le Fanu. Sequels: *Lust for a Vampire* and *Twins of Evil*. C: Ingrid Pitt, Pippa Steel, Madeleine Smith, Peter Cushing, Dawn Addams. D: Roy Ward Baker. HOR [R] 91m. v

Vampire's Kiss 1989 ★★★ A Manhattan yuppie (Cage) thinks he's becoming a vampire, but may just be going nuts. Attempt at dark satire is muddled, but Cage's peformance is memorable, to say the least. C: Nicolas Cage, Maria Conchita Alonso, Jennifer Beals, Elizabeth Ashley. D: Robert Bierman. COM [R] 103m. v

Vampyr 1931 French ★★★½ An evil vampire presides over a dark castle in this classic horror film that is more known for its choreography and style than for its plot or cast. Much more pleasing to the eye than most bloodsucker movies. One of director/cinematographer Dreyer's most disturbing films. C: Julian West, Sybille Schmitz. D: Carl-Theodore Dreyer. HOR 75m. v

Vampyres 1975 ★★★ Erotic chiller about two beautiful, bisexual vampires who lure male passers-by to fatal orgies in their crumbling castle. Tension mounts when one falls in love with a potential victim. Good of its kind, with heavy doses of blood and nudity. C: Marianne Morris, Anulka, Murray Brown. D: Joseph Larraz. HOR [R] 90m. V

Van Gogh 1991 French ★★★★½ Austerely beautiful film about the last months of the painter's life. Tastefully directed by Pialat, with an intelligent performance by Dutronc in the title role. C: Jacques Dutronc, Alexandra London, Gérard Sety, Bernard Le Coq, Corinne Bourdon. D: Maurice Pialat. DRA [R] 155m. V

Vanishing Point 1971 ★★½ Newman attempts to drive halfway across the country in 15 hours without getting caught by police. On the way, he teams up with blind deejay Little. Slightly more intelligent than most chase movies, but not as much fun. C: Barry Newman, Cleavon Little, Dean Jagger, Charlotte Rampling, Paul Koslo, Robert Donner, Severn Darden, Gilda Texter, Victoria Medlin. D: Richard Sarafian. ACT [PG] 107m. V

Vanishing Prairie, The 1954 ★★★★½ Disney's Oscar-winning documentary chronicles life on the American prairie between the Mississippi River and the Rocky Mountains. Breathtaking footage and intelligent narration present an absorbing portrait of nature; calf-birthing sequence is unforgettable. Interesting portrait for both adults and children. Narrated by Winston Hibler. D: James Algar. DOC [G] 75m. V

Vanishing, The 1988 French ★★★★½ When his girlfriend mysteriously disappears, a young man spends three years trying to find out why; then a stranger appears, willing to tell all—for a price. Absorbing suspense thriller, with unusual narrative style that builds to a blood-chilling conclusion. Remade in America (by the same director) in 1993. C: Bernard-Pierre Donnadieu, Gene Bervoets, Johanna Ter Steege. D: George Sluizer. CRI 101m. V

Vanishing, The 1993 ★★½ While vacationing, Sutherland finds his girlfriend has disappeared at a rest stop and he devotes the next three years trying to find out what happened to her. But the nice-guy psycho (Bridges) who kidnapped her can't resist finally making his presence known. Fair remake of the director's earlier effort. C: Jeff Bridges, Kiefer Sutherland, Nancy Travis, Sandra Bullock, Park Overall, Maggie Linderman, Lisa Eichhorn, George Hearn, Lynn Hamilton. D: George Sluizer. CRI [R] 110m. V

Vanishing Wilderness 1974 ★★★★ All-encompassing documentary that looks at endangered species in North America from polar bears to alligators. Great nature footage and thoughtful narration make for good family viewing, though overbearing music tends to dampen dramatic effect. Narrated by actor Rex Allen. D: Arthur Dubs, Heinz Seilmann. DOC [G] 93m.

Vanya on 42nd Street 1994 ★★★★ Chekhov's classic play is staged in deserted Times Square theatre, with actors in modern dress, using virtually no sets, props or costumes. Courageous gamble pays off, as performers and director illuminate complex tale of marital infidelity. Shawn, Gregory, and Malle previously collaborated on *My Dinner with Andre*. C: Wallace Shawn, Julianne Moore, Brooke Smith, Larry Pine, Andre Gregory. D: Louis Malle. DRA [PG] 119m. V

Variety Girl 1947 ★★★ Two starstruck young women (Hatcher and San Juan) seek success in Hollywood. Many of Paramount's contract players make appearances in this feature-length advertisement for the studio, which also features cartoon segments. Some sprightly stretches, thanks to guest stars. C: Mary Hatcher, Olga San Juan, DeForest Kelley, William Demarest, Frank Faylen, Frank Ferguson. D: George Marshall. COM 83m. V

Variety Lights 1951 Italian ★★★½ A lovely young woman (Del Poggio) slogs from music hall to music hall on the road to stardom with troupe of has-been players. Charming. Fellini's first try at direction. C: Peppino De Filippo, Carla Del Poggio, Giulietta Masina. D: Federico Fellini, Alberto Lattuada. DRA 93m. V

Varsity Show 1937 ★★★½ A Broadway producer (Powell) agrees to stage a musical revue at his old college. Flimsy story is really just an excuse for a series of musical numbers, some of them quite good, culminating in a Busby Berkeley knockout. C: Dick Powell, Priscilla Lane, Fred Waring, Walter Catlett, Ted Healy, Rosemary Lane. D: William Keighley. MUS 81m.

Vault of Horror 1973 ★★★★ Five frightful E. C. Comics stories guaranteed to keep you up at night. Bizarre is beautiful. (a.k.a. *Tales from the Crypt II*) HOR

Velvet Touch, The 1948 ★★★½ Murder melodrama about a stage actress (Russell) who commits the perfect crime. Nice theatrical ambiance. Stylish, well-acted mystery really satisfies. C: Rosalind Russell, Leo Genn, Claire Trevor, Sydney Greenstreet, Leon Ames, Frank McHugh. D: John Gage. DRA 97m. V

Velvet Vampire, The 1971 ★★½ Groovy version of the vampire tale has young swingers Miles and Blodgett cooped up in the Mojave desert home of hip vampire, Yarnall. Their stay turns into a sexy and dangerous acid trip; their only hope for escape is a bunch of Christian cultists. A mess, but goofy enough to provide some fun (a.k.a. *Cemetery Girls*). C: Michael Blodgett, Celeste Yarnall, Sherry Miles. D: Stephanie Rothman. HOR [R] 82m. V

Venga Prendere un Caffé da Noi 1970 *See* **Man Who Came for Coffee, The**

Vengeance 1965 *See* **Brain, The**

Venom 1982 British ★★½ A deadly snake is loose in London, terrorizing a gang of kidnappers and their hostages. Rattling good cast, suspenseless storytelling. C: Klaus Kinski, Nicol Williamson, Sarah Miles, Oliver Reed, Sterling Hayden (last film). D: Piers Haggard. HOR [R] 98m. v

Venus in Furs 1970 British ★★ A musician (Darren) is stunned when he sees the maimed body of a woman drift ashore, and more stunned still when he subsequently sees the woman is alive. Steamy but confusing mystery. C: James Darren, Barbara McNair, Maria Rohm, Klaus Kinski. D: Jess Franco. CRI [R] 90m. v

Vera Cruz 1954 ★★★½ Set in Mexico, rival mercenaries Cooper and Lancaster work together to oust Emperor Maximilan. Along the way, they also find time to vie for the attentions of Darcel. Methodical but reasonably entertaining. C: Gary Cooper, Burt Lancaster, Denise Darcel, Cesar Romero, Serita Montiel, George Macready. D: Robert Aldrich. WST 94m. v

Verboten! 1959 ★★★½ An American G.I. and a German woman fall in love amidst turmoil of occupied, post-WWII Berlin. Powerful, brashly directed action film includes battle sequences, Nuremberg trial footage, neo-Nazi machinations, and problems of basic human survival in a war-ravaged country. Unique directorial style. C: James Best, Susan Cummings, Tom Pittman, Paul Dubov, Dick Kallman, Steven Geray. D: Samuel Fuller. ACT 93m. v

Verdict 1974 *See* **Jury of One**

Verdict, The 1946 ★★★★ Enthralling film noir murder mystery set in Victorian England, with Greenstreet as retired Scotland Yard inspector who has a score to settle with his former assistant and a perplexing case still to unravel. Lorre plays a sinister artist. Suspenseful and satisfying. C: Peter Lorre, Sydney Greenstreet, Joan Lorring, George Coulouris, Arthur Shields, Rosalind Ivan, Holmes Herbert. D: Don Siegel. DRA 86m.

Verdict, The 1982 ★★★★½ Alcoholic ambulance-chaser gets one last shot at glory, fighting a big hospital and the church in a negligence suit. Lumet is a master at this kind of charged tale of redemption in the face of corruption; Newman never better. C: Paul Newman, Charlotte Rampling, Jack Warden, James Mason, Milo O'Shea, Edward Binns, Lindsay Crouse. D: Sidney Lumet. CRI [R] 129m. v

Verne Miller 1988 ★★ Based on the true story of a law officer from the prairie who turns into one of the most infamous gangsters of the Prohibition era. Lackluster biography has very little to offer. C: Scott Glenn, Barbara Stock, Thomas D. Waites, Lucinda Jenney, Sonny Carl Davis, Andrew Robinson. D: Rod Hewitt. WST [R] 95m. v

Veronika Voss 1982 German ★★★★ Fassbinder takes an unconventional approach to the true story of an aging German movie star, a close friend of Goebbels, who became a drug addict after WWII. Tragic story is engrossing, if not the director's best work. Final installment of his postwar trilogy, after *The Marriage of Maria Braun* and *Lola*. C: Rosel Zech, Hilmar Thate, Cornelia Froboess, Annemarie Duringer, Doris Schade, Volker Spengler. D: Rainer Werner Fassbinder. DRA [R] 105m. v

Vertigo 1958 ★★★★★ Hitchcock's inspired classic about an acrophobic former detective (Stewart) who's hired by a friend to follow the latter's wife and who gets far more involved with her than he should. Strong performances and complex plot, brilliantly directed and hauntingly photographed. A masterpiece. C: James Stewart, Kim Novak, Barbara Bell Geddes, Tom Helmore, Henry Jones. D: Alfred Hitchcock. CRI [PG] 126m. v

Very Curious Girl, A 1969 French ★★★½ Young woman in a rural French town rebels against licentious local males by charging them for her "services." Many amusing complications ensue. (a.k.a. *La Fiancée du Pirate*; *Dirty Mary*; and *Pirate's Fiancée*) C: Bernadette Lafont. D: Nelly Kaplan. COM [R] 105m. v

Very Private Affair, A 1962 French-Italian ★★★ A depressed movie star (Bardot) seeks privacy in the arms of an older man (Mastroianni). The stars are not at their best, despite some flashy Malle touches. (a.k.a. *La Vie Privee*) C: Brigitte Bardot, Marcello Mastroianni, Eleonore Hirt. D: Louis Malle. DRA 95m. v

Very Special Favor, A 1965 ★★½ A Frenchman (Boyer) hires a playboy (Hudson) to initiate his daughter (Caron) into romance. Swank production puts its glittery cast in shockingly sophomoric situations. Hudson has a now-notorious scene where his character pretends to be gay. C: Rock Hudson, Leslie Caron, Charles Boyer, Walter Slezak, Dick Shawn, Nita Talbot, Larry Storch. D: Michael Gordon. COM 104m.

V.I. Warshawski 1991 ★★ Turner portrays a tough private investigator who gets involved in a deadly fight for a valuable inheritance. Refreshing twist on classic detective story bungled by inept screenplay and direction. C: Kathleen Turner, Jay O. Sanders, Charles Durning. D: Jeff Kanew. CRI [R] 90m. v

Vibes 1988 ★ Two feuding psychics vie for discovery of Ecuadoran treasure. Noisy comedy was Lauper's film debut, who's the best thing in it. C: Cyndi Lauper, Jeff Goldblum, Julian Sands, Peter Falk. D: Ken Kwapis. COM [PG] 99m. v

Vice Squad 1953 ★★★½ During a routine day's work, a police detective (Robinson) tracks down the killers of a fellow cop. Crime drama gets power and style from a crackling Robinson performance. C: Edward G. Robinson, Paulette Goddard, Porter Hall. D: Arnold Laven. CRI 87m.

Vice Squad 1982 ★★½ Hubley is a prostitute who tries to help the cops catch a serial killer. Full of violence and sex, and not much else. C: Season Hubley, Gary Swanson, Wings Hauser, Pepe Serna. D: Gary A. Sherman. ACT [R] 95m. V

Vice Squad, The 1931 ★★★½ A respected citizen (Lukas) turns police informant, which ruins his life. Effective police corruption story. C: Paul Lukas, Kay Francis. D: John Cromwell. CRI 80m.

Vice Versa 1948 ★★★★ A stuffy stockbroker and his lively son exchange personalities after wishing on a magic rock. Charming comedy, set in Victorian London. Remade loosely in 1988. C: Roger Livesey, Anthony Newley, Kay Walsh, David Hutcheson, Petula Clark. D: Peter Ustinov. COM 111m.

Vice Versa 1988 ★★★½ A mysterious Asian skull, causes father (Reinhold) and son (Savage) to switch bodies. Dad fights schoolyard bullies while son runs corporate boardroom. Amiable fun, though lacks originality. Reinhold and Savage take turns upstaging each other. C: Judge Reinhold, Fred Savage, Swoosie Kurtz, David Proval. D: Brian Gilbert. COM [PG] 97m. V

Victim 1961 British ★★★★★ A closeted homosexual lawyer (Bogarde) risks disclosure of his private life while tracking down blackmailers responsible for his lover's death. Way-ahead-of-its-time treatment of gay subject matter; a stylish, gripping, beautifully acted thriller. C: Dirk Bogarde, Sylvia Sims, Dennis Price, Peter McEnery. D: Basil Dearden. CRI 100m. V

Victim of Beauty 1992 ★★ A shy school teacher becomes an overnight supermodel and finds herself the object of a serial killer's obsession. Too many suspects and too many twists but the whiny lead is unintentionally funny at times. C: Sally Kellerman, Jennifer Rubin. D: Paul Lynch. ACT 90m. TVM V

Victims 1982 ★★★ After Nelligan is raped and the offender (Hesseman) is released, she takes the law into her own hands and hunts him down with the help of other women he has attacked. Strong acting helps this movie overcome plot flaws. C: Kate Nelligan, Ken Howard, Howard Hesseman, Madge Sinclair, Jonelle Allen, Amy Madigan, Bert Remsen, Michael Gwynne. D: Jerrold Freedman. CRI 100m. TVM

Victor/Victoria 1982 ★★★★½ A struggling singer (Andrews) in '30s Paris, poses as a female impersonator with the help of a gay friend (Preston) and becomes the talk of the town. Sparkling, perceptive script about sexual identity, terrific musical numbers, and uproarious slapstick, including memorable melee in restaurant. Preston and Warren stand out in top-notch cast. C: Julie Andrews, James Garner, Robert Preston, Lesley Ann Warren, Alex Karras, John Rhys-Davies, Peter Arne. D: Blake Edwards. COM [PG] 133m. V

Victor Frankenstein 1975 Swedish ★★★½ Doctor Frankenstein brings a dead man back to life, leading to his own ruin. Sincere adaptation of Shelley novel is more low-key and character-driven than other Frankenstein films. C: Leon Vitali, Per Oscarsson. D: Calvin Floyd. HOR 92m. TVM

Victoria the Great 1937 British ★★★★ Historical drama about the life of Britain's longest-ruling queen, with a lot of time given to her romance with Prince Albert. Stellar performances by lovely Neagle as Victoria and Walbrook as the prince. Lavishly produced, but no speedster. C: Anna Neagle, Anton Walbrook, H.B. Warner, Walter Rilla, Mary Morris, C.V. France, Charles Carson, Felix Aylmer. D: Herbert Wilcox. DRA 118m.

Victors, The 1963 ★★★★ Colorful tale of U.S. infantrymen marching through the European theater in WWII. Terrific cast (especially Moreau) and solid direction make it work. C: George Hamilton, George Peppard, Vince Edwards, Eli Wallach, Melina Mercouri, Romy Schneider, Jeanne Moreau, Peter Fonda, Senta Berger, Elke Sommer, Albert Finney. D: Carl Foreman. DRA 156m.

Victory 1940 ★★★½ East Indies recluse (March) finds both love and danger when he encounters inhabitants on a neighboring island. Engrossing adaptation of Joseph Conrad's story, filmed in 1930 as *Dangerous Paradise.* C: Fredric March, Betty Field, Cedric Hardwicke, Jerome Cowan. D: John Cromwell. DRA 78m.

Victory 1981 ★★½ WWII story has Stallone as Yankee in German POW camp, who joins prisoners' soccer team to plot an escape during a game. Mediocre and sometimes silly adventure with a sports twist. C: Sylvester Stallone, Michael Caine, Max von Sydow, Pele. D: John Huston. ACT [PG] 117m. V

Victory at Sea 1954 ★★★★½ A compilation of television documentaries, this fast-moving historical film examines naval military conflicts of WWII. Surprisingly exciting, with stirring music by Richard Rogers. D: Henry Solomon. DOC 97m. V

Video Dead, The 1987 ★★ A possessed TV set is delivered to the wrong house; zombies emerge, kill the owner and terrorize a young couple who later move in. Competent, but nothing special; the camerawork is better than the special effects and makeup. C: Michael St. Michaels, Rocky Duvall, Roxanna Augesen. D: Robert Scott. HOR [R] 90m. V

Videodrome 1983 Canadian ★★★½ Woods is excellent as programming executive obsessed by enigmatic (and deadly) television show. Special effects are exciting, but climax is a letdown after well-paced setup. C: James Woods, Sonja Smits, Deborah Harry, Peter Dvorsky, Les Carlson, Jack Creley. D: David Cronenberg. HOR [R] 88m. V

Vienna Waltzes 1961 Austrian ★★★½ When

his son's talent threatens composer Johann Strauss, he pushes the young man out of his life. Biography of the waltz king offers look at creation of wonderful music and the birth of the waltz. C: Anton Walbrook, Marthe Harell, Lilly Stepanek. D: Emile Edwin Reinert. DRA 90m.

Viennese Nights 1930 ★★★½ Early Romberg and Hammerstein musical follows the fortunes of a composer and his love. Saved from over-sentimentality by music and charming performances. Fine singing by Walter Pidgeon! C: Alexander Gray, Vivienne Segal, Jean Hersholt, Walter Pidgeon. D: Alan Crosland. MUS 107m.

View From the Bridge, A 1962 French ★★★★ Jealous Brooklyn longshoreman (Vallone) lusts after his wife's niece (Lawrence), who's fallen in love with an undocumented immigrant (Sorel). Passionate drama based on Arthur Miller's successful Broadway play and enriched by a talented international cast. C: Raf Vallone, Maureen Stapleton, Carol Lawrence, Jean Sorel, Morris Carnovsky, Harvey Lembeck, Vincent Gardenia. D: Sidney Lumet. DRA 110m.

View to a Kill, A 1985 British ★★★ Bond returns to stop Walken and Jones from blowing up Silicon Valley and cornering the microchip market. Villains are good, but whole flick is stale. C: Roger Moore, Christopher Walken, Tanya Roberts, Grace Jones, Patrick Macnee, Patrick Bauchau, Fiona Fullerton, Desmond Llewellyn, Robert Brown, Lois Maxwell. D: John Glen. ACT [PG] 131m. v

Vigil 1984 New Zealand ★★★½ Sexual tension between a widow and the stranger working at her remote New Zealand sheep farm unexplainedly results in her daughter's having mysterious, symbolic dreams that blur the line between imagination and reality. Beautiful if baffling film is a visual treat. C: Bill Kerr, Fiona Kay, Penelope Stewart, Frank Whitten. D: Vincent Ward. DRA 90m. v

Vigil in the Night 1940 ★★★ Earnest medical drama about nurses in a British hospital, from a story by A.J. Cronin. Skillful, though downbeat. C: Carole Lombard, Anne Shirley, Brian Aherne. D: George Stevens. DRA 96m.

Vikings, The 1958 ★★★★ Big-budget epic follows the adventures of Douglas and a band of Norse warriors. The movie looks great and the screenplay is engrossing, but the characters are two-dimensional. C: Kirk Douglas, Tony Curtis, Ernest Borgnine, Janet Leigh, Alexander Knox, Frank Thring. D: Richard Fleischer. ACT 114m. v

Villa Rides 1968 ★★★½ In 1912 Mexico, an American gunrunner takes an active role in local revolution. Colorful, but simplistic hodgepodge of history. Star cast does the best it can. C: Yul Brynner, Robert Mitchum, Charles Bronson, Herbert Lom, Jill Ireland, Alexander Knox, Fernando Rey. D: Buzz Kulik. WST [R] 125m. v

Village of the Damned 1960 British ★★★★ Teacher Sanders discovers that a group of seemingly emotionless children in small British town have a terrifying secret. One of the first and best evil-kid movies, often genuinely frightening—watch out for those eyes! Based on John Wyndham novel *The Midwich Cuckoos.* C: George Sanders, Barbara Shelley, Michael Gwynne, Laurence Naismith, John Phillips, Richard Vernon. D: Wolf Rilla. SFI 78m. v

Village of the Giants 1965 ★★ Eight teenagers eat tainted food and grow into 30-foot giants. Weird musical/sci-fi hybrid has some funny moments; the special effects are too cheesy for words. Inspired by the H.G. Wells novel, *The Food of the Gods.* Remade by the same director in 1976. C: Tommy Kirk, Beau Bridges, Ronny Howard, Tisha Sterling. D: Bert I. Gordon. SFI 80m. v

Villain 1971 British ★★ Homosexual kingpin (Burton) of a British gang takes his followers on a nightmare ride of violence and deception. Lurid, seamy thriller. C: Richard Burton, Ian McShane, Nigel Davenport, Donald Sinden. D: Michael Tuchner. CRI [R] 98m.

Villain, The 1979 ★★★ This slapstick takeoff on classic good-guy vs. bad-guy Westerns stars Douglas as a humorously stubborn and resilient villain. Silly in parts but worth some chuckles. C: Kirk Douglas, Ann-Margret, Arnold Schwarzenegger, Paul Lynde, Foster Brooks, Ruth Buzzi, Jack Elam, Strother Martin. D: Hal Needham. COM [PG] 88m. v

Vincent 1986 *See* **Vincent: The Life and Death of Vincent Van Gogh**

Vincent & Theo 1990 ★★★½ Unconventional biography of artist Van Gogh and his brother captures the near-madness of the painter's creative impulses, but it takes forever to get there. Good performances help somewhat. C: Tim Roth, Paul Rhys, Johanna Ter Steege, Jip Wiingaarden. D: Robert Altman. DRA [PG-13] 138m. v

Vincent, Francois, Paul and the Others 1974 French ★★★★ Group of old pals get together for weekends in the country to escape pressures of life and work and lend each other moral support. Observant, well-acted study of friendship, with fine cast of top French actors. C: Yves Montand, Michel Piccoli, Serge Reggiani, Gerard Depardieu, Stephane Audran. D: Claude Sautet. DRA 118m. v

Vincent: The Life and Death of Vincent Van Gogh 1986 Australian ★★★★ Rich, insightful documentary uses the painter's letters as part of its exploration of his life and work. Above-average examination of the creative mind narrated by John Hurt. (a.k.a. *Vincent*) D: Paul Cox. DOC 99m. v

Vineyard, The 1989 ★ A reclusive winemaker (Hong) uses more than grapes in his world-renowned vino. Naturally, zombies turn up at the end. Hamhanded combo of horror and sexploitation, and veteran actor Hong co-directed and co-wrote. C: James Hong, Karen

Winter, Michael Wong. D: James Hong. HOR [R] 95m. v

Violent City 1970 *See* **The Family**

Violent Love 1967 *See* **Take Her By Surprise**

Violent Men, The 1955 ★★★½ Ford leads downtrodden locals against rich, tyrannical rancher Robinson. Simple story is well directed and the fight scenes are excellently choreographed. Based on novel by Donald Hamilton. C: Barbara Stanwyck, Glenn Ford, Edward G. Robinson, Dianne Foster, Brian Keith, Richard Jaeckel. D: Rudolph Maté. WST 95m. v

Violent Playground 1958 British ★★★½ A juvenile liaison officer (Baker) in a tough Liverpool neighborhood falls in love with the sister (Heywood) of a young arsonist (McCallum) in this gritty, sympathetic drama with a dynamic finale. C: Stanley Baker, Anne Heywood, David McCallum, Peter Cushing. D: Basil Dearden. DRA 108m. v

Violent Saturday 1955 ★★★★ Great cast buoys this tense tale of thieves sticking up a bank in a quiet Midwestern town. Violent and effective, with some very efficient writing. C: Victor Mature, Richard Egan, Stephen McNally, Virginia Leith, Tommy Noonan, Lee Marvin, Margaret Hayes, J. Carrol Naish, Sylvia Sidney, Ernest Borgnine, Brad Dexter. D: Richard Fleischer. CRI 91m.

Violent Summer 1961 French ★★★ A mentally handicapped young woman is found murdered at a resort hotel. Unconvincing mystery with too scattered a plot to be effective, but atmospheric. (a.k.a. *Un Soir Sur La Plage*) C: Martine Carol, Jean Desailly, Dahlia Lavi, Henri-Jacques Huet. D: Michel Boisrond. DRA 85m.

Violets Are Blue... 1986 ★★★½ High-school lovers reunite 15 years later and fall in love again; but one of them's married. Lovely, small-scale romantic drama with two charismatic stars. C: Kevin Kline, Sissy Spacek, Bonnie Bedelia. D: Jack Fisk. DRA [PG-13] 88m. v

Violette 1978 ★★★★ Stylish mystery, based on a true story, about a teenager accused of poisoning her parents. Huppert's expert performance made her an international star. One of Chabrol's better efforts. (a.k.a. *Violette Noziere*) C: Isabelle Huppert, Stephane Audran, Jean Carnet. D: Claude Chabrol. CRI [R] 122m.

Violette Noziere *See* **Violette**

Violin and Roller 1962 USSR ★★★★ Adventures of a tractor driver and his violin-playing buddy. Low-budget first effort from great Russian filmmaker Tarkovsky has lovely flourishes and vivid characterizations. C: Igor Fomchenko, V. Zamanskiy, Nina Arkhangelskaya. D: Andrey Tarkovskiy. DRA 55m.

V.I.P.s, The 1963 British ★★★★ Glossy soap opera set at London airport, as beautiful people sort out their troubles while waiting for delayed flight. Mindlessly entertaining. Smith is wonderful, as is Rutherford (the latter won Oscar for Best Supporting Actress). C: Elizabeth Taylor, Richard Burton, Louis Jourdan, Margaret Rutherford, Rod Taylor, Maggie Smith, Orson Welles, Linda Christian, Elsa Martinelli, Dennis Price, David Frost, Michael Hordern, Robert Coote. D: Anthony Asquith. DRA 119m. v

Virgin and the Gypsy, The 1970 British ★★★ An Anglican priest's daughter, in love with a gypsy, alienates all around her. D. H. Lawrence's story is altered into a sentimental romance, with some sequences resembling perfume commercials. C: Joanna Shimkus, Franco Nero, Honor Blackman, Maurice Denham. D: Christopher Miles. DRA [R] 92m.

Virgin High 1990 ★★ Guys sneak into a Catholic girls' boarding school. Silly, mindless sex farce. C: Richard Gabai, Burt Ward. D: Richard Gabai. COM [R] 90m. v

Virgin Queen, The 1955 ★★★★ Solid historical drama centers on the romantic triangle of Elizabeth, Sir Walter Raleigh (Todd), and one of the queen's ladies-in-waiting (Collins). Davis' second time out as Elizabeth, and she's very good. Engrossing, worth watching. C: Bette Davis, Richard Todd, Joan Collins, Herbert Marshall. D: Henry Koster. DRA 92m. v

Virgin Soldiers, The 1969 British ★★★½ Inexperienced British soldiers are stationed in Malaya, where they try to learn about war...and love. Amusingly episodic. Sequel: *Stand Up, Virgin Soldiers.* C: Hywel Bennett, Nigel Patrick, Lynn Redgrave, Nigel Davenport. D: John Dexter. COM [R] 96m. v

Virgin Spring, The 1959 Swedish ★★★★ Typically intense Bergman drama—based on a medieval ballad—about a farmer who seeks vengeance after his daughter is raped and murdered. Visually striking meditation on violence won Oscar for Best Foreign Film. C: Max von Sydow, Brigitta Valberg, Gunnel Lindblom, Brigitta Pettersson. D: Ingmar Bergman. DRA 88m. v

Virginia City 1940 ★★★ Nicely photographed Western has Flynn, a Civil War officer, and Bogart, a Mexican villain, fighting for the destiny of a spy (Hopkins). Casting Bogart as a bandito is only one of the mistakes made by the film makers. C: Errol Flynn, Miriam Hopkins, Randolph Scott, Humphrey Bogart, Frank McHugh, Alan Hale, Guinn Williams, John Litel. D: Michael Curtiz. WST 121m. v

Virginian, The 1929 ★★★½ Classic Western story about a man (Cooper) who must deal with a friend (Arlen) who goes bad—and is pursuing the same woman (Brinn). Huston is excellent as the unscrupulous villain. C: Gary Cooper, Richard Arlen, Walter Huston, Mary Brian. D: Victor Fleming. WST 92m. v

Virginian, The 1946 ★★★½ Famed western tale of a sturdy ranch hand who struggles to overcome the bad influences on the range. McCrea is fine in this colorful remake, though the quaint story wore best in 1929 with Gary

Cooper. C: Joel McCrea, Brian Donlevy, Sonny Tufts, Barbara Britton, Fay Bainter, William Frawley. D: Stuart Gilmore. WST 90m.

Viridiana 1961 Spanish ★★★★½ Young virgin (Pinal) about to take her final vows at a Spanish convent is corrupted by her wealthy, lecherous uncle (Rey); she then sets out to exact a punishing revenge. Surrealistic psychological study is perhaps Buñuel's darkest and most memorable film. C: Francisco Rabal, Silvia Pinal, Fernando Rey, Margarita Lozano. D: Luis Buñuel. DRA 90m. V

Virtue 1932 ★★½ A woman of the streets (Lombard) is rescued by a good man (O'Brien) and redeemed by love. Typical '30s potboiler, competently acted. C: Carole Lombard, Pat O'Brien. D: Edward Buzzell. DRA 87m.

Virus 1980 ★★★ Big-budget Japanese sci-fi drama has action star Chiba wandering through a frozen world ravaged by nuclear war and disease. Spectacular cinematography and grand cast keep this unfocused film from foundering. C: Sonny Chiba, Chuck Connors, Glenn Ford, Olivia Hussey, George Kennedy. D: Kinji Fukasaku. SFI [PG] 106m. V

Vision Quest 1985 ★★★½ High school wrestler gets both physical and metaphysical, but his focus on winning is disrupted by arrival of older woman. Ridiculous romance; decent wrestling footage. Based on the Terry Davis novel. C: Matthew Modine, Linda Fiorentino, Michael Schoeffling, Ronny Cox. D: Harold Becker. DRA [R] 107m. V

Visions of Eight 1973 ★★★½ Eight internationally renowned directors contribute short studies of the 1972 Olympics. Mixed bag unites sports and film aficionados. Schlesinger's marathon segment is best. D: Arthur Penn, Kon Ichikawa, Milos Forman, Claude Lelouch, John Schlesinger, Mai Zetterling, Juri Ozerov, Michael Pfleghar. DOC [G] 110m.

Visions of Light: The Art of Cinematography 1993 U.S.-Japanese ★★★★½ Eye-catching montage of over 100 clips illustrating the art of film cinematography. Fascinating commentary is provided by current masters of the craft. Best bit: Bill Butler (*Jaws*) explaining how he persuaded Steven Spielberg to allow innovative use of a hand-held camera. D: Arnold Glassman, Todd McCarthy, Stuart Samuels. DOC 90m. V

Visit, The 1964 German-French-Italian ★★★ Weak filming of Friedrich Durrenmatt's brilliant play, ruined by miscasting Bergman in the role of a wealthy woman returning to her home town to exact her revenge on the man who jilted her (Quinn). Desperately needs a remake. Meryl, are you listening? C: Ingrid Bergman, Anthony Quinn, Irina Demick. D: Bernhard Wicki. DRA 100m.

Visit to a Chief's Son 1974 ★★★½ American anthropologist and his son forget their differences on an adventure trip to Africa where they are privileged to witness and film tribal rituals. Stunningly photographed African vistas showcase well-acted family drama. C: Richard Mulligan, Johnny Sekka, John Philip Hogdon, Jesse Kinaru, Chief Lomoiro, Jock Anderson. D: Lamont Johnson. DRA [G] 92m.

Visit to a Small Planet 1960 ★★★½ Okay comedy about an alien (Lewis) who comes to Earth to study bizarre human behavior. With Jerry in the role, it's more ironic than hilarious. From Gore Vidal's play. C: Jerry Lewis, Joan Blackman, Earl Holliman, Fred Clark. D: Norman Taurog. COM 85m. V

Visitors from the Galaxy 1981 Yugoslavian ★★★½ Young writer's characters come to life and wreak havoc in a small town. Entertaining mix of live action and animation in family-oriented fantasy. C: Zarko Potocnjak, Ljubisa Samardzic, Lucie Zulova. D: Dusan Vukotic. SFI 90m.

Visitors, The 1972 ★★★½ Ex-con Vietnam vets invade home of fellow vet who ratted on them. Debut for Woods and Railsback. C: Patrick McVey, Patricia Joyce, James Woods, Chico Martinez, Steve Railsback. D: Elia Kazan. COM [R] 88m. V

Vital Signs 1990 ★★½ Formulaic tale of five medical students, each with a different problem to resolve in the pursuit of becoming a doctor. Dull. C: Adrian Pasdar, Diane Lane, Jimmy Smits, Norma Aleandro, Jack Gwaltney, Laura San Giacomo, William Devane. D: Marisa Silver. DRA [R] 102m. V

Vitelloni 1953 *See* **I Vitelloni**

Viva Knievel! 1977 ★★ Drug crime piece about the motorcycle daredevil foiling a plan to smuggle Mexican contraband into the U.S. Knievel plays himself, but George Hamilton (in 1972's *Evel Knievel*) did it better! C: Evel Knievel, Lauren Hutton, Gene Kelly, Marjoe Gortner, Red Buttons, Leslie Nielsen, Dabney Coleman, Frank Gifford. D: Gordon Douglas. CRI [PG] 106m. V

Viva Las Vegas 1964 ★★★★ Outstanding Presley musical features dynamic combustion between Elvis and sizzling Ann-Margret. Presley plays a race-car driver who shifts into high gear every time he runs into co-star. Songs include "I Need Somebody to Lean On," "The Lady Loves Me," title tune. C: Elvis Presley, Ann-Margret, Cesare Danova, William Demarest, Jack Carter, Nicky Blair. D: George Sidney. MUS 85m. V

Viva Maria! 1965 French ★★★½ Bardot and Moreau are entertainers who get mixed up with a Latin American revolution and dashing rebel leader (Hamilton). Cute self-parody, very funny in spots. C: Brigitte Bardot, Jeanne Moreau, George Hamilton, Gregor Von Rezzori, Paulette Dubost. D: Louis Malle. COM 119m. V

Viva Max! 1969 ★★★½ Ustinov as Mexican rebel reclaims the Alamo, much to the surprise of American park officials. Silly fun; Winters and Astin are great in supporting roles. C: Peter Ustinov, Pamela Tiffin, Jonathan Winters, John Astin, Keenan Wynn, Harry Morgan. D: Jerry Paris. COM [G] 93m. v

Viva Villa! 1934 ★★★★ Beery has the title role in story of Pancho Villa, courageous Mexican revolutionary leader of early 1900s. Supporting cast is excellent, and movie is consistently watchable, although not always historically accurate. C: Wallace Beery, Leo Carrillo, Fay Wray, Donald Cook, Stuart Erwin, George E. Stone, Henry B. Walthall, Joseph Schildkraut, Katherine DeMille. D: Jack Conway. WST 115m. v

Viva Zapata! 1952 ★★★★★ Brando plays tenant farmer who rose from folk-hero/revolutionary to president of Mexico until his betrayal by friends. Somber, epic historical drama glosses over facts but still plays effectively. Screenplay by John Steinbeck. Oscar to Quinn for Best Supporting Actor. C: Marlon Brando, Jean Peters, Anthony Quinn, Joseph Wiseman, Mildred Dunnock, Arnold Moss. D: Elia Kazan. DRA 112m. v

Vivacious Lady 1938 ★★★★ Cute comedy of mismatched mates Stewart and Rogers; she's a musical comedy star, he's a college prof. Now they have to face his family. C: James Stewart, Ginger Rogers, James Ellison, Beulah Bondi, Charles Coburn, Frances Mercer. D: George Stevens. COM 90m. v

Vogues 1937 *See* **Vogues of 1938**

Vogues of 1938 1937 ★★★½ Trying to embarrass her fiance (and boss) Baxter, Bennett becomes a fashion model. Amusing Manhattan-based musical comedy, typical for its time, replete with chichi humor and songs. (a.k.a. *Vogues*) C: Warner Baxter, Joan Bennett, Helen Vinson, Mischa Auer. D: Irving Cummings. MUS 110m. v

Voice in the Mirror, The 1958 ★★★½ Egan tries to come back from alcoholism, with the help of his loyal, patient spouse (London). Neatly played drama. C: Richard Egan, Julie London, Arthur O'Connell, Walter Matthau, Troy Donahue, Mae Clarke. D: Harry Keller. DRA 102m.

Voice of the Turtle, The 1947 ★★★★ While on leave in New York City, soldier (Reagan) becomes involved in whirlwind romance with struggling actress (Parker). Charming romantic comedy, adapted from popular Broadway play, gets boost from lively ensemble. Arden is especially good. (a.k.a. *One for the Book*). C: Ronald Reagan, Eleanor Parker, Eve Arden, Wayne Morris, Kent Smith. D: Irving Rapper. COM 103m.

Voice of the Whistler 1945 ★★★ Wealthy geezer (Dix) marries gold-digging nurse (Merrick) after she drops her fiance. Instead of wealthy happiness, Merrick ends up captive in Dix's mansion. Some genuine suspense in this creaky *Whistler* series entry. C: Richard Dix, Lynn Merrick, Rhys Williams, James Cardwell, Donald Woods, Gigi Perreau. D: William Castle. CRI 60m. v

Voices 1979 ★★★½ A hearing-impaired dancer (Irving) falls for Ontkean who longs to be a rock singer. Despite its reliance on familiar show business/romance/disability stereotypes, this works, thanks to good performances by leads. C: Michael Ontkean, Amy Irving, Alex Rocco, Barry Miller, Herbert Berghof, Viveca Lindfors. D: Robert Markowitz. DRA [PG] 107m.

Volcano 1953 Italian ★★★ Melodrama features scenery-chewing Magnani as one of two Italian sisters trying to win affections of unethical scuba diver. Lots of heavy passion mixed up with existential musings. C: Anna Magnani, Rossano Brazzi, Geraldine Brooks. D: William Dieterle. DRA 106m.

Volcano 1969 1969 *See* **Krakatoa, East of Java**

Volere Volare 1991 Italian ★★★½ Co-director Nichetti plays a movie sound engineer who finds himself turning into a cartoon character, complicating his romance with a lovable prostitute. Quirky, pleasant mix of live action and animation, just for adults. C: Maurizio Nichetti, Angela Finocchiaro. D: Maurizio Nichetti, Guido Manuli. COM [R] 92m. v

Volpone 1939 French ★★★★½ Entertaining adaptation of Ben Jonson period farce stars Baur as wealthy business dealer who decides to fake life-threatening illness in order to observe behavior of his would-be inheritors. Well played and intelligent, with beautiful period sets. C: Harry Baur, Louis Jouvet. D: Maurice Tourneur. COM 95m. v

Voltus 5 1983 ★★½ Kid-oriented animated science fiction adventure from Japan, pitting team of five youngsters against invaders from outer space. Lots of action, though story is undistinguished. FAM/SFI 75m. v

Volunteers 1985 ★★½ Trying to avoid creditors, rich volunteer (Hanks) joins Peace Corps in Thailand, where he struggles with CIA, blackmarketeers, and a buddy (Candy). Hanks and Candy are well teamed, but film relies on ugly humor for laughs. C: Tom Hanks, John Candy, Rita Wilson, Tim Thomerson. D: Nicholas Meyer. COM 106m. v

Von Richthofen and Brown 1971 ★★★½ Sturdy, intelligent, but curiously unmoving tale of the inevitable battle between two great WWI fighter aces. Corman tries for an "end of an era" feeling, but stolid actors weaken the picture's overall impact. Corman didn't direct again until *Frankenstein Unbound* (1990). C: John Philip Law, Barry Primus, Peter Masterson, Karen Huston, Hurd Hatfield. D: Roger Corman. ACT 97m.

Von Ryan's Express 1965 ★★★★ Sinatra, a WWII prisoner of war, attempts risky breakout that has him hijacking a freight train full of

Allied soldiers. Gritty, nail-biting action with superb acting. C: Frank Sinatra, Trevor Howard, Raffaella Carra, Brad Dexter, Edward Mulhare, James Brolin. D: Mark Robson. ACT 116m. v

Voodoo Dawn 1990 ★★ Two friends visit a buddy in the South and find that he has gotten a bit too friendly with a local voodoo priestess. Lacks either the budget or the ambition to create a sense of pervasive, black-magic evil, settles for cheap shocks instead. C: Raymond St. Jacques, Gina Gershon, Theresa Merritt. D: Steven Fierberg. HOR [R] 83m. v

Voyage of Terror: The Achille Lauro Affair 1990 U.S. ★★★★ Palestinians hijack a cruise ship, then torture and kill one of the passengers. Frightening version of true story. C: Burt Lancaster, Eva Marie Saint, Rebecca Schaeffer, Robert Culp, Brian Bloom. D: Alberto Negrin. ACT 200m. TVM v

Voyage of the Damned 1976 British ★★½ Soporific, poorly acted tale of an ocean liner with exclusively German-Jewish passengers in 1939, unable to dock in Havana or anywhere else. Shocking true story should have made powerful drama (a la *Ship of Fools*), but instead became an all-star travesty. Dunaway and Grant chew the most scenery. Cut from 158 minutes. C: Faye Dunaway, Oskar Werner, Max von Sydow, Lee Grant, James Mason, Orson Welles, Wendy Hiller, Jose Ferrer, Julie Harris, Katharine Ross, Malcolm McDowell, Ben Gazzara. D: Stuart Rosenberg. DRA [PG] 134m. v

Voyage, The 1973 Italian ★★½ Lukewarm, turn-of-the-century romance of star-crossed lovers (Loren and Burton). Sadly, the legendary De Sica's final film. C: Sophia Loren, Richard Burton, Ian Bannen. D: Vittorio De Sica. DRA [PG] 95m. v

Voyage to Italy 1953 Italian ★★★★½ A squabbling married couple (Sanders, Bergman) travel to Naples to inspect a newly inherited villa, a journey which changes their lives forever. Fine Bergman-Rossellini collaboration features her at her radiant best. (a.k.a. *The Strangers*) C: Ingrid Bergman, George Sanders, Maria Mauban. D: Roberto Rossellini. DRA 80m. v

Voyage to the Bottom of the Sea 1961 ★★★½ Mindless fun about atomic submarine bound for ocean bottom to neutralize potentially deadly radiation belt. Squabbles and intrigues aboard ship add to troubles faced by sub commander (Pidgeon). Good special effects, combined with some amusing overacting. C: Walter Pidgeon, Joan Fontaine, Robert Sterling, Barbara Eden, Peter Lorre. D: Irwin Allen. SFI 105m. v

Voyage to the End of the Universe 1963 Czechoslavakian ★★★ Scientists from 25th century investigate unusual signals emitted by strange black hole in outer space. Interesting science fiction. (a.k.a. *Ikarie XB 1*). C: Dennis Stephans, Francis Smolen, Dana Meredith, Irene Kova, Rodney Lucas, Otto Lack. D: Jack Pollack. SFI 81m.

Voyager 1991 German ★★★★ Drifting Shepard on aimless pilgrimage through '50s Europe lands in Greece where he has a romantic encounter with German woman (Delpy). Slow-moving but engaging adaptation of Max Frisch's novel *Homo Faber* features beautiful scenery and fine performance from Shepard. C: Sam Shepard, Julie Delpy, Barbara Sukowa, Dieter Kirchlechner, Traci Lind. D: Volker Schlondorff. DRA [PG-13] 113m. v

W

Wabash Avenue 1950 ★★★★ Grable reworks earlier film *Coney Island* as late 19th-century Chicago saloon chanteuse, whose romance with barkeep Harris is threatened by interloping Mature. Fluffy but entertaining and colorful musical. Vivacious performances by stars. C: Betty Grable, Victor Mature, Phil Harris, Reginald Gardiner, James Barton, Margaret Hamilton. D: Henry Koster. MUS 92m.

Wackiest Ship in the Army, The 1961 ★★★½ Rusting sailing ship with an inept misfit crew ends up playing a key role in confounding the Japanese in the Pacific arena during WWII. Unusual wartime comedy walks a fine line between comedy and drama with mixed results. C: Jack Lemmon, Ricky Nelson, John Lund, Chips Rafferty. D: Richard Murphy. COM 99m. V

Wackiest Wagon Train in the West, The 1976 ★★½ A pair of bumblers nearly drive a wagon train into oblivion. Goofy fun. C: Bob Denver, Forrest Tucker. FAM/WST [G] 88m. V

Wacky World of Mother Goose, The 1967 ★★½ Silly, animated spoof of famed nursery rhymes mixes secret agents with characters from the stories. Created for children. D: Jules Bass. FAM/COM 81m. V

Wages of Fear, The 1952 French ★★★★½ Seeking a way out of their squalid Central American town, four desperate men accept a suicide mission to drive nitroglycerin-filled trucks 300 miles through the jungle. Intense, nerve-wracking adventure film is also an absorbing character study; stunningly directed. Remade in English as *Sorcerer*. C: Yves Montand, Charles Vanel, Peter VonEyck, Vera Clouzot. D: Henri-Georges Clouzot. DRA 156m. V

Wagner 1983 British ★★½ Burton can't find the melody in this overlong film biography of composer Richard Wagner. Badly paced, to say the least. C: Richard Burton, Vanessa Redgrave, John Gielgud, Ralph Richardson, Laurence Olivier, Ronald Pickup, Franco Nero. D: Tony Palmer. DRA 300m. V

Wagon Master 1950 ★★★★½ Mormon pioneers, joined on their wagon train by two cowhands, are tested by elements and Navajos. Studied Western re-creates trailblazing hardships, with fine performances from talented ensemble. Excellent use of beautiful locations. C: Ben Johnson, Joanne Dru, Harry Carey Jr., Ward Bond, Alan Mowbray, Jane Darwell, James Arness, Charles Kemper. D: John Ford. WST 85m. V

Wagons Roll at Night, The 1941 ★★★½ Carnival boss (Bogart) tries to protect his convent-bred sister (Leslie) from circus atmosphere, but she falls for the novice liontamer (Albert). Minor Bogart fare with good cast provides some entertaining moments. C: Humphrey Bogart, Eddie Albert, Joan Leslie, Sig Ruman, Cliff Clark, Charley Foy, Frank Wilcox. D: Ray Enright. DRA 84m.

Waikiki Wedding 1937 ★★★★ Hawaiian pineapple company PR agent (Crosby) concocts phony beauty contest as publicity stunt. Unfortunately for Crosby, "winner" Raye arrives and proceeds to make life unbearable. Winsome comedy has naive charm thanks to appealing leads. Oscar for Best Song "Sweet Leilani." C: Bing Crosby, Martha Raye, Shirley Ross, Bob Burns, Leif Erickson, Grady Sutton, Anthony Quinn. D: Frank Tuttle. COM 89m.

Wait 'Til the Sun Shines, Nellie 1952 ★★★★ Wayne is small-town barber in early 20th-century America who observes Vlife's joys and disappointments from his unique perspective. Delicate and effective story benefits from deliberately understated telling. Wayne's performance is quietly moving. C: Jean Peters, David Wayne, Hugh Marlowe, Albert Dekker, Alan Hale, Warren Stevens. D: Henry King. DRA 108m.

Wait Until Dark 1967 ★★★★ Cleverly crafted thriller with Hepburn outstanding as blind housewife defending herself against drug traffickers in New York City. Broadway roots show in one-set, talky first half, but final showdown between Audrey and Arkin is a classic spine tingler. C: Audrey Hepburn, Alan Arkin, Richard Crenna, Efrem Zimbalist Jr., Jack Weston. D: Terence Young. DRA 108m. V

Waiting for the Light 1990 ★★★ During Cuban Missile Crisis, a medium (MacLaine, lampooning her own New Age image) weaves spell that brings changes to lives of anxious people. Some cute moments can't overcome predictable plotting. C: Shirley MacLaine, Terri Garr, Vincent Schiavelli, John Bedford Lloyd, Jeff McCracken. D: Christoper Monger. COM [PG] 95m. V

Waiting for the Moon 1987 ★★½ Film biography of relationship between Alice B. Toklas (Hunt) and Gertrude Stein (Basset). Well acted. Produced as part of the PBS *American Playhouse* series. C: Linda Hunt, Linda Bassett, Bruce McGill, Andrew McCarthy. D: Jill Godmilow. DRA [PG] 88m. TVM V

Wake in Fright 1971 *See* **Outback** TVM

Wake Island 1942 ★★★★ A beleaguered group of soldiers struggle to keep a strategic island in the Pacific out of enemy hands. Exciting action and thoughtfully conceived characters lift this WWII flick above the norm. C: Brian Donlevy, Robert Preston, Macdonald Carey, William Bendix. D: John Farrow. ACT 88m. V

Wake Me When It's Over 1960 ★★★★ When error lands military vet Shawn back in the Army, he uses military's supplies to open a hotel near his Asian base. Whacked-out nonsense played with zest by cast; Shawn and TV legend Kovacs are great fun. C: Dick Shawn, Ernie Kovacs, Margo Moore, Jack Warden, Don Knotts. D: Mervyn LeRoy. COM 126m.

Wake of the Red Witch 1948 ★★★ Wayne is a sea captain on the lookout for sunken treasure who has a formidable rival in a shipping magnate. Though visually pleasing, the story meanders. C: John Wayne, Gail Russell, Luther Adler, Gig Young, Henry Daniell. D: Edward Ludwig. ACT 106m. V

Wake Up and Live 1937 ★★★ Winchell and Bernie are two feuding radio legends (playing roles based on their airwave personas) struggling with young singer Haley, who suffers from severe microphone shyness. Cute if dated musical. C: Alice Faye, Walter Winchell, Ben Bernie, Jack Haley, Patsy Kelly, Joan Davis, Grace Bradley, Warren Hymer, Ned Sparks, Walter Catlett. D: Sidney Lanfield. MUS 91m.

Walk a Crooked Mile 1948 ★★★ Scotland Yard and the FBI join forces to foil spies who are after U.S. nuclear secrets. Uninvolving police investigation, with few surprises or suspenseful moments. C: Louis Hayward, Dennis O'Keefe, Louise Allbritton, Carl Esmond, Onslow Stevens, Raymond Burr. D: Gordon Douglas. CRI 91m.

Walk, Don't Run 1966 ★★★½ During 1964 Tokyo Olympics, business exec Grant uses apartment to play matchmaker with Eggar and Hutton. Cute remake of *The More the Merrier*, buoyed by good cast. C: Cary Grant, Samantha Eggar, Jim Hutton, John Standing. D: Charles Walters. COM 114m. V

Walk East on Beacon 1952 ★★★ When the Red Menace threatens Boston, FBI foils Communist plans. Heavy-handed and rather dated documentary-style tale, shot on location, typical of anti-Communist hysteria sweeping Hollywood at the time. C: George Murphy, Finlay Currie, Virginia Gilmore, George Hill. D: Alfred Werker. DRA 98m.

Walk in the Spring Rain, A 1970 ★★★ Middle-aged love in the Appalachians. Mild romance, pleasing but slight. C: Ingrid Bergman, Anthony Quinn, Fritz Weaver, Katharine Crawford. D: Guy Green. DRA [PG] 100m. V

Walk in the Sun, A 1945 ★★★★½ American WWII unit stationed in Italy must capture a group of German soldiers hiding in an abandoned barn. Excellent ensemble effort, marked by gritty performances. Based on novel by Harry Brown. C: Dana Andrews, Richard Conte, John Ireland, Norman Lloyd, Lloyd Bridges, Huntz Hall. D: Lewis Milestone. DRA 117m. V

Walk Into Hell 1957 ★★ "Civilized" Australians find their lives challenged by Aborigines. Shot on location. C: Chips Rafferty, Francoise Christophe, Reginald Lye, Pierre Cressoy. D: Lee Robinson. DRA 91m. V

Walk Like A Man 1987 ★ Feral child Mandel raised by wolves, becomes member of civilized society—but can't forget those lessons his animal parents taught him. Inane slapstick and a barely released career low for all involved. C: Howie Mandel, Christopher Lloyd, Cloris Leachman, Colleen Camp, Amy Steel. D: Melvin Frank. COM [PG] 86m. V

Walk on the Wild Side 1962 ★★★½ One of those "so bad, it's good" movies casts Stanwyck as a lesbian madame running a New Orleans house of ill repute, where Fonda, Capucine, and Baxter work. Suggested by Nelson Algren's bestseller. C: Laurence Harvey, Barbara Stanwyck, Jane Fonda, Capucine, Anne Baxter. D: Edward Dmytryk. DRA 114m. V

Walk Softly, Stranger 1950 ★★★★ Petty hood Cotten decides to give up his criminal life after encountering disabled child Valli. Despite cliched setup, this well-acted drama is effective and moving. C: Joseph Cotten, Alida Valli, Spring Byington, Paul Stewart, Jack Paar. D: Robert Stevenson. DRA 81m. V

Walk the Proud Land 1956 ★★★★ A government agent (Murphy) must settle disputes between white settlers and Native Americans, which ultimately leads to capture of Geronimo. Strong acting and intelligent dialogue make an entertaining action drama. C: Audie Murphy, Anne Bancroft, Pat Crowley, Charles Drake, Jay Silverheels. D: Jesse Hibbs. DRA 88m.

Walk With Love and Death, A 1969 ★★½ Stultifying romance between a nobleman and a peasant woman in 14th-century France. Anjelica (John's daughter) got dreadful notices in her film debut, but vindicated herself 16 years later, with *Prizzi's Honor*. C: Anjelica Huston, Assaf Dayan. D: John Huston. DRA [PG] 90m.

Walkabout 1971 Australian ★★★★½ After their father kills himself, two English children are left stranded in the Australian outback. They make it out with Aborigine help. Unusual and beautifully photographed; excellent performances. C: Jenny Agutter, Lucien John, David Gulpilil, John Meillon, John Illingworth. D: Nicolas Roeg. DRA [PG] 95m.

Walker 1988 ★★★ Stylized biography of William Walker, an American renegade who became President of Nicaragua in the 1800s. Fascinatingly inconsistent approach—keep a lookout for the distinctly 20th century props. C: Ed Harris, Marlee Matlin, Richard Masur, Peter Boyle. D: Alex Cox. DRA 90m. V

Walking Dead, The 1936 ★★★★ After wrongly being executed for a crime he didn't commit, Karloff is brought back to life and seeks revenge on those who set him up. Atmospheric horror story with good scares. Karloff is especially spooky. C: Boris Karloff, Edmund Gwenn, Marguerite Churchill, Ricardo Cortez, Barton MacLane, Warren Hull, Joe Sawyer. D: Michael Curtiz. HOR 66m.

Walking Dead, The 1995 ★★½ A predominantly black Vietnam platoon copes with war, disease, and discontent in an exploitative, simplistic treatment of a potentially powerful situation. All the black characters are victims; all the whites are villains. Wasted opportunity. C: Allen Payne, Joe Morton, Eddie Griffin. D: Preston A. Whitmore II. ACT [R] 90m. v

Walking Hills, The 1949 ★★★½ Scott leads ragtag group in the Old West to search for a gold mine. Well acted, especially by Scott. C: Randolph Scott, Ella Raines, William Bishop, Edgar Buchanan, Arthur Kennedy. D: John Sturges. WST 78m.

Walking My Baby Back Home 1953 ★★★ Three ex-GIs decide to form a Dixieland jazz combo. Good musical sequences, lively Hackett humor. C: Donald O'Connor, Buddy Hackett, Scatman Crothers, Janet Leigh. D: Lloyd Bacon. MUS 95m.

Walking Tall 1973 ★★★ Baker is powerful as a Tennessee sheriff who takes on a town full of criminals with nothing but determination and a baseball bat. Based on a true story, but excessive violence will make it hard for some to watch. C: Joe Don Baker, Elizabeth Hartman, Gene Evans, Noah Beery. D: Phil Karlson. ACT [R] 126m. v

Walking Tall, Part 2 1975 ★★½ Sequel to the popular, if violent, saga of real-life Tennessee sheriff, Buford Pusser, now played by Svenson, whose time is spent outwitting and out-muscling organized crime. Simple-minded action. Sequel: *Final Chapter—Walking Tall.* (a.k.a. *Part 2, Walking Tall*) C: Bo Svenson, Luke Askew, Bruce Glover, Richard Jaeckel. D: Earl Bellamy. ACT [PG] 109m. v

Walkover 1969 Polish ★★★★ An amateur fighter enters a local competition while trying to deal with a woman who reenters his life after a long absence. An intriguing character study, well acted and with some unusual flourishes. Sequel to *Identification Marks: None.* C: Aleksandra Zawieruszanka, Jerzy Skolimowski, Krzysztof Chamiec. D: Jerzy Skolimowski. DRA 77m.

Wall of Noise 1963 ★★★ Behind-the-scenes drama looks at the denizens of a race track, their affairs with gambling and each other. C: Suzanne Pleshette, Ty Hardin, Dorothy Provine, Ralph Meeker, Simon Oakland, Murray Matheson. D: Richard Wilson. DRA 112m.

Wall Street 1987 ★★★★ Young stock broker (C. Sheen) in the '80s cuts corners and gets rich but ends up selling his soul. Interesting view of business sharks on their own turf, though Stone takes everything a step too far. Great Oscar-winning performance by Douglas. C: Michael Douglas, Charlie Sheen, Daryl Hannah, Martin Sheen, Terence Stamp, Sean Young, Sylvia Miles, James Spader. D: Oliver Stone. DRA [R] 124m. v

Wall Street Cowboy 1939 ★★★ Cowboy Roy goes up against greedy Wall Street types hungry for his mineral-laden ranch. Rogers and Trigger are charmingly earnest, as usual. C: Roy Rogers, George "Gabby" Hayes, Jack Ingram. D: Joseph Kane. WST 54m. v

Wallflower 1948 ★★★ A shy young woman causes trouble when she becomes the love interest for her sister's beau. Somewhat dated, but still amusing. C: Joyce Reynolds, Robert Hutton, Janis Paige, Edward Arnold, Jerome Cowan, Barbara Brown. D: Frederick deCordova. COM 77m.

Walls of Jericho, The 1948 ★★★ Stuck in Midwestern town of Jericho, Kansas, Wilde dreams of bigger things but finds his goals continually shot down by his wife. Some good performances. C: Cornel Wilde, Linda Darnell, Anne Baxter, Kirk Douglas, Ann Dvorak, Marjorie Rambeau, Henry Hull, Colleen Townsend, Barton MacLane. D: John M. Stahl. DRA 106m.

Walls of Malapaga, The 1956 French ★★★★ In post-WWII Italy, French native on the run from law meets Italian waitress and they begin a healing romance. Fine performances in sweet and often touching story; simple telling belies ultimate power of the tale. C: Jean Gabin, Isa Miranda. D: Rene Clement. DRA 91m.

Walton's Thanksgiving Story, the ★★★ Sticky tale of 1963 family reunion on Walton's Mountain with original cast of popular TV series. Plotline deals with effect of Kennedy's assassination on clan. Lackluster, compared to original series. FAM/DRA TVM v

Waltz King, The 1963 ★★★ Disney's biography of composer Johann Strauss, Jr. (Mathews), follows his rise in 18th-century Europe. German scenery and familiar music give some life to an otherwise routine, slightly stagy story. C: Kerwin Mathews, Brian Aherne, Senta Berger, Peter Kraus. D: Steve Previn. FAM/DRA 94m. v

Waltz of the Toreadors 1962 British ★★★★ Sellers is a retired army official whose penchant for romance brings him trouble—time after time after time. Sellers is well cast in this clever, good-humored sex comedy. C: Peter Sellers, Dany Robin, Margaret Leighton, John Fraser. D: John Guillermin. COM 104m. v

Wanda 1971 ★★★★ Loden (who also wrote and directed) stars as a woman from small coal mining community who, tired of her endless string of abusive relationships, becomes involved with petty criminal (Higgins). An intriguing character study. C: Barbara Loden, Michael Higgins, Charles Dosinan, Frank Jourdano. D: Barbara Loden. DRA [PG] 105m.

Wanda Nevada 1979 ★★★ Grizzled drifter (Peter Fonda) acquires an adorable young tag-along (Shields). Meandering western notable only for its teaming of Peter with father Henry (in a small role). C: Peter Fonda, Brooke Shields, Fiona Lewis, Severn Darden, Henry Fonda. D: Peter Fonda. WST [PG] 105m. v

Wanderers, The 1979 ★★★½ Gritty, atmospheric depiction of youth gangs in early '60s Bronx is visually arresting, though plot is scattered. Based on the Richard Price novel. C: Ken Wahl, John Friedrich, Karen Allen, Toni Kalem, Linda Manz, Tony Ganios, Olympia Dukakis. D: Philip Kaufman. DRA [R] 113m. v

Wandering Jew, The 1931 ★★★½ Nazi propaganda film which shows how the interpretation of "Jewish influence" affects German society. Virulently anti-Semitic, the film is best viewed as part of National Socialism's baneful historical legacy. DOC

Wandering Jew, The 1933 ★★★½ Yiddish-language film looks at the struggles of a Jewish family in Germany at the time of the Nazis' rise. An invaluable historical record of a way of life soon annihilated by the Nazis. C: Jacob Ben-Ami, Ben Adler, Jacob Mestel. D: George Roland. DRA 68m.

Wannsee Conference, The 1984 German ★★★★½ Re-creation of 1942 Nazi meeting wherein the plans for the "Final Solution" were laid out. Based on minutes from the actual gathering, the film's running time is as long as the real session was. Disturbing in its calculated development and as an unforgettable depiction of the banality of evil. C: Dietrich Mattausch, Gerd Bockmann, Friedrich Beckhaus, Gunter Spoerrie, Martin Luttge, Peter Fritz. D: Heinz Schirk. DRA 87m. v

Wanted: Dead or Alive 1987 ★★ Action flick, supposedly connected to the TV series starring Steve McQueen, but the similarities end with the title. Hauer stars as the tough bounty hunter who shoots and explodes his way to an overkill climax. C: Rutger Hauer, Gene Simmons, Robert Guillaume, Mel Harris. D: Gary A. Sherman. ACT [R] 104m. v

Wanton Countess, The 1955 *See* **Senso**

War and Peace 1956 ★★★★ Lavish screen adaptation of Leo Tolstoy's novel, examining effect of Russia's Napoleonic wars on three families. The battle scenes are stunning, and Hepburn's performance is captivating. C: Audrey Hepburn, Henry Fonda, Mel Ferrer, Vittorio Gassman, John Mills, Anita Ekberg. D: King Vidor. DRA 208m. v

War and Peace 1968 Russian ★★★★★ Six-hour-plus film of Tolstoy's epic is worth the long sit; gorgeously produced film encompasses nearly all of the classic novel. Terrific battles and moving drama in this Oscar-winner for Best Foreign Film: beware alternate version that contains embarrassingly bad English dubbing. C: Ludmila Savelyeva, Vyacheslav Tihonov, Hira Ivanov-Golovko, Sergei Bondarchuk. D: Sergei Bondarchuk. DRA [PG] 507m. v

War Arrow 1953 ★★★ U.S. cavalry officer Chandler arrives at remote outpost to train Seminoles in battle against Kiowas. He also somehow manages to woo O'Hara. Action with a dabble of romance. C: Maureen O'Hara, Jeff Chandler, Suzan Ball, Charles Drake, Jay Silverheels. D: George Sherman. WST 78m.

War Between Men and Women, The 1972 ★★★½ Newlyweds Lemmon and Harris experience the battles that love brings as they try to build life together. Episodic rather than plot driven, the leads are quite good. Based on James Thurber's writings and cartoons. C: Jack Lemmon, Barbara Harris, Jason Robards, Herb Edelman, Lisa Gerritsen, Lisa Eilbacher, Severn Darden. D: Melville Shavelson. COM 110m.

War Between the Tates, The 1977 ★★★½ College professor (Crenna) has an affair with a student, leading to title battle with his wife (Ashley). Solid adaptation of the acerbic Alison Lurie novel. C: Elizabeth Ashley, Richard Crenna, Annette O'Toole, Ann Wedgeworth. D: Lee Philips. DRA 100m. TVM

War Cat 1988 ★ Another exploitative action cheapie about a beleaguered woman who trounces a bunch of sadistic creeps, this time a reporter treated as human prey by a group of survivalists. Lacks intrigue, wit, and surprises. (a.k.a. *Angel of Vengeance*) C: Jannina Poynter, David O'Hara, Macka Foley, Carl Irwin. D: Ted V. Mikels. ACT 78m. v

War Game, The 1966 British ★★★★½ Terrifying British film creates a graphic picture of world after a nuclear war. Remarkable in its vision and detail. Oscar for Best Documentary. Fascinating. D: Peter Watkins. DOC 50m. v

War Games *See* **Suppose They Gave a War and Nobody Came?**

War Hunt 1962 ★★★½ During the Korean War, an overzealous soldier (Saxon) makes friends with a boy, orphaned by the war. Punchy and violent; Redford's film debut. C: John Saxon, Robert Redford, Charles Aidman, Sydney Pollack. D: Denis Sanders. DRA 81m.

War Lord, The 1965 ★★★ Drama about 11th-century knight who falls for another man's bride and uses his rank to win her; ultimately, she returns his love. Well-produced and -acted adaptation of Leslie Stevens' play *The Lovers*. C: Charlton Heston, Rosemary Forsyth, Richard Boone, Maurice Evans, Guy Stockwell, Niall McGinnis, James Farentino, Henry Wilcoxon. D: Franklin Schaffner. DRA 123m. v

War Lover, The 1962 British ★★★½ Two American pilots, Wagner and McQueen, fly missions for British Royal Air Force and vie for the affections of the same woman. Dramatic scenes misfire, but footage of dogfighting war planes is well done. C: Steve McQueen, Robert Wagner, Shirley Ann Field, Gary Cockrell, Michael Crawford, Jerry Stavin, Al Waxman. D: Philip Leacock. DRA 105m. v

War of the Buttons 1963 French ★★★½ Two groups of French boys engage in a "war" in which they steal buttons, then belts, then suspenders from one another—until one decides to enter the battle naked. Innocuous comedy of kid-sized manners. C: Martin Lartique, Andre Treton, Michel Isella. D: Yves Robert. COM 92m.

War of the Colossal Beast 1958 ★★ In this cheap sequel to *The Amazing Colossal Man*, an insane giant humanoid wreaks havoc on everything in sight. Bad even by B-movie standards. C: Sally Fraser, Roger Pace, Dean Parkin, Russ Bender, Charles Stewart. D: Bert I. Gordon. SFI 68m. V

War of the Roses, The 1989 ★★★★ Brutal black comedy paints as bleak a picture of marriage as possible. Divorcing couple (Turner, Douglas) resort to physical violence as revenge tactics escalate under ruthless eye of divorce lawyer (DeVito). Terrific performances, even when the plot's relentless pessimism goes too far. C: Michael Douglas, Kathleen Turner, Danny DeVito, Marianne Sagebrecht, Sean Astin, Heather Fairfield, G. Spradlin, Peter Donat, Dan Castellaneta, Danitra Vance. D: Danny DeVito. COM [R] 116m. V

War of the Worlds 1953 ★★★★ Serious science fiction perfectly captures the intelligence and imagination of H.G. Wells' story of a Martian invasion of Earth. The film's special effects earned a well-deserved Oscar. C: Gene Barry, Les Tremayne, Ann Robinson, Robert Cornthwaite, Henry Brandon, Jack Kruschen, Lewis Martin. D: Byron Haskin. SFI 85m. V

War Paint 1953 ★★★½ U.S. cavalry overcomes all sorts of hazards and nefarious types in attempt to deliver peace treaty to warring parties. Lots of action in this fairly entertaining drama. C: Robert Stack, Joan Taylor, Charles McGraw, Peter Graves. D: Lesley Selander. WST 89m.

War Room, The 1993 ★★★★½ Behind-the-scenes documentary looks at Bill Clinton's 1992 presidential campaign through viewpoints of chief strategists George Stephanopoulos and James Carville. Alternately compelling, touching, and self-satirical view of political process and the many players involved. Nominated for Best Documentary Oscar. C: James Carville, George Stephanopoulos. D: D.A. Pennebaker, Chris Hegedus. DOC [PG] 94m. V

War, The 1994 ★★★★ Vietnam vet (Costner) helps son learn valuable lesson during altercation with town bullies involving tree house. Warm, literate coming of age story with solid performances from Wood and Costner. C: Kevin Costner, Elijah Wood, Mare Winningham, Lexi Randall. D: Jon Avnet. DRA [PG-13] 127m. V

War Wagon, The 1967 ★★★½ Western romp has Wayne and Douglas doing everything they can to hijack a stagecoach full of money. Adventure rolls along with a light touch and plenty of action. C: John Wayne, Kirk Douglas, Howard Keel, Robert Walker, Keenan Wynn, Bruce Cabot. D: Burt Kennedy. WST 101m. V

Warbirds 1988 ★★ Military hardware is the star when U.S. troops try to suppress a revolution in the Middle East. Mindless effort. C: Jim Eldert, Cully Holland, Bill Brinsfield, Timothy Hicks. D: Ulli Lommel. ACT [R] 88m. V

WarGames 1983 ★★★★ Broderick is an underachieving computer whiz kid who accidentally taps into the national defense's response system and inadvertently pushes the world toward nuclear confrontation. An inventive thriller; exciting and thought provoking. C: Matthew Broderick, Dabney Coleman, John Wood, Ally Sheedy, Barry Corbin, Dennis Lipscomb. D: John Badham. DRA [PG] 110m. V

Warlock 1959 ★★★★ Tired of being terrorized by a vicious band of horse thieves, the town of Warlock hires expert gunslinger Fonda to protect them. More thoughtful than most Westerns, and just as exciting. C: Richard Widmark, Henry Fonda, Anthony Quinn, Dorothy Malone. D: Edward Dmytryk. WST 122m. V

Warlock 1991 ★★★ About to be executed by Puritans, a warlock (Sands) time-leaps from 1691 Massachusetts to present-day L.A. in search of a holy book that will give him supreme power. Grant is a likable witch hunter who follows him through time and partners up with Singer to save the world. Not classy, but a lot of fun. C: Julian Sands, Lori Singer, Richard E. Grant. D: Steve Miner. SFI [R] 103m. V

Warlock 2: The Armageddon 1993 ★ Silly follow-up to 1991 *Warlock* with the feisty creature battling new enemies in countdown to the ultimate battle. Dumb combination of horror and action. C: Julian Sands, Paula Marshall, Chris Young, Joanna Pacula. D: Tony Hickox. HOR 98m. V

Warm December, A 1973 ★★★ African-American take on *Love Story* casts Poitier as a newlywed whose wife is dying of sickle cell anemia. Romantics might go for it, but cynics will howl at the most cosmetic death scene in film history! C: Sidney Poitier, Esther Anderson. D: Sidney Poitier. DRA [PG] 100m.

Warm Nights on a Slow Moving Train 1989 Australian ★★★½ To support her drug-addicted brother, a schoolteacher works as prostitute. Despite a good cast, the forced moral dilemma is ultimately undermined by the too-numerous sex sequences. C: Wendy Hughes, Colin Friels, Norman Kaye, John Clayton. D: Bob Ellis. DRA [R] 90m. V

Warm Summer Rain, A 1989 ★ After a failed suicide attempt, a distraught young woman (Lynch) picks up a man in a bar and engages in some odd behavior. Some say the featured five-legged iguana is the real star. C: Kelly Lynch, Barry Tubb. D: Joe Gayton. DRA [R] 82m. V

Warning from Space 1956 *See* **Mysterious Satellite, The**

Warning Shot 1967 ★★★★ After shooting a doctor, cop Janssen tries to clear his name—and finds out that his shooting victim may not have been as innocent as people imagined. Interesting detective thriller with nifty pacing keeps viewers on the edge. C: David Janssen, Ed Begley, Keenan Wynn, Lillian Gish, Eleanor Parker, Sam Wanamaker, Stefanie Powers, George Sanders, George Grizzard, Steve Allen, Carroll O'Connor, Joan Collins, Walter Pidgeon. D: Buzz Kulik. CRI 100m.

Warning Sign 1985 ★★★ Government research lab is exposed by the press when dangerous chemicals leak. Cautionary shocker delivers some jolts. C: Sam Waterston, Kathleen Quinlan, Jeffrey De Munn, Yaphet Kotto, Richard Dysart. D: Hal Barwood. SFI [R] 100m. v

Warpath 1951 ★★★½ After his fiance is murdered, O'Brien goes on the trail to seek revenge. Entertaining Western that's chock full of action includes an exciting conclusion with a fort under siege. C: Edmond O'Brien, Dean Jagger, Forrest Tucker, Harry Carey Jr., Wallace Ford, Polly Bergen. D: Byron Haskin. WST 95m.

Warrior and the Slave Girl, The 1958 Italian ★★ When Canale, a princess with a bad attitude, meets sword-wielding Manni, the steel flies. Lots of costumes and lots of action. C: Ettore Manni, Georges Marchal, Gianna Maria Canale, Rafael Calvo. D: Vittorio Cottafavi. ACT 84m.

Warrior Within, The 1980 ★★ Ostensible tribute to Bruce Lee features various lesser-known martial arts champs, with Chuck Norris showing up for a few minutes to add some cachet. Watch the real thing instead. C: Chuck Norris, Mike Stone. ACT [R] 85m. v

Warriors of the Wasteland 1983 Italian ★★ Pair of good-hearted wanderers become guardians of hapless group of victims who are constantly pillaged by marauding crew of meanies. No-budget *Road Warrior* rip-off. C: Timothy Brent, Fred Williamson, Anna Kanakis. D: Enzo Castellari. ACT [R] 92m. v

Warriors, The 1955 British ★★½ In Flynn's last swashbuckling adventure, he plays an English prince who must rescue Dru and her children from evil count Finch. Standard stuff, but still fun. (a.k.a. *The Dark Avenger*) C: Errol Flynn, Joanne Dru, Peter Finch, Patrick Holt. D: Henry Levin. ACT 85m. v

Warriors, The 1979 ★★★½ A NYC street gang, framed for murder of a rival gang leader, fight their way back to home turf against an almost endless series of enemies. Crisp, exciting action film was attacked as inflammatory and some elements are dated today, but still delivers. C: Michael Beck, James Remar, David Patrick Kelly, Brian Tyler, Deborah Van Valkenburgh, Mercedes Ruehl. D: Walter Hill. ACT [R] 94m. v

Washington Story 1952 ★★★ Assigned to find some dirt in Congress, journalist Neal goes after new representative Johnson, but instead of attacking him, Neal ends up falling in love. Political romance. C: Van Johnson, Patricia Neal, Louis Calhern, Sidney Blackmer, Elizabeth Patterson. D: Robert Pirosh. DRA 81m.

Wasp Woman, The 1960 ★★★½ Cosmetics tycoon, using insect jelly to retain her youth, turns into a hideous monster instead. Camp horror classic skewers the beauty industry, providing equal parts chills and laughter. C: Susan Cabot, Fred Eisley, Barboura Morris, Michael Mark. D: Roger Corman. HOR 66m. v

Watch It 1993 ★★★ Group of young men deal with the opposite sex with varying levels of maturity while playing a continuous series of practical jokes on each other. Alternates between the observant and the obvious, but sparked by a strong cast. C: Peter Gallagher, Suzy Amis, John C. McGinley, Jon Tenney, Cynthia Stevenson, Lili Taylor, Tom Sizemore. D: Tom Flynn. DRA [R] 102m. v

Watch on the Rhine 1943 ★★★★½ Earnest, well-acted adaptation of Lillian Hellman WWII play about two German refugees (Lukas, Davis) in Washington, pursued by Nazi agents. Lukas won Oscar for Best Actor. Script by Hellman and Dashiell Hammett. C: Bette Davis, Paul Lukas, Geraldine Fitzgerald, Lucile Watson, Beulah Bondi, George Coulouris. D: Herman Shumlin. DRA 109m. v

Watch the Birdie 1950 ★★★½ Mild-mannered comedy features father/grandfather/photographer Skelton whose lens-pointing leads to humorous trouble and a climactic chase in this amiable family picture. C: Red Skelton, Arlene Dahl, Ann Miller, Leon Ames, Pamela Britton, Richard Robert, Mike Mazurki. D: Jack Donohue. COM 71m. v

Watcher in the Woods, The 1980 ★★★ Spiritual possession haunts American family in English home, as Johnson begins to behave like Davis's long-dead daughter. Murky melodrama was recut several times to get it right. Almost! C: Bette Davis, Carroll Baker, David McCallum, Lynn-Holly Johnson, Kyle Richards. D: John Hough. HOR [PG] 100m. v

Watchers 1988 U.S. ★ Ineffective horror film based on Dean R. Koontz's book, with Haim taking in a stray dog, little knowing it's a lab escapee that serves as a living homing beacon for a murderous monster. Violent and absurd. C: Corey Haim, Michael Ironside, Barbara Williams, Lala. D: Jon Hess. HOR [R] 99m. v

Watchers 2 1990 U.S. ★★ Not really a sequel but a second try at adapting Koontz's novel. This one's slightly better; here, it's Singer who flees with experimental pooch while a deadly creature rampages one step behind. Competently done, though the monster needs some work. C: Marc Singer, Tracy Scoggins, Jonathan Farwell, Mary Woronov. D: Thierry Notz. HOR [R] 101m. v

Watchers III, The 1994 ★★ Yet another attempt to bring Dean Koontz's book to the screen turns the story into a *Predator* ripoff, with Hauser and his military comrades fighting a mutant creature in the jungle. Few scares and fewer surprises. C: Wings Hauser, Gregory Scott Cummins, Daryl Roach, John K. Linton, Lolita Ronalds. D: Jeremy Stanford. HOR [R] 80m.

Water Babies, The 1979 British ★★½ A young chimney sweep is transported into animated underwater world. Combination of live action and animation suffers from disjointed, often dull presentation. C: James Mason, Billie Whitelaw, Bernard Cribbins, Joan Greenwood, David Tomlinson, Samantha Gates. D: Lionel Jeffries. FAM/DRA 92m. V

Waterdance, The 1992 ★★★★½ Young writer falls while mountain climbing and faces the prospect of life in a wheelchair. Moving ensemble piece about the other patients in his ward coping with a similar future. C: C. Eric Stoltz, Wesley Snipes, William Forsythe, Helen Hunt, Elizabeth Pena. D: Di Neal Jimenez, Michael Steinberg. DRA [R] 106m. V

Waterfront 1944 ★★½ Carradine and Naish are Nazi spies working in San Francisco during WWII, committing murders while trying to recruit German-Americans to their cause. Minor potboiler. C: John Carradine, J. Carrol Naish, Maris Wrixon, Edwin Maxwell, Terry Frost. D: Steve Sekely. CRI 66m.

Waterhole #3 1967 ★★★½ Entertaining Western comedy (produced by Blake Edwards) with Coburn and two Confederate army buddies after a cache of stolen Union gold buried in title desert location. Fun cast and brisk pace deliver the laughs. C: James Coburn, Carroll O'Connor, Margaret Blye, Claude Akins, Bruce Dern, Joan Blondell, Timothy Carey. D: William Graham. WST 95m. V

Waterland 1993 British ★★★★½ Odd but moving story of British high school teacher in Pittsburgh, recalling the incidents of his youth, even as they make a tragic impact on his current life. Wonderful visuals, exceptional performances. Loosely based on the novel by Graham Swift. C: Jeremy Irons, Sinead Cusack, Ethan Hawke, John Heard, Cara Buono, Grant Warnock. D: Stephen Gyllenhaal. DRA [R] 95m. V

Waterloo 1971 Italian ★★ Historical epic from the Russian director of *War and Peace*, but it isn't nearly as good, partially due to heavy editing from four-hour original. Film chronicles the exploits of Napoleon up through his defeat at Waterloo; battle scenes are exciting. C: Rod Steiger, Christopher Plummer, Orson Welles, Jack Hawkins, Virginia McKenna, Dan O'Herlihy, Michael Wilding. D: Sergei Bondarchuk. DRA [G] 123m. V

Waterloo Bridge 1940 ★★★★★ While bombs fall on London during air raids, a ballerina (Leigh) and a soldier (Taylor) meet and fall in love. Beautiful, romantic story about love truly conquering all; Leigh and Taylor are exquisite. Previously filmed in 1931. Remade in 1956 as *Gaby*. C: Vivien Leigh, Robert Taylor, Lucile Watson, Virginia Field, Maria Ouspenskaya. D: Mervyn LeRoy. DRA 103m. V

Watermelon Man 1970 ★★★ A bigoted white man wakes up and finds that his skin has turned brown overnight. Now he learns the real lessons in prejudice. Cambridge is great as metamorphosed zealot, but film's moral message grows repetitious and preachy. C: Godfrey Cambridge, Estelle Parsons, Howard Caine, D'Urville Martin. D: Melvin Van Peebles. COM [R] 97m. V

Watership Down 1978 British ★★★★½ Richard Adams' popular book translates into a stunning and very adult animated film about a group of rabbits seeking safety at title locale and their travails along the way. Far from a whimsical Disney film, this gripping feature may be too much for young viewers. Voices of John Hurt, Richard Briers, Ralph Richardson, Harry Andrews. D: Martin Rosen. FAM/DRA [PG] 93m. V

Watts Monster, The 1976 *See* **Dr. Black and Mr. Hyde**

Waxwork 1988 ★ Teenagers venture into haunted wax museum and find out the hard way that when one enters the exhibits, the monsters become real. Poorly structured horror film is often gory but rarely scary, with ridiculous free-for-all climax. C: Zach Galligan, Deborah Foreman, David Warner, Michelle Johnson, Miles O'Keeffe. D: Anthony Hickox. HOR [R] 97m. V

Waxwork II—Lost in Time 1992 ★★ A couple (Galligan and Schnarre), attempting to clear her of murder actually committed by a severed hand, travel through time and encounter various fearsome characters. Watch for Drew Barrymore cameo in the vampire sketch. C: Zach Galligan, Alexander Godunov, Monika Schnarre. D: Anthony Hickox. HOR [R] 104m. V

Way Ahead, The 1944 *See* **Immortal Battalion, The**

Way Down East 1920 ★★★★½ Classic silent melodrama has virtuous Gish corrupted by Barthelmess, with tragic results. This is the one where Lillian sails down a partially frozen river, on an ice floe, towards those rapids! Remade with Henry Fonda in 1935. C: Lillian Gish, Richard Barthelmess, Lowell Sherman. D: D.W. Griffith. DRA 148m. V

Way Down South 1939 ★★★ One-of-a-kind musical about a boy in the pre-Civil War South who tries to prevent his family's slaves from being sold to another plantation. Antique curio inadvertantly says more about racism in the 1930s than the (18)50s. C: Bobby Breen, Alan Mowbray, Clarence Muse, Ralph Morgan, Hall Johnson Choir. D: Bernard Vorhaus. MUS 61m.

Way of All Flesh, The 1927 ★★★★ A pillar of society (Jannings) crumbles, due to an adulterous affair. Age-old story works in this silent version, thanks to Emil's shattering, Oscar-winning performance. Rarely shown in recent years, and may now be "lost." Remade in 1940. C: Emil Jannings, Belle Bennett, Phyllis Haver. D: Victor Fleming. DRA 94m.

Way of All Flesh, The 1940 ★★★½ A wayward husband (Tamiroff) falls victim to his own excesses. George is the stand-out in this remake of the 1927 silent classic. C: Akim Tamiroff, Gladys George. D: Louis King. DRA 86m.

Way Out West 1937 ★★★★½ Laurel and Hardy deliver dead man's mine deed to wrong woman in hilarious comedy, one of their best. The deed chase scene is brilliantly timed, with Stan's tickling fit a classic. C: Stan Laurel, Oliver Hardy, Sharon Lynne, James Finlayson, Stanley Fields, Vivien Oakland. D: James W. Horne. COM 64m. V

Way to the Gold, The 1957 ★★★ Convict tries to get at hidden cache of gold before others do. Suspenseful. C: Jeffrey Hunter, Sheree North, Barry Sullivan, Neville Brand, Walter Brennan. D: Robert D. Webb. ACT 94m.

Way to the Stars 1945 *See* **Johnny in the Clouds**

Way...Way Out 1966 ★★ An astronaut's romantic troubles don't stop even when he goes to the moon. Jerry Lewis gag-fest runs low on oxygen. C: Jerry Lewis, Connie Stevens, Robert Morley, Dennis Weaver, Anita Ekberg. D: Gordon Douglas. COM 106m.

Way We Were, The 1973 ★★★★ Classy soap opera is sparked by inspired casting of Redford and Streisand as mismatched lovers, whose ideological differences pull them apart during McCarthy era. Barbra captures liberal, prefeminist character to a T. Oscar-winning theme song by Marvin Hamlisch, Alan and Marilyn Bergman. C: Barbra Streisand, Robert Redford, Bradford Dillman, Murray Hamilton. D: Sydney Pollack. DRA [PG] 118m. V

Way West, The 1967 ★★ Misfired attempt at epic story, based on A.B. Guthrie, Jr.'s, Pulitzer Prize-winning novel, of a wagon train's journey to Oregon in the 1840s. The outstanding cast (including debuting Sally Field) is wasted in underheated, poorly developed film. C: Kirk Douglas, Robert Mitchum, Richard Widmark, Lola Albright, Michael Witney, Stubby Kaye, Sally Field, Jack Elam. D: Andrew V. McLaglen. WST 122m. V

Wayne's World 1992 ★★★½ Popular Saturday Night Live sketch becomes an intermittently funny feature, with Myers and Carvey as suburban "dudes" in search of "babes" and rock 'n' roll success. Gleeful party atmosphere and lots of goofy gags. C: Mike Myers, Dana Carvey, Rob Lowe, Tia Carrere, Brian Doyle-Murray, Lara Flynn Boyle, Kurt Fuller, Colleen Camp, Donna Dixon, Meat Loaf. D: Penelope Spheeris. COM [PG-13] 95m. V

Wayne's World 2 1993 ★★★ Myers, searching for meaning in his life, tries to get a "Waynestock" concert off the ground. Sequel to the surprise hit is uneven and sometimes downright sloppy, but several sequences are hysterically funny; Myers' kung fu battle with Hong is a highlight. C: Mike Myers, Dana Carvey, Christopher Walken, Tia Carrere, Ralph Brown, Kim Basinger, Chris Farley, James Hong, Ed O'Neill, Olivia D'Abo. D: Stephen Surjik. COM [PG-13] 94m. V

Wayward Bus, The 1957 ★★½ A varied bunch of bus passengers is stranded in a farmhouse after a mountain landslide. Talky adaptation of John Steinbeck novel. C: Joan Collins, Jayne Mansfield, Dan Dailey. D: Victor Vicas. DRA 89m.

W.C. Fields and Me 1976 ★★½ Pseudobiography of movie comedian W.C. Fields (Steiger), as seen through eyes of his mistress Carla Monti (Perrine). Steiger is the whole show. C: Rod Steiger, Valerie Perrine, John Marley, Jack Cassidy, Paul Stewart, Bernadette Peters, Billy Barty. D: Arthur Hiller. DRA [PG] 111m.

We All Loved Each Other So Much 1974 Italian ★★★★ An actress (Sandrelli) is the object of three men's affections over a 30-year period. Rollicking, often touching comedy works best for fans of the Fellini movies to which it pays tribute. C: Stefania Sandrelli, Vittorio Gassman, Nino Manfredi, Aldo Fabrizi. D: Ettore Scola. COM 124m. V

We Are All Murderers 1952 French ★★★★ After being honored for killing during war, befuddled young man is now on death row for murdering during peacetime. Intriguing philosophical drama with strong anti-capital punishment message. Well played by good cast. C: Marcel Mouloudji, Raymond Pellegrin, Louis Seigner, Antoine Balpetre, Claude Leydu, Georges Poujouly, Amedeo Nazzari. D: Andre Cayatte. DRA 113m.

We Are Not Alone 1939 ★★★★½ Muni falls for a governess and is subsequently accused of murdering his wife. Gripping, extremely suspenseful crime drama with strong performances. Adapted by James Hilton from his novel. C: Paul Muni, Jane Bryan, Flora Robson, Una O'Connor, Henry Daniell, Cecil Kellaway, Alan Napier. D: Edmund Goulding. CRI 112m.

We Dive at Dawn 1943 British ★★★★ Stiff-upper-lip drama of a submarine crew in WWII, focusing on the men's relationships as much as combat. Intelligent and well acted. C: John Mills, Eric Portman, Niall MacGinnis, Reginald Purdell, Louis Bradfield, Ronald Millar. D: Anthony Asquith. DRA 98m. V

We Live Again 1934 ★★★★ Russian 19th-century nobleman March believes life is missing something until he falls in love with Sten, a woman of the lower classes. Entertaining costume drama. One of many screen versions of Tolstoy's novel *Resurrection*. C: Fredric March, Anna Sten, Sam Jaffe, C. Aubrey

Smith, Jane Baxter, Ethel Griffies. D: Rouben Mamoulian. DRA 82m.

We of the Never Never 1982 Australian ★★★★ In 1900, McGregor moves with her husband to Australian Outback, known as the Never Never. There she proves herself capable, while forging friendship between white settlers and Aborigines. A thoughtful story, that is beautiful to look at. C: Angela Punch McGregor, Arthur Dignam, Tony Barry, Tommy Lewis, Martin Vaughan. D: Igor Auzins. DRA [G] 136m. V

We Still Kill the Old Way 1967 Italian ★★★½ Low-budget but entertaining crime drama looks at customs and traditions of Sicilian mob family, showing the psychological motivations behind revenge murders. Different and well played. C: Irene Papas, Gian Maria Volonte, Luigi Pistilli. D: Elio Petri. CRI 92m.

We Think the World of You 1988 British ★★★½ A lonely homosexual (Bates) tries to help the man he loves by befriending his dog. Charming comedy/drama for admirers of English style. C: Alan Bates, Gary Oldman, Frances Barber. D: Colin Gregg. COM [PG] 94m. V

We Three 1985 Italian ★★★½ Biography chronicles childhood days of Mozart and his tribulations as a child prodigy in music. Entertaining, great music. C: Christopher Davidson, Lino Capolicchio, Gianni Caino, Carlo Delle Piane, Ida Di Benedetto, Dario Parisini, Barbara Rebeschini. D: Pupi Avati. DRA 90m.

We Were Dancing 1942 ★★★½ While at her own engagement party, Her Royal Highness Princess Shearer takes off with someone other than her intended groom. A trifle with all the expected smiles, adapted from Noel Coward's play *Tonight at 8:30.* C: Norma Shearer, Melvyn Douglas, Gail Patrick, Marjorie Main, Reginald Owen, Connie Gilchrist, Sig Ruman. D: Robert Z. Leonard. COM 94m.

We Were Strangers 1949 ★★★★ During '30s Cuban revolt, Garfield and Jones join clandestine band that plots overthrow of corrupt government officials. Neatly played political drama, marked by good performances from leads; excellent direction. C: Jennifer Jones, John Garfield, Pedro Armendariz, Gilbert Roland, Ramon Novarro. D: John Huston. DRA 106m.

We Who Are Young 1940 ★★★½ Novice worker Turner falls for colleague Shelton, despite company policy against employee romances. Workable drama with touches of good humor. C: Lana Turner, John Shelton, Gene Lockhart, Grant Mitchell, Henry Armetta, Jonathan Hale, Clarence Wilson. D: Harold Bucquet. DRA 79m.

Weapon, The 1956 British ★★★ After accidentally shooting a friend, a boy goes on the run. Somewhat suspenseful. C: Steve Cochran, Lizabeth Scott, George Cole, Herbert Marshall, Nicole Maurey, Jon Whiteley. D: Val Guest. CRI 81m.

Weavers, The: Wasn't That a Time! 1982 ★★★★½ Legendary folk-singers of the 1940s, who inspired such later groups as Peter, Paul and Mary, reunite for a concert at Carnegie Hall. Thoughtful, entertaining musical documentary captures the spirited political commitment of the quartet especially well. C: Lee Hays, Pete Seeger, Fred Hellerman, Ronnie Gilbert. D: Jim Brown. DOC [PG] 78m. V

Web of Evidence 1959 British ★★★★ Johnson seeks to uncover evidence proving his father innocent of murder charges. Well acted story that benefits from good use of British locations. (a.k.a. *Beyond This Place*) C: Van Johnson, Vera Miles, Emlyn Williams, Bernard Lee, Jean Kent, Ralph Truman, Leo McKern. D: Jack Cardiff. CRI 88m.

Web of Fear 1963 French ★★★ A music teacher is wrongly accused of murder. Mild suspense. C: Michele Morgan, Dany Saval, Claude Rich, George Rigaud. D: Francois Villiers. CRI 92m.

Web, The 1947 ★★★★ After killing his boss's enemy, bodyguard O'Brien soon realizes he's fallen victim to an elaborate double cross. Tightly controlled and very suspenseful crime thriller, with a neat performance from O'Brien. C: Ella Raines, Edmond O'Brien, William Bendix, Vincent Price, Maria Palmer. D: Michael Gordon. CRI 87m.

Webb Wilder's Corn Flicks 1992 ★★★ Trio of comic shorts includes two featuring rock-and-roller Wilder investigating strange phenomena, plus another about a disease-phobic. Likable diversion is propelled by Wilder's laid-back charm and solid rock score. D: Stephen Mims. COM 64m. V

Wedding, A 1978 ★★★★ Another sprawling, star-studded Altman mosaic, this time focusing on an upper-crust wedding fraught with family crises. Always fun to watch, but don't expect a plot. C: Carol Burnett, Lillian Gish, Mia Farrow, Paul Dooley, Vittorio Gassman, Geraldine Chaplin, Lauren Hutton, Desi Arnaz, Amy Stryker. D: Robert Altman. COM [PG] 125m. V

Wedding Banquet, The 1993 Taiwanese ★★★★ A wedding arranged to please the homosexual groom's old-fashioned parents gets totally out of hand. Charming cross-cultural comedy gently pokes fun at Chinese and American attitudes about sexuality and relationships without stereotyping. C: Winston Chao, May Chin, Mitchell Lichtenstein, Sihung Lung, Ah-Loh Gua, Tine Pien. D: Ang Lee. COM [R] 111m.

Wedding in Galilee 1987 Israeli ★★★½ The interesting treatment of the Israeli/Palestinian conflict, set against preparations for the wedding of a Palestinian elder's son. Clash of traditional values and modern tensions is rendered in lengthy but entertaining fashion.

Subtitles. C: Ali M. Akili, Makram Khouri, Anna Achdian. D: Michel Khleifi. DRA 113m. v

Wedding March, The 1928 ★★★★½ Stunning silent tale of a penniless prince torn between the rich woman he should marry and the poor one he loves. Only the first half of von Stroheim's film survives, but it stands on its own plenty well, as one of the director's best. C: Erich von Stroheim, Fay Wray, ZaSu Pitts. D: Erich von Stroheim. DRA 113m. v

Wedding Night, The 1935 ★★★½ Sten, living in Connecticut countryside, inexplicably finds herself being romanced by a prosperous business exec. Light romance unfolds nicely. C: Gary Cooper, Anna Sten, Ralph Bellamy, Walter Brennan, Helen Vinson. D: King Vidor. DRA 84m.

Wedding Party, The 1969 ★★ After meeting prospective bride's family, uncertain groom reconsiders marriage. Made in 1963 but not released until 1969, film is poorly plotted, talky and dull. Inauspicious debuts for director De Palma, star Clayburgh, and supporting actor De Niro. C: Jill Clayburgh, Charles Pfluger, Valda Satterfield, Raymond McNally, Judy Thomas, Robert DeNiro. D: Cynthia Munroe, Brian De Palma. COM 90m. v

Wedding Rehearsal 1932 British ★★★½ An English aristrocrat (Young) manages to stay single by setting up all the young women his grandmother finds for him with his friends. Eventually, he falls for a commoner (Oberon, in an early film appearance). Atmospheric and light as a feather. C: Merle Oberon, Roland Young, Wendy Barrie. D: Alexander Korda. COM 84m.

Weddings and Babies 1960 ★★★★ A photographer and model have a brief affair in Manhattan. Small, delicate romance. C: Viveca Lindfors, John Myhers. D: Morris Engel. DRA 81m.

Wednesday's Child 1972 *See* **Family Life**

Wee Geordie 1956 British ★★★★ A small Scotsman gets into bodybuilding and becomes hammer thrower for Olympic competition. Slight but entertaining comedy with several charming moments. C: Bill Travers, Alastair Sim, Norah Gorsen, Molly Urquhart, Francis DeWolff. D: Frank Launder. COM 93m.

Wee Willie Winkie 1937 ★★★★ Temple and mother (Lang) head to British-occupied India where curly Shirley charms her crusty old grandfather (Smith), beguiles a soldier (McLaglan), and almost single-handedly stops a battle at Khyber Pass. One of Temple's better films, marked by talented cast and brisk direction from Ford. C: Shirley Temple, Victor McLaglen, C. Aubrey Smith, Cesar Romero, June Lang. D: John Ford. FAM/DRA 100m. v

Weeds 1987 ★★★★ Prison inmate discovers theater and uses playwriting and acting to rehabilitate himself and his friends. Occasionally clumsy but also enjoyable and frequently funny. C: Nick Nolte, Rita Taggart, John Toles-Bey, Joe Mantegna, Ernie Hudson. D: John Hancock. DRA [R] 109m. v

Week-end in Havana 1941 ★★★½ Faye, an American in Cuba, vies for affections of Romero and Payne. Inconsequential but enjoyable musical. Don't miss Carmen Miranda's colorful support. C: Alice Faye, Carmen Miranda, John Payne, Cesar Romero, Cobina Wright Jr., George Barbier, Leonid Kinskey, Sheldon Leonard, Billy Gilbert. D: Walter Lang. MUS 80m.

Weekend 1967 French ★★★★ Young couple on a drive into the country become increasingly caught up in violence they witness along the way. A disturbing, angry, often riveting film, which works as both a surrealist nightmare and an anticapitalist polemic. C: Mireille Darc, Jean Yanne, Jean-Pierre Leaud. D: Jean-Luc Godard. DRA 105m. v

Weekend at Bernie's 1989 ★★★½ Slapdash comedy is at its best when its taste is at its worst, with upwardly mobile McCarthy and Silverman traveling to their boss' beach house, only to find him dead. Kiser gets most of the laughs as the surprisingly limber corpse. C: Andrew McCarthy, Jonathan Silverman, Catherine Mary Stewart, Terry Kiser. D: Ted Kotcheff. COM [PG-13] 101m. v

Weekend at Bernie's II 1993 ★★½ Pointless sequel finds our two young heroes in St. Thomas searching for Bernie's cash stash, with his shambling corpse not far behind. Coasts by on Kiser's funny contortions and attractive scenery, but largely a retread of first film. C: Andrew McCarthy, Jonathan Silverman, Terry Kiser. D: Robert Klane. COM [PG] 89m. v

Weekend at the Waldorf 1945 ★★★½ Second-class retread of *Grand Hotel* switches setting to '50s New York and updates characters. Rogers comes off best as fading musical comedy star, but script is trite. C: Ginger Rogers, Lana Turner, Walter Pidgeon, Van Johnson, Edward Arnold, Phyllis Thaxter, Keenan Wynn, Robert Benchley, Leon Ames, Porter Hall, George Zucco, Xavier Cugat. D: Robert Z. Leonard. DRA 130m. v

Weekend With Father 1951 ★★★ Widow and widower marry and integrate, their respective families with comic results. Precursor to *Yours, Mine and Ours* and television's *The Brady Bunch* contains all the expected family situation laughs. C: Van Heflin, Patricia Neal, Virginia Field, Gigi Perreau, Richard Denning. D: Douglas Sirk. COM 83m.

Weekend With the Babysitter 1970 ★★ Middle-aged filmmaker making hip "youth" picture spends a weekend with the family babysitter to learn about younger generation. Cheap exploitation fare takes itself far too seriously. C: Susan Roman, George Carey. D: Don Henderson. DRA [R] 93m. v

Weird Science 1985 ★★ Two teenage nerds

(Hall and Mitchell-Smith) create a perfect woman (LeBrock) via computer. Not as smutty as it might have been, but even Hall's appeal can't carry it. C: Anthony Michael Hall, Kelly LeBrock, Ilan Mitchell—Smith, Suzanne Snyder, Robert Downey Jr. D: John Hughes. COM [PG-13] 94m. V

Weird Woman 1944 ★★★★ Chaney is a newly married groom who finds trouble waiting when he brings his tropical island bride home and his former lover disapproves. Strange and different suspense thriller has some good twisted moments. Remade as *Burn, Witch, Burn* and *Witches' Brew*. C: Lon Chaney Jr., Anne Gwynne, Evelyn Ankers, Ralph Morgan, Lois Collier. D: Reginald LeBorg. DRA 64m.

Welcome Home 1989 ★★½ Vietnam vet returns home after being thought dead 17 years. Slow-motion soap opera with scant story line. C: Kris Kristofferson, JoBeth Williams, Sam Waterston, Brian Keith, Trey Wilson. D: Franklin J. Schaffner. DRA [R] 92m. V

Welcome Home, Roxy Carmichael 1990 ★★½ Ryder shines as misfit teen in otherwise uninspired comedy/drama about a movie star's impending return to her hometown and the chaos it causes. The satire is awkward, but Ryder fans will enjoy it. C: Winona Ryder, Jeff Daniels, Laila Robins, Dinah Manoff. D: Jim Abrahams. COM [PG-13] 98m. V

Welcome in Vienna 1986 Austrian ★★★★½ Final film in Corti's superb trilogy about Austrian Jews and their reaction to Hitler. Brutally honest and very well made. The first two entries were *God Doesn't Believe in Us Anymore* and *Santa Fe*. C: Gabriel Barylli, Nicolas Brieger, Claudia Messner, Hubert Mann, Liliana Nelska. D: Axel Corti. DRA 126m.

Welcome Stranger 1947 ★★★★ Crosby substitutes for small town doctor on vacation, and romances local woman while soaking up rural ambiance. Well done, amiable feature. C: Bing Crosby, Barry Fitzgerald, Joan Caulfield, Wanda Hendrix, Frank Faylen, Elizabeth Patterson. D: Elliott Nugent. DRA 107m.

Welcome to Hard Times 1967 ★★★½ Western parable casts Fonda as the moral conscience of a small town terrorized by a killer (Ray). Gripping, well-acted oater. C: Henry Fonda, Janice Rule, Aldo Ray, Keenan Wynn, Janis Paige. D: Burt Kennedy. WST 105m.

Welcome to L.A. 1977 ★★★½ Lonely California hipsters spend their days whining and their nights dining. Strong ensemble cast makes this slice-of-life drama surprisingly compelling. C: Keith Carradine, Geraldine Chaplin, Harvey Keitel, Sally Kellerman, Lauren Hutton, Sissy Spacek, Denver Pyle. D: Alan Rudolph. DRA [R] 106m. V

Welfare 1975 ★★★★ Solid documentary about a day in the life of a New York City welfare office, including the frustrations and red tape that ensnare clients and case workers alike. Intelligent filmmaking on an important subject. D: Frederick Wiseman. DOC 167m.

Well-Digger's Daughter, The 1941 French ★★★★ Young French peasant woman becomes pregnant by her wealthy lover; when he is MIA during the war, she copes with her situation alone, while her father disapproves. Touching drama filled with pathos and gentle humor. C: Raimu, Fernandel, Josette Day, Charpin, George Grey. D: Marcel Pagnol. DRA 142m.

Well, The 1951 ★★★★ When a child disappears, residents of a small town turn ugly until she is discovered trapped in a well. Taut, neatly played psychological drama deals with delicate racial and social issues with insight. C: Richard Rober, Henry Morgan, Barry Kelley, Christine Larson, Maidie Norman, Ernest Anderson. D: Leo Popkin, Russell Rouse. DRA 85m. V

Wells Fargo 1937 ★★★½ McCrea devotes his life to building up his Wells Fargo transport service, but ignores wife Dee. Largely fictional history, full of action. C: Joel McCrea, Frances Dee, Bob Burns, Lloyd Nolan, Ralph Morgan, Johnny Mack Brown, Porter Hall, Robert Cummings, Harry Davenport. D: Frank Lloyd. DRA 94m.

We're Back: A Dinosaur's Story 1993 ★★★½ Dinosaurs come to Manhattan in this animated film. An evil scientist wants to put them in a zoo, but their human friend saves them. Strong animation, but the sentimental story works best with young children. Voices of John Goodman, Charles Fleischer, Rhea Perlman, Martin Short, Walter Cronkite, Julia Child, Jay Leno, Yeardly Smith. D: Dick Zondag, Ralph Zondag, Phil Nibbelink, Simon Wells. FAM/DRA [G] 72m. V

We're No Angels 1955 ★★★½ Trio of escaped convicts use a French family as cover to avoid capture and return to Devil's Island. Generally murky comedy has some very bright Bogart touches. Remade loosely in 1989. C: Humphrey Bogart, Aldo Ray, Peter Ustinov, Joan Bennett, Basil Rathbone. D: Michael Curtiz. COM 106m. V

We're No Angels 1989 ★★½ Lunkhead jailbirds (DeNiro, Penn) dress up as priests, and get involved in local miracle. Uneasy mix of comedy and violence gets little help from incessant mugging of two leads. Written (surprisingly) by David Mamet, from the 1955 film. C: Robert De Niro, Sean Penn, Demi Moore, Bruno Kirby. D: Neil Jordan. COM [PG-13] 106m. V

We're Not Dressing 1934 ★★★½ Rich folk are shipwrecked on a tropical island, where they become dependent on a lowly seaman (Crosby). Genial tuner, fabulous cast. C: Bing Crosby, Carole Lombard, George Burns, Gracie Allen, Ethel Merman, Ray Milland. D: Norman Taurog. MUS 77m. V

We're Not Married 1952 ★★★★ Six couples are happily married until each pair learns that the nuptials weren't legal. Episodic film rises and falls though overall cast has a good deal of fun. Rogers and Allen are the real standouts. C: Ginger Rogers, Fred Allen, Victor Moore, Marilyn Monroe, Paul Douglas, David Wayne, Eve Arden, Louis Calhern, Zsa Gabor, James Gleason, Jane Darwell, Eddie Bracken, Mitzi Gaynor. D: Edmund Goulding. COM 85m. V

Werewolf in a Girl's Dormitory 1961 Italian ★ Prim head of all-girls' school terrorizes students when he turns into a werewolf. Horribly dubbed. C: Carl Schell, Barbara Lass, Curt Lowens, Maurice Marsac. D: Richard Benson. HOR 84m. V

Werewolf of London 1935 ★★★ Botanist (Hull) infected with curse of lycanthropy in Tibet, terrorizes London. More historical interest than scares, but a competent mood piece nonetheless. C: Henry Hull, Warner Oland, Valerie Hobson, Lester Matthews, Spring Byington. D: Stuart Walker. HOR 75m. V

Werewolf Vs. the Vampire Woman 1970 Spanish ★★★★ Energetic, if illogical chiller in which a werewolf (Naschy) and a pair of students tangle with a bloodthirsty countess. One of the best-known—and most fun—of Naschy's horror films. C: Paul Naschy, Patty Shepard, Gaby Fuchs, Barbara Capell, Andres Resino. D: Leon Kilmovsky. HOR [R] 86m.

Werner Herzog's Woyzeck 1978 *See* **Woyzeck**

Wes Craven's New Nightmare 1994 ★★★★ Craven re-energizes the *Nightmare on Elm Street* franchise with this deliciously deceptive exercise in reality manipulation. Cast plays itself, working in the horror movie industry, gradually finding themselves terrorized by the fantasies they created in the previous *Elm Street* movies. Fans of the series will rejoice. C: Heather Langenkamp, Robert Englund, Miko Hughes, John Saxon, David Newsom, Wes Craven. D: Wes Craven. HOR [R] 112m. V

West of Shanghai 1937 ★★★ When American oil tycoon Oliver is given trouble by Chinese bandits, warlord Karloff comes to Oliver's aid to protect mutual interests. Colorful melodrama. C: Boris Karloff, Gordon Oliver, Beverly Roberts, Ricardo Cortez, Sheila Bromley, Vladimir Sokoloff, Richard Loo. D: John Farrow. DRA 64m.

West of the Divide 1934 ★★★ Wayne goes in search of his parents' murderers and his missing brother. Plenty of action in this B-Western, remake of *Remake of Partners of the Trail.* C: John Wayne, Virginia Brown Faire, George "Gabby" Hayes. D: Robert Bradbury. WST 54m. V

West of the Law 1942 ★★★½ Jones and McCoy battle a gold thief who seems to be a scion of the community. Last entry in *Rough Riders* series, with plenty of shoot-'em-up action. C: Buck Jones, Tim McCoy. D: Howard Bretherton. WST 60m.

West of the Pecos 1945 ★★★½ After a meat magnate's daughter is kidnapped by outlaws, Mitchum rides in to save the day. Action-filled Western adapted from Zane Grey tale. C: Robert Mitchum, Barbara Hale. D: Edward Killy. WST 66m.

West of Tombstone 1942 ★★★ When the stagecoach is robbed, the townspeople are sure that Billy the Kid, supposedly dead, was the perpetrator. One of endless series of efficiently made but undistinguished Starrett B-Westerns. C: Charles Starrett, Russell Hayden, Cliff Edwards, Lloyd Bridges. D: Howard Bretherton. WST 59m.

West of Zanzibar 1928 ★★★★ Maimed jungle recluse (Chaney) plots revenge on the man who crippled him. Horror master Browning (*Freaks*) serves up a silent, tingling tale of the grotesque with sentimental overtones. Remake: *Kongo.* C: Lon Chaney, Lionel Barrymore, Mary Nolan, Warner Baxter. D: Tod Browning. HOR 63m. V

West of Zanzibar 1954 British ★★★ Not to be confused with Lon Chaney silent, this is cinematic junk food about ivory hunters and angry native tribespeople. An insubstantial but momentarily pleasing diversion. Sequel to the 1951 *Ivory Hunters.* C: Anthony Steel, Sheila Sim, Edric Connor, Orlando Martins. D: Harry Watt. ACT 84m.

West Point of the Air 1935 ★★★½ Service drama of career sergeant (Beery) forcing his reluctant son (Young) into Army air corps. Studio gloss and production values raise it slightly above average. C: Wallace Beery, Robert Young, Maureen O'Sullivan, Lewis Stone, James Gleason, Rosalind Russell, Robert Taylor. D: Richard Rosson. DRA 100m.

West Point Story 1950 ★★★½ Hokey musical about Cagney going to the military academy to produce a show. He's fun and Day is vivacious as always. C: James Cagney, Virginia Mayo, Doris Day, Gordon MacRae, Gene Nelson. D: Roy Del Ruth. MUS 107m. V

West Side Story 1961 ★★★★★ Dynamic, near-perfect filming of Broadway musical update of *Romeo and Juliet,* putting tale of star-crossed lovers in context of Puerto Rican vs. American street-gang war. Emphasis is on brilliant Jerome Robbins choreography and exciting Leonard Bernstein/Stephen Sondheim score ("Tonight," "Maria," "Somewhere," "Something's Coming"). Leads Beymer and Wood are upstaged by Supporting Oscar-winners Chakiris and Moreno. Film won 10 Oscars in all, including Best Picture. C: Natalie Wood, Richard Beymer, George Chakiris, Rita Moreno, Russ Tamblyn. D: Robert Wise, Jerome Robbins. MUS 151m. V

Westbound 1959 ★★★ Scott helps Steele and husband Pate run stagecoach line in face of opposition from outlaws. The last of the seven Westerns Scott and Boetticher made together. C: Randolph Scott, Virginia Mayo,

Karen Steele, Michael Dante, Andrew Duggan, Michael Pate. D: Budd Boetticher. WST 72m.

Western Courage 1935 ★★★ Maynard is boss on a dude ranch, smitten with new guest (Mitchell), a spoiled socialite. Ken does his usual riding and roping tricks, but the film is most notable for having a strong leading lady. C: Ken Maynard, Geneva Mitchell. D: Spencer Gordon Bennett. WST 61m.

Western Union 1941 ★★★½ A Technicolor extravaganza with a big cast and numerous set pieces that has Young struggling to finish expanding the Western Union telegraph link to the Old West, with Scott as heroic outlaw. Trim, evocative direction keeps film moving. C: Robert Young, Randolph Scott, Dean Jagger, Virginia Gilmore, John Carradine, Slim Summerville, Chill Wills, Barton MacLane. D: Fritz Lang. WST 95m. V

Westerner, The 1940 ★★★★½ Brennan won well-deserved third Oscar for his multifaceted portrayal of Judge Roy Bean in this handsomely mounted Western. Cooper is stranger who rides into Bean's town and ongoing land war and is nearly hanged for his trouble. Alternately funny and thrilling. C: Gary Cooper, Walter Brennan, Fred Stone, Doris Davenport, Forrest Tucker, Dana Andrews. D: William Wyler. WST 100m. V

Westfront 1918 1930 German ★★★★ Morbid but powerful anti-war film about two soldiers from opposite sides having to share a trench during WWI. Silent master Pabst's first sound film. C: Gustav Diesl, Fritz Kampers. D: G.W. Pabst. DRA 90m. V

Westward Bound 1931 ★★★½ A spoiled rich kid is sent to work on a cattle drive by his father. This film, technically ahead of its time, had an unusually good script. C: Buffalo Bill, Jr., Buddy Roosevelt, Allene Ray. D: Harry S. Webb. WST 65m.

Westward Ho the Wagons! 1956 ★★★½ On the way out West, a wagon train is set upon by attacking Indians. Solid B-movie with budget is family fare that stays on track right to its destination. C: Fess Parker, Kathleen Crowley, Jeff York, Sebastian Cabot, George Reeves. D: William Beaudine. WST 94m. V

Westward Passage 1932 ★★★ Family melodrama in which Harding divorces to marry for true love. Interesting period piece with a very young Olivier. Debut of child star Bonita Granville. C: Ann Harding, Laurence Olivier, Irving Pichel, ZaSu Pitts, Juliette Compton, Irene Purcell, Don Alvarado, Florence Lake, Edgar Kennedy, Ethel Griffies. D: Robert Milton. DRA 73m.

Westward the Women 1951 ★★★★ Surprisingly effective Western has Taylor leading wagon train of women across plains to meet mail-order husbands. Set pieces take second-place to more intimate moments. Avoid colorized version, which looks like bad hand-painted postcards. C: Robert Taylor, Denise Darcel, Beverly Dennis, John McIntire, Hope Emerson, Lenore Longergan, Julie Bishop, Marilyn Erskine. D: William Wellman. WST 118m. V

Westworld 1973 ★★★★ Futuristic amusement park allows visitors to take part in various historical scenarios—until things start to go awry. Imaginative, scary tale, with a chilling performance by Brynner as deadly, malfunctioning robot gunslinger. C: Richard Benjamin, Yul Brynner, James Brolin, Norman Bartold, Alan Oppenheimer, Victoria Shaw, Dick VanPatten. D: Michael Crichton. SFI [PG] 90m. V

Wet Parade, The 1932 ★★★½ Upton Sinclair novel of Prohibition and corruption is treated with a strange mix of MGM gloss and pre-Production Code cynicism. Stone is dissipated Southerner, Huston crusades against booze and Durante is—improbably—a Prohibition agent. Strange, but well worth viewing. C: Walter Huston, Myrna Loy, Neil Hamilton, Lewis Stone, Dorothy Jordon, Robert Young, Jimmy Durante, Wallace Ford. D: Victor Fleming. DRA 120m.

Wetherby 1985 British ★★★★ Profoundly disturbing film about a young man who commits suicide in a stranger's home and the emotional havoc his act unleashes. Dark, effective directorial debut for Hare. C: Vanessa Redgrave, Joely Richardson, Judi Dench, Ian Holm, Tim McInnery. D: David Hare. DRA [R] 104m. V

We've Never Been Licked 1943 ★★★ Shrill WWII drama of American raised in Japan, who is forced to choose sides when war breaks out. Dated, but interesting for Quine and early Mitchum. C: Richard Quine, Noah Berry Jr., Robert Mitchum, Anne Gwynne, Martha O'Driscoll. D: John Rawlins. DRA 103m.

Whalers, The 1942 Swedish ★★★★ Excellent Swedish adventure film about last whaling expedition to Arctic before outbreak of WWII. Allan Bohlin is wastrel youth who learns lesson at sea. Amazing cinematography. C: Allan Bohlin, Hank Aabel, Tutia Rolf. D: Anders Henrikson. ACT 79m.

Whales of August, The 1987 ★★★★ Virtually plotless character study of a pair of elderly sisters, one who is blind, living hermetic existence on New England island. On the dull side, but must be seen for historic pairing of film legends Gish and Davis. C: Bette Davis, Lillian Gish, Vincent Price, Ann Sothern, Harry Carey Jr., Frank Grimes. D: Lindsay Anderson. DRA 90m. V

What a Carve Up! 1962 *See* **No Place Like Homocide!**

What a Way to Go! 1964 ★★★ Young widow (MacLaine) has trouble keeping a series of rich husbands in the pink. Colorful, lavish, star-studded comedy maintains its manic edge for most of its length. C: Shirley MacLaine, Paul Newman, Dean Martin, Gene Kelly, Robert Mitchum, Dick Van Dyke, Bob Cummings. D: J. Lee Thompson. COM 111m.

What About Bob? 1991 ★★★★ Hyperkinetic patient (Murray) can't live without psychiatrist (Dreyfuss). He crashes shrink's vacation home and becomes member of the family. Murray and Dreyfuss pull out the stops in manic comedy of ill-manners. Good star chemistry provides many laughs. C: Bill Murray, Richard Dreyfuss, Julie Hagerty, Charlie Korsmo. D: Frank Oz. COM [PG] 100m. V

What Did You Do in the War, Daddy? 1966 ★★½ WWII shenanigans as fun-loving soldiers try to invade an equally wacky village in Sicily. Episodic comedy provides slapstick and forced jokes. C: James Coburn, Dick Shawn, Sergio Fantoni, Aldo Ray, Harry Morgan, Carroll O'Connor, Leon Askin, Giovanna Ralli. D: Blake Edwards. COM 119m. V

What Do You Say to a Naked Lady? 1970 ★★★ Alan Funt brings his *Candid Camera* antics to feature film. Most of the vignettes deal with sex one way or another. Some funny moments. C: Alan Funt, Richard Roundtree. D: Allen Funt. COM [R] 85m. V

What Ever Happened to Baby Jane? 1962 ★★★★½ Two stars have a field day playing former film-star sisters at odds with each other—to say the least. Davis plays insane Jane, torturing crippled Crawford while she rehearses bizarre "comeback" act with Buono. Bette singing "I've Written a Letter to Daddy" is just one highlight. C: Bette Davis, Joan Crawford, Victor Buono. D: Robert Aldrich. HOR 132m. V

What Ever Happened to Baby Jane? 1991 ★★★ Sisters Lynn and Vanessa, together for the first time, pick the wrong vehicle in tame remake of 1962 camp horror classic. Every implausible plot device of original is magnified, while Lynn's Jane is hysterically funny. C: Vanessa Redgrave, Lynn Redgrave, John Glover, Bruce Young, Amy Steel, John Clough. D: David Greene. HOR 100m. TVM

What Every Woman Knows 1934 ★★★½ A woman pushes her husband into a political career for which he's ill-suited. Charmingly stagebound version of James Barrie play, a fine showcase for "the First Lady of the American Stage." C: Helen Hayes, Brian Aherne, Made Evans, Lucile Watson. D: Gregory La Cava. COM 92m.

What Every Woman Wants 1962 British ★★½ Tedious British comedy of women dealing with husbands' apparent philandering. C: William Fox, Hy Hazell, Dennis Lotis, Elizabeth Shepherd. D: Ernest Morris. COM 69m.

What Happened Was . . . 1994 ★★★½ Modest character study depicts the first date between two inarticulate losers. Film runs as long as their date, with a cinema verite feel to it. Sometimes dull, but it does offer some funny insights into human behavior. C: Tom Noonan, Karen Sillas. D: Tom Noonan. COM 91m.

What Have I Done to Deserve This? 1985 Spanish ★★★½ Housewife Maura rebels against the pressures of modern life, indulging in drugs, crime, and ultimately murder. Yet it's all played for laughs, and Almodovar succeeds in this original, irreverent black comedy. C: Carmen Maura, Chus Lampreave. D: Pedro Almodovar. COM 100m. V

What Next, Corporal Hargrove? 1945 ★★★ Competent sequel to *See Here, Private Hargrove* reteams charming Walker and con artist Wynn, now AWOL in Paris, as WWII drags on. C: Robert Walker, Keenan Wynn, Jean Porter, Chill Wills, Hugo Haas, William Phillips, Fred Essler, Cameron Mitchell. D: Richard Thorpe. COM 95m.

What, No Beer? 1933 ★★½ Two bootleggers weather the post-prohibition storm. Fine stars in quick, half-brewed material. Keaton's last starring American role. C: Buster Keaton, Jimmy Durante, Phyllis Barry. D: Edward Sedgwick. COM 66m. V

What Price Glory? 1926 ★★★★ Two American soldiers compete for the same woman during WWI. Rousing, silent comedy/drama, from Laurence Stallings-Maxwell Anderson play. Powerful anti-war message. Remade in 1952. C: Victor McLaglen, Edmund Lowe, Dolores Del Rio. D: Raoul Walsh. ACT 120m.

What Price Glory? 1952 ★★★ Unfortunate remake of Walsh silent classic is redeemed by Cagney and Dailey as perennially battling army buddies Quirt and Flagg. WWI antiwar message is undercut by director's bravado and mechanical performances of young Wagner and supporting cast. C: James Cagney, Corinne Calvet, Dan Dailey, Robert Wagner. D: John Ford. DRA 110m. V

What Price Hollywood? 1932 ★★★★ Forerunner of *A Star Is Born* takes surprisingly cynical look at Hollywood star-making machinery. Bennett is waitress propelled to fame by alcoholic director Shermann; he sinks while she rises. Mixes drama and comedy smoothly, anticipating Cukor's later, more acclaimed work. From story by Adela Rogers St. Johns. C: Constance Bennett, Lowell Shermann, Neil Hamilton, Gregory Ratoff, Brooks Benedict. D: George Cukor. DRA 88m. V

What Women Dream 1933 German ★★★½ Minor crime comedy has Lorre as detective tracking a kleptomaniac jewel thief. Early Billy Wilder script and Lorre are reason enough to watch, if you can find it. C: Nora Gregor, Gustav Frohlich, Otto Wallburg, Peter Lorre, Kurt Horwitz. D: Geza von Bolvary. COM 81m.

What Would You Do, Chums? 1939 British ★★½ Junk dealer is faced with moral dilemma when he tries to reform the fiancée of a friend; young man backslides and robs bank. Rather pedestrian treatment of an unusual premise. C: Syd Walker, Jean Gillie, Cyril Chamberlain. D: John Baxter. CRI 75m.

What Would You Say to Some Spinach 1976

Czechoslovakia ★★★★ A mad scientist invents a de-aging machine, which winds up in a beauty salon—but it isn't always used correctly (spinach can cause odd side effects). Charming comedy fantasy. (a.k.a. *A Nice Plate of Spinach*) C: Vladimir Mensik, Jiri Sovak. D: Vaclav Vorlicek, Milos Makourek. COM 90m.

Whatever Happened to Aunt Alice? 1969 ★★★½ When maids keep disappearing at Page's house, amateur detective Gordon hires on to solve mystery. Sprightly and lightweight. C: Geraldine Page, Ruth Gordon, Rosemary Forsyth, Robert Fuller. D: Lee H. Katzin. CRI [PG] 101m. v

What's Eating Gilbert Grape 1993 ★★★★ A young grocery clerk (Depp) with an unusual family is captivated by a young woman passing through his small Iowa town. Low-key and quite moving. C: Johnny Depp, Juliette Lewis, Mary Steenburgen, Leonardo DiCaprio, Darlene Cates, Laura Harrington, Kevin Tighe. D: Lasse Hallstrom. DRA 118m. v

What's Love Got to Do With It 1993 ★★★★ Brilliantly acted biography of singer Tina Turner, with Bassett and Fishburne remarkable as Tina and Ike. He's abusive and mean, but she's resilient and triumphs in the end. Absorbing and memorable. C: Angela Bassett, Laurence Fishburne, Vanessa Colloway, Jenifer Lewis, Phyllis Yvonne Stickney. D: Brian Gibson. DRA [R] 118m. v

What's New, Pussycat? 1965 ★★★½ Irreverent '60s comedy about quirky O'Toole seeking help from psychiatrist Sellers and discovering the shrink is a lunatic himself. Allen's debut film as an actor and writer, so it isn't surprising he ends up getting the biggest laughs. C: Peter Sellers, Peter O'Toole, Romy Schneider, Capucine, Paula Prentiss, Woody Allen. D: Clive Donner. COM 108m. v

What's So Bad About Feeling Good? 1968 ★★★ An exotic bird spreads a strange "happy virus" throughout New York. Silly, harmless fluff. World's first and only comedy about a toucan. C: George Peppard, Mary Tyler Moore, Dom DeLuise, Thelma Ritter. D: George Seaton. COM 94m.

What's the Matter with Helen? 1971 ★★★½ In '30s Hollywood, two women (Reynolds and Winters) who fled publicity after their sons were involved in a brutal murder now operate a finishing school for child actors, who are mysteriously dying. Melodramatic thriller, but extremely watchable. C: Debbie Reynolds, Shelley Winters, Dennis Weaver, Agnes Moorehead, Michael MacLiammoir. D: Curtis Harrington. HOR [PG] 101m. v

What's Up, Doc? 1972 ★★★★ Nutty, modern-day screwball involves Streisand with musicologist (O'Neal), whose bag of granite gets mixed up with bag of diamonds. Some marvelous sequences, most of them involving Kahn in film debut as Ryan's fiancée. Barbra sings "You're the Top," "As Time Goes By." May seem familiar to fans of *Bringing Up Baby*. C: Barbra Streisand, Ryan O'Neal, Kenneth Mars, Madeline Kahn, Austin Pendleton. D: Peter Bogdanovich. COM [G] 94m. v

What's Up, Tiger Lily? 1966 ★★★★ Woody Allen supervised redubbing of bargain basement Japanese spy flick *Key of Keys*, turning it into an international struggle for perfect egg salad. Rapid one-liners and truly offbeat ideas bubble throughout inventive silliness, and The Lovin' Spoonful's music. C: Tatsuya Mihashi, Miya Hana, Tadao Nakamura, Woody Allen. D: Woody Allen. COM [PG] 80m. v

Wheel of Fortune 1941 *See* **Man Betrayed, A**

Wheeler Dealers, The 1963 ★★★★ Garner is Texas oil baron who comes to Wall Street to raise some cash by playing the stock market but manages to get involved with stock analyst Remick in the process. Lively, energetic comedy with excellent supporting cast backing up two leads. C: Lee Remick, James Garner, Jim Backus, Phil Harris, Shelley Berman, Chill Wills, John Astin, Louis Nye. D: Arthur Hiller. COM 100m. v

Wheels of Terror 1986 *See* **Misfit Brigade, The**

When a Man Loves a Woman 1994 ★★★ A happy home is threatened by wife's alcoholism in this reworking of *Days of Wine and Roses*. Hold out for the original. C: Andy Garcia, Meg Ryan, Lauren Tom, Philip Seymour Hoffman, Tina Majorino, Mae Whitman, Ellen Burstyn, Egene Roche. D: Luis Mandoki. DRA [R] 124m.

When a Stranger Calls 1979 ★★★½ An evil baby killer terrorizes a young babysitter (Kane) over the phone—then he terrorizes her again years later when she has children of her own. Though familiar, the story still chills. (Have you checked the children?) C: Carol Kane, Charles Durning, Colleen Dewhurst, Tony Beckley. D: Fred Walton. CRI [R] 97m. v

When a Woman Ascends the Stairs 1960 Japanese ★★★★½ Moral dilemmas of 30ish widow (Takamine) who works as bartender to support her mother, divorced brother, and handicapped nephew. Typically low-key approach from Naruse and Takamine highlight this moving, if somewhat depressing drama. C: Hideko Takamine, Tatsuya Nakadai. D: Mikio Naruse. DRA 110m. v

When Comedy Was King 1960 ★★★★ Entertaining smorgasbord of silent comedy highlights, with emphasis on Chaplin and Keaton. Fine introduction to the period's treasures. C: Charlie Chaplin, Buster Keaton, Laurel and Hardy, Fatty Arbuckle, The Keystone Kops. D: Robert Youngson. COM 81m. v

When Dinosaurs Ruled the Earth 1970 British ★★★½ A man and a woman, once cast out of rival tribes, fall in love. Familiar story but novel setting in prehistory. It all looks pretty darn good, too, in this fine prehistoric family entertainment. C: Victoria Vetri, Robin Hawdon, Patrick Allen, Drewe Henley, Imogen Hassall. D: Val Guest. ACT [G] 96m. V

When Every Day Was the Fourth of July 1978 ★★★½ Principled lawyer puts everything he has into defending troubled veteran against murder charge. Often harrowing, with sensitive acting throughout. C: Dean Jones, Chris Peterson, Katy Kurtzman. D: Dan Curtis. DRA 98m. V

When Father Was Away on Business 1985 Yugoslav ★★★★ Set in Yugoslavia in the '50s, a moving child's-eye view of what happens when a six-year-old boy's father is imprisoned for adultery by the Communists. Story of everyday survival told in direct, lyrical fashion. Subtitled. C: Moreno D'EBartolli, Miki Manojlovic, Mirjana Karanovic. D: Emir Kusturica, V. DRA [R] 135m. V

When Harry Met Sally . . . 1989 ★★★★ Can a man and a woman remain friends, even though they're sexually attracted to each other? That's the question of charming romantic comedy with expert performances by two stars. Sometimes too cute for its own good, but pays off with touching New Year's Eve resolution. Highlight: faked orgasm scene in the deli. C: Billy Crystal, Meg Ryan, Carrie Fisher, Bruno Kirby. D: Rob Reiner. COM [R] 96m. V

When Hell Broke Loose 1958 ★★★ Axis assassins are loose in WWII Europe. Their target: General Eisenhower. Effective suspense smartly delivered. C: Charles Bronson, Violet Rensing, Richard Jaeckel, Arvid Nelson. D: Kenneth Crane. ACT 78m. V

When He's Not a Stranger 1989 ★★★★ College student suffers date rape and makes an effort to seek justice. Well-turned story has tension and believability in dealing with contemporary issue. C: Annabeth Gish, John Terlesky, Kevin Dillon, Kim Meyers, Paul Dooley. D: John Gray. CRI 100m. TVM V

When I Grow Up 1951 ★★★★ Likable minor film focuses on Driscoll's warm relationship with grandfather Grapewin and his estrangement from father Preston. Well-played and written. C: Bobby Driscoll, Robert Preston, Martha Scott, Sherry Jackson, Charley Grapewin, Henry Morgan. D: Michael Kanin. DRA 80m.

When in Rome 1952 ★★★½ Douglas masquerades as priest visiting Vatican during Holy Year, but is reformed by growing friendship with Johnson. Another con artist-goes-straight comedy, redeemed by the leads. C: Van Johnson, Paul Douglas, Joseph Calleia, Mimi Aguglia, Tudor Owen. D: Clarence Brown. COM 78m.

When Ladies Meet 1933 ★★★★ Two women discuss characters in one's novel, which has odd romantic parallels with their own mixed-up love lives. Fun soap opera material, with an unusual, intelligent script and marvelous performances by Harding and Loy. Remade in 1941. C: Ann Harding, Robert Montgomery, Myrna Loy, Alice Brady, Frank Morgan, Luis Alberni. D: Harry Beaumont. DRA 85m.

When Ladies Meet 1941 ★★★ Crawford and Garson discuss the former's new book, which contains the same strange romantic triangle the two friends are living. Talking remake looks good, but is somehow more dated than the original. (a.k.a. *Strange Skirts*) C: Joan Crawford, Robert Taylor, Greer Garson, Herbert Marshall, Spring Byington. D: Robert Z. Leonard. DRA 108m. V

When Love is Young 1937 ★★★½ Pleasant comedy of Bruce, college wallflower who becomes a Broadway star and then returns to campus. C: Virginia Bruce, Kent Taylor. D: Hal Mohr. COM 75m.

When Lovers Meet 1946 *See* **Lover Come Back**

When My Baby Smiles at Me 1948 ★★★ Burlesque stars Grable and Dailey break up when one goes to Broadway. Third film version of '20s Broadway hit *Burlesque* is strictly for Grable fans. C: Betty Grable, Dan Dailey, Jack Oakie, June Havoc, James Gleason, Richard Arlen. D: Walter Lang. MUS 98m.

When Strangers Marry 1944 ★★★★ Hunter's new husband (Jagger) may be a killer, but former beau (Mitchum) is around to straighten things out. Stylish film noir; B-movie sleeper hit of the '40s. Mitchum's first major role. (a.k.a. *Betrayed*) C: Robert Mitchum, Kim Hunter, Dean Jagger, Neil Hamilton, Lou Lubin, Milton Kibbee. D: William Castle. CRI 67m.

When the Bough Breaks 1986 ★★★★ Child psychologist begins investigating a series of murders on his own, with surprising results. Doesn't hang together all the way but remains compelling. Based on Jonathan Kellerman's solid novel. C: Ted Danson, Richard Masur, Rachel Ticotin, David Hudleston, James Noble, Kim Miyori, Merritt Butrick. D: Waris Hussein. CRI 100m. TVM V

When the Daltons Rode 1940 ★★★★ Incredible stuntwork highlights this brisk tale of famous outlaw brothers. Lots of action; great cast. C: Randolph Scott, Kay Francis, Brian Donlevy, George Bancroft, Andy Devine, Broderick Crawford, Stuart Erwin. D: George Marshall. WST 80m.

When the Legends Die 1972 ★★★★ Tasteful story of relationship between aging rodeo competitor Widmark and Ute youth (Forrest) he befriends. Restrained, intelligent handling of Hal Borland novel. C: Richard Widmark, Frederic Forrest, Luana Anders, Vito Scotti. D: Stuart Millar. WST [PG] 105m. V

When the Time Comes 1991 ★★★★½ When Bedelia learns she is terminally ill, she confronts her husband (O'Quinn) and friend (Davis) with plan to take her own life. Sensitive handling of difficult moral issue makes this compelling. Bedelia shines in the lead. C:

Bonnie Bedelia, Terry O'Quinn, Brad Davis. D: John Erman. DRA [PG-13] 94m. TVM V

When the Trees Were Tall 1965 Russian ★★★ Predictable Russian story of an alcoholic war vet who is redeemed by love of a teenager who believes he is her father. Earnest and plodding, but has definite historical interest. C: Inna Gulaya, Yuri Nikolin. D: Lev Kulidzhanov. DRA 100m.

When the Whales Came 1989 British ★★ Children on vacation island near Great Britain befriend deaf recluse obsessed with birds. Strictly for the birds. C: Paul Scofield, Helen Mirren, Helen Pearce, Max Rennie, David Suchet, David Threlfall, Jeremy Kemp. D: Clive Rees. DRA [PG] 100m. V

When the Wind Blows 1988 ★★★★ Animated satire about reaction of middle-class British couple to nuclear war. Superb voice work and excellent score by rockers Roger Waters, Paul Hardcastle, Squeeze, Genesis, and Bowie raise this above the level of clichés. COM

When Time Ran Out . . . 1980 ★★ Island volcano threatens its posh hotels and residents. Time ran out for the disaster film formula. (a.k.a. *Earth's Final Fury*) C: Paul Newman, Jacqueline Bisset, William Holden, James Franciscus, Edward Albert, Red Buttons, Ernest Borgnine, Burgess Meredith, Valentina Cortese, Veronica Hamel, Alex Karras, Barbara Carrera. D: James Goldstone. ACT [PG] 141m. V

When Tomorrow Comes 1939 ★★★½ A married man (Boyer) has a touching affair with a prim woman (Dunne). Classy, effective romantic weeper, from a story by James M. Cain. Re-teamed stars prove their *Love Affair* chemistry was no fluke. C: Irene Dunne, Charles Boyer, Barbara O'Neil. D: John M. Stahl. DRA 90m.

When Willie Comes Marching Home 1950 ★★★½ Dailey is first in town to volunteer for WWII duty but, to his dismay, gets assigned to home; then he's picked for secret mission in France. Minor comedy. C: Dan Dailey, Corinne Calvet, Colleen Townsend, William Demarest, Mae Marsh. D: John Ford. COM 82m.

When Wolves Cry *See* **The Christmas Tree**

When Worlds Collide 1951 ★★★½ Science fiction with an emphasis on human drama about rogue planet on collision course with Earth, and efforts to allow a handful of humans to escape. Intelligent, if occasionally talky. Oscar for special effects. C: Richard Derr, Barbara Rush, Peter Hanson, Larry Keating. D: Rudolph Mate. SFI 81m. V

When You're in Love 1937 ★★★½ Delightful screwball comedy has Moore hiring Grant to pose as her husband. Highlight is her lowbrow rendition of "Minnie the Moocher," cut from some TV prints. C: Grace Moore, Cary Grant, Aline MacMahon, Thomas Mitchell, Emma Dunn. D: Robert Riskin. COM 104m.

When's Your Birthday? 1937 ★★★ Brown is boxer who only fights when the stars are in the right position. Minor slapstick comedy is worth seeing for supporting cast headed by old reliables. C: Joe E. Brown, Marian Marsh, Edgar Kennedy, Fred Keating. D: Harry Beaumont. COM 76m. V

Where Angels Fear to Tread 1991 British ★★★ Impulsive Englishwoman marries while on vacation in Italy, to her family's chagrin; and their meddling causes trouble. One of the weaker E.M. Forster adaptations. C: Helena Bonham Carter, Judy Davis, Rupert Graves, Giovanni Guidelli, Barbara Jefford, Helen Mirren. D: Charles Sturridge. DRA [PG] 112m. V

Where Angels Go, Trouble Follows 1968 ★★★ Sequel to *The Trouble with Angels* has Mother Superior (Russell) confronting upstart novice (Stevens) over convent policies. Numerous guest star appearances fill out thin premise of one-joke comedy. C: Rosalind Russell, Stella Stevens, Binnie Barnes, Mary Wickes, Dolores Sutton, Barbara Hunter. D: James Neilson. FAM/COM [G] 94m. V

Where Danger Lives 1950 ★★★ Minor film noir has Mitchum falling for cunning Domergue with predictable results. C: Robert Mitchum, Faith Domergue, Claude Rains, Maureen O'Sullivan. D: John Farrow. DRA 84m.

Where Do We Go From Here? 1945 ★★★½ Peculiar wartime musical comedy has MacMurray transported through American history by genie (Sheldon). Superb score by Kurt Weill and Ira Gershwin was mostly cut before release, but "The Nina, the Pinta and the Santa Maria," a veritable one-act opera, is still intact. C: Fred MacMurray, June Haver, Joan Leslie, Gene Sheldon, Anthony Quinn, Carlos Ramirez, Otto Preminger. D: Gregory Ratoff. MUS 77m.

Where Eagles Dare 1969 ★★★★ Curious commando team (Burton, Eastwood) tries to rescue American general from Germans in the mountains of Bavaria. Strained credibility is more than compensated for by a thrill a minute. From the novel by Alistair MacLean, who also wrote the script. C: Richard Burton, Clint Eastwood, Mary Ure, Michael Hordern, Patrick Wymark, Anton Diffring. D: Brian G. Hutton. DRA [PG] 158m. V

Where Love Has Gone 1964 ★★★½ Prime trash, from the Harold Robbins roman á clef. The lover of a sculptor (Hayward) is killed by her daughter, á la Lana Turner-Cheryl Crane scandal of the '50s. Lurid and laughable, but worth seeing for diva showdowns between Hayward and Davis, playing her mother. C: Bette Davis, Susan Hayward, Michael Connors, Jane Greer, Joey Heatherton, George Macready. D: Edward Dmytryk. DRA 114m. V

Where No Vultures Fly 1951 *See* **Ivory Hunter**

Where Sleeping Dogs Lie 1993 ★★ Destitute author moves into old mansion to write a murder mystery, and soon discovers a creepy boarder he takes in might allow him some first-hand research. Uneasy mix of thriller elements and writer's angst, though it has some humorous moments, particularly a funny monologue about Mickey Rourke. C: Dylan McDermott, Tom Sizemore, Sharon Stone. D: Charles Finch. CRI [R] 92m. V

Where the Boys Are 1960 ★★★½ Pleasant sun-and-surf comedy with an attractive cast, led by Francis singing the title hit. Nichols is very funny as a dumb blonde. Spawned countless imitations, including the 1984 remake. C: Dolores Hart, George Hamilton, Yvette Mimieux, Jim Hutton, Paula Prentiss, Connie Francis, Barbara Nichols. D: Henry Levin. COM 100m. V

Where the Boys Are '84 1984 ★★ Four college women trek to Fort Lauderdale for spring break hijinks. Pretty awful remake/update of the 1960 musical. C: Lisa Hartman, Lorna Luft, Wendy Schaal, Lynn-Holly Johnson, Russell Todd. D: Hy Averback. COM [R] 93m. V

Where the Buffalo Roam 1980 ★★ The world of gonzo journalist Hunter S. Thompson (Murray), who throws himself into every story he writes and into copious amounts of booze and drugs. Despite Murray's frenzied performance, hopped-up comedy delivers pitifully few laughs. C: Peter Boyle, Bill Murray, Bruno Kirby, Rene Auberjonois. D: Art Linson. COM [R] 100m. V

Where the Day Takes You 1992 ★★★½ Young runaways on the streets of Los Angeles band together to cope with homelessness. Tough material, "who's who" cast includes cameos by Christian Slater and others. C: Dermot Mulroney, Sean Astin, Balthazar Getty, Will Smith, James Le Gros, Ricki Lake, Lara Flynn Boyle, Peter Dobson, Kyle Maclachley. D: Marc Rocco. DRA 107m. V

Where the Eagle Flies *See* **Pickup on 101**

Where the Green Ants Dream 1984 German ★★★ Clash between civilization and ancient traditions is well depicted in this low-key Australian-set film, centering on a mining company that wants to excavate aboriginal burial grounds. C: Bruce Spence, Wandjuk Marika, Roy Marika, Ray Barrett, Norman Kaye. D: Werner Herzog. DRA [R] 99m. V

Where the Heart Is 1990 ★★½ A father (Coleman) tries to teach his brood life lessons by forcing them to go homeless. Strange comedy that's uncomfortable to watch and fails as social satire, despite eager performances. C: Dabney Coleman, Uma Thurman, Joanna Cassidy, Crispin Glover, Suzy Amis, Christopher Plummer. D: John Boorman. COM [R] 107m. V

Where the Lilies Bloom 1974 ★★★★ When their father passes away, four children living in Appalachian mountains keep his death a secret so they won't be separated. Delicate premise handled with sensitivity in this unusual family film. Child cast handles difficult roles nicely. C: Julie Gholson, Jan Smithers, Matthew Burril, Helen Harmon, Harry Dean Stanton, Rance Howard. D: William A. Graham. FAM/DRA [G] 97m. V

Where the Red Fern Grows 1974 ★★★ Old-fashioned coming-of-age film set in Oklahoma in the '30s, when a young boy learns about life in the course of training a pair of hunting dogs. Nicely told, if occasionally too pat. C: James Whitmore, Beverly Garland, Jack Ging, Lonny Chapman, Stewart Peterson. D: Norman Tokar. FAM/DRA [G] 97m. V

Where the River Runs Black 1986 ★★½ Atmospheric tale of a young orphaned boy living in the jungles of Brazil (and apparently raised by dolphins) gives way to simplistic drama when a priest brings him into civilization. C: Charles Durning, Alessandro Rabelo, Marcelo Rabelo, Conchata Ferrell, Peter Horton, Ajay Naidu. D: Christopher Cain. DRA [PG] 96m. V

Where the Rivers Flow North 1994 ★★★★ Intelligent low-budget film, shot in Vermont, about an aging logger (Torn) fighting to save his livelihood when progress in the form of a hydroelectric dam threatens his forests. Cardinal is moving as his Native-American wife. C: Rip Torn, Tantoo Cardinal, Bill Raymond, Michael J. Fox, John Griesemer, Mark Margolis. D: Jay Craven. DRA 106m.

Where the Sidewalk Ends 1950 ★★★★½ Superb film noir features Andrews as a violent cop, haunted by the memory of his criminal father, who accidentallly kills a murder suspect and must cover his tracks. Dark and effective; scripted by Ben Hecht.. C: Dana Andrews, Gene Tierney, Gary Merrill, Karl Malden, Bert Freed, Tom Tully, Ruth Donnelly, Craig Stevens, Neville Brand. D: Otto Preminger. CRI 95m.

Where the Spies Are 1965 British ★★★½ An ex-spy turned doctor (Niven) is forced back into espionage work in Beirut. Light comedy pokes gentle fun at the spy genre at the dawn of the James Bond era. Stylish performances by leads. C: David Niven, Francoise Dorleac, John LeMesurier, Cyril Cusack, Eric Pohlmann, Reginald Beckwith. D: Val Guest. COM 110m.

Where There's a Will 1936 British ★★★ Popular British comic Hay plays a ne'er-do-well academic who sponges off his relatives during the holidays, then makes it all come out right by apprehending hoodlums. Mild, dated comedy. C: Will Hay, Gina Malo. D: William Beaudine. COM 80m.

Where There's Life 1947 ★★★½ Standard Hope vehicle, with star alternately cowardly and romantic as radio comic thought to be heir to mythical European throne. He dodges assassins while chasing Hasso. C: Bob Hope, Signe Hasso, William Bendix, George Coulouris. D: Sidney Lanfield. COM 75m.

Where Were You When the Lights Went Out? 1968 ★★ New York's infamous blackout of November 5, 1965 serves as basis for episodic Doris Day bedroom farce, complete with lots of slamming doors, mistaken identities, and unlikely couplings. C: Doris Day, Robert Morse, Terry—Thomas, Steve Allen, Lola Albright, Jim Backus, Patrick O'Neal, Pat Paulsen, Ben Blue, Earl Wilson. D: Hy Averback. COM [PG] 94m. v

Where's Charley? 1952 ★★★★ Remake of Broadway musical "Charley's Aunt" (already filmed three times) is mostly valuable for Bolger's delightful performance as Oxford student whose impersonation of friend's aunt leads to chaos. C: Ray Bolger, Allyn Ann McLerie, Robert Shackleton, Mary Germaine, Horace Cooper, Margaretta Scott. D: David Butler. MUS 97m.

Where's Poppa? 1970 ★★★★½ Beloved cult film features Segal as lawyer trying to induce fatal heart attack in nagging, senile mom Gordon. Meanwhile, New York City's best lunatics provide countless subplots. Black comedy at its finest, played with sick perfection by ensemble. Reiner's direction is right on target. (a.k.a *Going Ape*) C: George Segal, Ruth Gordon, Trish Van Devere, Ron Leibman. D: Carl Reiner. COM [R] 84m. v

Which Way Is Up? 1977 ★★★½ Loose American remake of Italian picture *The Seduction of Mimi* features Pryor in three roles—preacher, fruit picker, and dirty-minded geriatric, searching for love, lust, and other romantic trifles in southern California orange groves. Episodic tale provides nice showcase for Pryor's talents, but pacing never catches up to his boisterous performance. C: Richard Pryor, Lonette McKee, Margaret Avery, Dolph Sweet. D: Michael Schultz. COM [R] 94m. v

While the City Sleeps 1956 ★★★★½ Nightmarish minimalist cityscapes are used effectively in this deadpan thriller about callous newspaper reporters hunting a serial killer, using women as bait. Cast is uniformly excellent. C: Dana Andrews, Ida Lupino, Rhonda Fleming, George Sanders, Vincent Price, John Barrymore Jr., Thomas Mitchell, Sally Forrest, Howard Duff. D: Fritz Lang. CRI 100m. v

Whipsaw 1935 ★★★ Detective Tracy hunts gang of jewel thieves; gang member Loy recognizes him, but plays along, first for fun, then for love, with predictable results. Standard fare despite cast. C: Myrna Loy, Spencer Tracy, Harvey Stephens, William Harrigan, Clay Clement. D: Sam Wood. CRI 83m.

Whirlpool 1934 ★★★½ Carny owner Holt does long stretch in prison; emerges committed to caring for daughter he never met in serviceable vehicle for star. Arthur is charming in early performance as daughter. C: Jack Holt, Jean Arthur, Donald Cook, Lila Lee, Allen Jenkins, Rita LaRoy, John Miljan, Ward Bond. D: Roy William Neill. DRA 73m.

Whirlpool 1949 ★★★½ Ferrer hams it up as unscrupulous hypnotist who sends Tierney off to do his evil bidding in minor film noir. Taut, if implausible. C: Gene Tierney, Richard Conte, Jose Ferrer, Charles Bickford, Barbara O'Neil, Eduard Franz, Fortunio Bonanova, Constance Collier. D: Otto Preminger. DRA 97m.

Whiskey Galore! 1949 *See* **Tight Little Island**

Whisper Kill 1988 ★ A psychotic killer politely telephones his victims before he murders them. No-brainer is vehicle for Anderson to pose and practice screaming. C: Joe Penny, Loni Anderson, June Lockhart. D: Christian Nyby. CRI 96m. TVM v

Whisper to a Scream, A 1989 ★ Umpteenth thriller set in a strip club is boring, unscary story of an actress researching a role who attracts the attentions of the joint's psychopathic announcer. Nothing to scream about here. C: Nadia Capone, Yaphet Kotto, Lawrence Bayne. D: Robert Bergman. CRI [R] 96m. v

Whisperers, The 1966 British ★★★★ Elderly woman dreams of sudden wealth to escape her shabby London flat; when her no-good son hides proceeds of robbery in her spare room, and she finds it, she thinks her dreams have come true. Painful look at aging. Dame Edith brilliantly portrays the lonely woman. C: Edith Evans, Eric Portman, Nanette Newman, Avis Bunnage, Gerald Sim, Ronald Fraser. D: Bryan Forbes. DRA 106m.

Whispering City 1947 Canadian ★★★½ Compact thriller with well-paced suspense about reporter Anderson on trail of powerful lawyer with a dark past. C: Helmut Dantine, Mary Anderson, Paul Lukas. D: Fedor Ozep. CRI 89m.

Whispering Smith 1948 ★★★ Ladd is a soft-spoken railroad detective who finds that his best friend (Preston) can't stay out of trouble. Brisk but minor. C: Alan Ladd, Brenda Marshall, Robert Preston, Donald Crisp, William Demarest, Fay Holden, Frank Faylen. D: Leslie Fenton. DRA 88m.

Whispers 1989 Canadian ★★½ After Tennant kills goofball lunatic (LeClerc) in self-defense, she and detective (Sarandon) are bewildered to find the psycho is still alive, now with a perfect alibi in that he is presumed dead. Chiller with few surprises, but a great performance from LeCler. Based on the novel by Dean R. Koontz. C: Victoria Tennant, Chris Sarandon, Jean LeClerc. D: Douglas Jackson. CRI 96m. v

Whispers in the Dark 1992 ★★★½ When one of the patients of a psychiatrist (Sciorra) dies unexpectedly, she becomes obsessed with uncovering the reasons why. Middling thriller, hampered by too many plot twists, but buoyed by a splendid cast, especially Sciorra and Alda. C: Annabella Sciorra, Jamey Sheridan, Alan Alda, Jill Clayburgh, Anthony LaPaglia, John Leguizamo, Deborah Unger. D: Christopher Crowe. CRI 103m. v

Whistle at Eaton Falls, The 1951 ★★★½ Semi-documentary look at labor strife in small New England town caused by layoffs at local factory. Evocative location shooting and capable cast. C: Lloyd Bridges, Dorothy Gish, Carleton Carpenter, Murray Hamilton, Anne Francis, Ernest Borgnine, Doro Merande, Arthur O'Connell. D: Robert Siodmak. DRA 96m.

Whistle Blower, The 1987 British ★★★★½ A British spy (Caine) finds his leisurely retirement interrupted when his idealistic son (Havers) believes he's discovered government immorality. Superior, thinking person's thriller, with Caine outstanding. Based on John Hale's novel. C: Michael Caine, James Fox, Nigel Havers, Felicity Dean, John Gielgud. D: Simon Langton. CRI [PG] 99m. V

Whistle Down the Wind 1962 British ★★★★ Murderer (Bates) hides in barn and is discovered by kids who think he's Jesus. In his directorial debut, Forbes manages to play out premise inventively but never mawkishly. Mills and Bates are particularly good. From a novel by Mary Heyley Bell. C: Hayley Mills, Alan Bates, Bernard Lee, Norman Bird. D: Bryan Forbes. DRA 99m. V

Whistler, The "I am the Whistler, and I know many things." That opening graced a highly successful radio show of the '30s and '40s, a mystery anthology held together by its mysterious narrator, the Whistler. For film, the Whistler became Richard Dix, who would go through seven of eight moody little crime films in a variety of roles, from private detective to fall guy to villain. The anthology format allowed Columbia to draw on the eerie, atmospheric stories of Cornell Woolrich for most of the films. The result is several unusually intelligent and affecting B-movies.

The Whistler (1944)
Mark of the Whistler (1944)
Power of the Whistler (1945)
Voice of the Whistler (1945)
Mysterious Intruder (1946)
Secret of the Whistler (1946)
The 13th Hour (1947)
The Return of the Whistler (1948)

Whistler, The 1944 ★★★½ First film in series spun off from popular '30s and '40s radio program. Wracked by death of his wife, Dix hires a man to kill him, but when his wife reappears, Dix desperately tries to cancel the assassination contract he has ordered. C: Richard Dix, Gloria Stuart, Alan Dinehart, Joan Woodbury, J. Carrol Naish, Byron Foulger. D: William Castle. DRA 59m.

Whistling in Brooklyn 1943 ★★★★ Skelton returns as the pompous radio sleuth "The Fox" and once again scores high on the laugh meter as he gets mixed up in murder. Film climaxes on the baseball diamond with the comic going up against the Brooklyn Dodgers. Solid mix of laughs and thrills. C: Red Skelton, Ann Rutherford, Jean Rogers, Rags Ragland, Ray Collins, Henry O'Neill, William Frawley, Sam Levene. D: S. Sylvan Simon. COM 87m. V

Whistling in the Dark 1941 ★★★★ First appearance of Skelton's favorite film character, a blowhard popular radio sleuth named "The Fox" whom he brought back in two sequels. Here the would-be detective finds himself kidnapped and forced to plot the perfect murder. Fun-filled breezy comedy. C: Red Skelton, Ann Rutherford, Virginia Grey, Conrad Veidt, Rags Ragland, Eve Arden. D: S. Sylvan Simon. COM 78m. V

White *See* **Trois Couleurs: Blanc**

White Buffalo, The 1977 ★★½ A mythical buffalo brings together strange bedfellows. Wild Bill Hickok and Chief Crazy Horse unite to hunt it down. Old Western fantasy with a unique cast. C: Charles Bronson, Jack Warden, Will Sampson, Kim Novak, Clint Walker, Stuart Whitman, Slim Pickens, Cara Williams, John Carradine. D: J. Lee Thompson. WST [PG] 99m. V

White Cargo 1942 ★★★ Hilarious, dated miscegenation melodrama of Tondelayo who wreaks havoc at British outpost in Africa. Basically ridiculous. C: Hedy Lamarr, Walter Pidgeon, Frank Morgan, Richard Carlson, Reginald Owen. D: Richard Thorpe. DRA 90m. V

White Christmas 1954 ★★★½ Sentimental Irving Berlin holiday songfest with bunches of standards crammed into tired plot concerning army vets (Crosby and Kaye) putting on show for retired general at his failing ski lodge. Cast is game and numbers are lavish. C: Bing Crosby, Danny Kaye, Rosemary Clooney, Vera Ellen, Dean Jagger. D: Michael Curtiz. MUS 120m. V

White Cliffs of Dover, The 1944 ★★★★ Sentimental drama told in flashback about American woman (Dunne) who marries titled Englishman (Marshal) who's then killed in WWI; she loses her son in WWII. Glossy and uncomplicated. Based on poem by Alice Duer Miller. C: Irene Dunne, Alan Marshal, Van Johnson, Frank Morgan, C. Aubrey Smith, Dame May Whitty, Roddy McDowell, Gladys Cooper, Peter Lawford. D: Clarence Brown. DRA 127m. V

White Cradle Inn 1947 *See* **High Fury**

White Dawn, The 1974 ★★★ Conflict ensues when three 19th-century whalers are rescued by Eskimos. Fitfully engrossing tale with stunning visuals. C: Warren Oates, Timothy Bottoms, Lou Gossett Jr. D: Philip Kaufman. DRA [PG] 109m. V

White Demon, The 1932 ★★★½ Lorre plays a hunchbacked drug kingpin in this lumbering melodrama, with Albers fighting to break his opera singer sister's morphine habit. Strong drama has unfortunately become even more topical with time. C: Hans Albers, Gerda Maurus, Peter Lorre, Trudi von Molo. D: Kurt Gerron. DRA 106m.

White Dog 1982 ★★★½ Winfield, Ives, and McNichol trying to deprogram dog that has been trained to attack African-Americans. Pessimistic and disturbing. Adapted from Roman Gary novel. C: Kristy McNichol, Paul Winfield, Burl Ives, Jameson Parker, Lynn Moody, Marshall Thompson, Paul Bartel, Dick Miller, Parley Baer. D: Samuel Fuller. DRA [PG] 89m.

White Face 1933 British ★★★½ Reporter (Williams) trails a blackmailing murderer in this Edgar Wallace-based whodunit. Sturdy mystery. C: Hugh Williams, Norman McKinnel. D: T. Hayes Hunter. CRI 70m.

White Fang 1991 ★★★★ Jack London's adventure tale stars Hawke as a young prospector in search of his late father's claim. Once in frozen north he tangles with gold miner, dog trainer, and wolf-dog White Fang. Rousing family adventure features good cast sharply directed against gorgeous backdrop. Also filmed in 1936 and 1972. C: Klaus Maria Brandauer, Ethan Hawke, Seymour Cassel, James Remar. D: Randal Kleiser. FAM/DRA [PG] 109m. v

White Fang 2: Myth of the White Wolf 1994 ★★★½ The sequel Jack London did not write: Hawke is separated from White Fang on a dangerous prospecting trip downriver, finds romance with a beautiful Native-American woman. He also solves the mystery of why the caribou are disappearing. For kids. C: Scott Baristow, Charmaine Craig, Al Harrington, Anthony Michael Ruivivar, Victoria Racimo, Alfred Molina. D: Ken Olin. FAM/DRA [PG] 106m.

White Feather 1955 ★★★ Standard Western with Wagner trying to convince Paget, Hunter, and other Cheyennes to return to the reservation. C: Robert Wagner, Jeffrey Hunter, Debra Paget, John Lund, Eduard Franz, Noah Beery, Hugh O'Brian. D: Robert D. Webb. WST 102m.

White Heat 1949 ★★★★ Consumed by his relationship with his mother, a psychopathic mobster is brought down by a relentless government agent. Well-done gangland film loaded with violence. Cagney's electrifying final scene is a classic. C: James Cagney, Virginia Mayo, Edmond O'Brien, Margaret Wycherly, Steve Cochran. D: Raoul Walsh. ACT 114m. v

White Horse Inn, The 1959 German ★★★ Old-fashioned operetta about an inn full of lovelorn guests, the wacky owner, and the headwaiter who loves her. Unexceptional but enjoyable. C: Johanna Matz, Johannes Heesters, Walter Mueller. D: Willi Forst. MUS 99m.

White Hot: The Mysterious Murder of Thelma Todd 1991 ★★★ TV bio probes the still-mysterious murder of 1930s film actress Thelma Todd (Anderson), a former girlfriend of mobster Lucky Luciano. Slickly adapted from Andy Edmonds' bio, *Hot Toddy*. C: Loni Anderson, Scott Paulin, Robert Davi, Robin Strasser. D: Paul Wendkos. DRA 100m. TVM v

White Hunter, Black Heart 1990 ★★★½ Sharply-drawn portrait of maverick film director during difficult African shoot. Eastwood's character based on John Huston during the making of *The African Queen*. Good performances compensate for somewhat slow story. C: Clint Eastwood, Jeff Fahey, George Dzundza, Alun Armstrong, Marisa Berenson. D: Clint Eastwood. DRA [PG] 112m. v

White Lie 1991 ★★★½ New Yorker returns to Southern hometown and tries to uncover truth about his father's death. Interesting mystery gets overcomplicated with interracial love story. C: Gregory Hines, Annette O'Toole. D: Bill Condon. DRA [PG-13] 93m. v

White Lightning 1973 ★★★ Moonshiner ex-con (Reynolds) seeks vengeance on the dirty cop who killed his brother. Capable action and good driving sequences give this kick. C: Burt Reynolds, Jennifer Billingsley, Ned Beatty, Bo Hopkins. D: Joseph Sargent. ACT [PG] 101m. v

White Line Fever 1975 ★★★★ Independent trucker (Vincent) faces corruption in the long-haul business with considerable violence ensuing. Moves briskly, with good performances. C: Jan-Michael Vincent, Kay Lenz, Slim Pickens, L.Q. Jones. D: Jonathan Kaplan. ACT [PG] 92m. v

White Men Can't Jump 1992 ★★★★ Harrelson is basketball hustler, playing neighborhood courts for big bucks. After being swindled by fellow hustler Snipes, the pair team up for a big score. Funny and energetic. Perez, as Harrelson's girlfriend, steals the movie. C: Wesley Snipes, Woody Harrelson, Rosie Perez, Tyra Ferrell, Cylk Cozart, Kadeem Hardison, Ernest Harden Jr., John Marshall Jones. D: Ron Shelton. COM [R] 115m. v

White Mischief 1988 British ★★★★ In early days of WWII, trouble brews amidst British colonists living in Kenya: one official is murdered, while wife of another becomes involved with local resident. Coolly detached, elegantly played true story of upper-class decadence. Scacchi is cast standout. Based on James Fox's book. C: Sarah Miles, Joss Ackland, John Hurt, Greta Scacchi, Charles Dance, Trevor Howard. D: Michael Radford. DRA [R] 107m. v

White Nights 1957 Italian-French ★★★★ A young woman (Schell) waiting for her lover to return from a sea voyage is pursued by a shy man (Mastroianni). Short story by Dostoyevsky inspired this enigmatic, beautifully directed mood piece. C: Maria Schell, Marcello Mastroianni, Jean Marais. D: Luchino Visconti. DRA 94m.

White Nights 1985 ★★½ Russian expatriate ballet dancer winds up back in the Soviet Union, where he teams with African-American expatriate tap dancer in attempt to escape. Great dancing but weak plot. C: Mikhail Baryshnikov, Gregory Hines, Isabella Rossellini, Helen Mirren. D: Taylor Hackford. DRA [PG-13] 135m. V

White of the Eye 1987 British ★★★★ Ordinary guy (Keith) is the main suspect in a series of bizarre murders and his wife (Moriarty) is none too pleased. Inventive, chilling thriller goes for the jugular, with fascinating camerawork as a bonus. C: David Keith, Cathy Moriarty, Art Evans, Alan Rosenberg, Alberta Watson. D: Donald Cammell. CRI [R] 111m. V

White Palace 1990 ★★★★ Fortyish fast-food server (Sarandon) gets involved in torrid love affair with yuppie (Spader) half her age. Underrated romance makes some sharp points about class differences in modern-day America; Sarandon is exceptional. Based on Glenn Savan's novel. C: Susan Sarandon, James Spader, Jason Alexander, Kathy Bates, Eileen Brennan, Rachel Levin, Renee Taylor. D: Luis Mandoki. DRA [R] 103m. V

White Sands 1992 ★★★ New Mexico sheriff (Dafoe) leads a murder investigation that ends in a mess involving several government agencies, drugs, and weapons dealing. Confusing plot overwhelms a great cast and location. C: Willem Dafoe, Mary Elizabeth Mastrantonio, Mickey Rourke, Samuel L. Jackson, M. Emmet Walsh. D: Roger Donaldson. CRI [R] 101m. V

White Sheik, The 1951 Italian ★★★★ Fellini's first solo directorial effort is a charming comedy of new bride encountering heartthrob from *fumetti* (an Italian type of photonovel) and running off with him. Sordi is particularly winning as the hero who turns out to be schmo. Remade as *The World's Greatest Lover*. C: Alberto Sordi, Brunella Bova, Giulietta Masina. D: Federico Fellini. COM 86m. V

White Sister, The 1933 ★★★ Hayes joins convent when she thinks fiancée Gable has died. He comes back, entices her away from the order with disastrous results. Remake of silent classic doesn't hold up well, in large part due to hokey plot. C: Helen Hayes, Clark Gable, Lewis Stone, Louise Closser Hale, May Robson, Edward Arnold. D: Victor Fleming. DRA 110m.

White Tie and Tails 1946 ★★★½ Unusual casting has Duryea displaying comic skills as butler who poses as master when his employer is away. Pleasant diversion sparked by excellent supporting cast. C: Dan Duryea, William Bendix, Ella Raines, Clarence Kolb, Frank Jenks, John Miljan, Scotty Beckett. D: Charles Barton. COM 81m.

White Tower, The 1950 ★★★ Team of six sets out to conquer Alp peak, each showing his or her true colors when trouble hits. Allegorical tale of mountain climbers is pretty heavy going in spite of impressive scenery and taut action sequences. C: Glenn Ford, Claude Alida Rains, Valli, Oscar Homolka, Cedric Hardwicke. D: Ted Tetzlaff. DRA 98m. V

White Water Summer 1987 ★★★ Nature-loving tough guy (Bacon) teaches pack of young city slickers how to cope with the perils of the wild. Appealing *Outward Bound*-type adventure with convincing Bacon. Young teens will enjoy it most. (a.k.a. *Rites of Summer*) C: Kevin Bacon, Sean Astin, Jonathan Ward, Matt Adler. D: Jeff Bleckner. ACT [PG] 90m. V

White Wilderness 1958 ★★★ Disney nature film examines life in Arctic Circle, showcasing variety of plant and animal life. Undistinguished narration by Winston Hibler accompanies footage for largely routine documentary, though lemming sequence holds some interest. D: James Algar. DOC [G] 73m.

White Witch Doctor 1953 ★★★ While Mitchum and Slezak hunt for lost treasure, Hayward struggles to bring modern medicine to natives in this unexceptional action film set in Africa. Spiffy Bernard Herrmann score helps pass the time. C: Susan Hayward, Robert Mitchum, Walter Slezak, Timothy Carey. D: Henry Hathaway. ACT 96m.

White Zombie 1932 ★★★★★ Rich owner of Caribbean island (Lugosi) uses hypnotism and voodoo to control inhabitants of his domain. Intensely atmospheric zombie nightmare with excellent story, incredibly creepy sets, and outstanding performance by Lugosi. One of the great early horror films. (Avoid colorized version.) C: Bela Lugosi, Madge Bellamy, Robert Frazer. D: Victor Halperin. HOR 79m. V

Who Am I This Time? 1982 ★★★★ Short but sweet fable about a misfit (Walken) who can only connect to others while rehearsing or performing a play, and the new woman in town (Sarandon) who takes an interest in him. Walken does funny takeoff on Brando in *A Streetcar Named Desire*. From a Kurt Vonnegut short story. C: Christopher Walken, Susan Sarandon, Robert Ridgely. D: Jonathan Demme. DRA 60m. TVM V

Who Dares Wins 1982 *See* **Final Option, The**

Who Done It? 1942 ★★★½ The boys solve a rather routine mystery. A diverting comedy that contains some of their best patter. Wickes is a stand-out in good supporting cast. C: Bud Abbott, Lou Costello, Patric Knowles, William Bendix, Mary Wickes, Louise Allbritton, Jerome Cowan. D: Earle C. Kenton. COM 75m. V

Who Done It? 1956 British ★★ An early look at Britain's popular TV bad boy Hill in a slight comedy that features him as a bumbling amateur sleuth on the trail of international spies. Appealing mainly as a curiosity to Hill fans. C: Benny Hill, Belinda Lee, David Kossoff, Garry Marsh, George Margo, Ernest Thesiger. D: Basil Dearden. COM 85m.

Who Fears the Devil 1973 ★★★ Low-budget folk tale pits two Ozark natives—a young man and his grandfather—against Satan. Considered a cult classic. (a.k.a. *Legend of Hillbilly John*) C: Susan Strasberg, Percy Rodrigues. D: John Newland. DRA [G] 86m. V

Who Framed Roger Rabbit 1988 ★★★★½ Innovative, technically brilliant blending of live action and animation. Boozy detective (Hoskins) is hired by a cartoon rabbit to clear himself of a murder charge. Marvelous to behold (especially the side-splitting opening short), even if the story is less than original. Won Oscars for Special Visual Effects and a special Oscar for animation. C: Bob Hoskins, Christopher Lloyd, Joanna Cassidy, Stubby Kaye, Alan Tilvern. D: Robert Zemeckis. FAM/COM [PG] 106m. V

Who Goes There 1952 *See* **Passionate Sentry, The**

Who Has Seen the Wind? 1979 Canadian ★★★½ Painchaud comes of age during the Depression in Saskatchewan. Ferrer's flamboyant performance as a local bootlegger elevates it somewhat above the ordinary. C: Brian Painchaud, Douglas Junor, Gordon Pinsent, Jose Ferrer, Helen Shaver. D: Allan King. DRA 102m. V

Who Is Harry Kellerman and Why Is He Saying Those Terrible Things About Me? 1971 ★★★ Pop-rock composer/performer (Hoffman) can't find the meaning of life, no matter how successful he gets. Trendy comedy struggles to be "with it." Harris gives a deft, glowing performance. C: Dustin Hoffman, Jack Warden, Barbara Harris, David Burns, Dom DeLuise. D: Ulu Grosbard. COM [PG] 108m.

Who Is Killing the Great Chefs of Europe? 1978 ★★★★ Gourmet chefs are dropping like flies, while junk food magnate Segal heads to Europe and chases pastry designing ex-wife Bisset. Smart and funny whodunit, with sweet comic romance at the center; completely stolen by Morley as a gluttonous gourmet. C: George Segal, Jacqueline Bisset, Robert Morley. D: Ted Kotcheff. COM [PG] 112m. V

Who Murdered Joy Morgan? 1981 *See* **Killjoy**

Who Says I Can't Ride a Rainbow? 1971 ★★★ Saccharine tale of a man (Klugman) dedicated to the belief that the future of the world depends on children. A bit treacly, but has some surprises. C: Jack Klugman, Norma French, Reuben Figueroa, David Mann, Morgan Freeman, Esther Rolle. D: Edward Mann. DRA [G] 85m.

Who Was That Lady? 1960 ★★★½ Typical '60s sex farce with Curtis and Martin posing as secret agents to allay suspicions of Leigh, Curtis' perpetually jealous spouse. Glib, slick, and a little distasteful, but generally funny. From Norman Krasna's play. C: Tony Curtis, Dean Martin, Janet Leigh, James Whitmore, John McIntire, Barbara Nichols, Joi Lansing. D: George Sidney. COM 115m.

Who Will Love My Children? 1983 ★★★★ Gripping story of a sick mother (Ann-Margret) trying to find homes for her 10 children before she dies. Star's bravura performance makes this tearjerker memorable. C: Ann-Margret, Frederic Forrest, Cathryn Damon. D: John Erman. DRA 100m. TVM

Whole Shootin' Match, The 1978 ★★★★ Two Texas dreamers, losers on the wrong side of 30, still think they can strike it rich. A warm, often funny film, made for a mere $30,000. C: Lou Perry, Sonny Davis, Doris Hargrave, Eric Henshaw, David Weber. D: Eagle Pennell. COM 101m.

Whole Town's Talking, The 1935 ★★★★½ Winning, screwball comedy with Robinson delightful in dual role as mild bank clerk confused for gangster who he looks like. The fun is sparked by excellent cast. C: Edward G. Robinson, Jean Arthur, Wallace Ford, Arthur Hohl, Edward Brophy, Arthur Byron, Donald Meek. D: John Ford. COM 95m.

Whole Truth, The 1958 British ★★★½ Somebody is framing movie producer Granger for the murder of a young star. He spends film trying to track down real killer. Competent, mildly entertaining whodunit. C: Stewart Granger, Donna Reed, George Sanders, Gianna Canale. D: John Guillermin. CRI 84m.

Who'll Stop the Rain 1978 ★★★★ Vietnam vet (Nolte) is lured by the promise of easy drug money, not fully realizing the honor among thieves ethic isn't what it used to be. Effective, tension-filled foray into the sleazy underbelly of the crime world, with an excellent Nolte. Based on Robert Stone's novel. (a.k.a. *Dog Soldiers*) C: Nick Nolte, Tuesday Weld, Michael Moriarty, Anthony Zerbe, Richard Masur, Ray Sharkey. D: Karel Reisz. CRI [R] 126m. V

Wholly Moses 1980 ★★ Would-be biblical spoof features Moore as mistaken prophet trying to replicate deeds of Moses. Silly and occasionally tasteless humor. C: Dudley Moore, Laraine Newman, James Coco, Paul Sand, Jack Gilford, Dom DeLuise, Madeline Kahn. D: Gary Weis. COM [PG] 101m. V

Whom the Gods Destroy 1934 ★★★½ Theater producer (Connolly) on sinking ship throws on woman's coat to get into lifeboats. Thought to have gone down bravely with the ship, he abandons his real identity and family to avoid disgrace. Wildly improbable plot is helped by excellent cast. C: Walter Connolly, Robert Young, Doris Kenyon. D: Walter Lang. DRA 75m.

Whoopee! 1930 ★★★½ Cantor's first talkie is primitive and dated; mainly interesting for Cantor as world's greatest hypochondriac and Busby Berkeley choreography. Remake: *Up in Arms*. C: Eddie Cantor, Eleanor Hunt, Paul Gregory, John Rutherford. D: Thornton Freeland. MUS 93m. v

Whoopee Boys, The 1986 ★★ A pair of losers (Rodriguez and O'Keefe) lead a group of misfits who put the harm in charm school down in the Everglades. Crude, brainless, but occasionally amusing comedy. C: Michael O'Keefe, Paul Rodriguez, Denholm Elliott. D: John Byrum. COM [R] 89m. v

Whoops Apocalypse 1988 ★★ When British Prime Minister Cook launches a nuclear strike at Latin America, it's up to U.S. President Swit to stop the potential holocaust. Unfunny political satire weighted down by heavy subject and trite execution. C: Loretta Swit, Peter Cook, Rik Mayall, Alexei Sayle. D: Tom Bussman. COM [R] 93m.

Whore 1991 ★★ Russell's sordid, overbaked exploration of the life of a prostitute.(a.k.a. *If You Can't Say It, Just See It*) C: Theresa Russell, Benjamin Mouton, Antonio Fargas, Sanjay, Elizabeth Morehead, Michael Crabtree, John Diehl. D: Ken Russell. DRA [R] 84m. v

Who's Afraid of Virginia Woolf? 1966 ★★★★★ Vitriol, humiliation, and four-letter words highlight this exceptional adaptation of Albee's 1962 Broadway hit about a middle-aged professor and his wife (Burton and Taylor) whose alternately loving and loathsome relationship traumatizes their young guests (Segal and Dennis). Nichols' directorial debut. Oscars to Taylor and Dennis. C: Elizabeth Taylor, Richard Burton, George Segal, Sandy Dennis. D: Mike Nichols. DRA 131m. v

Who's Got the Action? 1962 ★★★½ Turner, fed up with husband Martin's constant playing of the ponies, decides to counteract his gambling by becoming a bookie. Lightweight situation comedy. C: Dean Martin, Lana Turner, Eddie Albert, Walter Matthau. D: Daniel Mann. COM 93m. v

Who's Harry Crumb? 1989 ★★ Candy is boorish private eye given the case of a lifetime when he goes on the trail of a kidnapped heiress. Weak caper comedy. C: John Candy, Jeffrey Jones, Annie Potts, Tim Thomerson, Barry Corbin, Shawnee Smith. D: Paul Flaherty. COM [PG-13] 91m. v

Who's Minding the Mint? 1967 ★★★★ Wonderful supporting cast highlights this attempt at '30s-style screwball comedy. U.S. Mint worker (Hutton) must replace $50,000 after he accidentally destroys it. His helpers turn out to be losers. C: Jim Hutton, Dorothy Provine, Milton Berle, Joey Bishop, Walter Brennan, Victor Buono, Jack Gilford. D: Howard Morris. COM 97m. v

Who's Minding the Store? 1963 ★★★½ A world-class klutz wreaks havoc in a department store when he gets a job as a clerk. Good Lewis vehicle features plenty of his trademark broad humor. C: Jerry Lewis, Agnes Moorehead, Ray Walston, Jill St. John. D: Frank Tashlin. COM 90m.

Who's That Girl? 1987 ★★ Madonna is released from prison and unsuspecting official Dunne must escort her out of town. Instead she takes him on the ride of his life. Best for serious Madonna fans. C: Madonna, Griffin Dunne, Haviland Morris, John McMartin, Bibi Besch, John Mills. D: James Foley. COM [PG] 94m. v

Who's That Knocking at My Door? 1968 ★★★½ Scorsese's first, a personal tale about young man (Keitel, in his debut) trying to break free from constraints of his strict religious upbringing. Interesting and gritty. C: Zina Bethune, Harvey Keitel, Anne Collette, Lennard Kuras, Michael Scala, Harry Northrup, Bill Minkin. D: Martin Scorsese. DRA [R] 90m. v

Who's the Man? 1993 ★★★ Updated Abbott and Costello plotting features rappers Ed Lover and Doctor Dre as Harlem barbers turned cops battling corrupt business interests. Funny in parts, with plenty of rap star cameos, but instantly dated. C: Ed Lover, Doctor Dre, Badja Djola, Colin Quinn, Denis Leary. D: Ted Demme. COM [R] 90m. v

Who's Your Lady Friend? 1937 British ★★★ Slight mistaken-identity farce, as a singer is confused with a plastic surgeon's wealthy client. C: Frances Day, Betty Stockfeld, Romney Brent, Margaret Lockwood. D: Carol Reed. COM 73m.

Whose Life Is It Anyway? 1981 ★★★★½ Uniformly excellent acting from a superb cast sparks this adaptation of Brian Clark's hit play about sculptor, paralyzed from neck down in auto accident, who argues for right to be taken off life-support. Dreyfuss is superb as lead; Lahti and Cassavetes are more than his match. C: Richard Dreyfuss, John Cassavetes, Christine Lahti, Bob Balaban, Kenneth McMillan, Kaki Hunter. D: John Badham. DRA [R] 118m. v

Why Bring That Up? 1929 ★★ Blackface comics Mack and Moran rise to fame in vaudeville, then are tormented by lover from Moran's past. Primitive musical represents rare film effort for Broadway legend George Abbott. Despite its appalling racism, a useful record of vaudeville comedy. C: George Moran, Charles Mack, Evelyn Brent. D: George Abbott. COM 80m.

Why Didn't They Ask Evans? 1980 ★★★½ In a '30s setting, a pair of amateur detectives tries to solve a mystery introduced by the death of a noted globe-trotter. Frothy performances by Annis and Warwick in this lighthearted British TV adaptation of an Agatha Christie story. C: Francesca Annis, James Warwick, Eric Porter, John Gielgud, Joan Hickson. D: John Davies, Tony Wharmby. CRI 180m. TVM v

Why Does Herr R. Run Amok? 1977 West German ★★★★½ Typically mordant Fassbinder look at put-upon office worker who finally goes berserk, murdering friends, colleagues, family. Not to all tastes, but director's deadpan treatment of material is jolting. C: Kurt Raab, Lilith Ungerer, Amadeus Fengler, Franz Maron. D: Rainer Werner Fassbinder, Michael Fengler. DRA 88m. V

Why Leave Home? 1929 ★★★½ Second film version of *The Cradle Snatchers* in which husbands go off to hunt, leaving wives to do the same, only for different game. Early talkie has a certain charm. C: Dixie Lee, Jean Barry, Sue Carol, Richard Keene. D: Raymond Cannon. COM 70m.

Why Must I Die? 1960 ★★★ Low-budget rip-off of *I Want to Live*, with Moore convicted for murder she didn't commit. Still surprisingly intense. C: Terry Moore, Debra Paget, Bert Freed, Julie Reding. D: Roy Del Ruth. CRI 86m.

Why Not! *See* **Pour quoi Pas!**

Why Shoot the Teacher? 1979 Canadian ★★★★ Cort is sent to far-off Saskatchewan to teach during the Depression. Rather heavy moral message, but the interaction with students is genuinely heartwarming. C: Bud Cort, Samantha Eggar, Chris Wiggins, Gary Reineke. D: Silvio Narizzano. DRA 101m. V

Wichita 1955 ★★★½ McCrea offers serviceable performance as Wyatt Earp, cleaning up the town, but stylish direction really carries the film. C: Joel McCrea, Vera Miles, Lloyd Bridges, Wallace Ford, Peter Graves. D: Jacques Tourneur. WST 81m.

Wicked Lady, The 1945 British ★★★★ Colorful, entertaining yarn of a 19th-century bandit, well-played by Lockwood. Notches above the 1980s remake. C: Margaret Lockwood, James Mason, Michael Rennie, Martita Hunt. D: Leslie Arliss. ACT 104m.

Wicked Lady, The 1983 British ★★★½ Sophisticated court lady leads a robber's life by night. Great talent and costumes, but a slow story. Remake of the 1945 film. C: Faye Dunaway, Alan Bates, John Gielgud, Denholm Elliott, Prunella Scales, Oliver Tobias. D: Michael Winner. ACT [R] 101m. V

Wicked Stepmother 1989 ★ Horror cheapie about the strange things that happen when a witch (Davis) marries widower Stander. Davis only worked one week on picture, her last film. C: Bette Davis, Barbara Carrera, Colleen Camp, David Rasche, Lionel Stander, Tom Bosley, Evelyn Keyes, Laurene Landon. D: Larry Cohen. HOR [PG-13] 90m. V

Wicked Woman, A 1934 ★★★½ Christians is excellent as woman who kills her abusive, alcoholic husband to protect their kids, then is forced to flee. Otherwise competent. C: Mady Christians, Jean Parker, Charles Bickford. D: Charles Brabin. DRA 72m.

Wicker Man, The 1973 British ★★★★½ The investigation of a British detective (Woodward) of a missing child leads him to an exotic island of modern pagans, where he learns horrible secrets. Unusual, effective, and eerie thriller with a chilling conclusion. A perennial cult favorite. C: Edward Woodward, Christopher Lee, Britt Ekland, Diane Cilento, Ingrid Pitt. D: Robin Hardy. CRI [R] 103m. V

Wide-Eyed and Legless 1993 British ★★★★½ Interesting, off-beat comedy/-drama about the relationship between a married couple (Walters and Broadbent) when she is stricken with a mysterious illness that leaves her bedridden and homebound. Notable for an excellent script by Jack Rosenthal, and superb performances. C: Julie Walters, Jim Broadbent, Thora Bird, Sian Thomas, Diniah Handley, Peter Whitfield, Candida Rundle. D: Richard Loncraine. COM 90m.

Wide Open 1930 ★★★½ Mouse of a bookkeeper (Horton) becomes a lion when the boss's daughter (Miller) comes into his life. Pleasant farce, carried by Horton's engaging presence and the manic script. C: Edward Everett Horton, Patsy Ruth Miller. D: Archie Mayo. COM 69m.

Wide Open Town 1941 ★★★ Boyd appears again as Hopalong Cassidy, this time helping honest mayor fight off crooked politician and saloon owner. Well mounted but standard. C: William Boyd, Evelyn Brent. D: Lesley Selander. WST 78m.

Wide Sargasso Sea 1993 U.S. ★★★ A young woman in the Caribbean gets into an arranged marriage, lust, and madness in the tropical night. The drama never really takes off, but there are some highly erotic sex scenes. Based on the Jean Rhys novel. C: Karina Lombard, Nathaniel Parker, Rachel Ward, Michael York. D: John Duigan. DRA [R] 98m. V

Widows' Peak 1994 ★★★★ A flamboyant newcomer (Richardson) to an Irish community of widows antagonizes a woman with a secret. Quirky comedy of manners, with a surprise ending. Great performances make it a very diverting trifle. C: Mia Farrow, Natasha Richardson, Joan Plowright, Jim Broadbent. D: John Irvin. COM [PG] 101m. V

Wife, Doctor and Nurse 1937 ★★★½ Doctor (Baxter) is caught between Young and Bruce. Predictable but efficient. C: Loretta Young, Warner Baxter, Virginia Bruce, Jane Darwell, Sidney Blackmer, Minna Gombell, Elisha Cook Jr., Lon Chaney Jr. D: Walter Lang. COM 85m.

Wife, Husband and Friend 1939 ★★★★ When Young wants to become an opera singer, husband Baxter decides to show her up. Very funny, with clever script from story by James M. Cain. Remade as *Everybody Does It*. C: Loretta Young, Warner Baxter, Binnie Barnes, George Barbier, Cesar Romero, J. Bromberg, Eugene Pallette. D: Gregory Ratoff. COM 80m.

Wife of General Ling, The 1938 British ★★★ Minor but well-done adventure of corruption and gunrunning. White wife of Chinese officer helps her former lover unmask her husband's dishonesty in '30s China. (a.k.a. *Revenge of General Ling*) C: Griffith Jones, Valery Inkijinoff, Adrianne Renn. D: Ladislas Vajda. DRA 72m.

Wife vs. Secretary 1936 ★★★★ Society wife (Loy) doesn't believe rumors about her publisher husband (Gable) and his devoted secretary (Harlow) but becomes suspicious when she thinks she's discovered proof. Breezy comedy with polished performances, especially Harlow in a rare down-to-earth role. C: Clark Gable, Jean Harlow, Myrna Loy, May Robson, George Barbier, James Stewart, Hobart Cavanaugh. D: Clarence Brown. COM 89m. V

Wifemistress 1979 Italian ★★★ Solid cast in effective, erotic comedy/drama set in the early 1900s about a woman who suffers under her husband's neglect; when he goes underground to escape a murder rap, she comes into her own. (a.k.a. *Lover, Wife*) C: Marcello Mastroianni, Laura Antonelli, Leonard Mann. D: Marco Vicario. DRA [R] 110m. V

Wilby Conspiracy, The 1975 ★★★½ An indifferent British engineer (Caine) and an African nationalist (Poitier) hit the road to flee apartheid. The unlikely pairing of characters on the run is the thrust of this decent chase flick. C: Sidney Poitier, Michael Caine, Nicol Williamson, Saeed Jaffrey, Rutger Hauer. D: Ralph Nelson. ACT [PG] 101m. V

Wild and the Free, The 1980 ★★★ Scientist saves laboratory-raised chimpanzees from radiation experiments by returning them to natural surroundings. Routine comedy with superficially presented message. C: Granville Van Dusen, Linda Gray, Frank Logan, Ray Forchion. D: James Hill. FAM/DRA 96m. V

Wild and the Innocent, The 1959 ★★★½ Moderately offbeat Western with Murphy a trapper who comes to town for July 4th celebration; finds himself involved with young woman from country (Dee) and outlaws. C: Audie Murphy, Joanne Dru, Gilbert Roland, Jim Backus, Sandra Dee, George Mitchell, Peter Breck. D: Jack Sher. WST 84m.

Wild and Wonderful 1964 ★★★ Curtis and Kauffman fall in love while chaperoning French poodle who is movie star. Not much here. C: Tony Curtis, Christine Kaufmann, Larry Storch, Marty Ingels, Jacques Aubuchon, Jules Munshin. D: Michael Anderson. COM 88m.

Wild and Woody 1963 ★★★½ Several Woody Woodpecker cartoons are strung together for loosely connected story involving the cackling redheaded bird fighting bad guys in Old West. Younger audiences and animation fans will probably enjoy this goofy, if somewhat disjointed romp. D: Walter Lantz. FAM/COM 51m. V

Wild and Woolly 1978 ★★½ Trio of women cowpunchers must break out of prison to prevent assassination of President Roosevelt in 1903. Tedious. C: Chris DeLisle, Susan Bigelow, Elyssa Davalos, Jessica Walter. D: Philip Leacock. WST 65m.

Wild Angels, The 1966 ★★½ Supercool Fonda leads his violent biker gang with an iron fist. Pre-*Easy Rider* Corman cheapie is running on fumes by the end, but may be of interest to fans of the genre and the inimitable Dern. C: Peter Fonda, Nancy Sinatra, Bruce Dern, Diane Ladd. D: Roger Corman. DRA [PG] 124m. V

Wild at Heart 1990 ★★★ A young woman (Dern) runs off with ex-convict Elvis worshipper (Cage), while her mother (Ladd, Dern's real-life mom) tries to stop them. Director Lynch's trademark weirdness ultimately drowns in its own excesses. Many cameos from Lynch's TV series *Twin Peaks*. C: Nicolas Cage, Laura Dern, Diane Ladd, Willem Dafoe, Isabella Rossellini, Harry Dean Stanton, Crispin Glover. D: David Lynch. DRA [R] 125m. V

Wild Beds 1979 *See* **Tigers in Lipstick**

Wild Blue Yonder, The 1951 ★★★½ War movie tribute to bomber crew. Dwan gives this some panache; Corey and Tucker are adequate as friends and romantic rivals. C: Wendell Corey, Vera Ralston, Forrest Tucker, Phil Harris, Walter Brennan, Ruth Donnelly. D: Allan Dwan. DRA 98m.

Wild Boys of the Road 1933 ★★★★½ Three youths turn hooligan to survive during the darkest days of the Depression. Searing melodrama pulls no punches; looks surprisingly fresh today. C: Frankie Darro, Rochelle Hudson, Dorothy Coonan, Edwin Philips, Ann Hovey, Arthur Hohl, Sterling Holloway. D: William Wellman. DRA 68m.

Wild Bunch, The 1969 ★★★★½ Peckinpah created a whole new genre with this film: the stylized bloodbath Western. Set during the early 1900s, a group of over-the-hill Texas bandits decide to retire after one last gambit only to be ambushed first by a long-forgotten enemy and, then, by a Mexican revolutionary. Exciting well-scripted action, with many memorable lines, is a paean to a lost code of violent macho camaraderie. Quite good from beginning to end. Not for the kiddies. A longer restored version is also available. C: William Holden, Ernest Borgnine, Robert Ryan, Edmond O'Brien, Warren Oates, Ben Johnson, Jaime Sanchez, Strother Martin, L.Q. Jones. D: Sam Peckinpah. WST [R] 144m. V

Wild Card 1992 ★★★½ Ex-clergyman (Boothe), investigating the death of a wealthy Texas land baron, must confront the close-lipped and shifty citizenry . . . and some local lugs. Standard mystery thriller helped out immeasurably by Boothe's solid presence. C: Powers Boothe, Rene Auberjonois, Cindy Pickett. D: Mel Damski. CRI [PG-13] 86m. TVM V

Wild Child, The 1969 *See* **L'Enfant Sauvage.**

Wild Country, The 1970 ★★★ Nineteenth-century clan experiences many adventures after relocating from urban Pittsburgh to rural Wyoming. Routine Disney family fare with good scenery that younger audiences will probably enjoy. Adapted from Ralph Moody's *Little Britches*. C: Steve Forrest, Vera Miles, Ron Howard, Jack Elam. D: Robert Totten. FAM/DRA [G] 92m. V

Wild Duck, The 1983 Australian ★★ Disappointing filming of Ibsen's play about a man who rejects his beloved daughter when he discovers her illegitimacy. The stars try hard...too hard. C: Liv Ullmann, Jeremy Irons, Lucinda Jones. D: Henri Safran. DRA [PG] 96m. V

Wild Frontier, The 1947 ★★★½ When his sheriff father is murdered Rocky Lane is determined to bring the killers to justice. Solid, fast-paced Western. C: Allan "Rocky" Lane, Jack Holt. D: Philip Ford. WST 59m.

Wild Geese, The 1978 British ★★★ British mercenaries are enlisted to rescue a political leader from central Africa. Compelling story with plenty of gore and action. Burton and Harris lead a cast of pros. C: Richard Burton, Roger Moore, Richard Harris, Hardy Kruger, Stewart Granger. D: Andrew V. McLaglen. ACT [R] 132m. V

Wild Harvest 1947 ★★★½ Zesty tale of migrant farm workers, with Ladd and Preston competing for Lamour's attentions. A lot of knockabout humor in between the romance. C: Alan Ladd, Dorothy Lamour, Robert Preston, Lloyd Nolan, Richard Erdman, Allen Jenkins. D: Tay Garnett. DRA 92m.

Wild Heart, The 1950 *See* **Gone to Earth**

Wild Hearts Can't Be Broken 1991 ★★★★½ Strong and unusual family drama about Depression-era young woman (Anwar) who runs away from foster home and joins traveling carnival where she becomes star "horse-diver"—leaping off 40-foot platform into water tub while astride horse. Spirited production marked by strong acting and fine re-creation of period. Based on a true story. C: Gabrielle Anwar, Michael Schoeffling, Cliff Robertson. D: Steve Miner. FAM/DRA [G] 90m. V

Wild in the Country 1961 ★★★★ A redneck youth (Presley) is desperate to become a respected writer. One of the King's strongest acting roles, and he shines in it. Screenplay by Clifford Odets. C: Elvis Presley, Hope Lange, Tuesday Weld, Millie Perkins, John Ireland. D: Philip Dunne. DRA 114m. V

Wild in the Sky 1972 *See* **Black Jack**

Wild in the Streets 1968 ★★★½ Youth satire seemed hip and biting in the '60s and still retains some of its kick. Rock star Jones is elected President when teens are given the vote, and imprisons all adults in internment camps where they're forced to drop acid. C: Christopher Jones, Shelley Winters, Diane Varsi, Hal Holbrook, Ed Begley, Richard Pryor. D: Barry Shear. DRA [PG] 97m. V

Wild is the Wind 1957 ★★★★ A wealthy Nevada sheep rancher (Quinn) marries his sister-in-law (Magnani) when his wife dies and he begins to confuse one with the other. Superb acting by Magnani and Quinn and sensitive direction transform potentially embarrassing melodrama. C: Anna Magnani, Anthony Quinn, Anthony Franciosa, Dolores Hart, Joseph Calleia. D: George Cukor. DRA 114m.

Wild Man of Borneo, The 1941 ★★★ Minor comedy of carnival life with Morgan improbably cast in title role. Other players are okay. C: Frank Morgan, Mary Howard, Billie Burke, Donald Meek, Marjorie Main, Connie Gilchrist, Bonita Granville, Walter Catlett, Phil Silvers, Dan Dailey. D: Robert Sinclair. COM 78m.

Wild One, The 1954 ★★★★½ The movie that ushered in a spate of generation gap and antihero dramas seems tame by today's standards, but still packs a punch due to brooding Brando as leader of the Black Rebels motorcycle gang that terrorizes a small town. Thoroughly enjoyable. C: Marlon Brando, Mary Murphy, Robert Keith, Lee Marvin. D: Laslo Benedek. DRA 79m. V

Wild Orchid 1990 ★★ While in Rio de Janeiro during Carnival, an attorney (Otis) becomes involved with a low-life (Rourke). What follows is sex, sex, and more sex. Sequel followed. C: Mickey Rourke, Jacqueline Bisset, Carre Otis, Bruce Greenwood. D: Zalman King. DRA [R] 111m. V

Wild Orchid 2—Two Shades of Blue 1992 ★★ Steamy and laughable erotica that bears little resemblance to original *Wild Orchid*. Scanty plot, reworked from *Angel*, involves a high school student who works in a bordello at night. A hot and heavy invitation to sleep. C: Nina Siemaszko, Wendy Hughes, Tom Skerritt, Robert Davi, Brent Fraser, Joe Dallesandro. D: Zalman King. DRA [R] 105m. V

Wild Orchids 1929 ★★★½ An adulterous shipboard affair results when a married woman (Garbo) falls for another man (Asther). Steamy silent melodrama, marked by a fine Garbo performance. C: Greta Garbo, Nils Asther, Lewis Stone. D: Sidney Franklin. DRA 102m. V

Wild Palms 1993 ★★★½ Oliver Stone's visually stunning, bizarre miniseries, set in the not-so-distant future, pits a powerful corporation bent on controlling the country through technology against rebels fighting for individual freedom. State-of-the art effects can't compensate for a confusing story that wastes the talented cast. C: James Belushi, Kim Cattrall, Dana Delany, Robert Loggia, Angie Dickinson. D: Kathryn Bigelow. SFI 300m. TVM V

Wild Party, The 1929 ★★★½ Early talkie has handsome new prof March at all-girls' school, dealing with Bow, who'd rather party than study. Hilarious, if not always intentionally so. C: Clara Bow, Fredric March, Shirley

O'Hara, Jack Oakie. D: Dorothy Arzner. COM 76m. V

Wild Party, The 1975 ★★★½ Silent film comic (Coco) throws an ill-fated orgy, ending in tragedy for both host and guests. Inspired by the real-life Fatty Arbuckle scandal, and one of the few movies based on a poem. Good performances. C: James Coco, Raquel Welch, Perry King. D: James Ivory. DRA [R] 95m. V

Wild Pony, The 1983 ★★ Young boy finds solace with his pony to avoid new stepfather he dislikes. Competent but unexceptional kids' fare. C: Marilyn Lightstone, Art Hindle, Josh Byrne. D: Kevin Sullivan. FAM/DRA 87m. V

Wild Ride, The 1960 ★★½ A loutish teenager goes on a murderous rampage. Low-budget shocker boasts a prehistoric Nicholson performance. C: Jack Nicholson, Georgianna Carter. D: Harvey Berman. CRI 63m. V

Wild River 1960 ★★★★★ Clift is Tennessee Valley Authority representative, trying to get families to move off land that will be inundated by new hydroelectric dam. While struggling with intransigent Van Fleet, he falls in love with Remick. Poignant and insightful recreation of '30s Tennessee. Bruce Dern's first film. C: Montgomery Clift, Lee Remick, Jo VanFleet, Albert Salmi, Jay C. Flippen, James Westerfield. D: Elia Kazan. DRA 110m.

Wild Rovers 1971 ★★★★ Two wildly different cowboys bond together while escaping the law. Warm, entertaining character western features one of Holden's best performances. C: William Holden, Ryan O'Neal, Karl Malden, Lynn Carlin. D: Blake Edwards. WST [PG] 136m. V

Wild Seed, The 1965 ★★★½ Kaye is teen on the run, heading for California; she is befriended by drifter Parks. Predictable, yet at times fascinating. C: Michael Parks, Celia Kaye, Ross Elliott, Woodrow Chambliss, Eva Novak. D: Brian G. Hutton. DRA 99m.

Wild Stallion 1952 ★★½ Flashback-strewn tale of romance and rivalries at a military academy. Tame, despite good supporting cast. C: Martha Hyer, Edgar Buchanan, Hugh Beaumont, Ben Johnson. D: Lewis Collins. DRA 72m.

Wild Strawberries 1957 Sweden ★★★★★ On his way to accept an honorary degree, an aging professor looks back on his life and attempts to come to terms with its disappointments. Bergman's classic is as moving now as ever, merging terrific performances with excellent use of flashbacks to create an overwhelming emotional experience. Subtitles. C: Victor Sjostrom, Ingrid Thulin, Bibi Andersson, Gunnar Bjornstrand. D: Ingmar Bergman. DRA 90m. V

Wild Wheels 1993 ★★★★ Unusual and extremely watchable documentary looks at car owners who create personal expression through eccentric customization. Extraordinary personalities and automobiles are dealt with matter-of-factly, creating fascinating portrait of American life. Don't miss the grassmobile! D: Harrod Blank. DOC [R] 64m. V

Wildcats 1986 ★★★½ Hawn becomes first woman coach for inner-city high school football team, leading rag-tag team of losers to victory. Though story follows familiar formula, Hawn's energy and cast of upcoming stars (including Wesley Snipes and Woody Harrelson) provide fresh moments of humor. C: Goldie Hawn, Swoosie Kurtz, James Keach, Bruce McGill, Nipsey Russell, M. Emmet Walsh. D: Michael Ritchie. COM [R] 106m. V

Wilder Napalm 1993 ★★★ Quaid and Howard are brothers, able to start fires mentally, who both have the hots for Howard's wife (Winger). Quirky comedy has inspired premise and dialogue, a good director and cast, but somehow doesn't quite deliver up to its potential. C: Debra Winger, Dennis Quaid, Arliss Howard. D: Glenn Gordon Caron. COM [PG-13] 109m. V

Wilderness Family Part 2, The 1978 ★★★½ Sequel to popular *Adventures of the Wilderness Family*, continuing the saga of the Robinsons, who opted for the good, outdoors life in Colorado, leaving evils of civilization behind. Good family drama. (a.k.a. *The Further Adventures of the Wilderness Family*) C: Robert Logan, Susan D. Shaw, Heather Rattray, Ham Larsen, George Flower, Brian Cutler. D: Frank Zuniga. FAM/DRA 105m. V

Wildflower 1992 ★★★★½ During 1930s, two teenagers find Arquette, thought to be demon-possessed because of epileptic seizures, locked up outside her cruel father's home. Sensitive telling of unusual tale, with excellent performances providing strength. Adapted by Sara Flanigan from her book, *Alice*. C: Beau Bridges, Susan Blakely, Patricia Arquette. D: Diane Keaton. DRA 94m. TVM V

Wildrose 1985 ★★★★ Excellent independent feature about divorcée (Eichhorn) taking job as iron-pit worker, coping with all-male work environment, finding romance with fellow employee. Evocative location shooting. C: Lisa Eichhorn, Tom Bower, Jim Cada, Cinda Jackson. D: John Hanson. DRA 96m. V

Will: G. Gordon Liddy 1982 ★★ Silly exercise in macho self-aggrandizement adapted from autobiography of former government agent turned dirty trickster. C: Robert Conrad, Katherine Cannon, Gary Bayer, Peter Ratray. D: Robert Lieberman. DRA 100m. TVM V

Will James' Sand 1949 *See* **Sand**

Will O' the Wisp 1958 *See* **Time to Love and a Time to Die, A**

Will Penny 1968 ★★★★ Classic tale of the cowboy as rugged individualist. Heston, as over-the-hill cowpuncher, is outstanding, and he's served quite well by a strong support cast. C: Charlton Heston, Joan Hackett, Donald Pleasence, Lee Majors, Bruce Dern, Ben Johnson. D: Tom Gries. WST 108m. V

Will Success Spoil Rock Hunter? 1957 ★★★★★ A wildly funny cartoonish satire on advertising, sex and success in the '50s. Randall is an ad exec who must convince movie queen Mansfield to endorse Stay-Put Lipstick. Memorable guest appearance by Groucho; Tashlin at his hysterical best. C: Tony Randall, Jayne Mansfield, Betsy Drake, Joan Blondell, John Williams, Henry Jones, Mickey Hargitay. D: Frank Tashlin. COM 94m.

Willard 1971 ★★★½ A disturbed young man (Davison) uses his pet rats to exact revenge on those who betrayed him. Gruesome, yet fascinating thriller was a surprise box-office hit. Best scene—Borgnine becomes lunch. Followed by sequel, *Ben.* C: Bruce Davison, Ernest Borgnine, Sondra Locke, Elsa Lanchester. D: Daniel Mann. HOR [PG] 95m. V

Willie and Phil 1980 ★★★★ Mazursky's take on *Jules and Jim* opens with the title characters watching that movie; they then go on to relive its "lover's triangle" plot (with Kidder in the Jeanne Moreau role). Surprisingly interesting, and a valentine to its predecessor. C: Michael Ontkean, Ray Sharkey, Margot Kidder. D: Paul Mazursky. COM [R] 115m. V

Willy Milly 1987 *See* **Something Special**

Willow 1988 ★★★½ Derivative but exciting and fast-paced fantasy casts Kilmer as a good-for-nothing warrior who rallies to help a little person (Davis) save his people. Great effects, but may be a bit too scary for young children. C: Val Kilmer, Joanne Whalley—Kilmer, Warwick Davis, Jean Marsh, Billy Barty. D: Ron Howard. SFI [PG] 125m. V

Willy McBean and his Magic Machine 1959 Japanese ★★★ Japanese-made kids film uses puppets to tell story of mad scientist experimenting with time travel. Harmless, with interesting technical effects. C: Larry Mann, Billie Richards, Alfie Scopp. D: Arthur Rankin Jr. FAM/SFI 94m. V

Willy Wonka and the Chocolate Factory 1971 ★★★½ Whimsical fantasy from Roald Dahl book, with Wilder perfect as "Candy Man" opening his secret kingdom to holders of five lucky tickets. Often delightful, but occasionally sticky, with too much moralizing. Attractive score by Anthony Newley and Leslie Bricusse. C: Gene Wilder, Jack Albertson, Peter Ostrum. D: Mel Stuart. MUS [G] 100m. V

Wilma 1977 ★★½ Film biography of noted Olympic star Wilma Rudolph blends tales of personal struggle with polio. Athletic sequences never soar. C: Cicely Tyson, Shirley Jo Finney, Jason Bernard. D: Bud Greenspan. DRA 100m. TVM V

Wilson 1944 ★★★★ Solid, expertly crafted biography of WWI-period President Woodrow Wilson (Knox), focusing on his postwar dream of League of Nations, and fatal illness which left wife Edith (Fitzgerald) virtually running the country. Sometimes too academic, but often moving. C: Alexander Knox, Charles Coburn, Geraldine Fitzgerald, Thomas Mitchell, Cedric Hardwicke, Vincent Price, Mary Anderson, Sidney Blackmer. D: Henry King. DRA 154m. V

Wilt 1989 *See* **Misadventures of Mr. Wilt, The**

Winchester '73 1950 ★★★★½ A stolid, aging cowpoke is relentless in a search for his stolen Winchester rifle. Quite sturdy and immensely entertaining. A very big film in every possible way. Remade in 1967. C: James Stewart, Shelley Winters, Dan Duryea, Stephen McNally, Millard Mitchell, John McIntire, Will Geer, Rock Hudson, Tony Curtis. D: Anthony Mann. WST 82m. V

Wind 1992 ★★★ Modine and Grey survive their turbulent relationship to compete in the America's Cup sailing contest. Magnificent racing footage dominates the story. C: Matthew Modine, Jennifer Grey, Cliff Robertson, Jack Thompson, Stellan Skarsgard, Rebecca Miller. D: Carroll Ballard. DRA [PG-13] 125m. V

Wind Across the Everglades 1958 ★★★★ Memorable and offbeat film pits Plummer as turn-of-the century game warden against bird poachers led by Ives. Spicy script; and Plummer and Ives are wonderful antagonists. Falk's first film. C: Burl Ives, Christopher Plummer, Gypsy Rose Lee, George Voskovec, Tony Galento, Emmett Kelly, Chana Eden, MacKinlay Kantor. D: Nicholas Ray. DRA 93m.

Wind and the Lion, The 1975 ★★★½ Exciting (if at times overdone and unbelievable) turn-of-the-century adventure based (very) loosely on real events. Connery is Moroccan sheik who abducts American Bergen, inspiring Teddy Roosevelt (Keith) to send in the Marines. C: Sean Connery, Candice Bergen, Brian Keith, John Huston, Steve Kanaly. D: John Milius. DRA [PG] 120m. V

Wind Cannot Read, The 1958 British ★★★½ British flier (Bogarde) in Burma and trained in Japanese in order to be able to interrogate POWs, marries Tani, his instructor. When he's captured by Japanese, he must escape to find her. Good acting by leads propels the romance; action is competent. C: Dirk Bogarde, Yoko Tani, Ronald Lewis, John Fraser, Anthony Bushell, Michael Medwin. D: Ralph Thomas. DRA 110m.

Wind, The 1928 ★★★★★ One of the great silent films, a stark rendition of the forces that drive a lonely pioneer woman mad. Gish has never been better. C: Lillian Gish, Lars Hanson, Montagu Love, Dorothy Cumming. D: Victor Seastrom. DRA 82m. V

Windom's Way 1957 British ★★★½ Dedicated doctor (Finch), working in Malaysia, becomes swept up in fight against Communists. He simultaneously juggles romantic attachments. Good cast saves overwrought material. C: Peter Finch, Mary Ure, Natasha Parry, Robert Flemyng. D: Ronald Neame. DRA 104m. V

Window Shopping 1986 *See* **Golden Eighties**

Window, The 1949 ★★★★ Boy with reputation as a compulsive liar witnesses real murder, but no one will believe him. Neat, claustrophobic Hitchcockian thriller. Driscoll won special Oscar for his performance. From Cornell Woolrich story. Remade as *The Boy Cried Murder* and *Cloak and Dagger*. C: Bobby Driscoll, Barbara Hale, Arthur Kennedy, Paul Stewart, Ruth Roman. D: Ted Tetzlaff. CRI 73m. v

Winds of Change 1979 ★★ Idea of animated retelling of five ancient Greek myths is promising, and some of the animation is colorful, but storytelling is uneven and disco score is awful. Watch *Fantasia*'s "Pastoral" sequence again instead. C: Peter Ustinov. FAM/DRA [PG] 82m. v

Winds of the Wasteland 1936 ★★★ Wayne tries to land government mail-hauling contract with partner Canutt; stymied by rivals led by Cosgrove. Decent early star vehicle. C: John Wayne, Yakima Canutt, Phyllis Fraser, Lane Chandler. D: Mack V. Wright. DRA 54m. v

Winds of War, The 1983 ★★★ An adaptation of the Herman Wouk novel, this huge WWII family saga began as a miniseries. Mitchum is outstanding as the former naval officer who is thrown into the turmoil of pre-WWII Germany. C: Robert Mitchum, Ali MacGraw, Jan-Michael Vincent, John Houseman, Polly Bergen, Lisa Eilibacher. D: Dan Curtis. DRA 883m. TVM v

Windwalker 1980 ★★★½ A dead Plains Indian returns to life to save his family from a tribal enemy: his evil twin raised by another tribe. Somewhat confusing story but beautiful Utah backdrops. C: Trevor Howard, Nick Ramus, James Remar, Serene Hedin. D: Kieth Merrill. WST [PG] 108m. v

Windy City 1984 ★★★ Thirty-somethings gather in Chicago to review their dreadfully failed lives. Uneven *Secaucus Seven* ripoff. C: John Shea, Kate Capshaw, Josh Mostel, Jim Borrelli, Jeffrey DeMunn, Eric Pierpoint. D: Armyan Bernstein. DRA [R] 103m. v

Wing and a Prayer 1944 ★★★★ Set on an aircraft carrier, this story of WWII pilots benefits from wartime footage. Good, action-packed adventure. C: Don Ameche, Dana Andrews, William Eythe, Richard Jaeckel, Charles Bickford, Richard Crane. D: Henry Hathaway. ACT 100m. v

Winged Victory 1944 ★★★½ Dated WWII propaganda film traces the training of young men who aspire to be Army pilots and the homefront lives of the women with whom they're involved. Young cast of then-unknowns provides some interest. C: Lon McCallister, Jeanne Crain, Edmond O'Brien, Don Taylor, Judy Holliday, Lee J. Cobb, Peter Lind Hayes, Red Buttons, Barry Nelson, Karl Malden, Gary Merrill, Martin Ritt. D: George Cukor. DRA 130m.

Wings 1927 ★★★★ Silent WWI adventure combines a love triangle plot with stupendous aerial battle scenes. First Oscar winner as Best Picture. C: Clara Bow, Charles "Buddy" Rogers, Richard Arlen, Gary Cooper. D: William A. Wellman. ACT 139m. v

Wings and the Woman 1942 British ★★★½ True tragic story of pioneering husband and wife aviators Amy Johnson (Neagle) and Jim Mollison (Newton), competently told. (a.k.a. *They Flew Alone*) C: Anna Neagle, Robert Newton. D: Herbert Wilcox. DRA 96m.

Wings in the Dark 1935 ★★★ Good aerial photography and stuntwork can't redeem this improbable soap opera about skywriter (Loy) falling for blind ex-pilot (Grant). C: Cary Grant, Myrna Loy, Dean Jagger, Roscoe Karns, Hobart Cavanaugh, Bert Hanlon. D: James Flood. DRA 77m.

Wings of Desire 1988 West German ★★★★ Angel Ganz comes to Earth and learns about human existence as he travels through Berlin, eventually falling for trapeze artist Dommartin. Deliberately paced, haunting and disturbing drama about the nature of humanity, with gorgeous cinematography in both b&w and color. Sequel: *Far Away, So Close*. C: Bruno Ganz, Solveig Dommartin, Otto Sander, Peter Falk. D: Wim Wenders. DRA [PG-13] 130m. v

Wings of Eagles, The 1957 ★★★★ Uneven, but ultimately moving tribute to screenwriter and Navy flier Frank "Spig" Wead. First half of film is hilarious slapstick, but when Wead is crippled in accident, it turns into a dark rumination on the nature of home. Bond plays a thinly disguised Ford to great comic effect. C: John Wayne, Maureen O'Hara, Dan Dailey, Ward Bond, Ken Curtis. D: John Ford. DRA 107m. v

Wings of the Morning 1937 British ★★★ The singing of legendary tenor McCormack is the best thing that this melodrama about Gypsies, horseracing, and romance has going for it. C: Annabella, Henry Fonda, John McCormack, Irene Vanbrugh, Philip Frost, Leslie Banks, Sam Livesey. D: Harold Schuster. DRA 89m.

Wings Over Wyoming 1937 *See* **Hollywood Cowboy**

Winner Never Quits, A 1993 ★★★★ TV biography about '40s professional baseball player Pete Gray, who succeeds despite his disability—one arm. Moving true life story strikes the right emotional chords. C: Keith Carradine, Mare Winningham, Dennis Weaver, Dana Delany. D: Mel Damski. DRA [PG] 96m. v

Winner Take All 1932 ★★★½ Bantamweight boxing champ (Cagney) is torn between two women. Typically good Warners prizefight yarn. C: James Cagney, Virginia Bruce, Marian Nixon, Guy Kibbee. D: Roy Del Ruth. ACT 68m.

Winners Take All 1987 ★★ Insecure, likable dirt bike racer shows what he's made of when he competes against an old friend turned rival. Standard root for underdog sports drama, buoyed by exciting motocross footage. C: Don Michael Paul, Kathleen York, Robert Krantz. D: Fritz Kiersch. ACT [PG-13] 103m. v

Winning 1969 ★★★★ Newman does his own driving in this exciting and briskly told tale of a ruthless driver who will do anything to get to the Indy 500. Woodward is his long-suffering wife. Thomas' first film. C: Paul Newman, Joanne Woodward, Richard Thomas, Robert Wagner. D: James Goldstone. DRA [PG] 123m. v

Winning Team, The 1953 ★★★★ Film biography of pitching great Grover Cleveland Alexander (Reagan), focuses mostly on his relationship with supportive wife (Day). The story addresses Alexander's alcoholism, but ignores his epilepsy, leading to complaints of distortion of facts. Overall, though, it's reasonably accurate, with fine performances. C: Doris Day, Ronald Reagan, Frank Lovejoy, Eve Miller, James Millican, Russ Tamblyn. D: Lewis Seiler. DRA 98m. v

Winning Way, The 1953 *See* **All American, The**

Winslow Boy, The 1950 British ★★★★ In pre-WWI England, a 13-year-old naval cadet is wrongly expelled for stealing a one-dollar postal order and his father takes the case all the way to Parliament to prove his son's innocence. Entertaining drama and fine performances, based on a true story. C: Robert Donat, Margaret Leighton, Cedric Hardwicke, Francis L. Sullivan. D: Anthony Asquith. DRA 112m. v

Winter Kills 1979 ★★★★ The brother of a slain President (Bridges), investigates the murder and finds it leads very close to home. Black comedy doesn't always hit the satiric mark, but the tremendous cast, especially Huston as the power-mad dad, is dead-on. Based on the Richard Condon novel. C: Jeff Bridges, John Huston, Anthony Perkins, Belinda Bauer. D: William Richert. CRI [R] 97m. v

Winter Light 1962 Swedish ★★★★ A small-town priest has a crisis of faith. Disturbing, allegorical drama, full of the director's trademark intensity. Second in Bergman's contemplative (but grim) 1960s trilogy, preceded by *Through a Glass Darkly* and followed by *The Silence*. C: Ingrid Thulin, Gunnar Bjornstrand, Max von Sydow. D: Ingmar Bergman. DRA 80m. v

Winter Meeting 1948 ★★½ Middle-aged poet (B. Davis) yearns after a bitter war veteran (J. Davis) who wants to become a priest. Feisty Bette is the highlight. C: Bette Davis, Janis Paige, Jim Davis, John Hoyt, Florence Bates. D: Bretaigne Windust. DRA 105m. v

Winter of Our Dreams, The 1981 Australian ★★★½ Bookshop keeper (Brown), unhappily wed to Downes, meets prostitute (Davis) after suicide of a mutual friend and the two begin an unlikely affair. Ponderous drama tries desperately for emotional depth, and succeeds occasionally. Good ensemble cant rise above script. C: Judy Davis, Bryan Brown, Cathy Downes, Baz Luhrmann. D: John Duigan. DRA 89m. v

Winter People 1989 ★★★ During the 1930s, a gentle clockmaker (Russell) returns to backwoods hometown where he finds a violent feud about to break loose because of McGillis' philandering. Despite good performances, old-fashioned Hatfields vs. McCoys plot just doesn't cut it nowadays. C: Kurt Russell, Kelly McGillis, Lloyd Bridges, Jeffrey Meek. D: Ted Kotcheff. DRA [PG-13] 109m. v

Winter Rates 1975 *See* **Out of Season**

Winter Wind 1970 French ★★★★ A violent anarchist in '30s Hungary has trouble with both the police and his frightened leftist comrades. Plays like a strange ballet, with little dialogue and much inexplicable but beautiful movement of people and camera. Not to all tastes, but some consider it a tour de force. Much nudity. C: Jacques Charrier. D: Miklos Jancso. DRA 80m.

Winterset 1936 ★★★ Meredith, re-creating Broadway role in his film debut, seeks justice for his father who was executed 15 years earlier for a crime he didn't commit. Dated, pretentious Maxwell Anderson play reworks the Sacco and Vanzetti case. C: Burgess Meredith, Margo, Eduardo Ciannelli, John Carradine, Myron McCormick, Mischa Auer. D: Alfred Santell. DRA 77m. v

Wired 1989 ★ Poorly conceived biography of self-destructive comic actor, John Belushi, who died of a drug overdose in 1982. Alters some facts, creates others all while ignoring Belushi's vital talent. Based on Bob Woodward's book. C: Michael Chiklis, Ray Sharkey, J.T. Walsh, Patti D'Arbanville, Lucinda Jenney, Alex Rocco, Gary Groomes. D: Larry Peerce. DRA [R] 108m. v

Wisdom 1987 ★★ Estevez wrote, directed, and stars in story of out-of-work young man who transforms himself into a '80s version of Robin Hood. No great shakes. C: Emilio Estevez, Demi Moore, Tom Skerritt, Veronica Cartwright. D: Emilio Estevez. DRA [R] 109m. v

Wise Blood 1979 ★★★★ Flannery O'Connor's dark gothic tale of fake religion and Southern dementia is brought chillingly to life. Dourif in compelling role, plays Hazel Motes, a preacher and sole member of The Church Without Christ. C: Brad Dourif, Daniel Shor, Amy Wright, Harry Dean Stanton, Ned Beatty. D: John Huston. DRA [PG] 106m. v

Wise Guys 1986 ★★ DeVito and Piscopo play small-time mobsters who get in all kinds of trouble when they try to rip off their boss. DeVito is good, but De Palma shouldn't do comedy. C: Danny DeVito, Joe Piscopo, Harvey Keitel, Ray Sharkey, Dan Hedaya, Patti LuPone. D: Brian De Palma. COM [R] 92m. v

Wisecracks 1992 Canadian ★★★★ Canadian documentary looks at stand-up comedy through eyes of female performers. Using archival footage, combined with interviews of modern practitioners, film gives feminist side of what is often perceived as male-dominated field. Enjoyable, funny, often insightful look at show business. D: Gail Singer. COM 93m. V

Wiser Age 1962 Japanese ★★★½ Family with five daughters faces myriad problems of domestic life in Tokyo. Two youngest vie for same man, oldest has faithless husband, while middle one eschews men for career, to everyone's dismay. Understated direction makes it work. (a.k.a. *A Woman's Place* or *Woman's Status*) C: Hideko Takamine, Tatsuya Mihashi, Akira Takarada, Yoko Tsukasa, Reiko Dan. D: Mikio Naruse. DRA 111m. V

Wish You Were Here 1987 British ★★★★ Teenage English girl (Lloyd) defies her father and established norms in suffocating post-WWII oceanside village. Tender, well-written coming-of-age tale. Fine lead performance by Lloyd. C: Emily Lloyd, Tom Bell, Jesse Birdsall, Geoffrey Durham. D: David Leland. DRA [R] 92m. V

Wishing Machine 1971 Czechoslavakian ★★★½ Czech fantasy film about boys who find a machine that grants wishes at a carnival. They want to go to the moon. Very good for children. C: Vit Weingaertner, Milan Zerman. D: Josef Pinkava. FAM/DRA [G] 75m.

Wistful Widow of Wagon Gap, The 1947 ★★★★ Abbott and Costello head to Montana and find themselves responsible for the care of Main and her brood of screaming brats when Lou gets blamed for shooting her alcoholic husband. Plenty of laughs in this hilarious well-plotted comedy. C: Bud Abbott, Lou Costello, Marjorie Main, George Cleveland, Gordon Jones, William Ching, Peter Thompson, Glenn Strange. D: Charles Barton. COM 78m. V

Witchboard 1987 ★★★½ Low-budget chiller, refreshingly free of gratuitous elements, follows Kitaen as she's haunted by a spirit residing in a Ouija board. Could have been scarier, but at least it's intelligent. Followed by sequel. C: Todd Allen, Tawny Kitaen, Stephen Nicholas, Rose Marie. D: Kevin S. Tenney. HOR [R] 97m. V

Witchboard 2: The Devil's Doorway 1993 ★★★ Hokey but diverting sequel in which protagonist fools around with Ouija board and unleashes a vengeful ghost. Nifty effects and stunt sequences, but pulpier than the first. C: Ami Dolenz, Laraine Newman, Timothy Gibbs, John Gatins. D: Kevin S. Tenney. HOR [R] 98m. V

Witchcraft 1988 British ★ Cheap, direct-to-video shocker centers on an evil cult out to claim a baby for diabolical purposes. Followed by several sequels. C: Gary Sloan, Lee Kisman. D: Roberta Spera. HOR 90m. V

Witchcraft II—The Temptress 1990 ★ Bedeviled infant from first film has grown up to become a reluctant young warlock, who must call upon his suppressed powers to deal with an evil succubus. Sexier but no scarier than the original. C: Charles Solomon, Mia Ruiz, Delia Sheppard. D: Mark Woods. HOR [R] 88m. V

Witchcraft III—The Kiss of Death 1991 ★★ Slightly improved characterizations and story make this the best of this low-budget bunch. This time, Solomon must defend himself and his girlfriend from a demon that sucks the life from his victims. C: Charles Solomon, Lisa Toothman, William L. Baker. D: R.L. Tillmanns. HOR [R] 85m. V

Witchcraft IV Virgin Heart 1992 ★ This series entry pits Solomon against a literal music promoter from hell. The subtitle is meaningless, but then so is the movie, which contains some of the worst dialogue in film history—which, of course, can be an attraction. C: Charles Solomon, Julie Strain, Clive Pearson. D: James Merendino. HOR [R] 92m. V

Witchcraft V: Dance With the Devil 1993 ★ Satan's emissary forces our heroic warlock to do his evil bidding, with exposed breasts and ripped-out hearts galore but no brains in sight and plenty of tacky effects. C: Nicole Sassaman, David Huffman, Lenny Rose. D: Talun Hsu. HOR [R] 94m. V

Witchcraft VI 1994 ★★ More satanic murders, more supernatural confrontations between amateur warlock Spicer and a devilish villain, more gratuitous nudity and violence, more cheapjack filmmaking. Please, no more! C: Jerry Spicer, Debra Beatty, Kurt Alan, John E. Holiday, Bryan Nutter. D: Julie Davis. HOR 89m.

Witchcraft Through the Ages (Haxan) 1920 Swedish ★★★★ Weird silent pseudodocumentary from Sweden blends history with scenes of satanic rituals, ritualistic torture, and a spectacular appearance by Satan himself. A one-of-a-kind experience, both insightful and spooky. (a.k.a. *Haxan*) C: Maren Pedersen, Clara Pontoppidah. D: Benjamin Christiansen. HOR [R] 85m. V

Witches' Brew 1980 ★★★½ A professor's wife (Garr) takes up witchcraft to further her hubby's failing career. Wan fantasy poofs into life whenever Turner's on screen, playing a scheming broomster; her last film to date. Remake of *Burn, Witch, Burn* and *Weird Woman*. C: Teri Garr, Lana Turner, Richard Benjamin. D: Richard Shorr, Herbert L. Strock. COM [PG] 99m. V

Witches of Eastwick, The 1987 ★★★½ Laden with special effects, film of John Updike's book is anything but subtle, but gets plenty of comic mileage from Nicholson as a charming Satan and Cher, Pfeiffer, and Sarandon as the frustrated women who conjure him up (and ultimately put him down) through witchcraft. C: Jack Nicholson, Cher, Susan Sarandon, Michelle Pfeiffer, Veronica Cartwright. D: George Miller. COM [R] 118m. V

Witches, The 1990 British ★★★★ Boy at English seaside hotel stumbles into witches' convention, led by Huston, and discovers their plan to turn the children of the world into mice. Huston is exceptional and Jim Henson's makeup is terrific, but beware of abrupt ending. C: Anjelica Huston, Mai Zetterling, Jasen Fisher, Rowan Atkinson, Bill Paterson, Jenny Runacre. D: Nicolas Roeg. FAM/DRA [PG] 92m. v

Witchfinder General, The 1968 *See* **Conqueror Worm, The**

Witching, The *See* **Necromancy**

With a Smile 1939 French ★★★½ Chevalier works his way up from doorman to director of the opera in this lightweight satire. Stylishly directed. C: Maurice Chevalier, Marie Glory, Andre Lefaur. D: Maurice Tourneur. DRA 80m.

With a Song in My Heart 1952 ★★★½ Well-made hokum about singer Jane Froman (Hayward) and her struggle to come back after a crippling air crash. Hayward works the role beautifully. C: Susan Hayward, Rory Calhoun, David Wayne, Thelma Ritter, Robert Wagner, Una Merkel. D: Walter Lang. DRA 117m.

With Honors 1994 ★★★½ Harvard student (Fraser) loses the only copy of his thesis; a homeless man (Pesci) finds it and will swap it for lodgings with Fraser and his apartment mates. He then turns their lives upside down, giving them an education in the university of the streets. Often very funny. C: Joe Pesci, Brendan Fraser, Moira Kelly, Patrick Dempsey, Josh Hamilton, Gore Vidal. D: Alek Keshishian. COM [PG-13] 100m.

With Love and Tenderness 1978 Bulgarian ★★★½ Muted story about Djakov, a sculptor, and his friends on retreat at a Black Sea resort. Intelligent examination of corruption and guilt among the prosperous. C: Alexander Dyakov. D: Rangel Vulchanov. DRA 100m.

With Six You Get Eggroll 1968 ★★★ Tedious, saccharine comedy of widow and widower remarrying, struggling to reconcile their large broods. On par with *The Brady Bunch.* C: Doris Day, Brian Keith, Pat Carroll, Barbara Hershey, George Carlin, Alice Ghostley. D: Howard Morris. COM 95m.

Withnail & I 1986 British ★★★★½ Hippies living in drug-infested London apartment head out to country for rest and relaxation, but find rural life has anxieties of its own. Offbeat coming-of-age film, based on life of director Robinson, follows breezy story with keen comic sensibilities. C: Richard E. Grant, Paul McGann, Richard Griffiths, Ralph Brown, Michael Elphick. D: Bruce Robinson. COM [R] 108m. v

Without a Clue 1988 British ★★★½ In this farce, Watson (Kingsley) is the real brains at 221B Baker Street. He's forced to hire a two-bit actor (Caine) to play the part of Sherlock Holmes, his illustrious fictional creation. Mildly interesting premise saved by the leads. C: Michael Caine, Ben Kingsley, Jeffrey Jones, Lysette Anthony, Paul Freeman. D: Thom Eberhardt. COM [PG] 106m. v

Without a Home 1939 Polish ★★★½ Competent Yiddish tearjerker about Kaminska trying to make home for family in U.S., thwarted by her husband's affair with a cabaret singer. The last Yiddish film produced in Poland before WWII. C: Alexander Marten, Ida Kaminska, Vera Gran. D: Alexander Marten. DRA 90m.

Without Love 1945 ★★★★ A widow (Hepburn) and her boarder (Tracy) originally marry out of convenience, but eventually fall in love. Charming, talky drama, not the best from the pairing, but a small gem all the same. Adapted from the play by Philip Barry. C: Spencer Tracy, Katharine Hepburn, Lucille Ball, Keenan Wynn, Carl Esmond, Patricia Morison, Felix Bressart, Gloria Grahame. D: Harold S. Bucquet. DRA 113m. v

Without Regret 1935 ★★★ Taylor, thought to be dead in China, turns up again, much to the dismay of his now-remarried wife. Blackmail and murder follow. Extremely complicated plot works if taken with a grain of salt. Loose remake of the 1928 *Interference.* C: Elissa Landi, Paul Cavanagh, Frances Drake, Kent Taylor. D: Harold Young. DRA 74m.

Without Reservations 1946 ★★★½ On a westbound train, a noted writer (Colbert) meets a Marine (Wayne) whom she wants to star in a film adaptation of her latest novel. Amiable romantic comedy takes a few pokes at Hollywood. C: Claudette Colbert, John Wayne, Don Defore, Anne Triola. D: Mervyn LeRoy. COM 101m. v

Without You I'm Nothing 1990 ★★★½ Mixed bag of sketches, monologues, and songs about popular culture and the media. Good showcase for Bernhard's writing/performing talents and born-to-shock style, from her one-woman stage show. C: Sandra Bernhard. D: John Boskovich. COM [R] 94m. v

Witness 1985 ★★★★★ After a young Amish boy witnesses a murder, the cop on the case (Ford) is forced to hide out with the child's family and becomes attracted to his widowed mother (McGillis). Terrific thriller (with an Oscar-winning script) succeeds as crime drama, tender romance, and a sympathetic portrayal of the Amish. C: Harrison Ford, Kelly McGillis, Josef Sommer, Lukas Haas, Alexander Godunov. D: Peter Weir. DRA [R] 112m. v

Witness for the Prosecution 1957 ★★★★★ Dandy Agatha Christie whodunit, with Power on trial for murdering old lady, and wife (Dietrich) turning state's evidence against him. Laughton is delightful as crotchety barrister for the defense, especially in scenes with Lancaster as his determined nurse. Surprise ending is one of Christie's most ingenious. Remade for TV in 1982. C: Marlene Dietrich, Tyrone Power, Charles Laughton, Elsa Lanchester, Una O'Connor, Ian Wolfe. D: Billy Wilder. DRA 114m. v

Witness for the Prosecution 1982 ★★★★ Outstanding TV production of Agatha Christie's courtroom mystery. Fabulous cast makes you forget the classic 1957 Billy Wilder film...almost. Best of the best: Rigg. C: Ralph Richardson, Diana Rigg, Deborah Kerr, Beau Bridges, Wendy Hiller, Donald Pleasence. D: Alan Gibson. CRI 100m.

Witness to Murder 1954 ★★★★ Stanwyck sees a murder and has to convince the police she didn't just imagine it. Taut suspense immeasurably aided by solid cast. C: Barbara Stanwyck, George Sanders, Gary Merrill, Jesse White. D: Roy Rowland. CRI 83m.

Wittgenstein 1993 British ★★★½ Stylized pseudobiography and pretentious probe into the thought of 20th-century philosopher Ludwig Wittgenstein. Daring, challenging, and bizarre. Effective as a mild introduction to the subject. No prerequisites, but two papers and a final required. C: Karl Johnson, Michael Gough, Tilda Swinton, John Quentin, Kevin Collins, Clancy Chassay, Jill Balcon. D: Derek Jarman. DRA 75m.

Wiz, The 1978 ★★★ African-American musical update of *The Wizard of Oz* uses disco rhythms and New York City locations to juice up old story of lion, straw man, tin man, and little girl off to see the wizard. Unfortunately, the "little girl" in this case is played by Ross, in her mid-30s, and that sinks the picture. Horne outstanding as Good Witch Glinda. C: Diana Ross, Michael Jackson, Nipsey Russell, Ted Ross, Lena Horne, Richard Pryor. D: Sidney Lumet. MUS [G] 133m. V

Wizard of Oz, The 1939 ★★★★★ Virtually an institution, this musical fantasy from the L. Frank Baum children's classic casts unique spell that will never be broken. Garland will always be Dorothy, transported to magical land of Oz but trying to get back home and escape the Wicked Witch (Hamilton). Flawless cast, and outstanding Harold Arlen-Yip Harburg score, including classic "Over the Rainbow," "If I Only Had a Brain," Lahr's hilarious "If I Were King of the Forest," and delightful munchkin sequence. Garland won special Oscar. C: Judy Garland, Ray Bolger, Bert Lahr, Jack Haley, Frank Morgan, Billie Burke, Margaret Hamilton, Charley Grapewin. D: Victor Fleming. FAM/MUS [G] 101m. V

Wizard, The 1989 ★★ Kid star (Savage) takes younger brother (Edwards) on cross-country trip to California's Universal Studios, where they enter national pinball championship. Feeble story only preps intended child audiences for overblown studio tour, inexhaustible product endorsements, and predictable pinball fest. C: Fred Savage, Luke Edwards, Jenny Lewis, Beau Bridges, Christian Slater. D: Todd Holland. FAM/DRA [PG] 100m. V

Wizards 1977 ★★½ Bakshi's striking animated visuals are highlight of this uneven, sometimes off-putting allegory set in postapocalyptic world, where a good magician battles his evil brother who's raising a Nazi-like army of mutants. C: Bob Holt, Jesse Wells, Richard Romanus, Mark Hamill. D: Ralph Bakshi. SFI [PG] 81m. V

Wolf 1994 ★★★★ Nicholson plays a prominent book editor who is also a werewolf (confirming most writers' worst fears). Nicholson plays it straight, with wit and intelligence in this thriller for adults. C: Michelle Pfeiffer, Jack Nicholson, James Spader, Kate Nelligan, Christopher Plummer. D: Mike Nichols. HOR [R] 109m.

Wolf Man, The 1941 ★★★★½ One of cinema's best, about a young man bitten by werewolf Lugosi, who succumbs to the dread curse himself. The role in which Chaney, Jr., nearly matched his father. C: Lon Chaney Jr., Evelyn Ankers, Claude Rains, Maria Ouspenskaya, Ralph Bellamy, Patric Knowles, Warren William, Bela Lugosi. D: George Waggner. HOR 69m. V

Wolfen 1981 ★★★½ Wolflike predators prowl Manhattan; detective Finney attempts to stop them. Stylish and scary, if a bit too heavily allegorical. Based on Whitley Strieber novel. C: Albert Finney, Diane Venora, Edward James Olmos, Gregory Hines. D: Michael Wadleigh. HOR [R] 114m. V

Woman Bait 1958 *See* **Inspector Maigret**

Woman Called Golda, A 1982 ★★★★½ An actress named Ingrid makes her last performance really count in this very satisfying biography of Israel's prime minister, Golda Meir. Posthumous Best Actress Emmy for Bergman. C: Ingrid Bergman, Judy Davis, Leonard Nimoy, Anne Jackson, Robert Loggia, Ned Beatty. D: Alan Gibson. DRA 200m. TVM V

Woman Called Moses, A 1978 ★★★★½ Historical TV biography of fugitive slave and abolitionist, Harriet Ross Tubman. Active in the 1850s underground railroad, she helps over 300 slaves escape to freedom. Tyson gives radiant performance. Based on Marcy Heldish novel. C: Cicely Tyson, Will Geer, Robert Hooks, James Wainwright, Dick Anthony Williams, Hari Rhodes. D: Paul Wendkos. DRA 200m. V

Woman, Her Men and Her Futon, A 1991 ★★★ Would-be movie director Rubin entertains her many boyfriends while dreaming of cinematic glory. Never dull tale of young artist learning the ropes suffers from spotty script, though Rubin gives it her best shot. C: Jennifer Rubin, Lance Edwards, Grant Show, Michael Cerveris, Robert Lipton, Delaune Michel. D: Mussef Sibay. DRA [R] 92m. V

Woman in a Dressing Gown 1957 British ★★★★ Stylish, intelligent triangle drama, with Quayle's fading marriage threatened when he becomes involved with a younger woman at work. Solid acting. C: Yvonne Mitchell, Anthony Quayle, Sylvia Syms, Andrew Ray, Carole Lesley. D: J. Lee Thompson. DRA 93m.

Woman in Flames, A 1984 German ★★★★ Tired of her stale marriage, a wealthy woman

(Landgrebe) leaves her husband, becomes a prostitute, and falls in love with a bisexual gigolo (Carriere). A complex film about societal roles and conflicts between women and men that makes effective use of its sordid arena. C: Gudrun Landgrebe, Mathieu Carriere, Gabriele Lafari, Hanns Zischler. D: Robert VanAckeren. DRA 106m. V

Woman in Green, The 1944 ★★★★ When Scotland Yard begins receiving the severed forefingers of several women, Holmes (Rathbone) investigates and finds archenemy Professor Moriarty (Daniell) at the bottom of it. Solid performances, especially Daniell's. C: Basil Rathbone, Nigel Bruce, Hillary Brooke, Henry Daniell. D: Roy William Neill. CRI 67m. V

Woman in Hiding 1949 ★★★ Lupino discovers her husband is a killer. Overwrought thriller. C: Ida Lupino, Howard Duff, Stephen McNally, Peggy Dow, John Litel, Joe Besser. D: Michael Gordon. DRA 92m.

Woman in Question, The 1950 British ★★★½ *Rashomon*-like murder mystery, with five suspects giving wildly varied accounts of the victim, a rapacious fortuneteller (Kent). Holds one's interest, but the climax is a letdown (a.k.a. Five Angles on Murder). C: Jean Kent, Dirk Bogarde. D: Anthony Asquith. DRA 82m.

Woman in Red, The 1984 ★★½ After glimpsing a beautiful model decked out in red (LeBrock), happily married Wilder goes nuts and starts pursuit. Remake of French film *Pardon Mon Affaire*. Includes Oscar-winning Stevie Wonder song, "I Just Called to Say I Love You." C: Gene Wilder, Kelly LeBrock, Gilda Radner, Joseph Bologna, Charles Grodin, Judith Ivey, Michael Huddleston. D: Gene Wilder. COM [PG-13] 87m. V

Woman in the Dunes (Suna No Onna) 1964 Japanese ★★★★½ Japanese classic is a beautifully filmed allegory about a scientist who becomes trapped by a woman living at the bottom of a sand pit while studying insects in the desert. Scenario sounds unpromising but yields rich psychological rewards. Subtitled. (a.k.a. *Woman of the Dunes*) C: Eiji Okada, Kyoko Kishida. D: Hiroshi Teshigahara. DRA 123m. V

Woman in the Window, The 1944 ★★★★½ A professor (Robinson) becomes involved with an attractive young woman (Bennett) and gets mixed up in a messy murder investigation. Effective, suspenseful thriller with neat surprise ending. C: Joan Bennett, Edward Robinson, Dan Duryea, Raymond Massey, Bobby Blake, Dorothy Peterson. D: Fritz Lang. CRI 99m.

Woman in White, The 1948 ★★★½ Classic Wilkie Collins gothic thriller of Parker tormented by Greenstreet and Moorehead in strange house. Efficiently acted and directed. C: Eleanor Parker, Alexis Smith, Sydney Greenstreet, Gig Young, Agnes Moorehead, John Emery, John Abbott. D: Peter Godfrey. DRA 109m.

Woman Is a Woman, A 1960 French ★★★★ Godard's first color, widescreen film is a delightful, loving send-up of MGM musicals, with Karina as a stripper who wants a baby. When lover Belmondo won't oblige, she goes to his best friend, Brialy. Film has a great deal of "charm," not a word usually associated with Godard. C: Jean-Paul Belmondo, Jean-Claude Brialy, Anna Karina. D: Jean-Luc Godard. MUS 88m. V

Woman Next Door, The 1981 French ★★★½ Solid Truffaut drama, one of his last, detailing what happens when married Depardieu resumes a relationship with old girlfriend Ardant, also married, when she becomes his neighbor. Sensitively-played and sincere. C: Gerard Depardieu, Fanny Ardant, Henri Garcin, Michele Baumgartner, Veronique Silver. D: Francois Truffaut. DRA [R] 106m. V

Woman Obsessed 1959 ★★★ A disturbed mother, having given up her baby for adoption, meets him as an adult and kidnaps him as surrogate for her dead husband. Bizarre psychodrama starts slowly but builds. C: Susan Hayward, Stephen Boyd, Barbara Nichols, Dennis Holmes, Theodore Bikel, Ken Scott. D: Henry Hathaway. CRI 102m.

Woman Obsessed, A 1989 *See* **Bad Blood**

Woman of Affairs, A 1928 ★★★★ Glossy, entertaining silent melodrama follows the exploits of a reckless rich woman. Fine romantic showcase for Garbo and Gilbert. C: Greta Garbo, John Gilbert, Lewis Stone, Douglas Fairbanks, Jr. D: Clarence Brown. DRA 96m. V

Woman of Distinction, A 1950 ★★★½ A college dean (Russell) is embarrassed by the arrival on campus of her former beau (Milland). Bright, energetic comedy, with an all-pro cast. C: Rosalind Russell, Ray Milland, Edmund Gwenn, Janis Carter, Francis Lederer. D: Edward Buzzell. COM 85m. V

Woman of Paris, A 1923 ★★★★ A virtuous French woman (Purviance) falls in with a dastardly rich man (Menjou) through unlucky circumstances. Silent weepie is a very moving Chaplin drama, rejected by audiences at the time of its release and withdrawn until the late 1970s. C: Edna Purviance, Adolphe Menjou, Carl Miller. D: Charles Chaplin. DRA 91m. V

Woman of Straw 1964 British ★★★ Connery, abused by his invalid multimillionaire uncle Richardson, plots murder with Lollobrigida. Tired whodunit. C: Sean Connery, Gina Lollobrigida, Ralph Richardson, Johnny Sekka, Alexander Knox. D: Basil Dearden. CRI 117m.

Woman of the Dunes 1964 *See* **Woman in the Dunes**

Woman of the Town, The 1943 ★★★★ Well-crafted Western, with Dekker as Bat Masterson, seeking justice after his woman is killed. Low-key and surprisingly realistic. C: Claire Trevor, Albert Dekker, Barry Sullivan,

Henry Hull, Marion Martin. D: George Archainbaud. WST 90m. V

Woman of the Year 1942 ★★★★½ Tracy and Hepburn, united for the first time, hit home run with battle-of-the-sexes comedy that can only be faulted for what now seems a sexist attitude. Hepburn plays famous journalist who everyone insists would be better off as docile, homemaking wife to sportswriter (Tracy). Two leads sparkle together. C: Spencer Tracy, Katharine Hepburn, Fay Bainter, Reginald Owen, Roscoe Karns, William Bendix. D: George Stevens. COM 112m. V

Woman on Pier 13, The 1950 *See* **I Married a Communist**

Woman on the Beach, The 1947 ★★★ Bennett is married to blind painter Bickford, falls in love with Coast Guard officer Ryan. In spite of excellent cast and acting, a minor effort, further hampered by script. C: Robert Ryan, Joan Bennett, Charles Bickford, Nan Leslie, Walter Sande, Irene Ryan. D: Jean Renoir. DRA 71m.

Woman on the Run 1950 ★★★½ Race against time as Sheridan searches for her husband, key witness to mob rubout, trying to beat the gangsters to him. Well paced and acted. C: Ann Sheridan, Dennis O'Keefe, Robert Keith, Ross Elliott, Frank Jenks. D: Norman Foster. CRI 77m.

Woman Rebels, A 1936 ★★★½ Earnest drama of a young woman in Victorian London who becomes a champion of female equality. Surprisingly engrossing; its commercial failure helped its star to earn the label "box-office poison" at the time. C: Katharine Hepburn, Herbert Marshall, Donald Crisp. D: Mark Sandrich. DRA 88m.

Woman Tamer *See* **She Couldn't Take It**

Woman Times Seven 1967 ★★★½ Seven short sketches provide a tour-de-force for MacLaine, in multiple roles. The last story, about a married woman's flirtation with a stranger (Caine) during a shopping trip, is best. C: Shirley MacLaine, Peter Sellers, Rossano Brazzi, Alan Arkin, Michael Caine, Vittorio Gassman. D: Vittorio De Sica. COM 99m. V

Woman Under the Influence, A 1974 ★★★★ To the dismay of her husband, a woman's overpowering identity crisis drives her closer to an emotional breakdown. Game drama with hard-hitting performance from Rowlands that helps diminish Cassavetes' typical excesses. C: Peter Falk, Gena Rowlands, Matthew Cassel, Matthew Laborteaux, Katherine Cassavetes. D: John Cassavetes. DRA [R] 155m. V

Woman's Face, A 1941 ★★★★ Stark, effective melodrama of scarred woman (Crawford) who undergoes plastic surgery that changes her life. Some of Crawford's best work with Veidt chilling as her nemesis. Original done in Swedish, *En Kvinnas Ansikate* (1938) as Ingrid Bergman vehicle. C: Joan Crawford, Melvyn Douglas, Conrad Veidt, Osa Massen. D: George Cukor. DRA 107m. V

Woman's Place, A 1962 *See* **Wiser Age**

Woman's Secret, A 1949 ★★★½ Singer whose voice has given out (O'Hara) grooms a coarse protégé (Graham) for stardom, but the student rebels against living out her patron's dreams, leading to tragic results. Offbeat, noir-flavored story told in flashbacks. Based on Vicki Baum novel. C: Maureen O'Hara, Melvyn Douglas, Gloria Grahame, Bill Williams, Victor Jory. D: Nicholas Ray. DRA 85m. V

Woman's Status 1962 *See* **Wiser Age**

Woman's Tale, A 1991 Australian ★★★★½ Tender story of engaging 80-year-old woman who will not conform to constraining social definitions of the aged. Evocative film brought to life with lively performance by Florance. C: Sheila Florance, Gosia Dobrowolska, Norman Kaye, Chris Haywood, Ernest Gray, Myrtle Woods. D: Paul Cox. DRA [PG-13] 93m. V

Woman's Vengeance, A 1947 ★★★★½ Terrific courtroom drama, with Boyer on trial when his wife dies under suspicious circumstances. Brilliant Aldous Huxley script spurs unusually intelligent film. C: Charles Boyer, Ann Blyth, Jessica Tandy, Cedric Hardwicke, Mildred Natwick. D: Zoltan Korda. DRA 96m.

Woman's World 1954 ★★★½ Glossy '50s melodrama about the dog-eat-dog corporate world, lifted above the commonplace by Webb's performance as corporate attorney and kingmaker, head of major auto company who is trying to pick new sales manager. C: Clifton Webb, June Allyson, Van Heflin, Arlene Dahl, Lauren Bacall, Fred MacMurray, Cornel Wilde, Elliott Reid. D: Jean Negulesco. DRA 94m.

Women & Men: In Love There Are No Rules 1991 ★★★★ Three more literary adaptations involving gender wars: "Return to Kansas City" by Irwin Shaw; "A Domestic Dilemma" by Carson McCullers; and "Mara" by Henry Miller. Fine ensemble acting makes this engaging. C: Matt Dillon, Kyra Sedgwick, Jerry Stiller, Ray Liotta, Andie MacDowell, Scott Glenn, Juliette Binoche. D: Walter Bernstein, Kristi Zea, Mike Figgis. DRA [R] 82m. TVM V

Women & Men: Stories of Seduction 1990 ★★★★½ Glossy trio of stories: "The Man in the Brooks Brothers Shirt" by Mary McCarthy, "Dusks before Fireworks" by Dorothy Parker, and "Hills Like White Elephants" by Ernest Hemingway. Entertaining and intelligent look at gender interactions, with uniformly excellent casting. A sequel anthology film followed. C: Beau Bridges, Elizabeth McGovern, Molly Ringwald, Peter Weller, James Woods, Melanie Griffith. D: Frederic Raphael, Ken Russell, Tony Richardson. DRA [R] 83m. TVM V

Women in Cages 1971 U.S. ★ Especially unpleasant film explained by its title, shot back to back with similar (and better) *Big Doll*

House. The usually heroic Grier is the villainess who tortures female inmates. (a.k.a. *Women's Penitentiary III*) C: Judy Brown, Pam Grier, Roberta Collins. D: Geraldo DeLeon. CRI [R] 78m. v

Women in Love 1969 British ★★★★½ Lyrical adaptation of D.H. Lawrence's romantic novel traces the course of two love affairs in late 19th-century England. Russell's vision of novel is frank and uncompromising, including a daring full-frontal male nudity wrestling scene. Excellent performances by Reed and Bates, while Jackson won her first Oscar for this. Followed 20 years later by prequel *The Rainbow*. C: Alan Bates, Oliver Reed, Glenda Jackson, Eleanor Bron. D: Ken Russell. DRA [R] 129m. v

Women of Brewster Place, The 1989 ★★★★ Entertaining, almost noble saga of black women in a small neighborhood, struggling with racism, poverty, and violence. Excellent cast, with Winfrey, Cole, and Jackée the standouts. Based on novel by Gloria Naylor. C: Oprah Winfrey, Mary Alice, Olivia Cole, Robin Givens, Moses Gunn, Jackee, Paula Kelly, Lonette McKee, Paul Winfield, Cicely Tyson. D: Donna Deitch. DRA 200m. v

Women of the Prehistoric Planet 1966 ★★★ A rocket ship crash-lands on a planet full of women. Middling science fiction. C: Wendell Corey, Keith Larsen, John Agar, Irene Tsu, Merry Anders. D: Arthur C. Pierce. SFI 87m. v

Women of Twilight 1953 *See* **Twilight Women**

Women on the Verge of a Nervous Breakdown 1988 Spanish ★★★★½ Brilliant, zany farce, with Maura a dazed Alice in the fabulously stylized Wonderland of downtown Madrid. The plot starts revolving when she loses her married lover, but that's just the beginning; look out for the mambo taxi and the spiked gazpacho. Very entertaining in quirky, surprising ways—Almodovar's most enjoyable film so far. C: Carmen Maura, Antonio Banderas, Julieta Serrano, Maria Barranco, Rossy De Palma. D: Pedro Almodovar. COM [R] 88m. v

Women, The 1939 ★★★★★ A rich woman's happy marriage goes up for grabs when it becomes grist for the gossip mill. Brutally funny all-star, all-woman comedy, from the Claire Boothe play. It sets out to skewer everyone, and succeeds sparklingly. Brilliant dialogue, marvelous cast. Features a fashion show in color (complete with *Jungle Red*!). C: Norma Shearer, Joan Crawford, Rosalind Russell, Paulette Goddard, Mary Boland, Joan Fontaine, Lucille Watson, Marjorie Main, Virginia Weidler. D: George Cukor. COM 132m. v

Women's Penitentiary I 1971 *See* **Big Doll House, The**

Women's Penitentiary III 1971 *See* **Women in Cages**

Women's Prison 1955 ★★★½ A heartless warden (Lupino) lords it over pitiful female prison inmates in this low-budget cult favorite. A lurid genre classic. C: Ida Lupino, Jan Sterling, Audrey Totter, Phyllis Thaxter, Howard Duff, Mae Clarke. D: Lewis Seiler. DRA 80m.

Women's Room, The 1980 ★★★★ Marvelous cast has a field day in this literate adaptation of Marilyn French's feminist novel, chronicling the consciousness-raising among a group of suburbanites. Dewhurst and Astin are stand-outs. C: Lee Remick, Colleen Dewhurst, Kathryn Harrold, Patty Duke Astin, Tovah Feldshuh, Tyne Daly, Ted Danson, Gregory Harrison. D: Glenn Jordan. DRA 150m. TVM

Won Ton Ton, the Dog Who Saved Hollywood 1976 ★★ Frantic satire of silent-era Tinseltown, ruled by a canine star and his unscrupulous manager (Dern). Elaborate misfire needed a shorter leash; zillions of cameos make it watchable. C: Madeline Kahn, Bruce Dern, Art Carney, Phil Silvers, Ron Leibman, Teri Garr. D: Michael Winner. COM [PG] 92m.

Wonder Bar 1934 ★★★½ One of Jolson's most overbearing and bizarre films, set in a Paris nightclub, with murder, romance, and the infamously racist Busby Berkeley "Goin' to Heaven on a Mule" thrown together. Tasteless and excessive, but sometimes hypnotic. C: Al Jolson, Kay Francis, Dolores DelRio, Dick Powell, Ricardo Cortez, Louise Fazenda, Hugh Herbert, Hal LeRoy, Guy Kibbee. D: Lloyd Bacon. MUS 84m.

Wonder Man 1945 ★★★★ Kaye is hilarious in dual role of serious fellow, forced to pose as his brother, a wild nightclub entertainer, after latter is murdered by gangsters. C: Danny Kaye, Virginia Mayo, Vera-Ellen, Donald Woods. D: H. Bruce Humberstone. COM 98m. v

Wonderful Country, The 1959 ★★★★ Underrated, lyrical Western about half-Irish-American, half-Mexican border gunrunner (Mitchum) who must choose between the two sides of the border. Excellent Mitchum. Strong supporting cast. C: Robert Mitchum, Julie London, Gary Merrill, Pedro Armendariz, Jack Oakie, Albert Dekker. D: Robert Parrish. WST 96m.

Wonderful, Horrible Life of Leni Riefenstahl, The 1993 German-Belgian ★★★★ Fascinating portrait of controversial Nazi-era filmmaker Riefenstahl, director of *Triumph of the Will* and *Olympia*. Interviews and clips probe the life of this unquestionably talented artist, whose work advanced Hitler's rise to power. D: Ray Muller. DOC 182m. v

Wonderful World of the Brothers Grimm, The 1962 ★★★★ Star-studded biography/-fantasy of storytellers Jacob and Wilhelm Grimm re-creates some of their best-loved tales. Pal's Puppetoons will delight both children and adults, while Hackett nearly steals show battling a dragon. Oscar winner for Best Costumes. C: Laurence Harvey, Claire Bloom, Karl Boehm, Oscar Homolka, Martita Hunt, Jim Backus, Yvette Mimieux, Barbara Eden, Walter Slezak, Russ Tamblyn, Buddy Hackett, Beulah Bondi, Terry Thomas. D: Henry Levin, George Pal. FAM/DRA [G] 129m. v

Wonderland *See* **Fruit Machine, The**

Wonders of Aladdin, The 1961 U.S. ★★½ O'Connor stars in this weak adaptation of *Arabian Nights* stories, fighting evil ruler with help of genie and flying carpet. Nothing original or fresh in this mundane reworking of oft-told tale. C: Donald O'Connor, Noelle Adam, Vittorio DeSica, Aldo Fabrizi. D: Henry Levin, Mario Bava. MUS 93m. v

Wooden Horse, The 1950 British ★★★★ Title refers to the gymnastic vaulting horse that British officers use for cover to tunnel their way out of German POW camp during WWII. Taut and understated. Based on a true story, recreated in Eric Williams' novel *The Tunnel Escape*. C: Leo Genn, David Tomlinson, Anthony Steel, Peter Burton, David Greene, Anthony Dawson, Bryan Forbes, Peter Finch. D: Jack Lee. DRA 101m.

Wooden Man's Bride, The 1995 Chinese ★★★★ Austere, beautifully acted tale of a bride widowed on her wedding day in 1920's China, then forced to spend the rest of her life "married" to a statue of her dead husband. Hard-edged look at the woman's role in society. C: Wang Lan, Chang Shih, Wang Yumei. D: Huang Jianxin. DRA 114m.

Woodstock 1970 ★★★★½ Classic four-day-long 1969 rock concert is brilliantly captured in this well-filmed documentary, which celebrates both the wonderful music (featuring artists from Joan Baez to The Who) and the spirit of peace and love it evoked. Only debit: video can't fully capture the stunning use of multiple images. C: Joan Baez, Richie Havens, Crosby, Stills and, Nash, Jefferson Airplane, Joe Cocker, Sly & the Family Stone, Santana. D: Michael Wadleigh. MUS [R] 184m. v

Words and Music 1948 ★★★ Biography of songwriter Lorenz Hart reduces his troubled life to a one-note obsession with his height. Rooney and Drake are irritating as Hart and Rodgers, but a few musical numbers somewhat redeem film. C: Mickey Rooney, Tom Drake, June Allyson, Ann Sothern, Judy Garland, Gene Kelly, Lena Horne. D: Norman Taurog. MUS 119m. v

Working Girl 1988 ★★★★½ Secretary (Griffith) can't get ahead by the rules, so she pretends to be her own boss, attracting biz whiz (Ford) along the way. Captivating romantic comedy, fueled by Melanie's star-making performance. Features Oscar-winning song "Let the River Run." C: Harrison Ford, Sigourney Weaver, Melanie Griffith, Alec Baldwin, Joan Cusack. D: Mike Nichols. COM [R] 115m. v

Working Girls 1986 ★★★★ Low-budget, surprisingly funny look at a typical day at a Manhattan call-girl establishment. Notable for its matter-of-fact tone and quirky performances. C: Louise Smith, Ellen McElduff, Marusia Zach, Amanda Goodwin. D: Lizzie Borden. COM 90m. v

Working Man, The 1933 ★★★½ Business exec (Arliss) becomes interested in the children of his foremost rival while on vacation. In disguise he goes to work for them, in competition with his own firm, now run by his nephew. Pleasant comedy is also good showcase for very young Bette Davis. C: George Arliss, Bette Davis, Hardie Albright, Theodore Newton, Gordon Westcott. D: John G. Adolfi. COM 75m.

World According to Garp, The 1982 ★★★★½ Splendid performances highlight sharp, satirical adaptation of John Irving's dark best-seller about the adventures of an illegitimate, eccentric young man bent on being a writer. Close's first film. C: Robin Williams, Mary Beth Hurt, Glenn Close, John Lithgow, Amanda Plummer. D: George Roy Hill. DRA [R] 136m. v

World Apart, A 1988 ★★★★ Fact-based story of a reporter incarcerated for her antiapartheid politics in '60s South Africa. Fine performances give vitality to family drama. C: Barbara Hershey, David Suchet, Jeroen Krabbe, Jodhi May, Paul Freeman, Linda Mvusi. D: Chris Menges. DRA [PG] 114m. v

World in His Arms, The 1952 ★★★½ Amiable action film set in 1850s about a sea captain (Peck) in love with Russian princess (Blyth). If nothing else, it moves quickly. C: Gregory Peck, Ann Blyth, John McIntire, Anthony Quinn, Andrea King, Eugenie Leontovich, Sig Ruman. D: Raoul Walsh. ACT 104m.

World in My Corner 1956 ★★★½ Atypical but okay Murphy vehicle has Audie as a boxer who fights his way out of poverty, only to nearly lose everything when he begins to enjoy the fruits of his labors too much. Loyal Rush keeps him from throwing it all away. C: Audie Murphy, Barbara Rush, Jeff Morrow, John McIntire, Tommy Rall, Howard John. D: Jesse Hibbs. DRA 82m.

World of Apu, The 1959 Indian ★★★★★ Ray's title hero matures into a struggling father in this third and last part of his magnificent series, preceded by *Pather Panchali* and *Aparajito*. One of the great masterworks of world cinema, with an unforgettable performance from Chatterjee. C: Soumitra Chatterjee, Sharmila Tagore. D: Satyajit Ray. DRA 103m. v

World of Hans Christian Andersen, The 1971 Japanese ★★★½ Japanese animated feature tells how Andersen became a world-famous storyteller. Brightly colored, engaging, and fine for small children. C: Hetty Galen. D: Al Kilgore, Chuck McCann. FAM/DRA [G] 75m. v

World of Henry Orient, The 1964 ★★★★½

Delightful comedy of Spaeth and Walker, teenagers infatuated with concert pianist (Sellers), going to insane lengths to follow him. A film of immense charm, with warm, likable characters and witty script by Nora Johnson (from her novel) and her father, Nunnally. C: Peter Sellers, Tippy Walker, Merrie Spaeth, Paula Prentiss, Angela Lansbury, Phyllis Thaxter, Tom Bosley. D: George Roy Hill. COM 106m. V

World of Suzie Wong, The 1960 ★★★ A struggling American artist (Holden) living in Hong Kong falls in love with a prostitute (Kwan). Dated romance relies on blatant stereotypes. Beautiful Hong Kong locations. Based on the popular Broadway play. C: William Holden, Nancy Kwan, Sylvia Syms, Michael Wilding, Laurence Naismith. D: Richard Quine. DRA 129m. V

World of Tomorrow, The 1984 ★★★★ Portrait of the 1939 New York World's Fair entertainingly captures the sense of wonder that fair-goers felt. Includes newsreels, home movies, and a filmed demonstration of a then unheard-of innovation: television! Narrated by Jason Robards. Also shown in a 60-minute version. D: Lance Bird, Tom Johnson. DOC 83m.

World Premiere 1941 ★★ Barrymore is producer with film about to premiere, fighting off Nazi saboteurs and engaging in other supposedly funny hijinks. Painful. C: John Barrymore, Frances Farmer, Eugene Pallette, Virginia Dale, Ricardo Cortez, Sig Ruman, Fritz Feld. D: Ted Tetzlaff. COM 70m.

World, the Flesh and the Devil, The 1959 ★★★½ Belafonte, Stevens, and Ferrer are last survivors of nuclear war, alone in Manhattan. Interesting idea runs out of gas midway. C: Harry Belafonte, Inger Stevens, Mel Ferrer. D: Ranald MacDougall. DRA 95m.

World Without Sun 1964 ★★★★½ Famed underwater explorer Cousteau takes his cameras to the depths, with thrilling results. Marvelous photography and informative narration by the director make it a cut above the many similar nature documentaries that have proliferated since. D: Jacques Cousteau. DOC 93m.

World's Greatest Athlete, The 1973 ★★★★ College coach (Amos) and assistant (Conway) discover Tarzan-like athlete (Vincent) while traveling through Africa. They bring him to America, where Vincent becomes unlikely star. Better than average Disney slapstick, with cameo appearance by sports announcer Cosell. Goofy fun. C: John Amos, Jan-Michael Vincent, Tim Conway, Roscoe Lee Browne. D: Robert Scheerer. FAM/COM [G] 92m. V

Worst Secret Agents 1966 *See* **Oh! Those Most Secret Agents**

Worst Woman in Paris?, The 1933 ★★★½ Hume leaves worldly Menjou and returns to the U.S., where she falls in love with innocent Stephens. Pleasant and stylish romance. C: Benita Hume, Adolphe Menjou, Harvey Stephens, Helen Chandler, Margaret Seddon. D: Monta Bell. DRA 78m.

Worth Winning 1989 ★★ Arrogant bachelor Harmon bets buddies he can con three different women into marrying him. Attractive cast makes this worth seeing. C: Mark Harmon, Madeleine Stowe, Lesley Ann Warren, Maria Holvoe, Mark Blum. D: Will MacKenzie. COM [PG-13] 103m. V

Woyzeck 1978 German ★★★½ Typically intense Herzog/Kinski collaboration, with the actor playing a German army official whose abusive superiors drive him to madness and murder. Claustrophobic but chilling; based on the Georg Büchner play. (a.k.a. *Werner Herzog's Woyzeck*) C: Klaus Kinski, Eva Mattes. D: Werner Herzog. DRA 82m. V

Wraith, The 1987 ★★ Slick but silly supernatural action film about a ghostly hot car that mows down a band of road pirates in the Southwest. The chase scenes are more compelling than the cast, which contains an inordinate number of celebrity relatives. C: Charlie Sheen, Nick Cassavetes, Randy Quaid, Sherilyn Fenn, Griffin O'Neal, Clint Howard. D: Mike Marvin. HOR [PG-13] 92m. V

Wreck of the Mary Deare, The 1959 U.S. ★★★½ Captain (Cooper) is the only one who believes the sinking of his ship was an act of insurance fraud. When he is blamed for the wreck, it's up to salvagers to find the truth. Slow going at times, but solidly acted with decent effects. C: Gary Cooper, Charlton Heston, Michael Redgrave, Emlyn Williams, Cecil Parker, Alexander Knox, Virginia McKenna, Richard Harris, Ben Wright. D: Michael Anderson. DRA 105m. V

Wrecking Crew, The 1969 ★★ Can our hero (Martin) stop organized crime from stealing a billion dollars worth of gold from a train? The fourth and last swingin' installment in the Matt Helm series. Watch close for Chuck Norris. C: Dean Martin, Elke Sommer, Sharon Tate, Nancy Kwan, Tina Louise. D: Phil Karlson. ACT [PG] 105m. V

Wrestling Ernest Hemingway 1993 ★★★ *Grumpy Old Men* without the laughs: Harris and Duvall (with a hilarious Cuban accent) are aging pals after the same woman. C: Robert Duvall, Richard Harris, Shirley MacLaine, Sandra Bullock, Nicole Mercurio, Marty Belafsky, Piper Laurie. D: Randa Haines. DRA [PG-13] 122m. V

Written on the Wind 1956 ★★★½ Lurid melodrama of rich brother/sister combo (Stack, Malone) messing up lives of noble Hudson and Bacall. Needless to say, the bad ones steal the picture, with slutty Malone winning Supporting Actress Oscar. C: Rock Hudson, Lauren Bacall, Robert Stack, Dorothy Malone, Robert Keith. D: Douglas Sirk. DRA 99m. V

Wrong Arm of the Law 1962 British ★★★★

Slick head of a London crime syndicate finds his nifty little operation in jeopardy when three outsiders, dressed as British Bobbies, start ripping him off. Consistently funny comedy maintains a high laugh level thanks to clever plotting and the comic talents of its cast. C: Peter Sellers, Lionel Jeffries, Bernard Cribbins, Nanette Newman. D: Cliff Owen. COM 94m. V

Wrong Bet 1990 *See* **Lionheart**

Wrong Box, The 1966 British ★★★★ Funny, well-done variation on "let's murder the relative for the inheritance" plot, with Mills attempting to do away with Richardson. Sellers steals movie with brief cameo as cat-crazy doctor. Based on a Robert Louis Stevenson story. C: John Mills, Ralph Richardson, Michael Caine, Peter Cook, Dudley Moore, Nanette Newman, Wilfred Lawson, Peter Sellers. D: Bryan Forbes. COM 105m. V

Wrong Guys, The 1988 ★★ Goodman is escaped con who stumbles onto campsite and thinks geriatric Cub Scout reunion is gathering of CIA operatives. Cast of stand-up comics end up fighting for punchlines. C: Louie Anderson, Richard Lewis, Richard Belzer, Franklyn Ajaye, Tim Thomerson, Brion James, John Goodman, Ernie Hudson. D: Danny Bilson. COM [PG] 86m. V

Wrong Kind of Girl 1956 *See* **Bus Stop**

Wrong Man, The 1956 ★★★★ Hitchcock found a true story perfectly suited to his innocent-in-trouble formula: A musician (well-played by Fonda) is wrongly charged with a series of Manhattan robberies. Told in documentary style, with strong acting and genuine suspense. C: Henry Fonda, Vera Miles, Anthony Quayle, Harold J. Stone. D: Alfred Hitchcock. DRA 105m. V

Wrong Move 1975 German ★★★½ Poet Vogler searches for the meaning of life while traveling across Germany, encountering various eccentrics as well as Kinski, in her film debut. One of three road movies Wenders made in the '70s, this one is sometimes slow but ultimately rewarding. Loosely based on Goethe's *Sorrows of Young Werther*. C: Rudiger Vogler, Hanna Schygulla, Nastassja Kinski. D: Wim Wenders. DRA 103m.

Wuthering Heights 1939 ★★★★★ Lush adaptation of some (but not all) of Brontë's great novel stars Olivier as the tortured Heathcliff, forever in love with the ethereal Cathy (Oberon). Atmospheric production remains a classic in screen romance; Olivier and Oberon are poignant as the lovers. The beautiful cinematography earned an Oscar. Filmed again in 1954 and 1970. C: Merle Oberon, Laurence Olivier, David Niven, Flora Robson, Donald Crisp, Geraldine Fitzgerald. D: William Wyler. DRA 103m. V

Wuthering Heights 1954 ★★★ The famed surrealist director does his take on Emily Bronte's classic novel about a headstrong woman who spurns her low-born true love. Striking visual effects. C: Irasema Dilian, Jorge Mistral. D: Luis Bunuel. DRA 90m. V

Wuthering Heights 1970 British ★★★★ Dalton and Calder-Marshall portray the doomed couple in this entertaining rendition of Brontë's novel, the third film version. Though story moves a little too quickly for its own good, film benefits from great use of English locations and strong lead performances, expecially Dalton's. C: Anna Marshall, Timothy Dalton, Harry Andrews, Pamela Browne, Judy Cornwell, Ian Ogilvy, Hugh Griffith, Julian Glover. D: Robert Fuest. DRA [G] 105m. V

W. W. and the Dixie Dancekings 1975 ★★★★ Low-level con artist (Reynolds) finds new challenges promoting struggling country-western band in '50s-era Nashville. Full of loopy humor and entertaining characters. Reynolds' tongue stays firmly in cheek throughout; excellent ensemble support. C: Burt Reynolds, Art Carney, Conny VanDyke, Jerry Reed, James Hampton, Ned Beatty. D: John G. Avildsen. COM [PG] 91m.

Wyatt Earp 1994 ★★★½ Costner plays title role as we follow the legend from youth to middle age, 1860s to the turn of the century. Quiet, understated drama—perhaps too quiet. C: Kevin Costner, Dennis Quaid, Gene Hackman, Jeff Fahey, Michael Madsen, Bill Pullman, JoBeth Williams, Mare Winningham, Mark Harmon. D: Lawrence Kasdan. WST [PG-13] 181m.

Wyoming 1940 ★★★½ Beery and Carrillo play Western genre for laughs as "good bad men" trying to make up their minds whether its time to go straight. Diverting. C: Wallace Beery, Leo Carrillo, Ann Rutherford, Marjorie Main, Lee Bowman, Joseph Calleia, Bobs Watson. D: Richard Thorpe. WST 89m.

Wyoming 1947 ★★★½ Typical Elliott Western pits homesteaders against ranchers in range war. Good of its kind. C: William Elliott, Vera Ralston, John Carroll, "Gabby" Hayes, Albert Dekker, Virginia Grey. D: Joseph Kane. WST 84m.

Wyoming Kid, The 1947 *See* **Cheyenne**

Wyoming Renegades 1955 ★★½ Low-budget junk Western about robber Carey who wants to give up his life of crime. C: Phil Carey, Gene Evans, Martha Hyer, William Bishop, Aaron Spelling. D: Fred F. Sears. WST 73m.

X, the Unknown 1956 British ★★★½ Intelligent and understated science fiction thriller about a radioactive substance found in Scotland, probably from outer space, that destroys Earth life forms. An American scientist (Jagger) tries to track it down. C: Dean Jagger, Leo McKern, William Lucas, Edward Chapman, Anthony Newley, Peter Hammond. D: Leslie Norman. SFI 80m.

X, Y and Zee 1972 British ★★ Over-the-top love triangle, fueled by lots of off-color dialogue. Self-consciously "modern" drama intends to shock, and it may succeed, depending on your tolerance for camp. (a.k.a. *Zee and Company*) C: Elizabeth Taylor, Susannah York, Michael Caine. D: Brian G. Hutton. DRA [PG] 110m. V

Xanadu 1980 ★★ Deliriously glitzy musical mess features Australian rocker Olivia Newton-John as an angel in roller skates, hoping to provide ethereal inspiration to a roller disco artist. Remake of *Down to Earth* features an appearance by Gene Kelly. C: Olivia Newton-John, Gene Kelly, Michael Beck. D: Robert Greenwald. MUS [PG] 96m. V

Xtro 1983 British ★★★ Years after his abduction by a UFO, a man returns to his son, in a decidedly altered state. Interesting horror premise gets lost in gross-out effects. C: Philip Sayer, Bernice Stegers, Danny Brainin, Simon Nash, Maryam D'Abo. D: Harry Bromley Davenport. HOR [R] 80m.

Xtro II: The Second Encounter 1991 Canadian ★★ Completely unrelated sequel is a shameless ripoff of *Aliens*, right down to the visual design. Here the setting is an underground lab terrorized by a beast from another dimension. C: Jan-Michael Vincent, Paul Koslo, Tara Buckman, Jano Frandsen, Nicholas Lea. D: Harry Bromley Davenport. SFI [R] 90m.

Y

Yakuza, The 1975 ★★★★½ Mitchum is terrific in thriller about American trying to find friend's kidnapped daughter in Japan. Interesting culture clash between hard-boiled Yankee and ice-cold Japanese gangsters. C: Robert Mitchum, Takakura Ken, Brian Keith, Herb Edelman, Richard Jordan. D: Sydney Pollack. CRI [R] 112m. v

Yanco 1964 Mexican ★★★ An outcast peasant boy teaches himself to play a homemade violin, and is befriended by older man who gives him lessons. Unusual Mexican film, done without dialogue. C: Jesus Medina, Maria Bustamantes, Ricardo Ancona. DRA 90m. v

Yank at Oxford, A 1938 U.S. ★★★★ Smart-alecky American student (Taylor) tries to adjust to life in the hallowed halls of Oxford University. He romances O'Sullivan, but Leigh also has a good part as a local student. Standard but winning. Remade as *Oxford Blues*. C: Robert Taylor, Lionel Barrymore, Maureen O'Sullivan, Vivien Leigh, Edmund Gwenn. D: Jack Conway. COM 100m.

Yank in the RAF, A 1941 ★★★½ Power is brash American flier who pitches in against the Nazis before U.S. entered WWII and falls for singer Grable. Dated, originally intended to drum up support for British war effort at height of Battle of Britain. C: Tyrone Power, Betty Grable, John Sutton, Reginald Gardiner, Donald Stuart, Richard Fraser. D: Henry King. DRA 98m. v

Yankee Doodle Dandy 1942 ★★★★½ The life and times of singer, dancer, composer George M. Cohan. Cagney pulls out all the stops, strutting his stuff with infectious exuberation. A joy to behold, superbly entertaining all the way. C: James Cagney, Joan Leslie, Walter Huston, Richard Whorf, Jeanne Cagney. D: Michael Curtiz. MUS 126m. v

Yankee Pasha 1954 ★★★½ Chandler mixes romance and adventure rescuing Fleming from Roberts' harem and the Barbary pirates. Unusual setting and lively action raise this a little above the ordinary. C: Jeff Chandler, Rhonda Fleming, Mamie Van Doren, Bart Roberts, Lee Cobb, Hal March. D: Joseph Pevney. ACT 84m.

Yanks 1979 ★★★½ While stationed in England during WWII, three American soldiers find themselves in romances with local women. Interesting performances and old-fashioned romantic air helps film, despite a rather predictable series of events. C: Richard Gere, Lisa Eichhorn, Vanessa Redgrave, William Devane, Chick Vennera, Arlen Dean Snyder, Rachel Roberts, Annie Ross. D: John Schlesinger. DRA [R] 139m. v

Yasemin 1988 West German ★★★½ Romey, a 17-year-old Turkish girl, falls in love with German boy, incensing her traditionalist father. Well played. C: Ayse Romey, Uwe Bohm, Sener Sen, Ithan Emirli, Katharina Lehmann, Nedim Hazar, Ssevigi Oezdamar. D: Hark Bohm. DRA 86m.

Year My Voice Broke, The 1987 Australian ★★★★ Intelligent, downbeat coming-of-age film set in Australia in the '60s. Protagonist suffers heartbreak when girl he loves becomes pregnant by older boy, then leaves town. Followed by the much-acclaimed *Flirting*. C: Noah Taylor, Loene Carmen, Ben Mendelsohn, Graeme Blundell, Lynette Curran, Bruce Spence. D: John Duigan. DRA [PG-13] 103m. v

Year of Living Dangerously, The 1983 Australian ★★★★ Riveting story set in Indonesia during the coup of 1965, where Australian journalist Gibson becomes romantically involved with British official Weaver in the midst of the bloodshed. Striking filmmaking is bolstered by solid acting, including Oscar-winning performance by Hunt as a male photographer. C: Mel Gibson, Sigourney Weaver, Linda Hunt, Michael Murphy. D: Peter Weir. DRA [PG] 115m. v

Year of the Comet 1992 ★★★½ When Miller inadvertently comes into possession of priceless bottle of booze, she finds herself the center of international shenanigans. Fun, slightly off-pace romp that has its moments. Miller is fun as a shy person turned manic by events swirling around her. C: Penelope Ann Miller, Timothy Daly, Louis Jourdan, Ian Richardson, Ian McNeice. D: Peter Yates. COM [PG-13] 135m. v

Year of the Dragon 1985 ★★½ Rourke as New York cop trying to shut down Chinese crime lord (Lone). Laughably overacted; watch Rourke's hair change color from scene to scene. C: Mickey Rourke, John Lone, Ariane, Leonard Termo, Ray Barry, Caroline Kava. D: Michael Cimino. CRI [R] 136m. v

Year of the Gun 1991 ★★★ While trying to liberate a woman from her abusive husband, a novelist in '70s Rome (McCarthy) discovers a plot by Italy's Red Brigade underground terrorist group to abduct then-Prime Minister Aldo Moro. Sloppy political intriguer, but with a decent performance by Stone. C: Andrew McCarthy, Valeria Golino, Sharon Stone, John Pankow, Marttia Sbragia, George Murcell. D: John Frankenheimer. CRI [R] 111m. v

Yearling, The 1946 ★★★★★ Classic juvenile tearjerker of boy's love for wild fawn, from Marjorie Kinnan Rawling's book. Impeccably produced, shot on location in Florida, with sterling cast headed by Peck as well-meaning father. Climax may be too emotionally painful for impressionable youngsters. Oscars for Cinematography and Art Direction, and a special one for Jarman. C: Gregory Peck, Jane Wyman, Claude Jarman Jr., Chill

Wills, Forrest Tucker, June Lockhart. D: Clarence Brown. FAM/DRA [G] 129m. v

Yellow Balloon, The 1952 British ★★★½ Little boy thinks he's accidentally killed his best friend; local hood takes advantage of misunderstanding, forcing him to steal from his parents. Solid cast of British stalwarts lifts it above the ordinary. C: Andrew Ray, Kenneth More, Veronica Hurst, William Sylvester, Bernard Lee. D: J. Lee Thompson. DRA 80m.

Yellow Cab Man, The 1950 ★★★★ Skelton shines in this inventive comedy about a bumbling taxi driver who comes up with a formula for unbreakable glass and then has to protect it from being stolen. Gag-filled screenplay proves a truckload of laughs. C: Red Skelton, Gloria DeHaven, Walter Slezak, Edward Arnold, James Gleason, Jay Flippen, Polly Moran. D: Jack Donohue. COM 85m. v

Yellow Cargo 1936 ★★★ Goofy, original B-movie crimer about smugglers using film extras as a front. Undercover cops crack their nefarious plan. C: Conrad Nagel, Eleanor Hunt. D: Crane Wilbur. CRI 70m. v

Yellow Earth 1986 Chinese ★★★★ Slow-moving, but ultimately compelling tale of folklorist sent to Chinese hinterlands in 1939 to collect songs of the people and falling in love with young peasant woman. Beautiful to look at. C: Xue Bai, Wang Xueqi, Tan Tuo, Liu Qiang. D: Chen Kaige. DRA 89m. v

Yellow Fin 1951 ★★★ Tuna-boat skipper (Morris) has problems with an unscrupulous rival, girlfriend, and father. After various adventures, everything works out. Unsurprising but well done. C: Wayne Morris, Adrian Booth, Damian O'Flynn. D: Frank McDonald. ACT 74m.

Yellow Jack 1938 ★★★ Somewhat dated adaptation of Sidney Howard's play about Dr. Walter Reed's battle to find a cure for yellow fever at the turn of the century. C: Robert Montgomery, Virginia Bruce, Lewis Stone, Stanley Ridges, Henry Hull, Charles Coburn, Buddy Ebsen, Andy Devine, Henry O'Neill, Sam Levene, Alan Curtis, William Henry. D: George B. Seitz. DRA 83m.

Yellow Rolls-Royce, The 1964 British ★★★★ Opulently produced trio of Terence Rattigan tales use the elegant title car as a common thread. Stories sometimes stall but never the car...or the high-octane cast. Best is last, with Bergman as a surprisingly resourceful socialite. C: Rex Harrison, Ingrid Bergman, Shirley MacLaine, Jeanne Moreau, George C. Scott, Alain Delon, Omar Sharif, Art Carney. D: Anthony Asquith. COM 122m.

Yellow Sky 1948 ★★★★½ Brisk Western, almost a version of *The Tempest*, with a gang of outlaws coming to a deserted town and finding Baxter and her father there. Taut, evocative. Remade in 1967 as *The Jackals*. Strong performances by all. C: Gregory Peck, Anne Baxter, Richard Widmark, Robert Arthur, John Russell, Harry Morgan, James Barton. D: William Wellman. WST 98m.

Yellow Submarine 1968 British ★★★★★ The Beatles lent their songs (but not their speaking voices) to this hugely enjoyable animated fantasy, in which the singers save the peaceful Pepperland from evil Blue Meanies. Great gags, memorable characters, and eye-popping visuals; the tunes are icing on the cake. Voices of The Beatles. D: George Dunning. MUS [G] 85m. v

Yellowbeard 1983 ★★ Chapman plays a 17th-century pirate in search of treasure. He's accompanied by his son, who has location of the loot tattooed on his noggin. Would-be movie parody features trmendous cast. C: Graham Chapman, Peter Boyle, Richard Marin, Tommy Chong, Peter Cook, Marty Feldman, Kenneth Mars, Eric Idle, Madeline Kahn, James Mason, John Cleese. D: Mel Damski. COM [PG] 97m. v

Yentl 1983 ★★★½ Streisand dominates musical she produced, directed, and co-wrote, as an intelligent young woman forced to pretend she's a man to study the Torah. Every scene, every song involves her, so her brilliance wears thin by end of movie. Score, mostly interior monologues for star, begins to sound the same as film drags to foregone conclusion. Devoted fans won't care. C: Barbra Streisand, Mandy Patinkin, Amy Irving, Nehemiah Persoff. D: Barbra Streisand. MUS [PG] 134m. v

Yes, Giorgio 1982 ★★½ No, Luciano! Misguided attempt to make a matinee idol of the corpulent opera star casts him as a singer with voice problems, seeking solace from an American doctor (Harrold). Their romance is as unbelievable as the plot of *Il Trovatore*! Anyway, it's different. C: Luciano Pavarotti, Kathryn Harrold, Eddie Albert. D: Franklin J. Schaffner. MUS [PG] 110m. v

Yesterday, Today and Tomorrow 1964 Italian ★★★★½ Loren is superb as three different sexy women in trio of comic stories: a black marketeer using her charms to avoid arrest, a wealthy flirt, and a prostitute involved with a seminary student. Often hilarious and frequently racy, including Loren's famous striptease. (a.k.a. *She Got What She Asked For*) C: Sophia Loren, Marcello Mastroianni, Tina Pica, Giovanni Ridolfi. D: Vittorio De Sica. COM 119m. v

Yojimbo 1961 Japanese ★★★★★ Violent, intense samurai film that works well as both comedy and tragedy. Itinerant warrior (Mifune superb, as usual) hires himself out to both sides of bitter dispute in small village. Makes interesting point about arbitrary nature of war, with no heroes, only buffoons. Extremely influential film that inspired Sergio Leone's *For a Fistful of Dollars*. Sequel: *Sanjuro*. C: Toshiro Mifune, Eijiro Tono, Seizaburo Kawazu, Isuzu Yamada. D: Akira Kurosawa. DRA 110m. v

Yol 1982 Turkish ★★★★ Stark drama of

five convicts on a week's furlough from a Turkish prison. Written by Yilmaz Guney, who was a political prisoner at the time. Grim but powerful. C: Tarik Akan, Serif Sezer. D: Serif Goren. DRA [PG] 126m. v

Yolanda and the Thief 1945 ★★★ MGM musical fantasy casts Astaire as a bogus "angel" pulling the wool over a wealthy young woman's eyes. Box-office fiasco has many deficiencies, but the lavish production design is not one of them. Some superb dance numbers, including "Coffee Time." C: Fred Astaire, Lucille Bremer, Frank Morgan, Mildred Natwick, Leon Ames. D: Vincente Minnelli. MUS 108m. v

Yor, the Hunter From the Future 1983 Italian ★★ A pumped-up amnesia victim (Brown) travels through time in search of his identity. Futuristic beefcake. C: Reb Brown, Corinne Clery, John Steiner. D: Anthony M. Dawson. SFI [PG] 88m. v

You and Me 1938 ★★★½ Man with a prison record (Raft) unknowingly marries a woman with a similar past (Sidney). Very well-acted mix of drama and comedy. The stars make it work. C: George Raft, Sylvia Sidney, Barton MacLane, Harry Carey. D: Fritz Lang. DRA 90m.

You Belong to Me 1941 ★★★ A doctor (Stanwyck) can't cure her husband's chronic jealousy. Screwball comedy's no jalopy, though it's not as smooth as the duo's 1941 Cadillac, *The Lady Eve*, either. Remake: *Emergency Wedding*. C: Henry Fonda, Barbara Stanwyck, Edgar Buchanan, Ruth Donnelly. D: Wesley Ruggles. COM 94m.

You Belong to My Heart *See* Mr. Imperium

You Can't Cheat an Honest Man 1939 ★★★★★ W.C. Fields (who wrote the original story under the name of Charles Bogle) teams with Edgar Bergen and Charlie McCarthy in an hysterical tale about a conniving circus owner frantically trying to stay a step ahead of the sheriff. Frantically funny, especially the show-stopping Ping-Pong match. C: W.C. Fields, Edgar Bergen, Constance Moore, James Bush. D: George Marshall. COM 76m. v

You Can't Run Away From It 1956 ★★★ A reporter (Lemmon) helps a runaway heiress (Allyson). So-so remake of classic *It Happened One Night*, with songs added. C: June Allyson, Jack Lemmon, Charles Bickford, Stubby Kaye. D: Dick Powell. MUS 95m.

You Can't Take It With You 1938 ★★★★ Adaptation of George S. Kaufman/Moss Hart Broadway hit is a delight, about the comic complications in the eccentric Sycamore family when daughter Arthur begins a romance with wealthy Stewart. Typically strong Capra cast and upbeat mood make this winning entertainment. Oscar-winner for Best Picture and Director. C: Jean Arthur, Lionel Barrymore, James Stewart, Edward Arnold. D: Frank Capra. COM 126m. v

You Can't Take Money 1937 *See* **Internes Can't Take Money**

You Light Up My Life 1977 ★★★ Struggling actress/singer (Conn) wrestles with her personal life. Sentimental show biz yarn, but helped by the charming Conn. Oscar-winning title song. C: Didi Conn, Joe Silver, Michael Zaslow, Melanie Mayron. D: Joseph Brooks. COM [PG] 90m. v

You Never Can Tell 1951 ★★★½ A dog is reincarnated as a detective (Powell) and tries to avenge his own murder. Don't let the premise put you off; this pleasing comedy has a lot of heart. C: Dick Powell, Peggy Dow, Charles Drake, Joyce Holden. D: Lou Breslow. COM 78m.

You Only Live Once 1937 ★★★★½ One of the best of the "young lovers on the lam" films, with Fonda and Sydney effective as victims of injustice who are forced to run from the law. An all-around terrific production. C: Sylvia Sidney, Henry Fonda, William Gargan, Barton MacLane, Jerome Cowan, Margaret Hamilton. D: Fritz Lang. CRI 86m. v

You Only Live Twice 1967 British ★★★★ James Bond (Connery) must stop SPECTRE madman Blofeld (Pleasence) from causing WWIII in this fast-paced, well-produced entry in the series. Good Japanese location photography and the usually fine special effects are pluses. C: Sean Connery, Donald Pleasence, Akiko Wakabayashi, Tetsuro Tamba, Lois Maxwell. D: Lewis Gilbert. ACT [PG] 116m. v

You Were Never Lovelier 1942 ★★★★½ Enjoyable Astaire/Hayworth musical with haunting music by Jerome Kern. Menjou is Hayworth's father, a wealthy South American anxious to see her married; Astaire is the man he proposes to get the job done. Entertaining, charming fluff. C: Fred Astaire, Rita Hayworth, Adolphe Menjou. D: William A. Seiter. MUS 98m. v

You'll Never Get Rich 1941 ★★★★ A musical comedy star (Astaire) is drafted, and tries to avoid it. The silly plot is no impediment to the marvelous dancing of Astaire and Hayworth, one of his favorite partners. Best Cole Porter song: "So Near and Yet So Far." C: Fred Astaire, Rita Hayworth, Robert Benchley, John Hubbard. D: Sidney Lanfield. MUS 88m. v

Young and Innocent 1937 British ★★★★ Charged with a murder he did not commit, a man flees for his life and, intent on finding the real killer, meets a young woman who agrees to help him. Hitchcock's taut thriller, based on the Josephine Tey mystery novel *A Shilling for Candles*, has good chase sequences and engaging characterizations. C: Derrick de Marney, Nova Pilbeam, Percy Marmont, Mary Clare. D: Alfred Hitchcock. CRI 80m. v

Young and the Damned, The 1950 *See* **Los Olvidados**

Young at Heart 1954 ★★★½ Unhappy musician Sinatra finds romance with small-town girl Day. Nice songs and appealing performances in this remake of Fannie Hurst's *Four Daughers.* C: Doris Day, Frank Sinatra, Gig Young, Ethel Barrymore. D: Gordon Douglas. DRA 117m. V

Young Bess 1953 ★★★★ Simmons is luminous as the young woman who was to become Elizabeth I; Laughton reprises his Henry VIII role. Sumptuous costume drama with impressive acting and commendable attention paid to historical detail. C: Jean Simmons, Stewart Granger, Charles Laughton, Deborah Kerr, Cecil Kellaway, Leo Carroll, Kay Walsh. D: George Sidney. DRA 112m. V

Young Bruce Lee, The ★★ One of many kung fu exploitation films to arrive in the wake of Lee's death, this one purports to demonstrate how he came by his amazing fighting skills. Hold out for the real thing. C: Bruce Lee, Hon Kwok Choi. ACT 90m. V

Young Cassidy 1965 British ★★★ Superb supporting cast makes this sturdy biography of Irish playwright Sean O'Casey (Taylor) worth watching. Director Cardiff took over mid-film for the ailing Ford. C: Rod Taylor, Julie Christie, Maggie Smith, Flora Robson, Michael Redgrave, Jack MacGowran, Edith Evans. D: Jack Cardiff, John Ford. DRA 110m.

Young Catherine 1991 British ★★★ Lavish film adds footage to tale detailing the early life of Catherine the Great, a German teenager who married into Russia's royal family in the 1700s. Dramatics aren't as impressive as the Russian location scenery. C: Vanessa Redgrave, Christopher Plummer, Franco Nero. D: Michael Anderson. DRA 200m. TVM V

Young Doctors, The 1961 ★★★★ Sprawling soap opera depicts the trials and tribulations of a city hospital's underpaid, overworked staff. Good performances from March, Gazarra, and Segal (in his film debut). From Arthur Hailey's best-selling novel. C: Fredric March, Ben Gazzara, Eddie Albert, George Segal, Arthur Hill, Ina Balin, Aline MacMahon. D: Phil Karlson. DRA 100m.

Young Doctors in Love 1982 ★ Parody film follows interns studying medicine and romance while encountering cast from popular TV soap opera *General Hospital* (including future film star Demi Moore!). One-joke idea that's two jokes short of being funny. Gags revolving around midget are completely tasteless. C: Michael McKean, Sean Young, Harry Dean Stanton, Patrick Macnee, Hector Elizondo, Dabney Coleman, Pamela Reed, Saul Rubinek. D: Garry Marshall. COM [R] 97m. V

Young Dr. Kildare 1938 ★★★ First in the Dr. Kildare series, with Ayres as the idealistic young physician who has to choose between a small-town practice or a position in a big-city hospital. Satisfying look at old-time values. C: Lew Ayres, Lionel Barrymore, Lynne Carver, Nat Pendleton, Jo Ann Sayers, Samuel S. Hinds, Emma Dunn, Walter Kingsford, Monty Woolley, Philip Terry, Donald Barry. D: Harold S. Bucquet. DRA 81m.

Young Dragons—Kung Fu Kids, The 1987 ★★ More miniature mayhem in this negligible sequel, which finds the little fighters torn between the grandfather who instructed them and their long-absent, equally skilled grandmother. Not much kick. C: Chen Shun Yun, Yen Chin Kwok. D: Chang Mei Jun. FAM/ACT 95m. V

Young Dragons—Kung Fu Kids II, The 1987 ★★ Cheapie adventure film for kids about wise old martial arts master who instructs his three grandsons in ancient fighting methods, which they soon get a chance to use. C: Chen Shun Yun, Yen Chin Kwok. D: Chen Che Hwa. FAM/ACT 100m. V

Young Einstein 1988 Australian ★★½ Yahoo Serious (his real name!) writes, produces, directs, and stars in Australian spoof biography of Albert Einstein, discoverer of relativity and rock 'n' roll music. Lots of energy and color in this conceptual comedy almost cover lack of substantial jokes. C: Yahoo Serious, John Howard, Pee Wee Wilson, Odile Le Clezio. D: Yahoo Serious. COM [PG] 90m. V

Young Frankenstein 1974 ★★★★★ Brooks' loving comic homage to Universal *Frankenstein* films stars co-writer Wilder as great-grandson of Victor Frankenstein who creates his own monster (Boyle) with help of beautiful Garr and bizarre Feldman. Wonderful loopy humor, packed with great set pieces and fine comic touches. "Putting On the Ritz" number is a classic. Brooks used actual lab machinery created for Karloff *Frankenstein.* Look for Gene Hackman's blind-man cameo. C: Gene Wilder, Peter Boyle, Marty Feldman, Teri Garr, Madeline Kahn, Cloris Leachman, Kenneth Mars. D: Mel Brooks. COM 106m. V

Young Girls of Rochefort, The 1968 French ★★★ Pretty musical romance about two sisters mixed up with an older song-and-dance man (Kelly). Same formula as director's immensely successful *Umbrellas of Cherbourg* doesn't quite click here, but it's Kelly's last big part and worth catching for that. Songs by Michel Legrand. C: Catherine Deneuve, Francoise Dorleac, Gene Kelly, George Chakiris, Danielle Darrieux. D: Jacques Demy. MUS 124m.

Young Guns 1988 ★★★½ Six young wiseguy gunslingers team up with Billy the Kid and the result is pure mayhem. Both the casting and language are contemporary, but it's fun and entertaining nonetheless. C: Emilio Estevez, Kiefer Sutherland, Lou Diamond Phillips, Charlie Sheen, Dermot Mulroney, Casey Siemaszko, Terence Stamp, Jack Palance, Terry O'Quinn. D: Christopher Cain. WST [R] 102m. V

Young Guns 2 1990 ★★★ The further adventures of a group of youthful gunslingers. This time they're traipsing down to Mexico in order to avoid determined government agents. C: Emilio Estevez, Kiefer Sutherland, Lou Diamond Phillips, Christian Slater, Alan Ruck, Leon Rippy, Tracy Walter, Balthazar Getty. D: Geoff Murphy. WST [PG-13] 105m. v

Young in Heart, The 1938 ★★★★½ Cute comedy about a free-spirited family of con artists who decide to go straight after they are befriended by a sweet old woman (Dupree) they'd intended to fleece. Funny, well-paced, and entertaining. C: Janet Gaynor, Douglas Fairbanks Jr., Paulette Goddard, Roland Young, Billie Burke. D: Richard Wallace. COM 91m. v

Young L.A. Nurses 3 1973 *See* **Young Nurses, The**

Young Lions, The 1958 ★★★★½ Story follows lives of three soldiers through WWII where they fight personal battles and enemies: Jewish G.I. Clift, reluctant draftee Martin, and disillusioned Nazi Brando. Adaptation of Irwin Shaw's novel manages effective examination of war and homefront from both sides. C: Marlon Brando, Montgomery Clift, Dean Martin, Hope Lange, Barbara Rush, Maximilian Schell. D: Edward Dmytryk. DRA 167m. v

Young Magician, The 1987 ★★ When young man taps into his conjuring talents, he finds the world opening up to him in unexpected ways. Minor and hackneyed story further hampered by obvious situations and bad English dubbing. C: Rusty Jedwab, Nastasza Maraszek, Edward Garson. D: Waldemar Dziki. FAM/DRA 99m. v

Young Man With a Horn 1950 ★★★★ Self-absorbed trumpet player (Douglas, with Harry James on the horn) gets involved with two women (Bacall and Day) who are couln't be more opposite. Keen, intelligently acted melodrama. C: Kirk Douglas, Lauren Bacall, Doris Day, Juano Hernandez, Hoagy Carmichael. D: Michael Curtiz. DRA 112m. v

Young Mr. Lincoln 1939 ★★★★½ Fledgling lawyer Abraham Lincoln (Fonda) argues a court case in Springfield, Illinois, with a combination of intuition, clear thinking, and old-fashioned common sense. Superb Fonda; a wonderful, inspirational film for the whole family. C: Henry Fonda, Alice Brady, Marjorie Weaver, Donald Meek, Richard Cromwell, Eddie Quillan, Milburn Stone, Ward Bond, Francis Ford. D: John Ford. FAM/DRA 100m. v

Young Mr. Pitt, The 1942 British ★★★½ Historical biography of Britain's youngest prime minister (Donat). When released, film proved to be of nominal interest to non-Britons—a shame, because Pitt was a fascinating and brilliant man, and Donat does him proud. C: Robert Donat, Robert Morley, Phyllis Calvert, John Mills, Max Adrian. D: Carol Reed. DRA 118m.

Young Nurses, The 1973 ★★ Typical shenanigans among the trio of sexy nurses from three previous films, this time discovering that their hospital is home base for a drug ring. Decent cast (including director Sam Fuller as villain) gives it some spark. (a.k.a. *Young L.A. Nurses 3* and *Nightingale*) C: Jean Manson, Ashley Porter, Angela Gibbs, Zack Taylor. D: Clinton Kimbrough. DRA [R] 77m. v

Young People 1940 ★★★ A song-and-dance team takes on an orphan (Temple), then tries to give up show biz. Routine Temple tuner. C: Shirley Temple, Jack Oakie, Charlotte Greenwood, George Montgomery. D: Allan Dwan. MUS 78m.

Young Philadelphians, The 1959 ★★★★ Ambitious lawyer (Newman) with a dark secret crashes upper-crust Philadelphia society, where he defends scion of wealthy family (Vaughn) accused of murder and makes play for young woman of society (Rush). Adaptation of Richard Powell's book ably handled with strong performances. C: Paul Newman, Barbara Rush, Alexis Smith, Brian Keith, Robert Vaughn. D: Vincent Sherman. DRA 148m. v

Young Savages, The 1961 ★★★½ Tough crime drama about a district attorney (Lancaster) trying to solve a youth gang murder. Gritty, street-smart atmosphere and good performances. Savalas's screen debut. C: Burt Lancaster, Shelly Winters, John David Chandler, Dina Merrill, Telly Savalas. D: John Frankenheimer. CRI 110m.

Young Sherlock Holmes 1986 ★★★½ Youthful Holmes (Rowe) and Watson (Cox) get into a series of adventures. Clever, foreshadowing references to the adult Sherlock Holmes overwhelmed by special effects. Plot continues throughout the final credits. C: Nicholas Rowe, Alan Cox, Sophie Ward, Anthony Higgins. D: Barry Levinson. CRI [PG-13] 109m. v

Young Stranger, The 1957 ★★★★ One of the better juvenile delinquent films of the '50s, with MacArthur in screen debut as troubled teenager with family problems. Frankenheimer's first film is understated and thoughtful. C: James MacArthur, James Daly, Kim Hunter, James Gregory, Marian Seldes, Whit Bissell. D: John Frankenheimer. DRA 84m.

Young Swordsman 1964 Japanese ★★★½ Dark, brooding samurai film about renegade swordsman (Ichikawa) who finds himself hunted by his own clan for violating laws against swordfighting. Excellent action sequences. C: Somegoro Ichikawa, Hiroyuki Nagato. D: Hiroshi Imagaki. ACT 108m.

Young Tiger, The 1980 ★ Only a few minutes of this film feature star Jackie Chan, and they depict him directing a film; the rest is a tedious Asian mobster movie that completely lacks Chan's involvement—as well as thrills. C: Jackie Chan, Meng Fei, Maggi Li. CRI 102m. v

Young Tom Edison 1940 ★★★★ Rooney holds forth as the teenage inventor in this pleasant mixture of fact and fantasy with a bit of melodrama tossed in. Later followed by *Edison the Man* with Spencer Tracy. C: Mickey Rooney, Fay Bainter, George Bancroft, Virginia Weidler, Eugene Palette, Victor Kilian. D: Norman Taurog. DRA 82m. V

Young Torless 1968 French ★★★★ An Austrian boarding school is used as a microcosm of pre-WWII society, and shows the seeds of Nazism underneath placid surface. Powerful production of Robert Musil's classic novel. C: Mathieu Carrier, Marian Seidowsky, Bernd Tischer, Alfred Dietz. D: Volker Schlondorff. DRA 90m.

Young, Willing and Eager 1962 British ★★★ A 17-year-old runs away from her abusive stepfather and encounters disastrous adventures in London's Soho district. Low-budget melodrama tries hard. C: Jess Conrad, Kenneth Griffith, Christina Gregg. D: Lance Comfort. DRA 77m.

Young Winston 1972 British ★★★★ Churchill's youth and early career are splendidly acted by Ward in sincere adaptation of Churchill's autobiography. Authentic historical detail offers little-known information about the British prime minister best known to Americans. Riveting action sequences. C: Simon Ward, Anne Bancroft, Robert Shaw, John Mills, Jack Hawkins. D: Richard Attenborough. DRA [PG] 124m. V

Young Wives' Tale 1951 British ★★★½ Wartime housing shortage forces two young couples to share lodgings with appropriately farcical action resulting. Greenwood is splendid; Hepburn has small supporting role as neighbor. C: Joan Greenwood, Nigel Patrick, Derek Farr, Helen Cherry, Guy Middleton, Athene Seyler, Audrey Hepburn. D: Henry Cass. DRA 78m.

Young Woodley 1930 British ★★½ Woodley (Lawton) is in love with his schoolmaster's wife (Carroll). Forerunner of *Tea and Sympathy* was scandalous in the '20s but looks dated today. C: Madeleine Carroll, Frank Lawton. D: Thomas Bentley. DRA 71m.

Youngblood 1986 ★★ Tyro hockey player (Lowe) on a bush league Canadian team must win approval of his peers. Watchable; fizzling fluff. C: Rob Lowe, Cynthia Gibb, Patrick Swayze, Ed Lauter, Jim Youngs. D: Peter Markle. DRA 109m. V

Youngblood Hawke 1964 ★★★½ An upstart Southern writer (Franciscus) claws his way to the top of the New York literary world. Very watchable melodrama, from the Herman Wouk bestseller. C: James Franciscus, Suzanne Pleshette, Genevieve Page, Eva Gabor, Mary Astor. D: Delmer Daves. DRA 137m.

Younger Brothers, The 1949 ★★★½ Two weeks from fulfilling the requirements of their parole, the Youngers (Morris, Bennett, Hutton, and Brown) are drawn back into a life of crime. Standard Western with solid supporting cast. C: Wayne Morris, Janis Paige, Bruce Bennett, Geraldine Brooks, Robert Hutton, Alan Hale, Fred Clark, Tom Tyler. D: Edwin L. Marin. WST 77m.

Youngest Profession, The 1943 ★★★½ Weidler and Porter are pushy, obnoxious fans pestering a raft of MGM stars for autographs. Worthwhile for Weidler and the many star cameos. C: Virginia Weidler, Jean Porter, Edward Arnold, John Carroll, Agnes Moorehead, Scotty Beckett. D: Edward Buzzell. COM 82m.

Youngest Spy, The 1962 *See* **My Name Is Ivan**

Your Cheatin' Heart 1964 ★★★★ Despite improbable casting, Hamilton is terrific as country-music legend Hank Williams in this somewhat bowdlerized biography. Williams is depicted as unable to cope with his success. Great music, dubbed by Hank Williams, Jr. C: George Hamilton, Susan Oliver, Red Buttons, Arthur O'Connell, Rex Ingram. D: Gene Nelson. DRA 99m.

Your Turn, Darling 1963 French ★★★ Constantine, intrepid U.S. secret agent, tries to break up a foreign spy ring. Boring. C: Eddie Constantine, Henri Cogan, Gaia Germani, Elga Andersen. D: Bernard Borderie. DRA 93m.

Your Uncle Dudley 1935 ★★★ Horton is small-town Milquetoast who finally rebels against his tyrannical sister and neighbors who have taken advantage of him. Mild comedy. C: Edward Everett Horton. D: James Tinling, Eugene Forde. COM 70m.

Your Witness 1950 *See* **Eye Witness**

You're a Big Boy Now 1966 ★★★★ Kastner, a young library clerk and long-suffering virgin, is buffeted by pressures from friends, family, and various NYC eccentrics. Funny, if mannered. C: Peter Kastner, Elizabeth Hartman, Geraldine Page, Julie Harris, Rip Torn, Michael Dunn, Tony Bill, Karen Black. D: Francis Ford Coppola. COM 98m. V

You're a Sweetheart 1937 ★★★ Murphy is promoter trying to invent publicity stunt for Faye's show in this standard musical. C: Alice Faye, George Murphy, Ken Murray, Andy Devine, William Gargan, Charles Winninger, Donald Meek, Bobby Watson. D: David Butler. MUS 96m.

You're in the Army Now 1941 ★★★ Vacuum cleaner sales reps Durante and Silvers unwittingly enlist in the Army. Silly and slapstick-rich film details their training and inept attempts to make it in the service. C: Jimmy Durante, Phil Silvers, Donald MacBride, Jane Wyman, Regis Toomey, Joe Sawyer. D: Lewis Seiler. COM 79m.

You're in the Navy Now 1951 ★★★ Minor comedy of Cooper getting assigned to broken-down bucket with clumsy crew whose members include Marvin and Charles Bronson in their film debuts. C: Gary Cooper, Jane Greer, Millard Mitchell, Eddie Albert, John McIntire, Ray Collins, Harry Von Zell, Lee

Marvin, Jack Webb. D: Henry Hathaway. COM 93m.

You're My Everything 1949 ★★★ Musical comedy of mismatched spouses Baxter and Dailey pursuing careers in vaudeville and movies during the '20s and '30s. Offers some excellent musical numbers. C: Dan Dailey, Anne Baxter, Anne Revere, Stanley Ridges, Alan Mowbray, Selena Royle. D: Walter Lang. MUS 94m.

You're Never Too Young 1955 ★★★½ Lewis has the Ginger Rogers part in this fast-paced remake of *The Major and the Minor*, he must disguise himself as a 12-year-old to escape from jewel thief Burr. C: Dean Martin, Jerry Lewis, Diana Lynn, Raymond Burr, Nina Foch, Veda Ann Borg. D: Norman Taurog. COM 102m.

You're Only Young Once 1938 ★★★½ Second *Andy Hardy* film finds the Hardys vacationing in Catalina where Rooney finds romance. Pleasant enough. C: Lewis Stone, Cecilia Parker, Mickey Rooney, Fay Holden, Frank Craven, Ann Rutherford. D: George B. Seitz. COM 78m.

You're Telling Me 1934 ★★★★½ Incomprehensible plot is merely clothesline on which to hang numerous classic Fields routines, including hilarious golf game sketch. Supposedly a remake of his silent film, *So's Your Old Man*. Brief, brisk, and a gem. C: W.C. Fields, Joan Marsh, Larry "Buster" Crabbe, Louise Carter, Kathleen Howard, Adrienne Ames. D: Erle C. Kenton. COM [R] 67m. V

Yours For the Asking 1936 ★★½ Gambler and roadhouse owner (Raft) makes socialite (Costello) his business partner, with predictable romantic results. Good supporting cast bolster gangster comedy. C: George Raft, Dolores Costello, Ida Lupino, Reginald Owen, James Gleason, Jynne Overman, Skeets Gallagher, Edgar Kennedy. D: Alexander Hall. COM 68m.

Yours, Mine and Ours 1968 ★★★½ Widow Ball (who has eight kids) weds widower Fonda (who's got ten) and there are endless complications. A light touch and likable cast make this a worthwhile family comedy. C: Lucille Ball, Henry Fonda, Van Johnson, Tom Bosley. D: Melville Shavelson. COM 114m. V

Youth and His Amulet, The 1963 Japanese ★★★½ Off-beat melodrama about a little boy whose Buddhist priest father remarries and then boards him with unsympathetic parishioner. Downbeat, but well crafted. C: Toru Koyanagi, Hisako Sakabe, Toshiro Mifune. D: Hiroshi Inagaki. DRA 111m.

Youth on Parade 1943 ★★★½ Frothy college musical in which prof (Hubbard) falls for student (O'Driscoll). Sweet Cahn/Styne score includes "I've Heard That Song Before." C: John Hubbard, Ruth Terry. D: Albert S. Rogell. MUS 72m.

You've Got to Have Heart 1977 ★★ Young couple's wedding night isn't all it's cracked up to be. Takes a sensitive subject and trashes it altogether. C: Carroll Baker. D: Franco Martinelli. COM [R] 98m. V

Yukon Flight 1940 ★★★ Intrepid Mounties hero (Newill) fights illegal mining in the Yukon. Entertaining entry in Renfrew of the Mounties B-movie series. C: James Newill, Louise Stanley. D: Ralph Staub. ACT 57m.

Yum-Yum Girls, The 1976 ★★ Low-budget comedy has its moments, as innocent young Landers and Roberts try to make it in the New York City fashion industry. Plenty of inside humor results in sporadic laughs, but this is far from penetrating satire. C: Judy Landers, Tanya Roberts, Michelle Dawn, Carey Poe, Stan Bernstein. D: Barry Rosen. COM [R] 93m. V

Z

Z 1969 French ★★★★ Angry, intense political thriller based on real-life assassination of Greek nationalist (Montand) and subsequent violent events. Played as a mystery thriller, it's occasionally long-winded but always involving; Oscar for Best Foreign Film and Best Editing. C: Yves Montand, Irene Papas, Jean-Louis Trintignant, Charles Denner. D: Costa-Gavras. CRI [PG] 127m. V

Zabriskie Point 1970 ★★½ Placid girl and unruly college boy take off for Death Valley. Papeir mâché social observation of youthful alienation produces arty escapism. C: Mark Frechette, Daria Halprin, Rod Taylor, Paul Fix. D: Michelangelo Antonioni. DRA [R] 112m. V

Zachariah 1971 ★★★ Rival outlaw gangs hire two gunslingers to shoot it out. Rock musical teeters between earnestness and outright parody. A cult favorite, scripted by members of the Firesign Theater troupe. Interesting "head" nostalgia. C: John Rubinstein, Don Johnson, Pat Quinn, Country Joe and the Fish, New York Rock Ensemble, The James Gang. D: George Englund. MUS [PG] 93m. V

Zandalee 1991 ★★ Anderson leaves her husband for his wild-minded pal, leading to unhappy circumstances. Plentiful sex can't overcome lack of plot logic in this New Orleans-based trifle. Good cast completely wasted. C: Nicolas Cage, Judge Reinhold, Erika Anderson. D: Sam Pillsbury. DRA [R] 95m. V

Zandy's Bride 1974 ★★½ A settler and his mail-order bride try to build a life on the frontier. The two stars are totally trashed in this sappy effort. C: Gene Hackman, Liv Ullmann, Eileen Heckart, Harry Dean Stanton, Susan Tyrrell, Sam Bottoms. D: Jan Troell. WST [PG] 97m. V

Zanzibar 1940 ★★★ Lane, Craig, and Fadden race the Nazis for a skull that confers power over restless African tribespeople. Snappy B-movie fodder, enlivened by stock footage of volcano eruption in last reel. The stuff Saturday afternoons were made of. C: Lola Lane, James Craig, Tom Fadden. D: Harold Schuster. ACT 69m.

Zapped! 1982 ★★ Student (Baio) discovers formula for telekinetic powers, which he uses to undress heartthrob (Thomas), among others. Silly *Carrie* spoof. C: Scott Baio, Willie Aames, Heather Thomas, Robert Mandan, Greg Bradford, Scatman Crothers. D: Robert J. Rosenthal. COM [R] 98m. V

Zapped Again 1990 ★★ Not so much a sequel as a remake, with slight alterations, of *Zapped!*, with a few bullies tossed in. C: Todd Eric Andrews, Kelli Williams, Linda Blair, Karen Black. D: Douglas Campbell. COM [R] 94m. V

Zarak 1957 British ★★★½ Wilding has stiff upper lip as British officer sent to India to fight outlaws led by Mature. Competent action fare. C: Victor Mature, Michael Wilding, Anita Ekberg, Bernard Miles, Finlay Currie. D: Terence Young. ACT 99m.

Zardoz 1973 British ★★★½ Strange but visually arresting action film about a future society ruled by remote intellectuals. Order is kept by a band of thugs called Brutals. Plot bobs and weaves, but Connery is in fine form. C: Sean Connery, Charlotte Rampling, Sara Kestelman, John Alderton. D: John Boorman. SFI [R] 105m. V

Zatoichi 1965 Japanese ★★★ A blind masseur who travels the roads of feudal-era Japan would be an easy mark for thieves; however, Zatoichi, embodied by Shintaro Katsu in over two dozen action films since 1962, is also a former samurai with an uncanny sense of hearing. But he's nearly indestructible, and his swordfighting abilities are at the center of this series of entertaining movies. C: Shintaro Katsu, Mikio Narita, Chizu Hayashi. D: Kenji Misumi. ACT 87m. V

Zatoichi Meets Yojimbo 1970 ★★★★ Mifune reprises his role as warrior Yojimbo from Kurosawa's film, becoming involved with blind samurai Zatoichi (star of his own series of Japanese movies), whose town has been overrun by bandits. Fast-paced, action-packed fun. ACT 90m. V

Zaza 1939 ★★★★ An amoral Parisian singer (Colbert) seduces an upstanding married man (Marshall). Familiar plot sparked by Colbert's bewitching performance, lovingly directed by Cukor. C: Claudette Colbert, Herbert Marshall, Bert Lahr, Constance Collier, Genevieve Tobin, Rex O'Malley. D: George Cukor. DRA 83m.

Zazie 1960 French ★★★ Comic tale of intelligent young girl and her adventures in Paris. (a.k.a. *Zazie Dans Le Metro*, *Zazie in the Subway*, and *Zazie in the Underground*) C: Catherine Demongeot, Philippe Noiret, Vittorio Caprioli. D: Louis Malle. COM 88m. V

Zazie Dans le Metro 1960 *See* **Zazie**

Zazie in the Subway 1960 *See* **Zazie**

Zazie in the Underground 1960 *See* **Zazie**

Zebra in the Kitchen 1965 ★★★ Animal-loving boy (North) takes in zoo dwellers after releasing them from cages. Animal antics are the featured attraction in this lightly amusing comedy for children. C: Jay North, Martin Milner, Andy Devine, Joyce Meadows, Jim Davis, Dorothy Green. D: Ivan Tors. FAM/COM [G] 92m. V

Zebrahead 1992 ★★½ Rapaport is strong as a white teenager who hangs out with black crowd, and whose romance with Wright (also good) leads to inevitable problems. But story eventually becomes pat and predictable, despite good intentions and some well-drawn moments. C: Michael Rapaport, DeShonn Castle, N'Bushe Wright, Ray Sharkey. D: Anthony Drazan. DRA [R] 102m. v

Zee and Company *See* **X, Y and Zee**

Zelig 1983 ★★★★ Conceptual Woody Allen pseudodocumentary about human chameleon who adapts himself into any situation from baseball to world politics. Blending of costumed Allen into existing newsreel footage is well done; nifty take on an intriguing subject. C: Woody Allen, Mia Farrow, Garreth Brown, Stephanie Farrow, Will Holt, Sol Lomita. D: Woody Allen. COM [PG] 79m. v

Zelly and Me 1988 ★★★ Elliptical narrative undermines this offbeat tale and, at times, confusing tale of overprotected orphan and her insanely possessive grandmother. C: Isabella Rossellini, Glynis Johns, Alexandra Johnes, David Lynch. D: Tina Rathborne. DRA [PG] 87m. v

Zenobia 1939 ★★★ When a kindly doctor (Hardy) treats a sick elephant, the cured animal won't forget—or leave him alone! Ollie's solo starrer without Stan is worth seeing for curiosity's sake, but it's a one-joke affair. C: Oliver Hardy, Harry Langdon, Billie Burke, Alice Brady, Chester Conklin, Stepin Fetchit, Hattie McDaniel. D: Gordon Douglas. COM 71m.

Zentropa 1992 Danish ★★★★ Enigmatic tale of skullduggery during WWII has a plot that barely matters; the imagery is all. Hypnotic visual style, mixing back projection and live action, will either fascinate you or put you to sleep. Narrated by Max von Sydow. C: Barbara Sukowa, Jean-Marc Barr, Eddie Constantine. D: Lars von Trier. DRA [R] 112m. v

Zeppelin 1971 British ★★★½ Entertaining action junk about York, a German-born British agent, stealing plans for airship during WWI. The title vehicle is particularly impressive. C: Michael York, Elke Sommer, Peter Carsten, Marius Goring, Anton Diffring, Andrew Keir. D: Etienne Perier. ACT [G] 101m. v

Zero de Conduite *See* **Zero for Conduct**

Zero for Conduct 1933 French ★★★★ Short but influential tale of boarding-school boys in revolt against their dictatorial headmaster. Surreal, funny forerunner of *If...* and other "youth and anarchy" movies. (a.k.a. *Zero de Conduite*) C: Jean Daste, Louis Lefebvre, Gibert Pruchon. D: Jean Vigo. COM 45m. v

Zero Hour 1957 ★★★½ When pilots are felled by food poisoning, someone must land the plane. Hokey but serviceable. C: Dana Andrews, Linda Darnell, Sterling Hayden, Elroy Hirsch, Geoffrey Toone, Jerry Paris, Peggy King, John Ashley. D: Hall Bartlett. DRA 81m.

Zero Population Growth 1972 *See* **Z.P.G.**

Ziegfeld Follies 1946 ★★★½ Flo Ziegfeld concocts a new revue from heaven, with a little help from other stars. Great musical treats include Astaire and Kelly together in "The Babbit and the Bromide" and Astaire in "Limehouse Blues." But comedy routines by Skelton, Brice and Cronyn, Arnold and Moore, are leaden and unfunny. C: William Powell, Judy Garland, Lucille Ball, Fred Astaire, Fanny Brice, Red Skelton, Gene Kelly. D: Vincente Minnelli. MUS 116m. v

Ziegfeld Girl 1941 ★★★★ Big, splashy MGM musical stars Turner, Lamarr, and Garland as Ziegfield girls coping with newfound stardom. Lavish musical numbers (including those by Busby Berkeley) are well worth watching. C: James Stewart, Lana Turner, Judy Garland, Hedy Lamarr, Tony Martin, Jackie Cooper, Ian Hunter, Edward Everett Horton, Al Shean, Eve Arden, Dan Dailey, Philip Dorn, Charles Winninger. D: Robert Z. Leonard. MUS 135m. v

Zigzag 1970 ★★★½ Wildly overcomplicated but moderately diverting thriller with Kennedy, dying from terminal disease, concocting scheme that will allow his family to collect reward money for his "murder." C: George Kennedy, Anne Jackson, Eli Wallach, Steve Ihnat, William Marshall, Joe Maross. D: Richard A. Colla. CRI [PG] 105m.

Zina 1985 British ★★★½ Beautifully mounted but slow-moving story of Trotsky's daughter undergoing psychoanalysis in Berlin before WWII. Offbeat film requires patience from viewers. C: Domiziana Giordano, Ian McKellen, Philip Madoc, Ron Anderson, Micha Bergese. D: Ken McMullen. DRA 90m.

Zombie 1980 Italian ★ Gross-out ripoff of *Dawn of the Dead* boasts plenty of gory makeup efffects, but little else. The setting is a tropical island, where voodoo has raised an army of vicious flesh-eaters. C: Tisa Farrow, Ian McCulloch, Richard Johnson, Al Cliver. D: Lucio Fulci. HOR 91m.

Zombies and Voodoo Blood Bath 1964 *See* **I Eat Your Skin**

Zombies on Broadway 1944 ★★★ Brown and Carney, Abbott and Costello imitators, are press agents sent to Caribbean to find talent; there they get mixed up with Lugosi and his weird experiments. Lugosi almost saves this horror/comedy mix. (a.k.a. *Loonies on Broadway*) C: Wally Brown, Alan Carney, Bela Lugosi, Anne Jeffreys, Sheldon Leonard, Frank Jenks. D: Gordon Douglas. COM 68m. v

Zoo in Budapest 1933 ★★★★½ Luminous, lovely romance of two misfits, runaway orphan (Young) and zookeeper (Raymond), finding love in the famous Budapest Zoo. Breathtakingly shot. C: Loretta Young, Gene Raymond, O.P. Heggie, Paul Fix, Wally Albright. D: Rowland V. Lee. DRA 85m.

Zoot Suit 1981 ★★★½ Intriguing filmed musical play revolves around true-life incident. Hispanic gang member is murdered in 1942, and rival group is framed for the crime.

Theatrical presentation occasionally distracts from what should be riveting story line, though performances are quite good throughout. C: Daniel Valdez, Edward James Olmos, Charles Aidman, Tyne Daly, John Anderson. D: Luis Valdez. MUS [R] 104m. v

Zorba the Greek 1964 ★★★★½ The lives of a passionate Greek peasant and a cerebral English writer become intertwined on the island of Crete. Magnetic performance from Quinn in stirring entertaining drama. From novel by Nikos Kazantzakis. Oscars for Best Supporting Actress (Kedrova), Cinematography and Art Direction-Set Direction. C: Anthony Quinn, Alan Bates, Irene Papas, Lila Kedrova, George Foundas. D: Michael Cacoyannis. DRA 142m. v

Zorro 1975 Italian-French ★★★★ A Latin American Robin Hood (Delon) crosses swords with aristocracy in his fight for the rights of the poor. Good version of the classic tale; Delon cuts a dashing figure in the title role. C: Alain Delon, Stanley Baker, Ottavia Piccolo. D: Duccio Tessari. ACT [G] 100m.

Zorro, the Gay Blade 1981 ★★ Hamilton stars in dual role as original Zorro's twin sons—one a dashing sword fighter, the other a stock movie gay man. When villainous scene-chewer Liebman threatens peaceful village, both brothers snap to action. Witless comedy relies too often on homophobia for cheap laughs. C: George Hamilton, Lauren Hutton, Brenda Vaccaro, Ron Leibman, Donovan Scott. D: Peter Medak. COM [PG] 93m. v

Zotz! 1962 ★★★ Yipes! A mild-mannered professor (Poston) has a magic coin that gives him control over others. Silly-chiller fantasy manages a few very charming moments. C: Tom Poston, Julia Meade, Jim Backus, Fred Clark, Margaret Dumont. D: William Castle. FAM/COM 87m. v

Zou Zou 1934 French ★★★★ Showcase for legendary Follies Bergere star Baker casts her as a laundry woman catapulted to stage stardom. Outlandish costumes and slick dance routines make it an eminently watchable introduction to the famous entertainer. C: Josephine Baker, Jean Gabin, Pierre Larquey. D: Marc Allegret. MUS 92m. v

Z.P.G. 1972 British ★★ Talky science fiction opus based on compelling idea of a future in which reproduction is a capital offense, but Reed and Chaplin decide to have a child regardless. Intriguing, detailed setup becomes uninteresting melodrama. (a.k.a. *Zero Population Growth*) C: Oliver Reed, Geraldine Chaplin, Don Gordon, Diane Cilento. D: Michael Campus. SFI [PG] 95m. v

Zuckerbaby 1987 *See* **Sugarbaby**

Zulu 1964 ★★★★ Gravely outnumbered, a British outpost tries to defend itself against thousands of Zulu warriors. Based on a true military episode; action-packed battle scenes dominate, and Caine is good, as usual, in his first big role. C: Stanley Baker, Jack Hawkins, Ulla Jacobsson, Michael Caine, Nigel Green, James Booth. D: Cy Endfield. ACT 138m. v

Zulu Dawn 1979 ★★★½ Prequel to *Zulu* details events that led to that film's action, as British government's increasingly ineffective dealings with African tribesmen ultimately lead to violence. Lavish production and solid cast make this worthwhile. C: Burt Lancaster, Peter O'Toole, Simon Ward, John Mills, Nigel Davenport, Denholm Elliott, Christopher Cazenove, Bob Hoskins. D: Douglas Hickox. DRA [PG] 117m. v

VIDEO-TRACKER INDEX

DIRECTORS

Abrahams, Jim ☐ Airplane! ☐ Big Business ☐ Hot Shots! ☐ Hot Shots! Part Deux ☐ Police Squad—Help Wanted ☐ Ruthless People ☐ Top Secret ☐ Welcome Home, Roxy Carmichael

Adlon, Percy ☐ Baghdad Cafe ☐ Celeste ☐ Rosalie Goes Shopping ☐ Sugarbaby

Akerman, Chantal ☐ Eighties, The ☐ Golden Eighties ☐ Les Rendezvous d'Anna ☐ News From Home ☐ Night and Day

Alda, Alan ☐ Betsy's Wedding ☐ Four Seasons, The ☐ M*A*S*H: Goodbye, Farewell and Amen ☐ New Life, A ☐ Sweet Liberty

Aldrich, Robert ☐ All the Marbles ☐ Angry Hills, The ☐ Apache ☐ Attack! ☐ Autumn Leaves ☐ Big Knife, The ☐ Big Leaguer, The ☐ Choirboys, The ☐ Dirty Dozen, The ☐ Emperor of the North ☐ Flight of the Phoenix, The ☐ Four for Texas ☐ Frisco Kid, The ☐ Grissom Gang, The ☐ Hush...Hush, Sweet Charlotte ☐ Hustle ☐ Killing of Sister George, The ☐ Kiss Me Deadly ☐ Last Sunset, The ☐ Legend of Lylah Clare, The ☐ Longest Yard, The ☐ Sodom and Gomorrah ☐ Ten Seconds to Hell ☐ Too Late the Hero ☐ Twilight's Last Gleaming ☐ Ulzana's Raid ☐ Vera Cruz ☐ What Ever Happened to Baby Jane?

Allen, Woody ☐ Alice ☐ Annie Hall ☐ Another Woman ☐ Bananas ☐ Broadway Danny Rose ☐ Bullets Over Broadway ☐ Crimes and Misdemeanors ☐ Everything You Always Wanted to Know About Sex (But Were Afraid to Ask) ☐ Hannah and Her Sisters ☐ Husbands and Wives ☐ Interiors ☐ Love and Death ☐ Manhattan ☐ Manhattan Murder Mystery ☐ Midsummer Night's Sex Comedy, A ☐ New York Stories ☐ Purple Rose of Cairo, The ☐ Radio Days ☐ September ☐ Shadows and Fog ☐ Sleeper ☐ Stardust Memories ☐ Take The Money And Run ☐ What's Up, Tiger Lily? ☐ Zelig

Almodóvar, Pedro ☐ Dark Habits ☐ High Heels ☐ Labyrinth of Passion ☐ Law of Desire ☐ Matador ☐ Pepi, Luci, Bom ☐ What Have I Done to Deserve This? ☐ Women on the Verge of a Nervous Breakdown

Altman, Robert ☐ Aria ☐ Beyond Therapy ☐ Brewster McCloud ☐ Buffalo Bill and the Indians ☐ Caine Mutiny Court-Martial, The ☐ California Split ☐ Come Back to the Five and Dime, Jimmy Dean, Jimmy Dean ☐ Countdown ☐ Delinquents, The ☐ Fool for Love ☐ H.E.A.L.T.H. ☐ Images ☐ James Dean Story, The ☐ Long Goodbye, The ☐ M*A*S*H ☐ McCabe & Mrs. Miller ☐ Nashville ☐ Ready to Wear ☐ O.C. & Stiggs ☐ Perfect Couple, A ☐ Player, The ☐ Popeye ☐ Quintet ☐ Secret Honor ☐ Short Cuts ☐ Streamers ☐ That Cold Day in the Park ☐ Thieves Like Us ☐ Three Women ☐ Vincent & Theo ☐ Wedding, A

Anderson, Lindsay ☐ Britannia Hospital ☐ Glory! Glory! ☐ If... ☐ In Celebration ☐ O Lucky Man! ☐ This Sporting Life ☐ Whales of August, The

Antonioni, Michelangelo ☐ Blowup ☐ Eclipse, The ☐ Identification of a Woman ☐ L'Avventura ☐ La Notte ☐ Lady Without Camellias, The ☐ Love in the City ☐ Outcry ☐ Passenger, The ☐ Red Desert ☐ Zabriskie Point

Apted, Michael ☐ 21 Up ☐ 28 Up ☐ 35 Up ☐ Agatha ☐ Blink ☐ Bring on the Night ☐ Class Action ☐ Coal Miner's Daughter ☐ Continental Divide ☐ Critical Condition ☐ Firstborn ☐ Gorillas in the Mist ☐ Gorky Park ☐ Incident at Oglala ☐ Kipperbang ☐ Nell ☐ Thunderheart

Ardolino, Emile ☐ Chances Are ☐ Dirty Dancing ☐ George Balanchine's The Nutcracker ☐ Gypsy ☐ Sister Act ☐ Three Men and a Little Lady

Argento, Dario ☐ Bird with the Crystal Plumage, The ☐ Cat o' Nine Tails ☐ Church, The ☐ Creepers ☐ Dario Argento's World of Horror ☐ Deep Red ☐ Suspiria ☐ Terror at the Opera ☐ Trauma ☐ Two Evil Eyes ☐ Unsane

Armstrong, Gillian ☐ Fires Within ☐ High Tide ☐ Last Days of Chez Nous, The ☐ Little Women ☐ Mrs. Soffel ☐ My Brilliant Career ☐ Starstruck

Arzner, Dorothy ☐ Bride Wore Red, The ☐ Christopher Strong ☐ Craig's Wife ☐ Dance, Girl, Dance ☐ First Comes Courage ☐ Merrily We Go to Hell ☐ Nana ☐ Paramount on Parade ☐ Sarah and Son ☐ Wild Party, The

Ashby, Hal ☐ 8 Million Ways to Die ☐ Being There ☐ Bound for Glory ☐ Coming Home ☐ Harold and Maude ☐ Landlord, The ☐ Last Detail, The ☐ Let's Spend the Night Together ☐ Lookin' to Get Out ☐ Shampoo ☐ Slugger's Wife, The

Attenborough, Richard ☐ Bridge Too Far, A ☐ Chaplin ☐ Chorus Line, A ☐ Cry Freedom ☐ Gandhi ☐ Magic ☐ Oh! What a Lovely War ☐ Shadowlands ☐ Young Winston

Avildsen, John G. ☐ 8 Seconds ☐ Cry Uncle! ☐ For Keeps ☐ Formula, The ☐ Happy New Year ☐ Joe ☐ Karate Kid, The ☐ Karate Kid, Part 2, The ☐ Karate Kid, Part 3, The ☐ Lean on Me ☐ Neighbors ☐ Night in Heaven, A ☐ Rocky ☐ Rocky 5 ☐ Save the Tiger ☐ Slow Dancing in the Big City ☐ W.W. and the Dixie Dancekings

Babenco, Hector ☐ At Play in the Fields of the Lord ☐ Ironweed ☐ Kiss of the Spider Woman ☐ Pixote

Bacon, Lloyd ☐ 42nd Street ☐ Action in the North Atlantic ☐ Affectionately Yours ☐ Boy Meets Girl ☐ Broadway Gondolier ☐ Brother Orchid ☐ Cain and Mabel ☐ Call Me Mister ☐ Captain Eddie ☐ Child Is Born, A ☐ Cowboy from Brooklyn, The ☐ Devil Dogs of the Air ☐ Espionage Agent ☐ Ever Since Eve ☐ Fireman, Save My Child ☐ Footlight Parade ☐ Footsteps in the Dark ☐ French Line, The ☐ Frisco Kid ☐ Frogmen, The ☐ Fuller Brush Girl, The ☐ Give My Regards to Broadway ☐ Gold Diggers of 1937 ☐ Gold Dust Gertie ☐ Golden Girl ☐ Good Humor Man, The ☐ Great Sioux Uprising ☐ He Was Her Man ☐ Here Comes the Navy ☐ Home, Sweet Homicide ☐ Honeymoon for Three ☐ I Don't Care Girl, The ☐ In Caliente ☐ Indianapolis Speedway ☐ Innocent Affair, An ☐ Invisible Stripes ☐ Irish in Us, The ☐ It Happens Every Spring ☐ Kill the Umpire ☐ Knute Rockne, All American ☐ Larceny, Inc. ☐ Marked Woman ☐ Miss Grant Takes Richmond ☐ Moby Dick ☐ Mother Is a Freshman ☐ Navy Blues ☐ Oklahoma Kid, The ☐ Other Tomorrow, The ☐ Picture Snatcher ☐ Racket Busters ☐ San Quentin ☐ Say It with Songs ☐ She Couldn't Say No ☐ Singing Fool, The ☐ Slight Case of Murder, A ☐ Sullivans, The ☐ Sunday Dinner for a Soldier ☐ Three Cheers for the Irish ☐ Walking My Baby Back Home ☐ Wonder Bar

Badham, John ☐ American Flyers ☐ Another Stakeout ☐ Bingo Long Traveling All-Stars & Motor Kings, The ☐ Bird on a Wire ☐ Blue Thunder ☐ Dracula ☐ Drop Zone ☐ Godchild, The ☐ Gun, The ☐ Hard Way, The ☐ Impatient Heart, The ☐ Isn't It Shocking? ☐ Point of No Return ☐ Reflections of Murder ☐ Saturday Night Fever ☐ Short Circuit ☐ Stakeout ☐ WarGames ☐ Whose Life Is It Anyway?

Baker, Roy Ward ☐ And Now the Screaming Starts ☐ Anniversary, The ☐ Asylum ☐ Don't Bother to Knock ☐ Dr. Jeykll and Sister Hyde ☐ Five Million Years to Earth ☐ Flame in the Streets ☐ Highly Dangerous ☐ I'll Never Forget You ☐ Inferno ☐ Jacqueline ☐ Masks of Death ☐ Monster Club, The ☐ Night to Remember, A ☐ Night Without Sleep ☐ October Man, The ☐ One That Got Away, The ☐ Operation Disaster ☐ Paper Orchid ☐ Passage Home ☐ Scars of Dracula ☐ Seven Brothers Meet Dracula, The ☐ Tiger in the Smoke ☐ Vampire Lovers, The

Bakshi, Ralph ☐ American Pop ☐ Cool World ☐ Coonskin ☐ Fire and Ice ☐ Heavy Traffic ☐ Hey Good Lookin' ☐ Lord of the Rings, The ☐ Wizards

Bartel, Paul ☐ Cannonball ☐ Death Race 2000 ☐ Eating Raoul ☐ Lust in the Dust ☐ Not for Publication ☐ Private Parts ☐ Scenes from the Class Struggle in Beverly Hills

Bava, Mario ☐ Baron Blood ☐ Bay of Blood ☐ Beyond the Door II ☐ Black Sabbath ☐ Black Sunday ☐ Blood and Black Lace ☐ Danger: Diabolik ☐ Dr. Goldfoot and the Girl Bombs ☐ Hatchet for the Honeymoon ☐ Hercules in the Haunted World ☐ Kill Baby Kill ☐ Lisa and the Devil ☐ Planet of the Vampires ☐ Wonders of Aladdin, The

Beatty, Warren ☐ Dick Tracy ☐ Heaven Can Wait ☐ Reds

Becker, Harold ☐ Black Marble, The ☐ Boost, The ☐ Malice ☐ Onion Field, The ☐ Ragman's Daughter, The ☐ Sea of Love ☐ Taps ☐ Vision Quest

Beineix, Jean-Jacques ☐ Betty Blue ☐ Diva ☐ Island of Pachyderms, The ☐ Moon in the Gutter, The

Bellocchio, Marco ☐ China Is Near ☐ Devil in the Flesh ☐ Eyes, the Mouth, The ☐ Fist in His Pocket ☐ Henry IV ☐ In the Name of the Father ☐ Leap into the Void

Benjamin, Richard ☐ City Heat ☐ Downtown ☐ Little Nikita ☐ Made in America ☐ Mermaids ☐ Milk Money ☐ Money Pit, The ☐ My Favorite Year ☐ My Stepmother Is an Alien ☐ Racing with the Moon

Benton, Robert ☐ Bad Company ☐ Billy Bathgate ☐ Kramer vs. Kramer ☐ Late Show, The ☐ Nadine ☐ Nobody's Fool ☐ Places in the Heart ☐ Still of the Night

Beresford, Bruce ☐ Adventures of Barry McKenzie, The ☐ Barry Mackenzie Holds His Own ☐ Black Robe, The ☐ Breaker Morant ☐ Crimes of the Heart ☐ Don's Party ☐ Driving Miss Daisy ☐ Fringe Dwellers, The ☐ Getting of Wisdom, The ☐ Good Man in Africa, A ☐ Her Alibi ☐ King David ☐ Mister Johnson ☐ Money Movers ☐ Puberty Blues ☐ Rich in Love ☐ Silent Fall ☐ Tender Mercies

Bergman, Andrew ☐ Freshman, The ☐ Honeymoon in Vegas ☐ It Could Happen to You ☐ So Fine

Bergman, Ingmar ☐ After the Rehearsal ☐ All These Women ☐ Autumn Sonata ☐ Brink of Life ☐ Cries and Whispers ☐ Devil's Eye, The ☐ Devil's Wanton, The ☐ Dreams ☐ Face to Face ☐ Fanny and Alexander ☐ From the Life of the Marionettes ☐ Hour of the Wolf ☐ Illicit Interlude ☐ Lesson in Love, A ☐ Magic Flute, The ☐ Magician, The ☐ Night Is My Future ☐ Passion of Anna, The ☐ Persona ☐ Port of Call ☐ Sawdust and Tinsel ☐ Scenes from a Marriage ☐ Secrets of Women ☐ Serpent's Egg, The ☐ Seventh Seal, The ☐ Shame ☐ Silence, The ☐ Smiles of a Summer Night ☐ Summer Interlude ☐ Through a Glass Darkly ☐ Touch, The ☐ Virgin Spring, The ☐ Wild Strawberries ☐ Winter Light

Berkeley, Busby ☐ Babes in Arms ☐ Babes on Broadway ☐ Bright Lights ☐ Cinderella Jones ☐ Comet Over Broadway ☐ Fast and Furious ☐ For Me and My Gal ☐ Forty Little Mothers ☐ Gang's All Here, The ☐ Garden of the Moon ☐ Gold Diggers of 1935 ☐ Hollywood Hotel ☐ I Live for Love ☐ Strike Up the Band ☐ Take Me Out to the Ballgame ☐ They Made Me a Criminal

Berri, Claude ☐ Germinal ☐ Je Vous Aime ☐ Jean de Florette ☐ Le Sex Shop ☐ Male of the Century, The ☐ Man with Connections, The ☐ Manon of the Spring ☐ Marry Me,

Marry Me ☐ One Wild Moment ☐ Tchao Pantin ☐ Two of Us, The ☐ Uranus

Bertolucci, Bernardo ☐ 1900 ☐ Before the Revolution ☐ Conformist, The ☐ Last Emperor, The ☐ Last Tango in Paris ☐ Little Buddha ☐ Luna ☐ Sheltering Sky, The ☐ Spider's Strategem, The ☐ Tragedy of a Ridiculous Man, The

Blier, Bertrand ☐ Beau Pere ☐ Buffet Froid ☐ Get Out Your Handkerchiefs ☐ Going Places ☐ My Best Friend's Girl ☐ Too Beautiful for You

Bluth, Don ☐ All Dogs Go to Heaven ☐ American Tail, An ☐ Land Before Time, The ☐ Rock-A-Doodle ☐ Secret of NIMH, The ☐ Thumbelina ☐ Troll in Central Park, A

Boetticher, Budd ☐ Arruza ☐ Bronco Buster ☐ Buchanan Rides Alone ☐ Bullfighter and the Lady, The ☐ Cimarron Kid, The ☐ City Beneath the Sea ☐ Comanche Station ☐ Decision at Sundown ☐ East of Sumatra ☐ Horizons West ☐ Killer Is Loose, The ☐ Magnificent Matador, The ☐ Man from the Alamo, The ☐ Ride Lonesome ☐ Rise and Fall of Legs Diamond, The ☐ Seminole ☐ Seven Men from Now ☐ Tall T, The ☐ Time For Dying, A ☐ Westbound

Bogdanovich, Peter ☐ At Long Last Love ☐ Daisy Miller ☐ Illegally Yours ☐ Last Picture Show, The ☐ Mask ☐ Nickelodeon ☐ Noises Off ☐ Paper Moon ☐ Saint Jack ☐ Targets ☐ Texasville ☐ They All Laughed ☐ Thing Called Love, The ☐ What's Up, Doc?

Boorman, John ☐ Deliverance ☐ Emerald Forest, The ☐ Excalibur ☐ Exorcist II: The Heretic ☐ Having a Wild Weekend ☐ Hell in the Pacific ☐ Hope and Glory ☐ Leo the Last ☐ Point Blank ☐ Where the Heart Is ☐ Zardoz

Borzage, Frank ☐ Bad Girl ☐ Big City, The ☐ Big Fisherman, The ☐ China Doll ☐ Desire ☐ Farewell to Arms, A ☐ Flight Command ☐ Flirtation Walk ☐ Green Light, The ☐ Hearts Divided ☐ His Butler's Sister ☐ History Is Made at Night ☐ I've Always Loved You ☐ Lazybones ☐ Liliom ☐ Little Man, What Now? ☐ Magnificent Doll ☐ Man's Castle ☐ Mannequin ☐ Moonrise ☐ Mortal Storm, The ☐ No Greater Glory ☐ Seven Sweethearts ☐ Seventh Heaven ☐ Shining Hour, The ☐ Shipmates Forever ☐ Smilin' Through ☐ Song o' My Heart ☐ Spanish Main, The ☐ Stage Door Canteen ☐ Strange Cargo ☐ Street Angel ☐ They Had to See Paris ☐ Three Comrades ☐ Till We Meet Again

Boulting, John ☐ Brighton Rock ☐ Fame Is the Spur ☐ Heavens Above ☐ I'm All Right, Jack ☐ Journey Together ☐ Lucky Jim ☐ Magic Box, The ☐ Risk, The ☐ Seven Days to Noon

Boulting, Roy ☐ Brothers in Law ☐ Fame Is the Spur ☐ Family Way, The ☐ Happy Is the Bride ☐ High Treason ☐ Man in a Cocked Hat ☐ Pastor Hall ☐ Risk, The ☐ There's a Girl in My Soup ☐ Thunder Rock

Branagh, Kenneth ☐ Dead Again ☐ Henry V ☐ Mary Shelley's Frankenstein ☐ Much Ado About Nothing ☐ Peter's Friends

Bresson, Robert ☐ Au Hasard Balthazar ☐ Diary of a Country Priest ☐ Four Nights of a Dreamer ☐ Gentle Creature, A ☐ L'Argent ☐ Lancelot of the Lake ☐ Man Escaped, A ☐ Mouchette ☐ Pickpocket ☐ Trial of Joan of Arc

Brest, Martin ☐ Beverly Hills Cop ☐ Going in Style ☐ Hot Tomorrows ☐ Midnight Run ☐ Scent of a Woman

Bridges, James ☐ Baby Maker, The ☐ Bright Lights, Big City ☐ China Syndrome, The ☐ Mike's Murder ☐ Paper Chase, The ☐ Perfect ☐ September 30, 1955 ☐ Urban Cowboy

Brooks, Albert ☐ Defending Your Life ☐ Lost in America ☐ Modern Romance ☐ Real Life

Brooks, James L. ☐ Broadcast News ☐ I'll Do Anything ☐ Terms of Endearment

Brooks, Mel ☐ Blazing Saddles ☐ High Anxiety ☐ History of the World Part I ☐ Life Stinks ☐ Producers, The ☐ Robin Hood: Men in Tights ☐ Silent Movie ☐ Spaceballs ☐ Twelve Chairs, The ☐ Young Frankenstein

Brooks, Richard ☐ $ (Dollars) ☐ Battle Circus ☐ Bite the Bullet ☐ Blackboard Jungle ☐ Brothers Karamazov, The ☐ Cat on a Hot Tin Roof ☐ Catered Affair, The ☐ Crisis ☐ Deadline U.S.A. ☐ Elmer Gantry ☐ Fever Pitch ☐ Flame and the Flesh, The ☐ Happy Ending, The ☐ In Cold Blood ☐ Last Hunt, The ☐ Last Time I Saw Paris, The ☐ Light Touch, The ☐ Looking For Mr. Goodbar ☐ Lord Jim ☐ Professionals, The ☐ Something of Value ☐ Sweet Bird of Youth

Brown, Clarence ☐ Ah, Wilderness ☐ Angels in the Outfield ☐ Anna Christie ☐ Anna Karenina ☐ Chained ☐ Come Live With Me ☐ Conquest ☐ Eagle, The ☐ Edison, the Man ☐ Emma ☐ Flesh and the Devil ☐ Free Soul, A ☐ Gorgeous Hussy, The ☐ Human Comedy, The ☐ Idiot's Delight ☐ Inspiration ☐ Intruder in the Dust ☐ Letty Lynton ☐ Looking Forward ☐ National Velvet ☐ Of Human Hearts ☐ Plymouth Adventure, The ☐ Possessed ☐ Rains Came, The ☐ Romance ☐ Sadie McKee ☐ Song of Love ☐ They Met in Bombay ☐ To Please a Lady ☐ When in Rome ☐ White Cliffs of Dover, The ☐ Wife vs. Secretary ☐ Woman of Affairs, A ☐ Yearling, The

Browning, Tod ☐ Devil-Doll, The ☐ Dracula ☐ Fast Workers ☐ Freaks ☐ Iron Man, The ☐ London After Midnight ☐ Mark of the Vampire ☐ Miracles for Sale ☐ Unholy Three, The ☐ West of Zanzibar

Buñuel, Luis ☐ Adventures of Robinson Crusoe, The ☐ Ascent to Heaven ☐ Belle de Jour ☐ Criminal Life of Archibaldo de la Cruz, The ☐ Diamond Hunters ☐ Diary of a Chambermaid ☐ Discreet Charm of the Bourgeoisie, The ☐ El Bruto ☐ Exterminating Angel, The ☐ Illusion Travels by Streetcar ☐ L'Age d'Or ☐ Los Olvidados ☐ Milky Way, The ☐ Nazarin ☐ Phantom of Liberty, The ☐ Simon of the Desert ☐ That Obscure Object of Desire ☐ Tristana ☐ Un Chien Andalou ☐ Viridiana ☐ Wuthering Heights

Burns, Ken ☐ Civil War, The ☐ Huey Long

Burton, Tim ☐ Batman ☐ Batman Returns ☐ Beetlejuice ☐ Ed Wood ☐ Edward Scissorhands ☐ Pee-wee's Big Adventure

Butler, David ☐ Ali Baba Goes to Town ☐ April in Paris ☐ Bright Eyes ☐ By the Light of the Silvery Moon ☐ C'Mon, Let's Live a Little ☐ Calamity Jane ☐ Captain January ☐ Caught in the Draft ☐ Command, The ☐ Connecticut Yankee, A ☐ Daughter of Rosie O'Grady, The ☐ Doubting Thomas ☐ Down to Earth ☐ East Side of Heaven ☐ Girl He Left Behind ☐ Glory ☐ Handy Andy ☐ If I Had My Way ☐ It's a Great Feeling ☐ John Loves Mary ☐ Jump into Hell ☐ Just Imagine ☐ Kentucky ☐ Kentucky Moonshine ☐ King Richard and the Crusaders ☐ Little Colonel, The ☐ Littlest Rebel, The ☐ Look for the Silver Lining ☐ Lullaby of Broadway ☐ My Weakness ☐ My Wild Irish Rose ☐ Painting the Clouds with Sunshine ☐ Pigskin Parade ☐ Princess and the Pirate, The ☐ Road to Morocco ☐ Salute ☐ San Antonio ☐ Shine on Harvest Moon ☐ Story of Seabiscuit, The ☐ Sunny Side Up ☐ Tea for Two ☐ Thank Your Lucky Stars ☐ They Got Me Covered ☐ Time, the Place, and the Girl, The ☐ Two Guys from Milwaukee ☐ Two Guys from Texas ☐ Where's Charley? ☐ You're a Sweetheart

Cacoyannis, Michael ☐ Day the Fish Came Out, The ☐ Iphigenia ☐ Matter of Dignity, A ☐ Sweet Country ☐ Trojan Women, The ☐ Zorba the Greek

Cameron, James ☐ Abyss, The ☐ Aliens ☐ Piranha II: The Spawning ☐ Terminator 2: Judgment Day ☐ Terminator, The ☐ True Lies

Campbell, Martin ☐ Cast a Deadly Spell ☐ Criminal Law ☐ Defenseless ☐ Edge of Darkness ☐ No Escape

Campion, Jane ☐ Angel at My Table, An ☐ Jane Campion Shorts ☐ Piano, The ☐ Sweetie

Capra, Frank ☐ American Madness ☐ Arsenic and Old Lace ☐ Bitter Tea of General Yen, The ☐ Broadway Bill ☐ Dirigible ☐ Donovan Affair, The ☐ Flight ☐ Forbidden ☐ Here Comes the Groom ☐ Hole in the Head, A ☐ It Happened One Night ☐ It's a Wonderful Life ☐ Ladies of Leisure ☐ Lady for a Day ☐ Lost Horizon ☐ Meet John Doe ☐ Miracle Woman, The ☐ Mr. Deeds Goes to Town ☐ Mr. Smith Goes to Washington ☐ Negro Soldier, The ☐ Platinum Blonde ☐ Pocketful of Miracles ☐ Rain or Shine ☐ Riding High ☐ State of the Union ☐ Strong Man, The ☐ You Can't Take it with You

Carne, Marcel ☐ Children of Paradise ☐ Devil's Envoys, The ☐ Gates of the Night ☐ Le Jour Se Leve ☐ Port of Shadows ☐

Carpenter, John ☐ Assault on Precinct 13 ☐ Big Trouble in Little China ☐ Christine ☐ Dark Star ☐ Elvis ☐ Escape from New York ☐ Fog, The ☐ Halloween ☐ In the Mouth of Madness ☐ Memoirs of an Invisible Man ☐ Prince of Darkness ☐ Starman ☐ They Live ☐ Thing, The

Cassavetes, John ☐ Big Trouble ☐ Child is Waiting, A ☐ Faces ☐ Gloria ☐ Husbands ☐ Killing of a Chinese Bookie, The ☐ Love Streams ☐ Minnie and Moskowitz ☐ Opening Night ☐ Shadows ☐ Too Late Blues ☐ Woman Under the Influence, A

Chabrol, Claude ☐ Alice, or the Last Escapade ☐ Betty ☐ Blood of Others, The ☐ Blood Relatives ☐ Bluebeard ☐ Champagne Murders, The ☐ Club Extinction ☐ Cop au Vin ☐ Cousins, The ☐ Dirty Hands ☐ Hatter's Ghost, The ☐ High Heels ☐ Horse Of Pride, The ☐ Inspector Lavardin ☐ Just Before Nightfall ☐ La Femme Infidele ☐ Le Beau Serge ☐ Le Boucher ☐ Le Cri du Hibou ☐ L'Enfer ☐ Les Biches ☐ Les Cousins ☐ Madame Bovary ☐ 7 Capital Sins ☐ Story of Women, The ☐ Ten Days Wonder ☐ This Man Must Die ☐ Twist, The ☐ Violette

Chaplin, Charles ☐ City Lights ☐ Countess from Hong Kong, A ☐ Gold Rush, The ☐ Great Dictator, The ☐ His Prehistoric Past/The Bank ☐ Kid, The ☐ King in New York, A ☐ Limelight ☐ Modern Times ☐ Monsieur Verdoux

Chopra, Joyce ☐ Lemon Sisters, The ☐ Murder in New Hampshire: The Pamela Smart Story

Cimino, Michael ☐ Deer Hunter, The ☐ Desperate Hours ☐ Heaven's Gate ☐ Sicilian, The ☐ Thunderbolt and Lightfoot ☐ Year of the Dragon

Clair, Rene ☐ All the Gold in the World ☐ And Then There Were None ☐ Beauties of the Night ☐ Break the News ☐ Crazy Ray, The ☐ Flame of New Orleans, The ☐ Forever and a Day ☐ Gates of Paris ☐ Ghost Goes West, The ☐ Grand Maneuver, The ☐ I Married a Witch ☐ It Happened Tomorrow ☐ Italian Straw Hat, The ☐ Last Millionaire, The ☐ Le Million ☐ Love and the Frenchwoman ☐ Man about Town ☐ Nous la Libert_, A ☐ Under the Roofs of Paris

Clark, Bob ☐ American Clock, The ☐ Black Christmas ☐ Breaking Point ☐ Christmas Story, A ☐ Deathdream ☐ From the Hip ☐ Loose Cannons ☐ Murder by Decree ☐ Porky's ☐ Porky's 2: The Next Day ☐ Rhinestone ☐ Tribute ☐ Turk 182!

Clayton, Jack ☐ Great Gatsby, The ☐ Innocents, The ☐ Lonely Passion of Judith Hearne, The ☐ Our Mother's House ☐ Pumpkin Eater, The ☐ Room at the Top ☐ Something Wicked This Way Comes

Clement, Rene ☐ And Hope to Die ☐ Babysitter, The ☐ Battle of the Rails ☐ Day and the Hour, The ☐ Forbidden Games ☐ Gervaise ☐ Is Paris Burning? ☐ Joy House ☐ Lovers, Happy Lovers ☐ Mr. Orchid ☐ Purple Noon ☐ Rider on the Rain ☐ This Angry Age ☐ Walls of Malapaga, The

Clouzot, Henri-Georges ☐ Diabolique ☐ Jenny Lamour ☐ La Prisionni_re ☐ Le Corbeau ☐ Murderer Lives at Number 21, The ☐ Wages of Fear, The

Cocteau, Jean ☐ Beauty and the Beast ☐ Blood of a Poet, The ☐ Les Parents Terribles ☐ Orpheus ☐ Testament of Orpheus

Coen, Joel ☐ Barton Fink ☐ Blood Simple ☐ Hudsucker Proxy, The ☐ Miller's Crossing ☐ Raising Arizona

Cohen, Larry ☐ Ambulance, The ☐ Black Caesar ☐ Demon ☐ Full Moon High ☐ Hell Up In Harlem ☐ It's Alive III: Island of the Alive ☐ It Lives Again ☐ It's Alive! ☐ Perfect Strangers ☐ Private Files of J. Edgar Hoover, The ☐ Q ☐ Return to Salem's Lot, A ☐ Wicked Stepmother

Columbus, Chris ☐ Adventures in Babysitting ☐ Heartbreak Hotel ☐ Home Alone ☐ Home Alone 2: Lost in New York ☐ Mrs. Doubtfire ☐ Only the Lonely

Comencini, Luigi ☐ Bebo's Girl ☐ Bread, Love and Dreams ☐ Frisky ☐ Goodnight, Ladies and Gentlemen ☐ Heidi ☐ History ☐ Misunderstood ☐ Till Marriage Do Us Part ☐ Three Nights of Love

Conway, Jack ☐ Arsene Lupin ☐ Assignment in Brittany ☐ Boom Town ☐ Crossroads ☐ Dragon Seed ☐ Easiest Way, The ☐ Gay Bride, The ☐ Girl from Missouri, The ☐ Hell Below ☐ High Barbaree ☐ Honky Tonk ☐ Hucksters, The ☐ Julia Misbehaves ☐ Lady of the Tropics ☐ Let Freedom Ring ☐ Libeled Lady ☐ Love Crazy ☐ One New York Night ☐ Our Modern Maidens ☐ Red-Headed Woman ☐ Saratoga ☐ Tale of Two Cities, A ☐ Tarzan and His Mate ☐ They Learned About Women ☐ Too Hot to Handle ☐ Unholy Three, The ☐ Untamed ☐ Viva Villa! ☐ Yank at Oxford, A

Cook, Fielder ☐ Big Hand for the Little Lady, A ☐ Eagle in a Cage ☐ Family Reunion ☐ From the Mixed-Up Files of Mrs. Basil E. Frankweiler ☐ Gauguin the Savage ☐ Home is the Hero ☐ Homecoming—A Christmas Story, The ☐ How to Save a Marriage (And Ruin Your Life) ☐ I Know Why the Caged Bird Sings ☐ Judge Horton and The Scottsboro Boys ☐ Love Affair, A: The Eleanor and Lou Gehrig Story ☐ Miracle on 34th Street ☐ Patterns ☐ Prudence and the Pill ☐ Seize the Day

Coolidge, Martha ☐ Angie ☐ Bare Essentials ☐ Best of Sledge Hammered, The ☐ City Girl ☐ Crazy in Love ☐ Joy of Sex ☐ Lost In Yonkers ☐ Plain Clothes ☐ Rambling Rose ☐ Real Genius ☐ Valley Girl

Coppola, Francis Ford ☐ Apocalypse Now ☐ Bram Stoker's Dracula ☐ Conversation, The ☐ Cotton Club, The ☐ Dementia 13 ☐ Finian's Rainbow ☐ Gardens of Stone ☐ Godfather, The ☐ Godfather, Part II, The ☐ Godfather, Part III, The ☐ New York Stories ☐ One from the Heart ☐ Outsiders, The ☐ Peggy Sue Got Married ☐ Rain People, The ☐ Rumble Fish ☐ Tucker: The Man and His Dream ☐ You're a Big Boy Now

Corbucci, Sergio ☐ Duel of the Titans ☐ Mercenary, The ☐ Minnesota Clay ☐ Navajo Joe ☐ Odds and Evens

Corman, Roger ☐ Apache Woman ☐ Atlas ☐ Attack of the Crab Monsters ☐ Bloody Mama ☐ Bucket of Blood, A ☐ Carnival Rock ☐ Creature from the Haunted Sea ☐ Day the World Ended, The ☐ Fall of the House of Usher ☐ Five Guns West ☐ Frankenstein Unbound ☐ Gas-s-s-s ☐ Gunslinger ☐ Haunted Palace, The ☐ I, Mobster ☐ Intruder, The ☐ It Conquered the World ☐ Last Woman on Earth, The ☐ Little Shop of Horrors, The ☐ Machine-Gun Kelly ☐ Masque of the Red Death, The ☐ Not of This Earth ☐ Oklahoma Woman, The ☐ Pit and the Pendulum ☐ Premature Burial, The ☐ Raven, The ☐ Rock All Night ☐ Secret Invasion, The ☐ Sorority Girl ☐ St. Valentine's Day Massacre, The ☐ Tales of Terror ☐ Terror, The ☐ Tomb of Ligeia ☐ Tower of London ☐ Trip, The ☐ Undead, The ☐ Von Richthofen and Brown ☐ Wasp Woman, The ☐ Wild Angels, The

Costa-Gavras, ☐ Betrayed ☐ Clair de Femme ☐ Family Business ☐ Hanna K ☐ Missing ☐ Sleeping Car Murders, The ☐ State of Siege ☐ Z

Cox, Alex ☐ Repo Man ☐ Sid and Nancy ☐ Straight to Hell ☐ Walker

Cox, Paul ☐ Cactus ☐ Golden Braid ☐ Kostas ☐ Man of Flowers, A ☐ My First Wife ☐ Vincent: The Life and Death of Vincent Van Gogh ☐ Woman's Tale, A

Craven, Wes ☐ Deadly Blessing ☐ Deadly Friend ☐ Hills Have Eyes Part II, The ☐ Hills Have Eyes, The ☐ Invitation to Hell ☐ Last House on the Left, The ☐ Night Visions ☐ Nightmare on Elm Street, A ☐ People Under the Stairs ☐ Serpent and the Rainbow, The ☐ Shocker ☐ Swamp Thing ☐ Wes Craven's New Nightmare: The Real Story

Crichton, Charles ☐ Against the Wind ☐ Battle of the Sexes, The ☐ Boy Who Stole a Million, The ☐ Dance Hall ☐ Dead of Night ☐ Decision Against Time ☐ Divided Heart, The ☐ Fish Called Wanda, A ☐ Floods of Fear ☐ For Those in Peril ☐ He Who Rides a Tiger ☐ Hue and Cry ☐ Lavender Hill Mob, The ☐ Love Lottery, The ☐ Third Secret, The ☐ Titfield Thunderbolt, The

Crichton, Michael ☐ Coma ☐ Great Train

Robbery, The ☐ Looker ☐ Physical Evidence ☐ Runaway ☐ Westworld
Cromwell, John ☐ Abe Lincoln In Illinois ☐ Algiers ☐ Ann Vickers ☐ Anna and the King of Siam ☐ Banjo on My Knee ☐ Caged ☐ Company She Keeps, The ☐ Dead Reckoning ☐ Enchanted Cottage, The ☐ For the Defense ☐ Fountain, The ☐ Goddess, The ☐ I Dream Too Much ☐ In Name Only ☐ Little Lord Fauntleroy ☐ Made for Each Other ☐ Matter of Morals, A ☐ Night Song ☐ Of Human Bondage ☐ Prisoner of Zenda, The ☐ Racket, The ☐ Rich Man's Folly ☐ Silver Cord, The ☐ Since You Went Away ☐ So Ends Our Night ☐ Son of Fury ☐ Spitfire ☐ This Man Is Mine ☐ Tom Sawyer ☐ Vice Squad ☐ Victory
Cronenberg, David ☐ Brood, The ☐ Dead Ringers ☐ Dead Zone, The ☐ Fly, The ☐ M. Butterfly ☐ Naked Lunch ☐ Rabid ☐ Scanners ☐ They Came from Within ☐ Videodrome
Cruze, James ☐ Covered Wagon, The ☐ David Harum ☐ Great Gabbo, The ☐ I Cover the Waterfront ☐ If I Had a Million ☐ Mr. Skitch ☐ Old Ironsides
Cukor, George ☐ Actress, The ☐ Adam's Rib ☐ Bhowani Junction ☐ Bill of Divorcement, A ☐ Blue Bird, The ☐ Born Yesterday ☐ Camille ☐ Chapman Report, The ☐ Corn Is Green, The ☐ David Copperfield ☐ Dinner at Eight ☐ Double Life, A ☐ Edward My Son ☐ Gaslight ☐ Girls About Town ☐ Grumpy ☐ Heller in Pink Tights ☐ Her Cardboard Lover ☐ Holiday ☐ It Should Happen to You ☐ Justine ☐ Keeper of the Flame ☐ Les Girls ☐ Let's Make Love ☐ Life of Her Own, A ☐ Little Women ☐ Love Among the Ruins ☐ Marrying Kind, The ☐ Model and the Marriage Broker, The ☐ My Fair Lady ☐ Our Betters ☐ Pat and Mike ☐ Philadelphia Story, The ☐ Rich and Famous ☐ Romeo and Juliet ☐ Royal Family of Broadway, The ☐ Song Without End ☐ Star Is Born, A ☐ Susan and God ☐ Sylvia Scarlett ☐ Travels with My Aunt ☐ Two-Faced Woman ☐ What Price Hollywood? ☐ Wild Is the Wind ☐ Winged Victory ☐ Woman's Face, A ☐ Women, The ☐ Zaza
Cummings, Irving ☐ Behind That Curtain ☐ Belle Starr ☐ Curly Top ☐ Dolly Sisters, The ☐ Double Dynamite ☐ Down Argentine Way ☐ Everything Happens at Night ☐ Girls' Dormitory ☐ Hollywood Cavalcade ☐ Impatient Years, The ☐ In Old Arizona ☐ Johnstown Flood, The ☐ Just Around the Corner ☐ Lillian Russell ☐ Little Miss Broadway ☐ Louisiana Purchase ☐ Merry Go Round of 1938 ☐ My Gal Sal ☐ Poor Little Rich Girl ☐ Springtime in the Rockies ☐ Story of Alexander Graham Bell, The ☐ Sweet Rosie O'Grady ☐ That Night in Rio ☐ Vogues of 1938
Curtiz, Michael ☐ 20,000 Years in Sing Sing ☐ Adventures of Huckleberry Finn, The ☐ Adventures of Robin Hood, The ☐ Angels with Dirty Faces ☐ Best Things in Life Are Free, The ☐ Black Fury ☐ Boy from Oklahoma, The ☐ Breaking Point ☐ Breath of Scandal, A ☐ Bright Leaf ☐ British Agent ☐ Cabin in the Cotton, The ☐ Captain Blood ☐ Captain of the Clouds ☐ Casablanca ☐ Case of the Curious Bride, The ☐ Charge of the Light Brigade, The ☐ Comancheros, The ☐ Daughters Courageous ☐ Dive Bomber ☐ Doctor X ☐ Dodge City ☐ Egyptian, The ☐ Female ☐ Flamingo Road ☐ Force of Arms ☐ Four Daughters ☐ Four Wives ☐ Four's a Crowd ☐ Francis of Assisi ☐ Front Page Woman ☐ Gold Is Where You Find It ☐ Hangman, The ☐ Helen Morgan Story, The ☐ I'll See You in My Dreams ☐ Janie ☐ Jazz Singer, The ☐ Jim Thorpe—All American ☐ Jimmy the Gent ☐ Kennel Murder Case, The ☐ Key, The ☐ Kid Galahad ☐ King Creole ☐ Lady Takes a Sailor, The ☐ Life with Father ☐ Mad Genius, The ☐ Mammy ☐ Man in the Net, The ☐ Man Killer ☐ Mandalay ☐ Mildred Pierce ☐ Mission to Moscow ☐ My Dream Is Yours ☐ Mystery of the Wax Museum, The ☐ Night and Day ☐ Noah's Ark ☐ Passage to Marseille ☐ Perfect Specimen, The ☐ Private Lives of Elizabeth and Essex, The ☐ Proud Rebel, The ☐ River's End ☐ Romance on the High Seas ☐ Santa Fe Trail ☐ Sea Hawk, The ☐ Sea Wolf, The ☐ Story of Will Rogers, The ☐ This Is the Army ☐ Trouble Along the Way ☐ Unsuspected, The ☐ Vagabond King, The ☐ Virginia City ☐ Walking Dead, The ☐ We're No Angels ☐ White Christmas ☐ Yankee Doodle Dandy ☐ Young Man with a Horn
Dante, Joe ☐ 'Burbs, The ☐ Amazon Women on the Moon ☐ Explorers ☐ Gremlins ☐ Gremlins 2—The New Batch ☐ Hollywood Boulevard ☐ Howling, The ☐ Innerspace ☐ Matinee ☐ Piranha ☐ Twilight Zone—The Movie
Dassin, Jules ☐ Brute Force ☐ Canterville Ghost, The ☐ Circle of Two ☐ Dream of Passion, A ☐ He Who Must Die ☐ Naked City, The ☐ Never on Sunday ☐ Night and the City ☐ Phaedra ☐ Promise at Dawn ☐ Reunion in France ☐ Rififi ☐ Topkapi
Daves, Delmer ☐ Badlanders, The ☐ Battle of the Villa Fiorita, The ☐ Bird of Paradise ☐ Broken Arrow ☐ Cowboy ☐ Dark Passage ☐ Demetrius and the Gladiators ☐ Destination Tokyo ☐ Drum Beat ☐ Hanging Tree, The ☐ Hollywood Canteen ☐ Jubal ☐ Kings Go Forth ☐ Kiss in the Dark, A ☐ Last Wagon, The ☐ Never Let Me Go ☐ Parrish ☐ Pride of the Marines ☐ Red House, The ☐ Return of the Texan ☐ Rome Adventure ☐ Susan Slade ☐ Spencer's Mountain ☐ Summer Place, A ☐ Task Force ☐ To the Victor ☐ Treasure of the Golden Condor ☐ Youngblood Hawke

Davies, Terence ☐ Distant Voices, Still Lives ☐ Long Day Closes, The
Davis, Andrew ☐ Above the Law ☐ Code of Silence ☐ Final Terror, The ☐ Fugitive, The ☐ Package, The ☐ Under Siege
De Broca, Philippe ☐ Cartouche ☐ Devil By the Tail, The ☐ Five Day Lover ☐ Give Her the Moon ☐ King of Hearts ☐ Le Cavaleur ☐ Le Magnifique ☐ 7 Capital Sins ☐ Up to His Ears
De Sica, Vittorio ☐ After the Fox ☐ Bicycle Thief, The ☐ Boccaccio Ô70 ☐ Brief Vacation, A ☐ Condemned of Altona, The ☐ Fast and Sexy ☐ Garden of the Finzi-Continis, The ☐ Gold of Naples, The ☐ Indiscretion of an American Wife ☐ Marriage Italian Style ☐ Miracle in Milan ☐ Place for Lovers, A ☐ Shoeshine ☐ Sunflower ☐ Two Women ☐ Umberto D. ☐ Woman Times Seven ☐ Yesterday, Today and Tomorrow
De Toth, Andre ☐ Bounty Hunter, The ☐ Carson City ☐ Dark Waters ☐ Gold for the Caesars ☐ Hidden Fear ☐ House of Wax ☐ Indian Fighter, The ☐ Last of the Comanches ☐ Man in the Saddle ☐ Man on a String ☐ Monkey on My Back ☐ Morgan the Pirate ☐ None Shall Escape ☐ Passport to Suez ☐ Pitfall, The ☐ Play Dirty ☐ Springfield Rifle
Dearden, Basil ☐ All Night Long ☐ Assassination Bureau, The ☐ Blue Lamp, The ☐ Cage of Gold ☐ Captive Heart, The ☐ Dead of Night ☐ Frieda ☐ Gentle Gunman, The ☐ Halfway House, The ☐ I Believe in You ☐ Khartoum ☐ League of Gentlemen, The ☐ Man in the Moon, The ☐ Man Who Haunted Himself, The ☐ Masquerade ☐ Mind Benders, The ☐ My Learned Friend ☐ Only When I Larf ☐ Pool of London ☐ Rainbow Jacket, The ☐ Sapphire ☐ Saraband ☐ Ship That Died Of Shame, The ☐ Smallest Show on Earth, The ☐ Square Ring, The ☐ They Came to a City ☐ Victim ☐ Violent Playground ☐ Who Done It? ☐ Woman of Straw
Del Ruth, Roy ☐ About Face ☐ Always Leave Them Laughing ☐ Babe Ruth Story, The ☐ Barbary Coast Gent ☐ Blessed Event ☐ Blonde Crazy ☐ Born to Dance ☐ Broadway Melody of 1936 ☐ Broadway Melody of 1938 ☐ Broadway Rhythm ☐ Bureau of Missing Persons ☐ Captured ☐ Chocolate Soldier, The ☐ Employees' Entrance ☐ Folies Berg_re ☐ Gold Diggers of Broadway ☐ Happy Landing ☐ He Married His Wife ☐ Here I Am a Stranger ☐ Hold Everything ☐ It Had to Happen ☐ It Happened on Fifth Avenue ☐ Kid Millions ☐ Lady Killer ☐ Little Giant, The ☐ Maisie Gets Her Man ☐ Maltese Falcon, The ☐ My Lucky Star ☐ My Past ☐ On Moonlight Bay ☐ On the Avenue ☐ Phantom of the Rue Morgue ☐ Starlift ☐ Taxi! ☐ Thanks a Million ☐ Three Faces East ☐ Three Sailors and a Girl ☐ Topper Returns ☐ Upperworld ☐ West Point Story ☐ Why Must I Die? ☐ Winner Take All
DeMille, Cecil B. ☐ Buccaneer, The ☐ Cleopatra ☐ Crusades, The ☐ Four Frightened People ☐ Greatest Show on Earth, The ☐ King of Kings ☐ Madam Satan ☐ Northwest Mounted Police ☐ Plainsman, The ☐ Reap the Wild Wind ☐ Samson and Delilah ☐ Sign of the Cross ☐ Squaw Man ☐ Story of Dr. Wassell, The ☐ Ten Commandments, The (1923 and 1956) ☐ This Day and Age ☐ Unconquered ☐ Union Pacific
Demme, Jonathan ☐ Caged Heat ☐ Citizens Band ☐ Cousin Bobby ☐ Crazy Mama ☐ Fighting Mad ☐ Handle with Care ☐ Last Embrace ☐ Married to the Mob ☐ Melvin and Howard ☐ Philadelphia ☐ Silence of the Lambs, The ☐ Something Wild ☐ Stop Making Sense ☐ Swimming to Cambodia ☐ Swing Shift
Demy, Jacques ☐ Donkey Skin ☐ Lola ☐ Model Shop, The ☐ Pied Piper, The ☐ 7 Capital Sins ☐ Slightly Pregnant Man, A ☐ Umbrellas of Cherbourg ☐ Young Girls of Rochefort, The
DePalma, Brian ☐ Carrie ☐ Casualties of War ☐ Dressed to Kill ☐ Fury, The ☐ Get to Know Your Rabbit ☐ Blow Out ☐ Body Double ☐ Bonfire of the Vanities, The ☐ Carlito's Way ☐ Greetings ☐ Hi, Mom! ☐ Home Movies ☐ Phantom of the Paradise ☐ Raising Cain ☐ Scarface 1983 ☐ Sisters ☐ Untouchables, The ☐ Wedding Party, The ☐ Wise Guys
Deutch, Howard ☐ Article 99 ☐ Getting Even with Dad ☐ Great Outdoors, The ☐ Pretty in Pink ☐ Some Kind of Wonderful ☐ Tales from the Crypt
Deville, Michel ☐ Benjamin ☐ Dossier 51 ☐ La Lectrice ☐ La Petite Bande ☐ Le Voyage en Douce ☐ Love at the Top ☐ Peril
DeVito, Danny ☐ Hoffa ☐ Ratings Game, The ☐ Throw Momma from the Train ☐ War of the Roses, The
Dieterle, William ☐ Accused, The ☐ Another Dawn ☐ Blockade ☐ Boots Malone ☐ Dark City ☐ Devil and Daniel Webster, The ☐ Devil's in Love, The ☐ Dispatch from Reuter's, A ☐ Dr. Ehrlich's Magic Bullet ☐ Dr. Socrates ☐ Elephant Walk ☐ Fashions ☐ Fog Over Frisco ☐ Grand Slam ☐ Great O'Malley, The ☐ Her Majesty, Love ☐ Hunchback of Notre Dame, The ☐ I'll Be Seeing You ☐ Jewel Robbery ☐ Juarez ☐ Kismet ☐ Last Flight, The ☐ Lawyer Man ☐ Life of Emile Zola, The ☐ Love Letters ☐ Magic Fire ☐ Midsummer Night's Dream, A ☐ Mistress Of The World ☐ Omar Khayyam ☐ Paid in Full ☐ Peking Express ☐ Portrait of Jennie ☐ Quick, Let's Get Married ☐ Red Mountain ☐ Salome ☐ Satan Met a Lady ☐ Scarlet Dawn, The ☐ Secret Bride, The ☐ September Affair ☐ Story of Louis Pasteur, The ☐ Tennessee Johnson ☐ This Love of Ours ☐ Turning Point, The ☐ Volcano
Dmytryk, Edward ☐ Alverez Kelly ☐ Anzio

☐ Back to Bataan ☐ Behind the Rising Sun ☐ Blue Angel, The ☐ Bluebeard ☐ Broken Lance ☐ Caine Mutiny, The ☐ Captive Wild Woman ☐ Carpetbaggers, The ☐ Confessions of Boston Blackie ☐ Cornered ☐ Crossfire ☐ Devil Commands, The ☐ Eight Iron Men ☐ End of the Affair, The ☐ Falcon Strikes Back, The ☐ He Is My Brother ☐ Hidden Room, The ☐ Hitler's Children ☐ Human Factor, The ☐ Juggler, The ☐ Left Hand of God, The ☐ Mirage ☐ Mountain, The ☐ Murder My Sweet ☐ Raintree County ☐ Salt to the Devil ☐ Secrets of the Lone Wolf ☐ Seven Miles from Alcatraz ☐ Shalako ☐ So Well Remembered ☐ Soldier of Fortune ☐ Sweetheart of the Campus ☐ Tender Comrade ☐ Till the End of Time ☐ Walk on the Wild Side ☐ Warlock ☐ Where Love Has Gone ☐ Young Lions, The

Donaldson, Roger ☐ Bounty, The ☐ Cadillac Man ☐ Cocktail ☐ Getaway, The ☐ Marie ☐ No Way Out ☐ Smash Palace ☐ White Sands

Donen, Stanley ☐ Arabesque ☐ Bedazzled ☐ Blame It on Rio ☐ Charade ☐ Damn Yankees ☐ Deep in My Heart ☐ Fearless Fagan ☐ Funny Face ☐ Give a Girl a Break ☐ Grass Is Greener, The ☐ Indiscreet ☐ It's Always Fair Weather ☐ Kiss Them For Me ☐ Little Prince, The ☐ Love Is Better Than Ever ☐ Lucky Lady ☐ Movie Movie ☐ On the Town ☐ Once More, With Feeling ☐ Pajama Game, The ☐ Royal Wedding ☐ Saturn 3 ☐ Seven Brides for Seven Brothers ☐ Singin' in the Rain ☐ Staircase ☐ Surprise Package ☐ Two for the Road

Donner, Clive ☐ Alfred the Great ☐ Babes in Toyland ☐ Charlie Chan and the Curse of the Dragon Queen ☐ Christmas Carol, A ☐ Dead Man's Folly ☐ Guest, The ☐ Here We Go Round the Mulberry Bush ☐ Luv ☐ Merlin and the Sword ☐ Not a Penny More, Not a Penny Less ☐ Nothing But the Best ☐ Nude Bomb, The ☐ Old Dracula ☐ Oliver Twist ☐ Scarlet Pimpernel, The ☐ Stealing Heaven ☐ Terror Stalks the Class Reunion ☐ Thief of Bagdad ☐ What's New, Pussycat?

Donner, Richard ☐ Bronk ☐ Goonies, The ☐ Inside Moves ☐ Ladyhawke ☐ Lethal Weapon ☐ Lethal Weapon 2 ☐ Lethal Weapon 3 ☐ Lola ☐ Maverick ☐ Omen, The ☐ Radio Flyer ☐ Scrooged ☐ Superman—The Movie ☐ Tales from the Crypt ☐ Toy, The

Douglas, Gordon ☐ Barquero ☐ Between Midnight and Dawn ☐ Big Land, The ☐ Bombers B-52 ☐ Broadway Limited ☐ Call Me Bwana ☐ Charge at Feather River, The ☐ Chuka ☐ Claudelle Inglish ☐ Come Fill the Cup ☐ Detective, The ☐ Doolins of Oklahoma, The ☐ Falcon in Hollywood, The ☐ Fiend Who Walked the West, The ☐ First Yank into Tokyo ☐ Follow That Dream ☐ Fortunes of Captain Blood, The ☐ General Spanky ☐ Gildersleeve on Broadway ☐ Gildersleeve's Ghost ☐ Great Gildersleeve, The ☐ Girl Rush ☐ Great Missouri Raid, The ☐ Harlow ☐ I Was a Communist for the FBI ☐ If You Knew Susie ☐ In Like Flint ☐ Iron Mistress, The ☐ Lady in Cement ☐ Mara Maru ☐ McConnell Story, The ☐ Nevadan, The ☐ Night of Adventure, A ☐ Only the Valiant ☐ Rio Conchos ☐ Road Show ☐ Robin and the 7 Hoods ☐ San Quentin ☐ Santiago ☐ Saps at Sea ☐ She's Back on Broadway ☐ Sincerely Yours ☐ Skullduggery ☐ Slaughter's Big Rip—Off ☐ So This Is Love ☐ Stagecoach ☐ Them! ☐ They Call Me MISTER Tibbs! ☐ Tony Rome ☐ Up Periscope ☐ Viva Knievel! ☐ Walk a Crooked Mile ☐ Way...Way Out ☐ Young at Heart ☐ Zenobia ☐ Zombies on Broadway

Dreyer, Carl-Theodor ☐ Day of Wrath ☐ Gertrude ☐ Leaves from Satan's Book ☐ Master of the House ☐ Ordet ☐ Passion of Joan of Arc, The ☐ Vampyr

Duffell, Peter ☐ England Made Me ☐ Experience Preferred...but Not Essential ☐ Far Pavilions, The ☐ House That Dripped Blood, The ☐ Inside Out ☐ King of the Wind ☐ Letters to an Unknown Lover

Duigan, John ☐ Dimboola ☐ Far East ☐ Flirting ☐ Mouth to Mouth ☐ Romero ☐ Sirens ☐ Wide Sargasso Sea ☐ Winter of Our Dreams, The ☐ Year My Voice Broke, The

Duke, Bill ☐ Cemetery Club, The ☐ Deep Cover ☐ Johnnie Mae Gibson: FBI ☐ Maximum Security ☐ Rage in Harlem, A ☐ Sister Act 2: Back in the Habit

Duke, Daryl ☐ Florence Nightingale ☐ Griffin and Phoenix: A Love Story ☐ Hard Feelings ☐ I Heard the Owl Call My Name ☐ Payday ☐ Silent Partner, The ☐ Tai-Pan ☐ Thorn Birds, The

Duvivier, Julien ☐ Anna Karenina ☐ Deadlier than the Male ☐ Devil and the Ten Commandments, The ☐ End of a Day, The ☐ Escape from Yesterday ☐ Flesh and Fantasy ☐ Golem, The ☐ Golgotha ☐ Great Waltz, The ☐ Heart of a Nation, The ☐ Highway Pickup ☐ Holiday For Henrietta ☐ Impostor, The ☐ Le Golem: The Legend of Prague ☐ Little World of Don Camillo, The ☐ Lovers of Paris ☐ Lydia ☐ Man in the Raincoat, The ☐ On Trial ☐ Panique ☐ Pepe Le Moko ☐ Poil de Carotte ☐ Tales of Manhattan ☐ They Were Five ☐ Un Carnet de Bal

Dwan, Allan ☐ Abroad with Two Yanks ☐ Angel in Exile ☐ Around the World ☐ Belle Le Grand ☐ Brewster's Millions ☐ Cattle Queen of Montana ☐ Chances ☐ Enchanted Island ☐ Escape to Burma ☐ Flight Nurse ☐ Frontier Marshal ☐ Getting Gertie's Garter ☐ Gorilla, The ☐ Heidi ☐ Here We Go Again ☐ High Tension ☐ Hold Back the Night ☐ I Dream of Jeannie ☐ Inside Story, The ☐ Iron Mask, The ☐ Josette ☐ Look Who's Laughing ☐ Man to Man ☐ Montana Belle ☐ Most Dangerous Man Alive, The ☐ Northwest Outpost ☐ Passion ☐ Pearl of the South Pacific ☐ Rebecca of Sunnybrook Farm ☐ Rendezvous with Annie ☐ Rise and Shine ☐ River's Edge, The ☐ Robin Hood ☐ Sands of Iwo Jima ☐ Silver Lode ☐ Slightly Scarlet ☐ Suez ☐ Tennessee's Partner ☐ Three Musketeers, The ☐ Up in Mabel's Room ☐ Wild Blue Yonder, The ☐ Young People

Eastwood, Clint ☐ Bird ☐ Breezy ☐ Bronco Billy ☐ Eiger Sanction, The ☐ Firefox ☐ Gauntlet, The ☐ Heartbreak Ridge ☐ High Plains Drifter ☐ Honkytonk Man ☐ Outlaw—Josey Wales, The ☐ Pale Rider ☐ Perfect World, A ☐ Play Misty for Me ☐ Rookie, The ☐ Sudden Impact ☐ Unforgiven ☐ White Hunter, Black Heart

Edwards, Blake ☐ Blind Date ☐ Breakfast at Tiffany's ☐ Bring Your Smile Along ☐ Carey Treatment, The ☐ Curse of the Pink Panther ☐ Darling Lili ☐ Days of Wine and Roses ☐ Experiment in Terror ☐ Fine Mess, A ☐ Great Race, The ☐ Gunn ☐ He Laughed Last ☐ High Time ☐ Justin Case ☐ Man Who Loved Women, The ☐ Micki + Maude ☐ Mister Cory ☐ Operation Petticoat ☐ Party, The ☐ Perfect Furlough, The ☐ Peter Gunn ☐ Pink Panther Strikes Again, The ☐ Pink Panther, The ☐ Return of the Pink Panther, The ☐ Revenge of the Pink Panther ☐ S.O.B. ☐ Shot in the Dark, A ☐ Skin Deep ☐ Son of the Pink Panther ☐ Sunset ☐ Switch ☐ Tamarind Seed, The ☐ 10 ☐ That's Life! ☐ This Happy Feeling ☐ Trail of the Pink Panther ☐ Victor/Victoria ☐ What Did You Do in the War, Daddy? ☐ Wild Rovers, The

Egoyan, Atom ☐ Adjuster, The ☐ Family Viewing

Eisenstein, Sergei ☐ Alexander Nevsky ☐ Battleship Potemkin ☐ General Line, The ☐ Ivan the Terrible, Part One ☐ Ivan the Terrible, Part Two ☐ October ☐ Strike

Farrow, John ☐ Alias Nick Beal ☐ Back from Eternity ☐ Beyond Glory ☐ Big Clock, The ☐ Bill of Divorcement, A ☐ Blaze of Noon ☐ Botany Bay ☐ Broadway Musketeers ☐ Bullet is Waiting, A ☐ Calcutta ☐ California ☐ China ☐ Commandos Strike at Dawn, The ☐ Copper Canyon ☐ Easy Come, Easy Go ☐ Five Came Back ☐ Full Confession ☐ His Kind of Woman ☐ Hitler Gang, The ☐ Hondo ☐ Invisible Menace, The ☐ John Paul Jones ☐ Night Has a Thousand Eyes ☐ Plunder of the Sun ☐ Red, Hot and Blue ☐ Reno ☐ Saint Strikes Back, The ☐ Sea Chase, The ☐ Sorority House ☐ Submarine Command ☐ Two Years Before the Mast ☐ Unholy Wife, The ☐ Wake Island ☐ West of Shanghai ☐ Where Danger Lives

Fassbinder, Rainer Werner ☐ Ali—Fear Eats the Soul ☐ American Soldier, The ☐ Berlin Alexanderplatz ☐ Beware of a Holy Whore ☐ Bitter Tears of Petra Von Kant, The ☐ Chinese Roulette ☐ Despair ☐ Effi Briest ☐ Fox and His Friends ☐ Gods of the Plague ☐ I Only Want You to Love Me ☐ In a Year of Thirteen Moons ☐ Jail Bait ☐ Katzelmacher ☐ Lili Marleen ☐ Lola ☐ Marriage of Maria Braun, The ☐ Merchant of Four Seasons, The ☐ Mother Kusters Goes to Heaven ☐ Querelle ☐ Stationmaster's Wife, The ☐ Third Generation, The ☐ Veronika Voss ☐ Why Does Herr R. Run Amok?

Fellini, Federico ☐ 8 1/2 ☐ Amarcord ☐ And the Ship Sails On ☐ Boccaccio '70 ☐ City of Women ☐ Fellini Satyricon ☐ Clowns, The ☐ Fellini's Casanova ☐ Fellini's Roma ☐ Ginger and Fred ☐ I Vitelloni ☐ Il Bidone ☐ Intervista ☐ Juliet of the Spirits ☐ La Dolce Vita ☐ La Strada ☐ Love in the City ☐ Nights of Cabiria ☐ Orchestra Rehearsal ☐ Spirits of the Dead ☐ Variety Lights ☐ White Sheik, The

Ferrara, Abel ☐ Bad Lieutenant ☐ Body Snatchers ☐ Cat Chaser ☐ China Girl ☐ Crime Story ☐ Dangerous Game ☐ Fear City ☐ Gladiator, The ☐ King of New York ☐ Ms. 45

Feyder, Jacques ☐ Carnival in Flanders ☐ Kiss, The ☐ Knight Without Armour

Figgis, Mike ☐ Browning Version, The ☐ Internal Affairs ☐ Liebestraum ☐ Mr. Jones ☐ Stormy Monday ☐ Women & Men: In Love there are No Rules

Fisher, Terence ☐ Astonished Heart, The ☐ Blackout ☐ Brides of Dracula ☐ Curse of Frankenstein, The ☐ Curse of the Werewolf, The ☐ Devil's Bride, The ☐ Dracula—Prince of Darkness ☐ Four Sided Triangle ☐ Frankenstein and the Monster from Hell ☐ Frankenstein Created Woman ☐ Frankenstein Must Be Destroyed! ☐ Girl in the Painting ☐ Gorgon, The ☐ Horror of Dracula ☐ Hound of the Baskervilles, The ☐ Island of Terror ☐ Island of the Burning Doomed ☐ Man Bait ☐ Man in Hiding ☐ Man Who Could Cheat Death, The ☐ Mummy, The ☐ Phantom of the Opera, The ☐ Race for Life ☐ Revenge of Frankenstein, The ☐ So Long at the Fair ☐ Stolen Face, A

Flaherty, Robert ☐ Elephant Boy ☐ Louisiana Story, The ☐ Man of Aran ☐ Moana ☐ Nanook of the North

Fleischer, Richard ☐ 20,000 Leagues Under the Sea ☐ Amityville 3-D ☐ Armored Car Robbery ☐ Ashanti: Land of No Mercy ☐ Bandido ☐ Barabbas ☐ Between Heaven and Hell ☐ Big Gamble, The ☐ Bodyguard ☐ Boston Strangler, The ☐ Che! ☐ Clay Pigeon, The ☐ Compulsion ☐ Conan the Destroyer ☐ Crack in the Mirror ☐ Crossed Swords ☐ Doctor Dolittle ☐ Don Is Dead, The ☐ Fantastic Voyage ☐ Follow Me Quietly ☐ Girl in the Red Velvet Swing, The ☐ Happy Time, The ☐ Incredible Sarah, The ☐ Jazz Singer, The ☐ Last Run, The ☐ Make Mine Laughs ☐ Mandingo ☐ Million Dollar Mystery ☐ Mr. Majestyk ☐ Narrow Margin, The ☐ New Centurions, The ☐ Red Sonja ☐ See

No Evil ☐ So This Is New York ☐ Soylent Green ☐ These Thousand Hills ☐ Tora! Tora! Tora! ☐ Vikings, The ☐ Violent Saturday
Fleming, Victor ☐ Adventure ☐ Bombshell ☐ Captains Courageous ☐ Dr. Jekyll and Mr. Hyde ☐ Farmer Takes a Wife, The ☐ Gone with the Wind ☐ Guy Named Joe, A ☐ Joan of Arc ☐ Reckless ☐ Red Dust ☐ Test Pilot ☐ Tortilla Flat ☐ Treasure Island ☐ Virginian, The ☐ Way of All Flesh, The ☐ Wet Parade, The ☐ White Sister, The ☐ Wizard of Oz, The
Florey, Robert ☐ Beast with Five Fingers, The ☐ Cocoanuts, The ☐ Danger Signal ☐ Dangerous to Know ☐ Dangerously They Live ☐ Daughter of Shanghai ☐ Ex-Lady ☐ Face Behind the Mask, The ☐ Florentine Dagger, The ☐ God is My Co-Pilot ☐ Hollywood Boulevard ☐ Hotel Imperial ☐ I Am a Thief ☐ Johnny One Eye ☐ King of Alcatraz ☐ Magnificent Fraud, The ☐ Man from Frisco, The ☐ Meet Boston Blackie ☐ Murders in the Rue Morgue ☐ Outcast ☐ Outpost in Morocco ☐ Tarzan and the Mermaids
Flynn, John ☐ Best Seller ☐ Brainscan ☐ Defiance ☐ Jerusalem File, The ☐ Lock Up ☐ Marilyn: The Untold Story ☐ Nails ☐ Out for Justice ☐ Outfit, The ☐ Rolling Thunder ☐ Scam ☐ Sergeant, The
Foley, James ☐ After Dark, My Sweet ☐ At Close Range ☐ Glengarry Glen Ross ☐ Reckless ☐ Two Bits ☐ Who's That Girl?
Forbes, Bryan ☐ Better Late Than Never ☐ Endless Game, The ☐ I Am a Dancer ☐ International Velvet ☐ King Rat ☐ L-Shaped Room, The ☐ Long Ago Tomorrow ☐ Madwoman of Chaillot, The ☐ Naked Face, The ☐ Seance on a Wet Afternoon ☐ Slipper and the Rose, The ☐ Stepford Wives, The ☐ Whisperers, The ☐ Whistle Down the Wind ☐ Wrong Box, The
Ford, John ☐ Air Mail ☐ Arrowsmith ☐ Battle of Midway ☐ Black Watch, The ☐ Cheyenne Autumn ☐ December 7th—The Movie ☐ Donovan's Reef ☐ Dr. Bull ☐ Drums Along the Mohawk ☐ Flesh ☐ Fort Apache ☐ Four Men and a Prayer ☐ Four Sons ☐ Fugitive, The ☐ Gideon of Scotland Yard ☐ Grapes of Wrath, The ☐ Hangman's House ☐ Horse Soldiers, The ☐ How Green Was My Valley ☐ How the West Was Won ☐ Hurricane, The ☐ Informer, The ☐ Iron Horse, The ☐ Judge Priest ☐ Last Hurrah, The ☐ Long Gray Line, The ☐ Long Voyage Home, The ☐ Lost Patrol, The ☐ Man Who Shot Liberty Valance, The ☐ Mary of Scotland ☐ Men without Women ☐ Mister Roberts ☐ Mogambo ☐ My Darling Clementine ☐ Pilgrimage ☐ Plough and the Stars, The ☐ Prisoner of Shark Island, The ☐ Quiet Man, The ☐ Rio Grande ☐ Rising of the Moon, The ☐ Salute ☐ Searchers, The ☐ Seas Beneath, The ☐ Sergeant Rutledge ☐ She Wore a Yellow Ribbon ☐ Stagecoach ☐ Steamboat 'Round the Bend ☐ Sun Shines Bright, The ☐ They Were Expendable ☐ Three Godfathers, The ☐ Tobacco Road ☐ Two Rode Together ☐ Up the River ☐ Up the River ☐ Wagon Master ☐ Wee Willie Winkie ☐ What Price Glory? ☐ When Willie Comes Marching Home ☐ Whole Town's Talking, The ☐ Wings of Eagles, The ☐ Young Cassidy ☐ Young Mr. Lincoln
Forman, Milos ☐ Amadeus ☐ Firemen's Ball, The ☐ Hair ☐ Loves of a Blonde ☐ One Flew Over the Cuckoo's Nest ☐ Ragtime ☐ Taking Off ☐ Valmont ☐ Visions of Eight
Forsyth, Bill ☐ Breaking In ☐ Comfort and Joy ☐ Gregory's Girl ☐ Housekeeping ☐ Local Hero ☐ That Sinking Feeling
Fosse, Bob ☐ All That Jazz ☐ Cabaret ☐ Lenny ☐ Star 80 ☐ Sweet Charity
Francis, Freddie ☐ Brain, The ☐ Creeping Flesh, The ☐ Doctor and the Devils, The ☐ Dr. Terror's House of Horrors ☐ Dracula Has Risen From the Grave ☐ Evil of Frankenstein, The ☐ Ghoul, The ☐ Girly ☐ Hysteria ☐ Legend of the Werewolf ☐ Paranoiac ☐ Psychopath, The ☐ Skull, The ☐ Tales from the Crypt ☐ Torture Garden ☐ Trog ☐ Vampire Happening, The
Franco, Jess ☐ Awful Dr. Orloff, The ☐ Castle of Fu Manchu ☐ Count Dracula ☐ Deadly Sanctuary ☐ Night of the Blood Monster ☐ Venus in Furs
Franju, Georges ☐ Horror Chamber of Dr. Faustus, The ☐ Judex ☐ Keepers, The
Frankenheimer, John ☐ 52 Pick-Up ☐ All Fall Down ☐ Birdman of Alcatraz ☐ Black Sunday ☐ Challenge, The ☐ Dead-Bang ☐ Extraordinary Seaman, The ☐ Fixer, The ☐ Fourth War, The ☐ French Connection II ☐ Grand Prix ☐ Gypsy Moths, The ☐ Holcroft Covenant, The ☐ Horsemen, The ☐ I Walk the Line ☐ Iceman Cometh, The ☐ Impossible Object ☐ Manchurian Candidate, The ☐ Prophecy ☐ Seconds ☐ Seven Days in May ☐ Train, The ☐ Year of the Gun ☐ Young Savages, The ☐ Young Stranger, The
Franklin, Carl ☐ Full Fathom Five ☐ One False Move
Franklin, Richard ☐ Cloak & Dagger ☐ F/X2 ☐ Link ☐ Patrick ☐ Psycho 2 ☐ Road Games
Frawley, James ☐ Assault and Matrimony ☐ Big Bus, The ☐ Christian Licorice Store, The ☐ Fraternity Vacation ☐ Great American Traffic Jam, The ☐ Gridlock ☐ Kid Blue ☐ Muppet Movie, The
Frears, Stephen ☐ Dangerous Liaisons ☐ Grifters, The ☐ Gumshoe ☐ Hero ☐ Hit, The ☐ My Beautiful Laundrette ☐ Prick Up Your Ears ☐ Sammy and Rosie ☐ Snapper, The
Friedkin, William ☐ Birthday Party, The ☐ Blue Chips ☐ Boys in the Band, The ☐ Brink's Job, The ☐ Cruising ☐ Deal of the Century ☐ Exorcist, The ☐ French Connection, The ☐ Good Times ☐ Guardian, The

☐ Night They Raided Minsky's, The ☐ Python Wolf ☐ Rampage ☐ Sorcerer ☐ Stalking Danger ☐ To Live and Die in L.A.

Fuller, Samuel ☐ Baron of Arizona, The ☐ Big Red One, The ☐ China Gate ☐ Crimson Kimono, The ☐ Fixed Bayonets ☐ Forty Guns ☐ Hell and High Water ☐ Hot Lead ☐ House of Bamboo ☐ I Shot Jesse James ☐ Meanest Men in the West, The ☐ Merrill's Marauders ☐ Naked Kiss, The ☐ Park Row ☐ Pickup on South Street ☐ Shark! ☐ Shock Corridor ☐ Steel Helmet, The ☐ Underworld U.S.A. ☐ Verboten! ☐ White Dog

Furie, Sidney J. ☐ Appaloosa, The ☐ Boys, The ☐ Boys in Company C, The ☐ Doctor Blood's Coffin ☐ Entity, The ☐ Gable and Lombard ☐ Hit ☐ Ipcress File, The ☐ Iron Eagle ☐ Iron Eagle II ☐ Lady Sings the Blues ☐ Ladybugs ☐ Leather Boys, The ☐ Little Fauss and Big Halsy ☐ Naked Runner, The ☐ Purple Hearts ☐ Sheila Levine is Dead and Living in New York ☐ Superman 4: The Quest for Peace ☐ Taking of Beverly Hills, The

Gance, Abel ☐ Battle of Austerlitz, The (1919 and 1937) ☐ Beethoven's Great Love ☐ J'Accuse ☐ Napoleon

Garnett, Tay ☐ Bad Company ☐ Bataan ☐ Black Knight, The ☐ Cattle King ☐ Cause for Alarm ☐ Challenge to Be Free ☐ Cheers for Miss Bishop ☐ China Seas ☐ Connecticut Yankee in King Arthur's Court ☐ Cross of Lorraine, The ☐ Eternally Yours ☐ Fireball, The ☐ Joy of Living ☐ Love Is News ☐ Main Street to Broadway ☐ Mrs. Parkington ☐ Night Fighters, The ☐ One Minute to Zero ☐ One Way Passage ☐ Postman Always Rings Twice, The ☐ Professional Soldier ☐ S.O.S. Iceberg ☐ Seven Sinners ☐ She Couldn't Take It ☐ Slave Ship ☐ Slightly Honorable ☐ Soldiers Three ☐ Stand-In ☐ Trade Winds ☐ Valley of Decision, The ☐ Wild Harvest

Garris, Mick ☐ Critters 2 ☐ Psycho IV: The Beginning ☐ Stand, The ☐ Stephen King's Sleepwalkers

Germi, Pietro ☐ Alfredo, Alfredo ☐ Birds, The Bees and the Italians, The ☐ Divorce—Italian Style ☐ Facts of Murder, The ☐ Four Ways Out ☐ Man of Iron ☐ Seduced and Abandoned ☐ Serafino

Gilliam, Terry ☐ Adventures of Baron Munchausen, The ☐ Brazil ☐ Fisher King, The ☐ Jabberwocky ☐ Monty Python and the Holy Grail ☐ Time Bandits

Godard, Jean-Luc ☐ Alphaville ☐ Aria ☐ Band of Outsiders ☐ Breathless ☐ Contempt ☐ Detective ☐ Every Man for Himself ☐ First Name: Carmen ☐ King Lear ☐ La Chinoise ☐ Le Gai Savior ☐ Le Petit Soldat ☐ Les Carabiniers ☐ Married Woman, A ☐ Masculine-Feminine ☐ My Life to Live ☐ Nouvelle Vague ☐ Numero Deux ☐ Passion ☐ Pierrot le Fou ☐ Tout Va Bien ☐ Weekend ☐ Woman Is a Woman, A

Golan, Menahem ☐ Delta Force, The ☐ Diamonds ☐ Enter the Ninja ☐ Escape to the Sun ☐ Hanna's War ☐ Hit the Dutchman ☐ Kazablan ☐ Lepke ☐ Lupo ☐ Magician of Lublin, The ☐ My Margo ☐ Over the Brooklyn Bridge ☐ Over the Top ☐ Silent Victim

Gordon, Bert I. ☐ Amazing Colossal Man, The ☐ Attack of the Puppet People ☐ Boy and the Pirates ☐ Beginning of the End ☐ Big Bet, The ☐ Earth vs. the Spider ☐ Empire of the Ants ☐ Food of the Gods, The ☐ King Dinosaur ☐ Mad Bomber, The ☐ Magic Sword, The ☐ Picture Mommy Dead ☐ War of the Colossal Beast, The

Gordon, Stuart ☐ Daughter of Darkness ☐ Dolls ☐ Fortress ☐ From Beyond ☐ Pit and the Pendulum, The ☐ Re-Animator ☐ Robot Jox

Goulding, Edmund ☐ Blondie of the Follies ☐ Claudia ☐ Constant Nymph, The ☐ Dark Victory ☐ Dawn Patrol, The ☐ Down Among the Sheltering Palms ☐ Everybody Does It ☐ Flame Within, The ☐ Grand Hotel ☐ Great Lie, The ☐ Love ☐ Mardi Gras ☐ Mister 880 ☐ Nightmare Alley ☐ Old Maid, The ☐ Paramount on Parade ☐ Razor's Edge, The ☐ Reaching for the Moon ☐ Riptide ☐ That Certain Woman ☐ 'Til We Meet Again ☐ Trespasser, The ☐ We Are Not Alone ☐ We're Not Married

Green, Alfred E. ☐ Adventure in Washington ☐ Baby Face ☐ Badlands of Dakota ☐ Colleen ☐ Copacabana ☐ Dangerous ☐ Dark Hazard ☐ Dark Horse ☐ Disraeli ☐ Duke of West Point, The ☐ East of the River ☐ Eddie Cantor Story, The ☐ Ella Cinders ☐ Fabulous Dorseys, The ☐ Flowing Gold ☐ Four Faces West ☐ Girl from 10th Avenue, The ☐ Girl from Manhattan, The ☐ Golden Arrow, The ☐ Goose and the Gander, The ☐ Gracie Allen Murder Case, The ☐ Green Goddess, The ☐ Housewife ☐ I Loved a Woman ☐ Invasion, U.S.A. ☐ It's Tough to Be Famous ☐ More Than a Secretary ☐ Smart Money ☐ Jackie Robinson Story, The ☐ Jolson Story, The ☐ Meet the Stewarts ☐ Mr. Winkle Goes to War ☐ Narrow Corner, The ☐ Old English ☐ Parachute Jumper ☐ Paris Model ☐ Silver Dollar ☐ South of Pago Pago ☐ Tars and Spars ☐ Thoroughbreds Don't Cry ☐ Thousand and One Nights, A ☐ Top Banana ☐ Union Depot

Griffith, D.W. ☐ Abraham Lincoln ☐ America ☐ Birth of a Nation, The ☐ Broken Blossoms ☐ Home Sweet Home ☐ Hearts of the World ☐ Intolerance ☐ Judith of Bethulia ☐ Lady of the Pavement ☐ Love Flower, The ☐ Musketeers of Pig Alley & Selected Biograph Shorts ☐ Orphans of the Storm ☐ True-Heart Susie

Guitry, Sacha ☐ Napoleon ☐ Pearls of the Crown ☐ Royal Affairs in Versailles

Gyllenhaal, Stephen ☐ Certain Fury ☐ Dangerous Woman, A ☐ Promised a Miracle

☐ Family of Spies ☐ Killing in a Small Town, A ☐ Losing Isaiah ☐ Paris Trout ☐ Question of Faith ☐ Waterland

Hall, Alexander ☐ Amazing Mr. Williams ☐ Because You're Mine ☐ Bedtime Story ☐ Doctor Takes a Wife, The ☐ Down to Earth ☐ Exclusive ☐ Forever Darling ☐ Girl in 419 ☐ Goin' To Town ☐ Good Girls Go to Paris ☐ Great Lover, The ☐ He Stayed for Breakfast ☐ Heavenly Body, The ☐ Here Comes Mr. Jordan ☐ I Am the Law ☐ Let's Do It Again ☐ Limehouse Blues ☐ Little Miss Marker ☐ Louisa ☐ Love That Brute ☐ Madame Racketeer ☐ Miss Fane's Baby Is Stolen ☐ My Sister Eileen ☐ Once Upon a Time ☐ Sinners in the Sun ☐ There's Always a Woman ☐ They All Kissed the Bride ☐ This Thing Called Love ☐ Up Front ☐ Yours for the Asking

Harrington, Curtis ☐ Cat Creature, The ☐ Dead Don't Die, The ☐ Games ☐ How Awful About Allan ☐ Killer Bees ☐ Killing Kind, The ☐ Mata Hari ☐ Night Tide ☐ Queen of Blood ☐ Ruby ☐ What's the Matter with Helen?

Haskin, Byron ☐ Armored Command ☐ Boss, The ☐ Captain Sinbad ☐ Conquest of Space ☐ First Texan, The ☐ From the Earth to the Moon ☐ His Majesty O'Keefe ☐ I Walk Alone ☐ Jet Over the Atlantic ☐ Long John Silver ☐ Man-Eater of Kumaon ☐ Naked Jungle, The ☐ Power, The ☐ Robinson Crusoe on Mars ☐ Silver City ☐ Too Late for Tears ☐ Treasure Island ☐ War of the Worlds, The ☐ Warpath

Hathaway, Henry ☐ 13 Rue Madeleine ☐ 23 Paces to Baker Street ☐ Black Rose, The ☐ Bottom of the Bottle, The ☐ Brigham Young ☐ Call Northside 777 ☐ China Girl ☐ Circus World ☐ Dark Corner, The ☐ Desert Fox, The ☐ Diplomatic Courier ☐ Down to the Sea in Ships ☐ Five Card Stud ☐ Fourteen Hours ☐ From Hell to Texas ☐ Garden of Evil ☐ Go West, Young Man ☐ Hangup ☐ Heritage of the Desert ☐ Home in Indiana ☐ House on 92nd Street ☐ How the West Was Won ☐ Johnny Apollo ☐ Kiss of Death ☐ Last Safari, The ☐ Legend of the Lost ☐ Lives of a Bengal Lancer, The ☐ Man of The Forest ☐ Nevada Smith ☐ Niagara ☐ Nob Hill ☐ North to Alaska ☐ Now and Forever ☐ O. Henry's Full House ☐ Peter Ibbetson ☐ Prince Valiant ☐ Racers, The ☐ Raid on Rommel ☐ Rawhide ☐ Real Glory, The ☐ Seven Thieves ☐ Sheperd of the Hills ☐ Sons of Katie Elder ☐ Souls at Sea ☐ Spawn of the North ☐ Sundown ☐ Thundering Herd, The ☐ Trail of the Lonesome Pine, The ☐ True Grit ☐ White Witch Doctor ☐ Wing and a Prayer, A ☐ Woman Obsessed, A ☐ You're in the Navy Now

Hawks, Howard ☐ Air Force ☐ Ball of Fire ☐ Barbary Coast ☐ Big Sky, The ☐ Big Sleep, The ☐ Bringing Up Baby ☐ Ceiling Zero ☐ Come and Get It ☐ Criminal Code, The ☐ Crowd Roars, The ☐ Dawn Patrol, The ☐ El Dorado ☐ Fazil ☐ Gentlemen Prefer Blondes ☐ Girl in Every Port, A ☐ Hatari! ☐ His Girl Friday ☐ I Was a Male War Bride ☐ Land of the Pharoahs ☐ Man's Favorite Sport? ☐ Monkey Business ☐ O. Henry's Full House ☐ Only Angels Have Wings ☐ Red Line 7000 ☐ Red River ☐ Rio Bravo ☐ Rio Lobo ☐ Road to Glory, The ☐ Scarface ☐ Sergeant York ☐ Song Is Born, A ☐ Tiger Shark ☐ To Have and Have Not ☐ Today We Live ☐ Twentieth Century

Heisler, Stuart ☐ Along Came Jones ☐ Among the Living ☐ Beachhead ☐ Biscuit Eater, The ☐ Blue Skies ☐ Burning Hills, The ☐ Chain Lightning ☐ Dallas ☐ Glass Key, The ☐ Hitler ☐ I Died a Thousand Times ☐ Island of Desire ☐ Journey into Light ☐ Lone Ranger, The ☐ Monster and the Girl, The ☐ Remarkable Andrew, The ☐ Smash-Up, the Story of a Woman ☐ Star, The ☐ Storm Warning ☐ Tokyo Joe ☐ Tulsa

Hellman, Monte ☐ Back Door to Hell ☐ Beast from Haunted Cave ☐ China 9, Liberty 37 ☐ Cockfighter ☐ Flight to Fury ☐ Shooting, The ☐ Silent Night, Deadly Night (Part III-Better Watch Out!) ☐ Two-Lane Blacktop

Herzog, Werner ☐ Aguirre: The Wrath of God ☐ Even Dwarfs Started Small ☐ Every Man For Himself and God Against All ☐ Fata Morgana ☐ Fitzcarraldo ☐ Heart of Glass ☐ Herdsmen Of The Sun ☐ La Soufri_re ☐ Land of Silence and Darkness ☐ Nosferatu the Vampyre ☐ Where the Green Ants Dream ☐ Woyzeck

Hill, George ☐ Big House, The ☐ Clear All Wires ☐ Hell Divers ☐ Min and Bill ☐ Secret Six, The

Hill, George Roy ☐ Butch Cassidy and the Sundance Kid ☐ Funny Farm ☐ Great Waldo Pepper, The ☐ Hawaii ☐ Little Drummer Girl, The ☐ Little Romance, A ☐ Period of Adjustment ☐ Slap Shot ☐ Slaughterhouse-Five ☐ Sting, The ☐ Thoroughly Modern Millie ☐ Toys in the Attic ☐ World According to Garp, The ☐ World of Henry Orient, The

Hill, Walter ☐ 48 Hrs. ☐ Another 48 Hours ☐ Brewster's Millions ☐ Crossroads ☐ Driver, The ☐ Extreme Prejudice ☐ Geronimo: An American Legend ☐ Hard Times ☐ Johnny Handsome ☐ Long Riders, The ☐ Red Heat ☐ Southern Comfort ☐ Streets of Fire ☐ Trespass ☐ Warriors, The

Hiller, Arthur ☐ Americanization of Emily, The ☐ Author! Author! ☐ Babe, The ☐ Hospital, The ☐ In-Laws, The ☐ Lonely Guy, The ☐ Love Story ☐ Making Love ☐ Man in the Glass Booth, The ☐ Man of La Mancha ☐ Married to It ☐ Miracle of the White Stallions ☐ Nightwing ☐ Out-of-Towners, The ☐ Outrageous Fortune ☐ Penelope ☐ Plaza Suite ☐ Popi ☐ Promise Her Anything ☐ Romantic Comedy ☐ See No Evil, Hear No Evil ☐ Silver Streak ☐ Taking Care of Business ☐ Teachers ☐ Tiger Makes Out, The ☐ Tobruk ☐ W.C. Fields and Me ☐ Wheeler Dealers, The

Hillyer, Lambert ☐ Dracula's Daughter ☐ Fighting Frontier ☐ Fighting Ranger, The ☐ Invisible Ray, The ☐ Narrow Trail, The ☐ Royal Mounted Patrol, The

Hitchcock, Alfred ☐ Birds, The ☐ Blackmail ☐ Champagne ☐ Dial M for Murder ☐ Downhill ☐ Easy Virtue ☐ Family Plot ☐ Farmer's Wife, The ☐ Foreign Correspondent ☐ Frenzy ☐ Hitchcock Collection, The ☐ I Confess ☐ Jamaica Inn ☐ Juno and the Paycock ☐ Lady Vanishes, The ☐ Lifeboat ☐ Lodger, The ☐ Man Who Knew Too Much, The (1934, 1956) ☐ Manxman, The ☐ Marnie ☐ Mr. and Mrs. Smith ☐ Murder! ☐ North by Northwest ☐ Notorious ☐ Number Seventeen ☐ Paradine Case ☐ Pleasure Garden, The ☐ Psycho ☐ Rear Window ☐ Rebecca ☐ Rich and Strange ☐ Rope ☐ Sabotage ☐ Saboteur ☐ Secret Agent ☐ Shadow of a Doubt ☐ Skin Game, The ☐ Spellbound ☐ Stage Fright ☐ Strangers on a Train ☐ Suspicion ☐ 39 Steps, The ☐ To Catch a Thief ☐ Topaz ☐ Torn Curtain ☐ Trouble with Harry, The ☐ Under Capricorn ☐ Vertigo ☐ Wrong Man, The ☐ Young and Innocent

Hodges, Mike ☐ Black Rainbow ☐ Flash Gordon ☐ Florida Straits ☐ Get Carter ☐ Morons from Outer Space ☐ Prayer for the Dying, A ☐ Pulp ☐ Terminal Man, The

Holland, Agnieszka ☐ Angry Harvest ☐ Europa Europa ☐ Olivier, Olivier ☐ Secret Garden, The

Honda, Inoshiro ☐ Battle in Outer Space ☐ Frankenstein Conquers the World ☐ Ghidrah: The Three-Headed Monster ☐ Godzilla's Revenge ☐ Godzilla vs. Monster Zero ☐ Gorath ☐ H-Man, The ☐ Human Vapor, The ☐ King Kong vs. Godzilla ☐ Mothra ☐ Mysterians, The ☐ Rodan ☐ Terror of Mechagodzilla

Howard, Ron ☐ Backdraft ☐ Cocoon ☐ Far and Away ☐ Grand Theft Auto ☐ Gung Ho ☐ Night Shift ☐ Paper, The ☐ Parenthood ☐ Splash ☐ Willow

Howard, William K. ☐ Cat and the Fiddle, The ☐ Evelyn Prentice ☐ Fire Over England ☐ First Year, The ☐ Johnny Come Lately ☐ This Side of Heaven ☐ Valiant, The

Hudson, Hugh ☐ Chariots of Fire ☐ Greystoke: The Legend of Tarzan, Lord of the Apes ☐ Lost Angels ☐ Revolution

Hughes, John ☐ Breakfast Club, The ☐ Curly Sue ☐ Ferris Bueller's Day Off ☐ Planes, Trains & Automobiles ☐ She's Having a Baby ☐ Sixteen Candles ☐ Uncle Buck ☐ Weird Science

Hunter, Tim ☐ Lies of the Twins ☐ Paint It Black ☐ River's Edge ☐ Saint of Fort Washington, The ☐ Sylvester ☐ Tex

Huston, John ☐ Across the Pacific ☐ African Queen, The ☐ Annie ☐ Asphalt Jungle, The ☐ Battle of San Pietro, The ☐ Barbarian and the Geisha, The ☐ Beat the Devil ☐ Bible, The ☐ Casino Royale ☐ Colors of War, The ☐ Dead, The ☐ Fat City ☐ Freud ☐ Heaven Knows, Mr. Allison ☐ In This Our Life ☐ Key Largo ☐ Kremlin Letter, The ☐ Let There Be Light ☐ Life and Times of Judge Roy Bean, The ☐ List of Adrian Messenger, The ☐ Mackintosh Man, The ☐ Maltese Falcon, The ☐ Man Who Would Be King, The ☐ Misfits, The ☐ Moby Dick ☐ Moulin Rouge ☐ Night of the Iguana, The ☐ Phobia ☐ Prizzi's Honor ☐ Red Badge of Courage, The ☐ Reflections in a Golden Eye ☐ Roots of Heaven, The ☐ Treasure of the Sierra Madre, The ☐ Under the Volcano ☐ Unforgiven, The ☐ Victory ☐ Walk with Love and Death, A ☐ We Were Strangers ☐ Wise Blood

Ichaso, Leon ☐ Crossover Dreams ☐ El Super ☐ Fear Inside, The ☐ Sugar Hill

Ichikawa, Kon ☐ Actors Revenge, An ☐ Alone on the Pacific ☐ Burmese Harp, The ☐ Conflagration ☐ Fires on the Plain ☐ Her Brother ☐ Makioka Sisters, The ☐ Odd Obsession ☐ Outcast, The Tokyo Olympiad ☐ Visions of Eight

Imamura, Shohei ☐ Ballad of Narayama, The ☐ Black Rain ☐ Eijanaika ☐ Insect Woman

Inagaki, Hiroshi ☐ Chushingura ☐ Rickshaw Man, The ☐ Rise Against the Sword ☐ Samurai 1—Musashi Miyamoto ☐ Samurai 2—Duel At Ichijoji Temple ☐ Samurai 3—Duel At Ganryu Island ☐ Secret Scrolls (Part I) ☐ Secret Scrolls (Part II) ☐ Youth and His Amulet, The

Itami, Juzo ☐ Funeral, The ☐ Minbo, or the Gentle Art of Japanese Extortion ☐ Tampopo ☐ Taxing Woman's Return, A ☐ Taxing Woman, A

Ivory, James ☐ Autobiography of a Princess ☐ Bombay Talkie ☐ Bostonians, The ☐ Europeans, The ☐ Guru, The ☐ Heat and Dust ☐ Householder, The ☐ Howards End ☐ Hullabaloo Over Georgie and Bonnie's Pictures ☐ Jane Austen in Manhattan ☐ Maurice ☐ Mr. & Mrs. Bridge ☐ Quartet ☐ Remains of the Day ☐ Room with A View, A ☐ Roseland ☐ Shakespeare Wallah ☐ Slaves of New York ☐ Wild Party, The

Jackson, Mick ☐ Bodyguard, The ☐ Chattahoochee ☐ Clean Slate ☐ L.A. Story

Jaglom, Henry ☐ Always ☐ Babyfever ☐ Can She Bake a Cherry Pie? ☐ Eating ☐ National Lampoon Goes to the Movies ☐ New Year's Day ☐ Sitting Ducks ☐ Someone to Love

Jancso, Miklos ☐ Red and the White, The ☐ Rome Wants Another Caesar ☐ Round Up, The ☐ Winter Wind

Jarman, Derek ☐ Caravaggio (English Language) ☐ Edward II ☐ Jubilee ☐ Last of England, The ☐ Wittgenstein

Jarmusch, Jim ☐ Down by Law ☐ Mystery

Train ☐ Night on Earth ☐ Stranger than Paradise

Jewison, Norman ☐ Agnes of God ☐ And Justice for All ☐ Art of Love, The ☐ Best Friends ☐ Cincinnati Kid, The ☐ F.I.S.T. ☐ Fiddler on the Roof ☐ Forty Pounds of Trouble ☐ Gaily, Gaily ☐ In Country ☐ In the Heat of the Night ☐ Jesus Christ Superstar ☐ Moonstruck ☐ Only You ☐ Other People's Money ☐ Rollerball ☐ Russians are Coming! The Russians are Coming! The ☐ Send Me No Flowers ☐ Soldier's Story, A ☐ Thomas Crown Affair, The ☐ Thrill of It All, The

Joffe, Roland ☐ City of Joy ☐ Fat Man and Little Boy ☐ Killing Fields, The ☐ Mission, The

Johnson, Lamont ☐ Cattle Annie and Little Britches ☐ Crisis at Central High ☐ Dangerous Company ☐ Ernie Kovacs: Between the Laughter ☐ Escape from Iran: The Canadian Caper ☐ Execution of Private Slovik, The ☐ Fear on Trial ☐ Gore Vidal's Lincoln ☐ Groundstar Conspiracy, The ☐ Gunfight, A ☐ Last American Hero, The ☐ Life of the Party: The Story of Beatrice ☐ Lipstick ☐ McKenzie Break, The ☐ My Sweet Charlie ☐ Off the Minnesota Strip ☐ One on One ☐ Paul's Case ☐ Spacehunter: Adventures in the Forbidden Zone ☐ That Certain Summer ☐ Unnatural Causes ☐ Visit to a Chief's Son

Jones, David ☐ 84 Charing Cross Road ☐ Betrayal ☐ Christmas Wife, The ☐ Fire in the Dark ☐ Jacknife

Jordan, Neil ☐ Company of Wolves, The ☐ Crying Game, The ☐ Danny Boy ☐ High Spirits ☐ Interview with the Vampire ☐ Miracle, The ☐ Mona Lisa ☐ We're No Angels

Kadar, Jan ☐ Angel Levine, The ☐ Blue Hotel, The ☐ Freedom Road ☐ Lies My Father Told Me ☐ Other Side of Hell, The ☐ Shop on Main Street, The

Kagan, Jeremy ☐ Big Fix, The ☐ Chosen, The ☐ Conspiracy: The Trial of the Chicago 8 ☐ Courage ☐ Descending Angel ☐ Heroes ☐ Journey of Natty Gann, The ☐ Judge Dee and the Monastery Murder ☐ Katherine ☐ Sting II, The

Kaige, Chen ☐ Big Parade, The ☐ Farewell My Concubine ☐ Life on a String ☐ Yellow Earth

Kanin, Garson ☐ Bachelor Mother ☐ Great Man Votes, The ☐ Man to Remember, A ☐ My Favorite Wife ☐ They Knew What They Wanted ☐ Tom, Dick and Harry

Kaplan, Jonathan ☐ Accused, The ☐ Bad Girls ☐ Gentleman Bandit, The ☐ Girls of the White Orchid ☐ Heart Like a Wheel ☐ Immediate Family ☐ Love Field ☐ Mr. Billion ☐ Night Call Nurses ☐ Over the Edge ☐ Project X ☐ Student Teachers, The ☐ Truck Turner ☐ Unlawful Entry ☐ White Line Fever

Karlson, Phil ☐ Ben ☐ Big Cat, The ☐ Black Gold ☐ Brigand, The ☐ Brothers Rico, The ☐ Down Memory Lane ☐ Five Against the House ☐ Framed ☐ Gunman's Walk ☐ Hell to Eternity ☐ Hell's Island ☐ Hornet's Nest ☐ Iroquois Trail, The ☐ Kansas City Confidential ☐ Key Witness ☐ Kid Galahad ☐ Ladies of the Chorus ☐ Live Wires ☐ Mask of the Avenger ☐ 99 River Street ☐ Phenix City Story, The ☐ Rampage ☐ Scandal Sheet ☐ Scarface Mob, The ☐ Shanghai Cobra, The ☐ Silencers, The ☐ Swing Parade of 1946 ☐ Texas Rangers, The ☐ Thunderhoof ☐ Tight Spot ☐ Time for a Killing, A ☐ Walking Tall ☐ Wrecking Crew, The ☐ Young Doctors, The

Kasdan, Lawrence ☐ Accidental Tourist, The ☐ Big Chill, The ☐ Body Heat ☐ Grand Canyon ☐ I Love You to Death ☐ Silverado ☐ Wyatt Earp

Kaufman, Philip ☐ Fearless Frank ☐ Great Northfield, Minnesota Raid, The ☐ Invasion of the Body Snatchers ☐ Right Stuff, The ☐ Rising Sun ☐ Unbearable Lightness of Being, The ☐ Wanderers, The ☐ White Dawn, The

Kaurismaki, Aki ☐ Ariel ☐ I Hired a Contract Killer ☐ La Vie de Boh_me ☐ Leningrad Cowboys Go America ☐ Match Factory Girl, The

Kazan, Elia ☐ America, America ☐ Arrangement, The ☐ Baby Doll ☐ Boomerang! ☐ East of Eden ☐ Face in the Crowd, A ☐ Gentleman's Agreement ☐ Last Tycoon, The ☐ Man on a Tightrope ☐ On the Waterfront ☐ Panic in the Streets ☐ Pinky ☐ Sea of Grass, The ☐ Splendor in the Grass ☐ Streetcar Named Desire, A ☐ Tree Grows in Brooklyn, A ☐ Visitors, The ☐ Viva Zapata! ☐ Wild River

Keaton, Buster ☐ General, The ☐ Our Hospitality ☐ Sherlock, Jr. ☐ Seven Chances

Kelly, Gene ☐ Cheyenne Social Club, The ☐ Gigot ☐ Guide for the Married Man, A ☐ Happy Road, The ☐ Hello, Dolly! ☐ Invitation to the Dance ☐ It's Always Fair Weather ☐ On the Town ☐ Singin' in the Rain ☐ That's Entertainment, Part 2 ☐ Tunnel of Love, The

Kennedy, Burt ☐ Alamo, The—Thirteen Days to Glory ☐ All the Kind Strangers ☐ Big Bad John ☐ Canadians, The ☐ Dirty Dingus Magee ☐ Good Guys and the Bad Guys, The ☐ Hannie Caulder ☐ Killer Inside Me, The ☐ Mail Order Bride ☐ Money Trap, The ☐ More Wild, Wild West ☐ Ramblin' Man ☐ Return of the Magnificent Seven ☐ Rounders, The ☐ Sidekicks ☐ Suburban Commando ☐ Support Your Local Gunfighter ☐ Support Your Local Sheriff ☐ Train Robbers, The ☐ War Wagon, The ☐ Welcome to Hard Times

Kershner, Irvin ☐ Empire Strikes Back, The ☐ Eyes of Laura Mars ☐ Face in the Rain, A ☐ Fine Madness, A ☐ Flim Flam Man, The ☐ Hoodlum Priest, The ☐ Loving ☐ Luck of Ginger Coffey, The ☐ Never Say Never Again

☐ Raid on Entebbe ☐ Return of a Man Called Horse, The ☐ Robocop 2 ☐ S.P.Y.S. ☐ Stake-out on Dope Street ☐ Up the Sandbox

Kidron, Beeban ☐ Antonia & Jane ☐ Used People

Kieslowski, Krzysztof ☐ Blue ☐ Camera Buff ☐ Double Life of Veronique, The ☐ Trois Couleurs: Blanc ☐ Trois Couleurs: Rouge

King, Henry ☐ Alexander's Ragtime Band ☐ Bell for Adano, A ☐ Beloved Infidel ☐ Black Swan, The ☐ Bravados, The ☐ Captain from Castile ☐ Carousel ☐ Chad Hanna ☐ Country Doctor, The ☐ David and Bathsheba ☐ Deep Waters ☐ Gunfighter, The ☐ I'd Climb the Highest Mountain ☐ In Old Chicago ☐ Jesse James ☐ King of the Khyber Rifles ☐ Little Old New York ☐ Lloyd's of London ☐ Love Is a Many Splendored Thing ☐ Margie ☐ Marie Galante ☐ Maryland ☐ Merely Mary Ann ☐ O. Henry's Full House ☐ One More Spring ☐ Over the Hill ☐ Prince of Foxes ☐ Ramona ☐ Seventh Heaven ☐ She Goes to War ☐ Snows of Kilimanjaro, The ☐ Song of Bernadette, The ☐ Stanley and Livingstone ☐ State Fair ☐ Sun Also Rises, The ☐ Tender Is the Night ☐ This Earth Is Mine ☐ Twelve O'Clock High ☐ Untamed ☐ Wait 'Til the Sun Shines, Nellie ☐ Wilson ☐ Yank in the RAF, A

Kleiser, Randal ☐ All Together Now ☐ Big Top Pee-Wee ☐ Blue Lagoon ☐ Boy in the Plastic Bubble, The ☐ Flight of the Navigator ☐ Gathering, The ☐ Getting It Right ☐ Grandview, U.S.A. ☐ Grease ☐ Honey, I Blew Up the Kid ☐ Summer Lovers ☐ White Fang

Klimov, Elem ☐ Come and See ☐ Rasputin

Kobayashi, Masaki ☐ Harakiri ☐ Human Condition, The (Part One: No Great) ☐ Human Condition, The (Part Three: A Sold) ☐ Human Condition, The (Part Two: The Road) ☐ Kwaidan ☐ Rebellion

Konchalovsky, Andrei ☐ Duet for One ☐ Homer & Eddie ☐ Inner Circle, The ☐ Maria's Lovers ☐ Runaway Train ☐ Shy People ☐ Tango and Cash ☐ Uncle Vanya

Korda, Alexander ☐ Ideal Husband, An ☐ Marius ☐ Private Life of Henry VIII, The ☐ Rembrandt ☐ Reserved for Ladies ☐ That Hamilton Woman ☐ Vacation from Marriage ☐ Wedding Rehearsal

Korda, Zoltan ☐ Counter-Attack ☐ Cry the Beloved Country ☐ Drums ☐ Elephant Boy ☐ Four Feathers, The ☐ If I Were Rich ☐ Jungle Book ☐ Macomber Affair, The ☐ Sahara ☐ Sanders of the River ☐ Woman's Vengeance, A

Korty, John ☐ Alex and the Gypsy ☐ Autobiography of Miss Jane Pittman ☐ Baby Girl Scott ☐ Christmas Without Snow, A ☐ Class of Ô63 ☐ Deadly Business, A ☐ Ewok Adventure, The ☐ Eye on the Sparrow ☐ Farewell to Manzanar ☐ Forever ☐ Funnyman ☐ Getting Out ☐ Go Ask Alice ☐ Haunting Passion, The ☐ Oliver's Story ☐ People, The ☐ Silence ☐ Twice Upon a Time

Kotcheff, Ted ☐ Apprenticeship of Duddy Kravitz, The ☐ Billy Two Hats ☐ First Blood ☐ Folks! ☐ Fun with Dick and Jane ☐ Joshua Then and Now ☐ Life at the Top ☐ North Dallas Forty ☐ Outback ☐ Switching Channels ☐ Uncommon Valor ☐ Weekend at Bernie's ☐ Who Is Killing the Great Chefs of Europe? ☐ Winter People

Kramer, Stanley ☐ Bless the Beasts and Children ☐ Defiant Ones, The ☐ Domino Principle, The ☐ Guess Who's Coming to Dinner ☐ Inherit the Wind ☐ It's a Mad Mad Mad Mad World ☐ Judgment at Nuremberg ☐ Not as a Stranger ☐ Oklahoma Crude ☐ On the Beach ☐ Pride and the Passion, The ☐ R.P.M. ☐ Runner Stumbles, The ☐ Secret of Santa Vittoria, The ☐ Ship of Fools

Kubrick, Stanley ☐ 2001: A Space Odyessy ☐ Barry Lyndon ☐ Clockwork Orange, A ☐ Dr. Strangelove or: How I Learned to Stop Worrying and Love the Bomb ☐ Full Metal Jacket ☐ Killer's Kiss ☐ Killing, The ☐ Lolita ☐ Paths of Glory ☐ Shining, The ☐ Spartacus

Kurosawa, Akira ☐ Akira Kurosawa's Dreams ☐ Bad Sleep Well, The ☐ Dersu Uzala ☐ Dodes'ka-den ☐ Drunken Angel ☐ Hidden Fortress, The ☐ High and Low ☐ I Live in Fear ☐ Idiot, The ☐ Ikiru ☐ Kagemusha ☐ Lower Depths, The ☐ Most Beautiful, The ☐ No Regrets for Our Youth ☐ Ran ☐ Rashomon ☐ Red Beard ☐ Rhapsody in August ☐ Sanjuro ☐ Seven Samurai, The ☐ Stray Dog ☐ Throne of Blood ☐ Yojimbo

Kurys, Diane ☐ C'est la Vie ☐ Cocktail Molotov ☐ Entre Nous ☐ Love After Love ☐ Man in Love, A ☐ Peppermint Soda

La Cava, Gregory ☐ Affairs of Cellini ☐ Bed of Roses ☐ Feel My Pulse ☐ 5th Avenue Girl ☐ Gabriel over the White House ☐ Gallant Lady ☐ Half-Naked Truth, The ☐ His First Command ☐ Living in a Big Way ☐ My Man Godfrey ☐ Running Wild ☐ She Married Her Boss ☐ Stage Door ☐ Symphony of Six Million ☐ Unfinished Business ☐ What Every Woman Knows

Landis, John ☐ Amazon Women on the Moon ☐ American Werewolf in London, An ☐ Animal House ☐ Beverly Hills Cop III ☐ Blues Brothers, The ☐ Coming Soon ☐ Coming to America ☐ Innocent Blood ☐ Into the Night ☐ Kentucky Fried Movie, The ☐ Oscar ☐ Schlock ☐ Spies Like Us ☐ Three Amigos! ☐ Trading Places ☐ Twilight Zone—The Movie

Lang, Fritz ☐ American Guerilla in the Philippines ☐ Beyond a Reasonable Doubt ☐ Big Heat, The ☐ Blue Gardenia ☐ Clash by Night ☐ Cloak and Dagger ☐ Die Niebelungen ☐ Doctor Mabuse, the Gambler ☐ Doctor Socrates ☐ Fury ☐ Hangmen Also Die

☐ House by the River, The ☐ Human Desire ☐ Indian Tomb, The ☐ M ('M') ☐ Man Hunt ☐ Metropolis ☐ Ministry of Fear ☐ Moonfleet ☐ Rancho Notorious ☐ Return of Frank James, The ☐ Scarlet Street ☐ Secret Beyond the Door ☐ Spies ☐ Testament of Dr. Mabuse, The ☐ Thousand Eyes of Dr. Mabuse, The ☐ Western Union ☐ While the City Sleeps ☐ Woman in the Window, The ☐ You and Me ☐ You Only Live Once

Lautner, Georges ☐ Great Spy Chase, The ☐ La Cage aux Folles III: The Wedding ☐ My Other Husband

Lean, David ☐ Blithe Spirit ☐ Breaking the Sound Barrier ☐ Bridge on the River Kwai, The ☐ Brief Encounter ☐ Doctor Zhivago ☐ Great Expectations ☐ Hobson's Choice ☐ In Which We Serve ☐ Lawrence of Arabia ☐ Madeleine ☐ Oliver Twist ☐ One Woman's Story ☐ Passage to India, A ☐ Ryan's Daughter ☐ Summertime ☐ This Happy Breed

Lee, Rowland V. ☐ Captain Kidd ☐ Count of Monte Cristo, The ☐ Bridge of San Luis Rey, The ☐ Cardinal Richelieu ☐ Love from a Stranger ☐ Toast of New York, The ☐ Tower of London, The☐ Mother Carey's Chickens ☐ Mysterious Dr. Fu Manchu, The ☐ One Rainy Afternoon ☐ Service De Luxe ☐ Son of Frankenstein ☐ Zoo in Budapest

Lee, Spike ☐ Crooklyn ☐ Do the Right Thing ☐ Jungle Fever ☐ Malcolm X ☐ Mo' Better Blues ☐ School Daze ☐ She's Gotta Have It

Leigh, Mike ☐ Four Days in July ☐ High Hopes ☐ Life Is Sweet ☐ Meantime ☐ Naked

Leisen, Mitchell ☐ Arise My Love ☐ Artists and Models Abroad ☐ Bedevilled ☐ Behold My Wife ☐ Big Broadcast of 1937, The ☐ Big Broadcast of 1938, The ☐ Bride of Vengeance ☐ Captain Carey, U.S.A. ☐ Darling, How Could You ☐ Death Takes a Holiday ☐ Dream Girl ☐ Easy Living ☐ Four Hours to Kill ☐ Frenchman's Creek ☐ Girl Most Likely, The ☐ Golden Earrings ☐ Hands Across the Table ☐ Hold Back the Dawn ☐ I Wanted Wings ☐ Kitty ☐ Lady in the Dark ☐ Lady Is Willing, The ☐ Masquerade in Mexico ☐ Mating Season, The ☐ Midnight ☐ Murder at the Vanities ☐ No Man of Her Own ☐ No Time for Love ☐ Practically Yours ☐ Remember the Night ☐ Suddenly, It's Spring ☐ Swing High, Swing Low ☐ Take a Letter, Darling ☐ Thirteen Hours by Air ☐ To Each His Own ☐ Tonight We Sing

Lelouch, Claude ☐ And Now My Love ☐ Another Man, Another Chance ☐ Bandits ☐ Bolero ☐ Cat and Mouse ☐ Crook, The ☐ Edith and Marcel ☐ Happy New Year ☐ Live for Life ☐ Man and a Woman, A ☐ Man and a Woman, A: 20 Years Later ☐ To Be a Crook ☐ Visions of Eight

Leonard, Robert Z. ☐ After Office Hours ☐ B.F.'s Daughter ☐ Bachelor Father, The ☐ Bribe, The ☐ Cynthia ☐ Everything I Have Is Yours ☐ King's Thief, The ☐ Nancy Goes to Rio ☐ Peg o' My Heart ☐ Broadway Serenade ☐ Clown, The ☐ Dancing Lady ☐ Divorcee, The ☐ Duchess of Idaho ☐ Firefly, The ☐ Five and Ten ☐ Girl of the Golden West, The ☐ Great Ziegfeld, The ☐ Grounds for Marriage ☐ Her Twelve Men ☐ In the Good Old Summertime ☐ Kelly and Me ☐ Man from Down Under, The ☐ Marianne ☐ Marriage Is a Private Affair ☐ Maytime ☐ New Moon ☐ Piccadilly Jim ☐ Pride and Prejudice ☐ Secret Heart, The ☐ Stand by for Action ☐ Strange Interlude ☐ Susan Lenox: Her Fall and Rise ☐ We Were Dancing ☐ Weekend at the Waldorf ☐ When Ladies Meet ☐ Ziegfeld Girl

Leone, Sergio ☐ Colossus of Rhodes, The ☐ Duck, You Sucker ☐ Fistful of Dollars, A ☐ For a Few Dollars More ☐ Good, the Bad and the Ugly, The ☐ Once Upon a Time in America (Long Version) ☐ Once Upon a Time in the West

LeRoy, Mervyn ☐ Big City Blues ☐ Broadminded ☐ Devil at 4 O'Clock, The ☐ East Side, West Side ☐ Elmer the Great ☐ Escape ☐ FBI Story, The ☐ Five Star Final ☐ Fools for Scandal ☐ Gentleman's Fate ☐ Gold Diggers of 1933 ☐ Happiness Ahead ☐ Hard to Handle ☐ Hi, Nellie! ☐ High Pressure ☐ Home Before Dark ☐ Homecoming ☐ I Am a Fugitive from a Chain Gang ☐ I Found Stella Parish ☐ Johnny Eager ☐ King and the Chorus Girl, The ☐ Latin Lovers ☐ Little Caesar ☐ Little Women ☐ Lovely to Look At ☐ Madame Curie ☐ Majority of One, A ☐ Mary, Mary ☐ Million Dollar Mermaid ☐ Mister Roberts ☐ No Time For Sergeants ☐ Oil for the Lamps of China ☐ Page Miss Glory ☐ Quo Vadis ☐ Random Harvest ☐ Rose Marie ☐ Strange Lady in Town ☐ Sweet Adeline ☐ They Won't Forget ☐ Thirty Seconds Over Tokyo ☐ Three on a Match ☐ Top Speed ☐ Toward the Unknown ☐ Tugboat Annie ☐ Two Seconds ☐ Unholy Partners ☐ Wake Me When It's Over ☐ Waterloo Bridge ☐ Without Reservations

Lester, Mark L. ☐ Armed and Dangerous ☐ Bobbie Jo and the Outlaw ☐ Class of 1984 ☐ Class of 1999 ☐ Commando ☐ Extreme Justice ☐ Firestarter ☐ Gold of the Amazon Women ☐ Showdown in Little Tokyo ☐ Steel Arena

Lester, Richard ☐ Bed-Sitting Room, The ☐ Butch and Sundance: The Early Days ☐ Cuba ☐ Finders Keepers ☐ Four Musketeers, The ☐ Funny Thing Happened on the Way to the Forum, A ☐ Get Back ☐ Hard Day's Night, A ☐ Help! ☐ How I Won the War ☐ Juggernaut ☐ Knack, and How to Get It, The ☐ Mouse on the Moon, The ☐ Petulia ☐ Return of the Musketeers, The ☐ Ring-a-Ding Rhythm ☐ Ritz, The ☐ Robin and

Marian ☐ Royal Flash ☐ Superman 2 ☐ Superman 3 ☐ Three Musketeers, The

Levinson, Barry ☐ Avalon ☐ Bugsy ☐ Diner ☐ Disclosure ☐ Good Morning, Vietnam! ☐ Jimmy Hollywood ☐ Natural, The ☐ Rain Man ☐ Tin Men ☐ Toys ☐ Young Sherlock Holmes

Lewin, Albert ☐ Moon and Sixpence, The ☐ Pandora and the Flying Dutchman ☐ Picture of Dorian Gray, The ☐ Private Affairs of Bel Ami, The

Lewis, Jerry ☐ Bellboy, The ☐ Big Mouth, The ☐ Cracking Up ☐ Errand Boy, The ☐ Family Jewels, The ☐ Hardly Working ☐ Ladies Man ☐ Nutty Professor, The ☐ One More Time ☐ Patsy, The ☐ Three on a Couch

Lewis, Joseph H. ☐ Big Combo, The ☐ Bombs Over Burma ☐ Boys of the City, The ☐ Courage of the West ☐ Cry of the Hunted ☐ Desperate Search ☐ Falcon in San Francisco, The ☐ Gun Crazy ☐ Halliday Brand, The ☐ Invisible Ghost, The ☐ Lady Without Passport, A ☐ Lawless Street, A ☐ Mad Doctor of Market Street, The ☐ My Name Is Julia Ross ☐ Retreat, Hell! ☐ Seventh Cavalry ☐ So Dark the Night ☐ Swordsman, The ☐ Terror in a Texas Town ☐ Undercover Man, The

Lindsay-Hogg, Michael ☐ As Is ☐ Let It Be ☐ Little Match Girl, The ☐ Master Harold and the Boys ☐ Murder By Moonlight ☐ Nasty Habits ☐ Running Mate

Linklater, Richard ☐ Before Sunrise ☐ Dazed and Confused ☐ Slacker

Loach, Ken ☐ Family Life ☐ Hidden Agenda ☐ Gamekeeper, The ☐ Ladybird, Ladybird ☐ Looks and Smiles ☐ Poor Cow ☐ Raining Stones ☐ Riff Raff

Logan, Joshua ☐ Bus Stop ☐ Camelot ☐ Ensign Pulver ☐ Fanny ☐ I Met My Love Again ☐ Paint Your Wagon ☐ Picnic ☐ Sayonara ☐ South Pacific ☐ Tall Story

Losey, Joseph ☐ Accident ☐ Assassination of Trotsky, The ☐ Big Night, The ☐ Boom! ☐ Boy With Green Hair, The ☐ Chance Meeting ☐ Concrete Jungle, The ☐ Doll's House, A ☐ Eva ☐ Figures in a Landscape ☐ Finger of Guilt ☐ Galileo ☐ Go-Between, The ☐ Gypsy and the Gentleman, The ☐ King and Country ☐ La Truite ☐ Lawless, The ☐ M ☐ Modesty Blaise ☐ Mr. Klein ☐ Prowler, The ☐ Romantic Englishwoman, The ☐ Secret Ceremony ☐ Servant, The ☐ Sleeping Tiger, The ☐ Steaming ☐ Stranger on the Prowl ☐ These Are the Damned ☐ Time Without Pity

Lubitsch, Ernst ☐ Angel ☐ Bluebeard's Eighth Wife ☐ Broken Lullaby ☐ Cluny Brown ☐ Design for Living ☐ Heaven Can Wait ☐ Lady Windemere's Fan ☐ Love Parade, The ☐ Marriage Circle, The ☐ Merry Widow, The ☐ Monte Carlo ☐ Ninotchka ☐ One Arabian Night ☐ One Hour with You ☐ Passion ☐ Royal Scandal, A ☐ Shop Around the Corner, The ☐ Smiling Lieutenant, The ☐ Student Prince in Old Heidelberg, The ☐ That Lady in Ermine ☐ That Uncertain Feeling ☐ To Be or Not to Be ☐ Trouble in Paradise

Lucas, George ☐ American Graffiti ☐ Star Wars ☐ THX 1138

Lumet, Sidney ☐ Anderson Tapes, The ☐ Appointment, The ☐ Bye Bye Braverman ☐ Child's Play ☐ Daniel ☐ Deadly Affair, The ☐ Deathtrap ☐ Dog Day Afternoon ☐ Equus ☐ Fail-Safe ☐ Family Business ☐ Fugitive Kind, The ☐ Garbo Talks ☐ Group, The ☐ Guilty as Sin ☐ Hill, The ☐ Just Tell Me What You Want ☐ King: A Filmed Record...Montgomery to Memphis ☐ Last of the Mobile Hot-Shots ☐ Long Day's Journey into Night ☐ Lovin' Molly ☐ Morning After, The ☐ Murder on the Orient Express ☐ Network ☐ Offence, The ☐ Pawnbroker, The ☐ Power ☐ Prince of The City ☐ Q & A ☐ Running on Empty ☐ Sea Gull, The ☐ Serpico ☐ Stage Struck ☐ Stranger Among Us, A ☐ That Kind of Woman ☐ Twelve Angry Men ☐ Verdict, The ☐ View from the Bridge, A ☐ Wiz, The

Lupino, Ida ☐ Bigamist, The ☐ Hard, Fast and Beautiful ☐ Hitch-Hiker, The ☐ Trouble With Angels, The

Lynch, David ☐ Blue Velvet ☐ Dune ☐ Elephant Man, The ☐ Eraserhead ☐ Twin Peaks ☐ Twin Peaks: Fire Walk With Me ☐ Wild at Heart

Lyne, Adrian ☐ 9 1/2 Weeks ☐ Fatal Attraction ☐ Flashdance ☐ Foxes ☐ Indecent Proposal ☐ Jacob's Ladder

Lynn, Jonathan ☐ Clue ☐ Greedy ☐ My Cousin Vinny ☐ Nuns on the Run

Mackendrick, Alexander ☐ Boy Ten Feet Tall, A ☐ Crash of Silence ☐ Don't Make Waves ☐ High and Dry ☐ High Wind in Jamaica, A ☐ Lady Killers, The ☐ Man in the White Suit, The ☐ Sweet Smell of Success ☐ Tight Little Island

Mackenzie, John ☐ Act of Vengeance ☐ Beyond the Limit ☐ Fourth Protocol, The ☐ Last of the Finest, The ☐ Long Good Friday, The ☐ Ruby ☐ Sense of Freedom, A ☐ Unman, Wittering and Zigo

McLeod, Norman Z. ☐ Here Comes Cookie ☐ It's a Gift ☐ Jackass Mail ☐ Alias Jesse James ☐ Alice in Wonderland ☐ Casanova's Big Night ☐ Early to Bed ☐ Horse Feathers ☐ Kid from Brooklyn, The ☐ Lady Be Good ☐ Let's Dance ☐ Little Men ☐ Many Happy Returns ☐ Many Happy Returns ☐ My Favorite Spy ☐ Paleface, The ☐ Panama Hattie ☐ Pennies from Heaven ☐ Public Pigeon No. One ☐ Road to Rio ☐ Secret Life of Walter Mitty, The ☐ There Goes My Heart ☐ Topper ☐ Topper Takes a Trip ☐ Touchdown! ☐ Merrily We Live ☐ Miracle Man, The ☐ Monkey Business ☐ Never Wave at a WAC

Makavejev, Dusan ☐ Coca-Cola Kid, The ☐ Man Is Not A Bird ☐ Manifesto ☐ Montenegro

Malle, Louis ☐ Alamo Bay ☐ Atlantic City ☐ Au Revoir, Les Enfants ☐ Black Moon ☐ Damage ☐ Fire Within, The ☐ Frantic ☐ God's Country ☐ Human, Too Human ☐ Lacombe, Lucien ☐ Lovers, The ☐ May Fools ☐ Murmur of the Heart ☐ My Dinner with Andr_ ☐ Pretty Baby ☐ Spirits of the Dead ☐ Vanya on 42nd Street ☐ Very Private Affair, A ☐ Viva Maria! ☐ Zazie

Mamet, David ☐ Homicide ☐ House of Games ☐ Oleanna ☐ Things Change

Mamoulian, Rouben ☐ Applause ☐ Becky Sharp ☐ Blood and Sand ☐ City Streets ☐ Dr. Jekyll and Mr. Hyde ☐ Gay Desperado, The ☐ Golden Boy ☐ High, Wide, and Handsome ☐ Love Me Tonight ☐ Mark of Zorro, The ☐ Queen Christina ☐ Silk Stockings ☐ Song of Songs ☐ Summer Holiday ☐ We Live Again

Mandoki, Luis ☐ Born Yesterday ☐ Gaby—A True Story ☐ Murderer In The Motel ☐ When a Man Loves a Woman ☐ White Palace

Mankiewicz, Joseph L. ☐ All About Eve ☐ Dragonwyck ☐ Escape ☐ 5 Fingers ☐ Barefoot Contessa, The ☐ Cleopatra ☐ Ghost and Mrs. Muir, The ☐ Guys and Dolls ☐ Honey Pot, The ☐ House of Strangers, The ☐ Julius Caesar ☐King: A Filmed Record...Montgomery to Memphis ☐ Late George Apley, The ☐ Letter to Three Wives, A ☐ No Way Out ☐ People Will Talk ☐ Quiet American, The ☐ Sleuth ☐ Somewhere in the Night ☐ Suddenly, Last Summer ☐ There Was a Crooked Man

Mann, Anthony ☐ Bend of the River ☐ Border Incident ☐ Cimarron ☐ Dandy in Aspic, A ☐ Desperate ☐ El Cid ☐ Fall of the Roman Empire ☐ Far Country, The ☐ Furies, The ☐ Glenn Miller Story, The ☐ God's Little Acre ☐ Great Flamarion, The ☐ Heroes of Telemark, The ☐ Last Frontier, The ☐ Man from Laramie, The ☐ Man of the West ☐ Men in War ☐ Naked Spur, The ☐ Railroaded ☐ Raw Deal ☐ Serenade ☐ Side Street ☐ Strategic Air Command ☐ T-Men ☐ Thunder Bay ☐ Tin Star, The ☐ Winchester 073

Mann, Daniel ☐ About Mrs. Leslie ☐ Ada ☐ Butterfield 8 ☐ Come Back, Little Sheba ☐ Dream of Kings, A ☐ Five Finger Exercise ☐ For Love of Ivy ☐ Hot Spell ☐ I'll Cry Tomorrow ☐ Interval ☐ Journey Into Fear ☐ Judith ☐ Last Angry Man, The ☐ Lost in the Stars ☐ Man Who Broke 1,000 Chains, The ☐ Matilda ☐ Maurie ☐ Mountain Road, The ☐ Our Man Flint ☐ Playing for Time ☐ Revengers, The ☐ Rose Tattoo, The ☐ Teahouse of the August Moon, The ☐ Who's Got the Action? ☐ Willard

Mann, Delbert ☐ Against Her Will: An Incident in Baltimore ☐ All Quiet on the Western Front ☐ April Morning ☐ Bachelor Party, The ☐ Birch Interval ☐ Bronte ☐ Dark at the Top of the Stairs, The ☐ David Copperfield ☐ Dear Heart ☐ Death in California, A ☐ Desire Under the Elms ☐ Fitzwilly ☐ Francis Gary Powers: The True Story of the U-2 Spy Incident ☐ Gathering of Eagles ☐ Gift of Love: A Christmas Story, The ☐ Girl Named Sooner, A ☐ Heidi ☐ Home to Stay ☐ Jane Eyre ☐ Last Days of Patton, The ☐ Love Leads the Way ☐ Lover Come Back ☐ Man without a Country, The ☐ Marty ☐ Middle of the Night ☐ Mister Buddwing ☐ Night Crossing ☐ No Place to Run ☐ Outsider, The ☐ Pink Jungle, The ☐ Quick, Before It Melts ☐ Separate Tables ☐ She Waits ☐ That Touch of Mink ☐ Torn Between Two Lovers

Mann, Michael ☐ Jericho Mile, The ☐ Keep, The ☐ Last of the Mohicans, The ☐ Manhunter ☐ Thief

Marker, Chris ☐ A.K. ☐ Le Joli Mal ☐ Letter from Siberia ☐ Sans Soleil

Markowitz, Robert ☐ Adam: His Song Continues ☐Afterburn ☐ Alex: The Life of a Child ☐ Belarus File, The ☐ Cry for Help: The Tracey Thurman Story, A ☐ Deadliest Season, The ☐ Decoration Day ☐ Phantom of the Opera, The ☐ Voices

Marshall, Garry ☐ Beaches ☐ Exit to Eden ☐ Flamingo Kid ☐ Frankie and Johnny ☐ Nothing in Common ☐ Overboard ☐ Pretty Woman ☐ Young Doctors in Love

Marshall, George ☐ Advance to the Rear ☐ And the Angels Sing ☐ Beyond Mombasa ☐ Blue Dahlia, The ☐ Boy, Did I Get a Wrong Number! ☐ Cry for Happy ☐ Destry ☐ Destry Rides Again ☐ Duel in the Jungle ☐ Eight on the Lam ☐ Fancy Pants ☐ Forest Rangers, The ☐ Gazebo, The ☐ Ghost Breakers, The ☐ Goldwyn Follies, The ☐ Guns of Fort Petticoat, The ☐ Happy Thieves ☐ Hazard ☐ Hold That Blonde ☐ Hold That Co-ed ☐ Hook, Line & Sinker ☐ Houdini ☐ How the West Was Won ☐ Imitation General ☐ In Old Kentucky ☐ Incendiary Blonde ☐ It Started with a Kiss ☐ Life Begins at Forty ☐ Love Under Fire ☐ Mating Game, The ☐ Message to Garcia, A ☐ Millionaire for Christy, A ☐ Money from Home ☐ Monsieur Beaucaire ☐ Murder, He Says ☐ Music Is Magic ☐ My Friend Irma ☐ Nancy Steele Is Missing ☐ Never a Dull Moment ☐ Off Limits ☐ Pack Up Your Troubles ☐ Papa's Delicate Condition ☐ Perils of Pauline, The ☐ Pillars of the Sky ☐ Red Garters ☐ Sad Sack, The ☐ Savage, The ☐ Scared Stiff ☐ Sheepman, The ☐ Show Them No Mercy! ☐ Star Spangled Rhythm ☐ Tap Roots ☐ Texas ☐ True to Life ☐ Valley of the Sun ☐ Variety Girl ☐ When the Daltons Rode ☐ You Can't Cheat an Honest Man

Marshall, Penny ☐ Awakenings ☐ Big ☐ Jumpin' Jack Flash ☐ League of Their Own, A ☐ Renaissance Man

Mate, Rudolph ☐ Black Shield of Falworth, The ☐ Branded ☐ D.O.A. ☐ Dark Past, The

☐ Deep Six, The ☐ Far Horizons, The ☐ Forbidden ☐ Green Glove, The ☐ It Had to Be You ☐ Miracle in the Rain ☐ Three Violent People ☐ When Worlds Collide

May, Elaine ☐ Heartbreak Kid, The ☐ Ishtar ☐ Mikey and Nicky ☐ New Leaf, A

Mayo, Archie ☐ Adventures of Marco Polo, The ☐ Angel on My Shoulder ☐ Black Legion ☐ Bordertown ☐ Call It a Day ☐ Case of the Lucky Legs, The ☐ Charley's Aunt ☐ Crash Dive ☐ Doorway to Hell ☐ Ever in My Heart ☐ Four Sons ☐ Gambling Lady ☐ Give Me Your Heart ☐ Go Into Your Dance ☐ Great American Broadcast, The ☐ House Across the Bay, The ☐ Illicit ☐ It's Love I'm After ☐ Life of Jimmy Dolan, The ☐ Man with Two Faces, The ☐ Mayor of Hell, The ☐ Moontide ☐ My Man ☐ Night After Night ☐ Night in Casablanca, A ☐ Oh! Sailor, Behave! ☐ Orchestra Wives ☐ Petrified Forest, The ☐ Svengali ☐ They Shall Have Music ☐ Wide Open

Mazursky, Paul ☐ Alex in Wonderland ☐ Blume In Love ☐ Bob & Carol & Ted & Alice ☐ Down and Out in Beverly Hills ☐ Enemies, A Love Story ☐ Harry and Tonto ☐ Moon Over Parador ☐ Moscow on the Hudson ☐ Next Stop, Greenwich Village ☐ Pickle, The ☐ Scenes from a Mall ☐ Tempest ☐ Unmarried Woman, An ☐ Willie and Phil

Mc Bride, Jim ☐ Big Easy, The ☐ Breathless ☐ David Holzman's Diary ☐ Glen and Randa ☐ Great Balls of Fire! ☐ Hot Times

McCarey, Leo ☐ Affair to Remember, An ☐ Awful Truth, The ☐ Belle of the Nineties ☐ Bells of St. Mary's, The ☐ Duck Soup ☐ Going My Way ☐ Good Sam ☐ Indiscreet ☐ Kid from Spain, The ☐ Love Affair ☐ Make Way for Tomorrow ☐ Milky Way, The ☐ My Son John ☐ Once Upon a Honeymoon ☐ Rally 'Round the Flag, Boys! ☐ Ruggles of Red Gap ☐ Satan Never Sleeps ☐ Six of a Kind

McLaglen, Andrew V. ☐ Abductors, The ☐ Ballad of Josie, The ☐ Bandolero ☐ Breakthrough ☐ Cahill—United States Marshal ☐ Chisum ☐ Devil's Brigade, The ☐ Dirty Dozen, The: The Next Mission ☐ ffolkes ☐ Fools' Parade ☐ Gun the Man Down ☐ Hellfighters ☐ Last Hard Men, The ☐ Man in the Vault ☐ McLintock! ☐ Mitchell ☐ Monkeys Go Home! ☐ On Wings of Eagles ☐ One More Train to Rob ☐ Rare Breed, The ☐ Sahara ☐ Sea Wolves, The ☐ Shadow Riders, The ☐ Shenandoah ☐ Undefeated, The ☐ Way West, The ☐ Wild Geese, The

McNaughton, John ☐ Borrower, The ☐ Mad Dog and Glory ☐ Sex, Drugs, Rock & Roll

McTiernan, John ☐ Die Hard ☐ Hunt for Red October, The ☐ Last Action Hero ☐ Medicine Man ☐ Nomads ☐ Predator

Medak, Peter ☐ Changeling, The ☐ Day in the Death of Joe Egg, A ☐ Ghost in the Noonday Sun ☐ Krays, The ☐ Let Him Have It ☐ Men's Club, The ☐ Negatives ☐ Odd Job, The ☐ Pontiac Man ☐ Romeo is Bleeding ☐ Ruling Class, The ☐ Zorro, the Gay Blade

Melville, Jean-Pierre ☐ Bob Le Flambeur ☐ Dirty Money ☐ Forgiven Sinner, The ☐ Godson, The ☐ L'Armee des Ombres ☐ Leon Morin, Priest ☐ Les Enfants Terribles

Meyer, Nicholas ☐ Company Business ☐ Day After, The ☐ Deceivers, The ☐ Star Trek II: The Wrath of Kahn ☐ Star Trek VI: The Undiscovered Country ☐ Time After Time ☐ Volunteers

Milestone, Lewis ☐ All Quiet on the Western Front ☐ Anything Goes ☐ Arch of Triumph ☐ Captain Hates the Sea, The ☐ Edge of Darkness ☐ Front Page, The ☐ General Died At Dawn, The ☐ Hallelujah, I'm a Bum ☐ Halls of Montezuma ☐ Kangaroo ☐ Les Miserables ☐ Lucky Partners ☐ Melba ☐ Mutiny on the Bounty ☐ My Life with Caroline ☐ No Minor Vices ☐ North Star, The ☐ Ocean's Eleven ☐ Of Mice and Men ☐ Pork Chop Hill ☐ Purple Heart, The ☐ Rain ☐ Red Pony, The ☐ Strange Love of Martha Ivers, The ☐ They Who Dare ☐ Walk in the Sun, A

Milius, John ☐ Big Wednesday ☐ Conan the Barbarian ☐ Dillinger ☐ Farewell to the King ☐ Flight of the Intruder ☐ Red Dawn ☐ Wind and the Lion, The

Miller, George ☐ Lorenzo's Oil ☐ Mad Max ☐ Mad Max Beyond Thunderdome ☐ Road Warrior, The ☐ Twilight Zone—The Movie ☐ Witches of Eastwick, The

Miller, George ☐ Anzacs: The War Down Under ☐ Aviator, The ☐ Christmas Visitor, The ☐ Far Country, The ☐ Frozen Assets ☐ Goodbye, Miss 4th of July ☐ Man from Snowy River, The ☐ Miracle Down Under ☐ Neverending Story II: The Next Chapter, The

Minnelli, Vincente ☐ American in Paris, An ☐ Bad and the Beautiful, The ☐ Band Wagon, The ☐ Bells Are Ringing ☐ Brigadoon ☐ Cabin in the Sky ☐ Clock, The ☐ Cobweb, The ☐ Courtship of Eddie's Father, The ☐ Designing Woman ☐ Father of the Bride ☐ Father's Little Dividend ☐ Four Horsemen of the Apocalypse ☐ Gigi ☐ Goodbye Charlie ☐ Home from the Hill ☐ I Dood It ☐ Kismet ☐ Long, Long Trailer, The ☐ Long, Long Trailer, The ☐ Lust for Life ☐ Madame Bovary ☐ Matter of Time, A ☐ Meet Me in St. Louis ☐ On a Clear Day You Can See Forever ☐ Pirate, The ☐ Reluctant Debutante, The ☐ Sandpiper, The ☐ Some Came Running ☐ Tea and Sympathy ☐ Undercurrent ☐ Yolanda and the Thief ☐ Ziegfeld Follies

Mizoguchi, Kenji ☐ Chikamatsu Monogatari ☐ Forty-Seven Ronin, The (Part One) ☐ Geisha, A ☐ Life of Oharu, The ☐ Osaka Elegy

Princess Yang Kwei Fei ☐ Sansho the Bailiff ☐ Ugetsu

Monicelli, Mario ☐ Big Deal on Madonna Street ☐ Casanova '70 ☐ Girl with a Pistol, The ☐ Great War, The ☐ High Infidelity ☐ Lady Liberty ☐ Let's Hope It's a Girl ☐ Lovers and Liars ☐ Organizer, The ☐ Passionate Thief, The ☐ Two Lives of Mattia Pascal, The

Morris, Errol ☐ Brief History of Time, A ☐ Dark Wind, The ☐ Gates of Heaven ☐ Thin Blue Line, The

Morrissey, Paul ☐ Andy Warhol's Dracula ☐ Andy Warhol's Frankenstein ☐ Beethoven's Nephew ☐ Forty Deuce ☐ Heat ☐ Hound of the Baskervilles, The ☐ Mixed Blood

Mulcahy, Russell ☐ Blue Ice ☐ Highlander ☐ Highlander II: The Quickening ☐ Razorback ☐ Real McCoy, The ☐ Ricochet ☐ Shadow, The

Mulligan, Robert ☐ Baby the Rain Must Fall ☐ Bloodbrothers ☐ Clara's Heart ☐ Come September ☐ Fear Strikes Out ☐ Great Imposter, The ☐ Inside Daisy Clover ☐ Kiss Me Goodbye ☐ Love with the Proper Stranger ☐ Man in the Moon, The ☐ Nickel Ride, The ☐ Other, The ☐ Rat Race, The ☐ Same Time, Next Year ☐ Stalking Moon ☐ Summer of '42 ☐ To Kill A Mockingbird ☐ Up the Down Staircase

Murnau, F.W. ☐ Faust ☐ Last Laugh, The ☐ Nosferatu ☐ Tabu

Murphy, Geoff ☐ Blind Side ☐ Freejack ☐ Goodbye Pork Pie ☐ Last Outlaw, The ☐ Quiet Earth, The ☐ Utu ☐ Young Guns II

Naruse, Mikio ☐ Late Chrysanthemums ☐ Mother (Okaasan) ☐ Thin Line, The ☐ Two in the Shadow ☐ When a Woman Ascends the Stairs ☐ Wiser Age

Negulesco, Jean ☐ Best of Everything, The ☐ Boy on a Dolphin ☐ Certain Smile, A ☐ Conspirators, The ☐ Count Your Blessings ☐ Daddy Long Legs ☐ Deep Valley ☐ Forbidden Street, The ☐ Gift of Love, The ☐ Hello-Goodbye ☐ How to Marry a Millionaire ☐ Humoresque ☐ Invincible Six, The ☐ Jessica ☐ Johnny Belinda ☐ Lure of the Wilderness ☐ Lydia Bailey ☐ Mask of Dimitrios, The ☐ Mudlark, The ☐ Nobody Lives Forever ☐ O. Henry's Full House ☐ Phone Call from a Stranger ☐ Pleasure Seekers, The ☐ Rains of Ranchipur, The ☐ Road House ☐ Three Came Home ☐ Three Coins in the Fountain ☐ Three Strangers ☐ Titanic ☐ Under My Skin ☐ Woman's World

Neill, Roy William ☐ Black Angel ☐ Black Room, The ☐ Circus Queen Murder, The ☐ Dressed to Kill ☐ Eight Bells ☐ Eyes of the Underworld ☐ Frankenstein Meets the Wolf Man ☐ Gypsy Wildcat ☐ Hoots Mon! ☐ House of Fear, The ☐ Lone Wolf Returns, The ☐ Pearl of Death, The ☐ Pursuit to Algiers ☐ Scarlet Claw, The ☐ Sherlock Holmes and the Spider Woman ☐ Sherlock Holmes Faces Death ☐ Sherlock Holmes in Washington ☐ Terror By Night ☐ Whirlpool ☐ Woman in Green, The

Newell, Mike ☐ Amazing Grace and Chuck ☐ Awakening, The ☐ Bad Blood ☐ Blood Feud ☐ Common Ground ☐ Dance With a Stranger ☐ Enchanted April ☐ Four Weddings and a Funeral ☐ Good Father, The ☐ Man in the Iron Mask

Newman, Paul ☐ Effect of Gamma Rays on Man-in-the-Moon Marigolds, The ☐ Glass Menagerie, The ☐ Harry and Son ☐ Rachel, Rachel ☐ Shadow Box, The ☐ Sometimes a Great Notion

Nichols, Mike ☐ Biloxi Blues ☐ Carnal Knowledge ☐ Catch-22 ☐ Day of the Dolphin, The ☐ Fortune, The ☐ Gilda Live ☐ Graduate, The ☐ Heartburn ☐ Postcards from the Edge ☐ Regarding Henry ☐ Silkwood ☐ Who's Afraid of Virginia Woolf? ☐ Wolf ☐ Working Girl

Nimoy, Leonard ☐ Funny About Love ☐ Good Mother, The ☐ Star Trek III: The Search for Spock ☐ Star Trek IV: The Voyage Home ☐ Three Men and a Baby

Noyce, Phillip ☐ Blind Fury ☐ Dead Calm ☐ Echoes of Paradise ☐ Heatwave ☐ Newsfront ☐ Patriot Games ☐ Sliver

Olivier, Laurence ☐ Hamlet ☐ Henry V ☐ Prince and the Showgirl, The ☐ Richard III ☐ Three Sisters

Olmi, Ermanno ☐ In the Summertime ☐ Legend of The Holy Drinker, The ☐ Man Named John, A ☐ Sound of Trumpets, The ☐ Tree of Wooden Clogs, The

Ophuls, Marcel ☐ Banana Peel ☐ Hotel Terminus: The Life and Times of Klaus Barbie ☐ Love at Twenty ☐ Memory of Justice, The ☐ Sorrow and the Pity, The

Ophuls, Max ☐ Caught ☐ Divine ☐ Earrings of Madame De..., The ☐ Exile, The ☐ La Ronde ☐ Le Plaisir ☐ Letter from an Unknown Woman ☐ Lola Montes ☐ Man Stolen ☐ Reckless Moment, The

Oshima, Nagisa ☐ Boy ☐ Cruel Story of Youth ☐ Max, Mon Amour ☐ Merry Christmas, Mr. Lawrence

Oswald, Gerd ☐ Agent for H.A.R.M. ☐ Brainwashed ☐ Brass Legend, The ☐ Bunny O'Hare ☐ Crime of Passion ☐ Fury at Showdown ☐ Kiss Before Dying, A ☐ Paris Holiday ☐ Three Moves to Freedom

Oz, Frank ☐ Dark Crystal, The ☐ Dirty Rotten Scoundrels ☐ House Sitter ☐ Little Shop of Horrors ☐ Muppets Take Manhattan, The ☐ What About Bob?

Ozu, Yasujiro ☐ Autumn Afternoon, An ☐ Early Spring ☐ Early Summer ☐ End of Summer, The ☐ Equinox Flower ☐ Flavor of Green Tea over Rice, The ☐ Floating Weeds ☐ Good Morning ☐ Late Autumn ☐ Late Spring ☐ Ohayo ☐ Tea and Rice ☐ Tokyo Story

Pabst, G.W. ☐ Diary of a Lost Girl ☐ From Top To Bottom ☐ Jackboot Mutiny ☐ Joyless Street, The ☐ Kameradschaft ☐ Last Ten Days, The ☐ Love of Jeanne Nay, The ☐ Mistress of Atlantis, The ☐ Pandora's Box ☐ Threepenny Opera, The ☐ Westfront 1918

Pagnol, Marcel ☐ Angele ☐ Baker's Wife, The ☐ Carnival ☐ Cesar ☐ Harvest ☐ Letters from My Windmill ☐ Nais ☐ Well-Digger's Daughter, The

Pakula, Alan J. ☐ All the President's Men ☐ Comes a Horseman ☐ Consenting Adults ☐ Dream Lover ☐ Klute ☐ Love and Pain (and the Whole Damn Thing) ☐ Orphans ☐ Parallax View, The ☐ Pelican Brief, The ☐ Presumed Innocent ☐ Rollover ☐ See You in the Morning ☐ Sophie's Choice ☐ Starting Over ☐ Sterile Cuckoo, The

Paradjanov, Sergei ☐ Ashik Kerib ☐ Color of Pomegranates, The ☐ Legend of Suram Fortress, The ☐ Shadows of Forgotten Ancestors

Parker, Alan ☐ Angel Heart ☐ Birdy ☐ Bugsy Malone ☐ Come See the Paradise ☐ Commitments, The ☐ Fame ☐ Midnight Express ☐ Mississippi Burning ☐ Road to Wellville, The ☐ Shoot the Moon

Parrish, Robert ☐ Assignment—Paris ☐ Bobo, The ☐ Casino Royale ☐ Cry Danger ☐ Destructors, The ☐ Duffy ☐ Fire Down Below ☐ In the French Style ☐ Journey to the Far Side of the Sun ☐ Lucy Gallant ☐ Mississippi Blues ☐ Mob, The ☐ Purple Plain, The ☐ Saddle the Wind ☐ San Francisco Story, The ☐ Up from the Beach ☐ Wonderful Country, The

Pasolini, Pier Paolo ☐ Accattone ☐ Gospel According to St. Matthew ☐ Love Meetings (Comizi D'Amore) ☐ Medea ☐ Oedipus Rex

Passer, Ivan ☐ Born to Win ☐ Creator ☐ Cutter's Way ☐ Fourth Story, The ☐ Haunted Summer ☐ Intimate Lighting ☐ Law and Disorder ☐ Stalin

Peckinpah, Sam ☐ Ballad of Cable Hogue, The ☐ Bring Me the Head of Alfredo Garcia ☐ Convoy ☐ Cross of Iron ☐ Deadly Companions, The ☐ Getaway, The ☐ Junior Bonner ☐ Killer Elite, The ☐ Major Dundee ☐ Osterman Weekend, The ☐ Pat Garrett and Billy the Kid ☐ Ride the High Country ☐ Straw Dogs ☐ Wild Bunch, The

Penn, Arthur ☐ Alice's Restaurant ☐ Bonnie and Clyde ☐ Chase, The ☐ Dead of Winter ☐ Four Friends ☐ Left-Handed Gun, The ☐ Little Big Man ☐ Mickey One ☐ Miracle Worker, The ☐ Missouri Breaks, The ☐ Night Moves ☐ Penn & Teller Get Killed ☐ Portrait, The ☐ Target ☐ Visions of Eight

Perry, Frank ☐ Compromising Positions ☐ David and Lisa ☐ Diary of a Mad Housewife ☐ Doc ☐ Hello Again ☐ Ladybug, Ladybug ☐ Last Summer ☐ Man on a Swing ☐ Mommie Dearest ☐ Monsignor ☐ Play It As It Lays ☐ Rancho Deluxe ☐ Swimmer, The ☐ Truman Capote's Trilogy

Petersen, Wolfgang ☐ Consequence, The ☐ Das Boat ☐ Enemy Mine ☐ For Your Love Only ☐ In the Line of Fire ☐ Neverending Story, The ☐ Outbreak ☐ Shattered

Pialat, Maurice ☐ Loulou ☐ Nos Amours, A ☐ Police ☐ Under the Sun of Satan ☐ Van Gogh

Poitier, Sidney ☐ Buck and the Preacher ☐ Fast Forward ☐ Ghost Dad ☐ Hanky Panky ☐ Let's Do it Again ☐ Piece of the Action, A ☐ Stir Crazy ☐ Uptown Saturday Nite ☐ Warm December, A

Polanski, Roman ☐ Bitter Moon ☐ Chinatown ☐ Cul-De-Sac ☐ Death and the Maiden ☐ Fearless Vampire Killers or: Pardon Me, But Your Teeth Are in My Neck ☐ Frantic ☐ Knife in the Water ☐ Macbeth ☐ Pirates ☐ Repulsion ☐ Rosemary's Baby ☐ Tenant, The ☐ Tess

Pollack, Sydney ☐ Absence of Malice ☐ Bobby Deerfield ☐ Castle Keep ☐ Electric Horseman, The ☐ Firm, The ☐ Havana ☐ Jeremiah Johnson ☐ Out of Africa ☐ Scalphunters, The ☐ Slender Thread, The ☐ They Shoot Horses, Don't They? ☐ This Property is Condemned ☐ Three Days of the Condor ☐ Tootsie ☐ Way We Were, The ☐ Yakuza, The

Polonsky, Abraham ☐ Force of Evil ☐ Tell Them Willy Boy Is Here

Powell, Michael ☐ 49th Parallel ☐ Age of Consent ☐ Black Narcissus ☐ Canterbury Tale, A ☐ Contraband ☐ Edge of the World, The ☐ Fighting Pimpernel, The ☐ Gone to Earth ☐ Honeymoon ☐ I Know Where I'm Going ☐ Ill Met by Moonlight ☐ Life and Death of Colonel Blimp, The ☐ Lion Has Wings, The ☐ Night Ambush ☐ One of Our Aircraft Is Missing ☐ Peeping Tom ☐ Pursuit of the Graf Spee ☐ Red Shoes, The ☐ Small Back Room, The ☐ Spy in Black, The ☐ Stairway to Heaven ☐ Tales of Hoffman ☐ They're a Weird Mob ☐ Thief of Bagdad, The

Preminger, Otto ☐ 13th Letter, The ☐ Advise and Consent ☐ Anatomy of a Murder ☐ Angel Face ☐ Bonjour Tristesse ☐ Bunny Lake Is Missing ☐ Cardinal, The ☐ Carmen Jones ☐ Centennial Summer ☐ Court-Martial of Billy Mitchell, The ☐ Daisy Kenyon ☐ Danger—Love At Work ☐ Exodus ☐ Fallen Angel ☐ Fan, The ☐ Forever Amber ☐ Human Factor, The ☐ Hurry Sundown ☐ In Harm's Way ☐ In the Meantime, Darling ☐ Laura ☐ Man with the Golden Arm ☐ Margin for Error ☐ Moon Is Blue, The ☐ Porgy and Bess ☐ River of No Return ☐ Royal Scandal, A ☐ Saint Joan ☐ Skiddoo ☐ Such Good Friends ☐ Tell Me That You Love Me, Junie Moon ☐ That Lady in Ermine ☐ Where the Sidewalk Ends ☐ Whirlpool

Pudovkin, V.I. ☐ General Suvorov

Rafelson, Bob ☐ Black Widow ☐ Five Easy Pieces ☐ Head ☐ King of Marvin Gardens, The ☐ Man Trouble ☐ Mountains of the

Moon ☐ Postman Always Rings Twice, The ☐ Stay Hungry

Raimi, Sam ☐ Army of Darkness ☐ Darkman ☐ Evil Dead 2, The ☐ Evil Dead, The ☐ Quick and the Dead, The

Rapper, Irving ☐ Adventures of Mark Twain, The ☐ Anna Lucasta ☐ Another Man's Poison ☐ Bad for Each Other ☐ Born Again ☐ Brave One, The ☐ Christine Jorgensen Story, The ☐ Corn Is Green, The ☐ Deception ☐ Forever Female ☐ Gay Sisters, The ☐ Glass Menagerie, The ☐ Joseph and His Brethren ☐ Marjorie Morningstar ☐ Miracle, The ☐ Now, Voyager ☐ One Foot in Heaven ☐ Rhapsody in Blue ☐ Voice of the Turtle, The

Ray, Fred Olen ☐ Alien Dead, The ☐ Alienator ☐ Armed Response ☐ Bad Girls from Mars ☐ Beverly Hills Vamp ☐ Haunting Fear ☐ Hollywood Chainsaw Hookers ☐ Mind Twister ☐ Mob Boss ☐ Phantom Empire ☐ Phantom Empire

Ray, Nicholas ☐ 55 Days at Peking ☐ Bigger than Life ☐ Bitter Victory ☐ Born To Be Bad ☐ Flying Leathernecks ☐ Hot Blood ☐ In a Lonely Place ☐ Johnny Guitar ☐ King of Kings ☐ Knock on Any Door ☐ Lusty Men, The ☐ On Dangerous Ground ☐ Party Girl ☐ Rebel Without a Cause ☐ Run for Cover ☐ Savage Innocents, The ☐ They Live By Night ☐ True Story of Jesse James, The ☐ Wind Across the Everglades ☐ Woman's Secret, A

Ray, Satyajit ☐ Adversary, The ☐ Aparajito ☐ Big City, The ☐ Chess Players, The ☐ Days and Nights in the Forest ☐ Devi ☐ Distant Thunder ☐ Enemy of the People, An ☐ Expedition ☐ Home and the World, The ☐ Music Room, The ☐ Pather Panchali ☐ Two Daughters ☐ World of Apu, The

Redford, Robert ☐ Milagro Beanfield War, The ☐ Ordinary People ☐ Quiz Show ☐ River Runs Through It, A

Reiner, Carl ☐ All of Me ☐ Bert Rigby, You're a Fool ☐ Comic, The ☐ Dead Men Don't Wear Plaid ☐ Enter Laughing ☐ Fatal Instinct ☐ Jerk, The ☐ Man with Two Brains, The ☐ Oh, God! ☐ One and Only, The ☐ Sibling Rivalry ☐ Summer Rental ☐ Summer School ☐ Where's Poppa?

Reiner, Rob ☐ Few Good Men, A ☐ Misery ☐ North ☐ Princess Bride, The ☐ Stand By Me ☐ Sure Thing, The ☐ This Is Spinal Tap ☐ When Harry Met Sally...

Reisz, Karel ☐ Everybody Wins ☐ French Lieutenant's Woman, The ☐ Gambler, The ☐ Isadora ☐ Morgan! ☐ Night Must Fall ☐ Saturday Night and Sunday Morning ☐ Sweet Dreams ☐ Who'll Stop the Rain

Renoir, Jean ☐ Boudu Saved from Drowning ☐ Crime of Monsieur Lange, The ☐ Day in the Country, A ☐ Diary of a Chambermaid ☐ Elusive Corporal, The ☐ French Cancan ☐ Golden Coach, The ☐ Grand Illusion ☐ La Bete Humaine ☐ La Chienne ☐ Little Theatre of Jean Renoir, The ☐ Lower Depths, The ☐ Madame Bovary ☐ Picnic On The Grass ☐ River, The ☐ Rules of the Game, The ☐ Southerner, The ☐ Swamp Water ☐ This Land Is Mine ☐ Toni ☐ Woman on the Beach, The

Resnais, Alain ☐ Hiroshima Mon Amour ☐ Je T'Aime, Je T'Aime ☐ La Guerre Est Finie ☐ Last Year at Marienbad ☐ Life Is a Bed of Roses ☐ Melo ☐ Mon Oncle D'Amerique ☐ Muriel ☐ Providence ☐ Stavisky

Richardson, Tony ☐ Beryl Markham: A Shadow on the Sun ☐ Border, The ☐ Blue Sky ☐ Charge of the Light Brigade, The ☐ Death in Canaan, A ☐ Delicate Balance, A ☐ Entertainer, The ☐ Hamlet ☐ Hotel New Hampshire, The ☐ Joseph Andrews ☐ Laughter in the Dark ☐ Loneliness of the Long Distance Runner, The ☐ Look Back in Anger ☐ Loved One, The ☐ Ned Kelly ☐ Penalty Phase ☐ Taste of Honey, A ☐ Tom Jones ☐ Women & Men: Stories of Seduction

Ritchie, Michael ☐ Almost Perfect Affair, An ☐ Bad News Bears, The ☐ Candidate, The ☐ Cops and Robbersons ☐ Couch Trip, The ☐ Diggstown ☐ Divine Madness ☐ Downhill Racer ☐ Fletch ☐ Fletch Lives ☐ Golden Child, The ☐ Island, The ☐ Outsider, The ☐ Positively True Adventures of the Alleged Texas Cheerleader- ☐ Prime Cut ☐ Scout, The ☐ Semi-Tough ☐ Smile ☐ Survivors, The ☐ Wildcats

Ritt, Martin ☐ Adventures of a Young Man ☐ Back Roads ☐ Black Orchid, The ☐ Brotherhood, The ☐ Casey's Shadow ☐ Conrack ☐ Cross Creek ☐ Edge of the City ☐ Five Branded Women ☐ Front, The ☐ Great White Hope, The ☐ Hombre ☐ Hud ☐ Long Hot Summer, The ☐ Molly Maguires, The ☐ Murphy's Romance ☐ No Down Payment ☐ Norma Rae ☐ Nuts ☐ Outrage, The ☐ Paris Blues ☐ Pete 'n' Tillie ☐ Sound and the Fury, The ☐ Sounder ☐ Spy Who Came In from the Cold, The ☐ Stanley and Iris

Rivette, Jacques ☐ Celine and Julie Go Boating ☐ L'Amour Fou ☐ La Belle Noiseuse ☐ Love on the Ground ☐ Nun, The ☐ Paris Belongs to Us

Roddam, Franc ☐ Bride, The ☐ K2—The Ultimate High ☐ Lords of Discipline, The ☐ Quadrophenia

Roeg, Nicolas ☐ Aria ☐ Bad Timing: A Sensual Obsession ☐ Castaway ☐ Cold Heaven ☐ Don't Look Now ☐ Eureka ☐ Heart of Darkness ☐ Insignificance ☐ Man Who Fell to Earth, The ☐ Performance ☐ Sweet Bird of Youth ☐ Track 29 ☐ Walkabout ☐ Witches, The

Rohmer, Eric ☐ Aviator's Wife, The ☐ Boyfriends and Girlfriends ☐ Chloe in the Afternoon ☐ Claire's Knee ☐ Four Adventures of Reinette and Mirabelle ☐ Full Moon in Paris ☐ La Collectioneuse ☐ Marquise of O, The ☐ My Night At Mauds ☐ Pauline at the Beach

☐ Summer ☐ Tale of Springtime, A ☐ Tale of Winter, A

Romero, George A. ☐ Crazies, The ☐ Dark Half, The ☐ Two Evil Eyes ☐ Creepshow ☐ Dawn of the Dead ☐ Day of the Dead ☐ Knightriders ☐ Martin ☐ Monkey Shines ☐ Night of the Living Dead ☐ Season of the Witch

Rosi, Francesco ☐ Carmen ☐ Eboli ☐ Illustrious Corpses ☐ Lucky Luciano ☐ Mattei Affair, The ☐ More than a Miracle ☐ Palermo Connection, The ☐ Salvatore Guiliano ☐ Three Brothers

Ross, Herbert ☐ Boys on the Side ☐ California Suite ☐ Dancers ☐ Footloose ☐ Funny Lady ☐ Goodbye Girl, The ☐ Goodbye, Mr. Chips ☐ I Ought to Be in Pictures ☐ Last of Sheila, The ☐ Max Dugan Returns ☐ My Blue Heaven ☐ Nijinsky ☐ Owl and the Pussycat, The ☐ Pennies From Heaven ☐ Play It Again, Sam ☐ Protocol ☐ Secret of My Success, The ☐ Seven-percent Solution, The ☐ Steel Magnolias ☐ Sunshine Boys, The ☐ True Colors ☐ Turning Point, The ☐ Undercover Blues

Rossellini, Roberto ☐ Amore ☐ Flowers of St. Francis ☐ General Della Rovere ☐ Germany Year Zero ☐ Greatest Love, The ☐ Open City ☐ Paisan ☐ Rise of Louis XIV ☐ Seven Deadly Sins ☐ Stromboli ☐ Voyage to Italy

Rossen, Robert ☐ Alexander the Great ☐ All the King's Men ☐ Body and Soul ☐ Brave Bulls, The ☐ Hustler, The ☐ Island in the Sun ☐ Johnny O'Clock ☐ Lilith ☐ Mambo ☐ They Came to Cordura

Roth, Bobby ☐ Baja Oklahoma ☐ Boss's Son, The ☐ Dead Solid Perfect ☐ Game Of Love, The ☐ Heartbreakers ☐ Keeper of the City ☐ Man Inside, The ☐ Rainbow Drive

Ruben, Joseph ☐ Dreamscape ☐ Good Son, The ☐ Gorp ☐ Joyride ☐ Our Winning Season ☐ Pom-Pom Girls ☐ Sleeping with the Enemy ☐ Stepfather, The ☐ True Believer

Rudolph, Alan ☐ Choose Me ☐ Endangered Species ☐ Equinox ☐ Love at Large ☐ Made in Heaven ☐ Moderns, The ☐ Mortal Thoughts ☐ Mrs. Parker and the Vicious Circle ☐ Roadie ☐ Songwriter ☐ Trouble in Mind ☐ Welcome to L.A.

Russell, Ken ☐ Altered States ☐ Billion Dollar Brain ☐ Boyfriend, The ☐ Crimes of Passion ☐ Devils, The ☐ Gothic ☐ Lair of the White Worm, The ☐ Lisztomania ☐ Mahler ☐ Music Lovers, The ☐ Prisoner of Honor ☐ Rainbow, The ☐ Salome's Last Dance ☐ Savage Messiah ☐ Tommy: The Movie ☐ Valentino ☐ Whore ☐ Women & Men: Stories of Seduction ☐ Women in Love

Sandrich, Mark ☐ Buck Benny Rides Again ☐ Carefree ☐ Cockeyed Cavaliers ☐ Follow the Fleet ☐ Gay Divorcee, The ☐ Here Come the Waves ☐ Hips, Hips, Hooray ☐ Holiday Inn ☐ I Love a Soldier ☐ Love Thy Neighbor ☐ Man about Town ☐ Melody Cruise ☐ Shall We Dance ☐ Skylark ☐ So Proudly We Hail ☐ Top Hat ☐ Woman Rebels, A

Sargent, Joseph ☐ Amber Waves ☐ Caroline? ☐ Coast to Coast ☐ Colossus: The Forbin Project ☐ Day One ☐ Freedom ☐ Friendly Persuasion ☐ Goldengirl ☐ Hell With Heroes, The ☐ Hustling ☐ Immortal, The ☐ Incident, The ☐ Jaws,The Revenge ☐ Karen Carpenter Story, The ☐ Last Elephant, The ☐ Love Is Never Silent ☐ Love She Sought, The ☐ MacArthur ☐ Man on a String ☐ Man Who Died Twice, The ☐ Man, The ☐ Manions of America, The ☐ Marcus-Nelson Murders, The ☐ Marion Rose White ☐ Maybe I'll Come Home in the Spring ☐ Memorial Day ☐ Miss Rose White ☐ Nazis, The: Of Pure Blood ☐ Never Forget ☐ Night that Panicked America, The ☐ Nightmares ☐ One Spy Too Many ☐ Skylark ☐ Taking of Pelham One Two Three, The ☐ Terrible Joe Moran ☐ There Must Be a Pony ☐ Tribes ☐ White Lightning

Sayles, John ☐ Baby, It's You ☐ Brother from Another Planet, The ☐ City of Hope ☐ Eight Men Out ☐ Lianna ☐ Matewan ☐ Passion Fish ☐ Return of the Secaucus Seven, The ☐ Secret of Roan Inish, The

Schaffner, Franklin J. ☐ Best Man, The ☐ Boys From Brazil, The ☐ Double Man, The ☐ War Lord, The ☐ Islands in the Stream ☐ Lionheart ☐ Nicholas And Alexandra ☐ Papillon ☐ Patton ☐ Planet of the Apes ☐ Sphinx ☐ Stripper ☐ Welcome Home

Schatzberg, Jerry ☐ Clinton and Nadine ☐ Honeysuckle Rose ☐ Misunderstood ☐ No Small Affair ☐ Panic in Needle Park, The ☐ Scarecrow ☐ Seduction of Joe Tynan, The ☐ Street Smart

Schepisi, Fred ☐ Barbarosa ☐ Chant of Jimmy Blacksmith, The ☐ Cry in the Dark, A ☐ Devil's Playground, The ☐ Iceman ☐ I.Q. ☐ Mr. Baseball ☐ Plenty ☐ Roxanne ☐ Russia House, The ☐ Six Degrees of Separation

Schlesinger, John ☐ Believers, The ☐ Billy Liar ☐ Darling ☐ Day of the Locust, The ☐ Falcon and the Snowman, The ☐ Far from the Madding Crowd ☐ Honky Tonk Freeway ☐ Kind of Loving, A ☐ Madame Sousatzka ☐ Marathon Man ☐ Midnight Cowboy ☐ Pacific Heights ☐ Sunday, Bloody Sunday ☐ Visions of Eight ☐ Yanks

Schlondorff, Volker ☐ Circle of Deceit ☐ Coup de Grace ☐ Death of a Salesman ☐ Free Woman, A ☐ Gathering of Old Men, A ☐ Handmaid's Tale, The ☐ Lost Honor of Katharina Blum, The ☐ Swann in Love ☐ Tin Drum, The ☐ Voyager ☐ Young Torless

Schrader, Paul ☐ American Gigolo ☐ Blue Collar ☐ Cat People ☐ Comfort of Strangers, The ☐ Hardcore ☐ Light of Day ☐ Light Sleeper ☐ Mishima ☐ Patty Hearst

Schroeder, Barbet ☐ Barfly ☐ General Idi Amin Dada ☐ Koko: A Talking Gorilla ☐ Maitresse ☐ Reversal of Fortune ☐ Single White Female ☐ Valley, The

Scola, Ettore ☐ Devil in Love, The ☐ Down and Dirty ☐ Family, The ☐ La Nuit des Varennes ☐ Le Bal ☐ Let's Talk About Women ☐ Macaroni ☐ Passion of Love ☐ Pizza Triangle, The ☐ Special Day, A ☐ We All Loved Each Other So Much

Scorsese, Martin ☐ After Hours ☐ Age of Innocence, The ☐ Alice Doesn't Live Here Anymore ☐ Amazing Stories: Book Four ☐ Boxcar Bertha ☐ Cape Fear ☐ Color Of Money, The ☐ GoodFellas ☐ King of Comedy, The ☐ Last Waltz, The ☐ Mean Streets ☐ New York Stories ☐ New York, New York ☐ Raging Bull ☐ Taxi Driver ☐ Who's That Knocking at My Door

Scott, Ridley ☐ 1492: Conquest of Paradise ☐ Alien ☐ Black Rain ☐ Blade Runner ☐ Duellists, The ☐ Legend ☐ Someone to Watch Over Me ☐ Thelma and Louise

Sherman, Lowell ☐ Bachelor Apartment ☐ Broadway Through a Keyhole ☐ Greeks Had a Word for Them, The ☐ Ladies of the Jury ☐ Morning Glory ☐ Night Life of the Gods ☐ She Done Him Wrong

Sherman, Vincent ☐ Adventures of Don Juan ☐ Affair in Trinidad ☐ All Through the Night ☐ Backfire ☐ Bogie ☐ Damned Don't Cry, The ☐ Fever in the Blood, A ☐ Flight from Destiny ☐ Garment Jungle, The ☐ Goodbye, My Fancy ☐ Hard Way, The ☐ Harriet Craig ☐ Hasty Heart, The ☐ Ice Palace ☐ In Our Time ☐ Janie Gets Married ☐ Lady of the House ☐ Last Hurrah, The ☐ Lone Star ☐ Man Who Talked Too Much, The ☐ Mr. Skeffington ☐ Nora Prentiss ☐ Old Acquaintance ☐ Pillow to Post ☐ Return of Dr. X, The ☐ Saturday's Children ☐ Second Time Around, The ☐ Underground ☐ Unfaithful, The ☐ Young Philadelphians, The

Shinoda, Masahiro ☐ Demon Pond ☐ Double Suicide ☐ Gonza The Spearman ☐ MacArthur's Children

Siegel, Don ☐ Annapolis Story, An ☐ Baby Face Nelson ☐ Beguiled, The ☐ Big Steal, The ☐ Black Windmill, The ☐ Charley Varrick ☐ China Venture ☐ Coogan's Bluff ☐ Crime in the Streets ☐ Dirty Harry ☐ Duel at Silver Creek, The ☐ Edge of Eternity ☐ Escape from Alcatraz ☐ Flaming Star ☐ Gun Runners, The ☐ Hanged Man, The ☐ Hell Is for Heroes ☐ Hound-Dog Man ☐ Invasion of the Body Snatchers ☐ Jinxed! ☐ Killers, The ☐ Lineup, The ☐ Madigan ☐ Night Unto Night ☐ No Time for Flowers ☐ Private Hell 36 ☐ Riot in Cell Block 11 ☐ Rough Cut ☐ Shootist, The ☐ Spanish Affair ☐ Stranger on the Run ☐ Telefon ☐ Two Mules for Sister Sara ☐ Verdict, The

Silver, Joan Micklin ☐ Between the Lines ☐ Big Girls Don't Cry...They Get Even ☐ Crossing Delancey ☐ Finnegan Begin Again ☐ Head Over Heels ☐ Hester Street ☐ Loverboy ☐ Prison Stories: Women on the Inside ☐ Private Matter, A

Singleton, John ☐ Boyz N the Hood ☐ Higher Learning ☐ Poetic Justice ☐ Siodmak, Robert ☐ Christmas Holiday ☐ Cobra Woman ☐ Crimson Pirate, The ☐ Criss Cross ☐ Cry of the City ☐ Custer of the West ☐ Dark Mirror, The ☐ Deported ☐ Fight for Rome ☐ File on Thelma Jordon, The ☐ Flesh and the Woman ☐ Great Sinner, The ☐ Killers, The ☐ Last Roman, The ☐ Magnificent Sinner ☐ Phantom Lady ☐ Rats, The ☐ Son of Dracula ☐ Spiral Staircase, The ☐ Uncle Harry ☐ Whistle at Eaton Falls

Sirk, Douglas ☐ All I Desire ☐ All That Heaven Allows ☐ Battle Hymn ☐ Captain Lightfoot ☐ Court Concert, The ☐ First Legion, The ☐ Has Anybody Seen My Gal? ☐ Hilter's Madman ☐ Imitation of Life ☐ Interlude ☐ Lady Pays Off, The ☐ Magnificent Obsession ☐ Meet Me at the Fair ☐ No Room for the Groom ☐ Personal Column ☐ Pillars of Society ☐ Scandal in Paris, A ☐ Shockproof ☐ Sign of the Pagan ☐ Sleep, My Love ☐ Summer Storm ☐ Take Me to Town ☐ Tarnished Angels, The ☐ Taza, Son of Cochise ☐ There's Always Tomorrow ☐ Thunder on the Hill ☐ Time to Love and a Time to Die, A ☐ Weekend with Father ☐ Written on the Wind

Skolimowski, Jerzy ☐ Adventures of Gerard, The ☐ Barrier ☐ Deep End ☐ Identification Marks: None ☐ King, Queen, Knave ☐ Lightship, The ☐ Moonlighting ☐ Shout, The ☐ Walkover

Soderbergh, Steven ☐ Kafka ☐ King of the Hill ☐ sex, lies and videotape

Spheeris, Penelope ☐ Beverly Hillbillies, The ☐ Boys Next Door, The ☐ Decline of Western Civilization, The ☐ Decline of Western Civilization Part II: The Metal Years, The ☐ Dudes ☐ Hollywood Vice Squad ☐ Little Rascals, The ☐ Wayne's World

Spielberg, Steven ☐ 1941 ☐ Always ☐ Close Encounters of the Third Kind ☐ Color Purple, The ☐ Columbo: Murder by the Book ☐ Duel ☐ E.T. The Extra-Terrestrial ☐ Empire of the Sun ☐ Hook ☐ Indiana Jones and the Last Crusade ☐ Indiana Jones and the Temple Of Doom ☐ Jaws ☐ Jurassic Park ☐ Night Gallery ☐ Raiders of the Lost Ark ☐ Schindler's List ☐ Sugarland Express, The ☐ Twilight Zone—The Movie

Stahl, John M. ☐ Back Street ☐ Eve of St. Mark ☐ Father Was a Fullback ☐ Foxes of Harrow, The ☐ Holy Matrimony ☐ Imitation of Life ☐ Immortal Sergeant, The ☐ Keys of the Kingdom ☐ Leave Her to Heaven ☐ Letter of Introduction, A ☐ Magnificent Obsession ☐ Oh, You Beautiful Doll ☐ Only Yesterday ☐ Our Wife ☐ Parnell ☐ Strictly Dishonorable ☐ Walls of Jericho ☐ When Tomorrow Comes

Stevens, George ☐ Alice Adams ☐ Annie Oakley ☐ Bachelor Bait ☐ Damsel in Distress, A ☐ Diary of Anne Frank, The ☐ Giant ☐ Greatest Story Ever Told, The ☐ Gunga Din ☐ I Remember Mama ☐ Kentucky Kernels ☐ More The Merrier, The ☐ Nitwits, The ☐ Only Game in Town, The ☐ Penny Serenade ☐ Place in the Sun, A ☐ Quality Street ☐ Shane ☐ Something to Live For ☐ Swing Time ☐ Talk of the Town, The ☐ Vivacious Lady ☐ Woman of the Year

Stillman, Whit ☐ Barcelona ☐ Metropolitan

Stone, Oliver ☐ Born on the Fourth of July ☐ Doors, The ☐ Hand, The ☐ Heaven and Earth ☐ JFK ☐ Natural Born Killers ☐ Platoon ☐ Salvador ☐ Seizure ☐ Talk Radio ☐ Wall Street

Streisand, Barbra ☐ Prince of Tides, The ☐ Yentl

Sturges, John ☐ Backlash ☐ Bad Day at Black Rock ☐ By Love Possessed ☐ Capture, The ☐ Chino ☐ Eagle Has Landed, The ☐ Escape from Fort Bravo ☐ Fast Company ☐ Girl in White, The ☐ Girl Named Tamiko, A ☐ Great Escape, The ☐ Gunfight at the O.K. Corral ☐ Hallelujah Trail, The ☐ Hour of the Gun ☐ Ice Station Zebra ☐ It's a Big Country ☐ Jeopardy ☐ Joe Kidd ☐ Kind Lady ☐ Last Train from Gun Hill ☐ Law and Jake Wade, The ☐ Magnificent Seven, The ☐ Magnificent Yankee, The ☐ Marooned ☐ McQ ☐ Mystery Street ☐ Never So Few ☐ Old Man and the Sea, The ☐ People Against O'Hara, The ☐ Right Cross ☐ Satan Bug, The ☐ Scarlet Coat, The ☐ Sergeants 3 ☐ Underwater! ☐ Walking Hills, The

Sturges, Preston ☐ Beautiful Blonde from Bashful Bend, The ☐ Christmas in July ☐ French, They Are A Funny Race, The ☐ Great McGinty, The ☐ Great Moment, The ☐ Hail the Conquering Hero ☐ Lady Eve, The ☐ Mad Wednesday ☐ Miracle of Morgan's Creek, The ☐ Palm Beach Story, The ☐ Sullivan's Travels ☐ Unfaithfully Yours

Szabo, Istvan ☐ Colonel Redl ☐ Confidence ☐ Father ☐ Hanussen ☐ Meeting Venus ☐ Mephisto

Tarantino, Quentin ☐ Pulp Fiction ☐ Reservoir Dogs

Tarkovsky, Andrei ☐ Andrei Rublev ☐ Mirror, The ☐ My Name Is Ivan ☐ Nostalghia ☐ Sacrifice, The ☐ Solaris ☐ Stalker ☐ Violin and Roller

Tashlin, Frank ☐ Alphabet Murders, The ☐ Artists and Models ☐ Bachelor Flat ☐ Caprice ☐ Cinderfella ☐ Disorderly Orderly, The ☐ First Time, The ☐ Geisha Boy, The ☐ Girl Can't Help It, The ☐ Glass Bottom Boat, The ☐ Hollywood or Bust ☐ It's Only Money ☐ Lieutenant Wore Skirts, The ☐ Man from the Diner's Club, The ☐ Marry Me Again ☐ Private Navy of Sgt. O'Farrell, The ☐ Rock-a-Bye Baby ☐ Say One for Me ☐ Son of Paleface ☐ Susan Slept Here ☐ Will Success Spoil Rock Hunter? ☐ Who's Minding the Store?

Tati, Jacques ☐ Jour de F_te ☐ Mon Oncle ☐ Mr. Hulot's Holiday ☐ Playtime ☐ Traffic

Tavernier, Bertrand ☐ Beatrice ☐ Clockmaker, The ☐ Coup de Torchon ☐ Daddy Nostalgia ☐ Deathwatch ☐ Judge and the Assassin, The ☐ Let Joy Reign Supreme ☐ Life And Nothing But ☐ Mississippi Blues ☐ Round Midnight ☐ Sunday in the Country, A

Taviani, Paolo ☐ Allonsanfan ☐ Good Morning, Babylon ☐ Kaos ☐ Night of the Shooting Stars, The ☐ Night Sun ☐ Padre Padrone

Taviani, Vittorio ☐ Allonsanfan ☐ Night of the Shooting Stars, The ☐ Night Sun ☐ Padre Padrone

Tourneur, Jacques ☐ Anne of the Indies ☐ Appointment in Honduras ☐ Berlin Express ☐ Canyon Passage ☐ Cat People ☐ Circle of Danger ☐ Comedy of Terrors, The ☐ Curse of the Demon ☐ Days of Glory ☐ Easy Living ☐ Experiment Perilous ☐ Fearmakers, The ☐ Flame and the Arrow, The ☐ Great Day in the Morning ☐ I Walked with a Zombie ☐ Leopard Man, The ☐ Nick Carter, Master Detective ☐ Nightfall ☐ Out of the Past ☐ Stars in My Crown ☐ Stranger on Horseback ☐ They All Come Out ☐ Wichita

Truffaut, Francois ☐ Bed and Board ☐ Bride Wore Black, The ☐ Confidentially Yours ☐ Day for Night ☐ Fahrenheit 451 ☐ Four Hundred Blows, The ☐ Green Room, The ☐ Jules and Jim ☐ Last Metro, The ☐ L'Enfant Sauvage ☐ Love at Twenty ☐ Love on the Run (L'Amour en Fuite) ☐ Man Who Loved Women, The ☐ Mississippi Mermaid ☐ Shoot the Piano Player ☐ Small Change ☐ Soft Skin ☐ Stolen Kisses ☐ Story of Adele H, The ☐ Such a Gorgeous Kid Like Me ☐ Two English Girls ☐ Woman Next Door, The

Ulmer, Edgar G. ☐ Amazing Transparent Man, The ☐ Amerikaner Schadohen ☐ Beyond the Time Barrier ☐ Black Cat, The ☐ Bluebeard ☐ Carnegie Hall ☐ Cavern, The ☐ Club Havana ☐ Daughter of Dr. Jekyll ☐ Detour ☐ Green Fields ☐ Hannibal ☐ Her Sister's Secret ☐ Isle of Forgotten Sins ☐ Light Ahead, The ☐ Man from Planet X, The ☐ Murder Is My Beat ☐ Naked Dawn, The ☐ Pirates of Capri, The ☐ Saint Benny The Dip ☐ Singing Blacksmith

Van Dyke II, W. S. ☐ After the Thin Man ☐ Andy Hardy Gets Spring Fever ☐ Another Thin Man ☐ Bitter Sweet ☐ Cairo ☐ Cuban Love Song, The ☐ Devil is a Sissy, The ☐ Dr. Kildare's Victory ☐ Feminine Touch, The ☐ Forsaking All Others ☐ Guilty Hands ☐ Hide-Out ☐ His Brother's Wife ☐ I Live My Life ☐ I Love You Again ☐ I Married an Angel ☐ I Take This Woman ☐ It's a Wonderful World ☐ Journey for Margaret ☐ Love on the Run ☐ Manhattan Melodrama ☐ Marie Antoinette ☐ Naughty Marietta ☐ Night Court ☐ Penthouse ☐ Personal Property ☐ Prizefighter and the Lady, The ☐ Rage in Heaven ☐ Rosalie ☐ Rose Marie ☐ San Francisco ☐ Shadow of the Thin Man ☐ Stand Up and Fight ☐ Sweethearts ☐ Tarzan, the Ape Man ☐ They Gave Him a Gun ☐ Thin Man, The ☐ Trader Horn

Varda, Agnes ☐ Cleo from 5 to 7 ☐ Jacquot ☐ Le Bonheur ☐ Le Petit Amour ☐ One Sings, The Other Doesn't ☐ Vagabond

Verhoeven, Paul ☐ Basic Instinct ☐ Flesh + Blood ☐ Fourth Man, The ☐ Judge and the Sinner ☐ Keetje Tippel ☐ Robocop ☐ Soldier of Orange ☐ Spetters ☐ Total Recall ☐ Turkish Delight

Vidor, King ☐ American Romance, An ☐ Beyond the Forest ☐ Big Parade, The ☐ Bird of Paradise ☐ Champ, The ☐ Citadel, The ☐ Comrade X ☐ Crowd, The ☐ Cynara ☐ Duel in the Sun ☐ Fountainhead, The ☐ H.M. Pulham, Esq. ☐ Hallelujah ☐ Jack Knife Man, The ☐ Japanese War Bride ☐ Man without a Star ☐ Northwest Passage ☐ On Our Merry Way ☐ Our Daily Bread ☐ Ruby Gentry ☐ Show People ☐ So Red the Rose ☐ Solomon and Sheba ☐ Stella Dallas ☐ Stranger's Return, A ☐ Street Scene ☐ Texas Rangers, The ☐ War and Peace ☐ Wedding Night, The

Vigo, Jean ☐ L'Atalante ☐ Zero for Conduct

Visconti, Luchino ☐ Bellissima ☐ Boccaccio '70 ☐ Conversation Piece ☐ Damned, The ☐ Death in Venice ☐ Innocent, The ☐ La Terra Trema ☐ Leopard, The ☐ Ludwig ☐ Of Life and Love ☐ Ossessione ☐ Rocco and His Brothers ☐ Senso ☐ Stranger, The ☐ White Nights

Von Sternberg, Josef ☐ American Tragedy, An ☐ Blonde Venus ☐ Blue Angel, The ☐ Crime and Punishment ☐ Jet Pilot ☐ King Steps Out, The ☐ Last Command, The ☐ Macao ☐ Morocco ☐ Scarlet Empress, The ☐ Sergeant Madden ☐ Shanghai Express ☐ Shanghai Gesture, The ☐ Thunderbolt ☐ Underworld

Von Stroheim, Erich ☐ Blind Husbands ☐ Foolish Wives ☐ Greed ☐ Hello Sister ☐ Merry Widow, The ☐ Queen Kelly ☐ Wedding March, The

Wajda, Andrzej ☐ Ashes and Diamonds ☐ Danton ☐ Everything for Sale ☐ Generation, A ☐ Innocent Sorcerers ☐ Kanal ☐ Korczak ☐ Land of Promise, The ☐ Love in Germany, A ☐ Maids Of Wilko ☐ Man of Iron ☐ Man of Marble ☐ Orchestra Conductor, The

Walsh, Raoul ☐ Along the Great Divide ☐ Artists and Models ☐ Baby Face Harrington ☐ Background to Danger ☐ Band of Angels ☐ Battle Cry ☐ Big Brown Eyes ☐ Big Trail, The ☐ Blackbeard, the Pirate ☐ Bowery, The ☐ Captain Horatio Hornblower ☐ Cheyenne ☐ College Swing ☐ Colorado Territory ☐ Dark Command ☐ Desperate Journey ☐ Distant Drums ☐ Distant Trumpet, A ☐ Esther and the King ☐ Every Night at Eight ☐ Fighter Squadron ☐ Gentleman Jim ☐ Glory Alley ☐ Going Hollywood ☐ Gun Fury ☐ High Sierra ☐ Hitting a New High ☐ Horn Blows at Midnight, The ☐ In Old Arizona ☐ King and Four Queens, The ☐ Klondike Annie ☐ Lawless Breed, The ☐ Lion Is in the Streets, A ☐ Man I Love, The ☐ Manpower ☐ Marines, Let's Go ☐ Me and My Gal ☐ Naked and the Dead, The ☐ Northern Pursuit ☐ Objective, Burma! ☐ One Sunday Afternoon ☐ Pursued ☐ Revolt of Mamie Stover, The ☐ Roaring Twenties, The ☐ Sadie Thompson ☐ Salty O'Rourke ☐ Saskatchewan ☐ Sea Devils ☐ Sheriff of Fractured Jaw, The ☐ Silver River ☐ Strawberry Blonde, The ☐ Tall Men, The ☐ They Died With Their Boots On ☐ They Drive by Night ☐ Thief of Bagdad, The ☐ Uncertain Glory ☐ Under Pressure ☐ What Price Glory? ☐ White Heat ☐ World in His Arms, The

Wang, Wayne ☐ Chan is Missing ☐ Dim Sum—A Little Bit of Heart ☐ Eat a Bowl of Tea ☐ Joy Luck Club, The ☐ Life Is Cheap...but Toilet Paper is Expensive ☐ Slam Dance

Waters, John ☐ Cry-Baby ☐ Divine Waters ☐ Female Trouble ☐ Hairspray ☐ Mondo Trasho ☐ Multiple Maniacs ☐ Polyester ☐ Serial Mom

Weir, Peter ☐ Cars that Ate Paris, The ☐ Dead Poets Society ☐ Fearless ☐ Gallipoli ☐ Green Card ☐ Last Wave, The ☐ Mosquito Coast, The ☐ Picnic at Hanging Rock ☐ Plumber, The ☐ Witness ☐ Year of Living Dangerously, The

Welles, Orson ☐ Chimes at Midnight ☐ Citizen Kane ☐ F for Fake ☐ Immortal Story, The ☐ Lady from Shanghai, The ☐ Macbeth ☐ Magnificent Ambersons, The ☐ Mr. Arkadin ☐ Othello ☐ Stranger, The ☐ Touch of Evil ☐ Trial, The

Wellman, William ☐ Across the Wide Missouri ☐ Battleground ☐ Beau Geste ☐ Beggars of Life ☐ Blood Alley ☐ Buffalo Bill ☐ Call of the Wild ☐ Central Airport ☐ College Coach ☐ Darby's Rangers ☐ Frisco Jenny ☐ Gallant Journey ☐ Good-bye, My Lady ☐ Great Man's Lady, The ☐ Happy Years, The ☐ Hatchet Man, The ☐ Heroes for Sale ☐ High and the Mighty, The ☐ Iron Curtain, The ☐ Island in the Sky ☐ Lady of Burlesque ☐ Lafayette Escadrille ☐ Light That Failed, The ☐ Love Is a Racket ☐ Magic Town ☐ Men with Wings ☐ My Man and I ☐ Next Voice You Hear, The ☐ Night Nurse ☐ Nothing Sacred ☐ Other Men's Women ☐ Ox-Bow Incident, The ☐ Public Enemy ☐ Reaching for the Sun ☐ Robin Hood of El Dorado, The ☐ Roxie Hart ☐ Small Town Girl ☐ Star Is Born, A ☐ Star Witness ☐ Story Of

G.I. Joe, The ☐ This Man's Navy ☐ Track of the Cat ☐ Westward the Women ☐ Wild Boys of the Road ☐ Yellow Sky
Wenders, Wim ☐ Alice in the Cities ☐ American Friend, The ☐ Faraway, So Close ☐ Goalie's Anxiety at the Penalty Kick, The ☐ Hammett ☐ Kings of the Road ☐ Lightning Over Water ☐ Notebook on Cities and Clothes ☐ Paris, Texas ☐ Scarlet Letter, The ☐ State of Things, The ☐ Until the End of the World ☐ Wings of Desire ☐ Wrong Move
Wertmuller, Lina ☐ All Screwed Up ☐ Camorra ☐ Joke of Destiny, A ☐ Let's Talk About Men ☐ Lizards, The ☐ Love and Anarchy ☐ Night Full of Rain, A ☐ Seduction of Mimi, The ☐ Seven Beauties ☐ Summer Night ☐ Swept Away
Whale, James ☐ Bride of Frankenstein, The ☐ By Candlelight ☐ Frankenstein (Restored) ☐ Great Garrick, The ☐ Green Hell ☐ Impatient Maiden, The ☐ Invisible Man, The ☐ Journey's End ☐ Kiss Before the Mirror, The ☐ Man in the Iron Mask, The ☐ Old Dark House, The ☐ One More River ☐ Port of Seven Seas ☐ Road Back, The ☐ Show Boat
Wilder, Billy ☐ Apartment, The ☐ Avanti! ☐ Big Carnival, The ☐ Buddy Buddy ☐ Double Indemnity ☐ Emperor Waltz, The ☐ Fedora ☐ Five Graves to Cairo ☐ Foreign Affair, A ☐ Fortune Cookie, The ☐ Front Page, The ☐ Irma la Douce ☐ Kiss Me, Stupid ☐ Lost Weekend, The ☐ Love in the Afternoon ☐ Major and the Minor, The ☐ One, Two, Three ☐ Private Life of Sherlock Holmes, The ☐ Sabrina ☐ Seven Year Itch, The ☐ Some Like It Hot ☐ Spirit of St. Louis, The ☐ Stalag 17 ☐ Sunset Boulevard ☐ Witness for the Prosecution
Wise, Robert ☐ Andromeda Strain, The ☐ Audrey Rose ☐ Blood on the Moon ☐ Body Snatcher, The ☐ Born to Kill ☐ Captive City, The ☐ Criminal Court ☐ Day the Earth Stood Still, The ☐ Desert Rats, The ☐ Destination Gobi ☐ Executive Suite ☐ Game of Death, A ☐ Haunting, The ☐ Helen of Troy ☐ Hindenberg, The ☐ House on Telegraph Hill ☐ I Want to Live! ☐ Mademoiselle Fifi ☐ Mystery in Mexico ☐ Odds Against Tomorrow ☐ Rooftops ☐ Run Silent, Run Deep ☐ Sand Pebbles, The ☐ Set-Up, The ☐ So Big ☐ Somebody Up There Likes Me ☐ Something for the Birds ☐ Sound of Music, The ☐ Star Trek: The Motion Picture ☐ Star! ☐ This Could Be the Night ☐ Three Secrets ☐ Tribute to a Bad Man ☐ Two Flags West ☐ Two for the Seesaw ☐ Until They Sail ☐ West Side Story
Wood, Jr., Edward D. ☐ Bride of the Monster ☐ Jail Bait ☐ Plan 9 from Outer Space ☐ Glen or Glenda
Wyler, William ☐ Ben-Hur ☐ Best Years of Our Lives, The ☐ Big Country, The ☐ Carrie ☐ Children's Hour, The ☐ Collector, The ☐ Come and Get It ☐ Counsellor-at-Law ☐ Dead End ☐ Desperate Hours, The ☐ Detective Story ☐ Dodsworth ☐ Friendly Persuasion ☐ Funny Girl ☐ Gay Deception, The ☐ Good Fairy, The ☐ Heiress, The ☐ Hell's Heroes ☐ House Divided, A ☐ How to Steal a Million ☐ Jezebel ☐ Letter, The ☐ Liberation of L.B. Jones, The ☐ Little Foxes, The ☐ Mrs. Miniver ☐ Roman Holiday ☐ These Three ☐ Westerner, The ☐ Wuthering Heights
Young, Robert ☐ Hostage ☐ Splitting Heirs
Young, Robert M. ☐ Alambrista! ☐ Ballad of Gregorio Cortez, The ☐ Dominick and Eugene ☐ Extremities ☐ One-Trick Pony ☐ Rich Kids ☐ Saving Grace ☐ Short Eyes ☐ Soldier's Home ☐ Talent for the Game
Zanussi, Krzysztof ☐ Camouflage ☐ Catamount Killing ☐ Constant Factor, The ☐ Contract ☐ From a Far Country: Pope John Paul II ☐ Illumination ☐ Imperative
Zeffirelli, Franco ☐ Brother Sun, Sister Moon ☐ Champ, The ☐ Endless Love ☐ Hamlet ☐ Jesus of Nazareth ☐ La Traviata ☐ Otello ☐ Romeo and Juliet ☐ Taming of the Shrew, The
Zemeckis, Robert ☐ Back to the Future ☐ Back to the Future Part II ☐ Back to the Future Part III ☐ Death Becomes Her ☐ Forrest Gump ☐ I Wanna Hold Your Hand ☐ Romancing the Stone ☐ Used Cars ☐ Who Framed Roger Rabbit?
Zieff, Howard ☐ Dream Team, The ☐ Hearts of the West ☐ House Calls ☐ Main Event, The ☐ My Girl ☐ My Girl 2 ☐ Private Benjamin ☐ Slither ☐ Unfaithfully Yours
Zinnemann, Fred ☐ Act of Violence ☐ Behold a Pale Horse ☐ Day of the Jackal, The ☐ Eyes in the Night ☐ Five Days One Summer ☐ From Here to Eternity ☐ Hatful of Rain, A ☐ High Noon ☐ Julia ☐ Kid Glove Killer ☐ Little Mr. Jim ☐ Man for All Seasons, A ☐ Member of the Wedding, The ☐ Men, The ☐ My Brother Talks to Horses ☐ Nun's Story, The ☐ Oklahoma! ☐ Search, The ☐ Seventh Cross, The ☐ Sundowners, The ☐ Teresa
Zucker, David ☐ Airplane! ☐ Naked Gun, The ☐ Naked Gun 2 1/2: The Smell of Fear, The ☐ Ruthless People ☐ Top Secret
Zucker, Jerry ☐ Airplane! ☐ Ghost ☐ Ruthless People ☐ Top Secret

ACTORS

Abbott, Bruce ☐ Bad Dreams ☐ Bride of Re-Animator ☐ Re-Animator ☐ Summer Heat
Abbott, Bud ☐ Abbott and Costello Go To Mars ☐ Abbott and Costello In Hollywood ☐ Abbott and Costello In The Foreign Legion ☐ Abbott and Costello Meet Captain Kidd ☐ Abbott and Costello Meet Dr Jekyll And Mr Hyde ☐ Abbott and Costello Meet Frankenstein ☐ Abbott and Costello Meet The Invisible Man ☐ Abbott and Costello Meet The Keystone Kops ☐ Abbott and Costello Meet the Killer ☐ Abbott and Costello Meet the Mummy ☐ Africa Screams ☐ Buck Privates ☐ Buck Privates Come Home ☐ Comin' Round the Mountain ☐ Dance with Me Henry ☐ Here Come the Co-eds ☐ Hey Abbott! ☐ Hit the Ice ☐ Hold That Ghost ☐ In Society ☐ In the Navy ☐ It Ain't Hay ☐ Jack and the Beanstalk ☐ Keep 'Em Flying ☐ Little Giant ☐ Lost in a Harem ☐ Lost in Alaska ☐ Mexican Hayride ☐ Naughty Nineties ☐ Noose Hangs High, The ☐ One Night in the Tropics ☐ Pardon My Sarong ☐ Ride 'Em Cowboy ☐ Rio Rita ☐ Time of Their Lives, The ☐ Who Done It? ☐ Wistful Widow of Wagon Gap, The
Abel, Walter ☐ Affairs of Susan, The ☐ Fabulous Joe, The ☐ Fury ☐ Glamour Boy ☐ Indian Fighter, The ☐ Island in the Sky ☐ Kiss and Tell ☐ Man Without a Country, The ☐ Men with Wings ☐ Michael Shayne, Private Detective ☐ Mirage ☐ Mr. Skeffington ☐ Night People ☐ Quick, Let's Get Married ☐ Racket Busters ☐ Skylark ☐ So Proudly We Hail! ☐ So This Is Love ☐ Three Musketeers, The
Abraham, F. Murray ☐ Amadeus ☐ Beyond the Stars ☐ Big Fix, The ☐ Innocent Man, An ☐ Intimate Power ☐ Last Action Hero ☐ Madman ☐ Mobsters ☐ Name of the Rose, The ☐ Ritz, The ☐ Slipstream ☐ Surviving the Game
Abril, Victoria ☐ High Heels ☐ Jimmy Hollywood ☐ L'Addition ☐ Lovers ☐ Max, Mon Amour ☐ Moon in the Gutter, The ☐ On the Line ☐ Our Father
Ackland, Joss ☐ Bill & Ted's Bogus Journey ☐ England Made Me ☐ Incident at Victoria Falls ☐ Jekyll & Hyde ☐ Man Who Lived at the Ritz, The ☐ Mighty Ducks, The ☐ Nowhere to Run ☐ Object of Beauty, The ☐ Operation Daybreak ☐ Princess and the Goblin, The ☐ Project: Shadowchaser ☐ Queenie ☐ Royal Flash ☐ Saint Jack ☐ Sicilian, The ☐ Spymaker—The Secret Life of Ian Fleming ☐ To Kill a Priest ☐ White Mischief
Ackroyd, David ☐ And I Alone Survived ☐ Cocaine: One Man's Seduction ☐ Dark Secret of Harvest Home ☐ Gun in the House, A
Adams, Brooke ☐ Almost You ☐ Cuba ☐ Days of Heaven ☐ Dead Zone, The ☐ F. Scott Fitzgerald and "The Last of the Belles" ☐ Gas, Food Lodging ☐ Haunted ☐ Invasion of the Body Snatchers ☐ Key Exchange ☐ Last Hit, The ☐ Man on Fire ☐ Man, a Woman and a Bank, A ☐ Shock Waves ☐ Sometimes They Come Back ☐ Tell Me a Riddle ☐ Unborn, The
Adams, Casey ☐ Indestructible Man, The ☐ Monster That Challenged the World, The ☐ Naked Alibi ☐ Niagara ☐ Summer and Smoke
Adams, Edie ☐ Best Man, The ☐ Call Me Bwana ☐ Cheech & Chong—Up in Smoke ☐ Ernie Kovacs: Between the Laughter ☐ Fast Friends ☐ Honey Pot, The ☐ It's a Mad Mad Mad Mad World ☐ Kovacs! ☐ Love with the Proper Stranger ☐ Lover Come Back ☐ Made in Paris ☐ Oscar, The ☐ Racquet ☐ Shooting Stars ☐ Under the Yum Yum Tree
Adams, Julie ☐ Away All Boats ☐ Bend of the River ☐ Black Roses ☐ Bright Victory ☐ Four Girls in Town ☐ Gunfight at Dodge City, The ☐ Last Movie, The ☐ McQ ☐ One Desire ☐ Private War of Major Benson, The ☐ Raymie ☐ Slaughter on Tenth Avenue ☐ Tarawa Beachhead ☐ Tickle Me
Adams, Mason ☐ F/X ☐ Final Conflict, The ☐ Flamingo Road ☐ Half Slave, Half Free ☐ Night They Saved Christmas, The ☐ Northstar ☐ Rage of Angels: The Story Continues ☐ Shining Season, A
Adams, Maud ☐ Angel III—Final Chapter, The ☐ Christian Licorice Store, The ☐ Girl in Blue, The ☐ Hell Hunters ☐ Jane and the Lost City ☐ Kill Reflex, The ☐ Killer Force ☐ Man with the Golden Gun, The ☐ Nairobi Affair ☐ Octopussy ☐ Playing for Time ☐ Rollerball ☐ Silent Night, Deadly Night (Part IV—The Initiation) ☐ Tattoo
Adams, Nick ☐ Die, Monster, Die! ☐ FBI Story, The ☐ Frankenstein Conquers the World ☐ Fury at Showdown ☐ Godzilla vs. Monster Zero ☐ Hell Is for Heroes ☐ Hook, The ☐ Interns, The ☐ Mission Mars ☐ Mosby's Marauders ☐ No Time for Sergeants ☐ Our Miss Brooks ☐ Rebel Without a Cause ☐ Strange Lady in Town
Addams, Dawn ☐ 20,000 Pound Kiss, The ☐ Alien Women ☐ Hour of 13, The ☐ House of Intrigue ☐ Khyber Patrol ☐ King in New York, A ☐ Silent Enemy, The ☐ Thousand Eyes of Dr. Mabuse, The ☐ Vampire Lovers, The
Adjani, Isabelle ☐ Brontë Sisters, The ☐ Camille Claudel ☐ Driver, The ☐ Ishtar ☐ Next Year if All Goes Well ☐ Nosferatu the Vampyre ☐ One Deadly Summer ☐ Posses-

sion ☐ Quartet ☐ Queen Margot ☐ Story of Adele H, The ☐ Subway ☐ Tenant, The

Adler, Luther ☐ Absence of Malice ☐ Brotherhood, The ☐ Cast a Giant Shadow ☐ D.O.A. ☐ Desert Fox, The ☐ Hot Blood ☐ House of Strangers, The ☐ M ☐ Magic Face, The ☐ Man in the Glass Booth, The ☐ Mean Johnny Barrows ☐ Under My Skin ☐ Wake of the Red Witch

Adorf, Mario ☐ Apache Gold ☐ Boomerang ☐ Fedora ☐ Invitation au Voyage ☐ Italian Connection, The ☐ Lola ☐ Lost Honor of Katharina Blum, The ☐ Major Dundee ☐ Rosemary ☐ Tin Drum, The

Adrian, Iris ☐ Bluebeard ☐ Errand Boy, The ☐ Fast and the Furious, The ☐ I Killed That Man ☐ It's a Pleasure! ☐ Juke Box Jenny ☐ Lady of Burlesque ☐ My Favorite Spy ☐ Paleface, The ☐ Roxie Hart ☐ Sky Dragon, The ☐ To the Shores of Tripoli

Adrian, Max ☐ Devils, The ☐ Dr. Terror's House of Horrors ☐ Music Lovers, The ☐ Pool of London ☐ Young Mr. Pitt, The

Agar, John ☐ Adventure in Baltimore ☐ Along the Great Divide ☐ Attack of the Puppet People ☐ Bait ☐ Brain from Planet Arous, The ☐ Breakthrough ☐ Daughter of Dr. Jekyll ☐ Fort Apache ☐ Golden Mistress, The ☐ Hold Back Tomorrow ☐ I Married a Communist ☐ Invisible Invaders ☐ Johnny Reno ☐ Journey to the Seventh Planet ☐ Magic Carpet, The ☐ Man of Conflict ☐ Miracle Mile ☐ Mole People, The ☐ Raymie ☐ Revenge of the Creature ☐ Sands of Iwo Jima ☐ She Wore a Yellow Ribbon ☐ Shield For Murder ☐ Stage to Thunder Rock ☐ Star in the Dust ☐ Tarantula ☐ Women of the Prehistoric Planet

Agren, Janet ☐ Gates of Hell, The ☐ Hands of Steel ☐ Karate Warrior ☐ Kidnapping of Baby John Doe, The ☐ Perfect Crime, The

Agutter, Jenny ☐ American Werewolf in London, An ☐ Amy ☐ Child's Play 2 ☐ China 9, Liberty 37 ☐ Dark Tower ☐ Dominique ☐ Eagle Has Landed, The ☐ Freddie as F.R.O.7 ☐ King of the Wind ☐ Logan's Run ☐ Man in the Iron Mask ☐ Mayflower: The Pilgrims' Adventure ☐ Not a Penny More, Not a Penny Less ☐ Railway Children, The ☐ Riddle of the Sands, The ☐ Secret Places ☐ Silas Marner ☐ Walkabout

Aherne, Brian ☐ Angel on the Amazon ☐ Beloved Enemy ☐ Best of Everything, The ☐ Bullet is Waiting, A ☐ Captain Fury ☐ Cavern, The ☐ First Comes Courage ☐ Fountain, The ☐ Great Garrick, The ☐ Hired Wife ☐ I Confess ☐ I Live My Life ☐ Juarez ☐ Lady in Question,The ☐ Locket, The ☐ Merrily We Live ☐ My Sister Eileen ☐ My Son, My Son ☐ Night to Remember, A ☐ Rosie ☐ Skylark ☐ Smilin' Through ☐ Song of Songs ☐ Sword of Lancelot ☐ Sylvia Scarlett ☐ Titanic ☐ Vigil in the Night ☐ Waltz King, The ☐ What Every Woman Knows

Ahn, Philip ☐ Fair Wind to Java ☐ I Was an American Spy ☐ Japanese War Bride ☐ Macao

Aidman, Charles ☐ Countdown ☐ Menace on the Mountain ☐ Picture of Dorian Gray, The ☐ War Hunt ☐ Zoot Suit

Aiello, Danny ☐ 29th Street ☐ Bang the Drum Slowly ☐ Blood Feud ☐ Bloodbrothers ☐ Cemetery Club, The ☐ Chu Chu and the Philly Flash ☐ Closer, The ☐ Defiance ☐ Do the Right Thing ☐ Fingers ☐ Fort Apache, The Bronx ☐ Harlem Nights ☐ Hudson Hawk ☐ Jacob's Ladder ☐ January Man, The ☐ Key Exchange ☐ Lovey: A Circle of Children, Part II ☐ Man on Fire ☐ Me and the Kid ☐ Mistress ☐ Moonstruck ☐ Old Enough ☐ Once Around ☐ Pick-up Artist, The ☐ Pickle, The ☐ Preppie Murder, The ☐ Professional, The ☐ Purple Rose of Cairo, The ☐ Radio Days ☐ Ready to Wear ☐ Ruby

Aimee, Anouk ☐ 8 1/2 ☐ Appointment, The ☐ Golden Salamander, The ☐ Justine ☐ Keepers, The ☐ La Dolce Vita ☐ Leap into the Void ☐ Lola ☐ Lovers of Montparnasse, The ☐ Man and a Woman, A ☐ Man and a Woman, A: 20 Years Later ☐ Model Shop, The ☐ Of Flesh and Blood ☐ Ready to Wear ☐ Sodom and Gomorrah ☐ Tragedy of a Ridiculous Man

Akins, Claude ☐ Battle for the Planet of the Apes ☐ Bitter Creek ☐ Black Gold ☐ Burning Hills, The ☐ Comanche Station ☐ Curse, The ☐ Distant Trumpet, A ☐ Eric ☐ Falling from Grace ☐ Farm, The ☐ First to Fight ☐ Flap ☐ Incident at Phantom Hill ☐ Incident at Victoria Falls ☐ Inherit the Wind ☐ Man Called Sledge, A ☐ Manhunt for Claude Dallas ☐ Medical Story ☐ Merrill's Marauders ☐ Monster in the Closet ☐ Night Stalker, The ☐ Norliss Tapes, The ☐ Raid, The ☐ Return of the Magnificent Seven ☐ Rio Bravo ☐ Shield For Murder ☐ Waterhole #3

Alberghetti, Anna Maria ☐ Cinderfella ☐ Duel at Apache Wells ☐ Here Comes the Groom ☐ Last Command, The ☐ Medium, The ☐ Ten Thousand Bedrooms

Albert, Eddie ☐ Actors and Sin ☐ Angel From Texas, An ☐ Attack! ☐ Beloved Infidel ☐ Beulah Land ☐ Birch Interval ☐ Blood Barrier ☐ Bombardier ☐ Borrowers, The ☐ Brother Rat ☐ Brother Rat and a Baby ☐ Burning Rage ☐ Captain Newman, M.D. ☐ Carrie ☐ Devil's Rain, The ☐ Dispatch from Reuters, A ☐ Dreamscape ☐ Dude Goes West, The ☐ Eagle Squadron ☐ Escape to Witch Mountain ☐ Evening in Byzantium, An ☐ Fireball Forward ☐ Foolin' Around ☐ Four Mothers ☐ Four Wives ☐ Fuller Brush Girl, The ☐ Girl from Mars, The ☐ Girl Rush, The ☐ Goliath Awaits ☐ Great Mr. Nobody, The ☐ Gun Runners, The ☐ Head Office ☐ Heartbreak Kid, The ☐ Hustle ☐ I'll Cry Tomorrow ☐ Joker is Wild, The ☐ Longest Yard, The ☐ Madison Avenue ☐ McQ ☐ Meet Me After the Show ☐ Miracle of the White Stallions ☐ Moving Violation ☐ My Love Came Back ☐ Oklahoma! ☐ On Your Toes ☐ Orders to Kill ☐ Out of the Fog ☐ Perfect Marriage, The ☐ Peter and Paul ☐ Rendezvous with Annie ☐ Roman Holiday ☐ Roots of Heaven, The ☐ Smash-Up, the Story of a Woman ☐ Sun Also Rises, The ☐ Teahouse of the August Moon, The ☐ Thieves Fall Out ☐ Two Little Bears, The ☐ Wagons Roll at Night, The ☐ Who's Got the Action? ☐ Yes, Giorgio ☐ You're in the Navy Now ☐ Young Doctors, The

Albert, Edward ☐ 40 Carats ☐ Accidents ☐ Blood Feud ☐ Body Language ☐ Butterflies Are Free ☐ Butterfly ☐ Demon Keeper ☐ Fist Fighter ☐ Fool Killer, The ☐ Galaxy of Terror ☐ Getting Even ☐ Girl from Mars, The ☐ Greek Tycoon, The ☐ Guarding Tess ☐ House Where Evil Dwells, The ☐ Ice Runner, The ☐ Killer Bees ☐ Mind Games ☐ Night School ☐ Out Of Sight, Out Of Mind ☐ Rescue, The ☐ Shootfighter: Fight to the Death ☐ Terminal Entry ☐ When Time Ran Out . . .

Albertson, Frank ☐ Connecticut Yankee, A ☐ Ever in My Heart ☐ Fury ☐ Here Comes Elmer ☐ It's a Wonderful Life ☐ Man Made Monster ☐ Men Without Women ☐ Mother Carey's Chickens ☐ Nightfall ☐ Room Service ☐ Salute ☐ Shepherd of the Ozarks ☐ Underground Agent

Albertson, Jack ☐ Big Business Girl ☐ Bring Your Smile Along ☐ Charlie and the Great Balloon Chase ☐ Dead and Buried ☐ Flim Flam Man, The ☐ Fox and the Hound, The ☐ Marriage Is Alive and Well ☐ Monkey on My Back ☐ My Body, My Child ☐ Once Upon a Dead Man ☐ Pickup on 101 ☐ Poseidon Adventure, The ☐ Rabbit, Run ☐ Subject Was Roses, The ☐ Unguarded Moment, The ☐ Willy Wonka and the Chocolate Factory

Albright, Hardie ☐ Cabin in the Cotton, The ☐ Jade Mask, The ☐ Jewel Robbery ☐ Match King, The ☐ Ninth Guest, The ☐ Scarlet Letter, The ☐ Song of Songs ☐ Successful Calamity, A ☐ Working Man, The

Albright, Lola ☐ Bodyhold ☐ Cold Wind in August, A ☐ Good Humor Man, The ☐ Impossible Years, The ☐ Joy House ☐ Kid Galahad ☐ Lord Love a Duck ☐ Magnificent Matador, The ☐ Monolith Monsters, The ☐ Oregon Passage ☐ Silver Whip, The ☐ Way West, The ☐ Where Were You When the Lights Went Out?

Alda, Alan ☐ And the Band Played On ☐ Betsy's Wedding ☐ California Suite ☐ Crimes and Misdemeanors ☐ Extraordinary Seaman, The ☐ Four Seasons, The ☐ Glass House, The ☐ Gone Are the Days ☐ Isn't It Shocking? ☐ Jenny ☐ Kill Me if You Can ☐ M*A*S*H—Goodbye, Farewell, Amen ☐ Manhattan Murder Mystery ☐ Mephisto Waltz, The ☐ New Life, A ☐ Paper Lion ☐ Playmates ☐ Same Time, Next Year ☐ Seduction of Joe Tynan, The ☐ Sweet Liberty ☐ To Kill a Clown ☐ Whispers in the Dark

Alda, Robert ☐ April Showers ☐ Beast with Five Fingers, The ☐ Bittersweet Love ☐ Cinderella Jones ☐ Cleopatra's Daughter ☐ Cloak and Dagger ☐ Imitation of Life ☐ Love by Appointment ☐ Man I Love, The ☐ Nora Prentiss ☐ Rhapsody in Blue

Aleandro, Norma ☐ Gaby—A True Story ☐ Official Story, The ☐ One Man's War ☐ Vital Signs

Alexander, Jane ☐ All the President's Men ☐ Betsy, The ☐ Blood & Orchids ☐ Brubaker ☐ Calamity Jane ☐ Circle of Children, A ☐ City Heat ☐ Daughter of the Streets ☐ Death Be Not Proud ☐ Eleanor and Franklin ☐ Eleanor and Franklin: The White House Years ☐ Friendship in Vienna ☐ Great White Hope, The ☐ Gunfight, A ☐ In Love and War ☐ In the Custody of Strangers ☐ Kramer vs. Kramer ☐ Lovey: A Circle of Children, Part II ☐ Malice in Wonderland ☐ Miracle on 34th Street ☐ New Centurions, The ☐ Night Crossing ☐ Open Admissions ☐ Playing for Time ☐ Question of Love, A ☐ Square Dance ☐ Sweet Country ☐ Testament

Alexander, Jason ☐ Brighton Beach Memoirs ☐ Burning, The ☐ I Don't Buy Kisses Anymore ☐ Jacob's Ladder ☐ North ☐ Paper, The ☐ Pretty Woman ☐ Return of Jafar, The ☐ White Palace

Alice, Mary ☐ Half Slave, Half Free 2 ☐ He Who Walks Alone ☐ Sparkle ☐ To Sleep With Anger ☐ Women of Brewster Place, The

Ali, Muhammad ☐ Body and Soul ☐ Freedom Road ☐ Greatest, The

Allan, Elizabeth ☐ Ace of Aces ☐ Brain Machine, The ☐ Folly to Be Wise ☐ Front Page Story ☐ Haunted Strangler, The ☐ Heart of the Matter, The ☐ If This Be Sin ☐ Insult ☐ Java Head ☐ Mark of the Vampire ☐ Men in White ☐ Mystery of Mr. X, The ☐ No Highway in the Sky ☐ Reserved for Ladies ☐ Slave Ship ☐ Tale of Two Cities, A

Allbritton, Louise ☐ Bowery to Broadway ☐ Doolins of Oklahoma, The ☐ Her Primitive Man ☐ Innocent Affair, An ☐ San Diego, I Love You ☐ Sitting Pretty ☐ Son of Dracula ☐ Walk a Crooked Mile ☐ Who Done It?

Allen, Fred ☐ It's in the Bag ☐ Love Thy Neighbor ☐ O. Henry's Full House ☐ Sally, Irene and Mary ☐ Thanks a Million ☐ We're Not Married

Allen, Gracie ☐ Big Broadcast of 1936, The ☐ Big Broadcast of 1937, The ☐ Big Broadcast, The ☐ College Holiday ☐ College Humor ☐ College Swing ☐ Damsel in Distress, A ☐ Gracie Allen Murder Case, The ☐ Here Comes Cookie ☐ Honolulu ☐ International House ☐ Love in Bloom ☐ Many Happy Returns ☐ Mr. and Mrs. North ☐ Six of a Kind ☐ Two Girls and a Sailor ☐ We're Not Dressing

Allen, Joan ☐ Compromising Positions ☐ Ethan Frome ☐ In Country ☐ Josh and S.A.M. ☐ Manhunter ☐ Peggy Sue Got Married ☐ Searching for Bobby Fischer ☐ Tucker—The Man and His Dream

Allen, Jonelle ☐ Come Back, Charleston Blue ☐ Grave Secrets ☐ Penalty Phase ☐ Victims

Allen, Judith ☐ Boots And Saddles ☐ Bright Eyes ☐ Old-Fashioned Way, The ☐ This Day and Age ☐ Thundering Herd, The ☐ Too Much Harmony

Allen, Karen ☐ Animal Behavior ☐ Backfire ☐ Challenger ☐ Cruising ☐ Ghost in the Machine ☐ Glass Menagerie, The ☐ King of the Hill ☐ Lovey: A Circle of Children, Part II ☐ Raiders of the Lost Ark ☐ Sandlot, The ☐ Scrooged ☐ Shoot the Moon ☐ Starman ☐ Until September ☐ Wanderers, The

Allen, Nancy ☐ 1941 ☐ Acting on Impulse ☐ Blow Out ☐ Buddy System, The ☐ Carrie ☐ Dressed to Kill ☐ Gladiator, The ☐ Home Movies ☐ I Wanna Hold Your Hand ☐ Limit Up ☐ Memories of Murder ☐ Not for Publication ☐ Philadelphia Experiment, The ☐ Poltergeist III ☐ Robocop ☐ Robocop 2 ☐ Robocop 3 ☐ Strange Invaders ☐ Terror in the Aisles

Allen, Steve ☐ Benny Goodman Story, The ☐ Big Circus, The ☐ College Confidential ☐ Down Memory Lane ☐ Lenny Bruce—Without Tears ☐ Steve Allen's Golden Age of Comedy ☐ Warning Shot ☐ Where Were You When the Lights Went Out?

Allen, Woody ☐ Annie Hall ☐ Bananas ☐ Broadway Danny Rose ☐ Casino Royale ☐ Crimes and Misdemeanors ☐ Everything You Always Wanted to Know About Sex (But Were Afraid to Ask) ☐ Front, The ☐ Hannah and Her Sisters ☐ Husbands and Wives ☐ King Lear ☐ Love and Death ☐ Manhattan ☐ Manhattan Murder Mystery ☐ Midsummer Night's Sex Comedy, A ☐ New York Stories ☐ Play It Again, Sam ☐ Scenes from a Mall ☐ Shadows and Fog ☐ Sleeper ☐ Stardust Memories ☐ Take the Money and Run ☐ What's New, Pussycat? ☐ What's Up, Tiger Lily? ☐ Zelig

Alley, Kirstie ☐ Bunny's Tale, A ☐ Champions ☐ Infidelity ☐ Look Who's Talking ☐ Look Who's Talking Now ☐ Look Who's Talking Too ☐ Loverboy ☐ Madhouse ☐ Prince of Bel Air ☐ Runaway ☐ Shoot to Kill ☐ Sibling Rivalry ☐ Summer School

Allgood, Sara ☐ Between Two Worlds ☐ Blackmail ☐ City Without Men ☐ Girl from Manhattan, The ☐ How Green Was My Valley ☐ It Happened in Flatbush ☐ It's Love Again ☐ Juno and the Paycock ☐ Life Begins at Eight-Thirty ☐ Lodger, The ☐ Storm in a Teacup ☐ That Hamilton Woman ☐ This Above All

Allyson, June ☐ Battle Circus ☐ Best Foot Forward ☐ Blackout ☐ Bride Goes Wild, The ☐ Curse of the Black Widow ☐ Executive Suite ☐ Girl Crazy ☐ Girl in White, The ☐ Glenn Miller Story, The ☐ Good News ☐ Her Highness and the Bellboy ☐ High Barbaree ☐ Interlude ☐ Kid with the Broken Halo, The ☐ Little Women ☐ McConnell Story, The ☐ Meet the People ☐ Music for Millions ☐ My Man Godfrey ☐ Opposite Sex, The ☐ Reformer and the Redhead, The ☐ Right Cross ☐ Secret Heart, The ☐ Shrike, The ☐ Stranger in My Arms ☐ Strategic Air Command ☐ Stratton Story, The ☐ They Only Kill Their Masters ☐ Three Musketeers, The ☐ Till the Clouds Roll By ☐ Two Girls and a Sailor ☐ Two Sisters From Boston ☐ Woman's World ☐ Words and Music ☐ You Can't Run Away From It

Alonso, Maria Conchita ☐ Blood Ties ☐ Colors ☐ Extreme Prejudice ☐ Fine Mess, A ☐ McBain ☐ Moscow on the Hudson ☐ Predator 2 ☐ Running Man, The ☐ Teamster Boss: The Jackie Presser Story ☐ Touch and Go ☐ Vampire's Kiss

Alvarado, Trini ☐ American Blue Note ☐ Babe, The ☐ Little Women ☐ Movie Star's Daughter, A ☐ Mrs. Soffel ☐ Nitti—The Enforcer ☐ Rich Kids ☐ Satisfaction ☐ Stella ☐ Sweet Lorraine ☐ Times Square

Ameche, Don ☐ Alexander's Ragtime Band ☐ Cocoon ☐ Cocoon: The Return ☐ Corinna, Corinna ☐ Down Argentine Way ☐ Feminine Touch, The ☐ Fever in the Blood, A ☐ Fifty Roads to Town ☐ Folks! ☐ Four Sons ☐ Gateway ☐ Gidget Gets Married ☐ Girl Trouble ☐ Greenwich Village ☐ Guest Wife ☐ Happy Land ☐ Happy Landing ☐ Harry and the Hendersons ☐ Heaven Can Wait ☐ Hollywood Cavalcade ☐ Homeward Bound: The Incredible Journey ☐ In Old Chicago ☐ It's in the Bag ☐ Josette ☐ Kiss the Boys Goodbye ☐ Ladies in Love ☐ Lillian Russell ☐ Love Is News ☐ Love Under Fire ☐ Magnificent Dope, The ☐ Masterpiece of Murder, A ☐ Midnight ☐ Moon Over Miami ☐ Oddball Hall ☐ One in a Million ☐ Oscar ☐ Pals ☐ Picture Mommy Dead ☐ Ramona ☐ Sleep My Love ☐ So Goes My Love ☐ Story of Alexander Graham Bell, The ☐ Sunstroke ☐ Suppose They Gave a War and Nobody Came? ☐ Swanee River ☐ That Night in Rio ☐ Things Change ☐ Three Musketeers, The ☐ Trading Places ☐ Wing and a Prayer

Ames, Leon ☐ Angel Face ☐ Big Hangover, The ☐ By the Light of the Silvery Moon ☐ Cattle Drive ☐ Charlie Chan on Broadway ☐ East Side Kids ☐ From the Terrace ☐ International Settlement ☐ Iron Major, The ☐ Jake Speed ☐ Marshal of Mesa City, The ☐ Meet Me in St. Louis ☐ Merton of the Movies ☐ Misadventures of Merlin Jones, The ☐ Monkey's Uncle, The ☐ Murders in the Rue Morgue ☐ Mysterious Mr. Moto ☐ On Moonlight Bay ☐ Panama Patrol ☐ Scene of the Crime ☐ Son of Lassie ☐ Suez ☐ Velvet

Touch, The ☐ Watch the Birdie ☐ Weekend at the Waldorf ☐ Yolanda and the Thief

Ames, Robert ☐ Holiday ☐ Rich Man's Folly ☐ Rich People ☐ Tomorrow and Tomorrow ☐ Trespasser, The

Amick, Madchen ☐ I'm Dangerous Tonight ☐ Love, Cheat & Steal ☐ Stephen King's Sleepwalkers ☐ Trapped in Paradise

Amis, Suzy ☐ Ballad of Little Jo, The ☐ Plain Clothes ☐ Rich in Love ☐ Rocket Gibraltar ☐ Watch It ☐ Where the Heart Is

Amos, John ☐ Beastmaster, The ☐ Coming to America ☐ Future Cop ☐ Jungle Heat ☐ Let's Do It Again ☐ Lock Up ☐ Mac ☐ Sweet Sweetback's Baadasssss Song ☐ World's Greatest Athlete, The

Amsterdam, Morey ☐ Beach Party ☐ Machine-Gun Kelly ☐ Murder, Inc. ☐ Muscle Beach Party ☐ Sooner or Later

Anders, Luana ☐ Border Radio ☐ Dementia 13 ☐ Greaser's Palace ☐ Killing Kind, The ☐ Manipulator, The ☐ Night Tide ☐ Pit and the Pendulum ☐ When the Legends Die

Anders, Merry ☐ Calypso Heat Wave ☐ Hear Me Good ☐ Hypnotic Eye, The ☐ Night Runner, The ☐ No Time to Be Young ☐ Quick Gun, The ☐ Time Travelers, The ☐ Women of the Prehistoric Planet

Anderson, Jr., Michael ☐ Legacy for Leonette, A ☐ Major Dundee ☐ Play It Cool ☐ Reach for Glory ☐ Sundowners, The

Anderson, Eddie "Rochester" ☐ Birth of the Blues ☐ Brewster's Millions ☐ Buck Benny Rides Again ☐ Cabin in the Sky ☐ Green Pastures, The ☐ I Love a Bandleader ☐ Love Thy Neighbor ☐ Man About Town ☐ Meanest Man in the World, The ☐ Stormy Weather ☐ Topper Returns

Anderson, John ☐ Deerslayer, The ☐ Executive Action ☐ In Broad Daylight ☐ In Search of Historic Jesus ☐ Last Hurrah, The ☐ Man Called Gannon, A ☐ Medicine Hat Stallion, The ☐ Namu, the Killer Whale ☐ Never Too Young to Die ☐ Smile Jenny, You're Dead ☐ Smokey and the Bandit, Part 2 ☐ Soldier Blue ☐ Specialist, The ☐ Stepmother, The ☐ Zoot Suit

Anderson, Judith ☐ All Through the Night ☐ And Then There Were None ☐ Blood Money ☐ Borrowers, The ☐ Cat on a Hot Tin Roof ☐ Cinderfella ☐ Diary of a Chambermaid ☐ Edge of Darkness ☐ Forty Little Mothers ☐ Furies, The ☐ Inn of the Damned ☐ Kings Row ☐ Lady Scarface ☐ Laura ☐ Man Called Horse, A ☐ Pursued ☐ Rebecca ☐ Red House, The ☐ Salome ☐ Spectre of the Rose ☐ Strange Love of Martha Ivers, The ☐ Ten Commandments, The ☐ Tycoon

Anderson, Kevin ☐ Hoffa ☐ In Country ☐ Liebestraum ☐ Miles from Home ☐ Night We Never Met, The ☐ Orphans ☐ Orpheus Descending ☐ Sleeping with the Enemy

Anderson, Loni ☐ All Dogs Go to Heaven ☐ Coins in the Fountain ☐ Jayne Mansfield Story, The ☐ Letter to Three Wives, A ☐ Munchie ☐ Sizzle ☐ Sorry, Wrong Number ☐ Stroker Ace ☐ Whisper Kill ☐ White Hot: The Mysterious Murder of Thelma Todd

Anderson, Mary ☐ Chicago Calling ☐ Henry Aldrich for President ☐ Henry and Dizzy ☐ Last of the Buccaneers, The ☐ Lifeboat ☐ To Each His Own ☐ Whispering City ☐ Wilson

Anderson, Melissa Sue ☐ Chattanooga Choo Choo ☐ Happy Birthday to Me ☐ Innocent Love, An ☐ James at 15

Anderson, Melody ☐ Dead and Buried ☐ Ernie Kovacs: Between the Laughter ☐ Final Notice ☐ Firewalker ☐ Flash Gordon ☐ Hitler's Daughter ☐ Landslide

Anderson, Richard ☐ Bionic Showdown: The Six Million Dollar Man and the Bionic Woman ☐ Fearless Fagan ☐ I Love Melvin ☐ Immigrants, The ☐ Johnny Cool ☐ Night Strangler, The ☐ Rich, Young and Pretty ☐ Ride to Hangman's Tree, The

Anderson, Warner ☐ Destination Moon ☐ Go for Broke ☐ Lawless Street, A ☐ Lineup, The ☐ My Reputation ☐ Star, The

Andersson, Bibi ☐ All These Women ☐ Babette's Feast ☐ Brink of Life ☐ Devil's Eye, The ☐ Duel at Diablo ☐ Enemy of the People, An ☐ Girls, The ☐ Hill on the Dark Side of the Moon, A ☐ I Never Promised You a Rose Garden ☐ Kremlin Letter, The ☐ Law of Desire ☐ Magician, The ☐ Passion of Anna, The ☐ Persona ☐ Quintet ☐ Scenes from a Marriage ☐ Seventh Seal, The ☐ Touch, The ☐ Wild Strawberries

Andersson, Harriet ☐ All These Women ☐ Cries and Whispers ☐ Deadly Affair, The ☐ Dreams ☐ Fight for Rome ☐ Girls, The ☐ Lesson in Love, A ☐ Monika ☐ Sawdust and Tinsel ☐ Smiles of a Summer Night ☐ Through a Glass Darkly

Andress, Ursula ☐ Anyone Can Play ☐ Blue Max, The ☐ Casino Royale ☐ Clash of the Titans ☐ Dr. No ☐ Fifth Musketeer, The ☐ Four for Texas ☐ Fun in Acapulco ☐ Loaded Guns ☐ Loves and Times of Scaramouche, The ☐ Man Against the Mob: The Chinatown Murders ☐ Once Before I Die ☐ Perfect Friday ☐ Red Sun ☐ Scaramouche ☐ Sensuous Nurse, The ☐ She ☐ Tenth Victim, The ☐ Tigers in Lipstick ☐ Up to His Ears

Andrews, Anthony ☐ Bluegrass ☐ Brideshead Revisited ☐ Hanna's War ☐ Holcroft Covenant, The ☐ Ivanhoe ☐ Scarlet Pimpernel, The ☐ Second Victory, The ☐ Suspicion ☐ Under the Volcano

Andrews, Dana ☐ Airport '75 ☐ Assignment—Paris ☐ Ball of Fire ☐ Battle of the Bulge ☐ Belle Starr ☐ Berlin Correspondent ☐ Best Years of Our Lives, The ☐ Beyond a Reasonable Doubt ☐ Boomerang! ☐ Born Again ☐ Canyon Passage ☐ Cobra, The ☐ Comanche ☐ Crack in the World ☐ Crash

Dive ☐ Crowded Sky, The ☐ Curse of the Demon ☐ Deep Waters ☐ Devil's Brigade, The ☐ Duel in the Jungle ☐ Edge of Doom ☐ Elephant Walk ☐ Enchanted Island ☐ Failing of Raymond, The ☐ Fallen Angel ☐ Fearmakers, The ☐ First 36 Hours of Dr. Durant, The ☐ Forbidden Street, The ☐ Frogmen, The ☐ Frozen Dead, The ☐ Good Guys Wear Black ☐ Hot Rods to Hell ☐ I Want You ☐ Ike: The War Years ☐ In Harm's Way ☐ Innocent Bystanders ☐ Iron Curtain, The ☐ Johnny Reno ☐ Kit Carson ☐ Last Hurrah, The ☐ Laura ☐ Madison Avenue ☐ My Foolish Heart ☐ Night Song ☐ No Minor Vices ☐ North Star, The ☐ Ox-Bow Incident, The ☐ Purple Heart, The ☐ Satan Bug, The ☐ Sealed Cargo ☐ State Fair ☐ Strange Lady in Town ☐ Swamp Water ☐ Sword in the Desert ☐ Take a Hard Ride ☐ Three Hours to Kill ☐ Tobacco Road ☐ Up in Arms ☐ Walk in the Sun, A ☐ Westerner, The ☐ Where the Sidewalk Ends ☐ While the City Sleeps ☐ Wing and a Prayer ☐ Zero Hour

Andrews, Harry ☐ 633 Squadron ☐ Agony and the Ecstasy, The ☐ Battle of Britain, The ☐ Best of Enemies, The ☐ Black Knight, The ☐ Brotherly Love ☐ Charge of the Light Brigade, The ☐ Circle of Deception, A ☐ Curse of King Tut's Tomb, The ☐ Entertaining Mr. Sloane ☐ Hell in Korea ☐ Hill, The ☐ I Want What I Want ☐ I'll Never Forget What's 'is Name ☐ Internecine Project, The ☐ Jokers, The ☐ Long Duel, The ☐ Mackintosh Man, The ☐ Man at the Top ☐ Man of La Mancha ☐ Man Who Loved Redheads, The ☐ Medusa Touch, The ☐ Mesmerized ☐ Moby Dick ☐ Modesty Blaise ☐ Nice Girl Like Me, A ☐ Nicholas and Alexandra ☐ Night They Raided Minsky's, The ☐ Nightcomers, The ☐ Nine Hours to Rama ☐ Nothing But the Best ☐ Paratrooper ☐ Passover Plot, The ☐ Play Dirty ☐ Reach for Glory ☐ Ruling Class, The ☐ Saint Joan ☐ Sands of the Kalahari ☐ Sea Gull, The ☐ Seven Dials Mystery, The ☐ Too Late the Hero ☐ Watership Down ☐ Wuthering Heights

Andrews, Julie ☐ 10 ☐ Americanization of Emily, The ☐ Darling Lili ☐ Duet for One ☐ Fine Romance, A ☐ Hawaii ☐ Little Miss Marker ☐ Man Who Loved Women, The ☐ Mary Poppins ☐ Our Sons ☐ S.O.B. ☐ Singing Princess, The ☐ Sound of Music, The ☐ Star! ☐ Tamarind Seed, The ☐ That's Life! ☐ Thoroughly Modern Millie ☐ Torn Curtain ☐ Victor/Victoria

Angel, Heather ☐ Arrest Bulldog Drummond ☐ Berkeley Square ☐ Bold Caballero, The ☐ Bulldog Drummond Escapes ☐ Bulldog Drummond in Africa ☐ Daniel Boone ☐ Informer, The ☐ Last of the Mohicans, The ☐ Mystery of Edwin Drood, The ☐ Pilgrimage ☐ Portia on Trial ☐ Saxon Charm, The ☐ Time to Kill

Angeli, Pier ☐ Angry Silence, The ☐ Battle of the Bulge ☐ Code Name, Red Roses ☐ Devil Makes Three, The ☐ Every Bastard a King ☐ Flame and the Flesh, The ☐ Light Touch, The ☐ Merry Andrew ☐ Octaman ☐ One Step to Hell ☐ Silver Chalice, The ☐ Sodom and Gomorrah ☐ Somebody Up There Likes Me ☐ Story of Three Loves, The ☐ Teresa

Anglade, Jean-Hugues ☐ Betty Blue ☐ Killing Zoe ☐ La Femme Nikita ☐ Queen Margot

Ankers, Evelyn ☐ Black Beauty ☐ Burma Convoy ☐ Captive Wild Woman ☐ Eagle Squadron ☐ Fatal Witness, The ☐ Flight to Nowhere ☐ French Key, The ☐ Frozen Ghost ☐ Great Impersonation, The ☐ Hold That Ghost ☐ Invisible Man's Revenge, The ☐ Jungle Woman ☐ Ladies Courageous ☐ Last of the Redmen ☐ Mad Ghoul, The ☐ Pardon My Rhythm ☐ Parole, Inc. ☐ Pearl of Death, The ☐ Sherlock Holmes and the Voice of Terror ☐ Weird Woman ☐ Wolf Man, The

Ankrum, Morris ☐ Earth vs. the Flying Saucers ☐ Half-Human ☐ Redhead and the Cowboy, The ☐ Short Grass ☐ Three Men from Texas

Ann-Margret ☐ Bus Riley's Back in Town ☐ Bye, Bye, Birdie ☐ C.C. and Company ☐ Carnal Knowledge ☐ Cheap Detective, The ☐ Cincinnati Kid, The ☐ 52 Pick-Up ☐ Joseph Andrews ☐ Grumpy Old Men ☐ I Ought to Be in Pictures ☐ Kitten with a Whip ☐ Last Remake of Beau Geste, The ☐ Lookin' to Get Out ☐ Made in Paris ☐ Magic ☐ Middle Age Crazy ☐ Murderers' Row ☐ New Life, A ☐ Newsies ☐ Nobody's Children ☐ Once a Thief ☐ Our Sons ☐ Outside Man, The ☐ Pleasure Seekers, The ☐ Pocketful of Miracles ☐ R.P.M. ☐ Return of the Soldier, The ☐ Stagecoach ☐ State Fair ☐ Streetcar Named Desire, A ☐ Swinger, The ☐ Tiger and the Pussycat, The ☐ Tiger's Tale, A ☐ Tommy ☐ Train Robbers, The ☐ Twice in a Lifetime ☐ Twist, The ☐ Two Mrs. Grenvilles, The ☐ Villain, The ☐ Viva Las Vegas ☐ Who Will Love My Children?

Annabella ☐ 13 Rue Madeleine ☐ Baroness and the Butler, The ☐ Dinner at the Ritz ☐ Escape from Yesterday ☐ Million, The ☐ Spring Shower ☐ Suez ☐ Tonight We Raid Calais ☐ Under the Red Robe ☐ Wings of the Morning

Annis, Francesca ☐ Agatha Christie—Affair Of The Pink Pearl, The ☐ Dune ☐ Krull ☐ Macbeth ☐ Maze, The ☐ Murder Most Foul ☐ Under the Cherry Moon ☐ Why Didn't They Ask Evans?

Ansara, Michael ☐ Abbott and Costello Meet the Mummy ☐ And Now Miguel ☐ Bayou Romance ☐ Bears and I, The ☐ Bengal Brigade ☐ Border Shootout ☐ Brave Warrior ☐ Day of the Animals ☐ Dear Dead Delilah ☐ Gun Brothers ☐ Harum Scarum ☐ Hill Number One ☐ It's Alive! ☐ KGB—the Secret War

☐ Manitou, The ☐ Message, The ☐ Pink Jungle, The ☐ Quick, Let's Get Married

Anspach, Susan ☐ Big Fix, The ☐ Blue Monkey ☐ Blume In Love ☐ Devil and Max Devlin, The ☐ Five Easy Pieces ☐ Gas ☐ I Want to Keep My Baby ☐ Into the Fire ☐ Mad Bull ☐ Montenegro ☐ Play It Again, Sam

Ant, Adam ☐ Cold Steel ☐ Nomads ☐ Slam Dance ☐ Spellcaster ☐ Sunset Heat ☐ Trust Me

Anthony, Lysette ☐ Face the Music ☐ Husbands and Wives ☐ Ivanhoe ☐ Krull ☐ Save Me ☐ Without a Clue

Antonelli, Laura ☐ Collector's Item ☐ Divine Nymph, The ☐ Dr. Goldfoot and the Girl Bombs ☐ High Heels ☐ How Funny Can Sex Be? ☐ Innocent, The ☐ Malicious ☐ Man Called Sledge, A ☐ Passion of Love ☐ Secret Fantasy ☐ Tigers in Lipstick ☐ Till Marriage Do Us Part ☐ Wifemistress

Anwar, Gabrielle ☐ Body Snatchers ☐ Fallen Angels—Volume 2 ☐ For Love or Money ☐ If Looks Could Kill ☐ Scent of a Woman ☐ Wild Hearts Can't Be Broken

Aratama, Michiyo ☐ Human Condition, The—Part One: No Greater Love ☐ Human Condition, The—Part Three: A Soldier's Prayer ☐ Human Condition, The—Part Two: The Road to Eternity ☐ Once a Rainy Day ☐ Thin Line, The

Arbuckle, Fatty ☐ Lizzies of Mack Sennett, The ☐ Mabel and Fatty ☐ When Comedy Was King

Archer, Anne ☐ All-American Boy, The ☐ Body of Evidence ☐ Check Is in the Mail, The ☐ Clear and Present Danger ☐ Eminent Domain ☐ Family Prayers ☐ Fatal Attraction ☐ Good Guys Wear Black ☐ Green Ice ☐ Harold Robbins' the Pirate ☐ Hero at Large ☐ Honkers, The ☐ Last of His Tribe, The ☐ Lifeguard ☐ Love at Large ☐ Mark of Zorro, The ☐ Nails ☐ Naked Face, The ☐ Narrow Margin ☐ Paradise Alley ☐ Patriot Games ☐ Question of Faith ☐ Raise the Titanic! ☐ Short Cuts

Archer, John ☐ Affair in Reno ☐ Bowery at Midnight ☐ Destination Moon ☐ Emergency Hospital ☐ Great Jewel Robber, The ☐ My Favorite Spy ☐ No Man's Woman ☐ Overland Stage Raiders ☐ Paper Bullets ☐ Sound Off

Ardant, Fanny ☐ Afraid of the Dark ☐ Colonel Chabert ☐ Confidentially Yours ☐ Family Business ☐ Family, The ☐ Love and Fear ☐ Melo ☐ Swann in Love ☐ Woman Next Door, The

Arden, Eve ☐ Anatomy of a Murder ☐ Arnelo Affair, The ☐ At the Circus ☐ Bedtime Story ☐ Change of Heart ☐ Child Is Born, A ☐ Cocoanut Grove ☐ Comrade X ☐ Cover Girl ☐ Dark at the Top of the Stairs, The ☐ Doughgirls, The ☐ Earl Carroll Vanities ☐ Forgotten Woman ☐ Goodbye, My Fancy ☐ Grease ☐ Grease 2 ☐ Guide for the Married Woman ☐ Having Wonderful Time ☐ Kid from Brooklyn, The ☐ Lady Takes a Sailor, The ☐ Lady Wants Mink, The ☐ Let's Face It ☐ Letter of Introduction, A ☐ Manpower ☐ Mildred Pierce ☐ My Dream Is Yours ☐ My Reputation ☐ Night and Day ☐ Obliging Young Lady ☐ One Touch of Venus ☐ Our Miss Brooks ☐ Paid in Full ☐ Pan Americana ☐ San Antonio Rose ☐ Sergeant Deadhead ☐ Slightly Honorable ☐ Stage Door ☐ Strongest Man in the World, The ☐ Tea for Two ☐ That Uncertain Feeling ☐ Three Husbands ☐ Under the Rainbow ☐ Unfaithful, The ☐ Voice of the Turtle, The ☐ We're Not Married ☐ Whistling in the Dark ☐ Ziegfeld Girl

Arkin, Alan ☐ Bad Medicine ☐ Big Trouble ☐ Catch-22 ☐ Chu Chu and the Philly Flash ☐ Coup de Ville ☐ Deadhead Miles ☐ Deadly Business, A ☐ Defection of Simas Kudirka, The ☐ Edward Scissorhands ☐ Escape from Sobibor ☐ Fire Sale ☐ Fourth Wise Man, The ☐ Freebie and the Bean ☐ Full Moon High ☐ Glengarry Glen Ross ☐ Havana ☐ Heart Is a Lonely Hunter, The ☐ Hearts of the West ☐ Improper Channels ☐ In-Laws, The ☐ Indian Summer ☐ Inspector Clouseau ☐ Jerky Boys, The ☐ Joshua Then and Now ☐ Last of the Red Hot Lovers ☐ Little Murders ☐ Magician of Lublin, The ☐ Matter of Principle, A ☐ Monitors, The ☐ Other Side of Hell, The ☐ Popi ☐ Rocketeer, The ☐ Russians Are Coming! The Russians Are Coming!, The ☐ Seven Percent Solution, The ☐ Simon ☐ Wait Until Dark ☐ Woman Times Seven

Arlen, Richard ☐ Aerial Gunner ☐ Alice in Wonderland ☐ Artists and Models ☐ Beggars of Life ☐ Behind the Front ☐ Black Spurs ☐ Blazing Forest, The ☐ Blonde Blackmailer ☐ Bounty Killer, The ☐ College Humor ☐ Conquering Horde, The ☐ Feel My Pulse ☐ Flying Blind ☐ Fort Utah ☐ French Key, The ☐ Golden Harvest ☐ Guilty as Hell ☐ Identity Unknown ☐ Island of Lost Souls ☐ Lady and the Monster, The ☐ Let 'Em Have It ☐ Mountain, The ☐ No Time to Marry ☐ Raymie ☐ Shepherd of the Hills, The ☐ Silver City ☐ Three-Cornered Moon ☐ Thunderbolt ☐ Tiger Shark ☐ Touchdown! ☐ Virginian, The ☐ When My Baby Smiles at Me ☐ Wings

Arliss, George ☐ Alexander Hamilton ☐ Cardinal Richelieu ☐ Disraeli ☐ Dr. Syn ☐ Green Goddess, The ☐ House of Rothschild, The ☐ Iron Duke, The ☐ King's Vacation, The ☐ Last Gentleman, The ☐ Man Who Played God, The ☐ Millionaire, The ☐ Mister Hobo ☐ Old English ☐ Successful Calamity, A ☐ Transatlantic Tunnel ☐ Working Man, The

Armendariz, Pedro ☐ Big Boodle, The ☐ Border River ☐ Conqueror, The ☐ Diane ☐ El Bruto ☐ Flor Silvestre ☐ Francis of Assisi ☐ From Russia with Love ☐ Fugitive, The ☐ Littlest Outlaw, The ☐ My Son, the Hero ☐ Pearl, The ☐ Three Godfathers, The

☐ Tulsa ☐ We Were Strangers ☐ Wonderful Country, The
Armetta, Henry ☐ Forbidden ☐ Imitation of Life ☐ Strangers May Kiss ☐ We Who Are Young
Armstrong, Bess ☐ High Road to China ☐ House of God, The ☐ How to Pick Up Girls! ☐ Jaws 3 ☐ Jekyll & Hyde . . . Together Again ☐ Nothing in Common ☐ Second Sight ☐ Skateboard Kid, The
Armstrong, Curtis ☐ Revenge of the Nerds ☐ Revenge of the Nerds 2: Nerds in Paradise ☐ Revenge of the Nerds 3: The Next Generation ☐ Risky Business
Armstrong, Louis ☐ Cabin in the Sky ☐ Every Day's a Holiday ☐ Five Pennies, The ☐ Glenn Miller Story, The ☐ Glory Alley ☐ Hello, Dolly! ☐ High Society ☐ Jam Session ☐ Jazz on a Summer's Day ☐ Man Called Adam, A ☐ New Orleans ☐ Paris Blues ☐ Pennies from Heaven ☐ Song is Born, A
Armstrong, Robert ☐ Action in Arabia ☐ Be Yourself ☐ Blood on the Sun ☐ Criminal Court ☐ Danger Lights ☐ Dive Bomber ☐ Enemy Agent ☐ Falcon in San Francisco, The ☐ Fall Guy ☐ Fast Workers ☐ Flying Irishman, The ☐ G-Men ☐ Girl in Every Port, A ☐ Iron Man, The ☐ Is My Face Red? ☐ It Happened in Flatbush ☐ King Kong ☐ Mad Ghoul, The ☐ Mighty Joe Young ☐ Most Dangerous Game, The ☐ Mr. Winkle Goes to War ☐ Mystery Man, The ☐ Nobody's Baby ☐ Paid ☐ Paleface, The ☐ Penguin Pool Murder, The ☐ Public Enemy's Wife ☐ Racketeer, The ☐ Son of Kong, The
Arnaz, Jr., Desi ☐ Billy Two Hats ☐ Fake-Out ☐ Gridlock ☐ House of the Long Shadows ☐ How to Pick Up Girls! ☐ Joyride ☐ Mambo Kings, The ☐ Marco ☐ Night the Bridge Fell Down, The ☐ Red Sky at Morning
Arnaz, Desi ☐ Bataan ☐ Cuban Pete ☐ Father Takes a Wife ☐ Forever Darling ☐ Four Jacks and a Jill ☐ Holiday in Havana ☐ Long, Long Trailer, The ☐ Too Many Girls ☐ Wedding, A
Arness, James ☐ Alamo, The—Thirteen Days to Glory ☐ Big Jim McLain ☐ Carbine Williams ☐ Cavalry Scout ☐ First Traveling Saleslady, The ☐ Flame of the Islands ☐ Girl in White, The ☐ Gun the Man Down ☐ Gunsmoke: Return to Dodge ☐ Gunsmoke: The Last Apache ☐ Hellgate ☐ Her Twelve Men ☐ Hondo ☐ Horizons West ☐ Island in the Sky ☐ Lone Hand, The ☐ Macahans, The ☐ Many Rivers to Cross ☐ Sea Chase, The ☐ Them ☐ Thing, The ☐ Wagon Master
Arnold, Edward ☐ Annie Get Your Gun ☐ Barbarian, The ☐ Belles on Their Toes ☐ Big Jack ☐ Biography of a Bachelor Girl ☐ Cardinal Richelieu ☐ City That Never Sleeps ☐ Come and Get It ☐ Crime and Punishment ☐ Crowd Roars, The ☐ Dear Ruth ☐ Dear Wife ☐ Design for Scandal ☐ Devil and Daniel Webster, The ☐ Diamond Jim ☐ Earl of Chicago, The ☐ Easy Living ☐ Eyes in the Night ☐ Glass Key, The ☐ Hidden Eye, The ☐ Hide-Out ☐ Houston Story, The ☐ I'm No Angel ☐ Idiot's Delight ☐ Janie ☐ Janie Gets Married ☐ Jennie Gerhardt ☐ John Meade's Woman ☐ Johnny Apollo ☐ Johnny Eager ☐ Kismet ☐ Lady from Cheyenne ☐ Lillian Russell ☐ Living It Up ☐ Main Street After Dark ☐ Man About Town ☐ Man of Conflict ☐ Meet John Doe ☐ Meet Nero Wolfe ☐ Mighty McGurk, The ☐ Mr. Smith Goes to Washington ☐ Mrs. Parkington ☐ My Brother Talks to Horses ☐ No Leave, No Love ☐ Nothing But the Truth ☐ Rasputin and the Empress ☐ Roman Scandals ☐ Sadie McKee ☐ Secret of the Blue Room ☐ Slightly Honorable ☐ Standing Room Only ☐ Thirty Day Princess ☐ Three Wise Fools ☐ Toast of New York, The ☐ Unholy Partners ☐ Wallflower ☐ Weekend at the Waldorf ☐ White Sister, The ☐ Yellow Cab Man, The ☐ You Can't Take It With You ☐ Youngest Profession, The
Arnoul, Francoise ☐ Forbidden Fruit ☐ French Cancan ☐ Little Theatre of Jean Renoir, The ☐ Sheep Has Five Legs, The
Arquette, Alexis ☐ Hollow Boy, The ☐ Jack Be Nimble ☐ Jumpin' at the Boneyard ☐ Threesome
Arquette, Patricia ☐ Ed Wood ☐ Ethan Frome ☐ Far North ☐ Indian Runner, The ☐ Inside Monkey Zetterland ☐ Nightmare on Elm Street 3: Dream Warriors ☐ Prayer of the Rollerboys ☐ Pretty Smart ☐ Trouble Bound ☐ True Romance ☐ Wildflower
Arquette, Rosanna ☐ 8 Million Ways to Die ☐ After Hours ☐ Almost ☐ Amazon Women on the Moon ☐ Aviator, The ☐ Baby, It's You ☐ Black Rainbow ☐ Dark Secret of Harvest Home ☐ Desperately Seeking Susan ☐ Executioner's Song, The ☐ Fathers and Sons ☐ Flight of the Intruder ☐ Gorp ☐ Having Babies II ☐ Johnny Belinda ☐ Linguini Incident, The ☐ New York Stories ☐ Nobody's Fool ☐ Nowhere to Run ☐ Off the Wall ☐ One Cooks, the Other Doesn't ☐ Parade, The ☐ Promised a Miracle ☐ Silverado ☐ Son of the Morning Star
Arthur, Jean ☐ Adventure in Manhattan ☐ Arizona ☐ Canary Murder Case ☐ Danger Lights ☐ Devil and Miss Jones, The ☐ Diamond Jim ☐ Easy Living ☐ Ex-Mrs. Bradford, The ☐ Foreign Affair, A ☐ Greene Murder Case, The ☐ History Is Made at Night ☐ If You Could Only Cook ☐ Impatient Years, The ☐ Lady Takes A Chance, A ☐ More Than a Secretary ☐ More the Merrier, The ☐ Mr. Deeds Goes to Town ☐ Mr. Smith Goes to Washington ☐ Mysterious Dr. Fu Manchu, The ☐ Only Angels Have Wings ☐ Paramount on Parade ☐ Party Wire ☐ Plainsman, The ☐ Public Hero No. 1 ☐ Shane ☐ Silver Horde ☐ Talk of the Town, The ☐ Too Many Hus-

bands ☐ Whirlpool ☐ Whole Town's Talking, The ☐ You Can't Take It With You
Ashcroft, Peggy ☐ 39 Steps, The ☐ Hullabaloo Over Georgie and Bonnie's Pictures ☐ Madame Sousatzka ☐ Nun's Story, The ☐ Passage to India, A ☐ Rhodes ☐ Sunday, Bloody Sunday ☐ Tell Me Lies ☐ Three Into Two Won't Go
Ashley, Elizabeth ☐ Carpetbaggers, The ☐ Coma ☐ Dragnet ☐ Face of Fear ☐ Golden Needles ☐ Great Scout and Cathouse Thursday ☐ Harpy ☐ Heist, The ☐ Magician, The ☐ Marriage of a Young Stockbroker, The ☐ One of My Wives Is Missing ☐ Paperback Hero ☐ Paternity ☐ Rancho Deluxe ☐ Ship of Fools ☐ Stagecoach ☐ Svengali ☐ Third Day, The ☐ Two Mrs. Grenvilles, The ☐ Vampire's Kiss ☐ War Between the Tates, The
Ashley, John ☐ Beast of the Dead, The ☐ Beasts ☐ Beyond Atlantis ☐ Eye Creatures, The ☐ Frankenstein's Daughter ☐ Hell on Wheels ☐ High School Caesar ☐ Hot Rod Gang ☐ Mad Doctor of Blood Island, The ☐ Motorcycle Gang ☐ Zero Hour
Ashton, John ☐ Beverly Hills Cop ☐ Dirty Work ☐ I Know My First Name Is Steven ☐ Last Resort ☐ Little Big League ☐ Midnight Run
Askew, Luke ☐ Angel Unchained ☐ Culpepper Cattle Co., The ☐ Flareup ☐ Great Northfield, Minnesota Raid, The ☐ Invasion of Johnson County, The ☐ Magnificent Seven Ride!, The ☐ Walking Tall, Part II
Aslan, Gregoire ☐ Fanatics, The ☐ Main Chance, The ☐ Red Inn, The ☐ Sea Fury
Asner, Edward ☐ Case of Libel, A ☐ Change of Habit ☐ Daniel ☐ El Dorado ☐ Fort Apache, The Bronx ☐ Friendship in Vienna ☐ Gathering, The ☐ Girl Most Likely To . . . , The ☐ Gunn ☐ Gus ☐ Gypsy ☐ Happily Ever After ☐ Haunts of the Very Rich ☐ Heads ☐ Hey, I'm Alive! ☐ Imposter, The ☐ Life and Assassination of the Kingfish, The ☐ Not a Penny More, Not a Penny Less ☐ O'Hara's Wife ☐ Roots ☐ Silent Motive ☐ Skin Game ☐ Slender Thread, The ☐ Todd Killings, The
Assante, Armand ☐ 1492: Conquest of Paradise ☐ Animal Behavior ☐ Belizaire the Cajun ☐ Deadly Business, A ☐ Eternity ☐ Fatal Instinct ☐ Hands of a Stranger ☐ Harold Robbins' the Pirate ☐ Hoffa ☐ I, the Jury ☐ Jack the Ripper ☐ Lady of the House ☐ Little Darlings ☐ Love and Money ☐ Mambo Kings, The ☐ Marrying Man, The ☐ Paradise Alley ☐ Passion in Paradise ☐ Penitent, The ☐ Private Benjamin ☐ Prophecy ☐ Q & A ☐ Rage of Angels ☐ Sophia Loren: Her Own Story ☐ Trial by Jury ☐ Unfaithfully Yours
Astaire, Fred ☐ Amazing Dobermans, The ☐ Band Wagon, The ☐ Barkleys of Broadway, The ☐ Belle of New York, The ☐ Blue Skies ☐ Broadway Melody of 1940 ☐ Carefree ☐ Daddy Long Legs ☐ Damsel in Distress, A ☐ Dancing Lady ☐ Easter Parade ☐ Family Upside Down, A ☐ Finian's Rainbow ☐ Flying Down to Rio ☐ Follow the Fleet ☐ Funny Face ☐ Gay Divorcee, The ☐ Ghost Story ☐ Holiday Inn ☐ Let's Dance ☐ Man in the Santa Claus Suit, The ☐ Midas Run ☐ Notorious Landlady, The ☐ On the Beach ☐ Over-the-Hill Gang Rides Again, The ☐ Pleasure of His Company, The ☐ Roberta ☐ Royal Wedding ☐ Second Chorus ☐ Shall We Dance ☐ Silk Stockings ☐ Sky's the Limit, The ☐ Story of Vernon and Irene Castle, The ☐ Swing Time ☐ That's Entertainment ☐ That's Entertainment, Part 2 ☐ Three Little Words ☐ Top Hat ☐ Towering Inferno, The ☐ Yolanda and the Thief ☐ You Were Never Lovelier ☐ You'll Never Get Rich ☐ Ziegfeld Follies
Asther, Nils ☐ Bitter Tea of General Yen, The ☐ Bluebeard ☐ By Candlelight ☐ Feathered Serpent, The ☐ If I Were Free ☐ Jealousy ☐ Letty Lynton ☐ Man in Half Moon Street, The ☐ Night Monster ☐ Night of January 16th, The ☐ Our Dancing Daughters ☐ Single Standard, The ☐ Son of Lassie ☐ Wild Orchids
Astin, John ☐ Addams Family, The—Vol. 1 ☐ Addams Family, The—Vol. 2 ☐ Addams Family, The—Vol. 3 ☐ Addams Family, The—Vol. 4 ☐ Addams Family, The—Vol. 5 ☐ Addams Family, The—Vol. 6 ☐ Brothers O'Toole, The ☐ Bunny O'Hare ☐ Candy ☐ Freaky Friday ☐ Get to Know Your Rabbit ☐ Operation Petticoat ☐ Pepper and His Wacky Taxi ☐ Return of the Killer Tomatoes ☐ Stepmonster ☐ Teen Wolf Too ☐ Viva Max! ☐ Wheeler Dealers, The
Astin, Patty Duke ☐ Absolute Strangers ☐ Amityville 4: The Evil Escapes ☐ Best Kept Secrets ☐ Billie ☐ By Design ☐ Call Me Anna ☐ Curse of the Black Widow ☐ Everybody's Baby: The Rescue of Jessica McClure ☐ Fight for Life ☐ Fire! ☐ 4 D Man ☐ Goddess, The ☐ Grave Secrets ☐ Happy Anniversary ☐ Having Babies III ☐ Last Wish ☐ Me, Natalie ☐ Miracle Worker, The (1962) ☐ Miracle Worker, The (1979) ☐ My Sweet Charlie ☐ Prelude to a Kiss ☐ She Waits ☐ Something Special ☐ Swarm, The ☐ Valley of the Dolls ☐ Women's Room, The
Astin, Sean ☐ Encino Man ☐ Goonies, The ☐ Rudy ☐ Safe Passage ☐ Staying Together ☐ Toy Soldiers ☐ War of the Roses, The ☐ Where the Day Takes You ☐ White Water Summer
Astor, Mary ☐ Across the Pacific ☐ Act of Violence ☐ And So They Were Married ☐ Any Number Can Play ☐ Blonde Fever ☐ Brigham Young ☐ Case of the Howling Dog, The ☐ Cass Timberlane ☐ Claudia and David ☐ Cynthia ☐ Desert Fury ☐ Devil's Hairpin, The ☐ Dodsworth ☐ Don Juan ☐ Don Q, Son of Zorro ☐ Fiesta ☐ Great Lie, The ☐ Holiday ☐ Hurricane, The ☐ Hush . . . Hush, Sweet Charlotte ☐ I Am a Thief ☐ Jennie Gerhardt

☐ Kennel Murder Case, The ☐ Kiss Before Dying, A ☐ Listen, Darling ☐ Little Giant, The ☐ Little Women ☐ Lost Squadron, The ☐ Maltese Falcon, The ☐ Man with Two Faces, The ☐ Meet Me in St. Louis ☐ Midnight ☐ No Time to Marry ☐ Other Men's Women ☐ Page Miss Glory ☐ Palm Beach Story, The ☐ Paradise for Three ☐ Prisoner of Zenda, The ☐ Red Dust ☐ Red Hot Tires ☐ Return to Peyton Place ☐ Stranger in My Arms ☐ Successful Calamity, A ☐ There's Always a Woman ☐ This Happy Feeling ☐ Turnabout ☐ Upperworld ☐ Youngblood Hawke

Ates, Roscoe ☐ Fair Exchange ☐ Father's Wild Game ☐ Freaks ☐ Ladies of the Jury

Atherton, William ☐ Chrome Soldiers ☐ Day of the Locust, The ☐ Die Hard 2 ☐ Grim Prairie Tales ☐ Looking for Mr. Goodbar ☐ Malibu ☐ Real Genius ☐ Sugarland Express, The

Atkins, Christopher ☐ Beaks—The Movie ☐ Blue Lagoon ☐ Child Bride of Short Creek ☐ Fatal Charm ☐ King's Ransom ☐ Mortuary Academy ☐ Night in Heaven, A ☐ Pirate Movie, The ☐ Shakma

Atkins, Eileen ☐ Dresser, The ☐ Inadmissible Evidence ☐ Let Him Have It ☐ Oliver Twist

Atkins, Tom ☐ Blind Justice ☐ Death in Canaan, A ☐ Lemon Sky ☐ Maniac Cop ☐ Special Delivery

Attenborough, Richard ☐ All Night Long ☐ Angry Silence, The ☐ Baby and the Battleship, The ☐ Bliss of Mrs. Blossom, The ☐ Brannigan ☐ Brighton Rock ☐ Brothers in Law ☐ Chess Players, The ☐ Conduct Unbecoming ☐ David Copperfield ☐ Doctor Dolittle ☐ Dulcimer Street ☐ Eight O'Clock Walk ☐ Flight of the Phoenix ☐ Gift Horse, The ☐ Glory at Sea ☐ Great Escape, The ☐ Guns at Batasi ☐ Human Factor, The ☐ I'm All Right, Jack ☐ In Which We Serve ☐ Journey Together ☐ Jurassic Park ☐ League of Gentlemen, The ☐ Loot ☐ Magic Box, The ☐ Man Upstairs, The ☐ Miracle on 34th Street ☐ Only Two Can Play ☐ Only When I Larf ☐ Operation Disaster ☐ Sand Pebbles, The ☐ School for Secrets ☐ Seance on a Wet Afternoon ☐ Severed Head, A ☐ Ship That Died of Shame, The ☐ Smugglers, the ☐ Stairway to Heaven ☐ Ten Little Indians ☐ Third Secret, The

Atwill, Lionel ☐ Boom Town ☐ Captain Blood ☐ Charlie Chan in Panama ☐ Charlie Chan's Murder Cruise ☐ Devil is a Woman, The ☐ Doctor X ☐ Firebird, The ☐ Fog Island ☐ Frankenstein Meets the Wolf Man ☐ Genius at Work ☐ Ghost of Frankenstein, The ☐ Gorilla, The ☐ Great Waltz, The ☐ High Command, The ☐ Hound of the Baskervilles, The ☐ Mad Doctor of Market Street, The ☐ Man Made Monster ☐ Man Who Reclaimed His Head, The ☐ Mark of the Vampire ☐ Mr. Moto Takes a Vacation ☐ Murder Man, The ☐ Murders in the Zoo ☐ Mystery of the Wax Museum, The ☐ Nana ☐ Night Monster ☐ Pardon My Sarong ☐ Rendezvous ☐ Road Back, The ☐ Secret of Dr. Kildare, The ☐ Secret of Madame Blanche, The ☐ Secret of the Blue Room ☐ Secret Weapon ☐ Son of Frankenstein ☐ Song of Songs ☐ Stamboul Quest ☐ Three Musketeers, The ☐ To Be or Not to Be ☐ Vampire Bat, The

Auberjonois, Rene ☐ Ballad of Little Jo, The ☐ Brewster McCloud ☐ Dark Secret of Harvest Home ☐ Eyes of Laura Mars ☐ Feud, The ☐ Images ☐ Little Mermaid, The ☐ Little Nemo: Adventures in Slumberland ☐ M*A*S*H ☐ McCabe and Mrs. Miller ☐ More Wild, Wild West ☐ My Best Friend Is a Vampire ☐ Panache ☐ Pete 'n' Tillie ☐ 3:15 ☐ Where the Buffalo Roam ☐ Wild Card

Aubrey, James ☐ Bouquet of Barbed Wire ☐ Forever Young ☐ Home Before Midnight ☐ Lord of the Flies ☐ Riders of the Storm

Aubuchon, Jacques ☐ McHale's Navy Joins the Air Force ☐ Operation Manhunt ☐ September Gun ☐ Wild and Wonderful

Auclair, Michel ☐ Fanatics, The ☐ French Provincial ☐ Holiday for Henrietta ☐ Justice Is Done ☐ One Step to Eternity ☐ Symphony for a Massacre

Audran, Stephane ☐ Babette's Feast ☐ Betty ☐ Black Bird, The ☐ Blood Relatives ☐ Bluebeard ☐ Champagne Charlie ☐ Champagne Murders, The ☐ Cop au Vin ☐ Coup de Torchon ☐ Discreet Charm of the Bourgeoisie, The ☐ Eagle's Wing ☐ Just Before Nightfall ☐ La Cage aux Folles III: The Wedding ☐ La Femme Infidele ☐ Lady in the Car with Glasses and a Gun, The ☐ Le Boucher ☐ Les Biches ☐ Ten Little Indians ☐ Turn of the Screw, The ☐ Twist, The ☐ Vincent, Francois, Paul and the Others ☐ Violette

Auer, Mischa ☐ And Then There Were None ☐ Around the World ☐ Benson Murder Case ☐ Brewster's Millions ☐ Christmas That Almost Wasn't, The ☐ Destry Rides Again ☐ East Side of Heaven ☐ Flame of New Orleans, The ☐ Gay Desperado, The ☐ Hellzapoppin ☐ Hold That Ghost ☐ Lady in the Dark ☐ Mam'zelle Pigalle ☐ Merry Go Round of 1938 ☐ Monster Walks, The ☐ Mr. Arkadin ☐ My Man Godfrey ☐ Rage of Paris, The ☐ Royal Scandal, A ☐ Sentimental Journey ☐ Service De Luxe ☐ Seven Sinners ☐ Sofia ☐ Spring Parade ☐ Stamboul Quest ☐ That Girl From Paris ☐ Three Smart Girls ☐ Up in Mabel's Room ☐ Vogues of 1938 ☐ Winterset

Auger, Claudine ☐ Associate, The ☐ Bay of Blood ☐ Devil in Love, The ☐ Fantastica ☐ Games of Desire ☐ In the French Style ☐ Killing Game, The ☐ Lobster for Breakfast ☐ Lovers and Liars ☐ Secret Places ☐ Thunderball

Aumont, Jean-Pierre ☐ Becoming Colette

☐ Beggarman, Thief ☐ Blackout ☐ Castle Keep ☐ Cat and Mouse ☐ Catherine & Co. ☐ Cauldron of Blood ☐ Cross of Lorraine, The ☐ Day for Night ☐ Devil at 4 O'Clock, The ☐ Five Miles to Midnight ☐ Gay Adventure, The ☐ Happy Hooker, The ☐ Heartbeat ☐ Hilda Crane ☐ Horse Without a Head, The ☐ John Paul Jones ☐ Lili ☐ Mahogany ☐ Man with the Transplanted Brain ☐ Memory of Eva Ryker, The ☐ Royal Affairs in Versailles ☐ 7 Capital Sins ☐ Sweet Country ☐ Three Hours

Aumont, Tina ☐ Fellini's Casanova ☐ Lifespan ☐ Malicious ☐ Man of Legend

Austin, Karen ☐ Assassin ☐ Far from Home ☐ Ladies Club, The ☐ Laura Lansing Slept Here ☐ Summer Rental

Auteuil, Daniel ☐ Elegant Criminal, The ☐ Few Days with Me, A ☐ Jean de Florette ☐ Mama, There's a Man in Your Bed ☐ Manon of the Spring ☐ Queen Margot ☐ Un Coeur en Hiver

Autry, Gene ☐ Bad Girls in the Movies ☐ Boots And Saddles ☐ Heart of The Rio Grande ☐ Man of The Frontier ☐ Melody Ranch ☐ Mexicali Rose ☐ Old Barn Dance, The ☐ Old Corral, The ☐ Public Cowboy No. 1 ☐ Ride, Ranger, Ride ☐ Ride, Tenderfoot, Ride ☐ Riders in the Sky ☐ Rim of the Canyon ☐ Robin of Texas ☐ Rootin' Tootin' Rhythm ☐ Roundup Time in Texas ☐ Sierra Sue ☐ Sioux City Sue ☐ Strawberry Roan, The

Avalon, Frankie ☐ Alakazam the Great ☐ Alamo, The ☐ Back to the Beach ☐ Beach Blanket Bingo ☐ Beach Party ☐ Bikini Beach ☐ Castillan, The ☐ Dr. Goldfoot and the Bikini Machine ☐ Fireball 500 ☐ Grease ☐ Guns of the Timberland ☐ Horror House ☐ I'll Take Sweden ☐ Jamboree ☐ Muscle Beach Party ☐ Operation Bikini ☐ Panic in Year Zero! ☐ Sail a Crooked Ship ☐ Sergeant Deadhead ☐ Skiddoo

Avery, Margaret ☐ Blueberry Hill ☐ Color Purple, The ☐ For Us, the Living ☐ Return of Superfly, The ☐ Sky Is Gray, The ☐ Which Way Is Up?

Axton, Hoyt ☐ Black Stallion, The ☐ Disorganized Crime ☐ Endangered Species ☐ Gremlins ☐ Heart Like a Wheel ☐ Liar's Moon ☐ Retribution

Aykroyd, Dan ☐ 1941 ☐ Blues Brothers, The ☐ Caddyshack II ☐ Chaplin ☐ Coneheads, The ☐ Couch Trip, The ☐ Doctor Detroit ☐ Dragnet ☐ Driving Miss Daisy ☐ Exit to Eden ☐ Ghostbusters ☐ Ghostbusters II ☐ Great Outdoors, The ☐ It Came From Hollywood ☐ Loose Cannons ☐ Love at First Sight ☐ Mr. Mike's Mondo Video ☐ My Girl ☐ My Girl 2 ☐ My Stepmother Is an Alien ☐ Neighbors ☐ Nothing But Trouble ☐ Nothing Lasts Forever ☐ Sneakers ☐ Spies Like Us ☐ This Is My Life ☐ Trading Places

Aylmer, Felix ☐ Angel Who Pawned Her Harp, The ☐ Becket ☐ Boys, The ☐ Dreaming Lips ☐ Edward, My Son ☐ Eye Witness ☐ Ghost of St. Michael's, The ☐ Hamlet ☐ Lady with a Lamp, The ☐ Master of Ballantrae, The ☐ Mummy, The ☐ Never Take Candy from a Stranger ☐ Night Train to Munich ☐ Smugglers, the ☐ So Long at the Fair ☐ Victoria the Great

Ayres, Lew ☐ Advise and Consent ☐ All Quiet on the Western Front ☐ Battlestar: Galactica ☐ Biscuit Eater, The ☐ Broadway Serenade ☐ Calling Dr. Kildare ☐ Capture, The ☐ Carpetbaggers, The ☐ Damien—Omen II ☐ Dark Mirror, The ☐ Donovan's Brain ☐ Doorway to Hell ☐ Dr. Kildare Goes Home ☐ Dr. Kildare's Crisis ☐ Dr. Kildare's Strange Case ☐ Dr. Kildare's Victory ☐ Dr. Kildare's Wedding Day ☐ Fingers at the Window ☐ Francis Gary Powers: The True Story of the U-2 Spy Incident ☐ Heat Wave! ☐ Hold 'Em Navy ☐ Holiday ☐ Ice Follies of 1939 ☐ Impatient Maiden, The ☐ Iron Man, The ☐ Johnny Belinda ☐ Kiss, The ☐ Last Train from Madrid, The ☐ Letters From Frank ☐ Maisie Was a Lady ☐ Man, The ☐ Marcus Welby, M.D. ☐ My Weakness ☐ Night World ☐ No Escape ☐ Of Mice and Men ☐ Rich Man, Poor Girl ☐ Salem's Lot: The Miniseries ☐ Secret of Dr. Kildare, The ☐ She Waits ☐ State Fair ☐ Unfaithful, The ☐ Young Dr. Kildare

Aznavour, Charles ☐ Blockhouse, The ☐ Candy ☐ Devil and the Ten Commandments, The ☐ Edith and Marcel ☐ Games, The ☐ Hatter's Ghost, The ☐ Heist, The ☐ High Infidelity ☐ Keepers, The ☐ Paris in the Month of August ☐ Shoot the Piano Player ☐ Ten Little Indians ☐ Twist, The

Bacall, Lauren ☐ All I Want for Christmas ☐ Appointment with Death ☐ Bacall on Bogart ☐ Big Sleep, The ☐ Blood Alley ☐ Bright Leaf ☐ Cobweb, The ☐ Confidential Agent ☐ Dark Passage ☐ Designing Woman ☐ Dinner at Eight ☐ Fan, The ☐ Flame over India ☐ Gift of Love, The ☐ H.E.A.L.T.H. ☐ Harper ☐ How to Marry a Millionaire ☐ Innocent Victim ☐ Key Largo ☐ Misery ☐ Mr. North ☐ Murder on the Orient Express ☐ Perfect Gentlemen ☐ Portrait, The ☐ Ready to Wear ☐ Sex and the Single Girl ☐ Shootist, The ☐ To Have and Have Not ☐ Woman's World ☐ Written on the Wind ☐ Young Man With a Horn

Bach, Barbara ☐ Caveman ☐ Force 10 from Navarone ☐ Give My Regards to Broad Street ☐ Great Alligator, The ☐ Jaguar Lives! ☐ Spy Who Loved Me, The

Bach, Catherine ☐ Driving Force ☐ Masters of Menace ☐ Matt Helm ☐ Midnight Man, The ☐ Nicole

Backus, Jim ☐ Above and Beyond ☐ Advance to the Rear ☐ Angel Face ☐ Angels' Brigade ☐ Big Operator, The ☐ Billie ☐ C.H.O.M.P.S. ☐ Castaways on Gilligan's

Island, The ☐ Cockeyed Cowboys of Calico County ☐ Crazy Mama ☐ Don't Make Waves ☐ Francis in the Navy ☐ Friday Foster ☐ Girl He Left Behind ☐ Good Guys Wear Black ☐ Great Man, The ☐ Harlem Globetrotters on Gilligan's Island, The ☐ Hello Down There ☐ High Cost of Loving, The ☐ His Kind of Woman ☐ Horizontal Lieutenant, The ☐ I Love Melvin ☐ I Want You ☐ Iron Man, The ☐ John Goldfarb, Please Come Home ☐ Johnny Cool ☐ Ma and Pa Kettle Go to Town ☐ Macabre ☐ Magic Pony, The ☐ Man of a Thousand Faces ☐ Man with a Cloak, The ☐ Meet Me in Las Vegas ☐ Mooch Goes To Hollywood ☐ Mr. Magoo In Sherwood Forest ☐ Mr. Magoo's Christmas Carol ☐ Mr. Magoo's Story Book ☐ Mr. Magoo—1001 Arabian Nights ☐ Mr. Magoo—Man of Mystery ☐ Now You See Him, Now You Don't ☐ Pat and Mike ☐ Rebel Without a Cause ☐ Slapstick of Another Kind ☐ Square Jungle, The ☐ Top Secret Affair ☐ Wheeler Dealers, The ☐ Where Were You When the Lights Went Out? ☐ Wild and the Innocent, The ☐ Wonderful World of the Brothers Grimm, The ☐ Zotz!

Bacon, Kevin ☐ Air Up There, The ☐ Big Picture, The ☐ Criminal Law ☐ Diner ☐ End of the Line ☐ Enormous Changes at the Last Minute ☐ Few Good Men, A ☐ Flatliners ☐ Footloose ☐ Forty Deuce ☐ Friday the 13th ☐ He Said, She Said ☐ JFK ☐ Lemon Sky ☐ Murder in the First ☐ Planes, Trains & Automobiles ☐ Pyrates ☐ Queens Logic ☐ Quicksilver ☐ River Wild, The ☐ She's Having a Baby ☐ Tremors ☐ White Water Summer

Baddeley, Hermione ☐ Belles of St. Trinians, The ☐ Brighton Rock ☐ Christmas Carol, A ☐ Do Not Disturb ☐ Information Received ☐ It Always Rains on Sunday ☐ Marriage on the Rocks ☐ Mary Poppins ☐ No Room at the Inn ☐ Passport to Pimlico ☐ Pickwick Papers, The ☐ Regal Cavalcade ☐ Room at the Top ☐ Time, Gentlemen, Please?

Badel, Alan ☐ Children of the Damned ☐ Day of the Jackal, The ☐ Magic Fire ☐ Nijinsky ☐ Otley ☐ Riddle of the Sands, The ☐ This Sporting Life ☐ Three Cases of Murder

Baez, Joan ☐ Big T.N.T. Show, The ☐ Celebration at Big Sur ☐ Don't Look Back ☐ Dynamite Chicken ☐ Renaldo and Clara ☐ Woodstock

Baggetta, Vincent ☐ Chicago Story ☐ I Want to Keep My Baby ☐ Man Who Wasn't There, The ☐ Ordeal of Bill Carney, The

Bailey, G.W. ☐ Burglar ☐ Mannequin ☐ Police Academy ☐ Police Academy 5: Assignment Miami Beach ☐ Rustlers' Rhapsody ☐ Short Circuit

Bailey, Pearl ☐ All the Fine Young Cannibals ☐ Carmen Jones ☐ Fox and the Hound, The ☐ Landlord, The ☐ Norman . . . Is That You? ☐ Peter Gunn ☐ Porgy and Bess ☐ St. Louis Blues ☐ That Certain Feeling

Bain, Barbara ☐ Goodnight, My Love ☐ Harlem Globetrotters on Gilligan's Island, The ☐ Space 1999: Alien Attack ☐ Space 1999: Journey Through Black Sun ☐ Space 1999—Vol. 1—Voyager's Return

Bainter, Fay ☐ Arkansas Traveler, The ☐ Babes on Broadway ☐ Bill of Divorcement, A ☐ Children's Hour, The ☐ Close to My Heart ☐ Cry Havoc ☐ Dark Waters ☐ Daughters Courageous ☐ Deep Valley ☐ Give My Regards to Broadway ☐ Heavenly Body, The ☐ Human Comedy, The ☐ Jezebel ☐ Journey for Margaret ☐ June Bride ☐ Lady and the Mob, The ☐ Make Way for Tomorrow ☐ Maryland ☐ Mother Carey's Chickens ☐ Our Town ☐ Presenting Lily Mars ☐ President's Lady, The ☐ Quality Street ☐ Secret Life of Walter Mitty, The ☐ Shining Hour, The ☐ State Fair ☐ This Side of Heaven ☐ Three Is a Family ☐ Virginian, The ☐ Woman of the Year ☐ Young Tom Edison

Baio, Scott ☐ Bugsy Malone ☐ Foxes ☐ I Love N.Y. ☐ Luke was There ☐ Zapped!

Baker, Blanche ☐ Awakening of Candra, The ☐ Cold Feet ☐ French Postcards ☐ Livin' Large ☐ Mary and Joseph: A Story of Faith ☐ Nobody's Child ☐ Shakedown

Baker, Carroll ☐ Andy Warhol's Bad ☐ Baby Doll ☐ Big Country, The ☐ Bridge to the Sun ☐ But Not For Me ☐ Captain Apache ☐ Carpetbaggers, The ☐ Cheyenne Autumn ☐ Easy to Love ☐ Giant ☐ Greatest Story Ever Told, The ☐ Harlow ☐ How the West Was Won ☐ Ironweed ☐ Jack of Diamonds ☐ Miracle, The ☐ Mr. Moses ☐ Next Victim, The ☐ On Fire ☐ Paranoia ☐ Quiet Place to Kill, A ☐ Secret Diary of Sigmund Freud, The ☐ Star 80 ☐ Station Six-Sahara ☐ Watcher in the Woods, The ☐ You've Got to Have Heart

Baker, Diane ☐ Adventures of a Young Man ☐ Baker's Hawk ☐ Best of Everything, The ☐ Horse in the Gray Flannel Suit, The ☐ Invaders—Volume I ☐ Krakatoa, East of Java ☐ Marnie ☐ Mirage ☐ Nine Hours to Rama ☐ Prize, The ☐ Silence of the Lambs, The ☐ Stolen Hours, The ☐ Tess of the Storm Country ☐ Twenty Bucks

Baker, George ☐ Feminine Touch, The ☐ No Time for Tears ☐ Ship That Died of Shame, The ☐ Sword of Lancelot

Baker, Joe Don ☐ Adam at 6 A.M. ☐ Cape Fear ☐ Charley Varrick ☐ Checkered Flag or Crash ☐ Children, The ☐ Citizen Cohn ☐ Criminal Law ☐ Distinguished Gentleman, The ☐ Edge of Darkness ☐ Final Justice ☐ Framed ☐ Golden Needles ☐ Joysticks ☐ Leonard Part 6 ☐ Mitchell ☐ Outfit, The ☐ Pack, The ☐ Reality Bites ☐ Walking Tall

Baker, Josephine ☐ French Way, The ☐ Princesse Tam Tam ☐ Zou Zou

Baker, Kathy ☐ Article 99 ☐ Clean and Sober □ Dad □ Edward Scissorhands □ Image, The □ Jacknife □ Jennifer 8 □ Killing Affair, A □ Mad Dog and Glory □ Mr. Frost □ Nobody's Child □ Street Smart

Baker, Stanley □ Accident □ Angry Hills, The □ Campbell's Kingdom □ Chance Meeting □ Checkpoint □ Child in the House □ Concrete Jungle, The □ Dingaka □ Eva □ Games, The □ Girl with a Pistol, The □ Guns of Navarone, The □ Hard Drivers □ Helen of Troy □ Hell Below Zero □ Hell Drivers □ Hell in Korea □ Hell Is a City □ In the French Style □ Innocent Bystanders □ Man Who Finally Died, The □ Perfect Friday □ Prize of Arms, A □ Robbery □ Sands of the Kalahari □ Sea Fury □ Sodom and Gomorrah □ Violent Playground □ Zorro □ Zulu

Baker, Tom □ Angels Die Hard □ Frankenstein: The True Story □ Golden Voyage of Sinbad, The □ Nicholas and Alexandra

Bakke, Brenda □ Dangerous Love □ Fast Gun □ Fist Fighter □ Scavengers □ Tales From the Crypt Presents Demon Knight

Balaban, Bob □ Absence of Malice □ Altered States □ End of the Line □ Making It □ Whose Life Is It Anyway?

Baldwin, Adam □ 3:15 □ Bad Guys □ Chocolate War, The □ Cohen and Tate □ D.C. Cab □ Family Hour Special—Out of Time □ Full Metal Jacket □ My Bodyguard □ Next of Kin □ Off Sides

Baldwin, Alec □ Alamo, The—Thirteen Days to Glory □ Alice □ Beetlejuice □ Code of Honor □ Dress Gray □ Forever, Lulu □ Getaway, The □ Glengarry Glen Ross □ Great Balls of Fire! □ Hunt for Red October, The □ Malice □ Married to the Mob □ Marrying Man, The □ Miami Blues □ Prelude to a Kiss □ Shadow, The □ She's Having a Baby □ Talk Radio □ Working Girl

Baldwin, Stephen □ 8 Seconds □ Beast, The □ Crossing the Bridge □ Last Exit to Brooklyn □ Posse □ Threesome

Baldwin, William □ Backdraft □ Flatliners □ Preppie Murder, The □ Sliver □ Three of Hearts

Bale, Christian □ Empire of the Sun □ Little Women □ Newsies □ Swing Kids □ Treasure Island

Balin, Ina □ Black Orchid, The □ Charro! □ Children of An Lac, The □ Comancheros, The □ Comeback Trail, The □ From the Terrace □ Immigrants, The □ Panic on the 5:22 □ Patsy, The □ Projectionist, The □ Young Doctors, The

Balk, Fairuza □ Gas, Food Lodging □ Imaginary Crimes □ Return to Oz □ Shame □ Valmont

Ballard, Kaye □ Falling in Love Again □ Fate □ Freaky Friday □ Girl Most Likely, The

Ball, Lucille □ Affairs of Annabel, The □ Annabel Takes A Tour □ Beauty for the Asking □ Best Foot Forward □ Big Street, The □ Chatterbox □ Critic's Choice □ Dance, Girl, Dance □ Dark Corner, The □ DuBarry Was a Lady □ Easy Living □ Easy to Wed □ Facts of Life, The □ Fancy Pants □ Five Came Back □ Forever Darling □ Fuller Brush Girl, The □ Girl, a Guy, and a Gob, A □ Go Chase Yourself □ Guide for the Married Man, A □ Having Wonderful Time □ Her Husband's Affairs □ Hitting a New High □ I Dream Too Much □ Joy of Living □ Long, Long Trailer, The □ Look Who's Laughing □ Lover Come Back □ Lucy's Lost Episodes □ Magic Carpet, The □ Mame □ Meet the People □ Miss Grant Takes Richmond □ Next Time I Marry □ Panama Lady □ Personal Column □ Roman Scandals □ Room Service □ Seven Days' Leave □ Sorrowful Jones □ Stage Door □ Stone Pillow □ That Girl From Paris □ Too Many Girls □ Valley of the Sun □ Without Love □ Yours, Mine and Ours □ Ziegfeld Follies

Balsam, Martin □ 12 Angry Men □ Ada □ After the Fox □ Al Capone □ All the President's Men □ Anderson Tapes, The □ Aunt Mary □ Bedford Incident, The □ Brand New Life, A □ Breakfast at Tiffany's □ Cape Fear □ Cape Fear □ Carpetbaggers, The □ Catch-22 □ Confessions of a Police Captain □ Conquered City, The □ Contract on Cherry Street □ Death Wish 3 □ Delta Force, The □ Good Guys and the Bad Guys, The □ Goodbye People, The □ Grown Ups □ Harlow □ Hombre □ House on Garibaldi Street, The □ Innocent Prey □ Lindbergh Kidnapping Case, The □ Little Big Man □ Little Gloria-Happy At Last □ Man, The □ Me, Natalie □ Middle of the Night □ Mitchell □ Murder in Space □ Murder on the Orient Express □ People vs. Jean Harris, The □ Psycho □ Queenie □ Raid on Entebbe □ Rainbow □ Salamander, The □ Season for Assassins □ Second Serve □ Sentinel, The □ Seven Days in May □ Summer Wishes, Winter Dreams □ Taking of Pelham One Two Three, The □ Thousand Clowns, A □ Time Limit □ Tora! Tora! Tora! □ Two Evil Eyes □ Two Minute Warning

Bancroft, Anne □ 'Night, Mother □ 84 Charing Cross Road □ Agnes of God □ Bert Rigby, You're a Fool □ Broadway Bound □ Demetrius and the Gladiators □ Don't Bother to Knock □ Elephant Man, The □ Fatso □ Garbo Talks □ Girl in Black Stockings, The □ Gorilla at Large □ Graduate, The □ Hindenburg, The □ Jesus of Nazareth □ Kid From Left Field, The □ Last Frontier, The □ Lipstick □ Love Potion No. 9 □ Miracle Worker, The □ Mr. Jones □ Naked Street, The □ Nightfall □ Oldest Living Confederate Widow Tells All □ Point of No Return □ Prisoner of Second Avenue, The □ Pumpkin Eater, The □ Raid, The □ Seven Women □ Slender Thread, The □ To Be or Not to Be □ Tonight We Sing □ Torch Song

Trilogy ☐ Treasure of the Golden Condor ☐ Turning Point, The ☐ Walk the Proud Land ☐ Young Winston

Bancroft, George ☐ Blood Money ☐ Docks of New York ☐ Each Dawn I Die ☐ Espionage Agent ☐ Little Men ☐ Mr. Deeds Goes to Town ☐ Northwest Mounted Police ☐ Rainbow Trail, The ☐ Rich Man's Folly ☐ Stagecoach ☐ Texas ☐ Thunderbolt ☐ Underworld ☐ When the Daltons Rode ☐ Young Tom Edison

Banderas, Antonio ☐ House of the Spirits ☐ Interview With the Vampire ☐ Labyrinth of Passion ☐ Law of Desire ☐ Mambo Kings, The ☐ Matador ☐ Miami Rhapsody ☐ Philadelphia ☐ Stilts, The ☐ Women on the Verge of a Nervous Breakdown

Bankhead, Tallulah ☐ Devil and the Deep ☐ Die Die My Darling ☐ Faithless ☐ Lifeboat ☐ Main Street to Broadway ☐ Royal Scandal, A

Banks, Leslie ☐ 21 Days Together ☐ Arsenal Stadium Mystery, The ☐ Big Blockade, The ☐ Chamber of Horrors ☐ Cottage to Let ☐ Eye Witness ☐ Farewell Again ☐ Fire Over England ☐ Haunted Honeymoon ☐ Henry V ☐ Jamaica Inn ☐ Madeleine ☐ Man Who Knew Too Much, The ☐ Most Dangerous Game, The ☐ Neutral Port ☐ Sanders of the River ☐ Transatlantic Tunnel ☐ Wings of the Morning

Bannen, Ian ☐ Bite the Bullet ☐ Crossing the Line ☐ Doomwatch ☐ Driver's Seat, The ☐ Eye of the Needle ☐ Flight of the Phoenix ☐ Fright ☐ Gathering Storm, The ☐ Hill, The ☐ Hope and Glory ☐ Inglorious Bastards ☐ Jane Eyre ☐ Lock Up Your Daughters! ☐ Mackintosh Man, The ☐ Man in a Cocked Hat ☐ Mr. Moses ☐ Night Crossing ☐ Offence, The ☐ Penelope ☐ Risk, The ☐ Sound and the Silence, The ☐ Station Six-Sahara ☐ Too Late the Hero ☐ Voyage, The

Bannon, Jim ☐ Devil's Mask, The ☐ I Love a Mystery ☐ Missing Juror, The ☐ Unknown World

Bansagi, Ildiko ☐ Brady's Escape ☐ Confidence ☐ Meeting Venus ☐ Mephisto

Barbeau, Adrienne ☐ Blood River ☐ Bridge Across Time ☐ Cannibal Women in the Avocado Jungle of Death ☐ Charlie and the Great Balloon Chase ☐ Creepshow ☐ Escape from New York ☐ Fog, The ☐ Having Babies ☐ Magic on Love Island ☐ Next One, The ☐ Open House ☐ Red Alert ☐ Seduced ☐ Swamp Thing ☐ Two Evil Eyes

Barbier, George ☐ Big Pond, The ☐ Early to Bed ☐ Merry Widow, The ☐ Milky Way, The ☐ No One Man ☐ She Loves Me Not ☐ Week-end in Havana ☐ Wife vs. Secretary ☐ Wife, Husband and Friend

Barclay, Joan ☐ Black Dragons ☐ Falcon Out West, The ☐ Lightning Carson Rides Again ☐ Shanghai Cobra, The

Barcroft, Roy ☐ In Old Amarillo ☐ Missourians, The ☐ Salt Lake Raiders ☐ Son of Zorro ☐ Under Mexicali Stars

Bardot, Brigitte ☐ ...And God Created Woman ☐ Act of Love ☐ Babette Goes to War ☐ Bride Is Much Too Beautiful, The ☐ Come Dance with Me! ☐ Contempt ☐ Doctor At Sea ☐ Grand Maneuver, The ☐ Helen of Troy ☐ La Parisienne ☐ Le Repos du Guerrier ☐ Legend of Frenchie King, The ☐ Light Across the Street, The ☐ Love Is My Profession ☐ Love on a Pillow ☐ Mam'zelle Pigalle ☐ Ms. Don Juan ☐ Night Heaven Fall, The ☐ Ravishing Idiot ☐ Shalako ☐ Spirits of the Dead ☐ Very Private Affair, A ☐ Viva Maria!

Bari, Lynn ☐ Abbott and Costello Meet The Keystone Kops ☐ Bridge of San Luis Rey, The ☐ Captain Eddie ☐ Charlie Chan in City in Darkness ☐ China Girl ☐ Falcon Takes Over, The ☐ Hello Frisco, Hello ☐ Home, Sweet Homicide ☐ I Dream of Jeannie ☐ I'd Climb the Highest Mountain ☐ I'll Give a Million ☐ Kit Carson ☐ Magnificent Dope, The ☐ Margie ☐ Mr. Moto's Gamble ☐ Nocturne ☐ On the Loose ☐ Pack Up Your Troubles ☐ Shock ☐ Six Gun Law ☐ Sun Valley Serenade ☐ Tampico

Barker, Lex ☐ Apache Gold ☐ Away All Boats ☐ Captain Falcon ☐ Code 7 Victim 5 ☐ Deerslayer, The ☐ Female Fiends ☐ Girl in Black Stockings, The ☐ Girl in the Kremlin, The ☐ Invisible Dr. Mabuse, The ☐ La Dolce Vita ☐ Man from Bitter Ridge, The ☐ Mr. Blandings Builds His Dream House ☐ Pirates of the Coast ☐ Price of Fear, The ☐ Return of Dr. Mabuse, The ☐ Twenty-Four Hours to Kill

Barkin, Ellen ☐ Act of Vengeance ☐ Adventures of Buckaroo Banzai Across the Eighth Dimension, The ☐ Bad Company ☐ Big Easy, The ☐ Clinton and Nadine ☐ Daniel ☐ Desert Bloom ☐ Diner ☐ Down by Law ☐ Eddie and the Cruisers ☐ Enormous Changes at the Last Minute ☐ Harry and Son ☐ Into the West ☐ Johnny Handsome ☐ Kent State ☐ Mac ☐ Man Trouble ☐ Sea of Love ☐ Siesta ☐ Switch ☐ Terrible Joe Moran ☐ This Boy's Life

Barnes, Binnie ☐ Adventures of Marco Polo, The ☐ Always Goodbye ☐ Barbary Coast Gent ☐ Broadway Melody of 1938 ☐ Call Out the Marines ☐ Day-Time Wife ☐ Decameron Nights ☐ Diamond Jim ☐ Divorce of Lady X, The ☐ Dude Goes West, The ☐ 40 Carats ☐ Frontier Marshal ☐ Fugitive Lady ☐ Gateway ☐ Getting Gertie's Garter ☐ Hour Before the Dawn ☐ I Married an Angel ☐ If Winter Comes ☐ In Old California ☐ It's in the Bag ☐ Last of the Mohicans, The ☐ Magnificent Brute, The ☐ Man About Town ☐ Man from Down Under, The ☐ Melody Master ☐ One Exciting Adventure ☐ Pirates of Capri, The ☐ Private Life of Henry VIII, The ☐ Rendezvous ☐ Skylark ☐ Small Town Girl ☐ Spanish Main, The ☐ This Thing Called

Love ☐ Three Musketeers, The ☐ Three Smart Girls ☐ Tight Shoes ☐ 'Til We Meet Again ☐ Time of Their Lives, The ☐ Where Angels Go, Trouble Follows ☐ Wife, Husband and Friend

Barnes, Priscilla ☐ Lords of the Deep ☐ Scruples ☐ Seniors, The ☐ Stepfather 3—Father's Day

Barnett, Vince ☐ Falcon's Alibi, The ☐ Fast Workers ☐ Overland Mail ☐ Paper Bullets ☐ Scarface

Barrat, Robert ☐ Distant Drums ☐ Exclusive Story ☐ I Loved a Woman ☐ Man from Dakota, The ☐ Massacre ☐ Murder Man, The ☐ Northwest Passage ☐ St. Louis Kid ☐ Strangler of the Swamp

Barrault, Jean-Louis ☐ Beethoven's Great Love ☐ Chappaqua ☐ Children of Paradise ☐ La Nuit des Varennes ☐ La Ronde ☐ Le Puritain ☐ Pearls of the Crown

Barrault, Marie-Christine ☐ Cousin, Cousine ☐ Love in Germany, A ☐ My Night at Maud's ☐ Table for Five

Barrie, Barbara ☐ Bell Jar, The ☐ Breaking Away ☐ End of the Line ☐ One Potato, Two Potato ☐ Real Men

Barrie, Mona ☐ Cairo ☐ First Time, The ☐ I Met Him in Paris ☐ I Take This Woman ☐ Secret of the Whistler ☐ Something to Sing About

Barrier, Edgar ☐ Cobra Woman ☐ Game of Death, A ☐ Macbeth ☐ Phantom of the Opera

Barrie, Wendy ☐ Big Broadcast of 1936, The ☐ Date With the Falcon, A ☐ Day-Time Wife ☐ Dead End ☐ Eyes of the Underworld ☐ Five Came Back ☐ Gay Falcon, The ☐ Girl with Ideas, A ☐ Hound of the Baskervilles, The ☐ I Am the Law ☐ If I Were Rich ☐ Pacific Liner ☐ Saint Strikes Back, The ☐ Saint Takes Over, The ☐ Speed ☐ Wedding Rehearsal

Barr, Patrick ☐ Brain Machine, The ☐ It's Never Too Late ☐ Marigold ☐ Next to No Time

Barry, Don ☐ Gunfire ☐ Jesse James's Women ☐ Ringside ☐ Sombrero Kid, The

Barry, Donald ☐ Frankenstein—1970 ☐ Seven Men from Now ☐ Shakiest Gun in the West, The ☐ Young Dr. Kildare

Barry, Gene ☐ 27th Day, The ☐ Atomic City, The ☐ China Gate ☐ Columbo: Prescription Murder ☐ Forty Guns ☐ Gambler Returns: The Luck of the Draw, The ☐ Guyana: Cult of the Damned ☐ Hong Kong Confidential ☐ Houston Story, The ☐ Istanbul Express ☐ Maroc 7 ☐ Naked Alibi ☐ Purple Mask, The ☐ Red Garters ☐ Soldier of Fortune ☐ Those Redheads From Seattle ☐ Thunder Road ☐ War of the Worlds

Barrymore, Jr., John ☐ Big Night, The ☐ High Lonesome ☐ Quebec ☐ Shadow on the Window, The ☐ Trojan Horse, The ☐ While the City Sleeps

Barrymore, Diana ☐ Between Us Girls ☐ Eagle Squadron ☐ Ladies Courageous ☐ Nightmare

Barrymore, Drew ☐ Amy Fisher Story, The ☐ Babes in Toyland ☐ Bad Girls ☐ Boys on the Side ☐ Cat's Eye ☐ E.T. The Extra-Terrestrial ☐ Far from Home ☐ Firestarter ☐ Guncrazy ☐ Irreconcilable Differences ☐ Motorama ☐ Poison Ivy ☐ See You in the Morning ☐ Sketch Artist

Barrymore, Ethel ☐ Deadline U.S.A ☐ Farmer's Daughter, The ☐ Great Sinner, The ☐ It's a Big Country ☐ Johnny Trouble ☐ Just for You ☐ Kind Lady ☐ Moonrise ☐ Night Song ☐ None But the Lonely Heart ☐ Paradine Case ☐ Pinky ☐ Portrait of Jennie ☐ Rasputin and the Empress ☐ Secret of Convict Lake, The ☐ Spiral Staircase, The ☐ Story of Three Loves, The ☐ That Midnight Kiss ☐ Young at Heart

Barrymore, John ☐ Arsene Lupin ☐ Beau Brummel ☐ Beloved Rogue, The ☐ Bill of Divorcement, A ☐ Bulldog Drummond Comes Back ☐ Counsellor-at-Law ☐ Dinner at Eight ☐ Don Juan ☐ Dr. Jekyll and Mr. Hyde ☐ Grand Hotel ☐ Great Man Votes, The ☐ Great Profile, The ☐ Hold That Co-ed ☐ Invisible Woman, The ☐ Long Lost Father ☐ Mad Genius, The ☐ Man From Blankley's, The ☐ Marie Antoinette ☐ Maytime ☐ Midnight ☐ Moby Dick ☐ Night Club Scandal ☐ Rasputin and the Empress ☐ Reunion in Vienna ☐ Romeo and Juliet ☐ Spawn of the North ☐ State's Attorney ☐ Svengali ☐ Tempest ☐ Topaze ☐ True Confession ☐ Twentieth Century ☐ World Premiere

Barrymore, Lionel ☐ Ah, Wilderness ☐ America ☐ Arsene Lupin ☐ Bad Man, The ☐ Bannerline ☐ Between Two Women ☐ Broken Lullaby ☐ Calling Dr. Gillespie ☐ Calling Dr. Kildare ☐ Camille ☐ Captains Courageous ☐ David Copperfield ☐ Devil-Doll, The ☐ Dinner at Eight ☐ Down to the Sea in Ships ☐ Dr. Gillespie's Criminal Case ☐ Dr. Gillespie's New Assistant ☐ Dr. Kildare Goes Home ☐ Dr. Kildare's Crisis ☐ Dr. Kildare's Strange Case ☐ Dr. Kildare's Victory ☐ Dr. Kildare's Wedding Day ☐ Duel in the Sun ☐ Family Affair, A ☐ Free and Easy ☐ Free Soul, A ☐ Girl from Missouri, The ☐ Gorgeous Hussy, The ☐ Grand Hotel ☐ Guilty Hands ☐ Guy Named Joe, A ☐ Hollywood Revue of 1929, The ☐ It's a Wonderful Life ☐ Key Largo ☐ Lady Be Good ☐ Let Freedom Ring ☐ Little Colonel, The ☐ Lone Star ☐ Looking Forward ☐ Main Street to Broadway ☐ Mark of the Vampire ☐ Mata Hari ☐ Navy Blue and Gold ☐ On Borrowed Time ☐ One Man's Journey ☐ Public Hero No. 1 ☐ Rasputin and the Empress ☐ Return of Peter Grimm, The ☐ Night Cross ☐ Road to Glory, The ☐ Sadie Thompson ☐ Saratoga ☐ Secret Heart, The ☐ Secret of Dr. Kildare, The ☐ Since You Went Away ☐ Stranger's Return, The ☐ Temptress, The ☐ Tennessee

Johnson ☐ Test Pilot ☐ This Side of Heaven ☐ Three Wise Fools ☐ Treasure Island ☐ Valley of Decision, The ☐ West of Zanzibar ☐ Yank at Oxford, A ☐ You Can't Take It With You ☐ Young Dr. Kildare

Barry, Patricia ☐ Kitten with a Whip ☐ Marriage of a Young Stockbroker, The ☐ Safe at Home ☐ Sammy, the Way-Out Seal

Barry, Tony ☐ Goodbye Pork Pie ☐ Jack Be Nimble ☐ Quest, The ☐ Shame ☐ We of the Never Never

Bartel, Paul ☐ Acting on Impulse ☐ Amazon Women on the Moon ☐ Chopping Mall ☐ Desire and Hell at Sunset Motel ☐ Eating Raoul ☐ Hollywood Boulevard ☐ Living End, The ☐ Pope Must Diet, The ☐ White Dog

Barthelmess, Richard ☐ Broken Blossoms ☐ Cabin in the Cotton, The ☐ Central Airport ☐ Dawn Patrol, The ☐ Finger Points, The ☐ Four Hours to Kill ☐ Heroes for Sale ☐ Idol Dancer, The ☐ Just Suppose ☐ Last Flight, The ☐ Love Flower, The ☐ Man Who Talked Too Much, The ☐ Massacre ☐ Only Angels Have Wings ☐ Way Down East

Bartholomew, Freddie ☐ Anna Karenina ☐ Captains Courageous ☐ David Copperfield ☐ Devil is a Sissy, The ☐ Kidnapped ☐ Listen, Darling ☐ Little Lord Fauntleroy ☐ Lloyd's of London ☐ Lord Jeff ☐ Professional Soldier ☐ St. Benny the Dip ☐ Swiss Family Robinson ☐ Tom Brown's School Days ☐ Two Bright Boys

Bartlett, Bennie ☐ Feudin' Fools ☐ Fighting Fools ☐ Here Come the Marines ☐ Jail Busters ☐ Jalopy ☐ Master Minds ☐ Smugglers' Cove

Bartok, Eva ☐ Assassin, The ☐ Blood and Black Lace ☐ Break in the Circle ☐ Crimson Pirate, The ☐ Front Page Story ☐ Gamma People, The ☐ Madeleine ☐ Operation Amsterdam ☐ Ten Thousand Bedrooms

Barty, Billy ☐ Foul Play ☐ Masters of the Universe ☐ Night Patrol ☐ Rumpelstiltskin ☐ Undead, The ☐ Under the Rainbow ☐ W.C. Fields and Me ☐ Willow

Baryshnikov, Mikhail ☐ Company Business ☐ Dancers ☐ Nutcracker, The ☐ That's Dancing ☐ Turning Point, The ☐ White Nights

Basehart, Richard ☐ And Millions Will Die ☐ Being There ☐ Bounty Man, The ☐ Brothers Karamazov, The ☐ Canyon Crossroads ☐ Chato's Land ☐ Cry Wolf ☐ Decision Before Dawn ☐ Finger of Guilt ☐ Five Branded Women ☐ Fixed Bayonets ☐ Flood! ☐ For the Love of Mike ☐ Fourteen Hours ☐ Good Die Young, The ☐ Great Bank Hoax, The ☐ Hans Brinker ☐ He Walked by Night ☐ Hitler ☐ House on Telegraph Hill ☐ Il Bidone ☐ Island of Dr. Moreau, The ☐ La Strada ☐ Maneater ☐ Mansion of the Doomed ☐ Marilyn: The Untold Story ☐ Moby Dick ☐ Outside the Wall ☐ Portrait in Black ☐ Rage ☐ Rebels, The ☐ Repeat Performance ☐ Satan Bug, The ☐ Savage Guns, The ☐ Stranger's Hand, The ☐ Tension ☐ Time Limit ☐ Titanic

Basinger, Kim ☐ 9 1/2 Weeks ☐ Batman ☐ Blind Date ☐ Cool World ☐ Final Analysis ☐ Fool for Love ☐ From Here to Eternity ☐ Getaway, The ☐ Hard Country ☐ Katie: Portrait of a Centerfold ☐ Killjoy ☐ Man Who Loved Women, The ☐ Marrying Man, The ☐ Mother Lode ☐ My Stepmother Is an Alien ☐ Nadine ☐ Natural, The ☐ Never Say Never Again ☐ No Mercy ☐ Ready to Wear ☐ Real McCoy, The ☐ Wayne's World 2

Bass, Alfie ☐ Carry on Admiral ☐ Fearless Vampire Killers or: Pardon Me, But Your Teeth Are in My Neck ☐ I Only Asked! ☐ It Always Rains on Sunday ☐ Lavender Hill Mob, The ☐ Night My Number Came Up, The

Basserman, Albert ☐ Foreign Correspondent ☐ Madame Curie ☐ Moon and Sixpence, The ☐ Rhapsody in Blue

Bassett, Angela ☐ Boyz N the Hood ☐ City of Hope ☐ Critters 4 ☐ Heroes of Desert Storm, The ☐ Jacksons: An American Dream, The ☐ Malcolm X ☐ What's Love Got to Do With It

Bateman, Jason ☐ Bates Motel ☐ Breaking the Rules ☐ Can You Feel Me Dancing? ☐ Necessary Roughness ☐ Taste for Killing, A ☐ Teen Wolf Too ☐ Thanksgiving Promise, The ☐ This Can't Be Love

Bateman, Justine ☐ Can You Feel Me Dancing? ☐ Closer, The ☐ Family Ties Vacation ☐ Fatal Image, The ☐ Night We Never Met, The ☐ Primary Motive ☐ Satisfaction

Bates, Alan ☐ Butley ☐ Club Extinction ☐ Day in the Death of Joe Egg, A ☐ Duet for One ☐ Entertainer, The ☐ Far from the Madding Crowd ☐ Fixer, The ☐ Georgy Girl ☐ Go-Between, The ☐ Guest, The ☐ Hamlet ☐ Impossible Object ☐ In Celebration ☐ Kind of Loving, A ☐ King of Hearts ☐ Mr. Frost ☐ Nijinsky ☐ Nothing But the Best ☐ Pack of Lies ☐ Prayer for the Dying, A ☐ Quartet ☐ Return of the Soldier, The ☐ Rose, The ☐ Royal Flash ☐ Secret Friends ☐ Shout, The ☐ Silent Tongue ☐ Story of a Love Story ☐ Unmarried Woman, An ☐ We Think the World of You ☐ Whistle Down the Wind ☐ Wicked Lady, The ☐ Women in Love ☐ Zorba the Greek

Bates, Barbara ☐ Apache Territory ☐ I'd Climb the Highest Mountain ☐ Inspector General, The ☐ June Bride ☐ Quicksand

Bates, Florence ☐ Chocolate Soldier, The ☐ Father Takes the Air ☐ Kismet ☐ Love Crazy ☐ Mask of Dimitrios, The ☐ Moon and Sixpence, The ☐ Mr. Lucky ☐ River Lady ☐ San Antonio ☐ San Francisco Story, The ☐ Saratoga Trunk ☐ Slightly Dangerous ☐ Time, the Place and the Girl, The ☐ Winter Meeting

Bates, Jeanne ☐ Eraserhead ☐ Mom ☐ Racket Man, The ☐ Strangler, The

Bates, Kathy ☐ Arthur 2—On the Rocks

☐ At Play in the Fields of the Lord ☐ Come Back to the Five and Dime, Jimmy Dean, Jimmy Dean ☐ Dolores Claiborne ☐ Fried Green Tomatoes ☐ High Stakes ☐ Home of Our Own, A ☐ Johnny Bull ☐ Men Don't Leave ☐ Misery ☐ No Place Like Home ☐ North ☐ Prelude to a Kiss ☐ Roe vs. Wade ☐ Shadows and Fog ☐ Summer Heat ☐ Used People ☐ White Palace

Bates, Ralph ☐ Dr. Jekyll and Sister Hyde ☐ Fear in the Night ☐ Graveyard, The ☐ Horror of Frankenstein, The ☐ Lust for a Vampire ☐ Second Chance

Bauchau, Patrick ☐ Double Identity ☐ La Collectioneuse ☐ Music Teacher, The ☐ Rapture, The ☐ State of Things, The ☐ View to a Kill, A

Bauer, Belinda ☐ Act of Piracy ☐ American Success Company, The ☐ Game of Love, The ☐ Robocop 2 ☐ Rosary Murders, The ☐ Samson and Delilah ☐ Servants of Twilight, The ☐ Sins of Dorian Gray, The ☐ Timerider ☐ Winter Kills

Bauer, Steven ☐ Beast, The ☐ Gleaming the Cube ☐ Raising Cain ☐ Running Scared ☐ Scarface ☐ Snapdragon ☐ Thief of Hearts

Baur, Harry ☐ Beethoven's Great Love ☐ Golgotha ☐ I Stand Condemned ☐ Le Golem: The Lend of Prague ☐ Poil de Carotte ☐ Un Carnet De Bal ☐ Volpone

Baxter, Anne ☐ 20 Mule Team ☐ All About Eve ☐ Angel on My Shoulder ☐ Bedevilled ☐ Blaze of Noon ☐ Blue Gardenia ☐ Busy Body, The ☐ Carnival Story ☐ Charley's Aunt ☐ Chase a Crooked Shadow ☐ Cimarron ☐ Come-On, The ☐ Crash Dive ☐ East of Eden ☐ Eve of St. Mark, The ☐ Five Graves to Cairo ☐ Follow the Sun ☐ Fools' Parade ☐ Great Profile, The ☐ Guest in the House ☐ Homecoming ☐ I Confess ☐ Jane Austen in Manhattan ☐ Lisa, Bright and Dark ☐ Magnificent Ambersons, The ☐ Marcus Welby, M.D. ☐ Masks of Death ☐ North Star, The ☐ O. Henry's Full House ☐ One Desire ☐ Outcasts of Poker Flat, The ☐ Pied Piper, The ☐ Razor's Edge, The ☐ Royal Scandal, A ☐ Season of Passion ☐ Smoky ☐ Spoilers, The ☐ Stranger on the Run ☐ Sullivans, The ☐ Sunday Dinner for a Soldier ☐ Swamp Water ☐ Ten Commandments, The ☐ Three Violent People ☐ Ticket to Tomahawk, A ☐ Walk on the Wild Side ☐ Walls of Jericho, The ☐ Yellow Sky ☐ You're My Everything

Baxter, Warner ☐ 42nd Street ☐ Adam Had Four Sons ☐ Barricade ☐ Behind That Curtain ☐ Broadway Bill ☐ Crime Doctor ☐ Gentleman from Nowhere, The ☐ Great Gatsby, The ☐ I'll Give a Million ☐ In Old Arizona ☐ Just Before Dawn ☐ Kidnapped ☐ King of Burlesque ☐ Lady in the Dark ☐ One More Spring ☐ Paddy, the Next Best Thing ☐ Penthouse ☐ Prisoner of Shark Island, The ☐ Road to Glory, The ☐ Robin Hood of El Dorado, The ☐ Romance of the Rio Grande ☐ Slave Ship ☐ Squaw Man, The ☐ Stand Up and Cheer ☐ Vogues of 1938 ☐ West of Zanzibar ☐ Wife, Doctor and Nurse ☐ Wife, Husband and Friend

Baxter-Birney, Meredith ☐ Ben ☐ Beulah Land ☐ Bittersweet Love ☐ Bump in the Night ☐ Burning Bridges ☐ Family Ties Vacation ☐ Invasion of Carol Enders, The ☐ Kissing Place, The ☐ Little Women ☐ Rape of Richard Beck, The

Baye, Nathalie ☐ Beau Pere ☐ Beethoven's Nephew ☐ C'est la Vie ☐ Detective ☐ Every Man for Himself ☐ Girl from Lorraine, A ☐ Green Room, The ☐ I Married a Shadow ☐ La Balance ☐ Man Inside, The ☐ Return of Martin Guerre, The

Beacham, Stephanie ☐ And Now the Screaming Starts ☐ Devil's Widow, The ☐ Dracula A.D. ☐ Foreign Affairs ☐ Horror Planet ☐ Nightcomers, The ☐ Troop Beverly Hills

Beal, John ☐ Break of Hearts ☐ Danger Patrol ☐ Edge of Darkness ☐ House That Cried Murder, The ☐ I Am the Law ☐ Little Minister, The ☐ Madame X ☐ My Six Convicts ☐ Ten Who Dared ☐ That Night

Beals, Jennifer ☐ Bride, The ☐ Caro Diario ☐ Club Extinction ☐ Flashdance ☐ Gamble, The ☐ In the Soup ☐ Indecency ☐ Terror Stalks the Class Reunion ☐ Vampire's Kiss

Bean, Sean ☐ Caravaggio ☐ Field, The ☐ Lorna Doone ☐ Stormy Monday

Beart, Emmanuelle ☐ Date with an Angel ☐ L'Enfer ☐ La Belle Noiseuse ☐ Manon of the Spring

Beatty, Ned ☐ 1941 ☐ Alambrista! ☐ All God's Children ☐ All the President's Men ☐ American Success Company, The ☐ Attack on Terror: The FBI vs. the Ku Klux Klan ☐ Back to Hannibal: The Return of Tom Sawyer and Huckleberry Finn ☐ Back to School ☐ Big Bad John ☐ Big Bus, The ☐ Big Easy, The ☐ Blind Vision ☐ Chattahoochee ☐ Cry in the Wild, A ☐ Deliverance ☐ Dying Room Only ☐ Execution of Private Slovik, The ☐ Fourth Protocol, The ☐ Friendly Fire ☐ Gray Lady Down ☐ Guyana Tragedy: The Story of Jim Jones ☐ Half Slave, Half Free 2 ☐ Hear My Song ☐ Hopscotch ☐ Hostage Flight ☐ Incredible Shrinking Woman, The ☐ Marcus-Nelson Murders, The ☐ Midnight Crossing ☐ Mikey and Nicky ☐ Ministry of Vengeance ☐ Nashville ☐ Network ☐ Our Town ☐ Physical Evidence ☐ Prelude to a Kiss ☐ Promises in the Dark ☐ Purple People Eater ☐ Question of Love, A ☐ Radioland Murders ☐ Repossessed ☐ Rudy ☐ Sex and Buttered Popcorn ☐ Shadows in the Storm ☐ Silver Streak ☐ Stroker Ace ☐ Superman 2 ☐ Superman—The Movie ☐ Switching Channels ☐ T Bone N Weasel ☐ Toy, The ☐ Tragedy of Flight 103, The: The Inside Story ☐ Unholy, The ☐ W. W. and the Dixie

Dancekings ☐ White Lightning ☐ Wise Blood ☐ Woman Called Golda, A

Beatty, Robert ☐ Against the Wind ☐ Break to Freedom ☐ Calling Bulldog Drummond ☐ Girl in the Painting ☐ Magic Box, The ☐ Man on a Tightrope ☐ Postmark for Danger ☐ Project M7 ☐ San Demetrio, London ☐ Square Ring, The

Beatty, Warren ☐ $ (Dollars) ☐ All Fall Down ☐ Bonnie and Clyde ☐ Bugsy ☐ Dick Tracy ☐ Fortune, The ☐ Heaven Can Wait ☐ Ishtar ☐ Kaleidoscope ☐ Lilith ☐ Love Affair ☐ McCabe and Mrs. Miller ☐ Mickey One ☐ Only Game in Town, The ☐ Parallax View, The ☐ Promise Her Anything ☐ Reds ☐ Roman Spring of Mrs. Stone, The ☐ Shampoo ☐ Splendor in the Grass

Beaumont, Hugh ☐ Blonde for a Day ☐ Flight Lieutenant ☐ Hell's Horizon ☐ Mexican Spitfire's Blessed Event ☐ Mole People, The ☐ Night Without Sleep ☐ Overland Telegraph ☐ Racket Man, The ☐ Railroaded ☐ Seventh Victim, The ☐ Wild Stallion

Beavers, Louise ☐ I Dream of Jeannie ☐ Imitation of Life ☐ Jackie Robinson Story, The ☐ Ladies of the Big House ☐ Make Way for Tomorrow ☐ Mr. Blandings Builds His Dream House ☐ Never Wave at a WAC

Beckett, Scotty ☐ Ali Baba and the Forty Thieves ☐ Dante's Inferno ☐ Gasoline Alley ☐ Happy Years, The ☐ My Favorite Wife ☐ My Son, My Son ☐ White Tie and Tails ☐ Youngest Profession, The

Beck, John ☐ Attack on Terror: The FBI vs. the Ku Klux Klan ☐ Audrey Rose ☐ Big Bus, The ☐ Call of the Wild, The ☐ Fire and Rain ☐ Flamingo Road ☐ Gridlock ☐ Other Side of Midnight, The ☐ Rollerball ☐ Sleeper

Beck, Michael ☐ Alcatraz: The Whole Shocking Story ☐ Blackout ☐ Golden Seal, The ☐ Madman ☐ Megaforce ☐ Rearview Mirror ☐ Triumphs of a Man Called Horse ☐ Warriors, The ☐ Xanadu

Beckley, Tony ☐ Fiend, The ☐ In the Devil's Garden ☐ Italian Job, The ☐ Lost Continent, The ☐ Penthouse, The ☐ When a Stranger Calls

Beddoe, Don ☐ Boy Who Caught a Crook ☐ Face Behind the Mask, The ☐ Island of Doomed Men ☐ Meet the Stewarts ☐ Notorious Lone Wolf, The ☐ Unholy Partners

Bedelia, Bonnie ☐ Alex: The Life of a Child ☐ Big Fix, The ☐ Boy Who Could Fly, The ☐ Death of an Angel ☐ Die Hard ☐ Die Hard 2 ☐ Fallen Angels—Volume 2 ☐ Fire Next Time, The ☐ Gypsy Moths, The ☐ Hawkins on Murder ☐ Heart Like a Wheel ☐ Heat Wave! ☐ Lovers and Other Strangers ☐ Memorial Day ☐ Message to My Daughter ☐ Needful Things ☐ Presumed Innocent ☐ Prince of Pennsylvania, The ☐ Salem's Lot: The Miniseries ☐ Somebody Has to Shoot the Picture ☐ Speechless ☐ Terms of Endearment ☐ They Shoot Horses, Don't They? ☐ Violets Are Blue . . . ☐ When the Time Comes

Beery, Jr., Noah ☐ 'Neath Brooklyn Bridge ☐ Cat Creeps, The ☐ Francis Gary Powers: The True Story of the U-2 Spy Incident ☐ Gung Ho! ☐ Her Lucky Night ☐ Indian Agent ☐ Inherit the Wind ☐ Mighty Treve, The ☐ Road Back, The ☐ Sergeant York ☐ We've Never Been Licked

Beery, Noah ☐ Bastard, The ☐ Kentucky Kernels ☐ Little Fauss and Big Halsy ☐ Mark of Zorro, The ☐ Mexicali Rose ☐ Millionaire, The ☐ Mysterious Two ☐ Mystery Liner ☐ Noah's Ark ☐ Oh! Sailor, Behave! ☐ Panamint's Badman ☐ Renegades ☐ She Done Him Wrong ☐ Soul of the Beast ☐ Thundering Herd, The ☐ Walking Tall ☐ White Feather

Beery, Wallace ☐ 20 Mule Team ☐ Ah, Wilderness ☐ Alias a Gentleman ☐ Bad Bascomb ☐ Bad Man of Brimstone ☐ Bad Man, The ☐ Barbary Coast Gent ☐ Barnacle Bill ☐ Beggars of Life ☐ Behind the Front ☐ Big House, The ☐ Big Jack ☐ Bowery, The ☐ Bugle Sounds, The ☐ Champ, The ☐ China Seas ☐ Date With Judy, A ☐ Dinner at Eight ☐ Flesh ☐ Four Horsemen of the Apocalypse, The ☐ Grand Hotel ☐ Hell Divers ☐ Jackass Mail ☐ Lady's Morals, A ☐ Last of the Mohicans, The ☐ Lost World, The ☐ Man from Dakota, The ☐ Message to Garcia, A ☐ Mighty Barnum, The ☐ Mighty McGurk, The ☐ Min and Bill ☐ O'Shaughnessy's Boy ☐ Old Hutch ☐ Old Ironsides ☐ Port of Seven Seas ☐ Rationing ☐ Robin Hood ☐ Secret Six, The ☐ Sergeant Madden ☐ Slave Ship ☐ Stablemates ☐ Stand Up and Fight ☐ This Man's Navy ☐ Treasure Island ☐ Tugboat Annie ☐ Viva Villa! ☐ West Point of the Air ☐ Wyoming

Begley, Ed ☐ 12 Angry Men ☐ Backfire ☐ Billion Dollar Brain ☐ Boomerang! ☐ Boots Malone ☐ Dark City ☐ Deadline U.S.A ☐ Deep Waters ☐ Dunwich Horror, The ☐ Firecreek ☐ Hang 'em High ☐ It Happens Every Spring ☐ Lone Star ☐ Odds Against Tomorrow ☐ Patterns ☐ Saddle Tramp ☐ Sitting Pretty ☐ Sorry, Wrong Number ☐ Stars in My Crown ☐ Street with No Name ☐ Sweet Bird of Youth ☐ Tulsa ☐ Turning Point, The ☐ Unsinkable Molly Brown, The ☐ Warning Shot ☐ Wild in the Streets

Begley, Jr., Ed ☐ Accidental Tourist, The ☐ Big One: The Great Los Angeles Earthquake, The ☐ Blue Collar ☐ Cat People ☐ Citizens Band ☐ Eating Raoul ☐ Get Crazy ☐ Great L.A. Earthquake, The ☐ Greedy ☐ In-Laws, The ☐ Meet the Applegates ☐ Not a Penny More, Not a Penny Less ☐ Now You See Him, Now You Don't ☐ Pagemaster, The ☐ Rascals and Robbers—The Secret Adventures ☐ Renaissance Man ☐ Running Mates ☐ Scenes from the Class Struggle in Beverly

Hills ☐ She-Devil ☐ Story Lady, The ☐ Streets of Fire ☐ Transylvania 6-5000

Belafonte, Harry ☐ Angel Levine, The ☐ Bright Road ☐ Buck and the Preacher ☐ Carmen Jones ☐ Grambling's White Tiger ☐ Harry Belafonte—Global Carnival ☐ Island in the Sun ☐ Odds Against Tomorrow ☐ Uptown Saturday Night ☐ World, the Flesh and the Devil, The

Belafonte, Shari ☐ Fire, Ice and Dynamite ☐ Midnight Hour, The ☐ Murder by Numbers ☐ Speed Zone!

Belford, Christine ☐ Banacek ☐ Groundstar Conspiracy, The ☐ Kenny Rogers as The Gambler ☐ Ladies Club, The ☐ Pocket Money

Bel Geddes, Barbara ☐ Blood on the Moon ☐ By Love Possessed ☐ Caught ☐ Five Branded Women ☐ Five Pennies, The ☐ Fourteen Hours ☐ I Remember Mama ☐ Long Night, The ☐ Panic in the Streets ☐ Summertree ☐ Todd Killings, The ☐ Vertigo

Bellamy, Ralph ☐ Ace of Aces ☐ Affectionately Yours ☐ Air Mail ☐ Amazon Women on the Moon ☐ Awful Truth, The ☐ Below the Sea ☐ Blind Alley ☐ Boy in the Plastic Bubble, The ☐ Boy Meets Girl ☐ Brother Orchid ☐ Cancel My Reservation ☐ Carefree ☐ Coast Guard ☐ Court-Martial of Billy Mitchell, The ☐ Dance, Girl, Dance ☐ Delightfully Dangerous ☐ Disorderlies ☐ Dive Bomber ☐ Doctor's Wives ☐ Eight Bells ☐ Ellery Queen and the Murder Ring ☐ Ellery Queen and the Perfect Crime ☐ Ellery Queen's Penthouse Mystery ☐ Ellery Queen, Master Detective ☐ Ever in My Heart ☐ Fools for Scandal ☐ Footsteps in the Dark ☐ Forbidden ☐ Fourth Wise Man, The ☐ Ghost of Frankenstein, The ☐ Girls' School ☐ Good Mother, The ☐ Great Impersonation, The ☐ Guest in the House ☐ Hands Across the Table ☐ His Girl Friday ☐ Immortal, The ☐ Lady in a Jam ☐ Lady on a Train ☐ Let Us Live ☐ Man Who Lived Twice, The ☐ McNaughton's Daughter ☐ Memory of Eva Ryker, The ☐ Men of Texas ☐ Missiles of October, The ☐ Murder on Flight 502 ☐ Narrow Corner, The ☐ Nightmare in Badham County ☐ Picture Snatcher ☐ Pretty Woman ☐ Queen of the Mob ☐ Roaming Lady ☐ Rosemary's Baby ☐ Secret Six, The ☐ Spitfire ☐ Sunrise at Campobello ☐ This Man Is Mine ☐ Trade Winds ☐ Trading Places ☐ Wedding Night, The ☐ Wolf Man, The

Beller, Kathleen ☐ Are You in the House Alone? ☐ Having Babies III ☐ Mary White ☐ No Place to Hide ☐ Promises in the Dark ☐ Surfacing ☐ Sword and the Sorcerer, The

Bell, Tom ☐ Ballad in Blue ☐ He Who Rides a Tiger ☐ In Enemy Country ☐ L-Shaped Room, The ☐ Let Him Have It ☐ Prime Suspect ☐ Prime Suspect 2 ☐ Prime Suspect 3 ☐ Prize of Arms, A ☐ Quest for Love ☐ Royal Flash ☐ Wish You Were Here

Belmondo, Jean-Paul ☐ Banana Peel ☐ Big Risk, The ☐ Borsalino ☐ Brain, The ☐ Breathless ☐ Burglars, The ☐ Cartouche ☐ Casino Royale ☐ Forgiven Sinner, The ☐ Greed in the Sun ☐ High Heels ☐ Is Paris Burning? ☐ La Viaccia ☐ Le Doulos ☐ Le Magnifique ☐ Les Tricheurs ☐ Love and the Frenchwoman ☐ Male Hunt ☐ Mississippi Mermaid ☐ Moderato Cantabile ☐ Monkey in Winter, A ☐ Pierrot le Fou ☐ Stavisky ☐ That Man From Rio ☐ Thief of Paris, The ☐ Two Women ☐ Up to His Ears ☐ Woman Is a Woman, A

Beltran, Robert ☐ Eating Raoul ☐ El Diablo ☐ Kiss Me a Killer ☐ Latino ☐ Night of the Comet ☐ Scenes from the Class Struggle in Beverly Hills ☐ Shadow Hunter

Belushi, James ☐ About Last Night... ☐ Abraxas, Guardian of the Universe ☐ Best Legs in the 8th Grade ☐ Curly Sue ☐ Diary of a Hitman ☐ Homer & Eddie ☐ K-9 ☐ Man with One Red Shoe ☐ Mr. Destiny ☐ Mutant Video ☐ Once Upon a Crime ☐ Only the Lonely ☐ Palermo Connection, The ☐ Principal, The ☐ Real Men ☐ Red Heat ☐ Salvador ☐ Taking Care of Business ☐ Thief ☐ Traces of Red ☐ Wild Palms

Belushi, John ☐ 1941 ☐ Animal House ☐ Blues Brothers, The ☐ Continental Divide ☐ Goin' South ☐ Neighbors ☐ Old Boyfriends ☐ Rutles, The

Benchley, Robert ☐ Bedtime Story ☐ Bride Wore Boots, The ☐ China Seas ☐ Dancing Lady ☐ Duffy's Tavern ☐ Flesh and Fantasy ☐ Foreign Correspondent ☐ Her Primitive Man ☐ Hired Wife ☐ I Married a Witch ☐ It's in the Bag ☐ Janie ☐ Janie Gets Married ☐ Kiss and Tell ☐ Major and the Minor, The ☐ Nice Girl? ☐ Pan Americana ☐ Practically Yours ☐ Reluctant Dragon, The ☐ See Here, Private Hargrove ☐ Sky's the Limit, The ☐ Snafu ☐ Song of Russia ☐ Take a Letter, Darling ☐ Weekend at the Waldorf ☐ You'll Never Get Rich

Bendix, William ☐ Abroad With Two Yanks ☐ Babe Ruth Story, The ☐ Battle Stations ☐ Bell for Adano, A ☐ Big Steal, The ☐ Blackbeard, the Pirate ☐ Blaze of Noon ☐ Blue Dahlia, The ☐ Calcutta ☐ China ☐ Connecticut Yankee in King Arthur's Court ☐ Crystal Ball, The ☐ Dangerous Mission ☐ Dark Corner, The ☐ Deep Six, The ☐ Detective Story ☐ For Love or Money ☐ Gambling House ☐ Girl in Every Port, A ☐ Glass Key, The ☐ Greenwich Village ☐ Guadalcanal Diary ☐ Hairy Ape, The ☐ Hostages ☐ I'll Be Yours ☐ It's in the Bag ☐ Johnny Holiday ☐ Johnny Nobody ☐ Kill the Umpire ☐ Law of the Lawless ☐ Life of Riley, The ☐ Lifeboat ☐ Macao ☐ Race Street ☐ Sentimental Journey ☐ Streets of Laredo ☐ Submarine Command ☐ Time of Your Life, The ☐ Two Years Before the Mast ☐ Wake Island ☐ Web, The ☐ Where There's Life ☐ White Tie and Tails ☐ Who Done It? ☐ Woman of the Year

Benedict, Billy ☐ Bowery Champs ☐ Come Out Fighting ☐ Fighting Fools ☐ Hold That Baby! ☐ Master Minds ☐ Mr. Muggs Steps Out ☐ Smugglers' Cove ☐ Trouble Makers
Benedict, Dirk ☐ Battlestar: Galactica ☐ Body Slam ☐ Demon Keeper ☐ Follow That Car ☐ Georgia, Georgia ☐ Scruples ☐ Shadow Force ☐ SSSSSSS
Benedict, Paul ☐ Billy in the Lowlands ☐ Deadhead Miles ☐ Goodbye Girl, The ☐ Man with Two Brains, The
Benedict, William ☐ Call a Messenger ☐ Ghost Chasers ☐ Let's Go Navy! ☐ Nyoka and the Tigerman
Benigni, Roberto ☐ Down by Law ☐ Johnny Stecchino ☐ Night on Earth ☐ Son of the Pink Panther
Bening, Annette ☐ Bugsy ☐ Great Outdoors, The ☐ Grifters, The ☐ Guilty by Suspicion ☐ Hostage ☐ Love Affair ☐ Regarding Henry ☐ Valmont
Benjamin, Paul ☐ Distance ☐ Education of Sonny Carson, The ☐ Escape from Alcatraz ☐ I Know Why the Caged Bird Sings ☐ Leadbelly ☐ Mr. Inside/Mr. Outside
Benjamin, Richard ☐ Catch-22 ☐ Diary of a Mad Housewife ☐ First Family ☐ Goodbye, Columbus ☐ House Calls ☐ How to Beat the High Cost of Living ☐ Last Married Couple in America, The ☐ Last of Sheila, The ☐ Love at First Bite ☐ Marriage of a Young Stockbroker, The ☐ No Room to Run ☐ Packin' It In ☐ Portnoy's Complaint ☐ Saturday the 14th ☐ Scavenger Hunt ☐ Sunshine Boys, The ☐ Westworld ☐ Witches' Brew
Bennent, Heinz ☐ From the Life of the Marionettes ☐ Last Metro, The ☐ Nea' ☐ Possession
Bennett, Bruce ☐ Before I Hang ☐ Big Tip Off, The ☐ Cosmic Man, The ☐ Daniel Boone, Trail Blazer ☐ Dark Passage ☐ Flaming Frontier ☐ Great Missouri Raid, The ☐ Last Outpost, The ☐ Man I Love, The ☐ Mildred Pierce ☐ More the Merrier, The ☐ Mystery Street ☐ Nora Prentiss ☐ Outsider, The ☐ Robber's Roost ☐ Sahara ☐ Silver River ☐ Sudden Fear ☐ To the Victor ☐ Treasure of the Sierra Madre, The ☐ Underground Agent ☐ Undertow ☐ Younger Brothers, The
Bennett, Constance ☐ Affairs of Cellini ☐ After Office Hours ☐ Angel on the Amazon ☐ As Young As You Feel ☐ Bed of Roses ☐ Centennial Summer ☐ Easiest Way, The ☐ Escape to Glory ☐ Everything Is Thunder ☐ Ladies in Love ☐ Lady with a Past ☐ Madame X ☐ Merrily We Live ☐ Our Betters ☐ Paris Underground ☐ Rich People ☐ Service De Luxe ☐ She Couldn't Take It ☐ Sin Takes a Holiday ☐ Three Faces East ☐ Topper ☐ Topper Takes a Trip ☐ Two-Faced Woman ☐ Unsuspected, The ☐ What Price Hollywood?
Bennett, Hywel ☐ Buttercup Chain, The ☐ Deadline ☐ Endless Night ☐ Family Way, The ☐ Murder Elite ☐ Virgin Soldiers, The
Bennett, Jill ☐ Anatomist, The ☐ Britannia Hospital ☐ For Your Eyes Only ☐ I Want What I Want ☐ Inadmissible Evidence ☐ Mr. Quilp ☐ Murders At Lynch Cross ☐ Nanny, The ☐ Sheltering Sky, The ☐ Skull, The
Bennett, Joan ☐ Arizona to Broadway ☐ Artists and Models Abroad ☐ Big Brown Eyes ☐ Bulldog Drummond ☐ Colonel Effingham's Raid ☐ Disraeli ☐ Divorce Wars: A Love Story ☐ Father of the Bride ☐ Father's Little Dividend ☐ For Heaven's Sake ☐ Gidget Gets Married ☐ Girl Trouble ☐ Green Hell ☐ Guy Who Came Back, The ☐ Highway Dragnet ☐ House Across the Bay, The ☐ House of Dark Shadows ☐ Housekeeper's Daughter, The ☐ I Met My Love Again ☐ Little Women ☐ Macomber Affair, The ☐ Man Hunt ☐ Man I Married, The ☐ Man in the Iron Mask, The ☐ Man Who Broke the Bank at Monte Carlo, The ☐ Man Who Reclaimed His Head, The ☐ Margin for Error ☐ Me and My Gal ☐ Mississippi ☐ Moby Dick ☐ Nob Hill ☐ Private Worlds ☐ Reckless Moment, The ☐ Scar, The ☐ Scarlet Street ☐ Secret Beyond the Door ☐ Suspiria ☐ There's Always Tomorrow ☐ Thirteen Hours By Air ☐ Trade Winds ☐ Two for Tonight ☐ Vogues of 1938 ☐ We're No Angels ☐ Woman in the Window, The ☐ Woman on the Beach, The
Bennett, Richard ☐ Arrowsmith ☐ Five and Ten ☐ Home Towners, The ☐ Madame Racketeer ☐ Magnificent Ambersons, The ☐ Nana
Benny, Jack ☐ Artists and Models ☐ Artists and Models Abroad ☐ Big Broadcast of 1937, The ☐ Broadway Melody of 1936 ☐ Buck Benny Rides Again ☐ Charley's Aunt ☐ College Holiday ☐ George Washington Slept Here ☐ Guide for the Married Man, A ☐ Hollywood Revue of 1929, The ☐ Horn Blows at Midnight, The ☐ It's in the Bag ☐ Love Thy Neighbor ☐ Man About Town ☐ Meanest Man in the World, The ☐ Medicine Man, The ☐ To Be or Not to Be ☐ Transatlantic Merry-Go-Round
Benson, Robby ☐ All the Kind Strangers ☐ Beauty and the Beast ☐ Chosen, The ☐ City Limits ☐ Death Be Not Proud ☐ Death of Richie, The ☐ Die Laughing ☐ End, The ☐ Harry and Son ☐ Homewrecker ☐ Ice Castles ☐ Invasion of Privacy ☐ Jeremy ☐ Jory ☐ Last of Mrs. Lincoln ☐ Modern Love ☐ National Lampoon Goes to the Movies ☐ Ode to Billy Joe ☐ One on One ☐ Our Town ☐ Rent-a-Cop ☐ Tribute
Bentley, John ☐ Escape in the Sun ☐ Istanbul ☐ Men Against the Sun ☐ Paper Gallows ☐ Submarine Seahawk
Bercovici, Luca ☐ Mirror Images II ☐ Mission of Justice ☐ Parasite ☐ Space Raiders
Berenger, Tom ☐ At Play in the Fields of the Lord ☐ Betrayed ☐ Beyond Obsession ☐ Big Chill, The ☐ Butch and Sundance: The Early

Days ☐ Dogs of War, The ☐ Eddie and the Cruisers ☐ Fear City ☐ Field, The ☐ Flesh & Blood ☐ Gettysburg ☐ In Praise of Older Women ☐ Last Rites ☐ Looking for Mr. Goodbar ☐ Love at Large ☐ Major League ☐ Major League II ☐ Platoon ☐ Rustlers' Rhapsody ☐ Shattered ☐ Shoot to Kill ☐ Sliver ☐ Someone to Watch Over Me

Berenson, Marisa ☐ Barry Lyndon ☐ Cabaret ☐ Death in Venice ☐ Night of the Cyclone ☐ Notorious ☐ Playing for Time ☐ Secret Diary of Sigmund Freud, The ☐ Sex on the Run ☐ Some Like It Cool ☐ White Hunter, Black Heart

Bergen, Candice ☐ 11 Harrowhouse ☐ Adventurers, The ☐ Bite the Bullet ☐ Carnal Knowledge ☐ Day the Fish Came Out, The ☐ Domino Principle, The ☐ Gandhi ☐ Getting Straight ☐ Group, The ☐ Hunting Party, The ☐ Live for Life ☐ Magus, The ☐ Mayflower Madam ☐ Merlin and the Sword ☐ Night Full of Rain, A ☐ Oliver's Story ☐ Rich and Famous ☐ Sand Pebbles, The ☐ Soldier Blue ☐ Starting Over ☐ Wind and the Lion, The

Bergen, Edgar ☐ Captain China ☐ Charlie McCarthy, Detective ☐ Don't Make Waves ☐ Fun and Fancy Free ☐ Goldwyn Follies, The ☐ Here We Go Again ☐ Homecoming—A Christmas Story, The ☐ I Remember Mama ☐ Letter of Introduction, A ☐ Look Who's Laughing ☐ Muppet Movie, The ☐ Mystery Lake ☐ Song of the Open Road ☐ Stage Door Canteen ☐ You Can't Cheat an Honest Man

Bergen, Polly ☐ Anatomy of Terror ☐ At War with the Army ☐ Cape Fear ☐ Caretakers, The ☐ Cry of the Hunted ☐ Cry-Baby ☐ Escape from Fort Bravo ☐ Fast Company ☐ Guide for the Married Man, A ☐ Haunting of Sarah Hardy, The ☐ Kisses for My President ☐ Lightning Incident, The ☐ Making Mr. Right ☐ Move Over, Darling ☐ Murder on Flight 502 ☐ Stooge, The ☐ That's My Boy ☐ Warpath ☐ Winds of War, The

Berger, Helmut ☐ Ash Wednesday ☐ Code Name—Emerald ☐ Conversation Piece ☐ Damned, The ☐ Dorian Gray ☐ Garden of the Finzi-Conntinis, The ☐ Great Battle, The ☐ Ludwig ☐ Romantic Englishwoman, The

Berger, Senta ☐ Ambush Murders, The ☐ Bang, Bang, You're Dead! ☐ Cast a Giant Shadow ☐ Cross of Iron ☐ Diabolically Yours ☐ Full Hearts & Empty Pockets ☐ Glory Guys, The ☐ Good Soldier Schweik, The ☐ Goodnight, Ladies and Gentlemen ☐ Istanbul Express ☐ Killing Cars ☐ Major Dundee ☐ Poppy Is Also a Flower, The ☐ Quiller Memorandum, The ☐ Scarlet Letter, The ☐ Treasure of San Gennaro, The ☐ Victors, The ☐ Waltz King, The

Berger, William ☐ Every Bastard a King ☐ Face to Face ☐ Sabata ☐ Superfly T.N.T.

Berggren, Thommy ☐ Broken Sky ☐ Elvira Madigan ☐ Hill on the Dark Side of the Moon, A ☐ Joe Hill ☐ Raven's End

Berghof, Herbert ☐ Mastermind ☐ Red Planet Mars ☐ Times Square ☐ Voices

Bergin, Patrick ☐ Frankenstein ☐ Highway to Hell ☐ Love Crimes ☐ Map of the Human Heart ☐ Mountains of the Moon ☐ Patriot Games ☐ Robin Hood ☐ Sleeping with the Enemy

Bergman, Ingrid ☐ Adam Had Four Sons ☐ Anastasia ☐ Arch of Triumph ☐ Autumn Sonata ☐ Bells of St. Mary's, The ☐ Cactus Flower ☐ Casablanca ☐ Dr. Jekyll and Mr. Hyde ☐ Elena and Her Men ☐ For Whom the Bell Tolls ☐ From the Mixed-Up Files of Mrs. Basil E. Frankweiler ☐ Gaslight ☐ Goodbye Again ☐ Greatest Love, The ☐ Indiscreet ☐ Inn of the Sixth Happiness, The ☐ Intermezzo ☐ Intermezzo ☐ Joan of Arc ☐ June Night ☐ Matter of Time, A ☐ Murder on the Orient Express ☐ Notorious ☐ Rage in Heaven ☐ Saratoga Trunk ☐ Spellbound ☐ Stromboli ☐ Swedenhielms ☐ Under Capricorn ☐ Visit, The ☐ Voyage to Italy ☐ Walk in the Spring Rain, A ☐ Woman Called Golda, A ☐ Yellow Rolls-Royce, The

Bergman, Sandahl ☐ Body of Influence ☐ Conan the Barbarian ☐ Getting Physical ☐ Hell Comes to Frogtown ☐ Kandyland ☐ Lipstick Camera, The ☐ Red Sonja ☐ She ☐ Stewardess School

Bergner, Elisabeth ☐ As You Like It ☐ Catherine the Great ☐ Cry of the Banshee ☐ Dreaming Lips ☐ Paris Calling

Berg, Peter ☐ Aspen Extreme ☐ Crooked Hearts ☐ Fire in the Sky ☐ Last Seduction, The ☐ Late for Dinner ☐ Midnight Clear, A ☐ Never on Tuesday ☐ Quiet Victory: The Charlie Wedemeyer Story ☐ Shocker

Berle, Milton ☐ Always Leave Them Laughing ☐ Can Hieronymus Merkin Ever Forget Mercy Humppe and Find True Happiness? ☐ Cracking Up ☐ For Singles Only ☐ Gentleman at Heart, A ☐ Happening, The ☐ Hey Abbott! ☐ It's a Mad Mad Mad Mad World ☐ Legend of Valentino, The ☐ Loved One, The ☐ Margin for Error ☐ Milton Berle's Mad World of Comedy ☐ Muppet Movie, The ☐ New Faces of 1937 ☐ Oscar, The ☐ Over My Dead Body ☐ Rise and Shine ☐ Sun Valley Serenade ☐ Tall, Dark and Handsome ☐ Who's Minding the Mint?

Berlin, Jeannie ☐ Baby Maker, The ☐ Heartbreak Kid, The ☐ In the Spirit ☐ Sheila Levine Is Dead and Living in New York

Bernardi, Herschel ☐ Cold Wind in August, A ☐ Front, The ☐ Green Fields ☐ Irma la Douce ☐ Love with the Proper Stranger ☐ No Deposit, No Return ☐ Stakeout on Dope Street

Bernhard, Sandra ☐ Bernhard, Sandra: Without You I'm Nothing ☐ Hudson Hawk ☐ Inside Monkey Zetterland ☐ King of Comedy, The ☐ Sesame Street Presents Follow That Bird ☐ Track 29 ☐ Without You I'm Nothing

Bernsen, Corbin ☐ Bert Rigby, You're a Fool ☐ Breaking Point ☐ Disorganized Crime ☐ Eat My Dust ☐ Frozen Assets ☐ Major League ☐ Major League II ☐ Shattered

Berridge, Elizabeth ☐ Amadeus ☐ Five Corners ☐ Funhouse, The ☐ Montana

Berry, Chuck ☐ Alice in the Cities ☐ American Hot Wax ☐ Chuck Berry Hail! Hail! Rock 'n' Roll ☐ Go, Johnny, Go! ☐ Jazz on a Summer's Day ☐ Let the Good Times Roll ☐ Rock, Rock, Rock!

Berry, Halle ☐ Boomerang ☐ Father Hood ☐ Flintstones, The ☐ Program, The ☐ Strictly Business

Berry, Jules ☐ Crime of Monsieur Lange, The ☐ Crossroads ☐ Devil's Envoy's, The ☐ Le Jour Se Leve

Berry, Richard ☐ C'est la Vie ☐ L'Addition ☐ La Balance ☐ Man and a Woman, A: 20 Years Later

Bertinelli, Valerie ☐ C.H.O.M.P.S. ☐ I Was a Mail Order Bride ☐ Number One with a Bullet ☐ Ordinary Heros ☐ Pancho Barnes ☐ Silent Witness

Berto, Juliet ☐ Céline and Julie Go Boating ☐ Le Gai Savoir ☐ Le Sex Shop ☐ Male of the Century, The ☐ Mr. Klein

Bessell, Ted ☐ Acorn People, The ☐ Breaking Up Is Hard to Do ☐ Don't Drink the Water ☐ McHale's Navy Joins the Air Force ☐ Scream, Pretty Peggy

Best, Edna ☐ Dispatch from Reuters, A ☐ Ghost and Mrs. Muir, The ☐ Intermezzo ☐ Iron Curtain, The ☐ Key, The ☐ Man Who Knew Too Much, The ☐ South Riding ☐ Swiss Family Robinson

Best, James ☐ Cole Younger, Gunfighter ☐ Francis Goes to West Point ☐ Killer Shrews, The ☐ Ma and Pa Kettle at the Fair ☐ Mountain Road, The ☐ Quick Gun, The ☐ Raid, The ☐ Ride Lonesome ☐ Rolling Thunder ☐ Seminole ☐ Seven Angry Men ☐ Shock Corridor ☐ Verboten!

Bettger, Lyle ☐ All I Desire ☐ Destry ☐ First Legion, The ☐ Forbidden ☐ Great Sioux Uprising ☐ Impasse ☐ Lone Ranger, The ☐ Sea Chase, The ☐ Showdown at Abilene ☐ Union Station

Betti, Laura ☐ Allonsanfan ☐ In the Name of the Father ☐ Jenatsch ☐ Teorema

Bey, Turhan ☐ Adventures of Casanova ☐ Ali Baba and the Forty Thieves ☐ Arabian Nights ☐ Bowery to Broadway ☐ Burma Convoy ☐ Climax, The ☐ Dragon Seed ☐ Falcon Takes Over, The ☐ Frisco Sal ☐ Gay Falcon, The ☐ Mad Ghoul, The ☐ Mummy's Tomb, The ☐ Out of the Blue ☐ Parole, Inc. ☐ Sudan

Beymer, Richard ☐ Adventures of a Young Man ☐ Bachelor Flat ☐ Cross Country ☐ Diary of Anne Frank, The ☐ Five Finger Exercise ☐ Indiscretion of an American Wife ☐ Silent Night, Deadly Night (Part III—Better Watch Out!) ☐ Stripper, The ☐ West Side Story

Bickford, Charles ☐ Anna Christie ☐ Babe Ruth Story, The ☐ Big Country, The ☐ Big Hand for the Little Lady, A ☐ Branded ☐ Brute Force ☐ Burma Convoy ☐ Captain Eddie ☐ Command Decision ☐ Court-Martial of Billy Mitchell, The ☐ Daughter of Shanghai ☐ Days of Wine and Roses ☐ Duel in the Sun ☐ Elopement ☐ Fallen Angel ☐ Farmer Takes a Wife, The ☐ Farmer's Daughter, The ☐ Fatal Confinement ☐ Four Faces West ☐ Guilty of Treason ☐ Hell's Heroes ☐ High, Wide, and Handsome ☐ Jim Thorpe—All American ☐ Johnny Belinda ☐ Last Posse, The ☐ Little Miss Marker ☐ Mister Cory ☐ Mr. Lucky ☐ Night Club Scandal ☐ Not as a Stranger ☐ Of Mice and Men ☐ Plainsman, The ☐ Prince of Players ☐ Raging Tide, The ☐ Riding High ☐ River's End ☐ Sea Bat, The ☐ Song of Bernadette, The ☐ Squaw Man, The ☐ Stand Up and Fight ☐ Star Is Born, A ☐ Tarzan's New York Adventure ☐ This Day and Age ☐ Thunder Trail ☐ Whirlpool ☐ Wicked Woman, A ☐ Wing and a Prayer ☐ Woman on the Beach, The ☐ You Can't Run Away From It

Bideau, Jean-Luc ☐ Inspector Lavardin ☐ Invitation, The ☐ Jonah Who Will Be 25 in the Year 2000 ☐ La Salamandre ☐ State of Siege

Biehn, Michael ☐ Abyss, The ☐ Aliens ☐ Coach ☐ Deadfall ☐ Fan, The ☐ Hog Wild ☐ In a Shallow Grave ☐ K2—The Ultimate High ☐ Navy SEALS ☐ Rampage ☐ Seventh Sign, The ☐ Strapped ☐ Taste for Killing, A ☐ Terminator, The ☐ Timebomb ☐ Tombstone

Bieri, Ramon ☐ Frisco Kid, The ☐ It's Good to Be Alive ☐ Matter of Life and Death, A ☐ Panic In Echo Park ☐ Sorcerer

Bikel, Theodore ☐ African Queen, The ☐ Angry Hills, The ☐ Assassination Game, The ☐ Blue Angel, The ☐ Colditz Story ☐ Dark Tower ☐ Darker than Amber ☐ Defiant Ones, The ☐ Dog of Flanders, A ☐ Enemy Below, The ☐ Final Days, The ☐ Forbidden Cargo ☐ I Bury the Living ☐ I Want To Live! ☐ Little Ark, The ☐ Madame Rosa ☐ Murder on Flight 502 ☐ My Fair Lady ☐ My Family Treasure ☐ My Side of the Mountain ☐ Pride and the Passion, The ☐ Sands of the Kalahari ☐ Sweet November ☐ Two Hundred Motels ☐ Woman Obsessed

Billingsley, Peter ☐ Arcade ☐ Beverly Hills Brats ☐ Christmas Story, A ☐ Christmas Story, A ☐ Dirt Bike Kid, The

Bill, Tony ☐ Are You in the House Alone? ☐ Come Blow Your Horn ☐ Flap ☐ Freedom ☐ Ice Station Zebra ☐ Initiation of Sarah, The ☐ Killing Mind, The ☐ Marriage on the Rocks ☐ None But the Brave ☐ Soldier in the Rain ☐ You're a Big Boy Now

Bing, Herman ☐ Every Day's a Holiday ☐ Every Night at Eight ☐ Flesh ☐ Jewel Robbery ☐ Maytime ☐ Merry Widow, The ☐ Mighty Barnum, The

Binoche, Juliette ☐ Bad Blood ☐ Blue ☐ Damage ☐ Rendez-vous ☐ Trois Couleurs: Blanc ☐ Trois Couleurs: Rouge ☐ Unbearable Lightness of Being, The ☐ Women & Men: In Love There Are No Rules

Birkin, Jane ☐ Beethoven's Nephew ☐ Catherine & Co. ☐ Daddy Nostalgia ☐ Dark Places ☐ Death on the Nile ☐ Dust ☐ Egon Schiele—Excess and Punishment ☐ Evil Under the Sun ☐ La Belle Noiseuse ☐ Le Petit Amour ☐ Leave All Fair ☐ Love at the Top ☐ Love on the Ground ☐ Make Room for Tomorrow ☐ Ms. Don Juan ☐ Seven Deaths in the Cat's Eye

Birney, David ☐ Dirty Knight's Work ☐ Five of Me, The ☐ Jacqueline Susann's Valley of the Dolls ☐ Night of the Fox ☐ Only with Married Men ☐ Ray Bradbury Chronicles: The Martian Episodes

Bishop, Joey ☐ Deep Six, The ☐ Delta Force, The ☐ Guide for the Married Man, A ☐ Johnny Cool ☐ Naked and the Dead, The ☐ Ocean's Eleven ☐ Sergeants 3 ☐ Texas Across the River ☐ Who's Minding the Mint?

Bishop, Julie ☐ Action in the North Atlantic ☐ Headline Hunters ☐ Hidden Hand, The ☐ International Squadron ☐ Murder in the Music Hall ☐ My Hero 1 ☐ Northern Pursuit ☐ Nurse's Secret, The ☐ Rhapsody in Blue ☐ Westward the Women

Bishop, William ☐ Anna Lucasta ☐ Basketball Fix, The ☐ Boss, The ☐ Oregon Trail, The ☐ Redhead from Wyoming, The ☐ Thunderhoof ☐ Walking Hills, The ☐ Wyoming Renegades

Bisley, Steve ☐ Chain Reaction ☐ Highest Honor, The ☐ Mad Max ☐ Silver City

Bissell, Whit ☐ F.B.I. Story, The—The FBI Versus Alvin Karpis, Public Enemy Number One ☐ I Was a Teenage Frankenstein ☐ I Was a Teenage Werewolf ☐ In Broad Daylight ☐ Incredible Rocky Mountain Race ☐ Man from Del Rio, The ☐ No Name on the Bullet ☐ Somewhere in the Night ☐ Young Stranger, The

Bisset, Jacqueline ☐ Airport ☐ Anna Karenina ☐ Believe in Me ☐ Bullitt ☐ Cape Town Affair, The ☐ Casino Royale ☐ Class ☐ Cul-De-Sac ☐ Day for Night ☐ Deep, The ☐ Detective, The ☐ End of the Game ☐ First Time, The ☐ Forbidden ☐ Grasshopper, The ☐ Greek Tycoon, The ☐ High Season ☐ Inchon ☐ Le Magnifique ☐ Life and Times of Judge Roy Bean, The ☐ Maid, The ☐ Mephisto Waltz, The ☐ Murder on the Orient Express ☐ Rich and Famous ☐ Scenes from the Class Struggle in Beverly Hills ☐ Secret World ☐ Secrets ☐ Spiral Staircase, The ☐ Thief Who Came to Dinner, The ☐ Together ☐ Under the Volcano ☐ When Time Ran Out . . . ☐ Who Is Killing the Great Chefs of Europe? ☐ Wild Orchid

Bixby, Bill ☐ Apple Dumpling Gang, The ☐ Barbary Coast, The ☐ Clambake ☐ Death of the Incredible Hulk, The ☐ Fantasy Island ☐ Incredible Hulk Returns, The ☐ Incredible Hulk, The ☐ Invasion of Johnson County, The ☐ Irma la Douce ☐ Kentucky Fried Movie, The ☐ Magician, The ☐ Speedway ☐ Trial of the Incredible Hulk, The

Bjornstrand, Gunnar ☐ Dreams ☐ Face to Face ☐ Girls, The ☐ Hagbard and Signe ☐ Lesson in Love, A ☐ Magician, The ☐ Persona ☐ Sawdust and Tinsel ☐ Secrets of Women ☐ Seventh Seal, The ☐ Shame ☐ Smiles of a Summer Night ☐ Through a Glass Darkly ☐ Wild Strawberries ☐ Winter Light

Black, Karen ☐ Addict ☐ Airport '75 ☐ Auntie Lee's Meat Pies ☐ Bad Manners ☐ Because He's My Friend ☐ Bound and Gagged: A Love Story ☐ Burnt Offerings ☐ Can She Bake a Cherry Pie? ☐ Capricorn One ☐ Chanel Solitaire ☐ Children of the Night ☐ Children, The ☐ Cisco Pike ☐ Come Back to the Five and Dime, Jimmy Dean, Jimmy Dean ☐ Day of the Locust, The ☐ Drive, He Said ☐ Easy Rider ☐ Eternal Evil ☐ Family Plot ☐ Final Judgment ☐ Five Easy Pieces ☐ Grass Is Singing, The ☐ Great Gatsby, The ☐ Gunfight, A ☐ Hard Contract ☐ Haunting Fear ☐ Hitz ☐ Homer & Eddie ☐ Hostage ☐ In Praise of Older Women ☐ Invaders from Mars ☐ Invisible Kid, The ☐ Island of the Alive ☐ It's Alive III: Island of the Alive ☐ Killer Fish ☐ Killer's Edge, The ☐ Law and Disorder ☐ Martin's Day ☐ Mirror, Mirror ☐ Miss Right ☐ Mr. Horn ☐ Nashville ☐ Night Angel ☐ Out of the Dark ☐ Outfit, The ☐ Portnoy's Complaint ☐ Pyx, The ☐ Quiet Fire ☐ Rhinoceros ☐ Savage Dawn ☐ Separate Ways ☐ Trilogy of Terror ☐ You're a Big Boy Now ☐ Zapped Again

Blackman, Honor ☐ Cat and the Canary, The ☐ Conspirator ☐ Fight for Rome ☐ First Olympics: Athens 1896, The ☐ Fright ☐ Goldfinger ☐ Green Grow the Rushes ☐ Jason and the Argonauts ☐ Last Roman, The ☐ Life at the Top ☐ Lola ☐ Matter of WHO, A ☐ Night to Remember, A ☐ Rainbow Jacket, The ☐ So Long at the Fair ☐ To the Devil A Daughter ☐ Twist of Sand, A ☐ Virgin and the Gypsy, The

Blackmer, Sidney ☐ Accused of Murder ☐ Beyond a Reasonable Doubt ☐ Count of Monte Cristo, The ☐ Deluge ☐ Fast and Loose ☐ From Hell to Heaven ☐ I Escaped from the Gestapo ☐ In Old Chicago ☐ It's a Wonderful World ☐ Johnny Dark ☐ Lady and the Monster, The ☐ Law of the Pampas ☐ Little Caesar ☐ Panther's Claw, The ☐ Quiet Please, Murder ☐ Rosemary's Baby ☐ San Francisco Story, The ☐ Suez ☐ Thank

You, Mr. Moto ☐ Washington Story ☐ Wife, Doctor and Nurse ☐ Wilson

Blades, Ruben ☐ Color of Night ☐ Crazy From the Heart ☐ Critical Condition ☐ Crossover Dreams ☐ Dead Man Out ☐ Disorganized Crime ☐ Fatal Beauty ☐ Josephine Baker Story, The ☐ Milagro Beanfield War, The ☐ One Man's War ☐ Predator 2 ☐ Super, The

Blaine, Vivian ☐ Cracker Factory, The ☐ Dark, The ☐ Doll Face ☐ Girl Trouble ☐ Greenwich Village ☐ Guys and Dolls ☐ If I'm Lucky ☐ Jitterbugs ☐ Katie: Portrait of a Centerfold ☐ Nob Hill ☐ Public Pigeon No. One ☐ Richard ☐ Skirts Ahoy! ☐ Something for the Boys ☐ State Fair ☐ Three Little Girls in Blue

Blain, Gerard ☐ American Friend, The ☐ Cousins, The ☐ Le Beau Serge ☐ Les Cousins

Blair, Betsy ☐ All Night Long ☐ Betrayed ☐ Delicate Balance, A ☐ Guilt of Janet Ames, The ☐ Halliday Brand, The ☐ Kind Lady ☐ Marcus Welby, M.D.: A Holiday Affair ☐ Marty ☐ Outcry, The

Blair, Janet ☐ Boys' Night Out ☐ Broadway ☐ Burn, Witch, Burn! ☐ Fabulous Dorseys, The ☐ Fuller Brush Man, The ☐ Gallant Journey ☐ I Love Trouble ☐ My Sister Eileen ☐ Once Upon a Time ☐ One and Only, Genuine, Original Family Band, The ☐ Public Pigeon No. One ☐ Tars and Spars ☐ Tonight and Every Night

Blair, Linda ☐ Airport '75 ☐ Bad Blood ☐ Bail Out ☐ Bedroom Eyes 2 ☐ Born Innocent ☐ Chained Heat ☐ Chilling, The ☐ Exorcist II: The Heretic ☐ Exorcist, The ☐ Grotesque ☐ Hell Night ☐ Night Patrol ☐ Nightforce ☐ Repossessed ☐ Savage Island ☐ Savage Streets ☐ Zapped Again

Blake, Bobby ☐ Marshal of Reno ☐ Return of Rin Tin Tin, The ☐ Rustlers of Devil's Canyon ☐ San Antonio Kid, The ☐ Slightly Dangerous ☐ Stagecoach To Denver ☐ Woman in the Window, The

Blake, Pamela ☐ Gunfire ☐ Live Wires ☐ Maisie Gets Her Man ☐ Mysterious Intruder

Blake, Robert ☐ Battle Flame ☐ Beast of Budapest, The ☐ Blood Feud ☐ Busting ☐ Coast to Coast ☐ Electra Glide in Blue ☐ Heart of a Champion: The Ray Mancini Story ☐ Hell Town ☐ In Cold Blood ☐ Murder in the Ring ☐ Of Mice and Men ☐ Purple Gang, The ☐ Revolt in the Big House ☐ Tell Them Willie Boy Is Here ☐ Town Without Pity ☐ Tucson Raiders

Blakely, Colin ☐ Alfred the Great ☐ All Things Bright and Beautiful ☐ Charlie Bubbles ☐ Day the Fish Came Out, The ☐ Decline and Fall of a Bird Watcher ☐ Dogs of War, The ☐ Equus ☐ Evil Under the Sun ☐ Galileo ☐ King Lear ☐ Little Lord Fauntleroy ☐ Loophole ☐ Love Among the Ruins ☐ Nijinsky ☐ Operation Julie ☐ Pink Panther Strikes Again, The ☐ Private Life of Sherlock Holmes, The ☐ This Sporting Life

Blakely, Susan ☐ Against Her Will: An Incident in Baltimore ☐ Airport '79—The Concorde ☐ April Morning ☐ Blood & Orchids ☐ Bunker, The ☐ Capone ☐ Dreamer ☐ Incident, The ☐ Intruders ☐ Ladykillers ☐ Lords of Flatbush, The ☐ Make Me an Offer ☐ My Mom's Werewolf ☐ Oklahoma City Dolls, The ☐ Out Of Sight, Out Of Mind ☐ Over the Top ☐ Report to the Commissioner ☐ Secrets ☐ Wildflower

Blakeney, Olive ☐ Henry Aldrich Gets Glamour ☐ Henry Aldrich, Boy Scout ☐ Henry Aldrich, Editor ☐ Mr. What's-His-Name

Blakley, Ronee ☐ Baltimore Bullet, The ☐ Murder by Numbers ☐ Nashville ☐ Nightmare on Elm Street, A ☐ Oklahoma City Dolls, The ☐ Renaldo and Clara ☐ She Came to the Valley ☐ Someone to Love

Blanchard, Mari ☐ Abbott and Costello Go To Mars ☐ Black Horse Canyon ☐ Cruel Tower, The ☐ Destry ☐ No Place to Land ☐ No Questions Asked ☐ Overland Telegraph ☐ Rails Into Laramie ☐ Twice-Told Tales

Blanchar, Pierre ☐ La Symphonie Pastorale ☐ Magnificent Sinner ☐ Man from Nowhere, The ☐ Symphonie Pastorale ☐ They Are Not Angels

Blanc, Mel ☐ Bugs Bunny Superstar ☐ Bugs Bunny's 3rd Movie—1001 Rabbit Tales ☐ Bugs Bunny/Road Runner Movie, The ☐ Daffy Duck's Movie: Fantastic Island ☐ Daffy Duck's Quackbusters ☐ Looney, Looney, Looney Bugs Bunny Movie, The ☐ Neptune's Daughter

Blanc, Michel ☐ Favor, the Watch, and the Very Big Fish, The ☐ I Hate Actors ☐ Monsieur Hire ☐ Prospero's Books ☐ Uranus

Blandick, Clara ☐ Frontier Gal ☐ Make Way for a Lady ☐ Romance ☐ Shopworn ☐ Tom Sawyer

Blane, Sally ☐ Advice to the Lovelorn ☐ Night of Terror ☐ No More Women ☐ Star Witness ☐ Vagabond Lover, The

Blier, Bernard ☐ Buffet Froid ☐ Counterfeiters of Paris, The ☐ I Hate Actors ☐ Jenny Lamour ☐ Les Miserables ☐ Let's Hope It's a Girl ☐ Magnificent Cuckold, The ☐ Man in the Raincoat, The ☐ Passion for Life ☐ Stranger, The ☐ Tall Blond Man with One Black Shoe ☐ Two Lives of Mattias Pascal, The

Blondell, Joan ☐ Advance to the Rear ☐ Adventure ☐ Amazing Mr. Williams ☐ Angel Baby ☐ Big Business Girl ☐ Big City Blues ☐ Blonde Crazy ☐ Blondie Johnson ☐ Blue Veil, The ☐ Broadway Bad ☐ Broadway Gondolier ☐ Bullets or Ballots ☐ Central Park ☐ Champ, The ☐ Christmas Eve ☐ Cincinnati Kid, The ☐ Colleen ☐ Corpse Came C.O.D., The ☐ Crowd Roars, The ☐ Cry Havoc ☐ Dames ☐ Death at Love House

☐ Desk Set ☐ East Side of Heaven ☐ Footlight Parade ☐ For Heaven's Sake ☐ Glove, The ☐ Gold Diggers of 1933 ☐ Gold Diggers of 1937 ☐ Good Girls Go to Paris ☐ Grease ☐ Greeks Had a Word for Them, The ☐ He Was Her Man ☐ I Want a Divorce ☐ Illicit ☐ King and the Chorus Girl, The ☐ Lady for a Night ☐ Lawyer Man ☐ Lizzie ☐ Model Wife ☐ My Past ☐ Night Nurse ☐ Nightmare Alley ☐ Opening Night ☐ Opposite Sex, The ☐ Other Men's Women ☐ Perfect Specimen, The ☐ Rebels, The ☐ Sinner's Holiday ☐ Stand-In ☐ Support Your Local Gunfighter ☐ There's Always a Woman ☐ This Could Be the Night ☐ Three Men on a Horse ☐ Three on a Match ☐ Topper Returns ☐ Traveling Saleslady ☐ Tree Grows in Brooklyn, A ☐ Two Girls on Broadway ☐ Union Depot ☐ Waterhole #3 ☐ Will Success Spoil Rock Hunter?

Bloom, Claire ☐ Alexander the Great ☐ Anastasia: The Mystery Of Anna ☐ Beryl Markham: A Shadow on the Sun ☐ Brainwashed ☐ Brideshead Revisited ☐ Brothers Karamazov, The ☐ Buccaneer, The ☐ Chapman Report, The ☐ Charly ☐ Clash of the Titans ☐ Crimes and Misdemeanors ☐ Deja Vu ☐ Doll's House, A ☐ Ellis Island ☐ Florence Nightingale ☐ Ghost Writer ☐ Haunting, The ☐ High Infidelity ☐ Hold the Dream ☐ Illustrated Man, The ☐ Innocents in Paris ☐ Intimate Contact ☐ Islands in the Stream ☐ Lady and the Highwayman, The ☐ Limelight ☐ Look Back in Anger ☐ Man Between, The ☐ Outrage, The ☐ Princess and the Goblin, The ☐ Queenie ☐ Red Sky at Morning ☐ Richard III ☐ Sammy and Rosie Get Laid ☐ Severed Head, A ☐ Spy Who Came In from the Cold, The ☐ Three Into Two Won't Go ☐ Three Moves to Freedom ☐ Wonderful World of the Brothers Grimm, The

Blore, Eric ☐ 'Til We Meet Again ☐ Abie's Irish Rose ☐ Adventures of Ichabod and Mr. Toad, The ☐ Bowery to Bagdad ☐ Boys from Syracuse, The ☐ Breakfast for Two ☐ Casino Murder Case ☐ Diamond Jim ☐ Ex-Mrs. Bradford, The ☐ Fancy Pants ☐ Flying Down to Rio ☐ Folies Bergere ☐ Gay Divorcee, The ☐ Hitting a New High ☐ I Dream Too Much ☐ I Live My Life ☐ Island of Lost Men ☐ It's Love I'm After ☐ Joy of Living ☐ Lady Eve, The ☐ Lady Scarface ☐ Limehouse Blues ☐ Lone Wolf in London, The ☐ Lone Wolf in Mexico, The ☐ Lone Wolf Keeps a Date, The ☐ Lone Wolf Meets a Lady, The ☐ Lone Wolf Strikes, The ☐ Lone Wolf Takes a Chance, The ☐ Love Happy ☐ Man Who Wouldn't Talk, The ☐ Moon and Sixpence, The ☐ Music in My Heart ☐ New York Town ☐ Notorious Lone Wolf, The ☐ One Dangerous Night ☐ Passport to Suez ☐ Piccadilly Jim ☐ Quality Street ☐ Road to Zanzibar ☐ Romance on the High Seas ☐ San Diego, I Love You ☐ Secrets of the Lone Wolf ☐ Shall We Dance ☐ Shanghai Gesture, The ☐ Sullivan's Travels ☐ Swing Time ☐ Swiss Miss ☐ Top Hat

Blossom, Roberts ☐ American Clock, The ☐ Deranged ☐ Escape from Alcatraz ☐ Family Reunion ☐ Resurrection

Blount, Lisa ☐ Blind Fury ☐ Cease Fire ☐ Femme Fatale ☐ Great Balls of Fire! ☐ Nightflyers ☐ Prince of Darkness ☐ Radioactive Dreams ☐ September 30, 1955

Blue, Ben ☐ Artists and Models ☐ Big Broadcast of 1938, The ☐ Cocoanut Grove ☐ College Swing ☐ For Me and My Gal ☐ Panama Hattie ☐ Where Were You When the Lights Went Out?

Blue, Monte ☐ Bells of San Fernando ☐ Born to the West ☐ Marriage Circle, The ☐ On Probation ☐ Ride, Ranger, Ride ☐ Road to Morocco ☐ Rootin' Tootin' Rhythm ☐ Silver River ☐ Treachery Rides the Range

Blye, Maggie ☐ Final Chapter—Walking Tall ☐ Italian Job, The ☐ Mayday at 40,000 Feet! ☐ Melvin Purvis—G-Man ☐ Waterhole #3

Blyth, Ann ☐ All the Brothers Were Valiant ☐ Another Part of the Forest ☐ Bowery to Broadway ☐ Brute Force ☐ Buster Keaton Story, The ☐ Chip Off the Old Block ☐ Free For All ☐ Golden Horde, The ☐ Great Caruso, The ☐ Helen Morgan Story, The ☐ I'll Never Forget You ☐ Katie Did It ☐ Killer McCoy ☐ King's Thief, The ☐ Kismet ☐ Merry Monahans, The ☐ Mildred Pierce ☐ Mr. Peabody and the Mermaid ☐ Once More My Darling ☐ One Minute to Zero ☐ Our Very Own ☐ Rose Marie ☐ Sally and Saint Anne ☐ Slander ☐ Student Prince, The ☐ Thunder on the Hill ☐ Top o' the Morning ☐ Woman's Vengeance, A ☐ World in His Arms, The

Boardman, Eleanor ☐ Crowd, The ☐ Great Meadow, The ☐ She Goes to War ☐ Squaw Man, The

Bochner, Hart ☐ And the Sea Will Tell ☐ Apartment Zero ☐ Batman: Mask of the Phantom ☐ Fellow Traveler ☐ Having It All ☐ Mad at the Moon ☐ Mr. Destiny ☐ Rich and Famous ☐ Terror Train

Bochner, Lloyd ☐ Crystal Heart ☐ Fine Gold ☐ Immigrants, The ☐ It Seemed Like a Good Idea at the Time ☐ Lonely Lady, The ☐ Mary and Joseph: A Story of Faith ☐ Night Walker, The ☐ Ulzana's Raid

Boehm, Karl ☐ Forever My Love ☐ Magnificent Rebel, The ☐ Peeping Tom ☐ Rififi in Tokyo ☐ Wonderful World of the Brothers Grimm, The

Bogarde, Dirk ☐ Accident ☐ Agent 8 3/4 ☐ Angel Wore Red, The ☐ Blue Lamp, The ☐ Bridge Too Far, A ☐ Campbell's Kingdom ☐ Cast a Dark Shadow ☐ Daddy Nostalgia ☐ Damn the Defiant! ☐ Damned, The ☐ Darling ☐ Death in Venice ☐ Despair ☐ Desperate Moment ☐ Doctor at Large ☐ Doctor At Sea ☐ Doctor in Distress ☐ Doctor in the

House ☐ Doctor's Dilemma ☐ Esther Waters ☐ Fixer, The ☐ For Better, For Worse ☐ Gentle Gunman, The ☐ I Could Go on Singing ☐ Ill Met by Moonlight ☐ Justine ☐ King and Country ☐ Libel ☐ McGuire, Go Home! ☐ Mind Benders, The ☐ Modesty Blaise ☐ Night Ambush ☐ Night Flight from Moscow ☐ Night Porter, The ☐ Oh! What a Lovely War ☐ Our Mother's House ☐ Password Is Courage, The ☐ Patricia Neal Story, The ☐ Penny Princess ☐ Permission to Kill ☐ Providence ☐ Sea Shall Not Have Them, The ☐ Sebastian ☐ Servant, The ☐ Sleeping Tiger, The ☐ So Long at the Fair ☐ Song Without End ☐ Spanish Gardener, The ☐ Tale of Two Cities, A ☐ They Who Dare ☐ Victim ☐ Wind Cannot Read, The ☐ Woman in Question, The

Bogart, Humphrey ☐ Across the Pacific ☐ Action in the North Atlantic ☐ African Queen, The ☐ All Through the Night ☐ Amazing Doctor Clitterhouse, The ☐ Angels with Dirty Faces ☐ Bacall on Bogart ☐ Barefoot Contessa, The ☐ Battle Circus ☐ Beat the Devil ☐ Big City Blues ☐ Big Shot, The ☐ Big Sleep, The ☐ Black Legion ☐ Brother Orchid ☐ Bullets or Ballots ☐ Caine Mutiny, The ☐ Casablanca ☐ Chain Lightning ☐ China Clipper ☐ Conflict ☐ Dark Passage ☐ Dark Victory ☐ Dead End ☐ Dead Reckoning ☐ Deadline U.S.A. ☐ Desperate Hours, The ☐ Enforcer, The ☐ Great O'Malley, The ☐ Harder They Fall, The ☐ High Sierra ☐ In a Lonely Place ☐ Invisible Stripes ☐ Isle of Fury ☐ It All Came True ☐ Key Largo ☐ Kid Galahad ☐ King of the Underworld ☐ Knock on Any Door ☐ Left Hand of God, The ☐ Maltese Falcon, The ☐ Marked Woman ☐ Oklahoma Kid, The ☐ Passage to Marseille ☐ Petrified Forest, The ☐ Racket Busters ☐ Return of Dr. X, The ☐ Roaring Twenties, The ☐ Sabrina ☐ Sahara ☐ San Quentin ☐ Sirocco ☐ Stand-In ☐ Swing Your Lady ☐ Thank Your Lucky Stars ☐ They Drive by Night ☐ Three on a Match ☐ To Have and Have Not ☐ Tokyo Joe ☐ Treasure of the Sierra Madre, The ☐ Two Mrs. Carrolls, The ☐ Up the River ☐ Virginia City ☐ Wagons Roll at Night, The ☐ We're No Angels

Bogosian, Eric ☐ Caine Mutiny Court-Martial, The ☐ Dolores Claiborne ☐ Sex, Drugs, Rock & Roll ☐ Talk Radio

Boland, Mary ☐ Artists and Models Abroad ☐ Big Broadcast of 1936, The ☐ College Holiday ☐ Danger—Love at Work ☐ Early to Bed ☐ Four Frightened People ☐ Guilty Bystander ☐ He Married His Wife ☐ If I Had a Million ☐ In Our Time ☐ Magnificent Fraud, The ☐ New Moon ☐ Night of June 13 ☐ One Night in the Tropics ☐ People Will Talk ☐ Pride and Prejudice ☐ Ruggles of Red Gap ☐ Six of a Kind ☐ Three-Cornered Moon ☐ Two for Tonight ☐ Women, The

Boles, John ☐ Back Street ☐ Between Us Girls ☐ Craig's Wife ☐ Curly Top ☐ Fazil ☐ Fight for Your Lady ☐ Frankenstein (Restored) ☐ King of Jazz, The ☐ Life of Vergie Winters, The ☐ Littlest Rebel, The ☐ Loves of Sunya, The ☐ Message to Garcia, A ☐ Music in the Air ☐ One Heavenly Night ☐ Only Yesterday ☐ Rio Rita ☐ Stand Up and Cheer ☐ Stella Dallas

Bolger, Ray ☐ April in Paris ☐ Babes in Toyland ☐ Daydreamer, The ☐ Entertainer, The ☐ Four Jacks and a Jill ☐ Great Ziegfeld, The ☐ Harvey Girls, The ☐ Just You and Me, Kid ☐ Look for the Silver Lining ☐ Make Mine Laughs ☐ Peter And The Wolf And Other Tales ☐ Runner Stumbles, The ☐ Sweethearts ☐ That's Dancing ☐ Where's Charley? ☐ Wizard of Oz, The

Bolkan, Florinda ☐ Brief Vacation, A ☐ Collector's Item ☐ Investigation of a Citizen Above Suspicion ☐ Last Valley, The ☐ Master Touch, The ☐ Royal Flash

Bolling, Tiffany ☐ Bonnie's Kids ☐ Centerfold Girls, The ☐ Kingdom of the Spiders ☐ Marriage of a Young Stockbroker, The

Bologna, Joseph ☐ Alligator II: The Mutation ☐ Big Bus, The ☐ Blame It on Rio ☐ Chapter Two ☐ Citizen Cohn ☐ Cops and Robbers ☐ Honor Thy Father ☐ Made for Each Other ☐ Mixed Company ☐ My Favorite Year ☐ Not Quite Human ☐ One Cooks, the Other Doesn't ☐ Rags to Riches ☐ Thanksgiving Day ☐ Torn Between Two Lovers ☐ Transylvania 6-5000 ☐ Woman in Red, The

Bonanova, Fortunio ☐ Bad Men of Tombstone ☐ Five Graves to Cairo ☐ For Whom the Bell Tolls ☐ Man Alive ☐ Nancy Goes to Rio ☐ Romance on the High Seas ☐ Whirlpool

Bondarchuk, Sergei ☐ Battle of Neretva, The ☐ Destiny of a Man ☐ Silence of Dr. Evans, The ☐ Uncle Vanya ☐ War and Peace

Bond, Derek ☐ Broken Journey ☐ Inheritance, The ☐ Nicholas Nickleby ☐ Press for Time ☐ Scott of the Antarctic ☐ Stranger From Venus ☐ Tony Draws a Horse

Bondi, Beulah ☐ And Now Tomorrow ☐ Arrowsmith ☐ Back to Bataan ☐ Baron of Arizona, The ☐ Breakfast in Hollywood ☐ Captain Is a Lady, The ☐ Case Against Mrs. Ames, The ☐ Finishing School ☐ Furies, The ☐ Good Fairy, The ☐ I Love a Soldier ☐ Invisible Ray, The ☐ It's a Wonderful Life ☐ Life of Riley, The ☐ Lone Star ☐ Maid of Salem ☐ Make Way for Tomorrow ☐ Moon's Our Home, The ☐ Mr. Smith Goes to Washington ☐ Of Human Hearts ☐ On Borrowed Time ☐ One Foot in Heaven ☐ Our Hearts Were Young and Gay ☐ Our Town ☐ Penny Serenade ☐ Remember the Night ☐ She Waits ☐ Shepherd of the Hills ☐ Sister Kenny ☐ Sisters, The ☐ So Dear to My Heart ☐ Southerner, The ☐ Stranger's Return, The ☐ Street Scene ☐ Tammy and the Doctor

☐ Tammy Tell Me True ☐ Tonight We Raid Calais ☐ Track of the Cat ☐ Trail of the Lonesome Pine ☐ Under-Pup, The ☐ Unholy Wife, The ☐ Vivacious Lady ☐ Watch on the Rhine ☐ Wonderful World of the Brothers Grimm, The

Bond, Ward ☐ Bob Mathias Story, The ☐ Dakota ☐ Falcon Takes Over, The ☐ Fort Apache ☐ Fugitive, The ☐ Guy Named Joe, A ☐ Gypsy Colt ☐ Hitler—Dead or Alive ☐ Hondo ☐ It Happened One Night ☐ It's a Wonderful Life ☐ Long Gray Line, The ☐ Long Voyage Home, The ☐ Made for Each Other ☐ Maltese Falcon, The ☐ Man Alone, A ☐ Man Betrayed, A ☐ Man Who Lived Twice, The ☐ Mister Roberts ☐ Moonlighter, The ☐ My Darling Clementine ☐ On Dangerous Ground ☐ Operation Pacific ☐ Pillars of the Sky ☐ Quiet Man, The ☐ Riding High ☐ Searchers, The ☐ Sergeant York ☐ Sullivans, The ☐ Tall in the Saddle ☐ Tap Roots ☐ They Came to Blow Up America ☐ They Were Expendable ☐ Three Godfathers, The ☐ Unconquered ☐ Wagon Master ☐ Whirlpool ☐ Wings of Eagles, The ☐ Young Mr. Lincoln

Bonerz, Peter ☐ Bastard, The ☐ Funnyman ☐ Jennifer on My Mind ☐ Medium Cool ☐ Nobody's Perfekt

Bonnaire, Sandrine ☐ A Nos Amours ☐ Few Days with Me, A ☐ Monsieur Hire ☐ Under the Sun of Satan ☐ Vagabond

Bonner, Tony ☐ Hurricane Smith ☐ Inn of the Damned ☐ Lighthorsemen, The ☐ Money Movers ☐ Sudden Terror

Bono, Sonny ☐ Balboa ☐ Dirty Laundry ☐ Good Times ☐ Hairspray ☐ Murder on Flight 502 ☐ Troll ☐ Under the Boardwalk

Booke, Sorrell ☐ Black Like Me ☐ Brenda Starr ☐ Bye Bye Braverman ☐ Gone Are the Days ☐ Mastermind ☐ Up the Down Staircase

Boone, Pat ☐ All Hands On Deck ☐ April Love ☐ Bernardine ☐ Goodbye Charlie ☐ Journey to the Center of the Earth, The ☐ Main Attraction, The ☐ Mardi Gras ☐ Perils of Pauline, The ☐ State Fair

Boone, Richard ☐ Against a Crooked Sky ☐ Alamo, The ☐ Battle Stations ☐ Big Jake ☐ Big Sleep, The ☐ Bushido Blade, The ☐ City of Bad Men ☐ Desert Fox, The ☐ Dragnet ☐ Garment Jungle, The ☐ God's Gun ☐ Goodnight, My Love ☐ Great Niagara, The ☐ Hombre ☐ I Bury the Living ☐ In Broad Daylight ☐ Kremlin Letter, The ☐ Last Dinosaur, The ☐ Lizzie ☐ Madron ☐ Man on a Tightrope ☐ Man Without a Star ☐ Night of the Following Day, The ☐ Raid, The ☐ Red Skies of Montana ☐ Return of the Texan ☐ Rio Conchos ☐ Robber's Roost ☐ Shootist, The ☐ Siege at Red River, The ☐ Star in the Dust ☐ Tall T, The ☐ War Lord, The

Booth, Connie ☐ American Friends ☐ Fawlty Towers—The Complete Set ☐ Leon, the Pig Farmer ☐ Past Caring ☐ Strange Case Of The End of Civilization As We Know It

Booth, James ☐ Bliss of Mrs. Blossom, The ☐ Evening in Byzantium, An ☐ Fraulein Doktor ☐ Inn of the Frightened People ☐ Jazz Boat ☐ Man Who Had Power Over Women, The ☐ Pray for Death ☐ Robbery ☐ Zulu

Booth, Shirley ☐ About Mrs. Leslie ☐ Come Back, Little Sheba ☐ Hot Spell ☐ Main Street to Broadway ☐ Matchmaker, The

Boothe, Powers ☐ Breed Apart, A ☐ By Dawn's Early Light ☐ Emerald Forest, The ☐ Extreme Prejudice ☐ Family of Spies ☐ Guyana Tragedy: The Story of Jim Jones ☐ Into the Homeland ☐ Phillip Marlowe: Smart-Aleck Kill ☐ Phillip Marlowe—Finger Man ☐ Rapid Fire ☐ Southern Comfort ☐ Tombstone ☐ Wild Card

Borchers, Cornell ☐ Big Lift, The ☐ Divided Heart, The ☐ Flood Tide ☐ Istanbul ☐ Never Say Goodbye ☐ Oasis

Borgnine, Ernest ☐ Adventurers, The ☐ All Quiet on the Western Front ☐ Any Man's Death ☐ Appearances ☐ Bad Day at Black Rock ☐ Badlanders, The ☐ Barabbas ☐ Best Things in Life Are Free, The ☐ Black Hole, The ☐ Blood Feud ☐ Bullet for Sandoval, A ☐ Bunny O'Hare ☐ Catered Affair, The ☐ China Corsair ☐ Chuka ☐ Codename—Wildgeese ☐ Convoy ☐ Crossed Swords ☐ Deadly Blessing ☐ Demetrius and the Gladiators ☐ Devil's Rain, The ☐ Dirty Dozen, The ☐ Dirty Dozen, The: The Next Mission ☐ Double McGuffin, The ☐ Emperor of the North, The ☐ Escape from New York ☐ Fire! ☐ Flight of the Phoenix ☐ From Here to Eternity ☐ Future Cop ☐ Go Naked in the World ☐ Greatest, The ☐ Hannie Caulder ☐ High Risk ☐ Ice Station Zebra ☐ Johnny Guitar ☐ Jubal ☐ Laser Mission ☐ Last Command, The ☐ Law and Disorder ☐ Legend of Lylah Clare, The ☐ Love by Appointment ☐ Man on a String ☐ Manhunt, The ☐ Marty ☐ McHale's Navy ☐ Mistress ☐ Mob, The ☐ Murder in the Ring ☐ Opponent, The ☐ Oscar, The ☐ Pay or Die ☐ Poseidon Adventure, The ☐ Rabbit Trap, The ☐ Ravagers ☐ Revengers, The ☐ Run for Cover ☐ Season of Passion ☐ Shoot ☐ Square Jungle, The ☐ Stranger Who Wore a Gun, The ☐ Suppose They Gave a War and Nobody Came? ☐ Three Brave Men ☐ Torpedo Run ☐ Vikings, The ☐ Violent Saturday ☐ When Time Ran Out . . . ☐ Whistle at Eaton Falls, The ☐ Wild Bunch, The ☐ Willard

Borg, Veda Ann ☐ Big Jim McLain ☐ Big Noise, The ☐ Fabulous Suzanne, The ☐ Falcon in Hollywood, The ☐ Fog Island ☐ Hold That Line ☐ Irish Eyes Are Smiling ☐ Isle of Forgotten Sins ☐ It's Love I'm After ☐ Mother Wore Tights ☐ San Quentin ☐ She's in the Army ☐ You're Never Too Young

Bosco, Philip ☐ Angie ☐ Children of a Lesser God ☐ F/X2 ☐ Luckiest Man In The

World, The ☐ Money Pit, The ☐ Quick Change ☐ Suspect ☐ Three Men and a Baby

Bosley, Tom ☐ Bang-Bang Kid, The ☐ Bastard, The ☐ Castaways on Gilligan's Island, The ☐ Divorce American Style ☐ Fatal Confession: A Father Dowling Mystery ☐ Fire and Rain ☐ Jesse Owens Story, The ☐ Love with the Proper Stranger ☐ Million Dollar Mystery ☐ Mixed Company ☐ Night Gallery ☐ Night That Panicked America, The ☐ Rebels, The ☐ Secret War of Harry Frigg, The ☐ Wicked Stepmother ☐ World of Henry Orient, The ☐ Yours, Mine and Ours

Bostwick, Barry ☐ Body of Evidence ☐ Challenger ☐ Jennifer on My Mind ☐ Megaforce ☐ Movie Movie ☐ Parent Trap III ☐ Rocky Horror Picture Show, The

Bottoms, Joseph ☐ Amore ☐ Black Hole, The ☐ Born to Race ☐ Cloud Dancer ☐ Dove, The ☐ High Rolling In A Hot Corvette ☐ Holocaust ☐ King of the Mountain ☐ Make Mine Chartreuse ☐ Open House ☐ Sins of Dorian Gray, The ☐ Surfacing

Bottoms, Timothy ☐ Drifter, The ☐ East of Eden ☐ Fantasist, The ☐ Gift of Love, The ☐ Hambone and Hillie ☐ High Country, The ☐ Husbands, Wives, Money & Murder ☐ In the Shadow of Kilimanjaro ☐ Invaders from Mars ☐ Istanbul ☐ Johnny Got His Gun ☐ Last Picture Show, The ☐ Love and Pain (and the Whole Damn Thing) ☐ Love Leads the Way ☐ Operation Daybreak ☐ Other Side of the Mountain (Part 2), The ☐ Paper Chase, The ☐ Rollercoaster ☐ Shining Season, A ☐ Small Town in Texas, A ☐ Texasville ☐ White Dawn, The

Bouquet, Carole ☐ For Your Eyes Only ☐ Jenatsch ☐ That Obscure Object of Desire ☐ Too Beautiful for You

Bouquet, Michel ☐ Beyond Fear ☐ Borsalino ☐ Bride Wore Black, The ☐ Cop au Vin ☐ Just Before Nightfall ☐ La Femme Infidele ☐ Le Complot ☐ Le Jouet ☐ Mississippi Mermaid ☐ Toto the Hero

Bourvil ☐ All the Gold in the World ☐ Brain, The ☐ Christmas Tree, The ☐ Four Bags Full ☐ Les Grandes Gueules ☐ Mirror Has Two Faces, The ☐ Sucker, The ☐ Thank Heaven for Small Favors

Bow, Clara ☐ Call Her Savage ☐ Dancing Mothers ☐ Down to the Sea in Ships ☐ It ☐ Paramount on Parade ☐ Wild Party, The ☐ Wings

Bowie, David ☐ Absolute Beginners ☐ Hunger, The ☐ Just a Gigolo ☐ Labyrinth ☐ Last Temptation of Christ, The ☐ Linguini Incident, The ☐ Man Who Fell to Earth, The ☐ Merry Christmas, Mr. Lawrence ☐ Twin Peaks: Fire Walk With Me

Bowman, Lee ☐ Buck Privates ☐ Cover Girl ☐ Fame Is the Name of the Game ☐ Florian ☐ Gold Rush Maisie ☐ Great Victor Herbert, The ☐ Having Wonderful Time ☐ House by the River, The ☐ I Met Him in Paris ☐ Impatient Years, The ☐ Internes Can't Take Money ☐ Kid Glove Killer ☐ Lady and the Mob, The ☐ Last Train from Madrid, The ☐ Love Affair ☐ Man to Remember, A ☐ Miracles for Sale ☐ Model Wife ☐ My Dream Is Yours ☐ Smash-Up, the Story of a Woman ☐ Third Finger, Left Hand ☐ Tonight and Every Night ☐ Up in Mabel's Room ☐ Wyoming

Boxleitner, Bruce ☐ Angel in Green ☐ Babe, The ☐ Baltimore Bullet, The ☐ Bare Essence ☐ Double Jeopardy ☐ East of Eden ☐ From the Dead of Night ☐ I Married Wyatt Earp ☐ Kenny Rogers as The Gambler ☐ Macahans, The ☐ Murderous Vision ☐ Perfect Family ☐ Tron

Boyd, Stephen ☐ Abandon Ship! ☐ Alligator Named Daisy, An ☐ Assignment K ☐ Ben-Hur ☐ Best of Everything, The ☐ Bible, The ☐ Big Gamble, The ☐ Billy Rose's Jumbo ☐ Bravados, The ☐ Caper of the Golden Bulls, The ☐ Fall of the Roman Empire ☐ Fantastic Voyage ☐ Genghis Khan ☐ Hell in Korea ☐ Imperial Venus ☐ Island in the Sun ☐ Kill! Kill! Kill! ☐ Lisa ☐ Man Who Never Was, The ☐ Night Heaven Fall, The ☐ Oscar, The ☐ Poppy Is Also a Flower, The ☐ Shalako ☐ Third Secret, The ☐ Woman Obsessed

Boyd, William ☐ Eagle's Brood, The ☐ False Colors ☐ False Paradise ☐ Flying Fool, The ☐ Frontiersman, The ☐ Heart of Arizona ☐ Heart of the West ☐ High Voltage ☐ His First Command ☐ Hopalong Cassidy ☐ Hopalong Cassidy Returns ☐ Hopalong Cassidy Rides Again ☐ Hoppy Serves a Writ ☐ Hoppy's Holiday ☐ Lady of the Pavements ☐ Law of the Pampas ☐ Leather Burners ☐ Lucky Devils ☐ Midnight Warning ☐ Murder by the Clock ☐ Painted Desert, The ☐ Partners of the Plains ☐ Riders of the Deadline ☐ Showdown, The ☐ Silent Conflict ☐ Silver on the Sage ☐ Sinister Journey ☐ Spoilers, The ☐ State's Attorney ☐ Three Men from Texas ☐ Unexpected Guest ☐ Wide Open Town

Boyer, Charles ☐ 13th Letter, The ☐ Adorable Julia ☐ Algiers ☐ All This and Heaven Too ☐ Appointment for Love ☐ April Fools, The ☐ Arch of Triumph ☐ Back Street ☐ Barefoot in the Park ☐ Batmania from Comics to Screen ☐ Battle of the Rails ☐ Battle, The ☐ Break of Hearts ☐ Buccaneer, The ☐ Caravan ☐ Casino Royale ☐ Cluny Brown ☐ Cobweb, The ☐ Confidential Agent ☐ Conquest ☐ Constant Nymph, The ☐ Day the Hot Line Got Hot, The ☐ Earrings of Madame de... ☐ Earrings of Madame de . . . , The ☐ Empress and I, The ☐ Fanny ☐ First Legion, The ☐ Flesh and Fantasy ☐ Four Horsemen of the Apocalypse ☐ Garden of Allah, The ☐ Gaslight ☐ Happy Time, The ☐ Heart of a Nation, The ☐ History Is Made at Night ☐ Hold Back the Dawn ☐ How to Steal a Million ☐ Is Paris Burning? ☐ La Parisienne ☐ Lost Horizon

☐ Love Affair ☐ Love Is a Ball ☐ Lucky to Be a Woman ☐ Madwoman of Chaillot, The ☐ Man from Yesterday, The ☐ Matter of Time, A ☐ Maxime ☐ Mayerling ☐ Private Worlds ☐ Red-Headed Woman ☐ Shanghai ☐ Stavisky ☐ Tales of Manhattan ☐ Thunder in the East ☐ Together Again ☐ Tovarich ☐ Very Special Favor, A ☐ When Tomorrow Comes ☐ Woman's Vengeance, A

Boyle, Lara Flynn ☐ Dark Backward, The ☐ Equinox ☐ Eye of the Storm ☐ How I Got Into College ☐ May Wine ☐ Mobsters ☐ Preppie Murder, The ☐ Red Rock West ☐ Rookie, The ☐ Temp, The ☐ Threesome ☐ Twin Peaks ☐ Wayne's World ☐ Where the Day Takes You

Boyle, Peter ☐ Beyond the Poseidon Adventure ☐ Brink's Job, The ☐ Candidate, The ☐ Challenger ☐ Conspiracy—The Trial of the Chicago 8 ☐ Disaster at Silo 7 ☐ Dream Team, The ☐ Echoes in the Darkness ☐ F.I.S.T. ☐ Friends of Eddie Coyle, The ☐ From Here to Eternity ☐ Ghost in the Noonday Sun ☐ Guts and Glory: The Rise and Fall of Oliver North ☐ Hammett ☐ Hardcore ☐ In God We Trust ☐ Joe ☐ Johnny Dangerously ☐ Kid Blue ☐ Man Who Could Talk to Kids, The ☐ Men of Respect ☐ Nervous Ticks ☐ Outland ☐ Red Heat ☐ Shadow, The ☐ Slither ☐ Solar Crisis ☐ Speed Zone! ☐ Steelyard Blues ☐ Surrender ☐ Swashbuckler ☐ Taxi Driver ☐ Tragedy of Flight 103, The: The Inside Story ☐ Walker ☐ Where the Buffalo Roam ☐ Yellowbeard ☐ Young Frankenstein

Bozyk, Max ☐ Catskill Honeymoon ☐ Der Purimshpiler ☐ God, Man and Devil ☐ Mamele

Bozzuffi, Marcel ☐ French Connection, The ☐ Illustrious Corpses ☐ Images ☐ Sky Above Heaven

Bracco, Lorraine ☐ Dream Team, The ☐ Getting Gotti ☐ GoodFellas ☐ Medicine Man ☐ Scam ☐ Sing ☐ Someone to Watch Over Me ☐ Switch ☐ Talent for the Game ☐ Traces of Red

Bracken, Eddie ☐ About Face ☐ American Clock, The ☐ Bring on the Girls ☐ Caught in the Draft ☐ Duffy's Tavern ☐ Fleet's In, The ☐ Fun on a Weekend ☐ Girl from Jones Beach, The ☐ Hail the Conquering Hero ☐ Happy Go Lucky ☐ Hold That Blonde ☐ Home Alone 2: Lost in New York ☐ Life with Henry ☐ Miracle of Morgan's Creek, The ☐ Out of This World ☐ Rainbow Island ☐ Reaching for the Sun ☐ Shinbone Alley ☐ Summer Stock ☐ Too Many Girls ☐ Two Tickets to Broadway ☐ We're Not Married

Bradford, Richard ☐ Enemy of the People, An ☐ Internal Affairs ☐ Man Against the Mob: The Chinatown Murders ☐ Milagro Beanfield War, The ☐ Night Game ☐ Scent of a Woman ☐ Untouchables, The

Brady, Alice ☐ Beauty for Sale ☐ Broadway to Hollywood ☐ Call It a Day ☐ Gay Divorcee, The ☐ Go West, Young Man ☐ Gold Diggers of 1935 ☐ In Old Chicago ☐ Joy of Living ☐ Let 'Em Have It ☐ Merry Go Round of 1938 ☐ Metropolitan ☐ Miss Fane's Baby is Stolen ☐ My Man Godfrey ☐ One Hundred Men and a Girl ☐ Three Smart Girls ☐ When Ladies Meet ☐ Young Mr. Lincoln ☐ Zenobia

Brady, Scott ☐ Ambush at Cimarron Pass ☐ Battle Flame ☐ Black Spurs ☐ Blood Arrow ☐ Bloodhounds of Broadway ☐ Bonnie's Kids ☐ Bronco Buster ☐ Canon City ☐ Castle of Evil ☐ China Syndrome, The ☐ Fort Utah ☐ Gal Who Took the West, The ☐ Gentlemen Marry Brunettes ☐ Gun Riders ☐ He Walked by Night ☐ Hell's Bloody Devils ☐ I Was a Shoplifter ☐ Johnny Guitar ☐ Journey to the Center of Time ☐ Maverick Queen, The ☐ Model and the Marriage Broker, The ☐ Mohawk ☐ Montana Belle ☐ Nightmare in Wax ☐ Operation Bikini ☐ Perilous Journey, A ☐ Port of New York ☐ Stage to Thunder Rock ☐ Undertow

Braga, Sonia ☐ Dona Flor and Her Two Husbands ☐ Gabriela ☐ I Love You (Eu Te Amo) ☐ Kiss of the Spider Woman ☐ Lady on the Bus ☐ Last Prostitute, The ☐ Man Who Broke 1,000 Chains, The ☐ Milagro Beanfield War, The ☐ Moon Over Parador ☐ Rookie, The

Branagh, Kenneth ☐ Coming Through ☐ Dead Again ☐ Fortunes of War ☐ Henry V ☐ Mary Shelley's Frankenstein ☐ Month in the Country, A ☐ Much Ado About Nothing ☐ Peter's Friends ☐ Swing Kids

Brandauer, Klaus Maria ☐ Becoming Colette ☐ Burning Secret ☐ Colonel Redl ☐ Hanussen ☐ Lightship, The ☐ Mephisto ☐ Never Say Never Again ☐ Out of Africa ☐ Quo Vadis? ☐ Russia House, The ☐ Salzburg Connection, The ☐ Streets of Gold ☐ White Fang

Brand, Neville ☐ Adventures of Huckleberry Finn, The ☐ Angels' Brigade ☐ Badman's Country ☐ Birdman of Alcatraz ☐ Bobby Ware Is Missing ☐ Cahill—United States Marshal ☐ Cry Terror ☐ Deadly Trackers, The ☐ Eaten Alive ☐ Five Days from Home ☐ Five Gates to Hell ☐ Fury at Gunsight Pass ☐ Gun Brothers ☐ Hero's Island ☐ Hijack ☐ Hitched ☐ Mad Bomber, The ☐ Man from the Alamo, The ☐ Mob, The ☐ Mohawk ☐ Ninth Configuration, The ☐ Prodigal, The ☐ Raw Edge ☐ Return from the Sea ☐ Riot in Cell Block 11 ☐ Scarface Mob, The ☐ Stalag 17 ☐ Tin Star, The ☐ Way to the Gold, The ☐ Where the Sidewalk Ends

Brando, Marlon ☐ Apocalypse Now ☐ Appaloosa, The ☐ Bedtime Story ☐ Burn! ☐ Candy ☐ Chase, The ☐ Christopher Columbus—The Discovery ☐ Countess from Hong Kong, A ☐ Desiree ☐ Dry White Season, A ☐ Formula, The ☐ Freshman, The ☐ Fugitive Kind, The ☐ Godfather, The

☐ Guys and Dolls ☐ Julius Caesar ☐ Last Tango in Paris ☐ Men, The ☐ Missouri Breaks, The ☐ Morituri ☐ Mutiny on the Bounty ☐ Night of the Following Day, The ☐ Nightcomers, The ☐ On the Waterfront ☐ One-Eyed Jacks ☐ Reflections in a Golden Eye ☐ Sayonara ☐ Streetcar Named Desire, A ☐ Superman—The Movie ☐ Teahouse of the August Moon, The ☐ Ugly American, The ☐ Viva Zapata! ☐ Wild One, The ☐ Young Lions, The

Brandon, Michael ☐ Change of Seasons, A ☐ FM ☐ Impatient Heart, The ☐ James Dean ☐ Jennifer on My Mind ☐ Queen of the Stardust Ballroom ☐ Red Alert

Brasselle, Keefe ☐ Bannerline ☐ Battle Stations ☐ Bring Your Smile Along ☐ Eddie Cantor Story, The ☐ Fighting Wildcats, The ☐ It's a Big Country ☐ Mad at the World ☐ Not Wanted ☐ Skirts Ahoy!

Brasseur, Claude ☐ Band of Outsiders ☐ Detective ☐ Elusive Corporal, The ☐ L'Etat Sauvage (The Savage State) ☐ La Boum ☐ La Boum 2 ☐ Lies Before Kisses ☐ Lobster for Breakfast ☐ Pardon Mon Affaire ☐ Simple Story, A ☐ Such a Gorgeous Kid Like Me

Brasseur, Pierre ☐ Carthage in Flames ☐ Children of Paradise ☐ Confessions of a Newlywed ☐ Gates of Paris ☐ Gates of the Night ☐ Horror Chamber of Dr. Faustus, The ☐ Keepers, The ☐ King of Hearts ☐ Matter of Resistance, A ☐ Oasis

Brazzi, Rossano ☐ Adventurers, The ☐ Barefoot Contessa, The ☐ Battle of the Villa Fiorita, The ☐ Bobo, The ☐ Bullet for Stefano ☐ Certain Smile, A ☐ Christmas That Almost Wasn't, The ☐ Count Your Blessings ☐ Final Conflict, The ☐ Final Justice ☐ Great Waltz, The ☐ Honeymoon with a Stranger ☐ Interlude ☐ Legend of the Lost ☐ Light in the Piazza ☐ Loser Takes All ☐ One Step to Hell ☐ Rome Adventure ☐ South Pacific ☐ Story of Esther Costello, The ☐ Summertime ☐ Three Coins in the Fountain ☐ Volcano ☐ Woman Times Seven

Brel, Jacques ☐ Assassins de l'Orde, Les Law Breakers ☐ Franz ☐ Jacques Brel Is Alive and Well and Living in Paris ☐ Pain in the A—, A

Brennan, Eileen ☐ At Long Last Love ☐ Babes in Toyland ☐ Blood Vows—The Story of a Mafia Wife ☐ Cheap Detective, The ☐ Clue ☐ Daisy Miller ☐ Death of Richie, The ☐ Divorce American Style ☐ FM ☐ Fourth Wise Man, The ☐ Funny Farm, The ☐ Great Smokey Roadblock, The ☐ Hustle ☐ I Don't Buy Kisses Anymore ☐ Incident at Crestridge ☐ Last Picture Show, The ☐ Murder by Death ☐ My Old Man ☐ New Adventures of Pippi Longstocking, The ☐ Night That Panicked America, The ☐ Pippi Longstocking—New Adventures of, The ☐ Private Benjamin ☐ Scarecrow ☐ Sticky Fingers ☐ Sting, The ☐ Texasville ☐ White Palace

Brennan, Walter ☐ Adventures of Tom Sawyer, The ☐ Along the Great Divide ☐ At Gunpoint ☐ Bad Day at Black Rock ☐ Barbary Coast ☐ Best of the Badmen ☐ Blood on the Moon ☐ Brimstone ☐ Buccaneer, The ☐ Centennial Summer ☐ Come and Get It ☐ Come Next Spring ☐ Cowboy and the Lady, The ☐ Dakota ☐ Far Country, The ☐ Four Guns to the Border ☐ Fury ☐ Glory ☐ Gnome-Mobile, The ☐ God Is My Partner ☐ Good-bye, My Lady ☐ Green Promise, The ☐ Hangmen Also Die ☐ Home for the Holidays ☐ Home in Indiana ☐ Joe and Ethel Turp Call on the President ☐ Kentucky ☐ Law and Order ☐ Lure of the Wilderness ☐ Man on the Flying Trapeze, The ☐ Maryland ☐ Meet John Doe ☐ Moon's Our Home, The ☐ Mother Carey's Chickens ☐ My Darling Clementine ☐ Nice Girl? ☐ Nobody Lives Forever ☐ North Star, The ☐ Northwest Passage ☐ One and Only, Genuine, Original Family Band, The ☐ Over-the-Hill Gang Rides Again, The ☐ Over-the-Hill Gang, The ☐ Pride of the Yankees, The ☐ Princess and the Pirate, The ☐ Proud Ones, The ☐ Red River ☐ Return of the Texan ☐ Rio Bravo ☐ Rise and Shine ☐ Scudda Hoo! Scudda Hay! ☐ Sea of Lost Ships ☐ Sergeant York ☐ Slightly Dangerous ☐ Stand by for Action ☐ Stanley and Livingstone ☐ Stolen Life, A ☐ Story of Vernon and Irene Castle, The ☐ Support Your Local Sheriff ☐ Swamp Water ☐ Tammy and the Bachelor ☐ Task Force ☐ These Three ☐ They Shall Have Music ☐ Those Calloways ☐ Three Godfathers ☐ To Have and Have Not ☐ Way to the Gold, The ☐ Wedding Night, The ☐ Westerner, The ☐ Who's Minding the Mint? ☐ Wild Blue Yonder, The

Brenner, Dori ☐ I Dream of Jeannie: 15 Years Later ☐ I Want to Keep My Baby ☐ Next Stop, Greenwich Village ☐ Oasis, The

Brent, Evelyn ☐ Broadway ☐ High Pressure ☐ Last Command, The ☐ Mr. Wong, Detective ☐ Night Club Scandal ☐ Nitwits, The ☐ Panama Lady ☐ Silver Horde ☐ Song of the Trail ☐ Symphony of Living ☐ Underworld ☐ Why Bring That Up? ☐ Wide Open Town

Brent, George ☐ 'Til We Meet Again ☐ 42nd Street ☐ Adventure in Diamonds ☐ Affairs of Susan, The ☐ Angel on the Amazon ☐ Baby Face ☐ Born Again ☐ Bride for Sale ☐ Case Against Mrs. Ames, The ☐ Christmas Eve ☐ Corpse Came C.O.D., The ☐ Dark Victory ☐ Experiment Perilous ☐ FBI Girl ☐ Female ☐ Fighting 69th, The ☐ Front Page Woman ☐ Gay Sisters, The ☐ Give Me Your Heart ☐ God's Country and the Woman ☐ Gold Is Where You Find It ☐ Golden Arrow, The ☐ Goose and the Gander, The ☐ Great Lie, The ☐ Honeymoon for Three ☐ Housewife

☐ Illegal Entry ☐ In Person ☐ In This Our Life ☐ International Lady ☐ Jezebel ☐ Lover Come Back ☐ Luxury Liner ☐ Man Bait ☐ Man Who Talked Too Much, The ☐ Montana Belle ☐ More Than a Secretary ☐ My Reputation ☐ Old Maid, The ☐ Out of the Blue ☐ Painted Veil, The ☐ Racket Busters ☐ Rains Came, The ☐ Special Agent ☐ Spiral Staircase, The ☐ Stamboul Quest ☐ Tomorrow Is Forever

Bressart, Felix ☐ Bitter Sweet ☐ Blonde Fever ☐ Blossoms in the Dust ☐ Comrade X ☐ Edison, the Man ☐ Escape ☐ Greenwich Village ☐ I've Always Loved You ☐ Iceland ☐ It All Came True ☐ Married Bachelor ☐ Ninotchka ☐ Seventh Cross, The ☐ Shop Around the Corner, The ☐ Song is Born, A ☐ Swanee River ☐ To Be or Not to Be ☐ Without Love

Brett, Jeremy ☐ Madame X ☐ My Fair Lady ☐ Sherlock Holmes, Adventures of, The ("Copper Beeches") ☐ Sherlock Holmes, Adventures of, The ("Final Problem") ☐ Sherlock Holmes, Adventures of, The ("Greek Interpreter") ☐ Sherlock Holmes, Adventures of, The ("Resident Patient") ☐ Sherlock Holmes, Adventures of, The ("Red Headed League") ☐ Sherlock Holmes, Casebook of, The ("Creeping Man") ☐ Sherlock Holmes, Return of, The ("Abbey Grange") ☐ Sherlock Holmes, Return of, The ("Empty House") ☐ Sherlock Holmes, Return of, The ("Man With the Twisted Lip") ☐ Sherlock Holmes, Return of, The ("Musgrave Ritual") ☐ Sherlock Holmes, Return of, The ("Priory School") ☐ Sherlock Holmes, Return of, The ("Second Stain") ☐ Sherlock Holmes, Return of, The ("Six Napoleons") ☐ Sherlock Holmes, Solitary Cyclist, The ☐ Sherlock Holmes: Dancing Men, The ☐ Sherlock Holmes: Scandal in Bohemia ☐ Sherlock Holmes: The Speckled Band

Brewster, Diane ☐ Black Patch ☐ Courage of Black Beauty ☐ Invisible Boy, The ☐ King of the Wild Stallions ☐ Man in the Net, The ☐ Quantrill's Raiders ☐ Torpedo Run

Brialy, Jean-Claude ☐ Bride Wore Black, The ☐ Circle of Love ☐ Claire's Knee ☐ Cousins, The ☐ Edith and Marcel ☐ Four Hundred Blows, The ☐ Inspector Lavardin ☐ King of Hearts ☐ La Notte Brava ☐ Le Beau Serge ☐ Les Cousins ☐ Levy and Goliath ☐ Male Hunt ☐ Nutty, Naughty Chateau ☐ Operation St. Peter's ☐ Phantom of Liberty, The ☐ Woman Is a Woman, A

Brian, David ☐ Accused of Murder ☐ Ambush at Tomahawk Gap ☐ Beyond the Forest ☐ Breakthrough ☐ First Traveling Saleslady, The ☐ Flamingo Road ☐ Fort Worth ☐ Fury at Gunsight Pass ☐ Ghost of the China Sea ☐ Great Jewel Robber, The ☐ Inside the Walls of Folsom Prison ☐ Intruder in the Dust ☐ Manhunter, The ☐ Million Dollar Mermaid ☐ Perilous Journey, A ☐ Rabbit Trap, The ☐ Springfield Rifle ☐ This Woman Is Dangerous

Brian, Mary ☐ Amazing Adventure ☐ Behind the Front ☐ Blessed Event ☐ Charlie Chan in Paris ☐ Front Page, The ☐ Hard to Handle ☐ I Escaped from the Gestapo ☐ It's Tough to Be Famous ☐ Man on the Flying Trapeze, The ☐ Marriage Playground, The ☐ Royal Family of Broadway, The ☐ Running Wild ☐ Virginian, The

Brice, Fanny ☐ Be Yourself ☐ Everybody Sing ☐ Great Ziegfeld, The ☐ My Man ☐ Ziegfeld Follies

Bridges, Beau ☐ Adam's Woman ☐ Child Stealer, The ☐ Child's Play ☐ Christian Licorice Store, The ☐ Daddy's Dyin'. . . Who's Got the Will? ☐ Dangerous Company ☐ Everybody's Baby: The Rescue of Jessica McClure ☐ Explosive Generation, The ☐ Fabulous Baker Boys, The ☐ Fifth Musketeer, The ☐ Fighting Choice ☐ For Love of Ivy ☐ Four Feathers, The ☐ Gaily, Gaily ☐ Greased Lightning ☐ Hammersmith Is Out ☐ Heart Like a Wheel ☐ Honky Tonk Freeway ☐ Hotel New Hampshire, The ☐ Incident, The ☐ Iron Triangle, The ☐ Kid from Nowhere, The ☐ Killing Time, The ☐ Landlord, The ☐ Love Child ☐ Lovin' Molly ☐ Man Without a Country, The ☐ Married to It ☐ Medical Story ☐ Night Crossing ☐ No Minor Vices ☐ Norma Rae ☐ One Summer Love ☐ Other Side of the Mountain, The ☐ Outrage ☐ Positively True Adventures of the Alleged Texas Cheerleader-Murdering Mom, The ☐ Runner Stumbles, The ☐ Seven Hours to Judgment ☐ Sidekicks ☐ Swashbuckler ☐ Thanksgiving Promise, The ☐ Two Minute Warning ☐ Village of the Giants ☐ Wildflower ☐ Witness for the Prosecution ☐ Wizard, The ☐ Women & Men: Stories of Seduction

Bridges, Jeff ☐ 8 Million Ways to Die ☐ Against All Odds ☐ American Heart ☐ American Success Company, The ☐ Bad Company ☐ Blown Away ☐ Cutter's Way ☐ Fabulous Baker Boys, The ☐ Fat City ☐ Fearless ☐ Fisher King, The ☐ Hearts of the West ☐ Heaven's Gate ☐ Iceman Cometh, The ☐ Jagged Edge ☐ King Kong ☐ Kiss Me Goodbye ☐ Last American Hero, The ☐ Last Picture Show, The ☐ Lolly Madonna XXX ☐ Morning After, The ☐ Nadine ☐ Rancho Deluxe ☐ See You in the Morning ☐ Starman ☐ Stay Hungry ☐ Texasville ☐ Thunderbolt and Lightfoot ☐ Tron ☐ Tucker—The Man and His Dream ☐ Vanishing, The ☐ Winter Kills

Bridges, Lloyd ☐ Abilene Town ☐ Airplane II, The Sequel ☐ Airplane! ☐ Apache Woman ☐ Around the World Under the Sea ☐ Attack on the Iron Coast ☐ Bear Island ☐ Blown Away ☐ Calamity Jane and Sam Bass ☐ Canyon Passage ☐ City of Bad Men ☐ Colt .45 ☐ Cross of Fire ☐ East of Eden ☐ Fifth Musketeer, The ☐ Flight Lieutenant ☐ Goddess,

The ☐ Grace Kelly ☐ Great Wallendas, The ☐ Happy Ending, The ☐ Haunts of the Very Rich ☐ High Noon ☐ Home of the Brave ☐ Honey, I Blew Up the Kid ☐ Hot Shots! ☐ Hot Shots! Part Deux ☐ Joe Versus the Volcano ☐ Kid From Left Field, The ☐ Last of the Comanches, The ☐ Leona Helmsley: The Queen of Mean ☐ Life of the Party: The Story of Beatrice ☐ Limping Man, The ☐ Little Big Horn ☐ Master Race, The ☐ Miss Susie Slagle's ☐ Mission Galactica: The Cylon Attack ☐ Moonrise ☐ Plymouth Adventure, The ☐ Rainmaker, The ☐ Rocket Ship X-M ☐ Roots ☐ Running Wild ☐ Sahara ☐ Shut My Big Mouth ☐ Silent Night, Lonely Night ☐ Sound of Fury, The ☐ Thanksgiving Promise, The ☐ Tucker—The Man and His Dream ☐ Walk in the Sun, A ☐ West of Tombstone ☐ Whistle at Eaton Falls, The ☐ Wichita ☐ Winter People

Brimley, Wilford ☐ Absence of Malice ☐ Act of Vengeance ☐ American Justice ☐ Billy the Kid ☐ Blood River ☐ Cocoon ☐ Cocoon: The Return ☐ Country ☐ End of the Line ☐ Eternity ☐ Firm, The ☐ Gore Vidal's Billy the Kid ☐ Hard Target ☐ Murder in Space ☐ Natural, The ☐ Remo Williams: The Adventure Begins ☐ Ten to Midnight ☐ Thing, The

Britt, May ☐ Blue Angel, The ☐ Fatal Desire ☐ Give 'Em Hell ☐ Haunts ☐ Hunters, The ☐ Murder, Inc. ☐ Ship of the Condemned Women, The

Britton, Barbara ☐ Albuquerque ☐ Bwana Devil ☐ Captain Kidd ☐ Fabulous Suzanne, The ☐ Fleet's In, The ☐ Great John L., The ☐ Gunfighters ☐ I Shot Jesse James ☐ Raiders, The ☐ Return of Monte Cristo, The ☐ So Proudly We Hail! ☐ Spoilers, The ☐ Till We Meet Again ☐ Virginian, The

Britton, Tony ☐ Dr. Syn, Alias the Scarecrow ☐ Operation Amsterdam ☐ Risk, The ☐ There's a Girl in My Soup

Broadbent, Jim ☐ Enchanted April ☐ Good Father, The ☐ Insurance Man, The ☐ Life Is Sweet ☐ Princess Caraboo ☐ Wide-Eyed and Legless ☐ Widow's Peak ☐ Widows' Peak

Broderick, Helen ☐ Because of Him ☐ Bride Walks Out, The ☐ Captain Is a Lady, The ☐ Chip Off the Old Block ☐ Father Takes a Wife ☐ Honeymoon in Bali ☐ Life of the Party, The ☐ Meet the Missus ☐ Naughty but Nice ☐ Service De Luxe ☐ Swing Time ☐ Three Is a Family ☐ Top Hat

Broderick, Matthew ☐ 1918 ☐ Biloxi Blues ☐ Family Business ☐ Ferris Bueller's Day Off ☐ Freshman, The ☐ Glory ☐ Ladyhawke ☐ Life in the Theater, A ☐ Lion King, The ☐ Master Harold and the Boys ☐ Max Dugan Returns ☐ Mrs. Parker and the Vicious Circle ☐ Night We Never Met, The ☐ On Valentine's Day ☐ Out on a Limb ☐ Project X ☐ Road to Wellville, The ☐ Torch Song Trilogy ☐ WarGames

Brodie, Steve ☐ Desperate ☐ Fighting Coast Guard ☐ Frankenstein Island ☐ Giant Spider Invasion, The ☐ Gun Duel in Durango ☐ Home of the Brave ☐ Sierra Baron ☐ Steel Helmet, The

Brolin, James ☐ Ambush Murders, The ☐ Amityville Horror, The ☐ And the Sea Will Tell ☐ Backstab ☐ Cape Town Affair, The ☐ Capricorn One ☐ Car, The ☐ Cheatin' Hearts ☐ Class of '63 ☐ Finish Line ☐ Gable and Lombard ☐ Gas, Food Lodging ☐ High Risk ☐ Mae West ☐ Marcus Welby, M.D. ☐ Night of the Juggler ☐ Nightmare on the 13th Floor ☐ Skyjacked ☐ Von Ryan's Express ☐ Westworld

Bromberg, J. Edward ☐ Charlie Chan on Broadway ☐ Devil Pays Off ☐ Four Men and a Prayer ☐ Hollywood Cavalcade ☐ I Shot Jesse James ☐ Lady of Burlesque ☐ Mark of Zorro, The ☐ Missing Corpse, The ☐ Mr. Moto Takes a Chance ☐ Salome, Where She Danced ☐ Seventh Heaven ☐ Suez ☐ Under Two Flags ☐ Wife, Husband and Friend

Bromfield, John ☐ Big Bluff, The ☐ Crime Against Joe ☐ Easy to Love ☐ Manfish ☐ Revenge of the Creature

Bron, Eleanor ☐ Bedazzled ☐ Help! ☐ National Health, The ☐ Thank You All Very Much ☐ Two for the Road ☐ Women in Love

Bronson, Betty ☐ Are Parents People? ☐ Ben-Hur ☐ Medicine Man, The ☐ Naked Kiss, The ☐ Singing Fool, The

Bronson, Charles ☐ Act of Vengeance ☐ Assassination ☐ Battle of the Bulge ☐ Big House, U.S.A. ☐ Borderline ☐ Breakheart Pass ☐ Breakout ☐ Caboblanco ☐ Chato's Land ☐ Chino ☐ Cold Sweat ☐ Crime Wave ☐ Death Hunt ☐ Death Wish ☐ Death Wish 3 ☐ Death Wish 4: The Crackdown ☐ Death Wish 5 ☐ Death Wish II ☐ Dirty Dozen, The ☐ Drum Beat ☐ Evil That Men Do ☐ Family, The ☐ Farewell Friend ☐ Four for Texas ☐ From Noon Till Three ☐ Gang War ☐ Great Escape, The ☐ Guns for San Sebastian ☐ Hard Times ☐ Honor Among Thieves ☐ Hot Lead ☐ Jubal ☐ Kid Galahad ☐ Kinjite: Forbidden Subjects ☐ Lola ☐ Love and Bullets ☐ Machine-Gun Kelly ☐ Magnificent Seven, The ☐ Master of the World ☐ Meanest Men in the West, The ☐ Mechanic, The ☐ Messenger of Death ☐ Miss Sadie Thompson ☐ Mob, The ☐ Mr. Majestyk ☐ Murphy's Law ☐ Never So Few ☐ Once Upon a Time in the West ☐ Raid on Entebbe ☐ Red Sun ☐ Rider on the Rain ☐ Sandpiper, The ☐ Sea Wolf, The ☐ Showdown at Boot Hill ☐ Someone Behind the Door ☐ Telefon ☐ Ten to Midnight ☐ This Property Is Condemned ☐ Valachi Papers, The ☐ Villa Rides ☐ When Hell Broke Loose ☐ White Buffalo, The

Brook, Clive ☐ Action for Slander ☐ Cavalcade ☐ Charming Sinners ☐ Gallant Lady ☐ If I Were Free ☐ List of Adrian Messenger, The ☐ Man from Yesterday, The ☐ Night of

June 13 ☐ On Approval ☐ Shanghai Express ☐ Shipbuilders, The ☐ Underworld
Brook, Lesley ☐ It's in the Blood ☐ Man Who Made Diamonds, The ☐ Night Alone ☐ Nursemaid Who Disappeared, The ☐ Side Street Angel
Brooke, Hillary ☐ Abbott and Costello Meet Captain Kidd ☐ Africa Screams ☐ Big Town ☐ Bodyhold ☐ Heatwave ☐ Lucky Losers ☐ Maze, The ☐ Ministry of Fear ☐ Never Wave at a WAC ☐ Road to Utopia ☐ Sherlock Holmes Faces Death ☐ Standing Room Only ☐ Strange Woman, The ☐ Woman in Green, The
Brooks, Albert ☐ Broadcast News ☐ Defending Your Life ☐ I'll Do Anything ☐ Lost in America ☐ Milton Berle's Mad World of Comedy ☐ Modern Romance ☐ Real Life ☐ Taxi Driver ☐ Unfaithfully Yours
Brooks, Louise ☐ Beggars of Life ☐ Canary Murder Case ☐ Diary of a Lost Girl ☐ Girl in Every Port, A ☐ Pandora's Box
Brooks, Mel ☐ High Anxiety ☐ History of the World Part I ☐ Life Stinks ☐ Muppet Movie, The ☐ Putney Swope ☐ Robin Hood: Men in Tights ☐ Silent Movie ☐ Spaceballs ☐ To Be or Not to Be ☐ Twelve Chairs, The
Brooks, Phyllis ☐ Charlie Chan in Honolulu ☐ Charlie Chan in Reno ☐ In Old Chicago ☐ Little Miss Broadway ☐ Silver Spurs ☐ Unseen, The
Brooks, Rand ☐ False Paradise ☐ Hoppy's Holiday ☐ Ladies of the Chorus ☐ Silent Conflict ☐ Sinister Journey ☐ Unexpected Guest
Brophy, Edward ☐ Falcon in San Francisco, The ☐ Falcon's Adventure, The ☐ It Happened Tomorrow ☐ Mad Love ☐ Night of Adventure, A ☐ Nine Lives Are Not Enough ☐ Show Them No Mercy! ☐ Slight Case of Murder, A ☐ Whole Town's Talking, The
Brosnan, Pierce ☐ Broken Chain, The ☐ Deceivers, The ☐ Entangled ☐ Fourth Protocol, The ☐ Heist, The ☐ Lawnmower Man, The ☐ Live Wire ☐ Love Affair ☐ Manions of America, The ☐ Mister Johnson ☐ Mrs. Doubtfire ☐ Murder 101 ☐ Nomads ☐ Taffin
Brown, Blair ☐ Altered States ☐ And I Alone Survived ☐ Bad Seed, The ☐ Child Stealer, The ☐ Continental Divide ☐ Eleanor and Franklin: The White House Years ☐ Extreme Close-Up ☐ Flash of Green ☐ Hands of a Stranger ☐ Lethal Innocence ☐ One-Trick Pony ☐ Oregon Trail, The ☐ Stealing Home ☐ Strapless
Brown, Bryan ☐ Blame It on the Bellboy ☐ Breaker Morant ☐ Cathy's Child ☐ Cocktail ☐ F/X ☐ F/X2 ☐ Far East ☐ Give My Regards to Broad Street ☐ Good Wife, The ☐ Gorillas in the Mist ☐ Irishman, The ☐ Kim ☐ Last Hit, The ☐ Money Movers ☐ Newsfront ☐ Odd Angry Shot, The ☐ Palm Beach ☐ Parker ☐ Rebel ☐ Tai-Pan ☐ Thorn Birds, The ☐ Winter of Our Dreams, The
Brown, Georgia ☐ Bawdy Adventures of Tom Jones, The ☐ Fixer, The ☐ Galileo ☐ Long Ago Tomorrow ☐ Nothing But the Night
Brown, James ☐ Adios Amigo ☐ Blues Brothers, The ☐ Corvette K-225 ☐ Objective, Burma! ☐ Targets
Brown, Jim ☐ Black Gunn ☐ Crack House ☐ Dark of the Sun ☐ Dirty Dozen, The ☐ El Condor ☐ Fingers ☐ Grasshopper, The ☐ I Escaped from Devil's Island ☐ I'm Gonna Git You Sucka ☐ Ice Station Zebra ☐ Kid Vengeance ☐ L.A. Heat ☐ One Down Two to Go ☐ 100 Rifles ☐ Pacific Inferno ☐ Rio Conchos ☐ Riot ☐ Slaughter ☐ Slaughter's Big Rip-Off ☐ Take a Hard Ride ☐ Three the Hard Way ☐ . . . tick . . . tick . . . tick . . .
Brown, Joe E. ☐ Beware, Spooks! ☐ Bright Lights ☐ Broadminded ☐ Casanova in Burlesque ☐ Chatterbox ☐ Circus Clown, The ☐ Comedy of Terrors, The ☐ Earthworm Tractors ☐ Elmer the Great ☐ Fireman, Save My Child ☐ Flirting with Fate ☐ Gladiator, The ☐ Hold Everything ☐ Lottery Bride, The ☐ Midsummer Night's Dream, A ☐ Pin Up Girl ☐ Riding on Air ☐ Show Boat ☐ Shut My Big Mouth ☐ Tenderfoot, The ☐ Top Speed ☐ When's Your Birthday?
Brown, Pamela ☐ Alice in Wonderland ☐ Becket ☐ Cleopatra ☐ Dracula ☐ Figures in a Landscape ☐ I Know Where I'm Going ☐ In this House of Brede ☐ Lust for Life ☐ Night Digger, The ☐ Scapegoat, The ☐ Second Mrs. Tanqueray, The ☐ Secret Ceremony
Brown, Peter ☐ Aurora Encounter ☐ Chrome and Hot Leather ☐ Foxy Brown ☐ Merrill's Marauders ☐ Rape Squad, The
Brown, Reb ☐ Cage ☐ Captain America ☐ Captain America II ☐ Distant Thunder ☐ Fast Break ☐ Firing Line, The ☐ Howling II: Your Sister Is a Werewolf ☐ Last Flight to Hell ☐ Mercenary Fighters ☐ Street Hunter ☐ Uncommon Valor ☐ Yor, the Hunter From the Future
Brown, Tom ☐ Adventures of Smilin' Jack ☐ Anne of Green Gables ☐ Buck Privates Come Home ☐ Central Airport ☐ Ex-Champ ☐ Gentle Julia ☐ Hell's Highway ☐ Hello Sucker ☐ I'd Give My Life ☐ In Old Chicago ☐ Judge Priest ☐ Man Who Cried Wolf, The ☐ Merrily We Live ☐ Navy Blue and Gold ☐ Ringside ☐ Sergeant Madden ☐ This Side of Heaven
Brown, Vanessa ☐ Basketball Fix, The ☐ Fighter, The ☐ Foxes of Harrow, The ☐ Late George Apley, The ☐ Mother Wore Tights
Browne, Coral ☐ American Dreamer ☐ Auntie Mame ☐ Courtney Affair, The ☐ Dream-Child ☐ Eleanor, First Lady of the World ☐ Killing of Sister George, The ☐ Nursemaid Who Disappeared, The ☐ Ruling Class, The ☐ Theatre of Blood
Brown, Georg Stanford ☐ Black Jack ☐ Jesse

Owens Story, The ☐ Night the City Screamed, The ☐ Roots: The Next Generation ☐ Stir Crazy

Browne, Roscoe Lee ☐ Black Like Me ☐ Brother Minister: The Assassination of Malcolm X ☐ Cowboys, The ☐ For Us, the Living ☐ King ☐ Liberation of L. B. Jones, The ☐ Naked in New York ☐ Nothing Personal ☐ Ra Expeditions, The ☐ Superfly T.N.T. ☐ World's Greatest Athlete, The

Bruce, Lenny ☐ Bruce, Lenny: The Performance Film ☐ Dance Hall Racket ☐ Lenny Bruce—Without Tears

Bruce, Nigel ☐ Adventure in Diamonds ☐ Adventures of Sherlock Holmes, The ☐ Blue Bird, The ☐ Bwana Devil ☐ Chocolate Soldier, The ☐ Coming-Out Party ☐ Corn Is Green, The ☐ Dressed to Kill ☐ Eagle Squadron ☐ Exile, The ☐ Follow the Boys ☐ Frenchman's Creek ☐ Gypsy Wildcat ☐ Hong Kong ☐ Hound of the Baskervilles, The ☐ House of Fear, The ☐ I Was a Spy ☐ Lassie Come Home ☐ Last of Mrs. Cheyney, The ☐ Limelight ☐ Man Who Broke the Bank at Monte Carlo, The ☐ Pearl of Death, The ☐ Pursuit to Algiers ☐ Rains Came, The ☐ Roxie Hart ☐ Scarlet Claw, The ☐ Scarlet Pimpernel, The ☐ Secret Weapon ☐ She ☐ Sherlock Holmes and the Spider Woman ☐ Sherlock Holmes and the Voice of Terror ☐ Sherlock Holmes Faces Death ☐ Sherlock Holmes in Washington ☐ Son of Lassie ☐ Spider Woman, The ☐ Suez ☐ Susan and God ☐ Suspicion ☐ Terror By Night ☐ This Above All ☐ Thunder in the City ☐ Trail of the Lonesome Pine ☐ Treasure Island ☐ Two Mrs. Carrolls, The ☐ Under Two Flags ☐ Woman in Green, The

Bruce, Virginia ☐ Action in Arabia ☐ Adventure in Washington ☐ Bad Man of Brimstone ☐ Born to Dance ☐ Dangerous Corner ☐ Downstairs ☐ Garden Murder Case, The ☐ Hired Wife ☐ Invisible Woman, The ☐ Jane Eyre ☐ Let 'Em Have It ☐ Let Freedom Ring ☐ Man Who Talked Too Much, The ☐ Metropolitan ☐ Mighty Barnum, The ☐ Murder Man, The ☐ Night Has a Thousand Eyes ☐ Pardon My Sarong ☐ There Goes My Heart ☐ When Love is Young ☐ Wife, Doctor and Nurse ☐ Winner Take All ☐ Yellow Jack

Bryan, Dora ☐ Apartment Zero ☐ Carry On Sergeant ☐ Child in the House ☐ Follow That Horse! ☐ Great St. Trinian's Train Robbery, The ☐ Intruder, The ☐ Mad About Men ☐ Man Who Wouldn't Talk, The ☐ Sandwich Man, The ☐ Taste of Honey, A

Bryan, Jane ☐ Brother Rat ☐ Brother Rat and a Baby ☐ Case of the Black Cat, The ☐ Each Dawn I Die ☐ Girls on Probation ☐ Invisible Stripes ☐ Old Maid, The ☐ Sisters, The ☐ Slight Case of Murder, A ☐ We Are Not Alone

Brynner, Yul ☐ Adios, Sabata ☐ Anastasia ☐ Battle of Neretva, The ☐ Brothers Karamazov, The ☐ Buccaneer, The ☐ Cast a Giant Shadow ☐ Catlow ☐ Double Man, The ☐ Escape from Zahrain ☐ File of the Golden Goose, The ☐ Flight from Ashiya ☐ Futureworld ☐ Fuzz ☐ Invitation to a Gunfighter ☐ Journey, The ☐ King and I, The ☐ Kings of the Sun ☐ Light at the Edge of the World, The ☐ Long Duel, The ☐ Madwoman of Chaillot, The ☐ Magnificent Seven, The ☐ Morituri ☐ Night Flight from Moscow ☐ Once More, With Feeling ☐ Poppy Is Also a Flower, The ☐ Port of New York ☐ Return of the Magnificent Seven ☐ Solomon and Sheba ☐ Sound and the Fury, The ☐ Surprise Package ☐ Taras Bulba ☐ Ten Commandments, The ☐ Triple Cross ☐ Villa Rides ☐ Westworld

Buchanan, Edgar ☐ Abilene Town ☐ Bandit of Sherwood Forest, The ☐ Benji ☐ Big Hangover, The ☐ Big Trees, The ☐ Cave of Outlaws ☐ City Without Men ☐ Desperadoes, The ☐ Edge of Eternity ☐ Fighting Guardsman ☐ Framed ☐ If I'm Lucky ☐ Impatient Years, The ☐ It Happens Every Thursday ☐ It Started with a Kiss ☐ Judge Roy Bean ☐ King of the Wild Stallions ☐ Make Haste to Live ☐ Man from Colorado, The ☐ Over-the-Hill Gang Rides Again, The ☐ Over-the-Hill Gang, The ☐ Penny Serenade ☐ Perilous Holiday ☐ Rage at Dawn ☐ Rawhide ☐ Ride the High Country ☐ Rounders, The ☐ Sea of Grass, The ☐ Shane ☐ Sheepman, The ☐ Swordsman, The ☐ Walking Hills, The ☐ Wild Stallion ☐ You Belong to Me

Buchholz, Horst ☐ Aces: Iron Eagle III ☐ Berlin Tunnel 21 ☐ Catamount Killing ☐ Code Name—Emerald ☐ Confessions of Felix Krull, The ☐ Empty Canvas, The ☐ Fanny ☐ Faraway, So Close ☐ From Hell to Victory ☐ Great Waltz, The ☐ Johnny Banco ☐ King in Shadow ☐ Magnificent Seven, The ☐ Marco the Magnificent ☐ Nine Hours to Rama ☐ One, Two, Three ☐ Raid on Entebbe ☐ Sahara ☐ Savage Bees, The ☐ Tiger Bay

Bujold, Genevieve ☐ Act of the Heart ☐ Alex and the Gypsy ☐ Anne of the Thousand Days ☐ Another Man, Another Chance ☐ Choose Me ☐ Coma ☐ Dead Ringers ☐ Earthquake ☐ False Identity ☐ Final Assignment ☐ Journey ☐ King of Hearts ☐ La Guerre Est Finie ☐ Last Flight of Noah's Ark, The ☐ Moderns, The ☐ Monsignor ☐ Murder by Decree ☐ Obsession ☐ Oh, What a Night ☐ Swashbuckler ☐ Tightrope ☐ Trojan Women, The ☐ Trouble in Mind

Bullock, Sandra ☐ Love Potion No. 9 ☐ Me and the Mob ☐ Speed ☐ Thing Called Love, The ☐ Vanishing, The ☐ Wrestling Ernest Hemingway

Buono, Victor ☐ Arnold ☐ Beneath the Planet of the Apes ☐ Boot Hill ☐ Brenda Starr ☐ Evil, The ☐ Four for Texas ☐ Hush . . . Hush, Sweet Charlotte ☐ Mad Butcher, the ☐ Man from Atlantis ☐ More Wild, Wild West ☐ Silencers, The ☐ Strangler, The ☐ What

Ever Happened to Baby Jane? ☐ Who's Minding the Mint?

Burke, Billie ☐ After Office Hours ☐ And Baby Makes Three ☐ Barkleys of Broadway, The ☐ Becky Sharp ☐ Bill of Divorcement, A ☐ Boy from Indiana ☐ Bride Wore Red, The ☐ Captain Is a Lady, The ☐ Cheaters, The ☐ Christopher Strong ☐ Craig's Wife ☐ Dinner at Eight ☐ Doubting Thomas ☐ Dulcy ☐ Everybody Sing ☐ Father of the Bride ☐ Father's Little Dividend ☐ Finishing School ☐ Forsaking All Others ☐ Ghost Comes Home, The ☐ Gildersleeve on Broadway ☐ Girl Trouble ☐ Hi Diddle Diddle ☐ Irene ☐ Man Who Came to Dinner, The ☐ Merrily We Live ☐ Navy Blue and Gold ☐ One Night in Lisbon ☐ Only Yesterday ☐ Parnell ☐ Piccadilly Jim ☐ She Couldn't Take It ☐ Small Town Girl ☐ They All Kissed the Bride ☐ Three Husbands ☐ Topper ☐ Topper Returns ☐ Topper Takes a Trip ☐ Wild Man of Borneo, The ☐ Wizard of Oz, The ☐ Young in Heart, The ☐ Zenobia

Burke, David ☐ Sherlock Holmes, Adventures of, The ("Copper Beeches") ☐ Sherlock Holmes, Adventures of, The ("Final Problem") ☐ Sherlock Holmes, Adventures of, The ("Greek Interpreter") ☐ Sherlock Holmes, Adventures of, The ("Resident Patient") ☐ Sherlock Holmes, Adventures of, The ("Red Headed League") ☐ Sherlock Holmes, Return of, The ("Abbey Grange") ☐ Sherlock Holmes, Return of, The ("Empty House") ☐ Sherlock Holmes, Return of, The ("Man With the Twisted Lip") ☐ Sherlock Holmes, Return of, The ("Musgrave Ritual") ☐ Sherlock Holmes, Return of, The ("Priory School") ☐ Sherlock Holmes, Return of, The ("Second Stain") ☐ Sherlock Holmes, Return of, The ("Six Napoleons") ☐ Sherlock Holmes, Solitary Cyclist, The ☐ Sherlock Holmes: Dancing Men, The ☐ Sherlock Holmes: Scandal in Bohemia ☐ Sherlock Holmes: The Speckled Band

Burke, Paul ☐ Anatomy of Terror ☐ Daddy's Gone A-Hunting ☐ Once You Kiss a Stranger ☐ South Sea Woman ☐ Thomas Crown Affair, The

Burke, Robert ☐ Far Off Place, A ☐ Simple Men ☐ Tombstone ☐ Unbelievable Truth, The

Burlinson, Tom ☐ Flesh + Blood ☐ Landslide ☐ Man from Snowy River, The ☐ Phar Lap ☐ Return to Snowy River ☐ Showdown at Williams Creek ☐ Time Guardian, The

Burnett, Carol ☐ Annie ☐ Between Friends ☐ Chu Chu and the Philly Flash ☐ Four Seasons, The ☐ Friendly Fire ☐ Front Page, The ☐ Grass Is Always Greener Over the Septic Tank, The ☐ H.E.A.L.T.H. ☐ Hostage ☐ Life of the Party: The Story of Beatrice ☐ Noises Off ☐ Pete 'n' Tillie ☐ Tenth Month, The ☐ Wedding, A

Burnette, Smiley ☐ Boots And Saddles ☐ Dude Ranger, The ☐ Frontier Outpost ☐ Heart of the Golden West ☐ Heart of The Rio Grande ☐ Idaho ☐ Man of The Frontier ☐ Mexicali Rose ☐ Old Barn Dance, The ☐ Old Corral, The ☐ Ride, Ranger, Ride ☐ Ride, Tenderfoot, Ride ☐ Rootin' Tootin' Rhythm ☐ Roundup Time in Texas ☐ Sierra Sue ☐ Silver Spurs ☐ Under Western Skies

Burns, Bob ☐ Arkansas Traveler, The ☐ Belle of the Yukon ☐ Big Broadcast of 1937, The ☐ I'm from Missouri ☐ Rhythm on the Range ☐ Waikiki Wedding ☐ Wells Fargo

Burns, David ☐ Knock on Wood ☐ Saint in London, The ☐ Tiger Makes Out, The ☐ Who Is Harry Kellerman and Why Is He Saying Those Terrible Things About Me?

Burns, George ☐ 18 Again! ☐ Big Broadcast of 1936, The ☐ Big Broadcast of 1937, The ☐ Big Broadcast, The ☐ College Holiday ☐ College Humor ☐ College Swing ☐ Damsel in Distress, A ☐ Going in Style ☐ Here Comes Cookie ☐ Honolulu ☐ International House ☐ Just You and Me, Kid ☐ Love in Bloom ☐ Many Happy Returns ☐ Oh God! Book II ☐ Oh, God! ☐ Oh, God! You Devil ☐ Sgt. Pepper's Lonely Hearts Club Band ☐ Six of a Kind ☐ Sunshine Boys, The ☐ We're Not Dressing

Burr, Raymond ☐ Abandoned ☐ Adventures of Don Juan ☐ Affair in Havana ☐ Bandits of Corsica, The ☐ Black Magic ☐ Blue Gardenia ☐ Borderline ☐ Brass Legend, The ☐ Bride of the Gorilla ☐ Bride of Vengeance ☐ Casanova's Big Night ☐ Count Three and Pray ☐ Crime of Passion ☐ Cry in the Night, A ☐ Curse of King Tut's Tomb, The ☐ Delirious ☐ Desperate ☐ FBI Girl ☐ Godzilla 1985 ☐ Godzilla, King of the Monsters ☐ Gorilla at Large ☐ His Kind of Woman ☐ Horizons West ☐ Jordan Chance, The ☐ Key to the City ☐ Khyber Patrol ☐ Magic Carpet, The ☐ Man Alone, A ☐ Mara Maru ☐ Meet Danny Wilson ☐ Night the City Screamed, The ☐ Out of the Blue ☐ Passion ☐ Perry Mason Returns ☐ Perry Mason: The Case of the Lost Love ☐ Peter and Paul ☐ Pitfall, The ☐ Place in the Sun, A ☐ Raw Deal ☐ Rear Window ☐ Sleep My Love ☐ Station West ☐ Walk a Crooked Mile ☐ You're Never Too Young

Burstyn, Ellen ☐ Act of Vengeance ☐ Alex in Wonderland ☐ Alice Doesn't Live Here Anymore ☐ Ambassador, The ☐ Cemetery Club, The ☐ Dream of Passion, A ☐ Dying Young ☐ Exorcist, The ☐ Getting Out ☐ Grand Isle ☐ Hanna's War ☐ Harry and Tonto ☐ Into Thin Air ☐ King of Marvin Gardens, The ☐ Last Picture Show, The ☐ Pack of Lies ☐ People vs. Jean Harris, The ☐ Providence ☐ Resurrection ☐ Roommates ☐ Same Time, Next Year ☐ Silence of the North ☐ Thursday's Game ☐ Twice in a Lifetime ☐ When a Man Loves a Woman

Burton, LeVar ☐ Acorn People, The ☐ Battered ☐ Grambling's White Tiger ☐ Hunter, The ☐ Jesse Owens Story, The ☐ Midnight

Hour, The ☐ One in a Million: The Ron LeFlore Story ☐ Roots ☐ Star Trek Generations

Burton, Richard ☐ Absolution ☐ Alexander the Great ☐ Anne of the Thousand Days ☐ Assassination of Trotsky, The ☐ Becket ☐ Bitter Victory ☐ Bluebeard ☐ Boom! ☐ Bramble Bush, The ☐ Breakthrough ☐ Brief Encounter ☐ Candy ☐ Circle of Two ☐ Cleopatra ☐ Comedians, The ☐ Desert Rats, The ☐ Divorce His, Divorce Hers ☐ Dr. Faustus ☐ Ellis Island ☐ Equus ☐ Exorcist II: The Heretic ☐ Gathering Storm, The ☐ Green Grow the Rushes ☐ Hammersmith Is Out ☐ Her Panelled Door ☐ Ice Palace ☐ Klansman, The ☐ Last Days of Dolwyn, The ☐ Longest Day, The ☐ Look Back in Anger ☐ Lovespell ☐ Massacre in Rome ☐ Medusa Touch, The ☐ My Cousin Rachel ☐ Night of the Iguana, The ☐ Prince of Players ☐ Raid on Rommel ☐ Rains of Ranchipur, The ☐ Robe, The ☐ Sandpiper, The ☐ Sea Wife ☐ Spy Who Came In from the Cold, The ☐ Staircase ☐ Taming of the Shrew, The ☐ Under Milk Wood ☐ V.I.P.s, The ☐ Villain ☐ Voyage, The ☐ Wagner ☐ Where Eagles Dare ☐ Who's Afraid of Virginia Woolf? ☐ Wild Geese, The

Burton, Robert ☐ I Was a Teenage Frankenstein ☐ Invasion of the Animal People ☐ Massacre At Fort Holman ☐ Reason to Live, a Reason to Die, A

Buscemi, Steve ☐ Floundering ☐ In the Soup ☐ Me and the Mob ☐ Mystery Train ☐ New York Stories ☐ Parting Glances ☐ Reservoir Dogs ☐ Twenty Bucks

Busch, Mae ☐ Blondie Johnson ☐ Fazil ☐ Foolish Wives ☐ Sons of the Desert ☐ Unholy Three, The

Busey, Gary ☐ Act of Piracy ☐ Angels Hard as They Come ☐ Barbarosa ☐ Bear, The ☐ Big Wednesday ☐ Buddy Holly Story, The ☐ Bulletproof ☐ Canvas ☐ Carny ☐ Chrome Soldiers ☐ Drop Zone ☐ Execution of Private Slovik, The ☐ Eye of the Tiger ☐ Fallen Angels—Volume 1 ☐ Firm, The ☐ Foolin' Around ☐ Half a Lifetime ☐ Hider in the House ☐ Insignificance ☐ Let's Get Harry ☐ Lethal Weapon ☐ My Heroes Have Always Been Cowboys ☐ Neon Empire, The ☐ Point Break ☐ Predator 2 ☐ Rookie of the Year ☐ Shrieking, The ☐ Silver Bullet ☐ South Beach ☐ Star Is Born, A ☐ Straight Time ☐ Surviving the Game ☐ Under Siege

Butterworth, Charles ☐ Baby Face Harrington ☐ Bermuda Mystery ☐ Cat and the Fiddle, The ☐ Every Day's a Holiday ☐ Forsaking All Others ☐ Illicit ☐ Mad Genius, The ☐ Magnificent Obsession ☐ Moon's Our Home, The ☐ My Weakness ☐ Penthouse ☐ Road Show ☐ Swing High, Swing Low

Buttons, Red ☐ 18 Again! ☐ Alice in Wonderland ☐ Ambulance, The ☐ Big Circus, The ☐ C.H.O.M.P.S. ☐ Five Weeks in a Balloon ☐ Gable and Lombard ☐ Gay Purr-ee ☐ Harlow ☐ Hatari! ☐ Imitation General ☐ Leave 'Em Laughing ☐ Movie Movie ☐ Pete's Dragon ☐ Poseidon Adventure, The ☐ Sayonara ☐ Side Show ☐ Stagecoach ☐ They Shoot Horses, Don't They? ☐ Up From the Beach ☐ Viva Knievel! ☐ When Time Ran Out . . . ☐ Winged Victory ☐ Your Cheatin' Heart

Byington, Spring ☐ Adventures of Tom Sawyer, The ☐ Angels in the Outfield ☐ Because You're Mine ☐ Big Wheel, The ☐ Blue Bird, The ☐ Charge of the Light Brigade, The ☐ Child Is Born, A ☐ Cynthia ☐ Devil and Miss Jones, The ☐ Dodsworth ☐ Dragonwyck ☐ Ellery Queen and the Perfect Crime ☐ Faithful in My Fashion ☐ Family Affair, A ☐ Green Light, The ☐ Heaven Can Wait ☐ Heavenly Body, The ☐ I'll Be Seeing You ☐ In the Good Old Summertime ☐ It Had to Be You ☐ It's Love I'm After ☐ Jezebel ☐ Little Women ☐ Louisa ☐ Love Me Forever ☐ Lucky Partners ☐ Meet John Doe ☐ My Brother Talks to Horses ☐ My Love Came Back ☐ No Room for the Groom ☐ Please Believe Me ☐ Please Don't Eat the Daisies ☐ Presenting Lily Mars ☐ Roxie Hart ☐ Salty O'Rourke ☐ Story of Alexander Graham Bell, The ☐ Theodora Goes Wild ☐ Thrill of a Romance ☐ Too Busy to Work ☐ Walk Softly, Stranger ☐ Werewolf of London ☐ When Ladies Meet

Byrne, Gabriel ☐ Christopher Columbus ☐ Cool World ☐ Dangerous Woman, A ☐ Dark Obsession ☐ Defence of the Realm ☐ Gothic ☐ Hanna K. ☐ Hello Again ☐ Into the West ☐ Julia and Julia ☐ Lionheart ☐ Little Women ☐ Miller's Crossing ☐ Point of No Return ☐ Shipwrecked ☐ Siesta ☐ Soldier's Tale, A ☐ Trial by Jury

Byrnes, Edd ☐ Back to the Beach ☐ Beach Ball ☐ Darby's Rangers ☐ Mankillers ☐ Reform School Girl ☐ Secret Invasion, The

Byron, Arthur ☐ 20,000 Years in Sing Sing ☐ Fog Over Frisco ☐ Man Killer ☐ Mayor of Hell, The ☐ Mummy, The ☐ Secret Bride, The ☐ Whole Town's Talking, The

Byron, Kathleen ☐ Black Narcissus ☐ From a Far Country: Pope John Paul II ☐ Prelude to Fame ☐ Small Back Room, The

Caan, James ☐ Alien Nation ☐ Another Man, Another Chance ☐ Bolero ☐ Brian's Song ☐ Bridge Too Far, A ☐ Chapter Two ☐ Cinderella Liberty ☐ Comes a Horseman ☐ Countdown ☐ Dark Backward, The ☐ El Dorado ☐ Flesh and Bone ☐ For the Boys ☐ Freebie and the Bean ☐ Funny Lady ☐ Gambler, The ☐ Games ☐ Gardens of Stone ☐ Glory Guys, The ☐ Godfather, The ☐ Harry and Walter Go to New York ☐ Hide in Plain Sight ☐ Honeymoon in Vegas ☐ Journey to Shiloh ☐ Killer Elite, The ☐ Kiss Me Goodbye ☐ Lady in a Cage ☐ Little Moon and Jud McGraw ☐ Misery ☐ Program, The ☐ Rabbit, Run ☐ Rain People, The

□ Red Line 7000 □ Rollerball □ Silent Movie □ Slither □ Submarine X-1 □ Thief

Cabot, Bruce □ Ann Vickers □ Bad Man of Brimstone □ Black Spurs □ Dodge City □ Fallen Angel □ Fancy Pants □ Finishing School □ Flame of New Orleans, The □ Fury □ Gallant Legion, The □ Girls Under Twenty-One □ Goliath and the Barbarians □ Homicide Bureau □ King Kong □ Last of the Mohicans, The □ Law of the Lawless □ Let 'Em Have It □ Lucky Devils □ McLintock! □ Murder on the Blackboard □ Quiet American, The □ Roadhouse Murder, The □ Robin Hood of El Dorado, The □ Salty O'Rourke □ Sheriff of Fractured Jaw, The □ Show Them No Mercy! □ Smoky □ Sorrowful Jones □ Sundown □ Susan and God □ Torso Murder Mystery, The □ Undefeated, The □ War Wagon, The

Cabot, Sebastian □ Black Patch □ Dragon Wells Massacre □ Family Jewels, The □ Johnny Tremain □ Jungle Book, The □ Miracle on 34th Street □ Sword in the Stone, The □ Terror in a Texas Town □ Time Machine, The □ Twice-Told Tales □ Westward Ho the Wagons!8

Cabot, Susan □ Carnival Rock □ Flame of Araby □ Fort Massacre □ Machine-Gun Kelly □ On the Isle of Samoa □ Ride Clear of Diablo □ Son of Ali Baba □ Sorority Girl □ Wasp Woman, The

Caesar, Adolph □ Club Paradise □ Color Purple, The □ Fortune Dane □ Hitter, The □ Soldier's Story, A

Caesar, Sid □ Airport '75 □ Amazing Stories: Book Four □ Barnaby and Me □ Busy Body, The □ Cheap Detective, The □ Fiendish Plot of Dr. Fu Manchu, The □ Fire Sale □ Grease □ Grease 2 □ Guide for the Married Man, A □ Guilt of Janet Ames, The □ History of the World Part I □ It's a Mad Mad Mad Mad World □ Love Is Never Silent □ Munsters' Revenge, The □ Over the Brooklyn Bridge □ Silent Movie □ Stoogemania □ Tars and Spars □ Ten From Your Show of Shows

Cage, Nicolas □ Amos and Andrew □ Birdy □ Boy in Blue, The □ Cotton Club, The □ Deadfall □ Firebirds □ Guarding Tess □ Honeymoon in Vegas □ It Could Happen To You □ Moonstruck □ Peggy Sue Got Married □ Racing With the Moon □ Raising Arizona □ Red Rock West □ Trapped in Paradise □ Valley Girl □ Vampire's Kiss □ Wild at Heart □ Zandalee

Cagney, James □ 13 Rue Madeleine □ Angels with Dirty Faces □ Blonde Crazy □ Blood on the Sun □ Boy Meets Girl □ Bride Came C.O.D., The □ Captain of the Clouds □ Ceiling Zero □ City for Conquest □ Come Fill the Cup □ Crowd Roars, The □ Devil Dogs of the Air □ Doorway to Hell □ Each Dawn I Die □ Fighting 69th, The □ Footlight Parade □ Frisco Kid □ G-Men □ Gallant Hours, The □ Great Guy □ Hard to Handle □ He Was Her Man □ Here Comes the Navy □ Irish in Us, The □ Jimmy the Gent □ Johnny Come Lately □ Lady Killer □ Lion Is in the Streets, A □ Love Me or Leave Me □ Man of a Thousand Faces □ Mayor of Hell, The □ Midsummer Night's Dream, A □ Millionaire, The □ Mister Roberts □ Never Steal Anything Small □ Oklahoma Kid, The □ One, Two, Three □ Other Men's Women □ Picture Snatcher □ Public Enemy, The □ Ragtime □ Roaring Twenties, The □ Run for Cover □ Seven Little Foys, The □ Shake Hands with the Devil □ Sinner's Holiday □ Smart Money □ Something to Sing About □ St. Louis Kid □ Strawberry Blonde, The □ Taxi! □ Terrible Joe Moran □ These Wilder Years □ Time of Your Life, The □ Torrid Zone □ Tribute to a Bad Man □ West Point Story □ What Price Glory? □ White Heat □ Winner Take All □ Yankee Doodle Dandy

Caine, Michael □ Alfie □ Ashanti: Land of No Mercy □ Battle of Britain, The □ Beyond the Limit □ Beyond the Poseidon Adventure □ Billion Dollar Brain □ Black Windmill, The □ Blame It on Rio □ Blue Ice □ Bridge Too Far, A □ Bullseye! □ California Suite □ Deathtrap □ Destructors, The □ Dirty Rotten Scoundrels □ Dressed to Kill □ Eagle Has Landed, The □ Educating Rita □ Fourth Protocol, The □ Foxhole in Cairo □ Funeral in Berlin □ Gambit □ Get Carter □ Half Moon Street □ Hand, The □ Hannah and Her Sisters □ Harry and Walter Go to New York □ Hell in Korea □ Holcroft Convenant, The □ Hurry Sundown □ Ipcress File, The □ Island, The □ Italian Job, The □ Jack the Ripper □ Jaws, The Revenge □ Jekyll & Hyde □ Jigsaw Man, The □ Last Valley, The □ Magus, The □ Man Who Would Be King, The □ Mona Lisa □ Mr. Destiny □ Muppet Christmas Carol, The □ Noises Off □ On Deadly Ground □ Peeper □ Play Dirty □ Pulp □ Romantic Englishwoman, The □ Shock to the System, A □ Sleuth □ Surrender □ Swarm, The □ Sweet Liberty □ Too Late the Hero □ Victory □ Whistle Blower, The □ Wilby Conspiracy, The □ Without a Clue □ Woman Times Seven □ Wrong Box, The □ X, Y and Zee □ Zulu

Calhern, Louis □ 20,000 Years in Sing Sing □ Annie Get Your Gun □ Arch of Triumph □ Asphalt Jungle, The □ Athena □ Betrayed □ Blackboard Jungle □ Blonde Crazy □ Bridge of San Luis Rey, The □ Charlie McCarthy, Detective □ Confidentially Connie □ Count of Monte Cristo, The □ Diplomaniacs □ Duck Soup □ Fast Company □ Forever Darling □ Frisco Jenny □ High Society □ I Take This Woman □ Invitation □ Juarez □ Julius Caesar □ Latin Lovers □ Life of Emile Zola, The □ Life of Her Own, A □ Magnificent Yankee, The □ Man with a Cloak, The

☐ Man with Two Faces, The ☐ Men of the Fighting Lady ☐ Nancy Goes to Rio ☐ Night After Night ☐ Notorious ☐ Prisoner of Zenda, The ☐ Prodigal, The ☐ Red Pony, The ☐ Rhapsody ☐ Student Prince, The ☐ Sweet Adeline ☐ Two Weeks with Love ☐ Washington Story ☐ We're Not Married

Calhoun, Rory ☐ Adventure Island ☐ Ain't Misbehavin' ☐ Angel ☐ Apache Territory ☐ Apache Uprising ☐ Avenging Angel ☐ Big Caper, The ☐ Black Spurs ☐ Bullet is Waiting, A ☐ Colossus of Rhodes, The ☐ Dawn at Socorro ☐ Domino Kid, The ☐ Face in the Rain, A ☐ Finger on the Trigger ☐ Flight to Hong Kong ☐ Four Guns to the Border ☐ Gun Hawk, The ☐ Hard Drivin' ☐ Hell Comes to Frogtown ☐ Hired Gun, The ☐ I'd Climb the Highest Mountain ☐ Marco Polo ☐ Massacre River ☐ Meet Me After the Show ☐ Midnight Auto Supply ☐ Motel Hell ☐ Night of the Lepus ☐ Nob Hill ☐ Operation Cross Eagles ☐ Our Men in Bagdad ☐ Powder River ☐ Raw Edge ☐ Red House, The ☐ River of No Return ☐ Sand ☐ Silver Whip, The ☐ Spoilers, The ☐ That Hagen Girl ☐ Ticket to Tomahawk, A ☐ With a Song in My Heart

Callan, Michael ☐ Because They're Young ☐ Bon Voyage! ☐ Cat and the Canary, The ☐ Cat Ballou ☐ Double Exposure ☐ Flying Fontaines, The ☐ Frasier, the Sensuous Lion ☐ Freeway ☐ Gidget Goes Hawaiian ☐ Interns, The ☐ Lepke ☐ Magnificent Seven Ride!, The ☐ Mysterious Island ☐ New Interns, The ☐ Photographer, The

Calleia, Joseph ☐ Exclusive Story ☐ Five Came Back ☐ For Whom the Bell Tolls ☐ Four Faces West ☐ Full Confession ☐ Iron Mistress, The ☐ Jungle Book ☐ Littlest Outlaw, The ☐ Monster and the Girl, The ☐ My Little Chickadee ☐ Noose Hangs High, The ☐ Public Hero No. 1 ☐ Riffraff ☐ Serenade ☐ Silk Noose, The ☐ Touch of Evil ☐ Tough Guy ☐ When in Rome ☐ Wild is the Wind ☐ Wyoming

Calloway, Cab ☐ Big Broadcast, The ☐ Blues Brothers, The ☐ Cincinnati Kid, The ☐ Manhattan Merry-Go-Round ☐ Minnie The Moocher ☐ Sensations ☐ St. Louis Blues ☐ Stormy Weather

Callow, Simon ☐ Amadeus ☐ Crucifer of Blood, The ☐ Four Weddings and a Funeral ☐ Manifesto ☐ Maurice ☐ Mr. & Mrs. Bridge ☐ Street Fighter

Calthrop, Donald ☐ I Was a Spy ☐ Number Seventeen ☐ Rome Express ☐ Scrooge

Calvert, Phyllis ☐ Appointment with Danger ☐ Battle of the Villa Fiorita, The ☐ Broken Journey ☐ Child in the House ☐ Crash of Silence ☐ Golden Madonna, The ☐ Her Panelled Door ☐ Indiscreet ☐ It's Never Too Late ☐ Kipps ☐ Madonna of the Seven Moons ☐ Magic Bow, The ☐ Man in Grey, The ☐ Man of Evil ☐ Mr. Denning Drives North ☐ Neutral Port ☐ Oscar Wilde ☐ Project M7 ☐ They Were Sisters ☐ Young Mr. Pitt, The

Calvet, Corinne ☐ Adventures of a Young Man ☐ Apache Uprising ☐ Far Country, The ☐ Flight to Tangier ☐ My Friend Irma Goes West ☐ On the Riviera ☐ One Step to Eternity ☐ Peking Express ☐ Powder River ☐ Quebec ☐ She's Dressed to Kill ☐ So This Is Paris ☐ Thunder in the East ☐ Too Hot to Handle ☐ What Price Glory? ☐ When Willie Comes Marching Home

Cambridge, Godfrey ☐ Biggest Bundle Of Them All ☐ Biscuit Eater, The ☐ Busy Body, The ☐ Bye Bye Braverman ☐ Come Back, Charleston Blue ☐ Cotton Comes to Harlem ☐ Five on the Black Hand Side ☐ Friday Foster ☐ Gone Are the Days ☐ President's Analyst, The ☐ Watermelon Man

Cameron, Rod ☐ Baron's African War, The ☐ Belle Starr's Daughter ☐ Black Dragon of Manzanar ☐ Bounty Killer, The ☐ Brimstone ☐ Cavalry Scout ☐ Electronic Monster, The ☐ Evel Knievel ☐ Fighting Chance, The ☐ Fleet's In, The ☐ Forest Rangers, The ☐ Fort Osage ☐ Frontier Gal ☐ Gun Hawk, The ☐ Headline Hunters ☐ Hell's Outpost ☐ Jungle, The ☐ Monster and the Girl, The ☐ Night of January 16th, The ☐ Oh! Susanna ☐ Panhandle ☐ Plunderers, The ☐ Requiem for a Gunfighter ☐ River Lady ☐ Salome, Where She Danced ☐ Santa Fe Passage ☐ Short Grass

Campanella, Joseph ☐ Ben ☐ Child Under a Leaf ☐ Earthbound ☐ Game, The ☐ Hit Lady ☐ Murder, Inc. ☐ My Body, My Child

Campbell, Beatrice ☐ I'll Never Forget You ☐ Last Holiday ☐ Master of Ballantrae, The ☐ Mudlark, The ☐ No Place for Jennifer

Campbell, Bruce ☐ Army of Darkness ☐ Evil Dead 2, The ☐ Evil Dead, The ☐ Hudsucker Proxy, The ☐ Lunatics: A Love Story ☐ Maniac Cop ☐ Maniac Cop 2 ☐ Mindwarp ☐ Moontrap ☐ Sundown, The Vampire in Retreat

Campbell, Cheryl ☐ Chariots of Fire ☐ McVicar ☐ Seven Dials Mystery, The ☐ Shooting Party, The

Campbell, Louise ☐ Bulldog Drummond Comes Back ☐ Men with Wings ☐ Night Club Scandal ☐ Star Maker, The

Campbell, Tisha ☐ House Party ☐ House Party 2 ☐ House Party III ☐ Rooftops ☐ School Daze

Campbell, William ☐ Blood Bath ☐ Cell 2455, Death Row ☐ Dementia 13 ☐ Man in the Vault ☐ Man Without a Star ☐ Naked and the Dead, The

Camp, Colleen ☐ Backfield in Motion ☐ City Girl ☐ Cloud Dancer ☐ Clue ☐ D.A.R.Y.L. ☐ Death Game ☐ Game of Death ☐ Illegally Yours ☐ Joy of Sex ☐ Midnight Auto Supply ☐ No-Tell Hotel, The ☐ Smile ☐ Smokey and the Bandit III ☐ Smokey and the Bandit, Part 3 ☐ Swinging Cheerleaders, The ☐ They All

Laughed ☐ Track 29 ☐ Vagrant, The ☐ Valley Girl ☐ Walk Like A Man ☐ Wayne's World ☐ Wicked Stepmother

Canale, Gianna Maria ☐ Adventures of Scaramouche ☐ Man from Cairo, The ☐ Nights of Rasputin ☐ Warrior and the Slave Girl, The

Canale, Gianna ☐ Clash of Steel ☐ Go for Broke ☐ Goliath and the Vampires ☐ Whole Truth, The

Candy, John ☐ Armed and Dangerous ☐ Blues Brothers, The ☐ Brewster's Millions ☐ Clown Murders, The ☐ Cool Runnings ☐ Delirious ☐ Find the Lady ☐ Going Berserk ☐ Great Outdoors, The ☐ Heavy Metal ☐ It Came From Hollywood ☐ It Seemed Like a Good Idea at the Time ☐ JFK ☐ Kavik the Wolf Dog ☐ Lost and Found ☐ Nothing But Trouble ☐ Once Upon a Crime ☐ Only the Lonely ☐ Planes, Trains & Automobiles ☐ Really Weird Tales ☐ Rescuers Down Under, The ☐ Sesame Street Presents Follow That Bird ☐ Shmenges, The—The Last Polka ☐ Silent Partner, The ☐ Spaceballs ☐ Speed Zone! ☐ Speed Zone! ☐ Splash ☐ Stripes ☐ Summer Rental ☐ Uncle Buck ☐ Volunteers ☐ Who's Harry Crumb?

Cannon, Dyan ☐ Anderson Tapes, The ☐ Author! Author! ☐ Based on an Untrue Story ☐ Bob & Carol & Ted & Alice ☐ Burglars, The ☐ Caddyshack II ☐ Child Under a Leaf ☐ Christmas in Connecticut ☐ Coast to Coast ☐ Deathtrap ☐ Doctor's Wives ☐ End of Innocence, The ☐ Having It All ☐ Heaven Can Wait ☐ Honeysuckle Rose ☐ Lady of the House ☐ Last of Sheila, The ☐ Love Machine, The ☐ Malibu ☐ Merlin and the Sword ☐ Pickle, The ☐ Revenge of the Pink Panther ☐ Shamus ☐ Such Good Friends

Canova, Judy ☐ Artists and Models ☐ Cannonball ☐ Carolina Cannonball ☐ Chatterbox ☐ Honeychile ☐ Joan of Ozark ☐ Oklahoma Annie

Cantor, Eddie ☐ Ali Baba Goes to Town ☐ Forty Little Mothers ☐ Glorifying the American Girl ☐ If You Knew Susie ☐ Kid from Spain, The ☐ Kid Millions ☐ Palmy Days ☐ Roman Scandals ☐ Show Business ☐ Story of Will Rogers, The ☐ Strike Me Pink ☐ Whoopee!

Canutt, Yakima ☐ 'Neath the Arizona Skies ☐ Code 645 ☐ Fighting Stallion, The ☐ Paradise Canyon ☐ Rocky Mountain ☐ Star Packer, The ☐ Texas Terror ☐ Trouble in Texas ☐ Winds of the Wasteland

Capshaw, Kate ☐ Best Defense ☐ Black Rain ☐ Dreamscape ☐ Her Secret Life ☐ Indiana Jones and the Temple of Doom ☐ Just Cause ☐ Little Sex, A ☐ Love Affair ☐ Love at Large ☐ My Heroes Have Always Been Cowboys ☐ Power ☐ Private Affairs ☐ Quick and the Dead, The ☐ Space Camp ☐ Windy City

Capucine ☐ Arabian Adventure ☐ Curse of the Pink Panther ☐ Fellini Satyricon ☐ Fraulein Doktor ☐ Honey Pot, The ☐ Lion, The ☐ North to Alaska ☐ Pink Panther, The ☐ Red Sun ☐ Song Without End ☐ Trail of the Pink Panther ☐ Walk on the Wild Side ☐ What's New, Pussycat?

Cara, Irene ☐ Aaron Loves Angela ☐ Caged in Paradiso ☐ Certain Fury ☐ City Heat ☐ D.C. Cab ☐ Fame ☐ For Us, the Living ☐ Guyana Tragedy: The Story of Jim Jones ☐ Happily Ever After ☐ Killing 'em Softly ☐ Magic Voyage, The ☐ Sister, Sister ☐ Sparkle

Cardinale, Claudia ☐ 8 1/2 ☐ Adventures of Gerard, The ☐ Battle of Austerlitz, The ☐ Bebo's Girl ☐ Bell' Antonio ☐ Blindfold ☐ Cartouche ☐ Circus World ☐ Conversation Piece ☐ Don't Make Waves ☐ Escape to Athena ☐ Facts of Murder, The ☐ Fine Pair, A ☐ Fitzcarraldo ☐ Gift, The ☐ Girl with a Suitcase ☐ Hell With Heroes, The ☐ Henry IV ☐ History ☐ Immortal Bachelor, The ☐ La Pelle ☐ La Viaccia ☐ Legend of Frenchie King, The ☐ Leopard, The ☐ Magnificent Cuckold, The ☐ Man in Love, A ☐ Once Upon a Time in the West ☐ Pink Panther, The ☐ Princess Daisy ☐ Professionals, The ☐ Red Tent, The ☐ Rocco and His Brothers ☐ Salamander, The ☐ Son of the Pink Panther ☐ Time of Indifference

Carey, Jr., Harry ☐ Challenge to White Fang ☐ Cherry 2000 ☐ Illegally Yours ☐ Mask ☐ Mister Roberts ☐ Public Affair, A ☐ Rio Grande ☐ Searchers, The ☐ She Wore a Yellow Ribbon ☐ Three Godfathers, The ☐ UFOria ☐ Wagon Master ☐ Warpath ☐ Whales of August, The

Carey, Harry ☐ Angel and the Badman ☐ Beyond Tomorrow ☐ China's Little Devils ☐ Danger Patrol ☐ Great Moment, The ☐ Happy Land ☐ King of Alcatraz ☐ Last Outlaw, The ☐ Man of the Forest ☐ Mr. Smith Goes to Washington ☐ Sea of Grass, The ☐ Shepherd of the Hills ☐ So Dear to My Heart ☐ Souls at Sea ☐ Spoilers, The ☐ Sundown ☐ They Knew What They Wanted ☐ Trader Horn ☐ Valiant Is the Word for Carrie ☐ You and Me

Carey, Macdonald ☐ Blue Denim ☐ Bride of Vengeance ☐ Cave of Outlaws ☐ Comanche Territory ☐ Copper Canyon ☐ Dream Girl ☐ Excuse My Dust ☐ Great Gatsby, The ☐ Great Missouri Raid, The ☐ Hannah Lee ☐ Hazard ☐ Lawless, The ☐ Let's Make It Legal ☐ Meet Me After the Show ☐ Odongo ☐ Rebels, The ☐ Shadow of a Doubt ☐ Streets of Laredo ☐ Suddenly, It's Spring ☐ Take a Letter, Darling ☐ Tammy and the Doctor ☐ These Are the Damned ☐ Wake Island

Carey, Michele ☐ Animals, The ☐ El Dorado ☐ In the Shadow of Kilimanjaro ☐ Live a Little, Love a Little ☐ Norliss Tapes, The ☐ Scandalous John

Carey, Philip ☐ Black Gold ☐ Calamity Jane ☐ Cattle Town ☐ Fighting Mad ☐ Great Sioux Massacre, The ☐ Gun Fury ☐ I Was a Communist for the FBI ☐ Inside the Walls of Folsom Prison ☐ Man Behind the Gun, The ☐ Monster ☐ Seven Minutes, The ☐ Time Travelers, The

Carey, Timothy ☐ Chesty Anderson, USN ☐ Fingerman ☐ Francis in the Haunted House ☐ Killing of a Chinese Bookie, The ☐ Revolt in the Big House ☐ Waterhole #3 ☐ White Witch Doctor

Carhart, Timothy ☐ Candyman: Farewell to the Flesh ☐ Manhattan Project, The ☐ Marie ☐ Pink Cadillac ☐ Quicksand: No Escape ☐ Sweet Liberty ☐ Thelma & Louise

Cariou, Len ☐ Four Seasons, The ☐ Killer in the Mirror ☐ Lady in White ☐ Little Night Music, A ☐ Madame X ☐ Sea Wolf, The

Carlin, George ☐ Bill & Ted's Bogus Journey ☐ Bill & Ted's Excellent Adventure ☐ Car Wash ☐ Justin Case ☐ Outrageous Fortune ☐ With Six You Get Eggroll

Carlisle, Kitty ☐ Here Is My Heart ☐ Murder at the Vanities ☐ Night at the Opera, A ☐ She Loves Me Not

Carlisle, Mary ☐ Beware, Spooks! ☐ College Humor ☐ Doctor Rhythm ☐ Dr. Rhythm ☐ Handy Andy ☐ Hold 'Em Navy ☐ Kind Lady ☐ Night Court ☐ One Frightened Night ☐ This Side of Heaven ☐ Tipp-Off Girls

Carlson, Richard ☐ All I Desire ☐ Back Street ☐ Behind Locked Doors ☐ Bengazi ☐ Beyond Tomorrow ☐ Blue Veil, The ☐ Creature From the Black Lagoon ☐ Duke of West Point, The ☐ Flat Top ☐ Ghost Breakers, The ☐ Helen Morgan Story, The ☐ Hold That Ghost ☐ It Came from Outer Space ☐ King Solomon's Mines ☐ Last Command, The ☐ Little Foxes, The ☐ Magnetic Monster, The ☐ Man from Down Under, The ☐ Maze, The ☐ Millionaire for Christy, A ☐ Power, The ☐ Presenting Lily Mars ☐ Retreat, Hell! ☐ Seminole ☐ So Well Remembered ☐ Sound of Fury, The ☐ Too Many Girls ☐ Valley of Gwangi ☐ White Cargo

Carmen, Julie ☐ Billy the Kid ☐ Finding the Way Home ☐ Fright Night, Part II ☐ Gore Vidal's Billy the Kid ☐ In the Mouth of Madness ☐ In the Mouth of Madness ☐ Kiss Me a Killer ☐ Last Plane Out ☐ Manhunt: Search for the Night Stalker ☐ Milagro Beanfield War, The ☐ Night of the Juggler

Carmet, Jean ☐ Alice, or the Last Escapade ☐ Black and White in Color ☐ Buffet Froid ☐ Elusive Corporal, The ☐ Investigation

Carmichael, Hoagy ☐ Belles on Their Toes ☐ Best Years of Our Lives, The ☐ Johnny Angel ☐ Las Vegas Story, The ☐ To Have and Have Not ☐ Young Man With a Horn

Carmichael, Ian ☐ Amorous Mr. Prawn, The ☐ Betrayed ☐ Brothers in Law ☐ Colditz Story ☐ From Beyond the Grave ☐ Happy Is the Bride ☐ I'm All Right, Jack ☐ Left Right and Center ☐ Lucky Jim ☐ Meet Mr. Lucifer ☐ Moment in Time, A ☐ School for Scoundrels

Carney, Art ☐ Alcatraz: The Whole Shocking Story ☐ Better Late Than Never ☐ Bitter Harvest ☐ Blue Yonder, The ☐ Death Scream ☐ Defiance ☐ Firestarter ☐ Going in Style ☐ Guide for the Married Man, A ☐ Harry and Tonto ☐ House Calls ☐ Izzy and Moe ☐ Katherine ☐ Last Action Hero ☐ Late Show, The ☐ Letters From Frank ☐ Miracle of the Heart: A Boys' Town Story ☐ Movie Movie ☐ Muppets Take Manhattan, The ☐ Naked Face, The ☐ Night Friend ☐ Night They Saved Christmas, The ☐ Ravagers ☐ Roadie ☐ Steel ☐ Sunburn ☐ Take this Job and Shove It ☐ Terrible Joe Moran ☐ W. W. and the Dixie Dancekings ☐ Won Ton Ton, the Dog Who Saved Hollywood ☐ Yellow Rolls-Royce, The

Carnovsky, Morris ☐ Address Unknown ☐ Cyrano de Bergerac ☐ Dead Reckoning ☐ Gambler, The ☐ Gun Crazy ☐ Life of Emile Zola, The ☐ Man-Eater of Kumaon ☐ Master Race, The ☐ Rhapsody in Blue ☐ Saigon ☐ View From the Bridge, A

Carol, Martine ☐ Action of the Tiger ☐ Adorable Creatures ☐ Battle of Austerlitz, The ☐ Beauties of the Night ☐ Counterfeiters of Paris, The ☐ French, They Are a Funny Race, The ☐ Lola Montes ☐ Ten Seconds to Hell ☐ Violent Summer

Caron, Leslie ☐ American in Paris, An ☐ Battle of Austerlitz, The ☐ Chandler ☐ Contract ☐ Courage Mountain ☐ Daddy Long Legs ☐ Damage ☐ Dangerous Moves ☐ Doctor's Dilemma ☐ Fanny ☐ Father Goose ☐ Funny Bones ☐ Gaby ☐ Gigi ☐ Glass Slipper, The ☐ Glory Alley ☐ Goldengirl ☐ Guns of Darkness ☐ Head of the Family, The ☐ Imperative ☐ Is Paris Burning? ☐ L-Shaped Room, The ☐ Lili ☐ Madron ☐ Man Who Lived at the Ritz, The ☐ Man Who Loved Women, The ☐ Man Who Understood Women, The ☐ Man with a Cloak, The ☐ Nicole ☐ Promise Her Anything ☐ Story of Three Loves, The ☐ Subterraneans, The ☐ Valentino ☐ Very Special Favor, A

Carradine, David ☐ Americana ☐ Animal Instincts ☐ Armed Response ☐ Bad Girls in the Movies ☐ Bad Seed, The ☐ Behind Enemy Lines ☐ Bird on a Wire ☐ Bound for Glory ☐ Boxcar Bertha ☐ Bus Riley's Back in Town ☐ Cannonball ☐ Circle of Iron ☐ Cloud Dancer ☐ Death Race 2000 ☐ Deathsport ☐ Fast Charlie, The Moonbeam Rider ☐ Field of Fire ☐ Film House Fever ☐ Future Force ☐ Future Zone ☐ Gambler Returns: The Luck of the Draw, The ☐ Gauguin the Savage ☐ Good Guys and the Bad Guys, The ☐ Gray Lady Down ☐ Heaven with a Gun ☐ High Noon, Part II: The Return of Will Kane ☐ Jealousy ☐ Karate Cop ☐ Kung Fu ☐ Kung Fu—

The Movie ☐ Lone Wolf McQuade ☐ Long Riders, The ☐ Macho Callahan ☐ Martial Law ☐ Maybe I'll Come Home in the Spring ☐ McMasters, The ☐ Midnight Fear ☐ Misfit Brigade, The ☐ Mr. Horn ☐ Night Children ☐ Oceans of Fire ☐ On the Line ☐ Q ☐ Ray Bradbury Chronicles: The Martian Episodes ☐ Serpent's Egg, The ☐ Sundown, The Vampire in Retreat

Carradine, John ☐ Adventures of Mark Twain, The ☐ Ali Baba Goes to Town ☐ Astro-Zombies ☐ Barbary Coast Gent ☐ Bees, The ☐ Billy the Kid vs. Dracula ☐ Black Sleep, The ☐ Blood and Sand ☐ Blood of Dracula's Castle ☐ Bluebeard ☐ Boogeyman, The ☐ Boxcar Bertha ☐ Bride of Frankenstein, The ☐ Brigham Young ☐ Buried Alive ☐ C-Man ☐ Captain Fury ☐ Captain Kidd ☐ Captains Courageous ☐ Captive Wild Woman ☐ Cat Creature, The ☐ Chad Hanna ☐ Cheyenne Autumn ☐ Cosmic Man, The ☐ Court Jester, The ☐ Danger—Love at Work ☐ Daniel Boone ☐ Death at Love House ☐ Drums Along the Mohawk ☐ Egyptian, The ☐ Everything You Always Wanted to Know About Sex (But Were Afraid to Ask) ☐ Face of Marble ☐ Fallen Angel ☐ Female Jungle, The ☐ Five Came Back ☐ Four Men and a Prayer ☐ Frankenstein Island ☐ Frontier Marshal ☐ Gallery of Horror ☐ Gangway for Tomorrow ☐ Garden of Allah, The ☐ Gateway ☐ Gatling Gun, The ☐ Goliath Awaits ☐ Good Guys and the Bad Guys, The ☐ Grapes of Wrath, The ☐ Gun Riders ☐ Half-Human ☐ Hell Ship Mutiny ☐ Hell's Bloody Devils ☐ Hillbillys in a Haunted House ☐ Hitler's Madman ☐ Hollywood Ghost Stories ☐ Horrors of the Red Planet ☐ Hostage, The ☐ Hound of the Baskervilles, The ☐ House of Dracula ☐ House of Frankenstein ☐ House of Seven Corpses, The ☐ House of the Black Death ☐ House of the Long Shadows ☐ Howling, The ☐ Hurricane, The ☐ I Escaped from the Gestapo ☐ I'll Give a Million ☐ Ice Pirates, The ☐ Incredible Petrified World, The ☐ Inspector General, The ☐ International Settlement ☐ Invisible Invaders ☐ Invisible Man's Revenge, The ☐ Isle of Forgotten Sins ☐ Jesse James ☐ Johnny Guitar ☐ Kentucky Moonshine ☐ Kidnapped ☐ Last Gangster, The ☐ Last Hurrah, The ☐ Love Under Fire ☐ Man Hunt ☐ Man Who Shot Liberty Valance, The ☐ Mary of Scotland ☐ Mary, Mary, Blood Mary ☐ McMasters, The ☐ Monster ☐ Monster Club, The ☐ Monster in the Closet ☐ Mr. Moto's Last Warning ☐ Mummy's Ghost, The ☐ Munster, Go Home ☐ Nancy Steel Is Missing ☐ Nesting, The ☐ Night Strangler, The ☐ Nocturna ☐ Of Human Hearts ☐ Patsy, The ☐ Prisoner of Shark Island, The ☐ Return of Frank James, The ☐ Return of the Ape Man ☐ Richard ☐ Satan's Cheerleaders ☐ Secret of NIMH, The ☐ Sentinel, The ☐ Seven Minutes, The ☐ Sex Kittens Go to College ☐ Shock Waves ☐ Showdown at Boot Hill ☐ Silver Spurs ☐ Son of Fury ☐ Stagecoach ☐ Superchick ☐ Swamp Water ☐ Tarzan the Magnificent ☐ Thank You, Mr. Moto ☐ This Is My Affair ☐ True Story of Jesse James, The ☐ Under Two Flags ☐ Vampire Hookers ☐ Waterfront ☐ Western Union ☐ White Buffalo, The ☐ Winterset

Carradine, Keith ☐ Almost Perfect Affair, An ☐ Backfire ☐ Ballad of the Sad Cafe, The ☐ Blackout ☐ Capone ☐ Chiefs ☐ Choose Me ☐ Cold Feet ☐ CrissCross ☐ Daddy's Dyin'. . . Who's Got the Will? ☐ Duellists, The ☐ Emperor of the North, The ☐ Eye on the Sparrow ☐ Forgotten, The ☐ Godchild, The ☐ Gunfight, A ☐ Half a Lifetime ☐ Idaho Transfer ☐ Inquiry, The ☐ Judgment ☐ Kung Fu ☐ Long Riders, The ☐ Lumière ☐ Man on a String ☐ Maria's Lovers ☐ McCabe and Mrs. Miller ☐ Moderns, The ☐ Nashville ☐ Old Boyfriends ☐ Payoff ☐ Pretty Baby ☐ Rumor of War, A ☐ Shrieking, The ☐ Southern Comfort ☐ Stones for Ibarra ☐ Thieves Like Us ☐ Trouble in Mind ☐ Welcome to L.A. ☐ Winner Never Quits, A

Carradine, Robert ☐ All's Fair ☐ As Is ☐ Big Red One, The ☐ Blackout ☐ Buy & Cell ☐ Clarence ☐ Coming Home ☐ Conspiracy—The Trial of the Chicago 8 ☐ Heartaches ☐ Incident, The ☐ Jackson County Jail ☐ Joyride ☐ Long Riders, The ☐ Massacre at Central High ☐ Monte Carlo ☐ Number One with a Bullet ☐ Pom-Pom Girls ☐ Revenge of the Nerds ☐ Revenge of the Nerds 2: Nerds in Paradise ☐ Revenge of the Nerds 3: The Next Generation ☐ Rude Awakening ☐ Somebody Has to Shoot the Picture

Carrera, Barbara ☐ Condorman ☐ Embryo ☐ I, the Jury ☐ Island of Dr. Moreau, The ☐ Lone Wolf McQuade ☐ Love at Stake ☐ Loverboy ☐ Masada ☐ Master Gunfighter, The ☐ Never Say Never Again ☐ Point of Impact ☐ When Time Ran Out . . . ☐ Wicked Stepmother

Carrere, Tia ☐ Aloha Summer ☐ Fatal Mission ☐ Showdown in Little Tokyo ☐ Wayne's World ☐ Wayne's World 2

Carrey, Jim ☐ Ace Ventura: Pet Detective ☐ Club Med ☐ Dumb and Dumber ☐ Earth Girls Are Easy ☐ Mask, The ☐ Once Bitten

Carrillo, Leo ☐ 20 Mule Team ☐ American Empire ☐ Barnacle Bill ☐ Blockade ☐ City Streets ☐ Flirting with Fate ☐ Four Frightened People ☐ Fugitive, The ☐ Gay Desperado, The ☐ History Is Made at Night ☐ Horror Island ☐ I Promise to Pay ☐ If You Could Only Cook ☐ In Caliente ☐ It Had to Happen ☐ Love Me Forever ☐ Manhattan Melodrama ☐ Manhattan Merry-Go-Round ☐ Parachute Jumper ☐ Viva Villa! ☐ Wyoming

Carroll, Diahann ☐ Carmen Jones ☐ Claudine ☐ Five Heartbeats, The ☐ From the Dead of

Night ☐ Goodbye Again ☐ Hurry Sundown ☐ I Know Why the Caged Bird Sings ☐ Paris Blues ☐ Porgy and Bess ☐ Sister, Sister

Carroll, Leo G. ☐ Bahama Passage ☐ Casino Murder Case ☐ Christmas Carol, A ☐ Clive of India ☐ Desert Fox, The ☐ Enchantment ☐ Father of the Bride ☐ First Legion, The ☐ From Nashville with Music ☐ Forever Amber ☐ House on 92nd Street ☐ Murder on a Honeymoon ☐ North by Northwest ☐ Sadie McKee ☐ Snows of Kilimanjaro, The ☐ So Evil My Love ☐ Song of Love ☐ Spellbound ☐ Strangers on a Train ☐ Tarantula ☐ Tower of London, The ☐ Treasure of the Golden Condor ☐ Young Bess

Carroll, Madeleine ☐ 39 Steps, The ☐ Bahama Passage ☐ Blockade ☐ Cafe Society ☐ Case Against Mrs. Ames, The ☐ Fan, The ☐ General Died at Dawn, The ☐ High Fury ☐ Honeymoon in Bali ☐ I Was a Spy ☐ Innocent Affair, An ☐ Lloyd's of London ☐ My Favorite Blonde ☐ My Son, My Son ☐ Northwest Mounted Police ☐ On the Avenue ☐ One Night in Lisbon ☐ Prisoner of Zenda, The ☐ Secret Agent ☐ Young Woodley

Carroll, Nancy ☐ Broken Lullaby ☐ Follow Thru ☐ Hot Saturday ☐ Kiss Before the Mirror, The ☐ Laughter ☐ Paramount on Parade ☐ Scarlet Dawn ☐ Shopworn Angel ☐ There Goes My Heart ☐ Transatlantic Merry-Go-Round

Carroll, Pat ☐ Brothers O'Toole, The ☐ Little Mermaid, The ☐ Tropic of Desire ☐ With Six You Get Eggroll

Carson, Jack ☐ Ain't Misbehavin' ☐ Always Together ☐ April Showers ☐ Arsenic and Old Lace ☐ Blood Beast from Outer Space ☐ Blues in the Night ☐ Bottom of the Bottle, The ☐ Bramble Bush, The ☐ Bride Came C.O.D., The ☐ Bright Leaf ☐ Carefree ☐ Cat on a Hot Tin Roof ☐ Dangerous When Wet ☐ Destry Rides Again ☐ Doughgirls, The ☐ Gentleman Jim ☐ Good Humor Man, The ☐ Groom Wore Spurs, The ☐ Hard Way, The ☐ Having Wonderful Time ☐ I Take This Woman ☐ It's a Great Feeling ☐ John Loves Mary ☐ King of the Roaring Twenties—The Story of Arnold Rothstein ☐ Larceny, Inc ☐ Love Crazy ☐ Lucky Partners ☐ Magnificent Roughnecks ☐ Maid's Night Out ☐ Make Your Own Bed ☐ Male Animal, The ☐ Mildred Pierce ☐ Mr. and Mrs. Smith ☐ My Dream Is Yours ☐ Navy Blues ☐ One More Tomorrow ☐ Phffft! ☐ Princess O'Rourke ☐ Queen of the Mob ☐ Rally 'Round the Flag, Boys! ☐ Red Garters ☐ Romance on the High Seas ☐ Saint in New York, The ☐ Sammy, the Way-Out Seal ☐ Shine On, Harvest Moon ☐ Stand-In ☐ Star Is Born, A ☐ Strawberry Blonde, The ☐ Tarnished Angels, The ☐ Time, the Place and the Girl, The ☐ Two Guys From Milwaukee ☐ Two Guys From Texas ☐ Typhoon

Carter, Helena Bonham ☐ Getting It Right ☐ Hamlet ☐ Hazard of Hearts, A ☐ Howards End ☐ Lady Jane ☐ Mary Shelley's Frankenstein ☐ Mask, The ☐ Room with a View, A ☐ Where Angels Fear to Tread

Carter, Janis ☐ Fighting Guardsman ☐ Flying Leathernecks ☐ Framed ☐ Half-Breed, The ☐ I Love Trouble ☐ I Married a Communist ☐ Mark of the Whistler ☐ Miss Grant Takes Richmond ☐ Missing Juror, The ☐ My Forbidden Past ☐ Night Editor ☐ Notorious Lone Wolf, The ☐ One Mysterious Night ☐ One Way to Love ☐ Woman of Distinction, A

Cartwright, Veronica ☐ Candyman: Farewell to the Flesh ☐ Flight of the Navigator ☐ Guyana Tragedy: The Story of Jim Jones ☐ Hitler's Daughter ☐ Invasion of the Body Snatchers ☐ Kid from Not So Big, The ☐ Man Trouble ☐ Mirror, Mirror 2: Raven Dance ☐ My Man Adam ☐ Nightmares ☐ One Man's Way ☐ Spencer's Mountain ☐ Wisdom ☐ Witches of Eastwick, The

Caruso, David ☐ Blue City ☐ First Blood ☐ King of New York ☐ Mad Dog and Glory ☐ Thief of Hearts

Carvey, Dana ☐ Clean Slate ☐ Moving ☐ Opportunity Knocks ☐ Road to Wellville, The ☐ Tough Guys ☐ Trapped in Paradise ☐ Wayne's World ☐ Wayne's World 2

Casey, Bernie ☐ Brothers ☐ Chains of Gold ☐ Cleopatra Jones ☐ Cornbread, Earl and Me ☐ Dr. Black and Mr. Hyde ☐ Fantastic World of D.C. Collins, The ☐ I'm Gonna Git You Sucka ☐ It Happened at Lakewood Manor ☐ Man Who Fell to Earth, The ☐ Mary Jane Harper Cried Last Night ☐ Maurie ☐ Panic on the 5:22 ☐ Sharky's Machine ☐ Sophisticated Gents, The

Cash, Johnny ☐ Baron and the Kid, The ☐ Gospel Road, The ☐ Gunfight, A ☐ Hootenanny Hoot ☐ Johnny Cash: The Man, His World, His Music ☐ Last Days of Frank and Jesse James, The ☐ Murder in Coweta County ☐ Stagecoach

Cassavetes, John ☐ Affair in Havana ☐ Brass Target, The ☐ Capone ☐ Crime in the Streets ☐ Dirty Dozen, The ☐ Edge of the City ☐ Flesh & Blood ☐ Fury, The ☐ Husbands ☐ Incubus, The ☐ Killers, The ☐ Love Streams ☐ Machine Gun McCain ☐ Marvin and Tige ☐ Mikey and Nicky ☐ Night Holds Terror, The ☐ Opening Night ☐ Rosemary's Baby ☐ Saddle the Wind ☐ Tempest ☐ Too Late Blues ☐ Two Minute Warning ☐ Whose Life Is It Anyway?

Cassavetes, Nick ☐ Body of Influence ☐ Quiet Cool ☐ Sins of the Night ☐ Under the Gun ☐ Wraith, The

Cassel, Jean-Pierre ☐ Alice ☐ Anyone Can Play ☐ Between Heaven and Earth ☐ Discreet Charm of the Bourgeoisie, The ☐ Elusive Corporal, The ☐ Fatal Image, The ☐ Five Day Lover ☐ High Infidelity ☐ Is

Paris Burning? ☐ Killing Game, The ☐ La Vie Continue ☐ Love at the Top ☐ Maid, The ☐ Murder on the Orient Express ☐ No Time for Breakfast ☐ Notorious ☐ Nudo di Donna ☐ Those Magnificent Men in Their Flying Machines ☐ Three Musketeers, The ☐ Twist, The

Cassel, Seymour ☐ Black Oak Conspiracy ☐ Death Game ☐ Eye of the Tiger ☐ Face of a Stranger ☐ Faces ☐ In the Soup ☐ Killing of a Chinese Bookie, The ☐ Minnie and Moskowitz ☐ Revolutionary, The ☐ Trouble Bound ☐ White Fang

Cassidy, Jack ☐ Bunny O'Hare ☐ Cockeyed Cowboys of Calico County ☐ Columbo: Murder By the Book ☐ Eiger Sanction, The ☐ W.C. Fields and Me

Cassidy, Joanna ☐ 1969 ☐ Bank Shot ☐ Barbarians at the Gate ☐ Don't Tell Mom the Babysitter's Dead ☐ Father's Revenge, A ☐ Fourth Protocol, The ☐ Girl of the Limberlost, A ☐ Glove, The ☐ Invitation to Hell ☐ Live From Death Row ☐ May Wine ☐ Night Games ☐ Nightmare at Bittercreek ☐ Package, The ☐ Perfect Family ☐ Tommyknockers, The ☐ Under Fire ☐ Where the Heart Is ☐ Who Framed Roger Rabbit

Castelnuovo, Nino ☐ Camille 2000 ☐ Five Man Army, The ☐ Loving in the Rain ☐ Umbrellas of Cherbourg, The

Castle, Peggie ☐ 99 River Street ☐ Back From the Dead ☐ Beginning of the End ☐ Finger Man, The ☐ Fingerman ☐ Harem Girl ☐ Hell's Crossroads ☐ Invasion, U.S.A. ☐ Jesse James's Women ☐ Oklahoma Woman, The ☐ Overland Pacific ☐ Payment on Demand ☐ Seven Hills of Rome, The ☐ Son of Belle Starr ☐ Two Gun Lady

Cates, Phoebe ☐ Bodies, Rest & Motion ☐ Bright Lights, Big City ☐ Date with an Angel ☐ Drop Dead Fred ☐ Fast Times at Ridgemont High ☐ Gremlins ☐ Gremlins 2—The New Batch ☐ Heart of Dixie ☐ Paradise ☐ Princess Caraboo ☐ Private School ☐ Shag, The Movie

Catlett, Walter ☐ Every Day's a Holiday ☐ Every Night at Eight ☐ Father Makes Good ☐ Father Takes the Air ☐ Father's Wild Game ☐ Florodora Girl, The ☐ Front Page, The ☐ Henry, the Rainmaker ☐ I Love a Bandleader ☐ It Started with Eve ☐ It's Tough to Be Famous ☐ Maisie Gets Her Man ☐ Manpower ☐ Mr. Deeds Goes to Town ☐ My Gal Sal ☐ Varsity Show ☐ Wake Up and Live ☐ Wild Man of Borneo, The

Cattrall, Kim ☐ Bastard, The ☐ Big Trouble in Little China ☐ Bonfire of the Vanities, The ☐ City Limits ☐ Double Vision ☐ Gossip Columnist, The ☐ Honeymoon Academy ☐ Mannequin ☐ Masquerade ☐ Midnight Crossing ☐ Miracle in the Wilderness ☐ Night Rider, The ☐ Police Academy ☐ Porky's ☐ Rebels, The ☐ Return of the Musketeers, The ☐ Smokescreen ☐ Split Second ☐ Star Trek VI: The Undiscovered Country ☐ Ticket to Heaven ☐ Turk 182! ☐ Wild Palms

Chakiris, George ☐ 633 Squadron ☐ Bebo's Girl ☐ Big Cube, The ☐ Day the Hot Line Got Hot, The ☐ Diamond Head ☐ Flight from Ashiya ☐ Kings of the Sun ☐ McGuire, Go Home! ☐ Pale Blood ☐ West Side Story ☐ Young Girls of Rochefort, The

Chamberlain, Richard ☐ Allan Quartermain And The Lost City Of Gold ☐ Bourne Identity, The ☐ Casanova ☐ Count of Monte Cristo, The ☐ F. Scott Fitzgerald and "The Last of the Belles" ☐ Four Musketeers, The ☐ Joy in the Morning ☐ Julius Caesar ☐ King Solomon's Mines ☐ Lady Caroline Lamb ☐ Last Wave, The ☐ Madwoman of Chaillot, The ☐ Man in the Iron Mask ☐ Music Lovers, The ☐ Night of the Hunter ☐ Petulia ☐ Return of the Musketeers, The ☐ Shogun ☐ Slipper and the Rose, The ☐ Swarm, The ☐ Thorn Birds, The ☐ Towering Inferno, The

Champion, Gower ☐ Give a Girl a Break ☐ Lovely to Look At ☐ Mr. Music ☐ Show Boat ☐ Three for the Show

Champion, Marge ☐ Cockeyed Cowboys of Calico County ☐ Everything I Have Is Yours ☐ Give a Girl a Break ☐ Lovely to Look At ☐ Mr. Music ☐ Party, The ☐ Show Boat ☐ Swimmer, The ☐ Three for the Show ☐ Jupiter's Darling

Chandler, Jeff ☐ Abandoned ☐ Away All Boats ☐ Battle at Apache Pass, The ☐ Because of You ☐ Bird of Paradise ☐ Broken Arrow ☐ Deported ☐ Drango ☐ East of Sumatra ☐ Female on the Beach ☐ Flame of Araby ☐ Foxfire ☐ Great Sioux Uprising ☐ Iron Man, The ☐ Jayhawkers, The ☐ Jeanne Eagels ☐ Johnny O'Clock ☐ Lady Takes a Flyer, The ☐ Man in the Shadow ☐ Merrill's Marauders ☐ Pillars of the Sky ☐ Plunderers, The ☐ Raw Wind in Eden ☐ Return to Peyton Place ☐ Sign of the Pagan ☐ Spoilers, The ☐ Stranger in My Arms ☐ Sword in the Desert ☐ Ten Seconds to Hell ☐ Thunder in the Sun ☐ Two Flags West ☐ War Arrow ☐ Yankee Pasha

Chaney, Jr., Lon ☐ Abbott and Costello Meet Frankenstein ☐ Albuquerque ☐ Alligator People, The ☐ Apache Uprising ☐ Behave Yourself ☐ Big House, U.S.A. ☐ Bird of Paradise ☐ Black Castle, The ☐ Black Pirates, The ☐ Black Spurs ☐ Boy from Oklahoma, The ☐ Bride of the Gorilla ☐ Buckskin ☐ Bushwackers, The ☐ Calling Dr. Death ☐ Captain China ☐ Cobra Woman ☐ Daniel Boone, Trail Blazer ☐ Defiant Ones, The ☐ Face of the Screaming Werewolf ☐ Frankenstein Meets the Wolf Man ☐ Ghost Catchers ☐ Ghost of Frankenstein, The ☐ Haunted Palace, The ☐ Here Come the Co-eds ☐ High Noon ☐ Hillbillys In a Haunted House ☐ House of Dracula ☐ House of Frankenstein ☐ House of the Black Death ☐ Indestructible Man, The ☐ Jivaro ☐ Man Made Monster ☐ Mummy's

Curse, The ☐ Mummy's Ghost, The ☐ Mummy's Tomb, The ☐ My Favorite Brunette ☐ Northwest Mounted Police ☐ Of Mice and Men ☐ Once a Thief ☐ One Million B.C. ☐ Passion ☐ San Antonio Rose ☐ Son of Dracula ☐ Weird Woman ☐ Wife, Doctor and Nurse ☐ Wolf Man, The

Chaney, Lon ☐ Black Sleep, The ☐ Eyes of the Underworld ☐ Frozen Ghost ☐ Gallery of Horror ☐ He Who Gets Slapped ☐ Hunchback of Notre Dame, The ☐ Indian Fighter, The ☐ Johnny Reno ☐ London After Midnight ☐ Manfish ☐ Monster, The ☐ Nomads of the North ☐ Not as a Stranger ☐ Oliver Twist ☐ Phantom of the Opera, The ☐ Springfield Rifle ☐ Stage to Thunder Rock ☐ Unholy Three, The ☐ Unholy Three, The ☐ West of Zanzibar

Chan, Jackie ☐ Big Brawl, The ☐ Deadliest Art, The: The Best of the Martial Arts Films, The ☐ Dragons Forever ☐ Fantasy Mission Force ☐ Fearless Hyena, The ☐ Fearless Hyena, The—Part 2 ☐ Half a Loaf of Kung Fu ☐ New Fist of Fury ☐ Ninja Thunderbolt ☐ Painted Faces ☐ Police Force ☐ Protector, The ☐ Snake Fist Fighter ☐ Spiritual Kung Fu ☐ To Kill With Intrigue ☐ Young Tiger, The

Channing, Carol ☐ Alice in Wonderland ☐ First Traveling Saleslady, The ☐ Happily Ever After ☐ Shinbone Alley ☐ Skiddoo ☐ Thoroughly Modern Millie ☐ Thumbelina

Channing, Stockard ☐ Big Bus, The ☐ Cheap Detective, The ☐ Echoes in the Darkness ☐ Fish that Saved Pittsburgh, The ☐ Fortune, The ☐ Girl Most Likely To . . ., The ☐ Grease ☐ Heartburn ☐ Married to It ☐ Meet the Applegates ☐ Not My Kid ☐ Perfect Witness ☐ Six Degrees of Separation ☐ Staying Together

Chaplin, Charlie ☐ Charlie Chaplin Carnival ☐ Chase Me Charlie ☐ Circus, The/A Day's Pleasure ☐ City Lights ☐ Days of Thrills and Laughter ☐ Gaslight Follies ☐ Gold Rush, The ☐ Great Dictator, The ☐ His Prehistoric Past/The Bank ☐ Kid, The ☐ King in New York, A ☐ Limelight ☐ Modern Times ☐ Monsieur Verdoux ☐ Tillie's Punctured Romance ☐ When Comedy Was King

Chaplin, Geraldine ☐ Ana and the Wolves ☐ Bolero ☐ Buffalo Bill and the Indians ☐ Chaplin ☐ Children, The ☐ Cria! ☐ Doctor Zhivago ☐ Duel of Hearts ☐ Hawaiians, The ☐ I Killed Rasputin ☐ Innocent Bystanders ☐ Le Voyage en Douce ☐ Life Is a Bed of Roses ☐ Love on the Ground ☐ Mama Turns 100 ☐ Moderns, The ☐ Nashville ☐ Return of the Musketeers, The ☐ Roseland ☐ Three Musketeers, The ☐ Wedding, A ☐ Welcome to L.A. ☐ Z.P.G.

Chapman, Graham ☐ And Now for Something Completely Different ☐ Monty Python and the Holy Grail ☐ Monty Python Live at the Hollywood Bowl ☐ Monty Python's Flying Circus—Vol. 1 ☐ Monty Python's Life of Brian ☐ Monty Python's Parrot Sketch Not Included ☐ Monty Python's The Meaning of Life ☐ Odd Job, The ☐ Secret Policeman's Other Ball, The ☐ Yellowbeard

Chapman, Marguerite ☐ Amazing Transparent Man, The ☐ Coroner Creek ☐ Counter-Attack ☐ Destroyer ☐ Flight to Mars ☐ Green Promise, The ☐ Kansas Raiders ☐ Man Bait ☐ One Dangerous Night ☐ One Way to Love ☐ Pardon My Past ☐ Spy Smasher

Charisse, Cyd ☐ Band Wagon, The ☐ Black Tights ☐ Brigadoon ☐ Deep in My Heart ☐ East Side, West Side ☐ Fiesta ☐ Five Golden Hours ☐ Harvey Girls, The ☐ It's Always Fair Weather ☐ Kissing Bandit, The ☐ Mark of the Renegade ☐ Maroc 7 ☐ Meet Me in Las Vegas ☐ On an Island with You ☐ Party Girl ☐ Silencers, The ☐ Silk Stockings ☐ Singin' in the Rain ☐ Tension ☐ Three Wise Fools ☐ Till the Clouds Roll By ☐ Twilight for the Gods ☐ Two Weeks in Another Town ☐ Unfinished Dance, The

Charleson, Ian ☐ Car Trouble ☐ Chariots of Fire ☐ Codename: Kyril ☐ Gandhi ☐ Greystoke: The Legend of Tarzan, Lord of the Apes ☐ Terror at the Opera

Charles, Ray ☐ Ballad in Blue ☐ Big T.N.T. Show, The ☐ Blues Brothers, The ☐ Fats Domino and Friends—Immortal Keyboards of Rock & Roll ☐ Limit Up

Chase, Chevy ☐ Caddyshack ☐ Caddyshack II ☐ Cops and Robbersons ☐ Deal of the Century ☐ Fletch ☐ Fletch Lives ☐ Foul Play ☐ Funny Farm ☐ Groove Tube, The ☐ L.A. Story ☐ Man of the House ☐ Memoirs of an Invisible Man ☐ Modern Problems ☐ National Lampoon's Christmas Vacation ☐ National Lampoon's European Vacation ☐ National Lampoon's Vacation ☐ Nothing But Trouble ☐ Oh, Heavenly Dog! ☐ Seems Like Old Times ☐ Sesame Street Presents Follow That Bird ☐ Spies Like Us ☐ Three Amigos! ☐ Tunnelvision ☐ Under the Rainbow

Chase, Ilka ☐ Animal Kingdom, The ☐ Big Knife, The ☐ Fast and Loose ☐ Florodora Girl, The ☐ Johnny Dark ☐ Miss Tatlock's Millions ☐ No Time for Love ☐ Now, Voyager

Chatterjee, Soumitra ☐ Days and Nights in the Forest ☐ Devi ☐ Distant Thunder ☐ Enemy of the People, An ☐ Expedition, The ☐ Home and the World, The ☐ Two Daughters ☐ World of Apu, The

Chen, Joan ☐ Blood of Heroes, The ☐ Deadlock ☐ Golden Gate ☐ Heaven and Earth ☐ Killing Beach, The ☐ Last Emperor, The ☐ On Deadly Ground ☐ Tai-Pan ☐ Twin Peaks

Cher ☐ Chastity ☐ Come Back to the Five and Dime, Jimmy Dean, Jimmy Dean ☐ Good Times ☐ Mask ☐ Mermaids ☐ Moonstruck ☐ Silkwood ☐ Suspect ☐ Witches of Eastwick, The

Chevalier, Maurice ☐ Aristocats, The ☐ Bedtime Story, A ☐ Big Pond, The ☐ Break the News ☐ Breath of Scandal, A ☐ Can-Can ☐ Count Your Blessings ☐ Fanny ☐ Folies Bergere ☐ Gigi ☐ I'd Rather Be Rich ☐ In Search of the Castaways ☐ Jessica ☐ Love in the Afternoon ☐ Love Me Tonight ☐ Love Parade, The ☐ Man About Town ☐ Merry Widow, The ☐ Monkeys, Go Home! ☐ My Seven Little Sins ☐ New Kind of Love, A ☐ One Hour with You ☐ Panic Button ☐ Paramount on Parade ☐ Playboy of Paris ☐ Royal Affair, A ☐ Smiling Lieutenant, The ☐ With a Smile

Chong, Rae Dawn ☐ Amazon ☐ American Flyers ☐ Badge of the Assassin ☐ Beat Street ☐ Borrower, The ☐ Cheech & Chong's The Corsican Brothers ☐ Choose Me ☐ City Limits ☐ Commando ☐ Common Bonds ☐ Curiosity Kills ☐ Denial ☐ Far Out Man ☐ Fear City ☐ Hideaway ☐ Principal, The ☐ Prison Stories: Women on the Inside ☐ Quest for Fire ☐ Soul Man ☐ Squeeze, The ☐ Tales From the Darkside: The Movie ☐ Time Runner

Chong, Tommy ☐ After Hours ☐ Cheech & Chong's Next Movie ☐ Cheech & Chong's Nice Dreams ☐ Cheech & Chong's The Corsican Brothers ☐ Cheech & Chong—Still Smokin' ☐ Cheech & Chong—Up in Smoke ☐ Cheech and Chong—Get Out of My Room ☐ Far Out Man ☐ FernGully . . . The Last Rainforest ☐ Yellowbeard

Christie, Julie ☐ Billy Liar ☐ Crooks Anonymous ☐ Dadah Is Death ☐ Darling ☐ Demon Seed ☐ Doctor Zhivago ☐ Don't Look Now ☐ Fahrenheit 451 ☐ Far from the Madding Crowd ☐ Fast Lady, The ☐ Fools of Fortune ☐ Go-Between, The ☐ Heat and Dust ☐ Heaven Can Wait ☐ In Search of Gregory ☐ McCabe and Mrs. Miller ☐ Memoirs of a Survivor ☐ Miss Mary ☐ Petulia ☐ Power ☐ Railway Station Man, The ☐ Return of the Soldier, The ☐ Secret Obsession ☐ Shampoo ☐ Sins of the Fathers ☐ Young Cassidy

Christopher, Dennis ☐ Breaking Away ☐ California Dreaming ☐ Don't Cry, It's Only Thunder ☐ Fade to Black ☐ False Arrest ☐ Jake Speed ☐ September 30, 1955 ☐ Stephen King's It

Ciannelli, Eduardo ☐ Dillinger ☐ Flight for Freedom ☐ Fugitive Lady ☐ Mambo ☐ Marked Woman ☐ Mask of Dimitrios, The ☐ Monster from Green Hell ☐ Mummy's Hand, The ☐ Mysterious Doctor Satan ☐ Scoundrel, The ☐ Secret of Santa Vittoria, The ☐ Strange Cargo ☐ Stranger's Hand, The ☐ Winterset

Cilento, Diane ☐ Admirable Crichton, The ☐ Agony and the Ecstasy, The ☐ Angel Who Pawned Her Harp, The ☐ Boy Who Had Everything, The ☐ Hitler: The Last Ten Days ☐ Hombre ☐ I Thank a Fool ☐ Naked Edge, The ☐ Negatives ☐ Passage Home ☐ Rattle of a Simple Man, The ☐ Third Secret, The ☐ Tom Jones ☐ Truth About Women, The ☐ Wicker Man, The ☐ Z.P.G.

Claire, Ina ☐ Claudia ☐ Greeks Had a Word for Them, The ☐ Ninotchka ☐ Royal Family of Broadway, The

Clark, Candy ☐ Amateur Night at the Dixie Bar and Grill ☐ American Graffiti ☐ Amityville 3D ☐ Big Sleep, The ☐ Blue Thunder ☐ Citizens Band ☐ Fat City ☐ Hambone and Hillie ☐ James Dean ☐ Johnny Belinda ☐ Man Who Fell to Earth, The ☐ More American Graffiti ☐ National Lampoon Goes to the Movies ☐ Original Intent ☐ Q

Clarke, Mae ☐ Fast Workers ☐ Frankenstein (Restored) ☐ Front Page, The ☐ Great Guy ☐ Hats Off ☐ Impatient Maiden, The ☐ King of the Rocket Men ☐ Lady Killer ☐ Man with Two Faces, The ☐ Nana ☐ Night World ☐ Penguin Pool Murder, The ☐ Penthouse ☐ Public Enemy, The ☐ This Side of Heaven ☐ Voice in the Mirror, The ☐ Women's Prison

Clark, Fred ☐ Abbott and Costello Meet The Keystone Kops ☐ Auntie Mame ☐ Bells Are Ringing ☐ Caddy, The ☐ Cry of the City ☐ Don't Go Near the Water ☐ Eagle and the Hawk, The ☐ Fuzzy Pink Nightgown, The ☐ Hazard ☐ Horse in the Gray Flannel Suit, The ☐ I Sailed to Tahiti with an All Girl Crew ☐ It Started with a Kiss ☐ Jackpot, The ☐ Mating Game, The ☐ Miracle in the Rain ☐ Ride the Pink Horse ☐ Skiddoo ☐ Solid Gold Cadillac, The ☐ Visit to a Small Planet ☐ Younger Brothers, The ☐ Zotz!

Clark, Matt ☐ Children Nobody Wanted, The ☐ Emperor of the North, The ☐ Execution of Private Slovik, The ☐ Frozen Assets ☐ Melvin Purvis-G-Man ☐ Out of the Darkness ☐ Return to Oz ☐ Tuff Turf

Clark, Petula ☐ Dance Hall ☐ Finian's Rainbow ☐ Goodbye, Mr. Chips ☐ Happiness of Three Women, The ☐ Made in Heaven ☐ Promoter, The ☐ Runaway Bus, The ☐ Vice Versa

Clark, Susan ☐ Amelia Earhart ☐ Apple Dumpling Gang, The ☐ Astronaut, The ☐ Babe ☐ Banning ☐ Choice, The ☐ City on Fire ☐ Colossus: The Forbin Project ☐ Coogan's Bluff ☐ Jimmy B. & Andre ☐ Madigan ☐ McNaughton's Daughter ☐ Midnight Man, The ☐ Night Moves ☐ Nobody's Perfekt ☐ North Avenue Irregulars, The ☐ Promises in the Dark ☐ Showdown ☐ Skin Game ☐ Skullduggery ☐ Tell Them Willie Boy Is Here ☐ Valdez Is Coming

Clayburgh, Jill ☐ First Monday in October ☐ Gable and Lombard ☐ Griffin and Phoenix: A Love Story ☐ Hanna K. ☐ Honor Thy Father and Mother: The True Story of the Menendez Murders ☐ Hustling ☐ I'm Dancing as Fast as I Can ☐ It's My Turn ☐ Luna ☐ Miles to Go ☐ Naked in New York ☐ Rich in Love ☐ Semi-Tough ☐ Shy People ☐ Silver Streak ☐ Starting Over ☐ Terminal Man, The

☐ Thief Who Came to Dinner, The ☐ Unmarried Woman, An ☐ Wedding Party, The ☐ Whispers in the Dark

Cleese, John ☐ American Tail: Fievel Goes West, An ☐ And Now for Something Completely Different ☐ Bliss of Mrs. Blossom, The ☐ Clockwise ☐ Erik the Viking ☐ Fawlty Towers—The Complete Set ☐ Fish Called Wanda, A ☐ Great Muppet Caper, The ☐ Interlude ☐ Monty Python and the Holy Grail ☐ Monty Python Live at the Hollywood Bowl ☐ Monty Python's Flying Circus—Vol. 1 ☐ Monty Python's Life of Brian ☐ Monty Python's Parrot Sketch Not Included ☐ Monty Python's The Meaning of Life ☐ Privates on Parade ☐ Secret Policeman's Other Ball, The ☐ Silverado ☐ Splitting Heirs ☐ Strange Case Of The End of Civilization As We Know It ☐ Swan Princess, The ☐ Time Bandits ☐ Yellowbeard

Clift, Montgomery ☐ Big Lift, The ☐ Defector, The ☐ Freud ☐ From Here to Eternity ☐ Heiress, The ☐ I Confess ☐ Indiscretion of an American Wife ☐ Judgment at Nuremberg ☐ Lonelyhearts ☐ Misfits, The ☐ Place in the Sun, A ☐ Raintree County ☐ Red River ☐ Search, The ☐ Suddenly, Last Summer ☐ Wild River ☐ Young Lions, The

Clive, Colin ☐ Bride of Frankenstein, The ☐ Christopher Strong ☐ Clive of India ☐ Frankenstein (Restored) ☐ Girl from 10th Avenue, The ☐ History Is Made at Night ☐ Jane Eyre ☐ Journey's End ☐ Key, The ☐ Mad Love ☐ Man Who Broke the Bank at Monte Carlo, The ☐ One More River

Clooney, Rosemary ☐ Deep in My Heart ☐ Here Come the Girls ☐ Red Garters ☐ White Christmas

Close, Glenn ☐ Big Chill, The ☐ Dangerous Liaisons ☐ Fatal Attraction ☐ Hamlet ☐ House of the Spirits ☐ Immediate Family ☐ Jagged Edge ☐ Maxie ☐ Meeting Venus ☐ Natural, The ☐ Paper, The ☐ Reversal of Fortune ☐ Sarah, Plain and Tall ☐ Skylark ☐ Something About Amelia ☐ Stone Boy, The ☐ Stones for Ibarra ☐ Too Far to Go ☐ World According to Garp, The

Cobb, Lee J. ☐ 12 Angry Men ☐ Anna and the King of Siam ☐ Blood Sweat and Fear ☐ Boomerang! ☐ Brothers Karamazov, The ☐ Buckskin Frontier ☐ But Not For Me ☐ Call Northside 777 ☐ Captain from Castile ☐ Come Blow Your Horn ☐ Coogan's Bluff ☐ Dark Past, The ☐ Exodus ☐ Exorcist, The ☐ Family Secret, The ☐ Fighter, The ☐ Four Horsemen of the Apocalypse ☐ Garment Jungle, The ☐ Golden Boy ☐ Gorilla at Large ☐ Great Ice Rip-Off, The ☐ Green Mansions ☐ Heat of Anger ☐ In Like Flint ☐ Johnny O'Clock ☐ Lawman ☐ Left Hand of God, The ☐ Liberation of L. B. Jones, The ☐ Macho Callahan ☐ Mackenna's Gold ☐ Man in the Gray Flannel Suit, The ☐ Man of the West ☐ Man Who Cheated Himself, The ☐ Man Who Loved Cat Dancing, The ☐ Meanest Men in the West, The ☐ Men of Boys Town ☐ Miracle of the Bells, The ☐ Moon Is Down, The ☐ On the Waterfront ☐ Our Man Flint ☐ Paris Calling ☐ Party Girl ☐ Racers, The ☐ Road to Denver, The ☐ Sirocco ☐ Song of Bernadette, The ☐ This Thing Called Love ☐ Three Faces of Eve, The ☐ Tonight We Raid Calais ☐ Winged Victory ☐ Yankee Pasha

Coburn, Charles ☐ B. F.'s Daughter ☐ Bachelor Mother ☐ Captain Is a Lady, The ☐ Colonel Effingham's Raid ☐ Constant Nymph, The ☐ Devil and Miss Jones, The ☐ Edison, the Man ☐ Everybody Does It ☐ Florian ☐ Gal Who Took the West, The ☐ Gentlemen Prefer Blondes ☐ George Washington Slept Here ☐ Green Grass of Wyoming ☐ Green Years, The ☐ H.M. Pulham, Esq. ☐ Has Anybody Seen My Gal? ☐ Heaven Can Wait ☐ Highwayman, The ☐ How to Be Very, Very Popular ☐ How to Murder a Rich Uncle ☐ Idiot's Delight ☐ Impact ☐ Impatient Years, The ☐ In Name Only ☐ In This Our Life ☐ John Paul Jones ☐ Kings Row ☐ Knickerbocker Holiday ☐ Lady Eve, The ☐ Lord Jeff ☐ Louisa ☐ Made for Each Other ☐ Monkey Business ☐ More the Merrier, The ☐ Mr. Music ☐ Of Human Hearts ☐ Our Wife ☐ Over 21 ☐ Paradine Case ☐ Peggy ☐ Personal Column ☐ Princess O'Rourke ☐ Remarkable Mr. Pennypacker, The ☐ Rhapsody in Blue ☐ Road to Singapore ☐ Royal Scandal, A ☐ Stanley and Livingstone ☐ Story of Alexander Graham Bell, The ☐ Story of Mankind, The ☐ Stranger in My Arms ☐ Three Faces West ☐ Together Again ☐ Town on Trial ☐ Trouble Along the Way ☐ Vivacious Lady ☐ Wilson ☐ Yellow Jack

Coburn, James ☐ Americanization of Emily, The ☐ Baltimore Bullet, The ☐ Bite the Bullet ☐ Candy ☐ Carey Treatment, The ☐ Charade ☐ Cross of Iron ☐ Dead Heat on a Merry-Go-Round ☐ Deadfall ☐ Death of a Soldier ☐ Draw! ☐ Duck, You Sucker ☐ Duffy ☐ Face of a Fugitive ☐ Firepower ☐ Great Escape, The ☐ Hard Contract ☐ Hard Times ☐ Harry in Your Pocket ☐ Hell Is for Heroes ☐ High Risk ☐ High Wind in Jamaica, A ☐ Honkers, The ☐ Hudson Hawk ☐ In Like Flint ☐ Internecine Project, The ☐ Jacqueline Susann's Valley of the Dolls ☐ Last Hard Men, The ☐ Last of Sheila, The ☐ Last of the Mobile Hot-Shots ☐ Looker ☐ Loving Couples ☐ Magnificent Seven, The ☐ Major Dundee ☐ Malibu ☐ Man from Galveston, The ☐ Martin's Day ☐ Massacre At Fort Holman ☐ Maverick ☐ Midway ☐ Our Man Flint ☐ Pat Garrett and Billy the Kid ☐ President's Analyst, The ☐ Reason to Live, a Reason to Die, A ☐ Ride Lonesome ☐ Sister Act 2: Back in the Habit ☐ Waterhole #3 ☐ What Did You Do in the War, Daddy?

Cochran, Steve ☐ Back to God's Country

☐ Big Operator, The ☐ Boston Blackie's Rendevous ☐ Carnival Story ☐ Chase, The ☐ Come Next Spring ☐ Copacabana ☐ Damned Don't Cry, The ☐ Deadly Companions, The ☐ Highway 301 ☐ I, Mobster ☐ Inside the Walls of Folsom Prison ☐ Of Love and Desire ☐ Outcry, The ☐ Private Hell 36 ☐ Quantrill's Raiders ☐ Raton Pass ☐ Shark River ☐ She's Back on Broadway ☐ Slander ☐ Song is Born, A ☐ Storm Warning ☐ Weapon, The ☐ White Heat

Coco, James ☐ Charleston ☐ Cheap Detective, The ☐ Diary of Anne Frank, The ☐ Ensign Pulver ☐ Generation ☐ Hunk ☐ Man of La Mancha ☐ Muppets Take Manhattan, The ☐ Murder by Death ☐ New Leaf, A ☐ Only When I Laugh ☐ Scavenger Hunt ☐ Such Good Friends ☐ Tell Me That You Love Me, Junie Moon ☐ There Must Be a Pony ☐ Wholly Moses ☐ Wild Party, The

Colbert, Claudette ☐ Arise, My Love ☐ Big Pond, The ☐ Bluebeard's Eighth Wife ☐ Boom Town ☐ Bride Comes Home, The ☐ Bride for Sale ☐ Cleopatra ☐ Daughters of Destiny ☐ Drums Along the Mohawk ☐ Egg and I, The ☐ Family Honeymoon ☐ Four Frightened People ☐ Gilded Lily, The ☐ Guest Wife ☐ His Woman ☐ I Cover the Waterfront ☐ I Met Him in Paris ☐ Imitation of Life ☐ It Happened One Night ☐ It's a Wonderful World ☐ Let's Make It Legal ☐ Maid of Salem ☐ Man from Yesterday, The ☐ Midnight ☐ Outpost in Malaya ☐ Palm Beach Story, The ☐ Parrish ☐ Phantom President, The ☐ Practically Yours ☐ Private Worlds ☐ Royal Affairs in Versailles ☐ Secret Fury, The ☐ Secret Heart, The ☐ She Married Her Boss ☐ Sign of the Cross, The ☐ Since You Went Away ☐ Skylark ☐ Sleep My Love ☐ Smiling Lieutenant, The ☐ So Proudly We Hail! ☐ Texas Lady ☐ Three Came Home ☐ Three-Cornered Moon ☐ Thunder on the Hill ☐ Tomorrow Is Forever ☐ Tovarich ☐ Two Mrs. Grenvilles, The ☐ Under Two Flags ☐ Without Reservations ☐ Zaza

Cole, George ☐ Adventures of Sadie, The ☐ Anatomist, The ☐ Belles of St. Trinians, The ☐ Blue Bird, The ☐ Blue Murder at St. Trinian's ☐ Dr. Syn, Alias the Scarecrow ☐ Flesh & Blood ☐ Fright ☐ Gone to Earth ☐ Green Man, The ☐ Mr. Potts Goes to Moscow ☐ My Brother's Keeper ☐ One Way Pendulum ☐ Pure Hell of St. Trinian's, The ☐ Quentin Durward ☐ Too Many Crooks ☐ Weapon, The

Cole, Nat King ☐ Blue Gardenia ☐ China Gate ☐ Istanbul ☐ Night of the Quarter Moon ☐ St. Louis Blues

Coleman, Dabney ☐ 9 to 5 ☐ Amos and Andrew ☐ Attack on Terror: The FBI vs. the Ku Klux Klan ☐ Baby M ☐ Bad Ronald ☐ Beverly Hillbillies, The ☐ Cinderella Liberty ☐ Clifford ☐ Cloak & Dagger ☐ Dove, The ☐ Downhill Racer ☐ Dragnet ☐ Guilty of Innocence: The Lenell Geter Story ☐ Hot to Trot ☐ I Love My . . . Wife ☐ Man with One Red Shoe ☐ Maybe Baby ☐ Meet the Applegates ☐ Melvin and Howard ☐ More Than Friends ☐ Muppets Take Manhattan, The ☐ Murrow ☐ Never Forget ☐ North Dallas Forty ☐ Nothing Personal ☐ On Golden Pond ☐ Rolling Thunder ☐ Scalphunters, The ☐ Short Time ☐ Slender Thread, The ☐ Tootsie ☐ Viva Knievel! ☐ WarGames ☐ Where the Heart Is ☐ Young Doctors in Love

Collins, Joan ☐ Adventures of Sadie, The ☐ Bawdy Adventures of Tom Jones, The ☐ Big Sleep, The ☐ Bitch, The ☐ Bravados, The ☐ Can Hieronymus Merkin Ever Forget Mercy Humppe and Find True Happiness? ☐ Dark Places ☐ Decameron Nights ☐ Empire of the Ants ☐ Esther and the King ☐ Executioner, The ☐ Fatal Charms ☐ Fear in the Night ☐ Game for Vultures ☐ Girl in the Red Velvet Swing, The ☐ Good Die Young, The ☐ Great Adventure, The ☐ Her Life as a Man ☐ Homework ☐ I Believe In You ☐ If It's Tuesday, This Must Be Belgium ☐ Inn of the Frightened People ☐ Island in the Sun ☐ Judgment Deferred ☐ Land of the Pharaohs ☐ Making of a Male Model ☐ Monte Carlo ☐ Oh, Alfie! ☐ Opposite Sex, The ☐ Paper Dolls ☐ Quest for Love ☐ Rally 'Round the Flag, Boys! ☐ Road to Hong Kong, The ☐ Sea Wife ☐ Seven Thieves ☐ Sins ☐ Square Ring, The ☐ Stud, The ☐ Sunburn ☐ Tales from the Crypt ☐ Up in the Cellar ☐ Virgin Queen, The ☐ Warning Shot ☐ Wayward Bus, The

Collins, Ray ☐ Badman's Territory ☐ Big Street, The ☐ Citizen Kane ☐ Commandos Strike at Dawn, The ☐ Free For All ☐ Good Sam ☐ Hidden Eye, The ☐ I Want You ☐ Invitation ☐ It Happens Every Spring ☐ Kill the Umpire ☐ Ma and Pa Kettle Back on the Farm ☐ Ma and Pa Kettle on Vacation ☐ Magnificent Ambersons, The ☐ Man from Colorado, The ☐ Miss Susie Slagle's ☐ Red Stallion in the Rockies, The ☐ Reformer and the Redhead, The ☐ Rose Marie ☐ Solid Gold Cadillac, The ☐ Whistling in Brooklyn ☐ You're in the Navy Now

Colman, Ronald ☐ Arrowsmith ☐ Bulldog Drummond ☐ Champagne for Caesar ☐ Clive of India ☐ Condemned ☐ Cynara ☐ Double Life, A ☐ If I Were King ☐ Kismet ☐ Lady Windemere's Fan ☐ Late George Apley, The ☐ Light that Failed, The ☐ Lost Horizon ☐ Lucky Partners ☐ Man Who Broke the Bank at Monte Carlo, The ☐ Masquerader, The ☐ My Life with Caroline ☐ Prisoner of Zenda, The ☐ Raffles ☐ Random Harvest ☐ Story of Mankind, The ☐ Tale of Two Cities, A ☐ Talk of the Town, The ☐ Under Two Flags

Connery, Sean ☐ Action of the Tiger ☐ Anderson Tapes, The ☐ Another Time, Another Place ☐ Bridge Too Far, A ☐ Cuba ☐ Darby

O'Gill and the Little People ☐ Diamonds Are Forever ☐ Dr. No ☐ Family Business ☐ Fine Madness, A ☐ Five Days One Summer ☐ Frightened City, The ☐ From Russia with Love ☐ Goldfinger ☐ Good Man in Africa, A ☐ Great Train Robbery, The ☐ Hard Drivers ☐ Hell Drivers ☐ Highlander ☐ Highlander II: The Quickening ☐ Hill, The ☐ Hunt for Red October, The ☐ Indiana Jones and the Last Crusade ☐ Just Cause ☐ Man Who Would Be King, The ☐ Marnie ☐ Medicine Man ☐ Meteor ☐ Molly Maguires, The ☐ Murder on the Orient Express ☐ Name of the Rose, The ☐ Never Say Never Again ☐ Next Man, The ☐ Offence, The ☐ Operation Snafu ☐ Outland ☐ Presidio, The ☐ Red Tent, The ☐ Rising Sun ☐ Robin and Marian ☐ Russia House, The ☐ Shalako ☐ Sword of the Valiant ☐ Tarzan's Greatest Adventure ☐ Thunderball ☐ Time Bandits ☐ Untouchables, The ☐ Wind and the Lion, The ☐ Woman of Straw ☐ You Only Live Twice ☐ Zardoz

Connolly, Walter ☐ 5th Avenue Girl ☐ Broadway Bill ☐ Captain Hates the Sea, The ☐ First Lady ☐ Girl Downstairs, The ☐ Good Earth, The ☐ Good Girls Go to Paris ☐ Great Victor Herbert, The ☐ Huckleberry Finn ☐ It Happened One Night ☐ King Steps Out, The ☐ Lady by Choice ☐ Man's Castle ☐ Nancy Steel Is Missing ☐ No More Orchids ☐ Nothing Sacred ☐ Paddy, the Next Best Thing ☐ She Couldn't Take It ☐ So Red the Rose ☐ Start Cheering ☐ Those High Grey Walls ☐ Twentieth Century ☐ Whom the Gods Destroy

Connors, Chuck ☐ Balboa ☐ Big Country, The ☐ Captain Nemo and the Underwater City ☐ Embassy ☐ Flipper ☐ Gambler Returns: The Luck of the Draw, The ☐ Geronimo ☐ Good Morning, Miss Dove ☐ High Desert Kill ☐ Hired Gun, The ☐ Hold Back the Night ☐ Last Flight to Hell ☐ Mad Bomber, The ☐ Move Over, Darling ☐ Naked Alibi ☐ Night They Took Miss Beautiful ☐ Nightmare in Badham County ☐ Pancho Villa ☐ South Sea Woman ☐ Soylent Green ☐ Standing Tall ☐ Support Your Local Gunfighter ☐ Synanon ☐ Virus

Conrad, Robert ☐ Adventures of Nick Carter ☐ Anything to Survive ☐ Assassin ☐ Breaking Up Is Hard to Do ☐ Coach of the Year ☐ Hard Knox ☐ High Mountain Rangers ☐ More Wild, Wild West ☐ Murph the Surf ☐ One Police Plaza ☐ Palm Springs Weekend ☐ Samurai Cowboy ☐ Will: G. Gordon Liddy

Conrad, William ☐ Alcatraz ☐ Body and Soul ☐ Cannon ☐ Conqueror, The ☐ Cry Danger ☐ Cry of the Hunted ☐ Five Against the House ☐ Johnny Concho ☐ Killing Cars ☐ Moonshine County Express ☐ Naked Jungle, The ☐ Racket, The ☐ Return of the King ☐ Ride Back, The ☐ Sorry, Wrong Number ☐ Sword of Monte Cristo, The

Conried, Hans ☐ 5,000 Fingers of Dr. T, The ☐ American Dream ☐ Behave Yourself ☐ Big Beat, The ☐ Big Jim McLain ☐ Big Street, The ☐ Brothers O'Toole, The ☐ Davy Crockett, King of the Wild Frontier ☐ Falcon Takes Over, The ☐ It's a Wonderful World ☐ Jet Pilot ☐ Monster That Challenged the World, The ☐ Nancy Goes to Rio ☐ Nightmare ☐ Rock-a-Bye Baby ☐ Senator Was Indiscreet, The ☐ Siren of Bagdad

Constantine, Eddie ☐ 7 Capital Sins ☐ Alphaville ☐ As If It Were Raining ☐ Beware of a Holy Whore ☐ Cleo From 5 to 7 ☐ Empire of the Night, The ☐ Flight to Berlin ☐ Follies Bergere ☐ Give 'Em Hell ☐ Hail, Mafia ☐ Headlines of Destruction ☐ Helsinki Napoli All Night Long ☐ It Lives Again ☐ Long Good Friday, The ☐ Third Generation, The ☐ Your Turn, Darling ☐ Zentropa

Constantine, Michael ☐ Beyond Fear ☐ Evita Peron ☐ Fear in the City ☐ If It's Tuesday, This Must Be Belgium ☐ Impatient Heart, The ☐ In the Mood ☐ Island of Love ☐ My Life ☐ Night That Panicked America, The ☐ Quick Before It Melts ☐ Reivers, The ☐ Say Goodbye, Maggie Cole ☐ Silent Rebellion ☐ Summer of My German Soldier

Conte, Richard ☐ 13 Rue Madeleine ☐ Bell for Adano, A ☐ Bengazi ☐ Big Combo, The ☐ Big Jack ☐ Big Tip Off, The ☐ Blue Gardenia ☐ Brothers Rico, The ☐ Call Northside 777 ☐ Case of the Red Monkey ☐ Circus World ☐ Cry of the City ☐ Explosion ☐ Fighter, The ☐ Full of Life ☐ Guadalcanal Diary ☐ Highway Dragnet ☐ Hollywood Story ☐ House of Strangers, The ☐ I'll Cry Tomorrow ☐ Lady in Cement ☐ Operation Cross Eagles ☐ Other Love, The ☐ Purple Heart, The ☐ Race for Life ☐ Raging Tide, The ☐ Raiders, The ☐ Somewhere in the Night ☐ Synanon ☐ This Angry Age ☐ Tony Rome ☐ Walk in the Sun, A ☐ Whirlpool

Conti, Tom ☐ American Dreamer ☐ Beyond Therapy ☐ Duellists, The ☐ Galileo ☐ Gospel According to Vic, The ☐ Haunting of Julia, The ☐ Merry Christmas, Mr. Lawrence ☐ Miracles ☐ Quick and the Dead, The ☐ Reuben, Reuben ☐ Saving Grace ☐ Shirley Valentine

Coogan, Jackie ☐ Addams Family, The—Vol. 1 ☐ Addams Family, The—Vol. 2 ☐ Addams Family, The—Vol. 3 ☐ Addams Family, The—Vol. 4 ☐ Addams Family, The—Vol. 5 ☐ Addams Family, The—Vol. 6 ☐ Big Operator, The ☐ Dr. Heckyl and Mr. Hype ☐ Girl Happy ☐ Huckleberry Finn ☐ Human Experiments ☐ Joker is Wild, The ☐ Kid, The ☐ Manchu Eagle Murder Caper Mystery, The ☐ Marlowe ☐ Million Dollar Legs ☐ Night of the Quarter Moon ☐ No Place to Land ☐ Oliver Twist ☐ Peck's Bad Boy ☐ Prey, The ☐ Sex Kittens Go to College ☐ Shakiest Gun in the West, The ☐ Space Children, The ☐ Tom Sawyer

Cook, Jr., Elisha ☐ Behave Yourself ☐ Big

Sleep, The ☐ Black Bird, The ☐ Born to Kill ☐ Dillinger ☐ Electra Glide in Blue ☐ Emperor of the North, The ☐ Falcon's Alibi, The ☐ Fall Guy ☐ Flaxy Martin ☐ Hammett ☐ Haunted Palace, The ☐ House on Haunted Hill ☐ I Wake Up Screaming ☐ It Came Upon the Midnight Clear ☐ Johnny Cool ☐ Killing, The ☐ Mad Bull ☐ Maltese Falcon, The ☐ Manila Calling ☐ Phantom Lady ☐ Plunder Road ☐ Shane ☐ Stranger on the Third Floor ☐ They Won't Forget ☐ Wife, Doctor and Nurse

Cook, Peter ☐ Adventures of Barry Mckenzie, The ☐ Bed-Sitting Room, The ☐ Bedazzled ☐ Find the Lady ☐ Getting It Right ☐ Hound of the Baskervilles, The ☐ Rise and Rise of Michael Rimmer, The ☐ Secret Policeman's Other Ball, The ☐ Those Daring Young Men in Their Jaunty Jalopies ☐ Whoops Apocalypse ☐ Wrong Box, The ☐ Yellowbeard

Cooper, Gary ☐ Adventures of Marco Polo, The ☐ Alice in Wonderland ☐ Along Came Jones ☐ Ball of Fire ☐ Beau Geste ☐ Blowing Wild ☐ Bluebeard's Eighth Wife ☐ Bright Leaf ☐ Casanova Brown ☐ City Streets ☐ Cloak and Dagger ☐ Court-Martial of Billy Mitchell, The ☐ Cowboy and the Lady, The ☐ Dallas ☐ Design for Living ☐ Desire ☐ Devil and the Deep ☐ Distant Drums ☐ Farewell to Arms, A ☐ Fighting Caravans ☐ For Whom the Bell Tolls ☐ Fountainhead, The ☐ Friendly Persuasion ☐ Garden of Evil ☐ General Died at Dawn, The ☐ Good Sam ☐ Hanging Tree, The ☐ High Noon ☐ His Woman ☐ If I Had a Million ☐ It's a Big Country ☐ Lives of a Bengal Lancer, The ☐ Love in the Afternoon ☐ Man of the West ☐ Meet John Doe ☐ Morocco ☐ Mr. Deeds Goes to Town ☐ Naked Edge, The ☐ Northwest Mounted Police ☐ Now and Forever ☐ Operator 13 ☐ Paramount on Parade ☐ Peter Ibbetson ☐ Plainsman, The ☐ Pride of the Yankees, The ☐ Real Glory, The ☐ Return to Paradise ☐ Saratoga Trunk ☐ Sergeant York ☐ Shopworn Angel ☐ Souls at Sea ☐ Spoilers, The ☐ Springfield Rifle ☐ Story of Dr. Wassell, The ☐ Task Force ☐ Ten North Frederick ☐ They Came to Cordura ☐ Today We Live ☐ Unconquered ☐ Vera Cruz ☐ Virginian, The ☐ Wedding Night, The ☐ Westerner, The ☐ Wings ☐ Wreck of the Mary Deare, The ☐ You're in the Navy Now

Cooper, Gladys ☐ Beware of Pity ☐ Bishop's Wife, The ☐ Black Cat, The ☐ Eagle Squadron ☐ Gay Falcon, The ☐ Green Dolphin Street ☐ Green Years, The ☐ Happiest Millionaire, The ☐ Iron Duke, The ☐ Kitty Foyle ☐ Love Letters ☐ Madame Bovary ☐ Mr. Lucky ☐ Mrs. Parkington ☐ My Fair Lady ☐ Nice Girl Like Me, A ☐ Now, Voyager ☐ Pirate, The ☐ Princess O'Rourke ☐ Secret Garden, The ☐ Separate Tables ☐ That Hamilton Woman ☐ This Above All ☐ Thunder on the Hill ☐ Valley of Decision, The ☐ White Cliffs of Dover, The

Cooper, Jackie ☐ Big Guy, The ☐ Bowery, The ☐ Boy of the Streets ☐ Broadway to Hollywood ☐ Champ, The ☐ Chosen Survivors ☐ Devil is a Sissy, The ☐ Glamour Boy ☐ Life with Henry ☐ Love Machine, The ☐ Maybe I'll Come Home in the Spring ☐ Men of Texas ☐ O'Shaughnessy's Boy ☐ Operation Petticoat ☐ Return of Frank James, The ☐ Seventeen ☐ Skippy ☐ Sunny Side Up ☐ Superman 2 ☐ Superman 3 ☐ Superman 4: The Quest for Peace ☐ Superman—The Movie ☐ That Certain Age ☐ Tough Guy ☐ Treasure Island ☐ Two Bright Boys ☐ Ziegfeld Girl

Coote, Robert ☐ Berlin Express ☐ Constant Husband, The ☐ Exile, The ☐ Fighting Pimpernel, The ☐ Macbeth ☐ Man Could Get Killed, A ☐ Merry Andrew ☐ Othello ☐ Prudence and the Pill ☐ Soldiers Three ☐ Stairway to Heaven ☐ Swinger, The ☐ Three Musketeers, The ☐ V.I.P.s, The

Corey, Wendell ☐ Accused, The ☐ Agent for H.A.R.M ☐ Alias Jesse James ☐ Any Number Can Play ☐ Astro-Zombies ☐ Big Knife, The ☐ Blood on the Arrow ☐ Bold and the Brave, The ☐ Buckskin ☐ Carbine Williams ☐ Desert Fury ☐ File on Thelma Jordon, The ☐ Furies, The ☐ Great Missouri Raid, The ☐ Harriet Craig ☐ Hell's Half Acre ☐ Holiday Affair ☐ I Walk Alone ☐ Jamaica Run ☐ Killer Is Loose, The ☐ Loving You ☐ Man-Eater of Kumaon ☐ My Man and I ☐ No Sad Songs for Me ☐ Rack, The ☐ Rainmaker, The ☐ Rear Window ☐ Rich, Young and Pretty ☐ Search, The ☐ Sorry, Wrong Number ☐ Wild Blue Yonder, The ☐ Women of the Prehistoric Planet

Cort, Bud ☐ Bates Motel ☐ Brain Dead ☐ Brave New World ☐ Brewster McCloud ☐ Chocolate War, The ☐ Gas-s-s-s ☐ Harold and Maude ☐ Invaders from Mars ☐ Love at Stake ☐ M*A*S*H ☐ Maria's Lovers ☐ Out of the Dark ☐ Secret Diary of Sigmund Freud, The ☐ She Dances Alone ☐ Why Shoot the Teacher?

Cortez, Ricardo ☐ Bad Company ☐ Big Business Girl ☐ Big Shakedown, The ☐ Broadway Bad ☐ Case of the Black Cat, The ☐ Charlie Chan in Reno ☐ Firebird, The ☐ Flesh ☐ Frisco Kid ☐ I Am a Thief ☐ I Killed That Man ☐ Illicit ☐ Is My Face Red? ☐ Make Your Own Bed ☐ Maltese Falcon, The ☐ Man with Two Faces, The ☐ Midnight Mary ☐ Montana Moon ☐ Mr. Moto's Last Warning ☐ Murder Over New York ☐ Mystery in Mexico ☐ No One Man ☐ Special Agent ☐ Symphony of Six Million ☐ Ten Cents a Dance ☐ Thirteen Women ☐ Torrent, The ☐ Walking Dead, The ☐ West of Shanghai ☐ Wonder Bar ☐ World Premiere

Cosby, Bill ☐ California Suite ☐ Devil and

Max Devlin, The ☐ Ghost Dad ☐ Hickey & Boggs ☐ I Spy Returns ☐ Leonard Part 6 ☐ Let's Do It Again ☐ Man and Boy ☐ Meteor Man ☐ Miles Ahead—The Music of Miles Davis ☐ Mother, Jugs & Speed ☐ Piece of the Action, A ☐ To All My Friends On Shore ☐ Uptown Saturday Night

Costello, Lou ☐ 30 Foot Bride of Candy Rock, The ☐ Abbott and Costello Go To Mars ☐ Abbott and Costello In Hollywood ☐ Abbott and Costello In The Foreign Legion ☐ Abbott and Costello Meet Captain Kidd ☐ Abbott and Costello Meet Dr Jekyll And Mr Hyde ☐ Abbott and Costello Meet Frankenstein ☐ Abbott and Costello Meet The Invisible Man ☐ Abbott and Costello Meet The Keystone Kops ☐ Abbott and Costello Meet the Killer ☐ Abbott and Costello Meet the Mummy ☐ Africa Screams ☐ Buck Privates ☐ Buck Privates Come Home ☐ Comin' Round the Mountain ☐ Dance with Me Henry ☐ Here Come the Co-eds ☐ Hey Abbott! ☐ Hit the Ice ☐ Hold That Ghost ☐ In Society ☐ In the Navy ☐ It Ain't Hay ☐ Jack and the Beanstalk ☐ Keep 'Em Flying ☐ Little Giant ☐ Lost in a Harem ☐ Lost in Alaska ☐ Mexican Hayride ☐ Naughty Nineties ☐ Noose Hangs High, The ☐ One Night in the Tropics ☐ Pardon My Sarong ☐ Ride 'Em Cowboy ☐ Rio Rita ☐ Time of Their Lives, The ☐ Who Done It? ☐ Wistful Widow of Wagon Gap, The

Costner, Kevin ☐ American Flyers ☐ Bodyguard, The ☐ Bull Durham ☐ Dances with Wolves ☐ Fandango ☐ Field of Dreams ☐ Gunrunner, The ☐ JFK ☐ Night Shift ☐ No Way Out ☐ Perfect World, A ☐ Revenge ☐ Robin Hood: Prince of Thieves ☐ Silverado ☐ Sizzle Beach, U.S.A. ☐ Table for Five ☐ Untouchables, The ☐ War, The ☐ Wyatt Earp

Cotten, Joseph ☐ Abominable Dr. Phibes, The ☐ Airport '77 ☐ Angel Wore Red, The ☐ Baron Blood ☐ Beyond the Forest ☐ Blueprint for Murder ☐ Bottom of the Bottle, The ☐ Brighty of the Grand Canyon ☐ Caravans ☐ Citizen Kane ☐ City Beneath the Sea ☐ Delicate Balance, A ☐ Delusion ☐ Duel in the Sun ☐ Farmer's Daughter, The ☐ From the Earth to the Moon ☐ Gaslight ☐ Grasshopper, The ☐ Great Sioux Massacre, The ☐ Guyana: Cult of the Damned ☐ Half Angel ☐ Halliday Brand, The ☐ Hearse, The ☐ Heaven's Gate ☐ Hers to Hold ☐ Hush . . . Hush, Sweet Charlotte ☐ I'll Be Seeing You ☐ Jack of Diamonds ☐ Journey into Fear ☐ Killer Is Loose, The ☐ Lady Frankenstein ☐ Last Sunset, The ☐ Latitude Zero ☐ Lindbergh Kidnapping Case, The ☐ Love Letters ☐ Lydia ☐ Magnificent Ambersons, The ☐ Man with a Cloak, The ☐ Money Trap, The ☐ Niagara ☐ Peking Express ☐ Perfect Crime, The ☐ Petulia ☐ Portrait of Jennie ☐ September Affair ☐ Shadow of a Doubt ☐ Since You Went Away ☐ Steel Trap, The ☐ Third Man, The ☐ Tora! Tora! Tora! ☐ Tramplers, The ☐ Twilight's Last Gleaming ☐ Two Flags West ☐ Under Capricorn ☐ Walk Softly, Stranger

Coulouris, George ☐ Citizen Kane ☐ Fury at Smugglers Bay ☐ Island Rescue ☐ It's Not the Size That Counts ☐ Lady on a Train ☐ Master Race, The ☐ Nobody Lives Forever ☐ None But the Lonely Heart ☐ Race for Life ☐ Skull, The ☐ Sleep My Love ☐ Song to Remember, A ☐ Southern Yankee, A ☐ Verdict, The ☐ Watch on the Rhine ☐ Where There's Life

Courtenay, Tom ☐ Billy Liar ☐ Catch Me a Spy ☐ Dandy in Aspic, A ☐ Day the Fish Came Out, The ☐ Doctor Zhivago ☐ Dresser, The ☐ Happy New Year ☐ I Heard the Owl Call My Name ☐ King and Country ☐ King Rat ☐ Last Butterfly, The ☐ Leonard Part 6 ☐ Let Him Have It ☐ Loneliness of the Long Distance Runner, The ☐ Night of the Generals, The ☐ One Day in the Life of Ivan Denisovich ☐ Operation Crossbow ☐ Otley

Court, Hazel ☐ Bond Street ☐ Curse of Frankenstein, The ☐ Doctor Blood's Coffin ☐ Ghost Ship ☐ Hour of Decision ☐ Man Who Could Cheat Death, The ☐ Masque of the Red Death ☐ Premature Burial, The ☐ Raven, The ☐ Shakedown, The

Cowan, Jerome ☐ Deadline at Dawn ☐ Exile Express ☐ Flight to Nowhere ☐ Fog Island ☐ Fuller Brush Girl, The ☐ Have Rocket, Will Travel ☐ Maltese Falcon, The ☐ Moontide ☐ Mr. Ace ☐ Mr. Skeffington ☐ New Faces of 1937 ☐ Shall We Dance ☐ Victory ☐ Wallflower ☐ Who Done It? ☐ You Only Live Once

Coward, Noel ☐ Astonished Heart, The ☐ Boom! ☐ Bunny Lake Is Missing ☐ In Which We Serve ☐ Italian Job, The ☐ Our Man in Havana ☐ Paris—when It Sizzles ☐ Scoundrel, The ☐ Surprise Package

Cox, Ronny ☐ Alcatraz: The Whole Shocking Story ☐ Beast Within, The ☐ Beverly Hills Cop ☐ Beverly Hills Cop II ☐ Bound for Glory ☐ Deliverance ☐ Demon Within, The ☐ Fallen Angel ☐ FBI Murders, The ☐ Girl Called Hatter Fox, The ☐ Hollywood Vice Squad ☐ In the Line of Duty: The F.B.I. Murders ☐ Jesse Owens Story, The ☐ Kavik the Wolf Dog ☐ Loose Cannons ☐ Lovey: A Circle of Children, Part II ☐ One Man Force ☐ Onion Field, The ☐ Our Town ☐ Reckless Disregard ☐ Robocop ☐ Scandal in a Small Town ☐ Scissors ☐ Some Kind of Hero ☐ Taps ☐ Total Recall ☐ Vision Quest

Coyote, Peter ☐ Baja Oklahoma ☐ Best Kept Secrets ☐ Bitter Moon ☐ Blue Yonder, The ☐ Crooked Hearts ☐ Cross Creek ☐ Die Laughing ☐ E.T. The Extra-Terrestrial ☐ Echoes in the Darkness ☐ Endangered Species ☐ Exposure ☐ Heart of Midnight ☐ Heartbreakers ☐ Isabel's Choice ☐ Jagged Edge

☐ Keeper of the City ☐ Man in Love, A ☐ Man Inside, The ☐ Out ☐ Outrageous Fortune ☐ People vs. Jean Harris, The ☐ Stacking ☐ Strangers Kiss ☐ Timerider

Crabbe, Buster ☐ Alien Dead, The ☐ Arizona Raiders ☐ Arizona Raiders, The ☐ Badman's Country ☐ Bounty Killer, The ☐ Caged Fury ☐ Call a Messenger ☐ Captive Girl ☐ Comeback Trail, The ☐ Daughter of Shanghai ☐ Gun Brothers ☐ His Brother's Ghost ☐ King of the Jungle ☐ Last of the Redmen ☐ Lawless Eighties, The ☐ Man of the Forest ☐ Million Dollar Legs ☐ Thundering Herd, The

Craig, James ☐ Devil and Daniel Webster, The ☐ Drums in the Deep South ☐ Fort Utah ☐ Fort Vengeance ☐ Ghost Diver ☐ Kitty Foyle ☐ Little Mister Jim ☐ Lost Angel ☐ Marriage Is a Private Affair ☐ Massacre ☐ Naked in the Sun ☐ Our Vines Have Tender Grapes ☐ Seven Miles from Alcatraz ☐ Side Street ☐ Valley of the Sun ☐ Zanzibar

Craig, Michael ☐ Angry Silence, The ☐ Brotherly Love ☐ Conquered City, The ☐ Doctor in Love ☐ High Tide at Noon ☐ Inn of the Damned ☐ Irishman, The ☐ Modesty Blaise ☐ Mysterious Island ☐ No My Darling Daughter ☐ Ride a Wild Pony ☐ Royal Hunt of the Sun, The ☐ Sapphire ☐ Silent Enemy, The ☐ Star! ☐ Stolen Hours, The

Crain, Jeanne ☐ Apartment for Peggy ☐ Belles on Their Toes ☐ Centennial Summer ☐ Cheaper by the Dozen ☐ City of Bad Men ☐ Dangerous Crossing ☐ Duel in the Jungle ☐ Fan, The ☐ Fastest Gun Alive, The ☐ Gentlemen Marry Brunettes ☐ Guns of the Timberland ☐ Home in Indiana ☐ Hot Rods to Hell ☐ In the Meantime, Darling ☐ Joker is Wild, The ☐ Leave Her to Heaven ☐ Letter to Three Wives, A ☐ Madison Avenue ☐ Man Without a Star ☐ Margie ☐ Model and the Marriage Broker, The ☐ Night God Screamed, The ☐ O. Henry's Full House ☐ People Will Talk ☐ Pinky ☐ Skyjacked ☐ State Fair ☐ Winged Victory

Crawford, Broderick ☐ Adventures of Nick Carter ☐ All the King's Men ☐ Anna Lucasta ☐ Bad Men of Tombstone ☐ Badlands of Dakota ☐ Beau Geste ☐ Between Heaven and Hell ☐ Big House, U.S.A. ☐ Black Angel ☐ Black Cat, The ☐ Born Yesterday ☐ Broadway ☐ Cargo to Capetown ☐ Castillan, The ☐ Convicts Four ☐ Decks Ran Red, The ☐ Embassy ☐ Fastest Gun Alive, The ☐ Flame, The ☐ Goliath and the Dragon ☐ Hell's Bloody Devils ☐ Human Desire ☐ I Can't Give You Anything But Love, Baby ☐ Il Bidone ☐ Island of Lost Men ☐ Kiss in the Dark, A ☐ Larceny, Inc ☐ Last of the Comanches, The ☐ Last Posse, The ☐ Liar's Moon ☐ Lone Star ☐ Mayday at 40,000 Feet! ☐ Men of Texas ☐ Mob, The ☐ Night People ☐ Night unto Night ☐ Not as a Stranger ☐ Private Files of J. Edgar Hoover, The ☐ Real Glory, The ☐ Scandal Sheet ☐ Seven Sinners ☐ Slightly Honorable ☐ Tight Shoes ☐ Time of Your Life, The ☐ When the Daltons Rode

Crawford, Joan ☐ Above Suspicion ☐ Autumn Leaves ☐ Berserk ☐ Best of Everything, The ☐ Bride Wore Red, The ☐ Caretakers, The ☐ Chained ☐ Daisy Kenyon ☐ Damned Don't Cry, The ☐ Dance, Fools, Dance ☐ Dancing Lady ☐ Fatal Confinement ☐ Female on the Beach ☐ Flamingo Road ☐ Forsaking All Others ☐ Goodbye, My Fancy ☐ Gorgeous Hussy, The ☐ Grand Hotel ☐ Harriet Craig ☐ Hollywood Revue of 1929, The ☐ Humoresque ☐ I Live My Life ☐ I Saw What You Did ☐ Ice Follies of 1939 ☐ Johnny Guitar ☐ Last of Mrs. Cheyney, The ☐ Laughing Sinners ☐ Letty Lynton ☐ Love on the Run ☐ Mannequin ☐ Mildred Pierce ☐ Montana Moon ☐ Night Gallery ☐ No More Ladies ☐ Our Blushing Brides ☐ Our Dancing Daughters ☐ Our Modern Maidens ☐ Paid ☐ Possessed ☐ Possessed ☐ Queen Bee ☐ Rain ☐ Reunion in France ☐ Sadie McKee ☐ Shining Hour, The ☐ Story of Esther Costello, The ☐ Strange Cargo ☐ Sudden Fear ☐ Susan and God ☐ They All Kissed the Bride ☐ This Modern Age ☐ This Woman Is Dangerous ☐ Today We Live ☐ Torch Song ☐ Trog ☐ Untamed ☐ What Ever Happened to Baby Jane? ☐ When Ladies Meet ☐ Woman's Face, A ☐ Women, The

Crawford, Michael ☐ Alice's Adventures in Wonderland ☐ Barnum ☐ Condorman ☐ Funny Thing Happened on the Way to the Forum, A ☐ Games, The ☐ Hello, Dolly! ☐ Hello-Goodbye ☐ How I Won the War ☐ Jokers, The ☐ Knack, and How to Get It, The ☐ Mouse on the Moon, The ☐ War Lover, The

Crenna, Richard ☐ After the Shock ☐ And the Sea Will Tell ☐ Body Heat ☐ Breakheart Pass ☐ Case of Deadly Force, A ☐ Case of the Hillside Stranglers, The ☐ Catlow ☐ Death Ship ☐ Dirty Money ☐ Doctor's Wives ☐ Evil, The ☐ First Blood ☐ First, You Cry ☐ Flamingo Kid ☐ Footsteps ☐ Girl Named Sooner, A ☐ Hillside Stranglers, The ☐ Honky Tonk ☐ Hot Shots! Part Deux ☐ Intruders ☐ It Grows on Trees ☐ John Goldfarb, Please Come Home ☐ Last Flight Out ☐ Leviathan ☐ Made in Paris ☐ Marooned ☐ Mayflower: The Pilgrims' Adventure ☐ Midas Run ☐ Montana ☐ On Wings of Eagles ☐ Ordeal of Bill Carney, The ☐ Our Miss Brooks ☐ Over-Exposed ☐ Pride of St. Louis, The ☐ Rambo III ☐ Rambo: First Blood, Part II ☐ Rape of Richard Beck, The ☐ Red Skies of Montana ☐ Red Sky at Morning ☐ Sand Pebbles, The ☐ Star! ☐ Summer Rental ☐ Table for Five ☐ Wait Until Dark ☐ War Between the Tates, The

Crisp, Donald ☐ Adventures of Mark Twain, The ☐ Amazing Doctor Clitterhouse, The

☐ Battle of Midway, The ☐ Beloved Enemy ☐ Black Pirate, The ☐ Bright Leaf ☐ Broken Blossoms ☐ Brother Orchid ☐ Challenge to Lassie ☐ Charge of the Light Brigade, The ☐ City for Conquest ☐ Comet Over Broadway ☐ Confession ☐ Daughters Courageous ☐ Dawn Patrol, The ☐ Dog of Flanders, A ☐ Don Q, Son of Zorro ☐ Dr. Ehrlich's Magic Bullet ☐ Dr. Jekyll and Mr. Hyde ☐ Drango ☐ Great O'Malley, The ☐ Greyfriars Bobby ☐ Hills of Home, The ☐ Hometown Story ☐ How Green Was My Valley ☐ Jezebel ☐ Juarez ☐ Knute Rockne, All American ☐ Lassie Come Home ☐ Life of Emile Zola, The ☐ Little Minister, The ☐ Long Gray Line, The ☐ Man from Laramie, The ☐ Mary of Scotland ☐ Mutiny on the Bounty ☐ National Velvet ☐ Oklahoma Kid, The ☐ Old Maid, The ☐ Pagan, The ☐ Parnell ☐ Private Lives of Elizabeth and Essex, The ☐ Ramrod ☐ Red Dust ☐ Saddle the Wind ☐ Sea Hawk, The ☐ Sisters, The ☐ Son of Lassie ☐ Spencer's Mountain ☐ Svengali ☐ That Certain Woman ☐ Uninvited, The ☐ Valley of Decision, The ☐ Whispering Smith ☐ Woman Rebels, A ☐ Wuthering Heights

Cronyn, Hume ☐ Age-Old Friends ☐ Arrangement, The ☐ batteries not included ☐ Brewster's Millions ☐ Bride Goes Wild, The ☐ Broadway Bound ☐ Brute Force ☐ Camilla ☐ Cleopatra ☐ Cocoon ☐ Cocoon: The Return ☐ Conrack ☐ Cross of Lorraine, The ☐ Day One ☐ Foxfire ☐ Gaily, Gaily ☐ Green Years, The ☐ Honky Tonk Freeway ☐ Impulse ☐ Lifeboat ☐ Main Street After Dark ☐ Parallax View, The ☐ Pelican Brief, The ☐ People Will Talk ☐ Postman Always Rings Twice, The ☐ Rollover ☐ Seventh Cross, The ☐ Shadow of a Doubt ☐ Sunrise at Campobello ☐ There Was a Crooked Man ☐ To Dance with the White Dog ☐ Top o' the Morning

Crosby, Bing ☐ Adventures of Ichabod and Mr. Toad, The ☐ Anything Goes ☐ Anything Goes ☐ Bells of St. Mary's, The ☐ Big Broadcast, The ☐ Birth of the Blues ☐ Blue Skies ☐ College Humor ☐ Connecticut Yankee in King Arthur's Court ☐ Country Girl, The ☐ Dixie ☐ Doctor Rhythm ☐ Double or Nothing ☐ Down Memory Lane ☐ Dr. Rhythm ☐ Duffy's Tavern ☐ East Side of Heaven ☐ Emperor Waltz, The ☐ Going Hollywood ☐ Going My Way ☐ Here Come the Waves ☐ Here Comes the Groom ☐ Here Is My Heart ☐ High Society ☐ High Time ☐ Holiday Inn ☐ If I Had My Way ☐ Just for You ☐ King of Jazz, The ☐ Little Boy Lost ☐ Man on Fire ☐ Mississippi ☐ Mr. Music ☐ Paris Honeymoon ☐ Pennies from Heaven ☐ Reaching for the Moon ☐ Rhythm on the Range ☐ Rhythm on the River ☐ Riding High ☐ Road to Bali ☐ Road to Hong Kong, The ☐ Road to Morocco ☐ Road to Rio ☐ Road to Singapore ☐ Road to Utopia ☐ Road to Zanzibar ☐ Robin and the Seven Hoods ☐ Say One for Me ☐ She Loves Me Not ☐ Sing, You Sinners ☐ Stagecoach ☐ Star Maker, The ☐ Star Spangled Rhythm ☐ That's Entertainment ☐ Too Much Harmony ☐ Top o' the Morning ☐ Two for Tonight ☐ Waikiki Wedding ☐ We're Not Dressing ☐ Welcome Stranger ☐ White Christmas

Crosby, Bob ☐ Five Pennies, The ☐ Kansas City Kitty ☐ Let's Make Music ☐ My Gal Loves Music ☐ Pardon My Rhythm ☐ See Here, Private Hargrove

Cross, Ben ☐ Assisi Underground, The ☐ Chariots of Fire ☐ Far Pavilions, The ☐ Lie, The ☐ Live Wire ☐ Nightlife ☐ Paperhouse ☐ Ray Bradbury Chronicles: The Martian Episodes ☐ Unholy, The

Crothers, Scatman ☐ Aristocats, The ☐ Black Belt Jones ☐ Bronco Billy ☐ Chesty Anderson, USN ☐ Coonskin ☐ Deadly Eyes ☐ Fortune, The ☐ Journey of Natty Gann, The ☐ Meet Me at the Fair ☐ Scavenger Hunt ☐ Shining, The ☐ Silver Streak ☐ Twilight Zone—The Movie ☐ Walking My Baby Back Home ☐ Zapped!

Cruise, Tom ☐ All the Right Moves ☐ Born on the Fourth of July ☐ Cocktail ☐ Color of Money, The ☐ Days of Thunder ☐ Endless Love ☐ Far and Away ☐ Few Good Men, A ☐ Firm, The ☐ Interview With the Vampire ☐ Legend ☐ Losin' It ☐ Outsiders, The ☐ Rain Man ☐ Risky Business ☐ Taps ☐ Top Gun

Crystal, Billy ☐ All-Star Salute to the Improv, An ☐ Animalympics ☐ Billy Crystal—Don't Get Me Started ☐ Billy Crystal—Midnight Train to Moscow ☐ Breaking Up Is Hard to Do ☐ City Slickers ☐ City Slickers 2: Legend of Curly's Gold ☐ Enola Gay ☐ Human Feelings ☐ Memories of Me ☐ Mr. Saturday Night ☐ Rabbit Test ☐ Running Scared ☐ Throw Momma From the Train ☐ When Harry Met Sally . . .

Cugat, Xavier ☐ Bathing Beauty ☐ Chicago Syndicate ☐ Date With Judy, A ☐ Heat's On, The ☐ Holiday in Mexico ☐ Luxury Liner ☐ On an Island with You ☐ Weekend at the Waldorf

Culkin, Macaulay ☐ George Balanchine's The Nutcracker ☐ Getting Even with Dad ☐ Good Son, The ☐ Home Alone ☐ Home Alone 2: Lost in New York ☐ My Girl ☐ Pagemaster, The ☐ Richie Rich ☐ Uncle Buck

Culp, Robert ☐ Big Bad Mama II ☐ Bob & Carol & Ted & Alice ☐ Breaking Point ☐ Castaway Cowboy, The ☐ Cold Night's Death, A ☐ Flood! ☐ Gladiator, The ☐ Goldengirl ☐ Great Scout and Cathouse Thursday ☐ Hanged Man, The ☐ Hannie Caulder ☐ Her Life as a Man ☐ Hickey & Boggs ☐ Hot Rod ☐ Houston, We've Got a Problem ☐ I Spy Returns ☐ Inside Out ☐ Killjoy ☐ Murderous Vision ☐ Name for Evil, A ☐ National Lampoon

Goes to the Movies ☐ Night the City Screamed, The ☐ Outrage ☐ PT 109 ☐ Raiders, The ☐ Rhino! ☐ Sammy, the Way-Out Seal ☐ Silent Night, Deadly Night (Part III—Better Watch Out!) ☐ Sunday in New York ☐ Timebomb ☐ Turk 182! ☐ Voyage of Terror: The Achille Lauro Affair

Culver, Roland ☐ Emperor Waltz, The ☐ Encore ☐ Folly to Be Wise ☐ Fragment of Fear ☐ Mad Little Island ☐ Man Could Get Killed, A ☐ Man Who Loved Redheads, The ☐ Next to No Time ☐ Night Train to Munich ☐ No Longer Alone ☐ Obsessed, The ☐ On Approval ☐ Secret Mission ☐ Ship That Died of Shame, The ☐ Spitfire ☐ To Each His Own ☐ Vacation From Marriage

Cummings, Constance ☐ Battle of the Sexes, The ☐ Behind the Mask ☐ Blithe Spirit ☐ Boy Ten Feet Tall, A ☐ Broadway Through a Keyhole ☐ Criminal Code, The ☐ Dead Man's Folly ☐ Finger of Guilt ☐ Foreman Went to France, The ☐ Haunted Honeymoon ☐ In the Cool of the Day ☐ Into the Blue ☐ John and Julie ☐ Movie Crazy ☐ Night After Night ☐ This Man Is Mine

Cummings, Robert ☐ Accused, The ☐ Barefoot Mailman, The ☐ Between Us Girls ☐ Bride Wore Boots, The ☐ Chase, The ☐ Devil and Miss Jones, The ☐ Dial M for Murder ☐ Everything Happens at Night ☐ First Time, The ☐ Five Golden Dragons ☐ Flesh and Fantasy ☐ For Heaven's Sake ☐ Free For All ☐ Heaven Only Knows ☐ Hollywood Boulevard ☐ How to Be Very, Very Popular ☐ It Started with Eve ☐ Kings Row ☐ Lost Moment, The ☐ Lucky Me ☐ Marry Me Again ☐ Moon Over Miami ☐ My Geisha ☐ My Hero 1 ☐ One Night in the Tropics ☐ Paid in Full ☐ Princess O'Rourke ☐ Saboteur ☐ Sleep My Love ☐ So Red the Rose ☐ Souls at Sea ☐ Spring Parade ☐ Tell It to the Judge ☐ Three Smart Girls Grow Up ☐ Under-Pup, The ☐ Wells Fargo

Cummins, Peggy ☐ Always a Bride ☐ Both Sides of the Law ☐ Captain's Table, The ☐ Carry on Admiral ☐ Curse of the Demon ☐ Escape ☐ Green Grass of Wyoming ☐ Gun Crazy ☐ Hell Drivers ☐ If This Be Sin ☐ Late George Apley, The ☐ Love Lottery, The ☐ March Hare, The ☐ Meet Mr. Lucifer ☐ Operation X ☐ Passionate Sentry, The

Curry, Tim ☐ Annie ☐ Clue ☐ FernGully . . . The Last Rainforest ☐ Home Alone 2: Lost in New York ☐ Legend ☐ Marzipan Pig, The ☐ Oliver Twist ☐ Oscar ☐ Pass the Ammo ☐ Ploughman's Lunch, The ☐ Rocky Horror Picture Show, The ☐ Shadow, The ☐ Shout, The ☐ Three Musketeers, The ☐ Times Square

Curtin, Jane ☐ Common Ground ☐ Coneheads, The ☐ Divorce Wars: A Love Story ☐ How to Beat the High Cost of Living ☐ Maybe Baby ☐ Mr. Mike's Mondo Video ☐ O.C. & Stiggs ☐ Suspicion

Curtis, Alan ☐ Buck Privates ☐ Destiny ☐ Flight to Nowhere ☐ Four Sons ☐ Frisco Sal ☐ High Sierra ☐ Hitler's Madman ☐ Inside Job ☐ Invisible Man's Revenge, The ☐ Mannequin ☐ Melody Master ☐ Naughty Nineties ☐ Phantom Lady ☐ Philo Vance's Secret Mission ☐ Pirates of Capri, The ☐ Sergeant Madden ☐ Yellow Jack

Curtis, Jamie Lee ☐ Amazing Grace and Chuck ☐ As Summers Die ☐ Blue Steel ☐ Coming Soon ☐ Death of a Centerfold: The Dorothy Stratten Story ☐ Dominick and Eugene ☐ Film House Fever ☐ Fish Called Wanda, A ☐ Fog, The ☐ Forever Young ☐ Grandview, U.S.A. ☐ Halloween ☐ Halloween II ☐ Love Letters ☐ Man in Love, A ☐ Mother's Boys ☐ My Girl ☐ My Girl 2 ☐ Perfect ☐ Prom Night ☐ Queens Logic ☐ Road Games ☐ Terror Train ☐ Trading Places ☐ True Lies

Curtis, Tony ☐ All American, The ☐ Arrivederci, Baby ☐ Bad News Bears Go To Japan, The ☐ Balboa ☐ Beachhead ☐ Black Shield of Falworth, The ☐ Boeing Boeing ☐ Boston Strangler, The ☐ Brainwaves ☐ Captain Newman, M.D. ☐ Center of the Web ☐ Christmas in Connecticut ☐ Count of Monte Cristo, The ☐ Defiant Ones, The ☐ Don't Make Waves ☐ Flesh and Fury ☐ Forbidden ☐ Forty Pounds of Trouble ☐ Goodbye Charlie ☐ Great Impostor, The ☐ Great Race, The ☐ Houdini ☐ Insignificance ☐ It Rained All Night the Day I Left ☐ Johnny Dark ☐ Kansas Raiders ☐ Kings Go Forth ☐ Last of Philip Banter, The ☐ Last Tycoon, The ☐ Lepke ☐ List of Adrian Messenger, The ☐ Little Miss Marker ☐ Lobsterman from Mars ☐ Mafia Princess ☐ Manitou, The ☐ Midnight ☐ Midnight Story, The ☐ Mirror Crack'd, The ☐ Mister Cory ☐ Naked in New York ☐ No Room for the Groom ☐ Not with My Wife You Don't! ☐ On My Way to the Crusades, I Met a Girl Who . . . ☐ Operation Petticoat ☐ Outsider, The ☐ Perfect Furlough, The ☐ Purple Mask, The ☐ Rat Race, The ☐ Rawhide Years, The ☐ Sex and the Single Girl ☐ Sex on the Run ☐ Sextette ☐ Six Bridges to Cross ☐ So This Is Paris ☐ Some Like It Cool ☐ Some Like It Hot ☐ Son of Ali Baba ☐ Spartacus ☐ Square Jungle, The ☐ Suppose They Gave a War and Nobody Came? ☐ Sweet Smell of Success ☐ Taras Bulba ☐ Tarzan in Manhattan ☐ Thanksgiving Day ☐ Those Daring Young Men in Their Jaunty Jalopies ☐ Trapeze ☐ Vikings, The ☐ Who Was That Lady? ☐ Wild and Wonderful ☐ Winchester '73

Cusack, Cyril ☐ Abdication, The ☐ All the Way, Boys ☐ Blue Lagoon, The ☐ Blue Veil, The ☐ Brotherly Love ☐ Catholics ☐ Day of the Jackal, The ☐ Devil's Widow, The ☐ Escape ☐ Esther Waters ☐ Fahrenheit 451 ☐ Fighting Pimpernel, The ☐ Floods of Fear ☐ Gideon of Scotland Yard ☐ Gone to Earth

☐ Harold and Maude ☐ Homecoming, The ☐ I Thank a Fool ☐ Ill Met by Moonlight ☐ Jacqueline ☐ King Lear ☐ Les Miserables ☐ Little Dorrit ☐ Lovespell ☐ March Hare, The ☐ Miracle in Soho ☐ My Left Foot ☐ Night Ambush ☐ Night Fighters, The ☐ Odd Man Out ☐ Oedipus the King ☐ Passage Home ☐ Rise of the Moon, The ☐ Sacco and Vanzetti ☐ Shake Hands with the Devil ☐ Soldiers Three ☐ Spanish Gardener, The ☐ Taming of the Shrew, The ☐ Tenth Man, The ☐ Time Lost and Time Remembered ☐ Where the Spies Are

Cusack, Joan ☐ Addams Family Values ☐ Allnighter, The ☐ Broadcast News ☐ Class ☐ Corinna, Corinna ☐ Hero ☐ Married to the Mob ☐ Men Don't Leave ☐ My Blue Heaven ☐ Stars and Bars ☐ Toys ☐ Working Girl

Cusack, John ☐ Better Off Dead ☐ Bullets Over Broadway ☐ Class ☐ Eight Men Out ☐ Fat Man and Little Boy ☐ Floundering ☐ Grifters, The ☐ Hot Pursuit ☐ Journey of Natty Gann, The ☐ Map of the Human Heart ☐ Money for Nothing ☐ One Crazy Summer ☐ Road to Wellville, The ☐ Say Anything . . . ☐ Shadows and Fog ☐ Sixteen Candles ☐ Sure Thing, The ☐ Tapeheads ☐ True Colors

Cusack, Sinead ☐ Bad Behavior ☐ Hoffman ☐ Inn of the Frightened People ☐ Waterland

Cushing, Peter ☐ And Now the Screaming Starts ☐ Arabian Adventure ☐ Asylum ☐ At the Earth's Core ☐ Beast Must Die, The ☐ Biggles: Adventures in Time ☐ Black Knight, The ☐ Bloodsuckers ☐ Brides of Dracula ☐ Call Him Mr. Shatter ☐ Creeping Flesh, The ☐ Curse of Frankenstein, The ☐ Daleks—Invasion Earth 2150 A.D. ☐ Dirty Knight's Work ☐ Dr. Phibes Rises Again ☐ Dr. Terror's House of Horrors ☐ Dr. Who and the Daleks ☐ Dracula A.D. ☐ End of the Affair, The ☐ Evil of Frankenstein, The ☐ Fear in the Night ☐ Flesh and the Fiends, The ☐ Frankenstein and the Monster From Hell ☐ Frankenstein Created Woman ☐ Frankenstein Must Be Destroyed! ☐ From Beyond the Grave ☐ Fury at Smugglers Bay ☐ Ghoul, The ☐ Gorgon, The ☐ Horror Express ☐ Horror of Dracula ☐ Hound of the Baskervilles, The ☐ House of the Long Shadows ☐ House That Dripped Blood, The ☐ I, Monster ☐ Island of Terror ☐ Island of the Burning Doomed ☐ John Paul Jones ☐ Land of the Minotaur ☐ Legend of the Werewolf ☐ Madhouse ☐ Man Who Finally Died, The ☐ Masks of Death ☐ Monster Island ☐ Moulin Rouge ☐ Mummy, The ☐ Nothing But the Night ☐ Revenge of Frankenstein, The ☐ Risk, The ☐ Satanic Rites of Dracula, The ☐ Scream and Scream Again ☐ Seven Brothers Meet Dracula, The ☐ She ☐ Shock Waves ☐ Skull, The ☐ Star Wars ☐ Sword of the Valiant ☐ Tale of Two Cities, A ☐ Tales from the Crypt ☐ Time Without Pity ☐ Top Secret ☐ Torture Garden ☐ Twins of Evil ☐ Vampire Lovers, The ☐ Violent Playground

D'Angelo, Beverly ☐ Big Trouble ☐ Coal Miner's Daughter ☐ Cold Front ☐ Daddy's Dyin'. . . Who's Got the Will? ☐ Every Which Way but Loose ☐ Finders Keepers ☐ First Love ☐ Hair ☐ Hands of a Stranger ☐ High Spirits ☐ Highpoint ☐ Honky Tonk Freeway ☐ In the Mood ☐ Lightning Jack ☐ Maid to Order ☐ Man Trouble ☐ Menendez: A Killing in Beverly Hills ☐ Miracle, The ☐ National Lampoon's Christmas Vacation ☐ National Lampoon's European Vacation ☐ National Lampoon's Vacation ☐ Paternity ☐ Pope Must Diet, The ☐ Slow Burn ☐ Streetcar Named Desire, A

da Silva, Howard ☐ 1776 ☐ Abe Lincoln In Illinois ☐ Blue Dahlia, The ☐ Border Incident ☐ David and Lisa ☐ Fourteen Hours ☐ I'm Still Alive ☐ Lost Weekend, The ☐ M ☐ Missiles of October, The ☐ Mommie Dearest ☐ Nine Lives Are Not Enough ☐ They Live by Night ☐ Three Husbands ☐ Tripoli ☐ Two Years Before the Mast ☐ Unconquered

Dafoe, Willem ☐ Body of Evidence ☐ Born on the Fourth of July ☐ Clear and Present Danger ☐ Faraway, So Close ☐ Flight of the Intruder ☐ Last Temptation of Christ, The ☐ Light Sleeper ☐ Loveless, The ☐ Mississippi Burning ☐ Off Limits ☐ Platoon ☐ Streets of Fire ☐ To Live and Die in L.A. ☐ Tom and Viv ☐ Triumph of the Spirit ☐ White Sands ☐ Wild at Heart

Dahl, Arlene ☐ Ambush ☐ Bengal Brigade ☐ Bride Goes Wild, The ☐ Caribbean ☐ Here Come the Girls ☐ Jamaica Run ☐ Journey to the Center of the Earth, The ☐ Kisses for My President ☐ Land Raiders ☐ My Wild Irish Rose ☐ Night of the Warrior ☐ No Questions Asked ☐ Scene of the Crime ☐ Slightly Scarlet ☐ Southern Yankee, A ☐ Three Little Words ☐ Watch the Birdie ☐ Woman's World

Dailey, Dan ☐ Adventures of a Young Man ☐ Best Things in Life Are Free, The ☐ Call Me Mister ☐ Captain Is a Lady, The ☐ Chicken Every Sunday ☐ Girl Next Door, The ☐ Give My Regards to Broadway ☐ I Can Get It for You Wholesale ☐ It's Always Fair Weather ☐ Kid From Left Field, The ☐ Lady Be Good ☐ Meet Me at the Fair ☐ Meet Me in Las Vegas ☐ Mother Wore Tights ☐ My Blue Heaven ☐ Oh, Men! Oh, Women! ☐ Panama Hattie ☐ Pepe ☐ Pride of St. Louis, The ☐ Private Files of J. Edgar Hoover, The ☐ There's No Business Like Show Business ☐ Ticket to Tomahawk, A ☐ Wayward Bus, The ☐ What Price Glory? ☐ When My Baby Smiles at Me ☐ When Willie Comes Marching Home ☐ Wild Man of Borneo, The ☐ Wings of Eagles, The ☐ You're My Everything ☐ Ziegfeld Girl

Dale, Jim ☐ Adventures of Huckleberry Finn ☐ American Clock, The ☐ Big Job, The

☐ Carry on Doctor ☐ Digby—The Biggest Dog in the World ☐ Follow That Camel ☐ Hot Lead & Cold Feet ☐ Joseph Andrews ☐ National Health, The ☐ Nurse on Wheels ☐ Pete's Dragon ☐ Scandalous ☐ Unidentified Flying Oddball

Dalio, Marcel ☐ Beethoven's Great Love ☐ Big Risk, The ☐ Mad Adventures of "Rabbi" Jacob, The ☐ Man Who Understood Women, The ☐ On the Riviera ☐ Rich, Young and Pretty ☐ Rules of the Game, The ☐ Sun Also Rises, The

Dalton, Timothy ☐ Agatha ☐ Brenda Starr ☐ Chanel Solitaire ☐ Cromwell ☐ Doctor and the Devils, The ☐ Flame Is Love, The ☐ Flash Gordon ☐ Florence Nightingale ☐ Hawks ☐ Jane Eyre ☐ King's Whore, The ☐ Licence to Kill ☐ Lion in Winter, The ☐ Living Daylights, The ☐ Mary, Queen of Scots ☐ Master of Ballantrae, The ☐ Mistral's Daughter ☐ Naked in New York ☐ Permission to Kill ☐ Rocketeer, The ☐ Sextette ☐ Sins ☐ Wuthering Heights

Daly, Tyne ☐ Angel Unchained ☐ Aviator, The ☐ Cagney & Lacey ☐ Enforcer, The ☐ Entertainer, The ☐ Face of a Stranger ☐ Intimate Strangers ☐ John and Mary ☐ Larry ☐ Last to Go ☐ Man Who Could Talk to Kids, The ☐ Matter of Life and Death, A ☐ Movers and Shakers ☐ On The Town ☐ Telefon ☐ Women's Room, The ☐ Zoot Suit

Dance, Charles ☐ Alien,3 ☐ China Moon ☐ Golden Child, The ☐ Hidden City ☐ Jewel in the Crown ☐ Last Action Hero ☐ McGuffin, The ☐ Out of the Shadows ☐ Out on a Limb ☐ Pascali's Island ☐ Plenty ☐ White Mischief

Dangerfield, Rodney ☐ Back to School ☐ Caddyshack ☐ Easy Money ☐ Ladybugs ☐ Projectionist, The ☐ Rover Dangerfield

Daniell, Henry ☐ Body Snatcher, The ☐ Camille ☐ Exile, The ☐ Firefly, The ☐ Four Skulls of Jonathan Drake, The ☐ Jane Eyre ☐ Madame X ☐ Madison Avenue ☐ My Fair Lady ☐ Nightmare ☐ Sea Hawk, The ☐ Sherlock Holmes and the Voice of Terror ☐ Sherlock Holmes in Washington ☐ Song of Love ☐ Sun Also Rises, The ☐ Unguarded Hour, The ☐ Wake of the Red Witch ☐ We Are Not Alone ☐ Woman in Green, The

Daniels, Bebe ☐ 42nd Street ☐ Counsellor-at-Law ☐ Dixiana ☐ Feel My Pulse ☐ Harold Lloyd's World of Comedy ☐ Maltese Falcon, The ☐ Music Is Magic ☐ My Past ☐ Reaching for the Moon ☐ Rio Rita ☐ Silver Dollar

Daniels, Jeff ☐ Arachnophobia ☐ Butcher's Wife, The ☐ Caine Mutiny Court-Martial, The ☐ Checking Out ☐ Disaster in Time ☐ Dumb and Dumber ☐ Gettysburg ☐ Heartburn ☐ House on Carroll Street, The ☐ Love Hurts ☐ Marie ☐ No Place Like Home ☐ Purple Rose of Cairo, The ☐ Radio Days ☐ Rain Without Thunder ☐ Something Wild ☐ Sweet Hearts Dance ☐ Teamster Boss: The Jackie Presser Story ☐ Terms of Endearment ☐ There Goes the Neighborhood ☐ Welcome Home, Roxy Carmichael

Danner, Blythe ☐ 1776 ☐ Alice ☐ Another Woman ☐ Are You in the House Alone? ☐ Brighton Beach Memoirs ☐ F. Scott Fitzgerald and "The Last of the Belles" ☐ Futureworld ☐ Great Santini, The ☐ Guilty Conscience, The ☐ Hearts of the West ☐ Helen Keller: The Miracle Continues ☐ In Defense of Kids ☐ Inside the Third Reich ☐ Judgment ☐ Love Affair, A: The Eleanor and Lou Gehrig Story ☐ Lovin' Molly ☐ Man, Woman and Child ☐ Mr. & Mrs. Bridge ☐ Never Forget ☐ Oldest Living Confederate Widow Tells All ☐ Prince of Tides, The ☐ To Kill a Clown ☐ Too Far to Go

Danson, Ted ☐ Body Heat ☐ Cousins ☐ Creepshow ☐ Dad ☐ Fine Mess, A ☐ Getting Even with Dad ☐ Just Between Friends ☐ Little Treasure ☐ Made in America ☐ Once Upon a Spy ☐ Our Family Business ☐ Pontiac Moon ☐ Something About Amelia ☐ Three Men and a Baby ☐ Three Men and a Little Lady ☐ When the Bough Breaks ☐ Women's Room, The

Dantine, Helmut ☐ Bring Me the Head of Alfredo Garcia ☐ Edge of Darkness ☐ Escape in the Desert ☐ Hell on Devil's Island ☐ Hotel Berlin ☐ Mrs. Miniver ☐ Northern Pursuit ☐ Stranger From Venus ☐ Whispering City

Danton, Ray ☐ George Raft Story, The ☐ Ice Palace ☐ Majority of One, A ☐ Night Runner, The ☐ Our Man Flint: Dead on Target ☐ Rise and Fall of Legs Diamond, The ☐ Tarawa Beachhead

Darby, Kim ☐ Better Off Dead ☐ Bus Riley's Back in Town ☐ Don't Be Afraid of the Dark ☐ Enola Gay ☐ First Steps ☐ Flatbed Annie & Sweetiepie: Lady Truckers ☐ Generation ☐ Grissom Gang, The ☐ Norwood ☐ One and Only, The ☐ People, The ☐ Teen Wolf Too ☐ True Grit

Darnell, Linda ☐ 13th Letter, The ☐ Angels of Darkness ☐ Anna and the King of Siam ☐ Black Spurs ☐ Blackbeard, the Pirate ☐ Blood and Sand ☐ Brigham Young ☐ Buffalo Bill ☐ Centennial Summer ☐ Chad Hanna ☐ City Without Men ☐ Dakota Incident ☐ Day-Time Wife ☐ Everybody Does It ☐ Fallen Angel ☐ Forever Amber ☐ Great John L., The ☐ Guy Who Came Back, The ☐ Hangover Square ☐ Hotel for Women ☐ Island of Desire ☐ It Happened Tomorrow ☐ Lady Pays Off, The ☐ Letter to Three Wives, A ☐ Loves of Edgar Allan Poe, The ☐ Mark of Zorro, The ☐ My Darling Clementine ☐ Night Without Sleep ☐ No Way Out ☐ Rise and Shine ☐ Second Chance ☐ Star Dust ☐ Summer Storm ☐ Two Flags West ☐ Unfaithfully Yours ☐ Walls of Jericho, The ☐ Zero Hour

Darrieux, Danielle ☐ 5 Fingers ☐ Adorable Creatures ☐ Alexander the Great ☐ Bluebeard

☐ Earrings of Madame de... ☐ Earrings of Madame de . . . , The ☐ Few Days with Me, A ☐ Her First Affair ☐ La Ronde ☐ Le Plaisir ☐ Le Rouge et le Noir ☐ Loss of Innocence ☐ Lovers of Paris ☐ Mayerling ☐ One Step to Eternity ☐ Rage of Paris, The ☐ Red and the Black, The ☐ Rich, Young and Pretty ☐ Scene of the Crime ☐ Young Girls of Rochefort, The

Darwell, Jane ☐ Affair with a Stranger ☐ All Through the Night ☐ Back Street ☐ Battle of Midway, The ☐ Before Dawn ☐ Bigamist, The ☐ Brigham Young ☐ Caged ☐ Captain Tugboat Annie ☐ Chad Hanna ☐ Craig's Wife ☐ Curly Top ☐ Daughter of Rosie O'Grady, The ☐ Design for Living ☐ Devil and Daniel Webster, The ☐ Father's Wild Game ☐ Fifty Roads to Town ☐ Girls in Prison ☐ Grapes of Wrath, The ☐ Great Gildersleeve, The ☐ Huckleberry Finn ☐ Impatient Years, The ☐ It Happened in Flatbush ☐ It Happens Every Thursday ☐ Jesse James ☐ Ladies of the Big House ☐ Lemon Drop Kid, The ☐ Life Begins at Forty ☐ Love Is News ☐ Loves of Edgar Allan Poe, The ☐ Nancy Steel Is Missing ☐ One More Spring ☐ Paddy O'Day ☐ Ramona ☐ Red Stallion, The ☐ Slave Ship ☐ Star for a Night ☐ Sun Shines Bright, The ☐ Tender Comrade ☐ Three Blind Mice ☐ Three Wise Fools ☐ Untamed ☐ Wagon Master ☐ We're Not Married ☐ Wife, Doctor and Nurse

Dauphin, Claude ☐ April in Paris ☐ Barbarella ☐ Casque D'or ☐ Conflict ☐ Curtain Rises, The ☐ Deported ☐ Eglantine ☐ Innocents in Paris ☐ Lady L ☐ Le Plaisir ☐ Les Miserables ☐ Little Boy Lost ☐ Madame Rosa ☐ Madwoman of Chaillot, The ☐ Phantom of the Rue Morgue ☐ Quiet American, The ☐ Symphony for a Massacre ☐ Two for the Road

Davidovich, Lolita ☐ Blaze ☐ Boiling Point ☐ Cobb ☐ Inner Circle, The ☐ Intersection ☐ Leap of Faith ☐ Object of Beauty, The ☐ Prison Stories: Women on the Inside ☐ Raising Cain

Davies, Marion ☐ Bachelor Father, The ☐ Blondie of the Follies ☐ Cain and Mabel ☐ Ever Since Eve ☐ Five and Ten ☐ Florodora Girl, The ☐ Going Hollywood ☐ Hearts Divided ☐ Hollywood Revue of 1929, The ☐ Marianne ☐ Operator 13 ☐ Page Miss Glory ☐ Peg o' My Heart ☐ Polly of the Circus ☐ Show People

Davis, Jr., Sammy ☐ Alice in Wonderland ☐ Anna Lucasta ☐ Cannonball Run II ☐ Cannonball Run, The ☐ Convicts Four ☐ Cracking Up ☐ Heidi's Song ☐ Johnny Cool ☐ Kid Who Loved Christmas, The ☐ Little Moon and Jud McGraw ☐ Man Called Adam, A ☐ Ocean's Eleven ☐ One More Time ☐ Porgy and Bess ☐ Robin and the Seven Hoods ☐ Sergeants 3 ☐ Sweet Charity ☐ Tap ☐ That's Dancing

Davis, Bette ☐ 20,000 Years in Sing Sing ☐ All About Eve ☐ All This and Heaven Too ☐ Anniversary, The ☐ Another Man's Poison ☐ As Summers Die ☐ Beyond the Forest ☐ Big Shakedown, The ☐ Bordertown ☐ Bride Came C.O.D., The ☐ Bunny O'Hare ☐ Bureau of Missing Persons ☐ Burnt Offerings ☐ Cabin in the Cotton, The ☐ Catered Affair, The ☐ Connecting Rooms ☐ Corn Is Green, The ☐ Dangerous ☐ Dark Horse ☐ Dark Secret of Harvest Home ☐ Dark Victory ☐ Dead Ringer ☐ Death on the Nile ☐ Deception ☐ Disappearance of Aimee, The ☐ Empty Canvas, The ☐ Ex-Lady ☐ Family Reunion ☐ Fashions ☐ Fog Over Frisco ☐ Front Page Woman ☐ Girl from 10th Avenue, The ☐ Golden Arrow, The ☐ Great Lie, The ☐ Hell's House ☐ Hollywood Canteen ☐ Housewife ☐ Hush . . . Hush, Sweet Charlotte ☐ In This Our Life ☐ It's Love I'm After ☐ Jezebel ☐ Jimmy the Gent ☐ John Paul Jones ☐ Juarez ☐ Judge and Jake Wyler, The ☐ June Bride ☐ Kid Galahad ☐ Letter, The ☐ Little Foxes, The ☐ Little Gloria-Happy At Last ☐ Madame Sin ☐ Man Who Came to Dinner, The ☐ Man Who Played God, The ☐ Marked Woman ☐ Menace, The ☐ Mr. Skeffington ☐ Murder with Mirrors ☐ Nanny, The ☐ Now, Voyager ☐ Of Human Bondage ☐ Old Acquaintance ☐ Old Maid, The ☐ Parachute Jumper ☐ Payment on Demand ☐ Petrified Forest, The ☐ Phone Call from a Stranger ☐ Piano for Mrs. Cimino, A ☐ Pocketful of Miracles ☐ Private Lives of Elizabeth and Essex, The ☐ Return from Witch Mountain ☐ Right of Way ☐ Satan Met a Lady ☐ Scapegoat, The ☐ Scream, Pretty Peggy ☐ Sisters, The ☐ Special Agent ☐ Star, The ☐ Stolen Life, A ☐ Storm Center ☐ Strangers: The Story of a Mother and Daughter ☐ Thank Your Lucky Stars ☐ That Certain Woman ☐ Three on a Match ☐ Virgin Queen, The ☐ Watch on the Rhine ☐ Watcher in the Woods, The ☐ Whales of August, The ☐ What Ever Happened to Baby Jane? ☐ Where Love Has Gone ☐ Wicked Stepmother ☐ Winter Meeting ☐ Working Man, The

Davis, Brad ☐ Blood Ties ☐ Caine Mutiny Court-Martial, The ☐ Chariots of Fire ☐ Chiefs ☐ Child of Darkness, Child of Light ☐ Cold Steel ☐ Greatest Man in the World, The ☐ Habitation of Dragons, The ☐ Heart ☐ Midnight Express ☐ Querelle ☐ Rosalie Goes Shopping ☐ Rumor of War, A ☐ Sybil ☐ When the Time Comes

Davis, Geena ☐ Accidental Tourist, The ☐ Angie ☐ Beetlejuice ☐ Earth Girls Are Easy ☐ Fletch ☐ Fly, The ☐ Hero ☐ League of Their Own, A ☐ Quick Change ☐ Speechless ☐ Thelma & Louise ☐ Transylvania 6-5000

Davis, Jim ☐ Apache Warrior ☐ Bad Company ☐ Badge of Marshal Brennan, The ☐ Blonde Bait ☐ Cavalry Scout ☐ Duel at

Apache Wells ☐ Flaming Frontier ☐ Fort Utah ☐ Gallant Bess ☐ Gun Riders ☐ Hellfire ☐ Jesse James Meets Frankenstein's Daughter ☐ Law of the Land ☐ Monster from Green Hell ☐ Monte Walsh ☐ Noose for a Gunman ☐ Outcast, The ☐ Outlaw's Daughter, The ☐ Winter Meeting ☐ Zebra in the Kitchen

Davis, Joan ☐ Around the World ☐ Day-Time Wife ☐ George White's Scandals ☐ Groom Wore Spurs, The ☐ Harem Girl ☐ Hold That Co-ed ☐ Hold That Ghost ☐ If You Knew Susie ☐ Josette ☐ Just Around the Corner ☐ Kansas City Kitty ☐ Life Begins in College ☐ Love That Brute ☐ Make Mine Laughs ☐ On the Avenue ☐ Sally, Irene and Mary ☐ Show Business ☐ Sun Valley Serenade ☐ Thin Ice ☐ Wake Up and Live

Davis, Judy ☐ Alice ☐ Amore ☐ Barton Fink ☐ Final Option, The ☐ Heatwave ☐ High Rolling In A Hot Corvette ☐ High Tide ☐ Hoodwink ☐ Husbands and Wives ☐ Impromptu ☐ Kangaroo ☐ My Brilliant Career ☐ Naked Lunch ☐ New Age, The ☐ One Against the Wind ☐ Passage to India, A ☐ Ref, The ☐ Where Angels Fear to Tread ☐ Winter of Our Dreams, The ☐ Woman Called Golda, A

Davis, Nancy ☐ Donovan's Brain ☐ East Side, West Side ☐ Hellcats of the Navy ☐ It's a Big Country ☐ Next Voice You Hear, The ☐ Night into Morning ☐ Shadow in the Sky ☐ Shadow on the Wall

Davison, Bruce ☐ Affair, The ☐ Been Down So Long It Looks Like Up to Me ☐ Brass Target, The ☐ Crimes of Passion ☐ Deadman's Curve ☐ Far From Home: The Adventures of Yellow Dog ☐ French Quarter ☐ Ghost Dancing ☐ Grand Jury ☐ High Risk ☐ Incident at Crestridge ☐ Jerusalem File, The ☐ Last Summer ☐ Lathe of Heaven, The ☐ Lies ☐ Live From Death Row ☐ Longtime Companion ☐ Mame ☐ Misfit Brigade, The ☐ Mother, Jugs & Speed ☐ Short Eyes ☐ Six Degrees of Separation ☐ Spies Like Us ☐ Summer of My German Soldier ☐ Ulzana's Raid ☐ Willard

Davis, Ossie ☐ All God's Children ☐ Avenging Angel ☐ Cardinal, The ☐ Countdown at Kusini ☐ Do the Right Thing ☐ Gladiator ☐ Gone Are the Days ☐ Grumpy Old Men ☐ Hill, The ☐ Hot Stuff ☐ House of God, The ☐ Joe Versus the Volcano ☐ Jungle Fever ☐ King ☐ Malcolm X ☐ Man Called Adam, A ☐ Night Gallery ☐ No Way Out ☐ Sam Whiskey ☐ Scalphunters, The ☐ School Daze

Day-Lewis, Daniel ☐ Age of Innocence, The ☐ Bounty, The ☐ Eversmile, New Jersey ☐ In the Name of the Father ☐ Insurance Man, The ☐ Last of the Mohicans, The ☐ My Beautiful Laundrette ☐ My Left Foot ☐ Room with a View, A ☐ Stars and Bars ☐ Unbearable Lightness of Being, The

Day, Doris ☐ April in Paris ☐ Ballad of Josie, The ☐ Billy Rose's Jumbo ☐ By the Light of the Silvery Moon ☐ Calamity Jane ☐ Caprice ☐ Do Not Disturb ☐ Glass Bottom Boat, The ☐ I'll See You in My Dreams ☐ It Happened to Jane ☐ It's a Great Feeling ☐ Julie ☐ Love Me or Leave Me ☐ Lover Come Back ☐ Lucky Me ☐ Lullaby of Broadway ☐ Man Who Knew Too Much, The ☐ Midnight Lace ☐ Move Over, Darling ☐ My Dream Is Yours ☐ On Moonlight Bay ☐ Pajama Game, The ☐ Pillow Talk ☐ Please Don't Eat the Daisies ☐ Romance on the High Seas ☐ Send Me No Flowers ☐ Storm Warning ☐ Tea for Two ☐ Teacher's Pet ☐ That Touch of Mink ☐ Thrill Of It All, The ☐ Tunnel of Love, The ☐ West Point Story ☐ Where Were You When the Lights Went Out? ☐ Winning Team, The ☐ With Six You Get Eggroll ☐ Young at Heart ☐ Young Man With a Horn

Day, Laraine ☐ Bad Man, The ☐ Calling Dr. Kildare ☐ Dr. Kildare Goes Home ☐ Dr. Kildare's Crisis ☐ Dr. Kildare's Strange Case ☐ Dr. Kildare's Wedding Day ☐ Fingers at the Window ☐ Foreign Correspondent ☐ High and the Mighty, The ☐ I Married a Communist ☐ I Take This Woman ☐ Journey for Margaret ☐ Kathleen ☐ Keep Your Powder Dry ☐ Locket, The ☐ Mr. Lucky ☐ Murder on Flight 502 ☐ My Dear Secretary ☐ My Son, My Son ☐ Secret of Dr. Kildare, The ☐ Sergeant Madden ☐ Story of Dr. Wassell, The ☐ Tarzan Finds a Son ☐ Tycoon ☐ Unholy Partners

de Banzie, Brenda ☐ Doctor At Sea ☐ Entertainer, The ☐ Flame in the Streets ☐ Happiness of Three Women, The ☐ Hobson's Choice ☐ Kid for Two Farthings, A ☐ Man Who Knew Too Much, The ☐ Mark, The ☐ Matter of Innocence, A ☐ 39 Steps, The ☐ Too Many Crooks

De Carlo, Yvonne ☐ American Gothic ☐ Bad Girls in the Movies ☐ Band of Angels ☐ Black Bart ☐ Border River ☐ Brute Force ☐ Buccaneer's Girl ☐ Calamity Jane and Sam Bass ☐ Captain's Paradise, The ☐ Casbah ☐ Cellar Dweller ☐ Criss Cross ☐ Death of a Scoundrel ☐ Desert Hawk, The ☐ Flame of the Islands ☐ Frontier Gal ☐ Gal Who Took the West, The ☐ Global Affair, A ☐ Guyana: Cult of the Damned ☐ Hostile Guns ☐ Hotel Sahara ☐ House of Shadows ☐ It Seemed Like a Good Idea at the Time ☐ Law of the Lawless ☐ Liar's Moon ☐ Magic Fire ☐ Mark of Zorro, The ☐ Masterpiece of Murder, A ☐ McLintock! ☐ Mirror, Mirror ☐ Munster, Go Home ☐ Munsters' Revenge, The ☐ Nocturna ☐ Passion ☐ Power, The ☐ Rainbow Island ☐ Raw Edge ☐ River Lady ☐ Road to Morocco ☐ Salome, Where She Danced ☐ San Francisco Story, The ☐ Satan's Cheerleaders ☐ Sea Devils ☐ Seven Minutes, The ☐ Shotgun ☐ Silver City ☐ Ten Commandments, The

De Cordova, Arturo ☐ El: This Strange Passion ☐ For Whom the Bell Tolls ☐ Frenchman's Creek ☐ Incendiary Blonde ☐ Masquerade in Mexico ☐ Medal for Benny, A ☐ New Orleans

de Corsia, Ted ☐ Inside the Mafia ☐ Inside the Walls of Folsom Prison ☐ It Happens Every Spring ☐ Man in the Dark ☐ Midnight Story, The ☐ Naked City, The ☐ Noose for a Gunman ☐ Quick Gun, The ☐ Savage, The ☐ Slightly Scarlet

De Funes, Louis ☐ Delusions of Grandeur ☐ Four Bags Full ☐ Innocents in Paris ☐ Mad Adventures of "Rabbi" Jacob, The ☐ Sucker, The

de Havilland, Olivia ☐ Adventurers, The ☐ Adventures of Robin Hood, The ☐ Airport '77 ☐ Ambassador's Daughter, The ☐ Anastasia: The Mystery Of Anna ☐ Anthony Adverse ☐ Call It a Day ☐ Captain Blood ☐ Charge of the Light Brigade, The ☐ Dark Mirror, The ☐ Devotion ☐ Dodge City ☐ Fifth Musketeer, The ☐ Four's a Crowd ☐ Gold Is Where You Find It ☐ Gone with the Wind ☐ Government Girl ☐ Great Garrick, The ☐ Hard to Get ☐ Heiress, The ☐ Hold Back the Dawn ☐ Hush . . . Hush, Sweet Charlotte ☐ In This Our Life ☐ Irish in Us, The ☐ It's Love I'm After ☐ Lady in a Cage ☐ Libel ☐ Light in the Piazza ☐ Male Animal, The ☐ Midsummer Night's Dream, A ☐ My Cousin Rachel ☐ My Love Came Back ☐ Not as a Stranger ☐ Pope Joan ☐ Princess O'Rourke ☐ Private Lives of Elizabeth and Essex, The ☐ Proud Rebel, The ☐ Raffles ☐ Roots: The Next Generation ☐ Santa Fe Trail ☐ Snake Pit, The ☐ Strawberry Blonde, The ☐ Swarm, The ☐ Thank Your Lucky Stars ☐ That Lady ☐ They Died With Their Boots On ☐ To Each His Own

De Mornay, Rebecca ☐ And God Created Woman ☐ Backdraft ☐ Blind Side ☐ By Dawn's Early Light ☐ Dealers ☐ Feds ☐ Getting Out ☐ Guilty as Sin ☐ Hand That Rocks the Cradle, The ☐ Inconvenient Woman, An ☐ Murders in the Rue Morgue, The ☐ Risky Business ☐ Runaway Train ☐ Slugger's Wife, The ☐ Three Musketeers, The ☐ Trip to Bountiful, The

De Niro, Robert ☐ 1900 ☐ Addict ☐ Angel Heart ☐ Awakenings ☐ Backdraft ☐ Bang the Drum Slowly ☐ Bloody Mama ☐ Brazil ☐ Bronx Tale, A ☐ Cape Fear ☐ Deer Hunter, The ☐ Falling in Love ☐ Gang That Couldn't Shoot Straight, The ☐ Godfather, Part II, The ☐ GoodFellas ☐ Greetings ☐ Guilty by Suspicion ☐ Hi, Mom! ☐ Jacknife ☐ King of Comedy, The ☐ Last Tycoon, The ☐ Mad Dog and Glory ☐ Mary Shelley's Frankenstein ☐ Mean Streets ☐ Midnight Run ☐ Mission, The ☐ Mistress ☐ New York, New York ☐ Night and the City ☐ Once Upon a Time in America ☐ Raging Bull ☐ Stanley & Iris ☐ Taxi Driver ☐ This Boy's Life ☐ True Confessions ☐ Untouchables, The ☐ Wedding Party, The ☐ We're No Angels

De Sica, Vittorio ☐ Amorous Adventures of Moll Flanders, The ☐ Andy Warhol's Dracula ☐ Angel in a Taxi ☐ Angel Wore Red, The ☐ Battle of Austerlitz, The ☐ Biggest Bundle Of Them All ☐ Bread, Love and Dreams ☐ Earrings of Madame de . . . , The ☐ Farewell to Arms, A ☐ Fast and Sexy ☐ Frisky ☐ General Della Rovere ☐ Gold of Naples, The ☐ Hello, Elephant ☐ It Started in Naples ☐ Lady Doctor ☐ Lafayette ☐ Millionairess, The ☐ Monte Carlo Story, The ☐ My Widow and I ☐ Peddlin' In Society ☐ Scandal in Sorrento ☐ Wonders of Aladdin, The

Dean, James ☐ East of Eden ☐ Fixed Bayonets ☐ Giant ☐ Hill Number One ☐ Rebel Without a Cause

DeCamp, Rosemary ☐ Big Hangover, The ☐ Blood on the Sun ☐ Bowery to Broadway ☐ By the Light of the Silvery Moon ☐ City Without Men ☐ Commandos Strike at Dawn, The ☐ Danger Signal ☐ Eyes in the Night ☐ From This Day Forward ☐ Jungle Book ☐ Life of Riley, The ☐ Main Street to Broadway ☐ Many Rivers to Cross ☐ Memories of a Fairy Godmother ☐ Merry Monahans, The ☐ Night into Morning ☐ Night unto Night ☐ Nora Prentiss ☐ Rhapsody in Blue ☐ Scandal Sheet ☐ So This Is Love ☐ Story of Seabiscuit, The ☐ Treasure of Lost Canyon, The

Dee, Frances ☐ American Tragedy, An ☐ Because of You ☐ Becky Sharp ☐ Blood Money ☐ Coast Guard ☐ Coming-Out Party ☐ Finishing School ☐ Four Faces West ☐ Gay Deception, The ☐ Gypsy Colt ☐ Happy Land ☐ I Walked with a Zombie ☐ If I Were King ☐ King of the Jungle ☐ Little Women ☐ Love Is a Racket ☐ Man Betrayed, A ☐ Meet the Stewarts ☐ Night of June 13 ☐ Of Human Bondage ☐ Payment on Demand ☐ Playboy of Paris ☐ Private Affairs of Bel Ami, The ☐ Reunion in Reno ☐ Rich Man's Folly ☐ Silver Cord, The ☐ Souls at Sea ☐ Wells Fargo

Dee, Ruby ☐ All God's Children ☐ Balcony, The ☐ Black Girl ☐ Buck and the Preacher ☐ Cat People ☐ Cop and a Half ☐ Countdown at Kusini ☐ Court-Martial of Jackie Robinson, The ☐ Decoration Day ☐ Do the Right Thing ☐ Edge of the City ☐ Go Tell It on the Mountain ☐ Gone Are the Days ☐ Gore Vidal's Lincoln ☐ I Know Why the Caged Bird Sings ☐ It's Good to Be Alive ☐ Jackie Robinson Story, The ☐ Jungle Fever ☐ Just Cause ☐ No Way Out ☐ Raisin in the Sun, A ☐ St. Louis Blues ☐ Stand, The ☐ Take a Giant Step

Dee, Sandra ☐ Come September ☐ Dunwich Horror, The ☐ Fantasy Island ☐ Gidget ☐ Houston, We've Got a Problem ☐ I'd Rather Be Rich ☐ If a Man Answers ☐ Imitation of Life ☐ Man Could Get Killed, A ☐ Manhunter, The ☐ Portrait in Black ☐ Reluctant Debutante, The ☐ Romanoff and

Juliet ☐ Rosie ☐ Stranger in My Arms ☐ Summer Place, A ☐ Take Her, She's Mine ☐ Tammy and the Doctor ☐ Tammy Tell Me True ☐ That Funny Feeling ☐ Until They Sail ☐ Wild and the Innocent, The

DeHaven, Gloria ☐ Best Foot Forward ☐ Between Two Women ☐ Bog ☐ Broadway Rhythm ☐ Down Among the Sheltering Palms ☐ Evening in Byzantium, An ☐ Girl Rush, The ☐ I'll Get By ☐ Off Sides ☐ Scene of the Crime ☐ So This Is Paris ☐ Step Lively ☐ Summer Holiday ☐ Susan and God ☐ Thin Man Goes Home, The ☐ Three Little Words ☐ Two Girls and a Sailor ☐ Two Tickets to Broadway ☐ Yellow Cab Man, The

Dekker, Albert ☐ Among the Living ☐ Buckskin Frontier ☐ Buy Me That Town ☐ Come Spy With Me ☐ Dr. Cyclops ☐ Experiment Perilous ☐ Forest Rangers, The ☐ French Key, The ☐ Furies, The ☐ Fury at Furnace Creek ☐ Gamera—The Invincible ☐ Hold That Blonde ☐ Illegal ☐ In Old California ☐ Incendiary Blonde ☐ Killers, The ☐ Kiss Me Deadly ☐ Once Upon a Honeymoon ☐ Pretender, The ☐ Rangers of Fortune ☐ Reaching for the Sun ☐ Salome, Where She Danced ☐ Seven Sinners ☐ Sound and the Fury, The ☐ Strange Cargo ☐ Suddenly, Last Summer ☐ Wait 'Til the Sun Shines, Nellie ☐ Woman of the Town, The ☐ Wonderful Country, The ☐ Wyoming

Del Rio, Dolores ☐ Accused ☐ Bird of Paradise ☐ Cheyenne Autumn ☐ Children of Sanchez, The ☐ Devil's Playground ☐ Flaming Star ☐ Flor Silvestre ☐ Flying Down to Rio ☐ Fugitive, The ☐ I Live for Love ☐ In Caliente ☐ International Settlement ☐ Journey into Fear ☐ Lancer Spy ☐ Man from Dakota, The ☐ More Than a Miracle ☐ What Price Glory? ☐ Wonder Bar

Dell, Gabriel ☐ Angels in Disguise ☐ Block Busters ☐ Blonde Dynamite ☐ Blues Busters ☐ Bowery Buckaroos ☐ Bowery Champs ☐ Come Out Fighting ☐ Dead End ☐ Fighting Fools ☐ Follow the Leader ☐ Framed ☐ Give Us Wings ☐ Hard Boiled Mahoney ☐ Hit the Road ☐ Hold That Baby! ☐ Kid Dynamite ☐ Lucky Losers ☐ Manchu Eagle Murder Caper Mystery, The ☐ Master Minds ☐ Million Dollar Kid ☐ Mr. Hex ☐ On Dress Parade ☐ Smugglers' Cove ☐ They Made Me a Criminal ☐ Trouble Makers

Delon, Alain ☐ Airport '79—The Concorde ☐ Any Number Can Win ☐ Assassination of Trotsky, The ☐ Borsalino ☐ Borsalino and Company ☐ Diabolically Yours ☐ Dirty Money ☐ Eclipse, The ☐ Farewell Friend ☐ Girl on a Motorcycle ☐ Godson, The ☐ Honor Among Thieves ☐ Hurried Man, The ☐ Is Paris Burning? ☐ Joy House ☐ Le Samourai ☐ Leopard, The ☐ Lost Command ☐ Mr. Klein ☐ Nouvelle Vague ☐ Once a Thief ☐ Purple Noon ☐ Red Sun ☐ Rocco and His Brothers ☐ Scorpio ☐ Sicilian Clan, The ☐ Spirits of the Dead ☐ Swann in Love ☐ Texas Across the River ☐ Yellow Rolls-Royce, The ☐ Zorro

Delon, Nathalie ☐ Bluebeard ☐ Game of Seduction ☐ Godson, The ☐ Le Samourai ☐ Le Sex Shop

Delpy, Julie ☐ Beatrice ☐ Before Sunrise ☐ Europa, Europa ☐ Killing Zoe ☐ Trois Couleurs: Blanc ☐ Trois Couleurs: Rouge ☐ Voyager

DeLuise, Dom ☐ Adventure of Sherlock Holmes' Smarter Brother, The ☐ All Dogs Go to Heaven ☐ Almost Pregnant ☐ American Tail, An ☐ American Tail: Fievel Goes West, An ☐ Best Little Whorehouse in Texas, The ☐ Busy Body, The ☐ Cannonball Run II ☐ Cannonball Run, The ☐ Cheap Detective, The ☐ Diary of a Young Comic ☐ End, The ☐ Fatso ☐ Glass Bottom Boat, The ☐ Going Bananas ☐ Happily Ever After ☐ Haunted Honeymoon ☐ History of the World Part I ☐ Hot Stuff ☐ Johnny Dangerously ☐ Loose Cannons ☐ Magic Voyage, The ☐ Munchie ☐ Norwood ☐ Only with Married Men ☐ Robin Hood: Men in Tights ☐ Secret of NIMH, The ☐ Sextette ☐ Silent Movie ☐ Smokey and the Bandit, Part 2 ☐ Twelve Chairs, The ☐ What's So Bad About Feeling Good? ☐ Who Is Harry Kellerman and Why Is He Saying Those Terrible Things About Me? ☐ Wholly Moses

Demarest, William ☐ After Office Hours ☐ All Through the Night ☐ Along Came Jones ☐ Behave Yourself ☐ Behind the Eight Ball ☐ Big City, The ☐ Blazing Forest, The ☐ Casino Murder Case ☐ Charlie Chan at the Opera ☐ Christmas in July ☐ Circus Clown, The ☐ Devil and Miss Jones, The ☐ Don't Be Afraid of the Dark ☐ Easy Living ☐ Escape from Fort Bravo ☐ Excuse My Dust ☐ Far Horizons, The ☐ First Legion, The ☐ Fog Over Frisco ☐ Fugitive Lady ☐ Girl in Every Port, A ☐ Glamour Boy ☐ Gracie Allen Murder Case, The ☐ Great Gambini, The ☐ Great Man Votes, The ☐ Great McGinty, The ☐ Great Moment, The ☐ Hail the Conquering Hero ☐ He's a Cockeyed Wonder ☐ Hell on Frisco Bay ☐ Jazz Singer, The ☐ Jolson Sings Again ☐ Jolson Story, The ☐ Josette ☐ Lady Eve, The ☐ Lady Wants Mink, The ☐ Little Men ☐ Lucy Gallant ☐ Miracle of Morgan's Creek, The ☐ Mountain, The ☐ Never a Dull Moment ☐ Night Has a Thousand Eyes ☐ Nine Girls ☐ Our Hearts Were Growing Up ☐ Palm Beach Story, The ☐ Pardon My Past ☐ Pardon My Sarong ☐ Perils of Pauline, The ☐ Private War of Major Benson, The ☐ Rawhide Years, The ☐ Red, Hot and Blue ☐ Riding High ☐ Salty O'Rourke ☐ Sincerely Yours ☐ Sorrowful Jones ☐ Sullivan's Travels ☐ That Darn Cat ☐ True to Life ☐ Variety Girl ☐ Viva Las Vegas ☐ When Willie Comes Marching Home ☐ Whispering Smith

Dempsey, Patrick ☐ Bank Robber ☐ Can't Buy Me Love ☐ Coup de Ville ☐ Face the Music ☐ Happy Together ☐ In a Shallow Grave ☐ In the Mood ☐ JFK: Reckless Youth ☐ Loverboy ☐ Meatballs III ☐ Mobsters ☐ Run ☐ With Honors

Dench, Judi ☐ 84 Charing Cross Road ☐ Handful of Dust, A ☐ He Who Rides a Tiger ☐ Henry V ☐ Midsummer Night's Dream, A ☐ Study in Terror, A ☐ Wetherby

Deneuve, Catherine ☐ April Fools, The ☐ Belle de Jour ☐ Benjamin ☐ Choice of Arms ☐ Dirty Money ☐ Donkey Skin ☐ Hunger, The ☐ Hustle ☐ Indochine ☐ It Only Happens to Others ☐ Je Vous Aime ☐ La Grande Bourgeoisie ☐ Last Metro, The ☐ Let's Hope It's a Girl ☐ Love Songs ☐ Lovers Like Us ☐ Male Hunt ☐ March or Die ☐ Matter of Resistance, A ☐ Mayerling ☐ Mississippi Mermaid ☐ Repulsion ☐ Scene of the Crime ☐ Slightly Pregnant Man, A ☐ Tristana ☐ Umbrellas of Cherbourg, The ☐ Young Girls of Rochefort, The

Dennehy, Brian ☐ Acceptable Risks ☐ Belly of an Architect, The ☐ Best Seller ☐ Blood Feud ☐ Burden of Proof, The ☐ Butch and Sundance: The Early Days ☐ Check Is in the Mail, The ☐ Cocoon ☐ Day One ☐ Death in Canaan, A ☐ F/X ☐ F/X2 ☐ Father's Revenge, A ☐ Finders Keepers ☐ First Blood ☐ Foreign Affairs ☐ Foul Play ☐ Gladiator ☐ Gorky Park ☐ I Take These Men ☐ In Broad Daylight ☐ Indio ☐ It Happened at Lakewood Manor ☐ Jericho Mile, The ☐ Killing in a Small Town, A ☐ Last of the Finest, The ☐ Legal Eagles ☐ Little Miss Marker ☐ Miles from Home ☐ Never Cry Wolf ☐ Off Sides ☐ Perfect Witness ☐ Presumed Innocent ☐ Real American Hero, A ☐ Return to Snowy River ☐ River Rat, The ☐ Semi-Tough ☐ Silverado ☐ Skokie ☐ Teamster Boss: The Jackie Presser Story ☐ To Catch a Killer ☐ To Love Again ☐ Twice in a Lifetime

Denning, Richard ☐ Affair to Remember, An ☐ Battle of Rogue River ☐ Beyond the Blue Horizon ☐ Black Beauty ☐ Black Scorpion, The ☐ Caged Fury ☐ Creature From the Black Lagoon ☐ Day the World Ended, The ☐ Fabulous Suzanne, The ☐ Farmer's Daughter, The ☐ Flame of Stamboul ☐ Girls in Prison ☐ Harbor of Missing Men ☐ Lady Takes a Flyer, The ☐ Magnificent Matador, The ☐ Million Dollar Legs ☐ No Man of Her Own ☐ Okinawa ☐ Oklahoma Woman, The ☐ Queen of the Mob ☐ Quiet Please, Murder ☐ Seventeen ☐ Weekend With Father

Dennis, Sandy ☐ 976-EVIL ☐ Another Woman ☐ Come Back to the Five and Dime, Jimmy Dean, Jimmy Dean ☐ Demon ☐ Four Seasons, The ☐ Fox, The ☐ Man Who Wanted to Live Forever, The ☐ Nasty Habits ☐ Out-of-Towners, The ☐ Parents ☐ Perfect Gentlemen ☐ Splendor in the Grass ☐ Sweet November ☐ Thank You All Very Much ☐ That Cold Day in the Park ☐ Up the Down Staircase ☐ Who's Afraid of Virginia Woolf?

Denny, Reginald ☐ Barbarian, The ☐ Bulldog Drummond Comes Back ☐ Bulldog Drummond in Africa ☐ Embarassing Moments ☐ Escape Me Never ☐ Eyes in the Night ☐ Fort Vengeance ☐ Four Men and a Prayer ☐ Lady's Morals, A ☐ Lost Patrol, The ☐ Macomber Affair, The ☐ Madam Satan ☐ Mr. Blandings Builds His Dream House ☐ Over My Dead Body ☐ Parlor, Bedroom and Bath ☐ Private Lives ☐ Richest Girl in the World, The ☐ Romeo and Juliet ☐ Sherlock Holmes and the Voice of Terror ☐ Vagabond Lady

Depardieu, Gerard ☐ All the Mornings of the World ☐ Buffet Froid ☐ Camille Claudel ☐ Choice of Arms ☐ Colonel Chabert ☐ Cyrano de Bergerac ☐ Danton ☐ 1492: Conquest of Paradise ☐ Germinal ☐ Get Out Your Handkerchiefs ☐ Going Places ☐ Green Card ☐ Holes, The ☐ Je Vous Aime ☐ Jean de Florette ☐ La Chevre ☐ Last Metro, The ☐ Les Comperes ☐ Loulou ☐ Maitresse ☐ Mon Oncle D'Amerique ☐ Moon in the Gutter, The ☐ My Father, the Hero ☐ 1900 ☐ One Woman or Two ☐ Police ☐ Return of Martin Guerre, The ☐ Stavisky ☐ Too Beautiful for You ☐ Under the Sun of Satan ☐ Uranus ☐ Vincent, Francois, Paul and the Others ☐ Woman Next Door, The

Depp, Johnny ☐ Benny & Joon ☐ Cry-Baby ☐ Ed Wood ☐ Edward Scissorhands ☐ Freddy's Dead: The Final Nightmare ☐ Nightmare on Elm Street, A ☐ Private Resort ☐ What's Eating Gilbert Grape

Derek, Bo ☐ 10 ☐ Bolero ☐ Change of Seasons, A ☐ Fantasies ☐ Ghosts Can't Do It ☐ Orca—the Killer Whale ☐ Tarzan, the Ape Man

Derek, John ☐ Adventures of Hajji Baba, The ☐ All the King's Men ☐ Annapolis Story, An ☐ Family Secret, The ☐ Fury at Showdown ☐ High Hell ☐ I'll Be Seeing You ☐ Knock on Any Door ☐ Last Posse, The ☐ Leather Saint, The ☐ Mask of the Avenger ☐ Omar Khayyam ☐ Once Before I Die ☐ Outcast, The ☐ Prince of Pirates ☐ Run for Cover ☐ Scandal Sheet ☐ Sea of Lost Ships

Dern, Bruce ☐ 'Burbs, The ☐ 1969 ☐ After Dark, My Sweet ☐ Big Town, The ☐ Black Sunday ☐ Bloody Mama ☐ Carolina Skeletons ☐ Castle Keep ☐ Coming Home ☐ Court-Martial of Jackie Robinson, The ☐ Cowboys, The ☐ Diggstown ☐ Drive, He Said ☐ Driver, The ☐ Family Plot ☐ Great Gatsby, The ☐ Harry Tracy, Desperado ☐ Incredible Two-Headed Transplant, The ☐ Into the Badlands ☐ King of Marvin Gardens, The ☐ Laughing Policeman, The ☐ Marnie ☐ Middle Age Crazy ☐ Number One ☐ On the Edge ☐ Posse ☐ Psych Out ☐ Rebel Rousers ☐ Silent Running ☐ Smile ☐ St. Valentine's Day Massacre, The ☐ Support Your Local

Sheriff ☐ Tattoo ☐ That Championship Season ☐ They Shoot Horses, Don't They? ☐ Trip, The ☐ Twist, The ☐ Uncle Tom's Cabin ☐ Waterhole #3 ☐ Wild Angels, The ☐ Will Penny ☐ Won Ton Ton, the Dog Who Saved Hollywood

Dern, Laura ☐ Afterburn ☐ Blue Velvet ☐ Fallen Angels—Volume 1 ☐ Fat Man and Little Boy ☐ Haunted Summer ☐ Jurassic Park ☐ Ladies and Gentlemen, The Fabulous Stains ☐ Mask ☐ Perfect World, A ☐ Rambling Rose ☐ Wild at Heart

Devane, William ☐ Bad News Bears in Breaking Training, The ☐ Chips, the War Dog ☐ Dark, The ☐ Family Plot ☐ Fear on Trial ☐ From Here to Eternity ☐ Hadley's Rebellion ☐ Honky Tonk Freeway ☐ Irish Whiskey Rebellion ☐ Jane Doe ☐ Lady Liberty ☐ Marathon Man ☐ Missiles of October, The ☐ My Old Man's Place ☐ Other Victim, The ☐ Red Alert ☐ Rolling Thunder ☐ Testament ☐ Vital Signs ☐ Yanks

Devine, Andy ☐ Ballad of Josie, The ☐ Bells of San Angelo ☐ Between Us Girls ☐ Big Cage, The ☐ Bowery to Broadway ☐ Buck Benny Rides Again ☐ Chance at Heaven ☐ Double or Nothing ☐ Dr. Bull ☐ Dr. Rhythm ☐ Eyes of Texas ☐ Far Frontier, The ☐ Fighting Youth ☐ Flame of New Orleans, The ☐ Frisco Sal ☐ Frontier Gal ☐ Gallant Legion, The ☐ Geronimo ☐ Hold 'Em Yale ☐ Impatient Maiden, The ☐ In Old Chicago ☐ Island in the Sky ☐ Law and Order ☐ Man from Yesterday, The ☐ Man Who Shot Liberty Valance, The ☐ Men with Wings ☐ Midnight Mary ☐ Montana Belle ☐ Never a Dull Moment ☐ Never Say Die ☐ Night Time in Nevada ☐ On the Old Spanish Trail ☐ Over-the-Hill Gang Rides Again, The ☐ Over-the-Hill Gang, The ☐ Road Back, The ☐ Robin Hood ☐ Romeo and Juliet ☐ Saturday's Millions ☐ Small Town Girl ☐ Smoke ☐ Springtime in the Sierras ☐ Stagecoach ☐ Sudan ☐ That's the Spirit ☐ Torrid Zone ☐ Two Rode Together ☐ Upperworld ☐ When the Daltons Rode ☐ Yellow Jack ☐ You're a Sweetheart ☐ Zebra in the Kitchen

DeVito, Danny ☐ Batman Returns ☐ Goin' South ☐ Going Ape! ☐ Head Office ☐ Hoffa ☐ Hurry Up, or I'll Be 30 ☐ Jack the Bear ☐ Jewel of the Nile ☐ Junior ☐ Lady Liberty ☐ Look Who's Talking Now ☐ Money, The ☐ My Little Pony—The Movie ☐ One Flew over the Cuckoo's Nest ☐ Other People's Money ☐ Ratings Game, The ☐ Renaissance Man ☐ Romancing the Stone ☐ Ruthless People ☐ Terms of Endearment ☐ Throw Momma From the Train ☐ Tin Men ☐ Twins ☐ War of the Roses, The ☐ Wise Guys

Dewhurst, Colleen ☐ And Baby Makes Six ☐ Anne of Avonlea ☐ Anne of Green Gables ☐ Annie Hall ☐ As Is ☐ Baby Comes Home ☐ Between Two Women ☐ Bigfoot ☐ Boy Who Could Fly, The ☐ Cowboys, The ☐ Dead Zone, The ☐ Dying Young ☐ Final Assignment ☐ Fine Madness, A ☐ Glitter Dome, The ☐ Ice Castles ☐ Johnny Bull ☐ Lantern Hill ☐ Last Run, The ☐ Man on a String ☐ Mary and Joseph: A Story of Faith ☐ McQ ☐ Nun's Story, The ☐ Obsessed ☐ Tribute ☐ When a Stranger Calls ☐ Women's Room, The

DeYoung, Cliff ☐ Awakening of Candra, The ☐ Dr. Giggles ☐ F/X ☐ Flashback ☐ Flight of the Navigator ☐ Forbidden Sun ☐ Fourth Story, The ☐ Immortal Sins ☐ In Dangerous Company ☐ Independence Day ☐ Lindbergh Kidnapping Case, The ☐ King ☐ Nails ☐ Night That Panicked America, The ☐ Pulse ☐ Reckless ☐ Shock Treatment ☐ Skateboard Kid, The

Dey, Susan ☐ Angel in Green ☐ Echo Park ☐ First Love ☐ I Love You Perfect ☐ Little Women ☐ Looker ☐ Love Leads the Way ☐ Malibu ☐ Mary Jane Harper Cried Last Night ☐ Trouble With Dick, The

DiCaprio, Leonardo ☐ Critters 3 ☐ Quick and the Dead, The ☐ This Boy's Life ☐ What's Eating Gilbert Grape

Dickinson, Angie ☐ Art of Love, The ☐ Big Bad Mama ☐ Big Bad Mama II ☐ Black Whip, The ☐ Bramble Bush, The ☐ Calypso Joe ☐ Captain Newman, M.D. ☐ Cast a Giant Shadow ☐ Charlie Chan and the Curse of the Dragon Queen ☐ Chase, The ☐ China Gate ☐ Cry Terror ☐ Death Hunt ☐ Dressed to Kill ☐ Even Cowgirls Get the Blues ☐ Fever in the Blood, A ☐ Fire and Rain ☐ Gun the Man Down ☐ Jealousy ☐ Jessica ☐ Killers, The ☐ Klondike Fever ☐ Last Challenge, The ☐ Man with the Gun, The ☐ Norliss Tapes, The ☐ Ocean's Eleven ☐ One Shoe Makes It Murder ☐ Outside Man, The ☐ Point Blank ☐ Poppy Is Also a Flower, The ☐ Pretty Maids All in a Row ☐ Resurrection of Zachary Wheeler, The ☐ Rio Bravo ☐ Rome Adventure ☐ Sam Whiskey ☐ Tension at Table Rock ☐ Texas Guns ☐ Wild Palms

Dietrich, Marlene ☐ Angel ☐ Blonde Venus ☐ Blue Angel, The ☐ Desire ☐ Destry Rides Again ☐ Devil is a Woman, The ☐ Dishonored ☐ Flame of New Orleans, The ☐ Follow the Boys ☐ Foreign Affair, A ☐ Garden of Allah, The ☐ Golden Earrings ☐ Judgment at Nuremberg ☐ Just a Gigolo ☐ Kismet ☐ Knight Without Armour ☐ Lady Is Willing, The ☐ Manpower ☐ Monte Carlo Story, The ☐ Morocco ☐ No Highway in the Sky ☐ Pittsburgh ☐ Rancho Notorious ☐ Scarlet Empress, The ☐ Seven Sinners ☐ Shanghai Express ☐ Song of Songs ☐ Spoilers, The ☐ Stage Fright ☐ Touch of Evil ☐ Witness for the Prosecution

Digges, Dudley ☐ Before Dawn ☐ Emperor Jones, The ☐ First Year, The ☐ Hatchet Man, The ☐ I Am a Thief ☐ Invisible Man, The ☐ King's Vacation, The ☐ Light that Failed, The ☐ Maltese Falcon, The ☐ Massacre ☐ Mayor of Hell, The ☐ Mutiny on the Bounty

☐ Narrow Corner, The ☐ Raffles ☐ Searching Wind, The ☐ Son of Fury ☐ Unguarded Hour, The

Diller, Phyllis ☐ Adding Machine, The ☐ Boy, Did I Get a Wrong Number! ☐ Eight on the Lam ☐ Happily Ever After ☐ Mad Monster Party? ☐ Maniac ☐ Nutcracker Prince, The ☐ Pink Floyd—The Wall ☐ Private Navy of Sgt. O'Farrell, The

Dillman, Bradford ☐ Amsterdam Kill, The ☐ Black Water Gold ☐ Bridge at Remagen, The ☐ Brother John ☐ Bug ☐ Certain Smile, A ☐ Circle of Deception, A ☐ Compulsion ☐ Crack in the Mirror ☐ Enforcer, The ☐ Escape from the Planet of the Apes ☐ Fear No Evil ☐ Francis of Assisi ☐ Gold ☐ Guyana: Cult of the Damned ☐ Heroes Stand Alone ☐ Iceman Cometh, The ☐ In Love and War ☐ Jennifer: A Woman's Story ☐ Jigsaw ☐ Legend of Walks Far Woman, The ☐ Lords of the Deep ☐ Man Outside ☐ Mastermind ☐ Moon of The Wolf ☐ Piranha ☐ Rage to Live, A ☐ Resurrection of Zachary Wheeler, The ☐ Sanctuary ☐ Sergeant Ryker ☐ Sudden Impact ☐ Way We Were, The

Dillon, Kevin ☐ Blob, The ☐ Doors, The ☐ Immediate Family ☐ Midnight Clear, A ☐ No Big Deal ☐ No Escape ☐ Rescue, The ☐ When He's Not a Stranger

Dillon, Matt ☐ Big Town, The ☐ Bloodhounds of Broadway ☐ Drugstore Cowboy ☐ Flamingo Kid ☐ Golden Gate ☐ Kansas ☐ Kiss Before Dying, A ☐ Liar's Moon ☐ Little Darlings ☐ Mr. Wonderful ☐ My Bodyguard ☐ Native Son ☐ Outsiders, The ☐ Over the Edge ☐ Rebel ☐ Rumble Fish ☐ Saint of Fort Washington, The ☐ Singles ☐ Target ☐ Tex ☐ Women & Men: In Love There Are No Rules

Dillon, Melinda ☐ Absence of Malice ☐ Bound for Glory ☐ Christmas Story, A ☐ Christmas Story, A ☐ Close Encounters of the Third Kind ☐ F.I.S.T. ☐ Fallen Angel ☐ Harry and the Hendersons ☐ Juggler of Notre Dame, The ☐ Marriage Is Alive and Well ☐ Nightbreaker ☐ Prince of Tides, The ☐ Right of Way ☐ Songwriter ☐ Spontaneous Combustion

Divine ☐ Divine Waters ☐ Female Trouble ☐ Hairspray ☐ I Wanna Be a Beauty Queen ☐ Lust in the Dust ☐ Mondo Trasho ☐ Multiple Maniacs ☐ Polyester ☐ Trouble in Mind

Dix, Richard ☐ Ace of Aces ☐ American Empire ☐ Badlands of Dakota ☐ Buckskin Frontier ☐ Cherokee Strip ☐ Cimarron ☐ Conquerors, The ☐ Devil's Playground ☐ Eyes of the Underworld ☐ Ghost Ship, The ☐ Hell's Highway ☐ Here I Am a Stranger ☐ Kansan, The ☐ Lost Squadron, The ☐ Man of Conquest ☐ Mark of the Whistler ☐ Mysterious Intruder ☐ Nothing But the Truth ☐ Reno ☐ Secret of the Whistler ☐ Shooting Straight ☐ Special Investigator ☐ Ten Commandments, The ☐ Transatlantic Tunnel ☐ Voice of the Whistler ☐ Whistler, The

Dodd, Claire ☐ Case of the Velvet Claws, The ☐ Elmer the Great ☐ Ex-Lady ☐ Fast Company ☐ Gambling Lady ☐ Glass Key, The ☐ If I Had My Way ☐ In the Navy ☐ Lawyer Man ☐ Mad Doctor of Market Street, The ☐ Massacre

Doherty, Shannen ☐ Beverly Hills, 90210 ☐ Beverly Hills, 90210—The Graduation ☐ Blindfold: Acts Of Obsession ☐ Heathers

Domingo, Placido ☐ Carmen ☐ La Traviata ☐ Madame Butterfly ☐ Maestro's Company, The—Vol. 1 ☐ Maestro's Company, The—Vol. 2 ☐ Otello ☐ Pagliacci

Domino, Fats ☐ Fats Domino and Friends—Immortal Keyboards of Rock & Roll ☐ Jamboree ☐ Rock, Rock, Rock! ☐ Shake, Rattle and Rock

Donahue, Troy ☐ Assault of the Party Nerds ☐ Bad Blood ☐ Chilling, The ☐ Cockfighter ☐ Come Spy With Me ☐ Crowded Sky, The ☐ Cry-Baby ☐ Distant Trumpet, A ☐ Dr. Alien ☐ Grandview, U.S.A. ☐ Hawkeye ☐ Hollywood Cop ☐ Love Thrill Murders ☐ Low Blow ☐ Omega Cop ☐ Palm Springs Weekend ☐ Parrish ☐ Rome Adventure ☐ Sexpot ☐ Shock 'em Dead ☐ Summer Place, A ☐ Susan Slade ☐ Tarnished Angels, The ☐ This Happy Feeling ☐ Voice in the Mirror, The

Donat, Robert ☐ 39 Steps, The ☐ Adventures of Tartu ☐ Citadel, The ☐ Count of Monte Cristo, The ☐ Ghost Goes West, The ☐ Goodbye, Mr. Chips ☐ If I Were Rich ☐ Inn of the Sixth Happiness, The ☐ Knight Without Armour ☐ Lease of Life ☐ Magic Box, The ☐ Private Life of Henry VIII, The ☐ Vacation From Marriage ☐ Winslow Boy, The ☐ Young Mr. Pitt, The

Donlevy, Brian ☐ Allegheny Uprising ☐ American Romance, An ☐ Beau Geste ☐ Big Combo, The ☐ Birth of the Blues ☐ Brigham Young ☐ Canyon Passage ☐ Command Decision ☐ Crack-Up ☐ Creeping Unknown, The ☐ Cry in the Night, A ☐ Destry Rides Again ☐ Duffy's Tavern ☐ Errand Boy, The ☐ Fighting Coast Guard ☐ Five Golden Dragons ☐ Gamera—The Invincible ☐ Gentleman After Dark, A ☐ Girl in Room 13 ☐ Glass Key, The ☐ Great Man's Lady, The ☐ Great McGinty, The ☐ Hangmen Also Die ☐ High Tension ☐ Hoodlum Empire ☐ How to Stuff a Wild Bikini ☐ I Wanted Wings ☐ Impact ☐ In Old Chicago ☐ Jesse James ☐ Juke Box Rhythm ☐ Kansas Raiders ☐ Killer McCoy ☐ Kiss of Death ☐ Lucky Stiff, The ☐ Mary Burns, Fugitive ☐ Miracle of Morgan's Creek, The ☐ Never So Few ☐ Nightmare ☐ Our Hearts Were Growing Up ☐ Remarkable Andrew, The ☐ Southern Yankee, A ☐ Stand by for Action ☐ Strike Me Pink ☐ Thirty-Six Hours to Kill ☐ This Is My Affair ☐ Two Years Before the Mast ☐ Union Pacific

☐ Virginian, The ☐ Wake Island ☐ When the Daltons Rode

Donnelly, Ruth ☐ Affairs of Annabel, The ☐ Amazing Mr. Williams ☐ Annabel Takes A Tour ☐ Bells of St. Mary's, The ☐ Blessed Event ☐ Bureau of Missing Persons ☐ Cain and Mabel ☐ Cinderella Jones ☐ Ever in My Heart ☐ Female ☐ Happiness Ahead ☐ Hard to Handle ☐ Housewife ☐ I'd Climb the Highest Mountain ☐ Ladies They Talk About ☐ Lawless Street, A ☐ Man Killer ☐ Mandalay ☐ Model Wife ☐ Pillow to Post ☐ Portia on Trial ☐ Rise and Shine ☐ Secret of Convict Lake, The ☐ Slight Case of Murder, A ☐ Thirteen Hours By Air ☐ Where the Sidewalk Ends ☐ Wild Blue Yonder, The ☐ You Belong to Me

Dooley, Paul ☐ Breaking Away ☐ Endangered Species ☐ Flashback ☐ Kiss Me Goodbye ☐ Lip Service ☐ Monster in the Closet ☐ Murder of Mary Phagan, The ☐ O.C. & Stiggs ☐ Perfect Couple, A ☐ Popeye ☐ Shakes the Clown ☐ Sixteen Candles ☐ Strange Brew ☐ Wedding, A ☐ When He's Not a Stranger

Dorn, Philip ☐ Blonde Fever ☐ Calling Dr. Gillespie ☐ Escape in the Desert ☐ Fighting Kentuckian, The ☐ I Remember Mama ☐ I've Always Loved You ☐ Passage to Marseille ☐ Random Harvest ☐ Reunion in France ☐ Sealed Cargo ☐ Undergound ☐ Ziegfeld Girl

Dors, Diana ☐ Adventures of a Private Eye ☐ Adventures of a Taxi Driver ☐ Alligator Named Daisy, An ☐ Amazing Mr. Blunden, The ☐ As Long As They're Happy ☐ Baby Love ☐ Berserk ☐ Code of Scotland Yard ☐ Dance Hall ☐ Deep End ☐ Hammerhead ☐ Hannie Caulder ☐ I Married a Woman ☐ Kid for Two Farthings, A ☐ King of the Roaring Twenties—The Story of Arnold Rothstein ☐ Lady Godiva Rides Again ☐ Man Bait ☐ Nothing But the Night ☐ On the Double ☐ Pied Piper, The ☐ Sandwich Man, The ☐ Scent of Mystery ☐ Steaming ☐ Theatre of Blood ☐ There's a Girl in My Soup ☐ Unholy Wife, The

Douglas, Kirk ☐ 20,000 Leagues Under the Sea ☐ Act of Love ☐ Along the Great Divide ☐ Amos ☐ Arrangement, The ☐ Bad and the Beautiful, The ☐ Big Carnival, The ☐ Big Sky, The ☐ Big Trees, The ☐ Brotherhood, The ☐ Cast a Giant Shadow ☐ Catch Me a Spy ☐ Champion ☐ Detective Story ☐ Devil's Disciple, The ☐ Draw! ☐ Eddie Macon's Run ☐ Final Countdown, The ☐ For Love or Money ☐ Fury, The ☐ Glass Menagerie, The ☐ Greedy ☐ Gunfight at the O.K. Corral ☐ Gunfight, A ☐ Heroes of Telemark, The ☐ Holocaust Survivors ☐ Holocaust 2000 ☐ Home Movies ☐ Hook, The ☐ I Walk Alone ☐ In Harm's Way ☐ Indian Fighter, The ☐ Inherit the Wind ☐ Is Paris Burning? ☐ Jacqueline Susann's Once Is Not Enough ☐ Juggler, The ☐ Last Sunset, The ☐ Last Train From Gun Hill ☐ Letter to Three Wives, A ☐ Light at the Edge of the World, The ☐ List of Adrian Messenger, The ☐ Lonely Are the Brave ☐ Lovely Way to Die, A ☐ Lust for Life ☐ Man from Snowy River, The ☐ Man Without a Star ☐ Master Touch, The ☐ Mourning Becomes Electra ☐ My Dear Secretary ☐ Out of the Past ☐ Paths of Glory ☐ Posse ☐ Queenie ☐ Racers, The ☐ Saturn 3 ☐ Scalawag ☐ Seven Days in May ☐ Spartacus ☐ Story of Three Loves, The ☐ Strange Love of Martha Ivers, The ☐ Strangers When We Meet ☐ There Was a Crooked Man ☐ Top Secret Affair ☐ Tough Guys ☐ Town Without Pity ☐ Two Weeks in Another Town ☐ Ulysses ☐ Vikings, The ☐ Villain, The ☐ Walls of Jericho, The ☐ War Wagon, The ☐ Way West, The ☐ Young Man With a Horn

Douglas, Melvyn ☐ Advance to the Rear ☐ Amazing Mr. Williams ☐ Americanization of Emily, The ☐ And So They Were Married ☐ Angel ☐ Annie Oakley ☐ As You Desire Me ☐ Being There ☐ Billy Budd ☐ Candidate, The ☐ Captains Courageous ☐ Changeling, The ☐ Counsellor-at-Law ☐ Dangerous Corner ☐ Fast Company ☐ Ghost Story ☐ Good Girls Go to Paris ☐ Gorgeous Hussy, The ☐ Great Sinner, The ☐ Guilt of Janet Ames, The ☐ Hard Frame ☐ He Stayed for Breakfast ☐ Hotel ☐ Hud ☐ I Met Him in Paris ☐ I Never Sang for My Father ☐ I'll Take Romance ☐ Intimate Strangers ☐ Lone Wolf Returns, The ☐ Mary Burns, Fugitive ☐ Mr. Blandings Builds His Dream House ☐ My Forbidden Past ☐ Ninotchka ☐ Old Dark House, The ☐ On the Loose ☐ One Is a Lonely Number ☐ Our Wife ☐ Rapture ☐ Sea of Grass, The ☐ She Married Her Boss ☐ Shining Hour, The ☐ Tell Me a Riddle ☐ Tenant, The ☐ That Certain Age ☐ That Uncertain Feeling ☐ Theodora Goes Wild ☐ There's Always a Woman ☐ They All Kissed the Bride ☐ Third Finger, Left Hand ☐ This Thing Called Love ☐ Too Many Husbands ☐ Twilight's Last Gleaming ☐ Two-Faced Woman ☐ Vampire Bat, The ☐ We Were Dancing ☐ Woman's Face, A ☐ Woman's Secret, A

Douglas, Michael ☐ Adam at 6 A.M. ☐ Basic Instinct ☐ Black Rain ☐ China Syndrome, The ☐ Chorus Line, A ☐ Coma ☐ Disclosure ☐ Falling Down ☐ Fatal Attraction ☐ Hail, Hero! ☐ It's My Turn ☐ Jewel of the Nile ☐ Napoleon and Samantha ☐ Romancing the Stone ☐ Shining Through ☐ Star Chamber, The ☐ Summertree ☐ Wall Street ☐ War of the Roses, The

Douglas, Paul ☐ Angels in the Outfield ☐ Beau James ☐ Big Lift, The ☐ Clash by Night ☐ Everybody Does It ☐ Forever Female ☐ Fourteen Hours ☐ Gamma People, The ☐ Green Fire ☐ Guy Who Came Back, The ☐ High and Dry ☐ It Happens Every

Spring ☐ Joe Macbeth ☐ Leather Saint, The ☐ Letter to Three Wives, A ☐ Love That Brute ☐ Mating Game, The ☐ Never Wave at a WAC ☐ Panic in the Streets ☐ Solid Gold Cadillac, The ☐ This Could Be the Night ☐ We're Not Married ☐ When in Rome

Douglas, Robert ☐ Adventures of Don Juan ☐ Fair Wind to Java ☐ Flame and the Arrow, The ☐ Flight to Tangier ☐ Fountainhead, The ☐ Ivanhoe ☐ Saskatchewan ☐ Thunder on the Hill

Dourif, Brad ☐ Body Parts ☐ Child's Play ☐ Common Bonds ☐ Critters 4 ☐ Dune ☐ Exorcist III, The ☐ Eyes of Laura Mars ☐ Fatal Beauty ☐ Final Judgment ☐ Graveyard Shift ☐ Grim Prairie Tales ☐ Hidden Agenda ☐ Horseplayer, The ☐ I, Desire ☐ Impure Thoughts ☐ London Kills Me ☐ Mississippi Burning ☐ Murder in the First ☐ One Flew over the Cuckoo's Nest ☐ Rage of Angels: The Story Continues ☐ Ragtime ☐ Sergeant Matlovich vs. the U.S. Air Force ☐ Spontaneous Combustion ☐ Wise Blood

Downey, Jr., Robert ☐ Air America ☐ Baby, It's You ☐ Back to School ☐ Chances Are ☐ Chaplin ☐ Firstborn ☐ Hail Caesar ☐ Heart & Souls ☐ Johnny Be Good ☐ Last Party, The ☐ Less than Zero ☐ Natural Born Killers ☐ 1969 ☐ Only You ☐ Pick-up Artist, The ☐ Soapdish ☐ True Believer ☐ Weird Science

Down, Lesley-Anne ☐ Arch of Triumph ☐ Betsy, The ☐ Brannigan ☐ Countess Dracula ☐ Death Wish 5 ☐ Great Train Robbery, The ☐ Hanover Street ☐ Hunchback of Notre Dame, The ☐ In the Devil's Garden ☐ Indiscreet ☐ Ladykillers ☐ Little Night Music, A ☐ Mardi Gras for the Devil ☐ Nomads ☐ North and South ☐ Pink Panther Strikes Again, The ☐ Rough Cut ☐ Scalawag ☐ Sphinx

Drake, Charles ☐ Bonzo Goes to College ☐ Female on the Beach ☐ Glenn Miller Story, The ☐ Harvey ☐ I Was a Shoplifter ☐ It Came from Outer Space ☐ Night in Casablanca, A ☐ Nine Lives Are Not Enough ☐ No Name on the Bullet ☐ Price of Fear, The ☐ To Hell and Back ☐ Until They Sail ☐ Walk the Proud Land ☐ War Arrow ☐ You Never Can Tell

Drake, Tom ☐ Alias a Gentleman ☐ Courage of Lassie ☐ Faithful in My Fashion ☐ FBI Girl ☐ Great Rupert, The ☐ Green Years, The ☐ Hills of Home, The ☐ I'll Be Yours ☐ Maisie Goes to Reno ☐ Mayday at 40,000 Feet! ☐ Meet Me in St. Louis ☐ Mr. Belvedere Goes to College ☐ Savage Abduction ☐ Scene of the Crime ☐ Singing Nun, The ☐ Sudden Danger ☐ This Man's Navy ☐ Words and Music

Dressler, Marie ☐ Anna Christie ☐ Dinner at Eight ☐ Emma ☐ Min and Bill ☐ One Romantic Night ☐ Tillie's Punctured Romance ☐ Tugboat Annie ☐ Vagabond Lover, The

Drew, Ellen ☐ Baron of Arizona, The ☐ Buck Benny Rides Again ☐ Cargo to Capetown ☐ China Sky ☐ Christmas in July ☐ Davy Crockett, Indian Scout ☐ Geronimo ☐ Gracie Allen Murder Case, The ☐ Great Missouri Raid, The ☐ If I Were King ☐ Impostor, The ☐ Isle of the Dead ☐ Mad Doctor, The ☐ Man Alive ☐ Man from Colorado, The ☐ Man in the Saddle ☐ Monster and the Girl, The ☐ Night of January 16th, The ☐ Night Plane from Chungking ☐ Our Wife ☐ Parson of Panamint, The ☐ Reaching for the Sun ☐ Remarkable Andrew, The ☐ Sing, You Sinners ☐ Stars in My Crown ☐ Swordsman, The

Dreyfuss, Richard ☐ Always ☐ American Graffiti ☐ Another Stakeout ☐ Apprenticeship Of Duddy Kravitz, The ☐ Big Fix, The ☐ Buddy System, The ☐ Close Encounters of the Third Kind ☐ Competition, The ☐ Dillinger ☐ Down and Out in Beverly Hills ☐ Goodbye Girl, The ☐ Hello Down There ☐ Jaws ☐ Let It Ride ☐ Lost in Yonkers ☐ Moon Over Parador ☐ Nuts ☐ Once Around ☐ Prisoner of Honor ☐ Rosencrantz and Guildenstern Are Dead ☐ Silent Fall ☐ Stakeout ☐ Stand by Me ☐ Tin Men ☐ What About Bob? ☐ Whose Life Is It Anyway?

Dru, Joanne ☐ 711 Ocean Drive ☐ Abie's Irish Rose ☐ All the King's Men ☐ Forbidden ☐ Hannah Lee ☐ Hell on Frisco Bay ☐ Mr. Belvedere Rings the Bell ☐ Pride of St. Louis, The ☐ Red River ☐ Return of the Texan ☐ She Wore a Yellow Ribbon ☐ Siege at Red River, The ☐ Sincerely Yours ☐ Three Ring Circus ☐ Thunder Bay ☐ Wagon Master ☐ Warriors, The ☐ Wild and the Innocent, The

Duff, Howard ☐ Blackjack Ketchum, Desperado ☐ Boys' Night Out ☐ Calamity Jane and Sam Bass ☐ Flame of the Islands ☐ Flamingo Road ☐ Illegal Entry ☐ Jennifer ☐ Johnny Stool Pigeon ☐ Lady from Texas ☐ Monster in the Closet ☐ Naked City, The ☐ No Way Out ☐ Panic in the City ☐ Private Hell 36 ☐ While the City Sleeps ☐ Woman in Hiding ☐ Women's Prison

Dukakis, Olympia ☐ Cemetery Club, The ☐ Dad ☐ Death Wish ☐ Fire in the Dark ☐ In the Spirit ☐ Look Who's Talking ☐ Look Who's Talking Too ☐ Lucky Day ☐ Made for Each Other ☐ Moonstruck ☐ Sinatra ☐ Steel Magnolias ☐ Wanderers, The

Dullea, Keir ☐ 2001: A Space Odyessy ☐ 2010: The Year We Make Contact ☐ Because He's My Friend ☐ Black Christmas ☐ Black Water Gold ☐ Brainwaves ☐ Brave New World ☐ Bunny Lake Is Missing ☐ David and Lisa ☐ Fox, The ☐ Haunting of Julia, The ☐ Hoodlum Priest, The ☐ Hostage Tower, The ☐ Law and Order ☐ Leopard in the Snow ☐ Mail Order Bride ☐ Naked

Hours, The ☐ Next One, The ☐ No Place to Hide ☐ Paperback Hero ☐ Paul and Michelle ☐ Pope Joan ☐ Thin Red Line, The

Dumont, Margaret ☐ Animal Crackers ☐ At the Circus ☐ Big Store, The ☐ Cocoanuts, The ☐ Dancing Masters, The ☐ Day at the Races, A ☐ Diamond Horseshoe ☐ Duck Soup ☐ Horn Blows at Midnight, The ☐ Life of the Party, The ☐ Little Giant ☐ Never Give a Sucker an Even Break ☐ Night at the Opera, A ☐ Shake, Rattle and Rock ☐ Zotz!

Dunaway, Faye ☐ Arrangement, The ☐ Barfly ☐ Bonnie and Clyde ☐ Burning Secret ☐ Casanova ☐ Champ, The ☐ Chinatown ☐ Christopher Columbus ☐ Cold Sassy Tree ☐ Disappearance of Aimee, The ☐ Doc ☐ Double Edge ☐ Ellis Island ☐ Evita Peron ☐ Extraordinary Seaman, The ☐ Eyes of Laura Mars ☐ First Deadly Sin, The ☐ Four Musketeers, The ☐ Gamble, The ☐ Handmaid's Tale, The ☐ Happening, The ☐ Hurry Sundown ☐ Little Big Man ☐ Midnight Crossing ☐ Mommie Dearest ☐ Network ☐ Oklahoma Crude ☐ Ordeal by Innocence ☐ Place for Lovers, A ☐ Scorchers ☐ Supergirl ☐ Temp, The ☐ Thirteen at Dinner ☐ Thomas Crown Affair, The ☐ Three Days of the Condor ☐ Three Musketeers, The ☐ Towering Inferno, The ☐ Voyage of the Damned ☐ Wicked Lady, The

Dunne, Griffin ☐ After Hours ☐ Almost You ☐ Amazon Women on the Moon ☐ American Werewolf in London, An ☐ Big Blue, The ☐ Big Girls Don't Cry . . . They Get Even ☐ Cold Feet ☐ I Like It Like That ☐ Johnny Dangerously ☐ Lip Service ☐ Me and Him ☐ My Girl ☐ Straight Talk ☐ Who's That Girl?

Dunne, Irene ☐ Ann Vickers ☐ Anna and the King of Siam ☐ Awful Truth, The ☐ Bachelor Apartment ☐ Back Street ☐ Cimarron ☐ Consolation Marriage ☐ Great Lover, The ☐ Guy Named Joe, A ☐ High, Wide, and Handsome ☐ I Remember Mama ☐ If I Were Free ☐ Invitation to Happiness ☐ It Grows on Trees ☐ Joy of Living ☐ Lady in a Jam ☐ Life with Father ☐ Love Affair ☐ Magnificent Obsession ☐ Mudlark, The ☐ My Favorite Wife ☐ Never a Dull Moment ☐ Over 21 ☐ Penny Serenade ☐ Roberta ☐ Secret of Madame Blanche, The ☐ Show Boat ☐ Silver Cord, The ☐ Sweet Adeline ☐ Symphony of Six Million ☐ Theodora Goes Wild ☐ Thirteen Women ☐ This Man Is Mine ☐ Together Again ☐ Unfinished Business ☐ When Tomorrow Comes ☐ White Cliffs of Dover, The

Dunnock, Mildred ☐ And Baby Makes Six ☐ Baby Comes Home ☐ Baby Doll ☐ Bad For Each Other ☐ Behold a Pale Horse ☐ Brand New Life, A ☐ Butterfield 8 ☐ Corn Is Green, The ☐ Death of a Salesman ☐ Girl in White, The ☐ I Want You ☐ Jazz Singer, The ☐ Nun's Story, The ☐ One Summer Love ☐ Patricia Neal Story, The ☐ Pick-up Artist, The ☐ Seven Women ☐ Spiral Staircase, The ☐ Story on Page One, The ☐ Sweet Bird of Youth ☐ Trouble With Harry, The ☐ Viva Zapata!

Durante, Jimmy ☐ Billy Rose's Jumbo ☐ Blondie of the Follies ☐ Cuban Love Song, The ☐ Forbidden Music ☐ Frosty the Snowman ☐ George White's Scandals ☐ Great Rupert, The ☐ Hell Below ☐ Hollywood Party ☐ It Happened in Brooklyn ☐ It's a Mad Mad Mad Mad World ☐ Little Miss Broadway ☐ Man Who Came to Dinner, The ☐ Meet the Baron ☐ Melody Ranch ☐ Milkman, The ☐ Music for Millions ☐ On an Island with You ☐ Palooka ☐ Passionate Plumber, The ☐ Phantom President, The ☐ Roadhouse Nights ☐ Sally, Irene and Mary ☐ Speak Easily ☐ Start Cheering ☐ Two Girls and a Sailor ☐ Two Sisters From Boston ☐ Wet Parade, The ☐ What, No Beer? ☐ You're in the Army Now

Durbin, Deanna ☐ Amazing Mrs. Holliday, The ☐ Because of Him ☐ Can't Help Singing ☐ Christmas Holiday ☐ First Love ☐ For the Love of Mary ☐ Hers to Hold ☐ His Butler's Sister ☐ I'll Be Yours ☐ It Started with Eve ☐ It's a Date ☐ Lady on a Train ☐ Mad about Music ☐ Nice Girl? ☐ One Hundred Men and a Girl ☐ Something in the Wind ☐ Spring Parade ☐ That Certain Age ☐ Three Smart Girls ☐ Three Smart Girls Grow Up ☐ Up In Central Park

Durning, Charles ☐ Attica ☐ Best Little Girl in The World, The ☐ Best Little Whorehouse in Texas, The ☐ Big Trouble ☐ Breakheart Pass ☐ Cat Chaser ☐ Choirboys, The ☐ Cop ☐ Crisis at Central High ☐ Deadhead Miles ☐ Dealing: or The Berkeley-to-Boston Forty-Brick Lost-Bag Blues ☐ Death of a Salesman ☐ Dick Tracy ☐ Die Laughing ☐ Dinner at Eight ☐ Dog Day Afternoon ☐ Enemy of the People, An ☐ Far North ☐ Final Countdown, The ☐ Front Page, The ☐ Fury, The ☐ Greek Tycoon, The ☐ Hadley's Rebellion ☐ Happy New Year ☐ Harry and Walter Go to New York ☐ Harvey Middleman, Fireman ☐ Hudsucker Proxy, The ☐ I Walk the Line ☐ Man Who Broke 1,000 Chains, The ☐ Man with One Red Shoe ☐ Mass Appeal ☐ Music of Chance, The ☐ North Dallas Forty ☐ Project: Alien ☐ Queen of the Stardust Ballroom ☐ Rosary Murders, The ☐ Sharky's Machine ☐ Sisters ☐ Starting Over ☐ Sting, The ☐ Story Lady, The ☐ Tiger's Tale, A ☐ To Be or Not to Be ☐ Tootsie ☐ Tough Guys ☐ True Confessions ☐ Twilight's Last Gleaming ☐ Two of a Kind ☐ V.I. Warshawski ☐ When a Stranger Calls ☐ Where the River Runs Black

Duryea, Dan ☐ Adventures of China Smith ☐ Al Jennings of Oklahoma ☐ Along Came Jones ☐ Another Part of the Forest ☐ Ball of Fire ☐ Bamboo Saucer, The ☐ Battle Hymn ☐ Black Angel ☐ Black Bart ☐ Bounty Killer,

The ☐ Chicago Calling ☐ Criss Cross ☐ Five Golden Dragons ☐ Flight of the Phoenix ☐ Foxfire ☐ Great Flamarion, The ☐ He Rides Tall ☐ Hills Run Red, The ☐ Incident at Phantom Hill ☐ Johnny Stool Pigeon ☐ Kathy O' ☐ Lady on a Train ☐ Larceny ☐ Little Foxes, The ☐ Main Street After Dark ☐ Man from Frisco, The ☐ Manhandled ☐ Marauders, The ☐ Ministry of Fear ☐ Mrs. Parkington ☐ Night Passage ☐ None But the Lonely Heart ☐ One-Way Street ☐ Pride of the Yankees, The ☐ Rails Into Laramie ☐ Ride Clear of Diablo ☐ River Lady ☐ Sahara ☐ Scarlet Street ☐ Silver Lode ☐ Slaughter on Tenth Avenue ☐ Stranger on the Run ☐ Thunder Bay ☐ Too Late for Tears ☐ Valley of Decision, The ☐ White Tie and Tails ☐ Winchester '73 ☐ Woman in the Window, The

Dutton, Charles ☐ Alien³ ☐ Crocodile Dundee II ☐ Distinguished Gentleman, The ☐ Foreign Student ☐ Jacknife ☐ Low Down Dirty Shame, A ☐ Menace II Society ☐ Mississippi Masala ☐ Murder of Mary Phagan, The ☐ Rudy ☐ Surviving the Game

Duvall, Robert ☐ Apocalypse Now ☐ Badge 373 ☐ Betsy, The ☐ Breakout ☐ Bullitt ☐ Captain Newman, M.D. ☐ Chase, The ☐ Colors ☐ Convicts ☐ Countdown ☐ Days of Thunder ☐ Detective, The ☐ Eagle Has Landed, The ☐ Falling Down ☐ Fame Is the Name of the Game ☐ Geronimo: An American Legend ☐ Godfather, Part II, The ☐ Godfather, The ☐ Great Northfield, Minnesota Raid, The ☐ Great Santini, The ☐ Greatest, The ☐ Handmaid's Tale, The ☐ Hotel Colonial ☐ Ike: The War Years ☐ Joe Kidd ☐ Killer Elite, The ☐ Lady Ice ☐ Lawman ☐ Let's Get Harry ☐ Lightship, The ☐ Lonesome Dove ☐ M*A*S*H ☐ Natural, The ☐ Network ☐ Newsies ☐ Outfit, The ☐ Paper, The ☐ Rain People, The ☐ Rambling Rose ☐ Revolutionary, The ☐ Seven Percent Solution, The ☐ Show of Force, A ☐ Stalin ☐ Stone Boy, The ☐ Tender Mercies ☐ THX 1138 ☐ To Kill a Mockingbird ☐ Tomorrow ☐ True Confessions ☐ True Grit ☐ Wrestling Ernest Hemingway

Duvall, Shelley ☐ 3 Women ☐ Annie Hall ☐ Brewster McCloud ☐ Frog ☐ McCabe and Mrs. Miller ☐ Mother Goose Rock 'n Rhyme ☐ Nashville ☐ Popeye ☐ Roxanne ☐ Shining, The ☐ Suburban Commando ☐ Thieves Like Us ☐ Time Bandits

Dvorak, Ann ☐ Abilene Town ☐ Blind Alley ☐ Bright Lights ☐ Case of the Stuttering Bishop, The ☐ College Coach ☐ Crowd Roars, The ☐ Doctor Socrates ☐ Dr. Socrates ☐ Flame of Barbary Coast ☐ Friends of Mr. Sweeney ☐ G-Men ☐ Girls of the Road ☐ Housewife ☐ I Was an American Spy ☐ Life of Her Own, A ☐ Long Night, The ☐ Love Is a Racket ☐ Manhattan Merry-Go-Round ☐ Masquerade in Mexico ☐ Massacre ☐ Merrily We Live ☐ Our Very Own ☐ Out of the Blue ☐ Private Affairs of Bel Ami, The ☐ Return of Jesse James, The ☐ Scarface ☐ Secret of Convict Lake, The ☐ Thanks a Million ☐ Three on a Match ☐ Walls of Jericho, The

Dysart, Richard ☐ Autobiography of Miss Jane Pittman ☐ Back to the Future Part III ☐ Being There ☐ Bitter Harvest ☐ Blood & Orchids ☐ Day of the Locust, The ☐ Day One ☐ Enemy of the People, An ☐ Hospital, The ☐ Last Days of Patton, The ☐ Malice in Wonderland ☐ Mask ☐ Ordeal of Dr. Mudd, The ☐ People vs. Jean Harris, The ☐ Prophecy ☐ Terminal Man, The ☐ Thing, The ☐ Warning Sign

Eastwood, Clint ☐ Ambush at Cimarron Pass ☐ Any Which Way You Can ☐ Beguiled, The ☐ Bronco Billy ☐ City Heat ☐ Coogan's Bluff ☐ Dead Pool, The ☐ Dirty Harry ☐ Eiger Sanction, The ☐ Enforcer, The ☐ Escapade in Japan ☐ Escape from Alcatraz ☐ Every Which Way but Loose ☐ Firefox ☐ First Traveling Saleslady, The ☐ Fistful of Dollars, A ☐ For a Few Dollars More ☐ Francis in the Navy ☐ Gauntlet, The ☐ Good, the Bad, and the Ugly, The ☐ Hang 'em High ☐ Heartbreak Ridge ☐ Here's Looking At You, Warner Bros. ☐ High Plains Drifter ☐ Honkytonk Man ☐ In the Line of Fire ☐ Joe Kidd ☐ Kelly's Heroes ☐ Lafayette Escadrille ☐ Magnum Force ☐ Outlaw—Josey Wales, The ☐ Paint Your Wagon ☐ Pale Rider ☐ Perfect World, A ☐ Pink Cadillac ☐ Play Misty for Me ☐ Revenge of the Creature ☐ Rookie, The ☐ Sudden Impact ☐ Thunderbolt and Lightfoot ☐ Tightrope ☐ Two Mules for Sister Sara ☐ Unforgiven ☐ Where Eagles Dare ☐ White Hunter, Black Heart

Ebsen, Buddy ☐ Andersonville Trial ☐ Bastard, The ☐ Between Heaven and Hell ☐ Born to Dance ☐ Breakfast at Tiffany's ☐ Broadway Melody of 1936 ☐ Broadway Melody of 1938 ☐ Captain January ☐ Davy Crockett and the River Pirates ☐ Davy Crockett, King of the Wild Frontier ☐ Girl of the Golden West, The ☐ Horror at 37,000 Feet ☐ Interns, The ☐ Mail Order Bride ☐ My Lucky Star ☐ Night People ☐ One and Only, Genuine, Original Family Band, The ☐ Red Garters ☐ Stone Fox ☐ Under Mexicali Stars ☐ Yellow Jack

Eddy, Nelson ☐ Balalaika ☐ Bitter Sweet ☐ Chocolate Soldier, The ☐ Dancing Lady ☐ Girl of the Golden West, The ☐ I Married an Angel ☐ Knickerbocker Holiday ☐ Let Freedom Ring ☐ Maytime ☐ Naughty Marietta ☐ New Moon ☐ Northwest Outpost ☐ Phantom of the Opera ☐ Rosalie ☐ Rose Marie ☐ Sweethearts

Eden, Barbara ☐ 7 Faces of Dr. Lao ☐ All Hands On Deck ☐ Amazing Dobermans, The ☐ Brass Bottle, The ☐ Chattanooga Choo Choo ☐ Feminist and the Fuzz, The ☐ Five Weeks in a Balloon ☐ Flaming Star ☐ From the Terrace ☐ Harper Valley P.T.A. ☐ How to Break Up a Happy Divorce ☐ Howling in the Woods, A ☐ I Dream of Jeannie: 15 Years Later ☐ New Interns, The ☐ Quick, Let's Get Married ☐ Ride the Wild Surf ☐ Stranger Within, The ☐ Voyage to the Bottom of the Sea ☐ Wonderful World of the Brothers Grimm, The

Edwards, Anthony ☐ Downtown ☐ El Diablo ☐ Going for the Gold: The Bill Johnson Story ☐ Gotcha! ☐ Hawks ☐ Hometown Boy Makes Good ☐ How I Got Into College ☐ Landslide ☐ Miracle Mile ☐ Mr. North ☐ Pet Sematary II ☐ Revenge of the Nerds ☐ Summer Heat ☐ Sure Thing, The ☐ Top Gun

Edwards, Cliff ☐ Dance, Fools, Dance ☐ Doughboys ☐ Falcon Strikes Back, The ☐ Fighting Frontier ☐ Flowing Gold ☐ Good News ☐ International Squadron ☐ Marianne ☐ Montana Moon ☐ Parlor, Bedroom and Bath ☐ Pinocchio ☐ Riders of the Badlands ☐ Saratoga ☐ Seven Miles from Alcatraz ☐ Sidewalks of New York ☐ Sin of Madelon Claudet, The ☐ West of Tombstone

Edwards, James ☐ Blood and Steel ☐ Bright Victory ☐ Home of the Brave ☐ Member of the Wedding, The ☐ Men in War ☐ Night of the Quarter Moon ☐ Steel Helmet, The

Edwards, Vince ☐ Cell 2455, Death Row ☐ Cellar Dweller ☐ City of Fear ☐ Deal of the Century ☐ Desperados, The ☐ Devil's Brigade, The ☐ Do Not Fold, Spindle or Mutilate ☐ Evening in Byzantium, An ☐ Firehouse ☐ Fix, The ☐ Gumshoe Kid, The ☐ Hammerhead ☐ Hiawatha ☐ Hired Gun, The ☐ Hit and Run ☐ Island Woman ☐ Killing, The ☐ Mad Bomber, The ☐ Night Holds Terror, The ☐ Return to Horror High ☐ Rogue Cop ☐ Seduction, The ☐ Serenade ☐ Space Raiders ☐ Too Late Blues ☐ Victors, The

Egan, Richard ☐ Amsterdam Kill, The ☐ Battle at Apache Pass, The ☐ Big Cube, The ☐ Blackbeard, the Pirate ☐ Chubasco ☐ Cripple Creek ☐ Damned Don't Cry, The ☐ Devil Makes Three, The ☐ Esther and the King ☐ Glory Brigade ☐ Gog ☐ Golden Horde, The ☐ Hollywood Story ☐ House That Would Not Die, The ☐ Hunters, The ☐ Khyber Patrol ☐ Love Me Tender ☐ Mission To Glory ☐ Mister Too Little ☐ One Minute to Zero ☐ Pollyanna ☐ Revolt of Mamie Stover, The ☐ Seven Cities of Gold ☐ Slaughter on Tenth Avenue ☐ Summer Place, A ☐ Tension at Table Rock ☐ These Thousand Hills ☐ Underwater! ☐ Untamed ☐ Up Front ☐ Violent Saturday ☐ Voice in the Mirror, The

Eggar, Samantha ☐ All the Kind Strangers ☐ Brood, The ☐ Collector, The ☐ Doctor Dolittle ☐ Doctor in Distress ☐ Exterminator, The ☐ Great Battle, The ☐ Inevitable Grace ☐ Lady in the Car with Glasses and a Gun, The ☐ Light at the Edge of the World, The ☐ Love Among Thieves ☐ Man Of Destiny ☐ Molly Maguires, The ☐ Name for Evil, A ☐ Seven Percent Solution, The ☐ Tales of the Unexpected ☐ Walk, Don't Run ☐ Why Shoot the Teacher?

Ekberg, Anita ☐ Alphabet Murders, The ☐ Back From Eternity ☐ Blood Alley ☐ Boccaccio '70 ☐ Call Me Bwana ☐ Cobra, The ☐ Four for Texas ☐ Glass Sphinx, The ☐ Gold of the Amazon Women ☐ Hollywood or Bust ☐ Intervista ☐ La Dolce Vita ☐ Man in the Vault ☐ Man Inside, The ☐ Paris Holiday ☐ War and Peace ☐ Way...*Way Out* ☐ *Zarak*

Ekland, Britt ☐ After the Fox ☐ Asylum ☐ Beverly Hills Vamp ☐ Bobo, The ☐ Double Man, The ☐ Endless Night ☐ Get Carter ☐ Great Wallendas, The ☐ High Velocity ☐ Jacqueline Susann's Valley of the Dolls ☐ Machine Gun McCain ☐ Man with the Golden Gun, The ☐ Marbella ☐ Monster Club, The ☐ Moon in Scorpio ☐ Night They Raided Minsky's, The ☐ Royal Flash ☐ Sex on the Run ☐ Slavers ☐ Some Like It Cool ☐ Wicker Man, The

Elam, Jack ☐ Aurora Encounter ☐ Big Bad John ☐ Dirty Dingus Magee ☐ Edge of Eternity ☐ Firecreek ☐ Four for Texas ☐ Girl, the Gold Watch and Dynamite, The ☐ Gun Runners, The ☐ Hannie Caulder ☐ High Lonesome ☐ Huckleberry Finn ☐ Last Rebel, The ☐ Lure of the Wilderness ☐ Moonlighter, The ☐ Night of the Grizzly ☐ Norseman, The ☐ Over-the-Hill Gang, The ☐ Rancho Notorious ☐ Red Pony, The ☐ Ride Clear of Diablo ☐ Rio Lobo ☐ Sacketts, The ☐ Sacred Ground ☐ Shadow Force ☐ Support Your Local Gunfighter ☐ Support Your Local Sheriff ☐ Villain, The ☐ Way West, The ☐ Wild Country, The

Elizondo, Hector ☐ Addict ☐ American Gigolo ☐ Beverly Hills Cop III ☐ Burden of Proof, The ☐ Chains of Gold ☐ Courage ☐ Cuba ☐ Deadhead Miles ☐ Fan, The ☐ Final Approach ☐ Finding the Way Home ☐ Flamingo Kid ☐ Forgotten Prisoners: The Amnesty Files ☐ Frankie and Johnny ☐ Impatient Heart, The ☐ Necessary Roughness ☐ Out of the Darkness ☐ Pretty Woman ☐ Private Resort ☐ Report to the Commissioner ☐ Taking of Pelham One Two Three, The ☐ There Goes the Neighborhood ☐ Valdez Is Coming ☐ Young Doctors in Love

Elliott, Denholm ☐ Alfie ☐ Apprenticeship Of Duddy Kravitz, The ☐ Bad Timing: A Sensual Obsession ☐ Bleak House ☐ Bourne Identity, The ☐ Boys From Brazil, The ☐ Breaking the Sound Barrier ☐ Brimstone and Treacle ☐ Camille ☐ Codename: Kyril ☐ Cruel Sea, The ☐ Cuba ☐ Defence of the Realm ☐ Doll's House, A ☐ Game for Vultures ☐ Hanna's War ☐ Heart of the Matter, The ☐ Here We Go Round the Mulberry Bush ☐ Holly and the Ivy, The ☐ Hotel du Lac ☐ Hound of the Baskervilles, The ☐ Hound of the Baskervilles, The

☐ House That Dripped Blood, The ☐ Indiana Jones and the Last Crusade ☐ It's Not the Size That Counts ☐ King Rat ☐ Lease of Life ☐ Love She Sought, The ☐ Madame Sin ☐ Man Who Loved Redheads, The ☐ Maurice ☐ McGuire, Go Home! ☐ Missionary, The ☐ Mrs. Delafield Wants to Marry ☐ Night My Number Came Up, The ☐ Night They Raided Minsky's, The ☐ Noises Off ☐ Nothing But the Best ☐ One Against the Wind ☐ Over Indulgence ☐ Pacific Destiny ☐ Past Caring ☐ Private Function, A ☐ Quest for Love ☐ Raiders of the Lost Ark ☐ Razor's Edge, The ☐ Rise and Rise of Michael Rimmer, The ☐ Robin and Marian ☐ Room with a View, A ☐ Saint Jack ☐ Scent of Mystery ☐ Scorchers ☐ Sea Gull, The ☐ September ☐ Station Six-Sahara ☐ Stealing Heaven ☐ They Who Dare ☐ To the Devil A Daughter ☐ Too Late the Hero ☐ Toy Soldiers ☐ Trading Places ☐ Whoopee Boys, The ☐ Wicked Lady, The ☐ Zulu Dawn

Elliott, Sam ☐ Blue Knight, The ☐ Conagher ☐ Death in California, A ☐ Fatal Beauty ☐ Frogs ☐ Games, The ☐ Gettysburg ☐ I Will Fight No More Forever ☐ Legacy, The ☐ Lifeguard ☐ Mask ☐ Murder in Texas ☐ Prancer ☐ Quick and the Dead, The ☐ Road House ☐ Rush ☐ Sacketts, The ☐ Shadow Riders, The ☐ Shakedown ☐ Sibling Rivalry ☐ Tombstone

Elwes, Cary ☐ Another Country ☐ Bram Stoker's Dracula ☐ Crush, The ☐ Glory ☐ Hot Shots! ☐ Lady Jane ☐ Leather Jackets ☐ Princess Bride, The ☐ Robin Hood: Men in Tights ☐ Rudyard Kipling's The Jungle Book

Englund, Robert ☐ Eaten Alive ☐ Freddy's Dead: The Final Nightmare ☐ Mangler, The ☐ Mysterious Two ☐ Never Too Young to Die ☐ Nightmare on Elm Street 2: Freddy's Revenge ☐ Nightmare on Elm Street 3: Dream Warriors ☐ Nightmare on Elm Street 4: The Dream Master ☐ Nightmare on Elm Street 5: The Dream Child ☐ Nightmare on Elm Street, A ☐ Phantom of the Opera ☐ V ☐ Wes Craven's New Nightmare

Erickson, Leif ☐ Abbott and Costello Meet Captain Kidd ☐ Abduction ☐ Arabian Nights ☐ Conquest ☐ Family Rico, The ☐ Fleet's In, The ☐ I Saw What You Did ☐ Invaders from Mars ☐ Kiss Them for Me ☐ Man and Boy ☐ New Lion of Sonora, The ☐ Night Monster ☐ Nothing But the Truth ☐ Once Upon a Horse ☐ One Third of a Nation ☐ Reunion in Reno ☐ Star in the Dust ☐ Tea and Sympathy ☐ Twilight for the Gods ☐ Waikiki Wedding

Estevez, Emilio ☐ Another Stakeout ☐ Breakfast Club, The ☐ D2: The Mighty Ducks ☐ Freejack ☐ In the Custody of Strangers ☐ Judgment Night ☐ Maximum Overdrive ☐ Men at Work ☐ Mighty Ducks, The ☐ National Lampoon's Loaded Weapon ☐ Nightbreaker ☐ Nightmares ☐ Outsiders, The ☐ Repo Man ☐ St. Elmo's Fire ☐ Stakeout ☐ Tex ☐ Wisdom ☐ Young Guns ☐ Young Guns 2

Evans, Dale ☐ Bells of Rosarita ☐ Bells of San Angelo ☐ Casanova in Burlesque ☐ Down Dakota Way ☐ Golden Stallion, The ☐ Helldorado ☐ Here Comes Elmer ☐ Hitchhike to Happiness ☐ Home in Oklahoma ☐ Roll on Texas Moon ☐ Song of Arizona ☐ Song of Nevada ☐ Under Nevada Skies ☐ Utah

Evans, Edith ☐ Chalk Garden, The ☐ Crooks and Coronets ☐ David Copperfield ☐ Doll's House, A ☐ Fitzwilly ☐ Importance of Being Earnest, The ☐ Last Days of Dolwyn, The ☐ Look Back in Anger ☐ Madwoman of Chaillot, The ☐ Nasty Habits ☐ Nun's Story, The ☐ Scrooge ☐ Slipper and the Rose, The ☐ Tom Jones ☐ Whisperers, The ☐ Young Cassidy

Evans, Gene ☐ Donovan's Brain ☐ Fixed Bayonets ☐ Force of Arms ☐ Giant Behemoth, The ☐ Golden Blade, The ☐ I Was an American Spy ☐ It Happens Every Spring ☐ Macahans, The ☐ Matt Helm ☐ Park Row ☐ Revolt in the Big House ☐ Shock Corridor ☐ Steel Helmet, The ☐ Support Your Local Sheriff ☐ Walking Tall ☐ Wyoming Renegades

Evans, Madge ☐ Beauty for Sale ☐ Broadway to Hollywood ☐ Dinner at Eight ☐ Exclusive Story ☐ Fugitive Lovers, The ☐ Greeks Had a Word for Them, The ☐ Guilty Hands ☐ Hallelujah, I'm a Bum ☐ Hell Below ☐ Mayor of Hell, The ☐ Pennies from Heaven ☐ Piccadilly Jim ☐ Sporting Blood ☐ Stand Up and Cheer ☐ Transatlantic Tunnel ☐ What Every Woman Knows

Evans, Maurice ☐ Androcles and the Lion ☐ Beneath the Planet of the Apes ☐ Caribbean Mystery, A ☐ Empress and I, The ☐ Girl, the Gold Watch and Everything, The ☐ Great Gilbert and Sullivan, The ☐ Jack of Diamonds ☐ Kind Lady ☐ Planet of the Apes ☐ Rosemary's Baby ☐ Scrooge ☐ War Lord, The

Everett, Chad ☐ Chapman Report, The ☐ Fever Pitch ☐ First to Fight ☐ Get Yourself a College Girl ☐ Heroes Stand Alone ☐ Impossible Years, The ☐ Johnny Tiger ☐ Last Challenge, The ☐ Made in Paris ☐ Malibu ☐ Rome Adventure ☐ Singing Nun, The

Everett, Rupert ☐ Another Country ☐ Comfort of Strangers, The ☐ Dance With a Stranger ☐ Duet for One ☐ Hearts of Fire ☐ Livin' the Life ☐ Madness of King George, The ☐ Right Hand Man, The

Ewell, Tom ☐ Adam's Rib ☐ American Guerilla in the Philippines ☐ Easy Money ☐ Finders Keepers ☐ Girl Can't Help It, The ☐ Great American Pastime, The ☐ Lieutenant Wore Skirts, The ☐ Life of Her Own, A ☐ Lost in Alaska ☐ Seven Year Itch, The ☐ State Fair ☐ Tender Is the Night ☐ They Only Kill Their Masters ☐ Up Front

Fabian ☐ High Time ☐ Hound-Dog Man ☐ Katie: Portrait of a Centerfold ☐ Kiss Daddy Goodbye ☐ Maryjane ☐ Mr. Hobbs Takes a Vacation ☐ North to Alaska ☐ Ride the Wild Surf ☐ Ten Little Indians

Fabray, Nanette ☐ Amy ☐ Band Wagon, The ☐ Cockeyed Cowboys of Calico County ☐ Fame Is the Name of the Game ☐ Happy Ending, The ☐ Harper Valley P.T.A. ☐ Private Matter, A

Fabrizi, Aldo ☐ Father's Dilemma ☐ Open City ☐ We All Loved Each Other So Much ☐ Wonders of Aladdin, The

Fabrizi, Franco ☐ Facts of Murder, The ☐ Ginger and Fred ☐ I Vitelloni ☐ Il Bidone

Fairbanks, Jr., Douglas ☐ Accused ☐ Angels over Broadway ☐ Captured ☐ Catherine the Great ☐ Chances ☐ Corsican Brothers, The ☐ Dawn Patrol, The ☐ Exile, The ☐ Fighting O'Flynn, The ☐ Ghost Story ☐ Great Manhunt, The ☐ Green Hell ☐ Gunga Din ☐ Having Wonderful Time ☐ Hostage Tower, The ☐ I Like Your Nerve ☐ It's Tough to Be Famous ☐ Jazz Age, The ☐ Joy of Living ☐ Life of Jimmy Dolan, The ☐ Little Caesar ☐ Love Is a Racket ☐ Mimi ☐ Morning Glory ☐ Narrow Corner, The ☐ One Night at Susie's ☐ Our Modern Maidens ☐ Outward Bound ☐ Parachute Jumper ☐ Prisoner of Zenda, The ☐ Rage of Paris, The ☐ Scarlet Dawn ☐ Sinbad the Sailor ☐ That Lady in Ermine ☐ Union Depot ☐ Woman of Affairs, A ☐ Young in Heart, The

Fairbanks, Douglas ☐ American Aristocracy, An ☐ Americano, The ☐ Black Pirate, The ☐ Don Q, Son of Zorro ☐ Gaslight Follies ☐ Great Chase, The ☐ His Picture In The Papers ☐ Iron Mask, The ☐ Mark of Zorro, The ☐ Mr. Robinson Crusoe ☐ Reaching for the Moon ☐ Robin Hood ☐ Taming of the Shrew, The ☐ Thief of Bagdad, The ☐ Three Musketeers, The

Falk, Peter ☐ All the Marbles ☐ Anzio ☐ Balcony, The ☐ Big Trouble ☐ Brink's Job, The ☐ Castle Keep ☐ Cheap Detective, The ☐ Columbo: Murder By the Book ☐ Columbo: Prescription Murder ☐ Cookie ☐ Faraway, So Close ☐ Great Race, The ☐ Griffin and Phoenix: A Love Story ☐ Happy New Year ☐ Husbands ☐ In the Spirit ☐ In-Laws, The ☐ It's a Mad Mad Mad Mad World ☐ Italiano Brava Gente ☐ Luv ☐ Machine Gun McCain ☐ Mikey and Nicky ☐ Murder by Death ☐ Murder, Inc. ☐ Operation Snafu ☐ Penelope ☐ Pocketful of Miracles ☐ Pressure Point ☐ Ransom for a Dead Man ☐ Robin and the Seven Hoods ☐ Roommates ☐ Scared Straight ☐ Tune In Tomorrow ☐ Vibes ☐ Wings of Desire ☐ Woman Under the Influence, A

Farentino, James ☐ Banning ☐ Common Ground ☐ Cradle Will Fall, The ☐ Dead and Buried ☐ Ensign Pulver ☐ Evita Peron ☐ Family Rico, The ☐ Family Sins ☐ Final Countdown, The ☐ Her Alibi ☐ Honor Thy Father and Mother: The True Story of the Menendez Murders ☐ Me, Natalie ☐ Pad and How to Use It, The ☐ Ride to Hangman's Tree, The ☐ Rosie ☐ War Lord, The

Farmer, Frances ☐ Among the Living ☐ Badlands of Dakota ☐ Ebb Tide ☐ Exclusive ☐ Flowing Gold ☐ Party Crashers, The ☐ Rhythm on the Range ☐ Son of Fury ☐ South of Pago Pago ☐ Toast of New York, The ☐ Too Many Parents ☐ World Premiere

Farrar, David ☐ Black Narcissus ☐ Black Shield of Falworth, The ☐ Cage of Gold ☐ Danny Boy ☐ Duel in the Jungle ☐ Escape to Burma ☐ For Those in Peril ☐ Frieda ☐ Golden Horde, The ☐ Gone to Earth ☐ Let's Make Up ☐ Mr. Perrin and Mr. Traill ☐ Night Invader, The ☐ Night Without Stars ☐ Obsessed, The ☐ Pearl of the South Pacific ☐ Sea Chase, The ☐ Small Back Room, The ☐ Tears for Simon

Farrell, Charles ☐ Big Shakedown, The ☐ Fazil ☐ Fighting Youth ☐ First Year, The ☐ Just Around the Corner ☐ Liliom ☐ Merely Mary Ann ☐ Moonlight Sonata ☐ Old Ironsides ☐ Seventh Heaven ☐ Street Angel ☐ Sunny Side Up

Farrell, Glenda ☐ Adventurous Blonde ☐ Apache War Smoke ☐ Big Shakedown, The ☐ Blondes at Work ☐ Breakfast for Two ☐ Bureau of Missing Persons ☐ Central Airport ☐ City Without Men ☐ Dark Hazard ☐ Disorderly Orderly, The ☐ Ever Since Venus ☐ Go Into Your Dance ☐ Gold Diggers of 1935 ☐ Gold Diggers of 1937 ☐ Grand Slam ☐ Heading for Heaven ☐ Hi, Nellie! ☐ High Tension ☐ Hollywood Hotel ☐ I Am a Fugitive from a Chain Gang ☐ I Love Trouble ☐ In Caliente ☐ Johnny Eager ☐ Kissin' Cousins ☐ Lady for a Day ☐ Life Begins ☐ Little Caesar ☐ Man's Castle ☐ Match King, The ☐ Middle of the Night ☐ Mystery of the Wax Museum, The ☐ Nobody's Fool ☐ Road to Reno, The ☐ Secret Bride, The ☐ Secret of the Incas ☐ Talk of the Town, The ☐ Three on a Match ☐ Traveling Saleslady

Farrow, Mia ☐ Alice ☐ Another Woman ☐ Avalanche ☐ Broadway Danny Rose ☐ Crimes and Misdemeanors ☐ Dandy in Aspic, A ☐ Death on the Nile ☐ Great Gatsby, The ☐ Guns at Batasi ☐ Hannah and Her Sisters ☐ Haunting of Julia, The ☐ Hurricane ☐ Husbands and Wives ☐ John and Mary ☐ Miami Rhapsody ☐ Midsummer Night's Sex Comedy, A ☐ New York Stories ☐ Purple Rose of Cairo, The ☐ Radio Days ☐ Rosemary's Baby ☐ Secret Ceremony ☐ See No Evil ☐ September ☐ Shadows and Fog ☐ Wedding, A ☐ Widow's Peak ☐ Widows' Peak ☐ Zelig

Fawcett, Farrah ☐ Between Two Women ☐ Burning Bed, The ☐ Cannonball Run, The ☐ Charlie's Angels ☐ Extremities ☐ Feminist and the Fuzz, The ☐ Girl Who Came Gift-Wrapped, The ☐ Great American Beauty Contest, The ☐ Logan's Run ☐ Man of the House ☐ Margaret Bourke-White ☐ Murder in Texas ☐ Murder on Flight 502 ☐ Myra Breckinridge ☐ Poor Little Rich Girl: The Barbara Hutton Story ☐ Saturn 3 ☐ See You in the Morning ☐ Small Sacrifices ☐ Sunburn

Faye, Alice ☐ Alexander's Ragtime Band ☐ Barricade ☐ Every Night at Eight ☐ Fallen Angel ☐ Four Jills in a Jeep ☐ Gang's All Here, The ☐ George White's Scandals ☐ George White's Scandals ☐ Great American Broadcast, The ☐ Hello Frisco, Hello ☐ Hollywood Cavalcade ☐ In Old Chicago ☐ King of Burlesque ☐ Lillian Russell ☐ Little Old New York ☐ Music Is Magic ☐ On the Avenue ☐ Poor Little Rich Girl ☐ Rose of Washington Square ☐ Sally, Irene and Mary ☐ Sing, Baby, Sing ☐ State Fair ☐ Stowaway ☐ That Night in Rio ☐ Tin Pan Alley ☐ Wake Up and Live ☐ Week-end in Havana ☐ You're a Sweetheart

Feldshuh, Tovah ☐ Amazing Howard Hughes, The ☐ Beggarman, Thief ☐ Blue Iguana, The ☐ Brewster's Millions ☐ Cheaper to Keep Her ☐ Citizen Cohn ☐ Daniel ☐ Day in October, A ☐ Idolmaker, The ☐ Nunzio ☐ Women's Room, The

Fellini, Federico ☐ Alex in Wonderland ☐ Amore ☐ Fellini's Roma ☐ Intervista

Fenn, Sherilyn ☐ Boxing Helena ☐ Desire and Hell at Sunset Motel ☐ Diary of a Hitman ☐ Fatal Instinct ☐ Meridian—Kiss of the Beast ☐ Of Mice and Men ☐ Ruby ☐ Three of Hearts ☐ Twin Peaks ☐ Two Moon Junction ☐ Wraith, The

Fernandel ☐ Angele ☐ Big Chief, The ☐ Carnival ☐ Cow and I ☐ Fernandel the Dressmaker ☐ Forbidden Fruit ☐ Gangster Boss ☐ Harvest ☐ Law Is the Law, The ☐ Little World of Don Camillo, The ☐ Man in the Raincoat, The ☐ Nais ☐ Pantaloons ☐ Paris Holiday ☐ Red Inn, The ☐ Sheep Has Five Legs, The ☐ Well-Digger's Daughter, The

Ferrer, Jose ☐ Anything Can Happen ☐ Banyon ☐ Being, The ☐ Berlin Tunnel 21 ☐ Big Brawl, The ☐ Big Bus, The ☐ Blood & Orchids ☐ Blood Feud ☐ Blood Tide ☐ Bloody Birthday ☐ Caine Mutiny, The ☐ Christopher Columbus ☐ Cockleshell Heroes, The ☐ Crisis ☐ Cyrano de Bergerac ☐ Deep in My Heart ☐ Dracula's Dog ☐ Dune ☐ Enter Laughing ☐ Evil That Men Do ☐ Evita Peron ☐ Fedora ☐ Fifth Musketeer, The ☐ Gideon's Trumpet ☐ Great Man, The ☐ Greatest Story Ever Told, The ☐ High Cost of Loving, The ☐ Hired to Kill ☐ Hitler's S.S.: Portrait in Evil ☐ I Accuse! ☐ Joan of Arc ☐ Lawrence of Arabia ☐ Life of Sin, A ☐ Marcus-Nelson Murders, The ☐ Medical Story ☐ Midsummer Night's Sex Comedy, A ☐ Miss Sadie Thompson ☐ Moulin Rouge ☐ Nine Hours to Rama ☐ Old Explorers ☐ Paco ☐ Peter and Paul ☐ Private Files of J. Edgar Hoover, The ☐ Samson and Delilah ☐ Sentinel, The ☐ Ship of Fools ☐ Shrike, The ☐ To Be or Not to Be ☐ Voyage of the Damned ☐ Whirlpool ☐ Who Has Seen the Wind?

Ferrer, Mel ☐ Blood and Roses ☐ Born To Be Bad ☐ Brannigan ☐ Brave Bulls, The ☐ Charge of the Black Lancers ☐ Eaten Alive ☐ El Greco ☐ Fall of the Roman Empire ☐ Fifth Floor, The ☐ Fraulein ☐ Great Alligator, The ☐ Hands of Orlac, The ☐ Hi-Riders ☐ Knights of the Round Table ☐ Lili ☐ Lili Marleen ☐ Lost Boundaries ☐ Memory of Eva Ryker, The ☐ Norseman, The ☐ One Shoe Makes It Murder ☐ Rancho Notorious ☐ Scaramouche ☐ Seduced ☐ Sex and the Single Girl ☐ Sun Also Rises, The ☐ Tempter, The ☐ War and Peace ☐ World, the Flesh and the Devil, The

Fetchit, Stepin ☐ David Harum ☐ Dimples ☐ Fifty Roads to Town ☐ Judge Priest ☐ Littlest Rebel, The ☐ Love Is News ☐ Marie Galante ☐ One More Spring ☐ Steamboat 'Round the Bend ☐ Sun Shines Bright, The ☐ Zenobia

Field, Betty ☐ Are Husbands Necessary? ☐ Birdman of Alcatraz ☐ Blues in the Night ☐ Bus Stop ☐ Butterfield 8 ☐ Coogan's Bluff ☐ Flesh and Fantasy ☐ Great Gatsby, The ☐ Great Moment, The ☐ Kings Row ☐ Of Mice and Men ☐ Peyton Place ☐ Picnic ☐ Seventeen ☐ Shepherd of the Hills ☐ Southerner, The ☐ Tomorrow the World ☐ Victory

Field, Sally ☐ Absence of Malice ☐ Back Roads ☐ Beyond the Poseidon Adventure ☐ End, The ☐ Forrest Gump ☐ Heroes ☐ Hitched ☐ Home for the Holidays ☐ Homeward Bound: The Incredible Journey ☐ Hooper ☐ Kiss Me Goodbye ☐ Marriage: Year One ☐ Maybe I'll Come Home in the Spring ☐ Mrs. Doubtfire ☐ Murphy's Romance ☐ Norma Rae ☐ Not Without My Daughter ☐ Places in the Heart ☐ Punchline ☐ Smokey and the Bandit ☐ Smokey and the Bandit, Part. 2 ☐ Soapdish ☐ Stay Hungry ☐ Steel Magnolias ☐ Surrender ☐ Sybil ☐ Way West, The

Fields, W.C. ☐ Alice in Wonderland ☐ Bank Dick, The ☐ Big Broadcast of 1938, The ☐ David Copperfield ☐ Down Memory Lane ☐ Follow the Boys ☐ Her Majesty, Love ☐ If I Had a Million ☐ International House ☐ It's a Gift ☐ Man on the Flying Trapeze, The ☐ Million Dollar Legs ☐ Mississippi ☐ Mrs. Wiggs of the Cabbage Patch ☐ My Little Chickadee ☐ Never Give a Sucker an Even Break ☐ Old-Fashioned Way, The ☐ Poppy ☐ Running Wild ☐ Sally of the Sawdust ☐ Sensations ☐ Six of a Kind ☐ Song of the Open Road ☐ Tillie and Gus ☐ You Can't Cheat an Honest Man ☐ You're Telling Me

Finch, Peter ☐ Abdication, The ☐ Detective,

The ☐ Elephant Walk ☐ England Made Me ☐ Far from the Madding Crowd ☐ Flight of the Phoenix ☐ Girl with Green Eyes, The ☐ Great Gilbert and Sullivan, The ☐ I Thank a Fool ☐ In the Cool of the Day ☐ Judith ☐ Kidnapped ☐ Legend of Lylah Clare, The ☐ Lost Horizon ☐ Make Me an Offer ☐ Man with the Green Carnation, The ☐ Miniver Story, The ☐ Nelson Affair, The ☐ Network ☐ No Love for Johnnie ☐ Nun's Story, The ☐ Operation Amsterdam ☐ Passage Home ☐ Pumpkin Eater, The ☐ Pursuit of the Graf Spee ☐ Raid on Entebbe ☐ Red Tent, The ☐ Shiralee, The ☐ Simon and Laura ☐ Story of Robin Hood and His Merrie Men, The ☐ Sunday, Bloody Sunday ☐ Town Like Alice, A ☐ Train of Events ☐ Warriors, The ☐ Windom's Way ☐ Wooden Horse, The

Finlay, Frank ☐ Arch of Triumph ☐ Bouquet of Barbed Wire ☐ Christmas Carol, A ☐ Cromwell ☐ Cthulhu Mansion ☐ Four Musketeers, The ☐ Gumshoe ☐ I'll Never Forget What's 'is Name ☐ In the Devil's Garden ☐ Inspector Clouseau ☐ Lifeforce ☐ Molly Maguires, The ☐ Mona ☐ Murder by Decree ☐ Othello ☐ Ploughman's Lunch, The ☐ Return of the Musketeers, The ☐ Robbery ☐ Shaft in Africa ☐ Three Musketeers, The

Finney, Albert ☐ Alpha Beta ☐ Annie ☐ Browning Version, The ☐ Charlie Bubbles ☐ Dresser, The ☐ Duellists, The ☐ Endless Game, The ☐ Entertainer, The ☐ Green Man, The ☐ Gumshoe ☐ Image, The ☐ Looker ☐ Loophole ☐ Man of No Importance, A ☐ Miller's Crossing ☐ Murder on the Orient Express ☐ Night Must Fall ☐ Orphans ☐ Picasso Summer, The ☐ Playboys, The ☐ Rich in Love ☐ Saturday Night and Sunday Morning ☐ Scrooge ☐ Shoot the Moon ☐ Tom Jones ☐ Two for the Road ☐ Under the Volcano ☐ Victors, The ☐ Wolfen

Fiorentino, Linda ☐ Acting on Impulse ☐ After Hours ☐ Gotcha! ☐ Last Seduction, The ☐ Moderns, The ☐ Neon Empire, The ☐ Queens Logic ☐ Shout ☐ Vision Quest

Firth, Colin ☐ Another Country ☐ Apartment Zero ☐ Camille ☐ Circle of Friends ☐ Femme Fatale ☐ Month in the Country, A ☐ Valmont

Firth, Peter ☐ Aces High ☐ Burndown ☐ Equus ☐ Fire and Sword ☐ Incident, The ☐ Innocent Victim ☐ Joseph Andrews ☐ King Arthur, the Young Warlord ☐ Letter to Brezhnev ☐ Lifeforce ☐ Prisoner of Honor ☐ Tess

Fishburne, Laurence ☐ Bad Company ☐ Boyz N the Hood ☐ Cadence ☐ Class Action ☐ Color Purple, The ☐ Cornbread, Earl and Me ☐ Death Wish II ☐ Decoration Day ☐ Deep Cover ☐ Higher Learning ☐ Just Cause ☐ King of New York ☐ Nightmare on Elm Street 3: Dream Warriors ☐ School Daze ☐ Searching for Bobby Fischer ☐ What's Love Got to Do With It

Fisher, Carrie ☐ 'Burbs, The ☐ Amazon Women on the Moon ☐ Appointment with Death ☐ Blues Brothers, The ☐ Drop Dead Fred ☐ Empire Strikes Back, The ☐ Garbo Talks ☐ Hannah and Her Sisters ☐ Hollywood Vice Squad ☐ Loverboy ☐ Man with One Red Shoe ☐ Mr. Mike's Mondo Video ☐ Paul Reiser—Out on a Whim ☐ Return of the Jedi, The ☐ Shampoo ☐ She's Back ☐ Sibling Rivalry ☐ Soapdish ☐ Star Wars ☐ This Is My Life ☐ Time Guardian, The ☐ Under the Rainbow ☐ When Harry Met Sally . . .

Fitzgerald, Barry ☐ Amazing Mrs. Holliday, The ☐ And Then There Were None ☐ Bringing Up Baby ☐ Broth of a Boy ☐ California ☐ Catered Affair, The ☐ Corvette K-225 ☐ Dawn Patrol, The ☐ Easy Come, Easy Go ☐ Ebb Tide ☐ Full Confession ☐ Going My Way ☐ How Green Was My Valley ☐ I Love a Soldier ☐ Incendiary Blonde ☐ Long Voyage Home, The ☐ Naked City, The ☐ None But the Lonely Heart ☐ Pacific Liner ☐ Plough and the Stars, The ☐ Quiet Man, The ☐ Rooney ☐ Saint Strikes Back, The ☐ Sea Wolf, The ☐ Silver City ☐ Story of Seabiscuit, The ☐ Tarzan's Secret Treasure ☐ Top o' the Morning ☐ Two Years Before the Mast ☐ Union Station ☐ Welcome Stranger

Fitzgerald, Ella ☐ Let No Man Write My Epitaph ☐ Pete Kelly's Blues ☐ Ride 'Em Cowboy ☐ St. Louis Blues

Fleming, Rhonda ☐ Abilene Town ☐ Adventure Island ☐ Alias Jesse James ☐ Big Circus, The ☐ Bullwhip ☐ Buster Keaton Story, The ☐ Connecticut Yankee in King Arthur's Court ☐ Crosswinds ☐ Crowded Sky, The ☐ Cry Danger ☐ Eagle and the Hawk, The ☐ Golden Hawk, The ☐ Great Lover, The ☐ Gun Glory ☐ Gunfight at the O.K. Corral ☐ Home Before Dark ☐ Hong Kong ☐ Inferno ☐ Jivaro ☐ Killer Is Loose, The ☐ Last Outpost, The ☐ Nude Bomb, The ☐ Odongo ☐ Out of the Past ☐ Pony Express ☐ Redhead and the Cowboy, The ☐ Slightly Scarlet ☐ Spellbound ☐ Tennessee's Partner ☐ Those Redheads From Seattle ☐ While the City Sleeps ☐ Yankee Pasha

Fletcher, Louise ☐ Best of the Best ☐ Blind Vision ☐ Blue Steel ☐ Brainstorm ☐ Cheap Detective, The ☐ Exorcist II: The Heretic ☐ Final Notice ☐ Firestarter ☐ Flowers in the Attic ☐ Invaders from Mars ☐ J. Edgar Hoover ☐ Karen Carpenter Story, The ☐ Lucky Star, The ☐ Magician of Lublin, The ☐ Mama Dracula ☐ Nightmare on the 13th Floor ☐ Nobody's Fool ☐ One Flew over the Cuckoo's Nest ☐ Return to Two Moon Junction ☐ Second Serve ☐ Shadowzone ☐ Strange Behavior ☐ Strange Invaders ☐ Thieves Like Us ☐ Two Moon Junction

Flynn, Errol ☐ Adventures of Captain Fabian ☐ Adventures of Don Juan ☐ Adventures of Robin Hood, The ☐ Against All Flags ☐ Another Dawn ☐ Assault of the Rebel Girls

☐ Big Boodle, The ☐ Captain Blood ☐ Charge of the Light Brigade, The ☐ Cry Wolf ☐ Dawn Patrol, The ☐ Desperate Journey ☐ Dive Bomber ☐ Dodge City ☐ Edge of Darkness ☐ Escape Me Never ☐ Footsteps in the Dark ☐ Four's a Crowd ☐ Gentleman Jim ☐ Green Light, The ☐ Istanbul ☐ Kim ☐ Let's Make Up ☐ Mara Maru ☐ Master of Ballantrae, The ☐ Montana ☐ Never Say Goodbye ☐ Northern Pursuit ☐ Objective, Burma! ☐ Perfect Specimen, The ☐ Prince and the Pauper, The ☐ Private Lives of Elizabeth and Essex, The ☐ Rocky Mountain ☐ Roots of Heaven, The ☐ San Antonio ☐ Santa Fe Trail ☐ Sea Hawk, The ☐ Silver River ☐ Sisters, The ☐ Sun Also Rises, The ☐ Thank Your Lucky Stars ☐ That Forsythe Woman ☐ They Died With Their Boots On ☐ Too Much, Too Soon ☐ Uncertain Glory ☐ Virginia City ☐ Warriors, The

Flynn, Joe ☐ Barefoot Executive, The ☐ Computer Wore Tennis Shoes, The ☐ How to Frame a Figg ☐ McHale's Navy ☐ McHale's Navy Joins the Air Force ☐ Million Dollar Duck ☐ My Dog the Thief ☐ Now You See Him, Now You Don't ☐ Rescuers, The ☐ Strongest Man in the World, The ☐ Superdad

Foch, Nina ☐ American in Paris, An ☐ Boston Blackie's Rendevous ☐ Cash McCall ☐ Columbo: Prescription Murder ☐ Dark Past, The ☐ Fast Company ☐ Four Guns to the Border ☐ Guilt of Janet Ames, The ☐ I Love a Mystery ☐ Illegal ☐ Jennifer ☐ Johnny O'Clock ☐ Mahogany ☐ My Name Is Julia Ross ☐ Nine Girls ☐ Return of the Vampire, The ☐ Song to Remember, A ☐ St. Benny the Dip ☐ Such Good Friends ☐ Ten Commandments, The ☐ Three Brave Men ☐ Undercover Man, The ☐ You're Never Too Young

Follows, Megan ☐ Anne of Avonlea ☐ Anne of Green Gables ☐ Back to Hannibal: The Return of Tom Sawyer and Huckleberry Finn ☐ Champagne Charlie ☐ Hockey Night ☐ Inherit the Wind ☐ Nutcracker Prince, The ☐ Stacking

Fonda, Bridget ☐ Aria ☐ Bodies, Rest & Motion ☐ Camilla ☐ Doc Hollywood ☐ End of Innocence, The ☐ Frankenstein Unbound ☐ Godfather, Part III, The ☐ Iron Maze ☐ It Could Happen To You ☐ Jacob Have I Loved ☐ Leather Jackets ☐ Little Buddha ☐ Out of the Rain ☐ Point of No Return ☐ Road to Wellville, The ☐ Scandal ☐ Shag, The Movie ☐ Single White Female ☐ Singles ☐ Strapless

Fonda, Henry ☐ 12 Angry Men ☐ Advise and Consent ☐ Alpha Caper, The ☐ Ash Wednesday ☐ Battle of Midway, The ☐ Battle of the Bulge ☐ Best Man, The ☐ Big Hand for the Little Lady, A ☐ Big Street, The ☐ Blockade ☐ Boston Strangler, The ☐ Chad Hanna ☐ Cheyenne Social Club, The ☐ City on Fire ☐ Collision Course ☐ Dirty Game, The ☐ Drums Along the Mohawk ☐ Fail-Safe ☐ Farmer Takes a Wife, The ☐ Fedora ☐ Firecreek ☐ Fort Apache ☐ Fugitive, The ☐ Gideon's Trumpet ☐ Grapes of Wrath, The ☐ Great Battle, The ☐ Great Smokey Roadblock, The ☐ Hollywood Retrospectives—Fonda on Fonda ☐ Home to Stay ☐ How the West Was Won ☐ I Dream Too Much ☐ I Met My Love Again ☐ Immortal Sergeant, The ☐ In Harm's Way ☐ Jesse James ☐ Jezebel ☐ Lady Eve, The ☐ Last Four Days, The ☐ Let Us Live ☐ Lillian Russell ☐ Long Night, The ☐ Longest Day, The ☐ Mad Miss Manton, The ☐ Madigan ☐ Magnificent Dope, The ☐ Main Street to Broadway ☐ Male Animal, The ☐ Man Who Understood Women, The ☐ Meteor ☐ Midway ☐ Mister Roberts ☐ Moon's Our Home, The ☐ My Darling Clementine ☐ My Name Is Nobody ☐ Night Flight from Moscow ☐ Oldest Living Graduate, The ☐ On Golden Pond ☐ On Our Merry Way ☐ Once Upon a Time in the West ☐ Ox-Bow Incident, The ☐ Red Pony, The ☐ Return of Frank James, The ☐ Rollercoaster ☐ Roots: The Next Generation ☐ Rounders, The ☐ Sex and the Single Girl ☐ Sometimes a Great Notion ☐ Spawn of the North ☐ Spencer's Mountain ☐ Stage Struck ☐ Story of Alexander Graham Bell, The ☐ Stranger on the Run ☐ Summer Solstice ☐ Swarm, The ☐ Tales of Manhattan ☐ That Certain Woman ☐ There Was a Crooked Man ☐ Tin Star, The ☐ Too Late the Hero ☐ Trail of the Lonesome Pine ☐ Wanda Nevada ☐ War and Peace ☐ Warlock ☐ Welcome to Hard Times ☐ Wings of the Morning ☐ Wrong Man, The ☐ You Belong to Me ☐ You Only Live Once ☐ Young Mr. Lincoln ☐ Yours, Mine and Ours

Fonda, Jane ☐ 9 to 5 ☐ Agnes of God ☐ Any Wednesday ☐ Barbarella ☐ Barefoot in the Park ☐ Blue Bird, The ☐ California Suite ☐ Cat Ballou ☐ Chapman Report, The ☐ Chase, The ☐ China Syndrome, The ☐ Circle of Love ☐ Comes a Horseman ☐ Coming Home ☐ Doll's House, A ☐ Dollmaker, The ☐ Electric Horseman, The ☐ F.T.A. ☐ Fun with Dick and Jane ☐ Game Is Over, The ☐ Hurry Sundown ☐ In the Cool of the Day ☐ Joy House ☐ Julia ☐ Klute ☐ Morning After, The ☐ No Nukes ☐ Old Gringo ☐ On Golden Pond ☐ Period of Adjustment ☐ Rollover ☐ Spirits of the Dead ☐ Stanley & Iris ☐ Steelyard Blues ☐ Sunday in New York ☐ Tall Story ☐ They Shoot Horses, Don't They? ☐ Tout Va Bien ☐ Walk on the Wild Side

Fonda, Peter ☐ 92 in the Shade ☐ Cannonball Run, The ☐ Certain Fury ☐ Deadfall ☐ Dirty Mary, Crazy Larry ☐ Easy Rider ☐ Fatal Mission ☐ Fighting Mad ☐ Futureworld ☐ Hawken's Breed ☐ High-Ballin' ☐ Hired Hand, The ☐ Hostage Tower, The ☐ Jungle Heat ☐ Killer Force ☐ Last Movie,

The ☐ Lilith ☐ Mercenary Fighters ☐ Molly and Gina ☐ Open Season ☐ Outlaw Blues ☐ Race With the Devil ☐ Signatures of the Soul ☐ South Beach ☐ Spasms ☐ Spirits of the Dead ☐ Tammy and the Doctor ☐ Trip, The ☐ Victors, The ☐ Wanda Nevada ☐ Wild Angels, The

Fontaine, Joan ☐ Affairs of Susan, The ☐ Beyond a Reasonable Doubt ☐ Bigamist, The ☐ Born To Be Bad ☐ Casanova's Big Night ☐ Certain Smile, A ☐ Constant Nymph, The ☐ Damsel in Distress, A ☐ Darling, How Could You ☐ Decameron Nights ☐ Devil's Own, The ☐ Duke of West Point, The ☐ Emperor Waltz, The ☐ Flight to Tangier ☐ Frenchman's Creek ☐ From This Day Forward ☐ Gunga Din ☐ Island in the Sun ☐ Ivanhoe ☐ Ivy ☐ Jane Eyre ☐ Kiss the Blood Off My Hands ☐ Letter from an Unknown Woman ☐ Maid's Night Out ☐ Man of Conquest ☐ Rebecca ☐ September Affair ☐ Serenade ☐ Something to Live For ☐ Suspicion ☐ Tender Is the Night ☐ This Above All ☐ Until They Sail ☐ Voyage to the Bottom of the Sea ☐ Women, The

Fonteyn, Margot ☐ Margot Fonteyn Story, The ☐ Most Beautiful Ballets, The ☐ Romeo and Juliet ☐ Swan Lake

Foran, Dick ☐ Atomic Submarine, The ☐ Behind the Eight Ball ☐ Black Legion ☐ Earthworm Tractors ☐ Easy Come, Easy Go ☐ Fearmakers, The ☐ Four Mothers ☐ Heart of the North ☐ Horror Island ☐ I Stole a Million ☐ Keep 'Em Flying ☐ Mummy's Hand, The ☐ Mummy's Tomb, The ☐ My Little Chickadee ☐ Rangers of Fortune ☐ Ride 'Em Cowboy ☐ Shipmates Forever ☐ Treachery Rides the Range

Ford, Glenn ☐ 3:10 to Yuma ☐ Advance to the Rear ☐ Adventures of Martin Eden, The ☐ Affair in Trinidad ☐ Americano, The ☐ Appointment in Honduras ☐ Beggarman, Thief ☐ Big Heat, The ☐ Blackboard Jungle ☐ Border Shootout ☐ Cimarron ☐ Courtship of Eddie's Father, The ☐ Cowboy ☐ Cry for Happy ☐ Dear Heart ☐ Desperadoes, The ☐ Destroyer ☐ Don't Go Near the Water ☐ Evening in Byzantium, An ☐ Experiment in Terror ☐ Fastest Gun Alive, The ☐ Fate Is the Hunter ☐ Final Verdict ☐ Flight Lieutenant ☐ Flying Missile, The ☐ Follow the Sun ☐ Four Horsemen of the Apocalypse ☐ Framed ☐ Gallant Journey ☐ Gazebo, The ☐ Gilda ☐ Greatest Gift, The ☐ Green Glove, The ☐ Happy Birthday to Me ☐ Heaven with a Barbed Wire Fence ☐ Heaven with a Gun ☐ Human Desire ☐ Imitation General ☐ Interrupted Melody ☐ Is Paris Burning? ☐ It Started with a Kiss ☐ Jarrett ☐ Jubal ☐ Lady in Question,The ☐ Last Challenge, The ☐ Love Is a Ball ☐ Loves of Carmen, The ☐ Lust for Gold ☐ Man from Colorado, The ☐ Man from the Alamo, The ☐ Mating of Millie, The ☐ Midway ☐ Money Trap, The ☐ Plunder of the Sun ☐ Pocketful of Miracles ☐ Rage ☐ Ransom ☐ Redhead and the Cowboy, The ☐ Rounders, The ☐ Sacketts, The ☐ Santee ☐ Secret of Convict Lake, The ☐ Sheepman, The ☐ Smith! ☐ So Ends Our Night ☐ Stolen Life, A ☐ Superman—The Movie ☐ Teahouse of the August Moon, The ☐ Texas ☐ Time for Killing, A ☐ Torpedo Run ☐ Trial ☐ Undercover Man, The ☐ Violent Men, The ☐ Virus ☐ White Tower, The

Ford, Harrison ☐ American Graffiti ☐ Blade Runner ☐ Clear and Present Danger ☐ Conversation, The ☐ Empire Strikes Back, The ☐ Force 10 from Navarone ☐ Frantic ☐ Frisco Kid, The ☐ Fugitive, The ☐ Hanover Street ☐ Heroes ☐ Indiana Jones and the Last Crusade ☐ Indiana Jones and the Temple of Doom ☐ James A. Michener's Dynasty ☐ Mosquito Coast, The ☐ Patriot Games ☐ Presumed Innocent ☐ Raiders of the Lost Ark ☐ Regarding Henry ☐ Return of the Jedi, The ☐ Star Wars ☐ Witness ☐ Working Girl

Ford, Paul ☐ Advise and Consent ☐ Big Hand for the Little Lady, A ☐ Comedians, The ☐ Matchmaker, The ☐ Missouri Traveler, The ☐ Music Man, The ☐ Never Too Late ☐ Richard ☐ Teahouse of the August Moon, The

Ford, Wallace ☐ Ape Man, The ☐ Back Door to Heaven ☐ Beast of The City, The ☐ Blood on the Sun ☐ Central Park ☐ Dark Sands ☐ Embraceable You ☐ Employees Entrance ☐ Exiled to Shanghai ☐ First Texan, The ☐ Flesh and Fury ☐ Freaks ☐ Furies, The ☐ He Ran All the Way ☐ Informer, The ☐ Lost Patrol, The ☐ Man Betrayed, A ☐ Man from Laramie, The ☐ Man Who Reclaimed His Head, The ☐ Mary Burns, Fugitive ☐ Matchmaker, The ☐ Men in White ☐ Mummy's Hand, The ☐ Mummy's Tomb, The ☐ Mysterious Mr. Wong, The ☐ Night of Terror ☐ One Frightened Night ☐ Possessed ☐ Red Stallion in the Rockies, The ☐ She Couldn't Say No ☐ Three-Cornered Moon ☐ Warpath ☐ Wet Parade, The ☐ Whole Town's Talking, The ☐ Wichita

Forrest, Frederic ☐ Adventures of Huckleberry Finn ☐ Apocalypse Now ☐ Beryl Markham: A Shadow on the Sun ☐ Best Kept Secrets ☐ Calamity Jane ☐ Citizen Cohn ☐ Conversation, The ☐ Deliberate Stranger, The ☐ Don Is Dead, The ☐ Falling Down ☐ Gotham ☐ Gravy Train, The ☐ Habitation of Dragons, The ☐ Hammett ☐ Hidden Fears ☐ It Lives Again ☐ Larry ☐ Lonesome Dove ☐ Margaret Bourke-White ☐ Missouri Breaks, The ☐ Music Box ☐ One from the Heart ☐ Parade, The ☐ Permission to Kill ☐ Quo Vadis? ☐ Rain Without Thunder ☐ Return ☐ Rose, The ☐ Stacking ☐ Stone Boy, The ☐ Trauma ☐ Tucker—The Man and His Dream ☐ Valley Girl ☐ When the Legends Die ☐ Who Will Love My Children?

Forrest, Steve ☐ Bedevilled ☐ Deerslayer, The ☐ Five Branded Women ☐ Flaming Star

☐ Heller in Pink Tights ☐ Hotline ☐ It Happened to Jane ☐ Last of the Mohicans, The ☐ Malibu ☐ Mommie Dearest ☐ Phantom of the Rue Morgue ☐ Rascal ☐ Rogue Cop ☐ Second Time Around, The ☐ So Big ☐ Spies Like Us ☐ Wild Country, The

Forsythe, John ☐ Ambassador's Daughter, The ☐ Amelia Earhart ☐ And Justice for All ☐ Captive City, The ☐ Escape from Fort Bravo ☐ Glass Web, The ☐ Happy Ending, The ☐ In Cold Blood ☐ It Happens Every Thursday ☐ Kitten with a Whip ☐ Lisa, Bright and Dark ☐ Madame X ☐ Mysterious Two ☐ On Fire ☐ Scrooged ☐ Sizzle ☐ Topaz ☐ Trouble With Harry, The

Forsythe, William ☐ American Me ☐ Dead-Bang ☐ Out for Justice ☐ Patty Hearst ☐ Raising Arizona ☐ Stone Cold ☐ Waterdance, The

Fosse, Bob ☐ Affairs of Dobie Gillis, The ☐ Give a Girl a Break ☐ Kiss Me Kate ☐ Little Prince, The ☐ My Sister Eileen

Fossey, Brigitte ☐ Enigma ☐ Farewell Friend ☐ Forbidden Games ☐ Imperative ☐ La Boum ☐ La Boum 2 ☐ Last Butterfly, The ☐ Man Who Died Twice, The ☐ Man Who Loved Women, The

Foster, Dianne ☐ Bad For Each Other ☐ Bamboo Prison, The ☐ Brothers Rico, The ☐ Deep Six, The ☐ Drive a Crooked Road ☐ Gideon of Scotland Yard ☐ King of the Roaring Twenties—The Story of Arnold Rothstein ☐ Last Hurrah, The ☐ Monkey on My Back ☐ Night Passage ☐ Three Hours to Kill ☐ Violent Men, The

Foster, Jodie ☐ Accused, The ☐ Alice Doesn't Live Here Anymore ☐ Backtrack ☐ Blood of Others, The ☐ Bugsy Malone ☐ Candleshoe ☐ Carny ☐ Echoes of a Summer ☐ Five Corners ☐ Foxes ☐ Freaky Friday ☐ Hotel New Hampshire, The ☐ Kansas City Bomber ☐ Little Girl Who Lives Down the Lane, The ☐ Little Man Tate ☐ Maverick ☐ Mesmerized ☐ Napoleon and Samantha ☐ Nell ☐ O'Hara's Wife ☐ Shadows and Fog ☐ Siesta ☐ Silence of the Lambs, The ☐ Smile Jenny, You're Dead ☐ Sommersby ☐ Stealing Home ☐ Svengali ☐ Taxi Driver ☐ Tom Sawyer

Foster, Meg ☐ Adam at 6 A.M. ☐ Backstab ☐ Best Kept Secrets ☐ Carny ☐ Different Story, A ☐ Emerald Forest, The ☐ Futurekick ☐ Hidden Fears ☐ James Dean ☐ Jezebel's Kiss ☐ Legend of Sleepy Hollow, The ☐ Masters of the Universe ☐ Project: Shadowchaser ☐ Relentless ☐ Relentless 2: Dead On ☐ Shrunken Heads ☐ Stepfather II ☐ They Live ☐ Ticket to Heaven ☐ To Catch a Killer

Foster, Preston ☐ American Empire ☐ Annie Oakley ☐ Bermuda Mystery ☐ Big Cat, The ☐ Big Gusher, The ☐ Big Night, The ☐ Doctor X ☐ Elmer the Great ☐ First Lady ☐ Gentleman After Dark, A ☐ Geronimo ☐ Guadalcanal Diary ☐ I Am a Fugitive from a Chain Gang ☐ I Shot Jesse James ☐ Informer, The ☐ Inside Job ☐ Kansas City Confidential ☐ Ladies They Talk About ☐ Last Days of Pompeii, The ☐ Last Mile, The ☐ Law and Order ☐ Love Before Breakfast ☐ Man from Galveston, The ☐ Man Who Dared, The ☐ Marshal's Daughter, The ☐ Missing Evidence ☐ My Friend Flicka ☐ Northwest Mounted Police ☐ Plough and the Stars, The ☐ Sea Devils ☐ Thunderhead—Son of Flicka ☐ Thunderhoof ☐ Time Travelers, The ☐ Two Seconds ☐ Unfinished Business ☐ Up The River ☐ Valley of Decision, The

Foster, Susanna ☐ Climax, The ☐ Frisco Sal ☐ Glamour Boy ☐ Phantom of the Opera ☐ This Is the Life

Fox, Edward ☐ Big Sleep, The ☐ Bounty, The ☐ Bridge Too Far, A ☐ Cat and the Canary, The ☐ Day of the Jackal, The ☐ Doll's House, A ☐ Dresser, The ☐ Duellists, The ☐ Force 10 from Navarone ☐ Frozen Dead, The ☐ Galileo ☐ Gandhi ☐ Hazard of Hearts, A ☐ I'll Never Forget What's 'is Name ☐ Mind Benders, The ☐ Naked Runner, The ☐ Shaka Zulu ☐ Shooting Party, The ☐ Soldier of Orange

Fox, James ☐ Absolute Beginners ☐ Afraid of the Dark ☐ Arabella ☐ Chase, The ☐ Crucifer of Blood, The ☐ Duffy ☐ Farewell to the King ☐ Greystoke: The Legend of Tarzan, Lord of the Apes ☐ Heart of Darkness ☐ High Season ☐ Hostage ☐ Isadora ☐ King Rat ☐ Loneliness of the Long Distance Runner, The ☐ Mighty Quinn, The ☐ No Longer Alone ☐ Passage to India, A ☐ Performance ☐ Remains of the Day ☐ Russia House, The ☐ Servant, The ☐ Thoroughly Modern Millie ☐ Those Magnificent Men in Their Flying Machines ☐ Whistle Blower, The

Fox, Michael J. ☐ Back to the Future ☐ Back to the Future Part II ☐ Back to the Future Part III ☐ Bright Lights, Big City ☐ Casualties of War ☐ Class of 1984 ☐ Doc Hollywood ☐ Family Ties Vacation ☐ For Love or Money ☐ Greedy ☐ Hard Way, The ☐ High School U.S.A. ☐ Homeward Bound: The Incredible Journey ☐ Letters From Frank ☐ Life with Mikey ☐ Light of Day ☐ Midnight Madness ☐ Poison Ivy ☐ Secret of My Success, The ☐ Teen Wolf ☐ Where the Rivers Flow North

Franciosa, Anthony ☐ Across 110th Street ☐ Assault on a Queen ☐ Blood Vows—The Story of a Mafia Wife ☐ Career ☐ Cricket, The ☐ Curse of the Black Widow ☐ Death Wish II ☐ Drowning Pool, The ☐ Face in the Crowd, A ☐ Fame Is the Name of the Game ☐ Fathom ☐ Ghost in the Noonday Sun ☐ Go Naked in the World ☐ Hatful of Rain, A ☐ Help Me Dream ☐ In Enemy Country ☐ Julie Darling ☐ Long Hot Summer, The ☐ Man Called Gannon, A ☐ Man Could Get Killed, A ☐ Matt Helm ☐ Naked Maja, The ☐ Period of Adjustment ☐ Pleasure Seekers,

The ☐ Rio Conchos ☐ Side Show ☐ Stagecoach ☐ Story on Page One, The ☐ Swinger, The ☐ This Could Be the Night ☐ Unsane ☐ Wild is the Wind

Francis, Anne ☐ Bad Day at Black Rock ☐ Battle Cry ☐ Beggarman, Thief ☐ Blackboard Jungle ☐ Born Again ☐ Don't Go Near the Water ☐ Dreamboat ☐ Elopement ☐ F.B.I. Story, The—The FBI Versus Alvin Karpis, Public Enemy Number One ☐ Forbidden Planet ☐ Funny Girl ☐ Girl Named Sooner, A ☐ Girl of the Night ☐ Great American Pastime, The ☐ Haunts of the Very Rich ☐ Hired Gun, The ☐ Hook, Line & Sinker ☐ Impasse ☐ Lion Is in the Streets, A ☐ Love God?, The ☐ Lydia Bailey ☐ Masterpiece of Murder, A ☐ More Dead Than Alive ☐ Rack, The ☐ Rebels, The ☐ Rogue Cop ☐ Satan Bug, The ☐ Scarlet Coat, The ☐ So Young, So Bad ☐ Summer Holiday ☐ Susan Slept Here ☐ Whistle at Eaton Falls, The

Franciscus, James ☐ Amazing Dobermans, The ☐ Beneath the Planet of the Apes ☐ Cat o' Nine Tails ☐ City on Fire ☐ Dario Argento's World of Horror ☐ Good Guys Wear Black ☐ I Passed for White ☐ Jacqueline Bouvier Kennedy ☐ Killer Fish ☐ Man Inside, The ☐ Marooned ☐ Miracle of the White Stallions ☐ Night Slaves ☐ Nightkill ☐ One of My Wives Is Missing ☐ Outsider, The ☐ Snow Treasure ☐ Valley of Gwangi ☐ When Time Ran Out . . . ☐ Youngblood Hawke

Francis, Kay ☐ Allotment Wives ☐ Always in My Heart ☐ Another Dawn ☐ Between Us Girls ☐ British Agent ☐ Charley's Aunt ☐ Cocoanuts, The ☐ Comet Over Broadway ☐ Confession ☐ Cynara ☐ Feminine Touch, The ☐ First Lady ☐ For the Defense ☐ Four Jills in a Jeep ☐ Girls About Town ☐ Give Me Your Heart ☐ Goose and the Gander, The ☐ Guilty Hands ☐ I Found Stella Parish ☐ I Loved a Woman ☐ In Name Only ☐ It's a Date ☐ Jewel Robbery ☐ King of the Underworld ☐ Ladies' Man ☐ Little Men ☐ Mandalay ☐ Marriage Playground, The ☐ One Way Passage ☐ Paramount on Parade ☐ Raffles ☐ Strangers in Love ☐ Trouble in Paradise ☐ Vice Squad, The ☐ When the Daltons Rode ☐ Wonder Bar

Franklin, Pamela ☐ Ace Eli and Rodger of the Skies ☐ And Soon the Darkness ☐ Eleanor and Franklin ☐ Flipper's New Adventure ☐ Food of the Gods, The ☐ Horse Without a Head, The ☐ Innocents, The ☐ Legend of Hell House, The ☐ Lion, The ☐ Nanny, The ☐ Necromancy ☐ Night of the Following Day, The ☐ Prime of Miss Jean Brodie, The ☐ Tiger Walks, A

Franz, Arthur ☐ Abbott and Costello Meet The Invisible Man ☐ Atomic Submarine, The ☐ Back From the Dead ☐ Battle Taxi ☐ Bobby Ware Is Missing ☐ Eight Iron Men ☐ Flame Barrier, The ☐ Flight Nurse ☐ Flight to Mars ☐ Invaders from Mars ☐ Jungle Patrol ☐ Member of the Wedding, The ☐ Rainbow 'Round My Shoulder ☐ Red Stallion in the Rockies, The ☐ Running Target ☐ Sisters of Death

Fraser, Brendan ☐ Dogfight ☐ Encino Man ☐ School Ties ☐ Scout, The ☐ Twenty Bucks ☐ With Honors

Frawley, William ☐ Babe Ruth Story, The ☐ Bolero ☐ Car 99 ☐ Desire ☐ Double or Nothing ☐ East Side, West Side ☐ Farmer's Daughter, The ☐ Fighting Seabees, The ☐ Flame of Barbary Coast ☐ General Died at Dawn, The ☐ Gentleman Jim ☐ High, Wide, and Handsome ☐ Hitchhike to Happiness ☐ Hold 'Em Yale ☐ Huckleberry Finn ☐ It Happened in Flatbush ☐ Joe Palooka in Winner Take All ☐ Kill the Umpire ☐ Lady on a Train ☐ Lemon Drop Kid, The ☐ Lemon Drop Kid, The ☐ Lone Wolf and His Lady, The ☐ Mad about Music ☐ Miss Fane's Baby is Stolen ☐ Persons in Hiding ☐ Princess Comes Across, The ☐ Professor Beware ☐ Rendezvous with Annie ☐ Rhubarb ☐ Rhythm on the River ☐ Rose of Washington Square ☐ Safe at Home ☐ Sandy Gets Her Man ☐ Something to Sing About ☐ Strike Me Pink ☐ Untamed ☐ Virginian, The ☐ Whistling in Brooklyn

Freeman, Morgan ☐ Atlanta Child Murders, The ☐ Attica ☐ Bonfire of the Vanities, The ☐ Brubaker ☐ Clean and Sober ☐ Clinton and Nadine ☐ Death of a Prophet ☐ Driving Miss Daisy ☐ Execution of Raymond Graham, The ☐ Eyewitness ☐ Fight for Life ☐ Glory ☐ Hollow Image ☐ Johnny Handsome ☐ Lean on Me ☐ Marie ☐ Marva Collins Story, The ☐ Outbreak ☐ Power of One, The ☐ Robin Hood: Prince of Thieves ☐ Roll of Thunder, Hear My Cry ☐ Shawshank Redemption, The ☐ Street Smart ☐ Teachers ☐ Unforgiven ☐ Who Says I Can't Ride a Rainbow?

Fresnay, Pierre ☐ Carnival of Sinners ☐ Cesar ☐ Fanatics, The ☐ Fanny ☐ Grand Illusion ☐ Le Corbeau ☐ Le Puritain ☐ Marius ☐ Monsieur Vincent ☐ Murderer Lives at Number 21, The

Fricker, Brenda ☐ Field, The ☐ Home Alone 2: Lost in New York ☐ Lethal Innocence ☐ Man of No Importance, A ☐ My Left Foot ☐ So I Married An Axe Murderer ☐ Sound and the Silence, The ☐ Utz

Friels, Colin ☐ Buddies ☐ Dingo ☐ Grievous Bodily Harm ☐ Ground Zero ☐ Kangaroo ☐ Malcolm ☐ Monkey Grip ☐ Warm Nights on a Slow Moving Train

Funicello, Annette ☐ Babes in Toyland ☐ Back to the Beach ☐ Beach Blanket Bingo ☐ Beach Party ☐ Bikini Beach ☐ Fireball 500 ☐ Horsemasters, The ☐ How to Stuff a Wild Bikini ☐ Lots of Luck ☐ Misadventures of Merlin Jones, The ☐ Monkey's Uncle, The ☐ Muscle Beach Party ☐ Pajama Party ☐ Shaggy Dog, The

Furneaux, Yvonne ☐ Charge of the Black Lancers ☐ La Dolce Vita ☐ Master of Ballantrae, The ☐ Mummy, The ☐ Repulsion
Furness, Betty ☐ Chance at Heaven ☐ Crossfire ☐ Dangerous Corner ☐ Here Comes Cookie ☐ Life of Vergie Winters, The ☐ Magnificent Obsession ☐ Swing Time
Gabin, Jean ☐ Any Number Can Win ☐ Case of Dr. Laurent, The ☐ Counterfeiters of Paris, The ☐ Deadlier than the Male ☐ Escape from Yesterday ☐ Four Bags Full ☐ French Cancan ☐ From Top to Bottom ☐ Golgotha ☐ Grand Illusion ☐ Grisbi ☐ Impostor, The ☐ Inspector Maigret ☐ Jury of One ☐ La Bete Humaine ☐ Le Cas du Docteur Laurent ☐ Le Gentleman D'Epsom ☐ Le Jour Se Leve ☐ Le Plaisir ☐ Les Miserables ☐ Love Is My Profession ☐ Lower Depths, The ☐ Monkey in Winter, A ☐ Moontide ☐ Pepe Le Moko ☐ Port of Shadows ☐ Sicilian Clan, The ☐ They Were Five ☐ Walls of Malapaga, The ☐ Zou Zou
Gable, Clark ☐ Across the Wide Missouri ☐ Adventure ☐ After Office Hours ☐ Any Number Can Play ☐ Band of Angels ☐ Betrayed ☐ Boom Town ☐ But Not For Me ☐ Cain and Mabel ☐ Call of the Wild ☐ Chained ☐ China Seas ☐ Command Decision ☐ Comrade X ☐ Dance, Fools, Dance ☐ Dancing Lady ☐ Finger Points, The ☐ Forsaking All Others ☐ Free Soul, A ☐ Gone with the Wind ☐ Hell Divers ☐ Hold Your Man ☐ Homecoming ☐ Honky Tonk ☐ Hucksters, The ☐ Idiot's Delight ☐ It Happened One Night ☐ It Started in Naples ☐ Key to the City ☐ King and Four Queens, The ☐ Laughing Sinners ☐ Lone Star ☐ Love on the Run ☐ Manhattan Melodrama ☐ Men in White ☐ MGM's Big Parade of Comedy ☐ Misfits, The ☐ Mogambo ☐ Mutiny on the Bounty ☐ Never Let Me Go ☐ Night Nurse ☐ No Man of Her Own ☐ Painted Desert, The ☐ Parnell ☐ Polly of the Circus ☐ Possessed ☐ Red Dust ☐ Run Silent, Run Deep ☐ San Francisco ☐ Saratoga ☐ Secret Six, The ☐ Soldier of Fortune ☐ Somewhere I'll Find You ☐ Sporting Blood ☐ Strange Cargo ☐ Strange Interlude ☐ Susan Lenox: Her Fall and Rise ☐ Tall Men, The ☐ Teacher's Pet ☐ Test Pilot ☐ They Met in Bombay ☐ To Please a Lady ☐ Too Hot to Handle ☐ White Sister, The ☐ Wife vs. Secretary
Gabor, Eva ☐ Aristocats, The ☐ Captain Kidd and the Slave Girl ☐ Don't Go Near the Water ☐ Gigi ☐ It Started with a Kiss ☐ Mad Magician, The ☐ Midnight Angel ☐ New Kind of Love, A ☐ Paris Model ☐ Rescuers Down Under, The ☐ Rescuers, The ☐ Truth About Women, The ☐ Youngblood Hawke
Gabor, Zsa Zsa ☐ Arrivederci, Baby ☐ Boys' Night Out ☐ Death of a Scoundrel ☐ For the First Time ☐ Girl in the Kremlin, The ☐ Happily Ever After ☐ Jack of Diamonds ☐ Lili ☐ Lovely to Look At ☐ Man Who Wouldn't Talk, The ☐ Moulin Rouge ☐ Picture Mommy Dead ☐ Queen of Outer Space ☐ Three Ring Circus ☐ We're Not Married
Gallagher, Peter ☐ Caine Mutiny Court-Martial, The ☐ DreamChild ☐ Fallen Angels—Volume 1 ☐ Fallen Angels—Volume 2 ☐ High Spirits ☐ I'll Be Home for Christmas ☐ Idolmaker, The ☐ Inconvenient Woman, An ☐ Late for Dinner ☐ Malice ☐ Mother's Boys ☐ Mrs. Parker and the Vicious Circle ☐ Murder of Mary Phagan, The ☐ Player, The ☐ sex, lies, and videotape ☐ Short Cuts ☐ Summer Lovers ☐ Terrible Joe Moran ☐ Watch It
Gambon, Michael ☐ Clean Slate ☐ Cook, the Thief, His Wife & Her Lover, The ☐ Man of No Importance, A ☐ Missing Link, The ☐ Mobsters ☐ Toys ☐ Turtle Diary
Ganz, Bruno ☐ American Friend, The ☐ Circle of Deceit ☐ Especially on Sunday ☐ Faraway, So Close ☐ Girl from Lorraine, A ☐ In the White City ☐ Knife in the Head ☐ Lady of the Camellias, The ☐ Last Days of Chez Nous, The ☐ Left-Handed Woman, The ☐ Marquise of O, The ☐ Nosferatu the Vampyre ☐ Sins of the Fathers ☐ Strapless ☐ Wings of Desire
Garbo, Greta ☐ Anna Christie ☐ Anna Karenina ☐ As You Desire Me ☐ Camille ☐ Conquest ☐ Flesh and the Devil ☐ Grand Hotel ☐ Inspiration ☐ Joyless Street, The ☐ Kiss, The ☐ Love ☐ Mata Hari ☐ MGM's Big Parade of Comedy ☐ Mysterious Lady, The ☐ Ninotchka ☐ Painted Veil, The ☐ Queen Christina ☐ Romance ☐ Single Standard, The ☐ Story Of Gosta Berling, The ☐ Susan Lenox: Her Fall and Rise ☐ Temptress, The ☐ Torrent, The ☐ Two-Faced Woman ☐ Wild Orchids ☐ Woman of Affairs, A
Garcia, Andy ☐ 8 Million Ways to Die ☐ American Roulette ☐ Black Rain ☐ Blue Skies Again ☐ Clinton and Nadine ☐ Dead Again ☐ Godfather, Part III, The ☐ Hero ☐ Internal Affairs ☐ Jennifer 8 ☐ Show of Force, A ☐ Stand and Deliver ☐ Untouchables, The ☐ When a Man Loves a Woman
Gardenia, Vincent ☐ Age-Old Friends ☐ Bang the Drum Slowly ☐ Cold Turkey ☐ Dark Mirror ☐ Death Wish ☐ Death Wish II ☐ Fire Sale ☐ Front Page, The ☐ Goldie and the Boxer ☐ Jenny ☐ Little Murders ☐ Little Shop of Horrors ☐ Mad Dog Coll ☐ Marciano ☐ Moonstruck ☐ Movers and Shakers ☐ Skin Deep ☐ Tragedy of Flight 103, The: The Inside Story ☐ View From the Bridge, A
Gardiner, Reginald ☐ Birds and the Bees, The ☐ Black Widow ☐ Christmas in Connecticut ☐ Claudia ☐ Doctor Takes a Wife, The ☐ Dolly Sisters, The ☐ Dulcy ☐ Flying Deuces, The ☐ Fury at Furnace Creek ☐ Girl Downstairs, The ☐ Great Dictator, The ☐ Horn Blows at Midnight, The ☐ Immortal Sergeant, The ☐ Molly and Me ☐ My Life

with Caroline ☐ Rock-a-Bye Baby ☐ Sweet Rosie O'Grady ☐ That Lady in Ermine ☐ That Wonderful Urge ☐ Wabash Avenue ☐ Yank in the RAF, A

Gardner, Ava ☐ 55 Days at Peking ☐ Angel Wore Red, The ☐ Barefoot Contessa, The ☐ Bhowani Junction ☐ Bible, The ☐ Blue Bird, The ☐ Bribe, The ☐ Cassandra Crossing, The ☐ City on Fire ☐ Devil's Widow, The ☐ Earthquake ☐ East Side, West Side ☐ Ghosts on the Loose ☐ Great Sinner, The ☐ Harem ☐ Hucksters, The ☐ Kidnapping of the President, The ☐ Killers, The ☐ Knights of the Round Table ☐ Life and Times of Judge Roy Bean, The ☐ Little Hut, The ☐ Lone Star ☐ Long Hot Summer, The ☐ Maisie Goes to Reno ☐ Mayerling ☐ Mogambo ☐ My Forbidden Past ☐ Naked Maja, The ☐ Night of the Iguana, The ☐ On the Beach ☐ One Touch of Venus ☐ Pandora and the Flying Dutchman ☐ Permission to Kill ☐ Priest of Love ☐ Seven Days in May ☐ Show Boat ☐ Snows of Kilimanjaro, The ☐ Sun Also Rises, The

Garfield, Allen ☐ Busting ☐ Conversation, The ☐ Cry Uncle! ☐ Front Page, The ☐ Gable and Lombard ☐ Hi, Mom! ☐ Jack and His Friends ☐ Marcus-Nelson Murders, The ☐ Mother, Jugs & Speed ☐ Night Visitor ☐ Nowhere to Run ☐ Paco ☐ Putney Swope ☐ Slither ☐ State of Things, The

Garfield, John ☐ Air Force ☐ Between Two Worlds ☐ Blackwell's Island ☐ Body and Soul ☐ Breaking Point ☐ Castle on the Hudson ☐ Dangerously They Live ☐ Daughters Courageous ☐ Destination Tokyo ☐ Dust Be My Destiny ☐ East of the River ☐ Fallen Sparrow ☐ Flowing Gold ☐ Force of Evil ☐ Four Daughters ☐ Four Wives ☐ Gentleman's Agreement ☐ He Ran All the Way ☐ Hollywood Canteen ☐ Humoresque ☐ Juarez ☐ Nobody Lives Forever ☐ Out of the Fog ☐ Postman Always Rings Twice, The ☐ Pride of the Marines ☐ Saturday's Children ☐ Sea Wolf, The ☐ Stepmother, The ☐ Thank Your Lucky Stars ☐ They Made Me a Criminal ☐ Tortilla Flat ☐ Under My Skin ☐ We Were Strangers

Garfunkel, Art ☐ Bad Timing: A Sensual Obsession ☐ Boxing Helena ☐ Carnal Knowledge ☐ Catch-22 ☐ Good to Go ☐ Short Fuse

Gargan, William ☐ Bells of St. Mary's, The ☐ Black Fury ☐ British Agent ☐ Cheers for Miss Bishop ☐ Close Call for Ellery Queen ☐ Four Frightened People ☐ House of Fear ☐ I Wake Up Screaming ☐ Lucky Devils ☐ Miss Annie Rooney ☐ Murder in the Music Hall ☐ Night Editor ☐ Rain ☐ Rawhide Years, The ☐ Star Dust ☐ Story of Temple Drake, The ☐ They Knew What They Wanted ☐ Traveling Saleslady ☐ You Only Live Once ☐ You're a Sweetheart

Garland, Beverly ☐ Alligator People, The ☐ Bitter Creek ☐ Chicago Confidential ☐ Finding the Way Home ☐ Gamble on Love ☐ Gunslinger ☐ It Conquered the World ☐ It's My Turn ☐ Mad Room, The ☐ Not of This Earth ☐ Pretty Poison ☐ Say Goodbye, Maggie Cole ☐ Sudden Danger ☐ Where the Red Fern Grows

Garland, Judy ☐ Andy Hardy Meets Debutante ☐ Babes in Arms ☐ Babes on Broadway ☐ Broadway Melody of 1938 ☐ Child Is Waiting, A ☐ Clock, The ☐ Easter Parade ☐ Everybody Sing ☐ For Me and My Gal ☐ Gay Purr-ee ☐ Girl Crazy ☐ Harvey Girls, The ☐ I Could Go on Singing ☐ In the Good Old Summertime ☐ Judgment at Nuremberg ☐ Life Begins for Andy Hardy ☐ Listen, Darling ☐ Little Nellie Kelly ☐ Love Finds Andy Hardy ☐ Meet Me in St. Louis ☐ Pigskin Parade ☐ Pirate, The ☐ Presenting Lily Mars ☐ Star Is Born, A ☐ Strike Up the Band ☐ Summer Stock ☐ Thoroughbreds Don't Cry ☐ Thousands Cheer ☐ Till the Clouds Roll By ☐ Wizard of Oz, The ☐ Words and Music ☐ Ziegfeld Follies ☐ Ziegfeld Girl

Garner, James ☐ 36 Hours ☐ Americanization of Emily, The ☐ Art of Love, The ☐ Barbarians at the Gate ☐ Boys' Night Out ☐ Breathing Lessons ☐ Cash McCall ☐ Castaway Cowboy, The ☐ Children's Hour, The ☐ Darby's Rangers ☐ Decoration Day ☐ Duel at Diablo ☐ Fan, The ☐ Fire in the Sky ☐ Girl He Left Behind ☐ Glitter Dome, The ☐ Grand Prix ☐ Great Escape, The ☐ H.E.A.L.T.H. ☐ Heartsounds ☐ Hour of the Gun ☐ How Sweet It Is! ☐ Long Summer of George Adams, The ☐ Man Called Sledge, A ☐ Man Could Get Killed, A ☐ Marlowe ☐ Maverick ☐ Mister Buddwing ☐ Move Over, Darling ☐ Murphy's Romance ☐ My Name is Bill W. ☐ One Little Indian ☐ Pink Jungle, The ☐ Promise, The ☐ Sayonara ☐ Skin Game ☐ Sunset ☐ Support Your Local Gunfighter ☐ Support Your Local Sheriff ☐ They Only Kill Their Masters ☐ Thrill Of It All, The ☐ Toward the Unknown ☐ Up Periscope ☐ Victor/Victoria ☐ Wheeler Dealers, The

Garner, Peggy Ann ☐ Black Widow ☐ Bomba the Jungle Boy ☐ Cat, The ☐ Daisy Kenyon ☐ Home, Sweet Homicide ☐ In Name Only ☐ Jane Eyre ☐ Junior Miss ☐ Lovable Cheat, The ☐ Nob Hill ☐ Pied Piper, The ☐ Teresa ☐ Tree Grows in Brooklyn, A

Garr, Teri ☐ After Hours ☐ Black Stallion, The ☐ Black Stallion Returns, The ☐ Close Encounters of the Third Kind ☐ Conversation, The ☐ Dumb and Dumber ☐ Escape Artist, The ☐ Firstborn ☐ Full Moon in Blue Water ☐ Head ☐ Honky Tonk Freeway ☐ Law and Order ☐ Let It Ride ☐ Maryjane ☐ Miracles ☐ Mom and Dad Save the World ☐ Mother Goose Rock 'n Rhyme ☐ Mr. Mom ☐ Oh, God! ☐ One from the Heart ☐ Out Cold ☐ Pack of Lies ☐ Paul Reiser—Out on a Whim ☐ Ready to Wear ☐ Short Time

☐ Sting II, The ☐ Tootsie ☐ Waiting for the Light ☐ Witches' Brew ☐ Won Ton Ton, the Dog Who Saved Hollywood ☐ Young Frankenstein

Garson, Greer ☐ Adventure ☐ Blossoms in the Dust ☐ Goodbye, Mr. Chips ☐ Happiest Millionaire, The ☐ Her Twelve Men ☐ Julia Misbehaves ☐ Julius Caesar ☐ Law and the Lady, The ☐ Little Women ☐ Madame Curie ☐ Miniver Story, The ☐ Mrs. Miniver ☐ Mrs. Parkington ☐ Pride and Prejudice ☐ Random Harvest ☐ Singing Nun, The ☐ Strange Lady in Town ☐ Sunrise at Campobello ☐ That Forsythe Woman ☐ Valley of Decision, The ☐ When Ladies Meet

Gassman, Vittorio ☐ Anna ☐ Big Deal on Madonna Street ☐ Bitter Rice ☐ Cry of the Hunted ☐ Devil in Love, The ☐ Dirty Game, The ☐ Easy Life, The ☐ Family, The ☐ Ghosts of Rome ☐ Ghosts—Italian Style ☐ Glass Wall, The ☐ Goodnight, Ladies and Gentlemen ☐ Great War, The ☐ Immortal Bachelor, The ☐ Let's Talk About Women ☐ Life Is a Bed of Roses ☐ Love and Larceny ☐ Lure of the Sila ☐ Mambo ☐ Miracle, The ☐ Nude Bomb, The ☐ Quintet ☐ Rhapsody ☐ Sharky's Machine ☐ Tempest ☐ Tempest ☐ Tiger and the Pussycat, The ☐ War and Peace ☐ We All Loved Each Other So Much ☐ Wedding, A ☐ Woman Times Seven

Gavin, John ☐ Back Street ☐ Behind the High Wall ☐ Breath of Scandal, A ☐ Four Girls in Town ☐ House of Shadows ☐ Imitation of Life ☐ Jennifer ☐ Madwoman of Chaillot, The ☐ Midnight Lace ☐ Murder For Sale ☐ New Adventures of Heidi, The ☐ Psycho ☐ Romanoff and Juliet ☐ Sophia Loren: Her Own Story ☐ Spartacus ☐ Tammy Tell Me True ☐ Thoroughly Modern Millie ☐ Time to Love and a Time to Die, A

Gaynor, Janet ☐ Bernardine ☐ Farmer Takes a Wife, The ☐ First Year, The ☐ Johnstown Flood, The ☐ Ladies in Love ☐ Merely Mary Ann ☐ One More Spring ☐ Paddy, the Next Best Thing ☐ Seventh Heaven ☐ Small Town Girl ☐ Star Is Born, A ☐ State Fair ☐ Street Angel ☐ Sunny Side Up ☐ Sunrise ☐ Young in Heart, The

Gaynor, Mitzi ☐ Anything Goes ☐ Birds and the Bees, The ☐ Bloodhounds of Broadway ☐ Down Among the Sheltering Palms ☐ For Love or Money ☐ Golden Girl ☐ Happy Anniversary ☐ I Don't Care Girl, The ☐ Joker is Wild, The ☐ Les Girls ☐ My Blue Heaven ☐ South Pacific ☐ Surprise Package ☐ There's No Business Like Show Business ☐ We're Not Married

Gazzara, Ben ☐ Anatomy of a Murder ☐ Blindsided ☐ Bloodline ☐ Bridge at Remagen, The ☐ Capone ☐ Conquered City, The ☐ Control ☐ Convicts Four ☐ Death of Richie, The ☐ Early Frost, An ☐ Family Rico, The ☐ Fireball Forward ☐ High Velocity ☐ Husbands ☐ Inchon ☐ Killing of a Chinese Bookie, The ☐ Maneater ☐ Opening Night ☐ Passionate Thief, The ☐ Question of Honor, A ☐ Rage to Live, A ☐ Road House ☐ Saint Jack ☐ Secret Obsession ☐ Sicilian Connection, The ☐ They All Laughed ☐ Trial of Lee Harvey Oswald, The ☐ Voyage of the Damned ☐ Young Doctors, The

Geer, Will ☐ Barefoot Mailman, The ☐ Billion Dollar Hobo, The ☐ Black Like Me ☐ Blue Bird, The ☐ Bright Victory ☐ Broken Arrow ☐ Brother John ☐ Comanche Territory ☐ Dear Dead Delilah ☐ Executive Action ☐ Honky Tonk ☐ Hurricane ☐ In Cold Blood ☐ Isn't It Shocking? ☐ Jeremiah Johnson ☐ Mafu Cage, The ☐ Manchu Eagle Murder Caper Mystery, The ☐ Moving Violation ☐ Napoleon and Samantha ☐ Night That Panicked America, The ☐ Reivers, The ☐ Salt of the Earth ☐ Seconds ☐ Silence ☐ Winchester '73 ☐ Woman Called Moses, A

Genn, Leo ☐ Beyond Mombasa ☐ Girls of Pleasure Island ☐ Green Scarf, The ☐ Henry V ☐ Immortal Battalion, The ☐ Martyr, The ☐ Miniver Story, The ☐ Missing Ten Days ☐ Moby Dick ☐ Night of the Blood Monster ☐ No Place for Jennifer ☐ Paratrooper ☐ Personal Affair ☐ Plymouth Adventure, The ☐ Quo Vadis? ☐ Snake Pit, The ☐ Strange Case of Dr. Jekyll And Mr. Hyde, The ☐ Ten Little Indians ☐ Velvet Touch, The ☐ Wooden Horse, The

George, Christopher ☐ Chisum ☐ Day of the Animals ☐ Dixie Dynamite ☐ El Dorado ☐ Enter the Ninja ☐ Exterminator, The ☐ Gates of Hell, The ☐ Gentle Rain, The ☐ Graduation Day ☐ Grizzly ☐ Heist, The ☐ House on Greenapple Road, The ☐ I Escaped from Devil's Island ☐ Immortal, The ☐ Man on a String ☐ Mayday at 40,000 Feet! ☐ Mortuary

George, Gladys ☐ Alias a Gentleman ☐ Best Years of Our Lives, The ☐ Child Is Born, A ☐ Christmas Holiday ☐ Crystal Ball, The ☐ Detective Story ☐ Flamingo Road ☐ Hard Way, The ☐ He Ran All the Way ☐ Here I Am a Stranger ☐ Hit the Road ☐ House Across the Bay, The ☐ I'm from Missouri ☐ Lady from Cheyenne ☐ Lullaby of Broadway ☐ Madame X ☐ Maltese Falcon, The ☐ Marie Antoinette ☐ Roaring Twenties, The ☐ Silver City ☐ They Gave Him a Gun ☐ Valiant Is the Word for Carrie ☐ Way of All Flesh, The

Gere, Richard ☐ American Gigolo ☐ And the Band Played On ☐ Baby Blue Marine ☐ Beyond the Limit ☐ Bloodbrothers ☐ Breathless ☐ Cotton Club, The ☐ Days of Heaven ☐ Final Analysis ☐ Internal Affairs ☐ Intersection ☐ King David ☐ Looking for Mr. Goodbar ☐ Miles from Home ☐ Mr. Jones ☐ No Mercy ☐ Officer and a Gentleman, An ☐ Power ☐ Pretty Woman ☐ Report to the Commissioner ☐ Rhapsody in August ☐ Sommersby ☐ Yanks

Gertz, Jami ☐ Crossroads ☐ Don't Tell Her

It's Me ☐ Endless Love ☐ Jersey Girl ☐ Less than Zero ☐ Listen to Me ☐ Quicksilver ☐ Renegades ☐ Sibling Rivalry ☐ Silence Like Glass ☐ This Can't Be Love

Giannini, Giancarlo ☐ American Dreamer ☐ Black Belly of the Tarantula ☐ Blood Feud ☐ Blood Red ☐ Fever Pitch ☐ Fraulein Doktor ☐ How Funny Can Sex Be? ☐ Immortal Bachelor, The ☐ Innocent, The ☐ La Grande Bourgeoisie ☐ Life Is Beautiful ☐ Lili Marleen ☐ Love and Anarchy ☐ Lovers and Liars ☐ New York Stories ☐ Night Full of Rain, A ☐ Pizza Triangle, The ☐ Saving Grace ☐ Secret of Santa Vittoria, The ☐ Seduction of Mimi, The ☐ Sensual Man, The ☐ Seven Beauties ☐ Swept Away

Gibson, Mel ☐ Air America ☐ Attack Force Z ☐ Bird on a Wire ☐ Bounty, The ☐ Forever Young ☐ Gallipoli ☐ Hamlet ☐ Lethal Weapon ☐ Lethal Weapon 2 ☐ Lethal Weapon 3 ☐ Mad Max ☐ Mad Max Beyond Thunderdome ☐ Man Without a Face, The ☐ Maverick ☐ Mrs. Soffel ☐ River, The ☐ Road Warrior, The ☐ Tequila Sunrise ☐ Tim ☐ Year of Living Dangerously, The

Gielgud, John ☐ 11 Harrowhouse ☐ Appointment with Death ☐ Arthur ☐ Arthur 2—On the Rocks ☐ Assignment to Kill ☐ Barretts of Wimpole Street, The ☐ Becket ☐ Caligula ☐ Camille ☐ Canterville Ghost, The ☐ Charge of the Light Brigade, The ☐ Chariots of Fire ☐ Chimes at Midnight ☐ Eagle in a Cage ☐ Elephant Man, The ☐ Far Pavilions, The ☐ Formula, The ☐ Frankenstein: The True Story ☐ Galileo ☐ Gandhi ☐ Getting It Right ☐ Gold ☐ Good Companions, The ☐ Human Factor, The ☐ Hunchback of Notre Dame, The ☐ Inside the Third Reich ☐ Insult ☐ Invitation To a Wedding ☐ Julius Caesar ☐ Julius Caesar ☐ Leave All Fair ☐ Les Miserables ☐ Lion of the Desert ☐ Lost Horizon ☐ Loved One, The ☐ Man for All Seasons, A ☐ Master of Ballantrae, The ☐ Murder on the Orient Express ☐ Oh! What a Lovely War ☐ Orchestra Conductor, The ☐ Plenty ☐ Portrait of the Artist as a Young Man, A ☐ Power of One, The ☐ Priest of Love ☐ Prospero's Books ☐ Providence ☐ Richard III ☐ Saint Joan ☐ Scandalous ☐ Scarlet and the Black, The ☐ Sebastian ☐ Secret Agent ☐ Seven Dials Mystery, The ☐ Shining Through ☐ Shoes of the Fisherman, The ☐ Shooting Party, The ☐ Sphinx ☐ Strike It Rich ☐ Wagner ☐ Whistle Blower, The ☐ Why Didn't They Ask Evans? ☐ Wicked Lady, The

Gilbert, Billy ☐ Block-Heads ☐ Destry Rides Again ☐ Fight for Your Lady ☐ Firefly, The ☐ Fun and Fancy Free ☐ Great Dictator, The ☐ Life of the Party, The ☐ Maid's Night Out ☐ Melody Master ☐ Million Dollar Legs ☐ Mistaken Identity ☐ Model Wife ☐ Noisy Neighbors ☐ On the Avenue ☐ Pack Up Your Troubles ☐ Peck's Bad Boy with the Circus ☐ Reaching for the Sun ☐ Song of the Islands ☐ Spotlight Scandals ☐ Star Maker, The ☐ Under-Pup, The ☐ Valley of the Sun ☐ Week-end in Havana

Gilbert, John ☐ Big Parade, The ☐ Captain Hates the Sea, The ☐ Downstairs ☐ Fast Workers ☐ Flesh and the Devil ☐ Gentleman's Fate ☐ He Who Gets Slapped ☐ Hollywood Revue of 1929, The ☐ Love ☐ Merry Widow, The ☐ Phantom of Paris, The ☐ Queen Christina ☐ Woman of Affairs, A

Gilbert, Melissa ☐ Blood Vows—The Story of a Mafia Wife ☐ Christmas Coal Mine Miracle, The ☐ Diary of Anne Frank, The ☐ Forbidden Nights ☐ Ice House ☐ Joshua's Heart ☐ Little House on the Prairie ☐ Lookalike, The ☐ Miracle Worker, The ☐ Nutcracker Fantasy ☐ Penalty Phase ☐ Sylvester

Gilford, Jack ☐ Anna to the Infinite Power ☐ Catch-22 ☐ Caveman ☐ Cheaper to Keep Her ☐ Cocoon ☐ Cocoon: The Return ☐ Daydreamer, The ☐ Enter Laughing ☐ Fixer, The ☐ Funny Thing Happened on the Way to the Forum, A ☐ Hey, Rookie ☐ Incident, The ☐ Save the Tiger ☐ They Might Be Giants ☐ Who's Minding the Mint? ☐ Wholly Moses

Gilliam, Terry ☐ And Now for Something Completely Different ☐ Monty Python and the Holy Grail ☐ Monty Python Live at the Hollywood Bowl ☐ Monty Python's Flying Circus—Vol. 1 ☐ Monty Python's Life of Brian ☐ Monty Python's Parrot Sketch Not Included ☐ Monty Python's The Meaning of Life

Gingold, Hermione ☐ Adventures of Sadie, The ☐ Bell, Book and Candle ☐ Garbo Talks ☐ Gay Purr-ee ☐ Gigi ☐ Harvey Middleman, Fireman ☐ I'd Rather Be Rich ☐ Little Night Music, A ☐ Munster, Go Home ☐ Music Man, The ☐ Naked Edge, The ☐ Pickwick Papers, The ☐ Promise Her Anything

Girardot, Annie ☐ Dear Detective ☐ Dirty Game, The ☐ Inspector Maigret ☐ La Vie Continue ☐ Le Cavaleur ☐ Live for Life ☐ Love and the Frenchwoman ☐ No Time for Breakfast ☐ Organizer, The ☐ Rocco and His Brothers

Gish, Annabeth ☐ Desert Bloom ☐ Hiding Out ☐ Last to Go ☐ Mystic Pizza ☐ Shag, The Movie ☐ When He's Not a Stranger

Gish, Dorothy ☐ Centennial Summer ☐ Hearts of the World ☐ Home Sweet Home ☐ Judith of Bethulia ☐ Orphans of the Storm ☐ Our Hearts Were Young and Gay ☐ Whistle at Eaton Falls, The

Gish, Lillian ☐ Adventures of Huckleberry Finn ☐ Birth of a Nation, The ☐ Broken Blossoms ☐ Cobweb, The ☐ Comedians, The ☐ Commandos Strike at Dawn, The ☐ Duel in the Sun ☐ Follow Me, Boys! ☐ Great Chase, The ☐ Hambone and Hillie ☐ Hearts of the World ☐ His Double Life ☐ Hobson's Choice ☐ Home Sweet Home ☐ Intolerance ☐ Judith of Bethulia ☐ Miss Susie Slagle's ☐ Night of the Hunter, The ☐ One Romantic Night ☐ Orders to Kill ☐ Orphans of the Storm ☐ Portrait of Jennie ☐ Scarlet Letter, The ☐ Sweet Liberty ☐ True-Heart Susie ☐ Unforgiven, The ☐ Warning Shot ☐ Way Down East ☐ Wedding, A ☐ Whales of August, The ☐ Wind, The

Gleason, Jackie ☐ All Through the Night ☐ Desert Hawk, The ☐ Don't Drink the Water ☐ Gigot ☐ How Do I Love Thee? ☐ How to Commit Marriage ☐ Hustler, The ☐ Izzy and Moe ☐ Mr. Billion ☐ Navy Blues ☐ Nothing in Common ☐ Papa's Delicate Condition ☐ Requiem for a Heavyweight ☐ Skiddoo ☐ Smokey and the Bandit ☐ Smokey and the Bandit III ☐ Smokey and the Bandit, Part 2 ☐ Smokey and the Bandit, Part 3 ☐ Soldier in the Rain ☐ Sting II, The ☐ Toy, The

Gleason, James ☐ Bad Boy ☐ Bishop's Wife, The ☐ Clear All Wires ☐ Clock, The ☐ Date With the Falcon, A ☐ Dude Goes West, The ☐ Ex-Mrs. Bradford, The ☐ Falcon Takes Over, The ☐ Forever Female ☐ Forty Naughty Girls ☐ Free Soul, A ☐ Here Comes Mr. Jordan ☐ Hoodlum Saint, The ☐ I'll See You in My Dreams ☐ Jackpot, The ☐ Joe Palooka in the Squared Circle ☐ Joe Palooka in Triple Cross ☐ Life of Riley, The ☐ Man in the Shadow ☐ Manhattan Merry-Go-Round ☐ Manila Calling ☐ Meet John Doe ☐ Miss Grant Takes Richmond ☐ Murder on a Honeymoon ☐ Murder on the Blackboard ☐ My Gal Sal ☐ Night of the Hunter, The ☐ Nine Lives Are Not Enough ☐ Once Upon a Time ☐ Orders Is Orders ☐ Penguin Pool Murder, The ☐ Riding High ☐ Rock-a-Bye Baby ☐ Star in the Dust ☐ Story of Will Rogers, The ☐ Suddenly ☐ Take One False Step ☐ This Man's Navy ☐ Tycoon ☐ We're Not Married ☐ West Point of the Air ☐ When My Baby Smiles at Me ☐ Yellow Cab Man, The ☐ Yours For the Asking

Glenn, Scott ☐ As Summers Die ☐ Baby Maker, The ☐ Backdraft ☐ Challenge, The ☐ Extreme Justice ☐ Fighting Mad ☐ Hunt for Red October, The ☐ Keep, The ☐ Man on Fire ☐ Miss Firecracker ☐ My Heroes Have Always Been Cowboys ☐ Off Limits ☐ Outside Woman, The ☐ Personal Best ☐ Right Stuff, The ☐ River, The ☐ Shadow Hunter ☐ She Came to the Valley ☐ Shrieking, The ☐ Silence of the Lambs, The ☐ Silverado ☐ Slaughter of the Innocents ☐ Tall Tale: The Unbelievable Adventures of Pecos Bill ☐ Urban Cowboy ☐ Verne Miller ☐ Women & Men: In Love There Are No Rules

Glover, Crispin ☐ At Close Range ☐ Back to the Future ☐ Friday the 13th: The Final Chapter ☐ Little Noises ☐ River's Edge ☐ Where the Heart Is ☐ Wild at Heart

Glover, Danny ☐ Bat 21 ☐ Bopha! ☐ Chu Chu and the Philly Flash ☐ Color Purple, The ☐ Dead Man Out ☐ Face of Rage, The ☐ Flight of the Intruder ☐ Grand Canyon ☐ Lethal Weapon ☐ Lethal Weapon 2 ☐ Lethal Weapon 3 ☐ Lonesome Dove ☐ Mandela ☐ Out ☐ Places in the Heart ☐ Predator 2 ☐ Pure Luck ☐ Rage in Harlem, A ☐ Raisin in the Sun, A ☐ Saint of Fort Washington, The ☐ Silverado ☐ Stand-In, The ☐ To Sleep With Anger

Glover, John ☐ 52 Pick-Up ☐ Apology ☐ Breaking Point ☐ Chocolate War, The ☐ David ☐ El Diablo ☐ Evil That Men Do ☐ Flash of Green ☐ Gremlins 2—The New Batch ☐ Last Embrace ☐ Little Sex, A ☐ Masquerade ☐ Meet The Hollowheads ☐ Mountain Men, The ☐ Rocket Gibraltar ☐ Scrooged ☐ Something Special ☐ What Ever Happened to Baby Jane?

Goddard, Paulette ☐ Anna Lucasta ☐ Bride of Vengeance ☐ Cat and the Canary, The ☐ Crystal Ball, The ☐ Diary of a Chambermaid ☐ Dramatic School ☐ Duffy's Tavern ☐ Forest Rangers, The ☐ Ghost Breakers, The ☐ Great Dictator, The ☐ Hazard ☐ Hold Back the Dawn ☐ I Love a Soldier ☐ Ideal Husband, An ☐ Kitty ☐ Lady Has Plans, The ☐ Modern Times ☐ Northwest Mounted Police ☐ Nothing But the Truth ☐ On Our Merry Way ☐ Paris Model ☐ Reap the Wild Wind ☐ Second Chorus ☐ So Proudly We Hail! ☐ Standing Room Only ☐ Star Spangled Rhythm ☐ Suddenly, It's Spring ☐ Time of Indifference ☐ Unconquered ☐ Vice Squad ☐ Women, The ☐ Young in Heart, The

Goldberg, Whoopi ☐ Boys on the Side ☐ Burglar ☐ Clara's Heart ☐ Color Purple, The ☐ Corinna, Corinna ☐ Fatal Beauty ☐ Ghost ☐ Homer & Eddie ☐ Jumpin' Jack Flash ☐ Kiss Shot ☐ Lion King, The ☐ Long Walk Home, The ☐ Made in America ☐ Pagemaster, The ☐ Player, The ☐ Sarafina! ☐ Sister Act ☐ Sister Act 2: Back in the Habit ☐ Soapdish ☐ Star Trek Generations ☐ Telephone, The

Goldblum, Jeff ☐ Adventures of Buckaroo Banzai Across the Eighth Dimension, The ☐ Between the Lines ☐ Beyond Therapy ☐ Big Chill, The ☐ Deep Cover ☐ Earth Girls Are Easy ☐ Ernie Kovacs: Between the Laughter ☐ Fathers and Sons ☐ Favor, the Watch, and the Very Big Fish, The ☐ Fly, The ☐ Framed ☐ Hideaway ☐ Into the Night ☐ Invasion of the Body Snatchers ☐ Jurassic Park ☐ Legend of Sleepy Hollow, The ☐ Mr. Frost ☐ Next Stop, Greenwich Village ☐ Shooting Elizabeth ☐ Tall Guy, The ☐ Thank God, It's Friday ☐ Threshold ☐ Transylvania 6-5000 ☐ Vibes

Gomez, Thomas ☐ Eagle and the Hawk, The ☐ Force of Evil ☐ Frisco Sal ☐ Furies, The ☐ Harlem Globetrotters, The ☐ I Married a Communist ☐ I'll Tell the World ☐ In Society ☐ Macao ☐ Magnificent Matador, The ☐ Phantom Lady ☐ Ride the Pink Horse ☐ Sellout, The ☐ Sherlock Holmes and the

Voice of Terror ☐ Sorrowful Jones ☐ Summer and Smoke

Gooding, Jr., Cuba ☐ Boyz N the Hood ☐ Few Good Men, A ☐ Gladiator ☐ Hitz ☐ Judgment Night ☐ Lightning Jack ☐ Losing Isaiah ☐ Outbreak

Goodman, John ☐ Always ☐ Arachnophobia ☐ Babe, The ☐ Barton Fink ☐ Big Easy, The ☐ Born Yesterday ☐ C.H.U.D. ☐ Everybody's All-American ☐ Flintstones, The ☐ Heart of Steel ☐ King Ralph ☐ Matinee ☐ Punchline ☐ Raising Arizona ☐ Sea of Love ☐ Stella ☐ Survivors, The ☐ True Stories ☐ We're Back: A Dinosaur's Story ☐ Wrong Guys, The

Gorcey, Leo ☐ Angels in Disguise ☐ Block Busters ☐ Blonde Dynamite ☐ Blues Busters ☐ Bowery Boys Meet the Monsters, The ☐ Bowery Buckaroos ☐ Bowery Champs ☐ Bowery to Bagdad ☐ Boys of the City, The ☐ Clipped Wings ☐ Come Out Fighting ☐ Dead End ☐ Feudin' Fools ☐ Fighting Fools ☐ Follow the Leader ☐ Ghost Chasers ☐ Hard Boiled Mahoney ☐ Here Come the Marines ☐ High Society ☐ Hold That Baby! ☐ Hold That Line ☐ Jail Busters ☐ Jalopy ☐ Kid Dynamite ☐ Let's Get Tough! ☐ Let's Go Navy! ☐ Live Wires ☐ Loose in London ☐ Lucky Losers ☐ Maisie Gets Her Man ☐ Mannequin ☐ Master Minds ☐ Million Dollar Kid ☐ Mr. Hex ☐ Mr. Muggs Steps Out ☐ No Holds Barred ☐ On Dress Parade ☐ Paris Playboys ☐ Smugglers' Cove ☐ So This Is New York ☐ They Made Me a Criminal ☐ Trouble Makers

Gordon, Gale ☐ 30 Foot Bride of Candy Rock, The ☐ Don't Give Up the Ship ☐ Dondi ☐ Francis Covers the Big Town ☐ Here Come the Nelsons ☐ Here We Go Again ☐ Our Miss Brooks ☐ Rally 'Round the Flag, Boys! ☐ Sergeant Deadhead ☐ Speedway

Gordon, Ruth ☐ Abe Lincoln In Illinois ☐ Action in the North Atlantic ☐ Any Which Way You Can ☐ Big Bus, The ☐ Boardwalk ☐ Don't Go to Sleep ☐ Dr. Ehrlich's Magic Bullet ☐ Edge of Darkness ☐ Every Which Way but Loose ☐ Great Houdinis, The ☐ Harold and Maude ☐ Inside Daisy Clover ☐ Isn't It Shocking? ☐ Jimmy the Kid ☐ Lord Love a Duck ☐ Maxie ☐ Mugsy's Girls ☐ My Bodyguard ☐ Perfect Gentlemen ☐ Rosemary's Baby ☐ Scavenger Hunt ☐ Two-Faced Woman ☐ Whatever Happened to Aunt Alice? ☐ Where's Poppa?

Goring, Marius ☐ Barefoot Contessa, The ☐ Big Blockade, The ☐ Break in the Circle ☐ Highly Dangerous ☐ I Was Monty's Double ☐ Ill Met by Moonlight ☐ Mr. Perrin and Mr. Traill ☐ Night Ambush ☐ Odette ☐ Paris Express, The ☐ Pastor Hall ☐ Quentin Durward ☐ Red Shoes, The ☐ Rembrandt ☐ Stairway to Heaven ☐ Up From the Beach ☐ Zeppelin

Gossett, Jr., Louis ☐ Aces: Iron Eagle III ☐ Benny's Place ☐ Bushbaby, The ☐ Carolina Skeletons ☐ Choirboys, The ☐ Deep, The ☐ Diggstown ☐ El Diablo ☐ Enemy Mine ☐ Father Clements Story, The ☐ Finders Keepers ☐ Firewalker ☐ Gathering of Old Men, A ☐ Good Man in Africa, A ☐ Goodbye, Miss 4th of July ☐ Guardian, The ☐ He Who Walks Alone ☐ Iron Eagle ☐ Iron Eagle II ☐ It Rained All Night the Day I Left ☐ It's Good to Be Alive ☐ J.D.'s Revenge ☐ Jaws 3 ☐ Josephine Baker Story, The ☐ Keeper of the City ☐ Landlord, The ☐ Laughing Policeman, The ☐ Lazarus Syndrome, The ☐ Monolith ☐ Murder on the Bayou ☐ Officer and a Gentleman, An ☐ Principal, The ☐ Punisher, The ☐ Raisin in the Sun, A ☐ River Niger, The ☐ Sadat ☐ Skin Game ☐ Sudie and Simpson ☐ Toy Soldiers ☐ White Dawn, The

Gough, Michael ☐ Black Zoo ☐ Blanche Fury ☐ Candidate for Murder ☐ Crucible of Horror ☐ Horror Hospital ☐ Horrors of the Black Museum ☐ House in the Woods, The ☐ I Like Money ☐ Man in the White Suit, The ☐ Memed My Hawk ☐ No Place Like Homicide! ☐ Rob Roy, the Highland Rogue ☐ Saraband ☐ Shell Seekers, The ☐ Skull, The ☐ Sword and the Rose, The ☐ To the Lighthouse ☐ Trog ☐ Wittgenstein

Gould, Elliott ☐ Beyond Justice ☐ Bob & Carol & Ted & Alice ☐ Bridge Too Far, A ☐ Bugsy ☐ Busting ☐ California Split ☐ Capricorn One ☐ Conspiracy—The Trial of the Chicago 8 ☐ Dangerous Love ☐ Devil and Max Devlin, The ☐ Falling in Love Again ☐ Frog ☐ Getting Straight ☐ Harry and Walter Go to New York ☐ Hitz ☐ I Love My . . . Wife ☐ I Will, I Will . . . For Now ☐ Inside Out ☐ Lady Vanishes, The ☐ Last Flight of Noah's Ark, The ☐ Lemon Sisters, The ☐ Lethal Obsession ☐ Little Murders ☐ Long Goodbye, The ☐ M*A*S*H ☐ Matilda ☐ Mean Johnny Barrows ☐ Move ☐ Muppets Take Manhattan, The ☐ My Wonderful Life ☐ Naked Face, The ☐ Night They Raided Minsky's, The ☐ Night Visitor ☐ Over the Brooklyn Bridge ☐ Paul Reiser—Out on a Whim ☐ Quick, Let's Get Married ☐ S.P.Y.S. ☐ Silent Partner, The ☐ Telephone, The ☐ Touch, The

Gould, Harold ☐ Aunt Mary ☐ Kenny Rogers as The Gambler ☐ Love and Death ☐ Mrs. Delafield Wants to Marry ☐ Mrs. Pollifax—Spy ☐ Ransom for a Dead Man ☐ Sting, The ☐ Strongest Man in the World, The

Grable, Betty ☐ Beautiful Blonde from Bashful Bend, The ☐ By Your Leave ☐ Call Me Mister ☐ College Swing ☐ Coney Island ☐ Diamond Horseshoe ☐ Dolly Sisters, The ☐ Down Argentine Way ☐ Farmer Takes a Wife, The ☐ Footlight Serenade ☐ Four Jills in a Jeep ☐ Gay Divorcee, The ☐ Give Me a Sailor ☐ Hold 'Em Jail ☐ How to Be Very, Very Popular ☐ How to Marry a Millionaire ☐ I Wake Up Screaming ☐ Man About Town

☐ Meet Me After the Show ☐ Million Dollar Legs ☐ Moon Over Miami ☐ Mother Wore Tights ☐ My Blue Heaven ☐ Nitwits, The ☐ Pigskin Parade ☐ Pin Up Girl ☐ Shocking Miss Pilgrim, The ☐ Song of the Islands ☐ Springtime in the Rockies ☐ Sweet Rosie O'Grady ☐ That Lady in Ermine ☐ Three for the Show ☐ Tin Pan Alley ☐ Wabash Avenue ☐ When My Baby Smiles at Me ☐ Yank in the RAF, A

Grahame, Gloria ☐ Bad and the Beautiful, The ☐ Big Heat, The ☐ Blonde Fever ☐ Blood and Lace ☐ Chandler ☐ Cobweb, The ☐ Crossfire ☐ Girl on the Late, Late Show, The ☐ Glass Wall, The ☐ Good Die Young, The ☐ Greatest Show on Earth, The ☐ Head over Heels ☐ Human Desire ☐ In a Lonely Place ☐ It Happened in Brooklyn ☐ It's a Wonderful Life ☐ Macao ☐ Mama's Dirty Girls ☐ Man on a Tightrope ☐ Man Who Never Was, The ☐ Mansion of the Doomed ☐ Mayfair Bank Caper, The ☐ Merry Wives of Windsor ☐ Merton of the Movies ☐ Naked Alibi ☐ Nesting, The ☐ Not as a Stranger ☐ Odds Against Tomorrow ☐ Oklahoma! ☐ Roughshod ☐ Song of the Thin Man ☐ Sudden Fear ☐ Todd Killings, The ☐ Without Love ☐ Woman's Secret, A

Granger, Farley ☐ Arnold ☐ Behave Yourself ☐ Edge of Doom ☐ Enchantment ☐ Girl in the Red Velvet Swing, The ☐ Hans Christian Andersen ☐ I Want You ☐ Imagemaker, The ☐ Naked Street, The ☐ North Star, The ☐ O. Henry's Full House ☐ Our Very Own ☐ Purple Heart, The ☐ Rope ☐ Senso ☐ Side Street ☐ Small Town Girl ☐ Story of Three Loves, The ☐ Strangers on a Train ☐ They Call Me Trinity ☐ They Live by Night

Granger, Stewart ☐ Adam and Evalyn ☐ All the Brothers Were Valiant ☐ Any Second Now ☐ Beau Brummel ☐ Bhowani Junction ☐ Blanche Fury ☐ Caesar and Cleopatra ☐ Captain Boycott ☐ Fine Gold ☐ Footsteps in the Fog ☐ Frontier Hellcat ☐ Green Fire ☐ Gun Glory ☐ Harry Black and the Tiger ☐ Hell Hunters ☐ Hound of the Baskervilles, The ☐ King Solomon's Mines ☐ Last Hunt, The ☐ Last Safari, The ☐ Light Touch, The ☐ Little Hut, The ☐ Madonna of the Seven Moons ☐ Magic Bow, The ☐ Man in Grey, The ☐ Man of Evil ☐ Moonfleet ☐ North to Alaska ☐ Prisoner of Zenda, The ☐ Salome ☐ Saraband ☐ Scaramouche ☐ Secret Invasion, The ☐ Secret Mission ☐ Sodom and Gomorrah ☐ Soldiers Three ☐ Whole Truth, The ☐ Wild Geese, The ☐ Young Bess

Grant, Cary ☐ Affair to Remember, An ☐ Alice in Wonderland ☐ Amazing Adventure ☐ Arsenic and Old Lace ☐ Awful Truth, The ☐ Bachelor and the Bobby-Soxer, The ☐ Big Brown Eyes ☐ Bishop's Wife, The ☐ Blonde Venus ☐ Bringing Up Baby ☐ Charade ☐ Crisis ☐ Destination Tokyo ☐ Devil and the Deep ☐ Dream Wife ☐ Eagle and the Hawk, The ☐ Enter Madame ☐ Every Girl Should Be Married ☐ Father Goose ☐ Grass is Greener, The ☐ Gunga Din ☐ His Girl Friday ☐ Holiday ☐ Hot Saturday ☐ Houseboat ☐ Howards of Virginia ☐ I Was a Male War Bride ☐ I'm No Angel ☐ In Name Only ☐ Indiscreet ☐ Kiss Them for Me ☐ Ladies Should Listen ☐ Last Outpost, The ☐ Madame Butterfly ☐ Monkey Business ☐ Mr. Blandings Builds His Dream House ☐ Mr. Lucky ☐ My Favorite Wife ☐ Night and Day ☐ None But the Lonely Heart ☐ North by Northwest ☐ Notorious ☐ Once Upon a Honeymoon ☐ Once Upon a Time ☐ Only Angels Have Wings ☐ Operation Petticoat ☐ Penny Serenade ☐ People Will Talk ☐ Philadelphia Story, The ☐ Pride and the Passion, The ☐ Room for One More ☐ She Done Him Wrong ☐ Sinners in the Sun ☐ Suspicion ☐ Suzy ☐ Sylvia Scarlett ☐ Talk of the Town, The ☐ That Touch of Mink ☐ Thirty Day Princess ☐ This Is the Night ☐ To Catch a Thief ☐ Toast of New York, The ☐ Topper ☐ Walk, Don't Run ☐ When You're in Love ☐ Wings in the Dark

Grant, Hugh ☐ Bitter Moon ☐ Champagne Charlie ☐ Crossing the Line ☐ Dawning, The ☐ Four Weddings and a Funeral ☐ Impromptu ☐ Lady and the Highwayman, The ☐ Lair of the White Worm, The ☐ Maurice ☐ Our Sons ☐ Remains of the Day ☐ Sirens

Grant, Lee ☐ Airport '77 ☐ Balcony, The ☐ Bare Essence ☐ Big Bounce, The ☐ Big Town, The ☐ Buona Sera, Mrs. Campbell ☐ Charlie Chan and the Curse of the Dragon Queen ☐ Citizen Cohn ☐ Damien—Omen II ☐ Defending Your Life ☐ Detective Story ☐ Divorce American Style ☐ For Ladies Only ☐ In the Heat of the Night ☐ Internecine Project, The ☐ Landlord, The ☐ Little Miss Marker ☐ Mafu Cage, The ☐ Marooned ☐ Middle of the Night ☐ Night Slaves ☐ Partners in Crime ☐ Plaza Suite ☐ Portnoy's Complaint ☐ Ransom for a Dead Man ☐ Shampoo ☐ Swarm, The ☐ Teachers ☐ Voyage of the Damned

Granville, Bonita ☐ Andy Hardy's Blonde Trouble ☐ Angels Wash Their Faces, The ☐ Breakfast in Hollywood ☐ Escape ☐ Guilty of Treason ☐ Guilty, The ☐ H.M. Pulham, Esq. ☐ Hard to Get ☐ Hitler's Children ☐ It's Love I'm After ☐ Lone Ranger, The ☐ Love Laughs at Andy Hardy ☐ Maid of Salem ☐ Merrily We Live ☐ Mortal Storm, The ☐ Nancy Drew and the Hidden Staircase ☐ Nancy Drew, Detective ☐ Nancy Drew, Reporter ☐ Nancy Drew, Troubleshooter ☐ Now, Voyager ☐ Seven Miles from Alcatraz ☐ Song of the Open Road ☐ These Three ☐ Those Were the Days ☐ Wild Man of Borneo, The

Grapewin, Charley ☐ Atlantic City ☐ Close Call for Ellery Queen ☐ Ellery Queen and the Murder Ring ☐ Ellery Queen and the Perfect Crime ☐ Ellery Queen's Penthouse Mystery

☐ Ellery Queen, Master Detective ☐ Family Affair, A ☐ Grapes of Wrath, The ☐ One Frightened Night ☐ Rhythm on the River ☐ Sand ☐ Stand Up and Fight ☐ Tobacco Road ☐ When I Grow Up ☐ Wizard of Oz, The

Graves, Peter ☐ Airplane II, The Sequel ☐ Airplane! ☐ Ballad of Josie, The ☐ Beginning of the End ☐ Black Tuesday ☐ Canyon River ☐ East of Sumatra ☐ Encore ☐ Five Man Army, The ☐ Fort Defiance ☐ Hold Back the Night ☐ I'll Never Forget What's 'is Name ☐ It Conquered the World ☐ Killers from Space ☐ Maytime in Mayfair ☐ Naked Street, The ☐ Night of the Hunter, The ☐ Number One with a Bullet ☐ Parts: The Clonus Horror ☐ Rage to Live, A ☐ Raid, The ☐ Rebels, The ☐ Red Planet Mars ☐ Robber's Roost ☐ Savannah Smiles ☐ Sergeant Ryker ☐ Stalag 17 ☐ Stranger in My Arms ☐ Texas Across the River ☐ War Paint ☐ Wichita

Gray, Coleen ☐ Apache Drums ☐ Arrow in the Dust ☐ Black Whip, The ☐ Fake, The ☐ Father Is a Bachelor ☐ Fury at Furnace Creek ☐ Johnny Rocco ☐ Kansas City Confidential ☐ Killing, The ☐ Kiss of Death ☐ Las Vegas Shakedown ☐ Leech Woman, The ☐ Lucky Nick Cain ☐ Nightmare Alley ☐ Red River ☐ Riding High ☐ Sand ☐ Star in the Dust ☐ Tennessee's Partner

Gray, Spalding ☐ Almost You ☐ Bad Company ☐ Clara's Heart ☐ King of the Hill ☐ Monster in a Box ☐ Paper, The ☐ Swimming to Cambodia ☐ True Stories ☐ Twenty Bucks

Grayson, Kathryn ☐ Anchors Aweigh ☐ Andy Hardy's Private Secretary ☐ Desert Song, The ☐ Grounds for Marriage ☐ It Happened in Brooklyn ☐ Kiss Me Kate ☐ Kissing Bandit, The ☐ Lovely to Look At ☐ Rio Rita ☐ Seven Sweethearts ☐ Show Boat ☐ So This Is Love ☐ That Midnight Kiss ☐ Thousands Cheer ☐ Till the Clouds Roll By ☐ Toast of New Orleans, The ☐ Two Sisters From Boston ☐ Vagabond King, The

Green, Nigel ☐ Africa—Texas Style ☐ Countess Dracula ☐ Face of Fu Manchu, The ☐ Fraulein Doktor ☐ Gawain and the Green Night ☐ Ipcress File, The ☐ Jason and the Argonauts ☐ Let's Kill Uncle ☐ Man Who Finally Died, The ☐ Masque of the Red Death ☐ Play Dirty ☐ Reach for the Sky ☐ Ruling Class, The ☐ Skull, The ☐ Tobruk ☐ Zulu

Greene, Ellen ☐ Dinner at Eight ☐ Glory! Glory! ☐ I'm Dancing as Fast as I Can ☐ Little Shop of Horrors ☐ Me and Him ☐ Naked Gun 33 1/3: The Final Insult ☐ Next Stop, Greenwich Village ☐ Pump Up the Volume ☐ Rock-a-Doodle ☐ Stepping Out ☐ Talk Radio

Greene, Lorne ☐ Alamo, The—Thirteen Days to Glory ☐ Autumn Leaves ☐ Bastard, The ☐ Battlestar: Galactica ☐ Buccaneer, The ☐ Conquest of the Earth ☐ Earthquake ☐ Gift of Love, The ☐ Hard Man, The ☐ Harness, The ☐ Heidi's Song ☐ Klondike Fever ☐ Man on the Outside ☐ Mission Galactica: The Cylon Attack ☐ Tight Spot ☐ Trial of Lee Harvey Oswald, The

Greene, Richard ☐ Bandits of Corsica, The ☐ Black Castle, The ☐ Captain Scarlett ☐ Castle of Fu Manchu, The ☐ Desert Hawk, The ☐ Don't Take It to Heart ☐ Fan, The ☐ Fighting O'Flynn, The ☐ Forever Amber ☐ Four Men and a Prayer ☐ Here I Am a Stranger ☐ Hound of the Baskervilles, The ☐ I Was an Adventuress ☐ If This Be Sin ☐ Island of the Lost ☐ Kentucky ☐ Little Princess, The ☐ My Lucky Star ☐ Operation X ☐ Showtime

Greenstreet, Sydney ☐ Across the Pacific ☐ Background to Danger ☐ Between Two Worlds ☐ Casablanca ☐ Christmas in Connecticut ☐ Conflict ☐ Conspirators, The ☐ Devotion ☐ Flamingo Road ☐ Hucksters, The ☐ Malaya ☐ Maltese Falcon, The ☐ Mask of Dimitrios, The ☐ Passage to Marseille ☐ Pillow to Post ☐ Three Strangers ☐ Velvet Touch, The ☐ Verdict, The ☐ Woman in White, The

Greenwood, Charlotte ☐ Dangerous When Wet ☐ Down Argentine Way ☐ Flying High ☐ Gang's All Here, The ☐ Glory ☐ Great Dan Patch, The ☐ Home in Indiana ☐ Moon Over Miami ☐ Oh, You Beautiful Doll ☐ Oklahoma! ☐ Opposite Sex, The ☐ Orders Is Orders ☐ Palmy Days ☐ Parlor, Bedroom and Bath ☐ Peggy ☐ Star Dust ☐ Tall, Dark and Handsome ☐ Up in Mabel's Room ☐ Young People

Greenwood, Joan ☐ Amorous Mr. Prawn, The ☐ Bad Lord Byron ☐ Detective, The ☐ Flesh & Blood ☐ Gentle Sex, The ☐ Girl in a Million, A ☐ Girl Stroke Boy ☐ Hound of the Baskervilles, The ☐ Importance of Being Earnest, The ☐ Kind Hearts and Coronets ☐ Little Dorrit ☐ Lovers, Happy Lovers ☐ Man in the White Suit, The ☐ Moonfleet ☐ Mysterious Island ☐ October Man, The ☐ Past Caring ☐ Saraband ☐ Smugglers, the ☐ Stage Struck ☐ Tight Little Island ☐ Tom Jones ☐ Water Babies, The ☐ Young Wives' Tale

Greer, Jane ☐ Big Steal, The ☐ Billie ☐ Clown, The ☐ Company She Keeps, The ☐ Desperate Search ☐ Down Among the Sheltering Palms ☐ Falcon's Alibi, The ☐ Man of a Thousand Faces ☐ Out of the Past ☐ Prisoner of Zenda, The ☐ Station West ☐ They Won't Believe Me ☐ Where Love Has Gone ☐ You're in the Navy Now

Gregory, James ☐ Al Capone ☐ Big Caper, The ☐ Francis Gary Powers: The True Story of the U-2 Spy Incident ☐ Main Event, The ☐ Manchurian Candidate, The ☐ Nightfall ☐ PT 109 ☐ Quick Before It Melts ☐ Rage to Live, A ☐ Secret War of Harry Frigg, The ☐ Sons of Katie Elder, The ☐ Strongest Man in the World, The ☐ Young Stranger, The

Gregson, John ☐ Above Us The Waves ☐ Angels One Five ☐ Captain's Table, The ☐ Cash on Delivery ☐ Faces in the Dark ☐ Fright ☐ Frightened City, The ☐ Fuss over Feathers ☐ Genevieve ☐ Hand in Hand ☐ Jacqueline ☐ Miracle in Soho ☐ Pursuit of the Graf Spee ☐ Rooney ☐ Three Cases of Murder ☐ Tight Little Island ☐ Titfield Thunderbolt, The ☐ Tomorrow at Ten

Grenfell, Joyce ☐ Belles of St. Trinians, The ☐ Blue Murder at St. Trinian's ☐ Forbidden Cargo ☐ Good Companions, The ☐ Happiest Days of Your Life, The ☐ Happy Is the Bride ☐ Laughter in Paradise ☐ Old Dark House, The ☐ Pure Hell of St. Trinian's, The ☐ Run for Your Money, A

Grey, Jennifer ☐ Bloodhounds of Broadway ☐ Criminal Justice ☐ Dirty Dancing ☐ Eyes of a Witness ☐ Murder in Mississippi ☐ Stroke of Midnight ☐ Wind

Grey, Joel ☐ About Face ☐ Buffalo Bill and the Indians ☐ Cabaret ☐ Calypso Heat Wave ☐ Come September ☐ Kafka ☐ Man on a String ☐ Man on a Swing ☐ Music of Chance, The ☐ Queenie ☐ Remo Williams: The Adventure Begins ☐ Seven Percent Solution, The

Grey, Virginia ☐ Another Thin Man ☐ Big Store, The ☐ Black Zoo ☐ Eternal Sea, The ☐ Fighting Lawman, The ☐ Flame of Barbary Coast ☐ Glamour Girl ☐ Grissly's Millions ☐ Highway 301 ☐ House of Horrors ☐ Idaho ☐ Idiot's Delight ☐ Jeanne Eagels ☐ Mr. and Mrs. North ☐ Naked Kiss, The ☐ No Name on the Bullet ☐ Perilous Journey, A ☐ Rose Tattoo, The ☐ Smooth as Silk ☐ So This Is New York ☐ Sweet Rosie O'Grady ☐ Tarzan's New York Adventure ☐ Threat, The ☐ Three Cheers for the Irish ☐ Whistling in the Dark ☐ Wyoming

Grier, Pam ☐ Above The Law ☐ Badge of the Assassin ☐ Beasts ☐ Big Bird Cage, The ☐ Big Doll House, The ☐ Bill & Ted's Bogus Journey ☐ Black Mama, White Mama ☐ Bucktown ☐ Class of 1999 ☐ Coffy ☐ Drum ☐ Foxy Brown ☐ Friday Foster ☐ Greased Lightning ☐ Scream, Blacula, Scream! ☐ Sheba Baby ☐ Women in Cages

Griffith, Andy ☐ Andy Griffith Show, The ☐ Andy Griffith Show, The—Special Holiday Release ☐ Angel in my Pocket ☐ Face in the Crowd, A ☐ Fatal Vision ☐ Girl in the Empty Grave, The ☐ Go Ask Alice ☐ Hearts of the West ☐ Murder in Coweta County ☐ Murder in Texas ☐ No Time for Sergeants ☐ Onionhead ☐ Return to Mayberry ☐ Rustlers' Rhapsody ☐ Second Time Around, The

Griffith, Hugh ☐ Abominable Dr. Phibes, The ☐ Beggar's Opera, The ☐ Ben-Hur ☐ Counterfeit Traitor, The ☐ Cry of the Banshee ☐ Day They Robbed the Bank of England, The ☐ Dr. Phibes Rises Again ☐ Fixer, The ☐ Gone to Earth ☐ Good Companions, The ☐ How to Steal a Million ☐ Last Days of Dolwyn, The ☐ Laughter in Paradise ☐ Legend of the Werewolf ☐ Lisa ☐ Lucky Jim ☐ Luther ☐ Mayfair Bank Caper, The ☐ Mutiny on the Bounty ☐ Oh Dad, Poor Dad, Mama's Hung You in the Closet and I'm Feeling So Sad ☐ On My Way to the Crusades, I Met a Girl Who . . . ☐ Passage Home ☐ Passover Plot, The ☐ Run for Your Money, A ☐ Sleeping Tiger, The ☐ So Evil My Love ☐ Start the Revolution Without Me ☐ Term of Trial ☐ Titfield Thunderbolt, The ☐ Tom Jones ☐ Wuthering Heights

Griffith, Melanie ☐ Body Double ☐ Bonfire of the Vanities, The ☐ Born Yesterday ☐ Cherry 2000 ☐ Drowning Pool, The ☐ Fear City ☐ In the Spirit ☐ Joyride ☐ Milagro Beanfield War, The ☐ Milk Money ☐ Night Moves ☐ Nobody's Fool ☐ Pacific Heights ☐ Paradise ☐ Shining Through ☐ Smile ☐ Something Wild ☐ Stormy Monday ☐ Stranger Among Us, A ☐ Women & Men: Stories of Seduction ☐ Working Girl

Grodin, Charles ☐ 11 Harrowhouse ☐ Beethoven ☐ Beethoven's 2nd ☐ Clifford ☐ Couch Trip, The ☐ Dave ☐ Grass Is Always Greener Over the Septic Tank, The ☐ Great Muppet Caper, The ☐ Grown Ups ☐ Heart & Souls ☐ Heartbreak Kid, The ☐ Heaven Can Wait ☐ Incredible Shrinking Woman, The ☐ Ishtar ☐ It's My Turn ☐ Just Me and You ☐ King Kong ☐ Last Resort ☐ Lonely Guy, The ☐ Meanest Men in the West, The ☐ Midnight Run ☐ Movers and Shakers ☐ Real Life ☐ Seems Like Old Times ☐ Sunburn ☐ Taking Care of Business ☐ Woman in Red, The

Guardino, Harry ☐ Adventures of Bullwhip Griffin, The ☐ Any Which Way You Can ☐ Capone ☐ Contract on Cherry Street ☐ Dirty Harry ☐ Enforcer, The ☐ Evening in Byzantium, An ☐ Fist of Honor ☐ Five Branded Women ☐ Flesh and Fury ☐ Get Christie Love ☐ Hell Is for Heroes ☐ Hell With Heroes, The ☐ Hold Back Tomorrow ☐ Houseboat ☐ Indict and Convict ☐ Jigsaw ☐ Lovers and Other Strangers ☐ Madigan ☐ Matilda ☐ Pigeon That Took Rome, The ☐ Pork Chop Hill ☐ Rhino! ☐ They Only Kill Their Masters ☐ Treasure of San Gennaro, The

Guest, Christopher ☐ Beyond Therapy ☐ Billy Crystal—Don't Get Me Started ☐ Death Wish ☐ Girlfriends ☐ Princess Bride, The ☐ Return of Spinal Tap, The ☐ This Is Spinal Tap

Guinness, Alec ☐ All at Sea ☐ Bridge on the River Kwai, The ☐ Brother Sun, Sister Moon ☐ Captain's Paradise, The ☐ Comedians, The ☐ Cromwell ☐ Damn the Defiant! ☐ Detective, The ☐ Doctor Zhivago ☐ Fall of the Roman Empire ☐ Great Expectations ☐ Handful of Dust, A ☐ Hitler: The Last Ten Days ☐ Horse's Mouth, The ☐ Hotel Paradiso ☐ Kafka ☐ Kind Hearts and Coronets ☐ Lady Killers, The ☐ Last Holiday ☐ Lavender Hill

Mob, The ☐ Lawrence of Arabia ☐ Little Dorrit ☐ Little Lord Fauntleroy ☐ Lovesick ☐ Majority of One, A ☐ Malta Story, The ☐ Man in the White Suit, The ☐ Monsignor Quixote ☐ Mudlark, The ☐ Murder by Death ☐ Oliver Twist ☐ Our Man in Havana ☐ Passage to India, A ☐ Prisoner, The ☐ Promoter, The ☐ Quiller Memorandum, The ☐ Raise the Titanic! ☐ Run for Your Money, A ☐ Scapegoat, The ☐ Scrooge ☐ Situation Hopeless—But Not Serious ☐ Star Wars ☐ Swan, The ☐ To Paris With Love ☐ Tunes of Glory

Gunn, Moses ☐ Aaron Loves Angela ☐ Amazing Grace ☐ Bates Motel ☐ Cornbread, Earl and Me ☐ Eagle in a Cage ☐ Great White Hope, The ☐ Heartbreak Ridge ☐ Iceman Cometh, The ☐ Killing Floor, The ☐ Neverending Story, The ☐ Ninth Configuration, The ☐ Ragtime ☐ Rollerball ☐ Shaft ☐ Shaft's Big Score! ☐ Women of Brewster Place, The

Guttenberg, Steve ☐ Amazon Women on the Moon ☐ Bad Medicine ☐ Bedroom Window, The ☐ Boys From Brazil, The ☐ Can't Stop the Music ☐ Chicken Chronicles, The ☐ Cocoon ☐ Cocoon: The Return ☐ Day After, The ☐ Diner ☐ Don't Tell Her It's Me ☐ High Spirits ☐ Man Who Wasn't There, The ☐ Miracle on Ice ☐ Players ☐ Police Academy ☐ Police Academy 2: Their First Assignment ☐ Police Academy 3: Back in Training ☐ Police Academy 4: Citizens on Patrol ☐ Short Circuit ☐ Surrender ☐ Three Men and a Baby ☐ Three Men and a Little Lady

Gwenn, Edmund ☐ Anthony Adverse ☐ Apartment for Peggy ☐ Between Two Worlds ☐ Bewitched ☐ Bigamist, The ☐ Bonzo Goes to College ☐ Challenge to Lassie ☐ Charley's Aunt ☐ Cheers for Miss Bishop ☐ Devil and Miss Jones, The ☐ Doctor Takes a Wife, The ☐ Earl of Chicago, The ☐ For Heaven's Sake ☐ Foreign Correspondent ☐ Good Companions, The ☐ Green Dolphin Street ☐ Hills of Home, The ☐ I Was a Spy ☐ If I Were Rich ☐ It's a Dog's Life ☐ Java Head ☐ Keys of the Kingdom ☐ Lassie Come Home ☐ Les Miserables ☐ Louisa ☐ Meanest Man in the World, The ☐ Miracle on 34th Street ☐ Mister 880 ☐ Parnell ☐ Peking Express ☐ Pride and Prejudice ☐ Sally and Saint Anne ☐ Skin Game, The ☐ Something for the Birds ☐ South Riding ☐ Student Prince, The ☐ Sylvia Scarlett ☐ Them ☐ Trouble With Harry, The ☐ Undercurrent ☐ Walking Dead, The ☐ Woman of Distinction, A ☐ Yank at Oxford, A

Gwynne, Fred ☐ Captains Courageous ☐ Cotton Club, The ☐ Disorganized Crime ☐ Fatal Attraction ☐ Ironweed ☐ Land Before Time, The ☐ Luna ☐ Munster, Go Home ☐ Munsters' Revenge, The ☐ Murder by the Book ☐ My Cousin Vinny ☐ Pet Sematary ☐ Shadows and Fog ☐ Simon

Haas, Hugo ☐ Bait ☐ Born To Be Loved ☐ Girl on the Bridge ☐ Hit and Run ☐ Lizzie ☐ Merton of the Movies ☐ My Girl Tisa ☐ One Girl's Confession ☐ What Next, Corporal Hargrove?

Haas, Lukas ☐ Alan & Naomi ☐ Convicts ☐ Lady in White ☐ Leap of Faith ☐ Music Box ☐ Perfect Tribute, The ☐ Rambling Rose ☐ See You in the Morning ☐ Testament ☐ Witness

Hackett, Buddy ☐ All Hands On Deck ☐ Bud and Lou ☐ Fireman Save My Child ☐ It's a Mad Mad Mad Mad World ☐ Love Bug, The ☐ Muscle Beach Party ☐ Music Man, The ☐ Walking My Baby Back Home ☐ Wonderful World of the Brothers Grimm, The

Hackett, Joan ☐ Assignment to Kill ☐ Class of '63 ☐ Escape Artist, The ☐ Flicks ☐ Group, The ☐ How Awful About Allan ☐ Last of Sheila, The ☐ Long Summer of George Adams, The ☐ Mackintosh and T.J. ☐ One-Trick Pony ☐ Only When I Laugh ☐ Other Man, The ☐ Paper Dolls ☐ Reflections of Murder ☐ Support Your Local Sheriff ☐ Terminal Man, The ☐ Treasure of Matecumbe ☐ Will Penny

Hackman, Gene ☐ All Night Long ☐ Another Woman ☐ Banning ☐ Bat 21 ☐ Bite the Bullet ☐ Bonnie and Clyde ☐ Bridge Too Far, A ☐ Cisco Pike ☐ Class Action ☐ Company Business ☐ Conversation, The ☐ Doctor's Wives ☐ Domino Principle, The ☐ Downhill Racer ☐ Eureka ☐ Firm, The ☐ First to Fight ☐ French Connection II ☐ French Connection, The ☐ Full Moon in Blue Water ☐ Geronimo: An American Legend ☐ Gypsy Moths, The ☐ Hawaii ☐ Hoosiers ☐ Hunting Party, The ☐ I Never Sang for My Father ☐ Loose Cannons ☐ Lucky Lady ☐ March or Die ☐ Marooned ☐ Mississippi Burning ☐ Misunderstood ☐ Narrow Margin ☐ Night Moves ☐ No Way Out ☐ Package, The ☐ Poseidon Adventure, The ☐ Postcards from the Edge ☐ Power ☐ Prime Cut ☐ Quick and the Dead, The ☐ Reds ☐ Riot ☐ Scarecrow ☐ Superman 2 ☐ Superman 4: The Quest for Peace ☐ Superman—The Movie ☐ Target ☐ Twice in a Lifetime ☐ Uncommon Valor ☐ Under Fire ☐ Unforgiven ☐ Wyatt Earp ☐ Zandy's Bride

Hagen, Jean ☐ Adam's Rib ☐ Ambush ☐ Asphalt Jungle, The ☐ Carbine Williams ☐ Half a Hero ☐ Night into Morning ☐ No Questions Asked ☐ Panic in Year Zero! ☐ Shadow in the Sky ☐ Shaggy Dog, The ☐ Side Street ☐ Singin' in the Rain ☐ Sunrise at Campobello

Hagman, Larry ☐ Alpha Caper, The ☐ Antonio ☐ Big Bus, The ☐ Cavern, The ☐ Checkered Flag or Crash ☐ Ensign Pulver ☐ Group, The ☐ Harry and Tonto ☐ Howling in the Woods, A ☐ Hurricane ☐ Intimate Strangers ☐ Mother, Jugs & Speed ☐ No Place to Run ☐ Up in the Cellar

Haim, Corey ☐ Anything for Love ☐ Dream

Machine, The ☐ Fast Getaway ☐ Firstborn ☐ Just One Of The Girls ☐ License to Drive ☐ Lost Boys, The ☐ Lucas ☐ Murphy's Romance ☐ Oh, What a Night ☐ Prayer of the Rollerboys ☐ Silver Bullet ☐ Watchers

Hale, Alan ☐ Action in the North Atlantic ☐ Adventures of Don Juan ☐ Adventures of Marco Polo, The ☐ Adventures of Mark Twain, The ☐ Adventures of Robin Hood, The ☐ Algiers ☐ Always Leave Them Laughing ☐ At Sword's Point ☐ Back to the Beach ☐ Captain of the Clouds ☐ Castaways on Gilligan's Island, The ☐ Cheyenne ☐ Covered Wagon, The ☐ Desperate Journey ☐ Destination Tokyo ☐ Dick Turpin ☐ Dodge City ☐ Dust Be My Destiny ☐ Escape in the Desert ☐ Fighting 69th, The ☐ Fog Over Frisco ☐ Footsteps in the Dark ☐ Four Days Leave ☐ Four Horsemen of the Apocalypse, The ☐ Four Men and a Prayer ☐ Gentleman Jim ☐ Gilligan's Island: The Collector's Edition, Vol. 1 ☐ God is My Co-Pilot ☐ Good Fairy, The ☐ Great Mr. Nobody, The ☐ Green Hell ☐ Hard Drivin' ☐ Harlem Globetrotters on Gilligan's Island, The ☐ Imitation of Life ☐ Inspector General, The ☐ Iron Glove, The ☐ It Happened One Night ☐ It Happens Every Spring ☐ Janie ☐ Lady in the Iron Mask ☐ Little Man, What Now? ☐ Lost Patrol, The ☐ Make Your Own Bed ☐ Man I Love, The ☐ Man in the Iron Mask, The ☐ Manpower ☐ Message to Garcia, A ☐ My Girl Tisa ☐ My Wild Irish Rose ☐ On Your Toes ☐ Our Relations ☐ Perilous Holiday ☐ Prince and the Pauper, The ☐ Robin Hood ☐ Sal of Singapore ☐ Santa Fe Trail ☐ Scarlet Letter, The ☐ Sea Hawk, The ☐ Stella Dallas ☐ Strawberry Blonde, The ☐ Susan Lenox: Her Fall and Rise ☐ Thieves Fall Out ☐ Thin Ice ☐ Three Cheers for the Irish ☐ Union Depot ☐ Up Periscope ☐ Virginia City ☐ Wait 'Til the Sun Shines, Nellie ☐ Younger Brothers, The

Hale, Barbara ☐ And Baby Makes Three ☐ Boy with Green Hair, The ☐ Clay Pigeon, The ☐ Falcon in Hollywood, The ☐ Falcon Out West, The ☐ Far Horizons, The ☐ First Time, The ☐ First Yank into Tokyo ☐ Flight of the Grey Wolf ☐ Giant Spider Invasion, The ☐ Heavenly Days ☐ Houston Story, The ☐ Jackpot, The ☐ Jolson Sings Again ☐ Last of the Comanches, The ☐ Lion Is in the Streets, A ☐ Lone Hand, The ☐ Oklahoman, The ☐ Perry Mason Returns ☐ Perry Mason: The Case of the Lost Love ☐ Seminole ☐ Seventh Cavalry ☐ West of the Pecos ☐ Window, The

Haley, Jack ☐ Alexander's Ragtime Band ☐ Beyond the Blue Horizon ☐ Danger—Love at Work ☐ Follow Thru ☐ George White's Scandals ☐ Girl Friend, The ☐ Higher and Higher ☐ Hold That Co-ed ☐ Navy Blues ☐ One Body Too Many ☐ People Are Funny ☐ Pigskin Parade ☐ Rebecca of Sunnybrook Farm ☐ Sitting Pretty ☐ Thanks for Everything ☐ Wake Up and Live ☐ Wizard of Oz, The

Hall, Anthony Michael ☐ Breakfast Club, The ☐ Edward Scissorhands ☐ Gnome Named Gnorm, A ☐ Hail Caesar ☐ Into the Sun ☐ Johnny Be Good ☐ National Lampoon's Vacation ☐ Out of Bounds ☐ Rascals and Robbers—The Secret Adventures ☐ Sixteen Candles ☐ Weird Science

Hall, Huntz ☐ Angels in Disguise ☐ Auntie Lee's Meat Pies ☐ Block Busters ☐ Blonde Dynamite ☐ Blues Busters ☐ Bowery Boys Meet the Monsters, The ☐ Bowery Buckaroos ☐ Bowery Champs ☐ Bowery to Bagdad ☐ Call a Messenger ☐ Clipped Wings ☐ Come Out Fighting ☐ Dead End ☐ Feudin' Fools ☐ Fighting Fools ☐ Fighting Trouble ☐ Follow the Leader ☐ Gas Pump Girls ☐ Ghost Chasers ☐ Give Us Wings ☐ Hard Boiled Mahoney ☐ Here Come the Marines ☐ High Society ☐ Hit the Road ☐ Hold That Baby! ☐ Hold That Hypnotist ☐ Hold That Line ☐ Jail Busters ☐ Jalopy ☐ Kid Dynamite ☐ Let's Get Tough! ☐ Let's Go Navy! ☐ Live Wires ☐ Loose in London ☐ Lucky Losers ☐ Manchu Eagle Murder Caper Mystery, The ☐ Master Minds ☐ Million Dollar Kid ☐ Mr. Hex ☐ Mr. Muggs Steps Out ☐ No Holds Barred ☐ On Dress Parade ☐ Paris Playboys ☐ Return of Dr. X, The ☐ Smugglers' Cove ☐ They Made Me a Criminal ☐ Trouble Makers ☐ Walk in the Sun, A

Halliday, John ☐ Bird of Paradise ☐ Desire ☐ Escape to Glory ☐ Finishing School ☐ Hollywood Boulevard ☐ Peter Ibbetson ☐ Scarlet Pages

Hall, Jon ☐ Ali Baba and the Forty Thieves ☐ Aloma of the South Seas ☐ Arabian Nights ☐ Brave Warrior ☐ China Corsair ☐ Cobra Woman ☐ Eagle Squadron ☐ Gypsy Wildcat ☐ Hell Ship Mutiny ☐ Hurricane Island ☐ Hurricane, The ☐ Invisible Agent ☐ Invisible Man's Revenge, The ☐ Kit Carson ☐ Lady in the Dark ☐ Last of the Redmen ☐ On the Isle of Samoa ☐ San Diego, I Love You ☐ South of Pago Pago ☐ Sudan ☐ Tuttles of Tahiti, The

Hall, Porter ☐ Big Carnival, The ☐ Double Indemnity ☐ Intruder in the Dust ☐ Make Way for Tomorrow ☐ Mark of the Whistler ☐ Miracle of Morgan's Creek, The ☐ Murder, He Says ☐ Satan Met a Lady ☐ Story of Louis Pasteur, The ☐ Sullivan's Travels ☐ Thin Man, The ☐ Unconquered ☐ Vice Squad ☐ Weekend at the Waldorf ☐ Wells Fargo

Halsey, Brett ☐ Atomic Submarine, The ☐ Backstab ☐ Blood and Steel ☐ Hot Rod Rumble ☐ Return of the Fly, The ☐ Return to Peyton Place ☐ Scruples ☐ Submarine Seahawk ☐ Twice-Told Tales

Hamill, Mark ☐ Batman: Mask of the Phantom ☐ Big Red One, The ☐ Black Magic

Woman ☐ Corvette Summer ☐ Empire Strikes Back, The ☐ Eric ☐ Guyver, The ☐ Night the Lights Went Out in Georgia, The ☐ Return of the Jedi, The ☐ Slipstream ☐ Star Wars ☐ Time Runner ☐ Wizards

Hamilton, George ☐ Act One ☐ All the Fine Young Cannibals ☐ Angel Baby ☐ By Love Possessed ☐ Crime & Punishment, USA ☐ Dead Don't Die, The ☐ Evel Knievel ☐ From Hell to Victory ☐ Godfather, Part III, The ☐ Happy Hooker Goes to Washington, The ☐ Home From the Hill ☐ Jack of Diamonds ☐ Jacqueline Susann's Once Is Not Enough ☐ Light in the Piazza ☐ Looking for Love ☐ Love at First Bite ☐ Malibu ☐ Man Who Loved Cat Dancing, The ☐ Medusa ☐ Monte Carlo ☐ Poker Alice ☐ Power, The ☐ Sextette ☐ Time for Killing, A ☐ Two Weeks in Another Town ☐ Victors, The ☐ Viva Maria! ☐ Where the Boys Are ☐ Your Cheatin' Heart ☐ Zorro, the Gay Blade

Hamilton, Linda ☐ Black Moon Rising ☐ Children of the Corn ☐ King Kong Lives ☐ Mr. Destiny ☐ Rape & Marriage: The Rideout Case ☐ Silent Fall ☐ Terminator 2—Judgment Day ☐ Terminator, The

Hamilton, Margaret ☐ 13 Ghosts ☐ Adventures of Tom Sawyer, The ☐ Anderson Tapes, The ☐ Angels Wash Their Faces, The ☐ Another Language ☐ Brewster McCloud ☐ Broadway Bill ☐ By Your Leave ☐ Chatterbox ☐ City Without Men ☐ Daydreamer, The ☐ George White's Scandals ☐ Guest in the House ☐ I'll Take Romance ☐ Letters From Frank ☐ Meet the Stewarts ☐ My Little Chickadee ☐ Night Strangler, The ☐ Riding High ☐ Saratoga ☐ Stablemates ☐ State of the Union ☐ These Three ☐ Wabash Avenue ☐ Wizard of Oz, The ☐ You Only Live Once

Hamilton, Murray ☐ Brubaker ☐ FBI Story, The ☐ Graduate, The ☐ If It's Tuesday, This Must Be Belgium ☐ Jaws ☐ Jaws 2 ☐ No Time for Sergeants ☐ No Way to Treat a Lady ☐ Seconds ☐ Spirit of St. Louis, The ☐ Way We Were, The ☐ Whistle at Eaton Falls, The

Hamilton, Neil ☐ America ☐ Dawn Patrol, The ☐ Father Takes a Wife ☐ Fugitive Lady ☐ Great Gatsby, The ☐ Laughing Sinners ☐ Mysterious Dr. Fu Manchu, The ☐ One Exciting Adventure ☐ Portia on Trial ☐ Sin of Madelon Claudet, The ☐ Strangers May Kiss ☐ Tarzan and His Mate ☐ This Modern Age ☐ Wet Parade, The ☐ What Price Hollywood? ☐ When Strangers Marry

Hamlin, Harry ☐ Blue Skies Again ☐ Clash of the Titans ☐ Deceptions ☐ Dinner at Eight ☐ King of the Mountain ☐ Laguna Heat ☐ Making Love ☐ Murder So Sweet ☐ Save Me

Hanks, Tom ☐ 'Burbs, The ☐ Bachelor Party ☐ Big ☐ Bonfire of the Vanities, The ☐ Dragnet ☐ Every Time We Say Goodbye ☐ Fallen Angels—Volume 2 ☐ Forrest Gump ☐ Joe Versus the Volcano ☐ League of Their Own, A ☐ Man with One Red Shoe ☐ Mazes and Monsters ☐ Money Pit, The ☐ Nothing in Common ☐ Philadelphia ☐ Punchline ☐ Sleepless in Seattle ☐ Splash ☐ Turner & Hooch ☐ Volunteers

Hannah, Daryl ☐ At Play in the Fields of the Lord ☐ Attack of the 50 Ft. Woman ☐ Blade Runner ☐ Clan of the Cave Bear, The ☐ Crazy People ☐ Final Terror, The ☐ Grumpy Old Men ☐ Hard Country ☐ High Spirits ☐ Legal Eagles ☐ Memoirs of an Invisible Man ☐ Paper Dolls ☐ Pope of Greenwich Village, The ☐ Reckless ☐ Roxanne ☐ Splash ☐ Steel Magnolias ☐ Summer Lovers ☐ Wall Street

Harden, Marcia Gay ☐ In Broad Daylight ☐ Late for Dinner ☐ Miller's Crossing ☐ Safe Passage ☐ Sinatra ☐ Used People

Harding, Ann ☐ Animal Kingdom, The ☐ Biography of a Bachelor Girl ☐ Christmas Eve ☐ Condemned ☐ Conquerors, The ☐ Enchanted April ☐ Eyes in the Night ☐ Flame Within, The ☐ Fountain, The ☐ Gallant Lady ☐ Holiday ☐ I've Lived Before ☐ It Happened on Fifth Avenue ☐ Janie ☐ Janie Gets Married ☐ Lady Consents, The ☐ Life of Vergie Winters, The ☐ Love from a Stranger ☐ Magnificent Yankee, The ☐ Mission to Moscow ☐ Nine Girls ☐ North Star, The ☐ Peter Ibbetson ☐ Two Weeks with Love ☐ Westward Passage ☐ When Ladies Meet

Hardwicke, Cedric ☐ Baby Face Nelson ☐ Becky Sharp ☐ Beware of Pity ☐ Botany Bay ☐ Caribbean ☐ Commandos Strike at Dawn, The ☐ Connecticut Yankee in King Arthur's Court ☐ Cross of Lorraine, The ☐ Diane ☐ Desert Fox, The ☐ Five Weeks in a Balloon ☐ Forever and a Day ☐ Gaby ☐ Ghost of Frankenstein, The ☐ Ghoul, The ☐ Green Glove, The ☐ Green Light, The ☐ Howards of Virginia ☐ Hunchback of Notre Dame, The ☐ I Remember Mama ☐ Imperfect Lady, The ☐ Invisible Agent ☐ Invisible Man Returns, The ☐ Ivy ☐ Keys of the Kingdom ☐ King Solomon's Mines ☐ Les Miserables ☐ Lodger, The ☐ Moon Is Down, The ☐ Nell Gwyn ☐ Nicholas Nickleby ☐ Nine Days A Queen ☐ On Borrowed Time ☐ Peg of Old Drury ☐ Pumpkin Eater, The ☐ Richard III ☐ Rope ☐ Salome ☐ Sentimental Journey ☐ Stanley and Livingstone ☐ Story of Mankind, The ☐ Suspicion ☐ Ten Commandments, The ☐ Things to Come ☐ Tom Brown's School Days ☐ Tycoon ☐ Vagabond King, The ☐ Valley of the Sun ☐ Victory ☐ White Tower, The ☐ Wilson ☐ Winslow Boy, The ☐ Woman's Vengeance, A

Hardy, Oliver ☐ A-Haunting We Will Go ☐ Air Raid Wardens ☐ Babes in Toyland ☐ Big Noise, The ☐ Block-Heads ☐ Bohemian Girl, The ☐ Bonnie Scotland ☐ Bullfighters, The ☐ Chump at Oxford, A ☐ Dancing Masters, The ☐ Days of Thrills and Laughter ☐ Devil's Brother, The ☐ Fighting Kentuckian, The ☐ Flying Deuces, The

☐ Four Clowns ☐ Further Perils of Laurel and Hardy, The ☐ Golden Age of Comedy, The ☐ Great Guns ☐ Hollywood Party ☐ Hollywood Revue of 1929, The ☐ Jitterbugs ☐ Laurel and Hardy's Laughing 20s ☐ MGM's Big Parade of Comedy ☐ Nothing But Trouble ☐ Our Relations ☐ Pack Up Your Troubles ☐ Pardon Us ☐ Saps at Sea ☐ Sons of the Desert ☐ Swiss Miss ☐ Utopia ☐ Way Out West ☐ When Comedy Was King ☐ Zenobia

Harewood, Dorian ☐ Against All Odds ☐ Ambush Murders, The ☐ American Christmas Carol, An ☐ Full Metal Jacket ☐ God Bless the Child ☐ Guilty of Innocence: The Lenell Geter Story ☐ High Ice ☐ I, Desire ☐ Jesse Owens Story, The ☐ Kiss Shot ☐ Polly ☐ Sparkle

Harlow, Jean ☐ Bombshell ☐ China Seas ☐ Dinner at Eight ☐ Girl from Missouri, The ☐ Hell's Angels ☐ Hold Your Man ☐ Iron Man, The ☐ MGM's Big Parade of Comedy ☐ Personal Property ☐ Platinum Blonde ☐ Public Enemy, The ☐ Reckless ☐ Red Dust ☐ Red-Headed Woman ☐ Riffraff ☐ Saratoga ☐ Secret Six, The ☐ Suzy ☐ Three Wise Girls ☐ Wife vs. Secretary

Harmon, Mark ☐ After the Promise ☐ Beyond the Poseidon Adventure ☐ Cold Heaven ☐ Comes a Horseman ☐ Deliberate Stranger, The ☐ Eleanor and Franklin: The White House Years ☐ Flamingo Road ☐ Fourth Story, The ☐ Goliath Awaits ☐ Let's Get Harry ☐ Presidio, The ☐ Prince of Bel Air ☐ Stealing Home ☐ Summer School ☐ Sweet Bird of Youth ☐ Till There Was You ☐ Worth Winning ☐ Wyatt Earp

Harper, Tess ☐ Amityville 3D ☐ Crimes of the Heart ☐ Criminal Law ☐ Daddy's Dyin'... Who's Got the Will? ☐ Far North ☐ Incident at Dark River ☐ Man in the Moon, The ☐ My Heroes Have Always Been Cowboys ☐ My New Gun ☐ Reckless Disregard ☐ Tender Mercies

Harrelson, Woody ☐ Cowboy Way ☐ Doc Hollywood ☐ Indecent Proposal ☐ Natural Born Killers ☐ White Men Can't Jump

Harris, Barbara ☐ Family Plot ☐ Freaky Friday ☐ Manchu Eagle Murder Caper Mystery, The ☐ Mixed Company ☐ Movie Movie ☐ Nashville ☐ Nice Girls Don't Explode ☐ North Avenue Irregulars, The ☐ Oh Dad, Poor Dad, Mama's Hung You in the Closet and I'm Feeling So Sad ☐ Peggy Sue Got Married ☐ Plaza Suite ☐ Seduction of Joe Tynan, The ☐ Thousand Clowns, A ☐ War Between Men and Women, The ☐ Who Is Harry Kellerman and Why Is He Saying Those Terrible Things About Me?

Harris, Ed ☐ Abyss, The ☐ Alamo Bay ☐ Borderline ☐ China Moon ☐ Creepshow ☐ Firm, The ☐ Flash of Green ☐ Glengarry Glen Ross ☐ Jacknife ☐ Just Cause ☐ Knightriders ☐ Last Innocent Man, The ☐ Milk Money ☐ Needful Things ☐ Paris Trout ☐ Places in the Heart ☐ Right Stuff, The ☐ Running Mates ☐ State of Grace ☐ Sweet Dreams ☐ Swing Shift ☐ To Kill a Priest ☐ Under Fire ☐ Walker

Harris, Julie ☐ Bell Jar, The ☐ Brontë ☐ Christmas Wife, The ☐ Dark Half, The ☐ East of Eden ☐ Gorillas in the Mist ☐ Greatest Gift, The ☐ Harper ☐ Haunting, The ☐ Hiding Place, The ☐ Home for the Holidays ☐ House on Greenapple Road, The ☐ Housesitter ☐ How Awful About Allan ☐ I Am a Camera ☐ Last of Mrs. Lincoln ☐ Member of the Wedding, The ☐ Nutcracker, The Motion Picture ☐ People Next Door, The ☐ Poacher's Daughter, The ☐ Reflections in a Golden Eye ☐ Requiem for a Heavyweight ☐ Truth About Women, The ☐ Voyage of the Damned ☐ You're a Big Boy Now

Harrison, Rex ☐ Agony and the Ecstasy, The ☐ Anastasia: The Mystery Of Anna ☐ Anna and the King of Siam ☐ Ashanti: Land of No Mercy ☐ Blithe Spirit ☐ Citadel, The ☐ Cleopatra ☐ Constant Husband, The ☐ Crossed Swords ☐ Doctor Dolittle ☐ Escape ☐ Fifth Musketeer, The ☐ Flea in Her Ear, A ☐ Four Poster, The ☐ Foxes of Harrow, The ☐ Ghost and Mrs. Muir, The ☐ Happy Thieves ☐ Heartbreak House ☐ Honey Pot, The ☐ King Richard and the Crusaders ☐ Long Dark Hall, The ☐ Main Street to Broadway ☐ Major Barbara ☐ Midnight Lace ☐ Missing Ten Days ☐ My Fair Lady ☐ Night Train to Munich ☐ Notorious Gentleman ☐ Over the Moon ☐ Reluctant Debutante, The ☐ Sidewalks of London ☐ Staircase ☐ Storm in a Teacup ☐ Unfaithfully Yours ☐ Yellow Rolls-Royce, The

Harris, Phil ☐ Aristocats, The ☐ Buck Benny Rides Again ☐ Good-bye, My Lady ☐ I Love a Bandleader ☐ Jungle Book, The ☐ Man About Town ☐ Melody Cruise ☐ Robin Hood ☐ Rock-a-Doodle ☐ Wabash Avenue ☐ Wheeler Dealers, The ☐ Wild Blue Yonder, The

Harris, Richard ☐ Bible, The ☐ Camelot ☐ Caprice ☐ Cassandra Crossing, The ☐ Cromwell ☐ Deadly Trackers, The ☐ Echoes of a Summer ☐ Field, The ☐ Game for Vultures ☐ Golden Rendezvous ☐ Gulliver's Travels ☐ Guns of Navarone, The ☐ Hawaii ☐ Hero, The ☐ Heroes of Telemark, The ☐ Highpoint ☐ Juggernaut ☐ King of the Wind ☐ Long and the Short and the Tall, The ☐ Mack the Knife ☐ Maigret ☐ Major Dundee ☐ Man Called Horse, A ☐ Man in the Wilderness ☐ Martin's Day ☐ Molly Maguires, The ☐ Mutiny on the Bounty ☐ Night Fighters, The ☐ Orca—the Killer Whale ☐ Ravagers ☐ Red Desert ☐ Return of a Man Called Horse, The ☐ Robin and Marian ☐ Shake Hands with the Devil ☐ Silent Tongue ☐ Tarzan, the Ape Man ☐ This Sporting Life ☐ Triumphs of a Man Called Horse ☐ Unforgiven

□ Wild Geese, The □ Wreck of the Mary Deare, The □ Wrestling Ernest Hemingway

Hart, William S. □ Disciple, The □ Hell's Hinges □ Narrow Trail, The □ Tumbleweeds

Harvey, Laurence □ Alamo, The □ Butterfield 8 □ Ceremony, The □ Dandy in Aspic, A □ Darling □ Escape to the Sun □ Expresso Bongo □ Fight for Rome □ Girl Named Tamiko, A □ Good Die Young, The □ I Am a Camera □ I Believe In You □ Innocents in Paris □ King Richard and the Crusaders □ Last Roman, The □ Life at the Top □ Long and the Short and the Tall, The □ Manchurian Candidate, The □ Night Watch □ Of Human Bondage □ Outrage, The □ Romeo and Juliet □ Room at the Top □ She and He □ Silent Enemy, The □ Summer and Smoke □ Truth About Women, The □ Two Loves □ Walk on the Wild Side □ Wonderful World of the Brothers Grimm, The

Hasso, Signe □ Crisis □ Double Life, A □ Evita Peron □ House on 92nd Street □ I Never Promised You a Rose Garden □ Johnny Angel □ Magician, The □ Reflection of Fear, A □ Scandal in Paris, A □ Seventh Cross, The □ Story of Dr. Wassell, The □ To the Ends of the Earth □ Where There's Life

Hatfield, Hurd □ Boston Strangler, The □ Diary of a Chambermaid □ Dragon Seed □ King of Kings □ Lies of the Twins □ Mickey One □ Norliss Tapes, The □ Picture of Dorian Gray, The □ Unsuspected, The □ Von Richthofen and Brown

Hatton, Raymond □ Arizona Raiders, The □ Behind the Front □ Fighting Ranger, The □ Flame of the West □ Forbidden Trails □ Ghost Town Law □ Hell's Heroes □ Invasion of the Saucer Men □ Motorcycle Gang □ Quick Gun, The □ Requiem for a Gunfighter □ Rough Riders' Roundup

Hauer, Rutger □ Beans of Egypt, Maine, The □ Beyond Justice □ Blade Runner □ Blind Fury □ Blind Side □ Blood of Heroes, The □ Bloodhounds of Broadway □ Breed Apart, A □ Buffy the Vampire Slayer □ Chanel Solitaire □ Deadlock □ Escape from Sobibor □ Eureka □ Fatal Error □ Flesh + Blood □ Hitcher, The □ Inside the Third Reich □ Keetje Tippel □ Ladyhawke □ Legend of the Holy Drinker, The □ Mysteries □ Nighthawks □ Osterman Weekend, The □ Past Midnight □ Soldier of Orange □ Spetters □ Split Second □ Surviving the Game □ Turkish Delights □ Wanted: Dead or Alive □ Wilby Conspiracy, The

Hauser, Wings □ Beastmaster 2: Through the Portal of Time □ Bedroom Eyes 2 □ Bump in the Night □ Carpenter, The □ Code of Honor □ Homework □ Hostage □ In Between □ Killer's Edge, The □ L.A. Bounty □ Living to Die □ Marked for Murder □ Mind, Body and Soul □ Mutant □ Out Of Sight, Out Of Mind □ Pale Blood □ Siege of Firebase Gloria, The □ Street Asylum □ Tough Guys Don't Dance □ Vice Squad □ Watchers III, The

Havers, Nigel □ Burke and Wills □ Chariots of Fire □ Empire of the Sun □ Farewell to the King □ Passage to India, A □ Whistle Blower, The

Havoc, June □ Brewster's Millions □ Casanova in Burlesque □ Chicago Deadline □ Follow the Sun □ Four Jacks and a Jill □ Hi Diddle Diddle □ Iron Curtain, The □ Lady Possessed □ Mother Didn't Tell Me □ My Sister Eileen □ No Time for Love □ Once a Thief □ Red, Hot and Blue □ Return to Salem's Lot, A □ When My Baby Smiles at Me

Hawke, Ethan □ Alive □ Before Sunrise □ Dad □ Dead Poets Society □ Explorers □ Floundering □ Midnight Clear, A □ Mystery Date □ Reality Bites □ Rich in Love □ Waterland □ White Fang

Hawkins, Jack □ Adventures of Gerard, The □ Angels One Five □ Ben-Hur □ Black Rose, The □ Bonnie Prince Charlie □ Bridge on the River Kwai, The □ Crash of Silence □ Cruel Sea, The □ Decision Against Time □ Fallen Idol, The □ Fighting Pimpernel, The □ Five Finger Exercise □ Fortune in Diamonds □ Front Page Story □ Gideon of Scotland Yard □ Great Catherine □ Great Manhunt, The □ Guns at Batasi □ Home at Seven □ I Lived with You □ Intruder, The □ Jane Eyre □ Judith □ Lafayette □ Land of the Pharaohs □ Lawrence of Arabia □ League of Gentlemen, The □ Lord Jim □ Malta Story, The □ Masquerade □ Nicholas and Alexandra □ No Highway in the Sky □ Outpost in Malaya □ Peg of Old Drury □ Prisoner, The □ Rampage □ Seekers, The □ Shalako □ Small Back Room, The □ Third Key, The □ Third Secret, The □ Two Loves □ Waterloo □ Young Winston □ Zulu

Hawn, Goldie □ $ (Dollars) □ Best Friends □ Bird on a Wire □ Butterflies Are Free □ Cactus Flower □ CrissCross □ Death Becomes Her □ Deceived □ Duchess and the Dirtwater Fox, The □ Foul Play □ Girl from Petrovka, The □ Here's Looking At You, Warner Bros. □ Housesitter □ Lovers and Liars □ One and Only, Genuine, Original Family Band, The □ Overboard □ Private Benjamin □ Protocol □ Seems Like Old Times □ Shampoo □ Sugarland Express, The □ Swing Shift □ There's a Girl in My Soup □ Wildcats

Hayakawa, Sessue □ Big Wave, The □ Bridge on the River Kwai, The □ Daughter of the Dragon □ Geisha Boy, The □ Green Mansions □ Hell to Eternity □ Three Came Home □ Tokyo Joe

Hayden, Russell □ 'Neath the Canadian Skies □ Gambler's Choice □ Heritage of the Desert □ Law of the Pampas □ Marshal of Gunsmoke □ Mysterious Rider, The □ Partners of the Plains ☐ Riders of the Badlands ☐ Royal Mounted Patrol, The ☐ Showdown, The ☐ Silver City Raiders ☐ Silver on the Sage ☐ Sons of Adventure ☐ Three Men from Texas ☐ West of Tombstone

Hayden, Sterling ☐ 1900 ☐ Arrow in the Dust ☐ Asphalt Jungle, The ☐ Bahama Passage ☐ Battle Taxi ☐ Blaze of Noon ☐ Come-On, The ☐ Crime of Passion ☐ Crime Wave ☐ Deadly Strangers ☐ Dr. Strangelove or: How I Learned To Stop Worrying and Love the Bomb ☐ Eternal Sea, The ☐ Fighter Attack ☐ Final Programme,.The ☐ Five Steps to Danger ☐ Flaming Feather ☐ Flat Top ☐ Gas ☐ Golden Hawk, The ☐ Gun Battle at Monterey ☐ Hellgate ☐ Iron Sheriff, The ☐ Johnny Guitar ☐ Journey into Light ☐ Kansas Pacific ☐ Killing, The ☐ King of the Gypsies ☐ Last Command, The ☐ Long Goodbye, The ☐ Loving ☐ Manhandled ☐ Naked Alibi ☐ Outsider, The ☐ Prince Valiant ☐ Shotgun ☐ So Big ☐ Star, The ☐ Suddenly ☐ Take Me to Town ☐ Terror in a Texas Town ☐ Venom ☐ Zero Hour

Hayes, George "Gabby" ☐ Albuquerque ☐ Arizona Kid, The ☐ Badman's Territory ☐ Bells of Rosarita ☐ Dark Command ☐ Emil ☐ Frontiersman, The ☐ Heart of Arizona ☐ Heart of the Golden West ☐ Heart of the West ☐ Helldorado ☐ Home in Oklahoma ☐ Hopalong Cassidy Returns ☐ Hopalong Cassidy Rides Again ☐ Lawless Frontier ☐ Lawless Nineties, The ☐ Lucky Texan, The ☐ Man from Utah, The ☐ Melody Ranch ☐ Randy Rides Alone ☐ Red River Valley ☐ Return of the Bad Men ☐ Riders of Destiny ☐ Riders of the Desert ☐ Ridin' Down the Canyon ☐ Roll on Texas Moon ☐ Saga Of Death Valley ☐ Silver on the Sage ☐ Song of Arizona ☐ Song of the Trail ☐ Sons of the Pioneers ☐ Tall in the Saddle ☐ Texas Terror ☐ Trail Street ☐ Tucson Raiders ☐ Under Nevada Skies ☐ Utah ☐ Wall Street Cowboy ☐ West of the Divide ☐ Wyoming

Hayes, Helen ☐ Airport ☐ Anastasia ☐ Another Language ☐ Arrowsmith ☐ Candleshoe ☐ Caribbean Mystery, A ☐ Do Not Fold, Spindle or Mutilate ☐ Family Upside Down, A ☐ Farewell to Arms, A ☐ Herbie Rides Again ☐ Main Street to Broadway ☐ Murder with Mirrors ☐ My Son John ☐ One of Our Dinosaurs is Missing ☐ Sin of Madelon Claudet, The ☐ Stage Door Canteen ☐ What Every Woman Knows ☐ White Sister, The

Hayes, Isaac ☐ Acting on Impulse ☐ Escape from New York ☐ Final Judgment ☐ I'm Gonna Git You Sucka ☐ It Seemed Like a Good Idea at the Time ☐ Robin Hood: Men in Tights ☐ Truck Turner

Haymes, Dick ☐ All Ashore ☐ Carnival in Costa Rica ☐ Diamond Horseshoe ☐ Do You Love Me? ☐ Four Jills in a Jeep ☐ Irish Eyes Are Smiling ☐ One Touch of Venus ☐ Shocking Miss Pilgrim, The ☐ St. Benny the Dip ☐ State Fair ☐ Up In Central Park

Hays, Robert ☐ Airplane! ☐ Airplane II, The Sequel ☐ Cat's Eye ☐ Fall of the House of Usher, The ☐ Fifty/Fifty ☐ Girl, the Gold Watch and Everything, The ☐ Homeward Bound: The Incredible Journey ☐ Honeymoon Academy ☐ Murder by the Book ☐ Running Against Time ☐ Scandalous ☐ Take this Job and Shove It ☐ Trenchcoat

Hayward, Louis ☐ And Then There Were None ☐ Anthony Adverse ☐ Captain Pirate ☐ Christmas Kid, The ☐ Chuka ☐ Dance, Girl, Dance ☐ Duke of West Point, The ☐ Flame Within, The ☐ Fortunes of Captain Blood, The ☐ House by the River, The ☐ Ladies in Retirement ☐ Lady in the Iron Mask ☐ Man in the Iron Mask, The ☐ My Son, My Son ☐ Pirates of Capri, The ☐ Rage of Paris, The ☐ Repeat Performance ☐ Return of Monte Cristo, The ☐ Saint in New York, The ☐ Saint's Girl Friday, The ☐ Strange Woman, The ☐ Walk a Crooked Mile

Hayward, Susan ☐ Ada ☐ Adam Had Four Sons ☐ Among the Living ☐ And Now Tomorrow ☐ Back Street ☐ Beau Geste ☐ Canyon Passage ☐ Change of Heart ☐ Conqueror, The ☐ David and Bathsheba ☐ Deadline at Dawn ☐ Demetrius and the Gladiators ☐ Fighting Seabees, The ☐ Forest Rangers, The ☐ Garden of Evil ☐ Girls on Probation ☐ Hairy Ape, The ☐ Heat of Anger ☐ Honey Pot, The ☐ House of Strangers, The ☐ I Can Get It for You Wholesale ☐ I Married a Witch ☐ I Thank a Fool ☐ I Want To Live! ☐ I'd Climb the Highest Mountain ☐ I'll Cry Tomorrow ☐ Jack London ☐ Lost Moment, The ☐ Lusty Men, The ☐ Marriage-Go-Round, The ☐ My Foolish Heart ☐ President's Lady, The ☐ Rawhide ☐ Reap the Wild Wind ☐ Revengers, The ☐ Saxon Charm, The ☐ Say Goodbye, Maggie Cole ☐ Smash-Up, the Story of a Woman ☐ Snows of Kilimanjaro, The ☐ Soldier of Fortune ☐ Star Spangled Rhythm ☐ Stolen Hours, The ☐ Tap Roots ☐ They Won't Believe Me ☐ Thunder in the Sun ☐ Top Secret Affair ☐ Tulsa ☐ Untamed ☐ Valley of the Dolls ☐ Where Love Has Gone ☐ White Witch Doctor ☐ With a Song in My Heart ☐ Woman Obsessed

Hayworth, Rita ☐ Affair in Trinidad ☐ Affectionately Yours ☐ Angels over Broadway ☐ Blood and Sand ☐ Charlie Chan in Egypt ☐ Circus World ☐ Cover Girl ☐ Dante's Inferno ☐ Down to Earth ☐ Fire Down Below ☐ Gilda ☐ Happy Thieves ☐ Hit The Saddle ☐ Homicide Bureau ☐ Lady from Shanghai, The ☐ Lady in Question,The ☐ Lone Wolf Spy Hunt, The ☐ Loves of Carmen, The ☐ Miss Sadie Thompson ☐ Money Trap, The ☐ Music in My Heart ☐ My Gal Sal ☐ Only Angels Have Wings ☐ Pal Joey ☐ Poppy Is Also a Flower, The ☐ Renegade Ranger ☐ Salome ☐ Separate Tables ☐ Shadow, The

☐ Story on Page One, The ☐ Strawberry Blonde, The ☐ Susan and God ☐ Tales of Manhattan ☐ They Came to Cordura ☐ Tonight and Every Night ☐ Trouble in Texas ☐ You Were Never Lovelier ☐ You'll Never Get Rich

Headly, Glenne ☐ And the Band Played On ☐ Dick Tracy ☐ Dirty Rotten Scoundrels ☐ Making Mr. Right ☐ Mortal Thoughts ☐ Nadine ☐ Ordinary Magic ☐ Paperhouse ☐ Seize the Day

Heard, John ☐ After Hours ☐ Beaches ☐ Betrayed ☐ Between the Lines ☐ Big ☐ C.H.U.D. ☐ Cat People ☐ Cross of Fire ☐ Cutter's Way ☐ Dead Ahead: The Exxon Valdez Disaster ☐ Deceived ☐ End of Innocence, The ☐ First Love ☐ Head over Heels ☐ Heart Beat ☐ Heaven Help Us ☐ Home Alone ☐ Home Alone 2: Lost in New York ☐ Legs ☐ Milagro Beanfield War, The ☐ Mindwalk ☐ On the Yard ☐ Out on a Limb ☐ Package, The ☐ Pelican Brief, The ☐ Telephone, The ☐ Trip to Bountiful, The ☐ Waterland

Heckart, Eileen ☐ Bad Seed, The ☐ Burnt Offerings ☐ Bus Stop ☐ Butterflies Are Free ☐ F.B.I. Story, The—The FBI Versus Alvin Karpis, Public Enemy Number One ☐ F.D.R., The Last Year ☐ Heartbreak Ridge ☐ Heller in Pink Tights ☐ Hiding Place, The ☐ Hot Spell ☐ Miracle in the Rain ☐ My Six Loves ☐ No Way to Treat a Lady ☐ Somebody Up There Likes Me ☐ Up the Down Staircase ☐ Zandy's Bride

Hedren, Tippi ☐ Birds, The ☐ Countess from Hong Kong, A ☐ Foxfire Light ☐ Harrad Experiment, The ☐ In the Cold of the Night ☐ Inevitable Grace ☐ Marnie

Heflin, Van ☐ 3:10 to Yuma ☐ Act of Violence ☐ Airport ☐ B. F.'s Daughter ☐ Back Door to Heaven ☐ Battle Cry ☐ Big Bounce, The ☐ Black Widow ☐ Count Three and Pray ☐ East Side, West Side ☐ Feminine Touch, The ☐ Five Branded Women ☐ Flight from Glory ☐ Golden Mask, The ☐ Grand Central Murder ☐ Green Dolphin Street ☐ Gunman's Walk ☐ H.M. Pulham, Esq. ☐ Johnny Eager ☐ Kid Glove Killer ☐ Madame Bovary ☐ Man Outside, The ☐ My Son John ☐ Once a Thief ☐ Patterns ☐ Possessed ☐ Presenting Lily Mars ☐ Prowler, The ☐ Raid, The ☐ Santa Fe Trail ☐ Seven Sweethearts ☐ Shane ☐ Stagecoach ☐ Strange Love of Martha Ivers, The ☐ Tap Roots ☐ Tempest ☐ Tennessee Johnson ☐ They Came to Cordura ☐ Three Musketeers, The ☐ Till the Clouds Roll By ☐ Under Ten Flags ☐ Weekend With Father ☐ Woman's World

Helmond, Katherine ☐ Autobiography of Miss Jane Pittman ☐ Baby Blue Marine ☐ Brazil ☐ Diary of a Teenage Hitchhiker ☐ Family Nobody Wanted, The ☐ First 36 Hours of Dr. Durant, The ☐ Lady in White ☐ Larry ☐ Overboard ☐ Time Bandits

Hemingway, Margaux ☐ Killer Fish ☐ Killing Machine ☐ Lipstick ☐ Over the Brooklyn Bridge ☐ They Call Me Bruce

Hemingway, Mariel ☐ Creator ☐ Delirious ☐ Falling from Grace ☐ I Want to Keep My Baby ☐ Into the Badlands ☐ Lipstick ☐ Manhattan ☐ Mean Season, The ☐ Personal Best ☐ Star 80 ☐ Suicide Club, The ☐ Superman 4: The Quest for Peace

Hemmings, David ☐ Alfred the Great ☐ Barbarella ☐ Be My Guest ☐ Beyond Reasonable Doubt ☐ Blowup ☐ Camelot ☐ Charge of the Light Brigade, The ☐ Charlie Muffin ☐ Dario Argento's World of Horror ☐ Deep Red ☐ Disappearance, The ☐ Eye of the Devil ☐ Fragment of Fear ☐ Heart Within, The ☐ Islands in the Stream ☐ Juggernaut ☐ Man, Woman and Child ☐ Mr. Quilp ☐ Murder by Decree ☐ Only When I Larf ☐ Rainbow, The ☐ Turn of the Screw, The ☐ Unman, Wittering and Zigo

Hendrix, Wanda ☐ Admiral Was a Lady, The ☐ Black Dakotas, The ☐ Boy Who Caught a Crook ☐ Captain Carey, U.S.A. ☐ Golden Mask, The ☐ Highway Dragnet ☐ Highwayman, The ☐ Johnny Cool ☐ Miss Tatlock's Millions ☐ Prince of Foxes ☐ Ride the Pink Horse ☐ Saddle Tramp ☐ Sea of Lost Ships ☐ Welcome Stranger

Henie, Sonja ☐ Everything Happens at Night ☐ Happy Landing ☐ Iceland ☐ It's a Pleasure! ☐ My Lucky Star ☐ One in a Million ☐ Second Fiddle ☐ Sun Valley Serenade ☐ Thin Ice

Henner, Marilu ☐ Between the Lines ☐ Bloodbrothers ☐ Cannonball Run II ☐ Chains of Gold ☐ Grown Ups ☐ Hammett ☐ Johnny Dangerously ☐ L.A. Story ☐ Ladykillers ☐ Love with a Perfect Stranger ☐ Man Who Loved Women, The ☐ Noises Off ☐ Perfect ☐ Rustlers' Rhapsody

Henreid, Paul ☐ Between Two Worlds ☐ Casablanca ☐ Conspirators, The ☐ Deception ☐ Devotion ☐ For Men Only ☐ Four Horsemen of the Apocalypse ☐ Goodbye, Mr. Chips ☐ Holiday for Lovers ☐ In Our Time ☐ Joan of Paris ☐ Last of the Buccaneers, The ☐ Madwoman of Chaillot, The ☐ Man in Hiding ☐ Meet Me in Las Vegas ☐ Never So Few ☐ Night Train to Munich ☐ Now, Voyager ☐ Pardon My French ☐ Scar, The ☐ Siren of Bagdad ☐ So Young, So Bad ☐ Song of Love ☐ Spanish Main, The ☐ Stolen Face, A ☐ Ten Thousand Bedrooms

Henry, Buck ☐ Defending Your Life ☐ Eating Raoul ☐ Gloria ☐ Grumpy Old Men ☐ Is There Sex After Death? ☐ Man Who Fell to Earth, The ☐ Taking Off

Hepburn, Audrey ☐ Always ☐ Bloodline ☐ Breakfast at Tiffany's ☐ Charade ☐ Children's Hour, The ☐ Funny Face ☐ Green Mansions ☐ How to Steal a Million ☐ Love Among Thieves ☐ Love in the Afternoon ☐ My Fair Lady ☐ Nun's Story, The

☐ Paris—when It Sizzles ☐ Robin and Marian ☐ Roman Holiday ☐ Sabrina ☐ They All Laughed ☐ Two for the Road ☐ Unforgiven, The ☐ Wait Until Dark ☐ War and Peace ☐ Young Wives' Tale

Hepburn, Katharine ☐ Adam's Rib ☐ African Queen, The ☐ Alice Adams ☐ Bill of Divorcement, A ☐ Break of Hearts ☐ Bringing Up Baby ☐ Christopher Strong ☐ Corn Is Green, The ☐ Delicate Balance, A ☐ Desk Set ☐ Dragon Seed ☐ Glass Menagerie, The ☐ Grace Quigley ☐ Guess Who's Coming to Dinner ☐ Holiday ☐ Iron Petticoat, The ☐ Keeper of the Flame ☐ Laura Lansing Slept Here ☐ Lion in Winter, The ☐ Little Minister, The ☐ Little Women ☐ Long Day's Journey into Night ☐ Love Affair ☐ Love Among the Ruins ☐ Madwoman of Chaillot, The ☐ Man Upstairs, The ☐ Mary of Scotland ☐ Morning Glory ☐ Mrs. Delafield Wants to Marry ☐ Olly, Olly, Oxen Free ☐ On Golden Pond ☐ Pat and Mike ☐ Philadelphia Story, The ☐ Quality Street ☐ Rainmaker, The ☐ Rooster Cogburn ☐ Sea of Grass, The ☐ Song of Love ☐ Spitfire ☐ Stage Door ☐ Stage Door Canteen ☐ State of the Union ☐ Suddenly, Last Summer ☐ Summertime ☐ Sylvia Scarlett ☐ This Can't Be Love ☐ Trojan Women, The ☐ Undercurrent ☐ Without Love ☐ Woman of the Year ☐ Woman Rebels, A

Herbert, Hugh ☐ Black Cat, The ☐ Danger Lights ☐ Eternally Yours ☐ Ever Since Venus ☐ Faithless ☐ Fashions ☐ Fog Over Frisco ☐ Four's a Crowd ☐ Friends and Lovers ☐ Hollywood Hotel ☐ It's a Great Life ☐ Meet the Chump ☐ Midsummer Night's Dream, A ☐ Million Dollar Legs ☐ On Our Merry Way ☐ One Rainy Afternoon ☐ Perfect Specimen, The ☐ So This Is New York ☐ Song is Born, A ☐ Sweet Adeline ☐ Traveling Saleslady ☐ Wonder Bar

Herrmann, Edward ☐ Big Business ☐ Born Yesterday ☐ Compromising Positions ☐ Eleanor and Franklin ☐ Eleanor and Franklin: The White House Years ☐ Foreign Student ☐ Freedom Road ☐ Harry's War ☐ Little Sex, A ☐ Love Affair, A: The Eleanor and Lou Gehrig Story ☐ Memorial Day ☐ Mrs. Soffel ☐ Murrow ☐ North Avenue Irregulars, The ☐ Overboard ☐ Reds ☐ Richie Rich ☐ Take Down

Hershey, Barbara ☐ Americana ☐ Angel on My Shoulder ☐ Baby Maker, The ☐ Beaches ☐ Boxcar Bertha ☐ Dangerous Woman, A ☐ Dealing: or The Berkeley-to-Boston Forty-Brick Lost-Bag Blues ☐ Defenseless ☐ Dirty Knight's Work ☐ Entity, The ☐ Falling Down ☐ Flood! ☐ Hannah and Her Sisters ☐ Heaven with a Gun ☐ Hoosiers ☐ Killing in a Small Town, A ☐ Last Hard Men, The ☐ Last Summer ☐ Last Temptation of Christ, The ☐ Liberation of L. B. Jones, The ☐ My Wicked, Wicked Ways—The Legend of Errol Flynn ☐ Natural, The ☐ Paris Trout ☐ Public Eye, The ☐ Right Stuff, The ☐ Shy People ☐ Splitting Heirs ☐ Stunt Man, The ☐ Swing Kids ☐ Take this Job and Shove It ☐ Tin Men ☐ Tune In Tomorrow ☐ With Six You Get Eggroll ☐ World Apart, A

Hersholt, Jean ☐ Beast of The City, The ☐ Break of Hearts ☐ Cat and the Fiddle, The ☐ Country Doctor, The ☐ Dinner at Eight ☐ Don Q, Son of Zorro ☐ Emma ☐ Flesh ☐ Fountain, The ☐ Four Horsemen of the Apocalypse, The ☐ Grand Hotel ☐ Greed ☐ Heidi ☐ His Brother's Wife ☐ I'll Give a Million ☐ Mark of the Vampire ☐ Mask of Fu Manchu, The ☐ Meet Dr. Christian ☐ Melody for Three ☐ Men in White ☐ Mr. Moto in Danger Island ☐ Night Court ☐ One in a Million ☐ Phantom of Paris, The ☐ Reunion ☐ Run for Cover ☐ Seventh Heaven ☐ Sin of Madelon Claudet, The ☐ Student Prince in Old Heidelberg, The ☐ Susan Lenox: Her Fall and Rise ☐ Viennese Nights

Hervey, Irene ☐ Boys from Syracuse, The ☐ Charlie Chan in Shanghai ☐ Dude Ranger, The ☐ East Side of Heaven ☐ Hard Rock Harrigan ☐ Manhandled ☐ Missing Evidence ☐ Mr. Peabody and the Mermaid ☐ Night Monster ☐ Three Godfathers

Hesseman, Howard ☐ Call Me Anna ☐ Clue ☐ Doctor Detroit ☐ Flight of the Navigator ☐ Inside Out ☐ More Than Friends ☐ Murder in New Hampshire: The Pamela Smart Story ☐ Private Lessons ☐ Steelyard Blues ☐ Tunnelvision ☐ Victims

Heston, Charlton ☐ 55 Days at Peking ☐ Agony and the Ecstasy, The ☐ Airport '75 ☐ Almost an Angel ☐ Antony and Cleopatra ☐ Arrowhead ☐ Awakening, The ☐ Bad For Each Other ☐ Ben-Hur ☐ Beneath the Planet of the Apes ☐ Big Country, The ☐ Buccaneer, The ☐ Call of the Wild ☐ Chiefs ☐ Counterpoint ☐ Crossed Swords ☐ Crucifer of Blood, The ☐ Dark City ☐ Diamond Head ☐ Earthquake ☐ El Cid ☐ Far Horizons, The ☐ Four Musketeers, The ☐ Gray Lady Down ☐ Greatest Show on Earth, The ☐ Greatest Story Ever Told, The ☐ Hawaiians, The ☐ In the Mouth of Madness ☐ In the Mouth of Madness ☐ Julius Caesar ☐ Khartoum ☐ Last Hard Men, The ☐ Little Kidnappers, The ☐ Lucy Gallant ☐ Major Dundee ☐ Man for All Seasons, A ☐ Midway ☐ Mother Lode ☐ Mountain Men, The ☐ Nairobi Affair ☐ Naked Jungle, The ☐ Number One ☐ Omega Man, The ☐ Pigeon That Took Rome, The ☐ Planet of the Apes ☐ Pony Express ☐ President's Lady, The ☐ Private War of Major Benson, The ☐ Proud Men ☐ Ruby Gentry ☐ Savage, The ☐ Secret of the Incas ☐ Skyjacked ☐ Solar Crisis ☐ Soylent Green ☐ Ten Commandments, The ☐ Three Musketeers, The ☐ Three Violent People ☐ Touch of Evil ☐ Treasure Island ☐ Two Minute Warning ☐ War Lord, The ☐ Will Penny ☐ Wreck of the Mary Deare, The

Hickey, William ☐ Any Man's Death ☐ Happy Birthday, Wanda June ☐ Jerky Boys, The ☐ Mob Boss ☐ My Blue Heaven ☐ Name of the Rose, The ☐ National Lampoon's Christmas Vacation ☐ Nightmare Before Christmas, The ☐ Pink Cadillac ☐ Prizzi's Honor ☐ Runestone, The ☐ Sea of Love ☐ Tales From the Darkside: The Movie

Hill, Arthur ☐ Andromeda Strain, The ☐ Angel Dusted ☐ Chairman, The ☐ Christmas Eve ☐ Death Be Not Proud ☐ Don't Let the Angels Fall ☐ Futureworld ☐ In the Cool of the Day ☐ Judge Horton and The Scottsboro Boys ☐ Killer Elite, The ☐ Little Romance, A ☐ Love Leads the Way ☐ Making Love ☐ Murder in Space ☐ Ordeal ☐ Other Man, The ☐ Rabbit, Run ☐ Tales of the Unexpected ☐ Young Doctors, The

Hiller, Wendy ☐ Cat and the Canary, The ☐ David Copperfield ☐ How to Murder a Rich Uncle ☐ I Know Where I'm Going ☐ Lonely Passion of Judith Hearne, The ☐ Major Barbara ☐ Making Love ☐ Man for All Seasons, A ☐ Murder on the Orient Express ☐ Outcast of the Islands ☐ Pygmalion ☐ Separate Tables ☐ Something of Value ☐ Sons and Lovers ☐ Toys in the Attic ☐ Voyage of the Damned ☐ Witness for the Prosecution

Hillerman, John ☐ Chinatown ☐ Ellery Queen ☐ Hands of a Murderer ☐ Invasion of Johnson County, The ☐ Lucky Lady ☐ Marathon ☐ Nickel Ride, The

Hilliard, Harriet ☐ Cocoanut Grove ☐ Falcon Strikes Back, The ☐ Hi, Good Lookin' ☐ Juke Box Jenny ☐ Life of the Party, The ☐ New Faces of 1937 ☐ Sweetheart of the Campus

Hilton-Jacobs, Lawrence ☐ Angels of the City ☐ Annihilators, The ☐ Chance ☐ Cooley High ☐ East L.A. Warriors ☐ Jacksons: An American Dream, The ☐ Killcrazy ☐ L.A. Heat ☐ L.A. Vice ☐ Quiet Fire

Hinds, Samuel S. ☐ Frisco Sal ☐ Gabriel over the White House ☐ I'll Remember April ☐ In Person ☐ It's a Date ☐ It's a Wonderful Life ☐ Man Made Monster ☐ Men in White ☐ Mighty Treve, The ☐ Raven, The ☐ Secret of Dr. Kildare, The ☐ Sequoia ☐ Young Dr. Kildare

Hines, Gregory ☐ Cotton Club, The ☐ Deal of the Century ☐ Eubie! ☐ Eve of Destruction ☐ History of the World Part I ☐ Muppets Take Manhattan, The ☐ Off Limits ☐ Rage in Harlem, A ☐ Renaissance Man ☐ Running Scared ☐ T Bone N Weasel ☐ Tap ☐ White Lie ☐ White Nights ☐ Wolfen

Hingle, Pat ☐ All the Way Home ☐ Batman ☐ Bloody Mama ☐ Brewster's Millions ☐ Carey Treatment, The ☐ Citizen Cohn ☐ Elvis ☐ Everybody's Baby: The Rescue of Jessica McClure ☐ Falcon and the Snowman, The ☐ Gauntlet, The ☐ Grifters, The ☐ Hang 'em High ☐ Invitation to a Gunfighter ☐ Land Before Time, The ☐ LBJ: The Early Years ☐ Lightning Jack ☐ Manhunt for Claude Dallas ☐ Maximum Overdrive ☐ No Down Payment ☐ Noon Wine ☐ Norma Rae ☐ Norwood ☐ Not of This World ☐ Of Mice and Men ☐ Rape of Richard Beck, The ☐ Running Wild ☐ Splendor in the Grass ☐ Stranger on My Land ☐ Sudden Impact ☐ Ugly American, The

Hirsch, Judd ☐ Fear on Trial ☐ First Steps ☐ Fury On Wheels ☐ Goodbye People, The ☐ Great Escape 2: The Untold Story, The ☐ King of the Gypsies ☐ Legend of Valentino, The ☐ Marriage Is Alive and Well ☐ Ordinary People ☐ Running on Empty ☐ Sooner or Later ☐ Teachers

Hobson, Valerie ☐ Adventures of Tartu ☐ Bride of Frankenstein, The ☐ Clouds over Europe ☐ Contraband ☐ Drums ☐ Great Expectations ☐ Interrupted Journey ☐ Kind Hearts and Coronets ☐ Lovers, Happy Lovers ☐ No Escape ☐ Passionate Sentry, The ☐ Promoter, The ☐ Rocking Horse Winner, The ☐ Spy in Black, The ☐ This Man in Paris ☐ This Man Is News ☐ Tonight at 8:30 ☐ Werewolf of London

Hodiak, John ☐ Across the Wide Missouri ☐ Ambush ☐ Ambush at Tomahawk Gap ☐ Arnelo Affair, The ☐ Battle Zone ☐ Battleground ☐ Bell for Adano, A ☐ Bribe, The ☐ Command Decision ☐ Desert Fury ☐ Harvey Girls, The ☐ Homecoming ☐ Lady without Passport, A ☐ Lifeboat ☐ Love from a Stranger ☐ Maisie Goes to Reno ☐ Marriage Is a Private Affair ☐ Miniver Story, The ☐ Night into Morning ☐ On the Threshold of Space ☐ People Against O'Hara, The ☐ Sellout, The ☐ Somewhere in the Night ☐ Song of Russia ☐ Sunday Dinner for a Soldier ☐ Trial

Hoffman, Dustin ☐ Agatha ☐ Alfredo, Alfredo ☐ All the President's Men ☐ Billy Bathgate ☐ Death of a Salesman ☐ Dick Tracy ☐ Family Business ☐ Graduate, The ☐ Hero ☐ Hook ☐ Ishtar ☐ John and Mary ☐ Kramer vs. Kramer ☐ Lenny ☐ Little Big Man ☐ Madigan's Million ☐ Marathon Man ☐ Midnight Cowboy ☐ Outbreak ☐ Papillon ☐ Rain Man ☐ Straight Time ☐ Straw Dogs ☐ Tootsie ☐ Who Is Harry Kellerman and Why Is He Saying Those Terrible Things About Me?

Hogan, Paul ☐ Almost an Angel ☐ Anzacs: The War Down Under ☐ Crocodile Dundee ☐ Crocodile Dundee II ☐ Lightning Jack

Holbrook, Hal ☐ All the President's Men ☐ Capricorn One ☐ Creepshow ☐ Day One ☐ Dress Gray ☐ Firm, The ☐ Fletch Lives ☐ Fog, The ☐ Girl from Petrovka, The ☐ Girls Nite Out ☐ Great White Hope, The ☐ Group, The ☐ I'll Be Home for Christmas ☐ Julia ☐ Kidnapping of the President, The ☐ Killing of Randy Webster, The ☐ Magnum Force ☐ Mario Puzo's "The Fortunate Pilgrim" ☐ Midway ☐ Off the Minnesota Strip ☐ People Next Door, The ☐ Sorry, Wrong Number ☐ Star Chamber, The ☐ That Certain Summer ☐ They Only Kill Their Masters ☐ Unholy, The ☐ Wild in the Streets

Holden, Fay ☐ Andy Hardy Comes Home ☐ Andy Hardy Gets Spring Fever ☐ Andy Hardy Meets Debutante ☐ Andy Hardy's Blonde Trouble ☐ Andy Hardy's Private Secretary ☐ Courtship of Andy Hardy, The ☐ Dr. Kildare's Wedding Day ☐ Exclusive ☐ Hardys Ride High, The ☐ Internes Can't Take Money ☐ Judge Hardy and Son ☐ Judge Hardy's Children ☐ Life Begins for Andy Hardy ☐ Love Finds Andy Hardy ☐ Out West with the Hardys ☐ Samson and Delilah ☐ Sergeant Madden ☐ Whispering Smith ☐ You're Only Young Once

Holden, William ☐ 21 Hours at Munich ☐ Alvarez Kelly ☐ Apartment for Peggy ☐ Arizona ☐ Ashanti: Land of No Mercy ☐ Blaze of Noon ☐ Blue Knight, The ☐ Boots Malone ☐ Born Yesterday ☐ Breezy ☐ Bridge on the River Kwai, The ☐ Bridges at Toko-Ri, The ☐ Casino Royale ☐ Christmas Tree, The ☐ Counterfeit Traitor, The ☐ Country Girl, The ☐ Damien—Omen II ☐ Dark Past, The ☐ Dear Ruth ☐ Dear Wife ☐ Devil's Brigade, The ☐ Earthling, The ☐ Escape from Fort Bravo ☐ Executive Suite ☐ Father Is a Bachelor ☐ Fedora ☐ Fleet's In, The ☐ Force of Arms ☐ Forever Female ☐ Golden Boy ☐ Horse Soldiers, The ☐ I Wanted Wings ☐ Invisible Stripes ☐ Key, The ☐ Lion, The ☐ Love Is a Many Splendored Thing ☐ Man from Colorado, The ☐ Meet the Stewarts ☐ Miss Grant Takes Richmond ☐ Moon Is Blue, The ☐ Network ☐ Open Season ☐ Our Town ☐ Paris—when It Sizzles ☐ Picnic ☐ Proud and Profane, The ☐ Rachel and the Stranger ☐ Remarkable Andrew, The ☐ Revengers, The ☐ S.O.B. ☐ Sabrina ☐ Satan Never Sleeps ☐ Stalag 17 ☐ Streets of Laredo ☐ Submarine Command ☐ Sunset Boulevard ☐ Texas ☐ Those Were the Days ☐ Toward the Unknown ☐ Towering Inferno, The ☐ Trespasser, The ☐ Turning Point, The ☐ Union Station ☐ When Time Ran Out . . . ☐ Wild Bunch, The ☐ Wild Rovers ☐ World of Suzie Wong, The

Holliday, Judy ☐ Adam's Rib ☐ Bells Are Ringing ☐ Born Yesterday ☐ Full of Life ☐ It Should Happen to You ☐ Marrying Kind, The ☐ Phffft! ☐ Solid Gold Cadillac, The ☐ Winged Victory

Holliman, Earl ☐ Alexander: The Other Side of Dawn ☐ Alias Smith and Jones ☐ Anzio ☐ Biscuit Eater, The ☐ Burning Hills, The ☐ Forbidden Planet ☐ I Died a Thousand Times ☐ I Love You, Goodbye ☐ Last Train From Gun Hill ☐ Rainmaker, The ☐ Smoke ☐ Sons of Katie Elder, The ☐ Summer and Smoke ☐ Tennessee Champ ☐ Tribes ☐ Visit to a Small Planet

Holloway, Stanley ☐ Alligator Named Daisy, An ☐ Beggar's Opera, The ☐ Brief Encounter ☐ Champagne Charlie ☐ Flight of the Doves ☐ Hamlet ☐ Immortal Battalion, The ☐ Lady Godiva Rides Again ☐ Lavender Hill Mob, The ☐ Lily of Killarney ☐ Magic Box, The ☐ Meet Mr. Lucifer ☐ Mrs. Brown, You've Got a Lovely Daughter ☐ My Fair Lady ☐ Nicholas Nickleby ☐ No Love for Johnnie ☐ No Trees in the Street ☐ Operation Snafu ☐ Passport to Pimlico ☐ Perfect Woman, The ☐ Sandwich Man, The ☐ Silk Noose, The ☐ Sing As We Go ☐ Ten Little Indians ☐ This Happy Breed ☐ Titfield Thunderbolt, The ☐ Tonight at 8:30

Holloway, Sterling ☐ Advice to the Lovelorn ☐ Alice in Wonderland ☐ Aristocats, The ☐ Beautiful Blonde from Bashful Bend, The ☐ Blondie Johnson ☐ Cheers for Miss Bishop ☐ Doctor Rhythm ☐ Doubting Thomas ☐ Dr. Rhythm ☐ Elmer the Great ☐ Fast Workers ☐ Hell Below ☐ Jungle Book, The ☐ Kentucky Rifle ☐ Live a Little, Love a Little ☐ Remember the Night ☐ Robin of Texas ☐ Shake, Rattle and Rock ☐ Sioux City Sue ☐ Super Seal ☐ Three Caballeros, The ☐ Wild Boys of the Road

Holm, Celeste ☐ All About Eve ☐ Bachelor Flat ☐ Bittersweet Love ☐ Carnival in Costa Rica ☐ Champagne for Caesar ☐ Chicken Every Sunday ☐ Cinderella ☐ Come to the Stable ☐ Everybody Does It ☐ Gentleman's Agreement ☐ High Society ☐ Midnight Lace ☐ Murder by the Book ☐ Polly ☐ Road House ☐ Snake Pit, The ☐ Tender Trap, The ☐ Three Little Girls in Blue ☐ Three Men and a Baby ☐ Tom Sawyer

Holm, Ian ☐ Alien ☐ All Quiet on the Western Front ☐ Another Woman ☐ Blue Ice ☐ Bofors Gun, The ☐ Brazil ☐ Chariots of Fire ☐ Dance With a Stranger ☐ DreamChild ☐ Endless Game, The ☐ Fixer, The ☐ Greystoke: The Legend of Tarzan, Lord of the Apes ☐ Hamlet ☐ Henry V ☐ Homecoming, The ☐ Kafka ☐ Madness of King George, The ☐ Man in the Iron Mask ☐ March or Die ☐ Mary, Queen of Scots ☐ Midsummer Night's Dream, A ☐ Naked Lunch ☐ Severed Head, A ☐ Singleton's Pluck ☐ Time Bandits ☐ Wetherby

Holt, Jack ☐ Behind the Mask ☐ Dirigible ☐ Donovan Affair, The ☐ End of the Trail ☐ Flight ☐ Flight into Nowhere ☐ Flight to Nowhere ☐ My Pal Trigger ☐ San Francisco ☐ Strawberry Roan, The ☐ They Were Expendable ☐ Trail of Robin Hood ☐ Whirlpool ☐ Wild Frontier, The

Holt, Tim ☐ 5th Avenue Girl ☐ Back Street ☐ Fighting Frontier ☐ Hitler's Children ☐ I Met My Love Again ☐ Indian Agent ☐ Magnificent Ambersons, The ☐ Monster That Challenged the World, The ☐ My Darling Clementine ☐ Mysterious Desperado, The ☐ Overland Telegraph ☐ Renegade Ranger ☐ Riders of the Range ☐ Riding the Wind

☐ Robbers of the Range ☐ Stella Dallas ☐ Swiss Family Robinson ☐ Treasure of the Sierra Madre, The ☐ Under the Tonto Rim

Homolka, Oscar ☐ Anna Lucasta ☐ Ball of Fire ☐ Billion Dollar Brain ☐ Code of Scotland Yard ☐ Comrade X ☐ Ebb Tide ☐ Everything Is Thunder ☐ Executioner, The ☐ Farewell to Arms, A ☐ Funeral in Berlin ☐ Hostages ☐ I Remember Mama ☐ Key, The ☐ Madwoman of Chaillot, The ☐ Mission to Moscow ☐ Mooncussers ☐ Mr. Potts Goes to Moscow ☐ Mr. Sardonicus ☐ One of Our Own ☐ Rage in Heaven ☐ Rhodes ☐ Sabotage ☐ Strange Case of Dr. Jekyll And Mr. Hyde, The ☐ White Tower, The ☐ Wonderful World of the Brothers Grimm, The

Hong, James ☐ Big Trouble in Little China ☐ Merlin ☐ Missing in Action ☐ Shadowzone ☐ Vineyard, The ☐ Wayne's World 2

Hooks, Kevin ☐ Aaron Loves Angela ☐ Can You Hear the Laughter? The Story of Freddie Prinze ☐ Greatest Thing That Almost Happened, The ☐ Just an Old Sweet Song ☐ Sounder

Hooks, Robert ☐ Aaron Loves Angela ☐ Hollow Image ☐ Hurry Sundown ☐ Just an Old Sweet Song ☐ Last of the Mobile Hot-Shots ☐ Madame X ☐ Sister, Sister ☐ Sophisticated Gents, The ☐ Supercarrier ☐ Woman Called Moses, A

Hope, Bob ☐ Alias Jesse James ☐ Bachelor in Paradise ☐ Beau James ☐ Big Broadcast of 1938, The ☐ Boy, Did I Get a Wrong Number! ☐ Call Me Bwana ☐ Cancel My Reservation ☐ Casanova's Big Night ☐ Cat and the Canary, The ☐ Caught in the Draft ☐ College Swing ☐ Critic's Choice ☐ Eight on the Lam ☐ Facts of Life, The ☐ Fancy Pants ☐ Ghost Breakers, The ☐ Give Me a Sailor ☐ Global Affair, A ☐ Great Lover, The ☐ Here Come the Girls ☐ How to Commit Marriage ☐ I'll Take Sweden ☐ Iron Petticoat, The ☐ Lemon Drop Kid, The ☐ Let's Face It ☐ Louisiana Purchase ☐ Masterpiece of Murder, A ☐ Milton Berle's Mad World of Comedy ☐ Monsieur Beaucaire ☐ My Favorite Blonde ☐ My Favorite Brunette ☐ My Favorite Spy ☐ Never Say Die ☐ Nothing But the Truth ☐ Off Limits ☐ Paleface, The ☐ Paris Holiday ☐ Princess and the Pirate, The ☐ Private Navy of Sgt. O'Farrell, The ☐ Road to Bali ☐ Road to Hong Kong, The ☐ Road to Morocco ☐ Road to Rio ☐ Road to Singapore ☐ Road to Utopia ☐ Road to Zanzibar ☐ Seven Little Foys, The ☐ Son of Paleface ☐ Sorrowful Jones ☐ Star Spangled Rhythm ☐ That Certain Feeling ☐ They Got Me Covered ☐ Where There's Life

Hopkins, Anthony ☐ 84 Charing Cross Road ☐ All Creatures Great and Small ☐ Arch of Triumph ☐ Audrey Rose ☐ Bounty, The ☐ Bram Stoker's Dracula ☐ Bridge Too Far, A ☐ Bunker, The ☐ Change of Seasons, A ☐ Chaplin ☐ Chorus of Disapproval, A ☐ Dark Victory ☐ Dawning, The ☐ Desperate Hours ☐ Doll's House, A ☐ Efficiency Expert, The ☐ Elephant Man, The ☐ Freejack ☐ Girl from Petrovka, The ☐ Good Father, The ☐ Guilty Conscience, The ☐ Hamlet ☐ Howards End ☐ Hunchback of Notre Dame, The ☐ International Velvet ☐ Juggernaut ☐ Legends of the Fall ☐ Lindbergh Kidnapping Case, The ☐ Lion in Winter, The ☐ Looking Glass War, The ☐ Magic ☐ Married Man, A ☐ Mayflower: The Pilgrims' Adventure ☐ Mussolini and I ☐ One Man's War ☐ Peter and Paul ☐ Remains of the Day ☐ Road to Wellville, The ☐ Shadowlands ☐ Silence of the Lambs, The ☐ Tenth Man, The

Hopkins, Bo ☐ Ballad of Little Jo, The ☐ Big Bad John ☐ Bounty Hunter, The ☐ Culpepper Cattle Co., The ☐ Fifth Floor, The ☐ Final Alliance ☐ Invasion of Johnson County, The ☐ Kansas City Massacre ☐ Killer Elite, The ☐ Man Who Loved Cat Dancing, The ☐ Midnight Express ☐ More American Graffiti ☐ Mutant ☐ Nickel Ride, The ☐ Posse ☐ Small Town in Texas, A ☐ Smoky Mountain Christmas, A ☐ White Lightning

Hopkins, Miriam ☐ All of Me ☐ Barbary Coast ☐ Becky Sharp ☐ Carrie ☐ Chase, The ☐ Children's Hour, The ☐ Design for Living ☐ Dr. Jekyll and Mr. Hyde ☐ Fast and Loose ☐ Gentleman After Dark, A ☐ Heiress, The ☐ Lady with Red Hair, The ☐ Old Acquaintance ☐ Old Maid, The ☐ Outcasts of Poker Flat, The ☐ Richest Girl in the World, The ☐ She Loves Me Not ☐ Smiling Lieutenant, The ☐ Story of Temple Drake, The ☐ Stranger's Return, The ☐ These Three ☐ Trouble in Paradise ☐ Virginia City

Hopper, Dennis ☐ American Friend, The ☐ Backtrack ☐ Black Widow ☐ Blood Red ☐ Blue Velvet ☐ Boiling Point ☐ Chattahoochee ☐ Cool Hand Luke ☐ Easy Rider ☐ Eye of the Storm ☐ Flashback ☐ From Hell to Texas ☐ Glory Stompers, The ☐ Hoosiers ☐ Human Highway ☐ Indian Runner, The ☐ Inside Man, The ☐ Key Witness ☐ Kid Blue ☐ King of the Mountain ☐ Last Movie, The ☐ Let It Rock ☐ Mad Dog Morgan ☐ My Science Project ☐ Nails ☐ Night Tide ☐ Osterman Weekend, The ☐ Out of the Blue ☐ Paris Trout ☐ Pick-up Artist, The ☐ Queen of Blood ☐ Rebel Without a Cause ☐ Red Rock West ☐ Riders of the Storm ☐ River's Edge ☐ Rumble Fish ☐ Speed ☐ Straight to Hell ☐ Sunset Heat ☐ Super Mario Bros. ☐ Superstar: The Life and Times of Andy Warhol ☐ Texas Chainsaw Massacre, The—Part 2 ☐ Trip, The ☐ True Grit ☐ True Romance

Hopper, Hedda ☐ As You Desire Me ☐ Barbarian, The ☐ Beauty for Sale ☐ Don Juan ☐ Downstairs ☐ Dracula's Daughter ☐ Flying High ☐ Holiday ☐ I Wanted Wings ☐ Life with Henry ☐ Little Man, What Now?

☐ Maid's Night Out ☐ Midnight ☐ Night World ☐ Racketeer, The ☐ Speak Easily

Hordern, Michael ☐ Baby and the Battleship, The ☐ Beachcomber, The ☐ Bed-Sitting Room, The ☐ Christmas Carol, A ☐ Constant Husband, The ☐ Dark Obsession ☐ England Made Me ☐ Flesh & Blood ☐ Freddie as F.R.O.7 ☐ Gauguin the Savage ☐ Girl in a Million, A ☐ Girl Stroke Boy ☐ Grand National Night ☐ Green Man, The ☐ How I Won the War ☐ I Was Monty's Double ☐ I'll Never Forget What's 'is Name ☐ Ivanhoe ☐ Jokers, The ☐ Joseph Andrews ☐ Lady Jane ☐ Mackintosh Man, The ☐ Malaga ☐ Man in the Moon, The ☐ Missionary, The ☐ Mr. Quilp ☐ Night My Number Came Up, The ☐ Oliver Twist ☐ Pacific Destiny ☐ Pied Piper, The ☐ Possession of Joel Delaney, The ☐ Royal Flash ☐ Secret Garden, The ☐ Slipper and the Rose, The ☐ Spanish Gardener, The ☐ Suspicion ☐ Taming of the Shrew, The ☐ Theatre of Blood ☐ V.I.P.s, The ☐ Where Eagles Dare

Horne, Lena ☐ Cabin in the Sky ☐ Death of a Gunfighter ☐ Duchess of Idaho ☐ I Dood It ☐ Meet Me in Las Vegas ☐ Panama Hattie ☐ Stormy Weather ☐ That's Entertainment 3 ☐ Thousands Cheer ☐ Till the Clouds Roll By ☐ Two Girls and a Sailor ☐ Wiz, The ☐ Words and Music

Horton, Edward Everett ☐ Alice in Wonderland ☐ All the King's Horses ☐ Angel ☐ Bedtime Story, A ☐ Biography of a Bachelor Girl ☐ Bluebeard's Eighth Wife ☐ Body Disappears, The ☐ Cinderella Jones ☐ College Swing ☐ Danger—Love at Work ☐ Design for Living ☐ Devil is a Woman, The ☐ Down to Earth ☐ Faithful in My Fashion ☐ Front Page, The ☐ Gang's All Here, The ☐ Gay Divorcee, The ☐ Great Garrick, The ☐ Hearts Divided ☐ Her Husband's Affairs ☐ Her Primitive Man ☐ Here Comes Mr. Jordan ☐ Hitting a New High ☐ Holiday ☐ Holiday ☐ I Married an Angel ☐ In Caliente ☐ King and the Chorus Girl, The ☐ Ladies Should Listen ☐ Lady on a Train ☐ Lonely Wives ☐ Lost Horizon ☐ Magnificent Dope, The ☐ Merry Widow, The ☐ Nobody's Fool ☐ Paris Honeymoon ☐ Perfect Specimen, The ☐ Reaching for the Moon ☐ San Diego, I Love You ☐ Shall We Dance ☐ Singing Kid, The ☐ Summer Storm ☐ Top Hat ☐ Trouble in Paradise ☐ Wide Open ☐ Your Uncle Dudley ☐ Ziegfeld Girl

Hoskins, Bob ☐ Beyond the Limit ☐ Brazil ☐ Cotton Club, The ☐ Dunera Boys, The ☐ Favor, the Watch, and the Very Big Fish, The ☐ Heart Condition ☐ Hook ☐ Inner Circle, The ☐ Lassiter ☐ Lonely Passion of Judith Hearne, The ☐ Long Good Friday, The ☐ Mermaids ☐ Mona Lisa ☐ Mussolini and I ☐ National Health, The ☐ Passed Away ☐ Prayer for the Dying, A ☐ Royal Flash ☐ Shattered ☐ Super Mario Bros. ☐ Sweet Liberty ☐ Who Framed Roger Rabbit ☐ Zulu Dawn

Houseman, John ☐ Bright Lights, Big City ☐ Cheap Detective, The ☐ Christmas Without Snow, A ☐ Fear on Trial ☐ Fog, The ☐ Ghost Story ☐ Gideon's Trumpet ☐ Gore Vidal's Lincoln ☐ Paper Chase, The ☐ Rollerball ☐ Seven Days in May ☐ Three Days of the Condor ☐ Winds of War, The

Howard, John ☐ Arrest Bulldog Drummond ☐ Bulldog Drummond Comes Back ☐ Bulldog Drummond in Africa ☐ Easy to Take ☐ Father Takes a Wife ☐ Four Hours to Kill ☐ Highest Honor, The ☐ Hold 'Em Navy ☐ I, Jane Doe ☐ Lost Horizon ☐ Love from a Stranger ☐ Mad Doctor, The ☐ Man from Dakota, The ☐ Thirteen Hours By Air ☐ Tight Shoes ☐ Valiant Is the Word for Carrie ☐ Young Einstein

Howard, Leslie ☐ 49th Parallel ☐ Animal Kingdom, The ☐ Berkeley Square ☐ British Agent ☐ Captured ☐ Five and Ten ☐ Free Soul, A ☐ Gone with the Wind ☐ Intermezzo ☐ It's Love I'm After ☐ Of Human Bondage ☐ Outward Bound ☐ Petrified Forest, The ☐ Pimpernel Smith ☐ Pygmalion ☐ Reserved for Ladies ☐ Romeo and Juliet ☐ Scarlet Pimpernel, The ☐ Smilin' Through ☐ Spitfire ☐ Stand-In

Howard, Ron ☐ American Graffiti ☐ Bitter Harvest ☐ Courtship of Eddie's Father, The ☐ Eat My Dust ☐ Grand Theft Auto ☐ Happy Mother's Day, Love George ☐ Huckleberry Finn ☐ Migrants, The ☐ More American Graffiti ☐ Music Man, The ☐ Return to Mayberry ☐ Shootist, The ☐ Smoke ☐ Village of the Giants ☐ Wild Country, The

Howard, Trevor ☐ 11 Harrowhouse ☐ Albino ☐ Battle of Britain, The ☐ Bawdy Adventures of Tom Jones, The ☐ Brief Encounter ☐ Catch Me a Spy ☐ Catholics ☐ Charge of the Light Brigade, The ☐ Christmas Eve ☐ Clouded Yellow, The ☐ Cockleshell Heroes, The ☐ Conduct Unbecoming ☐ Count of Monte Cristo, The ☐ Dawning, The ☐ Doll's House, A ☐ Dust ☐ Eliza Frazer ☐ Father Goose ☐ Foreign Body ☐ Gandhi ☐ Gift Horse, The ☐ Glory at Sea ☐ Golden Salamander, The ☐ Graveyard, The ☐ Green for Danger ☐ Heart of the Matter, The ☐ Hennessy ☐ I Became a Criminal ☐ I See a Dark Stranger ☐ Inside the Third Reich ☐ Key, The ☐ Last Remake of Beau Geste, The ☐ Light Years Away ☐ Lion, The ☐ Liquidator, The ☐ Lola ☐ Long Duel, The ☐ Ludwig ☐ Malaga ☐ Man in the Middle ☐ Mary, Queen of Scots ☐ Matter of Innocence, A ☐ Missionary, The ☐ Mutiny on the Bounty ☐ Night Visitor, The ☐ Odette ☐ Offence, The ☐ One Woman's Story ☐ Operation Crossbow ☐ Outcast of the Islands ☐ Pope Joan ☐ Poppy Is Also a Flower, The ☐ Roots of Heaven, The ☐ Ryan's Daughter ☐ Sea Wolves, The ☐ Shaka Zulu ☐ Shillingbury

Blowers, The ☐ Slavers ☐ So Well Remembered ☐ Sons and Lovers ☐ Stranger's Hand, The ☐ Superman—The Movie ☐ Sword of the Valiant ☐ Third Man, The ☐ Triple Cross ☐ Unholy, The ☐ Von Ryan's Express ☐ White Mischief ☐ Windwalker

Howell, C. Thomas ☐ Acting on Impulse ☐ Breaking the Rules ☐ Curiosity Kills ☐ Far Out Man ☐ Gettysburg ☐ Grandview, U.S.A. ☐ Hitcher, The ☐ Into the Homeland ☐ Kid ☐ Nickel & Dime ☐ Outsiders, The ☐ Red Dawn ☐ Return of the Musketeers, The ☐ Secret Admirer ☐ Side Out ☐ Soul Man ☐ That Night ☐ Tiger's Tale, A ☐ To Protect and Serve

Hudson, Rochelle ☐ Bachelor Bait ☐ Curly Top ☐ Dr. Bull ☐ Gallery of Horror ☐ Girls Under Twenty-One ☐ Hell's Highway ☐ Imitation of Life ☐ Island of Doomed Men ☐ Les Miserables ☐ Life Begins at Forty ☐ Meet Boston Blackie ☐ Mighty Barnum, The ☐ Mr. Moto Takes a Chance ☐ Mr. Skitch ☐ Poppy ☐ Reunion ☐ Show Them No Mercy! ☐ Wild Boys of the Road

Hudson, Rock ☐ Air Cadet ☐ All That Heaven Allows ☐ Ambassador, The ☐ Avalanche ☐ Back to God's Country ☐ Battle Hymn ☐ Bend of the River ☐ Bengal Brigade ☐ Blindfold ☐ Captain Lightfoot ☐ Come September ☐ Darling Lili ☐ Desert Hawk, The ☐ Embryo ☐ Farewell to Arms, A ☐ Fat Man, The ☐ Fine Pair, A ☐ Gathering of Eagles ☐ Giant ☐ Golden Blade, The ☐ Gun Fury ☐ Has Anybody Seen My Gal? ☐ Here Come the Nelsons ☐ Horizons West ☐ Hornet's Nest ☐ Ice Station Zebra ☐ Iron Man, The ☐ Last Sunset, The ☐ Lawless Breed, The ☐ Lover Come Back ☐ Magnificent Obsession ☐ Man's Favorite Sport? ☐ Martian Chronicles, The ☐ Mirror Crack'd, The ☐ Never Say Goodbye ☐ Once Upon a Dead Man ☐ One Desire ☐ Peggy ☐ Pillow Talk ☐ Pretty Maids All in a Row ☐ Sea Devils ☐ Seconds ☐ Seminole ☐ Send Me No Flowers ☐ Showdown ☐ Something of Value ☐ Strange Bedfellows ☐ Tarnished Angels, The ☐ Taza, Son of Cochise ☐ This Earth Is Mine ☐ Tobruk ☐ Twilight for the Gods ☐ Undefeated, The ☐ Very Special Favor, A ☐ Winchester '73 ☐ Written on the Wind

Hughes, Barnard ☐ Adventures of Huckleberry Finn ☐ Best Friends ☐ Borrowers, The ☐ Caribbean Mystery, A ☐ Cold Turkey ☐ Da ☐ Day One ☐ Deadhead Miles ☐ Doc Hollywood ☐ First Monday in October ☐ Guilty or Innocent: The Sam Sheppard Murder Case ☐ Guts and Glory: The Rise and Fall of Oliver North ☐ Hobo's Christmas, A ☐ Home Fires Burning ☐ Homeward Bound ☐ Hospital, The ☐ Incident, The ☐ Little Gloria-Happy At Last ☐ Lost Boys, The ☐ Maxie ☐ Night of Courage ☐ Rage ☐ See How She Runs ☐ Sister Act 2: Back in the Habit ☐ Sisters ☐ Under the Biltmore Clock

Hughes, Wendy ☐ Careful, He Might Hear You ☐ Dangerous Summer, A ☐ Echoes of Paradise ☐ Happy New Year ☐ Heist, The ☐ Indecent Obession, An ☐ Kostas ☐ My Brilliant Career ☐ My First Wife ☐ Newsfront ☐ Return to Eden ☐ Warm Nights on a Slow Moving Train ☐ Wild Orchid 2—Two Shades of Blue

Hulce, Tom ☐ Amadeus ☐ Black Rainbow ☐ Dominick and Eugene ☐ Echo Park ☐ Fearless ☐ Inner Circle, The ☐ Mary Shelley's Frankenstein ☐ Murder in Mississippi ☐ Parenthood ☐ September 30, 1955 ☐ Slam Dance ☐ Those Lips, Those Eyes

Hull, Henry ☐ Boys Town ☐ Buccaneer, The ☐ Colorado Territory ☐ Fighter Squadron ☐ Fool Killer, The ☐ Fountainhead, The ☐ Great Expectations ☐ Inferno ☐ Jesse James ☐ Lifeboat ☐ Man with the Gun, The ☐ Master of the World ☐ Miracles for Sale ☐ My Son, My Son ☐ Nick Carter, Master Detective ☐ Return of Jesse James, The ☐ Sheriff of Fractured Jaw, The ☐ Walls of Jericho, The ☐ Werewolf of London ☐ Woman of the Town, The ☐ Yellow Jack

Hunt, Helen ☐ Angel Dusted ☐ Bill: On His Own ☐ Child Bride of Short Creek ☐ Girls Just Want to Have Fun ☐ Incident at Dark River ☐ Into the Badlands ☐ Mr. Saturday Night ☐ Murder in New Hampshire: The Pamela Smart Story ☐ Next of Kin ☐ Only You ☐ Project X ☐ Quarterback Princess ☐ Trancers ☐ Trancers II—The Return of Jack Deth ☐ Trancers III—Deth Lives ☐ Waterdance, The

Hunt, Marsha ☐ Actors and Sin ☐ Arizona Raiders, The ☐ Blossoms in the Dust ☐ Blue Denim ☐ Bombers B-52 ☐ Born to the West ☐ Carnegie Hall ☐ Cry Havoc ☐ Easy to Take ☐ Ellery Queen, Master Detective ☐ Fear No Evil ☐ Gentle Julia ☐ Happy Time, The ☐ Hollywood Boulevard ☐ Human Comedy, The ☐ Inside Story, The ☐ Irene ☐ Joe Smith, American ☐ Johnny Got His Gun ☐ Kid Glove Killer ☐ Lost Angel ☐ Music for Millions ☐ None Shall Escape ☐ Plunderers, The ☐ Raw Deal ☐ Seven Sweethearts ☐ Smash-Up, the Story of a Woman ☐ Take One False Step ☐ Thunder Trail ☐ Unholy Partners

Hunt, Martita ☐ Admirable Crichton, The ☐ Anastasia ☐ Becket ☐ Brides of Dracula ☐ Bunny Lake Is Missing ☐ Folly to Be Wise ☐ Great Expectations ☐ I Like Money ☐ March Hare, The ☐ Melba ☐ So Evil My Love ☐ Song Without End ☐ Tonight at 8:30 ☐ Wicked Lady, The ☐ Wonderful World of the Brothers Grimm, The

Hunter, Ian ☐ Bedelia ☐ Broadway Serenade ☐ Call It a Day ☐ Comet Over Broadway ☐ Confession ☐ Dulcy ☐ Easy Virtue ☐ Edward, My Son ☐ Eight O'Clock Walk ☐ Girl from 10th Avenue, The ☐ High Fury ☐ I Found Stella Parish ☐ Long Voyage Home,

The ☐ Mad Little Island ☐ Order of the Black Eagle ☐ Phantom Light, The ☐ Sisters, The ☐ Smilin' Through ☐ Strange Cargo ☐ Ziegfeld Girl

Hunter, Holly ☐ Always ☐ Animal Behavior ☐ Broadcast News ☐ Crazy in Love ☐ End of the Line ☐ Firm, The ☐ Gathering of Old Men, A ☐ Miss Firecracker ☐ Murder on the Bayou ☐ Once Around ☐ Piano, The ☐ Positively True Adventures of the Alleged Texas Cheerleader-Murdering Mom, The ☐ Raising Arizona ☐ Roe vs. Wade ☐ Svengali ☐ Swing Shift

Hunter, Jeffrey ☐ Belles on Their Toes ☐ Call Me Mister ☐ Christmas Kid, The ☐ Count Five and Die ☐ Custer of the West ☐ Dreamboat ☐ Fourteen Hours ☐ Frogmen, The ☐ Gold for the Caesars ☐ Great Locomotive Chase, The ☐ Gun for a Coward ☐ Hell to Eternity ☐ In Love and War ☐ Key Witness ☐ King of Kings ☐ Kiss Before Dying, A ☐ Last Hurrah, The ☐ Longest Day, The ☐ Lure of the Wilderness ☐ Man from Galveston, The ☐ Man-Trap ☐ No Down Payment ☐ No Man Is an Island ☐ Princess of the Nile ☐ Private Navy of Sgt. O'Farrell, The ☐ Proud Ones, The ☐ Red Skies of Montana ☐ Searchers, The ☐ Sergeant Rutledge ☐ Seven Angry Men ☐ Seven Cities of Gold ☐ True Story of Jesse James, The ☐ Way to the Gold, The ☐ White Feather

Hunter, Kim ☐ Anything Can Happen ☐ Bad Ronald ☐ Beneath the Planet of the Apes ☐ Born Innocent ☐ Cross of Fire ☐ Deadline U.S.A ☐ Drop-Out Mother ☐ Ellery Queen ☐ Escape from the Planet of the Apes ☐ F.D.R., The Last Year ☐ Kindred, The ☐ Lilith ☐ Magician, The ☐ Planet of the Apes ☐ Seventh Victim, The ☐ Skokie ☐ Stairway to Heaven ☐ Storm Center ☐ Streetcar Named Desire, A ☐ Swimmer, The ☐ Tender Comrade ☐ Three Sovereigns For Sarah ☐ When Strangers Marry ☐ Young Stranger, The

Hunter, Tab ☐ Arousers, The ☐ Battle Cry ☐ Birds Do It ☐ Burning Hills, The ☐ Cameron's Closet ☐ Damn Yankees ☐ Fickle Finger of Fate, The ☐ Girl He Left Behind ☐ Grease 2 ☐ Grotesque ☐ Gunman's Walk ☐ Hostile Guns ☐ Island of Desire ☐ Katie: Portrait of a Centerfold ☐ Kid from Left Field, The ☐ Lafayette Escadrille ☐ Last Chance, The ☐ Life and Times of Judge Roy Bean, The ☐ Loved One, The ☐ Lust in the Dust ☐ Operation Bikini ☐ Pandemonium ☐ Pleasure of His Company, The ☐ Polyester ☐ Ride the Wild Surf ☐ Sea Chase, The ☐ That Kind of Woman ☐ They Came to Cordura ☐ Track of the Cat

Hunt, Linda ☐ Bostonians, The ☐ Dune ☐ Eleni ☐ If Looks Could Kill ☐ Kindergarten Cop ☐ Rain Without Thunder ☐ Ready to Wear ☐ She-Devil ☐ Silverado ☐ Twenty Bucks ☐ Waiting for the Moon ☐ Year of Living Dangerously, The

Huppert, Isabelle ☐ Bedroom Window, The ☐ Brontë Sisters, The ☐ Cactus ☐ Cesar and Rosalie ☐ Coup de Torchon ☐ Entre Nous ☐ Every Man for Himself ☐ Going Places ☐ Heaven's Gate ☐ Judge and the Assassin, The ☐ La Truite ☐ Lacemaker, The ☐ Lady of the Camellias, The ☐ Loulou ☐ Love After Love ☐ Madame Bovary ☐ My Best Friend's Girl ☐ Passion ☐ Story of Women, The ☐ Violette

Hurt, John ☐ Alien ☐ Aria ☐ Before Winter Comes ☐ Black Cauldron, The ☐ Champions ☐ Disappearance, The ☐ Elephant Man, The ☐ Field, The ☐ Frankenstein Unbound ☐ From the Hip ☐ Ghoul, The ☐ Heaven's Gate ☐ Hit, The ☐ In Search of Gregory ☐ Jake Speed ☐ King Lear ☐ King Ralph ☐ Little Malcolm ☐ Little Sweetheart ☐ Lord of the Rings, The ☐ Midnight Express ☐ Monolith ☐ Naked Civil Servant, The ☐ Night Crossing ☐ Osterman Weekend, The ☐ Partners ☐ Pied Piper, The ☐ Scandal ☐ Second Best ☐ Shout, The ☐ Watership Down ☐ White Mischief

Hurt, Mary Beth ☐ Baby Girl Scott ☐ Compromising Positions ☐ D.A.R.Y.L. ☐ Defenseless ☐ Head over Heels ☐ Light Sleeper ☐ Parents ☐ Six Degrees of Separation ☐ Slaves of New York ☐ World According to Garp, The

Hurt, William ☐ Accidental Tourist, The ☐ Alice ☐ Altered States ☐ Big Chill, The ☐ Body Heat ☐ Broadcast News ☐ Children of a Lesser God ☐ Doctor, The ☐ Eyewitness ☐ Gorky Park ☐ Kiss of the Spider Woman ☐ Mr. Wonderful ☐ Second Best ☐ Trial by Jury ☐ Until the End of the World

Hussey, Olivia ☐ Black Christmas ☐ Cat and the Canary, The ☐ Death on the Nile ☐ H-Bomb ☐ Harold Robbins' the Pirate ☐ Ivanhoe ☐ Lost Horizon ☐ Man with Bogart's Face, The ☐ Psycho IV: The Beginning ☐ Romeo and Juliet ☐ Save Me ☐ Virus

Hussey, Ruth ☐ Another Thin Man ☐ Blackmail ☐ Facts of Life, The ☐ Fast and Furious ☐ Flight Command ☐ H.M. Pulham, Esq. ☐ Hill Number One ☐ Honolulu ☐ I, Jane Doe ☐ Judge Hardy's Children ☐ Lady Wants Mink, The ☐ Louisa ☐ Madame X ☐ Maisie ☐ Man-Proof ☐ Marine Raiders ☐ Married Bachelor ☐ Mr. Music ☐ Northwest Passage ☐ Our Wife ☐ Philadelphia Story, The ☐ Rich Man, Poor Girl ☐ Stars and Stripes Forever ☐ Susan and God ☐ Tender Comrade ☐ Tennessee Johnson ☐ That's My Boy ☐ Uninvited, The

Huston, Anjelica ☐ Addams Family Values ☐ Addams Family, The ☐ And the Band Played On ☐ Crimes and Misdemeanors ☐ Dead, The ☐ Enemies, A Love Story ☐ Family Pictures ☐ Gardens of Stone ☐ Good to Go ☐ Grifters, The ☐ Handful of Dust, A ☐ Ice Pirates, The ☐ Lonesome Dove ☐ Manhattan Murder Mystery ☐ Mr. North

☐ Prizzi's Honor ☐ Walk With Love and Death, A ☐ Witches, The

Huston, John ☐ Angela ☐ Battle for the Planet of the Apes ☐ Bible, The ☐ Breakout ☐ Candy ☐ Cardinal, The ☐ Casino Royale ☐ Chinatown ☐ Fatal Attraction ☐ Great Battle, The ☐ Hobbit, The ☐ Hollywood on Trial ☐ Jaguar Lives! ☐ Life and Times of Judge Roy Bean, The ☐ List of Adrian Messenger, The ☐ Lovesick ☐ Man in the Wilderness ☐ Myra Breckinridge ☐ Return of the King ☐ Wind and the Lion, The ☐ Winter Kills

Huston, Walter ☐ Abraham Lincoln ☐ Always in My Heart ☐ American Madness ☐ And Then There Were None ☐ Ann Vickers ☐ Beast of The City, The ☐ Criminal Code, The ☐ December 7th—The Movie ☐ Devil and Daniel Webster, The ☐ Dodsworth ☐ Dragon Seed ☐ Dragonwyck ☐ Duel in the Sun ☐ Edge of Darkness ☐ Furies, The ☐ Gabriel over the White House ☐ Great Sinner, The ☐ Hell Below ☐ House Divided, A ☐ Kongo ☐ Law and Order ☐ Light that Failed, The ☐ Mission to Moscow ☐ Night Court ☐ North Star, The ☐ Of Human Hearts ☐ Outlaw, The ☐ Prizefighter and the Lady, The ☐ Rain ☐ Rhodes ☐ Shanghai Gesture, The ☐ Star Witness ☐ Summer Holiday ☐ Swamp Water ☐ Transatlantic Tunnel ☐ Treasure of the Sierra Madre, The ☐ Virginian, The ☐ Wet Parade, The ☐ Yankee Doodle Dandy

Hutton, Betty ☐ And the Angels Sing ☐ Annie Get Your Gun ☐ Dream Girl ☐ Duffy's Tavern ☐ Fleet's In, The ☐ Greatest Show on Earth, The ☐ Happy Go Lucky ☐ Here Come the Waves ☐ Incendiary Blonde ☐ Let's Dance ☐ Let's Face It ☐ Miracle of Morgan's Creek, The ☐ Perils of Pauline, The ☐ Red, Hot and Blue ☐ Sailor Beware

Hutton, Jim ☐ Bachelor in Paradise ☐ Don't Be Afraid of the Dark ☐ Ellery Queen ☐ Green Berets, The ☐ Hallelujah Trail, The ☐ Hellfighters ☐ Honeymoon Machine, The ☐ Horizontal Lieutenant, The ☐ Looking for Love ☐ Major Dundee ☐ Never Too Late ☐ Period of Adjustment ☐ Subterraneans, The ☐ Walk, Don't Run ☐ Where the Boys Are ☐ Who's Minding the Mint?

Hutton, Lauren ☐ American Gigolo ☐ Cradle Will Fall, The ☐ Fear ☐ Forbidden Sun ☐ Gambler, The ☐ Gator ☐ Guilty as Charged ☐ Lassiter ☐ Little Fauss and Big Halsy ☐ Malone ☐ Millions ☐ Monte Carlo ☐ My Father, the Hero ☐ Once Bitten ☐ Paper Lion ☐ Perfect People ☐ Scandal Sheet ☐ Scandalous ☐ Viva Knievel! ☐ Wedding, A ☐ Welcome to L.A. ☐ Zorro, the Gay Blade

Hutton, Robert ☐ Always Together ☐ And Baby Makes Three ☐ Big Bluff, The ☐ Hollywood Canteen ☐ Invisible Invaders ☐ Jailbreakers, The ☐ Janie ☐ Janie Gets Married ☐ Man on the Eiffel Tower, The ☐ Outcasts of the City ☐ Showdown at Boot Hill ☐ Steel Helmet, The ☐ Wallflower ☐ Younger Brothers, The

Hutton, Timothy ☐ And Baby Makes Six ☐ Best Place to Be, The ☐ Daniel ☐ Dark Half, The ☐ Everybody's All-American ☐ Falcon and the Snowman, The ☐ Father Figure ☐ Friendly Fire ☐ Iceman ☐ Made in Heaven ☐ Ordinary People ☐ Q & A ☐ Taps ☐ Temp, The ☐ Turk 182!

Hyde-White, Wilfrid ☐ Ada ☐ Adam and Evalyn ☐ Bang, Bang, You're Dead! ☐ Betrayed ☐ Browning Version, The ☐ Carry on Nurse ☐ Cat and the Canary, The ☐ Conspirator ☐ Crooks Anonymous ☐ Fanny Hill ☐ Fear No Evil ☐ Fragment of Fear ☐ Flame over India ☐ Forbidden Street, The ☐ In God We Trust ☐ In Search of the Castaways ☐ John and Julie ☐ Last Holiday ☐ Libel ☐ Man with a Million ☐ March Hare, The ☐ Mr. Potts Goes to Moscow ☐ Mudlark, The ☐ My Fair Lady ☐ Rainbow Jacket, The ☐ Sandwich Man, The ☐ Two Way Stretch

Hyer, Martha ☐ Abbott and Costello Go To Mars ☐ Battle Hymn ☐ Battle of Rogue River ☐ Best of Everything, The ☐ Big Fisherman, The ☐ Bikini Beach ☐ Blood on the Arrow ☐ Carpetbaggers, The ☐ Chase, The ☐ Clay Pigeon, The ☐ Cry Vengeance ☐ Delicate Delinquent, The ☐ First Men in the Moon ☐ Francis in the Navy ☐ Girl Named Tamiko, A ☐ House of 1,000 Dolls ☐ Houseboat ☐ Ice Palace ☐ Kelly and Me ☐ Last Time I Saw Archie, The ☐ Lucky Me ☐ Man from the Diner's Club, The ☐ Mister Cory ☐ Mistress of The World ☐ My Man Godfrey ☐ Night of the Grizzly ☐ Once Upon a Horse ☐ Once You Kiss a Stranger ☐ Paris Holiday ☐ Picture Mommy Dead ☐ Roughshod ☐ Sabrina ☐ Salt Lake Raiders ☐ Showdown at Abilene ☐ So Big ☐ Some Came Running ☐ Sons of Katie Elder, The ☐ Wild Stallion ☐ Wyoming Renegades

Idle, Eric ☐ Adventures of Baron Munchausen, The ☐ And Now for Something Completely Different ☐ Monty Python and the Holy Grail ☐ Monty Python Live at the Hollywood Bowl ☐ Monty Python's Flying Circus—Vol. 1 ☐ Monty Python's Life of Brian ☐ Monty Python's Parrot Sketch Not Included ☐ Monty Python's The Meaning of Life ☐ Nuns on the Run ☐ Rutles, The ☐ Splitting Heirs ☐ Transformers, The ☐ Yellowbeard

Ireland, Jill ☐ Assassination ☐ Battleaxe, The ☐ Breakheart Pass ☐ Breakout ☐ Carry on Nurse ☐ Chato's Land ☐ Chino ☐ Cold Sweat ☐ Death Wish II ☐ Family, The ☐ From Noon Till Three ☐ Girl, the Gold Watch and Everything, The ☐ Hard Drivers ☐ Hard Times ☐ Hell Drivers ☐ Love and Bullets ☐ Mechanic, The ☐ Rider on the Rain ☐ Someone Behind the Door ☐ Twice Around the Daffodils ☐ Valachi Papers, The ☐ Villa Rides

Ireland, John □ 55 Days at Peking □ All the King's Men □ Anna Lucasta □ Basketball Fix, The □ Bonanza: The Next Generation □ Bushwackers, The □ Cargo to Capetown □ Combat Squad □ Escape to the Sun □ Faces in the Dark □ Fall of the Roman Empire □ Farewell, My Lovely □ Fast and the Furious, The □ Fort Utah □ Gunfight at the O.K. Corral □ Gunslinger □ Guyana: Cult of the Damned □ Hannah Lee □ Hell's Horizon □ House of Seven Corpses, The □ I Saw What You Did □ I Shot Jesse James □ Incubus, The □ It Shouldn't Happen to a Dog □ Kavik the Wolf Dog □ Little Big Horn □ Marilyn: The Untold Story □ Martin's Day □ Messenger of Death □ Midnight Auto Supply □ Mission To Glory □ Mister Too Little □ My Darling Clementine □ No Place to Land □ No Time to Kill □ On the Air Live with Captain Midnight □ Party Girl □ Queen Bee □ Railroaded □ Raw Deal □ Red Mountain □ Red River □ Return of a Stranger □ Return of Jesse James, The □ Roughshod □ Satan's Cheerleaders □ Southern Yankee, A □ Sundown, The Vampire in Retreat □ Walk in the Sun, A □ Wild in the Country

Irons, Jeremy □ Betrayal □ Brideshead Revisited □ Chorus of Disapproval, A □ Damage □ Dead Ringers □ French Lieutenant's Woman, The □ House of the Spirits □ Kafka □ Lion King, The □ M. Butterfly □ Mission, The □ Moonlighting □ Nijinsky □ Reversal of Fortune □ Swann in Love □ Waterland □ Wild Duck, The

Ironside, Michael □ Cafe Romeo □ Common Bonds □ Cross Country □ Extreme Prejudice □ Ford: The Man and the Machine □ Hello Mary Lou—Prom Night II □ Hostile Takeover □ Killer Image □ Mardi Gras for the Devil □ McBain □ Mind Field □ Murder in Space □ Neon City □ Nowhere to Hide □ Point of Impact □ Surrogate, The □ Vagrant, The □ Watchers

Irving, Amy □ American Tail: Fievel Goes West, An □ Anastasia: The Mystery Of Anna □ Carrie □ Competition, The □ Crossing Delancey □ Far Pavilions, The □ Fury, The □ Heartbreak House □ Honeysuckle Rose □ James A. Michener's Dynasty □ James Dean □ Micki + Maude □ Rumpelstiltskin □ Show of Force, A □ Turn of the Screw, The □ Voices □ Yentl

Ives, Burl □ Baker's Hawk □ Big Country, The □ Brass Bottle, The □ Cat on a Hot Tin Roof □ Day of the Outlaw □ Desire Under the Elms □ Earthbound □ East of Eden □ Ensign Pulver □ Ewok Adventure, The □ Hugo the Hippo □ Just You and Me, Kid □ Let No Man Write My Epitaph □ Man Who Wanted to Live Forever, The □ McMasters, The □ New Adventures of Heidi, The □ Our Man in Havana □ Poor Little Rich Girl: The Barbara Hutton Story □ Smoky □ So Dear to My Heart □ Summer Magic □ Two Moon Junction □ White Dog □ Wind Across the Everglades

Ivey, Judith □ Brighton Beach Memoirs □ Compromising Positions □ Decoration Day □ Dixie: Changing Habits □ Everybody Wins □ Hello Again □ In Country □ Lonely Guy, The □ Long Hot Summer, The □ Love Hurts □ There Goes the Neighborhood □ Woman in Red, The

Iwashita, Shima □ Autumn Afternoon, An □ Double Suicide □ Gonza The Spearman □ Harakiri □ Red Lion □ Samurai from Nowhere □ Scarlet Camellia, The □ Through Days and Months □ Twin Sisters of Kyoto

Jackson, Anne □ Angel Levine, The □ Baby M □ Bell Jar, The □ Dirty Dingus Magee □ Folks! □ How to Save a Marriage (And Ruin Your Life) □ Journey, The □ Leave 'Em Laughing □ Lovers and Other Strangers □ Nasty Habits □ Out on a Limb □ Sam's Son □ Secret Life of an American Wife, The □ So Young, So Bad □ Tiger Makes Out, The □ Woman Called Golda, A □ Zigzag

Jackson, Glenda □ And Nothing But the Truth □ Beyond Therapy □ Business as Usual □ Class of Miss MacMichael, The □ Devil Is a Woman, The □ H.E.A.L.T.H. □ Hedda □ Hopscotch □ House Calls □ Incredible Sarah, The □ King of the Wind □ Lost and Found □ Maids, The □ Marat/Sade (Persecution and Assassination of Jean-Paul Marat Performed by the In □ Mary, Queen of Scots □ Music Lovers, The □ Nasty Habits □ Negatives □ Nelson Affair, The □ Patricia Neal Story, The □ Rainbow, The □ Return of the Soldier, The □ Romantic Englishwoman, The □ Salome's Last Dance □ Stevie □ Sunday, Bloody Sunday □ Tell Me Lies □ Touch of Class, A □ Turtle Diary □ Women in Love

Jackson, Gordon □ Against the Wind □ Captive Heart, The □ Fighting Prince of Donegal, The □ Foreman Went to France, The □ Hamlet □ Ipcress File, The □ Mad Little Island □ Meet Mr. Lucifer □ Millions Like Us □ Nine Men □ Prime of Miss Jean Brodie, The □ Run Wild, Run Free □ Scrooge □ Shooting Party, The □ Tight Little Island

Jackson, Kate □ Adrift □ Charlie's Angels □ Death at Love House □ Homewrecker □ James at 15 □ Killer Bees □ Limbo □ Loverboy □ Making Love □ Night of Dark Shadows

Jackson, Samuel L. □ Amos and Andrew □ Def By Temptation □ Hail Caesar □ Losing Isaiah □ Menace II Society □ National Lampoon's Loaded Weapon □ Pulp Fiction □ Return of Superfly, The □ White Sands

Jacobi, Derek □ Day of the Jackal, The □ Dead Again □ Enigma □ Henry V □ Human Factor, The □ Hunchback of Notre Dame, The □ Little Dorrit □ Odessa File, The □ Othello □ Secret Garden, The □ Secret of

NIMH, The ☐ Tenth Man, The ☐ Three Sisters

Jacobi, Lou ☐ Avalon ☐ Diary of Anne Frank, The ☐ Everything You Always Wanted to Know About Sex (But Were Afraid to Ask) ☐ I Don't Buy Kisses Anymore ☐ I. Q. ☐ Irma la Douce ☐ Lucky Star, The ☐ Magician of Lublin, The ☐ Next Stop, Greenwich Village ☐ Roseland ☐ Song Without End

Jaeckel, Richard ☐ Apache Ambush ☐ Awakening of Candra, The ☐ Big Leaguer, The ☐ Black Moon Rising ☐ Born Innocent ☐ Chosen Survivors ☐ City Across the River ☐ Cold River ☐ Come Back, Little Sheba ☐ Fighting Coast Guard ☐ Firehouse ☐ Fix, The ☐ Four for Texas ☐ Gallant Hours, The ☐ Ghetto Blaster ☐ Green Slime, The ☐ Grizzly ☐ King of the Kickboxers ☐ Latitude Zero ☐ Martial Outlaw ☐ My Son John ☐ Naked and the Dead, The ☐ Pacific Inferno ☐ Pat Garrett and Billy the Kid ☐ Red Pony, The ☐ Sands of Iwo Jima ☐ Sea of Lost Ships ☐ Starman ☐ Supercarrier ☐ Ulzana's Raid ☐ Violent Men, The ☐ Walking Tall, Part II ☐ When Hell Broke Loose ☐ Wing and a Prayer

Jaffe, Sam ☐ 13 Rue Madeleine ☐ Accused, The ☐ Asphalt Jungle, The ☐ Barbarian and the Geisha, The ☐ Battle Beyond the Stars ☐ Bedknobs and Broomsticks ☐ Ben-Hur ☐ Day the Earth Stood Still, The ☐ Dunwich Horror, The ☐ Gideon's Trumpet ☐ Gunga Din ☐ Guns for San Sebastian ☐ I Can Get It for You Wholesale ☐ Lost Horizon ☐ Night Gallery ☐ Nothing Lasts Forever ☐ On the Line ☐ Scarlet Empress, The ☐ We Live Again

Jagger, Dean ☐ Alligator ☐ Bad Day at Black Rock ☐ Bernardine ☐ Bombers B-52 ☐ Brigham Young ☐ C-Man ☐ Cash McCall ☐ Dark City ☐ Elmer Gantry ☐ Eternal Sea, The ☐ Exiled to Shanghai ☐ Firecreek ☐ First to Fight ☐ Forty Guns ☐ Game of Death ☐ Great Man, The ☐ Hootch County Boys, The ☐ I Escaped from the Gestapo ☐ I Heard the Owl Call My Name ☐ It Grows on Trees ☐ It's a Dog's Life ☐ King Creole ☐ Men in Her Life, The ☐ My Son John ☐ Nun's Story, The ☐ Parrish ☐ People Will Talk ☐ Proud Rebel, The ☐ Pursued ☐ Rawhide ☐ Sister Kenny ☐ Star for a Night ☐ Three Brave Men ☐ Twelve O'Clock High ☐ Valley of the Sun ☐ Vanishing Point ☐ Warpath ☐ Western Union ☐ When Strangers Marry ☐ White Christmas ☐ Wings in the Dark ☐ X, the Unknown

Jagger, Mick ☐ Burden of Dreams ☐ Freejack ☐ Mick Jagger—Running Out of Luck ☐ Ned Kelly ☐ Performance ☐ Rutles, The

James, Sidney ☐ Big Job, The ☐ Carry On Cabbie ☐ Carry on Camping ☐ Carry on Cleo ☐ Carry on Constable ☐ Carry on Henry VIII ☐ Carry On, Up the Khyber ☐ For Better, For Worse ☐ Heatwave ☐ Lavender Hill Mob, The ☐ Man Inside, The ☐ No Place Like Homicide! ☐ Paper Orchid ☐ Raising the Wind ☐ Shiralee, The ☐ Three Hats for Lisa

James, Steve ☐ American Ninja ☐ American Ninja 2: The Confrontation ☐ American Ninja 3: Blood Hunt ☐ Avenging Force ☐ Behind Enemy Lines ☐ Brother from Another Planet, The ☐ Exterminator, The ☐ Hero and the Terror, The ☐ Hoop Dreams ☐ I'm Gonna Git You Sucka ☐ McBain ☐ Stalking Danger ☐ Street Hunter

Jannings, Emil ☐ Blue Angel, The ☐ Faust ☐ Last Command, The ☐ Last Laugh, The ☐ Passion ☐ Way of All Flesh, The

Janssen, David ☐ Birds of Prey ☐ City in Fear ☐ Darby's Rangers ☐ Dondi ☐ Fer-de-Lance ☐ Francis Goes to West Point ☐ Francis in the Haunted House ☐ Francis in the Navy ☐ Generation ☐ Golden Gate Murders, The ☐ Golden Rendezvous ☐ Green Berets, The ☐ Hell to Eternity ☐ High Ice ☐ Jacqueline Susann's Once Is Not Enough ☐ King of the Roaring Twenties—The Story of Arnold Rothstein ☐ Lafayette Escadrille ☐ Macho Callahan ☐ Man-Trap ☐ Marooned ☐ Mayday at 40,000 Feet! ☐ Moon of The Wolf ☐ My Six Loves ☐ Never Say Goodbye ☐ Nowhere to Run ☐ Ring of Fire ☐ S.O.S. Titanic ☐ Shoes of the Fisherman, The ☐ Showdown at Abilene ☐ Smile Jenny, You're Dead ☐ Two Minute Warning ☐ Warning Shot

Jeffries, Lionel ☐ Arrivederci, Baby ☐ Chitty Chitty Bang Bang ☐ Colditz Story ☐ First Men in the Moon ☐ Further Up the Creek! ☐ Hellions, The ☐ Jazz Boat ☐ Jekyll & Hyde ☐ Man with the Green Carnation, The ☐ Murder Ahoy ☐ Notorious Landlady, The ☐ Prisoner of Zenda, The ☐ Revenge of Frankenstein, The ☐ Royal Flash ☐ Sudden Terror ☐ Truth About Spring, The ☐ Wrong Arm of the Law

Jenkins, Allen ☐ Blondie Johnson ☐ Bureau of Missing Persons ☐ Easy Come, Easy Go ☐ Employees Entrance ☐ Ever Since Eve ☐ Falcon Takes Over, The ☐ Five Came Back ☐ Fools for Scandal ☐ Footsteps in the Dark ☐ Fun on a Weekend ☐ Going Places ☐ I Live for Love ☐ I'd Rather Be Rich ☐ Irish in Us, The ☐ Jimmy the Gent ☐ Maisie Gets Her Man ☐ Marked Woman ☐ Mayor of Hell, The ☐ Racket Busters ☐ Ready, Willing and Able ☐ Slight Case of Murder, A ☐ St. Louis Kid ☐ Sweepstakes Winner ☐ Whirlpool ☐ Wild Harvest

Jergens, Adele ☐ Aaron Slick from Punkin Crick ☐ Abbott and Costello Meet The Invisible Man ☐ Armored Car Robbery ☐ Blonde Dynamite ☐ Corpse Came C.O.D., The ☐ Day the World Ended, The ☐ Edge of Doom ☐ Fighting Trouble ☐ Fireman Save My Child ☐ Fuller Brush Man, The ☐ Girls in Prison ☐ I Love Trouble ☐ Ladies of the Chorus ☐ Overland Pacific ☐ Thousand and One Nights, A

Jillian, Ann ☐ Ann Jillian Story, The ☐ Ellis Island ☐ Girls of the White Orchid ☐ Killer in the Mirror ☐ Little White Lies ☐ Mae West ☐ Malibu ☐ Mr. Mom

Jobert, Marlene ☐ Alexander ☐ Catch Me a Spy ☐ Masculine-Feminine ☐ Rider on the Rain ☐ Ten Days Wonder ☐ Ten Days' Wonder

Johns, Glynis ☐ 49th Parallel ☐ Adventures of Tartu ☐ All Mine to Give ☐ Another Time, Another Place ☐ Beachcomber, The ☐ Cabinet of Caligari, The ☐ Chapman Report, The ☐ Court Jester, The ☐ Dear Brigitte ☐ Don't Just Stand There ☐ Encore ☐ Flesh & Blood ☐ Frieda ☐ Great Manhunt, The ☐ Halfway House, The ☐ Ideal Husband, An ☐ Island Rescue ☐ Little Gloria-Happy At Last ☐ Lock Up Your Daughters! ☐ Loser Takes All ☐ Mad About Men ☐ Magic Box, The ☐ Mary Poppins ☐ Miranda ☐ No Highway in the Sky ☐ Nukie ☐ Papa's Delicate Condition ☐ Personal Affair ☐ Promoter, The ☐ Ref, The ☐ Rob Roy, the Highland Rogue ☐ Seekers, The ☐ Shake Hands with the Devil ☐ Sundowners, The ☐ Sword and the Rose, The ☐ Third Time Lucky ☐ This Man Is Mine ☐ Under Milk Wood ☐ Vacation From Marriage ☐ Zelly and Me

Johns, Mervyn ☐ 1984 ☐ Captive Heart, The ☐ Christmas Carol, A ☐ Echo of Barbara ☐ Edward, My Son ☐ Finger of Guilt ☐ Foreman Went to France, The ☐ Frightened Bride ☐ Halfway House, The ☐ Heroes of Telemark, The ☐ Jamaica Inn ☐ Men are Children Twice ☐ My Learned Friend ☐ No Love for Johnnie ☐ Romeo and Juliet ☐ San Demetrio, London

Johnson, Ben ☐ Bite the Bullet ☐ Breakheart Pass ☐ Champions ☐ Chase, The ☐ Cherry 2000 ☐ Chisum ☐ Dillinger ☐ Fort Bowie ☐ Fort Defiance ☐ Getaway, The ☐ Grayeagle ☐ Hustle ☐ Kid Blue ☐ Last Picture Show, The ☐ Major Dundee ☐ Mighty Joe Young ☐ My Heroes Have Always Been Cowboys ☐ One-Eyed Jacks ☐ Red Pony, The ☐ Rio Grande ☐ Sacketts, The ☐ Savage Bees, The ☐ Shadow Riders, The ☐ Shane ☐ She Wore a Yellow Ribbon ☐ Soggy Bottom USA ☐ Stranger on My Land ☐ Sugarland Express, The ☐ Terror Train ☐ Tex ☐ Town That Dreaded Sundown, The ☐ Train Robbers, The ☐ Undefeated, The ☐ Wagon Master ☐ Wild Bunch, The ☐ Wild Stallion ☐ Will Penny

Johnson, Celia ☐ Astonished Heart, The ☐ Brief Encounter ☐ Captain's Paradise, The ☐ Good Companions, The ☐ Holly and the Ivy, The ☐ Hostage Tower, The ☐ I Believe In You ☐ In Which We Serve ☐ Kid for Two Farthings, A ☐ Les Miserables ☐ Prime of Miss Jean Brodie, The ☐ This Happy Breed

Johnson, Don ☐ Amateur Night at the Dixie Bar and Grill ☐ Beulah Land ☐ Born Yesterday ☐ Boy and His Dog, A ☐ Cease Fire ☐ City, The ☐ Dead-Bang ☐ Elvis and the Beauty Queen ☐ First, You Cry ☐ G.I. Joe—The Movie ☐ Guilty as Sin ☐ Harley Davidson & the Marlboro Man ☐ Harrad Experiment, The ☐ Hot Spot, The ☐ Katie: Portrait of a Centerfold ☐ Law of the Land ☐ Long Hot Summer, The ☐ Magic Garden of Stanley Sweetheart, The ☐ Melanie ☐ Miami Vice ☐ Miami Vice 2: The Prodigal Son ☐ Paradise ☐ Rebels, The ☐ Snowblind ☐ Soggy Bottom USA ☐ Sweet Hearts Dance ☐ Tales of the Unexpected ☐ Zachariah

Johnson, Richard ☐ Amorous Adventures of Moll Flanders, The ☐ Beyond the Door ☐ Cairo ☐ Crucifer of Blood, The ☐ Deadlier than the Male ☐ Duel of Hearts ☐ Fifth Day of Peace, The ☐ Flame Is Love, The ☐ Great Alligator, The ☐ Haunting, The ☐ Hennessy ☐ Julius Caesar ☐ Khartoum ☐ Man for All Seasons, A ☐ Marquise, The ☐ Mayfair Bank Caper, The ☐ Monster Club, The ☐ Tomb of Ligeia ☐ Turtle Diary ☐ Twist of Sand, A ☐ Zombie

Johnson, Rita ☐ Appointment for Love ☐ Big Clock, The ☐ Broadway Serenade ☐ Edison, the Man ☐ Emergency Hospital ☐ Family Honeymoon ☐ Forty Little Mothers ☐ Here Comes Mr. Jordan ☐ Honolulu ☐ Innocent Affair, An ☐ Major and the Minor, The ☐ Man-Proof ☐ My Friend Flicka ☐ Naughty Nineties ☐ Nick Carter, Master Detective ☐ Rich Man, Poor Girl ☐ Sleep My Love ☐ They All Come Out ☐ They Won't Believe Me ☐ Thunderhead—Son of Flicka

Johnson, Van ☐ 23 Paces to Baker Street ☐ Action of the Tiger ☐ Battleground ☐ Between Two Women ☐ Big Hangover, The ☐ Bottom of the Bottle, The ☐ Bride Goes Wild, The ☐ Brigadoon ☐ Caine Mutiny, The ☐ Command Decision ☐ Confidentially Connie ☐ Divorce American Style ☐ Dr. Gillespie's Criminal Case ☐ Dr. Gillespie's New Assistant ☐ Duchess of Idaho ☐ Easy to Love ☐ Easy to Wed ☐ End of the Affair, The ☐ Girl on the Late, Late Show, The ☐ Go for Broke ☐ Grounds for Marriage ☐ Guy Named Joe, A ☐ High Barbaree ☐ Human Comedy, The ☐ In the Good Old Summertime ☐ Invitation ☐ It's a Big Country ☐ Kelly and Me ☐ Kidnapping of the President, The ☐ Last Blitzkrieg, The ☐ Last Time I Saw Paris, The ☐ Men of the Fighting Lady ☐ Miracle in the Rain ☐ Mother Is a Freshman ☐ No Leave, No Love ☐ Plymouth Adventure, The ☐ Romance of Rosy Ridge, The ☐ Scene of the Crime ☐ Siege at Red River, The ☐ Slander ☐ Somewhere I'll Find You ☐ State of the Union ☐ Subway in the Sky ☐ Thirty Seconds Over Tokyo ☐ Three Guys Named Mike ☐ Thrill of a Romance ☐ Two Girls and a Sailor ☐ Washington Story ☐ Web of Evidence ☐ Weekend at the Waldorf ☐ When in Rome ☐ White Cliffs of Dover, The ☐ Yours, Mine and Ours

Jolson, Al ☐ Big Boy ☐ Go Into Your Dance ☐ Hallelujah, I'm a Bum ☐ Hollywood Cavalcade ☐ Jazz Singer, The ☐ Mammy ☐ Rose of Washington Square ☐ Say It with Songs ☐ Singing Fool, The ☐ Singing Kid, The ☐ Swanee River ☐ Wonder Bar

Jones, Allan ☐ Boys from Syracuse, The ☐ Day at the Races, A ☐ Everybody Sing ☐ Firefly, The ☐ Great Victor Herbert, The ☐ Honeymoon in Bali ☐ Night at the Opera, A ☐ One Night in the Tropics ☐ Reckless ☐ Show Boat ☐ Stage to Thunder Rock

Jones, Carolyn ☐ Addams Family, The—Vol. 1 ☐ Addams Family, The—Vol. 2 ☐ Addams Family, The—Vol. 3 ☐ Addams Family, The—Vol. 4 ☐ Addams Family, The—Vol. 5 ☐ Addams Family, The—Vol. 6 ☐ Baby Face Nelson ☐ Bachelor Party, The ☐ Big Heat, The ☐ Career ☐ Color Me Dead ☐ Dance of Death ☐ Desiree ☐ Eaten Alive ☐ Good Luck, Miss Wyckoff ☐ Heaven with a Gun ☐ Hole in the Head, A ☐ House of Wax ☐ Ice Palace ☐ Invasion of the Body Snatchers ☐ Johnny Trouble ☐ King Creole ☐ Last Train From Gun Hill ☐ Man in the Net, The ☐ Marjorie Morningstar ☐ Midnight Lace ☐ Sail a Crooked Ship ☐ Saracen Blade, The ☐ Shield For Murder ☐ Tender Trap, The ☐ Three Hours to Kill ☐ Turning Point, The

Jones, Dean ☐ Any Wednesday ☐ Beethoven ☐ Blackbeard's Ghost ☐ Born Again ☐ Guess Who's Sleeping in My Bed? ☐ Handle with Care ☐ Herbie Goes to Monte Carlo ☐ Horse in the Gray Flannel Suit, The ☐ Imitation General ☐ Jailhouse Rock ☐ Love Bug, The ☐ Million Dollar Duck ☐ Mr. Superinvisible ☐ New Interns, The ☐ Night of the Quarter Moon ☐ Other People's Money ☐ Shaggy D.A., The ☐ Snowball Express ☐ That Darn Cat ☐ Ugly Dachshund, The ☐ Under the Yum Yum Tree ☐ Until They Sail ☐ When Every Day Was the Fourth of July

Jones, Freddie ☐ And the Ship Sails On ☐ Elephant Man, The ☐ Firefox ☐ Firestarter ☐ Frankenstein Must Be Destroyed! ☐ In the Devil's Garden ☐ Marat/Sade (Persecution and Assassination of Jean-Paul Marat Performed by the In ☐ Mystery of Edwin Drood, The

Jones, Gordon ☐ Feminine Touch, The ☐ Fight for Your Lady ☐ Green Hornet, The ☐ Heart of the Rockies ☐ North of the Great Divide ☐ Sea Devils ☐ Sons of Adventure ☐ Trail of Robin Hood ☐ Wistful Widow of Wagon Gap, The

Jones, Grace ☐ Boomerang ☐ Conan the Destroyer ☐ Siesta ☐ Straight to Hell ☐ Vamp ☐ View to a Kill, A

Jones, Henry ☐ 9 to 5 ☐ Butch Cassidy and the Sundance Kid ☐ Never Too Late ☐ Rabbit, Run ☐ Rascal ☐ Support Your Local Gunfighter ☐ Support Your Local Sheriff ☐ Vertigo ☐ Will Success Spoil Rock Hunter?

Jones, James Earl ☐ Allan Quartermain And The Lost City Of Gold ☐ Ambulance, The ☐ Atlanta Child Murders, The ☐ Bingo Long Traveling All-Stars & Motor Kings, The ☐ Blood Tide ☐ By Dawn's Early Light ☐ Claudine ☐ Clean Slate ☐ Clear and Present Danger ☐ Comedians, The ☐ Coming to America ☐ Conan the Barbarian ☐ Convicts ☐ Deadly Hero ☐ Excessive Force ☐ Exorcist II: The Heretic ☐ Field of Dreams ☐ Gardens of Stone ☐ Great White Hope, The ☐ Greatest Thing That Almost Happened, The ☐ Greatest, The ☐ Grim Prairie Tales ☐ Hard Road to Glory, A—The Black Athlete In America ☐ Heat Wave ☐ Hunt for Red October, The ☐ Last Elephant, The ☐ Last Flight Out ☐ Last Remake of Beau Geste, The ☐ Lion King, The ☐ Malcolm X ☐ Man, The ☐ Matewan ☐ Meteor Man ☐ Patriot Games ☐ Paul Robeson ☐ Percy and Thunder ☐ Piece of the Action, A ☐ River Niger, The ☐ Sandlot, The ☐ Scorchers ☐ Sommersby ☐ Soul Man ☐ Swashbuckler ☐ Three Fugitives

Jones, Jeffrey ☐ Amadeus ☐ Beetlejuice ☐ Ed Wood ☐ Ferris Bueller's Day Off ☐ Hanoi Hilton, The ☐ Houseguest ☐ Howard the Duck ☐ Mom and Dad Save the World ☐ Out on a Limb ☐ Over Her Dead Body ☐ Transylvania 6-5000 ☐ Valmont ☐ Who's Harry Crumb? ☐ Without a Clue

Jones, Jennifer ☐ Barretts of Wimpole Street, The ☐ Beat the Devil ☐ Carrie ☐ Cluny Brown ☐ Duel in the Sun ☐ Farewell to Arms, A ☐ Frontier Horizon ☐ Gone to Earth ☐ Good Morning, Miss Dove ☐ Idol, The ☐ Indiscretion of an American Wife ☐ Love Is a Many Splendored Thing ☐ Love Letters ☐ Madame Bovary ☐ Man in the Gray Flannel Suit, The ☐ Portrait of Jennie ☐ Ruby Gentry ☐ Since You Went Away ☐ Song of Bernadette, The ☐ Tender Is the Night ☐ Towering Inferno, The ☐ We Were Strangers

Jones, Shirley ☐ April Love ☐ Bedtime Story ☐ Beyond the Poseidon Adventure ☐ Bobbikins ☐ Carousel ☐ Cheyenne Social Club, The ☐ Children of An Lac, The ☐ Courtship of Eddie's Father, The ☐ Elmer Gantry ☐ Evening in Byzantium, An ☐ Family Nobody Wanted, The ☐ Fluffy ☐ Girl in Room 20 ☐ Girls of Huntington House, The ☐ Happy Ending, The ☐ Music Man, The ☐ Never Steal Anything Small ☐ Oklahoma! ☐ Pepe ☐ Silent Night, Lonely Night ☐ Two Rode Together

Jones, Terry ☐ And Now for Something Completely Different ☐ Monty Python and the Holy Grail ☐ Monty Python Live at the Hollywood Bowl ☐ Monty Python's Flying Circus—Vol. 1 ☐ Monty Python's Life of Brian ☐ Monty Python's Parrot Sketch Not Included ☐ Monty Python's The Meaning of Life ☐ Secret Policeman's Other Ball, The

Jones, Tommy Lee ☐ Amazing Howard

Hughes, The ☐ April Morning ☐ Back Roads ☐ Betsy, The ☐ Big Town, The ☐ Black Moon Rising ☐ Blown Away ☐ Blue Sky ☐ Cat on a Hot Tin Roof ☐ Client, The ☐ Coal Miner's Daughter ☐ Cobb ☐ Executioner's Song, The ☐ Eyes of Laura Mars ☐ Firebirds ☐ Fugitive, The ☐ Gotham ☐ Heaven and Earth ☐ House of Cards ☐ Jackson County Jail ☐ JFK ☐ Lonesome Dove ☐ Nate and Hayes ☐ Package, The ☐ Park Is Mine, The ☐ River Rat, The ☐ Rolling Thunder ☐ Stormy Monday ☐ Stranger on My Land ☐ Under Siege

Jordan, Richard ☐ Bunker, The ☐ Defection of Simas Kudirka, The ☐ Flash of Green ☐ Friends of Eddie Coyle, The ☐ Heaven Is a Playground ☐ Hunt for the Night Stalker, The ☐ Les Miserables ☐ Logan's Run ☐ Manhunt: Search for the Night Stalker ☐ Mayfair Bank Caper, The ☐ Mean Season, The ☐ Men's Club, The ☐ Murder of Mary Phagan, The ☐ Old Boyfriends ☐ Primary Motive ☐ Raise the Titanic! ☐ Romero ☐ Secret of My Success, The ☐ Shout ☐ Valdez Is Coming ☐ Yakuza, The

Jory, Victor ☐ Adventures of Tom Sawyer, The ☐ Bad Men of Missouri ☐ Blackjack Ketchum, Desperado ☐ Blackwell's Island ☐ Buckskin Frontier ☐ Bulldog Drummond at Bay ☐ Cariboo Trail ☐ Cat Women of the Moon ☐ Cave of Outlaws ☐ Charlie Chan in Rio ☐ Cherokee Strip ☐ Devil's in Love, The ☐ Fighting Man of the Plains ☐ First Lady ☐ Flap ☐ Frasier, the Sensuous Lion ☐ Fugitive Kind, The ☐ Glamorous Night ☐ He Was Her Man ☐ Highwayman, The ☐ I Stole a Million ☐ Kansan, The ☐ Lone Wolf Meets a Lady, The ☐ Loves of Carmen, The ☐ Man from the Alamo, The ☐ Man Who Turned to Stone, The ☐ Manfish ☐ Meet Nero Wolfe ☐ Midsummer Night's Dream, A ☐ Miracle Worker, The ☐ Papillon ☐ Party Wire ☐ River's End ☐ Secrets of the Lone Wolf ☐ Shut My Big Mouth ☐ Son of Ali Baba ☐ State Fair ☐ Susannah of the Mounties ☐ Time for Dying, A ☐ Woman's Secret, A

Josephson, Erland ☐ After the Rehearsal ☐ Brink of Life ☐ Cries and Whispers ☐ Face to Face ☐ Girls, The ☐ Hanussen ☐ Hour of the Wolf ☐ Meeting Venus ☐ Montenegro ☐ Ox, The ☐ Passion of Anna, The ☐ Prospero's Books ☐ Sacrifice, The ☐ Scenes from a Marriage ☐ To Forget Venice ☐ Unbearable Lightness of Being, The

Joslyn, Allyn ☐ Expensive Husbands ☐ Fast and Furious ☐ Great McGinty, The ☐ I Love Melvin ☐ If I Had My Way ☐ If You Knew Susie ☐ Immortal Sergeant, The ☐ Impostor, The ☐ Island in the Sky ☐ It Shouldn't Happen to a Dog ☐ Jazz Singer, The ☐ Junior Miss ☐ Moonrise ☐ My Sister Eileen ☐ Public Pigeon No. One ☐ Shining Hour, The ☐ This Thing Called Love

Jourdan, Louis ☐ Anne of the Indies ☐ Best of Everything, The ☐ Bird of Paradise ☐ Bride Is Much Too Beautiful, The ☐ Can-Can ☐ Count of Monte Cristo, The ☐ Dangerous Exile ☐ Decameron Nights ☐ Fear No Evil ☐ First Olympics: Athens 1896, The ☐ Flea in Her Ear, A ☐ Gigi ☐ Great American Beauty Contest, The ☐ Happy Time, The ☐ Julie ☐ Letter from an Unknown Woman ☐ Look Out Sister ☐ Madame Bovary ☐ Made in Paris ☐ Man in the Iron Mask ☐ No Minor Vices ☐ Octopussy ☐ Return of Swamp Thing ☐ Swamp Thing ☐ Swan, The ☐ Three Coins in the Fountain ☐ V.I.P.s, The ☐ Year of the Comet

Jouvet, Louis ☐ Carnival in Flanders ☐ Compliments of Mr. Flow ☐ Confessions of a Rogue ☐ Curtain Rises, The ☐ End of a Day, The ☐ Heart of a Nation, The ☐ Lower Depths, The ☐ Un Carnet De Bal ☐ Volpone

Joyce, Brenda ☐ Enchanted Forest ☐ Here I Am a Stranger ☐ I'll Tell the World ☐ Little Giant ☐ Little Old New York ☐ Maryland ☐ Rains Came, The ☐ Right to the Heart ☐ Tarzan and the Amazons ☐ Tarzan and the Mermaids ☐ Tarzan and the Leopard Woman

Julia, Raul ☐ Addams Family Values ☐ Addams Family, The ☐ Alamo, The—Thirteen Days to Glory ☐ Been Down So Long It Looks Like Up to Me ☐ Compromising Positions ☐ Death Scream ☐ Escape Artist, The ☐ Eyes of Laura Mars ☐ Florida Straits ☐ Frankenstein Unbound ☐ Gumball Rally, The ☐ Kiss of the Spider Woman ☐ La Gran Fiesta ☐ Life of Sin, A ☐ Mack the Knife ☐ McCloud: Who Killed Miss U.S.A.? ☐ Moon Over Parador ☐ Morning After, The ☐ Onassis: The Richest Man in the World ☐ One from the Heart ☐ Overdrawn At The Memory Bank ☐ Penitent, The ☐ Presumed Innocent ☐ Romero ☐ Rookie, The ☐ Street Fighter ☐ Tango Bar ☐ Tempest ☐ Tequila Sunrise

Jurado, Katy ☐ Arrowhead ☐ Badlanders, The ☐ Barabbas ☐ Broken Lance ☐ Bullfighter and the Lady, The ☐ Children of Sanchez, The ☐ Dragon Wells Massacre ☐ El Bruto ☐ Evita Peron ☐ High Noon ☐ Man from Del Rio, The ☐ Once Upon a Scoundrel ☐ One-Eyed Jacks ☐ Pat Garrett and Billy the Kid ☐ Trapeze ☐ Trial ☐ Under the Volcano

Jurgens, Curt ☐ . . . And God Created Woman ☐ Assassination Bureau, The ☐ Battle of Britain, The ☐ Battle of Neretva, The ☐ Bitter Victory ☐ Blue Angel, The ☐ Brainwashed ☐ Breakthrough ☐ Devil's General, The ☐ Enemy Below, The ☐ Ferry to Hong Kong ☐ Goldengirl ☐ Hello-Goodbye ☐ House of Intrigue ☐ I Aim at the Stars ☐ Inn of the Sixth Happiness, The ☐ Invincible Six, The ☐ Kill! Kill! Kill! ☐ Lord Jim ☐ Magnificent Sinner ☐ Me and the Colonel ☐ Mephisto Waltz, The ☐ Miracle of the White Stallions ☐ Murder For Sale ☐ Nutty, Naughty Chateau ☐ Of Love and Desire ☐ Rats, The ☐ Sleep of Death ☐ Spy Who

Loved Me, The ☐ Tamango ☐ This Happy Feeling ☐ Three Moves to Freedom ☐ Time Bomb ☐ Twist, The

Justice, James Robertson ☐ Alien Women ☐ Checkpoint ☐ Doctor at Large ☐ Doctor in Distress ☐ Doctor in Love ☐ Doctor in Trouble ☐ Face of Fu Manchu, The ☐ Fast Lady, The ☐ Foxhole in Cairo ☐ Iron Petticoat, The ☐ Land of the Pharaohs ☐ Le Repos du Guerrier ☐ Mayerling ☐ Murder, She Said ☐ Raising the Wind ☐ Rob Roy, the Highland Rogue ☐ Sword and the Rose, The

Kahn, Madeline ☐ Adventure of Sherlock Holmes' Smarter Brother, The ☐ American Tail, An ☐ At Long Last Love ☐ Betsy's Wedding ☐ Blazing Saddles ☐ Cheap Detective, The ☐ City Heat ☐ Clue ☐ First Family ☐ For Richer, For Poorer ☐ From the Mixed-Up Files of Mrs. Basil E. Frankweiler ☐ Happy Birthday, Gemini ☐ High Anxiety ☐ History of the World Part I ☐ Mixed Nuts ☐ My Little Pony—The Movie ☐ Paper Moon ☐ Simon ☐ Slapstick of Another Kind ☐ What's Up, Doc? ☐ Wholly Moses ☐ Won Ton Ton, the Dog Who Saved Hollywood ☐ Yellowbeard ☐ Young Frankenstein

Kane, Carol ☐ Annie Hall ☐ Baby on Board ☐ Drop-Out Mother ☐ Flashback ☐ Greatest Man in the World, The ☐ Hester Street ☐ In the Soup ☐ Ishtar ☐ Jumpin' Jack Flash ☐ Lemon Sisters, The ☐ License to Drive ☐ Mafu Cage, The ☐ My Blue Heaven ☐ Norman Loves Rose ☐ Pandemonium ☐ Racing With the Moon ☐ Scrooged ☐ Secret Diary of Sigmund Freud, The ☐ Sticky Fingers ☐ Transylvania 6-5000 ☐ Valentino ☐ When a Stranger Calls

Karina, Anna ☐ Alphaville ☐ Band of Outsiders ☐ Before Winter Comes ☐ Bread and Chocolate ☐ Chinese Roulette ☐ Cleo From 5 to 7 ☐ Justine ☐ Le Petit Soldat ☐ Magus, The ☐ My Life to Live ☐ Nun, The ☐ Pierrot le Fou ☐ Salzburg Connection, The ☐ Stranger, The ☐ Woman Is a Woman, A

Karloff, Boris ☐ Abbott and Costello Meet Dr Jekyll And Mr Hyde ☐ Abbott and Costello Meet the Killer ☐ Alien Terror ☐ Ape, The ☐ Bedlam ☐ Before I Hang ☐ Behind That Curtain ☐ Behind the Mask ☐ Black Castle, The ☐ Black Cat, The ☐ Black Friday ☐ Black Room, The ☐ Black Sabbath ☐ Body Snatcher, The ☐ Boogie Man Will Get You, The ☐ Bride of Frankenstein, The ☐ British Intelligence ☐ Cauldron of Blood ☐ Charlie Chan at the Opera ☐ Climax, The ☐ Comedy of Terrors, The ☐ Corridors of Blood ☐ Criminal Code, The ☐ Crimson Cult, The ☐ Devil Commands, The ☐ Devil's Island ☐ Dick Tracy Meets Gruesome ☐ Die, Monster, Die! ☐ Fatal Hour, The ☐ Fear Chamber, The ☐ Five Star Final ☐ Frankenstein (Restored) ☐ Frankenstein—1970 ☐ Ghost in the Invisible Bikini ☐ Ghoul, The ☐ Haunted Strangler, The ☐ House of Evil ☐ House of Frankenstein ☐ House of Rothschild, The ☐ I Like Your Nerve ☐ Invisible Menace, The ☐ Invisible Ray, The ☐ Isle of the Dead ☐ Lost Patrol, The ☐ Macabre Serenade ☐ Mad Genius, The ☐ Mad Monster Party? ☐ Man They Could Not Hang, The ☐ Man Who Lived Again, The ☐ Man with Nine Lives, The ☐ Mask of Fu Manchu, The ☐ Mr. Wong in Chinatown ☐ Mr. Wong, Detective ☐ Mummy, The ☐ Mystery of Mr. Wong, The ☐ Night Key ☐ Night World ☐ Old Dark House, The ☐ Personal Column ☐ Raven, The ☐ Raven, The ☐ Scarface ☐ Secret Life of Walter Mitty, The ☐ Son of Frankenstein ☐ Sorcerers, The ☐ Tap Roots ☐ Targets ☐ Terror, The ☐ Tower of London, The ☐ Unconquered ☐ Walking Dead, The ☐ West of Shanghai

Karns, Roscoe ☐ Beggars of Life ☐ Four Hours to Kill ☐ Front Page Woman ☐ Hi, Good Lookin' ☐ It Happened One Night ☐ Jazz Singer, The ☐ Night After Night ☐ Night of Mystery ☐ Red Hot Tires ☐ Saturday's Children ☐ Tipp-Off Girls ☐ Wings in the Dark ☐ Woman of the Year

Karras, Alex ☐ Against All Odds ☐ Alcatraz: The Whole Shocking Story ☐ Babe ☐ Blazing Saddles ☐ Hardcase ☐ Hootch County Boys, The ☐ Jacob Two-Two Meets the Hooded Fang ☐ Jimmy B. & Andre ☐ Mad Bull ☐ Mighty Moose and the Quarterback Kid ☐ Nobody's Perfekt ☐ Paper Lion ☐ Victor/Victoria ☐ When Time Ran Out . . .

Karyo, Tcheky ☐ Exposure ☐ Full Moon in Paris ☐ Husbands and Lovers ☐ La Femme Nikita ☐ Sketch Artist

Kaufman, Andy ☐ Andy Kaufman Special, The ☐ Andy Kaufman—Sound Stage ☐ Heartbeeps ☐ In God We Trust ☐ My Breakfast with Blassie

Kavner, Julie ☐ Awakenings ☐ Bad Medicine ☐ I'll Do Anything ☐ New York Stories ☐ No Other Love ☐ Shadows and Fog ☐ Surrender ☐ This Is My Life

Kaye, Danny ☐ Court Jester, The ☐ Five Pennies, The ☐ Hans Christian Andersen ☐ Inspector General, The ☐ Kid from Brooklyn, The ☐ Knock on Wood ☐ Madwoman of Chaillot, The ☐ Man from the Diner's Club, The ☐ Me and the Colonel ☐ Merry Andrew ☐ On the Double ☐ On the Riviera ☐ Pinocchio ☐ Secret Life of Walter Mitty, The ☐ Skokie ☐ Song is Born, A ☐ Up in Arms ☐ White Christmas ☐ Wonder Man

Kaye, Stubby ☐ Can Hieronymus Merkin Ever Forget Mercy Humppe and Find True Happiness? ☐ Forty Pounds of Trouble ☐ Guys and Dolls ☐ Li'l Abner ☐ Sweet Charity ☐ Way West, The ☐ Who Framed Roger Rabbit ☐ You Can't Run Away From It

Kazan, Lainie ☐ 29th Street ☐ Adventures of a Two-Minute Werewolf, The ☐ Beaches ☐ Cemetery Club, The ☐ Delta Force, The ☐ Eternity ☐ Harry and the Hendersons ☐ I

Don't Buy Kisses Anymore ☐ Jerk Too, The ☐ Journey of Natty Gann, The ☐ Lady in Cement ☐ Lust in the Dust ☐ My Favorite Year ☐ One from the Heart

Keach, James ☐ Blue Hotel, The ☐ Film House Fever ☐ Long Riders, The ☐ Love Letters ☐ Razor's Edge, The ☐ Wildcats

Keach, Stacy ☐ All the Kind Strangers ☐ Brewster McCloud ☐ Butterfly ☐ Cheech & Chong's Nice Dreams ☐ Cheech & Chong—Up in Smoke ☐ Class of 1999 ☐ Conduct Unbecoming ☐ Diary of a Young Comic ☐ Doc ☐ False Identity ☐ Fat City ☐ Forgotten, The ☐ Gravy Train, The ☐ Gray Lady Down ☐ Great Battle, The ☐ Heart Is a Lonely Hunter, The ☐ James A. Michener's Dynasty ☐ Killer Inside Me, The ☐ Life and Times of Judge Roy Bean, The ☐ Long Riders, The ☐ Luther ☐ Man Of Destiny ☐ Mission of the Shark ☐ Mistral's Daughter ☐ New Centurions, The ☐ Ninth Configuration, The ☐ Road Games ☐ Rumor of War, A ☐ That Championship Season

Keaton, Buster ☐ Beach Blanket Bingo ☐ Boom in the Moon ☐ Cameraman, The ☐ College ☐ Doughboys ☐ Four Clowns ☐ Free and Easy ☐ Funny Thing Happened on the Way to the Forum, A ☐ General, The ☐ God's Country ☐ Great Chase, The ☐ Hollywood Cavalcade ☐ Hollywood Revue of 1929, The ☐ How to Stuff a Wild Bikini ☐ In the Good Old Summertime ☐ Li'l Abner ☐ Limelight ☐ Lovable Cheat, The ☐ MGM's Big Parade of Comedy ☐ Old Spanish Custom, An ☐ Our Hospitality ☐ Pajama Party ☐ Parlor, Bedroom and Bath ☐ Passionate Plumber, The ☐ San Diego, I Love You ☐ Sergeant Deadhead ☐ Seven Chances ☐ Sherlock, Jr. ☐ Sidewalks of New York ☐ Speak Easily ☐ Spite Marriage ☐ Steamboat Bill, Jr. ☐ That's the Spirit ☐ What, No Beer? ☐ When Comedy Was King

Keaton, Diane ☐ Annie Hall ☐ Baby Boom ☐ Crimes of the Heart ☐ Father of the Bride ☐ Godfather, Part II, The ☐ Godfather, Part III, The ☐ Godfather, The ☐ Good Mother, The ☐ Harry and Walter Go to New York ☐ I Will, I Will . . . For Now ☐ Interiors ☐ Lemon Sisters, The ☐ Little Drummer Girl, The ☐ Look Who's Talking Now ☐ Looking for Mr. Goodbar ☐ Love and Death ☐ Manhattan ☐ Manhattan Murder Mystery ☐ Mrs. Soffel ☐ Play It Again, Sam ☐ Radio Days ☐ Reds ☐ Running Mates ☐ Shoot the Moon ☐ Sleeper

Keaton, Michael ☐ Batman ☐ Batman Returns ☐ Beetlejuice ☐ Clean and Sober ☐ Dream Team, The ☐ Gung Ho ☐ Johnny Dangerously ☐ Mr. Mom ☐ Much Ado About Nothing ☐ My Life ☐ Night Shift ☐ One Good Cop ☐ Pacific Heights ☐ Paper, The ☐ Speechless ☐ Squeeze, The ☐ Touch and Go

Keeler, Ruby ☐ 42nd Street ☐ Colleen ☐ Dames ☐ Flirtation Walk ☐ Footlight Parade ☐ Go Into Your Dance ☐ Gold Diggers of 1933 ☐ Mother Carey's Chickens ☐ Ready, Willing and Able ☐ Shipmates Forever ☐ Sweetheart of the Campus

Keel, Howard ☐ Annie Get Your Gun ☐ Armored Command ☐ Big Fisherman, The ☐ Calamity Jane ☐ Callaway Went Thataway ☐ Day of the Triffids, The ☐ Deep in My Heart ☐ Desperate Search ☐ Fast Company ☐ Floods of Fear ☐ Jupiter's Darling ☐ Kismet ☐ Kiss Me Kate ☐ Lovely to Look At ☐ Pagan Love Song ☐ Rose Marie ☐ Seven Brides for Seven Brothers ☐ Show Boat ☐ Texas Carnival ☐ Three Guys Named Mike ☐ War Wagon, The

Keitel, Harvey ☐ Alice Doesn't Live Here Anymore ☐ Bad Lieutenant ☐ Bad Timing: A Sensual Obsession ☐ Blue Collar ☐ Border, The ☐ Buffalo Bill and the Indians ☐ Bugsy ☐ Camorra ☐ Corrupt ☐ Dangerous Game ☐ Deathwatch ☐ Duellists, The ☐ Eagle's Wing ☐ Exposed ☐ Falling in Love ☐ Fingers ☐ Imaginary Crimes ☐ Inquiry, The ☐ January Man, The ☐ La Nuit des Varennes ☐ Last Temptation of Christ, The ☐ Mean Streets ☐ Men's Club, The ☐ Monkey Trouble ☐ Mortal Thoughts ☐ Mother, Jugs & Speed ☐ Piano, The ☐ Pick-up Artist, The ☐ Point of No Return ☐ Pulp Fiction ☐ Reservoir Dogs ☐ Rising Sun ☐ Saturn 3 ☐ Sister Act ☐ Star Knight ☐ Taxi Driver ☐ That's the Way of the World ☐ Thelma & Louise ☐ Two Evil Eyes ☐ Two Jakes, The ☐ Welcome to L.A. ☐ Who's That Knocking at My Door? ☐ Wise Guys

Keith, Brian ☐ Alamo, The—Thirteen Days to Glory ☐ Alaska Seas ☐ Arrowhead ☐ Bamboo Prison, The ☐ Charlie Chan and the Curse of the Dragon Queen ☐ Chicago Confidential ☐ Deadly Companions, The ☐ Death Before Dishonor ☐ Dino ☐ Gaily, Gaily ☐ Gambler Returns: The Luck of the Draw, The ☐ Hallelujah Trail, The ☐ Hell Canyon Outlaws ☐ Hooper ☐ Hot Lead ☐ In the Matter of Karen Ann Quinlan ☐ Jivaro ☐ Joe Panther ☐ Johnny Shiloh ☐ Krakatoa, East of Java ☐ Loneliest Runner, The ☐ McKenzie Break, The ☐ Meteor ☐ Moon Pilot ☐ Mountain Men, The ☐ Nevada Smith ☐ Nickelodeon ☐ Nightfall ☐ Parent Trap, The ☐ Pleasure Seekers, The ☐ Raiders, The ☐ Rare Breed, The ☐ Reflections in a Golden Eye ☐ Russians Are Coming! The Russians Are Coming!, The ☐ Savage Sam ☐ Scandalous John ☐ Sharky's Machine ☐ Sierra Baron ☐ Storm Center ☐ Suppose They Gave a War and Nobody Came? ☐ Ten Who Dared ☐ Those Calloways ☐ Tiger Walks, A ☐ Tight Spot ☐ Violent Men, The ☐ Welcome Home ☐ Wind and the Lion, The ☐ With Six You Get Eggroll ☐ Yakuza, The ☐ Young Philadelphians, The

Keith, David ☐ Back Roads ☐ Firestarter

☐ Further Adventures of Tennessee Buck, The ☐ Gulag ☐ Guts and Glory: The Rise and Fall of Oliver North ☐ Heartbreak Hotel ☐ Independence Day ☐ Liar's Edge ☐ Lords of Discipline, The ☐ Officer and a Gentleman, An ☐ Take this Job and Shove It ☐ White of the Eye

Kellaway, Cecil ☐ Beast from 20,000 Fathoms, The ☐ Burma Convoy ☐ Down to the Sea in Ships ☐ Easy to Wed ☐ Female on the Beach ☐ Fitzwilly ☐ Francis of Assisi ☐ Frenchman's Creek ☐ Guess Who's Coming to Dinner ☐ Half Angel ☐ Harvey ☐ Highwayman, The ☐ I Married a Witch ☐ Intermezzo ☐ Interrupted Melody ☐ Invisible Man Returns, The ☐ It Ain't Hay ☐ Johnny Trouble ☐ Just Across the Street ☐ Katie Did It ☐ Kitty ☐ Love Letters ☐ Maid's Night Out ☐ Mexican Spitfire ☐ Monsieur Beaucaire ☐ Mummy's Hand, The ☐ Night of January 16th, The ☐ Postman Always Rings Twice, The ☐ Proud Rebel, The ☐ Reformer and the Redhead, The ☐ Unconquered ☐ We Are Not Alone ☐ Young Bess

Keller, Marthe ☐ Amateur, The ☐ And Now My Love ☐ Black Sunday ☐ Bobby Deerfield ☐ Dark Eyes ☐ Fedora ☐ Femmes de Personne ☐ Formula, The ☐ Marathon Man ☐ Red Kiss

Kellerman, Sally ☐ All's Fair ☐ April Fools, The ☐ Back to School ☐ Big Bus, The ☐ Boris and Natasha ☐ Boston Strangler, The ☐ Brewster McCloud ☐ Dempsey ☐ Fatal Attraction ☐ Foxes ☐ It Rained All Night the Day I Left ☐ KGB—the Secret War ☐ Last of the Red Hot Lovers ☐ Little Romance, A ☐ Lost Horizon ☐ Loving Couples ☐ M*A*S*H ☐ Meatballs III ☐ Mirror, Mirror 2: Raven Dance ☐ Moving Violations ☐ Ready to Wear ☐ Reflection of Fear, A ☐ Reform School Girl ☐ Secret of the Ice Cave, The ☐ September Gun ☐ Serial ☐ Slither ☐ Someone to Love ☐ That's Life! ☐ Three for the Road ☐ Victim of Beauty ☐ Welcome to L.A.

Kelly, Gene ☐ 40 Carats ☐ American in Paris, An ☐ Anchors Aweigh ☐ Black Hand ☐ Brigadoon ☐ Christmas Holiday ☐ Cover Girl ☐ Cross of Lorraine, The ☐ Deep in My Heart ☐ Devil Makes Three, The ☐ DuBarry Was a Lady ☐ For Me and My Gal ☐ Happy Road, The ☐ Inherit the Wind ☐ Invitation to the Dance ☐ It's a Big Country ☐ It's Always Fair Weather ☐ Les Girls ☐ Living In a Big Way ☐ Marjorie Morningstar ☐ On the Town ☐ Pirate, The ☐ Singin' in the Rain ☐ Sins ☐ Summer Stock ☐ Take Me Out to the Ball Game ☐ That's Dancing ☐ That's Entertainment ☐ That's Entertainment 3 ☐ That's Entertainment, Part 2 ☐ Thousands Cheer ☐ Three Musketeers, The ☐ Viva Knievel! ☐ What a Way to Go! ☐ Words and Music ☐ Xanadu ☐ Young Girls of Rochefort, The ☐ Ziegfeld Follies

Kelly, Grace ☐ Bridges at Toko-Ri, The ☐ Country Girl, The ☐ Dial M for Murder ☐ Fourteen Hours ☐ Green Fire ☐ High Noon ☐ High Society ☐ Mogambo ☐ Rear Window ☐ Swan, The ☐ To Catch a Thief

Kelly, Patsy ☐ Broadway Limited ☐ C'mon, Let's Live a Little ☐ Cowboy and the Lady, The ☐ Crowded Sky, The ☐ Ever Since Eve ☐ Every Night at Eight ☐ Freaky Friday ☐ Ghost in the Invisible Bikini ☐ Girl from Missouri, The ☐ Go Into Your Dance ☐ Going Hollywood ☐ Gorilla, The ☐ Merrily We Live ☐ Nobody's Baby ☐ Pigskin Parade ☐ Road Show ☐ Sing, Baby, Sing ☐ Thanks a Million ☐ There Goes My Heart ☐ Topper Returns ☐ Transatlantic Merry-Go-Round ☐ Wake Up and Live

Kelly, Paul ☐ Adventure Island ☐ Allotment Wives ☐ Broadway Through a Keyhole ☐ China's Little Devils ☐ Fear in the Night ☐ File on Thelma Jordon, The ☐ Flight Command ☐ Flying Irishman, The ☐ Girl from Calgary, The ☐ Girls Under Twenty-One ☐ Glass Alibi, The ☐ Grissly's Millions ☐ Guilty of Treason ☐ Invisible Stripes ☐ Johnny Dark ☐ Join the Marines ☐ Mr. and Mrs. North ☐ Painted Hills, The ☐ San Antonio ☐ Secret Fury, The ☐ Side Street ☐ Springfield Rifle ☐ Square Jungle, The ☐ Star of Midnight

Kemp, Jeremy ☐ Belstone Fox, The ☐ Blue Max, The ☐ Darling Lili ☐ Evita Peron ☐ Feet Foremost ☐ Games, The ☐ Pope Joan ☐ Seven Percent Solution, The ☐ Twist of Sand, A ☐ When the Whales Came

Kendall, Kay ☐ Abdulla the Great ☐ Constant Husband, The ☐ Curtain Up ☐ Doctor in the House ☐ Genevieve ☐ Lady Godiva Rides Again ☐ Les Girls ☐ Meet Mr. Lucifer ☐ Once More, With Feeling ☐ Quentin Durward ☐ Reluctant Debutante, The ☐ Simon and Laura ☐ Square Ring, The

Kendall, Suzy ☐ 30 Is a Dangerous Age, Cynthia ☐ Adventures of a Private Eye ☐ Bird With the Crystal Plumage, The ☐ Darker than Amber ☐ Fear Is the Key ☐ Fraulein Doktor ☐ Gamblers, The ☐ In the Devil's Garden ☐ Penthouse, The ☐ To Sir with Love

Kennedy, Arthur ☐ Adventures of a Young Man ☐ Air Force ☐ Bad Men of Missouri ☐ Barabbas ☐ Bend of the River ☐ Boomerang! ☐ Bright Victory ☐ Champion ☐ Cheyenne ☐ Cheyenne Autumn ☐ Chicago Deadline ☐ City for Conquest ☐ Claudelle Inglish ☐ Desperate Hours, The ☐ Desperate Journey ☐ Devotion ☐ Elmer Gantry ☐ Girl in White, The ☐ Glass Menagerie, The ☐ Hail, Hero! ☐ High Sierra ☐ Home is the Hero ☐ Italiano Brava Gente ☐ Joy in the Morning ☐ Knockout ☐ Lawrence of Arabia ☐ Lusty Men, The ☐ Man from Laramie, The ☐ Mean Machine, The ☐ Minute to Pray, a Second to Die, A ☐ Murder, She Said ☐ My Old Man's Place ☐ Naked Dawn, The ☐ Nevada Smith

☐ Peyton Place ☐ Rancho Notorious ☐ Rawhide Years, The ☐ Red Mountain ☐ Shark! ☐ Some Came Running ☐ Summer Place, A ☐ Tempter, The ☐ They Died With Their Boots On ☐ Too Late for Tears ☐ Trial ☐ Twilight for the Gods ☐ Walking Hills, The ☐ Window, The

Kennedy, Douglas ☐ Amazing Transparent Man, The ☐ Flight of the Lost Balloon ☐ For Men Only ☐ Fort Osage ☐ I Was an American Spy ☐ Jack McCall, Desperado ☐ Lone Ranger and the Lost City of Gold, The ☐ Revenue Agent

Kennedy, Edgar ☐ Air Raid Wardens ☐ Captain Tugboat Annie ☐ Crossfire ☐ Double Wedding ☐ Duck Soup ☐ Falcon Strikes Back, The ☐ Hold 'Em Jail ☐ In Old California ☐ It Happened Tomorrow ☐ It's a Wonderful World ☐ Little Orphan Annie ☐ Murder on the Blackboard ☐ Peck's Bad Boy with the Circus ☐ Return of Jimmy Valentine, The ☐ Sandy Gets Her Man ☐ Tillie and Gus ☐ True Confession ☐ Westward Passage ☐ When's Your Birthday? ☐ Yours For the Asking

Kennedy, George ☐ . . . tick . . . tick . . . tick . . . ☐ Airport ☐ Airport '75 ☐ Airport '77 ☐ Airport '79—The Concorde ☐ Badge or the Cross, The ☐ Ballad of Josie, The ☐ Bandolero ☐ Bolero ☐ Born to Race ☐ Boston Strangler, The ☐ Brain Dead ☐ Brass Target, The ☐ Cahill—United States Marshal ☐ Charade ☐ Chattanooga Choo Choo ☐ Cool Hand Luke ☐ Creepshow 2 ☐ Death on the Nile ☐ Death Ship ☐ Delta Force, The ☐ Dirty Dingus Magee ☐ Dirty Dozen, The ☐ Double McGuffin, The ☐ Earthquake ☐ Eiger Sanction, The ☐ Fools' Parade ☐ Gaily, Gaily ☐ Good Guys and the Bad Guys, The ☐ Great American Tragedy, A ☐ Gunfighters, The ☐ Guns of the Magnificent Seven ☐ Hired to Kill ☐ Human Factor, The ☐ Hurry Sundown ☐ Island of the Blue Dolphins ☐ Lonely Are the Brave ☐ Lost Horizon ☐ Man from the Diner's Club, The ☐ McHale's Navy ☐ Mean Dog Blues ☐ Ministry of Vengeance ☐ Mirage ☐ Modern Romance ☐ Naked Gun 2 1/2: The Smell of Fear, The ☐ Naked Gun 33 1/3: The Final Insult ☐ Naked Gun, The ☐ Pink Jungle, The ☐ Radioactive Dreams ☐ Savage Dawn ☐ Sons of Katie Elder, The ☐ Steel ☐ Terror Within, The ☐ Virus ☐ Zigzag

Kensit, Patsy ☐ Absolute Beginners ☐ Blame It on the Bellboy ☐ Blue Bird, The ☐ Chicago Joe and the Showgirl ☐ Chorus of Disapproval, A ☐ Full Eclipse ☐ Kill Cruise ☐ Timebomb ☐ Turn of the Screw, The ☐ Twenty-One

Kerr, Deborah ☐ Affair to Remember, An ☐ Arrangement, The ☐ Assam Garden, The ☐ Beloved Infidel ☐ Black Narcissus ☐ Bonjour Tristesse ☐ Casino Royale ☐ Chalk Garden, The ☐ Count Your Blessings ☐ Day Will Dawn, The ☐ Dream Wife ☐ Edward, My Son ☐ End of the Affair, The ☐ Eye of the Devil ☐ From Here to Eternity ☐ Grass is Greener, The ☐ Gypsy Moths, The ☐ Hatter's Castle ☐ Heaven Knows, Mr. Allison ☐ Hold the Dream ☐ Hucksters, The ☐ I See a Dark Stranger ☐ If Winter Comes ☐ Innocents, The ☐ Journey, The ☐ Julius Caesar ☐ King and I, The ☐ King Solomon's Mines ☐ Life and Death of Colonel Blimp, The ☐ Love on the Dole ☐ Major Barbara ☐ Marriage on the Rocks ☐ Naked Edge, The ☐ Night of the Iguana, The ☐ Please Believe Me ☐ Prisoner of Zenda, The ☐ Proud and Profane, The ☐ Prudence and the Pill ☐ Quo Vadis? ☐ Separate Tables ☐ Sundowners, The ☐ Tea and Sympathy ☐ Thunder in the East ☐ Vacation From Marriage ☐ Witness for the Prosecution ☐ Young Bess

Kerr, John ☐ Cobweb, The ☐ Crowded Sky, The ☐ Gaby ☐ Pit and the Pendulum ☐ South Pacific ☐ Tea and Sympathy

Keyes, Evelyn ☐ 99 River Street ☐ Adventures of Martin Eden, The ☐ Before I Hang ☐ Desperadoes, The ☐ Enchantment ☐ Face Behind the Mask, The ☐ Flight Lieutenant ☐ Hell's Half Acre ☐ Here Comes Mr. Jordan ☐ Iron Man, The ☐ Johnny O'Clock ☐ Jolson Story, The ☐ Killer That Stalked New York, The ☐ Ladies in Retirement ☐ Mating of Millie, The ☐ Mrs. Mike ☐ Nine Girls ☐ One Big Affair ☐ Prowler, The ☐ Return to Salem's Lot, A ☐ Seven Year Itch, The ☐ Thousand and One Nights, A ☐ Union Pacific ☐ Wicked Stepmother

Kibbee, Guy ☐ Babbitt ☐ Babes in Arms ☐ Bad Man of Brimstone ☐ Big City Blues ☐ Captain Blood ☐ Captain January ☐ Central Park ☐ Chad Hanna ☐ City Streets ☐ Conquerors, The ☐ Crowd Roars, The ☐ Dames ☐ Dark Horse ☐ Design for Scandal ☐ Earthworm Tractors ☐ Fireman, Save My Child ☐ Flying High ☐ Footlight Parade ☐ Girl Crazy ☐ Gold Diggers of 1933 ☐ High Pressure ☐ Horn Blows at Midnight, The ☐ I Live for Love ☐ It Started with Eve ☐ It's a Wonderful World ☐ Joy of Living ☐ Lady for a Day ☐ Laughing Sinners ☐ Life of Jimmy Dolan, The ☐ Little Lord Fauntleroy ☐ Man of the World ☐ Miss Annie Rooney ☐ Mr. Smith Goes to Washington ☐ Of Human Hearts ☐ Rain ☐ Rich Man, Poor Girl ☐ Riding on Air ☐ Scattergood Baines ☐ Taxi! ☐ Three Men on a Horse ☐ Two Seconds ☐ Union Depot ☐ Winner Take All ☐ Wonder Bar

Kidder, Margot ☐ 92 in the Shade ☐ Amityville Horror, The ☐ Black Christmas ☐ Body of Evidence ☐ Bounty Man, The ☐ Gaily, Gaily ☐ Glitter Dome, The ☐ GoBots: Battle of the Rock Lords ☐ Gravy Train, The ☐ Heartaches ☐ Honky Tonk ☐ Keeping Track ☐ Little Treasure ☐ Miss Right ☐ Mob Story ☐ Quackser Fortune Has a Cousin in the Bronx ☐ Quiet Day in Belfast, A ☐ Reincarnation of Peter Proud, The ☐ Sisters ☐ Some Kind of Hero ☐ Superman 2 ☐ Superman 3 ☐ Superman 4: The Quest for Peace ☐ Superman—The Movie ☐ To Catch a Killer ☐ Trenchcoat ☐ Willie and Phil

Kidman, Nicole ☐ Archer's Adventure ☐ Billy Bathgate ☐ BMX Bandits ☐ Days of Thunder ☐ Dead Calm ☐ Far and Away ☐ Flirting ☐ Malice ☐ My Life

Kilbride, Percy ☐ Adventures of Mark Twain, The ☐ Black Bart ☐ Egg and I, The ☐ Feudin', Fussin' and A-Fightin' ☐ Free For All ☐ George Washington Slept Here ☐ Guest in the House ☐ Ma and Pa Kettle ☐ Ma and Pa Kettle at Home ☐ Ma and Pa Kettle at the Fair ☐ Ma and Pa Kettle at Waikiki ☐ Ma and Pa Kettle Back on the Farm ☐ Ma and Pa Kettle Go to Town ☐ Ma and Pa Kettle on Vacation ☐ Riding High

Kiley, Richard ☐ Absolute Strangers ☐ Angel on My Shoulder ☐ Bad Seed, The ☐ Blackboard Jungle ☐ Do You Remember Love? ☐ Eight Iron Men ☐ Endless Love ☐ Final Days, The ☐ Friendly Persuasion ☐ Gunsmoke: The Last Apache ☐ Incident in San Francisco ☐ Isabel's Choice ☐ Jigsaw ☐ Little Prince, The ☐ Looking for Mr. Goodbar ☐ Macahans, The ☐ Mob, The ☐ Night Gallery ☐ Pendulum ☐ Phenix City Story, The ☐ Pickup on South Street ☐ Separate But Equal ☐ Spanish Affair ☐ Thorn Birds, The

Kilmer, Val ☐ Billy the Kid ☐ Doors, The ☐ Gore Vidal's Billy the Kid ☐ Kill Me Again ☐ Man Who Broke 1,000 Chains, The ☐ Murders in the Rue Morgue, The ☐ Real Genius ☐ Real McCoy, The ☐ Thunderheart ☐ Tombstone ☐ Top Gun ☐ Top Secret ☐ True Romance ☐ Willow

King, Alan ☐ Anderson Tapes, The ☐ Author! Author! ☐ Bye Bye Braverman ☐ Cat's Eye ☐ Enemies, A Love Story ☐ Girl He Left Behind ☐ I, the Jury ☐ Just Tell Me What You Want ☐ Memories of Me ☐ Night and the City

King, Andrea ☐ Beast with Five Fingers, The ☐ Blackenstein ☐ God is My Co-Pilot ☐ Hotel Berlin ☐ House of the Black Death ☐ I Was a Shoplifter ☐ Man I Love, The ☐ Mr. Peabody and the Mermaid ☐ My Wild Irish Rose ☐ Red Planet Mars ☐ Ride the Pink Horse ☐ Southside 1-1000 ☐ World in His Arms, The

King, Perry ☐ Andy Warhol's Bad ☐ Choirboys, The ☐ City in Fear ☐ Class of 1984 ☐ Cracker Factory, The ☐ Different Story, A ☐ Disaster at Silo 7 ☐ Helen Keller: The Miracle Continues ☐ Jericho Fever ☐ Lipstick ☐ Lords of Flatbush, The ☐ Man Who Lived at the Ritz, The ☐ Mandingo ☐ Perfect People ☐ Possession of Joel Delaney, The ☐ Prize Pulitzer: The Roxanne Pulitzer Story, The ☐ Switch ☐ Wild Party, The

Kingsley, Ben ☐ Betrayal ☐ Bugsy ☐ Camille ☐ Children, The ☐ Dave ☐ Death and the Maiden ☐ Fear Is the Key ☐ Fifth Monkey, The ☐ Freddie as F.R.O.7 ☐ Gandhi ☐ Harem ☐ Maurice ☐ Murderers Among Us: The Simon Wiesenthal Story ☐ Pascali's Island ☐ Schindler's List ☐ Searching for Bobby Fischer ☐ Silas Marner ☐ Slipstream ☐ Sneakers ☐ Turtle Diary ☐ Without a Clue

Kinski, Klaus ☐ Aguirre: The Wrath of God ☐ Android ☐ Buddy Buddy ☐ Bullet for the General, A ☐ Burden of Dreams ☐ Codename—Wildgeese ☐ Count Dracula ☐ Crawlspace ☐ Creature ☐ Deadly Sanctuary ☐ Door with Seven Locks, The ☐ Fitzcarraldo ☐ Five for Hell ☐ For a Few Dollars More ☐ French Woman, The ☐ Gangsters' Law ☐ Grand Slam ☐ Heroes in Hell ☐ Indian Scarf, The ☐ Inn on the River, The ☐ Lifespan ☐ Little Drummer Girl, The ☐ Love and Money ☐ Nosferatu the Vampyre ☐ Schizoid ☐ Scotland Yard Hunts Dr. Mabuse ☐ Secret Diary of Sigmund Freud, The ☐ Shoot the Living Pray for the Dead ☐ Soldier, The ☐ Star Knight ☐ Venom ☐ Venus in Furs ☐ Woyzeck

Kinski, Nastassja ☐ Boarding School ☐ Cat People ☐ Exposed ☐ For Your Love Only ☐ Harem ☐ Hotel New Hampshire, The ☐ Magdalene ☐ Maria's Lovers ☐ Moon in the Gutter, The ☐ Night Sun ☐ One from the Heart ☐ Paris, Texas ☐ Revolution ☐ Spring Symphony ☐ Stay As You Are ☐ Terminal Velocity ☐ Tess ☐ To the Devil A Daughter ☐ Unfaithfully Yours ☐ Wrong Move

Kirby, Bruno ☐ Almost Summer ☐ City Slickers ☐ Fallen Angels—Volume 2 ☐ Freshman, The ☐ Golden Gate ☐ Good Morning, Vietnam ☐ Modern Romance ☐ We're No Angels ☐ When Harry Met Sally . . . ☐ Where the Buffalo Roam

Kirkland, Sally ☐ Anna ☐ Best of the Best ☐ Blue ☐ Bullseye! ☐ Cheatin' Hearts ☐ Cinderella Liberty ☐ Cold Feet ☐ Coming Apart ☐ Double Jeopardy ☐ Fatal Games ☐ Futz ☐ Haunted, The ☐ Heat Wave ☐ High Stakes ☐ Hit the Dutchman ☐ Hometown U.S.A. ☐ Human Highway ☐ In the Heat of Passion ☐ Paint It Black ☐ Primary Motive ☐ Revenge ☐ Two Evil Eyes

Kirk, Tommy ☐ Absent Minded Professor, The ☐ Bon Voyage! ☐ Ghost in the Invisible Bikini ☐ Horsemasters, The ☐ It's a Bikini World ☐ Mars Needs Women ☐ Misadventures of Merlin Jones, The ☐ Monkey's Uncle, The ☐ Moon Pilot ☐ Old Yeller ☐ Pajama Party ☐ Savage Sam ☐ Shaggy Dog, The ☐ Son of Flubber ☐ Village of the Giants

Kitt, Eartha ☐ Anna Lucasta ☐ Boomerang ☐ Erik the Viking ☐ Ernest Scared Stupid ☐ Friday Foster ☐ Mark of the Hawk, The ☐ Master of Dragonard Hill ☐ Naughty Knights ☐ New Faces ☐ St. Louis Blues ☐ Synanon ☐ Tropic of Desire

Klein, Robert ☐ All-Star Salute to the Improv, An ☐ Bell Jar, The ☐ Mixed Nuts ☐ No-

body's Perfekt ☐ Owl and the Pussycat, The ☐ Tales From the Darkside: The Movie
Klein-Rogge, Rudolf ☐ Dr. Mabuse, King of Crime ☐ Dr. Mabuse, the Gambler ☐ Metropolis ☐ Spies ☐ Testament of Dr. Mabuse, The
Klemperer, Werner ☐ Dark Intruder ☐ Five Steps to Danger ☐ High Cost of Loving, The ☐ Operation Eichmann
Kline, Kevin ☐ Big Chill, The ☐ Chaplin ☐ Consenting Adults ☐ Cry Freedom ☐ Dave ☐ Fish Called Wanda, A ☐ George Balanchine's The Nutcracker ☐ Grand Canyon ☐ I Love You to Death ☐ January Man, The ☐ Pirates of Penzance, The ☐ Princess Caraboo ☐ Silverado ☐ Soapdish ☐ Sophie's Choice ☐ Violets Are Blue...
Klugman, Jack ☐ 12 Angry Men ☐ Act One ☐ Cry Terror ☐ Days of Wine and Roses ☐ Detective, The ☐ Fame Is the Name of the Game ☐ Goodbye, Columbus ☐ Hail, Mafia ☐ I Could Go on Singing ☐ One of My Wives Is Missing ☐ Who Says I Can't Ride a Rainbow?
Knapp, Evalyn ☐ Confidential ☐ Fireman, Save My Child ☐ His Private Secretary ☐ In Old Santa Fe ☐ Madame Racketeer ☐ Millionaire, The ☐ Mistaken Identity ☐ Night Mayor, The ☐ Rawhide ☐ River's End ☐ Sinner's Holiday ☐ Smart Money ☐ Successful Calamity, A
Knight, Shirley ☐ 21 Hours at Munich ☐ Beyond the Poseidon Adventure ☐ Bump in the Night ☐ Champions: A Love Story ☐ Dark at the Top of the Stairs, The ☐ Defection of Simas Kudirka, The ☐ Dutchman ☐ Endless Love ☐ Five Gates to Hell ☐ Flight from Ashiya ☐ Friendly Persuasion ☐ Group, The ☐ House of Women ☐ Juggernaut ☐ Medical Story ☐ Petulia ☐ Playing for Time ☐ Rain People, The ☐ Sender, The ☐ Sweet Bird of Youth
Knotts, Don ☐ Apple Dumpling Gang Rides Again, The ☐ Apple Dumpling Gang, The ☐ Ghost and Mr. Chicken ☐ Gus ☐ Herbie Goes to Monte Carlo ☐ Hot Lead & Cold Feet ☐ How to Frame a Figg ☐ I Love a Mystery ☐ Incredible Mr. Limpet, The ☐ Love God?, The ☐ No Deposit, No Return ☐ No Time for Sergeants ☐ Private Eyes, The ☐ Prize Fighter, The ☐ Reluctant Astronaut, The ☐ Return to Mayberry ☐ Shakiest Gun in the West, The ☐ Wake Me When It's Over
Knowles, Patric ☐ Beauty for the Asking ☐ Charge of the Light Brigade, The ☐ Expensive Husbands ☐ Fair Exchange ☐ Five Came Back ☐ Flame of Calcutta ☐ Four's a Crowd ☐ Frankenstein Meets the Wolf Man ☐ From the Earth to the Moon ☐ It's Love I'm After ☐ Ivy ☐ Jamaica Run ☐ Kitty ☐ Lady in a Jam ☐ Masquerade in Mexico ☐ Mister Hobo ☐ Monsieur Beaucaire ☐ Mystery of Marie Roget, The ☐ No Man's Woman ☐ O.S.S. ☐ Quebec ☐ This Is the Life ☐ Three Came Home ☐ Who Done It? ☐ Wolf Man, The
Knox, Alexander ☐ Divided Heart, The ☐ Fraulein Doktor ☐ Greatest Love, The ☐ Hidden Fear ☐ High Tide at Noon ☐ I'd Climb the Highest Mountain ☐ Intent to Kill ☐ Judge Steps Out, The ☐ Man in the Middle ☐ Man in the Saddle ☐ Modesty Blaise ☐ Night My Number Came Up, The ☐ None Shall Escape ☐ Over 21 ☐ Paula ☐ Phantom Strikes, The ☐ Reach for the Sky ☐ Sea Wolf, The ☐ Share Out, The ☐ Sister Kenny ☐ Sleeping Tiger, The ☐ Tokyo Joe ☐ Vikings, The ☐ Villa Rides ☐ Wilson ☐ Woman of Straw ☐ Wreck of the Mary Deare, The
Korman, Harvey ☐ Americathon ☐ April Fools, The ☐ Based on an Untrue Story ☐ Betrayal of the Dove ☐ Blazing Saddles ☐ Bud and Lou ☐ Don't Just Stand There ☐ Herbie Goes Bananas ☐ High Anxiety ☐ History of the World Part I ☐ Huckleberry Finn ☐ Lord Love a Duck ☐ Munchies ☐ Trail of the Pink Panther
Koscina, Sylva ☐ Agent 8 3/4 ☐ Battle of Neretva, The ☐ Deadlier than the Male ☐ Deadly Sanctuary ☐ Fight for Rome ☐ Hercules ☐ Hercules Unchained ☐ Hornet's Nest ☐ Italian Connection, The ☐ Jessica ☐ Johnny Banco ☐ Juliet of the Spirits ☐ Last Roman, The ☐ Lisa and the Devil ☐ Little Nuns, The ☐ Lovely Way to Die, A ☐ Made in Italy ☐ Man of Iron ☐ Secret War of Harry Frigg, The ☐ Sex on the Run ☐ She and He ☐ Some Like It Cool
Kosleck, Martin ☐ Espionage Agent ☐ Flesh Eaters, The ☐ Frozen Ghost ☐ Hitler Gang, The ☐ International Lady ☐ Mad Doctor, The ☐ Manila Calling ☐ Mummy's Curse, The ☐ Smugglers' Cove ☐ Undergound
Kotto, Yaphet ☐ Across 110th Street ☐ After the Shock ☐ Badge of the Assassin ☐ Blue Collar ☐ Brubaker ☐ Extreme Justice ☐ Eye of the Tiger ☐ Fighting Back ☐ Freddy's Dead: The Final Nightmare ☐ Friday Foster ☐ In Self Defense ☐ Live and Let Die ☐ Midnight Run ☐ Monkey Hustle ☐ Nothing But a Man ☐ Park Is Mine, The ☐ Rage ☐ Report to the Commissioner ☐ Robert A. Heinlein's The Puppet Masters ☐ Running Man, The ☐ Sharks' Treasure ☐ Star Chamber, The ☐ Terminal Entry ☐ Truck Turner ☐ Warning Sign ☐ Whisper to a Scream, A
Kovacs, Ernie ☐ Bell, Book and Candle ☐ Five Golden Hours ☐ It Happened to Jane ☐ Kovacs! ☐ North to Alaska ☐ Operation Mad Ball ☐ Our Man in Havana ☐ Sail a Crooked Ship ☐ Strangers When We Meet ☐ Wake Me When It's Over
Krabbe, Jeroen ☐ Crossing Delancey ☐ Family of Spies ☐ Farinelli ☐ Flight of Rainbirds, A ☐ Fourth Man, The ☐ Fugitive, The ☐ Her Secret Life ☐ Immortal Beloved ☐ King of the Hill ☐ Living Daylights, The

☐ No Mercy ☐ Prince of Tides, The ☐ Punisher, The ☐ Robin Hood ☐ Soldier of Orange ☐ Stalin ☐ Till There Was You ☐ World Apart, A

Kristel, Sylvia ☐ Airport '79—The Concorde ☐ Alice, or the Last Escapade ☐ Arrogant, The ☐ Beauty School ☐ Big Bet, The ☐ Dracula's Widow ☐ Fifth Musketeer, The ☐ Game of Seduction ☐ Lady Chatterley's Lover ☐ Mata Hari ☐ Mysteries ☐ Nude Bomb, The ☐ Private Lessons ☐ Tigers in Lipstick

Kristofferson, Kris ☐ Alice Doesn't Live Here Anymore ☐ Another Pair of Aces: Three of a Kind ☐ Big Top Pee-Wee ☐ Blood & Orchids ☐ Blume In Love ☐ Bring Me the Head of Alfredo Garcia ☐ Cheatin' Hearts ☐ Christmas in Connecticut ☐ Cisco Pike ☐ Convoy ☐ Flashpoint ☐ Freedom Road ☐ Heaven's Gate ☐ Knights ☐ Last Days of Frank and Jesse James, The ☐ Last Movie, The ☐ Millennium ☐ Miracle in the Wilderness ☐ Night of the Cyclone ☐ Original Intent ☐ Pair of Aces ☐ Pat Garrett and Billy the Kid ☐ Rollover ☐ Sailor Who Fell from Grace with the Sea ☐ Semi-Tough ☐ Songwriter ☐ Stagecoach ☐ Star Is Born, A ☐ Trouble in Mind ☐ Welcome Home

Kruger, Hardy ☐ Barry Lyndon ☐ Blue Fin ☐ Boomerang ☐ Chance Meeting ☐ Confess, Dr. Corda ☐ Defector, The ☐ Flight of the Phoenix ☐ Hatari! ☐ Inside Man, The ☐ One That Got Away, The ☐ Paper Tiger ☐ Red Tent, The ☐ Rest Is Silence, The ☐ Secret of Santa Vittoria, The ☐ Sundays and Cybele ☐ Wild Geese, The

Kruger, Otto ☐ 711 Ocean Drive ☐ Allotment Wives ☐ Another Thin Man ☐ Beauty for Sale ☐ Chained ☐ Colossus of New York, The ☐ Corregidor ☐ Dr. Ehrlich's Magic Bullet ☐ Dracula's Daughter ☐ Earl Carroll Vanities ☐ Ever in My Heart ☐ Fabulous Suzanne, The ☐ Glamorous Night ☐ Hitler's Children ☐ Housemaster ☐ I Am the Law ☐ Magnificent Obsession ☐ Man I Married, The ☐ Men in Her Life, The ☐ Men in White ☐ Murder My Sweet ☐ Night Plane from Chungking ☐ On Stage Everybody ☐ Prizefighter and the Lady, The ☐ Saboteur ☐ Seventeen ☐ They Won't Forget

Krupa, Gene ☐ Ball of Fire ☐ Benny Goodman Story, The ☐ Glamour Girl ☐ Glenn Miller Story, The

Kurtz, Swoosie ☐ Against All Odds ☐ And the Band Played On ☐ Baja Oklahoma ☐ Bright Lights, Big City ☐ Caribbean Mystery, A ☐ Dangerous Liaisons ☐ Guilty Conscience, The ☐ Image, The ☐ Mating Season, The ☐ Positively True Adventures of the Alleged Texas Cheerleader-Murdering Mom, The ☐ Reality Bites ☐ Shock to the System, A ☐ Stanley & Iris ☐ True Stories ☐ Vice Versa ☐ Wildcats

Kwan, Nancy ☐ Arrivederci, Baby ☐ Blade in Hong Kong ☐ Dragon: The Bruce Lee Story ☐ Fate Is the Hunter ☐ Flower Drum Song ☐ Fowl Play ☐ Girl Who Knew Too Much ☐ Hawaii Five-O ☐ Honeymoon Hotel ☐ Lt. Robin Crusoe, USN ☐ Main Attraction, The ☐ McMasters, The ☐ Night Children ☐ Night Creature ☐ Nobody's Perfect ☐ Stickfighter ☐ World of Suzie Wong, The ☐ Wrecking Crew, The

Kyo, Machiko ☐ Floating Weeds ☐ Gate of Hell ☐ Odd Obsession ☐ Princess Yang Kwei Fei ☐ Rashomon ☐ Teahouse of the August Moon, The ☐ Ugetsu

Ladd, Alan ☐ All the Young Men ☐ And Now Tomorrow ☐ Appointment with Danger ☐ Badlanders, The ☐ Beyond Glory ☐ Big Land, The ☐ Black Knight, The ☐ Blue Dahlia, The ☐ Born to the West ☐ Botany Bay ☐ Boy on a Dolphin ☐ Branded ☐ Calcutta ☐ Captain Carey, U.S.A. ☐ Carpetbaggers, The ☐ Chicago Deadline ☐ China ☐ Deep Six, The ☐ Drum Beat ☐ Duffy's Tavern ☐ Glass Key, The ☐ Great Gatsby, The ☐ Guns of the Timberland ☐ Hell Below Zero ☐ Hell on Frisco Bay ☐ Iron Mistress, The ☐ Joan of Paris ☐ Lucky Jordan ☐ Man in the Net, The ☐ McConnell Story, The ☐ O.S.S. ☐ One Foot in Hell ☐ Paper Bullets ☐ Paratrooper ☐ Proud Rebel, The ☐ Red Mountain ☐ Saigon ☐ Salty O'Rourke ☐ Santiago ☐ Saskatchewan ☐ Shane ☐ Star Spangled Rhythm ☐ This Gun for Hire ☐ Thunder in the East ☐ Two Years Before the Mast ☐ Whispering Smith ☐ Wild Harvest

Ladd, Cheryl ☐ Bluegrass ☐ Changes ☐ Death in California, A ☐ Fulfillment ☐ Grace Kelly ☐ Jekyll & Hyde ☐ Millennium ☐ Now and Forever ☐ Purple Hearts

Ladd, Diane ☐ Alice Doesn't Live Here Anymore ☐ All Night Long ☐ Bluegrass ☐ Carnosaur ☐ Cemetery Club, The ☐ Chinatown ☐ Embryo ☐ Father Hood ☐ Grace Kelly ☐ Hold Me, Thrill Me, Kiss Me ☐ I Married a Centerfold ☐ Kiss Before Dying, A ☐ Lookalike, The ☐ National Lampoon's Christmas Vacation ☐ Plain Clothes ☐ Rambling Rose ☐ Rebel Rousers ☐ Something Wicked This Way Comes ☐ Wild Angels, The ☐ Wild at Heart

Lahr, Bert ☐ Always Leave Them Laughing ☐ Flying High ☐ Josette ☐ Just Around the Corner ☐ Meet the People ☐ Merry Go Round of 1938 ☐ Night They Raided Minsky's, The ☐ Rose Marie ☐ Ship Ahoy ☐ Wizard of Oz, The ☐ Zaza

Lahti, Christine ☐ And Justice for All ☐ Crazy From the Heart ☐ Doctor, The ☐ Executioner's Song, The ☐ Fear Inside, The ☐ Funny About Love ☐ Good Fight, The ☐ Gross Anatomy ☐ Henderson Monster, The ☐ Hideaway ☐ Housekeeping ☐ Just Between Friends ☐ Ladies and Gentlemen, The Fabulous Stains ☐ Leaving Normal ☐ No Place Like Home ☐ Running on Empty

☐ Stacking ☐ Swing Shift ☐ Whose Life Is It Anyway?

Lake, Ricki ☐ Babycakes ☐ Cookie ☐ Cry-Baby ☐ Hairspray ☐ Last Exit to Brooklyn ☐ Serial Mom ☐ Where the Day Takes You

Lake, Veronica ☐ Blue Dahlia, The ☐ Bring on the Girls ☐ Duffy's Tavern ☐ Flesh Feast ☐ Glass Key, The ☐ Hold That Blonde ☐ Hour Before the Dawn ☐ I Married a Witch ☐ I Wanted Wings ☐ Miss Susie Slagle's ☐ Out of This World ☐ Ramrod ☐ Saigon ☐ So Proudly We Hail! ☐ Star Spangled Rhythm ☐ Sullivan's Travels ☐ This Gun for Hire

Lamarr, Hedy ☐ Algiers ☐ Boom Town ☐ Come Live With Me ☐ Comrade X ☐ Conspirators, The ☐ Copper Canyon ☐ Crossroads ☐ Dishonored Lady ☐ Ecstasy ☐ Experiment Perilous ☐ Female Animal, The ☐ H.M. Pulham, Esq. ☐ Heavenly Body, The ☐ Her Highness and the Bellboy ☐ I Take This Woman ☐ Lady of the Tropics ☐ Lady without Passport, A ☐ Loves of Three Queens, The ☐ My Favorite Spy ☐ Samson and Delilah ☐ Story of Mankind, The ☐ Strange Woman, The ☐ Tortilla Flat ☐ White Cargo ☐ Ziegfeld Girl

Lambert, Christopher ☐ Fortress ☐ Greystoke: The Legend of Tarzan, Lord of the Apes ☐ Gunmen ☐ Highlander ☐ Highlander II: The Quickening ☐ Highlander: The Final Dimension ☐ Knight Moves ☐ Love Songs ☐ Priceless Beauty ☐ Sicilian, The ☐ Subway ☐ To Kill a Priest

Lamour, Dorothy ☐ Aloma of the South Seas ☐ And the Angels Sing ☐ Beyond the Blue Horizon ☐ Big Broadcast of 1938, The ☐ Caught in the Draft ☐ Chad Hanna ☐ Creepshow 2 ☐ Death at Love House ☐ Dixie ☐ Donovan's Reef ☐ Duffy's Tavern ☐ Fleet's In, The ☐ Girl from Manhattan, The ☐ Greatest Show on Earth, The ☐ Her Jungle Love ☐ High, Wide, and Handsome ☐ Hurricane, The ☐ Johnny Apollo ☐ Jungle Princess, The ☐ Last Train from Madrid, The ☐ Lucky Stiff, The ☐ Man About Town ☐ Manhandled ☐ Masquerade in Mexico ☐ Medal for Benny, A ☐ My Favorite Brunette ☐ On Our Merry Way ☐ Pajama Party ☐ Rainbow Island ☐ Road to Bali ☐ Road to Hong Kong, The ☐ Road to Morocco ☐ Road to Rio ☐ Road to Singapore ☐ Road to Utopia ☐ Road to Zanzibar ☐ Spawn of the North ☐ Star Spangled Rhythm ☐ Swing High, Swing Low ☐ They Got Me Covered ☐ Typhoon ☐ Wild Harvest

Lancaster, Burt ☐ 1900 ☐ Airport ☐ All My Sons ☐ Apache ☐ Atlantic City ☐ Birdman of Alcatraz ☐ Brute Force ☐ Buffalo Bill and the Indians ☐ Cassandra Crossing, The ☐ Castle Keep ☐ Cattle Annie and Little Britches ☐ Child Is Waiting, A ☐ Come Back, Little Sheba ☐ Control ☐ Conversation Piece ☐ Crimson Pirate, The ☐ Criss Cross ☐ Desert Fury ☐ Devil's Disciple, The ☐ Elmer Gantry ☐ Executive Action ☐ Field of Dreams ☐ Flame and the Arrow, The ☐ From Here to Eternity ☐ Go Tell the Spartans ☐ Gunfight at the O.K. Corral ☐ Gypsy Moths, The ☐ Hallelujah Trail, The ☐ His Majesty O'Keefe ☐ I Walk Alone ☐ Island of Dr. Moreau, The ☐ Jim Thorpe—All American ☐ Judgment at Nuremberg ☐ Kentuckian, The ☐ Killers, The ☐ Kiss the Blood Off My Hands ☐ La Pelle ☐ Lawman ☐ Leopard, The ☐ List of Adrian Messenger, The ☐ Little Treasure ☐ Local Hero ☐ Midnight Man, The ☐ Mister 880 ☐ Moses ☐ On Wings of Eagles ☐ Professionals, The ☐ Rainmaker, The ☐ Rocket Gibraltar ☐ Rose Tattoo, The ☐ Run Silent, Run Deep ☐ Scalphunters, The ☐ Scandal Sheet ☐ Scorpio ☐ Separate But Equal ☐ Separate Tables ☐ Seven Days in May ☐ Sins of the Fathers ☐ Sorry, Wrong Number ☐ South Sea Woman ☐ Sweet Smell of Success ☐ Swimmer, The ☐ Ten Tall Men ☐ Tough Guys ☐ Train, The ☐ Trapeze ☐ Twilight's Last Gleaming ☐ Ulzana's Raid ☐ Unforgiven, The ☐ Valdez Is Coming ☐ Vera Cruz ☐ Voyage of Terror: The Achille Lauro Affair ☐ Young Savages, The ☐ Zulu Dawn

Lanchester, Elsa ☐ Androcles and the Lion ☐ Arnold ☐ Beachcomber, The ☐ Bell, Book and Candle ☐ Bishop's Wife, The ☐ Blackbeard's Ghost ☐ Bride of Frankenstein, The ☐ Buccaneer's Girl ☐ Come to the Stable ☐ David Copperfield ☐ Die Laughing ☐ Dreamboat ☐ Easy Come, Easy Go ☐ Frenchie ☐ Ghost Goes West, The ☐ Girls of Pleasure Island ☐ Glass Slipper, The ☐ Hell's Half Acre ☐ Honeymoon Hotel ☐ Ladies in Retirement ☐ Lassie Come Home ☐ Me, Natalie ☐ Murder by Death ☐ My Dog the Thief ☐ Mystery Street ☐ Naughty Marietta ☐ Northwest Outpost ☐ Pajama Party ☐ Passport to Destiny ☐ Private Life of Henry VIII, The ☐ Rascal ☐ Rembrandt ☐ Secret Garden, The ☐ Son of Fury ☐ That Darn Cat ☐ Three Ring Circus ☐ Willard ☐ Witness for the Prosecution

Landau, Martin ☐ Alone in the Dark ☐ Being, The ☐ Black Gunn ☐ By Dawn's Early Light ☐ Crimes and Misdemeanors ☐ Ed Wood ☐ Empire State ☐ Fall of the House of Usher, The ☐ Firehead ☐ Hallelujah Trail, The ☐ Harlem Globetrotters on Gilligan's Island, The ☐ Intersection ☐ Legacy of Lies ☐ Max and Helen ☐ Mistress ☐ Neon Empire, The ☐ Nevada Smith ☐ North by Northwest ☐ Operation Snafu ☐ Paint It Black ☐ Sliver ☐ Space 1999: Alien Attack ☐ Space 1999: Journey Through Black Sun ☐ Space 1999—Vol. 1—Voyager's Return ☐ Stagecoach to Dancers' Rock ☐ They Call Me MISTER Tibbs! ☐ Tucker—The Man and His Dream

Landis, Carole ☐ Blondes at Work ☐ Dance Hall ☐ Four Jills in a Jeep ☐ Gentleman at Heart, A ☐ Having Wonderful Crime ☐ I

Wake Up Screaming ☐ It Happened in Flatbush ☐ It Shouldn't Happen to a Dog ☐ Manila Calling ☐ Moon Over Miami ☐ My Gal Sal ☐ One Million B.C. ☐ Orchestra Wives ☐ Out of the Blue ☐ Road Show ☐ Silk Noose, The ☐ Topper Returns ☐ Turnabout

Landis, Jessie Royce ☐ Critic's Choice ☐ Gidget Goes to Rome ☐ Girl He Left Behind ☐ Goodbye Again ☐ It Happens Every Spring ☐ Mother Didn't Tell Me ☐ Mr. Belvedere Goes to College ☐ My Foolish Heart ☐ My Man Godfrey ☐ North by Northwest ☐ To Catch a Thief

Landon, Michael ☐ I Was a Teenage Werewolf ☐ Little House on the Prairie ☐ Loneliest Runner, The ☐ Maracaibo ☐ Sam's Son

Lane, Diane ☐ Big Town, The ☐ Cattle Annie and Little Britches ☐ Chaplin ☐ Child Bride of Short Creek ☐ Cotton Club, The ☐ Descending Angel ☐ Fallen Angels—Volume 1 ☐ Indian Summer ☐ Knight Moves ☐ Ladies and Gentlemen, The Fabulous Stains ☐ Lady Beware ☐ Little Romance, A ☐ Lonesome Dove ☐ My New Gun ☐ National Lampoon Goes to the Movies ☐ Oldest Living Confederate Widow Tells All ☐ Outsiders, The ☐ Priceless Beauty ☐ Rumble Fish ☐ Six Pack ☐ Streets of Fire ☐ Touched by Love ☐ Vital Signs

Lane, Priscilla ☐ Arsenic and Old Lace ☐ Blues in the Night ☐ Bodyguard ☐ Brother Rat ☐ Brother Rat and a Baby ☐ Cowboy from Brooklyn, The ☐ Daughters Courageous ☐ Dust Be My Destiny ☐ Four Daughters ☐ Four Mothers ☐ Four Wives ☐ Fun on a Weekend ☐ Meanest Man in the World, The ☐ Million Dollar Baby ☐ Roaring Twenties, The ☐ Saboteur ☐ Three Cheers for the Irish ☐ Varsity Show

Lane, Richard ☐ Alias Boston Blackie ☐ Bullfighters, The ☐ Confessions of Boston Blackie ☐ Go Chase Yourself ☐ Jackie Robinson Story, The ☐ Meet Boston Blackie ☐ Meet the Chump ☐ Mr. Winkle Goes to War ☐ One Mysterious Night

Lane, Rosemary ☐ Angel From Texas, An ☐ Blackwell's Island ☐ Boys from Syracuse, The ☐ Chatterbox ☐ Daughters Courageous ☐ Four Daughters ☐ Four Mothers ☐ Four Wives ☐ Hollywood Hotel ☐ Oklahoma Kid, The ☐ Return of Dr. X, The ☐ Time Out for Rhythm ☐ Varsity Show

Lang, Stephen ☐ Another You ☐ Band of the Hand ☐ Crime Story ☐ Death of a Salesman ☐ Guilty as Sin ☐ Hard Way, The ☐ Last Exit to Brooklyn ☐ Manhunter ☐ Tall Tale: The Unbelievable Adventures of Pecos Bill ☐ Tombstone

Langan, Glenn ☐ Amazing Colossal Man, The ☐ Bell for Adano, A ☐ Fury at Furnace Creek ☐ Homestretch, The ☐ Iroquois Trail, The ☐ Margie ☐ One Girl's Confession ☐ Sentimental Journey ☐ Snake Pit, The ☐ Something for the Boys

Langdon, Harry ☐ Hallelujah, I'm a Bum ☐ His First Flame ☐ My Weakness ☐ Strong Man, The ☐ Zenobia

Lange, Hope ☐ Best of Everything, The ☐ Beulah Land ☐ Blue Velvet ☐ Bus Stop ☐ Death Wish ☐ Fer-de-Lance ☐ Ford: The Man and the Machine ☐ I Am the Cheese ☐ I Love You, Goodbye ☐ In Love and War ☐ Jigsaw ☐ Love Is a Ball ☐ Nightmare on Elm Street 2: Freddy's Revenge ☐ Peyton Place ☐ Pocketful of Miracles ☐ That Certain Summer ☐ True Story of Jesse James, The ☐ Wild in the Country ☐ Young Lions, The

Lange, Jessica ☐ All That Jazz ☐ Blue Sky ☐ Cape Fear ☐ Cat on a Hot Tin Roof ☐ Country ☐ Crimes of the Heart ☐ Everybody's All-American ☐ Far North ☐ Frances ☐ How to Beat the High Cost of Living ☐ King Kong ☐ Losing Isaiah ☐ Men Don't Leave ☐ Music Box ☐ Night and the City ☐ O Pioneers! ☐ Postman Always Rings Twice, The ☐ Sweet Dreams ☐ Tootsie

Langella, Frank ☐ 1492: Conquest of Paradise ☐ And God Created Woman ☐ Bad Company ☐ Body of Evidence ☐ Brainscan ☐ Dave ☐ Diary of a Mad Housewife ☐ Dracula ☐ Junior ☐ Mark of Zorro, The ☐ Masters of the Universe ☐ Men's Club, The ☐ Sphinx ☐ Those Lips, Those Eyes ☐ True Identity ☐ Twelve Chairs, The

Lansbury, Angela ☐ All Fall Down ☐ Amorous Adventures of Moll Flanders, The ☐ Beauty and the Beast ☐ Bedknobs and Broomsticks ☐ Blue Hawaii ☐ Breath of Scandal, A ☐ Company of Wolves, The ☐ Court Jester, The ☐ Dark at the Top of the Stairs, The ☐ Dear Heart ☐ Death on the Nile ☐ First Olympics: Athens 1896, The ☐ Gaslight ☐ Gift of Love: A Christmas Story, The ☐ Greatest Story Ever Told, The ☐ Harlow ☐ Harvey Girls, The ☐ Hoodlum Saint, The ☐ If Winter Comes ☐ In the Cool of the Day ☐ Kind Lady ☐ Lady Vanishes, The ☐ Lawless Street, A ☐ Little Gloria-Happy At Last ☐ Long Hot Summer, The ☐ Love She Sought, The ☐ Manchurian Candidate, The ☐ Mirror Crack'd, The ☐ Mister Buddwing ☐ Mrs. 'Arris Goes to Paris ☐ National Velvet ☐ Picture of Dorian Gray, The ☐ Pirates of Penzance, The ☐ Private Affairs of Bel Ami, The ☐ Purple Mask, The ☐ Rage of Angels: The Story Continues ☐ Reluctant Debutante, The ☐ Samson and Delilah ☐ Season of Passion ☐ Shell Seekers, The ☐ Something for Everyone ☐ State of the Union ☐ Sweeney Todd, the Demon Barber of Fleet Street ☐ Tenth Avenue Angel ☐ Three Musketeers, The ☐ Till the Clouds Roll By ☐ World of Henry Orient, The

Lanoux, Victor ☐ Cousin, Cousine ☐ Dog Day ☐ French Detective, The ☐ Investigation ☐ Make Room for Tomorrow ☐ National Lampoon's European Vacation ☐ One Wild Moment ☐ Pardon Mon Affaire ☐ Scene of the Crime ☐ Shameless Old Lady, The

Lanza, Mario ☐ Because You're Mine ☐ For the First Time ☐ Great Caruso, The ☐ Serenade ☐ Seven Hills of Rome, The ☐ That Midnight Kiss ☐ Toast of New Orleans, The

LaPaglia, Anthony ☐ Betsy's Wedding ☐ Black Magic ☐ Client, The ☐ Criminal Justice ☐ He Said, She Said ☐ Innocent Blood ☐ Keeper of the City ☐ Mixed Nuts ☐ Mortal Sins ☐ Nitti—The Enforcer ☐ One Good Cop ☐ So I Married An Axe Murderer ☐ 29th Street ☐ Whispers in the Dark

Larroquette, John ☐ Bare Essence ☐ Blind Date ☐ Cat People ☐ Choose Me ☐ Convicted ☐ Green Ice ☐ Hot Paint ☐ Madhouse ☐ Meatballs II ☐ Richie Rich ☐ Second Sight ☐ Stripes

Lasser, Louise ☐ Bananas ☐ Everything You Always Wanted to Know About Sex (But Were Afraid to Ask) ☐ For Ladies Only ☐ Frankenhooker ☐ In God We Trust ☐ Isn't It Shocking? ☐ Just Me and You ☐ Night We Never Met, The ☐ Sing ☐ Slither ☐ Such Good Friends

Laughton, Charles ☐ Abbott and Costello Meet Captain Kidd ☐ Advise and Consent ☐ Arch of Triumph ☐ Barretts of Wimpole Street, The ☐ Beachcomber, The ☐ Because of Him ☐ Big Clock, The ☐ Blue Veil, The ☐ Bribe, The ☐ Canterville Ghost, The ☐ Captain Kidd ☐ Devil and the Deep ☐ Epic that Never Was, The ☐ Forever and a Day ☐ Girl from Manhattan, The ☐ Hobson's Choice ☐ Hunchback of Notre Dame, The ☐ If I Had a Million ☐ Island of Lost Souls ☐ It Started with Eve ☐ Jamaica Inn ☐ Les Miserables ☐ Man from Down Under, The ☐ Man on the Eiffel Tower, The ☐ Mutiny on the Bounty ☐ O. Henry's Full House ☐ Old Dark House, The ☐ Paradine Case ☐ Payment Deferred ☐ Private Life of Henry VIII, The ☐ Rembrandt ☐ Ruggles of Red Gap ☐ Salome ☐ Sidewalks of London ☐ Sign of the Cross, The ☐ Spartacus ☐ Stand by for Action ☐ Tales of Manhattan ☐ They Knew What They Wanted ☐ This Land Is Mine ☐ Tuttles of Tahiti, The ☐ Under Ten Flags ☐ Witness for the Prosecution ☐ Young Bess

Laurel, Stan ☐ A-Haunting We Will Go ☐ Air Raid Wardens ☐ Babes in Toyland ☐ Big Noise, The ☐ Block-Heads ☐ Bohemian Girl, The ☐ Bonnie Scotland ☐ Bullfighters, The ☐ Chump at Oxford, A ☐ Dancing Masters, The ☐ Days of Thrills and Laughter ☐ Devil's Brother, The ☐ Flying Deuces, The ☐ Four Clowns ☐ Further Perils of Laurel and Hardy, The ☐ Golden Age of Comedy, The ☐ Great Guns ☐ Hollywood Party ☐ Hollywood Revue of 1929, The ☐ Jitterbugs ☐ Laurel and Hardy's Laughing 20s ☐ MGM's Big Parade of Comedy ☐ Nothing But Trouble ☐ Our Relations ☐ Pack Up Your Troubles ☐ Pardon Us ☐ Saps at Sea ☐ Sons of the Desert ☐ Swiss Miss ☐ Utopia ☐ Way Out West ☐ When Comedy Was King

Laurie, Piper ☐ Ain't Misbehavin' ☐ Appointment with Death ☐ Boss's Son, The ☐ Bunker, The ☐ Carrie ☐ Children of a Lesser God ☐ Dangerous Mission ☐ Dawn at Socorro ☐ Dream a Little Dream ☐ Francis Goes to the Races ☐ Golden Blade, The ☐ Has Anybody Seen My Gal? ☐ Hustler, The ☐ In the Matter of Karen Ann Quinlan ☐ Johnny Dark ☐ Kelly and Me ☐ Mae West ☐ Milkman, The ☐ Mississippi Gambler ☐ No Room for the Groom ☐ Other People's Money ☐ Promise, The ☐ Rainbow ☐ Return to Oz ☐ Rich in Love ☐ Ruby ☐ Son of Ali Baba ☐ Thorn Birds, The ☐ Tiger Warsaw ☐ Tim ☐ Trauma ☐ Twin Peaks ☐ Until They Sail ☐ Wrestling Ernest Hemingway

Lauter, Ed ☐ Chicken Chronicles, The ☐ Death Wish 3 ☐ Eureka ☐ Family Plot ☐ Finders Keepers ☐ Gleaming the Cube ☐ In the Custody of Strangers ☐ Jericho Mile, The ☐ Magic ☐ Midnight Man, The ☐ Raw Deal ☐ Revenge of the Nerds 2: Nerds in Paradise ☐ Stephen King's Golden Years ☐ Thanksgiving Promise, The ☐ Youngblood

Lavin, Linda ☐ Lena: My 100 Children ☐ Matter of Life and Death, A ☐ Morning After, The ☐ Muppets Take Manhattan, The

Law, John Phillip ☐ African Rage ☐ Alienator ☐ Attack Force Z ☐ Barbarella ☐ Danger: Diabolik ☐ Golden Voyage of Sinbad, The ☐ Hurry Sundown ☐ Love Machine, The ☐ Moon in Scorpio ☐ Open Season ☐ Sergeant, The ☐ Spiral Staircase, The ☐ Three Nights of Love ☐ Von Richthofen and Brown

Lawford, Peter ☐ Advise and Consent ☐ Angels' Brigade ☐ April Fools, The ☐ Body and Soul ☐ Buona Sera, Mrs. Campbell ☐ Canterville Ghost, The ☐ Cluny Brown ☐ Dead Ringer ☐ Easter Parade ☐ Exodus ☐ Fantasy Island ☐ Good News ☐ Harlow ☐ Hook, Line & Sinker ☐ Hour of 13, The ☐ How I Spent My Summer Vacation ☐ It Happened in Brooklyn ☐ It Should Happen to You ☐ Julia Misbehaves ☐ Kangaroo ☐ Little Women ☐ Mrs. Parkington ☐ My Brother Talks to Horses ☐ Mysterious Island of Beautiful Women ☐ Never So Few ☐ Ocean's Eleven ☐ On an Island with You ☐ One More Time ☐ Please Believe Me ☐ Sergeants 3 ☐ Skiddoo ☐ Son of Lassie ☐ That's Entertainment ☐ They Only Kill Their Masters ☐ Two Sisters From Boston ☐ White Cliffs of Dover, The

Lawrence, Barbara ☐ Jesse James vs. the Daltons ☐ Kronos ☐ Man with the Gun, The ☐ Margie ☐ Mother Is a Freshman ☐ Street with No Name ☐ Unfaithfully Yours

Lawrence, Bruno ☐ Efficiency Expert, The ☐ Grievous Bodily Harm ☐ Heart of the Stag ☐ Jack Be Nimble ☐ Quiet Earth, The ☐ Race to the Yankee Zephyr ☐ Smash Palace ☐ Utu

Lawrence, Jody ☐ Captain John Smith and Pocahontas ☐ Family Secret, The ☐ Leather

Saint, The ☐ Mask of the Avenger ☐ Stagecoach to Dancers' Rock ☐ Ten Tall Men

Lawrence, Marc ☐ Beware, Spooks! ☐ Eyes of the Underworld ☐ Foul Play ☐ Hurricane Island ☐ I Walk Alone ☐ Johnny Cool ☐ Rainbow Island ☐ Ruby ☐ Shadow, The ☐ Tall, Dark and Handsome

Lazenby, George ☐ Evening in Byzantium, An ☐ Hell Hunters ☐ Kentucky Fried Movie, The ☐ Man from Hong Kong, The ☐ Never Too Young to Die ☐ On Her Majesty's Secret Service

Leachman, Cloris ☐ Acorn People, The ☐ Beverly Hillbillies, The ☐ Brand New Life, A ☐ Breakfast with Les and Bess ☐ Butch Cassidy and the Sundance Kid ☐ Chapman Report, The ☐ Charley and the Angel ☐ Crazy Mama ☐ Daisy Miller ☐ Danielle Steel's Fine Things ☐ Death Sentence ☐ Dillinger ☐ Dixie: Changing Habits ☐ Dying Room Only ☐ Ernie Kovacs: Between the Laughter ☐ Facts of Life Down Under, The ☐ Foolin' Around ☐ Girl Named Sooner, A ☐ Hansel and Gretel ☐ Happy Mother's Day, Love George ☐ Haunts of the Very Rich ☐ Herbie Goes Bananas ☐ High Anxiety ☐ History of the World Part I ☐ In Broad Daylight ☐ It Happened One Christmas ☐ Kiss Me Deadly ☐ Last Picture Show, The ☐ Love Hurts ☐ Love Is Never Silent ☐ Lovers and Other Strangers ☐ Migrants, The ☐ Mrs. R's Daughter ☐ My Little Pony—The Movie ☐ People Next Door, The ☐ Prancer ☐ Rack, The ☐ S.O.S. Titanic ☐ Shadow Play ☐ Silent Night, Lonely Night ☐ Texasville ☐ Thursday's Game ☐ Troll in Central Park, A ☐ Walk Like A Man ☐ Young Frankenstein

Leaud, Jean-Pierre ☐ 36 Fillette ☐ Bed and Board ☐ Day for Night ☐ Detective ☐ Four Hundred Blows, The ☐ Help Me Dream ☐ I Hired a Contract Killer ☐ La Chinoise ☐ Last Tango in Paris ☐ Le Gai Savoir ☐ Love at Twenty ☐ Love on the Run ☐ Masculine-Feminine ☐ Mother and the Whore, The ☐ Oldest Profession, The ☐ Pierrot le Fou ☐ Stolen Kisses ☐ Testament of Orpheus ☐ Two English Girls ☐ Weekend

Lederer, Francis ☐ Bridge of San Luis Rey, The ☐ Confessions of a Nazi Spy ☐ Gay Deception, The ☐ Lone Wolf in Paris, The ☐ Madonna's Secret, The ☐ Man I Married, The ☐ Maracaibo ☐ Midnight ☐ One Rainy Afternoon ☐ Return of Dracula, The ☐ Woman of Distinction, A

Lee, Anna ☐ Bedlam ☐ Commandos Strike at Dawn, The ☐ Eleanor and Franklin ☐ Eleanor and Franklin: The White House Years ☐ Hangmen Also Die ☐ Man Who Lived Again, The ☐ My Life with Caroline ☐ Night Rider, The ☐ Non-Stop New York ☐ Passing of the Third Floor Back, The ☐ Secret Four, The

Lee, Bernard ☐ Across the Bridge ☐ Clue of the Silver Key ☐ Detective, The ☐ Elizabeth of Ladymead ☐ Fury at Smugglers Bay ☐ High Flight ☐ Island Rescue ☐ Kidnapped ☐ Man Upstairs, The ☐ Man Who Died Twice, The ☐ Nowhere to Go ☐ Purple Plain, The ☐ Rhodes ☐ Ring of Spies ☐ Share Out, The ☐ Ship That Died of Shame, The ☐ Spanish Gardener, The ☐ Web of Evidence ☐ Whistle Down the Wind ☐ Yellow Balloon, The

Lee, Brandon ☐ Crow, The ☐ Kung Fu—The Movie ☐ Laser Mission ☐ Rapid Fire ☐ Showdown in Little Tokyo

Lee, Bruce ☐ Bruce Lee Fights Back From The Grave ☐ Chinese Connection ☐ Deadliest Art, The: The Best of the Martial Arts Films, The ☐ Enter the Dragon ☐ Fists of Fury ☐ Furious, The ☐ Game of Death ☐ Goodbye Bruce Lee ☐ Marlowe ☐ Return of the Dragon ☐ Return of Fist of Fury ☐ True Game of Death ☐ Young Bruce Lee, The

Lee, Christopher ☐ 1941 ☐ Accursed, The ☐ Airport '77 ☐ Albino ☐ Arabian Adventure ☐ Bear Island ☐ Beyond Mombasa ☐ Bitter Victory ☐ Brides of Fu Manchu, The ☐ Captain America II ☐ Caravans ☐ Castle of Fu Manchu, The ☐ Castle of the Living Dead ☐ Charles & Diana: A Royal Love Story ☐ Circle of Iron ☐ Corridors of Blood ☐ Count Dracula ☐ Creeping Flesh, The ☐ Crimson Cult, The ☐ Crimson Pirate, The ☐ Curse of Frankenstein, The ☐ Dark Places ☐ Devil's Bride, The ☐ Devil-Ship Pirates, The ☐ Diagnosis: Murder ☐ Double Vision ☐ Dr. Terror's House of Horrors ☐ Dracula A.D. ☐ Dracula and Son ☐ Dracula Has Risen From the Grave ☐ Dracula—Prince of Darkness ☐ Eye for an Eye, An ☐ Face of Fu Manchu, The ☐ Five Golden Dragons ☐ Girl, The ☐ Goliath Awaits ☐ Gorgon, The ☐ Gremlins 2—The New Batch ☐ Hands of Orlac, The ☐ Hannie Caulder ☐ Harold Robbins' the Pirate ☐ Hercules in the Haunted World ☐ Horror Express ☐ Horror Hotel ☐ Horror of Dracula ☐ Hound of the Baskervilles, The ☐ House of the Long Shadows ☐ House That Dripped Blood, The ☐ Howling II: Your Sister Is a Werewolf ☐ I, Monster ☐ Incident at Victoria Falls ☐ Innocents in Paris ☐ Island of the Burning Doomed ☐ Jaguar Lives! ☐ Jocks ☐ Journey of Honor ☐ Keeper, The ☐ Killer Force ☐ Man Who Could Cheat Death, The ☐ Man with the Golden Gun, The ☐ Missiles from Hell ☐ Moulin Rouge ☐ Mummy, The ☐ My Brother's Keeper ☐ Night Ambush ☐ Night of the Blood Monster ☐ No-Tell Hotel, The ☐ Nothing But the Night ☐ Oblong Box, The ☐ Once Upon a Spy ☐ Pirates of Blood River, The ☐ Private Life of Sherlock Holmes, The ☐ Rasputin—the Mad Monk ☐ Raw Meat ☐ Return from Witch Mountain ☐ Return of the Musketeers, The ☐ Saraband ☐ Satanic Rites of Dracula, The ☐ Scars of Dracula ☐ Scott of the Antarctic ☐ Scream and

Scream Again ☐ Scream of Fear ☐ Shaka Zulu ☐ She ☐ Skull, The ☐ Starship Invasions ☐ Tale of Two Cities, A ☐ Taste the Blood of Dracula ☐ Theatre of Death ☐ Three Musketeers, The ☐ To the Devil A Daughter ☐ Treasure Island ☐ Wicker Man, The

Lee, Gypsy Rose ☐ Belle of the Yukon ☐ Over-the-Hill Gang, The ☐ Wind Across the Everglades

Lee, Michele ☐ Broadway Bound ☐ Bud and Lou ☐ Comic, The ☐ Dark Victory ☐ Fatal Image, The ☐ How to Succeed in Business Without Really Trying ☐ Letter to Three Wives, A ☐ Love Bug, The ☐ Nutcracker Fantasy ☐ Only with Married Men

Lee, Peggy ☐ Jazz Singer, The ☐ Lady and the Tramp ☐ Mr. Music ☐ Pete Kelly's Blues

Lee, Spike ☐ Backbeat ☐ Do the Right Thing ☐ Jungle Fever ☐ Malcolm X ☐ Mo' Better Blues ☐ School Daze ☐ She's Gotta Have It

Leibman, Ron ☐ Christmas Eve ☐ Door to Door ☐ Hot Rock, The ☐ Norma Rae ☐ Question of Guilt, A ☐ Romantic Comedy ☐ Seven Hours to Judgment ☐ Slaughterhouse-Five ☐ Up the Academy ☐ Where's Poppa? ☐ Won Ton Ton, the Dog Who Saved Hollywood ☐ Zorro, the Gay Blade

Leigh, Janet ☐ Act of Violence ☐ Angels in the Outfield ☐ Black Shield of Falworth, The ☐ Boardwalk ☐ Bye, Bye, Birdie ☐ Confidentially Connie ☐ Fearless Fagan ☐ Fog, The ☐ Grand Slam ☐ Harper ☐ Hello Down There ☐ Hills of Home, The ☐ Holiday Affair ☐ Honeymoon with a Stranger ☐ Houdini ☐ House on Greenapple Road, The ☐ If Winter Comes ☐ Jet Pilot ☐ Little Women ☐ Living It Up ☐ Manchurian Candidate, The ☐ My Sister Eileen ☐ Naked Spur, The ☐ Night of the Lepus ☐ One Is a Lonely Number ☐ Perfect Furlough, The ☐ Pete Kelly's Blues ☐ Prince Valiant ☐ Psycho ☐ Rogue Cop ☐ Romance of Rosy Ridge, The ☐ Scaramouche ☐ Strictly Dishonorable ☐ That Forsythe Woman ☐ Three on a Couch ☐ Touch of Evil ☐ Two Tickets to Broadway ☐ Vikings, The ☐ Walking My Baby Back Home ☐ Who Was That Lady?

Leigh, Jennifer Jason ☐ Angel City ☐ Backdraft ☐ Best Little Girl in The World, The ☐ Big Picture, The ☐ Crooked Hearts ☐ Dolores Claiborne ☐ Easy Money ☐ Eyes of a Stranger ☐ Fast Times at Ridgemont High ☐ Flesh + Blood ☐ Girls of the White Orchid ☐ Grandview, U.S.A. ☐ Heart of Midnight ☐ Hitcher, The ☐ Hudsucker Proxy, The ☐ Just Like Us ☐ Killing of Randy Webster, The ☐ Last Exit to Brooklyn ☐ Miami Blues ☐ Mrs. Parker and the Vicious Circle ☐ Rush ☐ Single White Female ☐ Under Cover

Leighton, Margaret ☐ Astonished Heart, The ☐ Best Man, The ☐ Bonnie Prince Charlie ☐ Calling Bulldog Drummond ☐ Constant Husband, The ☐ Court Martial ☐ Dirty Knight's Work ☐ Fighting Pimpernel, The ☐ Frankenstein: The True Story ☐ From Beyond the Grave ☐ Galileo ☐ Go-Between, The ☐ Good Die Young, The ☐ Great Expectations ☐ Holly and the Ivy, The ☐ Home at Seven ☐ Lady Caroline Lamb ☐ Madwoman of Chaillot, The ☐ Nelson Affair, The ☐ Novel Affair, A ☐ Seven Women ☐ Sound and the Fury, The ☐ Teckman Mystery, The ☐ Under Capricorn ☐ Waltz of the Toreadors ☐ Winslow Boy, The

Leigh, Vivien ☐ 21 Days Together ☐ Anna Karenina ☐ Caesar and Cleopatra ☐ Dark Journey ☐ Deep Blue Sea, The ☐ Fire Over England ☐ Gentlemen's Agreement ☐ Gone with the Wind ☐ Roman Spring of Mrs. Stone, The ☐ Ship of Fools ☐ Sidewalks of London ☐ Storm in a Teacup ☐ Streetcar Named Desire, A ☐ That Hamilton Woman ☐ Waterloo Bridge ☐ Yank at Oxford, A

LeMat, Paul ☐ aloha, bobby and rose ☐ American Graffiti ☐ Burning Bed, The ☐ Citizens Band ☐ Firehouse ☐ Grave Secrets ☐ Hanoi Hilton, The ☐ Into the Homeland ☐ Jimmy the Kid ☐ Melvin and Howard ☐ More American Graffiti ☐ Night They Saved Christmas, The ☐ On Wings of Eagles ☐ P.K. and the Kid ☐ Puppetmaster ☐ Rock & Rule ☐ Strange Invaders

Lemmon, Jack ☐ Airport '77 ☐ Alex and the Gypsy ☐ Apartment, The ☐ April Fools, The ☐ Avanti! ☐ Bell, Book and Candle ☐ Buddy Buddy ☐ China Syndrome, The ☐ Cowboy ☐ Dad ☐ Days of Wine and Roses ☐ Entertainer, The ☐ Fire Down Below ☐ For Richer, For Poorer ☐ Fortune Cookie, The ☐ Front Page, The ☐ Glengarry Glen Ross ☐ Good Neighbor Sam ☐ Great Race, The ☐ Grumpy Old Men ☐ How to Murder Your Wife ☐ Irma la Douce ☐ It Happened to Jane ☐ It Should Happen to You ☐ JFK ☐ Life in the Theater, A ☐ Luv ☐ Macaroni ☐ Mass Appeal ☐ Missing ☐ Mister Roberts ☐ Murder of Mary Phagan, The ☐ My Sister Eileen ☐ Notorious Landlady, The ☐ Odd Couple, The ☐ Operation Mad Ball ☐ Out-of-Towners, The ☐ Phffft! ☐ Prisoner of Second Avenue, The ☐ Save the Tiger ☐ Short Cuts ☐ Some Like It Hot ☐ That's Life! ☐ Three for the Show ☐ Tribute ☐ Under the Yum Yum Tree ☐ Wackiest Ship in the Army, The ☐ War Between Men and Women, The ☐ You Can't Run Away From It

Lennon, John ☐ Dynamite Chicken ☐ Hard Day's Night, A ☐ Help! ☐ How I Won the War ☐ Let It Be ☐ Magical Mystery Tour ☐ Yellow Submarine

Leno, Jay ☐ American Hot Wax ☐ Collision Course ☐ Jay Leno—The American Dream ☐ We're Back: A Dinosaur's Story

Lenya, Lotte ☐ Appointment, The ☐ From Russia with Love ☐ Roman Spring of Mrs. Stone, The ☐ Semi-Tough

Lenz, Kay ☐ Breezy ☐ Death Wish 4: The

Crackdown ☐ F.B.I. Story, The—The FBI Versus Alvin Karpis, Public Enemy Number One ☐ Falling from Grace ☐ Fast-Walking ☐ Headhunter ☐ House ☐ Initiation of Sarah, The ☐ Lisa, Bright and Dark ☐ Mean Dog Blues ☐ Moving Violation ☐ Stripped to Kill ☐ White Line Fever

Leonard, Robert Sean ☐ Dead Poets Society ☐ Married to It ☐ Mr. & Mrs. Bridge ☐ Much Ado About Nothing ☐ My Best Friend Is a Vampire ☐ Safe Passage ☐ Swing Kids

Lerner, Michael ☐ Amos and Andrew ☐ Anguish ☐ Barton Fink ☐ Coast to Coast ☐ Comrades of Summer, The ☐ Dark Victory ☐ Eight Men Out ☐ F. Scott Fitzgerald in Hollywood ☐ Hangup ☐ National Lampoon's Class Reunion ☐ Newsies ☐ Postman Always Rings Twice, The ☐ Radioland Murders ☐ Reflections of Murder

LeRoy, Baby ☐ Alice in Wonderland ☐ Bedtime Story, A ☐ It's a Gift ☐ Lemon Drop Kid, The ☐ Miss Fane's Baby is Stolen ☐ Old-Fashioned Way, The ☐ Tillie and Gus

Leslie, Joan ☐ Born To Be Bad ☐ Cinderella Jones ☐ Fire in the Dark ☐ Flight Nurse ☐ Great Mr. Nobody, The ☐ Hard Way, The ☐ Hell's Outpost ☐ Hellgate ☐ High Sierra ☐ Hollywood Canteen ☐ Janie Gets Married ☐ Jubilee Trail ☐ Male Animal, The ☐ Man in the Saddle ☐ Repeat Performance ☐ Revolt of Mamie Stover, The ☐ Rhapsody in Blue ☐ Sky's the Limit, The ☐ Thank Your Lucky Stars ☐ Thieves Fall Out ☐ This is the Army ☐ Two Guys From Milwaukee ☐ Wagons Roll at Night, The ☐ Where Do We Go From Here? ☐ Yankee Doodle Dandy

Levant, Oscar ☐ American in Paris, An ☐ Band Wagon, The ☐ Barkleys of Broadway, The ☐ Cobweb, The ☐ Humoresque ☐ I Don't Care Girl, The ☐ Kiss the Boys Goodbye ☐ O. Henry's Full House ☐ Rhapsody in Blue ☐ Rhythm on the River ☐ Romance on the High Seas

Levene, Sam ☐ Act One ☐ Action in the North Atlantic ☐ After the Thin Man ☐ Babe Ruth Story, The ☐ Big Street, The ☐ Boomerang! ☐ Crossfire ☐ Demon ☐ Designing Woman ☐ Dial 1119 ☐ Dream of Kings, A ☐ Guilty Bystander ☐ Gung Ho! ☐ Killers, The ☐ Mad Miss Manton, The ☐ Married Bachelor ☐ Purple Heart, The ☐ Shadow of the Thin Man ☐ Shopworn Angel, The ☐ Slaughter on Tenth Avenue ☐ Sweet Smell of Success ☐ Three Men on a Horse ☐ Three Sailors and a Girl ☐ Whistling in Brooklyn ☐ Yellow Jack

Lewis, Geoffrey ☐ Any Which Way You Can ☐ Bronco Billy ☐ Disturbed ☐ Double Impact ☐ Every Which Way but Loose ☐ Human Experiments ☐ Lucky Lady ☐ Macon County Line ☐ Man Without a Face, The ☐ Maverick ☐ Maximum Security ☐ My Name Is Nobody ☐ Night of the Comet ☐ Return of a Man Called Horse, The ☐ September Gun ☐ Thunderbolt and Lightfoot

Lewis, Jerry ☐ Artists and Models ☐ At Wa[r] with the Army ☐ Bellboy, The ☐ Big Mouth The ☐ Boeing Boeing ☐ Caddy, The ☐ Cinderfella ☐ Cookie ☐ Cracking Up ☐ Delicat[e] Delinquent, The ☐ Disorderly Orderly, The ☐ Don't Give Up the Ship ☐ Don't Raise the Bridge, Lower the River ☐ Errand Boy, The ☐ Family Jewels, The ☐ Fight for Life ☐ Funny Bones ☐ Geisha Boy, The ☐ Hardly Working ☐ Hollywood or Bust ☐ Hook, Line & Sinker ☐ It's Only Money ☐ Jumping Jacks ☐ King of Comedy, The ☐ Ladies' Man ☐ Living It Up ☐ Money From Home ☐ My Friend Irma ☐ My Friend Irma Goes West ☐ Nutty Professor, The ☐ Pardners ☐ Patsy, The ☐ Rock-a-Bye Baby ☐ Sad Sack, The ☐ Sailor Beware ☐ Scared Stiff ☐ Slapstick of Another Kind ☐ Stooge, The ☐ That's My Boy ☐ Three on a Couch ☐ Three Ring Circus ☐ Visit to a Small Planet ☐ Way . . . Way Out ☐ Who's Minding the Store? ☐ You're Never Too Young

Lewis, Juliette ☐ Cape Fear ☐ Crooked Hearts ☐ Husbands and Wives ☐ Kalifornia ☐ Meet The Hollowheads ☐ Mixed Nuts ☐ National Lampoon's Christmas Vacation ☐ Natural Born Killers ☐ Romeo is Bleeding ☐ That Night ☐ What's Eating Gilbert Grape

Li, Gong ☐ Farewell My Concubine ☐ Ju Dou ☐ Raise the Red Lantern ☐ Red Sorghum ☐ Story of a Cheat, The ☐ Story of Qiu Ju, The ☐ To Live

Linden, Hal ☐ Father Figure ☐ How to Break Up a Happy Divorce ☐ Mr. Inside/Mr. Outside ☐ My Wicked, Wicked Ways—The Legend of Errol Flynn ☐ New Life, A ☐ Ray Bradbury Chronicles: The Martian Episodes

Lindfors, Viveca ☐ Adventures of Don Juan ☐ Ann Jillian Story, The ☐ Backfire ☐ Best Little Girl in The World, The ☐ Cauldron of Blood ☐ Coming Apart ☐ Dark City ☐ Divorce Wars: A Love Story ☐ Flying Missile, The ☐ Four in a Jeep ☐ Going Undercover ☐ Gypsy Fury ☐ Halliday Brand, The ☐ Hand, The ☐ I Accuse! ☐ Journey into Light ☐ Lady Beware ☐ Marilyn: The Untold Story ☐ Moonfleet ☐ Night unto Night ☐ No Exit ☐ No Sad Songs for Me ☐ No Time for Flowers ☐ Playing for Time ☐ Rachel River ☐ Raiders, The ☐ Run for Cover ☐ Silent Madness ☐ Sure Thing, The ☐ Tempest ☐ These Are the Damned ☐ To the Victor ☐ Voices ☐ Weddings and Babies

Lindsay, Margaret ☐ Baby Face ☐ Bordertown ☐ British Intelligence ☐ Broadway Musketeers ☐ Captured ☐ Case of the Curious Bride, The ☐ Cavalcade ☐ Close Call for Ellery Queen ☐ Club Havana ☐ Crime Doctor ☐ Dangerous ☐ Devil Dogs of the Air ☐ Ellery Queen and the Murder Ring ☐ Ellery Queen and the Perfect Crime ☐ Ellery Queen's Penthouse Mystery ☐ Ellery Queen,

Master Detective ☐ Emergency Hospital ☐ Florentine Dagger, The ☐ Fog Over Frisco ☐ Frisco Kid ☐ G-Men ☐ Garden of the Moon ☐ Green Light, The ☐ Hell's Kitchen ☐ Her Sister's Secret ☐ House of the Seven Gables, The ☐ Isle of Fury ☐ Jezebel ☐ Lady Consents, The ☐ Lady Killer ☐ Man Killer ☐ Paddy, the Next Best Thing ☐ Public Enemy's Wife ☐ Scarlet Street ☐ Spoilers, The ☐ Under-Pup, The

Liotta, Ray ☐ Article 99 ☐ Corinna, Corinna ☐ Dominick and Eugene ☐ Field of Dreams ☐ GoodFellas ☐ No Escape ☐ Something Wild ☐ Unlawful Entry ☐ Women & Men: In Love There Are No Rules

Lisi, Virna ☐ Anyone Can Play ☐ Arabella ☐ Assault on a Queen ☐ Birds, the Bees and the Italians, The ☐ Bluebeard ☐ Casanova '70 ☐ Challenge to White Fang ☐ Christmas Tree, The ☐ Cricket, The ☐ Duel of the Titans ☐ Eva ☐ Girl Who Couldn't Say No, The ☐ Heist, The ☐ How to Murder Your Wife ☐ Kiss the Other Sheik ☐ Made in Italy ☐ Miss Right ☐ Night Flight from Moscow ☐ Not with My Wife You Don't! ☐ Queen Margot ☐ Secret of Santa Vittoria, The ☐ Statue, The

Litel, John ☐ Henry Aldrich Gets Glamour ☐ Henry Aldrich Swings It ☐ Henry Aldrich's Little Secret ☐ Henry and Dizzy ☐ I, Jane Doe ☐ Jack Slade ☐ Madonna's Secret, The ☐ Missing Witnesses ☐ Nancy Drew, Detective ☐ Nancy Drew, Reporter ☐ Nancy Drew, Troubleshooter ☐ Return of Dr. X, The ☐ San Antonio ☐ Secret Service of the Air ☐ Shamrock Hill ☐ Sitting Bull ☐ Slight Case of Murder, A ☐ Smooth as Silk ☐ Virginia City ☐ Woman in Hiding

Lithgow, John ☐ 2010: The Year We Make Contact ☐ Adventures of Buckaroo Banzai Across the Eighth Dimension, The ☐ All That Jazz ☐ At Play in the Fields of the Lord ☐ Baby Girl Scott ☐ Big Fix, The ☐ Blow Out ☐ Boys, The ☐ Cliffhanger ☐ Day After, The ☐ Dealing: or The Berkeley-to-Boston Forty-Brick Lost-Bag Blues ☐ Distant Thunder ☐ Footloose ☐ Glitter Dome, The ☐ Harry and the Hendersons ☐ I'm Dancing as Fast as I Can ☐ Last Elephant, The ☐ Love, Cheat & Steal ☐ Manhattan Project, The ☐ Mesmerized ☐ Not in Front of the Children ☐ Obsession ☐ Out Cold ☐ Pelican Brief, The ☐ Raising Cain ☐ Rich Kids ☐ Ricochet ☐ Santa Claus, The Movie ☐ Silent Fall ☐ Terms of Endearment ☐ Twilight Zone—The Movie ☐ World According to Garp, The

Little, Cleavon ☐ Blazing Saddles ☐ Fletch Lives ☐ FM ☐ Gig, The ☐ Gore Vidal's Lincoln ☐ Greased Lightning ☐ High Risk ☐ Homecoming—A Christmas Story, The ☐ Money to Burn ☐ Once Bitten ☐ Sky Is Gray, The ☐ Toy Soldiers ☐ Vanishing Point

Livesey, Roger ☐ Entertainer, The ☐ Finger of Guilt ☐ Girl in the News, The ☐ Green Grow the Rushes ☐ I Know Where I'm Going ☐ If This Be Sin ☐ League of Gentlemen, The ☐ Life and Death of Colonel Blimp, The ☐ Master of Ballantrae, The ☐ No My Darling Daughter ☐ Rembrandt ☐ Stairway to Heaven ☐ Vice Versa

Lloyd, Christopher ☐ Addams Family Values ☐ Addams Family, The ☐ Adventures of Buckaroo Banzai Across the Eighth Dimension, The ☐ Back to the Future ☐ Back to the Future Part II ☐ Back to the Future Part III ☐ Black Marble, The ☐ Clue ☐ Dead Ahead: The Exxon Valdez Disaster ☐ Dennis the Menace ☐ Dream Team, The ☐ Duck Tales: The Movie—Treasure of the Lost Lamp ☐ Eight Men Out ☐ Goin' South ☐ Joy of Sex ☐ Legend of the Lone Ranger, The ☐ Legend of the White Horse ☐ Miracles ☐ Mr. Mom ☐ One Flew over the Cuckoo's Nest ☐ Pagemaster, The ☐ Radioland Murders ☐ Schizoid ☐ September Gun ☐ Star Trek III: The Search for Spock ☐ Suburban Commando ☐ T Bone N Weasel ☐ To Be or Not to Be ☐ Track 29 ☐ Twenty Bucks ☐ Walk Like A Man ☐ Who Framed Roger Rabbit

Lloyd, Emily ☐ Chicago Joe and the Showgirl ☐ Cookie ☐ In Country ☐ River Runs Through It, A ☐ Scorchers ☐ Wish You Were Here

Lloyd, Harold ☐ Cat's Paw, The ☐ Feet First ☐ For Heaven's Sake ☐ Freshman, The ☐ Girl Shy ☐ Grandma's Boy ☐ Harold Lloyd's World of Comedy ☐ His Royal Slyness/Haunted Spooks ☐ Hot Water ☐ Kid Brother, The ☐ Mad Wednesday ☐ Milky Way, The ☐ Movie Crazy ☐ Professor Beware ☐ Safety Last

Locke, Sondra ☐ Any Which Way You Can ☐ Bronco Billy ☐ Death Game ☐ Every Which Way but Loose ☐ Gauntlet, The ☐ Heart Is a Lonely Hunter, The ☐ Outlaw—Josey Wales, The ☐ Ratboy ☐ Reflection of Fear, A ☐ Sudden Impact ☐ Willard

Lockhart, Gene ☐ Abe Lincoln In Illinois ☐ Action in Arabia ☐ Apartment for Peggy ☐ Blackmail ☐ Blondie ☐ By Your Leave ☐ Christmas Carol, A ☐ Confidentially Connie ☐ Down to the Sea in Ships ☐ Earthworm Tractors ☐ Edison, the Man ☐ Foxes of Harrow, The ☐ Francis Covers the Big Town ☐ Going My Way ☐ His Girl Friday ☐ House on 92nd Street ☐ I'd Climb the Highest Mountain ☐ I'm from Missouri ☐ I, Jane Doe ☐ Inspector General, The ☐ International Lady ☐ Jeanne Eagels ☐ Juke Girl ☐ Madame Bovary ☐ Man from Frisco, The ☐ Meet John Doe ☐ Mission to Moscow ☐ Northern Pursuit ☐ One Foot in Heaven ☐ Rhubarb ☐ Riding High ☐ Sea Wolf, The ☐ South of Pago Pago ☐ Star of Midnight ☐ Story of Alexander Graham Bell, The ☐ Strange Woman, The ☐ That's the Spirit ☐ We Who Are Young

Lockhart, June ☐ Easy to Wed ☐ Gift of

Love, The ☐ It's a Joke, Son ☐ Meet Me in St. Louis ☐ Night They Saved Christmas, The ☐ Sergeant York ☐ Son of Lassie ☐ T-Men ☐ Time Limit ☐ Whisper Kill ☐ Yearling, The

Lockwood, Margaret ☐ Bedelia ☐ Cast a Dark Shadow ☐ Dr. Syn ☐ Girl in the News, The ☐ Girl Must Live, A ☐ Highly Dangerous ☐ Hungry Hill ☐ Jassy ☐ Lady Vanishes, The ☐ Lorna Doone ☐ Man in Grey, The ☐ Night Train to Munich ☐ Place of One's Own, A ☐ Quiet Wedding ☐ Slipper and the Rose, The ☐ Stars Look Down, The ☐ Susannah of the Mounties ☐ Who's Your Lady Friend? ☐ Wicked Lady, The

Loder, John ☐ Abroad With Two Yanks ☐ Batmania from Comics to Screen ☐ Battle, The ☐ Brighton Strangler, The ☐ Dishonored Lady ☐ Dr. Syn ☐ Fighting Guardsman ☐ Game of Death, A ☐ Gorilla Man, The ☐ Hairy Ape, The ☐ Java Head ☐ Jealousy ☐ Lorna Doone ☐ Man Who Lived Again, The ☐ Non-Stop New York ☐ Old Acquaintance ☐ River of Unrest ☐ Sabotage ☐ Silent Passenger, The ☐ Sing As We Go

Loggia, Robert ☐ Afterburn ☐ Armed and Dangerous ☐ Bad Girls ☐ Believers, The ☐ Big ☐ Cattle King ☐ Che! ☐ Curse of the Pink Panther ☐ Echoes in the Darkness ☐ First Love ☐ Gaby—A True Story ☐ Gladiator ☐ Hot Pursuit ☐ Innocent Blood ☐ Jagged Edge ☐ Lifepod ☐ Marrying Man, The ☐ Necessary Roughness ☐ Nine Lives of Elfego Baca ☐ No Other Love ☐ Opportunity Knocks ☐ Over the Top ☐ Prizzi's Honor ☐ Psycho 2 ☐ Relentless ☐ Scarface ☐ Six Gun Law ☐ Somebody Up There Likes Me ☐ That's Life! ☐ Triumph of the Spirit ☐ Wild Palms ☐ Woman Called Golda, A

Lollobrigida, Gina ☐ Bad Man's River ☐ Beat the Devil ☐ Beauties of the Night ☐ Bread, Love and Dreams ☐ Buona Sera, Mrs. Campbell ☐ Come September ☐ Fanfan the Tulip ☐ Fast and Sexy ☐ Flesh and the Woman ☐ Four Ways Out ☐ Frisky ☐ Go Naked in the World ☐ Hotel Paradiso ☐ Hunchback of Notre Dame ☐ Imperial Venus ☐ King, Queen, Knave ☐ Never So Few ☐ Private Navy of Sgt. O'Farrell, The ☐ Solomon and Sheba ☐ Strange Bedfellows ☐ Trapeze ☐ Woman of Straw

Lom, Herbert ☐ Action of the Tiger ☐ And Now the Screaming Starts ☐ Assignment to Kill ☐ Asylum ☐ Bang, Bang, You're Dead! ☐ Big Fisherman, The ☐ Black Rose, The ☐ Cage of Gold ☐ Charleston ☐ Chase a Crooked Shadow ☐ Count Dracula ☐ Curse of the Pink Panther ☐ Dark Places ☐ Dead Zone, The ☐ Dorian Gray ☐ Fire Down Below ☐ Flame over India ☐ Frightened City, The ☐ Gambit ☐ Girl in the Painting ☐ Going Bananas ☐ Golden Salamander, The ☐ Good Time Girl ☐ Great Manhunt, The ☐ Hard Drivers ☐ Hell Drivers ☐ Horse Without a Head, The ☐ Hotel Reserve ☐ I Aim at the Stars ☐ I Like Money ☐ Intent to Kill ☐ Journey to the Far Side of the Sun ☐ King Solomon's Mines ☐ Lady Killers, The ☐ Lady Vanishes, The ☐ Love Lottery, The ☐ Mark of the Devil ☐ Master of Dragonard Hill ☐ Memed My Hawk ☐ Mysterious Island ☐ Night and the City ☐ No Trees in the Street ☐ Phantom of the Opera, The ☐ Pink Panther Strikes Again, The ☐ Pope Must Diet, The ☐ Project M7 ☐ Return of the Pink Panther, The ☐ Revenge of the Pink Panther ☐ Roots of Heaven, The ☐ Secret Mission ☐ Seventh Veil, The ☐ Shot in the Dark, A ☐ Son of the Pink Panther ☐ Ten Little Indians ☐ Ten Little Indians ☐ Third Man on the Mountain ☐ Trail of the Pink Panther ☐ Uncle Tom's Cabin ☐ Villa Rides

Lombard, Carole ☐ Bolero ☐ Eagle and the Hawk, The ☐ Fast and Loose ☐ Fools for Scandal ☐ From Hell to Heaven ☐ Gay Bride, The ☐ Golden Age of Comedy, The ☐ Hands Across the Table ☐ High Voltage ☐ In Name Only ☐ It Pays to Advertise ☐ Ladies' Man ☐ Lady by Choice ☐ Love Before Breakfast ☐ Made for Each Other ☐ Man of the World ☐ Mr. and Mrs. Smith ☐ My Man Godfrey ☐ No Man of Her Own ☐ No More Orchids ☐ No One Man ☐ Nothing Sacred ☐ Now and Forever ☐ Princess Comes Across, The ☐ Racketeer, The ☐ Sinners in the Sun ☐ Swing High, Swing Low ☐ They Knew What They Wanted ☐ To Be or Not to Be ☐ True Confession ☐ Twentieth Century ☐ Vigil in the Night ☐ Virtue ☐ We're Not Dressing

London, Julie ☐ Crime Against Joe ☐ Fat Man, The ☐ Fighting Chance, The ☐ George Raft Story, The ☐ Girl Can't Help It, The ☐ Great Man, The ☐ Man of the West ☐ Night of the Quarter Moon ☐ On Stage Everybody ☐ Question of Adultery, A ☐ Saddle the Wind ☐ Tap Roots ☐ Voice in the Mirror, The ☐ Wonderful Country, The

Lone, John ☐ Echoes of Paradise ☐ Iceman ☐ Last Emperor, The ☐ M. Butterfly ☐ Moderns, The ☐ Shadow of China, The ☐ Shadow, The ☐ Year of the Dragon

Long, Audrey ☐ Adventures of Gallant Bess ☐ Born to Kill ☐ Cavalry Scout ☐ Desperate ☐ Game of Death, A ☐ Indian Uprising ☐ Night of Adventure, A ☐ Pan Americana

Long, Richard ☐ All American, The ☐ Dark Mirror, The ☐ Fury at Gunsight Pass ☐ Girl Who Came Gift-Wrapped, The ☐ House on Haunted Hill ☐ Ma and Pa Kettle ☐ Ma and Pa Kettle Back on the Farm ☐ Ma and Pa Kettle Go to Town ☐ Saskatchewan ☐ Stranger, The

Long, Shelley ☐ Brady Bunch Movie, The ☐ Caveman ☐ Cracker Factory, The ☐ Don't Tell Her It's Me ☐ Frozen Assets ☐ Hello Again ☐ Irreconcilable Differences ☐ Losin' It ☐ Money Pit, The ☐ Night Shift ☐ Outrageous Fortune ☐ Troop Beverly Hills

Lords, Traci ☐ Cry-Baby ☐ Fast Food ☐ Ice ☐ Not of This Earth ☐ Serial Mom ☐ Shock 'em Dead ☐ Time to Die, A ☐ Tommyknockers, The

Loren, Sophia ☐ Aida ☐ Angela ☐ Arabesque ☐ Attila ☐ Aurora ☐ Black Orchid, The ☐ Blood Feud ☐ Boccaccio '70 ☐ Boy on a Dolphin ☐ Brass Target, The ☐ Breath of Scandal, A ☐ Brief Encounter ☐ Cassandra Crossing, The ☐ Condemned of Altona, The ☐ Countess from Hong Kong, A ☐ Courage ☐ Desire Under the Elms ☐ El Cid ☐ Fall of the Roman Empire ☐ Firepower ☐ Five Miles to Midnight ☐ Fortunate Pilgrim ☐ Ghosts—Italian Style ☐ Gold of Naples, The ☐ Heller in Pink Tights ☐ Houseboat ☐ It Started in Naples ☐ Judith ☐ Jury of One ☐ Key, The ☐ Lady L ☐ Lady Liberty ☐ Legend of the Lost ☐ Lucky to Be a Woman ☐ Madame ☐ Man of La Mancha ☐ Mario Puzo's "The Fortunate Pilgrim" ☐ Marriage Italian Style ☐ Millionairess, The ☐ More Than a Miracle ☐ Operation Crossbow ☐ Pride and the Passion, The ☐ Ready to Wear ☐ Scandal in Sorrento ☐ Sophia Loren: Her Own Story ☐ Special Day, A ☐ Sunflower ☐ That Kind of Woman ☐ Two Women ☐ Voyage, The ☐ Yesterday, Today and Tomorrow

Lorre, Peter ☐ 20,000 Leagues Under the Sea ☐ All Through the Night ☐ Arsenic and Old Lace ☐ Background to Danger ☐ Beast with Five Fingers, The ☐ Beat the Devil ☐ Big Circus, The ☐ Black Angel ☐ Boogie Man Will Get You, The ☐ Buster Keaton Story, The ☐ Casablanca ☐ Casbah ☐ Chase, The ☐ Comedy of Terrors, The ☐ Confidential Agent ☐ Conspirators, The ☐ Constant Nymph, The ☐ Crack-Up ☐ Crime and Punishment ☐ Cross of Lorraine, The ☐ F.P. 1 Doesn't Answer ☐ Face Behind the Mask, The ☐ Five Weeks in a Balloon ☐ Hell Ship Mutiny ☐ Hotel Berlin ☐ I Was an Adventuress ☐ I'll Give a Million ☐ Invisible Agent ☐ Island of Doomed Men ☐ Lancer Spy ☐ Lost One, The ☐ M ("M") ☐ Mad Love ☐ Maltese Falcon, The ☐ Man Who Knew Too Much, The ☐ Mask of Dimitrios, The ☐ Mr. Moto in Danger Island ☐ Mr. Moto Takes a Chance ☐ Mr. Moto Takes a Vacation ☐ Mr. Moto's Gamble ☐ Mr. Moto's Last Warning ☐ My Favorite Brunette ☐ Mysterious Mr. Moto ☐ Nancy Steel Is Missing ☐ Passage to Marseille ☐ Patsy, The ☐ Quicksand ☐ Raven, The ☐ Sad Sack, The ☐ Scent of Mystery ☐ Secret Agent ☐ Shot at Dawn ☐ Silk Stockings ☐ Strange Cargo ☐ Stranger on the Third Floor ☐ Tales of Terror ☐ Thank You, Mr. Moto ☐ They Met in Bombay ☐ Think Fast, Mr. Moto ☐ Three Strangers ☐ Trunks of Mr. O.F., The ☐ Verdict, The ☐ Voyage to the Bottom of the Sea ☐ What Women Dream ☐ White Demon, The

Louise, Anita ☐ Anthony Adverse ☐ Bandit of Sherwood Forest, The ☐ Bulldog Drummond at Bay ☐ Call It a Day ☐ Casanova Brown ☐ Devil's Mask, The ☐ Fighting Guardsman ☐ Firebird, The ☐ First Lady ☐ Going Places ☐ Gorilla, The ☐ Great Meadow, The ☐ Green Light, The ☐ Judge Priest ☐ Little Princess, The ☐ Love Letters ☐ Nine Girls ☐ Our Betters ☐ Reno ☐ Retreat, Hell! ☐ Sisters, The ☐ Story of Louis Pasteur, The ☐ That Certain Woman ☐ Tovarich

Louise, Tina ☐ Armored Command ☐ Day of the Outlaw ☐ Death Scream ☐ Dog Day ☐ For Those Who Think Young ☐ Friendships, Secrets, and Lies ☐ Gilligan's Island: The Collector's Edition, Vol. 1 ☐ God's Little Acre ☐ Good Guys and the Bad Guys, The ☐ Hangman, The ☐ Johnny Suede ☐ Mean Dog Blues ☐ Stepford Wives, The ☐ Wrecking Crew, The

Lovejoy, Frank ☐ Beachhead ☐ Breakthrough ☐ Charge at Feather River, The ☐ Cole Younger, Gunfighter ☐ Finger Man, The ☐ Fingerman ☐ Force of Arms ☐ Hitch-Hiker, The ☐ Home of the Brave ☐ House of Wax ☐ I Was a Communist for the FBI ☐ I'll See You in My Dreams ☐ In a Lonely Place ☐ Mad at the World ☐ Men of the Fighting Lady ☐ Retreat, Hell! ☐ Sound of Fury, The ☐ Strategic Air Command ☐ Three Brave Men ☐ Winning Team, The

Lovitz, Jon ☐ American Tail: Fievel Goes West, An ☐ Brave Little Toaster, The ☐ City Slickers 2: Legend of Curly's Gold ☐ Last Resort ☐ League of Their Own, A ☐ Mom and Dad Save the World ☐ Mr. Destiny ☐ My Stepmother Is an Alien ☐ National Lampoon's Loaded Weapon ☐ North ☐ Trapped in Paradise

Lowe, Edmund ☐ Call Out the Marines ☐ Chandu the Magician ☐ Dillinger ☐ Dinner at Eight ☐ Enchanted Forest ☐ Every Day's a Holiday ☐ Garden Murder Case, The ☐ Good Sam ☐ Guilty as Hell ☐ Hot Pepper ☐ I Love You Again ☐ In Old Arizona ☐ No More Women ☐ Painted Angel, The ☐ Under Pressure ☐ What Price Glory?

Lowe, Rob ☐ About Last Night . . . ☐ Bad Influence ☐ Class ☐ Dark Backward, The ☐ Finest Hour ☐ Hotel New Hampshire, The ☐ Illegally Yours ☐ Masquerade ☐ Outsiders, The ☐ Oxford Blues ☐ Square Dance ☐ St. Elmo's Fire ☐ Stand, The ☐ Stroke of Midnight ☐ Suddenly, Last Summer ☐ Wayne's World ☐ Youngblood

Loy, Myrna ☐ After the Thin Man ☐ Airport '75 ☐ Ambassador's Daughter, The ☐ Animal Kingdom, The ☐ Another Thin Man ☐ April Fools, The ☐ Arrowsmith ☐ Bachelor and the Bobby-Soxer, The ☐ Barbarian, The ☐ Belles on Their Toes ☐ Best Years of Our Lives, The ☐ Black Watch, The ☐ Broadway Bill ☐ Cheaper by the Dozen ☐ Connecticut Yankee, A ☐ Consolation Marriage ☐ Do Not Fold, Spindle or Mutilate ☐ Don Juan ☐ Double Wedding ☐ Emma ☐ End, The ☐ Evelyn Prentice ☐ From the Terrace ☐ Girl in Every Port, A ☐ Great Ziegfeld, The ☐ I Love You Again ☐ If This Be Sin ☐ It Happened at Lakewood Manor ☐ Just Tell Me What You Want ☐ Libeled Lady ☐ Lonelyhearts ☐ Love Crazy ☐ Love Me Tonight ☐ Lucky Night ☐ Man-Proof ☐ Manhattan Melodrama ☐ Mask of Fu Manchu, The ☐ Men in White ☐ Midnight Lace ☐ Mr. Blandings Builds His Dream House ☐ Noah's Ark ☐ Parnell ☐ Penthouse ☐ Petticoat Fever ☐ Prizefighter and the Lady, The ☐ Rains Came, The ☐ Red Pony, The ☐ Renegades ☐ Shadow of the Thin Man ☐ So Goes My Love ☐ Song of the Thin Man ☐ Stamboul Quest ☐ Summer Solstice ☐ Test Pilot ☐ Thin Man Goes Home, The ☐ Thin Man, The ☐ Third Finger, Left Hand ☐ Thirteen Women ☐ Too Hot to Handle ☐ Topaze ☐ Truth About Youth, The ☐ Wet Parade, The ☐ When Ladies Meet ☐ Whipsaw ☐ Wife vs. Secretary ☐ Wings in the Dark

Lucci, Susan ☐ Anastasia: The Mystery Of Anna ☐ Bride in Black, The ☐ Haunted by Her Past ☐ Hitwoman: The Double Edge ☐ Invitation to Hell ☐ Lady Mobster ☐ Mafia Princess ☐ Secret Passions

Luckinbill, Laurence ☐ Boys in the Band, The ☐ Death Sentence ☐ Ike: The War Years ☐ Mating Season, The ☐ Messenger of Death ☐ Money, The ☐ Not for Publication ☐ Star Trek V: The Final Frontier ☐ Such Good Friends

Lugosi, Bela ☐ Abbott and Costello Meet Frankenstein ☐ Ape Man, The ☐ Bela Lugosi Meets a Brooklyn Gorilla ☐ Black Camel, The ☐ Black Cat, The ☐ Black Cat, The ☐ Black Dragons ☐ Black Friday ☐ Black Sleep, The ☐ Body Snatcher, The ☐ Bowery at Midnight ☐ Bride of the Monster ☐ Broadminded ☐ Chandu the Magician ☐ Corpse Vanishes, The ☐ Death Kiss, The ☐ Devil Bat, The ☐ Devil's in Love, The ☐ Dracula ☐ Frankenstein Meets the Wolf Man ☐ Genius at Work ☐ Ghost of Frankenstein, The ☐ Ghosts on the Loose ☐ Glen or Glenda ☐ Gorilla, The ☐ Human Monster, The ☐ International House ☐ Invisible Ghost, The ☐ Invisible Ray, The ☐ Island of Lost Souls ☐ Mark of the Vampire ☐ Midnight Girl ☐ Murder by Television ☐ Murders in the Rue Morgue ☐ Mysterious Mr. Wong, The ☐ Night Monster ☐ Night of Terror ☐ Ninotchka ☐ One Body Too Many ☐ Phantom Ship ☐ Plan 9 from Outer Space ☐ Raven, The ☐ Renegades ☐ Return of the Ape Man ☐ Return of the Vampire, The ☐ Saint's Double Trouble, The ☐ Son of Frankenstein ☐ Spooks Run Wild ☐ White Zombie ☐ Wolf Man, The ☐ Zombies on Broadway

Lukas, Paul ☐ 20,000 Leagues Under the Sea ☐ 55 Days at Peking ☐ Address Unknown ☐ Benson Murder Case ☐ Berlin Express ☐ By Candlelight ☐ Captain Fury ☐ Captured ☐ Casino Murder Case ☐ City Streets ☐ Confessions of a Nazi Spy ☐ Deadline at Dawn ☐ Dinner at the Ritz ☐ Dodsworth ☐ Downstairs ☐ Experiment Perilous ☐ Fountain, The ☐ Fun in Acapulco ☐ Ghost Breakers, The ☐ Grand Slam ☐ Hostages ☐ I Found Stella Parish ☐ Kim ☐ Kiss Before the Mirror, The ☐ Ladies in Love ☐ Lady in Distress ☐ Lady Vanishes, The ☐ Monster and the Girl, The ☐ No One Man ☐ Right to Love, The ☐ Roots of Heaven, The ☐ Scent of Mystery ☐ Secret of the Blue Room ☐ Shopworn Angel ☐ Strictly Dishonorable ☐ Three Musketeers, The ☐ Tomorrow and Tomorrow ☐ Uncertain Glory ☐ Vice Squad, The ☐ Watch on the Rhine ☐ Whispering City

Luke, Keye ☐ Across the Pacific ☐ Alice ☐ Amsterdam Kill, The ☐ Andy Hardy's Blonde Trouble ☐ Barricade ☐ Battle Hell (Yangtse Incident) ☐ Between Two Women ☐ Burma Convoy ☐ Cat Creature, The ☐ Charlie Chan at Monte Carlo ☐ Charlie Chan at the Circus ☐ Charlie Chan at the Olympics ☐ Charlie Chan at the Opera ☐ Charlie Chan at the Race Track ☐ Charlie Chan in Paris ☐ Charlie Chan in Shanghai ☐ Charlie Chan on Broadway ☐ Dr. Gillespie's Criminal Case ☐ Dr. Gillespie's New Assistant ☐ Feathered Serpent, The ☐ First Yank into Tokyo ☐ Good Earth, The ☐ Green Hornet, The ☐ Hawaiians, The ☐ Kung Fu ☐ Mad Love ☐ Mr. Moto's Gamble ☐ Sky Dragon, The ☐ Sleep My Love

Lundigan, William ☐ Dishonored Lady ☐ Down Among the Sheltering Palms ☐ East of the River ☐ Elopement ☐ Follow Me Quietly ☐ Forgotten Woman ☐ Great Mr. Nobody, The ☐ House on Telegraph Hill ☐ I'd Climb the Highest Mountain ☐ I'll Get By ☐ Inferno ☐ Inside Story, The ☐ International Squadron ☐ Love Nest ☐ Man Who Talked Too Much, The ☐ Mother Didn't Tell Me ☐ Mystery in Mexico

Lund, John ☐ Affair in Reno ☐ Battle at Apache Pass, The ☐ Battle Stations ☐ Bride of Vengeance ☐ Bronco Buster ☐ Chief Crazy Horse ☐ Dakota Incident ☐ Darling, How Could You ☐ Duchess of Idaho ☐ Five Guns West ☐ Foreign Affair, A ☐ High Society ☐ If a Man Answers ☐ Just Across the Street ☐ Latin Lovers ☐ Mating Season, The ☐ Miss Tatlock's Millions ☐ My Friend Irma ☐ My Friend Irma Goes West ☐ Night Has a Thousand Eyes ☐ No Man of Her Own ☐ Perils of Pauline, The ☐ To Each His Own ☐ Wackiest Ship in the Army, The ☐ White Feather

Lupino, Ida ☐ Adventures of Sherlock Holmes, The ☐ Anything Goes ☐ Artists and Models ☐ Beware, My Lovely ☐ Big Knife, The ☐ Bigamist, The ☐ Deadhead Miles ☐ Deep Valley ☐ Devil's Rain, The ☐ Devotion ☐ Escape Me Never ☐ Fight for Your

Lady ☐ Food of the Gods, The ☐ Forever and a Day ☐ Gay Desperado, The ☐ Ghost Camera, The ☐ Hard Way, The ☐ High Sierra ☐ I Lived with You ☐ I Love a Mystery ☐ In Our Time ☐ Jennifer ☐ Junior Bonner ☐ Ladies in Retirement ☐ Lady and the Mob, The ☐ Letters, The ☐ Life Begins at Eight-Thirty ☐ Light that Failed, The ☐ Lone Wolf Spy Hunt, The ☐ Lust for Gold ☐ Man I Love, The ☐ Moontide ☐ On Dangerous Ground ☐ One Rainy Afternoon ☐ Out of the Fog ☐ Peter Ibbetson ☐ Pillow to Post ☐ Private Hell 36 ☐ Road House ☐ Sea Devils ☐ Sea Wolf, The ☐ Thank Your Lucky Stars ☐ They Drive by Night ☐ While the City Sleeps ☐ Woman in Hiding ☐ Women's Prison ☐ Yours For the Asking

LuPone, Patti ☐ Driving Miss Daisy ☐ Family Prayers ☐ Fighting Back ☐ LBJ: The Early Years ☐ Wise Guys

Lydon, Jimmy ☐ Gasoline Alley ☐ Henry Aldrich for President ☐ Henry Aldrich Gets Glamour ☐ Henry Aldrich Haunts a House ☐ Henry Aldrich Plays Cupid ☐ Henry Aldrich Swings It ☐ Henry Aldrich's Little Secret ☐ Henry Aldrich, Boy Scout ☐ Henry Aldrich, Editor ☐ Henry and Dizzy ☐ Life with Father ☐ Little Men ☐ Tom Brown's School Days

Lynch, John ☐ Cal ☐ In the Name of the Father ☐ Monkey Boy ☐ Railway Station Man, The ☐ Secret of Roan Inish, The

Lynch, Kelly ☐ Beans of Egypt, Maine, The ☐ Curly Sue ☐ Drugstore Cowboy ☐ Imaginary Crimes ☐ Road House ☐ Three of Hearts ☐ Warm Summer Rain, A

Lynde, Paul ☐ Beach Blanket Bingo ☐ Bye, Bye, Birdie ☐ Charlotte's Web ☐ For Those Who Think Young ☐ Gidget Grows Up ☐ Glass Bottom Boat, The ☐ How Sweet It Is! ☐ Hugo the Hippo ☐ New Faces ☐ Under the Yum Yum Tree ☐ Villain, The

Lynley, Carol ☐ Balboa ☐ Beasts Are in the Streets, The ☐ Blue Denim ☐ Bunny Lake Is Missing ☐ Cardinal, The ☐ Cat and the Canary, The ☐ Dark Tower ☐ Fantasy Island ☐ Four Deuces, The ☐ Harlow ☐ Having Babies II ☐ Holiday for Lovers ☐ Hound-Dog Man ☐ If It's a Man, Hang Up ☐ Immortal, The ☐ Last Sunset, The ☐ Light in the Forest, The ☐ Maltese Bippy, The ☐ Night Stalker, The ☐ Norwood ☐ Once You Kiss a Stranger ☐ Pleasure Seekers, The ☐ Poseidon Adventure, The ☐ Return to Peyton Place ☐ Stripper, The ☐ Under the Yum Yum Tree

Lynn, Diana ☐ And the Angels Sing ☐ Annapolis Story, An ☐ Bedtime for Bonzo ☐ Bride Wore Boots, The ☐ Easy Come, Easy Go ☐ Every Girl Should Be Married ☐ Henry Aldrich Gets Glamour ☐ Henry Aldrich Plays Cupid ☐ Kentuckian, The ☐ Major and the Minor, The ☐ Meet Me at the Fair ☐ Miracle of Morgan's Creek, The ☐ My Friend Irma ☐ My Friend Irma Goes West ☐ Our Hearts Were Growing Up ☐ Our Hearts Were Young and Gay ☐ Out of This World ☐ Paid in Full ☐ Peggy ☐ People Against O'Hara, The ☐ Plunder of the Sun ☐ Track of the Cat ☐ You're Never Too Young

Lynn, Jeffrey ☐ All This and Heaven Too ☐ Black Bart ☐ Body Disappears, The ☐ Child Is Born, A ☐ Espionage Agent ☐ Fighting 69th, The ☐ Flight from Destiny ☐ For the Love of Mary ☐ Four Daughters ☐ Four Mothers ☐ Four Wives ☐ Hometown Story ☐ It All Came True ☐ Letter to Three Wives, A ☐ Million Dollar Baby ☐ My Love Came Back ☐ Roaring Twenties, The ☐ Undergound ☐ Up Front

Lyon, Sue ☐ Alligator ☐ Evel Knievel ☐ Flim Flam Man, The ☐ Four Rode Out ☐ Lolita ☐ Night of the Iguana, The ☐ Seven Women

MacArthur, James ☐ Angry Breed, The ☐ Bedford Incident, The ☐ Interns, The ☐ Kidnapped ☐ Light in the Forest, The ☐ Mosby's Marauders ☐ Night the Bridge Fell Down, The ☐ Spencer's Mountain ☐ Swiss Family Robinson ☐ Third Man on the Mountain ☐ Truth About Spring, The ☐ Young Stranger, The

Macchio, Ralph ☐ Crossroads ☐ Dangerous Company ☐ Distant Thunder ☐ Karate Kid, Part 2, The ☐ Karate Kid, Part 3, The ☐ Karate Kid, The ☐ My Cousin Vinny ☐ Naked in New York ☐ Outsiders, The ☐ Teachers ☐ Up the Academy

MacDonald, J. Farrell ☐ County Fair ☐ Courage of the West ☐ Exclusive Story ☐ Fighting Youth ☐ Heritage of the Desert ☐ I Loved a Woman ☐ Iron Horse, The ☐ Madame Racketeer ☐ Me and My Gal ☐ Millionaire, The ☐ Painted Angel, The ☐ Peg o' My Heart ☐ Sporting Blood ☐ Star of Midnight ☐ Superman and the Mole Men ☐ Truth About Youth, The

MacDonald, Jeanette ☐ Bitter Sweet ☐ Broadway Serenade ☐ Cairo ☐ Cat and the Fiddle, The ☐ Firefly, The ☐ Follow the Boys ☐ Girl of the Golden West, The ☐ I Married an Angel ☐ Lottery Bride, The ☐ Love Me Tonight ☐ Love Parade, The ☐ Maytime ☐ Merry Widow, The ☐ Monte Carlo ☐ Naughty Marietta ☐ New Moon ☐ One Hour with You ☐ Rose Marie ☐ San Francisco ☐ Smilin' Through ☐ Sun Comes Up, The ☐ Sweethearts ☐ Three Daring Daughters ☐ Vagabond King, The

MacDowell, Andie ☐ Bad Girls ☐ Deception ☐ Four Weddings and a Funeral ☐ Green Card ☐ Greystoke: The Legend of Tarzan, Lord of the Apes ☐ Groundhog Day ☐ Hudson Hawk ☐ Object of Beauty, The ☐ sex, lies, and videotape ☐ Women & Men: In Love There Are No Rules

MacGinnis, Niall ☐ Edge of the World, The ☐ Face in the Rain, A ☐ Island of Terror ☐ Luck of the Irish, The ☐ Man Who Finally Died, The ☐ Martin Luther ☐ Never Take Candy from a Stranger ☐ We Dive at Dawn

MacGowran, Jack ☐ Exorcist, The ☐ Fearless Vampire Killers or: Pardon Me, But Your Teeth Are in My Neck ☐ How I Won the War ☐ King Lear ☐ Start the Revolution Without Me ☐ Young Cassidy

MacGraw, Ali ☐ Convoy ☐ Getaway, The ☐ Goodbye, Columbus ☐ Just Tell Me What You Want ☐ Love Story ☐ Murder Elite ☐ Players ☐ Winds of War, The

MacLaine, Shirley ☐ All in a Night's Work ☐ Apartment, The ☐ Around the World in 80 Days ☐ Artists and Models ☐ Ask Any Girl ☐ Being There ☐ Bliss of Mrs. Blossom, The ☐ Can-Can ☐ Cannonball Run II ☐ Career ☐ Change of Seasons, A ☐ Children's Hour, The ☐ Desperate Characters ☐ Gambit ☐ Guarding Tess ☐ Hot Spell ☐ Irma la Douce ☐ John Goldfarb, Please Come Home ☐ Loving Couples ☐ Madame Sousatzka ☐ Matchmaker, The ☐ My Geisha ☐ Out on a Limb ☐ Possession of Joel Delaney, The ☐ Postcards from the Edge ☐ Sheepman, The ☐ Some Came Running ☐ Steel Magnolias ☐ Sweet Charity ☐ Terms of Endearment ☐ Trouble With Harry, The ☐ Turning Point, The ☐ Two for the Seesaw ☐ Two Loves ☐ Two Mules for Sister Sara ☐ Used People ☐ Waiting for the Light ☐ What a Way to Go! ☐ Woman Times Seven ☐ Wrestling Ernest Hemingway ☐ Yellow Rolls-Royce, The

Mack, Helen ☐ Four Hours to Kill ☐ Girls of the Road ☐ I Promise to Pay ☐ Lemon Drop Kid, The ☐ Melody Cruise ☐ Milky Way, The ☐ Return of Peter Grimm, The ☐ She ☐ Son of Kong, The

MacLachlan, Kyle ☐ Blue Velvet ☐ Don't Tell Her It's Me ☐ Doors, The ☐ Dune ☐ Flintstones, The ☐ Hidden, The ☐ Rich in Love ☐ Twin Peaks ☐ Twin Peaks: Fire Walk With Me

MacLane, Barton ☐ Adventurous Blonde ☐ Big Street, The ☐ Blondes at Work ☐ Bullets or Ballots ☐ Dr. Socrates ☐ Ever Since Eve ☐ I Found Stella Parish ☐ Jack Slade ☐ Jaguar ☐ Jail Busters ☐ Maltese Falcon, The ☐ Man Is Armed, The ☐ Marine Raiders ☐ Mummy's Ghost, The ☐ Naked in the Sun ☐ Noose for a Gunman ☐ Rails Into Laramie ☐ San Quentin ☐ San Quentin ☐ Silver River ☐ Song of Texas ☐ Walking Dead, The ☐ Walls of Jericho, The ☐ Western Union ☐ You and Me ☐ You Only Live Once

MacMahon, Aline ☐ Ah, Wilderness ☐ All the Way Home ☐ Babbitt ☐ Back Door to Heaven ☐ Cimarron ☐ Diamond Head ☐ Dragon Seed ☐ Eddie Cantor Story, The ☐ Five Star Final ☐ Flame and the Arrow, The ☐ Gold Diggers of 1933 ☐ Guest in the House ☐ Heroes for Sale ☐ I Could Go on Singing ☐ I Live My Life ☐ Kind Lady ☐ Lady Is Willing, The ☐ Life Begins ☐ Life of Jimmy Dolan, The ☐ Man from Laramie, The ☐ Mouthpiece, The ☐ Once in a Lifetime ☐ One Way Passage ☐ Out of the Fog ☐ Search, The ☐ Silver Dollar ☐ TISH ☐ When You're in Love ☐ Young Doctors, The

MacMurray, Fred ☐ Above Suspicion ☐ Absent Minded Professor, The ☐ Alice Adams ☐ And the Angels Sing ☐ Apartment, The ☐ At Gunpoint ☐ Bon Voyage! ☐ Borderline ☐ Bride Comes Home, The ☐ Cafe Society ☐ Caine Mutiny, The ☐ Callaway Went Thataway ☐ Captain Eddie ☐ Car 99 ☐ Champagne Waltz ☐ Charley and the Angel ☐ Cocoanut Grove ☐ Day of the Bad Man ☐ Dive Bomber ☐ Double Indemnity ☐ Egg and I, The ☐ Exclusive ☐ Face of a Fugitive ☐ Fair Wind to Java ☐ Family Honeymoon ☐ Far Horizons, The ☐ Father Was a Fullback ☐ Flight for Freedom ☐ Follow Me, Boys! ☐ Forest Rangers, The ☐ Gilded Lily, The ☐ Good Day for a Hanging ☐ Gun for a Coward ☐ Hands Across the Table ☐ Happiest Millionaire, The ☐ Honeymoon in Bali ☐ Innocent Affair, An ☐ Invitation to Happiness ☐ Kisses for My President ☐ Lady Is Willing, The ☐ Little Old New York ☐ Maid of Salem ☐ Men with Wings ☐ Millionaire for Christy, A ☐ Miracle of the Bells, The ☐ Moonlighter, The ☐ Murder, He Says ☐ Never a Dull Moment ☐ New York Town ☐ No Time for Love ☐ On Our Merry Way ☐ One Night in Lisbon ☐ Oregon Trail, The ☐ Pardon My Past ☐ Practically Yours ☐ Princess Comes Across, The ☐ Pushover ☐ Rains of Ranchipur, The ☐ Rangers of Fortune ☐ Remember the Night ☐ Shaggy Dog, The ☐ Sing, You Sinners ☐ Smoky ☐ Son of Flubber ☐ Standing Room Only ☐ Suddenly, It's Spring ☐ Swing High, Swing Low ☐ Take a Letter, Darling ☐ Texas Rangers, The ☐ There's Always Tomorrow ☐ Thirteen Hours By Air ☐ Too Many Husbands ☐ Trail of the Lonesome Pine ☐ True Confession ☐ Where Do We Go From Here? ☐ Woman's World

MacNee, Patrick ☐ Battlestar: Galactica ☐ Bloodsuckers ☐ Down Under ☐ Evening in Byzantium, An ☐ Howling, The ☐ Incident at Victoria Falls ☐ Lobsterman from Mars ☐ Masque of the Red Death ☐ Matt Helm ☐ Pursuit of the Graf Spee ☐ Sorry, Wrong Number ☐ Until They Sail ☐ View to a Kill, A ☐ Young Doctors in Love

MacRae, Gordon ☐ About Face ☐ Backfire ☐ Best Things in Life Are Free, The ☐ Big Punch, The ☐ By the Light of the Silvery Moon ☐ Carousel ☐ Daughter of Rosie O'Grady, The ☐ Desert Song, The ☐ Look for the Silver Lining ☐ Oklahoma! ☐ On Moonlight Bay ☐ Tea for Two ☐ Three Sailors and a Girl ☐ West Point Story

Macready, George ☐ Abductors, The ☐ Alligator People, The ☐ Big Clock, The ☐ Desert Hawk, The ☐ Doolins of Oklahoma, The ☐ Fame Is the Name of the Game ☐ Fighting Guardsman ☐ Fortunes of Captain Blood, The ☐ Gilda ☐ Gunfire at Indian Gap ☐ I Beheld

His Glory ☐ I Love a Mystery ☐ Missing Juror, The ☐ My Name Is Julia Ross ☐ Nevadan, The ☐ Night Gallery ☐ Return of Monte Cristo, The ☐ Seven Days in May ☐ Seventh Cross, The ☐ Stranger Who Wore a Gun, The ☐ Swordsman, The ☐ Vera Cruz ☐ Where Love Has Gone

Madigan, Amy ☐ Alamo Bay ☐ Ambush Murders, The ☐ Dark Half, The ☐ Day After, The ☐ Field of Dreams ☐ Love Child ☐ Love Letters ☐ Lucky Day ☐ Nowhere to Hide ☐ Places in the Heart ☐ Prince of Pennsylvania, The ☐ Roe vs. Wade ☐ Streets of Fire ☐ Twice in a Lifetime ☐ Uncle Buck ☐ Victims

Madison, Guy ☐ Bang-Bang Kid, The ☐ Beast of Hollow Mountain, The ☐ Bullwhip ☐ Charge at Feather River, The ☐ Command, The ☐ Drums in the Deep South ☐ Five Against the House ☐ Gunmen of the Rio Grande ☐ Hard Man, The ☐ Hilda Crane ☐ Honeymoon ☐ Jet Over the Atlantic ☐ Last Frontier, The ☐ Massacre River ☐ On the Threshold of Space ☐ Till the End of Time

Madison, Noel ☐ Black Raven, The ☐ Bombs Over Burma ☐ Cocaine Fiends, The ☐ Four Hours to Kill ☐ Last Mile, The ☐ Man Who Made Diamonds, The ☐ Me and My Gal ☐ Sinner's Holiday

Madonna ☐ Bloodhounds of Broadway ☐ Body of Evidence ☐ Dangerous Game ☐ Desperately Seeking Susan ☐ Dick Tracy ☐ League of Their Own, A ☐ Madonna—Blond Ambition ☐ Madonna—The Girlie Show—Live Down Under ☐ Shadows and Fog ☐ Shanghai Surprise ☐ Truth or Dare ☐ Who's That Girl?

Madsen, Virginia ☐ Becoming Colette ☐ Candyman ☐ Creator ☐ Dune ☐ Fire with Fire ☐ Gotham ☐ Hearst and Davies Affair, The ☐ Heart of Dixie ☐ Highlander II: The Quickening ☐ Hot Spot, The ☐ Hot to Trot ☐ Linda ☐ Long Gone ☐ Love Kills ☐ Modern Girls ☐ Mr. North ☐ Slam Dance ☐ Third Degree Burn

Magee, Patrick ☐ And Now the Screaming Starts ☐ Barry Lyndon ☐ Birthday Party, The ☐ Clockwork Orange, A ☐ Dementia 13 ☐ Demons of the Mind ☐ Die, Monster, Die! ☐ Fiend, The ☐ Final Programme, The ☐ Killer in Every Corner, A ☐ King Lear ☐ Lady Ice ☐ Luther ☐ Marat/Sade (Persecution and Assassination of Jean-Paul Marat Performed by the In ☐ Masque of the Red Death ☐ Monster Club, The ☐ Seance on a Wet Afternoon ☐ Skull, The ☐ Sleep of Death ☐ Tales from the Crypt

Magnani, Anna ☐ Amore ☐ And the Wild, Wild Women ☐ Bellissima ☐ Fugitive Kind, The ☐ Golden Coach, The ☐ Made in Italy ☐ Mamma Roma ☐ Of Life and Love ☐ Open City ☐ Passionate Thief, The ☐ Peddlin' In Society ☐ Rose Tattoo, The ☐ Secret of Santa Vittoria, The ☐ Volcano ☐ Wild is the Wind

Maher, Bill ☐ Cannibal Women in the Avocado Jungle of Death ☐ Club Med ☐ Rags to Riches ☐ Ratboy

Mahoney, Jock ☐ I've Lived Before ☐ Joe Dakota ☐ Land Unknown, The ☐ Nevadan, The ☐ Overland Pacific ☐ Showdown at Abilene ☐ Tarzan the Magnificent ☐ Their Only Chance ☐ Time to Love and a Time to Die, A

Mahoney, John ☐ Betrayed ☐ Dinner at Eight ☐ Eight Men Out ☐ Frantic ☐ Hudsucker Proxy, The ☐ Image, The ☐ Love Hurts ☐ Manhattan Project, The ☐ Moonstruck ☐ Reality Bites ☐ Russia House, The ☐ Say Anything . . . ☐ Suspect ☐ Trapped in Silence

Main, Marjorie ☐ Angels Wash Their Faces, The ☐ Another Thin Man ☐ Bad Bascomb ☐ Barnacle Bill ☐ Belle of New York, The ☐ Big Jack ☐ Boy of the Streets ☐ Bugle Sounds, The ☐ Dark Command ☐ Dead End ☐ Egg and I, The ☐ Fast Company ☐ Feudin', Fussin' and A-Fightin' ☐ Friendly Persuasion ☐ Gentle Annie ☐ Harvey Girls, The ☐ Heaven Can Wait ☐ Honky Tonk ☐ I Take This Woman ☐ Jackass Mail ☐ Johnny Come Lately ☐ Kettles in the Ozarks, The ☐ Kettles on Old Macdonald's Farm, The ☐ Law and the Lady, The ☐ Long, Long Trailer, The ☐ Lucky Night ☐ Ma and Pa Kettle ☐ Ma and Pa Kettle at Home ☐ Ma and Pa Kettle at the Fair ☐ Ma and Pa Kettle at Waikiki ☐ Ma and Pa Kettle Back on the Farm ☐ Ma and Pa Kettle Go to Town ☐ Ma and Pa Kettle on Vacation ☐ Man Who Cried Wolf, The ☐ Meet Me in St. Louis ☐ Mr. Imperium ☐ Murder, He Says ☐ Rationing ☐ Roman Scandals ☐ Rose Marie ☐ Shadow, The ☐ Shepherd of the Hills ☐ Stella Dallas ☐ Summer Stock ☐ Susan and God ☐ Tennessee Johnson ☐ Test Pilot ☐ They Shall Have Music ☐ TISH ☐ Undercurrent ☐ We Were Dancing ☐ Wild Man of Borneo, The ☐ Wistful Widow of Wagon Gap, The ☐ Women, The ☐ Wyoming

Majors, Lee ☐ Agency ☐ Ballad of Andy Crocker, The ☐ Bionic Showdown: The Six Million Dollar Man and the Bionic Woman ☐ Francis Gary Powers: The True Story of the U-2 Spy Incident ☐ High Noon, Part II: The Return of Will Kane ☐ Keaton's Cop ☐ Killer Fish ☐ Last Chase, The ☐ Liberation of L. B. Jones, The ☐ Norseman, The ☐ Smoky Mountain Christmas, A ☐ Steel ☐ Will Penny

Makepeace, Chris ☐ Aloha Summer ☐ Captive Hearts ☐ Last Chase, The ☐ Mazes and Monsters ☐ My Bodyguard ☐ Oasis, The ☐ Savage Hunger, A ☐ Vamp

Mako ☐ Armed Response ☐ Behind Enemy Lines ☐ Bushido Blade, The ☐ Conan the Barbarian ☐ Conan the Destroyer ☐ Farewell to Manzanar ☐ Fatal Mission ☐ Hawaiians, The ☐ Highlander: The Final Dimension ☐ Hiroshima: Out of the Ashes ☐ Island at the Top of the World, The ☐ Judge Dee and the Monastery Murder ☐ Kung Fu—The Movie ☐ My Samurai ☐ Perfect Weapon, The ☐ Rising Sun ☐ Sand Pebbles, The ☐ Sidekicks ☐ Taking Care of Business ☐ Tucker—The Man and His Dream ☐ Unremarkable Life, An

Malden, Karl ☐ Absolute Strangers ☐ Adventures of Bullwhip Griffin, The ☐ All Fall Down ☐ Baby Doll ☐ Beyond the Poseidon Adventure ☐ Billion Dollar Brain ☐ Billy Galvin ☐ Birdman of Alcatraz ☐ Blue ☐ Bombers B-52 ☐ Boomerang! ☐ Call Me Anna ☐ Captains Courageous ☐ Cat o' Nine Tails ☐ Cheyenne Autumn ☐ Cincinnati Kid, The ☐ Come Fly with Me ☐ Dario Argento's World of Horror ☐ Dead Ringer ☐ Diplomatic Courier ☐ Fatal Vision ☐ Fear Strikes Out ☐ Great Impostor, The ☐ Gunfighter, The ☐ Gypsy ☐ Halls of Montezuma ☐ Hanging Tree, The ☐ Hot Millions ☐ Hotel ☐ I Confess ☐ Meteor ☐ Miracle on Ice ☐ Murderers' Row ☐ Nevada Smith ☐ Nuts ☐ On the Waterfront ☐ One-Eyed Jacks ☐ Operation Secret ☐ Parrish ☐ Patton ☐ Phantom of the Rue Morgue ☐ Pollyanna ☐ Ruby Gentry ☐ Sellout, The ☐ Sting II, The ☐ Streetcar Named Desire, A ☐ Where the Sidewalk Ends ☐ Wild Rovers ☐ Winged Victory

Malkovich, John ☐ Dangerous Liaisons ☐ Death of a Salesman ☐ Eleni ☐ Empire of the Sun ☐ Glass Menagerie, The ☐ Heart of Darkness ☐ In the Line of Fire ☐ Jennifer 8 ☐ Killing Fields, The ☐ Making Mr. Right ☐ Miles from Home ☐ Object of Beauty, The ☐ Of Mice and Men ☐ Places in the Heart ☐ Queens Logic ☐ Shadows and Fog ☐ Sheltering Sky, The

Malone, Dorothy ☐ Abduction ☐ Artists and Models ☐ At Gunpoint ☐ Basic Instinct ☐ Battle Cry ☐ Beach Party ☐ Being, The ☐ Big Sleep, The ☐ Bushwackers, The ☐ Colorado Territory ☐ Fast and the Furious, The ☐ Five Guns West ☐ Flaxy Martin ☐ Good Luck, Miss Wyckoff ☐ Jack Slade ☐ Janie Gets Married ☐ Katie: Portrait of a Centerfold ☐ Killer That Stalked New York, The ☐ Last Sunset, The ☐ Last Voyage, The ☐ Law and Order ☐ Man of a Thousand Faces ☐ Man Who Would Not Die, The ☐ Nevadan, The ☐ One Sunday Afternoon ☐ Pillars of the Sky ☐ Pushover ☐ Rest in Pieces ☐ Scared Stiff ☐ Sincerely Yours ☐ South of St. Louis ☐ Tarnished Angels, The ☐ Tension at Table Rock ☐ Tip on a Dead Jockey ☐ To the Victor ☐ Too Much, Too Soon ☐ Torpedo Alley ☐ Two Guys From Texas ☐ Warlock ☐ Written on the Wind

Mancuso, Nick ☐ Blame It on the Night ☐ Burning Bridges ☐ Death of an Angel ☐ Death Ship ☐ Double Identity ☐ Fatal Exposure ☐ Half a Lifetime ☐ Heartbreakers ☐ Mother Lode ☐ Nightwing ☐ Rapid Fire ☐ Ticket to Heaven

Manfredi, Nino ☐ Bread and Chocolate ☐ Cafe Express ☐ Down and Dirty ☐ Goodnight, Ladies and Gentlemen ☐ Head of the Family, The ☐ Helsinki Napoli All Night Long ☐ High Infidelity ☐ In the Name of the Pope King ☐ Let's Talk About Men ☐ Nudo di Donna ☐ Operation Snafu ☐ Treasure of San Gennaro, The ☐ We All Loved Each Other So Much

Mangano, Silvana ☐ Anna ☐ Barabbas ☐ Bitter Rice ☐ Conversation Piece ☐ Dark Eyes ☐ Death in Venice ☐ Dune ☐ Five Branded Women ☐ Gold of Naples, The ☐ Great War, The ☐ Ludwig ☐ Lure of the Sila ☐ Mambo ☐ Oedipus Rex ☐ Tempest ☐ Teorema ☐ This Angry Age ☐ Ulysses

Mansfield, Jayne ☐ Dog Eat Dog ☐ Female Jungle, The ☐ George Raft Story, The ☐ Girl Can't Help It, The ☐ Hell on Frisco Bay ☐ Illegal ☐ It Happened in Athens ☐ Kiss Them for Me ☐ Las Vegas Hillbillys ☐ Loves of Hercules, The ☐ Panic Button ☐ Pete Kelly's Blues ☐ Promises! Promises! ☐ Sheriff of Fractured Jaw, The ☐ Single Room Furnished ☐ Underwater! ☐ Wayward Bus, The ☐ Will Success Spoil Rock Hunter?

Mantegna, Joe ☐ Alice ☐ Baby's Day Out ☐ Body of Evidence ☐ Bugsy ☐ Compromising Positions ☐ Comrades of Summer, The ☐ Critical Condition ☐ Fallen Angels—Volume 2 ☐ Family Prayers ☐ Godfather, Part III, The ☐ Homicide ☐ House of Games ☐ Money Pit, The ☐ Off Beat ☐ Queens Logic ☐ Searching for Bobby Fischer ☐ Things Change ☐ Weeds

Marais, Jean ☐ Battle of Austerlitz, The ☐ Beauty and the Beast ☐ Captain Blood ☐ Donkey Skin ☐ Elena and Her Men ☐ Eternal Return, The ☐ Girl in His Pocket ☐ Julietta ☐ Les Parents Terribles ☐ Orpheus ☐ Royal Affairs in Versailles ☐ White Nights

March, Fredric ☐ . . . tick . . . tick . . . tick . . . ☐ Act of Murder, An ☐ Adventures of Mark Twain, The ☐ Affairs of Cellini ☐ Alexander the Great ☐ All of Me ☐ Anna Karenina ☐ Another Part of the Forest ☐ Anthony Adverse ☐ Barretts of Wimpole Street, The ☐ Bedtime Story ☐ Best Years of Our Lives, The ☐ Bridges at Toko-Ri, The ☐ Buccaneer, The ☐ Christopher Columbus ☐ Condemned of Altona, The ☐ Dark Angel, The ☐ Death of a Salesman ☐ Death Takes a Holiday ☐ Desperate Hours, The ☐ Dr. Jekyll and Mr. Hyde ☐ Eagle and the Hawk, The ☐ Executive Suite ☐ Good Dame ☐ Hombre ☐ I Married a Witch ☐ Iceman Cometh, The ☐ Inherit the Wind ☐ It's a Big Country ☐ Les Miserables ☐ Man in the Gray Flannel Suit, The ☐ Man on a Tightrope ☐ Marriage Playground, The ☐ Mary of Scotland ☐ Merrily We Go to Hell ☐ Middle of the Night ☐ Nothing Sacred

☐ One Foot in Heaven ☐ Paramount on Parade ☐ Road to Glory, The ☐ Royal Family of Broadway, The ☐ Sarah and Son ☐ Seven Days in May ☐ Sign of the Cross, The ☐ Smilin' Through ☐ So Ends Our Night ☐ Star Is Born, A ☐ Strangers in Love ☐ Susan and God ☐ There Goes My Heart ☐ Tomorrow the World ☐ Trade Winds ☐ Victory ☐ We Live Again ☐ Wild Party, The ☐ Young Doctors, The

Marin, Cheech ☐ After Hours ☐ Born in East L.A. ☐ Cheech & Chong's Next Movie ☐ Cheech & Chong's Nice Dreams ☐ Cheech & Chong's The Corsican Brothers ☐ Cheech & Chong—Still Smokin' ☐ Cheech & Chong—Up in Smoke ☐ Cheech and Chong—Get Out of My Room ☐ FernGully . . . The Last Rainforest ☐ Oliver and Co. ☐ Rude Awakening ☐ Shrimp on the Barbie, The

Marley, John ☐ Blade ☐ Deathdream ☐ Faces ☐ Falcon's Gold ☐ Framed ☐ In Broad Daylight ☐ Incident in San Francisco ☐ It Lives Again ☐ Jory ☐ Love Story ☐ Man Called Sledge, A ☐ Mob, The ☐ Mother Lode ☐ My Six Convicts ☐ On the Edge ☐ W.C. Fields and Me

Marlowe, Hugh ☐ All About Eve ☐ Black Whip, The ☐ Come to the Stable ☐ Day the Earth Stood Still, The ☐ Earth vs. the Flying Saucers ☐ Garden of Evil ☐ Illegal ☐ Marriage Is a Private Affair ☐ Mr. Belvedere Rings the Bell ☐ Night and the City ☐ Rawhide ☐ Twelve O'Clock High ☐ Wait 'Til the Sun Shines, Nellie

Marsh, Mae ☐ Birth of a Nation, The ☐ Blueprint for Murder ☐ Girls in Prison ☐ Hollywood Boulevard ☐ Intolerance ☐ Little Man, What Now? ☐ Man Who Wouldn't Talk, The ☐ Night Without Sleep ☐ Over the Hill ☐ Three Godfathers, The ☐ When Willie Comes Marching Home

Marsh, Jean ☐ Changeling, The ☐ Dark Places ☐ Eagle Has Landed, The ☐ Frenzy ☐ Jane Eyre ☐ Limping Man, The ☐ Return to Oz ☐ Unearthly Stranger, The ☐ Willow

Marshall, Brenda ☐ Background to Danger ☐ East of the River ☐ Espionage Agent ☐ Footsteps in the Dark ☐ Iroquois Trail, The ☐ Man Who Talked Too Much, The ☐ Paris After Dark ☐ Sea Hawk, The ☐ Whispering Smith

Marshall, E.G. ☐ At Mother's Request ☐ Bachelor Party, The ☐ Bamboo Prison, The ☐ Billy Jack Goes to Washington ☐ Bridge at Remagen, The ☐ Broken Lance ☐ Buccaneer, The ☐ Caine Mutiny, The ☐ Call Northside 777 ☐ Cash McCall ☐ Chase, The ☐ City, The ☐ Collision Course ☐ Compulsion ☐ Consenting Adults ☐ Creepshow ☐ Eleanor, First Lady of the World ☐ Journey, The ☐ Interiors ☐ Lazarus Syndrome, The ☐ Left Hand of God, The ☐ Man on Fire ☐ Money to Burn ☐ Mountain, The ☐ My Chauffeur ☐ National Lampoon's Christmas Vacation ☐ Poppy Is Also a Flower, The ☐ Power ☐ Pushover ☐ Tora! Tora! Tora! ☐ Town Without Pity ☐ 12 Angry Men ☐ Two Evil Eyes

Marshall, Herbert ☐ Accent on Youth ☐ Adventure in Washington ☐ Always Goodbye ☐ Andy Hardy's Blonde Trouble ☐ Angel ☐ Angel Face ☐ Anne of the Indies ☐ Bill of Divorcement, A ☐ Black Shield of Falworth, The ☐ Blonde Venus ☐ Breakfast for Two ☐ Captain Blackjack ☐ Caretakers, The ☐ College Confidential ☐ Crack-Up ☐ Dark Angel, The ☐ Duel in the Sun ☐ Enchanted Cottage, The ☐ Fever in the Blood, A ☐ Flame Within, The ☐ Flight for Freedom ☐ Fly, The ☐ Foreign Correspondent ☐ Forever and a Day ☐ Four Frightened People ☐ Girls' Dormitory ☐ Gog ☐ Good Fairy, The ☐ High Wall ☐ I Was a Spy ☐ If You Could Only Cook ☐ Ivy ☐ Kathleen ☐ Lady Consents, The ☐ Letter, The ☐ List of Adrian Messenger, The ☐ Little Foxes, The ☐ Mad about Music ☐ Make Way for a Lady ☐ Moon and Sixpence, The ☐ Murder! ☐ Painted Veil, The ☐ Razor's Edge, The ☐ Riptide ☐ Secret Garden, The ☐ Third Day, The ☐ Trouble in Paradise ☐ Unseen, The ☐ Virgin Queen, The ☐ Weapon, The ☐ When Ladies Meet ☐ Woman Rebels, A ☐ Zaza

Marshall, Tully ☐ Cat and the Canary, The ☐ Hunchback of Notre Dame, The ☐ Hurricane Express, The ☐ Invisible Stripes ☐ Let's Go ☐ Moontide ☐ Murder on the Blackboard ☐ Night of Terror ☐ One Night at Susie's ☐ Red Dust ☐ Thunderbolt

Marshall, William ☐ Abby ☐ Blacula ☐ Great Skycopter Rescue, The ☐ Honky ☐ Mask of Sheba, The ☐ Murder in the Music Hall ☐ Scream, Blacula, Scream! ☐ Zigzag

Mars, Kenneth ☐ Apple Dumpling Gang Rides Again, The ☐ Beer ☐ Butch Cassidy and the Sundance Kid ☐ Desperate Characters ☐ Fletch ☐ For Keeps ☐ Full Moon High ☐ Goin' Coconuts ☐ Illegally Yours ☐ Night Moves ☐ Producers, The ☐ What's Up, Doc? ☐ Yellowbeard ☐ Young Frankenstein

Martin, Andrea ☐ Big Beat, The ☐ Black Christmas ☐ Boris and Natasha ☐ Cannibal Girls ☐ Club Paradise ☐ Gypsy ☐ Stepping Out ☐ Up Periscope

Martin, Dean ☐ 5 Card Stud ☐ Ada ☐ Airport ☐ All in a Night's Work ☐ Ambush Murders, The ☐ Artists and Models ☐ At War with the Army ☐ Backfire ☐ Bandolero ☐ Bells Are Ringing ☐ Caddy, The ☐ Cannonball Run II ☐ Cannonball Run, The ☐ Career ☐ Four for Texas ☐ Hollywood or Bust ☐ How to Save a Marriage (And Ruin Your Life) ☐ Jumping Jacks ☐ Kiss Me, Stupid ☐ Living It Up ☐ Marriage on the Rocks ☐ Money From Home ☐ Murderers' Row ☐ My Friend Irma ☐ My Friend Irma Goes West ☐ Ocean's Eleven ☐ Pardners ☐ Rio Bravo ☐ Robin and the Seven Hoods

☐ Rough Night in Jericho ☐ Sailor Beware ☐ Scared Stiff ☐ Sergeants 3 ☐ Showdown ☐ Silencers, The ☐ Some Came Running ☐ Sons of Katie Elder, The ☐ Stooge, The ☐ Ten Thousand Bedrooms ☐ Texas Across the River ☐ That's My Boy ☐ Three Ring Circus ☐ Toys in the Attic ☐ What a Way to Go! ☐ Who Was That Lady? ☐ Who's Got the Action? ☐ Wrecking Crew, The ☐ You're Never Too Young ☐ Young Lions, The

Martin, Mary ☐ Birth of the Blues ☐ Great Victor Herbert, The ☐ Happy Go Lucky ☐ Kiss the Boys Goodbye ☐ Love Thy Neighbor ☐ Main Street to Broadway ☐ New York Town ☐ Night and Day ☐ Peter Pan ☐ Rhythm on the River ☐ Star Spangled Rhythm ☐ True to Life

Martin, Steve ☐ All of Me ☐ And the Band Played On ☐ Dead Men Don't Wear Plaid ☐ Dirty Rotten Scoundrels ☐ Father of the Bride ☐ Grand Canyon ☐ Housesitter ☐ Jerk, The ☐ L.A. Story ☐ Leap of Faith ☐ Little Shop of Horrors ☐ Lonely Guy, The ☐ Man with Two Brains, The ☐ Mixed Nuts ☐ Movers and Shakers ☐ Muppet Movie, The ☐ My Blue Heaven ☐ Parenthood ☐ Pennies From Heaven ☐ Planes, Trains & Automobiles ☐ Roxanne ☐ Sgt. Pepper's Lonely Hearts Club Band ☐ Simple Twist of Fate, A ☐ Steve Martin Live! ☐ Three Amigos!

Martin, Strother ☐ Brotherhood of Satan ☐ Butch Cassidy and the Sundance Kid ☐ Cheech & Chong—Up in Smoke ☐ Cool Hand Luke ☐ Eye for an Eye, An ☐ Fools' Parade ☐ Man Who Shot Liberty Valance, The ☐ Nightwing ☐ One of Our Own ☐ Pocket Money ☐ Rooster Cogburn ☐ Slap Shot ☐ SSSSSSS ☐ Villain, The ☐ Wild Bunch, The

Martin, Tony ☐ Ali Baba Goes to Town ☐ Big Store, The ☐ Casbah ☐ Easy to Love ☐ Here Come the Girls ☐ Hit the Deck ☐ Kentucky Moonshine ☐ Let's Be Happy ☐ Life Begins in College ☐ Music in My Heart ☐ Sally, Irene and Mary ☐ Sing, Baby, Sing ☐ Till the Clouds Roll By ☐ Two Tickets to Broadway ☐ Up The River ☐ Ziegfeld Girl

Martinelli, Elsa ☐ Blood and Roses ☐ Captain Blood ☐ Four Girls in Town ☐ Hail, Mafia ☐ Hatari! ☐ Indian Fighter, The ☐ Madigan's Million ☐ Marco the Magnificent ☐ Maroc 7 ☐ Oldest Profession, The ☐ Pigeon That Took Rome, The ☐ Rampage ☐ Tenth Victim, The ☐ Trial, The ☐ V.I.P.s, The

Marvin, Lee ☐ Attack! ☐ Avalanche Express ☐ Bad Day at Black Rock ☐ Big Heat, The ☐ Big Red One, The ☐ Caine Mutiny, The ☐ Cat Ballou ☐ Comancheros, The ☐ Death Hunt ☐ Delta Force, The ☐ Dirty Dozen, The ☐ Dirty Dozen, The: The Next Mission ☐ Dog Day ☐ Donovan's Reef ☐ Duel at Silver Creek, The ☐ Eight Iron Men ☐ Emperor of the North, The ☐ Glory Brigade ☐ Gorilla at Large ☐ Gorky Park ☐ Great Scout and Cathouse Thursday ☐ Gun Fury ☐ Hangman's Knot ☐ Hell in the Pacific ☐ I Died a Thousand Times ☐ Iceman Cometh, The ☐ Killers, The ☐ Klansman, The ☐ Man Who Shot Liberty Valance, The ☐ Meanest Men in the West, The ☐ Missouri Traveler, The ☐ Monte Walsh ☐ Not as a Stranger ☐ Paint Your Wagon ☐ Pete Kelly's Blues ☐ Pocket Money ☐ Point Blank ☐ Prime Cut ☐ Professionals, The ☐ Rack, The ☐ Raid, The ☐ Raintree County ☐ Seminole ☐ Sergeant Ryker ☐ Seven Men from Now ☐ Ship of Fools ☐ Stranger Who Wore a Gun, The ☐ Violent Saturday ☐ Wild One, The ☐ You're in the Navy Now

Marx, Chico ☐ Animal Crackers ☐ At the Circus ☐ Big Store, The ☐ Cocoanuts, The ☐ Day at the Races, A ☐ Go West ☐ Horse Feathers ☐ Love Happy ☐ MGM's Big Parade of Comedy ☐ Monkey Business ☐ Night at the Opera, A ☐ Night in Casablanca, A ☐ Story of Mankind, The

Marx, Groucho ☐ Animal Crackers ☐ At the Circus ☐ Big Store, The ☐ Cocoanuts, The ☐ Copacabana ☐ Day at the Races, A ☐ Double Dynamite ☐ Duck Soup ☐ Girl in Every Port, A ☐ Go West ☐ Horse Feathers ☐ Love Happy ☐ MGM's Big Parade of Comedy ☐ Milton Berle's Mad World of Comedy ☐ Monkey Business ☐ Mr. Music ☐ Night at the Opera, A ☐ Night in Casablanca, A ☐ Skiddoo ☐ Story of Mankind, The

Marx, Harpo ☐ Animal Crackers ☐ At the Circus ☐ Big Store, The ☐ Cocoanuts, The ☐ Day at the Races, A ☐ Duck Soup ☐ Go West ☐ Horse Feathers ☐ Love Happy ☐ MGM's Big Parade of Comedy ☐ Monkey Business ☐ Night at the Opera, A ☐ Night in Casablanca, A ☐ Stage Door Canteen ☐ Story of Mankind, The

Marx, Zeppo ☐ Animal Crackers ☐ Cocoanuts, The ☐ Duck Soup ☐ Horse Feathers ☐ MGM's Big Parade of Comedy ☐ Monkey Business ☐ Night at the Opera, A ☐ Night in Casablanca, A

Mason, James ☐ 11 Harrowhouse ☐ 20,000 Leagues Under the Sea ☐ 5 Fingers ☐ Age of Consent ☐ Assisi Underground, The ☐ Autobiography of a Princess ☐ Bad Man's River ☐ Bigger than Life ☐ Bloodline ☐ Blue Max, The ☐ Botany Bay ☐ Boys From Brazil, The ☐ Caught ☐ Child's Play ☐ Cold Sweat ☐ Cross of Iron ☐ Cry Terror ☐ Dangerous Summer, A ☐ Deadly Affair, The ☐ Decks Ran Red, The ☐ Desert Fox, The ☐ Desert Rats, The ☐ Destructors, The ☐ Duffy ☐ East Side, West Side ☐ Escape from Zahrain ☐ Evil Under the Sun ☐ Face to Face ☐ Fall of the Roman Empire ☐ ffolkes ☐ For Heaven's Sake ☐ Forever Darling ☐ Frankenstein: The True Story ☐ Genghis Khan ☐ Georgy Girl ☐ Great Expectations ☐ Hatter's Castle ☐ Heaven Can Wait ☐ Hero's Island ☐ High Command, The ☐ Hotel Reserve

☐ I Met a Murderer ☐ Inside Out ☐ Island in the Sun ☐ Ivanhoe ☐ Jesus of Nazareth ☐ Journey to the Center of the Earth, The ☐ Julius Caesar ☐ Kidnap Syndicate ☐ Kill! Kill! Kill! ☐ Lady Possessed ☐ Last of Sheila, The ☐ Lolita ☐ Lord Jim ☐ Mackintosh Man, The ☐ Madame Bovary ☐ Man Between, The ☐ Man in Grey, The ☐ Man of Evil ☐ Man with the Green Carnation, The ☐ Mandingo ☐ Marriage-Go-Round, The ☐ Mayerling ☐ Mill on the Floss, The ☐ Murder by Decree ☐ Night Has Eyes, The ☐ North by Northwest ☐ Odd Man Out ☐ One-Way Street ☐ Pandora and the Flying Dutchman ☐ Passage, The ☐ Place of One's Own, A ☐ Prince Valiant ☐ Prisoner of Zenda, The ☐ Pumpkin Eater, The ☐ Reckless Moment, The ☐ Salem's Lot: The Miniseries ☐ Sea Gull, The ☐ Secret Mission ☐ Seventh Veil, The ☐ Shooting Party, The ☐ Star Is Born, A ☐ Story of Three Loves, The ☐ They Were Sisters ☐ Thunder Rock ☐ Touch of Larceny, A ☐ Verdict, The ☐ Voyage of the Damned ☐ Water Babies, The ☐ Wicked Lady, The ☐ Yellowbeard

Mason, Marsha ☐ Audrey Rose ☐ Blume In Love ☐ Chapter Two ☐ Cheap Detective, The ☐ Cinderella Liberty ☐ Dinner at Eight ☐ Drop Dead Fred ☐ Goodbye Girl, The ☐ Heartbreak Ridge ☐ Image, The ☐ Lois Gibbs and the Love Canal ☐ Max Dugan Returns ☐ Only When I Laugh ☐ Promises in the Dark ☐ Stella ☐ Trapped in Silence

Massey, Anna ☐ Frenzy ☐ Hazard of Hearts, A ☐ Hotel du Lac ☐ Mansfield Park ☐ Peeping Tom ☐ Sacred Hearts

Massey, Raymond ☐ 49th Parallel ☐ Abe Lincoln In Illinois ☐ Action in the North Atlantic ☐ Arsenic and Old Lace ☐ Barricade ☐ Battle Cry ☐ Carson City ☐ Chain Lightning ☐ Come Fill the Cup ☐ Dallas ☐ Dangerously They Live ☐ David and Bathsheba ☐ Desert Song, The ☐ Desperate Journey ☐ Dreaming Lips ☐ Drums ☐ East of Eden ☐ Fiercest Heart, The ☐ Fire Over England ☐ Fountainhead, The ☐ God is My Co-Pilot ☐ Great Impostor, The ☐ Hotel Berlin ☐ Hurricane, The ☐ Mackenna's Gold ☐ Mourning Becomes Electra ☐ Naked and the Dead, The ☐ Omar Khayyam ☐ Possessed ☐ Prince of Players ☐ Prisoner of Zenda, The ☐ Santa Fe Trail ☐ Scarlet Pimpernel, The ☐ Seven Angry Men ☐ Stairway to Heaven ☐ Things to Come ☐ Under the Red Robe ☐ Woman in the Window, The

Masterson, Mary Stuart ☐ At Close Range ☐ Bad Girls ☐ Benny & Joon ☐ Chances Are ☐ Fried Green Tomatoes ☐ Funny About Love ☐ Gardens of Stone ☐ Heaven Help Us ☐ Immediate Family ☐ Mad at the Moon ☐ Married to It ☐ Mr. North ☐ Radioland Murders ☐ Some Kind of Wonderful

Mastrantonio, Mary Elizabeth ☐ Abyss, The ☐ Class Action ☐ Color of Money, The ☐ Consenting Adults ☐ Fools of Fortune ☐ January Man, The ☐ Robin Hood: Prince of Thieves ☐ Scarface ☐ Slam Dance ☐ Two Bits ☐ White Sands

Mastroianni, Marcello ☐ 8 1/2 ☐ Allonsanfan ☐ Assassin, The ☐ Bell' Antonio ☐ Beyond Obsession ☐ Big Deal on Madonna Street ☐ Blood Feud ☐ Casanova '70 ☐ City of Women ☐ Dark Eyes ☐ Diamonds for Breakfast ☐ Divine Nymph, The ☐ Divorce—Italian Style ☐ Everybody's Fine ☐ Fine Romance, A ☐ Gabriela ☐ Ghosts of Rome ☐ Ginger and Fred ☐ Goodnight, Ladies and Gentlemen ☐ Henry IV ☐ I Don't Want To Talk About It ☐ Intervista ☐ Island Princess, The ☐ It Only Happens to Others ☐ Kiss the Other Sheik ☐ La Dolce Vita ☐ La Notte ☐ La Nuit des Varennes ☐ La Pelle ☐ Leo the Last ☐ Lucky to Be a Woman ☐ Lunatics and Lovers ☐ Macaroni ☐ Man with the Balloons, The ☐ Marriage Italian Style ☐ Massacre in Rome ☐ Organizer, The ☐ Pizza Triangle, The ☐ Place for Lovers, A ☐ Poppy Is Also a Flower, The ☐ Ready to Wear ☐ Sensualita ☐ Slightly Pregnant Man, A ☐ Special Day, A ☐ Stay As You Are ☐ Stranger, The ☐ Sunflower ☐ Tenth Victim, The ☐ Two Lives of Mattias Pascal, The ☐ Used People ☐ Very Private Affair, A ☐ White Nights ☐ Wifemistress ☐ Yesterday, Today and Tomorrow

Masur, Richard ☐ Adam ☐ Adam: His Song Continues ☐ Big One: The Great Los Angeles Earthquake, The ☐ Bride of Boogedy, The ☐ Burning Bed, The ☐ Fallen Angel ☐ Far from Home ☐ Flight 90: Disaster on the Potomac ☐ George McKenna Story, The ☐ Great L.A. Earthquake, The ☐ I'm Dancing as Fast as I Can ☐ Mean Season, The ☐ My Girl ☐ My Girl 2 ☐ Nightmares ☐ Rent-a-Cop ☐ Risky Business ☐ Semi-Tough ☐ Thing, The ☐ Third Degree Burn ☐ Walker ☐ When the Bough Breaks ☐ Who'll Stop the Rain

Mathers, Jerry ☐ Back to the Beach ☐ Down the Drain ☐ Shadow on the Window, The ☐ That Certain Feeling

Matheson, Tim ☐ 1941 ☐ Almost Summer ☐ Animal House ☐ Apple Dumpling Gang Rides Again, The ☐ Best Legs in the 8th Grade ☐ Blind Justice ☐ Dreamer ☐ Drop Dead Fred ☐ Fallen Angels—Volume 1 ☐ Fletch ☐ Hitched ☐ House of God, The ☐ Impulse ☐ Joshua's Heart ☐ Little Sex, A ☐ Little White Lies ☐ Quicksand: No Escape ☐ Solar Crisis ☐ Sometimes They Come Back ☐ Speed Zone! ☐ To Be or Not to Be ☐ Up the Creek

Matlin, Marlee ☐ Bridge to Silence ☐ Children of a Lesser God ☐ Hear No Evil ☐ Walker

Mattes, Eva ☐ Bitter Tears of Petra Von Kant, The ☐ Celeste ☐ Germany, Pale Mother ☐ In a Year of Thirteen Moons ☐ Jail Bait ☐ Man Like Eva, A ☐ Stroszek ☐ Woyzeck

Matthau, Walter ☐ Against Her Will: An

Incident in Baltimore ☐ Bad News Bears, The ☐ Bigger than Life ☐ Buddy Buddy ☐ Cactus Flower ☐ California Suite ☐ Candy ☐ Casey's Shadow ☐ Charade ☐ Charley Varrick ☐ Couch Trip, The ☐ Dennis the Menace ☐ Ensign Pulver ☐ Face in the Crowd, A ☐ Fail-Safe ☐ First Monday in October ☐ Fortune Cookie, The ☐ Front Page, The ☐ Gangster Story ☐ Goodbye Charlie ☐ Grumpy Old Men ☐ Guide for the Married Man, A ☐ Hello, Dolly! ☐ Hopscotch ☐ House Calls ☐ I Ought to Be in Pictures ☐ I. Q. ☐ Incident, The ☐ Indian Fighter, The ☐ Island of Love ☐ JFK ☐ Kentuckian, The ☐ King Creole ☐ Kotch ☐ Laughing Policeman, The ☐ Little Miss Marker ☐ Lonely Are the Brave ☐ Mirage ☐ Movers and Shakers ☐ New Leaf, A ☐ Odd Couple, The ☐ Onionhead ☐ Pete 'n' Tillie ☐ Pirates ☐ Plaza Suite ☐ Secret Life of an American Wife, The ☐ Slaughter on Tenth Avenue ☐ Strangers When We Meet ☐ Sunshine Boys, The ☐ Survivors, The ☐ Taking of Pelham One Two Three, The ☐ Voice in the Mirror, The ☐ Who's Got the Action?

Mature, Victor ☐ Affair with a Stranger ☐ After the Fox ☐ Androcles and the Lion ☐ Bandit of Zhobe, The ☐ Betrayed ☐ Big Circus, The ☐ Captain Caution ☐ Chief Crazy Horse ☐ China Doll ☐ Cry of the City ☐ Dangerous Mission ☐ Demetrius and the Gladiators ☐ Easy Living ☐ Egyptian, The ☐ Footlight Serenade ☐ Fury at Furnace Creek ☐ Gambling House ☐ Glory Brigade ☐ Hannibal ☐ Housekeeper's Daughter, The ☐ I Wake Up Screaming ☐ Kiss of Death ☐ Las Vegas Story, The ☐ Last Frontier, The ☐ Million Dollar Mermaid ☐ My Darling Clementine ☐ My Gal Sal ☐ One Million B.C. ☐ Red, Hot and Blue ☐ Robe, The ☐ Samson and Delilah ☐ Samson and Delilah ☐ Seven Days' Leave ☐ Shanghai Gesture, The ☐ Something for the Birds ☐ Song of the Islands ☐ Violent Saturday ☐ Wabash Avenue ☐ Zarak

Mathews, Carole ☐ Betrayed Women ☐ Female Fiends ☐ I Love a Mystery ☐ Man with My Face, The ☐ Massacre River ☐ Meet Me at the Fair ☐ Shark River ☐ Showdown at Boot Hill

Mathews, Kerwin ☐ 7th Voyage of Sinbad, The ☐ Barquero ☐ Battle Beneath the Earth ☐ Boy Who Cried Werewolf, The ☐ Devil at 4 O'Clock, The ☐ Five Against the House ☐ Garment Jungle, The ☐ Jack the Giant Killer ☐ Killer Likes Candy, The ☐ Last Blitzkrieg, The ☐ Man on a String ☐ Maniac ☐ Nightmare in Blood ☐ Octaman ☐ Pirates of Blood River, The ☐ Tarawa Beachhead ☐ 3 Worlds of Gulliver, The ☐ Waltz King, The

Mathis, Samantha ☐ Extreme Close-Up ☐ FernGully . . . The Last Rainforest ☐ Little Women ☐ Pump Up the Volume ☐ Super Mario Bros. ☐ Thing Called Love, The ☐ This Is My Life

Maura, Carmen ☐ Ay, Carmela! ☐ Between Heaven and Earth ☐ Dark Habits ☐ Law of Desire ☐ Matador ☐ Pepi, Luci, Bom ☐ What Have I Done to Deserve This? ☐ Women on the Verge of a Nervous Breakdown

Maxwell, Marilyn ☐ Between Two Women ☐ Champion ☐ Critic's Choice ☐ East of Sumatra ☐ From Nashville with Music ☐ Lemon Drop Kid, The ☐ Lost in a Harem ☐ Off Limits ☐ Outside the Wall ☐ Paris Model ☐ Race Street ☐ Rock-a-Bye Baby ☐ Show-Off, The ☐ Stage to Thunder Rock ☐ Stand by for Action ☐ Summer Holiday

Mayo, Virginia ☐ Along the Great Divide ☐ Always Leave Them Laughing ☐ Backfire ☐ Best Years of Our Lives, The ☐ Big Land, The ☐ Captain Horatio Hornblower ☐ Castle of Evil ☐ Colorado Territory ☐ Flame and the Arrow, The ☐ Flaxy Martin ☐ Fort Utah ☐ French Quarter ☐ Girl from Jones Beach, The ☐ Great Day in the Morning ☐ Iron Mistress, The ☐ Jack London ☐ Jet Over the Atlantic ☐ Kid from Brooklyn, The ☐ King Richard and the Crusaders ☐ Out of the Blue ☐ Painting the Clouds with Sunshine ☐ Pearl of the South Pacific ☐ Princess and the Pirate, The ☐ Proud Ones, The ☐ Revolt of the Mercenaries ☐ Secret Life of Walter Mitty, The ☐ She's Back on Broadway ☐ She's Working Her Way Through College ☐ Silver Chalice, The ☐ Song is Born, A ☐ South Sea Woman ☐ Story of Mankind, The ☐ Up in Arms ☐ West Point Story ☐ Westbound ☐ White Heat ☐ Wonder Man

Mazurki, Mike ☐ Blood Alley ☐ Challenge to Be Free ☐ Four for Texas ☐ French Key, The ☐ Live Wires ☐ Mad Bull ☐ Mob Boss ☐ Murder My Sweet ☐ My Favorite Spy ☐ Mysterious Intruder ☐ Night and the City ☐ Nightmare Alley ☐ Noose Hangs High, The ☐ Requiem for a Gunfighter ☐ Shanghai Gesture, The ☐ Some Like It Hot ☐ Unconquered ☐ Watch the Birdie

Mazursky, Paul ☐ Blume In Love ☐ Man, a Woman and a Bank, A ☐ Miami Rhapsody ☐ Scenes from the Class Struggle in Beverly Hills ☐ Star Is Born, A

McAnally, Ray ☐ Empire State ☐ Jack the Ripper ☐ Mission, The ☐ My Left Foot ☐ No Surrender ☐ Taffin

McCallum, David ☐ Around the World Under the Sea ☐ Big T.N.T. Show, The ☐ Billy Budd ☐ Frankenstein: The True Story ☐ Freud ☐ Great Escape, The ☐ Hard Drivers ☐ Haunting of Morella, The ☐ Hear My Song ☐ Hell Drivers ☐ Kingfisher Caper, The ☐ Man Who Lived at the Ritz, The ☐ Night to Remember, A ☐ One Spy Too Many ☐ Ravine, The ☐ She Waits ☐ Slaughter ☐ Violent Playground ☐ Watcher in the Woods, The

McCambridge, Mercedes ☐ All the King's Men ☐ Angel Baby ☐ Cimarron ☐ Farewell to

Arms, A ☐ Giant ☐ Girls of Huntington House, The ☐ Johnny Guitar ☐ Sacketts, The ☐ Suddenly, Last Summer

McCartney, Paul ☐ Give My Regards to Broad Street ☐ Hard Day's Night, A ☐ Help! ☐ Let It Be ☐ Magical Mystery Tour ☐ Yellow Submarine

McCarthy, Andrew ☐ Beniker Gang, The ☐ Class ☐ Fresh Horses ☐ Heaven Help Us ☐ Kansas ☐ Less than Zero ☐ Mannequin ☐ Mrs. Parker and the Vicious Circle ☐ Only You ☐ Pretty in Pink ☐ St. Elmo's Fire ☐ Waiting for the Moon ☐ Weekend at Bernie's ☐ Weekend at Bernie's II ☐ Year of the Gun

McCarthy, Kevin ☐ Ace High ☐ Annapolis Story, An ☐ Big Hand for the Little Lady, A ☐ Buffalo Bill and the Indians ☐ Dan Candy's Law ☐ Death of a Salesman ☐ Drive a Crooked Road ☐ Duplicates ☐ Eve of Destruction ☐ Final Approach ☐ Flamingo Road ☐ Ghoulies 3—Ghoulies Go to College ☐ Hostage ☐ If He Hollers, Let Him Go ☐ Innerspace ☐ Invasion of the Body Snatchers ☐ Invitation to Hell ☐ Kansas City Bomber ☐ Making of a Male Model ☐ Mary Jane Harper Cried Last Night ☐ Masterpiece of Murder, A ☐ Mirage ☐ My Tutor ☐ Nightmare ☐ Piranha ☐ Poor Little Rich Girl: The Barbara Hutton Story ☐ Ratings Game, The ☐ Stranger on Horseback ☐ Those Lips, Those Eyes ☐ Twilight Zone—The Movie ☐ UHF

McClanahan, Rue ☐ After the Shock ☐ Agatha Christie's The Man in the Brown Suit ☐ Baby of the Bride ☐ Blade ☐ Dreamer of Oz, The: The Frank L. Baum Story ☐ Great American Traffic Jam, The ☐ Having Babies III ☐ Liberace ☐ Little Match Girl, The ☐ Modern Love ☐ Sergeant Matlovich vs. the U.S. Air Force

McClure, Doug ☐ At the Earth's Core ☐ Beau Geste ☐ Because They're Young ☐ Enemy Below, The ☐ Firebird 2015 A.D. ☐ House Where Evil Dwells, The ☐ Humanoids from the Deep ☐ Judge and Jake Wyler, The ☐ Land That Time Forgot ☐ Lively Set, The ☐ Nightside ☐ Nobody's Perfect ☐ Omega Syndrome ☐ People That Time Forgot, The ☐ Playmates ☐ Rebels, The ☐ Shenandoah ☐ Tapeheads

McCowen, Alec ☐ Assam Garden, The ☐ Cruel Sea, The ☐ Cry Freedom ☐ Devil's Own, The ☐ Forever Young ☐ Frenzy ☐ Good Companions, The ☐ Hanover Street ☐ Hawaiians, The ☐ Henry V ☐ Loneliness of the Long Distance Runner, The ☐ Never Say Never Again ☐ Night to Remember, A ☐ Personal Services ☐ Time Without Pity ☐ Town on Trial ☐ Travels With My Aunt

McCrea, Joel ☐ Adventure in Manhattan ☐ Banjo on My Knee ☐ Barbary Coast ☐ Bed of Roses ☐ Bird of Paradise ☐ Black Horse Canyon ☐ Border River ☐ Buffalo Bill ☐ Cattle Drive ☐ Cattle Empire ☐ Chance at Heaven ☐ Colorado Territory ☐ Come and Get It ☐ Cry Blood, Apache ☐ Dead End ☐ Espionage Agent ☐ First Texan, The ☐ Foreign Correspondent ☐ Fort Massacre ☐ Four Faces West ☐ Frenchie ☐ Gambling Lady ☐ Girls About Town ☐ Great Man's Lady, The ☐ Great Moment, The ☐ Gunfight at Dodge City, The ☐ Gunsight Ridge ☐ He Married His Wife ☐ Internes Can't Take Money ☐ Lone Hand, The ☐ Lost Squadron, The ☐ More the Merrier, The ☐ Most Dangerous Game, The ☐ Oklahoman, The ☐ One Man's Journey ☐ Our Little Girl ☐ Palm Beach Story, The ☐ Primrose Path, The ☐ Private Worlds ☐ Ramrod ☐ Reaching for the Sun ☐ Richest Girl in the World, The ☐ Ride the High Country ☐ Saddle Tramp ☐ San Francisco Story, The ☐ Silver Cord, The ☐ Silver Horde ☐ South of St. Louis ☐ Stars in My Crown ☐ Stranger on Horseback ☐ Sullivan's Travels ☐ These Three ☐ They Shall Have Music ☐ Three Blind Mice ☐ Union Pacific ☐ Unseen, The ☐ Virginian, The ☐ Wells Fargo ☐ Wichita

McDaniel, Hattie ☐ Alice Adams ☐ Bride Walks Out, The ☐ China Seas ☐ Gentle Julia ☐ George Washington Slept Here ☐ Gone with the Wind ☐ Great Lie, The ☐ In This Our Life ☐ Janie ☐ Johnny Come Lately ☐ Mad Miss Manton, The ☐ Male Animal, The ☐ Never Say Goodbye ☐ Saratoga ☐ Shopworn Angel, The ☐ Show Boat ☐ Since You Went Away ☐ Song of the South ☐ Three Is a Family ☐ Zenobia

McDermott, Dylan ☐ Blue Iguana, The ☐ Cowboy Way ☐ Fear Inside, The ☐ Hamburger Hill ☐ Hardware ☐ In the Line of Fire ☐ Into the Badlands ☐ Miracle on 34th Street ☐ Where Sleeping Dogs Lie

McDonnell, Mary ☐ American Clock, The ☐ Blue Chips ☐ Dances with Wolves ☐ Grand Canyon ☐ Matewan ☐ Passion Fish ☐ Sneakers

McDormand, Frances ☐ Blood Simple ☐ Butcher's Wife, The ☐ Chattahoochee ☐ Darkman ☐ Hidden Agenda ☐ Mississippi Burning

McDowall, Roddy ☐ 5 Card Stud ☐ Adventures of Bullwhip Griffin, The ☐ Alice in Wonderland ☐ Arnold ☐ Battle for the Planet of the Apes ☐ Cat From Outer Space, The ☐ Charlie Chan and the Curse of the Dragon Queen ☐ Circle of Iron ☐ Class of 1984 ☐ Cleopatra ☐ Conquest of the Planet of the Apes ☐ Cutting Class ☐ Dead of Winter ☐ Defector, The ☐ Dirty Mary, Crazy Larry ☐ Doin' Time on Planet Earth ☐ Embryo ☐ Escape from the Planet of the Apes ☐ Evil Under the Sun ☐ Fright Night ☐ Fright Night, Part II ☐ Funny Lady ☐ GoBots: Battle of the Rock Lords ☐ Hart to Hart ☐ Hello Down There ☐ Holiday in Mexico ☐ Hollywood's Children ☐ How Green Was My Valley ☐ Immigrants, The ☐ Inconvenient Woman, An

☐ Inside Daisy Clover ☐ It ☐ Keys of the Kingdom ☐ Lassie Come Home ☐ Legend of Hell House, The ☐ Life and Times of Judge Roy Bean, The ☐ Longest Day, The ☐ Lord Love a Duck ☐ Loved One, The ☐ Macbeth ☐ Mae West ☐ Man Hunt ☐ Martian Chronicles, The ☐ Mean Johnny Barrows ☐ Memory of Eva Ryker, The ☐ Midas Run ☐ Midnight Lace ☐ Miracle on 34th Street ☐ Molly and Me ☐ My Friend Flicka ☐ Night Gallery ☐ Nutcracker Fantasy ☐ Overboard ☐ Pied Piper, The ☐ Planet of the Apes ☐ Poseidon Adventure, The ☐ Rabbit Test ☐ Return of the King ☐ Shakma ☐ Son of Fury ☐ That Darn Cat ☐ Thief of Bagdad, The ☐ Third Day, The ☐ Thunderhead—Son of Flicka ☐ Tuna Clipper

McDowell, Malcolm ☐ Aces High ☐ Bedknobs and Broomsticks ☐ Blue Thunder ☐ Bopha! ☐ Britannia Hospital ☐ Buy & Cell ☐ Caligula ☐ Caller, The ☐ Carmilla ☐ Cat People ☐ Class of 1999 ☐ Clockwork Orange, A ☐ Disturbed ☐ Figures in a Landscape ☐ Get Crazy ☐ Gulag ☐ If . . . ☐ Jezebel's Kiss ☐ Light in the Jungle, The ☐ Long Ago Tomorrow ☐ Merlin and the Sword ☐ Milk Money ☐ Mirror, Mirror 2: Raven Dance ☐ Monte Carlo ☐ Moon 44 ☐ O Lucky Man! ☐ Passage, The ☐ Poor Cow ☐ Royal Flash ☐ Star Trek Generations ☐ Sunset ☐ Time After Time ☐ Voyage of the Damned ☐ White Cliffs of Dover, The

McEnery, John ☐ Bartleby ☐ Jamaica Inn ☐ Lady in the Car with Glasses and a Gun, The ☐ Land That Time Forgot ☐ Little Malcolm ☐ One Russian Summer

McGavin, Darren ☐ Airport '77 ☐ American Clock, The ☐ Banyon ☐ Beau James ☐ Billy Madison ☐ Bullet for a Badman ☐ By Dawn's Early Light ☐ Case Against Brooklyn, The ☐ Child in the Night ☐ Christmas Story, A ☐ Christmas Story, A ☐ Dead Heat ☐ Delicate Delinquent, The ☐ Firebird 2015 A.D. ☐ From the Hip ☐ Great Sioux Massacre, The ☐ Hangar 18 ☐ Hot Lead & Cold Feet ☐ Ike: The War Years ☐ Inherit the Wind ☐ Law and Order ☐ Man with the Golden Arm ☐ Mission Mars ☐ Mrs. Pollifax—Spy ☐ My Wicked, Wicked Ways—The Legend of Errol Flynn ☐ Natural, The ☐ Night Stalker, The ☐ Night Strangler, The ☐ No Deposit, No Return ☐ Outsider, The ☐ Perfect Harmony ☐ Raw Deal ☐ Ride the High Wind ☐ Say Goodbye, Maggie Cole ☐ Summer Magic ☐ Summertime ☐ Tribes

McGillis, Kelly ☐ Accused, The ☐ Babe, The ☐ Cat Chaser ☐ Code of Honor ☐ Grand Isle ☐ House on Carroll Street, The ☐ Made in Heaven ☐ Reuben, Reuben ☐ Top Gun ☐ Unsettled Land ☐ Winter People ☐ Witness

McGoohan, Patrick ☐ All Night Long ☐ Baby . . . Secret of the Lost Legend ☐ Brass Target, The ☐ Dr. Syn, Alias the Scarecrow ☐ Escape from Alcatraz ☐ Gypsy and the Gentleman, The ☐ Hard Drivers ☐ Hell Drivers ☐ Ice Station Zebra ☐ Jamaica Inn ☐ Kings and Desperate Men—A Hostage Incident ☐ Man in the Iron Mask ☐ Mary, Queen of Scots ☐ Nazis, The: Of Pure Blood ☐ Quare Fellow, The ☐ Scanners ☐ Silver Streak ☐ Three Lives of Thomasina, The ☐ Two Living, One Dead

McGovern, Elizabeth ☐ Bedroom Window, The ☐ Favor, The ☐ Handmaid's Tale, The ☐ Johnny Handsome ☐ King of the Hill ☐ Lovesick ☐ Me & Veronica ☐ Native Son ☐ Once Upon a Time in America ☐ Ordinary People ☐ Racing With the Moon ☐ Ragtime ☐ She's Having a Baby ☐ Shock to the System, A ☐ Women & Men: Stories of Seduction

McGuire, Dorothy ☐ Amos ☐ Callaway Went Thataway ☐ Caroline? ☐ Claudia ☐ Claudia and David ☐ Dark at the Top of the Stairs, The ☐ Enchanted Cottage, The ☐ Flight of the Doves ☐ Friendly Persuasion ☐ Gentleman's Agreement ☐ Ghost Dancing ☐ I Want You ☐ Incredible Journey of Doctor Meg Laurel, The ☐ Invitation ☐ Last Best Year, The ☐ Little Women ☐ Make Haste to Live ☐ Mister 880 ☐ Mother Didn't Tell Me ☐ Old Yeller ☐ Remarkable Mr. Pennypacker, The ☐ She Waits ☐ Spiral Staircase, The ☐ Summer Magic ☐ Summer Place, A ☐ Susan Slade ☐ Swiss Family Robinson ☐ This Earth Is Mine ☐ Three Coins in the Fountain ☐ Till the End of Time ☐ Tree Grows in Brooklyn, A ☐ Trial

McHugh, Frank ☐ All Through the Night ☐ Back Street ☐ Blessed Event ☐ Bowery to Broadway ☐ Boy Meets Girl ☐ Bullets or Ballots ☐ Carnegie Hall ☐ City for Conquest ☐ Corsair ☐ Crowd Roars, The ☐ Dark Horse ☐ Daughters Courageous ☐ Devil Dogs of the Air ☐ Dodge City ☐ Dust Be My Destiny ☐ Easy Come, Easy Go ☐ Easy Come, Easy Go ☐ Elmer the Great ☐ Ever Since Eve ☐ Ex-Lady ☐ Fashions ☐ Fighting 69th, The ☐ Four Mothers ☐ Four Wives ☐ Going My Way ☐ Gold Diggers of 1935 ☐ Grand Slam ☐ Happiness Ahead ☐ Her Cardboard Lover ☐ Here Comes the Navy ☐ High Pressure ☐ I Love You Again ☐ Indianapolis Speedway ☐ Irish in Us, The ☐ It Happens Every Thursday ☐ Manpower ☐ Marine Raiders ☐ Medal for Benny, A ☐ Midsummer Night's Dream, A ☐ Mighty Joe Young ☐ Miss Grant Takes Richmond ☐ My Son John ☐ Mystery of the Wax Museum, The ☐ On Your Toes ☐ One Way Passage ☐ Page Miss Glory ☐ Paid in Full ☐ Parachute Jumper ☐ State Fair ☐ Swing Your Lady ☐ Swing Your Lady ☐ Three Men on a Horse ☐ Top Speed ☐ Union Depot ☐ Velvet Touch, The ☐ Virginia City

McIntire, John ☐ Apache ☐ Far Country, The ☐ Flaming Star ☐ Honkytonk Man ☐ I've Lived Before ☐ Mark of the Hawk, The

☐ Mississippi Gambler ☐ President's Lady, The ☐ Rescuers, The ☐ Saddle Tramp ☐ Stranger on Horseback ☐ Summer and Smoke ☐ Westward the Women ☐ Who Was That Lady? ☐ Winchester '73 ☐ World in His Arms, The ☐ World in My Corner ☐ You're in the Navy Now

McIntire, Tim ☐ American Hot Wax ☐ Fast-Walking ☐ Gumball Rally, The ☐ Sacred Ground ☐ Sterile Cuckoo, The

McKean, Michael ☐ Big Picture, The ☐ Clue ☐ D.A.R.Y.L. ☐ Earth Girls Are Easy ☐ Hider in the House ☐ Man Trouble ☐ Memoirs of an Invisible Man ☐ Planes, Trains & Automobiles ☐ Return of Spinal Tap, The ☐ Short Circuit 2 ☐ This Is Spinal Tap ☐ Young Doctors in Love

McKee, Lonette ☐ Brewster's Millions ☐ Cotton Club, The ☐ Cuba ☐ Jungle Fever ☐ Round Midnight ☐ Sparkle ☐ Which Way Is Up? ☐ Women of Brewster Place, The

McKellen, Ian ☐ Alfred the Great ☐ And the Band Played On ☐ Ballad of Little Jo, The ☐ Keep, The ☐ Priest of Love ☐ Scandal ☐ Scarlet Pimpernel, The ☐ Shadow, The ☐ Thank You All Very Much ☐ Zina

McKenna, Siobhan ☐ Doctor Zhivago ☐ Fortune in Diamonds ☐ Hungry Hill ☐ King of Kings ☐ Memed My Hawk ☐ Of Human Bondage ☐ Playboy of the Western World

McKenna, Virginia ☐ Barretts of Wimpole Street, The ☐ Born Free ☐ Carve Her Name With Pride ☐ Christian the Lion ☐ Cruel Sea, The ☐ Gathering Storm, The ☐ Ring of Bright Water ☐ Second Mrs. Tanqueray, The ☐ Ship That Died of Shame, The ☐ Smallest Show on Earth, The ☐ Town Like Alice, A ☐ Two Living, One Dead ☐ Waterloo ☐ Wreck of the Mary Deare, The

McKeon, Doug ☐ At Mother's Request ☐ Heart of a Champion: The Ray Mancini Story ☐ Innocent Love, An ☐ Mischief ☐ Night Crossing ☐ Norman Rockwell's Breaking Home Ties ☐ On Golden Pond

McKeon, Nancy ☐ Cry for Help: The Tracey Thurman Story, A ☐ Facts of Life Down Under, The ☐ Facts of Life Goes to Paris, The ☐ High School U.S.A. ☐ Lightning Incident, The ☐ Poison Ivy

McKern, Leo ☐ Adventure of Sherlock Holmes' Smarter Brother, The ☐ Agent 8 3/4 ☐ Amorous Adventures of Moll Flanders, The ☐ Assignment K ☐ Blue Lagoon ☐ Candleshoe ☐ Day the Earth Caught Fire, The ☐ Decline and Fall of a Bird Watcher ☐ French Lieutenant's Woman, The ☐ Help! ☐ Horse Without a Head, The ☐ I Like Money ☐ Jolly Bad Fellow ☐ King and Country ☐ King Lear ☐ Ladyhawke ☐ Lisa ☐ Man for All Seasons, A ☐ Massacre in Rome ☐ Monsignor Quixote ☐ Mouse That Roared, The ☐ Murder with Mirrors ☐ Reilly: The Ace of Spies ☐ Scent of Mystery ☐ Shoes of the Fisherman, The ☐ Time Without Pity ☐ Traveling North ☐ Web of Evidence ☐ X, the Unknown

McLaglen, Victor ☐ Abductors, The ☐ Bengazi ☐ Big Guy, The ☐ Black Watch, The ☐ Broadway Limited ☐ Call Out the Marines ☐ Captain Fury ☐ Captain Hates the Sea, The ☐ China Girl ☐ City of Shadows ☐ Dishonored ☐ Ex-Champ ☐ Fair Wind to Java ☐ Fort Apache ☐ Foxes of Harrow, The ☐ Full Confession ☐ Girl in Every Port, A ☐ Guilty as Hell ☐ Gunga Din ☐ Hangman's House ☐ Hot Pepper ☐ Informer, The ☐ Klondike Annie ☐ Lady Godiva ☐ Let Freedom Ring ☐ Lost Patrol, The ☐ Magnificent Brute, The ☐ Many Rivers to Cross ☐ Murder at the Vanities ☐ Nancy Steel Is Missing ☐ No More Women ☐ Pacific Liner ☐ Prince Valiant ☐ Professional Soldier ☐ Quiet Man, The ☐ Rio Grande ☐ Sea Devils ☐ Sea Fury ☐ She Wore a Yellow Ribbon ☐ South of Pago Pago ☐ Tampico ☐ This Is My Affair ☐ Under Pressure ☐ Under Two Flags ☐ Unholy Three, The ☐ Wee Willie Winkie ☐ What Price Glory?

McMahon, Ed ☐ Full Moon High ☐ Fun with Dick and Jane ☐ Great American Traffic Jam, The ☐ Kid from Left Field, The ☐ Slaughter's Big Rip-Off

McNally, Stephen ☐ Air Cadet ☐ Apache Drums ☐ Battle Zone ☐ Black Castle, The ☐ City Across the River ☐ Duel at Silver Creek, The ☐ Eyes in the Night ☐ Fiend Who Walked the West, The ☐ Hell Bent for Leather ☐ Hell's Crossroads ☐ Hi-Riders ☐ Iron Man, The ☐ Johnny Rocco ☐ Lady Gambles, The ☐ Lady Pays Off, The ☐ Make Haste to Live ☐ Man from Bitter Ridge, The ☐ No Way Out ☐ Raging Tide, The ☐ Requiem for a Gunfighter ☐ Sword in the Desert ☐ Violent Saturday ☐ Winchester '73 ☐ Woman in Hiding

McQueen, Butterfly ☐ Adventures of Huckleberry Finn ☐ Duel in the Sun ☐ Gone with the Wind ☐ Mosquito Coast, The ☐ Polly

McNeil, Claudia ☐ Black Girl ☐ Incident in San Francisco ☐ Migrants, The ☐ Raisin in the Sun, A ☐ Roll of Thunder, Hear My Cry

McNichol, Kristy ☐ Baby of the Bride ☐ Dream Lover ☐ End, The ☐ Forgotten One, The ☐ Just the Way You Are ☐ Little Darlings ☐ My Old Man ☐ Night the Lights Went Out in Georgia, The ☐ Only When I Laugh ☐ Pirate Movie, The ☐ Summer of My German Soldier ☐ Two Moon Junction ☐ White Dog

McQueen, Steve ☐ Baby the Rain Must Fall ☐ Blob, The ☐ Bullitt ☐ Cincinnati Kid, The ☐ Enemy of the People, An ☐ Getaway, The ☐ Great Escape, The ☐ Great St. Louis Bank Robbery, The ☐ Hell Is for Heroes ☐ Honeymoon Machine, The ☐ Hunter, The ☐ Junior Bonner ☐ Le Mans ☐ Love with the Proper Stranger ☐ Magnificent Seven, The ☐ Nevada Smith ☐ Never So Few ☐ On Any Sunday ☐ Papillon ☐ Reivers, The ☐ Sand

Pebbles, The ☐ Soldier in the Rain ☐ Somebody Up There Likes Me ☐ Thomas Crown Affair, The ☐ Tom Horn ☐ Towering Inferno, The ☐ War Lover, The

Medina, Patricia ☐ Abbott and Costello In The Foreign Legion ☐ Aladdin and His Lamp ☐ Beast of Hollow Mountain, The ☐ Black Knight, The ☐ Botany Bay ☐ Captain Pirate ☐ Desperate Search ☐ Don't Take It to Heart ☐ Fighting O'Flynn, The ☐ Fortunes of Captain Blood, The ☐ Foxes of Harrow, The ☐ Francis ☐ Lady in the Iron Mask ☐ Latitude Zero ☐ Magic Carpet, The ☐ Missiles from Hell ☐ Mr. Arkadin ☐ Phantom of the Rue Morgue ☐ Plunder of the Sun ☐ Secret Heart, The ☐ Siren of Bagdad ☐ Snow White and the Three Stooges

Meatloaf ☐ Motorama ☐ Roadie ☐ Rocky Horror Picture Show, The ☐ Squeeze, The ☐ Wayne's World

Medford, Kay ☐ Angel in my Pocket ☐ Busy Body, The ☐ Butterfield 8 ☐ Ensign Pulver ☐ Fire Sale ☐ Funny Girl ☐ Girl of the Night ☐ Jamboree ☐ More Than Friends ☐ Rat Race, The

Meek, Donald ☐ Barnacle Bill ☐ Fabulous Joe, The ☐ Feminine Touch, The ☐ Informer, The ☐ Lost Angel ☐ Maid of Salem ☐ Maisie Gets Her Man ☐ Maisie Goes to Reno ☐ Make a Wish ☐ Man from Dakota, The ☐ Mrs. Wiggs of the Cabbage Patch ☐ Murder at the Vanities ☐ My Little Chickadee ☐ Nick Carter, Master Detective ☐ Rationing ☐ Return of Peter Grimm, The ☐ Rise and Shine ☐ Stagecoach ☐ Star Dust ☐ State Fair ☐ Whole Town's Talking, The ☐ Wild Man of Borneo, The ☐ You're a Sweetheart ☐ Young Mr. Lincoln

Meeker, Ralph ☐ Alpha Incident, The ☐ Big House, U.S.A. ☐ Birds of Prey ☐ Code Two ☐ Dead Don't Die, The ☐ Detective, The ☐ Food of the Gods, The ☐ Four in a Jeep ☐ Fuzzy Pink Nightgown, The ☐ Girl on the Late, Late Show, The ☐ Glory Alley ☐ Hot Lead ☐ I Walk the Line ☐ Jeopardy ☐ Kiss Me Deadly ☐ Naked Spur, The ☐ Night Stalker, The ☐ Paths of Glory ☐ Shadow in the Sky ☐ St. Valentine's Day Massacre, The ☐ Teresa ☐ Wall of Noise

Menjou, Adolphe ☐ Across the Wide Missouri ☐ Ambassador's Daughter, The ☐ Are Parents People? ☐ Bill of Divorcement, A ☐ Broadway Gondolier ☐ Bundle of Joy ☐ Cafe Metropole ☐ Circus Queen Murder, The ☐ Easiest Way, The ☐ Farewell to Arms, A ☐ Father Takes a Wife ☐ Forbidden ☐ Friends and Lovers ☐ Front Page, The ☐ Fuzzy Pink Nightgown, The ☐ Gold Diggers of 1935 ☐ Golden Boy ☐ Goldwyn Follies, The ☐ Great Lover, The ☐ Heartbeat ☐ Hi Diddle Diddle ☐ Housekeeper's Daughter, The ☐ Hucksters, The ☐ Human Side, The ☐ I Married a Woman ☐ I'll Be Yours ☐ Letter of Introduction, A ☐ Little Miss Marker ☐ Man Alive ☐ Man on a Tightrope ☐ Marriage Circle, The ☐ Mighty Barnum, The ☐ Milky Way, The ☐ Morning Glory ☐ Morocco ☐ My Dream Is Yours ☐ One Hundred Men and a Girl ☐ One in a Million ☐ Parisian, The ☐ Paths of Glory ☐ Pollyanna ☐ Road Show ☐ Roxie Hart ☐ Sheik, The ☐ Sing, Baby, Sing ☐ Stage Door ☐ Star Is Born, A ☐ State of the Union ☐ Step Lively ☐ Sweet Rosie O'Grady ☐ Thanks for Everything ☐ To Please a Lady ☐ Turnabout ☐ Woman of Paris, A ☐ Worst Woman in Paris?, The ☐ You Were Never Lovelier

Mercouri, Melina ☐ Dream of Passion, A ☐ Gaily, Gaily ☐ Gypsy and the Gentleman, The ☐ He Who Must Die ☐ Jacqueline Susann's Once Is Not Enough ☐ Man Could Get Killed, A ☐ Nasty Habits ☐ Never on Sunday ☐ Phaedra ☐ Promise at Dawn ☐ Topkapi ☐ Victors, The

Meredith, Burgess ☐ 92 in the Shade ☐ Advise and Consent ☐ Batman—The Movie ☐ Big Hand for the Little Lady, A ☐ Broken Rainbow ☐ Burnt Offerings ☐ Cardinal, The ☐ Castle on the Hudson ☐ Clash of the Titans ☐ Clay Pigeon ☐ Day of the Locust, The ☐ Diary of a Chambermaid ☐ Fan's Notes, A ☐ Final Assignment ☐ Foul Play ☐ Full Moon in Blue Water ☐ G.I. Joe—The Movie ☐ Gay Adventure, The ☐ Golden Needles ☐ Golden Rendezvous ☐ Great Bank Hoax, The ☐ Grumpy Old Men ☐ Hard Contract ☐ Hindenburg, The ☐ Hurry Sundown ☐ In Harm's Way ☐ Joe Butterfly ☐ Johnny, We Hardly Knew Ye ☐ King Lear ☐ Last Chase, The ☐ Mackenna's Gold ☐ Madame X ☐ Magic ☐ Magnificent Doll ☐ Man on the Eiffel Tower, The ☐ Man, The ☐ Mine Own Executioner ☐ Oddball Hall ☐ Of Mice and Men ☐ On Our Merry Way ☐ Outrage ☐ Rocky ☐ Rocky 2 ☐ Santa Claus, The Movie ☐ Second Chorus ☐ Story Of G.I. Joe, The ☐ Street of Chance ☐ Such Good Friends ☐ That Uncertain Feeling ☐ There Was a Crooked Man ☐ Tom, Dick and Harry ☐ Torture Garden ☐ True Confessions ☐ When Time Ran Out . . . ☐ Winterset

Merkel, Una ☐ Abraham Lincoln ☐ Baby Face Harrington ☐ Bank Dick, The ☐ Bat Whispers, The ☐ Beauty for Sale ☐ Biography of a Bachelor Girl ☐ Bombshell ☐ Born to Dance ☐ Bride Goes Wild, The ☐ Broadway Melody of 1936 ☐ Cat's Paw, The ☐ Checkers ☐ Clear All Wires ☐ Destry Rides Again ☐ Evelyn Prentice ☐ Fuzzy Pink Nightgown, The ☐ I Love Melvin ☐ Impatient Maiden, The ☐ It's a Joke, Son ☐ Kettles in the Ozarks, The ☐ Kill the Umpire ☐ Mad Doctor of Market Street, The ☐ Maltese Falcon, The ☐ Mating Game, The ☐ Merry Widow, The ☐ Merry Widow, The ☐ Midnight Mary ☐ My Blue Heaven ☐ On Borrowed Time ☐ One New York Night ☐ Private Lives ☐ Red-Headed Woman ☐ Rich, Young and

Pretty ☐ Riffraff ☐ Road to Zanzibar ☐ Sandy Gets Her Man ☐ Saratoga ☐ Secret of Madame Blanche, The ☐ Speed ☐ Spinout ☐ Summer and Smoke ☐ Summer Magic ☐ This Side of Heaven ☐ True Confession ☐ With a Song in My Heart

Merman, Ethel ☐ Alexander's Ragtime Band ☐ Anything Goes ☐ Art of Love, The ☐ Big Broadcast of 1936, The ☐ Call Me Madam ☐ Happy Landing ☐ It's a Mad Mad Mad Mad World ☐ Journey Back to Oz ☐ Kid Millions ☐ Strike Me Pink ☐ There's No Business Like Show Business ☐ We're Not Dressing

Merrill, Dina ☐ Anna to the Infinite Power ☐ Butterfield 8 ☐ Caddyshack II ☐ Courtship of Eddie's Father, The ☐ Desk Set ☐ Don't Give Up the Ship ☐ I'll Take Sweden ☐ Letters, The ☐ Operation Petticoat ☐ Running Wild ☐ Sundowners, The ☐ Tenth Month, The ☐ Twisted ☐ Young Savages, The

Merrill, Gary ☐ All About Eve ☐ Another Man's Poison ☐ Black Dakotas, The ☐ Blueprint for Murder ☐ Clambake ☐ Decision Before Dawn ☐ Frogmen, The ☐ Girl in White, The ☐ Girl Named Tamiko, A ☐ Great Impostor, The ☐ Human Jungle, The ☐ Last Challenge, The ☐ Missouri Traveler, The ☐ Mother Didn't Tell Me ☐ Mysterious Island ☐ Night Without Sleep ☐ Phone Call from a Stranger ☐ Twelve O'Clock High ☐ Where the Sidewalk Ends ☐ Winged Victory ☐ Witness to Murder ☐ Wonderful Country, The

Merrow, Jane ☐ Adam's Woman ☐ Appointment, The ☐ Girl-Getters, The ☐ Island of the Burning Doomed ☐ Lion in Winter, The

Metcalf, Laurie ☐ Blink ☐ Desperately Seeking Susan ☐ Execution of Raymond Graham, The ☐ Internal Affairs ☐ JFK ☐ Making Mr. Right ☐ Mistress

Michell, Keith ☐ All Night Long ☐ Dangerous Exile ☐ Deceivers, The ☐ Executioner, The ☐ Grendel, Grendel, Grendel ☐ Gypsy and the Gentleman, The ☐ Henry VIII and His Six Wives ☐ House of Cards ☐ Tenth Month, The

Midler, Bette ☐ Beaches ☐ Big Business ☐ Divine Madness ☐ Down and Out in Beverly Hills ☐ For the Boys ☐ Gypsy ☐ Hocus Pocus ☐ Jinxed! ☐ Oliver and Co. ☐ Outrageous Fortune ☐ Rose, The ☐ Ruthless People ☐ Scenes from a Mall ☐ Stella

Mifune, Toshiro ☐ 1941 ☐ Bad Sleep Well, The ☐ Bushido Blade, The ☐ Challenge, The ☐ Chushingura ☐ Drunken Angel ☐ Emperor and A General, The ☐ Grand Prix ☐ Hell in the Pacific ☐ Hidden Fortress, The ☐ High and Low ☐ I Live in Fear ☐ Idiot, The ☐ Important Man, The ☐ Inchon ☐ Journey of Honor ☐ Judo Saga ☐ Life of Oharu, The ☐ Lower Depths, The ☐ Midway ☐ Paper Tiger ☐ Picture Bride ☐ Rashomon ☐ Rebellion ☐ Red Beard ☐ Red Lion ☐ Red Sun ☐ Rickshaw Man, The ☐ Rise Against the Sword ☐ Saga of the Vagabonds ☐ Samurai 1—Musashi Miyamoto ☐ Samurai 2—Duel at Ichijoji Temple ☐ Samurai 3—Duel at Ganryu Island ☐ Sanjuro ☐ Secret Scrolls (Part I) ☐ Secret Scrolls: Part II ☐ Seven Samurai, The ☐ Shadow of the Wolf ☐ Shogun ☐ Stray Dog (Nora Inn) ☐ Sword of Doom ☐ Throne of Blood ☐ Tora! Tora! Tora! ☐ Yojimbo ☐ Youth and His Amulet, The

Miles, Sarah ☐ Big Sleep, The ☐ Blowup ☐ Ceremony, The ☐ Great Expectations ☐ Harem ☐ Hireling, The ☐ Hope and Glory ☐ James A. Michener's Dynasty ☐ Lady Caroline Lamb ☐ Man Who Loved Cat Dancing, The ☐ Ordeal by Innocence ☐ Priest of Love ☐ Queenie ☐ Ryan's Daughter ☐ Sailor Who Fell from Grace with the Sea ☐ Servant, The ☐ Steaming ☐ Term of Trial ☐ Those Magnificent Men in Their Flying Machines ☐ Time Lost and Time Remembered ☐ Venom ☐ White Mischief

Miles, Sylvia ☐ Critical Condition ☐ Crossing Delancey ☐ Farewell, My Lovely ☐ Funhouse, The ☐ Heat ☐ Last Movie, The ☐ Midnight Cowboy ☐ No Big Deal ☐ She-Devil ☐ Sleeping Beauty ☐ Superstar: The Life and Times of Andy Warhol ☐ Wall Street

Miles, Vera ☐ 23 Paces to Baker Street ☐ And I Alone Survived ☐ Autumn Leaves ☐ Back Street ☐ Baffled ☐ Beau James ☐ Brainwaves ☐ Cannon ☐ Castaway Cowboy, The ☐ Charge at Feather River, The ☐ FBI Story, The ☐ Fire! ☐ Five Branded Women ☐ Follow Me, Boys! ☐ For Men Only ☐ Gentle Giant ☐ Great American Tragedy, A ☐ Hanged Man, The ☐ Helen Keller: The Miracle Continues ☐ Hellfighters ☐ Howling in the Woods, A ☐ Initiation, The ☐ It Takes All Kinds ☐ Jigsaw ☐ Judge Horton and The Scottsboro Boys ☐ Man Who Shot Liberty Valance, The ☐ McNaughton's Daughter ☐ Mission Batangas ☐ One Little Indian ☐ Our Family Business ☐ Psycho ☐ Psycho 2 ☐ Searchers, The ☐ Sergeant Ryker ☐ Strange And Deadly Occurrence, The ☐ Those Calloways ☐ Tiger Walks, A ☐ Touch of Larceny, A ☐ Twilight's Last Gleaming ☐ Web of Evidence ☐ Wichita ☐ Wild Country, The ☐ Wrong Man, The

Milland, Ray ☐ Alias Nick Beal ☐ Ambassador Bill ☐ Are Husbands Necessary? ☐ Arise, My Love ☐ Attic, The ☐ Bachelor Father, The ☐ Battlestar: Galactica ☐ Beau Geste ☐ Big Broadcast of 1937, The ☐ Big Clock, The ☐ Blackout ☐ Blonde Crazy ☐ Bolero ☐ Bugles in the Afternoon ☐ Bulldog Drummond Escapes ☐ California ☐ Circle of Danger ☐ Close to My Heart ☐ Copper Canyon ☐ Crystal Ball, The ☐ Dead Don't Die, The ☐ Dial M for Murder ☐ Doctor Takes a Wife, The ☐ Easy Living ☐ Ebb Tide ☐ Ellery Queen ☐ Embassy ☐ Escape to Witch Mountain ☐ Everything Happens at Night ☐ Forever and a Day

☐ Four Hours to Kill ☐ Frogs ☐ Game for Vultures ☐ Gilded Lily, The ☐ Girl in the Red Velvet Swing, The ☐ Glass Key, The ☐ Gold ☐ Golden Earrings ☐ Her Jungle Love ☐ High Flight ☐ Hotel Imperial ☐ I Wanted Wings ☐ Imperfect Lady, The ☐ Irene ☐ It Happens Every Spring ☐ Jamaica Run ☐ Jungle Princess, The ☐ Kitty ☐ Lady Has Plans, The ☐ Lady in the Dark ☐ Last Tycoon, The ☐ Let's Do It Again ☐ Life of Her Own, A ☐ Lisbon ☐ Lost Weekend, The ☐ Love Story ☐ Major and the Minor, The ☐ Man Alone, A ☐ Man Who Played God, The ☐ Mayday at 40,000 Feet! ☐ Men with Wings ☐ Ministry of Fear ☐ Next Time We Love ☐ Night into Morning ☐ Oil ☐ Oliver's Story ☐ Our Family Business ☐ Panic in Year Zero! ☐ Payment Deferred ☐ Premature Burial, The ☐ Quick, Let's Get Married ☐ Reap the Wild Wind ☐ Rhubarb ☐ River's Edge, The ☐ Safecracker, The ☐ Skylark ☐ Slavers ☐ So Evil My Love ☐ Something to Live For ☐ Star Spangled Rhythm ☐ Three Brave Men ☐ Three Smart Girls ☐ Till We Meet Again ☐ Uninvited, The ☐ Untamed ☐ We're Not Dressing ☐ Woman of Distinction, A

Miller, Ann ☐ Deep in My Heart ☐ Easter Parade ☐ Eve Knew Her Apples ☐ Great American Pastime, The ☐ Hey, Rookie ☐ Hit the Deck ☐ Jam Session ☐ Kiss Me Kate ☐ Kissing Bandit, The ☐ Life of the Party, The ☐ Lovely to Look At ☐ On the Town ☐ Opposite Sex, The ☐ Reveille With Beverly ☐ Room Service ☐ Small Town Girl ☐ Stage Door ☐ Texas Carnival ☐ That's Entertainment 3 ☐ Time Out for Rhythm ☐ Too Many Girls ☐ Two Tickets to Broadway ☐ Watch the Birdie

Miller, Barry ☐ Chosen, The ☐ Journey of Natty Gann, The ☐ Peggy Sue Got Married ☐ Saturday Night Fever ☐ Voices

Miller, Colleen ☐ Four Guns to the Border ☐ Gunfight at Comanche Creek ☐ Hot Summer Night ☐ Man in the Shadow ☐ Night Runner, The ☐ Rawhide Years, The

Miller, Dennis ☐ Buddies ☐ Disclosure ☐ Hoodwink ☐ Live From Washington It's Dennis Miller ☐ Madhouse

Miller, Dick ☐ Bucket of Blood, A ☐ Carnival Rock ☐ Explorers ☐ Little Shop of Horrors, The ☐ Matinee ☐ National Lampoon Goes to the Movies ☐ New York, New York ☐ Night Call Nurses ☐ Rock All Night ☐ Sorority Girl ☐ Student Teachers, The ☐ Summer School Teachers ☐ Tales From the Crypt Presents Demon Knight ☐ White Dog

Miller, Jason ☐ Exorcist III, The ☐ Exorcist, The ☐ F. Scott Fitzgerald in Hollywood ☐ Henderson Monster, The ☐ Marilyn: The Untold Story ☐ Monsignor ☐ Nickel Ride, The ☐ Ninth Configuration, The ☐ Rudy ☐ Toy Soldiers

Miller, Kristine ☐ Domino Kid, The ☐ I Walk Alone ☐ Jungle Patrol ☐ Shadow on the Wall

Miller, Marvin ☐ Evita Peron ☐ Forbidden ☐ Hell Squad ☐ Kiss Daddy Goodbye ☐ Peking Express ☐ Red Planet Mars

Miller, Penelope Ann ☐ Adventures in Babysitting ☐ Awakenings ☐ Big Top Pee-Wee ☐ Biloxi Blues ☐ Carlito's Way ☐ Chaplin ☐ Dead-Bang ☐ Downtown ☐ Freshman, The ☐ Gun in Betty Lou's Handbag, The ☐ Kindergarten Cop ☐ Miles from Home ☐ Other People's Money ☐ Shadow, The ☐ Year of the Comet

Milligan, Spike ☐ Adventures of Barry Mckenzie, The ☐ Bed-Sitting Room, The ☐ Digby—The Biggest Dog in the World ☐ Ghost in the Noonday Sun ☐ Great Mc Gonagal ☐ Hound of the Baskervilles, The

Mills, Donna ☐ Bare Essence ☐ Bunco ☐ Curse of the Black Widow ☐ False Arrest ☐ Fire! ☐ Haunts of the Very Rich ☐ Hunted Lady, The ☐ Killer With Two Faces ☐ Murph the Surf ☐ Play Misty for Me

Mills, Hayley ☐ Appointment with Death ☐ Back Home ☐ Chalk Garden, The ☐ Deadly Strangers ☐ Endless Night ☐ Family Way, The ☐ Gypsy Girl ☐ In Search of the Castaways ☐ Kingfisher Caper, The ☐ Matter of Innocence, A ☐ Moon-Spinners, The ☐ Parent Trap II ☐ Parent Trap III ☐ Parent Trap, The ☐ Pollyanna ☐ Summer Magic ☐ That Darn Cat ☐ Tiger Bay ☐ Trouble With Angels, The ☐ Truth About Spring, The ☐ Whistle Down the Wind

Mills, John ☐ Above Us The Waves ☐ Adam's Woman ☐ Africa—Texas Style ☐ Baby and the Battleship, The ☐ Big Blockade, The ☐ Big Sleep, The ☐ Chalk Garden, The ☐ Charing Cross Road ☐ Chuka ☐ Colditz Story ☐ Cottage to Let ☐ Desert Attack ☐ Dirty Knight's Work ☐ Dunkirk ☐ End of the Affair, The ☐ Escapade ☐ Family Way, The ☐ Flame in the Streets ☐ Frankenstein ☐ Gandhi ☐ Gentle Gunman, The ☐ Ghost Camera, The ☐ Goodbye, Mr. Chips ☐ Great Expectations ☐ Green Cockatoo, The ☐ History of Mr. Polly, The ☐ Hobson's Choice ☐ Hold the Dream ☐ Human Factor, The ☐ I Was Monty's Double ☐ In Which We Serve ☐ Johnny in the Clouds ☐ King Rat ☐ Lady and the Highwayman, The ☐ Lady Caroline Lamb ☐ Long Memory, The ☐ Masks of Death ☐ Mr. Denning Drives North ☐ Murder with Mirrors ☐ Night of the Fox ☐ Nine Days A Queen ☐ October Man, The ☐ Oh! What a Lovely War ☐ Oklahoma Crude ☐ Operation Crossbow ☐ Operation Disaster ☐ Regal Cavalcade ☐ Rocking Horse Winner, The ☐ Run Wild, Run Free ☐ Ryan's Daughter ☐ Sahara ☐ Scott of the Antarctic ☐ Season of Passion ☐ So Well Remembered ☐ Swiss Family Robinson ☐ Thirty-Nine Steps, The ☐ This Happy Breed ☐ Tiger Bay ☐ Town on Trial ☐ Truth About Spring,

The ☐ Tunes of Glory ☐ War and Peace ☐ We Dive at Dawn ☐ Who's That Girl? ☐ Wrong Box, The ☐ Young Mr. Pitt, The ☐ Young Winston ☐ Zulu Dawn

Mimieux, Yvette ☐ Black Hole, The ☐ Caper of the Golden Bulls, The ☐ Dark of the Sun ☐ Diamond Head ☐ Forbidden Love ☐ Four Horsemen of the Apocalypse ☐ Hit Lady ☐ Jackson County Jail ☐ Journey Into Fear ☐ Joy in the Morning ☐ Light in the Piazza ☐ Monkeys, Go Home! ☐ Obsessive Love ☐ Outside Chance ☐ Picasso Summer, The ☐ Reward, The ☐ Skyjacked ☐ Snowbeast ☐ Three in the Attic ☐ Time Machine, The ☐ Toys in the Attic ☐ Where the Boys Are ☐ Wonderful World of the Brothers Grimm, The

Mineo, Sal ☐ Cheyenne Autumn ☐ Crime in the Streets ☐ Dino ☐ Escape from the Planet of the Apes ☐ Escape from Zahrain ☐ Exodus ☐ Family Rico, The ☐ Gene Krupa Story, The ☐ Giant ☐ Horse Named Comanche, A ☐ How to Steal an Airplane ☐ Krakatoa, East of Java ☐ Longest Day, The ☐ Private War of Major Benson, The ☐ Rebel Without a Cause ☐ Six Bridges to Cross ☐ Somebody Up There Likes Me ☐ Stranger on the Run

Minnelli, Liza ☐ Arthur ☐ Arthur 2—On the Rocks ☐ Cabaret ☐ Charlie Bubbles ☐ Journey Back to Oz ☐ Lucky Lady ☐ Matter of Time, A ☐ Muppets Take Manhattan, The ☐ New York, New York ☐ Rent-a-Cop ☐ Silent Movie ☐ Stepping Out ☐ Sterile Cuckoo, The ☐ Tell Me That You Love Me, Junie Moon ☐ That's Dancing ☐ That's Entertainment

Miranda, Carmen ☐ Copacabana ☐ Date With Judy, A ☐ Doll Face ☐ Down Argentine Way ☐ Four Jills in a Jeep ☐ Gang's All Here, The ☐ Greenwich Village ☐ If I'm Lucky ☐ Nancy Goes to Rio ☐ Scared Stiff ☐ Something for the Boys ☐ Springtime in the Rockies ☐ That Night in Rio ☐ Week-end in Havana

Mirren, Helen ☐ 2010: The Year We Make Contact ☐ Age of Consent ☐ Cal ☐ Caligula ☐ Comfort of Strangers, The ☐ Coming Through ☐ Cook, the Thief, His Wife & Her Lover, The ☐ Excalibur ☐ Fiendish Plot of Dr. Fu Manchu, The ☐ Gospel According to Vic, The ☐ Hussy ☐ Long Good Friday, The ☐ Madness of King George, The ☐ Midsummer Night's Dream, A ☐ Mosquito Coast, The ☐ O Lucky Man! ☐ Pascali's Island ☐ Prime Suspect ☐ Prime Suspect 2 ☐ Prime Suspect 3 ☐ Savage Messiah ☐ When the Whales Came ☐ Where Angels Fear to Tread ☐ White Nights

Mitchell, Cameron ☐ Adventures of Gallant Bess ☐ All Mine to Give ☐ As the Sea Rages ☐ Blood and Black Lace ☐ Buck and the Preacher ☐ Carousel ☐ Command Decision ☐ Death of a Salesman ☐ Desiree ☐ Dog Eat Dog ☐ Dulcinea ☐ Escapade in Japan ☐ Face of Fire ☐ Flight to Mars ☐ Frankenstein Island ☐ Garden of Evil ☐ Go for Gold ☐ Gorilla at Large ☐ Haunts ☐ High Barbaree ☐ Hombre ☐ Homecoming ☐ Inside the Mafia ☐ It's Called Murder, Baby ☐ Japanese War Bride ☐ Killers ☐ Killpoint ☐ Klansman, The ☐ Last Gun, The ☐ Last of the Vikings, The ☐ Last Reunion, The ☐ Love Me or Leave Me ☐ Low Blow ☐ Man on a Tightrope ☐ Man-Eater of Hydra ☐ Medusa ☐ Memorial Valley Massacre ☐ Messenger, The ☐ Midnight Man, The ☐ Minnesota Clay ☐ Mission Kill ☐ Monkey on My Back ☐ Nightmare in Wax ☐ No Down Payment ☐ Offspring, The ☐ Okinawa ☐ Outcasts of Poker Flat, The ☐ Pony Soldier ☐ Powder River ☐ Raw Force ☐ Rebel Rousers ☐ Sellout, The ☐ Slavers ☐ Strange Lady in Town ☐ Tall Men, The ☐ Tension at Table Rock ☐ Terror in Beverly Hills ☐ What Next, Corporal Hargrove?

Mitchell, Grant ☐ Impatient Years, The ☐ In Person ☐ It All Came True ☐ It Happened on Fifth Avenue ☐ Man to Man ☐ Man Who Came to Dinner, The ☐ Meet the Stewarts ☐ My Love Came Back ☐ New Moon ☐ No Man of Her Own ☐ One Exciting Adventure ☐ Secret Bride, The ☐ Secret of Dr. Kildare, The ☐ See Here, Private Hargrove ☐ Skylark ☐ Star Witness ☐ Successful Calamity, A ☐ We Who Are Young

Mitchell, Millard ☐ Everybody Does It ☐ Foreign Affair, A ☐ Gunfighter, The ☐ Mister 880 ☐ My Six Convicts ☐ Naked Spur, The ☐ Singin' in the Rain ☐ Strictly Dishonorable ☐ Winchester '73 ☐ You're in the Navy Now

Mitchell, Thomas ☐ Adventure ☐ Adventure in Manhattan ☐ Alias Nick Beal ☐ Angels over Broadway ☐ Bataan ☐ Big Wheel, The ☐ Black Swan, The ☐ Buffalo Bill ☐ By Love Possessed ☐ Captain Eddie ☐ Craig's Wife ☐ Dark Mirror, The ☐ Dark Waters ☐ Destry ☐ Flesh and Fantasy ☐ Flight from Destiny ☐ Gone with the Wind ☐ Handle with Care ☐ High Barbaree ☐ High Noon ☐ Hurricane, The ☐ I Promise to Pay ☐ Immortal Sergeant, The ☐ It's a Wonderful Life ☐ Joan of Paris ☐ Journey into Light ☐ Keys of the Kingdom ☐ Long Voyage Home, The ☐ Lost Horizon ☐ Make Way for Tomorrow ☐ Moontide ☐ Mr. Smith Goes to Washington ☐ Only Angels Have Wings ☐ Our Town ☐ Out of the Fog ☐ Outlaw, The ☐ Pocketful of Miracles ☐ Romance of Rosy Ridge, The ☐ Secret of the Incas ☐ Silver River ☐ Song of the Islands ☐ Stagecoach ☐ Sullivans, The ☐ Swiss Family Robinson ☐ Tales of Manhattan ☐ Theodora Goes Wild ☐ This Above All ☐ Three Cheers for the Irish ☐ Three Wise Fools ☐ Trade Winds ☐ When You're in Love ☐ While the City Sleeps ☐ Wilson

Mitchum, Robert ☐ 5 Card Stud ☐ Agency ☐ Ambassador, The ☐ Amsterdam Kill, The

☐ Angel Face ☐ Angry Hills, The ☐ Anzio ☐ Bandido ☐ Big Sleep, The ☐ Big Steal, The ☐ Blood on the Moon ☐ Breakthrough ☐ Brotherhood of the Rose ☐ Cape Fear ☐ Cape Fear ☐ Crossfire ☐ Desire Me ☐ El Dorado ☐ Enemy Below, The ☐ False Colors ☐ Family for Joe, A ☐ Farewell, My Lovely ☐ Fire Down Below ☐ Foreign Intrigue ☐ Friends of Eddie Coyle, The ☐ Girl Rush ☐ Going Home ☐ Good Guys and the Bad Guys, The ☐ Grass is Greener, The ☐ Gung Ho! ☐ Hearst and Davies Affair, The ☐ Heaven Knows, Mr. Allison ☐ His Kind of Woman ☐ Holiday Affair ☐ Home From the Hill ☐ Hoppy Serves a Writ ☐ Hunters, The ☐ Johnny Doesn't Live Here Any More ☐ Last Time I Saw Archie, The ☐ Last Tycoon, The ☐ Leather Burners ☐ List of Adrian Messenger, The ☐ Locket, The ☐ Longest Day, The ☐ Lusty Men, The ☐ Macao ☐ Man in the Middle ☐ Man with the Gun, The ☐ Maria's Lovers ☐ Matilda ☐ Midway ☐ Mr. Moses ☐ Mr. North ☐ My Forbidden Past ☐ Nevada ☐ Night Fighters, The ☐ Night of the Hunter, The ☐ Nightkill ☐ Not as a Stranger ☐ One Minute to Zero ☐ One Shoe Makes It Murder ☐ Out of the Past ☐ Pursued ☐ Rachel and the Stranger ☐ Racket, The ☐ Rampage ☐ Red Pony, The ☐ Riders of the Deadline ☐ River of No Return ☐ Ryan's Daughter ☐ Scrooged ☐ Second Chance ☐ Secret Ceremony ☐ She Couldn't Say No ☐ Story Of G.I. Joe, The ☐ Sundowners, The ☐ That Championship Season ☐ Thirty Seconds Over Tokyo ☐ Thunder Road ☐ Till the End of Time ☐ Track of the Cat ☐ Two for the Seesaw ☐ Undercurrent ☐ Villa Rides ☐ Way West, The ☐ We've Never Been Licked ☐ West of the Pecos ☐ What a Way to Go! ☐ When Strangers Marry ☐ Where Danger Lives ☐ White Witch Doctor ☐ Winds of War, The ☐ Wonderful Country, The ☐ Yakuza, The

Mix, Tom ☐ Dick Turpin ☐ Great K&A Train Robbery, The ☐ Hidden Gold ☐ Just Tony ☐ Miracle Rider, The ☐ My Pal, the King ☐ Rainbow Trail, The ☐ Rider of Death Valley ☐ Riders of the Purple Sage

Modine, Matthew ☐ And the Band Played On ☐ Baby, It's You ☐ Birdy ☐ Browning Version, The ☐ Bye Bye, Love ☐ Equinox ☐ Full Metal Jacket ☐ Gamble, The ☐ Gross Anatomy ☐ Hotel New Hampshire, The ☐ Married to the Mob ☐ Memphis Belle ☐ Mrs. Soffel ☐ Orphans ☐ Pacific Heights ☐ Private School ☐ Short Cuts ☐ Streamers ☐ Vision Quest ☐ Wind

Moffat, Donald ☐ Alamo Bay ☐ Best of Times, The ☐ Bourne Identity, The ☐ Call of the Wild, The ☐ Class Action ☐ Eleanor and Franklin: The White House Years ☐ Far North ☐ Housesitter ☐ Jacqueline Bouvier Kennedy ☐ Monster in the Closet ☐ Music Box ☐ On the Nickel ☐ Regarding Henry ☐ Trapped in Paradise ☐ Unbearable Lightness of Being, The

Mohr, Gerald ☐ Angry Red Planet, The ☐ Guns, Girls and Gangsters ☐ Invasion, U.S.A. ☐ Lone Wolf in London, The ☐ Lone Wolf in Mexico, The ☐ Notorious Lone Wolf, The

Monroe, Marilyn ☐ All About Eve ☐ As Young As You Feel ☐ Asphalt Jungle, The ☐ Bus Stop ☐ Clash by Night ☐ Don't Bother to Knock ☐ Fireball, The ☐ Gentlemen Prefer Blondes ☐ Hometown Story ☐ How to Marry a Millionaire ☐ Ladies of the Chorus ☐ Let's Make It Legal ☐ Let's Make Love ☐ Love Happy ☐ Love Nest ☐ Misfits, The ☐ Monkey Business ☐ Niagara ☐ O. Henry's Full House ☐ Prince and the Showgirl, The ☐ Right Cross ☐ River of No Return ☐ Seven Year Itch, The ☐ Some Like It Hot ☐ There's No Business Like Show Business ☐ We're Not Married

Montalban, Ricardo ☐ Across the Wide Missouri ☐ Adventures of a Young Man ☐ Badge or the Cross, The ☐ Battleground ☐ Black Water Gold ☐ Blue ☐ Border Incident ☐ Cannonball Run II ☐ Captains Courageous ☐ Cheyenne Autumn ☐ Conquest of the Planet of the Apes ☐ Escape from the Planet of the Apes ☐ Face of Fear ☐ Fantasy Island ☐ Fiesta ☐ Fireball Forward ☐ Joe Panther ☐ Kissing Bandit, The ☐ Latin Lovers ☐ Let No Man Write My Epitaph ☐ Love Is a Ball ☐ Madame X ☐ Mark of the Renegade ☐ Mark of Zorro, The ☐ McNaughton's Daughter ☐ Mission To Glory ☐ Mister Too Little ☐ Money Trap, The ☐ My Man and I ☐ Mystery Street ☐ Naked Gun, The ☐ Neptune's Daughter ☐ On an Island with You ☐ Rage of the Buccaneers, The ☐ Right Cross ☐ Saracen Blade, The ☐ Sayonara ☐ Singing Nun, The ☐ Star Trek II: The Wrath of Khan ☐ Sweet Charity ☐ Train Robbers, The ☐ Two Weeks with Love

Montand, Yves ☐ Cesar and Rosalie ☐ Choice of Arms ☐ Clair de Femme ☐ Confession, The ☐ Crucible, The ☐ Delusions of Grandeur ☐ Devil by the Tail, The ☐ Gates of the Night ☐ Goodbye Again ☐ Grand Prix ☐ Is Paris Burning? ☐ Island of Pachyderms, The ☐ Jean de Florette ☐ La Guerre Est Finie ☐ Let's Make Love ☐ Live for Life ☐ Lovers Like Us ☐ Man to Man Talk ☐ Manon of the Spring ☐ My Geisha ☐ Napoleon ☐ On a Clear Day You Can See Forever ☐ Sanctuary ☐ Sleeping Car Murders, The ☐ State of Siege ☐ Tout Va Bien ☐ Vincent, Francois, Paul and the Others ☐ Wages of Fear, The ☐ Z

Montez, Maria ☐ Ali Baba and the Forty Thieves ☐ Arabian Nights ☐ Bowery to Broadway ☐ Cobra Woman ☐ Exile, The ☐ Follow the Boys ☐ Gypsy Wildcat ☐ Mystery of Marie Roget, The ☐ Sudan ☐ Thief of Venice, The

Montgomery, Belinda ☐ Blackout ☐ Man from Atlantis ☐ Marciano ☐ Silent Madness ☐ Stone Fox

Montgomery, Elizabeth ☐ Act of Violence ☐ Amos ☐ Belle Starr ☐ Case of Rape, A ☐ Court-Martial of Billy Mitchell, The ☐ Dark Victory ☐ Jennifer: A Woman's Story ☐ Johnny Cool ☐ Legend of Lizzie Borden, The

Montgomery, George ☐ Badman's Country ☐ Battle of Rogue River ☐ Battle of the Bulge ☐ Belle Starr's Daughter ☐ Black Patch ☐ Bomb at 10:10 ☐ Brasher Doubloon, The ☐ Canyon River ☐ China Girl ☐ Coney Island ☐ Cripple Creek ☐ Davy Crockett, Indian Scout ☐ Fort Ti ☐ From Hell to Borneo ☐ Girl from Manhattan, The ☐ Guerrillas in Pink Lace ☐ Gun Duel in Durango ☐ Hallucination Generation ☐ Hostile Guns ☐ Huk ☐ Indian Uprising ☐ Iroquois Trail, The ☐ Jack McCall, Desperado ☐ King of the Wild Stallions ☐ Man from God's Country ☐ Masterson of Kansas ☐ Orchestra Wives ☐ Robber's Roost ☐ Roxie Hart ☐ Sword of Monte Cristo, The ☐ Texas Rangers, The ☐ Three Little Girls in Blue ☐ Young People

Montgomery, Robert ☐ Another Language ☐ Big House, The ☐ Biography of a Bachelor Girl ☐ Blondie of the Follies ☐ Divorcee, The ☐ Earl of Chicago, The ☐ Easiest Way, The ☐ Ever Since Eve ☐ Eye Witness ☐ Faithless ☐ Fast and Loose ☐ Forsaking All Others ☐ Free and Easy ☐ Fugitive Lovers, The ☐ Haunted Honeymoon ☐ Hell Below ☐ Here Comes Mr. Jordan ☐ Hide-Out ☐ Inspiration ☐ June Bride ☐ Lady in the Lake ☐ Last of Mrs. Cheyney, The ☐ Letty Lynton ☐ Live, Love and Learn ☐ Mr. and Mrs. Smith ☐ Mystery of Mr. X, The ☐ Night Must Fall ☐ No More Ladies ☐ Once More My Darling ☐ Our Blushing Brides ☐ Petticoat Fever ☐ Piccadilly Jim ☐ Private Lives ☐ Rage in Heaven ☐ Ride the Pink Horse ☐ Riptide ☐ Saxon Charm, The ☐ Strangers May Kiss ☐ They Were Expendable ☐ Unfinished Business ☐ Untamed ☐ When Ladies Meet ☐ Yellow Jack

Moody, Ron ☐ Dogpound Shuffle ☐ Dominique ☐ Five Golden Hours ☐ Flight of the Doves ☐ Follow a Star ☐ Legend of the Werewolf ☐ Mouse on the Moon, The ☐ Murder Most Foul ☐ Oliver! ☐ Sandwich Man, The ☐ Seaside Swingers ☐ Summer Holiday ☐ Twelve Chairs, The ☐ Unidentified Flying Oddball

Moon, Keith ☐ Sextette ☐ That'll Be the Day ☐ Tommy ☐ Two Hundred Motels

Moore, Clayton ☐ Black Dragons ☐ Code 645 ☐ Far Frontier, The ☐ International Lady ☐ Lone Ranger and the Lost City of Gold, The ☐ Lone Ranger, The ☐ Marshal of Amarillo ☐ Nyoka and the Tigerman ☐ Origin Of The Lone Ranger, The

Moore, Constance ☐ Argentine Nights ☐ Atlantic City ☐ Buy Me That Town ☐ Charlie McCarthy, Detective ☐ Delightfully Dangerous ☐ Earl Carroll Vanities ☐ Ex-Champ ☐ I Wanted Wings ☐ I'm Nobody's Sweetheart Now ☐ Take a Letter, Darling ☐ You Can't Cheat an Honest Man

Moore, Demi ☐ About Last Night . . . ☐ Blame It on Rio ☐ Butcher's Wife, The ☐ Choices ☐ Disclosure ☐ Few Good Men, A ☐ Ghost ☐ Indecent Proposal ☐ Master Ninja ☐ Mortal Thoughts ☐ No Small Affair ☐ Nothing But Trouble ☐ One Crazy Summer ☐ Parasite ☐ Seventh Sign, The ☐ St. Elmo's Fire ☐ We're No Angels ☐ Wisdom

Moore, Dickie ☐ Adventures of Martin Eden, The ☐ Bad Boy ☐ Blonde Venus ☐ Eve of St. Mark, The ☐ Gabriel over the White House ☐ Gallant Lady ☐ Gladiator, The ☐ Happy Land ☐ Man's Castle ☐ Million Dollar Legs ☐ Miss Annie Rooney ☐ Oliver Twist ☐ So Red the Rose ☐ Star Witness ☐ Tuna Clipper ☐ Upperworld

Moore, Dudley ☐ 10 ☐ 30 Is a Dangerous Age, Cynthia ☐ Adventures of Milo and Otis, The ☐ Alice's Adventures in Wonderland ☐ Arthur ☐ Arthur 2—On the Rocks ☐ Bed-Sitting Room, The ☐ Bedazzled ☐ Best Defense ☐ Blame It on the Bellboy ☐ Crazy People ☐ Foul Play ☐ Hound of the Baskervilles, The ☐ Like Father, Like Son ☐ Lovesick ☐ Micki + Maude ☐ Romantic Comedy ☐ Santa Claus, The Movie ☐ Six Weeks ☐ Those Daring Young Men in Their Jaunty Jalopies ☐ Unfaithfully Yours ☐ Wholly Moses ☐ Wrong Box, The

Moore, Grace ☐ I'll Take Romance ☐ King Steps Out, The ☐ Lady's Morals, A ☐ Love Me Forever ☐ One Night of Love ☐ When You're in Love

Moore, Juanita ☐ Dream for Christmas, A ☐ Foxstyle ☐ Green-Eyed Blonde, The ☐ Imitation of Life ☐ Lydia Bailey ☐ Singing Nun, The

Moore, Julianne ☐ Benny & Joon ☐ Cast a Deadly Spell ☐ Hand That Rocks the Cradle, The ☐ Roommates ☐ Short Cuts ☐ Vanya on 42nd Street

Moore, Kieron ☐ Anna Karenina ☐ Crack in the World ☐ Day of the Triffids, The ☐ Doctor Blood's Coffin ☐ Green Scarf, The ☐ I Thank a Fool ☐ Main Attraction, The ☐ Man About the House, A ☐ Man in Hiding ☐ Mine Own Executioner ☐ Naked Heart, The ☐ Ten Tall Men ☐ Thin Red Line, The

Moore, Mary Tyler ☐ Change of Habit ☐ Don't Just Stand There ☐ Finnegan Begin Again ☐ First, You Cry ☐ Gore Vidal's Lincoln ☐ Heartsounds ☐ Just Between Friends ☐ Last Best Year, The ☐ Ordinary People ☐ Six Weeks ☐ Stolen Babies ☐ Thanksgiving Day ☐ Thoroughly Modern Millie ☐ What's So Bad About Feeling Good?

Moore, Roger ☐ Bullseye! ☐ Cannonball Run, The ☐ Diane ☐ Escape to Athena

☐ ffolkes ☐ Fiction Makers, The ☐ Fire, Ice and Dynamite ☐ For Your Eyes Only ☐ Gold ☐ Interrupted Melody ☐ King's Thief, The ☐ Live and Let Die ☐ Man Who Haunted Himself, The ☐ Man with the Golden Gun, The ☐ Miracle, The ☐ Moonraker ☐ Naked Face, The ☐ Octopussy ☐ Sea Wolves, The ☐ Spy Who Loved Me, The ☐ View to a Kill, A ☐ Wild Geese, The

Moore, Terry ☐ Barefoot Mailman, The ☐ Beneath the 12 Mile Reef ☐ Bernardine ☐ Between Heaven and Hell ☐ Beverly Hills Brats ☐ Black Spurs ☐ Cast a Long Shadow ☐ City of Fear ☐ Come Back, Little Sheba ☐ Daddy Long Legs ☐ Gambling House ☐ Great Rupert, The ☐ He's a Cockeyed Wonder ☐ King of the Khyber Rifles ☐ Man Called Dagger, A ☐ Man on a Tightrope ☐ Mighty Joe Young ☐ Postmark for Danger ☐ Son of Lassie ☐ Why Must I Die?

Moore, Victor ☐ Gold Diggers of 1937 ☐ Heat's On, The ☐ It Happened on Fifth Avenue ☐ It's in the Bag ☐ Kiss in the Dark, A ☐ Life of the Party, The ☐ Louisiana Purchase ☐ Make Way for Tomorrow ☐ Meet the Missus ☐ On Our Merry Way ☐ Swing Time ☐ True to Life ☐ We're Not Married

Moorehead, Agnes ☐ Adventures of Captain Fabian ☐ All That Heaven Allows ☐ Bachelor in Paradise ☐ Ballad of Andy Crocker, The ☐ Bat, The ☐ Big Street, The ☐ Blazing Forest, The ☐ Blue Veil, The ☐ Caged ☐ Captain Blackjack ☐ Charlotte's Web ☐ Citizen Kane ☐ Conqueror, The ☐ Dark Passage ☐ Dear Dead Delilah ☐ Dragon Seed ☐ Fourteen Hours ☐ Frankenstein: The True Story ☐ Government Girl ☐ Her Highness and the Bellboy ☐ Hush . . . Hush, Sweet Charlotte ☐ Jane Eyre ☐ Jeanne Eagels ☐ Jessica ☐ Johnny Belinda ☐ Keep Your Powder Dry ☐ Left Hand of God, The ☐ Lost Moment, The ☐ Magnificent Ambersons, The ☐ Magnificent Obsession ☐ Meet Me in Las Vegas ☐ Mrs. Parkington ☐ Night of the Quarter Moon ☐ Opposite Sex, The ☐ Our Vines Have Tender Grapes ☐ Pardners ☐ Pollyanna ☐ Revolt of Mamie Stover, The ☐ Seventh Cross, The ☐ Show Boat ☐ Since You Went Away ☐ Singing Nun, The ☐ Station West ☐ Story of Mankind, The ☐ Story of Three Loves, The ☐ Stratton Story, The ☐ Summer Holiday ☐ Swan, The ☐ Tempest ☐ Those Redheads From Seattle ☐ Tomorrow the World ☐ True Story of Jesse James, The ☐ Untamed ☐ What's the Matter with Helen? ☐ Who's Minding the Store? ☐ Woman in White, The ☐ Youngest Profession, The

Moranis, Rick ☐ Club Paradise ☐ Flintstones, The ☐ Ghostbusters ☐ Ghostbusters II ☐ Head Office ☐ Hockey Night ☐ Honey, I Blew Up the Kid ☐ Honey, I Shrunk the Kids ☐ Little Giants ☐ Little Shop of Horrors ☐ My Blue Heaven ☐ Parenthood ☐ Spaceballs ☐ Splitting Heirs ☐ Strange Brew ☐ Strange Brew ☐ Streets of Fire ☐ Streets of Fire

More, Kenneth ☐ 39 Steps, The ☐ Admirable Crichton, The ☐ Adventures of Sadie, The ☐ Battle of Britain, The ☐ Chance of a Lifetime ☐ Clouded Yellow, The ☐ Dark of the Sun ☐ Deep Blue Sea, The ☐ Doctor in the House ☐ Flame over India ☐ Fraulein Doktor ☐ Genevieve ☐ Island Rescue ☐ Leopard in the Snow ☐ Loss of Innocence ☐ Man in the Moon, The ☐ Next to No Time ☐ Night to Remember, A ☐ No Highway in the Sky ☐ Reach for the Sky ☐ Scott of the Antarctic ☐ Scrooge ☐ Sheriff of Fractured Jaw, The ☐ Sink the Bismarck! ☐ Slipper and the Rose, The ☐ Tale of Two Cities, A ☐ Unidentified Flying Oddball ☐ Yellow Balloon, The

Moreau, Jeanne ☐ Alex in Wonderland ☐ Back to the Wall ☐ Banana Peel ☐ Bride Wore Black, The ☐ Chimes at Midnight ☐ Dangerous Liaisons 1960 ☐ Diary of a Chambermaid ☐ Eva ☐ Fire Within, The ☐ Five Branded Women ☐ Four Hundred Blows, The ☐ Frantic ☐ French Provincial ☐ Going Places ☐ Great Catherine ☐ Grisbi ☐ Heat of Desire ☐ Hu-Man ☐ Immortal Story, The ☐ Jules and Jim ☐ Julietta ☐ La Femme Nikita ☐ La Notte ☐ Last Tycoon, The ☐ Little Theatre of Jean Renoir, The ☐ Lovers, The ☐ Lumière ☐ Map of the Human Heart ☐ Mata Hari ☐ Moderato Cantabile ☐ Monte Walsh ☐ Mr. Klein ☐ Oldest Profession, The ☐ Querelle ☐ Summer House, The ☐ Train, The ☐ Trial, The ☐ Until the End of the World ☐ Victors, The ☐ Viva Maria! ☐ Yellow Rolls-Royce, The

Moreland, Mantan ☐ Black Magic ☐ Charlie Chan in the Secret Service ☐ Eyes in the Night ☐ Feathered Serpent, The ☐ Jade Mask, The ☐ Scarlet Clue, The ☐ Shanghai Cobra, The ☐ Sky Dragon, The

Morell, Andre ☐ Baby and the Battleship, The ☐ Black Knight, The ☐ Camp on Blood Island, The ☐ Flesh & Blood ☐ Frightened Bride ☐ Giant Behemoth, The ☐ High Treason ☐ Hound of the Baskervilles, The ☐ Plague of the Zombies, The ☐ Seven Days to Noon ☐ So Long at the Fair ☐ Stolen Face, A

Moreno, Rita ☐ Age Isn't Everything ☐ Anatomy of a Seduction ☐ Boss's Son, The ☐ Carnal Knowledge ☐ Cattle Town ☐ Deerslayer, The ☐ Evita Peron ☐ Fort Vengeance ☐ Four Seasons, The ☐ Garden of Evil ☐ Happy Birthday, Gemini ☐ I Like It Like That ☐ Jivaro ☐ Latin Lovers ☐ Lieutenant Wore Skirts, The ☐ Marlowe ☐ Night of the Following Day, The ☐ Pagan Love Song ☐ Popi ☐ Ritz, The ☐ Seven Cities of Gold ☐ Singin' in the Rain ☐ Summer and Smoke ☐ Untamed ☐ Vagabond King, The ☐ West Side Story

Morgan, Dennis ☐ Affectionately Yours ☐ Always Together ☐ Bad Men of Missouri

☐ Captain of the Clouds ☐ Cattle Town ☐ Cheyenne ☐ Christmas in Connecticut ☐ Fighting 69th, The ☐ God is My Co-Pilot ☐ Great Ziegfeld, The ☐ Gun That Won the West, The ☐ Hard Way, The ☐ I Conquer the Sea ☐ In This Our Life ☐ It's a Great Feeling ☐ Kitty Foyle ☐ Lady Takes a Sailor, The ☐ My Wild Irish Rose ☐ One More Tomorrow ☐ One Sunday Afternoon ☐ Painting the Clouds with Sunshine ☐ Pearl of the South Pacific ☐ Perfect Strangers ☐ Raton Pass ☐ Return of Dr. X, The ☐ River's End ☐ Shine On, Harvest Moon ☐ Thank Your Lucky Stars ☐ This Woman Is Dangerous ☐ Three Cheers for the Irish ☐ Time, the Place and the Girl, The ☐ To the Victor ☐ Two Guys From Milwaukee ☐ Two Guys From Texas

Morgan, Frank ☐ Affairs of Cellini ☐ Balalaika ☐ Bombshell ☐ Boom Town ☐ Broadway Melody of 1940 ☐ Broadway Serenade ☐ Broadway to Hollywood ☐ By Your Leave ☐ Casanova Brown ☐ Cat and the Fiddle, The ☐ Cockeyed Miracle, The ☐ Courage of Lassie ☐ Crowd Roars, The ☐ Dimples ☐ Emperor's Candlesticks, The ☐ Enchanted April ☐ Fast and Loose ☐ Ghost Comes Home, The ☐ Good Fairy, The ☐ Great Ziegfeld, The ☐ Green Dolphin Street ☐ Half-Naked Truth, The ☐ Hallelujah, I'm a Bum ☐ Honky Tonk ☐ Human Comedy, The ☐ I Live My Life ☐ Key to the City ☐ Kiss Before the Mirror, The ☐ Last of Mrs. Cheyney, The ☐ Laughter ☐ Mortal Storm, The ☐ Naughty Marietta ☐ Paradise for Three ☐ Piccadilly Jim ☐ Port of Seven Seas ☐ Reunion in Vienna ☐ Rosalie ☐ Saratoga ☐ Shop Around the Corner, The ☐ Stratton Story, The ☐ Summer Holiday ☐ Sweethearts ☐ Thousands Cheer ☐ Three Musketeers, The ☐ Tortilla Flat ☐ When Ladies Meet ☐ White Cargo ☐ White Cliffs of Dover, The ☐ Wild Man of Borneo, The ☐ Wizard of Oz, The ☐ Yolanda and the Thief

Morgan, Harry ☐ Against Her Will: An Incident in Baltimore ☐ Appointment with Danger ☐ Barefoot Executive, The ☐ Boots Malone ☐ Cat From Outer Space, The ☐ Charley and the Angel ☐ Dragnet ☐ Far Country, The ☐ Feminist and the Fuzz, The ☐ Flim Flam Man, The ☐ Frankie and Johnny ☐ Gentle Annie ☐ Incident, The ☐ Inherit the Wind ☐ It Started with a Kiss ☐ M*A*S*H—Goodbye, Farewell, Amen ☐ More Wild, Wild West ☐ Saxon Charm, The ☐ Scandalous John ☐ Snowball Express ☐ Support Your Local Gunfighter ☐ Support Your Local Sheriff ☐ Viva Max! ☐ What Did You Do in the War, Daddy? ☐ Yellow Sky

Morgan, Helen ☐ Applause ☐ Frankie and Johnny ☐ Glorifying the American Girl ☐ Go Into Your Dance ☐ Marie Galante ☐ Roadhouse Nights ☐ Show Boat

Morgan, Henry ☐ About Mrs. Leslie ☐ From This Day Forward ☐ High Noon ☐ It Shouldn't Happen to a Dog ☐ Moonrise ☐ Mountain Road, The ☐ Murder, Inc. ☐ My Six Convicts ☐ Not as a Stranger ☐ Ox-Bow Incident, The ☐ Race Street ☐ Scandal Sheet ☐ So This Is New York ☐ Somewhere in the Night ☐ Well, The ☐ When I Grow Up

Morgan, Michele ☐ Benjamin ☐ Bluebeard ☐ Cat and Mouse ☐ Chase, The ☐ Daughters of Destiny ☐ Fabiola ☐ Fallen Idol, The ☐ Grand Maneuver, The ☐ Heart of a Nation, The ☐ Heart of Paris ☐ Higher and Higher ☐ Joan of Paris ☐ La Symphonie Pastorale ☐ Lost Command ☐ Marie Antoinette ☐ Maxime ☐ Mirror Has Two Faces, The ☐ Naked Heart, The ☐ Oasis ☐ Passage to Marseille ☐ Port of Shadows ☐ Red and the Black, The ☐ Seven Deadly Sins ☐ Symphonie Pastorale ☐ Web of Fear

Morgan, Ralph ☐ Dr. Bull ☐ Exclusive ☐ Fast and Loose ☐ Forty Little Mothers ☐ Heart of the Rockies ☐ Impostor, The ☐ Mad Doctor, The ☐ Magnificent Obsession ☐ Mannequin ☐ Monster Maker, The ☐ Mother Carey's Chickens ☐ Night Monster ☐ Power and the Glory, The ☐ Rasputin and the Empress ☐ Sleep My Love ☐ Star of Midnight ☐ Strange Interlude ☐ Way Down South ☐ Weird Woman ☐ Wells Fargo

Moriarty, Cathy ☐ Burndown ☐ Gun in Betty Lou's Handbag, The ☐ Mambo Kings, The ☐ Matinee ☐ Me and the Kid ☐ Neighbors ☐ Pontiac Moon ☐ Raging Bull ☐ Soapdish ☐ White of the Eye

Moriarty, Michael ☐ Bang the Drum Slowly ☐ Dark Tower ☐ Deadliest Season, The ☐ Full Fathom Five ☐ Glass Menagerie, The ☐ Hanoi Hilton, The ☐ Holocaust ☐ Island of the Alive ☐ It's Alive III: Island of the Alive ☐ Last Detail, The ☐ My Old Man's Place ☐ Nitti—The Enforcer ☐ Odd Birds ☐ Pale Rider ☐ Q ☐ Report to the Commissioner ☐ Return to Salem's Lot, A ☐ Secret of the Ice Cave, The ☐ Shoot It Black, Shoot It Blue ☐ Too Far to Go ☐ Troll ☐ Who'll Stop the Rain

Morison, Patricia ☐ Dressed to Kill ☐ Fallen Sparrow ☐ Hitler's Madman ☐ I'm from Missouri ☐ Magnificent Fraud, The ☐ One Night in Lisbon ☐ Persons in Hiding ☐ Rangers of Fortune ☐ Sofia ☐ Song Without End ☐ Untamed ☐ Without Love

Morita, Pat ☐ Amos ☐ Auntie Lee's Meat Pies ☐ Babes in Toyland ☐ Captive Hearts ☐ Collision Course ☐ Do or Die ☐ Even Cowgirls Get the Blues ☐ Farewell to Manzanar ☐ Honeymoon in Vegas ☐ Karate Kid, The ☐ Karate Kid, Part 2, The ☐ Karate Kid, Part 3, The ☐ Lena's Holiday ☐ Next Karate Kid, The ☐ Slapstick of Another Kind

Morley, Karen ☐ Arsene Lupin ☐ Beloved Enemy ☐ Black Fury ☐ Flesh ☐ Framed ☐ Gabriel over the White House ☐ Girl from Scotland Yard, The ☐ Jealousy ☐ Littlest Rebel, The ☐ M ☐ Mask of Fu Manchu, The ☐ Our Daily Bread ☐ Outcast ☐ Scarface ☐ Sin of Madelon Claudet, The

Morley, Robert ☐ African Queen, The ☐ Agent 8 3/4 ☐ Alphabet Murders, The ☐ Battle of the Sexes, The ☐ Beat the Devil ☐ Beau Brummel ☐ Big Blockade, The ☐ Blue Bird, The ☐ Boys, The ☐ Cromwell ☐ Curtain Up ☐ Doctor in Trouble ☐ Doctor's Dilemma ☐ Final Test, The ☐ Foreman Went to France, The ☐ Genghis Khan ☐ Great Expectations ☐ Great Gilbert and Sullivan, The ☐ Great Muppet Caper, The ☐ Hot Millions ☐ Hotel Paradiso ☐ Hugo the Hippo ☐ Human Factor, The ☐ Istanbul ☐ Journey, The ☐ Lady and the Highwayman, The ☐ Libel ☐ Life at the Top ☐ Little Dorrit ☐ Lola ☐ Loophole ☐ Loser Takes All ☐ Major Barbara ☐ Marie Antoinette ☐ Melba ☐ Murder at the Gallop ☐ Nine Hours to Rama ☐ Of Human Bondage ☐ Oh, Heavenly Dog! ☐ Old Dark House, The ☐ Oscar Wilde ☐ Outcast of the Islands ☐ Quentin Durward ☐ Rainbow Jacket, The ☐ Road to Hong Kong, The ☐ Sheriff of Fractured Jaw, The ☐ Take Her, She's Mine ☐ Theatre of Blood ☐ Those Magnificent Men in Their Flying Machines ☐ Topkapi ☐ Way . . . Way Out ☐ Who Is Killing the Great Chefs of Europe? ☐ Young Mr. Pitt, The

Morris, Chester ☐ Aerial Gunner ☐ After Midnight With Boston Blackie ☐ Alias Boston Blackie ☐ Bat Whispers, The ☐ Big House, The ☐ Blind Alley ☐ Blind Spot ☐ Blondie Johnson ☐ Boston Blackie and the Law ☐ Boston Blackie Booked on Suspicion ☐ Boston Blackie Goes Hollywood ☐ Boston Blackie's Chinese Venture ☐ Boston Blackie's Rendevous ☐ Chance of a Lifetime, The ☐ Confessions of Boston Blackie ☐ Corsair ☐ Devil's Playground ☐ Divorcee, The ☐ Five Came Back ☐ Flight from Glory ☐ Frankie and Johnny ☐ Gambler's Choice ☐ Gay Bride, The ☐ Golden Harvest ☐ Great White Hope, The ☐ High Explosive ☐ I Promise to Pay ☐ Meet Boston Blackie ☐ Miracle Man, The ☐ No Hands on the Clock ☐ One Mysterious Night ☐ One Way to Love ☐ Pacific Liner ☐ Public Hero No. 1 ☐ Red-Headed Woman ☐ She Creature, The ☐ Sinners in the Sun ☐ Three Godfathers

Morris, Garrett ☐ Car Wash ☐ Children of the Night ☐ Coneheads, The ☐ Cooley High ☐ Husbands, Wives, Money & Murder ☐ Severed Ties

Morris, Howard ☐ Fluffy ☐ Forty Pounds of Trouble ☐ Life Stinks ☐ Munsters' Revenge, The ☐ Nutty Professor, The ☐ Ten From Your Show of Shows

Morris, Judy ☐ Best Enemies ☐ Between Wars ☐ In Search of Anna ☐ Phar Lap ☐ Plumber, The

Morrison, JoeMorris, Wayne ☐ Angel From Texas, An ☐ Bad Men of Missouri ☐ Big Gusher, The ☐ Big Punch, The ☐ Brother Rat ☐ Brother Rat and a Baby ☐ Bushwackers, The ☐ Deep Valley ☐ Fighting Lawman, The ☐ House Across the Street, The ☐ I Wanted Wings ☐ John Loves Mary ☐ Johnny One Eye ☐ Kid Galahad ☐ Marksman, The ☐ Plunder Road ☐ Return of Dr. X, The ☐ Task Force ☐ Time of Your Life, The ☐ Voice of the Turtle, The ☐ Yellow Fin ☐ Younger Brothers, The

Morrow, Vic ☐ Babysitter, The ☐ Bad News Bears, The ☐ Blackboard Jungle ☐ California Kid, The ☐ Cimarron ☐ Dirty Mary, Crazy Larry ☐ Funeral for an Assassin ☐ Glass House, The ☐ Humanoids from the Deep ☐ Man with the Power, The ☐ Men in War ☐ Message from Space ☐ Night That Panicked America, The ☐ Posse from Hell ☐ Tribute to a Bad Man ☐ Twilight Zone—The Movie

Morse, Robert ☐ Boatniks, The ☐ Guide for the Married Man, A ☐ Honeymoon Hotel ☐ How to Succeed in Business Without Really Trying ☐ Hunk ☐ Loved One, The ☐ Matchmaker, The ☐ Oh Dad, Poor Dad, Mama's Hung You in the Closet and I'm Feeling So Sad ☐ Quick Before It Melts ☐ Where Were You When the Lights Went Out?

Morton, Joe ☐ Brother from Another Planet, The ☐ City of Hope ☐ Crossroads ☐ File on Jill Hatch, The ☐ Howard Beach: Making a Case for Murder ☐ Inkwell, The ☐ Legacy of Lies ☐ Of Mice and Men ☐ Terminator 2—Judgment Day ☐ Trouble in Mind ☐ Walking Dead, The

Mostel, Zero ☐ Angel Levine, The ☐ DuBarry Was a Lady ☐ Enforcer, The ☐ Foreplay ☐ Front, The ☐ Funny Thing Happened on the Way to the Forum, A ☐ Great Bank Robbery, The ☐ Great Catherine ☐ Guy Who Came Back, The ☐ Hot Rock, The ☐ Journey Into Fear ☐ Marco ☐ Mastermind ☐ Model and the Marriage Broker, The ☐ Mr. Belvedere Rings the Bell ☐ Once Upon a Scoundrel ☐ Panic in the Streets ☐ Producers, The ☐ Rhinoceros ☐ Sirocco

Mowbray, Alan ☐ Charlie Chan in London ☐ Ever Since Venus ☐ I Wake Up Screaming ☐ In Person ☐ Innocent Affair, An ☐ Lone Wolf and His Lady, The ☐ Long Lost Father ☐ Lovable Cheat, The ☐ Ma and Pa Kettle at Home ☐ Man from Yesterday, The ☐ Man Who Knew Too Much, The ☐ Mary of Scotland ☐ Merrily We Live ☐ Merton of the Movies ☐ My Darling Clementine ☐ My Gal Loves Music ☐ Night Life of the Gods ☐ Personal Column ☐ Roman Scandals ☐ Slightly Dangerous ☐ Stand-In ☐ Terror By Night ☐ That Hamilton Woman ☐ That Uncertain Feeling ☐ There Goes My Heart ☐ Wagon Master ☐ Way Down South ☐ You're My Everything

Mueller-Stahl, Armin ☐ Angry Harvest ☐ Avalon ☐ Colonel Redl ☐ Forget Mozart

☐ House of the Spirits ☐ Love in Germany, A ☐ Midnight Cop ☐ Music Box ☐ Naked Among the Wolves ☐ Night on Earth ☐ Power of One, The ☐ Utz

Muldaur, Diana ☐ Beyond Reason ☐ McCloud: Who Killed Miss U.S.A.? ☐ McQ ☐ Miracle Worker, The ☐ Number One ☐ One More Train to Rob ☐ Ordeal ☐ Other, The

Mull, Martin ☐ Bad Manners ☐ Boss' Wife, The ☐ Clue ☐ Family Dog—Enemy Dog/Show Dog ☐ Far Out Man ☐ Flicks ☐ FM ☐ History Of White People In America, The—Vol. 2 ☐ History of White People In America, The—Vol. 1 ☐ Home Is Where the Hart Is ☐ Jerk Too, The ☐ Lots of Luck ☐ Mr. Mom ☐ My Bodyguard ☐ Out of Control ☐ Serial ☐ Ski Patrol ☐ Think Big

Mulligan, Richard ☐ Babes in Toyland ☐ Big Bus, The ☐ Fine Mess, A ☐ From the Mixed-Up Files of Mrs. Basil E. Frankweiler ☐ Having Babies III ☐ Irish Whiskey Rebellion ☐ Jealousy ☐ Malibu ☐ Meatballs II ☐ Micki + Maude ☐ One Potato, Two Potato ☐ Poker Alice ☐ S.O.B. ☐ Teachers ☐ Trail of the Pink Panther ☐ Visit to a Chief's Son

Mulroney, Dermot ☐ Bad Girls ☐ Bright Angel ☐ Career Opportunities ☐ Family Pictures ☐ Last Outlaw, The ☐ Long Gone ☐ Point of No Return ☐ Samantha ☐ Silent Tongue ☐ Staying Together ☐ Thing Called Love, The ☐ Where the Day Takes You ☐ Young Guns

Muni, Paul ☐ Angel on My Shoulder ☐ Black Fury ☐ Bordertown ☐ Commandos Strike at Dawn, The ☐ Counter-Attack ☐ Doctor Socrates ☐ Dr. Socrates ☐ Good Earth, The ☐ Hi, Nellie! ☐ Hudson's Bay ☐ I Am a Fugitive from a Chain Gang ☐ Juarez ☐ Last Angry Man, The ☐ Life of Emile Zola, The ☐ Scarface ☐ Song to Remember, A ☐ Story of Louis Pasteur, The ☐ Stranger on the Prowl ☐ Valiant, The ☐ We Are Not Alone

Murphy, Audie ☐ Apache Rifles ☐ Arizona Raiders ☐ Bad Boy ☐ Battle at Bloody Beach ☐ Bullet for a Badman ☐ Cast a Long Shadow ☐ Cimarron Kid, The ☐ Column South ☐ Destry ☐ Duel at Silver Creek, The ☐ Gun Runners, The ☐ Gunfight at Comanche Creek ☐ Gunpoint ☐ Guns of Fort Petticoat, The ☐ Hell Bent for Leather ☐ Joe Butterfly ☐ Kansas Raiders ☐ Night Passage ☐ No Name on the Bullet ☐ Posse from Hell ☐ Quick Gun, The ☐ Quiet American, The ☐ Red Badge of Courage, The ☐ Ride Clear of Diablo ☐ Time for Dying, A ☐ To Hell and Back ☐ Unforgiven, The ☐ Walk the Proud Land ☐ Wild and the Innocent, The ☐ World in My Corner

Murphy, Eddie ☐ 48 Hrs. ☐ Another 48 HRS ☐ Best Defense ☐ Beverly Hills Cop ☐ Beverly Hills Cop II ☐ Beverly Hills Cop III ☐ Boomerang ☐ Coming to America ☐ Distinguished Gentleman, The ☐ Eddie Murphy Raw ☐ Golden Child, The ☐ Harlem Nights ☐ Trading Places

Murphy, George ☐ Arnelo Affair, The ☐ Bataan ☐ Battleground ☐ Big City, The ☐ Border Incident ☐ Broadway Melody of 1940 ☐ Broadway Rhythm ☐ Cynthia ☐ For Me and My Gal ☐ Girl, a Guy, and a Gob, A ☐ Having Wonderful Crime ☐ Hold That Co-ed ☐ Kid Millions ☐ Little Miss Broadway ☐ Little Nellie Kelly ☐ No Questions Asked ☐ Rise and Shine ☐ Show Business ☐ Step Lively ☐ Tenth Avenue Angel ☐ This is the Army ☐ Tom, Dick and Harry ☐ Two Girls on Broadway ☐ Walk East on Beacon ☐ You're a Sweetheart

Murphy, Mary ☐ Beachhead ☐ Crime & Punishment, USA ☐ Electronic Monster, The ☐ Finger of Guilt ☐ Hell's Island ☐ Mad Magician, The ☐ Main Street to Broadway ☐ Make Haste to Live ☐ Man Alone, A ☐ Maverick Queen, The ☐ Sitting Bull ☐ Wild One, The

Murphy, Michael ☐ Brewster McCloud ☐ Class of Miss MacMichael, The ☐ Clean Slate ☐ Cloak & Dagger ☐ Front, The ☐ I Love You, Goodbye ☐ Manhattan ☐ McCabe and Mrs. Miller ☐ Mesmerized ☐ Nashville ☐ Phase IV ☐ Shocker ☐ Strange Behavior ☐ Unmarried Woman, An ☐ Year of Living Dangerously, The

Murphy, Rosemary ☐ Ace Eli and Rodger of the Skies ☐ Any Wednesday ☐ Attic, The ☐ Ben ☐ Eleanor and Franklin ☐ Eleanor and Franklin: The White House Years ☐ Fan's Notes, A ☐ That Night

Murray, Bill ☐ Caddyshack ☐ Ed Wood ☐ Ghostbusters ☐ Ghostbusters II ☐ Groundhog Day ☐ Mad Dog and Glory ☐ Meatballs ☐ Nothing Lasts Forever ☐ Quick Change ☐ Razor's Edge, The ☐ Scrooged ☐ Stripes ☐ Tootsie ☐ What About Bob? ☐ Where the Buffalo Roam

Murray, Don ☐ Advise and Consent ☐ Baby the Rain Must Fall ☐ Bachelor Party, The ☐ Borgia Stick, The ☐ Bus Stop ☐ Conquest of the Planet of the Apes ☐ Deadly Hero ☐ Endless Love ☐ From Hell to Texas ☐ Ghosts Can't Do It ☐ Girl Named Sooner, A ☐ Girl on the Late, Late Show, The ☐ Happy Birthday, Wanda June ☐ Hatful of Rain, A ☐ Hoodlum Priest, The ☐ I Am the Cheese ☐ If Things Were Different ☐ Justin Morgan Had a Horse ☐ Made in Heaven ☐ Mistress ☐ One Foot in Hell ☐ One Man's Way ☐ Quarterback Princess ☐ Rainbow ☐ Shake Hands with the Devil ☐ These Thousand Hills

Murray, Ken ☐ Juke Box Jenny ☐ Man Who Shot Liberty Valance, The ☐ Marshal's Daughter, The ☐ You're a Sweetheart

Murray, Stephen ☐ Four Sided Triangle ☐ Magnet, The ☐ Master of Bankdam, The ☐ Master Spy ☐ Silent Dust ☐ Stranger's Hand, The ☐ Tale of Two Cities, A

Musante, Tony ☐ Bird With the Crystal Plumage, The ☐ Collector's Item ☐ Grissom Gang, The ☐ High Ice ☐ Incident, The ☐ Last Run, The ☐ Mercenary, The ☐ Once a Thief ☐ Rearview Mirror

Muse, Clarence ☐ Black Stallion, The ☐ Invisible Ghost, The ☐ Night World ☐ Riding High ☐ Way Down South

Muti, Ornella ☐ Casanova ☐ Especially on Sunday ☐ Flash Gordon ☐ Life Is Beautiful ☐ Love and Money ☐ Oscar ☐ Swann in Love

Nabors, Jim ☐ Best Little Whorehouse in Texas, The ☐ Cannonball Run II ☐ Gomer Pyle U.S.M.C.—Vol. 1 ☐ Gomer Pyle U.S.M.C.—Vol. 2 ☐ Return to Mayberry ☐ Stroker Ace

Nader, George ☐ Away All Boats ☐ Beyond Atlantis ☐ Carnival Story ☐ Female Animal, The ☐ Flood Tide ☐ Four Girls in Town ☐ Four Guns to the Border ☐ House of 1,000 Dolls ☐ Human Duplicators, The ☐ Lady Godiva ☐ Man Afraid ☐ Monsoon ☐ Nowhere to Go ☐ Overland Telegraph ☐ Six Bridges to Cross ☐ Unguarded Moment, The

Nagel, Conrad ☐ All That Heaven Allows ☐ Dangerous Corner ☐ Du Barry, Woman of Passion ☐ Hell Divers ☐ Hidden Fear ☐ I Want a Divorce ☐ Kiss, The ☐ Kongo ☐ Man Who Understood Women, The ☐ Mysterious Lady, The ☐ One Romantic Night ☐ Stranger in My Arms ☐ Yellow Cargo

Naish, J. Carroll ☐ Beau Geste ☐ Behind the Rising Sun ☐ Black Hand ☐ Blood and Sand ☐ British Agent ☐ Bulldog Drummond in Africa ☐ Confidential ☐ Elmer the Great ☐ Fighter Attack ☐ Frisco Jenny ☐ Fugitive, The ☐ Hanged Man, The ☐ House of Frankenstein ☐ Humoresque ☐ Island of Lost Men ☐ Jackass Mail ☐ Joan of Arc ☐ King of Alcatraz ☐ Mark of the Renegade ☐ Medal for Benny, A ☐ Monster Maker, The ☐ Night Club Scandal ☐ Persons in Hiding ☐ Rage at Dawn ☐ Rebel in Town ☐ Robin Hood of El Dorado, The ☐ Saskatchewan ☐ Sitting Bull ☐ Southerner, The ☐ That Night in Rio ☐ Thunder Trail ☐ Tiger Shark ☐ Tipp-Off Girls ☐ Two Seconds ☐ Typhoon ☐ Upperworld ☐ Violent Saturday ☐ Waterfront ☐ Whistler, The

Naismith, Laurence ☐ Amazing Mr. Blunden, The ☐ Boy on a Dolphin ☐ Bushbaby, The ☐ Eye of the Cat ☐ Greyfriars Bobby ☐ Gypsy Girl ☐ Night to Remember, A ☐ Prince and the Pauper, The ☐ Quest for Love ☐ Scrooge ☐ Sink the Bismarck! ☐ Valley of Gwangi ☐ Village of the Damned ☐ World of Suzie Wong, The

Nakadai, Tatsuya ☐ Conflagration ☐ Face of Another, The ☐ Harakiri ☐ Human Condition, The—Part One: No Greater Love ☐ Human Condition, The—Part Three: A Soldier's Prayer ☐ Human Condition, The—Part Two: The Road to Eternity ☐ Kagemusha ☐ Ran ☐ Sanjuro ☐ Sword of Doom ☐ When a Woman Ascends the Stairs

Namath, Joe ☐ Avalanche Express ☐ C.C. and Company ☐ Chattanooga Choo Choo ☐ Last Rebel, The ☐ Marriage Is Alive and Well ☐ Norwood

Nakamura, Ganjiro ☐ Conflagration ☐ End of Summer, The ☐ Floating Weeds ☐ Odd Obsession

Napier, Alan ☐ Island of Lost Women ☐ Macbeth ☐ Mademoiselle Fifi ☐ Master Minds ☐ Ministry of Fear ☐ Uninvited, The ☐ We Are Not Alone

Napier, Charles ☐ Deep Space ☐ Homicidal Impulse ☐ In Search of a Golden Sky ☐ Instant Justice ☐ Married to the Mob ☐ Melvin and Howard ☐ Miami Blues ☐ Philadelphia ☐ Rambo: First Blood, Part II ☐ Skeeter ☐ Soldier's Fortune

Natwick, Mildred ☐ Against All Flags ☐ Barefoot in the Park ☐ Cheaper by the Dozen ☐ Court Jester, The ☐ Daisy Miller ☐ Dangerous Liaisons ☐ Do Not Fold, Spindle or Mutilate ☐ Enchanted Cottage, The ☐ If It's Tuesday, This Must Be Belgium ☐ Kiss Me Goodbye ☐ Kissing Bandit, The ☐ Long Voyage Home, The ☐ Maltese Bippy, The ☐ Money to Burn ☐ Quiet Man, The ☐ She Wore a Yellow Ribbon ☐ Tammy and the Bachelor ☐ Trouble With Harry, The ☐ Truman Capote's Trilogy ☐ Woman's Vengeance, A ☐ Yolanda and the Thief

Naughton, David ☐ American Werewolf in London, An ☐ Amityville—A New Generation ☐ Getting Physical ☐ Goddess of Love ☐ Hot Dog . . . The Movie ☐ I, Desire ☐ Midnight Madness ☐ Not for Publication ☐ Overexposed ☐ Private Affairs ☐ Separate Vacations ☐ Separate Ways

Neagle, Anna ☐ Bitter Sweet ☐ Courtney Affair, The ☐ Elizabeth of Ladymead ☐ Four Against Fate ☐ Irene ☐ Lady with a Lamp, The ☐ Let's Make Up ☐ Man Who Wouldn't Talk, The ☐ Maytime in Mayfair ☐ Nell Gwyn ☐ No Time for Tears ☐ Nurse Edith Cavell ☐ Odette ☐ Peg of Old Drury ☐ Sixty Glorious Years ☐ Spring in Park Lane ☐ Victoria the Great ☐ Wings and the Woman

Neal, Patricia ☐ All Quiet on the Western Front ☐ Breakfast at Tiffany's ☐ Breaking Point ☐ Bright Leaf ☐ Caroline? ☐ Day the Earth Stood Still, The ☐ Diplomatic Courier ☐ Eric ☐ Face in the Crowd, A ☐ Fountainhead, The ☐ Ghost Story ☐ Happy Mother's Day, Love George ☐ Hasty Heart, The ☐ Heidi ☐ Homecoming—A Christmas Story, The ☐ Hud ☐ In Harm's Way ☐ John Loves Mary ☐ Love Affair, A: The Eleanor and Lou Gehrig Story ☐ Love Leads the Way ☐ Night Digger, The ☐ Operation Pacific ☐ Passage, The ☐ Raton Pass ☐ Something for the Birds ☐ Stranger From Venus ☐ Subject Was Roses, The ☐ Three Secrets ☐ Unremarkable Life, An

☐ Washington Story ☐ Weekend With Father

Neeson, Liam ☐ Bounty, The ☐ Crossing the Line ☐ Darkman ☐ Dead Pool, The ☐ Deception ☐ Duet for One ☐ Ethan Frome ☐ Excalibur ☐ Good Mother, The ☐ High Spirits ☐ Hold the Dream ☐ Husbands and Wives ☐ Krull ☐ Leap of Faith ☐ Mission, The ☐ Nell ☐ Next of Kin ☐ Satisfaction ☐ Schindler's List ☐ Shining Through ☐ Suspect ☐ Under Suspicion

Neill, Sam ☐ Attack Force Z ☐ Blood of Others, The ☐ Cry in the Dark, A ☐ Dead Calm ☐ Enigma ☐ Family Pictures ☐ Final Conflict, The ☐ For Love Alone ☐ From a Far Country: Pope John Paul II ☐ Good Wife, The ☐ Hostage ☐ Hunt for Red October, The ☐ In the Mouth of Madness ☐ Ivanhoe ☐ Jurassic Park ☐ Memoirs of an Invisible Man ☐ My Brilliant Career ☐ One Against the Wind ☐ Piano, The ☐ Plenty ☐ Possession ☐ Question of Faith ☐ Reilly: The Ace of Spies ☐ Sirens ☐ Until the End of the World

Nelligan, Kate ☐ Bethune ☐ Control ☐ Count of Monte Cristo, The ☐ Dracula ☐ Eleni ☐ Eye of the Needle ☐ Fatal Instinct ☐ Frankie and Johnny ☐ Love and Hate: A Marriage Made in Hell ☐ Prince of Tides, The ☐ Shadows and Fog ☐ Terror Stalks the Class Reunion ☐ Victims ☐ Wolf

Nelson, Barry ☐ Borgia Stick, The ☐ Climb an Angry Mountain ☐ Eyes in the Night ☐ First Traveling Saleslady, The ☐ Island Claws ☐ Man with My Face, The ☐ Mary, Mary ☐ Pete 'n' Tillie ☐ Rio Rita ☐ Shadow of the Thin Man ☐ Winged Victory

Nelson, Craig T. ☐ Action Jackson ☐ Alex: The Life of a Child ☐ All the Right Moves ☐ And Justice for All ☐ Chicago Story ☐ Extreme Close-Up ☐ Fire Next Time, The ☐ Josephine Baker Story, The ☐ Killing Fields, The ☐ Man, Woman and Child ☐ Me and Him ☐ Murder in Texas ☐ Murderers Among Us: The Simon Wiesenthal Story ☐ Osterman Weekend, The ☐ Poltergeist ☐ Poltergeist II: The Other Side ☐ Rachel River ☐ Rage ☐ Red Riding Hood ☐ Silkwood ☐ Troop Beverly Hills ☐ Turner & Hooch

Nelson, Gene ☐ Atomic Man, The ☐ Brand New Life, A ☐ Crime Wave ☐ Daughter of Rosie O'Grady, The ☐ Lullaby of Broadway ☐ Oklahoma! ☐ Painting the Clouds with Sunshine ☐ She's Back on Broadway ☐ She's Working Her Way Through College ☐ So This Is Paris ☐ Tea for Two ☐ Three Sailors and a Girl ☐ West Point Story

Nelson, Harriet ☐ Adventures of Ozzie and Harriet, The ☐ Adventures of Ozzie and Harriet, The ☐ Confessions of Boston Blackie ☐ Here Come the Nelsons

Nelson, Judd ☐ Billionaire Boys Club ☐ Blindfold: Acts Of Obsession ☐ Blue City ☐ Breakfast Club, The ☐ Dark Backward, The ☐ Entangled ☐ Fandango ☐ From the Hip ☐ Hail Caesar ☐ Hiroshima: Out of the Ashes ☐ Making the Grade ☐ New Jack City ☐ Primary Motive ☐ Relentless ☐ St. Elmo's Fire

Nelson, Ozzie ☐ Adventures of Ozzie and Harriet, The ☐ Adventures of Ozzie and Harriet, The ☐ Here Come the Nelsons ☐ Hi, Good Lookin' ☐ Impossible Years, The ☐ People Are Funny ☐ Sweetheart of the Campus

Nelson, Ricky ☐ Here Come the Nelsons ☐ Rio Bravo ☐ Tale of Four Wishes, A ☐ Wackiest Ship in the Army, The

Nelson, Willie ☐ Another Pair of Aces: Three of a Kind ☐ Baja Oklahoma ☐ Barbarosa ☐ Electric Horseman, The ☐ Honeysuckle Rose ☐ Last Days of Frank and Jesse James, The ☐ Pair of Aces ☐ Red-Headed Stranger ☐ Songwriter ☐ Stagecoach ☐ Texas Guns ☐ Thief

Nero, Franco ☐ 21 Hours at Munich ☐ Battle of Neretva, The ☐ Bible, The ☐ Camelot ☐ Challenge to White Fang ☐ Confessions of a Police Captain ☐ Deaf Smith and Johnny Ears ☐ Die Hard 2 ☐ Don't Turn the Other Cheek ☐ Enter the Ninja ☐ Fifth Day of Peace, The ☐ Force 10 from Navarone ☐ Girl, The ☐ Harold Robbins' the Pirate ☐ High Crime ☐ Last Four Days, The ☐ Legend of Valentino, The ☐ Man with Bogart's Face, The ☐ Mercenary, The ☐ Pope Joan ☐ Querelle ☐ Salamander, The ☐ Sardinia: Kidnapped ☐ Shark Hunter, The ☐ Submission ☐ Sweet Country ☐ Tramplers, The ☐ Tristana ☐ Virgin and the Gypsy, The ☐ Wagner ☐ Young Catherine

Nesbitt, Cathleen ☐ Affair to Remember, An ☐ Black Widow ☐ Chamber of Horrors ☐ Desiree ☐ Family Plot ☐ French Connection II ☐ Passing of the Third Floor Back, The ☐ So Long at the Fair ☐ Staircase

Nettleton, Lois ☐ Any Second Now ☐ Bamboo Saucer, The ☐ Butterfly ☐ Come Fly with Me ☐ Deadly Blessing ☐ Dirty Dingus Magee ☐ Echoes of a Summer ☐ Fear on Trial ☐ Honkers, The ☐ Mail Order Bride ☐ Man in the Glass Booth, The ☐ Manhunt for Claude Dallas ☐ Period of Adjustment ☐ Soggy Bottom USA

Neville, John ☐ Adventures of Baron Munchausen, The ☐ Adventures of Gerard, The ☐ I Like Money ☐ Oscar Wilde ☐ Study in Terror, A ☐ Unearthly Stranger, The

Newhart, Bob ☐ Catch-22 ☐ Cold Turkey ☐ First Family ☐ Hell Is for Heroes ☐ Hot Millions ☐ Little Miss Marker ☐ Marathon ☐ On a Clear Day You Can See Forever ☐ Rescuers Down Under, The ☐ Rescuers, The ☐ Thursday's Game

Newley, Anthony ☐ Bandit of Zhobe, The ☐ Blade in Hong Kong ☐ Can Hieronymus Merkin Ever Forget Mercy Humppe and Find True Happiness? ☐ Cockleshell Heroes, The ☐ Coins in the Fountain ☐ Doctor Dolittle

☐ Family Hour Special—Animal Talk ☐ Garbage Pail Kids Movie, The ☐ Good Companions, The ☐ High Flight ☐ How to Murder a Rich Uncle ☐ It Seemed Like a Good Idea at the Time ☐ Jazz Boat ☐ Killers of Kilimanjaro ☐ Malibu ☐ Man Inside, The ☐ Mr. Quilp ☐ Oliver Twist ☐ Small World of Sammy Lee, The ☐ Stagecoach ☐ Sweet November ☐ Vice Versa ☐ X, the Unknown

Newman, Barry ☐ Amy ☐ City on Fire ☐ Fatal Vision ☐ Fear Is the Key ☐ Having It All ☐ Pretty Boy Floyd ☐ Salzburg Connection, The ☐ Vanishing Point

Newman, Laraine ☐ American Hot Wax ☐ Invaders from Mars ☐ Perfect ☐ Problem Child 2 ☐ Tunnelvision ☐ Wholly Moses ☐ Witchboard 2: The Devil's Doorway

Newman, Nanette ☐ Captain Nemo and the Underwater City ☐ Faces in the Dark ☐ House of Mystery ☐ International Velvet ☐ League of Gentlemen, The ☐ Long Ago Tomorrow ☐ Madwoman of Chaillot, The ☐ Man at the Top ☐ Mystery of Edwin Drood, The ☐ Seance on a Wet Afternoon ☐ Stepford Wives, The ☐ Twice Around the Daffodils ☐ Whisperers, The ☐ Wrong Arm of the Law ☐ Wrong Box, The

Newman, Paul ☐ Absence of Malice ☐ Adventures of a Young Man ☐ Blaze ☐ Buffalo Bill and the Indians ☐ Butch Cassidy and the Sundance Kid ☐ Cat on a Hot Tin Roof ☐ Color of Money, The ☐ Cool Hand Luke ☐ Drowning Pool, The ☐ Exodus ☐ Fat Man and Little Boy ☐ Fort Apache, The Bronx ☐ From the Terrace ☐ Harper ☐ Harry and Son ☐ Helen Morgan Story, The ☐ Hombre ☐ Hud ☐ Hudsucker Proxy, The ☐ Hustler, The ☐ Lady L ☐ Left-Handed Gun, The ☐ Life and Times of Judge Roy Bean, The ☐ Long Hot Summer, The ☐ Mackintosh Man, The ☐ Mr. & Mrs. Bridge ☐ New Kind of Love, A ☐ Nobody's Fool ☐ Outrage, The ☐ Paris Blues ☐ Pocket Money ☐ Prize, The ☐ Quintet ☐ Rack, The ☐ Rally 'Round the Flag, Boys! ☐ Secret War of Harry Frigg, The ☐ Silent Movie ☐ Silver Chalice, The ☐ Slap Shot ☐ Somebody Up There Likes Me ☐ Sometimes a Great Notion ☐ Sting, The ☐ Sweet Bird of Youth ☐ Torn Curtain ☐ Towering Inferno, The ☐ Until They Sail ☐ Verdict, The ☐ What a Way to Go! ☐ When Time Ran Out . . . ☐ Winning ☐ Young Philadelphians, The

Newton, Robert ☐ Androcles and the Lion ☐ Around the World in 80 Days ☐ Beachcomber, The ☐ Beachcomber, The ☐ Blackbeard, the Pirate ☐ Desert Rats, The ☐ Epic that Never Was, The ☐ Gaslight ☐ Green Cockatoo, The ☐ Hatter's Castle ☐ Haunted Honeymoon ☐ Henry V ☐ Hidden Room, The ☐ Jamaica Inn ☐ Kiss the Blood Off My Hands ☐ Les Miserables ☐ Long John Silver ☐ Major Barbara ☐ Odd Man Out ☐ Oliver Twist ☐ Poison Pen ☐ Soldiers Three ☐ This Happy Breed ☐ Tom Brown's Schooldays ☐ Treasure Island ☐ Wings and the Woman

Ngor, Haing S. ☐ Ambition ☐ Heaven and Earth ☐ In Love and War ☐ Iron Triangle, The ☐ Killing Fields, The ☐ Last Flight Out

Nichols, Barbara ☐ Dear Heart ☐ House of Women ☐ Human Duplicators, The ☐ Manfish ☐ Naked and the Dead, The ☐ Scarface Mob, The ☐ Sweet Smell of Success ☐ Ten North Frederick ☐ Where the Boys Are ☐ Who Was That Lady? ☐ Woman Obsessed

Nicholson, Jack ☐ Back Door to Hell ☐ Batman ☐ Border, The ☐ Broadcast News ☐ Broken Land, The ☐ Carnal Knowledge ☐ Chinatown ☐ Cry Baby Killer, The ☐ Easy Rider ☐ Elephant's Child ☐ Ensign Pulver ☐ Few Good Men, A ☐ Five Easy Pieces ☐ Flight to Fury ☐ Fortune, The ☐ Goin' South ☐ Head ☐ Heartburn ☐ Hell's Angels on Wheels ☐ Hoffa ☐ Ironweed ☐ King of Marvin Gardens, The ☐ Last Detail, The ☐ Last Tycoon, The ☐ Little Shop of Horrors, The ☐ Man Trouble ☐ Missouri Breaks, The ☐ On a Clear Day You Can See Forever ☐ One Flew over the Cuckoo's Nest ☐ Passenger, The ☐ Postman Always Rings Twice, The ☐ Prizzi's Honor ☐ Psych Out ☐ Raven, The ☐ Rebel Rousers ☐ Reds ☐ Shining, The ☐ Shooting, The ☐ Terms of Endearment ☐ Terror, The ☐ Tommy ☐ Two Jakes, The ☐ Wild Ride, The ☐ Witches of Eastwick, The ☐ Wolf

Nielsen, Leslie ☐ Airplane! ☐ All I Want for Christmas ☐ Amsterdam Kill, The ☐ And Millions Will Die ☐ Beau Geste ☐ Blade in Hong Kong ☐ Change of Mind ☐ City on Fire ☐ Counterpoint ☐ Creepshow ☐ Dangerous Curves ☐ Dark Intruder ☐ Day of the Animals ☐ Fatal Confession: A Father Dowling Mystery ☐ Forbidden Planet ☐ Four Rode Out ☐ Foxfire Light ☐ Grand Jury ☐ Gunfight in Abilene ☐ Hawaii Five-O ☐ Home Is Where the Hart Is ☐ Hot Summer Night ☐ Incident in San Francisco ☐ Letters, The ☐ Naked Gun 2 1/2: The Smell of Fear, The ☐ Naked Gun 33 1/3: The Final Insult ☐ Naked Gun, The ☐ Night Slaves ☐ Night the Bridge Fell Down, The ☐ Opposite Sex, The ☐ Patriot, The ☐ Police Squad!—Help Wanted ☐ Prom Night ☐ Reckless Disregard ☐ Reluctant Astronaut, The ☐ Repossessed ☐ Resurrection of Zachary Wheeler, The ☐ Sheepman, The ☐ Snatched ☐ Soul Man ☐ Surf Ninjas ☐ Tammy and the Bachelor ☐ Vagabond King, The ☐ Viva Knievel!

Nimoy, Leonard ☐ Alpha Caper, The ☐ Assault on the Wayne ☐ Baffled ☐ Balcony, The ☐ Catlow ☐ Invasion of the Body Snatchers ☐ Never Forget ☐ Pagemaster, The ☐ Rhubarb ☐ Satan's Satellites ☐ Star Trek 25th Anniversary Special ☐ Star Trek II: The Wrath of Khan ☐ Star Trek IV: The Voyage Home ☐ Star Trek V: The Final Frontier ☐ Star Trek VI: The Undiscovered Country ☐ Star Trek:

The Motion Picture ☐ Star Trek—Episode 1: The Cage ☐ Transformers, The ☐ Woman Called Golda, A

Niven, David ☐ 55 Days at Peking ☐ Around the World in 80 Days ☐ Ask Any Girl ☐ Bachelor Mother ☐ Bedtime Story ☐ Before Winter Comes ☐ Beloved Enemy ☐ Best of Enemies, The ☐ Better Late Than Never ☐ Birds and the Bees, The ☐ Bishop's Wife, The ☐ Bluebeard's Eighth Wife ☐ Bonjour Tristesse ☐ Bonnie Prince Charlie ☐ Brain, The ☐ Candleshoe ☐ Casino Royale ☐ Charge of the Light Brigade, The ☐ Conquered City, The ☐ Court Martial ☐ Curse of the Pink Panther ☐ Dawn Patrol, The ☐ Death on the Nile ☐ Dinner at the Ritz ☐ Dodsworth ☐ Enchantment ☐ Escape to Athena ☐ Eternally Yours ☐ Extraordinary Seaman, The ☐ Eye of the Devil ☐ Fighting Pimpernel, The ☐ Four Men and a Prayer ☐ Guns of Darkness ☐ Guns of Navarone, The ☐ Happy Anniversary ☐ Happy Go Lovely ☐ Immortal Battalion, The ☐ Impossible Years, The ☐ Island Rescue ☐ King's Thief, The ☐ King, Queen, Knave ☐ Kiss for Corliss, A ☐ Kiss in the Dark, A ☐ Lady L ☐ Lady Says No, The ☐ Little Hut, The ☐ Love Lottery, The ☐ Magnificent Doll ☐ Mayfair Bank Caper, The ☐ Moon Is Blue, The ☐ Murder by Death ☐ My Man Godfrey ☐ No Deposit, No Return ☐ Oh, Men! Oh, Women! ☐ Old Dracula ☐ Other Love, The ☐ Paper Tiger ☐ Perfect Marriage, The ☐ Pink Panther, The ☐ Please Don't Eat the Daisies ☐ Prudence and the Pill ☐ Raffles ☐ Real Glory, The ☐ Rough Cut ☐ Sea Wolves, The ☐ Separate Tables ☐ Soldiers Three ☐ Spitfire ☐ Stairway to Heaven ☐ Statue, The ☐ Three Blind Mice ☐ Toast of New Orleans, The ☐ Trail of the Pink Panther ☐ Where the Spies Are ☐ Wuthering Heights

Noiret, Philippe ☐ Alexander ☐ All the Gold in the World ☐ Assassination Bureau, The ☐ Aurora ☐ Birgit Haas Must Be Killed ☐ Cinema Paradiso ☐ Clockmaker, The ☐ Coup de Torchon ☐ Dear Detective ☐ Especially on Sunday ☐ Family, The ☐ Give Her the Moon ☐ Holes, The ☐ Judge and the Assassin, The ☐ Justine ☐ L'Etoile du Nord ☐ Le Secret ☐ Let Joy Reign Supreme ☐ Let's Hope It's a Girl ☐ Life and Nothing But ☐ Matter of Resistance, A ☐ Murphy's War ☐ My New Partner ☐ Night Flight from Moscow ☐ Three Brothers ☐ Topaz ☐ Uranus ☐ Zazie

Nolan, Lloyd ☐ Abandon Ship! ☐ Bad Boy ☐ Bataan ☐ Big Brown Eyes ☐ Blue, White and Perfect ☐ Blues in the Night ☐ Buy Me That Town ☐ Captain Eddie ☐ Circumstantial Evidence ☐ Circus World ☐ Crazylegs ☐ Dangerous to Know ☐ Easy Living ☐ Ebb Tide ☐ Every Day's a Holiday ☐ Exclusive ☐ Fire! ☐ Girl Hunters, The ☐ Girl of the Night ☐ Guadalcanal Diary ☐ Hannah and Her Sisters ☐ Hatful of Rain, A ☐ House Across the Bay, The ☐ House on 92nd Street ☐ Internes Can't Take Money ☐ Island in the Sky ☐ Isn't It Shocking? ☐ It Happened in Flatbush ☐ Johnny Apollo ☐ Just Off Broadway ☐ King of Alcatraz ☐ Lady in the Lake ☐ Last Hunt, The ☐ Lemon Drop Kid, The ☐ Magnificent Fraud, The ☐ Man I Married, The ☐ Man Who Wouldn't Die, The ☐ Man Who Wouldn't Talk, The ☐ Manila Calling ☐ Michael Shayne, Private Detective ☐ Never Too Late ☐ Peyton Place ☐ Portrait in Black ☐ Santiago ☐ She Couldn't Take It ☐ Somewhere in the Night ☐ Street with No Name ☐ Sun Comes Up, The ☐ Susan Slade ☐ Texas Rangers, The ☐ Time to Kill ☐ Tipp-Off Girls ☐ Toward the Unknown ☐ Tree Grows in Brooklyn, A ☐ Wells Fargo ☐ Wild Harvest

Nolte, Nick ☐ 48 Hrs. ☐ Another 48 HRS ☐ Blue Chips ☐ California Kid, The ☐ Cannery Row ☐ Cape Fear ☐ Deep, The ☐ Down and Out in Beverly Hills ☐ Everybody Wins ☐ Extreme Prejudice ☐ Farewell to the King ☐ Grace Quigley ☐ Heart Beat ☐ I'll Do Anything ☐ Lorenzo's Oil ☐ New York Stories ☐ North Dallas Forty ☐ Prince of Tides, The ☐ Q & A ☐ Teachers ☐ Three Fugitives ☐ Under Fire ☐ Weeds ☐ Who'll Stop the Rain

Noonan, Tommy ☐ Bundle of Joy ☐ Gentlemen Prefer Blondes ☐ Girl Most Likely, The ☐ Jungle Patrol ☐ Manhunter ☐ Monster Squad, The ☐ Promises! Promises! ☐ Robocop 2 ☐ Star Is Born, A ☐ Three Nuts in Search of a Bolt ☐ Violent Saturday ☐ What Happened Was . . .

Norris, Chuck ☐ Braddock: Missing in Action III ☐ Breaker! Breaker! ☐ Code of Silence ☐ Deadliest Art, The: The Best of the Martial Arts Films, The ☐ Delta Force 2—Operation Stranglehold ☐ Delta Force, The ☐ Eye for an Eye, An ☐ Firewalker ☐ Force of One, A ☐ Forced Vengeance ☐ Good Guys Wear Black ☐ Hero and the Terror, The ☐ Hitman, The ☐ Invasion, U.S.A. ☐ Lone Wolf McQuade ☐ Missing in Action ☐ Missing in Action 2: The Beginning ☐ Missing in Action III: Braddock ☐ Octagon, The ☐ One Riot, One Ranger ☐ Return of the Dragon ☐ Sidekicks ☐ Silent Rage ☐ Slaughter in San Francisco ☐ Warrior Within, The

North, Jay ☐ Maya ☐ Miracle of the Hills, The ☐ Teacher, The ☐ Zebra in the Kitchen

North, Sheree ☐ Amateur Night at the Dixie Bar and Grill ☐ Best Things in Life Are Free, The ☐ Breakout ☐ How to Be Very, Very Popular ☐ In Love and War ☐ Lawman ☐ Legs ☐ Lieutenant Wore Skirts, The ☐ Madigan ☐ Maneater ☐ Maniac Cop ☐ Mardi Gras ☐ Marilyn: The Untold Story ☐ No Down Payment ☐ Organization, The ☐ Trouble With Girls, The ☐ Way to the Gold, The

Nouri, Michael ☐ Between Two Women ☐ Changes ☐ Contract on Cherry Street ☐ Flashdance ☐ Gangster Wars ☐ GoBots: Battle of the Rock Lords ☐ Hidden, The ☐ Imagemaker, The ☐ Little Vegas ☐ Project: Alien ☐ Psychic ☐ Quiet Victory: The Charlie Wedemeyer Story ☐ Rage of Angels: The Story Continues ☐ Total Exposure

Novak, Kim ☐ Amorous Adventures of Moll Flanders, The ☐ Bell, Book and Candle ☐ Boys' Night Out ☐ Children, The ☐ Eddy Duchin Story, The ☐ Five Against the House ☐ Great Bank Robbery, The ☐ Jeanne Eagels ☐ Just a Gigolo ☐ Kiss Me, Stupid ☐ Legend of Lylah Clare, The ☐ Liebestraum ☐ Malibu ☐ Man with the Golden Arm ☐ Middle of the Night ☐ Mirror Crack'd, The ☐ Notorious Landlady, The ☐ Of Human Bondage ☐ Pal Joey ☐ Phffft! ☐ Picnic ☐ Pushover ☐ Strangers When We Meet ☐ Vertigo ☐ White Buffalo, The

Nureyev, Rudolf ☐ Don Quixote ☐ Exposed ☐ Most Beautiful Ballets, The ☐ Romeo and Juliet ☐ Swan Lake ☐ Valentino

Nuyen, France ☐ Black Water Gold ☐ Deathmoon ☐ Diamond Head ☐ Girl Named Tamiko, A ☐ In Love and War ☐ Joy Luck Club, The ☐ Last Time I Saw Archie, The ☐ Man in the Middle ☐ One More Train to Rob ☐ Passion to Kill, A ☐ Satan Never Sleeps ☐ South Pacific

O'Brian, Hugh ☐ Africa—Texas Style ☐ Ambush Bay ☐ Back to God's Country ☐ Battle at Apache Pass, The ☐ Brass Legend, The ☐ Broken Lance ☐ Cimarron Kid, The ☐ Come Fly with Me ☐ Doin' Time on Planet Earth ☐ Fantasy Island ☐ Fiend Who Walked the West, The ☐ Fighting Coast Guard ☐ Fireman Save My Child ☐ Gambler Returns: The Luck of the Draw, The ☐ Game of Death ☐ Harpy ☐ Killer Force ☐ Lawless Breed, The ☐ Love Has Many Faces ☐ Man from the Alamo, The ☐ Meet Me at the Fair ☐ Murder on Flight 502 ☐ Raiders, The ☐ Return of Jesse James, The ☐ Rocket Ship X-M ☐ Sally and Saint Anne ☐ Saskatchewan ☐ Seminole ☐ Shootist, The ☐ Son of Ali Baba ☐ Ten Little Indians ☐ White Feather

O'Brien, Edmond ☐ 1984 ☐ 711 Ocean Drive ☐ Act of Murder, An ☐ Admiral Was a Lady, The ☐ Amazing Mrs. Holliday, The ☐ Another Part of the Forest ☐ Backfire ☐ Barefoot Contessa, The ☐ Between Midnight and Dawn ☐ Big Land, The ☐ Bigamist, The ☐ Birdman of Alcatraz ☐ China Venture ☐ Cry in the Night, A ☐ D.O.A. ☐ Double Life, A ☐ Fantastic Voyage ☐ Fighter Squadron ☐ For the Love of Mary ☐ Girl Can't Help It, The ☐ Girl, a Guy, and a Gob, A ☐ Great Impostor, The ☐ Hanged Man, The ☐ Hitch-Hiker, The ☐ Isn't It Shocking? ☐ Julius Caesar ☐ Killers, The ☐ Last Voyage, The ☐ Love God?, The ☐ Lucky Luciano ☐ Man in the Dark ☐ Man Who Shot Liberty Valance, The ☐ Moon Pilot ☐ Obliging Young Lady ☐ Outsider, The ☐ Parachute Battalion ☐ Pete Kelly's Blues ☐ Rack, The ☐ Redhead and the Cowboy, The ☐ Seven Days in May ☐ Shield For Murder ☐ Silver City ☐ Synanon ☐ Turning Point, The ☐ Up Periscope ☐ Warpath ☐ Web, The ☐ White Heat ☐ Wild Bunch, The ☐ Winged Victory

O'Brien, George ☐ Daniel Boone ☐ Dude Ranger, The ☐ Fighting Gringo, The ☐ Fort Apache ☐ Gold Raiders ☐ Golden West, The ☐ Hard Rock Harrigan ☐ Hollywood Cowboy ☐ Iron Horse, The ☐ Johnstown Flood, The ☐ Marshal of Mesa City, The ☐ Mystery Ranch ☐ Noah's Ark ☐ Renegade Ranger ☐ Salute ☐ Seas Beneath, The ☐ She Wore a Yellow Ribbon ☐ Sunrise ☐ Thunder Mountain ☐ Trouble in Sundown

O'Brien, Margaret ☐ Amy ☐ Bad Bascomb ☐ Big City, The ☐ Canterville Ghost, The ☐ Dr. Gillespie's Criminal Case ☐ Glory ☐ Heller in Pink Tights ☐ Her First Romance ☐ Jane Eyre ☐ Journey for Margaret ☐ Little Women ☐ Lost Angel ☐ Meet Me in St. Louis ☐ Music for Millions ☐ Our Vines Have Tender Grapes ☐ Secret Garden, The ☐ Tenth Avenue Angel ☐ Three Wise Fools ☐ Unfinished Dance, The

O'Brien, Pat ☐ 'Til We Meet Again ☐ Air Mail ☐ Angels with Dirty Faces ☐ Bombardier ☐ Bombshell ☐ Boy Meets Girl ☐ Boy with Green Hair, The ☐ Broadway ☐ Bureau of Missing Persons ☐ Castle on the Hudson ☐ Ceiling Zero ☐ China Clipper ☐ College Coach ☐ Consolation Marriage ☐ Cowboy from Brooklyn, The ☐ Crack-Up ☐ Criminal Lawyer ☐ Devil Dogs of the Air ☐ End, The ☐ Escape to Glory ☐ Fighting 69th, The ☐ Fighting Father Dunne ☐ Fireball, The ☐ Flight Lieutenant ☐ Flirtation Walk ☐ Flowing Gold ☐ Flying High ☐ Front Page, The ☐ Gambling Lady ☐ Garden of the Moon ☐ Great O'Malley, The ☐ Having Wonderful Crime ☐ Hell's House ☐ Here Comes the Navy ☐ His Butler's Sister ☐ In Caliente ☐ Indianapolis Speedway ☐ Inside Detroit ☐ Irish in Us, The ☐ Iron Major, The ☐ Johnny One Eye ☐ Knute Rockne, All American ☐ Last Hurrah, The ☐ Man Alive ☐ Marine Raiders ☐ Oil for the Lamps of China ☐ Okinawa ☐ Over-the-Hill Gang, The ☐ Page Miss Glory ☐ People Against O'Hara, The ☐ Perilous Holiday ☐ Public Enemy's Wife ☐ San Quentin ☐ Slightly Honorable ☐ Some Like It Hot ☐ Torrid Zone ☐ Twenty Million Sweethearts ☐ Virtue

O'Connell, Arthur ☐ 7 Faces of Dr. Lao ☐ Anatomy of a Murder ☐ Ben ☐ Birds Do It ☐ Bus Stop ☐ Cimarron ☐ Follow That Dream ☐ Gidget ☐ Hiding Place, The ☐ Hound-Dog Man ☐ If He Hollers, Let Him Go ☐ Kissin' Cousins ☐ Man of the West ☐ Misty ☐ Monte Carlo Story, The ☐ Picnic ☐ Pocketful of Miracles ☐ Reluctant Astronaut, The ☐ Solid Gold Cadillac, The ☐ Third Day, The ☐ Voice in the Mirror, The ☐ Whistle at Eaton Falls, The ☐ Your Cheatin' Heart

O'Connor, Carroll ☐ All in the Family 20th Anniversary Special ☐ By Love Possessed ☐ Death of a Gunfighter ☐ Devil's Brigade, The ☐ Doctor's Wives ☐ Father Clements Story, The ☐ Fear No Evil ☐ Fever in the Blood, A ☐ For Love of Ivy ☐ Hawaii ☐ Lad: A Dog ☐ Last Hurrah, The ☐ Law and Disorder ☐ Lonely Are the Brave ☐ Marlowe ☐ Not with My Wife You Don't! ☐ Point Blank ☐ Warning Shot ☐ Waterhole #3 ☐ What Did You Do in the War, Daddy?

O'Connor, Donald ☐ Anything Goes ☐ Are You with It? ☐ Buster Keaton Story, The ☐ Call Me Madam ☐ Chip Off the Old Block ☐ Cry for Happy ☐ Feudin', Fussin' and A-Fightin' ☐ Francis ☐ Francis Covers the Big Town ☐ Francis Goes to the Races ☐ Francis Goes to West Point ☐ Francis in the Navy ☐ Francis Joins the Wacs ☐ Get Hep to Love ☐ I Love Melvin ☐ Merry Monahans, The ☐ Milkman, The ☐ Million Dollar Legs ☐ On Your Toes ☐ Sing, You Sinners ☐ Singin' in the Rain ☐ Something in the Wind ☐ That Funny Feeling ☐ That's Entertainment ☐ There's No Business Like Show Business ☐ This Is the Life ☐ Toys ☐ Walking My Baby Back Home ☐ Wonders of Aladdin, The

O'Connor, Una ☐ Adventures of Robin Hood, The ☐ Always in My Heart ☐ Barretts of Wimpole Street, The ☐ Bride of Frankenstein, The ☐ Canterville Ghost, The ☐ Cavalcade ☐ Chained ☐ Christmas in Connecticut ☐ Corpse Came C.O.D., The ☐ David Copperfield ☐ Fighting Father Dunne ☐ He Stayed for Breakfast ☐ Holy Matrimony ☐ Informer, The ☐ Invisible Man, The ☐ It All Came True ☐ Lost Honeymoon ☐ My Pal, Wolf ☐ Personal Property ☐ Plough and the Stars, The ☐ Return of Monte Cristo, The ☐ This Land Is Mine ☐ Unexpected Guest ☐ We Are Not Alone ☐ Witness for the Prosecution

O'Donnell, Chris ☐ Circle of Friends ☐ Fried Green Tomatoes ☐ Men Don't Leave ☐ Scent of a Woman ☐ School Ties ☐ Three Musketeers, The

O'Donnell, Rosie ☐ Another Stakeout ☐ Car 54, Where Are You? ☐ Exit to Eden ☐ Flintstones, The ☐ League of Their Own, A ☐ Sleepless in Seattle

O'Hara, Catherine ☐ After Hours ☐ Beetlejuice ☐ Home Alone ☐ Home Alone 2: Lost in New York ☐ Little Vegas ☐ Nightmare Before Christmas, The ☐ Paper, The ☐ Really Weird Tales ☐ Rock & Rule ☐ Shmenges, The—The Last Polka ☐ There Goes the Neighborhood

O'Hara, Maureen ☐ Against All Flags ☐ At Sword's Point ☐ Bagdad ☐ Battle of the Villa Fiorita, The ☐ Big Jake ☐ Bill of Divorcement, A ☐ Black Swan, The ☐ Buffalo Bill ☐ Comanche Territory ☐ Dance, Girl, Dance ☐ Deadly Companions, The ☐ Do You Love Me? ☐ Fallen Sparrow ☐ Father Was a Fullback ☐ Flame of Araby ☐ Forbidden Street, The ☐ Foxes of Harrow, The ☐ Homestretch, The ☐ How Do I Love Thee? ☐ How Green Was My Valley ☐ Hunchback of Notre Dame, The ☐ Immortal Sergeant, The ☐ Jamaica Inn ☐ Kangaroo ☐ Lady Godiva ☐ Lisbon ☐ Long Gray Line, The ☐ Magnificent Matador, The ☐ McLintock! ☐ Miracle on 34th Street ☐ Mr. Hobbs Takes a Vacation ☐ Only the Lonely ☐ Our Man in Havana ☐ Parent Trap, The ☐ Quiet Man, The ☐ Rare Breed, The ☐ Red Pony, The ☐ Redhead from Wyoming, The ☐ Rio Grande ☐ Sentimental Journey ☐ Sinbad the Sailor ☐ Sitting Pretty ☐ Spanish Main, The ☐ Spencer's Mountain ☐ This Land Is Mine ☐ To the Shores of Tripoli ☐ Tripoli ☐ War Arrow ☐ Wings of Eagles, The ☐ Woman's Secret, A

O'Herlihy, Dan ☐ 100 Rifles ☐ Actors and Sin ☐ Adventures of Robinson Crusoe, The ☐ At Sword's Point ☐ Bengal Brigade ☐ Big Cube, The ☐ Cabinet of Caligari, The ☐ Dead, The ☐ Fail-Safe ☐ Halloween III: Season of the Witch ☐ Home Before Dark ☐ Imitation of Life ☐ Invasion, U.S.A. ☐ Iroquois Trail, The ☐ Last Starfighter, The ☐ MacArthur ☐ Macbeth ☐ Night Fighters, The ☐ Odd Man Out ☐ Operation Secret ☐ People, The ☐ Purple Mask, The ☐ Robocop 2 ☐ Soldiers Three ☐ Waterloo

O'Keefe, Dennis ☐ Abandoned ☐ Abroad With Two Yanks ☐ Affairs of Susan, The ☐ All Hands On Deck ☐ Bad Man of Brimstone ☐ Brewster's Millions ☐ Broadway Limited ☐ Chaser, The ☐ Chicago Syndicate ☐ Company She Keeps, The ☐ Dishonored Lady ☐ Doll Face ☐ Dragon Wells Massacre ☐ Eagle and the Hawk, The ☐ Earl Carroll Vanities ☐ Everything I Have Is Yours ☐ Fake, The ☐ Fighting Seabees, The ☐ Follow the Sun ☐ Getting Gertie's Garter ☐ Great Dan Patch, The ☐ I'm Nobody's Sweetheart Now ☐ Inside Detroit ☐ Lady Scarface ☐ Lady Wants Mink, The ☐ Las Vegas Shakedown ☐ Leopard Man, The ☐ One Big Affair ☐ Passage West ☐ Raw Deal ☐ Sensations ☐ Story of Dr. Wassell, The ☐ T-Men ☐ Up in Mabel's Room ☐ Walk a Crooked Mile ☐ Woman on the Run

O'Keefe, Michael ☐ Bridge to Silence ☐ Caddyshack ☐ Dark Secret of Harvest Home ☐ Fear ☐ Finders Keepers ☐ Friendly Persuasion ☐ Great Santini, The ☐ Ironweed ☐ Me & Veronica ☐ Nate and Hayes ☐ Out of the Rain ☐ Rumor of War, A ☐ Slugger's Wife, The ☐ Whoopee Boys, The

O'Keefe, Miles ☐ Ator, the Fighting Eagle ☐ Blade Master, The ☐ Cartel ☐ Drifter, The ☐ Iron Warrior ☐ King's Ransom ☐ Liberty & Bash ☐ Sword of the Valiant ☐ Tarzan, the Ape Man ☐ Waxwork

O'Neal, Patrick ☐ Assignment to Kill ☐ Castle Keep ☐ El Condor ☐ Fine Madness, A ☐ For the Boys ☐ King Rat ☐ Kremlin Letter, The ☐ Mad Magician, The ☐ Maigret ☐ Matchless ☐ Matter of Morals, A ☐ Q & A ☐ Secret Life of an American Wife, The ☐ Stepford Wives, The ☐ Under Siege ☐ Where Were You When the Lights Went Out?

O'Neal, Ron ☐ Brothers ☐ Force of One, A ☐ Freedom Road ☐ Hitter, The ☐ Master Gunfighter, The ☐ Mercenary Fighters ☐ Sophisticated Gents, The ☐ Superfly ☐ Superfly T.N.T.

O'Neal, Ryan ☐ Barry Lyndon ☐ Big Bounce, The ☐ Bridge Too Far, A ☐ Chances Are ☐ Driver, The ☐ Fever Pitch ☐ Games, The ☐ Green Ice ☐ Irreconcilable Differences ☐ Love Story ☐ Main Event, The ☐ Man Upstairs, The ☐ Nickelodeon ☐ Oliver's Story ☐ Paper Moon ☐ Partners ☐ Small Sacrifices ☐ So Fine ☐ Thief Who Came to Dinner, The ☐ Tough Guys Don't Dance ☐ What's Up, Doc? ☐ Wild Rovers

O'Neal, Tatum ☐ Bad News Bears, The ☐ Certain Fury ☐ Circle of Two ☐ International Velvet ☐ Little Darlings ☐ Little Noises ☐ Nickelodeon ☐ Paper Moon

O'Neil, Barbara ☐ All This and Heaven Too ☐ Angel Face ☐ Stella Dallas ☐ Tower of London, The ☐ When Tomorrow Comes ☐ Whirlpool

O'Neill, Ed ☐ Adventures of Ford Fairlane, The ☐ Blue Chips ☐ Disorganized Crime ☐ Dutch ☐ Farrell for the People ☐ It's a Bundyful Life ☐ K-9 ☐ Little Giants ☐ Sibling Rivalry ☐ Wayne's World 2

O'Neill, Jennifer ☐ Caravans ☐ Carey Treatment, The ☐ Chase ☐ Cloud Dancer ☐ Force of One, A ☐ Full Exposure: The Sex Tape Scandals ☐ Innocent, The ☐ Invasion of Privacy ☐ Lady Ice ☐ Other Victim, The ☐ Perfect Family ☐ Reincarnation of Peter Proud, The ☐ Rio Lobo ☐ Scanners ☐ Steel ☐ Such Good Friends ☐ Summer of '42

O'Quinn, Terry ☐ Amityville—A New Generation ☐ Company Business ☐ Cutting Edge, The ☐ Forgotten One, The ☐ Good Fight, The ☐ Last to Go ☐ Lipstick Camera, The ☐ My Samurai ☐ Pin ☐ Roe vs. Wade ☐ Silver Bullet ☐ Son of the Morning Star ☐ Stepfather II ☐ Stepfather, The ☐ Stranger on My Land ☐ Tombstone ☐ When the Time Comes ☐ Young Guns

O'Ross, Ed ☐ Full Metal Jacket ☐ Hidden, The ☐ Play Nice ☐ Red Heat ☐ Universal Soldier

O'Shea, Michael ☐ Circumstantial Evidence ☐ Eve of St. Mark, The ☐ Fixed Bayonets ☐ It Should Happen to You ☐ It's a Pleasure! ☐ Jack London ☐ Lady of Burlesque ☐ Last of the Redmen ☐ Man from Frisco, The ☐ Model and the Marriage Broker, The ☐ Parole, Inc. ☐ Something for the Boys ☐ Threat, The

O'Shea, Milo ☐ Adding Machine, The ☐ Angel in Green ☐ Angel Levine, The ☐ Arabian Adventure ☐ Barbarella ☐ Carry On Cabbie ☐ Digby—The Biggest Dog in the World ☐ It's Not the Size That Counts ☐ Loot ☐ Medicine Hat Stallion, The ☐ Paddy ☐ Playboys, The ☐ Romeo and Juliet ☐ Sacco and Vanzetti ☐ Theatre of Blood ☐ Ulysses ☐ Verdict, The

O'Sullivan, Maureen ☐ All I Desire ☐ Anna Karenina ☐ Barretts of Wimpole Street, The ☐ Big Clock, The ☐ Bonzo Goes to College ☐ Cardinal Richelieu ☐ Connecticut Yankee, A ☐ Crowd Roars, The ☐ David Copperfield ☐ Day at the Races, A ☐ Devil-Doll, The ☐ Emperor's Candlesticks, The ☐ Flame Within, The ☐ Hannah and Her Sisters ☐ Hide-Out ☐ Just Imagine ☐ Let Us Live ☐ Maisie Was a Lady ☐ Never Too Late ☐ Payment Deferred ☐ Port of Seven Seas ☐ Pride and Prejudice ☐ So This Is London ☐ Song O' My Heart ☐ Strange Interlude ☐ Tall T, The ☐ Tarzan and His Mate ☐ Tarzan Escapes ☐ Tarzan Finds a Son ☐ Tarzan's New York Adventure ☐ Tarzan's Secret Treasure ☐ Tarzan, the Ape Man ☐ Thin Man, The ☐ Tugboat Annie ☐ West Point of the Air ☐ Where Danger Lives ☐ Yank at Oxford, A

O'Toole, Annette ☐ 48 Hrs. ☐ Best Legs in the 8th Grade ☐ Cat People ☐ Cross My Heart ☐ Dreamer of Oz, The: The Frank L. Baum Story ☐ Foolin' Around ☐ Girl of the Limberlost, A ☐ Guts and Glory: The Rise and Fall of Oliver North ☐ Kiss of a Killer ☐ One on One ☐ Smile ☐ Stephen King's It ☐ Superman 3 ☐ War Between the Tates, The ☐ White Lie

O'Toole, Peter ☐ Becket ☐ Bible, The ☐ Brotherly Love ☐ Caligula ☐ Club Paradise ☐ Creator ☐ Crossing to Freedom ☐ Day They Robbed the Bank of England, The ☐ Foxtrot ☐ Goodbye, Mr. Chips ☐ Great Catherine ☐ High Spirits ☐ How to Steal a Million ☐ Kidnapped ☐ Kim ☐ King Ralph ☐ Last Emperor, The ☐ Lawrence of Arabia ☐ Lion in Winter, The ☐ Lord Jim ☐ Man Friday ☐ Man of La Mancha ☐ Masada ☐ Murphy's War ☐ My Favorite Year ☐ Night of the Generals, The ☐ Nutcracker Prince, The ☐ Ruling Class, The ☐ Savage Innocents, The ☐ Seventh Coin, The ☐ Stunt Man, The ☐ Supergirl ☐ Svengali ☐ Under Milk Wood ☐ What's New, Pussycat? ☐ Zulu Dawn

Oakie, Jack ☐ Affairs of Annabel, The ☐ Alice in Wonderland ☐ Annabel Takes A Tour ☐ Big Broadcast of 1936, The ☐ Bowery to Broadway ☐ Call of the Wild ☐ Champagne Waltz ☐ Colleen ☐ College Humor ☐ Eagle and the Hawk, The ☐ Fight for Your Lady ☐ From Hell to Heaven ☐ Great American Broadcast, The ☐ Great Dictator, The ☐ Hello Frisco, Hello ☐ Hitting a New High ☐ Iceland ☐ If I Had a Million ☐ It Happened Tomorrow ☐ King of Burlesque ☐ Last of the

Buccaneers, The ☐ Little Men ☐ Merry Monahans, The ☐ Million Dollar Legs ☐ Murder at the Vanities ☐ Navy Blues ☐ On Stage Everybody ☐ Once in a Lifetime ☐ Paramount on Parade ☐ Rat Race, The ☐ Rise and Shine ☐ Sap from Syracuse, The ☐ Sitting Pretty ☐ Song of the Islands ☐ Texas Rangers, The ☐ Thanks for Everything ☐ That Girl From Paris ☐ That's the Spirit ☐ Tin Pan Alley ☐ Toast of New York, The ☐ Too Much Harmony ☐ Touchdown! ☐ When My Baby Smiles at Me ☐ Wild Party, The ☐ Wonderful Country, The ☐ Young People

Oates, Warren ☐ 1941 ☐ 92 in the Shade ☐ And Baby Makes Six ☐ Baby Comes Home ☐ Badlands ☐ Barquero ☐ Battleground ☐ Blue Thunder ☐ Border, The ☐ Bring Me the Head of Alfredo Garcia ☐ Brink's Job, The ☐ Chandler ☐ China 9, Liberty 37 ☐ Cockfighter ☐ Crooks and Coronets ☐ Dillinger ☐ Dixie Dynamite ☐ Drum ☐ Hired Hand, The ☐ In the Heat of the Night ☐ Kid Blue ☐ Mail Order Bride ☐ Major Dundee ☐ My Old Man ☐ Race With the Devil ☐ Return of the Magnificent Seven ☐ Rise and Fall of Legs Diamond, The ☐ Shooting, The ☐ Smith! ☐ Stripes ☐ There Was a Crooked Man ☐ Thief Who Came to Dinner, The ☐ Tom Sawyer ☐ Two-Lane Blacktop ☐ White Dawn, The ☐ Wild Bunch, The

Oberon, Merle ☐ 'Til We Meet Again ☐ Affair in Monte Carlo ☐ Affectionately Yours ☐ Batmania from Comics to Screen ☐ Battle, The ☐ Beloved Enemy ☐ Berlin Express ☐ Cowboy and the Lady, The ☐ Dark Angel, The ☐ Dark Waters ☐ Deep in My Heart ☐ Desiree ☐ Divorce of Lady X, The ☐ Epic that Never Was, The ☐ First Comes Courage ☐ Folies Bergere ☐ Forever and a Day ☐ Hotel ☐ Interval ☐ Lion Has Wings, The ☐ Lodger, The ☐ Lydia ☐ Night Song ☐ Of Love and Desire ☐ Over the Moon ☐ Pardon My French ☐ Price of Fear, The ☐ Private Life of Henry VIII, The ☐ Reserved for Ladies ☐ Scarlet Pimpernel, The ☐ Song to Remember, A ☐ That Uncertain Feeling ☐ These Three ☐ This Love of Ours ☐ Wedding Rehearsal ☐ Wuthering Heights

Oland, Warner ☐ Before Dawn ☐ Black Camel, The ☐ Charlie Chan at Monte Carlo ☐ Charlie Chan at the Circus ☐ Charlie Chan at the Olympics ☐ Charlie Chan at the Opera ☐ Charlie Chan at the Race Track ☐ Charlie Chan Carries On ☐ Charlie Chan in London ☐ Charlie Chan in Paris ☐ Charlie Chan in Shanghai ☐ Charlie Chan on Broadway ☐ Charlie Chan's Secret ☐ Daughter of the Dragon ☐ Dishonored ☐ Don Juan ☐ Don Q, Son of Zorro ☐ Jazz Singer, The ☐ Mandalay ☐ Mysterious Dr. Fu Manchu, The ☐ Painted Veil, The ☐ Riders of the Purple Sage ☐ Shanghai ☐ Shanghai Express ☐ Werewolf of London

Oldman, Gary ☐ Bram Stoker's Dracula ☐ Chattahoochee ☐ Criminal Law ☐ Fallen Angels—Volume 2 ☐ Immortal Beloved ☐ Meantime ☐ Murder in the First ☐ Prick Up Your Ears ☐ Professional, The ☐ Remembrance ☐ Romeo is Bleeding ☐ Rosencrantz and Guildenstern Are Dead ☐ Sid and Nancy ☐ State of Grace ☐ Track 29 ☐ True Romance ☐ We Think the World of You

Olin, Lena ☐ After the Rehearsal ☐ Enemies, A Love Story ☐ Havana ☐ Mr. Jones ☐ Romeo is Bleeding ☐ Unbearable Lightness of Being, The

Oliver, Edna May ☐ Alice in Wonderland ☐ Ann Vickers ☐ Conquerors, The ☐ David Copperfield ☐ Drums Along the Mohawk ☐ Half Shot at Sunrise ☐ Hold 'Em Jail ☐ Ladies of the Jury ☐ Last Gentleman, The ☐ Little Miss Broadway ☐ Little Women ☐ Meet the Baron ☐ Murder on a Honeymoon ☐ Murder on the Blackboard ☐ No More Ladies ☐ Nurse Edith Cavell ☐ Only Yesterday ☐ Paradise for Three ☐ Parnell ☐ Penguin Pool Murder, The ☐ Pride and Prejudice ☐ Romeo and Juliet ☐ Second Fiddle ☐ Story of Vernon and Irene Castle, The ☐ Tale of Two Cities, A

Olivier, Laurence ☐ 21 Days Together ☐ 49th Parallel ☐ As You Like It ☐ Battle of Britain, The ☐ Beggar's Opera, The ☐ Betsy, The ☐ Bounty, The ☐ Boys From Brazil, The ☐ Brideshead Revisited ☐ Bridge Too Far, A ☐ Bunny Lake Is Missing ☐ Carrie ☐ Clash of the Titans ☐ Clouds over Europe ☐ Dance of Death ☐ David Copperfield ☐ Devil's Disciple, The ☐ Divorce of Lady X, The ☐ Dracula ☐ Ebony Tower, The ☐ Entertainer, The ☐ Fire Over England ☐ Friends and Lovers ☐ Hamlet ☐ Henry V ☐ I Stand Condemned ☐ Inchon ☐ Jazz Singer, The ☐ Jesus of Nazareth ☐ Jigsaw Man, The ☐ Khartoum ☐ King Lear ☐ Lady Caroline Lamb ☐ Little Romance, A ☐ Love Among the Ruins ☐ Magic Box, The ☐ Marathon Man ☐ Merchant of Venice, The ☐ Nicholas and Alexandra ☐ Oh! What a Lovely War ☐ Othello ☐ Pride and Prejudice ☐ Prince and the Showgirl, The ☐ Rebecca ☐ Richard III ☐ Seven Percent Solution, The ☐ Shoes of the Fisherman, The ☐ Sleuth ☐ Spartacus ☐ Term of Trial ☐ That Hamilton Woman ☐ Wagner ☐ Westward Passage ☐ Wuthering Heights

Olmos, Edward James ☐ American Me ☐ Ballad of Gregorio Cortez, The ☐ Blade Runner ☐ Fortunate Pilgrim ☐ Mario Puzo's "The Fortunate Pilgrim" ☐ Menendez: A Killing in Beverly Hills ☐ Miami Vice 2: The Prodigal Son ☐ Saving Grace ☐ Stand and Deliver ☐ Talent for the Game ☐ Triumph of the Spirit ☐ Wolfen ☐ Zoot Suit

Olson, Nancy ☐ Absent Minded Professor, The ☐ Big Jim McLain ☐ Boy from Oklahoma, The ☐ Force of Arms ☐ Mr. Music

☐ Smith! ☐ Snowball Express ☐ So Big ☐ Son of Flubber ☐ Submarine Command ☐ Sunset Boulevard ☐ Union Station

Ontkean, Michael ☐ Allnighter, The ☐ Blood of Others, The ☐ Bye Bye Blues ☐ Clara's Heart ☐ Cold Front ☐ Girls on the Road ☐ In Defense of a Married Man ☐ Just the Way You Are ☐ Legacy of Lies ☐ Maid to Order ☐ Making Love ☐ Necromancy ☐ Pickup on 101 ☐ Right of the People, The ☐ Slap Shot ☐ Twin Peaks ☐ Voices ☐ Willie and Phil

Orbach, Jerry ☐ Beauty and the Beast ☐ Brewster's Millions ☐ Broadway Bound ☐ Crimes and Misdemeanors ☐ Delusion ☐ Dirty Dancing ☐ Fan's Notes, A ☐ Foreplay ☐ Gang That Couldn't Shoot Straight, The ☐ Imagemaker, The ☐ In Defense of a Married Man ☐ Last Exit to Brooklyn ☐ Love Among Thieves ☐ Mad Dog Coll ☐ Mr. Saturday Night ☐ Out for Justice ☐ Out on a Limb ☐ Prince of The City ☐ Someone to Watch Over Me ☐ Straight Talk ☐ Universal Soldier

Overman, Lynne ☐ Edison, the Man ☐ Enter Madame ☐ Forest Rangers, The ☐ Night Club Scandal ☐ Persons in Hiding ☐ Roxie Hart ☐ She Loves Me Not ☐ Spawn of the North ☐ Typhoon ☐ Union Pacific ☐ Yours For the Asking

Owen, Bill ☐ In Celebration ☐ My Brother's Keeper ☐ Rainbow Jacket, The ☐ Shakedown, The ☐ Ship That Died of Shame, The ☐ Square Ring, The

Owen, Reginald ☐ Above Suspicion ☐ Adventure in Manhattan ☐ Bride Wore Red, The ☐ Cairo ☐ Challenge to Lassie ☐ Christmas Carol, A ☐ Cluny Brown ☐ Conquest ☐ Downstairs ☐ Earl of Chicago, The ☐ Enchanted April ☐ Everybody Sing ☐ Fashions ☐ Fast and Loose ☐ Florian ☐ Green Dolphin Street ☐ Hotel Imperial ☐ Human Side, The ☐ If Winter Comes ☐ Imperfect Lady, The ☐ Kitty ☐ Love on the Run ☐ Madame X ☐ Mary Poppins ☐ Miniver Story, The ☐ Monsieur Beaucaire ☐ Moochie of the Little League ☐ Mrs. Miniver ☐ Music in the Air ☐ Personal Property ☐ Petticoat Fever ☐ Real Glory, The ☐ Reunion in France ☐ Rose Marie ☐ Somewhere I'll Find You ☐ Tale of Two Cities, A ☐ Tarzan's Secret Treasure ☐ Valley of Decision, The ☐ We Were Dancing ☐ White Cargo ☐ Woman of the Year ☐ Yours For the Asking

Pacino, Al ☐ And Justice for All ☐ Author! Author! ☐ Bobby Deerfield ☐ Carlito's Way ☐ Cruising ☐ Dick Tracy ☐ Dog Day Afternoon ☐ Frankie and Johnny ☐ Glengarry Glen Ross ☐ Godfather, Part II, The ☐ Godfather, Part III, The ☐ Godfather, The ☐ Me, Natalie ☐ Panic in Needle Park, The ☐ Revolution ☐ Scarecrow ☐ Scarface ☐ Scent of a Woman ☐ Sea of Love ☐ Serpico ☐ Two Bits

Pacula, Joanna ☐ Breaking Point ☐ Escape from Sobibor ☐ Gorky Park ☐ Husbands and Lovers ☐ Kiss, The ☐ Marked for Death ☐ Not Quite Paradise ☐ Options ☐ Warlock 2: The Armageddon

Page, Anita ☐ Big Cage, The ☐ Broadway Melody, The ☐ Easiest Way, The ☐ Free and Easy ☐ Gentleman's Fate ☐ Jungle Bride ☐ Night Court ☐ Our Blushing Brides ☐ Our Dancing Daughters ☐ Sidewalks of New York

Page, Gale ☐ Four Daughters ☐ Four Mothers ☐ Four Wives ☐ Heart of the North ☐ Indianapolis Speedway ☐ Knute Rockne, All American ☐ Naughty but Nice

Page, Genevieve ☐ Belle de Jour ☐ Beyond Therapy ☐ Buffet Froid ☐ Day and the Hour, The ☐ Decline and Fall of a Bird Watcher ☐ El Cid ☐ Foreign Intrigue ☐ Girl in His Pocket ☐ Mayerling ☐ Private Life of Sherlock Holmes, The ☐ Song Without End ☐ Youngblood Hawke

Page, Geraldine ☐ Beguiled, The ☐ Bride, The ☐ Day of the Locust, The ☐ Dear Heart ☐ Dollmaker, The ☐ Happiest Millionaire, The ☐ Harry's War ☐ Hondo ☐ Honky Tonk Freeway ☐ I'm Dancing as Fast as I Can ☐ Interiors ☐ J.W. Coop ☐ Nasty Habits ☐ Native Son ☐ Parade, The ☐ Pete 'n' Tillie ☐ Pope of Greenwich Village, The ☐ Rescuers, The ☐ Summer and Smoke ☐ Sweet Bird of Youth ☐ Toys in the Attic ☐ Trip to Bountiful, The ☐ Truman Capote's Trilogy ☐ Whatever Happened to Aunt Alice? ☐ You're a Big Boy Now

Paget, Debra ☐ Anne of the Indies ☐ Belles on Their Toes ☐ Bird of Paradise ☐ Broken Arrow ☐ Cleopatra's Daughter ☐ Cry of the City ☐ Demetrius and the Gladiators ☐ Fourteen Hours ☐ From the Earth to the Moon ☐ Gambler from Natchez, The ☐ Haunted Palace, The ☐ Indian Tomb, The ☐ Last Hunt, The ☐ Les Miserables ☐ Love Me Tender ☐ Most Dangerous Man Alive, The ☐ Omar Khayyam ☐ Prince Valiant ☐ Princess of the Nile ☐ River's Edge, The ☐ Seven Angry Men ☐ Stars and Stripes Forever ☐ Tales of Terror ☐ Ten Commandments, The ☐ White Feather ☐ Why Must I Die?

Paige, Janis ☐ Always Together ☐ Angel on My Shoulder ☐ Bachelor in Paradise ☐ Caretakers, The ☐ Cheyenne ☐ Follow the Boys ☐ Fugitive Lady ☐ Her Kind of Man ☐ House Across the Street, The ☐ One Sunday Afternoon ☐ Please Don't Eat the Daisies ☐ Romance on the High Seas ☐ Silk Stockings ☐ Time, the Place and the Girl, The ☐ Two Guys From Milwaukee ☐ Wallflower ☐ Welcome to Hard Times ☐ Winter Meeting ☐ Younger Brothers, The

Paige, Robert ☐ Abbott and Costello Go To Mars ☐ Can't Help Singing ☐ Flame, The ☐ Her Primitive Man ☐ Hi'ya Chum ☐ Homicide Bureau ☐ Marriage-Go-Round, The ☐ Monster and the Girl, The ☐ Red Stallion, The ☐ San Antonio Rose ☐ Son of Dracula

Paiva, Nestor ☐ Falcon in Mexico, The

☐ Flame of Stamboul ☐ Follow Me Quietly ☐ Mara Maru ☐ Mole People, The ☐ Revenge of the Creature

Palance, Jack ☐ Alone in the Dark ☐ Angels' Brigade ☐ Arrowhead ☐ Attack! ☐ Bagdad Cafe ☐ Barabbas ☐ Battle of Austerlitz, The ☐ Big Knife, The ☐ Bronk ☐ Chato's Land ☐ Che! ☐ City Slickers ☐ City Slickers 2: Legend of Curly's Gold ☐ Cocaine Cowboys ☐ Contempt ☐ Cops and Robbersons ☐ Deadly Sanctuary ☐ Desperados, The ☐ Dracula ☐ Flight to Tangier ☐ Four Deuces, The ☐ God's Gun ☐ Godchild, The ☐ Gor ☐ Great Adventure, The ☐ Halls of Montezuma ☐ Hawk the Slayer ☐ Hell's Brigade—The Final Assault ☐ Horsemen, The ☐ House of Numbers ☐ I Died a Thousand Times ☐ Ivory Ape, The ☐ Lonely Man, The ☐ Man in the Attic ☐ Man Inside, The ☐ McMasters, The ☐ Mercenary, The ☐ Monte Walsh ☐ Oklahoma Crude ☐ Once a Thief ☐ One Man Jury ☐ Outlaw of Gor ☐ Panic in the Streets ☐ Professionals, The ☐ Second Chance ☐ Sensuous Nurse, The ☐ Shane ☐ Sign of the Pagan ☐ Silver Chalice, The ☐ Solar Crisis ☐ Strange Case of Dr. Jekyll And Mr. Hyde, The ☐ Sudden Fear ☐ Swan Princess, The ☐ Tango & Cash ☐ Ten Seconds to Hell ☐ Torture Garden ☐ Young Guns

Palin, Michael ☐ American Friends ☐ And Now for Something Completely Different ☐ Brazil ☐ Fish Called Wanda, A ☐ Jabberwocky ☐ Missionary, The ☐ Monty Python and the Holy Grail ☐ Monty Python Live at the Hollywood Bowl ☐ Monty Python's Flying Circus—Vol. 1 ☐ Monty Python's Life of Brian ☐ Monty Python's Parrot Sketch Not Included ☐ Monty Python's The Meaning of Life ☐ Private Function, A ☐ Ripping Yarns-Vol. 1 ☐ Secret Policeman's Other Ball, The ☐ Time Bandits

Pallette, Eugene ☐ Adventures of Robin Hood, The ☐ All the King's Horses ☐ Baby Face Harrington ☐ Benson Murder Case ☐ Big Street, The ☐ Bordertown ☐ Bride Came C.O.D., The ☐ Cheaters, The ☐ Easy to Take ☐ First Love ☐ Follow Thru ☐ Forest Rangers, The ☐ Friends of Mr. Sweeney ☐ Ghost Goes West, The ☐ Girls About Town ☐ Golden Arrow, The ☐ Greene Murder Case, The ☐ Half-Naked Truth, The ☐ Heavenly Days ☐ Huckleberry Finn ☐ In the Meantime, Darling ☐ Intolerance ☐ It Ain't Hay ☐ It's a Date ☐ Kennel Murder Case, The ☐ Lady Eve, The ☐ Lady in a Jam ☐ Male Animal, The ☐ Mark of Zorro, The ☐ Mr. Skitch ☐ Mr. Smith Goes to Washington ☐ My Man Godfrey ☐ Night Mayor, The ☐ One Exciting Adventure ☐ Playboy of Paris ☐ Sensations ☐ Shanghai Express ☐ Slightly Dangerous ☐ Steamboat 'Round the Bend ☐ Three Musketeers, The ☐ Unfinished Business ☐ Wife, Husband and Friend ☐ World Premiere

Palmer, Lilli ☐ Adorable Julia ☐ Amorous Adventures of Moll Flanders, The ☐ Between Time And Eternity ☐ Beware of Pity ☐ Body and Soul ☐ Boys From Brazil, The ☐ But Not For Me ☐ Chamber of Horrors ☐ Cloak and Dagger ☐ Conspiracy of Hearts ☐ Counterfeit Traitor, The ☐ Four Poster, The ☐ Girl Must Live, A ☐ Glass Tower, The ☐ Hard Contract ☐ High Commissioner, The ☐ Holcroft Covenant, The ☐ House That Screamed, The ☐ Jack of Diamonds ☐ Long Dark Hall, The ☐ Lovers of Montparnasse, The ☐ Madchen in Uniform ☐ Main Street to Broadway ☐ Miracle of the White Stallions ☐ My Girl Tisa ☐ No Minor Vices ☐ Notorious Gentleman ☐ Oedipus the King ☐ Operation Crossbow ☐ Pleasure of His Company, The ☐ Sebastian

Pangborn, Franklin ☐ 5th Avenue Girl ☐ All Over Town ☐ Bank Dick, The ☐ Bed of Roses ☐ Call Out the Marines ☐ Carefree ☐ Christmas in July ☐ Cockeyed Cavaliers ☐ Design for Living ☐ Down Memory Lane ☐ Easy Living ☐ Eight Bells ☐ Flying Down to Rio ☐ George Washington Slept Here ☐ Girl, a Guy, and a Gob, A ☐ Great Moment, The ☐ Hail the Conquering Hero ☐ Hats Off ☐ Holy Matrimony ☐ Horn Blows at Midnight, The ☐ I'll Be Yours ☐ International House ☐ Life of the Party, The ☐ Mandarin Mystery, The ☐ My Dream Is Yours ☐ My Man Godfrey ☐ Never a Dull Moment ☐ Never Give a Sucker an Even Break ☐ Obliging Young Lady ☐ Palm Beach Story, The ☐ Reveille With Beverly ☐ Romance on the High Seas ☐ Star Is Born, A ☐ Sullivan's Travels ☐ Topper Takes a Trip

Pankin, Stuart ☐ Dirt Bike Kid, The ☐ Earthbound ☐ Mannequin Two: On the Move ☐ Second Sight ☐ Vagrant, The

Pankow, John ☐ Monkey Shines: An Experiment in Fear ☐ Mortal Thoughts ☐ Stranger Among Us, A ☐ To Live and Die in L.A. ☐ Year of the Gun

Pantoliano, Joe ☐ "In" Crowd, The ☐ Baby's Day Out ☐ Downtown ☐ Eddie and the Cruisers ☐ El Diablo ☐ Fugitive, The ☐ In Crowd, The ☐ Last of the Finest, The ☐ Me and the Kid ☐ Mean Season, The ☐ Nightbreaker ☐ Risky Business ☐ Running Scared ☐ Short Time ☐ Three of Hearts

Papas, Irene ☐ Anne of the Thousand Days ☐ Antigone ☐ Assisi Underground, The ☐ Attila ☐ Bloodline ☐ Brotherhood, The ☐ Dream of Kings, A ☐ Eboli ☐ Erendira ☐ Guns of Navarone, The ☐ High Season ☐ Into the Night ☐ Iphigenia ☐ Lion of the Desert ☐ Man from Cairo, The ☐ Message, The ☐ Moses ☐ Sweet Country ☐ Tribute to a Bad Man ☐ Trojan Women, The ☐ We Still Kill the Old Way ☐ Z ☐ Zorba the Greek

Pare, Michael ☐ Closer, The ☐ Eddie and the Cruisers ☐ Eddie and the Cruisers II—Eddie Lives! ☐ Moon 44 ☐ Philadelphia Experiment, The ☐ Point of Impact ☐ Streets of Fire ☐ Sunset Heat

Parillaud, Anne ☐ Innocent Blood ☐ La Femme Nikita ☐ Map of the Human Heart

Parker, Cecil ☐ 23 Paces to Baker Street ☐ Admirable Crichton, The ☐ Amorous Mr. Prawn, The ☐ Constant Husband, The ☐ Detective, The ☐ Follow That Horse! ☐ For Better, For Worse ☐ Heavens Above ☐ His Excellency ☐ I Believe In You ☐ I Was Monty's Double ☐ Indiscreet ☐ Isn't Life Wonderful! ☐ Lady Killers, The ☐ Magic Bow, The ☐ Man in the White Suit, The ☐ Man Who Lived Again, The ☐ Operation Snafu ☐ Pure Hell of St. Trinian's, The ☐ Saint's Vacation, The ☐ Storm in a Teacup ☐ Tale of Two Cities, A ☐ Tony Draws a Horse ☐ Under Capricorn ☐ Under Ten Flags ☐ Wreck of the Mary Deare, The

Parker, Cecilia ☐ Andy Hardy Comes Home ☐ Andy Hardy Gets Spring Fever ☐ Andy Hardy Meets Debutante ☐ Andy Hardy's Double Life ☐ Family Affair, A ☐ Grand Central Murder ☐ Hardys Ride High, The ☐ Hollywood Cowboy ☐ Judge Hardy and Son ☐ Judge Hardy's Children ☐ Love Finds Andy Hardy ☐ Mystery Ranch ☐ Old Hutch ☐ Out West with the Hardys ☐ Riders of Destiny ☐ You're Only Young Once

Parker, Eleanor ☐ Above and Beyond ☐ Between Two Worlds ☐ Caged ☐ Chain Lightning ☐ Detective Story ☐ Escape from Fort Bravo ☐ Escape Me Never ☐ Eye of the Cat ☐ Fantasy Island ☐ Great American Beauty Contest, The ☐ Hans Brinker ☐ Hole in the Head, A ☐ Home for the Holidays ☐ Home From the Hill ☐ Interrupted Melody ☐ King and Four Queens, The ☐ Lizzie ☐ Madame X ☐ Madison Avenue ☐ Man with the Golden Arm ☐ Many Rivers to Cross ☐ Maybe I'll Come Home in the Spring ☐ Millionaire for Christy, A ☐ Mission to Moscow ☐ Naked Jungle, The ☐ Never Say Goodbye ☐ Once Upon a Spy ☐ Oscar, The ☐ Panic Button ☐ Pride of the Marines ☐ Return to Peyton Place ☐ Scaramouche ☐ She's Dressed to Kill ☐ Sound of Music, The ☐ Three Secrets ☐ Tiger and the Pussycat, The ☐ Valley of the Kings ☐ Voice of the Turtle, The ☐ Warning Shot ☐ Woman in White, The

Parker, Fess ☐ Climb an Angry Mountain ☐ Davy Crockett and the River Pirates ☐ Davy Crockett, King of the Wild Frontier ☐ Great Locomotive Chase, The ☐ Hell Is for Heroes ☐ Jayhawkers, The ☐ Light in the Forest, The ☐ Old Yeller ☐ Westward Ho the Wagons!

Parker, Jameson ☐ American Justice ☐ Anatomy of a Seduction ☐ Caribbean Mystery, A ☐ Prince of Darkness ☐ White Dog

Parker, Jean ☐ Arkansas Traveler, The ☐ Beyond Tomorrow ☐ Black Tuesday ☐ Bluebeard ☐ Flying Blind ☐ Flying Deuces, The ☐ Ghost Goes West, The ☐ High Explosive ☐ Limehouse Blues ☐ Little Women ☐ No Hands on the Clock ☐ One Body Too Many ☐ Operator 13 ☐ Rasputin and the Empress ☐ Secret of Madame Blanche, The ☐ Sequoia ☐ Texas Rangers, The ☐ Wicked Woman, A

Parker, Lara ☐ Foxfire Light ☐ Hi, Mom! ☐ Night of Dark Shadows ☐ Race With the Devil

Parker, Mary-Louise ☐ Boys on the Side ☐ Bullets Over Broadway ☐ Client, The ☐ Fried Green Tomatoes ☐ Grand Canyon ☐ Longtime Companion ☐ Mr. Wonderful ☐ Naked in New York

Parker, Sarah Jessica ☐ Ed Wood ☐ Flight of the Navigator ☐ Girls Just Want to Have Fun ☐ Going for the Gold: The Bill Johnson Story ☐ Hocus Pocus ☐ Honeymoon in Vegas ☐ L.A. Story ☐ Miami Rhapsody ☐ Striking Distance

Parkins, Barbara ☐ Asylum ☐ Bear Island ☐ Breakfast in Paris ☐ Christina ☐ Mephisto Waltz, The ☐ Snatched ☐ Valley of the Dolls

Parks, Larry ☐ Boogie Man Will Get You, The ☐ Counter-Attack ☐ Down to Earth ☐ Flight Lieutenant ☐ Freud ☐ Hey, Rookie ☐ Jolson Sings Again ☐ Jolson Story, The ☐ Love Is Better Than Ever ☐ Racket Man, The ☐ Reveille With Beverly ☐ Swordsman, The

Parks, Michael ☐ Arizona Heat ☐ Bible, The ☐ Bus Riley's Back in Town ☐ Chase ☐ China Lake Murders, The ☐ Death Wish 5 ☐ ffolkes ☐ French Quarter Undercover ☐ Gore Vidal's Billy the Kid ☐ Happening, The ☐ Hard Country ☐ Hitman, The ☐ Idol, The ☐ Last Hard Men, The ☐ Midnight Auto Supply ☐ Rainbow ☐ Savage Bees, The ☐ Storyville ☐ Stranger on the Run ☐ Wild Seed, The

Parsons, Estelle ☐ American Clock, The ☐ Bonnie and Clyde ☐ Don't Drink the Water ☐ For Pete's Sake ☐ Foreplay ☐ Gentleman Bandit, The ☐ I Never Sang for My Father ☐ I Walk the Line ☐ Ladybug, Ladybug ☐ Open Admissions ☐ Rachel, Rachel ☐ Watermelon Man

Patinkin, Mandy ☐ Alien Nation ☐ Daniel ☐ Dick Tracy ☐ Doctor, The ☐ French Postcards ☐ House on Carroll Street, The ☐ Impromptu ☐ Maxie ☐ Music of Chance, The ☐ Night of the Juggler ☐ Princess Bride, The ☐ True Colors ☐ Yentl

Patric, Jason ☐ After Dark, My Sweet ☐ Beast, The ☐ Denial ☐ Frankenstein Unbound ☐ Geronimo: An American Legend ☐ Lost Boys, The ☐ Rush

Patrick, Gail ☐ Artists and Models ☐ Brewster's Millions ☐ Change of Heart ☐ Claudia and David ☐ Dangerous to Know ☐ Death Takes a Holiday ☐ Doctor Takes a Wife, The ☐ Doubting Thomas ☐ Early to Bed ☐ Inside Story, The ☐ John Meade's Woman ☐ King of Alcatraz ☐ Lone Wolf Returns, The ☐ Love

Crazy ☐ Mad about Music ☐ Madonna's Secret, The ☐ Man of Conquest ☐ Mississippi ☐ Murder at the Vanities ☐ Murders in the Zoo ☐ My Favorite Wife ☐ My Man Godfrey ☐ No More Ladies ☐ Quiet Please, Murder ☐ Rendezvous with Annie ☐ Reno ☐ Up in Mabel's Room ☐ We Were Dancing

Patrick, Lee ☐ Black Bird, The ☐ Caged ☐ Dangerously They Live ☐ Footsteps in the Dark ☐ Fuller Brush Girl, The ☐ Gambler's Choice ☐ Inner Sanctum ☐ Lawless, The ☐ Maltese Falcon, The ☐ Mrs. Parkington ☐ New Interns, The ☐ Now, Voyager ☐ Nurse's Secret, The ☐ Over 21 ☐ Saturday's Children ☐ Sisters, The ☐ Somewhere I'll Find You ☐ Summer and Smoke ☐ Take Me to Town

Patrick, Nigel ☐ Breaking the Sound Barrier ☐ Browning Version, The ☐ Count Five and Die ☐ Encore ☐ Forbidden Cargo ☐ Grand National Night ☐ Great Waltz, The ☐ How to Murder a Rich Uncle ☐ Johnny Nobody ☐ League of Gentlemen, The ☐ Mackintosh Man, The ☐ Man Inside, The ☐ Pandora and the Flying Dutchman ☐ Passionate Sentry, The ☐ Prize of Gold, A ☐ Sapphire ☐ Sea Shall Not Have Them, The ☐ Silent Dust ☐ Silk Noose, The ☐ Tonight at 8:30 ☐ Trio ☐ Virgin Soldiers, The ☐ Young Wives' Tale

Patterson, Elizabeth ☐ Intruder in the Dust ☐ Michael Shayne, Private Detective ☐ My Sister Eileen ☐ Night Club Scandal ☐ Night of Mystery ☐ No Man of Her Own ☐ Remember the Night ☐ Sing, You Sinners ☐ So Red the Rose ☐ Tobacco Road ☐ Washington Story ☐ Welcome Stranger

Paxinou, Katina ☐ Confidential Agent ☐ For Whom the Bell Tolls ☐ Hostages ☐ Inheritance, The ☐ Miracle, The ☐ Mourning Becomes Electra ☐ Mr. Arkadin ☐ Prince of Foxes

Paxton, Bill ☐ Boxing Helena ☐ Brain Dead ☐ Dark Backward, The ☐ Future Shock ☐ Impulse ☐ Indian Summer ☐ Monolith ☐ Mortuary ☐ Near Dark ☐ Next of Kin ☐ One False Move ☐ Pass the Ammo ☐ Slipstream ☐ Trespass ☐ True Lies ☐ Vagrant, The

Paymer, David ☐ City Slickers ☐ Mr. Saturday Night ☐ No Way Out ☐ Quiz Show ☐ Searching for Bobby Fischer

Payne, John ☐ 99 River Street ☐ Bailout at 43,000 ☐ Blazing Forest, The ☐ Boss, The ☐ Captain China ☐ Caribbean ☐ College Swing ☐ Crosswinds ☐ Dolly Sisters, The ☐ Eagle and the Hawk, The ☐ Footlight Serenade ☐ Garden of the Moon ☐ Great American Broadcast, The ☐ Great Profile, The ☐ Hats Off ☐ Hell's Island ☐ Hello Frisco, Hello ☐ Hidden Fear ☐ Hold Back the Night ☐ Iceland ☐ Indianapolis Speedway ☐ Kansas City Confidential ☐ Larceny ☐ Maryland ☐ Miracle on 34th Street ☐ Passage West ☐ Rails Into Laramie ☐ Rebel in Town ☐ Road to Denver, The ☐ Santa Fe Passage ☐ Saxon Charm, The ☐ Sentimental Journey ☐ Silver Lode ☐ Slightly Scarlet ☐ Springtime in the Rockies ☐ Star Dust ☐ Sun Valley Serenade ☐ Tennessee's Partner ☐ Tin Pan Alley ☐ To the Shores of Tripoli ☐ Tripoli ☐ Week-end in Havana

Pays, Amanda ☐ Cold Room, The ☐ Computer Dreams ☐ Exposure ☐ Flash, The ☐ Kindred, The ☐ Leviathan ☐ Off Limits ☐ Oxford Blues

Payton, Barbara ☐ Bride of the Gorilla ☐ Drums in the Deep South ☐ Four Sided Triangle ☐ Great Jesse James Raid, The ☐ Murder Is My Beat ☐ Only the Valiant

Peach, Mary ☐ Ballad in Blue ☐ Follow That Horse! ☐ Gathering of Eagles ☐ No Love for Johnnie

Peary, Harold ☐ Gildersleeve on Broadway ☐ Gildersleeve's Ghost ☐ Great Gildersleeve, The ☐ Here We Go Again ☐ Seven Days' Leave

Peck, Gregory ☐ Amazing Grace and Chuck ☐ Arabesque ☐ Behold a Pale Horse ☐ Beloved Infidel ☐ Big Country, The ☐ Billy Two Hats ☐ Boys From Brazil, The ☐ Bravados, The ☐ Cape Fear ☐ Cape Fear ☐ Captain Horatio Hornblower ☐ Captain Newman, M.D. ☐ Chairman, The ☐ David and Bathsheba ☐ Days of Glory ☐ Designing Woman ☐ Duel in the Sun ☐ Gentleman's Agreement ☐ Great Sinner, The ☐ Gunfighter, The ☐ Guns of Navarone, The ☐ How the West Was Won ☐ I Walk the Line ☐ Keys of the Kingdom ☐ MacArthur ☐ Mackenna's Gold ☐ Macomber Affair, The ☐ Man in the Gray Flannel Suit, The ☐ Man with a Million ☐ Marooned ☐ Mirage ☐ Moby Dick ☐ Night People ☐ Old Gringo ☐ Omen, The ☐ On the Beach ☐ Only the Valiant ☐ Other People's Money ☐ Paradine Case ☐ Pork Chop Hill ☐ Portrait, The ☐ Purple Plain, The ☐ Roman Holiday ☐ Scarlet and the Black, The ☐ Sea Wolves, The ☐ Snows of Kilimanjaro, The ☐ Spellbound ☐ Stalking Moon, The ☐ To Kill a Mockingbird ☐ Twelve O'Clock High ☐ Valley of Decision, The ☐ World in His Arms, The ☐ Yearling, The ☐ Yellow Sky

Pena, Elizabeth ☐ batteries not included ☐ El Super ☐ Fugutive Among Us ☐ Jacob's Ladder ☐ La Bamba ☐ Waterdance, The

Pendleton, Austin ☐ Front Page, The ☐ Guarding Tess ☐ Mr. & Mrs. Bridge ☐ Mr. Nanny ☐ My Cousin Vinny ☐ Rain Without Thunder ☐ Short Circuit ☐ Simon ☐ Starting Over ☐ What's Up, Doc?

Pendleton, Nat ☐ At the Circus ☐ Chaser, The ☐ Fast Company ☐ Flight Command ☐ Fugitive Lovers, The ☐ It's a Wonderful World ☐ Mad Doctor of Market Street, The ☐ Manhattan Melodrama ☐ Secret of Dr. Kildare, The ☐ Shopworn Angel, The ☐ Sign of the Cross, The ☐ Swing Your Lady ☐ Thin Man, The ☐ Young Dr. Kildare

Penn, Christopher ☐ At Close Range ☐ Best of the Best ☐ Footloose ☐ Futurekick ☐ Josh and S.A.M. ☐ Made in USA ☐ Mobsters ☐ Pale Rider ☐ Reservoir Dogs

Penn, Sean ☐ At Close Range ☐ Bad Boys ☐ Carlito's Way ☐ Casualties of War ☐ Colors ☐ Falcon and the Snowman, The ☐ Fast Times at Ridgemont High ☐ Judgment in Berlin ☐ Racing With the Moon ☐ Shanghai Surprise ☐ State of Grace ☐ Taps ☐ We're No Angels

Peppard, George ☐ Banacek ☐ Battle Beyond the Stars ☐ Blue Max, The ☐ Breakfast at Tiffany's ☐ Cannon for Cordoba ☐ Carpetbaggers, The ☐ Damnation Alley ☐ Executioner, The ☐ Five Days from Home ☐ From Hell to Victory ☐ Groundstar Conspiracy, The ☐ Guilty or Innocent: The Sam Sheppard Murder Case ☐ Home From the Hill ☐ House of Cards ☐ How the West Was Won ☐ Man Against the Mob ☐ Man Against the Mob: The Chinatown Murders ☐ Newman's Law ☐ Night of the Fox ☐ One More Train to Rob ☐ One of Our Own ☐ Operation Crossbow ☐ Pendulum ☐ Pork Chop Hill ☐ Race to the Yankee Zephyr ☐ Rough Night in Jericho ☐ Silence Like Glass ☐ Subterraneans, The ☐ Third Day, The ☐ Tobruk ☐ Torn Between Two Lovers ☐ Victors, The ☐ What's So Bad About Feeling Good?

Perez, Rosie ☐ Criminal Justice ☐ Do the Right Thing ☐ Fearless ☐ It Could Happen To You ☐ Night on Earth ☐ Untamed Heart ☐ White Men Can't Jump

Perkins, Anthony ☐ Actress, The ☐ Black Hole, The ☐ Catch-22 ☐ Champagne Murders, The ☐ Crimes of Passion ☐ Daughter of Darkness ☐ Desire Under the Elms ☐ Destroyer ☐ Edge of Sanity ☐ Fear Strikes Out ☐ ffolkes ☐ First, You Cry ☐ Five Miles to Midnight ☐ Fool Killer, The ☐ Friendly Persuasion ☐ Glory Boys, The ☐ Goodbye Again ☐ Green Mansions ☐ How Awful About Allan ☐ I'm Dangerous Tonight ☐ Les Miserables ☐ Life and Times of Judge Roy Bean, The ☐ Lonely Man, The ☐ Lovin' Molly ☐ Mahogany ☐ Matchmaker, The ☐ Murder on the Orient Express ☐ On the Beach ☐ Phaedra ☐ Play It As It Lays ☐ Pretty Poison ☐ Psycho ☐ Psycho 2 ☐ Psycho 3 ☐ Psycho IV: The Beginning ☐ Ravishing Idiot ☐ Sins of Dorian Gray, The ☐ Someone Behind the Door ☐ Tall Story ☐ Ten Days Wonder ☐ Ten Days' Wonder ☐ This Angry Age ☐ Tin Star, The ☐ Trial, The ☐ Winter Kills

Perkins, Elizabeth ☐ About Last Night . . . ☐ Avalon ☐ Big ☐ Doctor, The ☐ Flintstones, The ☐ From the Hip ☐ He Said, She Said ☐ Indian Summer ☐ Love at Large ☐ Miracle on 34th Street ☐ Over Her Dead Body ☐ Sweet Hearts Dance

Perkins, Millie ☐ Call Me Anna ☐ Diary of Anne Frank, The ☐ Dulcinea ☐ Ensign Pulver ☐ Love in the Present Tense ☐ Shooting, The ☐ Slam Dance ☐ Table for Five ☐ Thanksgiving Promise, The ☐ Wild in the Country

Perlman, Rhea ☐ Class Act ☐ Having Babies II ☐ I Want to Keep My Baby ☐ My Little Pony—The Movie ☐ Ratings Game, The ☐ Stamp of a Killer ☐ There Goes the Neighborhood ☐ We're Back: A Dinosaur's Story

Perreau, Gigi ☐ Bonzo Goes to College ☐ Dance with Me Henry ☐ Family Honeymoon ☐ Has Anybody Seen My Gal? ☐ Hell on Wheels ☐ Journey to the Center of Time ☐ Lady Pays Off, The ☐ Look in any Window ☐ My Foolish Heart ☐ Never a Dull Moment ☐ Reunion in Reno ☐ Shadow on the Wall ☐ Song of Love ☐ Voice of the Whistler ☐ Weekend With Father

Perrin, Jacques ☐ Cinema Paradiso ☐ Donkey Skin ☐ Flight of the Innocent, The ☐ Girl with a Suitcase ☐ Le Crabe Tambour ☐ Sleeping Car Murders, The

Perrine, Valerie ☐ Agency ☐ Boiling Point ☐ Border, The ☐ Bright Angel ☐ Can't Stop the Music ☐ Electric Horseman, The ☐ Last American Hero, The ☐ Lenny ☐ Magician of Lublin, The ☐ Maid to Order ☐ Malibu ☐ Mr. Billion ☐ Slaughterhouse-Five ☐ Superman—The Movie ☐ Sweet Bird of Youth ☐ W.C. Fields and Me

Perry, Joan ☐ International Squadron ☐ Lone Wolf Strikes, The ☐ Maisie Was a Lady ☐ Meet Nero Wolfe ☐ Mysterious Avenger, The ☐ Nine Lives Are Not Enough ☐ Start Cheering

Perry, Luke ☐ 8 Seconds ☐ Beverly Hills, 90210 ☐ Beverly Hills, 90210—The Graduation ☐ Buffy the Vampire Slayer ☐ Terminal Bliss

Pesci, Joe ☐ Betsy's Wedding ☐ Dear Mr. Wonderful ☐ Easy Money ☐ Famiy Enforcer ☐ GoodFellas ☐ Home Alone ☐ Home Alone 2: Lost in New York ☐ I'm Dancing as Fast as I Can ☐ JFK ☐ Jimmy Hollywood ☐ Lethal Weapon 2 ☐ Lethal Weapon 3 ☐ Man on Fire ☐ My Cousin Vinny ☐ Public Eye, The ☐ Raging Bull ☐ Super, The ☐ With Honors

Peters, Bernadette ☐ Ace Eli and Rodger of the Skies ☐ Alice ☐ Annie ☐ David ☐ Fall From Grace ☐ Heartbeeps ☐ Impromptu ☐ Jerk, The ☐ Last Best Year, The ☐ Longest Yard, The ☐ Martian Chronicles, The ☐ Pennies From Heaven ☐ Pink Cadillac ☐ Silent Movie ☐ Slaves of New York ☐ W.C. Fields and Me

Peters, Brock ☐ Ace High ☐ Adventures of Huckleberry, Finn, The ☐ Black Girl ☐ Framed ☐ Incident, The ☐ L-Shaped Room, The ☐ Lost in the Stars ☐ Major Dundee ☐ McMasters, The ☐ Pawnbroker, The ☐ Polly ☐ Porgy and Bess ☐ Slaughter's Big Rip-Off ☐ To Kill a Mockingbird

Peters, Jean ☐ Anne of the Indies ☐ Apache ☐ As Young As You Feel ☐ Blueprint for Murder ☐ Broken Lance ☐ Captain from Castile ☐ Deep Waters ☐ It Happens

Every Spring ☐ Love That Brute ☐ Lure of the Wilderness ☐ Man Called Peter, A ☐ Niagara ☐ O. Henry's Full House ☐ Peter and Paul ☐ Pickup on South Street ☐ Three Coins in the Fountain ☐ Viva Zapata! ☐ Wait 'Til the Sun Shines, Nellie

Petty, Lori ☐ Cadillac Man ☐ Free Willy ☐ League of Their Own, A ☐ Point Break

Pfeiffer, Michelle ☐ Age of Innocence, The ☐ Amazon Women on the Moon ☐ Batman Returns ☐ Charlie Chan and the Curse of the Dragon Queen ☐ Children Nobody Wanted, The ☐ Dangerous Liaisons ☐ Fabulous Baker Boys, The ☐ Falling in Love Again ☐ Frankie and Johnny ☐ Grease 2 ☐ Hollywood Knights, The ☐ Into the Night ☐ Ladyhawke ☐ Love Field ☐ Married to the Mob ☐ Russia House, The ☐ Scarface ☐ Sweet Liberty ☐ Tequila Sunrise ☐ Witches of Eastwick, The ☐ Wolf

Philipe, Gerard ☐ Beauties of the Night ☐ Beauty and the Devil ☐ Dangerous Liaisons 1960 ☐ Devil in the Flesh ☐ Fanfan the Tulip ☐ Grand Maneuver, The ☐ La Ronde ☐ Le Rouge et le Noir ☐ Lovers of Montparnasse, The ☐ Lovers of Paris ☐ Lovers, Happy Lovers ☐ Red and the Black, The ☐ Royal Affairs in Versailles ☐ Seven Deadly Sins

Phillips, Lou Diamond ☐ Ambition ☐ Dakota ☐ Dark Wind, The ☐ Disorganized Crime ☐ Extreme Justice ☐ First Power, The ☐ Harley ☐ La Bamba ☐ Renegades ☐ Shadow of the Wolf ☐ Show of Force, A ☐ Stand and Deliver ☐ Young Guns ☐ Young Guns 2

Phoenix, River ☐ Circle of Violence: A Family Drama, A ☐ Dogfight ☐ Explorers ☐ I Love You to Death ☐ Little Nikita ☐ Mosquito Coast, The ☐ My Own Private Idaho ☐ Night in the Life of Jimmy Reardon, A ☐ Running on Empty ☐ Silent Tongue ☐ Sneakers ☐ Stand by Me ☐ Thing Called Love, The

Phillips, Mackenzie ☐ American Graffiti ☐ Eleanor and Franklin ☐ Fast Friends ☐ Love Child ☐ More American Graffiti

Phillips, Michelle ☐ American Anthem ☐ Bloodline ☐ California Kid, The ☐ Dillinger ☐ Man with Bogart's Face, The ☐ Scissors ☐ Valentino

Phillips, Sian ☐ Clash of the Titans ☐ Dune ☐ Ewoks: The Battle for Endor ☐ Goodbye, Mr. Chips ☐ Heidi ☐ Murphy's War ☐ Valmont

Piccoli, Michel ☐ Atlantic City ☐ Bad Blood ☐ Belle de Jour ☐ Benjamin ☐ Beyond Obsession ☐ Contempt ☐ Danger: Diabolik ☐ Dangerous Moves ☐ Day and the Hour, The ☐ Diary of a Chambermaid ☐ Discreet Charm of the Bourgeoisie, The ☐ Eyes, the Mouth, The ☐ French Conspiracy, The ☐ Game Is Over, The ☐ Infernal Trio, The ☐ L'Etat Sauvage (The Savage State) ☐ La Belle Noiseuse ☐ La Guerre Est Finie ☐ La Passante ☐ Leap into the Void ☐ Leonor ☐ Lies Before Kisses ☐ Masquerade ☐ May Fools ☐ Milky Way, The ☐ Passion ☐ Peril ☐ Phantom of Liberty, The ☐ Sleeping Car Murders, The ☐ Ten Days Wonder ☐ Ten Days' Wonder ☐ Things of Life, The ☐ Topaz ☐ Vincent, Francois, Paul and the Others

Pichel, Irving ☐ Dracula's Daughter ☐ Madame Butterfly ☐ Most Dangerous Game, The ☐ Murder by the Clock ☐ Oliver Twist ☐ Westward Passage

Pickens, Slim ☐ Babe ☐ Blazing Saddles ☐ Bootleggers ☐ Charlie and the Great Balloon Chase ☐ Christmas Mountain ☐ Cowboys, The ☐ Dr. Strangelove or: How I Learned To Stop Worrying and Love the Bomb ☐ Eye for an Eye, An ☐ Flim Flam Man, The ☐ Gunsight Ridge ☐ Hitched ☐ Honeysuckle Rose ☐ Honkers, The ☐ J.C. ☐ JD and the Salt Flat Kid ☐ Legend of Earl Durand, The ☐ Major Dundee ☐ Mr. Billion ☐ Pink Floyd—The Wall ☐ Rancho Deluxe ☐ Rocky Mountain ☐ Rough Night in Jericho ☐ Sacketts, The ☐ Santa Fe Passage ☐ Stagecoach ☐ Sun Shines Bright, The ☐ White Buffalo, The ☐ White Line Fever

Pickford, Mary ☐ Coquette ☐ Gaslight Follies ☐ Little Annie Rooney ☐ Lonely Villa, The ☐ Pollyanna ☐ Rebecca of Sunnybrook Farm ☐ Suds ☐ Taming of the Shrew, The

Pidgeon, Walter ☐ Advise and Consent ☐ Bad and the Beautiful, The ☐ Big Brown Eyes ☐ Big Red ☐ Blossoms in the Dust ☐ Calling Bulldog Drummond ☐ Cinderella ☐ Command Decision ☐ Dark Command ☐ Deep in My Heart ☐ Design for Scandal ☐ Dream Wife ☐ Executive Suite ☐ Flight Command ☐ Forbidden Planet ☐ Funny Girl ☐ Girl of the Golden West, The ☐ Girl with Ideas, A ☐ Harry in Your Pocket ☐ Hit the Deck ☐ Holiday in Mexico ☐ House Across the Bay, The ☐ House on Greenapple Road, The ☐ How Green Was My Valley ☐ How I Spent My Summer Vacation ☐ If Winter Comes ☐ It's a Date ☐ Julia Misbehaves ☐ Kiss Before the Mirror, The ☐ Last Time I Saw Paris, The ☐ Listen, Darling ☐ Madame Curie ☐ Man Hunt ☐ Man-Proof ☐ Mask of Sheba, The ☐ Men of the Fighting Lady ☐ Million Dollar Mermaid ☐ Miniver Story, The ☐ Mrs. Miniver ☐ Mrs. Parkington ☐ Murder on Flight 502 ☐ Nick Carter, Master Detective ☐ Rack, The ☐ Saratoga ☐ Secret Heart, The ☐ Sellout, The ☐ Sextette ☐ Shopworn Angel, The ☐ Skyjacked ☐ Soldiers Three ☐ That Forsythe Woman ☐ These Wilder Years ☐ Too Hot to Handle ☐ Two Colonels, The ☐ Two Minute Warning ☐ Viennese Nights ☐ Voyage to the Bottom of the Sea ☐ Warning Shot ☐ Weekend at the Waldorf ☐ White Cargo

Piscopo, Joe ☐ Dead Heat ☐ Huck and the King of Hearts ☐ Johnny Dangerously ☐ Sidekicks ☐ Wise Guys

Pisier, Marie-France ☐ Brontë Sisters, The

☐ Céline and Julie Go Boating ☐ Chanel Solitaire ☐ Cousin, Cousine ☐ French Postcards ☐ French Provincial ☐ Love at Twenty ☐ Love on the Run ☐ Miss Right ☐ Other Side of Midnight, The

Pitt, Brad ☐ Across the Tracks ☐ Cool World ☐ Cutting Class ☐ Favor, The ☐ Interview With the Vampire ☐ Johnny Suede ☐ Kalifornia ☐ Legends of the Fall ☐ River Runs Through It, A ☐ Thelma & Louise ☐ True Romance

Pitts, ZaSu ☐ Back Street ☐ Blondie of the Follies ☐ Broadway Limited ☐ Broken Lullaby ☐ Dames ☐ Forty Naughty Girls ☐ Francis ☐ Francis Joins the Wacs ☐ Gay Bride, The ☐ Greed ☐ Guardsman, The ☐ Hello Sister ☐ Is My Face Red? ☐ It All Came True ☐ Let's Face It ☐ Life with Father ☐ Lottery Bride, The ☐ Meet the Baron ☐ Mexican Spitfire at Sea ☐ Mexican Spitfire's Baby ☐ Monte Carlo ☐ Mr. Skitch ☐ Mrs. Wiggs of the Cabbage Patch ☐ Naughty but Nice ☐ Nurse Edith Cavell ☐ Once in a Lifetime ☐ Out All Night ☐ River's End ☐ Ruggles of Red Gap ☐ Shopworn ☐ Sin Takes a Holiday ☐ Thirteen Hours By Air ☐ This Could Be the Night ☐ TISH ☐ Wedding March, The ☐ Westward Passage

Place, Mary Kay ☐ Big Chill, The ☐ Captain Ron ☐ Girl Who Spelled Freedom, The ☐ History Of White People In America, The—Vol. 2 ☐ History of White People In America, The—Vol. 1 ☐ Kansas City Bomber ☐ Modern Problems ☐ New Life, A ☐ New York, New York ☐ Samantha

Platt, Oliver ☐ Beethoven ☐ Benny & Joon ☐ Diggstown ☐ Flatliners ☐ Funny Bones ☐ Indecent Proposal ☐ Tall Tale: The Unbelievable Adventures of Pecos Bill ☐ Temp, The ☐ Three Musketeers, The

Pleasence, Donald ☐ 1984 ☐ All Quiet on the Western Front ☐ Alone in the Dark ☐ Ambassador, The ☐ American Tiger ☐ Arch of Triumph ☐ Barry Mackenzie Holds His Own ☐ Beachcomber, The ☐ Black Tent, The ☐ Black Windmill, The ☐ Blood Relatives ☐ Breed Apart, A ☐ Buried Alive ☐ Circus of Horrors ☐ Count of Monte Cristo, The ☐ Creepers ☐ Cul-De-Sac ☐ Dario Argento's World of Horror ☐ Decision Against Time ☐ Defection of Simas Kudirka, The ☐ Devonsville Terror, The ☐ Dirty Knight's Work ☐ Dracula ☐ Eagle Has Landed, The ☐ Escape from New York ☐ Escape to Witch Mountain ☐ Eye of the Devil ☐ Fantastic Voyage ☐ Flesh and the Fiends, The ☐ Freakmaker, The ☐ From Beyond the Grave ☐ Gold of the Amazon Women ☐ Goldenrod ☐ Good Luck, Miss Wyckoff ☐ Great Escape 2: The Untold Story, The ☐ Great Escape, The ☐ Ground Zero ☐ Guest, The ☐ Hallelujah Trail, The ☐ Halloween ☐ Halloween 4: The Return of Michael Myers ☐ Halloween 5: Revenge of Michael Myers, The ☐ Halloween II ☐ Hands of Orlac, The ☐ Hanna's War ☐ Hearts of the West ☐ Hell Is a City ☐ Henry VIII and His Six Wives ☐ Horsemasters, The ☐ Innocent Bystanders ☐ Into the Darkness ☐ Jaguar Lives! ☐ Jerusalem File, The ☐ Journey Into Fear ☐ Killers of Kilimanjaro ☐ Land of the Minotaur ☐ Last Tycoon, The ☐ Lisa ☐ Look Back in Anger ☐ Man Inside, The ☐ Matchless ☐ Monster Club, The ☐ Night Creature ☐ Night of the Generals, The ☐ No Love for Johnnie ☐ No Place Like Homicide! ☐ Operation Nam ☐ Outback ☐ Passover Plot, The ☐ Pied Piper, The ☐ Prince of Darkness ☐ Race to the Yankee Zephyr ☐ Raw Meat ☐ Risk, The ☐ Sgt. Pepper's Lonely Hearts Club Band ☐ Shadows and Fog ☐ Shakedown, The ☐ Soldier Blue ☐ Sons and Lovers ☐ Still Life ☐ Tale of Two Cities, A ☐ Telefon ☐ Ten Little Indians ☐ Terror in the Aisles ☐ THX 1138 ☐ Will Penny ☐ Witness for the Prosecution ☐ You Only Live Twice

Pleshette, Suzanne ☐ Adventures of Bullwhip Griffin, The ☐ Along Came a Spider ☐ Battling for Baby ☐ Belarus File, The ☐ Birds, The ☐ Blackbeard's Ghost ☐ Distant Trumpet, A ☐ Dixie: Changing Habits ☐ Fate Is the Hunter ☐ Flesh & Blood ☐ Forty Pounds of Trouble ☐ Geisha Boy, The ☐ Hard Frame ☐ Help Wanted: Male ☐ Hot Stuff ☐ If It's Tuesday, This Must Be Belgium ☐ If Things Were Different ☐ In Broad Daylight ☐ Law and Order ☐ Legend of Valentino, The ☐ Leona Helmsley: The Queen of Mean ☐ Mister Buddwing ☐ Nevada Smith ☐ Oh God! Book II ☐ One Cooks, the Other Doesn't ☐ Power, The ☐ Rage to Live, A ☐ Rome Adventure ☐ Shaggy D.A., The ☐ Support Your Local Gunfighter ☐ Suppose They Gave a War and Nobody Came? ☐ Ugly Dachshund, The ☐ Wall of Noise ☐ Youngblood Hawke

Plimpton, Martha ☐ Beans of Egypt, Maine, The ☐ Chantilly Lace ☐ Goonies, The ☐ Josh and S.A.M. ☐ Mosquito Coast, The ☐ Parenthood ☐ River Rat, The ☐ Rollover ☐ Running on Empty ☐ Samantha ☐ Shy People ☐ Silence Like Glass ☐ Stanley & Iris ☐ Stars and Bars

Plowright, Joan ☐ And a Nightingale Sang ☐ Avalon ☐ Brimstone and Treacle ☐ Britannia Hospital ☐ Dennis the Menace ☐ Diary of Anne Frank, The ☐ Dressmaker, The ☐ Drowning by Numbers ☐ Enchanted April ☐ Entertainer, The ☐ I Love You to Death ☐ Revolution ☐ Stalin ☐ Summer House, The ☐ Three Sisters ☐ Time Without Pity ☐ Widow's Peak ☐ Widows' Peak

Plummer, Amanda ☐ Cattle Annie and Little Britches ☐ Courtship ☐ Daniel ☐ Dollmaker, The ☐ Fisher King, The ☐ Freejack ☐ Hotel New Hampshire, The ☐ Last Light ☐ Made in Heaven ☐ Miss Rose White ☐ Needful Things ☐ Pulp Fiction ☐ So I Married An Axe

Murderer ☐ Tales from the Crypt ☐ World According to Garp, The

Plummer, Christopher ☐ Aces High ☐ Amateur, The ☐ American Tail, An ☐ Assignment, The ☐ Battle of Britain, The ☐ Boss' Wife, The ☐ Boy in Blue, The ☐ Conduct Unbecoming ☐ Disappearance, The ☐ Dolores Claiborne ☐ Dragnet ☐ Dreamscape ☐ Eyewitness ☐ Fall of the Roman Empire ☐ Firehead ☐ Hanover Street ☐ Hazard of Hearts, A ☐ High Commissioner, The ☐ Highpoint ☐ I Love N.Y. ☐ Inside Daisy Clover ☐ International Velvet ☐ Liar's Edge ☐ Lily in Love ☐ Little Gloria-Happy At Last ☐ Lock Up Your Daughters! ☐ Man Who Would Be King, The ☐ Mind Field ☐ Murder by Decree ☐ Night of the Generals, The ☐ Oedipus the King ☐ Ordeal by Innocence ☐ Pyx, The ☐ Return of the Pink Panther, The ☐ Rock-a-Doodle ☐ Royal Hunt of the Sun, The ☐ Scarlet and the Black, The ☐ Shadow Box, The ☐ Shadow Dancing ☐ Silent Partner, The ☐ Somewhere in Time ☐ Sound of Music, The ☐ Spiral Staircase, The ☐ Stage Struck ☐ Star Trek VI: The Undiscovered Country ☐ Starcrash ☐ Thorn Birds, The ☐ Triple Cross ☐ Waterloo ☐ Where the Heart Is ☐ Wind Across the Everglades ☐ Wolf ☐ Young Catherine

Poitier, Sidney ☐ All the Young Men ☐ Band of Angels ☐ Bedford Incident, The ☐ Blackboard Jungle ☐ Brother John ☐ Buck and the Preacher ☐ Cry the Beloved Country ☐ Defiant Ones, The ☐ Duel at Diablo ☐ Edge of the City ☐ For Love of Ivy ☐ Go, Man, Go! ☐ Good-bye, My Lady ☐ Greatest Story Ever Told, The ☐ Guess Who's Coming to Dinner ☐ In the Heat of the Night ☐ Let's Do It Again ☐ Lilies of the Field ☐ Little Nikita ☐ Long Ships, The ☐ Lost Man, The ☐ Mark of the Hawk, The ☐ No Way Out ☐ Organization, The ☐ Paris Blues ☐ Patch of Blue, A ☐ Piece of the Action, A ☐ Porgy and Bess ☐ Pressure Point ☐ Raisin in the Sun, A ☐ Separate But Equal ☐ Shoot to Kill ☐ Slender Thread, The ☐ Sneakers ☐ Something of Value ☐ They Call Me MISTER Tibbs! ☐ To Sir with Love ☐ Uptown Saturday Night ☐ Warm December, A ☐ Wilby Conspiracy, The

Polanski, Roman ☐ Back in the USSR ☐ Fearless Vampire Killers or: Pardon Me, But Your Teeth Are in My Neck ☐ Innocent Sorcerers ☐ Tenant, The

Pollack, Sydney ☐ Death Becomes Her ☐ Husbands and Wives ☐ Tootsie ☐ War Hunt

Pollak, Kevin ☐ Clean Slate ☐ Few Good Men, A ☐ Grumpy Old Men ☐ Indian Summer ☐ Miami Rhapsody ☐ Opposite Sex (And How to Live with Them), The

Pollan, Tracy ☐ Danielle Steel's Fine Things ☐ Great Love Experiment, The ☐ Promised Land ☐ Stranger Among Us, A

Pollard, Michael J. ☐ America ☐ American Gothic ☐ Bonnie and Clyde ☐ Fast Food ☐ Hannibal Brooks ☐ Heated Vengeance ☐ Legend of Frenchie King, The ☐ Little Fauss and Big Halsy ☐ Next of Kin ☐ Night Visitor ☐ Patriot, The ☐ Riders of the Storm ☐ Sleepaway Camp 3—Teenage Wasteland ☐ Split Second

Porter, Eric ☐ Antony and Cleopatra ☐ Belstone Fox, The ☐ Callan ☐ Day of the Jackal, The ☐ Hands of the Ripper ☐ Heroes of Telemark, The ☐ Hitler: The Last Ten Days ☐ Kaleidoscope ☐ Little Lord Fauntleroy ☐ Lost Continent, The ☐ Thirty-Nine Steps, The ☐ Why Didn't They Ask Evans?

Portman, Eric ☐ 49th Parallel ☐ Canterbury Tale, A ☐ Child in the House ☐ Colditz Story ☐ Corridor of Mirrors ☐ Daybreak ☐ Deep Blue Sea, The ☐ Good Companions, The ☐ Great Day ☐ His Excellency ☐ Magic Box, The ☐ Man Who Finally Died, The ☐ Millions Like Us ☐ Moonlight Sonata ☐ Naked Edge, The ☐ One of Our Aircraft Is Missing ☐ Spider and the Fly, The ☐ We Dive at Dawn ☐ Whisperers, The

Potts, Annie ☐ Bayou Romance ☐ Breaking the Rules ☐ Corvette Summer ☐ Crimes of Passion ☐ Flatbed Annie & Sweetiepie: Lady Truckers ☐ Ghostbusters ☐ Ghostbusters II ☐ Heartaches ☐ Pass the Ammo ☐ Pretty in Pink ☐ Texasville ☐ Who's Harry Crumb?

Pounder, CCH ☐ Bagdad Cafe ☐ Common Ground ☐ Ernest Green Story, The ☐ Murder in Mississippi ☐ No Place Like Home ☐ Robocop 3 ☐ Tales From the Crypt Presents Demon Knight

Powell, Dick ☐ 42nd Street ☐ Bad and the Beautiful, The ☐ Blessed Event ☐ Broadway Gondolier ☐ Christmas in July ☐ Colleen ☐ College Coach ☐ Cornered ☐ Cowboy from Brooklyn, The ☐ Cry Danger ☐ Dames ☐ Flirtation Walk ☐ Footlight Parade ☐ Going Places ☐ Gold Diggers of 1933 ☐ Gold Diggers of 1935 ☐ Gold Diggers of 1937 ☐ Happiness Ahead ☐ Happy Go Lucky ☐ Hard to Get ☐ Hearts Divided ☐ Hollywood Hotel ☐ I Want a Divorce ☐ In the Navy ☐ It Happened Tomorrow ☐ Johnny O'Clock ☐ King's Vacation, The ☐ Meet the People ☐ Midsummer Night's Dream, A ☐ Model Wife ☐ Mrs. Mike ☐ Murder My Sweet ☐ Naughty but Nice ☐ On the Avenue ☐ Page Miss Glory ☐ Pitfall, The ☐ Reformer and the Redhead, The ☐ Right Cross ☐ Shipmates Forever ☐ Star Spangled Rhythm ☐ Station West ☐ Susan Slept Here ☐ Thanks a Million ☐ To the Ends of the Earth ☐ True to Life ☐ Twenty Million Sweethearts ☐ Varsity Show ☐ Wonder Bar ☐ You Never Can Tell

Powell, Eleanor ☐ Born to Dance ☐ Broadway Melody of 1936 ☐ Broadway Melody of 1938 ☐ Broadway Melody of 1940 ☐ Duchess of Idaho ☐ George White's Scandals ☐ Honolulu ☐ I Dood It ☐ Lady Be Good

☐ Rosalie ☐ Sensations ☐ Ship Ahoy ☐ Thousands Cheer

Powell, Jane ☐ Athena ☐ Date With Judy, A ☐ Deep in My Heart ☐ Delightfully Dangerous ☐ Enchanted Island ☐ Female Animal, The ☐ Girl Most Likely, The ☐ Hit the Deck ☐ Holiday in Mexico ☐ Letters, The ☐ Luxury Liner ☐ Mayday at 40,000 Feet! ☐ Nancy Goes to Rio ☐ Rich, Young and Pretty ☐ Royal Wedding ☐ Seven Brides for Seven Brothers ☐ Small Town Girl ☐ Song of the Open Road ☐ Three Daring Daughters ☐ Three Sailors and a Girl ☐ Two Weeks with Love

Powell, Robert ☐ Asphyx ☐ Four Feathers, The ☐ Hunchback of Notre Dame, The ☐ Imperative ☐ Jane Austen in Manhattan ☐ Jesus of Nazareth ☐ Jigsaw Man, The ☐ Mahler ☐ Mystery of Edwin Drood, The ☐ Secrets ☐ Shaka Zulu ☐ Thirty-Nine Steps, The

Powell, William ☐ After the Thin Man ☐ Another Thin Man ☐ Baroness and the Butler, The ☐ Benson Murder Case ☐ Canary Murder Case ☐ Charming Sinners ☐ Crossroads ☐ Double Wedding ☐ Emperor's Candlesticks, The ☐ Evelyn Prentice ☐ Ex-Mrs. Bradford, The ☐ Fashions ☐ Feel My Pulse ☐ For the Defense ☐ Girl Who Had Everything, The ☐ Great Ziegfeld, The ☐ Greene Murder Case, The ☐ Heavenly Body, The ☐ High Pressure ☐ Hoodlum Saint, The ☐ How to Marry a Millionaire ☐ I Love You Again ☐ Jewel Robbery ☐ Kennel Murder Case, The ☐ Key, The ☐ Ladies' Man ☐ Last Command, The ☐ Last of Mrs. Cheyney, The ☐ Lawyer Man ☐ Libeled Lady ☐ Life with Father ☐ Love Crazy ☐ Man Killer ☐ Man of the World ☐ Manhattan Melodrama ☐ Mister Roberts ☐ Mr. Peabody and the Mermaid ☐ My Man Godfrey ☐ One Way Passage ☐ Paramount on Parade ☐ Pointed Heels ☐ Reckless ☐ Rendezvous ☐ Senator Was Indiscreet, The ☐ Shadow of the Law ☐ Shadow of the Thin Man ☐ Song of the Thin Man ☐ Star of Midnight ☐ Take One False Step ☐ Thin Man Goes Home, The ☐ Thin Man, The ☐ Treasure of Lost Canyon, The ☐ Ziegfeld Follies

Power, Tyrone ☐ Abandon Ship! ☐ Alexander's Ragtime Band ☐ American Guerilla in the Philippines ☐ Black Rose, The ☐ Black Swan, The ☐ Blood and Sand ☐ Brigham Young ☐ Cafe Metropole ☐ Captain from Castile ☐ Crash Dive ☐ Day-Time Wife ☐ Diplomatic Courier ☐ Eddy Duchin Story, The ☐ Girls' Dormitory ☐ I'll Never Forget You ☐ In Old Chicago ☐ Jesse James ☐ Johnny Apollo ☐ King of the Khyber Rifles ☐ Ladies in Love ☐ Lloyd's of London ☐ Long Gray Line, The ☐ Love Is News ☐ Marie Antoinette ☐ Mark of Zorro, The ☐ Mississippi Gambler ☐ Nightmare Alley ☐ Pony Soldier ☐ Prince of Foxes ☐ Rains Came, The ☐ Rawhide ☐ Razor's Edge, The ☐ Rose of Washington Square ☐ Second Fiddle ☐ Second Honeymoon ☐ Sinbad and the Eye of the Tiger ☐ Son of Fury ☐ Suez ☐ Sun Also Rises, The ☐ That Wonderful Urge ☐ Thin Ice ☐ This Above All ☐ Untamed ☐ Witness for the Prosecution ☐ Yank in the RAF, A

Powers, Mala ☐ City Beneath the Sea ☐ City That Never Sleeps ☐ Colossus of New York, The ☐ Cyrano de Bergerac ☐ Edge of Doom ☐ Flight of the Lost Balloon ☐ Rage at Dawn ☐ Rose of Cimarron ☐ Sierra Baron ☐ Tammy and the Bachelor

Powers, Stefanie ☐ At Mother's Request ☐ Boatniks, The ☐ Burden of Proof, The ☐ Death in Canaan, A ☐ Die Die My Darling ☐ Experiment in Terror ☐ Hardcase ☐ Hart to Hart ☐ Herbie Rides Again ☐ If a Man Answers ☐ Interns, The ☐ It Seemed Like a Good Idea at the Time ☐ Little Moon and Jud McGraw ☐ Love Has Many Faces ☐ Magnificent Seven Ride!, The ☐ Manhunter ☐ McLintock! ☐ New Interns, The ☐ No Place to Run ☐ Nowhere to Run ☐ Palm Springs Weekend ☐ Paper Man ☐ Stagecoach ☐ Warning Shot

Preminger, Otto ☐ Margin for Error ☐ Pied Piper, The ☐ Stalag 17 ☐ They Got Me Covered ☐ Where Do We Go From Here?

Prentiss, Paula ☐ Addict ☐ Bachelor in Paradise ☐ Black Marble, The ☐ Buddy Buddy ☐ Catch-22 ☐ Follow the Boys ☐ Friendships, Secrets, and Lies ☐ Having Babies II ☐ Honeymoon Machine, The ☐ Horizontal Lieutenant, The ☐ Last of the Red Hot Lovers ☐ Looking for Love ☐ M.A.D.D. ☐ Man's Favorite Sport? ☐ Move ☐ No Room to Run ☐ Packin' It In ☐ Parallax View, The ☐ Saturday the 14th ☐ Stepford Wives, The ☐ What's New, Pussycat? ☐ Where the Boys Are ☐ World of Henry Orient, The

Presle, Micheline ☐ Adventures of Captain Fabian ☐ Bride Is Much Too Beautiful, The ☐ Chance Meeting ☐ Devil in the Flesh ☐ Five Day Lover ☐ French Way, The ☐ If a Man Answers ☐ Imperial Venus ☐ Nun, The ☐ Royal Affairs in Versailles ☐ Time Out for Love ☐ Under My Skin

Presley, Elvis ☐ Blue Hawaii ☐ Change of Habit ☐ Charro! ☐ Clambake ☐ Double Trouble ☐ Easy Come, Easy Go ☐ Elvis on Tour ☐ Elvis: That's the Way It Is ☐ Flaming Star ☐ Follow That Dream ☐ Frankie and Johnny ☐ Fun in Acapulco ☐ G.I. Blues ☐ Girl Happy ☐ Girls! Girls! Girls! ☐ Harum Scarum ☐ It Happened at the World's Fair ☐ Jailhouse Rock ☐ Kid Galahad ☐ King Creole ☐ Kissin' Cousins ☐ Live a Little, Love a Little ☐ Love Me Tender ☐ Loving You ☐ Paradise Hawaiian Style ☐ Roustabout ☐ Speedway ☐ Spinout ☐ This Is Elvis

☐ Tickle Me ☐ Trouble With Girls, The ☐ Viva Las Vegas ☐ Wild in the Country
Presley, Priscilla ☐ Adventures of Ford Fairlane, The ☐ Naked Gun 2 1/2: The Smell of Fear, The ☐ Naked Gun 33 1/3: The Final Insult ☐ Naked Gun, The
Preston, Robert ☐ All the Way Home ☐ Beau Geste ☐ Best of the Badmen ☐ Big City, The ☐ Blood on the Moon ☐ Child's Play ☐ Cloudburst ☐ Dark at the Top of the Stairs, The ☐ Face to Face ☐ Finnegan Begin Again ☐ Island of Love ☐ Junior Bonner ☐ King of Alcatraz ☐ Lady from Cheyenne ☐ Lady Gambles, The ☐ Last Frontier, The ☐ Last Starfighter, The ☐ Macomber Affair, The ☐ Mame ☐ Midnight Angel ☐ Music Man, The ☐ New York Town ☐ Night of January 16th, The ☐ Night Plane from Chungking ☐ Northwest Mounted Police ☐ Outrage ☐ Parachute Battalion ☐ Reap the Wild Wind ☐ S.O.B. ☐ Semi-Tough ☐ September Gun ☐ This Gun for Hire ☐ Tulsa ☐ Typhoon ☐ Union Pacific ☐ Victor/Victoria ☐ Wake Island ☐ When I Grow Up ☐ Whispering Smith ☐ Wild Harvest
Price, Dennis ☐ Bad Lord Byron ☐ Five Golden Hours ☐ For Better, For Worse ☐ Fortune in Diamonds ☐ Good Time Girl ☐ High Wind in Jamaica, A ☐ Holiday Camp ☐ Horror House ☐ Hungry Hill ☐ I'll Never Forget You ☐ I'm All Right, Jack ☐ Intruder, The ☐ Jassy ☐ Kind Hearts and Coronets ☐ Lady Godiva Rides Again ☐ Magic Bow, The ☐ Master of Bankdam, The ☐ Millionairess, The ☐ Murder Most Foul ☐ Naked Truth, The ☐ No Love for Johnnie ☐ No Place Like Homicide! ☐ Place of One's Own, A ☐ Play It Cool ☐ Pot Carriers, The ☐ School for Scoundrels ☐ Tunes of Glory ☐ V.I.P.s, The ☐ Victim
Price, Vincent ☐ Abominable Dr. Phibes, The ☐ Adventures of Captain Fabian ☐ Backtrack ☐ Bagdad ☐ Baron of Arizona, The ☐ Bat, The ☐ Big Circus, The ☐ Bribe, The ☐ Brigham Young ☐ Casanova's Big Night ☐ Champagne for Caesar ☐ Comedy of Terrors, The ☐ Conqueror Worm, The ☐ Convicts Four ☐ Cry of the Banshee ☐ Dangerous Mission ☐ Dead Heat ☐ Diary of a Madman ☐ Dr. Goldfoot and the Bikini Machine ☐ Dr. Goldfoot and the Girl Bombs ☐ Dr. Phibes Rises Again ☐ Dragonwyck ☐ Edward Scissorhands ☐ Escapes ☐ Eve of St. Mark, The ☐ Fall of the House of Usher ☐ Fly, The ☐ Great Mouse Detective, The ☐ Green Hell ☐ Haunted Palace, The ☐ Here Comes Peter Cottontail ☐ His Kind of Woman ☐ House of 1,000 Dolls ☐ House of the Long Shadows ☐ House of the Seven Gables, The ☐ House of Wax ☐ House on Haunted Hill ☐ Hudson's Bay ☐ Invisible Man Returns, The ☐ It's Not the Size That Counts ☐ Jackals, The ☐ Journey Into Fear ☐ Keys of the Kingdom ☐ Las Vegas Story, The ☐ Last Man on Earth, The ☐ Laura ☐ Leave Her to Heaven ☐ Long Night, The ☐ Mad Magician, The ☐ Madhouse ☐ Masque of the Red Death ☐ Master of the World ☐ Monster Club, The ☐ Mooch Goes To Hollywood ☐ More Dead Than Alive ☐ Oblong Box, The ☐ Offspring, The ☐ Pit and the Pendulum ☐ Private Lives of Elizabeth and Essex, The ☐ Rage of the Buccaneers, The ☐ Raven, The ☐ Return of the Fly, The ☐ Royal Scandal, A ☐ Scream and Scream Again ☐ Serenade ☐ Service De Luxe ☐ Shock ☐ Song of Bernadette, The ☐ Story of Mankind, The ☐ Tales of Terror ☐ Theatre of Blood ☐ Three Musketeers, The ☐ Tingler, The ☐ Tomb of Ligeia ☐ Tower of London ☐ Tower of London, The ☐ Trouble With Girls, The ☐ Twice-Told Tales ☐ Up In Central Park ☐ Web, The ☐ Whales of August, The ☐ While the City Sleeps ☐ Wilson
Primus, Barry ☐ Been Down So Long It Looks Like Up to Me ☐ Boxcar Bertha ☐ Heart of Steel ☐ Heartland ☐ New York, New York ☐ Night Games ☐ Talking Walls ☐ Torn Apart ☐ Von Richthofen and Brown
Prince ☐ Graffiti Bridge ☐ Purple Rain ☐ Sign o' the Times ☐ Under the Cherry Moon
Prince, William ☐ Carnegie Hall ☐ Cyrano de Bergerac ☐ Greatest Man in the World, The ☐ Macabre ☐ Network ☐ Objective, Burma! ☐ Pillow to Post ☐ Soldier, The ☐ Spontaneous Combustion ☐ Stepford Wives, The
Principal, Victoria ☐ Burden of Proof, The ☐ I Will, I Will . . . For Now ☐ Life and Times of Judge Roy Bean, The ☐ Mistress ☐ Naked Ape, The
Prine, Andrew ☐ Centerfold Girls, The ☐ Donner Pass—The Road to Survival ☐ Evil, The ☐ Grizzly ☐ Last of the Mohicans, The ☐ Miracle Worker, The ☐ Mission of the Shark ☐ Night Slaves ☐ Simon, King Of The Witches ☐ They're Playing With Fire ☐ Town That Dreaded Sundown, The
Prochnow, Jurgen ☐ Beverly Hills Cop II ☐ Consequence, The ☐ Das Boat ☐ Forbidden ☐ Fourth War, The ☐ In the Mouth of Madness ☐ In the Mouth of Madness ☐ Kill Cruise ☐ Killing Cars ☐ Man Inside, The ☐ Robin Hood ☐ Seventh Sign, The
Prosky, Robert ☐ Age Isn't Everything ☐ Big Shots ☐ Broadcast News ☐ Christine ☐ Far and Away ☐ From the Dead of Night ☐ Green Card ☐ Gremlins 2—The New Batch ☐ Hoffa ☐ Home Fires Burning ☐ Into Thin Air ☐ Last Action Hero ☐ Lords of Discipline, The ☐ Love She Sought, The ☐ Mrs. Doubtfire ☐ Murder of Mary Phagan, The ☐ Outrageous Fortune ☐ Rudy ☐ Teamster Boss: The Jackie Presser Story ☐ Things Change
Provine, Dorothy ☐ 30 Foot Bride of Candy Rock, The ☐ Bonnie Parker Story, The

☐ Good Neighbor Sam ☐ Great Race, The ☐ It's a Mad Mad Mad Mad World ☐ Kiss the Girls and Make Them Die ☐ Never a Dull Moment ☐ That Darn Cat ☐ Wall of Noise ☐ Who's Minding the Mint?

Pryce, Jonathan ☐ Adventures of Baron Munchausen, The ☐ Barbarians at the Gate ☐ Brazil ☐ Breaking Glass ☐ Consuming Passions ☐ Doctor and the Devils, The ☐ Freddie as F.R.O.7 ☐ Glengarry Glen Ross ☐ Haunted Honeymoon ☐ Loophole ☐ Man on Fire ☐ Ploughman's Lunch, The ☐ Rachel Papers, The ☐ Something Wicked This Way Comes

Pryor, Richard ☐ Adios Amigo ☐ Another You ☐ Bingo Long Traveling All-Stars & Motor Kings, The ☐ Blue Collar ☐ Brewster's Millions ☐ Bustin' Loose ☐ Busy Body, The ☐ California Suite ☐ Car Wash ☐ Critical Condition ☐ Dynamite Chicken ☐ Greased Lightning ☐ Harlem Nights ☐ Hit ☐ In God We Trust ☐ Jo Jo Dancer—Your Life Is Calling ☐ Lady Sings the Blues ☐ Mack, The ☐ Motown 25—Yesterday, Today, Forever ☐ Moving ☐ Richard Pryor Here and Now ☐ Richard Pryor Live and Smokin' ☐ Richard Pryor Live on the Sunset Strip ☐ Richard Pryor—Live in Concert ☐ See No Evil, Hear No Evil ☐ Silver Streak ☐ Some Call It Loving ☐ Some Kind of Hero ☐ Stir Crazy ☐ Superman 3 ☐ Toy, The ☐ Uptown Saturday Night ☐ Which Way Is Up? ☐ Wild in the Streets ☐ Wiz, The

Pullman, Bill ☐ Brain Dead ☐ Favor, The ☐ Last Seduction, The ☐ Liebestraum ☐ Malice ☐ Nervous Ticks ☐ Newsies ☐ Rocket Gibraltar ☐ Serpent and the Rainbow, The ☐ Sibling Rivalry ☐ Singles ☐ Sleepless in Seattle ☐ Sommersby ☐ Spaceballs ☐ Wyatt Earp

Purcell, Dick ☐ Blackwell's Island ☐ Flight Command ☐ Flight into Nowhere ☐ Missing Witnesses

Purcell, Lee ☐ Adam at 6 A.M. ☐ Almost Summer ☐ Big Wednesday ☐ Eddie Macon's Run ☐ Girl, the Gold Watch and Dynamite, The ☐ Mr. Majestyk ☐ My Wicked, Wicked Ways—The Legend of Errol Flynn ☐ Necromancy ☐ Valley Girl

Purcell, Noel ☐ Island Rescue ☐ Jacqueline ☐ Mad About Men ☐ Mad Little Island ☐ Nurse on Wheels ☐ Rise of the Moon, The ☐ Seekers, The

Purdom, Edmund ☐ After the Fall of New York ☐ Athena ☐ Egyptian, The ☐ Fury of the Pagans ☐ Herod the Great ☐ King's Thief, The ☐ Last of the Vikings, The ☐ Malaga ☐ Nights of Rasputin ☐ Prodigal, The ☐ Student Prince, The

Purl, Linda ☐ Body Language ☐ Eleanor and Franklin ☐ Flame Is Love, The ☐ Having Babies ☐ High Country, The ☐ In Self Defense ☐ Jory ☐ Manions of America, The ☐ Night the City Screamed, The

Quaid, Dennis ☐ All Night Long ☐ Amateur Night at the Dixie Bar and Grill ☐ Are You in the House Alone? ☐ Big Easy, The ☐ Bill ☐ Bill: On His Own ☐ Breaking Away ☐ Caveman ☐ Come See the Paradise ☐ D.O.A. ☐ Dreamscape ☐ Enemy Mine ☐ Everybody's All-American ☐ Flesh and Bone ☐ Gorp ☐ Great Balls of Fire! ☐ Innerspace ☐ Jaws 3 ☐ Johnny Belinda ☐ Long Riders, The ☐ Night the Lights Went Out in Georgia, The ☐ Our Winning Season ☐ Postcards from the Edge ☐ Seniors, The ☐ September 30, 1955 ☐ Suspect ☐ Undercover Blues ☐ Wilder Napalm ☐ Wyatt Earp

Quaid, Randy ☐ Apprenticeship Of Duddy Kravitz, The ☐ Bloodhounds of Broadway ☐ Bound for Glory ☐ Breakout ☐ Bye Bye, Love ☐ Caddyshack II ☐ Choirboys, The ☐ Days of Thunder ☐ Dead Solid Perfect ☐ Fool for Love ☐ Foxes ☐ Frankenstein ☐ Freaked ☐ Great Niagara, The ☐ Heartbeeps ☐ Last Detail, The ☐ Last Picture Show, The ☐ LBJ: The Early Years ☐ Long Riders, The ☐ Martians Go Home ☐ Midnight Express ☐ Missouri Breaks, The ☐ Moving ☐ National Lampoon's Christmas Vacation ☐ National Lampoon's Vacation ☐ No Man's Land ☐ Of Mice and Men ☐ Out Cold ☐ Paper, The ☐ Parents ☐ Quick Change ☐ Slugger's Wife, The ☐ Streetcar Named Desire, A ☐ Sweet Country ☐ Texasville ☐ Wraith, The

Quayle, Anthony ☐ 21 Hours at Munich ☐ Anne of the Thousand Days ☐ Before Winter Comes ☐ Bourne Identity, The ☐ Buster ☐ Damn the Defiant! ☐ Desert Attack ☐ Great Expectations ☐ Guns of Navarone, The ☐ Immoral Charge ☐ Jarrett ☐ Lawrence of Arabia ☐ Legend of the Holy Drinker, The ☐ Mackenna's Gold ☐ Man Who Wouldn't Talk, The ☐ Misunderstood ☐ Moses ☐ Nelson Affair, The ☐ No Time for Tears ☐ Operation Crossbow ☐ Pursuit of the Graf Spee ☐ Saraband ☐ Study in Terror, A ☐ Tamarind Seed, The ☐ Tarzan's Greatest Adventure ☐ Woman in a Dressing Gown ☐ Wrong Man, The

Quigley, Linnea ☐ Assault of the Party Nerds ☐ Creepozoids ☐ Dr. Alien ☐ Hollywood Chainsaw Hookers ☐ Murder Weapon ☐ Night of the Demons ☐ Savage Streets ☐ Sorority Babes in the Slimeball Bowl-O-Rama

Quillan, Eddie ☐ Big City, The ☐ Gentleman from Louisiana ☐ Here Comes Kelly ☐ Hi, Good Lookin' ☐ It Ain't Hay ☐ Mandarin Mystery, The ☐ Mystery of the Riverboat ☐ Noisy Neighbors ☐ Young Mr. Lincoln

Quilley, Denis ☐ Evil Under the Sun ☐ In this House of Brede ☐ Memed My Hawk ☐ Privates on Parade

Quinlan, Kathleen ☐ Blackout ☐ Bodily Harm ☐ Clara's Heart ☐ Dreams Lost, Dreams Found ☐ Hanky Panky ☐ I Never Promised You a Rose Garden ☐ Independence Day ☐ Last Winter, The ☐ Lifeguard ☐ Man Outside ☐ Nightmare in Blood ☐ Promise, The ☐ Runner Stumbles, The ☐ Stolen Babies ☐ Strays ☐ Warning Sign

Quinn, Aidan ☐ At Play in the Fields of the Lord ☐ Avalon ☐ Benny & Joon ☐ Blink ☐ Crusoe ☐ Desperately Seeking Susan ☐ Early Frost, An ☐ Handmaid's Tale, The ☐ Legends of the Fall ☐ Lies of the Twins ☐ Mission, The ☐ Perfect Witness ☐ Playboys, The ☐ Private Matter, A ☐ Reckless ☐ Stakeout

Quinn, Anthony ☐ Across 110th Street ☐ African Rage ☐ Against All Flags ☐ Angels of Darkness ☐ Attila ☐ Back to Bataan ☐ Barabbas ☐ Behold a Pale Horse ☐ Black Gold ☐ Black Orchid, The ☐ Black Swan, The ☐ Blood and Sand ☐ Blowing Wild ☐ Brave Bulls, The ☐ Brigand, The ☐ Buccaneer, The ☐ Buffalo Bill ☐ Bulldog Drummond in Africa ☐ California ☐ Caravans ☐ Children of Sanchez, The ☐ China Sky ☐ City Beneath the Sea ☐ City for Conquest ☐ City, The ☐ Dangerous to Know ☐ Daughter of Shanghai ☐ Deaf Smith and Johnny Ears ☐ Destructors, The ☐ Don Is Dead, The ☐ Dream of Kings, A ☐ East of Sumatra ☐ Fatal Desire ☐ Flap ☐ Ghost Breakers, The ☐ Ghosts Can't Do It ☐ Greek Tycoon, The ☐ Guadalcanal Diary ☐ Guns for San Sebastian ☐ Guns of Navarone, The ☐ Happening, The ☐ Heller in Pink Tights ☐ High Risk ☐ High Wind in Jamaica, A ☐ Hot Spell ☐ Hunchback of Notre Dame ☐ Imperfect Lady, The ☐ Inheritance, The ☐ Irish Eyes Are Smiling ☐ Island of Lost Men ☐ Jungle Fever ☐ King of Alcatraz ☐ King of Chinatown ☐ Knockout ☐ La Strada ☐ Larceny, Inc ☐ Last Action Hero ☐ Last Train From Gun Hill ☐ Last Train from Madrid, The ☐ Lawrence of Arabia ☐ Lion of the Desert ☐ Lost Command ☐ Lust for Life ☐ Magnificent Matador, The ☐ Magus, The ☐ Man from Del Rio, The ☐ Marco the Magnificent ☐ Mask of the Avenger ☐ Message, The ☐ Mobsters ☐ Naked Street, The ☐ Onassis: The Richest Man in the World ☐ Only the Lonely ☐ Ox-Bow Incident, The ☐ Passage, The ☐ Portrait in Black ☐ R.P.M. ☐ Requiem for a Heavyweight ☐ Revenge ☐ Ride Back, The ☐ River's Edge, The ☐ Road to Morocco ☐ Road to Singapore ☐ Salamander, The ☐ Savage Innocents, The ☐ Secret of Santa Vittoria, The ☐ Seminole ☐ Seven Cities of Gold ☐ Shoes of the Fisherman, The ☐ Sinbad the Sailor ☐ They Died With Their Boots On ☐ Thieves Fall Out ☐ This Can't Be Love ☐ Tycoon ☐ Ulysses ☐ Union Pacific ☐ Visit, The ☐ Viva Zapata! ☐ Waikiki Wedding ☐ Walk in the Spring Rain, A ☐ Warlock ☐ Where Do We Go From Here? ☐ Wild is the Wind ☐ World in His Arms, The ☐ Zorba the Greek

Radford, Basil ☐ Captive Heart, The ☐ Chance of a Lifetime ☐ Dead of Night ☐ Galloping Major, The ☐ It's Not Cricket ☐ Lady Vanishes, The ☐ Millions Like Us ☐ Night Train to Munich ☐ Passport to Pimlico ☐ Tight Little Island

Radner, Gilda ☐ Animalympics ☐ First Family ☐ Gilda Live ☐ Hanky Panky ☐ Haunted Honeymoon ☐ It Came From Hollywood ☐ Movers and Shakers ☐ Rutles, The ☐ Woman in Red, The

Raft, George ☐ All of Me ☐ Background to Danger ☐ Black Widow ☐ Bolero ☐ Bowery, The ☐ Broadway ☐ Bullet for Joey, A ☐ Casino Royale ☐ Christmas Eve ☐ Deadhead Miles ☐ Each Dawn I Die ☐ Every Night at Eight ☐ Five Golden Dragons ☐ Follow the Boys ☐ Glass Key, The ☐ House Across the Bay, The ☐ I Stole a Million ☐ If I Had a Million ☐ Invisible Stripes ☐ It Had to Happen ☐ Jet Over the Atlantic ☐ Johnny Angel ☐ Limehouse Blues ☐ Lucky Nick Cain ☐ Madame Racketeer ☐ Man from Cairo, The ☐ Manpower ☐ Mr. Ace ☐ Night After Night ☐ Night World ☐ Nob Hill ☐ Nocturne ☐ Outpost in Morocco ☐ Palmy Days ☐ Quick Millions ☐ Race Street ☐ Rogue Cop ☐ Scarface ☐ Sextette ☐ She Couldn't Take It ☐ Some Like It Hot ☐ Souls at Sea ☐ Spawn of the North ☐ They Drive by Night ☐ You and Me ☐ Yours For the Asking

Railsback, Steve ☐ Angela ☐ Blue Monkey ☐ Forgotten, The ☐ From Here to Eternity ☐ Golden Seal, The ☐ Helter Skelter ☐ Lifeforce ☐ Nukie ☐ Private Wars ☐ Scenes from the Goldmine ☐ Scissors ☐ Stunt Man, The ☐ Sunstroke ☐ Visitors, The

Raimu ☐ Baker's Wife, The ☐ Cesar ☐ Confessions of a Newlywed ☐ Eternal Husband, The ☐ Fanny ☐ Heart of a Nation, The ☐ Heart of Paris ☐ Marius ☐ Strangers in the House ☐ Well-Digger's Daughter, The

Rainer, Luise ☐ Big City, The ☐ Dramatic School ☐ Emperor's Candlesticks, The ☐ Good Earth, The ☐ Great Waltz, The ☐ Great Ziegfeld, The ☐ Hostages

Raines, Cristina ☐ Duellists, The ☐ Flamingo Road ☐ Livin' the Life ☐ Nightmares ☐ Quo Vadis? ☐ Sentinel, The

Raines, Ella ☐ Corvette K-225 ☐ Cry Havoc ☐ Fighting Coast Guard ☐ Hail the Conquering Hero ☐ Impact ☐ Man in the Road, The ☐ Phantom Lady ☐ Senator Was Indiscreet, The ☐ Tall in the Saddle ☐ Uncle Harry ☐ Walking Hills, The ☐ Web, The ☐ White Tie and Tails

Rains, Claude ☐ Adventures of Robin Hood, The ☐ Angel on My Shoulder ☐ Anthony Adverse ☐ Battle of the Worlds ☐ Caesar and Cleopatra ☐ Casablanca ☐ Clairvoyant, The ☐ Crime Without Passion ☐ Daughters Courageous ☐ Deception ☐ Forever and a Day ☐ Four Daughters ☐ Four Mothers ☐ Four Wives ☐ Gold Is Where You Find It ☐ Greatest Story Ever Told, The ☐ Hearts Divided

☐ Here Comes Mr. Jordan ☐ Invisible Man, The ☐ Juarez ☐ Kings Row ☐ Lady with Red Hair, The ☐ Last Outpost, The ☐ Lawrence of Arabia ☐ Lisbon ☐ Lost World ☐ Man Who Reclaimed His Head, The ☐ Moontide ☐ Mr. Skeffington ☐ Mr. Smith Goes to Washington ☐ Mystery of Edwin Drood, The ☐ Notorious ☐ Now, Voyager ☐ One Woman's Story ☐ Paris Express, The ☐ Passage to Marseille ☐ Phantom of the Opera ☐ Prince and the Pauper, The ☐ Saturday's Children ☐ Sea Hawk, The ☐ Sealed Cargo ☐ They Made Me a Criminal ☐ They Won't Forget ☐ This Earth Is Mine ☐ This Love of Ours ☐ Unsuspected, The ☐ Where Danger Lives ☐ White Tower, The ☐ Wolf Man, The

Ralph, Jessie ☐ Affairs of Cellini ☐ After the Thin Man ☐ Bank Dick, The ☐ Cafe Society ☐ Camille ☐ David Copperfield ☐ Drums Along the Mohawk ☐ Enchanted April ☐ Good Earth, The ☐ I Found Stella Parish ☐ I Want a Divorce ☐ Last of Mrs. Cheyney, The ☐ Les Miserables ☐ Little Lord Fauntleroy ☐ One Night of Love ☐ Port of Seven Seas ☐ San Francisco ☐ They Met in Bombay ☐ Unguarded Hour, The

Ralston, Vera Hruba ☐ Accused of Murder ☐ Angel on the Amazon ☐ Belle Le Grand ☐ Dakota ☐ Fair Wind to Java ☐ Fighting Kentuckian, The ☐ Flame, The ☐ Gunfire at Indian Gap ☐ Hoodlum Empire ☐ I, Jane Doe ☐ Jubilee Trail ☐ Lady and the Monster, The ☐ Murder in the Music Hall ☐ Perilous Journey, A ☐ Wild Blue Yonder, The ☐ Wyoming

Rambeau, Marjorie ☐ 20 Mule Team ☐ Abandoned ☐ Bad For Each Other ☐ Broadway ☐ East of the River ☐ Inspiration ☐ Laughing Sinners ☐ Man Called Peter, A ☐ Man of a Thousand Faces ☐ Man's Castle ☐ Min and Bill ☐ Palooka ☐ Primrose Path, The ☐ Salome, Where She Danced ☐ Secret Six, The ☐ Slander ☐ Strangers May Kiss ☐ This Modern Age ☐ Tobacco Road ☐ Torch Song ☐ Under Pressure ☐ Walls of Jericho, The

Ramis, Harold ☐ Baby Boom ☐ Ghostbusters ☐ Ghostbusters II ☐ Heavy Metal ☐ Stealing Home ☐ Stripes

Rampling, Charlotte ☐ D.O.A. ☐ Farewell, My Lovely ☐ Foxtrot ☐ Georgy Girl ☐ Giordano Bruno ☐ Henry VIII and His Six Wives ☐ Long Duel, The ☐ Mascara ☐ Max, Mon Amour ☐ Night Porter, The ☐ Orca—the Killer Whale ☐ Sardinia: Kidnapped ☐ Stardust Memories ☐ Vanishing Point ☐ Verdict, The ☐ Zardoz

Randall, Tony ☐ 7 Faces of Dr. Lao ☐ Adventures of Huckleberry Finn, The ☐ Agatha Christie's The Man in the Brown Suit ☐ Alphabet Murders, The ☐ Bang, Bang, You're Dead! ☐ Boys' Night Out ☐ Brass Bottle, The ☐ Fluffy ☐ Foolin' Around ☐ Hello Down There ☐ Hitler's S.S.: Portrait in Evil ☐ Island of Love ☐ Let's Make Love ☐ Lover Come Back ☐ Mating Game, The ☐ My Little Pony—The Movie ☐ No Down Payment ☐ Off Sides ☐ Oh, Men! Oh, Women! ☐ Pillow Talk ☐ Send Me No Flowers ☐ Will Success Spoil Rock Hunter?

Randolph, John ☐ American Clock, The ☐ F. Scott Fitzgerald in Hollywood ☐ Lovely but Deadly ☐ Means and Ends ☐ National Lampoon's Christmas Vacation ☐ Nowhere to Run ☐ Number One ☐ Prizzi's Honor ☐ Right of the People, The ☐ Seconds ☐ Secrets ☐ Serpico

Rathbone, Basil ☐ Above Suspicion ☐ Adventures of Ichabod and Mr. Toad, The ☐ Adventures of Marco Polo, The ☐ Adventures of Robin Hood, The ☐ Adventures of Sherlock Holmes, The ☐ Anna Karenina ☐ Bathing Beauty ☐ Bishop Murder Case ☐ Black Cat, The ☐ Black Sleep, The ☐ Captain Blood ☐ Casanova's Big Night ☐ Comedy of Terrors, The ☐ Confession ☐ Court Jester, The ☐ Crossroads ☐ David Copperfield ☐ Dawn Patrol, The ☐ Dressed to Kill ☐ Fingers at the Window ☐ Frenchman's Creek ☐ Garden of Allah, The ☐ Ghost in the Invisible Bikini ☐ Heartbeat ☐ Hillbillys in a Haunted House ☐ Hound of the Baskervilles, The ☐ House of Fear, The ☐ If I Were King ☐ International Lady ☐ Kind Lady ☐ Last Days of Pompeii, The ☐ Last Hurrah, The ☐ Love from a Stranger ☐ Mad Doctor, The ☐ Magic Sword, The ☐ Make a Wish ☐ Mark of Zorro, The ☐ Paris Calling ☐ Pearl of Death, The ☐ Pursuit to Algiers ☐ Queen of Blood ☐ Rhythm on the River ☐ Romeo and Juliet ☐ Scarlet Claw, The ☐ Secret Weapon ☐ Sherlock Holmes and the Spider Woman ☐ Sherlock Holmes and the Voice of Terror ☐ Sherlock Holmes Faces Death ☐ Sherlock Holmes in Washington ☐ Sin Takes a Holiday ☐ Son of Frankenstein ☐ Spider Woman, The ☐ Tale of Two Cities, A ☐ Tales of Terror ☐ Terror By Night ☐ Tovarich ☐ Tower of London, The ☐ We're No Angels ☐ Woman in Green, The

Ratoff, Gregory ☐ Abdulla the Great ☐ All About Eve ☐ Broadway Through a Keyhole ☐ Cafe Metropole ☐ Great Profile, The ☐ Road to Glory, The ☐ Sally, Irene and Mary ☐ Seventh Heaven ☐ Sing, Baby, Sing ☐ Sitting Pretty ☐ Sun Also Rises, The ☐ Symphony of Six Million ☐ Under Two Flags ☐ What Price Hollywood?

Ray, Aldo ☐ Battle Cry ☐ Bog ☐ Centerfold Girls, The ☐ Day They Robbed the Bank of England, The ☐ Dead Heat on a Merry-Go-Round ☐ Executioner, Part II, The ☐ Four Desperate Men ☐ God's Little Acre ☐ Great Skycopter Rescue, The ☐ Green Berets, The ☐ Haunts ☐ Inside Out ☐ Johnny Nobody ☐ Let's Do It Again ☐ Little Moon and Jud McGraw ☐ Lucifer Complex, The ☐ Man Who Would Not Die, The ☐ Marrying Kind, The ☐ Men in War ☐ Miss Sadie Thompson ☐ Mission To Glory ☐ Mister Too Little ☐ Mongrel ☐ Naked and the Dead, The

☐ Nightfall ☐ Pat and Mike ☐ Riot on Sunset Strip ☐ Seven Alone ☐ Shock 'em Dead ☐ We're No Angels ☐ Welcome to Hard Times ☐ What Did You Do in the War, Daddy?

Raye, Martha ☐ Artists and Models ☐ Big Broadcast of 1937, The ☐ Big Broadcast of 1938, The ☐ Billy Rose's Jumbo ☐ Boys from Syracuse, The ☐ College Holiday ☐ College Swing ☐ Double or Nothing ☐ Farmer's Daughter, The ☐ Four Jills in a Jeep ☐ Give Me a Sailor ☐ Gossip Columnist, The ☐ Hellzapoppin ☐ Keep 'Em Flying ☐ Monsieur Verdoux ☐ Navy Blues ☐ Never Say Die ☐ Pin Up Girl ☐ Pippin ☐ Rhythm on the Range ☐ Waikiki Wedding

Raymond, Gene ☐ Behold My Wife ☐ Bride Walks Out, The ☐ Coming-Out Party ☐ Ex-Lady ☐ Flying Down to Rio ☐ Hooray for Love ☐ I'd Rather Be Rich ☐ Ladies of the Big House ☐ Life of the Party, The ☐ Mr. and Mrs. Smith ☐ Night of June 13 ☐ Plunder Road ☐ Red Dust ☐ Sadie McKee ☐ Smilin' Through ☐ Sofia ☐ That Girl From Paris ☐ Transatlantic Merry-Go-Round ☐ Zoo in Budapest

Raymond, Paula ☐ Bandits of Corsica, The ☐ Beast from 20,000 Fathoms, The ☐ Blood of Dracula's Castle ☐ Crisis ☐ Flight That Disappeared, The ☐ Gun That Won the West, The ☐ Human Jungle, The ☐ Sellout, The

Reagan, Ronald ☐ Accidents Will Happen ☐ Angel From Texas, An ☐ Angels Wash Their Faces, The ☐ Bad Man, The ☐ Bedtime for Bonzo ☐ Boy Meets Girl ☐ Brother Rat ☐ Brother Rat and a Baby ☐ Cattle Queen of Montana ☐ Code of the Secret Service ☐ Cowboy from Brooklyn, The ☐ Dark Victory ☐ Desperate Journey ☐ Girl from Jones Beach, The ☐ Girls on Probation ☐ Going Places ☐ Hasty Heart, The ☐ Hell's Kitchen ☐ Hellcats of the Navy ☐ Hong Kong ☐ International Squadron ☐ John Loves Mary ☐ Juke Girl ☐ Killers, The ☐ Kings Row ☐ Knute Rockne, All American ☐ Last Outpost, The ☐ Law and Order ☐ Louisa ☐ Million Dollar Baby ☐ Naughty but Nice ☐ Night unto Night ☐ Nine Lives Are Not Enough ☐ Santa Fe Trail ☐ Secret Service of the Air ☐ She's Working Her Way Through College ☐ Smashing the Money Ring ☐ Storm Warning ☐ Swing Your Lady ☐ Tennessee's Partner ☐ That Hagen Girl ☐ This is the Army ☐ Voice of the Turtle, The ☐ Winning Team, The

Rea, Stephen ☐ Angie ☐ Bad Behavior ☐ Company of Wolves, The ☐ Crying Game, The ☐ Danny Boy ☐ Doctor and the Devils, The ☐ Interview With the Vampire ☐ Life Is Sweet ☐ Loose Connections ☐ Princess Caraboo ☐ Ready to Wear

Redford, Robert ☐ All the President's Men ☐ Barefoot in the Park ☐ Bridge Too Far, A ☐ Brubaker ☐ Butch Cassidy and the Sundance Kid ☐ Candidate, The ☐ Chase, The ☐ Downhill Racer ☐ Electric Horseman, The ☐ Great Gatsby, The ☐ Great Waldo Pepper, The ☐ Havana ☐ Hot Rock, The ☐ Indecent Proposal ☐ Inside Daisy Clover ☐ Jeremiah Johnson ☐ Legal Eagles ☐ Little Fauss and Big Halsy ☐ Natural, The ☐ Out of Africa ☐ Situation Hopeless—But Not Serious ☐ Sneakers ☐ Sting, The ☐ Tell Them Willie Boy Is Here ☐ This Property Is Condemned ☐ Three Days of the Condor ☐ War Hunt ☐ Way We Were, The

Redgrave, Lynn ☐ Bad Seed, The ☐ Beggarman, Thief ☐ Big Bus, The ☐ Deadly Affair, The ☐ Don't Turn the Other Cheek ☐ Everything You Always Wanted to Know About Sex (But Were Afraid to Ask) ☐ Gauguin the Savage ☐ Georgy Girl ☐ Getting It Right ☐ Girl with Green Eyes, The ☐ Happy Hooker, The ☐ Here We Go Again ☐ Last of the Mobile Hot-Shots ☐ Midnight ☐ Morgan Stewart's Coming Home ☐ National Health, The ☐ Smashing Time ☐ Sooner or Later ☐ To Love Again ☐ Virgin Soldiers, The ☐ What Ever Happened to Baby Jane?

Redgrave, Michael ☐ 1984 ☐ Assignment K ☐ Battle of Britain, The ☐ Big Blockade, The ☐ Browning Version, The ☐ Captive Heart, The ☐ Connecting Rooms ☐ Dam Busters, The ☐ David Copperfield ☐ Dead of Night ☐ Fame Is the Spur ☐ Go-Between, The ☐ Goodbye, Mr. Chips ☐ Green Scarf, The ☐ Happy Road, The ☐ Heidi ☐ Heroes of Telemark, The ☐ Hill, The ☐ Importance of Being Earnest, The ☐ Innocents, The ☐ Jeannie ☐ Johnny in the Clouds ☐ Kipps ☐ Lady in Distress ☐ Lady Vanishes, The ☐ Loneliness of the Long Distance Runner, The ☐ Magic Box, The ☐ Mourning Becomes Electra ☐ Mr. Arkadin ☐ Nicholas and Alexandra ☐ Night My Number Came Up, The ☐ No My Darling Daughter ☐ Oh! What a Lovely War ☐ Quiet American, The ☐ Sea Shall Not Have Them, The ☐ Secret Beyond the Door ☐ Shake Hands with the Devil ☐ Smugglers, the ☐ Stars Look Down, The ☐ Thunder Rock ☐ Time Without Pity ☐ Wreck of the Mary Deare, The ☐ Young Cassidy

Redgrave, Vanessa ☐ Agatha ☐ Ballad of the Sad Cafe, The ☐ Bear Island ☐ Blowup ☐ Bostonians, The ☐ Camelot ☐ Charge of the Light Brigade, The ☐ Consuming Passions ☐ Devils, The ☐ House of the Spirits ☐ Howards End ☐ Isadora ☐ Julia ☐ Man for All Seasons, A ☐ Mary, Queen of Scots ☐ Morgan! ☐ Mother's Boys ☐ Murder on the Orient Express ☐ My Body, My Child ☐ Oh! What a Lovely War ☐ Orpheus Descending ☐ Out of Season ☐ Playing for Time ☐ Prick Up Your Ears ☐ Sea Gull, The ☐ Second Serve ☐ Seven Percent Solution, The ☐ Steaming ☐ Three Sovereigns For Sarah ☐ Trojan Women, The ☐ Wagner

☐ Wetherby ☐ What Ever Happened to Baby Jane? ☐ Yanks ☐ Young Catherine

Reed, Donna ☐ Babes on Broadway ☐ Backlash ☐ Benny Goodman Story, The ☐ Best Place to Be, The ☐ Beyond Glory ☐ Beyond Mombasa ☐ Bugle Sounds, The ☐ Caddy, The ☐ Calling Dr. Gillespie ☐ Chicago Deadline ☐ Courtship of Andy Hardy, The ☐ Dr. Gillespie's Criminal Case ☐ Eyes in the Night ☐ Faithful in My Fashion ☐ Far Horizons, The ☐ From Here to Eternity ☐ Gentle Annie ☐ Green Dolphin Street ☐ Gun Fury ☐ Hangman's Knot ☐ Human Comedy, The ☐ It's a Wonderful Life ☐ Last Time I Saw Paris, The ☐ Man from Down Under, The ☐ Picture of Dorian Gray, The ☐ Ransom ☐ Scandal Sheet ☐ See Here, Private Hargrove ☐ Shadow of the Thin Man ☐ They Were Expendable ☐ Three Hours to Kill ☐ Trouble Along the Way ☐ Whole Truth, The

Reed, Oliver ☐ Adventures of Baron Munchausen, The ☐ Assassination Bureau, The ☐ Big Sleep, The ☐ Blood in the Streets ☐ Brigand of Kandahar, The ☐ Brood, The ☐ Burnt Offerings ☐ Castaway ☐ Christopher Columbus ☐ Class of Miss MacMichael, The ☐ Condorman ☐ Crossed Swords ☐ Curse of the Werewolf, The ☐ Devils, The ☐ Dr. Heckyl and Mr. Hype ☐ Fanny Hill ☐ Four Musketeers, The ☐ Funny Bones ☐ Girl-Getters, The ☐ Gor ☐ Great Scout and Cathouse Thursday ☐ Hannibal Brooks ☐ Hired to Kill ☐ Hunting Party, The ☐ I'll Never Forget What's 'is Name ☐ Jokers, The ☐ Lady and the Highwayman, The ☐ Lady in the Car with Glasses and a Gun, The ☐ Lion of the Desert ☐ Maniac! ☐ Master of Dragonard Hill ☐ No Love for Johnnie ☐ Oliver! ☐ One Russian Summer ☐ Paranoiac ☐ Pirates of Blood River, The ☐ Prisoner of Honor ☐ Return of the Musketeers, The ☐ Royal Flash ☐ Severed Ties ☐ Spasms ☐ Sting II, The ☐ Ten Little Indians ☐ These Are the Damned ☐ Three Musketeers, The ☐ Tommy ☐ Treasure Island ☐ Two of a Kind ☐ Venom ☐ Women in Love ☐ Z.P.G.

Reed, Pamela ☐ Best of Times, The ☐ Cadillac Man ☐ Caroline? ☐ Chattahoochee ☐ Clan of the Cave Bear, The ☐ Goodbye People, The ☐ Heart of Steel ☐ Junior ☐ Kindergarten Cop ☐ Melvin and Howard ☐ Rachel River ☐ Scandal Sheet ☐ Young Doctors in Love

Reed, Philip ☐ Big Town ☐ Bodyguard ☐ Manhandled ☐ Take Me to Town

Reed, Robert ☐ Boy in the Plastic Bubble, The ☐ Brady Girls Get Married, The ☐ Bud and Lou ☐ Death of a Centerfold: The Dorothy Stratten Story ☐ Haunts of the Very Rich ☐ Hunted Lady, The ☐ Hurry Sundown ☐ Law and Order ☐ Maltese Bippy, The ☐ Man Who Could Talk to Kids, The ☐ Mandrake ☐ Nightmare in Badham County ☐ No Prince for My Cinderella ☐ Nurse ☐ Snatched ☐ Star!

Reed, Walter ☐ Emergency Hospital ☐ Government Agents vs. Phantom Legion ☐ How to Make a Monster ☐ Macumba Love ☐ Mexican Spitfire's Elephant ☐ Mystery in Mexico ☐ Seven Men from Now ☐ Superman and the Mole Men

Reese, Della ☐ Harlem Nights ☐ Kid Who Loved Christmas, The ☐ Let's Rock! ☐ Nightmare in Badham County

Rees, Roger ☐ Charles & Diana: A Palace Divided ☐ Christmas Carol, A ☐ Ebony Tower, The ☐ If Looks Could Kill ☐ Star 80 ☐ Stop! or My Mom Will Shoot

Reeve, Christopher ☐ Anna Karenina ☐ Aviator, The ☐ Bostonians, The ☐ Bump in the Night ☐ Deathtrap ☐ Great Escape 2: The Untold Story, The ☐ Monsignor ☐ Noises Off ☐ Remains of the Day ☐ Sea Wolf, The ☐ Somewhere in Time ☐ Speechless ☐ Street Smart ☐ Superman 2 ☐ Superman 3 ☐ Superman 4: The Quest for Peace ☐ Superman—The Movie ☐ Switching Channels

Reeves, George ☐ Blood and Sand ☐ Bugles in the Afternoon ☐ Hoppy Serves a Writ ☐ Rancho Notorious ☐ So Proudly We Hail! ☐ Superman and the Mole Men ☐ Westward Ho the Wagons!

Reeves, Keanu ☐ Act of Vengeance ☐ Babes in Toyland ☐ Bill & Ted's Bogus Journey ☐ Bill & Ted's Excellent Adventure ☐ Bram Stoker's Dracula ☐ Dangerous Liaisons ☐ Dream to Believe ☐ Even Cowgirls Get the Blues ☐ I Love You to Death ☐ Little Buddha ☐ Much Ado About Nothing ☐ My Own Private Idaho ☐ Night Before, The ☐ Parenthood ☐ Permanent Record ☐ Point Break ☐ Prince of Pennsylvania, The ☐ River's Edge ☐ Speed ☐ Tune In Tomorrow

Reeves, Steve ☐ Duel of the Titans ☐ Goliath and the Barbarians ☐ Hercules ☐ Hercules Unchained ☐ Jail Bait ☐ Last Days of Pompeii, The ☐ Morgan the Pirate ☐ Thief of Baghdad ☐ Trojan Horse, The

Reiner, Carl ☐ Dead Men Don't Wear Plaid ☐ End, The ☐ Gazebo, The ☐ Generation ☐ Gidget Goes Hawaiian ☐ Happy Anniversary ☐ Medical Story ☐ Russians Are Coming! The Russians Are Coming!, The ☐ Skokie ☐ Ten From Your Show of Shows

Reiner, Rob ☐ All in the Family 20th Anniversary Special ☐ Billy Crystal—Don't Get Me Started ☐ Bye Bye, Love ☐ Fire Sale ☐ Mixed Nuts ☐ More Than Friends ☐ Sleepless in Seattle ☐ This Is Spinal Tap ☐ Thursday's Game

Reinhold, Judge ☐ Baby on Board ☐ Bank Robber ☐ Beverly Hills Cop ☐ Beverly Hills Cop II ☐ Beverly Hills Cop III ☐ Black Magic ☐ Daddy's Dyin'. . . Who's Got the Will? ☐ Fast Times at Ridgemont High ☐ Four Eyes and Six-Guns ☐ Head Office ☐ Matter of Sex, A ☐ Off Beat ☐ Over Her Dead Body ☐ Promised a Miracle ☐ Rosalie Goes Shopping ☐ Ruthless People ☐ Santa Clause, The ☐ Soldier's Tale, A ☐ Vice Versa ☐ Zandalee

Reiser, Paul ☐ Aliens ☐ Bye Bye, Love ☐ Crazy People ☐ Cross My Heart ☐ Family Prayers ☐ Marrying Man, The ☐ Odd Jobs ☐ Paul Reiser—Out on a Whim

Remar, James ☐ 48 Hrs. ☐ Blink ☐ Boys on the Side ☐ Indecency ☐ Night Visions ☐ Quiet Cool ☐ Renaissance Man ☐ Warriors, The ☐ White Fang ☐ Windwalker

Remick, Lee ☐ Anatomy of a Murder ☐ Baby the Rain Must Fall ☐ Blue Knight, The ☐ Bridge to Silence ☐ Competition, The ☐ Days of Wine and Roses ☐ Delicate Balance, A ☐ Detective, The ☐ Europeans, The ☐ Experiment in Terror ☐ Face in the Crowd, A ☐ Gift of Love: A Christmas Story, The ☐ Girl Named Sooner, A ☐ Good Sport, A ☐ Hallelujah Trail, The ☐ Hard Contract ☐ Haywire ☐ Hennessy ☐ Hustling ☐ Ike: The War Years ☐ Jesse ☐ Letter, The ☐ Long Hot Summer, The ☐ Loot ☐ Medusa Touch, The ☐ Mistral's Daughter ☐ Nazis, The: Of Pure Blood ☐ No Way to Treat a Lady ☐ Omen, The ☐ Rearview Mirror ☐ Sanctuary ☐ Severed Head, A ☐ Sometimes a Great Notion ☐ Telefon ☐ These Thousand Hills ☐ Torn Between Two Lovers ☐ Tribute ☐ Wheeler Dealers, The ☐ Wild River ☐ Women's Room, The

Rennie, Michael ☐ 13th Letter, The ☐ 5 Fingers ☐ Assignment Terror ☐ Battle of El Alamein ☐ Big Blockade, The ☐ Black Rose, The ☐ Dangerous Crossing ☐ Day the Earth Stood Still, The ☐ Demetrius and the Gladiators ☐ Desiree ☐ Devil's Brigade, The ☐ Golden Madonna, The ☐ High Fury ☐ I'll Never Forget You ☐ Island in the Sun ☐ King of the Khyber Rifles ☐ Last Chance, The ☐ Les Miserables ☐ Lost World ☐ Mambo ☐ Mary, Mary ☐ Missiles from Hell ☐ Phone Call from a Stranger ☐ Princess of the Nile ☐ Rains of Ranchipur, The ☐ Robe, The ☐ Seven Cities of Gold ☐ Soldier of Fortune ☐ Third Man on the Mountain ☐ Trio ☐ Wicked Lady, The

Revere, Anne ☐ Body and Soul ☐ Carnival in Costa Rica ☐ Deep Waters ☐ Devil Commands, The ☐ Dragonwyck ☐ Falcon Takes Over, The ☐ Fallen Angel ☐ Forever Amber ☐ Gentleman's Agreement ☐ Great Missouri Raid, The ☐ Meet the Stewarts ☐ National Velvet ☐ Rainbow Island ☐ Scudda Hoo! Scudda Hay! ☐ Secret Beyond the Door ☐ Shocking Miss Pilgrim, The ☐ Standing Room Only ☐ Sunday Dinner for a Soldier ☐ Thin Man Goes Home, The ☐ You're My Everything

Revier, Dorothy ☐ Black Camel, The ☐ Donovan Affair, The ☐ Iron Mask, The ☐ Night World

Revill, Clive ☐ Avanti! ☐ Diary of Anne Frank, The ☐ Double Man, The ☐ Fathom ☐ Galileo ☐ Ghost in the Noonday Sun ☐ Headless Ghost ☐ High Commissioner, The ☐ Kaleidoscope ☐ Legend of Hell House, The ☐ Masterpiece of Murder, A ☐ Matilda ☐ Modesty Blaise ☐ One of Our Dinosaurs is Missing ☐ Rumpelstiltskin ☐ Sea Wolf, The

Rey, Alejandro ☐ Fun in Acapulco ☐ Moscow on the Hudson ☐ Mr. Majestyk ☐ Stepmother, The ☐ Synanon

Rey, Fernando ☐ Antony and Cleopatra ☐ Assignment, The ☐ Caboblanco ☐ Discreet Charm of the Bourgeoisie, The ☐ French Connection II ☐ French Connection, The ☐ Goliath Against the Giants ☐ High Crime ☐ Honey ☐ Illustrious Corpses ☐ Immortal Story, The ☐ La Grande Bourgeoisie ☐ Lady of the Camellias, The ☐ Light at the Edge of the World, The ☐ Monsignor ☐ Naked Tango ☐ Navajo Joe ☐ Our Father ☐ Pantaloons ☐ Quintet ☐ Rustlers' Rhapsody ☐ Saving Grace ☐ Seven Beauties ☐ Star Knight ☐ That Obscure Object of Desire ☐ Tristana ☐ Villa Rides ☐ Viridiana

Reynolds, Burt ☐ 100 Rifles ☐ All Dogs Go to Heaven ☐ Angel Baby ☐ Armored Command ☐ At Long Last Love ☐ Best Friends ☐ Best Little Whorehouse in Texas, The ☐ Breaking In ☐ Cannonball Run II ☐ Cannonball Run, The ☐ City Heat ☐ Cop and a Half ☐ Deliverance ☐ End, The ☐ Fade-In ☐ Fuzz ☐ Gator ☐ Hard Frame ☐ Heat ☐ Hooper ☐ Hustle ☐ Impasse ☐ Longest Yard, The ☐ Lucky Lady ☐ Malone ☐ Man Who Loved Cat Dancing, The ☐ Man Who Loved Women, The ☐ Modern Love ☐ Navajo Joe ☐ Nickelodeon ☐ Operation C.I.A. ☐ Paternity ☐ Physical Evidence ☐ Rent-a-Cop ☐ Rough Cut ☐ Sam Whiskey ☐ Semi-Tough ☐ Shamus ☐ Shark! ☐ Sharky's Machine ☐ Silent Movie ☐ Skullduggery ☐ Smokey and the Bandit ☐ Smokey and the Bandit, Part 2 ☐ Starting Over ☐ Stroker Ace ☐ Switching Channels ☐ W. W. and the Dixie Dancekings ☐ White Lightning

Reynolds, Debbie ☐ Affairs of Dobie Gillis, The ☐ Athena ☐ Battling for Baby ☐ Bundle of Joy ☐ Catered Affair, The ☐ Charlotte's Web ☐ Daughter of Rosie O'Grady, The ☐ Divorce American Style ☐ Gazebo, The ☐ Give a Girl a Break ☐ Goodbye Charlie ☐ Heaven and Earth ☐ Hit the Deck ☐ How Sweet It Is! ☐ How the West Was Won ☐ I Love Melvin ☐ It Started with a Kiss ☐ Mary, Mary ☐ Mating Game, The ☐ Mr. Imperium ☐ My Six Loves ☐ Pleasure of His Company, The ☐ Rat Race, The ☐ Say One for Me ☐ Second Time Around, The ☐ Singin' in the Rain ☐ Singing Nun, The ☐ Skirts Ahoy! ☐ Susan Slept Here ☐ Tammy and the Bachelor ☐ Tender Trap, The ☐ That's Entertainment ☐ This Happy Feeling ☐ Three Little Words ☐ Two Weeks with Love ☐ Unsinkable Molly Brown, The ☐ What's the Matter with Helen?

Reynolds, Gene ☐ Adventure in Washington

☐ Boys Town ☐ Flying Irishman, The ☐ In Old Chicago ☐ Of Human Hearts ☐ They Shall Have Music

Reynolds, Marjorie ☐ Bad Men of Tombstone ☐ Bring on the Girls ☐ Dixie ☐ Duffy's Tavern ☐ Enemy Agent ☐ Fatal Hour, The ☐ Great Jewel Robber, The ☐ Heaven Only Knows ☐ His Kind of Woman ☐ Holiday Inn ☐ Hometown Story ☐ Ministry of Fear ☐ Mr. Wong in Chinatown ☐ No Holds Barred ☐ Six Shootin' Sheriff ☐ Three Is a Family ☐ Time of Their Lives, The ☐ Up in Mabel's Room

Reynolds, William ☐ Big Beat, The ☐ Francis Goes to West Point ☐ No Questions Asked ☐ Raiders, The ☐ There's Always Tomorrow

Rhodes, Erik ☐ Charlie Chan in Paris ☐ Chatterbox ☐ Fight for Your Lady ☐ Gay Divorcee, The ☐ Mysterious Mr. Moto ☐ Nitwits, The ☐ Top Hat

Rhodes, Hari ☐ Dream for Christmas, A ☐ Matt Helm ☐ Nun and the Sergeant, The ☐ Shock Corridor ☐ Woman Called Moses, A

Rhys-Davies, John ☐ Best Revenge ☐ Canvas ☐ In the Shadow of Kilimanjaro ☐ Indiana Jones and the Last Crusade ☐ Kim ☐ Nairobi Affair ☐ Raiders of the Lost Ark ☐ Sadat ☐ Seventh Coin, The ☐ Sphinx ☐ Unnamable II, The ☐ Victor/Victoria

Ricci, Christina ☐ Addams Family Values ☐ Addams Family, The ☐ Cemetery Club, The ☐ Mermaids

Richard, Pierre ☐ La Chevre ☐ Le Jouet ☐ Les Comperes ☐ Return of the Tall Blond Man With One Black Shoe, The ☐ Tall Blond Man with One Black Shoe

Richardson, Ian ☐ Brazil ☐ Burning Secret ☐ Charlie Muffin ☐ Cry Freedom ☐ Gauguin the Savage ☐ Hound of the Baskervilles, The ☐ Ike: The War Years ☐ Marat/Sade (Persecution and Assassination of Jean-Paul Marat Performed by the In ☐ Midsummer Night's Dream, A ☐ Monsignor Quixote ☐ Sign of Four, The ☐ Year of the Comet

Richardson, Miranda ☐ Crying Game, The ☐ Damage ☐ Dance With a Stranger ☐ Empire of the Sun ☐ Enchanted April ☐ Tom and Viv

Richardson, Natasha ☐ Comfort of Strangers, The ☐ Favor, the Watch, and the Very Big Fish, The ☐ Gothic ☐ Handmaid's Tale, The ☐ Month in the Country, A ☐ Nell ☐ Past Midnight ☐ Patty Hearst ☐ Suddenly, Last Summer ☐ Widow's Peak

Richardson, Ralph ☐ Alice's Adventures in Wonderland ☐ Anna Karenina ☐ Battle of Britain, The ☐ Bed-Sitting Room, The ☐ Breaking the Sound Barrier ☐ Bulldog Jack ☐ Charlie Muffin ☐ Citadel, The ☐ Clouds over Europe ☐ David Copperfield ☐ Day Will Dawn, The ☐ Divorce of Lady X, The ☐ Doctor Zhivago ☐ Doll's House, A ☐ Dragonslayer ☐ Eagle in a Cage ☐ Exodus ☐ Fallen Idol, The ☐ Four Feathers, The ☐ Frankenstein: The True Story ☐ Ghoul, The ☐ Give My Regards to Broad Street ☐ Greystoke: The Legend of Tarzan, Lord of the Apes ☐ Heiress, The ☐ Holly and the Ivy, The ☐ Home at Seven ☐ Invitation To a Wedding ☐ Java Head ☐ Khartoum ☐ Lady Caroline Lamb ☐ Lion Has Wings, The ☐ Long Day's Journey into Night ☐ Looking Glass War, The ☐ Man in the Iron Mask ☐ Man Who Could Work Miracles, The ☐ Midas Run ☐ Novel Affair, A ☐ O Lucky Man! ☐ Oh! What a Lovely War ☐ Oscar Wilde ☐ Our Man in Havana ☐ Outcast of the Islands ☐ Richard III ☐ School for Secrets ☐ Silver Fleet, The ☐ Smiley ☐ South Riding ☐ Tales from the Crypt ☐ Things to Come ☐ Thunder in the City ☐ Time Bandits ☐ Wagner ☐ Watership Down ☐ Witness for the Prosecution ☐ Woman of Straw ☐ Wrong Box, The

Rickles, Don ☐ Beach Blanket Bingo ☐ Bikini Beach ☐ For the Love of It ☐ Innocent Blood ☐ Keaton's Cop ☐ Kelly's Heroes ☐ Milton Berle's Mad World of Comedy ☐ Muscle Beach Party ☐ Rabbit Trap, The ☐ Rat Race, The

Rickman, Alan ☐ Close My Eyes ☐ Closet Land ☐ Die Hard ☐ Fallen Angels—Volume 1 ☐ January Man, The ☐ Quigley Down Under ☐ Robin Hood: Prince of Thieves ☐ Shock! Shock! Shock! ☐ Truly Madly Deeply

Riegert, Peter ☐ Americathon ☐ Barbarians at the Gate ☐ City Girl ☐ Crossing Delancey ☐ Ellis Island ☐ Gypsy ☐ Head over Heels ☐ Local Hero ☐ Man in Love, A ☐ Mask, The ☐ National Lampoon Goes to the Movies ☐ News at Eleven ☐ Oscar ☐ Runestone, The ☐ Shock to the System, A ☐ Utz

Rigg, Diana ☐ Assassination Bureau, The ☐ Bleak House ☐ Evil Under the Sun ☐ Good Man in Africa, A ☐ Great Muppet Caper, The ☐ Hazard of Hearts, A ☐ Hospital, The ☐ In this House of Brede ☐ Julius Caesar ☐ King Lear ☐ Little Night Music, A ☐ Marquise, The ☐ Midsummer Night's Dream, A ☐ Mrs. 'Arris Goes to Paris ☐ On Her Majesty's Secret Service ☐ Snow White ☐ Theatre of Blood ☐ Witness for the Prosecution

Ringwald, Molly ☐ Betsy's Wedding ☐ Breakfast Club, The ☐ Face the Music ☐ For Keeps ☐ Fresh Horses ☐ King Lear ☐ P.K. and the Kid ☐ Packin' It In ☐ Pick-up Artist, The ☐ Pretty in Pink ☐ Sixteen Candles ☐ Spacehunter: Adventures in the Forbidden Zone ☐ Stand, The ☐ Strike It Rich ☐ Tempest ☐ Women & Men: Stories of Seduction

Ritter, John ☐ Americathon ☐ Barefoot Executive, The ☐ Dreamer of Oz, The: The Frank L. Baum Story ☐ Hero at Large ☐ In Love with an Older Woman ☐ Last Fling, The ☐ Letting Go ☐ Nickelodeon ☐ Night That Panicked America, The ☐ Noises Off ☐ Problem Child ☐ Problem Child 2 ☐ Real Men ☐ Skin Deep ☐ Stay Tuned ☐ Stephen King's It ☐ They All Laughed ☐ Unnatural Causes

Ritter, Tex ☐ Apache Ambush ☐ Hittin' The Trail ☐ Marshal of Gunsmoke ☐ Mystery of the Hooded Horsemen, The ☐ Riders of the Rockies ☐ Roll, Wagons, Roll ☐ Sing, Cowboy, Sing ☐ Song of the Buckaroo ☐ Tenting Tonight on the Old Camp Ground ☐ Trouble in Texas

Ritter, Thelma ☐ All About Eve ☐ As Young As You Feel ☐ Birdman of Alcatraz ☐ Boeing Boeing ☐ City Across the River ☐ Daddy Long Legs ☐ Farmer Takes a Wife, The ☐ Father Was a Fullback ☐ For Love or Money ☐ Hole in the Head, A ☐ I'll Get By ☐ Incident, The ☐ Letter to Three Wives, A ☐ Lucy Gallant ☐ Mating Season, The ☐ Misfits, The ☐ Model and the Marriage Broker, The ☐ Move Over, Darling ☐ New Kind of Love, A ☐ Perfect Strangers ☐ Pickup on South Street ☐ Pillow Talk ☐ Proud and Profane, The ☐ Rear Window ☐ Second Time Around, The ☐ Titanic ☐ What's So Bad About Feeling Good? ☐ With a Song in My Heart

Ritz Brothers, The ☐ Goldwyn Follies, The ☐ Gorilla, The ☐ Hi'ya Chum ☐ Kentucky Moonshine ☐ Life Begins in College ☐ On the Avenue ☐ One in a Million ☐ Pack Up Your Troubles ☐ Three Musketeers, The

Rivera, Chita ☐ Marcus-Nelson Murders, The ☐ Mayflower Madam ☐ Pippin ☐ Sweet Charity

Robards, Jr., Jason ☐ Burden of Dreams ☐ F.D.R., The Last Year ☐ Journey, The ☐ Long Day's Journey into Night ☐ Tender Is the Night

Robards, Jason ☐ Act One ☐ Adventures of Huck Finn, The ☐ All the President's Men ☐ Any Wednesday ☐ Atlanta Child Murders, The ☐ Ballad of Cable Hogue, The ☐ Big Hand for the Little Lady, A ☐ Black Rainbow ☐ Boy and His Dog, A ☐ Bright Lights, Big City ☐ By Love Possessed ☐ Caboblanco ☐ Chernobyl: The Final Warning ☐ Christmas to Remember, A ☐ Christmas Wife, The ☐ Comes a Horseman ☐ Day After, The ☐ Divorce American Style ☐ Dream a Little Dream ☐ Falcon's Alibi, The ☐ Fatal Hour, The ☐ Fools ☐ Game of Death, A ☐ Good Mother, The ☐ Haywire ☐ Heidi ☐ Hour of the Gun ☐ House Without a Christmas Tree, A ☐ Hurricane ☐ Inconvenient Woman, An ☐ Inherit the Wind ☐ Isadora ☐ Isle of Lost Ships ☐ Isle of the Dead ☐ Johnny Bull ☐ Johnny Got His Gun ☐ Julia ☐ Julius Caesar ☐ Laguna Heat ☐ Legend of the Lone Ranger, The ☐ Little Big League ☐ Long Hot Summer, The ☐ Mademoiselle Fifi ☐ Man Alive ☐ Mark Twain and Me ☐ Max Dugan Returns ☐ Melvin and Howard ☐ Miracle Rider, The ☐ Night They Raided Minsky's, The ☐ Norman Rockwell's Breaking Home Ties ☐ Once Upon a Time in the West ☐ Operation Snafu ☐ Paper, The ☐ Parenthood ☐ Perfect Tribute, The ☐ Philadelphia ☐ Quick Change ☐ Raise the Titanic! ☐ Something Wicked This Way Comes ☐ Square Dance ☐ St. Valentine's Day Massacre, The ☐ Storyville ☐ Thousand Clowns, A ☐ Tora! Tora! Tora! ☐ War Between Men and Women, The

Robbins, Tim ☐ Bob Roberts ☐ Bull Durham ☐ Cadillac Man ☐ Erik the Viking ☐ Five Corners ☐ Fraternity Vacation ☐ Howard the Duck ☐ Hudsucker Proxy, The ☐ I. Q. ☐ Jacob's Ladder ☐ Miss Firecracker ☐ Player, The ☐ Ready to Wear ☐ Shawshank Redemption, The ☐ Short Cuts ☐ Tapeheads

Roberts, Eric ☐ Ambulance, The ☐ Babyfever ☐ Best of the Best ☐ Blood Red ☐ Coca-Cola Kid, The ☐ Descending Angel ☐ Family Matter, A ☐ Final Analysis ☐ Fugutive Among Us ☐ King of the Gypsies ☐ Lost Capone, The ☐ Love, Cheat & Steal ☐ Nobody's Fool ☐ Paul's Case ☐ Pope of Greenwich Village, The ☐ Raggedy Man ☐ Rude Awakening ☐ Runaway Train ☐ Slow Burn ☐ Star 80

Roberts, Julia ☐ Baja Oklahoma ☐ Dying Young ☐ Flatliners ☐ Hook ☐ Mystic Pizza ☐ Pelican Brief, The ☐ Pretty Woman ☐ Ready to Wear ☐ Satisfaction ☐ Sleeping with the Enemy ☐ Steel Magnolias

Roberts, Pernell ☐ Four Rode Out ☐ High Noon, Part II: The Return of Will Kane ☐ Hot Rod ☐ Immigrants, The ☐ Incident at Crestridge ☐ Magic of Lassie, The ☐ Night Rider, The ☐ Night Train to Kathmandu, The ☐ Ride Lonesome

Roberts, Rachel ☐ Alpha Beta ☐ Baffled ☐ Belstone Fox, The ☐ Charlie Chan and the Curse of the Dragon Queen ☐ Circle of Children, A ☐ Doctor's Wives ☐ Flea in Her Ear, A ☐ Foul Play ☐ Good Companions, The ☐ Great Expectations ☐ Hostage Tower, The ☐ Limping Man, The ☐ Men are Children Twice ☐ Murder on the Orient Express ☐ O Lucky Man! ☐ Picnic at Hanging Rock ☐ Reckoning, The ☐ Saturday Night and Sunday Morning ☐ This Sporting Life ☐ Yanks

Roberts, Tanya ☐ Almost Pregnant ☐ Beastmaster, The ☐ Body Slam ☐ Fingers ☐ Hearts and Armour ☐ Legal Tender ☐ Night Eyes ☐ Purgatory ☐ Sheena ☐ Sins of Desire ☐ View to a Kill, A ☐ Yum-Yum Girls, The

Roberts, Tony ☐ 18 Again! ☐ American Clock, The ☐ Amityville 3D ☐ Annie Hall ☐ If Things Were Different ☐ Just Tell Me What You Want ☐ Midsummer Night's Sex Comedy, A ☐ Million Dollar Duck ☐ Packin' It In ☐ Play It Again, Sam ☐ Popcorn ☐ Question of Honor, A ☐ Radio Days ☐ Serpico ☐ Star Spangled Girl ☐ Stardust Memories ☐ Switch

Robertson, Cliff ☐ 633 Squadron ☐ Ace Eli and Rodger of the Skies ☐ All in a Night's Work ☐ As the Sea Rages ☐ Autumn Leaves ☐ Battle of the Coral Sea ☐ Best Man, The ☐ Big Show, The ☐ Brainstorm ☐ Charly

☐ Class ☐ Devil's Brigade, The ☐ Dominique ☐ Ford: The Man and the Machine ☐ Gidget ☐ Girl Most Likely, The ☐ Great Northfield, Minnesota Raid, The ☐ Honey Pot, The ☐ Interns, The ☐ J.W. Coop ☐ Key to Rebecca, The ☐ Love Has Many Faces ☐ Malone ☐ Man on a Swing ☐ Man Without a Country, The ☐ Masquerade ☐ Midway ☐ My Six Loves ☐ Naked and the Dead, The ☐ Obsession ☐ Out of Season ☐ Picnic ☐ PT 109 ☐ Renaissance Man ☐ Shoot ☐ Star 80 ☐ Sunday in New York ☐ Three Days of the Condor ☐ Too Late the Hero ☐ Underworld U.S.A. ☐ Up From the Beach ☐ Wild Hearts Can't Be Broken ☐ Wind

Robertson, Dale ☐ Blood on the Arrow ☐ Call Me Mister ☐ City of Bad Men ☐ Coast of Skeletons ☐ Dakota Incident ☐ Day of Fury, A ☐ Farmer Takes a Wife, The ☐ Fast and Sexy ☐ Gambler from Natchez, The ☐ Golden Girl ☐ Hell Canyon Outlaws ☐ High Terrace ☐ Kansas City Massacre ☐ Law of the Lawless ☐ Lydia Bailey ☐ Melvin Purvis-G-Man ☐ One-Eyed Soldiers ☐ Outcasts of Poker Flat, The ☐ Return of the Texan ☐ Silver Whip, The ☐ Sitting Bull

Robeson, Paul ☐ Body and Soul ☐ Dark Sands ☐ Emperor Jones, The ☐ King Solomon's Mines ☐ Native Land ☐ Sanders of the River ☐ Show Boat ☐ Song of Freedom ☐ Tales of Manhattan

Robinson, Bill ☐ Big Broadcast of 1936, The ☐ Dixiana ☐ Hooray for Love ☐ In Old Kentucky ☐ Just Around the Corner ☐ Little Colonel, The ☐ Littlest Rebel, The ☐ Rebecca of Sunnybrook Farm ☐ Stormy Weather

Robinson, Edward G. ☐ Actors and Sin ☐ All My Sons ☐ Amazing Doctor Clitterhouse, The ☐ Barbary Coast ☐ Big Leaguer, The ☐ Biggest Bundle Of Them All ☐ Black Tuesday ☐ Blackmail ☐ Boy Ten Feet Tall, A ☐ Brother Orchid ☐ Bullet for Joey, A ☐ ☐ Bullets or Ballots ☐ Cheyenne Autumn ☐ Cincinnati Kid, The Confessions of a Nazi Spy ☐ Dark Hazard ☐ Destroyer ☐ Dispatch from Reuters, A ☐ Double Indemnity ☐ Dr. Ehrlich's Magic Bullet ☐ Five Star Final ☐ Flesh and Fantasy ☐ Glass Web, The ☐ Good Neighbor Sam ☐ Grand Slam ☐ Hatchet Man, The ☐ Hell on Frisco Bay ☐ Hole in the Head, A ☐ House of Strangers, The ☐ I Am the Law ☐ I Loved a Woman ☐ Illegal ☐ It's Your Move ☐ Journey Together ☐ Key Largo ☐ Kid Galahad ☐ Larceny, Inc ☐ Last Gangster, The ☐ Little Caesar ☐ Little Giant, The ☐ Mackenna's Gold ☐ Man with Two Faces, The ☐ Manpower ☐ Mr. Winkle Goes to War ☐ My Geisha ☐ Never a Dull Moment ☐ Night Has a Thousand Eyes ☐ Nightmare ☐ Operation St. Peter's ☐ Operation X ☐ Our Vines Have Tender Grapes ☐ Outrage, The ☐ Prize, The ☐ Red House, The ☐ Scarlet Street ☐ Sea Wolf, The ☐ Seven Thieves ☐ Silver Dollar ☐ Slight Case of Murder, A ☐ Smart Money ☐ Song of Norway ☐ Soylent Green ☐ Stranger, The ☐ Tales of Manhattan ☐ Tampico ☐ Ten Commandments, The ☐ Thunder in the City ☐ Tiger Shark ☐ Tight Spot ☐ Two Seconds ☐ Two Weeks in Another Town ☐ Unholy Partners ☐ Vice Squad ☐ Violent Men, The ☐ Whole Town's Talking, The ☐ Woman in the Window, The

Robson, Flora ☐ 55 Days at Peking ☐ Alice's Adventures in Wonderland ☐ Bahama Passage ☐ Beast in the Cellar, The ☐ Black Narcissus ☐ Caesar and Cleopatra ☐ Catherine the Great ☐ Dominique ☐ Epic that Never Was, The ☐ Eye of the Devil ☐ Farewell Again ☐ Fire Over England ☐ Fragment of Fear ☐ Frieda ☐ Frightened Bride ☐ Good Time Girl ☐ Great Day ☐ Guns at Batasi ☐ Gypsy and the Gentleman, The ☐ High Tide at Noon ☐ Holiday Camp ☐ Invisible Stripes ☐ King's Story, A ☐ Les Miserables ☐ Murder at the Gallop ☐ No Time for Tears ☐ Poison Pen ☐ Romeo and Juliet ☐ Saraband ☐ Saratoga Trunk ☐ Sea Hawk, The ☐ Seven Women ☐ Tale of Two Cities, A ☐ We Are Not Alone ☐ Wuthering Heights ☐ Young Cassidy

Robson, May ☐ Adventures of Tom Sawyer, The ☐ Anna Karenina ☐ Beauty for Sale ☐ Bringing Up Baby ☐ Dancing Lady ☐ Daughters Courageous ☐ Four Mothers ☐ Four Wives ☐ Irene ☐ Joan of Paris ☐ Lady by Choice ☐ Lady for a Day ☐ Letty Lynton ☐ Little Orphan Annie ☐ Million Dollar Baby ☐ Nurse Edith Cavell ☐ One Man's Journey ☐ Perfect Specimen, The ☐ Reckless ☐ Red-Headed Woman ☐ Reunion in Vienna ☐ Star Is Born, A ☐ Strange Interlude ☐ They Made Me a Criminal ☐ White Sister, The ☐ Wife vs. Secretary

Rocco, Alex ☐ Badge of the Assassin ☐ Boris and Natasha ☐ Fire Sale ☐ Friends of Eddie Coyle, The ☐ Nobody's Perfekt ☐ P.K. and the Kid ☐ Pope Must Diet, The ☐ Question of Guilt, A ☐ Rabbit Test ☐ Return to Horror High ☐ Stunt Man, The ☐ Voices ☐ Wired

Roche, Eugene ☐ Corvette Summer ☐ Foul Play ☐ Newman's Law ☐ Rape & Marriage: The Rideout Case ☐ When a Man Loves a Woman

Rochefort, Jean ☐ Birgit Haas Must Be Killed ☐ Clockmaker, The ☐ Devil by the Tail, The ☐ French Postcards ☐ Hairdresser's Husband, The ☐ I Hate Blondes ☐ I Sent a Letter to My Love ☐ Le Cavaleur ☐ Le Complot ☐ Le Crabe Tambour ☐ Let Joy Reign Supreme ☐ Mean Frank & Crazy Tony ☐ Pardon Mon Affaire ☐ Symphony for a Massacre ☐ Tall Blond Man with One Black Shoe

Rogers, Ginger ☐ 42nd Street ☐ 5th Avenue Girl ☐ Bachelor Mother ☐ Barkleys of Broadway, The ☐ Black Widow ☐ Broadway Bad ☐ Carefree ☐ Chance at Heaven ☐ Cinderella

☐ Dreamboat ☐ Finishing School ☐ First Traveling Saleslady, The ☐ Flying Down to Rio ☐ Follow the Fleet ☐ Forever Female ☐ Gay Divorcee, The ☐ Gold Diggers of 1933 ☐ Groom Wore Spurs, The ☐ Harlow ☐ Having Wonderful Time ☐ Heartbeat ☐ I'll Be Seeing You ☐ In Person ☐ It Had to Be You ☐ Kitty Foyle ☐ Lady in the Dark ☐ Lucky Partners ☐ Magnificent Doll ☐ Major and the Minor, The ☐ Monkey Business ☐ Oh, Men! Oh, Women! ☐ Once Upon a Honeymoon ☐ Perfect Strangers ☐ Primrose Path, The ☐ Quick, Let's Get Married ☐ Roberta ☐ Roxie Hart ☐ Sap from Syracuse, The ☐ Shall We Dance ☐ Sitting Pretty ☐ Stage Door ☐ Star of Midnight ☐ Storm Warning ☐ Story of Vernon and Irene Castle, The ☐ Swing Time ☐ Tales of Manhattan ☐ Tender Comrade ☐ Tenderfoot, The ☐ Thirteenth Guest, The ☐ Tight Spot ☐ Tom, Dick and Harry ☐ Top Hat ☐ Twenty Million Sweethearts ☐ Upperworld ☐ Vivacious Lady ☐ We're Not Married ☐ Weekend at the Waldorf

Rogers, Mimi ☐ Blue Skies Again ☐ Deadlock ☐ Desperate Hours ☐ Far From Home: The Adventures of Yellow Dog ☐ Fourth Story, The ☐ Gung Ho ☐ Hider in the House ☐ Ladykiller ☐ Mighty Quinn, The ☐ Monkey Trouble ☐ Palermo Connection, The ☐ Rapture, The ☐ Shooting Elizabeth ☐ Someone to Watch Over Me ☐ Street Smart

Rogers, Roy ☐ Arizona Kid, The ☐ Bells of Rosarita ☐ Bells of San Angelo ☐ Dark Command ☐ Down Dakota Way ☐ Eyes of Texas ☐ Far Frontier, The ☐ Golden Stallion, The ☐ Hands Across The Border ☐ Heart of the Golden West ☐ Heart of the Rockies ☐ Helldorado ☐ Home in Oklahoma ☐ Idaho ☐ In Old Amarillo ☐ In Old Caliente ☐ Mackintosh and T.J. ☐ Melody Time ☐ My Pal Trigger ☐ Mysterious Avenger, The ☐ Night Time in Nevada ☐ North of the Great Divide ☐ On the Old Spanish Trail ☐ Red River Valley ☐ Ridin' Down the Canyon ☐ Roll on Texas Moon ☐ Rough Riders' Roundup ☐ Saga Of Death Valley ☐ Silver Spurs ☐ Son of Paleface ☐ Song of Arizona ☐ Song of Nevada ☐ Song of Texas ☐ Sons of the Pioneers ☐ Springtime in the Sierras ☐ Trail of Robin Hood ☐ Under Nevada Skies ☐ Under Western Skies ☐ Utah ☐ Wall Street Cowboy

Rogers, Will ☐ Ambassador Bill ☐ Connecticut Yankee, A ☐ County Chairman, The ☐ David Harum ☐ Doubting Thomas ☐ Down to Earth ☐ Dr. Bull ☐ Gaslight Follies ☐ Golden Age of Comedy, The ☐ Great Ziegfeld, The ☐ Handy Andy ☐ In Old Kentucky ☐ Judge Priest ☐ Life Begins at Forty ☐ Mr. Skitch ☐ So This Is London ☐ State Fair ☐ Steamboat 'Round the Bend ☐ They Had to See Paris

Roland, Gilbert ☐ Apache War Smoke ☐ Bad and the Beautiful, The ☐ Bandido ☐ Barbarosa ☐ Between God, the Devil and a Winchester ☐ Big Circus, The ☐ Bullfighter and the Lady, The ☐ Caboblanco ☐ Call Her Savage ☐ Cheyenne Autumn ☐ Christian Licorice Store, The ☐ Crisis ☐ French Line, The ☐ Furies, The ☐ Gateway ☐ Glory Alley ☐ Guns of the Timberland ☐ Islands in the Stream ☐ Johnny Hamlet ☐ Juarez ☐ Last Train from Madrid, The ☐ Mark of the Renegade ☐ Mark of Zorro, The ☐ Midnight Story, The ☐ Miracle of Our Lady of Fatima, The ☐ My Life with Caroline ☐ My Six Convicts ☐ New Lion of Sonora, The ☐ Our Betters ☐ Racers, The ☐ Rangers of Fortune ☐ Reward, The ☐ Running Wild ☐ Sacketts, The ☐ She Done Him Wrong ☐ Ten Tall Men ☐ That Lady ☐ Three Violent People ☐ Thunder Bay ☐ Thunder Trail ☐ Underwater! ☐ We Were Strangers ☐ Wild and the Innocent, The

Rolle, Esther ☐ Cleopatra Jones ☐ Driving Miss Daisy ☐ House of Cards ☐ I Know Why the Caged Bird Sings ☐ Kid Who Loved Christmas, The ☐ Raisin in the Sun, A ☐ Summer of My German Soldier ☐ To Dance with the White Dog ☐ Who Says I Can't Ride a Rainbow?

Romand, Beatrice ☐ Claire's Knee ☐ Four Adventures of Reinette and Mirabelle ☐ Le Beau Mariage ☐ Le Sex Shop ☐ Romantic Englishwoman, The ☐ Summer

Roman, Ruth ☐ Always Leave Them Laughing ☐ Baby, The ☐ Barricade ☐ Belle Starr's Daughter ☐ Beyond the Forest ☐ Bitter Victory ☐ Blowing Wild ☐ Bottom of the Bottle, The ☐ Champion ☐ Colt .45 ☐ Dallas ☐ Far Country, The ☐ Five Steps to Danger ☐ Great Day in the Morning ☐ Incident in San Francisco ☐ Invitation ☐ Joe Macbeth ☐ Killing Kind, The ☐ Ladies Courageous ☐ Look in any Window ☐ Love Has Many Faces ☐ Mara Maru ☐ Rebel in Town ☐ Strangers on a Train ☐ Three Secrets ☐ Window, The

Romero, Cesar ☐ Always Goodbye ☐ Americano, The ☐ Batman—The Movie ☐ Beautiful Blonde from Bashful Bend, The ☐ British Agent ☐ Captain from Castile ☐ Cardinal Richelieu ☐ Carnival in Costa Rica ☐ Castillan, The ☐ Charlie Chan at Treasure Island ☐ Clive of India ☐ Computer Wore Tennis Shoes, The ☐ Coney Island ☐ Crooks and Coronets ☐ Dance Hall ☐ Deep Waters ☐ Devil is a Woman, The ☐ Diamond Jim ☐ Donovan's Reef ☐ FBI Girl ☐ Frontier Marshal ☐ Gentleman at Heart, A ☐ Good Fairy, The ☐ Great American Broadcast, The ☐ Happy Go Lovely ☐ Happy Landing ☐ He Married His Wife ☐ Hold 'Em Yale ☐ Hot Millions ☐ If a Man Answers ☐ Julia Misbehaves ☐ Jungle, The ☐ Latitude Zero ☐ Leather Saint, The ☐ Little Princess, The ☐ Love Before Breakfast ☐ Love That Brute ☐ Lust in the Dust ☐ Madigan's Million ☐ Marriage on the Rocks ☐ Metropolitan ☐ Midas Run ☐ Mission To Glory ☐ Mister Too Little ☐ My Lucky Star ☐ Nobody's Fool ☐ Now You See Him, Now You Don't ☐ Once a Thief ☐ Orchestra Wives ☐ Public Enemy's Wife ☐ Racers, The ☐ Rendezvous ☐ Ride on Vaquero ☐ Sergeant Deadhead ☐ Show Them No Mercy! ☐ Simple Justice ☐ Springtime in the Rockies ☐ Strongest Man in the World, The ☐ Tales of Manhattan ☐ Tall, Dark and Handsome ☐ That Lady in Ermine ☐ Thin Man, The ☐ Vera Cruz ☐ Wee Willie Winkie ☐ Week-end in Havana ☐ Wife, Husband and Friend

Rooney, Mickey ☐ Ah, Wilderness ☐ All Ashore ☐ Ambush Bay ☐ Andy Hardy Comes Home ☐ Andy Hardy Gets Spring Fever ☐ Andy Hardy Meets Debutante ☐ Andy Hardy's Blonde Trouble ☐ Andy Hardy's Double Life ☐ Andy Hardy's Private Secretary ☐ Arabian Adventure ☐ Atomic Kid, The ☐ Babes in Arms ☐ Babes on Broadway ☐ Baby Face Nelson ☐ Beast of The City, The ☐ Big Cage, The ☐ Big Operator, The ☐ Big Wheel, The ☐ Bill ☐ Bill: On His Own ☐ Black Stallion, The ☐ Bluegrass ☐ Bold and the Brave, The ☐ Boys Town ☐ Breakfast at Tiffany's ☐ Bridges at Toko-Ri, The ☐ Broadway to Hollywood ☐ Captains Courageous ☐ Care Bears Movie, The ☐ Cockeyed Cowboys of Calico County ☐ Comic, The ☐ County Chairman, The ☐ Courtship of Andy Hardy, The ☐ Devil in Love, The ☐ Devil is a Sissy, The ☐ Domino Principle, The ☐ Drive a Crooked Road ☐ Erik the Viking ☐ Extraordinary Seaman, The ☐ Family Affair, A ☐ Find the Lady ☐ Fireball, The ☐ Fox and the Hound, The ☐ Francis in the Haunted House ☐ Gambler Returns: The Luck of the Draw, The ☐ Girl Crazy ☐ Hardys Ride High, The ☐ He's a Cockeyed Wonder ☐ Hide-Out ☐ Home for Christmas ☐ Hoosier Schoolboy ☐ How to Stuff a Wild Bikini ☐ Huckleberry Finn ☐ Human Comedy, The ☐ It Came Upon the Midnight Clear ☐ It's a Mad Mad Mad Mad World ☐ Judge Hardy and Son ☐ Judge Hardy's Children ☐ Killer McCoy ☐ King of the Roaring Twenties—The Story of Arnold Rothstein ☐ Last Mile, The ☐ Leave 'Em Laughing ☐ Life Begins for Andy Hardy ☐ Lightning, the White Stallion ☐ Little Lord Fauntleroy ☐ Little Nemo: Adventures in Slumberland ☐ Live, Love and Learn ☐ Lord Jeff ☐ Love Finds Andy Hardy ☐ Love Laughs at Andy Hardy ☐ Magic of Lassie, The ☐ Magnificent Roughnecks ☐ Manhattan Melodrama ☐ Manipulator, The ☐ Men of Boys Town ☐ Midsummer Night's Dream, A ☐ My Heroes Have Always Been Cowboys ☐ My Kidnapper, My Love ☐ My Pal, the King ☐ National Velvet ☐ Odyssey of the Pacific ☐ Off Limits ☐ Operation Mad Ball ☐ Out West with the Hardys ☐ Pete's Dragon ☐ Pulp ☐ Quicksand ☐ Reckless ☐ Requiem for a Heavyweight ☐ Richard ☐ Riffraff ☐ Secret Invasion, The ☐ Silent Night, Deadly Night (Part V—The Toy Maker) ☐ Skiddoo ☐ Slave Ship ☐ Sound Off ☐ Stablemates ☐ Strike Up the Band ☐ Summer Holiday ☐ That's Entertainment ☐ That's Entertainment 3 ☐ Thoroughbreds Don't Cry ☐ Thousands Cheer ☐ Twenty-Four Hours to Kill ☐ Upperworld ☐ Words and Music ☐ You're Only Young Once ☐ Young Tom Edison

Rossellini, Isabella ☐ Blue Velvet ☐ Cousins ☐ Death Becomes Her ☐ Fallen Angels—Volume 1 ☐ Fearless ☐ Immortal Beloved ☐ Last Elephant, The ☐ Lies of the Twins ☐ Red Riding Hood ☐ Siesta ☐ Tough Guys Don't Dance ☐ White Nights ☐ Wild at Heart ☐ Zelly and Me

Ross, Katharine ☐ Betsy, The ☐ Butch Cassidy and the Sundance Kid ☐ Conagher ☐ Final Countdown, The ☐ Fools ☐ Games ☐ Get to Know Your Rabbit ☐ Graduate, The ☐ Hellfighters ☐ Legacy, The ☐ Mister Buddwing ☐ Murder in Texas ☐ Red-Headed Stranger ☐ Shadow Riders, The ☐ Singing Nun, The ☐ Stepford Wives, The ☐ Swarm, The ☐ Tell Them Willie Boy Is Here ☐ They Only Kill Their Masters ☐ Voyage of the Damned

Roth, Tim ☐ Bodies, Rest & Motion ☐ Heart of Darkness ☐ Hit, The ☐ Jumpin' at the Boneyard ☐ Meantime ☐ Pulp Fiction ☐ Reservoir Dogs ☐ Rosencrantz and Guildenstern Are Dead ☐ Vincent & Theo

Roundtree, Richard ☐ Amityville—A New Generation ☐ Angel III—Final Chapter, The ☐ Banker, The ☐ Big Score, The ☐ Bloodfist III—Forced to Fight ☐ Charley One-Eye ☐ City Heat ☐ Crack House ☐ Diamonds ☐ Embassy ☐ Eye for an Eye, An ☐ Firehouse ☐ Game for Vultures ☐ Gypsy Angels ☐ Inchon ☐ Jocks ☐ Killpoint ☐ Man Friday ☐ Maniac Cop ☐ Miami Cops ☐ Mind Twister ☐ One Down Two to Go ☐ Opposing Force ☐ Party Line ☐ Q ☐ Shaft ☐ Shaft in Africa ☐ Shaft's Big Score! ☐ Time to Die, A ☐ What Do You Say to a Naked Lady?

Rourke, Mickey ☐ 9 1/2 Weeks ☐ Angel Heart ☐ Barfly ☐ Body Heat ☐ City in Fear ☐ Desperate Hours ☐ Diner ☐ Eureka ☐ Harley Davidson & the Marlboro Man ☐ Homeboy ☐ Johnny Handsome ☐ Last Outlaw, The ☐ Pope of Greenwich Village, The ☐ Prayer for the Dying, A ☐ Rape & Marriage: The Rideout Case ☐ Rumble Fish ☐ White Sands ☐ Wild Orchid ☐ Year of the Dragon

Rowlands, Gena ☐ Another Woman ☐ Betty Ford Story, The ☐ Brink's Job, The ☐ Child Is Waiting, A ☐ Crazy in Love ☐ Early Frost, An ☐ Face of a Stranger ☐ Faces ☐ Gloria ☐ High Cost of Loving, The ☐ Light of Day ☐ Lonely Are the Brave ☐ Love Streams ☐ Machine Gun McCain ☐ Minnie and Moskowitz ☐ Montana ☐ Night on Earth ☐ Once Around ☐ Opening Night ☐ Question of Love, A ☐ Strangers: The Story of a Mother and Daughter ☐ Tempest ☐ Tony Rome ☐ Two

Minute Warning ☐ Woman Under the Influence, A

Ruehl, Mercedes ☐ 84 Charing Cross Road ☐ Another You ☐ Big ☐ Crazy People ☐ Fisher King, The ☐ Last Action Hero ☐ Leader of the Band ☐ Lost in Yonkers ☐ Married to the Mob ☐ Slaves of New York ☐ Warriors, The

Ruggles, Charlie ☐ All in a Night's Work ☐ Anything Goes ☐ Balalaika ☐ Big Broadcast of 1936, The ☐ Bringing Up Baby ☐ Early to Bed ☐ Exclusive ☐ Farmer's Daughter, The ☐ Follow Me, Boys! ☐ Friends of Mr. Sweeney ☐ Gallant Journey ☐ Give My Regards to Broadway ☐ Hearts Divided ☐ Honeymoon for Three ☐ I'd Rather Be Rich ☐ If I Had a Million ☐ Incendiary Blonde ☐ Invitation to Happiness ☐ It Happened on Fifth Avenue ☐ Lovable Cheat, The ☐ Love Me Tonight ☐ Madame Butterfly ☐ Melody Cruise ☐ Model Wife ☐ Murders in the Zoo ☐ My Brother Talks to Horses ☐ Night of June 13 ☐ No More Ladies ☐ No Time for Comedy ☐ Our Hearts Were Young and Gay ☐ Papa's Delicate Condition ☐ Parson of Panamint, The ☐ People Will Talk ☐ Perfect Marriage, The ☐ Ramrod ☐ Roadhouse Nights ☐ Ruggles of Red Gap ☐ Service De Luxe ☐ Six of a Kind ☐ Smiling Lieutenant, The ☐ This Is the Night ☐ Three Is a Family

Rule, Janice ☐ 3 Women ☐ Alvarez Kelly ☐ Ambush Murders, The ☐ Doctor's Wives ☐ Gumshoe ☐ Gun for a Coward ☐ Holiday for Sinners ☐ Invitation to a Gunfighter ☐ Kid Blue ☐ L.A. Bad ☐ Starlift ☐ Subterraneans, The ☐ Swimmer, The ☐ Welcome to Hard Times

Ruman, Sig ☐ Berlin Correspondent ☐ Bitter Sweet ☐ Bold Caballero, The ☐ Confessions of a Nazi Spy ☐ Day at the Races, A ☐ Emperor Waltz, The ☐ Errand Boy, The ☐ Faithful in My Fashion ☐ Father Is a Bachelor ☐ Girls on Probation ☐ Honolulu ☐ I Was an Adventuress ☐ It Happened Tomorrow ☐ Ma and Pa Kettle on Vacation ☐ Marie Galante ☐ Maytime ☐ Night at the Opera, A ☐ Night in Casablanca, A ☐ Ninotchka ☐ Nothing Sacred ☐ Saint in New York, The ☐ Stalag 17 ☐ Suez ☐ Summer Storm ☐ Thank You, Mr. Moto ☐ Think Fast, Mr. Moto ☐ To Be or Not to Be ☐ Wagons Roll at Night, The ☐ We Were Dancing ☐ World in His Arms, The ☐ World Premiere

Runyon, Jennifer ☐ "In" Crowd, The ☐ 18 Again! ☐ Blue de Ville ☐ Falcon and the Snowman, The ☐ In Crowd, The ☐ Man Called Sarge, A ☐ Up the Creek

Rush, Barbara ☐ Between Friends ☐ Bigger than Life ☐ Black Shield of Falworth, The ☐ Bramble Bush, The ☐ Captain Lightfoot ☐ Come Blow Your Horn ☐ First Legion, The ☐ Flaming Feather ☐ Flamingo Road ☐ Flight to Hong Kong ☐ Goldbergs, The ☐ Harry Black and the Tiger ☐ Hombre ☐ It Came from Outer Space ☐ Magnificent Obsession ☐ Man, The ☐ Moon of The Wolf ☐ No Down Payment ☐ Oh, Men! Oh, Women! ☐ Prince of Pirates ☐ Quebec ☐ Strangers When We Meet ☐ Summer Lovers ☐ Superdad ☐ Taza, Son of Cochise ☐ When Worlds Collide ☐ World in My Corner ☐ Young Lions, The ☐ Young Philadelphians, The

Russell, Jane ☐ Darker than Amber ☐ Double Dynamite ☐ Fate Is the Hunter ☐ Foxfire ☐ French Line, The ☐ Fuzzy Pink Nightgown, The ☐ Gentlemen Marry Brunettes ☐ Gentlemen Prefer Blondes ☐ His Kind of Woman ☐ Hot Blood ☐ Johnny Reno ☐ Las Vegas Story, The ☐ Macao ☐ Montana Belle ☐ Outlaw, The ☐ Paleface, The ☐ Revolt of Mamie Stover, The ☐ Son of Paleface ☐ Tall Men, The ☐ Underwater!

Russell, Kurt ☐ Amber Waves ☐ Backdraft ☐ Barefoot Executive, The ☐ Best of Times, The ☐ Big Trouble in Little China ☐ Captain Ron ☐ Charley and the Angel ☐ Christmas Coal Mine Miracle, The ☐ Computer Wore Tennis Shoes, The ☐ Elvis ☐ Escape from New York ☐ Fools' Parade ☐ Fox and the Hound, The ☐ Horse in the Gray Flannel Suit, The ☐ Mean Season, The ☐ Mosby's Marauders ☐ Now You See Him, Now You Don't ☐ One and Only, Genuine, Original Family Band, The ☐ Overboard ☐ Silkwood ☐ Stargate ☐ Strongest Man in the World, The ☐ Superdad ☐ Swing Shift ☐ Tango & Cash ☐ Tequila Sunrise ☐ Thing, The ☐ Tombstone ☐ Unlawful Entry ☐ Used Cars ☐ Winter People

Russell, Rosalind ☐ Auntie Mame ☐ Casino Murder Case ☐ China Seas ☐ Citadel, The ☐ Craig's Wife ☐ Design for Scandal ☐ Evelyn Prentice ☐ Fast and Loose ☐ Feminine Touch, The ☐ Five Finger Exercise ☐ Flight for Freedom ☐ Forsaking All Others ☐ Four's a Crowd ☐ Girl Rush, The ☐ Guilt of Janet Ames, The ☐ Gypsy ☐ Hired Wife ☐ His Girl Friday ☐ It Had to Happen ☐ Live, Love and Learn ☐ Majority of One, A ☐ Man-Proof ☐ Mourning Becomes Electra ☐ Mrs. Pollifax—Spy ☐ My Sister Eileen ☐ Never Wave at a WAC ☐ Night Must Fall ☐ No Time for Comedy ☐ Oh Dad, Poor Dad, Mama's Hung You in the Closet and I'm Feeling So Sad ☐ Picnic ☐ Reckless ☐ Rendezvous ☐ Rosie ☐ Sister Kenny ☐ Take a Letter, Darling ☐ Tell It to the Judge ☐ They Met in Bombay ☐ This Thing Called Love ☐ Trouble With Angels, The ☐ Under Two Flags ☐ Velvet Touch, The ☐ West Point of the Air ☐ Where Angels Go, Trouble Follows ☐ Woman of Distinction, A ☐ Women, The

Russell, Theresa ☐ Aria ☐ Bad Timing: 'A Sensual Obsession ☐ Black Widow ☐ Cold Heaven ☐ Eureka ☐ Impulse ☐ Insignificance ☐ Kafka ☐ Physical Evidence ☐ Razor's Edge, The ☐ Straight Time ☐ Track 29 ☐ Whore

Russo, Rene ☐ Freejack ☐ In the Line of Fire ☐ Lethal Weapon 3 ☐ Mr. Destiny ☐ One Good Cop ☐ Outbreak

Rutherford, Ann ☐ Adventures of Don Juan ☐ Andy Hardy Gets Spring Fever ☐ Andy Hardy Meets Debutante ☐ Andy Hardy's Double Life ☐ Badlands of Dakota ☐ Bermuda Mystery ☐ Christmas Carol, A ☐ Courtship of Andy Hardy, The ☐ Ghost Comes Home, The ☐ Happy Land ☐ Hardys Ride High, The ☐ Inside Job ☐ Judge Hardy and Son ☐ Judge Hardy's Children ☐ Life Begins for Andy Hardy ☐ Love Finds Andy Hardy ☐ Madonna's Secret, The ☐ Murder in the Music Hall ☐ Operation Haylift ☐ Orchestra Wives ☐ Out West with the Hardys ☐ Whistling in Brooklyn ☐ Whistling in the Dark ☐ Wyoming ☐ You're Only Young Once

Rutherford, Margaret ☐ Alligator Named Daisy, An ☐ Arabella ☐ Blithe Spirit ☐ Chimes at Midnight ☐ Countess from Hong Kong, A ☐ Curtain Up ☐ Happiest Days of Your Life, The ☐ Her Man Gilbey ☐ Hideout in the Alps ☐ I'm All Right, Jack ☐ Importance of Being Earnest, The ☐ Innocents in Paris ☐ Mad About Men ☐ Magic Box, The ☐ Miranda ☐ Mouse on the Moon, The ☐ Murder Ahoy ☐ Murder at the Gallop ☐ Murder Most Foul ☐ Murder, She Said ☐ On the Double ☐ Passport to Pimlico ☐ Runaway Bus, The ☐ Smallest Show on Earth, The ☐ Spring Meeting ☐ Trouble in Store ☐ V.I.P.s, The

Ryan, Meg ☐ Amityville 3D ☐ Armed and Dangerous ☐ D.O.A. ☐ Doors, The ☐ Flesh and Bone ☐ I. Q. ☐ Innerspace ☐ Joe Versus the Volcano ☐ Prelude to a Kiss ☐ Presidio, The ☐ Promised Land ☐ Sleepless in Seattle ☐ When a Man Loves a Woman ☐ When Harry Met Sally . . .

Ryan, Mitchell ☐ Choice, The ☐ Christmas Coal Mine Miracle, The ☐ Five of Me, The ☐ Flesh & Blood ☐ Friends of Eddie Coyle, The ☐ Magnum Force ☐ Margaret Bourke-White ☐ Medicine Hat Stallion, The ☐ Monte Walsh ☐ My Old Man's Place ☐ Northstar

Ryan, Peggy ☐ All Ashore ☐ Chip Off the Old Block ☐ Here Come the Co-eds ☐ Merry Monahans, The ☐ On Stage Everybody ☐ Shamrock Hill ☐ That's the Spirit ☐ This Is the Life

Ryan, Robert ☐ About Mrs. Leslie ☐ Act of Violence ☐ Alaska Seas ☐ And Hope to Die ☐ Anzio ☐ Back From Eternity ☐ Bad Day at Black Rock ☐ Battle of the Bulge ☐ Behind the Rising Sun ☐ Berlin Express ☐ Best of the Badmen ☐ Beware, My Lovely ☐ Billy Budd ☐ Bombardier ☐ Born To Be Bad ☐ Boy with Green Hair, The ☐ Busy Body, The ☐ Canadians, The ☐ Captain Nemo and the Underwater City ☐ Caught ☐ City Beneath the Sea ☐ Clash by Night ☐ Crossfire ☐ Custer of the West ☐ Day of the Outlaw ☐ Dirty Dozen, The ☐ Dirty Game, The ☐ Escape to Burma ☐ Executive Action ☐ Feminine Touch, The ☐ Flying Leathernecks ☐ Gangway for Tomorrow ☐ God's Little Acre ☐ Her Twelve Men ☐ Horizons West ☐ Hour of the Gun ☐ House of Bamboo ☐ I Married a Communist ☐ Ice Palace ☐ Iceman Cometh, The ☐ Inferno ☐ Iron Major, The ☐ King of Kings ☐ Lawman ☐ Lolly Madonna XXX ☐ Lonelyhearts ☐ Longest Day, The ☐ Love Machine, The ☐ Man Without a Country, The ☐ Marine Raiders ☐ Men in War ☐ Minute to Pray, a Second to Die, A ☐ Naked Spur, The ☐ Northwest Mounted Police ☐ Odds Against Tomorrow ☐ On Dangerous Ground ☐ Outfit, The ☐ Professionals, The ☐ Proud Ones, The ☐ Racket, The ☐ Return of the Bad Men ☐ Secret Fury, The ☐ Set-Up, The ☐ Sky's the Limit, The ☐ Tall Men, The ☐ Tender Comrade ☐ Trail Street ☐ Wild Bunch, The ☐ Woman on the Beach, The

Ryder, Winona ☐ 1969 ☐ Age of Innocence, The ☐ Beetlejuice ☐ Bram Stoker's Dracula ☐ Edward Scissorhands ☐ Great Balls of Fire! ☐ Heathers ☐ House of the Spirits ☐ Little Women ☐ Lucas ☐ Mermaids ☐ Night on Earth ☐ Reality Bites ☐ Square Dance ☐ Welcome Home, Roxy Carmichael

Ryu, Chishu ☐ Autumn Afternoon, An ☐ Early Summer ☐ Emperor and A General, The ☐ Good Morning ☐ Human Condition, The—Part Three: A Soldier's Prayer ☐ Late Spring ☐ Ohayo ☐ Tokyo Story

Sabu ☐ Arabian Nights ☐ Black Narcissus ☐ Cobra Woman ☐ Drums ☐ Elephant Boy ☐ End of the River, The ☐ Hello, Elephant ☐ Jaguar ☐ Jungle Book ☐ Man-Eater of Kumaon ☐ Mistress of The World ☐ Rampage ☐ Thief of Bagdad, The ☐ Tiger Walks, A

Sagebrecht, Marianne ☐ Bagdad Cafe ☐ Rosalie Goes Shopping ☐ Sugarbaby ☐ War of the Roses, The

Sahl, Mort ☐ All the Young Men ☐ Don't Make Waves ☐ In Love and War ☐ Johnny Cool ☐ Lenny Bruce—Without Tears ☐ Nothing Lasts Forever

Saint, Eva Marie ☐ 36 Hours ☐ All Fall Down ☐ Best Little Girl in The World, The ☐ Cancel My Reservation ☐ Christmas to Remember, A ☐ Curse of King Tut's Tomb, The ☐ Exodus ☐ Fatal Vision ☐ Grand Prix ☐ Hatful of Rain, A ☐ I'll Be Home for Christmas ☐ Jane Doe ☐ Kiss of a Killer ☐ Last Days of Patton, The ☐ Love Leads the Way ☐ Loving ☐ Macahans, The ☐ Norman Rockwell's Breaking Home Ties ☐ North by Northwest ☐ Nothing in Common ☐ On the Waterfront ☐ Raintree County ☐ Russians Are Coming! The Russians Are Coming!, The ☐ Sandpiper, The ☐ Stalking Moon, The ☐ That Certain Feeling ☐ Voyage of Terror: The Achille Lauro Affair

Sakall, S.Z. ☐ April Showers ☐ Ball of Fire ☐ Broadway ☐ Casablanca ☐ Christmas in Connecticut ☐ Cinderella Jones ☐ Cynthia

☐ Daughter of Rosie O'Grady, The ☐ Devil and Miss Jones, The ☐ Dolly Sisters, The ☐ Embraceable You ☐ In the Good Old Summertime ☐ It's a Date ☐ Lullaby of Broadway ☐ Montana ☐ My Dream Is Yours ☐ Never Say Goodbye ☐ Oh, You Beautiful Doll ☐ Romance on the High Seas ☐ San Antonio ☐ Seven Sweethearts ☐ Shine On, Harvest Moon ☐ Tea for Two ☐ That Night in Rio ☐ Time, the Place and the Girl, The ☐ Two Guys From Milwaukee

San Giacomo, Laura ☐ Once Around ☐ Pretty Woman ☐ Quigley Down Under ☐ sex, lies, and videotape ☐ Under Suspicion ☐ Vital Signs

Sanda, Dominique ☐ 1900 ☐ Caboblanco ☐ Conformist, The ☐ Damnation Alley ☐ First Love ☐ Garden of the Finzi-Conntinis, The ☐ Gentle Creature, A ☐ Impossible Object ☐ Inheritance, The ☐ Le Voyage en Douce ☐ Mackintosh Man, The ☐ Nobody's Children ☐ Steppenwolf ☐ Story of a Love Story

Sanders, George ☐ Action in Arabia ☐ All About Eve ☐ Allegheny Uprising ☐ Amorous Adventures of Moll Flanders, The ☐ Assignment—Paris ☐ Bitter Sweet ☐ Black Swan, The ☐ Cairo ☐ Call Me Madam ☐ Candy Man, The ☐ Captain Blackjack ☐ Confessions of a Nazi Spy ☐ Date With the Falcon, A ☐ Death of a Scoundrel ☐ Doomwatch ☐ Endless Night ☐ Falcon Takes Over, The ☐ Falcon's Brother, The ☐ Fan, The ☐ Five Golden Hours ☐ Foreign Correspondent ☐ Forever Amber ☐ Four Men and a Prayer ☐ From the Earth to the Moon ☐ Gay Falcon, The ☐ Ghost and Mrs. Muir, The ☐ Good Times ☐ Green Hell ☐ Hangover Square ☐ Her Cardboard Lover ☐ House of the Seven Gables, The ☐ I Can Get It for You Wholesale ☐ In Search of the Castaways ☐ International Settlement ☐ Ivanhoe ☐ Jungle Book, The ☐ Jupiter's Darling ☐ King Richard and the Crusaders ☐ King's Thief, The ☐ Kremlin Letter, The ☐ Lancer Spy ☐ Last Voyage, The ☐ Light Touch, The ☐ Lloyd's of London ☐ Lodger, The ☐ Love Is News ☐ Man Hunt ☐ Man Who Could Work Miracles, The ☐ Moon and Sixpence, The ☐ Moonfleet ☐ Mr. Moto's Last Warning ☐ Never Say Goodbye ☐ Nurse Edith Cavell ☐ One Step to Hell ☐ Operation Snatch ☐ Paris After Dark ☐ Personal Column ☐ Picture of Dorian Gray, The ☐ Private Affairs of Bel Ami, The ☐ Quiet Please, Murder ☐ Rage in Heaven ☐ Rebecca ☐ Saint in London, The ☐ Saint Strikes Back, The ☐ Saint Takes Over, The ☐ Saint's Double Trouble, The ☐ Samson and Delilah ☐ Scandal in Paris, A ☐ Scarlet Coat, The ☐ Shot in the Dark, A ☐ Slave Ship ☐ Solomon and Sheba ☐ Son of Fury ☐ Strange Woman, The ☐ Summer Storm ☐ Sundown ☐ Tales of Manhattan ☐ That Certain Feeling ☐ That Kind of Woman ☐ They Came to Blow Up America ☐ This Land Is Mine ☐ Touch of Larceny, A ☐ Uncle Harry ☐ Village of the Damned ☐ Voyage to Italy ☐ Warning Shot ☐ While the City Sleeps ☐ Whole Truth, The ☐ Witness to Murder

Sands, Julian ☐ Arachnophobia ☐ Boxing Helena ☐ Doctor and the Devils, The ☐ Gothic ☐ Grand Isle ☐ Husbands and Lovers ☐ Impromptu ☐ Killing Fields, The ☐ Married Man, A ☐ Murder by Moonlight ☐ Naked Lunch ☐ Night Sun ☐ Oxford Blues ☐ Room with a View, A ☐ Siesta ☐ Turn of the Screw, The ☐ Vibes ☐ Warlock ☐ Warlock 2: The Armageddon

Sarandon, Chris ☐ Child's Play ☐ Dog Day Afternoon ☐ Forced March ☐ Fright Night ☐ Goodbye, Miss 4th of July ☐ Lipstick ☐ Mayflower Madam ☐ Nightmare Before Christmas, The ☐ Princess Bride, The ☐ Protocol ☐ Resurrected, The ☐ Sentinel, The ☐ Slaves of New York ☐ Tale of Two Cities, A ☐ Whispers

Sarandon, Susan ☐ Atlantic City ☐ Buddy System, The ☐ Bull Durham ☐ Checkered Flag or Crash ☐ Client, The ☐ Compromising Positions ☐ Dry White Season, A ☐ F. Scott Fitzgerald and "The Last of the Belles" ☐ Front Page, The ☐ Great Smokey Roadblock, The ☐ Great Waldo Pepper, The ☐ Hunger, The ☐ January Man, The ☐ Joe ☐ King of the Gypsies ☐ Light Sleeper ☐ Little Women ☐ Lorenzo's Oil ☐ Lovin' Molly ☐ Loving Couples ☐ Monkey People, The ☐ Mussolini and I ☐ One Summer Love ☐ Other Side of Midnight, The ☐ Pretty Baby ☐ Rocky Horror Picture Show, The ☐ Safe Passage ☐ Sweet Hearts Dance ☐ Tempest ☐ Thelma & Louise ☐ White Palace ☐ Who Am I This Time? ☐ Witches of Eastwick, The

Sargent, Dick ☐ Fluffy ☐ Ghost and Mr. Chicken ☐ Parts: The Clonus Horror ☐ Teen Witch

Sarrazin, Michael ☐ Believe in Me ☐ Beulah Land ☐ Caravans ☐ Eye of the Cat ☐ Fighting Back ☐ Flim Flam Man, The ☐ For Pete's Sake ☐ Frankenstein: The True Story ☐ Groundstar Conspiracy, The ☐ Gumball Rally, The ☐ Gunfight in Abilene ☐ Harry in Your Pocket ☐ In Search of Gregory ☐ Joshua Then and Now ☐ Journey to Shiloh ☐ Keeping Track ☐ Loves and Times of Scaramouche, The ☐ Malarek ☐ Man Called Gannon, A ☐ Mascara ☐ Phone Call, The ☐ Reincarnation of Peter Proud, The ☐ Scaramouche ☐ Seduction, The ☐ Sometimes a Great Notion ☐ They Shoot Horses, Don't They?

Savage, John ☐ All the Kind Strangers ☐ Amateur, The ☐ Any Man's Death ☐ Beat, The ☐ Brady's Escape ☐ Deer Hunter, The ☐ Eric ☐ Hair ☐ Hotel Colonial ☐ Inside Moves ☐ Killing Kind, The ☐ Maria's Lovers ☐ Nairobi Affair ☐ Onion Field, The ☐ Primary Motive ☐ Salvador ☐ Silent Witness ☐ Soldier's Revenge ☐ Steelyard Blues

Savalas, Telly ☐ Alcatraz: The Whole Shocking Story ☐ Alice in Wonderland ☐ Assassination Bureau, The ☐ Battle of the Bulge ☐ Battleground ☐ Beau Geste ☐ Belarus File, The ☐ Beyond Reason ☐ Beyond the Poseidon Adventure ☐ Birdman of Alcatraz ☐ Blood Barrier ☐ Buona Sera, Mrs. Campbell ☐ Cannonball Run II ☐ Cape Fear ☐ Capricorn One ☐ Clay Pigeon ☐ Crooks and Coronets ☐ Dirty Dozen, The ☐ Escape to Athena ☐ Fake-Out ☐ Family, The ☐ Genghis Khan ☐ GoBots: Battle of the Rock Lords ☐ Greatest Story Ever Told, The ☐ Hollywood Detective, The ☐ Horror Express ☐ Inside Out ☐ Johnny Cool ☐ Kelly's Heroes ☐ Killer Force ☐ Land Raiders ☐ Lisa and the Devil ☐ Love Is a Ball ☐ Mackenna's Gold ☐ Mad Dog Coll ☐ Man from the Diner's Club, The ☐ Marcus-Nelson Murders, The ☐ Massacre At Fort Holman ☐ Mind Twister ☐ New Interns, The ☐ On Her Majesty's Secret Service ☐ Pancho Villa ☐ Pretty Maids All in a Row ☐ Reason to Live, a Reason to Die, A ☐ Scalphunters, The ☐ Scenes from a Murder ☐ Silent Rebellion ☐ Slender Thread, The ☐ Young Savages, The

Saxon, John ☐ Animal Instincts ☐ Appaloosa, The ☐ Arrival, The ☐ Baby Doll Murders, The ☐ Battle Beyond the Stars ☐ Bees, The ☐ Beyond Evil ☐ Big Fisherman, The ☐ Big Score, The ☐ Black Christmas ☐ Blood Beach ☐ Blood Beast from Outer Space ☐ Blood Salvage ☐ Cardinal, The ☐ Cavern, The ☐ Death of a Gunfighter ☐ Enter the Dragon ☐ Final Alliance ☐ For Singles Only ☐ Glove, The ☐ Hands of Steel ☐ Hellmaster ☐ Immigrants, The ☐ Invasion of the Flesh Hunters ☐ Istanbul Express ☐ Joe Kidd ☐ Maximum Force ☐ Mitchell ☐ Moonshine County Express ☐ Mr. Hobbs Takes a Vacation ☐ My Mom's Werewolf ☐ Nightmare on Elm Street 3: Dream Warriors ☐ Nightmare on Elm Street, A ☐ Payoff ☐ Plunderers, The ☐ Portrait in Black ☐ Posse from Hell ☐ Queen of Blood ☐ This Happy Feeling ☐ Unguarded Moment, The ☐ Unsane ☐ War Hunt ☐ Wes Craven's New Nightmare

Sayles, John ☐ City of Hope ☐ Hard Choices ☐ Matinee ☐ Unnatural Causes

Sbarge, Raphael ☐ Back to Hannibal: The Return of Tom Sawyer and Huckleberry Finn ☐ Billionaire Boys Club ☐ Hidden II, The ☐ Murder 101 ☐ My Man Adam ☐ My Science Project ☐ Risky Business

Scacchi, Greta ☐ Browning Version, The ☐ Burke and Wills ☐ Camille ☐ Coca-Cola Kid, The ☐ Defence of the Realm ☐ Ebony Tower, The ☐ Fires Within ☐ Good Morning, Babylon ☐ Heat and Dust ☐ Killing Beach, The ☐ Love and Fear ☐ Man in Love, A ☐ Player, The ☐ Presumed Innocent ☐ Shattered ☐ White Mischief

Scheider, Roy ☐ 2010: The Year We Make Contact ☐ 52 Pick-Up ☐ All That Jazz ☐ Blue Thunder ☐ Cohen and Tate ☐ Fourth War, The ☐ French Connection, The ☐ French Conspiracy, The ☐ Jacobo Timerman: Prisoner Without a Name, Cell Without a Number ☐ Jaws ☐ Jaws 2 ☐ Klute ☐ Last Embrace ☐ Listen to Me ☐ Marathon Man ☐ Men's Club, The ☐ Naked Lunch ☐ Night Game ☐ Outside Man, The ☐ Romeo is Bleeding ☐ Russia House, The ☐ Seven-Ups, The ☐ Sheila Levine Is Dead and Living in New York ☐ Somebody Has to Shoot the Picture ☐ Sorcerer ☐ Still of the Night ☐ Tiger Town

Schell, Maria ☐ As the Sea Rages ☐ Brothers Karamazov, The ☐ Christmas Lilies of the Field ☐ Cimarron ☐ Devil by the Tail, The ☐ End of Desire ☐ Gervaise ☐ Hanging Tree, The ☐ Heart of the Matter, The ☐ Inside the Third Reich ☐ Just a Gigolo ☐ La Passante ☐ Last Bridge, The ☐ Magic Box, The ☐ Mark, The ☐ Napoleon ☐ Night of the Blood Monster ☐ Odessa File, The ☐ Rats, The ☐ White Nights

Schell, Maximilian ☐ Assisi Underground, The ☐ Avalanche Express ☐ Black Hole, The ☐ Bridge Too Far, A ☐ Castle, The ☐ Chosen, The ☐ Condemned of Altona, The ☐ Counterpoint ☐ Cross of Iron ☐ Deadly Affair, The ☐ Diary of Anne Frank, The ☐ Far Off Place, A ☐ First Love ☐ Five Finger Exercise ☐ Heidi ☐ Judgment at Nuremberg ☐ Julia ☐ Krakatoa, East of Java ☐ Man in the Glass Booth, The ☐ Man Under Suspicion ☐ Miss Rose White ☐ Odessa File, The ☐ Pedestrian, The ☐ Phantom of the Opera, The ☐ Players ☐ Pope Joan ☐ Simon Bolivar ☐ Stalin ☐ Together ☐ Topkapi ☐ Young Lions, The

Schildkraut, Joseph ☐ Baroness and the Butler, The ☐ Cheaters, The ☐ Cleopatra ☐ Diary of Anne Frank, The ☐ Flame of Barbary Coast ☐ Gallant Legion, The ☐ Garden of Allah, The ☐ King of Kings, The ☐ Lady of the Tropics ☐ Lancer Spy ☐ Life of Emile Zola, The ☐ Man in the Iron Mask, The ☐ Marie Antoinette ☐ Monsieur Beaucaire ☐ Mr. Moto Takes a Vacation ☐ Northwest Outpost ☐ Orphans of the Storm ☐ Pack Up Your Troubles ☐ Parson of Panamint, The ☐ Rains Came, The ☐ Rangers of Fortune ☐ Shop Around the Corner, The ☐ Slave Ship ☐ Souls at Sea ☐ Suez ☐ Viva Villa!

Schneider, Romy ☐ Assassination of Trotsky, The ☐ Bloodline ☐ Boccaccio '70 ☐ Cardinal, The ☐ Cesar and Rosalie ☐ Clair de Femme ☐ Deathwatch ☐ Dirty Hands ☐ Forever My Love ☐ Garde A Vue ☐ Good Neighbor Sam ☐ Hero, The ☐ Infernal Trio, The ☐ Inquisitor, The ☐ La Passante ☐ Love at the Top ☐ Loving in the Rain ☐ Ludwig ☐ Madchen in Uniform ☐ Magnificent Sinner ☐ Otley ☐ Simple Story, A ☐ Things of Life, The ☐ Trial, The ☐ Triple Cross ☐ Victors, The ☐ What's New, Pussycat?

Schoeffling, Michael ☐ Belizaire the Cajun ☐ Let's Get Harry ☐ Mermaids ☐ Sixteen Candles ☐ Sylvester ☐ Vision Quest ☐ Wild Hearts Can't Be Broken

Schwarzenegger, Arnold ☐ Commando ☐ Conan the Barbarian ☐ Conan the Destroyer ☐ Jayne Mansfield Story, The ☐ Junior ☐ Kindergarten Cop ☐ Last Action Hero ☐ Predator ☐ Pumping Iron ☐ Raw Deal ☐ Red Heat ☐ Red Sonja ☐ Running Man, The ☐ Stay Hungry ☐ Terminator, The ☐ Terminator 2—Judgment Day ☐ Total Recall ☐ True Lies ☐ Twins ☐ Villain, The

Schygulla, Hanna ☐ Berlin Alexanderplatz ☐ Beware of a Holy Whore ☐ Bitter Tears of Petra Von Kant, The ☐ Casanova ☐ Circle of Deceit ☐ Dead Again ☐ Delta Force, The ☐ Effi Briest ☐ Forever, Lulu ☐ Friends and Husbands ☐ Gods of the Plague ☐ Jail Bait ☐ Katzelmacher ☐ La Nuit des Varennes ☐ Lili Marleen ☐ Love in Germany, A ☐ Marriage of Maria Braun, The ☐ Merchant of Four Seasons, The ☐ Passion ☐ Sheer Madness ☐ Third Generation, The ☐ Wrong Move

Sciorra, Annabella ☐ Cadillac Man ☐ Hand That Rocks the Cradle, The ☐ Hard Way, The ☐ Jungle Fever ☐ Mario Puzo's "The Fortunate Pilgrim" ☐ Mr. Wonderful ☐ Night We Never Met, The ☐ Prison Stories: Women on the Inside ☐ Reversal of Fortune ☐ Romeo is Bleeding ☐ True Love ☐ Whispers in the Dark

Scofield, Paul ☐ Anna Karenina ☐ Attic, The: The Hiding of Anne Frank ☐ Bartleby ☐ Carve Her Name With Pride ☐ Delicate Balance, A ☐ Hamlet ☐ Henry V ☐ King Lear ☐ Man for All Seasons, A ☐ Quiz Show ☐ Scorpio ☐ Tell Me Lies ☐ That Lady ☐ Train, The ☐ Utz ☐ When the Whales Came

Scott, Campbell ☐ Dying Young ☐ Longtime Companion ☐ Mrs. Parker and the Vicious Circle ☐ Perfect Tribute, The ☐ Sheltering Sky, The ☐ Singles

Scott, George C. ☐ Anatomy of a Murder ☐ Bank Shot ☐ Bible, The ☐ Changeling, The ☐ Christmas Carol, A ☐ Crossed Swords ☐ Day of the Dolphin, The ☐ Descending Angel ☐ Dr. Strangelove or: How I Learned To Stop Worrying and Love the Bomb ☐ Exorcist III, The ☐ Fear on Trial ☐ Finding the Way Home ☐ Firestarter ☐ Flim Flam Man, The ☐ Formula, The ☐ Hanging Tree, The ☐ Hardcore ☐ Hindenburg, The ☐ Hospital, The ☐ Hustler, The ☐ Indomitable Teddy Roosevelt, The ☐ Islands in the Stream ☐ Jane Eyre ☐ Last Days of Patton, The ☐ Last Run, The ☐ List of Adrian Messenger, The ☐ Movie Movie ☐ Murders in the Rue Morgue, The ☐ New Centurions, The ☐ Oklahoma Crude ☐ Oliver and Co. ☐ Oliver Twist ☐ Pals ☐ Patton ☐ Petulia ☐ Rage ☐ Savage is Loose, The ☐ Taps ☐ They Might Be Giants ☐ This Savage Land ☐ Yellow Rolls-Royce, The

Scott, Gordon ☐ Duel of the Titans ☐ Goliath and the Vampires ☐ Tarzan the Magnificent ☐ Tarzan's Greatest Adventure ☐ Tramplers, The

Scott, Janette ☐ As Long As They're Happy ☐ Crack in the World ☐ Devil's Disciple, The ☐ Galloping Major, The ☐ Good Companions, The ☐ Happy Is the Bride ☐ Old Dark House, The ☐ Paranoiac ☐ School for Scoundrels ☐ Siege of the Saxons

Scott, Lizabeth ☐ Bad For Each Other ☐ Company She Keeps, The ☐ Dark City ☐ Dead Reckoning ☐ Desert Fury ☐ Easy Living ☐ I Walk Alone ☐ Loving You ☐ Paid in Full ☐ Pitfall, The ☐ Pulp ☐ Racket, The ☐ Red Mountain ☐ Scared Stiff ☐ Silver Lode ☐ Stolen Face, A ☐ Strange Love of Martha Ivers, The ☐ Too Late for Tears ☐ Weapon, The

Scott, Martha ☐ Adam ☐ Adam: His Song Continues ☐ Ben-Hur ☐ Cheers for Miss Bishop ☐ Daughter of the Streets ☐ Desperate Hours, The ☐ Father Figure ☐ Hi Diddle Diddle ☐ Howards of Virginia ☐ Medical Story ☐ One Foot in Heaven ☐ Our Town ☐ So Well Remembered ☐ Ten Commandments, The ☐ When I Grow Up

Scott, Randolph ☐ Abilene Town ☐ Albuquerque ☐ Badman's Territory ☐ Belle of the Yukon ☐ Belle Starr ☐ Bombardier ☐ Bounty Hunter, The ☐ Buchanan Rides Alone ☐ Canadian Pacific ☐ Captain Kidd ☐ Cariboo Trail ☐ Carson City ☐ China Sky ☐ Christmas Eve ☐ Coast Guard ☐ Colt .45 ☐ Comanche Station ☐ Coroner Creek ☐ Corvette K-225 ☐ Decision at Sundown ☐ Desperadoes, The ☐ Doolins of Oklahoma, The ☐ Fighting Man of the Plains ☐ Fort Worth ☐ Frontier Marshal ☐ Go West, Young Man ☐ Gunfighters ☐ Gung Ho! ☐ Hangman's Knot ☐ Heritage of the Desert ☐ High, Wide, and Handsome ☐ Home, Sweet Homicide ☐ Hot Saturday ☐ Jesse James ☐ Last of the Mohicans, The ☐ Lawless Street, A ☐ Man Behind the Gun, The ☐ Man in the Saddle ☐ Man of the Forest ☐ Murders in the Zoo ☐ My Favorite Wife ☐ Nevadan, The ☐ Paris Calling ☐ Pittsburgh ☐ Rage at Dawn ☐ Rebecca of Sunnybrook Farm ☐ Return of the Bad Men ☐ Ride Lonesome ☐ Ride the High Country ☐ Road to Reno, The ☐ Roberta ☐ Rocky Mountain Mystery ☐ Seven Men from Now ☐ Seventh Cavalry ☐ She ☐ So Red the Rose ☐ Spoilers, The ☐ Stranger Who Wore a Gun, The ☐ Successful Calamity, A ☐ Susannah of the Mounties ☐ Tall T, The ☐ Thundering Herd, The ☐ To the Shores of Tripoli ☐ Trail Street ☐ Virginia City ☐ Walking Hills, The ☐ Westbound ☐ Western Union ☐ When the Daltons Rode

Scott, Zachary ☐ Appointment in Honduras ☐ Bandido ☐ Born To Be Bad ☐ Cass Timberlane ☐ Colt .45 ☐ Danger Signal ☐ Flame of the Islands ☐ Flamingo Road ☐ Flaxy Martin ☐ Guilty Bystander ☐ Her Kind of Man ☐ It's Only Money ☐ Let's Make It Legal ☐ Mask of Dimitrios, The ☐ Mildred Pierce ☐ One Last Fling ☐ Secret of Convict Lake, The ☐ Shadow on the Wall ☐ Shotgun ☐ South of St. Louis ☐ Southerner, The ☐ Unfaithful, The

Seagal, Steven ☐ Above The Law ☐ Hard to Kill ☐ Marked for Death ☐ On Deadly Ground ☐ Out for Justice ☐ Under Siege

Seberg, Jean ☐ Airport ☐ Bonjour Tristesse ☐ Breathless ☐ Fine Madness, A ☐ Five Day Lover ☐ French Conspiracy, The ☐ In the French Style ☐ Kill! Kill! Kill! ☐ Let No Man Write My Epitaph ☐ Lilith ☐ Macho Callahan ☐ Mouse That Roared, The ☐ Paint Your Wagon ☐ Pendulum ☐ Saint Joan ☐ Time Out for Love

Sedgwick, Kyra ☐ Born on the Fourth of July ☐ Family Pictures ☐ Heart & Souls ☐ Lemon Sky ☐ Man Who Broke 1,000 Chains, The ☐ Miss Rose White ☐ Mr. & Mrs. Bridge ☐ Pyrates ☐ Singles ☐ Tai-Pan ☐ Women & Men: In Love There Are No Rules

Segal, George ☐ Act One ☐ Addict ☐ All's Fair ☐ Black Bird, The ☐ Blume In Love ☐ Bridge at Remagen, The ☐ Bye Bye Braverman ☐ California Split ☐ Carbon Copy ☐ Cold Room, The ☐ Duchess and the Dirtwater Fox, The ☐ Endless Game, The ☐ For the Boys ☐ Fun with Dick and Jane ☐ Girl Who Couldn't Say No, The ☐ Hot Rock, The ☐ Invitation to a Gunfighter ☐ Killing 'em Softly ☐ King Rat ☐ Last Married Couple in America, The ☐ Look Who's Talking ☐ Lost and Found ☐ Lost Command ☐ Loving ☐ Many Happy Returns ☐ New Interns, The ☐ No Way to Treat a Lady ☐ Not My Kid ☐ Owl and the Pussycat, The ☐ Quiller Memorandum, The ☐ Rollercoaster ☐ Ship of Fools ☐ St. Valentine's Day Massacre, The ☐ Terminal Man, The ☐ Touch of Class, A ☐ Where's Poppa? ☐ Who Is Killing the Great Chefs of Europe? ☐ Who's Afraid of Virginia Woolf? ☐ Young Doctors, The

Sellars, Elizabeth ☐ Cloudburst ☐ Day They Robbed the Bank of England, The ☐ Decision Against Time ☐ Forbidden Cargo ☐ Gentle Gunman, The ☐ Long Memory, The ☐ Madeleine ☐ Never Let Go ☐ Shiralee, The

Sellecca, Connie ☐ Brotherhood of the Rose ☐ Captain America II ☐ Last Fling, The ☐ Turn Back the Clock

Selleck, Tom ☐ Bunco ☐ Christopher Columbus—The Discovery ☐ Daughters of Satan ☐ Divorce Wars: A Love Story ☐ Folks! ☐ Gypsy Warriors, The ☐ Her Alibi ☐ High Road to China ☐ Innocent Man, An ☐ Lassiter ☐ Most Wanted ☐ Mr. Baseball ☐ Quigley Down Under ☐ Ramblin' Man ☐ Runaway ☐ Sacketts, The ☐ Shadow Riders, The ☐ Terminal Island ☐ Three Men and a Baby ☐ Three Men and a Little Lady

Sellers, Peter ☐ After the Fox ☐ Alice's Adventures in Wonderland ☐ Battle of the Sexes, The ☐ Being There ☐ Blockhouse, The ☐ Bobo, The ☐ Casino Royale ☐ Dr. Strangelove or: How I Learned To Stop Worrying and Love the Bomb ☐ Fiendish Plot of Dr. Fu Manchu, The ☐ Ghost in the Noonday Sun ☐ Great Mc Gonagal ☐ Heavens Above ☐ Hoffman ☐ I Like Money ☐ I Love You, Alice B. Toklas ☐ I'm All Right, Jack ☐ King Lear ☐ Lady Killers, The ☐ Lolita ☐ Magic Christian, The ☐ Man in a Cocked Hat ☐ Millionairess, The ☐ Mouse That Roared, The ☐ Murder by Death ☐ Naked Truth, The ☐ Never Let Go ☐ Only Two Can Play ☐ Optimists, The ☐ Orders Are Orders ☐ Party, The ☐ Pink Panther Strikes Again, The ☐ Pink Panther, The ☐ Prisoner of Zenda, The ☐ Return of the Pink Panther, The ☐ Revenge of the Pink Panther ☐ Shot in the Dark, A ☐ Smallest Show on Earth, The ☐ There's a Girl in My Soup ☐ Tom Thumb ☐ Trail of the Pink Panther ☐ Two Way Stretch ☐ Waltz of the Toreadors ☐ What's New, Pussycat? ☐ Woman Times Seven ☐ World of Henry Orient, The ☐ Wrong Arm of the Law ☐ Wrong Box, The

Sennett, Mack ☐ Abbott and Costello Meet The Keystone Kops ☐ Down Memory Lane ☐ Hollywood Cavalcade ☐ Lonely Villa, The

Serrault, Michel ☐ Associate, The ☐ Garde A Vue ☐ Get Out Your Handkerchiefs ☐ Hatter's Ghost, The ☐ Inquisitor, The ☐ La Cage aux Folles ☐ La Cage aux Folles II ☐ La Cage aux Folles III: The Wedding

Seymour, Jane ☐ Battlestar: Galactica ☐ Dark Mirror ☐ East of Eden ☐ Four Feathers, The ☐ Frankenstein: The True Story ☐ Haunting Passion, The ☐ Head Office ☐ Heidi ☐ Jack the Ripper ☐ Jamaica Inn ☐ Lassiter ☐ Live and Let Die ☐ Matters of the Heart ☐ Oh! What a Lovely War ☐ Oh, Heavenly Dog! ☐ Onassis: The Richest Man in the World ☐ Only Way, The ☐ Phantom of the Opera, The ☐ Scarlet Pimpernel, The ☐ Sinbad and the Eye of the Tiger ☐ Somewhere in Time ☐ Sunstroke

Seyrig, Delphine ☐ Accident ☐ Black Windmill, The ☐ Daughters of Darkness ☐ Day of the Jackal, The ☐ Discreet Charm of the Bourgeoisie, The ☐ Doll's House, A ☐ Donkey Skin ☐ Golden Eighties ☐ I Sent a Letter to My Love ☐ India Song ☐ Last Year at Marienbad ☐ Milky Way, The ☐ Muriel ☐ Stolen Kisses

Sharif, Omar ☐ Anastasia: The Mystery Of Anna ☐ Appointment, The ☐ Ashanti: Land of No Mercy ☐ Baltimore Bullet, The ☐ Behold a Pale Horse ☐ Beyond Justice ☐ Bloodline ☐ Burglars, The ☐ Che! ☐ Doctor Zhivago ☐ Fall of the Roman Empire ☐ Far Pavilions, The ☐ Funny Girl ☐ Funny Lady ☐ Genghis

Khan □ Green Ice □ Harem □ Horsemen, The □ Juggernaut □ Last Valley, The □ Lawrence of Arabia □ Mackenna's Gold □ Marco the Magnificent □ Mayerling □ More Than a Miracle □ Mrs. 'Arris Goes to Paris □ Night of the Generals, The □ Oh, Heavenly Dog! □ Tamarind Seed, The □ Top Secret □ Yellow Rolls-Royce, The

Sharkey, Ray □ Act of Piracy □ Capone □ Chrome Soldiers □ Cop and a Half □ Dubeat-e-o □ Heart Beat □ Hellhole □ Hot Tomorrows □ Idolmaker, The □ Love and Money □ Neon Empire, The □ Ordeal of Bill Carney, The □ Relentless 2: Dead On □ Scenes from the Class Struggle in Beverly Hills □ Some Kind of Hero □ Who'll Stop the Rain □ Willie and Phil □ Wired □ Wise Guys □ Zebrahead

Shatner, William □ Airplane II, The Sequel □ Andersonville Trial □ Barbary Coast, The □ Big Bad Mama □ Brothers Karamazov, The □ Devil's Rain, The □ Explosive Generation, The □ Go Ask Alice □ Horror at 37,000 Feet □ Hound of the Baskervilles, The □ Indict and Convict □ Intruder, The □ Kidnapping of the President, The □ Kingdom of the Spiders □ Little Women □ National Lampoon's Loaded Weapon □ Outrage, The □ People, The □ Star Trek 25th Anniversary Special □ Star Trek Generations □ Star Trek II: The Wrath of Khan □ Star Trek III: The Search for Spock □ Star Trek IV: The Voyage Home □ Star Trek V: The Final Frontier □ Star Trek VI: The Undiscovered Country □ Star Trek: The Motion Picture □ Star Trek—Episode 1: The Cage

Shaver, Helen □ Amazing Stories: Book Four □ Believers, The □ Color of Money, The □ Desert Hearts □ Harry Tracy, Desperado □ High-Ballin' □ In Praise of Older Women □ Innocent Victim □ Land Before Time, The □ Many Happy Returns □ Murder So Sweet □ Pair of Aces □ Park Is Mine, The □ Shoot □ Starship Invasions □ That Night □ Who Has Seen the Wind?

Shaw, Robert □ Avalanche Express □ Battle of Britain, The □ Battle of the Bulge □ Birthday Party, The □ Black Sunday □ Custer of the West □ Deep, The □ Diamonds □ End of the Game □ Figures in a Landscape □ Force 10 from Navarone □ From Russia with Love □ Guest, The □ Hell in Korea □ Hireling, The □ Jaws □ Luck Of Ginger Coffey, The □ Man for All Seasons, A □ Reflection of Fear, A □ Robin and Marian □ Royal Hunt of the Sun, The □ Sea Fury □ Sting, The □ Swashbuckler □ Taking of Pelham One Two Three, The □ Tomorrow at Ten □ Young Winston

Shawn, Dick □ Angel □ Beer □ Check Is in the Mail, The □ Fast Friends □ Goodbye Cruel World □ Happy Ending, The □ It's a Mad Mad Mad Mad World □ Love at First Bite □ Maid to Order □ Penelope □ Producers, The □ Secret Diary of Sigmund Freud, The □ Very Special Favor, A □ Wake Me When It's Over □ What Did You Do in the War, Daddy?

Shawn, Wallace □ Bedroom Window, The □ Micki + Maude □ Moderns, The □ My Dinner with Andre □ Nice Girls Don't Explode □ Nickel & Dime □ Prick Up Your Ears □ Princess Bride, The □ Scenes from the Class Struggle in Beverly Hills □ She's Out of Control □ Vanya on 42nd Street

Shea, John □ Baby M □ Case of Deadly Force, A □ Family Reunion □ Hitler's S.S.: Portrait in Evil □ Hussy □ Impossible Spy, The □ Ladykiller □ Missing □ Nativity, The □ New Life, A □ Notorious □ Small Sacrifices □ Stealing Home □ Unsettled Land □ Windy City

Shearer, Moira □ Black Tights □ Man Who Loved Redheads, The □ Peeping Tom □ Red Shoes, The □ Story of Three Loves, The □ Tales of Hoffman

Shearer, Norma □ Barretts of Wimpole Street, The □ Divorcee, The □ Escape □ Free Soul, A □ He Who Gets Slapped □ Her Cardboard Lover □ Hollywood Revue of 1929, The □ Idiot's Delight □ Marie Antoinette □ Private Lives □ Riptide □ Romeo and Juliet □ Smilin' Through □ Strange Interlude □ Strangers May Kiss □ Student Prince in Old Heidelberg, The □ Trial of Mary Dugan, The □ We Were Dancing □ Women, The

Sheedy, Ally □ Bad Boys □ Betsy's Wedding □ Blue City □ Breakfast Club, The □ Chantilly Lace □ Fear □ Heart of Dixie □ Lost Capone, The □ Maid to Order □ Man's Best Friend □ Only the Lonely □ Oxford Blues □ Short Circuit □ St. Elmo's Fire □ Twice in a Lifetime □ WarGames

Sheen, Charlie □ Backtrack □ Boys Next Door, The □ Cadence □ Chase, The □ Courage Mountain □ Deadfall □ Eight Men Out □ Hot Shots! □ Hot Shots! Part Deux □ Lucas □ Major League □ Major League II □ Men at Work □ National Lampoon's Loaded Weapon □ Navy SEALS □ No Man's Land □ Platoon □ Red Dawn □ Rookie, The □ Terminal Velocity □ Three for the Road □ Three Musketeers, The □ Wall Street □ Wraith, The □ Young Guns

Sheen, Martin □ Andersonville Trial □ Apocalypse Now □ Atlanta Child Murders, The □ Badlands □ Believers, The □ Beverly Hills Brats □ Beyond the Stars □ Cadence □ California Kid, The □ Cassandra Crossing, The □ Catch-22 □ Catholics □ Cold Front □ Consenting Adult □ Conspiracy—The Trial of the Chicago 8 □ Da □ Dead Zone, The □ Eagle's Wing □ Enigma □ Execution of Private Slovik, The □ Final Countdown, The □ Firestarter □ Fourth Wise Man, The □ Gandhi □ Gettysburg □ Guardian, The □ Hear No Evil □ In the Custody of Strangers □ In the King of Prussia □ Incident, The □ Judgment in Berlin □ Legend of Earl

Durand, The ☐ Little Girl Who Lives Down the Lane, The ☐ Loophole ☐ Maid, The ☐ Man, Woman and Child ☐ Message to My Daughter ☐ Missiles of October, The ☐ News at Eleven ☐ Nightbreaker ☐ No Drums, No Bugles ☐ Original Intent ☐ Out of the Darkness ☐ Pickup on 101 ☐ Rage ☐ Samaritan: The Mitch Snyder Story ☐ Siesta ☐ Subject Was Roses, The ☐ That Certain Summer ☐ That Championship Season ☐ Wall Street

Sheffer, Craig ☐ Babycakes ☐ Eye of the Storm ☐ Fire in the Sky ☐ Fire with Fire ☐ Instant Karma ☐ Night Breed ☐ Program, The ☐ River Runs Through It, A ☐ Sleep With Me

Sheffield, Johnny ☐ African Treasure ☐ Bomba and the Elephant Stampede ☐ Bomba and the Jungle Girl ☐ Bomba on Panther Island ☐ Bomba the Jungle Boy ☐ Golden Idol, The ☐ Tarzan and the Amazons ☐ Tarzan and the Leopard Woman ☐ Tarzan Finds a Son ☐ Tarzan Triumphs ☐ Tarzan's New York Adventure ☐ Tarzan's Secret Treasure

Shelley, Barbara ☐ Blood of the Vampire ☐ Cat Girl ☐ Dracula—Prince of Darkness ☐ Five Million Years to Earth ☐ Gorgon, The ☐ Maigret ☐ Rasputin—the Mad Monk ☐ Secret of Blood Island, The ☐ Village of the Damned

Shepard, Sam ☐ Baby Boom ☐ Bright Angel ☐ Country ☐ Crimes of the Heart ☐ Days of Heaven ☐ Defenseless ☐ Fool for Love ☐ Frances ☐ Pelican Brief, The ☐ Raggedy Man ☐ Renaldo and Clara ☐ Resurrection ☐ Right Stuff, The ☐ Safe Passage ☐ Steel Magnolias ☐ Thunderheart ☐ Voyager

Shepherd, Cybill ☐ At Long Last Love ☐ Chances Are ☐ Daisy Miller ☐ Guide for the Married Woman ☐ Heartbreak Kid, The ☐ Lady Vanishes, The ☐ Last Picture Show, The ☐ Long Hot Summer, The ☐ Married to It ☐ Moonlighting ☐ Once Upon a Crime ☐ Seduced ☐ Special Delivery ☐ Taxi Driver ☐ Texasville

Sheridan, Ann ☐ Angels Wash Their Faces, The ☐ Angels with Dirty Faces ☐ Appointment in Honduras ☐ Behold My Wife ☐ Black Legion ☐ Broadway Musketeers ☐ Car 99 ☐ Castle on the Hudson ☐ City for Conquest ☐ Come Next Spring ☐ Cowboy from Brooklyn, The ☐ Dodge City ☐ Doughgirls, The ☐ Edge of Darkness ☐ Fighting Youth ☐ George Washington Slept Here ☐ Good Sam ☐ Great O'Malley, The ☐ Honeymoon for Three ☐ I Was a Male War Bride ☐ Indianapolis Speedway ☐ It All Came True ☐ Juke Girl ☐ Just Across the Street ☐ Kings Row ☐ Ladies Should Listen ☐ Man Who Came to Dinner, The ☐ Naughty but Nice ☐ Navy Blues ☐ Nora Prentiss ☐ One More Tomorrow ☐ Opposite Sex, The ☐ San Quentin ☐ Shine On, Harvest Moon ☐ Silver River ☐ Take Me to Town ☐ Thank Your Lucky Stars ☐ They Drive by Night ☐ They Made Me a Criminal ☐ Torrid Zone ☐ Unfaithful, The ☐ Woman on the Run

Shields, Brooke ☐ Alice, Sweet Alice ☐ Blue Lagoon ☐ Brenda Starr ☐ Endless Love ☐ Freaked ☐ Just You and Me, Kid ☐ Muppets Take Manhattan, The ☐ Pretty Baby ☐ Sahara ☐ Wanda Nevada

Shimura, Takashi ☐ Drunken Angel ☐ Emperor and A General, The ☐ Godzilla, King of the Monsters ☐ I Live in Fear ☐ Idiot, The ☐ Ikiru ☐ Most Beautiful, The ☐ No Regrets for Our Youth ☐ Rashomon ☐ Saga of the Vagabonds ☐ Seven Samurai, The ☐ Stray Dog (Nora Inn) ☐ Throne of Blood

Shire, Talia ☐ Chantilly Lace ☐ Cold Heaven ☐ Deadfall ☐ For Richer, For Poorer ☐ Gas-s-s-s ☐ Godfather, Part II, The ☐ Godfather, Part III, The ☐ Godfather, The ☐ Kill Me if You Can ☐ Mark Twain and Me ☐ New York Stories ☐ Old Boyfriends ☐ Prophecy ☐ Rad ☐ Rocky ☐ Rocky 2 ☐ Rocky 3 ☐ Rocky 4 ☐ Rocky 5

Shirley, Anne ☐ Anne of Green Gables ☐ Anne of Windy Poplars ☐ Bombardier ☐ Chatterbox ☐ Devil and Daniel Webster, The ☐ Four Jacks and a Jill ☐ Girls' School ☐ Government Girl ☐ Make Way for a Lady ☐ Man from Frisco, The ☐ Man to Remember, A ☐ Meet the Missus ☐ Mother Carey's Chickens ☐ Murder My Sweet ☐ Saturday's Children ☐ Sorority House ☐ Steamboat 'Round the Bend ☐ Stella Dallas ☐ Vigil in the Night

Shore, Dinah ☐ Aaron Slick from Punkin Crick ☐ Belle of the Yukon ☐ Follow the Boys ☐ Fun and Fancy Free ☐ Till the Clouds Roll By ☐ Up in Arms

Short, Martin ☐ Captain Ron ☐ Clifford ☐ Cross My Heart ☐ Father of the Bride ☐ Innerspace ☐ Lost and Found ☐ Pure Luck ☐ Really Weird Tales ☐ Three Amigos! ☐ Three Fugitives ☐ We're Back: A Dinosaur's Story

Shue, Elisabeth ☐ Adventures in Babysitting ☐ Back to the Future Part II ☐ Back to the Future Part III ☐ Cocktail ☐ Heart & Souls ☐ Karate Kid, The ☐ Link ☐ Marrying Man, The ☐ Soapdish ☐ Twenty Bucks

Sidney, Sylvia ☐ Accent on Youth ☐ American Tragedy, An ☐ Beetlejuice ☐ Behind the High Wall ☐ Behold My Wife ☐ Blood on the Sun ☐ City Streets ☐ Corrupt ☐ Damien—Omen II ☐ Dead End ☐ Death at Love House ☐ Demon ☐ Do Not Fold, Spindle or Mutilate ☐ Early Frost, An ☐ Finnegan Begin Again ☐ Fury ☐ Good Dame ☐ Having It All ☐ I Never Promised You a Rose Garden ☐ Jennie Gerhardt ☐ Ladies of the Big House ☐ Les Miserables ☐ Love from a Stranger ☐ Madame Butterfly ☐ Mary Burns, Fugitive ☐ Merrily We Go to Hell ☐ Miracle Man, The ☐ Mr. Ace ☐ One Third of a Nation ☐ Pals ☐ Sabotage ☐ Searching Wind, The ☐ Street

Scene ☐ Summer Wishes, Winter Dreams ☐ Thirty Day Princess ☐ Trail of the Lonesome Pine ☐ Used People ☐ Violent Saturday ☐ You and Me ☐ You Only Live Once

Signoret, Simone ☐ Adolescent, The ☐ Against the Wind ☐ Casque D'or ☐ Confession, The ☐ Crucible, The ☐ Day and the Hour, The ☐ Deadly Affair, The ☐ Diabolique ☐ Diamond Hunters ☐ Four Days Leave ☐ Games ☐ I Sent a Letter to My Love ☐ Is Paris Burning? ☐ L'Armee des Ombres ☐ L'Etoile du Nord ☐ La Ronde ☐ Madame Rosa ☐ Room at the Top ☐ Sea Gull, The ☐ Ship of Fools ☐ Sleeping Car Murders, The ☐ Term of Trial

Silva, Henry ☐ Above The Law ☐ Allan Quartermain And The Lost City Of Gold ☐ Animals, The ☐ Bulletproof ☐ Code of Silence ☐ Escape from the Bronx ☐ Hail, Mafia ☐ Italian Connection, The ☐ Jayhawkers, The ☐ Johnny Cool ☐ Manchurian Candidate, The ☐ Manhunt, The ☐ Matchless ☐ Megaforce ☐ Never a Dull Moment ☐ Return of Mr. Moto, The ☐ Reward, The ☐ Secret Invasion, The ☐ Sharky's Machine ☐ Shoot

Silver, Ron ☐ Best Friends ☐ Blind Side ☐ Blue Steel ☐ Enemies, A Love Story ☐ Entity, The ☐ Father's Revenge, A ☐ Fellow Traveler ☐ Forgotten Prisoners: The Amnesty Files ☐ Garbo Talks ☐ Goodbye People, The ☐ Lifepod ☐ Live Wire ☐ Married to It ☐ Mr. Saturday Night ☐ Oh, God! You Devil ☐ Reversal of Fortune ☐ Silent Rage ☐ Timecop ☐ Trapped in Silence ☐ Tunnelvision

Silverheels, Jay ☐ Brave Warrior ☐ Feathered Serpent, The ☐ Indian Paint ☐ Jack McCall, Desperado ☐ Last of the Comanches, The ☐ Lone Ranger and the Lost City of Gold, The ☐ Lone Ranger, The ☐ Origin Of The Lone Ranger, The ☐ Saskatchewan ☐ Walk the Proud Land ☐ War Arrow

Silverman, Jonathan ☐ Age Isn't Everything ☐ Breaking the Rules ☐ Brighton Beach Memoirs ☐ Broadway Bound ☐ Caddyshack II ☐ Class Action ☐ For Richer, For Poorer ☐ Girls Just Want to Have Fun ☐ Little Big League ☐ Stealing Home ☐ Weekend at Bernie's ☐ Weekend at Bernie's II

Silvers, Phil ☐ All Through the Night ☐ Boatniks, The ☐ Buona Sera, Mrs. Campbell ☐ Cheap Detective, The ☐ Chicken Chronicles, The ☐ Coney Island ☐ Cover Girl ☐ Diamond Horseshoe ☐ Follow That Camel ☐ Footlight Serenade ☐ Forty Pounds of Trouble ☐ Four Jills in a Jeep ☐ Funny Thing Happened on the Way to the Forum, A ☐ Happy Hooker Goes Hollywood, The ☐ Hey Abbott! ☐ If I'm Lucky ☐ It's a Mad Mad Mad Mad World ☐ Just Off Broadway ☐ Lady Takes A Chance, A ☐ Lucky Me ☐ My Gal Sal ☐ Night They Took Miss Beautiful ☐ Racquet ☐ Roxie Hart ☐ Something for the Boys ☐ Strongest Man in the World, The ☐ Summer Stock ☐ Thousand and One Nights, A ☐ Tom, Dick and Harry ☐ Top Banana ☐ Wild Man of Borneo, The ☐ Won Ton Ton, the Dog Who Saved Hollywood ☐ You're in the Army Now

Sim, Alastair ☐ Anatomist, The ☐ Belles of St. Trinians, The ☐ Blue Murder at St. Trinian's ☐ Captain Boycott ☐ Christmas Carol, A ☐ Cottage to Let ☐ Doctor's Dilemma ☐ Dulcimer Street ☐ Escapade ☐ Folly to Be Wise ☐ Green for Danger ☐ Green Man, The ☐ Happiest Days of Your Life, The ☐ Hue and Cry ☐ Innocents in Paris ☐ Inspector Calls, An ☐ Inspector Hornleigh ☐ Inspector Hornleigh on Holiday ☐ Lady Godiva Rides Again ☐ Laughter in Paradise ☐ Left Right and Center ☐ Littlest Horse Thieves, The ☐ Millionairess, The ☐ Royal Flash ☐ Ruling Class, The ☐ School for Scoundrels ☐ Stage Fright ☐ This Man in Paris ☐ This Man Is News ☐ Wee Geordie

Simmons, Jean ☐ Actress, The ☐ Adam and Evalyn ☐ Affair with a Stranger ☐ All the Way Home ☐ Androcles and the Lion ☐ Angel Face ☐ Beggarman, Thief ☐ Big Country, The ☐ Black Narcissus ☐ Blue Lagoon, The ☐ Bullet is Waiting, A ☐ Cage of Gold ☐ Clouded Yellow, The ☐ Dawning, The ☐ Desiree ☐ Divorce American Style ☐ Dominique ☐ Egyptian, The ☐ Elmer Gantry ☐ Footsteps in the Fog ☐ Going Undercover ☐ Grass is Greener, The ☐ Great Expectations ☐ Guys and Dolls ☐ Hamlet ☐ Happy Ending, The ☐ Heidi ☐ Hilda Crane ☐ Home Before Dark ☐ Hungry Hill ☐ Inherit the Wind ☐ Inheritance, The ☐ Jacqueline Susann's Valley of the Dolls ☐ Life at the Top ☐ Mister Buddwing ☐ Moment in Time, A ☐ Robe, The ☐ Rough Night in Jericho ☐ Say Hello to Yesterday ☐ She Couldn't Say No ☐ So Long at the Fair ☐ Spartacus ☐ This Could Be the Night ☐ This Earth Is Mine ☐ Thorn Birds, The ☐ Trio ☐ Until They Sail ☐ Young Bess

Simon, Simone ☐ Cat People ☐ Curse of the Cat People, The ☐ Devil and Daniel Webster, The ☐ Girls' Dormitory ☐ Johnny Doesn't Live Here Any More ☐ Josette ☐ La Bete Humaine ☐ La Ronde ☐ Le Plaisir ☐ Mademoiselle Fifi ☐ Seventh Heaven

Simpson, O.J. ☐ C.I.A.: Code Name Alexa ☐ Capricorn One ☐ Cassandra Crossing, The ☐ Firepower ☐ Goldie and the Boxer ☐ Goldie and the Boxer Go to Hollywood ☐ Hambone and Hillie ☐ Naked Gun, The ☐ Naked Gun 2 1/2: The Smell of Fear, The ☐ Naked Gun 33 1/3: The Final Insult

Sinatra, Frank ☐ Anchors Aweigh ☐ Assault on a Queen ☐ Can-Can ☐ Cast a Giant Shadow ☐ Come Blow Your Horn ☐ Contract on Cherry Street ☐ Detective, The ☐ Devil at 4 O'Clock, The ☐ Dirty Dingus Magee ☐ Double Dynamite ☐ First Deadly Sin, The ☐ Four for Texas ☐ From Here to Eternity ☐ Guys and Dolls ☐ High Society ☐ Higher and

Higher ☐ Hole in the Head, A ☐ It Happened in Brooklyn ☐ Johnny Concho ☐ Joker is Wild, The ☐ Kings Go Forth ☐ Kissing Bandit, The ☐ Lady in Cement ☐ List of Adrian Messenger, The ☐ Man with the Golden Arm ☐ Manchurian Candidate, The ☐ Marriage on the Rocks ☐ Meet Danny Wilson ☐ Miracle of the Bells, The ☐ Naked Runner, The ☐ Never So Few ☐ None But the Brave ☐ Not as a Stranger ☐ Ocean's Eleven ☐ On the Town ☐ Pal Joey ☐ Pride and the Passion, The ☐ Robin and the Seven Hoods ☐ Sergeants 3 ☐ Ship Ahoy ☐ Some Came Running ☐ Step Lively ☐ Suddenly ☐ Take Me Out to the Ball Game ☐ Tender Trap, The ☐ That's Entertainment ☐ Till the Clouds Roll By ☐ Tony Rome ☐ Von Ryan's Express ☐ Young at Heart

Sinatra, Nancy ☐ Get Yourself a College Girl ☐ Ghost in the Invisible Bikini ☐ Last of the Secret Agents?, The ☐ Marriage on the Rocks ☐ Speedway ☐ Wild Angels, The

Sinclair, Madge ☐ Coming to America ☐ Conrack ☐ High Ice ☐ Leadbelly ☐ One in a Million: The Ron LeFlore Story ☐ Victims

Sinden, Donald ☐ Above Us The Waves ☐ Alligator Named Daisy, An ☐ Beachcomber, The ☐ Black Tent, The ☐ Captain's Table, The ☐ Cruel Sea, The ☐ Doctor at Large ☐ Doctor in the House ☐ Island at the Top of the World, The ☐ Mad About Men ☐ Mad Little Island ☐ Mogambo ☐ National Health, The ☐ Tiger in the Smoke ☐ Twice Around the Daffodils ☐ Villain

Singer, Lori ☐ Equinox ☐ Falcon and the Snowman, The ☐ Footloose ☐ Made in USA ☐ Man with One Red Shoe ☐ Storm and Sorrow ☐ Summer Heat ☐ Trouble in Mind ☐ Warlock

Singer, Marc ☐ Beastmaster 2: Through the Portal of Time ☐ Beastmaster, The ☐ Berlin Conspiracy, The ☐ Body Chemistry ☐ Born to Race ☐ Go Tell the Spartans ☐ Her Life as a Man ☐ High Desert Kill ☐ If You Could See What I Hear ☐ Man Called Sarge, A ☐ Sea Wolf, The ☐ Sergeant Matlovich vs. the U.S. Air Force ☐ Two Worlds of Jennie Logan, The ☐ V ☐ Watchers 2

Singleton, Penny ☐ Beware of Blondie ☐ Blondie ☐ Blondie Brings Up Baby ☐ Footlight Glamour ☐ It's a Great Life ☐ Leave It to Blondie ☐ Life with Blondie ☐ Mad Miss Manton, The ☐ Outside of Paradise ☐ Racket Busters ☐ Swing Your Lady

Sinise, Gary ☐ Forrest Gump ☐ Jack the Bear ☐ Midnight Clear, A ☐ My Name is Bill W. ☐ Of Mice and Men ☐ Quick and the Dead, The ☐ Stand, The

Sizemore, Tom ☐ Flight of the Intruder ☐ Heart & Souls ☐ Passenger 57 ☐ Watch It ☐ Where Sleeping Dogs Lie

Skala, Lilia ☐ Charly ☐ Eleanor and Franklin ☐ End of August, The ☐ Flashdance ☐ Heartland ☐ House of Games ☐ Lilies of the Field

Skelton, Red ☐ Bathing Beauty ☐ Clown, The ☐ Dr. Kildare's Wedding Day ☐ DuBarry Was a Lady ☐ Excuse My Dust ☐ Flight Command ☐ Fuller Brush Man, The ☐ Great Diamond Robbery, The ☐ Half a Hero ☐ I Dood It ☐ Lady Be Good ☐ Lovely to Look At ☐ Maisie Gets Her Man ☐ Merton of the Movies ☐ Neptune's Daughter ☐ Panama Hattie ☐ Public Pigeon No. One ☐ Ship Ahoy ☐ Show-Off, The ☐ Southern Yankee, A ☐ Texas Carnival ☐ Thousands Cheer ☐ Three Little Words ☐ Watch the Birdie ☐ Whistling in Brooklyn ☐ Whistling in the Dark ☐ Yellow Cab Man, The ☐ Ziegfeld Follies

Skerritt, Tom ☐ Alien ☐ Big Bad Mama ☐ Big Town, The ☐ Child in the Night ☐ China Lake Murders, The ☐ Dangerous Summer, A ☐ Dead Zone, The ☐ Devil's Rain, The ☐ Fighting Back ☐ Fuzz ☐ Heist, The ☐ Ice Castles ☐ Knight Moves ☐ M*A*S*H ☐ Maid to Order ☐ Miles to Go ☐ Nightmare at Bittercreek ☐ Opposing Force ☐ Parent Trap II ☐ Poison Ivy ☐ Poker Alice ☐ Poltergeist III ☐ River Runs Through It, A ☐ Silence of the North ☐ Space Camp ☐ Steel Magnolias ☐ Turning Point, The ☐ Wild Orchid 2—Two Shades of Blue ☐ Wisdom

Skipworth, Alison ☐ Casino Murder Case ☐ Coming-Out Party ☐ Devil is a Woman, The ☐ Doubting Thomas ☐ If I Had a Million ☐ Madame Racketeer ☐ Night After Night ☐ Princess Comes Across, The ☐ Raffles ☐ Satan Met a Lady ☐ Sinners in the Sun ☐ Six of a Kind ☐ Song of Songs ☐ Tillie and Gus

Skye, Ione ☐ Carmilla ☐ Gas, Food Lodging ☐ Guncrazy ☐ Mindwalk ☐ Night in the Life of Jimmy Reardon, A ☐ Rachel Papers, The ☐ River's Edge ☐ Samantha ☐ Say Anything . . .

Slater, Christian ☐ Beyond the Stars ☐ FernGully . . . The Last Rainforest ☐ Gleaming the Cube ☐ Heathers ☐ Interview With the Vampire ☐ Jimmy Hollywood ☐ Kuffs ☐ Legend of Billie Jean, The ☐ Mobsters ☐ Murder in the First ☐ Name of the Rose, The ☐ Pump Up the Volume ☐ Robin Hood: Prince of Thieves ☐ Tales From the Darkside: The Movie ☐ True Romance ☐ Twisted ☐ Untamed Heart ☐ Wizard, The ☐ Young Guns 2

Slater, Helen ☐ Betrayal of the Dove ☐ Chantilly Lace ☐ Happy Together ☐ Legend of Billie Jean, The ☐ Ruthless People ☐ Secret of My Success, The ☐ Sticky Fingers ☐ Supergirl

Slezak, Walter ☐ Abbott and Costello In The Foreign Legion ☐ Bedtime for Bonzo ☐ Black Beauty ☐ Born to Kill ☐ Come September ☐ Confidentially Connie ☐ Cornered ☐ Emil and the Detectives ☐ Fallen Sparrow ☐ Inspector General, The ☐ Lifeboat ☐ Magic Legend of the Juggler ☐ Miracle, The ☐ Mysterious House of Dr. C., The ☐ Once Upon a Honeymoon ☐ People Will Talk ☐ Pirate, The ☐ Princess and the Pirate, The ☐ Salome, Where She Danced ☐ Sinbad the Sailor ☐ Spanish Main, The ☐ Ten Thousand Bedrooms ☐ This Land Is Mine ☐ Till We Meet Again ☐ Twenty-Four Hours to Kill ☐ Very Special Favor, A ☐ White Witch Doctor ☐ Wonderful World of the Brothers Grimm, The ☐ Yellow Cab Man, The

Smith, Alexis ☐ Adventures of Mark Twain, The ☐ Always Together ☐ Any Number Can Play ☐ Beau James ☐ Casey's Shadow ☐ Cave of Outlaws ☐ Conflict ☐ Constant Nymph, The ☐ Death in California, A ☐ Dive Bomber ☐ Doughgirls, The ☐ Eternal Sea, The ☐ Gentleman Jim ☐ Here Comes the Groom ☐ Horn Blows at Midnight, The ☐ Jacqueline Susann's Once Is Not Enough ☐ Little Girl Who Lives Down the Lane, The ☐ Marcus Welby, M.D.: A Holiday Affair ☐ Montana ☐ Night and Day ☐ One Last Fling ☐ One More Tomorrow ☐ Rhapsody in Blue ☐ San Antonio ☐ Sleeping Tiger, The ☐ South of St. Louis ☐ This Happy Feeling ☐ Tough Guys ☐ Turning Point, The ☐ Two Mrs. Carrolls, The ☐ Woman in White, The ☐ Young Philadelphians, The

Smith, Bubba ☐ Fist of Honor ☐ My Samurai ☐ Police Academy 2: Their First Assignment ☐ Police Academy 3: Back in Training ☐ Police Academy 4: Citizens on Patrol ☐ Police Academy 5: Assignment Miami Beach ☐ Police Academy 6: City Under Siege

Smith, C. Aubrey ☐ And Then There Were None ☐ Another Thin Man ☐ Bachelor Father, The ☐ Barbarian, The ☐ Beyond Tomorrow ☐ Bill of Divorcement, A ☐ Bombshell ☐ China Seas ☐ Cleopatra ☐ Clive of India ☐ Cluny Brown ☐ Crusades, The ☐ East Side of Heaven ☐ Eternally Yours ☐ Firebird, The ☐ Five Came Back ☐ Florentine Dagger, The ☐ Four Men and a Prayer ☐ Gilded Lily, The ☐ Guilty Hands ☐ Hurricane, The ☐ Ideal Husband, An ☐ Little Lord Fauntleroy ☐ Madame Curie ☐ Maisie Was a Lady ☐ Morning Glory ☐ Polly of the Circus ☐ Queen Christina ☐ Rendezvous with Annie ☐ Romeo and Juliet ☐ Scarlet Empress, The ☐ Scotland Yard Investigator ☐ Sensations ☐ Sixty Glorious Years ☐ Tarzan, the Ape Man ☐ Thoroughbreds Don't Cry ☐ Unconquered ☐ Under-Pup, The ☐ We Live Again ☐ Wee Willie Winkie ☐ White Cliffs of Dover, The

Smith, Jaclyn ☐ Bootleggers ☐ Bourne Identity, The ☐ Charlie's Angels ☐ Deja Vu ☐ Florence Nightingale ☐ Jacqueline Bouvier Kennedy ☐ Night They Saved Christmas, The ☐ Nightkill ☐ Rage of Angels ☐ Rage of Angels: The Story Continues

Smith, Kent ☐ Cat People ☐ Comanche ☐ Curse of the Cat People, The ☐ Damned Don't Cry, The ☐ Distant Trumpet, A ☐ Forever and a Day ☐ Fountainhead, The ☐ Hitler's Children ☐ Imitation General ☐ Magic Town ☐ My Foolish Heart ☐ Nora Prentiss ☐ Paula ☐ Spiral Staircase, The ☐ Voice of the Turtle, The

Smith, Maggie ☐ Better Late Than Never ☐ California Suite ☐ Clash of the Titans ☐ Death on the Nile ☐ Evil Under the Sun ☐ Honey Pot, The ☐ Hook ☐ Hot Millions ☐ Lily in Love ☐ Lonely Passion of Judith Hearne, The ☐ Love and Pain (and the Whole Damn Thing) ☐ Missionary, The ☐ Mrs. Silly ☐ Murder by Death ☐ Nowhere to Go ☐ Oh! What a Lovely War ☐ Othello ☐ Prime of Miss Jean Brodie, The ☐ Private Function, A ☐ Pumpkin Eater, The ☐ Quartet ☐ Room with a View, A ☐ Secret Garden, The ☐ Sister Act ☐ Suddenly, Last Summer ☐ Travels With My Aunt ☐ V.I.P.s, The ☐ Young Cassidy

Smith, William ☐ Angels Die Hard ☐ B.O.R.N. ☐ Blood & Guts ☐ Chrome and Hot Leather ☐ East L.A. Warriors ☐ Emperor of the Bronx ☐ Evil Altar ☐ Grave of the Vampire ☐ Hollywood Man ☐ Invasion of the Bee Girls ☐ Jungle Assault ☐ L.A. Vice ☐ Last of the Warriors ☐ Last Riders ☐ Manhunter, The ☐ Maniac Cop ☐ Moon in Scorpio ☐ Scorchy ☐ Seven ☐ Spirit of the Eagle

Smits, Jimmy ☐ Believers, The ☐ Fires Within ☐ Glitz ☐ Old Gringo ☐ Stamp of a Killer ☐ Switch ☐ Tommyknockers, The ☐ Vital Signs

Snipes, Wesley ☐ Boiling Point ☐ Demolition Man ☐ Drop Zone ☐ Jungle Fever ☐ King of New York ☐ Mo' Better Blues ☐ New Jack City ☐ Passenger 57 ☐ Rising Sun ☐ Streets of Gold ☐ Sugar Hill ☐ Waterdance, The ☐ White Men Can't Jump

Snodgress, Carrie ☐ Across the Tracks ☐ Attic, The ☐ Ballad of Little Jo, The ☐ Blueberry Hill ☐ Diary of a Mad Housewife ☐ 8 Seconds ☐ Fast Friends ☐ Fury, The ☐ Homework ☐ Impatient Heart, The ☐ L.A. Bad ☐ Mission of the Shark ☐ Murphy's Law ☐ Nadia ☐ Night in Heaven, A ☐ Pale Rider ☐ Rabbit, Run ☐ Silent Night, Lonely Night

Soles, P.J. ☐ Alienator ☐ Awakening of Cassie, The ☐ B.O.R.N. ☐ Halloween ☐ Innocent Prey ☐ Rock 'n' Roll High School ☐ Stripes

Sommer, Elke ☐ Anastasia: The Mystery Of Anna ☐ Art of Love, The ☐ Baron Blood ☐ Boy, Did I Get a Wrong Number! ☐ Deadlier than the Male ☐ Double McGuffin, The ☐ Frontier Hellcat ☐ Invincible Six, The ☐ It's Not the Size That Counts ☐ Left for Dead ☐ Lily in Love ☐ Lisa and the Devil ☐ Mayfair Bank Caper, The ☐ Money Trap, The ☐ Oscar, The ☐ Prisoner of Zenda, The ☐ Prize, The ☐ Severed Ties ☐ Shot in the Dark, A ☐ Ten Little Indians ☐ Victors, The ☐ Wrecking Crew, The ☐ Zeppelin

Sondergaard, Gale ☐ Anna and the King of

Siam ☐ Anthony Adverse ☐ Black Cat, The ☐ Blue Bird, The ☐ Cat and the Canary, The ☐ Cat Creature, The ☐ Christmas Holiday ☐ Climax, The ☐ East Side, West Side ☐ Follow the Boys ☐ Gypsy Wildcat ☐ Invisible Man's Revenge, The ☐ Isle of Forgotten Sins ☐ Juarez ☐ Letter, The ☐ Life of Emile Zola, The ☐ Lord Jeff ☐ Maid of Salem ☐ Mark of Zorro, The ☐ My Favorite Blonde ☐ Never Say Die ☐ Night to Remember, A ☐ Paris Calling ☐ Return of a Man Called Horse, The ☐ Road to Rio ☐ Seventh Heaven ☐ Sherlock Holmes and the Spider Woman ☐ Spider Woman, The ☐ Time of Their Lives, The

Sorvino, Paul ☐ Age Isn't Everything ☐ Bloodbrothers ☐ Brink's Job, The ☐ Chiefs ☐ Cruising ☐ Day of the Dolphin, The ☐ Dick Tracy ☐ Fine Mess, A ☐ Gambler, The ☐ GoodFellas ☐ I Will, I Will . . . For Now ☐ I, the Jury ☐ Lost and Found ☐ Made for Each Other ☐ Melanie ☐ Off the Wall ☐ Oh, God! ☐ Question of Honor, A ☐ Rocketeer, The ☐ Slow Dancing in the Big City ☐ That Championship Season ☐ Touch of Class, A

Sothern, Ann ☐ April Showers ☐ Best Man, The ☐ Blue Gardenia ☐ Brother Orchid ☐ Chubasco ☐ Crazy Mama ☐ Cry Havoc ☐ Danger—Love at Work ☐ Dulcy ☐ Eight Bells ☐ Fast and Furious ☐ Fifty Roads to Town ☐ Folies Bergere ☐ Girl Friend, The ☐ Gold Rush Maisie ☐ Golden Needles ☐ Hooray for Love ☐ Hotel for Women ☐ Joe and Ethel Turp Call on the President ☐ Judge Steps Out, The ☐ Kid Millions ☐ Killing Kind, The ☐ Lady Be Good ☐ Lady in a Cage ☐ Letter to Three Wives, A ☐ Letter to Three Wives, A ☐ Maisie ☐ Maisie Gets Her Man ☐ Maisie Goes to Reno ☐ Maisie Was a Lady ☐ Manitou, The ☐ Nancy Goes to Rio ☐ Panama Hattie ☐ Shadow on the Wall ☐ Trade Winds ☐ Whales of August, The ☐ Words and Music

Spacek, Sissy ☐ 'Night, Mother ☐ 3 Women ☐ Badlands ☐ Carrie ☐ Coal Miner's Daughter ☐ Crimes of the Heart ☐ Ginger in the Morning ☐ Girls of Huntington House, The ☐ Hard Promises ☐ Heart Beat ☐ JFK ☐ Katherine ☐ Long Walk Home, The ☐ Marie ☐ Migrants, The ☐ Missing ☐ Prime Cut ☐ Private Matter, A ☐ Raggedy Man ☐ River, The ☐ Trading Mom ☐ Violets Are Blue . . . ☐ Welcome to L.A.

Spader, James ☐ Baby Boom ☐ Bad Influence ☐ Endless Love ☐ Jack's Back ☐ Less than Zero ☐ Music of Chance, The ☐ New Kids, The ☐ Pretty in Pink ☐ Rachel Papers, The ☐ sex, lies, and videotape ☐ Stargate ☐ Storyville ☐ True Colors ☐ Tuff Turf ☐ Wall Street ☐ White Palace ☐ Wolf

Spano, Vincent ☐ Alive ☐ Alphabet City ☐ And God Created Woman ☐ Baby, It's You ☐ Black Stallion Returns, The ☐ Blood Ties ☐ City of Hope ☐ Creator ☐ Double McGuffin, The ☐ Good Morning, Babylon ☐ High Frequency ☐ Indian Summer

Squire, Ronald ☐ Action for Slander ☐ Footsteps in the Fog ☐ Hideout in the Alps ☐ Inn of the Sixth Happiness, The ☐ Man with a Million ☐ My Cousin Rachel ☐ Rocking Horse Winner, The ☐ Scotch on the Rocks ☐ Unfinished Symphony, The

St. Jacques, Raymond ☐ Book of Numbers ☐ Born Again ☐ Change of Mind ☐ Come Back, Charleston Blue ☐ Comedians, The ☐ Cotton Comes to Harlem ☐ Green Berets, The ☐ Kill Castro ☐ Lost in the Stars ☐ Voodoo Dawn

St. James, Susan ☐ Carbon Copy ☐ Don't Cry, It's Only Thunder ☐ Fame Is the Name of the Game ☐ How to Beat the High Cost of Living ☐ I Take These Men ☐ Kid from Nowhere, The ☐ Love at First Bite ☐ Once Upon a Dead Man ☐ Outlaw Blues ☐ S.O.S. Titanic

St. John, Jill ☐ Banning ☐ Brenda Starr ☐ Come Blow Your Horn ☐ Concrete Jungle, The ☐ Diamonds Are Forever ☐ Eight on the Lam ☐ Fame Is the Name of the Game ☐ Hart to Hart ☐ Holiday for Lovers ☐ Honeymoon Hotel ☐ Liquidator, The ☐ Lost World ☐ Mooch Goes To Hollywood ☐ Oscar, The ☐ Remarkable Mr. Pennypacker, The ☐ Roman Spring of Mrs. Stone, The ☐ Tender Is the Night ☐ Tony Rome ☐ Who's Minding the Store?

Stack, Robert ☐ 1941 ☐ Airplane! ☐ Badlands of Dakota ☐ Big Trouble ☐ Bullfighter and the Lady, The ☐ Bwana Devil ☐ Caddyshack II ☐ Caretakers, The ☐ Dangerous Curves ☐ Date With Judy, A ☐ Eagle Squadron ☐ Fighter Squadron ☐ First Love ☐ Gift of Love, The ☐ Good Morning, Miss Dove ☐ Great Day in the Morning ☐ High and the Mighty, The ☐ House of Bamboo ☐ Iron Glove, The ☐ Is Paris Burning? ☐ Joe Versus the Volcano ☐ John Paul Jones ☐ Last Voyage, The ☐ Men of Texas ☐ Miss Tatlock's Millions ☐ Mortal Storm, The ☐ Most Wanted ☐ Murder on Flight 502 ☐ Nice Girl? ☐ Plain Clothes ☐ Scarface Mob, The ☐ Strange And Deadly Occurrence, The ☐ Tarnished Angels, The ☐ To Be or Not to Be ☐ Transformers, The ☐ Uncommon Valor ☐ War Paint ☐ Written on the Wind

Stallone, Frank ☐ Lethal Games ☐ Midnight Cop ☐ Order of the Eagle ☐ Ten Little Indians ☐ Terror in Beverly Hills

Stallone, Sylvester ☐ Capone ☐ Cliffhanger ☐ Cobra ☐ Death Race 2000 ☐ Demolition Man ☐ F.I.S.T. ☐ First Blood ☐ Lock Up ☐ Lords of Flatbush, The ☐ Nighthawks ☐ Oscar ☐ Over the Top ☐ Paradise Alley ☐ Rambo III ☐ Rambo: First Blood, Part II ☐ Rhinestone ☐ Rocky ☐ Rocky 2 ☐ Rocky 3 ☐ Rocky 4 ☐ Rocky 5 ☐ Specialist, The ☐ Stop! or My Mom Will Shoot ☐ Tango & Cash ☐ Victory

Stamp, Terence ☐ Adventures of Priscilla,

Queen of the Desert, The □ Alamut Ambush, The □ Alien Nation □ Billy Budd □ Blue □ Collector, The □ Divine Nymph, The □ Far from the Madding Crowd □ Hit, The □ Human □ Legal Eagles □ Link □ Meetings With Remarkable Men □ Mind of Mr. Soames, The □ Modesty Blaise □ Monster Island □ Poor Cow □ Real McCoy, The □ Sicilian, The □ Spirits of the Dead □ Superman 2 □ Teorema □ Term of Trial □ Thief of Bagdad, The □ Together □ Wall Street □ Young Guns

Stander, Lionel □ Beyond the Law □ Black Bird, The □ Boot Hill □ Cookie □ Crowd Roars, The □ Cul-De-Sac □ Dandy in Aspic, A □ Gang That Couldn't Shoot Straight, The □ Hart to Hart □ Ice Follies of 1939 □ If You Could Only Cook □ Last Gangster, The □ Meet Nero Wolfe □ Milky Way, The □ More Than a Secretary □ Mr. Deeds Goes to Town □ New York, New York □ No Time to Marry □ Professor Beware □ Promise Her Anything □ Pulp □ Scoundrel, The □ St. Benny the Dip □ Star Is Born, A □ Unfaithfully Yours □ Wicked Stepmother

Stanley, Kim □ Frances □ Goddess, The □ Seance on a Wet Afternoon

Stanton, Harry Dean □ 92 in the Shade □ Alien □ Bear, The □ Black Marble, The □ Christine □ Cisco Pike □ Cockfighter □ Cool Hand Luke □ Count Your Bullets □ Deathwatch □ Dillinger □ Dream a Little Dream □ Flatbed Annie & Sweetiepie: Lady Truckers □ Fool for Love □ Fourth War, The □ Hero's Island □ Hostage, The □ Man Trouble □ Missouri Breaks, The □ Mr. North □ Oldest Living Graduate, The □ One Magic Christmas □ Paris, Texas □ Payoff □ Pretty in Pink □ Rancho Deluxe □ Rebel Rousers □ Repo Man □ Slam Dance □ Stars and Bars □ Straight Time □ UFOria □ Where the Lilies Bloom □ Wild at Heart □ Wise Blood □ Young Doctors in Love □ Zandy's Bride

Stanwyck, Barbara □ All I Desire □ Always Goodbye □ Annie Oakley □ B. F.'s Daughter □ Baby Face □ Ball of Fire □ Banjo on My Knee □ Bitter Tea of General Yen, The □ Blowing Wild □ Breakfast for Two □ Bride Walks Out, The □ Bride Wore Boots, The □ California □ Cattle Queen of Montana □ Christmas in Connecticut □ Clash by Night □ Crime of Passion □ Cry Wolf □ Double Indemnity □ East Side, West Side □ Escape to Burma □ Ever in My Heart □ Executive Suite □ File on Thelma Jordon, The □ Flesh and Fantasy □ Forbidden □ Forty Guns □ Furies, The □ Gambling Lady □ Gay Sisters, The □ Golden Boy □ Great Man's Lady, The □ His Brother's Wife □ House That Would Not Die, The □ Illicit □ Internes Can't Take Money □ Jeopardy □ Ladies of Leisure □ Ladies They Talk About □ Lady Eve, The □ Lady Gambles, The □ Lady of Burlesque □ Letters, The □ Mad Miss Manton, The □ Man with a Cloak, The □ Maverick Queen, The □ Meet John Doe □ Message to Garcia, A □ Miracle Woman, The □ Moonlighter, The □ My Reputation □ Night Nurse □ Night Walker, The □ No Man of Her Own □ Other Love, The □ Plough and the Stars, The □ Remember the Night □ Roustabout □ Secret Bride, The □ Shopworn □ Sorry, Wrong Number □ Stella Dallas □ Strange Love of Martha Ivers, The □ Ten Cents a Dance □ There's Always Tomorrow □ These Wilder Years □ This Is My Affair □ Thorn Birds, The □ Titanic □ To Please a Lady □ Two Mrs. Carrolls, The □ Union Pacific □ Violent Men, The □ Walk on the Wild Side □ Witness to Murder □ You Belong to Me

Stapleton, Jean □ All in the Family 20th Anniversary Special □ Angel Dusted □ Aunt Mary □ Bells Are Ringing □ Buddy System, The □ Cold Turkey □ Damn Yankees □ Dead Man's Folly □ Eleanor, First Lady of the World □ Fire in the Dark □ Grown Ups □ Habitation of Dragons, The □ Isabel's Choice □ Matter of Sex, A □ Up the Down Staircase

Stapleton, Maureen □ Airport □ Bye, Bye, Birdie □ Cocoon □ Cocoon: The Return □ Cosmic Eye, The □ Doin' Time on Planet Earth □ Fan, The □ Fugitive Kind, The □ Gathering, Part II, The □ Gathering, The □ Heartburn □ Interiors □ Last Wish □ Letters From Frank □ Liberace: Behind the Music □ Little Gloria-Happy At Last □ Lonelyhearts □ Lost and Found □ Made in Heaven □ Miss Rose White □ Money Pit, The □ Nuts □ On the Right Track □ Passed Away □ Plaza Suite □ Queen of the Stardust Ballroom □ Reds □ Runner Stumbles, The □ Sweet Lorraine □ Trading Mom □ Truman Capote's Trilogy □ View From the Bridge, A

Starr, Ringo □ Blindman □ Candy □ Caveman □ Concert for Bangladesh, The □ Give My Regards to Broad Street □ Hard Day's Night, A □ Help! □ Let It Be □ Lisztomania □ Magic Christian, The □ Princess Daisy □ Sextette □ That'll Be the Day □ Two Hundred Motels

Starrett, Charles □ Cowboy Canteen □ Fast and Loose □ Frontier Outpost □ Jungle Bride □ Mask of Fu Manchu, The □ Mysterious Avenger, The □ One Man Justice □ Our Betters □ Outlaws of the Prairie □ Riders of the Badlands □ Riding West □ Royal Family of Broadway, The □ Royal Mounted Patrol, The □ Start Cheering □ Texas Stampede □ Two-Fisted Sheriff □ West of Tombstone

Steele, Barbara □ 8 1/2 □ Black Sunday □ Caged Heat □ Castle of Blood □ Crimson Cult, The □ Ghost, The □ Honeymoon with a Stranger □ Horrible Dr. Hichcock, The □ Hours of Love, The □ Nightmare Castle □ Pit and the Pendulum □ She-Beast, The □ They Came From Within

Steenburgen, Mary □ Attic, The: The Hiding of

Anne Frank ☐ Back to the Future Part III ☐ Butcher's Wife, The ☐ Clifford ☐ Cross Creek ☐ Dead of Winter ☐ End of the Line ☐ Goin' South ☐ Melvin and Howard ☐ Midsummer Night's Sex Comedy, A ☐ Miss Firecracker ☐ One Magic Christmas ☐ Parenthood ☐ Philadelphia ☐ Pontiac Moon ☐ Ragtime ☐ Romantic Comedy ☐ Time After Time ☐ What's Eating Gilbert Grape

Steiger, Rod ☐ Across the Bridge ☐ Al Capone ☐ American Gothic ☐ Amityville Horror, The ☐ Back From Eternity ☐ Ballad of the Sad Cafe, The ☐ Big Knife, The ☐ Breakthrough ☐ Cattle Annie and Little Britches ☐ Chosen, The ☐ Convicts Four ☐ Court-Martial of Billy Mitchell, The ☐ Cry Terror ☐ Dirty Hands ☐ Doctor Zhivago ☐ Duck, You Sucker ☐ F.I.S.T. ☐ Glory Boys, The ☐ Guilty as Charged ☐ Happy Birthday, Wanda June ☐ Harder They Fall, The ☐ Hennessy ☐ Heroes, The ☐ Hot Lead ☐ Illustrated Man, The ☐ In the Heat of the Night ☐ January Man, The ☐ Jesus of Nazareth ☐ Jubal ☐ Kindred, The ☐ Klondike Fever ☐ Last Four Days, The ☐ Lion of the Desert ☐ Lolly Madonna XXX ☐ Longest Day, The ☐ Love and Bullets ☐ Loved One, The ☐ Lucky Luciano ☐ Lucky Star, The ☐ Man Named John, A ☐ Mark, The ☐ Men of Respect ☐ Naked Face, The ☐ Neighbor, The ☐ No Way to Treat a Lady ☐ Oklahoma! ☐ On the Waterfront ☐ Passion in Paradise ☐ Pawnbroker, The ☐ Sergeant, The ☐ Seven Thieves ☐ Sinatra ☐ Specialist, The ☐ Three Into Two Won't Go ☐ Time of Indifference ☐ Unholy Wife, The ☐ W.C. Fields and Me ☐ Waterloo

Sten, Anna ☐ Exile Express ☐ Girl with the Hatbox, The ☐ Karamazov ☐ Man I Married, The ☐ Nana ☐ Nun and the Sergeant, The ☐ They Came to Blow Up America ☐ We Live Again ☐ Wedding Night, The

Stephens, Robert ☐ Asphyx ☐ Fruit Machine, The ☐ Morgan! ☐ Prime of Miss Jean Brodie, The ☐ Private Life of Sherlock Holmes, The ☐ Searching for Bobby Fischer ☐ Shout, The ☐ Small World of Sammy Lee, The ☐ Taste of Honey, A ☐ Travels With My Aunt

Stephenson, Henry ☐ Baroness and the Butler, The ☐ Conquest ☐ If I Were Free ☐ Mr. Lucky ☐ Return of Monte Cristo, The ☐ Richest Girl in the World, The ☐ She Loves Me Not ☐ Song of Love ☐ Spring Parade ☐ Suez ☐ Tarzan and the Amazons

Stephenson, James ☐ Calling Philo Vance ☐ Confessions of a Nazi Spy ☐ Devil's Island ☐ Espionage Agent ☐ Flight from Destiny ☐ International Squadron ☐ It's in the Blood ☐ King of the Underworld ☐ Letter, The ☐ Man Who Made Diamonds, The ☐ Nancy Drew, Detective ☐ Secret Service of the Air

Sterling, Jan ☐ 1984 ☐ Alaska Seas ☐ Angry Breed, The ☐ Appointment with Danger ☐ Big Carnival, The ☐ Caged ☐ Female Animal, The ☐ Female on the Beach ☐ Flesh and Fury ☐ Harder They Fall, The ☐ High and the Mighty, The ☐ High School Confidential ☐ Human Jungle, The ☐ Johnny Belinda ☐ Kathy O' ☐ Man with the Gun, The ☐ Mystery Street ☐ Pony Express ☐ Return from the Sea ☐ Rhubarb ☐ Slaughter on Tenth Avenue ☐ Union Station ☐ Women's Prison

Stern, Daniel ☐ Blue Thunder ☐ Born in East L.A. ☐ Boss' Wife, The ☐ Breaking Away ☐ C.H.U.D. ☐ City Slickers ☐ City Slickers 2: Legend of Curly's Gold ☐ Coup de Ville ☐ Court-Martial of Jackie Robinson, The ☐ D.O.A. ☐ Diner ☐ Friends, Lovers & Lunatics ☐ Get Crazy ☐ Home Alone ☐ Home Alone 2: Lost in New York ☐ I'm Dancing as Fast as I Can ☐ Key Exchange ☐ Leviathan ☐ Little Monsters ☐ Milagro Beanfield War, The ☐ Rookie of the Year ☐ Stardust Memories

Sternhagen, Frances ☐ At Mother's Request ☐ Bright Lights, Big City ☐ Communion ☐ Doc Hollywood ☐ Fedora ☐ Independence Day ☐ Misery ☐ Outland ☐ Raising Cain ☐ Romantic Comedy ☐ Starting Over ☐ Stephen King's Golden Years

Stevens, Connie ☐ Back to the Beach ☐ Bring Me the Head of Dobie Gillis ☐ Grease 2 ☐ Grissom Gang, The ☐ Never Too Late ☐ Palm Springs Weekend ☐ Parrish ☐ Party Crashers, The ☐ Playmates ☐ Rock-a-Bye Baby ☐ Scorchy ☐ Susan Slade ☐ Tapeheads ☐ Way . . . Way Out

Stevens, Fisher ☐ Baby, It's You ☐ Boss' Wife, The ☐ Flamingo Kid ☐ Marrying Man, The ☐ My Science Project ☐ Mystery Date ☐ Only You ☐ Reversal of Fortune ☐ Short Circuit ☐ Short Circuit 2

Stevens, Inger ☐ 5 Card Stud ☐ Borgia Stick, The ☐ Buccaneer, The ☐ Cry Terror ☐ Dream of Kings, A ☐ Firecreek ☐ Guide for the Married Man, A ☐ Hang 'em High ☐ House of Cards ☐ Madigan ☐ Man on Fire ☐ Mask of Sheba, The ☐ New Interns, The ☐ Time for Killing, A ☐ World, the Flesh and the Devil, The

Stevens, Mark ☐ Between Midnight and Dawn ☐ Cry Vengeance ☐ From This Day Forward ☐ Gunsmoke in Tucson ☐ Jack Slade ☐ Katie Did It ☐ Oh, You Beautiful Doll ☐ Reunion in Reno ☐ Sand ☐ Snake Pit, The ☐ Street with No Name ☐ Timetable ☐ Torpedo Alley

Stevenson, Parker ☐ Baywatch: Panic at Malibu Pier ☐ Lifeguard ☐ Our Time ☐ Separate Peace, A ☐ Shooting Stars ☐ Stroker Ace

Stevens, Onslow ☐ Flight from Glory ☐ Man Who Wouldn't Talk, The ☐ Mark of the Gorilla ☐ Peg o' My Heart ☐ Revenue Agent ☐ Sealed Cargo ☐ Secret of the Blue Room

☐ Those High Grey Walls ☐ Walk a Crooked Mile

Stevens, Stella ☐ Advance to the Rear ☐ Arnold ☐ Ballad of Cable Hogue, The ☐ Chained Heat ☐ Cleopatra Jones and the Casino of Gold ☐ Courtship of Eddie's Father, The ☐ Down the Drain ☐ Flamingo Road ☐ Friendships, Secrets, and Lies ☐ Girls! Girls! Girls! ☐ Honky Tonk ☐ How to Save a Marriage (And Ruin Your Life) ☐ In Broad Daylight ☐ Jordan Chance, The ☐ Las Vegas Lady ☐ Last Call ☐ Li'l Abner ☐ Mad Room, The ☐ Make Me an Offer ☐ Man Against the Mob ☐ Man-Trap ☐ Masterpiece of Murder, A ☐ Molly and Gina ☐ Mom ☐ Monster in the Closet ☐ Nickelodeon ☐ Night They Took Miss Beautiful ☐ Nutty Professor, The ☐ Poseidon Adventure, The ☐ Rage ☐ Say One for Me ☐ Silencers, The ☐ Slaughter ☐ Synanon ☐ Terror Within II, The ☐ Terror Within II, The ☐ Too Late Blues ☐ Where Angels Go, Trouble Follows

Stewart, James ☐ After the Thin Man ☐ Airport '77 ☐ American Tail: Fievel Goes West, An ☐ Anatomy of a Murder ☐ Bandolero ☐ Bell, Book and Candle ☐ Bend of the River ☐ Big Sleep, The ☐ Born to Dance ☐ Broken Arrow ☐ Call Northside 777 ☐ Carbine Williams ☐ Cheyenne Autumn ☐ Cheyenne Social Club, The ☐ Come Live With Me ☐ Dear Brigitte ☐ Destry Rides Again ☐ Far Country, The ☐ FBI Story, The ☐ Firecreek ☐ Flight of the Phoenix ☐ Fools' Parade ☐ Glenn Miller Story, The ☐ Gorgeous Hussy, The ☐ Greatest Show on Earth, The ☐ Harvey ☐ Hawkins on Murder ☐ How the West Was Won ☐ Ice Follies of 1939 ☐ It's a Wonderful Life ☐ It's a Wonderful World ☐ Jackpot, The ☐ Last Gangster, The ☐ Made for Each Other ☐ Magic of Lassie, The ☐ Magic Town ☐ Malaya ☐ Man from Laramie, The ☐ Man Who Knew Too Much, The ☐ Man Who Shot Liberty Valance, The ☐ Mortal Storm, The ☐ Mountain Road, The ☐ Mr. Hobbs Takes a Vacation ☐ Mr. Smith Goes to Washington ☐ Murder Man, The ☐ Naked Spur, The ☐ Navy Blue and Gold ☐ Next Time We Love ☐ Night Passage ☐ No Highway in the Sky ☐ No Time for Comedy ☐ Of Human Hearts ☐ On Our Merry Way ☐ Philadelphia Story, The ☐ Rare Breed, The ☐ Rear Window ☐ Right of Way ☐ Rope ☐ Rose Marie ☐ Seventh Heaven ☐ Shenandoah ☐ Shootist, The ☐ Shop Around the Corner, The ☐ Shopworn Angel, The ☐ Small Town Girl ☐ Speed ☐ Spirit of St. Louis, The ☐ Strategic Air Command ☐ Stratton Story, The ☐ Take Her, She's Mine ☐ That's Entertainment ☐ Thunder Bay ☐ Two Rode Together ☐ Vertigo ☐ Vivacious Lady ☐ Wife vs. Secretary ☐ Winchester '73 ☐ You Can't Take It With You ☐ Ziegfeld Girl

Stewart, Patrick ☐ Doctor and the Devils, The ☐ Excalibur ☐ Hedda ☐ L.A. Story ☐ Lady Jane ☐ Pagemaster, The ☐ Star Trek Generations

Stewart, Paul ☐ Appointment with Danger ☐ Citizen Kane ☐ In Cold Blood ☐ Joe Louis Story, The ☐ Kiss Me Deadly ☐ Mr. Lucky ☐ Nobody's Perfekt ☐ Top Secret Affair ☐ W.C. Fields and Me ☐ Walk Softly, Stranger ☐ Window, The

Stiers, David Ogden ☐ Accidental Tourist, The ☐ Bad Company ☐ Bad Seed, The ☐ Beauty and the Beast ☐ Better Off Dead ☐ Circle of Children, A ☐ Final Days, The ☐ Final Notice ☐ First Olympics: Athens 1896, The ☐ Harry's War ☐ J. Edgar Hoover ☐ Kissing Place, The ☐ M*A*S*H—Goodbye, Farewell, Amen ☐ Mrs. Delafield Wants to Marry

Stockwell, Dean ☐ Abbott and Costello In Hollywood ☐ Adventures of Nick Carter ☐ Alsino and the Condor ☐ Anchors Aweigh ☐ Arnelo Affair, The ☐ Backtrack ☐ Banzai Runner ☐ Beverly Hills Cop II ☐ Blue Iguana, The ☐ Blue Velvet ☐ Boy with Green Hair, The ☐ Buying Time ☐ Cattle Drive ☐ Compulsion ☐ Deep Waters ☐ Down to the Sea in Ships ☐ Dunwich Horror, The ☐ Failing of Raymond, The ☐ Gardens of Stone ☐ Green Years, The ☐ Gun for a Coward ☐ Happy Years, The ☐ Home, Sweet Homicide ☐ Human Highway ☐ Kim ☐ Limit Up ☐ Long Day's Journey into Night ☐ Married to the Mob ☐ Mighty McGurk, The ☐ Paper Man ☐ Paris, Texas ☐ Psych Out ☐ Rapture ☐ Secret Garden, The ☐ Shame ☐ She Came to the Valley ☐ Smokescreen ☐ Son of the Morning Star ☐ Song of the Thin Man ☐ Sons and Lovers ☐ Stars in My Crown ☐ Stickfighter ☐ Time Guardian, The ☐ Tucker—The Man and His Dream

Stole, Mink ☐ Female Trouble ☐ Mondo Trasho ☐ Multiple Maniacs ☐ Polyester ☐ Serial Mom

Stoltz, Eric ☐ Bodies, Rest & Motion ☐ Code Name—Emerald ☐ Fly II, The ☐ Foreign Affairs ☐ Haunted Summer ☐ Killing Zoe ☐ Lionheart ☐ Manifesto ☐ Mask ☐ Memphis Belle ☐ Naked in New York ☐ Sleep With Me ☐ Some Kind of Wonderful ☐ Waterdance, The

Stone, Lewis ☐ All the Brothers Were Valiant ☐ Andy Hardy Gets Spring Fever ☐ Andy Hardy Meets Debutante ☐ Andy Hardy's Blonde Trouble ☐ Andy Hardy's Double Life ☐ Andy Hardy's Private Secretary ☐ Angels in the Outfield ☐ Any Number Can Play ☐ Bad Man of Brimstone ☐ Bannerline ☐ Big House, The ☐ Bugle Sounds, The ☐ Bureau of Missing Persons ☐ Chaser, The ☐ China Seas ☐ Courtship of Andy Hardy, The ☐ David Copperfield ☐ Girl from Missouri, The ☐ Grand Hotel ☐ Grounds for Marriage ☐ Hardys Ride High, The ☐ Hoodlum Saint, The ☐ Ice Follies of 1939 ☐ Inspiration

☐ Joe and Ethel Turp Call on the President ☐ Judge Hardy and Son ☐ Judge Hardy's Children ☐ Letty Lynton ☐ Life Begins for Andy Hardy ☐ Looking Forward ☐ Lost World, The ☐ Love Finds Andy Hardy ☐ Love Laughs at Andy Hardy ☐ Madame X ☐ Man Who Cried Wolf, The ☐ Mask of Fu Manchu, The ☐ Mata Hari ☐ My Past ☐ Mystery of Mr. X, The ☐ Night Court ☐ Night into Morning ☐ Nomads of the North ☐ Out West with the Hardys ☐ Outcast ☐ Phantom of Paris, The ☐ Queen Christina ☐ Red-Headed Woman ☐ Romance ☐ Secret Six, The ☐ Shipmates Forever ☐ Sin of Madelon Claudet, The ☐ Small Town Girl ☐ State of the Union ☐ Strictly Dishonorable ☐ Sun Comes Up, The ☐ Suzy ☐ Three Godfathers ☐ Three Wise Fools ☐ Treasure Island ☐ Trial of Mary Dugan, The ☐ Unguarded Hour, The ☐ West Point of the Air ☐ Wet Parade, The ☐ White Sister, The ☐ Wild Orchids ☐ Woman of Affairs, A ☐ Yellow Jack ☐ You're Only Young Once

Stone, Sharon ☐ Above The Law ☐ Action Jackson ☐ Allan Quartermain And The Lost City Of Gold ☐ Basic Instinct ☐ Beyond the Stars ☐ Blood and Sand ☐ Cold Steel ☐ Deadly Blessing ☐ Diary of a Hitman ☐ He Said, She Said ☐ Intersection ☐ Irreconcilable Differences ☐ King Solomon's Mines ☐ Police Academy 4: Citizens on Patrol ☐ Quick and the Dead, The ☐ Scissors ☐ Sliver ☐ Specialist, The ☐ Total Recall ☐ Where Sleeping Dogs Lie ☐ Year of the Gun

Storch, Larry ☐ Adventures of Huckleberry, Finn, The ☐ Bus Riley's Back in Town ☐ Captain Newman, M.D. ☐ Forty Pounds of Trouble ☐ Great Race, The ☐ Incredible Rocky Mountain Race ☐ Monitors, The ☐ Very Special Favor, A ☐ Wild and Wonderful

Storm, Gale ☐ Abandoned ☐ Al Jennings of Oklahoma ☐ Between Midnight and Dawn ☐ Dude Goes West, The ☐ It Happened on Fifth Avenue ☐ Red River Valley ☐ Swing Parade of 1946 ☐ Texas Rangers, The ☐ Tom Brown's School Days

Stowe, Madeleine ☐ Bad Girls ☐ Blink ☐ China Moon ☐ Closet Land ☐ Deerslayer, The ☐ Last of the Mohicans, The ☐ Nativity, The ☐ Revenge ☐ Short Cuts ☐ Stakeout ☐ Two Jakes, The ☐ Unlawful Entry ☐ Worth Winning

Strasberg, Lee ☐ And Justice for All ☐ Boardwalk ☐ Godfather, Part II, The ☐ Going in Style ☐ Skokie

Strasberg, Susan ☐ Adventures of a Young Man ☐ And Millions Will Die ☐ Bloody Birthday ☐ Chubasco ☐ Cobweb, The ☐ Delta Force, The ☐ Frankenstein ☐ Immigrants, The ☐ In Praise of Older Women ☐ Kapo ☐ Light in the Jungle, The ☐ Manitou, The ☐ Marcus Welby, M.D. ☐ McGuire, Go Home! ☐ Picnic ☐ Psych Out ☐ Rollercoaster ☐ Scream of Fear ☐ Stage Struck ☐ Trip, The ☐ Who Fears the Devil

Strathairn, David ☐ Big Girls Don't Cry . . . They Get Even ☐ City of Hope ☐ Dangerous Woman, A ☐ Day One ☐ Dolores Claiborne ☐ Eight Men Out ☐ Enormous Changes at the Last Minute ☐ Feud, The ☐ Firm, The ☐ Iceman ☐ League of Their Own, A ☐ Losing Isaiah ☐ Lost in Yonkers ☐ O Pioneers! ☐ Passion Fish ☐ Return of the Secaucus Seven, The ☐ River Wild, The ☐ Sneakers ☐ Son of the Morning Star

Strauss, Peter ☐ Angel on My Shoulder ☐ Brotherhood of the Rose ☐ Flight of Black Angel ☐ Fugutive Among Us ☐ Heart of Steel ☐ Jericho Mile, The ☐ Man of Legend ☐ Man Without a Country, The ☐ Masada ☐ Penalty Phase ☐ Peter Gunn ☐ Proud Men ☐ Secret of NIMH, The ☐ Soldier Blue ☐ Spacehunter: Adventures in the Forbidden Zone

Streep, Meryl ☐ Cry in the Dark, A ☐ Deadliest Season, The ☐ Death Becomes Her ☐ Deer Hunter, The ☐ Defending Your Life ☐ Falling in Love ☐ French Lieutenant's Woman, The ☐ Heartburn ☐ Holocaust ☐ House of the Spirits ☐ Ironweed ☐ Julia ☐ Kramer vs. Kramer ☐ Manhattan ☐ Out of Africa ☐ Plenty ☐ Postcards from the Edge ☐ River Wild, The ☐ Seduction of Joe Tynan, The ☐ She-Devil ☐ Silkwood ☐ Sophie's Choice ☐ Still of the Night

Streisand, Barbra ☐ All Night Long ☐ For Pete's Sake ☐ Funny Girl ☐ Funny Lady ☐ Hello, Dolly! ☐ Here's Looking At You, Warner Bros. ☐ My Name Is Barbra ☐ Nuts ☐ On a Clear Day You Can See Forever ☐ Owl and the Pussycat, The ☐ Prince of Tides, The ☐ Star Is Born, A ☐ Up the Sandbox ☐ Way We Were, The ☐ What's Up, Doc? ☐ Yentl

Strode, Woody ☐ Black Stallion Returns, The ☐ Boot Hill ☐ Gatling Gun, The ☐ Italian Connection, The ☐ Kill Castro ☐ Kingdom of the Spiders ☐ Last Rebel, The ☐ Loaded Guns ☐ Man Who Shot Liberty Valance, The ☐ Oil ☐ Professionals, The ☐ Quick and the Dead, The ☐ Ravagers ☐ Revengers, The ☐ Sergeant Rutledge ☐ Super Brother

Sullavan, Margaret ☐ Appointment for Love ☐ Back Street ☐ Cry Havoc ☐ Good Fairy, The ☐ Little Man, What Now? ☐ Moon's Our Home, The ☐ Mortal Storm, The ☐ Next Time We Love ☐ No Sad Songs for Me ☐ Only Yesterday ☐ Shining Hour, The ☐ Shop Around the Corner, The ☐ Shopworn Angel, The ☐ So Ends Our Night ☐ So Red the Rose ☐ Three Comrades

Sullivan, Barry ☐ And Now Tomorrow ☐ Another Time, Another Place ☐ Bad and the Beautiful, The ☐ Bad Men of Tombstone ☐ Buckskin ☐ Cause for Alarm ☐ China Venture ☐ Cry of the Hunted ☐ Dragon Wells Massacre ☐ Duffy's Tavern ☐ Forty Guns

☐ Framed ☐ Gangster, The ☐ Getting Gertie's Garter ☐ Great Gatsby, The ☐ Grounds for Marriage ☐ Harlow ☐ Her Twelve Men ☐ High Explosive ☐ Hurricane ☐ Immigrants, The ☐ Immortal, The ☐ It Takes All Kinds ☐ Jeopardy ☐ Julie ☐ Kung Fu ☐ Lady in the Dark ☐ Magician, The ☐ Man in the Middle ☐ Maverick Queen, The ☐ Mr. Imperium ☐ Nancy Goes to Rio ☐ Night Gallery ☐ No Questions Asked ☐ No Room to Run ☐ Payment on Demand ☐ Planet of the Vampires ☐ Playgirl ☐ Purple Gang, The ☐ Queen Bee ☐ Rainbow Island ☐ Shark! ☐ Skirts Ahoy! ☐ Stage to Thunder Rock ☐ Strategic Air Command ☐ Tell Them Willie Boy Is Here ☐ Tension ☐ Texas Lady ☐ This Savage Land ☐ Three Guys Named Mike ☐ Way to the Gold, The ☐ Woman of the Town, The

Sutherland, Donald ☐ 1900 ☐ Act of the Heart ☐ Alex in Wonderland ☐ Animal House ☐ Backdraft ☐ Bear Island ☐ Bedford Incident, The ☐ Bethune ☐ Blood Relatives ☐ Buffy the Vampire Slayer ☐ Castle of the Living Dead ☐ Dan Candy's Law ☐ Day of the Locust, The ☐ Die Die My Darling ☐ Dirty Dozen, The ☐ Disappearance, The ☐ Disclosure ☐ Don't Look Now ☐ Dr. Terror's House of Horrors ☐ Dry White Season, A ☐ Eagle Has Landed, The ☐ Eminent Domain ☐ End of the Game ☐ Eye of the Needle ☐ F.T.A. ☐ Fellini's Casanova ☐ Gas ☐ Great Train Robbery, The ☐ Heaven Help Us ☐ Interlude ☐ Invasion of the Body Snatchers ☐ JFK ☐ Joanna ☐ Johnny Got His Gun ☐ Kelly's Heroes ☐ Kentucky Fried Movie, The ☐ Klute ☐ Lady Ice ☐ Little Murders ☐ Lock Up ☐ Lost Angels ☐ M*A*S*H ☐ Man, a Woman and a Bank, A ☐ Max Dugan Returns ☐ Murder by Decree ☐ Nothing Personal ☐ Oedipus the King ☐ Oldest Living Confederate Widow Tells All ☐ Ordeal by Innocence ☐ Ordinary People ☐ Outbreak ☐ Quicksand: No Escape ☐ Railway Station Man, The ☐ Revolution ☐ Robert A. Heinlein's The Puppet Masters ☐ Rosary Murders, The ☐ S.P.Y.S. ☐ Savage and Beautiful ☐ Shadow of the Wolf ☐ Six Degrees of Separation ☐ Start the Revolution Without Me ☐ Steelyard Blues ☐ Threshold

Sutherland, Kiefer ☐ 1969 ☐ Article 99 ☐ At Close Range ☐ Bay Boy, The ☐ Bright Lights, Big City ☐ Chicago Joe and the Showgirl ☐ Cowboy Way ☐ Few Good Men, A ☐ Flashback ☐ Flatliners ☐ Killing Time, The ☐ Last Light ☐ Lost Boys, The ☐ Nutcracker Prince, The ☐ Promised Land ☐ Renegades ☐ Stand by Me ☐ Three Musketeers, The ☐ Trapped in Silence ☐ Vanishing, The ☐ Young Guns ☐ Young Guns 2

Svenson, Bo ☐ Breaking Point ☐ Curse II: The Bite ☐ Deadly Impact ☐ Final Chapter—Walking Tall ☐ Frankenstein ☐ Gold of the Amazon Women ☐ Great Waldo Pepper, The ☐ Inglorious Bastards ☐ Jealousy ☐ Kill Reflex, The ☐ Manhunt, The ☐ Maurie ☐ Night Warning ☐ North Dallas Forty ☐ Snowbeast ☐ Special Delivery ☐ Steele's Law ☐ Walking Tall, Part II

Swanson, Gloria ☐ Airport '75 ☐ Father Takes a Wife ☐ Indiscreet ☐ Killer Bees ☐ Loves of Sunya, The ☐ Music in the Air ☐ Queen Kelly ☐ Sadie Thompson ☐ Shifting Sands ☐ Sunset Boulevard ☐ Trespasser, The

Swayze, Patrick ☐ City of Joy ☐ Dirty Dancing ☐ Father Hood ☐ Ghost ☐ Grandview, U.S.A. ☐ Next of Kin ☐ North and South ☐ Outsiders, The ☐ Point Break ☐ Red Dawn ☐ Road House ☐ Steel Dawn ☐ Tall Tale: The Unbelievable Adventures of Pecos Bill ☐ Tiger Warsaw ☐ Uncommon Valor ☐ Youngblood

Sweeney, D.B. ☐ Cutting Edge, The ☐ Day in October, A ☐ Eight Men Out ☐ Fire in the Sky ☐ Gardens of Stone ☐ Hear No Evil ☐ Heaven Is a Playground ☐ Leather Jackets ☐ Memphis Belle ☐ No Man's Land ☐ Roommates

Swit, Loretta ☐ Beer ☐ Cagney & Lacey ☐ Deadhead Miles ☐ Freebie and the Bean ☐ Kid from Nowhere, The ☐ M*A*S*H—Goodbye, Farewell, Amen ☐ Miracle at Moreaux ☐ Race With the Devil ☐ S.O.B. ☐ Whoops Apocalypse

Syms, Sylvia ☐ Big Job, The ☐ Chorus of Disapproval, A ☐ Conspiracy of Hearts ☐ Desert Attack ☐ Desperados, The ☐ Expresso Bongo ☐ Ferry to Hong Kong ☐ Flame in the Streets ☐ Intimate Contact ☐ No Trees in the Street ☐ Operation Crossbow ☐ Quare Fellow, The ☐ Run Wild, Run Free ☐ Woman in a Dressing Gown ☐ World of Suzie Wong, The

Tagore, Sharmila ☐ Days and Nights in the Forest ☐ Devi ☐ Mississippi Masala ☐ World of Apu, The

Talbot, Lyle ☐ 20,000 Years in Sing Sing ☐ African Treasure ☐ City of Fear ☐ Falcon Out West, The ☐ Feudin' Fools ☐ Fighting Fools ☐ Fog Over Frisco ☐ Fury of the Congo ☐ Glen or Glenda ☐ Jail Bait ☐ Jail Busters ☐ Lucky Losers ☐ Mandalay ☐ Oil for the Lamps of China ☐ One Night of Love ☐ Parole, Inc. ☐ Plan 9 from Outer Space ☐ Red Hot Tires ☐ Second Fiddle ☐ Second Honeymoon ☐ She's in the Army ☐ Sky Dragon, The ☐ Sudden Danger ☐ Thirteenth Guest, The

Tamblyn, Russ ☐ B.O.R.N. ☐ Cimarron ☐ Fastest Gun Alive, The ☐ Follow the Boys ☐ Haunting, The ☐ High School Confidential ☐ Human Highway ☐ Long Ships, The ☐ Necromancer—Satan's Servant ☐ Peyton Place ☐ Phantom Empire ☐ Retreat, Hell! ☐ Seven Brides for Seven Brothers ☐ Tom Thumb ☐ West Side Story ☐ Winning Team, The ☐ Wonderful World of the Brothers Grimm, The

Tamiroff, Akim ☐ Alphaville ☐ Anastasia ☐ Anthony Adverse ☐ Battle Hell (Yangtse Incident) ☐ Black Magic ☐ Black Sleep, The ☐ Bridge of San Luis Rey, The ☐ Buccaneer, The ☐ Can't Help Singing ☐ Captain Hates the Sea, The ☐ Chained ☐ Corsican Brothers, The ☐ Dangerous to Know ☐ Deadly Sanctuary ☐ Desire ☐ Dragon Seed ☐ Fiesta ☐ Five Graves to Cairo ☐ For Whom the Bell Tolls ☐ Gangster, The ☐ Gay Deception, The ☐ General Died at Dawn, The ☐ Girl Who Couldn't Say No, The ☐ Great Gambini, The ☐ Great McGinty, The ☐ Honeymoon in Bali ☐ Hotel Paradiso ☐ Jungle Princess, The ☐ King of Chinatown ☐ Lt. Robin Crusoe, USN ☐ Magnificent Fraud, The ☐ Marco the Magnificent ☐ Miracle of Morgan's Creek, The ☐ Mr. Arkadin ☐ My Girl Tisa ☐ New York Town ☐ Northwest Mounted Police ☐ Outpost in Morocco ☐ Pardon My Past ☐ Paris Honeymoon ☐ Romanoff and Juliet ☐ Sabra ☐ Sadie McKee ☐ Spawn of the North ☐ They Who Dare ☐ Touch of Evil ☐ Union Pacific ☐ Untamed ☐ Way of All Flesh, The

Tanaka, Kinuyo ☐ Alone on the Pacific ☐ Ballad of Narayama, The ☐ Equinox Flower ☐ Life of Oharu, The ☐ Mother (Okaasan) ☐ Sandakan 8 ☐ Sansho the Bailiff

Tandy, Jessica ☐ Adventures of a Young Man ☐ batteries not included ☐ Best Friends ☐ Birds, The ☐ Bostonians, The ☐ Butley ☐ Camilla ☐ Cocoon ☐ Cocoon: The Return ☐ Desert Fox, The ☐ Dragonwyck ☐ Driving Miss Daisy ☐ Forever Amber ☐ Foxfire ☐ Fried Green Tomatoes ☐ Green Years, The ☐ Honky Tonk Freeway ☐ House on Carroll Street, The ☐ Light in the Forest, The ☐ Nobody's Fool ☐ September Affair ☐ Seventh Cross, The ☐ Still of the Night ☐ Story Lady, The ☐ To Dance with the White Dog ☐ Used People ☐ Valley of Decision, The ☐ Woman's Vengeance, A

Tati, Jacques ☐ Devil in the Flesh ☐ Jour de Fête ☐ Mon Oncle ☐ Mr. Hulot's Holiday ☐ Playtime ☐ Sylvia and the Phantom ☐ Traffic

Taylor, Don ☐ Bold and the Brave, The ☐ Destination Gobi ☐ Father of the Bride ☐ Father's Little Dividend ☐ Flying Leathernecks ☐ For the Love of Mary ☐ Girls of Pleasure Island ☐ Japanese War Bride ☐ Johnny Dark ☐ Men of Sherwood Forest ☐ Naked City, The ☐ Savage Guns, The ☐ Stalag 17 ☐ Submarine Command ☐ Winged Victory

Taylor, Elizabeth ☐ Ash Wednesday ☐ Beau Brummel ☐ Between Friends ☐ Big Hangover, The ☐ Blue Bird, The ☐ Boom! ☐ Butterfield 8 ☐ Cat on a Hot Tin Roof ☐ Cleopatra ☐ Comedians, The ☐ Conspirator ☐ Courage of Lassie ☐ Cynthia ☐ Date With Judy, A ☐ Divorce His, Divorce Hers ☐ Dr. Faustus ☐ Driver's Seat, The ☐ Elephant Walk ☐ Father of the Bride ☐ Father's Little Dividend ☐ Flintstones, The ☐ Genocide ☐ Giant ☐ Girl Who Had Everything, The ☐ Hammersmith Is Out ☐ Ivanhoe ☐ Jane Eyre ☐ Julia Misbehaves ☐ Lassie Come Home ☐ Last Time I Saw Paris, The ☐ Life with Father ☐ Little Night Music, A ☐ Little Women ☐ Love Is Better Than Ever ☐ Malice in Wonderland ☐ Mirror Crack'd, The ☐ National Velvet ☐ Night Watch ☐ Only Game in Town, The ☐ Place in the Sun, A ☐ Poker Alice ☐ Raintree County ☐ Reflections in a Golden Eye ☐ Rhapsody ☐ Sandpiper, The ☐ Scent of Mystery ☐ Secret Ceremony ☐ Suddenly, Last Summer ☐ Sweet Bird of Youth ☐ Taming of the Shrew, The ☐ That's Entertainment ☐ There Must Be a Pony ☐ Under Milk Wood ☐ V.I.P.s, The ☐ Who's Afraid of Virginia Woolf? ☐ X, Y and Zee

Taylor, Kent ☐ Broken Land, The ☐ County Chairman, The ☐ Fort Bowie ☐ Gang War ☐ Girl with Ideas, A ☐ Harbor Lights ☐ I Take This Woman ☐ I'm No Angel ☐ I'm Still Alive ☐ Iron Sheriff, The ☐ Mrs. Wiggs of the Cabbage Patch ☐ Ramona ☐ Slightly Scarlet ☐ Smooth as Silk ☐ When Love is Young ☐ Without Regret

Taylor, Lili ☐ Bright Angel ☐ Dogfight ☐ Household Saints ☐ Mystic Pizza ☐ Rudy ☐ Say Anything . . . ☐ Watch It

Taylor, Renee ☐ Jennifer on My Mind ☐ Last of the Red Hot Lovers ☐ Made for Each Other ☐ White Palace

Taylor, Robert ☐ Above and Beyond ☐ All the Brothers Were Valiant ☐ Ambush ☐ Bataan ☐ Bribe, The ☐ Broadway Melody of 1936 ☐ Broadway Melody of 1938 ☐ Camille ☐ Cattle King ☐ Conspirator ☐ Crowd Roars, The ☐ D-Day the Sixth of June ☐ Day the Hot Line Got Hot, The ☐ Escape ☐ Flight Command ☐ Glass Sphinx, The ☐ Gorgeous Hussy, The ☐ Handy Andy ☐ Hangman, The ☐ Her Cardboard Lover ☐ High Wall ☐ His Brother's Wife ☐ Ivanhoe ☐ Johnny Eager ☐ Johnny Tiger ☐ Killers of Kilimanjaro ☐ Knights of the Round Table ☐ Lady of the Tropics ☐ Last Hunt, The ☐ Law and Jake Wade, The ☐ Lucky Night ☐ Magnificent Obsession ☐ Many Rivers to Cross ☐ Miracle of the White Stallions ☐ Night Walker, The ☐ Party Girl ☐ Personal Property ☐ Quentin Durward ☐ Quo Vadis? ☐ Rogue Cop ☐ Saddle the Wind ☐ Savage Pampas ☐ Small Town Girl ☐ Song of Russia ☐ Stand by for Action ☐ Stand Up and Fight ☐ This Is My Affair ☐ Three Comrades ☐ Tip on a Dead Jockey ☐ Undercurrent ☐ Valley of the Kings ☐ Waterloo Bridge ☐ West Point of the Air ☐ Westward the Women ☐ When Ladies Meet ☐ Yank at Oxford, A

Taylor, Rod ☐ 36 Hours ☐ Ask Any Girl ☐ Birds, The ☐ Catered Affair, The ☐ Charles & Diana: A Royal Love Story ☐ Chuka ☐ Dark of the Sun ☐ Darker than Amber ☐ Deadly Trackers, The ☐ Do Not Disturb ☐ Fate Is the

Hunter ☐ Gathering of Eagles ☐ Glass Bottom Boat, The ☐ Hell River ☐ Hell With Heroes, The ☐ Heroes, The ☐ High Commissioner, The ☐ Hotel ☐ Jacqueline Bouvier Kennedy ☐ Liquidator, The ☐ Man Who Had Power Over Women, The ☐ Marbella ☐ Oregon Trail, The ☐ Picture Show Man, The ☐ Sunday in New York ☐ Time Machine, The ☐ Train Robbers, The ☐ V.I.P.s, The ☐ Young Cassidy ☐ Zabriskie Point

Temple, Shirley ☐ Adventure in Baltimore ☐ Baby Take a Bow ☐ Bachelor and the Bobby-Soxer, The ☐ Blue Bird, The ☐ Bright Eyes ☐ Captain January ☐ Curly Top ☐ Dimples ☐ Fort Apache ☐ Heidi ☐ Honeymoon ☐ I'll Be Seeing You ☐ Just Around the Corner ☐ Kathleen ☐ Kiss and Tell ☐ Kiss for Corliss, A ☐ Little Colonel, The ☐ Little Miss Broadway ☐ Little Miss Marker ☐ Little Princess, The ☐ Littlest Rebel, The ☐ Miss Annie Rooney ☐ Mr. Belvedere Goes to College ☐ Now and Forever ☐ Our Little Girl ☐ Out All Night ☐ Poor Little Rich Girl ☐ Rebecca of Sunnybrook Farm ☐ Since You Went Away ☐ Stand Up and Cheer ☐ Story of Seabiscuit, The ☐ Stowaway ☐ Susannah of the Mounties ☐ That Hagen Girl ☐ Wee Willie Winkie ☐ Young People

Tennant, Victoria ☐ All of Me ☐ Best Seller ☐ Flowers in the Attic ☐ Handmaid's Tale, The ☐ Holcroft Convenant, The ☐ L.A. Story ☐ Maigret ☐ Ragman's Daughter, The ☐ Strangers Kiss ☐ Whispers

Terry-Thomas ☐ Abominable Dr. Phibes, The ☐ Arabella ☐ Bachelor Flat ☐ Bang, Bang, You're Dead! ☐ Bawdy Adventures of Tom Jones, The ☐ Blue Murder at St. Trinian's ☐ Brothers in Law ☐ Danger: Diabolik ☐ Don't Raise the Bridge, Lower the River ☐ Dr. Phibes Rises Again ☐ Green Man, The ☐ Happy Is the Bride ☐ Heroes, The ☐ How Sweet It Is! ☐ How to Murder Your Wife ☐ I Love a Mystery ☐ I'm All Right, Jack ☐ It's Your Move ☐ Kiss the Girls and Make Them Die ☐ Last Remake of Beau Geste, The ☐ Lucky Jim ☐ Make Mine Mink ☐ Man in a Cocked Hat ☐ Matter of WHO, A ☐ Mouse on the Moon, The ☐ Munster, Go Home ☐ Mysterious House of Dr. C., The ☐ Naked Truth, The ☐ Operation Snatch ☐ Perils of Pauline, The ☐ Robin Hood ☐ Sandwich Man, The ☐ School for Scoundrels ☐ Strange Bedfellows ☐ Those Daring Young Men in Their Jaunty Jalopies ☐ Those Magnificent Men in Their Flying Machines ☐ Tom Thumb ☐ Too Many Crooks ☐ Where Were You When the Lights Went Out? ☐ Wonderful World of the Brothers Grimm, The

Thaxter, Phyllis ☐ Act of Violence ☐ Bewitched ☐ Blood on the Moon ☐ Breaking Point ☐ Come Fill the Cup ☐ Fort Worth ☐ Incident in San Francisco ☐ Jim Thorpe—All American ☐ Man Afraid ☐ No Man of Her Own ☐ Operation Secret ☐ Sea of Grass, The ☐ She's Working Her Way Through College ☐ Springfield Rifle ☐ Superman—The Movie ☐ Tenth Avenue Angel ☐ Thirty Seconds Over Tokyo ☐ Three Sovereigns For Sarah ☐ Weekend at the Waldorf ☐ Women's Prison ☐ World of Henry Orient, The

Thomas, Danny ☐ Big City, The ☐ Call Me Mister ☐ I'll See You in My Dreams ☐ Jazz Singer, The ☐ Journey Back to Oz ☐ Looking for Love ☐ Unfinished Dance, The

Thomas, Henry ☐ Cloak & Dagger ☐ E.T. The Extra-Terrestrial ☐ Legends of the Fall ☐ Misunderstood ☐ Psycho IV: The Beginning ☐ Quest, The ☐ Raggedy Man ☐ Taste for Killing, A ☐ Valmont

Thomas, Richard ☐ All Quiet on the Western Front ☐ Battle Beyond the Stars ☐ Berlin Tunnel 21 ☐ Common Ground ☐ Glory! Glory! ☐ Hobson's Choice ☐ Homecoming—A Christmas Story, The ☐ Johnny Belinda ☐ Last Summer ☐ Linda ☐ Master of Ballantrae, The ☐ Mission of the Shark ☐ No Other Love ☐ Red Sky at Morning ☐ September 30, 1955 ☐ Stephen King's It ☐ Todd Killings, The ☐ Winning

Thompson, Emma ☐ Dead Again ☐ Fortunes of War ☐ Henry V ☐ Howards End ☐ Impromptu ☐ In the Name of the Father ☐ Junior ☐ Much Ado About Nothing ☐ Peter's Friends ☐ Remains of the Day ☐ Tall Guy, The

Thompson, Jack ☐ Bad Blood ☐ Because He's My Friend ☐ Breaker Morant ☐ Burke and Wills ☐ Caddie ☐ Chant of Jimmy Blacksmith, The ☐ Deception ☐ Earthling, The ☐ Far Off Place, A ☐ Flesh + Blood ☐ Ground Zero ☐ Killing Beach, The ☐ Letter, The ☐ Mad Dog Morgan ☐ Man from Snowy River, The ☐ Merry Christmas, Mr. Lawrence ☐ Petersen ☐ Trouble in Paradise ☐ Wind

Thompson, Lea ☐ All the Right Moves ☐ Article 99 ☐ Back to the Future ☐ Back to the Future Part II ☐ Back to the Future Part III ☐ Casual Sex? ☐ Dennis the Menace ☐ Going Undercover ☐ Howard the Duck ☐ Jaws 3 ☐ Montana ☐ Nightbreaker ☐ Red Dawn ☐ Some Kind of Wonderful ☐ Space Camp ☐ Stolen Babies ☐ Tales from the Crypt

Thorndike, Sybil ☐ Big Gamble, The ☐ Forbidden Street, The ☐ Gone to Earth ☐ Hand in Hand ☐ Melba ☐ Nicholas Nickleby ☐ Prince and the Showgirl, The ☐ Shake Hands with the Devil ☐ Smiley Gets a Gun ☐ Stage Fright

Thulin, Ingrid ☐ After the Rehearsal ☐ Brink of Life ☐ Cries and Whispers ☐ Damned, The ☐ Foreign Intrigue ☐ Four Horsemen of the Apocalypse ☐ Games of Desire ☐ La Guerre Est Finie ☐ Magician, The ☐ Moses ☐ Silence, The ☐ Wild Strawberries ☐ Winter Light

Thurman, Uma ☐ Adventures of Baron Munchausen, The ☐ Dangerous Liaisons ☐ Even

Cowgirls Get the Blues ☐ Final Analysis ☐ Jennifer 8 ☐ Johnny Be Good ☐ Kiss Daddy Good Night ☐ Mad Dog and Glory ☐ Pulp Fiction ☐ Robin Hood ☐ Where the Heart Is

Tierney, Gene ☐ Advise and Consent ☐ Bell for Adano, A ☐ Belle Starr ☐ Black Widow ☐ China Girl ☐ Close to My Heart ☐ Dragonwyck ☐ Egyptian, The ☐ Ghost and Mrs. Muir, The ☐ Heaven Can Wait ☐ Hudson's Bay ☐ Iron Curtain, The ☐ Laura ☐ Leave Her to Heaven ☐ Left Hand of God, The ☐ Mating Season, The ☐ Never Let Me Go ☐ Night and the City ☐ On the Riviera ☐ Personal Affair ☐ Pleasure Seekers, The ☐ Plymouth Adventure, The ☐ Razor's Edge, The ☐ Return of Frank James, The ☐ Secret of Convict Lake, The ☐ Shanghai Gesture, The ☐ Son of Fury ☐ Sundown ☐ That Wonderful Urge ☐ Tobacco Road ☐ Toys in the Attic ☐ Where the Sidewalk Ends ☐ Whirlpool

Tilly, Meg ☐ Agnes of God ☐ Big Chill, The ☐ Body Snatchers ☐ Carmilla ☐ Fallen Angels—Volume 2 ☐ Girl in a Swing, The ☐ Impulse ☐ Leaving Normal ☐ Masquerade ☐ Off Beat ☐ One Dark Night ☐ Psycho 2 ☐ Sleep With Me ☐ Tex ☐ Two Jakes, The ☐ Valmont

Tobias, George ☐ Everybody Does It ☐ Gallant Bess ☐ Judge Steps Out, The ☐ Magic Carpet, The ☐ Make Your Own Bed ☐ Man Who Talked Too Much, The ☐ Mission to Moscow ☐ My Sister Eileen ☐ My Wild Irish Rose ☐ New Kind of Love, A ☐ Nobody Lives Forever ☐ Objective, Burma! ☐ River's End ☐ Saturday's Children ☐ Sergeant York ☐ Set-Up, The ☐ Seven Little Foys, The ☐ Southside 1-1000 ☐ Strawberry Blonde, The

Tobias, Oliver ☐ Abduction from the Seraglio, The ☐ King Arthur, the Young Warlord ☐ Mata Hari ☐ Mayfair Bank Caper, The ☐ Operation Nam ☐ Stud, The ☐ Wicked Lady, The

Tobin, Genevieve ☐ By Your Leave ☐ Case of the Lucky Legs, The ☐ Dark Hazard ☐ Dramatic School ☐ Golden Harvest ☐ Goose and the Gander, The ☐ Great Gambini, The ☐ I Loved a Woman ☐ Ninth Guest, The ☐ No Time for Comedy ☐ One Hour with You ☐ Zaza

Todd, Ann ☐ Action for Slander ☐ Breaking the Sound Barrier ☐ Danny Boy ☐ Daybreak ☐ Fiend, The ☐ Green Scarf, The ☐ How Green Was My Valley ☐ Human Factor, The ☐ Madeleine ☐ One Woman's Story ☐ Paradine Case ☐ Poison Pen ☐ Scream of Fear ☐ Seventh Veil, The ☐ Showtime ☐ So Evil My Love ☐ Son of Captain Blood ☐ South Riding ☐ Things to Come ☐ Three Daring Daughters ☐ Time Without Pity ☐ Vacation From Marriage

Todd, Richard ☐ Affair in Monte Carlo ☐ Assassin, The ☐ Asylum ☐ Battle Hell (Yangtse Incident) ☐ Battle of the Villa Fiorita, The ☐ Boys, The ☐ Chase a Crooked Shadow ☐ Coast of Skeletons ☐ D-Day the Sixth of June ☐ Dam Busters, The ☐ Dorian Gray ☐ Flesh & Blood ☐ Hasty Heart, The ☐ Hellions, The ☐ Incident at Victoria Falls ☐ Intent to Kill ☐ Interrupted Journey ☐ Long and the Short and the Tall, The ☐ Man Called Peter, A ☐ Marie Antoinette ☐ Never Let Go ☐ Number 1 of the Secret Service ☐ Operation Crossbow ☐ Rob Roy, the Highland Rogue ☐ Saint Joan ☐ Stage Fright ☐ Story of Robin Hood and His Merrie Men, The ☐ Sword and the Rose, The ☐ Virgin Queen, The

Todd, Thelma ☐ Bohemian Girl, The ☐ Broadminded ☐ Call Her Savage ☐ Cockeyed Cavaliers ☐ Corsair ☐ Counsellor-at-Law ☐ Devil's Brother, The ☐ Follow Thru ☐ Hips, Hips, Hooray ☐ Horse Feathers ☐ Maltese Falcon, The ☐ Monkey Business ☐ Palooka ☐ Sitting Pretty ☐ Speak Easily ☐ This Is the Night ☐ Two for Tonight

Tognazzi, Ugo ☐ Conjugal Bed, The ☐ Crazy Desire ☐ Fascist, The ☐ Goodnight, Ladies and Gentlemen ☐ High Infidelity ☐ Hours of Love, The ☐ Joke of Destiny, A ☐ La Cage aux Folles ☐ La Cage aux Folles II ☐ La Cage aux Folles III: The Wedding ☐ Love in the City ☐ Magnificent Cuckold, The ☐ Man Who Came for Coffee, The ☐ Tragedy of a Ridiculous Man

Toler, Sidney ☐ Adventures of Smilin' Jack ☐ Black Magic ☐ Castle in the Desert ☐ Charlie Chan at the Wax Museum ☐ Charlie Chan at Treasure Island ☐ Charlie Chan in City in Darkness ☐ Charlie Chan in Honolulu ☐ Charlie Chan in Panama ☐ Charlie Chan in Reno ☐ Charlie Chan in Rio ☐ Charlie Chan in the Secret Service ☐ Charlie Chan's Murder Cruise ☐ Chinese Cat, The ☐ If I Were King ☐ Is My Face Red? ☐ Isle of Forgotten Sins ☐ It's in the Bag ☐ Jade Mask, The ☐ King of Chinatown ☐ King of the Jungle ☐ Madame X ☐ Murder Over New York ☐ Mysterious Rider, The ☐ Narrow Corner, The ☐ Night to Remember, A ☐ Our Relations ☐ Phantom President, The ☐ Scarlet Clue, The ☐ Shanghai Cobra, The ☐ Speak Easily ☐ Spitfire ☐ Upperworld

Tomei, Marisa ☐ Chaplin ☐ Equinox ☐ My Cousin Vinny ☐ Only You ☐ Paper, The ☐ Untamed Heart

Tomlin, Lily ☐ 9 to 5 ☐ All of Me ☐ And the Band Played On ☐ Beverly Hillbillies, The ☐ Big Business ☐ Incredible Shrinking Woman, The ☐ Late Show, The ☐ Moment by Moment ☐ Nashville ☐ Search for Signs of Intelligent Life in the Universe, The ☐ Shadows and Fog ☐ Short Cuts

Tone, Franchot ☐ Advise and Consent ☐ Because of Him ☐ Bombshell ☐ Bride Wore Red, The ☐ Dancing Lady ☐ Danger-

☐ Man Without a Star ☐ Marjorie Morningstar ☐ Mountain, The ☐ Murder My Sweet ☐ My Man and I ☐ Norman Rockwell's Breaking Home Ties ☐ Raw Deal ☐ Second Honeymoon ☐ Stagecoach ☐ Star for a Night ☐ Stranger Who Wore a Gun, The ☐ Street of Chance ☐ Stripper, The ☐ Texas ☐ Two Weeks in Another Town ☐ Velvet Touch, The ☐ Woman of the Town, The

Trintignant, Jean-Louis ☐ . . . And God Created Woman ☐ 7 Capital Sins ☐ And Hope to Die ☐ Confidentially Yours ☐ Conformist, The ☐ Crook, The ☐ Dangerous Liaisons 1960 ☐ Easy Life, The ☐ Femmes de Personne ☐ French Conspiracy, The ☐ Je Vous Aime ☐ Le Secret ☐ Les Biches ☐ Les Violins du Bal ☐ Love at the Top ☐ Man and a Woman, A ☐ Man and a Woman, A: 20 Years Later ☐ Man Who Lies, The ☐ Mata Hari ☐ My Night at Maud's ☐ Nutty, Naughty Chateau ☐ Outside Man, The ☐ Rendez-vous ☐ Sleeping Car Murders, The ☐ Trois Couleurs: Rouge ☐ Z

Tucker, Forrest ☐ Adventures of Huckleberry, Finn, The ☐ Auntie Mame ☐ Barquero ☐ Big Cat, The ☐ Blood Feud ☐ Boston Blackie Goes Hollywood ☐ Break in the Circle ☐ Brimstone ☐ Bugles in the Afternoon ☐ Chisum ☐ Crawling Eye, The ☐ Crosswinds ☐ Deerslayer, The ☐ Fighting Coast Guard ☐ Final Chapter—Walking Tall ☐ Finger Man, The ☐ Fingerman ☐ Flaming Feather ☐ Flight Nurse ☐ Fort Massacre ☐ Girl in the Woods ☐ Gunfighters ☐ Gunsmoke in Tucson ☐ Hellfire ☐ Hoodlum Empire ☐ Incredible Rocky Mountain Race ☐ Jarrett ☐ Jubilee Trail ☐ Montana Belle ☐ Nevadan, The ☐ Night They Raided Minsky's, The ☐ Oh! Susanna ☐ Outtakes ☐ Plunderers, The ☐ Pony Express ☐ Rage at Dawn ☐ Real American Hero, A ☐ Sands of Iwo Jima ☐ Shut My Big Mouth ☐ Three Violent People ☐ Two Guys From Texas ☐ Wackiest Wagon Train in the West, The ☐ Warpath ☐ Westerner, The ☐ Wild Blue Yonder, The ☐ Yearling, The

Tucker, Sophie ☐ Broadway Melody of 1938 ☐ Follow the Boys ☐ Joker is Wild, The ☐ Sensations ☐ Thoroughbreds Don't Cry

Turner, Kathleen ☐ Accidental Tourist, The ☐ Body Heat ☐ Breed Apart, A ☐ Crimes of Passion ☐ House of Cards ☐ Jewel of the Nile ☐ Julia and Julia ☐ Man with Two Brains, The ☐ Naked in New York ☐ Peggy Sue Got Married ☐ Prizzi's Honor ☐ Romancing the Stone ☐ Serial Mom ☐ Switching Channels ☐ Undercover Blues ☐ V.I. Warshawski ☐ War of the Roses, The

Turner, Lana ☐ Another Time, Another Place ☐ Bachelor in Paradise ☐ Bad and the Beautiful, The ☐ Betrayed ☐ Big Cube, The ☐ Bittersweet Love ☐ By Love Possessed ☐ Calling Dr. Kildare ☐ Cass Timberlane ☐ Diane ☐ Dr. Jekyll and Mr. Hyde ☐ Dramatic School ☐ Flame and the Flesh, The ☐ Graveyard, The ☐ Great Garrick, The ☐ Green Dolphin Street ☐ Homecoming ☐ Honky Tonk ☐ Imitation of Life ☐ Johnny Eager ☐ Keep Your Powder Dry ☐ Lady Takes a Flyer, The ☐ Latin Lovers ☐ Life of Her Own, A ☐ Love Finds Andy Hardy ☐ Love Has Many Faces ☐ Madame X ☐ Marriage Is a Private Affair ☐ Merry Widow, The ☐ Mr. Imperium ☐ Peyton Place ☐ Portrait in Black ☐ Postman Always Rings Twice, The ☐ Prodigal, The ☐ Rains of Ranchipur, The ☐ Rich Man, Poor Girl ☐ Sea Chase, The ☐ Slightly Dangerous ☐ Somewhere I'll Find You ☐ They Won't Forget ☐ Three Musketeers, The ☐ Two Girls on Broadway ☐ We Who Are Young ☐ Weekend at the Waldorf ☐ Who's Got the Action? ☐ Witches' Brew ☐ Ziegfeld Girl

Turturro, John ☐ Backtrack ☐ Barton Fink ☐ Brain Donors ☐ Color of Money, The ☐ Do the Right Thing ☐ Five Corners ☐ Fortunate Pilgrim ☐ Gung Ho ☐ Jungle Fever ☐ Mac ☐ Mario Puzo's "The Fortunate Pilgrim" ☐ Men of Respect ☐ Miller's Crossing ☐ Mo' Better Blues ☐ Quiz Show ☐ Sicilian, The ☐ To Live and Die in L.A.

Tushingham, Rita ☐ Bed-Sitting Room, The ☐ Diamonds for Breakfast ☐ Doctor Zhivago ☐ Dream to Believe ☐ Girl with Green Eyes, The ☐ Green Eyes ☐ Guru, The ☐ Human Factor, The ☐ Judgment in Stone, A ☐ Knack, and How to Get It, The ☐ Leather Boys, The ☐ Mysteries ☐ Paper Marriage ☐ Slaughter Day ☐ Smashing Time ☐ Taste of Honey, A

Twiggy ☐ Boy Friend, The ☐ Club Paradise ☐ Doctor and the Devils, The ☐ Istanbul ☐ Madame Sousatzka

Tyson, Cicely ☐ Acceptable Risks ☐ Autobiography of Miss Jane Pittman ☐ Benny's Place ☐ Blue Bird, The ☐ Bustin' Loose ☐ Comedians, The ☐ Duplicates ☐ Fried Green Tomatoes ☐ Heart Is a Lonely Hunter, The ☐ Heat Wave ☐ Hero Ain't Northin' But a Sandwich, A ☐ Just an Old Sweet Song ☐ Kid Who Loved Christmas, The ☐ King ☐ Man Called Adam, A ☐ Marva Collins Story, The ☐ Oldest Living Confederate Widow Tells All ☐ River Niger, The ☐ Samaritan: The Mitch Snyder Story ☐ Sounder ☐ Wilma ☐ Woman Called Moses, A ☐ Women of Brewster Place, The

Ullmann, Liv ☐ Abdication, The ☐ Autumn Sonata ☐ Bay Boy, The ☐ Bridge Too Far, A ☐ Cold Sweat ☐ Cries and Whispers ☐ Dangerous Moves ☐ Emigrants, The ☐ Face to Face ☐ 40 Carats ☐ Gaby—A True Story ☐ Hour of the Wolf ☐ Jacobo Timerman: Prisoner Without a Name, Cell Without a Number ☐ Leonor ☐ Let's Hope It's a Girl ☐ Lost Horizon ☐ Mindwalk ☐ New Land, The ☐ Night Visitor, The ☐ Ox, The ☐ Passion of Anna, The ☐ Persona ☐ Pope Joan

☐ Richard's Things ☐ Scenes from a Marriage ☐ Serpent's Egg, The ☐ Shame ☐ Wild Duck, The ☐ Zandy's Bride

Ullman, Tracey ☐ Bullets Over Broadway ☐ Give My Regards to Broad Street ☐ Happily Ever After ☐ Happy Since I Met You ☐ Household Saints ☐ I Love You to Death ☐ I'll Do Anything ☐ Plenty ☐ Ready to Wear ☐ Robin Hood: Men in Tights

Urich, Robert ☐ April Morning ☐ Blind Faith ☐ Blind Man's Bluff ☐ Bunco ☐ Endangered Species ☐ His Mistress ☐ Hitwoman: The Double Edge ☐ Ice Pirates, The ☐ In a Stranger's Hand ☐ Invitation to Hell ☐ Lonesome Dove ☐ Magnum Force ☐ Mistral's Daughter ☐ Princess Daisy ☐ Scandal Sheet ☐ Shadow Box, The ☐ Turk 182!

Ustinov, Peter ☐ Appointment with Death ☐ Ashanti: Land of No Mercy ☐ Beau Brummel ☐ Billy Budd ☐ Blackbeard's Ghost ☐ Charlie Chan and the Curse of the Dragon Queen ☐ Comedians, The ☐ Dead Man's Folly ☐ Death on the Nile ☐ Egyptian, The ☐ Evil Under the Sun ☐ Grandpa ☐ Great Muppet Caper, The ☐ Grendel, Grendel, Grendel ☐ Hammersmith Is Out ☐ Hot Millions ☐ Hotel Sahara ☐ John Goldfarb, Please Come Home ☐ Last Remake of Beau Geste, The ☐ Logan's Run ☐ Lola Montes ☐ Lorenzo's Oil ☐ Magic Box, The ☐ Man Who Wagged His Tail, The ☐ Memed My Hawk ☐ Odette ☐ One of Our Dinosaurs is Missing ☐ Quo Vadis? ☐ Robin Hood ☐ Romanoff and Juliet ☐ Spartacus ☐ Sundowners, The ☐ Thief of Bagdad, The ☐ Thirteen at Dinner ☐ Topkapi ☐ Treasure of Matecumbe ☐ Viva Max! ☐ We're No Angels ☐ Winds of Change

Valentino, Rudolph ☐ Blood and Sand ☐ Eagle, The ☐ Four Horsemen of the Apocalypse, The ☐ Sheik, The ☐ Son of the Sheik

Vallee, Rudy ☐ Admiral Was a Lady, The ☐ Bachelor and the Bobby-Soxer, The ☐ Beautiful Blonde from Bashful Bend, The ☐ Fabulous Suzanne, The ☐ Father Was a Fullback ☐ Gentlemen Marry Brunettes ☐ George White's Scandals ☐ Glorifying the American Girl ☐ Happy Go Lucky ☐ How to Succeed in Business Without Really Trying ☐ I Remember Mama ☐ It's in the Bag ☐ Live a Little, Love a Little ☐ Man Alive ☐ Mother Is a Freshman ☐ My Dear Secretary ☐ Palm Beach Story, The ☐ People Are Funny ☐ Second Fiddle ☐ So This Is New York ☐ Time Out for Rhythm ☐ Unfaithfully Yours ☐ Vagabond Lover, The

Valli, Alida ☐ Castillan, The ☐ Happy Thieves ☐ Horror Chamber of Dr. Faustus, The ☐ Inferno ☐ Lisa and the Devil ☐ Long Absence, The ☐ Luna ☐ Miracle of the Bells, The ☐ Night Heaven Fall, The ☐ Oedipus Rex ☐ Outcry, The ☐ Paradine Case ☐ Schoolgirl Diary ☐ Senso ☐ Spider's Stratagem, The ☐ Stranger's Hand, The ☐ Suspiria ☐ Tempter, The ☐ Third Man, The ☐ This Angry Age ☐ Walk Softly, Stranger

Van Cleef, Lee ☐ Armed Response ☐ Bad Man's River ☐ Badge of Marshal Brennan, The ☐ Bandits of Corsica, The ☐ Barquero ☐ Beast from 20,000 Fathoms, The ☐ Beyond the Law ☐ Captain Apache ☐ Codename—Wildgeese ☐ Deadliest Art, The: The Best of the Martial Arts Films, The ☐ El Condor ☐ Escape from New York ☐ For a Few Dollars More ☐ God's Gun ☐ Good, the Bad, and the Ugly, The ☐ Grand Duel, The ☐ Gun Battle at Monterey ☐ Gunfight at the O.K. Corral ☐ Guns, Girls and Gangsters ☐ High Noon ☐ It Conquered the World ☐ Kid Vengeance ☐ Killing Machine ☐ Magnificent Seven Ride!, The ☐ Man Alone, A ☐ Man Who Shot Liberty Valance, The ☐ Master Ninja ☐ Mean Frank & Crazy Tony ☐ Octagon, The ☐ Rails Into Laramie ☐ Ride Lonesome ☐ Road to Denver, The ☐ Sabata ☐ Take a Hard Ride

Van Damme, Jean-Claude ☐ Black Eagle ☐ Bloodsport ☐ Cyborg ☐ Deadliest Art, The: The Best of the Martial Arts Films, The ☐ Death Warrant ☐ Double Impact ☐ Hard Target ☐ Kickboxer ☐ Lionheart ☐ Nowhere to Run ☐ Street Fighter ☐ Timecop ☐ Universal Soldier

Van Doren, Mamie ☐ Ain't Misbehavin' ☐ All American, The ☐ Big Operator, The ☐ Born Reckless ☐ College Confidential ☐ Francis Joins the Wacs ☐ Girl in Black Stockings, The ☐ Girls Town ☐ Guns, Girls and Gangsters ☐ High School Confidential ☐ Las Vegas Hillbillys ☐ Navy vs. the Night Monsters, The ☐ Sex Kittens Go to College ☐ Star in the Dust ☐ Teacher's Pet ☐ Three Nuts in Search of a Bolt ☐ Yankee Pasha

Van Dyke, Dick ☐ Art of Love, The ☐ Breakfast with Les and Bess ☐ Bye, Bye, Birdie ☐ Chitty Chitty Bang Bang ☐ Cold Turkey ☐ Comic, The ☐ Divorce American Style ☐ Fitzwilly ☐ Lt. Robin Crusoe, USN ☐ Mary Poppins ☐ Morning After, The ☐ Never a Dull Moment ☐ Runner Stumbles, The ☐ What a Way to Go!

Van Peebles, Mario ☐ Exterminator II ☐ New Jack City ☐ Full Eclipse ☐ Gunmen ☐ Highlander: The Final Dimension ☐ Identity Crisis ☐ Jaws, The Revenge ☐ Facts of Life Down Under, The ☐ Posse ☐ Rappin ☐ South Bronx Heroes

Vanel, Charles ☐ Alice, or the Last Escapade ☐ Crossroads ☐ Diabolique ☐ Rififi in Tokyo ☐ Symphony for a Massacre ☐ They Were Five ☐ Three Brothers ☐ Wages of Fear, The

Vaughn, Robert ☐ Babysitter, The ☐ Battle Beyond the Stars ☐ Big Show, The ☐ Black Moon Rising ☐ Brass Target, The ☐ Bridge at Remagen, The ☐ Brutal Glory ☐ Bullitt ☐ Buried Alive ☐ C.H.U.D. II ☐ City in Fear ☐ Clay Pigeon ☐ Good Day for a Hanging

☐ Good Luck, Miss Wyckoff ☐ Gossip Columnist, The ☐ Hangar 18 ☐ Hell's Crossroads ☐ Hour of the Assassin ☐ Julius Caesar ☐ Kill Castro ☐ Last Bastion, The ☐ Lucifer Complex, The ☐ Magnificent Seven, The ☐ Mind of Mr. Soames, The ☐ No Time to Be Young ☐ Nobody's Perfect ☐ One Spy Too Many ☐ Prince of Bel Air ☐ Question of Honor, A ☐ Rebels, The ☐ S.O.B. ☐ Starship Invasions ☐ Statue, The ☐ Superman 3 ☐ Young Philadelphians, The

Veidt, Conrad ☐ Above Suspicion ☐ All Through the Night ☐ Beloved Rogue, The ☐ Cabinet of Dr. Caligari, The ☐ Casablanca ☐ Congress Dances ☐ Contraband ☐ Dark Journey ☐ Escape ☐ F.P. 1 ☐ I Was a Spy ☐ Men in Her Life, The ☐ Passing of the Third Floor Back, The ☐ Rome Express ☐ Spy in Black, The ☐ Thief of Bagdad, The ☐ Under the Red Robe ☐ Whistling in the Dark ☐ Woman's Face, A

Velez, Lupe ☐ Cuban Love Song, The ☐ Girl from Mexico, The ☐ Half-Naked Truth, The ☐ Hollywood Party ☐ Hot Pepper ☐ Kongo ☐ Lady of the Pavements ☐ Mexican Spitfire ☐ Mexican Spitfire at Sea ☐ Mexican Spitfire Out West ☐ Mexican Spitfire Sees a Ghost ☐ Mexican Spitfire's Baby ☐ Mexican Spitfire's Blessed Event ☐ Mexican Spitfire's Elephant ☐ Palooka ☐ Squaw Man, The

Vera-Ellen ☐ Belle of New York, The ☐ Big Leaguer, The ☐ Call Me Madam ☐ Carnival in Costa Rica ☐ Happy Go Lovely ☐ Kid from Brooklyn, The ☐ Let's Be Happy ☐ Love Happy ☐ On the Town ☐ Three Little Girls in Blue ☐ Three Little Words ☐ White Christmas ☐ Wonder Man

Verdon, Gwen ☐ Cocoon ☐ Cocoon: The Return ☐ Cotton Club, The ☐ Damn Yankees ☐ Jerk Too, The ☐ Legs ☐ Nadine

Vereen, Ben ☐ All That Jazz ☐ Buy & Cell ☐ Ellis Island ☐ Funny Lady ☐ Gas-s-s-s ☐ Intruders ☐ Jesse Owens Story, The ☐ Kid Who Loved Christmas, The ☐ Pippin ☐ Sweet Charity

Vincent, Jan-Michael ☐ Alienator ☐ Animal Instincts ☐ Baby Blue Marine ☐ Big Wednesday ☐ Bite the Bullet ☐ Born in East L.A. ☐ Buster and Billie ☐ Damnation Alley ☐ Defiance ☐ Going Home ☐ Hard Country ☐ Haunting Fear ☐ Hidden Obsession ☐ Hit List ☐ Hooper ☐ Last Plane Out ☐ Mechanic, The ☐ Midnight Witness ☐ Sins of Desire ☐ Tarzan in Manhattan ☐ Tribes ☐ White Line Fever ☐ Winds of War, The ☐ World's Greatest Athlete, The ☐ Xtro II: The Second Encounter

Voight, Jon ☐ All-American Boy, The ☐ Catch-22 ☐ Champ, The ☐ Chernobyl: The Final Warning ☐ Coming Home ☐ Conrack ☐ Deliverance ☐ Desert Bloom ☐ End of the Game ☐ Eternity ☐ Fearless Frank ☐ Hour of the Gun ☐ Last of His Tribe, The ☐ Lookin' to Get Out ☐ Midnight Cowboy ☐ Odessa File, The ☐ Out of It ☐ Revolutionary, The ☐ Runaway Train ☐ Table for Five

Volonte, Gian Maria ☐ Bullet for the General, A ☐ Eboli ☐ Face to Face ☐ Fistful of Dollars, A ☐ For a Few Dollars More ☐ French Conspiracy, The ☐ Giordano Bruno ☐ Investigation of a Citizen Above Suspicion ☐ Lady of the Camellias, The ☐ Lucky Luciano ☐ Mattei Affair, The ☐ Moro Affair, The ☐ Open Doors ☐ Sacco and Vanzetti ☐ We Still Kill the Old Way

Von Stroheim, Erich ☐ As You Desire Me ☐ Blind Husbands ☐ Crimson Romance ☐ Five Graves to Cairo ☐ Foolish Wives ☐ Friends and Lovers ☐ Grand Illusion ☐ Great Flamarion, The ☐ Great Gabbo, The ☐ Heart of Humanity, The ☐ Lost Squadron, The ☐ Mask of Dijon, The ☐ Napoleon ☐ North Star, The ☐ Scotland Yard Investigator ☐ So Ends Our Night ☐ Sunset Boulevard ☐ Three Faces East ☐ Wedding March, The

Von Sydow, Max ☐ Awakenings ☐ Belarus File, The ☐ Best Intentions, The ☐ Brass Target, The ☐ Brink of Life ☐ Christopher Columbus ☐ Code Name—Emerald ☐ Conan the Barbarian ☐ Deathwatch ☐ Dreamscape ☐ Duet for One ☐ Dune ☐ Foxtrot ☐ Pelle the Conqueror ☐ Quiller Memorandum, The ☐ Embassy ☐ Emigrants, The ☐ Exorcist II: The Heretic ☐ Exorcist, The ☐ Flash Gordon ☐ Flight of the Eagle, The ☐ Greatest Story Ever Told, The ☐ Hannah and Her Sisters ☐ Hawaii ☐ Hiroshima: Out of the Ashes ☐ Hour of the Wolf ☐ Hurricane ☐ Illustrious Corpses ☐ Kiss Before Dying, A ☐ Kremlin Letter, The ☐ Magician, The ☐ March or Die ☐ Needful Things ☐ Never Say Never Again ☐ New Land, The ☐ Night Visitor, The ☐ Ox, The ☐ Passion of Anna, The ☐ Quo Vadis? ☐ Reward, The ☐ Samson and Delilah ☐ Second Victory, The ☐ Seventh Seal, The ☐ Shame ☐ She Dances Alone ☐ Steppenwolf ☐ Strange Brew ☐ Three Days of the Condor ☐ Through a Glass Darkly ☐ Touch, The ☐ Until the End of the World ☐ Victory ☐ Virgin Spring, The ☐ Voyage of the Damned ☐ Winter Light

Wagner, Robert ☐ Affair, The ☐ Airport '79—The Concorde ☐ All the Fine Young Cannibals ☐ Banning ☐ Beneath the 12 Mile Reef ☐ Between Heaven and Hell ☐ Biggest Bundle Of Them All ☐ Broken Lance ☐ City Beneath the Sea ☐ Condemned of Altona, The ☐ Curse of the Pink Panther ☐ Death at Love House ☐ Don't Just Stand There ☐ Dragon: The Bruce Lee Story ☐ False Arrest ☐ Frogmen, The ☐ Getting Physical ☐ Halls of Montezuma ☐ Harper ☐ Hart to Hart ☐ How I Spent My Summer Vacation ☐ Hunters, The ☐ I Am the Cheese ☐ In Love and War ☐ Indiscreet ☐ Kiss Before Dying, A ☐ Let's Make It Legal ☐ Love Among Thieves ☐ Madame Sin ☐ Midway ☐ Mountain, The ☐ Pink Panther, The ☐ Prince Valiant ☐ Sail a Crooked Ship ☐ Say One for Me ☐ Silver Whip, The ☐ Stars and Stripes Forever ☐ There Must Be a Pony ☐ Titanic ☐ Towering Inferno, The ☐ Trail of the Pink Panther ☐ True Story of Jesse James, The ☐ War Lover, The ☐ What Price Glory? ☐ White Feather ☐ Winning ☐ With a Song in My Heart

Waits, Tom ☐ At Play in the Fields of the Lord ☐ Big Time ☐ Bram Stoker's Dracula ☐ Candy Mountain ☐ Cold Feet ☐ Down by Law ☐ Face of Rage, The ☐ Ironweed ☐ Outsiders, The ☐ Paradise Alley ☐ Queens Logic

Walburn, Raymond ☐ Christmas in July ☐ Father Makes Good ☐ Father Takes the Air ☐ Father's Wild Game ☐ Flowing Gold ☐ Hail the Conquering Hero ☐ Heaven with a Barbed Wire Fence ☐ Henry, the Rainmaker ☐ I'll Tell the World ☐ Mr. Deeds Goes to Town ☐ Professor Beware ☐ Rendezvous with Annie ☐ Riding High ☐ Rise and Shine ☐ She Married Her Boss ☐ Spoilers, The ☐ State of the Union

Walken, Christopher ☐ All-American Murder ☐ Anderson Tapes, The ☐ Annie Hall ☐ At Close Range ☐ Batman Returns ☐ Biloxi Blues ☐ Brainstorm ☐ Comfort of Strangers, The ☐ Communion ☐ Dead Zone, The ☐ Deadline ☐ Deer Hunter, The ☐ Demon Within, The ☐ Dogs of War, The ☐ Heaven's Gate ☐ Homeboy ☐ King of New York ☐ Last Embrace ☐ McBain ☐ Mistress ☐ Next Stop, Greenwich Village ☐ Pennies From Heaven ☐ Puss in Boots ☐ Sarah, Plain and Tall ☐ Scam ☐ Skylark ☐ True Romance ☐ View to a Kill, A ☐ Wayne's World 2 ☐ Who Am I This Time?

Walker, Clint ☐ Baker's Hawk ☐ Bounty Man, The ☐ Great Bank Robbery, The ☐ Hardcase ☐ Maya ☐ More Dead Than Alive ☐ Mysterious Island of Beautiful Women ☐ Night of the Grizzly ☐ None But the Brave ☐ Pancho Villa ☐ Sam Whiskey ☐ Send Me No Flowers ☐ White Buffalo, The

Walker, Robert ☐ Clock, The ☐ Devonsville Terror, The ☐ Happening, The ☐ Her Highness and the Bellboy ☐ Madame Curie ☐ My Son John ☐ One Touch of Venus ☐ Please Believe Me ☐ Sea of Grass, The ☐ See Here, Private Hargrove ☐ Since You Went Away ☐ Song of Love ☐ Strangers on a Train ☐ Thirty Seconds Over Tokyo ☐ Till the Clouds Roll By ☐ War Wagon, The ☐ What Next, Corporal Hargrove?

Wallach, Eli ☐ Ace High ☐ Act One ☐ Adventures of a Young Man ☐ Adventures of Gerard, The ☐ Angel Levine, The ☐ Article 99 ☐ Baby Doll ☐ Brain, The ☐ Christopher Columbus ☐ Cinderella Liberty ☐ Circle of Iron ☐ Cold Night's Death, A ☐ Deep, The ☐ Domino Principle, The ☐ Don't Turn the Other Cheek ☐ Executioner's Song, The ☐ Family Matter, A ☐ Firepower ☐ Genghis Khan ☐ Girlfriends ☐ Godfather, Part III, The ☐ Good, the Bad, and the Ugly, The ☐ Harold Robbins' the Pirate ☐ How to Save a Marriage (And Ruin Your Life) ☐ How to Steal a Million ☐ Hunter, The ☐ Impossible Spy, The ☐ Indict and Convict ☐ Kisses for My President ☐ Legacy of Lies ☐ Lineup, The ☐ Lord Jim ☐ Lovely Way to Die, A ☐ Mackenna's Gold ☐ Magnificent Seven, The ☐ Misfits, The ☐ Mistress ☐ Moon-Spinners, The ☐ Movie Movie ☐ Night and the City ☐ Nuts ☐ People Next Door, The ☐ Sam's Son ☐ Seven Thieves ☐ Skokie ☐ Teamster Boss: The Jackie Presser Story ☐ Tiger Makes Out, The ☐ Tough Guys ☐ Two Jakes, The ☐ Victors, The ☐ Zigzag

Walsh, Kay ☐ Connecting Rooms ☐ Devil's Own, The ☐ Encore ☐ Greyfriars Bobby ☐ Horse's Mouth, The ☐ Last Holiday ☐ Lease of Life ☐ Luck of the Irish, The ☐ Magnet, The ☐ Oliver Twist ☐ Rainbow Jacket, The ☐ Reach for Glory ☐ Scrooge ☐ This Happy Breed ☐ Tonight at 8:30 ☐ Tunes of Glory ☐ Vice Versa ☐ Young Bess

Walsh, M. Emmet ☐ Brotherhood of the Rose ☐ Critters ☐ Fast-Walking ☐ Four Eyes and Six-Guns ☐ Killer Image ☐ Mighty Quinn, The ☐ Missing in Action ☐ Music of Chance, The ☐ Red Scorpion ☐ Right of the People, The ☐ Straight Time ☐ Tales from the Crypt ☐ White Sands ☐ Wildcats

Walston, Ray ☐ Apartment, The ☐ Blood Relations ☐ Blood Salvage ☐ Caprice ☐ Convicts Four ☐ Damn Yankees ☐ Fall of the House of Usher, The ☐ Fast Times at Ridgemont High ☐ Fine Gold ☐ Galaxy of Terror ☐ Happy Hooker Goes to Washington, The ☐ I Know My First Name Is Steven ☐ Jerk Too, The ☐ Kiss Me, Stupid ☐ Paint Your Wagon ☐ Popcorn ☐ Popeye ☐ Say One for Me ☐ Silver Streak ☐ Ski Patrol ☐ South Pacific ☐ Sting, The ☐ Tall Story ☐ Who's Minding the Store?

Walthall, Henry B. ☐ Birth of a Nation, The ☐ Dante's Inferno ☐ Men in White ☐ Scarlet Letter, The ☐ Scarlet Letter, The ☐ Somewhere in Sonora ☐ Strange Interlude ☐ Viva Villa!

Wanamaker, Sam ☐ Aviator, The ☐ Baby Boom ☐ Billy Jack Goes to Washington ☐ Charlie Muffin ☐ Competition, The ☐ Concrete Jungle, The ☐ Day the Fish Came Out, The ☐ From Hell to Victory ☐ Guilty by Suspicion ☐ Heartsounds ☐ Irreconcilable Differences ☐ Judgment in Berlin ☐ Mr. Denning Drives North ☐ My Girl Tisa ☐ Our Family Business ☐ Pure Luck ☐ Raw Deal ☐ Running Against Time ☐ Salt to the Devil ☐ Spiral Staircase, The ☐ Spy Who Came In from the Cold, The ☐ Warning Shot

Warden, Jack ☐ 12 Angry Men ☐ All the President's Men ☐ And Justice for All ☐ Apprenticeship Of Duddy Kravitz, The ☐ Aviator, The ☐ Bachelor Party, The ☐ Being There

☐ Beyond the Poseidon Adventure ☐ Billy Two Hats ☐ Blindfold ☐ Brian's Song ☐ Bye Bye Braverman ☐ Carbon Copy ☐ Champ, The ☐ Chu Chu and the Philly Flash ☐ Darby's Rangers ☐ Dead Solid Perfect ☐ Death on the Nile ☐ Donovan's Reef ☐ Dreamer ☐ Edge of the City ☐ Escape from Zahrain ☐ Everybody Wins ☐ Face of Fear ☐ Frogmen, The ☐ From Here to Eternity ☐ Godchild, The ☐ Guilty as Sin ☐ Heaven Can Wait ☐ Helen Keller: The Miracle Continues ☐ Hobson's Choice ☐ Hoover vs. the Kennedys: The Second Civil War ☐ Judgment ☐ Man on a String ☐ Man Who Loved Cat Dancing, The ☐ Night and the City ☐ Passed Away ☐ Presidio, The ☐ Problem Child ☐ Problem Child 2 ☐ Run Silent, Run Deep ☐ September ☐ Shampoo ☐ So Fine ☐ Sound and the Fury, The ☐ Summertree ☐ That Kind of Woman ☐ Thin Red Line, The ☐ Toys ☐ Used Cars ☐ Verdict, The ☐ Wake Me When It's Over ☐ White Buffalo, The ☐ Who Is Harry Kellerman and Why Is He Saying Those Terrible Things About Me?

Ward, Rachel ☐ After Dark, My Sweet ☐ Against All Odds ☐ And the Sea Will Tell ☐ Black Magic ☐ Christopher Columbus—The Discovery ☐ Dead Men Don't Wear Plaid ☐ Double Jeopardy ☐ Final Terror, The ☐ Fortress ☐ Good Wife, The ☐ Hotel Colonial ☐ How to Get Ahead in Advertising ☐ Night School ☐ Sharky's Machine ☐ Thorn Birds, The ☐ Wide Sargasso Sea

Warner, H.B. ☐ Arrest Bulldog Drummond ☐ Bulldog Drummond in Africa ☐ Five Star Final ☐ Gracie Allen Murder Case, The ☐ Green Goddess, The ☐ High Wall ☐ In Old Santa Fe ☐ It's a Wonderful Life ☐ Jennie Gerhardt ☐ King of Kings, The ☐ Journey into Light ☐ Lost Horizon ☐ Menace, The ☐ Mr. Deeds Goes to Town ☐ New Moon ☐ Trial of Mary Dugan, The ☐ Victoria the Great

Warner, Jack ☐ Against the Wind ☐ Blue Lamp, The ☐ Break to Freedom ☐ Captive Heart, The ☐ Carve Her Name With Pride ☐ Christmas Carol, A ☐ Final Test, The ☐ Forbidden Cargo ☐ Game of Danger ☐ Hue and Cry ☐ Hundred Hour Hunt ☐ It Always Rains on Sunday ☐ My Brother's Keeper ☐ Square Ring, The ☐ Tonight at 8:30 ☐ Train of Events

Warren, Lesley Ann ☐ Apology ☐ Baja Oklahoma ☐ Beulah Land ☐ Burglar ☐ Choose Me ☐ Cinderella ☐ Clue ☐ Color of Night ☐ Cop ☐ Family of Spies ☐ Fight for Jenny, A ☐ Happiest Millionaire, The ☐ Harry and Walter Go to New York ☐ Legend of Valentino, The ☐ Life Stinks ☐ Night in Heaven, A ☐ One and Only, Genuine, Original Family Band, The ☐ Pickup on 101 ☐ Pure Country ☐ Race to the Yankee Zephyr ☐ Songwriter ☐ Victor/Victoria ☐ Worth Winning

Warrick, Ruth ☐ China Sky ☐ Citizen Kane ☐ Corsican Brothers, The ☐ Daisy Kenyon ☐ Great Dan Patch, The ☐ Guest in the House ☐ Iron Major, The ☐ Let's Dance ☐ Mr. Winkle Goes to War ☐ Obliging Young Lady ☐ Perilous Holiday ☐ Song of the South ☐ Three Husbands

Washbourne, Mona ☐ Adventure in the Hopfields ☐ Bed-Sitting Room, The ☐ Billy Liar ☐ Cast a Dark Shadow ☐ Charles & Diana: A Royal Love Story ☐ Collector, The ☐ Driver's Seat, The ☐ Fragment of Fear ☐ Good Companions, The ☐ If . . . ☐ Mrs. Brown, You've Got a Lovely Daughter ☐ My Fair Lady ☐ Night Must Fall ☐ One Way Pendulum ☐ Stevie ☐ Third Day, The

Washington, Denzel ☐ Carbon Copy ☐ Cry Freedom ☐ Flesh & Blood ☐ For Queen and Country ☐ George McKenna Story, The ☐ Glory ☐ Heart Condition ☐ John Henry ☐ Malcolm X ☐ Mighty Quinn, The ☐ Mississippi Masala ☐ Mo' Better Blues ☐ Much Ado About Nothing ☐ Pelican Brief, The ☐ Philadelphia ☐ Power ☐ Ricochet ☐ Soldier's Story, A

Waters, Ethel ☐ Cabin in the Sky ☐ Cairo ☐ Member of the Wedding, The ☐ Sound and the Fury, The ☐ Tales of Manhattan

Waters, John ☐ Alice to Nowhere ☐ Breaker Morant ☐ Christmas Visitor, The ☐ End Play ☐ Grievous Bodily Harm ☐ Miracle Down Under ☐ True Colors

Waterston, Sam ☐ Amazing Stories: Book Four ☐ Capricorn One ☐ Crimes and Misdemeanors ☐ Dempsey ☐ Eagle's Wing ☐ Finnegan Begin Again ☐ Fitzwilly ☐ Friendly Fire ☐ Generation ☐ Glass Menagerie, The ☐ Gore Vidal's Lincoln ☐ Great Gatsby, The ☐ Hannah and Her Sisters ☐ Hopscotch ☐ In Defense of Kids ☐ Journey Into Fear ☐ Just Between Friends ☐ Killing Fields, The ☐ Lantern Hill ☐ Man in the Moon, The ☐ Mindwalk ☐ Rancho Deluxe ☐ Reflections of Murder ☐ September ☐ Serial Mom ☐ Warning Sign ☐ Welcome Home

Watson, Lucile ☐ Emperor Waltz, The ☐ Everybody Does It ☐ Florian ☐ Harriet Craig ☐ Ivy ☐ Made for Each Other ☐ Model Wife ☐ Mr. and Mrs. Smith ☐ My Reputation ☐ Never Say Goodbye ☐ Rage in Heaven ☐ Rhythm on the Range ☐ Song of the South ☐ Thin Man Goes Home, The ☐ Tomorrow Is Forever ☐ Uncertain Glory ☐ Watch on the Rhine ☐ Waterloo Bridge ☐ What Every Woman Knows ☐ Women, The

Wayne, David ☐ Adam's Rib ☐ American Christmas Carol, An ☐ Andromeda Strain, The ☐ As Young As You Feel ☐ Big Gamble, The ☐ Down Among the Sheltering Palms ☐ Ellery Queen ☐ Finders Keepers ☐ Front Page, The ☐ Gift of Love, The ☐ Huckleberry Finn ☐ I Don't Care Girl, The ☐ Last Angry Man, The ☐ M ☐ My Blue Heaven ☐ Naked Hills, The ☐ Prize Fighter, The ☐ Reformer and the Redhead, The ☐ Sad Sack, The

☐ Tender Trap, The ☐ Three Faces of Eve, The ☐ Tonight We Sing ☐ Up Front ☐ Wait 'Til the Sun Shines, Nellie ☐ We're Not Married ☐ With a Song in My Heart

Wayne, John ☐ 'Neath the Arizona Skies ☐ Alamo, The ☐ Allegheny Uprising ☐ Angel and the Badman ☐ Baby Face ☐ Back to Bataan ☐ Barbarian and the Geisha, The ☐ Big Jake ☐ Big Jim McLain ☐ Big Trail, The ☐ Blood Alley ☐ Born to the West ☐ Brannigan ☐ Cahill—United States Marshal ☐ California Straight Ahead ☐ Cast a Giant Shadow ☐ Chisum ☐ Circus World ☐ Comancheros, The ☐ Conqueror, The ☐ Cowboys, The ☐ Dakota ☐ Dark Command ☐ Donovan's Reef ☐ El Dorado ☐ Fighting Kentuckian, The ☐ Fighting Seabees, The ☐ Flame of Barbary Coast ☐ Flying Leathernecks ☐ Fort Apache ☐ Frontier Horizon ☐ Greatest Story Ever Told, The ☐ Green Berets, The ☐ Hatari! ☐ Haunted Gold ☐ Hellfighters ☐ High and the Mighty, The ☐ His Private Secretary ☐ Hondo ☐ Horse Soldiers, The ☐ How the West Was Won ☐ Hurricane Express, The ☐ I Cover the War ☐ Idol of the Crowds ☐ In Harm's Way ☐ In Old California ☐ Island in the Sky ☐ Jet Pilot ☐ King of the Pecos ☐ Lady for a Night ☐ Lady from Louisiana ☐ Lady Takes A Chance, A ☐ Lawless Frontier ☐ Lawless Nineties, The ☐ Lawless Range ☐ Legend of the Lost ☐ Long Voyage Home, The ☐ Longest Day, The ☐ Lucky Texan, The ☐ Man Betrayed, A ☐ Man from Monterey ☐ Man from Utah, The ☐ Man Who Shot Liberty Valance, The ☐ McLintock! ☐ McQ ☐ North to Alaska ☐ Operation Pacific ☐ Overland Stage Raiders ☐ Pals of the Saddle ☐ Paradise Canyon ☐ Pittsburgh ☐ Quiet Man, The ☐ Randy Rides Alone ☐ Reap the Wild Wind ☐ Red River ☐ Reunion in France ☐ Ride Him, Cowboy ☐ Riders of Destiny ☐ Rio Bravo ☐ Rio Grande ☐ Rio Lobo ☐ Rooster Cogburn ☐ Salute ☐ Sands of Iwo Jima ☐ Santa Fe Stampede ☐ Sea Chase, The ☐ Searchers, The ☐ Seven Sinners ☐ Shadow of the Eagle ☐ She Wore a Yellow Ribbon ☐ Shepherd of the Hills ☐ Shootist, The ☐ Somewhere in Sonora ☐ Sons of Katie Elder, The ☐ Spoilers, The ☐ Stagecoach ☐ Star Packer, The ☐ Tall in the Saddle ☐ Texas Terror ☐ They Were Expendable ☐ Three Faces West ☐ Three Godfathers, The ☐ Train Robbers, The ☐ Trouble Along the Way ☐ True Grit ☐ Tycoon ☐ Undefeated, The ☐ Wake of the Red Witch ☐ War Wagon, The ☐ West of the Divide ☐ Winds of the Wasteland ☐ Wings of Eagles, The ☐ Without Reservations

Wayne, Naunton ☐ Dead of Night ☐ Hidden Room, The ☐ Lady Vanishes, The ☐ Millions Like Us ☐ Night Train to Munich ☐ Passport to Pimlico ☐ Titfield Thunderbolt, The

Weaver, Sigourney ☐ 1492: Conquest of Paradise ☐ Alien ☐ Alien^3 ☐ Aliens ☐ Dave ☐ Deal of the Century ☐ Death and the Maiden ☐ Eyewitness ☐ Ghostbusters ☐ Ghostbusters II ☐ Gorillas in the Mist ☐ Half Moon Street ☐ Madman ☐ One Woman or Two ☐ Working Girl ☐ Year of Living Dangerously, The

Webb, Clifton ☐ Boy on a Dolphin ☐ Cheaper by the Dozen ☐ Dark Corner, The ☐ Dreamboat ☐ Elopement ☐ For Heaven's Sake ☐ Holiday for Lovers ☐ Laura ☐ Man Who Never Was, The ☐ Mr. Belvedere Goes to College ☐ Mr. Belvedere Rings the Bell ☐ Razor's Edge, The ☐ Remarkable Mr. Pennypacker, The ☐ Satan Never Sleeps ☐ Sitting Pretty ☐ Stars and Stripes Forever ☐ Three Coins in the Fountain ☐ Titanic ☐ Woman's World

Webber, Robert ☐ 10 ☐ 12 Angry Men ☐ Big Bounce, The ☐ Bring Me the Head of Alfredo Garcia ☐ Casey's Shadow ☐ Don't Make Waves ☐ Final Option, The ☐ Highway 301 ☐ Hysteria ☐ Nun and the Sergeant, The ☐ Nuts ☐ Private Benjamin ☐ Revenge of the Pink Panther ☐ Sandpiper, The ☐ Silencers, The

Webb, Jack ☐ Appointment with Danger ☐ D.I., The ☐ Dark City ☐ Dragnet ☐ He Walked by Night ☐ Last Time I Saw Archie, The ☐ Men, The ☐ Original "Dragnet" 1 ☐ Pete Kelly's Blues ☐ You're in the Navy Now

Weidler, Virginia ☐ All This and Heaven Too ☐ Babes on Broadway ☐ Barnacle Bill ☐ Best Foot Forward ☐ Gold Rush Maisie ☐ Great Man Votes, The ☐ Lone Wolf Spy Hunt, The ☐ Maid of Salem ☐ Men with Wings ☐ Mother Carey's Chickens ☐ Outside These Walls ☐ Philadelphia Story, The ☐ Souls at Sea ☐ Under-Pup, The ☐ Women, The ☐ Young Tom Edison ☐ Youngest Profession, The

Weissmuller, Johnny ☐ Cannibal Attack ☐ Captive Girl ☐ Fury of the Congo ☐ Jungle Jim in the Forbidden Land ☐ Jungle Man-Eaters ☐ Jungle Manhunt ☐ Mark of the Gorilla ☐ Tarzan and His Mate ☐ Tarzan and the Amazons ☐ Tarzan and the Leopard Woman ☐ Tarzan and the Mermaids ☐ Tarzan Escapes ☐ Tarzan Finds a Son ☐ Tarzan Triumphs ☐ Tarzan's New York Adventure ☐ Tarzan's Secret Treasure ☐ Tarzan, the Ape Man

Welch, Raquel ☐ 100 Rifles ☐ Bandolero ☐ Bedazzled ☐ Biggest Bundle Of Them All ☐ Bluebeard ☐ Crossed Swords ☐ Fantastic Voyage ☐ Fathom ☐ Flareup ☐ Four Musketeers, The ☐ Fuzz ☐ Hannie Caulder ☐ Kansas City Bomber ☐ Lady in Cement ☐ Last of Sheila, The ☐ Legend of Walks Far Woman, The ☐ Mother, Jugs & Speed ☐ Myra Breckinridge ☐ Oldest Profession, The ☐ One Million Years B.C. ☐ Scandal in a Small Town ☐ Three Musketeers, The ☐ Trouble in Paradise ☐ Wild Party, The

Weld, Tuesday ☐ Author! Author! ☐ Bachelor Flat ☐ Because They're Young ☐ Cincinnati Kid, The ☐ Circle of Violence: A Family Drama, A ☐ F. Scott Fitzgerald in Hollywood ☐ Falling Down ☐ Five Pennies, The ☐ Heartbreak Hotel ☐ High Time ☐ I Walk the Line ☐ I'll Take Sweden ☐ Looking for Mr. Goodbar ☐ Lord Love a Duck ☐ Madame X ☐ Once Upon a Time in America ☐ Play It As It Lays ☐ Pretty Poison ☐ Question of Guilt, A ☐ Rally 'Round the Flag, Boys! ☐ Reflections of Murder ☐ Return to Peyton Place ☐ Rock, Rock, Rock! ☐ Serial ☐ Sex Kittens Go to College ☐ Soldier in the Rain ☐ Thief ☐ Who'll Stop the Rain ☐ Wild in the Country

Weller, Peter ☐ Adventures of Buckaroo Banzai Across the Eighth Dimension, The ☐ Apology ☐ Cat Chaser ☐ Fifty/Fifty ☐ Firstborn ☐ Just Tell Me What You Want ☐ Killing Affair, A ☐ Leviathan ☐ Naked Lunch ☐ New Age, The ☐ Of Unknown Origin ☐ Rainbow Drive ☐ Robocop ☐ Robocop 2 ☐ Shakedown ☐ Shoot the Moon ☐ Women & Men: Stories of Seduction

Welles, Orson ☐ Battle of Austerlitz, The ☐ Battle of Neretva, The ☐ Black Magic ☐ Black Rose, The ☐ Butterfly ☐ Casino Royale ☐ Catch-22 ☐ Chimes at Midnight ☐ Citizen Kane ☐ Compulsion ☐ Crack in the Mirror ☐ Ferry to Hong Kong ☐ Fight for Rome ☐ Finest Hours, The ☐ Follow the Boys ☐ Genocide ☐ Get to Know Your Rabbit ☐ House of Cards ☐ I'll Never Forget What's 'is Name ☐ Immortal Story, The ☐ It Happened One Christmas ☐ It's All True ☐ Jane Eyre ☐ Journey into Fear ☐ King's Story, A ☐ Kremlin Letter, The ☐ Lady from Shanghai, The ☐ Lafayette ☐ Last Roman, The ☐ Long Hot Summer, The ☐ Macbeth ☐ Man for All Seasons, A ☐ Man in the Shadow ☐ Man Who Saw Tomorrow, The ☐ Marco the Magnificent ☐ Moby Dick ☐ Mr. Arkadin ☐ Napoleon ☐ Necromancy ☐ Oedipus the King ☐ Orson Welles' Ghost Story ☐ Othello ☐ Prince of Foxes ☐ Roots of Heaven, The ☐ Royal Affairs in Versailles ☐ Salvador Dali—A Soft-Self Portrait ☐ Someone to Love ☐ Stranger, The ☐ Ten Days Wonder ☐ Ten Days' Wonder ☐ Third Man, The ☐ Three Cases of Murder ☐ Tomorrow Is Forever ☐ Touch of Evil ☐ Transformers, The ☐ Trial, The ☐ V.I.P.s, The ☐ Voyage of the Damned ☐ Waterloo

Werner, Oskar ☐ Decision Before Dawn ☐ Fahrenheit 451 ☐ Interlude ☐ Jules and Jim ☐ Last Ten Days, The ☐ Lola Montes ☐ Ship of Fools ☐ Shoes of the Fisherman, The ☐ Spy Who Came In from the Cold, The ☐ Voyage of the Damned

West, Mae ☐ Belle of the Nineties ☐ Every Day's a Holiday ☐ Go West, Young Man ☐ Goin' to Town ☐ Heat's On, The ☐ I'm No Angel ☐ Klondike Annie ☐ My Little Chickadee ☐ Myra Breckinridge ☐ Night After Night ☐ Sextette ☐ She Done Him Wrong

Weston, Jack ☐ Cactus Flower ☐ Cincinnati Kid, The ☐ Cuba ☐ Dirty Dancing ☐ Fame Is the Name of the Game ☐ Four Seasons, The ☐ Fuzz ☐ Gator ☐ I Love a Mystery ☐ Incredible Mr. Limpet, The ☐ Ishtar ☐ It's Only Money ☐ Marco ☐ Mirage ☐ New Leaf, A ☐ Rad ☐ Ritz, The ☐ Short Circuit 2 ☐ Wait Until Dark

Wheeler, Bert ☐ Cockeyed Cavaliers ☐ Diplomaniacs ☐ Dixiana ☐ Half Shot at Sunrise ☐ Hips, Hips, Hooray ☐ Hold 'Em Jail ☐ Kentucky Kernels ☐ Nitwits, The ☐ Rio Rita

Whitaker, Forest ☐ Article 99 ☐ Bird ☐ Bloodsport ☐ Blown Away ☐ Body Snatchers ☐ Consenting Adults ☐ Criminal Justice ☐ Crying Game, The ☐ Diary of a Hitman ☐ Downtown ☐ Fast Times at Ridgemont High ☐ Good Morning, Vietnam ☐ Jason's Lyric ☐ Last Light ☐ Platoon ☐ Rage in Harlem, A ☐ Ready to Wear

Whitelaw, Billie ☐ Adding Machine, The ☐ Bobbikins ☐ Camille ☐ Charlie Bubbles ☐ Dressmaker, The ☐ Duel of Hearts ☐ Eagle in a Cage ☐ Freddie as F.R.O.7 ☐ Frenzy ☐ Gumshoe ☐ Hell Is a City ☐ I Like Money ☐ Jamaica Inn ☐ Krays, The ☐ Leo the Last ☐ Leopard in the Snow ☐ Lorna Doone ☐ Make Mine Mink ☐ Maurice ☐ Murder Elite ☐ Night Watch ☐ Omen, The ☐ Secret Garden, The ☐ Sleeping Tiger, The ☐ Start the Revolution Without Me ☐ Strange Case of Dr. Jekyll And Mr. Hyde, The ☐ Tale of Two Cities, A ☐ Water Babies, The

Whitman, Stuart ☐ Battleground ☐ Call Him Mr. Shatter ☐ Captain Apache ☐ Cat Creature, The ☐ China Doll ☐ City Beneath the Sea ☐ Comancheros, The ☐ Convicts Four ☐ Crazy Mama ☐ Darby's Rangers ☐ Day and the Hour, The ☐ Decks Ran Red, The ☐ Eaten Alive ☐ Fiercest Heart, The ☐ Francis of Assisi ☐ Guyana: Cult of the Damned ☐ Hound-Dog Man ☐ Invincible Six, The ☐ Johnny Trouble ☐ Kill Castro ☐ Las Vegas Lady ☐ Man Who Died Twice, The ☐ Man Who Wanted to Live Forever, The ☐ Maniac! ☐ Mark, The ☐ Mean Johnny Barrows ☐ Mob Boss ☐ Monster Club, The ☐ Murder, Inc. ☐ Night of the Lepus ☐ Oil ☐ Omega Cop ☐ Private Wars ☐ Rio Conchos ☐ Ruby ☐ Sands of the Kalahari ☐ Smoothtalker ☐ Sound and the Fury, The ☐ Story of Ruth, The ☐ Ten North Frederick ☐ These Thousand Hills ☐ Those Magnificent Men in Their Flying Machines ☐ White Buffalo, The

Whitmore, James ☐ Above and Beyond ☐ Adventures of Mark Twain, The ☐ All the Brothers Were Valiant ☐ Asphalt Jungle, The ☐ Battle Cry ☐ Battleground ☐ Because You're Mine ☐ Black Like Me ☐ Chuka ☐ Command, The ☐ Crime in the Streets ☐ Deep Six, The ☐ Eddy Duchin Story, The

☐ Face of Fire ☐ First Deadly Sin, The ☐ Girl Who Had Everything, The ☐ Give 'em Hell, Harry! ☐ Glory! Glory! ☐ Golden Honeymoon, The ☐ Great Diamond Robbery, The ☐ Guns of the Magnificent Seven ☐ Harrad Experiment, The ☐ High Crime ☐ I Will Fight No More Forever ☐ It's a Big Country ☐ Kiss Me Kate ☐ Last Frontier, The ☐ Madigan ☐ McConnell Story, The ☐ Next Voice You Hear, The ☐ Nobody's Perfect ☐ Nuts ☐ Old Explorers ☐ Please Believe Me ☐ Serpent's Egg, The ☐ Shadow in the Sky ☐ Shawshank Redemption, The ☐ Them ☐ Undercover Man, The ☐ Where the Red Fern Grows ☐ Who Was That Lady?

Whitty, Dame May ☐ Bill of Divorcement, A ☐ Conquest ☐ Constant Nymph, The ☐ Crash Dive ☐ Devotion ☐ Gaslight ☐ Green Dolphin Street ☐ I Met My Love Again ☐ If Winter Comes ☐ Lady Vanishes, The ☐ Lassie Come Home ☐ Mrs. Miniver ☐ My Name Is Julia Ross ☐ Night Must Fall ☐ Raffles ☐ Slightly Dangerous ☐ White Cliffs of Dover, The

Wickes, Mary ☐ Actress, The ☐ By the Light of the Silvery Moon ☐ Dear Heart ☐ Good Morning, Miss Dove ☐ Half a Hero ☐ Higher and Higher ☐ It Happened to Jane ☐ June Bride ☐ Little Women ☐ Ma and Pa Kettle at Home ☐ Man Who Came to Dinner, The ☐ Now, Voyager ☐ On Moonlight Bay ☐ Sister Act ☐ Sister Act 2: Back in the Habit ☐ Touched by Love ☐ Trouble With Angels, The ☐ Where Angels Go, Trouble Follows ☐ Who Done It?

Widmark, Richard ☐ Against All Odds ☐ Alamo, The ☐ All God's Children ☐ Alvarez Kelly ☐ Backlash ☐ Bear Island ☐ Bedford Incident, The ☐ Blackout ☐ Broken Lance ☐ Cheyenne Autumn ☐ Cobweb, The ☐ Cold Sassy Tree ☐ Coma ☐ Death of a Gunfighter ☐ Destination Gobi ☐ Domino Principle, The ☐ Don't Bother to Knock ☐ Down to the Sea in Ships ☐ Final Option, The ☐ Flight from Ashiya ☐ Frogmen, The ☐ Garden of Evil ☐ Gathering of Old Men, A ☐ Halls of Montezuma ☐ Hanky Panky ☐ Hell and High Water ☐ Judgment at Nuremberg ☐ Kiss of Death ☐ Last Wagon, The ☐ Law and Jake Wade, The ☐ Long Ships, The ☐ Madigan ☐ Mr. Horn ☐ Murder on the Bayou ☐ Murder on the Orient Express ☐ Night and the City ☐ No Way Out ☐ O. Henry's Full House ☐ Panic in the Streets ☐ Pickup on South Street ☐ Prize of Gold, A ☐ Red Skies of Montana ☐ Road House ☐ Rollercoaster ☐ Saint Joan ☐ Street with No Name ☐ Swarm, The ☐ Texas Guns ☐ Time Limit ☐ To the Devil A Daughter ☐ True Colors ☐ Tunnel of Love, The ☐ Twilight's Last Gleaming ☐ Two Rode Together ☐ Warlock ☐ Way West, The ☐ When the Legends Die ☐ Yellow Sky

Wiest, Dianne ☐ Bright Lights, Big City ☐ Bullets Over Broadway ☐ Cookie ☐ Cops and Robbersons ☐ Edward Scissorhands ☐ Face of Rage, The ☐ Falling in Love ☐ Footloose ☐ Hannah and Her Sisters ☐ I'm Dancing as Fast as I Can ☐ Independence Day ☐ Little Man Tate ☐ Lost Boys, The ☐ Parenthood ☐ Radio Days ☐ Scout, The ☐ September

Wilde, Cornel ☐ At Sword's Point ☐ Bandit of Sherwood Forest, The ☐ Beach Red ☐ Beyond Mombasa ☐ Big Combo, The ☐ California Conquest ☐ Centennial Summer ☐ Comic, The ☐ Constantine and the Cross ☐ Devil's Hairpin, The ☐ Edge of Eternity ☐ Forever Amber ☐ Four Days Leave ☐ Gargoyles ☐ Greatest Show on Earth, The ☐ Homestretch, The ☐ Hot Blood ☐ It Had to Be You ☐ Knockout ☐ Leave Her to Heaven ☐ Life Begins at Eight-Thirty ☐ Manila Calling ☐ Maracaibo ☐ Naked Prey, The ☐ Norseman, The ☐ Omar Khayyam ☐ Operation Secret ☐ Passion ☐ Road House ☐ Scarlet Coat, The ☐ Sharks' Treasure ☐ Shockproof ☐ Song to Remember, A ☐ Sword of Lancelot ☐ Thousand and One Nights, A ☐ Treasure of the Golden Condor ☐ Two Flags West ☐ Walls of Jericho, The ☐ Woman's World

Wilder, Gene ☐ Adventure of Sherlock Holmes' Smarter Brother, The ☐ Another You ☐ Blazing Saddles ☐ Everything You Always Wanted to Know About Sex (But Were Afraid to Ask) ☐ Frisco Kid, The ☐ Funny About Love ☐ Hanky Panky ☐ Haunted Honeymoon ☐ Little Prince, The ☐ Producers, The ☐ Quackser Fortune Has a Cousin in the Bronx ☐ Rhinoceros ☐ See No Evil, Hear No Evil ☐ Silver Streak ☐ Start the Revolution Without Me ☐ Stir Crazy ☐ Thursday's Game ☐ Willy Wonka and the Chocolate Factory ☐ Woman in Red, The ☐ Young Frankenstein

Wilding, Michael ☐ Best of Enemies, The ☐ Big Blockade, The ☐ Cottage to Let ☐ Courtney Affair, The ☐ Egyptian, The ☐ Four Against Fate ☐ Frankenstein: The True Story ☐ Glass Slipper, The ☐ Ideal Husband, An ☐ Into the Blue ☐ Lady with a Lamp, The ☐ Law and the Lady, The ☐ Maytime in Mayfair ☐ Naked Edge, The ☐ Scarlet Coat, The ☐ Secret Mission ☐ Spring in Park Lane ☐ Spring Meeting ☐ Stage Fright ☐ Three Cockeyed Sailors ☐ Torch Song ☐ Under Capricorn ☐ Waterloo ☐ World of Suzie Wong, The ☐ Zarak

Williams, Billy Dee ☐ Alien Intruder ☐ Bingo Long Traveling All-Stars & Motor Kings, The ☐ Brian's Song ☐ Chiefs ☐ Children of Divorce ☐ Christmas Lilies of the Field ☐ Courage ☐ Empire Strikes Back, The ☐ Fear City ☐ Final Comedown, The ☐ Giant Steps ☐ Glass House, The ☐ Hit ☐ Hostage Tower, The ☐ Imposter, The ☐ Jacksons: An American Dream, The ☐ Lady Sings the Blues ☐ Mahogany ☐ Marvin and Tige ☐ Nighthawks ☐ Number One with a Bullet ☐ Oceans of Fire ☐ Percy and Thunder

☐ Return of the Jedi, The ☐ Right of the People, The ☐ Shooting Stars

Williams, Emlyn ☐ Another Man's Poison ☐ Citadel, The ☐ David Copperfield ☐ Deep Blue Sea, The ☐ Epic that Never Was, The ☐ Eye of the Devil ☐ Girl in the News, The ☐ Hatter's Castle ☐ I Accuse! ☐ Iron Duke, The ☐ Ivanhoe ☐ Jamaica Inn ☐ L-Shaped Room, The ☐ Last Days of Dolwyn, The ☐ Magic Box, The ☐ Major Barbara ☐ My Song for You ☐ Night Alone ☐ Past Caring ☐ Stars Look Down, The ☐ Three Husbands ☐ Web of Evidence ☐ Wreck of the Mary Deare, The

Williams, Esther ☐ Andy Hardy's Double Life ☐ Bathing Beauty ☐ Big Show, The ☐ Dangerous When Wet ☐ Duchess of Idaho ☐ Easy to Love ☐ Easy to Wed ☐ Fiesta ☐ Guy Named Joe, A ☐ Hoodlum Saint, The ☐ Jupiter's Darling ☐ Million Dollar Mermaid ☐ Neptune's Daughter ☐ On an Island with You ☐ Pagan Love Song ☐ Raw Wind in Eden ☐ Skirts Ahoy! ☐ Take Me Out to the Ball Game ☐ Texas Carnival ☐ Thrill of a Romance ☐ Unguarded Moment, The

Williams, JoBeth ☐ Adam ☐ Adam: His Song Continues ☐ American Dreamer ☐ Baby M ☐ Big Chill, The ☐ Chantilly Lace ☐ Child in the Night ☐ Day After, The ☐ Desert Bloom ☐ Dutch ☐ Endangered Species ☐ Memories of Me ☐ My Name is Bill W. ☐ Poltergeist ☐ Poltergeist II: The Other Side ☐ Stir Crazy ☐ Stop! or My Mom Will Shoot ☐ Switch ☐ Teachers ☐ Welcome Home ☐ Wyatt Earp

Williams, John ☐ Dial M for Murder ☐ Emil ☐ Island in the Sun ☐ Sabrina ☐ Secret War of Harry Frigg, The ☐ Solid Gold Cadillac, The ☐ Will Success Spoil Rock Hunter?

Williamson, Fred ☐ Adios Amigo ☐ Big Score, The ☐ Black Caesar ☐ Blind Rage ☐ Boss Nigger ☐ Bucktown ☐ Deadly Impact ☐ Fear in the City ☐ Foxtrap ☐ Hammer ☐ Hell Up In Harlem ☐ Inglorious Bastards ☐ Joshua ☐ Kill Reflex, The ☐ Legend of Nigger Charley, The ☐ Mean Johnny Barrows ☐ Messenger, The ☐ New Gladiators, The ☐ One Down Two to Go ☐ South Beach ☐ Steele's Law ☐ Take a Hard Ride ☐ Three the Hard Way ☐ Warriors of the Wasteland

Williams, Robin ☐ Aladdin ☐ All-Star Salute to the Improv, An ☐ Awakenings ☐ Best of Times, The ☐ Cadillac Man ☐ Can I Do It . . . 'Til I Need Glasses? ☐ Club Paradise ☐ Dead Again ☐ Dead Poets Society ☐ FernGully . . . The Last Rainforest ☐ Fisher King, The ☐ Good Morning, Vietnam ☐ Hook ☐ Moscow on the Hudson ☐ Mrs. Doubtfire ☐ Popeye ☐ Seize the Day ☐ Survivors, The ☐ Toys ☐ World According to Garp, The

Williams, Treat ☐ 1941 ☐ Dead Heat ☐ Deadly Hero ☐ Dempsey ☐ Final Verdict ☐ Flashpoint ☐ Hair ☐ Heart of Dixie ☐ J. Edgar Hoover ☐ Max and Helen ☐ Men's Club, The ☐ Prince of The City ☐ Ritz, The ☐ Streetcar Named Desire, A ☐ Third Degree Burn ☐ Till Death Us Do Part

Williams, Vanessa ☐ Another You ☐ Candyman ☐ D.R.O.P. Squad ☐ Full Exposure: The Sex Tape Scandals ☐ Harley Davidson & the Marlboro Man ☐ Jacksons: An American Dream, The ☐ Kid Who Loved Christmas, The ☐ New Jack City ☐ Pick-up Artist, The ☐ Under the Gun

William, Warren ☐ Case of the Curious Bride, The ☐ Case of the Howling Dog, The ☐ Case of the Lucky Legs, The ☐ Case of the Velvet Claws, The ☐ Cleopatra ☐ Dark Horse ☐ Day-Time Wife ☐ Employees Entrance ☐ Fear ☐ Firefly, The ☐ Go West, Young Man ☐ Gold Diggers of 1933 ☐ Gracie Allen Murder Case, The ☐ Imitation of Life ☐ Lady for a Day ☐ Lone Wolf Keeps a Date, The ☐ Lone Wolf Meets a Lady, The ☐ Lone Wolf Spy Hunt, The ☐ Lone Wolf Strikes, The ☐ Lone Wolf Takes a Chance, The ☐ Madame X ☐ Man in the Iron Mask, The ☐ Match King, The ☐ Mouthpiece, The ☐ One Dangerous Night ☐ Outcast ☐ Passport to Suez ☐ Satan Met a Lady ☐ Secret Bride, The ☐ Secrets of the Lone Wolf ☐ Three on a Match ☐ Upperworld ☐ Wolf Man, The

Willis, Bruce ☐ Billy Bathgate ☐ Blind Date ☐ Bonfire of the Vanities, The ☐ Color of Night ☐ Death Becomes Her ☐ Die Hard ☐ Die Hard 2 ☐ Hudson Hawk ☐ In Country ☐ Last Boy Scout, The ☐ Look Who's Talking ☐ Look Who's Talking Too ☐ Moonlighting ☐ Mortal Thoughts ☐ Nobody's Fool ☐ North ☐ Pulp Fiction ☐ Striking Distance ☐ Sunset

Wills, Chill ☐ Alamo, The ☐ Allegheny Uprising ☐ Barbary Coast Gent ☐ Boom Town ☐ Bronco Buster ☐ Cattle Drive ☐ City That Never Sleeps ☐ Deadly Companions, The ☐ Fireball 500 ☐ Francis ☐ Francis Covers the Big Town ☐ Francis Goes to the Races ☐ Francis Goes to West Point ☐ Francis in the Haunted House ☐ Francis in the Navy ☐ Francis Joins the Wacs ☐ From Hell to Texas ☐ Gallant Bess ☐ Giant ☐ Gun for a Coward ☐ Gun Glory ☐ Guns of a Stranger ☐ Hell's Outpost ☐ High Lonesome ☐ Kentucky Rifle ☐ Man from the Alamo, The ☐ McLintock! ☐ Mr. Billion ☐ Oh! Susanna ☐ Over-the-Hill Gang Rides Again, The ☐ Rio Grande ☐ Rounders, The ☐ Sad Horse, The ☐ Santiago ☐ Sunday Dinner for a Soldier ☐ Trouble in Sundown ☐ Tulsa ☐ Western Union ☐ What Next, Corporal Hargrove? ☐ Wheeler Dealers, The ☐ Yearling, The

Wilson, Marie ☐ Boy Meets Girl ☐ Broadway Musketeers ☐ China Clipper ☐ Fabulous Joe, The ☐ Flying Blind ☐ Fools for Scandal ☐ Girl in Every Port, A ☐ Invisible Menace, The ☐ Marry Me Again ☐ My Friend Irma ☐ My Friend Irma Goes West ☐ Never Wave at a WAC ☐ No Leave, No Love ☐ Satan Met a Lady ☐ Shine On, Harvest Moon ☐ Sweepstakes Winner

Windsor, Marie ☐ Abbott and Costello Meet the Mummy ☐ Bounty Hunter, The ☐ Cat Women of the Moon ☐ Eddie Cantor Story, The ☐ Fighting Kentuckian, The ☐ Force of Evil ☐ Frenchie ☐ Hellfire ☐ Hurricane Island ☐ Island Woman ☐ Japanese War Bride ☐ Little Big Horn ☐ Lovely but Deadly ☐ Mail Order Bride ☐ Narrow Margin, The ☐ No Man's Woman ☐ Outlaw Women ☐ Outpost in Morocco ☐ Parson and the Outlaw, The ☐ Support Your Local Gunfighter ☐ Trouble Along the Way ☐ Two Gun Lady

Winfield, Paul ☐ Angel City ☐ Back to Hannibal: The Return of Tom Sawyer and Huckleberry Finn ☐ Big Shots ☐ Blue City ☐ Brother John ☐ Carbon Copy ☐ Cliffhanger ☐ Conrack ☐ Damnation Alley ☐ Death Before Dishonor ☐ Dennis the Menace ☐ For Us, the Living ☐ Go Tell It on the Mountain ☐ Gordon's War ☐ Greatest, The ☐ Green Eyes ☐ Guilty of Innocence: The Lenell Geter Story ☐ Hero Ain't Northin' But a Sandwich, A ☐ High Velocity ☐ Huckleberry Finn ☐ Hustle ☐ It's Good to Be Alive ☐ King ☐ Mighty Pawns, The ☐ Mike's Murder ☐ Presumed Innocent ☐ R.P.M. ☐ Serpent and the Rainbow, The ☐ Sister, Sister ☐ Sophisticated Gents, The ☐ Sounder ☐ Terminator, The ☐ Twilight's Last Gleaming ☐ White Dog ☐ Women of Brewster Place, The

Winfrey, Oprah ☐ Color Purple, The ☐ Native Son ☐ Women of Brewster Place, The

Winger, Debra ☐ Betrayed ☐ Black Widow ☐ Cannery Row ☐ Dangerous Woman, A ☐ Everybody Wins ☐ French Postcards ☐ Leap of Faith ☐ Legal Eagles ☐ Made in Heaven ☐ Mike's Murder ☐ Officer and a Gentleman, An ☐ Shadowlands ☐ Sheltering Sky, The ☐ Slumber Party '57 ☐ Terms of Endearment ☐ Thank God, It's Friday ☐ Urban Cowboy ☐ Wilder Napalm

Winninger, Charles ☐ Babes in Arms ☐ Barricade ☐ Belle of the Yukon ☐ Beyond Tomorrow ☐ Broadway Rhythm ☐ Cafe Metropole ☐ Champ for a Day ☐ Coney Island ☐ Destry Rides Again ☐ Every Day's a Holiday ☐ Flesh and Fantasy ☐ Flying High ☐ Give My Regards to Broadway ☐ Hard to Get ☐ Hers to Hold ☐ If I Had My Way ☐ Inside Story, The ☐ Lady Takes A Chance, A ☐ Las Vegas Shakedown ☐ Little Nellie Kelly ☐ Living In a Big Way ☐ Lover Come Back ☐ My Life with Caroline ☐ My Love Came Back ☐ Night Nurse ☐ Nothing Sacred ☐ Raymie ☐ Show Boat ☐ Something in the Wind ☐ State Fair ☐ Sun Shines Bright, The ☐ Sunday Dinner for a Soldier ☐ Three Smart Girls ☐ Torpedo Alley ☐ You're a Sweetheart ☐ Ziegfeld Girl

Winningham, Mare ☐ Amber Waves ☐ Crossing to Freedom ☐ Eye on the Sparrow ☐ Fatal Exposure ☐ God Bless the Child ☐ Helen Keller: The Miracle Continues ☐ Intruders ☐ Love Is Never Silent ☐ Made in Heaven ☐ Miracle Mile ☐ Nobody's Fool ☐ Off the Minnesota Strip ☐ Shy People ☐ St. Elmo's Fire ☐ Thorn Birds, The ☐ Threshold ☐ Turner & Hooch ☐ War, The ☐ Winner Never Quits, A ☐ Wyatt Earp

Winters, Jonathan ☐ Alakazam the Great ☐ Alice in Wonderland ☐ Eight on the Lam ☐ Fish that Saved Pittsburgh, The ☐ It's a Mad Mad Mad Mad World ☐ Jonathan Winters on the Ledge ☐ Loved One, The ☐ Moon Over Parador ☐ More Wild, Wild West ☐ Now You See It, Now You Don't ☐ Oh Dad, Poor Dad, Mama's Hung You in the Closet and I'm Feeling So Sad ☐ Penelope ☐ Russians Are Coming! The Russians Are Coming!, The ☐ Say Yes ☐ Shadow, The ☐ Viva Max!

Winters, Shelley ☐ Adventures of Nick Carter ☐ Alfie ☐ Balcony, The ☐ Behave Yourself ☐ Big Knife, The ☐ Bloody Mama ☐ Blume In Love ☐ Buona Sera, Mrs. Campbell ☐ Cash on Delivery ☐ Chapman Report, The ☐ City on Fire ☐ Cleopatra Jones ☐ Cry of the City ☐ Deja Vu ☐ Delta Force, The ☐ Diamonds ☐ Diary of Anne Frank, The ☐ Double Life, A ☐ Elvis ☐ Enter Laughing ☐ Fanny Hill ☐ Flap ☐ Frenchie ☐ Gangster, The ☐ Great Gatsby, The ☐ Harper ☐ He Ran All the Way ☐ Heartbreak Motel ☐ How Do I Love Thee? ☐ I Am a Camera ☐ I Died a Thousand Times ☐ Initiation of Sarah, The ☐ Johnny Stool Pigeon ☐ Journey Into Fear ☐ King of the Gypsies ☐ Knickerbocker Holiday ☐ Larceny ☐ Let No Man Write My Epitaph ☐ Lolita ☐ Mad Room, The ☐ Magician of Lublin, The ☐ Mambo ☐ Meet Danny Wilson ☐ My Man and I ☐ Next Stop, Greenwich Village ☐ Night of the Hunter, The ☐ Odds Against Tomorrow ☐ Over the Brooklyn Bridge ☐ Patch of Blue, A ☐ Pete's Dragon ☐ Phone Call from a Stranger ☐ Pickle, The ☐ Place in the Sun, A ☐ Playgirl ☐ Poseidon Adventure, The ☐ Purple People Eater ☐ Raging Tide, The ☐ S.O.B. ☐ Saskatchewan ☐ Scalphunters, The ☐ Stepping Out ☐ Take One False Step ☐ Tenant, The ☐ Tennessee Champ ☐ Time of Indifference ☐ Unremarkable Life, An ☐ What's the Matter with Helen? ☐ Wild in the Streets ☐ Winchester '73 ☐ Young Savages, The

Withers, Jane ☐ Bright Eyes ☐ Checkers ☐ Farmer Takes a Wife, The ☐ Gentle Julia ☐ Giant ☐ Golden Hoofs ☐ Pack Up Your Troubles ☐ Paddy O'Day ☐ This Is the Life

Wolfe, Ian ☐ 99 River Street ☐ Bedlam ☐ Fountain, The ☐ Homebodies ☐ Invisible Man's Revenge, The ☐ Moonfleet ☐ Mr. Blandings Builds His Dream House ☐ Witness for the Prosecution

Wolfit, Donald ☐ Accursed, The ☐ Becket ☐ Blood of the Vampire ☐ Guilty? ☐ Isn't Life Wonderful! ☐ Man in the Road, The ☐ Mark, The ☐ Silent Passenger, The

Wong, Anna May ☐ Bombs Over Burma ☐ Dangerous to Know ☐ Daughter of Shanghai ☐ Daughter of the Dragon ☐ Ellery Queen's Penthouse Mystery ☐ Island of Lost Men ☐ Java Head ☐ King of Chinatown ☐ Limehouse Blues ☐ Savage Innocents, The ☐ Shanghai Express ☐ Thief of Bagdad, The

Wong, Victor ☐ Dim Sum—A Little Bit of Heart ☐ Eat a Bowl of Tea ☐ Forbidden Nights ☐ Ice Runner, The ☐ Son of Kong, The ☐ Three Ninjas Kick Back

Wood, Natalie ☐ Affair, The ☐ All the Fine Young Cannibals ☐ Blue Veil, The ☐ Bob & Carol & Ted & Alice ☐ Bombers B-52 ☐ Brainstorm ☐ Bride Wore Boots, The ☐ Burning Hills, The ☐ Cash McCall ☐ Chicken Every Sunday ☐ Cracker Factory, The ☐ Cry in the Night, A ☐ Father Was a Fullback ☐ From Here to Eternity ☐ Ghost and Mrs. Muir, The ☐ Girl He Left Behind ☐ Great Race, The ☐ Green Promise, The ☐ Gypsy ☐ Inside Daisy Clover ☐ Jackpot, The ☐ Just for You ☐ Kings Go Forth ☐ Last Married Couple in America, The ☐ Love with the Proper Stranger ☐ Marjorie Morningstar ☐ Memory of Eva Ryker, The ☐ Meteor ☐ Miracle on 34th Street ☐ Never a Dull Moment ☐ No Sad Songs for Me ☐ One Desire ☐ Our Very Own ☐ Peeper ☐ Penelope ☐ Rebel Without a Cause ☐ Scudda Hoo! Scudda Hay! ☐ Searchers, The ☐ Sex and the Single Girl ☐ Splendor in the Grass ☐ Star, The ☐ This Property Is Condemned ☐ Tomorrow Is Forever ☐ West Side Story

Woodard, Alfre ☐ Ambush Murders, The ☐ Blue Chips ☐ Bopha! ☐ Code of Honor ☐ Crooklyn ☐ Cross Creek ☐ Extremities ☐ Freedom Road ☐ Go Tell It on the Mountain ☐ Grand Canyon ☐ Gun in Betty Lou's Handbag, The ☐ H.E.A.L.T.H. ☐ Heart & Souls ☐ Killing Floor, The ☐ Mandela ☐ Miss Firecracker ☐ Passion Fish ☐ Rich in Love ☐ Scrooged ☐ Sophisticated Gents, The ☐ Unnatural Causes

Woods, Donald ☐ 13 Ghosts ☐ Anthony Adverse ☐ Bells of San Fernando ☐ Big Town Girl ☐ Case of the Stuttering Bishop, The ☐ Corregidor ☐ Florentine Dagger, The ☐ Fog Over Frisco ☐ Frisco Kid ☐ Girl from Mexico, The ☐ Heritage of the Desert ☐ Isle of Fury ☐ Mexican Spitfire ☐ Mexican Spitfire Out West ☐ Return of Rin Tin Tin, The ☐ Sea Devils ☐ Story of Louis Pasteur, The ☐ Sweet Adeline ☐ Voice of the Whistler ☐ Wonder Man

Woods, James ☐ Against All Odds ☐ Alex and the Gypsy ☐ Badge of the Assassin ☐ Best Seller ☐ Black Marble, The ☐ Boost, The ☐ Boys, The ☐ Cat's Eye ☐ Choirboys, The ☐ Citizen Cohn ☐ Cop ☐ Diggstown ☐ Disappearance of Aimee, The ☐ Distance ☐ Eyewitness ☐ F. Scott Fitzgerald in Hollywood ☐ Fallen Angels—Volume 1 ☐ Fast-Walking ☐ Gambler, The ☐ Getaway, The ☐ Gift of Love, The ☐ Great American Tragedy, A ☐ Hard Way, The ☐ Holocaust ☐ Immediate Family ☐ In Love and War ☐ Incredible Journey of Doctor Meg Laurel, The ☐ Joshua Then and Now ☐ My Name is Bill W. ☐ Night Moves ☐ Once Upon a Time in America ☐ Onion Field, The ☐ Promise, The ☐ Salvador ☐ Specialist, The ☐ Straight Talk ☐ True Believer ☐ Videodrome ☐ Visitors, The ☐ Women & Men: Stories of Seduction

Woodward, Joanne ☐ Big Hand for the Little Lady, A ☐ Blind Spot ☐ Breathing Lessons ☐ Christmas to Remember, A ☐ Count Three and Pray ☐ Crisis at Central High ☐ Do You Remember Love? ☐ Drowning Pool, The ☐ Effect of Gamma Rays on Man-in-the-Moon Marigolds, The ☐ End, The ☐ Fine Madness, A ☐ Foreign Affairs ☐ From the Terrace ☐ Fugitive Kind, The ☐ Glass Menagerie, The ☐ Harry and Son ☐ Kiss Before Dying, A ☐ Long Hot Summer, The ☐ Mr. & Mrs. Bridge ☐ New Kind of Love, A ☐ No Down Payment ☐ Paris Blues ☐ Rachel, Rachel ☐ Rally 'Round the Flag, Boys! ☐ See How She Runs ☐ Shadow Box, The ☐ Sound and the Fury, The ☐ Stripper, The ☐ Summer Wishes, Winter Dreams ☐ Sybil ☐ They Might Be Giants ☐ Three Faces of Eve, The ☐ Winning

Woolley, Monty ☐ As Young As You Feel ☐ Bishop's Wife, The ☐ Holy Matrimony ☐ Irish Eyes Are Smiling ☐ Kismet ☐ Life Begins at Eight-Thirty ☐ Live, Love and Learn ☐ Man About Town ☐ Man Who Came to Dinner, The ☐ Midnight ☐ Miss Tatlock's Millions ☐ Molly and Me ☐ Never Say Die ☐ Night and Day ☐ Pied Piper, The ☐ Since You Went Away ☐ Young Dr. Kildare

Wray, Fay ☐ Adam Had Four Sons ☐ Affairs of Cellini ☐ Below the Sea ☐ Bowery, The ☐ Bulldog Jack ☐ Clairvoyant, The ☐ Conquering Horde, The ☐ Crime of Passion ☐ Dirigible ☐ Doctor X ☐ Finger Points, The ☐ Gideon's Trumpet ☐ Hell on Frisco Bay ☐ King Kong ☐ Melody for Three ☐ Most Dangerous Game, The ☐ Mystery of the Wax Museum, The ☐ Pointed Heels ☐ Queen Bee ☐ Richest Girl in the World, The ☐ Roaming Lady ☐ Small Town Girl ☐ Tammy and the Bachelor ☐ Thunderbolt ☐ Treasure of the Golden Condor ☐ Vampire Bat, The ☐ Viva Villa! ☐ Wedding March, The

Wright, Robin ☐ Denial ☐ Forrest Gump ☐ Playboys, The ☐ Princess Bride, The ☐ State of Grace ☐ Toys

Wright, Teresa ☐ Actress, The ☐ Best Years of Our Lives, The ☐ Bill: On His Own ☐ California Conquest ☐ Capture, The ☐ Casanova Brown ☐ Enchantment ☐ Escapade in Japan ☐ Golden Honeymoon, The ☐ Good Mother, The ☐ Hail, Hero! ☐ Happy Ending, The ☐ Imperfect Lady, The ☐ Lethal Innocence ☐ Little Foxes, The ☐ Men, The ☐ Mrs. Miniver ☐ Pride of the Yankees, The ☐ Pursued ☐ Roseland ☐ Shadow of a Doubt ☐ Something to Live For ☐ Somewhere in Time ☐ Steel Trap, The ☐ Track of the Cat

Wyman, Jane ☐ All That Heaven Allows ☐ Angel From Texas, An ☐ Bad Men of Missouri ☐ Blue Veil, The ☐ Body Disappears, The ☐ Bon Voyage! ☐ Brother Rat ☐ Brother Rat and a Baby ☐ Cheyenne ☐ Crowd Roars, The ☐ Doughgirls, The ☐ Failing of Raymond, The ☐ Glass Menagerie, The ☐ Here Comes the Groom ☐ Holiday for Lovers ☐ Honeymoon for Three ☐ How to Commit Marriage ☐ Incredible Journey of Doctor Meg Laurel, The ☐ Johnny Belinda ☐ Just for You ☐ King and the Chorus Girl, The ☐ Kiss in the Dark, A ☐ Lady Takes a Sailor, The ☐ Larceny, Inc ☐ Let's Do It Again ☐ Lost Weekend, The ☐ Lucy Gallant ☐ Magic Town ☐ Magnificent Obsession ☐ Make Your Own Bed ☐ Miracle in the Rain ☐ My Love Came Back ☐ Night and Day ☐ One More Tomorrow ☐ Pollyanna ☐ Princess O'Rourke ☐ So Big ☐ Stage Fright ☐ Story of Will Rogers, The ☐ Three Guys Named Mike ☐ Yearling, The ☐ You're in the Army Now

Wynn, Keenan ☐ Absent Minded Professor, The ☐ All the Brothers Were Valiant ☐ Americanization of Emily, The ☐ Angels in the Outfield ☐ Animals, The ☐ Annie Get Your Gun ☐ Around the World Under the Sea ☐ B. F.'s Daughter ☐ Battle Circus ☐ Bay of Saint Michel, The ☐ Belle of New York, The ☐ Best Friends ☐ Between Two Women ☐ Bikini Beach ☐ Black Jack ☐ Cancel My Reservation ☐ Cannon ☐ Clock, The ☐ Coach ☐ Cockeyed Miracle, The ☐ Code Two ☐ Dark, The ☐ Deep Six, The ☐ Desperate Search ☐ Devil's Rain, The ☐ Don't Go Near the Water ☐ Dr. Strangelove or: How I Learned To Stop Worrying and Love the Bomb ☐ Easy to Wed ☐ Fearless Fagan ☐ Finian's Rainbow ☐ For Me and My Gal ☐ Fuzzy Pink Nightgown, The ☐ Glass Slipper, The ☐ Glove, The ☐ Great Man, The ☐ Great Race, The ☐ He Is My Brother ☐ Herbie Rides Again ☐ High Velocity ☐ Holiday for Sinners ☐ Honeymoon Hotel ☐ Hucksters, The ☐ Hyper Sapien—People from Another Star ☐ Internecine Project, The ☐ It's a Big Country ☐ Joe Butterfly ☐ Johnny Concho ☐ Just Tell Me What You Want ☐ Killer Inside Me, The ☐ Kind Lady ☐ Kiss Me Kate ☐ Legend of Earl Durand, The ☐ Long, Long Trailer, The ☐ Lost Angel ☐ Love That Brute ☐ Loving ☐ Lucifer Complex, The ☐ Mackenna's Gold ☐ Man in the Gray Flannel Suit, The ☐ Man in the Middle ☐ Man Who Would Not Die, The ☐ Manipulator, The ☐ Marauders, The ☐ Marriage Is a Private Affair ☐ Mechanic, The ☐ Men of the Fighting Lady ☐ Mirros ☐ Monitors, The ☐ Monster ☐ My Dear Secretary ☐ Naked Hills, The ☐ Neptune's Daughter ☐ Night of the Grizzly ☐ No Leave, No Love ☐ Orca—the Killer Whale ☐ Patsy, The ☐ Perfect Furlough, The ☐ Phone Call from a Stranger ☐ Piano for Mrs. Cimino, A ☐ Piranha ☐ Point Blank ☐ Promise Her Anything ☐ Royal Wedding ☐ Scarface Mob, The ☐ See Here, Private Hargrove ☐ Shaggy D.A., The ☐ Since You Went Away ☐ Smith! ☐ Snowball Express ☐ Son of Flubber ☐ Song of the Thin Man ☐ Stage to Thunder Rock ☐ Stagecoach ☐ Tennessee Champ ☐ Texas Carnival ☐ That Kind of Woman ☐ That Midnight Kiss ☐ Three Little Words ☐ Three Musketeers, The ☐ Time to Love and a Time to Die, A ☐ Viva Max! ☐ War Wagon, The ☐ Warning Shot ☐ Weekend at the Waldorf ☐ Welcome to Hard Times ☐ What Next, Corporal Hargrove? ☐ Without Love

York, Michael ☐ Accident ☐ Alfred the Great ☐ Cabaret ☐ Conduct Unbecoming ☐ Duel of Hearts ☐ England Made Me ☐ Far Country, The ☐ Fedora ☐ Final Assignment ☐ Four Musketeers, The ☐ Great Expectations ☐ Guru, The ☐ Island of Dr. Moreau, The ☐ Justine ☐ Lady and the Highwayman, The ☐ Last Remake of Beau Geste, The ☐ Lethal Obsession ☐ Logan's Run ☐ Lost Horizon ☐ Master of Ballantrae, The ☐ Midnight Cop ☐ Night of the Fox ☐ Phantom of the Opera, The ☐ Return of the Musketeers, The ☐ Riddle of the Sands, The ☐ Romeo and Juliet ☐ Smashing Time ☐ Something for Everyone ☐ Still Life ☐ Taming of the Shrew, The ☐ Three Musketeers, The ☐ Wide Sargasso Sea ☐ Zeppelin

York, Susannah ☐ Alice ☐ American Roulette ☐ Awakening, The ☐ Battle of Britain, The ☐ Brotherly Love ☐ Christmas Carol, A ☐ Conduct Unbecoming ☐ Duffy ☐ Eliza Frazer ☐ Falling in Love Again ☐ Freud ☐ Gold ☐ Golden Gate Murders, The ☐ Happy Birthday, Wanda June ☐ Images ☐ Jane Eyre ☐ Kaleidoscope ☐ Killing of Sister George, The ☐ Lock Up Your Daughters! ☐ Loophole ☐ Loss of Innocence ☐ Maids, The ☐ Man for All Seasons, A ☐ Oh! What a Lovely War ☐ Sands of the Kalahari ☐ Sebastian ☐ Second Chance ☐ Shout, The ☐ Silent Partner, The ☐ Summer Story, A ☐ Superman—The Movie ☐ They Shoot Horses, Don't They? ☐ Tom Jones ☐ Tunes of Glory ☐ X, Y and Zee

Young, Gig ☐ Air Force ☐ Ask Any Girl ☐ Bring Me the Head of Alfredo Garcia ☐ City That Never Sleeps ☐ Come Fill the Cup ☐ Desk Set ☐ Desperate Hours, The ☐ Escape Me Never ☐ Five Miles to Midnight ☐ For Love or Money ☐ Gay Sisters, The ☐ Girl Who Had Everything, The ☐ Great Ice Rip-Off, The ☐ Hindenburg, The ☐ Holiday for Sinners ☐ Hunt the Man Down ☐ Kid Galahad ☐ Lovers and Other Strangers ☐ Lust for Gold ☐ Old Acquaintance ☐ Only the Valiant ☐ Story on Page One, The ☐ Strange Bedfellows ☐ Teacher's Pet ☐ Tell It to the Judge ☐ That Touch of Mink ☐ They

Shoot Horses, Don't They? ☐ Three Musketeers, The ☐ Torch Song ☐ Tunnel of Love, The ☐ Wake of the Red Witch ☐ Woman in White, The ☐ Young at Heart

Young, Loretta ☐ Accused, The ☐ Along Came Jones ☐ And Now Tomorrow ☐ Because of You ☐ Bedtime Story ☐ Big Business Girl ☐ Bishop's Wife, The ☐ Cafe Metropole ☐ Call of the Wild ☐ Caravan ☐ Cause for Alarm ☐ China ☐ Christmas Eve ☐ Clive of India ☐ Come to the Stable ☐ Crusades, The ☐ Devil's in Love, The ☐ Doctor Takes a Wife, The ☐ Employees Entrance ☐ Eternally Yours ☐ Farmer's Daughter, The ☐ Four Men and a Prayer ☐ Grand Slam ☐ Half Angel ☐ Hatchet Man, The ☐ He Stayed for Breakfast ☐ Heroes for Sale ☐ House of Rothschild, The ☐ I Like Your Nerve ☐ It Happens Every Thursday ☐ Kentucky ☐ Key to the City ☐ Ladies Courageous ☐ Ladies in Love ☐ Lady from Cheyenne ☐ Life Begins ☐ Life of Jimmy Dolan, The ☐ Love Is News ☐ Love Under Fire ☐ Man From Blankley's, The ☐ Man's Castle ☐ Men in Her Life, The ☐ Midnight Mary ☐ Mother Is a Freshman ☐ Night to Remember, A ☐ Paula ☐ Perfect Marriage, The ☐ Platinum Blonde ☐ Rachel and the Stranger ☐ Ramona ☐ Second Honeymoon ☐ Shanghai ☐ Story of Alexander Graham Bell, The ☐ Stranger, The ☐ Suez ☐ Taxi! ☐ Three Blind Mice ☐ Truth About Youth, The ☐ Unguarded Hour, The ☐ Wife, Doctor and Nurse ☐ Wife, Husband and Friend ☐ Zoo in Budapest

Young, Robert ☐ Adventure in Baltimore ☐ And Baby Makes Three ☐ Black Camel, The ☐ Bride Comes Home, The ☐ Bride for Sale ☐ Bride Walks Out, The ☐ Bride Wore Red, The ☐ Cairo ☐ Canterville Ghost, The ☐ Claudia ☐ Claudia and David ☐ Crossfire ☐ Dr. Kildare's Crisis ☐ Emperor's Candlesticks, The ☐ Enchanted Cottage, The ☐ Florian ☐ Goodbye, My Fancy ☐ H.M. Pulham, Esq. ☐ Half-Breed, The ☐ Honolulu ☐ I Met Him in Paris ☐ It's Love Again ☐ Joe Smith, American ☐ Josette ☐ Journey for Margaret ☐ Kid from Spain, The ☐ Lady Be Good ☐ Little Women ☐ Maisie ☐ Marcus Welby, M.D. ☐ Marcus Welby, M.D.: A Holiday Affair ☐ Married Bachelor ☐ Miracles for Sale ☐ Mortal Storm, The ☐ Navy Blue and Gold ☐ Northwest Passage ☐ Paradise for Three ☐ Rich Man, Poor Girl ☐ Saturday's Millions ☐ Searching Wind, The ☐ Secret Agent ☐ Secret of the Incas ☐ Shining Hour, The ☐ Sin of Madelon Claudet, The ☐ Sitting Pretty ☐ Slightly Dangerous ☐ Spitfire ☐ Stowaway ☐ Strange Interlude ☐ Sweet Rosie O'Grady ☐ That Forsythe Woman ☐ They Won't Believe Me ☐ Three Comrades ☐ Today We Live ☐ Tugboat Annie ☐ Vagabond Lady ☐ West Point of the Air ☐ Western Union ☐ Wet Parade, The ☐ Whom the Gods Destroy

Young, Roland ☐ Ali Baba Goes to Town ☐ And Then There Were None ☐ Bishop Murder Case ☐ Bond Street ☐ Dulcy ☐ Flame of New Orleans, The ☐ Give Me Your Heart ☐ Great Lover, The ☐ Guardsman, The ☐ Gypsy ☐ Here I Am a Stranger ☐ Here Is My Heart ☐ His Double Life ☐ Irene ☐ King Solomon's Mines ☐ Lady Has Plans, The ☐ Let's Dance ☐ Madam Satan ☐ Man Who Could Work Miracles, The ☐ One Rainy Afternoon ☐ Philadelphia Story, The ☐ Squaw Man, The ☐ St. Benny the Dip ☐ Standing Room Only ☐ Star Dust ☐ They All Kissed the Bride ☐ This Is the Night ☐ Topper ☐ Topper Returns ☐ Topper Takes a Trip ☐ Two-Faced Woman ☐ Unguarded Hour, The ☐ Wedding Rehearsal ☐ Young in Heart, The

Young, Sean ☐ Baby . . . Secret of the Lost Legend ☐ Blade Runner ☐ Blood & Orchids ☐ Blue Ice ☐ Boost, The ☐ Cousins ☐ Fatal Instinct ☐ Firebirds ☐ Hold Me, Thrill Me, Kiss Me ☐ Kiss Before Dying, A ☐ Love Crimes ☐ No Way Out ☐ Once Upon a Crime ☐ Sketch Artist ☐ Stripes ☐ Under the Biltmore Clock ☐ Wall Street ☐ Young Doctors in Love

Zetterling, Mai ☐ Abandon Ship! ☐ Bad Lord Byron ☐ Bay of Saint Michel, The ☐ Desperate Moment ☐ Faces in the Dark ☐ Frieda ☐ Frightened Bride ☐ Girl in the Painting ☐ Knock on Wood ☐ Main Attraction, The ☐ Man Who Finally Died, The ☐ Night Is My Future ☐ Only Two Can Play ☐ Prize of Gold, A ☐ Torment ☐ Truth About Women, The ☐ Witches, The

Zimbalist, Jr., Efrem ☐ Airport '75 ☐ Avenging, The ☐ Band of Angels ☐ Batman: Mask of the Phantom ☐ Best Place to Be, The ☐ Bombers B-52 ☐ By Love Possessed ☐ Chapman Report, The ☐ Crowded Sky, The ☐ Deep Six, The ☐ Family Upside Down, A ☐ Fever in the Blood, A ☐ Gathering, Part II, The ☐ Harlow ☐ Reward, The ☐ Too Much, Too Soon ☐ Wait Until Dark

Zimbalist, Stephanie ☐ Agatha Christie's The Man in the Brown Suit ☐ Caroline? ☐ Elvis and the Beauty Queen ☐ Forever ☐ Jericho Fever ☐ Killing Mind, The ☐ Letter to Three Wives, A ☐ Magic of Lassie, The ☐ Story Lady, The

Zucco, George ☐ Adventures of Sherlock Holmes, The ☐ Black Raven, The ☐ Desire Me ☐ Fast Company ☐ Firefly, The ☐ Flying Serpent, The ☐ Fog Island ☐ Mad Ghoul, The ☐ Mad Monster, The ☐ Man Who Could Work Miracles, The ☐ Monster and the Girl, The ☐ Mummy's Ghost, The ☐ Mummy's Hand, The ☐ Mummy's Tomb, The ☐ My Favorite Blonde ☐ New Moon ☐ Return of the Ape Man ☐ Saratoga ☐ Seventh Cross, The ☐ Sherlock Holmes in Washington ☐ Souls at Sea ☐ Sudan ☐ Suez ☐ Weekend at the Waldorf

FILMS BY CATEGORY

ACTION

Abdulla the Great
Above The Law
Above Us The Waves
Ace Eli and Rodger of the Skies
Ace of Aces
Aces High
Aces: Iron Eagle III
Across 110th Street
Across the Bridge
Across the Great Divide
Act of Piracy
Action in the North Atlantic
Action Jackson
Action of the Tiger
Adventure Island
Adventures of Babar
Adventures of Babar—Vol. 2
Adventures of Babar—Vol. 3
Adventures of Captain Fabian
Adventures of Casanova
Adventures of China Smith
Adventures of Don Juan
Adventures of Hajji Baba, The
Adventures of Ichabod and Mr. Toad, The
Adventures of Robin Hood, The
Adventures of Scaramouche
Adventures of Sinbad, The
Adventures of Smilin' Jack
Adventures of Superman
Adventures of Teddy Ruxpin
Aerial Gunner
Africa—Texas Style
African Rage
African Treasure
After the Shock
Against All Flags
Against the Drunken Cat Paws
Air America
Air Force
Air Mail
Aladdin and His Magic Lamp
Alakazam the Great
Alamut Ambush, The
Albino
Alcatraz: The Whole Shocking Story
Alexa: A Prostitute's Own Story
Alfred the Great
Ali Baba and the Forty Thieves
Alice to Nowhere
Alien Women
Alive
Allan Quartermain And The Lost City Of Gold
Allegheny Uprising
Alone on the Pacific
Amateur, The
Amazing Dobermans, The
Ambush Bay
American Cyborg—Steel Warrior
American Guerilla in the Philippines
American Ninja
American Ninja 2: The Confrontation
American Ninja 3: Blood Hunt
American Ninja 4: The Annihilation
American Tiger
Americano, The (1916)
Americano, The (1955)
Amsterdam Kill, The
And Millions Will Die
And Then You Die
Anderson Tapes, The
Angel
Angel River
Angel III—Final Chapter, The
Angel Town
Angel Unchained
Angels' Brigade
Angels Die Hard
Angels From Hell
Angels Hard as They Come
Angels of the City
Angels One Five
Angry Hills, The
Anne of the Indies
Annihilators, The
Anzacs: The War Down Under
Arabesque
Arabian Adventure
Arabian Nights
Archer's Adventure
Arizona Heat
Ark of the Sun God . . . Temple of Hell, The
Around the World in 80 Days
Arrogant, The
Assassin
Assassination
Assassination Game, The
Assassination Run, The
Assault of the Rebel Girls
Assault on Agathon
Assault on Precinct 13
Assault on the Wayne
Assault with a Deadly Weapon
Assignment in Brittany
Assignment K
Assignment—Paris
Assignment to Kill
At Gunpoint
At Sword's Point
Atlantis, the Lost Continent
Atlas
Atomic City, The
Ator, the Fighting Eagle
Attack Force Z
Attack on the Iron Coast
Attila
Avalanche
Avalanche Express
Avenging Angel
Avenging Force
Away All Boats
Baby . . . Secret of the Lost Legend
Back Door to Hell
Back From Eternity
Back to Bataan
Back to God's Country
Background to Danger
Bad Attitude
Bad Company
Bad Georgia Road
Bad Girls Dormitory
Badge 373
Baffled
Bagdad
Bail Out
Ballad of a Bounty Hunter
Ballad of Death Valley
Bamboo Prison, The
Band of the Hand
Bandit of Sherwood Forest, The
Bandit of Zhobe, The
Bandits of Corsica, The
Barbarians, The
Barbary Coast
Barefoot Mailman, The
Baron Münchausen
Baron's African War, The
Barricade
Barry Mackenzie Holds His Own
Batman
Batman: Mask of the Phantom
Batman Returns
Batman—The Movie
Batmen of Africa
Battle at Bloody Beach
Battle Cry
Battle Hell (Yangtse Incident)
Battle Hymn
Battle of Austerlitz, The
Battle of El Alamein
Battle of the Bulge
Battle of the Coral Sea
Battle Stations
Battle Taxi
Battle Zone
Bay of Saint Michel, The
Baywatch: Panic at Malibu Pier
Beach Red

Beachhead
Bear Island
Beast, The
Beastmaster, The
Beastmaster 2: Through the Portal of Time
Beau Geste (1939)
Beau Geste (1966)
Bedford Incident, The
Behind Enemy Lines
Behind the Rising Sun
Below the Sea
Bengal Brigade
Bengazi
Berlin Conspiracy, The
Beryl Markham: A Shadow on the Sun
Best of the Best
Best Revenge
Betrayal from the East
Better Tomorrow, A
Between Midnight and Dawn
Beverly Hills Cop
Beverly Hills Cop II
Beverly Hills Cop III
Beyond Atlantis
Beyond Fear
Beyond Justice
Beyond Mombasa
Beyond the Poseidon Adventure
Big Bad John
Big Bad Mama
Big Bad Mama II
Big Bird Cage, The
Big Brawl, The
Big Bust-Out, The
Big Cage, The
Big Combo, The
Big House, U.S.A.
Big Jim McLain
Big Land, The
Big Parade, The
Big Red One, The
Big Score, The
Big Trouble in Little China
Big Wheel, The
Biggles: Adventures in Time
Billy Jack
Billy Jack Goes to Washington
Bionic Showdown: The Six Million Dollar Man and the Bionic Woman
Bird With the Crystal Plumage, The
Birds of Prey
Birgit Haas Must Be Killed
Black Belt Jones
Black Castle, The
Black Cross
Black Dragon of Manzanar
Black Eagle
Black Force
Black Gestapo, The
Black Gold
Black Gunn
Black Knight, The
Black Mama, White Mama
Black Pirate, The
Black Pirates, The
Black Rain
Black Rose, The
Black Shield of Falworth, The
Black Six, The
Black Stallion, The
Black Stallion Returns, The
Black Sunday
Black Swan, The
Black Watch, The
Black Water Gold
Blackbeard, the Pirate
Blackout
Blade
Blind Fury
Blind Rage
Blind Vengeance
Blood Alley
Blood Barrier
Blood in the Streets
Blood of Heroes, The
Bloodfist
Bloodfist 2
Bloodfist III—Forced to Fight
Bloodmatch
Bloodsport
Blown Away
Blue Fin
Blue Steel
Blue Thunder
Blue, White and Perfect
Blue Yonder, The
BMX Bandits
Boatniks, The
Bobbie Jo and the Outlaw
Boiling Point
Bold and the Brave, The
Bold Caballero, The
Bomba and the Elephant Stampede
Bomba and the Jungle Girl
Bomba on Panther Island
Bomba the Jungle Boy
Bombardier
Bonnie Parker Story, The
Borderline
Born American
Born Losers
Born to Race
Bounty Hunter, The (1954)
Bounty Hunter, The (1989)
Bounty Man, The
Bounty Tracker
Boy and the Pirates
Boy from Indiana
Braddock: Missing in Action III
Brady's Escape
Brannigan
Brass Target, The
Brave Little Toaster, The
Breaker! Breaker!
Breaking Loose
Breaking Point (1976)
Breaking Point (1989)
Breakout
Breathing Fire
Brenda Starr (1976)
Brenda Starr (1992)
Brides of Fu Manchu, The
Bridge at Remagen, The
Bridges at Toko-Ri, The
Bring Me the Head of Alfredo Garcia
Bronk
Brotherhood of the Rose
Brothers in Arms
Brothers Lionheart, The
Bruce Lee Fights Back From The Grave
Buccaneer, The (1938)
Buccaneer, The (1958)
Buccaneer's Girl
Bucktown
Bullet for Stefano
Bulletproof
Bullies
Bullitt
Burglar
Burma Convoy
Burn!
Bury Me an Angel
Bush Christmas
Bushido Blade, The
Cage
Caged Heat
Caged in Paradiso
Caged Terror
California Straight Ahead
Call Him Mr. Shatter
Call of the Wild
Callan
Camel Boy, The
Canadian Pacific
Canadians, The
Canaris
Candy Tangerine Man, The
Cannibal Attack
Cannonball
Cape Town Affair, The
Capricorn One
Captain America
Captain America II
Captain Blackjack
Captain Blood (1935)
Captain Blood (1960)
Captain Caution
Captain Falcon
Captain from Castile
Captain Fury
Captain Horatio Hornblower
Captain Kidd
Captain Kidd and the Slave Girl
Captain Lightfoot
Captain Nemo and the Underwater City
Captain of the Clouds
Captain Pirate
Captain Scarlett
Captain Sinbad
Captive Girl
Cargo to Capetown
Caribbean
Cartel
Carthage in Flames
Cassandra Crossing, The
Castillan, The
Castle Keep
Castle of Cagliostro
Catch Me a Spy
Center of the Web
Central Airport
Chain Gang Killings, The
Chained Heat
Chained Heat 2
Challenge
Challenge for Robin

Hood, A
Challenge of the Masters
Challenge, The
Challenge to White Fang
Chance
Charge of the Black Lancers
Charge of the Light Brigade, The (1936)
Charge of the Light Brigade, The (1968)
Charlie Muffin
Charlie, the Lonesome Cougar
Chase, The
Checkered Flag or Crash
China Clipper
China Corsair
China Gate
China Girl
China Lake Murders, The
China Venture
Chinese Boxes
Chinese Connection
Christmas Comes to Willow Creek
Chrome and Hot Leather
Chrome Soldiers
C.I.A.: Code Name Alexa
Circle of Iron
City Beneath the Sea
City on Fire
Clash of Steel
Class of 1999
Claw Monsters, The
Clear and Present Danger
Cleopatra Jones
Cleopatra Jones and the Casino of Gold
Cliffhanger
Cloak & Dagger
Clouds over Europe
Coast Guard
Coast of Skeletons
Cobra
Cobra, The
Cocaine Wars
Cockleshell Heroes, The
Code Name—Emerald
Code Name, Red Roses
Code of Silence
Code of the Secret Service
Code 7 Victim 5
Code 645
Codename: Kyril
Codename—Wildgeese
Coffy
Cold River
Cold Sweat
Colditz Story
Colossus of Rhodes, The
Combat Squad
Come Spy With Me
Command Decision
Commando
Commandos Strike at Dawn, The
Company Business
Conan the Barbarian
Conan the Destroyer
Concrete Jungle, The
Condorman
Convoy
Cops and Robbers
Corsican Brothers, The
Corvette K-225
Count Five and Die
Count of Monte Cristo, The
Counter-Attack
Crash Dive
Crimson Pirate, The
Cross of Lorraine, The
Crow, The
Crowded Sky, The
Cry Danger
Cry Havoc
Cry in the Wild, A
Damn the Defiant!
Dan Candy's Law
Dangerous Exile
Dangerous Summer, A
Daniel Boone
Daring Dobermans, The
Dark of the Sun
Darkman
Dawn Patrol, The
Day of the Dolphin, The
Day Will Dawn, The
Dead Reckoning
Deadline
Deadlock
Deadly Vengeance
Death Before Dishonor
Death Hunt
Death of the Incredible Hulk, The
Death Race 2000
Death Warrant
Death Wish
Death Wish II
Death Wish 3
Death Wish 4: The Crackdown
Death Wish 5
Deathsport
Deceivers, The
Decision Against Time
Decks Ran Red, The
Deep Cover
Deep Six, The
Deep, The
Deerslayer, The (1957)
Deerslayer, The (1978)
Defiance
Delta Force, The
Delta Force 2—Operation Stranglehold
Deluge
Demolition Man
Desert Attack
Desert Hawk, The
Desperate
Destination Gobi
Destructors, The
Devil Dogs of the Air
Devil-Ship Pirates, The
Devil's Brigade, The
Devil's Hairpin, The
Devil's Playground
Devlin
Diamond Jim
Diamonds Are Forever
Dick Turpin
Die Hard
Die Hard 2
Dirty Dozen, The
Dirty Dozen, The: The Next Mission
Dirty Mary, Crazy Larry
Dirty Work
Disco Godfather
Dixie Dynamite
Do or Die
Doberman Gang, The
Doc Savage: The Man of Bronze
Dog Eat Dog
Dogs of War, The
Dolemite
Dolemite II: The Human Tornado
Dollman
Don Q, Son of Zorro
Double Dragon
Double Impact
Down Twisted
Dr. Minx
Dr. No
Dr. Syn
Dr. Syn, Alias the Scarecrow
Dragon Fist
Dragon: The Bruce Lee Story
Dragon vs. Needles of Death
Dragon's Showdown, The
Driver, The
Driving Force
Drop Zone
Drums Along the Mohawk
Duck, You Sucker
Duel
Duel of the Seven Tigers
Duel of the Titans
Dynamo
Eagle and the Hawk, The (1933)
Eagle and the Hawk, The (1950)
Eagle Squadron
Earthquake
East L.A. Warriors
East of Sumatra
Ebony, Ivory and Jade
Eddie Macon's Run
Eiger Sanction, The
Eighteen Jade Arhats, The
84 Charlie Mopic
El Mariachi
Embassy
Emperor Caligula
Emperor of the Bronx
Emperor of the North, The
Empire State
Enemy Agent
Enigma
Entangled
Enter the Dragon
Enter the Game of Death
Enter the Ninja
Escape from Alcatraz
Escape from New York
Escape from Sobibor
Escape from the Bronx
Escape from Yesterday
Escape from Zahrain
Escape in the Desert
Escape to Athena
Escape to the Sun
Espionage Agent
Esther Waters
Eternal Sea, The
Eve of Destruction

Every Bastard a King
Everything Is Thunder
Evil That Men Do
Ewoks: The Battle for Endor
Excessive Force
Executioner, Part II, The
Exit Dragon, Enter Tiger
Exterminator, The
Exterminator II
Extreme Justice
Extreme Prejudice
Eye for an Eye, An
Eye of the Tiger
F/X
F/X2
Fabiola
Fabulous Baron Munchausen, The
Face in the Rain, A
Face of the Frog
Fair Game
Fair Wind to Java
Fake-Out
Falcon's Gold
Family of Spies
Family Rico, The
Family, The
Famous Five Get Into Trouble, The
Far From Home: The Adventures of Yellow Dog
Far Off Place, A
Farewell Again
Farmer, The
Fast and the Furious, The
Fast Charlie, The Moonbeam Rider
Fast Lane Fever
Fast Money
Faster Pussycat . . . Kill! Kill!
Fatal Confession: A Father Dowling Mystery
Fatal Justice
Fatal Mission
Fatal Witness, The
Fate of Lee Khan, The
FBI Girl
FBI Story, The
F.B.I. Story, The—The FBI Versus Alvin Karpis, Public Enemy Number One
Fear City
Fear Stalk
Fearless Fighters
Fearless Hyena, The
Fearless Hyena, The—Part 2
Fearless Young Boxer
Federal Agents vs. Underworld, Inc.
Federal Manhunt
Fer-de-Lance
Ferry to Hong Kong
ffolkes
Fiction Makers, The
Field of Fire
Fiercest Heart, The
Fifth Musketeer, The
Fight for Us
Fight for Your Life
Fight to the Death
Fight to Win
Fighter Attack
Fighter Squadron
Fighting Back
Fighting Black Kings
Fighting Devil Dogs, The
Fighting Guardsman
Fighting Kentuckian, The
Fighting Mad
Fighting O'Flynn, The
Fighting Pimpernel, The
Fighting Prince of Donegal, The
Fighting Seabees, The
Fighting 69th, The
Fighting Wildcats, The
Final Alliance
Final Approach
Final Comedown, The
Final Cut
Final Impact
Final Justice
Final Option, The
Finest Hour
Finger on the Trigger
Fire!
Fire and Sword
Fire, Ice and Dynamite
Fire in the Stone, The
Fire! Trapped on the 37th Floor
Fireback
Fireball 500
Fireball Forward
Firebirds
Firecracker
Firefight
Firefox
Firehead
Firehouse
Firepower
Firewalker
Firing Line, The
First Blood
First to Fight
Fist Fighter
Fist of Honor
Fist of Steel
Fist of Vengeance
Fists of Blood
Fists of Bruce Lee
Fists of Dragons
Fists of Fury
Fists of Fury 2
Fit to Kill
Five Came Back
Five Fighters from Shaolin
Five Fingers of Death
Five for Hell
Five Golden Dragons
Five Graves to Cairo
Five Steps to Danger
Five Weeks in a Balloon
Fix, The
Fixed Bayonets
Flame and the Arrow, The
Flame of Araby
Flame of Calcutta
Flame of Stamboul
Flame over India
Flaming Feather
Flaming Frontier
Flash and the Firecat
Flashback
Flashpoint
Flatfoot
Flaxy Martin
Flesh + Blood
Flesh & Blood
Fleshburn
Flight
Flight into Nowhere
Flight Lieutenant
Flight 90: Disaster on the Potomac
Flight Nurse
Flight of Black Angel
Flight of the Lost Balloon
Flight, The
Flight to Fury
Flight to Nowhere
Flood!
Florida Straits
Flying Blind
Flying Fool, The
Flying Leathernecks
Flying Missile, The
Follow That Car
For Your Eyes Only
Force: Five
Force of One, A
Force on Thunder Mountain
Force 10 from Navarone
Forced Vengeance
Forever Fairytales—Rudyard Kipling
Forgotten, The
Forgotten Warrior
Fort Ti
Fortress
Fortune in Diamonds
Fortunes of Captain Blood, The
49th Parallel
Forty Thousand Horsemen
Four Deuces, The
Four Feathers, The
Four Musketeers, The
Fourth Man, The
Foxhole in Cairo
Foxtrap
Foxy Brown
Francis Gary Powers: The True Story of the U-2 Spy Incident
Free Ride
French Connection, The
French Connection II
French Conspiracy, The
Frenchman's Creek
Frenchman's Farm
Fresh Kill
Friday Foster
Frogmen, The
From Hell to Borneo
From Hell to Victory
From Russia with Love
Full Contact
Full Metal Ninja
Furious
Furious Avenger, The
Furious, The
Fury at Smugglers Bay
Fury of Hercules, The
Fury of King Boxer
Fury of the Congo
Fury of the Pagans
Fury On Wheels
G-Men
Gallagher's Travels
Gallant Hours, The
Game of Death
Game of Death, A
Game, The
Gang War
Gang Wars
Gator
Gator Bait
Gator Bait II
Ghetto Blaster
Ghost Diver
Ghost in the Machine

His Kind of Woman
Hit
Hit List
Hitchhikers, The
Hitler—Dead or Alive
Hitler's S.S.: Portrait in Evil
Hitman, The
Hitter, The
Hockey Night
Holcroft Convenant, The
Hollywood Man
Home in Indiana
Homeward Bound: The Incredible Journey
Honeybaby
Hong Kong Affair
Hong Kong Nights
Honky Tonk
Honor and Glory
Hooked Generation
Hornet's Nest
Horse Without a Head, The
Hostage (1987)
Hostage (1992)
Hostage Flight
Hostage Tower, The
Hostile Takeover
Hot Box, The
Hot Potato
Hot Rod
Hot Rods to Hell
Hour of the Assassin
House by the Lake, The
House of Bamboo
House of Numbers
House of Women
How to Steal an Airplane
Howards of Virginia
Huck and the King of Hearts
Human Factor, The
Human Shield, The
Hundra
Hunt for Red October, The
Hunt, The
Hunted
Hunter, The
Hunter's Blood
Hunters of the Golden Cobra
Hurricane
Hurricane Island
Hurricane Smith
I Come in Peace
I Escaped from Devil's Island
I Escaped from the Gestapo
I Spit On Your Corpse
I Spy Returns
Ice
Ice Palace
Ice Pirates, The
Ice Runner, The
Ill Met by Moonlight
Image of Bruce Lee, The
Immortal Battalion, The
Impasse
Imposter, The
In Enemy Country
In Hot Pursuit
In Like Flint
In Search of the Castaways
In the Shadow of Kilimanjaro
In Too Deep
In Your Face
Inchon
Incredible Hulk, The
Incredible Hulk Returns, The
Incredible Journey, The
Incredible Master Beggars
Indian Tomb, The
Indiana Jones and the Last Crusade
Indiana Jones and the Temple of Doom
Indio
Indio 2: The Revolt
Inferno in Paradise
Infinity
Inglorious Bastards
Innocent Bystanders
Inside Out
Inside the Walls of Folsom Prison
Instant Justice
Instructor, The
Insult
Intent to Kill
International Lady
International Settlement
Into the Badlands
Into the Homeland
Invasion, U.S.A.
Invincible Gladiators, The
Invincible Sword, The
Invisible Man Returns, The
Ipcress File, The
Iron Dragon Strikes Back
Iron Eagle
Iron Eagle II
Iron Glove, The
Iron Thunder
Iron Warrior
Island at the Top of the World, The
Island, The
Island Trader
Island Warriors
Istanbul
Istanbul Express
It Couldn't Happen Here
Ivanhoe (1952)
Ivanhoe (1982)
Jackson County Jail
Jaguar (1956)
Jaguar (1977)
Jaguar Lives!
Jakarta
Jake Speed
Jamaica Inn
Jarrett
Jason and the Argonauts
Jaws
Jaws 2
Jaws 3
Jaws of Justice
Jaws of the Dragon
Jaws, The Revenge
Jazz Age, The
Jet Over the Atlantic
Jewel of the Nile
Jigsaw
Jivaro
Jive Turkey
Joe Palooka, Champ
Joe Palooka in the Big Fight
Joe Palooka in the Counterpunch
Joe Palooka in the Squared Circle
Joe Palooka in Triple Cross
Joe Palooka in Winner Take All
Joe Palooka Meets Humphrey
Johnny Dark
Joniko and the Kush Ta Ta
Journey of Honor
Journey's End
Joyride
Joyride to Nowhere
Judgment Night
Judo Saga
Judo Showdown
Juggernaut
Jungle Assault
Jungle Bride
Jungle Gold
Jungle Jim in the Forbidden Land
Jungle Man-Eaters
Jungle Manhunt
Jungle Master, The
Jungle Princess, The
Jungle Warriors
Jungle Woman
Junkman
Jurassic Park
Just Tell Me You Love Me
K2—The Ultimate High
Karate Cop
Karate Cops
Karate Warrior
Keeper of the City
Kelly's Heroes
Key to Rebecca, The
KGB—the Secret War
Khartoum
Khyber Patrol
Kick or Die
Kickboxer
Kickboxer 3—The Art of War
Kid
Kid Colter
Kid Galahad
Kidnap Syndicate
Kidnapped (1938)
Kidnapped (1960)
Kidnapping of the President, The
Kill and Kill Again
Kill Castro
Kill! Kill! Kill!
Kill Line
Kill or Be Killed
Kill Reflex, The
Kill Slade
Kill the Ninja
Killcrazy
Killer Elephants, The
Killer Elite, The
Killer Fish
Killer Force
Killer Likes Candy, The
Killer, The
Killers
Killer's Edge, The
Killers of Kilimanjaro
Killing Cars
Killing Device, The
Killpoint
Killzone
Kim (1950)
Kim (1984)
King Arthur, the Young Warlord
King Boxer
King Boxers, The
King Kong
King Kung Fu
King of the Forest Rangers

King of the Jungle
King of the Khyber Rifles
King of the Kickboxers
King of the Mountain
King Solomon's Mines (1937)
King Solomon's Mines (1950)
King Solomon's Mines (1985)
Kings of the Sun
King's Ransom
Kinjite: Forbidden Subjects
Kiss Daddy Goodbye
Kiss the Night
Klansman, The
Klondike Fever
Knightriders
Knights of the City
Knights of the Round Table
Kowloon Assignment
Krakatoa, East of Java
Krull
Kuffs
Kung Fu
Kung Fu Genius
Kung Fu—The Movie
L.A. Heat
L.A. Vice
Ladies Club, The
Lady and the Highwayman, The
Lady Avenger
Lady Cocoa
Lady Dragon
Lady Dragon 2
Lady Ice
Lady in the Iron Mask
Lady Terminator
Ladyhawke
Lafayette
Laguna Heat
Laser Mission
Lassiter
Last Action Hero
Last Bastion, The
Last Boy Scout, The
Last Chase, The
Last Day of the War, The
Last Days of Pompeii, The
Last Dragon, The
Last Flight Out
Last Flight to Hell
Last Hunter, The
Last Man Standing
Last of the Buccaneers, The
Last of the Finest, The
Last of the Mohicans, The (1920)
Last of the Mohicans, The (1936)
Last of the Mohicans, The (1977)
Last of the Mohicans, The (1992)
Last of the Redmen
Last of the Ski Bums
Last of the Vikings, The
Last Outpost, The
Last Plane Out
Last Reunion, The
Last Riders
Last Roman, The
Last Safari, The
Last Season, The
Last Warrior, The
Laughing Policeman, The
Le Secret
Left Hand of God, The
Legend of Billie Jean, The
Legend of Black Thunder Mountain, The
Legend of the Eight Samurai
Legend of Wisely
Legendary Weapons of Kung Fu
Legion of Iron
Lepke
Lethal Games
Lethal Pursuit
Lethal Weapon
Lethal Weapon 2
Lethal Weapon 3
Lethal Woman
Let's Get Harry
Liberty & Bash
Life Is Beautiful
Light at the Edge of the World, The
Lighthorsemen, The
Lights! Cameras! Murder!
Linda
Lion of the Desert
Lionheart (1989)
Lionheart (1990)
Lion's Share, The
Lipstick
Liquidator, The
Lisa
Little Fauss and Big Halsy
Little Ninjas
Live and Let Die
Live Wire
Live Wires
Lives of a Bengal Lancer, The
Living Daylights, The
Living to Die
Loaded Guns
Lock and Load
Lock Up
Lockdown
Lone Wolf Returns, The
Lone Wolf Spy Hunt, The
Long John Silver
Long Ships, The
Lost Command
Lost in The Barrens
Lost Patrol, The
Lost Samurai Sword, The
Lost Squadron, The
Love and Bullets
Love by Appointment
Low Down Dirty Shame, A
Lydia Bailey
MacArthur
Maciste—the Mighty
Mack, The
Mad Dog Morgan
Mad Wax—The Surf Movie
Madame Sin
Mafia vs. Ninja
Magic Carpet, The
Magical Princess Gigi, The
Magical Wonderland
Magician, The
Magnificent Kick, The
Malone
Malta Story, The
Man Called Dagger, A
Man Could Get Killed, A
Man-Eater of Kumaon
Man Escaped, A
Man from Deep River, The
Man from Hong Kong, The
Man in the Iron Mask
Man in the Vault
Man in the Wilderness
Man Inside, The (1976)
Man Inside, The (1990)
Man Is Armed, The
Man of Violence
Man on a String (1960)
Man on a String (1971)
Man on the Outside
Man Who Cheated Himself, The
Manchurian Avenger, The
Mandrake
Manhunt in the Jungle
Manhunt: Search for the Night Stalker
Manhunter (1974)
Manhunter (1983)
Manhunter, The
Maniac!
Manila Calling
Manipulator, The
Man's Best Friend
Mara Maru
Maracaibo
Marathon Man
Marbella
March or Die
Mark of the Beast
Mark of the Gorilla
Mark of the Renegade
Mark of the Scorpion
Mark of Zorro, The (1920)
Mark of Zorro, The (1974)
Marked for Death
Marked for Murder
Maroc 7
Martial Law
Martial Law 2—Undercover
Martial Outlaw
Marvel Comics Video Library
Mask of Sheba, The
Mask of the Avenger
Masquerade
Massacre at Central High
Massarati and the Brain
Master Blaster
Master Killer
Master Killers, The
Master Ninja
Master of Ballantrae, The (1953)
Master of Ballantrae, The (1984)
Master of Dragonard Hill
Master Touch, The
Masters of Menace
Masters of the Universe
Matt Helm
Matusalem
Maximum Breakout

Mayday at 40,000 Feet!
Mayhem
McBain
McGuire, Go Home!
Me and the Mob
Mechanic, The
Medicine Hat Stallion, The
Mediterranean in Flames, The
Megaforce
Megaville
Melinda
Men in War
Men of Steel
Men of the Fighting Lady
Men of the Sea
Men Without Women
Menace on the Mountain
Menace II Society
Mercenary Fighters
Merchants of War
Merlin and the Sword
Merrill's Marauders
Message to Garcia, A
Messalina Vs. The Son of Hercules
Messenger, The
Miami Beach Cops
Miami Vice
Miami Vice 2: The Prodigal Son
Midas Run
Midnight Clear, A
Midnight Kiss
Midnight Warrior
Mighty Jack
Mighty Mouse in the Great Space Chase
Mind, Body and Soul
Mind Games
Mines of Kilimanjaro
Ministry of Vengeance
Minotaur, The
Missiles from Hell
Missing in Action
Missing in Action 2: The Beginning
Mission Batangas
Mission Kill
Mission Manila
Mission of Justice
Mission Phantom
Mission To Glory
Mississippi Gambler
Mistress Of The Apes
Mohawk
Molly and Gina
Monkey in the Master's Eye
Monkey Kung Fu
Moonfleet
Moonraker
Morgan the Pirate
Most Dangerous Game, The
Most Dangerous Man Alive, The
Mother Lode
Mother's Boys
Mountain Road, The
Moving Violation
Mr. Majestyk
Mr. Moses
Murder For Sale
Murder Masters of Kung Fu
Murderers' Row
Murders At Lynch Cross
Murph the Surf
Muthers, The
My Dog Shep
My Samurai
My Son, the Hero
My 12 Kung Fu Kicks
Mystery Island
Mystery Mountain
Mystery of the Million Dollar Hockey Puck, The
Mystery on Bird Island
Naked Angels
Naked Killer
Naked Runner, The
Nam Angels
Narrow Margin
Nasty Hero
Nate and Hayes
Navy Blue and Gold
Navy SEALS
Ned Kelly
Neutral Port
Never a Dull Moment
Never Say Never Again
Never Too Young to Die
New Adventures of Pippi Longstocking, The
New Adventures of Tarzan, The
New Fist of Fury
New Gladiators, The
Night Ambush
Night of the Fox
Night of the Warrior
Night Plane from Chungking
Night Rider, The
Nightforce
9 1/2 Ninjas
Ninja—American Warrior
Ninja Brothers of Blood
Ninja Champion
Ninja Commandments
Ninja Condors
Ninja Destroyer
Ninja in the Claws of the C.I.A.
Ninja Massacre
Ninja Phantom Heroes
Ninja Strike Force
Ninja 3—The Domination
Ninja Thunderbolt
Ninja Turf
Ninja Vengeance
No Dead Heroes
No Escape, No Return
No Holds Barred (1952)
No Holds Barred (1989)
No Man Is an Island
No More Women
No Way Out (1950)
No Way Out (1987)
Noozles—Adventures in Koalawalla Land
Noozles—Blinky and Pinky's Excellent Adventure
Noozles—Fuzzy Was a Noozle
Noozles—Koala Bear Magic
Noozles—Nuzzling with the Noozles
Norseman, The
North Star, The
Northville Cemetery Massacre, The
Northwest Mounted Police
Northwest Passage
Nowhere to Hide
Nowhere to Run
Number 1 of the Secret Service
Nun and the Sergeant, The
Nyoka and the Tigerman
Oasis
Oasis, The
Objective, Burma!
Oceans of Fire
Octagon, The
Octopussy
Odongo
Off on a Comet
Oil
Okinawa
Old Ironsides
Olly, Olly, Oxen Free
Omega Cop
Omega Syndrome
On Deadly Ground
On Her Majesty's Secret Service
On Wings of Eagles
Once A Hero
Once a Thief
Once Before I Die
One Down Two to Go
One Little Indian
One Man Jury
One Riot, One Ranger
One That Got Away, The
Only One Survived
Only the Strong
Open Season
Operation Amsterdam
Operation Bottleneck
Operation C.I.A.
Operation Conspiracy
Operation Cross Eagles
Operation Crossbow
Operation Daybreak
Operation Disaster
Operation Eichmann
Operation Haylift
Operation Julie
Operation Kid Brother
Operation Manhunt
Operation Nam
Operation Pacific
Operation Secret
Operation War Zone
Opponent, The
Opposing Force
Orca—the Killer Whale
Order of the Black Eagle
Order of the Eagle
Ordinary Magic
Original "Dragnet" 1
O.S.S.
O.S.S. 117—Mission for a Killer
Osterman Weekend, The
Our Man Flint
Our Man Flint: Dead on Target
Out For Blood
Out of Bounds
Out of Control
Out of Order
Out of the Shadows
Outlaw of Gor
Outpost in Morocco

Overkill
Pacific Inferno
Package, The
Pair of Aces
Panache
Panama Patrol
Paper Man
Paper Tiger
Papillon
Parker
Passage, The
Passage to Marseille
Passenger 57
Passion for Power
Password Is Courage, The
Patriot Games
Patriot, The
Payback
Peanut Butter Solution
Penitentiary
Penitentiary II
Penitentiary III
Perfect Crime, The
Perfect Weapon, The
Perils of Gwendoline
Perils of the Darkest Jungle
Peter Pan
Philadelphia Experiment 2, The
Phillip Marlowe—Finger Man
Phillip Marlowe: Smart-Aleck Kill
Picasso Trigger
Pickwick Papers
Pinchcliffe Grand Prix
Pink Jungle, The
Pippi Longstocking
Pirates of Blood River, The
Pirates of Capri, The
Pirates of the Coast
Play Dirty
Point Blank
Point Break
Point of No Return
Police Force
Poseidon Adventure, The
Pray for Death
Prayer of the Rollerboys
Predator
Predator 2
Prince of Foxes
Prince of Pirates
Princess of the Nile
Prisoner of Zenda, The (1937)
Prisoner of Zenda, The (1952)
Private Wars
Professional, The—Golgo 13
Protector, The
Provoked
Punisher, The
Purgatory
Pursuit of the Graf Spee
Pushed to the Limit
Python Wolf
Queen Boxer
Quiet Cool
Quiet Fire
Quo Vadis?
Race for Life
Race to the Yankee Zephyr
Racing Fever
Rad
Rage and Honor
Rage of Honor
Rage of the Buccaneers, The
Rage of the Master
Raid on Entebbe
Raid on Rommel
Raid, The
Raiders of the Buddhist Kung Fu
Raiders of the Lost Ark
Rainbow Jacket, The
Raise the Titanic!
Ramblin' Man
Rambo: First Blood, Part II
Rambo III
Rapid Fire
Rat Pfink and Boo Boo
Ravine, The
Raw Deal
Raw Force
R.C.M.P. & the Treasure of Genghis Khan
Reach for the Sky
Rebellion
Red Alert
Red Dawn
Red Dust
Red Heat
Red Hot Tires
Red Line 7000
Red Scorpion
Red Skies of Montana
Red Sonja
Red Tent, The
Reform School Girl
Reform School Girls
Remo Williams: The Adventure Begins
Renegades
Rent-a-Cop
Rescue, The
Return of Fist of Fury
Return of Monte Cristo, The
Return of Superfly, The
Return of the Chinese Boxer
Return of the Dragon
Return of the Musketeers, The
Revenge
Revenge of Fist of Fury
Revenge of the Ninja
Revenge of the Ninja Warrior
Revolt in the Big House
Revolt of the Mercenaries
Rhino!
Ring of Fire
Riot
Riot in Cell Block 11
Riot on Sunset Strip
Rise Against the Sword
Risk, The
River Wild, The
Road House
Road Warrior, The
Roaming Lady
Roaring Twenties, The
Robin Hood (1922)
Robin Hood (1991)
Robin Hood: Prince of Thieves
Rocketeer, The
Rollercoaster
Rolling Thunder
Romancing the Stone
Rough Waters
Royal Flash
Royal Hunt of the Sun, The
Royal Mounted Patrol, The
Run
Running Target
Safecracker, The
Saga of the Vagabonds
Sahara
Saigon
Saigon Commandos
Samson
Samurai from Nowhere
Samurai 3—Duel at Ganryu Island
Sanjuro
Santiago
Sardinia: Kidnapped
Sartana's Here . . . Trade Your Pistol For A Coffin
Savage Attraction
Savage Beach
Savage Bees, The
Savage Dawn
Savage Hunger, A
Savage is Loose, The
Savage Island
Savage Justice
Savage Streets
Scandalous
Scaramouche
Scarlet Pimpernel, The
Scarred
Scorpio
Sea Bat, The
Sea Devils (1937)
Sea Devils (1953)
Sea Fury
Sea Hawk, The
Sea of Lost Ships
Sea Shall Not Have Them, The
Sea Wolf, The (1941)
Sea Wolf, The (1993)
Sea Wolves, The
Sealed Cargo
Search and Destroy
Seas Beneath, The
Season for Assassins
Season of Fear
Second Victory, The
Secret Four, The
Secret Invasion, The
Secret Mission
Secret of Blood Island, The
Secret of the Golden Eagle, The
Secret of the Ice Cave, The
Secret of the Incas
Secret Scrolls: Part I
Secret Scrolls: Part II
Secret Service of the Air
Self-Defense
Serpent Island
Serpent of Death, The
Seven
Seven Blows of the Dragon
Seven Cities of Gold
Seven Days to Noon
Seven Indignant
Seven Magnificent Gladiators, The
Seven Miles from Alcatraz
Seven Women
7th Voyage of Sinbad, The
Severance
Shadow Force
Shadow Hunter

Shadow Killers
Shadow Man
Shadow of the Eagle
Shadow of the Wolf
Shadow World
Shadows in the Storm
Shaft in Africa
Shake Hands with the Devil
Shame (1988)
Shame (1992)
Shaolin Devil: Shaolin Angel
Shaolin Drunk Fighter
Shaolin Executioner
Shaolin Temple Strikes Back
Shaolin Traitor
Shaolin vs. Lama
Share Out, The
Shark!
Shark Hunter, The
Shark River
Sheba Baby
Sheena
Shinobi Ninja, The
Ship That Died of Shame, The
Shipwrecked
Shogun
Shogun Assassin
Shogun's Ninja
Shoot to Kill
Shootfighter: Fight to the Death
Shooting Stars
Showdown
Showdown At The Equator
Showdown in Little Tokyo
Sicilian Connection, The
Sidekicks
Siege of Firebase Gloria, The
Siege of the Saxons
Sign of the Pagan
Sign of Zorro, The
Silencer, The
Silencers, The
Silent Enemy, The
Silent Rage
Silk
Silk 2/Circle of Fear
Silver Fleet, The
Simple Justice
Sinai Commandos
Sinbad and the Eye of the Tiger
Sinbad Of The Seven Seas
Sinbad the Sailor
Single Fighter
Sink the Bismarck!
Siren of Bagdad
Sirocco
633 Squadron
Ski School
Skier's sDream
Skyjacked
Slaughter
Slaughter Day
Slaughter in San Francisco
Slaughter of the Innocents
Slaughter's Big Rip-Off
Slave Ship
Sleeping Fist, The
Slipping Into Darkness
Sloane
Snake Eater
Snake Eater 2—The Drug Buster
Snake Eater 3—His Law
Snake Fist Fighter
Snake in the Eagle's Shadow—2
Snow Treasure
Soldier of Fortune
Soldier, The
Soldier's Fortune
Soldier's Revenge
Soldiers Three
Sole Survivor
Solo
Son of Ali Baba
Son of Captain Blood
Son of the Sheik
Sorceress
S.O.S. Iceberg
Soul of Samurai
Souls at Sea
Sourdough
South Bronx Heroes
South of Pago Pago
Southern Comfort
Spanish Main, The
Spawn of the North
Special Delivery
Special Investigator
Specialist, The (1975)
Specialist, The (1994)
Speed (1936)
Speed (1994)
Spider-Man (The Amazing Spider-Man)
Spiderman Vol. 1
Spiderman Vol. 2
Spiritual Kung Fu
Spittin' Image
Spook Who Sat By the Door, The
Sporting Blood
Spring, The
Spy Smasher
Spy Who Loved Me, The
Spymaker—The Secret Life of Ian Fleming
St. Valentine's Day Massacre, The
Stakeout
Stalking Danger
Stand by for Action
Stand-In, The
Steel
Steel Arena
Steel Dawn
Steel Fisted Dragon
Steel Helmet, The
Steele's Law
Stickfighter
Sticks Of Death
Sting of the Dragon Masters
Stone Cold
Stone Fox
Storm and Sorrow
Stormquest
Story of Drunken Master, The
Story of 15 Boys, The
Story Of G.I. Joe, The
Straightline
Straw Dogs
Street Crimes
Street Fighter
Street Fighter's Last Revenge, The
Street Girls
Street Hunter
Street Knight
Street Soldiers
Striking Distance
Stripped to Kill
Stripped to Kill II—Live Girls
Sudden Impact
Sundown
Super Mario Bros.
Supercarrier
Superchick
Superfly
Superfly T.N.T.
Superman—The Movie
Superman 2
Superman 3
Superman 4: The Quest for Peace
Surviving the Game
Swamp Thing
Swarm, The
Swashbuckler
Sweet Sea
Sweet Sugar
Sword and the Dragon
Sword in the Desert
Sword of Doom
Sword of Lancelot
Sword of Monte Cristo, The
Sword of the Valiant
Take a Hard Ride
Taking of Beverly Hills, The
Taking of Pelham One Two Three, The
Tall Tale: The Unbelievable Adventures of Pecos Bill
Tarzan and the Amazons
Tarzan and the Leopard Woman
Tarzan and the Mermaids
Tarzan Finds a Son
Tarzan in Manhattan
Tarzan of the Apes
Tarzan, the Ape Man
Tarzan the Magnificent
Tarzan Triumphs
Tarzan's Greatest Adventure
Task Force
Teckman Mystery, The
Telefon
Ten Tall Men
Ten Tigers of Shaolin
Ten to Midnight
Ten Who Dared
Terminal Velocity
Terror in Beverly Hills
Terror of Rome Against the Son of Hercules
Texas
That Man From Rio
These Are the Damned
They Are Not Angels
They Came to Blow Up America
They Met in Bombay
They Were Expendable
They Who Dare
Thief of Bagdad, The (1924)
Thief of Bagdad, The (1978)
Thin Red Line, The
13 Rue Madeleine
Thirteen, The
Thirty-Nine Steps,

The 36 Hours
Thomasine & Bushrod
Thrashin'
Three Avengers, The
Three Caballeros, The
3:15
Three Musketeers, The (1921)
Three Musketeers, The (1935)
Three Musketeers, The (1948)
Three Musketeers, The (1974)
Three Musketeers, The (1993)
3 Ninjas
Three Ninjas Kick Back
Three the Hard Way
Thunder Bay
Thunder in the East
Thunderball
Thundering Mantis, The
Tiger vs. Dragon
Timebomb
Timecop
Tintorera
T.N.T. Jackson
To Have and Have Not
To Hell and Back
To Kill With Intrigue
To the Shores of Tripoli
Tobruk
Together Brothers
Tonight We Raid Calais
Too Hot to Handle
Too Late the Hero
Top Fights of Kung Fu
Top Gun
Tor—Mighty Warrior
Tora! Tora! Tora!
Torpedo Alley
Torpedo Run
Tour of Duty
Tour of Duty II—Bravo Company
Toward the Unknown
Towering Inferno, The
Toy Soldiers (1984)
Toy Soldiers (1991)
Trader Horn
Train of Events
Train, The
Trapped in a Submarine
Treasure at the Mill
Treasure of Lost Canyon, The
Treasure of Matecumbe
Treasure of the Sierra Madre, The
Trespass
Trial of the Incredible Hulk, The
Triple Cross
Tripoli
Triumph of Hercules, The
Truck Turner
True Lies
Tuff Turf
Twice Upon a Time
Twist of Sand, A
Two Great Cavaliers, The
2020 Texas Gladiators
Two Wondrous Tigers
Tycoon
Unbeaten 28, The
Uncertain Glory
Uncommon Valor
Unconquered
Under Cover
Under Fire
Under Siege
Under Ten Flags
Under the Gun
Under the Red Robe
Under Two Flags
Undergound
Underwater!
Universal Soldier
Untamed
Up Periscope
Vanishing Point
Verboten!
Vice Squad
Victim of Beauty
Victory
View to a Kill, A
Vikings, The
Von Richthofen and Brown
Von Ryan's Express
Voyage of Terror: The Achille Lauro Affair
Wake Island
Wake of the Red Witch
Walking Dead, The
Walking Tall
Walking Tall, Part II
Wanted: Dead or Alive
War Cat
Warbirds
Warrior and the Slave Girl, The
Warrior Within, The
Warriors of the Wasteland
Warriors, The (1955)
Warriors, The (1979)
Way to the Gold, The
West of Zanzibar
Whalers, The
What Price Glory?
When Dinosaurs Ruled the Earth
When Hell Broke Loose
When Time Ran Out . . .
White Heat
White Lightning
White Line Fever
White Water Summer
White Witch Doctor
Wicked Lady, The (1945)
Wicked Lady, The (1983)
Wilby Conspiracy, The
Wild Geese, The
Wing and a Prayer
Wings
Winner Take All
Winners Take All
World in His Arms, The
Wrecking Crew, The
Yankee Pasha
Yellow Fin
You Only Live Twice
Young Bruce Lee, The
Young Dragons—Kung Fu Kids, The
Young Dragons—Kung Fu Kids II, The
Young Swordsman
Yukon Flight
Zanzibar
Zarak
Zatoichi
Zatoichi Meets Yojimbo
Zeppelin
Zorro
Zulu

COMEDY

A-Haunting We Will Go
Abbott and Costello Go To Mars
Abbott and Costello In Hollywood
Abbott and Costello In The Foreign Legion
Abbott and Costello Meet Captain Kidd
Abbott and Costello Meet Dr Jekyll And Mr Hyde
Abbott and Costello Meet Frankenstein
Abbott and Costello Meet The Invisible Man
Abbott and Costello Meet The Keystone Kops
Abbott and Costello Meet the Killer
Abbott and Costello Meet the Mummy
About Last Night . . .
Abroad With Two Yanks
Absent Minded Professor, The
Absolutely the Best of the Soupy Sales Show
Academy Awarded Winners—Animated Short Films
Accent on Youth
Ace Ventura: Pet Detective
Aces Go Places 2
Adam's Rib
Addams Family—Ghost Town
Addams Family—Left in the Lurch
Addams Family, The
Addams Family, The—Vol. 1
Addams Family, The—Vol. 2
Addams Family, The—Vol. 3
Addams Family, The—Vol. 4
Addams Family, The—Vol. 6

Addams Family, The—Vol. 5
Addams Family Values
Addict
Adding Machine, The
Adios Amigo
Admirable Crichton, The
Admiral Was a Lady, The
Adorable Creatures
Adventure
Adventure in Baltimore
Adventure of Sherlock Holmes' Smarter Brother, The
Adventures in Babysitting
Adventures of a Private Eye
Adventures of a Taxi Driver
Adventures of a Two-Minute Werewolf, The
Adventures of Barry Mckenzie, The
Adventures of Bullwhip Griffin, The
Adventures of Droopy Featuring "Wags to Riches," The
Adventures of Ford Fairlane, The
Adventures of Gerard, The
Adventures of Milo and Otis, The
Adventures of Ozzie and Harriet, The (1956)
Adventures of Ozzie and Harriet, The (1964)
Adventures of Picasso, The
Adventures of Priscilla, Queen of the Desert, The
Adventures of Sadie, The
Adventurous Blonde
Affairs of Annabel, The
Affairs of Susan, The
Affairs of the Heart
Affectionately Yours
Africa Screams
After Hours
After the Fox
Age Isn't Everything
Agent 8 3/4
Agent for H.A.R.M
Air Raid Wardens
Air Up There, The
Airplane!
Airplane II, The Sequel
Alex in Wonderland
Alfie
Alfredo, Alfredo
Alias a Gentleman
Alias Jesse James
Alias Smith and Jones
Alice
Alice's Restaurant
Alien from L.A.
All About Eve
All at Sea
All in a Night's Work
All in the Family 20th Anniversary Special
All Night Long
All of Me
All Over Town
All Screwed Up
All-Star Salute to the Improv, An
All the Marbles
All the Way, Boys
All These Women
All Tied Up
Allegro Non Troppo
Alligator Named Daisy, An
Allnighter, The
All's Fair
Almost
Almost an Angel
Almost Perfect Affair, An
Almost Pregnant
Almost Summer
Almost You
Alone in the T-Shirt Zone
Along Came Jones
Alvin Purple
Alvin Rides again
Always
Always a Bride
Always Together
Amarcord
Amateur Night at the Dixie Bar and Grill
Amazing Adventure
Amazing Doctor Clitterhouse, The
Amazing Grace
Amazing Mr. Williams
Amazon Women on the Moon
Ambassador Bill
Ambassador's Daughter, The
Ambush Murders, The
America
America 3000
American Aristocracy, An
American Boyfriends
American Dreamer
American Graffiti
American Success Company, The
American Tail: Fievel Goes West, An
Americanization of Emily, The
Americathon
Amore
Amorous Adventures of Moll Flanders, The
Amorous Mr. Prawn, The
Amos and Andrew
And Baby Makes Three
. . . And God Spoke
And Now for Something Completely Different
And So They Were Married
And You Thought Your Parents Were Weird!
Andrew Dice Clay—"No Apologies"
Androcles and the Lion
Andy Griffith Show, The
Andy Griffith Show, The—Special Holiday Release
Andy Hardy Comes Home
Andy Hardy Gets Spring Fever
Andy Hardy Meets Debutante
Andy Hardy's Blonde Trouble
Andy Hardy's Double Life
Andy Hardy's Private Secretary
Andy Kaufman—Sound Stage
Andy Kaufman Special, The
Andy Warhol's Bad
Angel From Texas, An
Angel in my Pocket
Angel on My Shoulder
Angel Who Pawned Her Harp, The
Angels in Disguise
Angels in the Outfield
Animal Behavior
Animal Crackers
Animal House
Animalympics
Annabel Takes A Tour
Annie Hall
Anniversary, The
Another Chance
Another 48 HRS
Another You
Antonia & Jane
Any Number Can Win
Any Wednesday
Any Which Way You Can
Anyone Can Play
Anything for Love
Apartment for Peggy
Apartment, The
Apple Dumpling Gang, The
Apple Dumpling Gang Rides Again, The
Appointment for Love
Apprenticeship Of Duddy Kravitz, The
April Fools, The
Arabella
Archie: To Riverdale and Back Again
Are Husbands Necessary?
Are Parents People?
Armed and Dangerous
Army Brats
Arnold
Around the World in 80 Ways
Arrivederci, Baby
Arsenic and Old Lace
Art of Love, The
Art of Tom and Jerry III: The Chuck Jones Years
Arthur
Arthur 2—On the Rocks
Artists and Models
As You Like It
As Young As You Feel
Ascent to Heaven
Ask Any Girl
Assassination Bureau, The

Blondie's Big Deal
Blondie's Big Moment
Blondie's Blessed Event
Blondie's Hero
Blondie's Holiday
Blondie's Lucky Day
Blondie's Reward
Blondie's Secret
Bloodhounds of Broadway (1952)
Bloodhounds of Broadway (1989)
Blue Iguana, The
Blue Movies
Blue Murder at St. Trinian's
Bluebeard's Eighth Wife
Blues Brothers, The
Blues Busters
Blume In Love
Boarding School
Bob & Carol & Ted & Alice
Bob Roberts
Bobbikins
Bobo, The
Boccaccio '70
Body Beat
Body Disappears, The
Body Slam
Boeing Boeing
Bohemian Girl, The
Bombs Away
Bombshell
Bon Voyage!
Bon Voyage Charlie Brown (and Don't Come Back!)
Bonnie Scotland
Bonzo Goes to College
Boob Tube, The
Book of Love
Boom in the Moon
Boomerang
Bootleggers
Boris and Natasha
Born in East L.A.
Born Yesterday (1950)
Born Yesterday (1993)
Bowery Blitzkrieg
Bowery Bombshell
Bowery Boys Meet the Monsters, The
Bowery Buckaroos
Bowery Champs
Bowery to Bagdad
Boy, Did I Get a Wrong Number!
Boy Meets Girl
Boy Named Charlie Brown, A
Boy Who Stole a Million, The
Boyfriends and Girlfriends
Boys' Night Out
Boys of the City, The
Boys on the Side
Brady Bunch Movie, The
Brady Girls Get Married, The
Brain Donors
Brain Smasher: A Love Story
Brain, The
Brass Bottle, The
Brazil
Bread and Chocolate
Bread, Love and Dreams
Breakfast at Tiffany's
Breakfast for Two
Breakfast with Les and Bess
Breaking All the Rules
Breaking In
Breath of Scandal, A
Brewster McCloud
Brewster's Millions (1935)
Brewster's Millions (1945)
Brewster's Millions (1985)
Bride Came C.O.D., The
Bride Comes Home, The
Bride for Sale
Bride Goes Wild, The
Bride of Boogedy, The
Bride Walks Out, The
Bride Wore Boots, The
Brighton Beach Memoirs
Bring Me the Head of Dobie Gillis
Bringing Up Baby
Brink's Job, The
Britannia Hospital
Broadcast News
Broadminded
Broadway Bill
Broadway Bound
Broadway Danny Rose
Bronco Billy
Broth of a Boy
Brother Orchid
Brother Rat
Brother Rat and a Baby
Brotherly Love
Brothers in Law
Bruce, Lenny: The Performance Film
B.S. I Love You
Buck Benny Rides Again
Buck Privates
Buck Privates Come Home
Bud and Lou
Buddy Buddy
Buddy System, The
Buffy the Vampire Slayer
Bugs Bunny/Road Runner Movie, The
Bugs Bunny's 3rd Movie—1001 Rabbit Tales
Bull Durham
Bullets Over Broadway
Bullfighters, The
Bullseye!
Bullshot
Bunco
Bundle of Joy
Bunny O'Hare
Buona Sera, Mrs. Campbell
'Burbs, The
Bureau of Missing Persons
Bus Stop
Bushbaby, The
Bustin' Loose
Busy Body, The
Butcher's Wife, The
Butterflies Are Free
Buy & Cell
Buy Me That Town
By Candlelight
By Design
By Your Leave
Bye Bye Braverman
Bye Bye Brazil
Bye Bye, Love
Cabbage Patch Kids First Christmas
Cabin Boy
Cactus Flower
Caddy, The
Caddyshack
Caddyshack II
Cadillac Man
Cafe Au Lait
Cafe Express
Cafe Metropole
Cafe Society
Calendar Girl
California Suite
Call a Messenger
Call It a Day
Call Me Bwana
Call Out the Marines
Callaway Went Thataway
Came a Hot Friday
Camera Buff
Cameraman, The
Camilla
Camouflage
Camp Cucamonga
Campus Man
Can I Do It . . . 'Til I Need Glasses?
Can It Be Love
Can She Bake a Cherry Pie?
Cancel My Reservation
Candid Candid Camera
Candy
Candy Stripe Nurses
Cannery Row
Cannibal Girls
Cannibal Women in the Avocado Jungle of Death
Cannonball Run, The
Cannonball Run II
Can't Buy Me Love
Canterville Ghost, The (1944)
Canterville Ghost, The (1986)
Caprice
Capricious Summer
Captain from Koepenick
Captain Hates the Sea, The
Captain Is a Lady, The
Captain Ron
Captain Tugboat Annie
Captain's Paradise, The
Captain's Table, The
Car 54, Where Are You?
Car Trouble
Car Wash
Carbon Copy
Career Opportunities
Caro Diario
Carolina Cannonball
Carry on Admiral
Carry On Cabbie
Carry on Camping
Carry on Cleo
Carry on Constable
Carry on Doctor
Carry on Henry VIII
Carry on Nurse
Carry On Sergeant
Carry on Spying

Crossing Delancey
Cry for Happy
Cry Uncle!
Crystal Ball, The
Curly Sue
Curse of the Pink Panther
Curse of the Queerwolf
Curtain Up
D2: The Mighty Ducks
Daddy's Dyin'. . . Who's Got the Will?
Daffy Duck's Movie: Fantastic Island
Daffy Duck's Quackbusters
Dance Hall
Dance with Me Henry
Dancing Masters, The
Dancing Mothers
Danger—Love at Work
Dangerous Curves
Dare to Be Truthful
Dark Backward, The
Dark Habits
Darling, How Could You
Date with an Angel
Dave
David Harum
Day at the Races, A
Day in the Death of Joe Egg, A
Day the Hot Line Got Hot, The
Day-Time Wife
Days of Thrills and Laughter
Dazed and Confused
D.C. Cab
Dead End Kids
Dead Men Don't Wear Plaid
Dead Solid Perfect
Deal of the Century
Dealing: or The Berkeley-to-Boston Forty-Brick Lost-Bag Blues
Dear Brigitte
Dear Michael
Dear Ruth
Dear Wife
Death Becomes Her
Death of a Bureaucrat
Decline and Fall of a Bird Watcher
Defending Your Life
Delicate Delinquent, The
Delicatessen
Delirious
Delusions of Grandeur
Dennis the Menace
Design for Living
Design for Scandal
Designing Woman
Desire
Desire and Hell at Sunset Motel
Desk Set
Desperately Seeking Susan
Detective, The
Devil and Max Devlin, The
Devil and Miss Jones, The
Devil by the Tail, The
Devil in Love, The
Devil's Disciple, The
Devil's Eye, The
Diamonds for Breakfast
Diary of a Young Comic
Die Laughing
Digby—The Biggest Dog in the World
Dim Sum—A Little Bit of Heart
Dimboola
Dining Room, The
Dinner at Eight (1933)
Dinner at Eight (1990)
Dinner for Adele
Dirty Dishes
Dirty Knight's Work
Dirty Laundry
Dirty Rotten Scoundrels
Discreet Charm of the Bourgeoisie, The
Disorderlies
Disorderly Orderly, The
Disorganized Crime
Distinguished Gentleman, The
Divine Madness
Divorce American Style
Divorce—Italian Style
Divorce of Lady X, The
Dixie: Changing Habits
Do Not Disturb
Doc Hollywood
Doctor at Large
Doctor At Sea
Doctor Detroit
Doctor in Distress
Doctor in Love
Doctor in the House
Doctor in Trouble
Doctor Takes a Wife, The
Doctor's Dilemma
Doin' Time on Planet Earth
Doing Time
$ (Dollars)
Don Juan, My Love
Dona Flor and Her Two Husbands
Dona Herlinda and Her Son
Donovan Affair, The
Donovan's Reef
Don's Party
Don't Drink the Water
Don't Give Up the Ship
Don't Go Near the Water
Don't Just Stand There
Don't Make Waves
Don't Raise the Bridge, Lower the River
Don't Take It to Heart
Don't Tell Her It's Me
Don't Tell Mom the Babysitter's Dead
Door to Door
Double Dynamite
Double Wedding
Doubting Thomas
Doughboys
Doughgirls, The
Down and Out in Beverly Hills
Down by Law
Down Memory Lane
Down the Drain
Down to Earth
Dr. Goldfoot and the Bikini Machine
Dr. Heckyl and Mr. Hype
Dr. Otto and the Riddle of the Gloom Beam
Dr. Strangelove or: How I Learned To Stop Worrying and Love the Bomb
Dracula and Son
Dragnet
Dragons Forever
Dream a Little Dream
Dream Date
Dream Girl
Dream Machine, The
Dream Team, The
Dream Wife
Dreamboat
Drive-In
Drop Dead Fred
Drop-Out Mother
Du-beat-e-o
Duck Soup
Duck Tales: The Movie—Treasure of the Lost Lamp
Dude Goes West, The
Dudes
Duffy
Duffy's Tavern
Dulcy
Dumb and Dumber
Dutch
Dynamite Chicken
Earl of Chicago, The
Early to Bed
Earth Girls Are Easy
Earthworm Tractors
East and West
Easy Living
Easy Money
Easy to Take
Eat a Bowl of Tea
Eat Drink Man Woman
Eat My Dust
Eat the Peach
Eat the Rich
Eating
Eating Raoul
Echo Park
Ed Wood
Eddie Murphy Raw
Educating Rita
Efficiency Expert, The
Egg and I, The
Eight on the Lam
18 Again!
El Manosanta Esta Cargado
El Professor Hippie
El: This Strange Passion
Electric Dreams
Elena and Her Men
11 Harrowhouse
Eliza Frazer
Ella Cinders
Elmer the Great
Elopement
Elvira, Mistress of the Dark
Embarassing Moments
Enchanted April
Encino Man
End, The
Endurance
Ensign Pulver

Enter Laughing
Enter Madame
Entertaining Mr. Sloane
Erik the Viking
Ernest Goes to Camp
Ernest Goes to Jail
Ernest Rides Again
Ernest Saves Christmas
Ernest Scared Stupid
Errand Boy, The
Escape Artist, The
Eternally Yours
Eve Wants to Sleep
Even Cowgirls Get the Blues
Ever Since Eve
Every Day's a Holiday
Every Girl Should Be Married
Every Which Way but Loose
Everybody Does It
Everything Happens at Night
Everything You Always Wanted to Know About Sex (But Were Afraid to Ask)
Exclusive
Exit to Eden
Experts, The
Exquisite Corpses
Exterminating Angel, The
Extra Girl, The
Extraordinary Seaman, The
Eyes of the Amaryllis, The
Fabulous Joe, The
Fabulous Suzanne, The
Face the Music
Facts of Life Down Under, The
Facts of Life Goes to Paris, The
Facts of Life, The
Fair Exchange
Faithful in My Fashion
Family Affair, A
Family Business
Family Circus Christmas, A
Family Circus Easter, A
Family Dog—Enemy Dog/Show Dog
Family for Joe, A
Family Game, The
Family Honeymoon
Family Jewels, The
Family Ties Vacation
Fan, The
Fancy Pants
Fanfan the Tulip
Fangface II Spooky Spoofs
Fantasies
Fantastic Animation Festival
Fantastic Comedy
Fantastic World of D.C. Collins, The
Far Out Man
Far Out Space Nuts
Farmer's Daughter, The (1940)
Farmer's Daughter, The (1947)
Farmer's Other Daughter, The
Farmer's Wife, The
Fast and Loose
Fast and Sexy
Fast Break
Fast Food
Fast Getaway
Fast Lady, The
Fast Talking
Fast Times at Ridgemont High
Fastest Guitar Alive, The
Fatal Beauty
Fatal Instinct
Fate
Father Goose
Father Guido Sarducci Goes to College
Father Hood
Father Is a Bachelor
Father Makes Good
Father of the Bride (1950)
Father of the Bride (1991)
Father Takes a Wife
Father Takes the Air
Father Was a Fullback
Father's Dilemma
Father's Wild Game
Fathom
Fatso
Favor, The
Favor, the Watch, and the Very Big Fish, The
Fawlty Towers—The Complete Set
Fe-Fi-Fo-Fun
Fear, Anxiety and Depression
Fear of a Black Hat
Fearless Fagan
Fearless Frank
Feds
Feel My Pulse
Feet First
Felix in Outer Space
Felix the Cat—Movie, The
Felix's Magic Bag of Tricks
Female Trouble
Feminine Touch, The
Feminist and the Fuzz, The
Femme Fatale
Fernandel the Dressmaker
Ferocious Female Freedom Fighters
Ferris Bueller's Day Off
Feud of the West
Feud, The
Feudin' Fools
Few Days with Me, A
Fickle Finger of Fate, The
Fiendish Plot of Dr. Fu Manchu, The
Fievel's American Tails Vol. 1—The Gift & A Case of the Hiccups
5th Avenue Girl
Fifty/Fifty
Fifty Roads to Town
Fighting Fools
Fighting Trouble
Fighting Youth
Final Programme, The
Final Test, The
Find the Lady
Finders Keepers (1951)
Finders Keepers (1984)
Fine Madness, A
Fine Mess, A
Fine Pair, A
Fine Romance, A
Finnegan Begin Again
Fire Sale
Fireballs
Fireman, Save My Child (1932)
Fireman Save My Child (1954)
Firemen's Ball, The
First Date
First Family
First Lady
First Monday in October
First Nudie Musical, The
First Time, The (1952)
First Time, The (1983)
First Traveling Saleslady, The
First Turn-On, The
Fish Called Wanda, A
Fish that Saved Pittsburgh, The
Fitzwilly
Five Day Lover
Five Golden Hours
Five on the Black Hand Side
5,000 Fingers of Dr. T, The
Flame of New Orleans, The
Flamingo Kid
Flea in Her Ear, A
Flesh and the Woman
Fletch
Fletch Lives
Flicks
Flight of Rainbirds, A
Flim Flam Man, The
Flintstone Christmas, A
Flintstone Files, The
Flintstones, The
Flirting
Flirting with Fate
Florian
Fluffy
Flustered Comedy of Leon Errol, The
Flying Deuces, The
FM
Folks!
Follow a Star
Follow That Camel
Follow That Horse!
Follow the Leader
Folly to Be Wise
Foolin' Around
Fools for Scandal
Footlight Glamour
For Better, For Worse
For Heaven's Sake (1926)
For Heaven's Sake (1950)
For Keeps
For Love of Ivy
For Love or Money (1963)
For Love or Money (1993)
For Pete's Sake
For Richer, For Poorer
For Singles Only
For the Love of It
For the Love of Mary
For Those Who Think Young
For Valor

Foreign Affair, A
Foreign Affairs
Foreign Body
Foreign Student
Foreplay
Forever Darling
Forever Female
Forgotten Tune for the Flute, A
Fortune Cookie, The
Fortune, The
40 Carats
48 Hrs.
Forty Pounds of Trouble
Foul Play
Four Against Fate
Four Bags Full
Four Clowns
Four Days in July
Four Days Leave
Four Seasons, The
Four Weddings and a Funeral
Four's a Crowd
Fowl Play
Fox and the Hound, The
Framed
Francis
Francis Covers the Big Town
Francis Goes to the Races
Francis Goes to West Point
Francis in the Haunted House
Francis in the Navy
Francis Joins the Wacs
Frasier, the Sensuous Lion
Fraternity Vacation
Frauds
Freaked
Freaky Friday
Freddie as F.R.O.7
Free For All
Freebie and the Bean
French Postcards
French, They Are a Funny Race, The
Freshman, The (1925)
Freshman, The (1990)
Friends, Lovers & Lunatics
Friends of Mr. Sweeney
Frisco Kid, The
Frog
From Pluto with Love
From the Hip
From the Mixed-Up Files of Mrs. Basil E. Frankweiler
From Top to Bottom
Front Page, The (1931)
Front Page, The (1974)
Front Page Woman
Frosty the Snowman
Frozen Assets
Frozen Limits, The
Fruit Machine, The
Fugitive Lovers, The
Full Hearts & Empty Pockets
Full Moon High
Full Moon in Paris
Full of Life
Fuller Brush Girl, The
Fuller Brush Man, The
Fun at St. Fanny's
Fun on a Weekend
Fun with Dick and Jane
Funeral, The
Funland
Funny About Love
Funny Bones
Funny Dirty Little War
Funny Farm
Funny Farm, The
Funny Money
Funny Thing Happened on the Way to the Forum, A
Funnyman
Further Perils of Laurel and Hardy, The
Further Up the Creek!
Fuzzy Pink Nightgown, The
Gaily, Gaily
Gal Who Took the West, The
Galactic Gigolo
Galloping Major, The
Gambler Returns: The Luck of the Draw, The
Game Show Models
Games Girls Play
Gang That Couldn't Shoot Straight, The
Gangster Boss
Garbage Pail Kids Movie, The
Gas
Gas Pump Girls
Gaslight Follies
Gay Bride, The
Gay Deception, The
Gay Desperado, The
Gazebo, The
Geisha Boy, The
General Spanky
General, The
Generals without Buttons
Generation
Genevieve
Genius at Work
Gentleman at Heart, A
Gentleman Jim
Gentlemen Prefer Blondes
Gentlemen's Agreement
George and Margaret
George Washington Slept Here
Georgia Peaches, The
Georgy Girl
Get Charlie Tully
Get Crazy
Get on with It
Get Out Your Handkerchiefs
Get Smart, Again!
Get to Know Your Rabbit
Getting Even with Dad
Getting Gertie's Garter
Getting It On
Getting It Right
Getting Over
Getting Straight
Getting Wasted
Ghost and Mr. Chicken
Ghost and the Guest
Ghost Breakers, The
Ghost Catchers
Ghost Chase
Ghost Chasers
Ghost Comes Home, The
Ghost Dad
Ghost Fever
Ghost Goes West, The
Ghost in the Invisible Bikini
Ghost in the Noonday Sun
Ghost of Dragstrip Hollow, The
Ghost of St. Michael's, The
Ghost Writer
Ghostbusters
Ghostbusters II
Ghosts Can't Do It
Ghosts on the Loose
Gidget
Gidget Gets Married
Gidget Goes Hawaiian
Gidget Goes to Rome
Gidget Grows Up
Gidget's Summer Reunion
Gift, The
Gilda Live
Gilded Lily, The
Gildersleeve on Broadway
Gildersleeve's Ghost
Gilligan's Island: The Collector's Edition, Vol. 1
Gimme an "F"
Ginger Ale Afternoon
Ginger in the Morning
Girl, a Guy, and a Gob, A
Girl Can't Help It, The
Girl Downstairs, The
Girl Friend, The
Girl from Jones Beach, The
Girl from Manhattan, The
Girl from Mexico, The
Girl from Missouri, The
Girl from Petrovka, The
Girl-Getters, The
Girl He Left Behind
Girl in a Million, A
Girl in Blue, The
Girl in Every Port, A (1928)
Girl in Every Port, A (1952)
Girl in His Pocket
Girl in the Picture, The
Girl Most Likely To . . . , The
Girl Must Live, A
Girl Rush
Girl Shy
Girl Stroke Boy
Girl Trouble
Girl Who Came Gift-Wrapped, The
Girl Who Couldn't Say No, The
Girl with a Pistol, The
Girl with a Suitcase
Girl with Ideas, A
Girl with the Hatbox, The
Girlfriend from Hell
Girls About Town
Girls Just Want to

Have Fun
Girls of Pleasure Island
Girls on the Beach, The
Girls' School
Girls, The
Girls Town
Girls Will Be Boys
Give Her the Moon
Give Us Wings
Glamour Boy
Glass Bottom Boat, The
Glitch
Global Affair, A
Glory! Glory!
Glory Years
Gnome-Mobile, The
Go Chase Yourself
Go West
Go West, Young Man
Gods Must Be Crazy, The
Gods Must Be Crazy II, The
Goin' All the Way
Goin' to Town
Going Ape!
Going Bananas
Going Berserk
Going Hollywood
Going in Style
Going Places
Going Undercover
Gold Dust Gertie
Gold Raiders
Gold Rush, The
Goldbergs, The
Golden Age of Comedy, The
Golden Arrow, The
Golden Child, The
Golden Coach, The
Golden Madonna, The
Goldstein
Gomer Pyle U.S.M.C.—Vol. 1
Gomer Pyle U.S.M.C.—Vol. 2
Gone Are the Days
Gong Show Movie, The
Good Companions, The
Good Fairy, The
Good Girls Go to Paris
Good Humor Man, The
Good Man in Africa, A
Good Morning
Good Morning, Vietnam
Good Neighbor Sam
Good Sam
Good Soldier Schweik, The
Good Sport, A
Goodbye Charlie
Goodbye, Columbus
Goodbye Cruel World
Goodbye Girl, The
Goodbye, New York
Goodbye Pork Pie
Goodnight, Ladies and Gentlemen
Goof Balls
Gorilla, The
Gorp
Gospel According to Vic, The
Gotcha!
Government Girl
Grace Quigley
Gracie Allen Murder Case, The
Grad Night
Graduate, The
Grand Slam
Grand Theft Auto
Grandma's Boy
Grass Is Always Greener Over the Septic Tank, The
Grass is Greener, The
Gravy Train, The
Greaser's Palace
Great American Beauty Contest, The
Great American Pastime, The
Great American Traffic Jam, The
Great American Tragedy, A
Great Bank Hoax, The
Great Bank Robbery, The
Great Catherine
Great Chase, The
Great Diamond Robbery, The
Great Dictator, The
Great Garrick, The
Great Gildersleeve, The
Great Gleason, The
Great Guns
Great Love Experiment, The
Great Lover, The
Great Man Votes, The
Great Mc Gonagal
Great McGinty, The
Great Mike, The
Great Mr. Nobody, The
Great Muppet Caper, The
Great Outdoors, The
Great Race, The
Great Rupert, The
Great Scout and Cathouse Thursday
Great Spy Chase, The
Great St. Trinian's Train Robbery, The
Great War, The
Greedy
Greeks Had a Word for Them, The
Green Card
Green Grow the Rushes
Green Man, The
Greetings
Gregory's Girl
Gremlins
Gremlins 2—The New Batch
Greyfriars Bobby
Gridlock
Groom Wore Spurs, The
Groove Tube, The
Gross Anatomy
Gross Jokes
Group Marriage
Grumpy Old Men
Grunt! The Wrestling Movie
Guarding Tess
Guerrillas in Pink Lace
Guess Who's Sleeping in My Bed?
Guest Wife
Guide for the Married Man, A
Guilty as Charged
Gumball Rally, The
Gumshoe
Gumshoe Kid, The
Gun in Betty Lou's Handbag, The
Gung Ho
Gus
Hail
Hail Caesar
Hail the Conquering Hero
Half a Hero
Half Angel
Half-Naked Truth, The
Half Shot at Sunrise
Hallelujah the Hills
Hamburger . . . The Motion Picture
Hammersmith Is Out
Hands Across the Table
Handy Andy
Hangin' with the Homeboys
Hanky Panky
Hannah and Her Sisters
Happening, The
Happiest Days of Your Life, The
Happiness
Happiness of Three Women, The
Happy Anniversary
Happy Birthday, Wanda June
Happy Ever After
Happy Gigolo, The
Happy Hooker, The
Happy Hooker Goes Hollywood, The
Happy Hooker Goes to Washington, The
Happy Hour
Happy Is the Bride
Happy New Year (1974)
Happy New Year (1987)
Happy New Year!, A
Happy Road, The
Happy Since I Met You
Happy Thieves
Happy Together
Hard Promises
Hard to Get
Hard to Handle
Hardbodies
Hardbodies 2
Hardhat and Legs
Hardly Working
Hardware Wars
Hardys Ride High, The
Harem Girl
Harlem Globetrotters on Gilligan's Island, The
Harlem Nights
Harold and Maude
Harold Lloyd's World of Comedy
Harper Valley P.T.A.
Harry and the Hendersons
Harry and Walter Go to New York
Harry in Your Pocket
Harry's War
Harvey
Harvey Middleman, Fireman
Has Anybody Seen My Gal?

Haunted Honeymoon
Have Picnic Basket Will Travel
Have Rocket, Will Travel
Having It All
Having Wonderful Crime
Having Wonderful Time
Hawks
Hawmps!
Hazard
He Laughed Last
He Married His Wife
He Said, She Said
He Stayed for Breakfast
Head Office
Heads
H.E.A.L.T.H.
Hear My Song
Heart & Souls
Heart Condition
Heart to Heart
Heartaches
Heartbeeps
Heartbreak Hotel
Heartbreak Kid, The
Heat
Heathers
Heaven Can Wait (1943)
Heaven Can Wait (1978)
Heaven Help Us
Heavenly Body, The
Heavenly Days
Heavenly Kid, The
Heavens Above
Heavy Petting
Heavyweights
Hello Again
Hello Down There
Hello, Elephant
Hello Sucker
Help Wanted: Kids
Help Wanted: Male
Henry Aldrich, Boy Scout
Henry Aldrich, Editor
Henry Aldrich for President
Henry Aldrich Gets Glamour
Henry Aldrich Haunts a House
Henry Aldrich Plays Cupid
Henry Aldrich Swings It
Henry Aldrich's Little Secret
Henry and Dizzy
Henry, the Rainmaker
Her Alibi
Her Cardboard Lover
Her First Affair
Her Highness and the Bellboy
Her Husband's Affairs
Her Life as a Man
Her Primitive Man
Herbie Goes Bananas
Herbie Goes to Monte Carlo
Herbie Rides Again
Here Come the Co-eds
Here Come the Girls
Here Come the Littles
Here Come the Marines
Here Come the Nelsons
Here Comes Bugs
Here Comes Cookie
Here Comes Kelly
Here Comes Mr. Jordan
Here Comes Peter Cottontail
Here Comes the Groom
Here We Go Again
Here We Go Round the Mulberry Bush
Here's George
Hero
Hero at Large
Hero in the Family
He's a Cockeyed Wonder
He's Fired, She's Hired
He's My Girl
Hexed
Hey Abbott!
Hey Cinderella
Hey There, It's Yogi Bear
Hi-Di-Hi
Hi Diddle Diddle
Hi, Mom!
Hiding Out
High and Dry
High Anxiety
High Cost of Loving, The
High Heels
High Hopes
High Infidelity
High Pressure
High School U.S.A.
High Season
High Spirits
High Tension
Higher Education
Highway 61
Hillbilly Bears
Hillbillys in a Haunted House
Hired Wife
His Double Life
His First Flame
His Girl Friday
His Majesty O'Keefe
His Picture In The Papers
His Prehistoric Past/The Bank
His Private Secretary
His Royal Slyness/Haunted Spooks
His Wife's Lover
History of Mr. Polly, The
History of the World Part I
History of White People In America, The—Vol. 1
History Of White People In America, The—Vol. 2
Hit, The
Hit the Ice
Hi'ya Chum
Hobson's Choice
Hocus Pocus
Hog Wild
Hold 'Em Jail
Hold 'Em Yale
Hold Me, Thrill Me, Kiss Me
Hold That Baby!
Hold That Blonde
Hold That Ghost
Hold That Girl
Hold That Hypnotist
Hold That Line
Hole in the Head, A
Holiday
Holiday Camp
Holiday for Henrietta
Holiday for Lovers
Holiday Hotel
Hollywood Boulevard
Hollywood Chaos
Hollywood Detective, The
Hollywood Harry
Hollywood High
Hollywood High, Part 2
Hollywood Hot Tubs
Hollywood Knights, The
Hollywood or Bust
Hollywood Salutes Canadian Animation
Hollywood Shuffle
Hollywood Vice Squad
Hollywood Zap
Holy Matrimony
Home Alone
Home Alone 2: Lost in New York
Home Free All
Home Is Where the Hart Is
Home Movies
Home Remedy
Homebodies
Hometown Boy Makes Good
Hometown U.S.A.
Homework
Honey, I Blew Up the Kid
Honey, I Shrunk the Kids
Honey Pot, The
Honeychile
Honeymoon Academy
Honeymoon for Three
Honeymoon Hotel
Honeymoon in Bali
Honeymoon in Vegas
Honeymoon Machine, The
Honky Tonk Freeway
Hook
Hook, Line & Sinker
Hootch County Boys, The
Hoots Mon!
Hope and Glory
Hopscotch
Horizontal Lieutenant, The
Horn Blows at Midnight, The
Horror Hospital
Horse Feathers
Horse in the Gray Flannel Suit, The
Horse's Mouth, The
Hospital, The
Hot Dog . . . The Movie
Hot Ice
Hot Millions
Hot Paint
Hot Pepper
Hot Pursuit
Hot Resort
Hot Rock, The
Hot Saturday
Hot Shots!
Hot Shots! Part Deux
Hot Stuff
Hot T-Shirts
Hot Times

Hot to Trot
Hot Tomorrows
Hot Water
Hotel Paradiso
Hotel Sahara
Hothead
H.O.T.S.
Hound of the Baskervilles, The
Hours of Love, The
House Calls
House of Angels
House of God, The
House Party
House Party 2
House Party III
Houseboat
Houseguest
Householder, The
Housekeeper's Daughter, The
Housekeeping
Housemaster
Housesitter
How Funny Can Sex Be?
How I Got Into College
How I Won the War
How Sweet It Is!
How Tasty Was My Little Frenchman
How to Be Very, Very Popular
How to Beat the High Cost of Living
How to Break Up a Happy Divorce
How to Commit Marriage
How to Frame a Figg
How to Get Ahead in Advertising
How to Make Love to a Negro Without Getting Tired
How to Marry a Millionaire
How to Murder a Rich Uncle
How to Murder Your Wife
How to Pick Up Girls!
How to Save a Marriage (And Ruin Your Life)
How to Steal a Million
How to Stuff a Wild Bikini
How U Like Me Now
Howard the Duck
Hudsucker Proxy, The
Hue and Cry
Hullabaloo Over Georgie and Bonnie's Pictures
Human Feelings
Human Highway
Human Side, The
Hunk
Hurry Up, or I'll Be '30
Husbands, Wives, Money & Murder
Hyde Park Corner
Hysterical
I Can Get It for You Wholesale
I Could Never Have Sex With Any Man Who Has So Little Respect for My Husband
I Don't Buy Kisses Anymore
I Don't Want To Talk About It
I Dream of Jeannie: 15 Years Later
I Hate Actors
I Hate Blondes
I Hired a Contract Killer
I Killed Einstein, Gentlemen
I Know Where I'm Going
I Like It Like That
I Like Money
I Like Your Nerve
I Live My Life
I Love a Mystery
I Love My . . . Wife
I Love N.Y.
I Love You Again
I Love You, Alice B. Toklas
I Love You, Rosa
I Love You to Death
I Married a Centerfold
I Married a Witch
I Married a Woman
I Met Him in Paris
I Only Asked!
I Ought to Be in Pictures
I. Q.
I Sailed to Tahiti with an All Girl Crew
I Take These Men
I Wanna Be a Beauty Queen
I Wanna Hold Your Hand
I Want a Divorce
I Was a Male War Bride
I Was a Teenage TV Terrorist
I Was a Teenage Zombie
I Was an Adventuress
I Will, I Will . . . For Now
I Wonder Who's Killing Her Now
Icicle Thief, The
I'd Rather Be Rich
Ideal Husband, An
Identity Crisis
If a Man Answers
If I Had a Million
If I Were Rich
If It's Tuesday, This Must Be Belgium
If Looks Could Kill
If This Be Sin
If You Could Only Cook
I'll Do Anything
I'll Give a Million
I'll Never Forget What's 'is Name
I'll Take Sweden
I'll Tell the World
Illegally Yours
I'm All Right, Jack
I'm from Missouri
I'm Gonna Git You Sucka
I'm No Angel
Imitation General
Immortal Bachelor, The
Impatient Maiden, The
Impatient Years, The
Importance of Being Earnest, The
Imported Bridegroom, The
Impossible Years, The
Improper Channels
Impure Thoughts
In Between
In Fast Company
In God We Trust
In-Laws, The
In Love with an Older Woman
In Name Only
In Old Kentucky
In Person
In Praise of Older Women
In Search of the Perfect 10
In Society
In the Meantime, Darling
In the Mood
In the Name of the Father
In the Navy
In the Soup
In the Spirit
In the Summertime
Incident at Crestridge
Incoming Freshmen
Incredible Manitoba Animation
Incredible Mr. Limpet, The
Incredible Rocky Mountain Race
Incredible Shrinking Woman, The
Indian Summer
Indiscreet (1958)
Indiscreet (1988)
Infernal Trio, The
Innerspace
Innocent Affair, An
Innocent Sorcerers
Innocents in Paris
Inside Monkey Zetterland
Inside Story, The
Inspector Clouseau
Inspector General, The
Inspector Hornleigh
Inspector Lavardin
Instant Karma
International House
Intimate Lighting
Into the Blue
Into the Night
Into the Sun
Invasion of the Space Preachers
Invisible Kid, The
Invitation To a Wedding
Irish in Us, The
Irma la Douce
Iron Petticoat, The
Irreconcilable Differences
Is My Face Red?
Is There Sex After Death?
Ishtar
Island of Love
Island Rescue
Isn't Life Wonderful!
It Ain't Hay
It Came From Hollywood
It Could Happen to You (1937)
It Could Happen To You (1994)
It Grows on Trees
It Had to Be You
It Happened in Athens

It Happened on Fifth Avenue
It Happened One Night
It Happened to Jane
It Happened Tomorrow
It Happens Every Spring
It Happens Every Thursday
It Pays to Advertise
It Seemed Like a Good Idea at the Time
It Should Happen to You
It Shouldn't Happen to a Dog
It Started in Naples
It Started with a Kiss
It Started with Eve
It Takes Two
Italian Job, The
Italian Straw Hat, The
It's a Bet
It's a Bikini World
It's a Bundyful Life
It's a Dog's Life
It's a Gift
It's a Great Life
It's a Joke, Son
It's a Mad Mad Mad Mad World
It's a Wonderful World
It's in the Bag
It's Love I'm After
It's Never Too Late
It's Not Cricket (1937)
It's Not Cricket (1949)
It's Not the Size That Counts
It's Only Money
It's Pat: The Movie
It's Showtime
It's Tough to Be Famous
It's Your Move
J-Men Forever!
Jabberwocky
Jack and His Friends
Jack and the Beanstalk
Jackass Mail
Jackpot, The
Jacob Two-Two Meets the Hooded Fang
Jail Busters
Jalopy
Jamon Jamon
Jane and the Lost City
Jane Campion Shorts
Janie
Janie Gets Married
Jay Leno—The American Dream
JD and the Salt Flat Kid
Je T'Aime, Je T'Aime
Jeannie
Jekyll & Hyde . . . Together Again
Jerk, The
Jerk Too, The
Jerky Boys, The
Jersey Girl
Jetsons: The Movie
Jewel Robbery
Jewish Luck
Jimmy and Sally
Jimmy Hollywood
Jimmy the Gent
Jimmy the Kid
Jinx Money
Jinxed!
Jitterbugs
Joan of Ozark
Jocks
Joe Bob Briggs: Bad Girls Go to Hell
Joe Bob Briggs: Deadly Weapons
Joe Butterfly
Joe Versus the Volcano
Joey Breaker
John and Julie
John and Mary
John Goldfarb, Please Come Home
John Loves Mary
Johnny Banco
Johnny Be Good
Johnny Come Lately
Johnny Dangerously
Johnny Doesn't Live Here Any More
Johnny Steals Europe
Johnny Stecchino
Johnny Suede
Join the Marines
Joke of Destiny, A
Jokers, The
Jolly Bad Fellow
Jonathan Winters on the Ledge
Joseph Andrews
Josh and S.A.M.
Joshua Then and Now
Jour de Fête
Joy of Living
Joy of Sex
Joysticks
Jubilee
Judge Hardy's Children
Judge Priest
Julia Misbehaves
Julietta
Jumpin' Jack Flash
Jumping Jacks
June Bride
Jungle Gents
Junior
Junior Bonner
Junior Miss
Just Across the Street
Just Me and You
Just One Of The Girls
Just One of the Guys
Just Suppose
Just Tell Me What You Want
Just the Way You Are
Just You and Me, Kid
K-9
Kadoyng
Kaleidoscope
Kathleen
Kathy O'
Katie Did It
Keaton's Cop
Keep 'Em Flying
Keep Your Seats Please
Kentucky Fried Movie, The
Kentucky Kernels
Kettles in the Ozarks, The
Kettles on Old Macdonald's Farm, The
Key Exchange
Kid Blue
Kid Brother, The
Kid Dynamite
Kid from Brooklyn, The
Kid From Left Field, The
Kid, The
Kill the Umpire
Kind Hearts and Coronets
Kindergarten Cop
King and the Chorus Girl, The
King in New York, A
King of Comedy, The
King Ralph
King's Vacation, The
Kiss and Tell
Kiss for Corliss, A
Kiss in the Dark, A
Kiss Me Goodbye
Kiss Me, Stupid
KISS Meets the Phantom of the Park
Kiss Shot
Kiss the Girls and Make Them Die
Kiss the Other Sheik
Kiss Them for Me
Kisses for My President
Klondike Annie
Klutz, The
Knack, and How to Get It, The
Knock on Wood
Kotch
Kovacs!
La Cage aux Folles
La Cage aux Folles II
La Cage aux Folles III: The Wedding
La Chevre
La Chinoise
La Lectrice
La Parisienne
La Soufrière
L.A. Story
Labyrinth of Passion
Ladies in Love
Ladies' Man
Ladies of the Jury
Ladies Should Listen
Lady and the Mob, The
Lady Doctor
Lady Eve, The
Lady for a Day
Lady from Texas
Lady Godiva Rides Again
Lady Has Plans, The
Lady in a Jam
Lady Is Willing, The
Lady Killers, The
Lady L
Lady Liberty
Lady of the Pavements
Lady on a Train
Lady Says No, The
Lady Takes A Chance, A
Lady Takes a Flyer, The
Lady Takes a Sailor, The
Lady Wants Mink, The
Lady Windemere's Fan
Lady with a Past
Lady with Red Hair, The
Ladybugs
L'Age d'Or
Lana in Love
Landlord, The

Larceny, Inc
Las Vegas Hillbillys
Las Vegas Lady
Las Vegas Weekend
Laserman, The
Last American Virgin, The
Last Fling, The
Last Gentleman, The
Last Holiday
Last Married Couple in America, The
Last Millionaire, The
Last of Mrs. Cheyney, The
Last of the Red Hot Lovers
Last of the Secret Agents?, The
Last Outlaw, The
Last Porno Flick, The
Last Remake of Beau Geste, The
Last Resort
Last Time I Saw Archie, The
Late George Apley, The
Late Show, The
Lauderdale
Laughter
Laughter in Paradise
Laura Lansing Slept Here
Laurel and Hardy's Laughing 20s
Lavender Hill Mob, The
Law and Disorder
Law and the Lady, The
Law Is the Law, The
Law of Desire
Lawyer Man
Le Cavaleur
Le Gentleman D'Epsom
Le Jouet
Le Magnifique
Le Sex Shop
Leader of the Band
League of Gentlemen, The
League of Their Own, A
Leap into the Void
Leave It to Blondie
Leaving Normal
Lecheria De Zacarias, La
Left Right and Center
Legal Eagles
Lemon Drop Kid, The (1934)
Lemon Drop Kid, The (1951)
Lemonade Joe
Lena's Holiday
Leningrad Cowboys Go America
Leon, the Pig Farmer
Leonard Part 6
Les Carabiniers
Les Comperes
Lesson in Love, A
Let Freedom Ring
Let It Ride
Let's Do It Again
Let's Face It
Let's Get Tough!
Let's Go Navy!
Let's Make It Legal
Let's Make Love
Let's Make Up
Let's Talk About Men
Let's Talk About Women
Letter of Introduction, A
Letter to Brezhnev
Letting Go
Levy and Goliath
Libeled Lady
License to Drive
Lieutenant Wore Skirts, The
Life and Times of the Chocolate Killer, The
Life Begins at Forty
Life Begins for Andy Hardy
Life Begins in College
Life in the Theater, A
Life Is a Long Quiet River
Life Is Sweet
Life of Riley, The
Life Stinks
Life Upside Down
Life with Blondie
Life with Father
Life with Henry
Life with Mikey
Lifetaker
Lightning Jack
Like Father, Like Son
Li'l Abner
Lily in Love
Limelight
Limit Up
Linguini Incident, The
Liquid Sky
Listen to Me
Little Annie Rooney
Little Big League
Little Cigars
Little Darlings
Little Giant
Little Giant, The
Little Giants
Little Hut, The
Little Miss Marker (1934)
Little Miss Marker (1980)
Little Monsters
Little Murders
Little Nuns, The
Little Orphan Annie
Little Rascals, The
Little Romance, A
Little Sex, A
Little Vegas
Little White Lies
Little World of Don Camillo, The
Live From Washington It's Dennis Miller
Live, Love and Learn
Lively Set, The
Livin' Large
Livin' the Life
Living End, The
Living It Up
Living on Tokyo Time
Lizards, The
Lizzies of Mack Sennett, The
Lobster for Breakfast
Lobsterman from Mars
Local Hero
Lock Up Your Daughters!
Lonely Guy, The
Lonely in America
Lonely Wives
Long Gone
Long, Long Trailer, The
Longest Yard, The
Look Who's Laughing
Look Who's Talking
Look Who's Talking Now
Look Who's Talking Too
Lookin' to Get Out
Looking for Love
Looney, Looney, Looney Bugs Bunny Movie, The
Loose Cannons
Loose Connections
Loose in London
Loose Screws
Loot
Lord Love a Duck
Lords of Flatbush, The
Loser Takes All
Losin' It
Lost and Found
Lost in a Harem
Lost in Alaska
Lost in America
Louisa
Lovable Cheat, The
Love Among Thieves
Love and Death
Love and Larceny
Love and the Frenchwoman
Love at First Bite
Love at First Sight
Love at Large
Love at Stake
Love at the Top
Love Before Breakfast
Love Bug, The
Love Crazy
Love Finds Andy Hardy
Love God?, The
Love Happy
Love in a Taxi
Love in Bloom
Love Is a Ball
Love Is a Racket
Love Is News
Love Laughs at Andy Hardy
Love Lottery, The
Love Nest
Love on a Pillow
Love on the Run
Love Potion No. 9
Love That Brute
Love Thrill Murders
Love Thy Neighbor
Loved One, The
Lovelines
Lover Come Back (1946)
Lover Come Back (1962)
Loverboy
Lovers and Liars
Lovers and Lollipops
Lovers and Other Strangers
Lovers, Happy Lovers
Lovers Like Us
Lovers of Paris
Loves and Times of Scaramouche, The
Loves of a Blonde
Lovesick
Loving Couples
Lt. Robin Crusoe, USN
Lucas
Luck of the Irish, The
Luckiest Man In The World, The
Lucky Devils
Lucky Jim
Lucky Lady

Lucky Losers
Lucky Night
Lucky Partners
Lucky Stiff
Lucky to Be a Woman
Lucy's Lost Episodes
Luggage of the Gods!
Lunatic, The
Lunatics: A Love Story
Lunatics and Lovers
Lunch Wagon
Lupo
Lust in the Dust
Luz—Cama—Accion
M*A*S*H
M*A*S*H—Goodbye, Farewell, Amen
Ma and Pa Kettle
Ma and Pa Kettle at Home
Ma and Pa Kettle at the Fair
Ma and Pa Kettle at Waikiki
Ma and Pa Kettle Back on the Farm
Ma and Pa Kettle Go to Town
Ma and Pa Kettle on Vacation
Mabel and Fatty
Mack Sennett Comedies—Vol. 1
Mack Sennett Comedies—Vol. 2
Mad About Men
Mad about Music
Mad about You
Mad Adventures of "Rabbi" Jacob, The
Mad Dog and Glory
Mad Little Island
Mad Mission 3
Mad Monster Party?
Mad Wednesday
Madame
Madame Racketeer
Made for Each Other
Made in America
Made in Heaven (1952)
Made in Heaven (1987)
Made in Italy
Made in Paris
Madhouse
Madigan's Million
Magic Adventure
Magic Christian, The
Magic Show, The
Magic Town
Magic Voyage, The
Magic World of Topo Gigio, The
Magnificent Cuckold, The
Magnificent Dope, The
Magnificent Fraud, The
Magnificent Magical Magnet of Santa Mesa, The
Magnificent Roughnecks
Magnificent Seven Deadly Sins, The
Maid in Paris
Maid, The
Maid to Order
Maid's Night Out
Main Event, The
Maisie
Maisie Gets Her Man
Maisie Goes to Reno
Maisie Was a Lady
Major and the Minor, The
Major Barbara
Major League
Major League II
Major Payne
Make Me an Offer
Make Mine Mink
Make Room for Tomorrow
Make Way for a Lady
Make Your Own Bed
Making It
Making Mr. Right
Making of a Male Model
Making the Grade
Malcolm
Male Animal, The
Male Hunt
Male of the Century, The
Malibu Beach
Malibu Bikini Shop, The
Malicious
Maltese Bippy, The
Mama, There's a Man in Your Bed
Mama Turns 100
Man/Woman Wanted
Man, a Woman and a Bank, A
Man About Town
Man Alive
Man Called Flintstone, The
Man Called Sarge, A
Man From Blankley's, The
Man from Clover Grove, The
Man from Down Under, The
Man from Nowhere, The
Man from the Diner's Club, The
Man in a Cocked Hat
Man in the Moon, The
Man in the White Suit, The
Man of Flowers, A
Man of No Importance, A
Man of the House
Man on Fire
Man on the Flying Trapeze, The
Man Trouble
Man Upstairs, The
Man Who Broke the Bank at Monte Carlo, The
Man Who Came for Coffee, The
Man Who Came to Dinner, The
Man Who Could Work Miracles, The
Man Who Had Power Over Women, The
Man Who Loved Redheads, The
Man Who Loved Women, The (1977)
Man Who Loved Women, The (1983)
Man Who Wagged His Tail, The
Man Who Wasn't There, The
Man with a Million
Man with Connections, The
Man with One Red Shoe
Man with the Balloons, The
Man with Two Brains, The
Manchu Eagle Murder Caper Mystery, The
Manhattan Murder Mystery
Manifesto
Mannequin
Mannequin Two: On the Move
Manny's Orphans
Man's Best Friend
Man's Favorite Sport?
Many Happy Returns (1934)
Many Happy Returns (1986)
Many Thanks to Mr. Atkins
Marathon
March on Paris 1914—of Generaloberst Alexander von Kluck—and His Memory
Margin for Error
Marianne
Marquise, The
Marriage Circle, The
Marriage-Go-Round, The
Marriage Is Alive and Well
Marriage Italian Style
Marriage of Balzaminov, The
Marriage on the Rocks
Marriage: Year One
Married Bachelor
Married to It
Married to the Mob
Marry Me Again
Marry Me, Marry Me
Marrying Kind, The
Marrying Man, The
Martha's Attic, Vols. 1-6
Martians Go Home
Marx Brothers In a Nutshell, The
Mary, Mary
Masala
Mask, The (1988)
Mask, The (1994)
Master Minds
Master of the House
Mastermind
Masterpiece of Murder, A
Matador
Match Factory Girl, The
Matchless
Matchmaker, The
Matilda
Matinee
Mating Game, The
Mating Season, The (1951)
Mating Season, The (1980)
Matter of Degrees, A
Matter of Resistance, A
Matter of WHO, A

Express
Moonstruck
More American Graffiti
More Milton Berle's Mad World of Comedy
More Roobarb
More Than a Miracle
More Than a Secretary
More Than Friends
More the Merrier, The
Morgan!
Morgan Stewart's Coming Home
Moron Movies
Moron Movies, More
Morons from Outer Space
Moscow on the Hudson
Most Eligible Bachelor
Mother Didn't Tell Me
Mother Is a Freshman
Mother, Jugs & Speed
Mother Kusters Goes to Heaven
Motorama
Mouse on the Moon, The
Mouse That Roared, The
Mouth to Mouth
Move
Move Over, Darling
Movers and Shakers
Movie Crazy
Movie Movie
Moving
Moving Violations
Mr. and Mrs. North
Mr. and Mrs. Smith
Mr. Baseball
Mr. Belvedere Goes to College
Mr. Belvedere Rings the Bell
Mr. Bill Looks Back
Mr. Billion
Mr. Blandings Builds His Dream House
Mr. Cohen Takes a Walk
Mr. Destiny
Mr. Hex
Mr. Hobbs Takes a Vacation
Mr. Hulot's Holiday
Mr. Imperium
Mr. Love
Mr. Lucky
Mr. Magoo In Sherwood Forest
Mr. Magoo—Man of Mystery
Mr. Magoo—1001 Arabian Nights
Mr. Magoo's Christmas Carol
Mr. Magoo's Story Book
Mr. Mike's Mondo Video
Mr. Mom
Mr. Muggs Steps Out
Mr. Nanny
Mr. North
Mr. Peabody and the Mermaid
Mr. Potts Goes to Moscow
Mr. Quincey of Monte Carlo
Mr. Robinson Crusoe
Mr. Saturday Night
Mr. Scoutmaster
Mr. Skitch
Mr. Superinvisible
Mr. Winkle Goes to War
Mr. Wonderful
Mrs. 'Arris Goes to Paris
Mrs. Delafield Wants to Marry
Mrs. Doubtfire
Much Ado About Nothing
Mugsy's Girls
Multiple Maniacs
Munchie
Munchies
Munster, Go Home
Munsters' Revenge, The
Murder by Death
Murder, Czech Style
Murder, He Says
Murderer Lives at Number 21, The
Muriel's Wedding
Murmur of the Heart
Murphy's Fault
Muscle Beach Party
Mutant Video
Mutants in Paradise
My Best Friend Is a Vampire
My Best Friend's Girl
My Blue Heaven
My Boyfriend's Back (1989)
My Boyfriend's Back (1993)
My Breakfast with Blassie
My Brother Talks to Horses
My Chauffeur
My Cousin Vinny
My Dear Secretary
My Demon Lover
My Dog the Thief
My Father, the Hero
My Favorite Blonde
My Favorite Brunette
My Favorite Spy
My Favorite Wife
My Favorite Year
My Friend Irma
My Friend Irma Goes West
My Gal Loves Music
My Geisha
My Girl
My Hero 1
My Hobo
My Learned Friend
My Life with Caroline
My Little Chickadee
My Love Came Back
My Man
My Man Adam
My Man Godfrey (1936)
My Man Godfrey (1957)
My Mom's Werewolf
My New Gun
My New Partner
My Pleasure Is My Business
My Seven Little Sins
My Sister Eileen
My Six Loves
My Stepmother Is an Alien
My Therapist
My Tutor
My Widow and I
My Wonderful Life
Mystery Date
Mystery Train
Mystic Pizza
Nadine
Naked Ape, The
Naked Gun, The
Naked Gun 2 1/2: The Smell of Fear, The
Naked Gun 33 1/3: The Final Insult
Naked in New York
Naked Truth, The
Nasty Habits
Nasty Rabbit, The
National Exposure
National Health, The
National Lampoon Goes to the Movies
National Lampoon's Christmas Vacation
National Lampoon's Class Reunion
National Lampoon's European Vacation
National Lampoon's Loaded Weapon
National Lampoon's Vacation
Naughty Knights
Naughty Nineties
Necessary Roughness
Neighborhood Thief, The
Neighbors
Nervous Ticks
Network
Neurotic Cabaret
Never a Dull Moment (1943)
Never a Dull Moment (1950)
Never Give a Sucker an Even Break
Never on Tuesday
Never Say Die
Never Say Goodbye
Never Steal Anything Small
Never Too Late
Never Wave at a WAC
New Age, The
New Leaf, A
New Life, A
New York Town
New York's Finest
Next Stop, Greenwich Village
Next Time I Marry
Next to No Time
Next Year if All Goes Well
Nice Girl Like Me, A
Nice Girls Don't Explode
Nickel & Dime
Nickelodeon
Night Alone
Night and Day
Night at the Opera, A
Night Before, The
Night Call Nurses
Night in Casablanca, A
Night in Heaven, A
Night in the Life of Jimmy Reardon, A
Night Life of the Gods
Night Like This, A
Night on Earth

Night Patrol
Night Shift
Night They Raided Minsky's, The
Night to Remember, A
Night Visitor
Night We Never Met, The
Nightlife
Nightmare Before Christmas, The
Nightmare in Blood
Nine Lives of Fritz the Cat, The
9 to 5
1941
92 in the Shade
Ninja Academy
Ninotchka
Nitwits, The
No Leave, No Love
No Limit
No Minor Vices
No More Ladies
No My Darling Daughter
No Place Like Homicide!
No Place to Land
No Room for the Groom
No Sex Please—We're British
No Small Affair
No Surrender
No-Tell Hotel, The
No Time for Comedy
No Time for Flowers
No Time for Love
No Time for Sergeants
No Time to Marry
No Way to Treat a Lady
Nobody's Baby
Nobody's Fool (1936)
Nobody's Fool (1986)
Nobody's Fool (1994)
Nobody's Perfect (1968)
Nobody's Perfect (1990)
Nobody's Perfekt
Noises Off
Noisy Neighbors
Noose Hangs High, The
Norman . . . Is That You?
Norman Loves Rose
Norman's Awesome Experience
North
North Avenue Irregulars, The
North Dallas Forty
North to Alaska
Not a Penny More, Not a Penny Less
Not for Publication
Not of This World
Not Quite Human
Not Quite Human II
Not So Dusty
Not So Quiet on the Western Front
Not with My Wife You Don't!
Nothing But the Best
Nothing But the Truth (1929)
Nothing But the Truth (1941)
Nothing But Trouble (1944)
Nothing But Trouble (1991)
Nothing Lasts Forever
Nothing Personal
Nothing Sacred
Notorious Landlady, The
Novel Affair, A
Now You See Him, Now You Don't
Now You See It, Now You Don't
Nude Bomb, The
Nudo di Donna
Nuisance, The
Nuns on the Run
Nutty, Naughty Chateau
Nutty Professor, The
O Lucky Man!
Object of Beauty, The
Obliging Young Lady
O.C. & Stiggs
Ocean Drive Weekend
Odd Couple, The
Odd Job, The
Odd Jobs
Oddball Hall
Odds and Evens
Off Beat
Off Limits
Off Sides
Off the Dole
Off the Mark
Off the Wall
Office Picnic, The
Oh Dad, Poor Dad, Mama's Hung You in the Closet and I'm Feeling So Sad
Oh, God!
Oh God! Book II
Oh, God! You Devil
Oh, Heavenly Dog!
Oh, Men! Oh, Women!
Oh! Sailor, Behave!
Oh! Those Most Secret Agents
Oh, What a Night
Ohayo
Old Bones of the River
Old Dracula
Old Enough
Old-Fashioned Way, The
Old Hutch
Old Mother Riley
Old Spanish Custom, An
Oldest Profession, The
On Approval
On Dress Parade
On My Way to the Crusades, I Met a Girl Who . . .
On Our Merry Way
On Our Selection
On the Air Live with Captain Midnight
On the Beat
On the Double
On the Isle of Samoa
Once Around
Once Bitten
Once in a Lifetime
Once in Paris . . .
Once More My Darling
Once More, With Feeling
Once Upon a Crime
Once Upon a Honeymoon
Once Upon a Scoundrel
Once Upon a Spy
Once Upon a Time
One and Only, The
One Big Affair
One Body Too Many
One Cooks, the Other Doesn't
One Crazy Night
One Crazy Summer
One Exciting Adventure
One Last Fling
One More Saturday Night
One More Spring
One More Time
One More Tomorrow
One Night in Lisbon
One Night Only!
One Rainy Afternoon
One, Two, Three
One Way Pendulum
One Way to Love
One Wild Moment
One Woman or Two
Onionhead
Only the Lonely
Only Two Can Play
Only When I Larf
Only When I Laugh
Only with Married Men
Only You (1992)
Only You (1994)
Open All Hours
Open the Door and See All the People
Operation Bikini
Operation Mad Ball
Operation Petticoat (1959)
Operation Petticoat (1977)
Operation Snafu (1961)
Operation Snafu (1970)
Operation Snatch
Operation St. Peter's
Opportunity Knocks
Opposite Sex (And How to Live with Them), The
Optimists, The
Options
Orders Are Orders
Orders Is Orders
Oscar
Other People's Money
Otley
Our Betters
Our Blushing Brides
Our Father
Our Gang
Our Gang Comedies
Our Hearts Were Growing Up
Our Hearts Were Young and Gay
Our Hospitality
Our Man in Havana
Our Miss Brooks
Our Relations
Our Wife
Out All Night
Out Cold
Out of It
Out of the Blue
Out-of-Towners, The
Out on a Limb
Out West with the Hardys
Outback Bound
Outlaws Is Coming, The

Outrageous
Outrageous Fortune
Outtakes
Over Her Dead Body
Over My Dead Body
Over She Goes
Over the Brooklyn Bridge
Over-the-Hill Gang, The
Over-the-Hill Gang Rides Again, The
Over the Moon
Over the Odds
Over 21
Overboard
Overnight
Ovide And The Gang
Owl and the Pussycat, The
Pack Up Your Troubles (1932)
Pack Up Your Troubles (1939)
Packin' It In
Pad and How to Use It, The
Paddy
Paddy, the Next Best Thing
Page Miss Glory
Pain in the A—, A
Pajama Party
Paleface, The
Palm Beach Story, The
Palm Springs Weekend
Palombella Rossa
Palooka
Pals
Panama Lady
Pandemonium
Panic Button
Pantaloons
Papa's Delicate Condition
Paper Lion
Paper Marriage
Paper Moon
Paradise for Three
Paradisio
Pardners
Pardon Mon Affaire
Pardon My French
Pardon My Past
Pardon My Sarong
Pardon Us
Parent Trap, The
Parent Trap III
Parent Trap II
Parenthood
Parents
Paris Holiday
Paris in the Month of August
Paris Playboys
Paris—when It Sizzles
Parlor, Bedroom and Bath
Part-Time Wife
Partners
Party Camp
Party Favors
Party Incorporated
Party, The
Party Wire
Pass the Ammo
Passed Away
Passionate Plumber, The
Passionate Sentry, The
Passionate Thief, The
Passport to Pimlico
Pat and Mike
Paternity
Patsy, The
Paul Reiser—Out on a Whim
Pauline at the Beach
P.C.U.
Peck's Bad Boy
Peck's Bad Boy with the Circus
Pee-Wee Herman Show, The
Pee-wee's Big Adventure
Peeper
Peg o' My Heart
Peggy
Peggy Sue Got Married
Peking Opera Blues
Penelope
Penn & Teller Get Killed
Penn and Teller's Cruel Tricks for Dear Friends
Penny Princess
Penthouse
People Are Funny
People Will Talk (1935)
People Will Talk (1951)
Pepe
Pepi, Luci, Bom
Pepper and His Wacky Taxi
Perfect Couple, A
Perfect Friday
Perfect Furlough, The
Perfect Gentlemen
Perfect Marriage, The
Perfect Match, The
Perfect People
Perfect Specimen, The
Perfect Woman, The
Perfectly Normal
Perfumed Nightmare, The
Period of Adjustment
Personal Foul
Personal Property
Personal Services
Personals, The
Peter's Friends
Petit Con
Petticoat Fever
Phantom Empire
Phantom of Liberty, The
Phantom of the Paradise
Phffft!
Philadelphia Story, The
Piccadilly Jim
Pick-up Artist, The
Pickle, The
Pickles Make Me Cry
Picture Show Man, The
Piece of the Action, A
Pigeon That Took Rome, The
Pillow Talk
Pillow to Post
Pink Panther Strikes Again, The
Pink Panther, The
Pinocchio
Pinocchio's Christmas
Pinocchio's Storybook Adventures
Pippi Longstocking—New Adventures of, The
Pirates
Pizza Triangle, The
Plain Clothes
Planes, Trains & Automobiles
Platinum Blonde
Play It Again, Sam
Playboy of the Western World
Playful Little Audrey
Playmates
Playtime
Plaza Suite
Please Believe Me
Please Don't Eat the Daisies
Please Turn Over
Pleasure of His Company, The
Plot Against Harry, The
Plumber, The
Poacher's Daughter, The
Pocket Money
Pocketful of Miracles
Poison Ivy
Police Academy
Police Academy 2: Their First Assignment
Police Academy 3: Back in Training
Police Academy 4: Citizens on Patrol
Police Academy 5: Assignment Miami Beach
Police Academy 6: City Under Siege
Police Squad!—Help Wanted
Polyester
Pom-Pom Girls
Pontiac Moon
Pope Must Diet, The
Popeye
Poppy
Porky's
Porky's 2: The Next Day
Porky's Revenge
Positively True Adventures of the Alleged Texas Cheerleader-Murdering Mom, The
Postcards from the Edge
Pourquoi Pas!
Power
Powwow Highway
Practically Yours
Prelude to a Kiss
President's Analyst, The
Press for Time
Pretty in Pink
Pretty Poison
Pretty Smart
Pretty Woman
Primo Baby
Prince and the Pauper, The (1937)
Prince and the Pauper, The (1962)
Prince and the Showgirl, The
Prince of Bel Air
Prince of Pennsylvania, The
Princess and the Pirate, The
Princess Bride, The

Princess Caraboo
Princess Comes Across, The
Princess O'Rourke
Prisoner of Second Avenue, The
Prisoner of Zenda, The
Private Affairs
Private Benjamin
Private Duty Nurses
Private Eyes, The
Private Function, A
Private Lessons
Private Lives
Private Navy of Sgt. O'Farrell, The
Private Resort
Private School
Private War of Major Benson, The
Privates on Parade
Prize Fighter, The
Problem Child
Problem Child 2
Producers, The
Professor Beware
Projectionist, The
Promise Her Anything
Promises! Promises!
Promoter, The
Protocol
Prudence and the Pill
Psych Out
Public Pigeon No. One
Puppetoon Movie, The
Pure Hell of St. Trinian's, The
Pure Luck
Purple People Eater
Purple Rose of Cairo, The
Putney Swope
Pygmalion
Quackser Fortune Has a Cousin in the Bronx
Quality Street
Quick Before It Melts
Quick Change
Quick, Let's Get Married
Quiet Little Neighborhood, A Perfect Little Murder, A
Quiet Wedding
Quiet Weekend
Rabbit Test
Race for Your Life, Charlie Brown
Radio Days
Radioland Murders
Rage of Paris, The
Rags to Riches
Raining Stones
Raising Arizona
Raising the Wind
Rally 'Round the Flag, Boys!
Ranch, The
Rancho Deluxe
Rascals, The
Rat Race, The
Ratings Game, The
Rationing
Rattle of a Simple Man, The
Ravishing Idiot
Reaching for the Moon
Reaching for the Sun
Ready to Wear
Real Genius
Real Life
Real Men
Reality Bites
Really Weird Tales
Red Inn, The
Reefer Madness
Ref, The
Reformer and the Redhead, The
Reivers, The
Reluctant Astronaut, The
Reluctant Debutante, The
Reluctant Dragon, The
Remarkable Andrew, The
Remarkable Mr. Pennypacker, The
Remember the Night
Renaissance Man
Rendezvous with Annie
Rent Control
Repo Man
Repossessed
Reserved for Ladies
Return of Jafar, The
Return of Spinal Tap, The
Return of the Killer Tomatoes
Return of the Pink Panther, The
Return of the Tall Blond Man With One Black Shoe, The
Return to Mayberry
Reuben, Reuben
Reunion in Vienna
Revenge of the Nerds
Revenge of the Nerds 2: Nerds in Paradise
Revenge of the Nerds 3: The Next Generation
Revenge of the Pink Panther
Revenge of the Teenage Vixens from Outer Space
Reversal of Fortune
Rhinestone
Rhubarb
Rich in Love
Rich Man, Poor Girl
Richard
Richard Pryor Here and Now
Richard Pryor Live and Smokin'
Richard Pryor—Live in Concert
Richard Pryor Live on the Sunset Strip
Richest Girl in the World, The
Richie Rich
Ride 'Em Cowboy
Ride the Wild Surf
Riders of the Storm
Riding on Air
Riff Raff
Rikki and Pete
Ring-a-Ding Rhythm
Ring Around the Clock
Rio Rita
Ripping Yarns-Vol. 1
Rise and Rise of Michael Rimmer, The
Rising Damp
Risky Business
Ritz, The
Road Scholar
Road Show
Road to Bali
Road to Hong Kong, The
Road to Morocco
Road to Reno, The
Road to Rio
Road to Singapore
Road to Utopia
Road to Wellville, The
Road to Zanzibar
Robin Hood: Men in Tights
Rock-a-Bye Baby
Rock 'n' Roll High School
Rock, Rock, Rock!
Roman Holiday
Romanoff and Juliet
Romantic Comedy
Romantic Englishwoman, The
Rookie of the Year
Room for One More
Room Service
Roommates
Rooney
Rosalie Goes Shopping
Rosencrantz and Guildenstern Are Dead
Rover Dangerfield
Roxanne
Roxie Hart
Royal Affair, A
Royal Family of Broadway, The
Royal Scandal, A
Rude Awakening
Ruggles of Red Gap
Rules of the Game, The
Ruling Class, The
Run for Your Money, A
Runaway Bus, The
Running Mates
Running Wild
Russians Are Coming! The Russians Are Coming!, The
Rustlers' Rhapsody
Ruthless People
Rutles, The
Sabrina
Sad Sack, The
Safety Last
Sail a Crooked Ship
Sailor Beware
Saint Jack
Sallah
Sally and Saint Anne
Sally of the Sawdust
Salty O'Rourke
Sam Kinison Live!
Samantha
Same Time, Next Year
Sammy and Rosie Get Laid
Sammy, the Way-Out Seal
San Diego, I Love You
Sandwich Man, The
Sandy Gets Her Man
Santa Clause, The
Saps at Sea
Saratoga
Saturday the 14th
Saturday's Children
Savannah Smiles
Saving Grace
Say Anything . . .

Say Yes
Scalphunters, The
Scandal in Sorrento
Scandalous
Scandalous John
Scaramouche
Scared Stiff
Scattergood Baines
Scavenger Hunt
Scenes from a Mall
Scenes from the Class Struggle in Beverly Hills
School Daze
School for Scoundrels
School Spirit
Score
Scotch on the Rocks
Scoundrel, The
Scout, The
Screwballs
Scrooged
Scudda Hoo! Scudda Hay!
Search for Signs of Intelligent Life in the Universe, The
Second Best Bed
Second Best Secret Agent in the Whole Wide World
Second Fiddle
Second Honeymoon
Second Sight
Second Time Around, The
Secret Admirer
Secret Diary of Sigmund Freud, The
Secret Fantasy
Secret Honor
Secret Ingredient
Secret Life of an American Wife, The
Secret Life of Walter Mitty, The
Secret of My Success, The
Secret of Santa Vittoria, The
Secret War of Harry Frigg, The
Seduced and Abandoned
Seduction of Mimi, The
See Here, Private Hargrove
See No Evil, Hear No Evil
Seems Like Old Times
Semi-Tough
Senator Was Indiscreet, The
Send Me No Flowers
Senior Week
Seniors, The
Sensual Man, The
Sensuous Nurse, The
Separate Vacations
Serafino
Serenade for Two Spies
Sergeants 3
Serial
Service De Luxe
Sesame Street: Big Bird in China
Sesame Street: Big Bird in Japan
Sesame Street Presents Follow That Bird
7 Capital Sins
Seven Chances
Seven Sinners
Seven Year Itch, The
Severed Head, A
Sex and Buttered Popcorn
Sex and the Single Girl
Sex Kittens Go to College
Sex Machine, The
Sex on the Run
Sex with a Smile
Sexpot
Sextette
Sez O'Reilly to McNab
Shadows and Fog
Shag, The Movie
Shaggy D.A., The
Shaggy Dog, The
Shakes the Clown
Shakiest Gun in the West, The
Shampoo
She Couldn't Take It
She-Devil
She Didn't Say No!
She Done Him Wrong
She Goes to War
She Married Her Boss
Sheep Has Five Legs, The
Sheila Levine Is Dead and Living in New York
She'll Be Wearing Pink Pajamas
Shepherd of the Ozarks
Sheriff of Fractured Jaw, The
Sherlock, Jr.
She's Back
She's Gotta Have It
She's Having a Baby
She's in the Army
She's Out of Control
Shirley Valentine
Shmenges, The—The Last Polka
Shooting Elizabeth
Shooting Party, The
Shop Around the Corner, The
Short Circuit
Short Circuit 2
Short Time
Shot in the Dark, A
Show-Off, The
Show People
Shrimp on the Barbie, The
Shut My Big Mouth
Sibling Rivalry
Side Street Angel
Sidewalks of New York
Silent Movie
Silver Streak
Simchon Family, The
Simon
Simon and Laura
Simon of the Desert
Simple Case of Money, A
Simple Twist of Fate, A
Sing As We Go
Singles
Sinners
Sister Act
Sister Act 2: Back in the Habit
Sitting Ducks
Sitting Pretty
Situation Hopeless—But Not Serious
Six of a Kind
Six Pack
Sixteen Candles
Sizzle Beach, U.S.A.
Skateboard Kid, The
Ski Patrol
Skiddoo
Skin Deep
Skin Game
Skylark (1941)
Skylark (1993)
Slacker
Slap Shot
Slapstick of Another Kind
Slave Girls from Beyond Infinity
Slaves of New York
Sleeper
Sleepless in Seattle
Sleuth
Slight Case of Murder, A
Slightly Dangerous
Slightly Honorable
Slightly Pregnant Man, A
Slither
Slugger's Wife, The
Slumber Party '57
Small Town Girl
Smallest Show on Earth, The
Smashing Time
Smile
Smiles of a Summer Night
Smiley
Smiley Gets a Gun
Smokey and the Bandit
Smokey and the Bandit, Part 2
Smokey and the Bandit III
Smugglers' Cove
Smurfs and the Magic Flute, The
Smurfs, The
Snafu
Snapper, The
Snoopy, Come Home
Snow—The Movie
Snow White and the Three Stooges
Snowball Express
So Fine
So Goes My Love
So I Married An Axe Murderer
So This Is London
So This Is New York
So This Is Washington
Soapdish
S.O.B.
Soggy Bottom USA
Solid Gold Cadillac, The
Some Like It Cool
Some Like It Hot
Someone Like You
Something for—Everyone
Something for the Birds
Something Special
Something Wild
Son-In-Law
Son of Flubber
Son of Paleface
Son of the Pink Panther

Song is Born, A
Sons of the Desert
Sooner or Later
Sorrowful Jones
Soul Man
Sound of Trumpets, The
South Sea Woman
Southern Yankee, A
Spaceballs
Spaced Invaders
Spaced Out
Sparkle
Speak Easily
Speechless
Speed Zone!
Spies Like Us
Spite Marriage
Splash
Splitting Heirs
Spook Buster
Spooks Run Wild
Spring Break
Spring in Park Lane
Spring Meeting
S.P.Y.S.
Squeeze Play
Squeeze, The
St. Benny the Dip
St. Louis Kid
Stage Door
Staircase
Stand-In
Standing Room Only
Star Spangled Girl
Stardust Memories
Stars and Bars
Start the Revolution Without Me
Starting Over
Statue, The
Stay Hungry
Stay Tuned
Steamboat Bill, Jr.
Steelyard Blues
Stepmonster
Steve Allen's Golden Age of Comedy
Steve Martin Live!
Stewardess School
Stick Up, The
Sticky Fingers
Still Not Quite Human
Sting, The
Sting II, The
Stir Crazy
Stoned Age, The
Stoogemania
Stop! Look! and Laugh!
Stop! or My Mom Will Shoot
Storm in a Teacup
Story of Boys and Girls, The
Straight Talk
Straight to Hell
Strange Bedfellows
Strange Brew
Strange Case Of The End of Civilization As We Know It
Stranger Than Paradise
Strawberry and Chocolate
Strictly Ballroom
Strictly Business
Strike It Rich
Stripes
Stroker Ace
Strong Man, The
Strongest Man in the World, The
Stuck On You!
Student Nurses, The
Student Prince in Old Heidelberg, The
Student Teachers, The
Successful Calamity, A
Such a Gorgeous Kid Like Me
Such Good Friends
Sucker, The
Suddenly, It's Spring
Sugarland Express, The
Sullivan's Travels
Summer House, The
Summer Job
Summer Night, with Greek Profile, Almond Eyes and Scent of Basil
Summer Rental
Summer School
Summer School Teachers
Sunburn
Sunday in New York
Sunset
Sunshine Boys, The
Super, The
Superdad
Support Your Local Gunfighter
Support Your Local Sheriff
Suppose They Gave a War and Nobody Came?
Sure Thing, The
Surf Nazis Must Die
Surf Ninjas
Surprise Package
Surrender
Survivors, The
Susan Slept Here
Sweepstakes Winner
Sweet and Sour
Sweet Devil
Sweet Liberty
Sweet November
Sweet Perfection
Swimming to Cambodia
Swinger, The
Swinging Cheerleaders, The
Swinging Wives
Swiss Miss
Switch
Switching Channels
Sylvia Scarlett
T Bone N Weasel
Take a Letter, Darling
Take Down
Take Her, She's Mine
Take Me to Town
Take the Money and Run
Take this Job and Shove It
Taking Care of Business
Tale of Springtime, A
Talk of the Town, The
Talkin' Dirty After Dark
Tall Blond Man with One Black Shoe
Tall, Dark and Handsome
Tall Guy, The
Tall Story
Taming of the Shrew, The (1929)
Taming of the Shrew, The (1967)
Tammy and the Bachelor
Tammy and the Doctor
Tammy Tell Me True
Tampopo
Tap
Tapeheads
Tatie Danielle
Tawny Pipit
Taxi!
Taxing Woman, A
Taxing Woman's Return, A
Teachers
Teacher's Pet
Teahouse of the August Moon, The
Teen Witch
Teen Wolf
Teen Wolf Too
Teenage Mutant Ninja Turtles—The Movie
Teenage Mutant Ninja Turtles 2: The Secret of the Ooze
Teenage Mutant Ninja Turtles III
Telephone, The
Tell It to the Judge
10
Ten From Your Show of Shows
Ten Thousand Bedrooms
Tender Loving Care
Tender Trap, The
Tenderfoot, The
Tendres Cousines
Texas Across the River
Thank Heaven for Small Favors
Thanks for Everything
Thanksgiving Day
Thark
That Certain Feeling
That Darn Cat
That Funny Feeling
That Kind of Woman
That Obscure Object of Desire
That Sinking Feeling
That Touch of Mink
That Uncertain Feeling
That Wonderful Urge
That's Life!
That's My Boy
That's the Way of the World
Theatre Royal
Theodora Goes Wild
There Goes My Heart
There Goes the Neighborhood
There's a Girl in My Soup
There's Always a Woman
They All Kissed the Bride
They All Laughed
They Call Me Bruce
They Call Me Trinity
They Got Me Covered
They Had to See Paris
They Might Be Giants
They Still Call Me Bruce
They're a Weird Mob
Thief of Paris, The
Thief Who Came to Dinner, The
Things Change

Think Big
Thinkin Big'
Third Finger, Left Hand
Third Generation, The
Thirty Day Princess
30 Foot Bride of Candy Rock, The
30 Is a Dangerous Age, Cynthia
36 Fillette
Thirty-Six Hours to Kill
This Can't Be Love
This Could Be the Night
This Green Hell
This Happy Feeling
This Is My Life
This Is Spinal Tap
This Is the Life
This Is the Night
This Man in Paris
This Man Is News
This Side of Heaven
This Thing Called Love
This Week of Grace
Those Daring Young Men in Their Jaunty Jalopies
Those Magnificent Men in Their Flying Machines
Those Were the Days (1934)
Those Were the Days (1940)
Thousand Clowns, A
Three Amigos!
Three Blind Mice
Three Cheers for the Irish
Three Cockeyed Sailors
Three-Cornered Moon
Three Crowns of the Sailor
Three Daring Daughters
Three for the Road
Three Fugitives
Three Guys Named Mike
Three Husbands
Three in the Attic
Three Into Two Won't Go
Three Is a Family
Three Men and a Baby
Three Men and a Cradle
Three Men and a Little Lady
Three Men on a Horse
Three Nuts in Search of a Bolt
Three O'Clock High
Three on a Couch
Three Ring Circus
Three Stooges Go Around the World in a Daze, The
Three Stooges in Orbit, The
Three Stooges Meet Hercules, The
Three Wise Fools
Three Wise Girls
Threesome
Thrill Of It All, The
Throw Momma From the Train
Thursday's Game
Tiger and the Pussycat, The
Tiger Makes Out, The
Tigers in Lipstick
Tight Little Island
Tight Shoes
Tiki Tiki
Till Marriage Do Us Part
Tillie and Gus
Tillie's Punctured Romance
Time Bandits
Time, Gentlemen, Please?
Time of Their Lives, The
Tin Men
TISH
Titfield Thunderbolt, The
To Be or Not to Be (1942)
To Be or Not to Be (1983)
To Paris With Love
Together Again
Tom and Jerry: The Movie
Tom, Dick and Harry
Tom Jones
Tons of Trouble
Tony Draws a Horse
Too Beautiful for You
Too Busy to Work
Too Hot to Handle
Too Many Crooks
Too Many Girls
Too Many Husbands
Too Outrageous!
Tootsie
Top Banana
Top Secret
Top Secret Affair
Topper
Topper Returns
Topper Takes a Trip
Touch and Go
Touch of Class, A
Touch of Larceny, A
Tough Guys
Tovarich
Toy, The
Toys
Trading Mom
Trading Places
Traffic
Trail of the Pink Panther
Train Goes East, The
Transatlantic Merry-Go-Round
Transylvania 6-5000
Trapped in Paradise
Traveling Saleslady
Trenchcoat
Troop Beverly Hills
Trouble Brewing
Trouble in Paradise (1932)
Trouble in Paradise (1988)
Trouble in Store
Trouble Makers
Trouble With Angels, The
Trouble With Dick, The
True Confession
True Identity
True Stories
True to Life
Truly Madly Deeply
Trunks of Mr. O.F., The
Trust
Trust Me
Truth About Women, The
Tune In Tomorrow
Tunes of Glory
Tunnel of Love, The
Tunnelvision
Turk 182!
Turkey Time
Turnabout
Turner & Hooch
Twelfth Night
Twelve Chairs, The
Twelve-Handed Men of Mars, The
12 Tasks of Asterix, The
Twentieth Century
29th Street
Twice Around the Daffodils
Twins
Twist, The
Two-Faced Woman
Two for the Seesaw
Two Guys From Milwaukee
Two Kouney Lemels
Two Little Bears, The
Two Lives of Mattias Pascal, The
Two of a Kind
Two of Us, The
2000 Year Old Man, The
Two Way Stretch
Two Weeks with Love
Typhoon
Ugly Dachshund, The
UHF
Unbelievable Truth, The
Uncle Buck
Uncle, The
Under the Biltmore Clock
Under the Boardwalk
Under the Cherry Moon
Under the Rainbow
Under the Yum Yum Tree
Unfaithfully Yours (1948)
Unfaithfully Yours (1984)
Unfinished Business
Unidentified Flying Oddball
Unmarried Woman, An
Up for the Cup
Up Front
Up in Mabel's Room
Up in the Cellar
Up the Academy
Up the Creek
Up the River (1930)
Up The River (1938)
Up the Sandbox
Up to His Ears
Up to the Neck
Uptown Saturday Night
Used Cars
Used People
Utopia
Vacation From Marriage
Vagrant, The
Valley Girl
Vampire's Kiss
Vanya on 42nd Street
Variety Girl
Very Curious Girl, A
Very Special Favor, A
Vibes
Vice Versa (1948)
Vice Versa (1988)

Victor/Victoria
Villain, The
Virgin High
Virgin Soldiers, The
Visit to a Small Planet
Visitors, The
Viva Maria!
Viva Max!
Vivacious Lady
Voice of the Turtle, The
Volere Volare
Volpone
Volunteers
W. W. and the Dixie Dancekings
Wackiest Ship in the Army, The
Wacky World of Mother Goose, The
Waikiki Wedding
Waiting for the Light
Wake Me When It's Over
Walk, Don't Run
Walk Like A Man
Wallflower
Waltz of the Toreadors
War Between Men and Women, The
War of the Buttons
War of the Roses, The
Watch the Birdie
Watermelon Man
Way Out West
Way . . . Way Out
Wayne's World
Wayne's World 2
We All Loved Each Other So Much
We Think the World of You
We Were Dancing
Webb Wilder's Corn Flicks
Wedding, A
Wedding Banquet, The
Wedding Party, The
Wedding Rehearsal
Wee Geordie
Weekend at Bernie's
Weekend at Bernie's II
Weekend With Father
Weird Science
Welcome Home, Roxy Carmichael
We're No Angels (1955)
We're No Angels (1989)
We're Not Married
What a Way to Go!
What About Bob?
What Did You Do in the War, Daddy?
What Do You Say to a Naked Lady?
What Every Woman Knows
What Every Woman Wants
What Happened Was . . .
What Have I Done to Deserve This?
What Next, Corporal Hargrove?
What, No Beer?
What Women Dream
What Would You Say to Some Spinach
What's New, Pussycat?
What's So Bad About Feeling Good?
What's Up, Doc?
What's Up, Tiger Lily?
Wheeler Dealers, The
When Comedy Was King
When Harry Met Sally . . .
When in Rome
When Love is Young
When the Wind Blows
When Willie Comes Marching Home
When You're in Love
When's Your Birthday?
Where Angels Go, Trouble Follows
Where the Boys Are
Where the Boys Are '84
Where the Buffalo Roam
Where the Heart Is
Where the Spies Are
Where There's a Will
Where There's Life
Where Were You When the Lights Went Out?
Where's Poppa?
Which Way Is Up?
Whistling in Brooklyn
Whistling in the Dark
White Men Can't Jump
White Sheik, The
White Tie and Tails
Who Done It? (1942)
Who Done It? (1956)
Who Framed Roger Rabbit
Who Is Harry Kellerman and Why Is He Saying Those Terrible Things About Me?
Who Is Killing the Great Chefs of Europe?
Who Was That Lady?
Whole Shootin' Match, The
Whole Town's Talking, The
Wholly Moses
Whoopee Boys, The
Whoops Apocalypse
Who's Got the Action?
Who's Harry Crumb?
Who's Minding the Mint?
Who's Minding the Store?
Who's That Girl?
Who's the Man?
Who's Your Lady Friend?
Why Bring That Up?
Why Leave Home?
Wide-Eyed and Legless
Wide Open
Widows' Peak
Wife, Doctor and Nurse
Wife, Husband and Friend
Wife vs. Secretary
Wild and Wonderful
Wild and Woody
Wild Man of Borneo, The
Wild Party, The
Wildcats
Wilder Napalm
Will Success Spoil Rock Hunter?
Willie and Phil
Wise Guys
Wisecracks
Wistful Widow of Wagon Gap, The
Witches' Brew
Witches of Eastwick, The
With Honors
With Six You Get Eggroll
Withnail & I
Without a Clue
Without Reservations
Without You I'm Nothing
Woman in Red, The
Woman of Distinction, A
Woman of the Year
Woman Times Seven
Women on the Verge of a Nervous Breakdown
Women, The
Won Ton Ton, the Dog Who Saved Hollywood
Wonder Man
Working Girl
Working Girls
Working Man, The
World of Henry Orient, The
World Premiere
World's Greatest Athlete, The
Worth Winning
Wrong Arm of the Law
Wrong Box, The
Wrong Guys, The
Yank at Oxford, A
Year of the Comet
Yellow Cab Man, The
Yellow Rolls-Royce, The
Yellowbeard
Yesterday, Today and Tomorrow
You Belong to Me
You Can't Cheat an Honest Man
You Can't Take It With You
You Light Up My Life
You Never Can Tell
Young Doctors in Love
Young Einstein
Young Frankenstein
Young in Heart, The
Youngest Profession, The
Your Uncle Dudley
You're a Big Boy Now
You're in the Army Now
You're in the Navy Now
You're Never Too Young
You're Only Young Once
You're Telling Me
Yours For the Asking
Yours, Mine and Ours
You've Got to Have Heart
Yum-Yum Girls, The

Zapped!
Zapped Again
Zazie
Zebra in the Kitchen
Zelig
Zenobia
Zero for Conduct
Zombies on Broadway
Zorro, the Gay Blade
Zotz!

CRIME

Abandoned
Abducted
Abductors, The
Absolution
Accattone
Accidents
Accursed, The
Accused, The
Acorraldo
Acting on Impulse
Adam
Adventure in Diamonds
Adventure in Manhattan
Adventures of Nick Carter
Adventures of Sherlock Holmes, The
Affair in Havana
Afraid of the Dark
After Midnight With Boston Blackie
After the Thin Man
Agatha
Agatha Christie—Affair Of The Pink Pearl, The
Agatha Christie's The Man in the Brown Suit
Agent on Ice
Al Capone
Alex and the Gypsy
Alias Boston Blackie
All-American Murder
Aloma of the South Seas
Alpha Caper, The
Alphabet City
Alphabet Murders, The
Ambition
Ambulance, The
Ambush in Leopard Street
Ambush Murders, The
American Me
American Soldier, The
Amongst Friends
Amor Bandido
Amsterdam Affair, The
And Hope to Die
And Then There Were None
Angel Face
Angel Heart
Another Pair of Aces: Three of a Kind
Another Thin Man
Apology
Appointment with Death
Armed Response
Armored Car Robbery
Arnelo Affair, The
Arrest Bulldog Drummond
Arsenal Stadium Mystery, The
Arsene Lupin
Asphalt Jungle, The
Assassin, The (1953)
Assassin, The (1961)
Assassins de l'Orde, Les Law Breakers
Assault on a Queen
At Close Range
At Mother's Request
Baby Doll Murders, The
Baby Face Nelson
Babysitter, The
Back Door to Heaven
Back in the USSR
Back to the Wall
Backfire (1950)
Backfire (1988)
Backlash
Backtrack
Bad Blood
Bad Boys
Bad Company (1931)
Bad Company (1995)
Bad Influence
Bad Lieutenant
Badge of the Assassin
Badlands
Ballbuster
Banacek
Band of Outsiders
Banker, The
Banyon
Banzai Runner
Basic Instinct
Beast of The City, The
Bedroom Eyes
Bedroom Eyes 2
Bedroom Window, The
Before Dawn
Behind the High Wall
Behind the Mask
Bellman and True
Benson Murder Case
Bermuda Mystery
Best Seller
Betrayed
Bewitched
Beyond a Reasonable Doubt
Beyond Reasonable Doubt
Big Boodle, The
Big Brown Eyes
Big Clock, The
Big Doll House, The
Big Easy, The
Big Fix, The
Big Heat, The
Big House, The
Big Shot, The
Big Sleep, The (1946)
Big Sleep, The (1978)
Big Steal, The
Bimbo the Great
Bishop Murder Case
Black Angel
Black Caesar
Black Camel, The
Black Hand
Black Jack
Black Magic (1944)
Black Magic (1991)
Black Moon Rising
Black Rainbow
Black Raven, The
Black Tuesday
Black Widow
Black Windmill, The
Blackmail (1929)
Blackmail (1939)
Blackwell's Island
Blade in Hong Kong
Blind Alley
Blind Faith
Blind Fear
Blind Side
Blind Spot
Blind Vision
Blindfold
Blindsided
Blink
Blonde Blackmailer
Blood Relatives
Blood Simple
Blood Sweat and Fear
Blood Ties
Blood Vows—The Story of a Mafia Wife
Blow Out
Blue City
Blue Collar
Blue Dahlia, The
Blue Gardenia
Blue Ice
Blue Knight, The
Blue Lamp, The
Blue Velvet
Blueprint for Murder
Blueprint for Robbery, A
Bob Le Flambeur
Bobby Ware Is Missing
Body Chemistry
Body Chemistry 2 (Voice of a Stranger)
Body Double
Body Heat
Body Language
Body of Evidence (1988)
Body of Evidence (1993)
Body of Influence
Bodyguard
Bodyhold
Bomb in the High Street
Bonnie and Clyde
Bonnie's Kids
Book of Numbers
Boomerang
Boomerang!
Boomerang
Bootleg
Border Incident
Borderline
Borgia Stick, The
Born to Kill
Borsalino
Borsalino and Company
Boss, The
Boston Blackie and the Law
Boston Blackie Booked on Suspicion
Boston Blackie Goes Hollywood

Boston Blackie's Chinese Venture
Boston Blackie's Rendevous
Boston Strangler, The
Boulevard Nights
Bound by Honor
Bourne Identity, The
Boy Cried Murder, The
Boy Who Caught a Crook
Boys Next Door, The
Brasher Doubloon, The
Breaking the Rules
Breathless (1959)
Breathless (1983)
Bride Wore Black, The
Bridge Across Time
Brighton Rock
Brighton Strangler, The
Brothers Rico, The
Brute Force
Buffet Froid
Bugsy
Bulldog Drummond at Bay (1937)
Bulldog Drummond at Bay (1947)
Bulldog Drummond Comes Back
Bulldog Drummond Escapes
Bulldog Drummond in Africa
Bulldog Drummond Strikes Back
Bulldog Drummond's Bride
Bulldog Drummond's Peril
Bulldog Drummond's Revenge
Bulldog Drummond's Secret Police
Bulldog Jack
Bullet for Joey, A
Bullet for Pretty Boy, A
Bullets or Ballots
Bump in the Night
Bunny Lake Is Missing
Burglars, The
Burndown
Busting
Butterfly
Buying Time
By Whose Hand?
C-Man
Caged Fury
Cagney & Lacey
Cairo
California Kid, The
Call Northside 777
Calling Bulldog Drummond
Calling Dr. Death
Calling Homicide
Calling Philo Vance
Camorra
Canary Murder Case
Candidate for Murder
Candy Man, The
Cannon
Canon City
Canvas
Cape Fear (1961)
Cape Fear (1991)
Caper of the Golden Bulls, The
Capone (1975)
Capone (1989)
Captive City, The
Car 99
Cardiac Arrest
Carey Treatment, The
Caribbean Mystery, A
Carlito's Way
Carolina Skeletons
Case Against Brooklyn, The
Case Against Mrs. Ames, The
Case of Deadly Force, A
Case of the Black Cat, The
Case of the Curious Bride, The
Case of the Hillside Stranglers, The
Case of the Howling Dog, The
Case of the Lucky Legs, The
Case of the Red Monkey
Case of the Stuttering Bishop, The
Case of the Velvet Claws, The
Casino Murder Case
Cast a Dark Shadow
Castle in the Desert
Castle on the Hudson
Cat and Mouse
Cat and the Canary, The
Cat o' Nine Tails
Catamount Killing
Cause for Alarm
Cell 2455, Death Row
Centerfold Girls, The
Ceremony, The
Certain Sacrifice, A
Chain of Evidence
Champ for a Day
Champagne Murders, The
Chance Meeting
Chance of a Lifetime, The
Chandler
Charley Varrick
Charlie Chan at Monte Carlo
Charlie Chan at the Circus
Charlie Chan at the Olympics
Charlie Chan at the Opera
Charlie Chan at the Race Track
Charlie Chan at the Wax Museum
Charlie Chan at Treasure Island
Charlie Chan Carries On
Charlie Chan in City in Darkness
Charlie Chan in Egypt
Charlie Chan in Honolulu
Charlie Chan in London
Charlie Chan in Panama
Charlie Chan in Paris
Charlie Chan in Reno
Charlie Chan in Rio
Charlie Chan in Shanghai
Charlie Chan in the Secret Service
Charlie Chan on Broadway
Charlie Chan's Murder Cruise
Charlie Chan's Secret
Charlie's Angels
Chase
Chase a Crooked Shadow
Chase, The (1946)
Chase, The (1991)
Chicago Joe and the Showgirl
Chiefs
Child in the Night
China Moon
Chinatown
Chinese Cat, The
Chinese Ring, The
C.H.O.M.P.S.
Circumstantial Evidence
Circus Queen
Murder, The
Cisco Pike
City Heat
City in Fear
City Streets
City, The
Client, The
Clinton and Nadine
Clockmaker, The
Close Call for Boston Blackie, A
Close Call for Ellery Queen
Cloudburst
Clouded Yellow, The
Clown Murders, The
Club Extinction
Clue of the New Pin
Clue of the Silver Key
Cobra Strikes, The
Code Two
Cohen and Tate
Cold Front
Cold Steel
Color Me Dead
Color of Night
Colors
Columbo: Murder By the Book
Columbo: Prescription Murder
Come Back, Charleston Blue
Come-On, The
Comeback, The
Compulsion
Concerning Mr. Martin
Concrete Jungle, The
Confess, Dr. Corda
Confession
Confessions of a Police Captain
Confessions of Boston Blackie
Confidential
Confidentially Yours
Consenting Adults
Contract on Cherry Street
Coogan's Bluff
Cop
Cop au Vin
Cornered
Corrupt
Cottage to Let
Counterfeiters of Paris, The
Coup de Torchon
Court Martial
Crack-Up
Cradle Will Fall, The
Crime Against Joe
Crime Doctor
Crime in the Streets

Crime Story
Crime Wave
Crime Without Passion
Criminal Code, The
Criminal Court
Criminal Justice
Criminal Law
Crimson Kimono, The
Criss Cross
Crook, The
Cross Country
Crowd Roars, The
Crucifer of Blood, The
Crush, The
Cry Baby Killer, The
Cry of the City
Cry of the Hunted
Cry Terror
Cry Vengeance
Curiosity Kills
Curtain Rises, The
Daddy's Gone A-Hunting
Dandy in Aspic, A
Danger: Diabolik
Dangerous Company
Dangerous Corner
Dangerous Love
Dangerous Mission
Dangerous to Know
Dark Corner, The
Dark Intruder
Dark Past, The
Dark Waters
Dark Wind, The
Darker than Amber
Date With the Falcon, A
Daughter of the Dragon
Day of the Jackal, The
Day They Robbed the Bank of England, The
Dead Again
Dead Calm
Dead Connection
Dead Heat
Dead Heat on a Merry-Go-Round
Dead Man's Folly
Dead Pool, The
Deadfall
Deadlier than the Male
Deadliest Sin, The
Deadline at Dawn
Deadly Affair, The
Deadly Business, A
Deadly Hero
Deadly Impact
Deadly Strangers
Dear Detective (1977)
Dear Detective (1979)
Death Game
Death in California, A
Death in Canaan, A
Death Kiss, The
Death of a Scoundrel
Deathtrap
Deceived
Deception
Deceptions
Decoy, The
Defector, The
Defenseless
Defiant Ones, The
Deliberate Stranger, The
Delusion
Descending Angel
Desperate Hours
Detective, The
Detour
Devil Thumbs a Ride, The
Devil's Mask, The
Diabolically Yours
Diabolique
Diagnosis: Murder
Dial: Help
Dial M for Murder
Diamonds
Dick Tracy (1945)
Dick Tracy (1990)
Dick Tracy Meets Gruesome
Dillinger (1945)
Dillinger (1973)
Dinner at the Ritz
Dirt Bike Kid, The
Dirty Hands
Dirty Harry
Dirty Money
Disappearance, The
Dishonored Lady
Distortions
Diva
Do Not Fold, Spindle or Mutilate
D.O.A.
Dog Day
Dog Day Afternoon
Dominique
Domino Principle, The
Don Is Dead, The
Doorway to Hell
Dossier 51
Double Exposure
Double Indemnity
Double Man, The
Double McGuffin, The
Double Vision
Downtown
Dr. Gillespie's Criminal Case
Dr. Mabuse, the Gambler
Dr. Socrates
Dragnet
Dream Lover
Dressed to Kill (1946)
Dressed to Kill (1980)
Drifter, The
Drowning Pool, The
Dying Room Only
Edge of Darkness
8 Million Ways to Die
Elegant Criminal, The
Element of Crime, The
Ellery Queen
Ellery Queen and the Murder Ring
Ellery Queen and the Perfect Crime
Ellery Queen, Master Detective
Ellery Queen's Penthouse Mystery
Emil
Emil and the Detectives
Empire of the Night, The
End of the Game
Endless Game, The
Endless Night
Enforcer, The (1951)
Enforcer, The (1976)
Enrapture
Everybody Wins
Evil Under the Sun
Ex-Mrs. Bradford, The
Executioner, The
Executive Action
Experiment in Terror
Experiment Perilous
Exposure
Eye of the Storm
Eye Witness
Eyes in the Night
Eyes of Laura Mars
Eyes of the Underworld
Eyewitness
Falcon and the Co-eds, The
Falcon in Danger, The
Falcon in Hollywood, The
Falcon in Mexico, The
Falcon in San Francisco, The
Falcon Out West, The
Falcon Strikes Back, The
Falcon Takes Over, The
Falcon's Adventure, The
Falcon's Alibi, The
Falcon's Brother, The
Fall Guy
Fallen Angel
False Arrest
False Witness
Family Business
Family Matter, A
Family Plot
Famiy Enforcer
Fan, The
Fantasist, The
Far from Home
Farewell, My Lovely
Fass Black
Fast and Furious
Fast and Loose
Fast Company
Fast Gun
Fast-Walking
Fat Man, The
Fatal Attraction
Fatal Exposure
Fatal Games
Fatal Hour, The
Fatal Image, The
Fatal Images
Fatal Vision
Fathers and Sons
FBI Murders, The
Fear
Fear in the City
Fear in the Night (1947)
Fear in the Night (1972)
Fear Inside, The
Feathered Serpent, The
Female Jungle, The
Fever
52 Pick-Up
Fighting Rookie, The
Fighting Trouper
File of the Golden Goose, The
Final Analysis
Final Embrace
Final Extra, The
Final Judgment
Final Mission
Final Notice
Finger Man, The
Finger of Guilt
Finger Points, The
Fingers
Fingers at the Window
Firm, The

Five Miles to Midnight
Flame, The
Flareup
Flesh and Bone
Flight of the Innocent, The
Flight to Hong Kong
Flood Tide
Florentine Dagger, The
Follow Me Quietly
Footsteps in the Dark
Footsteps in the Fog
Forbidden Cargo
Forbidden Sun
Foreign Correspondent
Forgotten Woman
Formula, The
Fort Apache, The Bronx
Fortune Dane
Forty Naughty Girls
Four Desperate Men
Four Hours to Kill
Four Men and a Prayer
Fragment of Fear
Framed
Frantic
Freeway
French Detective, The
Frenzy
Friends of Eddie Coyle, The
Frightened City, The
From Hollywood to Deadwood
Fugitive Lady (1934)
Fugitive Lady (1951)
Fugitive Among Us
Future Force
Fuzz
Gambit
Gambler, The
Games
Gangster Story
Gangster, The
Gangster Wars
Garde A Vue
Garden Murder Case, The
Gauntlet, The
Gay Falcon, The
Gentleman from Louisiana
Gentleman from Nowhere, The
Gentleman's Fate
Get Carter
Get Christie Love
Get out of Town
Getaway, The (1972)
Getaway, The (1994)
Getting Even
Getting Gotti
Girl Hunters, The
Girl in a Swing, The
Girl in Black Stockings, The
Girl in 419
Girl in the Empty Grave, The
Girl on the Late, Late Show, The
Girl, The
Girls on the Loose
Girls Under Twenty-One
Give 'Em Hell
Glass Alibi, The
Glass Key, The (1935)
Glass Key, The (1942)
Glass Web, The
Glitter Dome, The
Glitz
Gloria
Godfather, Part II, The
Godfather, Part III, The
Godfather, The
Gods of the Plague
Godson, The
Golden Link, The
Good to Go
GoodFellas
Goodnight, My Love
Gordon's War
Gorky Park
Gotham
Grand Central Murder
Great Flamarion, The
Great Gambini, The
Great Manhunt, The
Great Texas Dynamite Chase, The
Great Train Robbery, The
Green for Danger
Green Ice
Grievous Bodily Harm
Grifters, The
Grisbi
Grissom Gang, The
Guilty?
Guilty as Hell
Guilty as Sin
Gun Crazy
Gun, The
Hail, Mafia
Hammett
Hand That Rocks the Cradle, The
Hanged Man, The
Hangup
Harper
Haunted Honeymoon
He Walked by Night
He Who Rides a Tiger
Hear No Evil
Hearse, The
Heatwave
Heist, The (1979)
Heist, The (1989)
Hell Is a City
Hell Up In Harlem
Hell's Highway
Helter Skelter
Helter Skelter Murders, The
Hennessy
Heroes, The
Heroes Three
Hi, Nellie!
Hidden Eye, The
Hidden Fear
Hidden Homicide
Hidden Room, The
Hide-Out
High and Low
High Frequency
High Sierra
High Stakes
High Terrace
Highly Dangerous
Highway Dragnet
Highway Pickup
Hit and Run
Hit the Dutchman
Hitwoman: The Double Edge
Hitz
Hollywood Cop
Home, Sweet Homicide
Homeboys
Homicidal Impulse
Homicide
Homicide Bureau
Honeymoon Killers, The
Hong Kong
Honor Among Thieves
Honor Thy Father
Honor Thy Father and Mother: The True Story of the Menendez Murders
Hooch
Hooded Terror, The
Hoodlum Empire
Hoodlum, The
Hoodwink
Horseplayer, The
Hostage
Hostage, The
Hot Child in the City
Hot Spot, The
Hound of the Baskervilles, The
Hour of 13, The
House of Fear, The
House of Games
House of the Arrow, The
House of the Long Shadows
House of the Rising Sun
House on Carroll Street, The
Human Desire
Human Jungle, The
Hunt for the Night Stalker, The
Hunt the Man Down
Hunted Men
Hustle
Hysteria
I Am a Thief
I Became a Criminal
I Confess
I Died a Thousand Times
I Killed That Man
I Love a Mystery
I Love Trouble
I Met a Murderer
I, Mobster
I Shot Jesse James
I Stole a Million
I Was a Shoplifter
Idol of the Crowds
If He Hollers, Let Him Go
I'll Remember April
Illegal Entry
Illicit Behavior
Illustrious Corpses
Impossible Spy, The
Impulse
In a Lonely Place
In Broad Daylight
In Cold Blood
In Defense of a Married Man
In Self Defense
In the Cold of the Night
In the Heat of Passion
In the Heat of the Night
In the Line of Duty: The F.B.I. Murders
In the Mouth of Madness
Inadmissible Evidence
Incident
Incident at Midnight
Incident at Victoria Falls
Incident in San Francisco
Incident on a Dark

Street
Incident, The
Indian Scarf, The
Indict and Convict
Inevitable Grace
Information Received
Inn on the River, The
Inner Sanctum
Innocent Man, An
Inquest
Inside Job
Inside the Mafia
Inside the Room
Inspector Hornleigh on Holiday
Inspector Maigret
Internal Affairs
Intimate Stranger
Into the Fire
Invasion of Privacy
Invisible Agent
Invisible Creature, The
Iron Maze
Ironheart
Island of Lost Men
Isn't It Shocking?
It Takes All Kinds
Italian Connection, The
It's Called Murder, Baby
It's in the Blood
Ivy
J. Edgar Hoover
Jack's Back
Jade Mask, The
Jagged Edge
Jail Bait
Jailbreakers, The
January Man, The
Jazz Boat
Jazzband Five, The
Jennifer
Jennifer 8
Jenny Lamour
Jeopardy
Jigsaw (1949)
Jigsaw (1971)
Joe Dakota
Johnnie Mae Gibson: FBI
Johnny Angel
Johnny Apollo
Johnny Cool
Johnny Eager
Johnny Handsome
Johnny Holiday
Johnny Nobody
Johnny O'Clock
Johnny One Eye
Johnny Rocco
Johnny Stool Pigeon
Jordan Chance, The
Journey Into Fear
Joy House
Joy Ride
Judex
Judge and Jake Wyler, The
Judge Dee and the Monastery Murder
Judge, The
Judgment Deferred
Judgment in Stone, A
Juice
Julie Darling
Just Before Dawn
Just Cause
Just Off Broadway
Kalifornia
Kamikaze
Kansas City Confidential
Kansas City Massacre
Keeping Track
Kennel Murder Case, The
Kid Glove Killer
Kill Me Again
Killer Image
Killer Instinct
Killer Is Loose, The
Killer That Stalked New York, The
Killing 'em Softly
Killing in a Small Town, A
Killing Kind, The
Killing Mind, The
Killing of a Chinese Bookie, The
Killing, The
Killing Time, The
Killing Zoe
Killjoy
Kind Lady (1936)
Kind Lady (1951)
King of Alcatraz
King of Chinatown
King of New York
King of the Roaring Twenties—The Story of Arnold Rothstein
King of the Underworld
Kirlian Witness, The
Kiss Before Dying, A (1956)
Kiss Before Dying, A (1991)
Kiss Before the Mirror, The
Kiss Daddy Good Night
Kiss Me Deadly
Kiss of a Killer
Kiss of Death
Kiss the Blood Off My Hands
Knight Moves
Krays, The
Kremlin Letter, The
La Balance
La Bete Humaine
L.A. Bounty
L.A. Crackdown
L.A. Crackdown 2
La Femme Nikita
La Grande Bourgeoisie
La Passante
L.A. Wars
L'Addition
Lady Beware
Lady for a Night
Lady from Shanghai, The
Lady in a Cage
Lady in Cement
Lady in Distress
Lady in the Lake
Lady in White
Lady Killer
Lady Mobster
Lady of Burlesque
Lady Scarface
Lady Vanishes, The (1938)
Lady Vanishes, The (1979)
Ladykiller
Ladykillers
Las Vegas Story, The
Last Embrace
Last Hit, The
Last Hour, The
Last House on the Left, The
Last of Sheila, The
Last Rites
Last Seduction, The
Laura
Le Boucher
Le Complot
Le Cri du Hibou
Le Doulos
Le Samourai
Leather Jackets
Left for Dead
Legacy of Lies
Legal Tender
Let 'Em Have It
Lethal Obsession
Let's Kill Uncle
Lies
Lies Before Kisses
Light Touch, The
Lightship, The
Limping Man, The
Lineup, The
Liquid Dreams
List of Adrian Messenger, The
Little Caesar
Lone Wolf and His Lady, The
Lone Wolf in London, The
Lone Wolf in Mexico, The
Lone Wolf in Paris, The
Lone Wolf Keeps a Date, The
Lone Wolf Meets a Lady, The
Lone Wolf Strikes, The
Lone Wolf Takes a Chance, The
Lonely Villa, The
Long Goodbye, The
Long Memory, The
Looker
Loophole
Love Crimes
Love from a Stranger (1937)
Love from a Stranger (1947)
Lovely Way to Die, A
Lucky Luciano
Lucky Nick Cain
Lucky Stiff, The
Lure of the Wilderness
M ("M")
M
Ma Barker's Killer Brood
Machine-Gun Kelly
Machine Gun McCain
Mackintosh Man, The
Mad Bomber, The
Mad Dog Coll
Mad Executioners, The
Madigan
Madonna's Secret, The
Magnum Force
Maigret
Mailbag Robbery
Make Haste to Live
Malarek
Malibu Express
Maltese Falcon, The (1931)
Maltese Falcon, The (1941)
Man at the Carlton Tower
Man Bait
Man Hunt
Man in the Dark
Man in the Net, The
Man in the Raincoat, The
Man in the Road, The

Man Inside, The
Man Killer
Man on a Swing
Man on the Eiffel Tower, The
Man on the Roof
Man Who Couldn't Walk, The
Man Who Cried Wolf, The
Man Who Knew Too Much, The
Man Who Made Diamonds, The
Man Who Was Sherlock Holmes, The
Man Who Would Not Die, The
Man Who Wouldn't Die, The
Mandalay
Mandarin Mystery, The
Manhandled
Manhattan Melodrama
Manhunt for Claude Dallas
Manhunter
Mankillers
Margin for Murder
Mark of the Whistler
Marked Woman
Marlowe
Mary Burns, Fugitive
Mascara
Mask of Dijon, The
Mask of Dimitrios, The
Mask of Fu Manchu, The
Masks of Death
Masquerade
Matter of Morals, A
Maximum Force
Mayfair Bank Caper, The
Maze, The
McGuffin, The
McNaughton's Daughter
McVicar
Mean Dog Blues
Mean Frank & Crazy Tony
Mean Johnny Barrows
Mean Machine, The
Mean Season, The
Mean Streets
Medusa
Meet Boston Blackie
Meet Nero Wolfe
Melvin Purvis-G-Man
Memories of Murder
Men of Respect
Menace, The
Menendez: A Killing in Beverly Hills
Miami Blues
Miami Cops
Miami Vendetta
Michael Shayne, Private Detective
Midnight Angel
Midnight Cop
Midnight Crossing
Midnight Fear
Midnight Lace (1960)
Midnight Lace (1980)
Midnight Man, The
Midnight Mary
Midnight Story, The
Midnight Witness
Midnite Spares
Mighty Quinn, The
Mike's Murder
Mikey and Nicky
Miller's Crossing
Miracle Man, The
Miracles for Sale
Mirage
Mirror Crack'd, The
Mirror Images
Miss Fane's Baby is Stolen
Missing Corpse, The
Missing Juror, The
Missing Witnesses
Mitchell
Mob Boss
Mob, The
Mob War
Mobsters
Mona Lisa
Money, The
Money to Burn
Money Trap, The
Monique
Monsieur Hire
Moonlighting
Moonrise
Morning After, The
Mortal Passions
Mortal Sins
Mortal Thoughts
Most Wanted
Mr. and Mrs. North
Mr. Denning Drives North
Mr. Frost
Mr. Moto in Danger Island
Mr. Moto Takes a Chance
Mr. Moto Takes a Vacation
Mr. Moto's Gamble
Mr. Moto's Last Warning
Mr. Wong, Detective
Mr. Wong in Chinatown
Mrs. Pollifax—Spy
Murder!
Murder Ahoy
Murder at the Gallop
Murder at the Vanities
Murder by Moonlight
Murder by Numbers
Murder by Television
Murder by the Book
Murder in Coweta County
Murder in Space
Murder in Texas
Murder Is My Beat
Murder Man, The
Murder Most Foul
Murder My Sweet
Murder of Mary Phagan, The
Murder on a Honeymoon
Murder on Line One
Murder on the Blackboard
Murder on the Orient Express
Murder 101
Murder Over New York
Murder, She Said
Murder So Sweet
Murder with Mirrors
Murderer In The Motel
Murderous Vision
Murders in the Rue Morgue, The
Murphy's Law
My Cousin Rachel
My Gun is Quick
Mystery Man, The
Mystery of Edwin Drood, The (1935)
Mystery of Edwin Drood, The (1993)
Mystery of Marie Roget, The
Mystery of Mr. Wong, The
Mystery of Mr. X, The
Mystery of the Third Planet
Mystic Hour, The
Nails
Naked Alibi
Naked Edge, The
Naked Face, The
Nancy Drew—A Haunting We Will Go
Nancy Drew and the Hidden Staircase
Nancy Drew, Detective
Nancy Drew, Reporter
Nancy Drew—Secret of the Whispering Walls
Nancy Drew—The Mysery of the Solid Gold Kicker
Nancy Drew—The Mystery of Pirate's Cove
Nancy Drew—The Mystery of the Diamond Triangle
Nancy Drew—The Mystery of the Fallen Angels
Nancy Drew, Troubleshooter
Narrow Margin, The
Nashville Beat
Natural Born Killers
'Neath Brooklyn Bridge
Never Too Late to Mend
New Centurions, The
New Jack City
Newman's Law
Next of Kin
Next Victim, The
Nick Carter, Master Detective
Night after Halloween, The
Night After Night After Night (He Kills)
Night and the City
Night Children
Night Court
Night Editor
Night Game
Night Moves
Night Must Fall
Night Nurse
Night of Adventure, A
Night of Courage
Night of January 16th, The
Night of Mystery
Night of the Cyclone
Night of the Following Day, The
Night of the Hunter
Night Rhythms
Night Strangler, The
Night Visions
Night Visitor, The
Night Watch
Night Without Sleep
Night Without Stars
Nighthawks
Nightkill

Nine Girls
99 River Street
Ninth Guest, The
Nitti—The Enforcer
No Escape (1936)
No Escape (1953)
No Hands on the Clock
No Man's Land
No Man's Woman
No Mercy
No One Cries Forever
No Trace
Nocturne
North by Northwest
Notorious (1946)
Notorious (1992)
Nowhere to Run
Nude in a White Car
Number One with a Bullet
Nursemaid Who Disappeared, The
Obsessed, The
Ocean's Eleven
Off Limits
Offence, The
On Dangerous Ground
On the Yard
Once Upon a Time in America
Once You Kiss a Stranger
One Armed Swordsmen, The
One Dangerous Night
One False Move
One Good Cop
One Man Force
One Mysterious Night
One New York Night
One of My Wives Is Missing
One Police Plaza
One Shoe Makes It Murder
One Spy Too Many
One Step to Eternity
Onion Field, The
Ordeal by Innocence
Organization, The
Other Woman, The
Out for Justice
Out of the Darkness
Out of the Fog
Out of the Past
Outfit, The
Outrage
Outside Chance
Outside Man, The
Outside the Wall
Outsider, The
Overexposed
Paco
Paid to Kill
Paint It Black
Paint Job, The
Palermo Connection, The
Panic on the 5:22
Panique
Panther's Claw, The
Paper Bullets
Paper Gallows
Paperback Hero
Parachute Jumper
Paradine Case
Parallax View, The
Parole, Inc.
Partners in Crime
Party Crashers, The
Pascali's Island
Passion in Paradise
Passion to Kill, A
Passport to Suez
Past Midnight
Payoff
Pearl of Death, The
Pelican Brief, The
Penalty Phase
Pendulum
Penguin Pool Murder, The
Penthouse, The (1967)
Penthouse, The (1989)
People's Hero
Perfect Strangers (1950)
Perfect Strangers (1985)
Perfect Victims
Perfect Witness
Peril
Perilous Holiday
Perry Mason Returns
Perry Mason: The Case of the Lost Love
Personal Affair
Personal Column
Persons in Hiding
Peter Gunn
Phantom Lady
Phantom Strikes, The
Phenix City Story, The
Philo Vance Returns
Philo Vance's Secret Mission
Phobia
Physical Evidence
Pickup on South Street
Picture Snatcher
Pierrot le Fou
Pink Cadillac
Play Misty for Me
Play Nice
Playgirl Killer
Plunder Road
Point of Impact
Pope of Greenwich Village, The
Portrait in Black
Possessed
Postman Always Rings Twice, The (1946)
Postman Always Rings Twice, The (1981)
Pot Luck
Preppie Murder, The
Presidio, The
Presumed Innocent
Pretty Maids All in a Row
Prime Cut
Prime Suspect
Prime Suspect 2
Prime Suspect 3
Prince of The City
Prison Stories: Women on the Inside
Private Hell 36
Prizzi's Honor
Professional, The
Psychic
Public Enemy, The
Public Enemy's Wife
Public Eye, The
Public Hero No. 1
Pulp
Purple Gang, The
Pursuit to Algiers
Pushover
Q & A
Queen of the Mob
Quick Millions
Quiet Please, Murder
Race Street
Racket Busters
Racket, The
Raffles
Rage in Harlem, A
Railroaded
Rainbow Drive
Raising Cain
Rampage
Ransom for a Dead Man
Raw Deal
Real McCoy, The
Rear Window
Rebecca
Red Rock West
Reflections of Murder
Relentless
Relentless 2: Dead On
Renegades
Reservoir Dogs
Return of the Rat, The
Revenue Agent
Ricochet
Ride the Pink Horse
Rider on the Rain
Rififi
Rififi in Tokyo
Rise and Fall of Legs Diamond, The
Rising Sun
River's Edge, The
Road Games
Road House
Roadblock
Roadhouse Murder, The
Roadhouse Nights
Robbery
Rogue Cop
Rome Express
Romeo is Bleeding
Rookie, The
Rope
Rosary Murders, The
Rosemary
Rough Cut
Running Scared
Rush
Saboteur
Sabra
Saint in London, The
Saint in New York, The
Saint Takes Over, The
Saint's Double Trouble, The
Saint's Girl Friday, The
Saint's Vacation, The
Salvatore Guiliano
Sapphire
Satan Met a Lady
Scandal in Paris, A
Scandal Sheet
Scapegoat, The
Scarface (1932)
Scarface (1983)
Scarface Mob, The
Scarlet Camellia, The
Scarlet Claw, The
Scarlet Clue, The
Scarlet Street
Scene of the Crime (1949)
Scene of the Crime (1987)
Scent of Mystery
Schizoid
Scissors
Scotland Yard Hunts Dr. Mabuse
Scotland Yard Investigator
Scream for Help

Sea of Love
Secret Agent
Secret Beyond the Door
Secret of the Telegian, The
Secret Six, The
Secret Weapon
Serial Mom
Serpico
Seven Dials Mystery, The
Seven Doors to Death
711 Ocean Drive
Seven Thieves
Seven-Ups, The
Sexton Blake and the Hooded Terror
Shadow Between, The
Shadow of a Doubt
Shadow of the Thin Man
Shadow, The (1937)
Shadow, The (1994)
Shaft
Shaft's Big Score!
Shakedown
Shamus
Shanghai Cobra, The
Sharky's Machine
Sherlock Holmes, Adventures of, The ("Copper Beeches")
Sherlock Holmes, Adventures of, The ("Final Problem")
Sherlock Holmes, Adventures of, The ("Greek Interpreter")
Sherlock Holmes, Adventures of, The ("Red Headed League")
Sherlock Holmes, Adventures of, The ("Resident Patient")
Sherlock Holmes and the Spider Woman
Sherlock Holmes and the Voice of Terror
Sherlock Holmes—Baskerville Curse,The
Sherlock Holmes, Casebook of, The ("Creeping Man")
Sherlock Holmes, Casebook of, The ("Disappearance of")
Sherlock Holmes, Casebook of, The ("Illustious Client")
Sherlock Holmes, Casebook of, The ("Problem of Thor Bridge")
Sherlock Holmes, Casebook of, The ("Shoscombe Old Place")
Sherlock Holmes: Dancing Men, The
Sherlock Holmes Faces Death
Sherlock Holmes in Washington
Sherlock Holmes, Return of, The ("Abbey Grange")
Sherlock Holmes, Return of, The ("Bruce Partington")
Sherlock Holmes, Return of, The ("Empty House")
Sherlock Holmes, Return of, The ("Man With the Twisted Lip")
Sherlock Holmes, Return of, The ("Musgrave Ritual")
Sherlock Holmes, Return of, The ("Priory School")
Sherlock Holmes, Return of, The ("Second Stain")
Sherlock Holmes, Return of, The ("Six Napoleons")
Sherlock Holmes, Return of, The ("Wisteria Lodge")
Sherlock Holmes: Scandal in Bohemia
Sherlock Holmes, Solitary Cyclist, The
Sherlock Holmes: The Speckled Band
She's Dressed to Kill
Shield For Murder
Shock
Shock Corridor
Shock to the System, A
Short Fuse
Shot at Dawn
Show Them No Mercy!
Sicilian Clan, The
Sicilian, The
Side Street
Sign of Four, The
Silence of the Lambs, The
Silent Partner, The
Silent Witness
Silk Noose, The
Sins of the Night
Six Bridges to Cross
Sketch Artist
Sky Dragon, The
Slam Dance
Slaughter on Tenth Avenue
Sleeping Car Murders, The
Slightly Scarlet
Sliver
Slow Burn
Snapdragon
Sneakers
So Dark the Night
Soldier's Story, A
Somebody Has to Shoot the Picture
Someone Behind the Door
Someone to Watch Over Me
Song of the Thin Man
Sons of Adventure
Sorry, Wrong Number (1948)
Sorry, Wrong Number (1989)
Sound of Fury, The
Southside 1-1000
Spellbound
Spider Woman, The
Spies
Spiral Staircase, The
Stakeout on Dope Street
Star of Midnight
Star Witness
Stavisky
Steel Trap, The
Stepmother, The
Still of the Night
Straight Out of Brooklyn
Straight Time
Stranger Among Us, A
Stranger Is Watching, A
Stranger on the Prowl
Stranger on the Run
Stranger on the Third Floor
Strangers on a Train
Streets
Study in Terror, A
Subway
Subway in the Sky
Sudden Danger
Sudden Fear
Sugar Hill
Suicide Club, The
Surrogate, The
Suspect
Suspicion (1941)
Suspicion (1987)
Suture
Swordsman, The
Symphony for a Massacre
T-Men
Take Her by Surprise
Take One False Step
Tamarind Seed, The
Tango & Cash
Target
Targets
Teacher, The
Tears for Simon
Tell Them Willie Boy Is Here
Temp, The
Ten Days Wonder
Ten Little Indians (1965)
Ten Little Indians (1975)
Ten Little Indians (1989)
Tension
Tequila Sunrise
Terminal Entry
Terror By Night
Testament of Dr. Mabuse, The
Thank You, Mr. Moto
They Call Me MISTER Tibbs!
They Drive by Night
They Live by Night
They Only Kill Their Masters
They Won't Believe Me
Thief
Thieves Like Us
Thin Man Goes Home, The
Thin Man, The
Think Fast, Mr. Moto
Third Alibi, The
Third Degree Burn
Third Man, The
Third Secret, The
Thirteen at Dinner
Thirteen Women
Thirteenth Guest, The
39 Steps, The
Thousand Eyes of Dr. Mabuse, The

Threat, The
Thunder Road
Thunderbolt
Thunderbolt and Lightfoot
Tight Spot
Tightrope
Till Death Us Do Part
Till There Was You
Time to Kill
Tip on a Dead Jockey
Tipp-Off Girls
To Be a Crook
To Catch a Killer
To Live and Die in L.A.
Todd Killings, The
Too Late for Tears
Topkapi
Total Exposure
Touch of Evil
Tough Guys Don't Dance
Traces of Red
Trade Winds
Treasure of San Gennaro, The
Trial
Trial by Jury
Trouble Bound
Trouble Preferred
True Believer
True Confessions
True Story of Lynn Stuart, The
Turning Point, The
Twenty-Four Hours to Kill
20,000 Pound Kiss, The
20,000 Years in Sing Sing
23 Paces to Baker Street
Twilight Women
Two Jakes, The
Two Living, One Dead
Two Minute Warning
Ulterior Motives
Under Suspicion
Undercover Blues
Undercover Man, The
Undercurrent
Undertow
Underworld
Underworld U.S.A.
Unguarded Hour, The
Unholy Three, The
Unlawful Entry
Untouchables, The
Utu
Vanishing, The (1988)
Vanishing, The (1993)
Venus in Furs
Verdict, The
Vertigo
V.I. Warshawski
Vice Squad
Vice Squad, The
Victim
Victims
Villain
Violent Saturday
Violette
Viva Knievel!
Voice of the Whistler
Walk a Crooked Mile
Warning Shot
Waterfront
We Are Not Alone
We Still Kill the Old Way
Weapon, The
Web of Evidence
Web of Fear
Web, The
What Would You Do, Chums?
Whatever Happened to Aunt Alice?
When a Stranger Calls
When He's Not a Stranger
When Strangers Marry
When the Bough Breaks
Where Sleeping Dogs Lie
Where the Sidewalk Ends
While the City Sleeps
Whipsaw
Whisper Kill
Whisper to a Scream, A
Whispering City
Whispers
Whispers in the Dark
Whistle Blower, The
White Face
White of the Eye
White Sands
Whole Truth, The
Who'll Stop the Rain
Why Didn't They Ask Evans?
Why Must I Die?
Wicker Man, The
Wild Card
Wild Ride, The
Window, The
Winter Kills
Witness for the Prosecution
Witness to Murder
Woman in Green, The
Woman in the Window, The
Woman Obsessed
Woman of Straw
Woman on the Run
Women in Cages
Yakuza, The
Year of the Dragon
Year of the Gun
Yellow Cargo
You Only Live Once
Young and Innocent
Young Savages, The
Young Sherlock Holmes
Young Tiger, The
Z
Zigzag

DOCUMENTARY

Abraham Lincoln—The New Birth of Freedom
Absolutely Positive
African Elephant, The
African Lion, The
A.K.
AKA Cassius Clay
Aku Aku
Alcatraz
Aliens, Dragons, Monsters & Me
America at the Movies
American Dream
American Gangster, The
Anderson Platoon, The
Andrei Tarkovsky, the Genius, the Man, the Legend
Andrzej Wajda—A Portrait
Antonia: A Portrait of a Woman
Architecture of Frank Lloyd Wright, The
Arruza
Artur Rubinstein—Love of Life
Atomic Cafe, The
Bacall on Bogart
Backstage at the Kirov
Baraka
Basic Training
Batmania from Comics to Screen
Battle of Midway, The
Battle of San Pietro, The
Beach Boys: An American Band, The
Beer Drinker's Guide to Fitness and Filmmaking, The
Before Stonewall
Benefit of the Doubt, The
Berkeley in the Sixties
Bermuda Triangle, The
Best Boy
Big Bang, The
Black Fox: Adolph Hitler
Black Rodeo
Blood in the Face
Blue Water, White Death
Bosna!
Boys of St. Vincent, The
Brief History of Time, A
Bring 'Em Back Alive
Bring on the Night
Broken Rainbow
Brother, Can You Spare a Dime?
Brother Minister: The Assassination of Malcolm X
Brother's Keeper
Bugs Bunny Superstar
Bugsy, Dutch, and Al—The Gangsters
Burden of Dreams
Burroughs
Can Tropical Rainforests Be Saved?
Catastrophe
Celebration at Big Sur
Central Park
Challenger

Champions Forever
Chang
Children of Theatre Street, The
Chopper Wars
Chronique d'un Ete
Chronos
Chuck Berry Hail! Hail! Rock 'n' Roll
Ciao! Manhattan
Civil War, The
Cliff Cemetery
Cliffhangers—Adventures from the Thrill Factory
Colors of War, The
Comic Book Confidential
Common Threads: Stories From the Quilt
Compleat Beatles, The
Computer Dreams
Computer Visions
Congress of Penguins, The
Conquest of Everest, The
Cousin Bobby
Dario Argento's World of Horror
David Holzman's Diary
Deaf and Blind
Decline of the American Empire, The
Decline of Western Civilization, The Part II: The Metal Years
Derby
Divine Waters
D.O.A.—A Right of Passage
Down Under
80 Blocks from Tiffany's
Eleanor Roosevelt Story, The
Encounter with the Unknown
Endless Summer, The
Endless Summer II—The Journey Continues
Enthusiasm
Epic that Never Was, The
F for Fake
Face of War, A
Faithkeeper, The
Falklands Task Force South
Fall of the Berlin Wall, The
Fallen Champ: The Untold Story of Mike Tyson
Falling for the Stars
Farrebique
Fata Morgana
Fear in the Dark
Fighters, The
Finest Hours, The
Flying Saucers over Hollywood: The Plan 9 Companion
For All Mankind
From Mao to Mozart: Isaac Stern in China
F.T.A.
Gates of Heaven
General Idi Amin Dada
Genocide
George Stevens: A Filmmaker's Journey
Gizmo
Glacier Fox, The
God's Country
Good Fight, The
Grass
Great American Cowboy, The
Great Rock 'n Roll Swindle, The
Grey Gardens
Guns of August, The
Hands That Picked Cotton
Happy Anniversary 007—25 Years Of James Bond
Hard Act to Follow, A
Hard Road to Glory, A—The Black Athlete In America
Harlan County, U.S.A.
He Makes Me Feel Like Dancin'
Heart of Tibet—An Intimate Portrait of the 14th Dalai Lama
Hearts and Minds
Hearts of Darkness: A Filmmaker's Apocalypse
Heartworn Highways
Heaven
Heirs of the Vikings, The
Helen Keller—Separate Views
Hell's Angels Forever
Hellstrom Chronicle, The
Helmut Newton—Frames from the Edge
Herdsmen Of The Sun
Here Comes Every Body
Here We Go Again
Here's Looking At You, Warner Bros.
Hidden Memories—Are You a UFO Abductee?
High School
High School II
Hitler: A Career
Hitler's Henchmen
Hitler's Master Race—The Mad Dream of the S.S.
Hollywood on Trial
Hollywood Remembers—Gary Cooper: American Life, American
Hollywood Retrospectives—Fonda on Fonda
Hollywood's Children
Hoop Dreams
Hotel Terminus: The Life and Times of Klaus Barbie
Hour of the Furnaces
Huey Long
Human, Too Human
I Am a Dancer
I Am My Films: A Portrait of Werner Herzog
I Was Stalin's Bodyguard
I.F. Stone's Weekly
Imagine: John Lennon
Improper Conduct
In Our Hands
In Search of Noah's Ark
In the Shadow of the Stars
In the Year of the Pig
Incident at Oglala
Indomitable Teddy Roosevelt, The
It Started with a Mouse
It's All True
Jack Johnson
Jacquot
James Dean Story, The
Janis
Jazz on a Summer's Day
Jimi Hendrix
John F. Kennedy: Years of Lighting, Day of Drums
John Huston: The Man, the Movies, the Maverick
Johnny Cash: The Man, His World, His Music
Journey Together
Jud Suss
Jungle Cat
Jungle Cavalcade
Kaddish
Kerouac
King: A Filmed Record . . . Montgomery to Memphis
King's Story, A
Kitty: Return to Auschwitz
Koko: A Talking Gorilla
Kon-Tiki
Koyaanisqatsi
Land of Silence and Darkness
Land of the Indians, The
Last of England, The
Last Party, The
Last Waltz, The
Latcho Drom
Le Joli Mai
Legendary Champions, The
Lenny Bruce—Without Tears
Let It Be
Let the Good Times Roll
Let There Be Light
Let's Get Lost
Let's Spend the Night Together
Letter from Siberia
Life and Times of Harvey Milk, The
Life and Times of Rosie the Riveter, The
Lightning over Water
Lily Tomlin
Listen to Britain
Listen Up: The Lives of Quincy Jones
Living Desert, The
Louisiana Story, The
Love Goddesses, The
Love Meetings (Comizi D'Amore)
Love Without Fear

Lowell Thomas Remembers—The Roaring Twenties—Vol. 1
Lowell Thomas Remembers—The Roaring Twenties—Vol. 2
Lowell Thomas Remembers—The New Deal—The Thirties
Lowell Thomas Remembers—The War Years—The Forties—Vol. 1
Lowell Thomas Remembers—The War Years—The Forties—Vol. 2
Lowell Thomas Remembers—The Fabulous Fifties
Lulu in Berlin
Madhur Jaffrey's Far Eastern Cooking
Madhur Jaffrey's Indian Cookery
Madrid
Magellan Meridian GPS
Magic Memories on Ice
Magic of Bing Crosby, The—Part 1
Malcolm X
Man in Space
Man In The Silk Hat, The
Man Like Eva, A
Man Named John, A
Man of Aran
Man of Peace, The
Man Who Skied Down Everest, The
Mandela in America
Mandela—The Man And His Country
Manson
Many Faces of Sherlock Holmes, The
Marcel Duchamp—A Game Of Chess
Marching Out
Margaret Mead And Samoa
Margot Fonteyn Story, The
Marilyn
Marilyn Monroe—Beyond the Legend
Marilyn—Say Goodbye to the President
Marjoe
Marlene
Martha Graham—An American Original In Performance
Martin Luther
Martin Luther King, Jr.: Commemorative Collection
Mein Kampf
Memory of Justice, The
Men of Bronze
Mercenary Game, The
Merchants And Masterpieces
Millennium—Tribal Wisdom and the Modern World
Miners '88
Mingus
Mini Dragons—Hong Kong
Minnelli On Minnelli
Minnie The Moocher
Miracle Of Intervale Avenue, The
Mississippi Blues
Moana
Modern World, the—Ten Great Writers
Mondo Africa
Mondo Cane
Mondo New York
Mondo World War II—Short Memory
Monkey People, The
Monocacy, the Battle that Saved Washington
Monster Forces of Nature
Moshe Dayan: A Portrait
Mother Teresa
Murder By Numbers—Inside the Serial Killers
Murder, No Apparent Motive
Mutiny on the Western Front
Mysterious Egypt
Nanook of the North
NASA—The 25th Year
Near Death
Negro Soldier
News from Home
Night Mail
Nobody Waved Goodbye
Notebook on Cities and Clothes
Olympia
On Any Sunday
On Any Sunday II
Operation Shark Attack
Our Hitler
Panama Deception, The
Paris Is Burning
Petit a Petit
Powaqqatsi
Primary
Pumping Iron
Pumping Iron II: The Women
Punk Rock Movie, The
Ra Expeditions, The
Radium City
Rain Makers, The
Rise and Fall of the Third Reich, The
Roger & Me
Salesman
Salvador Dali—A Soft-Self Portrait
Sans Soleil
Sartre by Himself (Sartre Par Lui Meme)
Savage and Beautiful
Say Amen, Somebody
Scared Straight
Scotland Yard's Chamber of Crime
Scream of Fear
Seapower
Secret File on J. Edgar Hoover, The
Sherman's March
Shoah
Signatures of the Soul
Sky Above, The Mud Below, The
Sorrow and the Pity, The
Spirit of Crazy Horse, The
Stalking the President
Streetwise
Superstar: The Life and Times of Andy Warhol
Superstorms
Target for Today
Terror in the Aisles
Testament
Texas Chainsaw Massacre—A Documentary Family Portrait
Thin Blue Line, The
35 Up
Thirty Two Short Films About Glenn Gould
This Is Elvis
Time Indefinite
Tokyo Olympiad
Top Guns: The Real Story
Troika
True Game of Death
Truth or Dare
28 Up
21 Up
Unfinished Journey of Robert F. Kennedy, The
Vanishing Prairie, The
Vanishing Wilderness
Victory at Sea
Vincent: The Life and Death of Vincent Van Gogh
Visions of Eight
Visions of Light: The Art of Cinematography
Wandering Jew, The
War Game, The
War Room, The
Weavers, The: Wasn't That a Time!
Welfare
White Wilderness
Wild Wheels
Wonderful, Horrible Life of Leni Riefenstahl, The
World of Tomorrow, The
World Without Sun

DRAMA

A Brivele der Mamen
A Nos Amours
Aaron Loves Angela
Abandon Ship!
Abdication, The
Abduction
Abe Lincoln In Illinois
Abie's Irish Rose
About Mrs. Leslie
Above and Beyond
Above Suspicion
Above the Rim
Abraham Lincoln
Absence of Malice
Absolute Strangers
Acapulco Gold
Acceptable Levels
Acceptable Risks
Accident
Accidental Tourist, The
Accidents Will Happen
Accomplices, The
Accused
Accused of Murder
Accused, The
Acorn People, The
Across the Pacific
Across the Tracks
Act of Love
Act of Murder, An
Act of the Heart
Act of Vengeance
Act of Violence (1949)
Act of Violence (1979)
Act One
Action for Slander
Action in Arabia
Actors and Sin
Actor's Revenge, An
Actress, The
Ada
Adam and Evalyn
Adam at 6 A.M.
Adam Had Four Sons
Adam: His Song Continues
Adam's Rib
Adam's Woman
Address Unknown
Adjuster, The
Adolescent, The
Adorable Julia
Adrift
Adventure in the Hopfields
Adventure in Washington
Adventurers, The
Adventures of a Young Man
Adventures of Arsene Lupin
Adventures of Charlie and Cubby, The
Adventures of Frontier Freemont, The
Adventures of Huck Finn, The
Adventures of Huckleberry Finn
Adventures of Huckleberry Finn, The
Adventures of Huckleberry, Finn, The
Adventures of Marco Polo, The
Adventures of Mark Twain, The (1944)
Adventures of Mark Twain, The (1985)
Adventures of Martin Eden, The
Adventures of Robinson Crusoe, The
Adventures of Tartu
Adventures of the Wilderness Family, The
Adventures of Tom Sawyer, The
Adversary, The
Advice to the Lovelorn
Advise and Consent
Aerograd
Affair in Monte Carlo
Affair in Reno
Affair in Trinidad
Affair, The
Affair to Remember, An
Affair with a Stranger
Affairs of Cellini
Africa Addio
African Dream, An
African Queen, The
After Dark, My Sweet
After Midnight
After Office Hours
After the Promise
After the Rehearsal
Afterburn
Aftermath: A Test of Love
Against All Odds
Against Her Will: An Incident in Baltimore
Against the Wind
Age of Consent
Age of Innocence, The
Age-Old Friends
Agency
Agnes of God
Agony and the Ecstasy, The
Aguirre: The Wrath of God
Ah, Wilderness
Air Cadet
Airborne
Airport
Airport '75
Airport '77
Airport '79—The Concorde
Akira Kurosawa's Dreams
Alambrista!
Alamo Bay
Alan & Naomi
Alaska Seas
Alex: The Life of a Child
Alexander
Alexander Hamilton
Alexander Nevsky
Alexander the Great
Alexander: The Other Side of Dawn
Algiers
Ali—Fear Eats the Soul
Alias Nick Beal
Alice Adams
Alice Doesn't Live Here Anymore
Alice in the Cities
Alice in Wonderland (1933)
Alice in Wonderland (1950)
Alice in Wonderland (1951)
Alice in Wonderland (1985)
Alice, or the Last Escapade
All About Ah Long
All-American Boy, The
All American, The
All Creatures Great and Small
All Fall Down
All God's Children
All I Desire
All I Want for Christmas
All Mine to Give
All My Sons
All Night Long
All of Me
All Quiet on the Western Front (1930)
All Quiet on the Western Front (1978)
All That Heaven Allows
All the Brothers Were Valiant
All the Fine Young Cannibals
All the Gold in the World
All the King's Men
All the Mornings of the World
All the President's Men
All the Right Moves
All the Vermeers in New York
All the Way Home
All the Young Men
All Things Bright and Beautiful
All This and Heaven Too
All Through the Night
All Together Now
Alligator Eyes
Alligator Shoes
Allonsanfan
Allotment Wives
Almanac of Fall
Almost Angels
aloha, bobby and rose
Aloha Summer
Along Came a Spider
Alpha Beta
Alpine Fire
Alsino and the Condor
Always
Always Goodbye
Always in My Heart
Always Leave Them Laughing
Amadeus
Amazing Grace and Chuck
Amazing Howard Hughes, The
Amazing Mr. Blunden, The
Amazon
Ambassador, The
Amber Waves

Amelia Earhart
America
America, America
American Anthem
American Autobahn
American Blue Note
American Christmas Carol, An
American Clock, The
American Dream
American Eagle
American Flyers
American Friend, The
American Friends
American Gigolo
American Heart
American Justice
American Madness
American Nightmare
American Pop
American Romance, An
American Roulette
American Summer, An
American Tail, An
American Tragedy, An
Americana
Amin—The Rise and Fall
Among the Living
Amore
Amos
Amy
Amy Fisher: My Story
Amy Fisher Story, The
Ana and the Wolves
Anastasia
Anastasia: The Mystery Of Anna
Anatomy of a Marriage
Anatomy of a Murder
Anatomy of a Seduction
Anatomy of Terror
And a Nightingale Sang
And Baby Makes Six
. . . And God Created Woman
And God Created Woman
And I Alone Survived
And Justice for All
And No One Could Save Her
And Nothing But the Truth
And Now Miguel
And Now My Love
And Now Tomorrow
And Quiet Flows the Don
And Soon the Darkness
And the Band Played On
And the Sea Will Tell
And the Ship Sails On
And the Wild, Wild Women
Andersonville Trial
Andrei Rublev
Andy
Angel
Angel at My Table, An
Angel Baby
Angel City
Angel Dusted
Angel in a Taxi
Angel in Green
Angel Levine, The
Angel on My Shoulder
Angel on the Amazon
Angel Wore Red, The
Angela
Angele
Angelo, My Love
Angels' Alley
Angels of Darkness
Angels over Broadway
Angels Wash Their Faces, The
Angels with Dirty Faces
Angi Vera
Angie
Angry Breed, The
Angry Harvest
Angry Joe Bass
Angry Silence, The
Animal Farm
Animal Instincts
Animal Kingdom, The
Anita—Dances of Vice
Ann Jillian Story, The
Ann Vickers
Anna (1951)
Anna (1987)
Anna Akhmatova File, The
Anna and the King of Siam
Anna Christie (1923)
Anna Christie (1930)
Anna Karenina (1935)
Anna Karenina (1948)
Anna Karenina (1985)
Anna Lucasta (1949)
Anna Lucasta (1958)
Annapolis Story, An
Anne of Avonlea
Anne of Green Gables (1934)
Anne of Green Gables (1985)
Anne of the Thousand Days
Anne of Windy Poplars
Another Country
Another Dawn
Another Language
Another Man, Another Chance
Another Man's Poison
Another Part of the Forest
Another Stakeout
Another Time, Another Place
Another Woman
Antarctica
Anthony Adverse
Antigone
Antonio
Antony and Cleopatra
Any Man's Death
Any Number Can Play
Any Second Now
Anything Can Happen
Anything to Survive
Anzio
Aparajito
Apartment Zero
Apocalypse Now
Appearances
Applause
Appointment in Honduras
Appointment, The
Appointment with Danger
April Morning
April Showers
Arch of Triumph (1948)
Arch of Triumph (1985)
Ariel
Arise, My Love
Arizona to Broadway
Arkansas Traveler, The
Armored Command
Around the World Under the Sea
Arousers, The
Arrangement, The
Arrowsmith
Arthur and the Square Knights of the Round Table
Arthur's Hallowed Ground
Article 99
As If It Were Raining
As Is
As Summers Die
As the Sea Rages
As You Desire Me
Ash Wednesday
Ashanti: Land of No Mercy
Ashes and Diamonds
Ashes and Embers
Ashik Kerib
Aspen Extreme
Assam Garden, The
Assassin of Youth
Assassination of Trotsky, The
Assault, The
Assignment, The
Assisi Underground, The
Astonished Heart, The
Astronaut, The
At Play in the Fields of the Lord
Atalia
Atlanta Child Murders, The
Atlantic City
Attack!
Attack on Terror: The FBI vs. the Ku Klux Klan
Attic, The
Attic, The: The Hiding of Anne Frank
Attica
Au Hasard, Balthazar
Au Revoir, Les Enfants
Aunt Mary
Aurora
Austeria (The Inn)
Autobiography of a Princess
Autobiography of Miss Jane Pittman
Autumn Afternoon, An
Autumn Born
Autumn Leaves
Autumn Marathon
Autumn Sonata
Autumn's Tale, An
Avalon
Avant Garde and Experimental Films
Aviator, The
Awakening of

Candra, The
Awakening of
Cassie, The
Awakenings
Ay, Carmela!
B. F.'s Daughter
Babar: The Movie
Babbitt
Babe
Babe Ruth Story, The
Babe, The
Babette's Feast
Baby Blue Marine
Baby Comes Home
Baby Doll
Baby Face
Baby Girl Scott
Baby Love
Baby M
Baby Maker, The
Baby the Rain Must
Fall
Babycakes
Bach and Broccoli
Bachelor Father, The
Bachelor Party, The
Back Home
Back Street (1932)
Back Street (1941)
Back Street (1961)
Back to Hannibal:
The Return of
Tom Sawyer and
Huckleberry Finn
Back to the Forest
Backdraft
Backlash
Backstab
Bad and the
Beautiful, The
Bad Blood (1987)
Bad Blood (1989)
Bad Boy
Bad For Each Other
Bad Girl
Bad Girls in the
Movies
Bad Lord Byron
Bad Seed, The (1956)
Bad Seed, The (1985)
Bad Sleep Well, The
Bad Timing: A
Sensual
Obsession
Badge or the Cross,
The
Bahama Passage
Bailout at 43,000
Bait
Baja Oklahoma
Balboa
Balcony, The
Ballad in Blue
Ballad of A Soldier
Ballad of Andy
Crocker, The
Ballad of Little Jo,
The
Ballad of Narayama,
The (1958)
Ballad of Narayama,
The (1983)
Ballad of the Sad
Cafe, The
Bambi
Band of Angels
Bandits
Bandits of Orgosolo
Bang the Drum
Slowly
Bannerline
Banning
Barabbas
Barbarian and the
Geisha, The
Barbarian, The
Bare Essence
Barefoot Contessa,
The
Barfly
Baritone
Barjo
Barnacle Bill
Barnum
Baron and the Kid,
The
Barretts of Wimpole
Street, The (1934)
Barretts of Wimpole
Street, The (1957)
Barrier
Barry Lyndon
Bartleby
Bashful Elephant, The
Basileus Quartet
Basketball Fix, The
Bastard, The
Bat 21
Bataan
Battered
Battle Circus
Battle Flame
Battle for the
Falklands
Battle of Algiers
Battle of Britain, The
Battle of Neretva, The
Battle of the Rails
Battle of the Villa
Fiorita, The
Battle, The
Battleground
Battleship Potemkin
Battling for Baby
Baxter
Bay Boy, The
Bayou Romance
Be Beautiful but Shut
Up
Be Yourself
Beachcomber, The
(1938)
Beachcomber, The
(1955)
Beaches
Beans of Egypt,
Maine, The
Bear, The (1984)
Bear, The (1989)
Bear Who Slept
through
Christmas, The
Bears and I, The
Beast of Budapest,
The
Beat, The
Beatrice
Beau Brummel
(1924)
Beau Brummel
(1954)
Beau James
Beau Pere
Beauties of the Night
Beauty and the Beast
(1946)
Beauty and the Beast
(1963)
Beauty and the Devil
Beauty for Sale
Beauty for the Asking
Bebo's Girl
Because He's My
Friend
Because of You
Because They're
Young
Becket
Becky Sharp
Becoming Colette
Bed and Board
Bedelia
Bedevilled
Been Down So Long
It Looks Like Up
to Me
Beethoven Lives
Upstairs
Beethoven's Great
Love
Beethoven's Nephew
Beezbo
Before the Revolution
Before Winter Comes
Beggarman, Thief
Beggars of Life
Beguiled, The
Behind Locked Doors
Behind That Curtain
Behold a Pale Horse
Behold My Wife
Belarus File, The
Believe in Me
Belizaire the Cajun
Bell for Adano, A
Bell Jar, The
Belle de Jour
Bellissima
Bells of St. Mary's,
The
Belly of an Architect,
The
Beloved Enemy
Beloved Infidel
Beloved Rogue, The
Below the Belt
Belstone Fox, The
Ben-Hur (1926)
Ben-Hur (1959)
Beneath the 12 Mile
Reef
Beniker Gang, The
Benjamin
Benji
Benji the Hunted
Benny Goodman
Story, The
Benny's Place
Berkeley Square
Berlin Affair, The
Berlin Alexanderplatz
Berlin Blues
Berlin Correspondent
Berlin Express
Berlin Tunnel 21
Bernadette of
Lourdes
Berry Gordy's the
Last Dragon
Best Enemies
Best Intentions, The
Best Kept Secrets
Best Little Girl in The
World, The
Best Man, The
Best of Everything,
The
Best Place to Be, The
Best Years of Our
Lives, The
Bethune
Betrayal
Betrayal of the Dove
Betrayed
Betrayed Women
Betsy, The
Betty
Betty Blue
Betty Ford Story, The
Between Friends
Between Heaven and
Earth
Between Heaven and
Hell
Between Time And
Eternity
Between Two
Women (1944)
Between Two
Women (1986)
Between Two Worlds
Between Wars
Beulah Land
Beverly Hills, 90210

Beverly Hills, 90210—The Graduation
Beware, My Lovely
Beware of a Holy Whore
Beware of Pity
Beyond Glory
Beyond Obsession
Beyond Reason
Beyond the Forest
Beyond the Limit
Beyond the Walls
Bhowani Junction
Bible, The
Bicycle Thief, The
Big Blockade, The
Big Blue, The
Big Bluff, The
Big Bounce, The
Big Caper, The
Big Carnival, The
Big Chill, The
Big Circus, The
Big City Blues
Big City, The (1937)
Big City, The (1963)
Big Cube, The
Big Fisherman, The
Big Gusher, The
Big Guy, The
Big Knife, The
Big Leaguer, The
Big Lift, The
Big Night, The
Big One: The Great Los Angeles Earthquake, The
Big Operator, The
Big Parade, The
Big Punch, The
Big Red
Big Risk, The
Big Shakedown, The
Big Show, The
Big Street, The
Big Tip Off, The
Big Town
Big Town Girl
Big Town, The
Big Wave, The
Big Wednesday
Bigamist, The
Bigger than Life
Bilitis
Bill
Bill and Coo
Bill of Divorcement, A (1932)
Bill of Divorcement, A (1940)
Bill: On His Own
Billion Dollar Brain
Billionaire Boys Club
Billy Bathgate
Billy Budd
Billy Galvin
Billy in the Lowlands
Billy Liar
Bingo
Biography of a Bachelor Girl
Biquefarre
Birch Interval
Bird
Bird of Paradise (1932)
Bird of Paradise (1951)
Birdman of Alcatraz
Birdy
Birth of a Nation, The
Birthday Party, The
Biscuit Eater, The (1940)
Biscuit Eater, The (1972)
Bitch, The
Bitter Harvest
Bitter Moon
Bitter Rice
Bitter Tea of General Yen, The
Bitter Tears of Petra Von Kant, The
Bitter Victory
Bittersweet Love
Black and White in Color
Black Beauty (1946)
Black Beauty (1971)
Black Belly of the Tarantula
Black Fury
Black Girl
Black Gold
Black Klansman, the
Black Legion
Black Like Me
Black Lizard
Black Magic
Black Marble, The
Black Narcissus
Black Oak Conspiracy
Black Orchid, The
Black Orpheus
Black Rain
Black Robe, The
Black Shampoo
Black Starlet
Black Tent, The
Black Venus
Black Widow
Blackboard Jungle
Blackout
Blades of Courage
Blanche Fury
Blaze
Blaze of Noon
Blazing Forest, The
Bleak House
Bless the Beasts and Children
Blind Husbands
Blind Justice
Blind Spot
Blind Trust
Blindfold: Acts Of Obsession
Blockade
Blockhouse, The
Blonde Bait
Blonde Venus
Blood & Guts
Blood & Orchids
Blood and Sand (1922)
Blood and Sand (1941)
Blood and Sand (1989)
Blood and Steel
Blood Feud (1979)
Blood Feud (1983)
Blood Mania
Blood Money
Blood of a Poet, The
Blood of Others, The
Blood of the Condor
Blood on the Sun
Blood Wedding
Bloodbrothers
Bloodline
Bloody Mama
Blossoms in the Dust
Blowing Wild
Blowup
Blue
Blue Angel, The (1930)
Blue Angel, The (1959)
Blue Blood
Blue Chips
Blue de Ville
Blue Denim
Blue Fyre Lady
Blue Grass of Kentucky
Blue Hotel, The
Blue Hour, The
Blue Lagoon
Blue Lagoon, The
Blue Light, The
Blue Max, The
Blue Skies Again
Blue Sky
Blue Sunshine
Blue Veil, The
Bluebeard (1962)
Bluebeard (1972)
Blueberry Hill
Bluegrass
Boardwalk
Boat is Full, The
Boat People
Bob Mathias Story, The
Bobby Deerfield
Bodies, Rest & Motion
Body and Soul (1926)
Body and Soul (1947)
Body and Soul (1981)
Body Rock
Bodyguard, The
Bofors Gun, The
Bogie
Bolero (1934)
Bolero (1982)
Bolero (1984)
Bomb at 10:10
Bombay Talkie
Bombers B-52
Bombs Over Burma
Bond Street
Bonfire of the Vanities, The
Bonjour Tristesse
Bonnie Prince Charlie
Boom!
Boom Town
Boost, The
Boots Malone
Bopha!
Border Heat
Border Radio
Border Street
Border, The
Bordertown
Born Again
Born Free
Born Innocent
Born on the Fourth of July
Born Reckless
Born To Be Bad
Born To Be Loved
Borrowers, The
Boss' Wife, The
Boss's Son, The
Bostonians, The
Botany Bay
Both Sides of the Law
Bottom of the Bottle, The
Boudu Saved From Drowning
Bound and Gagged: A Love Story
Bound for Glory
Bounty, The
Bouquet of Barbed Wire
Bowery, The
Boxcar Bertha
Boxing Helena
Boy
Boy in Blue, The

Boy in the Plastic Bubble, The
Boy Meets Girl
Boy of the Streets
Boy on a Dolphin
Boy Ten Feet Tall, A
Boy Who Could Fly, The
Boy Who Cried Bitch, The
Boy Who Had Everything, The
Boy with Green Hair, The
Boys From Brazil, The
Boys in Company C, The
Boys in the Band, The
Boys of Paul Street
Boys, The (1961)
Boys, The (1991)
Boys Town
Boyz N the Hood
Brainwashed
Bramble Bush, The
Brand New Life, A
Brave Bulls, The
Brave One, The
Break in the Circle
Break of Hearts
Break to Freedom
Breaker Morant
Breakfast Club, The
Breakfast in Paris
Breaking Away
Breaking Point
Breaking the Sound Barrier
Breaking Up Is Hard to Do
Breaking with Old Ideas
Breakthrough (1950)
Breakthrough (1978)
Breathing Lessons
Breed Apart, A
Breezy
Brian's Song
Bribe, The
Bridal Path, The
Bride in Black, The
Bride Is Much Too Beautiful, The
Bride of Vengeance
Bride Wore Red, The
Brideshead Revisited
Bridge of San Luis Rey, The
Bridge on the River Kwai, The
Bridge, The
Bridge to Silence
Bridge to the Sun
Bridge Too Far, A

Brief Encounter (1945)
Brief Encounter (1974)
Brief Vacation, A
Brigand of Kandahar, The
Brigand, The
Brigham Young
Bright Angel
Bright Eyes
Bright Leaf
Bright Lights
Bright Lights, Big City
Bright Road
Bright Victory
Brimstone and Treacle
Brink of Life
British Agent
British Intelligence
Broadway
Broadway Bad
Broadway Limited
Broadway Musketeers
Broadway Through a Keyhole
Broken Blossoms
Broken Chain, The
Broken Journey
Broken Lullaby
Broken Sky
Brontë
Brontë Sisters, The
Bronx Tale, A
Bronx War, The
Brother John
Brother Sun, Sister Moon
Brotherhood, The
Brothers
Brothers Karamazov, The
Browning Version, The (1951)
Browning Version, The (1994)
Brubaker
Brutal Glory
Brute Man
Buddies
Bugle Sounds, The
Bulldog Drummond
Bullfighter and the Lady, The
Bunker, The
Bunny's Tale, A
Burden of Proof, The
Burke and Wills
Burmese Harp, The
Burning an Illusion
Burning Bed, The
Burning Bridges
Burning Rage

Burning Secret
Bus Is Coming, The
Bus Riley's Back in Town
Business as Usual
Buster and Billie
Buster Keaton Story, The
But Not For Me
Butley
Buttercup Chain, The
Butterfield 8
Bwana Devil
By Dawn's Early Light
By Love Possessed
Bye Bye Blues
Cabeza de Vaca
Cabin in the Cotton, The
Cabiria
Caboblanco
Cactus
Caddie
Cadence
Caesar and Cleopatra
Cafe Romeo
Cage of Gold
Cage of Nightingales
Caged
Caine Mutiny Court-Martial, The
Caine Mutiny, The
Cal
Calamity Jane
Calcutta
California Dreaming
California Split
Caligula
Call Her Savage
Call Me
Call Me Anna
Call of the Wild
Call of the Wild, The
Caller, The
Calling Dr. Gillespie
Calling Dr. Kildare
Camila
Camille (1936)
Camille (1984)
Camille Claudel
Camille 2000
Camp on Blood Island, The
Can Hieronymus Merkin Ever Forget Mercy Humppe and Find True Happiness?
Can You Feel Me Dancing?
Can You Hear the Laughter? The Story of Freddie Prinze
Candidate, The

Candleshoe
Candy Mountain
Canterbury Tale, A
Captain Boycott
Captain Carey, U.S.A.
Captain China
Captain Eddie
Captain John Smith and Pocahontas
Captain Newman, M.D.
Captains Courageous (1937)
Captains Courageous (1977)
Captive Heart, The
Captive Hearts
Capture, The
Captured
Caravaggio
Caravans
Carbine Williams
Cardinal Richelieu
Cardinal, The
Care Bears Adventure in Wonderland!, The
Care Bears Movie, The
Care Bears Movie II: A New Generation
Career
Career Girl
Careful, He Might Hear You
Caretakers, The
Cariboo Trail
Carl Sandburg—Echoes and Silences
Carnal Knowledge
Carnival
Carnival in Flanders
Carnival of Sinners
Carnival Story
Carny
Caroline?
Carpetbaggers, The
Carrie
Carrier, The
Carve Her Name With Pride
Casablanca
Casanova
Case of Dr. Laurent, The
Case of Libel, A
Case of Rape, A
Casey's Shadow
Cash McCall
Cash on Delivery
Casque D'or
Cass Timberlane
Cast a Giant Shadow

Castaway
Castaway Cowboy, The
Castle, The
Casualties of Love: The "Long Island Lolita" Story
Casualties of War
Cat Chaser
Cat on a Hot Tin Roof (1958)
Cat on a Hot Tin Roof (1984)
Cat, The
Catch-22
Catered Affair, The
Catherine the Great
Catholics
Cathy's Child
Caught
Cavalcade
Cavern, The
Cease Fire
Ceiling Zero
Celeste
Celia—Child of Terror
Céline and Julie Go Boating
Central Park
Certain Fury
Certain Smile, A
Cesar
Cesar and Rosalie
C'est la Vie
Chad Hanna
Chain Lightning
Chain Reaction
Chained
Chains of Gold
Chairman, The
Chalk Garden, The
Challenge to Be Free
Challenge to Lassie
Champ, The (1931)
Champ, The (1979)
Champagne
Champagne Charlie
Champion
Champions
Champions: A Love Story
Chance at Heaven
Chance of a Lifetime
Chances
Chanel Solitaire
Change of Habit
Change of Mind
Changes
Chant of Jimmy Blacksmith, The
Chantilly Lace
Chapayev
Chaplin
Chapman Report, The
Chappaqua
Chariots of Fire
Charles & Diana: A Palace Divided
Charles & Diana: A Royal Love Story
Charles and Lucie
Charles, Dead or Alive
Charley and the Angel
Charlie and the Great Balloon Chase
Charlie Bubbles
Charlotte's Web
Charly
Charming Sinners
Chase, The
Chasing Dreams
Chastity
Chattahoochee
Che!
Cheaper to Keep Her
Cheatin' Hearts
Checkpoint
Cheers for Miss Bishop
Cheetah
Chernobyl: The Final Warning
Chess Players, The
Chicago Calling
Chicago Confidential
Chicago Deadline
Chicago Story
Chicago Syndicate
Chikamatsu Monogatari
Child Bride of Short Creek
Child in the House
Child Is Born, A
Child Is Waiting, A
Child Stealer, The
Child Under a Leaf
Children Nobody Wanted, The
Children of a Lesser God
Children of An Lac, The
Children of Divorce
Children of Hiroshima
Children of Paradise
Children of Sanchez, The
Children, The
Children's Hour, The
Child's Play
Chimes at Midnight
China
China Cry
China Doll
China Girl
China Seas
China Sky
China Syndrome, The
China's Little Devils
Chinese Ghost Story, A
Chocolat
Chocolate War, The
Choice of Arms
Choice, The
Choices
Choirboys, The
Choose Me
Chosen, The
Christian the Lion
Christiane F.
Christina
Christine Jorgensen Story, The
Christmas Carol, A (1938)
Christmas Carol, A (1951)
Christmas Carol, A (1984)
Christmas Coal Mine Miracle, The
Christmas Eve (1947)
Christmas Eve (1986)
Christmas Holiday
Christmas Lilies of the Field
Christmas to Remember, A
Christmas Tree, The
Christmas Visitor, The
Christmas Wife, The
Christmas Without Snow, A
Christopher Columbus (1949)
Christopher Columbus (1985)
Christopher Columbus—The Discovery
Christopher Strong
Chubasco
Chushingura
Cincinnati Kid, The
Cinderella Liberty
Cinema Paradiso
Circle of Children, A
Circle of Danger
Circle of Deceit
Circle of Deception, A
Circle of Love
Circle of Violence: A Family Drama, A
Circus World
Citadel, The
Citizen Cohn
Citizen Kane
City Across the River
City for Conquest
City Girl
City of Fear (1959)
City of Fear (1966)
City of Hope
City of Joy
City of Sadness, A
City of Shadows
City Streets
City That Never Sleeps
City, The
City Without Men
Civilization
Clair de Femme
Claire of the Moon
Clairvoyant, The
Clan of the Cave Bear, The
Clara's Heart
Clarence and Angel
Clarence, the Cross-Eyed Lion
Clash by Night
Clash of the Titans
Class Action
Class of '44
Class of Miss MacMichael, The
Class of 1984
Class of '63
Claudelle Inglish
Claudia and David
Clay Pigeon
Clay Pigeon, The
Clean and Sober
Clearcut
Cleo From 5 to 7
Cleopatra (1934)
Cleopatra (1963)
Cleopatra's Daughter
Climax, The
Clive of India
Cloak and Dagger
Clock, The
Close My Eyes
Close to Eden
Close to My Heart
Closer, The
Closet Land
Cloud Dancer
Clown, The
Clowns, The
Club Havana
Club Med
Coach of the Year
Coal Miner's Daughter
Cobb
Cobra Woman
Cobweb, The
Cocaine Cowboys
Cocaine Fiends, The
Cocaine: One Man's

Seduction
Cockfighter
Cocktail
Cocktail Molotov
Code of Honor
Code of Scotland Yard
Coins in the Fountain
Cold Heaven
Cold Room, The
Cold Sassy Tree
Cold Wind in August, A
Collector, The
Collector's Item
College Coach
College Confidential
Collision Course
Colonel Chabert
Colonel Redl
Color of Money, The
Color of Pomegranates, The
Color Purple, The
Coma
Come and Get It
Come and See
Come Back, Little Sheba
Come Back to the Five and Dime, Jimmy Dean, Jimmy Dean
Come Fill the Cup
Come Next Spring
Come See the Paradise
Come to the Stable
Comedians, The
Comet Over Broadway
Comfort of Strangers, The
Comic, The
Coming Apart
Coming Home
Coming-Out Party
Coming Through
Commissar
Commitments, The
Common Bonds
Common Ground
Company She Keeps, The
Competition, The
Concentration Camp
Condemned
Condemned of Altona, The
Conduct Unbecoming
Conductor, The
Confession, The
Confessions of a Nazi Spy
Confessions of Amans, The
Confidence
Confidential Agent
Conflagration
Conflict (1939)
Conflict (1945)
Conformist, The
Connecting Rooms
Connection, The
Conquered City, The
Conqueror, The
Conquerors, The
Conquest
Conrack
Consenting Adult
Consequence, The
Consolation Marriage
Conspiracy of Hearts
Conspiracy—The Trial of the Chicago 8
Conspirator
Conspirators, The
Constance
Constant Factor, The
Constant Nymph, The
Constantine and the Cross
Contraband
Control
Conversation Piece
Conversation, The
Convicted
Convicts
Convicts Four
Cook, the Thief, His Wife & Her Lover, The
Cool as Ice
Cool Hand Luke
Cool World
Cooley High
Coquette
Cordelia
Corinna, Corinna
Corn Is Green, The (1945)
Corn Is Green, The (1978)
Cornbread, Earl and Me
Corpse Came C.O.D., The
Corregidor
Corridor of Mirrors
Corsair
Cotton Club, The
Counsellor-at-Law
Count of Monte Cristo, The
Count Three and Pray
Countdown
Countdown at Kusini
Counterfeit Traitor, The
Counterpoint
Countess from Hong Kong, A
Country
Country Doctor, The
Country Girl, The
County Fair
Coup de Grace
Courage
Courage Mountain
Courage of Black Beauty
Courage of Lassie
Court-Martial of Billy Mitchell, The
Court-Martial of Jackie Robinson, The
Court Martial of Major Keller, The
Courtney Affair, The
Courtship
Cousin Angelica
Cousins, The
Cowboy from Brooklyn, The
Crack House
Crack in the Mirror
Crack-Up
Cracker Factory, The
Craig's Wife
Cranes Are Flying, The
Crash of Silence
Crazy From the Heart
Cria!
Cricket, The
Cries and Whispers
Crime and Punishment (1935)
Crime and Punishment (1970)
Crime & Punishment, USA
Crime of Monsieur Lange, The
Crime of Passion
Crimes at the Dark House
Crimes of Passion
Criminal Lawyer
Criminal Life of Archibaldo de la Cruz, The
Crimson Romance
Crisis
Crisis at Central High
CrissCross
Cromwell
Crooked Hearts
Crooklyn
Cross Creek
Cross of Fire
Cross of Iron
Crossed Swords
Crossfire
Crossing, The
Crossing the Bridge
Crossing the Line
Crossing to Freedom
Crossroads (1938)
Crossroads (1942)
Crosswinds
Crowd Roars, The
Crowd, The
Crucible, The
Cruel Sea, The
Cruel Story of Youth
Cruel Tower, The
Cruising
Crusades, The
Crusoe
Cry for Help: The Tracey Thurman Story, A
Cry Freedom
Cry from the Mountain
Cry from the Streets, A
Cry in the Dark, A
Cry in the Night, A
Cry the Beloved Country
Cry Wolf
Crying Game, The
Crystal Heart
Cuba
Cul-De-Sac
Cup Final
Cutter's Way
Cutting Edge, The
Cynara
Cynthia
Cyrano de Bergerac (1950)
Cyrano de Bergerac (1990)
D-Day the Sixth of June
Da
Dad
Dadah Is Death
Daddy Nostalgia
Daisy Kenyon
Daisy Miller
Dakota
Dam Busters, The
Damage
Damned Don't Cry, The
Damned, The
Dance, Fools, Dance
Dance Hall Racket
Dance of Death
Dance With a Stranger
Dances with Wolves
Dancing in the Dark
Danger Lights

Danger Patrol
Danger Signal
Dangerous
Dangerous Crossing
Dangerous Game
Dangerous Liaisons
Dangerous Liaisons 1960
Dangerous Moonlight
Dangerous Moves
Dangerous Woman, A
Dangerously Close
Dangerously They Live
Daniel
Danielle Steel's Fine Things
Danny
Danny Boy
Dante's Inferno
Danton
Danzon
Darby O'Gill and the Little People
Darby's Rangers
Dark Angel, The
Dark at the Top of the Stairs, The
Dark City
Dark End of the Street, The
Dark Eyes
Dark Hazard
Dark Horse
Dark Journey
Dark Mirror
Dark Mirror, The
Dark Obsession
Dark Passage
Dark Sands
Dark Victory (1939)
Dark Victory (1976)
Darktown Strutters
Darling
Das Boat
Daughter of Shanghai
Daughter of the Streets
Daughters Courageous
Daughters of Destiny
Daughters of the Dust
David (1976)
David (1988)
David and Bathsheba
David and Lisa
David Copperfield (1935)
David Copperfield (1970)
Dawn Patrol, The
Dawning, The
Day After, The
Day and the Hour, The
Day for Night
Day for Thanks on Waltons' Mountain, A
Day in October, A
Day in the Country, A
Day of the Locust, The
Day of Wrath
Day One
Day the Fish Came Out, The
Daybreak
Daydreamer, The
Days and Nights in the Forest
Days of Glory
Days of Heaven
Days of Thunder
Days of Wine and Roses
Dead Ahead: The Exxon Valdez Disaster
Dead-Bang
Dead End
Dead Man Out
Dead of Winter
Dead Poets Society
Dead Ringer
Dead Ringers
Dead, The
Deadhead Miles
Deadlier than the Male
Deadliest Art, The: The Best of the Martial Arts Films, The
Deadliest Season, The
Deadline U.S.A
Deadly Breed
Deadly Surveillance
Dealers
Dear America: Letters Home from Vietnam
Dear Heart
Dear Mr. Wonderful
Death and the Maiden
Death Be Not Proud
Death Drug
Death in Venice
Death of a Centerfold: The Dorothy Stratten Story
Death of a Cyclist
Death of a Prophet
Death of a Salesman (1951)
Death of a Salesman (1985)
Death of a Soldier
Death of an Angel
Death of Richie, The
Death of Tarzan, The
Death of the Empedocles, The
Death on the Nile
Death Scream
Death Sentence
Death Takes a Holiday
Debajo del Mundo (Under Earth)
Decameron Nights
December
December 7th—The Movie
Deception
Decision Before Dawn
Decline of Western Civilization, The
Decoration Day
Deep Blue Sea, The
Deep End
Deep in the Heart
Deep Valley
Deep Waters
Deer Hunter, The
Defection of Simas Kudirka, The
Defence of the Realm
Deja Vu
Delicate Balance, A
Delinquents, The
Deliverance
Deluge, The
Delusion
Demetrius and the Gladiators
Demon Within, The
Demons in the Garden
Dempsey
Denial
Deported
Deputy, The
Dersu Uzala
Desert Bloom
Desert Fox, The
Desert Hearts
Desert Rats, The
Desire Me
Desire Under the Elms
Desiree
Despair
Desperate Characters
Desperate Hours, The
Desperate Journey
Desperate Moment
Desperate Search
Destination Tokyo
Destiny
Destiny of a Man
Destroyer
Detective
Detective Story
Devi
Devil and Daniel Webster, The
Devil and the Deep
Devil and the Ten Commandments, The
Devil at 4 O'Clock, The
Devil Hunter Yohko
Devil in the Flesh (1946)
Devil in the Flesh (1986)
Devil is a Sissy, The
Devil is a Woman, The
Devil Makes Three, The
Devil on Horseback, The
Devil Pays Off
Devil Probably, The
Devil Strikes at Night, The
Devil's Envoys, The
Devil's General, The
Devil's in Love, The
Devil's Island
Devil's Playground, The
Devils, The
Devil's Wanton, The
Devil's Widow, The
Devotion
D.I., The
Dial 1119
Diamond Head
Diamond Hunters
Diamonds of the Night
Diana: Her True Story
Diane
Diary for My Children
Diary of a Chambermaid (1946)
Diary of a Chambermaid (1964)
Diary of a Country Priest
Diary of a Hitman
Diary of a Lost Girl
Diary of a Mad Housewife
Diary of a Teenage Hitchhiker
Diary of Anne Frank, The (1959)

Diary of Anne Frank, The (1980)
Die Niebelungen
Different Story, A
Diggstown
Dime with a Halo
Diner
Dingaka
Dingo
Dino
Dinosaur!
Diplomatic Courier
Dirigible
Dirty Game, The
Disappearance of Aimee, The
Disaster at Silo 7
Disclosure
Dishonored
Disorder and Early Torment
Dispatch from Reuters, A
Disraeli
Distance
Distant Thunder (1973)
Distant Thunder (1988)
Distant Voices, Still Lives
Dive Bomber
Divided Heart, The
Divine
Divine Nymph, The
Divorce His, Divorce Hers
Divorce Wars: A Love Story
Divorcee, The
Do the Right Thing
Do You Remember Love?
D.O.A.
Docks of New York
Doctor Socrates
Doctor, The
Doctor Zhivago
Doctor's Wives
Dodes'ka-den
Dodsworth
Dog of Flanders, A
Dogfight
Dogpound Shuffle
Doll, The
Dollmaker, The
Doll's House, A (1973, Losey)
Doll's House, A (1973, Garland)
Dominick and Eugene
Domino
Don Juan
Dondi
Donkey Skin
Don't Bother to Knock
Don't Cry, It's Only Thunder
Don't Let the Angels Fall
Doomwatch
Dorian Gray
Dorothy and Alan at Norma Place
Dorothy in the Land of Oz
Dot and the Bunny
Double Edge
Double Identity
Double Jeopardy
Double Life, A
Double Life of Veronique, The
Double Revenge
Double Suicide
Dove, The
Down and Dirty
Down to the Sea in Ships (1922)
Down to the Sea in Ships (1949)
Downhill
Downhill Racer
Downstairs
Dr. Bull
Dr. Ehrlich's Magic Bullet
Dr. Faustus
Dr. Gillespie's New Assistant
Dr. Kildare Goes Home
Dr. Kildare's Crisis
Dr. Kildare's Strange Case
Dr. Kildare's Victory
Dr. Kildare's Wedding Day
Dr. Mabuse, King of Crime
Dragon Chow
Dragon Seed
Dramatic School
Draughtsman's Contract, The
Dream for Christmas, A
Dream of Kings, A
Dream of Passion, A
DreamChild
Dreamer
Dreamer of Oz, The: The Frank L. Baum Story
Dreaming Lips
Dreams
Dreams Lost, Dreams Found
Dress Gray
Dresser, The
Dressmaker, The
Drifting
Drive a Crooked Road
Drive, He Said
Driver's Seat, The
Driving Miss Daisy
D.R.O.P. Squad
Drowning by Numbers
Drugstore Cowboy
Drum
Drums
Drums in the Deep South
Drunken Angel
Dry White Season, A
Du Barry, Woman of Passion
Duel in the Jungle
Duel of Hearts
Duel, The
Duellists, The
Duet for One
Duke of West Point, The
Dulcimer Street
Dulcinea
Dunera Boys, The
Dunkirk
Dust
Dust Be My Destiny
Dusty
Dutchman
Dybbuk, The
Dying Young
Each Dawn I Die
Eagle Has Landed, The
Eagle in a Cage
Eagle, The
Early Frost, An
Early Spring
Early Summer
Earrings of Madame de...
Earth
Earth Entranced
Earthbound
Earthling, The
Easiest Way, The
East of Eden (1955)
East of Eden (1981)
East of the River
East Side Kids
East Side, West Side
Easy Come, Easy Go
Easy Life, The
Easy Living
Easy Rider
Easy Virtue
Ebb Tide
Eboli
Ebony Tower, The
Echo of Barbara
Echoes in the Darkness
Echoes of a Summer
Echoes of Paradise
Eclipse, The
Ecstasy
Ecstasy of Young Love
Eddie Cantor Story, The
Edge of Darkness
Edge of Doom
Edge of the City
Edge of the World, The
Edge, The
Edison, the Man
Edith and Marcel
Education of Sonny Carson, The
Edvard Munch
Edward and Caroline
Edward, My Son
Edward Scissorhands
Edward II
Effect of Gamma Rays on Man-in-the-Moon Marigolds, The
Effi Briest
Egg
Eglantine
Egon Schiele—Excess and Punishment
Egyptian, The
8 1/2
Eight Bells
Eight Iron Men
Eight Men Out
Eight O'Clock Walk
8 Seconds
Eighth Day of the Week, The
84 Charing Cross Road
Eijanaika
El Bruto
El Cid
El Greco
El Nino Y El Papa
El Norte
El Super
Eleanor and Franklin
Eleanor and Franklin: The White House Years
Eleanor, First Lady of the World
Electra Glide in Blue
Electric Horseman, The
Eleni
Elephant Boy
Elephant Man, The
Elephant Walk
Elephant's Child
Elizabeth of

Ladymead
Ellis Island
Elmer Gantry
Elusive Corporal, The
Elvira Madigan
Elvis
Elvis and the Beauty Queen
Embraceable You
Emerald Forest, The
Emergency Hospital
Emigrants, The
Emily
Eminent Domain
Emma
Emma's Shadow
Emperor and A General, The
Emperor Jones, The
Emperor's Candlesticks, The
Empire of the Sun
Employees' Entrance
Empty Canvas, The
Enchanted April
Enchanted Cottage, The
Enchanted Forest
Enchanted Island
Enchantment
Encore
End of a Day, The
End of August, The
End of Desire
End of Innocence, The
End of St. Petersburg, The
End of Summer, The
End of the Affair, The
End of the Line
End of the River, The
End of the Road, The
End Play
Endangered Species
Endless Love
Enemies, A Love Story
Enemies of Progress
Enemy Below, The
Enemy of the People, An (1977)
Enemy of the People, An (1989)
England Made Me
Enola Gay
Enormous Changes at the Last Minute
Entertainer, The (1960)
Entertainer, The (1975)
Entre Nous
Equinox
Equinox Flower
Equus
Erendira
Eric
Ernest Green Story, The
Ernie Kovacs: Between the Laughter
Eroica
Escapade
Escapade in Japan
Escape (1940)
Escape (1948)
Escape from Iran: The Canadian Caper
Escape in the Sun
Escape Me Never
Escape to Burma
Escape to Glory
Escape to Love
Especially on Sunday
Esther and the King
Eternal Husband, The
Eternal Mask, The
Eternal Return, The
Eternity
Eternity of Love
Ethan Frome
Eureka
Europa, Europa
Europeans, The
Eva
Eve of St. Mark, The
Evel Knievel
Evelyn Prentice
Even Dwarfs Started Small
Evening in Byzantium, An
Event, An
Events
Ever in My Heart
Eversmile, New Jersey
Every Man for Himself
Every Man for Himself and God Against All
Every Time We Say Goodbye
Everybody's All-American
Everybody's Baby: The Rescue of Jessica McClure
Everybody's Fine
Everything for Sale
Evita Peron
Ex-Champ
Ex-Lady
Exclusive Story
Execution of Private Slovik, The
Execution of Raymond Graham, The
Executioner's Song, The
Executive Suite
Exile Express
Exile, The
Exiled to Shanghai
Exodus
Expedition, The
Expensive Husbands
Explosion
Explosive Generation, The
Exposed
Expresso Bongo
Extreme Close-Up
Extremities
Eye of the Needle
Eye on the Sparrow
Eyes of a Witness
Eyes, the Mouth, The
Eyes, the Sea and a Ball, The
F. Scott Fitzgerald and "The Last of the Belles"
F. Scott Fitzgerald in Hollywood
Fable, A
Fabulous Baker Boys, The
Face in the Crowd, A
Face of a Stranger
Face of Another, The
Face of Fear
Face of Fire
Face of Rage, The
Face to Face (1952)
Face to Face (1976)
Faces
Faces in the Dark
Facts of Murder, The
Fade-In
Fail-Safe
Failing of Raymond, The
Faithful City
Faithless
Fake, The
Falcon and the Snowman, The
Fall From Grace
Fall of the Roman Empire
Fallen Angel
Fallen Angels—Volume 1
Fallen Angels—Volume 2
Fallen Idol, The
Fallen Sparrow
Falling Down
Falling from Grace
Falling in Love
Falling in Love Again
False Identity
Fame Is the Name of the Game
Fame Is the Spur
Family Hour Special—Animal Talk
Family Hour Special—Out of Time
Family Life
Family Nobody Wanted, The
Family Pictures
Family Prayers
Family Reunion
Family Secret, The
Family Sins
Family, The
Family Upside Down, A
Family Viewing
Family Way, The
Fanatics, The
Fandango
Fangface
Fanny (1932)
Fanny (1961)
Fanny and Alexander
Fanny Hill
Fan's Notes, A
Fantastica
Fantasy Island
Fantasy Mission Force
Far and Away
Far Country, The
Far East
Far from the Madding Crowd
Far Horizons, The
Far North
Far Pavilions, The
Faraway, So Close
Farewell Friend
Farewell My Concubine
Farewell to Arms, A (1932)
Farewell to Arms, A (1957)
Farewell to Manzanar
Farewell to the King
Farinelli
Farmer Takes a Wife, The
Farrell for the People
Fascist, The
Fast Friends
Fast Workers
Fat City
Fat Man and Little Boy
Fatal Attraction
Fatal Charms
Fatal Confinement
Fatal Desire

Fatal Error
Fatal Skies
Fate Is the Hunter
Fate Takes a Hand
Father
Father Clements Story, The
Father Figure
Father of a Soldier
Father's Little Dividend
Father's Revenge, A
Faust (1926)
Faust (1994)
Favorites of the Moon
Fazil
F.D.R., The Last Year
Fear
Fear Is the Key
Fear on Trial
Fear Strikes Out
Fearless
Fearmakers, The
Federal Hill
Fedora
Fellini Satyricon
Fellini's Casanova
Fellini's Roma
Fellow Traveler
Female
Female Animal, The
Female Fiends
Female on the Beach
Feminine Touch, The
Femmes de Personne
FernGully ...The Last Rainforest
Fever in the Blood, A
Fever Pitch
Few Good Men, A
Field of Dreams
Field, The
Fields of Endless Day
Fifth Day of Peace, The
Fifth Horseman Is Fear, The
Fifth Monkey, The
Fifth Seal, The
55 Days at Peking
Fight for Jenny, A
Fight for Life
Fight for Rome
Fighter, The
Fighting Chance, The
Fighting Choice
Fighting Coast Guard
Fighting Father Dunne
Figures in a Landscape
File on Jill Hatch, The
File on Thelma Jordon, The
Final Assignment
Final Chapter—Walking Tall
Final Days, The
Final Verdict
Final War, The
Finding the Way Home
Fine Gold
Fingerman
Finish Line
Finishing School
Finnegan's Wake
Fiorile
Fire Alarm
Fire and Ice
Fire and Rain
Fire Down Below
Fire in the Dark
Fire in the Night
Fire in the Straw
Fire Next Time, The
Fire Over England
Fire with Fire
Fire Within, The
Fireball, The
Firebird, The
Firehawk
Fires on the Plain
Fires Were Started
Fires Within
First Comes Courage
First Deadly Sin, The
First Legion, The
First Love (1939)
First Love (1970)
First Love (1977)
First Name: Carmen
First Olympics: Athens 1896, The
First Steps
First Teacher, The
First 36 Hours of Dr. Durant, The
First Time, The
First Yank into Tokyo
First Year, The
First, You Cry
Firstborn
Fish Hawk
Fisher King, The
F.I.S.T.
Fist in His Pocket
Fitzcarraldo
Five
Five Against the House
Five and Ten
Five Branded Women
Five Corners
Five Days from Home
Five Days One Summer
Five Easy Pieces
Five Finger Exercise
5 Fingers
Five Gates to Hell
Five of Me, The
Five Star Final
Fixer, The
F.J. Holden, The
Flame and the Flesh, The
Flame in the Streets
Flame Is Love, The
Flame of the Islands
Flame over Vietnam
Flame Within, The
Flamingo Road (1949)
Flamingo Road (1980)
Flap
Flash of Green
Flat Top
Flatbed Annie & Sweetiepie: Lady Truckers
Flatliners
Flavor of Green Tea over Rice, The
Flaxfield, The
Flesh
Flesh & Blood
Flesh and Fantasy
Flesh and Fury
Flesh and the Devil
Flight Command
Flight for Freedom
Flight from Ashiya
Flight from Destiny
Flight from Glory
Flight of Dragons
Flight of the Doves
Flight of the Eagle, The
Flight of the Grey Wolf
Flight of the Intruder
Flight of the Phoenix
Flight to Berlin
Flight to Tangier
Flipper
Flipper's New Adventure
Flipper's Odyssey
Floating Weeds
Floods of Fear
Flor Silvestre
Florence Nightingale
Floundering
Flowers in the Attic
Flowers of St. Francis
Flowing Gold
Fly with the Hawk
Flying Fontaines, The
Flying Irishman, The
Fog Over Frisco
Follow Me, Boys!
Follow the Sun
Follow Your Heart
Following the Fuhrer
Fool for Love
Fool Killer, The
Foolish Wives
Fools
Fools of Fortune
Fools' Parade
Footsteps
For Freedom
For Ladies Only
For Love Alone
For Men Only
For Queen and Country
For the Defense
For the First Time
For the Love of Angela
For the Love of Benji
For the Love of Mike
For Those in Peril
For Us, the Living
For Whom the Bell Tolls
For Your Love Only
Forbidden (1932)
Forbidden (1953)
Forbidden (1985)
Forbidden Fruit
Forbidden Games
Forbidden Love
Forbidden Nights
Forbidden Relations
Forbidden Street, The
Force of Arms
Force of Evil
Forced March
Ford: The Man and the Machine
Foreign Affairs
Foreign Intrigue
Foreigner
Foreman Went to France, The
Forest Rangers, The
Forever
Forever Amber
Forever and a Day
Forever Fairytales—Brothers Grimm
Forever Fairytales—Charles Perrault
Forever Fairytales—Hans Christian Andersen
Forever, Lulu
Forever Mary
Forever My Love
Forever Young (1983)
Forever Young (1992)
Forget Mozart
Forgiven Sinner, The
Forgotten Prisoners:

The Amnesty Files
Forrest Gump
Forsaking All Others
Fortunate Pilgrim
Fortune and Men's Eyes
Fortune's Fool
Fortunes of War
Forty Deuce
Forty Little Mothers
47 Ronin, The
Fountain, The
Fountainhead, The
Four Adventures of Reinette and Mirabelle
Four Daughters
Four Feathers, The
Four Friends
Four Frightened People
Four Girls in Town
Four Horsemen of the Apocalypse
Four Horsemen of the Apocalypse, The
Four Hundred Blows, The
Four in a Jeep
Four Infernos to Cross
Four Mothers
Four Nights of a Dreamer
Four Poster, The
Four Sons (1928)
Four Sons (1940)
Four Ways Out
Four Wives
Fourteen Hours
1492: Conquest of Paradise
Fourth Protocol, The
Fourth Story, The
Fourth War, The
Fourth Wise Man, The
Fox and His Friends
Fox, The
Foxes
Foxes of Harrow, The
Foxfire (1955)
Foxfire (1987)
Foxfire Light
Foxstyle
Foxtrot
F.P. 1
F.P. 1 Doesn't Answer
Fragrance of Wild Flowers, The
Framed
Fran
Frances
Francis of Assisi
Frankie and Johnny
Frantic
Franz
Fraternity Row
Fraulein
Fraulein Doktor
Free Soul, A
Free, White and 21
Free Willy
Free Woman, A
Freedom
Freedom Road
Freeze—Die—Come to Life
French Key, The
French Lesson, The
French Lieutenant's Woman, The
French Provincial
French Quarter
French Quarter Undercover
French Way, The
French Woman, The
Fresh
Fresh Horses
Freud
Frida
Fried Green Tomatoes
Frieda
Friendly Fire
Friendly Persuasion (1956)
Friendly Persuasion (1975)
Friends
Friends and Husbands
Friends and Lovers
Friendship in Vienna
Friendships, Secrets, and Lies
Frightened Bride
Fringe Dwellers, The
Frisco Jenny
Frisco Kid
Frisky
From a Far Country: Pope John Paul II
From Hell to Heaven
From Here to Eternity (1953)
From Here to Eternity (1979)
From the Life of the Marionettes
From the Terrace
From This Day Forward
Front Page Story
Front, The
Fugitive from Justice, A
Fugitive Kind, The
Fugitive, The (1947)
Fugitive, The (1993)
Fulfillment
Full Confession
Full Exposure: The Sex Tape Scandals
Full Fathom Five
Full Metal Jacket
Full Moon in Blue Water
Fun and Fancy Free
Fun Down There
Funeral for an Assassin
Funeral in Berlin
Further Adventures of Tennessee Buck, The
Fury
Fuss over Feathers
Futz
Gable and Lombard
Gabriel over the White House
Gabriela
Gaby
Gaby—A True Story
Gaijin
Gal Young 'Un
Galileo
Gallant Bess
Gallant Journey
Gallant Lady
Gallipoli
Gamble on Love
Gamble, The
Gamblers, The
Gambling House
Gambling Lady
Game for Vultures
Game Is Over, The
Game of Danger
Game of Love, The
Game of Seduction
Gamekeeper, The
Games of Desire
Games, The
Gandhi
Gang Busters
Gangsters' Law
Gangway for Tomorrow
Garbo Talks
Garden of Allah, The
Garden of Delights, The
Garden of the Finzi-Continis, The
Gardens of Stone
Garment Jungle, The
Garnet Bracelet, The
Garnet Princess, The
Gas, Food Lodging
Gaslight (1940)
Gaslight (1944)
Gasoline Alley
Gate of Hell
Gates of Paris
Gates of the Night
Gateway
Gathering of Eagles
Gathering of Old Men, A
Gathering, The
Gathering, Part II, The
Gathering Storm, The
Gauguin the Savage
Gay Adventure, The
Gay Intruders, The
Gay Lady, The
Gay Sisters, The
Geisha, A
General Della Rovere
General Died at Dawn, The
General Line, The
General Suvorov
Generation, A
Genghis Khan
Gentle Creature, A
Gentle Giant
Gentle Gunman, The
Gentle Julia
Gentle Rain, The
Gentle Sex, The
Gentleman After Dark, A
Gentleman Bandit, The
Gentleman's Agreement
George McKenna Story, The
George Raft Story, The
Georgia, Georgia
German Sisters, The
Germany, Pale Mother
Germany Year Zero
Germinal
Gertrud
Gervaise
Getting of Wisdom, The
Getting Out
Getting Physical
Gettysburg
Ghost
Ghost and Mrs. Muir, The
Ghost Camera, The
Ghost Dancing
Ghost of the China Sea
Ghost Ship, The
Ghost Walks, The
Ghost Writer
Ghosts of Rome
Giant

Giant Steps
Gideon's Trumpet
Gift for Heidi, A
Gift of Love: A Christmas Story, The
Gift of Love, The (1958)
Gift of Love, The (1978)
Gig, The
Gigot
Gilda
Gilsodom
Ginger and Fred
Giordano Bruno
Girl from Calgary, The
Girl from Chicago
Girl from Hunan
Girl from Lorraine, A
Girl from 10th Avenue, The
Girl in Room 20
Girl in the News, The
Girl in the Painting
Girl in the Red Velvet Swing, The
Girl in White, The
Girl Named Sooner, A
Girl Named Tamiko, A
Girl of the Limberlost, A
Girl of the Night
Girl on a Motorcycle
Girl on the Bridge
Girl Who Had Everything, The
Girl Who Spelled Freedom, The
Girl with Green Eyes, The
Girl with the Red Hair, The
Girlfriends
Girls' Dormitory
Girls of Huntington House, The
Girls of the Night
Girls of the Road
Girls of the White Orchid
Girls on Probation
Girls Riot
Git
Give 'em Hell, Harry!
Give Me Your Heart
Given Word, The
Gladiator, The
Glass Menagerie, The (1950)
Glass Menagerie, The (1973)
Glass Menagerie, The (1987)
Glass Tower, The
Glass Wall, The
Gleaming the Cube
Glen or Glenda
Glengarry Glen Ross
Glory (1956)
Glory (1989)
Glory Alley
Glory at Sea
Glory Brigade
Gnomes
Go Ask Alice
Go-Between, The
Go for Broke
Go for Gold
Go, Man, Go!
Go Masters, The
Go Naked in the World
Go Tell It on the Mountain
Go Tell the Spartans
Goalie's Anxiety at the Penalty Kick, The
God Bless the Child
God Is My Partner
God, Man and Devil
Godchild, The
Goddess of Love (1960)
Goddess of Love (1988)
Goddess, The
God's Country and the Woman
God's Little Acre
Goha
Goin' Down the Road
Goin' Home
Going for the Gold: The Bill Johnson Story
Going Home
Going My Way
Going Steady
Gold for the Caesars
Gold of Naples, The
Golden Boy
Golden Braid
Golden Demon
Golden Earrings
Golden Gate
Golden Gloves Story, The
Golden Goose, The
Golden Harvest
Golden Honeymoon, The
Golden Hoofs
Golden Seal, The
Goldengirl
Goldenrod
Goldie and the Boxer
Goldie and the Boxer Go to Hollywood
Golgotha
Gone to Earth
Gone with the Wind
Gonza The Spearman
Good-bye, My Lady
Good Dame
Good Dissonance Like a Man, A
Good Earth, The
Good Father, The
Good Fight, The
Good Luck, Miss Wyckoff
Good Morning, Babylon
Good Morning, Miss Dove
Good Mother, The
Good Son, The
Good Time Girl
Good Wife, The
Goodbye Again
Goodbye Bird, The
Goodbye, Franklin High
Goodbye, Miss 4th of July
Goodbye, Mr. Chips
Goodbye, My Fancy
Goodbye, Norma Jean
Goodbye People, The
Goodnight, Sweet Marilyn
Goose and the Gander, The
Goose Girl, The
Gore Vidal's Lincoln
Gorgeous Hussy, The
Gorilla at Large
Gorillas in the Mist
Gospel According to St. Matthew
Gossip Columnist, The
Grace Kelly
Grambling's White Tiger
Grand Canyon
Grand Hotel
Grand Illusion
Grand Isle
Grand Jury
Grand Maneuver, The
Grandma's House
Grandpa
Grandview, U.S.A.
Grapes of Wrath, The
Grass Is Singing, The
Grasshopper, The
Great Adventure, The
Great Balls of Fire!
Great Battle, The
Great Brain, The
Great Dan Patch, The
Great Day
Great Expectations (1934)
Great Expectations (1946)
Great Expectations (1974)
Great Expectations (1981)
Great Gabbo, The
Great Gatsby, The (1926)
Great Gatsby, The (1949)
Great Gatsby, The (1974)
Great Gay Road, The
Great Guy
Great Hope, The
Great Houdinis, The
Great Impersonation, The
Great Impostor, The
Great John L., The
Great Lie, The
Great Locomotive Chase, The
Great Lover, The
Great Man, The
Great Moment, The
Great, My Parents Are Divorcing
Great Niagara, The
Great O'Malley, The
Great Profile, The
Great Santini, The
Great Sinner, The
Great Waldo Pepper, The
Great Wall, A
Great Wallendas, The
Great Waltz, The
Great White Hope, The
Greatest Gift, The
Greatest Love, The
Greatest Man in the World, The
Greatest Show on Earth, The
Greatest Story Ever Told, The
Greatest, The
Greatest Thing That Almost Happened, The
Greed
Greed in the Sun
Greek Tycoon, The
Green Dolphin Street
Green-Eyed Blonde, The
Green Eyes
Green Fields
Green Goddess, The
Green Grass of

Hell on Wheels
Hell River
Hell Squad
Hell to Eternity
Hell Town
Hell With Heroes, The
Hellbent
Hellfighters
Hellgate
Hello-Goodbye
Hello Sister
Hell's Brigade—The Final Assault
Hell's Half Acre
Hell's House
Hell's Kitchen
Hell's Long Road
Hell's Outpost
Helsinki Napoli All Night Long
Henderson Monster, The
Henry IV
Henry V (1945)
Henry V (1989)
Henry VIII and His Six Wives
Her Brother
Her First Romance
Her Kind of Man
Her Man Gilbey
Her Panelled Door
Her Secret Life
Her Sister's Secret
Her Twelve Men
Here Comes Santa Claus
Here Comes the Navy
Here I Am a Stranger
Hero Ain't Nothin' But a Sandwich, A
Hero Banker
Hero of the Year (Top Dog Part 2)
Hero, The
Herod the Great
Heroes
Heroes Die Young
Heroes for Sale
Heroes in Hell
Heroes of Desert Storm, The
Heroes Stand Alone
Hero's Island
He's Not Your Son
Hester Street
Hey Babu Riba
Hey Good Lookin'
Hey, I'm Alive!
Hide in Plain Sight
Hideout in the Alps
Hideout, The
Hider in the House
Hiding Place, The
High Barbaree
High Commissioner, The
High Country, The
High Explosive
High Flight
High Fury
High Heels
High Hell
High Road to China
High School Caesar
High School Confidential
High Tide
High Tide at Noon
High Wall
Higher Learning
Highest Honor, The
Highwayman, The
Hilda Crane
Hildur and the Magician
Hill Number One
Hill on the Dark Side of the Moon, A
Hill, The
Hill 24 Doesn't Answer
Hills of Home, The
Hillside Stranglers, The
Himatsuri
Himmo, King of Jerusalem
Hindenburg, The
Hippodrome
Hireling, The
Hiroshima, Mon Amour
Hiroshima: Out of the Ashes
His Brother's Wife
His Excellency
His First Command
His Mistress
His Woman
History
History Is Made at Night
History Lessons
Hit and Run
Hit Lady
Hit the Road
Hitch-Hiker, The
Hitchcock Collection, The
Hitchhike to Happiness
Hitler
Hitler Gang, The
Hitler: The Last Ten Days
Hitler's Children
Hitler's Daughter
Hitler's Madman
H.M. Pulham, Esq.
Hoa-Binh
Hobo's Christmas, A
Hobson's Choice
Hoffa
Hoffman
Hold Back the Dawn
Hold Back the Night
Hold Back Tomorrow
Hold 'Em Navy
Hold the Dream
Hold Your Man
Holes, The
Holiday
Holiday Affair
Holiday for Sinners
Hollow Boy, The
Hollow Image
Holly and the Ivy, The
Hollywood Boulevard
Hollywood In Trouble
Hollywood Story
Holocaust
Holocaust Survivors
Holy Innocents
Home and the World, The
Home at Seven
Home Before Dark
Home Before Midnight
Home Fires Burning
Home for Christmas
Home for the Holidays
Home From the Hill
Home is the Hero
Home of Our Own, A (1975)
Home of Our Own, A (1993)
Home of the Brave
Home Sweet Home
Home to Stay
Home Towners, The
Homeboy
Homecoming
Homecoming—A Christmas Story, The
Homecoming, The
Homer
Homer & Eddie
Homestretch, The
Hometown Story
Homeward Bound
Honey
Honeyboy
Honeymoon
Honeymoon Merry-Go-Round
Honeymoon with a Stranger
Hong Kong Confidential
Honky
Honkytonk Man
Hoodlum Priest, The
Hoodlum Saint, The
Hook, The
Hooligans, The
Hooper
Hoosier Schoolboy
Hoosiers
Hoover vs. the Kennedys: The Second Civil War
Hoppity Goes to Town
Horse of Pride, The
Horse, The
Horse Thief, The
Horsemasters, The
Horsemen, The
Hostages
Hot Hours
Hot News
Hot Rod Rumble
Hot Spell
Hot Summer in Barefoot County
Hot Summer Night
Hotel
Hotel Berlin
Hotel Colonial
Hotel du Lac
Hotel for Women
Hotel Imperial
Hotel New Hampshire, The
Hotel Reserve
Hotline
Hotshot
Houdini
Hound of the Baskervilles, The
Hour Before the Dawn
Hour of Decision
Hour of the Star, The
Hour of the Wolf
House Across the Bay, The
House Across the Street, The
House by the River, The
House Divided, A
House in the Woods, The
House of Cards (1969)
House of Cards (1993)
House of Fear
House of Intrigue
House of Rothschild, The
House of Strangers, The
House of the Seven Gables, The
House of the Spirits
House on Garibaldi Street, The
House on

Greenapple Road, The
House on 92nd Street
House on Telegraph Hill
House on the Front Line, The
House with an Attic, The
House Without a Christmas Tree, A
Household Saints
Housewife
Houston Story, The
Houston, We've Got a Problem
How Awful About Allan
How Do I Love Thee?
How Green Was My Valley
How I Spent My Summer Vacation
How Many Miles to Babylon
Howard Beach: Making a Case for Murder
Howards End
Howling in the Woods, A
Huckleberry Finn (1931)
Huckleberry Finn (1939)
Huckleberry Finn (1975)
Hucksters, The
Hud
Hudson Hawk
Hudson's Bay
Huk
Human Comedy, The
Human Condition, The—Part One: No Greater Love
Human Condition, The—Part Two: The Road to Eternity
Human Condition, The—Part Three: A Soldier's Prayer
Human Factor, The
Humoresque
Hunchback of Notre Dame
Hunchback of Notre Dame, The (1923)
Hunchback of Notre Dame, The (1939)
Hunchback of Notre Dame, The (1982)
Hundred Hour Hunt
Hungarian Fairy Tale, A
Hunger
Hungry Hill
Hunted Lady, The
Hunters, The
Hurricane
Hurricane, The
Hurried Man, The
Hurry Sundown
Husbands
Husbands and Lovers
Husbands and Wives
Hussy
Hustler of Muscle Beach, The
Hustler, The
Hustling
Hypnotic Eye, The
I Accuse!
I Aim at the Stars
I Am a Camera
I Am a Fugitive from a Chain Gang
I Am the Cheese
I Am the Law
I Beheld His Glory
I Believe In You
I Conquer the Sea
I Cover the War
I Cover the Waterfront
I Deal in Danger
I Dream of Jeannie
I Found Stella Parish
I Heard the Owl Call My Name
I, Jane Doe
I Killed Rasputin
I Know My First Name Is Steven
I Know Why the Caged Bird Sings
I Live in Fear
I Live with Me Dad
I Lived with You
I Love a Soldier
I Love You (Eu Te Amo)
I Love You, Goodbye
I Love, You Love
I Love You Perfect
I Loved a Woman
I Married a Communist
I Married a Shadow
I Met My Love Again
I Never Promised You a Rose Garden
I Never Sang for My Father
I Only Want You to Love Me
I Passed for White
I Posed for Playboy
I Promise to Pay
I Remember Mama
I See a Dark Stranger
I Sent a Letter to My Love
I Stand Condemned
I Take This Woman
I Thank a Fool
I, the Jury
I Vitelloni
I Walk Alone
I Walk the Line
I Want to Keep My Baby
I Want To Live!
I Want What I Want
I Want You
I Wanted Wings
I Was a Communist for the FBI
I Was a Mail Order Bride
I Was a Spy
I Was an American Spy
I Was Monty's Double
I Will Fight No More Forever
Ice Castles
Ice House
Ice Pawn
Ice Station Zebra
Iceman Cometh, The
I'd Climb the Highest Mountain
I'd Give My Life
Identification Marks: None
Identification of a Woman
Identity Unknown
Idiot, The (1951)
Idiot, The (1960)
Idiot's Delight
Idol Dancer, The
Idol, The
If . . .
If Ever I See You Again
If I Were Free
If I Were King
If It's a Man, Hang Up
If Things Were Different
If Winter Comes
If You Could See What I Hear
Ike: The War Years
Ikiru
Il Bidone
Il Ladro di Bambini
Il Mare
I'll Be Home for Christmas
I'll Be Seeing You
I'll Cry Tomorrow
I'll Never Forget You
I'll Turn to You
Illegal
Illicit
Illumination
Illusion Travels by Streetcar
Illustrious Energy
I'm Dancing as Fast as I Can
I'm Still Alive
I'm the Girl He Wants to Kill
I'm the One You're Looking For
Image of Passion
Image, The
Imagemaker, The
Images
Imaginary Crimes
Imitation of Life (1934)
Imitation of Life (1959)
Immediate Family
Immigrants, The
Immoral Charge
Immortal Beloved
Immortal Gentlemen
Immortal Sergeant, The
Immortal Story, The
Immortal Vagabond
Impact
Impatient Heart, The
Imperative
Imperfect Lady, The
Imperial Venus
Important Man, The
Impossible Object
Imposter, The
Impostor, The
Impromptu
Impulse
In a Glass Cage
In A Moment Of Passion
In a Shallow Grave
In a Stranger's Hand
In a Year of Thirteen Moons
In Broad Daylight
In Celebration
In Country
In Dangerous Company
In Defense of Kids
In for Treatment
In Harm's Way
In Love and War (1958)
In Love and War (1987)
In Old Chicago

In Our Time
In Search of a Golden Sky
In Search of Anna
In Search of Gregory
In Search of Historic Jesus
In the Cool of the Day
In the Custody of Strangers
In the Devil's Garden
In the French Style
In the King of Prussia
In the Line of Duty: Ambush in Waco
In the Line of Fire
In the Matter of Karen Ann Quinlan
In the Name of Life
In the Name of the Father
In the Name of the Pope King
In the White City
In this House of Brede
In This Our Life
In Which We Serve
Incendiary Blonde
Incident at Dark River
Incident, The
Inconvenient Woman, An
Incredible Journey of Doctor Meg Laurel, The
Incredible Sarah, The
Indecent Behavior
Indecent Obession, An
Indecent Proposal
Independence Day
India Song
Indian Runner, The
Indianapolis Speedway
Indiscreet
Indiscretion of an American Wife
Indochine
Inferno
Infidelity
Informer, The
Inherit the Wind (1960)
Inherit the Wind (1988)
Inheritance, The (1947)
Inheritance, The (1978)
Inheritor, The
Inheritors, The
Inkwell, The
Inn of the Sixth Happiness, The
Inner Circle, The
Innocent Love, An
Innocent, The
Innocent Victim
Innocents, The
Inquiry, The
Inquisitor, The
Insect Woman
Inside Daisy Clover
Inside Detroit
Inside Man, The
Inside Moves
Inside Out
Inside the Third Reich
Insignificance
Inspector Calls, An
Inspiration
Insurance Man, The
Interiors
Interlude (1957)
Interlude (1968)
Intermezzo (1936)
Intermezzo (1939)
International Squadron
International Velvet
Internecine Project, The
Internes Can't Take Money
Interns, The
Interrogation
Interrupted Journey
Interrupted Melody
Intersection
Interval
Intervista
Intimate Contact
Intimate Moments
Intimate Obsession
Intimate Power
Intimate Strangers
Into the Darkness
Into Thin Air
Intolerance
Intruder in the Dust
Intruder, The (1955)
Intruder, The (1961)
Invasion Force
Investigation
Investigation of a Citizen Above Suspicion
Invincible Six, The
Invisible Adversaries
Invisible Menace, The
Invisible Stripes
Invitation
Invitation au Voyage
Invitation, The
Invitation to Happiness
Invitation to Hell
Iphigenia
Irezumi: Spirit of Tatoo
Irish Whiskey Rebellion
Irishman, The
Iron and Silk
Iron Curtain, The
Iron Duke, The
Iron Horse, The
Iron Major, The
Iron Man, The (1931)
Iron Man, The (1951)
Iron Mask, The
Iron Triangle, The
Ironweed
Is Paris Burning?
Isabel's Choice
Isadora
Ishi: The Last of His Tribe
Island in the Sky
Island in the Sun
Island of Desire
Island of Pachyderms, The
Island of Procida, The
Island of the Blue Dolphins
Island of the Lost
Island Princess, The
Island Sons
Island, The
Island Woman
Islands
Islands in the Stream
Isle of Forgotten Sins
Isle of Fury
Isle of Lost Ships
Isle of Secret Passion
Isle of Sin
Istanbul
It
It All Came True
It Always Rains on Sunday
It Came Upon the Midnight Clear
It Had to Happen
It Happened Here
It Happened in Flatbush
It Happened One Christmas
It Only Happens to Others
It Rained All Night the Day I Left
Italiano Brava Gente
It's a Big Country
It's a Pleasure!
It's a Wonderful Life
It's Good to Be Alive
It's My Turn
It's Never Too Late to Mend
Ivan
Ivan the Terrible, Part One
Ivan the Terrible, Part Two
I've Always Loved You
I've Heard the Mermaids Singing
I've Lived Before
Ivory Hunter
Izzy and Moe
J'Accuse (1919)
J'Accuse (1937)
Jack Frost
Jack Knife Man, The
Jack London
Jack of Diamonds
Jack the Bear
Jack the Ripper
Jackal of Nahueltoro, The
Jackals, The
Jackboot Mutiny
Jackie Robinson Story, The
Jackknife
Jacksons: An American Dream, The
Jacob Have I Loved
Jacob, Man Who Fought with God
Jacob the Liar
Jacobo Timerman: Prisoner Without a Name, Cell Without a Number
Jacob's Ladder
Jacqueline
Jacqueline Bouvier Kennedy
Jacqueline Susann's Once Is Not Enough
Jacqueline Susann's Valley of the Dolls
Jacques and November
Jail Bait
Jailbird Rock
Jamaica Inn
Jamaica Run
James A. Michener's Dynasty
James at 15
James Dean
James Joyce's Women
Jane Austen in Manhattan
Jane Doe
Jane Eyre (1934)
Jane Eyre (1944)
Jane Eyre (1971)
Jane Eyre (1983)

Japanese War Bride
Jason's Lyric
Jassy
Java Head
Jayne Mansfield Story, The
J.C.
Je Vous Aime
Jealousy (1945)
Jealousy (1984)
Jean de Florette
Jeanne Eagels
Jenatsch
Jennie Gerhardt
Jennifer: A Woman's Story
Jennifer on My Mind
Jenny
Jeremy
Jericho Fever
Jericho Mile, The
Jerusalem File, The
Jesse
Jesse Owens Story, The
Jessica
Jesus
Jesus of Montreal
Jesus of Nazareth
Jesus Trip, The
Jet Pilot
Jewel in the Crown
Jewish King Lear, The
Jezebel
Jezebel's Kiss
JFK
JFK: Reckless Youth
Jigsaw Man, The
Jim Thorpe—All American
Jimmy B. & Andre
Jo Jo Dancer—Your Life Is Calling
Joan of Arc
Joan of Paris
Joan of the Angels
Joanna
Joe
Joe and Ethel Turp Call on the President
Joe Hill
Joe Louis Story, The
Joe Macbeth
Joe Panther
Joe Smith, American
John and the Missus
John and Yoko: A Love Story
John Henry
John Meade's Woman
John of the Fair
John Paul Jones
John Wesley
Johnny Belinda (1948)
Johnny Belinda (1982)
Johnny Bull
Johnny Got His Gun
Johnny in the Clouds
Johnny Shiloh
Johnny Tiger
Johnny Trouble
Johnny Vic
Johnny, We Hardly Knew Ye
Johnstown Flood, The
Jonah Who Will Be 25 in the Year 2000
Jonathan Livingston Seagull
Joni
Joseph and His Brethren
Josephine Baker Story, The
Joshua's Heart
Journey
Journey Back to Oz
Journey for Margaret
Journey from Berlin
Journey into Fear
Journey into Light
Journey of Hope
Journey of Natty Gann, The
Journey, The
Journey to Freedom
Journey to Shiloh
Journey to Spirit Island
Joy in the Morning
Joy Luck Club, The
Joyless Street, The
Ju Dou
Juarez
Jud
Judge and the Assassin, The
Judge and the Sinner
Judge Hardy and Son
Judge Horton and The Scottsboro Boys
Judge Steps Out, The
Judgment
Judgment at Nuremberg
Judgment in Berlin
Judith
Judith of Bethulia
Juggler of Notre Dame, The
Juggler, The
Juke Girl
Jules and Jim
Julia
Julia and Julia
Julia Has Two Lovers
Julie
Juliet of the Spirits
Julius Caesar (1953)
Julius Caesar (1970)
Jump into Hell
Jumpin' at the Boneyard
June Night
Jungle Book
Jungle Book, The
Jungle Fever
Juno and the Paycock
Jury of One
Just a Gigolo
Just an Old Sweet Song
Just Another Girl on the I.R.T.
Just Before Nightfall
Just Between Friends
Just Like Us
Justice Is Done
Justin Case
Justin Morgan Had a Horse
Justine
J.W. Coop
Kafka
Kagemusha
Kameradschaft
Kamilla
Kanal
Kandyland
Kangaroo
Kansas
Kansas City Bomber
Kaos
Kapo
Karamazov
Karate Kid, The
Karate Kid, Part 2, The
Karate Kid, Part 3, The
Karen Carpenter Story, The
Karma
Katerina Izmailova
Katherine
Katie: Portrait of a Centerfold
Katzelmacher
Kavik the Wolf Dog
Kaya, I'll Kill You
Keep Your Powder Dry
Keeper of the Flame
Keepers, The
Keetje Tippel
Kenny & Co.
Kent State
Kentucky
Key Largo
Key, The (1934)
Key, The (1958)
Key to the City
Key Witness
Keys of the Kingdom
Kid for Two Farthings, A
Kid from Left Field, The
Kid from Not So Big, The
Kid from Nowhere, The
Kid Who Loved Christmas, The
Kid with the Broken Halo, The
Kid with the 200 I.Q., The
Kidco
Kidnapping of Baby John Doe, The
Kill Cruise
Kill Me if You Can
Killer in the Mirror
Killer Inside Me, The
Killer McCoy
Killer's Kiss
Killers, The (1946)
Killers, The (1964)
Killing Affair, A
Killing Beach, The
Killing Fields, The
Killing Floor, The
Killing Game, The
Killing Machine
Killing of Angel Street, The
Killing of Randy Webster, The
Killing of Sister George, The
Kind of Loving, A
King
King and Country
King David
King in Shadow
King Lear (1971)
King Lear (1983)
King Lear (1987)
King of Hearts
King of Kings
King of Kings, The
King of Marvin Gardens, The
King of the Grizzlies
King of the Gypsies
King of the Hill
King of the Wild Stallions
King of the Wind
King, Queen, Knave
King Rat
King Richard and the Crusaders
Kingfisher Caper, The

Kings and Desperate Men—A Hostage Incident
Kings Go Forth
Kings of the Road
Kings Row
King's Thief, The
King's Whore, The
Kipperbang
Kipps
Kismet
Kiss Me a Killer
Kiss of the Spider Woman
Kiss, The
Kissing Place, The
Kitchen Toto, The
Kitten with a Whip
Kitty
Kitty Foyle
Klute
Knife in the Head
Knife in the Water
Knight Without Armour
Knights and Emeralds
Knock on Any Door
Knockout
Knute Rockne, All American
Kongo
Korczak
Kostas
Kramer vs. Kramer
Kuroneko
L-Shaped Room, The
L.A. Bad
La Bamba
La Belle Noiseuse
La Boum
La Boum 2
La Chienne
La Collectioneuse
La Cuisine Polonaise
La Discrete
La Dolce Vita
La Femme Infidele
L.A. Goddess
La Gran Fiesta
La Guerre Est Finie
La Mafia
La Marseillaise
La Maternelle
La Notte
La Notte Brava
La Nuit des Varennes
La Pelle
La Petite Bande
La Prisonniére
La Ronde
La Salamandre
La Signora di Tutti
La Strada
La Symphonie Pastorale
La Terra Trema
La Truite
La Viaccia
La Vie Continue
La Vie de Bohème
Lacemaker, The
Lacombe, Lucien
Lad: A Dog
Ladies Courageous
Ladies in Retirement
Ladies' Man
Ladies of Leisure
Ladies of the Big House
Ladies of the Chorus
Ladies They Talk About
Lady by Choice
Lady Caroline Lamb
Lady Chatterley's Lover
Lady Consents, The
Lady from Louisiana
Lady Gambles, The
Lady Godiva
Lady Grey
Lady in Question,The
Lady in the Car with Glasses and a Gun, The
Lady in the Dark
Lady Jane
Lady of the Camellias, The
Lady of the House
Lady of the Tropics
Lady on the Bus
Lady Pays Off, The
Lady Possessed
Lady Sings the Blues
Lady with a Dog, The
Lady with a Lamp, The
Lady without Camellias, The
Lady without Passport, A
Ladybird, Ladybird
Ladybug, Ladybug
Ladykiller of Rome, The
Lafayette Escadrille
Lai Shi: China's Last Eunuch
L'Amour Fou
Lancelot of the Lake
Lancer Spy
Land Before Time, The
Land of Promise, The
Land of the Pharaohs
Landlord Blues
Landscape in the Mist
Landslide
Lantern Hill
Larceny
L'Argent
L'Armee des Ombres
Larry
Las Vegas Shakedown
Lassie
Lassie Come Home
Last American Hero, The
Last Angry Man, The
Last Best Year, The
Last Blitzkrieg, The
Last Bridge, The
Last Butterfly, The
Last Call
Last Chance, The
Last Command, The
Last Days of Chez Nous, The
Last Days of Dolwyn, The
Last Days of Patton, The
Last Days of Pompeii, The
Last Detail, The
Last Elephant, The
Last Emperor, The
Last Exit to Brooklyn
Last Flight of Noah's Ark, The
Last Flight, The
Last Four Days, The
Last Game, The
Last Gangster, The
Last Hurrah, The (1958)
Last Hurrah, The (1977)
Last Innocent Man, The
Last Laugh, The
Last Light
Last Metro, The
Last Mile, The (1932)
Last Mile, The (1959)
Last Movie, The
Last Night at the Alamo
Last of His Tribe, The
Last of Mrs. Lincoln
Last of Philip Banter, The
Last of the Mobile Hot-Shots
Last of the Red Hot Dragons
Last Picture Show, The
Last Prostitute, The
Last Run, The
Last Summer
Last Supper, The
Last Tango in Paris
Last Temptation of Christ, The
Last Ten Days, The
Last Time I Saw Paris, The
Last to Go
Last Train from Madrid, The
Last Tycoon, The
Last Valley, The
Last Voyage, The
Last Wave, The
Last Winter, The
Last Wish
Last Year at Marienbad
L'Atalante
Late Autumn
Late Chrysanthemums
Late for Dinner
Late Spring
Late Summer Blues
Latin Lovers
Latino
Laughing Sinners
L'Avventura
Law and Order
Lawless, The
Lawrence of Arabia
Laws of Gravity
Lazarus Syndrome, The
Lazybones
LBJ: The Early Years
Le Bal
Le Beau Mariage
Le Beau Serge
Le Bonheur
Le Cas du Docteur Laurent
Le Caviar Rouge
Le Corbeau
Le Crabe Tambour
Le Gai Savoir
Le Golem: The Lend of Prague
Le Grand Chemin
Le Jour Se Leve
Le Mans
Le Petit Amour
Le Petit Soldat
Le Plaisir
Le Puritain
Le Repos du Guerrier
Le Rouge et le Noir
Le Voyage en Douce
Lean on Me
Leap of Faith
Learning Curve
Learning Tree, The
Lease of Life
Leather Boys, The
Leather Saint, The
Leave All Fair
Leave 'Em Laughing
Leave Her to Heaven

Marva Collins Story, The
Marvelous Land of Oz (1981)
Marvelous Land of Oz (1988)
Marvin and Tige
Mary and Joseph: A Story of Faith
Mary Jane Harper Cried Last Night
Mary of Scotland
Mary, Queen of Scots
Mary White
Maryjane
Maryland
Marzipan Pig, The
Masada
Masculine-Feminine
Mask
Masoch
Masquerade
Masquerader, The
Mass Appeal
Massacre in Rome
Massive Retaliation
Master Harold and the Boys
Master of Bankdam, The
Master Race, The
Master Spy
Mata Hari (1932)
Mata Hari (1965)
Mata Hari (1985)
Mata Hari's Daughter
Match King, The
Matchmaking of Anna, The
Matewan
Mating of Millie, The
Matt the Gooseboy
Mattei Affair, The
Matter of Cunning, A
Matter of Days, A
Matter of Dignity, A
Matter of Innocence, A
Matter of Life and Death, A
Matter of Love, A
Matter of Principle, A
Matter of Sex, A
Matter of Time, A
Matters of the Heart
Maurice
Maurie
Max and Helen
Max Havelaar
Maximum Security
May Fools
Maya (1966)
Maya (1982)
Maybe I'll Come Home in the Spring
Mayerling (1936)
Mayerling (1968)
Mayflower Madam
Mayflower: The Pilgrims' Adventure
Mayor of Hell, The
McCabe and Mrs. Miller
McCloud: Who Killed Miss U.S.A.?
McConnell Story, The
McKenzie Break, The
McQ
Me and Marlborough
Me & Veronica
Me, Natalie
Means and Ends
Meantime
Medal for Benny, A
Medea
Medical Story
Medicine Man
Medium Cool
Medium, The
Meet Danny Wilson
Meet Dr. Christian
Meet John Doe
Meeting Venus
Meetings With Remarkable Men
Melanie
Melo
Melody
Melody for Three
Melody in Love
Melody Master
Melvin and Howard
Member of the Wedding, The
Memed My Hawk
Memoirs of a Survivor
Memorial Day
Memories of a Fairy Godmother
Memories of a Marriage
Memories of Underdevelopment
Memory of Eva Ryker, The
Memphis Belle
Men Against the Sun
Men Don't Leave
Men in Her Life, The
Men In Love
Men in White
Men of Boys Town
Men of Sherwood Forest
Men of Yesterday
Men, The
Men with Wings
Men's Club, The
Mephisto
Merchant of Four Seasons, The
Merchant of Venice, The
Merely Mary Ann
Merry Christmas, Mr. Lawrence
Mesmerized
Message, The
Message to My Daughter
Messaline
Messenger of Death
Metropolitan
MIA—We Can Keep You Here Forever
Mickey One
Middle Age Crazy
Middle Age Spread
Middle of the Night
Middleton Family at the 1939 New York World's Fair, The
Midnight Auto Supply
Midnight Cowboy
Midnight Dancer
Midnight Express
Midnight Girl
Midnight Warning
Midway
Mighty Barnum, The
Mighty Ducks, The
Mighty Joe Young
Mighty McGurk, The
Mighty Moose and the Quarterback Kid
Mighty Pawns, The
Mighty Treve, The
Migrants, The
Mikey
Milagro Beanfield War, The
Mildred Pierce
Miles from Home
Miles to Go
Milestones
Military Secret
Milky Way, The
Mill on the Floss, The
Millionairess, The
Millions
Millions Like Us
Mimi
Min and Bill
Mind Field
Mindwalk
Mine Own Executioner
Ministry of Fear
Miniver Story, The
Miracle at Moreaux
Miracle Down Under
Miracle in Milan
Miracle in Soho
Miracle in the Rain
Miracle in the Wilderness
Miracle of Our Lady of Fatima, The
Miracle of the Bells, The
Miracle of the Heart: A Boys' Town Story
Miracle of the White Stallions
Miracle on Ice
Miracle on 34th Street (1947)
Miracle on 34th Street (1994)
Miracle, The (1959)
Miracle, The (1991)
Miracle Woman, The
Miracle Worker, The (1962)
Miracle Worker, The (1979)
Mirror Has Two Faces, The
Mirror Images II
Mirror, The
Mirros
Misfit Brigade, The
Misfits, The
Mishima
Miss A and Miss M
Miss Annie Rooney
Miss Julie
Miss Mary
Miss Melody Jones
Miss Rose White
Missiles of October, The
Missing
Missing Evidence
Missing Link, The
Missing Ten Days
Mission of the Shark
Mission, The
Mission to Moscow
Mississippi Burning
Mississippi Masala
Mississippi Mermaid
Missouri Traveler, The
Mister Brown
Mister Buddwing
Mister Cory
Mister Johnson
Mister Too Little
Mistral's Daughter
Mistress
Mistress of Atlantis, The
Mistress, The
Misty
Misunderstood (1983)

Misunderstood (1988)
Mixed Blood
Moby Dick (1930)
Moby Dick (1956)
Model Behavior
Model Shop, The
Moderato Cantabile
Modern Girls
Moderns, The
Mogambo
Molly Maguires, The
Moment by Moment
Moment in Time, A
Mommie Dearest
Mon Oncle Antoine
Mon Oncle D'Amerique
Mona
Money Movers
Monika
Monkey Grip
Monkey in Winter, A
Monkey on My Back
Monsieur Vincent
Monsignor
Monsignor Quixote
Monsoon
Monte Carlo
Montenegro
Month in the Country, A
Moochie of the Little League
Moon and Sixpence, The
Moon in the Gutter, The
Moon Is Down, The
Moon-Spinners, The
Mooncussers
Moonlighting
Moon's Our Home, The
Moontide
More
Morituri
Morning After, The
Morning Glory
Moro Affair, The
Morocco
Mortal Storm, The
Mosby's Marauders
Moscow Does Not Believe in Tears
Moses
Mosquito Coast, The
Most Beautiful, The
Mother (Okaasan)
Mother and the Whore, The
Mother Carey's Chickens
Mother of Kings
Motorcycle Gang
Mouchette
Moulin Rouge
Mountain Family Robinson
Mountain Man
Mountain, The
Mountains of the Moon
Mourning Becomes Electra
Mouse and His Child, The
Mouthpiece, The
Movie Star's Daughter, A
Moving Out
Moving Targets
Mowgli's Brothers
Mozart—A Childhood Chronicle
Mr. Ace
Mr. & Mrs. Bridge
Mr. Arkadin
Mr. Deeds Goes to Town
Mr. Inside/Mr. Outside
Mr. Jones
Mr. Klein
Mr. Mean
Mr. Orchid
Mr. Perrin and Mr. Traill
Mr. Skeffington
Mr. Smith Goes to Washington
Mr. What's-His-Name
Mrs. Mike
Mrs. Miniver
Mrs. Parker and the Vicious Circle
Mrs. Parkington
Mrs. R's Daughter
Mrs. Silly
Mrs. Soffel
Mrs. Wiggs of the Cabbage Patch
Ms. Don Juan
Ms. 45
Muddy River
Mudhoney
Mudlark, The
Muppet Christmas Carol, The
Murder at Midnight
Murder at the Baskervilles
Murder by Decree
Murder Elite
Murder in Harlem
Murder in Mississippi
Murder in New Hampshire: The Pamela Smart Story
Murder in the First
Murder in the Music Hall
Murder in the Ring
Murder, Inc.
Murder on Flight 502
Murder on Lenox Avenue
Murder on the Bayou
Murder Rap
Murder Without Motive
Murderers Among Us
Murderers Among Us: The Simon Wiesenthal Story
Murderlust
Muriel
Murphy's Romance
Murphy's War
Murrow
Music Box
Music Lovers, The
Music of Chance, The
Music Room, The
Music Teacher, The
Mussketeers of Pig Alley & Selected Biograph Shorts
Mussolini and I
Mutiny on the Bounty (1935)
Mutiny on the Bounty (1962)
My American Cousin
My Beautiful Laundrette
My Body, My Child
My Bodyguard
My Brilliant Career
My Brother's Keeper
My Brother's Wedding
My Champion
My Childhood
My Dinner with Andre
My Family Treasure
My Father's Glory
My First Wife
My Foolish Heart
My Forbidden Past
My Friend Flicka
My Girl
My Girl 2
My Girl Tisa
My Heroes Have Always Been Cowboys
My Kidnapper, My Love
My Left Foot
My Life
My Life As a Dog
My Life to Live
My Little Pony—The Movie
My Man and I
My Margo
My Michael
My Mother's Castle
My Name is Bill W.
My Name Is Ivan
My Name Is Julia Ross
My Neighbor Totoro
My Night at Maud's
My Old Man
My Old Man's Place
My Other Husband
My Own Private Idaho
My Pal, Wolf
My Past
My Reputation
My Side of the Mountain
My Six Convicts
My Son Is a Criminal
My Son John
My Son, My Son
My Sweet Charlie
My Sweet Little Village
My Twentieth Century
My Wicked, Wicked Ways—The Legend of Errol Flynn
Myra Breckinridge
Mysteries
Mysterious Dr. Fu Manchu, The
Mysterious Intruder
Mysterious Lady, The
Mysterious Mr. Moto
Mysterious Mr. Wong, The
Mystery in Mexico
Mystery Lake
Mystery Liner
Mystery Mansion
Mystery of Alexina, The
Mystery of the Riverboat
Mystery Street
Nadia
Nadie Te Quierra Como Yo
Nairobi Affair
Nais
Naked
Naked Among the Wolves
Naked and the Dead, The
Naked Cage, The

Naked City, The
Naked Civil Servant, The
Naked Country, The
Naked Dawn, The
Naked General, The
Naked Heart, The
Naked Hours, The
Naked Jungle, The
Naked Kiss, The
Naked Lunch
Naked Maja, The
Naked Obsession
Naked Prey, The
Naked Street, The
Naked Tango
Naked Vengeance
Name of the Rose, The
Namu, the Killer Whale
Nana
Nanami, First Love
Nancy Steel Is Missing
Nanny, The
Napoleon (1927)
Napoleon (1955)
Napoleon and Samantha
Narrow Corner, The
Nashville
Nasty Girl, The
National Velvet
Native Land
Native Son (1950)
Native Son (1987)
Nativity, The
Natural, The
Nazarin
Nazis, The: Of Pure Blood
Nea'
Negatives
Neighbor, The
Nell
Nell Gwyn
Nelson Affair, The
Neon Empire, The
Nest, The
Never Cry Wolf
Never Forget
Never Let Go
Never Let Me Go
Never on Sunday
Never Say Goodbye
Never So Few
Never Take Candy from a Stranger
Never Take No for an Answer
New Adventures of Heidi, The
New Interns, The
New Kids, The
New Kind of Love, A
New Land, The
New Year's Day
New York Stories
News at Eleven
Newsfront
Next Karate Kid, The
Next Man, The
Next Time We Love
Next Voice You Hear, The
Ngati
Niagara
Nice Neighbor, The
Nicholas and Alexandra
Nicholas Nickleby
Nickel Mountain
Nickel Ride, The
Nicole
Night After Night
Night and the City
Night Angels
Night Club Scandal
Night Creature
Night Crossing
Night Eyes
Night Eyes 2
Night Fighters, The
Night Flight
Night Flight from Moscow
Night Friend
Night Full of Rain, A
Night Games
Night Has a Thousand Eyes
Night Has Eyes, The
Night Heaven Fell, The
Night Holds Terror, The
Night into Morning
Night Invader, The
Night Is My Future
Night Key
Night Mayor, The
'Night, Mother
Night Must Fall
Night My Number Came Up, The
Night of June 13
Night of the Blood Monster
Night of the Generals, The
Night of the Hunter, The
Night of the Iguana, The
Night of the Juggler
Night of the Quarter Moon
Night of the Shooting Stars, The
Night People
Night Porter, The
Night Song
Night Sun
Night That Panicked America, The
Night the Bridge Fell Down, The
Night the City Screamed, The
Night the Lights Went Out in Georgia, The
Night They Saved Christmas, The
Night They Took Miss Beautiful
Night Tide
Night to Remember, A
Night Train
Night Train to Kathmandu, The
Night Train to Munich
Night unto Night
Night World
Night Zoo
Nightbreaker
Nightcomers, The
Nightfall
Nightmare (1942)
Nightmare (1956)
Nightmare Alley
Nightmare at Bittercreek
Nightmare in Badham County
Nights of Cabiria
Nights of Prague
Nights of Rasputin
Nights of Shame
Nightside
Nijinsky
Nikki, Wild Dog of the North
9 1/2 Weeks
Nine Days A Queen
Nine Days of One Year
Nine Hours to Rama
Nine Lives Are Not Enough
Nine Men
1900
1918
1969
1984
Ninth Circle, The
Ninth Configuration, The
No Big Deal
No Deposit, No Return
No Down Payment
No Drums, No Bugles
No Exit
No Greater Glory
No Greater Love
No Greater Love Than This
No Highway in the Sky
No Longer Alone
No Love for Johnnie
No Man of Her Own (1933)
No Man of Her Own (1950)
No More Orchids
No One Man
No Other Love
No Place for Jennifer
No Place Like Home
No Place to Hide
No Place to Run
No Prince for My Cinderella
No Questions Asked
No Regrets for Our Youth
No Return Address
No Room at the Inn
No Room to Run
No Sad Songs for Me
No Time for Breakfast
No Time for Ecstasy
No Time for Tears
No Time to Be Young
No Time to Kill
No Trees in the Street
Noah's Ark
Nobody Lives Forever
Nobody's Child
Nobody's Children
Nomads of the North
Non-Stop New York
None But the Brave
None But the Lonely Heart
None Shall Escape
Noon Wine
Nora Prentiss
Norma Rae
Norman Rockwell's Breaking Home Ties
North and South
North Shore
Northern Lights
Northern Pursuit
Norwood
Nostalghia
Not as a Stranger
Not in Front of the Children
Not Mine to Love
Not My Kid
Not Quite Paradise
Not Wanted
Not Without My Daughter

Nothing But a Man
Nothing in Common
Notorious Gentleman
Notorious Lone Wolf, The
Notorious Sophie Lang
Nouvelle Vague
Now and Forever (1934)
Now and Forever (1982)
Now, Voyager
Nowhere to Go
Nuclear Conspiracy
Number One
Number Seventeen
Number Six
Numero Deux
Nun, The
Nun's Story, The
Nunzio
Nurse
Nurse Edith Cavell
Nurse on Wheels
Nurse's Secret, The
Nutcracker Fantasy
Nuts
O. Henry's Full House
O Pioneers!
Oak, The
Oblomov
Obsessed
Obsession
Obsessive Love
Occurrence at Owl Creek Bridge, An
Octavia
October
October Man, The
October Moth
Odd Angry Shot, The
Odd Birds
Odd Man Out
Odd Obsession
Odds Against Tomorrow
Ode to Billy Joe
Odessa File, The
Odette
Odyssey of the Pacific
Oedipus Rex (1957)
Oedipus Rex (1967)
Oedipus the King
Of Flesh and Blood
Of Human Bondage (1934)
Of Human Bondage (1964)
Of Human Hearts
Of Life and Love
Of Love and Desire
Of Mice and Men (1939)
Of Mice and Men (1981)
Of Mice and Men (1992)
Of Stars and Men
Off the Minnesota Strip
Offering, The
Officer and a Gentleman, An
Official Story, The
Oh, Alfie!
Oh, Bloody Life! . . .
O'Hara: U.S. Treasury
O'Hara's Wife
OHMS
Oil for the Lamps of China
Oklahoma City Dolls, The
Old Acquaintance
Old Boyfriends
Old Curiosity Shop, The
Old English
Old Explorers
Old Gringo
Old Maid, The
Old Man and the Sea, The
Old Yeller
Oldest Living Confederate Widow Tells All
Oldest Living Graduate, The
Oleanna
Oliver and Co.
Oliver Twist (1922)
Oliver Twist (1933)
Oliver Twist (1948)
Oliver Twist (1982)
Oliver's Story
Olivier, Olivier
Omar Khayyam
On Borrowed Time
On Fire
On Golden Pond
On Probation
On the Beach
On the Edge
On the Line
On the Loose
On the Nickel
On the Right Track
On the Threshold of Space
On the Waterfront
On Thin Ice: The Tai Babilonia Story
On Trial
On Valentine's Day
On Your Toes
Onassis: The Richest Man in the World
Once a Rainy Day
Once a Thief
Once There Was a Girl
Once Upon a Dead Man
Once Upon a Forest
One Against the Wind
One and Only, Genuine, Original Family Band, The
One Arabian Night
One Day in the Life of Ivan Denisovich
One Deadly Summer
One Desire
One-Eyed Soldiers
One Flew over the Cuckoo's Nest
One Foot in Heaven
One Frightened Night
One Girl's Confession
One Hundred and One Dalmatians
One in a Million
One in a Million: The Ron LeFlore Story
One Is a Lonely Number
One Magic Christmas
One Man's Journey
One Man's War
One Man's Way
One Million B.C.
One Million Years B.C.
One Minute to Zero
One More River
One Night at Susie's
One of Our Aircraft Is Missing
One of Our Dinosaurs is Missing
One of Our Own
One on One
One Potato, Two Potato
One Romantic Night
One Russian Summer
One Sings, The Other Doesn't
One Step to Hell
One Summer Love
One Third of a Nation
One Way Passage
One-Way Street
One Wish Too Many
One Woman's Story
Onibaba
Only Angels Have Wings
Only Game in Town, The
Only Way, The
Only Yesterday
Open Admissions
Open City
Open Doors
Opening Night
Opera Do Malandro
Operation X
Operator 13
Orchestra Conductor, The
Orchestra Rehearsal
Ordeal
Ordeal of Bill Carney, The
Ordeal of Dr. Mudd, The
Ordeal of Patty Hearst, The
Ordered to Love
Orders, The
Orders to Kill
Ordet
Ordinary Heros
Ordinary People
Organizer, The
Oriane
Original Intent
Original Sin
Orion's Belt
Orlando
Orphan Train, The
Orphans
Orphans of the Storm
Orphans of the Street
Orpheus
Orpheus Descending
Osaka Elegy
Oscar, The
Oscar Wilde
O'Shaughnessy's Boy
Ossessione
Othello (1952)
Othello (1965)
Other Love, The
Other Lover, The
Other Man, The
Other Men's Women
Other Side of Hell, The
Other Side of Midnight, The
Other Side of the Mountain (Part 2), The
Other Side of the Mountain, The
Other Tomorrow, The
Other Victim, The
Our Daily Bread
Our Dancing

Daughters
Our Family Business
Our Little Girl
Our Men in Bagdad
Our Modern Maidens
Our Mother's House
Our Silent Love
Our Sons
Our Time
Our Town (1940)
Our Town (1977)
Our Very Own
Our Vines Have Tender Grapes
Our Winning Season
Out
Out of Africa
Out of Darkness
Out of Season
Out of the Blue
Out of the Rain
Out on a Limb
Out On Bail
Outback
Outcast
Outcast of the Islands
Outcast, The
Outcasts of Poker Flat, The
Outcasts of the City
Outcry, The
Outlaw And His Wife, The
Outlaw Blues
Outpost in Malaya
Outrage
Outside Chance of Maximilian Glick, The
Outside In
Outside These Walls
Outside Woman, The
Outsider, The (1949)
Outsider, The (1961)
Outsider, The (1979)
Outsiders, The
Outward Bound
Over-Exposed
Over Indulgence
Over the Edge
Over the Hill
Over the Summer
Over the Top
Overcoat, The
Overlanders, The
Overlord
Overseas
Overture to Glory
Ox, The
Oxford Blues
Pace That Kills, The
Pacific Destiny
Pacific Heights
Pacific Liner
Pack of Lies
Padre Padrone
Pagan, The
Pagans, The
Pagemaster, The
Paid
Paid in Full
Painted Faces
Painted Hills, The
Painted Veil, The
Paisan
Palm Beach
Pancho Barnes
Panda and the Magic Serpent
Pandora and the Flying Dutchman
Pandora's Box
Panic In Echo Park
Panic in Needle Park, The
Panic in the City
Panic in the Streets
Paper Chase, The
Paper Dolls
Paper Mask
Paper, The
Parachute Battalion
Parade, The
Paradise (1981)
Paradise (1991)
Paradise Alley
Paradise Isle
Paranoia
Paratrooper
Paris After Dark
Paris Belongs to Us
Paris Blues
Paris Calling
Paris Express, The
Paris Model
Paris, Texas
Paris Trout
Paris Underground
Parisian, The
Park Is Mine, The
Park Row
Parking
Parnell
Parrish
Parting Glances
Party Girl
Passage Home
Passage to India, A
Passenger, The (1963)
Passenger, The (1975)
Passing of the Third Floor Back, The
Passing Through
Passion (1919)
Passion (1954)
Passion (1982)
Passion (1986)
Passion Fish
Passion for Life
Passion Island
Passion of Anna, The
Passion of Joan of Arc, The
Passion of Love
Passion of Slow Fire, The
Passover Plot, The
Passport to Destiny
Past Caring
Pastime
Pastor Hall
Patch of Blue, A
Patchwork Girl of Oz, The
Pather Panchali
Pathfinder
Paths of Glory
Patricia Neal Story, The
Patterns
Pattes Blanches (White Paws)
Patti Rocks
Patton
Patty Hearst
Paul and Michelle
Paul Robeson
Paula
Paul's Case
Pawnbroker, The
Pay or Die
Payday
Payment Deferred
Payment on Demand
Pearl of the South Pacific
Pearl, The
Pearls of the Crown
Peddlin' In Society
Pedestrian, The
Peeping Tom
Peg of Old Drury
Peking Express
Pelle the Conqueror
Penitent, The
Penny Serenade
People Against O'Hara, The
People Next Door, The
People That Time Forgot, The
People vs. Jean Harris, The
Pepe Le Moko
Peppermint Soda
Percy and Thunder
Perfect
Perfect Bride, The
Perfect Family
Perfect Harmony
Perfect Tribute, The
Perfect World, A
Performance
Perfume
Perils of Pauline, The
Permanent Record
Permission to Kill
Perri
Persona
Personal Best
Pete Kelly's Blues
Pete 'n' Tillie
Peter and Paul
Peter And The Wolf And Other Tales
Peter Ibbetson
Petersen
Pete's Dragon
Petite Sirene, La (The Little Mermaid)
Petrified Forest, The
Petulia
Peyton Place
Phaedra
Phantom Light, The
Phantom of Paris, The
Phantom Tollbooth, The
Phar Lap
Philadelphia
Philadelphia Experiment, The
Phone Call from a Stranger
Phone Call, The
Photographer, The
Piaf—The Early Years
Piano for Mrs. Cimino, A
Piano, The
Picasso Summer, The
Pickpocket
Pickup on 101
Pickwick Papers, The
Picnic
Picnic at Hanging Rock
Picnic On The Grass
Picture Bride
Picture of Dorian Gray, The
Pied Piper, The
Pigs
Pigs, The
Pilgrimage
Pillars of Society
Pimpernel Smith
Pink Floyd—The Wall
Pinky
Pinocchio and the Emperor of the Night
Pinocchio in Outer Space
Pipe Dreams
Pippi Goes on Board

Pippi in the South Seas
Pippi On The Run
Pistol—The Birth of a Legend, The
Pitfall, The
Pittsburgh
Pixote
P.K. and the Kid
Place for Lovers, A
Place in the Sun, A
Place of One's Own, A
Place of Weeping
Places in the Heart
Plague Dogs, The
Plague, The
Platoon
Platoon Leader
Play It As It Lays
Play It Cool
Playboy of Paris
Playboys, The
Player, The
Players
Playgirl
Playing for Time
Pleasure Garden, The
Plenty
Plough and the Stars, The
Ploughman's Lunch, The
Plunder of the Sun
Plymouth Adventure, The
Poetic Justice
Poil de Carotte
Point, The
Pointed Heels
Poison Ivy
Poison Pen
Police
Polly of the Circus
Pollyanna (1920)
Pollyanna (1960)
Pool of London
Poor Cow
Poor Little Rich Girl: The Barbara Hutton Story
Pope Joan
Popi
Poppy Is Also a Flower, The
Pork Chop Hill
Port of Call
Port of New York
Port of Seven Seas
Port of Shadows
Portia on Trial
Portnoy's Complaint
Portrait of Jennie
Portrait of the Artist as a Young Man, A
Portrait, The
Possessed
Postmark for Danger
Pot Carriers, The
Power and the Glory, The
Power of One, The
Prancer
Prayer for the Dying, A
Prelude to Fame
President's Lady, The
Pressure Point
Pretender, The
Pretty Baby
Pretty Boy Floyd
Prey of the Chameleon
Price of Fear, The
Priceless Beauty
Prick Up Your Ears
Pride and Prejudice (1940)
Pride and Prejudice (1985)
Pride and the Passion, The
Pride of St. Louis, The
Pride of the Marines
Pride of the Yankees, The
Priest
Priest of Love
Primary Motive
Prime of Miss Jean Brodie, The
Prime Risk
Primrose Path, The
Prince of Players
Prince of Tides, The
Prince Valiant
Princess Daisy
Princess Yang Kwei Fei
Principal, The
Prisoner of Honor
Prisoner of Shark Island, The
Prisoner, The
Private Affairs of Bel Ami, The
Private Files of J. Edgar Hoover, The
Private Life of Henry VIII, The
Private Life of Sherlock Holmes, The
Private Lives of Elizabeth and Essex, The
Private Matter, A
Private Worlds
Prize of Arms, A
Prize of Gold, A
Prize Pulitzer: The Roxanne Pulitzer Story, The
Prize, The
Prizefighter and the Lady, The
Prodigal, The
Professional Soldier
Program, The
Project M7
Project X
Promise at Dawn
Promise, The (1978)
Promise, The (1986)
Promised a Miracle
Promised Land
Promises in the Dark
Proof
Prospero's Books
Prostitute
Proud and Profane, The
Proud Men
Proud Rebel, The
Providence
Prowler, The
PT 109
Puberty Blues
Public Affair, A
Pulp Fiction
Pump Up the Volume
Pumpkin Eater, The
Punchline
Pure Country
Purple Heart, The
Purple Hearts
Purple Mask, The
Purple Noon
Purple Plain, The
Puss in Boots
Pyrates
Quadrophenia
Quantrill's Raiders
Quare Fellow, The
Quarterback Princess
Quartet
Quebec
Queen Bee
Queen Christina
Queen Kelly
Queen Margot
Queen of Hearts
Queenie
Queens Logic
Quentin Durward
Querelle
Quest for Fire
Quest, The
Question of Adultery, A
Question of Faith
Question of Guilt, A
Question of Honor, A
Question of Love, A
Question of Silence, A
Quicksand
Quicksand: No Escape
Quicksilver
Quiet American, The
Quiet Day in Belfast, A
Quiet Man, The
Quiet Place to Kill, A
Quiet Victory: The Charlie Wedemeyer Story
Quiller Memorandum, The
Quintet
Quiz Show
Quo Vadis?
Rabbit, Run
Rabbit Trap, The
Racers, The
Rachel and the Stranger
Rachel Papers, The
Rachel, Rachel
Rachel River
Racing With the Moon
Rack, The
Racket Man, The
Racketeer, The
Racquet
Radio Flyer
Radio On
Raffles
Rage (1966)
Rage (1972)
Rage (1980)
Rage in Heaven
Rage of Angels
Rage of Angels: The Story Continues
Rage to Live, A
Raggedy Man
Raging Bull
Raging Tide, The
Ragman's Daughter, The
Ragtime
Railway Children, The
Railway Station Man, The
Rain
Rain Man
Rain or Shine
Rain People, The
Rain Without Thunder
Rainbow
Rainbow, The
Rainmaker, The
Rains Came, The
Rains of Ranchipur, The

Raintree County
Raise the Red Lantern
Raisin in the Sun, A (1961)
Raisin in the Sun, A (1989)
Rambling Rose
Rampage
Ramparts of Clay
Ran
Random Harvest
Ransom
Rape & Marriage: The Rideout Case
Rape of Love
Rape of Richard Beck, The
Rape Squad, The
Rapture
Rapture, The
Rapunzel
Rascal
Rascals and Robbers—The Secret Adventures
Rashomon
Rasputin
Rasputin and the Empress
Rasputin—the Mad Monk
Ratboy
Rats, The
Raven's End
Raw Wind in Eden
Raymie
Razor's Edge, The (1946)
Razor's Edge, The (1984)
Reach for Glory
Real American Hero, A
Real Glory, The
Reap the Wild Wind
Rearview Mirror
Rebecca of Sunnybrook Farm (1917)
Rebecca of Sunnybrook Farm (1938)
Rebel Love
Rebel Rousers
Rebel Without a Cause
Rebels, The
Reckless (1935)
Reckless (1984)
Reckless Disregard
Reckless Moment, The
Reckoning, The
Red and the Black, The
Red and the White, The
Red Badge of Courage, The
Red Balloon, The
Red Beard
Red Desert
Red-Headed Woman
Red House, The
Red Kiss
Red Lanterns
Red Lion
Red Pony, The (1949)
Red Pony, The (1973)
Red Sky at Morning
Red Sorghum
Red Stallion, The
Reds
Reflecting Skin, The
Reflection of Fear, A
Reflections in a Golden Eye
Regal Cavalcade
Regarding Henry
Reilly: The Ace of Spies
Remains of the Day
Rembrandt
Remembrance
Removalists, The
Rendez-vous
Rendezvous
Repeat Performance
Repentance
Report to the Commissioner
Requiem for a Heavyweight
Rescuers Down Under, The
Rescuers, The
Resistance
Rest Is Silence, The
Resurrection
Retreat, Hell!
Return
Return from the Sea
Return from Witch Mountain
Return of a Stranger
Return of Dr. Mabuse, The
Return of Jimmy Valentine, The
Return of Martin Guerre, The
Return of Mr. Moto, The
Return of Peter Grimm, The
Return of Rin Tin Tin, The
Return of the King
Return of the Secaucus Seven, The
Return of the Soldier, The
Return to Eden
Return to Oz
Return to Paradise
Return to Peyton Place
Return to the Blue Lagoon
Return to Two Moon Junction
Reunion (1932)
Reunion (1936)
Reunion in France
Reunion in Reno
Revolt of Job, The
Revolt of Mamie Stover, The
Revolution
Revolutionary, The
Rhapsody
Rhapsody in August
Rhinoceros
Rhodes
Rich and Famous
Rich and Strange
Rich Kids
Rich Man's Folly
Rich People
Richard III
Richard's Things
Rickshaw Man, The
Riddle of the Sands, The
Ride a Wild Pony
Ride the High Wind
Riding Bean
Riffraff
Right Cross
Right Hand Man, The
Right of the People, The
Right of Way
Right Stuff, The
Right to Love, The
Right to the Heart
Ring of Bright Water
Ring of Spies
Ring of Terror
Ringside
Riptide
Rise and Shine
Rise of Louis XIV
Rise of the Moon, The
Risk
River Changes, The
River Lady
River Niger, The
River of No Return
River of Unrest
River Rat, The
River Runs Through It, A
River, The (1951)
River, The (1961)
River, The (1984)
River's Edge
Road Back, The
Road to Glory, The
Road to Life
Rob Roy, the Highland Rogue
Robber Symphony, The
Robe, The
Robin and Marian
Rocco and His Brothers
Rocket Gibraltar
Rocking Horse Winner, The
Rocky
Rocky 2
Rocky 3
Rocky 4
Rocky 5
Roe vs. Wade
Roll of Thunder, Hear My Cry
Rollover
Roman Spring of Mrs. Stone, The
Romance
Romance of Rosy Ridge, The
Romance of the Rio Grande
Rome Adventure
Rome Wants Another Caesar
Romeo and Juliet (1936)
Romeo and Juliet (1954)
Romeo and Juliet (1966)
Romeo and Juliet (1968)
Romero
Romper Stomper
Room at the Top
Room with a View, A
Roots
Roots of Heaven, The
Roots: The Next Generation
Rose Tattoo, The
Rose, The
Roseland
Rosie
Round Up, The
Royal Affairs in Versailles
R.P.M.
Ruby
Ruby Gentry
Ruby in Paradise
Rudy
Rudyard Kipling's

Someone to Love
Something About Amelia
Something of Value
Something to Live For
Sometimes a Great Notion
Somewhere I'll Find You
Somewhere in the Night
Somewhere in Time
Sommersby
Son of Fury
Son of Lassie
Song of Bernadette, The
Song of Love
Song of Russia
Song of Songs
Song to Remember, A
Sons
Sons and Lovers
Sons and Mothers
Sophia Loren: Her Own Story
Sophie's Choice
Sophisticated Gents, The
Sorcerer
Sorority Girl
Sorority House
S.O.S. Titanic
Soul of the Beast
Sound and the Fury, The
Sound and the Silence, The
Sounder
Sounder, Part Two
South Beach
South Central
South Riding
Southerner, The
Spanish Affair
Spanish Gardener, The
Spartacus
Special Agent
Special Day, A
Spectre of the Rose
Spencer's Mountain
Spetters
Sphinx
Spider and the Fly, The
Spider's Stratagem, The
Spiral Staircase, The
Spirit of St. Louis, The
Spirit of the Beehive
Spirit of the Eagle
Spitfire (1934)
Spitfire (1942)
Splendor in the Grass
Spring Shower
Springtime on the Volga
Spy in Black, The
Spy Who Came In from the Cold, The
Square Dance
Square Jungle, The
Square Ring, The
Square Shoulders
Squaw Man, The
St. Elmo's Fire
Stablemates
Stacking
Stage Fright
Stage Struck
Stairway to Heaven
Stalag 17
Stalin
Stalker
Stalking Moon, The
Stamboul Quest
Stammheim
Stamp of a Killer
Stand and Deliver
Stand by Me
Stand, The
Stanley & Iris
Stanley and Livingstone
Star Chamber, The
Star Dust
Star 80
Star Fairies
Star for a Night
Star Is Born, A (1937)
Star Is Born, A (1976)
Star, The
Starlight Hotel
Stars in My Crown
Stars Look Down, The
State of Grace
State of Siege
State of the Union
State of Things, The
State's Attorney
Station Six-Sahara
Stationmaster's Wife, The
Stay As You Are
Stay Tuned For Murder
Staying Together
Stealing Heaven
Stealing Home
Steamboat 'Round the Bend
Steaming
Steel Magnolias
Stella
Stella Dallas
Steppenwolf
Sterile Cuckoo, The
Stevie
Stigma
Stilts, The
Stocks and Blondes
Stolen Babies
Stolen Face, A
Stolen Hours, The
Stolen Kisses
Stolen Life, A
Stone Boy, The
Stone Pillow
Stones for Ibarra
Stooge, The
Storm Boy
Storm Center
Storm Warning
Stormy Monday
Story Lady, The
Story of a Cheat, The
Story of a Three-Day Pass, The
Story of Adele H, The
Story of Alexander Graham Bell, The
Story of Dr. Wassell, The
Story of Esther Costello, The
Story Of Gosta Berling, The
Story of Louis Pasteur, The
Story of Mankind, The
Story of Qiu Ju, The
Story of Robin Hood and His Merrie Men, The
Story of Ruth, The
Story of Seabiscuit, The
Story of Sin
Story of Temple Drake, The
Story of Three Loves, The
Story of Will Rogers, The
Story of Women, The
Story on Page One, The
Storyville
Stowaway
Straight Through the Heart
Strange Cargo
Strange Interlude
Strange Love of Martha Ivers, The
Strange Woman, The
Stranger in My Arms
Stranger on My Land
Stranger, The (1946)
Stranger, The (1967)
Stranger's Hand, The
Strangers in Good Company
Strangers in Love
Strangers in the City
Strangers in the House
Strangers Kiss
Strangers May Kiss
Stranger's Return, The
Strangers: The Story of a Mother and Daughter
Strangers When We Meet
Strapless
Strapped
Strategic Air Command
Stratton Story, The
Strawberry Blonde, The
Strawberry Roan, The
Stray Dog (Nora Inn)
Streamers
Street Angel
Street Music
Street of Chance
Street Scene
Street Smart
Street with No Name
Streetcar Named Desire, A (1951)
Streetcar Named Desire, A (1984)
Streets of Fire
Streets of Gold
Strike
Stripper, The
Stroke of Midnight
Stromboli
Stroszek
Stud, The
Stunt Man, The
Subject Was Roses, The
Submarine Command
Submarine Seahawk
Submarine X-1
Submission
Subterraneans, The
Sudan
Sudden Fury
Sudden Terror
Suddenly
Suddenly, Last Summer (1959)
Suddenly, Last Summer (1992)
Sudie and Simpson
Suds

Suez
Sugar Cane Alley
Sugar Hill
Sugarbaby
Sullivans, The
Summer
Summer and Smoke
Summer Fantasy
Summer Heat
Summer Interlude
Summer Lovers
Summer Magic
Summer of '42
Summer of My German Soldier
Summer Place, A
Summer Solstice
Summer Storm
Summer Story, A
Summer Wishes, Winter Dreams
Summerdog
Summertime
Summertree
Sun Also Rises, The
Sun Comes Up, The
Sun Shines Bright, The
Sunday, Bloody Sunday
Sunday Dinner for a Soldier
Sunday in the Country, A
Sundays and Cybele
Sundowners, The
Sunflower
Sunrise
Sunrise at Campobello
Sunset Boulevard
Sunset Heat
Sunstroke
Super Brother
Super Seal
Surfacing
Susan and God
Susan Lenox: Her Fall and Rise
Susan Slade
Susannah of the Mounties
Suzy
Svengali
Swamp Water
Swan, The
Swann in Love
Swedenhielms
Swedish Wedding Night
Sweet Bird of Youth (1962)
Sweet Bird of Youth (1989)
Sweet Country
Sweet Dreams
Sweet 15
Sweet Hearts Dance
Sweet Lorraine
Sweet Smell of Success
Sweet Sweetback's Baadasssss Song
Sweetie
Swept Away
Swimmer, The
Swing High, Swing Low
Swing Kids
Swing Shift
Swiss Family Robinson (1940)
Swiss Family Robinson (1960)
Swoon
Sword and the Rose, The
Swordkill
Sybil
Sylvester
Sylvia
Sylvia and the Phantom
Symphonie Pastorale
Symphony of Living
Symphony of Six Million
Synanon
Table for Five
Tabu
Taffin
Tai-Pan
Take a Giant Step
Taking Off
Tale of Four Wishes, A
Tale of Ruby Rose, The
Tale of Two Cities, A (1935)
Tale of Two Cities, A (1958)
Tale of Two Cities, A (1980)
Tale of Winter, A
Talent for the Game
Tales of Manhattan
Tales of Robin Hood
Tales of the Uncanny
Tales of the Unexpected
Talk Radio
Talking Walls
Tall Timbers
Tamango
Tampico
Tangled Destinies
Tanya's Island
Tap Roots
Taps
Taras Bulba
Tarawa Beachhead
Tarka the Otter
Tarnished Angels, The
Tarzan and His Mate
Tarzan Escapes
Tarzan, the Ape Man
Tarzan's New York Adventure
Tarzan's Secret Treasure
Taste for Killing, A
Taste of Honey, A
Tattoo
Taxi Blues
Taxi Driver
Tchao Pantin
Tea and Rice
Tea and Sympathy
Teacher and the Miracle, The
Teamster Boss: The Jackie Presser Story
Tears and Laughter: The Joan and Melissa Rivers Story
Tell Me a Riddle
Tell Me Lies
Tell Me That You Love Me, Junie Moon
Tempest (1928)
Tempest (1959)
Tempest (1982)
Temptress, The
Ten Cents a Dance
Ten Commandments, The (1923)
Ten Commandments, The (1956)
Ten North Frederick
Ten Seconds to Hell
Tender Comrade
Tender Is the Night
Tender Mercies
Tennessee Champ
Tennessee Johnson
Tenth Avenue Angel
Tenth Man, The
Tenth Month, The
Teorema
Teresa
Term of Trial
Terminal Bliss
Terminal Island
Terms of Endearment
Terrible Joe Moran
Terror Stalks the Class Reunion
Tess
Tess of the Storm Country
Test Pilot
Testament
Testament of Orpheus
Tevye
Tex
Texasville
Thank You All Very Much
Thanksgiving Promise, The
That Certain Summer
That Certain Woman
That Championship Season
That Cold Day in the Park
That Forsythe Woman
That Hagen Girl
That Hamilton Woman
That Lady
That Night (1957)
That Night (1993)
That'll Be the Day
Their Only Chance
Thelma & Louise
There Must Be a Pony
There Was an Old Couple
There's Always Tomorrow
Therese
These Three
These Wilder Years
They All Come Out
They Gave Him a Gun
They Knew What They Wanted
They Made Me a Criminal
They Shoot Horses, Don't They?
They Were Five
They Were Sisters
They Won't Forget
They're Playing With Fire
Thief of Bagdad, The
Thief of Baghdad
Thief of Hearts
Thief of Venice, The
Thieves Fall Out
Thin Line, The
Thing Called Love, The
Things of Life, The
Third Day, The
Third Key, The
Third Man on the Mountain
Third Time Lucky
Thirteen Hours By Air
13 Lead Soldiers
13th Letter, The

Tuck Everlasting
Tucker—The Man and His Dream
Tugboat Annie
Tulsa
Tuna Clipper
Turkish Delights
Turn Back the Clock
Turning Point, The
Turtle Diary
Tuttles of Tahiti, The
12 Angry Men
Twelve Months
Twelve O'Clock High
Twenty Bucks
Twenty-One
21 Days Together
21 Hours at Munich
27th Day, The
20,000 Leagues Under the Sea
Twice in a Lifetime
Twice-Told Tales
Twilight for the Gods
Twilight Story, The
Twilight's Last Gleaming
Twin Peaks
Twin Peaks: Fire Walk With Me
Twin Sisters of Kyoto
Twist and Shout
Two Bits
Two Bright Boys
Two Colonels, The
Two Daughters
Two English Girls
Two Eyes, Twelve Hands
Two Flags West
Two for the Road
Two in the Shadow
Two-Lane Blacktop
Two Loves
Two Moon Junction
Two Mrs. Carrolls, The
Two Mrs. Grenvilles, The
Two Mules for Sister Sara
Two Seconds
Two Weeks in Another Town
Two Women
Two Worlds of Jennie Logan, The
Two Years Before the Mast
Ugetsu
Ugly American, The
Ulysses (1955)
Ulysses (1967)
Umberto D
Un Carnet De Bal
Un Chien Andalou
Un Coeur en Hiver
Unbearable Lightness of Being, The
Uncle Harry
Uncle Tom's Cabin (1970)
Uncle Tom's Cabin (1987)
Uncle Vanya
Undefeated, The
Under Capricorn
Under Milk Wood
Under My Skin
Under Pressure
Under the Roofs of Paris
Under the Sun of Rome
Under the Sun of Satan
Under the Volcano
Underground Agent
Unfaithful, The
Unfinished Dance, The
Unfinished Symphony, The
Unguarded Moment, The
Unholy Partners
Unholy Three, The
Unholy Wife, The
Union Depot
Union Station
University of Life
Unman, Wittering and Zigo
Unnatural Causes
Unremarkable Life, An
Unsettled Land
Unsuspected, The
Untamed
Untamed Heart
Until September
Until the End of the World
Until They Sail
Up Against the Wall
Up From the Beach
Up the Down Staircase
Upperworld
Uptown Angel
Uranus
Urban Cowboy
Utz
Vagabond
Vagabond Lady
Valachi Papers, The
Valentino
Valhalla
Valiant Is the Word for Carrie
Valiant, The
Valley of Decision, The
Valley of Hunted Men
Valley of the Dolls
Valley of the Kings
Valley, The
Valmont
Van Gogh
Variety Lights
Velvet Touch, The
Verdict, The
Veronika Voss
Very Private Affair, A
Victoria the Great
Victors, The
Victory
Vienna Waltzes
View From the Bridge, A
Vigil
Vigil in the Night
Vincent & Theo
Vincent, Francois, Paul and the Others
Violent Playground
Violent Summer
Violets Are Blue...
Violin and Roller
V.I.P.s, The
Virgin and the Gypsy, The
Virgin Queen, The
Virgin Spring, The
Viridiana
Virtue
Vision Quest
Visit, The
Visit to a Chief's Son
Vital Signs
Viva Zapata!
Voice in the Mirror, The
Voices
Volcano
Voyage of the Damned
Voyage, The
Voyage to Italy
Voyager
Wages of Fear, The
Wagner
Wagons Roll at Night, The
Wait 'Til the Sun Shines, Nellie
Wait Until Dark
Waiting for the Moon
Walk East on Beacon
Walk in the Spring Rain, A
Walk in the Sun, A
Walk Into Hell
Walk on the Wild Side
Walk Softly, Stranger
Walk the Proud Land
Walk With Love and Death, A
Walkabout
Walker
Walkover
Wall of Noise
Wall Street
Walls of Jericho, The
Walls of Malapaga, The
Walton's Thanksgiving Story, the
Waltz King, The
Wanda
Wanderers, The
Wandering Jew, The
Wannsee Conference, The
War and Peace (1956)
War and Peace (1968)
War Between the Tates, The
War Hunt
War Lord, The
War Lover, The
War, The
WarGames
Warm December, A
Warm Nights on a Slow Moving Train
Warm Summer Rain, A
Washington Story
Watch It
Watch on the Rhine
Water Babies, The
Waterdance, The
Waterland
Waterloo
Waterloo Bridge
Watership Down
Way Down East
Way of All Flesh, The (1927)
Way of All Flesh, The (1940)
Way We Were, The
Wayward Bus, The
W.C. Fields and Me
We Are All Murderers
We Dive at Dawn
We Live Again
We of the Never Never
We Three
We Were Strangers
We Who Are Young
Wedding in Galilee
Wedding March, The
Wedding Night, The
Weddings and Babies

Wee Willie Winkie
Weeds
Weekend
Weekend at the Waldorf
Weekend With the Babysitter
Weird Woman
Welcome Home
Welcome in Vienna
Welcome Stranger
Welcome to L.A.
Well-Digger's Daughter, The
Well, The
Wells Fargo
We're Back: A Dinosaur's Story
West of Shanghai
West Point of the Air
Westfront 1918
Westward Passage
Wet Parade, The
Wetherby
We've Never Been Licked
Whales of August, The
What Price Glory?
What Price Hollywood?
What's Eating Gilbert Grape
What's Love Got to Do With It
When a Man Loves a Woman
When a Woman Ascends the Stairs
When Every Day Was the Fourth of July
When Father Was Away on Business
When I Grow Up
When Ladies Meet (1933)
When Ladies Meet (1941)
When the Time Comes
When the Trees Were Tall
When the Whales Came
When Tomorrow Comes
Where Angels Fear to Tread
Where Danger Lives
Where Eagles Dare
Where Love Has Gone
Where the Day Takes You
Where the Green Ants Dream
Where the Lilies Bloom
Where the Red Fern Grows
Where the River Runs Black
Where the Rivers Flow North
Whirlpool (1934)
Whirlpool (1949)
Whisperers, The
Whispering Smith
Whistle at Eaton Falls, The
Whistle Down the Wind
Whistler, The
White Cargo
White Cliffs of Dover, The
White Dawn, The
White Demon, The
White Dog
White Fang
White Fang 2: Myth of the White Wolf
White Hot: The Mysterious Murder of Thelma Todd
White Hunter, Black Heart
White Lie
White Mischief
White Nights (1957)
White Nights (1985)
White Palace
White Sister, The
White Tower, The
Who Am I This Time?
Who Fears the Devil
Who Has Seen the Wind?
Who Says I Can't Ride a Rainbow?
Who Will Love My Children?
Whom the Gods Destroy
Whore
Who's Afraid of Virginia Woolf?
Who's That Knocking at My Door?
Whose Life Is It Anyway?
Why Does Herr R. Run Amok?
Why Shoot the Teacher?
Wicked Woman, A
Wide Sargasso Sea
Wife of General Ling, The
Wifemistress
Wild and the Free, The
Wild Angels, The
Wild at Heart
Wild Blue Yonder, The
Wild Boys of the Road
Wild Country, The
Wild Duck, The
Wild Harvest
Wild Hearts Can't Be Broken
Wild in the Country
Wild in the Streets
Wild is the Wind
Wild One, The
Wild Orchid
Wild Orchid 2—Two Shades of Blue
Wild Orchids
Wild Party, The
Wild Pony, The
Wild River
Wild Seed, The
Wild Stallion
Wild Strawberries
Wilderness Family Part 2, The
Wildflower
Wildrose
Will: G. Gordon Liddy
Wilma
Wilson
Wind
Wind Across the Everglades
Wind and the Lion, The
Wind Cannot Read, The
Wind, The
Windom's Way
Winds of Change
Winds of the Wasteland
Winds of War, The
Windy City
Winged Victory
Wings and the Woman
Wings in the Dark
Wings of Desire
Wings of Eagles, The
Wings of the Morning
Winner Never Quits, A
Winning
Winning Team, The
Winslow Boy, The
Winter Light
Winter Meeting
Winter of Our Dreams, The
Winter People
Winter Wind
Winterset
Wired
Wisdom
Wise Blood
Wiser Age
Wish You Were Here
Wishing Machine
Witches, The
With a Smile
With a Song in My Heart
With Love and Tenderness
Without a Home
Without Love
Without Regret
Witness
Witness for the Prosecution
Wittgenstein
Wizard, The
Woman Called Golda, A
Woman Called Moses, A
Woman, Her Men and Her Futon, A
Woman in a Dressing Gown
Woman in Flames, A
Woman in Hiding
Woman in Question, The
Woman in the Dunes (Suna No Onna)
Woman in White, The
Woman Next Door, The
Woman of Affairs, A
Woman of Paris, A
Woman on the Beach, The
Woman Rebels, A
Woman Under the Influence, A
Woman's Face, A
Woman's Secret, A
Woman's Tale, A
Woman's Vengeance, A
Woman's World
Women & Men: In Love There Are No Rules
Women & Men: Stories of Seduction
Women in Love
Women of Brewster Place, The

Women's Prison
Women's Room, The
Wonderful World of the Brothers Grimm, The
Wooden Horse, The
Wooden Man's Bride, The
World According to Garp, The
World Apart, A
World in My Corner
World of Apu, The
World of Hans Christian Andersen, The
World of Suzie Wong, The
World, the Flesh and the Devil, The
Worst Woman in Paris?, The
Woyzeck
Wreck of the Mary Deare, The
Wrestling Ernest Hemingway
Written on the Wind
Wrong Man, The
Wrong Move
Wuthering Heights (1939)
Wuthering Heights (1954)
Wuthering Heights (1970)
X, Y and Zee
Yanco
Yank in the RAF, A
Yanks
Yasemin
Year My Voice Broke, The
Year of Living Dangerously, The
Yearling, The
Yellow Balloon, The
Yellow Earth
Yellow Jack
Yojimbo
Yol
You and Me
Young at Heart
Young Bess
Young Cassidy
Young Catherine
Young Doctors, The
Young Dr. Kildare
Young Lions, The
Young Magician, The
Young Man With a Horn
Young Mr. Lincoln
Young Mr. Pitt, The
Young Nurses, The
Young Philadelphians, The
Young Stranger, The
Young Tom Edison
Young Torless
Young, Willing and Eager
Young Winston
Young Wives' Tale
Young Woodley
Youngblood
Youngblood Hawke
Your Cheatin' Heart
Your Turn, Darling
Youth and His Amulet, The
Zabriskie Point
Zandalee
Zaza
Zebrahead
Zelly and Me
Zentropa
Zero Hour
Zina
Zoo in Budapest
Zorba the Greek
Zulu Dawn

HORROR

Abby
Abominable Dr. Phibes, The
Alchemist, The
Alice, Sweet Alice
Alien Dead, The
Alien Terror
Alison's Birthday
All the Kind Strangers
Alligator
Alligator People, The
Alligator II: The Mutation
Alone in the Dark
Alpha Incident, The
American Gothic
American Werewolf in London, An
Amityville—A New Generation
Amityville Curse, The
Amityville 4: The Evil Escapes
Amityville Horror, The
Amityville 1992: It's About Time
Amityville 3D
Amityville II: The Possession
Amsterdamned
Anatomist, The
And Now the Screaming Starts
Andy Warhol's Dracula
Andy Warhol's Frankenstein
Anguish
Ape Man, The
Ape, The
Appointment, The
Appointment with Fear
April Fool's Day
Arachnophobia
Are You in the House Alone?
Army of Darkness
Arrival, The
Asphyx
Assignment Terror
Astro-Zombies
Asylum
Asylum of Satan
Atom Age Vampire
Attack of the Beast Creatures
Attack of the Crab Monsters
Attack of the Giant Leeches
Attack of the Mayan Mummy
Attack of the Puppet People
Attack of the Swamp Creature
Audrey Rose
Autopsy
Awakening, The
Awful Dr. Orloff, The
Baby, The
Back From the Dead
Bad Channels
Bad Dreams
Bad Ronald
Baron Blood
Basket Case
Basket Case 2
Basket Case 3
Bat People
Bat, The
Bat Whispers, The
Bates Motel
Bay of Blood
Beaks—The Movie
Beast from Haunted Cave
Beast in the Cellar, The
Beast Must Die, The
Beast of Hollow Mountain, The
Beast of the Dead, The
Beast of Yucca Flats, The
Beast with Five Fingers, The
Beast Within, The
Beasts (1972)
Beasts (1983)
Beasts Are in the Streets, The
Bedlam
Bees, The
Before I Hang
Being, The
Believers, The
Bellman, The
Ben
Berserk
Berserker
Beyond Evil
Beyond the Door
Beyond the Door II
Billy the Kid vs. Dracula
Birds, The
Black Abbot, The
Black Cat, The (1934)
Black Cat, The (1941)
Black Christmas
Black Dragons
Black Friday
Black Magic Woman
Black Room, The
Black Roses
Black Sabbath
Black Scorpion, The
Black Sleep, The
Black Sunday
Black Vampire
Black Zoo
Blackenstein
Blacula
Blade in the Dark, A
Blades
Blind Man's Bluff
Blood and Black Lace
Blood and Lace
Blood and Roses
Blood Bath
Blood Beach
Blood from the Mummy's Tomb
Blood of Dracula
Blood of Dracula's Castle
Blood of the Vampire

Blood on Satan's Claw, The
Blood Relations
Blood Rose
Blood Salvage
Blood Sisters
Blood Tide
Bloodeaters
Bloodstone—Subspecies II
Bloodsuckers
Bloody Birthday
Blue Monkey
Bluebeard
Bodily Harm
Body Beneath, The
Body Melt
Body Parts
Body Snatcher, The
Bog
Boggy Creek II
Boogens, The
Boogeyman, The
Boogeyman II
Boogie Man Will Get You, The
B.O.R.N.
Borrower, The
Bowery at Midnight
Boy Who Cried Werewolf, The
Brain Damage
Brain Dead
Brain from Planet Arous, The
Brain Machine, The
Brain That Wouldn't Die, The
Brain, The
Brainwaves
Bram Stoker's Dracula
Bride of Frankenstein, The
Bride of Re-Animator
Bride of the Gorilla
Bride of the Monster
Bride, The
Brides of Dracula
Brood, The
Brotherhood of Satan
Bucket of Blood, A
Bug
Buried Alive (1984)
Buried Alive (1990)
Burn, Witch, Burn!
Burning, The
Burnt Offerings
Cabinet of Caligari, The
Cabinet of Dr. Caligari, The
Caltiki, the Immortal Monster
Cameron's Closet
Candyman
Candyman: Farewell to the Flesh
Cape Canaveral Monsters
Captain Kronos: Vampire Hunter
Captive Wild Woman
Capture of Big Foot
Car, The
Carmilla
Carnival of Souls
Carnosaur
Carpenter, The
Carrie
Cast a Deadly Spell
Castle of Blood
Castle of Evil
Castle of Fu Manchu, The
Castle of the Living Dead
Cat and the Canary, The
Cat Creature, The
Cat Creeps, The
Cat Girl
Cat People (1942)
Cat People (1982)
Cathy's Curse
Catman of Paris
Cat's Eye
Cauldron of Blood
Cellar Dweller
Chamber of Horrors
Changeling, The
Child of Darkness, Child of Light
Children of the Corn
Children of the Corn II
Children of the Damned
Children of the Night
Children Shouldn't Play with Dead Things
Children, The
Child's Play
Child's Play 2
Child's Play 3
Chilling, The
Chopping Mall
Chosen Survivors
Christine
C.H.U.D.
C.H.U.D. II
Church, The
Circus of Horrors
City of Blood
Class of Nuke 'Em High Part II: Subhumanoid Meltdown
Claws
Club, The
Cold Night's Death, A
Comedy of Terrors, The
Coming Soon
Company of Wolves, The
Confessions of a Serial Killer
Conqueror Worm, The
Contagion
Corpse Vanishes, The
Corridors of Blood
Count Dracula
Count Yorga, Vampire
Countess Dracula
Crater Lake Monster, The
Craving, The
Crawlspace
Crazies, The
Creature From the Black Lagoon
Creature Walks Among Us, The
Creepers
Creeping Flesh, The
Creepozoids
Creepshow
Creepshow 2
Crimson Cult, The
Critters 3
Critters 4
Crocodile
Cronos
Crucible of Horror
Cry of the Banshee
Crystal Force
Cthulhu Mansion
Cujo
Curse 4
Curse of Frankenstein, The
Curse of King Tut's Tomb, The
Curse of the Black Widow
Curse of the Cat People, The
Curse of the Demon
Curse of the Werewolf, The
Curse, The
Curse II: The Bite
Cutting Class
Damien—Omen II
Dance of the Damned
Dark Angel: The Ascent
Dark Half, The
Dark of the Night
Dark Places
Dark Secret of Harvest Home
Dark Shadows
Dark, The (1979)
Dark, The (1994)
Dark Tower
Daughter of Darkness
Daughter of Dr. Jekyll
Daughters of Darkness
Daughters of Satan
Dawn of the Dead
Day of the Animals
Day of the Dead
Dead-Alive
Dead and Buried
Dead Don't Die, The
Dead of Night
Dead People
Dead Pit
Dead Zone, The
Deadly Blessing
Deadly Eyes
Deadly Sanctuary
Deadly Spawn, The
Deadtime Stories
Dear Dead Delilah
Death at Love House
Death Ship
Deathdream
Deathmoon
Deep Red
Def By Temptation
Dementia 13
Demon
Demon Keeper
Demon of Paradise
Demon Wind
Demonic Toys
Demons
Demons of the Mind
Demons 2
Deranged
Destroy All Monsters!
Destroyer
Devil Bat, The
Devil Commands, The
Devil Doll
Devil-Doll, The
Devil Is a Woman, The
Devil's Bride, The
Devil's Daughter, The
Devil's Nightmare, The
Devil's Own, The
Devil's Rain, The
Devonsville Terror, The
Diary of a Madman
Die Die My Darling
Die, Monster, Die!
Disturbance, The
Disturbed
Doctor and the

Devils, The
Doctor Blood's Coffin
Doctor of Doom
Doctor X
Dogs of Hell
Dollman vs. Demonic Toys
Dolls
Dolores Claiborne
Donovan's Brain
Don't Answer the Phone
Don't Be Afraid of the Dark
Don't Go to Sleep
Don't Look in the Basement
Don't Look Now
Doom Asylum
Door with Seven Locks, The
Dr. Alien
Dr. Black and Mr. Hyde
Dr. Giggles
Dr. Jekyll and Mr. Hyde (1920)
Dr. Jekyll and Mr. Hyde (1932)
Dr. Jekyll and Mr. Hyde (1941)
Dr. Jekyll and Sister Hyde
Dr. Phibes Rises Again
Dr. Tarr's Torture Dungeon
Dr. Terror's House of Horrors
Dracula (1931)
Dracula (1973)
Dracula (1979)
Dracula A.D.
Dracula Has Risen From the Grave
Dracula—Prince of Darkness
Dracula's Daughter
Dracula's Dog
Dracula's Widow
Dragonwyck
Dunwich Horror, The
Dust Devil
Eaten Alive
Edge of Sanity
Elvira—Alabama's Ghost
Entity, The
Eraserhead
Eternal Evil
Evil Altar
Evil Dead, The
Evil Dead 2, The
Evil of Frankenstein, The
Evil, The
Evil Within, The
Evilspeak
Exorcist, The
Exorcist II: The Heretic
Exorcist III, The
Experience Preferred . . . but Not Essential
Eye Creatures, The
Eye of the Cat
Eye of the Devil
Eyes of a Stranger
Eyes of Hell
Face at the Window, The
Face Behind the Mask, The
Face of Fu Manchu, The
Face of Marble
Face of the Screaming Werewolf
Fade to Black
Fall of the House of Usher
Fall of the House of Usher, The
Farm, The
Fatal Charm
Fatal Pulse
Fear Chamber, The
Fear No Evil (1969)
Fear No Evil (1981)
Fearless Vampire Killers or: Pardon Me, But Your Teeth Are in My Neck
Feast of the Devil
Feet Foremost
Fiend
Fiend, The
Fifth Floor, The
Film House Fever
Filmgore
Final Conflict, The
Final Terror, The
Firestarter
First Power, The
Flesh and the Fiends, The
Flesh Eating Mothers
Flesh Feast
Fly, The
Fly II, The
Flying Serpent, The
Fog Island
Fog, The
Food of the Gods, The
Food of the Gods, The (Part 2)
Forest, The
Forever Evil
Forgotten One, The
Four Skulls of Jonathan Drake, The
Frankenhooker
Frankenstein (Restored)
Frankenstein (1972)
Frankenstein (1993)
Frankenstein and the Monster From Hell
Frankenstein Conquers the World
Frankenstein Created Woman
Frankenstein Island
Frankenstein Meets the Space Monster
Frankenstein Meets the Wolf Man
Frankenstein Must Be Destroyed!
Frankenstein—1970
Frankenstein: The True Story
Frankenstein Unbound
Frankenstein's Daughter
Freakmaker, The
Freaks
Freddy's Dead: The Final Nightmare
Freeway Maniac, The
Friday the 13th
Friday the 13th, Part 2
Friday the 13th, Part 3
Friday the 13th, Part V: A New Begining
Friday the 13th, Part VI: Jason Lives
Friday the 13th, Part VII: The New Blood
Friday the 13th, Part VIII: Jason Takes Manhattan
Friday the 13th: The Orphan
Friday the 13th: The Final Chapter
Fright
Fright Night
Fright Night, Part II
Frightmare (1974)
Frightmare (1983)
Frogs
From Beyond
From Beyond the Grave
From the Dead of Night
Frozen Ghost
Full Eclipse
Funhouse, The
Fury, The
Galaxy of Terror
Gallery of Horror
Gargoyles
Gate, The
Gate II—Return to the Nightmare
Gates of Hell, The
Ghost Dance
Ghost Keeper
Ghost of Frankenstein, The
Ghost Story
Ghost, The
Ghost Town
Ghosthouse
Ghostriders
Ghosts—Italian Style
Ghoul, The (1933)
Ghoul, The (1975)
Ghoulies
Ghoulies 2
Ghoulies 3—Ghoulies Go to College
Ghoulies IV
Giant Behemoth, The
Giant Gila Monster, The
Girl Called Hatter Fox, The
Girl in Room 2A
Girls Nite Out
Girls on the Road
Girls School Screamers
Girly
Glen and Randa
Goblin
Godsend, The
Gog
Golem, The
Goodnight God Bless
Gorgon, The
Gothic
Graduation Day
Grave of the Vampire
Grave Secrets (1989)
Grave Secrets (1992)
Graveyard of Horrors
Graveyard Shift (1987)
Graveyard Shift (1990)
Graveyard, The
Great Alligator, The
Great Ride, A
Greed of William Hart, The
Green Man, The
Green Slime, The
Grim Prairie Tales

Grim Reaper, The
Grizzly
Grotesque
Growing Pains
Gruesome Twosome, The
Guardian, The
Halloween
Halloween II
Halloween III: Season of the Witch
Halloween 4: The Return of Michael Myers
Halloween 5: Revenge of Michael Myers, The
Hand of the Night, The
Hand, The
Hands of a Stranger
Hands of Orlac, The
Hands of the Ripper
Hanging Woman, The
Hangover Square
Happy Birthday to Me
Happy Mother's Day, Love George
Hard Rock Zombies
Harpy
Hatchet for the Honeymoon
Haunted by Her Past
Haunted Palace, The
Haunted Strangler, The
Haunted, The
Haunting Fear
Haunting of Julia, The
Haunting of Morella, The
Haunting of Sarah Hardy, The
Haunting, The
Haunts
He Knows You're Alone
Head, The
Headhunter
Headless Ghost
Heartbreak Motel
Heartstopper
Hell High
Hell Night
Hellbound: Hellraiser II
Hellmaster
Hello Mary Lou—Prom Night II
Hellraiser
Hellraiser III: Hell on Earth
Hidden City
Hidden Fears
Hidden Hand, The
Hidden Obsession
Hide and Go Shriek
High Desert Kill
Highway to Hell
Hills Have Eyes, The
Hills Have Eyes Part II, The
Hitcher, The
Hollow Gate
Hollywood Chainsaw Hookers
Hollywood Ghost Stories
Hollywood Strangler
Hollywood's New Blood
Holocaust: 2000
Homicidal
Horrible Dr. Hichcock, The
Horror at 37,000 Feet
Horror Chamber of Dr. Faustus, The
Horror Express
Horror Hotel
Horror House
Horror Island
Horror of Dracula
Horror of Frankenstein, The
Horror of It All, The
Horror of Party Beach, The
Horror Show, The
Horrors of the Black Museum
Hound of the Baskervilles, The (1939)
Hound of the Baskervilles, The (1959)
House
House by the Cemetery
House IV: Home Deadly Home
House of Dark Shadows
House of Dracula
House of Evil
House of Frankenstein
House of Horrors
House of Mystery
House of 1,000 Dolls
House of Seven Corpses, The
House of Shadows
House of Terror
House of the Black Death
House of the Living Dead
House of Wax
House on Haunted Hill
House on Skull Mountain
House on Straw Hill, The
House That Cried Murder, The
House That Dripped Blood, The
House That Screamed, The
House That Vanished, The
House That Would Not Die, The
House II: The Second Story
House Where Evil Dwells, The
How to Make a Monster
Howling, The
Howling II: Your Sister Is a Werewolf
Howling III: The Marsupials
Howling IV: The Original Nightmare
Howling V: The Rebirth
Howling VI: The Freaks
Human Experiments
Human Monster, The
Humanoids from the Deep
Humongous
Hunger, The
Hush . . . Hush, Sweet Charlotte
I Bury the Living
I, Desire
I Dismember Mama
I Drink Your Blood
I Eat Your Skin
I, Madman
I Married a Vampire
I, Monster
I Saw What You Did
I Spit On Your Grave
I Wake Up Screaming
I Walked with a Zombie
I Was a Teenage Frankenstein
I Was a Teenage Werewolf
Iceman
Igor and the Lunatics
I'm Dangerous Tonight
Immortal Sins
Immortalizer, The
Impersonator, The
Incredible Two-Headed Transplant, The
Incredibly Strange Creatures Who Stopped Living and Became Mixed up Zombies
Incubus, The
Indecency
Indestructible Man, The
Inferno
Initiation of Sarah, The
Initiation, The
Inn of the Damned
Inn of the Frightened People
Innocent Blood
Innocent Prey
Interview With the Vampire
Invasion of Carol Enders, The
Invasion of the Body Snatchers (1956)
Invasion of the Body Snatchers (1978)
Invasion of the Flesh Hunters
Invisible Dr. Mabuse, The
Invisible Ghost, The
Invisible Maniac, The
Invisible Man's Revenge, The
Invisible Ray, The
Island Claws
Island of Doomed Men
Island of Dr. Moreau, The
Island of Lost Souls
Island of Lost Women
Island of Terror
Isle of the Dead
It
It Happened at Lakewood Manor
It Lives Again
It's Alive!
It's Alive III: Island of the Alive
Ivory Ape, The
Jack Be Nimble
Jack the Ripper
Jar, The

Jason Goes to Hell: The Final Friday
Jaws of Satan
J.D.'s Revenge
Jekyll & Hyde
Jennifer
Jesse James Meets Frankenstein's Daughter
Judgment Day
Jugular Wine: A Vampire Odyssey
Jungle Heat
K-9000
Keep, The
Keeper, The
Kemek
Kill Baby Kill
Killer Bees
Killer in Every Corner, A
Killer Shrews, The
Killer With Two Faces
Killer's Moon
Kindred, The
King Kong
King of Kong Island
Kingdom of the Spiders
Kiss and Be Killed
Kiss, The
Kwaidan
Lady and the Monster, The
Lady Dracula
Lady Frankenstein
Lair of the White Worm, The
Land of the Minotaur
Last Call For Murder
Last Dance
Last Dinosaur, The
Last Horror Film, The
Last Man on Earth, The
Last Slumber Party, The
Leatherface: Texas Chainsaw Massacre III
Leech Woman, The
Legacy, The
Legend of Boggy Creek
Legend of Hell House, The
Legend of the Dinosaurs
Legend of the Werewolf
Legend of the Wolfwoman
Leonor
Leopard Man, The
Leprechaun
Leprechaun 2
Let's Scare Jessica to Death
Leviathan
Liar's Edge
Lift, The
Lisa and the Devil
Little Girl Who Lives Down the Lane, The
Little Shop of Horrors, The
Little Sweetheart
Loch Ness Horror, The
Lodger, The (1926)
Lodger, The (1944)
London After Midnight
Lost Boys, The
Lost Platoon, The
Love & Murder
Love Butcher, The
Love Kills
Love Me Deadly
Lucifer Complex, The
Lurking Fear
Lust for a Vampire
Luther the Geek
Macabre
Mad at the Moon
Mad Butcher, the
Mad Doctor of Blood Island, The
Mad Doctor of Market Street, The
Mad Ghoul, The
Mad Love
Mad Magician, The
Mad Monster, The
Madhouse (1974)
Madhouse (1981)
Madhouse Mansion
Madman
Magic
Majorettes, The
Making Contact
Mama Dracula
Mama's Dirty Girls
Man-Eater of Hydra
Man in Half Moon Street, The
Man in the Attic
Man Made Monster
Man They Could Not Hang, The
Man Who Could Cheat Death, The
Man Who Turned to Stone, The
Man with Nine Lives, The
Mangler, The
Manhattan Baby
Maniac (1934)
Maniac (1963)
Maniac (1981)
Maniac Cop
Maniac Cop 2
Maniac Cop 3: Badge of Silence
Manitou, The
Mansion of the Doomed
Mardi Gras for the Devil
Mardi Gras Massacre
Mark of Cain
Mark of the Devil
Mark of the Vampire
Martin
Mary, Mary, Blood Mary
Mary Shelley's Frankenstein
Masque of the Red Death (1964)
Masque of the Red Death (1989)
Mausoleum
Maxim Xul
Maximum Overdrive
Maze, The
Mazes and Monsters
Medusa Touch, The
Memorial Valley Massacre
Mephisto Waltz, The
Meridian—Kiss of the Beast
Microwave Massacre
Midnight
Midnight Cabaret
Midnight Faces
Midnight Movie Massacre
Midnight's Child
Mind Twister
Mindkiller
Mirror, Mirror
Mirror, Mirror 2: Raven Dance
Mirror of Death
Mirrors
Misery
Mom
Mongrel
Monkey Boy
Monkey Shines: An Experiment in Fear
Monster
Monster and the Girl, The
Monster Club, The
Monster Dog
Monster in the Closet
Monster Maker, The
Monster of Piedras Blancas, The
Monster That Challenged the World, The
Monster, The
Monster Walks, The
Moon in Scorpio
Moon of The Wolf
Mortuary
Mortuary Academy
Motel Hell
Mother's Day
Mountaintop Motel Massacre
Mr. Sardonicus
Mummy, The (1932)
Mummy, The (1959)
Mummy's Curse, The
Mummy's Ghost, The
Mummy's Hand, The
Mummy's Tomb, The
Murder by the Clock
Murder Mansion, The
Murder Motel
Murder on the Midnight Express
Murder Weapon
Murders in the Rue Morgue
Murders in the Zoo
Mutant
Mutator
My Bloody Valentine
My Grandpa Is a Vampire
Mystery of the Wax Museum, The
Nail Gun Massacre
Name for Evil, A
Natas: The Reflection
Navy vs. the Night Monsters, The
Near Dark
Necromancer—Satan's Servant
Necromancy
Necropolis
Needful Things
Nesting, The
Netherworld
New Year's Evil
New York Ripper
Newlydeads, The
Next of Kin
Next Victim, The
Night Angel
Night Breed
Night Brings Charlie, The
Night Digger, The
Night God Screamed, The
Night Monster
Night of Dark Shadows
Night of Terror
Night of the Creeps
Night of the Demons
Night of the Demons 2

Night of the Living Dead (1968)
Night of the Living Dead (1990)
Night Runner, The
Night School
Night Stalker, The
Night Walker, The
Night Warning
Nightmare Castle
Nightmare in Wax
Nightmare on Elm Street, A
Nightmare on Elm Street 2: Freddy's Revenge
Nightmare on Elm Street 3: Dream Warriors
Nightmare on Elm Street 4: The Dream Master
Nightmare on Elm Street 5: The Dream Child
Nightmare on the 13th Floor
Nightmares
Nightwing
Nightwish
976-EVIL
976-EVIL II
No Secrets
Nocturna
Nomads
Norliss Tapes, The
Nosferatu
Nosferatu the Vampyre
Not of This Earth
Nothing But the Night
Nudist Colony of the Dead
Oblong Box, The
Of Unknown Origin
Offspring, The
Old Dark House, The (1932)
Old Dark House, The (1963)
Omen, The
Omen IV—The Awakening
On the Third Day
One Dark Night
Open House
Orson Welles' Ghost Story
Other, The
Out Of Sight, Out Of Mind
Out Of The Body
Out of the Dark
Outcast, The
Outing, The
Pack, The
Pale Blood
Paperboy, The
Paperhouse
Paranoiac
Parasite
Party Line
Passing, The
Patrick
People Under the Stairs
Pet Sematary
Pet Sematary II
Phantasm
Phantasm II
Phantasm III: Lord of the Dead
Phantom of the Mall—Eric's Revenge
Phantom of the Opera (1943)
Phantom of the Opera (1989)
Phantom of the Opera, The (1925)
Phantom of the Opera, The (1962)
Phantom of the Opera, The (1983)
Phantom of the Ritz
Phantom of the Rue Morgue
Phantom Ship
Picture Mommy Dead
Picture of Dorian Gray, The
Pied Piper, The
Pin
Piranha
Piranha II: The Spawning
Pit and the Pendulum
Pit and the Pendulum, The
Pit, The
Plague of the Zombies, The
Playroom
Poltergeist
Poltergeist II: The Other Side
Poltergeist III
Poor White Trash II
Popcorn
Possession
Possession of Joel Delaney, The
Premature Burial, The
Premonition, The
Prey, The
Prince of Darkness
Prison
Private Parts
Prom Night
Prom Night III: The Last Kiss
Prom Night IV: Deliver Us From Evil
Prophecy
Psycho
Psycho 2
Psycho 3
Psycho IV: The Beginning
Psychopath, The
Pulse
Pumpkinhead
Pumpkinhead II: Blood Wings
Puppetmaster
Puppetmaster II
Puppet Master III: Toulon's Revenge
Puppetmaster 4
Puppetmaster 5
Pyx, The
Q
Rabid
Rabid Grannies
Race With the Devil
Rattlers
Raven, The (1935)
Raven, The (1963)
Raw Meat
Rawhead Rex
Razorback
Re-Animator
Regenerated Man, The
Reincarnation of Peter Proud, The
Repulsion
Rest in Pieces
Resurrected, The
Retribution
Return of Dr. X, The
Return of Dracula, The
Return of the Ape Man
Return of the Living Dead, The
Return of the Living Dead: Part II
Return of the Living Dead 3
Return of the Vampire, The
Return to Boggy Creek
Return to Horror High
Return to Salem's Lot, A
Revenge of Frankenstein, The
Revenge of the Creature
Rosemary's Baby
Ruby
Runestone, The
Salem's Lot: The Miniseries
Satan Killer, The
Satanic Rites of Dracula, The
Satan's Black Wedding
Satan's Cheerleaders
Satanwar
Savage Abduction
Savage Lust
Savage Weekend
Scanners
Scanners III—The Takeover
Scanners II—The New Order
Scar, The
Scarecrows
Scared Stiff
Scared to Death
Scars of Dracula
Schlock
Scream and Scream Again
Scream, Blacula, Scream!
Scream Bloody Murder
Scream Dream
Scream, Pretty Peggy
Season of the Witch
Secret of the Blue Room
See No Evil
Seedpeople
Seizure
Sender, The
Sentinel, The
Serpent and the Rainbow, The
Servants of Twilight, The
Seven Brothers Meet Dracula, The
Seven Deaths in the Cat's Eye
7 Doors of Death
Seventh Sign, The
Seventh Victim, The
Severed Arm, The
Severed Ties
Shadow Play
Shakma
Shallow Grave
Shaman, The
She-Beast, The
She Creature, The
She Demons
She Freaks
She Waits
She Wolf

Shining, The
Shock 'em Dead
Shock! Shock! Shock!
Shock Waves
Shocker
Shredder Orpheus
Shrieking, The
Shrunken Heads
Silent Madness
Silent Motive
Silent Night, Deadly Night
Silent Night, Deadly Night (Part II)
Silent Night, Deadly Night (Part III—Better Watch Out!)
Silent Night, Deadly Night (Part IV—The Initiation)
Silent Night, Deadly Night (Part V—The Toy Maker)
Silver Bullet
Simon, King Of The Witches
Single White Female
Sins of Dorian Gray, The
Sisters
Sisters of Death
Sketches of a Strangler
Skinned Alive
Skull, The
Slaughter
Slaughter High
Sleep of Death
Sleepaway Camp
Sleepaway Camp 2—Unhappy Campers
Sleepaway Camp 3—Teenage Wasteland
Slugs
Slumber Party Massacre II
Slumber Party Massacre, The
Snowbeast
Society
Sometimes They Come Back
Son of Dracula
Son of Frankenstein
Sorcerers, The
Sorority Babes in the Slimeball Bowl-O-Rama
Sorority House Massacre
Sorority House Massacre 2
Soultaker
Spasms
Spellbinder
Spellcaster
Spirits of the Dead
Splatter University
Spontaneous Combustion
Spookies
SSSSSSS
Stepfather, The
Stepfather II
Stepfather 3—Father's Day
Stepford Wives, The
Stephen King's Golden Years
Stephen King's It
Stephen King's Sleepwalkers
Still Life
Stones of Death
Strange And Deadly Occurrence, The
Strange Behavior
Strange Case of Dr. Jekyll And Mr. Hyde, The
Strangeness, The
Stranger Within, The
Strangers In Paradise
Strangler of the Swamp
Strangler, The
Strays
Street Asylum
Subspecies
Sundown, The Vampire in Retreat
Suspiria
Syngenor
Tales from the Crypt (1972)
Tales from the Crypt (1989)
Tales from the Crypt (1990)
Tales From the Crypt Presents Demon Knight
Tales From the Darkside: The Movie
Tales of Terror
Tarantula
Taste the Blood of Dracula
Teenage Exorcist
Tempter, The
Tenant, The
Terror at the Opera
Terror House
Terror, The
Terror Train
Terror Within II, The
Texas Chainsaw Massacre, The—Part 2
Texas Chainsaw Massacre, The
Theatre of Blood
Theatre of Death
They Saved Hitler's Brain
13 Ghosts
Ticks
Tingler, The
To Die For
To Die For 2—Son of Darkness
To Sleep With a Vampire
To the Devil A Daughter
Tomb of Ligeia
Torture Garden
Tower of London
Tower of London, The
Town That Dreaded Sundown, The
Toxic Avenger, The
Toxic Avenger—Part II, The
Toxic Avenger—Part III, The: The Last Temptation of Toxie
Trauma
Tremors
Trick or Treat
Trilogy of Terror
Trog
Troll II
Turn of the Screw, The (1989)
Turn of the Screw, The (1992)
Twins of Evil
Twisted
Two Evil Eyes
2,000 Maniacs
Unborn, The
Unborn II, The
Undead, The
Unholy, The
Uninvited, The
Unnameable, The
Unnamable II, The
Unsane
Unseen, The
Vamp
Vampire Bat, The
Vampire Happening, The
Vampire Hookers
Vampire Lovers, The
Vampyr
Vampyres
Vault of Horror
Velvet Vampire, The
Venom
Victor Frankenstein
Video Dead, The
Videodrome
Vineyard, The
Voodoo Dawn
Walking Dead, The
Warlock 2: The Armageddon
Wasp Woman, The
Watcher in the Woods, The
Watchers
Watchers 2
Watchers III, The
Waxwork
Waxwork II—Lost in Time
Werewolf in a Girl's Dormitory
Werewolf of London
Werewolf Vs. the Vampire Woman
Wes Craven's New Nightmare
West of Zanzibar
What Ever Happened to Baby Jane? (1962)
What Ever Happened to Baby Jane? (1991)
What's the Matter with Helen?
White Zombie
Wicked Stepmother
Willard
Witchboard
Witchboard 2: The Devil's Doorway
Witchcraft
Witchcraft II—The Temptress
Witchcraft III—The Kiss of Death
Witchcraft IV Virgin Heart
Witchcraft V: Dance With the Devil
Witchcraft VI
Witchcraft Through the Ages (Haxan)
Wolf
Wolf Man, The
Wolfen
Wraith, The
Xtro
Zombie

MUSIC

A Nous La Liberté
Aaron Slick from Punkin Crick
Abduction from the Seraglio, The
About Face
Absolute Beginners
Aerosmith—The Making of "Pump"
Aerosmith—Things That Go Pump in the Night
Affairs of Dobie Gillis, The
Agrippina
Aida (1953)
Aida (1983)
Ain't Misbehavin'
Air Supply—Live in Hawaii
Aladdin
Aladdin and His Lamp
Alexander's Ragtime Band
Ali Baba Goes to Town
Alice
Alice's Adventures in Wonderland
All Ashore
All Dogs Go to Heaven
All Hands On Deck
All-Star Reggae Session
All That Jazz
All the King's Horses
All This and World War II
Allman Brothers Band, The—Live at Great Woods
Amazing Mrs. Holliday, The
American Hot Wax
American in Paris, An
Amerikaner Schadchen
Anchors Aweigh
And the Angels Sing
Annie
Annie Get Your Gun
Anything Goes (1936)
Anything Goes (1956)
April in Paris
April Love
Arabella
Are You with It?
Aretha Franklin—The Queen of Soul
Argentine Nights
Aria
Aristocats, The
Around the World
Artists and Models
Artists and Models Abroad
As Long As They're Happy
At Long Last Love
At the Jazz Band Ball
Athena
Atlantic City
Babes in Arms
Babes in Toyland (1934)
Babes in Toyland (1961)
Babes in Toyland (1986)
Babes on Broadway
Baby Snakes
Baby Take a Bow
Back to the Beach
Backbeat
Balalaika
Band Wagon, The
Banjo on My Knee
Barber of Seville
Barkleys of Broadway, The
Bathing Beauty
Bawdy Adventures of Tom Jones, The
Be My Guest
Beach Ball
Beach Blanket Bingo
Beach Party
Beat Street
Beatlemania
Beauty and the Beast
Because You're Mine
Bedtime Story, A
Beggar's Opera, The
Behind the Eight Ball
Belle of New York, The
Belle of the Yukon
Bells Are Ringing
Bert Rigby, You're a Fool
Best Foot Forward
Best Little Whorehouse in Texas, The
Best Things in Life Are Free, The
Beverly Sills in Verdi's La Traviata
Big Beat, The
Big Boy
Big Broadcast, The
Big Broadcast of 1936, The
Big Broadcast of 1937, The
Big Broadcast of 1938, The
Big Meat Eater, The
Big Pond, The
Big Time
Big T.N.T. Show, The
Billy Joel—Live at Yankee Stadium
Billy Rose's Jumbo
Birth of the Beatles
Birth of the Blues
Bitter Sweet (1933)
Bitter Sweet (1940)
Bix: An Interpretation of a Legend
Black Tights
Blame It on the Night
Blaze O'Glory
Blue Bird, The (1940)
Blue Bird, The (1976)
Blue Hawaii
Blue Skies
Blues in the Night
Bop Girl
Boris Godunov
Born to Dance
Bottoms Up
Bowery to Broadway
Boy Friend, The
Boy! What a Girl
Boys from Syracuse, The
Break the News
Breakfast in Hollywood
Breakin'
Breakin' II: Electric Boogaloo
Breaking Glass
Brigadoon
Bring on the Girls
Bring Your Smile Along
Broadway
Broadway Gondolier
Broadway Melody, The
Broadway Melody of 1936
Broadway Melody of 1938
Broadway Melody of 1940
Broadway Rhythm
Broadway Serenade
Broadway to Hollywood
Buddy Holly Story, The
Bugsy Malone
Buster
By the Light of the Silvery Moon
Bye, Bye, Birdie
Cabaret
Cabin in the Sky
Cain and Mabel
Cairo
Calamity Jane
Call Me Madam
Call Me Mister
Calypso Heat Wave
Calypso Joe
Camelot
Can-Can
Can't Help Singing
Can't Stop the Music
Captain January
Caravan
Carefree
Carmen (1983)
Carmen (1984)
Carmen Jones
Carnegie Hall
Carnival in Costa Rica
Carnival Rock
Carousel
Casbah
Cat and the Fiddle, The
Centennial Summer
Champagne Charlie
Champagne Waltz
Change of Heart
Charing Cross Road
Chitty Chitty Bang Bang
Chocolate Soldier, The
Chorus Line, A
Christmas That Almost Wasn't, The
Cinderella (1950)
Cinderella (1964)
Cindy
Clambake
C'mon, Let's Live a Little
Cocoanut Grove
Colleen
College Humor
College Swing
Concert for Bangladesh, The
Coney Island
Congress Dances

Copacabana
Court Concert, The
Cover Girl
Crossover Dreams
Crossroads
Cry-Baby
Cuban Love Song, The
Cuban Pete
Curly Top
Daddy Long Legs
Dames
Damn Yankees
Damsel in Distress, A
Dance, Girl, Dance
Dance Hall
Dancers
Dancing Lady
Dangerous When Wet
Danny Boy
Darling Lili
Date With Judy, A
Daughter of Rosie O'Grady, The
Deadman's Curve
Deep in My Heart
Delightfully Dangerous
Der Purimshpiler
Desert Song, The
Devil's Brother, The
Diamond Horseshoe
Dimples
Diplomaniacs
Dirty Dancing
Distant Harmony—Pavarotti in China
Dixiana
Dixie
Do You Love Me?
Doctor Dolittle
Doctor Rhythm
Dogs in Space
Doll Face
Dolly Sisters, The
Don Giovanni
Don Quixote
Don't Knock the Rock
Don't Look Back
Doors, The
Double or Nothing
Double Trouble
Down Among the Sheltering Palms
Down Argentine Way
Down to Earth
Dr. Demento: 20th Anniversary Collection
Dr. Rhythm
Dream to Believe
DuBarry Was a Lady
Duchess of Idaho
Dumbo
Earl Carroll Vanities
East Side of Heaven
Easter Parade
Easy Come, Easy Go
Easy to Love
Easy to Wed
Eddie and the Cruisers
Eddie and the Cruisers II—Eddie Lives!
Eddy Duchin Story, The
Eighties, The
El Amor Brujo
Elvis and Me
Elvis on Tour
Elvis: That's the Way It Is
Emperor Waltz, The
Empress and I, The
End of the Road, The
Eubie!
Eve Knew Her Apples
Ever Since Venus
Evergreen
Every Night at Eight
Everybody Sing
Everything I Have Is Yours
Excuse My Dust
Fabulous Dorseys, The
Falstaff (1976)
Falstaff (1983)
Fame
Fantasia
Fantasy Double Bill, A
Farewell to Love
Farmer Takes a Wife, The
Fashions
Fast Company
Fast Forward
Fats Domino and Friends—Immortal Keyboards of Rock & Roll
Ferry Cross the Mersey
Feudin', Fussin' and A-Fightin'
Fiddler on the Roof
Fiesta
Fight for Your Lady
Fillmore
Final Romance, The
Finian's Rainbow
Firefly, The
Five Heartbeats, The
Five Pennies, The
Flashdance
Fleet's In, The
Flirtation Walk
Florodora Girl, The
Flower Drum Song
Flying Down to Rio
Flying High
Folies Bergere
Follies Bergere
Follow That Dream
Follow the Boys (1944)
Follow the Boys (1963)
Follow the Fleet
Follow Thru
Footlight Parade
Footlight Serenade
Footloose
For Me and My Gal
For the Boys
Forbidden Dance, The
Forbidden Music
42nd Street
Four Jacks and a Jill
Four Jills in a Jeep
Frankie and Johnny (1936)
Frankie and Johnny (1965)
Free and Easy
French Cancan
French Line, The
Frisco Sal
From Nashville with Music
Fun in Acapulco
Funny Face
Funny Girl
Funny Lady
Gang's All Here, The
Garden of the Moon
Gay Divorcee, The
Gay Purr-ee
Gene Krupa Story, The
Gentlemen Marry Brunettes
George Balanchine's The Nutcracker
George White's Scandals (1934)
George White's Scandals (1935)
George White's Scandals (1945)
Get Back
Get Hep to Love
Get Yourself a College Girl
G.I. Blues
Gigi
Gimme Shelter
Girl Crazy
Girl Happy
Girl Most Likely, The
Girl Next Door, The
Girl of the Golden West, The
Girl Rush, The
Girls! Girls! Girls!
Giselle
Give a Girl a Break
Give Me a Sailor
Give My Regards to Broad Street
Give My Regards to Broadway
Glamorous Night
Glamour Girl
Glass Mountain, The
Glass Slipper, The
Glenn Miller Story, The
Glorifying the American Girl
Go Into Your Dance
Go, Johnny, Go!
Godspell
Goin' Coconuts
Going Places
Gold Diggers of Broadway
Gold Diggers of 1933
Gold Diggers of 1935
Gold Diggers of 1937
Golden Eighties
Golden Girl
Goldwyn Follies, The
Good Companions, The
Good News (1930)
Good News (1947)
Good Times
Goodbye, Mr. Chips
Gospel
Gospel Road, The
Graffiti Bridge
Grateful Dead—Dead Ahead
Grateful Dead Movie, The
Grease
Grease 2
Great American Broadcast, The
Great Caruso, The
Great Gilbert and Sullivan, The
Great Victor Herbert, The
Great Waltz, The
Great Ziegfeld, The
Greenwich Village
Grounds for Marriage
Gulliver's Travels
Guys and Dolls
Gypsy (1962)
Gypsy (1993)
Hair
Hairspray
Half a Sixpence
Hallelujah
Hallelujah, I'm a Bum
Hans Brinker
Hans Christian

Porgy and Bess
Presenting Lily Mars
Princesse Tam Tam
Purple Rain
Queen of the Stardust Ballroom
Raggedy Ann and Andy
Rainbow Island
Rainbow 'Round My Shoulder
Rappin
Ready, Willing and Able
Rebel
Red Garters
Red, Hot and Blue
Red Riding Hood
Red Shoes, The
Renaldo and Clara
Reveille With Beverly
Rhapsody in Blue
Rhythm on the Range
Rhythm on the River
Rich, Young and Pretty
Rio Rita
Roadie
Roberta
Robin and the Seven Hoods
Robin Hood
Rock-a-Doodle
Rock All Night
Rock & Read
Rock & Rule
Rock Around the Clock
Rocky Horror Picture Show, The
Rogue Song, The
Rolling Stones, The: In the Park
Roman Scandals
Romance on the High Seas
Rooftops
Rosalie
Rose Marie (1936)
Rose Marie (1954)
Rose of Washington Square
Round Midnight
Roustabout
Royal Wedding
Sacred Music Of Duke Ellington, The
Sally, Irene and Mary
Salsa
San Antonio Rose
Sap from Syracuse, The
Sarafina!
Satisfaction
Saturday Night Fever
Say It with Music
Say It with Songs
Say One for Me
Scarecrow in a Garden of Cucumbers
Scrooge
Seaside Swingers
Second Chorus
Secret Policeman's Other Ball, The
Sensations
Serenade
Sergeant Deadhead
Seven Brides for Seven Brothers
Seven Days' Leave
Seven Hills of Rome, The
Seven Little Foys, The
Seven Sweethearts
1776
Sex Pistols—Great Rock 'n' Roll Swindle
Sgt. Pepper's Lonely Hearts Club Band
Shake, Rattle and Rock
Shall We Dance
Shamrock Hill
She Loves Me Not
She's Back on Broadway
She's Working Her Way Through College
Shillingbury Blowers, The
Shinbone Alley
Shine On, Harvest Moon
Ship Ahoy
Shipmates Forever
Shock Treatment
Shocking Miss Pilgrim, The
Shout
Show Boat (1936)
Show Boat (1951)
Show Business
Showtime
Sign o' the Times
Silk Stockings
Sinatra
Sincerely Yours
Sing
Sing, Baby, Sing
Sing, You Sinners
Singin' in the Rain
Singing Kid, The
Singing Princess, The
Sioux City Sue
Sitting Pretty
Skirts Ahoy!
Sky's the Limit, The (1937)
Sky's the Limit, The (1943)
Slipper and the Rose, The
Small Town Girl
Smiling Lieutenant, The
Smoky Mountain Christmas, A
So This Is Love
So This Is Paris
Soldiers Of Music
Something for the Boys
Something in the Wind
Something to Sing About
Song O' My Heart
Song of Freedom
Song of Norway
Song of the Islands
Song of the Open Road
Song of the South
Song Remains the Same, The
Song Without End
Songwriter
Sophisticated Ladies
Sound of Music, The
Sound Off
South Pacific
Speedway
Spinout
Spotlight Scandals
Spring Parade
Spring Symphony
Springtime in the Rockies
St. Louis Blues
Stage Door Canteen
Stand Up and Cheer
Star!
Star Is Born, A
Star Maker, The
Star Spangled Rhythm
Starlift
Stars and Stripes Forever
Starstruck
Start Cheering
State Fair (1933)
State Fair (1945)
State Fair (1962)
Staying Alive
Step Lively
Stepping Out
Stop Making Sense
Stormy Weather
Story of Vernon and Irene Castle, The
Strictly Dishonorable (1931)
Strictly Dishonorable (1951)
Strike Me Pink
Strike Up the Band
Student Prince, The
Summer Holiday (1948)
Summer Holiday (1963)
Summer Stock
Sun Valley Serenade
Sunny
Sunny Side Up
Svengali
Swan Lake
Swan Princess, The
Swanee River
Sweeney Todd, the Demon Barber of Fleet Street
Sweet Adeline
Sweet Charity
Sweet Rosie O'Grady
Sweetheart of the Campus
Sweethearts
Swing It, Professor
Swing Parade of 1946
Swing Time
Swing Your Lady
Take Me Out to the Ball Game
Tales of Beatrix Potter, The
Tales of Hoffman
Tango Bar
Tars and Spars
Tea for Two
Terror of Tiny Town, The
Texas Carnival
Thank God, It's Friday
Thank Your Lucky Stars
Thanks a Million
That Certain Age
That Girl From Paris
That Lady in Ermine
That Midnight Kiss
That Night in Rio
That's Dancing
That's Entertainment
That's Entertainment, Part 2
That's Entertainment 3
That's the Spirit
There's No Business

Like Show Business
They Learned About Women
They Shall Have Music
Thin Ice
This is the Army
This Is the Life (1935)
This Is the Life (1944)
Thoroughly Modern Millie
Those Lips, Those Eyes
Those Redheads From Seattle
Thousand and One Nights, A
Thousands Cheer
Three for the Show
Three Hats for Lisa
Three Little Girls in Blue
Three Little Words
Three Musketeers, The
Three Sailors and a Girl
Three Smart Girls
Three Smart Girls Grow Up
Threepenny Opera, The
Thrill of a Romance
Tickle Me
Till the Clouds Roll By
Time Out for Rhythm
Time, the Place and the Girl, The
Times Square
Tin Pan Alley
Toast of New Orleans, The
Tokyo Pop
Tommy
Tonight and Every Night
Tonight We Sing
Too Late Blues
Too Much Harmony
Top Hat
Top o' the Morning
Top Speed
Trouble With Girls, The
Tsar's Bride, The
Tune, The
Twenty Million Sweethearts
Twist Around the Clock
Two for Tonight
Two Girls and a Sailor
Two Girls on Broadway
Two Guys From Texas
Two Hundred Motels
Two Sisters From Boston
Two Tickets to Broadway
U2: Rattle and Hum
Umbrellas of Cherbourg, The
Under-Pup, The
Unsinkable Molly Brown, The
Up in Arms
Up In Central Park
Vagabond King, The (1930)
Vagabond King, The (1956)
Vagabond Lover, The
Varsity Show
Viennese Nights
Viva Las Vegas
Vogues of 1938
Wabash Avenue
Wake Up and Live
Walking My Baby Back Home
Way Down South
Week-end in Havana
We're Not Dressing
West Point Story
West Side Story
When My Baby Smiles at Me
Where Do We Go From Here?
Where's Charley?
White Christmas
White Horse Inn, The
Whoopee!
Willy Wonka and the Chocolate Factory
Wiz, The
Wizard of Oz, The
Woman Is a Woman, A
Wonder Bar
Wonders of Aladdin, The
Woodstock
Words and Music
Xanadu
Yankee Doodle Dandy
Yellow Submarine
Yentl
Yes, Giorgio
Yolanda and the Thief
You Can't Run Away From It
You Were Never Lovelier
You'll Never Get Rich
Young Girls of Rochefort, The
Young People
You're a Sweetheart
You're My Everything
Youth on Parade
Zachariah
Ziegfeld Follies
Ziegfeld Girl
Zoot Suit
Zou Zou

SCIENCE FICTION

Abraxas, Guardian of the Universe
Abyss, The
Adventures of Baron Munchausen, The
Adventures of Buckaroo Banzai Across the Eighth Dimension, The
After the Fall of New York
Aftershock
Akira
Alien
Alien Contamination
Alien Factor, The
Alien Intruder
Alien Nation
Alien Prey
Alien Private Eye
Alien Seed
Alien Space Avenger
Alien^3
Alienator
Aliens
Aliens Are Coming, The
Alphaville
Altered States
Amazing Colossal Man, The
Amazing Spiderman, The
Amazing Stories: Book Four
Amazing Transparent Man, The
Amazons
Android
Andromeda Strain, The
Angry Red Planet, The
Anna to the Infinite Power
Appleseed
Aquaman
Arcade
Assassin
Asterix and Cleopatra
Asterix in Britain
Asterix the Gaul
Asterix vs. Caesar
At the Earth's Core
Atom Man vs. Superman—Complete
Atomic Man, The
Atomic Submarine, The
Attack of the 50 Ft. Woman (1958)
Attack of the 50 Ft. Woman (1993)
Aurora Encounter
Bad Girls from Mars
Bad Taste
Bamboo Saucer, The
Barbarella
Barbarian Queen
Barbarian Queen II—The Empress Strikes Back
batteries not included
Battle Angel
Battle Beneath the Earth
Battle Beyond the Stars
Battle Beyond the Sun
Battle for the Planet of the Apes
Battle in Outer Space
Battle of the Worlds
Battlestar: Galactica
Beach Babes from Beyond
Beast from 20,000 Fathoms, The
Beginning of the End
Beneath the Planet of the Apes
Beyond the Stars
Beyond the Time Barrier
Black Cauldron, The
Black Hole, The
Black Magic M-66
Black Moon
Blade Master, The
Blade Runner
Blob, The (1958)

Blob, The (1988)
Blood Beast from Outer Space
Body Snatchers
Boy and His Dog, A
Brain Eaters, The
Brainscan
Brainstorm
Brave New World
Bronx Executioner, The
Brother from Another Planet, The
Buck Rogers in the 25th Century
Buck Rogers: Space Vampire
Cat From Outer Space, The
Cat Women of the Moon
Chandu the Magician
Chariots of the Gods?
Cherry 2000
Chinese Web, The
Chronicles of Narnia—Prince Caspian and the Voyage of the Dawn Treader
Chronicles of Narnia—Silver Chair, The
Chronicles of Narnia—The Lion, the Witch and the Wardrobe,
Chronopolis
Circuitry Man
City Beneath the Sea
City Limits
Class of Nuke 'Em High
Clockwork Orange, A
Close Encounters of the Third Kind
Cocoon
Cocoon: The Return
Colossus of New York, The
Colossus: The Forbin Project
Communion
Conquest
Conquest of Space
Conquest of the Earth
Conquest of the Planet of the Apes
Cosmic Eye, The
Cosmic Man, The
Crack in the World
Crash and Burn
Crawling Eye, The
Creation of the Humanoids
Creature
Creature From the Haunted Sea
Creeping Unknown, The
Critters
Critters 2
Cyborg
Daleks—Invasion Earth 2150 A.D.
Damnation Alley
Dark Crystal, The
Dark Side of the Moon, The
Dark Star
D.A.R.Y.L.
Day of the Triffids, The
Day the Earth Caught Fire, The
Day the Earth Stood Still, The
Day the World Ended, The
Dead End Drive-In
Deadly Friend
Deadly Mantis, The
Deathstalker
Deathstalker II—Duel of the Titans
Deathstalker III
Deathstalker IV
Deathwatch
Deep Space
DeepStar Six
Def-Con 4
Demon Pond
Demon Seed
Destination Moon
Dinosaurus!
Disaster in Time
Doctor Mordrid—Master of the Unknown
Dog Soldier: Shadows of the Past
Dr. Cyclops
Dr. Goldfoot and the Girl Bombs
Dr. Strange
Dr. Who and the Daleks
Dragonslayer
Dreamscape
Dune
Dungeonmaster, The
Duplicates
Earth vs. the Flying Saucers
Earth vs. the Spider
Eegah!
El Mundo Del Talisman
Electronic Monster, The
Embryo
Empire of the Ants
Empire Strikes Back, The
Encounter at Raven's Gate
Enemy Mine
Equinox
Escape from the Planet of the Apes
Escape to Witch Mountain
Escapes
E.T. The Extra-Terrestrial
Ewok Adventure, The
Excalibur
Explorers
Fabulous World of Jules Verne, The
Fahrenheit 451
Fantastic Invasion of Planet Earth
Fantastic Planet
Fantastic Voyage
Final Combat, The
Final Countdown, The
Final Executioner, The
Fire and Ice
Fire in the Sky
Fire Maidens of Outer Space
Firebird 2015 A.D.
First Man into Space
First Men in the Moon
First Spaceship on Venus
Five Million Years to Earth
Flame Barrier, The
Flash Gordon
Flash, The
Flesh Eaters, The
Flight of the Navigator
Flight That Disappeared, The
Flight to Mars
Fly, The
Flying Saucer, The
Forbidden Planet
Forbidden World
Forbidden Zone
Fortress
4 D Man
Four Sided Triangle
Freejack
From Hell It Came
From the Earth to the Moon
Frozen Dead, The
Future Cop
Future Hunters
Future Shock
Future Zone
Futurekick
Futureworld
Galaxina
Galaxy Express
Galaxy Invader, The
Game of Survival
Gamera—The Invincible
Gamma People, The
Ganjasaurus Rex
Gas-s-s-s
Gawain and the Green Night
Gemini Man
Ghidrah: The Three-Headed Monster
Giant Claw, The
Giant from the Unknown
Giant of Metropolis, The
Giant Spider Invasion, The
Gigantis, the Fire Monster
Girl from Mars, The
Girl, the Gold Watch and Dynamite, The
Girl, the Gold Watch and Everything, The
Glitterball, The
Godzilla, King of the Monsters
Godzilla 1985
Godzilla vs. Biolante
Godzilla vs. Gigan
Godzilla vs. Mechagodzilla
Godzilla vs. Megalon
Godzilla vs. Monster Zero
Godzilla vs. Mothra
Godzilla vs. the Sea Monster
Godzilla vs. the Smog Monster
Godzilla's Revenge
Gor
Gorath
Gorgo
Great Big World and Little Children, The
Green Hornet, The
H-Man, The
Half-Human
Hands of Steel

Hangar 18
Heavy Metal
Hell Comes to Frogtown
Hercules Against the Moon Men
Hidden, The
Hidden II, The
Hideaway
Hideous Sun Demon, The
Highlander
Highlander II: The Quickening
Highlander: The Final Dimension
Hitch in Time, A
Hitchhiker's Guide to the Galaxy
Hitchhiker's Guide to the Galaxy, Making of, The
Hobbit, The
Homewrecker
Horror Planet
Horrors of the Red Planet
Hu-Man
Human Duplicators, The
Human Vapor, The
Humanoid Defender
Hyper Sapien—People from Another Star
I-Man
I Married a Monster from Outer Space
Idaho Transfer
Illustrated Man, The
Immortal, The
Impossible Voyage, The
In the Aftermath
Incredible Petrified World, The
Incredible Shrinking Man, The
Infra-Man
Interface
Into the West
Intruders
Invader
Invaders from Mars (1953)
Invaders from Mars (1986)
Invaders—Volume I
Invasion
Invasion of the Animal People
Invasion of the Bee Girls
Invasion of the Girl Snatchers
Invasion of the Neptune Men
Invasion of the Saucer Men
Invasion, U.S.A.
Invisible Boy, The
Invisible Invaders
Invisible Man, The
Invisible Monster, The
Invisible Woman, The
Ironmaster
Island of the Burning Doomed
It Came from Beneath the Sea
It Came from Outer Space
It Conquered the World
It! The Terror from Beyond Space
Jack the Giant Killer
Jitters, The
Journey to the Beginning of Time
Journey to the Center of the Earth, The
Journey to the Center of Time
Journey to the Far Side of the Sun
Journey to the Seventh Planet
Jungle, The
Killer Klowns from Outer Space
Killers from Space
King Dinosaur
King Kong Lives
King Kong vs. Godzilla
King of the Rocket Men
Knights
Kronos
Laboratory
Labyrinth
Land of Doom
Land of Faraway, The
Land That Time Forgot
Land Unknown, The
Last of the Warriors
Last Starfighter, The
Last Woman on Earth, The
Lathe of Heaven, The
Latitude Zero
Lawless Land, The
Lawnmower Man, The
Le Dernier Combat
Legend
Legend of Big Foot, The
Legend of the White Horse
Lensman
Lifeforce
Lifepod
Light Years
Lightblast
Link
Logan's Run
Lord of the Rings, The
Lords of the Deep
Lost Continent, The
Lost World
Lost World, The
Loves of Hercules, The
Mac and Me
Maciste in Hell
Mad Max
Mad Max Beyond Thunderdome
Magic Sword, The
Magnetic Monster, The
Man Beast
Man Called Rage, A
Man from Atlantis
Man from Planet X, The
Man Of Destiny
Man Who Fell to Earth, The
Man Who Haunted Himself, The
Man Who Lived Again, The
Man Who Lived Twice, The
Man with the Power, The
Man with the Transplanted Brain
Mandroid
Maniac Warriors
Marooned
Mars Needs Women
Martian Chronicles, The
Massacre In Dinosaur Valley
Master of the World (1961)
Master of the World (1976)
Maximum Thrust
MD Geist—The Most Dangerous Ever
Merlin
Mermaid Forest
Message from Space
Metallica
Metalstorm—The Destruction of Jared-Syn
Metamorphosis: The Alien Factor
Meteor
Meteor Monster
Metropolis
Millennium
Mind Benders, The
Mind of Mr. Soames, The
Mindwarp
Miracle Mile
Misfits of Science
Missile to the Moon
Mission Galactica: The Cylon Attack
Mission Mars
Mission Stardust
Mister Rossi Looks for Happiness
Mistress of The World
Mole People, The
Monitors, The
Monkey House
Monolith
Monolith Monsters, The
Monster a Go-Go
Monster from a Prehistoric Planet
Monster from Green Hell
Monster From the Ocean Floor, The
Monster High
Monster Island
Moon 44
Moon Pilot
Moontrap
Mothra
Mutant Hunt
My Science Project
Mysterians, The
Mysterious Doctor Satan
Mysterious Island
Mysterious Island of Beautiful Women
Mysterious Satellite, The
Mysterious Two
Navigator, The: A Medieval Odyssey
Nemesis
Neon City
Neverending Story, The
Neverending Story II: The Next Chapter, The
Next One, The
Night Gallery
Night of the Blood Beast
Night of the Comet

Night of the Lepus
Night Slaves
Night the World Exploded, The
Nightflyers
Ninth Heart, The
No Escape
Northstar
Not of This Earth
Nothing Venture
Nukie
Octaman
Omega Man, The
On the Comet
Operation Ganymed
Outbreak
Outland
Overdrawn At The Memory Bank
Panic in Year Zero!
Parts: The Clonus Horror
Peacemaker
People, The
Peppermint Rose
Phantom Treehouse, The
Phase IV
Phoenix The Warrior
Pirates of Dark Water, The—The Saga Begins
Plan 9 from Outer Space
Planet of the Apes
Planet of the Vampires
Power, The
Prehysteria!
Princess and the Goblin, The
Project A-Ko
Project: Alien
Project: Shadowchaser
Prototype X29A
Quarantine
Queen of Blood
Queen of Outer Space
Quest for Love
Quiet Earth, The
Radioactive Dreams
Raiders of Atlantis
Ravagers
Ray Bradbury Chronicles: The Martian Episodes
Red Planet Mars
Remote
Reptilicus
Resurrection of Zachary Wheeler, The
Return of Swamp Thing
Return of the Fly, The
Return of the Jedi, The
Robert A. Heinlein's The Puppet Masters
Robinson Crusoe on Mars
Robocop
Robocop 2
Robocop 3
Robot Jox
Robot Wars
Rocket Ship X-M
Rocket to Nowhere
Rodan
Rollerball
Runaway
Running Against Time
Running Man, The
Sand Castle, The
Santa Claus Conquers the Martians
Satan Bug, The
Satan's Satellites
Saturn 3
Scanner Cop
7 Faces of Dr. Lao
Shadowzone
She (1935)
She (1965)
She (1983)
Silence of Dr. Evans, The
Silent Running
Sisterhood, The
Skeeter
Slipstream
Slithis
Solar Crisis
Solaris
Something Wicked This Way Comes
Son of Godzilla
Son of Kong, The
Soylent Green
Space Camp
Space Children, The
Space Firebird
Space 1999: Alien Attack
Space 1999: Journey Through Black Sun
Space 1999—Vol. 1—Voyager's Return
Space Ninja—Sword of the Space Ark
Space Raiders
Spacehunter: Adventures in the Forbidden Zone
Spidcrman: The Deadly Dust
Split
Split Second
Star Crystal
Star Knight
Star Quest
Star Trek—Episode 1: The Cage
Star Trek—Episode 2: Where No Man Has Gone Before
Star Trek—Episode 3: The Corbomite Manuever
Star Trek—Episode 4: Mudd's Women
Star Trek—Episode 5: The Enemy Within
Star Trek—Episode 6: The Man Trap
Star Trek—Episode 7: The Naked Time
Star Trek—Episode 8: Charlie X
Star Trek—Episode 9: Balance of Terror
Star Trek—Episode 10: What Are Little Girls Made Of
Star Trek—Episode 11: Dagger of The Mind
Star Trek—Episode 12: Miri
Star Trek—Episode 13: The Conscience of the King
Star Trek—Episode 14: The Galileo Seven
Star Trek—Episode 15: Court Martial
Star Trek—Episode 16: The Menagerie, Parts I and II
Star Trek—Episode 17: Shore Leave
Star Trek—Episode 18: The Squire of Gothos
Star Trek—Episode 19: Arena
Star Trek—Episode 20: The Alternative Factor
Star Trek—Episode 21: Tomorrow is Yesterday
Star Trek—Episode 22: Return of the Archons
Star Trek—Episode 23: A Taste of Armageddon
Star Trek—Episode 24: Space Seed
Star Trek—Episode 25: This Side of Paradise
Star Trek—Episode 26: The Devil in the Dark
Star Trek—Episode 27: Errand of Mercy
Star Trek—Episode 28: The City on the Edge of Forever
Star Trek—Episode 29: Operation-Annihilate
Star Trek—Episode 30: Catspaw
Star Trek—Episode 31: Metamorphosis
Star Trek—Episode 32: Friday's Child
Star Trek—Episode 33: Who Mourns for Adonis
Star Trek—Episode 34: Amok Time
Star Trek—Episode 35: The Doomsday Machine
Star Trek—Episode 36: Wolf in the Fold
Star Trek—Episode 37: The Changeling
Star Trek—Episode 38: The Apple
Star Trek—Episode 39: Mirror, Mirror
Star Trek—Episode 40: The Deadly Years
Star Trek—Episode 41: I. Mudd
Star Trek—Episode 42: The Trouble With Tribbles
Star Trek—Episode 43: Bread and Circuses
Star Trek—Episode 44: Journey to Babel
Star Trek—Episode 45: A Private Little War
Star Trek—Episode

WESTERN

Gallant Bess
Against a Crooked Sky
Al Jennings of Oklahoma
Alamo, The
Alamo, The—Thirteen Days to Glory
Albuquerque
Along the Great Divide
Alvarez Kelly
Ambush
Ambush at Cimarron Pass
Ambush at Tomahawk Gap
American Empire
Angel and the Badman
Angel in Exile
Animal Called Man, An
Animals, The
Annie Oakley
Antonio das Mortes
Apache
Apache Ambush
Apache Drums
Apache Gold
Apache Rifles
Apache Territory
Apache Uprising
Apache War Smoke
Apache Warrior
Apache Woman
Appaloosa, The
Arizona
Arizona Kid, The
Arizona Raiders
Arizona Raiders, The
Arrow in the Dust
Arrowhead
At Gunpoint
Avenging, The
Backlash
Bad Bascomb
Bad Day at Black Rock
Bad Girls
Bad Man of Brimstone
Bad Man, The
Bad Man's River
Bad Men of Missouri
Bad Men of Tombstone
Badge of Marshal Brennan, The
Badlanders, The
Badlands of Dakota
Badman's Country
Badman's Territory
Baker's Hawk
Ballad of a Gunfighter
Ballad of Cable Hogue, The
Ballad of Gregorio Cortez, The
Ballad of Josie, The
Bandido
Bandolero
Barbarosa
Barbary Coast Gent
Barbary Coast, The
Baron of Arizona, The
Barquero
Barricade
Battle at Apache Pass, The
Battle of Rogue River
Belle Le Grand
Belle Starr (1941)
Belle Starr (1980)
Belle Starr's Daughter
Bells of Rosarita
Bells of San Angelo
Bells of San Fernando
Bend of the River
Best of the Badmen
Between God, the Devil and a Winchester
Beyond the Law
Big Cat, The
Big Country, The
Big Hand for the Little Lady, A
Big Jake
Big Sky, The
Big Trail, The
Big Trees, The
Billy the Kid
Billy Two Hats
Bite the Bullet
Bitter Creek
Black Bart
Black Dakotas, The
Black Horse Canyon
Black Patch
Black Spurs
Black Whip, The
Blackjack Ketchum, Desperado
Blindman
Blood Arrow
Blood on the Arrow
Blood on the Moon
Blood Red
Blood River
Blue
Bonanza: The Next Generation
Boot Hill
Boots And Saddles
Border Phantom
Border River
Border Shootout
Born to the West
Boss Nigger
Bounty Killer, The
Boy from Oklahoma, The
Branded
Brass Legend, The
Bravados, The
Brave Warrior
Breakheart Pass
Brighty of the Grand Canyon
Brimstone
Broken Arrow
Broken Lance
Broken Land, The
Bronco Buster
Brothers O'Toole, The
Buchanan Rides Alone
Buck and the Preacher
Buckeye and Blue
Buckskin
Buckskin Frontier
Buffalo Bill
Buffalo Bill and the Indians
Bugles in the Afternoon
Bullet for a Badman
Bullet for Sandoval, A
Bullet for the General, A
Bullet is Waiting, A
Bullwhip
Burning Hills, The
Bushwackers, The
Butch and Sundance: The Early Days
Butch Cassidy and the Sundance Kid
Cahill—United States Marshal
Calamity Jane and Sam Bass
California
California Conquest
Campbell's Kingdom
Cannon for Cordoba
Canyon Crossroads
Canyon Passage
Canyon River
Captain Apache
Carson City
Cast a Long Shadow
Cat Ballou
Catlow
Cattle Annie and Little Britches
Cattle Drive
Cattle Empire
Cattle King
Cattle Queen of Montana
Cattle Town
Cavalier, The
Cavalry Scout
Cave of Outlaws
Charge at Feather River, The
Charley One-Eye
Charro!
Chato's Land
Cherokee Strip
Cheyenne
Cheyenne Autumn
Cheyenne Social Club, The
Chief Crazy Horse
China 9, Liberty 37
Chino
Chisum
Christmas Kid, The
Christmas Mountain
Chuka
Cimarron (1931)
Cimarron (1960)
Cimarron Kid, The
City of Bad Men
Climb an Angry Mountain
Cole Younger, Gunfighter
Colorado Territory
Colt .45
Column South
Comanche
Comanche Station
Comanche Territory
Comancheros, The
Comes a Horseman
Comin' at Ya!
Command, The
Conagher
Conquering Horde, The
Copper Canyon
Coroner Creek
Count Your Bullets
Courage of the West
Covered Wagon, The
Cowboy
Cowboy Canteen
Cowboys, The
Cripple Creek
Crossfire
Cry Blood, Apache
Culpepper Cattle Co., The
Custer of the West
Dakota
Dakota Incident
Dallas
Daniel Boone, Trail Blazer
Dark Command
Davy Crockett and

the River Pirates
Davy Crockett, Indian Scout
Davy Crockett, King of the Wild Frontier
Dawn at Socorro
Day of Fury, A
Day of the Bad Man
Day of the Outlaw
Deadly Companions, The
Deadly Trackers, The
Deaf Smith and Johnny Ears
Death of a Gunfighter
Decision at Sundown
Desert Fury
Desperadoes, The
Desperados, The
Destry
Destry Rides Again
Dirty Dingus Magee
Disciple, The
Distant Drums
Distant Trumpet, A
Doc
Dodge City
Domino Kid, The
Donner Pass—The Road to Survival
Don't Turn the Other Cheek
Doolins of Oklahoma, The
Down Dakota Way
Dragon Wells Massacre
Drango
Draw!
Drum Beat
Duchess and the Dirtwater Fox, The
Dude Ranger, The
Duel at Apache Wells
Duel at Diablo
Duel at Silver Creek, The
Duel in the Sun
Eagle's Brood, The
Eagle's Wing
Edge of Eternity
El Condor
El Diablo
El Dorado
End of the Trail (1932)
End of the Trail (1936)
Escape from Fort Bravo
Eye for an Eye, An
Eyes of Texas
Face of a Fugitive
Face to Face
False Colors
False Paradise
Fangs of Fate
Far Country, The
Far Frontier, The
Fastest Gun Alive, The
Fiend Who Walked the West, The
Fighting Caravans
Fighting Frontier
Fighting Gringo, The
Fighting Lawman, The
Fighting Man of the Plains
Fighting Ranger, The
Fighting Stallion, The
Firecreek
First Texan, The
Fistful of Dollars, A
5 Card Stud
Five Guns West
Five Man Army, The
Flame of Barbary Coast
Flame of the West
Flaming Star
For a Few Dollars More
Forbidden Trails
Fort Apache
Fort Bowie
Fort Defiance
Fort Massacre
Fort Osage
Fort Utah
Fort Vengeance
Fort Worth
Forty Guns
Four Eyes and Six-Guns
Four Faces West
Four for Texas
Four Guns to the Border
Four Rode Out
Frenchie
From Hell to Texas
From Noon Till Three
Frontier Gal
Frontier Hellcat
Frontier Horizon
Frontier Marshal
Frontier Outpost
Frontiersman, The
Fugitive from Sonora
Furies, The
Fury at Furnace Creek
Fury at Gunsight Pass
Fury at Showdown
Gallant Legion, The
Galloping Thru
Gambler from Natchez, The
Gambler's Choice
Garden of Evil
Gatling Gun, The
Gentle Annie
Geronimo (1939)
Geronimo (1962)
Geronimo (1993)
Geronimo: An American Legend
Ghost Town Law
Ghost Town Renegades
Ghost Valley
Glory Guys, The
God Forgives, I Don't
God's Country
God's Gun
Goin' South
Gold Is Where You Find It
Golden Stallion, The
Golden West, The
Good Day for a Hanging
Good Guys and the Bad Guys, The
Good, the Bad, and the Ugly, The
Gore Vidal's Billy the Kid
Grand Duel, The
Grayeagle
Great Day in the Morning
Great Gundown, The
Great Jesse James Raid, The
Great K&A Train Robbery, The
Great Man's Lady, The
Great Meadow, The
Great Missouri Raid, The
Great Northfield, Minnesota Raid, The
Great Sioux Massacre, The
Great Sioux Uprising
Great Treasure Hunt, The
Grey Fox, The
Gun Battle at Monterey
Gun Brothers
Gun Code
Gun Duel in Durango
Gun for a Coward
Gun Fury
Gun Glory
Gun Hawk, The
Gun Riders
Gun That Won the West, The
Gun the Man Down
Gunfight, A
Gunfight at Comanche Creek
Gunfight at Dodge City, The
Gunfight at the O.K. Corral
Gunfight in Abilene
Gunfighter, The
Gunfighters
Gunfighters, The
Gunfire
Gunfire at Indian Gap
Gunman's Walk
Gunmen from Laredo
Gunmen of the Rio Grande
Gunpoint
Guns in the Dark
Guns of a Stranger
Guns of Fort Petticoat, The
Guns of the Magnificent Seven
Gunsight Ridge
Gunslinger
Gunsmoke in Tucson
Gunsmoke: Return to Dodge
Gunsmoke: The Last Apache
Half-Breed, The
Hallelujah Trail, The
Halliday Brand, The
Hands Across The Border
Hang 'em High
Hanging Tree, The
Hangman, The
Hangman's Knot
Hannah Lee
Hannie Caulder
Hard Man, The
Hardcase
Harlem Rides the Range
Harry Tracy, Desperado
Haunted Gold
Haunted Ranch
Have A Good Funeral, My Friend
Hawken's Breed
He Rides Tall
Heart of Arizona
Heart of the Golden West
Heart of The Rio Grande
Heart of the Rockies
Heart of the West
Heartland
Hearts of the West
Heaven Only Knows
Heaven with a Gun
Heaven's Gate
Hell Bent for Leather

Hell Canyon Outlaws
Helldorado
Heller in Pink Tights
Hellfire
Hell's Crossroads
Hell's Heroes
Hell's Hinges
Heritage of the Desert (1933)
Heritage of the Desert (1939)
Heroes of the Hills
Hiawatha
Hidden Gold
High Lonesome
High Noon
High Noon, Part II: The Return of Will Kane
High Plains Drifter
Hills Run Red, The
Hired Gun, The
Hired Hand, The
His Brother's Ghost
His Fighting Blood
Hit The Saddle
Hitched
Hittin' The Trail
Hollywood Cowboy
Hombre
Home in Oklahoma
Hondo
Honkers, The
Honky Tonk
Hopalong Cassidy
Hopalong Cassidy Returns
Hopalong Cassidy Rides Again
Hoppy Serves a Writ
Hoppy's Holiday
Horizons West
Horse Named Comanche, A
Horse Soldiers, The
Hostile Guns
Hot Lead
Hot Lead & Cold Feet
Hour of the Gun
How the West Was Won
Hunting Party, The
Hurricane Express, The
I Married Wyatt Earp
Idaho
In Old Amarillo
In Old Arizona
In Old Caliente
In Old California
In Old Montana
In Old New Mexico
In Old Santa Fe
Incident at Phantom Hill
Independence
Indian Agent
Indian Fighter, The
Indian Paint
Indian Uprising
Invasion of Johnson County, The
Invitation to a Gunfighter
Iron Mistress, The
Iron Sheriff, The
Iroquois Trail, The
Jack McCall, Desperado
Jack Slade
Jayhawkers, The
Jeremiah Johnson
Jesse James
Jesse James vs. the Daltons
Jesse James's Women
Jessi's Girls
Joe Kidd
Johnny Concho
Johnny Guitar
Johnny Hamlet
Johnny Reno
Johnny Yuma
Jory
Joshua
Journey Through Rosebud
Jubal
Jubilee Trail
Judge Roy Bean
Just Tony
Kangaroo
Kansan, The
Kansas Cyclone
Kansas Pacific
Kansas Raiders
Kansas Territory
Kenny Rogers as The Gambler
Kentuckian, The
Kentucky Rifle
Kid Vengeance
King and Four Queens, The
King of the Pecos
King of the Texas Rangers
Kit Carson
Lady from Cheyenne
Land Raiders
Last Challenge, The
Last Command, The
Last Days of Frank and Jesse James, The
Last Frontier, The
Last Gun, The
Last Hard Men, The
Last Hunt, The
Last of the Comanches, The
Last Outlaw, The
Last Outpost, The
Last Posse, The
Last Rebel, The
Last Sunset, The
Last Train From Gun Hill
Last Wagon, The
Law and Jake Wade, The
Law and Order (1932)
Law and Order (1953)
Law of the Land
Law of the Lawless
Law of the Pampas
Lawless Breed, The
Lawless Eighties, The
Lawless Frontier
Lawless Nineties, The
Lawless Range
Lawless Street, A
Lawman
Leather Burners
Left-Handed Gun, The
Legend of Alfred Packer, The
Legend of Earl Durand, The
Legend of Frenchie King, The
Legend of Jedediah Carver, The
Legend of Nigger Charley, The
Legend of the Lone Ranger, The
Legend of Walks Far Woman, The
Legends of the Fall
Life and Times of Judge Roy Bean, The
Lightning Carson Rides Again
Little Big Horn
Little Big Man
Little Moon and Jud McGraw
Lone Hand, The
Lone Justice
Lone Ranger and the Lost City of Gold, The
Lone Ranger, The
Lone Star
Lone Texan
Lone Wolf McQuade
Lonely Are the Brave
Lonely Man, The
Lonesome Dove
Long Riders, The
Look Out Sister
Lucky Texan, The
Lusty Men, The
Macahans, The
Macho Callahan
Mackenna's Gold
Mackintosh and T.J.
Madron
Magnificent Seven Ride!, The
Magnificent Seven, The
Mail Order Bride
Major Dundee
Man Alone, A
Man Behind the Gun, The
Man Called Gannon, A
Man Called Horse, A
Man Called Sledge, A
Man from Bitter Ridge, The
Man from Colorado, The
Man from Dakota, The
Man from Del Rio, The
Man from Galveston, The
Man from God's Country
Man from Laramie, The
Man from Monterey
Man from the Alamo, The
Man from Utah, The
Man in the Saddle
Man in the Shadow
Man of Conquest
Man of the Forest
Man of The Frontier
Man of the West
Man Who Loved Cat Dancing, The
Man Who Shot Liberty Valance, The
Man with the Gun, The
Man Without a Star
Manhunt, The
Many Rivers to Cross
Marauders, The (1947)
Marauders, The (1955)
Marksman, The
Marshal of Amarillo
Marshal of Cedar Rock
Marshal of Gunsmoke
Marshal of Mesa City, The

Marshal of Reno
Marshal's Daughter, The
Masked Rider, The
Massacre (1934)
Massacre (1956)
Massacre At Fort Holman
Massacre River
Master Gunfighter, The
Masterson of Kansas
Maverick
Maverick Queen, The
McLintock!
McMasters, The
Meanest Men in the West, The
Melody Ranch
Men of Texas
Mercenary, The
Mexicali Rose
Minnesota Clay
Minute to Pray, a Second to Die, A
Miracle of the Hills, The
Miracle Rider, The
Missouri Breaks, The
Missourians, The
Montana (1950)
Montana (1990)
Montana Belle
Montana Moon
Monte Walsh
Moonlighter, The
More Dead Than Alive
More Wild, Wild West
Mountain Men, The
Mr. Horn
Murder on the Yukon
My Darling Clementine
My Name Is Nobody
My Pal, the King
My Pal Trigger
Mysterious Avenger, The
Mysterious Desperado, The
Mysterious Rider, The (1933)
Mysterious Rider, The (1938)
Mystery of the Hooded Horsemen, The
Mystery Ranch
Naked Hills, The
Naked in the Sun
Naked Spur, The
Narrow Trail, The
Navajo
Navajo Joe
'Neath the Arizona Skies
'Neath the Canadian Skies
Nevada
Nevada Smith
Nevadan, The
New Lion of Sonora, The
Night of the Grizzly
Night Passage
Night Time in Nevada
Nine Lives of Elfego Baca
No Name on the Bullet
Noose for a Gunman
North of the Great Divide
Oh! Susanna
Oklahoma Annie
Oklahoma Crude
Oklahoma Kid, The
Oklahoma Territory
Oklahoma Woman, The
Oklahoman, The
Old Barn Dance, The
Old Corral, The
On the Old Spanish Trail
Once Upon a Horse
Once Upon a Time in the West
One-Eyed Jacks
One Foot in Hell
100 Rifles
One Man Justice
One More Train to Rob
Only the Valiant
Oregon Passage
Oregon Trail, The (1959)
Oregon Trail, The (1976)
Origin Of The Lone Ranger, The
Outcast, The
Outlaw Country
Outlaw Deputy, The
Outlaw—Josey Wales, The
Outlaw, The
Outlaw Women
Outlaw's Daughter, The
Outlaws of Texas
Outlaws of the Prairie
Outlaw's Son
Outrage, The
Overland Mail
Overland Pacific
Overland Stage Raiders
Overland Telegraph
Ox-Bow Incident, The
Painted Desert, The
Painted Stallion, The
Painted Trail, The
Pale Rider
Pals of the Pecos
Pals of the Saddle
Panamint's Badman
Pancho Villa
Panhandle
Paper Orchid
Paradise Canyon
Parson and the Outlaw, The
Parson of Panamint, The
Partners of the Plains
Passage West
Pat Garrett and Billy the Kid
Perilous Journey, A
Pillars of the Sky
Pistol for Ringo, A
Plainsman, The
Plunderers, The (1948)
Plunderers, The (1960)
Poker Alice
Pony Express
Pony Express Rider, The
Pony Soldier
Posse (1975)
Posse (1993)
Posse from Hell
Powder River
Professionals, The
Proud Ones, The
Public Cowboy No. 1
Pursued
Quick and the Dead, The (1987)
Quick and the Dead, The (1995)
Quick Gun, The
Quigley Down Under
Rage at Dawn
Raiders, The (1952)
Raiders, The (1963)
Rails Into Laramie
Rainbow Trail, The
Ramona
Ramrod
Rancho Notorious
Randy Rides Alone
Rangers of Fortune
Rare Breed, The
Raton Pass
Raw Edge
Rawhide (1938)
Rawhide (1951)
Rawhide Trail, The
Rawhide Years, The
Reason to Live, a Reason to Die, A
Rebel in Town
Red-Headed Stranger
Red Mountain
Red River
Red River Valley
Red Rope, The
Red Stallion in the Rockies, The
Red Sun
Redhead and the Cowboy, The
Redhead from Wyoming, The
Renegade Ranger
Reno
Requiem for a Gunfighter
Return of a Man Called Horse, The
Return of Frank James, The
Return of Jesse James, The
Return of the Bad Men
Return of the Magnificent Seven
Return of the Texan
Return to Snowy River
Revengers, The
Revolt at Fort Laramie
Reward, The
Ride Back, The
Ride Clear of Diablo
Ride Him, Cowboy
Ride Lonesome
Ride on Vaquero
Ride, Ranger, Ride
Ride, Tenderfoot, Ride
Ride the High Country
Ride to Hangman's Tree, The
Rider of Death Valley
Riders in the Sky
Riders of Destiny
Riders of the Badlands
Riders of the Black Hills
Riders of the Deadline
Riders of the Desert
Riders of the Purple Sage
Riders of the Range
Riders of the Rockies
Riders of the Whistling Skull
Ridin' Down the Canyon
Ridin' for Justice
Riding High

Riding the Sunset Trail
Riding the Wind
Riding Tornado, The
Riding West
Rim of the Canyon
Rio Bravo
Rio Conchos
Rio Grande
Rio Grande Raiders
Rio Lobo
River's End (1931)
River's End (1940)
Road to Denver, The
Robbers of the Range
Robber's Roost
Robin Hood of El Dorado, The
Robin of Texas
Rocky Mountain
Rocky Mountain Mystery
Roll on Texas Moon
Roll, Wagons, Roll
Rooster Cogburn
Rootin' Tootin' Rhythm
Rose of Cimarron
Rough Night in Jericho
Rough Riders' Roundup
Roughshod
Rounders, The
Roundup Time in Texas
Run for Cover
Rustlers of Devil's Canyon
Sabata
Sacketts, The
Sacred Ground
Saddle the Wind
Saddle Tramp
Saga Of Death Valley
Salt Lake Raiders
Sam Whiskey
San Antonio
San Antonio Kid, The
Sandflow
Santa Fe Passage
Santa Fe Stampede
Santa Fe Trail
Santee
Savage Guns, The
Savage Pampas
Savage, The
Scalps
Searchers, The
Seminole
September Gun
Seven Men from Now
Seventh Cavalry
Shadow of Chikara, The
Shadow Riders, The
Shalako
Shane
She Came to the Valley
She Wore a Yellow Ribbon
Sheepman, The
Shenandoah
Shepherd of the Hills
Sheriff of Cimarron
Shoot the Living Pray for the Dead
Shooting Straight
Shooting, The
Shootist, The
Short Grass
Shotgun
Showdown
Showdown at Abilene
Showdown at Boot Hill
Showdown at Williams Creek
Showdown, The
Siege at Red River, The
Sierra Baron
Sierra Sue
Silent Conflict
Silent Tongue
Silver City
Silver City Raiders
Silver Dollar
Silver Lode
Silver on the Sage
Silver River
Silver Spurs
Silver Trails
Silver Whip, The
Silverado
Simon Bolivar
Sing, Cowboy, Sing
Sinister Journey
Sitting Bull
Six Gun Law
Six Shootin' Sheriff
Soldier Blue
Sombrero Kid, The
Somewhere in Sonora
Son of a Badman
Son of Belle Starr
Son of the Morning Star
Son of Zorro
Song of Arizona
Song of Nevada
Song of Texas
Song of the Buckaroo
Song of the Trail
Sons of Katie Elder, The
Sons of the Pioneers
South of St. Louis
Spoilers, The (1930)
Spoilers, The (1942)
Spoilers, The (1955)
Springfield Rifle
Springtime in the Sierras
Stage to Thunder Rock
Stagecoach (1939)
Stagecoach (1966)
Stagecoach (1986)
Stagecoach Buckaroo
Stagecoach to Dancers' Rock
Stagecoach To Denver
Stand Up and Fight
Standing Tall
Star in the Dust
Star Packer, The
Station West
Strange Lady in Town
Stranger In Paso Bravo, A
Stranger on Horseback
Stranger Who Wore a Gun, The
Stranger's Gold
Streets of Laredo
Talisman, The
Tall in the Saddle
Tall Men, The
Tall T, The
Taza, Son of Cochise
Tennessee's Partner
Tension at Table Rock
Tenting Tonight on the Old Camp Ground
Terror in a Texas Town
Texas Guns
Texas Lady
Texas Ranger, The
Texas Rangers, The (1936)
Texas Rangers, The (1951)
Texas Stampede
Texas Terror
There Was a Crooked Man
These Thousand Hills
They Came to Cordura
They Died With Their Boots On
This Savage Land
Three Faces West
Three Godfathers
Three Godfathers, The
Three Hours to Kill
Three Men from Texas
3:10 to Yuma
Three Violent People
Thunder in the Sun
Thunder Mountain
Thunder Trail
Thunderhoof
Thundering Herd, The
Ticket to Tomahawk, A
Time for Dying, A
Time for Killing, A
Tin Star, The
Tom Horn
Tombstone
Tombstone Canyon
Topeka
Trail of Robin Hood
Trail Riders
Trail Street
Train Robbers, The
Tramplers, The
Treachery Rides the Range
Tribute to a Bad Man
Trouble in Sundown
Trouble in Texas
True Grit
True Story of Jesse James, The
Tucson Raiders
Tumbledown Ranch in Arizona
Tumbleweeds
20 Mule Team
Two-Fisted Sheriff
Two Gun Lady
Two Rode Together
Ulzana's Raid
Under Mexicali Stars
Under Nevada Skies
Under the Tonto Rim
Under Western Skies
Unexpected Guest
Unforgiven
Unforgiven, The
Union Pacific
Untamed
Utah
Valdez Is Coming
Valley of Gwangi
Valley of the Sun
Vera Cruz
Verne Miller
Villa Rides
Violent Men, The
Virginia City
Virginian, The (1929)
Virginian, The (1946)
Viva Villa!
Wackiest Wagon Train in the West,

FAMILY/CHILDREN BY CATEGORY

ACTION

Abdulla the Great
Adventures of Babar
Adventures of Babar—Vol. 2
Adventures of Babar—Vol. 3
Adventures of Ichabod and Mr. Toad, The
Adventures of Sinbad, The
Adventures of Superman
Adventures of Teddy Ruxpin
African Treasure
Aladdin and His Magic Lamp
Alakazam the Great
Amazing Dobermans, The
Archer's Adventure
Baby . . . Secret of the Lost Legend
Batman—The Movie
Black Stallion Returns, The
Black Stallion, The
Blue Fin
Blue Yonder, The
BMX Bandits
Boatniks, The
Bomba and the Elephant Stampede
Bomba and the Jungle Girl
Bomba on Panther Island
Bomba the Jungle Boy
Boy and the Pirates
Boy from Indiana
Brave Little Toaster, The
Brothers Lionheart, The
Bush Christmas
Camel Boy, The
Captain Sinbad
Castle of Cagliostro
Challenge for Robin Hood, A
Challenge to White Fang
Charlie, the Lonesome Cougar
Cloak & Dagger
Cold River
Condorman
Cry in the Wild, A
Daring Dobermans, The
Deerslayer, The (1957)
Deerslayer, The (1978)
Doberman Gang, The
Dr. Syn, Alias the Scarecrow
Ewoks: The Battle for Endor
Fabulous Baron Munchausen, The
Famous Five Get Into Trouble, The
Far From Home: The Adventures of Yellow Dog
Far Off Place, A
Fighting Prince of Donegal, The
Fire in the Stone, The
Five Weeks in a Balloon
Force on Thunder Mountain
Forever Fairytales—Rudyard Kipling
G.I. Joe—The Movie
Gigantor: Volumes 1-3
GoBots: Battle of the Rock Lords
Golden Voyage of Sinbad, The
Great Adventure, The
Great Bear Scare, The
Great Mouse Detective, The
Gulliver's Travels
Beyond the Moon
Hawk Jones
Here Comes the Grump
Heroic Adventures of John the Fearless, The
Hockey Night
Home in Indiana
Homeward Bound: The Incredible Journey
Horse Without a Head, The
In Search of the Castaways
Incredible Journey, The
Island at the Top of the World, The
Jason and the Argonauts
Joniko and the Kush Ta Ta
Kid Colter
Kidnapped
Legend of Black Thunder Mountain, The
Lionheart
Magical Princess Gigi, The
Magical Wonderland
Marvel Comics Video Library
Massarati and the Brain
Matusalem
Medicine Hat Stallion, The
Mighty Jack
Mighty Mouse in the Great Space Chase
My Dog Shep
Mystery Island
Mystery on Bird Island
Never a Dull Moment
New Adventures of Pippi Longstocking, The
Noozles—Adventures in Koalawalla Land
Noozles—Blinky and Pinky's Excellent Adventure
Noozles—Fuzzy Was a Noozle
Noozles—Koala Bear Magic
Noozles—Nuzzling with the Noozles
Off on a Comet
Olly, Olly, Oxen Free
Once A Hero
One Little Indian
Peter Pan
Pickwick Papers
Pinchcliffe Grand Prix
Pippi Longstocking
Rough Waters
7th Voyage of Sinbad, The
Shadow World
Sidekicks
Sign of Zorro, The
Stone Fox
Story of 15 Boys, The
Super Mario Bros.
Sweet Sea
Tall Tale: The Unbelievable Adventures of Pecos Bill
Three Caballeros, The
3 Ninjas
Treasure at the Mill
Treasure of Matecumbe
Twice Upon a Time
Young Dragons—Kung Fu Kids, The
Young Dragons—Kung Fu Kids II, The

COMEDY

Absent Minded Professor, The
Addams Family—Ghost Town
Addams Family—Left in the Lurch
Addams Family, The—Vol. 1
Addams Family, The—Vol. 2
Addams Family, The—Vol. 3
Addams Family, The—Vol. 4

Addams Family, The—Vol. 5
Addams Family, The—Vol. 6
Adventures of a Two-Minute Werewolf, The
Adventures of Bullwhip Griffin, The
Adventures of Droopy Featuring "Wags to Riches," The
Adventures of Milo and Otis, The
Adventures of Ozzie and Harriet, The
American Tail: Fievel Goes West, An
And You Thought Your Parents Were Weird!
Androcles and the Lion
Andy Griffith Show, The
Andy Hardy Comes Home
Andy Hardy Gets Spring Fever
Andy Hardy Meets Debutante
Andy Hardy's Blonde Trouble
Andy Hardy's Double Life
Andy Hardy's Private Secretary
Animal Behavior
Animalympics
Apple Dumpling Gang, The
Apple Dumpling Gang Rides Again, The
Bang-Bang Kid, The
Barefoot Executive, The
Barnaby and Me
Bedknobs and Broomsticks
Beethoven
Big Chief, The
Big Top Pee-Wee
Bigfoot
Birds Do It
Blackbeard's Ghost
Bon Voyage!
Bon Voyage Charlie Brown (and Don't Come Back!)
Boy Named Charlie Brown, A
Boy Who Stole a Million, The
Brady Girls Get Married, The
Bugs Bunny/Road Runner Movie, The
Bugs Bunny Superstar
Bugs Bunny's 3rd Movie—1001 Rabbit Tales
Bushbaby, The
Cabbage Patch Kids First Christmas
Canterville Ghost, The (1944)
Canterville Ghost, The (1986)
Charge of the Model Ts, The
Checkers
Chicken Every Sunday
Chips, the War Dog
Circus Clown, The
City Lights
Cool Runnings
Daffy Duck's Movie: Fantastic Island
Daffy Duck's Quackbusters
Devil and Max Devlin, The
Digby—The Biggest Dog in the World
Duck Tales: The Movie—Treasure of the Lost Lamp
Ernest Goes to Camp
Ernest Goes to Jail
Ernest Rides Again
Ernest Saves Christmas
Ernest Scared Stupid
Eyes of the Amaryllis, The
Family Affair, A
Family Circus Christmas, A
Family Circus Easter, A
Family Dog—Enemy Dog/Show Dog
Fantastic World of D.C. Collins, The
Fast Talking
Fe-Fi-Fo-Fun
Felix in Outer Space
Felix the Cat—Movie, The
Felix's Magic Bag of Tricks
Fievel's American Tails Vol. 1—The Gift & A Case of the Hiccups
5,000 Fingers of Dr. T, The
Flintstone Christmas, A
Flintstone Files, The
Flintstones, The
Fluffy
Fox and the Hound, The
Freaky Friday
Freddie as F.R.O.7
From Pluto with Love
Frosty the Snowman
General Spanky
Ghost and Mr. Chicken
Gidget
Gidget Gets Married
Gidget Goes Hawaiian
Gidget Goes to Rome
Gidget Grows Up
Gidget's Summer Reunion
Gnome-Mobile, The
Great Muppet Caper, The
Greyfriars Bobby
Gus
Have Picnic Basket Will Travel
Heavyweights
Henry Aldrich, Boy Scout
Henry Aldrich, Editor
Henry Aldrich for President
Henry Aldrich Gets Glamour
Henry Aldrich Haunts a House
Henry Aldrich Swings It
Henry Aldrich's Little Secret
Henry and Dizzy
Henry, the Rainmaker
Herbie Goes Bananas
Herbie Goes to Monte Carlo
Herbie Rides Again
Here Come the Littles
Here Come the Nelsons
Here Comes Bugs
Here Comes Peter Cottontail
Hero in the Family
Hey Cinderella
Hey There, It's Yogi Bear
Hillbilly Bears
Honey, I Blew Up the Kid
Honey, I Shrunk the Kids
Horse in the Gray Flannel Suit, The
Isn't Life Wonderful!
It Shouldn't Happen to a Dog
Jack and the Beanstalk
Jacob Two-Two Meets the Hooded Fang
Jetsons: The Movie
Jimmy the Kid
John and Julie
Judge Hardy's Children
Kadoyng
Life Begins for Andy Hardy
Little Big League
Little Miss Marker
Little Rascals, The
Looney, Looney, Looney Bugs Bunny Movie, The
Love Bug, The
Love Finds Andy Hardy
Lt. Robin Crusoe, USN
Mad Monster Party?
Magic Adventure
Magic Show, The
Magic Voyage, The
Magnificent Magical Magnet of Santa Mesa, The
Major Payne
Man Called Flintstone, The
Man's Best Friend
Martha's Attic, Vols. 1-6
Matilda
Max Fleischer's Koko The Clown Cartoons
Max Fleischer's Popeye Cartoons
Maxie's World—Dancin' & Romancin'
Maxie's World—Surfs Up In Surfside
Me and the Kid
Mickey Mouse and Donald Duck Cartoons
Mickey Mouse—the Black and White Years, Vol. 1
Million Dollar Duck
Misadventures of Merlin Jones, The
Monkeys, Go Home!
Monkey's Uncle, The
Mooch Goes To

Hollywood
More Roobarb
Mr. Magoo In Sherwood Forest
Mr. Magoo—Man of Mystery
Mr. Magoo—1001 Arabian Nights
Mr. Magoo's Christmas Carol
Mr. Magoo's Story Book
Mr. Robinson Crusoe
Mr. Scoutmaster
Mr. Superinvisible
North
North Avenue Irregulars, The
Not Quite Human
Not Quite Human II
Now You See Him, Now You Don't
Now You See It, Now You Don't
Our Gang
Our Gang Comedies
Ovide And The Gang
Parent Trap, The
Parent Trap II
Parent Trap III
Peck's Bad Boy
Peck's Bad Boy with the Circus
Pinocchio
Pinocchio's Christmas
Pinocchio's Storybook Adventures
Pippi Longstocking—New Adventures of, The
Playful Little Audrey
Popeye
Private Eyes, The
Private War of Major Benson, The
Prize Fighter, The
Puppetoon Movie, The
Purple People Eater
Race for Your Life, Charlie Brown
Return of Jafar, The
Return to Mayberry
Richie Rich
Rover Dangerfield
Sally and Saint Anne
Sammy, the Way-Out Seal
Santa Clause, The
Savannah Smiles
Sesame Street: Big Bird in China
Sesame Street: Big Bird in Japan
Sesame Street Presents Follow That Bird
Shaggy D.A., The
Shaggy Dog, The
Six Pack
Skylark
Smiley
Smiley Gets a Gun
Smurfs and the Magic Flute, The
Smurfs, The
Snoopy, Come Home
Snowball Express
Son of Flubber
Stepmonster
Still Not Quite Human
Stop! Look! and Laugh!
Strongest Man in the World, The
Superdad
Teenage Mutant Ninja Turtles—The Movie
Teenage Mutant Ninja Turtles 2: The Secret of the Ooze
Teenage Mutant Ninja Turtles III
That Darn Cat
Three Wise Fools
Tiki Tiki
Tom and Jerry: The Movie
Trouble With Angels, The
12 Tasks of Asterix, The
Ugly Dachshund, The
Wacky World of Mother Goose, The
Where Angels Go, Trouble Follows
Who Framed Roger Rabbit
Wild and Woody
World's Greatest Athlete, The
Zebra in the Kitchen
Zotz!

CRIME

C.H.O.M.P.S.
Dick Tracy
Dick Tracy Meets Gruesome
Dirt Bike Kid, The
Emil
Emil and the Detectives
Invisible Agent
Mystery of the Third Planet
Sherlock Holmes—Baskerville Curse,The

DRAMA

Adventure in the Hopfields
Adventures of Charlie and Cubby, The
Adventures of Frontier Freemont, The
Adventures of Huck Finn, The
Adventures of Huckleberry Finn
Adventures of Huckleberry Finn, The
Adventures of Huckleberry, Finn, The
Adventures of Mark Twain, The
Adventures of the Wilderness Family, The
Adventures of Tom Sawyer, The
Alan & Naomi
Alice in Wonderland (1933)
Alice in Wonderland (1950)
Alice in Wonderland (1951)
Alice in Wonderland (1985)
All Creatures Great and Small
All I Want for Christmas
All Mine to Give
Almost Angels
Amazing Grace and Chuck
Amazing Mr. Blunden, The
American Tail, An
Amy
And Now Miguel
Anne of Avonlea
Anne of Green Gables (1934)
Anne of Green Gables (1985)
Around the World Under the Sea
Babar: The Movie
Bach and Broccoli
Back to the Forest
Bambi
Bashful Elephant, The
Bear, The
Bear Who Slept through Christmas, The
Bears and I, The
Beauty and the Beast
Beethoven Lives Upstairs
Beezbo
Belstone Fox, The
Beniker Gang, The
Benji
Benji the Hunted
Big Red
Bill: On His Own
Bingo
Birch Interval
Biscuit Eater, The (1940)
Biscuit Eater, The (1972)
Black Beauty (1946)
Black Beauty (1971)
Born Free
Borrowers, The
Boy of the Streets
Boy Ten Feet Tall, A
Brave One, The
Bright Eyes
Call of the Wild
Call of the Wild, The
Candleshoe

Captains Courageous
Care Bears Adventure in Wonderland!, The
Care Bears Movie, The
Care Bears Movie II: A New Generation
Casey's Shadow
Castaway Cowboy, The
Challenge to Lassie
Charley and the Angel
Charlie and the Great Balloon Chase
Charlotte's Web
Cheetah
Chosen, The
Christian the Lion
Christmas Carol, A (1938)
Christmas Carol, A (1951)
Christmas Carol, A (1984)
Christmas Coal Mine Miracle, The
Christmas to Remember, A
Christmas Visitor, The
Cinema Paradiso
Clara's Heart
Clarence and Angel
Clarence, the Cross-Eyed Lion
Come to the Stable
Courage Mountain
Courage of Black Beauty
Crossed Swords
Cry from the Mountain
Cynthia
Danny
Darby O'Gill and the Little People
Dark Horse
Day for Thanks on Waltons' Mountain, A
Daydreamer, The
Decoration Day
Dog of Flanders, A
Dondi
Dorothy in the Land of Oz
Dot and the Bunny
Dream for Christmas, A
Dreamer of Oz, The: The Frank L. Baum Story
Elephant's Child
Family Hour Special—Animal Talk
Family Hour Special—Out of Time
Fangface
FernGully . . . The Last Rainforest
Field of Dreams
Fish Hawk
Flight of Dragons
Flight of the Grey Wolf
Flipper
Flipper's New Adventure
Flipper's Odyssey
Follow Me, Boys!
For the Love of Benji
For the Love of Mike
Forever Fairytales—Brothers Grimm
Forever Fairytales—Charles Perrault
Forever Fairytales—Hans Christian Andersen
Free Willy
Friendly Persuasion
Fun and Fancy Free
Gallant Bess
Gentle Giant
Gift for Heidi, A
Gift of Love, The
Girl Named Sooner, A
Girl of the Limberlost, A
Girl Who Spelled Freedom, The
Git
Glory
Gnomes
Go Tell It on the Mountain
Goin' Home
Golden Goose, The
Golden Hoofs
Golden Seal, The
Good-bye, My Lady
Goodbye, Miss 4th of July
Grandpa
Great Adventure, The
Great Locomotive Chase, The
Green Grass of Wyoming
Gulliver's Travels
Gypsy Colt
Hambone and Hillie
Hand in Hand
Hans Christian Andersen's Day Dreamer
Hansel and Gretel
Happily Ever After
Heidi (1937)
Heidi (1952)
Heidi (1968)
Heidi (1993)
Heidi and Peter
Her First Romance
Here Comes Santa Claus
Hildur and the Magician
Hills of Home, The
Hobo's Christmas, A
Home for Christmas
Home of Our Own, A
Hoppity Goes to Town
Horsemasters, The
House Without a Christmas Tree, A
Huckleberry Finn (1931)
Huckleberry Finn (1939)
Huckleberry Finn (1975)
International Velvet
Island of the Blue Dolphins
Island of the Lost
It Came Upon the Midnight Clear
Jack Frost
Jacob Have I Loved
Joe Panther
John Henry
Johnny Shiloh
Jonathan Livingston Seagull
Joseph and His Brethren
Journey Back to Oz
Journey of Natty Gann, The
Journey to Spirit Island
Judge Hardy and Son
Juggler of Notre Dame, The
Jungle Book
Jungle Book, The
Justin Morgan Had a Horse
Kavik the Wolf Dog
Kid from Left Field, The
Kid from Not So Big, The
Kid from Nowhere, The
Kid Who Loved Christmas, The
Kid with the Broken Halo, The
Kid with the 200 I.Q., The
King of Kings
King of Kings, The
King of the Grizzlies
King of the Wild Stallions
L.A. Bad
La Petite Bande
Lad: A Dog
Land Before Time, The
Lantern Hill
Lassie
Lassie Come Home
Last Flight of Noah's Ark, The
Last of the Red Hot Dragons
Legend of Lobo, The
Legend of Sleepy Hollow, The
Legend of the Northwest
Lies My Father Told Me
Life and Times of Grizzly Adams, The
Light in the Forest, The
Lightning, the White Stallion
Lion King, The
Little Ark, The
Little House on the Prairie
Little Kidnappers, The (1953)
Little Kidnappers, The (1990)
Little Lord Fauntleroy (1936)
Little Lord Fauntleroy (1980)
Little Match Girl, The
Little Men
Little Nemo: Adventures in Slumberland
Little Women (1933)
Little Women (1949)
Little Women (1978)
Little Women (1994)
Littlest Horse Thieves, The
Littlest Outlaw, The
Living Free
Lord Jeff
Lost Angel
Magic Cloak of Oz, The
Magic Legend of the Juggler
Magic of Lassie, The
Magic Pony, The
Magic Snowman, The

Magnet, The
Man and Boy
Man from Snowy River, The
Mark Twain and Me
Martin's Day
Marvelous Land of Oz (1981)
Marvelous Land of Oz (1988)
Marzipan Pig, The
Matt the Gooseboy
Maya
Meet Dr. Christian
Memories of a Fairy Godmother
Mighty Ducks, The
Mighty Moose and the Quarterback Kid
Mighty Treve, The
Miracle Down Under
Miracle in the Wilderness
Miracle of the Heart: A Boys' Town Story
Miracle of the White Stallions
Miracle on 34th Street (1947)
Miracle on 34th Street (1994)
Miss Annie Rooney
Mister Too Little
Misty
Moochie of the Little League
Moon-Spinners, The
Mooncussers
Mountain Family Robinson
Mouse and His Child, The
Mowgli's Brothers
Muppet Christmas Carol, The
My Girl
My Girl 2
My Little Pony—The Movie
My Neighbor Totoro
My Pal, Wolf
My Side of the Mountain
Mystery Mansion
Namu, the Killer Whale
Napoleon and Samantha
National Velvet
Native Land
Nativity, The
Never Cry Wolf
New Adventures of Heidi, The
Night Crossing
Night They Saved Christmas, The
Night Train to Kathmandu, The
Nikki, Wild Dog of the North
No Deposit, No Return
Now and Forever
Nutcracker Fantasy
Of Stars and Men
Old Yeller
Oliver and Co.
On the Right Track
Once Upon a Forest
One and Only, Genuine, Original Family Band, The
One Hundred and One Dalmatians
One Magic Christmas
One of Our Dinosaurs is Missing
One Wish Too Many
Orphan Train, The
Orphans of the Street
Our Little Girl
Outside Chance of Maximilian Glick, The
Outsiders, The
Pagemaster, The
Painted Hills, The
Panda and the Magic Serpent
Patchwork Girl of Oz, The
Perfect Harmony
Perfect Tribute, The
Perri
Peter And The Wolf And Other Tales
Pete's Dragon
Phantom Tollbooth, The
Phar Lap
Pinocchio in Outer Space
Pippi Goes on Board
Pippi in the South Seas
Pippi On The Run
Plague Dogs, The
Point, The
Pollyanna (1920)
Pollyanna (1960)
Prancer
Prince Valiant
Puss in Boots
Quarterback Princess
Quest, The
Railway Children, The
Rapunzel
Rascal
Rascals and Robbers—The Secret Adventures
Raymie
Rebecca of Sunnybrook Farm (1917)
Rebecca of Sunnybrook Farm (1938)
Red Balloon, The
Red Pony, The (1949)
Red Pony, The (1973)
Rescuers Down Under, The
Rescuers, The
Return from Witch Mountain
Return of the King
Return to Oz
Ride a Wild Pony
Ring of Bright Water
Rob Roy, the Highland Rogue
Rudyard Kipling's The Jungle Book
Rumpelstiltskin
Run Wild, Run Free
Running Wild
Sad Horse, The
Safe at Home
Salvage Gang, The
Sand
Sand Fairy, The
Sandlot, The
Sandu Follows the Sun
Santa Claus, The Movie
Saul and David
Savage Sam
Scalawag
Scary Tales
Scruffy
Sea Gypsies, The
Searching for Bobby Fischer
Secret Garden, The (1949)
Secret Garden, The (1987)
Secret Garden, The (1993)
Secret of NIMH, The
Secret of Roan Inish, The
Secret Of The Seal, The
Sequoia
Seven Alone
Seventh Coin, The
Seventh Continent, The
Shoemaker and the Elves, The
Silence Has No Wings
Singing Nun, The
Skippy
Sleeping Beauty (1959)
Sleeping Beauty (1988)
Smith!
Smoke
Smoky
Snow White
Snow White and the Seven Dwarfs
So Dear to My Heart
Son of Lassie
Spencer's Mountain
Spirit of the Eagle
Star Fairies
Story of Robin Hood and His Merrie Men, The
Story of Seabiscuit, The
Stowaway
Strawberry Roan, The
Summer Magic
Summerdog
Sun Comes Up, The
Sundowners, The
Super Seal
Susannah of the Mounties
Sweet 15
Swiss Family Robinson (1940)
Swiss Family Robinson (1960)
Sword and the Rose, The
Sylvester
Sylvia and the Phantom
Tale of Four Wishes, A
Tarka the Otter
Tenth Avenue Angel
Thanksgiving Promise, The
Their Only Chance
Thief of Bagdad, The
Third Man on the Mountain
Those Calloways
Three Lives of Thomasina, The
3 Worlds of Gulliver, The
Thumbelina (1970)
Thumbelina (1994)
Thunderhead—Son of Flicka
Tiger Town

Tiger Walks, A
Toby Tyler
Tom Brown's Schooldays
Tom Sawyer (1930)
Tom Sawyer (1973)
Tom Thumb
Treasure Island (1934)
Treasure Island (1950)
Treasure Island (1989)
Tree Grows in Brooklyn, A
Troll in Central Park, A
Tuck Everlasting
Twelve Months
20,000 Leagues Under the Sea
Two Bright Boys
Walton's Thanksgiving Story, the
Waltz King, The
Water Babies, The
Watership Down
Wee Willie Winkie
We're Back: A Dinosaur's Story
Where the Lilies Bloom
Where the Red Fern Grows
White Fang
White Fang 2: Myth of the White Wolf
Wild and the Free, The
Wild Country, The
Wild Hearts Can't Be Broken
Wild Pony, The
Wilderness Family Part 2, The
Winds of Change
Wishing Machine
Witches, The
Wizard, The
Wonderful World of the Brothers Grimm, The
World of Hans Christian Andersen, The
Yearling, The
Young Magician, The
Young Mr. Lincoln

MUSIC

Aladdin
Aladdin and His Lamp
Alice's Adventures in Wonderland
All Dogs Go to Heaven
Aristocats, The
Babes in Arms
Babes in Toyland (1961)
Babes in Toyland (1986)
Baby Take a Bow
Beauty and the Beast
Blue Bird, The (1940)
Blue Bird, The (1976)
Brigadoon
Bugsy Malone
Cinderella
Dimples
Doctor Dolittle
Dumbo
Fantasia
Fantasy Double Bill, A
Goin' Coconuts
Hans Brinker
Hansel and Gretel
Happiest Millionaire, The
Heidi's Song
Hocus Pocus It's Magic
Huckleberry Finn
Johnny Tremain
Lady and the Tramp
Lili
Little Mermaid, The
Little Miss Broadway
Maestro's Company, The—Vol. 1
Maestro's Company, The—Vol. 2
Man From Button Willow, The
Marco
Melody Time
Miss Ewa's Follies
Mother Goose Rock 'n Rhyme
Muppet Movie, The
Muppets Take Manhattan, The
Newsies
Oliver!
Peter Pan
Pinocchio (1940)
Pinocchio (1977)
Raggedy Ann and Andy
Red Riding Hood
Robin Hood
Rock-a-Doodle
Rock & Read
Singing Princess, The
Slipper and the Rose, The
Song of the South
Sound of Music, The
Swan Princess, The
Tales of Beatrix Potter, The
Wizard of Oz, The

SCIENCE FICTION

Aquaman
batteries not included
Black Cauldron, The
Buck Rogers in the 25th Century
Buck Rogers: Space Vampire
Cat From Outer Space, The
Chronicles of Narnia—Prince Caspian and the Voyage of the Dawn Treader
Chronicles of Narnia—Silver Chair, The
Chronicles of Narnia—The Lion, the Witch and the Wardrobe,
D.A.R.Y.L.
El Mundo Del Talisman
Escape to Witch Mountain
E.T. The Extra-Terrestrial
Explorers
Flight of the Navigator
Galaxy Express
Girl from Mars, The
Girl, the Gold Watch and Dynamite, The
Girl, the Gold Watch and Everything, The
Glitterball, The
Hitch in Time, A
Hobbit, The
Hyper Sapien—People from Another Star
Into the West
Invisible Boy, The
Jack the Giant Killer
Journey to the Beginning of Time
Journey to the Center of the Earth, The
Land of Faraway, The
Legend of the White Horse
Lensman
Lord of the Rings, The
Magic Sword, The
Mister Rossi Looks for Happiness
Moon Pilot
Neverending Story, The
Neverending Story II: The Next Chapter, The
Ninth Heart, The
Nothing Venture
Peppermint Rose
Phantom Treehouse, The
Pirates of Dark Water, The—The Saga Begins
Prehysteria!
Princess and the Goblin, The
Rocket to Nowhere
Sand Castle, The
Starbirds
Suburban Commando
Sword in the Stone, The
Transformers, The
Voltus 5
Willy McBean and his Magic Machine

WESTERN

Against a Crooked Sky
Brighty of the Grand Canyon
Christmas Mountain
Davy Crockett and the River Pirates
Davy Crockett, King of the Wild Frontier
Hot Lead & Cold Feet
Saddle Tramp
Wackiest Wagon Train in the West, The